The New York Times
Directory of the Film

The New York Times Directory of the Film

Introduction by
ARTHUR KNIGHT

ARNO PRESS

A NEW YORK TIMES COMPANY

1974

INTRODUCTION

Perhaps one of the reasons for the tremendous popularity of old movies is the fact that they tell us so much about ourselves as we were when those movies were new. The celluloid may deteriorate, but whatever images that remain are the very ones we saw when we were kids, or when we were courting, or when we were in the Army, or when the first baby came. We see them again in the perspective of today, but with the added enhancement of all those varied emotions that surrounded our original viewing. As Iris Barry, who founded the Museum of Modern Art Film Library, once observed, it isn't the pictures that have changed, "it is we who have changed, and the world we live in."

Paradoxically, while this may be all very well for nostalgia, it makes the work of the film scholar or the film historian doubly difficult. A picture from the past comes freighted not only with our recollections of that past, but with an entirely new set of values drawn from the contemporary scene. "Camp," for example, is a contemporary concept, but it has cast its own special coloration over those lavish Busby Berkeley musicals of the Thirties, or has accentuated certain aspects of such stars as Bette Davis, Humphrey Bogart, Judy Garland and Ruby Keeler—to name a few—that were not visible, or at least not risible, in their original incarnation. On the other hand, Mae West, who was pure "camp" from the start, has been in effect rediscovered by the "camp"-followers, and the distance has lent enchantment without distortion to what was there all along. But who can be sure?

Because the work of the daily reviewer is to get down on paper as quickly as possible his immediate reactions to a movie, the collected reviews of The New York Times, published by The Times and Arno Press in 1969, afforded the scholar an unparalleled opportunity to check out his own, current impressions of a picture against those of responsible, responsive critics writing at the time of release. It hardly matters whether or not they were the best critics of their day; they were always good journalists. And The Times gave them the space and the encouragement to write lengthy and considered appraisals of virtually every picture released here since 1913. To have all of these reviews available in a single source, together with pertinent Sunday features and news items, was almost too good to be true (particularly for anyone who hitherto has been forced to strain his eyes deciphering these same articles in microfilm). Not since the "make-work," precomputerized days of W.P.A. has such an invaluable research tool been placed in the hands of film students and historians—and, fortunately or unfortunately, the Great Depression of the Thirties ended before the New York City Writers' Project could publish more than one of the three planned volumes of its own *Film Index*, an invaluable guide to the literature of the film as an art form.

But where *The Film Index* and the six volumes of *The New York Times Film Reviews* were conceived as primarily for film scholarship, and to be used as library reference works, this *New York Times Directory of the Film* has been pointed to that rising generation of film buffs who can name all the actors who ever played Charlie Chan, and throw in their Number One Sons for good measure. Essentially, the *Directory* is an enlargement of the original Index to the reviews, with such "extras" as up-datings of The Times' annual "Ten Best" lists (from 1924), the Academy Award winners (from 1927), and the New York Film Critics' Award selections (from 1935). Carried over from the Index is the Portrait Gallery, with photos of around 2,000 stars, starlets and child actors (some of the child actors who grew up on the screen, like Jackie Coogan, Jackie Cooper and Natalie Wood, are glimpsed twice), and also the Personal Name Index.

Probably the most useful, as well as the most fun, will be the Personal Name section. Through the miracle of the computer, every name that has ever appeared in the credits of a Time review—actors, directors, producers, writers, cameramen, composers, even animals—has been lifted from the columns and placed alphabetically under the proper heading, with their films arranged chronologically. This leads to some pleasant discoveries, like Akka (chimpanzee), or Dostoevski, Feodor (original author), or the surprising number of films made by, say, Jean Arthur and Gary Cooper before either was officially "discovered."

Obviously, this section is destined to become as indispensable to the settling of disputes and wagers as Hoyle in games of chance or Roberts' *Rules of Order* for more serious matters.

Perhaps the real importance of the appearance of this volume, however, lies in the evident conviction of Arno Press that general interest in the motion picture medium has now reached a level that warrants the labor and expense of such a publication. For this is a far cry from the fan books of yesteryear—and also a far cry, it might be noted, from such industry stand-bys as the *International Motion Picture Almanac* to which one had hitherto been forced to turn for biographical information, even though that information (sketchy at best) was supplied by the biographees themselves. Eminently more readable, but not necessarily more reliable or complete, have been the several, constantly expanding editions of Leslie Halliwell's *The Filmgoer's Companion*, the first major effort to reach the film buff as opposed to the mere film fan, and to provide him with solid, factual information.

This is not to disparage the fans who, after all, brought along the medium from the first nickelodeons to the age of the vast picture palaces. But this audience has tended to remain static, or now to find its entertainment on the tube. In fact, one of the reasons for the industry's current decline has been is tendency in the past few years to outpace its fans, turning out pictures that demand more than merely passive acceptance. At the same time, as witnessed by the increase in film schools and the huge leap forward in the number of film appreciation classes now being offered all the way from grammar school to the university level, a new generation is being prepared to look on motion pictures as more than just an entertainment, more than just a means of whiling away a few idle hours. Their interest is in film as a creative art form—and hence, quite properly, they are also interested in the artists who have shaped that form, and in those who continue to do so. Significantly, the emphasis has shifted from film star to film director for this new, more sophisticated breed of film buffs, and there are also signs that cameramen and even writers are beginning to receive their long-overdue recognition.

Recognition, oddly enough, is just as important to the film maker as his out-sized salary checks—in the long run, perhaps even more so. Today's stars, directors, producers and writers no longer hole up in their Beverly Hills mansions or Malibu beach homes between assignments. They are out touring the campuses, visiting film festivals, appearing on TV "talk" shows. They not only want to keep their visibility high and to enjoy at first hand the fruits of their labors; they also want the "feedback" that comes from personal contact with this new, knowledgeable and highly articulate generation of film enthusiasts. "Why, they know more about my pictures than I do myself!" exclaimed veteran director King Vidor after addressing a cinema class at the University of Southern California. And he was not altogether wrong.

With the film buff replacing the film fan, the accent is no longer so relentlessly placed upon the new. The pioneering work of the Museum of Modern Art, which at one time was virtually the only source for old movies, has finally begun to pay off. Not only are there now long lines waiting to get into the Museum itself, but revival houses are springing up in every major city in America, supplemented by innumerable campus film societies—and not forgetting the nightly range of fare offered on television's popular "late, late" shows. The fact that the pictures themselves are now available in such abundance is reason enough for this present volume, which supplies the kinds of specific information that the intelligent, inquisitive viewer would certainly want to know about the films he has just seen, and about the people who made them. For further information, each entry refers to the date of the original review in The New York Times.

These original reviews are rather like butterfly specimens that have been pinned for all time in spectacular array. But the films themselves are not butterflies; unlike the reviews, they are not to be pinned down to one time and one place. Whether produced as entertainment, art or propaganda, they live a life of their own, with a continuing power to affect us as they impinge upon our lives at one time or another. They become, in effect, the gauge to our own degree of change, with these reviews at hand to remind us what the films were like—and we—when they were first released. *The New York Times Directory of the Film* can only enrich the film viewing experience of all of us.

—*Arthur Knight*

Contents

	Introduction	
I	Listings of Awards	1
	The Times "10 Best"	3
	The New York Film Critics Circle Awards	6
	The Academy Awards	8
II	Portrait Gallery	11
III	Index	59
	Personal Name Index	61

I Listing of Awards

NOTE: In this section will be found listings of The New York Times selections of each year's ten best films (by title only) and of filmdom's two principal series of honors, the New York Film Critics Circle annual awards and the "Oscars" of the Academy of Motion Picture Arts and Sciences. The Film Critics Circle and Academy awards are listed by year, and within each year by category. It should be noted, however, that these categories varied over the years, and that not every year was an award given in each category.

The Times "10 Best"

1924

The Dramatic Life of Abraham Lincoln
The Thief of Bagdad
Beau Brummel
Merton of the Movies
The Sea Hawk
He Who Gets Slapped
The Marriage Circle
In Hollywood With Potash and Perlmutter
Peter Pan
Isn't Life Wonderful?

1925

The Big Parade
The Last Laugh
The Unholy Three
The Gold Rush
The Merry Widow
The Dark Angel
Don Q, Son of Zorro
Ben-Hur
Stella Dallas
A Kiss for Cinderella

1926

Variety
Beau Geste
What Price Glory
Potemkin
The Grand Duchess and the Waiter
The Black Pirate
Old Ironsides
Moana
La Bohème
So This Is Paris

1927

The King of Kings
Chang
The Way of All Flesh
Wings
Seventh Heaven
Sunrise
Service for Ladies
Quality Street
Underworld
Stark Love

1928

The Circus
Street Angel
Czar Ivan the Terrible
The Last Command
White Shadows of the South Seas
The Patriot
The End of St. Petersburg
Show People
Homecoming
Four Devils

1929.

The Love Parade
Disraeli

Hallelujah
The Passion of Jeanne d'Arc
The Taming of the Shrew
Bulldog Drummond
They Had to See Paris
The Sky Hawk
The Virginian
Sally

1930

With Byrd at the South Pole
All Quiet on the Western Front
Journey's End
Lightnin'
The Devil to Pay
Outward Bound
Tom Sawyer
Holiday
Abraham Lincoln
Anna Christie

1931

The Guardsman
City Lights
The Smiling Lieutenant
Arrowsmith
Tabu
Bad Girl
Frankenstein
Skippy
Private Lives
A Connecticut Yankee

1932

Maedchen in Uniform
Trouble in Paradise
Der Raub der Mona Lisa
Grand Hotel
Dr. Jekyll and Mr. Hyde
The Mouthpiece
One Hour With You
A Bill of Divorcement
The Doomed Battalion
Reserved for Ladies

1933

Cavalcade
Reunion in Vienna
Morgenrot
State Fair
Dinner at Eight
Berkeley Square
The Private Life of Henry VIII
Little Women
The Invisible Man
His Double Life

1934

It Happened One Night
The House of Rothschild
The Battle
The Thin Man
Catherine the Great

The First World War
One Night of Love
The Lost Patrol
Man of Aran
Our Daily Bread

1935

The Informer
Ruggles of Red Gap
David Copperfield
Lives of a Bengal Lancer
Les Miserables
The Scoundrel
Chapayev
The Man Who Knew Too Much
Sequoia
Love Me Forever

1936

La Kermesse Heroique; or, Carnival in
    Flanders
Fury
Dodsworth
Mr. Deeds Goes to Town
Winterset
Romeo and Juliet
The Green Pastures
The Ghost Goes West
The Story of Louis Pasteur
These Three
The Great Ziegfeld

1937

The Life of Emile Zola
The Good Earth
Stage Door
Captains Courageous
They Won't Forget
Make Way for Tomorrow
I Met Him in Paris
A Star Is Born
Camille
Lost Horizon

1938

Snow White and the Seven Dwarfs
The Citadel
To the Victor
Pygmalion
A Slight Case of Murder
Three Comrades
The Lady Vanishes
The Adventures of Robin Hood
A Man to Remember
Four Daughters

1939

Made for Each Other
Stagecoach
Wuthering Heights
Dark Victory
Juarez
Goodbye, Mr. Chips

The Women
Mr. Smith Goes to Washington
Ninotchka
Gone With the Wind

1940

The Grapes of Wrath
The Baker's Wife
Rebecca
Our Town
The Mortal Storm
Pride and Prejudice
The Great McGinty
The Long Voyage Home
The Great Dictator
Fantasia

1941

The Lady Eve
Citizen Kane
Major Barbara
Sergeant York
The Stars Look Down
Here Comes Mr. Jordan
Target for Tonight
Dumbo
How Green Was My Valley
One Foot in Heaven

1942

In Which We Serve
Journey for Margaret
Casablanca
One of Our Aircraft Is Missing
Wake Island
Mrs. Miniver
Yankee Doodle Dandy
The Gold Rush
Woman of the Year
Sullivan's Travels

1943

Air Force
Desert Victory
The Ox-Bow Incident
The More the Merrier
For Whom the Bell Tolls
Report From the Aleutians
Watch on the Rhine
Corvette K-225
Sahara
Madame Curie

1944

Destination Tokyo
The Miracle of Morgan's Creek
The Purple Heart
Going My Way
Wilson
Hail the Conquering Hero
Thirty Seconds Over Tokyo
None But the Lonely Heart
Meet Me in St. Louis
National Velvet

1945

A Tree Grows in Brooklyn
The Way Ahead
Anchors Aweigh
Pride of the Marines
The House on Ninety-Second Street
Story of G. I. Joe
Spellbound
The Last Chance
The Lost Weekend
They Were Expendable

1946

Open City
Road to Utopia
The Green Years
Henry V
Notorious
Brief Encounter
The Well-Digger's Daughter
The Best Years of Our Lives
My Darling Clementine
Stairway to Heaven

1947

The Yearling
Great Expectations
Miracle on 34th Street
Crossfire
Life with Father
Shoe Shine
Gentleman's Agreement
To Live in Peace
The Bishop's Wife
The Fugitive

1948

Treasure of Sierra Madre
The Pearl
The Search
A Foreign Affair
Louisiana Story
Hamlet
Johnny Belinda
Apartment for Peggy
The Red Shoes
The Snake Pit

1949

Command Decision
A Letter to Three Wives
The Quiet One
Lost Boundaries
Pinky
The Heiress
All the King's Men
Battleground
The Fallen Idol
Intruder in the Dust

1950

The Titan — Story of Michelangelo
Twelve O'Clock High
Father of the Bride
The Asphalt Jungle
Destination Moon
The Men
Sunset Boulevard
Trio
All About Eve
Born Yesterday

1951

Fourteen Hours
The Brave Bulls
Oliver Twist
A Place in the Sun
People Will Talk
A Streetcar Named Desire
An American in Paris
Detective Story
Death of a Salesman
Decision Before Dawn

Best Foreign Film: Rasho-Mon

1952

The Greatest Show on Earth
Cry, the Beloved Country

Viva Zapata!
Five Fingers
High Noon
Ivanhoe
The Quiet Man
Limelight
Breaking Through the Sound Barrier
Come Back, Little Sheba

1953

Moulin Rouge
Lili
Shane
Julius Caesar
Man on a Tightrope
Stalag 17
From Here to Eternity
Roman Holiday
Martin Luther
The Conquest of Everest

1954

The Glenn Miller Story
Genevieve
Knock on Wood
Mr. Hulot's Holiday
Seven Brides for Seven Brothers
On the Waterfront
The Little Kidnappers
Sabrina
The Country Girl
Romeo and Juliet

1955

The Bridges at Toko-Ri
Bad Day at Black Rock
A Man Called Peter
Marty
The Great Adventure
Mister Roberts
The Phenix City Story
It's Always Fair Weather
Oklahoma!
The Prisoner

1956

Richard III
The King and I
Moby Dick
Bus Stop
Lust for Life
The Silent World
Giant
Around the World in 80 Days
Friendly Persuasion
Anastasia

Best Foreign Films: The Proud and the
  Beautiful (French); Rififi (French); La
  Strada (Italian); The Grand Maneuver
  (French) The Magnificent Seven (Japan-
  ese)

1957

The Great Man
Funny Face
12 Angry Men
The Green Man
A Hatful of Rain
Silk Stockings
Love in the Afternoon
Les Girls
Sayonara
The Bridge on the River Kwai

Best Foreign Films: We Are All Murderers
  (French); Gold of Naples (Italian); The
  Red Balloon (French); Torero! (Mexican);

Passionate Summer (French); The Last Bridge (German); Cabiria (Italian); Gervaise (French); Odet (Danish); Smiles of a Summer Night (Swedish)

1958

Teacher's Pet
Gigi
The Goddess
God's Little Acre
Cat On a Hot Tin Roof
The Defiant Ones
Damn Yankees
The Horse's Mouth
I Want to Live!
A Night to Remember

Best Foreign Films: Gates of Paris (French); Rouge et Noir (French); Case of Dr. Laurent (French); The Captain from Koepenick (German); Panther Panchali (Indian); Inspector Maigret (French); The Seventh Seal (Swedish); My Uncle (French); Witches of Salem (French); He Who Must Die (French)

1959

The Diary of Anne Frank
Room at the Top
The Nun's Story
Porgy and Bess
Anatomy of a Murder
A Hole in the Head
North by Northwest
Pillow Talk
Ben-Hur
On the Beach

Best Foreign Films: The Devil Strikes at Night (German); Forbidden Fruit (French); Aparajito (Indian); The Roof (Italian); Wild Strawberries (Swedish); The Magician (Swedish); The Lovers (French); The 400 Blows (French); The Cousins (French); Black Orpheus (French-Brazilian)

1960

I'm All Right, Jack
The Apartment
Psycho
Elmer Gantry
Sunrise at Campobello
The Entertainer
Inherit the Wind
The Angry Silence
Exodus
Tunes of Glory

Best Foreign Films: Rosemary (German); Ikiru (Japanese); The Cranes Are Flying (Russian); Hiroshima Mon Amour (French); The World of Apu (Indian); Never on Sunday (Greek); The Virgin Spring (Swedish); General della Rovere (Italian); The Big Deal on Madonna Street (Italian); The Ballad of a Soldier (Russian)

1961

The Facts of Life
A Raisin in the Sun
Saturday Night and Sunday Morning
Fanny
The Hustler
Splendor in the Grass
West Side Story
El Cid
Judgment at Nuremberg
One, Two, Three

Best Foreign Films: Don Quixote (Russian); Breathless (French); La Dolce Vita (Italian); The Bridge (German); Two Women (Italian); Ashes and Diamonds (Polish); Rocco and His Brothers (Italian); Purple Noon (French); Girl With a Suitcase (Italian); A Summer to Remember (Russian)

1962

Lover Come Back
Last Year at Marienbad
Whistle Down the Wind
A Taste of Honey
Divorce — Italian Style
The Longest Day
Long Day's Journey Into Night
Sundays and Cybele
Freud
Electra

1963

Heavens Above!
The L-Shaped Room
Hud
Cleopatra
8-½
Tom Jones
Any Number Can Win
The Sound of Trumpets
It's a Mad, Mad, Mad, Mad World
America, America

1964

Dr. Strangelove, or How I Learned to Stop Worrying and Love the Bomb
The Servant
That Man From Rio
One Potato, Two Potato
A Hard Day's Night
Woman in the Dunes
Mary Poppins
My Fair Lady
The Americanization of Emily
Marriage Italian Style

1965

The Pawnbroker
Ship of Fools
Darling
Repulsion
Juliet of the Spirits
The Eleanor Roosevelt Story

Red Desert
Kwaidan
To Die in Madrid
Thunderball

1966

The Shop on Main Street
The Gospel According to St. Matthew
Dear John
Morgan!
The Russians Are Coming, The Russians Are Coming
Who's Afraid of Virginia Woolf
Georgy Girl
Loves of a Blonde
A Man for All Seasons
Blow-Up

1967

La Guerre Est Finie
Ulysses
The Hunt
In the Heat of the Night
Father
Elvira Madigan
Closely Watched Trains
Cool Hand Luke
In Cold Blood
The Graduate

1968

Charlie Bubbles
The Two of Us
Belle de Jour
Faces
Les Carabiniers
The Bride Wore Black
The Fifth Horseman Is Fear
Petulia
Rosemary's Baby
A Report on the Party and the Guests

1969

Alice's Restaurant
The Damned
If...
La Femme Infidele
Midnight Cowboy
Stolen Kisses
Topaz
True Grit
The Wild Bunch
"Z"

1970

The Ballad of Cable Hogue
Catch-22
Fellini Satyricon
Little Big Man
Loving
M*A*S*H*
Ma Nuit Chez Maud (My Night at Maud's)
The Passion of Anna
Tristana
The Wild Child

The New York Film Critics Circle Awards

1935

Best Motion Picture: The Informer (director, John Ford; producer, Cliff Reid)
Best Actor: Charles Laughton (Mutiny on the Bounty and Ruggles of Red Gap)
Best Actress: Greta Garbo (Anna Karenina)
Best Direction: John Ford (The Informer)

1936

Best Motion Picture: Mr. Deeds Goes to Town (director, Frank Capra; producer, Columbia)
Best Actor: Walter Huston (Dodsworth)
Best Actress: Luise Rainer (The Great Ziegfeld)
Best Direction: Rouben Mamoulian (The Gay Desperado)
Best Foreign Film: La Kermesse Heroique (director, Jacques Feyder; producer, Tobis; French)

1937

Best Motion Picture: The Life of Emile Zola (director, William Dieterle; producer, Warner Brothers)
Best Actor: Paul Muni (The Life of Emile Zola)
Best Actress: Greta Garbo (Camille)
Best Direction: Gregory La Cava (Stage Door)
Best Foreign Film: Mayerling (director, Anatole Litvak; French)

1938

Best Motion Picture: The Citadel (director, King Vidor; producer, Victor Saville)
Best Actor: James Cagney (Angels With Dirty Faces)
Best Actress: Margaret Sullavan (Three Comrades)
Best Direction: Alfred Hitchcock (The Lady Vanishes)
Best Foreign Film: Grande Illusion (director, Jean Renoir; producer, R.C.A.; French)

1939

Best Motion Picture: Wuthering Heights (director, William Wyler; producer, Samuel Goldwyn)
Best Actor: James Stewart (Mr. Smith Goes to Washington)
Best Actress: Vivien Leigh (Gone With the Wind)
Best Direction: John Ford (Stagecoach)

1940

Best Motion Picture: The Grapes of Wrath (director, John Ford; producer, Twentieth Century-Fox)
Best Actor: Charles Chaplin (The Great Dictator)
Best Actress: Katharine Hepburn (The Philadelphia Story)
Best Direction: John Ford (The Grapes of Wrath and The Long Voyage Home)

1941

Best Motion Picture: Citizen Kane (director and producer, Orson Welles)
Best Actor: Gary Cooper (Sergeant York)
Best Actress: Joan Fontaine (Suspicion)
Best Direction: John Ford (How Green Was My Valley)

1942

Best Motion Picture: In Which We Serve (directors, Noel Coward and David Lean; producer, Noel Coward)
Best Actor: James Cagney (Yankee Doodle Dandy)
Best Actress: Agnes Moorehead (The Magnificent Ambersons)
Best Direction: John Farrow (Wake Island)

1943

Best Motion Picture: Watch on the Rhine (director, Herman Shumlin; producer, Warner Brothers)
Best Actor: Paul Lukas (Watch on the Rhine)
Best Actress: Ida Lupino (The Hard Way)
Best Direction: George Stevens (The More the Merrier)

1944

Best Motion Picture: Going My Way (director, Leo McCarey; producer, Paramount)
Best Actor: Barry Fitzgerald (Going My Way)
Best Actress: Tallulah Bankhead (Lifeboat)
Best Direction: Leo McCarey (Going My Way)

1945

Best Motion Picture: The Lost Weekend (director, Billy Wilder; producer, Charles Brackett)
Best Actor: Ray Milland (The Lost Weekend)
Best Actress: Ingrid Bergman (Spellbound and The Bells of St. Mary's)
Best Direction: Billy Wilder (The Lost Weekend)

1946

Best Motion Picture: The Best Years of Our Lives (director, William Wyler; producer, Samuel Goldwyn)
Best Actor: Laurence Olivier (Henry V)
Best Actress: Celia Johnson (Brief Encounter)
Best Direction: William Wyler (The Best Years of Our Lives)

1947

Best Motion Picture: Gentleman's Agreement (director, Elia Kazan; producer, Darryl F. Zanuck)
Best Actor: William Powell (Life With Father and The Senator Was Indiscreet)
Best Actress: Deborah Kerr (Black Narcissus and The Adventuress)
Best Direction: Elia Kazan (Gentleman's Agreement and Boomerang)
Best Foreign Film: To Live in Peace (director, Luigi Zampa; producer, Carlo Ponti; Italian)

1948

Best Motion Picture: Treasure of Sierra Madre (director, John Huston; producer, Henry Blanke)
Best Actor: Laurence Olivier (Hamlet)
Best Actress: Olivia de Havilland (The Snake Pit)
Best Direction: John Huston (Treasure of Sierra Madre)
Best Foreign Film: Paisan (director and producer, Roberto Rosellini; Italian)

1949

Best Motion Picture: All the King's Men (director and producer, Robert Rossen)
Best Actor: Broderick Crawford (All the King's Men)
Best Actress: Olivia de Havilland (The Heiress)
Best Direction: Carol Reed (The Fallen Idol)
Best Foreign Film: The Bicycle Thief (director and producer, Vittorio De Sica; Italian)

1950

Best Motion Picture: All About Eve (director, Joseph L. Mankiewicz; producer, Darryl F. Zanuck)
Best Actor: Gregory Peck (Twelve O'Clock High)
Best Actress: Bette Davis (All About Eve)
Best Direction: Joseph L. Mankiewicz (All About Eve)
Best Foreign Film: Ways of Love (directors, Rosselini, Pagnol, Renoir; Italian/French)

1951

Best Motion Picture: A Streetcar Named Desire (director, Elia Kazan; producer, Charles K. Feldman)
Best Actor: Arthur Kennedy (Bright Victory)
Best Direction: Elia Kazan (A Streetcar Named Desire)
Best Foreign Film: Miracle in Milan (director, Vittorio De Sica; Italian)

1952

Best Motion Picture: High Noon (director, Fred Zinnemann; producer, Stanley Kramer)
Best Actor: Ralph Richardson (Breaking Through the Sound Barrier)

Best Actress: Shirley Booth (Come Back, Little Sheba)
Best Direction: Fred Zinnemann (High Noon)
Best Foreign Film: Forbidden Games (director, René Clement; producer, Robert Dorfman; French)

1953

Best Motion Picture: From Here to Eternity (director, Fred Zinnemann; producer, Buddy Adler)
Best Actor: Burt Lancaster (From Here to Eternity)
Best Actress: Audrey Hepburn (Roman Holiday)
Best Direction: Fred Zinnemann (From Here to Eternity)
Best Foreign Film: Justice is Done (director, André Cayatte; producer, Robert Dorfman; French)

1954

Best Motion Picture: On the Waterfront (director, Elia Kazan; producer, Sam Spiegel)
Best Actor: Marlon Brando (On the Waterfront)
Best Actress: Grace Kelly (The Country Girl)
Best Direction: Elia Kazan (On the Waterfront)
Best Foreign Film: Gate of Hell (director, Teinosuke Kinugasa; producer, Masaichi Nagata; Japanese)

1955

Best Motion Picture: Marty (director, Delbert Mann; producer, Harold Hecht)
Best Actor: Ernest Borgnine (Marty)
Best Actress: Anna Magnani (The Rose Tattoo)
Best Direction: David Lean (Summertime)
Best Foreign Film: A tie between Umberto D (director, Vittorio De Sica; Italian) and Diabolique (director and producer, Henri-Georges Clouzot; French)

1956

Best Motion Picture: Around the World in 80 Days (director, Michael Anderson; producer, Michael Todd)
Best Actor: Kirk Douglas (Lust for Life)
Best Actress: Ingrid Bergman (Anastasia)
Best Direction: John Huston (Moby Dick)
Best Foreign Film: La Strada (director, Federico Fellini; producer, Dino de Laurentiis; Italian)

1957

Best Motion Picture: The Bridge on the River Kwai (director, David Lean; producer, Sam Spiegel)
Best Actor: Alec Guinness (The Bridge on the River Kwai)
Best Actress: Deborah Kerr (Heaven Knows, Mr. Allison)
Best Direction: David Lean (The Bridge on the River Kwai)
Best Foreign Film: Gervaise (director, René Clement; producer, Annie Dorfmann; French)

1958

Best Motion Picture: The Defiant Ones (director and producer, Stanley Kramer)
Best Actor: David Niven (Separate Tables)
Best Actress: Susan Hayward (I Want to Live)
Best Direction: Stanley Kramer (The Defiant Ones)
Best Foreign Film: My Uncle, Mr. Hulot (director and producer, Jacques Tati; French)

1959

Best Motion Picture: Ben-Hur (director, William Wyler; producer, Sam Zimbalist)
Best Actor: James Stewart (Anatomy of a Murder)
Best Actress: Audrey Hepburn (The Nun's Story)
Best Direction: Fred Zinnemann (The Nun's Story)
Best Foreign Film: The 400 Blows (director and producer, François Truffaut; French)

1960

Best Motion Picture: A tie between The Apartment (director and producer, Billy Wilder) and Sons and Lovers (director, Jack Cardiff; producer, Jerry Wald)
Best Actor: Burt Lancaster (Elmer Gantry)
Best Actress: Deborah Kerr (The Sundowners)
Best Directors: A tie between Billy Wilder (The Apartment) and Jack Cardiff (Sons and Lovers)
Best Foreign Film: Hiroshima, Mon Amour (director and producer, Alain Resnais; French-Japanese)

1961

Best Motion Picture: West Side Story (directors, Robert Wise and Jerome Robbins; producer, Robert Wise)
Best Actor: Maximilian Schell (Judgment at Nuremberg)
Best Actress: Sophia Loren (Two Women)
Best Director: Robert Rossen (The Hustler)
Best Foreign Film: La Dolce Vita (director, Federico Fellini; producer, Giuseppe Amato; Italian)

1962

None

1963

Best Motion Picture: Tom Jones (director and producer, Tony Richardson)
Best Actor: Albert Finney (Tom Jones)
Best Actress: Patricia Neal (Hud)
Best Direction: Tony Richardson (Tom Jones)
Best Foreign Film: 8-½ (director, Federico Fellini; producer, Angelo Rizzoli; Italian)

1964

Best Motion Picture: My Fair Lady (director, George Cukor; producer, Jack L. Warner)
Best Actor: Rex Harrison (My Fair Lady)
Best Actress: Kim Stanley (Seance on a Wet Afternoon)
Best Direction: Stanley Kubrick (Dr. Strangelove, or How I Learned to Stop Worrying and Love the Bomb)
Best Foreign Film: That Man From Rio (director, Philippe De Broca; producers, Alexandre Mnouchkine and Georges Dancigers; French)

1965

Best Motion Picture: Darling (director, John Schlesinger; producer, Joseph Janni)
Best Actor: Oskar Werner (Ship of Fools)
Best Actress: Julie Christie (Darling)
Best Direction: John Schlesinger (Darling)
Best Foreign Film: Juliet of the Spirits (director, Federico Fellini; producer, Angelo Rizzoli; Italian)

1966

Best Motion Picture: A Man for All Seasons (director, Fred Zinnemann; producers, Fred Zinnemann and William N. Graf)
Best Actor: Paul Scofield (A Man for All Seasons)
Best Actress: A tie between Elizabeth Taylor (Who's Afraid of Virginia Woolf?) and Lynn Redgrave (Georgy Girl)
Best Direction: Fred Zinnemann (A Man for All Seasons)
Best Foreign Film: The Shop on Main Street (directors, Jan Kadar and Elmer Klos; producer, Barrandov Studios; Czechoslovakian)

1967

Best Motion Picture: In the Heat of the Night (director, Norman Jewison; producer, Walter Mirisch)
Best Actor: Rod Steiger (In the Heat of the Night)
Best Actress: Edith Evans (The Whisperers)
Best Direction: Mike Nichols (The Graduate)
Best Foreign Film: La Guerre Est Finie (director, Alain Resnais; producers, Sofracima/Europa—Film; French)

1968

Best Motion Picture: The Lion in Winter (director, Anthony Harvey; producers, Martin Poll and Joseph E. Levine)
Best Actor: Alan Arkin (The Heart Is a Lonely Hunter)
Best Actress: Joanne Woodward (Rachel, Rachel)
Best Direction: Paul Newman (Rachel, Rachel)
Best Foreign Film: War and Peace (director, Sergei Boudarchuk; producer, Moscow Studios; Russian)

1969

Best Motion Picture: "Z" (director, Costa-Gavras; producers, Jacques Perrin and Hamed Rachedi)
Best Actor: Jon Voight (Midnight Cowboy)
Best Actress: Jane Fonda (They Shoot Horses, Don't They?)
Best Direction: Costa-Gavras ("Z")

1970

Best Motion Picture: Five Easy Pieces (director, Bob Rafelson; producers, Bob Rafelson and Richard Wechsler)
Best Actor: George C. Scott (Patton)
Best Actress: Glenda Jackson (Women in Love)
Best Direction: Bob Rafelson (Five Easy Pieces)

Academy Awards

1927–1928

Best Motion Pictures: Wings (director, William A. Wellman; producer, Paramount); Sunrise (director, F. W. Murnau; producer, Fox)
Best Actor: Emil Jannings (Way of All Flesh, Last Command)
Best Actress: Janet Gaynor (Seventh Heaven, Street Angel, Sunrise)
Best Direction: Frank Borzage (Seventh Heaven); Lewis Milestone (Two Arabian Knights)

1928–1929

Best Motion Picture: The Broadway Melody (director, Harry Beaumont; producer, Metro-Goldwyn-Mayer)
Best Actor: Warner Baxter (In Old Arizona)
Best Actress: Mary Pickford (Coquette)
Best Direction: Frank Lloyd (Weary River, Divine Lady, Drag)

1929–1930

Best Motion Picture: All Quiet on the Western Front (director, Lewis Milestone; producer, Universal)
Best Actor: George Arliss (Disraeli)
Best Actress: Norma Shearer (The Divorcee)
Best Direction: Lewis Milestone (All Quiet on the Western Front)

1930–1931

Best Motion Picture: Cimarron (director, Wesley Ruggles; producer, RKO Radio Pictures)
Best Actor: Lionel Barrymore (A Free Soul)
Best Actress: Marie Dressler (Min and Bill)
Best Direction: Norman Taurog (Skippy)

1931–1932

Best Motion Picture: Grand Hotel (director, Edmund Goulding; producer, Metro-Goldwyn-Mayer)
Best Actor: Fredric March (Dr. Jekyll and Mr. Hyde)
Best Actress: Helen Hayes (Sin of Madelon Claudet)
Best Direction: Frank Borzage (Bad Girl)

1932–1933

Best Motion Picture: Cavalcade (director, Frank Lloyd; producer, Fox)
Best Actor: Charles Laughton (The Private Life of Henry VIII)
Best Actress: Katharine Hepburn (Morning Glory)
Best Direction: Frank Lloyd (Cavalcade)

1934

Best Motion Picture: It Happened One Night (director, Frank Capra; producer, Columbia)
Best Actor: Clark Gable (It Happened One Night)
Best Actress: Claudette Colbert (It Happened One Night)
Best Direction: Frank Capra (It Happened One Night)

1935

Best Motion Picture: Mutiny on the Bounty (director, Frank Lloyd; producer, Metro-Goldwyn-Mayer)
Best Actor: Victor McLaglen (The Informer)
Best Actress: Bette Davis (Dangerous)
Best Direction: John Ford (The Informer)

1936

Best Motion Picture: The Great Ziegfeld (director, Robert Z. Leonard; producer, Hunt Stromberg)
Best Actor: Paul Muni (The Story of Louis Pasteur)
Best Actress: Luise Rainer (The Great Ziegfeld)
Best Supporting Actor: Walter Brennan (Come and Get It)
Best Supporting Actress: Gail Sondergaard (Anthony Adverse)
Best Direction: Frank Capra (Mr. Deeds Goes to Town)

1937

Best Motion Picture: The Life of Emile Zola (director, William Dieterle; producer, Warner Brothers)
Best Actor: Spencer Tracy (Captains Courageous)
Best Actress: Luise Rainer (The Good Earth)
Best Supporting Actor: Joseph Schildkraut (The Life of Emile Zola)
Best Supporting Actress: Alice Brady (In Old Chicago)
Best Direction: Leo McCarey (The Awful Truth)

1938

Best Motion Picture: You Can't Take It With You (director, Frank Capra; producer, Columbia)
Best Actor: Spencer Tracy (Boys Town)
Best Actress: Bette Davis (Jezebel)
Best Supporting Actor: Walter Brennan (Kentucky)
Best Supporting Actress: Fay Bainter (Jezebel)
Best Direction: Frank Capra (You Can't Take It With You)

1939

Best Motion Picture: Gone With the Wind (director, Victor Fleming; producer, David Selznick)
Best Actor: Robert Donat (Goodbye, Mr. Chips)
Best Actress: Vivien Leigh (Gone With the Wind)
Best Supporting Actor: Thomas Mitchell (Stagecoach)
Best Supporting Actress: Hattie McDaniel (Gone With the Wind)
Best Direction: Victor Fleming (Gone With the Wind)

1940

Best Motion Picture: Rebecca (director, Alfred Hitchcock; producer, Selznick-International)
Best Actor: James Stewart (The Philadelphia Story)
Best Actress: Ginger Rogers (Kitty Foyle)
Best Supporting Actor: Walter Brennan (The Westerner)
Best Supporting Actress: Jane Darwell (The Grapes of Wrath)
Best Direction: John Ford (The Grapes of Wrath)

1941

Best Motion Picture: How Green Was My Valley (director, John Ford; producer, Twentieth Century-Fox)
Best Actor: Gary Cooper (Sergeant York)
Best Actress: Joan Fontaine (Suspicion)
Best Supporting Actor: Donald Crisp (How Green Was My Valley)
Best Supporting Actress: Mary Astor (The Great Lie)
Best Direction: John Ford (How Green Was My Valley)

1942

Best Motion Picture: Mrs. Miniver (director, William Wyler; producer, Metro-Goldwyn-Mayer)
Best Actor: James Cagney (Yankee Doodle Dandy)
Best Actress: Greer Garson (Mrs. Miniver)
Best Supporting Actor: Van Heflin (Johnny Eager)
Best Supporting Actress: Teresa Wright (Mrs. Miniver)
Best Direction: William Wyler (Mrs. Miniver)

1943

Best Motion Picture: Casablanca (director, Michael Curtiz; producer, Hal Wallis)
Best Actor: Paul Lukas (Watch on the Rhine)
Best Actress: Jennifer Jones (The Song of Bernadette)
Best Supporting Actor: Charles Coburn (The More the Merrier)
Best Supporting Actress: Katina Paxinou (For Whom the Bell Tolls)
Best Direction: Michael Curtiz (Casablanca)

1944

Best Motion Picture: Going My Way (director, Leo McCarey; producer, Paramount)

Best Actor: Bing Crosby (Going My Way)
Best Actress: Ingrid Bergman (Gaslight)
Best Supporting Actor: Barry Fitzgerald (Going My Way)
Best Supporting Actress: Ethel Barrymore (None but the Lonely Heart)
Best Direction: Leo McCarey (Going My Way)

1945

Best Motion Picture: The Lost Weekend (director, Billy Wilder; producer, Charles Brackett)
Best Actor: Ray Milland (The Lost Weekend)
Best Actress: Joan Crawford (Mildred Pierce)
Best Supporting Actor: James Dunn (A Tree Grows in Brooklyn)
Best Supporting Actress: Ann Revere (National Velvet)
Best Direction: Billy Wilder (The Lost Weekend)

1946

Best Motion Picture: The Best Years of Our Lives (director, William Wyler; producer, Samuel Goldwyn)
Best Actor: Fredric March (The Best Years of Our Lives)
Best Actress: Olivia de Havilland (To Each His Own)
Best Supporting Actor: Harold Russell (The Best Years of Our Lives)
Best Supporting Actress: Anne Baxter (The Razor's Edge)
Best Direction: William Wyler (The Best Years of Our Lives)

1947

Best Motion Picture: Gentleman's Agreement (director, Elia Kazan; producer, Darryl F. Zanuck)
Best Actor: Ronald Colman (A Double Life)
Best Actress: Loretta Young (The Farmer's Daughter)
Best Supporting Actor: Edmund Gwenn (Miracle on 34th Street)
Best Supporting Actress: Celeste Holm (Gentleman's Agreement)
Best Direction: Elia Kazan (Gentleman's Agreement)

1948

Best Motion Picture: Hamlet (director and producer, Laurence Olivier)
Best Actor: Laurence Olivier (Hamlet)
Best Actress: Jane Wyman (Johnny Belinda)
Best Supporting Actor: Walter Huston (The Treasure of Sierra Madre)
Best Supporting Actress: Claire Trevor (Key Largo)
Best Direction: John Huston (The Treasure of Sierra Madre)
Best Foreign Film: Monsieur Vincent (director, Maurice Cloche; producer, E.D.I.C.-U.G.C. of Paris; French)

1949

Best Motion Picture: All The King's Men (director and producer, Robert Rossen)
Best Actor: Broderick Crawford (All the King's Men)
Best Actress: Olivia de Havilland (The Heiress)
Best Supporting Actor: Dean Jagger (Twelve O'Clock High)

Best Supporting Actress: Mercedes McCambridge (All the King's Men)
Best Direction: Joseph L. Mankiewicz (A Letter to Three Wives)
Best Foreign Film: The Bicycle Thief (director and producer, Vittorio De Sica; Italian)

1950

Best Motion Picture: All About Eve (director, Joseph L. Mankiewicz; producer, Darryl F. Zanuck)
Best Actor: Jose Ferrer (Cyrano de Bergerac)
Best Actress: Judy Holliday (Born Yesterday)
Best Supporting Actor: George Sanders (All About Eve)
Best Supporting Actress: Josephine Hull (Harvey)
Best Direction: Joseph L. Mankiewicz (All About Eve)

1951

Best Motion Picture: An American in Paris (director, Vincente Minnelli; producer, Arthur Freed)
Best Actor: Humphrey Bogart (The African Queen)
Best Actress: Vivien Leigh (A Streetcar Named Desire)
Best Supporting Actor: Karl Malden (A Streetcar Named Desire)
Best Supporting Actress: Kim Hunter (A Streetcar Named Desire)
Best Direction: George Stevens (A Place in the Sun)

1952

Best Motion Picture: The Greatest Show on Earth (director and producer, Cecil B. DeMille)
Best Actor: Gary Cooper (High Noon)
Best Actress: Shirley Booth (Come Back, Little Sheba)
Best Supporting Actor: Anthony Quinn (Viva Zapata!)
Best Supporting Actress: Gloria Grahame (The Bad and the Beautiful)
Best Direction: John Ford (The Quiet Man)

1953

Best Motion Picture: From Here to Eternity (director, Fred Zinnemann; producer, Buddy Adler)
Best Actor: William Holden (Stalag 17)
Best Actress: Audrey Hepburn (Roman Holiday)
Best Supporting Actor: Frank Sinatra (From Here to Eternity)
Best Supporting Actress: Donna Reed (From Here to Eternity)
Best Direction: Fred Zinnemann (From Here to Eternity)

1954

Best Motion Picture: On The Waterfront (director, Elia Kazan; producer, Sam Spiegel)
Best Actor: Marlon Brando (On The Waterfront)
Best Actress: Grace Kelly (The Country Girl)
Best Supporting Actor: Edmond O'Brien (The Barefoot Contessa)
Best Supporting Actress: Eva Marie Saint (On The Waterfront)

Best Direction: Elia Kazan (On The Waterfront)
Best Foreign Film: Gate of Hell (director, Teinosuke Kinugasa; producer, Masaichi Nagata; Japanese)

1955

Best Motion Picture: Marty (director, Delbert Mann; producer, Harold Hecht)
Best Actor: Ernest Borgnine (Marty)
Best Actress: Anna Magnani (The Rose Tattoo)
Best Supporting Actor: Jack Lemmon (Mister Roberts)
Best Supporting Actress: Jo Van Fleet (East of Eden)
Best Direction: Delbert Mann (Marty)

1956

Best Motion Picture: Around the World in 80 Days (director, Michael Anderson; producer, Michael Todd)
Best Actor: Yul Brynner (The King and I)
Best Actress: Ingrid Bergman (Anastasia)
Best Supporting Actor: Anthony Quinn (Lust for Life)
Best Supporting Actress: Dorothy Malone (Written on the Wind)
Best Direction: George Stevens (Giant)
Best Foreign Film: La Strada (director, Federico Fellini; producer, Dino de Laurentiis; Italian)

1957

Best Motion Picture: The Bridge on the River Kwai (director, David Lean; producer, Sam Spiegel)
Best Actor: Alec Guinness (The Bridge on the River Kwai)
Best Actress: Joanne Woodward (The Three Faces of Eve)
Best Supporting Actor: Red Buttons (Sayonara)
Best Supporting Actress: Miyoshi Umeki (Sayonara)
Best Direction: David Lean (The Bridge on the River Kwai)
Best Foreign Film: The Nights of Cabiria (director, Federico Fellini; producer, Dino de Laurentiis; Italian)

1958

Best Motion Picture: Gigi (director, Vincente Minnelli; producer, Arthur Freed)
Best Actor: David Niven (Separate Tables)
Best Actress: Susan Hayward (I Want to Live)
Best Supporting Actor: Burl Ives (The Big Country)
Best Supporting Actress: Wendy Hiller (Separate Tables)
Best Direction: Vincente Minnelli (Gigi)
Best Foreign Film: My Uncle (director and producer, Jacques Tati; French)

1959

Best Motion Picture: Ben-Hur (director, William Wyler; producer Sam Zimbalist)
Best Actor: Charlton Heston (Ben-Hur)
Best Actress: Simone Signoret (Room at the Top)
Best Supporting Actor: Hugh Griffith (Ben-Hur)
Best Supporting Actress: Shelley Winters (The Diary of Anne Frank)
Best Direction: William Wyler (Ben-Hur)
Best Foreign Film: Black Orpheus (director, Marcel Camus; producer, Sacha Gordine; French-Brazilian)

1960

Best Motion Picture: The Apartment (director and producer, Billy Wilder)
Best Actor: Burt Lancaster (Elmer Gantry)
Best Actress: Elizabeth Taylor (Butterfield 8)
Best Supporting Actor: Peter Ustinov (Spartacus)
Best Supporting Actress: Shirley Jones (Elmer Gantry)
Best Direction: Billy Wilder (The Apartment)
Best Foreign Film: The Virgin Spring (director, Ingmar Bergman; producer, A. B. Svensk Filmindustri; Swedish)

1961

Best Motion Picture: West Side Story (directors, Robert Wise and Jerome Robbins; producer, Robert Wise)
Best Actor: Maximillian Schell (Judgment at Nuremberg)
Best Actress: Sophia Loren (Two Women)
Best Supporting Actor: George Chakiris (West Side Story)
Best Supporting Actress: Rita Moreno (West Side Story)
Best Direction: Robert Wise, Jerome Robbins (West Side Story)
Best Foreign Film: Through A Glass Darkly (director, Ingmar Bergman; producer, A. B. Svensk Filmindustri; Swedish)

1962

Best Motion Picture: Lawrence of Arabia (director, David Lean; producer, Sam Spiegel)
Best Actor: Gregory Peck (To Kill a Mockingbird)
Best Actress: Anne Bancroft (The Miracle Worker)
Best Supporting Actor: Ed Begley (Sweet Bird of Youth)
Best Supporting Actress: Patty Duke (The Miracle Worker)
Best Direction: David Lean (Lawrence of Arabia)
Best Foreign Film: Sundays and Cybele (director, Serge Bourgnignon; producer, Romain Pines; French)

1963

Best Motion Picture: Tom Jones (director and producer, Tony Richardson)
Best Actor: Sidney Poitier (Lilies of the Field)
Best Actress: Patricia Neal (Hud)
Best Supporting Actor: Melvyn Douglas (Hud)
Best Supporting Actress: Margaret Rutherford (The V.I.P.'s)

Best Direction: Tony Richardson (Tom Jones)
Best Foreign Film: 8-½ (director, Federico Fellini; producer, Angelo Rizzoli; Italian)

1964

Best Motion Picture: My Fair Lady (director, George Cukor; producer, Jack L. Warner)
Best Actor: Rex Harrison (My Fair Lady)
Best Actress: Julie Andrews (Mary Poppins)
Best Supporting Actor: Peter Ustinov (Topkapi)
Best Supporting Actress: Lila Kedrova (Zorba The Greek)
Best Direction: George Cukor (My Fair Lady)
Best Foreign Film: Yesterday, Today and Tomorrow (director, Vittorio De Sica; producer, Champion-Concordia Productions; Italian)

1965

Best Motion Picture: The Sound of Music (director and producer, Robert Wise)
Best Actor: Lee Marvin (Cat Ballou)
Best Actress: Julie Christie (Darling)
Best Supporting Actor: Martin Balsam (A Thousand Clowns)
Best Supporting Actress: Shelley Winters (A Patch of Blue)
Best Direction: Robert Wise (The Sound of Music)
Best Foreign Film: The Shop on Main Street (directors, Jan Kadar and Elmer Klos; producer, Barrandov Studios; Czechoslovakian)

1966

Best Motion Picture: A Man for All Seasons (director, Fred Zinnemann; producers, Fred Zinnemann and William N. Graf)
Best Actor: Paul Scofield (A Man for All Seasons)
Best Actress: Elizabeth Taylor (Who's Afraid of Virginia Woolf?)
Best Supporting Actor: Walter Matthau (The Fortune Cookie)
Best Supporting Actress: Sandy Dennis (Who's Afraid of Virginia Woolf?)
Best Direction: Fred Zinnemann (A Man for All Seasons)
Best Foreign Film: A Man and a Woman (director, Claude Lelouch; producer, a Les Films 13; French)

1967

Best Motion Picture: In the Heat of the Night (director, Norman Jewison; producer, Walter Mirisch)

Best Actor: Rod Steiger (In the Heat of the Night)
Best Actress: Katharine Hepburn (Guess Who's Coming to Dinner)
Best Supporting Actor: George Kennedy (Cool Hand Luke)
Best Supporting Actress: Estelle Parsons (Bonnie and Clyde)
Best Direction: Mike Nichols (The Graduate)
Best Foreign Film: Closely Watched Trains (director, Jiri Menzel; producer, Barrandov Studios; Czechoslovakian)

1968

Best Motion Picture: Oliver (director, Carol Reed; producer, John Wolf)
Best Actor: Cliff Robertson (Charly)
Best Actress: Katharine Hepburn (The Lion in Winter) tied; Barbra Streisand (Funny Girl) tied
Best Supporting Actor: Jack Albertson (The Subject Was Roses)
Best Supporting Actress: Ruth Gordon (Rosemary's Baby)
Best Direction: Carol Reed (Oliver)
Best Foreign Film: War and Peace (director, Sergei Bondarchuk; producer, Moscow Film Studios; Russian)

1969

Best Motion Picture: Midnight Cowboy (director, John Schlesinger; producer, Jerome Hellman)
Best Actor: John Wayne (True Grit)
Best Actress: Maggie Smith (The Prime of Miss Jean Brodie)
Best Supporting Actor: Gig Young (They Shoot Horses, Don't They?)
Best Supporting Actress: Goldie Hawn (Cactus Flower)
Best Direction: John Schlesinger (Midnight Cowboy)
Best Foreign Film: ''Z'' (director, Costa-Gavras; producers, Jacques Perrin and Hamed Rachedi)

1970

Best Motion Picture: Patton (director, Franklin J. Schaffner; producer, Frank McCarthy)
Best Actor: George C. Scott (Patton)
Best Actress: Glenda Jackson (Women in Love)
Best Supporting Actor: John Mills (Ryan's Daughter)
Best Supporting Actress: Helen Hayes (Airport)
Best Direction: Franklin J. Schaffner (Patton)
Best Foreign Film: Investigation of a Citizen Above Suspicion (director, Elio Petri; producer, Daniele Senatore)

II Portrait Gallery

NOTE: This section consists of the portraits of almost 2,000 movie stars. They are grouped by sex, and within each group alphabetically by name. Children are included in the appropriate adult grouping. In a few cases, two portraits of the same person, as child and as adult, are given.

This section serves the obvious purpose of providing a way in which a user can easily find out what a certain actor or actress looked like; it also provides a finding tool for those who would recognize a performer's face but cannot recall his or her name.

Only portraits owned by or readily available to The Times were used. To qualify for inclusion, a performer had to appear in at least 15 reviews, although exceptions were made in cases (such as James Dean) where unusual public interest was recognized.

PICTURE CREDITS

Abbott, Bud

Abel, Walter

Acuff, Eddie

Adams, Nick

Adler, Jay

Adler, Luther

Agar, John

Aherne, Brian

Albert, Eddie

Albertson, Frank

Albertson, Jack

Alda, Alan

Alda, Robert

Aldredge, Thomas

Alerme

Alexander, Ben

Alexander, John

Alexander, Ross

Allen, Fred

Allen, Robert

Allen, Steve

Alvarado, Don

Ameche, Don

Ames, Leon

Ames, Robert

Anderson, Eddie (Rochester)

Anderson, Richard

Anderson, Warner

Andrews, Dana

Andrews, Edward

Andrews, Harry

Ansara, Michael

Antrim, Harry

Arbuckle, Roscoe

Archer, John

Arkin, Alan

Arlen, Richard

Arliss, George

Armendariz, Pedro

Armetta, Henry

Armstrong, Louis (Satchmo)

Armstrong, Robert

Arness, James

Arno, Sig

Arnold, Edward

Arthur, George K.

Aslan, Gregoire

Astaire, Fred

Asther, Nils

Ates, Rosco

Attenborough, Richard

Atwill, Lionel

Auer, Mischa

Aumont, Jean Pierre

Avalon, Frankie

Aylmer, Felix

Ayres, Lew

Backus, Jim

Bacon, Irving

Baer, Buddy

Baker, Art

Baker, Benny

Baker, Kenny

Baker, Stanley

Balpetre

Balsam, Martin

Bancroft, George

Banks, Leslie

Bannen, Ian

Banner, John

Barbier, George

Barker, Lex

Barlow, Reginald

Barnes, T. Roy

Barnett, Griff

Barnett, Vince

Barrier, Edgar

Barry, Donald

Barry, Gene

Barry, Wesley

Barrymore, John

Barrymore, Lionel

Barthelmess, Richard

Bartholomew, Freddie

Barton, James
Basehart, Richard
Basserman, Albert
Bates, Alan
Baur, Harry
Baxter, Alan
Baxter, Warner

Beal, John
Beatty, Robert
Beatty, Warren
Beaumont, Hugh
Beck, Thomas
Beckett, Scotty
Beery, Noah

Beery, Noah, Jr
Beery, Wallace
Begley, Ed
Belafonte, Harry
Belasco, Leon
Bell, James
Bellamy, Ralph

Bellaver, Harry
Belmondo, Jean-Paul
Benchley, Robert
Bendix, William
Benedict, Richard
Bennett, Bruce
Bennett, Richard

Benny, Jack
Bergen, Edgar
Berle, Milton
Bey, Turhan
Bickford, Charles
Bickel, Theodore
Bing, Herman

Bishop, Joey
Bissell, Whit
Blackmer, Sidney
Blier, Bernard
Blore, Eric
Blue, Ben
Blue, Monte

Bogarde, Dirk

Bogart, Humphrey

Boles, John

Bolger, Ray

Bond, Derek

Bond, Ward

Boone, Pat

Boone, Richard

Borgnine, Ernest

Bosworth, Hobart

Bowman, Lee

Boyd, Stephen

Boyd, William

Boyer, Charles

Bracken, Eddie

Brady, Scott

Brando, Marlon

Brasseur, Pierre

Brazzi, Rossano

Brecher, Egon

Breese, Edmund

Brendel, El

Brennan, Walter

Brent, George

Brent, Romney

Brialy, Jean-Claude

Brian, David

Bridges, Lloyd

Briggs, Don

Briggs, Harlan

Brodie, Steve

Bromberg, J. Edward

Bronson, Charles

Brook, Clive

Brown, Joe E.

Brown, Tom

Bruce, Nigel

Brynner, Yul

Buchanan, Edgar

Bull, Peter

Burns, Bob

Burns, David

Burns, George   Burr, Raymond   Burton, Richard   Bushman, Francis X   Butterworth, Charles   Butler, Jimmie   Buttons, Red

Byron, Arthur   Cabot, Bruce   Cabot, Sebastian   Caesar, Sid   Cagney, James   Caine, Michael   Calhern, Louis

Calhoun, Rory   Callan, Michael   Calleia, Joseph   Cameron, Rod   Cantinflas   Cantor, Eddie   Carey, Harry

Carey, Harry Jr   Carey, Leonard   Carey, MacDonald   Carlson, Richard   Carlyle, Richard   Carmichael, Hoagy   Carmichael, Ian

Carminati, Tullio   Carnovsky, Morris   Carradine, John   Carrillo, Leo   Carroll, John   Carroll, Leo G   Carson, Jack

Carter, Ben   Caruso, Enrico   Cassavetes, John   Cassel, Jean-Pierre   Catlett, Walter   Cavanagh, Paul   Cavanaugh, Hobart

Cawthorn, Joseph   Celi, Adolfo   Cervi, Gino   Chadwick, Cyril   Chandler, George   Chandler, Jeff   Chandler, Lane

Chaplin, Charlie   Chaney, Lon   Chaney, Lon Jr   Chevalier, Maurice   Chiari, Walter   Churchill, Berton   Clark, Dane

Clark, Fred   Clements, Stanley (Stash)   Clift, Montgomery   Clive, Colin   Clive, E E   Clyde, Andy   Cobb, Lee J

Coburn, Charles   Coburn, James   Cochran, Steve   Cody, Lew   Cole, George   Cole, Nat (King)   Colleano, Bonar

Collier, William   Collièr, William Jr   Collins, Eddie   Collins, Ray   Colman, Ronald   Colonna, Jerry   Conklin, Chester

Connery, Sean   Connolly, Walter   Connors, Chuck   Conrad, William   Conreid, Hans   Conroy, Frank   Conte, Richard

Conway, Morgan   Conway, Tim   Coogan, Jackie   Coogan, Jackie   Cook, Donald   Cooper, Gary   Cooper, Jackie

Cooper, Jackie   Cooper, Melville   Coote, Robert   Corey, Wendell   Cossart, Ernest   Cortez, Ricardo   Costello, Lou

Cotten, Joseph   Coulouris, George   Cowan, Jerome   Coward, Noel   Cox, Wally   Crabbe, Buster (Larry)   Craig, James

Craig, Michael   Craven, Frank   Crawford, Broderick   Crehan, Joseph   Cregar, Laird   Crisp, Donald   Cromwell, Richard

Cronyn, Hume   Crosby, Bing   Culver, Roland   Cummings, Robert   Currie, Finlay   Curtis, Alan   Curtis, Tony

Cushing, Peter   da Silva, Howard   Dailey, Dan   Daniell, Henry   Dano, Royal   Dantine, Helmut   D'Arcy, Roy

Darin, Bobby   Darro, Frankie   Darrow, John   Dassin, Jules   Dauphin, Claude   Davenport, Harry   Davis, Ossie

Davis, Sammy Jr   Davidson, John   Dean, James   De Cordova, Arturo   de Corsia, Ted   DeFore, Don   Dekker, Albert

Demarest, William   Denham, Maurice   Denning, Richard   Dennis, Nick   Denny, Reginald   Derek, John   De Sica, Vittorio

Devine, Andy   Dexter, Brad   Digges, Dudley   Dinehart, Allan   Dix, Richard   Donahue, Troy   Donald, James

Donat, Robert   Donath, Ludwig   Donovan, King   Donlevy, Brian   Dorn, Philip   Douglas, Don   Douglas, Kirk

Douglas, Melvyn   Douglas, Paul   Douglas, Robert   Drake, Charles   Drake, Tom   Driscoll, Bobby   Duff, Howard

Duggan, Andrew   Dumbrille, Douglas   Dumke, Ralph   Dunn, Eddie   Dunn, James   Durante, Jimmy   Duryea, Dan

Eastwood, Clint   Ebsen, Buddy   Eddy, Nelson   Edeson, Robert   Edwards, Cliff   Edwards, Jimmy   Egan, Richard

Eldredge, John   Elliott, Denholm   Ellis, Edward   Ellison, James   Emery, Gilbert   Emery, John   Erickson, Leif

Errol, Leon   Erwin, Stuart   Esmond, Carl   Evans, Clifford   Evans, Gene   Ewell, Tom   Fabrizi, Aldo

Fairbanks, Douglas   Fairbanks, Douglas Jr   Falk, Peter   Farley, Morgan   Farnum, William   Farr, Derek   Farrar, David

Farrell, Charles   Fawcett, George   Faylen, Frank   Feld, Fritz   Fernandel   Ferguson, Frank   Ferrer, Jose

Ferrer, Mel · Fetchit, Stepin · Fields, Sidney · Fields, W C · Finch, Peter · Finlayson, James H · Fitzgerald, Barry

Flippen, Jay C · Flynn, Errol · Fonda, Henry · Foran, Dick · Forbes, Ralph · Ford, Francis · Ford, Glenn

Ford, Paul · Ford, Wallace · Foster, Norman · Foster, Preston · Fowley, Douglas · Forrest, Steve · Foy, Eddie Jr

Francen, Victor · Franciosa, Anthony · Francis, Alec B · Franz, Arthur · Franz, Eduard · Frawley, William · Frazer, Robert

Freed, Bert · Freeman, Howard · Fresnay, Pierre · Fritsch, Willy · Frobe, Gert · Gabin, Jean · Gable, Clark

Gaines, Richard · Gallagher, Richard S · Gallaudet, John · Gardiner, Reginald · Garfield, John · Gargan, William · Garner, James

Gassman, Vittorio   Gates, Larry   Gazzara, Ben   Geer, Will   Gelin, Daniel   Genn, Leo   Gilbert, Billy

Gilbert, John   Gillingwater, Claude   Gilmore, Lowell   Givot, George   Glass, Gaston   Gleason, Jackie   Gleason, James

Gleckler, Robert   Gobel, George   Gomez, Thomas   Goodwin, Bill   Gorcey, Leo   Gordon, C Henry   Gordon, Gavin

Goring, Marius   Gottschalk, Ferdinand   Gough, Lloyd   Gough, Michael   Graff, Wilton   Granger, Farley   Grant, Cary

Grapewin, Charley   Greene, Richard   Greenstreet, Sydney   Gregson, John   Griffith, Hugh   Guinness, Sir Alec   Gwenn, Edmund

Haas, Hugo   Hackett, Buddy   Hadley, Reed   Haines, William   Hale, Allan   Hale, Creighton   Haley, Jack

Hall, Huntz   Hall, Jon   Hall, Thurston   Halliday, John   Halop, Billy   Hamilton, George   Hamilton, Hale

Hamilton, Mahlon   Hamilton, Murray   Hamilton, Neil   Hampden, Walter   Hanley, Jimmy   Hardie, Russell   Hardwicke, Sir Cedric

Hardy, Oliver   Hardy, Sam   Harlan, Kenneth   Harrigan, William   Harris, Phil   Harrison, Rex   Harron, Donald

Hart, Teddy   Hart, William S   Hartnell, William   Harvey, Laurence   Harvey, Paul   Hatton, Raymond   Hawkins, Jack

Hayakawa, Sessue   Hayden, Sterling   Haydn, Richard   Hayes, Gabby   Hayward, Louis   Healy, Ted   Heflin, Van

Heggie, O P   Henreid, Paul   Henry, William   Herbert, Henry   Herbert, Hugh   Hersholt, Jean   Heston, Charlton

Heydt, Louis Jean   Hicks, Russell   Hiers, Walter   Hinds, Samuel S   Hitchcock, Alfred   Hobbes, Halliwell   Hodiak, John

Hoey, Dennis   Hohl, Arthur   Holden, William   Holloway, Stanley   Holloway, Sterling   Holmes, Phillips   Holmes, Taylor

Holt, Jack   Holt, Tim   Homeier, Skip   Homolka, Oscar   Hope, Bob   Hopton, Russell   Hordern, Michael

Horton, Edward Everett   Houston, Donald   Howard, John   Howard, Leslie   Howard, Ronald   Howard, Trevor   Huber, Harold

Hudd, Walter   Hudson, Rock   Hughes, Lloyd   Hull, Henry   Hunter, Ian   Hunter, Jeffrey   Hunter, Tab

Hurst, Brandon   Huston, John   Huston, Walter   Hutton, Robert   Hyde-White, Wilfrid   Ichikawa, Somegoro   Ichikawa, Utaemon

Imhof, Roger	Ince, Ralph	Ingram, Rex	Interlenghi, Franco	Ireland, John	Irving, George S	Ives, Burl
Iwatare, Yukhiro	Jackson, Thomas	Jaffe, Sam	Jagger, Dean	Jannings, Emil	Janssen, David	Jenkins, Allen
Johns, Mervyn	Jolson, Al	Johnson, Van	Jones, Barry	Jones, Dean	Jones, Gordon	Jordan, Bobby
Jory, Victor	Joslyn, Allyn	Jourdan, Louis	Jouvet, Louis	—Joy, Nicholas	Jurgens, Curt	Justice, James Robertson
Kaliz, Armand	Karloff, Boris	Karns, Roscoe	Kasznar, Kurt	Katch, Kurt	Kaye, Danny	Keane, Robert Emmett
Keating, Larry	Keaton, Buster	Keel, Howard	Keith, Brian	Keith, Ian	Kellaway, Cecil	Kelly, Gene

Kelly, Paul   Kennedy, Arthur   Kennedy, Edgar   Kennedy, George   Kennedy, Tom   Kent, Robert   Kerrigan, J M

Kerry, Norman   Kibbee, Guy   Kilbride, Percy   Kilian, Victor   King, Claude   Kingsford, Walter   Kinskey, Leonid

Knotts, Don   Knox, Alexander   Kohler, Fred   Kolb, Clarence   Kolker, Henry   Kortner, Fritz   Kosleck, Martin

Kossoff, David   Kovaks, Ernie   Krauss, Werner   Kroeger, Berry   Kruger, Otto   Ladd, Alan   Ladd, David

Lahr, Bert   Lake, Arthur   Lamas, Fernando   Lancaster, Burt   Langan, Glenn   Langdon, Harry   Lanza, Mario

La Rocque, Rod   La Rue, Jack   Laughton, Charles   Laurel, Stan   Lawford, Peter   Lawrence, Marc   Lawson, Wilfrid

Lawton, Frank   Lebedeff, Ivan   Lederer, Francis   Lee, Billy   Lee, Christopher   Leiber, Fritz   Leister, Frederick

Lembeck, Harvey   Lemmon, Jack   Leonard, Sheldon   Lessey, George   Levene, Sam   Lewis, George   Lewis, Jerry

Lewis, Mitchell   Liberace   Linden, Eric   Litel, John   Livesey, Roger   Lloyd, Harold   Lloyd, Norman

Lockhart, Gene   Loder, John   Long, Richard   Longden, John   Lorre, Peter   Louis, Willard   Love, Montagu

Lovejoy, Frank   Lovell, Raymond   Lowe, Edmund   Lowery, Robert   Lugosi, Bela   Lukas, Paul   Luke, Keye

Lulli, Folco   Lund, John   Lundigan, William   Lydon, Jimmy   Lyon, Ben   Lynn, Jeffrey   Lytell, Bert

MacArthur, James   MacBride, Donald   McCarthy, Kevin   McCrea, Joel   MacDonald, J Farrell   McDowall, Roddy   McGiver, John

McGlynn, Frank   McGrail, Walter   McGraw, Charles   McHugh, Frank   McIntire, John   McIntosh, Burr   McKern, Leo

McKim, Robert   McLaglen, Victor   MacLane, Barton   MacMahon, Horace   MacMurray, Fred   McNally, Stephen   McQueen, Steve

MacRae, Gordon   Macready, George   McWade, Robert   Malden, Karl   Malleson, Miles   Manners, David   March, Fredric

Marion, George   Marlowe, Hugh   Marmont, Percy   Marshal, Alan   Marshall, E G   Marshall, Herbert   Marshall, Tully

Martin, Dean   Martin, Tony   Marvin, Lee   Marx, Groucho   Marx, Harpo   Mason, James   Massey, Raymond

Massie, Paul   Mastroianni, Marcello   Mather, Aubrey   Matieson, Otto   Matthau, Walter   Matthews, A E   Matthews, Lester

Mature, Victor   Maxwell, Edwin   Mazurki, Mike   Meek, Donald   Meeker, George   Meeker, Ralph   Meighan, Thomas

Menjou, Adolphe   Meredith, Burgess   Merrill, Gary   Middleton, Charles   Middleton, Guy   Middleton, Robert   Mifune, Toshiro

Miles, Bernard   Miljan, John   Milland, Ray   Miller, Glenn   Mills, John   Milner, Martin   Mineo, Sal

Mitchell, Cameron   Mitchell, Grant   Mitchell, Millard   Mitchell, Thomas   Mitchum, Robert   Mix, Tom   Mohr, Gerald

Montalban, Ricardo   Montand, Yves   Montgomery, George   Montgomery, Robert   Moore, Dickie   Moore, Kieron   Moore, Tom

Moore, Victor   More, Kenneth   Moreno, Antonio   Morgan, Dennis   Morgan, Frank   Morgan, Gene   Morgan, Henry

Morgan, Ralph   Morley, Robert   Morris, Chester   Morris, Wayne   Morse, Robert   Mostel, Zero   Mowbray, Alan

Muir, Gavin   Mulhall, Jack   Mundin, Herbert   Muni, Paul   Murat, Jean   Murphy, Audie   Murphy, George

Murray, Charles   Murray, Don   Murray, James   Muse, Clarence   Nagel, Conrad   Naish, J Carrol   Naismith, Laurence

Newley, Anthony   Newman, Paul   Newton, Robert   Newton, Theodore   Nichols, George   Nicol, Alex   Niven, David

Nolan, Lloyd   Norton, Barry   Novarro, Ramon   Novello, Jay   Nugent, Edward   Oakie, Jack   Ober, Philip

O'Brian, Hugh

O'Brien, Edmond

O'Brien, George

O'Brien, Pat

O'Connell, Arthur

O'Connell, Hugh

O'Connor, Donald

O'Dea, Denis

O'Herlihy, Dan

O'Keefe, Dennis

Oland, Warner

Olivier, Sir Laurence

O'Malley, Pat

O'Neill, Henry

Opatoshu, David

Oscar, Henry

Oscarsson, Per

O'Shea, Michael

O'Toole, Peter

Overman, Lynne

Owen, Reginald

Owsley, Monroe

Page, Bradley

Palance, Jack

Pallette, Eugene

Pangborn, Franklin

Parker, Barnett

Parker, Cecil

Parker, Willard

Parks, Larry

Pate, Michael

Patrick, Nigel

Pawley, Edward

Payne, John

Peck, Gregory

Pendleton, Nat

Penner, Joe

Peppard, George

Percy, Esme

Perier, Francois

Perkins, Anthony

Persoff, Nehemiah

Persson, Edvard	Petrie, Hay	Petrie, Howard	Philipe, Gerard	Piccoli, Michel	Pidgeon, Walter	Pinza, Ezio
Pleasance, Donald	Plummer, Christopher	Poitier, Sidney	Portman, Eric	Powell, Dick	Powell, William	Power, Tyrone
Powers, Tom	Presley, Elvis	Preston, Robert	Price, Dennis	Price, Vincent	Prival, Lucien	Prouty, Jed
Pryor, Roger	Purcell, Dick	Purcell, Noel	Purdom, Edmund	Qualen, John	Quayle, Anthony	Quinn, Anthony
Quillan, Eddie	Radford, Basil	Raft, George	Ragland, "Rags"	Raimu, Jules	Rains, Claude	Randall, Tony
Randell, Ron	Randolph, Donald	Rasumny, Mikhail	Rathbone, Basil	Ratoff, Gregory	Rawlinson, Herbert	Ray, Aldo

Ray, Charles   Raymond, Gene   Reagan, Ronald   Redgrave, Michael   Redmond, Liam   Reed, Alan   Reed, George

Reed, Philip   Reeves, George   Reeves, Steve   Regan, Phil   Reggiani, Serge   Reicher, Frank   Reid, Carl Benton

Rennie, James   Rennie, Michael   Rhodes, Erik   Richardson, Sir Ralph   Ricciardi, William   Richmond, Kane   Ridgely, John

Ridges, Stanley   Rigby, Edward   Ritz Brothers   Robards, Jason Sr   Robards, Jason Jr   Rober, Richard   Roberts, Theodore

Robertson, Cliff   Robertson, Dale   Robertson, Willard   Robeson, Paul   Robinson, Dewey   Robinson, Edward G   Rogers, Paul

Rogers, Will   Roland, Gilbert   Rolfe, Guy   Romero, Cesar   Rooney, Mickey   Rooney, Mickey   Rorke, Hayden

Rubinstein, Artur

Ruggles, Charles

Rumann, Siegfried

Russell, Harold

Russell, John

Ryan, Robert

Sabu

St John, Howard

Sakall, S Z

Sande, Walter

Sanders, George

Sands, Tommy

Savalas, Telly

Sawyer, Joe

Schell, Maximilian

Schildkraut, Joseph

Scott, George C

Scott, Randolph

Scott, Zachary

Scourby, Alexander

Searl, Jackie

Seay, James

Segal, George

Seigner, Louis

Sellers, Peter

Sharif, Omar

Shatner, William

Shaughnessy, Mickey

Shean, Al

Sheehan, John Jr

Sheffield, Reginald

Sherman, Lowell

Shields, Arthur

Sidney, George

Siegmann, George

Sills, Milton

Silva, Henry

Silvers, Phil

Sim, Alastair

Simon, Michel

Simon, Robert

Simpson, Ivan

Sinatra, Frank

Skelton, Red

Slezak, Leo

Slezak, Walter

Sloane, Everett

Smith, Art

Smith, C Aubrey

Smith, Kent

Sofaer, Abraham

Sokoloff, Vladimir

Soler, Julian

Sparks, Ned

Spencer, Douglas

Squire, Ronald

Stack, Robert

Stack, William

Stander, Lionel

Standing, Sir Guy

Starrett, Charles

Steel, Anthony

Steiger, Rod

Stepanek, Karl

Stephens, Harvey

Stephenson, Henry

Stephenson, James

Sterling, Ford

Sterling, Robert

Stevens, Craig

Stevens, Mark

Stevens, Onslow

Stewart, James

Stockwell, Dean

Stockwell, Dean

Stone, George E

Stone, Lewis

Stone, Milburn

Strauss, Robert

Strong, Leonard

Strudwick, Shepperd

Sullivan, Barry

Sullivan, Francis L

Summerville, Slim

Sundberg, Clinton   Sydney, Basil   Sydow, Max von   Talbot, Lyle   Tamblyn, Russ   Tamiroff, Akim   Tannen, William

Tapley, Colin   Taylor, Don   Taylor, Kent   Taylor, Robert   Taylor, Rod   Taylor, Vaughn   Tearle, Conway

Tellegen, Lou   Terry-Thomas   Thatcher, Torin   Thomas, Danny   Thomas, Jameson   Thompson, Marshall   Tibbett, Lawrence

Tierney, Lawrence   Tobias, George   Todd, Richard   Toler, Sidney   Tombes, Andrew   Tone, Franchot   Toomey, Regis

Torrence, Ernest   Tracy, Lee   Tracy, Spencer   Tracy, William   Travers, Henry   Treacher, Arthur   Triesault, Ivan

Truex, Ernest   Tryon, Glenn   Tucker, Forrest   Tucker, Richard   Tufts, Sonny   Tully, Tom   Tyler, Tom

Ustinov, Peter	Valentino, Rudolph	Vallee, Rudy	Vallone, Raf	Van Cleef, Lee	Van Dyke, Dick	Van Eyck, Peter
Varconi, Victor	Veidt, Conrad	Vincent, Allen	Vincent, Romo	Vinton, Arthur	Von Eltz, Theodore	Von Stroheim, Eric
Vye, Murvyn	Wadsworth, Henry	Wagner, Robert	Walbrook, Anton	Walburn, Raymond	Waldridge, Harold	Waldron, Charles
Walker, Robert	Wallach, Eli	Walthall, Henry B	Walton, Douglas	Warden, Jack	Warner, H B	Warner, Jack
Warren, E Alyn	Warwick, Robert	Washburn, Bryant	Wayne, David	Wayne, John	Wayne, John	Webb, Clifton
Webb, Jack	Webb, Richard	Wegener, Paul	Wengraf, John	Weismuller, Johnny	Welles, Orson	Werner, Oskar

Westcott, Gordon

Whalen, Michael

Wheeler, Bert

White, Jesse

Whitman, Stuart

Whitmore, James

Widmark, Richard

Wilcoxon, Henry

Wilde, Cornel

Wilder, Billy

Wilding, Michael

William, Warren

Williams, Bill

Williams, Emlyn

Williams, Guinn

Williams, Hugh

Williams, John

Williams, Rhys

Willock, Dave

Wills, Chill

Winninger, Charles

Winninger, Charles

Winters, Jonathan

Winters, Roland

Wolheim, Louis

Woods, Donald

Woolley, Monty

Woolsey, Robert

Worlock, Frederic

Wray, John

Wynn, Ed

Wynn, Keenan

Young, Gig

Young, Robert

Young, Roland

Zimbalist, Efrem Jr

Zucco, George

Adams, Julie	Addams, Dawn	Adoree, Renee	Adrian, Iris	Aguglia, Mimi	Aimee, Anouk	Aked, Muriel
Alberghetti, Anna Maria	Albright, Lola	Alexander, Katharine	Allan, Elizabeth	Allbritton, Louise	Allen, Gracie	Allen, Judith
Allgood, Sara	Allwyn, Astrid	Allyson, June	Ames, Adrienne	Anderson, Dame Judith	Anderson, Mary	Andress, Ursula
Andrews, Julie	Angel, Heather	Angeli, Pier	Ankers, Evelyn	Ann-Margret	Annabella	Arden, Eve
Armida	Arnoul, Francoise	Arthur, Jean	Astor, Mary	Aubert, Lenore	Ayres, Agnes	Bacall, Lauren
Baclanova, Olga	Baddeley, Hermione	Bainter, Fay	Baker, Carroll	Baker, Diane	Ball, Lucille	Bancroft, Anne

Bankhead, Tallulah	Banky, Vilma	Bara, Theda	Bardot, Brigitte	Bari, Lynn	Barnes, Binnie	Barondess, Barbara
Barrett, Edith	Barrie, Mona	Barrie, Wendy	Barry, Phyllis	Barrymore, Ethel	Bartok, Eva	Basquette, Lina
Bates, Florence	Baxter, Anne	Beavers, Louise	Bedford, Barbara	Beecher, Janet	Bel Geddes, Barbara	Bell, Marie
Bellamy, Madge	Bennett, Belle	Bennett, Constance	Bennett, Joan	Bergen, Polly	Bergman, Ingrid	Best, Edna
Blaine, Vivian	Blair, Janet	Blane, Sally	Blondell, Joan	Bloom, Claire	Blyth, Ann	Blyth, Betty
Boardman, Eleanor	Boland, Mary	Bondi, Beulah	Booth, Shirley	Borden, Olive	Borg, Veda Ann	Bow, Clara

Bradley, Grace	Bradna, Olympe	Brady, Alice	Brent, Evelyn	Brian, Mary	Britt, May	Britton, Barbara
Broderick, Helen	Bronson, Betty	Brooke, Hilary	Brooks, Phyllis	Brown, Vanessa	Browne, Coral	Bruce, Virginia
Bryan, Dora	Bryant, Nana	Burgess, Dorothy	Burke, Billie	Burke, Kathleen	Busch, Mae	Byington, Spring
Byron, Kathleen	Byron, Marion	Calvet, Corinne	Calvert, Phyllis	Campbell, Beatrice	Campbell, Judy	Capucine
Cardinale, Claudia	Carey, Joyce	Carlisle, Kitty	Carlisle, Mary	Carol, Martine	Carol, Sue	Caron, Leslie
Carr, Mary	Carroll, Madeleine	Carroll, Nancy	Carter, Janis	Carton, Pauline	Carver, Lynne	Castle, Peggie

Caulfield, Joan | Chadwick, Helene | Champion, Marge | Chandler, Helen | Charisse, Cyd | Chase, Ilka | Chatterton, Ruth

Christian, Linda | Christians, Mady | Christie, Julie | Christine, Virginia | Churchill, Marguerite | Clark, Petula | Clarke, Mae

Clayworth, June | Clifford, Ruth | Clooney, Rosemary | Clyde, June | Colbert, Claudette | Coleman, Nancy | Collier, Constance

Collins, Joan | Collyer, June | Compton, Fay | Compton, Joyce | Compton, Juliette | Cortese, Valentina | Courtney, Inez

Crain, Jeanne | Crawford, Joan | Crews, Laura Hope | Cristal, Linda | Crosman, Henrietta | Cummings, Constance | Cummins, Peggy

Dahl, Arlene | Dale, Esther | Dandridge, Dorothy | Daniels, Bebe | Darcel, Denise | Darnell, Linda | Darrieux, Danielle

Darwell, Jane   Davies, Marion   Davis, Bette   Davis, Joan   D'Avril, Yola   Daw, Marjorie   Day, Doris

Day, Laraine   Day, Marceline   De Camp, Rosemary   De Carlo, Yvonne   Dee, Frances   Dee, Ruby   Dee, Sandra

De Haven, Gloria   De Havilland, Olivia   Del Rio, Dolores   Demongeot, Mylène   Deyers, Lien   Dickinson, Angie   Dietrich, Marlene

Dodd, Claire   Donnelly, Ruth   Doran, Mary   Dors, Diana   Dorziat, Gabrielle   Doucet, Catherine   Dove, Billie

Drago, Eleonora Rossi   Drake, Betsy   Drake, Frances   Dresser, Louise   Dressler, Marie   Drew, Ellen   Dru, Joanne

Duke, Patty   Dumont, Margaret   Dunaway, Faye   Duncan, Mary   Dunn, Emma   Dunn, Josephine   Dunne, Irene

Dunnock, Mildred	Durbin, Deanna	Dvorak, Ann	Eaton, Shirley	Edwards, Sarah	Eggerth, Marta	Eilers, Sally
Ekberg, Anita	Eldridge, Florence	Ellis, Patricia	Elsom, Isobel	Emerson, Faye	Emerson, Hope	Esmond, Jill
Evans, Dame Edith	Evans, Madge	Farmer, Frances	Farrell, Glenda	Farrow, Mia	Faye, Alice	Faye, Julia
Fazenda, Louise	Ferguson, Elsie	Feuillere, Edwige	Field, Betty	Field, Virginia	Fields, Gracie	Fitzgerald, Geraldine
Fleming, Rhonda	Flint, Helen	Foch, Nina	Fonda, Jane	Fontaine, Joan	Fonteyn, Margot	Forrest, Sally
Foster, Susanna	Francis, Anne	Francis, Kay	Francis, Noel	Fraser, Elisabeth	Freeman, Helen	Freeman, Mona

Furness, Betty

Gam, Rita

Garbo, Greta

Gardner, Ava

Garland, Judy

Garner, Peggy Ann

Garson, Greer

Gates, Nancy

Gateson, Marjorie

Gaynor, Janet

Gaynor, Mitzi

George, Gladys

Gibson, Wynne

Gifford, Frances

Gish, Dorothy

Gish, Lillian

Goddard, Paulette

Gombell, Minna

Gordon, Mary

Grable, Betty

Grahame, Gloria

Gray, Nadia

Grayson, Kathryn

Greenwood, Charlotte

Greenwood, Joan

Greer, Jane

Grey, Nan

Haden, Sara

Hagen, Jean

Haid, Liane

Hale, Barbara

Hale, Louise Closser

Hamilton, Margaret

Harlow, Jean

Harris, Julie

Hart, Dolores

Harvey, Lilian

Haver, June

Haver, Phyllis

Havoc, June

Hayes, Bernadine

Hayes, Helen

Hayward, Susan	Hayworth, Rita	Helm, Brigitte	Hendrix, Wanda	Henie, Sonja	Hepburn, Audrey	Hepburn, Katharine
Hervey, Irene	Hiller, Wendy	Hobart, Rose	Hobson, Valerie	Holden, Fay	Holden, Gloria	Holliday, Judy
Holm, Celeste	Hopkins, Miriam	Hoppe, Marianne	Hopper, Hedda	Horn, Camilla	Howland, Jobyna	Hudson, Rochelle
Hume, Benita	Hughes, Mary Beth	Hunt, Marsha	Hunt, Martita	Hussey, Ruth	Hutchinson, Josephine	Hutton, Betty
Hyams, Leila	Hyer, Martha	Hylton, Jane	Inescort, Frieda	Irving, Margaret	Jergens, Adele	Jewell, Isabel
Johns, Glynis	Johnson, Kay	Johnson, Rita	Jones, Carolyn	Jones, Jennifer	Jones, Shirley	Jordan, Dorothy

Joy, Leatrice	Joyce, Alice	Joyce, Brenda	Judge, Arlene	Karina, Anna	Keeler, Ruby	Keller, Helen
Kelly, Grace	Kelly, Kitty	Kelly, Nancy	Kelly, Patsy	Kendall, Kay	Kennedy, Madge	Kent, Barbara
Kent, Dorothea	Kent, Jean	Kenyon, Doris	Kerr, Deborah	Keyes, Evelyn	King, Andrea	Kitt, Eartha
Knapp, Evalyn	Koscina, Sylva	Kruger, Alma	Kwan, Nancy	Kyo, Machiko	Lake, Florence	Lake, Veronica
Lamarr, Hedy	Lamont, Molly	Lamour, Dorothy	Lanchester, Elsa	Landi, Elissa	Landis, Carole	Landis, Jessie Royce
Lane, Lola	Lane, Nora	Lane, Priscilla	Lane, Rosemary	Lang, June	Langford, Frances	Lansbury, Angela

La Plante, Laura

La Verne, Lucille

Lawrence, Barbara

Lawrence, Gertrude

Lee, Anna

Lee, Dorothy

Lee, Gwen

Lee, Lila

Leigh, Janet

Leigh, Vivien

Leighton, Margaret

Leslie, Joan

Lindfors, Viveca

Lindsay, Margaret

Lister, Moira

Lloyd, Doris

Lockhart, Kathleen

Lockwood, Margaret

Logan, Jacqueline

Lohr, Marie

Lollobrigida, Gina

Lombard, Carole

London, Julie

Loren, Sophia

Louise, Anita

Love, Bessie

Lowell, Helen

Loy, Myrna

Lualdi, Antonella

Lupino, Ida

Lynley, Carol

Lynn, Diana

Lynn, Sharon

McAvoy, May

McCambridge, Mercedes

McDaniel, Hattie

MacDonald, Jeanette

McGuire, Dorothy

Mack, Helen

MacLaine, Shirley

MacMahon, Aline

Magnani, Anna

Main, Marjorie   Malone, Dorothy   Mangano, Silvana   Mansfield, Jayne   Maricle, Leona   Maris, Mona   Marsh, Joan

Marsh, Mae   Marsh, Marian   Marshall, Brenda   Martin, Mary   Martinelli, Elsa   Massey, Ilona   Mattox, Martha

Maxwell, Lois   Maxwell, Marilyn   Mayo, Virginia   Medina, Patricia   Mercer, Beryl   Mercouri, Melina   Merkel, Una

Merman, Ethel   Methot, Mayo   Meyer, Greta   Michael, Gertrude   Miles, Vera   Miller, Ann   Miller, Patsy Ruth

Mills, Hayley   Miranda, Carmen   Miranda, Isa   Mitchell, Geneva   Monroe, Marilyn   Montez, Maria   Moore, Colleen

Moore, Constance   Moore, Dennie   Moore, Grace   Moore, Terry   Moorehead, Agnes   Moran, Lois   Moran, Peggy

Moran, Polly

Moreau, Jeanne

Moreno, Rosita

Morgan, Michele

Morison, Patricia

Morlay, Gaby

Morley, Karen

Mueller, Renate

Muir, Jean

Munsel, Patrice

Munson, Ona

Murphy, Mary

Myers, Carmel

Nagel, Anne

Natwick, Mildred

Nazimova, Alla

Neagle, Anna

Neal, Patricia

Neff, Hildegarde

Negri, Pola

Nesbitt, Cathleen

Newmar, Julie

Nilsson, Anna Q

Nissen, Greta

Nixon, Marian

Nolan, Mary

North, Sheree

Novak, Kim

Oberon, Merle

O'Brien, Margaret

O'Connor, Una

O'Hara, Maureen

Oliver, Edna May

Olmsted, Gertrude

Ondra, Anny

O'Neil, Nance

Osborne, Vivienne

O'Sullivan, Maureen

Ottiano, Rafaela

Ouspenskaya, Maria

Page, Anita

Page, Gale

Page, Geraldine   Paget, Debra   Paige, Janis   Paige, Mabel   Palmer, Lilli   Papas, Irene   Parker, Cecilia

Parker, Eleanor   Parker, Jean   Parker, Suzy   Parrish, Helen   Patrick, Gail   Patrick, Lee   Patterson, Elizabeth

Pepper, Barbara   Percy, Eileen   Perreau, Gigi   Peters, Jean   Peters, Susan   Peterson, Dorothy   Peterson, Dorothy

Pickford, Mary   Pilbeam, Nova   Pitts, Zasu   Pleshette, Suzanne   Powell, Eleanor   Powell, Jane   Presle, Micheline

Prevost, Marie   Pringle, Aileen   Printemps, Yvonne   Prowse, Juliette   Quigley, Juanita   Rainer, Louise   Raines, Ella

Ralph, Jessie   Ralston, Esther   Ralston, Vera   Rambeau, Marjorie   Raye, Martha   Redgrave, Lynn   Reed, Donna

Remick, Lee	Revere, Anne	Revier, Dorothy	Reynolds, Debbie	Reynolds, Marjorie	Reynolds, Vera	Riano, Renie
Rice, Florence	Rich, Irene	Rich, Lillian	Risdon, Elizabeth	Ritter, Thelma	Roberts, Beverly	Roberts, Florence
Robin, Dany	Robinson, Madeleine	Robson, Dame Flora	Robson, May	Roc, Patricia	Rogers, Ginger	Rogers, Jean
Roman, Ruth	Rosay, Francoise	Ross, Shirley	Royle, Selena	Rush, Barbara	Russell, Gail	Russell, Jane
Russell, Rosalind	Rutherford, Ann	Rutherford, Margaret	Ryan, Peggy	Saint, Eva Marie	St. John, Betta	St. John, Jill
Sale, Virginia	Schafer, Natalie	Schell, Maria	Schneider, Magda	Schneider, Romy	Scott, Lizabeth	Scott, Martha

Sebastian, Dorothy

Seberg, Jean

Shannon, Peggy

Shearer, Moira

Shearer, Norma

Sheridan, Ann

Shirley, Anne

Shoemaker, Ann

Sidney, Sylvia

Signoret, Simone

Simmons, Jean

Simon, Simone

Singleton, Penny

Skipworth, Alison

Sleeper, Martha

Smith, Alexis

Sommer, Elke

Sondergaard, Gale

Sothern, Ann

Stanwyck, Barbara

Starke, Pauline

Stedman, Myrtle

Sten, Anna

Sterling, Jan

Stevens, Connie

Stevens, Rise

Strasberg, Susan

Streisand, Barbra

Stuart, Gloria

Sullavan, Margaret

Swanson, Gloria

Swarthout, Gladys

Sweet, Blanche

Swinburne, Nora

Sylvie

Talmadge, Constance

Tandy, Jessica

Tashman, Lilyan

Taylor, Elizabeth

Taylor, Estelle

Tell, Olive

Temple, Shirley

Terry, Alice	Terry, Sheila	Thatcher, Heather	Thaxter, Phyllis	Thulin, Ingrid	Tierney, Gene	Tobin, Genevieve
Todd, Ann	Todd, Thelma	Totter, Audrey	Travis, June	Tree, Dorothy	Treen, Mary	Trevor, Claire
Turner, Lana	Tushingham, Rita	Tuttle, Lurene	Twelvetrees, Helen	Valerie, Joan	Valli, Alida	Varden, Norma
Vaughn, Hilda	Velez, Lupe	Venable, Evelyn	Vidor, Florence	Vera-Ellen	Vinson, Helen	Vitti, Monica
Walker, Cheryl	Walker, Nella	Wall, Geraldine	Walsh, Kay	Ware, Helen	Warren, Katharine	Warrick, Ruth
Watson, Lucile	Weaver, Marjorie	Weidler, Virginia	Welch, Raquel	Wells, Jacqueline	West, Mae	Westley, Helen

Westman, Nydia

White, Alice

Whitty, Dame May

Wickes, Mary

Williams, Esther

Wilson, Lois

Wilson, Marie

Windsor, Claire

Windsor, Marie

Winters, Shelley

Winton, Jane

Withers, Googie

Withers, Jane

Witherspoon, Cora

Wong, Anna May

Wood, Natalie

Wood, Natalie

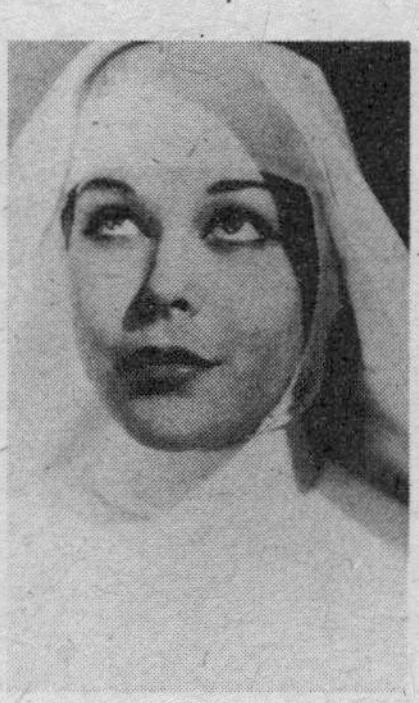

Woodbury, Joan

Woodward, Joanne

Wray, Fay

Wright, Teresa

Wyatt, Jane

Wyman, Jane

Wycherly, Margaret

Wynyard, Diana

Wynter, Dana

York, Susannah

Young, Loretta

Yurka, Blanche

Zetterling, Mai

III Index

NOTE: This index covers all the film reviews printed in The New York Times during the period 1913–1968. It is divided into two sections: Personal Name Index and Corporate Index.

The Personal Name Index lists every performer, producer, director, screenwriter, etc. mentioned in the reviews, with the function, if other than performer, in parenthesis following the name, and the titles of the movies with which the person was connected in chronological order.

The Corporate Index lists all producing, distributing and otherwise participating companies mentioned in the reviews by name, again with the function in parenthesis following the name, and the titles of the movies with which they were associated, in chronological order.

Additional explanations are given on the two sectional title pages.

Citations in this index refer to the publication in The New York Times, giving the year, month, section of the newspaper (if applicable), day, page and column; for example, 1919, O 5, IV, 5:3 indicates that the review appeared on October 5, 1919, Section IV, page 5, column 3. It thus permits the interested reader to locate the review in the bound volumes and microfilm editions of The Times as well as in the volumes containing exclusively the reprints of all Times film reviews.

In the preparation of an index of such scope—some 18,000 films were covered—inevitably some incorrect citations have occurred. The reader will find the correct citation in parenthesis following the incorrect entry. The remark "(In Addenda)" appended to some of the entries refers to another edition and should be disregarded by the reader of the present volume.

The months are abbreviated as follows:

Ja—January	My—May	S—September
F—February	Je—June	O—October
Mr—March	Jl—July	N—November
Ap—April	Ag—August	D—December

Persons

NOTE: All persons mentioned in the film reviews are listed here alphabetically, last name first. Their function in the films is listed after the name in parentheses, such as director, producer, screenwriter, etc. In entries where no such qualifier appears, the person was a performer (actor, actress, singer). A person with multiple functions will have multiple entries; for example, an actor who later turned producer or director will have two listings. A person having two functions in the same film will also have two listings. Functions that are very uncommon or are given imprecisely in the reviews are designated miscellaneous (misc).

During the compilation of this index it was found that many names appeared in variant spellings and with different surnames, nicknames and middle initials. An intensive effort was undertaken to reconcile such differences and to assure that all names appear accurately and unambiguously. Cross references between variants are used when unavoidable, generally when the variants are spaced far apart in the alphabet.

Names beginning with Mc are alphabetized as though spelled Mac.

Entries under each name are by title of film, in chronological order.

For an explanation of the Index generally and of the citations, see page 268.

A

Aabel, Hauk
En Glad Gutt 1933,N 24,25:7
Aadland, Beverly
Cuban Rebel Girls 1959,D 26,7:3
Aaker, Lee
Atomic City, The 1952,My 2,21:1
No Room for the Groom 1952,Je 14,12:2
Jeopardy 1953,Mr 31,36:2
Take Me to Town 1953,Je 20,8:6
Arena 1953,Jl 23,20:2
Hondo 1953,N 27,99:9
Aalten, Truus van
Geschichten aus dem Wienerwald; Tales From the
Vienna Woods 1935,N 2,13:3
Aames, Marlene
Best Years of our Lives, The 1946,N 22,27:2
Aaron, Charles
Do You Love Me 1946,My 25,12:2
Aaron, Levy
Guide, The 1965,F 10,44:2
Aasen, Johan
Why Worry? 1923,S 3,9:3
Aason, John
Legionnaires in Paris 1927,D 26,26:6
Abad, Nati
Heroes del Barrio, Los 1936,D 28,12:4
Abarbanel
Cantor's Son, The 1937,D 27,11:1
Abarbanel, Judith
Americaner Shadchen; American Matchmaker
1940,My 7,31:3
Abarbanel, Sam X (Producer)
Prehistoric Women 1950,D 29,15:5
Abarbanel, Sam X (Screenwriter)
Prehistoric Women 1950,D 29,15:5
Abashidze, D
Dragonfly, The 1955,Je 27,18:2
Abashidze, L
Dragonfly, The 1955,Je 27,18:2
Dragonfly, The 1955,Je 27,18:2
Scrapper, The 1959,D 14,42:2
Abba, Marta
Loyalty of Love 1937,Mr 1,15:1
Abbas, K A (Director)
Journey Beyond Three Seas 1960,Ap 11,42:6
Abbas, K A (Original Author)
Vagabond, The 1956,Ap 16,30:4
Abbas, K A (Screenwriter)
Vagabond, The 1956,Ap 16,30:4
Journey Beyond Three Seas 1960,Ap 11,42:6
Abbe, Charles
Cappy Ricks 1921,Ag 22,13:6
Homeward Bound 1923,Jl 31,12:4
West of the Water Tower 1923,D 31,9:3
Abbe, Jack
Tale of Two Worlds, A 1921,Mr 14,9:2
Abbe, James
White Sister, The 1923,S 6,10:2
Abbey, Edward (Original Author)
Lonely are the Brave 1962,Je 28,21:2
Abbey, William
Hawaii Calls 1938,Ap 29,17:2
ABBOT
See Also ABBOTT
Abbot, Anthony (Original Author)
Night Club Lady, The 1932,Ag 27,13:4
Circus Queen Murder, The 1933,My 9,20:5
President's Mystery, The 1936,O 19,22:1
Boomerang 1947,Mr 6,36:2
ABBOTT
See Also ABBOT
Abbott, Brian
Wild Innocence 1938,N 11,31:2
Abbott, Bud
One Night in the Tropics 1940,D 20,33:2
Buck Privates 1941,F 14,15:2
In the Navy 1941,Je 12,29:2
Hold That Ghost 1941,Ag 8,13:3
Keep 'Em Flying 1941,N 27,29:2
Ride 'Em Cowboy 1942,Mr 5,27:3
Rio Rita 1942,My 8,27:3
Pardon my Sarong 1942,Ag 27,15:1
Who Done It 1942,D 3,35:2
It Ain't Hay 1943,Mr 11,17:3
Hit the Ice 1943,S 23,27:2
In Society 1944,Ag 17,20:2
Lost in a Harem 1944,N 9,23:2
Here Come the Co-Eds 1945,F 19,21:1
Naughty Nineties, The 1945,Je 21,16:2
Abbott and Costello in Hollywood
1945,N 23,26:2
Little Giant 1946,My 9,27:5
Time of Their Lives, The 1946,N 28,40:2
Buck Privates Come Home 1947,Ap 12,11:3
Wistful Widow of Wagon Gap, The
1947,N 21,36:2
Noose Hangs High, The 1948,My 29,8:6
Abbott and Costello Meet Frankenstein
1948,Jl 29,17:2
Mexican Hayride 1949,Ja 12,33:3

Africa Screams 1949,My 5,34:2
Abbott and Costello Meet the Killer Boris Karloff
1949,S 19,18:3
Abbott and Costello in the Foreign Legion
1950,Ag 14,14:4
Abbott and Costello Meet the Invisible Man
1951,Ap 13,18:6
Comin' Round the Mountain 1951,Jl 27,15:2
Jack and the Beanstalk 1952,Ap 8,35:3
Dance With Me Henry 1956,D 24,8:2
Abbott, Dorothy
Gathering of Eagles, A 1963,Jl 11,21:2
Abbott, Eleanor Hallowell (Original Author)
Molly Make Believe 1916,Ap 17,9:3
Abbott, Elizabeth
Chad Hanna 1940,D 26,23:1
Abbott, George (Director)
Why Bring That Up? 1929,O 5,22:5
Half Way to Heaven 1929,D 7,19:3
Sea God, The 1930,S 6,9:2
Stolen Heaven 1931,F 14,11:4
Secrets of a Secretary 1931,Ag 29,16:3
My Sin 1931,S 11,24:2
Cheat, The 1931,D 12,23:3
Too Many Girls 1940,N 21,43:1
Pajama Game, The 1957,Ag 30,12:2
Damn Yankees 1958,S 27,12:7
Abbott, George (Miscellaneous)
All Quiet on The Western Front 1930,Ap 30,29:1
Abbott, George (Original Author)
Love 'Em and Leave 'Em 1926,D 8,24:3
Four Walls 1928,Ag 20,21:3
Coquette 1929,Ap 6,14:4 (In Addenda)
Broadway 1929,My 28,36:2
Saturday Night Kid, The 1929,N 16,25:2
Lilly Turner 1933,Je 15,21:2
Heat Lightning 1934,Mr 8,23:2
Straight Is the Way 1934,Ag 29,13:2
Three Men on a Horse 1936,N 26,39:1
On Your Toes 1939,O 21,12:2
Boys From Syracuse, The 1940,Ag 1,25:2
Highway West 1941,Ag 8,13:4
Broadway 1942,Je 5,23:2
Pajama Game, The 1957,Ag 30,12:2
Damn Yankees 1958,S 27,12:7
Abbott, George (Producer)
Boy Meets Girl 1938,Ag 27,7:2
Room Service 1938,S 22,27:1
Primrose Path 1940,Mr 23,16:2
Too Many Girls 1940,N 21,43:1
Pajama Game, The 1957,Ag 30,12:2
Damn Yankees 1958,S 27,12:7
Abbott, George (Screenwriter)
Pajama Game, The 1957,Ag 30,12:2
Damn Yankees 1958,S 27,12:7
Abbott, Gregory (Miscellaneous)
World in Flames, The 1940,O 24,31:2
Abbott, John
Missing Ten Days 1941,Ap 21,15:5 (In Addenda)
Joan of Paris 1942,Ja 26,18:2
Mrs Miniver 1942,Je 5,23:1
Get Help to Love 1942,O 19,15:3
Nightmare 1942,D 4,31:2
Gorilla Man, The 1943,Ja 15,21:4
They Got Me Covered 1943,Mr 5,20:2
Mission to Moscow 1943,Ap 30,25:2
Jane Eyre 1944,F 4,12:5
Mask of Dimitrios, The 1944,Je 24,16:2
Cry of the Werewolf, The 1944,Ag 12,16:5
Summer Storm 1944,O 23,14:3
Abroad With two Yanks 1944,O 26,19:7
Falcon in Hollywood, The 1944,D 9,21:2
Pursuit to Algiers 1945,O 27,12:2
Saratoga Trunk 1945,N 22,39:2
Bandit of Sherwood Forest, The 1946,Mr 23,8:4
One More Tomorrow 1946,My 25,12:2
Anna and the King of Siam 1946,Je 21,20:2
Deception 1946,O 19,15:3
Humoresque 1946,D 26,28:1
Time Out of Mind 1947,Ap 7,20:1
Web, The 1947,Je 5,32:1
Adventure Island 1947,O 20,29:2
If Winter Comes 1948,Ja 23,28:4
Woman in White, The 1948,My 8,12:2
Madame Bovary 1949,Ag 26,15:2
Her Wonderful Lie 1950,Jl 17,15:2
Thunder on the Hill 1951,O 18,32:3
Crosswinds 1951,D 7,35:4
Merry Widow, The 1952,S 25,38:1
Thunder in the East 1953,F 4,32:2
Sombrero 1953,Ap 23,37:2
Public Pigeon No 1 1957,My 18,23:2
Gigi 1958,My 16,21:1
Who's Minding the Store? 1963,N 29,67:6
(Incorrect in this edition; use 1963,N 28,67:6
elsewhere)
Greatest Story Ever Told, The 1965,F 16,40:2
Gambit 1966,D 22,40:2
Abbott, Marion
Backbone 1923,Ap 30,11:2
Abbott, Merriel Dancers
Smiling Faces 1932,Ag 31,12:3

Abbott, Merriel DAncers
Love Thy Neighbor 1940,D 18,32:5
Abbott, Merriel Dancers
Swing Fever 1944,Ja 28,14:1
Abbott, Norman (Director)
Last of the Secret Agents, The? 1966,Je 23,29:1
Abbott, Norman (Producer)
Last of the Secret Agents, The? 1966,Je 23,29:1
Abbott, Philip
Bachelor Party, The 1957,Ap 10,37:2
Sweet Bird of Youth 1962,Mr 29,28:2
Spiral Road, The 1962,Ag 4,11:2
Miracle of the White Stallions 1963,My 23,31:2
Those Calloways 1965,Ap 15,38:2
Abbott, Richard
Fountain, The 1934,Ag 31,14:1
Abdallah
Eagle with Two Heads 1948,D 30,24:2
Abduliah, Mohammed
Africa-Texas Style! 1967,Jl 13,30:2
Abdulla
I Cover the War 1937,Ag 2,10:2
Abdullah, Achmed (Original Author)
Hatchet Man, The 1932,F 4,25:2
Abdullah, Achmed (Screenwriter)
Lives of a Bengal Lancer, The 1935,Ja 12,12:2
Abdulov, O
Paris Commune 1937,Je 2,20:4
Gobsek 1937,Jl 16,22:1
Oppenheim Family, The 1939,My 24,29:2
Tanya 1942,Mr 5,27:1
Marriage 1945,F 22,31:3
Abdy, Harry
Wild Innocence 1938,N 11,31:2
Forty Thousand Horsemen 1941,Ag 15,13:2
Abe, Kobo (Screenwriter)
Woman in the Dunes; Suno no Onna
1964,S 17,52:1
Abe, Toru
Human Condition, The 1959,D 16,56:1
ABEL
See Also ABELL
Abel, Alfred
Metropolis 1927,Mr 7,16:3
Dr Nabuse 1927,Ag 10,21:4
Argent, L' 1929,Mr 3,VII,7:2 (Incorrect in this
edition; use 1929,Mr 3,VIII,8:5 in film)
Strauss, The Waltz King 1929,Jl 22,17:1
Dolly Macht Karriere; Dolly's Way to Stardom
1930,N 23,IX,6:2
Dolly Macht Karriere 1931,Jl 18,16:6
Meine Frau, Die Hochstaplerin 1932,F 6,14:4
Der Herr Buerovorsteher 1932,Je 17,24:1
1914: The Last Days Before the War 1932,S 5,9:6
Das Schicksal der Renate Langen 1933,N 4,18:4
Die Galavorstellung 1933,D 11,23:4
Maria, Die Magd 1937,My 22,19:2
Seltsamer Gast, Ein 1937,Jl 10,18:2
Salon Dora Green 1937,Jl 26,15:3
Sieben Ohrfeigen; Seven Slaps 1938,F 12,20:5
Kater Lampe 1938,Ap 23,19:3
Alle stehen Kopf; General Confusion
1940,Je 22,18:4
Argent, L' 1968,S 23,42:5
Abel, Alfred (Director)
Alles um Eine Frau 1935,D 21,11:1
Glueckliche Reise 1936,Ja 20,22:3
Abel, Allen (S I N A)
No More Excuses 1968,My 22,53:1
Abel, Fritz
Guardsman, The 1927,S 7,35:2
Abel, Michael (Producer)
Blueprint for Murder, A 1953,Jl 25,8:2
Abel, Walter
Liliom 1930,O 4,15:2
Three Musketeers, The 1935,N 1,25:1
Two in the Dark 1936,F 1,9:2
Lady Consents, The 1936,F 6,23:4
Witness Chair, The 1936,Ap 18,19:2
Fury 1936,Je 6,21:1
We Went to College 1936,Jl 27,20:2
Second Wife 1936,Ag 29,16:3
Green Light 1937,F 13,9:1
Portia on Trial 1937,D 3,29:2
Wise Girl 1938,Ja 10,13:3
Law of the Underworld 1938,Ap 28,27:2
Racket Busters 1938,Ag 11,13:1
Men With Wings 1938,O 27,27:2
King of the Turf 1939,My 8,21:2
Dance, Girl, Dance 1940,O 11,25:2
Arise my Love 1940,O 17,33:2
Michael Shayne, Private Detective
1940,D 19,33:2
Hold Back the Dawn 1941,O 2,29:1
Skylark 1941,N 20,39:2
Beyond the Blue Horizon 1942,Je 25,27:2
Holiday Inn 1942,Ag 5,16:1
Wake Island 1942,S 2,19:2
Star Spangled Rhythm 1942,D 31,20:1
So Proudly We Hail 1943,S 10,29:1
Fired Wife 1943,O 1,15:2
Mr Skeffington 1944,My 26,23:2
American Romance, An 1944,N 24,19:1

Abel, Walter— Cont
  Affairs of Susan, The 1945,Mr 29,18:2
  Duffy's Tavern 1945,S 6,23:3
  Kiss and Tell 1945,O 26,16:2
  Kid From Brooklyn, The 1946,Ap 19,25:2
  13 Rue Madeleine 1947,Ja 16,30:2
  Dream Girl 1948,Je 17,29:2
  That Lady in Ermine 1948,Ag 25,31:2
  So This Is Love 1953,Ag 12,22:1
  Island in the Sky 1953,S 10,22:2
  Night People 1954,Mr 13,11:2
  Indian Fighter, The 1955,D 22,20:1
  Steel Jungle, The 1956,Mr 10,9:5
  Bernardine 1957,Jl 25,28:1
  Raintree County 1957,D 21,22:1
  Mirage 1965,My 27,28:1
ABELL
  See Also ABEL
Abell, Walter
  North Wind's Malice, The 1920,O 18,13:1
Aber, Billy
  Born to the West 1926,Je 30,18:1 (In Addenda)
Aber, Nestor
  Half Way to Heaven 1929,D 7,19:3
  Penrod and Sam 1931,S 26,25:3
  Chandu the Magician 1932,O 1,10:4
Aberschal, Frank
  Torn Curtain 1966,Jl 28,23:1
Aberson, Helen (Original Author)
  Dumbo 1941,O 24,27:2
Abgulayev, L
  Arshin Takes a Wife 1950,Jl 31,13:6
Abich, Hans (Producer)
  Sins of Rose Bernd, The 1959,Ja 24,13:4 (In Addenda)
Abingdon, W L
  Manon Lescaut 1914,Je 14,15:1
Aboyneau, Robert
  Oh, Amelia 1951,D 3,22:2
Abraham, David
  Nine Hours to Rama 1963,Ap 4,58:2
Abraham, Johnston Dr (Original Author)
  Norah O'Neale 1934,O 25,26:3
Abraham, Paul (Composer)
  Privatsekretaerin, Der 1931,Je 12,27:1
  3:1 a Szerelem Javara; 3 to 1 for Love 1939,Mr 25,19:3
  Seeds of Freedom 1943,Ag 25,17:2
Abraham, Paul (Miscellaneous)
  Viktoria und Ihr Husar 1933,Ap 10,8:3
  Affairs of Maupassant, The 1938,F 12,20:2
Abraham, Zaky
  Little Miss Devil 1951,D 8,9:2
ABRAHAMSON
  See Also ABRAMSON
Abrahamson, Eric
  Rena Rama Sanningen; Nothing but the Truth 1939,O 7,11:2
Abraikosof
  Anna 1936,Jl 17,20:2
Abramov, A (Screenwriter)
  Alego 1954,D 27,22:7
Abramov, Vasili
  Girl From Leningrad 1941,D 20,25:2
Abramov, Viktor
  Sailor From the Comet, The 1959,Ag 3,21:2
Abramova, A (Screenwriter)
  Mussorgsky 1951,Ag 20,14:3
  Rimsky-Korsakov 1954,Mr 1,16:3
  Khovanshchina 1960,S 19,41:2
Abramovitch-Bleck, S (Screenwriter)
  Heroes of the Sea 1941,Ap 28,11:2
Abramowitz, Bina
  Broken Hearts 1926,Mr 3,26:1
Abrams, Leon (Original Author)
  Heat Lightning 1934,Mr 8,23:2
  Highway West 1941,Ag 8,13:4
  Mummy's Curse, The 1945,Mr 31,16:1
Abrams, Margaret (Original Author)
  Uncle, The 1966,Jl 19,34:1
Abrams, Margaret (Screenwriter)
  Uncle, The 1966,Jl 19,34:1
ABRAMSON
  See Also ABRAHAMSON
Abramson, Ivan (Director)
  Enlighten Thy Daughter 1917,Ja 29,11:2
  I Am the Man 1925,Mr 6,23:1
  Lying Wives 1925,Je 17,16:2
Abramson, Ivan (Original Author)
  Enlighten Thy Daughter 1917,Ja 29,11:2
Abramson, Ivan (Screenwriter)
  I Am the Man 1925,Mr 6,23:1
  Lying Wives 1925,Je 17,16:2
Abramson, Robert
  8 X 8 1957,Mr 16,13:2
Abrham, Josef
  Transport From Paradise 1967,F 8,22:1
  Happy End 1968,Je 11,54:4
Abrikosof, A
  Grain 1936,Ja 16,25:2
Abrikosof, D
  Pozor 1933,Mr 11,18:4

Abrikosof, M
  Cossacks of the Don 1932,Mr 19,11:2
Abrikosov, A
  Paris Commune 1937,Je 2,20:4
Abrikosov, Alexander
  Girl From Leningrad 1941,D 20,25:2
  Ivan the Terrible, Part I 1947,Mr 10,25:2
Abrikosov, Andrei
  Turning Point, The 1946,O 28,19:4
  Ivan the Terrible, Part II 1959,N 25,22:4
  Sword and the Dragon, The 1960,N 17,46:3
Abrikossov, A L
  Alexander Nevsky 1939,Mr 23,27:1
Abriksov, C
  Wrestler and the Clown, The 1959,Ja 1,38:1
Absolon, A
  Seven Brave Men 1936,Je 15,24:2
Abuladze, Tenghiz (Director)
  Magdana's Donkey 1958,Ja 27,21:7
  Stepchildren 1962,Jl 2,22:2
Abuladze, Tenghiz (Producer)
  Stepchildren 1962,Jl 2,22:2
Abuladze, Tenghiz (Screenwriter)
  Magdana's Donkey 1958,Ja 27,21:7
  Stepchildren 1962,Jl 2,22:2
Accursi, Claude (Screenwriter)
  Voyage Surprise 1948,F 14,17:3
  Theodora, Slave Empress 1955,Ja 12,24:2
Ace, Goodman (Screenwriter)
  I Married a Woman 1958,N 5,42:5
Ace (Dog)
  Blind Alibi 1938,My 20,17:2
  Girl From God's Country 1940,S 9,18:5
Acero, Ricardo
  Mad Queen, The 1950,O 27,24:3
Acevedo, Manuel (Original Author)
  Song of Dolores 1951,Je 16,9:2
Achard, Marcel (Director)
  Paris Waltz, The 1950,Ag 23,35:2
Achard, Marcel (Miscellaneous)
  Twilight 1949,D 30,13:2
  Days of our Years 1951,D 6,42:2
Achard, Marcel (Original Author)
  Heart of Paris 1939,Ja 13,17:3
  Alibi, L' 1939,Ap 10,13:3
  Lady in Question, The 1940,D 10,33:2
  Paris Waltz, The 1950,Ag 23,35:2
  Shot in the Dark, A 1964,Je 24,28:1
  Friend of the Family 1965,N 18,55:3
Achard, Marcel (Screenwriter)
  Heart of a Nation, The 1943,Ap 8,27:2
  Female, The 1960,Ap 28,29:1
Achi, Kamaunani
  White Heat 1934,Je 16,20:2
Acho, M Torres
  Manhunt in the Jungle 1958,Ap 12,13:1
Acker, Jean
  Checkers 1919,Ag 25,8:5
  Spellbound 1945,N 2,22:2
Acker, Sharon
  Lucky Jim 1958,S 1,8:6
  Point Blank 1967,S 19,53:1
Ackerman, Jack
  Shadows 1961,Mr 22,37:1
Ackerman, Leonard J (Producer)
  Al Capone 1959,Mr 26,27:1
Ackerman, Walter
  Back to God's Country 1927,O 24,24:3
Ackland, Joss
  Midsummer Night's Dream, A 1961,D 19,39:1
Ackland, Rodney (Miscellaneous)
  Lady Surrenders, A 1947,Je 20,25:6
Ackland, Rodney (Original Author)
  Three on a Week-End 1938,Je 2,19:3
Ackland, Rodney (Screenwriter)
  Three on a Week-End 1938,Je 2,19:3
  Continental Express 1942,Ap 7,26:3
  Wanted for Murder 1946,D 12,38:4
  Temptation Harbor 1949,My 11,34:7
  Queen of Spades, The 1949,Jl 1,14:4
  Bond Street 1950,Mr 30,40:6
Ackles, Ken
  Bodyhold 1949,D 12,29:4
Acklund, Rodney (Screenwriter)
  Invaders, The 1942,Mr 6,17:1
Ackroyd, Jack
  Convoy 1927,My 9,26:4
  Desired Woman, The 1927,Ag 30,21:3
  Lion and the Mouse, The 1928,Je 16,11:4
  Dawn Patrol, The 1930,Jl 11,22:1
Acola, Ettore (Screenwriter)
  Vista, La; Visit, The 1966,Ag 10,32:1
Acosta, Enrique
  Don Q, Son of Zorro 1925,Je 16,24:1
  Texan, The 1930,My 17,21:2
  Thunder Below 1932,Je 20,11:2
  Cantante de Napoles, El; Singer of Naples, The 1935,F 25,13:4
  Message to Garcia, A 1936,Ap 10,27:1
  Desire 1936,Ap 13,15:1
Acosta, Fraser
  Tundra 1936,D 3,31:2

Acosta, Lina d'
  Grande Appello, Il; Last Roll-Call, The 1939,Ap 11,18:6
Acosta, Rodolfo
  One Way Street 1950,My 12,33:3
  Pancho Villa Returns 1950,O 24,34:6
  Bullfighter and the Lady, The 1951,Ap 27,19:2
  Destination Gobi 1953,My 30,7:1
  Wings of the Hawk 1953,Ag 27,22:1
  Appointment in Honduras 1953,N 19,41:4
  Hondo 1953,N 27,99:9
  Drum Beat 1954,N 18,42:1
  Passion 1954,D 11,11:1
  Littlest Outlaw, The 1955,D 27,31:1
  Proud Ones, The 1956,Ag 11,10:2
  From Hell to Texas 1958,Je 5,39:2
  Rio Conchos 1964,O 29,38:1
  Reward, The 1965,S 16,55:1
Acosta, Rudolfo
  Life in the Balance, A 1955,Jl 14,19:1
  Trooper Hook 1957,Jl 13,11:2
Acosta, Rudolph
  Walk Like a Dragon 1960,S 16,24:1
  Let no Man Write my Epitaph 1960,N 11,36:2
  Flaming Star 1960,D 17,19:1
  One Eyed Jacks 1961,Mr 31,21:1
  Second Time Around, The 1961,D 23,16:1
Acqua, Antonio
  Divorce-Italian Style 1962,S 18,34:1
Acquanetta
  Captive Wild Woman 1943,Je 7,9:4
  Jungle Woman 1944,Jl 15,19:6
  Tarzan and the Leopard Woman 1946,F 11,25:2
Acremant, Germaine (Original Author)
  Ces Dames aux Chapeaux Verts; Ladies in the Green Hats, The 1945,Ap 5,26:2
Acton, Wallace
  Marrying Kind, The 1952,Mr 14,27:1
Acuff, Eddie
  Shipmates Forever 1935,O 17,29:3
  I Found Stella Parish 1935,N 4,24:4
  Miss Pacific Fleet 1935,D 7,22:2
  Petrified Forest, The 1936,F 7,14:2
  Walking Dead, The 1936,Mr 2,13:2
  Boulder Dam 1936,Mr 30,17:5
  Golden Arrow, The 1936,My 4,16:1
  Law in her Hands, The 1936,Je 6,21:2
  Jailbreak 1936,Ag 6,22:1
  Crash Donovan 1936,Ag 10,10:3
  Case of the Velvet Claws, The 1936,Ag 29,16:3
  Black Legion 1937,Ja 18,21:1
  What Price Vengeance 1937,My 26,30:3
  Singing Marine, The 1937,Jl 1,33:2
  They Won't Forget 1937,Jl 15,16:1
  Back in Circulation 1937,O 4,17:1
  Love Is on the Air 1937,N 12,27:3
  Outer Gate, The 1937,N 22,15:2
  She Loved a Fireman 1938,Ja 21,15:3
  Invisible Menace, The 1938,F 14,20:6
  Law of the Underworld 1938,Ap 28,27:2
  Four Daughters 1938,Ag 19,13:3
  Meet Doctor Christian 1939,D 1,27:2
  Street of Missing Women 1940,Ja 8,11:2
  Blondie Goes Latin 1941,F 26,17:3
  People vs Dr Kildare, The 1941,My 8,21:1
  Dr Kildare's Victory 1942,F 5,25:2
  Guadalcanal Diary 1943,N 18,29:1
  It Happened Tomorrow 1944,My 29,18:2
  She Gets her Man 1945,F 9,20:5
Acze, Ilona Cs
  Nagymama 1935,D 30,15:1
Adair, Alice
  Private Life of Helen of Troy, The 1927,D 10,14:7
  Wild Party, The 1929,Ap 2,28:4
  Pick Up 1933,Mr 25,13:4
Adair, Jean
  Advice to the Lovelorn 1933,D 14,28:2
  Arsenic and old Lace 1944,S 2,17:2
  Something in the Wind 1947,Ag 29,14:3
  Living in a Big Way 1947,O 10,31:4
Adair, John
  Muss 'Em Up 1936,F 3,21:2
  Ramparts We Watch, The 1940,S 20,27:1
Adair, Josephine
  Third Alarm, The 1923,Ja 10,28:5
Adair, Robert
  Journey's End 1930,Ap 9,25:1
  King of the Jungle 1933,F 25,20:3
  Kiss Before the Mirror, The 1933,My 15,16:2
  Where Sinners Meet 1934,My 25,25:2
  Limehouse Blues 1934,D 12,28:2
  Prince and the Pauper, The 1937,My 6,23:1
Adalbert, Max
  Schlacht von Bademuende, Die 1931,N 21,20:4
  Das Ekel 1932,Ja 30,13:2
  Hauptmann von Koepenick, Der; Captain of Koepenick, The 1932,F 28,VIII,6:1
  Mein Leopold 1932,Ap 1,17:4
  Hurra! Ein Junge! 1932,Je 21,19:6
  Der Herr Finanzdirektor 1932,Je 25,18:2
  Mad Idea, A; Toller Einfall, Ein 1932,Jl 31,IX,3:4
  Kyritz-Pyritz 1932,Ag 9,20:5

Adalbert, Max — Cont

Hauptmann von Koepenick, Der 1933,Ja 17,22:6
Schuetzen Koenig, Der 1933,My 3,15:5 (In Addenda)
Drei Tage Mittelarrest 1933,My 18,17:4
Hellseher, Der 1933,S 11,20:4
Lachende Erben 1933,N 18,18:6
Die Galavorstellung 1933,D 11,23:4
Tante Gusti Kommandiert 1934,My 4,24:4
Toller Einfall, Ein 1934,My 21,20:3

Adam, Alfred

Kermesse Heroique, La 1936,S 23,29:1
Angel and Sinner 1947,F 24,16:5
Vie de Boheme, La 1947,N 28,37:4
Royal Affair, A; (Roi, Le) 1950,Mr 9,25:2
Caroline Cherie 1954,My 25,23:1
What Price Murder 1958,N 11,26:1
Witches of Salem 1958,D 9,54:2
Belle Americaine, La 1961,D 18,42:1

Adam, Alfred (Original Author)

Sylvie and the Phantom 1950,O 16,30:5

Adam, Alfred (Screenwriter)

Belle Americaine, La 1961,D 18,42:1

Adam, Klara

Tommy 1937,O 16,22:3
Sutyi, a Szerencseqyerek; Sutyi, the Lucky Child 1938,Ja 22,19:2

Adam, Nelle

Wonders of Aladdin, The 1961,D 23,16:1

Adam, Noelle

Crazy in the Noodle 1957,D 15,45:4 (Incorrect in this edition; use 1957,D 17,45:4 elsewhere)

Adam, Ronald

Drums 1938,S 30,24:4
Inspector Hornleigh 1939,Je 15,27:3
Hell's Cargo 1940,S 16,15:2
Take my Life 1949,Ja 19,34:2
All Over the Town 1949,My 26,34:4
Under Capricorn 1949,S 9,28:3
Hidden Room, The 1950,Ja 9,19:2
Operation X 1950,D 11,31:2
Seven Days to Noon 1950,D 19,41:3
Lavender Hill Mob, The 1951,O 16,35:2
Laughter in Paradise 1951,N 12,21:2
Bonnie Prince Charlie 1952,Ja 7,14:3
Angels One Five 1954,Ap 30,28:2
Malta Story 1954,Jl 17,7:2
Black Knight, The 1954,O 29,27:2
Lust for Life 1956,S 18,39:1
Reach for the Sky 1957,My 1,40:1
Ship Was Loaded, The 1958,Ja 20,20:1
Man in a Cocked Hat 1960,Je 15,50:2

Adamaitis, A

Jimmie Higgins 1933,F 22,25:3

Adamaitis, E

Flames on the Volga 1958,Ja 27,21:7

Adami, Giuseppe

Carnevale di Venezia, Il; Carnival of Venice, The 1940,O 11,25:2

Adamira, Jiri

Fifth Horseman is Fear, The 1968,My 7,52:1

Adamov, J (Narrator)

Great is my Country 1959,Jl 1,26:1

Adamovic, Olga

Ljubav I Strast 1932,D 16,25:5

Adams, Bernard

Murder Ahoy 1964,S 23,55:3

Adams, Betty

Dalton Gang, The 1949,N 25,27:5

Adams, Beverly

Silencers, The 1966,Mr 17,35:1
Murderers' Row 1966,D 22,40:3
How to Stuff a Wild Bikini 1967,Ja 12,48:1
Kiss the Girls and Make Them Die 1967,Ja 26,25:1
Devil's Angels 1967,O 5,46:1
Ambushers, The 1967,D 23,29:1
Torture Garden 1968,Jl 20,18:2
Hammerhead 1968,S 12,54:3

Adams, Carol

Sis Hopkins 1941,My 1,27:5
Ice-Capades 1941,S 25,29:1

Adams, Casey

What Price Glory 1952,Ag 23,10:2
My Wife's Best Friend 1952,O 11,17:2
Niagara 1953,Ja 22,20:3
Destination Gobi 1953,My 30,7:1
Vickie 1953,S 8,26:3
Dangerous Crossing 1953,S 30,37:2
Night People 1954,Mr 13,11:2
Down Three Dark Streets 1954,S 4,6:4
Naked Alibi 1954,O 2,21:2
Return of Jack Slade, The 1955,N 24,41:3
Bus Stop 1956,S 1,19:2
Dragoon Wells Massacre 1957,My 6,25:2
Naked and the Dead, The 1958,Ag 7,21:1
Summer and Smoke 1961,N 17,41:1

Adams, Claire

Riders of the Dawn 1920,My 3,18:1
When Romance Rides 1922,Ap 10,18:2
Just Tony 1922,Ag 7,14:2
Where the North Begins 1923,Ag 27,14:3
Daddies 1924,F 11,18:3
Fast Set, The 1924,N 18,22:1

Devil's Cargo, The 1925,F 3,24:1
Men and Women 1925,Mr 30,21:3
Souls for Sables 1925,S 15,12:1 (Incorrect in this edition; use 1925,S 15,29:1 elsewhere)

Adams, Clay (Screenwriter)

Honeymoon's Over, The 1939,D 15,33:3
Girl in 313 1940,Je 14,25:3

Adams, Diana

Knock on Wood 1954,Ap 15,34:2
Invitation to the Dance (Ring Around the Rosy); Ring Around the Rosy (Invitation to the Dance) 1956,My 23,35:7

Adams, Donald

Mikado, The 1967,Mr 15,53:1

Adams, Dora Mills

His Children's Children 1923,N 5,15:1

Adams, Dorothy

Broadway Musketeers 1938,O 14,27:1
Fight for Life, The 1940,Mr 7,19:2
Devil Commands, The 1941,F 14,15:3
Bedtime Story 1942,Mr 20,25:4
Lady Gangster 1942,Jl 10,13:2
So Proudly We Hail 1943,S 10,29:1
Laura 1944,O 12,24:1
Circumstantial Evidence 1945,Ap 21,18:3
Miss Susie Slagle's 1946,F 7,29:2
Sentimental Journey 1946,Mr 7,33:2
Best Years of our Lives, The 1946,N 22,27:2
That's my Man 1947,Ap 7,20:2
Sainted Sisters, The 1948,My 20,35:2
Not Wanted 1949,Jl 25,11:4
First Legion, The 1951,Ap 28,9:2
Winning Team, The 1952,Je 21,12:2
Carrie 1952,Jl 17,20:2
Three for Jamie Dawn 1956,Jl 7,11:3
Johnny Concho 1956,Ag 16,30:1
Big Country, The 1958,O 2,44:1

Adams, Eadie

Sinner Take All 1937,F 3,27:1
Thirteenth Man, The 1938,Ja 1,11:2

Adams, Edie

Apartment, The 1960,Je 16,37:2
Lover Come Back 1962,F 9,21:1
Call Me Bwana 1963,Jl 4,9:1
It's a Mad, Mad, Mad, Mad World 1963,N 19,47:1
Under the Yum Yum Tree 1963,N 21,43:2
Love With the Proper Stranger 1963,D 26,33:1
Best Man, The 1964,Ap 7,29:1
Made in Paris 1966,F 17,29:1
Oscar, The 1966,Mr 5,16:1
Honey Pot, The 1967,My 23,52:1

Adams, Ernie

Regular Girl, A 1919,N 11,13:3
Beloved Brute, The 1924,N 10,20:1
Best People 1925,O 21,21:3
Black Bird, The 1926,F 1,16:1
Pals in Paradise 1926,N 24,26:4
Main Event, The 1927,O 31,22:1
Gay Defender, The 1927,D 26,26:6
Tenth Avenue 1928,O 9,35:1
What a Night! 1928,D 24,11:1
For the Defense 1930,Jl 19,7:5
Gang Buster, The 1931,Ja 24,15:1
Tip Off, The 1931,O 26,22:1
Panama Flo 1932,Ja 20,17:4
West of Singapore 1933,Ap 1,18:3
Perfect Clue, The 1935,Mr 14,18:1
Three on the Trail 1936,My 5,26:5
Hopalong Rides Again 1938,Ja 22,19:1
Man With Nine Lives, The 1940,Ap 29,12:3
Invisible Ghost, The 1941,My 8,21:2
Pride of the Yankees, The 1942,Jl 16,23:1
Frisco Sal 1945,F 17,11:2
Pretender, The 1947,Ag 12,26:2

Adams, Eustace L (Original Author)

Sixteen Fathoms Deep 1934,Ja 19,24:3
Down Under the Sea 1936,Ag 10,10:2
16 Fathoms Deep 1948,O 7,35:2

Adams, Frank R (Original Author)

Marriage Cheat, The 1921,Je 2,14:3
Love Piker, The 1923,Jl 16,14:2
Stage Struck 1925,N 16,19:4
Love in Bloom 1935,Ap 20,16:2
Outcast 1937,Mr 3,27:2
Cowboy and the Lady, The 1938,N 25,19:3

Adams, Frank R (Screenwriter)

Trade Winds 1939,Ja 13,17:2

Adams, Frankie

Forgotten Commandments 1932,Je 2,25:2

Adams, Gerald Drayson (Original Author)

Dead Reckoning 1947,Ja 23,31:2
Between Midnight and Dawn 1950,O 2,19:2
Flame of Araby 1951,D 20,41:7
Battle at Apache Pass, The 1952,My 10,16:4
Son of Ali Baba 1952,Ag 16,7:4
Wings of the Hawk 1953,Ag 27,22:1
Princess of the Nile 1954,Je 12,13:2

Adams, Gerald Drayson (Screenwriter)

Old Los Angeles 1948,Jl 12,11:2
Plunders, The 1948,N 1,28:2
Big Steal, The 1949,Jl 11,13:2
Desert Hawk, The 1950,Ag 26,9:2

Adams, Gerald Drayson (Screenwriter) — Cont

Prince Who Was a Thief, The 1951,Jl 4,13:2
Flame of Araby 1951,D 20,41:7
Battle at Apache Pass, The 1952,My 10,16:4
Steel Town 1952,My 10,16:4
Duel at Silver Creek 1952,Ag 2,7:6
Son of Ali Baba 1952,Ag 16,7:4
Untamed Frontier 1952,Ag 23,10:2
Three Young Texans 1954,Ap 17,8:2
Gambler From Natchez, The 1954,Ag 14,8:2
Chief Crazy Horse 1955,Ap 28,25:1
Three bad Sisters 1956,F 13,24:1
Kissin' Cousins 1964,Ap 2,28:3
Harum Scarum 1965,D 16,63:3

Adams, Glyn

Mikado, The 1967,Mr 15,53:1

Adams, H Austin (Original Author)

Out of the Fog 1919,F 10,11:3

Adams, Harold

Hold 'Em Navy 1937,N 6,14:2

Adams, Harvey

Forty Thousand Horsemen 1941,Ag 15,13:2
His Majesty O'Keefe 1954,F 6,17:2
Long John Silver 1955,Ap 7,24:1

Adams, Jane

House of Dracula 1945,D 22,16:3

Adams, Jill

Chance Meeting 1955,Ap 20,38:1
Doctor at Sea 1956,Mr 1,37:3
Private's Progress 1956,Jl 24,19:2
Green Man, The 1957,My 23,40:1
Value for Money 1957,Ag 1,20:4
Brothers in Law 1957,Ag 20,22:1

Adams, Jimmie

Triumph 1924,Ap 21,21:4
Stop Flirting 1925,Je 18,16:3

Adams, Joe

Carmen Jones 1954,O 29,27:2

Adams, Joey

Ringside 1949,S 17,10:8
Singing in the Dark 1956,Mr 8,32:5

Adams, Julia

Hollywood Story 1951,Je 7,40:6
Bright Victory 1951,Ag 1,19:2
Bend of the River 1952,Ap 10,37:1
Horizons West 1952,N 22,16:5
Mississippi Gambler, The 1953,Ja 30,25:1
Wings of the Hawk 1953,Ag 27,22:1
Man From the Alamo, The 1953,S 12,13:2
Creature from the Black Lagoon 1954,My 1,13:4
Francis Joins the Wacs 1954,Jl 31,6:3

Adams, Julie

Six Bridges to Cross 1955,Ja 22,8:2
Private War of Major Benson, The 1955,Ag 3,27:2
One Desire 1955,S 3,9:1
Away all Boats 1956,Ag 17,14:2
Four Girls in Town 1957,Ja 17,34:5
Slaughter on Tenth Avenue 1957,N 6,43:1
Tickle Me 1965,Je 24,28:3

Adams, Kathryn

Forbidden Woman, The 1920,F 23,11:2
Best of Luck, The 1920,Jl 5,12:4
Pampered Youth 1925,F 10,20:1
Fifth Avenue Girl 1939,Ag 25,12:2
If I Had my Way 1940,My 6,13:2
Ski Patrol 1940,My 21,29:4
Black Diamonds 1940,S 10,26:6
Argentine Nights 1940,O 11,25:3
Meet the Chump 1941,F 27,23:4
Unfinished Business 1941,S 2,20:2
Saboteur 1942,My 8,27:2

Adams, Kitty

Lawless Woman, The 1931,Je 8,21:1

Adams, Leslie

Crime Without Passion 1934,S 1,16:2

Adams, Lionel

Success 1923,Jl 10,22:5

Adams, Lowden

Silent Witness, The 1932,F 8,21:1

Adams, Margaret

My Sin 1931,S 11,24:2

Adams, Maria

Splendor in the Grass 1961,O 11,53:1

Adams, Mary

Executive Suite 1954,My 7,19:1

Adams, Neile

This Could Be the Night 1957,My 15,39:1

Adams, Nick

Mister Roberts 1955,Jl 15,14:1
Picnic 1956,F 17,13:3
Last Wagon, The 1956,S 22,20:2
Fury at Showdown 1957,Ap 20,21:3
Sing Boy Sing 1958,F 22,9:4
Teacher's Pet 1958,Mr 20,33:1
No Time for Sergeants 1958,My 30,13:2
F B I Story, The 1959,S 25,23:1
Pillow Talk 1959,O 7,47:2
Hell is for Heroes 1962,Jl 12,19:3
Interns, The 1962,Ag 9,17:5
Hook, The 1963,F 16,5:6
Twilight of Honor 1963,N 14,41:2
Young Lovers, The 1965,F 11,45:1
Young Dillinger 1965,My 13,32:3

Adams, Peggy
Spirit of the Red Cross, The 1918,Ap 21,IV,11:8
Adams, Peter
Donovan's Brain 1954,Ja 21,28:2
Big Fisherman, The 1959,Ag 6,18:1
Adams, Richard
East Side Kids 1940,F 19,21:6
Adams, Robert
King Solomon's Mines 1937,Jl 3,18:1
Kisenga, Man of Africa 1952,Mr 7,18:2
Sapphire 1959,N 3,27:1
Adams, Sam
Million Dollar Legs 1932,Jl 9,7:5
Pick a Star 1937,My 28,17:2
Adams, Samuel Hopkins (Original Author)
Siege 1925,Je 16,24:1
It Happened One Night 1934,F 23,23:2
In Person 1935,D 13,31:5
Gorgeous Hussy, The 1936,S 5,7:1
President's Mystery, The 1936,O 19,22:1
Perfect Specimen, The 1937,O 28,29:2
Harvey Girls, The 1946,Ja 25,26:2
Adams, Sosnick (Composer)
Sioux City Sue 1947,Jl 23,19:3
Adams, Stanley
Hell on Frisco Bay 1956,Ja 7,21:1
North to Alaska 1960,N 11,36:1
Breakfast at Tiffany's 1961,O 6,28:1
Outsider, The 1962,F 8,25:1
Requiem for a Heavyweight 1962,O 17,35:1
Lilies of the Field 1963,O 2,51:1
Thunder Valley 1967,S 14,55:1
Thunder Alley 1967,S 14,55:1
Every Day's a Holiday 1938,Ja 27,17:2
Road Show 1941,F 19,25:2
Adams, Stella
Me, Gangster 1928,O 22,29:1
Vampire Bat, The 1933,Ja 23,9:1
Adams, Ted
Three on the Trail 1936,My 5,26:5
Billy the Kid 1941,Je 20,28:2
Adams, Tom
2nd Best Secret Agent in the Whole Wide World,
    The 1966,Ap 28,49:1
Fighting Prince of Donegal, The 1966,N 10,64:1
Where the Bullets Fly 1967,S 7,50:4
Fathom 1967,D 14,62:1
Adams, Tommye
Tahiti Honey 1943,My 13,17:2
Adams, Victor
Counsellor-At-Law 1933,D 8,31:2
Holy Terror, The 1937,Ja 30,21:2
Adams, William
House on Ninety-Second Street, The
    1945,S 27,24:7
Adamson, Ewart (Miscellaneous)
Gingham Girl, The 1927,Jl 19,27:2
Adamson, Ewart (Original Author)
Annie Oakley 1935,D 24,10:5
Walking Dead, The 1936,Mr 2,13:2
Adamson, Ewart (Screenwriter)
Go Straight 1925,O 6,30:1
Walking Dead, The 1936,Mr 2,13:2
Adamson, Harold (Composer)
Dancing Lady 1933,D 1,23:2
Bottoms Up 1934,Mr 23,29:2
Strictly Dynamite 1934,Jl 4,18:2
Folies Bergere 1935,F 25,13:2
Reckless 1935,Ap 20,16:1
Great Ziegfeld, The 1936,Ap 9,21:2
Top of the Town 1937,Mr 27,19:2
When Love Is Young 1937,Ap 17,15:1
Merry-Go-Round of 1938 1937,N 26,27:2
You're a Sweetheart 1937,D 25,10:5
Hitting a new High 1937,D 27,11:1
Mad About Music 1938,Mr 12,13:2
Dance Hall 1941,Jl 19,16:2
Hold That Ghost 1941,Ag 8,13:3
Hit Parade of 1943 1943,Ap 16,24:3
Thousands Cheer 1943,S 14,27:1
Around the World 1943,N 25,39:2
Four Jills in a Jeep 1944,Ap 6,27:2
Something for the Boys 1944,N 30,19:1
Bring on the Girls 1945,Mr 1,25:5
Nob Hill 1945,Jl 4,10:3
Doll Face 1946,Mr 28,35:3
Do You Love Me 1946,My 25,12:2
Hit Parade of 1947 1947,My 5,32:8
If You Knew Susie 1948,F 23,19:2
Date with Judy, A 1948,Ag 7,8:2
Three for the Show 1955,F 25,16:1
Adamson, Harold (Miscellaneous)
Kid Millions 1934,N 12,17:2
Escapade 1935,Je 6,16:2
Suzy 1936,Jl 25,16:1
Banjo on My Knee 1936,D 12,15:1
Adamson, James
Jungle Siren 1942,O 10,11:3
Adamson, Joy (Original Author)
Born Free 1966,Je 23,29:1
Adamson, Robert
Temptress, The 1926,O 11,18:1

Adashevsky, Konstantin
Girl From Leningrad 1941,D 20,25:2
Adcock, Chris
Treasure Island 1950,Ag 16,24:2
Addams, Dawn
Night Into Morning 1951,Je 11,20:7
Hour of 13, The 1952,O 28,37:1
Plymouth Adventure 1952,N 14,20:3
Young Bess 1953,My 22,31:1
Moon Is Blue, The 1953,Jl 9,18:3
Robe, The 1953,S 17,32:6
Khyber Patrol 1954,S 20,19:2
Bed, The (The Divorce); Divorce, The (The Bed)
    1955,Je 8,26:4
House of Intrigue, The 1960,Mr 10,36:3
Prisoner of the Volga 1960,Je 2,27:2
Come Dance With Me!; Voulez-Vous Danser Avec
    Moi 1960,N 8,32:6
House of Fright 1961,Ag 24,25:4
Temptation 1962,N 10,16:2
Come Fly With Me 1963,My 2,40:2
Blues for Lovers 1966,S 8,43:1
Where the Bullets Fly 1967,S 7,50:4
Addams, James
Avventura, L' 1961,Ap 5,30:1
Addington, Sarah (Original Author)
Dance Team 1932,Ja 16,13:1
And So They Were Married 1936,My 14,29:3
Addis, H B (Screenwriter)
Young One, The 1961,Ja 19,26:1
Addison, Edward
Escape 1930,N 1,23:2
Addy, Wesley
First Legion, The 1951,Ap 28,9:2
Big Knife, The 1955,N 9,41:2
Timetable 1956,Mr 17,13:2
Second to Hell 1959,Jl 18,6:3
Hush...Hush, Sweet Charlotte 1965,Mr 4,36:1
Seconds 1966,O 6,56:1
Mister Buddwing 1966,O 12,36:1
Ade, George (Original Author)
Old Home Week 1925,My 25,21:3
Fair Co-ed, The 1927,O 24,24:3
College Widow, The 1927,N 7,26:4
Young as You Feel 1931,Ag 8,16:3
County Chairman, The 1935,Ja 19,8:1
Freshman Love 1936,Ja 25,18:5
Ade, George (Screenwriter)
Our Leading Citizen 1922,Je 12,16:2 (Incorrect in
    this edition; use 1922,Je 12,10:2 elsewhere)
Back Home and Broke 1922,D 25,21:1
Woman Proof 1923,O 30,16:1
Fish 1936,Ja 25,18:5
Adelgeim, T
Seeds of Freedom 1929,S 9,30:2
Adelson, Maude
Obession 1968,Ag 29,46:3
Ader, Jack
Pawnbroker, The 1965,Ap 21,51:1
Adiarte, Patrick
King and I, The 1956,Je 29,15:6
High Time 1960,S 17,15:1
Flower Drum Song 1961,N 10,40:1
John Goldfarb, Please Come Home
    1965,Mr 25,42:4
Adleman, Robert H (Original Author)
Devil's Brigade, The 1968,My 23,56:2
Adler, Allen (Original Author)
Forbidden Planet 1956,My 4,21:2
Adler, Ben
Wandering Jew, The 1933,O 21,11:2
Adler, Buddy (Producer)
Dark Past, The 1948,D 23,25:2
Woman of Distinction, A 1950,Mr 17,28:2
No Sad Songs for Me 1950,Ap 28,26:2
Saturday's Hero 1951,S 12,37:2
Paula 1952,Jl 16,21:2
Salome 1953,Mr 25,37:1
From Here to Eternity 1953,Ag 6,16:2
Violent Saturday 1955,My 12,32:2
Soldier of Fortune 1955,My 28,7:4
House of Bamboo 1955,Jl 2,13:2
Love Is a Many-Splendored Thing
    1955,Ag 19,10:1
Left Hand of God, The 1955,S 22,34:5
Lieutenant Wore Skirts, The 1956,Ja 12,22:1
Bottom of the Bottle, The 1956,F 2,19:2
Revolt of Mamie Stover, The 1956,My 12,12:7
Bus Stop 1956,S 1,19:2
Anastasia 1956,D 14,35:6
Heaven Knows Mr Allison 1957,Mr 15,22:1
Hatful of Rain, A 1957,Jl 18,19:2
South Pacific 1958,Mr 20,33:1
Inn of the Sixth Happiness, The 1958,D 14,2:7
Adler, Charles
Victims of Persecution 1933,Je 17,16:6
Adler, Felix (Original Author)
Block-Heads 1938,Ag 30,14:2
Chump at Oxford, A 1940,F 20,17:3
Adler, Felix (Screenwriter)
Movie Crazy 1932,S 15,19:3
Our Relations 1936,N 11,55:1
Way out West 1937,My 4,29:1

Adler, Felix (Screenwriter) — Cont
Swiss Miss 1938,Je 4,18:2
Block-Heads 1938,Ag 30,14:2
Chump at Oxford, A 1940,F 20,17:3
Saps at Sea 1940,Ap 29,12:2
Adler, Hans (Original Author)
That Night in Rio 1941,Mr 10,21:2
On the Riviera 1951,My 24,47:1
Adler, Jay
No Time to Marry 1938,F 23,27:2
Cry Danger 1951,F 22,27:3
Scandal Sheet 1952,Ja 17,23:1
My Six Convicts 1952,Mr 28,27:3
Dreamboat 1952,Jl 26,9:2
Juggler, The 1953,My 6,39:2
Vice Squad 1953,Ag 26,23:2
99 River Street 1953,O 3,14:2
Big Combo, The 1955,Mr 26,13:2
Illegal 1955,O 29,12:6
Killing, The 1956,My 21,20:1
Catered Affair, The 1956,Je 15,32:4
Lust for Life 1956,S 18,39:1
Sweet Smell of Success 1957,Je 28,29:2
Brothers Karamazov, The 1958,F 21,18:2
Story of Page One, The 1960,Ja 14,28:1
Family Jewels, The 1965,Ag 12,30:4
Adler, Julius
Broken Hearts 1926,Mr 3,26:1
Tevya 1939,D 22,15:3
Catskill Honeymoon 1950,Ja 28,10:3
Adler, Larry
Singing Marine, The 1937,Jl 1,33:2
Sidewalks of London 1940,F 15,15:1
Music for Millions 1944,D 22,12:4
Adler, Luther
Lancer Spy 1937,N 4,29:1
Cornered 1945,D 26,15:1
Saigon 1948,Ap 1,30:5
Loves of Carmen, The 1948,S 3,16:2
Wake of the Red Witch 1949,Ja 10,19:2
House of Strangers 1949,Jl 2,8:2
South Sea Sinner 1950,Ja 16,18:4
Under my Skin 1950,Mr 18,9:2
D O A 1950,My 1,18:2
Kiss Tomorrow Goodbye 1950,Ag 5,9:2
M 1951,Je 11,20:7
Magic Face, The 1951,O 1,19:2
Desert Fox, The 1951,O 18,32:1
Desert Fox, The 1951,O 28,II,1:8
Hoodlum Empire 1952,Mr 6,25:6
Tall Texan, The 1953,Ap 13,32:4
Miami Story, The 1954,My 15,13:2
Crashout 1955,Jl 9,9:2
Girl in the Red Velvet Swing, The
    1955,O 20,41:2
Hot Blood 1956,Mr 24,14:2
Last Angry Man, The 1959,O 23,24:1
Cast a Giant Shadow 1966,Mr 31,43:3
Adler, Polly (Original Author)
House is not a Home, A 1964,S 2,33:1
Adler, Richard (Composer)
Damn Yankees 1958,S 27,12:7
Adler, Robert
Smoky 1946,Je 27,29:1
Brasher Doubloon, The 1947,My 22,34:5
Green Grass of Wyoming 1948,Je 10,28:3
Yellow Sky 1949,F 2,36:1
Broken Arrow 1950,Jl 21,15:2
No Way Out 1950,Ag 17,23:1
Frogmen, The 1951,Je 30,8:6
How to Marry a Millionaire 1953,N 11,37:1
Hell and High Water 1954,F 2,20:6
Broken Lance 1954,Jl 30,9:1
Virgin Queen, The 1955,Ag 6,13:2
These Thousand Hills 1959,My 7,36:1
Journey to the Center of the Earth
    1959,D 17,51:1
Adler, Stanislaw (Producer)
Kanal 1961,My 10,52:1
Adler, Stella
Shadow of the Thin Man 1941,N 21,23:2
My Girl Tisa 1948,F 21,9:2
Adler, Toby
Good Morning and Goodbye! 1968,F 20,53:1
Adler, William (Cinematographer)
Shipwrecked Among Cannibals 1920,Jl 5,12:4
Adlon, Duke
Iceland 1942,O 15,27:1
Adlon, Louis
Mystery Sea Raider 1940,Ag 26,11:4
Counter-Attack 1945,My 17,15:2
Adolfas (Director)
Brig, The 1964,S 21,37:4
Adolfi, Dr
Waltz Time in Vienna 1934,N 19,13:2
Adolfi, John (Director)
Midnight Taxi, The 1928,O 29,29:1
Evidence 1929,O 5,22:5
Show of Shows 1929,N 21,24:5
Recaptured Love 1930,Ag 9,16:5
Sinners' Holiday 1930,O 11,21:3
College Lovers 1930,N 28,23:1
Millionaire, The 1931,Ap 9,30:5
Alexander Hamilton 1931,S 17,21:4

Adolfi, John (Director) — Cont
Compromised 1931,N 7,16:5
Man Who Played God, The 1932,F 11,16:1
Successful Calamity, A 1932,S 23,22:2
Central Park 1932,D 7,29:3
King's Vacation, The 1933,Ja 20,21:2
Working Man, The 1933,Ap 21,20:3
Voltaire 1933,Ag 23,21:2

Adolphson, Edvin
Dream Waltz, The 1930,D 27,16:3
Paa Solsidan 1936,Ag 26,16:3
John Ericsson Victor of Hampton Roads
  1938,My 18,17:2
En Enda Natt 1942,D 7,22:2
One Summer of Happiness 1955,Mr 22,35:2
Of Love and Lust (On Payment); On Payment (Of
  Love and Lust) 1959,My 26,31:2
Swedish Wedding Night 1965,N 15,48:1

Adolphson, Edvin (Director)
Brokiga Blad 1931,N 30,16:2
Klart till Drabbning; Cleared for Action
  1937,D 10,33:3

Adoree, Renee
Eternal Struggle, The 1923,O 16,21:3
Women Who Give 1924,Je 3,22:1
Bandolero, The 1924,O 27,27:1
Excuse Me 1925,Ja 27,11:2
Man and Maid 1925,Ap 7,17:3
Parisian Nights 1925,Je 2,16:3
Exchange of Wives 1925,O 5,25:2
Big Parade, The 1925,N 20,18:1 (In Addenda)
Black Bird, The 1926,F 1,16:1
Boheme, La 1926,F 25,26:2
Tin Gods 1926,S 20,21:3
Flaming Forest, The 1926,N 22,28:3
Show, The 1927,Mr 14,16:1
Mr Wu 1927,My 16,24:2
Back to God's Country 1927,O 24,24:3
Certain Young Man, A 1928,Je 11,27:1
Cossacks, The 1928,Je 25,27:1
Michigan Kid, The 1928,Jl 2,11:2
Forbidden Hours 1928,Jl 23,11:2
Mating Call, The 1928,O 8,14:2
Spieler, The 1929,F 25,16:1
Pagan, The 1929,My 14,29:1
Redemption 1930,My 3,23:1
Call of the Flesh 1930,S 13,9:3

Adorf, Mario
Devil Strikes at Night, The 1959,Ja 30,31:3
Rosemary 1960,Ja 19,40:2
Station Six-Sahara 1964,N 12,40:2
Major Dundee 1965,Ap 8,45:1
Ten Little Indians 1966,F 10,33:1
That Man in Istanbul 1966,My 19,51:2
Vista, La; Visit, The 1966,Ag 10,32:1
Rose for Everyone, A 1967,Je 30,30:1
Treasure of San Gennaro 1968,F 27,36:1

Adrian, Iris
Rumba 1935,F 25,13:2
Stolen Harmony 1935,Ap 20,16:2
Our Relations 1936,N 11,55:1
One Third of a Nation 1939,F 11,13:2
Horror Island 1941,Mr 31,11:3
Road to Zanzibar 1941,Ap 10,29:2
Wild Geese Calling 1941,Ag 30,10:2
Roxie Hart 1942,F 20,21:1
To the Shores of Tripoli 1942,Mr 26,27:2
Juke Box Jenny 1942,Ap 17,21:3
Rings on her Fingers 1942,Ap 24,21:4
Broadway 1942,Je 5,23:2
Thunder Birds 1942,O 29,19:2
Crystal Ball, The 1943,F 19,22:2
Ladies' Day 1943,Mr 26,14:3
Taxi, Mister 1943,Ap 15,20:2
Lady of Burlesque 1943,My 14,17:2
Action in the North Atlantic 1943,My 22,10:2
Calaboose 1943,Jl 30,19:2
It's a Pleasure 1945,My 4,23:3
Stork Club, The 1945,D 20,18:2
Cross my Heart 1946,D 19,42:3
Trouble With Women, The 1947,Jl 14,14:4
Paleface, The 1948,D 16,41:2
Always Leave Them Laughing 1949,N 24,48:2
There's a Girl in my Heart 1950,Ja 20,29:2
Once a Thief 1951,Ja 19,21:3
My Favorite Spy 1951,D 26,19:3
Highway Dragnet 1954,F 20,8:7
Buccaneer, The 1958,D 24,00:0
That Darn Cat 1965,D 3,44:1

Adrian, Max
Macushla 1940,Ja 6,9:2
Kipps 1942,My 25,11:2
Young Mr Pitt, The 1943,Mr 11,17:1
Courageous Mr Penn 1943,D 23,26:5
Henry V 1946,Je 18,30:2
Pool of London 1951,N 28,37:2
Deadly Affair, The 1967,Ja 27,31:1

Adrienne, Jean
After the Ball 1933,Mr 20,18:3
Father O'Flynn 1938,D 26,29:2

Ady, Gudrun
Annemarie, Die Braut der Kompanie
  1934,D 8,18:6

Ael, Mme
Mystere de la Villa Rose, Le 1932,Ja 11,28:5

Afford, Max (Original Author)
Pacific Adventure 1947,N 26,18:2

Afonso, Yves
Weekend 1968,S 28,36:1

Afritsch, Viktor
Gottes Muehlen mahlen Langsam; Mills of the
  Gods, The 1939,F 18,12:4

Afton, Effie
Middle of the Night 1959,Je 18,36:1
Pretty Boy Floyd 1960,N 3,49:2

Agadati, B (Director)
ThIs is the Land 1936,Jl 10,15:2

Agadatl, Izhak (Producer)
Pillar of Fire, The 1963,Ap 8,35:2

Agafanova, D
Springtime on the Volga 1961,D 25,27:4

Agai, Irene
Iza Neni 1934,Je 5,28:6
My Wife, The Miss 1934,S 13,26:2
Mindent a Noert! 1934,O 17,26:3
Buzavirag 1935,Ja 14,11:3
Huszarszerelem 1935,Ap 23,24:5
Lila Akac 1935,My 15,26:3
Cimzett Ismeretlen 1936,F 7,14:2
Naszut Felaron 1937,F 13,9:2
Szensacio 1937,Mr 1,15:2
Segitseg Oeroekoeltem; Help, I'm an Heiress
  1937,O 28,29:2
Maga Lesz a Ferjem; You Will Be my Husband
  1938,O 12,35:3
Ket Fogoly; Two Prisoners 1938,D 31,7:3

Agamben, Giorgio
Gospel According to St Matthew, The
  1966,F 18,23:1

Agamirova, T
Don Quixote 1961,Ja 21,18:1

Aganbekova, N
Eagle of the Caucasus, The 1932,S 17,18:4

Agar, John
Fort Apache 1948,Je 25,26:2
Adventure in Baltimore 1949,Ap 29,27:2
She Wore a Yellow Ribbon 1949,N 18,35:2
Sands of Iwo Jima 1949,D 31,9:2
Woman on Pier 13, The 1950,Je 16,28:4
Breakthrough 1950,N 18,10:2
Along the Great Divide 1951,My 17,38:3
Woman of the North Country 1952,Ag 30,6:2
Bait 1954,F 24,21:3
Shield for Murder 1954,Ag 28,8:3
Golden Mistress, The 1954,O 30,15:6
Revenge of the Creature 1955,My 14,10:7
Joe Butterfly 1957,My 30,23:2
Journey to the Seventh Planet 1962,My 25,28:3
Of Love and Desire 1963,S 12,32:1
Law of the Lawless 1964,Ag 27,28:2
Johnny Reno 1966,Mr 10,26:3

Agarov, V (Composer)
Two Soldiers 1944,Jl 27,14:2

Agate, Mary
French Leave 1931,D 7,16:1

Agate, May
I Was a Spy 1934,Ja 15,12:2
Are You a Mason? 1934,O 30,23:5

Agay, Denes (Composer)
Ecstasy 1940,D 25,33:2

Age (Miscellaneous)
Bigamist, The 1958,My 12,25:1

Age (Screenwriter)
Birds, the Bees and the Italians, The
  1967,Ag 8,33:2

Agee, James
Bride Comes to Yellow Sky, The 1953,Ja 14,27:2

Agee, James (Narrator)
Quiet One, The 1949,F 14,15:2

Agee, James (Screenwriter)
African Queen, The 1952,F 21,24:3
Bride Comes to Yellow Sky, The 1953,Ja 14,27:2
Green Magic 1955,My 17,32:1
Night of the Hunter, The 1955,S 30,23:1

Ager, Milton (Composer)
King of Jazz 1930,My 3,23:1
Listen, Darling 1938,N 24,37:2

Aggebrecht, Exel (Screenwriter)
Operetta 1949,Je 6,15:4

Agiman, Paul (Producer)
Respectful Prostitute, The 1957,Jl 11,21:1

Agliani, Giorgio G (Producer)
Most Wonderful Moment, The 1959,Je 1,23:6

Agnel, Louis
They Met on Skis 1940,D 23,23:2

Agnew, Robert
Little Child Shall Lead Them, A 1922,S 2,10:4
Clarence 1922,O 16,20:2
Kick In 1922,D 18,22:2
Bluebeard's 8th Wife 1923,Ag 7,20:2
Spanish Dancer, The 1923,O 8,20:1
Woman Proof 1923,O 30,16:1
Love's Whirlpool 1924,Mr 11,16:2
Those Who Dance 1924,Je 30,16:1
Broken Barriers 1924,Ag 4,16:3
Wine of Youth 1924,Ag 11,16:1

Agnew, Robert — Cont
Denial, The 1925,Mr 10,19:3
Lost-a Wife 1925,Je 22,10:2
Private Affairs 1925,Jl 15,22:3
Fourth Commandment, The 1927,Ap 6,25:1
Heart of a Salome, The 1927,Je 6,27:2
Prince of Head-Waiters 1927,Jl 11,23:5
College Hero, The 1927,N 22,32:2
Midnight Taxi, The 1928,O 29,29:1
Extravagance 1930,D 9,31:3
Naughty Flirt, The 1931,Ap 13,17:1
Gold Diggers of 1933 1933,Je 8,22:3

Ago (Screenwriter)
Mafioso 1964,Jl 1,42:1

Agranenko, Z (Director)
Immortal Garrison, The 1957,Mr 4,30:2
Leningrad Symphony 1958,Je 23,19:6

Agranenko, Z (Original Author)
Leningrad Symphony 1958,Je 23,19:6

Aguet, William
Grandeur et Decadence 1937,My 31,11:3

Aguglia, Mimi
El Ultimo Varon Sobre la Tierra 1933,Je 12,20:4
Su Ultimo Amor 1933,Ag 19,14:5
Tres Amores 1934,N 5,23:1
Carnival in Costa Rica 1947,Mr 29,21:2
Outlaw, The 1947,S 12,18:4
Cry of the City 1948,S 30,32:4
That Midnight Kiss 1949,S 23,28:2
Black Hand 1950,Mr 13,15:2
Deported 1950,N 2,39:3
Right Cross 1950,N 16,39:2
Man Who Cheated Himself, The 1951,F 9,21:2
When in Rome 1952,My 12,21:2
Rose Tattoo, The 1955,D 13,55:1

Aguila, Guz (Screenwriter)
Asi Se Quiere En Jalisco 1943,Ag 7,6:2

Aguilar, Alfredo
Brave Bulls, The 1951,Ap 19,39:2

Aguilar, Antonio
Cucaracha, La 1961,N 2,42:1
Important Man, The; El Mayordoma
  1962,Je 26,25:2

Aguilar, Rinaldo (Director)
Madres del Mundo 1936,Ag 17,9:3

Aguilar, Rolando (Director)
Esos Hombres 1937,Ag 21,7:3
Cancion del Milagro, La; Miracle Song, The
  1940,My 11,15:2

Ahearn, Danny (Original Author)
Picture Snatcher 1933,My 19,20:3
Wild Boys of the Road 1933,S 22,14:1
Escape From Crime 1942,O 12,12:3

Ahearn, Thomas (Original Author)
Behind the Headlines 1937,Je 1,27:2
Big Shot, The 1937,Ag 13,13:1
Swing That Cheer 1938,N 11,31:2

Ahen, R Paul (Cinematographer)
Endless Summer, The 1966,Je 16,53:2

Ahern, Lassie Lou
Uncle Tom's Cabin 1927,N 5,16:2

Ahern, Michael J Rev (Narrator)
Monastery 1938,Mr 10,16:3

Aherne, Brian
Shooting Stars 1928,Mr 4,IX,7:7
Shooting Stars 1928,Je 11,27:1
Underground 1928,Ag 12,VII,4:3 (In Addenda)
Underground 1929,F 26,31:1
W Plan, The 1931,Mr 23,24:7
Song of Songs 1933,Jl 20,22:2
Constant Nymph, The 1934,Ap 7,19:1
Fountain, The 1934,Ag 31,14:1
What Every Woman Knows 1934,O 27,20:2
I Live my Life 1935,O 12,12:2
Sylvia Scarlett 1936,Ja 10,16:2
Beloved Enemy 1936,D 26,15:2
Great Garrick, The 1937,O 25,23:1
Merrily We Live 1938,Mr 18,23:3
Juarez 1939,Ap 26,27:1
Captain Fury 1939,My 26,20:2
Vigil in the Night 1940,Mr 9,19:2
My Son, My Son! 1940,My 10,26:6
Hired Wife 1940,S 14,11:2
Lady in Question, The 1940,D 10,33:2
Skylark 1941,N 20,39:2
Smilin' Through 1941,D 5,29:2
My Sister Eileen 1942,O 23,15:1
Night to Remember, A 1943,Ja 1,27:2
Forever and a Day 1943,Mr 13,9:2
First Comes Courage 1943,S 3,15:3
What a Woman 1943,D 3,27:2
Locket, The 1947,Mr 20,38:2
Angel on the Amazon 1948,D 27,16:4
I Confess 1953,Mr 23,28:2
Titanic 1953,My 28,27:5
Prince Valiant 1954,Ap 7,40:2
Bullet is Waiting, A 1954,N 12,17:2
Swan, The 1956,Ap 27,21:5
Best of Everything 1959,O 9,24:2
Susan Slade 1961,N 11,14:6
Sword of Lancelot 1963,O 10,49:2
Cavern, The 1965,D 25,17:2
Rosie 1968,F 8,36:1

Aherne, Pat
Green Dolphin Street 1947,O 16,34:2
Bwana Devil 1953,F 19,20:5
Court Jester, The 1956,F 2,19:1
Aherne, Richard
Christopher Columbus 1949,O 13,33:2
Pardners 1956,Jl 26,20:2
Buster Keaton Story, The 1957,Ap 22,31:6
Ahiberg, Mac (Director)
I, A Woman 1966,O 12,36:3
Ahlers, Anni
Wahre Jakob, Der 1931,Ag 7,20:2
Marquise von Pompadour, Die 1936,F 3,21:3
Ahlersmeyer, Mathieu
Marriage of Figaro 1950,N 3,31:2
Ahmang
Samarang 1933,Je 29,22:2
Ahn, Philip
General Died at Dawn, The 1936,S 3,17:2
Stowaway 1936,D 19,16:1
China Passage 1937,Ap 16,27:2
Roaring Timber 1937,Ag 19,23:1
Something to Sing About 1937,S 21,29:4
Daughter of Shanghai 1937,D 24,21:2
Thank You, Mr Moto 1938,Ja 3,16:2
Hawaii Calls 1938,Ap 29,17:2
Charlie Chan in Honolulu 1938,D 31,7:3
King of Chinatown 1939,Mr 16,27:2
Barricade 1939,D 9,18:2
Yank on the Burma Road, A 1942,Ja 29,25:3
China Girl 1943,Ja 21,27:2
They Got Me Covered 1943,Mr 5,20:2
Story of Dr Wassell, The 1944,Je 7,13:2
Keys of the Kingdom, The 1944,D 30,15:2
Betrayal From the East 1945,Ap 25,27:2
China Sky 1945,My 25,22:3
Back to Bataan 1945,S 13,26:3
Woman in the Night 1948,Ja 10,16:2
Miracle of the Bells, The 1948,Mr 17,30:1
Intrigue 1948,Ap 24,11:2
Rogues' Regiment 1948,D 20,31:2
State Department-File 649 1949,F 21,20:2
Impact 1949,Mr 21,19:2
Big Hangover, The 1950,My 26,20:3
Halls of Montezuma, The 1951,Ja 6,9:6
Japanese War Bride 1952,Ja 30,22:6
Macao 1952,My 1,34:2
Battle Zone 1952,N 1,17:2
His Majesty O'Keefe 1954,F 6,17:2
Hell's Half Acre 1954,F 27,11:3
Love Is a Many-Splendored Thing
1955,Ag 19,10:1
Left Hand of God, The 1955,S 22,34:5
Battle Hymn 1957,F 16,14:1
Never so Few 1960,Ja 22,15:2
Yesterday's Enemy 1960,Mr 4,19:1
Great Impostor, The 1961,Mr 30,24:1
Diamond Head 1963,F 21,5:2
Girl Named Tamiku, A 1963,Mr 15,8:2
Shock Corridor 1963,S 12,32:1
Thoroughly Modern Millie 1967,Mr 23,25:1
Ahn, Pock Rock
Ugly American, The 1963,Ap 12,30:2
Ahn, Ralph
Prisoner of War 1954,My 10,20:2
Aho, Betty
Case of Lena Smith, The 1929,Ja 15,22:4
Ahrens, Monique
Dog of Flanders, A 1960,Ap 1,37:1
Ahrens, Thekla
Eternal Mask, The 1937,Ja 13,20:3
Postillon of Lonjumeau, The 1937,N 20,21:3
Alles Fuer Veronika 1939,F 4,11:2
Ahuet, Julio
Maria Candelaria 1944,S 12,23:7
Ahumate, Harold (Original Author)
Counterfeit Lady 1937,Ja 11,15:6
Ai, Li Ling (Miscellaneous)
Kukan 1941,Je 24,17:2
Aichbichler, Thea
Bei der Blonden Kathrein 1934,D 3,15:2
Aidman, Charles
Countdown 1968,My 2,57:3
AIKEN
See Also AITKEN
Aiken, Spottiswoode
White Circle, The 1920,Ag 23,9:2
Birth of a Nation, The 1922,D 5,24:3
Birth of a Nation, The 1930,D 22,16:2
Aimee, Anouk
Lovers of Verona, The 1951,Mr 12,20:2
Golden Salamander 1951,Mr 24,8:3
Paris Express, The 1953,Je 6,8:6
Pot Bouille 1958,O 28,39:1
Chasers, The; Draguers, Les 1960,My 3,43:1
Modigliani of Montparnasse 1961,Mr 1,27:3
Dolce Vita, La 1961,Ap 20,30:1
Joker, The; (Farceur, Le) 1961,Ag 8,32:2
Lola 1962,O 15,32:2
Sodom and Gomorrah 1963,Ja 24,5:3
Eight and One Half 1963,Je 26,36:1
White Voices; Voci Blanche 1965,Ap 13,32:2
Successo, Il 1965,Ap 29,40:2

Fuga, La 1966,Mr 22,33:1
Man and a Woman, A; Homme et une Femme,
Un 1966,Jl 13,35:1
Very Handy Man, A 1966,D 15,60:1
Aimes, Robert
Tomorrow and Tomorrow 1932,Ja 30,13:2
Aimogor, Gila
Sallah 1965,O 13,39:1
Aimos
Golem, The 1937,Mr 22,27:2
Escape From Yesterday 1939,My 3,27:2
Port of Shadows 1939,O 30,13:2
Katia 1939,D 23,9:2
S O S Mediterranean -1940,Ja 1,29:2
Ultimatum 1940,F 5,13:2
Mayerling to Sarajevo 1940,O 30,27:6
Man of the Hour, The 1940,N 21,43:2
Nine Bachelors 1942,F 9,19:2
Fire in the Straw 1943,Jl 2,15:2
Three Hours 1944,O 30,16:5
Symphonie d'Amour 1946,Mr 11,19:2
Midnight in Paris 1947,O 9,32:3
Aimos, Raymond
Quatorez Juillet 1933,O 20,14:2
Ainley, Henry
First Mrs Fraser, The 1932,My 29,VIII,4:5 (In
Addenda)
As You Like It 1936,N 6,29:3
Ainley, Lynn
Undercover Girl 1950,N 8,37:2
Man With my Face, The 1951,Je 15,27:5
Ainley, Richard
As You Like It 1936,N 6,29:3
Stolen Life 1939,Je 15,27:2
Lady With red Hair 1940,D 6,28:2
Singapore Woman 1941,My 12,13:6
Shining Victory 1941,My 31,14:1
Bullets for O'Hara 1941,Jl 28,16:4
Smiling Ghost, The 1941,S 26,26:5
White Cargo 1942,N 27,27:2
Three Hearts for Julia 1943,My 21,22:4
Above Suspicion 1943,Ag 6,10:3
I Dood It 1943,N 11,29:1
Ainsley, Ian
Invasion Quartet 1961,D 11,41:2
Ainsley, Mary
Pride of the Bowery 1941,Ja 24,15:2
Sis Hopkins 1941,My 1,27:5
Ainsley, Norman
Notorious Sophie Lang, The 1934,Jl 21,14:2
Shadow Strikes, The 1937,S 13,17:1
Adventure in Diamonds 1940,Ap 4,27:2
Ainsworth, Cupid
Tip Off, The 1931,O 26,22:1
Cafe Society 1939,F 23,19:2
Ainsworth, Sydney
Man and his Money, A 1919,Ap 14,11:4
Crimson Gardenia, The 1919,Je 16,11:2
Heartsease 1919,Ag 25,8:5
Girl From Outside, The 1919,N 10,18:2
Madame X 1920,S 27,18:1
Doubling for Romeo 1921,O 24,13:1
Ainsworth, Virginia
Why Girls Go Back Home 1926,My 18,28:2
Aird, Jane
Stranger in Between, The 1952,Ag 20,21:3
Dance Little Lady 1955,D 26,23:3
Aisha
Itto 1936,Ja 29,15:5
Aisner, Robert (Original Author)
Cross of Lorraine, The 1943,D 3,27:4
Aitariba, Beatrice
Crazy Desire 1964,Jl 3,13:2
AITKEN
See Also AIKEN
Aitken, Mary
Sinners in Silk 1924,S 8,15:3
Aitken, Spottiswood
Captain Kidd,-Jr 1919,Ap 21,13:4
White Heather, The 1919,My 5,11:1
Hay Foot, Straw Foot 1919,Je 23,10:3
Her Kingdom of Dreams 1919,S 22,8:1
Nomads of the North 1920,S 27,18:1
Monte Cristo 1922,Ag 15,20:3
Triumph 1924,Ap 21,21:4
Ajala, Mashood
White Witch Doctor 1953,Jl 2,19:3
Ajoret, Daniele
Bernadette of Lourdes 1962,Ja 30,20:2
Ajtay, Andor
Doentoe Pillanat, A; Crucial Moment, The
1938,S 17,20:3
Rad Bizom a Felesegem; I Entrust my Wife to
You 1939,My 6,21:3
Ajubey, A (Screenwriter)
Song and Dance Over the Vistula 1956,Je 25,19:7
Akal, Saeed (Screenwriter)
Broken Wings, The 1968,Mr 16,34:1
Akar, John J
Something of Value 1957,My 11,24:6
Akasakov, Sergei (Original Author)
Adventure in Odessa 1954,Je 21,19:6

Akawansh, Chief
Silent Enemy, The 1930,My 20,32:3
Aked, Muriel
Middle Watch, The 1930,D 20,20:6
Magic Night 1932,N 3,25:3
Rome Express 1933,F 27,11:2
No Funny Business 1934,Mr 9,22:4
Friday the 13th 1934,My 15,18:1
Autumn Crocus 1934,O 25,26:2
Evensong 1934,N 17,12:1
Continental Express 1942,Ap 7,26:3
Life and Death of Colonel Blimp, The
1945,Mr 30,18:2
Adventure for Two 1945,D 14,24:5
Happiest Days of Your Life, The 1950,S 18,19:2
Wonder Boy 1951,D 26,19:5
Gilbert and Sullivan 1953,O 28,36:3
Akers, Andra
Murder a la Mod 1968,My 2,57:1
Akert, Pamela
Blue Hawaii 1962,F 22,20:2
Akiki, Philip
Broken Wings, The 1968,Mr 16,34:1
Akimoff, Nicolai
Kampf, Der 1936,S 11,29:3
Akin, Mary
Charley's Aunt 1925,F 9,15:3
Akins, Claude
From Here to Eternity 1953,Ag 6,16:2
Caine Mutiny, The 1954,Je 25,17:1
Burning Hills, The 1956,Ag 24,15:2
Defiant Ones, The 1958,S 25,29:1
Onionhead 1958,O 2,44:1
Rio Bravo 1959,Mr 19,40:2
Inherit the Wind 1960,O 13,41:1
Claudelle Inglish 1961,S 21,40:2
Merrill's Marauders 1962,Je 14,23:4
Distant Trumpet, A 1964,My 28,40:1
Killers, The 1964,Jl 18,10:4
Ride Beyond Vengance 1966,S 29,60:1
Return of the Seven 1966,O 20,52:5
First to Fight 1967,Mr 30,55:1
Waterhole #3 1967,O 11,41:4
Devil's Brigade, The 1968,My 23,56:2
Akins, Zoe (Original Author)
Daddy's Gone A-Hunting 1925,F 24,17:3
Declassee 1925,Mr 23,14:2
Furies, The 1930,Ap 19,15:1
Ladies Love Brutes 1930,My 16,20:4
Women Love Once 1931,Je 27,20:3
Girls About Town 1931,N 2,27:1
Greeks Had a Word for Them, The 1932,F 4,25:2
Morning Glory 1933,Ag 18,18:2
Accused 1936,D 17,35:1
Old Maid, The 1939,Ag 12,16:2
How to Marry a Millionaire 1953,N 11,37:1
Stage Struck 1958,Ap 23,40:1
Akins, Zoe (Screenwriter)
Eve's Secret 1925,Je 11,14:3
Outcast Lady 1934,N 3,20:3
Lady of Secrets 1936,F 22,12:1
Accused 1936,D 17,35:1
Camille 1937,Ja 23,13:1
Toy Wife, The 1938,Je 24,15:1
Desire Me 1947,S 26,28:3
Akiyama, Yukio
Angry Island 1960,F 28,31:1
Akka (chimpanzee)
Missing Link, The 1927,My 7,15:2
Akkerman, Willem
Silver Fleet, The 1945,Mr 24,22:6
Akmakjian, Martin (Cinematographer)
Hunters of the Deep 1954,D 17,37:4
Aksenov, V
General Suvorov 1941,S 20,11:2
Akst, Georgia
Song of Russia 1944,F 11,17:2
Akst, Harry
June Moon 1931,Mr 14,23:2
42d Street 1933,Mr 10,19:3
Akst, Harry (Composer)
Under the Pampas Moon 1935,My 31,11:1
Paddy O'Day 1936,F 8,19:2
Music Goes 'Round, The 1936,F 22,12:1
Holy Terror, The 1937,Ja 30,21:2
Sing and Be Happy 1937,Je 19,20:2
She Had to Eat 1937,Jl 24,12:1
Big Town Girl 1937,D 13,23:4
Battle of Broadway 1938,Ap 25,19:2
Rascals 1938,My 27,12:2
Akst, Harry (Miscellaneous)
Diplomaniacs 1933,Ap 29,14:2
Aksyonov, Vsevolod
My Daughter 1960,N 28,40:2
Akutagawa, Hiroshi
Mistress, The 1959,F 3,36:2
Rikisha Man, The 1960,My 4,57:1
Akutagawa, Ryunosuke (Original Author)
Rasho-Mon 1951,D 27,18:3
Akzanof, I
Zemlya Zhazhdet 1932,My 6,15:3

Aladar, Laszlo (Original Author)
Trouble in Paradise 1932,N 9,28:5
Aladi
Paraiso Recobrado, El 1936,Ap 27,19:3
Alai, Nadine
Bernadette of Lourdes 1962,Ja 30,20:2
Alain
Maternite 1937,Je 8,30:2
Alain, Claude
Portrait of a Woman 1946,Ap 22,26:2
ALAN
See Also ALLAN, ALLEN
Alandh, Lissi
Miss Julie 1952,Ap 8,35:2
Unmarried Mothers 1956,F 23,32:5
Alaniz, Rico
Appointment in Honduras 1953,N 19,41:4
Siege at Red River, The 1954,Ap 3,19:2
Green Fire 1954,D 25,7:1
Alari, Nadine
Mr Orchid; Pere Tranquille, Le 1948,Mr 29,17:3
Caroline Cherie 1954,My 25,23:1
Sleeping Car Murder, The 1966,Mr 8,45:1
Alatriste, Gustavo (Producer)
Viridiana 1962,Mr 20,43:4
Exterminating Angel, The 1967,Ag 22,33:1
Alazraki, Betnito (Director)
Roots, The (The Filly); Filly, The (The Roots)
1957,S 3,23:2
Roots, The (Our Lady); Our Lady (The Roots)
1957,S 3,23:2
Roots, The (The One-Eyed Boy); One-Eyed Boy,
The (The Roots) 1957,S 3,23:2
Roots, The (The Cows); Cows, The (The Roots)
1957,S 3,23:2
Alazraki, Betnito (Screenwriter)
Roots, The (The Filly); Filly, The (The Roots)
1957,S 3,23:2
Roots, The (The Cows); Cows, The (The Roots)
1957,S 3,23:2
Roots, The (The One-Eyed Boy); One-Eyed Boy,
The (The Roots) 1957,S 3,23:2
Roots, The (Our Lady); Our Lady (The Roots)
1957,S 3,23:2
Alazraki, Olympia
Roots, The (Our Lady); Our Lady (The Roots)
1957,S 3,23:2
Alba
Bedazzled 1967,D 11,65:2
Alba, Armando Orive (Producer)
Macario 1961,S 28,48:6
Alba, Irene Caba
Nail, The 1949,Jl 1,14:6
Alba, Luz
Sofia 1948,S 4,8:7
Alba, Maria
Hell's Heroes 1929,D 28,11:1
Just a Gigolo 1931,Je 13,20:4
Goldie 1931,Je 29,20:3
Mr Robinson Crusoe 1932,S 22,25:4
Hypnotized 1933,Ja 16,13:3
Ley Del Haren, La 1933,Je 17,16:7
West of the Pecos 1934,D 29,11:2
Great God Gold 1935,My 6,22:3
Albach-Retty, Rosa
Mozart Story, The 1948,N 15,21:5
Albach-Retty, Wolf
Zwei Herzen und ein Schlag 1932,S 9,17:5
Das Schoene Abenteuer 1932,D 8,25:3
Schwartze Husar, Der 1932,D 23,20:1
Und Es Leuchtet die Puszta 1934,Ja 30,17:2
Liebe Muss Verstanden Sein 1934,Mr 21,24:3
Einmal Eine Grosse Dame Sein 1934,O 27,20:3
Geschichten aus dem Wienerwald; Tales From the
Vienna Woods 1935,N 2,13:3
Freuhling im Wien 1937,F 6,15:2
Rendezvous in Wien 1938,F 19,19:4
Gross Reinemachen; General Housecleaning
1938,Je 23,27:2
Gluecklichste Ehe von Wien, Die; Happiest
Married Couple in Vienna, The 1938,O 8,10:2
Hotel Sacher 1939,Je 10,14:2
Heimatland; Homeland 1939,O 28,11:2
Albanese, Francesco
Lost One, The; La Traviata 1948,Mr 30,26:2
Albanese, Licia
Serenade 1956,Mr 24,21:1 (Incorrect in this
edition; use 1956,Mr 23,21:1 elsewhere)
Albani, Marcella
Russia-1908 1929,Ja 7,36:2
Behind the Altar 1929,Ja 29,27:1
Fight for Matterhorn, The 1929,Jl 29,23:3
Theatre 1929,Ag 25,VIII,5:1
Secrets of the Orient 1932,Ja 4,27:3
Albano, F (Miscellaneous)
Zappatore 1932,Mr 28,11:2
Albee, Edward (Original Author)
Who's Afraid of Virginia Woolf? 1966,Je 30,28:1
Who's Afraid of Virginia Woolf? 1966,Jl 10,II,1:5
Albee, George Sumner (Original Author)
Next Voice You Hear, The 1950,Je 30,18:2

Alberg, Mildred Freed (Producer)
Hot Millions 1968,S 20,42:1
Alberg, Somer
Shrike, The 1955,Jl 8,15:2
Alberghetti, Anna Maria
Medium, The 1951,S 6,39:2
Here Comes the Groom 1951,S 21,19:2
Stars Are Singing, The 1953,Mr 12,24:2
Ten Thousand Bedrooms 1957,Ap 4,37:1
Cinderfella 1960,D 17,19:2
Alberi, Guido
Shoot Loud, Louder... I Don't Understand
1967,S 21,56:4
Alberni, Luis
Sante Fe Trail, The 1930,O 18,23:2
Svengali 1931,My 1,30:3
Side Show 1931,S 19,10:2
Mad Genius, The 1931,O 24,20:3
Men in her Life 1931,N 30,16:2
Manhattan Parade 1931,D 25,29:2
Cock of the Air 1932,Ja 25,20:3
High Pressure 1932,F 1,22:3
Cohens and Kellys in Hollywood, The
1932,Ap 22,23:2
Woman in Room 13, The 1932,My 21,9:2
Week-End Marriage 1932,Je 4,9:2
Hypnotized 1933,Ja 16,13:3
Topaze 1933,F 10,12:2
Child of Manhattan 1933,F 13,11:4
Men Must Fight 1933,Mr 11,18:3
Trick for Trick 1933,Je 10,16:4
When Ladies Meet 1933,Je 24,16:2
Sphinx, The 1933,Jl 6,26:5
Ciudad de Carton, La 1934,F 28,23:3
I Believed in You 1934,Ap 11,25:3
Glamour 1934,My 12,12:3
Black Cat, The 1934,My 19,18:4
One Night of Love 1934,S 7,25:3
Buenaventura, La 1934,S 15,20:3
Count of Monte Cristo, The 1934,S 27,25:2
Captain Hates the Sea, The 1934,N 29,33:2
Gilded Lily, The 1935,F 9,11:2
Winning Ticket, The 1935,F 11,14:2
Roberta 1935,Mr 8,25:2
Let's Live Tonight 1935,Mr 18,14:4
Goin' to Town 1935,My 11,21:2
In Caliente 1935,Je 27,16:1
Love Me Forever 1935,Je 28,24:1
Gay Deception, The 1935,O 11,31:1
Metropolitan 1935,O 18,27:4
Bad Boy 1935,O 28,16:3
Colleen 1936,Mr 9,20:2
Dancing Pirate 1936,Je 18,19:1
Ticket to Paradise 1936,Ag 8,5:3
Anthony Adverse 1936,Ag 27,16:1
Follow Your Heart 1936,O 22,31:1
When You're in Love 1937,F 19,15:2
King and the Chorus Girl, The 1937,Mr 29,14:4
Sing and Be Happy 1937,Je 19,20:2
Easy Living 1937,Jl 8,20:1
Great Garrick, The 1937,O 25,23:1
Madame X 1937,O 25,23:1
Under Suspicion 1937,D 20,23:2 (In Addenda)
Hitting a new High 1937,D 27,11:1
Manhattan Merry-Go-Round 1937,D 31,9:3
I'll Give a Million 1938,Jl 16,7:2
Great Man Votes, The 1939,Ja 20,15:2
Naughty but Nice 1939,Je 23,23:2
Housekeeper's Daughter, The 1939,D 2,21:4
Enemy Agent 1940,Ap 22,13:3
Public Deb No 1 1940,S 18,19:2
Lady Eve, The 1941,F 26,17:1
That Hamilton Woman 1941,Ap 4,25:1
Road to Zanzibar 1941,Ap 10,29:2
They Met in Bombay 1941,Jl 4,17:1
World Premiere 1941,Ag 21,15:2
Babes on Broadway 1942,Ja 1,37:1
Obliging Young Lady 1942,F 13,24:4
Mexican Spitfire's Elephant 1942,S 18,25:2
Voice in the Wind 1944,Mr 16,17:2
Bell for Adano, A 1945,Jl 6,8:3
Captain Carey U S A 1950,Mr 30,40:5
Alberoni, Sherri
Dance With Me Henry 1956,D 24,8:2
Three Worlds of Gulliver, The 1960,D 17,19:3
Albers, Hans
Rasputin 1929,O 21,30:1
Nacht Gehoert Uns, Die; Night Belongs to Us,
The 1930,My 11,IX,4:2 (In Addenda)
Blue Angel, The 1930,D 6,21:3
Drei Tage Liebe; Three Days of Love
1931,Mr 15,IX,6:1
Bomben auf Monte Carlo; Bombardment of Monte
Carlo, The 1931,S 27,VIII,7:1
Monte Carlo Madness 1931,N 15,VIII,6:1
Draufganger, Der; Daredevil, The
1932,Ja 17,VIII,6:1
Sieger, Der; Victor, The 1932,My 15,VIII,4:4 (In
Addenda)
Liebe Ist Liebe 1932,Je 2,25:2
Monte Carlo Madness 1932,Je 4,9:2
Koenigin der Unterwelt 1932,D 9,26:5
Quick, Koenig der Clowns 1933,D 9,18:3

Albers, Hans— Cont
Ein Gewisser Herr Gran 1934,F 24,18:5
Fluechtlinge 1934,O 15,20:5
Gold 1934,O 22,12:3
Zwei lustige Abenteurer; Two Merry Adventures
1938,Ja 1,11:2
Peer Gynt 1939,N 11,12:2
Henker Fraven und Soldaten; Hangmen, Women
and Soldiers 1940,Ja 13,11:3
City of Torment 1950,Je 10,11:4
White Hell of Pitz Palu, The 1953,N 14,14:2
Albert, Arnold (Producer)
Man I Love, The 1947,Ja 25,12:2
Albert, Eddie
Brother Rat 1938,N 5,15:2
On Your Toes 1939,O 21,12:2
Four Wives 1939,D 23,9:1
Brother Rat and a Baby 1940,Ja 27,9:4
Angel From Texas, An 1940,My 10,26:7
My Love Came Back 1940,Jl 13,16:5
Dispatch From Reuters, A 1940,D 12,37:2
Four Mothers 1941,Ja 11,12:7
Wagons Roll at Night, The 1941,My 10,20:4
Out of the Fog 1941,Je 21,20:2
Treat 'Em Rough 1942,Ja 19,21:3
Eagle Squadron 1942,Jl 3,12:5
Ladies' Day 1943,Mr 26,14:3
Bombardier 1943,Jl 2,15:2
Rendezvous With Annie 1946,S 23,29:3
Perfect Marriage, The 1947,Ja 16,30:3
Time Out of Mind 1947,Ap 7,20:1
Smash-Up, The Story of a Woman
1947,Ap 11,31:2
Hit Parade of 1947 1947,My 5,32:8
You Gotta Stay Happy 1948,N 5,29:2
Every Girl Should be Married 1948,D 24,14:2
Fuller Brush Girl, The 1950,O 6,23:2
U S S Teakettle 1951,F 24,11:2
Meet Me After the Show 1951,Ag 16,23:2
Actors and Sin; (Woman of Sin) 1952,My 30,11:3
Carrie 1952,Jl 17,20:2
Roman Holiday 1953,Ag 28,13:1
Oklahoma! 1955,O 11,49:1
I'll Cry Tomorrow 1956,Ja 13,18:1
Attack! 1956,S 20,29:4
Teahouse of the August Moon, The
1956,N 30,19:1
Sun Also Rises, The 1957,Ag 24,12:2
Joker Is Wild, The 1957,S 27,16:6
Roots of Heaven, The 1958,O 16,46:1
Orders to Kill 1958,N 18,41:2
Beloved Infidel 1959,N 18,46:1
Young Doctors, The 1961,Ag 24,25:2
Madison Avenue 1962,Mr 29,28:2
Longest Day, The 1962,O 5,28:1
Who's Got the Action? 1962,D 26,5:4
Miracle of the White Stallions 1963,My 23,31:2
Captain Newman, MD 1964,F 21,36:1
7 Women 1966,My 5,59:1
Albert, Emmerich
Rebel, The 1933,Jl 25,17:2
Albert, Frank
Air Mail 1932,N 7,20:3
Albert, Germaine
Dr Knock 1937,My 1,16:4
Albert, Julius
Daisies 1967,O 26,54:2
Albert, Katherine (Original Author)
How to Marry a Millionaire 1953,N 11,37:1
Albert, Katherine (Screenwriter)
Star, The 1953,Ja 29,25:1
Sabre Jet 1953,N 3,34:1
Albert, Marvin H (Original Author)
Law and Jake Wade, the 1958,Je 7,11:1
Duel at Diablo 1966,Je 16,53:1
Tony Rome 1967,N 16,58:1
Lady in Cement 1968,N 21,41:1
Albert, Marvin H (Screenwriter)
Duel at Diablo 1966,Je 16,53:1
Rough Night in Jericho 1967,N 9,56:4
Lady in Cement 1968,N 21,41:1
Albertano, Linda
Beach Red 1967,Ag 4,18:1
Albertazzi, Giorgio
Last Year at Marienbad 1962,Mr 8,26:1
Red Lips 1964,Mr 19,28:2
Eva 1965,Je 5,21:2
Alberti, Fritz
Aftermath 1927,D 6,27:1
U-Boat 9 1929,Ja 22,23:1
Man Who Cheated Life, The 1929,F 11,26:3
Eleven Who Were Loyal 1929,My 20,22:6
Rasputin 1929,O 21,30:1
Because I Loved You 1930,Ja 25,13:2
Docks of Hamburg 1930,Jl 7,22:3
Student Sein 1931,My 4,16:2
Karamazof 1931,S 21,20:2
Zwei Menschen 1931,D 23,27:3
1914: The Last Days Before the War 1932,S 5,9:6
Herzblut 1932,O 3,15:2
Salon Dora Green 1937,Jl 26,15:3
Alberti, Guido
Eight and One Half 1963,Je 26,36:1
Not on Your Life; Verdugo, El 1965,Mr 30,52:1

Albertini, Edda
  Before Him all Rome Trembled 1947,F 22,16:2
Albertini, Franscini
  Eine Liebesnacht 1933,My 15,16:2
Albertini, Giampiero
  Organizer, The 1964,My 7,31:2
Albertson, Frank
  Prep and Pep 1928,D 24,11:1
  Salute 1929,O 5,22:5
  Son of the Gods 1930,Ja 31,24:1
  Men Without Women 1930,F 1,15:1
  Happy Days 1930,F 14,20:1
  So This Is London 1930,My 24,21:2
  Born Reckless 1930,Je 7,10:4
  Wild Company 1930,Jl 19,7:5
  Just Imagine 1930,N 22,21:3
  Connecticut Yankee, A 1931,Ap 13,17:1
  Big Business Girl 1931,Je 12,27:1
  Traveling Husbands 1931,Ag 8,16:3
  Brat, The 1931,Ag 24,13:4
  Way Back Home 1932,Ja 16,13:1
  Huddle 1932,Je 17,24:1
  Billion Dollar Scandal, The 1933,Ja 9,23:1
  Cohens and Kellys in Trouble, The
    1933,Ap 17,16:4
  Ann Carver's Profession 1933,Je 9,20:2
  Ever in my Heart 1933,O 13,25:3
  Midshipman Jack 1933,N 20,18:2
  King for a Night 1933,D 11,23:4
  Life of Vergie Winters, The 1934,Je 15,26:1
  Last Gentleman, The 1934,O 18,26:5
  Enter Madame 1935,Ja 12,12:1
  Doubting Thomas 1935,Jl 11,24:2
  Alice Adams 1935,Ag 16,11:3
  Ah, Wilderness! 1935,D 25,30:2
  Farmer in the Dell, The 1936,Mr 7,11:4
  Connecticut Yankee at the Court of King Arthur,
    A 1936,My 4,16:1
  Fury 1936,Je 6,21:1
  Plainsman, The 1937,Ja 14,16:2
  Navy Blue and Gold 1937,D 24,21:2
  Hold That Kiss 1938,Je 11,9:1
  Mother Carey's Chickens 1938,Ag 5,11:1
  Fugitives for a Night 1938,S 21,30:4
  Room Service 1938,S 22,27:1
  Spring Madness 1938,D 1,29:3
  Shining Hour, The 1939,Ja 20,15:2
  Bachelor Mother 1939,Je 30,17:2
  When the Daltons Rode 1940,Ag 23,13:3
  Behind the News 1941,Ja 16,25:3
  Ellery Queen's Penthouse Mystery
    1941,Mr 7,17:2
  Man Made Monster 1941,Mr 19,25:4
  Burma Convoy 1941,O 7,26:7
  Flying Cadets 1941,O 14,29:2
  Louisiana Purchase 1942,Ja 1,37:1
  And the Angels Sing 1944,Jl 13,14:2
  I Love a Soldier 1944,N 2,22:2
  It's a Wonderful Life 1946,D 23,19:2
  Hucksters, The 1947,Jl 18,21:2
  Nightfall 1957,Ja 24,34:1
  Enemy Below, The 1957,D 26,23:2
  Last Hurrah, The 1958,O 24,40:1
  Psycho 1960,Je 17,37:1
  Bye Bye Birdie 1963,Ap 5,27:3
Albertson, Jack
  Top Banana 1954,F 20,8:6
  Harder They Fall, The 1956,My 10,26:3
  Monkey on my Back 1957,My 30,23:2
  Man of a Thousand Faces 1957,Ag 14,21:1
  Don't Go Near the Water 1957,N 15,37:1
  Teacher's Pet 1958,Mr 20,33:1
  Never Steal Anything Small 1959,F 12,23:1
  Lover Come Back 1962,F 9,21:1
  Convicts 4 1962,O 4,44:2
  Period of Adjustment 1962,N 1,34:1
  Kissin' Cousins 1964,Ap 2,28:3
  Tiger Walks, A 1964,Ag 27,28:2
  How to Murder Your Wife 1965,Ja 27,26:1
  Flim Flam Man, The 1967,Ag 23,40:1
  How to Save a Marriage - And Ruin Your Life
    1968,Ja 19,30:1
  Subject Was Roses, The 1968,O 14,53:2
Albertson, Lillian
  Greatest Show on Earth, The 1952,Ja 11,17:2
Albertson, Mabel
  Mutiny on the Blackhawk 1939,Ag 2,17:2
  She's Back on Broadway 1953,Mr 12,24:2
  So This Is Love 1953,Ag 12,22:1
  Ransom 1956,Ja 25,28:3
  Forever, Darling 1956,F 10,18:1
  Long, Hot Summer, The 1958,Ap 4,16:1
  Home Before Dark 1958,N 7,23:1
  Don't Give up the Ship 1959,Jl 9,22:1
  Gazebo, The 1960,Ja 16,14:4
  All in a Nights Work 1961,Mr 23,28:1
  Period of Adjustment 1962,N 1,34:1
  Barefoot in the Park 1967,My 26,51:1
Alberty, Fritz
  White Devil, The 1931,Ag 28,20:1
Albicocco, Jean Gabriel (Director)
  Girl With the Golden Eyes, The 1962,Ag 21,36:2

Albiin, Elsy
  Crime and Punishment 1948,Mr 1,17:2
  Incorrigible 1949,Jl 2,8:2
  Rapture 1950,D 14,51:3
  Intimate Relations 1954,F 22,15:4
Albrand, Martha (Original Author)
  Captain Carey U S A 1950,Mr 30,40:5
  Desperate Moment 1953,S 1,19:4
Albright, Hardie
  Young Sinners 1931,My 9,15:4
  Hush Money 1931,Jl 11,7:6
  Skyline 1931,O 5,17:3
  Heartbreak 1931,O 17,20:1
  So Big 1932,Ap 30,19:3
  Purchase Price, The 1932,Jl 16,5:5
  Jewel Robbery 1932,Jl 23,6:6
  Crash, The 1932,S 9,17:5
  Successful Calamity, A 1932,S 23,22:2
  Cabin in the Cotton 1932,S 30,17:3
  This Sporting Age 1932,O 1,10:4
  Match King, The 1932,D 8,25:3
  Working Man, The 1933,Ap 21,20:3
  Song of Songs 1933,Jl 20,22:2
  Three-Cornered Moon 1933,Ag 12,14:2
  House on 56th Street, The 1933,D 2,9:3
  Ninth Guest, The 1934,Mr 3,8:5
  White Heat 1934,Je 16,20:2
  Crimson Romance 1934,O 13,10:1
  Silver Streak, The 1935,Ja 16,21:1
  Sing Sing Nights 1935,Ja 26,13:2
  Red Salute 1935,S 30,13:1
  Ski Patrol 1940,My 21,29:4
  Flight From Destiny 1941,Mr 28,26:7
  Marry the Boss's Daughter 1941,D 4,33:4
  Pride of the Yankees, The 1942,Jl 16,23:1
  Loves of Edgar Allan Poe, The 1942,S 21,19:2
  Angel on my Shoulder 1946,O 21,27:2
  Mom and Dad 1957,Ja 31,21:1
Albright, Lois
  What Price Vengeance 1937,My 26,30:3
Albright, Lola
  Champion 1949,Ap 11,29:2
  Bodyhold 1949,D 12,29:4
  Good Humor Man, The 1950,Jl 14,17:2
  Beauty on Parade 1950,Ag 18,17:2
  Killer That Stalked New York, The
    1951,Ja 5,17:2
  Magnificent Matador, The 1955,My 25,38:1
  Tender Trap, The 1955,N 11,29:6
  Cold Wind in August, A 1961,Jl 27,23:2
  Kid Galahad 1963,Mr 7,8:5
  Joy House 1965,F 18,29:1
  Lord Love a Duck 1966,F 22,14:6
  Way West, The 1967,My 25,54:1
  Where Were You When the Lights Went Out?
    1968,Ag 9,30:2
  Impossible Years, The 1968,D 6,54:1
Albright, Vicky
  Wild Wild Winter 1966,Ja 6,20:2
Albright, Wally
  Thunder 1929,Jl 8,17:3
  Wonder of Women 1929,Jl 22,17:1
  East Lynne 1931,F 21,15:2
  Prodigal, The 1931,Je 27,20:3
  Salvation Nell 1931,Jl 6,24:4
  Sob Sister 1931,O 3,20:2
  Rebecca of Sunnybrook Farm 1932,Jl 30,16:5
  Thirteen Women 1932,O 15,13:1
  Zoo in Budapest 1933,Ap 28,15:2
  As the Earth Turns 1934,Ap 12,27:2
  Count of Monte Cristo, The 1934,S 27,25:2
  Black Fury 1935,Ap 11,27:2
  Woman I Love, The 1937,Ap 16,27:2
  What Price Vengeance 1937,My 26,30:3
  Sons of the Legion 1938,S 30,24:3
Albritton, Louise
  Parachute Nurse 1942,Jl 27,18:2
  Walk a Crooked Mile 1948,O 13,31:2
Albuquerque, Janet
  Amazon Trader, The 1956,N 17,17:6
Alcaide, Chris
  Glass Menagerie, The 1950,S 29,31:5
  Big Heat, The 1953,O 15,43:2
  Miami Story, The 1954,My 15,13:2
  Chicago Syndicate 1955,Je 21,37:1
Alcaide, Mario
  Crowded Paradise 1956,Je 22,15:1
Alcaide, Rafael
  Castillos en el Aire; Castles in the Air
    1938,My 21,9:3
  Adventures of Casanova 1948,Mr 22,18:3
Alcaniz, Luana
  Devil With Women, A 1930,O 20,28:2
  Primavera en Otono 1933,My 18,17:3
  Nada Mas Que Una Mujer 1934,N 26,12:2
  Julieta Compra un Hijo; Julieta Buys a Baby
    1935,Mr 25,12:3
  Ultima Cita, La 1936,Ja 22,15:6
  Contra la Corriente 1936,Mr 10,27:3
  Pasado Acusa, El; Accusing Past, The
    1938,O 15,21:4
  Verbena Tragica; Tragic Festival, The
    1939,Mr 13,12:3

Alcon, Alfredo
  Summerskin 1962,My 29,22:2
Alcoriza, Luis
  Virgin of Guadalupe, The 1943,My 15,13:3
  St Francis of Assisi 1947,Ap 5,12:5
Alcoriza, Luis (Original Author)
  Exterminating Angel, The 1967,Ag 22,33:1
Alcoriza, Luis (Screenwriter)
  Young and the Damned, The 1952,Mr 25,23:2
  This Strange Passion 1955,D 5,34:2
  Exterminating Angel, The 1967,Ag 22,33:1
Alcorn, Olive Ann
  Up the Ladder 1925,My 12,26:2
  Phantom of the Opera, The 1925,S 7,15:3
Alcorn, R W (Producer)
  Johnny Holiday 1950,My 17,36:1
Alcorn, Ron (Producer)
  Armored Command 1961,O 7,14:3
Alcorn, Ron (Screenwriter)
  Armored Command 1961,O 7,14:3
Alcorn, Ronald W (Original Author)
  Johnny Holiday 1950,My 17,36:1
Alcott, Louisa May (Original Author)
  Little Women 1918,N 11,13:3
  Little Women 1933,N 17,22:3
  Little Men 1935,F 18,19:3
  Little Men 1940,D 9,23:2
  Little Women 1949,Mr 11,33:2
Alcover
  Argent, L' 1929,Mr 3,VII,7:2 (Incorrect in this
    edition; use 1929,Mr 3,VIII,8:5 in film)
  Bizarre, Bizarre 1939,Mr 21,27:2
  Argent, L' 1968,S 23,42:5
Alcover, M
  Courier of Lyons, The 1938,Je 3,17:1
Alcover, Pedro
  Liliom 1935,Mr 18,14:4
Alda, Alan
  Gone are the Days! 1963,S 24,43:2
  Paper Lion 1968,O 24,54:1
Alda, Robert
  Rhapsody in Blue 1945,Je 28,22:2
  Cinderella Jones 1946,Mr 16,9:6
  Cloak and Dagger 1946,O 5,13:2
  Beast With Five Fingers, The 1946,D 26,28:3
  Man I Love, The 1947,Ja 25,12:2
  Nora Prentiss 1947,F 22,16:2
  April Showers 1948,Mr 27,10:2
  Tarzan and the Slave Girl 1950,Je 24,7:3
  Mr Universe 1951,Mr 23,16:2
  Beautiful but Dangerous 1958,F 6,24:1
  Imitation of Life 1959,Ap 18,18:1
Aldas, Luid
  Night of the Mayas 1941,Ja 14,16:7
Alden, Betty
  Fountain, The 1934,Ag 31,14:1
  Nut Farm, The 1935,Ap 8,23:3
Alden, Eric
  Little Lord Fauntleroy 1936,Ap 3,27:1
  Broadway Limited 1941,Je 16,11:6
Alden, Mary
  Hell-to-Pay Austin 1916,Ag 7,9:5
  Unpardonable Sin, The 1919,My 3,11:3
  Honest Hutch 1920,S 26,VI,2:1 (In Addenda)
  Birth of a Nation, The 1921,My 2,12:1
  Snowblind 1921,My 23,16:3
  Old Nest, The 1921,Je 29,10:3
  Bond Boy, The 1922,O 9,10:2
  Birth of a Nation, The 1922,D 5,24:3
  Pleasure Mad 1924,Ja 7,23:1
  Painted People 1924,Ja 29,16:1
  Babbitt 1924,Jl 15,9:4
  Beloved Brute, The 1924,N 10,20:1
  Siege 1925,Je 16,24:1
  Happy Warrior, The 1925,Jl 7,24:2
  Under the Rouge 1925,Jl 22,14:4
  Brown of Harvard 1926,My 3,27:1
  Lovey Mary 1926,Je 21,17:2
  Plastic Age, The 1926,Jl 19,13:1
  Potters, The 1927,Ja 18,23:1
  Joy Girl, The 1927,S 6,34:3
  Fools for Luck 1928,Je 12,33:5
  Ladies of the Mob 1928,Je 18,13:2
  Cossacks, The 1928,Je 25,27:1
  Sawdust Paradise, The 1928,Ag 27,23:1
  Some One to Love 1928,D 4,29:1
  Birth of a Nation, The 1930,D 22,16:2
  Politics 1931,Ag 1,16:4
  Hell's House 1932,F 12,24:5
  Strange Interlude 1932,S 1,24:3
Alden, Norman
  Portrait of a Mobster 1961,Ap 20,30:4
  Operation Bottleneck 1961,S 7,40:2
  Secret of Deep Harbor 1961,O 26,39:7
  Man's Favorite Sport? 1964,F 20,22:1
  Andy 1965,Ja 22,21:2
  Red Line 7000 1965,D 9,60:4
  Wild Angels, The 1966,D 22,40:4
  Good Times 1967,Ag 3,26:4
Alden, Richard
  Howards of Virginia, The 1940,S 27,27:1

Alden, Robert
Maker of Men 1931,D 19,16:4
Shopworn 1932,Ap 4,13:6
Alder, W F (Producer)
Isle of Vanishing Men, The 1925,Mr 9,21:1
Alderette, Clorinda
Salt of the Earth 1954,Mr 15,20:2
Alderson, Erville
Isn't Life Wonderful? 1924,D 1,17:3
Fortune Hunter, The 1928,Ja 10,28:4
Fazil 1928,Je 5,21:1
Guilty 1930,Ap 7,21:1
Lash, The 1931,Ja 1,31:3
Cabin in the Cotton 1932,S 30,17:3
They Call It Sin 1932,O 21,25:4
I Am a Fugitive From a Chain Gang
1932,N 11,17:2
Lazy River 1934,Ap 4,26:2
Scralet Empress, The 1934,S 15,20:2
County Chairman, The 1935,Ja 19,8:1
Seven Keys to Baldpate 1935,D 14,11:2
Educating Father 1936,Je 20,22:2
Jesse James 1939,Ja 14,13:1
Andy Hardy Gets Spring Fever 1939,Jl 19,23:2
Santa Fe Trail 1940,D 21,21:2
Sergeant York 1941,Jl 3,15:1
Bad Men of Missouri 1941,Ag 16,18:2
Parachute Battalion 1941,Ag 29,13:2
My Favorite Blonde 1942,Ap 2,27:2
Loves of Edgar Allan Poe, The 1942,S 21,19:2
You Can't Escape Forever 1942,O 17,11:1
First Comes Courage 1943,S 3,15:3
Along Came Jones 1945,Jl 19,8:7
Smash-Up, The Story of a Woman
1947,Ap 11,31:2
Commandos Strike at Dawn 1954,Ja 14,25:1
Alderson, George
Dial M for Murder 1954,My 29,13:2
Alderson, John
Against all Flags 1952,D 25,34:6
South Sea Woman 1953,Je 4,33:6
Violent Saturday 1955,My 12,32:2
Don't Go Near the Water 1957,N 15,37:1
Young Lions, The 1958,Ap 3,23:1
Alderton, John
Duffy 1968,S 17,50:3
Aldine, James
Wreck of the Hesperus, The 1927,N 28,18:5
Aldinger, Bertl
1A in Oberbayern; 1A in Upper Bavaria
1939,N 18,22:6
Aldins, Zoe (Screenwriter)
Zaza 1939,Ja 5,17:1
Aldinyan, Arthur
Heart Sings, The 1958,Ag 18,15:2
Aldman, Charles
War Hunt 1962,Ag 8,35:2
Hour of the Gun 1967,N 2,58:4
Aldon, Mari
Tanks are Coming, The 1951,D 6,42:4
Distant Drums 1951,D 26,19:3
ThIs Woman is Dangerous 1952,F 28,23:2
Barefoot Contessa, The 1954,S 30,37:1
Summertime 1955,Je 22,25:1
Aldor, Bernd
Zwei Menschen 1931,D 23,27:3
Aldredge, Tom
Mouse on the Moon, The 1963,Je 18,32:1
Troublemaker, The 1964,Je 23,25:1
Aldrich, Bess Streeter (Original Author)
Cheers for Miss Bishop 1941,Mr 14,17:2
Aldrich, Darragh (Original Author)
Prince There Was 1921,N 14,18:1
Aldrich, Fred
Mrs Mike 1950,F 9,36:5
711 Ocean Drive 1950,Jl 20,21:2
Aldrich, Mariska
Lady by Choice 1934,N 17,12:1
You're the One 1941,F 20,23:2
Whistling in the Dark 1941,Ag 28,23:2
Aldrich, Meeka
Loves of Ricardo, The 1926,Ag 16,10:1
Aldrich, Robert (Director)
World for Ransom 1954,Je 5,11:2
Apache 1954,Jl 10,7:2
Vera Cruz 1954,D 27,22:4
Big Knife, The 1955,N 9,41:2
Autumn Leaves 1956,Ag 2,21:2
Attack! 1956,S 20,29:4
Angry Hills, The 1959,Jl 16,31:3
Second to Hell 1959,Jl 18,6:3
Last Sunset, The 1961,Je 15,51:1
What Ever Happened to Baby Jane?
1962,N 7,48:1
Sodom and Gomorrah 1963,Ja 24,5:3
4 for Texas 1963,D 26,33:3
Hush...Hush, Sweet Charlotte 1965,Mr 4,36:1
Flight of the Phoenix, The 1966,F 1,26:1
Dirty Dozen 1967,Je 16,36:1
Legend of Lylah Clare, The 1968,Ag 23,33:1
Killing of Sister George, The 1968,D 17,58:4

Aldrich, Robert (Producer)
World for Ransom 1954,Je 5,11:2
Big Knife, The 1955,N 9,41:2
Attack! 1956,S 20,29:4
What Ever Happened to Baby Jane?
1962,N 7,48:1
4 for Texas 1963,D 26,33:3
Hush...Hush, Sweet Charlotte 1965,Mr 4,36:1
Flight of the Phoenix, The 1966,F 1,26:1
Legend of Lylah Clare, The 1968,Ag 23,33:1
Killing of Sister George, The 1968,D 17,58:4
Aldrich, Robert (Screenwriter)
Second to Hell 1959,Jl 18,6:3
4 for Texas 1963,D 26,33:3
Aldrich, Roma
Parachute Nurse 1942,Jl 27,18:2
Aldrich, William
Flight of the Phoenix, The 1966,F 1,26:1
Aldriche, Jesse J
Drivin' Fool, The 1923,O 29,18:1
Aldridge, Katharine
Hotel for Women 1939,Ag 26,20:2
Here I Am a Stranger 1939,S 30,11:2
Free, Blonde and 21 1940,Ap 5,25:2
Shooting High 1940,Ap 12,19:2
Girl in 313 1940,Je 14,25:3
Sailor's Lady 1940,Je 29,12:2
Down Argentine Way 1940,O 18,25:1
Dead Men Tell 1941,Ap 17,29:3
Navy Blues 1941,S 20,11:2
Aldridge, Michael
Murder in the Cathedral 1952,Mr 26,35:2
Falstaff; Chimes at Midnight 1967,Mr 18,19:2
Aleazaba, Jose
Relicario, El; Reliquary, The 1935,D 31,11:3
Alehina, Mme
Broken Shoes 1934,Mr 31,8:3
Aleichem, Sholem (Original Author)
Tevya 1939,D 22,15:3
Aleinikov, Peter
Ski Battalion 1938,Mr 14,13:1
City of Youth 1938,S 5,30:4
No Greater Love 1944,F 25,23:3
Moscow Skies 1945,Ja 22,22:5
Ural Front, The 1945,Je 7,25:3
Aleinikova, Ava
Welcome Kostya! 1965,N 22,48:2
Alejandro, Julio (Screenwriter)
Nazarin 1968,Je 21,48:1
Alekseyev, A
Lad From our Town 1943,O 7,26:2
Alekseyev, K
Fate of Man 1961,Jl 11,28:1
Alekseyev, V (Screenwriter)
Miners of the Don 1951,N 12,21:2
Aleksic, Mila
I Even Met Happy Gypsies 1968,Mr 21,57:1
Aleksic, Zivojin Dr
Affair of the Heart, An 1967,S 23,20:3
Alen, Harry
Rich Man's Folly 1931,N 27,29:3
Alennikov, P
Peasants 1935,Ag 29,25:2
Aleong, Aki
No Down Payment 1957,O 31,41:1
Never so Few 1960,Ja 22,15:2
Alerme
Mam'zelle Nitouche 1933,N 20,18:3
Pension Mimosas 1936,My 6,27:1
Kermesse Heroique, La 1936,S 23,29:1
Avocate d'Amour 1938,S 8,27:2
Mademoiselle ma Mere 1939,S 19,29:2
Man of the Hour, The 1940,N 21,43:2
Man Who Seeks the Truth, The 1941,O 7,26:6
Four Flights to Love 1942,Ap 13,12:2
Barge-Keeper's Daughter, The 1945,S 6,23:3
Symphonie d'Amour 1946,Mr 11,19:2
Blue Veil, The 1947,O 2,32:6
Passionnelle 1948,Mr 1,17:2
Noah's Ark 1950,Ag 21,15:1
Hoboes in Paradise 1950,O 9,21:5
Alers, Christian
Other One, The 1967,S 29,53:1
Aleshnikova, Lilia
Sun Shines for All 1961,Jl 10,25:3
Alessandrini, Goffredo
Rapture 1950,D 14,51:3
Alessandrini, Goffredo (Director)
Don Bosco 1936,My 27,27:3
Between Two Worlds 1940,F 9,15:2
Foria 1948,Ja 21,30:2
Furia 1948,Ja 21,30:2
Wandering Jew, The 1949,Mr 11,33:2
Rapture 1950,D 14,51:3
Anita Garibaldi 1954,Mr 19,19:4
Alessandrini, Goffredo (Screenwriter)
Foria 1948,Ja 21,30:2
Furia 1948,Ja 21,30:2
Wandering Jew, The 1949,Mr 11,33:2
Alessi, Ottavio (Screenwriter)
Woman in the Painting, The 1959,Ja 15,27:1
Nude Odyssey 1962,O 27,14:6

Alessi, Rino (Screenwriter)
Loyalty of Love 1937,Mr 1,15:1
Aletter, Frank
Mister Roberts 1955,Jl 15,14:1
Alexander, A L
War Is a Racket 1934,D 10,16:2
Alexander, A L (Miscellaneous)
War Is a Racket 1934,D 10,16:2
Alexander, Arthur (Producer)
International Crime 1938,My 16,14:4
Alexander, Ben
Hearts of the World 1918,Ap 5,13:1
Turn in the Road, The 1919,Mr 30,IV,6:1
White Heather, The 1919,My 5,11:1
Penrod and Sam 1923,Je 25,16:5
Boy of Mine 1923,D 24,12:1 (In Addenda)
Flaming Love 1925,Ja 19,14:1
Pampered Youth 1925,F 10,20:1
All Quiet on The Western Front 1930,Ap 30,29:1
It's a Wise Child 1931,My 16,13:3
Are These our Children 1931,N 14,15:3
Suicide Fleet 1931,N 23,22:1
High Pressure 1932,F 1,22:3
Strange Love of Molly Louvain, The
1932,My 9,19:5
Tom Brown of Culver 1932,Jl 30,16:5
What Price Innocence? 1933,Je 26,16:3
This Day and Age 1933,S 1,15:4
Stage Mother 1933,S 30,18:5
Once to Every Woman 1934,Mr 26,22:3
Life of Vergie Winters, The 1934,Je 15,26:1
Grand Old Girl 1935,F 26,16:4
Outer Gate, The 1937,N 22,15:2
Spy Ring, The 1938,Ja 15,19:1
Mr Doodle Kicks Off 1938,S 28,29:4
Dragnet 1954,Ag 21,10:2
Man With a Shadow 1958,Ja 23,24:3
Alexander, Curt (Screenwriter)
Twilight 1949,D 30,13:2
Alexander, David
Vicious Circle, The 1948,Jl 22,27:2
Alexander, Denise
Crime in the Streets 1956,My 24,27:4
Alexander, Dick
Leopard Lady, The 1928,F 27,16:2
See America Thirst 1930,D 12,35:3
Front Page, The 1931,Mr 20,29:1
Freckles 1935,O 26,12:2
Frontier Marshal 1939,Jl 29,18:2
Alexander, Donald (Director)
Monkey Into Man 1941,My 31,14:1
Alexander, E Grubb (Screenwriter)
Passionate Youth 1925,Je 30,14:3
Alexander, Elizabeth (Original Author)
Changing Husbands 1924,Je 23,22:4
Second Choice 1930,Ja 4,21:1
You Belong to Me 1934,S 13,26:1
Alexander, Georg
Carnival Crime, The 1929,Jl 8,17:3
Liebeswalzer 1931,My 4,15:3
Acht Tage Glueck 1931,Jl 24,22:1
Opernredoute; Opera ball 1931,O 4,VIII,7:1
Opern-Ball; Der; Opera Ball 1931,N 6,28:3
Leutnant Warst Du Einst bei den Husaren
1932,Mr 14,13:3
Ein Prinz Verliebt Sich 1932,Ap 29,13:4
Hurra! Ein Junge! 1932,Je 21,19:6
Madame Wuenscht Keine Kinder 1933,Je 2,22:4
Wenn die Liebe Mode Macht 1933,O 30,14:3
Wie Sag' Ich's Meinem Mann? 1934,Ja 23,22:4
Liebe Muss Verstanden Sein 1934,Mr 21,24:3
Frau wie Du, Eine 1934,D 24,17:3
Und Wer Kuesst Mich? 1935,Ja 28,10:5
Zigeunerblut 1935,Ap 8,23:5
Geschichten aus dem Wienerwald; Tales From the
Vienna Woods 1935,N 2,13:3
Alte und der Junge Koenig, Der 1935,D 10,31:2
Tanzmusik 1936,My 26,27:2
Mein Liebster Ist ein Jaegersmann 1936,S 15,37:6
Letzte Rose 1936,O 10,21:3
Ist Mein Mann Nicht Fabelhaft 1936,D 8,31:3
Idealer Gatte, Ein 1937,Ja 11,15:7
Falscher Fuffziger, Ein 1937,F 13,9:1
Schloss im Flandern, Das 1937,Ag 7,7:3
For Her Country's Sake 1937,N 27,21:3
Rendezvous in Wien 1938,F 19,19:4
Meadehen von Gestern Nacht, Das; Girl of Last
Night, The 1938,Je 18,18:2
Magda 1938,S 10,20:2
Krach und Glueckum Kuennemann; Row and Joy
About Kuennemann 1938,S 17,20:3
Teufelskerl, Ein; Devil of a Fellow, A
1938,O 1,10:3
Klapperstorchverband, Der; Stork Society, The
1938,O 29,15:3
Zweimal zwei im Himmelbett; Twice Two in a
Four-Post Bed 1939,F 5,19:3
Ueber Alles die Treue 1939,F 13,13:3
Solo per Danne 1939,My 30,13:3
Kluge Schwiegermutter, Die; Wise Mother-in-Law,
The 1939,O 9,15:3
Arme Millionar, Der; Poor Millionaire, The
1939,D 30,9:2

71

Alexander, Georg— Cont

Our Little Wife 1940,Ja 27,9:2

Alexander, George

Love Makes Us Blind 1927,Ag 23,29:4
Lady From Paris, The 1927,S 28,28:3
Jealousy 1928,D 4,29:1
Die Singende Stadt 1932,My 10,25:4
Whispering City 1948,My 10,25:5
Thirteenth Letter, The 1951,F 22,27:2

Alexander, Gus

Safe for Democracy 1918,N 4,11:3
Alice in Wonderland 1931,D 28,22:1

Alexander, James

Jack and the Beanstalk 1952,Ap 8,35:3

Alexander, Janie

Great Man, The 1957,Ja 2,28:2

Alexander, John

Petrified Forest, The 1936,F 7,14:2
Flowing Gold 1940,S 2,19:3
Mr Skeffington 1944,My 26,23:2
Doughgirls, The 1944,Ag 31,14:1
Arsenic and old Lace 1944,S 2,17:2
Tree Grows in Brooklyn, A 1945,Mr 1,25:5
Horn Blows at Midnight, The 1945,Ap 21,18:2
Junior Miss 1945,Je 18,15:4
It Shouldn't Happen to a Dog 1946,S 7,11:2
Jolson Story, The 1946,O 11,28:2
New Orleans 1947,Je 20,25:6
Living in a Big Way 1947,O 10,31:4
Cass Timberlane 1947,N 7,20:2
Where There's Life 1947,D 25,32:1
Summer Holiday 1948,Je 12,8:5
Night Has a Thousand Eyes 1948,O 14,38:3
Winchester 73 1950,Je 8,38:2
Fancy Pants 1950,Ag 31,21:2
Sleeping City, The 1950,S 21,20:2
Model and the Marriage Broker, The
    1952,Ja 12,10:6
Marrying Kind, The 1952,Mr 14,27:1
Man in the Net, The 1959,Je 11,36:2

Alexander, Julie

Pure Hell of St Trinian's, The 1961,S 26,31:1

Alexander, Katharine

Should Ladies Behave? 1933,D 18,24:3
Death Takes a Holiday 1934,F 24,18:4
Operator 13 1934,Je 23,16:5
Barretts of Wimpole Street, The 1934,S 29,12:2
Painted Veil, The 1934,D 7,29:1
Enchanted April 1935,Mr 9,19:1
After Office Hours 1935,Mr 9,19:1
Cardinal Richelieu 1935,Ap 19,24:2
Girl From 10th Avenue, The 1935,My 27,20:6
Alias Mary Dow 1935,Je 29,16:2
Ginger 1935,Jl 19,13:2
She Married her Boss 1935,S 27,25:3
Splendor 1935,N 23,23:2
Sutter's Gold 1936,Mr 27,25:2
Moonlight Murder 1936,Mr 28,11:2
Devil is a Sissy, The 1936,O 17,21:2
Reunion 1936,N 27,27:1
As Good as Married 1937,My 22,19:2
Girl From Scotland Yard, The 1937,My 31,11:2
That Certain Woman 1937,S 16,29:1
Double Wedding 1937,O 22,27:2
Rascals 1938,My 27,12:2
Great Man Votes, The 1939,Ja 20,15:2
Broadway Serenade 1939,Ap 7,25:2
In Name Only 1939,Ag 4,11:3
Three Sons 1939,N 24,29:3
Hunchback of Notre Dame, The 1940,Ja 1,29:2
Anne of Windy Poplars 1940,Ag 23,13:3
Dance, Girl, Dance 1940,O 11,25:2
Play Girl 1941,Ja 30,19:3
Sis Hopkins 1941,My 1,27:5
Vanishing Virginian, The 1942,My 28,13:3
Now, Voyager 1942,O 23,25:3
Human Comedy, The 1943,Mr 3,19:2
Kiss and Tell 1945,O 26,16:2
For the Love of Mary 1948,S 23,37:2
John Loves Mary 1949,F 5,11:2

Alexander, Kurt (Screenwriter)

Tender Enemy, The 1938,Mr 31,15:2 (In
    Addenda)

Alexander, Louis

Prince of Players 1955,Ja 12,24:2

Alexander, Major (Original Author)

Dress Parade 1927,O 31,22:1

Alexander, Mara

Rains Came, The 1939,S 9,11:2

Alexander, Max (Producer)

International Crime 1938,My 16,14:4
Swamp Woman 1941,D 27,15:2
Amazon Quest 1949,My 14,9:3

Alexander, Nick

Love With the Proper Stranger 1963,D 26,33:1

Alexander, Paris

Day the Fish Came Out, The 1967,O 3,57:1

Alexander, Patrick (Screenwriter)

Room 43 1959,D 3,46:1

Alexander, Peter

Fledermaus, Die 1964,F 8,15:2
How to Seduce a Playboy 1968,My 16,53:2

Alexander, R Howard (Original Author)

Dance Little Lady 1955,D 26,23:3

Alexander, Richard

Mysterious Lady, The 1928,Ag 6,15:2
Viking, The 1928,N 29,32:4
All Quiet on The Western Front 1930,Ap 30,29:1
Donovan's Kid 1931,My 22,28:5
Law and Order 1932,F 29,21:3
Scarlet Dawn 1932,N 4,25:4
Sign of the Cross, The 1932,D 1,25:1
Destination Unknown 1933,Ap 8,16:2
Kentucky Kernels 1935,Ja 5,20:2
Big Broadcast of 1936, The 1935,S 16,15:2
Dangerous Waters 1936,Ja 22,15:5
Silly Billies 1936,Ap 6,18:1
Mars Attacks the World 1938,N 8,26:3
Dangerous When Wet 1953,Je 19,18:1

Alexander, Ronald (Original Author)

Holiday for Lovers 1959,Jl 25,10:2

Alexander, Ronald (Screenwriter)

Return to Peyton Place 1961,My 6,26:1
Billie 1965,S 16,55:3

Alexander, Ross

Wiser Sex, The 1932,Mr 12,19:5
Gentlemen are Born 1934,N 22,27:2
Flirtation Walk 1934,N 29,33:1
Maybe It's Love 1935,F 11,14:2
Midsummer Night's Dream, A 1935,O 10,31:1
Shipmates Forever 1935,O 17,29:3
Captain Blood 1935,D 27,14:1
Brides are Like That 1936,Mr 23,22:5
Boulder Dam 1936,Mr 30,17:5
I Married a Doctor 1936,Ap 20,17:1
Hot Money 1936,Jl 25,16:2
China Clipper 1936,Ag 12,14:3
Here Comes Carter 1936,N 14,23:3
Ready, Willing and Able 1937,Mr 15,27:1

Alexander, Shana (Original Author)

Slender Thread, The 1965,D 24,24:2

Alexander, Sidney (Screenwriter)

Pirates of Capri, The 1949,D 26,33:5

Alexander, Stephen (Producer)

Slender Thread, The 1965,D 24,24:2

Alexander, Suzanne

Cat-Women of the Moon 1954,Mr 20,10:7

Alexander, Tad

Ambassador Bill 1931,N 14,15:3
Tomorrow and Tomorrow 1932,Ja 30,13:2
Strange Interlude 1932,S 1,24:3
Rasputin and the Empress 1932,D 24,11:4
Stranger's Return, The 1933,Jl 28,18:2
Broadway to Hollywood 1933,S 2,14:4
Bureau of Missing Persons 1933,S 9,9:2
You Can't Buy Everything 1934,F 3,9:2
I Give my Love 1934,Jl 17,24:2
Little Men 1935,F 18,19:3

Alexander, Terence

Runaway Bus, The 1954,O 25,30:7
One That Got Away, The 1958,Ap 23,40:2
Doctor's Dilemma, A 1958,D 18,2:7
League of Gentlemen, The 1961,Ja 25,30:4
Only When I Larf 1968,O 24,55:3

Alexander, William (Miscellaneous)

Truth About Africa, The 1933,Ap 17,16:3

Alexander, William (Producer)

Kukan 1941,Je 24,17:2

Alexanders, Flying

Big Circus, The 1959,Jl 18,6:1

Alexandrakis, Alexos

Stella 1957,Je 11,40:1
Lily of the Harbor 1958,Ap 16,38:3
Madame X 1960,O 3,34:5

Alexandre, Curt (Screenwriter)

Mayerling to Sarajevo 1940,O 30,27:6

Alexandre, Robert (Director)

Cloistered 1936,My 20,25:1

Alexandre, Roland

Perfectionist, The 1952,My 2,21:3
House of Ricordi 1956,Mr 13,32:1

Alexandresco

Arab, The 1924,Jl 14,11:5

Alexandroski, Serge

End of St Petersberg, The 1928,My 31,21:2 (In
    Addenda)

Alexandrou, Victor (Screenwriter)

Damned, The; Maudits, Les 1948,Ap 26,27:2

Alexandrov, A (Composer)

Lenin in October 1938,Ap 2,18:1

Alexandrov, George V (Director)

Old and New 1930,My 3,23:1

Alexandrov, Gregori (Producer)

Tanya 1942,Mr 5,27:1

Alexandrov, Gregory (Director)

Moscow Laughs 1935,Mr 25,12:2
Volga-Volga 1941,My 17,19:2
Tanya 1942,Mr 5,27:1
Spring 1948,Mr 15,26:2
Man of Music 1953,My 11,25:2

Alexandrov, Gregory (Screenwriter)

Moscow Laughs 1935,Mr 25,12:2
Volga-Volga 1941,My 17,19:2
Spring 1948,Mr 15,26:2
Man of Music 1953,My 11,25:2

Alexandrov, N G

Station Master, The 1928,Je 18,13:2

Alexandrovskaya, Yekaterina

Fathers and Sons 1960,D 26,27:2

Alexeeff, Nathalie

Lower Depths, The 1937,S 11,20:1

Alexeyev, Andrei

Days and Nights 1946,Ap 29,24:4
Heroes of Shipka 1956,S 3,10:5

Alexeyev, Grigori

They Met in Moscow 1944,Je 7,13:2

Alexeyeva, E

Childhood of Maxim Gorky 1938,S 28,29:3

Alexeyeva, T

Land, The 1955,Ap 11,29:3

Alexiou, Nicos

Day the Fish Came Out, The 1967,O 3,57:1

Alexis, Dimitri

Red Dance, The 1928,Je 26,29:1

Aley, Albert (Screenwriter)

Hound that Thought he was a Racoon, The
    1960,Ag 18,19:2
Ugly Dachshund, The 1966,Ap 7,45:1

Aley, Maxwell (Original Author)

You're not so Tough 1940,Jl 9,25:3

Aleynikov, Peter

Great Glinka, The 1947,D 22,30:2

Alfa, Michele

Dame de Pique, La 1944,O 19,19:2
Winner's Circle, The 1957,My 6,25:2

Alfieri, Ferdinando

Tosca 1958,O 24,40:3

Alfonsi, Lidia

Hercules 1959,Jl 23,32:2
Morgan the Pirate 1961,Jl 20,32:2

Alfonsino

Paisan 1948,Mr 30,26:2

Alfonso, Mercedes

Gunfighters of Casa Grande 1965,S 2,36:1

Alfonso, Yves

Made in U S A 1967,S 28,58:2

Alford, Philip

Shenandoah 1965,Jl 29,18:3

Alford, Phillip

To Kill a Mockingbird 1963,F 15,10:2

Alfredo, Colella

House of Ricordi 1956,Mr 13,32:1

Alfven, Margita

Doctor's Women, The 1929,Je 3,27:2
Nar Rosorna Sla Ut 1931,F 10,24:4

Algar, James (Director)

Adventures of Ichabod and Mr Toad, The
    1949,O 10,18:2
Living Desert, The 1953,N 10,38:1
Vanishing Prairie, The 1954,Ag 17,17:3
African Lion, The 1955,S 15,39:2
Secrets of Life 1956,N 21,20:1
White Wilderness 1958,Ag 13,22:1
Jungle Cat 1960,Ag 18,19:2

Algar, James (Original Author)

Secrets of Life 1956,N 21,20:1

Algar, James (Producer)

Incredible Journey, The 1963,N 21,43:2

Algar, James (Screenwriter)

Living Desert, The 1953,N 10,38:1
Vanishing Prairie, The 1954,Ag 17,17:3
African Lion, The 1955,S 15,39:2
White Wilderness 1958,Ag 13,22:1
Jungle Cat 1960,Ag 18,19:2
Legend of Lobo, The 1962,N 10,16:2
Incredible Journey, The 1963,N 21,43:2

Algazy, Andre E (Producer)

Symphonie d'Amour 1946,Mr 11,19:2

Algezy, Andre E (Producer)

Katia 1939,D 23,9:2

Algood, Sara

Man From Texas 1948,Ag 12,16:5

Algotsson, Sven

491 1967,D 21,45:1

Algren, Nelson

Goldstein 1965,My 8,19:7

Algren, Nelson (Original Author)

Man With the Golden Arm, The 1955,D 16,38:2
Walk on the Wild Side 1962,F 22,20:1

Algy, Antonio D'

Soul Mates 1926,Ja 4,16:1

Algy, Helena D'

Daddy's Gone A-Hunting 1925,F 24,17:3
Confessions of a Queen 1925,Mr 24,20:6

Algy, Tony D'

Semana de Felicidad, Una; One Week of
    Happiness 1935,Je 15,20:3

Ali

Rango 1931,F 19,20:4

Ali, Fatima Bint

Island of Allah 1956,Je 27,35:1

Ali, George

Peter Pan 1924,D 29,11:4

Ali, Hadji

Scarlet Dawn 1932,N 4,25:4

Ali, Useff

Falcon in Hollywood, The 1944,D 9,21:2

Aliaga, Amparo
Boliche 1935,My 28,30:2
Aliaga, Nieves
Relicario, El; Reliquary, The 1935,D 31,11:3
Aliardice, James (Screenwriter)
Money From Home 1954,F 27,11:3
Alibali, Adivie
Skanderbeg 1954,Jl 5,6:4
Alibert, Louis
Million, Le 1931,My 21,33:2
Aligrudic, Slobodan
Affair of the Heart, An 1967,S 23,20:3
Love Affair, or the Case of the Missing
Switchboard Operator; Affair of the Heart, An
1968,F 7,38:3
Alington, Adrian (Screenwriter)
My Brother Jonathan 1949,Je 29,34:4
Portrait of Clare 1951,D 26,19:6
Alippi, Elias
Cadetes de San Martin 1939,Jl 3,10:6
Viento Norte; North Wind 1939,S 16,20:3
Asi es la Vida; Such Is Life 1940,Ag 6,15:1
Alison, Dave
Disputed Passage 1939,O 26,27:2
Alison, Dorothy
Turn the Key Softly 1954,F 4,21:6
High and Dry 1954,Ag 31,25:5
Purple Plain, The 1955,Ap 11,29:1
Reach for the Sky 1957,My 1,40:1
Third Key, The 1957,Je 3,30:2
Silken Affair, The 1957,O 31,41:1
Man Upstairs, The 1959,Ag 11,23:2
Georgy Girl 1966,O 18,48:1
Matter of Innocence, A 1968,F 22,36:1
Alison, Joan (Original Author)
Casablanca 1942,N 27,27:1
Alisova, Natalia
Rainbow, The 1944,O 23,14:3
Ivan Pavlov 1950,F 13,15:2
Alisova, Nina
Without Dowry 1946,Ap 15,22:2
Lady With the Dog, The 1962,N 7,48:1
1929 All-American football team
Maybe It's Love 1930,O 18,23:2
Allain, Marcel (Original Author)
Fantomas 1934,Mr 13,27:4
Allain, Raymonde
Paris Waltz, The 1950,Ag 23,35:2
ALLAN
See Also ALAN, ALLEN
Allan, Anthony
Out West With the Hardys 1938,D 9,31:2
Dramatic School 1938,D 9,31:2
Fast and Loose 1939,Mr 9,18:1
Maisie 1939,Je 23,23:1
Allan, David
Fear and Desire 1953,Ap 1,35:2
Allan, Elizabeth
Michael and Mary 1932,Mr 5,11:2
Reserved for Ladies 1932,My 21,9:2
Looking Forward 1933,My 1,10:2
No Marriage Ties 1933,Ag 4,18:2
Solitaire Man, The 1933,S 23,11:5
Ace of Aces 1933,N 11,10:4
Mystery of Mr X, The 1934,F 26,21:3
Men in White 1934,Je 9,18:2
Outcast Lady 1934,N 3,20:3
David Copperfield 1935,Ja 19,8:1
Phantom Fiend 1935,Ap 22,14:2
Mark of the Vampire 1935,My 3,23:4
Java Head 1935,Jl 31,21:4
Tale of Two Cities, A 1935,D 26,21:2
Woman Rebels, A 1936,O 30,27:2
Camille 1937,Ja 23,13:1
Soldier and the Lady, The 1937,Ap 10,11:1
Slave Ship 1937,Je 17,19:2
Great Mr Handel, The 1943,S 10,29:3
48 Hours 1944,Je 26,21:2
No Highway in the Sky 1951,S 22,8:6
Folly to be Wise 1953,D 28,17:2
Heart of the Matter, The 1954,N 19,20:2
Front Page Story 1955,Ap 19,28:1
Haunted Strangler, The 1958,Jl 4,15:3
Allan, Hugh
What Fools Men 1925,S 29,31:3
Dress Parade 1927,O 31,22:1
Beware of Married Men 1928,Ap 10,33:2
Allan, Igor
Cinerama-South Seas Adventure 1958,Jl 16,26:1
Allan, Lewis (Composer)
Romance of Rosy Ridge, The 1947,S 12,18:3
Allan, Lewis (Miscellaneous)
Roosevelt Story, The 1947,Ag 22,11:2
Allan, Marguerite
April Romance 1937,Ja 27,17:4
Allan, Michael
Broken Journey 1949,My 26,34:3
While the Sun Shines 1950,Jl 1,9:2
Allan, Richard
Frogmen, The 1951,Je 30,8:6
With a Song in my Heart 1952,Ap 5,20:2
Snows of Kilimanjaro, The 1952,S 19,19:2
Bloodhounds of Broadway 1952,N 15,15:2

Niagara 1953,Ja 22,20:3
Rest Is Silence, The 1960,Ag 2,22:6
Allan, Vicky
House of Fright 1961,Ag 24,25:4
Alland, Rose (Original Author)
Train, The 1965,Mr 18,25:1
Alland, William
Citizen Kane 1941,My 2,25:1
Macbeth 1950,D 28,22:6
Alland, William (Director)
Look in any Window 1962,Mr 22,40:1
Alland, William (Original Author)
Flesh and Fury 1952,Mr 28,27:4
Revenge of the Creature 1955,My 14,10:7
Alland, William (Producer)
Raiders, The 1952,D 13,19:2
Black Castle, The 1952,D 26,20:4
It Came From Outer Space 1953,Je 18,38:2
Creature from the Black Lagoon 1954,My 1,13:4
Johnny Dark 1954,Je 26,7:2
Dawn at Socorro 1954,Ag 28,8:2
Four Guns to the Border 1954,N 6,15:3
Chief Crazy Horse 1955,Ap 28,25:1
Revenge of the Creature 1955,My 14,10:7
This Island Earth 1955,Je 11,8:7
Creature Walks among Us, The 1956,Ap 27,21:6
Gun for a Coward 1957,Ja 31,21:1
Lady Takes a Flyer, The 1958,Ja 30,19:2
Raw Wind in Eden 1958,S 20,10:6
Look in any Window 1962,Mr 22,40:1
Lively Set, The 1964,O 15,54:1
Rare Breed, The 1966,Ap 14,42:3
Allardice, James B (Original Author)
At War With the Army 1951,Ja 25,21:5
Allardice, James B (Screenwriter)
Sailor Beware 1952,F 1,17:1
Francis Joins the Wacs 1954,Jl 31,6:3
Allardt, Arthur
Louisiana 1919,Jl 21,12:3
Allasio, Marisa
Seven Hills of Rome 1958,Ja 28,24:2 (Incorrect
in this edition; use 1958,Ja 31,24:2 elsewhere)
Poor but Beautiful 1958,Je 11,39:4
Sword and the Cross, The 1960,Jl 7,26:1
Allbright, Wally
Trespasser, The 1929,N 2,14:6
Allbritton, Louise
Who Done It 1942,D 3,35:2
It Comes up Love 1943,Ja 22,25:3
Pittsburgh 1943,F 25,27:2
Good Morning, Judge 1943,Ap 30,25:4
Fired Wife 1943,O 1,15:2
Son of Dracula 1943,N 6,16:4
Her Primitive Man 1944,Ap 1,11:1
ThIs is the Life 1944,Ap 28,23:3
San Diego, I Love You 1944,N 10,25:1
Bowery to Broadway 1944,N 30,19:2
Men in her Diary 1945,S 24,16:5
That Night With You 1945,N 9,16:2
Tangier 1946,Je 7,II,16:4
Egg and I, The 1947,Ap 25,29:2
Sitting Pretty 1948,Mr 11,35:2
Innocent Affair, An 1948,S 29,36:2
Allegret, Catherine
Sleeping Car Murder, The 1966,Mr 8,45:1
Lady L 1966,My 19,51:1
Allegret, Marc
Blood and Roses 1961,O 12,41:4
Allegret, Marc (Director)
Luc Aux Dames 1936,Ja 15,14:4
Razumov 1937,Mr 9,27:2
Orage 1938,D 12,26:2
Heart of Paris 1939,Ja 13,17:3
Curtain Rises, The 1939,Ap 22,15:2
Fanny 1948,F 13,26:2
Blanche Fury 1948,N 24,20:2
Twilight 1949,D 30,13:2
Naked Heart, The 1955,Mr 9,22:4
Julietta 1957,Je 18,38:2
Please Mr Balzac 1957,N 18,37:2
Lady Chatterley's Lover 1959,Jl 11,11:1
Tales of Paris (The Tale of Sophie); Tale of Sophie,
The (Tales of Paris) 1962,Ag 27,18:1
Allegret, Marc (Miscellaneous)
Tales of Paris (The Tale of Sophie); Tale of Sophie,
The (Tales of Paris) 1962,Ag 27,18:1
Allegret, Marc (Screenwriter)
Naked Heart, The 1955,Mr 9,22:4
Please Mr Balzac 1957,N 18,37:2
Lady Chatterley's Lover 1959,Jl 11,11:1
Allegret, Yves (Director)
Dedee 1949,Ap 9,9:2
Cheat, The 1950,O 2,19:3
Riptide 1951,Ap 7,9:2
Seven Deadly Sins, The (Lust); Lust (The Seven
Deadly Sins) 1953,My 12,31:3
Desperate Decision 1954,N 9,31:5
Proud and the Beautiful, The 1956,My 29,32:2
Young Girls Beware 1959,Ag 22,8:2
Oasis 1960,Jl 7,26:1
Port of Desire 1960,N 3,49:2

Allegret, Yves (Screenwriter)
Dedee 1949,Ap 9,9:2
Allegrini, Olga
Parlami d'Amore Mariu 1934,O 20,20:3
ALLEN
See Also ALLAN, ALAN
Allen, Adrianne
Loose Ends 1930,O 18,23:2
Merrily We Go to Hell 1932,Je 11,9:3
Night of June 13th, The 1932,S 17,18:4
Morals of Marcus, The 1936,Ja 13,14:2
October Man, The 1948,Ap 16,29:2
Bond Street 1950,Mr 30,40:6
Final Test, The 1954,Ja 26,21:5
Allen, Alfred
Old Fashioned Boy, An 1920,N 1,13:2
O'Malley of the Mounted 1921,F 7,8:2
Dangerous Innocence 1925,Je 8,19:1
Rolling Home 1926,Je 8,22:1
Out all Night 1927,S 27,31:1
Hot News 1928,Jl 23,11:2
Flying Fleet, The 1929,F 11,26:3
Allen, Arthur
Ebb Tide 1937,N 18,27:2
Our Town 1940,Je 14,25:3
Rangers of Fortune 1940,S 19,27:2
Allen, Austen (Original Author)
Pleasure Cruise 1933,Ap 3,13:3
Allen, Barbara
Melody Ranch 1940,D 26,23:3
Mad Doctor, The 1941,F 27,23:4
Kiss the Boys Goodbye 1941,Ag 14,21:2
Buy Me That Town 1941,O 23,27:2
Allen, Barbara Jo (Vera Vague)
Ice-Capades 1941,S 25,29:1
Design for Scandal 1942,F 6,23:3
Larceny, Inc 1942,Ap 25,9:1
Opposite Sex, The 1956,N 16,23:2
Allen, Barry
Sunny 1930,D 27,16:3
Allen, Bebe
Operation Mad Ball 1957,N 21,38:1
Allen, Christine
One, Two, Three 1961,D 22,17:1
Allen, Corey
Rebel without a Cause 1955,O 27,28:3
Big Caper, The 1957,Mr 29,16:1
Darby's Rangers 1958,F 13,23:2
Party Girl 1958,O 29,30:1
Private Property 1960,Ap 25,40:2
Chapman Report, The 1962,O 18,49:2
Allen, Diana
Heliotrope 1920,N 29,20:3
Exciters, The 1923,Je 4,13:3
Allen, Dorothy
Over the Hill to the Poor House 1920,S 18,16:2
Hoosier Schoolmaster, The 1924,Mr 18,25:2
School for Wives 1925,Ap 1,21:3
Allen, Drew
Song of my Heart 1948,Mr 5,17:3
Allen, Edith
Scaramouche 1923,O 12,7:2 (Incorrect in this
edition; use 1927,O 1,7:2 elsewhere)
Virtuous Liars 1924,Mr 31,20:1
Allen, Elizabeth
If This Be Sin 1950,Jl 1,9:2
From the Terrace 1960,Jl 16,10:1
Diamond Head 1963,F 21,5:2
Donovan's Reef 1963,Jl 25,14:1
Cheyenne Autumn 1964,D 24,8:1
Allen, Ethan
Border Legion, The 1930,Je 30,22:6
Flood, The 1931,Ap 27,25:1
Allen, Ethan (Director)
Safe at Home 1941,N 26,31:2
Allen, Ethan (Screenwriter)
Safe at Home 1941,N 26,31:2
Allen, Florence
Lone Wolf's Daughter, The 1929,Mr 4,20:2
Allen, Fred
Thanks a Million 1935,N 14,17:1
Sally, Irene and Mary 1938,F 26,9:2
Love Thy Neighbor 1940,D 18,32:5
It's in the Bag 1945,Je 11,12:1
We're not Married 1952,Jl 12,16:2
Allen, Frederick Lewis (Miscellaneous)
Golden Twenties, The 1950,Ap 10,15:2
Allen, Frederick Lewis (Original Author)
Only Yesterday 1933,N 10,25:1
Allen, Gene (Screenwriter)
Chapman Report, The 1962,O 18,49:2
Allen, Glen
Burning Cross, The 1948,F 20,19:1
Allen, Gracie
International House 1933,My 27,11:5
College Humor 1933,Je 23,15:4
Six of a Kind 1934,Mr 10,18:3
We're not Dressing 1934,Ap 26,27:2
Many Happy Returns 1934,Je 9,18:2
Love in Bloom 1935,Ap 20,16:2
Big Broadcast of 1936, The 1935,S 16,15:2
Here Comes Cookie 1935,O 12,12:2
Big Broadcast of 1937, The 1936,O 22,31:1

Allen, Gracie— Cont

College Holiday 1936,D 24,21:2
Damsel in Distress, A 1937,N 25,37:1
College Swing 1938,Ap 28,27:2
Honolulu 1939,F 23,19:2
Gracie Allen Murder Case, The 1939,Je 8,31:3
Mr and Mrs North 1942,Ja 22,13:2
Two Girls and a Sailor 1944,Je 15,16:1

Allen, Harry

Corporal Kate 1926,D 15,30:4
Two Lovers 1928,Mr 23,24:4
Strange Cargo 1929,F 18,28:1
Hell Harbor 1930,Mr 28,22:6
Chances 1931,Je 12,27:1
Silver Streak, The 1935,Ja 16,21:1
Anna Karenina 1935,Ag 31,16:2
White Angel, The 1936,Je 25,24:1
Little Princess, The 1939,Mr 11,21:1
Moon Over Burma 1940,D 12,37:4
Hour Before the Dawn, The 1944,My 11,25:6
Swordsman, The 1947,O 17,18:4
Thunder in the Valley 1947,N 28,30:1

Allen, Henry

Dawn Patrol, The 1930,Jl 11,22:1

Allen, Hervey (Original Author)

Anthony Adverse 1936,Ag 27,16:1

Allen, Hugh

Good Time Charley 1927,N 21,20:1
At Yale 1928,Jl 30,21:2
Plastered in Paris 1928,S 24,25:1

Allen, Irving (Director)

Avalanche 1946,Jl 8,25:2
16 Fathoms Deep 1948,O 7,35:2

Allen, Irving (Producer)

16 Fathoms Deep 1948,O 7,35:2
Man on the Eiffel Tower, The 1950,Ja 30,12:2
New Mexico 1951,Jl 14,7:2
Paratrooper 1953,D 31,9:3
Hell Below Zero 1954,Jl 17,7:3
Black Knight, The 1954,O 29,27:2
Prize of Gold, A 1955,O 15,19:2
Cockleshell Heroes, The 1956,Je 4,25:2
Zarak 1956,D 27,22:1
Fire Down Below 1957,Ag 9,11:2
Man Inside, The 1959,F 5,24:7
Long Ships, The 1964,Je 25,25:1
Murderers' Row 1966,D 22,40:3
Ambushers, The 1967,D 23,29:1
Hammerhead 1968,S 12,54:3

Allen, Irwin (Director)

Animal World, The 1956,My 31,21:6
Story of Mankind, The 1957,N 9,31:2
Lost World, The 1960,Jl 14,23:1
Voyage to the Bottom of the Sea 1961,Jl 20,32:2
Five Weeks in a Balloon 1962,Ag 27,18:1

Allen, Irwin (Miscellaneous)

Sea Around Us, The 1953,Jl 8,24:4

Allen, Irwin (Original Author)

Big Circus, The 1959,Jl 18,6:1

Allen, Irwin (Producer)

Girl in Every Port, A 1952,F 14,23:1
Sea Around Us, The 1953,Jl 8,24:4
Dangerous Mission 1954,Mr 6,13:5
Animal World, The 1956,My 31,21:6
Story of Mankind, The 1957,N 9,31:2
Big Circus, The 1959,Jl 18,6:1
Lost World, The 1960,Jl 14,23:1
Voyage to the Bottom of the Sea 1961,Jl 20,32:2
Five Weeks in a Balloon 1962,Ag 27,18:1

Allen, Irwin (Screenwriter)

Animal World, The 1956,My 31,21:6
Story of Mankind, The 1957,N 9,31:2
Big Circus, The 1959,Jl 18,6:1
Lost World, The 1960,Jl 14,23:1
Voyage to the Bottom of the Sea 1961,Jl 20,32:2
Five Weeks in a Balloon 1962,Ag 27,18:1

Allen, Jack

Four Feathers 1939,Ag 4,11:1
Conspirator 1950,Ap 28,26:2
Breaking Through the Sound Barrier 1952,N 7,19:1

Allen, Jack Major

Bear Hunt, The 1919,Jl 21,12:3

Allen, Jack Major (Producer)

Montana Mountain Adventures 1919,Ja 13,9:3
Lion Trapping 1919,Ag 11,9:1

Allen, Jane (Original Author)

She Knew All the Answers 1941,Je 20,28:4
Without Reservations 1946,Je 8,17:2

Allen, Jay Presson (Screenwriter)

Marnie 1964,Je 23,19:1

Allen, Jimmie

Sky Parade, The 1936,Ap 20,17:1

Allen, Joel

Story of Dr Wassell, The 1944,Je 7,13:2
Sign of the Cross 1944,D 21,16:3
Objective Burma 1945,Ja 27,15:2

Allen, Johannes (Director)

Young Have no Time, The 1959,N 23,41:2

Allen, Johannes (Original Author)

Young Have no Time, The 1959,N 23,41:2

Allen, Johannes (Screenwriter)

Girls are Willing, The 1959,My 11,30:1
Young Have no Time, The 1959,N 23,41:2

Allen, John

One, Two, Three 1961,D 22,17:1

Allen, John H

Charlie Chan at the Race Track 1936,Ag 15,6:2
Give Me a Sailor 1938,Ag 11,31:1

Allen, Joseph

Seven Keys to Baldpate 1929,D 26,21:1
Gambling 1934,D 4,22:3
Lucky Night 1939,My 5,29:3

Allen, Joseph Jr

Death of a Champion 1939,Ag 24,17:3
Our Leading Citizen 1939,Ag 24,17:1
Night Before the Divorce, The 1942,Ap 10,21:3
Who Is Hope Schuyler 1942,My 22,27:1
It Happened in Flatbush 1942,Jl 3,12:8

Allen, Judith

This Day and Age 1933,S 1,15:4
Too Much Harmony 1933,S 23,11:5
Hell and Highwater 1933,D 18,24:4
Witching Hour, The 1934,Ap 28,11:3
Old-Fashioned Way, The 1934,Jl 14,16:5
Dancing Man 1934,Jl 16,11:3
She Loves Me Not 1934,S 8,18:5
Young and Beautiful 1934,S 18,18:4
Bright Eyes 1934,D 21,31:1
Behind the Green Lights 1935,Ap 22,14:2
Navy Spy 1937,Mr 22,27:3
It Happened Out West 1937,Je 7,22:3
Boots and Saddles 1937,N 8,19:2
Port of Missing Girls, The 1938,Ap 4,12:5

Allen, June

Forbidden Street, The 1949,My 14,9:2

Allen, Lee

Funny Girl 1968,S 20,42:1

Allen, Leigh

Rebound 1931,Ag 29,16:3
Sooky 1931,D 21,28:4
Double Harness 1933,Jl 21,20:2

Allen, Lester

Heat's on, The 1943,N 26,29:2
Great Flamario, The 1945,Ja 15,15:5
Dolly Sisters, The 1945,N 15,24:6
Dark Mirror, The 1946,O 19,15:2
Pirate, The 1948,My 21,19:2
That Lady in Ermine 1948,Ag 25,31:2
Ma and Pa Kettle 1949,Ag 12,13:2

Allen, Lewis (Director)

Uninvited, The 1944,F 21,19:3
Our Hearts Were Young and Gay 1944,O 12,24:2
Unseen, The 1945,My 14,20:5
Those Endearing Young Charms 1945,Je 20,26:5
Perfect Marriage, The 1947,Ja 16,30:3
Imperfect Lady, The 1947,My 22,34:5
Desert Fury 1947,S 25,35:4
So Evil my Love 1948,Jl 22,27:2
Sealed Verdict 1948,N 3,36:2
Chicago Deadline 1949,N 3,37:2
Valentino 1951,Ap 20,25:1
Appointment With Danger 1951,My 10,38:2
At Swords Point 1952,Ap 10,37:1
Suddenly 1954,O 8,27:2
Bullet for Joey, A 1955,Ap 16,12:1
Illegal 1955,O 29,12:6
Another Time Another Place 1958,My 3,10:4

Allen, Lewis (Producer)

Connection, The 1962,O 4,44:1
Lord of the Flies 1963,Ag 20,37:1
Fahrenheit 451 1966,N 15,53:1

Allen, Marguerite

Widecombe Fair 1929,O 28,20:1
Sleeping Partners 1930,D 13,22:2

Allen, Marty

Last of the Secret Agents, The? 1966,Je 23,29:1

Allen, Maude

Whispering Smith Speaks 1936,F 17,21:1
Secret Valley 1937,Ja 25,22:2
Painted Desert 1938,S 14,26:5
Black Diamonds 1940,S 10,26:6

Allen, Patrick

Dial M for Murder 1954,My 29,13:2
1984 1956,O 1,31:1
Mark of the Hawk, The 1958,Mr 6,32:1
Traitors, The 1963,Je 27,23:4
Night of the Generals, The 1967,F 3,38:1

Allen, R S (Original Author)

Man Called Flintstone, The 1967,N 25,42:1

Allen, R S (Screenwriter)

Girl Happy 1965,My 27,28:1
Who's Minding the Mint? 1967,D 7,60:3
With Six You Get Egg Roll 1968,O 10,59:6

Allen, Rae

Damn Yankees 1958,S 27,12:7
Tiger Makes Out, The 1967,S 19,53:1

Allen, Rex

Dream of Jeanie, I 1952,Je 26,26:2

Allen, Rex (Narrator)

Hound that Thought he was a Racoon, The 1960,Ag 18,19:2
Run, Appaloosa, Run! 1966,Jl 14,28:1

Allen, Ricca

Close Harmony 1929,Ap 29,29:2
Pursuit of Happiness, The 1934,O 26,25:1
Trail of the Lonesome Pine, The 1936,F 20,23:5

Allen, Richard (Screenwriter)

Belle Sommers 1962,My 31,23:2

Allen, Robert

Menace 1934,N 22,27:2
I'll Love You Always 1935,Mr 30,11:2
Air Hawks 1935,Je 4,26:5
Love Me Forever 1935,Je 28,24:1
Crime and Punishment 1935,N 22,18:2
Lady of Secrets 1936,F 22,12:1
Pride of the Marines 1936,Ap 27,19:2
Craig's Wife 1936,O 2,29:3
Awful Truth, The 1937,N 5,19:3
Keep Smiling 1938,Ag 10,15:2
Meet the Girls 1938,S 3,16:6
Up the River 1938,D 3,11:2
Tail Spin 1939,F 11,13:2
Winter Carnival 1939,Jl 28,14:2
City of Chance 1940,Ja 22,11:3
Terror in the City 1966,N 9,43:4

Allen, Roger

Student Prince, The 1954,Je 16,18:2
Lord of the Flies 1963,Ag 20,37:1

Allen, Ronald

A Night to Remember 1958,D 17,2:7

Allen, Sam

Sea Hunt, The 1926,Ja 16,8:5
Sea Beast, The 1926,Ja 16,8:5
Mother 1927,My 4,29:2
Death Valley 1927,N 22,32:2

Allen, Sheila

Alphabet Murders, The 1966,Jl 12,36:2

Allen, Steve

I'll Get by 1950,N 2,39:3
Benny Goodman Story 1956,F 22,22:1
Big Circus, The 1959,Jl 18,6:1
College Confidential 1960,Ag 22,23:1
Warning Shot 1967,Je 8,52:2
Where Were You When the Lights Went Out? 1968,Ag 9,30:2

Allen, Ted (Original Author)

Great Rupert, The 1950,Ap 14,27:2

Allen, Tom

Shadows 1961,Mr 22,37:1

Allen, Valerie

Hot Spell 1958,S 18,37:2
Five Pennies, The 1959,Je 19,30:1
Bells Are Ringing 1960,Je 24,31:2

Allen, Vera

Doctor Bull 1933,O 6,21:2

Allen, Viktor

Brig, The 1964,S 21,37:4

Allen, Winifred

Second Youth 1924,Ap 22,19:3

Allen, Woody

What's New Pussycat? 1965,Je 23,49:1
Casino Royale 1967,Ap 29,25:1

Allen, Woody (Miscellaneous)

What's Up, Tiger Lily? 1966,N 18,33:1

Allen, Woody (Screenwriter)

What's New Pussycat? 1965,Je 23,49:1

Allenby, Frank

Return of the Scarlet Pimpernel, The 1938,Ap 11,12:2
Madame Bovary 1949,Ag 26,15:2
Flame and the Arrow, The 1950,Jl 8,7:2
Soldiers Three 1951,Mr 30,28:5

Alleney, Tamba

Moby Dick 1956,Jl 5,18:1

Allensworth, Carl (Director)

Pilgrimage for Peace: Pope Paul VI Visits America, A 1966,Jl 21,20:2

Allensworth, Carl (Screenwriter)

Pilgrimage for Peace: Pope Paul VI Visits America, A 1966,Jl 21,20:2

Alley, S

Beachcomber, The 1938,D 26,29:3

Allgood, Sara

To What Red Hell 1929,O 6,IX,9:4 (In Addenda)
Blackmail 1929,O 7,22:1
Juno and the Paycock 1930,Je 30,22:6
Bride of the Lake, The 1934,S 11,24:5
Passing of the Third Floor Back, The 1936,Ap 29,19:2
It's Love Again 1936,My 23,12:1
Kathleen 1938,Ja 24,17:1
Storm in a Teacup 1938,Mr 22,18:4
Fugitive, The 1940,Jl 23,22:2
That Hamilton Woman 1941,Ap 4,25:1
Dr Jekyll and Mr Hyde 1941,Ag 13,13:2
Lydia 1941,S 19,27:1
How Green Was my Valley 1941,O 29,27:2
Roxie Hart 1942,F 20,21:1
This Above All 1942,My 13,14:3
It Happened in Flatbush 1942,Jl 3,12:8
War Against Mrs Hadley, The 1942,N 26,40:2
Life Begins at Eight-Thirty 1942,D 10,35:2
Lodger, The 1944,Ja 20,15:3
Jane Eyre 1944,F 4,12:5
Between Two Worlds 1944,My 6,11:2
Keys of the Kingdom, The 1944,D 30,15:2
Uncle Harry 1945,Ag 24,14:5
Spiral Staircase, The 1946,F 7,29:3
Kitty 1946,Ap 1,23:1

Allgood, Sara— Cont
Cluny Brown 1946,Je 3,27:3
Fabulous Dorseys, The 1947,My 30,25:3
Ivy 1947,Je 26,19:1
Mother Wore Tights 1947,Ag 21,33:2
Mourning Becomes Electra 1947,N 20,38:2
My Wild Irish Rose 1947,D 25,32:2
One Touch of Venus 1948,O 29,29:5
Accused, The 1949,Ja 13,26:2
Cheaper by the Dozen 1950,Ap 1,12:2
Challenge to Lassie 1950,Ap 7,22:3

Allhoff, Fred (Original Author)
I Am the Law 1938,Ag 26,14:2
Allibert, Jean-Louis
Marseillaise 1939,N 6,20:2
Allibert, Louis
Milady 1933,S 8,22:3
Allieres, Annick
Love Is my Profession 1959,Ap 28,41:1
Allin, Alex
Horse Ate the Hat, The 1931,S 1,30:6
Allinson, Vera (Original Author)
Broken Melody, The 1934,O 31,17:3
Allio, Rene (Director)
Shameless old Lady, The 1966,S 19,57:1
Shameless Old Lady, The 1966,S 27,52:1
Other One, The 1967,S 29,53:1
Allio, Rene (Screenwriter)
Shameless Old Lady, The 1966,S 27,52:1
Other One, The 1967,S 29,53:1
Allison, May
Youth for Sale 1924,S 3,17:1
I Want my Man 1925,Ap 6,17:3
Greater Glory, The 1926,My 4,31:1
Men of Steel 1926,Jl 12,24:4
Telephone Girl, The 1927,My 16,24:2
Allison, Paul (Original Author)
Main Event, The 1927,O 31,22:1
Allison, Perk
Massacre Hill 1950,D 14,51:3
Allister, Claude
Trial of Mary Dugan, The 1929,Mr 29,21:1
Bulldog Drummond 1929,My 3,23:2
Charming Sinners 1929,Jl 8,17:3
Three Live Ghosts 1929,S 30,23:1
Slightly Scarlet 1930,Mr 1,23:1
Such Men Are Dangerous 1930,Mr 8,21:1
In the Next Room 1930,Ap 7,21:1
Murder Will Out 1930,Ap 14,24:2
Ladies Love Brutes 1930,My 16,20:4
Florodora Girl, The 1930,My 31,19:4
Czar of Broadway, The 1930,Je 30,22:6
Monte Carlo 1930,Ag 28,22:4
Reaching for the Moon 1930,D 30,24:2
I Like Your Nerve 1931,S 12,15:4
Platinum Blonde 1931,O 31,22:2
Blame the Woman 1932,O 25,24:5
Private Life of Henry VIII, The 1933,O 13,25:2
Lady is Willing, The 1934,Ag 11,16:5
Dark Angel, The 1935,S 6,12:2
Dracula's Daughter 1936,My 18,14:2
Bulldog Drummond at Bay 1937,O 25,23:2
Awful Truth, The 1937,N 5,19:3
Men Are Such Fools 1938,Je 17,25:1
Arrest Bulldog Drummond 1939,Ja 12,23:2
Captain Fury 1939,My 26,20:2
Lillian Russell 1940,My 18,11:2
Reluctant Dragon, The 1941,Jl 25,12:2
Charley's Aunt 1941,Ag 2,18:2
Confirm or Deny 1941,D 19,35:2
Hong Kong 1952,Ap 5,20:3
Kiss Me Kate 1953,N 6,23:2
Allister, Claude (Miscellaneous)
Adventures of Ichabod and Mr Toad, The
1949,O 10,18:2
Allman, Elvia
Night at Earl Carroll's, A 1941,Ja 23,19:1
Sis Hopkins 1941,My 1,27:5
Pleasure of his Company, The 1961,Je 2,36:1
Breakfast at Tiffany's 1961,O 6,28:1
Honeymoon Hotel 1964,Je 4,28:1
Allman, Sheldon
Hud 1963,My 29,36:1
Allred, Julie
What Ever Happened to Baby Jane?
1962,N 7,48:1
Allworth, Frank
Manhandled 1924,Jl 29,9:2
That Royle Girl 1926,Ja 4,33:1
East Side, West Side 1927,O 18,33:2
Allwyn, Astrid
Lady With a Past 1932,F 22,23:2
Night Mayor, The 1932,N 25,19:2
Iron Master, The 1933,F 4,11:3
Beggars in Ermine 1934,Ap 25,25:3
Servants' Entrance 1934,S 27,25:2
White Parade, The 1934,N 10,19:1
One More Spring 1935,F 22,27:1
Accent on Youth 1935,Ag 12,10:3
Way Down East 1935,O 31,16:2
Hands Across the Table 1935,N 2,13:2
Charlie Chan's Secret 1936,Ja 18,19:4
Follow the Fleet 1936,F 21,21:2

Star for a Night 1936,S 5,7:2
Dimples 1936,O 10,21:2
Flying Hostess 1936,D 14,29:4
Stowaway 1936,D 19,16:1
Woman Wise 1937,Ja 23,13:1
Love Takes Flight 1937,S 27,24:3
Westland Case, The 1937,O 23,14:2
International Crime 1938,My 16,14:4
Love Affair 1939,Mr 17,25:2
Miracles for Sale 1939,Ag 10,15:2
Honeymoon in Bali 1939,S 21,21:1
Mr Smith Goes to Washington 1939,O 20,27:2
Reno 1939,D 21,29:2
Lone Wolf Strikes, The 1940,F 5,13:2
Gangs of Chicago 1940,Je 13,29:2
Unexpected Uncle 1941,S 25,29:1
No Hands on the Clock 1941,D 22,24:6
Hit Parade of 1943 1943,Ap 16,24:3
Allyson, June
Best Foot Forward 1943,Je 30,25:2
Thousands Cheer 1943,S 14,27:1
Girl Crazy 1943,D 3,27:2
Two Girls and a Sailor 1944,Je 15,16:1
Meet The People 1944,S 8,16:2
Music for Millions 1944,D 22,12:4
Her Highness and the Bellboy 1945,S 28,16:2
Sailor Takes a Wife, The 1946,Mr 1,17:2
Two Sisters From Boston 1946,Je 7,16:2
Till the Clouds Roll By 1946,D 6,27:4
Secret Heart, The 1946,D 26,28:2
High Barbaree 1947,Je 6,27:2
Good News 1947,D 5,33:2
Bride Goes Wild, The 1948,Je 4,27:2
Three Musketeers, The 1948,O 21,33:2
Words and Music 1948,D 10,34:2
Little Women 1949,Mr 11,33:2
Stratton Story, The 1949,My 13,29:1
Reformer and the Redhead, The 1950,Ap 10,15:2
Right Cross 1950,N 16,39:2
Too Young to Kiss 1951,N 23,32:2
Girl in White, The 1952,My 31,12:5
Battle Circus 1953,My 28,27:5
Glenn Miller Story, the 1954,F 11,33:2
Executive Suite 1954,My 7,19:1
Woman's World 1954,S 29,23:4
Strategic Air Command 1955,Ap 21,33:1
Shrike, The 1955,Jl 8,15:2
McConnell Story, The 1955,S 30,23:1
Opposite Sex, The 1956,N 16,23:2
My Man Godfrey 1957,O 12,23:1
Stranger in my Arms 1959,Mr 4,34:2
Almada, Guillermina
Tierra, Amor y Dolor 1935,Ag 10,16:5
Almas, Joseph
Secret Flight 1952,Jl 3,16:2
Almazan, Humberto
Inside a Girls' Dormitory 1956,F 6,27:7
Almer, Ann
Cold Wind in August, A 1961,Jl 27,23:2
Almirante
Three Caballeros, The 1945,F 5,20:1
Almirante, Ada C
Richiamo del Cuore, Il; Appeal of the Heart, The
1931,Mr 2,19:1
Almirante, Ernesto
Marco Visconti 1947,S 20,12:4
To Live in Peace 1947,N 25,37:2
Angelina 1948,Ap 6,27:2
Difficult Years 1950,Ag 22,31:2
Father's Dilemma 1952,S 23,25:1
White Line, The 1952,D 6,17:2
Almirante, Luigi
Stella del Mare; Star of the Sea 1940,My 3,17:6
Dream of Butterfly, The 1941,F 13,25:2
Cavalleria Rusticana 1947,D 20,21:2
My Widow and I 1950,Ag 30,27:5
Almlof, Charles
Karl Fredrik Reigns 1938,F 2,15:2
Almond, Paul (Director)
Isabel 1968,Jl 24,47:1
Almond, Paul (Producer)
Isabel 1968,Jl 24,47:1
Almond, Paul (Screenwriter)
Isabel 1968,Jl 24,47:1
Almos
French Way, The 1952,S 6,12:6
Almos, Lubina
Vida es un Tango, La; Life is a Tango
1939,Jl 8,20:5
Almos, Raymond
They Were Five 1938,Je 1,19:5
Almroth, Greta
Witch Woman, The 1929,Ap 8,32:1
Aloes, Goesti Poetoe
Legong 1935,O 2,27:1
Alon, Ygal
Clouds Over Israel 1966,My 10,48:6
Alonso, Arsenio
Walls of Hell, The 1965,N 18,55:3
Alonso, Chelo
Sign of the Gladiator 1959,D 3,46:1
Goliath and the Barbarians 1960,Ja 7,24:6
Son of Samson 1962,S 27,33:4

Alonso, Victoria
En un Burro Tres Baturros; Three Rustics on one
Donkey 1940,S 21,13:3
Alonzo, Trini
Weekend, Italian Style 1968,My 23,56:2
Aloshnikova, Lily
Grown-Up Children 1963,Ap 15,36:5
Alov, Aleksandr (Director)
Peace to Him Who Enters 1963,N 25,23:5
Alov, Aleksandr (Producer)
Peace to Him Who Enters 1963,N 25,23:5
Alovand, Aleksandr (Screenwriter)
Peace to Him Who Enters 1963,N 25,23:5
Alpar, Gitta
Gitta Entdeckt Ihr Herz 1932,S 30,17:3
Die oder Keine; Her or Nobody
1932,N 13,IX,4:2
Die-oder Keine 1934,O 29,14:3
Loves of Madame Dubarry, The 1938,Ap 4,12:5
Alpe, James
Cyanamide 1954,Mr 26,17:6
Alper, Murray
Royal Family of Broadway, The 1930,D 23,25:1
Little Big Shot 1935,O 7,11:2
Seven Keys to Baldpate 1935,D 14,11:2
Panic on the Air 1936,Ap 20,17:1
Two in Revolt 1936,Ap 25,21:1
High Tension 1936,Jl 11,11:4
Winterset 1936,D 4,31:1
You Can't Buy Luck 1937,My 14,21:2
23 1/2 Hours Leave 1937,My 17,23:2
Big Town Girl 1937,D 13,23:4
Next Time I Marry 1938,D 2,27:2
Tail Spin 1939,F 11,13:2
Twelve Crowded Hours 1939,F 24,15:2
Night of Nights, The 1939,D 28,17:1
Big Guy, The 1940,Ja 1,29:2
Black Friday 1940,Mr 22,23:3
Turnabout 1940,Jl 27,17:6
Maltese Falcon, The 1941,O 4,18:2
My Life With Caroline 1941,O 30,27:1
Lady is Willing, The 1942,Ap 24,21:2
Saboteur 1942,My 8,27:2
Big Shot, The 1942,Jl 18,8:2
Corvette K-225 1943,O 21,30:1
No Time for Love 1943,D 2,30:1
Eve of St Mark, The 1944,My 31,22:2
Roger Touhy, Gangster 1944,Je 5,14:7
Wing and a Prayer 1944,Ag 31,14:1
They Were Expendable 1945,D 21,25:2
Up Goes Maisie 1946,Ja 25,26:7
Angel on my Shoulder 1946,O 21,27:2
Gallant Bess 1946,D 6,27:6
Alperson, Edward L (Producer)
Dakota Lil 1950,Mr 3,21:5
Sword of Monte Cristo, The 1951,Ap 23,21:2
3 for Bedroom C 1952,Je 27,18:3
Invaders From Mars 1953,My 30,7:1
New Faces 1954,F 20,8:7
September Storm 1960,O 29,26:7
Alperstein, Chava
Dream no More 1950,Ja 6,25:2
Alpert, David
Death of a Salesman 1951,D 21,21:3
Star, The 1953,Ja 29,25:1
Gog 1954,Ag 14,8:2
Alpha, Aliki
Anna of Rhodes 1950,Mr 23,34:2
Alphin, Patricia
White Tie and Tails 1946,N 8,28:2
I'll Be Yours 1947,F 22,16:2
Something in the Wind 1947,Ag 29,14:3
Larceny 1948,S 4,8:6
Ma and Pa Kettle 1949,Ag 12,13:2
Yes Sir, That's my Baby 1949,N 11,31:2
Alpi, Domenico
Before the Revolution; Prima della Revolutiona
1964,S 25,32:1
Alsen, Elsa
Rogue Song, The 1930,Ja 29,26:4
Alston, Bill
Bank Dick, The 1940,D 13,29:2
Alta, Vincenzo
Marriage Italian Style 1964,D 21,42:1
Altaiskaya, B
Mashenka 1942,N 21,10:7
Altaiskaya, Vera
Tanya 1942,Mr 5,27:1
Ural Front, The 1945,Je 7,25:3
Once There Was a Girl 1945,D 24,19:2
Altamirano, Lucha
Juan Soldado, o Venganza; John the Soldier or
Vengeance 1939,Jl 24,9:3
Altan, Francesco Tullio (Screenwriter)
Tropics 1968,S 24,52:1
Altariba, Beatrice
Young Racers, The 1963,O 10,49:3
Altemus, Edneh
As Man Desires 1925,F 10,20:1
Alten, Ferdinand V
1914: The Last Days Before the War 1932,S 5,9:6
Die-oder Keine 1934,O 29,14:3

Alten, Frank
  This Land Is Mine 1943,My 28,19:1
Alten, Juergen von (Director)
  Togger 1937,Mr 14,XI,4:5 (In Addenda)
  Susanne im Bade; Susanna in the Bath
    1937,S 11,20:1
  Stronger Than the Rule 1937,S 25,10:2
  Biberpelz, Der; Beaver Coat, The 1939,S 9,11:3
Altenkirch, F (Original Author)
  Man Braucht Kein Geld 1932,N 16,15:3
Alter, Ferdinand
  All for a Woman 1921,D 5,20:1
Alter, Louis (Composer)
  Take a Chance 1933,N 27,20:3
  Rainmakers, The 1935,N 2,13:2
  Vogues of 1938 1937,Ag 20,21:1
  Las Vegas Nights 1941,Mr 20,25:2
Alter, Louis (Miscellaneous)
  Sing, Baby, Sing 1936,S 12,20:1
  Make a Wish 1937,S 23,33:1
Althoff, Gustav (Producer)
  Keine Feier Ohne Meyer 1932,O 29,18:4
  Meine Frau, Die Schuetzenkoenigin
    1935,Ja 7,13:3
  Kalte Mamsell, Die 1935,Ja 12,12:2
  Gretl Zieht das Grosse Los 1935,F 11,14:2
  Aschermittwoch; Ash Wednesday
    1935,Mr 11,15:2
  Unschuld vom Lande, Die 1935,My 13,18:6
  Landstreicher, Die; Hoboes, The 1938,N 26,18:1
  Dahinten in der Heide; Back in the Country
    1939,Ja 21,19:3
Altieri, Elena
  Bicycle Thief, The 1949,D 13,44:2
  His Last Twelve Hours 1953,N 13,24:7
  Golden Coach, The 1954,Ja 22,30:2
Altieri, James Capt (Screenwriter)
  This Is Your Army 1954,D 15,41:1
Altieri, James Captain (Miscellaneous)
  This Is Your Army 1954,D 15,41:1
Altieri, James Major (Original Author)
  Darby's Rangers 1958,F 13,23:2
Altimus, Henry (Original Author)
  Man Who Lived Twice, The 1936,O 12,23:2
  Crime Takes a Holiday 1938,N 28,11:2
  Man in the Dark 1953,Ap 9,31:5
Altimus, Henry (Screenwriter)
  Crime Takes a Holiday 1938,N 28,11:2
  They all Kissed the Bride 1942,Jl 31,11:1
Altman, Frieda
  Go, Man, Go 1954,Mr 10,29:5
Altman, Robert (Director)
  James Dean Story, The 1957,O 19,16:7
  Countdown 1968,My 2,57:3
Altman, Robert (Producer)
  James Dean Story, The 1957,O 19,16:7
Altman, William (Screenwriter)
  That Certain Felling 1956,Je 21,35:2
Altolaguirre, Manuel (Producer)
  Mexican Bus ride 1954,Jl 21,18:3
Altolaguirre, Manuel (Screenwriter)
  Mexican Bus ride 1954,Jl 21,18:3
Alton, Bob
  Two Faced Woman 1942,Ja 1,37:2
Alton, Kenneth
  Kronos 1957,My 11,24:6
  Time Limit 1957,O 24,37:2
Alton, Robert (Composer)
  Till the Clouds Roll By 1946,D 6,27:4
Alton, Robert (Director)
  Merton of the Movies 1947,N 7,20:3
  Pagan Love Song 1950,D 26,19:1
Alton, Robert (Miscellaneous)
  You'll Never Get Rich 1941,O 24,27:2
  Pirate, The 1948,My 21,19:2
  Easter Parade 1948,Jl 1,19:3
Altringen, Heinz
  Life of Beethoven, The 1929,Mr 12,26:3
Altschul, Lutiz
  Rosenmontag 1931,Mr 28,15:3
Altschuler, Alice (Original Author)
  Woman Doctor 1939,Mr 24,27:3
  Mickey, the Kid 1939,Jl 6,27:1
Altschuler, Alice (Screenwriter)
  Sabotage 1939,N 16,29:5
Altus, E
  Great Citizen, The 1939,Ja 16,11:2
Altzeva, Tatania
  Zoya 1945,Ap 16,18:6
Alustiza, Frank
  Big Game, The 1936,O 24,23:1
Alva, Popi
  Girl From Corfu, The 1957,My 20,28:2
Alvarado, Crox
  St Francis of Assisi 1947,Ap 5,12:5
  Rosanna 1956,My 17,37:2
Alvarado, Don
  Wife Who Wasn't Wanted, The 1925,S 9,23:1
  Satan in Sables 1925,O 15,27:3
  Night Cry, The 1926,Ap 7,26:6
  Monkey Talks, The 1927,Ap 5,30:7
  Loves of Carmen 1927,S 27,31:1
  Breakfast at Sunrise 1927,N 14,26:1

  Drums of Love 1928,Ja 25,20:4
  Scarlet Lady, The 1928,Ag 15,19:4
  Battle of The Sexes, The 1928,O 15,16:1
  Bridge of San Luis Rey, The 1929,My 20,22:6
  Rio Rita 1929,O 7,22:1
  Bad One, The 1930,Je 13,28:3
  Beau Ideal 1931,Ja 19,25:1
  Captain Thunder 1931,My 11,15:4
  Lady With a Past 1932,F 22,23:2
  Bachelor's Affairs 1932,Je 25,18:2
  Morning Glory 1933,Ag 18,18:2
  Sweet Adeline 1935,Ja 7,13:2
  Devil is a Woman, The 1935,My 4,17:2
  I Live for Love 1935,O 19,21:2
  Rose of the Rancho 1936,Ja 9,25:2
  Spy 77 1936,F 10,15:1
  Red Wagon 1936,Je 22,22:1
  Nobody's Baby 1937,My 20,17:3
  Love Under Fire 1937,Ag 28,8:2
  Rose of the Rio Grande 1938,Jl 9,10:3
  Cafe Society 1939,F 23,19:2
  One Night in the Tropics 1940,D 20,33:2
  Big Steal, The 1949,Jl 11,13:2
Alvarado, Fernando
  Barrier, The 1937,N 27,21:2
  Falcon in Mexico, The 1944,Ag 5,16:2
  Medal for Benny, A 1945,My 24,15:2
  Thrill of a Romance 1945,My 25,22:2
  Stallion Road 1947,Ap 5,12:5
  Jewels of Brandenburg 1947,My 24,10:5
  Tycoon 1947,D 26,22:6
Alvarez, Angel
  Not on Your Life; Verdugo, El 1965,Mr 30,52:1
Alvarez, Carmen
  Li'l Abner 1959,D 12,19:2
Alvarez, Elrol
  Dark River 1956,F 27,19:4
Alvarez, Juanita
  Curse of the Cat People, The 1944,Mr 4,11:1
Alvarez, Luis
  Manhunt in the Jungle 1958,Ap 12,13:1
Alvarez, Paquito
  Vidas Rotas 1935,Ag 3,16:3
Alvarez, Robert
  Illiac Passion, The 1968,Ap 19,40:1
Alvaro, Corrado (Screenwriter)
  Tragic Hunt 1948,O 22,30:2
Alventosa, Ricardo (Director)
  Inheritance, The; Herencia, La 1964,S 16,36:3
Alventosa, Ricardo (Screenwriter)
  Inheritance, The; Herencia, La 1964,S 16,36:3
Alves, Lidia
  Native Son 1951,Je 18,19:2
Alves, Vern (Producer)
  Big Night, The 1960,F 18,37:4
Alvey, Glenn H Jr (Director)
  Door in the Wall 1965,Ja 22,21:2
Alvey, Glenn H Jr (Screenwriter)
  Door in the Wall 1965,Ja 22,21:2
Alvin, John
  Destination Tokyo 1944,Ja 1,9:2
  Sullivans, The 1944,F 10,19:2
  Very Thought of You, The 1944,N 18,16:7
  Objective Burma 1945,Ja 27,15:2
  Roughly Speaking 1945,F 1,18:4
  San Antonio 1945,D 29,19:5
  Three Strangers 1946,F 23,20:2
  Beast With Five Fingers, The 1946,D 26,28:3
  Love and Learn 1947,My 3,10:3
  Open Secret 1948,F 2,15:2
  Two Guys From Texas 1948,Ag 28,8:6
  This Side of the Law 1950,Jl 7,15:2
  Come Fill the Cup 1951,N 22,47:2
  Carrie 1952,Jl 17,20:2
  April in Paris 1952,D 25,34:5
Alvirez, Alfonso
  Brave Bulls, The 1951,Ap 19,39:2
Alwyn, William (Composer)
  Desert Victory 1943,Ap 14,1:6
  True Glory, The 1945,S 7,1:2
Alycia, Marthe
  24 Hours in a Woman's Life 1968,S 25,39:1
Alyn, Glen
  Ware Case, The 1939,Jl 22,12:2
  Lady in Distress 1942,F 16,21:2
Alyn, Kirk
  Pistol Packin' Mama 1943,D 20,27:4
Alyoshina, Tatania
  Girl From Leningrad 1941,D 20,25:2
Alzamora, Armand
  Sergeants 3 1962,F 12,28:2
Alzcona, Raphel (Screenwriter)
  Mafioso 1964,Jl 1,42:1
Amade, Raymond
  Barber of Seville 1949,Jl 21,21:2
Amadio, Silvio (Director)
  Minotaur, The 1961,N 8,41:1
  All the Other Girls Do! 1967,My 30,12:1
Amadio, Silvio (Screenwriter)
  All the Other Girls Do! 1967,My 30,12:1
Amadori, Luis Cesar (Director)
  Poor Perez 1937,N 1,24:6
  Canillita y la Dama, El; Newsie and the Lady,

Amadori, Luis Cesar (Director)— Cont
  The 1939,F 18,12:2
  Madreselva; Honeysuckle 1939,Ag 19,18:4
  Maestro Leuita, El 1940,Je 10,21:2
**Amalgamated Clothing Workers of America, AFL-CIO
                              /(Miscellaneous)**
  Inheritance, The 1964,N 9,42:2
Amalu, Josef
  Daybreak in Udi 1950,Je 2,26:2
Amamoto, Eisei
  King Kong Escapes 1968,Jl 11,30:1
Amanda, Lia
  Three Forbidden Stories 1953,N 16,21:4
Amann, Betty
  Asphalt 1930,My 6,33:4
  White Devil, The 1931,Ag 28,20:1
  O Alte Burschenherrlichkeit 1932,Je 18,9:2
  Grosse Bluff, Der; Big Bluff, The 1937,S 6,20:2
Amaral, Nestor
  Three Caballeros, The 1945,F 5,20:1
Amaral, Nestor Samba Band
  Pan-Americana 1945,Mr 23,13:2
Amaranto, Maruja
  Relicario, El; Reliquary, The 1935,D 31,11:3
Amargo, Henry
  Naked and the Dead, The 1958,Ag 7,21:1
Amateau, Rodney (Director)
  Monsoon 1953,S 26,15:2
Amato
  Francis the First 1947,N 20,38:4
  Devil's Daughter 1949,F 26,11:2
Amato, Giuseppe (Director)
  Malia 1952,F 2,11:4
  Angels of Darkness 1956,N 22,51:1
Amato, Giuseppe (Original Author)
  Seven Hills of Rome 1958,Ja 28,24:2 (Incorrect
    in this edition; use 1958,Ja 31,24:2 elsewhere)
Amato, Giuseppe (Producer)
  Eternal Melodies 1948,F 14,17:3
  Peddler and the Lady, The 1949,S 30,28:4
  Escape into Dreams 1950,Ap 13,34:5
  Tomorrow is too Late 1952,Ap 14,22:2
  Mademoiselle Gobette 1955,F 5,13:3
  Angels of Darkness 1956,N 22,51:1
  Facts of Murder, The 1965,Jl 1,34:1
Amato, Giuseppe (Screenwriter)
  Four Steps in the Clouds 1948,N 22,25:2
  Peddler and the Lady, The 1949,S 30,28:4
  Escape into Dreams 1950,Ap 13,34:5
  Malia 1952,F 2,11:4
Amato, Pasquale
  Glorious Betsy 1928,Ap 27,16:4
Amaya, Carmen
  Knickerbocker Holiday 1944,Ap 20,22:7
  Tarantos, Los 1964,Je 30,22:1
Amaya, Carmen and Co
  Follow the Boys 1944,Ap 26,24:6
Amber, Eve
  Suspect, The 1945,F 1,18:5
  Woman in Green, The 1945,Je 16,10:3
Ambesi, Adriana
  Bible, The 1966,S 29,60:1
Ambler, Eric (Original Author)
  Journey Into Fear 1943,Mr 19,15:3
  Background to Danger 1943,Jl 3,11:2
  Mask of Dimitrios, The 1944,Je 24,16:2
  Way Ahead, The 1945,Je 4,22:3
  Topkapi 1964,S 18,25:1
Ambler, Eric (Producer)
  October Man, The 1948,Ap 16,29:2
Ambler, Eric (Screenwriter)
  Way Ahead, The 1944,Jl 16,II,3:4
  Way Ahead, The 1945,Je 4,22:3
  October Man, The 1948,Ap 16,29:2
  One Woman's Story 1949,My 18,33:2
  Encore (The Ant and the Grasshopper); Ant and
    the Grasshopper, The (Encore) 1952,Ap 3,45:1
  Encore (Gigolo and Gigolette); Gigolo and
    Gigolette (Encore) 1952,Ap 3,45:1
  Encore (Winter Cruise); Winter Cruise (Encore)
    1952,Ap 3,45:1
  Magic Box, The 1952,S 24,40:2
  Promoter, The 1952,O 29,36:2
  Cruel Sea, The 1953,Ag 11,18:5
  Purple Plain, The 1955,Ap 11,29:1
  Lease of Life 1956,F 10,18:1
  Battle Hell 1957,Ag 22,23:1
  A Night to Remember 1958,D 17,2:7
  Wreck of the Mary Deare, The 1959,N 7,27:1
Ambler, Joan
  Battle for Music 1945,O 15,13:2
Ambler, Joss
  Citadel, The 1938,N 4,27:2
  Break the News 1941,Ja 2,24:2
  Flying Fortress 1942,D 19,22:2
  Courageous Mr Penn 1943,D 23,26:5
  Silver Fleet, The 1945,Mr 24,22:6
  Years Between, The 1947,Mr 10,25:2
  Mine Own Executioner 1949,Ja 19,34:2
  Agitator, The 1949,Ag 19,12:5
Ambricourt, Mme d'
  Humming Bird, The 1924,Ja 14,2:1

Ambrogi, Adriano
  Deported 1950,N 2,39:3
  Three Steps North 1951,Je 29,14:2
Ambrosio, Arturo (Director)
  Theodora 1921,O 15,16:2
Ambrosio, Arturo (Producer)
  Story of Tosca, The 1947,D 19,34:2
Ambrosio, Arturo (Screenwriter)
  Story of Tosca, The 1947,D 19,34:2
Ambrus, Irene
  Wien Du Stadt der Lieder; (Vienna City of Song)
    1931,Mr 20,29:1
  Lumpenball 1931,Ap 27,25:1
  Opern-Ball, Der; Opera Ball 1931,N 6,28:3
  Marquise von Pompadour, Die 1936,F 3,21:3
Ameche, Don
  Sins of Man 1936,Je 19,17:2
  Ramona 1936,O 7,32:4
  Ladies in Love 1936,O 29,31:1
  One in a Million 1937,Ja 1,19:3
  Love Is News 1937,Mr 6,10:1
  Fifty Roads to Town 1937,Je 5,21:1
  You Can't Have Everything 1937,Ag 4,15:2
  Love Under Fire 1937,Ag 28,8:2
  In Old Chicago 1938,Ja 7,15:2
  Happy Landing 1938,Ja 22,19:1
  Josette 1938,Je 11,9:1
  Alexander's Ragtime Band 1938,Ag 6,7:2
  Gateway 1938,Ag 8,9:2
  Three Musketeers, The 1939,F 18,12:2
  Story of Alexander Graham Bell, The
    1939,Ap 1,17:2
  Midnight 1939,Ap 6,31:1
  Hollywood Cavalcade 1939,O 14,13:2
  Swanee River 1939,D 30,9:2
  Lillian Russell 1940,My 18,11:2
  Four Sons 1940,Je 8,18:4
  Down Argentine Way 1940,O 18,25:1
  That Night in Rio 1941,Mr 10,21:2
  Moon Over Miami 1941,Jl 5,14:2
  Kiss the Boys Goodbye 1941,Ag 14,21:2
  Feminine Touch, The 1941,D 12,35:3
  Confirm or Deny 1941,D 19,35:2
  Magnificent Dope, The 1942,Jl 3,12:5
  Girl Trouble 1942,O 8,31:2
  Something to Shout About 1943,Ap 8,27:3
  Heaven Can Wait 1943,Ag 12,15:1
  Happy Land 1943,D 9,33:3
  Wing and a Prayer 1944,Ag 31,14:1
  Greenwich Village 1944,S 28,26:2
  It's in the Bag 1945,Je 11,12:1
  Guest Wife 1945,O 18,21:2
  So Goes my Love 1946,My 2,3:7
  That's my Man 1947,Ap 7,20:2
  Sleep, My Love 1948,F 19,29:4
  Slightly French 1949,My 27,25:3
  Fever in the Blood 1961,Ap 20,30:4
  Picture Mommy Dead 1966,N 3,45:4
  Rings Around the World 1967,D 7,60:3
Amedee
  Forbidden Games 1952,D 9,43:2
  Gates of Paris 1958,Ja 15,24:1
Amendola, M (Screenwriter)
  Teacher and the Miracle, The 1961,Ap 24,36:4
Amendolla (Director)
  Padre Mercader; Merchant Father 1939,Jl 15,8:3
Amendt, Rudolph
  When Strangers Marry 1933,My 25,24:3
  Stamboul Quest 1934,Jl 14,16:6
  Fountain, The 1934,Ag 31,14:1
  Hell in the Heavens 1934,D 12,28:2
  I Met Him in Paris 1937,Je 3,29:2
Ament, Walton C (Miscellaneous)
  Fifty Years Before your Eyes 1950,Je 30,18:2
    (Incorrect in this edition; use 1950,Je 28,32:3
    elsewhere)
America, Paul
  My Hustler 1967,Jl 11,29:2
American Ballet of the Metropolitan Opera
  Goldwyn Follies, The 1938,F 21,15:1
American GI Chorus
  Northwest Outpost 1947,Ag 8,10:2
Ames, Adrienne
  Twenty-Four Hours 1931,O 3,20:2
  Girls About Town 1931,N 2,27:1
  Husband's Holiday 1931,D 25,29:2
  Two Kinds of Women 1932,Ja 16,13:1
  Sinners in the Sun 1932,My 14,11:5
  Guilty as Hell 1932,Ag 6,14:5
  Death Kiss, The 1933,F 5,IX,5:3
  Broadway Bad 1933,Mr 6,16:6
  From Hell to Heaven 1933,Mr 18,9:3
  Bedtime Story, A 1933,Ap 20,20:3
  Disgraced 1933,Jl 15,14:2
  Avenger, The 1933,O 3,28:3
  George White's Scandals 1934,Mr 16,24:2
  You're Telling Me 1934,Ap 7,19:1
  Gigolette 1935,My 13,18:6
  Black Sheep 1935,Je 28,34:1
  Harmony Lane 1935,O 24,19:4
  Abdul the Damned 1936,My 11,16:2
  City Girl 1938,F 4,17:3
  Fugitives for a Night 1938,S 21,30:4

  Zero Hour, The 1939,Jl 5,20:3
Ames, Allyson
  House is not a Home, A 1964,S 2,33:1
Ames, Barbara
  Bachelor Party, The 1957,Ap 10,37:2
Ames, Christine (Original Author)
  Human Side, The 1934,S 15,20:3
Ames, Florenz
  Viva Zapata 1952,F 8,19:2
  Human Jungle, The 1954,N 26,24:6
  Man With the Gun 1955,D 23,14:2
  That Certain Felling 1956,Je 21,35:2
  Fastest Gun Alive, The 1956,Jl 13,23:3
  Girl He Left Behind, The 1956,O 27,17:1
  Teacher's Pet 1958,Mr 20,33:1
Ames, Janet
  Winter Kept Us Warm 1968,F 9,55:3
Ames, Jean
  All Through the Night 1942,Ja 24,13:2
  Male Animal, The 1942,Mr 28,11:1
  Larceny, Inc 1942,Ap 25,9:1
  Powers Girl, The 1943,Mr 26,14:2 (In Addenda)
Ames, Jimmy
  Whistle Stop 1946,Mr 18,24:2
  Lucky Stiff, The 1949,Ja 31,14:2
Ames, Judith
  When Worlds Collide 1952,F 7,30:2
Ames, Leon
  Charlie Chan on Broadway 1937,S 20,19:1
  Dangerously Yours 1937,O 18,14:2
  Murder in Greenwich Village 1937,O 30,22:2
  45 Fathers 1937,D 11,22:2
  Spy Ring, The 1938,Ja 15,19:1
  International Settlement 1938,F 12,20:3
  Mr Moto in Danger Island 1938,Mr 20,13:3
  Island in the Sky 1938,My 14,18:1
  Come on Leathernecks 1938,S 15,29:3
  Mysterious Mr Moto of Devil's Island
    1938,S 19,16:2
  Suez 1938,O 15,21:2
  Secrets of a Nurse 1938,D 12,26:2
  Cipher Bureau 1938,D 14,32:6
  I Was a Convict 1939,Mr 23,27:2
  Risky Business 1939,Mr 23,27:2
  Man of Conquest 1939,Ap 28,31:2
  Calling All Marines 1939,O 26,27:2
  Pack up Your Troubles 1939,O 27,27:2
  Legion of Lost Flyers 1939,O 30,13:3
  Fugitive at Large 1939,N 13,15:2
  East Side Kids 1940,F 19,21:6
  No Greater Sin 1941,Ag 29,18:2
  Ellery Queen and the Murder Ring
    1941,O 21,29:4
  Crime Doctor 1943,Jl 5,11:4
  Iron Major, The 1943,N 1,12:5
  Thirty Seconds Over Tokyo 1944,N 16,19:1
  Meet Me in St Louis 1944,N 29,20:2
  Thin Man Goes Home, The 1945,Ja 26,16:5
  Son of Lassie 1945,Je 11,12:1
  Week-End at the Waldorf 1945,O 5,27:2
  Yolanda and the Thief 1945,N 23,26:2
  They Were Expendable 1945,D 21,25:2
  Postman Always Rings Twice, The
    1946,My 3,15:3
  No Leave, No Love 1946,O 18,29:2
  Cockeyed Miracle, The 1946,O 25,28:1
  Lady in the Lake 1947,Ja 24,18:3
  Show-Off, The 1947,Mr 20,38:2
  Song of the Thin Man 1947,Ag 29,14:2
  Merton of the Movies 1947,N 7,20:3
  On an Island With You 1948,Jl 30,13:2
  Date with Judy, A 1948,Ag 7,8:2
  Velvet Touch, The 1948,Ag 26,16:2
  Little Women 1949,Mr 11,33:2
  Any Number Can Play 1949,Jl 1,14:4
  Scene of the Crime 1949,Jl 29,12:2
  Battleground 1949,N 12,8:4
  Ambush 1950,Ja 19,35:2
  Big Hangover, The 1950,My 26,20:3
  Skipper Surprised his Wife, The 1950,Je 30,18:2
  Crisis 1950,Jl 4,10:2
  Dial 1119 1950,D 4,32:6
  Watch the Birdie 1950,D 12,46:4
  On Moonlight Bay 1951,Jl 27,15:2
  Cattle Drive 1951,Ag 9,17:5
  It's a big Country 1952,Ja 9,25:2
  By the Light of the Silvery Moon
    1953,Mr 27,28:2
  Angel Face 1953,Ap 25,11:5
  Let's Do It Again 1953,O 14,34:3
  Sabre Jet 1953,N 3,34:1
  Peyton Place 1957,D 13,35:1
  From the Terrace 1960,Jl 16,10:1
  Absent-Minded Professor, The 1961,Mr 16,44:2
  Son of Flubber 1963,F 9,5:2
  Misadventures of Merlin Jones, The
    1964,Mr 26,40:4
  Monkey's Uncle, The 1965,Ag 19,35:4
Ames, Lionel
  Why Must I Die? 1960,S 15,45:4
Ames, Michael
  Bullet Scars 1942,Ap 24,21:4
  Murder in the Big House 1942,My 8,27:3

Ames, Michael — Cont
  I Was Framed 1942,Je 12,16:6
  Spy Ship 1942,Jl 11,8:2
  Now, Voyager 1942,O 23,25:3
  Truck Busters 1943,Ja 29,23:5
  Action in the North Atlantic 1943,My 22,10:2
  Heaven Can Wait 1943,Ag 12,15:1
Ames, Percy
  Soul Fire 1925,My 6,26:3
  Gambling 1934,D 4,22:3
Ames, Ramsay
  Two Senoritas From Chicago 1943,Ag 6,10:4
  Calling Dr Death 1944,F 12,11:3
  Ali Baba and the Forty Thieves 1944,Mr 16,17:3
  Follow the Boys 1944,Ap 26,24:6
  Mummy's Ghost, The 1944,Jl 1,10:7
  Wave, A Wac and a Marine, A 1944,Ag 14,11:4
  Running Man, The 1963,O 3,31:1
Ames, Robert
  Three Faces West 1926,F 16,22:4
  Crown of Lies 1926,Mr 30,20:6
  Voice of the City, The 1929,Ap 29,29:2
  Trespasser, The 1929,N 2,14:6
  Nix on Dames 1929,N 23,18:5
  Lady to Love, A 1930,Mr 1,23:1
  Double Cross Roads 1930,Ap 29,31:1
  Not Damaged 1930,Je 9,23:3
  Holiday 1930,Jl 3,25:4
  War Nurse 1930,O 24,31:1
  Madonna of the Streets 1930,N 29,21:4
  Millie 1931,F 7,11:1
  Behind Office Doors 1931,Mr 21,15:1
  Rebound 1931,Ag 29,16:3
  Smart Woman 1931,O 12,28:2
  Rich Man's Folly 1931,N 27,29:3
Ames, Rosemary
  I Believed in You 1934,Ap 11,25:3
  Such Women Are Dangerous 1934,Je 9,18:3
  One More Spring 1935,F 22,27:1
  Great Hotel Murder, The 1935,F 28,17:4
  Our Little Girl 1935,Je 7,24:4
Ames, Stephen (Producer)
  Sinbad the Sailor 1947,Ja 23,31:2
  Tycoon 1947,D 26,22:6
  Boy With Green Hair, The 1949,Ja 13,26:2
  Man With a Cloak, The 1951,N 28,37:2
  Wild North, The 1952,My 12,21:2
  My Man and I 1952,S 6,12:6
  Ride Vaquero 1953,Jl 16,17:2
Ames, Totty
  In Like Flint 1967,Mr 16,53:2
Ames, Trudi
  Gidget Goes to Rome 1963,S 12,32:2
  Impossible Years, The 1968,D 6,54:1
Ami, Bat
  Tel Aviv Taxi 1956,D 31,10:7
Amico, Gianni (Director)
  Tropics 1968,S 24,52:1
Amico, Gianni (Screenwriter)
  Tropics 1968,S 24,52:1
  Partner 1968,S 24,52:2
Amidei, Sergio (Miscellaneous)
  Stromboli 1950,F 16,28:2
  Bigamist, The 1958,My 12,25:1
Amidei, Sergio (Original Author)
  Three Girls From Rome 1953,O 14,34:2
  Daughters of Destiny (Elizabeth); Elizabeth
    (Daughters of Destiny) 1954,Jl 6,19:1
  It Happened in the Park 1957,Ag 13,23:2
Amidei, Sergio (Producer)
  Picasso 1955,D 23,14:4
Amidei, Sergio (Screenwriter)
  Open City; Citta Aperta 1946,F 26,21:2
  Shoe-Shine 1947,Ag 27,19:2
  Paisan 1948,Mr 30,26:2
  Under the Sun of Rome 1949,O 6,40:4
  Difficult Years 1950,Ag 22,31:2
  Three Girls From Rome 1953,O 14,34:2
  Bed, The (The Divorce); Divorce, The (The Bed)
    1955,Je 8,26:4
  Picasso 1955,D 23,14:2
  It Happened in the Park 1957,Ag 13,23:2
  Bigamist, The 1958,My 12,25:1
  Most Wonderful Moment, The 1959,Je 1,23:6
  General Della Rovere 1960,N 22,41:1
  Fuga, La 1966,Mr 22,33:1
  Very Handy Man, A 1966,D 15,60:1
Amidei, Signor (Original Author)
  Most Wonderful Moment, The 1959,Je 1,23:6
Amidou
  To be a Crook 1967,F 7,33:2
Amidou, Souad
  Man and a Woman, A; Homme et une Femme,
    Un 1966,Jl 13,35:1
Amigo, Cesar (Screenwriter)
  Walls of Hell, The 1965,N 18,55:3
Amikura
  Ana-Ta-Han 1954,My 18,38:2
Aminoff, Marianne
  John Ericsson Victor of Hampton Roads
    1938,My 18,17:2
Amiot, Martial P
  Moscow Nights 1938,My 3,19:3

Amiot, Paul
Bouquets From Nicholas 1939,Mr 2,19:1
That They May Live 1939,N 7,31:2
Entente Cordiale 1939,D 26,23:2
King, The 1941,O 23,29:3
Midnight in Paris 1947,O 9,32:3
Ruy Blas 1948,O 4,14:2
Amiranayhvili, P
Keto and Kote 1954,Ap 5,21:4
Amis, Kingsley (Original Author)
Lucky Jim 1958,S 1,8:6
Only Two Can Play 1962,Mr 21,33:2
Amis, Martin
High Wind in Jamaica, A 1965,Je 17,27:2
Amman, Betty
Temptation 1929,Jl 14,IX,4:5
Ammen, Bernhard
Marie-Louise 1945,N 13,24:2
Ammon, Vanessa Princess
Tin Pan Alley 1940,N 22,27:3
Amodio, Francesco
Paraninfo, Il; Matchmaker, The 1940,Ja 23,17:2
Amoit, Paul
Dawn Over France 1945,Mr 17,17:2
Amon, Robert (Producer)
Devil and the 10 Commandments, The (Episode 5) 1963,O 15,44:1
Devil and the 10 Commandments, The (Episode 7) 1963,O 15,44:1
Devil and the 10 Commandments, The (Episode 6) 1963,O 15,44:1
Devil and the 10 Commandments, The (Episode 4) 1963,O 15,44:1
Devil and the 10 Commandments, The (Episode 3) 1963,O 15,44:1
Devil and the 10 Commandments, The (Episode 2) 1963,O 15,44:1
Devil and the 10 Commandments, The (Episode 1) 1963,O 15,44:1
Amonsin, Viraj
Pork Chop Hill 1959,My 30,9:2
Echoes of Silence 1967,Ap 7,32:2
Amont, Marcel
Bride Is Much too Beautiful, The 1958,Ja 21,35:1
Amor, Carlos
Ramona 1928,My 15,17:3
Amos, Beth
Incredible Journey, The 1963,N 21,43:2
Ampeles, Piere
Electra 1962,D 18,5:2
Amsten, Jane
Slow Run 1968,O 11,39:1
Amsterdam, Morey
Beach Party 1963,S 26,40:2
Horse in the Gray Flannel Suit, The 1968,D 21,49:3
Amy, George (Director)
She Had to Say Yes 1933,Jl 29,14:2
Kid Nightingale 1939,D 8,33:6
Amys, Julian
High Treason 1952,My 21,23:3
Anais
Claudine 1940,Ap 1,15:2
Anam, F D (Screenwriter)
Madchen in Uniform 1965,Ag 18,41:2
Anand, Dev
Guide, The 1965,F 10,44:2
Ananda, Jafeth
Ivory Hunter 1952,Ag 19,19:1
Anauo, Jim
Ambush Bay 1966,S 15,51:4
Anazhevskaya, Y
Diary of a Nazi 1943,Mr 25,25:3
Ancelin, Robert
Amour Maitre des Choses, L' 1931,Mr 30,25:2
Ancona, Ricardo
Yanco 1964,Je 18,29:2
Anda, de (Director)
Tierra del Mariachi, La; Country of the Mariachi, The 1938,D 3,11:2
Anda, Raul de
Rebel Souls 1937,N 13,11:2
Tierra del Mariachi, La; Country of the Mariachi, The 1938,D 3,11:2
Virgen de la Sierra, La 1939,Mr 6,11:3
A lo Macho; In Rough Style 1939,Je 3,11:3
Anda, Raul de (Producer)
Con los Dorados de Villa; With Villa's Veterans 1939,N 20,15:8
Ande, Michael
Reaching for the Stars 1958,My 24,18:2
Marianne of my Youth; (Marianne de ma Jeunesse) 1959,Ja 20,43:1
Anden, Mathew
David and Lisa 1962,D 27,5:5
Ander, Charlotte
Nacht Gehoert Uns, Die; Night Belongs to Us, The 1930,My 11,IX,4:2 (In Addenda)
Wien Du Stadt der Lieder; (Vienna City of Song) 1931,Mr 20,29:1
Elisabeth von Oesterreich 1931,D 11,35:1
Theaternaechte von Berlin 1932,Ja 11,28:5
Wenn Herzen Sich Finden 1934,N 12,17:3

Graefin Mariza 1935,Ja 26,13:3
Ein Lied Geht um die Welt 1936,S 25,20:3
Drei Blaue Jungs-Ein Blondes Maedel 1936,D 29,16:3
Zwei im Sonnenschein 1937,Jl 31,6:2
Anton der Letzte; Anthony the Last 1940,Mr 30,11:2
Joseph Schmidt Story, The 1951,Mr 5,24:2
Ander, Lisl
Amicizia; Friendship 1940,Mr 1,17:3
Anderberg, Bertil
Hour of the Wolf 1968,Ap 10,50:2
Andere, Jacqueline
Exterminating Angel, The 1967,Ag 22,33:1
Andergast, Maria
Mein Leben fuer Maria Isabell; My Life for Maria Isabell 1935,N 5,33:5
Liebe und Trompetenklang 1936,Ap 13,15:2
Drei Maeoerl um Schubert 1937,Je 5,21:2
Endstation 1937,Jl 17,18:1
Husaren Heraus 1938,Mr 19,11:3
Seine Tochter Ist der Peter; His Daughter is Peter 1938,Mr 28,19:3
Gluecklichste Ehe von Wien, Die; Happiest Married Couple in Vienna, The 1938,O 8,10:2
Unsterblicher Walzer; Immortal Waltz 1939,N 18,22:6
Drei um Christine, Die; Three After Christine, The 1940,My 4,13:2
Anders, Charlotte
Wenn die Soldaten 1932,O 31,18:4
Glueckszylinder, Der 1934,Mr 10,18:4
Anders, Glenn
Laughter 1930,N 15,15:3
Nothing but the Truth 1941,O 23,27:1
Lady From Shanghai, The 1948,Je 10,28:2
Nancy Goes to Rio 1950,Ap 7,22:2
M 1951,Je 11,20:7
Behave Yourself 1951,N 8,35:2
Anders, Gunther (Cinematographer)
Verraeter; Traitors 1936,N 22,XI,4:2 (In Addenda)
Anders, Helga
How to Seduce a Playboy 1968,My 16,53:2
Anders, Ina
Blue Angel, The 1959,S 5,11:4
Anders, Keith
Clash by Night 1952,Je 19,32:6
Anders, Lew (Director)
Truth About Murder, The 1946,Jl 27,12:6
Anders, Luana
Pit and the Pendulum, The 1961,Ag 24,25:3
Night Tide 1963,Je 7,37:1
Young Racers, The 1963,O 10,49:3
Dementia 13 1963,O 24,37:1
Anders, Lynn
Girl From Scotland Yard, The 1937,My 31,11:2
Shadow Strikes, The 1937,S 13,17:1
Anders, Merry
Wait Till the Sun Shines, Nellie 1952,Je 28,12:2
Farmer Takes a Wife, The 1953,Je 13,11:2
Phffft 1954,N 11,43:2
All That Heaven Allows 1956,F 29,35:1
Desk Set 1957,My 16,28:2
Young Jesse James 1960,Ag 25,25:1
20,000 Eyes 1961,Je 19,30:1
Secret of Deep Harbor 1961,O 26,39:7
FBI Code 98 1964,Ap 9,25:6
Tiger Walks, A 1964,Ag 27,28:2
Tickle Me 1965,Je 24,28:3
Anders, Richard
Savage Seven, The 1968,Ag 22,47:1
Anders, Rudolph
Escape in the Desert 1945,My 12,10:2
Counter-Attack 1945,My 17,15:2
Her Sister's Secret 1947,Ja 23,31:3
Dangerous Millions 1947,Mr 15,10:3
Actors and Sin; (Actor's Blood) 1952,My 30,11:3
Private's Affair, A 1959,Ag 15,8:7
On the Double 1961,My 20,12:1
Pigeon That Took Rome, The 1962,Ag 23,25:1
Prize, The 1964,Ja 24,21:1
ANDERSEN
See Also ANDERSON
Andersen, Clinton
Quiet American, The 1958,F 6,24:1
Andersen, Elga
Bonjour Tristesse 1958,Ja 16,32:1
Frantic 1961,Je 12,34:1
Andersen, Gerald
Amazing Mr Beecham, The 1949,D 26,33:4
Horrors of the Black Museum 1959,Ap 30,37:2
Andersen, Hans Christian (Original Author)
Emperor's Nightingale, The 1951,My 14,29:1
Snow Queen, The 1960,Ap 14,34:1
Andersen, Suzy
Magnificent Cuckold 1965,Ap 20,42:1
ANDERSON
See Also ANDERSEN, ANDERSSON
Anderson, Agnes
Wedding Night, The 1935,Mr 16,19:1
Vanessa: Her Love Story 1935,Ap 13,11:3
Plot Thickens, The 1936,D 9,35:2

Anderson, Augusta
Belle of the Nineties 1934,S 22,12:2
Ruggles of Red Gap 1935,Mr 7,26:1
Anderson, Beaudine
No Greater Glory 1934,My 5,22:2
Band Plays on, The 1934,D 22,21:2
Anderson, Bill (Producer)
Swiss Family Robinson 1960,D 24,8:4
Savage Sam 1963,Ag 1,17:3
Tiger Walks, A 1964,Ag 27,28:2
Fighting Prince of Donegal, The 1966,N 10,64:1
Adventures of Bullwhip Griffin, The 1967,Mr 9,43:2
Happiest Millionaire, The 1967,D 1,56:1
One and Only Genuine Original Family Band, The 1968,Mr 22,55:1
Anderson, Bruce
Cry, the Beloved Country 1952,Ja 24,23:2
Anderson, Bull
Mystery of the Wax Museum, The 1933,F 18,13:3
Milky Way, The 1936,Mr 26,27:2
Anderson, C E
Let Freedom Ring 1939,Mr 10,19:2
Anderson, Captain
Our Daily Bread 1934,O 3,25:2
Anderson, Charles
Winds of Chance 1925,Ag 17,10:3
Anderson, Charles E
Eagle of the Sea, The 1926,N 17,21:6
Anderson, Daphne
Beggar's Opera, The 1953,Ag 25,18:2
Hobson's Choice 1954,Je 15,37:1
Kid for two Farthings, A 1956,Ap 18,25:1
Prince and the Showgirl 1957,Je 14,22:2
Anderson, Delbert
Hansel and Gretel 1954,O 11,33:1
Anderson, Donna
Inherit the Wind 1960,O 13,41:1
Anderson, Doris (Screenwriter)
Ten Modern Commandments 1927,Jl 11,23:4
True to the Navy 1930,My 24,21:2
And So They Were Married 1936,My 14,29:3
Girl From Scotland Yard, The 1937,My 31,11:2
King of Gamblers 1937,Jl 3,18:1
Sophie Lang Goes West 1937,S 30,19:2
Give Me a Sailor 1938,Ag 11,31:1
Beauty for the Asking 1939,F 10,19:1
Women in War 1940,My 30,21:2
That Brennan Girl 1946,D 9,34:3
Never a Dull Moment 1950,N 22,20:2
Anderson, Dusty
Tonight and Every Night 1945,Mr 9,16:2
Thousand and one Nights, A 1945,Jl 12,8:2
Anderson, Eddie (Rochester)
What Price Hollywood 1932,Jl 16,5:5
Green Pastures, The 1936,Jl 17,20:1
Three Men on a Horse 1936,N 26,39:1
Melody for Two 1937,My 21,19:5
One Mile From Heaven 1937,Ag 19,23:1
Over the Goal 1937,O 16,22:2
Jezebel 1938,Mr 11,15:2
Gold Diggers in Paris 1938,Je 2,19:2
You Can't Take It With You 1938,S 2,21:2
Exposed 1938,N 21,14:5
Thanks for the Memory 1938,D 8,34:3
Kentucky 1938,D 24,12:1
Going Places 1939,Ja 7,6:1
You Can't Cheat an Honest Man 1939,F 20,13:2
Honolulu 1939,F 23,19:2
Man About Town 1939,Je 29,19:1
Gone With the Wind 1939,D 20,31:2
Buck Benny Rides Again 1940,Ap 25,28:4
Love Thy Neighbor 1940,D 18,32:5
Topper Returns 1941,Mr 28,26:6
Kiss the Boys Goodbye 1941,Ag 14,21:2
Birth of the Blues 1941,D 11,39:1
Tales of Manhattan 1942,S 25,25:1
Star Spangled Rhythm 1942,D 31,20:1
Meanest Man in the World, The 1943,F 25,27:3
Cabin in the Sky 1943,My 28,19:3
What's Buzzin Cousin 1943,Jl 23,21:4
Broadway Rhythm 1944,Ap 14,24:6
Brewster's Millions 1945,Ap 27,23:2
Sailor Takes a Wife, The 1946,Mr 1,17:2
Show-Off, The 1947,Mr 20,38:2
It's a Mad, Mad, Mad, Mad World 1963,N 19,47:1
Anderson, Edward (Original Author)
They Live by Night 1949,N 4,33:2
Anderson, Effie
Fight for Life, The 1940,Mr 7,19:2
Pop Always Pays 1940,Ag 30,16:6
Anderson, Elbridge
That's my Boy 1932,N 21,21:1
Anderson, Elga
Global Affair, A 1964,My 7,31:2
Anderson, Erica (Cinematographer)
Grandma Moses 1950,O 24,34:6
Anderson, Erica (Miscellaneous)
Albert Schweitzer 1957,Ja 21,20:2

Anderson, Ernest
In This our Life 1942,My 9,10:2
Well, The 1951,S 27,37:2
3 for Bedroom C 1952,Je 27,18:3
Anderson, Erville
White Rose, The 1923,My 23,18:3
America 1924,F 22,20:1
White Black Sheep, The 1926,D 21,20:2
Girl From Chicago, The 1927,D 20,33:2
Speakeasy 1929,Mr 11,22:2
Tobacco Road 1941,F 21,16:2
Anderson, Esther
Touchables, The 1968,N 21,41:1
Anderson, Freddy
Half Way to Heaven 1929,D 7,19:3
Anderson, Frederick Irving (Original Author)
Notorious Sophie Lang, The 1934,Jl 21,14:2
Return of Sophie Lang, The 1936,Jl 24,13:1
Sophie Lang Goes West 1937,S 30,19:2
Anderson, Gene
Day the Earth Caught Fire, The 1962,Mr 16,25:1
Anderson, George
Under Suspicion 1937,D 20,23:2 (In Addenda)
King of Chinatown 1939,Mr 16,27:2
Lady's From Kentucky, The 1939,Ap 27,31:1
Our Neighbors-The Carters 1940,F 15,15:2
Secret Seven, The 1940,Ag 12,11:6
Palm Beach Story, The 1942,D 11,33:1
Anderson, Gerd
Secrets of Woman 1961,Jl 12,36:1
Anderson, Gilbert
Shootin' Mad 1918,O 21,15:1
Anderson, Guy
Battleground 1949,N 12,8:4
Yellow Cab Man, The 1950,Mr 27,19:2
Lawless, The 1950,Je 23,29:2
Magnificent Yankee, The 1951,Ja 19,21:2
Excuse my Dust 1951,Je 28,21:2
Girl in White, The 1952,My 31,12:5
Anderson, Herbert
'Til We Meet Again 1940,Ap 14,14:2
No Time for Comedy 1940,S 7,9:2
Honeymoon for Three 1941,F 8,19:2
Bride Came C O D, The 1941,Jl 26,18:2
Dive Bomber 1941,Ag 30,10:2
Navy Blues 1941,S 20,11:2
Body Disappears, The 1942,Ja 31,13:2
Male Animal, The 1942,Mr 28,11:1
This Is the Army 1943,Jl 29,11:6
That Way With Women 1947,F 15,20:4
Love and Learn 1947,My 3,10:3
You Were Meant for Me 1948,Ja 29,27:5
Give my Regards to Broadway 1948,Je 23,32:2
Benny Goodman Story 1956,F 22,22:1
Spring Reunion 1957,My 6,25:2
Night Passage 1957,Jl 25,28:1
Sunrise at Campobello 1960,S 29,32:1
Hold On! 1966,Je 23,29:4
Anderson, Irvil
Exciters, The 1923,Je 4,13:3
Anderson, Ivie
Day at the Races, A 1937,Je 18,25:2
Anderson, James
Freshman, The 1925,S 21,12:4
Butterflies in the Rain 1926,D 25,10:5
Tight Little Island 1949,D 26,33:2
Five 1951,Ap 26,34:2
Along the Great Divide 1951,My 17,38:3
Ruby Gentry 1952,D 26,20:2
Freshman, The 1953,Ap 28,31:6
Riot in Cell Block 11 1954,F 19,24:5
Rawhide Years, The 1956,Je 16,12:2
Connection, The 1962,O 4,44:1
Pressure Point 1962,O 11,49:3
To Kill a Mockingbird 1963,F 15,10:2
Anderson, Jean
White Corridors 1952,Jl 16,21:1
Little Kidnappers, The 1954,S 2,18:1
Lease of Life 1956,F 10,18:1
Barretts of Wimpole Street, The 1957,Ja 18,15:3
Lucky Jim 1958,S 1,8:6
Town Like Alice, A 1958,S 22,27:1
S O S Pacific 1960,O 13,41:3
Waltz of the Toreadors 1962,Ag 14,34:1
Three Lives of Thomasina, The 1963,D 12,46:1
Anderson, Jim
Brig, The 1964,S 21,37:4
Anderson, John
Target Zero 1955,N 16,43:2
Walk on the Wild Side 1962,F 22,20:1
Ride the High Country 1962,Je 21,26:2
Satan Bug, The 1965,Ap 15,38:1
Hallelujah Trail, The 1965,Jl 2,17:1
Welcome to Hard Times 1967,My 2,56:1
Day of the Evil Gun 1968,Ap 25,53:2
Anderson, John Murray (Director)
King of Jazz 1930,My 3,23:1
Anderson, Joseph
Anderson Platoon, The 1967,D 18,70:4
Anderson, Judith
Blood Money 1933,N 16,30:5
Rebecca 1940,Mr 29,25:2
Forty Little Mothers 1940,Ap 19,25:2

Free and Easy 1941,Ap 3,29:4
Lady Scarface 1941,Ag 4,16:6
All Through the Night 1942,Ja 24,13:2
Kings Row 1942,F 3,23:2
Edge of Darkness 1943,Ap 10,12:4
Stage Door Canteen 1943,Je 25,13:2
Laura 1944,O 12,24:1
And Then There Were None 1945,N 1,20:2
Diary of a Chambermaid, The 1946,Je 23,28:2
Strange Love of Martha Ivers, The
1946,Jl 25,18:4
Specter of the Rose 1946,S 2,12:4
Pursued 1947,Mr 8,10:2
Red House, The 1947,Mr 17,27:2
Tycoon 1947,D 26,22:6
Furies, The 1950,Ag 17,23:2
Salome 1953,Mr 25,37:1
Ten Commandments, The 1956,N 9,35:2
Cat on a Hot Tin Roof 1958,S 19,24:1
Cinderfella 1960,D 17,19:2
Why Bother to Knock 1965,F 4,24:2
Anderson, Katherine
Tight Spot 1955,Mr 19,11:7
Queen Bee 1955,N 23,18:2
Anderson, Ken (Miscellaneous)
one Hundred and One Dalmations
1961,F 11,27:1
Anderson, Lawrence
Nell Gwyn 1935,Je 20,16:2
Man of Affairs 1937,F 20,9:2
Gangway 1937,Ag 21,7:3
Anderson, Lindsay (Director)
This Sporting Life 1963,Jl 17,19:2
Anderson, Ludwig
D-Zug 13 Hat Verspaetung 1931,Ag 10,18:3
Anderson, Margaret
Barefoot Contessa, The 1954,S 30,37:1
Anderson, Marius (Producer)
Nomadie 1931,Je 13,20:4
Anderson, Mary
Two Minutes to Go 1921,O 24,13:1
Gone With the Wind 1939,D 20,31:2
Flight Angels 1940,My 27,23:2
Cheers for Miss Bishop 1941,Mr 14,17:2
Henry Aldrich for President 1941,O 18,22:2
Bahama Passage 1942,F 19,23:2
Lifeboat 1944,Ja 13,17:1
Song of Bernadette, The 1944,Ja 27,15:2
Wilson 1944,Ag 2,18:1
Within These Walls 1945,Jl 16,8:4
Behind Green Lights 1946,F 16,10:2
To Each his Own 1946,My 24,15:2
Whispering City 1948,My 10,25:5
Underworld Story, The 1950,Jl 27,29:4
Last of the Buccaneers 1950,D 15,43:2
Passage West 1951,Ag 31,12:2
I, The Jury 1953,Ag 22,8:2
Dangerous Crossing 1953,S 30,37:2
Anderson, Maxwell (Composer)
Knickerbocker Holiday 1944,Ap 20,22:7
Never Steal Anything Small 1959,F 12,23:1
Anderson, Maxwell (Miscellaneous)
All Quiet on The Western Front 1930,Ap 30,29:1
Daybreak in Udi 1950,Je 2,26:2
Anderson, Maxwell (Original Author)
What Price Glory 1926,N 24,26:4
Saturday's Children 1929,Ap 29,29:2
Washington Merry-Go-Round 1932,O 24,18:5
Maybe It's Love 1935,F 11,14:2
Mary of Scotland 1936,Jl 31,22:2
Winterset 1936,D 4,31:1
Private Lives of Elizabeth and Essex, The
1939,D 2,21:2
Saturday's Children 1940,My 4,13:1
Eve of St Mark, The 1944,My 31,22:2
Key Largo 1948,Jl 17,6:6
Joan of Arc 1948,N 12,30:5
What Price Glory 1952,Ag 23,10:2
Bad Seed, The 1956,S 13,39:6
Wrong Man, The 1956,D 24,8:1
Never Steal Anything Small 1959,F 12,23:1
Anderson, Maxwell (Screenwriter)
We Live Again 1934,N 2,27:2
So Red the Rose 1935,N 28,39:1
Joan of Arc 1948,N 12,30:5
Wrong Man, The 1956,D 24,8:1
Anderson, Michael (Director)
Will any Gentleman? 1955,S 28,70:6
1984 1956,O 1,31:1
Around the World in 80 Days 1956,O 18,37:1
Battle Hell 1957,Ag 22,23:1
Chase a Crooked Shadow 1958,Mr 25,28:4
Shake Hands With the Devil 1959,Je 25,20:7
Wreck of the Mary Deare, The 1959,N 7,27:1
All the Fine Young Cannibals 1960,S 23,33:1
Naked Edge 1961,Jl 1,9:1
Flight From Ashiya 1964,Ap 23,34:1
Wild and Wonderful 1964,Je 11,27:4
Operation Crossbow 1965,Ap 2,29:1
Quiller Memorandum, The 1966,D 16,59:1
Shoes of the Fisherman, The 1968,N 15,40:3

Anderson, Michael (Producer)
Shake Hands With the Devil 1959,Je 25,20:7
Anderson, Michael Jr
Sundowners, The 1960,D 9,39:1
In Search of the Castaways 1962,D 22,5:2
Play it Cool 1963,Jl 18,15:3
Reach for Glory 1963,S 10,46:1
Greatest Story Ever Told, The 1965,F 16,40:2
Dear Heart 1965,Mr 8,33:1
Major Dundee 1965,Ap 8,45:1
Sons of Katie Elder, The 1965,Ag 26,40:3
Anderson, Myrtle
Green Pastures, The 1936,Jl 17,20:1
White Witch Doctor 1953,Jl 2,19:3
Anderson, Nancy
Come September 1961,S 8,34:1
Anderson, Olga
Sara Laer Sig Folkvett 1938,F 16,17:1
Anderson, Philip
Man, Woman and Sin 1927,D 5,26:2
Redskin 1929,Ja 28,21:1
Anderson, R Alex (Composer)
Pick a Star 1937,My 28,17:2
Anderson, Relyea
Should a Woman Tell? 1920,Ja 5,15:1
Anderson, Richard
Twelve O'Clock High 1950,Ja 28,10:2
Magnificent Yankee, The 1951,Ja 19,21:2
Payment on Demand 1951,F 16,21:2
Rich, Young and Pretty 1951,Jl 26,17:3
No Questions Asked 1951,Ag 10,13:2
Across the Wide Missouri 1951,N 7,35:4
Unknown Man, The 1951,N 17,9:5
Just This Once 1952,Mr 18,22:3
Scaramouche 1952,My 9,20:2
Holiday for Sinners 1952,S 20,13:2
Story of Three Loves, The (Equilibrium);
Equilibrium (The Story of Three Loves)
1953,Mr 6,29:2
Equilibrium 1953,Mr 6,29:2
I Love Melvin 1953,Ap 10,18:4
Dream Wife 1953,Jl 30,20:1
Escape from Fort Bravo 1954,Ja 23,11:2
Student Prince, The 1954,Je 16,18:2
Hit the Deck 1955,Mr 4,17:1
It's a Dog's Life 1955,D 23,14:3
Forbidden Planet 1956,My 4,21:2
Cry in the Night, A 1956,S 1,19:4
Buster Keaton Story, The 1957,Ap 22,31:6
Paths of Glory 1957,D 26,23:2
Long, Hot Summer, The 1958,Ap 4,16:1
Compulsion 1959,Ap 2,26:2
Wackiest Ship in the Army, The 1961,F 9,36:1
Johnny Cool 1963,O 3,31:1
Seven Days in May 1964,F 20,22:1
Kitten With a Whip 1964,N 5,50:4
Seconds 1966,O 6,56:1
Anderson, Robert
Hearts of the World 1918,Ap 5,13:1
Heart of Humanity, The 1918,D 22,17:3
Fires of Faith 1919,My 6,16:2
Hearts of the World 1919,Ag 12,7:6
Eternal Struggle, The 1923,O 16,21:3
Love Me and the World Is Mine 1928,F 6,12:3
White Shadows of the South Seas 1928,Ag 1,13:3
Young People 1940,Ag 24,16:2
Action in Arabia 1944,F 19,18:7
Marine Raiders 1944,Jl 1,10:7
Bride by Mistake 1944,S 16,20:2
It's a Wonderful Life 1946,D 23,19:2
Ruthless 1948,S 4,8:7
Two of a Kind 1951,Je 30,8:6
Crowning Experience, The 1960,O 24,25:3
Anderson, Robert (Director)
Feeling of Rejection, The 1948,D 27,16:4
Anderson, Robert (Producer)
Feeling of Rejection, The 1948,D 27,16:4
Anderson, Robert (Screenwriter)
Tea and Sympathy 1956,S 28,24:4
Until They Sail 1957,O 9,41:2
Nun's Story, The 1959,Je 19,30:1
Sand Pebbles, The 1966,D 21,48:1
Anderson, Roger
Not Wanted 1949,Jl 25,11:4
Twelve O'Clock High 1950,Ja 28,10:2
Rancho Notorious 1952,My 15,39:5
Anderson, Rona
Sleeping Car to Trieste 1949,Ap 18,18:6
Christmas Carol, A 1951,N 29,41:2
Anderson, Stuart
Texas Across the River 1966,N 24,65:1
Anderson, U S (Original Author)
Highway Dragnet 1954,F 20,8:7
Anderson, W R (Original Author)
Take It From Me 1926,N 2,35:1
Anderson, Warner
Destination Tokyo 1944,Ja 1,9:2
Objective Burma 1945,Ja 27,15:2
Dangerous Partners 1945,N 2,22:4
Abbott and Costello in Hollywood
1945,N 23,26:2
My Reputation 1946,Ja 26,19:2
Bad Bascomb 1946,My 23,18:4

Anderson, Warner— Cont
Three Wise Fools 1946,S 27,19:2
Beginning or the End, The 1947,F 21,15:1
Dark Delusion 1947,Je 26,19:2
Song of the Thin Man 1947,Ag 29,14:2
Arnelo Affair, The 1947,S 13,8:5
High Wall 1947,D 26,22:2
Command Decision 1949,Ja 20,34:2
Lucky Stiff, The 1949,Ja 31,14:2
Doctor and the Girl, The 1949,O 31,20:2
Destination Moon 1950,Je 28,32:2
Only the Valiant 1951,Ap 14,9:6
Santa Fe 1951,My 4,31:2
Go for Broke 1951,My 25,31:2
Detective Story 1951,N 7,35:2
Star, The 1953,Ja 29,25:1
Lion Is in the Streets, A 1953,S 24,39:2
Caine Mutiny, The 1954,Je 25,17:1
Drum Beat 1954,N 18,42:1
Violent Men, The 1955,Ja 27,17:2
Blackboard Jungle 1955,Mr 21,21:5
Armored Command 1961,O 7,14:3
Rio Conchos 1964,O 29,38:1
Anderson, William H (Producer)
Third Man on the Mountain 1959,N 12,27:1
Sign of Zorro, The 1961,S 5,37:6
Andersson, Bibi
Seventh Seal 1958,O 14,44:1
Wild Strawberries 1959,Je 23,37:1
Brink of Life; (Nara Livet) 1959,N 9,36:2
Devil's Eye, The 1961,O 31,27:4
All These Women 1964,O 6,35:1
Duel at Diablo 1966,Je 16,53:1
Persona 1966,O 20,52:7
My Sister, My Love 1967,F 20,45:2
Persona 1967,Mr 7,46:2
Viol, Le 1968,S 20,42:1
Andersson, Bo
491 1967,D 21,45:1
Andersson, Harriet
Naked Night, The 1956,Ap 10,27:5
Smiles of a Summer Night 1957,D 24,11:1
Lesson in Love, A 1960,Mr 15,46:1
Dreams; Kvinnodrom 1960,Je 1,42:1
Through a Glass Darkly 1962,Mr 14,45:1
To Love; Att Alska 1964,S 23,45:3 (Incorrect in
   this edition; use 1964,S 23,54:1 elsewhere)
All These Women 1964,O 6,35:1
Loving Couples 1966,S 20,38:1
Deadly Affair, The 1967,Ja 27,31:1
Andersson, Morgan
Dear John 1966,Mr 9,46:1
Andersson, Viktor
Sara Laer Sig Folkvett 1938,F 16,17:1
Andes, Keith
Farmer's Daughter, The 1947,Mr 26,31:2
Blackbeard the Pirate 1952,D 26,20:3
Split Second 1953,My 13,34:2
Second Greatest Sex, The 1956,F 11,12:2
Away all Boats 1956,Ag 17,14:2
Back From Eternity 1956,S 8,20:6
Pillars of the Sky 1956,O 13,15:2
Girl Most Likely, The 1958,O 9,47:1
Andeyenko, J (Director)
Ukraine in Flames 1944,Ap 3,18:2
Andjaparidze, Z (Composer)
Yolanta 1964,D 23,22:3
Ando, Eiko
Barbarian and the Geisha 1958,O 3,25:1
Andor, Ajtay
Urilany Szobat Keres; Lady Seeks Room
   1938,Mr 19,11:2
Andor, Charlotte
All for a Woman 1921,D 5,20:1
Andor, Paul
Enemy of Women 1944,S 12,23:6
Hotel Berlin 1945,Mr 3,11:2
Counter-Attack 1945,My 17,15:2
Walk East on Beacon 1952,My 29,17:2
Singing in the Dark 1956,Mr 8,32:5
Andra, Fern
Eyes of the World 1930,Ag 15,20:5
Andrade, Cisco
World in my Corner 1956,F 18,12:5
Andral, Paule
Ronde des Heures, La 1932,Ja 25,20:3
David Golder 1932,O 20,24:2
With a Smile 1939,F 6,8:4
Andre, Anette
Funny Thing Happened on the Way to the Forum,
   A 1966,O 17,48:1
Andre, Charles
Seven Days' Leave 1942,D 11,33:2
I Confess 1953,Mr 23,28:2
Andre, Claire
River of no Return 1954,My 1,13:2
Andre, E J
Battle at Bloody Beach, The 1961,Ag 17,18:2
Andre, Gaby
End of a Day, The 1939,S 12,28:4
Please Believe Me 1950,Je 12,19:4
Hoboes in Paradise 1950,O 9,21:5
Highway 301 1950,D 9,13:2
Green Glove, The 1952,Ap 24,38:1

Life and Music of Giuseppe Verdi, The
   1957,My 2,26:2
Cosmic Monster, The 1959,Ja 1,38:1
Andre, George
Once in a Blue Moon 1936,D 2,35:1
Andre, Gwili
Roar of the Dragon 1932,Jl 25,11:2
Secrets of the French Police 1932,D 12,18:4
No Other Woman 1933,Ja 30,9:4 (In Addenda)
Girl Said No, The 1937,O 18,14:1
Woman's Face, A 1941,My 16,21:2
Falcon's Brother, The 1942,O 3,9:5
Andre, Lona
Woman Accused, The 1933,Mr 13,18:2
College Humor 1933,Je 23,15:4
Take a Chance 1933,N 27,20:3
Come on Marines 1934,Mr 24,20:3
Murder at the Vanities 1934,My 21,20:2
Under the Pampas Moon 1935,My 31,11:1
Our Relations 1936,N 11,55:1
Crusade Against Rackets 1937,Jl 26,15:3
Taxi, Mister 1943,Ap 15,20:2
Andre, Marcel
Chance, La 1932,My 28,18:2
Agonie des Aigles, L' 1934,D 1,8:5
Heart of Paris 1939,Ja 13,17:3
Ultimatum 1940,F 5,13:2
Marthe Richard 1944,N 9,23:2
Beauty and the Beast 1947,D 24,12:2
Friend Will come Tonight, A; Ami Viendra Ce
   Soir, Un 1948,Jl 12,11:2
Room Upstairs, The 1948,S 4,8:6
Storm Within, The; (Parents Terribles, Les)
   1950,Ap 24,21:2
Andre, Michael
Idiot, The 1948,F 5,26:2
Andre, Michel
Vierge Folle, La 1938,D 30,11:3
Every Second Counts 1957,O 15,39:4
Andre, Pierre
My Wild Irish Rose 1947,D 25,32:2
Andreas, Demitri
Night Ambush 1958,Ap 25,32:4
Andreas, Harry
Helen of Troy 1956,Ja 27,21:4
Andrecota, Paul (Miscellaneous)
Companions of the Night 1954,N 25,44:2
Andree, Aline
Man to Men 1949,F 21,20:2
Andree, Ingrid
Confessions of Felix Krull, The 1958,Mr 5,38:1
Rest Is Silence, The 1960,Ag 2,22:6
Andreguy, Serge
Devil's Daughter 1949,F 26,11:2
Andrei, Franco
No Sun in Venice 1958,Je 10,40:2
Big Show, The 1961,My 11,42:4
Andrei, M (Screenwriter)
Eye of the Needle, The 1965,Je 22,25:2
Andrei, Marcello (Director)
Eye of the Needle, The 1965,Je 22,25:2
Andrejewska, Jadzia
Dziewczeta z Nowolipek; Girls of Nowolipek
   1938,N 25,19:2
Andreota, Paul (Miscellaneous)
Tempest in the Flesh 1957,Ja 19,12:2
Andreota, Paul (Screenwriter)
Julie the Redhead 1963,O 15,44:1
Andreota (Screenwriter)
Bed, The (Riviera Express); Riviera Express (The
   Bed) 1955,Je 8,26:4
Andres, Rudolph
South Sea Woman 1953,Je 4,33:6
Andress, Ursula
Dr No 1963,My 30,20:1
4 for Texas 1963,D 26,33:3
Fun in Acapulco 1964,F 20,22:4
What's New Pussycat? 1965,Je 23,49:1
She 1965,S 2,36:1
10th Victim, The 1965,D 21,46:1
Up to his Ears 1966,My 18,37:1
Blue Max, The 1966,Je 22,38:1
Casino Royale 1967,Ap 29,25:1
Andrew, Annette
He Who Rides a Tiger 1968,S 10,39:1
Andrew, Sylvia
Three Came Home 1950,F 21,22:5
Andrews, Adora
Smiling Faces 1932,Ag 31,12:3
Andrews, Andy
23 1/2 Hours Leave 1937,My 17,23:2
Andrews, Ann
Cheat, The 1931,D 12,23:3
Andrews, Betti
Madison Avenue 1962,Mr 29,28:2
Andrews, C E (Original Author)
Innocents of Paris 1929,Ap 27,16:5
Andrews, Carol
Bullfighters, The 1945,My 12,10:3
Guilty, The 1947,My 19,27:2
Andrews, Charles
Green Pastures, The 1936,Jl 17,20:1

Andrews, Charlton (Original Author)
Bluebeard's Eighth Wife 1938,Mr 24,21:2
Andrews, Charlton (Screenwriter)
Ladies' Night in a Turkish Bath 1928,Ap 9,18:2
Andrews, Clark (Screenwriter)
Pier 13 1940,Ag 9,19:3
Andrews, Daisy H (Original Author)
Shanghai Lady 1929,N 11,20:2
Andrews, Dana
Lucky Cisco Kid 1940,Je 24,19:5
Sailor's Lady 1940,Je 29,12:2
Westerner, The 1940,O 25,25:2
Kit Carson 1940,N 15,25:3
Tobacco Road 1941,F 21,16:2
Belle Starr 1941,N 1,20:2
Swamp Water 1941,N 17,15:2
Ball of Fire 1942,Ja 16,25:2
Berlin Correspondent 1942,S 4,19:2
Crash Dive 1943,Ap 29,25:2
Ox-Bow Incident, The 1943,My 10,15:2 (In
   Addenda)
North Star, The 1943,N 5,23:1
Up in Arms 1944,Mr 3,19:2
Purple Heart, The 1944,Mr 9,15:2
Wing and a Prayer 1944,Ag 31,14:1
Laura 1944,O 12,24:1
State Fair 1945,Ag 31,14:3
Walk in the Sun, A 1946,Ja 12,10:6
Fallen Angel 1946,F 7,29:4
Canyon Passage 1946,Ag 8,18:2
Best Years of our Lives, The 1946,N 22,27:2
Boomerang 1947,Mr 6,36:2
Daisy Kenyon 1947,D 25,32:1
Night Song 1948,Ja 29,27:5
Iron Curtain, The 1948,My 13,31:2
Deep Waters 1948,Jl 23,12:4
No Minor Vices 1949,F 26,11:2
Forbidden Street, The 1949,My 14,9:2
Sword in the Desert 1949,Ag 25,20:2
My Foolish Heart 1950,Ja 20,29:2
Where the Sidewalk Ends 1950,Jl 8,7:4
Edge of Doom 1950,Ag 4,13:2
Sealed Cargo 1951,My 24,47:1
Frogmen, The 1951,Je 30,8:6
I Want You 1951,D 24,9:1
Assignment-Paris 1952,O 25,12:6
Elephant Walk 1954,Ap 22,37:2
Duel in the Jungle 1954,Ag 9,13:2
Three Hours to Kill 1954,S 4,6:4
Strange Lady in Town 1955,My 21,11:1
While the City Sleeps 1956,My 17,37:1
Beyond a Reasonable Doubt 1956,S 14,27:2
Spring Reunion 1957,My 6,25:2
Zero Hour 1957,N 14,41:1
Crowded Sky, The 1961,F 11,27:2
Madison Avenue 1962,Mr 29,28:2
In Harm's Way 1965,Ap 7,36:1
Satan Bug, The 1965,Ap 15,38:1
Crack in the World 1965,My 13,32:2
Brainstorm 1965,Je 10,38:1
Loved One, The 1965,O 12,57:1
Battle of the Bulge 1965,D 18,36:1
Johnny Reno 1966,Mr 10,26:3
Hot Rods to Hell 1967,Ag 10,45:5
Frozen Dead, The 1967,N 16,58:1
Cobra, The 1968,Mr 28,52:3
Devil's Brigade, The 1968,My 23,56:2
Andrews, Del (Director)
Hottentot, The 1923,F 19,10:1
Andrews, Edward
Phenix City Story, The 1955,S 3,9:1
Harder They Fall, The 1956,My 10,26:3
These Wilder Years 1956,Ag 18,11:2
Tea and Sympathy 1956,S 28,24:4
Tattered Dress, The 1957,Mr 15,22:3
Three Brave Men 1957,Mr 16,13:2
Trooper Hook 1957,Jl 13,11:2
Elmer Gantry 1960,Jl 8,16:1
Absent-Minded Professor, The 1961,Mr 16,44:2
Young Savages, The 1961,My 25,31:1
Love in a Goldfish Bowl 1961,Jl 13,26:3
Young Doctors, The 1961,Ag 24,25:2
Advise and Consent 1962,Je 7,31:2
40 Pounds of Trouble 1963,Ja 24,5:2
Son of Flubber 1963,F 9,5:2
Thrill of it All, The 1963,Ag 2,15:3
Man From Galveston, The 1964,Ja 23,26:3
Brass Bottle, The 1964,My 21,42:1
Good Neighbor Sam 1964,Jl 23,19:1
Kisses for my President 1964,Ag 22,13:1
Tiger Walks, A 1964,Ag 27,28:2
Youngblood Hawke 1964,N 6,30:1
Send Me no Flowers 1964,N 13,30:1
Fluffy 1965,O 21,57:2
Glass Bottom Boat, The 1966,Je 10,54:1
Andrews, Frank
Hoosier Schoolmaster, The 1924,Mr 18,25:2
Andrews, Harry
Paratrooper 1953,D 31,9:3
Black Knight, The 1954,O 29,27:2
Man Who Loved Redheads, The 1955,Jl 26,29:2
Alexander the Great 1956,Mr 29,23:1
Moby Dick 1956,Jl 5,18:1

Andrews, Harry— Cont

Saint Joan 1957,Je 27,21:1
I Accuse! 1958,Mr 6,32:1
Devil's Disciple, The 1959,Ag 21,12:1
Solomon and Sheba 1959,D 26,7:2
Touch of Larceny, A 1960,Mr 17,28:1
Circle of Deception 1961,F 18,12:2
Desert Attack 1961,Mr 23,28:1
Lisa 1962,My 25,28:1
Best of Enemies, The 1962,Ag 7,35:2
Barabbas 1962,O 11,49:1
Nine Hours to Rama 1963,Ap 4,58:2
55 Days at Peking 1963,My 30,20:1
Reach for Glory 1963,S 10,46:1
633 Squadron 1964,Je 25,25:1
Nothing but the Best 1964,Jl 14,28:1
Truth About Spring, The 1965,Je 17,27:2
Hill, The 1965,O 4,00:0
Agony and the Ecstacy, The 1965,O 9,5:6
Underworld Informers 1965,O 14,53:1
Sands of the Kalahari 1965,N 25,64:5
Modesty Blaise 1966,Ag 11,27:1
Deadly Affair, The 1967,Ja 27,31:1
Jokers, The 1967,My 16,50:1
Long Duel, The 1967,N 2,58:3
Dandy in Aspic, A 1968,Ap 3,40:1
I'll Never Forget What's 'Isname
    1968,Ap 15,51:1
Danger Route 1968,Je 6,54:2
Charge of the Light Brigade, The 1968,O 7,59:1
Night They Raided Minsky's, The
    1968,D 23,43:1
Sea Gull, The 1968,D 24,14:1

Andrews, Jack (Original Author)
Born Reckless 1937,Jl 30,22:6
Cadet Girl 1941,D 11,39:1
Chetniks 1943,Mr 19,15:3

Andrews, Jack (Screenwriter)
Maryland 1940,Jl 13,16:5
Marry the Boss's Daughter 1941,D 4,33:4
Berlin Correspondent 1942,S 4,19:2
Chetniks 1943,Mr 19,15:3
Caribbean Mystery, The 1945,Ag 20,22:4
Dark Delusion 1947,Je 26,19:2
Johnny Holiday 1950,My 17,36:1

Andrews, Julie
Mary Poppins 1964,S 25,34:1
Americanization of Emily, The 1964,O 28,51:1
Sound of Music, The 1965,Mr 3,34:1
Torn Curtain 1966,Jl 28,23:1
Hawaii 1966,O 11,54:1
Thoroughly Modern Millie 1967,Mr 23,25:1
Star! 1968,O 23,36:2

Andrews, Lois
Dixie Dugan 1943,Ap 9,25:5
Roger Touhy, Gangster 1944,Je 5,14:7
Desert Hawk, The 1950,Ag 26,9:2
Meet Me After the Show 1951,Ag 16,23:2

Andrews, Robert
Fascinating Youth 1926,My 10,19:1
Rubber Heels 1927,Je 28,29:4

Andrews, Robert (Original Author)
I Live for Love 1935,O 19,21:2
Mayor of Forty-Fourth Street, The
    1942,Je 11,27:4

Andrews, Robert (Screenwriter)
Little Big Shot 1935,O 7,11:2
I Live for Love 1935,O 19,21:2
Walking Dead, The 1936,Mr 2,13:2
Longest Night, The 1936,O 17,21:2
Mutiny in the Big House 1939,D 11,26:2

Andrews, Robert B (Original Author)
Streets of New York 1939,My 1,21:1

Andrews, Robert B (Screenwriter)
Streets of New York 1939,My 1,21:1

Andrews, Robert D (Original Author)
Three Girls Lost 1931,My 2,23:4
If I Had a Million 1932,D 3,21:4
Flight From Glory 1937,S 11,20:1
Gangster's Boy 1938,N 7,23:6
Before I Hang 1940,O 3,31:3
Salute to the Marines 1943,Ag 30,11:3

Andrews, Robert D (Screenwriter)
Jailbreak 1936,Ag 6,22:1
Gangster's Boy 1938,N 7,23:6
I Was a Convict 1939,Mr 23,27:2
Men Without Souls 1940,My 13,21:2
Island Of Doomed Men 1940,Je 10,21:2
Girls of the Road 1940,Jl 22,20:2
Before I Hang 1940,O 3,31:3
Devil Commands, The 1941,F 14,15:3
Road to Happiness 1942,Mr 27,27:4
Bataan 1943,Je 4,17:2
Cross of Lorraine, The 1943,D 3,27:4
Hairy Ape, The 1944,Jl 3,8:3
Man From Colorado 1949,Ja 21,24:3

Andrews, Robert Hardy (Original Author)
Bad Boy 1949,Mr 23,35:2
Kid From Texas, The 1950,Je 2,26:2
Wyoming Mail 1950,O 23,26:5
Best of the Badmen 1951,Ag 10,13:2
Trouble Along the Way 1953,My 7,37:2
King's Thief, The 1955,Ag 13,7:2
Great Day in the Morning 1956,My 19,12:6

Andrews, Robert Hardy (Screenwriter)
Bad Boy 1949,Mr 23,35:2
Bagdad 1949,D 24,11:4
Kid From Texas, The 1950,Je 2,26:2
Woman on Pier 13, The 1950,Je 16,28:4
Best of the Badmen 1951,Ag 10,13:2
Mark of the Renegade 1951,S 7,24:2
Tanks are Coming, The 1951,D 6,42:4
Tarzan Goes to India 1962,S 6,37:2

Andrews, Sisters
Road to Rio 1948,F 19,29:3

Andrews, Stanley
All the King's Horses 1935,Mr 9,19:1
Private Worlds 1935,Mr 28,25:2
Hold 'Em Yale 1935,Ap 27,20:6
Escape from Devil's Island 1935,N 25,22:2
Desire 1936,Ap 13,15:1
In His Steps 1936,O 29,31:1
Devil's Playground 1937,F 15,12:5
John Meade's Woman 1937,F 18,19:1
High, Wide and Handsome 1937,Jl 22,15:1
Buccaneer, The 1938,F 17,17:2
When G-Men Step In 1938,Mr 14,13:2
I'll Give a Million 1938,Jl 16,7:2
Alexander's Ragtime Band 1938,Ag 6,7:2
Adventure in Sahara 1938,D 19,19:2
Kentucky 1938,D 24,12:1
Homicide Bureau 1939,F 2,17:2
Blue Bird, The 1940,Ja 20,11:2
Little Old New York 1940,F 3,9:2
Geronimo 1940,F 8,18:3
Brigham Young - Frontiersman 1940,S 21,13:2
Kit Carson 1940,N 15,25:3
Play Girl 1941,Ja 30,19:3
Meet John Doe 1941,Mr 13,25:2
Strange Alibi 1941,Ap 28,11:2
Time Out for Rhythm 1941,Jl 10,16:3
Wild Geese Calling 1941,Ag 30,10:2
North to the Klondike 1942,Mr 12,24:3
Canal Zone 1942,Mr 30,21:2
My Gal Sal 1942,My 1,23:1
Ten Gentlemen From West Point 1942,Je 5,23:3
Crash Dive 1943,Ap 29,25:2
Princess and the Pirate, The 1945,F 10,16:2
Michigan Kid 1947,F 22,16:3
Northwest Stampede 1948,D 10,34:3
Paleface, The 1948,D 16,41:2
Man From Colorado 1949,Ja 21,24:3
Last Bandit, The 1949,Mr 21,19:2
Brimstone 1949,O 7,35:3
Short Grass 1951,Ja 13,10:4
Vengeance Valley 1951,F 16,21:2
Al Jennings of Oklahoma 1951,My 18,34:6
Dangerous Crossing 1953,S 30,37:2
Appointment in Honduras 1953,N 19,41:4
Southwest Passage 1954,S 11,11:2

Andrews, Tige
Wings of Eagles, The 1957,F 1,28:1
Until They Sail 1957,O 9,41:2
Imitation General 1958,Ag 21,22:2
Onionhead 1958,O 2,44:1
China Doll 1958,D 4,52:1
Private's Affair, A 1959,Ag 15,8:7

Andrews, Tiger
Mister Roberts 1955,Jl 15,14:1

Andrews, Tod
Outrage 1950,O 16,30:5
In Harm's Way 1965,Ap 7,36:1

Andrews, William
Sealed Cargo 1951,My 24,47:1

Andrews Sisters, The
Argentine Nights 1940,O 11,25:3
Buck Privates 1941,F 14,15:2
In the Navy 1941,Je 12,29:2
Hold That Ghost 1941,Ag 8,13:3
What's Cookin' 1942,F 26,15:5
Private Buckaroo 1942,Je 25,27:4
Give Out, Sisters 1942,Ag 28,22:3
Swingtime Johnny 1943,D 17,23:3
Follow the Boys 1944,Ap 26,24:6
Hollywood Canteen 1944,D 16,19:2

Andrex
Amours de Toni, Les 1936,N 5,35:1
Heart of Paris 1939,Ja 13,17:3
Heartbeat 1939,S 5,21:3
Marseillaise 1939,N 6,20:2
32 Rue de Montmartre 1944,S 28,26:3
Fric-Frac 1948,My 29,8:6
Ignace 1950,S 19,39:4
Virtuous Bigamist, The 1959,My 28,34:3
My Wife's Husband 1965,Ja 27,26:1
Toni 1968,S 19,62:2

Andreyev, A
Mexican, The 1957,Ap 3,28:2

Andreyev, Boris
Two Soldiers 1944,Jl 27,14:2
Last Hill, The 1945,Je 26,13:2
Dark Is The Night 1946,Mr 18,24:3
Symphony of Life 1948,D 28,19:7
Cossacks of the Kuban 1950,O 30,22:4
Fall of Berlin 1952,Je 9,19:2
Maximka 1953,O 12,30:4

Andreyev, Boris— Cont

Big Family, A 1955,Je 6,24:1
Poem of the Sea 1959,D 21,34:4
Sword and the Dragon, The 1960,N 17,46:3
Optimistic Tragedy, The 1964,F 24,20:2

Andreyev, Leonid (Original Author)
He Who Gets Slapped 1924,N 10,20:1

Andreyev, P
Poet and Tsar 1938,Ag 25,15:1

Andreyev (Original Author)
Lash of the Czar, The 1929,F 12,23:1

Andreyor, Yvette
Friend Will come Tonight, A; Ami Viendra Ce
    Soir, Un 1948,Jl 12,11:2

Andriane, Marayat
Sand Pebbles, The 1966,D 21,48:1

Andriani, Oscar
Theodora, Slave Empress 1955,Ja 12,24:2

Andric, Ivo (Original Author)
Legends of Anika 1956,Ap 19,35:1

Andric, Miodrag
Affair of the Heart, An 1967,S 23,20:3

Andrieux
They Are not Angels 1948,My 22,8:3

Andrievsky, Pavel
Turning Point, The 1946,O 28,19:4

Andriot, Poupee
All Quiet on The Western Front 1930,Ap 30,29:1

Andrisson
Marseillaise 1939,N 6,20:2

Andronikashvilli, Kira
Caucasian Love 1929,D 3,28:4

Androniskova, Kiba
Zemlya Zhazhdet 1932,My 6,15:3

Androsky, Carol
Funnyman 1967,S 25,56:3

Androvskaya, Olga
Jubilee 1945,F 22,31:3

Andrusco, Richie
Little Fugitive 1953,O 7,35:1

Andrzejewski, Jerzy (Original Author)
Ashes and Diamonds 1961,My 30,8:1

Andrzejewski, Jerzy (Screenwriter)
Ashes and Diamonds 1961,My 30,8:1

Anduze, Carlos
Illiac Passion, The 1968,Ap 19,40:1

Andzhaparidze, V
Twenty-Six Commissars 1933,Jl 1,16:6
Fall of Berlin 1952,Je 9,19:2

Anee, James (Original Author)
All the Way Home 1963,O 30,46:1

Anerobi, Harford
Daybreak in Udi 1950,Je 2,26:2

Anet, Claude (Original Author)
Ariane 1934,Mr 7,23:4
Mayerling 1937,S 14,27:1
Love in the Afternoon 1957,Ag 24,12:1

Anet, Genica
Don Quixote 1934,D 24,17:1

Angarola, Richard
Gambit 1966,D 22,40:2

Ange, Julie
Teenage Mother 1968,S 19,62:4

Angel, Daniel M (Producer)
Another Man's Poison 1952,Ja 7,14:3
Mister Drake's Duck 1952,Ja 28,15:2
Reach for the Sky 1957,My 1,40:1
Escapade 1957,Ag 6,30:2
Cast a Dark Shadow 1957,N 28,57:1
Sheriff of Fractured Jaw, The 1959,Mr 14,27:4

Angel, Heather
Man Who Won, The 1933,F 27,11:2
Pilgrimage 1933,Jl 13,17:5
Berkeley Square 1933,S 14,26:2
Charlie Chan's Greatest Case 1933,O 7,18:4
Farewell to Love 1933,N 25,10:2
Orient Express 1934,F 28,23:2
Murder in Trinidad 1934,My 16,22:2
Romance in the Rain 1934,S 8,18:5
Mystery of Edwin Drood, The 1935,Mr 21,27:1
It Happened in New York 1935,Ap 6,10:1
Informer, The 1935,My 10,25:2
Three Musketeers, The 1935,N 1,25:1
Perfect Gentleman, The 1935,D 19,33:4
Last of the Mohicans, The 1936,S 3,17:3
Daniel Boone 1936,O 24,23:2
Portia on Trial 1937,D 3,29:2
Army Girl 1938,Ag 12,11:1
Bulldog Drummond in Africa 1938,Ag 25,15:1
Arrest Bulldog Drummond 1939,Ja 12,23:2
Bulldog Drummond's Secret Police
    1939,Mr 30,19:3
Undercover Doctor 1939,Je 1,31:2
Bulldog Drummond's Bride 1939,Jl 13,17:2
Pride and Prejudice 1940,Ag 9,19:1
That Hamilton Woman 1941,Ap 4,25:1
Singapore Woman 1941,My 12,13:6
Suspicion 1941,N 21,23:2
Time to Kill 1942,D 25,15:4
Cry Havoc 1943,N 24,16:2
Lifeboat 1944,Ja 13,17:1
Saxon Charm, The 1948,S 30,32:3
Premature Burial, The 1962,My 24,29:2

Angel, Marguerite
Affair Lafont, The; Conflit 1939,O 9,15:2
Angel-Engelowna, Stanislawa
Wrzos; Heather 1938,N 7,23:4
Rena 1939,Ja 27,17:3
Angeletti, Marietto
Behold a Pale Horse 1964,Ag 14,16:1
Angeli, Pier
Teresa 1951,Ap 6,31:2
Light Touch, The 1952,Ja 17,23:1
Tomorrow is too Late 1952,Ap 14,22:2
Devil Makes Three, The 1952,Ag 30,6:2
Story of Three Loves, The (Equilibrium);
  Equilibrium (The Story of Three Loves)
  1953,Mr 6,29:2
Equilibrium 1953,Mr 6,29:2
Sombrero 1953,Ap 23,37:2
Flame and the Flesh 1954,My 3,21:2
Silver Chalice, The 1954,D 27,22:5
Somebody up There Likes Me 1956,Jl 6,16:1
Port Afrique 1956,N 3,27:5
Vintage, The 1957,My 9,36:5
Merry Andrews 1958,Mr 21,17:1
S O S Pacific 1960,O 13,41:3
Angry Silence, The 1960,D 13,25:2
Sodom and Gomorrah 1963,Ja 24,5:3
Battle of the Bulge 1965,D 18,36:1
Angelillo, Luciana
Girl With a Suitcase 1961,S 12,36:2
Easy Life, The 1963,D 23,18:2
Love and Marriage (The First Night); First Night,
  The (Love and Marriage) 1966,Ag 5,20:1
Wild Eye, The 1968,Ag 22,47:1
Angelis, Enrique de
Nuestra Tierra de Paz; Our Land of Peace
  1940,Je 1,12:3
Angelle, Simone
Demoniaque 1958,Mr 4,34:5
Angelo, Jean
Nana 1928,Ja 22,VIII,7:7
Java, Une 1928,Jl 15,VIII,3:4 (In Addenda)
Vierge Folle, La 1929,Ja 13,VIII,7:4
Nana 1929,Jl 30,19:4
Strange Case of District Attorney M, The
  1930,Mr 17,20:3
Atlantide, L' 1932,Ag 7,IX,2:1
Angelo, Little
Mister Wong in Chinatown 1939,Jl 31,9:2 (In
  Addenda)
Angelo 1951,Mr 26,19:4
Angelo, Salvo d' (Producer)
Fabiola 1951,My 30,14:2
Angelotti, Mario
It's Forever Springtime 1951,D 29,7:7
Angelus, Muriel
Night Birds 1931,Ja 3,21:2
Light That Failed, The 1939,D 25,19:1
Way of all Flesh, The 1940,Je 6,33:2
Safari 1940,Je 20,29:2
Great McGinty, The 1940,Ag 15,23:1
Angers, Avril
Green Man, The 1957,My 23,40:1
Family Way, The 1967,Je 29,32:1
Angioletti, G B (Original Author)
Wandering Jew, The 1949,Mr 11,33:2
Angioletti, G B (Screenwriter)
Wandering Jew, The 1949,Mr 11,33:2
Anglade, France
Oldest Profession, The (Paris Today); Paris Today
  (The Oldest Profession) 1968,N 8,42:1
Angold, Edit
Tomorrow the World 1944,D 22,12:4
Suspense 1946,Jl 5,15:3
White Tower, The 1950,Jl 3,9:2
Molly 1951,My 8,37:2
Blue Angel, The 1959,S 5,11:4
Angst, Richard (Cinematographer)
Ski Chase, The 1938,Mr 26,12:1
Angus, Robert (Original Author)
Timetable 1956,Mr 17,13:2
Anhalt, Edna (Original Author)
Panic in the Streets 1950,Ag 5,9:2
Sniper, The 1952,My 10,16:3
Anhalt, Edna (Screenwriter)
Younger Brothers, The 1949,My 28,11:2
Return of the Frontiersman 1950,Je 10,11:3
Sierra 1950,S 15,31:2
Member of the Wedding, The 1952,D 31,10:2
Not as a Stranger 1955,Je 29,24:1
Pride and the Passion, The 1957,Je 29,10:6
Anhalt, Edward (Original Author)
Panic in the Streets 1950,Ag 5,9:2
Sniper, The 1952,My 10,16:3
Anhalt, Edward (Screenwriter)
Member of the Wedding, The 1952,D 31,10:2
Not as a Stranger 1955,Je 29,24:1
Pride and the Passion, The 1957,Je 29,10:6
Young Lions, The 1958,Ap 3,23:1
In Love and War 1958,N 1,14:2
Sins of Rachel Cade, The 1961,Ap 6,30:3
Young Savages, The 1961,My 25,31:1
Girl Named Tamiku, A 1963,Mr 15,8:2
Wives and Lovers 1963,Ag 29,36:1

Becket 1964,Mr 12,40:2
Satan Bug, The 1965,Ap 15,38:1
Boeing Boeing 1965,D 24,24:4
Hour of the Gun 1967,N 2,58:4
Boston Strangler, The 1968,O 17,52:1
Anibhebe, Oso
Daybreak in Udi 1950,Je 2,26:2
Anicelli, Corrado
Secret Conclave, The 1953,My 16,10:1
Anil
Kanchenjungha 1966,Jl 26,27:2
Anima
Kanchenjungha 1966,Jl 26,27:2
Animals, The
Go Go Mania 1965,My 20,52:4
Anjaparidze, Veriko
Skanderbeg 1954,Jl 5,6:4
Anka, Paul
Look in any Window 1962,Mr 22,40:1
Longest Day, The 1962,O 5,28:1
Ankers, Evelyn
Hit the Road 1941,Jl 3,15:3
Hold That Ghost 1941,Ag 8,13:3
Burma Convoy 1941,O 7,26:7
Wolf Man, The 1941,D 22,24:5
North to the Klondike 1942,Mr 12,24:3
Ghost of Frankenstein, The 1942,Ap 4,19:2
Eagle Squadron 1942,Jl 3,12:5
Pierre of the Plains 1942,Jl 30,17:3
Sherlock Holmes and the Voice Of Terror
  1942,S 19,9:2
Captive Wild Woman 1943,Je 7,9:4
All by Myself 1943,Jl 16,20:3
Hers to Hold 1943,Jl 22,15:1
Son of Dracula 1943,N 6,16:4
Mad Ghoul, The 1943,D 11,11:2
His Butler's Sister 1943,D 30,13:2
Ladies Courageous 1944,Mr 16,17:2
Weird Woman 1944,Ap 1,11:1
Invisible Man's Revenge, The 1944,Je 10,12:2
Jungle Woman 1944,Jl 15,19:6
Pearl of Death 1944,Ag 26,15:2
Bowery to Broadway 1944,N 30,19:2
Frozen Ghost, The 1945,Jl 28,7:3
Black Beauty 1946,Ag 30,13:2
Last of the Redmen 1947,Ag 30,8:6
Lone Wolf in London, The 1947,N 22,10:3
Tarzan's Magic Fountain 1949,F 7,15:2
Ankrum, Morris
Cherokee Strip 1940,N 4,23:2
Roundup, The 1941,Mr 13,25:4
This Woman Is Mine 1941,O 13,21:2
I Wake up Screaming 1942,Ja 17,13:2
Ride 'Em Cowboy 1942,Mr 5,27:3
Loves of Edgar Allan Poe, The 1942,S 21,19:2
Tales of Manhattan 1942,S 25,25:1
Time to Kill 1942,D 25,15:4
Tennessee Johnson 1943,Ja 13,18:2
Reunion in France 1943,Mr 5,20:3
Swing Fever 1944,Ja 28,14:1
Heavenly Body, The 1944,Mr 24,17:3
Rationing 1944,Ap 10,14:2
Meet The People 1944,S 8,16:2
Barbary Coast Gent 1944,S 29,18:2
Marriage Is a Private Affair 1944,O 27,17:7
Gentle Annie 1945,My 5,11:5
Harvey Girls, The 1946,Ja 25,26:2
Courage of Lassie 1946,Jl 25,18:5
Cockeyed Miracle, The 1946,O 25,28:1
Lady in the Lake 1947,Ja 24,18:3
Sea of Grass, The 1947,F 28,27:2
Mighty McGurk, The 1947,Ap 4,19:4
Cynthia 1947,S 19,27:2
Desire Me 1947,S 26,28:3
Good News 1947,D 5,33:2
High Wall 1947,D 26,22:2
For the Love of Mary 1948,S 23,37:2
We Were Strangers 1949,Ap 28,28:2
Colorado Territory 1949,Je 25,8:6
Slattery's Hurricane 1949,Ag 13,6:6
Chain Lightning 1950,F 20,21:2
Borderline 1950,Mr 6,17:2
Damned Don't Cry, The 1950,Ap 8,9:2
In a Lonely Place 1950,My 18,37:2
Rocketship X-M 1950,My 27,10:6
Southside 1-1000 1950,N 3,31:2
Short Grass 1951,Ja 13,10:4
Along the Great Divide 1951,My 17,38:3
Redhead and the Cowboy, The 1951,Je 6,37:2
Tomorrow Is Another Day 1951,Ag 9,17:5
My Favorite Spy 1951,D 26,19:3
Red Planet Mars 1952,Je 16,15:2
Son of Ali Baba 1952,Ag 16,7:4
Raiders, The 1952,D 13,19:2
Hiawatha 1952,D 26,20:4
Invaders From Mars 1953,My 30,7:1
Arena 1953,Jl 23,20:2
Moonlighter, The 1953,S 23,37:2
Southwest Passage 1954,S 11,11:2
Vera Cruz 1954,D 27,22:4
Cattle Queen of Montana 1955,Ja 26,22:1
Tennessee's Partner 1955,N 5,22:8
Earth vs the Flying Saucers 1956,Ag 2,21:2

Ankrum, Morris— Cont
Walk the Proud Land 1956,S 8,20:6 (In
  Addenda)
Death of a Scoundrel 1956,N 6,30:1
Kronos 1957,My 11,24:6
Beginning of the End 1957,Jl 4,16:1
Most Dangerous Man Alive 1961,Jl 5,29:2
Ankwicz, Krystyna
Przysieglas 1932,My 16,19:5
Ann, Anny
Lumpenball 1931,Ap 27,25:1
Ann, Bruce
Bike Boy 1967,O 6,31:2
Ann, George
Bike Boy 1967,O 6,31:2
Ann, Philip
China 1943,Ap 22,31:2
Ann-Margret
Pocketful of Miracles 1961,D 19,39:1
State Fair 1962,Ap 12,41:4
Bye Bye Birdie 1963,Ap 5,27:3
Viva Las Vegas 1964,My 21,42:1
Kitten With a Whip 1964,N 5,50:4
Pleasure Seekers, The 1964,D 26,9:1
Bus Riley's Back in Town 1965,Ap 8,45:2
Once a Thief 1965,S 9,36:1
Cincinnati Kid, The 1965,O 28,48:1
Made in Paris 1966,F 17,29:1
Stagecoach 1966,Je 16,53:1
Swinger, The 1966,D 15,60:1
Murderers' Row 1966,D 22,40:3
Tiger and the Pussycat, The 1967,S 21,56:4
Annabella
Million, Le 1931,My 21,33:2
Million, The 1931,Jl 19,VIII,4:3
Soir de Rafle, Un 1931,O 16,27:1
Paris-Mediterranee 1932,Mr 27,VIII,6:2
July 14th 1933,Mr 19,IX,4:1 (In Addenda)
Marie 1933,Mr 19,IX,4:2 (In Addenda)
On Demande un Compaznon 1933,Je 5,18:5
Quatorez Juillet 1933,O 20,14:2
Wings of the Morning 1937,Mr 12,19:1
Under the Red Robe 1937,Je 1,27:2
Dinner at the Ritz 1937,D 4,21:1
Baroness and the Butler, The 1938,F 19,19:2
Moscow Nights 1938,My 3,19:3
Suez 1938,O 15,21:2
Flight Into Darkness (L'Equipage)
  1938,O 17,12:1
Sacrifice d'Honneur 1938,D 2,27:2
Escape From Yesterday 1939,My 3,27:2
Bridal Suite 1939,My 26,20:2
Citadel of Silence, The 1939,D 25,29:1
Hotel du Nord 1940,D 30,21:2
Tonight We Raid Calais 1943,Ap 15,20:2
Bomber's Moon 1943,Jl 31,8:2
13 Rue Madeleine 1947,Ja 16,30:2
Annakin, Ken (Director)
Holiday Camp 1948,Ja 24,11:2
Quartet (The Colonel's Lady); Colonel's Lady, The
  (Quartet) 1949,Mr 29,30:3
Miranda 1949,Ap 25,20:2
Broken Journey 1949,My 26,34:3
Trio 1950,O 11,42:1
Here Come the Huggetts 1950,D 25,25:3
Hotel Sahara 1952,Ja 1,21:4
Story of Robin Hood, The 1952,Je 27,18:3
Outpost in Malaya 1952,N 27,49:2
Double Confession 1953,My 1,17:2
Landfall 1953,My 11,25:2
Sword and the Rose, The 1953,Ag 20,18:3
Land of Fury 1955,My 3,37:4
Value for Money 1957,Ag 1,20:4
Across the Bridge 1957,O 30,24:1
Elephant Gun 1959,Je 20,11:2
3 Men in a Boat 1959,Jl 29,33:2
Third Man on the Mountain 1959,N 12,27:1
Swiss Family Robinson 1960,D 24,8:4
Hellions, The 1962,Mr 15,28:2
Coming-Out Party, A 1962,Jl 31,19:2
Longest Day, The 1962,O 5,28:1
Crooks Anonymous 1963,O 31,26:3
Those Magnificent Men in Their Flying Machines
  (Or How I Flew From London to Paris in 25
  Hours and 11 Minutes) 1965,Je 17,27:1
Underworld Informers 1965,O 14,53:1
Battle of the Bulge 1965,D 18,36:1
Long Duel, The 1967,N 2,58:3
Biggest Bundle of Them All, The 1968,Ja 18,46:1
Annakin, Ken (Producer)
Long Duel, The 1967,N 2,58:3
Annakin, Ken (Screenwriter)
Those Magnificent Men in Their Flying Machines
  (Or How I Flew From London to Paris in 25
  Hours and 11 Minutes) 1965,Je 17,27:1
Annensky, I (Director)
Marriage 1945,F 22,31:3
Anna Cross, The 1954,O 25,30:7
Sailor From the Comet, The 1959,Ag 3,21:2
Annensky, I (Screenwriter)
Marriage 1945,F 22,31:3
Anna Cross, The 1954,O 25,30:7

Annensky, Isidore (Producer)
Sailor From the Comet, The 1959,Ag 3,21:2
Annette
Monkey's Uncle, The 1965,Ag 19,35:4
Annicchiarico, Vito
Open City; Citta Aperta 1946,F 26,21:2
Annis, Francesca
Cleopatra 1963,Je 13,29:1
Eyes of Annie Jones, The 1964,My 14,39:1
Flipper's New Adventure 1964,Ag 27,28:2
Murder Most Foul 1965,My 24,36:2
Pleasure Girls, The 1966,Ap 21,43:1
Annixfer, Paul (Original Author)
Those Calloways 1965,Ap 15,38:2
Annunzio, Gabriel D (Director)
Quo Vadis 1925,F 16,24:1
Anofriev, O
Behind the Show Window 1957,Ap 17,37:1
Anore, Charles
Paris Underground 1945,O 20,8:2
Anouilh, Jean (Miscellaneous)
Monsieur Vincent 1948,D 21,33:2
Anouilh, Jean (Original Author)
Monsoon 1953,S 26,15:2
Waltz of the Toreadors 1962,Ag 14,34:1
Becket 1964,Mr 12,40:2
Anouilh, Jean (Screenwriter)
Anna Karenina 1948,Ap 28,32:2
Monsieur Vincent 1948,D 21,33:2
Caroline Cherie 1954,My 25,23:1
Passion of Slow Fire, The 1962,O 12,26:1
Circle of Love 1965,Mr 25,42:4
Anouk
See Aimee, Anouk
Anoulth, Catherine
Grand Maneuver, The 1956,O 2,39:1
Anousaki, Eleni
Zorba, The Greek 1964,D 18,25:1
Anoussaki, Elena
Red Lanterns 1965,Ap 1,30:1
Anrzejewska, Jadzia
Cabman No 13 1937,N 1,24:6
Ansara, Michael
Action in Arabia 1944,F 19,18:7
Soldiers Three 1951,Mr 30,28:5
Diplomatic Courier 1952,Je 14,12:2
Golden Hawk, The 1952,O 18,16:4
White Witch Doctor 1953,Jl 2,19:3
Diamond Queen, The 1954,Ja 27,24:2
Three Young Texans 1954,Ap 17,8:2
Saracen Blade, The 1954,My 15,13:4
Princess of the Nile 1954,Je 12,13:2
New Orleans Uncensored 1955,Ap 30,10:8
Diane 1956,Ja 13,18:1
Pillars of the Sky 1956,O 13,15:2
Quantez 1957,S 7,12:7
Sad Sack, The 1957,N 28,57:1
Voyage to the Bottom of the Sea 1961,Jl 20,32:2
Comancheros, The 1961,N 2,42:1
Harum Scarum 1965,D 16,63:3
...And Now Miguel 1966,S 8,43:1
Texas Across the River 1966,N 24,65:1
Sol Madrid 1968,Je 14,43:1
Pink Jungle, The 1968,O 17,52:1
Ansell, Eric (Composer)
I Met a Murderer 1939,O 2,15:2
Ansell, Louis A (Producer)
Woman in the Night 1948,Ja 10,16:2
Anselmi, Rosina
Eredita dello Zio, L' 1935,Je 29,16:3
Milizia Territoriale 1936,Ap 6,18:2
Signora Fortuna; Lady Luck 1937,N 29,19:3
Aria del Continente, L'; Continental Atmosphere 1939,N 17,17:3
Re di Danari; Money King 1939,D 22,15:2
Paraninfo, Il; Matchmaker, The 1940,Ja 23,17:2
Ansen, Joseph (Original Author)
Cinerama-South Seas Adventure 1958,Jl 16,26:1
Ansen, Joseph (Screenwriter)
Jungle Headhunters 1951,D 6,42:5
Ansky, S (Original Author)
Dybbuk, The 1938,Ja 28,17:2
Ansley, F (Original Author)
Brass Bottle, The 1964,My 21,42:1
Anslinger, Harry J Commissioner
To the Ends of the Earth 1948,F 13,26:2
Anson, A E
Road to Singapore, The 1931,O 1,25:2
Arrowsmith 1931,D 8,36:4
Anson, Ina
Shooting of Dan McGrew, The 1924,Je 9,14:3
Anson, Joe (Screenwriter)
Babes in Bagdad 1954,Ap 5,21:3
Anstey, F (Original Author)
Brass Bottle, The 1923,Jl 23,13:4
Man From Blankley's, The 1930,Mr 29,23:1
Antal, Pagor
Csokolj Meg Edes 1932,N 25,19:2
Antamoro, Giulio (Director)
Passion of St Francis, The 1932,D 17,22:3
Antes, Jerry
Opposite Sex, The 1956,N 16,23:2

Antheil, George (Composer)
Buccaneer, The 1938,F 17,17:2
Hunters of the Deep 1954,D 17,37:4
Dementia 1955,D 23,14:4
Antheil, George (Miscellaneous)
Once in a Blue Moon 1936,D 2,35:1
Plainsman, The 1937,Ja 14,16:2
Anthelme, Paul (Original Author)
I Confess 1953,Mr 23,28:2
Anthony, C L (Original Author)
Looking Forward 1933,My 1,10:2
Autumn Crocus 1934,O 25,26:2
Anthony, David
Touchables, The 1968,N 21,41:1
Anthony, Edward (Original Author)
Big Cage, The 1933,My 9,20:5
Anthony, Emmett (Original Author)
Make a Million 1935,N 9,19:3
Anthony, Jack
Hell-Ship Bronson 1928,Je 19,31:1
Anthony, Joseph
Shadow of the Thin Man 1941,N 21,23:2
Joe Smith, American 1942,Ap 2,27:4
Anthony, Joseph (Director)
Rainmaker, The 1956,D 13,51:1
Matchmaker, The 1958,Ag 13,22:1
Career 1959,O 9,24:1
All in a Nights Work 1961,Mr 23,28:1
Anthony, Joseph (Original Author)
Spellbinder, The 1939,Ag 24,17:3
Anthony, Joseph (Screenwriter)
Crime and Punishment 1935,N 22,18:2
One Way Ticket 1936,Ja 1,35:2
Lady of Secrets 1936,F 22,12:1
And So They Were Married 1936,My 14,29:3
Meet Nero Wolfe 1936,Jl 16,20:1
Anthony, Michael
Ideal Husband, An 1948,Ja 15,28:2
To Paris With Love 1955,Mr 29,33:4
Khartoum 1966,Jl 14,28:1
Anthony, Ray
Girl Can't Help It, The 1957,F 9,12:7
High School Confidential 1958,My 31,6:6
Five Pennies, The 1959,Je 19,30:1
Anthony, Stuart (Original Author)
Fame Street 1932,Ap 2,13:2
Illegal Traffic 1938,N 17,29:3
Anthony, Stuart (Screenwriter)
Charlie Chan in Paris 1935,Ja 22,23:2
Border Flight 1936,Je 22,22:1
Thunder Trail 1938,F 5,19:3
Tip-Off Girls 1938,Mr 25,15:3
Prison Farm 1938,Jl 15,13:3
Highway Patrol 1938,Ag 4,15:2
Illegal Traffic 1938,N 17,29:3
Biscuit Eater, The 1940,My 23,28:5
Monster and the Girl, The 1941,Mr 20,25:3
Shepherd of the Hills, The 1941,Jl 31,13:2
Anthony, Tony
Engagement Italiano 1966,Je 21,35:1
Stranger in Town, A 1968,Ap 25,53:4
Stranger Returns, The 1968,S 12,54:3
Anthony, Tony (Original Author)
Stranger Returns, The 1968,S 12,54:3
Anthony-Havelock-Allan (Producer)
Chance Meeting 1955,Ap 20,38:1
Antimonv, Sergei
Volga-Volga 1941,My 17,19:2
Antinea, Maria
Games Men Play, The 1968,Mr 15,30:1
Antjaparidze, Mary (Director)
Skanderbeg 1954,Jl 5,6:4
Antneil, George (Composer)
Make Way for Tomorrow 1937,My 10,23:1
Antoine, A P (Original Author)
Tender Enemy, The 1938,Mr 31,15:2 (In Addenda)
Antoine, Andre-Paul (Miscellaneous)
Mayerling to Sarajevo 1940,O 30,27:6
Star Without Light; Etoile Sans Lumiere 1947,Ag 4,14:2
Antoine, Andre Paul (Original Author)
Theodora, Slave Empress 1955,Ja 12,24:2
French-Cancan 1956,Ap 17,26:2
Antoine, Andre-Paul (Screenwriter)
Miracle of the Wolves, The 1925,F 24,17:3
Golem, The 1937,Mr 22,27:2
Sins of Paris 1954,Ja 30,9:6
Antomov, A
Adventure in Odessa 1954,Je 21,19:6
Anton, Charles (Director)
Chasseur de Chez Maxim's, Le 1935,F 4,11:4
Anton, Edoardo (Screenwriter)
Angela 1954,Je 4,9:2
Anton, Jose De San
Heroina 1965,N 11,58:2
Anton, Karel (Director)
Criez-Le sur les Toits; Shout it From the Housetops 1935,Je 22,18:5
Anton, Karl (Director)
Maedel von der Reeperbahn, Das 1931,Ja 31,15:1
Fall des Oberst Redl, Der 1932,Ag 18,23:3
Letzte Rose 1936,O 10,21:3

Anton, Karl (Director) — Cont
Weisse Sklaven 1937,Jl 31,6:2
Mit versiegelter Order; Under Sealed Orders 1938,Jl 30,10:2
Anton, Ronald
Diane 1956,Ja 13,18:1
Antonelli, Roberto
Taming of the Shrew, The 1967,Mr 9,43:1
Antoniani, Victor (Director)
Eclipse 1962,D 21,5:1
Antonini, Gabriel
Tailor's Maid, The; (Patri e Figli) 1959,S 2,35:4
Hercules Unchained 1960,Jl 14,23:1
Antonio
Ziegfeld Girl 1941,Ap 25,17:2
Pan-Americana 1945,Mr 23,13:2
Neapolitan Carousel 1961,O 12,41:3
Antonio, Jose de San
Harbor Lights 1964,F 13,25:3
Antonio, Lou
America America 1963,D 16,44:1
Hawaii 1966,O 11,54:1
Cool Hand Luke 1967,N 2,58:1
Antonio, Marco
Chuka 1967,N 2,58:3
Antonio and Luisa Triana
World Dances 1954,N 8,24:6
Antonioni, Michelangelo (Director)
Avventura, L' 1961,Ap 5,30:1
Night, The; Notte, La 1962,F 20,29:4
Grido, Il 1962,O 23,42:1
Deserto Rossa; Red Desert 1964,S 8,32:4
Red Desert 1965,F 9,43:1
Camille Without Camelias 1965,S 11,16:1
Blow-Up 1966,D 19,52:2
Antonioni, Michelangelo (Original Author)
Grido, Il 1962,O 23,42:1
Antonioni, Michelangelo (Screenwriter)
Avventura, L' 1961,Ap 5,30:1
Night, The; Notte, La 1962,F 20,29:4
Grido, Il 1962,O 23,42:1
Eclipse 1962,D 21,5:1
Red Desert 1965,F 9,43:1
Blow-Up 1966,D 19,52:2
Antonov, A
General Suvorov 1941,S 20,11:2
Mistress, The 1954,My 31,9:2
Frigid Sea, The 1955,N 21,23:4
Twelfth Night 1956,Mr 5,21:1
Antonovich, D
Mass Struggle 1934,S 17,20:3
Antonucci, Vittorio
Bicycle Thief, The 1949,D 13,44:2
Antrim, Harry
Miracle on 34th Street 1947,Je 5,32:1
Larceny 1948,S 4,8:6
Let's Live a Little 1948,D 10,34:2
Words and Music 1948,D 10,34:2
Act of Violence 1949,Ja 24,16:2
Johnny Allegro 1949,My 31,19:2
Ma and Pa Kettle 1949,Ag 12,13:2
Intruder in the Dust 1949,N 23,19:1
Thelma Jordon 1950,Ja 19,35:2
I'll Get by 1950,N 2,39:3
Devil's Doorway 1950,N 10,35:1
Appointment With Danger 1951,My 10,38:2
Night Into Morning 1951,Je 11,20:7
Mr Belvedere Rings the Bell 1951,Ag 2,18:1
Tomorrow Is Another Day 1951,Ag 9,17:5
I'll See You in my Dreams 1951,D 7,35:1
Lion and the Horse, The 1952,My 19,12:2
Solid Gold Cadillac, The 1956,O 25,40:3
Teacher's Pet 1958,Mr 20,33:1
Antropova, Maria
Road to Life 1932,Ja 28,24:2
Antsi-Polovski (Director)
If War Comes Tomorrow 1938,Jl 14,17:2
Antwerp, Van
Uncertain Glory 1944,Ap 8,9:2
Antzsch, Walter L
Mit dir Durch Dick und Duenn 1934,N 24,19:2
Anufirov, O
Girl With the Guitar, The 1960,F 1,22:4
Anwar, Rafik
Lord Jim 1965,F 26,18:1
Anys, Georgette
Fanfan the Tulip 1953,My 5,34:2
Little Boy Lost 1953,S 22,38:2
To Catch a Thief 1955,Ag 5,14:2
Four Bags Full 1957,S 5,32:1
Premier May 1958,S 17,44:2
Mirror Has two Faces, The 1959,My 27,31:1
Fanny 1961,Jl 7,16:1
Jessica 1962,Ap 20,20:2
Bon Voyage! 1962,My 18,34:2
Love Is a Ball 1963,Ap 25,38:1
Anzal, Kyoko
Battle in Outer Space 1960,Jl 9,10:5
Anzani, Governor
Tanga Tika 1953,O 6,34:4
Anzed, Toula
Prosfygopoula; Girl Refugee, The 1938,S 27,25:3

Anziani, Yvette
Lola 1962,O 15,32:2
Anzures, Miguel
American Guerrilla in the Philippines 1950,N 8,37:2
Aoki, Tsuro
Breath of the Gods, The 1920,Jl 26,9:5
Hell to Eternity 1960,O 13,41:1
Aoki, Tsuru
Dragon Painter, The 1919,O 5,IV,5:3 (In Addenda)
Aoki, Yoshio
Harakiri 1964,Ag 5,24:2
Aoyama, Kyoko
Naked General, The 1964,D 16,51:2
Aoyama, Yoshihiko
Majin 1968,Ag 10,15:5
Apagon, Art
World in my Corner 1956,F 18,12:5
Aparicio, Manuel
Jigsaw 1949,My 30,9:4
Apathy, Imre
Leanyvari Boszorkany; Witch of Leanyvar 1939,N 25,13:2
Apellan, H
Honor 1929,S 10,27:1
Apesteguy, Pierre (Screenwriter)
Sextette (Part 6-Ski Champ); Ski Champ (Sextette) 1953,Mr 2,19:2
Sextette (Part 5-Seducer's Fate); Seducer's Fate (Sextette) 1953,Mr 2,19:2
Sextette (Part 3-The Key to Sin); Key to Sin, The (Sextette) 1953,Mr 2,19:2
Sextette (Part 4-Snow Queen); Snow Queen (Sextette) 1953,Mr 2,19:2
Sextette (Part I-The Gun); Gun, The (Sextette) 1953,Mr 2,19:2
Sextette (Part 2-Female Affair); Female Affair (Sextette) 1953,Mr 2,19:2
Foxiest Girl in Paris 1958,S 20,10:6
Apfel, Oscar
Romance of the Underworld 1929,Ja 7,36:2
True Heaven 1929,F 11,26:3
Not Quite Decent 1929,My 6,30:4
Half Way to Heaven 1929,D 7,19:3
Texan, The 1930,My 17,21:2
Abraham Lincoln 1930,Ag 26,24:1
Spoilers, The 1930,S 20,15:4
Right to Love, The 1931,Ja 2,25:1
Inspiration 1931,F 9,25:3
Finger Points, The 1931,Mr 28,15:3
Maltese Falcon, The 1931,My 29,26:5
Big Business Girl 1931,Je 12,27:1
Huckleberry Finn 1931,Ag 8,16:3
Bargain, The 1931,S 5,7:4
Five Star Final 1931,S 11,24:2
Wicked 1931,S 19,10:2
Men in her Life 1931,N 30,16:2
Sooky 1931,D 21,28:4
Way Back Home 1932,Ja 16,13:1
Man Who Played God, The 1932,F 11,16:1
Business and Pleasure 1932,F 13,23:4
Heart of New York, The 1932,Mr 2,15:3
Alias the Doctor 1932,Mr 3,22:3
Shopworn 1932,Ap 4,13:6
It's Tough to be Famous 1932,Ap 9,18:1
State's Attorney 1932,My 6,15:3
World and the Flesh, The 1932,My 7,11:5
When a Feller Needs a Friend 1932,My 14,11:5
Make Me a Star 1932,Jl 1,19:3
Madame Racketeer 1932,Jl 23,6:6
Two Against the World 1932,Ag 19,20:6
Hell's Highway 1932,S 26,18:2
Hot Saturday 1932,N 5,12:5
I Am a Fugitive From a Chain Gang 1932,N 11,17:2
You Said a Mouthful 1932,N 18,23:2
False Faces 1932,N 25,19:2
Tomorrow at Seven 1933,Jl 3,14:6
One Man's Journey 1933,S 1,15:2
Bowery, The 1933,O 5,24:2
Before Dawn 1933,O 17,26:2
World Changes, The 1933,O 27,22:3
Only Yesterday 1933,N 10,25:1
Madame Spy 1934,F 10,20:1
House of Rothschild, The 1934,Mr 15,27:2
Whirlpool 1934,My 5,22:3
Are We Civilized? 1934,Je 14,28:5
Romance in Manhattan 1935,Ja 18,29:2
Nut Farm, The 1935,Ap 8,23:3
Man on the Flying Trapeze 1935,Ag 3,16:2
O'Shaughnessy's Boy 1935,O 5,18:2
His Night Out 1935,N 16,19:2
Every Saturday Night 1936,Mr 14,10:2
Sudden Death, And 1936,Jl 18,18:2
Plot Thickens, The 1936,D 9,35:2
Crack-Up 1937,Ja 4,20:4
Trouble in Morocco 1937,Mr 15,27:1
Soldier and the Lady, The 1937,Ap 10,11:1
Toast of New York, The 1937,Jl 23,16:2
Shadows of the Orient 1937,O 11,26:6

Apfel, Oscar (Director)
Sporting Chance, The 1925,Je 24,14:3
Aphenos, Pamis
Castle in Greece 1960,D 12,38:2
Apicella, Tina
Bellissima 1953,My 18,26:2
Apitz, Bruno (Original Author)
Naked Among the Wolves 1967,Ap 19,54:7
Aplon, Boris
Citizen Saint 1948,My 28,28:2
Apollo Boys Choir
Hansel and Gretel 1954,O 11,33:1
Apollon, Dave and his orchestra
Merry-Go-Round of 1938 1937,N 26,27:2
Apolloni, Camillo (Original Author)
Terra Madre 1931,O 31,22:2
APPEL
See Also APPELL
Appel, Anna
Broken Hearts 1926,Mr 3,26:1
Heart of New York, The 1932,Mr 2,15:3
Symphony of Six Million 1932,Ap 15,23:1
Faithless 1932,N 19,20:2
Green Fields 1937,O 12,31:4
Singing Blacksmith, The 1938,N 3,27:1
Appel, Benjamin (Original Author)
Cry of Battle 1963,O 12,27:2
Appel, David (Original Author)
Tonka 1959,Mr 26,27:1
Appel, Sam
Long Live the King 1923,D 4,24:1
White Black Sheep, The 1926,D 21,20:2
Revenge 1928,D 10,25:1
Under a Texas Moon 1930,Ap 4,22:1
Appelgren, Britta
Troette Teodor 1932,Ja 18,18:4
APPELL
See Also APPEL
Appell, Dave
Don't Knock the Rock 1957,F 23,13:1
Appels, Hendrik
Brand in der Oper 1932,Jl 11,11:4
Appian (Miscellaneous)
Cleopatra 1963,Je 13,29:1
Appiegate, Eddie
Ticklish Affair, A 1963,Ag 22,19:2
Appleby, Basil
Mister V 1942,F 13,24:4
Invaders, The 1942,Mr 6,17:1
Appleby, Dorothy
Under Eighteen 1931,D 26,15:5
As the Earth Turns 1934,Ap 12,27:2
I Give my Love 1934,Jl 17,24:2
Charlie Chan in Paris 1935,Ja 22,23:2
Making the Headlines 1938,Ap 1,17:2
Flying Irishman, The 1939,Ap 12,27:2
Convicted Woman 1940,F 26,11:2
Manpower 1941,Jl 5,14:2
Appleby, Lucy
Blues for Lovers 1966,S 8,43:1
Applegarth, Jonas
Battle Cry 1955,F 3,18:1
Applegate, Roy
Yolanda 1924,F 20,23:1
Applegren, Brita
Youth 1927,N 30,22:4
Appleton, Louis B Jr (Producer)
Never Trust a Gambler 1951,Jl 20,14:2
Apra, Pieriuigi
China Is Near 1968,Ja 9,37:1
Apsolon, Alex
Wait for Me 1945,Mr 19,23:3
Aquilar, Rolando (Director)
Noches de Gloria; Glorious Nights 1938,Ap 23,19:3
Millones de Chaflan, Los 1938,S 13,28:3
Aquilliere
End of a Day, The 1939,S 12,28:4
Aquistapace, M
Mon Coeur Balance 1933,F 3,21:4
Aracheguesne, Michel
Adolescents, The (Marie-France and Veronica); Marie-France and Veronica (The Adolescents) 1967,Ap 14,33:1
Arafama, Michio
Samurai Assassin 1965,Mr 19,27:5
Aragon, Art
Off Limits 1953,Mr 30,25:5
To Hell and Back 1955,S 23,21:2
Arakon, A (Director)
Conquest of Constantinople 1954,Ap 13,39:3
Aranda, Angel
Last Days of Pompeii, The 1960,Ag 11,19:1
Colossus of Rhodes, The 1961,D 14,55:6
Aranio, Roque
Tropics 1968,S 24,52:1
Arata, Luis
Fuera de la Ley; Outside the Law 1940,My 13,21:2
Amor Manda, El; Love Commands 1940,My 18,11:3

Aratama, Michiyo
Human Condition, The 1959,D 16,56:1
Prodigal Son 1964,Ja 30,24:3 (Incorrect in this edition; use 1964,Ja 31,16:1 elsewhere)
Enjo 1964,S 23,54:1
Kwaidan (Black Hair); Black Hair (Kwaidan) 1965,N 23,51:1
Arbeid, Ben (Producer)
Murder Most Foul 1965,My 24,36:2
Jokers, The 1967,My 16,50:1
Assignment K 1968,Jl 20,18:2
Arbenna, Stella
Stolen Life 1939,Je 15,27:2
Arbessier
Thirst of Men, The 1952,O 28,37:1
Demoniaque 1958,Mr 4,34:5
Arbin, Marta
Torment 1947,Ap 22,34:2
Arbo, Manuel
Mad Queen, The 1950,O 27,24:3
Arbuckle, Andrew
Name the Man 1924,F 4,23:3
Arbuckle, Maclyn
Prodigal Judge, The 1922,F 5,VI,3:1 (In Addenda)
Yolanda 1924,F 20,23:1
Janice Meredith 1924,Ag 6,13:3
Arbuckle, Roscoe (Fatty)
Moonshine 1918,My 13,11:3
Good Night, Nurse 1918,Jl 1,9:3
Fatty and Mabel Adrift 1918,Jl 8,9:4
Waiters' Ball, The 1918,Jl 22,9:1
Cook, The 1918,S 16,9:3
Love 1919,Mr 3,11:2
Desert Hero, A 1919,Je 16,11:2
Back Stage 1919,S 29,16:1
Life of the Party, The 1920,N 22,13:3
When Comedy Was King 1960,Mr 30,42:1
Days of Thrills and Laughter 1961,Mr 22,37:1
Arbuthnot, Thomas S Dr (Miscellaneous)
Wild Heart of Africa, The 1929,My 27,22:1
Arcand, Bernard
Adolescents, The (Genevieve); Genevieve (The Adolescents) 1967,Ap 14,33:1
Arcella, Salvador
Besos Brujos; Bewitching Kisses 1939,O 21,12:3
Archainbaud, George (Director)
One Week of Love 1923,Ja 8,22:1
For Sale 1924,Jl 14,11:5
Single Wives 1924,Jl 29,9:2
Christine of the Hungry Heart 1924,D 8,13:3
Enticement 1925,Mr 21,16:3
What Fools Men 1925,S 29,31:3
Men of Steel 1926,Jl 12,24:4
Silent Lover, The 1926,N 15,19:1
Easy Pickings 1927,Mr 25,25:3
Night Life 1927,D 20,33:2
College Coquette, The 1929,Ag 26,17:1
Broadway Scandals 1929,O 29,35:1
Framed 1930,Mr 29,23:1
Alias French Gertie 1930,Ap 14,24:2
Silver Horde, The 1930,O 25,20:6
Men of Chance 1931,D 28,22:1
Lost Squadron, The 1932,Mr 11,15:4
State's Attorney 1932,My 6,15:3
Thirteen Women 1932,O 15,13:1
Penguin Pool Murder, The 1932,D 26,26:2
Big Brain, The 1933,Ag 5,9:5
After Tonight 1933,N 3,23:2
Murder on the Blackboard 1934,Je 20,24:2
My Marriage 1936,F 22,12:2
Return of Sophie Lang, The 1936,Jl 24,13:1
Hideaway Girl 1937,Ja 13,20:4
Blonde Trouble 1937,Ag 7,7:2
Thrill of a Lifetime 1937,D 9,30:2
Her Jungle Love 1938,Ap 14,27:2
Campus Confessions 1938,S 23,35:1
Thanks for the Memory 1938,D 8,34:3
Some Like It Hot 1939,My 25,31:2
Untamed 1940,Jl 25,14:3
Comin' Round the Mountain 1940,S 26,27:3
Kansan, The 1943,O 1,15:3
Woman of the Town, The 1944,Mr 6,17:2
Big Bonanza, The 1945,F 26,14:5
Archainbaud, George (Original Author)
One Week of Love 1923,Ja 8,22:1
Archainbaud, George (Screenwriter)
Common Law, The 1923,O 29,18:1
Archangelskaya, Nina
Violin and Roller 1962,Ag 20,18:2
Archard, Bernard
Spy With a Cold Nose, The 1966,D 20,58:2
Archard, Marcel (Screenwriter)
Orage 1938,D 12,26:2
Earrings of Madame De, The 1954,Jl 20,15:5
Archdale, Alexander
His Majesty O'Keefe 1954,F 6,17:2
Headless Ghost, The 1959,Ap 30,37:2
Invasion Quartet 1961,D 11,41:2
Archduke Leopold of Austria
Four Sons 1928,F 14,27:1

Archer, Barbara
  Horror of Dracula 1958,My 29,24:4
  In the Wake of a Stranger 1961,Je 22,23:3
  Rattle of a Simple Man 1964,D 21,42:2
Archer, Bernard
  List of Adrian Messenger, The 1963,My 30,20:1
Archer, Jeri
  Sweet Love, Bitter 1967,Ja 31,50:1
Archer, John
  Career 1939,Jl 28,14:2
  Curtain Call 1940,Ap 19,25:2
  Scattergood Baines 1941,Ap 4,25:2
  Gangs Incorporated 1941,Ag 4,16:6
  Hello, Frisco, Hello 1943,Mr 25,25:1
  Crash Dive 1943,Ap 29,25:2
  Guadalcanal Diary 1943,N 18,29:1
  Eve of St Mark, The 1944,My 31,22:2
  Roger Touhy, Gangster 1944,Je 5,14:7
  Lost Moment, The 1947,N 22,10:2
  Colorado Territory 1949,Je 25,8:6
  White Heat 1949,S 3,7:2
  Destination Moon 1950,Je 28,32:2
  Great Jewel Robber, The 1950,Ag 4,13:2
  High Lonesome 1950,D 8,40:4
  Santa Fe 1951,My 4,31:2
  Best of the Badmen 1951,Ag 10,13:2
  My Favorite Spy 1951,D 26,19:3
  Big Trees, The 1952,F 6,24:2
  Stars Are Singing, The 1953,Mr 12,24:2
  Ten Thousand Bedrooms 1957,Ap 4,37:1
  Blue Hawaii 1962,F 22,20:2
Archer, Mel
  Undercover Girl 1950,N 8,37:2
Archer, Sandra
  Funnyman 1967,S 25,56:3
Archer, William (Original Author)
  Green Goddess, The 1930,F 14,20:1
Archer, William (Screenwriter)
  Green Goddess, The 1923,Ag 15,21:1
Archibald, Myra
  Ramparts We Watch, The 1940,S 20,27:1
Archibald, William (Screenwriter)
  I Confess 1953,Mr 23,28:2
  Innocents, The 1961,D 26,15:2
Archie, Will
  Wildfire 1925,Je 10,18:2
Archie Savage Dancers
  Glenn Miller Story, the 1954,F 11,33:2
Archuletta, Beulah
  Searchers, The 1956,My 31,21:4
Arco, Louis
  Underground 1941,Je 23,13:2
Arcos, Carmen Gentil
  En un Burro Tres Baturros; Three Rustics on one
    Donkey 1940,S 21,13:3
Arcos, Guillermo
  Cuesta Abajo 1934,Ag 15,13:5
Arcos, Pilar
  Castillos en el Aire; Castles in the Air
    1938,My 21,9:3
  Verbena Tragica; Tragic Festival, The
    1939,Mr 13,12:3
Arcos, Rafael
  Mercedes 1935,My 14,17:5
  Relicario, El; Reliquary, The 1935,D 31,11:3
Arcos, Raphael
  Boliche 1935,My 28,30:2
Arcy, Roy d'
  Merry Widow, The 1925,Ag 27,14:1
Ardan, Michel
  Panic 1947,N 27,50:2
  Fire Under Her Skin 1958,Je 28,13:6
Ardavin, Cesar (Director)
  Lazarillo 1963,Ap 5,27:6
Ardavin, Cesar (Screenwriter)
  Lazarillo 1963,Ap 5,27:6
Ardavin, Eusebio F (Director)
  Agua en el Suelo, El 1935,F 4,11:4
  Vidas Rotas 1935,Ag 3,16:3
Ardell, Alice
  Notorious Gentleman, A 1935,F 16,9:1
  Ruggles of Red Gap 1935,Mr 7,26:1
  Go West, Young Man 1936,N 19,31:3
Ardell, Franklyn
  Palooka 1934,F 28,23:2
  Looking for Trouble 1934,Ap 12,27:2
  She Loves Me Not 1934,S 8,18:5
  Mark of the Vampire 1935,My 3,23:4
  Metropolitan 1935,O 18,27:4
Ardell, Lillian
  Alice in Wonderland 1931,D 28,22:1
Ardelli, Norberto
  Ueber Alles die Treue 1939,F 13,13:3
Arden, Clive (Original Author)
  Sinners in Heaven 1924,S 10,21:3
  Enticement 1925,Mr 21,16:3
Arden, Edwin
  Virtuous Wives 1918,D 30,7:3
Arden, Elaine
  Headin' East 1938,Ja 15,19:2
Arden, Enoch (Original Author)
  Derecho y el Deber, El 1938,Jl 9,10:4

Arden, Eve
  Oh, Doctor 1937,Je 19,20:3
  Stage Door 1937,O 8,27:2
  Cocoanut Grove 1938,Je 16,21:2
  Having Wonderful Time 1938,Jl 8,11:2
  Letter of Introduction 1938,S 1,17:1
  Women in the Wind 1939,Ap 13,27:2
  Big Town Czar 1939,My 4,27:3
  Forgotten Woman, The 1939,Ag 4,11:2
  Eternally Yours 1939,O 7,11:2
  At the Circus 1939,N 17,17:2
  Child Is Born, A 1940,Ja 11,19:2
  Slightly Honorable 1940,My 17,23:4
  No, No, Nanette 1940,D 20,33:1
  Comrade X 1940,D 26,23:1
  She Couldn't Say No 1941,Ja 17,21:3
  Ziegfeld Girl 1941,Ap 25,17:2
  That Uncertain Feeling 1941,My 2,25:1
  She Knew All the Answers 1941,Je 20,28:4
  Manpower 1941,Jl 5,14:2
  Whistling in the Dark 1941,Ag 28,23:2
  Sing for Your Supper 1941,D 1,15:5
  Obliging Young Lady 1942,F 13,24:4
  Bedtime Story 1942,Mr 20,25:4
  Hit Parade of 1943 1943,Ap 16,24:3
  Let's Face It 1943,Ag 5,18:1
  Cover Girl 1944,Mr 31,26:1
  Doughgirls, The 1944,Ag 31,14:1
  Pan-Americana 1945,Mr 23,13:2
  Earl Carroll Vanities 1945,Ap 2,15:6
  Patrick the Great 1945,Ap 13,15:2
  Mildred Pierce 1945,S 29,12:2
  My Reputation 1946,Ja 26,19:2
  Kid From Brooklyn, The 1946,Ap 19,25:2
  Night and Day 1946,Jl 26,16:2
  Song of Scheherazade 1947,F 27,26:2
  Unfaithful, The 1947,Je 28,10:2
  Arnelo Affair, The 1947,S 13,8:5
  Voice of the Turtle, The 1947,D 26,22:4
  One Touch of Venus 1948,O 29,29:5
  Whiplash 1948,D 27,16:3
  My Dream Is Yours 1949,Ap 16,11:3
  Lady Takes a Sailor, The 1949,D 17,15:2
  Paid in Full 1950,F 16,28:2
  Tea for Two 1950,S 2,11:2
  Curtain Call at Cactus Creek 1950,S 22,35:4
  Three Husbands 1951,Mr 9,30:2
  Goodbye, my Fancy 1951,My 30,14:2
  We're not Married 1952,Jl 12,16:2
  Lady Wants Mink, The 1953,Ap 6,24:2
  Anatomy of a Murder 1959,Jl 3,10:1
  Khovanschina 1960,S 23,33:1
  Sergeant Deadhead 1965,O 23,17:3
Arden, Jane
  Separation 1968,Mr 26,41:2
Arden, Jane (Original Author)
  Separation 1968,Mr 26,41:2
Arden, Jane (Screenwriter)
  Separation 1968,Mr 26,41:2
Arden, Mary
  Blood and Black Lace 1965,N 11,58:3
Arden, Mildred
  Janice Meredith 1924,Ag 6,13:3
Arden, Patty Lou
  Dear Brat 1951,Jl 5,21:2
Arden, Robert
  Mr Arkadin 1962,O 12,26:1
Ardi, N
  Peter Vinogradof 1935,Je 28,24:1
Ardisson
  S O S Mediterranean 1940,Ja 1,29:2
  Wild Oat, The 1956,Je 28,33:2
  My Wife's Husband 1965,Ja 27,26:1
Ardley, Robert (Screenwriter)
  Wonderful Country, The 1959,N 5,39:7
Ardov, V (Screenwriter)
  Tanya 1942,Mr 5,27:1
Ardrey, Robert (Original Author)
  Thunder Rock 1944,S 15,16:1
Ardrey, Robert (Screenwriter)
  They Knew What They Wanted 1940,O 11,25:2
  Lady Takes a Chance, A 1943,S 16,25:2
  Green Years, The 1946,Ap 5,21:2
  Song of Love 1947,O 10,31:2
  Three Musketeers, The 1948,O 21,33:2
  Madame Bovary 1949,Ag 26,15:2
  Quentin Durward 1955,N 24,41:1
  Power and The Prize, the 1956,S 27,42:1
  4 Horsemen of the Apocalypse, The
    1962,Mr 10,10:2
  Khartoum 1966,Jl 14,28:1
Arduini, Suzanne (Screenwriter)
  Lafayette 1963,Ap 11,29:1
Arecidiacono, Saro
  Path of Hope, The (Il Cammino Della Speranza)
    1952,Ag 5,15:5
Arena, Maurizio
  It Happened in the Park 1957,Ag 13,23:2
  Poor but Beautiful 1958,Je 11,39:4
  Man Who Wagged his Tail, The 1961,S 19,39:1
  Bambole; Dolls, The (Treatise on Eugenics);
    Treatise on Eugenics (The Dolls)
    1965,Je 29,26:1

Arena, Maurizio— Cont
  Corrupt Ones, The 1967,F 23,41:3
Arenas, Miguel
  Mas Alla de la Muerta 1936,Mr 2,13:3
  El Misterio del Rostro Palido 1937,Ja 4,20:5
  no Basta ser Madre; Motherhood Is Not Enough
    1938,Ja 31,15:2
  Abnegacion 1938,My 31,8:3
  Domingo en la Tarde, Un; On a Sunday
    Afternoon 1939,Ja 7,6:3
  Maria 1939,Ap 10,13:4
  Herencia Macabra; Macabre Legacy, A
    1940,My 4,13:2
  Vivire Otra Vez; I Shall Live Again
    1940,O 23,27:2
  El Conde de Monte Cristo 1943,N 9,26:2
  Dama de las Camelias, La 1944,S 26,16:1
  Toast to Love 1951,N 7,35:5
Arendt, Ekkehard
  Elisabeth von Oesterreich 1931,D 11,35:1
  Luise, Koenigin von Preussen 1932,O 5,26:6
  Brave Suender, Der 1933,Mr 29,13:2
  Rosen aus dem Sueden; Roses from the South
    1935,Ap 23,24:5
  Glueckliche Reise 1936,Ja 20,22:3
Arene (Original Author)
  King, The 1941,O 23,29:3
  Royal Affair, A; (Roi, Le) 1950,Mr 9,25:2
Arenstein, Marek (Screenwriter)
  Dybbuk, The 1938,Ja 28,17:2
Arent, Arthur (Original Author)
  One Third of a Nation 1939,F 11,13:2
Arepina, I
  Big Family, A 1955,Je 6,24:1
  Captain's Daughter, The 1959,N 23,41:3
Argal, Else
  Club De Femmes 1937,O 20,27:2
  Kathleen 1941,D 19,35:3
Argentin
  King, The 1941,O 23,29:3
Argentina, Imperio
  Melodia de Arrabal 1933,Ag 5,9:5
  Nobleza Baturra; Rustic Chivalry
    1938,Mr 28,19:3
  Morena Clara 1938,Je 18,18:3
  Andalusische Naechte; Nights in Andalusia
    1938,S 24,13:2
  Carmen de la Triana 1940,Je 15,12:2
  Goyescas 1944,My 29,18:3
  Story of Tosca, The 1947,D 19,34:2
  Song of Dolores 1951,Je 16,9:2
Arghyris, John
  Antigone 1962,S 19,30:1
Argilano, Nicola
  Great War; (Grande Guerra, La) 1961,Ag 31,22:3
Argus, Edward
  Janice Meredith 1924,Ag 6,13:3
Argus, Edwin
  Scaramouche 1923,O 12,7:2 (Incorrect in this
    edition; use 1927,O 1,7:2 elsewhere)
  Smart Money 1931,Je 19,21:1
Argyle, John (Director)
  Human Monster, The 1940,Mr 25,11:2
Argyle, John (Producer)
  Kathleen 1938,Ja 24,17:1
  Human Monster, The 1940,Mr 25,11:2
  Tower of Terror 1942,Je 29,11:4
  Patient Vanishes, The 1947,My 23,31:2
Argyle, John (Screenwriter)
  Human Monster, The 1940,Mr 25,11:2
  Patient Vanishes, The 1947,My 23,31:2
Argyle, Pearl
  Chu Chin Chow 1934,S 22,12:2
  Things to Come 1936,Ap 18,19:2
Arias, Pepe
  Puerto Nuevo; New Port 1937,F 20,9:3
  Poor Perez 1937,N 1,24:6
  Loco Serenata, El; Crazy Musician, The
    1940,Ap 22,13:2
  Maestro Leuita, El 1940,Je 10,21:2
Arien, Harold (Composer)
  Slightly French 1949,My 27,25:3
Arietty
  Pension Mimosas 1936,My 6,27:1
  Pearls of the Crown, The 1938,Ap 12,26:2
  Daybreak 1940,Jl 30,16:2
Arima, Ineko
  Human Condition, The 1959,D 16,56:1
Arinendariz, Pedro
  Conqueror, The 1956,Mr 31,13:3
Aris, Bengy
  Tom Brown's School Days 1952,Ja 8,23:5
Ariss, Christopher
  Uncle, The 1966,Jl 19,34:1
Aristarco, Guido (Screenwriter)
  Outcry 1949,Mr 14,15:5
Aristedes, John
  Moonlighting Wives 1968,My 9,54:4
Aristophanes (Original Author)
  Lysistrata 1948,Je 19,19:2
Arita, Noriko
  She Was Like a Wild Chrysanthemum
    1960,Ja 22,15:2

Arius
Nais 1948,Je 16,37:2
Savage Triangle 1952,S 30,38:2
Virtuous Bigamist, The 1959,My 28,34:3
Arius, Henri
My Wife's Husband 1965,Ja 27,26:1
Arjanov, P
Secret Agent 1949,F 10,37:3
Arkadev, A A
Heroes of the Sea 1941,Ap 28,11:2
Arkadin, I I
Last Night, The 1937,Ap 28,18:3
Arkangelskaya, Natalya
And Quiet Flows the Don 1960,My 25,45:2
Arkanof, I P
Rivals 1933,Ap 5,22:6
Arkanoff, M
Czar Ivan the Terrible 1928,Mr 12,26:1
Arkell, Mme
Diary of a Country Priest 1954,Ap 6,35:2
Arkhipova, Nina
Bountiful Summer 1951,D 24,9:1
Arkin, Alan
Russians are Coming the Russians are Coming, The 1966,My 26,55:1
Last Mohican, The 1966,S 13,51:2
Woman Times Seven 1967,Je 28,38:1
Wait Until Dark 1967,O 27,48:1
Inspector Clouseau 1968,Jl 25,26:1
Heart is a Lonely Hunter, The 1968,Ag 1,24:1
Arkin, David
I Love You Alice B Toklas! 1968,O 8,40:1
Arkoff, Samuel Z (Producer)
Comedy of Terrors, The 1964,Ja 23,26:2
Bikini Beach 1964,S 17,52:6
Sergeant Deadhead 1965,O 23,17:3
Dr Goldfoot and the Bikini Machine 1966,F 17,29:3
Fireball 500 1966,N 24,65:4
How to Stuff a Wild Bikini 1967,Ja 12,48:1
Wild in the Streets 1968,My 30,21:1
Arkrum, Morris
Ten Gentlemen From West Point 1942,Je 5,23:3
Arlan, Iris
Barberina, Die Taenzerin Von Sans-Souci 1932,O 26,15:4
Kirschen in Nachbars Garten 1937,My 15,23:6
Sextanerin, Die; Erste Liebe; First Love 1938,S 12,13:3
Arland, R M (Screenwriter)
Inspector Maigret 1958,O 9,47:1
Paris in the Month of August 1968,Ag 26,46:4
Arledge, John
Young Sinners 1931,My 9,15:4
Daddy Long Legs 1931,Je 6,15:5
Spider, The 1931,S 5,7:4
Heartbreak 1931,O 17,20:1
Careless Lady 1932,Ap 18,19:2
Huddle 1932,Je 17,24:1
Week Ends Only 1932,Je 18,9:2
Jimmy and Sally 1933,D 16,12:3
Flirtation Walk 1934,N 29,33:1
Devil Dogs of the Air 1935,F 7,23:2
Shipmates Forever 1935,O 17,29:3
We're Only Human 1936,Ja 18,19:2
You may Be Next 1936,F 24,14:1
Murder on a Bridle Path 1936,Ap 11,19:2
Two in Revolt 1936,Ap 25,21:1
Don't Turn 'em Loose 1936,S 25,20:2
Big Game, The 1936,O 24,23:1
Big City 1937,S 17,29:2
Saturday's Heroes 1937,O 16,22:2
County Fair 1937,D 27,11:1
Prison Nurse 1938,Mr 4,17:5
Campus Confessions 1938,S 23,35:1
You Can't Cheat an Honest Man 1939,F 20,13:2
Twelve Crowded Hours 1939,F 24,15:2
Six Thousand Enemies 1939,Je 9,26:2
Grapes of Wrath, The 1940,Ja 25,17:2
Strange Cargo 1940,Ap 26,25:2
Ski Patrol 1940,My 21,29:4
Flight Angels 1940,My 27,23:2
City for Conquest 1940,S 28,9:2
Cheers for Miss Bishop 1941,Mr 14,17:2
Arleen, Joyce
Our Neighbors-The Carters 1940,F 15,15:2
Arlen, Don (Cinematographer)
Living Desert, The 1953,N 10,38:1
Arlen, Harold (Composer)
Let's Fall in Love 1934,Ja 22,12:3
Love Affair 1939,Mr 17,25:2
Wizard of Oz, The 1939,Ag 18,16:2
Babes in Arms 1939,O 20,27:2
At the Circus 1939,N 17,17:2
Blues in the Night 1941,D 12,35:2
Rio Rita 1942,My 8,27:3
Cairo 1942,N 6,27:2
Star Spangled Rhythm 1942,D 31,20:1
Cabin in the Sky 1943,My 28,19:3
Riding High 1943,D 23,26:4
Here Come the Waves 1944,D 28,25:2
Casbah 1948,My 3,27:4
My Blue Heaven 1950,S 16,12:6

Mr Imperium 1951,O 15,22:2
Star is Born, A 1954,O 12,23:1
Arlen, Harold (Miscellaneous)
Strike Me Pink 1936,Ja 17,15:2
Singing Kid, The 1936,Ap 4,11:1
Stage Struck 1936,S 28,14:4
Gold Diggers of 1937 1936,D 25,19:2
Artists and Models 1937,Ag 5,19:2
Arlen, Michael (Original Author)
Dancers of Paris, The 1926,Mr 29,24:3
Ace of Cads, The 1926,O 18,18:1 (In Addenda)
Woman of Affairs, A 1929,Ja 21,18:4
Lily Christine 1932,My 29,VIII,4:4 (In Addenda)
Outcast Lady 1934,N 3,20:3
Golden Arrow, The 1936,My 4,16:1
Falcon takes Over, The 1942,My 30,9:2
Falcon's Brother, The 1942,O 3,9:5
Falcon Strikes Back, The 1943,Ap 2,17:4
Falcon in Danger, The 1943,Jl 23,21:2
Falcon out West, The 1944,Mr 18,18:2
Falcon in Mexico, The 1944,Ag 5,16:2
Falcon in San Francisco, The 1945,Jl 21,7:2
Falcon's Alibi, The 1946,Ap 13,23:2
Falcon's Adventure, The 1946,D 14,19:2
Arlen, Michael (Screenwriter)
Heavenly Body, The 1944,Mr 24,17:3
Arlen, Richard
In the Name of Love 1925,Ag 27,14:1
Enchanted Hill, The 1925,D 29,19:2 (In Addenda)
Behind the Front 1926,F 10,16:2
Padlocked 1926,Ag 2,21:2
Rolled Stockings 1927,Jl 19,27:2
Blood Ship, The 1927,Jl 19,27:2
Wings 1927,Ag 13,10:4
She's a Shiek 1927,N 21,20:1
Feel my Pulse 1928,F 27,16:2
Ladies of the Mob 1928,Je 18,13:2
Beggars of Life 1928,S 24,25:1
Manhattan Cocktail 1928,N 26,30:2
Man I Love, The 1929,My 28,36:2
Four Feathers, The 1929,Je 13,35:4
Thunderbolt 1929,Je 21,17:2
Dangerous Curves 1929,Jl 15,25:1
Virginian, The 1929,D 23,18:2
Burning Up 1930,F 8,12:5
Dangerous Paradise 1930,F 16,III,8:1
Light of Western Stars, The 1930,Ap 26,11:1
Border Legion, The 1930,Je 30,22:6
Sea God, The 1930,S 6,9:2
Sante Fe Trail, The 1930,O 18,23:2
Only Saps Work 1930,D 13,22:2
Conquering Horde, The 1931,Mr 30,25:2
Gun Smoke 1931,Ap 24,27:1
Lawyer's Secret, The 1931,My 30,9:2
Secret Call, The 1931,Jl 13,13:5
Touchdown 1931,N 16,23:1
Wayward 1932,F 15,13:1
Sky Bride 1932,Ap 23,11:5
Guilty as Hell 1932,Ag 6,14:5
Tiger Shark 1932,S 23,22:2
All American, The 1932,O 22,18:4
Island of Lost Souls 1933,Ja 13,19:2
Song of the Eagle 1933,Ap 29,14:3
College Humor 1933,Je 23,15:4
Three-Cornered Moon 1933,Ag 12,14:2
Hell and Highwater 1933,D 18,24:4
Alice in Wonderland 1933,D 23,19:1
Come on Marines 1934,Mr 24,20:3
She Made her Bed 1934,Ap 27,25:1
She Made her Bed 1934,Ap 27,25:1
Helldorado 1935,Ja 7,13:2
Let 'Em Have It 1935,My 30,21:1
Calling of Dan Matthews, The 1936,Ja 25,18:4
Mine With the Iron Door, The 1936,Jl 11,11:3
Secret Valley 1937,Ja 25,22:2
Great Barrier, The 1937,F 5,17:5
Silent Barriers 1937,Mr 26,25:1
Artists and Models 1937,Ag 5,19:2
Murder in Greenwich Village 1937,O 30,22:2
No Time to Marry 1938,F 23,27:2
Call of the Yukon 1938,My 6,27:1
Straight, Place and Show 1938,O 1,10:2
Missing Daughters 1939,Je 12,14:5
Mutiny on the Blackhawk 1939,Ag 2,17:2
Tropic Fury 1939,S 8,28:4
Legion of Lost Flyers 1939,O 30,13:3
Hot Steel 1940,Je 21,25:3
Black Diamonds 1940,S 10,26:6
Devil's Pipeline, The 1940,N 11,22:4
Mutiny in the Arctic 1941,My 3,20:5
Power Dive 1941,My 29,15:4
Aerial Gunner 1943,Je 26,10:2
Lady and the Monster, The 1944,Ap 8,9:2
Storm Over Lisbon 1944,S 11,14:1
Big Bonanza, The 1945,F 26,14:5
When my Baby Smiles at Me 1948,N 24,20:2
Kansas Raiders 1951,Ja 26,19:2
Hurricane Smith 1952,O 4,15:2
Sabre Jet 1953,N 3,34:1
Mountain, The 1956,N 15,44:6
Warlock 1959,My 1,34:1
Last Time I Saw Archie, The 1961,My 29,9:6

Arlen, Richard— Cont
Best Man, The 1964,Ap 7,29:1
Law of the Lawless 1964,Ag 27,28:2
Black Spurs 1965,My 29,17:1
Fort Utah 1967,My 25,54:3
Arlen, Roxanne
Best Things in Life are Free, The 1956,S 29,12:2
Big Caper, The 1957,Mr 29,16:1
Bachelor Flat 1962,Ja 13,14:1
Gypsy 1962,N 2,24:1
Arless, Jean
Homicidal 1961,Jl 27,23:4
Arletty
Hotel du Nord 1940,D 30,21:2
Extenuating Circumstances; Circostances Attenuantes 1946,S 24,41:3
Enfants du Paradis, Les 1947,F 20,32:2
Devil's Own Envoy, The 1947,Ag 30,8:6
Fric-Frac 1948,My 29,8:6
Longest Day, The 1962,O 5,28:1
Maxime 1962,O 25,48:3
Arley, Catherine (Original Author)
Woman of Straw 1964,O 1,30:6
Arlin, Georg
Swedish Wedding Night 1965,N 15,48:1
Arling, Joyce
Romance of Rosy Ridge, The 1947,S 12,18:3
Ruthless 1948,S 4,8:7
Arliss, Florence
Disraeli 1929,O 3,27:5
Millionaire, The 1931,Ap 9,30:5
King's Vacation, The 1933,Ja 20,21:2
House of Rothschild, The 1934,Mr 15,27:2
Arliss, George
Devil, The 1921,Ja 17,9:1
Disraeli 1921,Ag 22,13:6
Ruling Passion, The 1922,Ja 23,11:4
Man Who Played God, The 1922,O 2,21:2
Green Goddess, The 1923,Ag 15,21:1
$20 a Week 1924,Je 10,24:4
Disraeli 1929,O 3,27:5
Green Goddess, The 1930,F 14,20:1
Millionaire, The 1931,Ap 9,30:5
Alexander Hamilton 1931,S 17,21:4
Man Who Played God, The 1932,F 11,16:1
Successful Calamity, A 1932,S 23,22:2
King's Vacation, The 1933,Ja 20,21:2
Working Man, The 1933,Ap 21,20:3
Voltaire 1933,Ag 23,21:2
House of Rothschild, The 1934,Mr 15,27:2
Last Gentleman, The 1934,O 18,26:5
Cardinal Richelieu 1935,Ap 19,24:2
Transatlantic Tunnel 1935,O 28,16:2
Mister Hobo 1936,F 8,19:2
East Meets West 1936,O 31,24:2
Man of Affairs 1937,F 20,9:2
Dr Syn 1937,N 15,15:1
Arliss, George (Original Author)
Alexander Hamilton 1931,S 17,21:4
Arliss, George Mrs
Devil, The 1921,Ja 17,9:1
Arliss, Leslie (Director)
Man in Grey, The 1945,N 30,18:6
Wicked Lady, The 1946,D 23,19:5
Lady Surrenders, A 1947,Je 20,25:6
Man About the House, A 1949,Mr 9,33:2
Saints and Sinners 1949,S 12,17:2
Woman's Angle, The 1954,Ag 27,11:6
Arliss, Leslie (Producer)
Saints and Sinners 1949,S 12,17:2
Arliss, Leslie (Screenwriter)
Jack Ahoy 1935,F 9,11:2
Rhodes 1936,F 29,11:1
Sez O'Reilly to MacNab 1938,F 19,19:4
Pastor Hall 1940,S 21,13:2
Somewhere in France 1943,Jl 12,11:2
Man in Grey, The 1945,N 30,18:6
Wicked Lady, The 1946,D 23,19:5
Lady Surrenders, A 1947,Je 20,25:6
Saints and Sinners 1949,S 12,17:2
Woman's Angle, The 1954,Ag 27,11:6
Arliss, Pam
Saints and Sinners 1949,S 12,17:2
Arlorio, Giorgio (Screenwriter)
...And Suddenly It's Murder! 1964,Ja 24,21:1
Arlsberg, Max (Screenwriter)
Voruntersuchung; Inquest 1931,My 24,VIII,4:1
Arluck, Elliot
Yank in London, A 1946,Ap 20,16:3
Armand, Alice
Wife, Husband and Friend 1939,F 25,19:2
Lillian Russell 1940,My 18,11:2
Armand, Corinne
Anatomy of a Marriage; My Days With Jean Marc; My Nights With Francoise 1964,O 27,42:2
Armand, Jacques (Screenwriter)
Tales of Paris (The Tale of Francoise); Tale of Francoise, The (Tales of Paris) 1962,Ag 27,18:1
Armando Curcio Company's Players
Tarantella Napoletana 1954,Ap 19,19:3
Armandy, Andre (Original Author)
Renegades 1930,N 8,21:3

Armen, Kay
Hit the Deck 1955,Mr 4,17:1
Hey, Lets Twist 1962,F 8,25:1
Armendariz, Pedro
Rosario 1936,Ap 20,17:2
Jalisco Nunca Pierde; Jalisco Never Loses
  1937,N 20,21:3
Mi Candidato; My Candidate 1938,O 31,12:3
Indio, El 1939,My 13,11:5
China Hilaria, La 1939,Ag 12,16:3
Olvidados de Dios, Los; Those Forgotten by God
  1940,Ja 15,11:2
Reina del Rio, La; Queen of the River, The
  1940,F 24,9:3
Passion Island 1943,My 1,11:2
Guadalajara 1943,Je 12,9:3
Life of Simon Bolivar, The 1943,Je 18,16:5
Maria Candelaria 1944,S 12,23:7
Tierra de Pasiones 1944,N 7,24:3
Flor Sylvestre 1945,Ja 16,17:2
Fugitive, The 1947,D 26,22:2
Pearl, The 1948,F 18,36:4
Fort Apache 1948,Je 25,26:2
Three Godfathers 1949,Mr 4,25:2
We Were Strangers 1949,Ap 28,28:2
Tulsa 1949,My 27,25:2
Enamorada 1949,D 3,8:6
Torch, The 1950,Ag 21,15:2
Lovers of Toledo, The 1954,Ap 10,11:3
Littlest Outlaw, The 1955,D 27,31:1
Diane 1956,Ja 13,18:1
Sins of the Borgias 1956,Mr 5,21:1
Big Boodle, The 1957,Mr 12,38:1
Stowaway Girl 1957,N 6,43:3
Wonderful Country, The 1959,N 5,39:7
Francis of Assisi 1961,Jl 29,8:2
Captain Sindbad 1963,Jl 4,9:1
My Son, The Hero 1963,S 19,23:1
From Russia with Love 1964,Ap 9,25:1
Armengod, Pedro
Adelita, La 1938,O 12,35:2
Armengod, Ramon
Que Hago con la Criatura? 1936,Mr 17,25:6
Familia Dressel, La 1936,My 4,16:2
Hoy Comienza la Vida 1936,Je 27,21:2
Alma Jarocha 1938,Ap 30,18:2
Nobleza Ranchero; Rural Chivalry
  1939,F 20,13:3
Viejo Amor, Un; Old Love, An 1940,Ja 29,11:6
Herencia Macabra; Macabre Legacy, A
  1940,My 4,13:2
Vivire Otra Vez; I Shall Live Again
  1940,O 23,27:2
Armenkino (Producer)
Pepo 1935,O 10,31:6
Armetiz, Henry
Passionate Plumber, The 1932,Mr 12,19:5
Armetler, Estela
Tras la Reja 1937,Ja 11,15:7
Armetta, Enrico
Sei tu l'Amore 1930,N 18,28:4
Armetta, Henry
Silent Command, The 1923,S 5,15:3
Street Angel 1928,Ap 10,33:2
In old Arizona 1929,Ja 21,18:4
Lady of the Pavements 1929,Mr 11,22:2
Jazz Heaven 1929,O 30,29:2
Love, Live and Laugh 1929,N 2,14:6
Lovin' the Ladies 1930,Mr 22,22:6
Little Accident 1930,Ag 4,13:4
Romance 1930,Ag 23,7:3
Strangers May Kiss 1931,Ap 13,17:1
Tailor-Made Man, A 1931,Ap 25,23:4
Five and Ten 1931,Jl 11,7:6
Unholy Garden, The 1931,O 29,27:1
Arsene Lupin 1932,F 27,22:1
Scarface, The Shame of the Nation
  1932,My 20,22:3
Doomed Battalion, The 1932,Je 11,9:3
Huddle 1932,Je 17,24:1
Week Ends Only 1932,Je 18,9:2
Speak Easily 1932,Ag 19,20:6
Okay America 1932,S 10,18:5
Prosperity 1932,N 26,11:4
Central Park 1932,D 7,29:3
Farewell to Arms, A 1932,D 9,26:5
Uptown New York 1932,D 10,19:3
Deception 1933,Ja 10,26:2
What! No Beer? 1933,F 11,11:3
They Just Had to Get Married 1933,F 13,11:4
Cohens and Kellys in Trouble, The
  1933,Ap 17,16:4
So This Is Africa! 1933,Ap 24,11:3
Devil's Brother, The 1933,Je 10,16:4
Her First Mate 1933,S 2,14:5
Cross Country Cruise 1934,Ja 20,12:3
Cat and the Fiddle, The 1934,F 17,20:2
Hide-Out 1934,Ag 25,16:5
One Night of Love 1934,S 7,25:3
Gift of Gab 1934,S 26,17:6
Wake up and Dream 1934,O 11,28:3
Imitation of Life 1934,N 24,19:1
Man Who Reclaimed his Head, The

  1935,Ja 9,22:1
Night Life of the Gods 1935,F 23,14:6
After Office Hours 1935,Mr 9,19:1
Princess O'Hara 1935,Ap 13,11:3
Three Kids and a Queen 1935,N 9,19:2
Magnificent Obsession 1935,D 31,11:2
Let's Sing Again 1936,My 9,11:2
Poor Little Rich Girl, The 1936,Je 26,16:1
Crime of Dr Forbes, The 1936,Jl 6,11:4
Two in a Crowd 1936,O 5,25:1
Magnificent Brute, The 1936,O 24,23:1
Top of the Town 1937,Mr 27,19:2
Make a Wish 1937,S 23,33:1
Manhattan Merry-Go-Round 1937,D 31,9:3
Everybody Sing 1938,Mr 11,15:3
Speed to Burn 1938,S 9,25:1
Submarine Patrol 1938,N 19,9:2
Fisherman's Wharf 1939,F 24,15:2
Winner Take All 1939,Mr 31,19:3
I Stole a Million 1939,Ag 7,11:2
Dust Be my Destiny 1939,O 7,11:2
Escape, The 1939,N 3,17:4
Three Cheers for the Irish 1940,Mr 9,19:2
Man Who Talked too Much, The 1940,Je 29,12:2
You're not so Tough 1940,Jl 9,25:3
We Who Are Young 1940,S 13,27:2
Big Store, The 1941,Je 27,14:4
Stage Door Canteen 1943,Je 25,13:2
Thank Your Lucky Stars 1943,O 2,19:2
Bell for Adano, A 1945,Jl 6,8:3
Colonel Effingham's Raid 1946,Ap 5,21:3
Armetta, Tony
Let's Talk It Over 1934,Je 16,20:2
Armida
General Crack 1929,D 4,36:6
On the Border 1930,F 3,17:1
Under a Texas Moon 1930,Ap 4,22:1
Border Romance 1930,My 26,25:3
Marines are Coming, The 1935,F 23,14:7
Under the Pampas Moon 1935,My 31,11:1
Border Cafe 1937,Je 8,30:2
Conga Nights, La 1940,Je 5,33:5
South of Tahiti 1941,N 10,21:3
Always in my Heart 1942,Mr 14,19:2
Armillita
Gavilan, El; Hawk, The 1940,Ja 22,11:2
Armitage, Buford
Stolen Heaven 1931,F 14,11:4
Armitage, Walter
Love Habit, The 1931,F 2,23:1
Bombay Mail 1934,Ja 6,18:2
Where Sinners Meet 1934,My 25,25:2
British Agent 1934,S 20,20:1
Armont, Paul (Original Author)
Love Me Tonight 1932,Ag 19,20:6
Face to the Wind 1951,Ja 16,34:2
French Touch, The 1954,S 2,18:2
Purple Mask, The 1955,Je 16,35:7
Armontel
Scandals of Clochemerle, The 1950,Mr 28,28:2
Face to the Wind 1951,Ja 16,34:2
Lovers of Verona, The 1951,Mr 12,20:2
Minne 1951,Ap 17,35:2
Oh, Amelia 1951,D 3,22:2
Pantaloons 1956,D 26,34:1
Razzi 1957,N 19,39:4
Senechal the Magnificent 1958,O 14,44:1
Armontel, M
Dame aux Camelias, La 1935,Mr 21,27:1
Armontel, Roland
Man About Town 1947,O 22,37:1
Arms, Russell
Man Who Came to Dinner, The 1942,Ja 2,25:2
Captains of the Clouds 1942,F 13,24:2
Always in my Heart 1942,Mr 14,19:2
Wings for the Eagle 1942,Ag 1,14:2
By the Light of the Silvery Moon
  1953,Mr 27,28:2
Armstrong, Anthony (Original Author)
Orders Is Orders 1934,My 7,20:2
Armstrong, Anthony (Screenwriter)
Girl Was Young, The 1938,F 11,27:2
Armstrong, Arnold B (Original Author)
Raw Deal 1948,Jl 9,11:4
Armstrong, Byron
Adventures of Tom Sawyer, The 1938,F 18,23:1
Armstrong, Charlotte (Original Author)
Unsuspected, The 1947,O 4,9:2
Don't Bother to Knock 1952,Jl 19,8:2
Armstrong, Edwina
Once in a Blue Moon 1936,D 2,35:1
Armstrong, Henry
Pittsburgh Kid, The 1941,S 23,27:4
Armstrong, Hugh
Prudence and the Pill 1968,My 24,37:1
Armstrong, Louis
Pennies From Heaven 1936,D 10,35:2
Artists and Models 1937,Ag 5,19:2
Doctor Rhythm 1938,My 19,25:2
Going Places 1939,Ja 7,6:1
Cabin in the Sky 1943,My 28,19:3
New Orleans 1947,Je 20,25:6
Song Is Born, A 1948,O 20,37:2

Armstrong, Louis — Cont
Here Comes the Groom 1951,S 21,19:2
Glory Alley 1952,Jl 30,20:8
Glenn Miller Story, the 1954,F 11,33:2
High Society 1956,Ag 10,9:2
Satchmo the Great 1958,Mr 1,12:1
Five Pennies, The 1959,Je 19,30:1
Jazz on a Summer's Day 1960,Mr 29,46:2
Paris Blues 1961,N 8,41:1
Man Called Adam, A 1966,Ag 4,24:2
Armstrong, Louis and His Orchestra
Pennies From Heaven 1936,D 10,35:2
Jam Session 1944,My 3,25:3
Atlantic City 1944,Ag 14,11:4
Armstrong, Margaret
Tomorrow and Tomorrow 1932,Ja 30,13:2
She Loves Me Not 1934,S 8,18:5
Our Little Girl 1935,Je 7,24:4
Annie Oakley 1935,D 24,10:5
Trail of the Lonesome Pine, The 1936,F 20,23:5
M'liss 1936,Ag 8,5:2
Soldier and the Lady, The 1937,Ap 10,11:1
Women in Prison 1938,Mr 1,19:3
Armstrong, Paul (Original Author)
Escape, The 1914,Je 2,11:5
Alias Jimmy Valentine 1920,Ap 19,13:3
Paths to Paradise 1925,Je 30,14:3
Paths to Paradise 1925,Jl 5,VII,2:1
Escape, The 1928,My 7,29:1
Alias Jimmy Valentine 1928,N 16,28:6
Romance of the Underworld 1929,Ja 7,36:2
Ever Since Eve 1934,Mr 28,27:5
Hold That Blonde 1945,N 8,17:2
Armstrong, R G
Garden of Eden 1957,D 18,45:3
From Hell to Texas 1958,Je 5,39:2
Never Love a Stranger 1958,N 22,27:4
Fugitive Kind, The 1960,Ap 15,13:1
Ride the High Country 1962,Je 21,26:2
He Rides Tall 1964,F 27,28:1
Dorado, El 1967,Je 29,32:1
Armstrong, Richard
10th Victim, The 1965,D 21,46:1
Armstrong, Robert
Main Event, The 1927,O 31,22:1
Girl in Every Port, A 1928,F 20,14:1
Leopard Lady, The 1928,F 27,16:2
Cop, The 1928,N 6,35:1
Show Folks 1928,D 10,25:1
Ned McCobb's Daughter 1929,F 18,28:1
Shady Lady, The 1929,Mr 25,32:2
Leatherneck, The 1929,Ap 22,23:1
Big News 1929,O 7,22:1
Racketeer, The 1930,Je 6,30:8
Be Yourself 1930,Mr 7,20:5
Dumbbells in Ermine 1930,Jl 28,22:1
Big Money 1930,N 22,21:3
Danger Lights 1930,D 15,29:1
Paid 1931,Ja 3,21:2
Iron Man 1931,Ap 18,17:3
Tip Off, The 1931,O 26,22:1
Suicide Fleet 1931,N 23,22:1
Panama Flo 1932,Ja 20,17:4
Lost Squadron, The 1932,Mr 11,15:4
Is my Face red 1932,Je 11,9:3
Radio Patrol 1932,Jl 14,24:2
Most Dangerous Game, The 1932,N 21,21:1
Billion Dollar Scandal, The 1933,Ja 9,23:1
King Kong 1933,Mr 3,12:1
Fast Workers 1933,Mr 20,18:2
I Love That Man 1933,Jl 10,11:7
Blind Adventure 1933,O 31,24:3
Son of Kong 1933,D 30,9:2
Search for Beauty 1934,F 10,20:2
Palooka 1934,F 28,23:2
She Made her Bed 1934,Ap 27,25:1
Hell Cat, The 1934,Jl 7,16:5
Kansas City Princess 1934,N 5,23:1
Sweet Music 1935,F 21,23:2
G Men 1935,My 2,17:1
Gigolette 1935,My 13,18:6
Little Big Shot 1935,O 7,11:2
Remember Last Night? 1935,N 21,27:2
Dangerous Waters 1936,Ja 22,15:5
Ex-Mrs Bradford, The 1936,My 28,19:2
Public Enemy's Wife 1936,Jl 9,17:2
Without Orders 1936,N 4,41:3
Nobody's Baby 1937,My 20,17:3
Three Legionnaires 1937,Jl 10,18:2
It Can't Last Forever 1937,Jl 30,22:5
Girl Said No, The 1937,O 18,14:1
She Loved a Fireman 1938,Ja 21,15:3
Flying Irishman, The 1939,Ap 12,27:2
Man of Conquest 1939,Ap 28,31:2
Winter Carnival 1939,Jl 28,14:2
Flight at Midnight 1939,S 7,29:2
Enemy Agent 1940,Ap 22,13:3
San Francisco Docks 1940,D 26,23:3
Behind the News 1941,Ja 16,25:3
Mr Dynamite 1941,Mr 13,25:2
Bride Wore Crutches, The 1941,My 26,15:3
Dive Bomber 1941,Ag 30,10:2
My Favorite Spy 1942,My 29,13:4
It Happened in Flatbush 1942,Jl 3,12:8

Armstrong, Robert— Cont

Kansan, The 1943,O 1,15:3
Mad Ghoul, The 1943,D 11,11:2
Action in Arabia 1944,F 19,18:7
Mr Winkle Goes to War 1944,Ag 3,16:1
Belle of the Yukon 1945,Mr 30,18:4
Blood on the Sun 1945,Je 29,12:2
Falcon in San Francisco, The 1945,Jl 21,7:2
Decoy 1946,N 2,12:2
Criminal Court 1946,N 16,15:3
Sea of Grass, The 1947,F 28,27:2
Fugitive, The 1947,D 26,22:2
Return of the Badmen 1948,Ag 5,16:2
Paleface, The 1948,D 16,41:2
Lucky Stiff, The 1949,Ja 31,14:2
Mighty Joe Young 1949,Jl 28,19:3
Captain China 1950,Mr 2,33:2
Las Vegas Shakedown 1955,Je 18,14:2

Armstrong, Sam (Screenwriter)

Sequoia 1935,F 23,14:6

Armstrong, Thomas (Original Author)

Master of Bankdam 1949,O 17,18:2

Armstrong, Todd

Walk on the Wild Side 1962,F 22,20:1
Jason and the Argonauts 1963,Ag 8,19:1
King Rat 1965,O 28,48:1
Dead Heat on a Merry-Go-Round
1966,O 13,50:1

Armstrong, Will

Clancy's Kosher Wedding 1927,S 7,35:2

Armus, Sidney

Thomas Crown Affair, The 1968,Je 27,48:2

Arna, Lissi

Prince of Rogues, The 1929,Jl 30,19:4
Those Who Dance; Tanz Geht Weiter, Der
1930,D 7,IX,6:4
Tanz Geht Weiter, Der 1931,Ja 6,25:1
Beyond Victory 1931,Ap 6,24:1
Ungetreue Eckehart, Der 1932,Ja 23,18:4
Theodor Koerner 1933,My 6,11:2
Schwebende Jungfrau, Die 1937,Ag 7,7:2

Arnac, Marcel (Original Author)

Extenuating Circumstances; Circostances
Attenuantes 1946,S 24,41:3

Arnall, Julia

Tears for Simon 1957,Ap 18,35:2
Triple Deception 1957,O 7,23:2
Trunk, The 1962,N 1,34:3

Arnatt, John

Only Two Can Play 1962,Mr 21,33:2
Whistle Down the Wind 1962,Ap 23,34:2
Dr Crippen 1964,F 15,14:1
2nd Best Secret Agent in the Whole Wide World,
The 1966,Ap 28,49:1

Arnaud, Georges (Original Author)

Wages of Fear, The 1955,F 17,23:1

Arnaud, Leo (Miscellaneous)

Girl of the Golden West, The 1938,Mr 25,15:2
Babes in Arms 1939,O 20,27:2

Arnaud, Marie-Helene

Fantomas 1966,Ap 6,36:2

Arnaud, Yvonne

Princess Charming 1935,Je 22,18:5
At Dawn We Die 1943,My 8,19:2
My Uncle 1958,N 4,30:2

Arnaudy, M

Prince Jean, Le 1936,D 12,15:2

Arnaz, Desi

Too Many Girls 1940,N 21,43:1
Father takes a Wife 1941,S 5,19:3
Navy Comes Through, The 1942,N 12,30:3
Bataan 1943,Je 4,17:2
Holiday in Havana 1949,O 14,33:5
Long, Long Trailer, The 1954,F 19,24:3
Forever, Darling 1956,F 10,18:1

Arnaz, Desi (Producer)

Forever, Darling 1956,F 10,18:1

Arndt, Charles

Sun Sets at Dawn, The 1951,Ja 15,13:1

Arne, Peter

Purple Plain, The 1955,Ap 11,29:1
Cockleshell Heroes, The 1956,Je 4,25:2
Tarzan and the Lost Safari 1957,Ap 13,12:3
Scent of Mystery 1960,F 19,23:1
Conspiracy of Hearts 1960,Ap 8,24:1
Model Murder Case, The 1964,N 25,45:1
Khartoum 1966,Jl 14,28:1
Battle Beneath the Earth 1968,S 12,54:3

Arnell, France

Suitor, The; Soupirant, Le 1963,S 18,35:1

Arness, James

Farmer's Daughter, The 1947,Mr 26,31:2
Roses Are Red 1947,N 15,11:2
Battleground 1949,N 12,8:4
Wagonmaster 1950,Je 19,17:2
Wyoming Mail 1950,O 23,26:5
Thing, The 1951,My 3,34:4
Cavalry Scout 1951,Je 8,32:2
Iron Man 1951,Ag 20,14:2
People Against O'Hara, The 1951,S 6,39:3
Carbine Williams 1952,My 8,37:2
Girl in White, The 1952,My 31,12:5
Big Jim McLain 1952,S 18,35:2
Horizons West 1952,N 22,16:5

Lone Hand 1953,Je 27,7:2
Island in the Sky 1953,S 10,22:2
Hondo 1953,N 27,99:9
Veils of Bagdad, The 1953,N 27,99:9
Them 1954,Je 17,36:2
Her Twelve Men 1954,Ag 12,23:2
Many Rivers to Cross 1955,F 24,21:2
Sea Chase, The 1955,Je 11,8:7
Flame of the Islands 1956,F 25,12:4

Arniche, Don Carlos (Original Author)

Asi Se Quiere En Jalisco 1943,Ag 7,6:2

Arnna, Jacques

Passion Of Joan Of Arc, The 1929,Mr 29,21:1
Passion of Jeanne d'Arc, The 1929,Mr 31,VIII,7:1

Arno, Lisay

Inge und die Millionen 1934,Ap 13,25:1

Arno, Nelly

So Long at the Fair 1951,Ja 22,14:2

Arno, Siegfried

Manon Lescaut 1926,N 30,27:1
Wien Du Stadt der Lieder; (Vienna City of Song)
1931,Mr 20,29:1
Die vom Rummelplatz 1932,Ja 2,14:2
Der Storch Streikt 1932,My 2,13:2
Ein Ausgekochter Junge 1932,My 3,25:5
Schubert's Fruehlingstraum 1932,Je 22,19:4
Keine Feier Ohne Meyer 1932,O 29,18:4
Moritz Macht Sein Glueck 1932,D 24,11:4
Zapfenstreich am Rhein 1933,F 2,21:6
Heute Nacht-Eventuell 1933,Je 24,16:3
Die Grosse Attraktion 1933,Jl 24,11:2
Mummy's Hand, The 1940,S 20,27:2
Diamond Frontiers 1940,O 4,29:2
Dark Streets of Cairo 1940,D 2,19:3

Arno, Sig

This Thing Called Love 1941,F 14,15:2
New Wine 1942,F 2,11:2
Two Yanks in Trinidad 1942,Ap 6,19:4
Juke Box Jenny 1942,Ap 17,21:3
Tales of Manhattan 1942,S 25,25:1
Devil With Hitler, The 1942,O 19,15:2
Palm Beach Story, The 1942,D 11,33:1
Crystal Ball, The 1943,F 19,22:2
Taxi, Mister 1943,Ap 15,20:2
His Butler's Sister 1943,D 30,13:2
Up in Arms 1944,Mr 3,19:2
Song of the Open Road 1944,Je 7,13:3
Song to Remember, A 1945,Ja 26,16:4
Bring on the Girls 1945,Mr 1,25:5
One More Tomorrow 1946,My 25,12:2
Holiday in Havana 1949,O 14,33:5
Great Lover, The 1949,N 24,48:2
Duchess of Idaho 1950,Jl 21,15:3
Toast of New Orleans, The 1950,S 30,13:3
Diplomatic Courier 1952,Je 14,12:2

Arnoic, Phil

Good Times 1967,Ag 3,26:4

Arnold, Danny

Breakthrough 1950,N 18,10:2
Jumping Jacks 1952,Jl 24,30:2

Arnold, Danny (Director)

Lady Takes a Flyer, The 1958,Ja 30,19:2

Arnold, Danny (Screenwriter)

Caddy, The 1953,S 18,16:6
Desert Sands 1955,N 19,22:7
Lady Takes a Flyer, The 1958,Ja 30,19:2

Arnold, Dorothy

Storm, The 1938,O 31,12:2
Secrets of a Nurse 1938,D 12,26:2
Unexpected Father 1939,Ag 11,12:2
Lizzie 1957,Ap 5,24:2

Arnold, Edward

Okay America 1932,S 10,18:5
Afraid to Talk 1932,D 19,19:5
Rasputin and the Empress 1932,D 24,11:4
Whistling in the Dark 1933,F 5,IX,5:1
White Sister, The 1933,Mr 18,9:3
Barbarian, The 1933,My 13,16:2
Jennie Gerhardt 1933,Je 9,20:2
Her Bodyguard 1933,Ag 7,18:2
Secret of the Blue Room, The 1933,S 13,22:1
I'm no Angel 1933,O 14,18:2
Roman Scandals 1933,D 25,28:2
Madame Spy 1934,F 10,20:1
Unknown Blonde 1934,Ap 24,27:2
Thirty Day Princess 1934,My 12,12:3
Sadie McKee 1934,My 18,18:3 (Incorrect in this
edition; use 1934,My 19,18:3 elsewhere)
Hide-Out 1934,Ag 25,16:5
Million Dollar Ransom 1934,S 19,15:2
President Vanishes, The 1934,D 8,18:5
Wednesday's Child 1934,D 15,9:3
Biography of a Bachelor Girl 1935,Mr 2,18:2
Cardinal Richelieu 1935,Ap 19,24:2
Glass Key, The 1935,Je 15,20:2
Diamond Jim 1935,Ag 24,18:2
Remember Last Night? 1935,N 21,27:2
Crime and Punishment 1935,N 22,18:2
Sutter's Gold 1936,Mr 27,25:2
Meet Nero Wolfe 1936,Jl 16,20:1
Come and Get It 1936,N 12,31:1
John Meade's Woman 1937,F 18,19:1
Easy Living 1937,Jl 8,20:1

Arnold, Edward— Cont

Toast of New York, The 1937,Jl 23,16:2
Blossoms On Broadway 1937,D 3,29:2
Crowd Roars, The 1938,Ag 5,11:1
You Can't Take It With You 1938,S 2,21:2
Idiot's Delight 1939,F 3,13:1
Let Freedom Ring 1939,Mr 10,19:2
Man About Town 1939,Je 29,19:1
Mr Smith Goes to Washington 1939,O 20,27:2
Earl of Chicago, The 1940,Mr 14,29:3
Johnny Apollo 1940,Ap 13,21:2
Slightly Honorable 1940,My 17,23:4
Lillian Russell 1940,My 18,11:2
Meet John Doe 1941,Mr 13,25:2
Penalty, The 1941,Ap 10,29:3
Lady From Cheyenne, The 1941,Ap 18,18:2
All That Money Can Buy 1941,O 17,27:2
Nothing but the Truth 1941,O 23,27:1
Unholy Partners 1941,D 29,21:4
Design for Scandal 1942,F 6,23:3
Johnny Eager 1942,F 20,21:2
Eyes in the Night 1942,O 16,23:1
War Against Mrs Hadley, The 1942,N 26,40:2
Youngest Profession, The 1943,Je 25,13:3
Standing Room Only 1944,F 23,17:2
Janie 1944,Ag 5,16:2
Kismet 1944,Ag 23,16:1
Mrs Parkington 1944,O 13,16:1
Main Street After Dark 1945,Ja 13,15:4
Hidden Eye, The 1945,Ag 31,14:3
Week-End at the Waldorf 1945,O 5,27:2
Ziegfeld Follies 1946,Mr 23,8:3
Janie Gets Married 1946,Je 15,24:2
Three Wise Fools 1946,S 27,19:2
No Leave, No Love 1946,O 18,29:2
Mighty McGurk, The 1947,Ap 4,19:4
Dear Ruth 1947,Je 11,33:3
My Brother Talks to Horses 1947,Je 19,27:4
Hucksters, The 1947,Jl 18,21:2
Three Daring Daughters 1948,F 13,26:3
Big City 1948,My 17,23:3
Wallflower 1948,Je 12,8:5
Command Decision 1949,Ja 20,34:2
John Loves Mary 1949,F 5,11:2
Take Me Out to the Ball Game 1949,Mr 10,35:2
Big Jack 1949,My 23,27:4
Dear Wife 1950,F 2,31:2
Yellow Cab Man, The 1950,Mr 27,19:2
Annie Get Your Gun 1950,My 18,37:1
Skipper Surprised his Wife, The 1950,Je 30,18:2
Dear Brat 1951,Jl 5,21:2
Belles on Their Toes 1952,My 3,17:5
City That Never Sleeps 1953,Ag 8,14:2
Living It Up 1954,Jl 24,6:6
Ambassador's Daughter, The 1956,Ag 30,19:1

Arnold, Elliott (Original Author)

First Comes Courage 1943,S 3,15:3
Broken Arrow 1950,Jl 21,15:2
Deep in my Heart 1954,D 10,35:2
Flight From Ashiya 1964,Ap 23,34:1

Arnold, Elliott (Screenwriter)

King of the Sun 1963,D 26,33:4
Flight From Ashiya 1964,Ap 23,34:1

Arnold, Franz (Original Author)

It's a Boy 1934,Je 8,18:2

Arnold, Gertrud

Rosenmontag 1931,Mr 28,15:3
Brand in der Oper 1932,Jl 11,11:4

Arnold, Grace

Girl in the Canal, The 1947,O 9,32:3
Jassy 1948,F 20,19:2
Caretaker's Daughter, The 1953,Ag 20,18:5
Eight O'Clock Walk 1955,Ap 30,10:6

Arnold, Jack

Danger Patrol 1937,N 19,27:3
Law of the Underworld 1938,Ap 28,27:2
Blind Alibi 1938,My 20,17:2
Crime Ring 1938,Jl 22,10:3
Tarnished Angel 1938,N 15,27:2
Fixer Dugan 1939,My 6,21:2
Day the Bookies Wept, The 1939,S 14,18:2
Sued for Libel 1940,Ja 19,15:3
Enemy Agent 1940,Ap 22,13:3
Millionaires in Prison 1940,Jl 16,21:3
Juke Box Jenny 1942,Ap 17,21:3

Arnold, Jack (Director)

With These Hands 1950,Je 16,28:4
Girls in the Night 1953,Ja 16,19:3
It Came From Outer Space 1953,Je 18,38:2
Glass Web, The 1953,N 12,37:5
Creature from the Black Lagoon 1954,My 1,13:4
Revenge of the Creature 1955,My 14,10:7
Incredible Shrinking Man, The 1957,F 23,13:1
Tattered Dress, The 1957,Mr 15,22:3
Man With a Shadow 1958,Ja 23,24:3
High School Confidential 1958,My 31,6:6
Mouse That Roared, The 1959,O 27,40:1
Bachelor in Paradise 1961,N 17,41:2
Global Affair, A 1964,My 7,31:2
Lively Set, The 1964,O 15,54:1

Arnold, Jack (Producer)

With These Hands 1950,Je 16,28:4

Arnold, James
Strangers on a Honeymoon 1937,Mr 13,23:2
Arnold, Jeanne
Munster, Go Home 1966,Je 16,53:4
What's so bad About Feeling Good?
1968,My 25,27:1
Arnold, Jess (Original Author)
Eagle and the Hawk, The 1950,Jl 6,31:2
Arnold, Jessie
Playing With Souls 1925,Ap 20,18:1 (Incorrect in
this edition; use 1925,Ap 28,18:1 elsewhere)
Brothers 1930,N 15,15:3
Stranger in Town 1932,Jl 8,22:5
Hot Saturday 1932,N 5,12:5
Bitter Tea of General Yen, The 1933,Ja 12,20:6
We Live Again 1934,N 2,27:2
Ape, The 1940,N 28,28:3
Strange Woman, The 1947,F 24,16:4
Arnold, John
Silver Fleet, The 1945,Mr 24,22:6
Arnold, John (Producer)
Time Without Pity 1957,N 23,11:2
Arnold, Lester
This Day and Age 1933,S 1,15:4
Arnold, Marcelle
Mr Peek-A-Boo 1951,S 19,37:1
Night is my Kingdom, The 1953,S 30,37:1
Bride Is Much too Beautiful, The 1958,Ja 21,35:1
7 Capital Sins (Gluttony); Gluttony (7 Capital
Sins) 1963,Ja 17,5:2
Arnold, Marilee
Babes in Toyland 1961,D 15,49:1
Arnold, Melanie
Babes in Toyland 1961,D 15,49:1
Arnold, Phil
Court-Martial of Billy Mitchell, The
1955,D 23,14:2
Arnold, Seth
Lost Boundaries 1949,Jl 1,14:4
Arnold, Tom (Producer)
Strauss's Great Waltz 1935,Ap 8,23:3
Arnold, Victor
Incident, The 1967,N 6,65:1
Arnold, Wilfred (Composer)
Escape me Never 1935,My 24,24:2
Arnold, William
Gun Smoke 1931,Ap 24,27:1
Vice Squad, The 1931,Je 6,15:5
Rich Man's Folly 1931,N 27,29:3
Crowd Roars, The 1932,Mr 23,25:4
In Love With Life 1934,My 12,12:3
Arnoul, Francoise
Strollers, The 1952,Jl 22,22:7
Lovers of Toledo, The 1954,Ap 10,11:3
Companions of the Night 1954,N 25,44:2
Bed, The (Riviera Express); Riviera Express (The
Bed) 1955,Je 8,26:4
Sheep Has Five Legs, The 1955,Ag 10,19:2
Inside a Girls' Dormitory 1956,F 6,27:7
French-Cancan 1956,Ap 17,26:2
Tempest in the Flesh 1957,Ja 19,12:2
Lover's Net 1957,Jl 23,23:1
No Sun in Venice 1958,Je 10,40:2
Forbidden Fruit 1959,F 23,19:1
Cat, The 1959,Ap 13,35:1
Paris Hotel 1959,S 12,12:3
Tales of Paris (The Tale of Francoise); Tale of
Francoise, The (Tales of Paris) 1962,Ag 27,18:1
Season for Love, The 1963,My 9,40:2
Devil and the 10 Commandments, The (Episode
4) 1963,O 15,44:1
Arnould, Vana (Screenwriter)
Gioconda, La 1958,O 13,33:4
Arnoux, Alexander (Miscellaneous)
Song of the Street 1939,S 5,21:2
Ultimatum 1940,F 5,13:2
Arnoux, Alexander (Screenwriter)
Song of the Street 1939,S 5,21:2
drame De Shanghai; Shanghai Drama, The
1945,Ja 11,19:2
Arnoux, Robert
Mademoiselle ma Mere 1939,S 19,29:2
Whirlpool; (Remous) 1940,O 8,31:2
Between Eleven and Midnight 1950,F 23,33:3
Au Grand Balcon 1951,My 5,14:2
Night is my Kingdom, The 1953,S 30,37:1
Four Bags Full 1957,S 5,32:1
Deadlier Than the Male 1957,O 9,41:1
Bernadette of Lourdes 1962,Ja 30,20:2
Arnova, Alba
Miracle in Milan 1951,D 18,42:2
Times Gone By (Less Than a Day); Less Than a
Day (Times Gone By) 1953,D 30,16:2
Arnow, Mordecai
Sallah 1965,O 13,39:1
Arnshtam, Lev (Director)
Soviets Greet New Turkey 1934,S 3,16:6
Three Women 1936,F 12,25:4
Friends 1939,Ja 2,28:3
Zoya 1945,Ap 16,18:6
Great Glinka, The 1947,D 22,30:2
Ballet of Romeo and Juliet, The 1956,Ap 3,31:2

Arnshtam, Lev (Screenwriter)
Friends 1939,Ja 2,28:3
Zoya 1945,Ap 16,18:6
Great Glinka, The 1947,D 22,30:2
Ballet of Romeo and Juliet, The 1956,Ap 3,31:2
Bolshoi Ballet 67 1966,S 30,54:1
Arnst, Bobbe
Night Club 1929,Ag 12,22:2
Wine, Women and Song 1934,Mr 21,24:3
Arnstaedt, Hansi
Wahre Jakob, Der 1931,Ag 7,20:2
Kyritz-Pyritz 1932,Ag 9,20:5
Bettelstudent, Der 1933,O 14,18:3
Feldherrnhuegel, Der 1934,Ap 20,17:2
Meadehen von Gestern Nacht, Das; Girl of Last
Night, The 1938,Je 18,18:2
Hurra! Ich bin Papa; Hurrah! I'm a Papa
1940,Je 1,12:3
Arnt, Charles
Ladies Should Listen 1934,Jl 28,16:6
Here is my Heart 1934,D 22,21:1
Stolen Harmony 1935,Ap 20,16:2
Two for Tonight 1935,Ag 31,16:2
Witness Chair, The 1936,Ap 18,19:2
Bunker Bean 1936,Je 27,21:2
Sudden Death, And 1936,Jl 18,18:2
Swing High, Swing Low 1937,Ap 15,19:1
It Happened in Hollywood 1937,O 2,18:1
Remember the Night 1940,Ja 18,27:2
I Love You Again 1940,Ag 16,11:2
Pot o'Gold 1941,Ap 4,25:2
Mr District Attorney 1941,Ap 17,29:3
Blossoms in the Dust 1941,Je 27,14:4
Dressed to Kill 1941,Ag 22,19:3
Great Guns 1941,O 3,27:2
Marry the Boss's Daughter 1941,D 4,33:4
Ball of Fire 1942,Ja 16,25:2
Paris Calling 1942,Ja 19,21:2
Lady Has Plans, The 1942,Mr 5,27:1
Twin Beds 1942,My 1,23:4
My Gal Sal 1942,My 1,23:1
Take a Letter Darling 1942,My 28,13:2
Falcon's Brother, The 1942,O 3,9:5
Great Gildersleeve, The 1942,D 18,36:8
Reunion in France 1943,Mr 5,20:3
Gildersleeve's Bad Day 1943,Je 11,23:1
Up in Arms 1944,Mr 3,19:2
Impatient Years, The 1944,S 20,20:1
My Pal, Wolf 1944,O 9,17:2
Crime Doctor's Courage, The 1945,Mr 3,11:3
Sudan 1945,Ap 19,22:8
Christmas in Connecticut 1945,Jl 28,7:2
She Wouldn't Say Yes 1946,Ja 12,10:7
Pardon my Past 1946,Ja 28,15:5
Miss Susie Slagle's 1946,F 7,29:2
Cinderella Jones 1946,Mr 16,9:6
Somewhere in the Night 1946,Je 13,24:2
That Brennan Girl 1946,D 9,34:3
That Way With Women 1947,F 15,20:4
Sitting Pretty 1948,Mr 11,35:2
Hollow Triumph 1948,O 29,29:5
That Wonderful Urge 1948,D 22,29:6
Bride for Sale 1949,N 21,29:4 (In Addenda)
Wabash Avenue 1950,Ap 29,8:3
He's a Cockeyed Wonder 1950,O 20,32:4
Man Who Cheated Himself, The 1951,F 9,21:2
Wild in the Country 1961,Je 10,12:2
Sweet Bird of Youth 1962,Mr 29,28:2
Aro, Ritova
Jaakarin Morsian; Soldiers' Bride 1939,D 18,29:3
Aron, Jean
Poupee, La 1963,Ag 28,39:1
Arora, Prakash (Director)
Boot Polish 1958,Ag 18,15:2
Aroseva, Olga
Uncommon Thief, An 1967,D 1,56:2
Arout, G (Screenwriter)
Every Second Counts 1957,O 15,39:4
Riff Raff Girls 1962,O 20,13:5
Arozamena, Amparo
Almas Encontradas 1933,Je 27,13:5
Rayo, El 1935,O 19,21:3
Arozamena, Eduardo
Perjura 1939,Ja 16,11:2
Capitan Aventurero, El; Adventureous Captain,
The 1939,O 3,19:5
Flor Sylvestre 1945,Ja 16,17:2
Hidden River 1950,D 1,31:2
Arp, Jean
8 X 8 1957,Mr 16,13:2
Arquette, Cliff
Comin' Round the Mountain 1940,S 26,27:3
Arrau, Claudio
Sueno de Amor 1936,Ja 11,9:3
Arriaga, Rosita
Cruz Diablo 1935,Ap 6,10:1
Tribu 1935,Je 10,14:7
Familia Dressel, La 1936,My 4,16:2
Arrieta, Santiago
Que Tiempos Aquellos; Those Were the Days
1938,Mr 7,13:2
Ley que Olvidaron, La; Law They Forgot, The
1940,Ja 13,11:3

Arrieta, Santiago— Cont
Alma del Bandoneon, El; Soul of the Accordion,
The 1940,Ap 27,9:3
Arrighi, Nike
Devil's Bride, The 1968,D 19,60:1
Arrova, Alba
Gioconda, La 1958,O 13,33:4
Arrow, Jack
Treasure Island 1950,Ag 16,24:2
Arroyo, Luis
Young Savages, The 1961,My 25,31:1
Arruza, Carlos
Torero! 1957,My 22,29:2
Alamo, The 1960,O 27,45:1
Arski, N
Lenin in October 1938,Ap 2,18:1
Alexander Nevsky 1939,Mr 23,27:1
Arslan, Sylvia
Moon Over her Shoulder 1941,N 5,31:2
Mr Skeffington 1944,My 26,23:2
Artaud, Antonin
Passion Of Joan Of Arc, The 1929,Mr 29,21:1
Passion of Jeanne d'Arc, The 1929,Mr 31,VIII,7:1
Serment, Le 1934,Mr 14,23:2
Argent, L' 1968,S 23,42:5
Artault
Lucrezia Borgia 1937,O 13,27:2
Artega, Sophia
Sadie Thompson 1928,F 6,12:3
Artemovski, Gulak (Original Author)
Cossack Beyond the Danube, A 1954,F 8,18:5
Artemovsky, S (Original Author)
Cossacks in Exile 1939,Ja 28,19:2
Artero, Matilde
Esperame 1933,Jl 3,14:6
Arthur, Art (Original Author)
Charlie Chan on Broadway 1937,S 20,19:1
Love and Hisses 1938,Ja 1,11:1
Sun Valley Serenade 1941,S 6,20:1
Clarence, the Cross-Eyed Lion 1965,Ag 5,15:3
Arthur, Art (Screenwriter)
Love and Hisses 1938,Ja 1,11:1
Kentucky Moonshine 1938,My 21,9:2
Thanks For Everything 1938,D 10,13:2
Daytime Wife 1939,N 24,29:1
Everything Happens at Night 1939,D 16,12:6
Tight Shoes 1941,Je 19,25:2
True to the Army 1942,Je 15,15:4
Dr Broadway 1942,Je 25,27:3
Priorities on Parade 1942,Jl 23,19:2
Riding High 1943,D 23,26:4
Fabulous Dorseys, The 1947,My 30,25:3
Northwest Stampede 1948,D 10,34:3
Song of India 1949,Je 10,32:3
Flipper's New Adventure 1964,Ag 27,28:2
Rhino! 1964,Ag 27,28:2
Around the World Under the Sea 1966,Jl 21,20:2
Arthur, Bob
Ace in the Hole 1951,Je 30,8:6
System, The 1953,My 23,19:3
Arthur, George (Producer)
Last Train from Madrid, The 1937,Je 19,20:2
Her Jungle Love 1938,Ap 14,27:2
Cocoanut Grove 1938,Je 16,21:2
Arkansas Traveler, The 1938,N 17,29:2
Our Leading Citizen 1939,Ag 24,17:1
Night of Nights, The 1939,D 28,17:1
I Want a Divorce 1940,O 3,31:2
Mad Doctor, The 1941,F 27,23:4
Arthur, George K
Salvation Hunters, The 1925,F 2,14:1
Lady of the Night 1925,Mr 2,14:1
Sun Up 1925,Ag 18,14:3
Lights of Old Broadway 1925,N 2,20:1
Irene 1926,Mr 1,17:1
Kiki 1926,Ap 6,26:4
Waning Sex, The 1926,S 21,33:1
Bardelys The Magnificent 1926,N 1,28:1 (In
Addenda)
Lovers 1927,Ap 19,24:4
Rookies 1927,Ap 25,20:4
Tillie the Toiler 1927,Je 7,27:4
Gingham Girl, The 1927,Jl 19,27:2
Spring Fever 1927,O 18,33:2
Baby Mine 1928,Ja 9,20:1
Circus Rookies 1928,My 14,25:1
Last of Mrs Cheyney, The 1929,Ag 12,22:2
Chasing Rainbows 1930,F 22,13:1
Oliver Twist 1933,Ap 13,15:3
Looking Forward 1933,My 1,10:2
Blind Adventure 1933,O 31,24:3
Riptide 1934,Mr 31,8:2
Vanessa: Her Love Story 1935,Ap 13,11:3
Arthur, George M (Director)
Crooks Can't Win 1928,My 29,17:2
Arthur, Indus
Slender Thread, The 1965,D 24,24:2
Arthur, Jean
Poor Nut, The 1927,Jl 19,27:2
Warming Up 1928,Jl 16,25:3
Sins of the Fathers 1929,Ja 28,21:1
Canary Murder Case, The 1929,Mr 11,22:2
Insidious Dr Fu Manchu, The 1929,Jl 22,17:1
Mysterious Dr Fu Manchu, The

Arthur, Jean— Cont

1929,Jl 28,VIII,3:7 (In Addenda)
Greene Murder Case, The 1929,Ag 10,11:3
Saturday Night Kid, The 1929,N 16,25:2
Half Way to Heaven 1929,D 7,19:3
Street of Chance 1930,F 3,17:1
Young Eagles 1930,Mr 22,22:6
New Adventures of Dr Fu Manchu, The
  1930,My 3,23:1
Silver Horde, The 1930,O 25,20:6
Danger Lights 1930,D 15,29:1
Gang Buster, The 1931,Ja 24,15:1
Virtuous Husband 1931,My 8,30:2
Lawyer's Secret, The 1931,My 30,9:2
Past of Mary Holmes, The 1933,My 1,10:3
Whirlpool 1934,My 5,22:3
Defense Rests, The 1934,Ag 16,20:3
Whole Town's Talking, The 1935,Mr 1,16:2
Public Hero No 1 1935,Je 8,12:2
Diamond Jim 1935,Ag 24,18:2
If You Could Only Cook 1935,D 26,21:4
Mr Deeds Goes to Town 1936,Ap 17,17:2
Ex-Mrs Bradford, The 1936,My 28,19:2
Adventure in Manhattan 1936,O 23,27:5
More Than a Secretary 1936,D 11,35:2
Plainsman, The 1937,Ja 14,16:2
History Is Made at Night 1937,Mr 29,14:2
Easy Living 1937,Jl 8,20:1
You Can't Take It With You 1938,S 2,21:2
Only Angels Have Wings 1939,My 12,25:2
Mr Smith Goes to Washington 1939,O 20,27:2
Too Many Husbands 1940,Mr 8,25:2
Arizona 1941,F 7,23:3
Devil and Miss Jones, The 1941,My 16,21:2
Talk of the Town, The 1942,Ag 28,22:3
More the Merrier, The 1943,My 14,17:1
Lady Takes a Chance, A 1943,S 16,25:2
Impatient Years, The 1944,S 20,20:1
Foreign Affair, A 1948,Jl 1,19:3
Shane 1953,Ap 24,30:3

Arthur, Johnny

Unknown Purple, The 1924,Mr 24,13:1
Mademoiselle Midnight 1924,My 27,14:1
Monster, The 1925,F 16,24:1
On Trial 1928,N 15,26:5
Desert Song, The 1929,My 2,20:6
Gamblers, The 1929,Ag 24,11:5
Aviator, The 1930,Ja 11,21:3
She Couldn't Say No 1930,F 16,III,8:1
Going Wild 1931,Ja 26,21:1
It's a Wise Child 1931,My 16,13:3
Penrod and Sam 1931,S 26,25:3
Convention City 1933,D 25,28:2
20 Million Sweethearts 1934,Ap 27,25:1
Many Happy Returns 1934,Je 9,18:2
Hell in the Heavens 1934,D 12,28:2
Traveling Saleslady 1935,Mr 29,26:2
Ghost Walks, The 1935,Mr 30,11:2
Doubting Thomas 1935,Jl 11,24:2
Crime and Punishment 1935,N 22,18:2
Bride Comes Home, The 1935,D 25,30:2
Murder of Dr Harrigan, The 1936,Ja 21,27:5
Fish 1936,Ja 25,18:5
Freshman Love 1936,Ja 25,18:5
King Steps Out, The 1936,My 29,15:2
Stage Struck 1936,S 28,14:4
Pick a Star 1937,My 28,17:2
It Happened Out West 1937,Je 7,22:3
Something to Sing About 1937,S 21,29:4
Blossoms On Broadway 1937,D 3,29:2
Road to Singapore 1940,Mr 14,29:2
That Nazty Nuisance 1943,My 29,10:3

Arthur, Julia

Woman the Germans Shot, The 1918,O 28,11:1

Arthur, Louise (Narrator)

Snow Queen, The 1960,Ap 14,34:1

Arthur, Maureen

How to Succeed in Business Without Really
  Trying 1967,Mr 10,30:1
Wicked Dreams of Paula Schultz, The
  1968,Ja 4,28:1

Arthur, Robert

Too Young to Know 1945,D 8,21:2
Nora Prentiss 1947,F 22,16:2
Mother Wore Tights 1947,Ag 21,33:2
Green Grass of Wyoming 1948,Je 10,28:3
Yellow Sky 1949,F 2,36:1
Mother is a Freshman 1949,Mr 12,10:2
You're my Everything 1949,Jl 23,7:2
Twelve O'Clock High 1950,Ja 28,10:2
September Affair 1951,F 2,19:2
Air Cadet 1951,My 11,32:3
Belles on Their Toes 1952,My 3,17:5
Just for You 1952,O 9,40:6
Young Bess 1953,My 22,31:1
Take the High Ground 1953,N 20,19:2

Arthur, Robert (Original Author)

Chip off the Old Block 1944,Mr 17,14:2
Francis Goes to the Races 1951,Jl 25,19:2

Arthur, Robert (Producer)

Buck Privates Come Home 1947,Ap 12,11:3
Wistful Widow of Wagon Gap, The
  1947,N 21,36:2
Are You With It? 1948,Ap 15,31:2

Abbott and Costello Meet Frankenstein
  1948,Jl 29,17:2
For the Love of Mary 1948,S 23,37:2
Mexican Hayride 1949,Ja 12,33:3
Abbott and Costello Meet the Killer Boris Karloff
  1949,S 19,18:3
Bagdad 1949,D 24,11:4
Francis 1950,Mr 16,40:2
Buccaneer's Girl 1950,Mr 27,19:2
Abbott and Costello in the Foreign Legion
  1950,Ag 14,14:4
Curtain Call at Cactus Creek 1950,S 22,35:4
Louisa 1950,O 25,45:2
Starlift 1951,D 15,11:2
Story of Will Rogers, The 1952,Jl 18,10:5
Big Heat, The 1953,O 15,43:2
Black Shield of Falworth, The 1954,O 7,16:2
Long Gray Line, The 1955,F 11,19:2
Lady Godiva 1955,D 3,13:3
Francis in the Haunted House 1956,Jl 21,9:2
Pillars of the Sky 1956,O 13,15:2
Mister Cory 1957,F 23,13:1
Midnight Story, The 1957,Jl 5,14:2
Man of a Thousand Faces 1957,Ag 14,21:1
Time to Love and a Time to Die, A
  1958,Jl 10,22:1
Perfect Furlough, The 1959,Ja 22,27:4
Operation Petticoat 1959,D 6,38:1
Great Impostor, The 1961,Mr 30,24:1
Come September 1961,S 8,34:1
That Touch of Mink 1962,Je 15,16:2
Spiral Road, The 1962,Ag 4,11:2
For Love or Money 1963,Ag 8,19:1
Captain Newman, MD 1964,F 21,36:1
Brass Bottle, The 1964,My 21,42:1
Father Goose 1964,D 11,55:1
Shenandoah 1965,Jl 29,18:3
Man Could Get Killed, A 1966,My 12,54:2
Blindfold 1966,My 26,55:2

Arthur, Robert (Screenwriter)

New Moon 1940,Jl 19,22:2

Arthy, Judith

Shuttered Room, The 1968,F 15,47:1

Artigas, Jose

Age d'Or, L'; Golden Age, The 1964,S 22,44:1

Artur, Jose

Mr Orchid; Pere Tranquille, Le 1948,Mr 29,17:3

Artur, Monique

Dirty Hands 1954,My 11,25:5

Artus, Raymond (Producer)

Blue Veil, The 1947,O 2,32:6

Aruillo, Colette D'

Tango-Bar 1935,Jl 6,16:3

Arundale, Sybil

Loose Ends 1930,O 18,23:2

Arundel, Sidney

Sensation Seekers 1927,Mr 16,28:2

Arundell, Dennis

Courageous Mr Penn 1943,D 23,26:5
Man From Morocco, The 1946,N 25,38:2
End of the River, The 1948,Je 21,18:2
History of Mr Polly, The 1951,O 25,36:3

Arvan, Jan

Brass Bottle, The 1964,My 21,42:1

Arvedson, Ragnar

For Her Sake 1930,N 11,29:1

Arvedson, Ragner (Director)

Kustens Glada Kavaljerer; Coast's Happy
  Cavaliers, The 1939,My 23,27:2

Arvel

Avocate d'Amour 1938,S 8,27:2

Arvide, Manuel

Marvels of the Bull Ring 1943,Jl 3,11:3
Honeymoon 1947,My 19,27:2

Arvizu, Juan

Infidelidad 1939,My 8,21:3
Ahora Seremos Felices; Now We Shall Be Happy
  1940,Mr 16,8:2

Arys-Nissotti, M (Producer)

They Were Five 1938,Je 1,19:5

Arzner, Dorothy (Director)

Fashions For Women 1927,Mr 28,26:4
Ten Modern Commandments 1927,Jl 11,23:4
Get Your Man 1927,D 5,26:2
Manhattan Cocktail 1928,N 26,30:2
Wild Party, The 1929,Ap 2,28:4
Sarah and Son 1930,Mr 13,22:4
Anybody's Woman 1930,Ag 16,8:3
Honor Among Lovers 1931,F 28,15:2
Merrily We Go to Hell 1932,Je 11,9:3
Christopher Strong 1933,Mr 10,19:2
Nana 1934,F 2,20:3
Craig's Wife 1936,O 2,29:3
Bride Wore Red, The 1937,O 15,18:4
Dance, Girl, Dance 1940,O 11,25:2
First Comes Courage 1943,S 3,15:3

Asagaroff, Georg (Director)

Eva and the Grasshopper 1928,N 19,16:7
Escaped From Hell 1929,Ja 29,27:1
Tolle Bomberg, Der 1935,O 26,12:2

Asaji, Shinobu

Sword for Hire 1957,S 5,32:1

Asander, Birger

Children, The 1949,D 23,17:1

Asaoka, Ruriko

Alone on the Pacific 1964,S 24,46:2

Asatian, L

Dragonfly, The 1955,Je 27,18:2

Asbury, Herbert (Original Author)

Gangs of New York 1938,My 28,9:2

ASCHE

See Also ASH, ASHE

Asche, Oscar

Don Quixote 1934,D 24,17:1
Scrooge 1935,D 14,11:1
Robber Symphony 1937,Ja 27,17:2

Asche, Oscar (Original Author)

Chu Chin Chow 1934,S 22,12:2

Asche, Oscar (Screenwriter)

Chu Chin Chow 1925,F 11,19:4

Ascher, Diane

Do You Love Me 1946,My 25,12:2

Ascot, J M Garcia (Screenwriter)

Roots, The (The Filly); Filly, The (The Roots)
  1957,S 3,23:2
Roots, The (The One-Eyed Boy); One-Eyed Boy,
  The (The Roots) 1957,S 3,23:2
Roots, The (Our Lady); Our Lady (The Roots)
  1957,S 3,23:2
Roots, The (The Cows); Cows, The (The Roots)
  1957,S 3,23:2

Asguith, Anthony (Director)

V I P's, The 1963,S 20,29:1

ASH

See Also ASCHE, ASHE

Ash, Frances (Composer)

Call Me Mister 1951,F 1,21:2

Ash, Sam

Girl Without a Room 1933,D 7,26:3
Some Like It Hot 1939,My 25,31:2
Heat's on, The 1943,N 26,29:2
Dancing Masters, The 1943,D 2,30:2
Oh, You Beautiful Doll 1949,N 12,8:4

Ashbridge, Bryan

Royal Ballet, The (Swan Lake Act II); Swan Lake
  Act II (The Royal Ballet) 1960,O 5,45:2

Ashcroft, Peggy

Wandering Jew, The 1935,Ja 14,11:3
Thirty-Nine Steps, The 1935,S 14,8:4
Rhodes 1936,F 29,11:1
Quiet Wedding 1941,D 29,27:4
Nun's Story, The 1959,Je 19,30:1
Secret Ceremony 1968,O 24,55:1

Ashdown, Anthony

Tobruk 1967,F 9,33:2

Ashdown, Nadene

Shadow in the Sky 1952,Jl 19,8:2
Bridges at Toko-Ri, The 1955,Ja 21,20:2

ASHE

See Also ASCHE, ASH

Ashe, Robert (Director)

Follow a Star 1961,Ap 26,34:1

Ashe, Warren

Military Academy 1940,Ag 5,10:4
Face Behind the Mask, The 1941,F 7,23:2
Naval Academy 1941,Je 5,27:3
Harmon of Michigan 1941,O 2,29:2
What's Buzzin Cousin 1943,Jl 23,21:4
Destroyer 1943,S 2,15:3

Ashelbe (Original Author)

Algiers 1938,Jl 15,13:2
Dedee 1949,Ap 9,9:2

Asher, E M (Producer)

Wings Over Honolulu 1937,My 29,20:1
Some Blondes Are Dangerous 1937,N 3,29:3

Asher, Irving (Producer)

Clouds Over Europe 1939,Je 16,27:2
U-Boat 29 1939,O 6,31:3
Missing Ten Days 1941,Ap 21,15:5 (In Addenda)
Billy the Kid 1941,Je 20,28:2
Blossoms in the Dust 1941,Je 27,14:4
Mr and Mrs North 1942,Ja 22,13:2
Nazi Agent 1942,Je 13,11:2
War Against Mrs Hadley, The 1942,N 26,40:2
Redhead and the Cowboy, The 1951,Je 6,37:2
Turning Point, The 1952,N 15,15:2
Stars Are Singing, The 1953,Mr 12,24:2
Elephant Walk 1954,Ap 22,37:2

Asher, Jane

Loss of Innocence 1961,N 22,27:1
Masque of the Red Death, The 1964,S 17,52:6
Model Murder Case, The 1964,N 25,45:1
Alfie 1966,Ag 25,42:1

Asher, Max

Courtship of Myles Standish, The 1923,D 31,9:3
Shooting of Dan McGrew, The 1924,Je 9,14:3
Lost at the Front 1927,Je 14,33:2
Painting the Town 1927,Ag 2,19:2
Little Man, What Now? 1934,Je 1,29:1

Asher, Nils

If I Were Free 1934,Ja 5,25:2

Asher, Peter

Outpost in Malaya 1952,N 27,49:2
Escapade 1957,Ag 6,30:2

Asher, Robert (Director)
Make Mine Mink 1960,D 20,43:4
Asher, William (Director)
Beach Party 1963,S 26,40:2
Johnny Cool 1963,O 3,31:1
Muscle Beach Party 1964,My 28,40:1
Bikini Beach 1964,S 17,52:6
Fireball 500 1966,N 24,65:4
How to Stuff a Wild Bikini 1967,Ja 12,48:1
Asher, William (Screenwriter)
Bikini Beach 1964,S 17,52:6
Fireball 500 1966,N 24,65:4
How to Stuff a Wild Bikini 1967,Ja 12,48:1
Asherov, Mischa
Impossible on Saturday 1966,F 17,29:1
Asherson, Renee
Johnny in the Clouds 1945,N 16,16:2
Henry V 1946,Je 18,30:2
Caesar and Cleopatra 1946,S 6,18:2
Pool of London 1951,N 28,37:2
Malta Story 1954,Jl 17,7:2
Day the Earth Caught Fire, The 1962,Mr 16,25:1
Asherton, Renee
Small Back Room, The 1952,F 2,11:3
Ashford, Donald
Return to Paradise 1953,S 11,24:2
Ashley, Audrey (Original Author)
Raw Deal 1948,Jl 9,11:4
Ashley, Edward
Pride and Prejudice 1940,Ag 9,19:1
Sky Murder 1940,N 14,28:3
Bitter Sweet 1940,N 22,27:1
Gallant Sons 1940,D 12,37:2
Maisie Was a Lady 1941,F 13,25:2
Come Live With Me 1941,F 28,17:3
Black Swan, The 1942,D 24,18:3
Love, Honor and Goodbye 1945,S 8,12:2
Nocturne 1946,N 11,42:2
Other Love, The 1947,My 15,32:4
Dick Tracy and Gruesome 1947,S 27,11:2
Tarzan and the Mermaids 1948,Mr 30,26:4
Macao 1952,My 1,34:2
Elephant Walk 1954,Ap 22,37:2
Court Jester, The 1956,F 2,19:1
Ashley, Elizabeth
Carpetbaggers, The 1964,Jl 2,24:4
Ship of Fools 1965,Jl 29,18:1
Third Day, The 1965,Ag 5,15:3
Ashley, Herbert
King of Burlesque 1936,Ja 16,25:2
League of Frightened Men, The 1937,Jl 2,25:1
Hotel for Women 1939,Ag 26,20:2
Little Old New York 1940,F 3,9:2
Ashley, Iris
Charming Deceiver, The 1933,D 9,18:3
Loves of Madame Dubarry, The 1938,Ap 4,12:5
Ashley, John
Frankenstein's Daughter 1958,N 17,37:2
Hud 1963,My 29,36:1
Beach Party 1963,S 26,40:2
Muscle Beach Party 1964,My 28,40:1
Ashley, Lyn
I'll Never Forget What's 'Isname 1968,Ap 15,51:1
Ashley, Norman
Immortal Story, The 1968,S 19,62:2
Ashley, Ray (Director)
Little Fugitive 1953,O 7,35:1
Ashley, Ray (Producer)
Little Fugitive 1953,O 7,35:1
Ashley, Ray (Screenwriter)
Little Fugitive 1953,O 7,35:1
Ashley, Rosalie
Too Many Crooks 1959,Ap 25,14:2
Ashmore, Jonathan
Kid for two Farthings, A 1956,Ap 18,25:1
Ashoke
Kanchenjungha 1966,Jl 26,27:2
Ashrafova, L
Othello 1960,My 16,39:1
Ashton, Frederick
Tales of Hoffmann 1951,Ap 5,34:2
Ashton, Frederick (Miscellaneous)
Tales of Hoffmann 1951,Ap 5,34:2
Royal Ballet, The (Ondine); Ondine (The Royal Ballet) 1960,O 5,45:2
Ashton, Helen (Original Author)
White Corridors 1952,Jl 16,21:1
Ashton, Herbert
Me, Gangster 1928,O 22,29:1
Ashton, Herbert Jr (Original Author)
Brothers 1930,N 15,15:3
Ashton, Sylvia
Don't Change Your Husband 1919,F 3,13:2
Men, Women and Money 1919,Je 16,11:2
Lottery Man, The 1919,O 6,15:1
Jenny, Be Good 1920,Je 28,13:2
Conrad in Quest of his Youth 1920,N 8,20:2
Sham 1921,My 6,20:2
Prince There Was 1921,N 14,18:1
Is Matrimony a Failure 1922,Ap 17,22:3
Borderland 1922,Jl 24,10:2
Greed 1924,D 5,28:1

Women's Wares 1927,N 15,27:1
Cheating Cheaters 1927,D 6,27:1
Leopard Lady, The 1928,F 27,16:2
Ladies' Night in a Turkish Bath 1928,Ap 9,18:2
Barker, The 1928,D 6,35:1
Ashton, Warwick
Touch and go 1956,Mr 20,13:2
Dunkirk 1958,S 11,42:2
Ashton-Warner, Sylvia (Original Author)
Two Loves 1961,Je 22,23:2
Ashton-Wolfe, H (Original Author)
Secrets of the French Police 1932,D 12,18:4
Ashwood, Terry (Director)
Elizabeth is Queen 1953,Je 29,20:4
Asian, Gregoire
Invasion Quartet 1961,D 11,41:2
Paris When it Sizzles 1964,Ap 9,25:3
Moment to Moment 1966,Mr 3,28:1
Asimakopoulos, G (Screenwriter)
Castle in Greece 1960,D 12,38:2
Askam, Perry
Sweet Kitty Bellairs 1930,S 6,9:2
Askenas, Paul
Hands of Orlac, The 1928,Je 5,21:1
Askew, Luke
Hurry Sundown 1967,Mr 24,22:1
Cool Hand Luke 1967,N 2,58:1
Green Berets, The 1968,Je 20,49:1
Askin, Leon
Road to Bali 1953,Ja 30,25:1
Desert Legion 1953,My 9,13:2
South Sea Woman 1953,Je 4,33:6
Robe, The 1953,S 17,32:6
Veils of Bagdad, The 1953,N 27,99:9
Knock on Wood 1954,Ap 15,34:2
Secret of the Incas 1954,My 29,13:3
Valley of the Kings 1954,Jl 22,15:2
Son of Sinbad 1955,Jl 28,18:2
Last Blitzkrieg, The 1959,Ja 31,13:5
One, Two, Three 1961,D 22,17:1
John Goldfarb, Please Come Home 1965,Mr 25,42:4
Do Not Disturb 1965,D 25,17:2
What Did You Do in the War, Daddy? 1966,S 1,28:1
Double Trouble 1967,My 25,54:2
Wicked Dreams of Paula Schultz, The 1968,Ja 4,28:1
Guns for San Sebastian 1968,Mr 21,57:2
Askley, Edward
Spies of the Air 1940,Jl 4,12:3
Aslan, Coco
Sleeping Car to Trieste 1949,Ap 18,18:6
Last Holiday 1950,N 14,39:4
Oh, Amelia 1951,D 3,22:2
Cairo Road 1952,N 1,17:2
Aslan, Gregoire
Act of Love 1954,F 12,20:5
Red Inn, The 1954,Je 8,25:2
Joe Macbeth 1956,Ap 7,13:1
Snorkel, The 1958,S 18,37:2
Windom's Way 1958,O 1,45:1
Roots of Heaven, The 1958,O 16,46:1
He Who Must Die 1958,D 29,21:1
Our Man in Havana 1960,Ja 28,26:1
Killers of Kilimanjaro 1960,Ap 7,46:1
Oasis 1960,Jl 7,26:1
Under ten Flags 1960,S 16,24:1
Three Worlds of Gulliver, The 1960,D 17,19:3
King of Kings 1961,O 12,41:2
Call Me Genius 1961,O 17,47:1
Devil at 4 O'Clock, The 1961,O 19,39:3
Happy Thieves, The 1962,F 5,19:4
Mr Arkadin 1962,O 12,26:1
Cleopatra 1963,Je 13,29:1
Man Could Get Killed, A 1966,My 12,54:2
Lost Command 1966,S 15,51:1
Marco the Magnificent 1966,D 15,60:1
Bang, Bang, You're Dead 1967,Ja 19,41:2
25th Hour, The 1967,F 17,45:1
Flea in her Ear, A 1968,N 28,66:1
Aslan, Raoul
Floetenkonzert von Sanssouci, Das 1931,O 17,20:1
Yorck 1932,N 24,35:2
Aslanian, Jacques
Shoot the Piano Player 1962,Jl 24,19:1
Aslanov, N
Paris Commune 1937,Je 2,20:4
Aslim, Rita
Uncivilized 1937,N 17,27:4
Asmondi, Herbert
Young Torless 1967,S 25,56:2
Young Torless 1968,Jl 23,27:2
Asner, Edward
Satan Bug, The 1965,Ap 15,38:1
Slender Thread, The 1965,D 24,24:2
Venetian Affair, The 1967,Ja 19,41:2
Dorado, El 1967,Je 29,32:1
Gunn 1967,Je 29,32:1
Asoka
Diamond Queen The 1954,Ja 27,24:2

Aspegren, Anders (Producer)
Flamboyant Sex, The 1963,Ag 13,25:1
Asquitapace
Prenez Garde a la Peinture 1935,Ag 17,18:6
Asquith, Anthony (Director)
Underground 1929,F 26,31:1
Escaped From Dartmoor 1930,Ap 12,23:1
Tell England 1931,Ap 19,VIII,6:1
Battle of Gallipoli, The 1931,D 7,16:1
I Stand Condemned 1936,Jl 2,27:2
Pygmalion 1938,D 8,34:2
French Without Tears 1940,Ap 29,12:2
Voice in the Night, The 1941,My 23,25:4
Quiet Wedding 1941,D 29,27:4
Johnny in the Clouds 1945,N 16,16:2
Adventure for Two 1945,D 14,24:5
Man of Evil 1948,Mr 26,26:2
Winslow Boy, The 1950,Je 7,34:4
While the Sun Shines 1950,Jl 1,9:2
Browning Version, The 1951,O 30,33:2
Woman in Question, The 1952,F 19,24:2
Importance of Being Earnest, The 1952,D 23,17:2
Project M 7 1953,N 27,22:5
Final Test, The 1954,Ja 26,21:5
Chance Meeting 1955,Ap 20,38:1
Court Martial 1955,Ag 2,17:1
Orders to Kill 1958,N 18,41:2
Doctor's Dilemma, A 1958,D 18,2:7
Libel 1959,O 24,12:4
Millionairess, The 1961,F 10,19:1
Guns of Darkness 1962,Ag 18,10:1
Yellow Rolls-Royce, The 1965,My 14,42:2
Evening With the Royal Ballet, An 1965,D 9,60:1
Asquith, Anthony (Producer)
Underground 1928,Ag 12,VII,4:3 (In Addenda)
Asquith, Anthony (Screenwriter)
Shooting Stars 1928,Mr 4,IX,7:7
Shooting Stars 1928,Je 11,27:1
Underground 1929,F 26,31:1
Importance of Being Earnest, The 1952,D 23,17:2
Asro, Alexander
Room Service 1938,S 22,27:1
Asselin, Henry (Director)
Oppressed, The 1929,Jl 15,25:1
Asselin, Henry (Screenwriter)
Oppressed, The 1929,Jl 15,25:1
Asselin, Paul
Crime et Chatiment; Crime and Punishment 1935,N 13,25:3
Assia
They Met on Skis 1940,D 23,23:2
Assimakopoulos, G (Screenwriter)
Anna of Rhodes 1950,Mr 23,34:2
Wind of Hate; (O Anemos Tou Missous) 1958,N 17,37:2
Assmann, Arno
Original Sin, The 1950,Ag 21,15:2
Last Illusion, The 1951,Mr 8,37:2
Assy, Pierre
Story of a Cheat, The 1938,S 27,25:2
Thirst of Men, The 1952,O 28,37:1
Asta
Another Thin Man 1939,N 24,29:1
Thin Man Goes Home, The 1945,Ja 26,16:5
Astaflyef, Maxim
False Uniforms 1932,N 19,20:2
Astaire, Fred
Dancing Lady 1933,D 1,23:2
Flying Down to Rio 1933,D 22,25:2
Gay Divorcee, The 1934,N 16,27:1
Roberta 1935,Mr 8,25:2
Top Hat 1935,Ag 30,12:2
Follow the Fleet 1936,F 21,21:2
Swing Time 1936,Ag 28,21:2
Shall We Dance 1937,My 14,21:1
Damsel in Distress, A 1937,N 25,37:1
Carefree 1938,S 23,35:1
Story of Vernon and Irene Castle, The 1939,Mr 31,19:2
Broadway Melody of 1940 1940,Mr 29,25:3
Second Chorus 1941,Ja 16,25:2
You'll Never Get Rich 1941,O 24,27:2
Holiday Inn 1942,Ag 5,16:1
You Were Never Lovelier 1942,D 4,31:1
Sky's the Limit, The 1943,S 3,15:2
Yolanda and the Thief 1945,N 23,26:2
Ziegfeld Follies 1946,Mr 23,8:3
Blue Skies 1946,O 17,28:2
Easter Parade 1948,Jl 1,19:3
Barkleys of Broadway, The 1949,My 5,34:2
Three Little Words 1950,Ag 10,21:2
Let's Dance 1950,N 30,42:2
Royal Wedding 1951,Mr 9,30:2
Belle of New York, The 1952,Mr 6,25:6
Band Wagon, The 1953,Jl 10,10:2
Daddy Long Legs 1955,My 6,17:5
Funny Face 1957,Mr 29,16:1
Silk Stockings 1957,Jl 19,11:1
On the Beach 1959,D 18,34:1
Pleasure of his Company, The 1961,Je 2,36:1
Notorious Landlady, The 1962,Jl 27,15:2
Finian's Rainbow 1968,O 10,59:5

Astaire, Marie
Last Man on Earth, The 1924,D 13,12:4
Price of Pleasure, The 1925,My 26,24:2
Mad Whirl, The 1925,Jl 1,16:1
Grand Parade, The 1930,F 1,15:1
Millie 1931,F 7,11:1
Soldiers Plaything, A 1931,My 2,23:4

Astangor, M
Prisoners 1937,F 20,9:2
Oppenheim Family, The 1939,My 24,29:2
We Will Come Back 1943,O 15,15:2

Astangov, M
First Front, The 1949,N 14,19:2
Victors and the Vanquished, The 1950,My 1,18:2
Sadko 1953,Je 1,18:6
Maxima 1953,O 12,30:4

Astar, Ben
Five Fingers 1952,F 23,7:5
Fort Ti 1953,My 30,7:1
Marriage-Go-Round 1961,Ja 7,12:2
On the Double 1961,My 20,12:1
Honeymoon Machine, The 1961,Ag 24,25:2
Bye Bye Birdie 1963,Ap 5,27:3
Walk, Don't Run 1966,Ag 25,42:3
Dead Heat on a Merry-Go-Round
1966,O 13,50:1

Astarita, Luigi
Two Cents Worth of Hope 1952,D 16,44:2

Asther, Nils
Topsy and Eva 1927,Ag 8,10:3
Sorrell and Son 1927,N 14,26:1
Blue Danube, The 1928,Ap 30,18:3
Laugh, Clown, Laugh 1928,My 28,23:2
Cossacks, The 1928,Je 25,27:1
Loves of an Actress 1928,Jl 30,21:2
Cardboard Lover, The 1928,S 3,14:2
Our Dancing Daughters 1928,O 8,14:2
Dream of Love 1928,D 24,11:1
Wild Orchids 1929,Ap 1,22:1
Single Standard, The 1929,Jl 29,23:3
Wrath of the Seas, The 1929,Ag 19,22:1
But the Flesh Is Weak 1932,Ap 16,11:2
Letty Lynton 1932,Ap 30,19:3
Washington Masquerade, The 1932,Jl 22,18:2
Bitter Tea of General Yen, The 1933,Ja 12,20:6
Storm at Daybreak 1933,Jl 22,14:2
Right to Romance, The 1933,D 15,28:2
By Candlelight 1934,Ja 6,18:2
Madame Spy 1934,F 10,20:1
Crime Doctor, The 1934,My 11,24:3
Love Captive, The 1934,Je 8,18:1
Abdul the Damned 1936,My 11,16:2
Dr Kildare's Wedding Day 1941,S 18,31:1
Night of January 16th, The 1941,D 19,35:1
Night Before the Divorce, The 1942,Ap 10,21:3
Sweater Girl 1942,Jl 13,18:3
Night Monster 1942,N 30,18:5
Hour Before the Dawn, The 1944,My 11,25:6
Man in Half Moon Street, The 1945,Ja 20,16:2
Son of Lassie 1945,Je 11,12:1

Asti, Adriana
Before the Revolution; Prima della Revolutiona
1964,S 25,32:1
Accattone! 1968,Ap 5,56:1

Astin, John
West Side Story 1961,O 19,39:3
That Touch of Mink 1962,Je 15,16:2
Wheeler Dealers, The 1963,N 15,25:2
Move Over Darling 1963,D 26,33:1
Candy 1968,D 18,54:2

Aston, George Major-Gen Sir K C B (Producer)
Battle of Jutland, The 1921,N 21,20:1

Aston, M Smedley (Producer)
Two-Way Stretch 1961,Ja 24,20:3

Astor, Betty
Hurrah I'm Alive 1930,Je 16,25:3
Docks of Hamburg 1930,Jl 7,22:3
O Alte Burschenherrlichkeit 1932,Je 18,9:2

Astor, Gertrude
Concert, The 1921,F 21,16:1
Wall Flower, The 1922,Je 26,16:2
Impossible Mrs Bellew, The 1922,O 23,10:1
Ne'er Do-Well, The 1923,My 1,24:3
Rupert of Hentzau 1923,Jl 9,8:4
Flaming Youth 1923,N 26,15:6
Secrets 1924,Mr 25,25:2
Charmer, The 1925,Ap 6,17:3
Wife Who Wasn't Wanted, The 1925,S 9,23:1
Satan in Sables 1925,O 15,27:3
Stage Struck 1925,N 16,19:4
Kiki 1926,Ap 6,26:4
Strong Man, The 1926,S 7,44:2
Cheerful Fraud, The 1926,D 28,17:1
Taxi Dancer, The 1927,Mr 8,18:4
Cat and the Canary, The 1927,S 10,9:4
Shanghaied 1927,S 13,36:2
Irresistible Lover, The 1927,O 19,24:4
Uncle Tom's Cabin 1927,N 5,16:2
Cohens and the Kellys In Paris, The
1928,F 6,12:3
Hit of the Show 1928,Jl 9,25:1
Butter and Egg Man, The 1928,Ag 28,27:4
Stocks and Blondes 1928,O 23,33:1

Synthetic Sin 1929,Ja 7,36:2
Fall of Eve, The 1929,Je 18,29:4
Two Weeks Off 1929,Je 24,27:1
Twin Beds 1929,Jl 15,25:1
Frozen Justice 1929,O 26,15:1
Untamed 1929,N 30,23:1
Be Yourself 1930,Mr 7,20:5
Dames Ahoy 1930,Mr 29,23:1
Hell Bound 1931,My 9,15:4
Western Limited 1932,D 12,18:4
I Have Lived 1933,S 6,24:4
Wine, Women and Song 1934,Mr 21,24:3
My Dear Secretary 1949,F 14,15:4

Astor, Junie
Lower Depths, The 1937,S 11,20:1
Club De Femmes 1937,O 20,27:2
Entente Cordiale 1939,D 26,23:2
Carnevale di Venezia, Il; Carnival of Venice, The
1940,O 11,25:2
Eternal Return, The; Eternel Retour, L'
1948,Ja 5,15:2

Astor, Mary
Beggar Maid, The 1921,S 26,18:1
Young Painter, The 1922,F 26,VI,3:1 (In
Addenda)
Bright Shawl, The 1923,Ap 23,18:3
Success 1923,Jl 10,22:5
Hollywood 1923,Jl 30,11:4
Puritan Passions 1923,O 15,15:4
Woman Proof 1923,O 30,16:1
Fighting Coward, The 1924,Mr 17,19:1
Beau Brummell 1924,Mr 31,20:1
Fighting American, The 1924,My 13,24:1
Unguarded Women 1924,Je 24,18:2
Price of a Party, The 1924,N 26,17:3
Inez From Hollywood 1924,D 16,28:1
Oh, Doctor! 1925,F 23,24:1
Enticement 1925,Mr 21,16:3
Playing With Souls 1925,Ap 20,18:1 (Incorrect in
this edition; use 1925,Ap 28,18:1 elsewhere)
Don Q, Son of Zorro 1925,Je 16,24:1
Don Juan 1926,Ag 7,6:1 (In Addenda)
Forever After 1926,N 9,31:1
Rough Riders, The 1927,Mr 16,28:2
Rose of the Golden West 1927,S 26,27:1
Two Arabian Knights 1927,O 24,24:3
Sailors' Wives 1928,F 28,18:4
Dressed to Kill 1928,Mr 12,26:1
Heart to Heart 1928,S 10,29:2
Dry Martini 1928,N 5,26:5 (In Addenda)
Romance of the Underworld 1929,Ja 7,36:2
Ladies Love Brutes 1930,My 16,20:4
Runaway Bride 1930,My 17,21:2
Holiday 1930,Jl 3,25:4
Lash, The 1931,Ja 1,31:3
Royal Bed, The 1931,Ja 31,15:1
Behind Office Doors 1931,Mr 21,15:1
Other Men's Women 1931,Ap 20,16:3
White Shoulders 1931,Je 5,26:5
Smart Woman 1931,O 12,28:2
Men of Chance 1931,D 28,22:1
Lost Squadron, The 1932,Mr 11,15:4
Successful Calamity, A 1932,S 23,22:2
Red Dust 1932,N 5,12:5
Little Giant, The 1933,My 27,11:5
Jennie Gerhardt 1933,Je 9,20:2
World Changes, The 1933,O 27,22:3
Kennel Murder Case, The 1933,O 30,14:2
Convention City 1933,D 25,28:2
Easy to Love 1934,Ja 15,12:2
Upper World 1934,My 25,25:4
Return of the Terror 1934,Jl 11,20:2
Man With two Faces, The 1934,Jl 12,20:2
Case of the Howling Dog, The 1934,O 18,26:5
I am a Thief 1935,Ja 1,24:1
Red Hot Tires 1935,Mr 1,16:3
Page Miss Glory 1935,Ag 29,25:2
Man of Iron 1935,D 7,22:2
Murder of Dr Harrigan, The 1936,Ja 21,27:5
And So They Were Married 1936,My 14,29:3
Trapped by Television 1936,Je 15,24:3
Dodsworth 1936,S 24,29:1
Lady From Nowhere 1936,D 21,19:2
Prisoner of Zenda, The 1937,S 3,12:1
Hurricane, The 1937,N 10,31:2
Paradise for Three 1938,F 16,17:1
No Time to Marry 1938,F 23,27:2
There's Always a Woman 1938,Ap 29,17:2
Woman Against Woman 1938,Ag 23,20:6
Listen, Darling 1938,N 24,37:2
Midnight 1939,Ap 6,31:1
Turnabout 1940,Jl 27,17:6
Brigham Young - Frontiersman 1940,S 21,13:2
Great Lie, The 1941,Ap 12,19:2
Maltese Falcon, The 1941,O 4,18:2
Across the Pacific 1942,S 5,9:2
Palm Beach Story, The 1942,D 11,33:1
Thousands Cheer 1943,S 14,27:1
Meet Me in St Louis 1944,N 29,20:2
Claudia and David 1946,Ag 15,19:2
Fiesta 1947,Je 27,17:3
Cynthia 1947,S 19,27:2
Desert Fury 1947,S 25,35:4

Astor, Mary— Cont
Cass Timberlane 1947,N 7,20:2
Act of Violence 1949,Ja 24,16:2
Little Women 1949,Mr 11,33:2
Any Number Can Play 1949,Jl 1,14:4
Power and The Prize, the 1956,S 27,42:1
This Happy Feeling 1958,Je 19,28:2
Stranger in my Arms 1959,Mr 4,34:2
Return to Peyton Place 1961,My 6,26:1
Youngblood Hawke 1964,N 6,30:1
Hush...Hush, Sweet Charlotte 1965,Mr 4,36:1

Astor, Raoul
Way of a Gaucho 1952,N 5,36:2

Astrologo, Pacifico
Shoe-Shine 1947,Ag 27,19:2

Astruc, A (Miscellaneous)
Respectful Prostitute, The 1957,Jl 11,21:1

Astruc, Alexandre (Director)
End of Desire 1962,Jl 10,29:2

Asturias, Carpi
Walls of Hell, The 1965,N 18,55:3

Asztalos, Bela
Age of Illusions 1967,Mr 30,55:1

Atalov, V
Nightingale 1936,N 4,41:2

Atamanov, Lev (Director)
Adventure in Odessa 1954,Je 21,19:6

Atasheva, Pera (Director)
Czechoslovakia 1946,Jl 15,21:1

Atchley, Hooper
Sante Fe Trail, The 1930,O 18,23:2
Men in her Life 1931,N 30,16:2
Secret Witness, The 1931,D 21,28:4
Hell's House 1932,F 12,24:5
Hunted Men 1938,My 21,9:2
Mr Wong, Detective 1938,N 21,14:4
Gay Caballero, The 1940,O 25,25:3

Ateinza, Edward
Romanoff and Juliet 1961,Je 9,26:1

Ates, Roscoe
South Sea Rose 1929,D 7,19:3
Big House, The 1930,Je 25,31:2
Love in the Rough 1930,S 27,21:3
Billy the Kid 1930,O 18,23:2
Cimarron 1931,Ja 27,20:5
Politics 1931,Ag 1,16:4
Too Many Cooks 1931,Ag 17,18:2
Great Lover, The 1931,Ag 24,13:4
Champ, The 1931,N 10,29:4
Big Shot, The 1932,Ja 2,14:2
Rainbow Trail, The 1932,Ja 30,13:2
Ladies of the Jury 1932,Ap 2,13:2
Love Starved 1932,Ap 15,23:1
Roadhouse Murder 1932,Ap 29,13:4
Freaks 1932,Jl 9,7:5
Hold 'Em Jail! 1932,Ag 20,7:4
What! No Beer? 1933,F 11,11:3
Lucky Devils 1933,F 20,11:5
Past of Mary Holmes, The 1933,My 1,10:3
Alice in Wonderland 1933,D 23,19:1
She Made her Bed 1934,Ap 27,25:1
People's Enemy, The 1935,Ap 30,13:7
God's Country and the Woman 1937,Ja 11,15:5
Untamed 1940,Jl 25,14:3
Captain Caution 1940,O 21,21:3
Chad Hanna 1940,D 26,23:1
Bad Men of Missouri 1941,Ag 16,18:2
One Foot in Heaven 1941,N 14,28:3
Palm Beach Story, The 1942,D 11,33:1
Stranger Wore a Gun, The 1953,Jl 30,20:3
Those Redheads From Seattle 1953,O 1,34:2

Athanas, Verne (Original Author)
Proud Ones, The 1956,Ag 11,10:2

Athens, Vi
Crime Doctor 1943,Jl 5,11:4

Athens Corps de Ballet
Shepherd's Daughter, The 1956,My 14,23:3

Atherton, Gertrude (Original Author)
Avalanche, The 1919,Je 30,16:3
Black Oxen 1924,Ja 7,23:1
Crystal Cup, The 1927,O 25,33:3
Woman Accused, The 1933,Mr 13,18:2

Atherton, Gertrude (Screenwriter)
Dont Neglect Your Wife 1921,Jl 31,VI,2:1 (In
Addenda)

Atkins, Eileen
Inadmissible Evidence 1968,Je 24,44:1

Atkins, Geoffrey
Hell's Cargo 1940,S 16,15:2
Young Mr Pitt, The 1943,Mr 11,17:1

Atkins, Gregory
Yours, Mine and Ours 1968,Ap 25,53:1

Atkins, Laurence
Pearls of the Crown, The 1938,Ap 12,26:2

Atkins, Lynnell
Yours, Mine and Ours 1968,Ap 25,53:1

Atkins, Robert
Peg of Old Drury 1936,Ap 13,15:1
Stairway to Heaven 1946,D 26,28:1
Black Magic 1949,N 9,37:2

Atkins, Thomas (Director)
Silver Streak, The 1935,Ja 16,21:1

Atkinson, Dione
Black Oxen 1924,Ja 7,23:1
Atkinson, Doris
Desirable 1934,S 15,20:5
Atkinson, Eleanor (Original Author)
Challenge to Lassie 1950,Ap 7,22:3
Greyfriars' Bobby 1961,O 12,41:4
Atkinson, Frank
Ladies' Man 1931,My 1,30:3
Cavalcade 1933,Ja 6,23:2
Sailor's Luck 1933,Mr 17,21:2
Pleasure Cruise 1933,Ap 3,13:3
Green Cockatoo, The 1947,Jl 19,10:2
Kitchen, The 1961,N 2,42:1
Atkinson, George
Conquering Power, The 1921,Jl 10,VI,2:1 (In Addenda)
Atkinson, John
Trunk, The 1962,N 1,34:3
Atkinson, Owen (Original Author)
Twenty-Mule Team 1940,My 10,26:6
Atkinson, Rosalind
Tom Jones 1963,O 8,48:1
Pumpkin Eater, The 1964,N 10,58:1
Atlas, Leopold (Miscellaneous)
Hand in Hand 1961,F 7,41:3
Atlas, Leopold (Original Author)
Wednesday's Child 1934,D 15,9:3
Atlas, Leopold (Screenwriter)
Notorious Gentleman, A 1935,F 16,9:1
Mystery of Edwin Drood, The 1935,Mr 21,27:1
Tomorrow the World 1944,D 22,12:4
Story of G I Joe 1945,O 6,9:6
Her Kind of Man 1946,My 4,10:6
Raw Deal 1948,Jl 9,11:4
My Forbidden Past 1951,Ap 26,34:2
Atouna, Mlle
Siroco 1931,N 26,37:2
Atoyedze, M
Red and White 1932,N 29,23:5
Atrache, Farid M (Producer)
Little Miss Devil 1951,D 8,9:2
Attanasio, Ugo
Mafioso 1964,Jl 1,42:1
Attaway, Ruth
President's Lady, The 1953,My 22,31:1
Young Don't Cry, The 1957,Jl 27,10:7
Porgy and Bess 1959,Je 25,20:3
Terror in the City 1966,N 9,43:4
Atteberry, Duke (Screenwriter)
Mountain Music 1937,Je 24,30:3
Tropic Holiday 1938,Je 30,21:2
I'm From Missouri 1939,Mr 23,27:1
Attenborough, Richard
In Which We Serve 1942,D 24,18:1
Journey Together 1946,Mr 4,16:5
Stairway to Heaven 1946,D 26,28:1
Smugglers, The 1948,Mr 29,17:1
Dulcimer Street 1948,N 8,24:2
Guinea Pig, The 1949,My 2,20:2
Lost People, The 1950,O 2,19:4
Operation Disaster 1951,Ja 15,13:1
Young Scarface 1951,N 8,35:2
Secret Flight 1952,Jl 3,16:2
Glory at Sea 1953,Mr 11,36:7
Eight O'Clock Walk 1955,Ap 30,10:6
Private's Progress 1956,Jl 24,19:2
Ship That Died of Shame, The 1956,Ag 21,33:2
Brothers in Law 1957,Ag 20,22:1
Baby and the Battleship, The 1957,O 1,37:2
Dunkirk 1958,S 11,42:2
Man Upstairs, The 1959,Ag 11,23:2
I'm All Right Jack 1960,Ap 26,40:2
Breakout 1960,My 9,44:3
S O S Pacific 1960,O 13,41:3
Angry Silence, The 1960,D 13,25:2
League of Gentlemen, The 1961,Ja 25,30:4
Desert Patrol 1962,Ja 18,23:5
Only Two Can Play 1962,Mr 21,33:2
Trial and Error 1962,N 17,17:2
Great Escape, The 1963,Ag 8,19:1
Third Secret, The 1964,Ap 29,27:1
Seance on a Wet Afternoon 1964,N 6,30:1
Guns at Batasi 1964,N 17,47:1
Flight of the Phoenix, The 1966,F 1,26:1
Sand Pebbles, The 1966,D 21,48:1
Doctor Dolittle 1967,D 20,55:1
Only When I Larf 1968,O 24,55:3
Bliss of Mrs Blossom, The 1968,D 12,62:6
Attenborough, Richard (Producer)
Angry Silence, The 1960,D 13,25:2
Whistle Down the Wind 1962,Ap 23,34:2
L-Shaped Room, The 1963,My 28,32:1
Seance on a Wet Afternoon 1964,N 6,30:1
Attenhofer, Elsie
Heidi 1953,D 21,27:2
Atterbury, Duke (Screenwriter)
Double or Nothing 1937,S 2,17:3
Comin' Round the Mountain 1940,S 26,27:3
Atterbury, Malcolm
Crime in the Streets 1956,My 24,27:4
Toward the Unknown 1956,S 28,24:4
From Hell to Texas 1958,Je 5,39:2

Rio Bravo 1959,Mr 19,40:2
Wild River 1960,My 27,22:1
Summer and Smoke 1961,N 17,41:1
Seven Days in May 1964,F 20,22:1
Hawaii 1966,O 11,54:1
Attiwill, Ken (Original Author)
Non-Stop New York 1937,N 29,19:2
Attwood, Bill
Hoodlum Priest, The 1961,Ap 3,28:5
Atvos, A Dorian (Screenwriter)
Merry-Go-Round of 1938 1937,N 26,27:2
Atwater, Barry
Nightmare 1956,My 12,12:7
Rack, The 1956,N 6,30:1
Pork Chop Hill 1959,My 30,9:2
Battle at Bloody Beach, The 1961,Ag 17,18:2
Sweet Bird of Youth 1962,Mr 29,28:2
Atwater, Edith
We Went to College 1936,Jl 27,20:2
Body Snatcher, The 1945,My 26,18:3
C-Man 1949,My 28,11:4
Teresa 1951,Ap 6,31:2
Sweet Smell of Success 1957,Je 28,29:2
It Happened at the World's Fair 1963,My 30,20:1
Strait Jacket 1964,Ja 23,26:1
Strange Bedfellows 1965,Mr 11,38:1
Atwater, Gladys (Original Author)
Argentine Nights 1940,O 11,25:3
In old California 1942,Je 18,25:3
American Empire 1943,Ja 14,25:4
El Paso 1949,Mr 24,35:2
Siege at Red River, The 1954,Ap 3,19:2
Naked Alibi 1954,O 2,21:2
Atwater, Gladys (Screenwriter)
Criminal Lawyer 1937,Ja 27,17:3
Man Who Found Himself, The 1937,Ap 9,19:3
Crashing Hollywood 1938,Ja 8,19:2
Crime Ring 1938,Jl 22,10:3
Parents on Trial 1939,S 18,15:5
American Empire 1943,Ja 14,25:4
First Yank into Tokyo 1945,O 25,18:2
Great Sioux Uprising, The 1953,Jl 18,6:2
Atwell, Roy
Red Hot Romance 1922,Ja 23,11:4
Grand Larceny 1922,F 27,13:4
Harvester, The 1936,Jl 4,18:2
Varsity Show 1937,S 2,17:2
People Are Funny 1946,Ja 28,15:6
Atwill, Lionel
Marriage Price, The 1919,Mr 17,13:2
Silent Witness, The 1932,F 8,21:1
Doctor X 1932,Ag 4,17:2
Vampire Bat, The 1933,Ja 23,9:1
Secret of Madame Blanche, The 1933,F 4,11:3
Mystery of the Wax Museum, The 1933,F 18,13:3
Murders in the Zoo 1933,Ap 3,13:4
Sphinx, The 1933,Jl 6,26:5
Song of Songs 1933,Jl 20,22:2
Secret of the Blue Room, The 1933,S 13,22:1
Solitaire Man, The 1933,S 23,11:5
Nana 1934,F 2,20:3
Beggars in Ermine 1934,Ap 25,25:3
Stamboul Quest 1934,Jl 14,16:6
One More River 1934,Ag 10,21:1
Age of Innocence, The 1934,O 19,27:1
Firebird, The 1934,N 15,25:2
Man Who Reclaimed his Head, The 1935,Ja 9,22:1
Mark of the Vampire 1935,My 3,23:4
Devil is a Woman, The 1935,My 4,17:2
Murder Man, The 1935,Jl 27,16:2
Rendezvous 1935,O 26,12:2
Captain Blood 1935,D 27,14:1
Lady of Secrets 1936,F 22,12:1
Absolute Quiet 1936,My 2,11:1
Till We Meet Again 1936,My 9,11:2
Road Back, The 1937,Je 18,25:2
Last Train from Madrid, The 1937,Je 19,20:2
Great Garrick, The 1937,O 25,23:1
Lancer Spy 1937,N 4,29:1
Three Comrades 1938,Je 3,17:1
Great Waltz, The 1938,N 25,19:1
Son of Frankenstein 1939,Ja 30,9:2
Three Musketeers, The 1939,F 18,12:2
Hound of the Baskervilles, The 1939,Mr 25,19:2
Gorilla, The 1939,My 28,6:2
Sun Never Sets, The 1939,Je 9,26:2
Mr Moto Takes a Vacation 1939,Je 19,12:6
Secret of Dr Kildare, The 1939,D 8,33:5
Balalaika 1939,D 15,33:2
Mad Empress, The 1940,F 15,15:1
Johnny Apollo 1940,Ap 13,21:2
Charlie Chan's Murder Cruise 1940,My 3,17:5
Girl in 313 1940,Je 14,25:3
Boom Town 1940,S 6,25:2
Great Profile, The 1940,O 18,25:1
Man Made Monster 1941,Mr 19,25:4
Mad Doctor of Market Street, The 1942,Ja 5,21:5
To Be or not to Be 1942,Mr 7,13:2
Strange Case of Dr Rx 1942,Mr 28,11:2
Ghost of Frankenstein, The 1942,Ap 4,19:2
Pardon my Sarong 1942,Ag 27,15:1

Atwill, Lionel— Cont
Cairo 1942,N 6,27:2
Night Monster 1942,N 30,18:5
Sherlock Holmes and the Secret Weapon 1943,Ja 5,15:2
Frankenstein Meets the Wolf Man 1943,Mr 6,8:3
House of Frankenstein 1944,D 16,19:3
Crime Incorporated 1945,Je 23,9:7
House of Dracula 1945,D 22,16:3
Atwill, Lionel (Miscellaneous)
Mad Empress, The 1940,F 15,15:1
Atwood, Richard
This Freedom 1923,N 28,15:1
Auber, Brigitte
Under the Paris Sky 1952,My 6,35:1
To Catch a Thief 1955,Ag 5,14:2
Auber (Composer)
Fra Diavolo 1931,N 23,22:1
Auber (Original Author)
Devil's Brother, The 1933,Je 10,16:4
Auberge, Maurice (Miscellaneous)
Anatomy of a Marriage; My Days With Jean Marc; My Nights With Francoise 1964,O 27,42:2
Auberge, Maurice (Screenwriter)
Paris Frills 1946,N 25,38:3
Bed, The (The Billet); Billet, The (The Bed) 1955,Je 8,26:4
Doctors, The 1956,Ag 7,19:2
Port of Desire 1960,N 3,49:2
Aubert, Carmelita
Mercedes 1935,My 14,17:5
Aubert, Georges
Mademoiselle 1966,Ag 2,23:1
Aubert, Jane
Possession, La 1929,D 1,X,8:6
Aubert, Jeanne
Symphonie d'Amour 1946,Mr 11,19:2
Senechal the Magnificent 1958,O 14,44:1
Aubert, Lenore
They Got Me Covered 1943,Mr 5,20:2
Action in Arabia 1944,F 19,18:7
Having Wonderful Crime 1945,Ap 13,15:2
Wife of Monte Cristo, The 1946,Ap 8,31:2
Catman of Paris, The 1946,Jl 13,12:2
Other Love, The 1947,My 15,32:4
I Wonder Who's Kissing Her Now 1947,Jl 24,27:2
Abbott and Costello Meet Frankenstein 1948,Jl 29,17:2
Abbott and Costello Meet the Killer Boris Karloff 1949,S 19,18:3
Barbary Pirate 1949,O 28,29:3
Aubiberti, Jacques (Screenwriter)
Poupee, La 1963,Ag 28,39:1
Aubin, Henry
Dark Sands 1938,Ag 17,23:4
Aubray, Laurence
Face to the Wind 1951,Ja 16,34:2
Aubrey, Anne
Killers of Kilimanjaro 1960,Ap 7,46:1
Hellions, The 1962,Mr 15,28:2
Aubrey, Dennis
Legend of William Tell, The 1935,O 2,27:1
Aubrey, Diane
Haunted Strangler, The 1958,Jl 4,15:3
Aubrey, James
Women Men Marry 1931,Jl 13,13:5
Lord of the Flies 1963,Ag 20,37:1
Aubrey, Jimmy
Make a Million 1935,N 9,19:3
Swamp Woman 1941,D 27,15:2
Aubry, Cecile
Black Rose, The 1950,S 2,11:2
Manon 1950,D 26,19:1
Aubry, Simon
Poil de Carotte 1933,My 26,24:2
Aubuchon, Jacques
So Big 1953,O 22,34:2
Beneath the 12-Mile Reef 1953,D 17,52:2
Silver Chalice, The 1954,D 27,22:5
Big Boodle, The 1957,Mr 12,38:1
Way to the Gold, The 1957,My 11,24:6
Gun Glory 1957,Jl 20,8:7
Wild and Wonderful 1964,Je 11,27:4
Auburn, Dennis D
Captain Blood 1935,D 27,14:1
Auburn, Jane
Her Love Story 1924,O 7,26:1
Auclair, Michel
Beauty and the Beast 1947,D 24,12:2
Damned, The; Maudits, Les 1948,Ap 26,27:2
Manon 1950,D 26,19:1
Justice Is Done 1953,Mr 3,23:2
Anita Garibaldi 1954,Mr 19,19:4
Holiday for Henrietta 1955,Ja 25,21:1
One Step to Eternity 1955,O 3,22:2
Funny Face 1957,Mr 29,16:1
Mistress for the Summer, A 1964,Mr 28,13:5
Symphony for a Massacre 1965,My 28,40:1
Audiard, Michel (Miscellaneous)
There's Always a Price Tag 1958,My 26,25:2
Monkey in Winter 1963,F 1,7:2

Audiard, Michel (Screenwriter)
Mr Peek-A-Boo 1951,S 19,37:1
Inspector Maigret 1958,O 9,47:1
Possessors, The 1959,Jl 21,24:1
Speaking of Murder 1959,O 12,14:1
Babette Goes to War 1960,Je 8,46:1
Rue de Paris 1960,D 23,14:3
Love and the Frenchwoman; (Francaise et l'Amour, La) 1961,F 28,38:2
Night Affair 1961,O 13,27:1
Magnificent Tramp, The 1962,Ap 25,30:1
Money, Money, Money 1962,Jl 18,20:1
Any Number Can Win 1963,O 9,47:2
Devil and the 10 Commandments, The (Episode 4) 1963,O 15,44:1
Devil and the 10 Commandments, The (Episode 3) 1963,O 15,44:1
Devil and the 10 Commandments, The (Episode 7) 1963,O 15,44:1
Devil and the 10 Commandments, The (Episode 1) 1963,O 15,44:1
Devil and the 10 Commandments, The (Episode 2) 1963,O 15,44:1
Devil and the 10 Commandments, The (Episode 6) 1963,O 15,44:1
Devil and the 10 Commandments, The (Episode 5) 1963,O 15,44:1
Taxi for Tobruk 1965,Mr 30,52:1
Greed in the Sun 1965,Ag 19,35:3
Great Spy Chase, The 1966,O 6,56:4
Audiberti, Jacques (Original Author)
Poupee, La 1963,Ag 28,39:1
Audiero, Gaitano
Summertime 1955,Je 22,25:1
Audley, Eleanor
Pretty Baby 1950,S 23,11:2
Gambling House 1951,Mr 19,23:2
Full of Life 1957,F 13,38:1
Second Time Around, The 1961,D 23,16:1
Audley, Maxine
Sleeping Tiger, The 1954,O 9,8:7
Barretts of Wimpole Street, The 1957,Ja 18,15:3
Prince and the Showgirl 1957,Je 14,22:2
Dunkirk 1958,S 11,42:2
Trials of Oscar Wilde, The 1960,Je 28,26:1
They all Died Laughing 1964,Mr 16,37:2
Battle of the Villa Fiorita, The 1965,My 27,28:1
Audley, Michael (Director)
Mark of the Hawk, The 1958,Mr 6,32:1
Audouard, Yvan (Screenwriter)
Crazy in the Noodle 1957,D 15,45:4
Audouy, Pierre (Producer)
Fire Under Her Skin 1958,Je 28,13:6
Audran, Stephane
Landru 1963,Ap 10,31:1
Third Lover, The 1963,Je 25,23:3
Bonnes Femmes, Les 1966,My 13,32:1
Champagne Murders, The 1968,Ap 25,53:1
Biches, Les 1968,S 27,34:1
Audret, Pascale
Eye for an Eye, An 1961,F 10,19:1
Lafayette 1963,Ap 11,29:1
Two Are Guilty 1964,F 29,12:1
Audrey Share's English Folk Dancers
World Dances 1954,N 8,24:6
Audry, Colette (Screenwriter)
Battle of the Rails; (Bataille Du Rail) 1949,D 27,27:2
Audry, Jacqueline (Director)
Gigi 1950,Ja 31,20:2
Minne 1951,Ap 17,35:2
Pit of Loneliness 1954,Ap 9,19:2
Mitsou 1958,Ap 15,42:5
Auen, Carl
Horst Wessel 1939,Mr 4,18:5
AUER
See Also OUR
Auer, Florence
Heart of a Siren, The 1925,Ap 8,24:3
Beautiful City, The 1925,N 23,25:4
That Royle Girl 1926,Ja 4,33:1
State of the Union 1948,Ap 23,28:1
Auer, John (Director)
Una Vida Por Otra 1933,F 11,11:3
Vida por Otra, Una 1933,F 11,11:3
Su Ultima Cancion 1934,My 9,23:4
Crime of Dr Crespi, The 1936,Ja 13,14:3
Invisible Enemy 1938,Ap 30,18:2
I Stand Accused 1939,Ja 5,17:1
S O S Tidal Wave 1939,Je 22,19:3
Calling All Marines 1939,O 26,27:2
Thou Shalt Not Kill 1940,Ja 8,11:2
Women in War 1940,My 30,21:2
Hit Parade of 1941 1940,D 5,33:2
Man Betrayed, A 1941,Mr 27,29:5
Johnny Doughboy 1943,My 6,25:3
Tahiti Honey 1943,My 13,17:2
Seven Days Ashore 1944,Ap 26,24:7
Music in Manhattan 1944,O 7,11:2
Pan-Americana 1945,Mr 23,13:2
Flame, The 1948,F 20,19:2
I, Jane Doe 1948,Jl 5,8:4
Angel on the Amazon 1948,D 27,16:4

Thunderbirds 1953,Mr 12,24:4
City That Never Sleeps 1953,Ag 8,14:2
Hell's Half Acre 1954,F 27,11:3
Eternal Sea, The 1955,Je 10,16:2
Auer, John H (Original Author)
Crime of Dr Crespi, The 1936,Ja 13,14:3
Pan-Americana 1945,Mr 23,13:2
Auer, John H (Producer)
Crime of Dr Crespi, The 1936,Ja 13,14:3
Seven Days Ashore 1944,Ap 26,24:7
Music in Manhattan 1944,O 7,11:2
Pan-Americana 1945,Mr 23,13:2
Flame, The 1948,F 20,19:2
Angel on the Amazon 1948,D 27,16:4
City That Never Sleeps 1953,Ag 8,14:2
Hell's Half Acre 1954,F 27,11:3
Auer, Ludwig
Drei Kaiserjaeger 1935,Mr 16,19:1
Auer, Mischa
Something Always Happens 1928,My 21,25:1
Marquis Preferred 1929,Ja 21,18:4
Benson Murder Case, The 1930,Ap 12,23:1
Inside the Lines 1930,Jl 5,17:4
Just Imagine 1930,N 22,21:3
Women Love Once 1931,Je 27,20:3
Unholy Garden, The 1931,O 29,27:1
Yellow Ticket, The 1931,O 31,22:2
Delicious 1931,D 26,15:5
Midnight Patrol, The 1932,My 7,11:5
No Greater Love 1932,My 14,11:5
Scarlet Dawn 1932,N 4,25:4
Dangerously Yours 1933,F 23,20:3
Sucker Money 1933,Ap 7,22:5
Infernal Machine 1933,Ap 8,16:3
Corruption 1933,Je 20,22:7
After Tonight 1933,N 3,23:2
Cradle Song 1933,N 20,18:2
Girl Without a Room 1933,D 7,26:3
Wharf Angel 1934,Ap 21,12:1
Stamboul Quest 1934,Jl 14,16:6
Bulldog Drummond Strikes Back 1934,Ag 16,20:2
Mystery Woman 1935,Ja 9,22:2
Lives of a Bengal Lancer, The 1935,Ja 12,12:2
Clive of India 1935,Ja 18,29:1
Murder in the Fleet 1935,Je 3,22:2
House of a Thousand Candles, The 1936,Ap 2,29:2
One Rainy Afternoon 1936,My 14,29:2
Princess Comes Across, The 1936,Je 4,27:2
My Man Godfrey 1936,S 19,18:1 (Incorrect in this edition; use 1936,S 18,18:1 elsewhere)
Gay Desperado, The 1936,O 9,31:4
Winterset 1936,D 4,31:1
That Girl From Paris 1937,Ja 1,19:1
Three Smart Girls 1937,Ja 25,22:2
Top of the Town 1937,Mr 27,19:2
We Have our Moments 1937,Ap 30,17:3
Pick a Star 1937,My 28,17:2
Marry the Girl 1937,Jl 31,6:2
Vogues of 1938 1937,Ag 20,21:1
100 Men and a Girl 1937,S 18,15:2
Merry-Go-Round of 1938 1937,N 26,27:2
It's all Yours 1938,Ja 7,15:3
Rage of Paris 1938,Jl 2,10:2
You Can't Take It With You 1938,S 2,21:2
Service de Luxe 1938,O 24,13:2
Little Tough Guys in Society 1938,N 21,14:4
Sweethearts 1938,D 23,16:2
East Side of Heaven 1939,My 5,29:3
Unexpected Father 1939,Ag 11,12:2
Destry Rides Again 1939,N 30,25:1
Alias the Deacon 1940,My 14,27:5
Sandy Is a Lady 1940,Je 28,22:2
Public Deb No 1 1940,S 18,19:2
Spring Parade 1940,O 4,29:2
Seven Sinners 1940,N 18,23:2
Trail of the Vigilantes 1940,D 7,13:2
Flame of New Orleans, The 1941,Ap 26,20:2
Hold That Ghost 1941,Ag 8,13:3
Moonlight in Hawaii 1941,O 10,26:6
Hellzapoppin 1941,D 26,21:4
Twin Beds 1942,My 1,23:4
Around the World 1943,N 25,39:2
Lady in the Dark 1944,F 23,17:1
Up in Mabel's Room 1944,Ap 22,8:6
Royal Scandal, A 1945,Ap 12,19:2
Brewster's Millions 1945,Ap 27,23:2
And Then There Were None 1945,N 1,20:2
Sentimental Journey 1946,Mr 7,33:2
She Wrote the Book 1946,Je 20,20:3
Sofia 1948,S 4,8:7
Sky Is Red, The 1952,My 27,30:2
Monte Carlo Story, The 1958,F 13,23:2
Mam'zelle Pigalle 1958,Ap 19,10:4
Foxiest Girl in Paris 1958,S 20,10:6
Dog, a Mouse and a Sputnik, A; Pied, a Cheval et un Sputnik, A 1960,N 1,46:2
Mr Arkadin 1962,O 12,26:1
Christmas That Almost Wasn't 1966,N 24,65:2
Auerbach, George (Original Author)
His Brother's Wife 1936,Ag 15,6:2

Auffay, Patrick
400 Blows, The; (Les Quatre Cents Coups) 1959,N 17,41:1
Auger, Claudine
In the French Style 1963,S 19,23:1
Thunderball 1965,D 22,23:1
Yo Yo 1967,Mr 1,50:1
Triple Cross 1967,Jl 20,20:2
Treasure of San Gennaro 1968,F 27,36:1
Devil in Love, The 1968,Jl 4,13:4
Killing Game, The 1968,Ag 27,36:1
Auger, Germaine
Rothchild 1938,O 12,35:2
August, Adelle
Women's Prison 1955,F 3,18:5
August, Edwin
Over my Dead Body 1942,D 26,15:2
August, Helen (Screenwriter)
Misadventures of Merlin Jones, The 1964,Mr 26,40:4
Monkey's Uncle, The 1965,Ag 19,35:4
August, Kim
No Way to Treat a Lady 1968,Mr 21,56:1
August, Tom (Screenwriter)
Misadventures of Merlin Jones, The 1964,Mr 26,40:4
Monkey's Uncle, The 1965,Ag 19,35:4
Auila, Lucha Maria
Alla en el Rancho Chico; Out on the Little Ranch 1939,F 25,19:3
Auld, Aggie
Hawaii Calls 1938,Ap 29,17:2
Aulin, Ewa
Candy 1968,D 18,54:2
Aulinger, Elise
S A Mann Brand 1934,My 28,16:2
Ehestreik 1935,Ag 31,16:3
Golden Plaque, The 1963,Ag 10,8:6
Ault, Marie
Woman to Woman 1924,Ap 1,19:3
Kitty 1929,Je 11,27:2
Fanny Hawthorn 1929,N 11,20:2
Major Barbara 1941,My 15,27:1
Love on the Dole 1945,O 13,11:2
Aumont, Genevieve
Affair to Remember, An 1957,Jl 20,8:5
Aumont, Jean-Pierre
Maria Chapdelaine 1935,S 25,18:2
Luc Aux Dames 1936,Ja 15,14:4
Dark Eyes 1938,Ap 19,24:5
Flight Into Darkness (L'Equipage) 1938,O 17,12:1
Bizarre, Bizarre 1939,Mr 21,27:2
Song of the Street 1939,S 5,21:2
Hotel du Nord 1940,D 30,21:2
Great Temptation, The 1942,Jl 10,13:3
Assignment in Brittany 1943,Ap 22,31:2
Cross of Lorraine, The 1943,D 3,27:4
Three Hours 1944,O 30,16:5
Heartbeat 1946,My 11,22:4
Song of Scheherazade 1947,F 27,26:2
Siren of Atlantis 1949,Ag 22,13:1
Life Begins Tomorrow 1952,N 18,37:2
Lili 1953,Mr 11,36:7
Gay Adventure, The 1954,S 16,35:7
Hilda Crane 1956,My 3,35:2
Royal Affairs in Versailles 1957,Mr 9,16:1
Seventh Sin, The 1957,Je 29,10:6
John Paul Jones 1959,Je 17,39:1
Enemy General, The 1960,O 20,42:2
Devil at 4 O'Clock, The 1961,O 19,39:3
7 Capital Sins (Pride); Pride (7 Capital Sins) 1963,Ja 17,5:2
Five Miles to Midnight 1963,Mr 21,8:6
Aumont, Tina
Partner 1968,S 24,52:2
Aurain, Mark (Miscellaneous)
Tales of Paris (The Tale of Ella); Tale of Ella, The (Tales of Paris) 1962,Ag 27,18:1
Auray, Jacques d'
Humming Bird, The 1924,Ja 14,2:1
Four Horsemen of the Apocalypse, The 1926,S 27,27:3
Aureil, Katherine (Screenwriter)
Of Love and Lust (On Payment); On Payment (Of Love and Lust) 1959,My 26,31:2
Of Love and Lust (Doll's House, A); Doll's House, A (Of Love and Lust) 1959,My 26,31:2
Aureil, Tage (Screenwriter)
Of Love and Lust (Doll's House, A); Doll's House, A (Of Love and Lust) 1959,My 26,31:2
Of Love and Lust (On Payment); On Payment (Of Love and Lust) 1959,My 26,31:2
Aurel, Jean (Miscellaneous)
Over There, 1914-1918 1965,Mr 11,38:2
Aurel, Jean (Screenwriter)
Parisienne, La 1958,Jl 31,27:1
Night Watch, The; Trou, Le 1964,My 27,46:1
Aurel, Jean-Claude (Original Author)
Tempest in the Flesh 1957,Ja 19,12:2
Aureli, Andrea
Last of the Vikings 1962,S 27,33:4

Aurenche, Jean (Miscellaneous)
Forbidden Games 1952,D 9,43:2
Proud and the Beautiful, The 1956,My 29,32:2
Aurenche, Jean (Original Author)
Red Inn, The 1954,Je 8,25:2
Daughters of Destiny (Jeanne); Jeanne (Daughters of Destiny) 1954,Jl 6,19:1
Aurenche, Jean (Screenwriter)
Courier of Lyons, The 1938,Je 3,17:1
Hotel du Nord 1940,D 30,21:2
Symphonie Pastorale 1948,S 14,34:3
Devil in the Flesh 1949,My 10,29:2
Walls of Malapaga, The 1950,Mr 21,34:2
Sylvie and the Phantom 1950,O 16,30:5
God Needs Men 1951,Mr 27,35:1
Oh, Amelia 1951,D 3,22:2
Seven Deadly Sins (Pride); Pride (The Seven Deadly Sins) 1953,My 12,31:3
Seven Deadly Sins, The (The Eighth Sin); Eighth Sin, The (The Seven Deadly Sins) 1953,My 12,31:3
Seven Deadly Sins, The (Lust); Lust (The Seven Deadly Sins) 1953,My 12,31:3
Daughters of Destiny (Jeanne); Jeanne (Daughters of Destiny) 1954,Jl 6,19:1
Game of Love, The 1954,D 15,41:1
Proud and the Beautiful, The 1956,My 29,32:2
Four Bags Full 1957,S 5,32:1
Gervaise 1957,N 12,46:1
Hunchback of Notre Dame, The 1957,D 12,35:1
Rouge et Noir 1958,Ap 9,42:1
Love Is my Profession 1959,Ap 28,41:1
Green Mare, The; Jument Verte, La 1961,O 24,41:2
Enough Rope 1966,Jl 15,34:3
This Special Friendship 1967,N 8,56:1
Oldest Profession, The (Paris Today); Paris Today (The Oldest Profession) 1968,N 8,42:1
Auric, Georges (Composer)
Orage 1938,D 12,26:2
Mystery of Picasso, The 1957,O 8,41:2
Auriol, Jean-Georges (Miscellaneous)
Children of Chaos 1950,Ap 20,37:2
Auritano, Alberto
Pirates of Capri, The 1949,D 26,33:5
Auritano, Mario
Pirates of Capri, The 1949,D 26,33:5
Aurora
Chucho el Roto 1935,Mr 30,11:3
Phantom Lady 1944,F 18,15:2
Aurthur, Robert Alan (Original Author)
Edge of the City 1957,Ja 30,33:2
Spring Reunion 1957,My 6,25:2
Aurthur, Robert Alan (Screenwriter)
Edge of the City 1957,Ja 30,33:2
Warlock 1959,My 1,34:1
Grand-Prix 1966,D 22,40:1
For Love of Ivy 1968,Jl 18,26:1
Aussey, Germaine
A Nous la Liberte 1932,Ja 10,VIII,5:1
Nous, la Liberte, A 1932,My 18,25:2
Golem, The 1937,Mr 22,27:2
Pearls of the Crown, The 1938,Ap 12,26:2
AUSTEN
See Also AUSTIN
Austen, Ray
Loneliness of the Long Distance Runner, The 1962,O 9,44:1
Auster, Islin (Original Author)
Mayor of Hell, The 1933,Jl 1,16:5
Auster, Islin (Producer)
Navy Comes Through, The 1942,N 12,30:3
Suspect, The 1945,F 1,18:5
Auster, Islin (Screenwriter)
Bride for Sale 1949,N 21,29:4 (In Addenda)
AUSTIN
See Also AUSTEN
Austin, Alan
Pay or Die 1960,My 27,22:2
Austin, Albert
Suds 1920,Je 28,13:2
Austin, Anne (Original Author)
Wicked Woman, A 1935,Ja 1,24:1
Austin, Burt
Cat Ballou 1965,Je 25,36:1
Austin, Charles
Another Dawn 1937,Je 18,25:3
Austin, Charlotte
Farmer Takes a Wife, The 1953,Je 13,11:2
Gorilla at Large 1954,Je 12,13:2
Desiree 1954,N 18,42:1
Daddy Long Legs 1955,My 6,17:5
How to be Very, Very Popular 1955,Jl 23,10:1
Austin, Clare
Abandon Ship 1957,Ap 18,35:1
Austin, F Britten (Original Author)
Last Outpost, The 1935,O 5,18:2
Austin, Frank
Sea Horses 1926,F 23,26:5
Terror, The 1928,Ag 16,25:3
Swamp Water 1941,N 17,15:2

Austin, Gene
Sadie McKee 1934,My 18,18:3 (Incorrect in this edition; use 1934,My 19,18:3 elsewhere)
Gift of Gab 1934,S 26,17:6
Austin, Gene (Composer)
Klondike Annie 1936,Mr 12,18:2
Three for the Show 1955,F 25,16:1
Austin, George
Monster, The 1925,F 16,24:1
Austin, Harold
Love Master, The 1924,My 19,14:2
Austin, Harold (Producer)
Monster of the Deep 1931,My 18,21:2
Eat 'Em Alive 1933,N 6,24:4
Austin, J W
Hangover Square 1945,F 8,15:2
Austin, Jerry
Single Wives 1924,Jl 29,9:2
Sundown 1924,D 1,17:3
Regular Fellow, A 1925,O 5,25:2
Saratoga Trunk 1945,N 22,39:2
Adventures of Don Juan 1948,D 25,10:1
Austin, Leslie
Democracy, The Vision Restored 1920,Ag 25,6:4
Let Not Man Put Asunder 1924,Ja 15,16:1
Sandra 1924,D 22,20:2
Young Man of Manhattan 1930,Ap 19,15:1
Austin, Lois
Swamp Woman 1941,D 27,15:2
Spider Woman Strikes Back, The 1946,Mr 23,8:3
Night Unto Night 1949,Je 11,11:2
Mom and Dad 1957,Ja 31,21:1
Austin, Pam
Kissin' Cousins 1964,Ap 2,28:3
Perils of Pauline, The 1967,Ag 3,26:3
Austin, Phyllis Konstam
Crowning Experience, The 1960,O 24,25:3
Austin, Ronald (Original Author)
Happening, The 1967,My 18,56:3
Austin, Ronald (Screenwriter)
Happening, The 1967,My 18,56:3
Austin, Vivian
Destiny 1945,F 3,16:5
She Gets her Man 1945,F 9,20:5
Men in her Diary 1945,S 24,16:5
Austin, William
Ruggles of Red Gap 1923,S 10,15:4
Reckless Age, The 1924,Je 10,24:4
Garden of Weeds, The 1924,N 4,24:1
Seven Days 1925,Ag 31,19:3
Best People 1925,O 21,21:3
What Happened to Jones 1926,F 9,22:1
Her big Night 1926,O 13,21:1
Flaming Forest, The 1926,N 22,28:3
Ritzy 1927,Je 20,25:3
Swim, Girl, Swim 1927,S 5,13:2
Silk Stockings 1927,N 29,31:1
Honeymoon Hate 1927,D 31,31:1
Drums of Love 1928,Ja 25,20:4
Red Hair 1928,Mr 26,26:2
Fifty-Fifty Girl, The 1928,My 14,25:1
Just Married 1928,Ag 13,23:2
Some One to Love 1928,D 4,29:1
What a Night! 1928,D 24,11:1
Insidious Dr Fu Manchu, The 1929,Jl 22,17:1
Illusion 1929,S 28,17:3
Sweetie 1929,O 26,15:1
Marriage Playground, The 1929,D 14,22:4
Man From Blankley's, The 1930,Mr 29,23:1
New Adventures of Dr Fu Manchu, The 1930,My 3,23:1
Flirting Widow, The 1930,Ag 2,16:4
Let's Go Native 1930,Ag 30,7:4
Tailor-Made Man, A 1931,Ap 25,23:4
Chances 1931,Je 12,27:1
Corsair 1931,N 19,27:5
Private Life of Henry VIII, The 1933,O 13,25:2
Alice in Wonderland 1933,D 23,19:1
Goose and the Gander, The 1935,S 12,29:2
$1,000 a Minute 1935,D 21,11:1
Renfrew of the Royal Mounted 1937,N 3,29:4
Doctor Rhythm 1938,My 19,25:2
Adventures of Sherlock Holmes, The 1939,S 2,20:1
Charley's Aunt 1941,Ag 2,18:2
Return of the Vampire, The 1944,Ja 29,10:1
Autant Lara, Claude
Ciboulette 1936,S 12,20:2
Autant-Lara, Claude (Director)
Ciboulette 1934,Ja 7,X,4:2
Love Story 1949,Je 27,18:4
Sylvie and the Phantom 1950,O 16,30:5
Oh, Amelia 1951,D 3,22:2
Seven Deadly Sins (Pride); Pride (The Seven Deadly Sins) 1953,My 12,31:3
Red Inn, The 1954,Je 8,25:2
Game of Love, The 1954,D 15,41:1
Four Bags Full 1957,S 5,32:1
Rouge et Noir 1958,Ap 9,42:1
Love Is my Profession 1959,Ap 28,41:1
Green Mare, The; Jument Verte, La 1961,O 24,41:2
Story of Monte Cristo, The 1962,N 7,48:1

Autant-Lara, Claude (Director)— Cont
Enough Rope 1966,Jl 15,34:3
Oldest Profession, The (Paris Today); Paris Today (The Oldest Profession) 1968,N 8,42:1
Autant-Lara, Claude (Producer)
Love Story 1949,Je 27,18:4
Green Mare, The; Jument Verte, La 1961,O 24,41:2
Autant-Lara, Claude (Screenwriter)
Love Story 1949,Je 27,18:4
Seven Deadly Sins (Pride); Pride (The Seven Deadly Sins) 1953,My 12,31:3
Game of Love, The 1954,D 15,41:1
Auten, Harold Captain (Miscellaneous)
Q Ships 1928,S 17,27:1
Q Ships 1928,S 17,27:1
Battle of Mons, The 1929,Mr 18,30:6
Savage Gold 1933,Jl 25,17:2
Auten, Harold Captain (Screenwriter)
Q Ships 1928,S 17,27:1
Autry, Gene
Boots and Saddles 1937,N 8,19:2
Manhattan Merry-Go-Round 1937,D 31,9:3
Shooting High 1940,Ap 12,19:2
Melody Ranch 1940,D 26,23:3
Sioux City Sue 1947,Jl 23,19:3
Autry, Gene (Composer)
Under Western Stars 1938,Je 25,7:3
Autry, Gene (Miscellaneous)
Manhattan Merry-Go-Round 1937,D 31,9:3
Auzat, Maurice
We Lived Through Buchenwald 1947,Jl 24,27:3
Auzinger, Theodor
Schimmelkrieg von Holledau, Der 1938,Jl 19,15:4
Avakian, Aram (Director)
Lad: A Dog 1963,My 2,40:2
Avalon, Frankie
Alamo, The 1960,O 27,45:1
Voyage to the Bottom of the Sea 1961,Jl 20,32:2
Sail a Crooked Ship 1962,F 3,12:6
Drums of Africa 1963,Jl 4,9:1
Beach Party 1963,S 26,40:2
Castilian, The 1963,O 3,31:1
Muscle Beach Party 1964,My 28,40:1
Bikini Beach 1964,S 17,52:6
I'll Take Sweden 1965,Ag 12,30:4
Sergeant Deadhead 1965,O 23,17:3
Ski Party 1965,O 23,17:3
Dr Goldfoot and the Bikini Machine 1966,F 17,29:3
Fireball 500 1966,N 24,65:4
How to Stuff a Wild Bikini 1967,Ja 12,48:1
Avalon Boys, The
Way out West 1937,My 4,29:1
Avanzo, Renzo
Paisan 1948,Mr 30,26:2
Avanzo, Renzo (Screenwriter)
Golden Coach, The 1954,Ja 22,30:2
Avdeyeva, L
Boris Godunov 1956,Ja 23,21:4
Tsar's Bride, The 1966,Mr 12,13:2
Avdiushko, Viktor
Heroes of Shipka 1956,S 3,10:5
Fathers and Sons 1960,D 26,27:2
Peace to Him Who Enters 1963,N 25,23:5
Red and the White, The 1968,S 21,26:1
Avedon, Doe
Deep in my Heart 1954,D 10,35:2
Avellana, Bert
No Man is an Island 1962,O 11,49:2
Avellana, Lamberto V (Director)
Badjao 1962,S 21,35:1
Averback, Hy
Benny Goodman Story 1956,F 22,22:1
Averback, Hy (Director)
Chamber of Horrors 1966,O 20,52:5
Where Were You When the Lights Went Out? 1968,Ag 9,30:2
I Love You Alice B Toklas! 1968,O 8,40:1
Averback, Hy (Producer)
Chamber of Horrors 1966,O 20,52:5
Averill, Anthony
Torchy Blane in Panama 1938,Ap 18,11:1
When Were You Born? 1938,Je 9,27:2
Mystery House 1938,Je 29,15:5
Racket Busters 1938,Ag 11,13:1
Broadway Musketeers 1938,O 14,27:1
Girls on Probation 1938,O 21,27:3
Heart of the North 1938,D 21,29:2
Blackwell's Island 1939,Mr 2,19:1
Secret Service of the Air 1939,Mr 2,19:2
Averin, Y
Fate of Man 1961,Jl 11,28:1
Averman, Jack
Johnny One-Eye 1950,N 17,31:2
Aversa, Andre
Pardon my French 1952,Mr 31,17:2
Avery, Bettye
They Got Me Covered 1943,Mr 5,20:2
Avery, Brian
Graduate, The 1967,D 22,44:4
Avery, Margaret
Curtain Up 1953,F 2,17:3

Avery, Patricia
Annie Laurie 1927,My 12,24:3
Alex The Great 1928,My 1,33:3
Avery, Phyllis
Ruby Gentry 1952,D 26,20:2
Best Things in Life are Free, The 1956,S 29,12:2
Avery, Stephen Morehouse (Original Author)
Annapolis Farewell 1935,Ag 24,18:2
I'll Take Romance 1937,D 17,33:2
Hard To Get 1938,N 14,15:2
Avery, Stephen Morehouse (Screenwriter)
Our Little Girl 1935,Je 7,24:4
Gay Deception, The 1935,O 11,31:1
One Rainy Afternoon 1936,My 14,29:2
Georgeous Hussy, The 1936,S 5,7:1
Four Mothers 1941,Ja 11,12:7
Male Animal, The 1942,Mr 28,11:1
Deep Valley 1947,Ag 23,7:2
Woman in White, The 1948,My 8,12:2
Every Girl Should be Married 1948,D 24,14:2
Avery, Ted
Night People 1954,Mr 13,11:2
Avery, Tol
I'll Cry Tomorrow 1956,Ja 13,18:1
Twist Around the Clock 1962,Ja 27,13:4
Hotel 1967,Ja 20,27:1
Avery, Val
Harder They Fall, The 1956,My 10,26:3
Edge of the City 1957,Ja 30,33:2
Long, Hot Summer, The 1958,Ap 4,16:1
Too Late Blues 1962,Mr 1,27:4
Hud 1963,My 29,36:1
Hallelujah Trail, The 1965,Jl 2,17:1
Nevada Smith 1966,Je 24,28:1 (Incorrect in this edition; use 1966,Je 30,28:1 elsewhere)
Hombre 1967,Mr 22,41:1
Faces 1968,S 23,42:4
Avidsen, John
Greenwich Village Story 1963,Jl 12,14:3
Avila, Lucha Maria
Juntos pero no Revueltos; United but not Mixed 1939,O 23,15:3
Avins, Lorraine
Small Hours, The 1962,Ag 14,34:1
Avitabile, Enzo (Screenwriter)
Cliff of Sin, The 1952,N 22,16:5
Avlonitis, Basil
Fortune Teller, The 1961,My 22,37:5
We Have Only one Life 1963,Je 24,21:4
Avlonitis, Vassilis
Horse and Carriage 1958,Je 30,23:3
Hurdy Gurdy, The 1958,S 22,27:1
Avonde, Richard
Captain Carey U S A 1950,Mr 30,40:5
Cyrano De Bergerac 1950,N 17,31:2
Avraham, Anshel
Dream no More 1950,Ja 6,25:2
Avramenko, V (Producer)
Cossacks in Exile 1939,Ja 28,19:2
Avril, Mag
My Wife's Husband 1965,Ja 27,26:1
Awaji, Keiko
Bridges at Toko-Ri, The 1955,Ja 21,20:2
Stray Dog 1964,Mr 4,32:7
Utamaro, Painter of Women 1964,D 2,57:1
Awashima, Chikage
Human Condition, The 1959,D 16,56:1
Utamaro, Painter of Women 1964,D 2,57:1
Awazi, Keiko
When a Woman Ascends the Stairs 1963,Je 26,36:4
Awdjuschko, Viktor
Naked Among the Wolves 1967,Ap 19,54:7
Awes, Alena
South Sea Woman 1953,Je 4,33:6
Axberg, Eddie
Here's Your Life 1968,D 20,60:1
Axberg, Ric
Doll, The 1964,Ja 14,27:1
Axel, Gabriel (Director)
Girls are Willing, The 1959,My 11,30:1
Crazy Paradise 1965,Ag 11,41:2
Hagbard and Signe 1968,My 17,56:1
Axel, Gabriel (Screenwriter)
Crazy Paradise 1965,Ag 11,41:2
Axel-Branner, Per (Director)
Kryss med Albertina, Paa; Cruise in the Albertina, A 1940,Mr 25,11:3
Axel-Branner, Per (Original Author)
Kryss med Albertina, Paa; Cruise in the Albertina, A 1940,Mr 25,11:3
Axelbank, Herman (Producer)
Tsar to Lenim 1937,Mr 9,27:2
Tsar to Lenin 1966,My 27,33:3
Axelle, Carl
Chicago After Midnight 1928,Mr. 6,20:3
Axelrod, George (Director)
Lord Love a Duck 1966,F 22,14:6
Secret Life of an American Wife, The 1968,Je 26,42:2
Axelrod, George (Original Author)
Seven Year Itch, The 1955,Je 4,9:1
Will Success Spoil Rock Hunter 1957,S 12,37:5

Goodbye, Charlie 1964,N 19,49:1
Axelrod, George (Producer)
Manchurian Candidate, The 1962,O 25,48:3
Paris When it Sizzles 1964,Ap 9,25:3
How to Murder Your Wife 1965,Ja 27,26:1
Lord Love a Duck 1966,F 22,14:6
Secret Life of an American Wife, The 1968,Je 26,42:2
Axelrod, George (Screenwriter)
Phffft 1954,N 11,43:2
Seven Year Itch, The 1955,Je 4,9:1
Bus Stop 1956,S 1,19:2
Breakfast at Tiffany's 1961,O 6,28:1
Manchurian Candidate, The 1962,O 25,48:3
Paris When it Sizzles 1964,Ap 9,25:3
How to Murder Your Wife 1965,Ja 27,26:1
Lord Love a Duck 1966,F 22,14:6
Secret Life of an American Wife, The 1968,Je 26,42:2
Axelson, Einar
Ungdom Av I Dag 1936,Je 23,27:7
Paa Solsidan 1936,Ag 26,16:3
Axelson, Mary McDougal (Original Author)
Life Begins 1932,Ag 26,20:3
Child Is Born, A 1940,Ja 11,19:2
Axiotis, George
Barefoot Battalion 1954,My 29,13:4
Axlyer, Felix
Rat, The 1938,F 28,19:1
Axman, Hanne
Red Menace, The 1949,Je 27,18:2
Axmann-Rezzori, Hanne
Young Torless 1967,S 25,56:2
Axt, William (Composer)
Ben Hur 1925,D 31,10:5 (In Addenda)
Fire Brigade, The 1926,D 21,20:2
Camille 1927,Ap 22,19:1
Trail of '98, The 1928,Mr 21,30:3
Storm at Daybreak 1933,Jl 22,14:2
O'Shaughnessy's Boy 1935,O 5,18:2
Parnell 1937,Je 4,27:2
Yellow Jack 1938,My 20,17:2
Axt, William (Miscellaneous)
Trail of '98, The 1928,Mr 21,30:3
Axzell, Evelyn
Sainted Devil, A 1924,N 24,15:3
Axzelle, Violet
Wedding Night, The 1935,Mr 16,19:1
Ayala, Fernando (Producer)
No Exit 1962,D 6,55:2
Ayars, Ann
Nazi Agent 1942,Je 13,11:2
Human Comedy, The 1943,Mr 3,19:2
Reunion in France 1943,Mr 5,20:3
Youngest Profession, The 1943,Je 25,13:3
Tales of Hoffmann 1951,Ap 5,34:2
Aye, Jimmy
Fourflusher, The 1928,Ja 16,24:1
Aye, Maryon
Eternal Three, The 1923,O 12,7:2 (Incorrect in this edition; use 1927,O 1,7:2 elsewhere)
Roughneck, The 1924,D 3,14:1
Last Man on Earth, The 1924,D 13,12:4
Irene 1926,Mr 1,17:1
Ayer, Harold
Desperate Moment 1953,S 1,19:4
Ayerbach, Hy
Cry Danger 1951,F 22,27:3
AYERS
See Also AYRES
Ayers, Robert
A Night to Remember 1958,D 17,2:7
Ayerton, Robert
Regular Girl, A 1919,N 11,13:3
Aylesworth, Arthur
Key, The 1934,My 30,14:3
Man With two Faces, The 1934,Jl 12,20:2
Dames 1934,Ag 16,20:2
Dragon Murder Case, The 1934,Ag 23,13:3
Desirable 1934,S 15,20:5
British Agent 1934,S 20,20:1
Case of the Howling Dog, The 1934,O 18,26:5
St Louis Kid, The 1934,N 1,25:2
6-Day Bike Rider 1934,N 3,20:3
Gentlemen are Born 1934,N 22,27:2
Babbitt 1934,D 17,24:2
I am a Thief 1935,Ja 1,24:1
Secret Bride, The 1935,F 2,10:1
Men Without Names 1935,Je 29,16:2
Man on the Flying Trapeze 1935,Ag 3,16:2
Escape from Devil's Island 1935,N 25,22:2
Rose of the Rancho 1936,Ja 9,25:2
To Mary-With Love 1936,Ag 27,16:1
Love Begins at 20 1936,S 19,20:1
Dimples 1936,O 10,21:2
Plot Thickens, The 1936,D 9,35:2
That Man's Here Again 1937,My 6,23:3
Of Human Hearts 1938,F 18,23:1
Test Pilot 1938,Ap 16,17:1
King of the Underworld 1939,Ja 7,6:2
Jesse James 1939,Ja 14,13:1
Oklahoma Kid, The 1939,Mr 11,21:1
Return of the Cisco Kid, The 1939,Ap 29,13:2

Aylesworth, Arthur— Cont
Six Thousand Enemies 1939,Je 9,26:2
Dust Be my Destiny 1939,O 7,11:2
Drums Along the Mohawk 1939,N 4,11:2
Return Of Doctor X, The 1939,N 23,38:5
Grapes of Wrath, The 1940,Ja 25,17:2
Little Old New York 1940,F 3,9:2
Edison the Man 1940,Je 7,27:2
Young People 1940,Ag 24,16:2
Brigham Young - Frontiersman 1940,S 21,13:2
Moontide 1942,Ap 30,14:1
Aylesworth, Douglas
I Wanted Wings 1941,Mr 27,29:4
Aylmer, Felix
Wandering Jew, The 1935,Ja 14,11:3
Iron Duke, The 1935,Ja 25,27:2
Seven Sinners 1936,Ag 22,6:1
Nine Days a Queen 1936,O 3,21:1
As You Like It 1936,N 6,29:3
Dreaming Lips 1937,My 20,17:1
Victoria the Great 1937,O 29,19:1
Citadel, The 1938,N 4,27:2
Sixty Glorious Years 1938,N 18,25:2
Mill On the Floss, The 1939,N 15,19:3
Spies of the Air 1940,Jl 4,12:3
Night Train 1940,D 30,21:1
Girl in the News, The 1941,My 5,13:2
Saint's Vacation, The 1941,Je 13,22:2
Frightened Lady 1941,N 10,21:3
She Shall Have Music 1942,O 31,11:2
Young Mr Pitt, The 1943,Mr 11,17:1
Young Man's Fancy, A 1943,D 4,11:2
Mr Emmanuel 1945,Ja 8,15:2
Life and Death of Colonel Blimp, The 1945,Mr 30,18:2
Johnny in the Clouds 1945,N 16,16:2
Adventure for Two 1945,D 14,24:5
Henry V 1946,Je 18,30:2
Wicked Lady, The 1946,D 23,19:5
Years Between, The 1947,Mr 10,25:2
Smugglers, The 1948,Mr 29,17:1
October Man, The 1948,Ap 16,29:2
Hamlet 1948,S 30,32:2
Man About the House, A 1949,Mr 9,33:2
Quartet (The Colonel's Lady); Colonel's Lady, The (Quartet) 1949,Mr 29,30:3
Edward my Son 1949,Je 3,21:2
Christopher Columbus 1949,O 13,33:2
Prince of Foxes 1949,D 24,11:2
Laughing Lady, The 1950,Ja 23,16:3
Eye Witness 1950,Ag 28,13:2
Verger, The 1950,O 11,42:1
So Long at the Fair 1951,Ja 22,14:2
Alice in Wonderland 1951,Jl 27,15:2
Quo Vadis 1951,N 9,22:2
Ivanhoe 1952,Ag 1,8:2
Paris Express, The 1953,Je 6,8:6
Master of Ballantrae, The 1953,Ag 6,16:2
Knights of the Round Table 1954,Ja 8,17:2
Angel Who Pawned her Harp, The 1956,F 29,35:2
Anastasia 1956,D 14,35:6
Saint Joan 1957,Je 27,21:1
I Accuse! 1958,Mr 6,32:1
Doctor's Dilemma, A 1958,D 18,2:7
Separate Tables 1958,D 19,2:7
Two-Headed Spy, The 1959,Mr 3,38:4
Mummy, The 1959,D 17,51:4
From the Terrace 1960,Jl 16,10:1
Exodus 1960,D 16,44:1
Road to Hong Kong, The 1962,Je 28,21:1
Running Man, The 1963,O 3,31:1
Becket 1964,Mr 12,40:2
Chalk Garden, The 1964,My 22,42:2
Aylmer, Mimi
Avventura di Giacomo Casanova 1938,D 2,27:3
Aylsworth, Arthur
President's Mystery, The 1936,O 19,22:1
I Cover the War 1937,Ag 2,10:2
What a Life 1939,O 12,33:1
Sin Town 1942,O 17,11:2
Ayme, Jean
Passion Of Joan Of Arc, The 1929,Mr 29,21:1
Passion of Jeanne d'Arc, The 1929,Mr 31,VIII,7:1
End of a Day, The 1939,S 12,28:4
Ayme, Marcel (Original Author)
Mr Peek-A-Boo 1951,S 19,37:1
Four Bags Full 1957,S 5,32:1
Green Mare, The; Jument Verte, La 1961,O 24,41:2
Ayme, Marcel (Screenwriter)
Mama, Papa, the Maid and I 1956,Ag 28,31:1
Love and the Frenchwoman; (Francaise et l'Amour, La) 1961,F 28,38:2
Aynesworth, Allan
Just Smith 1934,Ap 23,20:2
Iron Duke, The 1935,Ja 25,27:2
Brewster's Millions 1935,Ap 8,23:3
Dolwyn 1949,Ag 30,18:4
AYRES
See Also AYERS
Ayres, Agnes
Go and Get It 1920,Jl 19,16:3
Forbidden Fruit 1921,Ja 24,16:2

Ayres, Agnes— Cont

Love Special, The 1921,Mr 21,11:3
Too Much Speed 1921,Je 6,16:4
Cappy Ricks 1921,Ag 22,13:6
Affairs of Anatol, The 1921,S 12,16:1
Sheik, The 1921,N 7,20:1
Lane That had no Turning, The 1922,Ja 9,15:2
Bought and Paid For 1922,Mr 13,18:2
Borderland 1922,Jl 24,10:2
Clarence 1922,O 16,20:2
Heart Raider, The 1923,Je 6,24:5
Don't Call it Love 1923,D 25,26:1
Bluff 1924,Ap 28,18:2
Guilty One, The 1924,Je 17,22:4
Story Without a Name, The 1924,O 6,25:1
Worldly Goods 1924,N 3,20:1
Tomorrow's Love 1925,Ja 7,33:5
Awful Truth, The 1925,Jl 2,12:4
Donovan Affair, The 1929,Ap 29,29:2

Ayres, Ann

Dr Kildare's Victory 1942,F 5,25:2

Ayres, John H Police Captain (Original Author)

Bureau of Missing Persons 1933,S 9,9:2

Ayres, Lew

Kiss, The 1929,N 16,25:2
All Quiet on The Western Front 1930,Ap 30,29:1
Common Clay 1930,Ag 2,16:4
East Is West 1930,N 1,23:2
Doorway to Hell, The 1930,N 1,23:2
Iron Man 1931,Ap 18,17:3
Up for Murder 1931,My 30,9:2
Spirit of Notre Dame, The 1931,O 16,27:1
Heaven on Earth 1931,D 19,16:4
Mississippi 1931,D 27,VIII,5:4 (In Addenda)
Impatient Maiden, The 1932,Mr 4,17:3
Night World 1932,My 28,18:2
Okay America 1932,S 10,18:5
State Fair 1933,Ja 27,13:2
Don't Bet on Love 1933,Jl 31,16:2
My Weakness 1933,S 22,14:1
Cross Country Cruise 1934,Ja 20,12:3
She Learned About Sailors 1934,Jl 30,9:4
Servants' Entrance 1934,S 27,25:2
Silk Hat Kid 1935,Ag 7,22:5
Leathernecks Have Landed, The 1936,Mr 23,22:5
Panic on the Air 1936,Ap 20,17:1
Shakedown 1936,Ag 17,9:2
Lady, Be Careful 1936,O 10,21:1
Murder With Pictures 1936,N 21,21:4
Crime Nobody Saw, The 1937,Ap 5,17:2
Last Train from Madrid, The 1937,Je 19,20:2
Hold 'Em Navy 1937,N 6,14:2
Scandal Street 1938,F 5,19:2 (In Addenda)
King of the Newsboys 1938,Ap 2,18:2
Holiday 1938,Je 24,15:1
Rich Man, Poor Girl 1938,Ag 19,13:3
Young Doctor Kildare 1938,O 28,27:1
Spring Madness 1938,D 1,29:3
Ice Follies of 1939 1939,Mr 17,25:2
Broadway Serenade 1939,Ap 7,25:2
Calling Dr Kildare 1939,My 12,25:4
These Glamour Girls 1939,Ag 31,14:2
Secret of Dr Kildare, The 1939,D 8,33:5
Remember? 1939,D 15,33:4
Dr Kildare's Strange Case 1940,Ap 12,19:2
Dr Kildare Goes Home 1940,S 19,27:4
Golden Fleecing, The 1940,N 7,33:4
Dr Kildare's Crisis 1940,D 19,33:1
Maisie Was a Lady 1941,F 13,25:2
People vs Dr Kildare, The 1941,My 8,21:1
Dr Kildare's Wedding Day 1941,S 18,31:1
Fingers at the Window 1942,Ap 23,27:3
Dark Mirror, The 1946,O 19,15:2
Unfaithful, The 1947,Je 28,10:2
Johnny Belinda 1948,O 2,11:2
Capture, The 1950,My 20,8:6
New Mexico 1951,Jl 14,7:2
Donovan's Brain 1954,Ja 21,28:2
Advise and Consent 1962,Je 7,31:2
Carpetbaggers, The 1964,Jl 2,24:4

Ayres, Mitchell and His Orchestra

Swingtime Johnny 1943,D 17,23:3

Ayres, Robert

Night Without Stars 1953,Jl 14,19:4
Battle Beneath the Earth 1968,S 12,54:3

Ayrton, Randle

Chu Chin Chow 1925,F 11,19:4
Nell Gwyn 1926,Jl 19,13:1
Manxman, The 1929,D 17,28:7
Hate Ship, The 1930,N 15,15:3
Two Worlds 1930,N 22,21:3
Dreyfus Case, The 1931,Ag 31,11:5
Talk of the Devil 1937,My 15,23:5

Azais, Paul

Fantomas 1934,Mr 13,27:4
Cette Vieille Canaille 1935,Ja 12,12:2
Celle Vieille Canaille 1935,Ja 12,12:2
Pension Mimosas 1936,My 6,27:1

Azana, Mariano

Marcelino 1956,O 23,39:1

Azanchevski, S

Conquerors of the Night 1933,Jl 31,16:3
Poet and Tsar 1938,Ag 25,15:1

Azarov, Villen (Director)

Grown-Up Children 1963,Ap 15,36:5

Azcona, Rafael (Original Author)

Conjugal Bed, The 1963,S 17,30:1
Man With the Balloons, The 1968,Je 25,33:2

Azcona, Rafael (Screenwriter)

Conjugal Bed, The 1963,S 17,30:1
Ape Woman, The 1964,S 23,55:1
Not on Your Life; Verdugo, El 1965,Mr 30,52:1
Man With the Balloons, The 1968,Je 25,33:2

Azevedo, Dionizio

Given Word, The 1964,Mr 25,47:1

Azikri, Nissim

They Were Ten; (Heym Hayu Assara) 1961,Ap 18,44:2

Aznavour, Charles

Chasers, The; Draguers, Les 1960,My 3,43:1
Tomorrow Is my Turn 1962,F 2,24:2
Testament of Orpheus 1962,Ap 10,48:1
Shoot the Piano Player 1962,Jl 24,19:1
Three Fables of Love (Two Pigeons); Two Pigeons (Three Fables of Love) 1963,Ag 21,38:1
Devil and the 10 Commandments, The (Episode 3) 1963,O 15,44:1
Taxi for Tobruk 1965,Mr 30,52:1
High Infidelity (Sin in the Afternoon); Sin in the Afternoon (High Infidelity) 1965,Jl 2,17:1
Cloportes 1966,Ap 19,36:1
Paris in the Month of August 1968,Ag 26,46:4
Candy 1968,D 18,54:2

Azuful, Hadara

Clouds Over Israel 1966,My 10,48:6

B

Baal, Karin

Rosemary 1960,Ja 19,40:2
Judge and the Sinner, The 1964,Je 6,14:2

Baarova, Lida

Einer zu viel an Bord 1936,Ja 25,18:5
Barcarole 1936,O 21,35:3
Verraeter 1937,Ja 23,13:1
Patriots 1937,S 18,15:3
Teufelskerl, Ein; Devil of a Fellow, A 1938,O 1,10:3
Vitelloni 1956,O 24,43:1

Baart, Lottina

Why Cry at Parting 1930,F 4,28:3

Baay, Chris

Last Blitzkrieg, The 1959,Ja 31,13:5

Baba, Princess

You Can't Cheat an Honest Man 1939,F 20,13:2

Babayevsky, S (Original Author)

Dream of a Cossack 1952,F 18,15:2

Babb, Dorothy

Earl Carroll Sketchbook 1946,Ag 30,13:2

Babb, Kroger (Producer)

Prince of Peace, The 1951,Mr 24,8:3
Mom and Dad 1957,Ja 31,21:1

Babbitt, Harry

That's Right, You're Wrong 1939,N 30,25:3
You'll Find Out 1940,N 15,25:2
Playmates 1941,D 26,21:3
Around the World 1943,N 25,39:2

Babcock, Dwight V (Miscellaneous)

River Gang 1945,O 6,9:7

Babcock, Dwight V (Original Author)

Mummy's Curse, The 1945,Mr 31,16:1
Jungle Captive 1945,Jl 7,7:5
Pillow of Death 1946,Ja 26,19:3
House of Horrors 1946,F 23,20:3
She Wolf of London 1946,Ap 6,10:6
Loophole 1954,Mr 13,11:3

Babcock, Dwight V (Screenwriter)

Dead Man's Eyes 1944,O 7,11:2
Jungle Captive 1945,Jl 7,7:5
So Dark the Night 1946,D 7,16:2
Corpse came C O D, The 1947,Ag 19,27:2
Bury Me Dead 1947,O 25,13:3

Babcock, Theodore

Silent Command, The 1923,S 5,15:3
Shock Punch, The 1925,My 11,14:3

Babet, Doudou

If all the Guys in the World 1957,Ap 23,34:1

Babeuf, Howard Loeb

Edge, The 1968,Mr 28,52:1

Babies, Dionne

Country Doctor, The 1936,Mr 13,32:2 (Incorrect in this edition; use 1936,Mr 13,27:2 elsewhere)

Babin

Adventure in Music 1944,Mr 6,17:3

Babochkin, Boris

Return of Nathan Becker, The 1933,Ap 15,16:3
Three Women 1936,F 12,25:4
Friends 1939,Ja 2,28:3
Fortress on the Volga 1942,D 25,15:3

Babynin, G

Village of Sin, The 1929,My 21,29:3

Bacall, Lauren

To Have and Have Not 1944,O 12,24:1
Confidential Agent 1945,N 3,11:2
Big Sleep, The 1946,Ag 24,6:6

Bacall, Lauren— Cont

Dark Passage 1947,S 6,11:2
Key Largo 1948,Jl 17,6:6
Young Man With a Horn 1950,F 10,18:4
Bright Leaf 1950,Je 17,7:2
How to Marry a Millionaire 1953,N 11,37:1
Woman's World 1954,S 29,23:4
Cobweb, The 1955,Ag 6,13:3
Blood Alley 1955,O 6,25:3
Written on the Wind 1957,Ja 12,12:6
Designing Woman 1957,My 17,20:2
Gift of Love, The 1958,F 12,32:2
Flame Over India 1960,Ap 30,14:1
Shock Treatment 1964,Jl 23,19:1
Sex and the Single Girl 1964,D 26,9:2
Harper 1966,Mr 31,43:1

Baccaloni

Full of Life 1957,F 13,38:1
Merry Andrews 1958,Mr 21,17:1
Rock-a-Bye Baby 1958,Jl 24,18:1
Fanny 1961,Jl 7,16:1
Pigeon That Took Rome, The 1962,Ag 23,25:1

Bacchelli, Ricardo (Original Author)

Mill on the Po, The 1951,O 23,35:2

Bacchelli, Ricardo (Screenwriter)

Mill on the Po, The 1951,O 23,35:2

Bacchion, De Mori (Screenwriter)

Secret Conclave, The 1953,My 16,10:1

Baccus, Lionel

Our Daily Bread 1934,O 3,25:2

BACH

See Also BACHE, BOCK

Bach, Annette

Merchant of Slaves 1949,O 27,35:4
Voice of Love, The 1950,Ja 7,11:2
Man With the Grey Glove, The 1953,Ja 3,11:2
Duel Without Honor 1953,F 28,8:8

Bach, Ernest (Original Author)

It's a Boy 1934,Je 8,18:2

Bach, Ernest Curt

Trouble With Harry, The 1955,O 18,46:2

Bach, Johann Sebastian (Composer)

St Matthew Passion 1952,My 29,17:4

Bach, Olaf

Krach um Iolanthe 1935,My 11,21:3
Wenn am Sonntagabend die Dorfmusik Spielt 1935,D 9,25:3
Verlorene Tal, Das 1936,My 30,7:3

Bach, Simone

What Price Murder 1958,N 11,26:1

Bach, Vivi

Mozambique 1966,F 10,33:1

BACHE

See Also BACH, BOCK

Bache, Gordon (Screenwriter)

Blonde Savage 1947,O 4,9:2

Bachelor, Stephanie

Lady of Burlesque 1943,My 14,17:2
Her Primitive Man 1944,Ap 1,11:1
Man From Frisco 1944,Je 16,14:7
Lake Placid Serenade 1944,D 25,15:6
Experiment Perilous 1944,D 30,15:2
Earl Carroll Vanities 1945,Ap 2,15:6
I've Always Loved You 1946,S 7,11:1
Blackmail 1947,Ag 5,26:3

Bacher, William A (Producer)

Wing and a Prayer 1944,Ag 31,14:1
Carnival in Costa Rica 1947,Mr 29,21:2
Foxes of Harrow, The 1947,S 25,35:4
Untamed 1955,Mr 12,11:6
Tall Men, The 1955,O 12,36:2

Bacher, William A (Screenwriter)

Untamed 1955,Mr 12,11:6

BACHMAN

See Also BACHMANN

Bachman, Larry (Original Author)

Speed 1936,My 16,11:2

Bachman, Larry (Screenwriter)

Jalna 1935,S 14,8:4

BACHMANN

See Also BACHMAN

Bachmann, Lawrence (Original Author)

People vs Dr Kildare, The 1941,My 8,21:1
Dr Kildare's Wedding Day 1941,S 18,31:1
Shadow on the Wall 1950,My 19,31:3
Devil Makes Three, The 1952,Ag 30,6:2
Second to Hell 1959,Jl 18,6:3
Follow the Boys 1963,F 28,8:2

Bachmann, Lawrence (Producer)

Follow the Boys 1963,F 28,8:2
Murder at the Gallop 1963,Je 25,23:2
Children of the Damned 1964,Ja 30,24:2
Murder Ahoy 1964,S 23,55:3
Alphabet Murders, The 1966,Jl 12,36:2

Bachmann, Lawrence (Screenwriter)

Fingers at the Window 1942,Ap 23,27:3

Bachrach, Jacques (Original Author)

Nur am Rhein 1931,S 25,28:7
Opern-Ball, Der; Opera Ball 1931,N 6,28:3
Give Us This Night 1936,Ap 6,18:1

Bachwitz, Hans (Original Author)

For Wives Only 1926,D 1,24:5

Bacianova, Olga
Man I Love, The 1929,My 28,36:2
Claudia 1943,N 5,23:2
Bacigalupi, Louis
Dancing in the Dark 1949,D 3,8:6
Double Crossbones 1951,Ap 27,19:2
Backer, Herbert (Screenwriter)
Don't Give up the Ship 1959,Jl 9,22:1
Backes, Alice
I Want to Live 1958,N 19,45:1
It Started With a Kiss 1959,Ag 20,14:2
Backlar, Marshal (Producer)
Pretty Poison 1968,O 25,55:1
Backlin, Helen
Amazing Mr Beecham, The 1949,D 26,33:4
Backlin, Ingrid
Incorrigible 1949,Jl 2,8:2
Backus, Georgia
Citizen Kane 1941,My 2,25:1
Suddenly It's Spring 1947,F 27,26:2
Force of Evil 1948,D 27,16:2
Copper Canyon 1950,N 16,39:2
Cause for Alarm 1951,Mr 30,28:5
Apache Drums 1951,My 7,22:2
Mark of the Renegade 1951,S 7,24:2
Backus, Henny
Great Man, The 1957,Ja 2,28:2
Backus, Jim
One Last Fling 1949,Jl 1,14:6
Father Was a Fullback 1949,O 13,33:3
Great Lover, The 1949,N 24,48:2
Dangerous Profession, A 1949,D 12,29:4
Emergency Wedding 1950,D 22,19:2
Hollywood Story 1951,Je 7,40:6
M 1951,Je 11,20:7
Half Angel 1951,Je 16,9:2
Bright Victory 1951,Ag 1,19:2
Iron Man 1951,Ag 20,14:2
His Kind of Woman 1951,Ag 30,20:2
Man With a Cloak, The 1951,N 28,37:2
I'll See You in my Dreams 1951,D 7,35:1
I Want You 1951,D 24,9:1
Deadline U S A 1952,Mr 15,8:2
Pat and Mike 1952,Je 19,32:6
Don't Bother to Knock 1952,Jl 19,8:2
Androcles and the Lion 1953,Ja 15,23:2
Above and Beyond 1953,Ja 31,10:6
I Love Melvin 1953,Ap 10,18:4
Deep in my Heart 1954,D 10,35:2
Francis in the Navy 1955,Ag 6,13:4
Rebel without a Cause 1955,O 27,28:3
Square Jungle, The 1955,D 31,17:2
Meet Me in Las Vegas 1956,Mr 14,39:2
Girl He Left Behind, The 1956,O 27,17:1
Opposite Sex, The 1956,N 16,23:2
Great Man, The 1957,Ja 2,28:2
Top Secret Affair 1957,Ja 31,21:1
Man of a Thousand Faces 1957,Ag 14,21:1
Eighteen and Anxious 1957,D 14,16:6
High Cost of Loving, The 1958,My 17,12:1
Macabre 1958,Jl 24,18:1
Ask any Girl 1959,My 22,32:1
Private's Affair, A 1959,Ag 15,8:7
Ice Palace 1960,Je 30,22:1
Horizontal Lieutenant, The 1962,My 12,15:3
Boys' Night Out 1962,Je 22,15:2
Wonderful World of the Brothers Grimm, The
    (The Dancing Princess); Dancing Princess, The
    (The Wonderful World of the Brothers Grimm)
    1962,Ag 8,35:1
Zotz! 1962,O 4,44:3
My Six Loves 1963,Ap 4,58:4
Critic's Choice 1963,My 2,40:2
Johnny Cool 1963,O 3,31:1
Wheeler Dealers, The 1963,N 15,25:2
It's a Mad, Mad, Mad, Mad World
    1963,N 19,47:1
Sunday in New York 1964,F 12,30:2
Advance to the Rear 1964,Je 11,27:3
John Goldfarb, Please Come Home
    1965,Mr 25,42:4
Billie 1965,S 16,55:3
Where Were You When the Lights Went Out?
    1968,Ag 9,30:2
Backus, Michael
Rainmaker, The 1956,D 13,51:1
Backy, Don
Violent Four, The 1968,Ag 15,46:2
Baclanova, Olga
Three Sinners 1928,Ap 23,20:2
Man Who Laughs, The 1928,Ap 28,12:3
Forgotten Faces 1928,Ag 6,15:2
Docks of New York, The 1928,S 17,28:2
Wolf of Wall Street, The 1929,Ja 28,21:1
Dangerous Woman, A 1929,My 20,22:6
Great Lover, The 1931,Ag 24,13:4
Freaks 1932,Jl 9,7:5
Downstairs 1932,O 8,15:4
Billion Dollar Scandal, The 1933,Ja 9,23:1
Bacon, David
Ten Gentlemen From West Point 1942,Je 5,23:3
Crash Dive 1943,Ap 29,25:2
Gals, Inc 1943,Ag 13,13:4

Bacon, Frank (Original Author)
Lightnin 1925,Jl 22,14:4
Bacon, Irving
Good-Bye Kiss, The 1928,N 12,18:2
Half Way to Heaven 1929,D 7,19:3
Street of Chance 1930,F 3,17:1
Branded Men 1931,D 12,23:3
No One Man 1932,Ja 23,18:4
File No 113 1932,F 20,11:2
This is the Night 1932,Ap 16,11:2
Million Dollar Legs 1932,Jl 9,7:5
Central Park 1932,D 7,29:3
Hello, Everybody 1933,Ja 30,9:4
Miss Fane's Baby is Stolen 1934,Ja 20,12:2
Shadows of Sing Sing 1934,F 21,23:2
Hell Cat, The 1934,Jl 7,16:5
Hat, Coat and Glove 1934,Jl 27,21:2
You Belong to Me 1934,S 13,26:1
Pursuit of Happiness, The 1934,O 26,25:1
Private Worlds 1935,Mr 28,25:2
Here Comes Cookie 1935,O 12,12:2
Millions in the Air 1935,D 12,33:4
Petticoat Fever 1936,Mr 21,13:2
Three Cheers for Love 1936,Ag 1,16:2
Internes Can't Take Money 1937,My 6,23:2
Big City 1937,S 17,29:2
Big Town Girl 1937,D 13,23:4
Tip-Off Girls 1938,Mr 25,15:3
First 100 Years, The 1938,My 13,17:2
Amazing Dr Clitterhouse, The 1938,Jl 21,14:2
Chaser, The 1938,Ag 2,15:3
There Goes my Heart 1938,O 14,27:1
Tail Spin 1939,F 11,13:2
Oklahoma Kid, The 1939,Mr 11,21:1
Lucky Night 1939,My 5,29:3
Second Fiddle 1939,Jl 1,11:2
Indianapolis Speedway 1939,Jl 15,8:2
I Stole a Million 1939,Ag 7,11:2
Rio 1939,O 27,27:2
Man Who Wouldn't Talk, The 1940,Ja 12,13:3
Grapes of Wrath, The 1940,Ja 25,17:2
Dr Ehrlich's Magic Bullet 1940,F 24,9:2
Star Dust 1940,My 4,13:1
You Can't Fool Your Wife 1940,My 24,23:4
Return of Frank James, The 1940,Ag 10,16:4
Young People 1940,Ag 24,16:2
Gold Rush Maisie 1940,S 2,19:2
Howards of Virginia, The 1940,S 27,27:1
She Couldn't Say No 1941,Ja 17,21:3
Western Union 1941,F 7,23:2
Blondie Goes Latin 1941,F 26,17:3
Meet John Doe 1941,Mr 13,25:2
Girl, a Guy and a Gob, A 1941,Ap 24,25:3
Caught in the Draft 1941,Je 26,27:3
It Started With Eve 1941,O 3,27:1
Great Guns 1941,O 3,27:2
Henry Aldrich for President 1941,O 18,22:2
Moon Over her Shoulder 1941,N 5,31:2
Cadet Girl 1941,D 11,39:1
Give Out, Sisters 1942,Ag 28,22:3
Footlight Serenade 1942,S 10,30:3
Between Us Girls 1942,S 25,25:3
Get Help to Love 1942,O 19,15:3
Shadow of a Doubt 1943,Ja 13,18:2
Happy Go Lucky 1943,Mr 25,25:1
Hers to Hold 1943,Jl 22,15:1
In old Oklahoma 1943,D 6,21:1
Heavenly Days 1944,O 21,15:2
Patrick the Great 1945,Ap 13,15:2
Out of This World 1945,Je 7,25:2
Guest Wife 1945,O 18,21:2
Wake up and Dream 1947,Ja 24,18:4
My Brother Talks to Horses 1947,Je 19,27:4
Bachelor and the Bobby-Soxer, The
    1947,Jl 25,12:5
State of the Union 1948,Ap 23,28:1
Good Sam 1948,S 17,28:2
John Loves Mary 1949,F 5,11:2
Family Honeymoon 1949,F 25,28:2
Moonrise 1949,Mr 7,17:2
Manhandled 1949,My 26,34:2
Night Unto Night 1949,Je 11,11:2
Green Promise, The 1949,Je 24,29:2
Big Cat, The 1949,Jl 29,12:2
It's a Great Feeling 1949,Ag 13,6:6
Dear Wife 1950,F 2,31:2
Woman in Hiding 1950,F 23,33:2
Wabash Avenue 1950,Ap 29,8:3
Emergency Wedding 1950,D 22,19:2
Cause for Alarm 1951,Mr 30,28:5
Room for One More 1952,Ja 16,21:2
Fort Ti 1953,My 30,7:1
Duffy of San Quentin 1954,F 10,38:5
Glenn Miller Story, the 1954,F 11,33:2
Star is Born, A 1954,O 12,23:1
Run for Cover 1955,Ap 30,10:6
Dakota Incident 1956,N 10,14:2
Bacon, Lloyd (Director)
Private Izzy Murphy 1926,N 10,25:1
White Flannels 1927,Mr 22,31:2
Lion and the Mouse, The 1928,Je 16,11:4
Singing Fool, The 1928,S 20,33:2
Honky Tonk 1929,Je 5,32:3

Say It With Songs 1929,Ag 7,29:2
So Long Letty 1930,F 8,12:5
She Couldn't Say No 1930,F 16,III,8:1
Notorious Affair, A 1930,Ap 26,11:1
Moby Dick 1930,Ag 15,20:5
Office Wife, The 1930,S 27,21:3
Sit Tight 1931,F 19,20:4
Kept Husbands 1931,Mr 24,31:2
Fifty Million Frenchmen 1931,Mr 26,31:2
Gold Dust Gertie 1931,My 30,9:2
Honor of the Family 1931,O 17,20:1
Manhattan Parade 1931,D 25,29:2
Fireman, Save My Child 1932,F 18,25:3
Alias the Doctor 1932,Mr 3,22:3
Famous Ferguson Case, The 1932,Ap 25,18:6
Miss Pinkerton 1932,Jl 9,7:5
Crooner 1932,Ag 20,7:4
You Said a Mouthful 1932,N 18,23:2
42d Street 1933,Mr 10,19:3
Picture Snatcher 1933,My 19,20:3
Mary Stevens, M D 1933,Ag 5,9:6
Footlight Parade 1933,O 6,21:3
Son of a Sailor 1933,N 30,38:4
Wonder Bar 1934,Mr 1,23:2
He Was her Man 1934,My 17,28:2
Here Comes the Navy 1934,Jl 21,14:2
6-Day Bike Rider 1934,N 3,20:3
Devil Dogs of the Air 1935,F 7,23:2
In Caliente 1935,Je 27,16:1
Broadway Gondolier 1935,Jl 18,15:2
Irish in US, The 1935,Ag 1,15:1
Frisco Kid 1935,N 25,22:1
Sons o'Guns 1936,My 14,29:2
Cain and Mabel 1936,O 19,22:1
Gold Diggers of 1937 1936,D 25,19:2
Marked Woman 1937,Ap 12,15:2
Ever Since Eve 1937,Je 25,25:2
San Quentin 1937,Ag 4,15:2
Submarine D-1 1937,D 30,15:4
Slight Case of Murder, A 1938,F 28,19:1
Cowboy From Brooklyn 1938,Jl 14,17:1
Racket Busters 1938,Ag 11,13:1
Boy Meets Girl 1938,Ag 27,7:2
Wings of the Navy 1939,F 4,11:1
Oklahoma Kid, The 1939,Mr 11,21:1
Indianapolis Speedway 1939,Jl 15,8:2
Espionage Agent 1939,S 23,22:2
Child Is Born, A 1940,Ja 11,19:2
Invisible Stripes 1940,Ja 13,11:2
Three Cheers for the Irish 1940,Mr 9,19:2
Brother Orchid 1940,Je 8,18:2
Knute Rockne-All American 1940,O 19,21:2
Honeymoon for Three 1941,F 8,19:2
Footsteps in the Dark 1941,Mr 15,13:2
Affectionally Yours 1941,My 24,18:2
Navy Blues 1941,S 20,11:2
Larceny, Inc 1942,Ap 25,9:1
Wings for the Eagle 1942,Ag 1,14:2
Silver Queen 1943,Ja 11,18:4
Action in the North Atlantic 1943,My 22,10:2
Sullivans, The 1944,F 10,19:2
Sunday Dinner for a Soldier 1945,Ja 25,16:2
Captain Eddie 1945,Ag 9,24:2
Home Sweet Homicide 1946,S 12,5:7
Wake up and Dream 1947,Ja 24,18:4
I Wonder Who's Kissing Her Now
    1947,Jl 24,27:2
You Were Meant for Me 1948,Ja 29,27:5
Give my Regards to Broadway 1948,Je 23,32:2
Innocent Affair, An 1948,S 29,36:2
Mother is a Freshman 1949,Mr 12,10:2
It Happens Every Spring 1949,Je 11,11:2
Kill the Umpire 1950,My 29,10:6
Good Humor Man, The 1950,Jl 14,17:2
Fuller Brush Girl, The 1950,O 6,23:2
Call Me Mister 1951,F 1,21:2
Frogmen, The 1951,Je 30,8:6
Golden Girl 1951,N 21,20:3
Great Sioux Uprising, The 1953,Jl 18,6:2
Walking my Baby Back Home 1954,Ja 16,10:5
She Couldn't Say No 1954,F 27,11:3
French Line, The 1954,My 15,13:2
Bacon, Max
Pool of London 1951,N 28,37:2
Privilege 1967,Jl 25,30:2
Bacon, Robert
Stolen Hours 1963,O 17,39:1
Bacon, Roger
If a Man Answers 1962,N 22,43:1
Baconnet
Prize, The 1952,Ap 30,33:2
Baconnet, Georges
Crazy for Love 1960,N 26,13:2
Marriage of Figaro, The 1963,Ap 30,26:1
Bacque, Andrew
Maria Chapdelaine 1935,S 25,18:2
Bacquet, Maurice
Youth in Revolt 1939,My 16,27:3
Baddeley, Angela
Speckled Band, The 1931,N 7,16:5
Ghost Train, The 1933,F 18,13:3
Quartet (The Facts of Life); Facts of Life, The
    (Quartet) 1949,Mr 29,30:3

Baddeley, Angela— Cont
Tom Jones 1963,O 8,48:1
Baddeley, Hermione
No Room at the Inn 1949,D 26,33:4
Dear Mr Prohack 1950,Jl 15,7:2
Young Scarface 1951,N 8,35:2
Christmas Carol, A 1951,N 29,41:2
Tom Brown's School Days 1952,Ja 8,23:5
Woman in Question, The 1952,F 19,24:2
Wall of Death 1952,My 19,12:4
Time, Gentlemen, Please 1953,S 24,39:2
Pickwick Papers, The 1954,Ap 5,21:2
Belles of St Trinian's, The 1954,D 23,13:4
Room at the Top 1959,Mr 31,26:1
Expresso Bongo 1960,Ap 13,44:1
Midnight Lace 1960,O 14,27:1
Unsinkable Molly Brown, The 1964,Jl 17,15:1
Mary Poppins 1964,S 25,34:1
Harlow 1965,My 15,18:1
Marriage on the Rocks 1965,S 16,00:0
Do Not Disturb 1965,D 25,17:2
Adventures of Bullwhip Griffin, The 1967,Mr 9,43:2
Happiest Millionaire, The 1967,D 1,56:1
Badel, Alan
Salome 1953,Mr 25,37:1
Three Cases of Murder (Lord Mountdrago); Lord Mountdrago (Three Cases of Murder) 1955,Mr 16,39:4
Three Cases of Murder (You Killed Elizabeth); You Killed Elizabeth (Three Cases of Murder) 1955,Mr 16,39:4
Three Cases of Murder (In the Picture); In the Picture (Three Cases of Murder) 1955,Mr 16,39:4
Will any Gentleman? 1955,S 28,70:6
This Sporting Life 1963,Jl 17,19:2
Children of the Damned 1964,Ja 30,24:2
Arabesque 1966,My 6,54:1
Badey, Peggy
Let's Dance 1950,N 30,42:2
Badger, Clarence (Director)
Perfect Lady, A 1918,D 2,11:3
Leave It to Susan 1919,My 26,19:4
Through the Wrong Door 1919,Jl 21,12:3
Strictly Confidential 1919,O 6,15:1
Almost a Husband 1919,O 13,16:3
Jes' Call Me Jim 1920,My 24,20:3
Man Who Lost Himself, The 1920,My 31,14:2
Cupid, the Cowpuncher 1920,Jl 26,9:5
Honest Hutch 1920,S 26,VI,2:1 (In Addenda)
Guile of Women 1921,F 28,16:2
Boys Will Be Boys 1921,My 6,20:2 (Incorrect in this edition; use 1921,My 16,20:2 elsewhere)
Doubling for Romeo 1921,O 24,13:1
Quincy Adams Sawyer 1922,D 18,22:2
Red Lights 1923,S 10,15:4
Shooting of Dan McGrew, The 1924,Je 9,14:3
New Lives for Old 1925,F 25,16:7
Eve's Secret 1925,Je 11,14:3
Paths to Paradise 1925,Je 30,14:3
Paths to Paradise 1925,Jl 5,VII,2:1
Golden Princess 1925,S 7,15:3
Hands Up 1926,Ja 18,26:2
Miss Brewster's Millions 1926,Mr 8,17:1
Rainmaker, The 1926,My 18,28:2
Campus Flirt, The 1926,S 22,31:1
Kiss in a Taxi, A 1927,Mr 15,29:2
Senorita 1927,My 9,26:4
Swim, Girl, Swim 1927,S 5,13:2
She's a Shiek 1927,N 21,20:1
Red Hair 1928,Mr 26,26:2
Three Week Ends 1928,D 10,25:1
No, No, Nanette 1930,Ja 4,21:1
Murder Will Out 1930,Ap 14,24:2
Sweethearts and Wives 1930,Je 28,9:2
Bad Man, The 1930,S 27,21:3
Hot Heiress, The 1931,Mr 14,23:2
Woman Hungry 1931,Mr 23,24:7
Party Husband 1931,My 16,13:3
When Strangers Marry 1933,My 25,24:3
Badham, Mary
To Kill a Mockingbird 1963,F 15,10:2
This Property is Condemned 1966,Ag 4,24:1
Let's Kill Uncle 1966,N 19,26:1
Badias, Carlos
Romance del Palmar, El 1939,My 1,21:2
Badie, Laura
Virtuous Scoundrel, The 1957,O 23,37:1
Badie, Laurence
Forbidden Games 1952,D 9,43:2
Lust for Life 1956,S 18,39:1
Four Bags Full 1957,S 5,32:1
Muriel 1963,O 31,26:1
Badigin, K (Screenwriter)
Frigid Sea, The 1955,N 21,23:4
Badiole, Charles
Miserables, Les 1926,Jl 9,17:1
Miserables, Les 1927,Ag 23,29:4
Badioli, Carla
Boheme, La 1965,O 20,51:2
Badirev, Kapan
Amangeldy 1939,Je 16,27:4

Badolati, Luigi
Life and Miracles of Blesses Mother Cabrini, The 1946,Jl 8,25:2
Badolati, Mario
Parlami d'Amore Mariu 1934,O 20,20:3
Badyk, Pam
Zero in the Universe 1966,O 12,36:3
Badyrov, K
Horsemen, The 1951,Ja 29,14:5
BAEHR
See Also BAER, BAIR, BEAR, BEYER, BYER
Baehr, Nicholas E (Original Author)
Incident, The 1967,N 6,65:1
Baehr, Nicholas E (Screenwriter)
Incident, The 1967,N 6,65:1
Baena, Carlos
This Strange Passion 1955,D 5,34:2
Alexander the Great 1956,Mr 29,23:1
BAER
See Also BAEHR, BAIR, BEAR, BEYER, BYER
Baer, (Bugs)
Great White Way, The 1924,Ja 4,10:1
Baer, (Bugs) (Miscellaneous)
Headin' Home 1920,S 20,13:1
Baer, Abel (Composer)
Love, Live and Laugh 1929,N 2,14:6
Baer, Buddy
Africa Screams 1949,My 5,34:2
Quo Vadis 1951,N 9,22:2
Two Tickets to Broadway 1951,N 22,47:2
Flame of Araby 1951,D 20,41:7
Jack and the Beanstalk 1952,Ap 8,35:3
Big Sky, The 1952,Ag 20,21:1
Dream Wife 1953,Jl 30,20:1
Fair Wind to Java 1953,Ag 28,13:3
Jubilee Trail 1954,My 1,13:3
Slightly Scarlet 1956,Mr 17,13:2
Snow White and the Three Stooges 1961,Jl 1,9:1
Baer, Emil
William Tell 1925,My 20,26:2
Baer, John
About Face 1952,My 24,15:3
Mississippi Gambler, The 1953,Ja 30,25:1
Miami Story, The 1954,My 15,13:2
We're no Angels 1955,Jl 8,15:2
Huk! 1956,D 15,20:4
Baer, Mary
Bride for Sale 1949,N 21,29:4 (In Addenda)
Baer, Max
Prizefighter and the Lady, The 1933,N 11,11:3
Navy Comes Through, The 1942,N 12,30:3
Ladies' Day 1943,Mr 26,14:3
Africa Screams 1949,My 5,34:2
Bride for Sale 1949,N 21,29:4 (In Addenda)
Harder They Fall, The 1956,My 10,26:3
Baer, Parley
Union Station 1950,O 5,38:3
Air Cadet 1951,My 11,32:3
Frogmen, The 1951,Je 30,8:6
People Will Talk 1951,Ag 30,20:1
Vickie 1953,S 8,26:3
Young Lions, The 1958,Ap 3,23:1
F B I Story, The 1959,S 25,23:1
Wake Me When It's Over 1960,Ap 9,17:2
Adventures of Huckleberry Fin, The 1960,Ag 4,17:1
Gypsy 1962,N 2,24:1
Brass Bottle, The 1964,My 21,42:1
Bedtime Story 1964,Je 11,27:1
Bus Riley's Back in Town 1965,Ap 8,45:2
Follow Me, Boys! 1966,D 2,46:1
Day of the Evil Gun 1968,Ap 25,53:2
Baerlein, Henry (Original Author)
Charmer, The 1925,Ap 6,17:3
Baez, Joan
Don't Look Back 1967,S 7,50:2
Festival 1967,O 24,53:2
Bafalov, Alexei
Nine Days of one Year 1964,D 29,19:1
Baffico, Mario (Director)
Terra di Nessuno; Nobody's Land 1940,O 25,25:4
Bagar, Andres
Janosik 1936,D 25,19:3
Bagashvili, F
They Wanted Peace 1940,Ja 8,11:3
Bagdasarian, Ross
Destination Gobi 1953,My 30,7:1
Alaska Seas 1954,Mr 6,13:5
Rear Window 1954,Ag 5,18:2
Proud and Profane, The 1956,Je 14,41:2
Baggett, Lynne
Time of Their Lives, The 1946,N 28,40:2
D O A 1950,My 1,18:2
Flame and the Arrow, The 1950,Jl 8,7:2
Baggott, King
Moonlight Follies 1921,S 19,12:1
Going Straight 1922,Mr 28,17:4
Tumbleweeds 1925,D 21,27:2
Lovey Mary 1926,Je 21,17:2
Notorious Lady, The 1927,Ap 11,18:3
Czar of Broadway, The 1930,Je 30,22:6
Once a Gentleman 1930,O 4,15:2
Sweepstakes 1931,Je 25,23:5

Baggott, King— Cont
Fame Street 1932,Ap 2,13:2
Mississippi 1935,Ap 18,27:2
Come Live With Me 1941,F 28,17:3
Baggott, King (Director)
Home Maker, The 1925,Ag 10,8:2
Baggott, King (Original Author)
Sporting Chance 1931,N 28,20:4
Baghetti, Aristide
Zio d'America, Lo; Uncle From America, The 1939,S 15,26:5
Amicizia; Friendship 1940,Mr 1,17:3
Bagley, Bob (Cinematographer)
Endless Summer, The 1966,Je 16,53:2
Bagley, Richard (Miscellaneous)
On the Bowery 1957,Mr 19,44:1
Bagni, Gwen (Original Author)
Captain China 1950,Mr 2,33:2
With Six You Get Egg Roll 1968,O 10,59:6
Bagni, Gwen (Screenwriter)
Captain China 1950,Mr 2,33:2
Untamed Frontier 1952,Ag 23,10:2
With Six You Get Egg Roll 1968,O 10,59:6
Bagni, John
Bombay Clipper 1942,Ja 12,23:3
Pretender, The 1947,Ag 12,26:2
Captain China 1950,Mr 2,33:2
Bagni, John (Original Author)
Captain China 1950,Mr 2,33:2
Bagni, Margherita
Eternal Melodies 1948,F 14,17:3
Too Bad She's Bad 1955,D 26,23:2
Bagnold, Enid (Original Author)
National Velvet 1944,D 15,25:2
Chalk Garden, The 1964,My 22,42:2
Bagolini, Silvio
Four Steps in the Clouds 1948,N 22,25:2
Bagratide
Occident, L' 1928,D 16,IX,8:2
Baguez, Salvador
Second Chance 1953,Jl 23,20:2
Americano, The 1955,Ja 20,35:1
First Texan, The 1956,Je 23,20:2
From Hell to Texas 1958,Je 5,39:2
Bahelfer, M (Producer)
We Live Again 1948,S 6,17:2
Bahl, Ellen
Tender Scoundrel 1967,N 16,58:2
Bahquells, Rafael
Marvels of the Bull Ring 1943,Jl 3,11:3
BAHR
See Also BARR
Bahr, Herman (Original Author)
Concert, The 1921,F 21,16:1
Romance in the Dark 1938,Mr 21,18:2
Bai, Akhtari
Music Room, The 1963,O 16,50:6
Baidukov, Georgi (Screenwriter)
Wings of Victory 1941,N 17,15:2
Baigum, Princess
Charge of the Light Brigade, The 1936,N 2,24:1
Bailargeon, J J
Requiem for a Heavyweight 1962,O 17,35:1
Baile, C
Mating Game, The 1959,Ap 30,37:1
Mating Game, The 1959,Ap 30,37:1
BAILEY
See Also BAILY, BAYLEY
Bailey, Bill
Cabin in the Sky 1943,My 28,19:3
Bailey, Bob
Jitterbugs 1943,Je 5,12:2
Bailey, Charles W 2d (Original Author)
Seven Days in May 1964,F 20,22:1
Bailey, Claude
Yellow Canary, The 1944,Ap 14,24:7
Hatter's Castle 1948,Jl 3,8:6
Bailey, Cliff
Between Midnight and Dawn 1950,O 2,19:2
Bailey, Dave
Subterraneans, The 1960,Jl 7,26:1
Bailey, Frankie
Thank You 1925,O 6,30:1
Crown of Lies 1926,Mr 30,20:6
Bailey, Harry
Bertha, The Sewing Machine Girl 1927,Ja 4,21:1
Touchdown Army 1938,O 28,27:2
Some Like It Hot 1939,My 25,31:2
Bailey, Hilda
Carnival 1921,Je 27,16:3
Bailey, Jeff (Original Author)
Bengazi 1955,O 8,13:4
Bailey, John
Circle of Danger 1951,Jl 12,21:6
High Treason 1952,My 21,23:3
Cairo Road 1952,N 1,17:2
Assassin, The 1953,Ap 18,17:2
So Little Time 1953,Jl 28,23:2
Never Let Go 1963,Je 15,10:2
Bailey, Pearl
Isn't It Romantic? 1948,O 7,35:2
Carmen Jones 1954,O 29,27:2
That Certain Felling 1956,Je 21,35:2
St Louis Blues 1958,Ap 12,13:1

Bailey, Pearl— Cont
Porgy and Bess 1959,Je 25,20:3
All the Fine Young Cannibals 1960,S 23,33:1
Bailey, Raymond
S O S Tidal Wave 1939,Je 22,19:3
Flight at Midnight 1939,S 7,29:2
Picnic 1956,F 17,13:3
I've Lived Before 1956,Ag 4,13:1
Girl He Left Behind, The 1956,O 27,17:1
Incredible Shrinking Man, The 1957,F 23,13:1
Band of Angels 1957,Jl 11,21:1
No Time for Sergeants 1958,My 30,13:2
I Want to Live 1958,N 19,45:1
Al Capone 1959,Mr 26,27:1
Gallant Hours, The 1960,Je 23,19:4
From the Terrace 1960,Jl 16,10:1
Bailey, Richard
Night in Paradise 1946,Je 6,16:3
Young Widow 1946,Jl 29,12:8
Burning Cross, The 1948,F 20,19:1
Bailey, Robert
Dancing Masters, The 1943,D 2,30:2
Eve of St Mark, The 1944,My 31,22:2
Tampico 1944,Je 2,21:2
Wing and a Prayer 1944,Ag 31,14:1
Sunday Dinner for a Soldier 1945,Ja 25,16:2
Bailey, Robert B (Original Author)
Underwater! 1955,F 10,27:2
Bailey, Robin
Glory at Sea 1953,Mr 11,36:7
Sailor of the King 1953,S 3,15:2
His Excellency 1956,F 2,19:3
Having a Wild Weekend 1965,Ag 19,35:1
Bailey, Sherwood
Devil is a Sissy, The 1936,O 17,21:2
Quality Street 1937,Ap 9,19:2
Bailey, William Norton
Desert Flower, The 1925,Je 1,10:3
Ranson's Folly 1926,My 31,10:2
High School Hero 1927,O 24,24:3
Hit of the Show 1928,Jl 9,25:1
Waterfront 1928,O 22,29:1
Midnight Patrol, The 1932,My 7,11:5
George White's Scandals 1934,Mr 16,24:2
Thunder Mountain 1935,O 2,27:2
Charlie Chan's Secret 1936,Ja 18,19:4
Bailly, Auguste (Original Author)
Kiss of Fire, The 1940,N 20,27:4
Flame and the Flesh 1954,My 3,21:2
BAILY
See Also BAILEY, BAYLEY
Baily, Leslie (Screenwriter)
Gilbert and Sullivan 1953,O 28,36:3
Baim, Karyn
Two for the Road 1967,Ap 28,36:2
Bainbridge, Hazel
Family Way, The 1967,Je 29,32:1
Baines, John (Original Author)
Dead of Night 1946,Je 29,22:6
Baines, John (Screenwriter)
Dead of Night 1946,Je 29,22:6
Blue Lagoon, The 1949,O 3,13:2
Simba 1955,O 22,24:2
Bainter, Fay
This Side of Heaven 1934,F 10,21:2
Quality Street 1937,Ap 9,19:2
Soldier and the Lady, The 1937,Ap 10,11:1
Make Way for Tomorrow 1937,My 10,23:1
Jezebel 1938,Mr 11,15:2
White Banners 1938,Je 23,27:1
Mother Carey's Chickens 1938,Ag 5,11:1
Arkansas Traveler, The 1938,N 17,29:2
Shining Hour, The 1939,Ja 20,15:2
Yes, My Darling Daughter 1939,F 27,11:2
Daughters Courageous 1939,Je 24,14:2
Our Neighbors-The Carters 1940,F 15,15:2
Young Tom Edison 1940,Mr 15,27:2
Our Town 1940,Je 14,25:3
Bill of Divorcement, A 1940,Jl 12,11:2
Maryland 1940,Jl 13,16:5
Babes on Broadway 1942,Ja 1,37:1
Woman of the Year 1942,F 6,23:2
War Against Mrs Hadley, The 1942,N 26,40:2
Journey for Margaret 1942,D 18,36:7
Human Comedy, The 1943,Mr 3,19:2
Presenting Lily Mars 1943,Ap 30,25:3
Salute to the Marines 1943,Ag 30,11:3
Cry Havoc 1943,N 24,16:2
Heavenly Body, The 1944,Mr 24,17:3
Dark Waters 1944,N 22,25:2
3 Is a Family 1944,D 20,20:3
State Fair 1945,Ag 31,14:3
Virginian, The 1946,Ap 18,22:2
Kid From Brooklyn, The 1946,Ap 19,25:2
Secret Life of Walter Mitty, The 1947,Ag 15,12:2
Deep Valley 1947,Ag 23,7:2
Give my Regards to Broadway 1948,Je 23,32:2
June Bride 1948,O 30,10:2
President's Lady, The 1953,My 22,31:1
Childrens Hour, The 1962,Mr 15,28:2
BAIR
See Also BAEHR, BAER, BEAR, BEYER, BYER

Bair, David
Reckless Moment, The 1949,D 30,13:2
Enemy Below, The 1957,D 26,23:2
Baird, Anthony
Dead of Night 1946,Je 29,22:6
Baird, E Wing Comdr
School for Danger 1947,N 10,21:3
Baird, E Wing Commander (Director)
School for Danger 1947,N 10,21:3
Baird, Harry
Sapphire 1959,N 3,27:1
Mark, The 1961,O 3,46:2
Small World of Sammy Lee, The 1963,Ag 14,28:1
Whisperers, The 1967,Ag 1,24:1
Story of a Three Day Pass, The 1968,Jl 9,31:1
Touchables, The 1968,N 21,41:1
Baird, Jeanne
Andy Hardy Comes Home 1958,D 24,00:0
Baird, Jimmie
Seven Little Foys, The 1955,Je 30,18:2
Black Orchid, The 1959,F 13,33:2
Baird, Leah
Lady Gangster 1942,Jl 10,13:2
Baird, Leah (Original Author)
Jungle Bride 1933,My 13,16:3
Baird, Sharon
Bloodhounds of Broadway 1952,N 15,15:2
Baird, Teddy (Producer)
Browning Version, The 1951,O 30,33:2
Woman in Question, The 1952,F 19,24:2
Importance of Being Earnest, The 1952,D 23,17:2
Court Martial 1955,Ag 2,17:1
Simon and Laura 1956,Jl 3,17:2
Bairnsfather, Capt (Original Author)
Better 'Ole, The 1919,F 24,11:3
Bairstow, David (Director)
Royal Journey 1952,F 29,19:2
Baisseitov, Kanabek
Amangeldy 1939,Je 16,27:4
Bajor, Gizi
Ket Fogoly; Two Prisoners 1938,D 31,7:3
Bak, Cheong Yul
Cease Fire! 1953,N 25,17:1
Bakaleinikoff, Constantin (Director)
Let's Fall in Love 1934,Ja 22,12:3
Bakalyan, Richard
Delicate Delinquent, The 1957,Jl 4,16:1
Up Periscope 1959,Mr 5,35:4
Von Ryan's Express 1965,Je 24,28:1
St Valentine's Day Massacre, The 1967,Jl 27,29:2
Never a Dull Moment 1968,Ag 15,46:2
Baker, Allen
West of the Water Tower 1923,D 31,9:3
Baker, Art
Once Upon a Time 1944,Je 30,17:2
Spellbound 1945,N 2,22:2
Abie's Irish Rose 1946,D 23,19:4
Beginning or the End, The 1947,F 21,15:1
Farmer's Daughter, The 1947,Mr 26,31:2
Dark Delusion 1947,Je 26,19:2
Daisy Kenyon 1947,D 25,32:1
State of the Union 1948,Ap 23,28:1
Silver River 1948,My 22,8:3
Walls of Jericho, The 1948,Ag 5,16:2
Walk a Crooked Mile 1948,O 13,31:2
Southern Yankee, A 1948,N 25,47:2
Decision of Christopher Blake, The 1948,D 11,12:2
Impact 1949,Mr 21,19:2
Night Unto Night 1949,Je 11,11:2
Take one False Step 1949,Je 23,33:2
Any Number Can Play 1949,Jl 1,14:4
Massacre River 1949,Jl 15,17:2
Task Force 1949,O 1,8:6
Easy Living 1949,O 13,33:3
Underworld Story, The 1950,Jl 27,29:4
Cause for Alarm 1951,Mr 30,28:5
Baker, Belle
Song of Love, The 1929,N 14,24:3
Atlantic City 1944,Ag 14,11:4
Baker, Benny
Hell Cat, The 1934,Jl 7,16:5
Belle of the Nineties 1934,S 22,12:2
Annapolis Farewell 1935,Ag 24,18:2
Big Broadcast of 1936, The 1935,S 16,15:2
Thanks a Million 1935,N 14,17:1
Millions in the Air 1935,D 12,33:4
Rose of the Rancho 1936,Ja 9,25:2
Give Us This Night 1936,Ap 6,18:1
Panic on the Air 1936,Ap 20,17:1
Lady, Be Careful 1936,O 10,21:1
Murder With Pictures 1936,N 21,21:4
Rose Bowl 1936,D 2,35:2
Champagne Waltz 1937,F 4,17:2
Crime Nobody Saw, The 1937,Ap 5,17:2
Blonde Trouble 1937,Ag 7,7:2
Double or Nothing 1937,S 2,17:3
Hold 'Em Navy 1937,N 6,14:2
Tip-Off Girls 1938,Mr 25,15:3
Touchdown Army 1938,O 28,27:2
Sing for Your Supper 1941,D 1,15:5
Captains of the Clouds 1942,F 13,24:2
Stage Door Canteen 1943,Je 25,13:2

Baker, Benny— Cont
Up in Arms 1944,Mr 3,19:2
My Girl Tisa 1948,F 21,9:2
Inspector General, The 1949,D 31,9:2
Models, Inc 1952,My 26,18:4
Public Pigeon No 1 1957,My 18,23:2
Boy, Did I Get a Wrong Number! 1966,Je 9,54:2
Baker, Bob
Singing Outlaw 1937,D 27,11:1
Chip of the Flying U 1940,Ja 22,11:3
West of Carson City 1940,My 7,31:3
Baker, Bob (Cinematographer)
Untitled-Adventure, Lion Hunting 1918,My 27,11:3
Baker, Bonnie
You're the One 1941,F 20,23:2
Baker, C Graham (Original Author)
Personality Kid, The 1934,Ag 1,14:2
Baker, C Graham (Screenwriter)
Masters of Men 1923,My 15,22:1
Baker, Carroll
Easy to Love 1953,N 27,99:9
Giant 1956,O 11,51:1
Baby Doll 1956,D 19,40:2
But Not for Me 1959,O 3,14:6
Miracle, The 1959,N 13,25:4
Bridge to the Sun 1961,O 18,50:1
Something Wild 1961,D 24,30:6
How the West Was Won 1963,Ap 1,54:1
Carpetbaggers, The 1964,Jl 2,24:4
Station Six-Sahara 1964,N 12,40:2
Cheyenne Autumn 1964,D 24,8:1
Sylvia 1965,F 11,45:1
Greatest Story Ever Told, The 1965,F 16,40:2
Mister Moses 1965,My 13,32:1
Harlow 1965,Jl 22,24:1
Baker, Diane
Diary of Anne Frank, The 1959,Mr 19,40:1
Best of Everything 1959,O 9,24:2
Journey to the Center of the Earth 1959,D 17,51:1
Wizard of Baghdad, The 1961,Mr 4,16:1
Hemingway's Adventures of a Young Man 1962,Jl 26,17:1
300 Spartans, The 1962,S 20,29:2
Nine Hours to Rama 1963,Ap 4,58:2
Stolen Hours 1963,O 17,39:1
Strait Jacket 1964,Ja 23,26:1
Prize, The 1964,Ja 24,21:1
Marnie 1964,Je 23,19:1
Mirage 1965,My 27,28:1
Sands of Beersheba 1966,My 6,54:2
Horse in the Gray Flannel Suit, The 1968,D 21,49:3
Baker, Doris
Ella Cinders 1926,Je 7,23:2
Baker, Dorothy (Original Author)
Young Man With a Horn 1950,F 10,18:4
Baker, Dottie Bee
Rainmaker, The 1956,D 13,51:1
Baker, Eddie
Elmer and Elsie 1934,Ag 4,14:5
Baker, Edward
Land of Fury 1955,My 3,37:4
Baker, Elaine
Secret Call, The 1931,Jl 13,13:5
Baker, Elliott (Screenwriter)
Fine Madness, A 1966,Je 30,28:2
Luv 1967,Jl 27,29:1
Baker, Evadne
Seven Women From Hell 1962,F 1,22:2
Sound of Music, The 1965,Mr 3,34:1
Baker, Fay
No Minor Vices 1949,F 26,11:2
Chain Lightning 1950,F 20,21:2
Company She Keeps, The 1951,Ja 29,14:4
House on Telegraph Hill, The 1951,My 14,29:1
Deadline U S A 1952,Mr 15,8:2
Star, The 1953,Ja 29,25:1
Don't Knock the Rock 1957,F 23,13:1
Baker, Florence
Waterloo Bridge 1940,My 17,23:2
Baker, Frank
New Adventures of Tarzan, The 1935,O 15,19:3
Mary of Scotland 1936,Jl 31,22:2
Baroness and the Butler, The 1938,F 19,19:2
Four Men and a Prayer 1938,My 7,18:1
Chump at Oxford, A 1940,F 20,17:3
Donovan's Reef 1963,Jl 25,14:1
Baker, Frank (Original Author)
Lease of Life 1956,F 10,18:1
Baker, George
Waltz Time 1933,S 29,24:2
Ship That Died of Shame, The 1956,Ag 21,33:2
Baker, George (Original Author)
Sad Sack, The 1957,N 28,57:1
Baker, George (Screenwriter)
One Million BC 1940,Ap 27,9:2
Baker, George D (Director)
Heliotrope 1920,N 29,20:3
Buried Treasure 1921,F 14,12:2
Without Limit 1921,Mr 21,11:3
Slave of Desire 1923,D 11,26:2
Revelation 1924,Je 24,18:2

Baker, Graham (Original Author)
Billion Dollar Scandal, The 1933,Ja 9,23:1
Song of the Eagle 1933,Ap 29,14:3
I Love That Man 1933,Jl 10,11:7
Shanghai 1935,Jl 20,16:2
Girl Friend, The 1935,S 28,12:2
Grand Exit 1935,N 4,24:5
She Couldn't Take It 1935,N 7,27:1
Mary Burns, Fugitive 1935,N 16,19:2
You Only Live Once 1937,F 1,15:2
History Is Made at Night 1937,Mr 29,14:2
Ali Baba Goes to Town 1937,O 23,14:1
Baker, Graham (Producer)
Swiss Family Robinson 1940,F 9,15:3
Little Men 1940,D 9,23:2
Valley of the Sun 1942,Mr 19,29:2
Baker, Graham (Screenwriter)
Girl From Chicago, The 1927,D 20,33:2
Air Circus, The 1928,S 3,14:2
Shanghai 1935,Jl 20,16:2
Every Night at Eight 1935,Ag 3,16:2
Mary Burns, Fugitive 1935,N 16,19:2
Case Against Mrs Ames, The 1936,My 28,19:2
History Is Made at Night 1937,Mr 29,14:2
Stand-In 1937,N 19,27:2
Joy of Living 1938,My 6,27:1
Eternally Yours 1939,O 7,11:2
Swiss Family Robinson 1940,F 9,15:3
Tom Brown's School Days 1940,Je 28,22:2
Crime Doctor 1943,Jl 5,11:4
Danger Signal 1945,N 22,39:2
Ramrod 1947,Je 30,25:6
Four Faces West 1948,Ag 4,18:3
Tennessee's Partner 1955,N 5,22:8
Baker, Herbert (Director)
Jumping Jacks 1952,Jl 24,30:2
Baker, Herbert (Screenwriter)
Dream Wife 1953,Jl 30,20:1
Artists and Models 1955,D 22,20:1
Girl Can't Help It, The 1957,F 9,12:7
King Creole 1958,Jl 4,15:2
Murderers' Row 1966,D 22,40:3
Ambushers, The 1967,D 23,29:1
Hammerhead 1968,S 12,54:3
Baker, Hylda
Saturday Night and Sunday Morning
  1961,Ap 4,44:2
Baker, Jennifer
Funny Thing Happened on the Way to the Forum,
  A 1966,O 17,48:1
Baker, Joby
Last Angry Man, The 1959,O 23,24:1
Wackiest Ship in the Army, The 1961,F 9,36:1
Gidget Goes to Rome 1963,S 12,32:2
Girl Happy 1965,My 27,28:1
When the Boys Meet the Girls 1966,Ja 20,29:1
Adventures of Bullwhip Griffin, The
  1967,Mr 9,43:2
Blackbeard's Ghost 1968,Ap 11,51:3
Baker, Joe
Where the Bullets Fly 1967,S 7,50:4
Baker, Josephine
Moulin Rouge 1944,N 23,38:2
French Way, The 1952,S 6,12:6
Baker, Kenny
King of Burlesque 1936,Ja 16,25:2
King and the Chorus Girl, The 1937,Mr 29,14:4
Mr Dodd Takes the Air 1937,Ag 12,14:2
52d Street 1937,N 15,15:1
Goldwyn Follies, The 1938,F 21,15:1
Radio City Revels 1938,Mr 21,18:3
Mikado, The 1939,Je 2,27:2
At the Circus 1939,N 17,17:2
Hit Parade of 1941 1940,D 5,33:2
Silver Skates 1943,Mr 19,15:3
Stage Door Canteen 1943,Je 25,13:2
Harvey Girls, The 1946,Ja 25,26:2
Baker, Lee
Fighting Blade, The 1923,O 15,15:4
Soul Fire 1925,My 6,26:3
Mourning Becomes Electra 1947,N 20,38:2
Baker, Lorin
Mother's Boy 1929,My 8,34:6
Impatient Maiden, The 1932,Mr 4,17:3
No Hands on the Clock 1941,D 22,24:6
Baker, Louis (Original Author)
Her Twelve Men 1954,Ag 12,23:2
Baker, Mark
Across the Bridge 1957,O 30,24:1
Baker, Melville (Original Author)
Zoo in Budapest 1933,Ap 28,15:2
Now and Forever 1934,O 13,10:1
Gilded Lily, The 1935,F 9,11:2
Last Days of Pompeii, The 1935,O 17,29:2
Baker, Melville (Screenwriter)
Next Time We Love 1936,Ja 31,16:2
Ladies in Love 1936,O 29,31:1
Seventh Heaven 1937,Mr 26,25:1
First 100 Years, The 1938,My 13,17:2
Joe and Ethel Turp Call on the President
  1940,Ja 4,19:2
Above Suspicion 1943,Ag 6,10:3

Baker, Mickey (Composer)
Story of a Three Day Pass, The 1968,Jl 9,31:1
Baker, Nellie Bly
Goldfish, The 1924,My 20,15:2
Snob, The 1924,D 15,14:1
Red Kimono, The 1926,F 3,23:1
Breakfast at Sunrise 1927,N 14,26:1
Bishop Murder Case, The 1930,F 1,15:1
Baker, Phil
Gift of Gab 1934,S 26,17:6
Goldwyn Follies, The 1938,F 21,15:1
Gang's All Here, The 1943,D 23,26:4
Take It or Leave It 1944,Jl 13,14:2
Baker, Robert (Director)
Jack the Ripper 1960,F 18,37:4
Baker, Robert (Screenwriter)
Scared Stiff 1953,Jl 3,10:2
Baker, Robert S (Producer)
Murder Will Out 1953,Ap 6,24:2
Crawling Eye, The 1959,Ja 1,38:1
Jack the Ripper 1960,F 18,37:4
Home Is the Hero 1961,Ja 26,32:1
Desert Patrol 1962,Ja 18,23:5
No Place Like Homicide 1962,S 13,32:1
Baker, Roy (Director)
October Man, The 1948,Ap 16,29:2
Weaker Sex, The 1949,Jl 11,13:2
Operation Disaster 1951,Ja 15,13:1
I'll Never Forget You 1951,D 8,9:2
Don't Bother to Knock 1952,Jl 19,8:2
Night Without Sleep 1952,S 27,13:2
Inferno 1953,Ag 12,22:2
One That Got Away, The 1958,Ap 23,40:2
A Night to Remember 1958,D 17,2:7
Singer not the Song, The 1962,My 3,25:4
Valiant, The 1962,Je 14,23:4
Flame in the Streets 1962,S 13,32:1
Anniversary, The 1968,Mr 21,57:2
Five Million Years to Earth 1968,My 30,21:4
Baker, Roy (Producer)
Flame in the Streets 1962,S 13,32:1
Baker, Ruth
Persecution and Assassination of Jean-Paul Marat
  as Performed by the Inmates of the Asylum of
  Charenton Under the Direction of the Marquis
  De Sade, The 1967,F 23,41:1
Baker, Sam
Sea Hunt, The 1926,Ja 16,8:5
Sea Beast, The 1926,Ja 16,8:5
Missing Link, The 1927,My 7,15:2
King of the Jungle 1933,F 25,20:3
Public Hero No 1 1935,Je 8,12:2
Baker, Stanley
Lilli Marlene 1952,Mr 29,19:2
Cruel Sea, The 1953,Ag 11,18:5
Paratrooper 1953,D 31,9:3
Knights of the Round Table 1954,Ja 8,17:2
Hell Below Zero 1954,Jl 17,7:3
Helen of Troy 1956,Ja 27,21:4
Richard III 1956,Mr 12,1:4
Alexander the Great 1956,Mr 29,23:1
Checkpoint 1957,S 19,25:2
Angry Hills, The 1959,Jl 16,31:3
Campbell's Kingdom 1960,Ja 11,35:5
Yesterday's Enemy 1960,Mr 4,19:1
Chance Meeting 1960,O 27,45:2
Hell is a City 1961,Ja 19,26:3
Guns of Navarone, The 1961,Je 23,19:1
Sodom and Gomorrah 1963,Ja 24,5:3
In the French Style 1963,S 19,23:1
Zulu 1964,Jl 8,38:1
Eva 1965,Je 5,21:2
Dingaka 1965,Jl 1,34:1
Sands of the Kalahari 1965,N 25,64:5
Accident 1967,Ap 18,33:1
Robbery 1967,S 28,58:2
Baker, Stanley (Producer)
Zulu 1964,Jl 8,38:1
Sands of the Kalahari 1965,N 25,64:5
Robbery 1967,S 28,58:2
Baker, Susan
Funny Thing Happened on the Way to the Forum,
  A 1966,O 17,48:1
Baker, Tom
I, A Man 1967,Ag 25,28:1
Baker, Tom (Screenwriter)
Conqueror Worm, The 1968,Ag 15,46:2
Baker, Tommy
Blue Bird, The 1940,Ja 20,11:2
Brother Orchid 1940,Je 8,18:2
Baker, Tony
Cry From the Streets, A 1959,F 24,32:2
Baker, Virginia
Second to Hell 1959,Jl 18,6:3
Bakewell, William
Heart Thief, The 1927,Ap 27,22:5
Mother 1927,My 4,29:2
West Point 1928,Ja 2,28:1
Latest From Paris, The 1928,F 27,16:2
Harold Teen 1928,Ag 14,15:4
Battle of The Sexes, The 1928,O 15,16:1
Iron Mask, The 1929,F 22,18:6
Hot Stuff 1929,My 13,27:2

Bakewell, William— Cont
On With the Show 1929,My 29,28:6
Gold Diggers of Broadway, The 1929,Ag 31,13:4
Show of Shows 1929,N 21,24:5
Lummox 1930,Mr 24,25:1
Playing Around 1930,Mr 31,24:3
All Quiet on The Western Front 1930,Ap 30,29:1
Paid 1931,Ja 3,21:2
Bat Whispers, The 1931,Ja 16,27:1
Reducing 1931,Ja 17,23:1
Dance, Fools, Dance 1931,Mr 21,15:1
Daybreak 1931,Je 1,15:1
Woman of Experience, A 1931,Jl 9,26:5
Politics 1931,Ag 1,16:4
Guilty Hands 1931,Ag 29,16:3
Spirit of Notre Dame, The 1931,O 16,27:1
Cheaters at Play 1932,F 27,22:1
Back Street 1932,Ag 29,9:2
Lucky Devils 1933,F 20,11:5
Three-Cornered Moon 1933,Ag 12,14:2
You Can't Buy Everything 1934,F 3,9:2
Quitter, The 1934,Mr 14,23:3
Straight Is the Way 1934,Ag 29,13:2
Crimson Romance 1934,O 13,10:1
Sons of Steel 1935,Ap 15,16:3
Quality Street 1937,Ap 9,19:2
Trapped by G-Men 1937,N 4,29:1
Duke of West Point, The 1938,D 16,33:2
King of the Turf 1939,My 8,21:2
Beyond Tomorrow 1940,S 27,27:1
Seven Sinners 1940,N 18,23:2
Cheers for Miss Bishop 1941,Mr 14,17:2
Loves of Edgar Allan Poe, The 1942,S 21,19:2
Fabulous Dorseys, The 1947,My 30,25:3
Bachelor and the Bobby-Soxer, The
  1947,Jl 25,12:5
Romance on the High Seas 1948,Je 26,10:5
You Gotta Stay Happy 1948,N 5,29:2
Come Fill the Cup 1951,N 22,47:2
Davy Crockett, King of the Wild Frontier
  1955,My 26,36:1
Bakiga and Batwa Tribes, Members of
Man of Africa 1956,O 11,51:1
Bakker, Piet (Original Author)
Ciske 1963,Ag 3,8:2
Baklanov, G (Original Author)
Forty-Nine Days 1964,Ja 27,19:1
Baklanova, Olga
Street of Sin, The 1928,My 28,23:2
Baksheev, D
Yellow Ticket, The 1928,D 10,25:1
Bakshy, Alexander (Miscellaneous)
No Greater Love 1944,F 25,23:3
Baky, Josef von (Director)
Kleine und die Grosse Liebe, Die; Minor Love and
  the Real Thing, The 1938,Jl 23,10:5
Ihr Erstes Erlebnis; Her First Experience
  1940,Je 8,18:3
Bal, Anny
Girl From Corfu, The 1957,My 20,28:2
Bala, Rani
Light of Asia, The 1928,My 12,8:4
Balaban, Bruce (Producer)
Place Called Glory, A 1966,Ag 11,27:4
Balaban, Burt (Director)
Murder, Inc 1960,Je 29,26:6
Mad Dog Coll 1961,My 13,10:1
Balaban, Burt (Producer)
Murder, Inc 1960,Je 29,26:6
Baladimes, K
Phaedra 1962,O 19,24:1
Balanchine, George (Miscellaneous)
Goldwyn Follies, The 1938,F 21,15:1
Midsummer Night's Dream, A 1967,Ap 18,32:1
Balandin, S
Lust for Gold 1958,Jl 24,18:1
Balanoff, Simcha
Vilna Legend, A (Russian-Jewish Cast)
  1949,S 26,17:1
Balasco, Leon
Can-Can 1960,Mr 10,36:1
Balash, Bela (Miscellaneous)
Karl Brunner 1936,D 6,XII,8:5 (In Addenda)
Balashov, V
Oppenheim Family, The 1939,My 24,29:2
Heroes Are Made 1944,Mr 11,10:2
Girl No 217 1945,S 3,17:2
Ivan Pavlov 1950,F 13,15:2
Secret Brigade 1951,Mr 19,23:2
Mussorgsky 1951,Ag 20,14:3
New Number Comes to Moscow, A
  1959,Jl 6,23:1
Ivan the Terrible, Part II 1959,N 25,22:4
Balashova, Emma
Village Teacher 1948,Jl 5,8:4
Balazs, Bela (Screenwriter)
Threepenny Opera, The 1960,Jl 11,24:4
Balazs, Maria (Director)
Pokhalo 1938,My 7,18:2
Balbina
Belles of St Trinian's, The 1954,D 23,13:4
Balch, Slim
Hollywood Cowboy 1937,Jl 24,12:1

Balchin, Nigel (Original Author)
Mine Own Executioner 1949,Ja 19,34:2
Small Back Room, The 1952,F 2,11:3
Risk, The 1961,S 25,41:2
Balchin, Nigel (Screenwriter)
Mine Own Executioner 1949,Ja 19,34:2
Fame Is the Spur 1949,N 8,34:2
Story of Mandy, The 1953,F 24,21:3
Malta Story 1954,Jl 17,7:2
Man Who Never Was, The 1956,Ap 4,24:1
23 Paces to Baker Street 1956,My 19,12:6
Blue Angel, The 1959,S 5,11:4
Circle of Deception 1961,F 18,12:2
Risk, The 1961,S 25,41:2
Singer not the Song, The 1962,My 3,25:4
Balcon, Jill
Nicholas Nickleby 1947,D 1,27:2
Saraband 1949,Je 13,16:3
Good Time Girl 1950,S 25,18:5
Balcon, Michael (Director)
Ware Case, The 1939,Jl 22,12:2
Balcon, Michael (Miscellaneous)
Rome Express 1932,D 18,X,6:5
Balcon, Michael (Producer)
Yank at Oxford, A 1938,F 25,15:1
Secret Four, The 1940,Ap 22,13:2
Let George Do It 1940,O 14,25:5
Convoy 1941,Ja 17,21:2
Proud Valley 1941,My 17,19:2
Three Cockeyed Sailors 1942,Ja 26,18:3
Ships With Wings 1942,My 25,11:2
Next of Kin 1943,My 6,25:2
Somewhere in France 1943,Jl 12,11:2
Shrine of Victory 1943,Ag 20,13:2
Young Man's Fancy, A 1943,D 4,11:2
48 Hours 1944,Je 26,21:2
They Came to a City 1945,F 19,21:3
Half-Way House 1945,Ag 13,22:4
Dead of Night 1946,Je 29,22:6
Johnny Frenchman 1946,O 21,27:3
Overlanders, The 1946,D 20,31:2
Captive Heart, The 1947,Ap 28,27:2
Frieda 1947,Ag 15,12:3
Girl in the Canal, The 1947,O 9,32:3
Nicholas Nickleby 1947,D 1,27:2
Champagne Charlie 1948,Ag 7,8:2
It Always Rains on Sunday 1949,F 14,15:5
Saraband 1949,Je 13,16:3
Against the Wind 1949,Je 27,18:3
Run for Your Money, A 1950,Ap 10,15:3
Kind Hearts and Coronets 1950,Je 15,41:2
Pink String and Sealing Wax 1950,O 4,38:2
Hue and Cry 1951,Ja 9,25:2
Blue Lamp, The 1951,Ja 9,25:1
Scott of the Antarctic 1951,F 26,20:2
Magnet, The 1951,F 27,22:6
Lavender Hill Mob, The 1951,O 16,35:2
Pool of London 1951,N 28,37:2
Case of Gold 1952,Ja 19,13:3
Cage of Gold 1952,Ja 19,13:3
Man in the White Suit, The 1952,Ap 1,35:2
Train of Events 1952,My 26,18:4
Ivory Hunter 1952,Ag 19,19:1
Night my Number Came up, The 1955,D 20,39:5
Lease of Life 1956,F 10,18:1
All at Sea 1957,D 23,18:2
Dunkirk 1958,S 11,42:2
Scapegoat, The 1959,Ag 7,28:1
Baldanello, Dora
Avvocato Difensore, L'; Attorney for the Defense,
    The 1935,N 13,25:4
Balderas, Francisco
Brave Bulls, The 1951,Ap 19,39:2
Balderston, John L (Original Author)
Frankenstein 1931,D 5,21:2
Berkeley Square 1933,S 14,26:2
Little Old New York 1940,F 3,9:2
I'll Never Forget You 1951,D 8,9:2
Red Planet Mars 1952,Je 16,15:2
Balderston, John L (Screenwriter)
Lives of a Bengal Lancer, The 1935,Ja 12,12:2
Mystery of Edwin Drood, The 1935,Mr 21,27:1
Bride of Frankenstein, The 1935,My 11,21:2
Mad Love 1935,Ag 5,20:2
Last of the Mohicans, The 1936,S 3,17:3
Man Who Lived Again, The 1936,D 16,35:4
Beloved Enemy 1936,D 26,15:2
Prisoner of Zenda, The 1937,S 3,12:1
Victory 1940,D 23,23:2
Scotland Yard 1941,Ap 9,33:3
Smilin' Through 1941,D 5,29:2
Tennessee Johnson 1943,Ja 13,18:2
Stand by for Action 1943,Mr 12,12:2
Gaslight 1944,My 5,17:2
Red Planet Mars 1952,Je 16,15:2
Prisoner of Zenda, The 1952,N 5,36:2
Baldi, Ferdinando (Director)
David and Goliath 1961,O 7,14:3
Baldi, Gian Vittorio (Director)
Adolescents, The (Flammetta); Flammetta (The
    Adolescents) 1967,Ap 14,33:1

Baldi, Gian Vittorio (Producer)
Chronicle of Anna Magdalena Bach
    1968,S 20,37:7
Baldi, Gian Vittorio (Screenwriter)
Adolescents, The (Flammetta); Flammetta (The
    Adolescents) 1967,Ap 14,33:1
Baldini, Renato
Angelo 1951,Mr 26,19:4
Behind Closed Shutters 1952,Je 10,22:7
Theodora, Slave Empress 1955,Ja 12,24:2
Wayward Wife, The 1955,Ap 11,29:3
Girls of the Night 1959,Mr 21,13:2
See Naples and Die 1959,Ag 31,16:2
White Warrior, The 1961,F 11,27:2
Girl With a Suitcase 1961,S 12,36:2
Head of a Tyrant 1962,Je 7,31:2
Baldock, Alvin
Saturday's Hero 1951,S 12,37:2
Baldour, Charles (Producer)
Secret Door, The 1964,Je 4,28:1
Baldova, Zdenka
Inspector General, The 1937,N 25,37:1
Distant Journey 1950,Ag 28,13:3
Baldra, Chuck
Lawless Nineties, The 1936,Je 29,11:1
Balducci, Franco
Stranger on the Prowl 1953,N 10,38:1
Viaccia, La 1962,S 21,35:1
Tramplers, The 1966,D 8,64:1
Baldwin, Alan
Winter Carnival 1939,Jl 28,14:2
Prison Camp 1940,Ag 3,9:3
Baldwin, Bill
Once a Thief 1951,Ja 19,21:3
Baldwin, Dick
Life Begins In College 1937,O 9,16:1
Love and Hisses 1938,Ja 1,11:1
International Settlement 1938,F 12,20:3
Mr Moto's Gamble 1938,Ap 8,17:2
One Wild Night 1938,Je 3,17:2
Spring Madness 1938,D 1,29:3
Baldwin, Earl (Original Author)
Naughty Flirt, The 1931,Ap 13,17:1
Blondie Johnson 1933,F 27,11:2
Havana Widows 1933,N 23,24:3
6-Day Bike Rider 1934,N 3,20:3
Breakfast in Hollywood 1946,Jl 15,21:1
Lullaby of Broadway 1951,Mr 27,35:2
Baldwin, Earl (Screenwriter)
6-Day Bike Rider 1934,N 3,20:3
Devil Dogs of the Air 1935,F 7,23:2
Go Into Your Dance 1935,My 4,17:2
Irish in US, The 1935,Ag 1,15:1
Ever Since Eve 1937,Je 25,25:2
Slight Case of Murder, A 1938,F 28,19:1
Gold Diggers in Paris 1938,Je 2,19:2
Cowboy From Brooklyn 1938,Jl 14,17:1
Off the Record 1939,F 18,12:2
Brother Orchid 1940,Je 8,18:2
Man Who Talked too Much, The 1940,Je 29,12:2
My Love Came Back 1940,Jl 13,16:5
She Couldn't Say No 1941,Ja 11,21:3
Honeymoon for Three 1941,F 8,19:2
Unholy Partners 1941,D 29,21:4
Navy Comes Through, The 1942,N 12,30:3
Pin Up Girl 1944,My 11,25:6
Greenwich Village 1944,S 28,26:2
Irish Eyes Are Smiling 1944,N 8,27:1
Hold That Blonde 1945,N 8,17:2
Breakfast in Hollywood 1946,Jl 15,21:1
Africa Screams 1949,My 5,34:2
South Sea Woman 1953,Je 4,33:6
Baldwin, Evelyn
Struggle, The 1931,D 11,35:1
Baldwin, Faith (Original Author)
Office Wife, The 1930,S 27,21:3
Week-End Marriage 1932,Je 4,9:2
Skyscraper Souls 1932,Ag 5,17:2
Beauty for Sale 1933,S 16,9:3
Wife vs Secretary 1936,F 29,11:1
Love Before Breakfast 1936,Mr 14,10:1
Moon's our Home, The 1936,My 13,29:2
Portia on Trial 1937,D 3,29:2
Men Are Such Fools 1938,Je 17,25:1
Comet over Broadway 1938,D 16,33:3
Apartment for Peggy 1948,O 16,9:2
Baldwin, Harry
Buck Benny Rides Again 1940,Ap 25,28:4
Baldwin, Peter
Girls of Pleasure Island, The 1953,My 16,10:1
Stalag 17 1953,Jl 2,19:2
Houdini 1953,Jl 3,10:2
Little Boy Lost 1953,S 22,38:2
Tin Star, The 1957,O 24,37:2
Teacher's Pet 1958,Mr 20,33:1
Trap, The 1959,Ja 29,18:4
Baldwin, Robert
Girl From Scotland Yard, The 1937,My 31,11:2
Midnight Madonna 1937,Jl 17,18:1
Main Street Lawyer 1939,N 9,27:2
Meet Doctor Christian 1939,D 1,27:2
Courageous Dr Christian, The 1940,Mr 29,25:3

Baldwin, Walter
Devil Commands, The 1941,F 14,15:3
Look Who's Laughing 1941,D 25,33:2
Mr Winkle Goes to War 1944,Ag 3,16:1
Together Again 1944,N 24,19:2
Why Girls Leave Home 1945,Ag 4,7:3
Best Years of our Lives, The 1946,N 22,27:2
Unsuspected, The 1947,O 4,9:2
Mourning Becomes Electra 1947,N 20,38:2
Winter Meeting 1948,Ap 8,31:2
Rachel and the Stranger 1948,S 20,21:2
Cry of the City 1948,S 30,32:4
Come to the Stable 1949,Jl 28,19:1
Special Agent 1949,Ag 22,13:1
Thieves' Highway 1949,S 24,8:6
Cheaper by the Dozen 1950,Ap 1,12:2
Stella 1950,Ag 19,9:2
Jackpot, The 1950,N 23,55:2
Storm Warning 1951,Mr 3,8:2
Racket, The 1951,D 13,44:2
I Want You 1951,D 24,9:1
Winning Team, The 1952,Je 21,12:2
Carrie 1952,Jl 17,20:2
Scandal at Scourie 1953,Je 16,24:2
Long, Long Trailer, The 1954,F 19,24:3
Interrupted Melody 1955,My 6,18:1
Baledon, Rafael
El Conde de Monte Cristo 1943,N 9,26:2
Balestrieri, Virginia
Malia 1952,F 2,11:4
Balfe, William (Original Author)
Bohemian Girl, The 1923,F 5,18:2
Bohemian Girl, The 1936,F 17,21:1
Balfour, Betty
Paradise 1929,N 4,28:1
Evergreen 1935,Ja 11,29:1
Born for Glory 1935,O 21,22:4
Facts of Love, The 1949,O 31,20:2
Balfour, Katherine
Music for Millions 1944,D 22,12:4
America America 1963,D 16,44:1
Balfour, Lorna
Merely Mary Ann 1931,S 12,15:4
Balfour, Michael
Hidden Room, The 1950,Ja 9,19:2
Prelude to Fame 1950,N 10,35:3
No Orchids for Miss Blandish 1951,F 23,33:2
Assassin, The 1953,Ap 18,17:2
Fiend Without a Face 1958,Jl 4,15:3
Balhaus, Carl
Abel Mit Der Mundharmonika 1934,S 1,16:3
Anna und Elisabeth 1936,Je 13,13:1
Balhous, Carl
Wackere Schustermeister, Der 1936,Jl 7,22:4
Balieff, Nikita
Once in a Blue Moon 1936,D 2,35:1
Balik, Jaroslav (Director)
Death of Tarzan, The 1968,Jl 4,13:2
Balik, Jaroslav (Screenwriter)
Death of Tarzan, The 1968,Jl 4,13:2
Balikhin, Victor
Without Dowry 1946,Ap 15,22:2
Balin, Ina
Black Orchid, The 1959,F 13,33:2
From the Terrace 1960,Jl 16,10:1
Young Doctors, The 1961,Ag 24,25:2
Comancheros, The 1961,N 2,42:1
Patsy, The 1964,Ag 13,24:2
Greatest Story Ever Told, The 1965,F 16,40:2
Balin, Mireille
Kiss of Fire, The 1940,N 20,27:4
Pepe le Moko 1941,Mr 4,20:2
Balint, Andras
Age of Illusions 1967,Mr 30,55:1
Father 1967,S 29,53:1
Balkin, Karen
Childrens Hour, The 1962,Mr 15,28:2
Ball, Ernest (Composer)
Marriage of Molly-O, The 1916,Jl 24,7:4
Ball, J A (Cinematographer)
Toll of the Sea, The 1922,N 27,18:1
Ball, Jane
Winged Victory 1944,D 21,16:2
Keys of the Kingdom, The 1944,D 30,15:2
Forever Amber 1947,O 23,31:2
Ball, John (Original Author)
In the Heat of the Night 1967,Ag 3,26:1
Ball, Lucille
Carnival 1935,F 16,9:1
I Dream too Much 1935,N 29,24:1
Chatterbox 1936,F 15,18:6
Follow the Fleet 1936,F 21,21:2
Bunker Bean 1936,Je 27,21:2
That Girl From Paris 1937,Ja 1,19:1
Don't Tell the Wife 1937,F 19,15:2
Stage Door 1937,O 8,27:2
Joy of Living 1938,My 6,27:1
Go Chase Yourself 1938,Je 15,27:1
Having Wonderful Time 1938,Jl 8,11:2
Room Service 1938,S 22,27:1
Affairs of Annabel, The 1938,O 13,29:2
Next Time I Marry 1938,D 2,27:2
Annabel Takes a Tour 1938,D 29,15:3

Ball, Lucille — Cont

Beauty for the Asking 1939,F 10,19:1
Twelve Crowded Hours 1939,F 24,15:2
Five came Back 1939,Jl 5,20:2
That's Right, You're Wrong 1939,N 30,25:3
You Can't Fool Your Wife 1940,My 24,23:4
Dance, Girl, Dance 1940,O 11,25:2
Too Many Girls 1940,N 21,43:1
Girl, a Guy and a Gob, A 1941,Ap 24,25:3
Look Who's Laughing 1941,D 25,33:2
Valley of the Sun 1942,Mr 19,29:2
Big Street, The 1942,Ag 14,13:1
Seven Days' Leave 1942,D 11,33:2
Best Foot Forward 1943,Je 30,25:2
Du Barry Was a Lady 1943,Ag 20,13:1
Thousands Cheer 1943,S 14,27:1
Meet The People 1944,S 8,16:2
Without Love 1945,Mr 23,13:1
Ziegfeld Follies 1946,Mr 23,8:3
Dark Corner, The 1946,My 9,27:3
Lover Come Back 1946,Je 20,20:3
Easy to Wed 1946,Jl 12,14:2
Two Smart People 1947,F 15,20:4
Lured 1947,Ag 29,14:4
Her Husband's Affairs 1947,N 14,29:2
Sorrowful Jones 1949,Je 6,15:2
Easy Living 1949,O 13,33:3
Fancy Pants 1950,Ag 31,21:2
Fuller Brush Girl, The 1950,O 6,23:2
Long, Long Trailer, The 1954,F 19,24:3
Forever, Darling 1956,F 10,18:1
Facts of Life, The 1961,F 11,27:1
Critic's Choice 1963,My 2,40:2
Guide for the Married Man, A 1967,My 27,16:1
Yours, Mine and Ours 1968,Ap 25,53:1

Ball, Susan
Untamed Frontier 1952,Ag 23,10:2
City Beneath the Sea 1953,Mr 12,24:3
Chief Crazy Horse 1955,Ap 28,25:1

Ball, Vincent
You Can't Beat the Irish 1952,My 1,34:4
Town Like Alice, A 1958,S 22,27:1
Desert Patrol 1962,Ja 18,23:5
Matter of Who, A 1962,Jl 25,29:2

Balla, Lici
Mindent a Noert! 1934,O 17,26:3
Egy ej Velencebzn 1935,D 27,14:2

Balla, Zsuzsi
Sportszerelem; Love of Sport 1938,F 14,20:8

Ballah, Miriam
Which Shall It Be? 1924,Ap 7,15:3

Ballantine, Carl
McHale's Navy 1964,Jl 11,15:2
Speedway 1968,Je 14,43:1
Shakiest Gun in the West, The 1968,Jl 11,30:1

Ballantine, E J
Moon Is Down, The 1943,Mr 27,8:6
Tampico 1944,Je 2,21:2
Miss Susie Slagle's 1946,F 7,29:2
Magic Town 1947,O 8,29:2

Ballantyne, Nell
Mr Emmanuel 1945,Ja 8,15:2
Scotch on the Rocks 1954,Je 14,18:2
Bridal Path, The 1959,D 21,34:2

Ballard, Elmer
Alibi 1929,Ap 9,29:1
Her Private Affair 1930,Ja 11,21:3
Fall Guy, The 1930,My 27,27:2

Ballard, Fred (Original Author)
Ladies of the Jury 1932,Ap 2,13:2
Young America 1932,My 7,11:5
We're on the Jury 1937,F 10,18:5
When's Your Birthday? 1937,Mr 19,27:2

Ballard, Kaye
Girl Most Likely, The 1958,O 9,47:1
House is not a Home, A 1964,S 2,33:1

Ballard, Manuela
Francis of Assisi 1961,Jl 29,8:2

Ballard, Shirley
Second Woman, The 1951,F 2,19:2
Cop Hater 1958,O 2,44:3

Ballas, Demetris
Casablan 1964,D 14,50:1

Ballasko, Viktoria
Freiheit und Liebe, Um; For Freedom and Love
  1938,F 5,19:3
Kleine Suenderin, Die; Little Sinner, The
  1938,D 3,11:3
Robert Koch 1939,N 25,13:2

Ballbusch, Peter
Body Is a Shell, The 1957,S 9,21:2

Ballbusch, Peter (Original Author)
Body Is a Shell, The 1957,S 9,21:2

Ballbusch, Peter (Screenwriter)
Body Is a Shell, The 1957,S 9,21:2

Ballerin, Piero (Director)
Lucia di Lammermoor 1947,N 1,11:3

Ballerini, Piero (Screenwriter)
Lucia di Lammermoor 1947,N 1,11:3
Cinderella 1953,My 15,20:2

Ballerini, Ugo Col
Roman Holiday 1953,Ag 28,13:1

Ballester, Amparo
That Midnight Kiss 1949,S 23,28:2

Ballet, Corps de of Monte Carlo
Lover's Return, A; Revenant, Le 1948,Ja 26,15:2

Ballet, Corps de of the Bolshoy Theater
Spring 1948,Mr 15,26:2

Ballet, Corps de of the Kirghizian State Opera Co
Morning Star 1962,Ag 20,18:2

Ballet, Corps de of the Leningrad Kirov Ballet
Sleeping Beauty, The 1966,My 4,50:1

Ballet, Moscow, Members of
Lenin in 1918 1939,Je 27,27:2

Ballet, New York City
Midsummer Night's Dream, A 1967,Ap 18,32:1

Ballet, School of Amrican
Midsummer Night's Dream, A 1967,Ap 18,32:1

Ballet de l'Etoile
Belles and Ballets 1960,N 15,45:3

Ballew, Smith
Rawhide 1938,Ap 25,19:2

Ballhaus, Carl
Comrades of 1918 1931,F 20,18:5

Ballier, Guenther
Heideschulmeister uwe Karsten 1934,Ap 14,18:3

Ballin, Hugo (Director)
Vanity Fair 1923,My 7,19:3

Ballin, Hugo (Producer)
Journey's End, The 1921,Jl 18,16:3
Jane Eyre 1922,Ja 29,VI,2:1 (In Addenda)

Ballin, Mabel
Lord and Lady Algy 1919,S 29,16:1
Journey's End, The 1921,Jl 18,16:3
Jane Eyre 1922,Ja 29,VI,2:1 (In Addenda)
Vanity Fair 1923,My 7,19:3
Barriers Burned Away 1925,Mr 12,17:2
Code of the West 1925,Ap 13,24:1
Riders of the Purple Sage 1925,Ap 15,16:1

Balling, Erik (Producer)
Girls are Willing, The 1959,My 11,30:1

Ballinger, Bill S (Screenwriter)
Strangler, The 1964,Je 11,27:4

Ballinger, William S (Original Author)
Pushover 1954,Jl 31,6:3

Ballista, Gigi
Birds, the Bees and the Italians, The
  1967,Ag 8,33:2
Climax, The 1967,S 12,55:1

Ballot, Nadine
Adolescents, The (Marie-France and Veronica);
  Marie-France and Veronica (The Adolescents)
  1967,Ap 14,33:1

BALLOU
See Also BELLEW

Ballou, Marion
Big Pond, The 1930,My 19,21:1
Cradle Song 1933,N 20,18:2
Melody Lingers on, The 1935,N 7,27:1
Camille 1937,Ja 23,13:1

Bally, Michele
Steppe, The 1963,O 1,33:1
Mafioso 1964,Jl 1,42:1

Balmer, Edwin (Original Author)
That Royle Girl 1926,Ja 4,33:1
Party Girl 1930,Ja 2,28:2
When Worlds Collide 1952,F 7,30:2

Balmer, Edwin (Screenwriter)
Breath of Scandal, The 1924,N 26,17:3

Balogh, Bela (Director)
Edes Mostoha 1935,N 21,27:2
Salary, 200 a Month 1937,Ja 15,17:3
Tommy 1937,O 16,22:3
Sutyi, a Szerencseqyerek; Sutyi, the Lucky Child
  1938,Ja 22,19:2
Urilany Szobat Keres; Lady Seeks Room
  1938,Mr 19,11:2
Keseru Mezeshetek; Bitter Honeymoon
  1939,O 9,15:3
Vadroza; Wild Rose 1940,Ja 29,11:6

Balpetre, Antoine
Dawn Over France 1945,Mr 17,17:2
Carnival of Sinners 1947,Ap 8,34:2
Corbeau, Le; Raven, The 1948,F 24,21:1
Tainted 1950,Ja 21,10:2
Justice Is Done 1953,Mr 3,23:2
Diary of a Country Priest 1954,Ap 6,35:2
Snow Was Black, The 1956,O 16,36:5
We Are all Murderers 1957,Ja 9,27:2
Rouge et Noir 1958,Ap 9,42:1
Money, Money, Money 1962,Jl 18,20:1
Magnificent Sinner 1963,Ap 25,38:1
Burning Court, The 1963,Ag 1,17:2
Mistress for the Summer, A 1964,Mr 28,13:5

Balpo
Panic 1947,N 27,50:2

Balque, Erica
Seven Journeys 1951,Mr 12,20:2
Devil's General, The 1957,Ap 16,38:2

Balsam, Martin
On the Waterfront 1954,Jl 29,18:1
12 Angry Men 1957,Ap 15,24:1
Time Limit 1957,O 24,37:2
Marjorie Morningstar 1958,Ap 25,32:2
Al Capone 1959,Mr 26,27:1

Balsam, Martin — Cont
Middle of the Night 1959,Je 18,36:1
Psycho 1960,Je 17,37:1
Ada 1961,Ag 26,15:1
Breakfast at Tiffany's 1961,O 6,28:1
Cape Fear 1962,Ap 19,35:2
Everybody go Home!; Tutti a Casa 1962,N 6,38:1
Who's Been Sleeping in My Bed? 1963,D 26,33:2
Seven Days in May 1964,F 20,22:1
Carpetbaggers, The 1964,Jl 2,24:4
Harlow 1965,Jl 22,24:1
Bedford Incident, The 1965,N 3,43:1
Thousand Clowns, A 1965,D 14,54:2
After the Fox 1966,D 24,11:1
Hombre 1967,Mr 22,41:1

Balsamo, Ignazio
Mafia; (In Nome Della Legge) 1950,Mr 2,33:2
What Price Innocence? 1953,My 2,13:3
Genoese Dragnet 1954,F 12,20:5
Eye of the Needle, The 1965,Je 22,25:2

Balser, Ewald
Jana, Das Maedchen aus dem Boehmerwald
  1936,Je 20,22:3
Eroica; (The Beethoven Story) 1951,O 29,19:2
Dreimaederlhaus, Das; (House of Three Girls,
  The) 1961,N 18,15:1

Balser, George (Composer)
Are You With It? 1948,Ap 15,31:2

Balsetti, Alessandro (Director)
Patria, Amore e Dovere 1937,Ap 8,21:1

Balter, Sam
Pittsburgh Kid, The 1941,S 23,27:4
Abbott and Costello Meet the Invisible Man
  1951,Ag 13,18:6

Balthoff, Alfred
Marriage in the Shadows 1948,S 17,28:3
Escape from East Berlin 1962,D 6,55:3

Baltzell, J Thomas (Producer)
Washington's Sky Patrol 1918,D 30,7:3

Balustein, Julian (Producer)
Take Care of my Little Girl 1951,Jl 19,20:2

Balutin, Jacques
Army Game, The; Tire Au Flanc
  1963,Ap 24,40:1
Great Spy Chase, The 1966,O 6,56:4

Balzac, Honore de (Original Author)
Gobsek 1937,Jl 16,22:1
Colonel Chabert 1947,Je 21,11:2
Wicked Duchess, The 1949,N 5,10:5
Girl With the Golden Eyes, The 1962,Ag 21,36:2

Balzac (Original Author)
Conquering Power, The 1921,Jl 10,VI,2:1 (In
  Addenda)
Eternal Flame, The 1922,S 18,14:2
Slave of Desire 1923,D 11,26:2
Cousine Bette, La 1928,Ag 12,VII,3:4
Survival 1930,Ja 13,21:1
Honor of the Family 1931,O 17,20:1
Vautrin, the Thief 1949,N 11,31:2

Balzer, Karl Michael
Bridge, The; (Bruecke, Die) 1961,My 2,42:1

Bamattre, Martha
American in Paris, An 1951,O 5,24:2

Bamberger, Peter (Producer)
Always Victorious 1960,Ap 7,46:1

Bamberger, Rudolph (Miscellaneous)
Cinderella 1926,Ap 5,24:1

Ban, Frigyes (Director)
Treasured Earth 1950,D 14,51:3

Banal, Ehud
Clouds Over Israel 1966,My 10,48:6

Banas, Robert
King and I, The 1956,Je 29,15:6

Banbury, Frith
Life and Death of Colonel Blimp, The
  1945,Mr 30,18:2

Bancrjce, Haradhan
Mahanagar; Big City, The 1964,S 28,19:1

Bancroft, Anne
Don't Bother to Knock 1952,Jl 19,8:2
Tonight We Sing 1953,F 13,17:2
Treasure of the Golden Condor 1953,My 23,19:2
Kid From Left Field, The 1953,S 26,15:3
Gorilla at Large 1954,Je 12,13:2
Demetrius and the Gladiators 1954,Je 19,9:1
Raid, The 1954,Ag 21,10:4
New York Confidential 1955,F 19,18:1
Life in the Balance, A 1955,Jl 14,19:1
Naked Street, The 1955,O 1,11:2
Last Frontier, The 1955,D 8,45:1
Walk the Proud Land 1956,S 8,20:6 (In
  Addenda)
Nightfall 1957,Ja 24,34:1
Miracle Worker, The 1962,My 24,29:2
Pumpkin Eater, The 1964,N 10,58:1
Slender Thread, The 1965,D 24,24:2
7 Women 1966,My 5,59:1
Graduate, The 1967,D 22,44:4

Bancroft, George
Journey's End, The 1921,Jl 18,16:3
Driven 1923,F 12,13:4
Deadwood Coach, The 1925,Ja 21,19:3
Code of the West 1925,Ap 13,24:1
Rainbow Trail, The 1925,Je 3,26:4

Bancroft, George— Cont
Pony Express, The 1925,S 14,16:1
Enchanted Hill, The 1925,D 29,19:2 (In Addenda)
Sea Horses 1926,F 23,26:5
Runaway, The 1926,Ap 27,23:2
Splendid Road, The 1926,Je 13,31:1
Old Ironsides 1926,D 7,21:2
Rough Riders, The 1927,Mr 16,28:2
White Gold 1927,Ap 11,18:3
Underworld 1927,Ag 22,21:3
Tell It to Sweeney 1927,O 17,20:2
Showdown, The 1928,Mr 5,21:1
Drag Net, The 1928,Je 4,13:2
Docks of New York, The 1928,S 17,28:2
Wolf of Wall Street, The 1929,Ja 28,21:1
Thunderbolt 1929,Je 21,17:2
Mighty, The 1929,D 30,16:4
Nuits de Chicago; Underworld 1930,Ap 20,VIII,6:5
Docks of New York; Damnees de l'Ocean, Les 1930,Ap 20,VIII,6:5
Paramount on Parade 1930,Ap 21,20:4
Ladies Love Brutes 1930,My 16,20:4
Derelict 1930,N 22,21:3
Scandal Sheet 1931,F 9,25:3
Skin Game, The 1931,Je 20,20:4
Rich Man's Folly 1931,N 27,29:3
World and the Flesh, The 1932,My 7,11:5
Lady and Gent 1932,Jl 16,5:5
Blood Money 1933,N 16,30:5
Elmer and Elsie 1934,Ag 4,14:5
Mr Deeds Goes to Town 1936,Ap 17,17:2
Wedding Present 1936,N 19,31:3
Doctor's Diary, A 1937,F 17,16:4
John Meade's Woman 1937,F 18,19:1
Racketeers in Exile 1937,Ap 12,15:3
Submarine Patrol 1938,N 19,9:2
Angels With Dirty Faces 1938,N 26,18:1
Stagecoach 1939,Mr 3,21:1
Each Dawn I Die 1939,Jl 22,12:2
Espionage Agent 1939,S 23,22:2
Rulers of the Sea 1939,N 9,27:1
Green Hell 1940,Ja 30,15:6
Young Tom Edison 1940,Mr 15,27:2
When the Daltons Rode 1940,Ag 23,13:3
North West Mounted Police 1940,N 7,33:2
Little Men 1940,D 9,23:2
Texas 1941,O 17,27:3
Bugle Sounds, The 1942,Ap 3,25:2
Syncopation 1942,My 29,13:3
Whistling in Dixie 1942,D 31,20:4
Bancroft, George Pleydell (Original Author)
Ware Case, The 1939,Jl 22,12:2
Bancroft, Roy
Hoodlum Empire 1952,Mr 6,25:6
Rogue Cop 1954,S 18,12:2
Band, Albert (Director)
Tramplers, The 1966,D 8,64:1
Band, Albert (Original Author)
Minute to Pray, A Second to Die, A 1968,My 23,56:2
Band, Albert (Producer)
Tramplers, The 1966,D 8,64:1
Minute to Pray, A Second to Die, A 1968,My 23,56:2
Band, Albert (Screenwriter)
Red Badge of Courage, The 1951,O 19,22:2
Tramplers, The 1966,D 8,64:1
Bandini, Armando
Mandragola 1966,Je 7,50:2
Bando, Kotaro
Gate of Hell 1954,D 14,45:2
Bandob, J
Slums of Tokyo 1930,Jl 7,22:3
Bandopadhaya, B (Original Author)
Pather Panchali 1958,S 23,37:2
Bandopadyaya, Bibhutibhushan (Original Author)
Aparajito 1959,Ap 29,30:1
Banducci, Eliana
Bandit, The 1949,Je 7,26:3
Banerjee, Tarashankar (Original Author)
Music Room, The 1963,O 16,50:6
Banerji, Karuna
Pather Panchali 1958,S 23,37:2
Aparajito 1959,Ap 29,30:1
Aparajito 1959,Ap 29,30:1
Kanchenjungha 1966,Jl 26,27:2
Banerji, Runki
Pather Panchali 1958,S 23,37:2
Banerji, Subir
Pather Panchali 1958,S 23,37:2
Bang, Axel
Girls are Willing, The 1959,My 11,30:1
Bang, Herman (Original Author)
4 Devils 1928,O 4,26:3
Banguels, Roberto
Domingo en la Tarde, Un; On a Sunday Afternoon 1939,Ja 7,6:3
Banin, Vassili
Road Home, The 1947,My 2,28:3
Banke, Leslie
Man Who Knew too Much, The 1935,Mr 23,11:2

Banker, Bill
Man to Man 1931,Ja 3,21:2
Bankhead, Tallulah
Tarnished Lady 1931,Ap 30,29:3
My Sin 1931,S 11,24:2
Cheat, The 1931,D 12,23:3
Thunder Below 1932,Je 20,11:2
Devil and the Deep 1932,Ag 20,7:4
Faithless 1932,N 19,20:2
Stage Door Canteen 1943,Je 25,13:2
Lifeboat 1944,Ja 13,17:1
Royal Scandal, A 1945,Ap 12,19:2
Main Street to Broadway 1953,O 14,34:1
Die! Die! My Darling 1965,My 20,52:1
Banks, Aaron
Greenwich Village Story 1963,Jl 12,14:3
Banks, Emily
Plainsman, The 1966,N 19,26:1
Banks, Joan
Cry Danger 1951,F 22,27:3
Bright Victory 1951,Ag 1,19:2
Washington Story 1952,Jl 2,22:3
Banks, Leslie
Most Dangerous Game, The 1932,N 21,21:1
I Am Suzanne 1934,Ja 19,24:3
Sanders of the River 1935,Je 27,16:1
Transatlantic Tunnel 1935,O 28,16:2
Fire Over England 1937,Mr 5,16:2
Wings of the Morning 1937,Mr 12,19:1
Troopship 1938,Ap 26,18:2
Jamaica Inn 1939,O 12,33:1
21 Days Together 1940,My 23,28:4
Haunted Honeymoon 1940,O 31,28:2
Ships With Wings 1942,My 25,11:2
48 Hours 1944,Je 26,21:2
Henry V 1946,Je 18,30:2
Mrs Fitzherbert 1950,My 11,37:2
Eye Witness 1950,Ag 28,13:2
Madeleine 1950,S 1,17:2
Small Back Room, The 1952,F 2,11:3
Banks, Lynne Reid (Original Author)
L-Shaped Room, The 1963,My 28,32:1
Banks, Montagle
Bell for Adano, A 1945,Jl 6,8:3
Banks, Monty
Atlantic 1930,Ja 26,VIII,6:2
Compulsory Husband, The 1930,Mr 23,IX,6:1
Atlantic 1930,O 6,21:1
Blood and Sand 1941,My 23,25:3
Days of Thrills and Laughter 1961,Mr 22,37:1
Banks, Monty (Director)
Compulsory Husband, The 1930,Mr 23,IX,6:1
Money for Nothing 1932,F 21,VIII,5:2 (In Addenda)
Charming Deceiver, The 1933,D 9,18:3
You Made Me Love You 1934,My 30,14:3
Trouble Ahead 1936,S 21,26:5
We're Going to Be Rich 1938,Jl 4,10:2
Smiling Along 1939,F 20,13:2
Great Guns 1941,O 3,27:2
Banks, Polan (Original Author)
Street of Women 1932,My 30,16:5
Woman Accused, The 1933,Mr 13,18:2
Great Lie, The 1941,Ap 12,19:2
My Forbidden Past 1951,Ap 26,34:2
Banks, Polan (Producer)
My Forbidden Past 1951,Ap 26,34:2
Banks, Sydney (Miscellaneous)
Whispering City 1948,My 10,25:5
Banky, Suzy
It Happened in Europe 1949,O 4,32:4
Banky, Vilma
Dark Angel, The 1925,O 12,19:3
Eagle, The 1925,N 9,25:1
Son of the Sheik, The 1926,Jl 26,13:2
Winning of Barbara Worth, The 1926,N 29,16:3
Night of Love, The 1927,Ja 25,18:4
Magic Flame, The 1927,S 19,30:3
Lady From Paris, The 1927,S 28,28:3
Two Lovers 1928,Mr 23,24:4
Awakening, The 1928,D 31,9:1
This Is Heaven 1929,My 27,22:1
Lady to Love, A 1930,Mr 1,23:1
Rebel, The 1933,Jl 25,17:2
Bannard, Robert
Incident, The 1967,N 6,65:1
Bannen, Ian
Private's Progress 1956,Jl 24,19:2
Third Key, The 1957,Je 3,30:2
Tale of Two Cities, A 1958,Ag 5,23:1
Man in a Cocked Hat 1960,Je 15,50:2
French Mistress, A 1960,D 19,34:2
Risk, The 1961,S 25,41:2
World in my Pocket, The 1962,My 10,30:2
Psyche 39 1964,Ap 30,30:1
Station Six-Sahara 1964,N 12,40:2
Rotten to the Core 1965,Jl 20,39:2
Hill, The 1965,O 4,00:0
Flight of the Phoenix, The 1966,F 1,26:1
Penelope 1966,N 11,36:6
Sailor From Gibraltar, The 1967,Ap 25,38:2

Banner, Jill
President's Analyst, The 1967,D 22,44:4
Stranger Returns, The 1968,S 12,54:3
Banner, John
Once Upon a Honeymoon 1942,N 13,28:1
Seven Miles From Alcatraz 1942,N 19,31:3
Moon Is Down, The 1943,Mr 27,8:6
Tonight We Raid Calais 1943,Ap 15,20:2
Fallen Sparrow, The 1943,Ag 20,13:1
My Girl Tisa 1948,F 21,9:2
To the Victor 1948,Ap 17,11:2
Guilty of Treason 1950,Ap 11,26:2
Juggler, The 1953,My 6,39:2
Rains of Ranchipur, The 1955,D 16,38:2
Blue Angel, The 1959,S 5,11:4
Story of Ruth, The 1960,Je 18,12:3
Operation Eichmann 1961,My 4,40:7
20,000 Eyes 1961,Je 19,30:1
Yellow Canary, The 1963,My 16,42:1
36 Hours 1965,Ja 29,25:2
Wicked Dreams of Paula Schultz, The 1968,Ja 4,28:1
Bannerjee, Chandana
Two Daughters (The Postman); Postman, The (Two Daughters) 1963,My 1,35:1
Bannerjee, Karuna
Devi 1962,O 8,19:1
Bannerji
Kanchenjungha 1966,Jl 26,27:2
Bannerji, Bibhutibhusan (Original Author)
World of Apu; Apur Sansar 1960,O 5,45:1
Bannerman, Kay (Original Author)
Pair of Briefs, A 1964,F 3,22:2
Bannerman, Margaret
Loves of Madame Dubarry, The 1938,Ap 4,12:5
Cluny Brown 1946,Je 3,27:3
Homestretch, The 1947,Ap 24,30:2
Banning, Leslie
Girl's School 1950,F 3,29:2
Banning, Leslye
His Kind of Woman 1951,Ag 30,20:2
Banning, Margaret Culkin (Original Author)
Woman Against Woman 1938,Ag 23,20:6
Bannister, Harry
Her Private Affair 1930,Ja 11,21:3
Girl of the Golden West, The 1930,O 27,17:1
Suicide Fleet 1931,N 23,22:1
Husband's Holiday 1931,D 25,29:2
Bannister, Monica
Mystery of the Wax Museum, The 1933,F 18,13:3
Bannon, Jim
Soul of a Monster, The 1944,S 9,12:4
Tonight and Every Night 1945,Mr 9,16:2
Renegades 1946,Jl 11,18:2
Unknown, The 1946,Jl 20,10:3
Johnny O'Clock 1947,Mr 27,39:2
Framed 1947,My 26,24:2
Corpse came C O D, The 1947,Ag 19,27:2
T-Men 1948,Ja 23,28:3
Miraculous Journey 1948,S 20,21:2
Man From Colorado 1949,Ja 21,24:3
Kill the Umpire 1950,My 29,10:6
Jack Slade 1953,O 29,42:6
They Came to Cordura 1959,O 22,47:2
Gathering of Eagles, A 1963,Jl 11,21:2
Bannon, Jim (Narrator)
I Married Adventure 1940,S 24,26:5
Banos, Ricardo (Director)
Relicario, El; Reliquary, The 1935,D 31,11:3
Banovitch, Milenko
Lovers of Teruel, The 1962,D 15,5:1
Banquells, Rafael
This Strange Passion 1955,D 5,34:2
Bansal, R (Producer)
Mahanagar; Big City, The 1964,S 28,19:1
Charulata 1965,S 11,16:1
Banth, Benjamin
William Tell 1925,My 20,26:2
Banthim, Larry
Hot Stuff 1929,My 13,27:2
Banton, Travis (Miscellaneous)
Crusades, The 1935,Ag 22,21:3
Banuet, Conchita
Héroe de Nacozari, El 1935,S 23,20:4
Banyard, Beatrice
What Price Innocence? 1933,Je 26,16:3
Banyard, Beatrice (Original Author)
Myrt and Marge 1934,Ja 17,23:2
Bao, Miguel G
Madreselva; Honeysuckle 1939,Ag 19,18:4
Baptiste, Thomas
Ipcress File, The 1965,Ag 3,35:1
Baqer, Herb (Screenwriter)
Loving You 1957,Jl 18,19:2
Baqueriza, Guillermo (Director)
Desheredados, Los 1936,Mr 23,22:6
Baquet, Maurice
Voyage Surprise 1948,F 14,17:3
Sextette (Part 6-Ski Champ); Ski Champ (Sextette) 1953,Mr 2,19:2
Stowaway in the Sky 1962,Je 19,28:1
Crime of Monsieur Lange, The 1964,Ap 4,15:5

Bar, Jacques (Producer)
Mr Peek-A-Boo 1951,S 19,37:1
Fernandel the Dressmaker 1957,Jl 1,19:2
Man in the Raincoat, The 1958,Jl 15,21:2
Virtuous Bigamist, The 1959,My 28,34:3
Where the Hot Wind Blows 1960,N 12,15:1
Bridge to the Sun 1961,O 18,50:1
Swordsman of Siena 1962,D 6,55:3
Any Number Can Win 1963,O 9,47:2
Day and the Hour, The 1964,F 20,22:2
Joy House 1965,F 18,29:1
Once a Thief 1965,S 9,36:1
Guns for San Sebastian 1968,Mr 21,57:2
Bar-Adon
Chalutzim 1934,Ap 2,13:3
Bara, Jean
Ne Sirj Edesanyam 1936,N 24,35:4
Queen and the Cardinal, The 1944,Je 1,17:3
Bara, Lori (Original Author)
Samarang 1933,Je 29,22:2
Bara, Nina
Missle to the Moon 1958,N 17,37:2
Bara, Theda
Carmen 1915,N 1,11:1
Serpent, The 1916,Ja 24,12:3
Gold and the Woman 1916,Mr 13,5:5
Eternal Sapho, The 1916,My 8,7:2
East Lynne 1916,Je 19,9:5 (In Addenda)
Her Double Life 1916,S 11,11:4
Romeo and Juliet 1916,O 23,10:3
Cleopatra 1917,O 15,11:2
Salome 1918,O 7,11:3
Kathleen Mavourneen 1919,Ag 20,12:3
Baracco, Adriano (Original Author)
Danger Diabolik 1968,D 12,62:6
Baracco, Adriano (Screenwriter)
Treasure of San Gennaro 1968,F 27,36:1
Baragrey, John
Loves of Carmen, The 1948,S 3,16:2
Four Days' Leave 1950,Je 9,29:4
Pardners 1956,Jl 26,20:2
Fugitive Kind, The 1960,Ap 15,13:1
Barakat (Screenwriter)
Little Miss Devil 1951,D 8,9:2
Baral, Eileen
Mirage 1965,My 27,28:1
Barancey
As du Turf, Les; Acres of Turf 1935,My 11,21:3
Baranov, Alexei
In the Rear of the Enemy 1942,O 10,11:2
Baranowska, Anna
End of St Petersberg, The 1928,My 31,21:2 (In Addenda)
Barany, Baroness
Rembrandt 1936,D 3,31:1
Baras, Marguerite (Original Author)
This Angry Age 1958,Je 26,23:3
Barasch, Norman (Original Author)
Send Me no Flowers 1964,N 13,30:1
Baratashvili, M (Screenwriter)
Dragonfly, The 1955,Je 27,18:2
Baratier, Jacques (Director)
Poupee, La 1963,Ag 28,39:1
Sweet and Sour 1964,D 28,34:2
Baratier, Jacques (Screenwriter)
Sweet and Sour 1964,D 28,34:2
Baratoff, Ben-Zvi
Singing Blacksmith, The 1938,N 3,27:1
Baratoff, Paul
Men In her Life, The 1941,D 12,35:1
Baratti, Bruno (Screenwriter)
Love and Marriage (Saturday, July 18); Saturday, July 18 (Love and Marriage) 1966,Ag 5,20:1
Love and Marriage (The First Night); First Night, The (Love and Marriage) 1966,Ag 5,20:1
Love and Marriage (The Last Resort); Last Resort, The (Love and Marriage) 1966,Ag 5,20:1
Love and Marriage (One Moment Is Enough); One Moment Is Enough (Love and Marriage) 1966,Ag 5,20:1
Baratz, Gideon
Dream no More 1950,Ja 6,25:2
Baraud, Daniele
7 Capital Sins (Greed); Greed (7 Capital Sins) 1963,Ja 17,5:2
Barbachano, Manuel (Producer)
Roots, The (The Filly); Filly, The (The Roots) 1957,S 3,23:2
Roots, The (The One-Eyed Boy); One-Eyed Boy, The (The Roots) 1957,S 3,23:2
Roots, The (The Cows); Cows, The (The Roots) 1957,S 3,23:2
Roots, The (Our Lady); Our Lady (The Roots) 1957,S 3,23:2
Barbachano, Manuel (Screenwriter)
Roots, The (The Filly); Filly, The (The Roots) 1957,S 3,23:2
Roots, The (The Cows); Cows, The (The Roots) 1957,S 3,23:2
Roots, The (The One-Eyed Boy); One-Eyed Boy, The (The Roots) 1957,S 3,23:2
Roots, The (Our Lady); Our Lady (The Roots) 1957,S 3,23:2

Barbara, Paola
Trionfo dell'Amore, Il; Love's Triumph 1938,Mr 29,18:4
Eravamo Sette Sorelle; We Were Seven Sisters 1939,Mr 3,21:3
Per Vomini Soli; For Men Only 1939,Ap 21,27:4
Napoli che mon Muore; Naples That Never Dies 1940,Mr 4,11:3
King's Jester, The 1947,Je 26,19:3
Rossini 1948,Ja 31,14:2
Barbarita, Maria
Loves of Ricardo, The 1926,Ag 16,10:1
Barbaro, Umberto (Director)
Ultima Nemica, L'; Last Enemy, The 1940,Ap 18,28:5
Barbaro, Umberto (Screenwriter)
Tragic Hunt 1948,O 22,30:2
Barbaud, Pierre
Hiroshima, Mon Amour 1960,My 17,43:1
BARBER
See Also BARBOUR
Barber, Elsie Oaks (Original Author)
Angel Baby 1961,O 5,43:1
Barber, Red (Narrator)
Safe at Home 1941,N 26,31:2
Barber, Rowland (Original Author)
Somebody up There Likes Me 1956,Jl 6,16:1
Night They Raided Minsky's, The 1968,D 23,43:1
Barbera, Joseph (Director)
Hey There, It's Yogi Bear 1964,Jl 30,16:1
Man Called Flintstone, The 1967,N 25,42:1
Barbera, Joseph (Producer)
Hey There, It's Yogi Bear 1964,Jl 30,16:1
Man Called Flintstone, The 1967,N 25,42:1
Barberis, Rene (Director)
Ramuntcho 1953,Mr 2,19:2
Barberis, Rene (Screenwriter)
Ramuntcho 1953,Mr 2,19:2
Barbetti, Carlo
Eternal Melodies 1948,F 14,17:3
Barbetti, Cesare
Faust and the Devil 1950,My 1,18:2
Barbetti, Cesarino
Man of the Sea 1948,Ja 24,11:2
Barbier, Christian
Trans-Europ-Express 1968,My 13,52:1
Barbier, George
Big Pond, The 1930,My 19,21:1
Sap From Syracuse, The 1930,Jl 26,16:4
Smiling Lieutenant, The 1931,My 23,13:4
Twenty-Four Hours 1931,O 3,20:2
Girls About Town 1931,N 2,27:1
Touchdown 1931,N 16,23:1
No One Man 1932,Ja 23,18:4
Strangers in Love 1932,Mr 5,11:2
One Hour with You 1932,Mr 24,17:5
Broken Wing, The 1932,Mr 26,17:2
Strange Case of Clara Deane, The 1932,My 6,15:3
Million Dollar Legs 1932,Jl 9,7:5
Skyscraper Souls 1932,Ag 5,11:2
Phantom President, The 1932,O 1,10:4
Big Broadcast, The 1932,O 15,13:1
Evenings for Sale 1932,N 12,20:5
No Man of her Own 1932,D 31,10:1
Hello, Everybody 1933,Ja 30,9:4
Lady's Profession, A 1933,Mr 25,13:3
Mama Loves Papa 1933,Jl 24,11:2
Turn Back the Clock 1933,Ag 26,14:2
This Day and Age 1933,S 1,15:4
Love, Honor and Oh, Baby! 1933,O 28,20:3
Tillie and Gus 1933,N 13,21:1
Miss Fane's Baby is Stolen 1934,Ja 20,12:2
Journal of a Crime 1934,Ap 28,11:3
Many Happy Returns 1934,Je 9,18:2
Ladies Should Listen 1934,Jl 28,16:6
Elmer and Elsie 1934,Ag 4,14:5
Cat's Paw, The 1934,Ag 17,12:2
She Loves Me Not 1934,S 8,18:5
Merry Widow, The 1934,O 12,33:1
College Rhythm 1934,N 24,19:1
McFadden's Flats 1935,Mr 13,16:2
Life Begins at 40 1935,Ap 5,21:3
Hold 'Em Yale 1935,Ap 27,20:6
Broadway Gondolier 1935,Jl 18,15:2
Crusades, The 1935,Ag 22,21:3
Here Comes Cookie 1935,O 12,12:2
Millions in the Air 1935,D 12,33:4
Wife vs Secretary 1936,F 29,11:1
Preview Murder Mystery, The 1936,Mr 21,13:2
Milky Way, The 1936,Mr 26,27:2
Princess Comes Across, The 1936,Je 4,27:2
Early to Bed 1936,Jl 16,20:2
Spendthrift 1936,Jl 23,24:1
On the Avenue 1937,F 5,17:3
Waikiki Wedding 1937,Mr 25,29:1
It's Love I'm After 1937,N 11,31:2
Girl With Ideas, A 1938,Ja 1,11:2
Tarzan's Revenge 1938,Ja 10,13:3
Hold That Kiss 1938,Je 11,9:1
Little Miss Broadway 1938,Jl 23,10:4
My Lucky Star 1938,S 10,20:2

Barbier, George—Cont
Hold That Co-ed 1938,S 24,13:1
Straight, Place and Show 1938,O 1,10:2
Thanks For Everything 1938,D 10,13:2
Sweethearts 1938,D 23,16:2
Wife, Husband and Friend 1939,F 25,19:2
S O S Tidal Wave 1939,Je 22,19:3
News Is Made at Night 1939,Jl 13,17:2
Remember? 1939,D 15,33:4
Return of Frank James, The 1940,Ag 10,16:4
Million Dollar Baby 1941,Je 7,20:2
Week-End in Havana 1941,N 8,11:2
Marry the Boss's Daughter 1941,D 4,33:4
Man Who Came to Dinner, The 1942,Ja 2,25:2
Song of the Islands 1942,Mr 12,24:4
Yankee Doodle Dandy 1942,My 30,9:1
Magnificent Dope, The 1942,Jl 3,12:5
Thunder Birds 1942,O 29,19:2
Adventures of Marco Polo, The 1965,Ap 8,17:2
Barbieri, Fedora
Cinderella 1953,My 15,20:2
Barbin, Charles J (Director)
While New York Sleeps 1920,Ag 24,6:2
Barbini, Luigi
Gospel According to St Matthew, The 1966,F 18,23:1
BARBOUR
See Also BARBER
Barbour, Dave
Secret Fury, The 1950,Je 22,34:2
Barbour, Joyce
Woman Alone, The 1937,F 27,9:2
Housemaster 1939,Ap 10,13:2
Barbulee, Madeleine
Seven Deadly Sins, The (Sloth); Sloth (The Seven Deadly Sins) 1953,My 12,31:3
Caroline Cherie 1954,My 25,23:1
Love Is my Profession 1959,Ap 28,41:1
How Not to Rob a Department Store 1965,D 29,23:1
Barcelata, Lorenzo
Alla en el Rancho Grande 1936,N 23,17:3
Tierra Brava 1938,O 29,15:6
Supremo Sacrificio; Supreme Sacrifice 1938,N 29,27:2
Rancho Grande 1938,D 2,27:2
Barcelata, Lorenzo (Composer)
Rancho Grande 1938,D 2,27:2
Barcelata, Lorenzo (Miscellaneous)
Rancho Grande 1938,D 2,27:2
Barcelata (Composer)
Reina del Rio, La; Queen of the River, The 1940,F 24,9:3
Barcelata (Producer)
Reina del Rio, La; Queen of the River, The 1940,F 24,9:3
Barcelloni, Gianni (Producer)
Tropics 1968,S 24,52:1
Barcelos, Joel
Tropics 1968,S 24,52:1
Barcena, Catalina
Primavera en Otono 1933,My 18,17:3
Mama 1933,Jl 8,14:6
Viuda Romantica, La 1933,S 4,9:6
IO... TU... Y...; (I... Thou... and... She) 1933,D 5,31:6
Ciudad de Carton, La 1934,F 28,23:3
Julieta Compra un Hijo; Julieta Buys a Baby 1935,Mr 25,12:3
Barcklind, Carl
Ungdom Av I Dag 1936,Je 23,27:7
Familjen Som Var En Karusel 1937,My 22,19:3
John Ericsson Victor of Hampton Roads 1938,My 18,17:2
Vi Tvaa; We Two 1939,D 2,21:3
BARCLAY
See Also BARKLEY
Barclay, David
Renfrew of the Royal Mounted 1937,N 3,29:4
Barclay, Don
Murder of Dr Harrigan, The 1936,Ja 21,27:5
Man Hunt 1936,Ja 30,14:2
Fugitive in the Sky 1937,Ja 16,21:1
Navy Spy 1937,Mr 22,27:3
I Cover the War 1937,Ag 2,10:2
Spy Ring, The 1938,Ja 15,19:1
Accidents Will Happen 1938,Ap 25,19:2
Sing Your Worries Away 1942,My 15,25:2
Mexican Spitfire Sees a Ghost 1942,Jl 31,11:2
Falcon's Brother, The 1942,O 3,9:5
Frankenstein Meets the Wolf Man 1943,Mr 6,8:3
Good Morning, Judge 1943,Ap 30,25:4
Mr Perrin and Mr Traill 1949,Ja 17,15:2
Whispering Smith 1949,F 15,28:2
Long Gray Line, The 1955,F 11,19:2
Mary Poppins 1964,S 25,34:1
Barclay, Eric
Faust 1926,D 7,21:2
Charlotte Loewenskoeld 1932,F 22,23:2
Barclay, George (Screenwriter)
Village of the Damned 1960,D 8,43:3
Barclay, Jerry
Untamed Youth 1957,My 11,24:6

Barclay, Joan
Flying Wild 1941,Ap 12,19:3
Mr Wise Guy 1942,Mr 5,27:2
Ladies' Day 1943,Mr 26,14:3
Falcon out West, The 1944,Mr 18,18:2
Barclay, John
Mikado, The 1939,Je 2,27:2
Dr Jekyll and Mr Hyde 1941,Ag 13,13:2
Aloma of the South Seas 1941,Ag 28,23:4
Barclay, Stephen
Great Flamario, The 1945,Ja 15,15:5
Barclay, Steve (Producer)
Dark Purpose 1964,F 6,36:4
Barcroft, Roy
Big Bonanza, The 1945,F 26,14:5
Dakota 1945,D 17,17:2
My Pal Trigger 1946,Ag 17,16:3
Wyoming 1947,Jl 25,12:5
Blackmail 1947,Ag 5,26:3
Fabulous Texan, The 1947,D 26,22:5
Old Los Angeles 1948,Jl 12,11:2
Rock Island Trail 1950,Je 5,19:3
Surrender 1950,O 9,21:5
Man Without a Star 1955,Mr 25,19:3
Oklahoma! 1955,O 11,49:1
Spoilers, The 1955,D 24,10:2
6 Black Horses 1962,Ap 25,30:1
Barcynska, Countess (Original Author)
Woman in the Night, A 1929,Mr 11,22:2
Barczy, Katerine
Sutyi, a Szerencseqyerek; Sutyi, the Lucky Child 1938,Ja 22,19:2
Bard, Bardson
My Own Pal 1926,Mr 15,18:3
Bard, Ben
Seventh Heaven 1927,My 26,22:1
Secret Studio, The 1927,Je 15,31:4
Two Girls Wanted 1927,N 14,26:1
Come to My House 1928,Ja 16,24:1
Dressed to Kill 1928,Mr 12,26:1
Romance of the Underworld 1929,Ja 7,36:2
Born Reckless 1930,Je 7,10:4
Bat Whispers, The 1931,Ja 16,27:1
Meet the Baron 1933,O 28,20:3
Hollywood Party 1934,My 26,12:2
Leopard Man, The 1943,My 20,26:4
Ghost Ship, The 1943,D 25,19:4
Youth Runs Wild 1944,S 2,17:2
Black Angel 1946,S 26,32:4
Bard, Benna
I Can Get It for You Wholesale 1951,Ap 5,34:4
Bard, Katharine
Decks Ran Red, The 1958,O 11,18:2
Interns, The 1962,Ag 9,17:5
Inside Daisy Clover 1966,F 18,23:1
How to Save a Marriage - And Ruin Your Life 1968,Ja 19,30:1
Bard, Maria
Mensch Ohne Namen 1932,N 7,20:3
Berlin-Alexanderplatz 1933,My 11,14:1
Liebe im Gleitflug; Love in Stunt Flying 1938,Je 18,18:3
Bard, Mary (Original Author)
Mother Didn't Tell Me 1950,Mr 4,11:2
Bard, Migo
Husbands or Lovers 1927,N 22,32:2
Barda, Antonio
White Sister, The 1923,S 6,10:2
Barddell, Maurice
Flesh 1968,S 27,36:1
Bardem, Juan (Director)
Lovemaker, The 1958,Mr 11,33:4
Age of Infidelity 1958,Ag 19,23:2
Uninhibited, The 1968,Je 13,57:2
Bardem, Juan (Screenwriter)
Pantaloons 1956,D 26,34:1
Lovemaker, The 1958,Mr 11,33:4
Age of Infidelity 1958,Ag 19,23:2
Barden, Juan (Screenwriter)
Uninhibited, The 1968,Je 13,57:2
Bardette, Trevor
They Won't Forget 1937,Jl 15,16:1
Great Garrick, The 1937,O 25,23:1
Mystery House 1938,Je 29,15:5
Let Freedom Ring 1939,Mr 10,19:2
Oklahoma Kid, The 1939,Mr 11,21:1
Charlie Chan at Treasure Island 1939,S 1,15:5
Abe Lincoln in Illinois 1940,F 23,19:2
Dark Command 1940,My 11,15:2
Wagons Westward 1940,Jl 8,13:2
Three Faces West 1940,Ag 19,13:2
Romance of the Rio Grande 1940,D 25,33:4
Topper Returns 1941,Mr 28,26:6
Mystery Ship 1941,Ag 16,18:3
Wild Bill Hickok Rides 1942,F 7,13:5
Flight Lieutenant 1942,Jl 31,11:1
None Shall Escape 1944,Ap 7,23:2
Whistler, The 1944,Ap 29,12:2
Tampico 1944,Je 2,21:2
Counter-Attack 1945,My 17,15:2
Dick Tracy 1946,Ja 12,10:7
Hoodlum Saint, The 1946,Je 27,29:1
Sea of Grass, The 1947,F 28,27:2

Slave Girl 1947,Jl 18,21:3
Wyoming 1947,Jl 25,12:5
Hellfire 1949,My 30,9:4
Song of India 1949,Je 10,32:3
Lady Without Passport, A 1950,Ag 4,13:2
Lone Star 1952,F 2,11:4
San Francisco Story, The 1952,My 10,16:4
Thunder Over the Plains 1953,D 10,64:4
Run for Cover 1955,Ap 30,10:6
Rack, The 1956,N 6,30:1
Dragoon Wells Massacre 1957,My 6,25:2
Mating Game, The 1959,Ap 30,37:1
Bardi, Mariemma
Bitter Rice 1950,S 19,39:2
Bardini, Alexander
Long Is the Road 1948,N 12,30:5
Bardot, Brigitte
Act of Love 1954,F 12,20:5
Helen of Troy 1956,Ja 27,21:4
Doctor at Sea 1956,Mr 1,37:3
Grand Maneuver, The 1956,O 2,39:1
Light Across the Street, The; Lumiere d'en Face, La 1957,Jl 30,20:2
And God Created Woman 1957,O 22,41:1
Please Mr Balzac 1957,N 18,37:2
Bride Is Much too Beautiful, The 1958,Ja 21,35:1
Mam'zelle Pigalle 1958,Ap 19,10:4
Parisienne, La 1958,Jl 31,27:1
Night Heaven Fell, The 1958,O 22,40:4
Girl in the Bikini, The 1958,O 25,16:3
Love Is my Profession 1959,Ap 28,41:1
Female, The 1960,Ap 28,29:1
Babette Goes to War 1960,Je 8,46:1
Come Dance With Me!; Voulez-Vous Danser Avec Moi 1960,N 8,32:6
Crazy for Love 1960,N 26,13:2
Truth, The 1961,Je 27,23:2
Very Private Affair, A 1962,S 29,15:1
Love on a Pillow 1963,D 17,49:1
Contempt 1964,D 19,25:2
Dear Brigitte 1965,Ja 28,20:1
Viva Maria 1965,D 20,48:2
Masculine Feminine 1966,S 19,57:1
Shalako 1968,N 6,32:1
Bardy, George
It Happened in Europe 1949,O 4,32:4
Bare, Bobby
Distant Trumpet, A 1964,My 28,40:1
Bare, Richard (Director)
House Across the Street 1949,S 2,14:4
Return of the Frontiersman 1950,Je 10,11:3
This Side of the Law 1950,Jl 7,15:2
This Rebel Breed 1960,My 5,41:2
Bareket, Yitchak
They Were Ten; (Heym Hayu Assara) 1961,Ap 18,44:2
Barella, Giovanni
Cuore Napoletano; Neapolitan Heart 1940,O 8,31:2
Baret, Dora
Terrace, The 1964,N 25,45:1
Barett, Edith
In Love and War 1958,N 1,14:2
Barezzi, Margherita
Life of Giuseppe Verdi 1940,Ap 3,19:2
Barge, Paul
Casque D'Or 1952,Ag 19,19:1
Barginan, Ben (Screenwriter)
Boy With Green Hair, The 1949,Ja 13,26:2
Bari, Lynn
Baroness and the Butler, The 1938,F 19,19:2
Walking Down Broadway 1938,Ap 1,17:3
Mr Moto's Gamble 1938,Ap 8,17:2
Battle of Broadway 1938,Ap 25,19:2
Josette 1938,Je 11,9:1
Always Goodbye 1938,Je 25,7:2
I'll Give a Million 1938,Jl 16,7:2
Meet the Girls 1938,S 3,16:6
Speed to Burn 1938,S 9,25:1
Sharpshooters 1938,D 5,19:2
Return of the Cisco Kid, The 1939,Ap 29,13:2
News Is Made at Night 1939,Jl 13,17:2
Hotel for Women 1939,Ag 26,20:2
Pack up Your Troubles 1939,O 27,27:2
Charlie Chan in City in Darkness 1939,D 18,29:2
City of Chance 1940,Ja 22,11:3
Free, Blonde and 21 1940,Ap 5,25:2
Lillian Russell 1940,My 18,11:2
Earthbound 1940,Je 7,27:4
Pier 13 1940,Ag 9,19:3
Kit Carson 1940,N 15,25:3
Sleepers West 1941,Mr 20,25:3
Blood and Sand 1941,My 23,25:3
Sun Valley Serenade 1941,S 6,20:1
Moon Over her Shoulder 1941,N 5,31:2
Secret Agent of Japan 1942,Mr 23,19:3
Night Before the Divorce, The 1942,Ap 10,21:3
Falcon takes Over, The 1942,My 30,9:2
Magnificent Dope, The 1942,Jl 3,12:5
Orchestra Wives 1942,S 24,23:2
China Girl 1943,Ja 21,27:2
Hello, Frisco, Hello 1943,Mr 25,25:1
Bridge of San Luis Rey, The 1944,Mr 4,11:1

Bari, Lynn— Cont
Tampico 1944,Je 2,21:2
Sweet and Low Down 1944,O 19,19:2
Captain Eddie 1945,Ag 9,24:2
Shock 1946,Mr 9,10:2
Home Sweet Homicide 1946,S 12,5:7
Margie 1946,O 17,28:3
Nocturne 1946,N 11,42:2
Man From Texas 1948,Ag 12,16:5
Kid From Cleveland, The 1949,S 13:2
I'd Climb the Highest Mountain 1951,My 10,38:1
Dream of Jeanie, I 1952,Je 26,26:2
Has Anybody Seen My Gal 1952,Jl 5,7:2
Francis Joins the Wacs 1954,Jl 31,6:3
Young Runaways, The 1968,S 12,54:3
Bari, Tania
Belles and Ballets 1960,N 15,45:3
Barik, Nimai
River, The 1951,S 11,33:2
Barile, Chiarina
Weddings and Babies 1960,O 6,51:3
Barillet, Pierre (Screenwriter)
Beauties of the Night 1954,Mr 23,23:5
Barilli, Cecrope
Before the Revolution; Prima della Revolutiona 1964,S 25,32:1
Barilli, Francesco
Before the Revolution; Prima della Revolutiona 1964,S 25,32:1
Baring, Aubrey (Producer)
Snowbound 1949,F 21,20:2
Bad Lord Byron, The 1952,Mr 20,37:5
Spider and the Fly, The 1952,Jl 29,17:3
Cairo Road 1952,N 1,17:2
So Little Time 1953,Jl 28,23:2
Golden Mask, The 1954,Mr 20,10:5
Trouble in the Sky 1961,Jl 13,26:3
Baring, Nora
Underground 1928,Ag 12,VII,4:3 (In Addenda)
Underground 1929,F 26,31:1
Escaped From Dartmoor 1930,Ap 12,23:1
Mystery at the Villa Rose 1930,Je 2,25:4
Baring, Norah
Murder 1930,O 25,20:6
Two Worlds 1930,N 22,21:3
Should a Doctor Tell 1931,Ag 22,7:5
Baringer, A B (Screenwriter)
One Glorious Day 1922,Ja 30,16:2
Barishova, Tania
Girl No 217 1945,S 3,17:2
Barisse, Rita (Screenwriter)
Midnight Episode 1955,My 19,25:5
Barjavel, Rene (Screenwriter)
Little World of Don Camillo, The 1953,Ja 14,27:1
Case of Dr Laurent, The 1958,Je 26,23:2
Devil and the 10 Commandments, The (Episode 5) 1963,O 15,44:1
Devil and the 10 Commandments, The (Episode 7) 1963,O 15,44:1
Devil and the 10 Commandments, The (Episode 6) 1963,O 15,44:1
Devil and the 10 Commandments, The (Episode 3) 1963,O 15,44:1
Devil and the 10 Commandments, The (Episode 4) 1963,O 15,44:1
Devil and the 10 Commandments, The (Episode 2) 1963,O 15,44:1
Devil and the 10 Commandments, The (Episode 1) 1963,O 15,44:1
Barjavet, Rene (Screenwriter)
Return of Don Camillo, The 1956,Mr 27,41:1
Barkas, Geoffrey (Director)
Q Ships 1928,S 17,27:1
Battle of Gallipoli, The 1931,D 7,16:1
Barkas, Geoffrey (Miscellaneous)
Tell England 1931,Ap 19,VIII,6:1
Barkeley, Ballard
Quiet Week-End 1948,Ag 20,13:2
Barker, Abe
Doctor at Large 1957,Jl 29,15:5
Battle of the Sexes, The 1960,Ap 19,40:4
Barker, Ambrose
Unfaithful 1931,Mr 7,17:2
Peter Ibbetson 1935,N 8,18:2
Barker, Betty
Cheaper by the Dozen 1950,Ap 1,12:2
Barker, Bradley
Master Mind, The 1920,S 13,12:1
Fighting Blade, The 1923,O 15,15:4
Twenty-One 1924,F 18,13:1
Into the Net 1924,Ag 23,10:2
Crackerjack, The 1925,My 18,12:1
Brown Derby, The 1926,Je 14,24:1
Potters, The 1927,Ja 18,23:1
Rubber Heels 1927,Je 28,29:4
Barker, Bradley (Director)
Mother's Boy 1929,My 8,34:6
Barker, Corinne
Peace of Roaring River, The 1919,Ag 11,9:1
Barker, Daphne
Showtime 1948,My 20,35:3
Encore (Gigolo and Gigolette); Gigolo and Gigolette (Encore) 1952,Ap 3,45:1

Barker, Eric
Brothers in Law 1957,Ag 20,22:1
Happy is the Bride 1959,Je 30,27:2
Carry on Sergeant 1959,O 28,40:5
Left, Right and Centre 1961,F 10,19:1
Pure Hell of St Trinian's, The 1961,S 26,31:1
Ferry Cross the Mersey 1965,F 20,16:2
Barker, Horton
Festival 1967,O 24,53:2
Barker, Jess
Government Girl 1944,Ja 7,13:2
Cover Girl 1944,Mr 31,26:1
Jam Session 1944,My 3,25:3
Keep Your Powder Dry 1945,Mr 12,22:6
This Love of Ours 1945,N 1,20:2
Daltons Ride Again, The 1945,D 8,21:2
Scarlet Street 1946,F 15,29:2
Time of Their Lives, The 1946,N 28,40:2
Take one False Step 1949,Je 23,33:2
Black Book, The 1949,O 17,18:2
Milkman, The 1951,Ja 1,13:6
Shack out on 101 1956,Ja 10,26:2
Three bad Sisters 1956,F 13,24:1
Barker, Lex
Farmer's Daughter, The 1947,Mr 26,31:2
Crossfire 1947,Jl 23,19:2
Return of the Badmen 1948,Ag 5,16:2
Tarzan's Magic Fountain 1949,F 7,15:2
Tarzan and the Slave Girl 1950,Je 24,7:3
Thunder Over the Plains 1953,D 10,64:4
Away all Boats 1956,Ag 17,14:2
Girl in the Kremlin, The 1957,My 22,29:2
Dolce Vita, La 1961,Ap 20,30:1
Code 7...Victim 5 1965,My 20,52:1
Place Called Glory, A 1966,Ag 11,27:4
Woman Times Seven 1967,Je 28,38:1
Shatterhand 1968,Je 6,54:1
Barker, Patricia
Blossoms in the Dust 1941,Je 27,14:4
Presenting Lily Mars 1943,Ap 30,25:3
Frenchman's Creek 1944,S 21,26:2
Barker, Reginald (Director)
Shadows 1919,F 10,11:3
Brand, The 1919,Mr 17,13:2
Crimson Gardenia, The 1919,Je 16,11:2
Flame of the Desert 1919,O 27,9:3
Bonds of Love 1919,N 3,13:3
Woman and the Puppet 1920,Ap 5,20:1
Bunty Pulls the Strings 1921,Ja 9,VI,2:1 (In
    Addenda)
Godless Men 1921,Ja 31,11:1
Snowblind 1921,My 23,16:3
Old Nest, The 1921,Je 29,10:3
Eternal Struggle, The 1923,O 16,21:3
Pleasure Mad 1924,Ja 7,23:1
Women Who Give 1924,Je 3,22:1
Broken Barriers 1924,Ag 4,16:3
Dixie Handicap, The 1924,D 30,15:3
Great Divide, The 1925,F 11,19:4
White Desert, The 1925,Jl 8,12:4
Flaming Forest, The 1926,N 22,28:3
Body and Soul 1927,N 8,33:1
Mississippi Gambler, The 1929,O 28,20:1
Seven Keys to Baldpate 1929,D 26,21:1
Great Divide, The 1930,F 17,17:6
Hide Out 1930,Ap 12,23:1
Barkhatov, Borya
Summer to Remember, A; (Seryozha)
    1961,N 7,38:1
BARKLEY
See Also BARCLAY
Barkley, Lucille
Frenchie 1951,F 12,19:2
Bedtime for Bonzo 1951,Ap 6,31:4
Fat Man, The 1951,My 25,31:2
Barkley, Roxanne
Irene 1940,My 24,23:3
Barklind, Carl
Vi Som Gar Koeksvaegen 1933,O 7,18:5
Kaera Slaekten 1934,My 14,20:4
Barko, Hildegard
Musketier Meier III 1938,D 31,7:2
Gluck auf den Lande; Rural Happiness
    1940,F 10,19:3
Barkoulis, Andrew
Moment of Passion 1960,N 21,34:1
Take Me Away, My Love 1962,Jl 30,15:5
You Came too Late 1962,N 12,35:8
Barkoutis, Andreas
Moussitsa 1960,O 31,25:2
Barkow, Hildegard
Wenn der Hahn Kraeht 1936,N 14,23:3
Barkworth, Peter
Touch of Larceny, A 1960,Mr 17,28:1
No Love for Johnnie 1961,D 13,55:1
Barlacchi, Cesare (Director)
Favorita, La 1953,O 30,27:4
Barlett, Peter
Countess from Hong Kong, A 1967,Mr 17,35:1
Barlick, Al
Safe at Home 1941,N 26,31:2

Barlow, James (Original Author)
Term of Trial 1963,Ja 31,5:2
Barlow, Jeff
Chu Chin Chow 1925,F 11,19:4
Barlow, Kitty
Night Life 1927,D 20,33:2
Barlow, Reginald
Clothes Make the Pirate 1925,N 30,17:1
Woman From Monte Carlo, The 1931,D 31,17:6
This Reckless Age 1932,Ja 9,21:1
Alias the Doctor 1932,Mr 3,22:3
Wet Parade, The 1932,Ap 22,23:2
World and the Flesh, The 1932,My 7,11:5
Sinners in the Sun 1932,My 14,11:5
Washington Masquerade, The 1932,Jl 22,18:2
Horse Feathers 1932,Ag 11,12:2
Age of Consent, The 1932,S 3,16:2
Afraid to Talk 1932,D 19,19:5
Grand Slam 1933,F 22,25:2
Big Cage, The 1933,My 9,20:5
You Can't Buy Everything 1934,F 3,9:2
Half a Sinner 1934,Je 23,16:5
Romance in Manhattan 1935,Ja 18,29:2
Bride of Frankenstein, The 1935,My 11,21:2
Little Lord Fauntleroy 1936,Ap 3,27:1
O'Malley of the Mounted 1936,Ap 6,18:1
Lloyds of London 1936,N 26,39:1
It Happened Out West 1937,Je 7,22:3
Witness Vanishes, The 1939,O 23,15:2
Courageous Dr Christian, The 1940,Mr 29,25:3
Barlow, William
Circus Days 1923,Ag 6,14:2
Greed 1924,D 5,28:1
Barlowe, Joy
Big Sleep, The 1946,Ag 24,6:6
Barlowe, Violet
Flood, The 1931,Ap 27,25:1
Barma, Claude (Director)
Tales of Paris (The Tale of Francoise); Tale of
    Francoise, The (Tales of Paris) 1962,Ag 27,18:1
Barma, Claude (Miscellaneous)
Tales of Paris (The Tale of Francoise); Tale of
    Francoise, The (Tales of Paris) 1962,Ag 27,18:1
Barnabe, Bruno
Dreaming Lips 1937,My 20,17:1
Barnabo, Guglielmo
Scipio Africanus 1939,S 23,22:2
Manon Lescaut 1941,Ap 14,23:5
Marco Visconti 1947,S 20,12:4
Loves of Don Juan, The 1948,S 2,18:4
Voice of Love, The 1950,Ja 7,11:2
Miracle in Milan 1951,D 18,42:2
BARNARD
See Also BERNARD, BERNHARD,
    BERNHARDT
Barnard, Charles (Original Author)
Forest Ring, The 1930,Ap 26,11:1
Barnard, Ivor
Waltz Time 1933,S 29,24:2
Wandering Jew, The 1935,Ja 14,11:3
Princess Charming 1935,Je 22,18:5
Victoria the Great 1937,O 29,19:1
Storm in a Teacup 1938,Mr 22,18:4
Mill On the Floss, The 1939,N 15,19:3
Saint's Vacation, The 1941,Je 13,22:2
Stars Look Down, The 1941,Jl 24,15:2
Silver Fleet, The 1945,Mr 24,22:6
So Well Remembered 1947,N 5,34:3
Dulcimer Street 1948,N 8,24:2
Don't Take it to Heart 1948,D 25,10:3
Mrs Fitzherbert 1950,My 11,37:2
Madeleine 1950,S 1,17:2
Sea Devils 1953,Jl 31,11:5
Beat the Devil 1954,Mr 13,11:2
Barner, Maurice
Rise of Louis XIV, The 1967,S 26,54:2
Barnes, A W (Director)
White Cargo 1930,F 24,18:1
Barnes, Alan
Whistle Down the Wind 1962,Ap 23,34:2
Barnes, Barry
Return of the Scarlet Pimpernel, The
    1938,Ap 11,12:2
Prison Without Bars 1939,Ap 10,13:2
This Man Is News 1939,Jl 20,16:4
Ware Case, The 1939,Jl 22,12:2
Spies of the Air 1940,Jl 4,12:3
Girl in the News, The 1941,My 5,13:2
Bedelia 1947,F 8,10:2
Barnes, Binnie
Private Life of Henry VIII, The 1933,O 13,25:2
Charming Deceiver, The 1933,D 9,18:3
Lady is Willing, The 1934,Ag 11,16:5
There's Always Tomorrow 1934,N 10,19:2
Diamond Jim 1935,Ag 24,18:2
Rendezvous 1935,O 26,12:2
Sutter's Gold 1936,Mr 27,25:2
Small Town Girl 1936,Ap 11,19:1
Last of the Mohicans, The 1936,S 3,17:3
Magnificent Brute, The 1936,O 24,23:1
Three Smart Girls 1937,Ja 25,22:2
Breezing Home 1937,Mr 20,23:5
Broadway Melody of 1938 1937,S 3,12:1

Barnes, Binnie— Cont
Divorce of Lady X, The 1938,Ap 1,17:2
First 100 Years, The 1938,My 13,17:2
Three Blind Mice 1938,Je 18,18:2
Holiday 1938,Je 24,15:1
Always Goodbye 1938,Je 25,7:2
Tropic Holiday 1938,Je 30,21:2
Gateway 1938,Ag 8,9:2
Thanks For Everything 1938,D 10,13:2
Three Musketeers, The 1939,F 18,12:2
Wife, Husband and Friend 1939,F 25,19:2
Man About Town 1939,Je 29,19:1
Frontier Marshal 1939,Jl 29,18:2
Daytime Wife 1939,N 24,29:1
'Til We Meet Again 1940,Ap 14,14:2
This Thing Called Love 1941,F 14,15:2
Tight Shoes 1941,Je 19,25:2
Skylark 1941,N 20,39:2
Call out the Marines 1942,Ja 26,18:3
New Wine 1942,F 2,11:2
In old California 1942,Je 18,25:3
I Married an Angel 1942,Jl 10,13:2
Man From Down Under, The 1943,S 27,23:2
Up in Mabel's Room 1944,Ap 22,8:6
Hour Before the Dawn, The 1944,My 11,25:6
Barbary Coast Gent 1944,S 29,18:2
It's in the Bag 1945,Je 11,12:1
Spanish Main, The 1945,N 7,20:2
Getting Gertie's Garter 1946,F 4,21:2
Time of Their Lives, The 1946,N 28,40:2
If Winter Comes 1948,Ja 23,28:4
My Own True Love 1949,F 3,27:3
Pirates of Capri, The 1949,D 26,33:5
Fugitive Lady 1951,Ag 25,7:2
Decameron Nights 1953,N 17,38:2
Fire over Africa 1954,N 22,29:5
Adventures of Marco Polo, The 1965,Ap 8,17:2
Trouble With Angels, The 1966,Ap 7,45:1
Where Angels Go-Trouble Follows
    1968,Ap 11,51:1
Barnes, Bobby
Male Animal, The 1942,Mr 28,11:1
Barnes, Charles
Intruder, The 1962,My 15,48:1
Barnes, Charles Mercer
Saturday's Hero 1951,S 12,37:2
Barnes, Frank
General, The 1927,F 8,21:1
Barnes, Geoffrey (Original Author)
Party Husband 1931,My 16,13:3
Barnes, Howard McKent (Original Author)
She-Wolf 1931,My 28,30:6
Barnes, Jane
Your Uncle Dudley 1935,D 12,33:4
Man of the People 1937,F 23,25:4
Barnes, Joanna
Home Before Dark 1958,N 7,23:1
Auntie Mame 1958,D 5,39:1
Spartacus 1960,O 7,28:1
Parent Trap, The 1961,Je 22,23:1
Goodbye, Charlie 1964,N 19,49:1
Don't Make Waves 1967,Je 21,36:2
Barnes, Mae
Odds Against Tomorrow 1959,O 16,27:1
Barnes, Margaret Ayer (Original Author)
Westward Passage 1932,Je 4,9:2
Dishonored Lady 1947,My 24,10:5
Barnes, Peter (Screenwriter)
Ring of Treason 1964,My 28,40:3 (Incorrect in
    this edition; use 1964,My 29,15:1 elsewhere)
Not With my Wife, You Don't! 1966,N 3,45:2
Barnes, Rayford
Three Stooges in Orbit, The 1962,Jl 12,19:4
Barnes, Rosamond
Housemaster 1939,Ap 10,13:2
Barnes, T Roy
Scratch my Back 1920,Je 5,19:3
Is Matrimony a Failure 1922,Ap 17,22:3
Old Homestead, The 1922,O 9,10:2
Go-Getter 1923,Ag 9,14:3 (In Addenda)
Hollywood 1923,Jl 30,11:4
Great White Way, The 1924,Ja 4,10:1
Seven Chances 1925,Mr 17,18:1
Crowded Hour, The 1925,Ap 27,15:2
Price of Pleasure, The 1925,My 26,24:2
Tender Hour, The 1927,Je 7,27:4
Body and Soul 1927,N 8,33:1
Chicago 1927,D 24,9:1
Dangerous Curves 1929,Jl 15,25:1
Sally 1929,D 24,14:4
Wide Open 1930,My 22,22:6
Caught Short 1930,Je 21,20:5
Women of all Nations 1931,My 30,9:2
Kansas City Princess 1934,N 5,23:1
It's a Gift 1935,Ja 5,20:2
Doubting Thomas 1935,Jl 11,24:2
Barnes, Walter
Big Gundown, The 1968,Ag 23,33:1
BARNET
See Also BARNETT
Barnet, Boris
Dark Is The Night 1946,Mr 18,24:3
Secret Agent 1949,F 10,37:3

Barnet, Boris (Director)
Dark Is The Night 1946,Mr 18,24:3
Secret Agent 1949,F 10,37:3
Bountiful Summer 1951,D 24,9:1
Wrestler and the Clown, The 1959,Ja 1,38:1
Barnet, Charlie
Jam Session 1944,My 3,25:3
Song Is Born, A 1948,O 20,37:2
Barnet, Charlie and Orchestra
Music in Manhattan 1944,O 7,11:2
Barnet, M (Director)
Moscow in October 1927,N 1,27:1
BARNETT
See Also BARNET
Barnett, B (Director)
Patrioty 1933,S 25,18:5
Barnett, Gilbert
David and Bathsheba 1951,Ag 15,23:2
Barnett, Griff
To Each his Own 1946,My 24,15:2
Possessed 1947,My 30,25:2
Gunfighters 1947,Jl 25,12:5
Cass Timberlane 1947,N 7,20:2
Wild Harvest 1947,N 13,33:2
Daisy Kenyon 1947,D 25,32:1
Fighting Father Dunne 1948,Je 25,26:2
Fury at Furnace Creek 1948,Jl 12,11:2
Walls of Jericho, The 1948,Ag 5,16:2
Tap Roots 1948,Ag 26,16:3
For the Love of Mary 1948,S 23,37:2
Apartment for Peggy 1948,O 16,9:2
Criss Cross 1949,Mr 12,10:2
Mother is a Freshman 1949,Mr 12,10:2
Pinky 1949,S 30,28:2
Holiday Affair 1949,N 24,48:2
Peggy 1950,Jl 21,15:4
Two of a Kind 1951,Je 30,8:6
Passage West 1951,Ag 31,12:2
Scandal Sheet 1952,Ja 17,23:1
Marrying Kind, The 1952,Mr 14,27:1
Barneti, Jackie
Eddie Cantor Story, The 1953,D 26,10:2
Barnett, S H (Original Author)
Father Goose 1964,D 11,55:1
Barnett, Vince
One Heavenly Night 1931,Ja 10,19:2
Scarface, The Shame of the Nation
1932,My 20,22:3
Tiger Shark 1932,S 23,22:2
Rackety Rax 1932,N 5,12:5
Night Mayor, The 1932,N 25,19:2
Flesh 1932,D 10,19:3
Death Kiss, The 1933,F 5,IX,5:3
Heritage of the Desert 1933,Mr 11,18:3
Fast Workers 1933,Mr 20,18:2
Big Cage, The 1933,My 9,20:5
Girl in 419 1933,My 20,11:5
Made on Broadway 1933,Jl 8,14:5
Prizefighter and the Lady, The 1933,N 11,11:3
Madame Spy 1934,F 10,20:1
Ninth Guest, The 1934,Mr 3,8:5
Thirty Day Princess 1934,My 12,12:3
Now I'll Tell 1934,My 26,12:2
Affairs of Cellini, The 1934,S 6,22:3
She Loves Me Not 1934,S 8,18:5
Young and Beautiful 1934,S 18,18:4
Crimson Romance 1934,O 13,10:1
Hell in the Heavens 1934,D 12,28:2
Black Fury 1935,Ap 11,27:2
Princess O'Hara 1935,Ap 13,11:3
Don't Bet on Blondes 1935,Jl 20,16:2
Silk Hat Kid 1935,Ag 7,22:5
Riffraff 1936,Ja 13,14:2
Dancing Feet 1936,Mr 28,11:2
Down Under the Sea 1936,Ag 10,10:2
Woman I Love, The 1937,Ap 16,27:2
Star Is Born, A 1937,Ap 23,25:1
Exile Express 1939,Ag 16,21:3
East Side Kids 1940,F 19,21:6
Ghost Creeps, The 1940,Ag 19,13:3
Seven Sinners 1940,N 18,23:2
Gangs Incorporated 1941,Ag 4,16:6
Captive Wild Woman 1943,Je 7,9:4
Thrill of a Romance 1945,My 25,22:2
River Gang 1945,O 6,9:7
Falcon's Alibi, The 1946,Ap 13,23:2
Virginian, The 1946,Ap 18,22:2
Killers, The 1946,Ag 29,24:2
No Leave, No Love 1946,O 18,29:2
Shoot to Kill 1947,My 17,8:5
Brute Force 1947,Jl 17,16:2
High Wall 1947,D 26,22:2
Red Planet Mars 1952,Je 16,15:2
Springfield Rifle 1952,O 23,40:2
Barnette, Griff
Arizona 1941,F 7,23:3
Barney, Jay
Shrike, The 1955,Jl 8,15:2
Mister Rock and Roll 1957,O 17,42:2
Blueprint for Robbery 1961,F 2,24:3
Barnitz, Michael Baby
Butch Minds the Baby 1942,My 1,23:3

Barnum, Franklyn
Sunset Boulevard 1950,Ag 11,15:2
Barnwell, John (Director)
Huk! 1956,D 15,20:4
Barnwell, John (Producer)
Five Against the House 1955,Je 11,8:7
Barnwell, John (Screenwriter)
Five Against the House 1955,Je 11,8:7
BARON
See Also BARRON
Baron, Allen
Blast of Silence 1961,D 30,12:1
Baron, Allen (Director)
Blast of Silence 1961,D 30,12:1
Terror in the City 1966,N 9,43:4
Baron, Allen (Producer)
Terror in the City 1966,N 9,43:4
Baron, Allen (Screenwriter)
Blast of Silence 1961,D 30,12:1
Terror in the City 1966,N 9,43:4
Baron, Elizabeth (Screenwriter)
Gay Intruders, The 1946,Mr 18,24:2
Baron, Emma
Viaccia, La 1962,S 21,35:1
Baron, Joan
Neapolitan Carousel 1961,O 12,41:3
Baron, Lita
Jungle Jim 1949,Ja 1,9:2
Jesse James' Women 1954,S 29,23:4
Baron, Pauline
Satan in Sables 1925,O 15,27:3
Baron, Sandy
Sweet November 1968,F 9,55:1
Targets 1968,Ag 14,34:1
Baron Jr
Mystere de la Villa Rose, Le 1932,Ja 11,28:5
Baroncelli, de (Director)
Cessez le Feu; Cease Firing 1934,Ag 12,IX,2:1
Baroncelli, J (Director)
Forbidden Love 1948,Ag 26,16:4
Baroncelli, Jacques de (Director)
Crainquebille 1934,D 10,16:3
Wicked Duchess, The 1949,N 5,10:5
French Way, The 1952,S 6,12:6
Baroncelli, Jacques de (Producer)
French Way, The 1952,S 6,12:6
Barondess, Barbara
Soldiers of the Storm 1933,My 17,15:3
When Strangers Marry 1933,My 25,24:3
Hold Your Man 1933,Jl 1,16:6
Devil's Mate 1933,S 23,11:7
Eight Girls in a Boat 1934,Ja 13,16:3
Unknown Blonde 1934,Ap 24,27:2
Change of Heart 1934,My 11,24:2
Fountain, The 1934,Ag 31,14:1
Pursuit of Happiness, The 1934,O 26,25:1
Plot Thickens, The 1936,D 9,35:2
Baronova, Irina
Florian 1940,Je 6,33:2
Toast to Love 1951,N 7,35:5
Train of Events 1952,My 26,18:4
Baronovitch, Elene D
Passion of St Francis, The 1932,D 17,22:3
Baronovskaya, V
Mother 1928,Ja 8,VIII,3:2
Mother, 1905 1934,My 30,14:4
Barouh, Pierre
Man and a Woman, A; Homme et une Femme,
Un 1966,Jl 13,35:1
To be a Crook 1967,F 7,33:2
Baroux, Lucien
Soir de Rafle, Un 1931,O 16,27:1
Charlemagne 1935,Ag 24,18:3
Mysteres de Paris, Les 1937,Ja 30,21:2
Forty Little Mothers 1938,D 23,16:3
Champs-Elysees 1939,F 28,17:2
Fire in the Straw 1943,Jl 2,15:2
32 Rue de Montmartre 1944,S 28,26:3
Moulin Rouge 1944,N 23,38:2
French Way, The 1952,S 6,12:6
Father's Dilemma 1952,S 23,25:1
Naughty Martine 1953,Ap 13,32:4
Devil and the 10 Commandments, The (Episode
1) 1963,O 15,44:1
BARR
See Also BAHR
Barr, Betty
Forest Ring, The 1930,Ap 26,11:1
Barr, Byron
Double Indemnity 1944,S 7,21:1
Affairs of Susan, The 1945,Mr 29,18:2
Love Letters 1945,Ag 27,22:3
Pitfall 1948,Ag 25,31:2
Thelma Jordon 1950,Ja 19,35:2
Barr, Douglas
Madeleine 1950,S 1,17:2
Hue and Cry 1951,Ja 9,25:2
Barr, George
Safe at Home 1941,N 26,31:2
Barr, George (Original Author)
Up From the Beach 1965,Je 10,38:1

Barr, Jeanne
Long Day's Journey Into Night 1962,O 10,57:2
Barr, Mel (Screenwriter)
Murder, Inc 1960,Je 29,26:6
Barr, Patrick
Norah O'Neale 1934,O 25,26:3
Return of the Scarlet Pimpernel, The
1938,Ap 11,12:2
Frightened Lady 1941,N 10,21:3
Blue Lagoon, The 1949,O 3,13:2
Story of Robin Hood, The 1952,Je 27,18:3
Sailor of the King 1953,S 3,15:2
Duel in the Jungle 1954,Ag 9,13:2
Crest of the Wave 1954,N 11,43:2
Saint Joan 1957,Je 27,21:1
Next to no Time 1960,My 28,13:2
Billy Liar 1963,D 17,49:1
Barr, Robert (Original Author)
Horse's Mouth, The 1954,Ja 20,33:4
Third Key, The 1957,Je 3,30:2
Barr, Robert (Screenwriter)
Third Key, The 1957,Je 3,30:2
Barr, Tony
Mozart Story, The 1948,N 15,21:5
Between Midnight and Dawn 1950,O 2,19:2
Scared Stiff 1953,Jl 3,10:2
Barra, Cappy Harmonica Band
Mad About Music 1938,Mr 12,13:2
Barracaracciolo, Vittoria
Neapolitan Carousel 1961,O 12,41:3
Barrangon, Eloise (Original Author)
Spring Madness 1938,D 1,29:3
Barrat, Maxine
Thousands Cheer 1943,S 14,27:1
Barrat, Pierre
Rise of Louis XIV, The 1967,S 26,54:2
Barrat, Robert
King of the Jungle 1933,F 25,20:3
Picture Snatcher 1933,My 19,20:3
Ann Carver's Profession 1933,Je 9,20:2
Lilly Turner 1933,Je 15,21:2
Baby Face 1933,Je 24,16:2
Silk Express, The 1933,Je 28,24:2
Mayor of Hell, The 1933,Jl 1,16:5
Heroes for Sale 1933,Jl 22,14:3
Captured 1933,Ag 18,18:3
Secret of the Blue Room, The 1933,S 13,22:1
I Loved a Woman 1933,S 22,14:2
Wild Boys of the Road 1933,S 22,14:1
Kennell Murder Case, The 1933,O 30,14:2
From Headquarters 1933,N 17,22:4
Massacre 1934,Ja 18,19:2
Hi, Nellie! 1934,F 1,15:5
Dark Hazard 1934,F 23,23:3
Wonder Bar 1934,Mr 1,23:2
Gambling Lady 1934,Ap 5,25:2
Upper World 1934,My 25,25:4
Fog over Frisco 1934,Je 7,26:2
Midnight Alibi 1934,Jl 4,18:3
Return of the Terror 1934,Jl 11,20:2
Here Comes the Navy 1934,Jl 21,14:2
Friends of Mr Sweeney 1934,Jl 31,20:4
Housewife 1934,Ag 10,21:2
Dragon Murder Case, The 1934,Ag 23,13:3
St Louis Kid, The 1934,N 1,25:2
Big Hearted Herbert 1934,N 14,23:2
Firebird, The 1934,N 15,25:2
I Sell Anything 1934,D 27,25:2
I am a Thief 1935,Ja 24,22:5
Bordertown 1935,Ja 24,22:5
Devil Dogs of the Air 1935,F 7,23:2
While the Patient Slept 1935,Mr 2,18:2
Florentine Dagger, The 1935,Ap 27,20:6
Stranded 1935,Je 20,16:2
Murder Man, The 1935,Jl 27,16:2
Special Agent 1935,S 19,28:1
Dr Socrates 1935,O 3,29:2
Captain Blood 1935,D 27,14:1
Exclusive Story 1936,Ja 18,19:2
Trail of the Lonesome Pine, The 1936,F 20,23:5
Country Doctor, The 1936,Mr 13,32:2 (Incorrect
in this edition; use 1936,Mr 13,27:2 elsewhere)
I Married a Doctor 1936,Ap 20,17:1
Sons o'Guns 1936,My 14,29:2
Mary of Scotland 1936,Jl 31,22:2
Last of the Mohicans, The 1936,S 3,17:3
Charge of the Light Brigade, The 1936,N 2,24:1
God's Country and the Woman 1937,Ja 11,15:5
Black Legion 1937,Ja 18,21:1
Mountain Justice 1937,My 13,31:2
Life of Emile Zola, The 1937,Ag 12,14:2
Confession 1937,Ag 19,23:1
Love Is on the Air 1937,N 12,27:3
Barrier, The 1937,N 27,21:2
Bad Man of Brimstone, The 1938,F 4,17:2
Buccaneer, The 1938,F 17,17:2
Penitentiary 1938,Mr 7,13:2
Texans, The 1938,Jl 28,23:2
Breaking the Ice 1938,S 23,35:3
Shadows Over Shanghai 1938,D 1,29:2
Charlie Chan in Honolulu 1938,D 31,7:3
Man of Conquest 1939,Ap 28,31:2
Return of the Cisco Kid, The 1939,Ap 29,13:2

Bad Lands 1939,Ag 9,15:2
Conspiracy 1939,Ag 23,19:2
Allegheny Uprising 1939,N 10,27:3
Cisco Kid and the Lady, The 1939,D 25,29:2
Man From Dakota, The 1940,F 22,29:2
Northwest Passage 1940,Mr 8,25:1
Prison Camp 1940,Ag 3,9:3
Captain Caution 1940,O 21,21:3
Go West 1941,F 21,16:2
Parachute Battalion 1941,Ag 29,13:2
American Empire 1943,Ja 14,25:4
Fall In 1943,My 15,13:3
They Came to Blow up America
  1943,My 15,13:2
Bomber's Moon 1943,Jl 31,8:2
Johnny Come Lately 1943,S 24,26:1
Adventures of Mark Twain, The 1944,My 4,25:5
Enemy of Women 1944,S 12,23:6
Great John L; The 1945,Jl 9,14:6
Wanderer of the Wasteland 1945,S 29,12:2
Dakota 1945,D 17,17:2
They Were Expendable 1945,D 21,25:2
San Antonio 1945,D 29,19:5
Road to Utopia 1946,F 28,20:2
Time of Their Lives, The 1946,N 28,40:2
Magnificent Doll ·1946,D 9,34:2
Sea of Grass, The 1947,F 28,27:2
Dangerous Millions 1947,Mr 15,10:3
Fabulous Texan, The 1947,D 26,22:5
Relentless 1948,Mr 6,17:3
Joan of Arc 1948,N 12,30:5
Canadian Pacific 1949,My 20,32:4
Song of India 1949,Je 10,32:3
Davy Crockett, Indian Scout 1950,Mr 17,28:3
Kid From Texas, The 1950,Je 2,26:2
Baron of Arizona, The 1950,Je 23,29:2
American Guerrilla in the Philippines
  1950,N 8,37:2
Double Crossbones 1951,Ap 27,19:2
Distant Drums 1951,D 26,19:3
Barratt, Watson (Miscellaneous)
Smiling Faces 1932,Ag 31,12:3
Barratto, Larry (Original Author)
Crash, The 1932,S 9,17:5
Barraud, George
Little Old New York 1923,Ag 2,10:3
Flaming Youth 1923,N 26,15:6
Bellamy Trial, The 1929,Ja 24,30:5
Strange Cargo 1929,F 18,28:1
Ned McCobb's Daughter 1929,F 18,28:1
Last of Mrs Cheyney, The 1929,Ag 12,22:2
Woman to Woman 1929,N 12,34:4
Road to Paradise 1930,S 30,23:1
Road to Paradise, The 1931,Ja 20,21:3
Stingaree 1934,My 18,27:1
Charlie Chan in London 1934,S 13,26:1
Mystery Woman 1935,Ja 9,22:2
Dark Sands 1938,Ag 17,23:4
Barraud, George (Miscellaneous)
Adam and Evalyn 1950,My 12,33:4
Barraud, George (Screenwriter)
Accused 1936,D 17,35:1
Dark Sands 1938,Ag 17,23:4
Barrault, Jean-Louis
Razumov 1937,Mr 9,27:2
Helene 1938,Ja 22,19:1
Pearls of the Crown, The 1938,Ap 12,26:2
Orage 1938,D 12,26:2
Bizarre, Bizarre 1939,Mr 21,27:2
Youth in Revolt 1939,My 16,27:3
Enfants du Paradis, Les 1947,F 20,32:2
Symphonie Fantastique, La 1947,D 8,35:2
Blind Desire 1948,Je 10,28:4
Homme a Hommes D' 1948,Ag 30,14:8
Mlle Desiree 1948,N 19,35:2
Street of Shadows 1948,N 20,9:2
Man to Men 1949,F 21,20:2
Ronde, La 1954,Mr 17,27:2
Longest Day, The 1962,O 5,28:1
Chappaqua 1967,N 6,65:2
Barray, Gerard
Adventures of Scaramouche, The 1964,N 23,34:1
  (Incorrect in this edition; use 1964,N 21,34:1
  elsewhere)
Barreara, Antonio (Director)
Kif Tebbi 1929,My 20,22:6
Barreett, Katherine
Eighteen and Anxious 1957,D 14,16:6
Barreiro, Luis G
Mano in Mano 1933,F 20,11:6
Sombra de Pancho Villa, La 1934,Ja 8,20:3
Tiburon 1934,Ap 18,23:3
Pecados de Amor 1934,Ap 24,27:2
Prisionero 13, El 1934,Ap 30,11:4
Sangre Manda, La 1934,My 15,18:2
Compadre Mendoza, El 1934,N 19,13:2
Payasada de la Vida; Tricks of Life
  1935,Mr 18,14:5
Rayo, El 1935,O 19,21:3
Isla Maldita, La 1935,D 2,18:3
Todo un Hombre 1936,Ja 6,20:5
Esos Hombres 1937,Ag 21,7:3
Perjura 1939,Ja 16,11:2

Estrellita; Starlet 1939,Ap 12,27:3
Luna Criolla; Creole Moon 1940,Ap 8,15:3
Bestia Negra, La; Black Beast, The 1940,Je 3,11:2
Barrell, Joseph
Love Master, The 1924,My 19,14:2
Barrella, Giovanni
Loyalty of Love 1937,Mr 1,15:1
Barren, Tony (Screenwriter)
Good Times 1967,Ag 3,26:4
Barret, Andre (Original Author)
Day and the Hour, The 1964,F 20,22:2
Barreto, Lima (Director)
Cangaceiro 1954,S 3,13:2
Barreto, Lima (Screenwriter)
Cangaceiro 1954,S 3,13:2
Barrett, Adrienne
Dementia 1955,D 23,14:4
Barrett, Claudia
Last Time I Saw Archie, The 1961,My 29,9:6
Barrett, Edith
Ladies in Retirement 1941,N 7,27:1
Lady for a Night 1942,F 12,27:2
Give Out, Sisters 1942,Ag 28,22:3
Get Help to Love 1942,O 19,15:3
I Walked With a Zombie 1943,Ap 22,31:5
Ghost Ship, The 1943,D 25,19:4
Song of Bernadette, The 1944,Ja 27,15:2
Jane Eyre 1944,F 4,12:5
Keys of the Kingdom, The 1944,D 30,15:2
Molly and Me 1945,My 26,18:2
That's the Spirit 1945,Je 2,11:2
Ruthless 1948,S 4,8:7
Lady Gambles, The 1949,My 21,9:2
Holiday for Sinners 1952,S 20,13:2
Swan, The 1956,Ap 27,21:5
Barrett, James Lee (Screenwriter)
D'I, The 1957,Je 6,35:2
Greatest Story Ever Told, The 1965,F 16,40:2
Truth About Spring, The 1965,Je 17,27:2
Shenandoah 1965,Jl 29,18:3
Green Berets, The 1968,Je 20,49:1
Bandolero 1968,Jl 18,26:2
Barrett, Jane
Massacre Hill 1950,D 14,51:3
Sword and the Rose, The 1953,Ag 20,18:3
Time, Gentlemen, Please 1953,S 24,39:2
Barrett, Jerry
Under a Texas Moon 1930,Ap 4,22:1
Barrett, John
Far From the Madding Crowd 1967,O 19,59:1
Barrett, Judith
Flying Hostess 1936,D 14,29:4
Good Old Soak 1937,Ap 20,25:3
Let Them Live 1937,Je 8,30:3
Armored Car 1937,Jl 26,15:2
Illegal Traffic 1938,N 17,29:3
I'm From Missouri 1939,Mr 23,27:1
Gracie Allen Murder Case, The 1939,Je 8,31:3
Disputed Passage 1939,O 26,27:2
Great Victor Herbert, The 1939,D 7,35:1
Road to Singapore 1940,Mr 14,29:2
Women Without Names 1940,My 9,26:4
Those Were the Days 1940,Jl 15,18:4
Barrett, Laurinda
Wrong Man, The 1956,D 24,8:1
Heart is a Lonely Hunter, The 1968,Ag 1,24:1
Barrett, Louise
Payment in Blood 1968,D 5,59:1
Barrett, Majel
Track of Thunder 1968,F 1,28:4
Barrett, Michael (Original Author)
Reward, The 1965,S 16,55:1
Barrett, Pat
Comin' Round the Mountain 1940,S 26,27:3
Barrett, Paul
Border Flight 1936,Je 22,22:1
Barrett, Sean
Four Sided Triangle 1953,My 16,10:1
Dunkirk 1958,S 11,42:2
Cry From the Streets, A 1959,F 24,32:2
Sink the Bismarck! 1960,F 12,22:3
Sons and Lovers 1960,Ag 3,35:1
Barrett, Tim
Boy Cried Murder, The 1966,Ap 14,42:3
Psycopath, The 1966,S 29,60:1
Where the Bullets Fly 1967,S 7,50:4
Barrett, Tony
San Quentin 1947,F 10,24:3
Born to Kill 1947,My 1,34:2
Dick Tracy's Dilemma 1947,Jl 14,14:5
Dick Tracy and Gruesome 1947,S 27,11:2
Impact 1949,Mr 21,19:2
Barrett, Vince
Kansas City Princess 1934,N 5,23:1
Barrett, W Capt
Life and Death of Colonel Blimp, The
  1945,Mr 30,18:2
Barrett, William E (Original Author)
Left Hand of God, The 1955,S 22,34:5
Lilies of the Field 1963,O 2,51:1
Barrett, Wilson (Original Author)
Sign of the Cross, The 1932,D 1,25:1

Barri, Mario
Huk! 1956,D 15,20:4
Steel Claw, The 1961,S 21,40:2
Yank in Vietnam, A 1964,F 6,36:4
BARRIE
See Also BARRY, BERRY
Barrie, Amanda
Pair of Briefs, A 1964,F 3,22:2
Carry on Cleo 1965,O 23,17:2
Barrie, Barbara
Caretakers, The 1963,Ag 22,19:2
Caretakers, The 1963,Ag 22,19:2
One Potato, Two Potato 1964,Jl 30,16:1
Barrie, Elaine
Midnight 1939,Ap 6,31:1
Barrie, H E (Screenwriter)
Missle to the Moon 1958,N 17,37:2
Frankenstein's Daughter 1958,N 17,37:2
Barrie, Harry
Every Night at Eight 1935,Ag 3,16:2
Barrie, J M (Original Author)
Peter Pan 1953,F 12,23:1
Forever Female 1954,Ja 13,26:2
Barrie, James (Original Author)
Male and Female 1919,N 24,13:1
Sentimental Tommy 1921,My 9,16:2
Little Minister, The 1921,D 26,13:3
Peter Pan 1924,D 29,11:4
Kiss for Cinderella, A 1925,D 26,11:2
Quality Street 1927,N 2,24:5
Doctor's Secret, The 1929,F 4,20:1
Seven Days' Leave 1930,Ja 25,13:2
What Every Woman Knows 1934,O 27,20:2
Little Minister, The 1934,D 28,25:1
Quality Street 1937,Ap 9,19:2
Darling, How Could You! 1951,N 9,22:4
Admirable Crichton, The 1957,D 15,45:4
  (Incorrect in this edition; use 1957,D 17,45:4
  elsewhere)
Barrie, James (Screenwriter)
Real Thing at Last, The 1916,Mr 9,11:2
Barrie, John
Victim 1962,F 6,27:2
Walk in the Shadow 1966,S 12,52:5
Barrie, Judith
Party Girl 1930,Ja 2,28:2
Ex-Flame 1931,Ja 24,15:1
Barrie, Leslie
Iron Curtain, The 1948,My 13,31:2
Barrie, Lina
Pastor Hall 1940,S 21,13:2
Barrie, Mona
Carolina 1934,F 16,17:2
Such Women Are Dangerous 1934,Je 9,18:3
One Night of Love 1934,S 7,25:3
Charlie Chan in London 1934,S 13,26:1
I'll Fix It 1934,N 12,17:3
Mystery Woman 1935,Ja 9,22:2
Melody Lingers on, The 1935,N 7,27:1
King of Burlesque 1936,Ja 16,25:2
Message to Garcia, A 1936,Ap 10,27:1
Love on the Run 1936,N 28,13:3
Mountain Justice 1937,My 13,31:2
I Met Him in Paris 1937,Je 3,29:2
Something to Sing About 1937,S 21,29:4
Love, Honor and Behave 1938,Mr 21,18:2
Men Are Such Fools 1938,Je 17,25:1
Say It in French 1938,D 1,29:1
I Take This Woman 1940,F 16,23:3
Lady With red Hair 1940,D 6,28:2
When Ladies Meet 1941,S 5,19:2
Ellery Queen and the Murder Ring
  1941,O 21,29:4
Never Give a Sucker an Even Break
  1941,O 27,21:2
Skylark 1941,N 20,39:2
Road to Happiness 1942,Mr 27,27:4
Strange Case of Dr Rx 1942,Mr 28,11:2
Cairo 1942,N 6,27:2
Storm Over Lisbon 1944,S 11,14:1
Cass Timberlane 1947,N 7,20:2
Plunder of the Sun 1953,Ag 27,22:1
Barrie, Nigel
Widow by Proxy 1919,S 22,8:1
Charge It 1921,Ag 29,14:4
Prince There Was 1921,N 14,18:1
Stranger's Banquet, The 1923,Ja 1,18:1
Peg o'my Heart 1923,Ja 22,10:1
Hogan's Alley 1925,N 24,28:4
Steel Preferred 1925,D 22,13:1
Amateur Gentleman, The 1926,Ag 17,15:3
Climbers, The 1927,My 4,29:2
Shield of Honor 1927,D 13,33:2
Lone Eagle, The 1927,D 20,33:2
Dreyfus Case, The 1931,Ag 31,11:5
Barrie, Wendy
Private Life of Henry VIII, The 1933,O 13,25:2
It's a Boy 1934,Je 8,18:2
For Love or Money 1934,Jl 26,14:2
Big Broadcast of 1936, The 1935,S 16,15:2
Feather in her Hat, A 1935,O 25,24:5
Millions in the Air 1935,D 12,33:4
Love on a Bet 1936,Mr 5,25:2

Barrie, Wendy— Cont
  Speed 1936,My 16,11:2
  Ticket to Paradise 1936,Ag 8,5:3
  Under Your Spell 1936,N 7,15:2
  Breezing Home 1937,Mr 20,23:5
  What Price Vengeance 1937,My 26,30:3
  Wings Over Honolulu 1937,My 29,20:1
  Dead End 1937,Ag 25,25:1
  Girl With Ideas, A 1938,Ja 1,11:2
  I Am the Law 1938,Ag 26,14:2
  Pacific Liner 1939,Ja 18,17:3
  Newsboys' Home 1939,Ja 23,8:2
  Saint Strikes Back, The 1939,Mr 9,18:2
  Hound of the Baskervilles, The 1939,Mr 25,19:2
  Five came Back 1939,Jl 5,20:2
  Witness Vanishes, The 1939,O 23,15:2
  Daytime Wife 1939,N 24,29:1
  Saint Takes Over, The 1940,My 28,29:3
  Women in War 1940,My 30,21:2
  Cross Country Romance 1940,Jl 19,22:3
  Men Against the Sky 1940,S 12,31:2
  Saint in Palm Springs, The 1941,Ja 31,15:5
  Date With the Falcon, A 1941,N 25,33:2
  Eyes of the Underworld 1942,O 5,15:2
  It Should Happen to You 1954,Ja 16,10:5

Barrier, Edgar
  Escape 1940,N 1,33:1
  Comrade X 1940,D 26,23:1
  They Dare not Love 1941,My 16,21:4
  Eagle Squadron 1942,Jl 3,12:5
  Arabian Nights 1942,D 26,15:1
  Journey Into Fear 1943,Mr 19,15:3
  We've Never Been Licked 1943,Ag 19,23:1
  Phantom of the Opera, The 1943,O 15,15:2
  Flesh and Fantasy 1943,N 18,29:1
  Cobra Woman 1944,My 18,17:2
  Nob Hill 1945,Jl 4,10:3
  Game of Death, A 1945,N 24,22:4
  Cornered 1945,D 26,15:1
  Tarzan and the Leopard Woman 1946,F 11,25:2
  To the Ends of the Earth 1948,F 13,26:2
  Rogues' Regiment 1948,D 20,31:2
  Cyrano De Bergerac 1950,N 17,31:2
  Last of the Buccaneers 1950,D 15,43:2
  Macbeth 1950,D 28,22:6
  Destination Gobi 1953,My 30,7:1
  Count the Hours 1953,Je 24,30:4
  Princess of the Nile 1954,Je 12,13:2
  On the Double 1961,My 20,12:1
  Snow White and the Three Stooges 1961,Jl 1,9:1

Barringer, Dale
  Do You Love Me 1946,My 25,12:2
Barringer, Emily Dunning (Original Author)
  Girl in White, The 1952,My 31,12:5
Barringer, Michael (Director)
  Q Ships 1928,S 17,27:1
Barringer, Michael (Miscellaneous)
  In a Monastery Garden 1935,Mr 13,16:2
Barringer, Michael (Screenwriter)
  Rhodes 1936,F 29,11:1
  Silent Barriers 1937,Mr 26,25:1
Barrington, Phyllis
  Ten Nights in a Barroom 1931,F 28,15:2
  Sucker Money 1933,Ap 7,22:5
Barris, Harry
  Spirit of Notre Dame, The 1931,O 16,27:1
  Man I Marry, The 1936,O 31,24:3
  Something to Sing About 1937,S 21,29:4
  Cowboy From Brooklyn 1938,Jl 14,17:1
  Shining Hour, The 1939,Ja 20,15:2
  Some Like It Hot 1939,My 25,31:2
  Birth of the Blues 1941,D 11,39:1
  Priorities on Parade 1942,Jl 23,19:2
Barriscale, Bessie
  Plain Jane 1916,Ag 28,7:5
  Show Folks 1928,D 10,25:1
  Man Who Reclaimed his Head, The
    1935,Ja 9,22:1
Barrois, Charles
  Carmen 1928,My 7,29:1
  Shadows of Fear 1928,N 6,35:1
BARRON
  See Also BARON
Barron, Baynes
  War Is Hell 1964,Ja 23,26:1
  Strangler, The 1964,Je 11,27:4
Barron, Bebe (Miscellaneous)
  8 X 8 1957,Mr 16,13:2
Barron, Isabel
  Toda una Vida 1933,O 23,18:3
Barron, Louis (Miscellaneous)
  8 X 8 1957,Mr 16,13:2
Barron, Marcus
  Loyalties 1934,O 26,25:1
  Strauss's Great Waltz 1935,Ap 8,23:3
Barron, Richard
  Dementia 1955,D 23,14:4
Barron, Robert
  Pittsburgh Kid, The 1941,S 23,27:4
  Song of my Heart 1948,Mr 5,17:3
Barror, Cecil
  Broth of a Boy 1959,D 28,18:1

Barroso, Ary (Composer)
  Brazil 1944,N 20,25:2
  Three Caballeros, The 1945,F 5,20:1
Barrow, Barbara
  Mountain, The 1956,N 15,44:6
Barrow, Bernard
  Rachel Rachel 1968,Ag 27,36:1
Barrows, Henry
  Sporting Youth 1924,Ap 2,16:1
  Between Friends 1924,My 12,14:4
  Sea Hawk, The 1924,Je 3,22:1
  Captain Blood 1924,S 9,19:1
  Drusilla With a Million 1925,My 25,21:3
  His Majesty Bunker Bean 1925,S 15,12:1
  Man on the Box, The 1925,S 28,24:1
  Cobra 1925,D 7,19:1
  Oh! What a Nurse! 1926,F 22,14:1
  Skinner's Dress Suit 1926,My 3,27:1
  Little Irish Girl, The 1926,My 11,24:3
  All Abroad 1927,Ap 19,24:4
  Three's a Crowd 1927,O 3,20:1
  Drake Case, The 1929,S 16,30:1
  Guilty Hands 1931,Ag 29,16:3
Barrows, James O
  Stephen Steps Out 1923,N 19,19:3
  Signal Tower, The 1924,Jl 21,14:4
  Daddy's Gone A-Hunting 1925,F 24,17:3
  Price of Pleasure, The 1925,My 26,24:2
  Goose Woman, The 1925,Ag 4,14:3
  Sea Hunt, The 1926,Ja 16,8:5
  Sea Beast, The 1926,Ja 16,8:5
Barrows, Leslie S (Original Author)
  Honky Tonk 1929,Je 5,32:3
Barrows, Leslie S (Screenwriter)
  Singing Fool, The 1928,S 20,33:2
Barrows, Nicholas T (Screenwriter)
  I'm From the City 1938,Ag 19,13:4
BARRY
  See Also BARRIE, BARY, BERRY
Barry, Barta
  Gladiators Seven 1964,My 7,31:2
Barry, Dave
  Some Like It Hot 1959,Mr 30,23:1
Barry, Donald
  Night Waitress 1936,D 18,31:5
  Woman I Love, The 1937,Ap 16,27:2
  Sinners in Paradise 1938,My 20,17:2
  Crowd Roars, The 1938,Ag 5,11:1
  Duke of West Point, The 1938,D 16,33:2
  Calling Dr Kildare 1939,My 12,25:4
  Only Angels Have Wings 1939,My 12,25:2
  S O S Tidal Wave 1939,Je 22,19:3
  Calling All Marines 1939,O 26,27:2
  Remember Pearl Harbor 1942,Je 4,22:4
  Purple Heart, The 1944,Mr 9,15:2
  Chicago Kid, The 1945,F 12,24:3
  Last Crooked Mile, The 1946,S 14,10:8
  Plainsman and the Lady, The 1946,N 4,33:1
  Ringside 1949,S 17,10:8
  Dalton Gang, The 1949,N 25,27:5
  Jesse James' Women 1954,S 29,23:4
  I'll Cry Tomorrow 1956,Ja 13,18:1
  Walk on the Wild Side 1962,F 22,20:1
  Twilight of Honor 1963,N 14,41:2
  Alvarez Kelly 1966,N 17,55:2
  Fort Utah 1967,My 25,54:3
  Shakiest Gun in the West, The 1968,Jl 11,30:1
Barry, Donald (Director)
  Jesse James' Women 1954,S 29,23:4
Barry, Gene
  Atomic City, The 1952,My 2,21:1
  Girls of Pleasure Island, The 1953,My 16,10:1
  War of the Worlds, The 1953,Ag 14,10:2
  Those Redheads From Seattle 1953,O 1,34:2
  Alaska Seas 1954,Mr 6,13:5
  Red Garters 1954,Mr 27,13:5
  Naked Alibi 1954,O 2,21:2
  Soldier of Fortune 1955,My 28,7:4
  Purple Mask, The 1955,Je 16,35:7
  Back From Eternity 1956,S 8,20:6
  China Gate 1957,My 23,40:2
Barry, Gerard
  His Glorious Night 1929,O 5,22:5
Barry, Henrietta
  Long Dark Hall, The 1951,My 10,38:3
Barry, Jean
  Why Leave Home 1929,S 16,30:1
  Rome Express 1932,D 18,X,6:5
  Strictly Personal 1933,Mr 20,18:2
Barry, Jimmie
  These Thirty Years 1934,My 24,28:3
Barry, Joan
  Blackmail 1929,Jl 14,IX,4:5
  Atlantic 1930,Ja 26,VIII,6:2
  Atlantic 1930,O 6,21:1
  Outsider, The 1931,Je 7,VIII,6:1
  First Mrs Fraser, The 1932,My 29,VIII,4:5 (In
    Addenda)
  Rome Express 1933,F 27,11:2
Barry, Joe
  Man With the Gun 1955,D 23,14:2
  Bell, Book and Candle 1958,D 27,2:7

Barry, John
  Dream Maker, The 1964,Ap 23,34:1
Barry, John (Composer)
  Born Free 1966,Je 23,29:1
Barry, Kevin (Screenwriter)
  Saintly Sinners 1962,Mr 29,28:2
Barry, Leon
  Three Musketeers, The 1921,Ag 29,14:4
  Suzanna 1923,Mr 26,16:2
  Temple of Venus, The 1923,N 1,24:3
  Iron Mask, The 1929,F 22,18:6
Barry, Maurice (Screenwriter)
  Three Sinners 1952,Jl 8,23:2
Barry, Patricia
  Show Boat 1936,My 15,29:4
  Safe at Home 1962,Ap 14,14:1
  Kitten With a Whip 1964,N 5,50:4
  Send Me no Flowers 1964,N 13,30:1
  Dear Heart 1965,Mr 8,33:1
Barry, Paul
  Body Is a Shell, The 1957,S 9,21:2
Barry, Philip (Original Author)
  Paris Bound 1929,S 21,17:1
  Holiday 1930,Jl 3,25:4
  Bargain, The 1931,S 5,7:4
  Tomorrow and Tomorrow 1932,Ja 30,13:2
  Animal Kingdom, The 1932,D 30,14:2
  Holiday 1938,Je 24,15:1
  Spring Madness 1938,D 1,29:3
  Philadelphia Story, The 1940,D 27,22:2
  Without Love 1945,Mr 23,13:1
  One More Tomorrow 1946,My 25,12:2
  High Society 1956,Ag 10,9:2
Barry, Philip Jr (Producer)
  Mating Game, The 1959,Ap 30,37:1
Barry, Phillip (Producer)
  Sail a Crooked Ship 1962,F 3,12:6
Barry, Phyllis
  Cynara 1932,D 26,26:2
  What! No Beer? 1933,F 11,11:3
  Diplomaniacs 1933,Ap 29,14:2
  Blind Adventure 1933,O 31,24:3
  Long Lost Father 1934,F 19,18:2
  Where Sinners Meet 1934,My 25,25:2
  One Rainy Afternoon 1936,My 14,29:2
  Prince and the Pauper, The 1937,My 6,23:1
  Invisible Menace, The 1938,F 14,20:6
  Marriage Forbidden 1938,Jl 16,7:2
  Trade Winds 1939,Ja 13,17:2
  Case of the Black Parrot, The 1941,Ja 10,23:3
  Unfinished Business 1941,S 2,20:2
  Mysterious Doctor, The 1943,My 20,26:4
Barry, Richard
  Satan in Sables 1925,O 15,27:3
Barry, Tom (Original Author)
  Song O' my Heart 1930,Mr 12,32:6
  Courage 1930,My 23,21:1
  My Bill 1938,Jl 7,22:4
Barry, Violaine
  Paris-Beguin 1932,D 31,10:1
Barry, Wesley
  Unpardonable Sin, The 1919,My 3,11:3
  Dinty 1920,N 22,13:3
  Bits of Life 1921,O 17,18:1
  Penrod 1922,F 20,7:1
  Country Kid, The 1923,O 30,16:1
  Midshipman, The 1925,O 13,20:1
  In old Kentucky 1927,N 21,20:1
  Wild Geese 1927,D 5,26:2
  Sunny Skies 1930,My 17,21:2
  Border Romance 1930,My 26,25:3
  Life of Vergie Winters, The 1934,Je 15,26:1
  Night Life of the Gods 1935,F 23,14:6
  Plough and the Stars, The 1937,Ja 29,15:1
  Pick a Star 1937,My 28,17:2
Barry, Wesley (Producer)
  From Rags to Riches 1922,S 25,10:2
Barry, Yane
  To be a Crook 1967,F 7,33:2
Barrymore, Diana
  Eagle Squadron 1942,Jl 3,12:5
  Between Us Girls 1942,S 25,25:3
  Nightmare 1942,D 4,31:2
  Frontier Badmen 1943,Ag 14,12:8
  Fired Wife 1943,O 1,15:2
  Ladies Courageous 1944,Mr 16,17:2
Barrymore, Diana (Original Author)
  Too Much, Too Soon 1958,My 10,19:2
Barrymore, Dolores Costello
  Little Lord Fauntleroy 1936,Ap 3,27:1
  Yours for the Asking 1936,Ag 20,14:2
Barrymore, Ethel
  White Raven, The 1917,Ja 15,7:2
  Call of her People, The 1917,My 28,11:2
  Our Mrs McChesney 1918,Ag 19,7:1
  Rasputin and the Empress 1932,D 24,11:4
  None but the Lonely Heart 1944,N 18,16:6
  None but the Lonely Heart 1944,D 3,II,1:8
  Spiral Staircase, The 1946,F 7,29:3
  Farmer's Daughter, The 1947,Mr 26,31:2
  Moss Rose 1947,Jl 3,14:2
  Paradine Case, The 1948,Ja 9,26:2
  Night Song 1948,Ja 29,27:5

Barrymore, Ethel— Cont

Moonrise 1949,Mr 7,17:2
Portrait of Jennie 1949,Mr 30,31:2
Great Sinner, The 1949,Je 30,19:2
That Midnight Kiss 1949,S 23,28:2
Pinky 1949,S 30,28:2
Red Danube, The 1949,D 9,37:3
Secret of Convict Lake, The 1951,Ag 4,7:2
Kind Lady 1951,Ag 8,21:2
It's a big Country 1952,Ja 9,25:2
Deadline U S A 1952,Mr 15,8:2
Just for You 1952,O 9,40:6
Story of Three Loves, The (Mademoiselle);
    Mademoiselle (The Story of Three Loves)
    1953,Mr 6,29:2
Main Street to Broadway 1953,O 14,34:1
Young at Heart 1955,Ja 20,35:1

Barrymore, John

Lost Bridegroom, The 1916,Mr 20,9:4
Red Widow, The 1916,Ap 24,11:2
Raffles 1918,F 19,9:2 (Incorrect in this edition;
    use 1918,F 18,9:2 elsewhere)
On the Quiet 1918,Ag 26,9:1
Here Comes the Bride 1919,F 3,13:2
Test of Honor, The 1919,Ap 7,11:5
Dr Jekyll and Mr Hyde 1920,Mr 29,18:1
Lotus Eater, The 1921,N 28,16:1
Sherlock Holmes 1922,My 8,14:3
Beau Brummell 1924,Mr 31,20:1
Sea Hunt, The 1926,Ja 16,8:5
Sea Beast, The 1926,Ja 16,8:5
Don Juan 1926,Ag 7,6:1 (In Addenda)
When a Man Loves 1927,F 4,16:6
Beloved Rogue, The 1927,Mr 14,16:1
Tempest 1928,My 18,27:3
Eternal Love 1929,My 13,27:2
Show of Shows 1929,N 21,24:5
General Crack 1929,D 4,36:6
Man From Blankley's, The 1930,Mr 29,23:1
Handsome Gigolo, Poor Gigolo 1930,Ag 3,4:1
Moby Dick 1930,Ag 15,20:5
Svengali 1931,My 1,30:3
Mad Genius, The 1931,O 24,20:3
Arsene Lupin 1932,F 27,22:1
Grand Hotel 1932,Ap 13,23:2
State's Attorney 1932,My 6,15:3
Bill of Divorcement, A 1932,O 3,15:2
Rasputin and the Empress 1932,D 24,11:4
Topaze 1933,F 10,12:2
Reunion in Vienna 1933,Ap 29,14:2
Dinner at Eight 1933,Ag 24,18:1
Night Flight 1933,O 7,18:4
Counsellor-At-Law 1933,D 8,31:2
Long Lost Father 1934,F 19,18:2
20th Century 1934,My 4,24:2
Romeo and Juliet 1936,Ag 21,12:2
Maytime 1937,Mr 19,27:1
Bulldog Drummond Comes Back 1937,S 4,8:3
Night Club Scandal 1937,N 12,27:2
True Confession 1937,D 16,35:2
Bulldog Drummond's Revenge 1937,D 17,33:2
Bulldog Drummond's Peril 1938,Mr 18,23:2
Romance in the Dark 1938,Mr 21,18:2
Marie Antoinette 1938,Ag 17,23:2
Spawn of the North 1938,S 8,27:1
Hold That Co-ed 1938,S 24,13:1
Great Man Votes, The 1939,Ja 20,15:2
Midnight 1939,Ap 6,31:1
Great Profile, The 1940,O 18,25:1
Invisible Woman, The 1941,Ja 9,27:2
World Premiere 1941,Ag 21,15:2
Playmates 1941,D 26,21:3

Barrymore, John Drew

High School Confidential 1958,My 31,6:6
Never Love a Stranger 1958,N 22,27:4
Night of the Quarter Moon 1959,Mr 5,35:5
Cossacks, The 1960,S 6,41:4
Pharaohs' Woman, The 1962,Ap 19,35:2

Barrymore, John Jr

Sundowners, The 1950,My 5,17:2
High Lonesome 1950,D 8,40:4
Quebec 1951,Mr 16,34:2
Big Night, The 1952,Mr 20,37:5
Thunderbirds 1953,Mr 12,24:4
While the City Sleeps 1956,My 17,37:1

Barrymore, Lionel

Copperhead, The 1920,F 9,10:3
Master Mind, The 1920,S 13,12:1
Enemies of Women 1923,Ap 1,5:4
Unseeing Eyes 1923,O 22,17:1
Eternal City, The 1924,Ja 21,20:1
America 1924,F 22,20:1
I Am the Man 1925,Mr 6,23:1
Barrier, The 1926,Mr 22,16:1
Splendid Road, The 1926,Je 13,31:1
Temptress, The 1926,O 11,18:1
Show, The 1927,Mr 14,16:1
Body and Soul 1927,N 8,33:1
Thirteenth Hour, The 1927,N 28,18:5
Drums of Love 1928,Ja 25,20:4
Sadie Thompson 1928,F 6,12:3
Decameron Nights 1928,My 29,17:2
Lion and the Mouse, The 1928,Je 16,11:4
Alias Jimmy Valentine 1928,N 16,28:6

West of Zanzibar 1928,D 31,9:1
Mysterious Island, The 1929,D 21,17:1
Free Soul, A 1931,Je 3,29:2
Guilty Hands 1931,Ag 29,16:3
Yellow Ticket, The 1931,O 31,22:2
Mata Hari 1932,Ja 1,31:1
Man I Killed, The 1932,Ja 20,17:4
Arsene Lupin 1932,F 27,22:1
Grand Hotel 1932,Ap 13,23:2
Washington Masquerade, The 1932,Jl 22,18:2
Rasputin and the Empress 1932,D 24,11:4
Sweepings 1933,Mr 24,22:3
Looking Forward 1933,My 1,10:2
Grand Hotel 1933,Je 4,IX,2:1 (In Addenda)
Stranger's Return, The 1933,Jl 28,18:2
Dinner at Eight 1933,Ag 24,18:1
One Man's Journey 1933,S 1,15:2
Night Flight 1933,O 7,18:4
Christopher Bean 1933,N 25,10:2
Should Ladies Behave? 1933,D 18,24:3
This Side of Heaven 1934,F 10,21:2
Carolina 1934,F 16,17:2
Girl From Missouri, The 1934,Ag 4,14:6
Treasure Island 1934,Ag 18,5:5
David Copperfield 1935,Ja 19,8:1
Little Colonel, The 1935,Mr 22,26:2
Mark of the Vampire 1935,My 3,23:4
Public Hero No 1 1935,Je 8,12:2
Return of Peter Grimm, The 1935,O 4,25:2
Ah, Wilderness! 1935,D 25,30:2
Voice of Bugle Ann, The 1936,F 27,23:1
Road to Glory, The 1936,Ag 6,22:1
Devil Doll, The 1936,Ag 8,5:2
Gorgeous Hussy, The 1936,S 5,7:1
Camille 1937,Ja 23,13:1
Family Affair, A 1937,Ap 20,29:2
Captains Courageous 1937,My 12,27:1
Saratoga 1937,Jl 23,16:3
Navy Blue and Gold 1937,D 24,21:2
Yank at Oxford, A 1938,F 25,15:1
Test Pilot 1938,Ap 16,17:1
You Can't Take It With You 1938,S 2,21:2
Young Doctor Kildare 1938,O 28,27:1
Let Freedom Ring 1939,Mr 10,19:2
Calling Dr Kildare 1939,My 12,25:4
On Borrowed Time 1939,Jl 7,13:2
Secret of Dr Kildare, The 1939,D 8,33:5
Dr Kildare's Strange Case 1940,Ap 12,19:2
Dr Kildare Goes Home 1940,S 19,27:4
Dr Kildare's Crisis 1940,D 19,33:1
Bad Man, The 1941,Ap 4,25:1
Penalty, The 1941,Ap 10,29:3
People vs Dr Kildare, The 1941,My 8,21:1
Dr Kildare's Wedding Day 1941,S 18,31:1
Lady Be Good 1941,S 19,27:1
Dr Kildare's Victory 1942,F 5,25:2
Calling Dr Gillespie 1942,Jl 9,17:4
Tennessee Johnson 1943,Ja 13,18:2
Guy Named Joe, A 1943,D 24,17:2
Three Men in White 1944,My 26,23:3
Since You Went Away 1944,Jl 21,16:2
Between Two Women 1945,Mr 29,18:3
Valley of Decision, The 1945,My 4,23:2
Three Wise Fools 1946,S 27,19:2
It's a Wonderful Life 1946,D 23,19:2
Secret Heart, The 1946,D 26,28:2
Duel in the Sun 1947,My 8,30:2
Dark Delusion 1947,Je 26,19:2
Key Largo 1948,Jl 17,6:6
Down to the Sea in Ships 1949,F 23,31:2
Malaya 1950,F 23,33:1
Right Cross 1950,N 16,39:2
Lone Star 1952,F 2,11:4
Main Street to Broadway 1953,O 14,34:1

Barrymore, Lionel (Director)

Confession 1929,F 9,15:3
Madame X 1929,Ap 25,32:3
His Glorious Night 1929,O 5,22:5
Unholy Night, The 1929,O 12,11:1
Rogue Song, The 1930,Ja 29,26:4
Ten Cents a Dance 1931,Mr 7,17:2

Barrymore, Lionel (Narrator)

Dragon Seed 1944,Jl 21,16:4

Barsac, Madame

Living Dead Man, The 1927,Mr 7,16:3

Barsacq, Yves

Love on a Pillow 1963,D 17,49:1

Barsamian, Louise

Arshin Mal Alan; Peddler, Lover, The
    1937,Mr 8,22:2

Barsha, Leon (Director)

Who Killed Gail Preston? 1938,My 6,27:2
Convicted 1938,Ag 22,9:3

Barsha, Leon (Producer)

Sing for Your Supper 1941,D 1,15:5

Barsi, Bela

Merry Go-Round 1958,Ap 3,23:3

Barska, M

Polish Terror, The 1933,Mr 13,18:3

Barskaya, Margarita (Director)

Broken Shoes 1934,Mr 31,8:3

Barsony, Elsie

Salary, 200 a Month 1937,Ja 15,17:3

Barsony, Rose

Mad Idea, A; Toller Einfall, Ein 1932,Jl 31,IX,3:4
Und Es Leuchtet die Puszta 1934,Ja 30,17:2
Liebe Muss Verstanden Sein 1934,Mr 21,24:3
Toller Einfall, Ein 1934,My 21,20:3
Waltz Time in Vienna 1934,N 19,13:2
Jo as a Haznal; Father Knows Best 1935,F 5,22:4
Hello Budapest 1935,N 14,17:4
Viki 1937,N 29,19:3
Harapos Ferj; Biting Husbank 1939,Ja 28,19:2
3:1 a Szerelem Javara; 3 to 1 for Love
    1939,Mr 25,19:3

Barszczewska, Elzbieta

Tredowata 1936,D 31,21:2
Hearts Aflame 1937,O 14,22:3
Znachor; Miracle Man, The 1938,F 21,15:2
Znachor 1938,N 24,37:2
Dziewczeta z Nowolipek; Girls of Nowolipek
    1938,N 25,19:2
Kosciuszki 1938,D 27,13:2
Dzien Upragniony; Anticipated Day, The
    1939,Mr 13,12:3

Bart, Jan

Catskill Honeymoon 1950,Ja 28,10:3

Bart, Jean (Original Author)

Man Who Reclaimed his Head, The
    1935,Ja 9,22:1
Strange Confession 1945,N 8,17:3

Bart, Jean (Screenwriter)

Man Who Reclaimed his Head, The
    1935,Ja 9,22:1
Mad Empress, The 1940,F 15,15:1

Bart, Lionel (Composer)

Oliver! 1968,D 11,57:1

Bart, Lionel (Original Author)

Oliver! 1968,D 11,57:1

Bart, Una

Nicholas Nickleby 1947,D 1,27:2

Bartashevich, K

Ladies 1955,Je 27,18:2

Barteaux, Morton (Original Author)

Six Hours to Live 1932,O 22,18:4

Barteaux, Morton (Screenwriter)

Till We Meet Again 1936,My 9,11:2

Bartel, Eddie

Every Night at Eight 1935,Ag 3,16:2

Bartel, Jean

Sanctuary 1961,F 22,31:1

Bartel, Paul (Director)

Secret Cinema, The 1968,My 2,57:1

Bartel, Paul (Producer)

Secret Cinema, The 1968,My 2,57:1

Bartel, Paul (Screenwriter)

Secret Cinema, The 1968,My 2,57:1

Bartell, Dick

Untitled-Baseball Technique 1941,Ja 17,11:3

Bartell, Harry

Johnny Concho 1956,Ag 16,30:1
Voice in the Mirror 1958,Ag 14,23:2
Decks Ran Red, The 1958,O 11,18:2

Bartels, Louis John

Broadway Nights 1927,Je 28,29:4
Dance Magic 1927,Jl 13,21:2
Canary Murder Case, The 1929,Mr 11,22:2
Nothing but the Truth 1929,Ap 22,23:1
Florodora Girl, The 1930,My 31,19:4
Sin Takes a Holliday 1930,N 28,23:1
Cohens and Kellys in Africa, The 1930,D 20,20:6
Prodigal, The 1931,Je 27,20:3
Big Shot, The 1932,Ja 2,14:2

Bartenieff, George

Brig, The 1964,S 21,37:4
Zero in the Universe 1966,O 12,36:3

Barth, Moglia (Director)

Riachuelo 1934,D 8,18:5
Dancing, El 1935,Ja 28,10:6
Ultimo Encventro, El; Last Meeting, The
    1939,Ag 26,20:3
Doce Mujeres; Twelve Women 1940,Mr 11,11:3
Huella; Trial 1940,O 22,27:3

Bartheel, Carla

Bride 68 1930,Ap 15,28:5
Tanz Geht Weiter, Der 1931,Ja 6,25:1

Barthelmess, Richard

Hope Chest, The 1919,Ja 6,11:3
Boots 1919,Mr 10,9:3
Girl Who Stayed Home, The 1919,Mr 24,11:3
Three Men and a Girl 1919,Mr 31,11:3
Peppy Polly 1919,Ap 7,11:5
Broken Blossoms 1919,My 14,15:5
I'll Get Him yet 1919,My 19,20:5
Scarlet Days 1919,N 10,18:2
Idol Dancer, The 1920,Mr 22,12:1
Love Flower, The 1920,Ag 23,9:2
Experience 1921,Ag 8,12:2
Tol'able David 1922,Ja 2,20:1
Seventh Day, The 1922,Mr 13,18:2
Sonny 1922,My 29,14:1
Bond Boy, The 1922,O 9,10:2
Bright Shawl, The 1923,Ap 23,18:3
Fighting Blade, The 1923,O 15,15:4

Barthelmess, Richard— Cont
Twenty-One 1924,F 18,13:1
Enchanted Cottage, The 1924,Ap 14,14:1
Classmates 1924,D 30,15:3
New Toys 1925,F 17,18:1
Soul Fire 1925,My 6,26:3
Shore Leave 1925,S 14,16:1
Beautiful City, The 1925,N 23,25:4
Just Suppose 1926,Ja 18,26:2
Ranson's Folly 1926,My 31,10:2
Amateur Gentleman, The 1926,Ag 17,15:3
White Black Sheep, The 1926,D 21,20:2
Patent Leather Kid, The 1927,Ag 16,31:2
Drop Kick, The 1927,S 20,32:2
Noose, The 1928,Mr 19,26:4
Kentucky Courage 1928,My 14,25:1
Wheels of Chance 1928,Jl 2,11:2
Out of the Ruins 1928,Ag 20,21:3
Scarlet Seas 1928,D 31,9:1
Weary River 1929,Ja 25,20:6
Drag 1929,Je 21,17:2
Young Nowheres 1929,O 2,28:4
Show of Shows 1929,N 21,24:5
Son of the Gods 1930,Ja 31,24:1
Dawn Patrol, The 1930,Jl 11,22:1
Lash, The 1931,Ja 1,31:3
Way Down East 1931,Mr 16,25:1
Finger Points, The 1931,Mr 28,15:3
Last Flight, The 1931,Ag 20,17:4
Alias the Doctor 1932,Mr 3,22:3
Cabin in the Cotton 1932,S 30,17:3
Central Airport 1933,My 4,20:5
Heroes for Sale 1933,Jl 22,14:3
Massacre 1934,Ja 18,19:2
Modern Hero, A 1934,Ap 20,17:1
Midnight Alibi 1934,Jl 4,18:3
Four Hours to Kill 1935,Ap 11,27:3
Only Angels Have Wings 1939,My 12,25:2
Spy of Napoleon 1939,Ag 19,18:4
Man Who Talked too Much, The 1940,Je 29,12:2
Spoilers, The 1942,My 22,27:2
Mayor of Forty-Fourth Street, The
1942,Je 11,27:4
Bartholomew, Freddie
David Copperfield 1935,Ja 19,8:1
Anna Karenina 1935,Ag 31,16:2
Professional Soldier 1936,Ja 30,14:2
Little Lord Fauntleroy 1936,Ap 3,27:1
Devil is a Sissy, The 1936,O 17,21:2
Lloyds of London 1936,N 26,39:1
Captains Courageous 1937,My 12,27:1
Kidnapped 1938,My 28,9:2
Lord Jeff 1938,Jl 1,22:2
Listen, Darling 1938,N 24,37:2
Spirit of Culver 1939,Mr 9,18:1
Two Bright Boys 1939,S 22,27:3
Swiss Family Robinson 1940,F 9,15:3
Tom Brown's School Days 1940,Je 28,22:2
Naval Academy 1941,Je 5,27:3
Yank at Eton, A 1942,O 16,23:1
Barti, Marina
Deported 1950,N 2,39:3
Bartlett, Sy (Producer)
Cape Fear 1962,Ap 19,35:2
Bartik, Stefan
Eve Wants to Sleep 1961,Je 6,42:2
Bartl, Pavel
Joseph Kilian 1966,Jl 19,34:1
Bartlam, Dorothy
Ringer, The 1932,Je 2,25:2
Fires of Fate 1933,Ap 3,13:4
Bartlett, Bennie
Millions in the Air 1935,D 12,33:4
Sky Parade, The 1936,Ap 20,17:1
13 Hours by Air 1936,Ap 30,17:2
Texas Rangers, The 1936,S 24,29:1
Maid of Salem 1937,Mr 4,27:2
Time Out for Romance 1937,Mr 13,23:2
Let Them Live 1937,Je 8,30:3
Danger-Love at Work 1937,D 11,22:2
Bulldog Drummond's Revenge 1937,D 17,33:2
Penrod and his Twin Brother 1938,Ag 18,11:1
Sons of the Legion 1938,S 30,24:3
Just Around the Corner 1938,D 3,11:2
Great Man Votes, The 1939,Ja 20,15:2
Family Next Door, The 1939,Ap 28,31:2
Honeymoon in Bali 1939,S 21,21:1
What a Life 1939,O 12,33:1
Our Neighbors-The Carters 1940,F 15,15:2
Alias the Deacon 1940,My 14,27:5
Let's Make Music 1941,Ja 23,19:2
Meet John Doe 1941,Mr 13,25:2
Next of Kin 1943,My 6,25:2
He Hired the Boss 1943,Je 4,17:4
Cheaper by the Dozen 1950,Ap 1,12:2
Scapegoat, The 1959,Ag 7,28:1
Bartlett, Bob Captain
Viking, The 1931,Je 17,32:5
Bartlett, Elise
Angel of Broadway 1927,N 1,21:1 (In Addenda)
Bartlett, Elsie
Show Boat 1929,Ap 18,32:3

Bartlett, Hall
Navajo 1952,F 21,24:4
Bartlett, Hall (Director)
Unchained 1955,Ja 28,15:2
Zero Hour 1957,N 14,41:1
All the Young Men 1960,Ag 27,8:6
Caretakers, The 1963,Ag 22,19:2
Bartlett, Hall (Original Author)
Unchained 1955,Ja 28,15:2
Bartlett, Hall (Producer)
Navajo 1952,F 21,24:4
Unchained 1955,Ja 28,15:2
Zero Hour 1957,N 14,41:1
All the Young Men 1960,Ag 27,8:6
Caretakers, The 1963,Ag 22,19:2
Global Affair, A 1964,My 7,31:2
Sol Madrid 1968,Je 14,43:1
Bartlett, Hall (Screenwriter)
Zero Hour 1957,N 14,41:1
All the Young Men 1960,Ag 27,8:6
Caretakers, The 1963,Ag 22,19:2
Bartlett, Jeanne
Werewolf of London, The 1935,My 10,25:2
Bartlett, Jeanne (Screenwriter)
Son of Lassie 1945,Je 11,12:1
Gallant Bess 1946,D 6,27:6
Man-Eater of Kumaon 1948,Jl 2,24:2
Bartlett, Martine
Splendor in the Grass 1961,O 11,53:1
Prize, The 1964,Ja 24,21:1
No Way to Treat a Lady 1968,Mr 21,56:1
Bartlett, Michael
Love Me Forever 1935,Je 28,24:1
She Married her Boss 1935,S 27,25:3
Follow Your Heart 1936,O 22,31:1
Bartlett, Richard
Hiawatha 1952,D 26,20:4
Bartlett, Richard (Director)
I've Lived Before 1956,Ag 4,13:1
Bartlett, Sy (Original Author)
Big Brain, The 1933,Ag 5,9:5
Kansas City Princess 1934,N 5,23:1
Under Your Spell 1936,N 7,15:2
Cocoanut Grove 1938,Je 16,21:2
Amazing Mr Williams, The 1940,Ja 19,15:2
Road to Zanzibar 1941,Ap 10,29:2
Two Yanks in Trinidad 1942,Ap 6,19:4
Bullet Scars 1942,Ap 24,21:4
Down to the Sea in Ships 1949,F 23,31:2
Twelve O'Clock High 1950,Ja 28,10:2
Gathering of Eagles, A 1963,Jl 11,21:2
Bartlett, Sy (Producer)
Outsider, The
That Lady 1955,Je 11,8:7
Pork Chop Hill 1959,My 30,9:2
Gathering of Eagles, A 1963,Jl 11,21:2
Bartlett, Sy (Screenwriter)
Kansas City Princess 1934,N 5,23:1
Murder of Dr Harrigan, The 1936,Ja 21,27:5
Boulder Dam 1936,Mr 30,17:5
Danger Patrol 1937,N 19,27:3
Cocoanut Grove 1938,Je 16,21:2
Amazing Mr Williams, The 1940,Ja 19,15:2
Two Yanks in Trinidad 1942,Ap 6,19:4
13 Rue Madeleine 1947,Ja 16,30:2
Down to the Sea in Ships 1949,F 23,31:2
Twelve O'Clock High 1950,Ja 28,10:2
Paratrooper 1953,D 31,9:3
That Lady 1955,Je 11,8:7
Big Country, The 1958,O 2,44:1
Beloved Infidel 1959,N 18,46:1
Bartlett, T
Happy Road, The 1957,Je 21,20:2
Bartlett, William (Screenwriter)
Call of the Yukon 1938,My 6,27:1
Bartley, Betty
Laughing Lady, The 1930,Ja 4,21:1
Bartley, James
Ulysses 1967,Mr 14,55:1
Bartley, Nalbro (Original Author)
Devil's Lottery 1932,Ap 2,13:2
Bartok, Eva
Crimson Pirate, The 1952,Ag 28,21:2
Tale of Five Women, A 1953,Ja 16,19:2
Assassin, The 1953,Ap 18,17:2
Front Page Story 1955,Ap 19,28:1
Ten Thousand Bedrooms 1957,Ap 4,37:1
Last Waltz, The 1958,Ap 12,13:1
Circus of Love 1958,Ag 16,10:2
Operation Amsterdam 1960,Jl 7,26:1
S O S Pacific 1960,O 13,41:3
Blood and Black Lace 1965,N 11,58:3
Bartold, Norman
She's Working her Way Through College
1952,Jl 10,27:2
Bartoleschi, Valerio
Red Desert 1965,F 9,43:1
Bartoletti, Walter
Too Bad She's Bad 1955,D 26,23:2
Bartoli, Leon
Cieca di Sorrento, La 1936,Ag 3,11:3

Bartolini, Elio (Screenwriter)
Grido, Il 1962,O 23,42:1
Very Handy Man, A 1966,D 15,60:1
Bartolini, Luigi (Original Author)
Bicycle Thief, The 1949,D 13,44:2
Barton, Anne
Pressure Point 1962,O 11,49:3
Barton, Charles (Director)
Wagon Wheels 1934,O 4,19:1
Car 99 1935,F 23,14:7
Last Outpost, The 1935,O 5,18:2
Timothy's Quest 1936,F 29,11:2
Sudden Death, And 1936,Jl 18,18:2
Murder With Pictures 1936,N 21,21:4
Rose Bowl 1936,D 2,35:2
Crime Nobody Saw, The 1937,Ap 5,17:2
Thunder Trail 1938,F 5,19:3
Behind Prison Gates 1939,Ag 21,9:3
My Son Is Guilty 1940,Ja 15,11:2
Island Of Doomed Men 1940,Je 10,21:2
Phantom Submarine, The 1941,F 12,25:3
Harmon of Michigan 1941,O 2,29:2
Sing for Your Supper 1941,D 1,15:5
Parachute Nurse 1942,Jl 27,18:2
Reveille With Beverly 1943,Ap 24,17:2
What's Buzzin Cousin 1943,Jl 23,21:4
Jam Session 1944,My 3,25:3
Men in her Diary 1945,S 24,16:5
Time of Their Lives, The 1946,N 28,40:2
Noose Hangs High, The 1948,My 29,8:6
Africa Screams 1949,My 5,34:2
Ma and Pa Kettle at the Fair 1952,Jl 12,16:2
Dance With Me Henry 1956,D 24,8:2
Shaggy Dog, The 1959,Mr 20,26:2
Toby Tyler 1960,Ap 20,45:2
Swingin' Along 1962,Ag 27,18:1
Barton, Charles (Producer)
Noose Hangs High, The 1948,My 29,8:6
Barton, Charles T (Director)
White Tie and Tails 1946,N 8,28:2
Buck Privates Come Home 1947,Ap 12,11:3
Wistful Widow of Wagon Gap, The
1947,N 21,36:2
Abbott and Costello Meet Frankenstein
1948,Jl 29,17:2
Mexican Hayride 1949,Ja 12,33:3
Abbott and Costello Meet the Killer Boris Karloff
1949,S 19,18:3
Milkman, The 1951,Ja 1,13:6
Double Crossbones 1951,Ap 27,19:2
Barton, Dan
Sailor Beware 1952,F 1,17:1
Onionhead 1958,O 2,44:1
Barton, Finis
My Pal the King 1932,O 4,26:4
Becky Sharp 1935,Je 14,27:2
Barton, Grace
Town That Forgot God, The 1922,N 1,16:3
Barton, Gregg
Flying Tigers 1942,O 23,25:2
Not Wanted 1949,Jl 25,11:4
Far Country, The 1955,F 14,24:2
Man From Laramie, The 1955,S 1,20:2
Barton, James
Shepherd of the Hills, The 1941,Jl 31,13:2
Time of your Life, The 1948,My 27,29:2
Yellow Sky 1949,F 2,36:1
Daughter of Rosie O'Grady, The
1950,Mr 31,36:2
Wabash Avenue 1950,Ap 29,8:3
Screen, The 1951,Ap 23,21:2
Here Comes the Groom 1951,S 21,19:2
Golden Girl 1951,N 21,20:3
Quantez 1957,S 7,12:7
Misfits, The 1961,F 2,24:2
Barton, Joan
Angel and the Badman 1947,Mr 3,28:4
Barton, Joe
McFadden's Flats 1935,Mr 13,16:2
Barton, Margaret
Brief Encounter 1946,Ag 26,21:2
Temptation Harbor 1949,My 11,34:7
Good Time Girl 1950,S 25,18:5
Mr Lord Says No! 1952,F 12,22:5
Landfall 1953,My 11,25:2
Barton, Sir
Race of the Age, The 1920,N 1,13:2
Bartowna, Pani
Za Winy niepopelnione; For Crimes Not Theirs
1939,F 20,13:3
Bartowna, Wanda
Za Winy niepopelnione; For Crimes Not Theirs
1939,F 20,13:3
Last Stop, The 1949,Mr 22,31:2
Barty, Billy
Alice in Wonderland 1933,D 23,19:1
Gift of Gab 1934,S 26,17:6
Midsummer Night's Dream, A 1935,O 10,31:1
Barty, Jack
Angel Street 1952,N 11,25:2
Barwise, Patrick
Doctor Faustus 1968,F 7,38:1

Barwyn, Max
Beverly of Graustark 1926,Ap 19,24:3
Bardelys The Magnificent 1926,N 1,28:1 (In Addenda)
Valencia 1926,D 27,20:3
Fighting Eagle, The 1927,Ag 15,22:5
Beyond Victory 1931,Ap 6,24:1
Chocolate Soldier, The 1941,N 1,20:2
Bary, Jean
Cock Eyed World, The 1929,Ag 5,25:2
June Moon 1931,Mr 14,23:2
Florida Special 1936,My 29,15:2
Bary, Marcelle
Ces Dames aux Chapeaux Verts; Ladies in the Green Hats, The 1945,Ap 5,26:2
Bary, Regine
Crise est Finie, La 1935,Mr 14,18:1
Barzani, Baronessa
General Della Rovere 1960,N 22,41:1
Barzell, Wolfe
Blue Angel, The 1959,S 5,11:4
Sands of Beersheba 1966,My 6,54:2
Barzila, Joe (Original Author)
Blood and Black Lace 1965,N 11,58:3
Barzila, Joe (Screenwriter)
Blood and Black Lace 1965,N 11,58:3
Barzilai, Itzhak
Clouds Over Israel 1966,My 10,48:6
Barzizza, Isa
Lucky Five, The 1953,N 27,22:5
Barzman, Ben (Original Author)
True to Life 1943,O 14,26:1
Meet The People 1944,S 8,16:2
Barzman, Ben (Screenwriter)
Back to Bataan 1945,S 13,26:3
Give Us This Day 1949,D 21,41:2
Time Without Pity 1957,N 23,11:2
He Who Must Die 1958,D 29,21:1
Chance Meeting 1960,O 27,45:2
Fall of the Roman Empire, The 1964,Mr 27,14:2
Ceremony, The 1964,My 14,39:1
Visit, The 1964,O 22,44:1
Heroes of Telemark, The 1966,Mr 10,26:1
Barzman, Sol (Original Author)
True to Life 1943,O 14,26:1
Meet The People 1944,S 8,16:2
Basch, Felix
Pacific Rendezvous 1942,Jl 8,27:4
Enemy Agents meet Ellery Queen 1942,Ag 22,16:2
Desperate Journey 1942,S 26,11:2
Destination Unknown 1942,O 29,19:3
Chetniks 1943,Mr 19,15:3
Hitler-Dead or Alive 1943,Mr 31,23:3
Mission to Moscow 1943,Ap 30,25:2
Falcon in Danger, The 1943,Jl 23,21:2
Bomber's Moon 1943,Jl 31,8:2
Hostages 1943,O 11,23:2
Woman in Bondage 1944,Mr 27,17:2
Uncertain Glory 1944,Ap 8,9:2
Basch, Felix (Director)
Two Neckties; Zwei Kravatten 1930,N 30,IX,6:5
Baschiera, Bruno
Roman Holiday 1953,Ag 28,13:1
Baseggio, Cesco
Alpine Love 1936,Je 8,22:5
Bertoldo, Bertoldino, Cacasenno 1937,D 22,32:3
Carnevale di Venezia, Il; Carnival of Venice, The 1940,O 11,25:2
White Line, The 1952,D 6,17:2
Basehart, Richard
Repeat Performance 1947,Jl 2,19:2
Cry Wolf 1947,Jl 19,10:2
He Walked by Night 1949,F 7,15:2
Roseanna McCoy 1949,O 13,33:2
Black Book, The 1949,O 17,18:2
Tension 1950,Ja 12,32:4
Outside the Wall 1950,Mr 15,34:8
Fourteen Hours 1951,Mr 7,43:2
House on Telegraph Hill, The 1951,My 14,29:1
Fixed Bayonets 1951,N 21,20:2
Decision Before Dawn 1951,D 22,12:2
Titanic 1953,My 28,27:5
Stranger's Hand, The 1955,F 16,24:5
Moby Dick 1956,Jl 5,18:1
Strada, La 1956,Jl 17,19:2
Time Limit 1957,O 24,37:2
Brothers Karamazov, The 1958,F 21,18:2
Five Branded Women 1960,Je 2,27:2
Portrait in Black 1960,Jl 28,19:1
Passport to China 1961,Mr 23,28:1
King of the Sun 1963,D 26,33:4
Bidone, Il 1964,N 20,42:1
Satan Bug, The 1965,Ap 15,38:1
Basevi, James (Miscellaneous)
Blockade 1938,Je 17,25:1
Bash, John (Producer)
Woman's Devotion, A 1957,Mr 22,26:1
Bashkirtseff, Marie (Original Author)
Affairs of Maupassant, The 1938,F 12,20:2
Basie, Count
Reveille With Beverly 1943,Ap 24,17:2
Cinderfella 1960,D 17,19:2

Basie, Count (Composer)
I Dood It 1943,N 11,29:1
Basie, Count and His Band
Hit Parade of 1943 1943,Ap 16,24:3
Stage Door Canteen 1943,Je 25,13:2
Top Man 1943,O 29,23:2
Crazy House 1943,D 16,33:3
Basilashvili, O
Garnet Bracelet, The 1966,My 28,11:6
Basile, Nadine
Snow Was Black, The 1956,O 16,36:5
Fire Under Her Skin 1958,Je 28,13:6
Crazy for Love 1960,N 26,13:2
Basiliadi, D (Screenwriter)
House on Stournara Street, The 1960,O 17,33:4
Baskcomb, A W
Good Companions, The 1933,O 10,24:1
Phantom Fiend 1935,Ap 22,14:2
Baskcomb, Lawrence
Escape 1930,N 1,23:2
Drums 1938,S 30,24:4
Baskett, James
Song of the South 1946,N 28,40:2
Baskette, Billy (Composer)
Tin Pan Alley 1940,N 22,27:3
Basor, Vladimir (Director)
Stillness 1964,Ja 28,25:1 (In Addenda)
Basov, V (Director)
School of Courage 1957,S 9,21:2
Basov, Vladimir (Director)
No Ordinary Summer 1958,O 6,36:3
Basov, Vladimir (Producer)
No Ordinary Summer 1958,O 6,36:3
Basquette, Lina
Serenade 1927,D 19,30:1
Noose, The 1928,Mr 19,26:4
Wheels of Chance 1928,Jl 2,11:2
Show Folks 1928,D 10,25:1
Younger Generation, The 1929,Mr 11,22:2
Godless Girl, The 1929,Ap 1,22:1
Goldie 1931,Je 29,20:3
Morals for Women 1931,N 16,23:1
Midnight Lady, The 1932,Jl 1,19:3
Final Hour, The 1936,Ag 1,16:3
Ebb Tide 1937,N 18,27:2
Four Men and a Prayer 1938,My 7,18:1
Rose of the Rio Grande 1938,Jl 9,10:3
Bass, Alfie
Always Rains on Sunday, It 1949,F 14,15:5
Hasty Heart, The 1950,Ja 21,10:5
Lavender Hill Mob, The 1951,O 16,35:2
Pool of London 1951,N 28,37:2
Galloping Major, The 1951,D 17,27:2
Brandy for the Parson 1952,Ag 18,13:4
Svengali 1955,S 26,18:2
Night my Number Came up, The 1955,D 20,39:5
Make Me an Offer 1956,F 29,35:2
Angel Who Pawned her Harp, The 1956,F 29,35:2
Bespoke Overcoat, The 1956,O 8,31:1
Tale of Two Cities, A 1958,Ag 5,23:1
Millionairess, The 1961,F 10,19:1
Alfie 1966,Ag 25,42:1
Fearless Vampire Killers, The, or Pardon Me but Your Teeth are in my Neck 1967,N 14,52:1
Bass, George Houston (Original Author)
Now Cinema! (The Game); Game, The (Now Cinema!) 1968,Ap 9,56:1
Bassac, Robert
Baker's Wife, The 1940,F 27,17:2
Bassani, Giorgio (Screenwriter)
Stranger's Hand, The 1955,F 16,24:5
Wayward Wife, The 1955,Ap 11,29:3
Woman of Rome 1956,N 6,30:1
It Happened in the Park 1957,Ag 13,23:2
Basse, Wilfried (Producer)
Germany Between Yesterday and Today 1934,O 14,X,4:2 (In Addenda)
Basserman, Albert
Voruntersuchung; Inquest 1931,My 24,VIII,4:1
1914: The Last Days Before the War 1932,S 5,9:6
Kadetten 1933,D 26,19:3
Heroes of the Marne; (Famille Lefrancois, Le) 1939,Ap 24,13:2
Dr Ehrlich's Magic Bullet 1940,F 24,9:2
Foreign Correspondent 1940,Ag 28,15:2
Knute Rockne-All American 1940,O 19,21:2
Moon Over Burma 1940,D 12,37:4
Dispatch From Reuters, A 1940,D 12,37:2
Shanghai Gesture, The 1941,D 26,21:2
New Wine 1942,F 2,11:2
Invisible Agent 1942,Ag 6,23:2
Desperate Journey 1942,S 26,11:2
Moon and Sixpence, The 1942,O 28,26:4
Once Upon a Honeymoon 1942,N 13,28:1
Madame Curie 1943,D 17,23:1
Since You Went Away 1944,Jl 21,16:2
Rhapsody in Blue 1945,Je 28,22:2
Searching Wind, The 1946,Je 27,29:1
Private Affairs of Bel Ami, The 1947,Je 16,25:4
Escape me Never 1947,N 8,11:2
Red Shoes, The 1948,O 23,9:2

Basserman, Elsa
Escape 1940,N 1,33:1
Desperate Journey 1942,S 26,11:2
Madame Curie 1943,D 17,23:1
Bassermann, Albert
Ein Gewisser Herr Gran 1934,F 24,18:5
Alraune 1934,My 5,22:4
Letzte Liebe; Last; Last Love 1938,Jl 19,15:4
Dreyfus Case, The 1940,O 30,29:3
Escape 1940,N 1,33:1
Woman's Face, A 1941,My 16,21:2
Reunion in France 1943,Mr 5,20:3
Bassermann, Else
Letzte Liebe; Last; Last Love 1938,Jl 19,15:4
Basset, Gaby
Fire in the Straw 1943,Jl 2,15:2
My Seven Little Sins 1956,My 2,27:1
Deadlier Than the Male 1957,O 9,41:1
Bassett, James (Original Author)
In Harm's Way 1965,Ap 7,36:1
Bassett, Ronald (Original Author)
Conqueror Worm, The 1968,Ag 15,46:2
Bassi, Parsifal (Screenwriter)
Rossini 1948,Ja 31,14:2
Bassiak, Boris
Jules and Jim 1962,Ap 24,32:1
Bassier, Robert (Producer)
Black Swan, The 1942,D 24,18:3
Thunderhead 1945,Mr 16,21:2
Girl Next Door, The 1953,S 5,7:4
Dangerous Crossing 1953,S 30,37:2
Bassing, Eileen (Original Author)
Home Before Dark 1958,N 7,23:1
Bassing, Eileen (Screenwriter)
Home Before Dark 1958,N 7,23:1
Bassing, Robert (Screenwriter)
Home Before Dark 1958,N 7,23:1
Bassler, Robert (Miscellaneous)
Gentlemen Marry Brunettes 1955,O 31,31:5
Bassler, Robert (Producer)
My Gal Sal 1942,My 1,23:1
Girl Trouble 1942,O 8,31:2
Lodger, The 1944,Ja 20,15:3
Tampico 1944,Je 2,21:2
Hangover Square 1945,F 8,15:2
Molly and Me 1945,My 26,18:2
Smoky 1946,Je 27,29:1
Homestretch, The 1947,Ap 24,30:2
Thunder in the Valley 1947,N 28,30:1
Green Grass of Wyoming 1948,Je 10,28:3
Snake Pit, the 1948,N 5,29:2
Sand 1949,Ag 5,23:2
Thieves' Highway 1949,S 24,8:6
Ticket to Tomahawk, A 1950,My 20,8:6
Halls of Montezuma 1951,Ja 6,9:6
House on Telegraph Hill, The 1951,My 14,29:1
Let's Make It Legal 1951,N 7,35:3
Kangaroo 1952,My 17,22:7
Night Without Sleep 1952,S 27,13:2
Beneath the 12-Mile Reef 1953,D 17,52:2
Suddenly 1954,O 8,27:2
Bassman, George (Miscellaneous)
Babes in Arms 1939,O 20,27:2
Basso, Hamilton (Original Author)
Holiday for Sinners 1952,S 20,13:2
View From Pompey's Head, The 1955,N 5,22:5
Bassoff, Olga
Schoen Ist die Manoeverzeit 1932,Ag 19,20:6
Bassoli, Carlo J (Director)
Avventura di Giacomo Casanova 1938,D 2,27:3
Bassoli, Renato (Producer)
Three Forbidden Stories 1953,N 16,21:4
Bassoli, Vittorio (Producer)
Three Forbidden Stories 1953,N 16,21:4
Bast, William (Screenwriter)
Hammerhead 1968,S 12,54:3
Bastable, Bart
Broth of a Boy 1959,D 28,18:1
Basthy, Lajos
Szent Peter Esernyoeje 1936,Ja 8,22:2
Meltosagos Kisasszony, A; Superior Maiden, The 1937,S 6,20:2
120 Kilometers an Hour 1937,N 23,27:4
Pillanatnyi Pezzavar; Temporarily Broke 1939,My 20,11:3
Keseru Mezeshetek; Bitter Honeymoon 1939,O 9,15:3
Bastian, Jack
Loves of Carmen 1927,S 27,31:1
Baston, J Thorton
Virgin Paradise, A 1921,Ag 4,18:3
Baston, Jack
Snow Bride, The 1923,Je 12,22:2
Circus Ace, The 1927,Jl 6,23:2
Bastos, Oihon
Given Word, The 1964,Mr 25,47:1
Bataillie, Nicholas
Zazie 1961,N 21,45:5
Very Private Affair, A 1962,S 29,15:1
Bataille, Henri (Original Author)
Vierge Folle, La 1929,Ja 13,VIII,7:4
Possession, La 1929,D 1,X,8:6
Tenderness 1930,Jl 27,VIII,4:2 (In Addenda)

Bataille, Henri (Original Author)— Cont
Scandale, Le 1934,Ag 12,IX,2:1
Vierge Folle, La 1938,D 30,11:3
Bataille, Henry (Original Author)
Naked Woman, The 1950,Ja 21,10:2
Bataille, Sylvia
Courier of Lyons, The 1938,Je 3,17:1
Gates of the Night 1950,Mr 16,40:2
Ways of Love (A Day in the Country); Day in the
Country, A (Ways of Love) 1950,D 13,50:2
Batalof, M
Mother 1928,Ja 8,VIII,3:2
Batalof, Nikolai
Road to Life 1932,Ja 28,24:2
Horizon, The Wandering Jew 1933,My 12,20:4
Mother, 1905 1934,My 30,14:4
Tovaristchi 1935,My 25,12:2
Batalov, A
1905 1956,Jl 9,27:2
Batalov, Alexei
My Beloved 1959,Je 15,31:4
Cranes are Flying, The 1960,Mr 22,31:2
Lady With the Dog, The 1962,N 7,48:1
Batalov, Alexei (Director)
Overcoat, The 1965,Mr 2,31:2
Batalov, Andrei
Big Family, A 1955,Je 6,24:1
Batanides, Arthur
Cry Tough 1959,S 17,48:4
Batapoulos, Takis (Director)
Youth of Athens 1949,O 31,20:4
Batcheller, George R (Miscellaneous)
World Accuses, The 1935,Mr 21,27:2
Batcheller, George R (Producer)
Sons of Steel 1935,Ap 15,16:3
Missing Girls 1936,O 5,25:1
Batchelor, Joy (Director)
Animal Farm 1954,D 30,14:1
Batchelor, Joy (Producer)
Animal Farm 1954,D 30,14:1
Here Comes the Mad Martian 1965,Je 4,39:1
Batchelor, Joy (Screenwriter)
Animal Farm 1954,D 30,14:1
Batchoff, Pierre
Chess Player, The 1930,My 19,21:1
Love in Morocco 1933,Mr 20,18:3
Batelli, Iva (Original Author)
Psycosissimo 1962,S 8,16:2
Bateman, Anthony
Hatter's Castle 1948,Jl 3,8:6
Bateman, Edwin (Original Author)
Narrow Street, The 1925,Ja 5,19:1
Bateman, Gwen
Man From Morocco, The 1946,N 25,38:2
Bateman, Victory
Eternal Three, The 1923,O 12,7:2 (Incorrect in
this edition; use 1927,O 1,7:2 elsewhere)
Tess of the D'Urbervilles 1924,Jl 28,12:2
Bates, Alan
Entertainer, The 1960,O 4,49:2
Whistle Down the Wind 1962,Ap 23,34:2
Kind of Loving, A 1962,O 2,46:1
Running Man, The 1963,O 3,31:1
Guest, The 1964,Ja 21,25:2
Nothing but the Best 1964,Jl 14,28:1
Zorba, The Greek 1964,D 18,25:1
Georgy Girl 1966,O 18,48:1
King of Hearts 1967,Je 20,34:1
Far From the Madding Crowd 1967,O 19,59:1
Fixer, The 1968,D 9,59:1
Bates, Barbara
Strange Holiday 1945,O 20,8:2
This Love of Ours 1945,N 1,20:2
June Bride 1948,O 30,10:2
House Across the Street 1949,S 2,14:4
Inspector General, The 1949,D 31,9:2
Cheaper by the Dozen 1950,Ap 1,12:2
Quicksand 1950,Je 16,28:4
All About Eve 1950,O 14,13:2
I'd Climb the Highest Mountain 1951,My 10,38:1
Secret of Convict Lake, The 1951,Ag 4,7:2
Let's Make It Legal 1951,N 7,35:3
Belles on Their Toes 1952,My 3,17:5
Outcasts of Poker Flat 1952,My 16,19:3
Caddy, The 1953,S 18,16:6
Rhapsody 1954,Mr 12,17:1
Triple Deception 1957,O 7,23:2
Bates, Blanche
Border Legion, The 1918,Jl 29,9:3
Bates, Charles
Shadow of a Doubt 1943,Ja 13,18:2
Strange Death of Adolf Hitler, The 1943,O 9,11:5
San Diego, I Love You 1944,N 10,25:1
Pursued 1947,Mr 8,10:2
Bates, Florence
Rebecca 1940,Mr 29,25:2
Son of Monte Cristo, The 1940,D 5,33:1
Kitty Foyle 1941,Ja 9,27:2
Hudson's Bay 1941,Ja 10,23:2
Strange Alibi 1941,Ap 28,11:2
Devil and Miss Jones, The 1941,My 16,21:2
Love Crazy 1941,Je 6,25:5
Chocolate Soldier, The 1941,N 1,20:2
Tuttles of Tahiti, The 1942,Ap 30,14:1

We Were Dancing 1942,My 1,23:2
Mexican Spitfire at Sea 1942,Je 26,16:5
Moon and Sixpence, The 1942,O 28,26:4
They Got Me Covered 1943,Mr 5,20:2
Slightly Dangerous 1943,Ap 2,17:2
Mister Big 1943,Je 14,13:4
His Butler's Sister 1943,D 30,13:2
Mask of Dimitrios, The 1944,Je 24,16:2
Kismet 1944,Ag 23,16:1
Tonight and Every Night 1945,Mr 9,16:2
Belle of the Yukon 1945,Mr 30,18:4
Out of This World 1945,Je 7,25:2
Saratoga Trunk 1945,N 22,39:2
San Antonio 1945,D 29,19:5
Whistle Stop 1946,Mr 18,24:2
Cluny Brown 1946,Je 3,27:3
Diary of a Chambermaid, The 1946,Je 23,28:2
Claudia and David 1946,Ag 15,19:2
Time, The Place And The Girl, The
1946,D 27,14:3
Love and Learn 1947,My 3,10:3
Brasher Doubloon, The 1947,My 22,34:5
Secret Life of Walter Mitty, The 1947,Ag 15,12:2
I Remember Mama 1948,Mr 12,29:2
Winter Meeting 1948,Ap 8,31:2
River Lady 1948,My 21,19:5
Letter to Three Wives, A 1949,Ja 21,24:2
My Dear Secretary 1949,F 14,15:4
Portrait of Jennie 1949,Mr 30,31:2
Judge Steps Out, The 1949,Je 3,21:4
Girl from Jones Beach, The 1949,Jl 30,9:2
On the Town 1949,D 9,37:2
Second Woman, The 1951,F 2,19:2
Lullaby of Broadway 1951,Mr 27,35:2
Tall Target, The 1951,S 28,26:2
San Francisco Story, The 1952,My 10,16:4
Miserables, Les 1952,Ag 15,11:2
Bates, Granville
Sap From Syracuse, The 1930,Jl 26,16:4
Smiling Lieutenant, The 1931,My 23,13:4
Wiser Sex, The 1932,Mr 12,19:5
Midnight 1934,Mr 10,18:3
O'Shaughnessy's Boy 1935,O 5,18:2
Chatterbox 1936,F 15,18:6
13 Hours by Air 1936,Ap 30,17:2
Times Square Playboy 1936,My 2,11:2
Poppy 1936,Je 18,19:1
Beloved Enemy 1936,D 26,15:2
Sing Me a Love Song 1936,D 26,15:2
Plainsman, The 1937,Ja 14,16:2
Green Light 1937,F 13,9:1
Nancy Steele is Missing 1937,Mr 8,22:1
When's Your Birthday? 1937,Mr 19,27:2
Waikiki Wedding 1937,Mr 25,29:1
Mountain Justice 1937,My 13,31:2
They Won't Forget 1937,Jl 15,16:1
It Happened in Hollywood 1937,O 2,18:1
Back in Circulation 1937,O 4,17:1
Perfect Specimen, The 1937,O 28,29:2
Under Suspicion 1937,D 20,23:2 (In Addenda)
Wells Fargo 1937,D 30,15:2
Jury's Secret, The 1938,F 4,17:2
Gold Is Where You Find It 1938,F 14,20:6
Go Chase Yourself 1938,Je 15,27:1
Cowboy From Brooklyn 1938,Jl 14,17:1
Garden of the Moon 1938,S 24,13:1
Affairs of Annabel, The 1938,O 13,29:2
Youth Takes a Fling 1938,O 17,12:1
Man to Remember, A 1938,N 7,23:2
Hard To Get 1938,N 14,15:2
Next Time I Marry 1938,D 2,27:2
Great Man Votes, The 1939,Ja 20,15:2
Twelve Crowded Hours 1939,F 24,15:2
Blackwell's Island 1939,Mr 2,19:1
Naughty but Nice 1939,Je 23,23:2
Indianapolis Speedway 1939,Jl 15,8:2
Eternally Yours 1939,O 7,11:2
Fast And Furious 1939,O 12,33:3
Thou Shalt Not Kill 1940,Ja 8,11:2
Our Neighbors-The Carters 1940,F 15,15:2
Of Mice and Men 1940,F 17,9:2
My Favorite Wife 1940,My 31,15:2
Brother Orchid 1940,Je 8,18:2
Mortal Storm, The 1940,Je 21,25:2
Private Affairs 1940,Jl 5,10:3
Flowing Gold 1940,S 2,19:3
Men Against the Sky 1940,S 12,31:2
Bates, H E (Original Author)
Mating Game, The 1959,Ap 30,37:1
Bates, H E (Screenwriter)
Summertime 1955,Je 22,25:1
Bates, Harry (Original Author)
Day the Earth Stood Still, The 1951,S 19,37:1
Bates, Jeanne
Shadows in the Night 1944,Jl 29,16:2
Soul of a Monster, The 1944,S 9,12:4
Bates, Les
Buck Privates 1928,Ja 30,18:1
Bates, Michael
Court Martial 1955,Ag 2,17:1
Bedazzled 1967,D 11,65:2
Here We Go Around the Mulberry Bush
1968,Mr 5,34:5

Bates, Michael— Cont
Don't Raise the Bridge, Lower the River
1968,Jl 13,18:1
Hammerhead 1968,S 12,54:3
Salt and Pepper 1968,S 19,62:3
Bates, Peggy
Alcatraz Island 1937,O 14,22:2
Bates, Scotty
Varsity Show 1937,S 2,17:2
Bates, Tom
Huckleberry Finn 1920,F 23,11:2
In the Palace of the King 1923,D 3,14:1
Through the Dark 1924,Ja 8,27:1
Bateson, Timothy
Nicholas Nickleby 1947,D 1,27:2
Guinea Pig, The 1949,My 2,20:2
White Corridors 1952,Jl 16,21:1
Mouse That Roared, The 1959,O 27,40:1
Our Man in Havana 1960,Ja 28,26:1
Bathieson, Muir
Magic Box, The 1952,S 24,40:2
Bathory, Gisell
Hungarian Rhapsody 1929,Ag 5,25:2
Bathory, Giza
Szerelmi Almok 1937,Ja 5,19:2
Bathurst, Peter
Babes in Bagdad 1954,Ap 5,21:3
Baticock, Gregory
Illiac Passion, The 1968,Ap 19,40:1
Batie, Franklin
Big Boy 1930,S 13,9:3
Batista, Aurora
Tia Tula, A 1965,Je 3,24:1
Batley, Dorothy
Blue Lagoon, The 1949,O 3,13:2
Bato-Ochir
Son of Mongolia 1936,N 21,21:4
Battaglia, Aurelius (Screenwriter)
Pinocchio 1940,F 8,18:3
Battaglia, Guillermo
Casa del Angel, La 1960,Ag 30,25:1
Battaglia, Rick
Raw Wind in Eden 1958,S 20,10:6
Hannibal 1960,Ag 4,17:1
Esther and the King 1960,N 19,13:4
Mighty Crusaders, The 1961,S 23,17:1
From a Roman Balcony 1961,O 16,33:5
Minotaur, The 1961,N 8,41:1
Sodom and Gomorrah 1963,Ja 24,5:3
Why Bother to Knock 1965,F 4,24:2
Batten, John
Battle of The Sexes, The 1928,O 15,16:1
Batten, Tommy
Rationing 1944,Ap 10,14:2
Batterini, Cesare
Pierpin, La Figlia Ritrovata 1936,Mr 27,25:3
Batti, Jeanette
Four Bags Full 1957,S 5,32:1
Battier, Robert
Love and Hisses 1938,Ja 1,11:1
Battille, Sylvia
Crime of Monsieur Lange, The 1964,Ap 4,15:5
Battista, Lloyd
Flipper's New Adventure 1964,Ag 27,28:2
Battista, Miriam
Steadfast Heart, The 1923,D 25,26:1
Battisti, Carlo
Umberto D 1955,N 8,37:1
Battistoni, Aurelio (Director)
Life and Miracles of Blesses Mother Cabrini, The
1946,Jl 8,25:2
Battle, John Tucker (Original Author)
Man Alive 1945,N 17,14:5
Battle, John Tucker (Screenwriter)
Irish Eyes Are Smiling 1944,N 8,27:1
Captain Eddie 1945,Ag 9,24:2
So Dear to my Heart 1949,Ja 31,14:2
Frogmen, The 1951,Je 30,8:6
Lisbon 1956,Ag 30,19:2
Battley, David
Hotel Paradiso 1966,O 15,34:2
Batty, Archibald
Drums 1938,S 30,24:4
Four Feathers 1939,Ag 4,11:1
Baturin, A
Life is Beautiful 1933,F 13,11:5
Batycka, Zofja
Dziesieciu z Pawiaka 1932,Ap 21,25:2
Batzygaris, Helen
Shepherd's Daughter, The 1956,My 14,23:3
Bau, Miguel Gomez
Canillita y la Dama, El; Newsie and the Lady,
The 1939,F 18,12:2
Baucquet, Harold S (Director)
Dr Kildare's Wedding Day 1941,S 18,31:1
Baucum, Paul
Quiet One, The 1949,F 14,15:2
Baude, Anna-Lisa
Nar Rosorna Sla Ut 1931,F 10,24:4
Baudet, Louise
Sally 1925,Mr 16,16:1
Baudin, Henri
Pawns of Passion 1929,My 27,22:1
Walzerkoenig, Der 1932,D 5,21:2

Baudo, Serge (Composer)
World Without Sun 1964,D 23,22:1
Baudrier, Yves (Composer)
Silent World, The 1956,S 25,30:1
Bauduc, Ray (Composer)
Let's Make Music 1941,Ja 23,19:2
BAUER
See Also BAUR, BOWER
Bauer, Georg
1A in Oberbayern; 1A in Upper Bavaria
1939,N 18,22:6
Bauer, Willi
Gottes Muehlen mahlen Langsam; Mills of the
Gods, The 1939,F 18,12:4
Bauge, Andre
Ronde des Heures, La 1932,Ja 25,20:3
Barbier de Seville, Le 1936,S 23,29:2
Baum, L Frank (Original Author)
Wizard of Oz, The 1939,Ag 18,16:2
Baum, Ralph (Director)
Paris Nights 1952,F 21,24:5
Baum, Ralph (Producer)
Big Chief, The 1960,Ap 27,32:1
Modigliani of Montparnasse 1961,Mr 1,27:3
Baum, Vicki (Original Author)
Grand Hotel 1932,Ap 13,23:2
Woman Accused, The 1933,Mr 13,18:2
I Give my Love 1934,Jl 17,24:2
Night is Young, The 1935,Ja 14,11:2
Helene 1938,Ja 22,19:1
Dance, Girl, Dance 1940,O 11,25:2
Powder Town 1942,Je 8,11:2
Girl Trouble 1942,O 8,31:2
Great Flamario, The 1945,Ja 15,15:5
Hotel Berlin 1945,Mr 3,11:2
Week-End at the Waldorf 1945,O 5,27:2
Honeymoon 1947,My 19,27:2
She Returned at Dawn; Retour a l'Aube
1947,Ag 1,21:5
Bauman, Anne-Marie
Last Days of Pompeii, The 1960,Ag 11,19:1
Season for Love, The 1963,My 9,40:2
Bauman, S (Director)
Flickorna Fran Gamla Stan 1934,D 27,25:4
Larsson I Andra Giftet 1935,O 19,21:3
Loerdagskvaellar 1936,F 13,25:3
Raggen, Det Aer Jag Det 1936,My 22,19:1
Familjen Som Var En Karusel 1937,My 22,19:3
Vi Tvaa; We Two 1939,D 2,21:3
Hennes Lilla Majestat; Her Little Majesty
1940,Ap 20,14:2
Bauman, S (Miscellaneous)
Old Gods Still Live, The 1937,N 5,19:4
Baumann, Eric (Composer)
Sun Over Sweden 1938,Ap 9,11:2
Lasse-Maja 1943,Mr 22,15:4
Baumann, Franz
Student Sein 1931,My 4,15:3
Baumann, Karl
Acht Tage Glueck 1931,Jl 24,22:1
Baumeister, Ernst
Life of Beethoven, The 1929,Mr 12,26:3
Baumer, Jacques
Heart of Paris 1939,Ja 13,17:3
Crime in the Maginot Line 1939,My 8,21:2
Rasputin 1939,O 17,31:4
Entente Cordiale 1939,D 26,23:2
Daybreak 1940,Jl 30,16:2
Great Temptation, The 1942,Jl 10,13:3
32 Rue de Montmartre 1944,S 28,26:3
Colonel Chabert 1947,Je 21,11:2
Private Life of an Actor; En Scene 1948,S 7,21:3
Strangers in the House 1949,O 13,33:3
Cheat, The 1950,O 2,19:3
Ma Pomme 1951,O 15,22:2
Simple Case of Money, A 1952,F 2,11:2
Baumer, Marie (Original Author)
Sinners' Holiday 1930,O 11,21:3
BAUR
See Also BAUER, BOWER
See Also BOWER, BAUER
Baur, Esperanza
Jalisco Nunca Pierde; Jalisco Never Loses
1937,N 20,21:3
Guadalajara 1943,Je 12,9:3
El Conde de Monte Cristo 1943,N 9,26:2
Baur, Harry
David Golder 1932,O 20,24:2
Trois Mousquetaires, Les 1933,My 1,10:2
Poil de Carotte 1933,My 26,24:2
Miserables, Les 1934,Mr 25,X,4:2
Celle Vielle Canaille 1935,Ja 12,12:2
Cette Vielle Canaille 1935,Ja 21,27:2
Crime et Chatiment; Crime and Punishment
1935,N 13,25:3
I Stand Condemned 1936,Jl 2,27:2
Miserables, Les 1936,O 28,31:2
Golem, The 1937,Mr 22,27:2
Juif Polonais, Le 1937,S 17,29:3
Life and Loves of Beethoven, The
1937,N 22,15:1
Carnet de Bal, Un 1938,Mr 26,12:1
Dark Eyes 1938,Ap 19,24:5

Moscow Nights 1938,My 3,19:3
Rothchild 1938,O 12,35:2
Man and his Wife, A 1939,Mr 28,20:1
Rasputin 1939,O 17,31:4
Hatred 1941,Ja 27,11:2
Mad Emperor, The 1941,Mr 10,21:3
Postmaster's Daughter, The 1946,Ag 19,17:6
Miserables, Les 1946,D 26,28:4
Volpone 1947,D 27,9:3
Who Killed Santa Claus? 1948,Ap 21,33:2
Forbidden Love 1948,Ag 26,16:4
Baus, Manuel Tamayo y (Original Author)
Mad Queen, The 1950,O 27,24:3
Bautista, Aurora
Mad Queen, The 1950,O 27,24:3
Bautista, Lucha Maria
Desheredados, Los 1936,Mr 23,22:6
Novillero 1939,Mr 4,18:5
Bava, Mario (Director)
Black Sunday 1961,Mr 9,23:1
Blood and Black Lace 1965,N 11,58:3
Danger Diabolik 1968,D 12,62:6
Bava, Mario (Original Author)
Blood and Black Lace 1965,N 11,58:3
Bava, Mario (Screenwriter)
Black Sunday 1961,Mr 9,23:1
Blood and Black Lace 1965,N 11,58:3
Danger Diabolik 1968,D 12,62:6
Bavier, Frances
Day the Earth Stood Still, The 1951,S 19,37:1
Lady Says No, The 1952,Ja 7,14:3
Bend of the River 1952,Ap 10,37:1
My Wife's Best Friend 1952,O 11,17:2
Horizons West 1952,N 22,16:5
Stooge, The 1953,F 5,19:2
Man in the Attic 1954,F 6,17:2
Nice Little Bank That Should Be Robbed, A
1958,D 11,17:4
It Started With a Kiss 1959,Ag 20,14:2
Baviera, Jose
Romeo and Juliet 1944,Je 17,10:3
Tierra de Pasiones 1944,N 7,24:3
Exterminating Angel, The 1967,Ag 22,33:1
Bawers, William (Screenwriter)
Imitation General 1958,Ag 21,22:2
Bax, Clifford (Screenwriter)
Gateway of the Moon, The 1928,Ja 9,20:1
Bax, Roger (Original Author)
Never Let Me Go 1953,Je 11,37:2
Baxley, Barbara
Savage Eye, The 1960,Je 7,27:1
All Fall Down 1962,Ap 12,41:3
No Way to Treat a Lady 1968,Mr 21,56:1
Countdown 1968,My 2,57:3
Baxley, Jack
Our Little Girl 1935,Je 7,24:4
Woman Chases Man 1937,Je 11,26:2
International Crime 1938,My 16,14:4
Gracie Allen Murder Case, The 1939,Je 8,31:3
Baxt, George (Screenwriter)
Circus of Horrors 1960,S 1,31:1
Shadow of the Cat, The 1961,Je 8,40:2
Payroll 1963,My 11,15:2
Horror Hotel 1963,Je 20,29:1
Baxter, Alan
Mary Burns, Fugitive 1935,N 16,19:2
Trail of the Lonesome Pine, The 1936,F 20,23:5
13 Hours by Air 1936,Ap 30,17:2
Big Brown Eyes 1936,My 2,11:1
Case Against Mrs Ames, The 1936,My 28,19:2
Parole 1936,Je 27,21:1
Breezing Home 1937,Mr 20,23:5
Night Key 1937,Ap 19,27:2
Last Gangster, The 1937,D 10,33:2
Big Town Girl 1937,D 13,23:4
I Met my Love Again 1938,Ja 15,19:1
Wide Open Faces 1938,Ap 15,23:2
Gangs of New York 1938,My 28,9:2
Boy Slaves 1939,F 9,17:3
Off the Record 1939,F 18,12:2
Let Us Live 1939,Mr 30,19:2
Each Dawn I Die 1939,Jl 22,12:2
Lone Wolf Strikes, The 1940,F 5,13:2
Abe Lincoln in Illinois 1940,F 23,19:2
Free, Blonde and 21 1940,Ap 5,25:2
Santa Fe Trail 1940,D 21,21:2
Submarine Zone; (Escape To Glory)
1941,Ap 7,13:2
Bad Men of Missouri 1941,Ag 16,18:2
Pittsburgh Kid, The 1941,S 23,27:4
Shadow of the Thin Man 1941,N 21,23:2
Saboteur 1942,My 8,27:2
China Girl 1943,Ja 21,27:2
Human Comedy, The 1943,Mr 3,19:2
Pilot No 5 1943,Je 25,13:4
Woman in Bondage 1944,Mr 27,17:2
Winged Victory 1944,D 21,16:2
Close-Up 1948,Ap 5,24:2
Set-Up, The 1949,Mr 30,31:2
She Shoulda Said No 1957,Ja 31,21:1
True Story of Jesse James, The 1957,Mr 23,17:2
Judgment at Nuremberg 1961,D 20,36:1
This Property is Condemned 1966,Ag 4,24:1

Baxter, Anne
Twenty-Mule Team 1940,My 10,26:6
Great Profile, The 1940,O 18,25:1
Charley's Aunt 1941,Ag 2,18:2
Swamp Water 1941,N 17,15:2
Pied Piper, The 1942,Ag 13,15:3
Magnificent Ambersons, The 1942,Ag 14,13:3
Crash Dive 1943,Ap 29,25:2
Five Graves to Cairo 1943,My 27,21:2
North Star, The 1943,N 5,23:1
Sullivans, The 1944,F 10,19:2
Eve of St Mark, The 1944,My 31,22:2
Sunday Dinner for a Soldier 1945,Ja 25,16:2
Guest in the House 1945,F 16,19:2
Royal Scandal, A 1945,Ap 12,19:2
Smoky 1946,Je 27,29:1
Angel on my Shoulder 1946,O 21,27:2
Razor's Edge, The 1946,N 20,42:2
Blaze of Noon 1947,Mr 5,31:2
Homecoming 1948,Ap 30,28:4
Walls of Jericho, The 1948,Ag 5,16:2
Luck of the Irish, The 1948,S 16,34:1
Yellow Sky 1949,F 2,36:1
You're my Everything 1949,Jl 23,7:2
Ticket to Tomahawk, A 1950,My 20,8:6
All About Eve 1950,O 14,13:2
Follow the Sun 1951,Ap 26,34:4
Outcasts of Poker Flat 1952,My 16,19:3
My Wife's Best Friend 1952,O 11,17:2
O Henry's Full House (The Last Leaf
1952,O 17,33:1
I Confess 1953,Mr 23,28:2
Blue Gardenia, The 1953,Ap 28,31:1
Carnival Story 1954,Ap 17,8:2
Bedevilled 1955,Ap 23,23:1
One Desire 1955,S 3,9:1
Spoilers, The 1955,D 24,10:2
Come on, The 1956,Ap 7,13:1
Ten Commandments, The 1956,N 9,35:2
Three Violent People 1957,F 11,34:2
Chase a Crooked Shadow 1958,Mr 25,28:4
Cimarron 1961,F 17,12:2
Walk on the Wild Side 1962,F 22,20:1
Busy Body, The 1967,Je 8,52:2
Baxter, Clive
Four Feathers 1939,Ag 4,11:1
Guinea Pig, The 1949,My 2,20:2
Baxter, David
Mr Emmanuel 1945,Ja 8,15:2
Baxter, Deborah
High Wind in Jamaica, A 1965,Je 17,27:2
Baxter, George
Marianne 1929,O 19,22:6
Right to Love, The 1931,Ja 2,25:1
Woman Commands, A 1932,Ja 28,13:2
Dinner at Eight 1933,Ag 24,18:1
Thirty Day Princess 1934,My 12,12:3
Great Flirtation, The 1934,Je 22,16:5
Sing Sing Nights 1935,Ja 26,13:2
Sofia 1948,S 4,8:7
Lili 1953,Mr 11,36:7
Baxter, Jane
Constant Nymph, The 1934,Ap 7,19:1
We Live Again 1934,N 2,27:2
Enchanted April 1935,Mr 9,19:1
Clairvoyant, The 1935,Je 8,12:2
April Romance 1937,Ja 27,17:4
Ware Case, The 1939,Jl 22,12:2
Chinese Den 1941,Mr 26,27:3
Ships With Wings 1942,My 25,11:2
Baxter, Jimmy
Dark Angel, The 1935,S 6,12:2
Baxter, John (Director)
Love on the Dole 1945,O 13,11:2
Baxter, John (Producer)
Love on the Dole 1945,O 13,11:2
Baxter, Keith
Barretts of Wimpole Street, The 1957,Ja 18,15:3
Falstaff; Chimes at Midnight 1967,Mr 18,19:2
Baxter, Stanley
Wee Geordie 1956,O 8,31:1
Coming-Out Party, A 1962,Jl 31,19:2
Crooks Anonymous 1963,O 31,26:3
Baxter, Warner
Those Who Dance 1924,Je 30,16:1
Female, The 1924,S 2,19:2
Garden of Weeds, The 1924,N 4,24:1
Christine of the Hungry Heart 1924,D 8,13:3
Golden Bed, The 1925,Ja 20,18:2
Air Mail, The 1925,Mr 17,18:1
Welcome Home 1925,My 18,12:1
Awful Truth, The 1925,Jl 2,12:4
Son of his Father, A 1925,S 29,31:3
Best People 1925,O 21,21:3
Mannequinn 1926,Ja 12,27:5
Miss Brewster's Millions 1926,Mr 8,17:1
Runaway, The 1926,Ap 27,23:2
Aloma of the South Seas 1926,My 17,19:1
Great Gatsby, The 1926,N 22,28:3
Telephone Girl, The 1927,My 16,24:2
Singed 1927,Jl 12,29:3
Three Sinners 1928,Ap 23,20:2
Ramona 1928,My 15,17:3

Baxter, Warner— Cont

Danger Street 1928,S 25,29:4 (In Addenda)
Craig's Wife 1928,D 4,29:1
West of Zanzibar 1928,D 31,9:1
In old Arizona 1929,Ja 21,18:4
Thru Different Eyes 1929,Ap 15,22:6
Behind That Curtain 1929,Jl 1,31:2
Romance of Rio Grande 1929,N 9,22:5
Happy Days 1930,F 14,20:1
Such Men Are Dangerous 1930,Mr 8,21:1
Arizona Kid, The 1930,My 17,21:2
Renegades 1930,N 8,21:3
Doctors' Wives 1931,Ap 25,23:4
Daddy Long Legs 1931,Je 6,15:5
Squaw Man, The 1931,S 19,10:2
Cisco Kid, The 1931,O 24,20:3
Surrender 1931,N 28,20:4
Amateur Daddy 1932,Ap 23,11:5
Man About Town 1932,My 28,18:2
Six Hours to Live 1932,O 22,18:4
Dangerously Yours 1933,F 23,20:3
42d Street 1933,Mr 10,19:3
I Loved You Wednesday 1933,Je 16,20:2
Paddy the Next Best Thing 1933,Ag 25,12:2
Penthouse 1933,S 9,9:2
As Husbands Go 1934,Ja 26,20:3
Stand up and Cheer 1934,Ap 20,17:1
Such Women Are Dangerous 1934,Je 9,18:3
Grand Canary 1934,Jl 20,11:1
Broadway Bill 1934,N 30,22:2
Hell in the Heavens 1934,D 12,28:2
One More Spring 1935,F 22,27:1
Under the Pampas Moon 1935,My 31,11:1
King of Burlesque 1936,Ja 16,25:2
Prisoner of Shark Island, The 1936,F 13,25:2
Robin Hood of El Dorado, The 1936,Mr 14,10:1
Road to Glory, The 1936,Ag 6,22:1
To Mary-With Love 1936,Ag 27,16:1
White Hunter 1936,N 26,39:2
Slave Ship 1937,Je 17,19:2
Vogues of 1938 1937,Ag 20,21:1
Wife, Doctor and Nurse 1937,O 11,26:5
Kidnapped 1938,My 28,9:2
I'll Give a Million 1938,Jl 16,7:2
Wife, Husband and Friend 1939,F 25,19:2
Return of the Cisco Kid, The 1939,Ap 29,13:2
Barricade 1939,D 9,18:2
Earthbound 1940,Je 7,27:4
Adam Had Four Sons 1941,Mr 28,26:6
Crime Doctor 1943,Jl 5,11:4
Lady in the Dark 1944,F 23,17:1
Shadows in the Night 1944,Jl 29,16:2
Crime Doctor's Courage, The 1945,Mr 3,11:3
Prison Warden 1949,O 21,31:2

Bay, Susan
Big Mouth, The 1967,Jl 13,30:2
Bayer, Oliver Weld (Original Author)
Dangerous Partners 1945,N 2,22:4
Bayer, Rolf
No Man is an Island 1962,O 11,49:2
Bayer, Rolf (Screenwriter)
Badjao 1962,S 21,35:1
Bayidon, Geoffrey
They all Died Laughing 1964,Mr 16,37:2
To Sir, With Love 1967,Je 15,56:1
BAYLEY
See Also BAILEY, BAILY
Bayley, Helen
Jeannie 1943,S 13,14:2
Bayley, Hilda
Madonna of the Seven Moons 1946,My 23,18:4
Baylis, Peter (Director)
Finest Hours, The 1964,N 11,38:1
Bayliss, Peter
Darling 1965,Ag 4,20:1
Matter of Innocence, A 1968,F 22,36:1
30 Is a Dangerous Age, Cynthia 1968,Mr 5,34:1
Baylor, Hal
Wild Blue Yonder, The 1952,Ja 2,20:1
Big Jim McLain 1952,S 18,35:2
Island in the Sky 1953,S 10,22:2
River of no Return 1954,My 1,13:2
ThIs is my Love 1954,D 25,7:3
Young Lions, The 1958,Ap 3,23:1
Baylor, Steve
Marines, Lets Go! 1961,Ag 16,37:2
Comancheros, The 1961,N 2,42:1
Baylos, Gene
Family Jewels, The 1965,Ag 12,30:4
Bayly, Johnson
How to Murder a Rich Uncle 1957,O 26,19:2
Bayne, Al
Stadium Murders, The 1938,Ap 9,11:2
Bayne, Beverly
Romeo and Juliet 1916,O 23,10:3
Passionate Youth 1925,Je 30,14:3
Bayon, Antonio
Goyescas 1944,My 29,18:3
Bazelian, Y (Director)
House With an Attic 1964,D 21,42:5
Bazhenova, Irina
Sleeping Beauty, The 1966,My 4,50:1

Bazhov, Pavel (Screenwriter)
Stone Flower 1946,D 30,15:2
Baziga
King Solomon's Mines 1950,N 10,35:1
Bazlen, Brigid
Honeymoon Machine, The 1961,Ag 24,25:2
King of Kings 1961,O 12,41:2
How the West Was Won 1963,Ap 1,54:1
Bazolon, David T (Miscellaneous)
Point of Order 1964,Ja 15,27:2
Bazuet, Maurice
Lower Depths, The 1937,S 11,20:1
Bdankfort, Michael (Screenwriter)
Untamed 1955,Mr 12,11:6
Bea, John
That Night 1957,O 15,39:3
Beach, Ann
Horror Hotel 1963,Je 20,29:1
Hotel Paradiso 1966,O 15,34:2
Beach, Brandon
Under Western Stars 1938,Je 25,7:3
Beach, Edward L Comdr (Original Author)
Run Silent, Run Deep 1958,Mr 28,29:1
Beach, Gerard (Screenwriter)
Fearless Vampire Killers, The, or Pardon Me but
Your Teeth are in my Neck 1967,N 14,52:1
Beach, Guy
Smoky 1946,Je 27,29:1
In a Lonely Place 1950,My 18,37:2
Beach, John
Partners of the Plains 1938,F 12,20:4
Heart of Arizona 1938,Ap 16,17:1
Cisco Kid and the Lady, The 1939,D 25,29:2
Beach, Lewis (Original Author)
This Reckless Age 1932,Ja 9,21:1
Handy Andy 1934,Ag 4,14:5
Young as You Feel 1940,Mr 8,25:3
Beach, Rex (Original Author)
Barrier, The 1917,F 26,10:2
Laughing Bill Hyde 1918,S 23,7:1
Too Fat to Fight 1918,D 2,11:3
Brand, The 1919,Mr 17,13:2
Crimson Gardenia, The 1919,Je 16,11:2
Girl From Outside, The 1919,N 10,18:2
Silver Horde, The 1920,My 10,18:2
North Wind's Malice, The 1920,O 18,13:1
Iron Trail, The 1921,O 31,19:3
Ne'er Do-Well, The 1923,My 1,24:3
Spoilers, The 1923,Ag 6,14:2
Big Brother 1923,D 24,12:1 (In Addenda)
Flowing Gold 1924,Mr 10,18:2
Recoil, The 1924,Je 30,16:1
Sainted Devil, A 1924,N 24,15:3
Goose Woman, The 1925,Ag 4,14:3
Auction Block, The 1926,F 15,16:4
Barrier, The 1926,Mr 22,16:1
Mating Call, The 1928,O 8,14:2
Son of the Gods 1930,Ja 31,24:1
Spoilers, The 1930,S 20,15:4
Silver Horde, The 1930,O 25,20:6
Donovan's Kid 1931,My 22,28:5
White Shoulders 1931,Je 5,26:5
Past of Mary Holmes, The 1933,My 1,10:3
Barrier, The 1937,N 27,21:2
Flowing Gold 1940,S 2,19:3
Spoilers, The 1942,My 22,27:2
Michigan Kid 1947,F 22,16:3
Spoilers, The 1955,D 24,10:2
Beachcomber, Don
Cinerama-South Seas Adventure 1958,Jl 16,26:1
Beahan, Charles (Original Author)
Ladies in Love 1930,Je 14,9:4
Dangerous Nan McGrew 1930,Je 21,20:5
Night Court 1932,My 27,27:5
Society Girl 1932,Je 10,22:3
One Night of Love 1934,S 7,25:3
White Tie and Tails 1946,N 8,28:2
Beaird, Barbara
Man in the Net, The 1959,Je 11,36:2
Toby Tyler 1960,Ap 20,45:2
BEAL
See Also BEALE, BEALL
Beal, Frank
Best Bad Man, The 1925,D 2,23:1
Stolen Bride, The 1927,Ag 10,21:4
Cimarron 1931,Ja 27,20:5
Everything's Rosie 1931,My 22,28:5
Beal, John
Another Language 1933,Ag 5,9:5
Hat, Coat and Glove 1934,Jl 27,21:2
Little Minister, The 1934,D 28,25:1
Miserables, Les 1935,Ap 22,14:2
Laddie 1935,My 6,22:3
Break of Hearts 1935,My 17,24:3
We Who Are About to Die 1937,Ja 2,15:1
Man Who Found Himself, The 1937,Ap 9,19:3
Border Cafe 1937,Je 8,30:2
Double Wedding 1937,O 22,27:2
Madame X 1937,O 25,23:1
Danger Patrol 1937,N 19,27:3
Beg, Borrow or Steal 1937,D 10,33:2
Port of Seven Seas 1938,Jl 15,13:2
I Am the Law 1938,Ag 26,14:2

Beal, John— Cont

Arkansas Traveler, The 1938,N 17,29:2
Cat and the Canary, The 1939,N 23,38:5
Ellery Queen and the Perfect Crime
1941,Ag 11,17:3
Atlantic Convoy 1942,Jl 6,18:5
Great Commandment, The 1942,O 17,11:1
Edge of Darkness 1943,Ap 10,12:4
Key Witness 1947,Jl 30,27:6
Alimony 1949,Jl 22,16:3
Chicago Deadline 1949,N 3,37:2
My Six Convicts 1952,Mr 28,27:3
Sound and the Fury, The 1959,Mr 28,11:1
Beal, Royal
Lost Boundaries 1949,Jl 1,14:4
Death of a Salesman 1951,D 21,21:3
Joe Louis Story, The 1953,N 4,29:4
Anatomy of a Murder 1959,Jl 3,10:1
BEALE
See Also BEAL, BEALL
Beale, Charlie
New Orleans 1947,Je 20,25:6
BEALL
See Also BEALE, BEAL
Beall, Betty
Day Mars Invaded Earth, The 1964,Ap 2,28:3
BEAN
See Also BEIN
Bean, Orson
How to be Very, Very Popular 1955,Jl 23,10:1
Anatomy of a Murder 1959,Jl 3,10:1
Beane, Reginald
Time of your Life, The 1948,My 27,29:2
BEAR
See Also BAEHR, BAER, BAIR, BEYER, BYER
Bear, Mary
That Lady in Ermine 1948,Ag 25,31:2
Singing Guns 1950,Je 5,19:3
Stella 1950,Ag 19,9:2
Beard, Peter H
Hallelujah the Hills 1963,D 17,49:1
Beard, Renee
Foxes of Harrow, The 1947,S 25,35:4
Bright Road 1953,Ap 29,33:5
Beard, Stymie
Kid Millions 1934,N 12,17:2
Rainbow on the River 1936,D 18,31:4
Jezebel 1938,Mr 11,15:2
Beloved Brat 1938,My 2,13:2
Way Down South 1939,Ag 18,16:4
Return of Frank James, The 1940,Ag 10,16:4
Bearden, Basil (Director)
League of Gentlemen, The 1961,Ja 25,30:4
Bearden, Gene
Stratton Story, The 1949,My 13,29:1
Beardmore, Diane
Cinerama-South Seas Adventure 1958,Jl 16,26:1
Beardsley, Aubrey (Miscellaneous)
Salome 1923,Ja 1,18:1
Bears, Fiddler
Festival 1967,O 24,53:2
Beatles, The
Go Go Mania 1965,My 20,52:4
Beaton, Betsy (Original Author)
Boy With Green Hair, The 1949,Ja 13,26:2
Beaton, Kenneth C (Miscellaneous)
America's Answer 1918,Jl 30,9:3
Under Four Flags 1918,N 18,13:3
BEATTY
See Also BEATTIE, BEATY
Beatty, Bunny
Becky Sharp 1935,Je 14,27:2
Beatty, Clyde
Big Cage, The 1933,My 9,20:5
Lost Jungle, The 1934,Je 8,18:1
Africa Screams 1949,My 5,34:2
Ring of Fear 1954,Jl 29,18:3
Beatty, Clyde (Original Author)
Big Cage, The 1933,My 9,20:5
Beatty, Edgar (Director)
Hippie Revolt, The 1967,D 20,53:1
Beatty, George (Screenwriter)
You're in the Army Now 1941,D 26,21:4
Beatty, Lauri
Libeled Lady 1936,O 31,24:2
Wee Willie Winkie 1937,Jl 24,12:1
Bill of Divorcement, A 1940,Jl 12,11:2
Beatty, May
Benson Murder Case, The 1930,Ap 12,23:1
Ex-Flame 1931,Ja 24,15:1
Becky Sharp 1935,Je 14,27:2
Mad Love 1935,Ag 5,20:2
Little Lord Fauntleroy 1936,Ap 3,27:1
Show Boat 1936,My 15,29:4
Lloyds of London 1936,N 26,39:1
She Loved a Fireman 1938,Ja 21,15:3
Adventures of Sherlock Holmes, The
1939,S 2,20:1
Eternally Yours 1939,O 7,11:2
We Are not Alone 1939,D 1,27:1
My Son, My Son! 1940,My 10,26:6
Pride and Prejudice 1940,Ag 9,19:1

Beatty, Robert
Odd Man Out 1947,Ap 24,30:2
Against the Wind 1949,Je 27,18:3
Girl in the Painting, The 1949,Ag 22,13:1
Another Shore 1951,F 12,19:3
Appointment With Crime 1951,F 19,19:3
Captain Horatio Hornblower 1951,S 14,21:2
Man on a Tightrope 1953,Je 5,19:1
Devil's Plot 1953,Je 19,18:1
Gentle Gunman, The 1953,O 1,34:3
Project M 7 1953,N 27,22:5
Horse's Mouth, The 1954,Ja 20,33:4
Tarzan and the Lost Safari 1957,Ap 13,12:3
Out of the Clouds 1957,Ag 1,20:4
2001 A Space Odyssey 1968,Ap 4,58:1
Beatty, Warren
Splendor in the Grass 1961,O 11,53:1
Roman Spring of Mrs Stone, The 1961,D 29,11:1
All Fall Down 1962,Ap 12,41:3
Lilith 1964,S 21,37:2
Mickey One 1965,S 9,36:1
Promise her Anything 1966,F 23,46:1
Kaleidoscope 1966,S 23,45:1
Bonnie and Clyde 1967,Ag 14,36:1
Beatty, Warren (Producer)
Bonnie and Clyde 1967,Ag 14,36:1
BEATY
See Also BEATTY
Beaty, David (Original Author)
Trouble in the Sky 1961,Jl 13,26:3
Beaty, May
Vanity Street 1932,O 15,13:1
Beauchamp
Louise 1940,F 3,9:4
Tainted 1950,Ja 21,10:2
Savage Triangle 1952,S 30,38:2
Beauchamp, Catherine (Original Author)
Desperate Decision 1954,N 9,31:5
Beauchamp, D D (Original Author)
Wistful Widow of Wagon Gap, The
1947,N 21,36:2
Abbott and Costello in the Foreign Legion
1950,Ag 14,14:4
Port of Hell 1954,D 18,12:2
Beauchamp, D D (Screenwriter)
River Lady 1948,My 21,19:5
Belle le Grand 1951,My 18,34:6
San Francisco Story, The 1952,My 10,16:4
Man From the Alamo, The 1953,S 12,13:2
She Couldn't Say No 1954,F 27,11:3
Rails Into Laramie 1954,My 13,34:2
Jesse James' Women 1954,S 29,23:4
Man Without a Star 1955,Mr 25,19:3
Tennessee's Partner 1955,N 5,22:8
Massacre 1956,Je 2,13:5
Rawhide Years, The 1956,Je 16,12:2
Alias Jesse James 1959,My 18,31:2
Beauchamp, Edmond
Beau Serge, Le 1959,Ag 3,21:1
Beaudet, Rolland Joseph
Quebec 1951,Mr 16,34:2
Beaudine, Helen
Penrod and Sam 1931,S 26,25:3
Beaudine, William (Director)
Penrod and Sam 1923,Je 25,16:5
Boy of Mine 1923,D 24,12:1 (In Addenda)
Narrow Street, The 1925,Ja 5,19:1
Little Annie Rooney 1925,O 19,26:1
That's My Baby 1926,Ap 12,18:4
Social Highwayman, The 1926,Je 15,23:3
Hold That Lion 1926,S 6,16:2
Sparrows 1926,S 20,21:3
Canadian, The 1926,N 30,27:1
Frisco Sally Levy 1927,Ap 13,29:4
Life of Riley, The 1927,S 5,13:2
Irresistible Lover, The 1927,O 19,24:4
Cohens and the Kellys In Paris, The
1928,F 6,12:3
Heart to Heart 1928,S 10,29:2
Home James 1928,S 11,31:3
Give and Take 1928,D 27,27:1
Hard to Get 1929,S 28,17:3
Girl From Woolworth's, The 1929,D 21,17:1
Wedding Rings 1930,My 10,25:3
Road to Paradise 1930,S 30,23:1
Father's Son 1931,F 21,15:2
Lady Who Dared, The 1931,Je 6,15:5
Mad Parade, The 1931,S 19,10:2
Penrod and Sam 1931,S 26,25:3
Men in her Life 1931,N 30,16:2
Three Wise Girls 1932,F 6,14:4
Make Me a Star 1932,Jl 1,19:3
Crime of the Century, The 1933,Mr 13,18:2
Her Bodyguard 1933,Ag 7,18:2
Old-Fashioned Way, The 1934,Jl 14,16:5
Mr Cohen Takes a Walk 1936,F 13,25:2
Sez O'Reilly to MacNab 1938,F 19,19:4
Torchy Gets her Man 1938,N 18,25:3
Torchy Blane in Chinatown 1939,F 3,13:2
Black Market Babies 1946,Ap 1,23:1
Blue Grass of Kentucky 1950,Ja 27,29:2
Prince of Peace, The 1951,Mr 24,8:3
Mom and Dad 1957,Ja 31,21:1

**Beaumarchais, Pierre Augustin Caron de (Original
/Author)**
Marriage of Figaro, The 1963,Ap 30,26:1
Beaumarchais (Original Author)
Figaro 1929,N 25,22:1
Beaumont, Charles
Intruder, The 1962,My 15,48:1
Beaumont, Charles (Original Author)
Intruder, The 1962,My 15,48:1
Beaumont, Charles (Screenwriter)
Intruder, The 1962,My 15,48:1
Premature Burial, The 1962,My 24,29:2
Burn, Witch, Burn 1962,Jl 5,21:2 (In Addenda)
Wonderful World of the Brothers Grimm, The
(The Cobbler and the Elves); Cobbler and the
Elves, The (The Wonderful World of the
Brothers Grimm) 1962,Ag 8,35:1
Wonderful World of the Brothers Grimm, The
(The Singing Bone); Singing Bone, The (The
Wonderful World of the Brothers Grimm)
1962,Ag 8,35:1
Wonderful World of the Brothers Grimm, The
1962,Ag 8,35:1
Wonderful World of the Brothers Grimm, The
(The Dancing Princess); Dancing Princess, The
(The Wonderful World of the Brothers Grimm)
1962,Ag 8,35:1
Haunted Palace, The 1964,Ja 30,24:1
7 Faces of Dr Lao 1964,Jl 23,19:1
Masque of the Red Death, The 1964,S 17,52:6
Mister Moses 1965,My 13,32:1
Beaumont, Dan (Screenwriter)
For Those Who Think Young 1964,Jl 9,27:1
Beaumont, Diana
Autumn Crocus 1934,O 25,26:2
Black Limelight 1939,Je 26,12:2
Let George Do It 1940,O 14,25:5
Murder on Monday 1953,O 7,35:2
Beaumont, Gerald (Original Author)
Dixie Handicap, The 1924,D 30,15:3
My Own Pal 1926,Mr 15,18:3
Rainmaker, The 1926,My 18,28:2
Girl from Coney Island or Just Another Blonde
1926,D 13,27:1
Winner Take All 1932,Je 18,9:2
Frisco Jenny 1933,Ja 7,11:2
Silk Hat Kid 1935,Ag 7,22:5
Pride of the Marines 1936,Ap 27,19:2
Great O'Malley, The 1937,Mr 6,10:1
Girl and the Gambler, The 1939,Je 28,17:3
Beaumont, Gerald (Screenwriter)
Sporting Venus, The 1925,My 11,14:3
Beaumont, Harry (Director)
Man and his Money, A 1919,Ap 14,11:4
Lord and Lady Algy 1919,S 29,16:1
Toby's Bow 1919,D 15,20:1
Main Street 1923,Je 12,22:2
Beau Brummell 1924,Mr 31,20:1
Babbitt 1924,Jl 15,9:4
Lover of Camille, The 1924,N 11,14:1
Lost Lady, A 1925,Ja 19,14:1
Recompense 1925,Ap 20,22:1
His Majesty Bunker Bean 1925,S 15,12:1
Rose of the World 1925,N 10,25:3
Our Dancing Daughters 1928,O 8,14:2
Broadway Melody, The 1929,F 9,15:3
Two Weeks Off 1929,Je 24,27:1
Speedway 1929,S 21,17:1
Lord Byron of Broadway 1930,Mr 8,21:1
Florodora Girl, The 1930,My 31,19:4
Our Blushing Brides 1930,Ag 2,16:4
Those Three French Girls 1930,O 11,21:3
Dance, Fools, Dance 1931,Mr 21,15:1
Laughing Sinners 1931,Jl 4,11:5
Great Lover, The 1931,Ag 24,13:4
Unashamed 1932,Jl 15,13:4
Faithless 1932,N 19,20:2
When Ladies Meet 1933,Je 24,16:2
Made on Broadway 1933,Jl 8,14:5
Should Ladies Behave? 1933,D 18,24:3
Enchanted April 1935,Mr 9,19:1
Girl on the Front Page, The 1936,N 7,15:2
When's Your Birthday? 1937,Mr 19,27:2
Maisie Goes to Reno 1944,S 29,18:1
Twice Blessed 1945,Jl 7,7:5
Up Goes Maisie 1946,Ja 25,26:7
Show-Off, The 1947,Mr 20,38:2
Beaumont, Hugh
Flight Lieutenant 1942,Jl 31,11:1
He Hired the Boss 1943,Je 4,17:4
Fallen Sparrow, The 1943,Ag 20,13:1
Seventh Victim, The 1943,S 18,11:3
Objective Burma 1945,Ja 27,15:2
Blue Dahlia, The 1946,My 9,27:3
Guilt of Janet Ames, The 1947,My 23,31:2
Bury Me Dead 1947,O 25,13:3
Last Outpost, The 1951,Je 22,16:3
Phone Call From a Stranger 1952,F 2,11:2
Night Without Sleep 1952,S 27,13:2
Mississippi Gambler, The 1953,Ja 30,25:1
Night Passage 1957,Jl 25,28:1

Beaumont, Kathryn
On an Island With You 1948,Jl 30,13:2
Beaumont, Lucy
Ashes of Vengeance 1923,Ag 7,20:2
Lucretia Lombard 1923,D 17,23:1
Man Without a Country, The 1925,F 12,16:1
Trouble With Wives, The 1925,Ag 5,12:4
Ibanez's Torrent 1926,F 22,14:1
Greater Glory, The 1926,My 4,31:1
Beloved Rogue, The 1927,Mr 14,16:1
Resurrection 1927,My 17,27:2
Crowd, The 1928,F 20,14:1
Sonny Boy 1929,Mr 9,24:3
Free Soul, A 1931,Je 3,29:2
Caught Plastered 1931,S 12,15:4
Three Wise Girls 1932,F 6,14:4
Midnight Lady, The 1932,Jl 1,19:3
His Double Life 1933,D 16,12:3
Devil Doll, The 1936,Ag 8,5:2
Maid of Salem 1937,Mr 4,27:2
Beaumont, Roger
Judith 1966,Ja 21,22:1
Bible, The 1966,S 29,60:1
Beaumont, Tessa
Belles and Ballets 1960,N 15,45:3
Beaumont (Director)
City of Comrades, The 1919,Jl 14,12:2
Beaune, Michele
Backfire 1965,Ap 27,27:1
Beauregard, Georges de (Producer)
Breathless 1961,F 8,26:1
Carabiniers, Les 1968,Ap 26,31:1
Beauregard, Ponti de (Producer)
Woman Is a Woman, A 1964,S 19,19:1
Beauvais
Jour de Fete 1952,F 20,26:4
Beauvais, David
Illiac Passion, The 1968,Ap 19,40:1
Beauvais, Paul
Petit Soldat, Le 1967,Ap 21,48:1
Beauvais, Richard
Illiac Passion, The 1968,Ap 19,40:1
Beauvy, Nicolas
Camelot 1967,O 26,54:1
Beaver, Lee W (Director)
Hills Run Red, The 1967,N 11,26:3
Beavers, Louise
Coquette 1929,Ap 6,14:4 (In Addenda)
Nix on Dames 1929,N 23,18:5
Up for Murder 1931,My 30,9:2
Annabelle's Affairs 1931,Je 29,20:3
Girls About Town 1931,N 2,27:1
Good Sport 1931,D 12,23:3
Ladies of the Big House 1932,Ja 1,31:1
Expert, The 1932,F 27,22:1
It's Tough to be Famous 1932,Ap 9,18:1
Young America 1932,My 7,11:5
Night World 1932,My 28,18:2
Street of Women 1932,My 30,16:5
Unashamed 1932,Jl 15,13:4
What Price Hollywood 1932,Jl 16,5:5
Too Busy to Work 1932,D 3,21:4
She Done Him Wrong 1933,F 10,12:3
Pick Up 1933,Mr 25,13:4
Girl Missing 1933,Ap 1,18:2
What Price Innocence? 1933,Je 26,16:3
Her Bodyguard 1933,Ag 7,18:2
Bombshell 1933,O 21,11:2
Cheaters 1934,My 12,12:4
Hat, Coat and Glove 1934,Jl 27,21:2
Imitation of Life 1934,N 24,19:1
West of the Pecos 1934,D 29,11:2
Annapolis Farewell 1935,Ag 24,18:2
Bullets or Ballots 1936,My 27,27:1
Wives Never Know 1936,O 31,24:2
Rainbow on the River 1936,D 18,31:4
Make Way for Tomorrow 1937,My 10,23:1
Wings Over Honolulu 1937,My 29,20:1
Last Gangster, The 1937,D 10,33:2
Scandal Street 1938,F 5,19:2 (In Addenda)
Brother Rat 1938,N 5,15:2
Peck's bad Boy With the Circus 1939,Ja 11,17:4
Made for Each Other 1939,F 17,17:2
Lady's From Kentucky, The 1939,Ap 27,31:1
Women Without Names 1940,My 9,26:4
No Time for Comedy 1940,S 7,9:2
I Want a Divorce 1940,O 3,31:2
Virginia 1941,Ja 29,21:2
Belle Starr 1941,N 1,20:2
Shadow of the Thin Man 1941,N 21,23:2
Reap the Wild Wind 1942,Mr 27,27:2
Vanishing Virginian, The 1942,My 28,13:3
Holiday Inn 1942,Ag 5,16:1
Big Street, The 1942,Ag 14,13:1
Seven Sweethearts 1942,N 13,28:1
Good Morning, Judge 1943,Ap 30,25:4
All by Myself 1943,Jl 16,20:3
Du Barry Was a Lady 1943,Ag 20,13:1
Jack London 1944,Mr 3,19:4
Barbary Coast Gent 1944,S 29,18:2
Delightfully Dangerous 1945,Je 9,17:3
Lover Come Back 1946,Je 20,20:3
Mr Blandings Builds his Dream House

Beavers, Louise— Cont
1948,Mr 26,26:2
Good Sam 1948,S 17,28:2
For the Love of Mary 1948,S 23,37:2
Jackie Robinson Story, The 1950,My 17,36:1
My Blue Heaven 1950,S 16,12:6
Never Wave at a Wac 1953,Ap 24,30:2
Teenage Rebel 1956,N 17,17:6
Tammy and the Bachelor 1957,Je 15,10:7
Goddess, The 1958,Je 25,24:1
All the Fine Young Cannibals 1960,S 23,33:1
Facts of Life, The 1961,F 11,27:1
Beban, George
Pasquale 1916,My 22,20:4
Greatest Love of All, The 1924,N 11,14:1
Loves of Ricardo, The 1926,Ag 16,10:1
Fabulous Texan, The 1947,D 26,22:5
Beban, George (Director)
Greatest Love of All, The 1924,N 11,14:1
Loves of Ricardo, The 1926,Ag 16,10:1
Beban, George (Screenwriter)
Greatest Love of All, The 1924,N 11,14:1
Loves of Ricardo, The 1926,Ag 16,10:1
Bebb, Richard
Final Test, The 1954,Ja 26,21:5
Bebutova, Marina
Bountiful Summer 1951,D 24,9:1
Bechdolt, Jack (Original Author)
Fog Bound 1923,My 29,10:3
Bechervaise, Lynden
Isabel 1968,Jl 24,47:1
Bechi, Gino
When Love Calls 1948,O 9,12:6
Voice of Love, The 1950,Ja 7,11:2
Aida 1954,N 12,17:1
Traviata, La 1968,F 28,43:2
Bechtal, William
Jazz Age, The 1929,Ja 7,36:2
Bechtel, William
Spite Marriage 1929,Mr 25,32:2
Social Lion, The 1930,Je 14,9:4
Beck, Billy
Irma la Douce 1963,Je 6,39:1
Beck, Dan
Birth of the Blues 1941,D 11,39:1
Beck, Danny
Man of a Thousand Faces 1957,Ag 14,21:1
Beck, George (Director)
Behave Yourself 1951,N 8,35:2
Beck, George (Original Author)
There Goes my Girl 1937,Je 12,8:2
Hired Wife 1940,S 14,11:2
Take a Letter Darling 1942,My 28,13:2
Behave Yourself 1951,N 8,35:2
Boy, Did I Get a Wrong Number! 1966,Je 9,54:2
Beck, George (Screenwriter)
Behave Yourself 1951,N 8,35:2
Beck, Glenn
Dr Strangelove or: How I Learned to Stop
Worrying and Love the Bomb 1964,Ja 31,16:1
(Incorrect in this edition; use 1964,Ja 30,24:1
elsewhere)
Beck, Horst
Great British Train Robbery, The 1967,Ap 6,45:2
Beck, J Emmett
Broadway Melody, The 1929,F 9,15:3
Beck, James
Outsider, The 1962,F 8,25:1
Beck, John
Cock O' the Walk 1930,Ap 12,23:1
Billy the Kid 1930,O 18,23:2
Wet Parade, The 1932,Ap 22,23:2
Trail of the Lonesome Pine, The 1936,F 20,23:5
Beck, John (Producer)
Family Honeymoon 1949,F 25,28:2
Kill the Umpire 1950,My 29,10:6
Harvey 1950,D 22,19:1
Fury at Showdown 1957,Ap 20,21:3
King Kong vs. Godzilla 1963,Je 27,23:4
Singing Nun, The 1966,Mr 18,33:1
Private Navy of Sgt O'Farrell, The
1968,My 9,54:1
Beck, Jorgen
Weekend 1964,Ap 27,24:1
Beck, Kimberly
Yours, Mine and Ours 1968,Ap 25,53:1
Beck, Pierre-Michel
Savage Triangle 1952,S 30,38:2
Game of Love, The 1954,D 15,41:1
Beck, Reginald (Director)
Long Dark Hall, The 1951,My 10,38:3
Beck, Reginald (Miscellaneous)
Henry V 1946,Je 18,30:2
Beck, Thomas
Charlie Chan in Paris 1935,Ja 22,23:2
Life Begins at 40 1935,Ap 5,21:3
Charlie Chan in Egypt 1935,Je 24,12:2
My Marriage 1936,F 22,12:2
Every Saturday Night 1936,Mr 14,10:2
Under Two Flags 1936,My 1,19:1
Champagne Charlie 1936,My 7,21:2
White Fang 1936,Jl 18,18:2
Charlie Chan at the Race Track 1936,Ag 15,6:2
Charlie Chan at the Opera 1936,D 5,16:2

Crack-Up 1937,Ja 4,20:4
Woman Wise 1937,Ja 23,13:1
Seventh Heaven 1937,Mr 26,25:1
Thirteenth Chair, The 1937,Je 18,25:3
Great Hospital Mystery, The 1937,Jl 16,22:2
Think Fast, Mr Moto 1937,Ag 16,15:3
Heidi 1937,N 6,14:2
45 Fathers 1937,D 11,22:2
Thank You, Mr Moto 1938,Ja 3,16:2
I Stand Accused 1939,Ja 5,17:1
Family Next Door, The 1939,Ap 28,31:2
They Asked for It 1939,Je 30,17:4
Beck, Vincent
Santa Claus Conquers the Martians
1964,D 17,50:2
Beck-Gaden, Hans
Judas von Tirol, Der 1935,Ap 27,20:7
Grenzfeuer 1936,D 19,16:1
Fuerst Sepp'l 1937,Jl 17,18:1
Beck-Gaden, Hans (Director)
Grenzfeuer 1936,D 19,16:1
Becker, Arnold (Screenwriter)
Go, Man, Go 1954,Mr 10,29:5
Becker, Fred
Man Without a Country, The 1925,F 12,16:1
Black Pirate, The 1926,Mr 9,21:4
Becker, Hazel Lee
Prince of Peace, The 1951,Mr 24,8:3
Becker, Israel
Long Is the Road 1948,N 12,30:5
Becker, Israel (Original Author)
Long Is the Road 1948,N 12,30:5
Becker, Israel (Screenwriter)
Long Is the Road 1948,N 12,30:5
Becker, Jacques
Boudu Saved From Drowning; Boudu Sauve Des
Eaux 1967,F 24,26:2
Becker, Jacques (Director)
It Happened at the Inn; Goupi Mains Rouge
1945,D 22,16:2
Paris Frills 1946,N 25,38:3
Antoine and Antoinette 1948,Ap 16,29:2
Edward and Caroline 1952,Ap 30,33:3
Casque D'Or 1952,Ag 19,19:1
Grisbi 1959,Jl 13,23:1
Modigliani of Montparnasse 1961,Mr 1,27:3
Night Watch, The; Trou, Le 1964,My 27,46:1
Becker, Jacques (Miscellaneous)
Antoine and Antoinette 1948,Ap 16,29:2
Becker, Jacques (Screenwriter)
Paris Frills 1946,N 25,38:3
Antoine and Antoinette 1948,Ap 16,29:2
Edward and Caroline 1952,Ap 30,33:3
Casque D'Or 1952,Ag 19,19:1
Grisbi 1959,Jl 13,23:1
Night Watch, The; Trou, Le 1964,My 27,46:1
Becker, Jean (Director)
Tender Scoundrel 1967,N 16,58:2
Becker, Jean (Screenwriter)
Tender Scoundrel 1967,N 16,58:2
Becker, Stephen (Original Author)
Covenant with Death, A 1967,F 16,32:3
Becker, Terry
Compulsion 1959,Ap 2,26:2
Becker, Vernon P (Producer)
Flame and the Fire 1966,Mr 29,37:1
Becker, Zivia
Dream no More 1950,Ja 6,25:2
Beckers, Paul
Im Heidekrug 1934,D 31,9:7
Gruen ist die Heide 1935,O 14,21:2
Traum vom Rhein, Der 1935,D 9,25:2
Alte Kameraden 1936,Ap 27,19:3
Wackere Schustermeister, Der 1936,Jl 7,22:4
Beckersachs, Carl
Waltz Dream, The 1926,Jl 26,13:2
Beckett, James
Rotten to the Core 1965,Jl 20,39:2
Beckett, Samuel (Screenwriter)
Film 1965,S 15,41:1
Now Cinema! (Film); Film (Now Cinema!)
1968,Ap 9,56:1
Beckett, Scotty
Whom the Gods Destroy 1934,Jl 13,14:2
Dante's Inferno 1935,Ag 1,15:1
I Dream too Much 1935,N 29,24:1
Case Against Mrs Ames, The 1936,My 28,19:2
Anthony Adverse 1936,Ag 27,16:1
Charge of the Light Brigade, The 1936,N 2,24:1
Conquest 1937,N 5,19:1
Devil's Party, The 1938,My 31,8:3
Four's a Crowd 1938,Ag 12,11:1
Listen, Darling 1938,N 24,37:2
Flying Irishman, The 1939,Ap 12,27:2
Blind Alley 1939,My 23,27:2
Mickey, the Kid 1939,Jl 6,27:1
Escape, The 1939,N 3,17:4
Blue Bird, The 1940,Ja 20,11:2
Our Neighbors-The Carters 1940,F 15,15:2
My Son, My Son! 1940,My 10,26:6
My Favorite Wife 1940,My 31,15:2
Gold Rush Maisie 1940,S 2,19:2
Aloma of the South Seas 1941,Ag 28,23:4

Beckett, Scotty— Cont
Kings Row 1942,F 3,23:2
Vanishing Virginian, The 1942,My 28,13:3
It Happened in Flatbush 1942,Jl 3,12:8
Between Us Girls 1942,S 25,25:3
Youngest Profession, The 1943,Je 25,13:3
Ali Baba and the Forty Thieves 1944,Mr 16,17:3
Climax, The 1944,D 14,28:5
Circumstantial Evidence 1945,Ap 21,18:3
Junior Miss 1945,Je 18,15:4
My Reputation 1946,Ja 26,19:2
Jolson Story, The 1946,O 11,28:2
White Tie and Tails 1946,N 8,28:2
Cynthia 1947,S 19,27:2
Date with Judy, A 1948,Ag 7,8:2
Battleground 1949,N 12,8:4
Nancy Goes to Rio 1950,Ap 7,22:2
Louisa 1950,O 25,45:2
Three for Jamie Dawn 1956,Jl 7,11:3
Beckhard, Arthur (Screenwriter)
West Point of the Air 1935,Ap 6,10:1
Curly Top 1935,Ag 2,22:3
Sky Parade, The 1936,Ap 20,17:1
Border Flight 1936,Je 22,22:1
Beckhardt, Fred
Cyanamide 1954,Mr 26,17:6
Beckhardt, Israel (Original Author)
Violators, The 1959,Ag 4,32:5
Becklen, Fredrik
Hugo and Josephine 1968,S 30,60:1
Beckley, Christine
Royal Ballet, The (Swan Lake Act II); Swan Lake
Act II (The Royal Ballet) 1960,O 5,45:2
Beckley, Tony
Falstaff; Chimes at Midnight 1967,Mr 18,19:2
Penthouse, The 1967,O 4,38:3
Long Day's Dying, The 1968,My 29,20:1
Lost Continent, The 1968,Je 20,50:2
Beckman, Henry
Caper of the Golden Bulls, The 1967,Je 22,46:1
Beckman, Margit (Screenwriter)
Pimpernel Svensson 1953,F 6,16:4
Beckwith, Bainard
Sun Up 1925,Ag 18,14:3
Beckwith, Frank (Miscellaneous)
Secret Service of the Air 1939,Mr 2,19:2
Beckwith, Reginald
Voice in the Night, The 1941,My 23,25:4
Scott of the Antarctic 1951,F 26,20:2
Circle of Danger 1951,Jl 12,21:6
Another Man's Poison 1952,Ja 7,14:3
Mister Drake's Duck 1952,Ja 28,15:2
Penny Princess 1953,Mr 25,37:3
Titfield Thunderbolt, The 1953,O 6,34:2
Man With a Million 1954,Je 29,21:2
Dance Little Lady 1955,D 26,23:3
Ship Was Loaded, The 1958,Ja 20,20:1
Law and Disorder 1958,Ag 6,20:1
Up the Creek 1958,N 11,26:2
Horse's Mouth, The 1958,N 12,41:1
Mad Little Island 1958,D 31,12:1
Expresso Bongo 1960,Ap 13,44:1
Next to no Time 1960,My 28,13:2
Captain's Table, The 1960,S 27,40:1
39 Steps, The 1960,O 11,55:2
Double Bunk 1961,N 17,41:3
Day the Earth Caught Fire, The 1962,Mr 16,25:1
Password Is Courage, The 1962,D 22,5:2
Shot in the Dark, A 1964,Je 24,28:1
Mister Moses 1965,My 13,32:1
Beckworth, Reginald
Lease of Life 1956,F 10,18:1
Becourt, Alain
My Uncle 1958,N 4,30:2
Bedard, Rolland
Big Red 1962,S 3,11:2
Beddell, Charles
Are You With It? 1948,Ap 15,31:2
Beddoe, Don
There's That Woman Again 1939,Ja 6,25:4
Lone Wolf Spy Hunt, The 1939,Mr 6,11:3
Blondie Meets the Boss 1939,Ap 27,31:1
Missing Daughters 1939,Je 12,14:5
Golden Boy 1939,S 8,28:2
Those High Grey Walls 1939,O 19,27:2
Beware, Spooks 1939,N 3,17:4
My Son Is Guilty 1940,Ja 15,11:2
Amazing Mr Williams, The 1940,Ja 19,15:2
Lone Wolf Strikes, The 1940,F 5,13:2
Charlie Chan's Murder Cruise 1940,My 3,17:5
Men Without Souls 1940,My 13,21:2
Island Of Doomed Men 1940,Je 10,21:2
Girls of the Road 1940,Jl 22,20:2
Military Academy 1940,Ag 5,10:4
Secret Seven, The 1940,Ag 12,11:6
Before I Hang 1940,O 3,31:3
Lone Wolf Keeps a Date, The 1941,Ja 2,24:3
Face Behind the Mask, The 1941,F 7,23:2
This Thing Called Love 1941,F 14,15:2
Submarine Zone; (Escape To Glory)
1941,Ap 7,13:2
Lone Wolf Takes a Chance, The 1941,Ap 7,13:2
Texas 1941,O 17,27:3
Sing for Your Supper 1941,D 1,15:5

Beddoe, Don— Cont
Unholy Partners 1941,D 29,21:4
Sabotage Squad 1942,Ag 5,16:1
Talk of the Town, The 1942,Ag 28,22:3
Boogie Man Will Get You, The 1942,O 12,12:4
Crime Incorporated 1945,Je 23,9:7
Midnight Manhunt 1945,Ag 18,12:5
Behind Green Lights 1946,F 16,10:2
O S S 1946,My 27,15:5
Best Years of our Lives, The 1946,N 22,27:2
Farmer's Daughter, The 1947,Mr 26,31:2
Buck Privates Come Home 1947,Ap 12,11:3
They Won't Believe Me 1947,Jl 17,16:2
Bachelor and the Bobby-Soxer, The
    1947,Jl 25,12:5
Welcome Stranger 1947,Ag 7,15:2
Black Bart 1948,Mr 4,30:4
Another Part of the Forest 1948,My 19,30:2
Live Today for Tomorrow 1948,D 6,29:2
Lady Gambles, The 1949,My 21,9:2
Once More, my Darling 1949,S 26,17:1
Dancing in the Dark 1949,D 3,8:6
Dear Wife 1950,F 2,31:2
Woman in Hiding 1950,F 23,33:2
Great Rupert, The 1950,Ap 14,27:2
Cyrano De Bergerac 1950,N 17,31:2
Enforcer, The 1951,Ja 26,19:2
Company She Keeps, The 1951,Ja 29,14:4
Scandal Sheet 1952,Ja 17,23:1
Hoodlum Empire 1952,Mr 6,25:6
Narrow Margin, The 1952,My 5,18:7
Carrie 1952,Jl 17,20:2
Don't Bother to Knock 1952,Jl 19,8:2
Iron Mistress, The 1952,N 20,39:2
Stop, You're Killing Me 1952,D 11,45:3
Clown, The 1953,Ja 29,25:1
System, The 1953,My 23,19:3
Loophole 1954,Mr 13,11:3
River of no Return 1954,My 1,13:2
Night of the Hunter, The 1955,S 30,23:1
Warlock 1959,My 1,34:1
Saintly Sinners 1962,Mr 29,28:2
Impossible Years, The 1968,D 6,54:1
Bedford, Barbara
Last of the Mohicans, The 1921,Ja 3,20:2
Spoilers, The 1923,Ag 6,14:2
Acquittal, The 1923,D 12,24:5
Women Who Give 1924,Je 3,22:1
Percy 1925,Mr 25,24:2
Talker, The 1925,My 12,26:2
Mad Whirl, The 1925,Jl 1,16:1
What Fools Men 1925,S 29,31:3
Tumbleweeds 1925,D 21,27:2
Old Loves and New 1926,Ap 20,24:7
Notorious Lady, The 1927,Ap 11,18:3
Mockery 1927,Ag 22,21:3
Man's Past, A 1927,O 4,34:2
Port of Missing Girls, The 1928,Jl 31,13:4
Cavalier, The 1928,O 31,28:4
Haunted House, The 1928,D 17,23:1
Tol'able David 1930,N 17,29:1
Sunny 1930,D 27,16:3
Lash, The 1931,Ja 1,31:3
Death Kiss, The 1933,F 5,IX,5:3
Found Alive 1934,F 12,19:2
Girl of the Limberlost, A 1934,N 9,24:6
World Accuses, The 1935,Mr 21,27:2
Keeper of the Bees, The 1935,Ag 17,18:5
Mine With the Iron Door, The 1936,Jl 11,11:3
Bedford, Basil
Just Smith 1934,Ap 23,20:2
Bedford, Brian
Angry Silence, The 1960,D 13,25:2
Pad, The (And How to Use It) 1966,Ag 18,27:2
Grand-Prix 1966,D 22,40:1
Bedford, Patrick
Up the Down Staircase 1967,Ag 18,36:2
Bedford-Jones, H (Original Author)
Garden of the Moon 1938,S 24,13:1
Bedogni, Odette
Difficult Years 1950,Ag 22,31:2
Bedos, Guy
Elusive Corporal, The 1963,F 19,5:1
Sweet and Sour 1964,D 28,34:2
Bedos, Guy (Screenwriter)
Sweet and Sour 1964,D 28,34:2
Bedoya, Alfonso
Treasure of Sierra Madre 1948,Ja 24,11:2
Pearl, The 1948,F 18,36:4
Angel on the Amazon 1948,D 27,16:4
Streets of Laredo 1949,My 12,28:2
Border Incident 1949,N 21,29:2
Fortunes of Captain Blood 1950,Je 10,11:3
Black Rose, The 1950,S 2,11:2
California Conquest 1952,Je 7,22:6
Stranger Wore a Gun, The 1953,Jl 30,20:3
Bee, Molly
Summer Love 1958,Je 26,23:4
Beebe, Ford (Director)
Big Pay-Off, The 1933,Ja 17,22:7
Laughing at Life 1933,Jl 15,14:2
Mars Attacks the World 1938,N 8,26:3
Night Monster 1942,N 30,18:5
Invisible Man's Revenge, The 1944,Je 10,12:2

Enter Arsene Lupin 1944,D 2,17:6
Bomba, the Jungle Boy 1949,Ap 16,11:4
Dalton Gang, The 1949,N 25,27:5
Beebe, Ford (Original Author)
Laughing at Life 1933,Jl 15,14:2
Davy Crockett, Indian Scout 1950,Mr 17,28:3
Beebe, Ford (Producer)
Night Monster 1942,N 30,18:5
Enter Arsene Lupin 1944,D 2,17:6
Beebe, Ford (Screenwriter)
Dalton Gang, The 1949,N 25,27:5
Beebe, Lloyd (Cinematographer)
Jungle Cat 1960,Ag 18,19:2
Beebe, Lloyd (Miscellaneous)
White Wilderness 1958,Ag 13,22:1
Beebe, Marjorie
Ankles Preferred 1927,Ap 18,21:2
Rich but Honest 1927,My 18,29:3
Very Confidential 1927,N 29,31:1
Love Hungry 1928,Ap 16,20:5
Speakeasy 1929,Mr 11,22:2
Not Quite Decent 1929,My 6,30:4
Rackety Rax 1932,N 5,12:5
Hypnotized 1933,Ja 16,13:3
Beebe, Marshall V
Bridges at Toko-Ri, The 1955,Ja 21,20:2
Beech, Frances
Mirandy Smiles 1918,D 16,13:3
Beecham, Thomas Sir (Composer)
Mozart 1940,O 4,29:2
Tales of Hoffmann 1951,Ap 5,34:2
Beecher, Janet
Gallant Lady 1934,Ja 22,12:3
Last Gentleman, The 1934,O 18,26:5
President Vanishes, The 1934,D 8,18:5
Mighty Barnum, The 1934,D 24,17:1
Let's Live Tonight 1935,Mr 18,14:4
Dark Angel, The 1935,S 6,12:2
So Red the Rose 1935,N 28,39:1
Love Before Breakfast 1936,Mr 14,10:1
I'd Give my Life 1936,Ag 17,9:1
Longest Night, The 1936,O 17,21:2
Good Old Soak 1937,Ap 20,25:3
Thirteenth Chair, The 1937,Je 18,25:3
Between Two Women 1937,Ag 6,21:1
Big City 1937,S 17,29:2
Beg, Borrow or Steal 1937,D 10,33:2
Rosalie 1937,D 31,9:2
Judge Hardy's Children 1938,Ap 8,17:2
Yellow Jack 1938,My 20,17:2
Woman Against Woman 1938,Ag 23,20:6
Say It in French 1938,D 1,19:1
I Was a Convict 1939,Mr 23,27:2
Story of Vernon and Irene Castle, The
    1939,Mr 31,19:2
Man of Conquest 1939,Ap 28,31:2
Career 1939,Jl 28,14:2
Slightly Honorable 1940,My 17,23:4
All This and Heaven, Too 1940,Jl 5,10:2
Gay Caballero, The 1940,O 25,25:3
Mark of Zorro, The 1940,N 4,23:2
Bitter Sweet 1940,N 22,27:1
Lady Eve, The 1941,F 26,17:1
Parson of Panamint, The 1941,Jl 26,18:2
West Point Widow 1941,S 11,21:5
Reap the Wild Wind 1942,Mr 27,27:2
Men of Texas 1942,Jl 13,18:3 (In Addenda)
Silver Queen 1943,Ja 11,18:4
Beecher, Sylvia
Innocents of Paris 1929,Ap 27,16:5
Beecroft, Chester (Original Author)
Three Kids and a Queen 1935,N 9,19:2
Beeding, Francis (Original Author)
Dead Men Tell no Tales 1939,Jl 24,9:2
Spellbound 1945,N 2,22:2
Beeny, Christopher
Little Kidnappers, The 1954,S 2,18:1
Beer, Erica
Counterfeit Traitor, The 1962,Ap 18,28:1
Beer, Gustav (Miscellaneous)
Hampelmann, Der 1931,S 8,38:7
Beer, Jack
Nobody Waved Goodbye 1964,S 17,52:1
Beer, Jacqueline
Prize, The 1964,Ja 24,21:1
Made in Paris 1966,F 17,29:1
Beerblock, Maurice
Man Escaped, A 1957,Ag 27,33:2
Beernstein, Roger (Composer)
Moulin Rouge 1944,N 23,38:2
Beers, Ethel Lynn (Original Author)
Which Shall It Be? 1924,Ap 7,15:3
Beery, Carol Ann
China Seas 1935,Ag 10,16:4
Rationing 1944,Ap 10,14:2
Beery, Noah
Red Lantern, The 1919,My 5,11:1
Woman Next Door, The 1919,My 19,20:5
Louisiana 1919,Jl 21,12:3
In Mizzoura 1919,O 13,16:3
Fighting Shepherdess, The 1920,Mr 29,18:1
Go and Get It 1920,Jl 19,16:3
Dinty 1920,N 22,13:3

Beery, Noah— Cont
Mark of Zorro, The 1920,N 29,20:3
Bob Hampton of Placer 1921,My 2,12:1
Bits of Life 1921,O 17,18:1
Wild Honey 1922,F 28,17:4
Crossroads of New York, The 1922,My 22,18:4
Ebb Tide 1922,N 20,21:3
Soul of the Beast, The 1923,My 22,14:4
Main Street 1923,Je 12,22:2
Wandering Daughters 1923,Jl 2,16:2
Spoilers, The 1923,Ag 6,14:2
Stephen Steps Out 1923,N 19,19:3
Call of the Canyon, The 1923,D 17,23:1
Heritage of the Desert, The 1924,Ja 24,15:1
Fighting Coward, The 1924,Mr 17,19:1
Wanderer of the Wasteland, The 1924,Jl 8,14:2
Lily of the Dust 1924,Ag 25,16:2
Female, The 1924,S 2,19:2
Welcome Stranger 1924,O 14,21:5
North of 36 1924,D 8,13:3
East of Suez 1925,Ja 26,22:1
Contraband 1925,Mr 24,20:6
Light of the Western Stars, The 1925,Je 24,14:3
Wild Horse Mesa 1925,Ag 10,8:2
Coming of Amos, The 1925,S 8,29:1
Vanishing American, The 1925,O 16,18:2
Lord Jim 1925,N 16,19:4
Enchanted Hill, The 1925,D 29,19:2 (In
    Addenda)
Crown of Lies 1926,Mr 30,20:6
Padlocked 1926,Ag 2,21:2
Beau Geste 1926,Ag 26,17:3
Paradise 1926,O 4,20:2
Rough Riders, The 1927,Mr 16,28:2
Evening Clothes 1927,Mr 21,10:4
Love Mart, The 1927,D 26,16:6
Dove, The 1928,Ja 3,28:2
Beau Sabreur 1928,Ja 23,18:3
Two Lovers 1928,Mr 23,24:4
Hell-Ship Bronson 1928,Je 19,31:1
Noah's Ark 1929,Mr 13,28:6
Godless Girl, The 1929,Ap 1,22:1
Careers 1929,Je 10,23:1
Four Feathers, The 1929,Je 13,35:4
Isle of Lost Ships, The 1929,O 26,15:1
Isle of Escape 1930,Mr 31,24:3
Under a Texas Moon 1930,Ap 4,22:1
Murder Will Out 1930,Ap 14,24:2
Song of the Flame 1930,My 7,24:5
Golden Dawn 1930,Jl 26,16:4
Way of all Men, The 1930,S 20,15:4
Renegades 1930,N 8,21:3
Tol'able David 1930,N 17,29:1
Bright Lights 1931,F 10,24:4
Millionaire, The 1931,Ap 9,30:5
Soldiers Plaything, A 1931,My 2,23:4
Honeymoon Lane 1931,Ag 1,16:4
Riders of the Purple Sage 1931,S 26,25:3
Homicide Squad 1931,O 19,28:1
Stranger in Town 1932,Jl 8,22:5
Stoker, The 1932,Jl 16,5:5
Kid From Spain, The 1932,N 18,23:2
She Done Him Wrong 1933,F 10,12:3
Woman I Stole, The 1933,Je 28,24:3
Madame Spy 1934,F 10,20:1
David Harum 1934,Mr 2,23:2
Cockeyed Cavaliers 1934,Jl 25,22:2
Caravan 1934,S 28,27:1
Kentucky Kernels 1935,Ja 5,20:2
Sweet Adeline 1935,Ja 7,13:2
King of the Damned 1936,F 1,9:2
Crimson Circle, The 1936,D 28,12:3
Strangers on a Honeymoon 1936,Mr 13,23:2
Bad Man of Brimstone, The 1938,F 4,17:2
Mutiny on the Blackhawk 1939,Ag 2,17:2
Torpedoed 1939,S 26,20:5
Tennessee Johnson 1943,Ja 13,18:2
Salute to the Marines 1943,Ag 30,11:3
Barbary Coast Gent 1944,S 29,18:2
This Man's Navy 1945,Ap 16,18:6
Beery, Noah Jr
Parole 1936,Je 27,21:1
Road Back, The 1937,Je 18,25:2
Some Blondes Are Dangerous 1937,N 3,29:3
Girls' School 1938,N 3,27:1
Only Angels Have Wings 1939,My 12,25:2
Bad Lands 1939,Ag 9,15:2
Flight at Midnight 1939,S 7,29:2
Parents on Trial 1939,S 18,15:5
Of Mice and Men 1940,F 17,9:2
Twenty-Mule Team 1940,My 10,26:6
Passport to Alcatraz 1940,Je 15,12:2
Little Bit of Heaven, A 1940,N 8,24:2
Sergeant York 1941,Jl 3,15:1
Tanks a Million 1941,O 9,27:2
Prairie Chickens 1943,Jl 9,21:6
Calaboose 1943,Jl 30,19:2
Frontier Badmen 1943,Ag 14,12:8
We've Never Been Licked 1943,Ag 19,23:1
Corvette K-225 1943,O 21,30:1
Top Man 1943,O 29,23:2
Gung Ho! 1944,Ja 26,23:2
See my Lawyer 1945,My 4,23:4
Cat Creeps, The 1946,My 18,12:4

Beery, Noah Jr— Cont

Red River 1948,O 1,31:2
Davy Crockett, Indian Scout 1950,Mr 17,28:3
Rocketship X-M 1950,My 27,10:6
Two Flags West 1950,O 13,23:2
Last Outpost, The 1951,Je 22,16:3
Texas Rangers, The 1951,Jl 14,7:2
Story of Will Rogers, The 1952,Jl 18,10:5
Wings of the Hawk 1953,Ag 27,22:1
Black Dakotas, The 1954,O 2,21:2
Jubal 1956,Ap 25,39:1
Fastest Gun Alive, The 1956,Jl 13,23:3
Inherit the Wind 1960,O 13,41:1

Beery, Rita

Dark Waters 1944,N 22,25:2

Beery, Wallace

Unpardonable Sin, The 1919,My 3,11:3
Love Burglar, The 1919,Jl 28,8:5
Life Line, The 1919,S 29,16:1
Victory 1919,D 28,4:4
Behind the Door 1920,Ja 5,15:1
Virgin of Stamboul, The 1920,Mr 28,V,9:1
Mollycoddle, The 1920,Je 14,13:2
Rookie's Return, The 1920,D 27,11:3
Last of the Mohicans, The 1921,Ja 3,20:2
Tale of Two Worlds, A 1921,Mr 14,9:2
Golden Snare, The 1921,Jl 11,9:3
Wild Honey 1922,F 28,17:4
Robin Hood 1922,O 31,15:4 (In Addenda)
Ashes of Vengeance 1923,Ag 7,20:2
Drifting 1923,Ag 20,4:2
Spanish Dancer, The 1923,O 8,20:1
Eternal Struggle, The 1923,O 16,21:3
Richard the Lion-Hearted 1923,O 22,17:1
Sea Hawk, The 1924,Je 3,22:1
Signal Tower, The 1924,Jl 21,14:4
Red Lily, The 1924,S 29,10:1
So Big 1925,Ja 5,19:1
Devil's Cargo, The 1925,F 3,24:1
Lost World, The 1925,F 9,15:3
Great Divide, The 1925,F 11,19:4
Coming Through 1925,F 18,17:3
Adventure 1925,Ap 15,16:1
Night Club, The 1925,My 5,24:2
Wanderer, The 1925,Ag 20,22:1
In the Name of Love 1925,Ag 27,14:1
Pony Express, The 1925,S 14,16:1
Behind the Front 1926,F 10,16:2
Volcano 1926,My 24,24:3
Four Horsemen of the Apocalypse, The
  1926,S 27,27:3
We're in the Navy Now 1926,N 8,19:2
Old Ironsides 1926,D 7,21:2
Casey at the Bat 1927,Ap 4,30:5
Fireman, Save My Child 1927,O 10,24:1
We're in the Air Now 1927,D 31,31:1
Wife Savers 1928,Ja 17,23:2
Partners in Crime 1928,Ap 30,18:3
Big Killing, The 1928,Jl 2,11:2
Beggars of Life 1928,S 24,25:1
Chinatown Nights 1929,Ap 1,22:1
River of Romance, The 1929,Jl 29,23:3
Big House, The 1930,Je 25,31:2
Billy the Kid 1930,O 18,23:2
Lady's Morals, A 1930,N 8,21:3
Min and Bill 1930,N 24,26:5
Way for a Sailor 1930,D 13,22:2
Stolen Jools 1931,Ap 4,23:1
Secret Six, The 1931,My 2,23:4
Champ, The 1931,N 10,29:4
Hell Divers 1931,D 23,27:3
Grand Hotel 1932,Ap 13,23:2
Flesh 1932,D 10,19:3
Tugboat Annie 1933,Ag 12,14:2
Dinner at Eight 1933,Ag 24,18:1
Bowery, The 1933,O 5,24:2
Viva Villa! 1934,Ap 11,25:2
Treasure Island 1934,Ag 18,5:5
Mighty Barnum, The 1934,D 24,17:1
West Point of the Air 1935,Ap 6,10:1
China Seas 1935,Ag 10,16:4
O'Shaughnessy's Boy 1935,O 5,18:2
Ah, Wilderness! 1935,D 25,30:2
Message to Garcia, A 1936,Ap 10,27:1
Old Hutch 1936,D 7,27:4
Good Old Soak 1937,Ap 20,25:3
Slave Ship 1937,Je 17,19:2
Bad Man of Brimstone, The 1938,F 4,17:2
Port of Seven Seas 1938,Jl 15,13:2
Stablemates 1938,O 21,27:2
Sergeant Madden 1939,Mr 24,27:2
Thunder Afloat 1939,O 13,27:2
Man From Dakota, The 1940,F 22,29:2
Twenty-Mule Team 1940,My 10,26:6
Wyoming 1940,O 3,31:4
Bad Man, The 1941,Ap 4,25:1
Barnacle Bill 1941,Jl 25,12:4
Bugle Sounds, The 1942,Ap 3,25:2
Jackass Mail 1942,Jl 2,25:2
Salute to the Marines 1943,Ag 30,11:3
Rationing 1944,Ap 10,14:2
Barbary Coast Gent 1944,S 29,18:2
This Man's Navy 1945,Ap 16,18:6
Bad Bascomb 1946,My 23,18:4

Mighty McGurk, The 1947,Ap 4,19:4
Date with Judy, A 1948,Ag 7,8:2
Big Jack 1949,My 23,27:4
When Comedy Was King 1960,Mr 30,42:1

Beery, William

Soldiers of Fortune 1919,N 24,13:1

Beethoven (Composer)

Fidelio 1961,My 13,10:1

Begg, Gordon

Bandolero, The 1924,O 27,27:1
Sherlock Holmes's Fatal Hour 1931,Jl 13,13:5

Beggiani, Serge

Casque D'Or 1952,Ag 19,19:1

Beggs, Lee

America 1924,F 22,20:1
Janice Meredith 1924,Ag 6,13:3

Beggs, Malcolm Lee

Houdini 1953,Jl 3,10:2
Botany Bay 1953,O 30,27:2

Beghi, Luisella

Eternal Melodies 1948,F 14,17:3
Angelo in the Crowd 1952,O 4,15:2

Begley, Ed

Boomerang 1947,Mr 6,36:2
Sitting Pretty 1948,Mr 11,35:2
Street with no Name, The 1948,Jl 15,26:6
Deep Waters 1948,Jl 23,12:4
Sorry, Wrong Number 1948,S 2,18:2
Tulsa 1949,My 27,25:2
It Happens Every Spring 1949,Je 11,11:2
Great Gatsby, The 1949,Jl 14,20:5
Backfire 1950,Ja 27,29:2
Dark City 1950,O 19,40:5
Wyoming Mail 1950,O 23,26:5
Stars in my Crown 1950,D 22,19:1
U S S Teakettle 1951,F 24,11:2
Lone Star 1952,F 2,11:4
On Dangerous Ground 1952,F 13,35:2
Boots Malone 1952,Mr 13,26:2
Deadline U S A 1952,Mr 15,8:2
Turning Point, The 1952,N 15,15:2
Patterns 1956,Mr 28,26:1
12 Angry Men 1957,Ap 15,24:1
Odds Against Tomorrow 1959,O 16,27:1
Green Helmet, The 1961,Jl 20,32:2
Sweet Bird of Youth 1962,Mr 29,28:2
Unsinkable Molly Brown, The 1964,Jl 17,15:1
Oscar, The 1966,Mr 5,16:1
Warning Shot 1967,Je 8,52:2
Billion Dollar Brain 1967,D 23,29:1
Firecreek 1968,F 22,36:2
Wild in the Streets 1968,My 30,21:1
Hang 'Em High 1968,Ag 8,27:3

Begley, Ed (Narrator)

Roosevelt Story, The 1947,Ag 22,11:2

Begley, Elizabeth

Sons and Lovers 1960,Ag 3,35:1

Behan, Brendan (Original Author)

Quare Fellow 1963,F 20,6:1

Behivedes, Teddy

Huk! 1956,D 15,20:4

Behm, Marc (Original Author)

Charade 1963,D 6,40:1
Help! 1965,Ag 24,25:1

Behm, Marc (Screenwriter)

Help! 1965,Ag 24,25:1
Trunk to Cairo 1966,D 29,22:1

Behmer, Ernst

Student Sein 1931,My 4,15:3
Blonde Nachtigall, Die 1931,Ag 22,7:5
Rheinlandmaedel, Das 1931,S 18,29:1
Der Schrecken der Garnison 1932,Je 1,19:5
Bettelstudent, Der 1936,D 28,12:3

Behn-Grund, Friedel (Director)

Sajenko, The Soviet 1929,Ja 15,22:4

Behna Brothers (Producer)

Dr Epameinondas 1938,Ap 5,19:6

Behrendt, Hans (Director)

Royal Scandal, A 1929,S 23,24:3
Danton 1931,S 7,19:3
Gloria 1932,O 28,22:4
Ich Geh' aus und Du Bleibst da 1932,N 21,21:1
Hochzeit am Wolfgangsee 1934,N 17,12:2
Dona Francisquita 1935,Ap 27,20:6
Gruen ist die Heide 1935,O 14,21:2

Behrens, Manja

Susanne im Bade; Susanna in the Bath
  1937,S 11,20:1
Stronger Than the Rule 1937,S 25,10:2

Behrle, Fred

Big News 1929,O 7,22:1

Behrman, S N (Narrator)

Stowaway in the Sky 1962,Je 19,28:1

Behrman, S N (Original Author)

He Knew Women 1930,Ap 23,24:1
Brief Moment 1933,S 30,18:5
Biography of a Bachelor Girl 1935,Mr 2,18:2
No Time for Comedy 1940,S 7,9:2
Pirate, The 1948,My 21,19:2
Me and the Colonel 1958,Ag 27,33:1

Behrman, S N (Screenwriter)

Tale of Two Cities, A 1935,D 26,21:2
Parnell 1937,Je 4,27:2

Behrman, S N (Screenwriter)— Cont

Conquest 1937,N 5,19:1
Cowboy and the Lady, The 1938,N 25,19:3
Waterloo Bridge 1940,My 17,23:2
Two Faced Woman 1942,Ja 1,37:2
Quo Vadis 1951,N 9,22:2
Gaby 1956,My 10,26:3
Me and the Colonel 1958,Ag 27,33:1

Behrmann, Josef

Kitchen, The 1961,N 2,42:1

Behrs, Pati

Apartment for Peggy 1948,O 16,9:2
Beautiful Blonde From Bashful Bend, The
  1949,My 28,11:2

Bei, Heliane

Flying Classroom, The 1958,Je 28,13:7

Beibutov, L

Arshin Takes a Wife 1950,Jl 31,13:6

Beich, Albert (Miscellaneous)

Chicago Kid, The 1945,F 12,24:3

Beich, Albert (Original Author)

Lieutenant Wore Skirts, The 1956,Ja 12,22:1

Beich, Albert (Screenwriter)

Bride Goes Wild, The 1948,Je 4,27:2
Yellow Cab Man, The 1950,Mr 27,19:2
Milkman, The 1951,Ja 1,13:6
Lieutenant Wore Skirts, The 1956,Ja 12,22:1
Dead Ringer 1964,F 20,22:3
Perils of Pauline, The 1967,Ag 3,26:3

Beierle, Alfred

D-Zug 13 Hat Verspaetung 1931,Ag 10,18:3
Avalanche 1932,Mr 26,17:2
O Alte Burschenherrlichkeit 1932,Je 18,9:2
Hauptmann von Koepenick, Der 1933,Ja 17,22:6
Burning Secret 1933,My 28,IX,2:5 (In Addenda)
Gruen ist die Heide 1935,O 14,21:2

Beil, Marie

Bonne Soupe, La 1964,Mr 16,37:1

Beilbey, Walter

State Fair 1962,Ap 12,41:4

BEIN

See Also BEAN

Bein, Albert (Original Author)

Boy Slaves 1939,F 9,17:3

Bein, Albert (Screenwriter)

Boy Slaves 1939,F 9,17:3

Beint, Michael

Conqueror Worm, The 1968,Ag 15,46:2

Beir, Fred

Violators, The 1959,Ag 4,32:5

Beirute, Yerye

Woman's Devotion, A 1957,Mr 22,26:1

Beisenalyev, Bolot

Red and the White, The 1968,S 21,26:1

Beitman, Vincent (Miscellaneous)

Beyond Endurance 1946,My 20,18:8

Bejart, Maurice

Belles and Ballets 1960,N 15,45:3

Bejart, Maurice (Miscellaneous)

Belles and Ballets 1960,N 15,45:3

Bek-Mazaroff (Director)

Pepo 1935,O 10,31:6

Bek-Nazarov, Amo (Director)

Igdenbu 1930,D 9,31:3

Bekassy, Stephen

Pesti Mese; Tales of Budapest 1938,Ja 3,16:3
Song to Remember, A 1945,Ja 26,16:4
Arch of Triumph 1948,Ap 21,33:2
Black Magic 1949,N 9,37:2
Hell and High Water 1954,F 2,20:6
Prisoner of War 1954,My 10,20:2
Interrupted Melody 1955,My 6,18:1
Bachelor Flat 1962,Ja 13,14:1
4 Horsemen of the Apocalypse, The
  1962,Mr 10,10:2

Bekeffi, Istvan (Screenwriter)

Man Who Wagged his Tail, The 1961,S 19,39:1
Shadows Grow Longer, The 1962,Je 11,36:4
Judge and the Sinner, The 1964,Je 6,14:2

Bekeffi, Stephen (Original Author)

Kiss and Make-Up 1934,Je 29,17:1

Bekker, Albert

Last Warning, The 1938,D 8,34:4

Beklaris, Apostolis

Barefoot Battalion 1954,My 29,13:4

Bel Geddes, Barbara

Long Night, The 1947,S 17,31:2
I Remember Mama 1948,Mr 12,29:2
Blood on the Moon 1948,N 12,30:5
Caught 1949,F 18,26:4
Panic in the Streets 1950,Ag 5,9:2
Fourteen Hours 1951,Mr 7,43:2
Vertigo 1958,My 29,24:2
Five Pennies, The 1959,Je 19,30:1
Five Branded Women 1960,Je 2,27:2
By Love Possessed 1961,Jl 20,32:2

Bel Geddes, Norman (Original Author)

Dead End 1937,Ag 25,25:1

Bela, Gaal (Director)

Csokolj Meg Edes 1932,N 25,19:2

Bela, Nicholas

Night Watch, The 1928,O 8,14:2
Adoration 1929,Ja 14,20:1

Bela, Salamon
Csokolj Meg Edes 1932,N 25,19:2
Belafonte, Harry
Bright Road 1953,Ap 29,33:5
Carmen Jones 1954,O 29,27:2
Island in the Sun 1957,Je 13,37:1
World, The Flesh and the Devil, The
1959,My 21,35:1
Odds Against Tomorrow 1959,O 16,27:1
Belajeff, Olga
Three Way Works, The 1926,Mr 19,25:1
Belanger, Adrian
Quebec 1951,Mr 16,34:2
Belanger, Juliette
Don Q, Son of Zorro 1925,Je 16,24:1
Belasco, Arthur
Penthouse 1933,S 9,9:2
Belasco, David
Star Overnight, A 1919,N 17,20:1
Belasco, David (Original Author)
Heart of Maryland, The 1915,Mr 21,II,12:4
Case of Becky, The 1921,O 10,16:1
Girl of the Golden West, The 1923,My 21,12:2
Daddies 1924,F 11,18:3
Men and Women 1925,Mr 30,21:3
Kiki 1926,Ap 6,26:4
Laugh, Clown, Laugh 1928,My 28,23:2
Laugh, Clown, Laugh! 1928,Je 3,VIII,5:1
Girl of the Golden West, The 1930,O 27,17:1
Kiki 1931,Mr 6,16:1
Hatchet Man, The 1932,F 4,25:2
Son-Daughter, The 1933,Ja 2,29:2
Return of Peter Grimm, The 1935,O 4,25:2
Rose of the Rancho 1936,Ja 9,25:2
Girl of the Golden West, The 1938,Mr 25,15:2
Belasco, David (Screenwriter)
Forty Winks 1925,F 3,24:1
Belasco, Jay
Woman Accused, The 1933,Mr 13,18:2
Belasco, Leon
Fisherman's Wharf 1939,F 24,15:2
Legion of Lost Flyers 1939,O 30,13:3
Lucky Partners 1940,S 6,25:2
Mummy's Hand, The 1940,S 20,27:2
Tall, Dark and Handsome 1941,Ja 24,15:2
I'll Wait for You 1941,Je 2,13:6
Nothing but the Truth 1941,O 23,27:1
Design for Scandal 1942,F 6,23:3
Night Before the Divorce, The 1942,Ap 10,21:3
Road to Morocco 1942,N 12,30:1
Over my Dead Body 1942,D 26,15:2
It Comes up Love 1943,Ja 22,25:3
Gang's All Here, The 1943,D 23,26:4
Storm Over Lisbon 1944,S 11,14:1
Earl Carroll Vanities 1945,Ap 2,15:6
I, Jane Doe 1948,Jl 5,8:4
For the Love of Mary 1948,S 23,37:2
Adventures of Don Juan 1948,D 25,10:1
Everybody Does It 1949,O 26,32:2
Bagdad 1949,D 24,11:4
Love Happy 1950,Ap 8,9:4
Love That Brute 1950,My 27,10:6
Please Believe Me 1950,Je 12,19:4
Abbott and Costello in the Foreign Legion
1950,Ag 14,14:4
Son of Ali Baba 1952,Ag 16,7:4
Call Me Madam 1953,Mr 26,37:1
Belasco (Original Author)
Big Fight, The 1930,Je 28,9:2
Du Barry, Woman of Passion 1930,N 3,19:3
Belasko, Viktoria von
Dr Engel, Child Specialist 1937,S 20,19:2
Belayeff (Producer)
Sixty-Ninth Parallel 1942,D 13,29:1
Belcher, Charles
Rosita 1923,S 4,14:1
Thief of Bagdad, The 1924,Mr 19,19:1
Fools in the Dark 1924,Ag 18,8:2
Ben Hur 1925,D 31,10:5 (In Addenda)
Black Pirate, The 1926,Mr 9,21:4
King of Kings, The 1927,Ap 20,29:2
Ben Hur 1931,D 4,28:2
Belcher, Frank
Gloria's Romance 1916,My 23,9:2
Belden, Charles
Widow From Monte Carlo, The 1936,Ja 23,25:2
Belden, Charles (Miscellaneous)
Widow From Monte Carlo, The 1936,Ja 23,25:2
Belden, Charles (Original Author)
Mystery of the Wax Museum, The
1933,F 18,13:3
World Accuses, The 1935,Mr 21,27:2
Ghost Walks, The 1935,Mr 30,11:2
Sons of Steel 1935,Ap 15,16:3
We Have our Moments 1937,Ap 30,17:3
Bullet Scars 1942,Ap 24,21:4
Sing Your Worries Away 1942,My 15,25:2
House of Wax 1953,Ap 11,15:2
Belden, Charles (Screenwriter)
Shot in the Dark, A 1935,My 22,23:2
God's Country and the Woman 1937,Ja 11,15:5
Charlie Chan on Broadway 1937,S 20,19:1
Charlie Chan at Monte Carlo 1937,D 18,18:1

Mr Moto's Gamble 1938,Ap 8,17:2
One Wild Night 1938,Je 3,17:2
Charlie Chan in Honolulu 1938,D 31,7:3
Kid Nightingale 1939,D 8,33:6
Tear Gas Squad 1940,My 31,15:3
Beldon, Charles P (Screenwriter)
Charlie Chan at the Opera 1936,D 5,16:2
Belenda, Carla
Sealed Cargo 1951,My 24,47:1
Belenradska, Jana (Original Author)
Fifth Horseman is Fear, The 1968,My 7,52:1
Belerle, Alfred
Das Nachtigall Maedel 1933,Ja 23,9:2
Beleyev, Vassili (Director)
Russia on Parade 1946,S 9,20:1
Belfger, Lyle
Greatest Show on Earth, The 1952,Ja 11,17:2
Belfrage, Bruce
Scarlet Pimpernel, The 1935,F 8,27:2
Corridor of Mirrors 1949,Mr 23,35:3
Galloping Major, The 1951,D 17,27:2
Belfrage, Cedric (Screenwriter)
Invisible Man Returns, The 1940,Ja 16,19:2
Belgard, Arnold (Original Author)
Block-Heads 1938,Ag 30,14:2
That Night With You 1945,N 9,16:2
Belgard, Arnold (Screenwriter)
Block-Heads 1938,Ag 30,14:2
Road Show 1941,F 19,25:2
My Life With Caroline 1941,O 30,27:1
Prairie Chickens 1943,Jl 9,21:6
Calaboose 1943,Jl 30,19:2
Second Chance 1947,S 20,12:4
Invisible Wall, The 1947,N 1,11:2
Tarzan and the Slave Girl 1950,Je 24,7:3
Belhomne, Marie
Claudine 1940,Ap 1,15:2
Beliah, James Warner (Original Author)
Command, The 1954,Ja 16,10:5
Beliakov (Cinematographer)
Moscow Today 1929,My 13,27:2
Beliaver, Harry
One Potato, Two Potato 1964,Jl 30,16:1
Belier, Bernard
Carmen 1946,N 27,20:2
Belieres, Leo
Charlemagne 1935,Ag 24,18:3
Affair Lafont, The; Conflit 1939,O 9,15:2
Simple Case of Money, A 1952,F 2,11:2
Beling, Maria
Schwarzwaldmaedel 1935,O 12,12:3
Stimme der Liebe, Die 1936,My 16,11:2
Eine Frau die Weiss Was sie Will 1936,Jl 18,18:3
Belinsky, Bo
C'mon Let's Live a Little 1967,My 4,34:1
Belita
Ice-Capades 1941,S 25,29:1
Silver Skates 1943,Mr 19,15:3
Suspense 1946,Jl 5,15:3
Gangster, The 1947,O 31,29:3
Man on the Eiffel Tower, The 1950,Ja 30,12:2
Never Let Me Go 1953,Je 11,37:2
Invitation to the Dance (Ring Around the Rosy);
Ring Around the Rosy (Invitation to the
Dance) 1956,My 23,35:7
Terrace, The 1964,N 25,45:1
Belkin, Bestruce
Versailles 1929,N 16,25:2
BELL
See Also BELLE
Bell, Ann
Midsummer Night's Dream, A 1961,D 19,39:1
Devil's Own, The 1967,Mr 16,53:2
Bell, Arnold
Star of India 1956,Ap 28,11:1
Seance on a Wet Afternoon 1964,N 6,30:1
Bell, Bob (Composer)
See my Lawyer 1945,My 4,23:4
Bell, Cynthia
Those Redheads From Seattle 1953,O 1,34:2
Bell, Frederic
Paths of Glory 1957,D 26,23:2
Bell, Hank
Terror Trail 1933,F 11,11:3
Trail of the Lonesome Pine, The 1936,F 20,23:5
Geronimo 1940,F 8,18:3
Valley of the Sun 1942,Mr 19,29:2
Flame of Barbary Coast 1945,My 28,22:2
Bell, James
I Am a Fugitive From a Chain Gang
1932,N 11,17:2
King's Vacation, The 1933,Ja 20,21:2
Infernal Machine 1933,Ap 8,16:3
Private Detective 62 1933,Jl 7,20:2
White Woman 1933,N 18,18:5
I Walked With a Zombie 1943,Ap 22,31:5
Leopard Man, The 1943,My 20,26:4
My Friend Flicka 1943,My 27,21:4
So Proudly We Hail 1943,S 10,29:1
I Love a Soldier 1944,N 2,22:2
Thunderhead 1945,Mr 16,21:2
Blood on the Sun 1945,Je 29,12:2
Spiral Staircase, The 1946,F 7,29:3

Bell, James— Cont
Unknown, The 1946,Jl 20,10:3
Dead Reckoning 1947,Ja 23,31:2
Sea of Grass, The 1947,F 28,27:2
Brute Force 1947,Jl 17,16:2
Romance of Rosy Ridge, The 1947,S 12,18:3
Killer McCoy 1948,F 12,31:2
I, Jane Doe 1948,Jl 5,8:4
Sealed Verdict 1948,N 3,36:2
Streets of Laredo 1949,My 12,28:2
Roughshod 1949,Je 17,27:2
Dial 1119 1950,D 4,32:6
Company She Keeps, The 1951,Ja 29,14:4
Flying Leathernecks 1951,S 20,37:1
Japanese War Bride 1952,Ja 30,22:6
Red Mountain 1952,Ap 26,19:2
Million Dollar Mermaid 1952,D 5,35:2
All the Brothers Were Valiant 1953,D 29,19:2
Crime Wave 1954,Ja 13,26:2
Glenn Miller Story, the 1954,F 11,33:2
Riding Shotgun 1954,Ap 2,22:2
About Mrs Leslie 1954,Je 28,16:2
Black Tuesday 1955,Ja 1,16:2
Strategic Air Command 1955,Ap 21,33:1
Sincerely Yours 1955,N 3,37:1
Tribute to a Bad Man 1956,Mr 31,13:3
Huk! 1956,D 15,20:4
Tin Star, The 1957,O 24,37:2
In Love and War 1958,N 1,14:2
30 1959,N 12,27:1
Twilight of Honor 1963,N 14,41:2
Bell, Joanie
This Love of Ours 1945,N 1,20:2
Bell, Jorge (Director)
Pulpo Humano, El 1935,My 6,22:4
Bell, Karina
David Copperfield 1923,N 6,23:3
Heart of a Clown 1928,Ja 17,23:2
Last Night, The 1930,Ja 27,18:4
Bell, Kay
Those Redheads From Seattle 1953,O 1,34:2
Bell, Marie
Madame Recamier 1928,Jl 15,VIII,3:3
Chason de Paris, La; Innocents of Paris
1929,Ag 25,VIII,5:1
Figaro 1929,N 25,22:1
Nuit est a Nous, La; (Night is Ours, The)
1931,F 21,15:2
Chance, La 1932,My 28,18:2
Carnet de Bal, Un 1938,Mr 26,12:1
Charrette Fantome, La 1940,My 28,29:2
Colonel Chabert 1947,Je 21,11:2
Sandra 1966,Ja 17,32:1
Hotel Paradiso 1966,O 15,34:2
Bell, Marion
Ziegfeld Follies 1946,Mr 23,8:3
Bell, Mary
Shrike, The 1955,Jl 8,15:2
Bell, Mary Hayley (Original Author)
Whistle Down the Wind 1962,Ap 23,34:2
Bell, Monta (Director)
Broadway After Dark 1924,My 20,15:2
Snob, The 1924,D 15,14:1
Lady of the Night 1925,Mr 2,14:1
Pretty Ladies 1925,Jl 14,14:1
King on Main Street, The 1925,O 26,25:2
Lights of Old Broadway 1925,N 2,20:1
Ibanez's Torrent 1926,F 22,14:1
Upstage 1926,N 15,19:1
After Midnight 1927,Ag 16,31:2
Man, Woman and Sin 1927,D 5,26:2
Bellamy Trial, The 1929,Ja 24,30:5
Young Man of Manhattan 1930,Ap 19,15:1
East Is West 1930,N 1,23:2
Up for Murder 1931,My 30,9:2
Personal Maid 1931,S 5,7:4
Downstairs 1932,O 8,15:4
Worst Woman in Paris, The 1933,N 25,10:3
Bell, Monta (Original Author)
Popular Sin, The 1926,D 20,28:3
Worst Woman in Paris, The 1933,N 25,10:3
Bell, Monta (Producer)
West Point of the Air 1935,Ap 6,10:1
Bell, Monta (Screenwriter)
After Midnight 1927,Ag 16,31:2
Man, Woman and Sin 1927,D 5,26:2
Bell, Pearl Doles (Original Author)
Sandra 1924,D 22,20:2
Bell, Ralph
Edge of the City 1957,Ja 30,33:2
Bell, Rex
Pleasure Crazed 1929,Jl 15,25:1
Salute 1929,O 5,22:5
They Had to See Paris 1929,O 12,11:1
Courage 1930,My 23,21:1
True to the Navy 1930,My 24,21:2
Lightnin' 1930,N 29,21:4
Tombstone, The Town too Tough to Die
1942,Jl 27,18:2
Bell, Rodney
Hitch-Hiker, The 1953,Ap 30,39:3
Bell, Spencer
Midnight Taxi, The 1928,O 29,29:1

Bell, Thomas (Original Author)
From This Day Forward 1946,Ap 20,16:2
Bell, Tom
Kitchen, The 1961,N 2,42:1
Damn the Defiant 1962,S 20,29:2
Payroll 1963,My 11,15:2
L-Shaped Room, The 1963,My 28,32:1
Sands of Beersheba 1966,My 6,54:2
Blues for Lovers 1966,S 8,43:1
Long Day's Dying, The 1968,My 29,20:1
He Who Rides a Tiger 1968,S 10,39:1
Bell, Tom (Miscellaneous)
Kelly the Second 1936,O 3,21:2
Bell, Tula
Blue Bird, The 1918,Ap 1,9:3
Deliverance 1919,Ag 19,10:1
Bell, Valdemar D (Miscellaneous)
Don Quixote 1934,D 24,17:1
Bell, Vereen (Original Author)
Swamp Water 1941,N 17,15:2
Lure of the Wilderness 1952,O 4,15:2
Bella, Nicholas
Lady in Question, The 1940,D 10,33:2
Bellah, James Warner (Original Author)
Dancing Lady 1933,D 1,23:2
Fort Apache 1948,Je 25,26:2
She Wore a Yellow Ribbon 1949,N 18,35:2
Rio Grande 1950,N 20,21:2
Ten Tall Men 1951,O 27,10:5
Target Zero 1955,N 16,43:2
Bellah, James Warner (Screenwriter)
Sea Chase, The 1955,Je 11,8:7
Sergeant Rutledge 1960,My 26,37:1
Thunder of Drums, A 1961,S 27,35:1
X-15 1962,Ap 5,30:2
Man Who Shot Liberty Valance, The
1962,My 24,29:2
Bellamann, Henry (Original Author)
Kings Row 1942,F 3,23:2
Bellamy, Earl (Director)
Blackjack Ketchum Desperado 1956,Ap 5,26:2
Fluffy 1965,O 21,57:2
Munster, Go Home 1966,Je 16,53:4
Bellamy, Franklyn
Wanted Men 1936,Jl 8,15:2
Bellamy, Madge
Hail the Woman 1922,Ja 16,18:3
Lorna Doone 1922,D 4,20:2
Hottentot, The 1923,F 19,10:1
Soul of the Beast, The 1923,My 22,14:4
Garrison's Finish 1923,My 28,18:2
Love's Whirlpool 1924,Mr 11,16:2
Love and Glory 1924,Ag 5,10:2
Iron Horse, The 1924,Ag 29,6:1
Dancers, The 1925,Ja 26,22:1
Parasite, The 1925,F 16,24:1
Wings of Youth 1925,Ap 20,18:1 (Incorrect in
this edition; use 1925,Ap 28,18:1 elsewhere)
Lightnin 1925,Jl 22,14:4
Summer Bachelors 1926,D 20,28:3
Bertha, The Sewing Machine Girl 1927,Ja 4,21:1
Ankles Preferred 1927,Ap 18,21:2
Telephone Girl, The 1927,My 16,24:2
Very Confidential 1927,N 29,31:1
Silk Legs 1927,D 26,26:6
Soft Living 1928,F 27,16:2
Play Girl, The 1928,Ap 23,20:2
Mother Knows Best 1928,S 17,27:1
Tonight at Twelve 1929,S 23,24:3
White Zombie 1932,Jl 29,18:2
Charlie Chan in London 1934,S 13,26:1
Great Hotel Murder, The 1935,F 28,17:4
Daring Young Man, The 1935,Jl 18,15:2
Bellamy, Ralph
Secret Six, The 1931,My 2,23:4
Magnificent Lie, The 1931,Jl 25,11:6
Surrender 1931,N 28,20:4
Forbidden 1932,Ja 11,28:5
Disorderly Conduct 1932,Ap 11,19:2
Young America 1932,My 7,11:5
Woman in Room 13, The 1932,My 21,9:2
Rebecca of Sunnybrook Farm 1932,Jl 30,16:5
Air Mail 1932,N 7,20:3
Second Hand Wife 1933,Ja 14,8:4
Destination Unknown 1933,Ap 8,16:2
Parole Girl 1933,Ap 10,8:2
Picture Snatcher 1933,My 19,20:3
Below the Sea 1933,Je 3,16:4
Narrow Corner, The 1933,Jl 14,15:3
Flying Devils 1933,Ag 26,14:3
Ever in my Heart 1933,O 13,25:3
Headline Shooters 1933,O 23,18:3
Blind Adventure 1933,O 31,24:3
Ace of Aces 1933,N 11,10:4
Before Midnight 1934,Ja 10,24:3
Spitfire 1934,Mr 9,22:3
Once to Every Woman 1934,Mr 26,22:3
This Man is Mine 1934,Ap 13,25:1
Helldorado 1935,Ja 7,13:2
Wedding Night, The 1935,Mr 16,19:1
Gigolette 1935,My 13,18:6
Air Hawks 1935,Je 4,26:5
Hands Across the Table 1935,N 2,13:2

Final Hour, The 1936,Ag 1,16:3
Man Who Lived Twice, The 1936,O 12,23:2
Counterfeit Lady 1937,Ja 11,15:6
It Can't Last Forever 1937,Jl 30,22:5
Awful Truth, The 1937,N 5,19:3
Crime of Dr Hallet, The 1938,Mr 24,21:3
Fools for Scandal 1938,Mr 25,15:3
Boy Meets Girl 1938,Ag 27,7:2
Carefree 1938,S 23,35:1
Girls' School 1938,N 3,27:1
Trade Winds 1939,Ja 13,17:2
Let Us Live 1939,Mr 30,19:2
Blind Alley 1939,My 23,27:2
His Girl Friday 1940,Ja 12,13:2
Flight Angels 1940,My 27,23:2
Brother Orchid 1940,Je 8,18:2
Queen of the Mob 1940,Jl 1,23:2
Dance, Girl, Dance 1940,O 11,25:2
Meet the Wildcat 1940,O 23,27:2
Ellery Queen, Master Detective 1940,D 19,33:1
Ellery Queen's Penthouse Mystery
1941,Mr 7,17:2
Footsteps in the Dark 1941,Mr 15,13:2
Affectionaly Yours 1941,My 24,18:2
Ellery Queen and the Perfect Crime
1941,Ag 11,17:3
Dive Bomber 1941,Ag 30,10:2
Ellery Queen and the Murder Ring
1941,O 21,29:4
Wolf Man, The 1941,D 22,24:5
Men of Texas 1942,Jl 13,18:3 (In Addenda)
Lady in a Jam 1942,S 11,25:2
Stage Door Canteen 1943,Je 25,13:2
Guest in the House 1945,F 16,19:2
Delightfully Dangerous 1945,Je 9,17:3
Lady on a Train 1945,S 15,21:2
Court-Martial of Billy Mitchell, The
1955,D 23,14:2
Sunrise at Campobello 1960,S 29,32:1
Professionals, The 1966,N 3,45:1
Rosemary's Baby 1968,Je 13,57:1
Bellanova, Piero Prof (Screenwriter)
Fuga, La 1966,Mr 22,33:1
Bellaskaya, L
Storm Over Asla 1930,S 8,17:1
Bellaver, Harry
Another Thin Man 1939,N 24,29:1
House on Ninety-Second Street, The
1945,S 27,24:7
Perfect Strangers 1950,Mr 11,8:2
Side Street 1950,Mr 24,29:2
No Way Out 1950,Ag 17,23:1
Lemon Drop Kid, The 1951,Mr 22,41:2
Stage to Tucson 1951,My 5,14:2
Tanks are Coming, The 1951,D 6,42:4
Something to Live For 1952,Mr 8,11:2
From Here to Eternity 1953,Ag 6,16:2
Miss Sadie Thompson 1953,D 24,9:1
Love Me or Leave Me 1955,My 27,14:1
Serenade 1956,Mr 24,21:1 (Incorrect in this
edition; use 1956,Mr 23,21:1 elsewhere)
Birds and the Bees, The 1956,Ap 23,22:1
Slaughter on Tenth Avenue 1957,N 6,43:1
Old Man and the Sea, The 1958,O 8,41:1
BELLE
See Also BELL
Belle, Yva
Portrait of a Woman 1946,Ap 22,26:2
Bellem, Robert Leslie (Original Author)
Blackmail 1947,Ag 5,26:3
Belles, Herbert
Red Mountain 1952,Ap 26,19:2
BELLEW
See Also BALLOU
Bellew, Anita
Lummox 1930,Mr 24,25:1
Bellew, Kyrle
Summer Bachelors 1926,D 20,28:3
Hit of the Show 1928,Jl 9,25:1
Strange Cargo 1929,F 18,28:1
Disraeli 1929,O 3,27:5
Lummox 1930,Mr 24,25:1
Lady Who Dared, The 1931,Je 6,15:5
Norah O'Neale 1934,O 25,26:3
Bellia, Aida
Gesuzza, La Sposa Garibaldina 1936,N 3,33:4
Bellini, Carlo
Hell Raiders of the Deep 1954,Jl 3,9:2
Bellini, Francesca
Bachelor Flat 1962,Ja 13,14:1
Who's Minding the Store? 1963,N 29,67:6
(Incorrect in this edition; use 1963,N 28,67:6
elsewhere)
Bellis, Guy
Cardinal Richelieu 1935,Ap 19,24:2
Little Princess, The 1939,Mr 11,21:1
Adventure in Diamonds 1940,Ap 4,27:2
Kathleen 1941,D 19,35:3
Bellmore, Lionel
Service de Luxe 1938,O 24,13:2
Belloc-Lowndes, Marie Mrs (Original Author)
Lodger, The 1944,Ja 20,15:3

Bellocchio, Marco (Director)
Fist in his Pocket 1968,My 28,40:1
Bellocchio, Marco (Original Author)
China Is Near 1968,Ja 9,37:1
Bellocchio, Marco (Screenwriter)
China Is Near 1968,Ja 9,37:1
Fist in his Pocket 1968,My 28,40:1
Belloise, Steve
Requiem for a Heavyweigh 1962,O 17,35:1
Bellon, Loleh
Skipper Next to God 1953,Ja 13,24:2
Bellran, Pedro (Miscellaneous)
Moment of Truth, The 1965,Ag 10,18:1
Belluscio, Daniel
Huella; Trial 1940,O 22,27:3
Belmondo, Jean-Paul
Breathless 1961,F 8,26:1
Love and the Frenchwoman; (Francaise et
l'Amour, La) 1961,F 28,38:2
Two Women; (Ciociara, La) 1961,My 9,43:2
Cheaters, The; (Tricheurs, Les) 1961,Je 5,37:4
Leda 1961,Jl 19,33:1
Viaccia, La 1962,S 21,35:1
Monkey in Winter 1963,F 1,7:2
Moderato Cantabile 1964,Ja 7,24:1
Doulos-The Finger Man 1964,Mr 3,31:1
That Man From Rio 1964,Je 9,30:1
Cartouche 1964,Jl 22,39:1
Woman Is a Woman, A 1964,S 19,19:1
Sweet and Sour 1964,D 28,34:2
Banana Peel; Peau de Banane 1965,Ja 19,29:1
Male Hunt; Chasse a l'Homme, La
1965,Ap 20,42:1
Backfire 1965,Ap 27,27:1
Greed in the Sun 1965,Ag 19,35:3
Up to his Ears 1966,My 18,37:1
Weekend at Dunkirk 1966,My 19,51:2
Pierre le Fou; Peter the Crazy 1966,S 22,57:2
Is Paris Burning? 1966,N 11,36:1
Casino Royale 1967,Ap 29,25:1
Thief of Paris, The 1967,Ag 24,43:2
Tender Scoundrel 1967,N 16,58:2
Belmont, Baldy
Young April 1926,Ag 31,15:3
Belmont, Eleanor Robeson (Original Author)
Case of the Black Parrot, The 1941,Ja 10,23:3
Belmont, Gladys
Redskin 1929,Ja 28,21:1
Belmont, Joan (Producer)
Burma Chapter 1945,Ag 7,10:6
Belmont, Morgan Mrs
Way Down East 1931,Mr 16,25:1
Belmont, Terry
Men Against the Sky 1940,S 12,31:2
Belmont, Virginia
Pirates of Capri, The 1949,D 26,33:5
Dead Woman's Kiss, A 1951,O 6,16:4
Singing Taxi Driver 1953,My 16,10:1
Belmore, Bertha
Are You a Mason? 1934,O 30,23:5
Broken Blossoms 1937,Ja 14,16:3
Belmore, Daisy
We Americans 1928,Mr 29,25:3
Seven Days' Leave 1930,Ja 25,13:2
Alias French Gertie 1930,Ap 14,24:2
Scarlet Pages 1930,D 6,21:3
My Past 1931,Mr 12,22:7
Born to Love 1931,Ap 25,23:4
Belmore, Lionel
Jes' Call Me Jim 1920,My 24,20:3
Madame X 1920,S 27,18:1
Moonlight Follies 1921,S 19,12:1
Two Minutes to Go 1921,O 24,13:1
Kindred of the Dust 1922,Ag 28,14:1
Peg o'my Heart 1923,Ja 22,10:1
Within the Law 1923,Ap 30,11:2
Red Lights 1923,S 10,15:4
Boy of Flanders, A 1924,Ap 15,24:1
Sea Hawk, The 1924,Je 3,22:1
Man Who Fights Alone, The 1924,Jl 28,12:2
Eve's Secret 1925,Je 11,14:3
Never the Twain Shall Meet 1925,Jl 29,24:4
Bardelys The Magnificent 1926,N 1,28:1 (In
Addenda)
Sorrell and Son 1927,N 14,26:1
Rose-Marie 1928,F 13,16:2
Play Girl, The 1928,Ap 23,20:2
Matinee Idol, The 1928,Ap 24,29:3
Good-Bye Kiss, The 1928,N 12,18:2
Circus Kid, The 1928,D 17,23:1
Redeeming Sin, The 1929,F 16,14:6
Love Parade, The 1929,N 20,32:6
Rogue Song, The 1930,Ja 29,26:4
Captain of the Guard 1930,Mr 29,23:1
Playing Around 1930,Mr 31,24:3
Hell's Island 1930,Jl 19,7:5
Sweet Kitty Bellairs 1930,S 6,9:2
Boudoir Diplomat, The 1930,D 8,26:1
One Heavenly Night 1931,Ja 10,19:2
Ten Nights in a Barroom 1931,F 28,15:2
Alexander Hamilton 1931,S 17,21:4

Belmore, Lionel— Cont

Frankenstein 1931,D 5,21:2
Fame Street 1932,Ap 2,13:2
So Big 1932,Ap 30,19:3
Vampire Bat, The 1933,Ja 23,9:1
Oliver Twist 1933,Ap 13,15:3
Warrior's Husband, The 1933,My 12,20:4
I Am Suzanne 1934,Ja 19,24:3
Count of Monte Cristo, The 1934,S 27,25:2
Caravan 1934,S 28,27:1
Vanessa: Her Love Story 1935,Ap 13,11:3
Mary of Scotland 1936,Jl 31,22:2
Toast of New York, The 1937,Jl 23,16:2
Tower of London 1939,D 12,37:2
My Son, My Son! 1940,My 10,26:6
Diamond Frontiers 1940,O 4,29:2

Belogoskino (Producer)

Rubicon 1931,S 21,20:2

Beloin, Edmund

Paris Holiday 1958,My 10,19:2

Beloin, Edmund (Original Author)

Because of Him 1946,Ja 25,26:6
Road to Rio 1948,F 19,29:3
Lemon Drop Kid, The 1951,Mr 22,41:2
My Favorite Spy 1951,D 26,19:3
Donovan's Reef 1963,Jl 25,14:1

Beloin, Edmund (Producer)

Great Lover, The 1949,N 24,48:2

Beloin, Edmund (Screenwriter)

Buck Benny Rides Again 1940,Ap 25,28:4
Love Thy Neighbor 1940,D 18,32:5
Lady on a Train 1945,S 15,21:2
Because of Him 1946,Ja 25,26:6
Harvey Girls, The 1946,Ja 25,26:2
Ladies' Man 1947,Ja 13,18:5
My Favorite Brunette 1947,Mr 20,38:2
Road to Rio 1948,F 19,29:3
Connecticut Yankee in King Arthur's Court, A
  1949,Ap 8,31:2
Top o' the Morning 1949,S 1,25:2
Great Lover, The 1949,N 24,48:2
Sad Sack, The 1957,N 28,57:1
Don't Give up the Ship 1959,Jl 9,22:1
Visit to a Small Planet 1960,Ap 14,34:1
G I Blues 1960,N 5,28:1
All in a Nights Work 1961,Mr 23,28:1

Belokurov, V

House of Death 1932,Ag 13,18:6
Paris Commune 1937,Je 2,20:4
Wings of Victory 1941,N 17,15:2

Belot, Marthe

Living Dead Man, The 1927,Mr 7,16:3

Belousow, Serge

No Way Back 1955,My 19,25:5

Belov, Goigori

Life in Bloom 1949,My 9,20:4
Country Doctor, The 1953,F 16,16:2
Rimsky-Korsakov 1954,Mr 1,16:3
Gift for Music 1957,Jl 15,15:2

Belov, Yuri

Carnival in Moscow 1957,N 4,40:1

Belsky, Leno

Country Doctor, The 1953,F 16,16:2

Belsnick, Myron (Director)

Common Law, The 1923,O 29,18:1

Belson, Jerry (Producer)

How Sweet It Is 1968,Ag 22,47:1

Belson, Jerry (Screenwriter)

How Sweet It Is 1968,Ag 22,47:1

Belson, Jordan (Director)

Phenomena 1968,Jl 19,30:1

Beltarini, Cesare

Destino, Il 1938,F 8,17:3

Belton, Eve

Time Lost and Time Remembered
  1966,Ag 30,35:2

Beltram, Ray

This Woman Is Mine 1941,O 13,21:2

Beltran, Alma

Dragoon Wells Massacre 1957,My 6,25:2

Beltran, Guillermo

Pandora and the Flying Dutchman 1951,D 7,35:2

Beltran, Henry

High Wind in Jamaica, A 1965,Je 17,27:2

Beltran, Neftali (Screenwriter)

Rosanna 1956,My 17,37:2

Belusova, M

Life is Beautiful 1933,F 13,11:5

Belyaev, V (Director)

Black Sea Fighters 1943,Jl 28,18:3
People's Avengers 1944,Je 15,16:3
Lenin 1950,Mr 13,15:2

Belyaev, V (Screenwriter)

Lenin 1950,Mr 13,15:2

Belyavsky, Aleksandr

Yolanta 1964,D 23,22:3

Bemelmans, Ludwig (Original Author)

Yolanda and the Thief 1945,N 23,26:2

Ben

Gentle Giant 1968,Ap 20,26:1

Ben-Ami, Jacob

Wandering Jew, The 1933,O 21,11:2

Ben-Ami, Jacob (Director)

Green Fields 1937,O 12,31:4

Ben Carter Choir

Mister Big 1943,Je 14,13:4

Benaderet, Bea

Tender is the Night 1962,Ja 20,13:2

Benanova, Fortunio

Bad Men of Tombstone 1949,Mr 5,10:2

Benard, Raymond

Night Life of the Gods 1935,F 23,14:6

Benardino, John

Naked and the Dead, The 1958,Ag 7,21:1

Benari, Carlo (Screenwriter)

Four Days of Naples, The 1963,Mr 20,5:1
Climax, The 1967,S 12,55:1

Benassi, Memo

Signora di Tutti, La 1936,Mr 26,27:3
Signora Paradiso 1937,Jl 22,15:2
Scipio Africanus 1939,S 23,22:2
Rossini 1948,Ja 31,14:2

Benatzky, Ralph (Composer)

Der Unsterbliche Lump 1932,My 20,22:3

Benatzky, Ralph (Miscellaneous)

White Horse Inn, The 1957,D 4,50:3

Benavente, Lolita

Esperame 1933,Jl 3,14:6

Benavides, Jose

En un Burro Tres Baturros; Three Rustics on one
  Donkey 1940,S 21,13:3

Benavides, Jose (Director)

Tierra de Pasiones 1944,N 7,24:3

Benazeraf, Jose (Producer)

Port of Desire 1960,N 3,49:2

Bence, Amelia

Matrero, El; Outlaw, The 1940,Mr 18,13:2

Benchley, Nathaniel (Original Author)

Sail a Crooked Ship 1962,F 3,12:6

Benchley, Robert

Headline Shooters 1933,O 23,18:3
Dancing Lady 1933,D 1,23:2
China Seas 1935,Ag 10,16:4
Piccadilly Jim 1936,Ag 31,19:1
Broadway Melody of 1938 1937,S 3,12:1
Live, Love and Learn 1937,N 19,27:2
Foreign Correspondent 1940,Ag 28,15:2
Hired Wife 1940,S 14,11:2
Nice Girl 1941,Mr 27,29:6
Reluctant Dragon, The 1941,Jl 25,12:2
You'll Never Get Rich 1941,O 24,27:2
Bedtime Story 1942,Mr 20,25:4
Take a Letter Darling 1942,My 28,13:2
Major and the Minor, The 1942,S 17,21:3
I Married a Witch 1942,N 20,27:2
Sky's the Limit, The 1943,S 3,15:2
Song of Russia 1944,F 11,17:2
See Here Private Hargrove 1944,Mr 22,17:2
Her Primitive Man 1944,Ap 1,11:1
Janie 1944,Ag 5,16:2
Pan-Americana 1945,Mr 23,13:2
Practically Yours 1945,Mr 29,18:2
It's in the Bag 1945,Je 11,12:1
Duffy's Tavern 1945,S 6,23:3
Week-End at the Waldorf 1945,O 5,27:2
Kiss and Tell 1945,O 26,16:2
Stork Club, The 1945,D 20,18:2
Snafu 1945,D 26,15:2
Road to Utopia 1946,F 28,20:2
Bride Wore Boots, The 1946,Je 6,16:3
Janie Gets Married 1946,Je 15,24:2

Benchley, Robert (Miscellaneous)

Foreign Correspondent 1940,Ag 28,15:2
Reluctant Dragon, The 1941,Jl 25,12:2

Benchley, Robert (Screenwriter)

Murder on a Honeymoon 1935,Mr 4,12:2

Benda, W T

American Venus, The 1926,Ja 26,25:2

Bendani, Poldo

Viva Maria 1965,D 20,48:2

Bender, Dawn

Actress, The 1953,O 13,34:1

Bender, Erich F (Director)

Helga 1968,O 5,40:1

Bender, Erich F (Screenwriter)

Helga 1968,O 5,40:1

Bender, Henry

Ein Ausgekochter Junge 1932,My 3,25:5
Kyritz-Pyritz 1932,Ag 9,20:5
Zu Befehl, Herr Unteroffizier 1934,Je 16,20:3

Bender, Russ

Amazing Colossal Man, The 1957,O 26,19:2
Compulsion 1959,Ap 2,26:2
Gathering of Eagles, A 1963,Jl 11,21:2
Satan Bug, The 1965,Ap 15,38:1
Born Wild 1968,D 12,62:6

Bendi, Alexis

Horse Ate the Hat, The 1931,S 1,30:6

Bendick, Robert (Director)

Cinerama Holiday 1955,F 9,31:1

Bendix, William

Woman of the Year 1942,F 6,23:2
Wake Island 1942,S 2,19:2
Glass Key, The 1942,O 16,23:1
Who Done It 1942,D 3,35:2

Bendix, William— Cont

Star Spangled Rhythm 1942,D 31,20:1
Crystal Ball, The 1943,F 19,22:2
Taxi, Mister 1943,Ap 15,20:2
China 1943,Ap 22,31:2
Hostages 1943,O 11,23:2
Guadalcanal Diary 1943,N 18,29:1
Lifeboat 1944,Ja 13,17:1
Hairy Ape, The 1944,Jl 3,8:3
Greenwich Village 1944,S 28,26:2
Abroad With two Yanks 1944,O 26,19:7
It's in the Bag 1945,Je 11,12:1
Bell for Adano, A 1945,Jl 6,8:3
Don Juan Quilligan 1945,Jl 30,16:2
Sentimental Journey 1946,Mr 7,33:2
Dark Corner, The 1946,My 9,27:3
Blue Dahlia, The 1946,My 9,27:3
Two Years Before the Mast 1946,S 25,39:2
White Tie and Tails 1946,N 8,28:2
I'll Be Yours 1947,F 22,16:2
Blaze of Noon 1947,Mr 5,31:2
Calcutta 1947,Ap 24,30:2
Web, The 1947,Je 5,32:1
Where There's Life 1947,D 25,32:1
Time of your Life, The 1948,My 27,29:2
Babe Ruth Story, The 1948,Jl 29,17:2
Race Street 1948,Ag 23,13:3
Connecticut Yankee in King Arthur's Court, A
  1949,Ap 8,31:2
Life of Riley, The 1949,Ap 18,18:4
Streets of Laredo 1949,My 12,28:2
Big Steal, The 1949,Jl 11,13:2
Johnny Holiday 1950,My 17,36:1
Kill the Umpire 1950,My 29,10:6
Gambling House 1951,Mr 19,23:2
Detective Story 1951,N 7,35:2
Submarine Command 1952,Ja 19,13:2
Girl in Every Port, A 1952,F 14,23:1
Macao 1952,My 1,34:2
Blackbeard the Pirate 1952,D 26,20:3
Dangerous Mission 1954,Mr 6,13:5
Crashout 1955,Jl 9,9:2
Deep Six, The 1958,Ja 16,32:1
Portrait of a Sinner 1961,D 7,52:1
Boys' Night Out 1962,Je 22,15:2
For Love or Money 1963,Ag 8,19:1
Law of the Lawless 1964,Ag 27,28:2
Johnny Nobody 1965,N 24,35:1

Bendova, Jirka

Closely Watched Trains 1967,O 16,59:2

Bendow, Wilhelm

Blonde Nachtigall, Die 1931,Ag 22,7:5
Kaiserliebchen 1931,N 12,30:2
Schuechterne Casanova, Der 1936,Ag 22,6:2
Familie Schimek 1939,S 2,20:2

Benedek, Laslo (Director)

Kissing Bandit, The 1948,N 19,35:2
Port of New York 1950,F 3,29:2
Death of a Salesman 1951,D 21,21:3
Wild One, The 1953,D 31,9:2
Bengal Brigade 1954,N 13,13:2
Malaga 1962,F 22,20:3

Benedek, Laslo (Producer)

Mask of the Himalayas 1953,Ag 12,22:3

Benedet, Julian

Di que me Quieres; Say That You Love Me
  1939,Ap 24,13:2

Benedetti, A (Director)

Zio d'America, Lo; Uncle From America, The
  1939,S 15,26:5

Benedetti, Adriana

Doctor, Beware 1951,Ap 30,16:3

Benedetti, Wanda

Too Bad She's Bad 1955,D 26,23:2

Benedic, Jule

Go, Man, Go 1954,Mr 10,29:5

Benedico, Augusto

Exterminating Angel, The 1967,Ag 22,33:1

Benedict, Billy

Hold That Co-ed 1938,S 24,13:1
Confessions of Boston Blackie 1941,D 8,31:2
Aerial Gunner 1943,Je 26,10:2

Benedict, Brooks

Only Woman, The 1924,N 3,20:1
Freshman, The 1925,S 21,12:4
Why Girls Go Back Home 1926,My 18,28:2
Tramp, Tramp, Tramp 1926,My 24,24:3
Ranson's Folly 1926,My 31,10:2
White Flannels 1927,Mr 22,31:2
Orchids and Ermine 1927,Ap 19,24:4
Lost at the Front 1927,Je 14,33:2
Drop Kick, The 1927,S 20,32:2
Gorilla, The 1927,N 21,20:1
Speedy 1928,Ap 7,20:4
Moran of the Marines 1928,O 15,16:1
Clear the Decks 1929,Ap 1,22:1
Sophomore, The 1929,Ag 24,11:5
Street of Chance 1930,F 3,17:1
Office Wife, The 1930,S 27,21:3
Widow From Chicago, The 1930,D 20,20:6
Gun Smoke 1931,Ap 24,27:1
Reckless Living 1931,D 5,21:2
What Price Hollywood 1932,Jl 16,5:5
No Other Woman 1933,Ja 30,9:4 (In Addenda)

Benedict, Brooks— Cont
Cheating Blondes 1933,My 20,11:4
Murder on a Honeymoon 1935,Mr 4,12:2
Follow the Fleet 1936,F 21,21:2
Love Takes Flight 1937,S 27,24:3
Freshman, The 1953,Ap 28,31:6
Benedict, Harold
Paths of Glory 1957,D 26,23:2
Benedict, Howard (Producer)
Curtain Call 1940,Ap 19,25:2
Saint Takes Over, The 1940,My 28,29:3
Millionaires in Prison 1940,Jl 16,21:3
Men Against the Sky 1940,S 12,31:2
Let's Make Music 1941,Ja 23,19:2
Saint in Palm Springs, The 1941,Ja 31,15:5
Parachute Battalion 1941,Ag 29,13:2
Hurry, Charlie, Hurry 1941,N 12,31:3
Date With the Falcon, A 1941,N 25,33:2
Call out the Marines 1942,Ja 26,18:3
Obliging Young Lady 1942,F 13,24:4
Falcon takes Over, The 1942,My 30,9:2
Sherlock Holmes and the Secret Weapon 1943,Ja 5,15:2
Patrick the Great 1945,Ap 13,15:2
This Love of Ours 1945,N 1,20:2
White Tie and Tails 1946,N 8,28:2
Benedict, Jean
Slight Case of Murder, A 1938,F 28,19:1
Patient in Room 18, The 1938,Ap 22,15:6
Benedict, Kingsley
Man of Action, A 1923,Je 4,13:3
Fast and Furious 1927,Jl 4,20:3
Benedict, Richard
See my Lawyer 1945,My 4,23:4
Walk in the Sun, A 1946,Ja 12,10:6
O S S 1946,My 27,15:5
Till the End of Time 1946,Jl 24,24:1
Guilt of Janet Ames, The 1947,My 23,31:2
Backlash 1947,My 24,10:5
Crossfire 1947,Jl 23,19:2
Race Street 1948,Ag 23,13:3
City Across the River 1949,Ap 8,31:3
Scene of the Crime 1949,Jl 29,12:2
Ace in the Hole 1951,Je 30,8:6
Okinawa 1952,Ap 24,38:3
Juggler, The 1953,My 6,39:2
Act of Love 1954,F 12,20:5
Shrike, The 1955,Jl 8,15:2
Monkey on my Back 1957,My 30,23:2
Beginning of the End 1957,Jl 4,16:1
Ocean's Eleven 1960,Ag 11,19:1
Benedict, Robert L (Producer)
ThIs is Cinerama 1952,O 1,1:7
Benedict, William
Doubting Thomas 1935,Jl 11,24:2
Silk Hat Kid 1935,Ag 7,22:5
Way Down East 1935,O 31,16:2
Three Kids and a Queen 1935,N 9,19:2
Show Them no Mercy 1935,D 9,25:2
Your Uncle Dudley 1935,D 12,33:4
Country Doctor, The 1936,Mr 13,32:2 (Incorrect in this edition; use 1936,Mr 13,27:2 elsewhere)
Witness Chair, The 1936,Ap 18,19:2
Ramona 1936,O 7,32:4
Libeled Lady 1936,O 31,24:2
King of the Newsboys 1938,Ap 2,18:2
Little Tough Guys in Society 1938,N 21,14:4
Newsboys' Home 1939,Ja 23,8:2
Melody Ranch 1940,D 26,23:3
Benedictus, David (Original Author)
You're a Big Boy Now 1967,Mr 21,35:3
Beneditti, Nelly
Soft Skin, The; Peau Douce, La 1964,O 13,49:2
Benefield, Barry (Original Author)
Valiant Is the Word for Carrie 1936,O 8,27:2
Benerji, Kanu
Pather Panchali 1958,S 23,37:2
Benes, Jara
Versuchen Sie Meine Schwester 1931,Je 20,20:4
Benes, Karel J (Original Author)
Stolen Life 1939,Je 15,27:2
Stolen Life, A 1946,My 2,27:4
Benes, Mark
Far for Moscow 1951,Jl 2,16:6
Benesh, Natalie
Babes in Bagdad 1954,Ap 5,21:3
Benet, Brenda
Track of Thunder 1968,F 1,28:4
Benet, Marianne
Night Fighters, The 1960,D 15,59:1
Boy Who Stole a Million, The 1960,D 22,18:3
Benet, Stephen Vincent (Original Author)
Love, Honor and Behave 1938,Mr 21,18:2
All That Money Can Buy 1941,O 17,27:2
Just for You 1952,O 9,40:6
Seven Brides for Seven Brothers 1954,Jl 23,8:3
Benet, Stephen Vincent (Screenwriter)
Cheers for Miss Bishop 1941,Mr 14,17:2
All That Money Can Buy 1941,O 17,27:2
Benetti, Adriana
Foria 1948,Ja 21,30:2
Furia 1948,Ja 21,30:2
Four Steps in the Clouds 1948,N 22,25:2
Fear No Evil 1949,Mr 31,31:2

Tombolo 1949,D 31,9:4
Dark River 1956,F 27,19:4
Benevuti, Anna (Screenwriter)
Woman 1950,F 9,36:6
Benfer, Friedrich
Pechmarie 1935,Ap 22,14:3
Signora di Tutti, La 1936,Mr 26,27:3
Drei Blaue Jungs-Ein Blondes Maedel 1936,D 29,16:3
Nacht mit dem Kaiser, Die 1937,Ag 14,16:5
Andalusische Naechte; Nights in Andalusia 1938,S 24,13:2
Bengal, Ben (Original Author)
Illegal Entry 1949,Je 11,11:2
Bengal, Ben (Screenwriter)
Crack-Up 1946,S 7,11:1
Benge, Wilson
Fast and Furious 1927,Jl 4,20:3
That's my Daddy 1928,F 13,16:2
Bulldog Drummond 1929,My 3,23:2
Untamed 1929,N 30,23:1
This Thing Called Love 1929,D 14,22:4
Raffles 1930,Jl 25,20:4
Her Wedding Night 1930,S 29,19:1
Charley's Aunt 1930,D 26,18:4
Bat Whispers, The 1931,Ja 16,27:1
Men in her Life 1931,N 30,16:2
Cynara 1932,D 26,26:2
Ghost Walks, The 1935,Mr 30,11:2
Shadow Strikes, The 1937,S 13,17:1
Trade Winds 1939,Ja 13,17:2
Bengell, Norma
Given Word, The 1964,Mr 25,47:1
Mafioso 1964,Jl 1,42:1
Benglia, Habib
Roots of Heaven, The 1958,O 16,46:1
Bengston, Eric (Composer)
Karl Fredrik Reigns 1938,F 2,15:2
John Ericsson Victor of Hampton Roads 1938,My 18,17:2
Bengtsson, Bengt-Ake
Dreams; Kvinnodrom 1960,Je 1,42:1
Bengtsson, Frans (Original Author)
Long Ships, The 1964,Je 25,25:1
Benham, Albert (Original Author)
Adventure in Washington 1941,Ag 1,11:3
Benham, Harry
Town That Forgot God, The 1922,N 1,16:3
Benham, Joan
Man Who Loved Redheads, The 1955,Jl 26,29:2
Bridal Path, The 1959,D 21,34:2
Murder Ahoy 1964,S 23,55:3
Benier, Guy (Producer)
Naked Childhood 1968,S 28,36:1
Benio, Serge
Biches, Les 1968,S 27,34:1
Benita, Ina
Maryjka 1934,D 3,15:2
Milosc Wszystko Zwycieza 1936,Ja 28,15:3
Benjamin, Adrian
Doctor Faustus 1968,F 7,38:1
Benjamin, Benny (Composer)
Melody Time 1948,My 28,28:2
Benjamin, Bernie (Composer)
Fun and Fancy Free 1947,S 29,17:2 (In Addenda)
Benjamin, James (Miscellaneous)
Jonas 1959,Ap 30,37:1
Benjamin, Philip (Original Author)
Quick, Before it Melts 1965,Ap 1,30:2
Benjamin, Richard
Thunder Over the Plains 1953,D 10,64:4
Benjamin, Sonjia
Return of Mr Moto 1965,D 2,48:1
Benjamin, William (Miscellaneous)
Champagne Murders, The 1968,Ap 25,53:1
Benkhoff, Fita
Beiden Seehunde, Die 1935,Mr 9,19:2
Schwarzer Jaeger Johanna 1935,Ap 1,17:2
Schwarzer Jaeger Johanna 1935,Ap 1,17:2
Pantoffelhelden 1935,O 21,22:5
Alte Kameraden 1936,Ap 27,19:3
Koenigin der Liebe 1936,My 4,16:2
Schuechterne Casanova, Der 1936,Ag 22,6:2
Boccaccio 1937,F 27,9:3
Werf zum Graven Hecht, Die; Gray Pikes Wharf, The 1938,Ap 18,11:2
Liebe im Gleitflug; Love in Stunt Flying 1938,Je 18,18:3
Henker Fraven und Soldaten; Hangmen, Women and Soldiers 1940,Ja 13,11:3
Opernball; Opera Ball 1940,O 15,29:2
Beggar Student, The 1958,Ja 25,14:3
Benkhoff, Rudolf
Diskretion-Ehrensache; Discretion with Honor 1939,Mr 13,12:3
Benko, Gyula
Varju a Toronyoran; Crow on the Tower 1939,N 18,22:6
Benltez Sisters
I Love, You Love 1962,N 10,16:2

Bennati, Giuseppe (Director)
Red Lips 1964,Mr 19,28:2
Benner, Priscilla
Red Kimono, The 1926,F 3,23:1
Bennett, Alma
Lilies of the Field 1924,Mr 17,19:1
Dawn of a Tomorrow, The 1924,Mr 26,19:2
Triumph 1924,Ap 21,21:4
Why Men Leave Home 1924,My 12,14:4
Lost World, The 1925,F 9,15:3
Light of the Western Stars, The 1925,Je 24,14:3
Silent Lover, The 1926,N 15,19:1
Long Pants 1927,Mr 29,23:2
Orchids and Ermine 1927,Ap 19,24:4
Good-Bye Kiss, The 1928,N 12,18:2
Bennett, Arnold (Original Author)
Piccadilly 1929,Jl 15,25:1
His Double Life 1933,D 16,12:3
Holy Matrimony 1943,S 16,25:2
Dear Mr Prohack 1950,Jl 15,7:2
Promoter, The 1952,O 29,36:2
Bennett, Barbara
Syncopation 1929,Ap 8,32:1
Mother's Boy 1929,My 8,34:6
Love Among the Millionaires 1930,Jl 5,17:4
Bennett, Belle
In Hollywood with Potash and Perlmutter 1924,S 30,27:3
His Supreme Moment 1925,Ap 13,24:1
Playing With Souls 1925,Ap 20,18:1 (Incorrect in this edition; use 1925,Ap 28,18:1 elsewhere)
If Marriage Fails 1925,Je 2,16:3
Stella Dallas 1925,N 17,30:2
Reckless Lady, The 1926,Ja 25,21:2
Fourth Commandment, The 1927,Ap 6,25:1
Mother 1927,My 4,29:2
Way of all Flesh, The 1927,Je 27,25:2
Wild Geese 1927,D 5,26:2
Mother Machree 1928,N 6,20:3
Battle of The Sexes, The 1928,O 15,16:1
Iron Mask, The 1929,F 22,18:6
Their own Desire 1929,Ja 25,13:2
Courage 1930,My 23,21:1
Recaptured Love 1930,Ag 9,16:5
Big Shot, The 1932,Ja 2,14:2
Bennett, Billie
Robin Hood 1922,O 31,15:4 (In Addenda)
Eternal Three, The 1923,O 12,7:2 (Incorrect in this edition; use 1927,O 1,7:2 elsewhere)
Ranson's Folly 1926,My 31,10:2
Amateur Gentleman, The 1926,Ag 17,15:3
Claw, The 1927,My 11,28:3
Fashions in Love 1929,Jl 1,31:2
One Romantic Night 1930,My 31,19:4
Bennett, Bruce
Street of Missing Women 1940,Ja 8,11:2
My Son Is Guilty 1940,Ja 15,11:2
Man With Nine Lives, The 1940,Ap 29,12:3
Lone Wolf Meets a Lady, The 1940,Je 17,19:2
Girls of the Road 1940,Jl 22,20:2
Secret Seven, The 1940,Ag 12,11:6
Before I Hang 1940,O 3,31:3
Lone Wolf Keeps a Date, The 1941,Ja 2,24:3
Phantom Submarine, The 1941,F 12,25:3
Officer and the Lady, The 1941,Ag 11,17:4
Atlantic Convoy 1942,Jl 6,18:5
Sabotage Squad 1942,Ag 5,16:1
More the Merrier, The 1943,My 14,17:1
Murder in Times Square 1943,My 31,13:2
Sahara 1943,N 12,25:2
Mildred Pierce 1945,S 29,12:2
Danger Signal 1945,N 22,39:2
Stolen Life, A 1946,My 2,27:4
Man I Love, The 1947,Ja 25,12:2
Nora Prentiss 1947,F 22,16:2
Cheyenne 1947,Je 7,9:2
Dark Passage 1947,S 6,11:2
Treasure of Sierra Madre 1948,Ja 24,11:2
To the Victor 1948,Ap 17,11:2
Silver River 1948,My 22,8:3
Younger Brothers, The 1949,My 28,11:2
House Across the Street 1949,S 2,14:4
Task Force 1949,O 1,8:6
Doctor and the Girl, The 1949,O 31,20:2
Undertow 1949,D 16,37:2
Without Honor 1950,Jl 3,9:2
Mystery Street 1950,Jl 28,12:5
Shakedown 1950,S 4,11:2
Second Face, The 1951,Mr 2,21:3
Great Missouri Raid, The 1951,Ap 9,31:2
Last Outpost, The 1951,Je 22,16:3
Angels in the Outfield 1951,O 18,32:1
Sudden Fear 1952,Ag 8,9:2
Dream Wife 1953,Jl 30,20:1
Strategic Air Command 1955,Ap 21,33:1
Bottom of the Bottle, The 1956,F 2,19:2
Love Me Tender 1956,N 16,23:1
Three Violent People 1957,F 11,34:2
Outsider, The 1962,F 8,25:1

Bennett, Charles
America 1924,F 22,20:1
Bennett, Charles (Director)
Madness of the Heart 1950,O 12,43:2
Bennett, Charles (Original Author)
Blackmail 1929,O 7,22:1
Man Who Knew too Much, The 1935,Mr 23,11:2
Forever and a Day 1943,Mr 13,9:2
Green Glove, The 1952,Ap 24,38:1
Man Who Knew too Much, The 1956,My 17,37:1
Bennett, Charles (Screenwriter)
Thirty-Nine Steps, The 1935,S 14,8:4
King of the Damned 1936,F 1,9:2
Secret Agent 1936,Je 13,13:1
Woman Alone, The 1937,F 27,9:2
King Solomon's Mines 1937,Jl 3,18:1
Girl Was Young, The 1938,F 11,27:2
Young in Heart, The 1938,N 4,27:2
Balalaika 1939,D 15,33:2
Foreign Correspondent 1940,Ag 28,15:2
They Dare not Love 1941,My 16,21:4
Joan of Paris 1942,Ja 26,18:2
Reap the Wild Wind 1942,Mr 27,27:2
Story of Dr Wassell, The 1944,Je 7,13:2
Ivy 1947,Je 26,19:1
Unconquered 1947,O 11,11:2
Sign of the Ram, The 1948,Mr 4,30:2
Black Magic 1949,N 9,37:2
Madness of the Heart 1950,O 12,43:2
Where Danger Lives 1951,Ja 1,13:6
Kind Lady 1951,Ag 8,21:2
Green-Glove, The 1952,Ap 24,38:1
Story of Mankind, The 1957,N 9,31:2
Big Circus, The 1959,Jl 18,6:1
Lost World, The 1960,Jl 14,23:1
Voyage to the Bottom of the Sea 1961,Jl 20,32:2
Five Weeks in a Balloon 1962,Ag 27,18:1
War Gods of the Deep 1965,Je 3,24:3
Bennett, Chester (Director)
Divorce 1923,Je 26,14:2
Bennett, Compton (Director)
Seventh Veil, The 1945,D 26,15:1
Years Between, The 1947,Mr 10,25:2
My Own True Love 1949,F 3,27:3
Daybreak 1949,Jl 4,9:2
That Forsyte Woman 1949,N 11,31:2
King Solomon's Mines 1950,N 10,35:1
Glory at Sea 1953,Mr 11,36:7
It Started in Paradise 1953,Jl 25,8:2
So Little Time 1953,Jl 28,23:2
Desperate Moment 1953,S 1,19:4
Bennett, Constance
Cytherea 1924,My 26,21:1
Into the Net 1924,Ag 23,10:2
Goose Hangs High, The 1925,Mr 10,19:3
Code of the West 1925,Ap 13,24:1
My Wife and I 1925,My 20,26:2
Goose Woman, The 1925,Ag 4,14:3
Sally, Irene and Mary 1925,D 7,19:1
This Thing Called Love 1929,D 14,22:4
Son of the Gods 1930,Ja 31,24:1
Common Clay 1930,Ag 2,16:4
Three Faces East 1930,S 6,9:2
Sin Takes a Holliday 1930,N 28,23:1
Easiest Way, The 1931,F 28,15:2
Born to Love 1931,Ap 25,23:4
Common Law, The 1931,Jl 20,20:4
Bought 1931,Ag 15,18:3
Lady With a Past 1932,F 22,23:2
What Price Hollywood 1932,Jl 16,5:5
Two Against the World 1932,Ag 19,20:6
Rockabye 1932,D 5,21:2
Our Betters 1933,F 24,13:2
Bed of Roses 1933,Je 30,20:3
After Tonight 1933,N 3,23:2
Moulin Rouge 1934,F 8,14:4
Affairs of Cellini, The 1934,S 6,22:3
Outcast Lady 1934,N 3,20:3
After Office Hours 1935,Mr 9,19:1
Ladies in Love 1936,O 29,31:1
Topper 1937,Ag 20,21:2
Merrily We Live 1938,Mr 18,23:3
Service de Luxe 1938,O 24,13:2
Topper Takes a Trip 1938,D 30,11:2
Tail Spin 1939,F 11,13:2
Submarine Zone; (Escape To Glory) 1941,Ap 7,13:2
Law of the Tropics 1941,O 10,26:5
Two Faced Woman 1942,Ja 1,37:2
Wild Bill Hickok Rides 1942,F 7,13:5
Sin Town 1942,O 17,11:2
Paris Underground 1945,O 20,8:2
Centennial Summer 1946,Jl 18,20:2
Unsuspected, The 1947,O 4,9:2
Angel on the Amazon 1948,D 27,16:4
As Young as You Feel 1951,Ag 3,10:6
It Should Happen to You 1954,Ja 16,10:5
Madame X 1966,Ap 28,49:1
Bennett, Constance (Producer)
Paris Underground 1945,O 20,8:2
Bennett, Dorothy (Original Author)
Daughters Courageous 1939,Je 24,14:2
Always in my Heart 1942,Mr 14,19:2

All by Myself 1943,Jl 16,20:3
Bennett, Dorothy (Screenwriter)
It Comes up Love 1943,Ja 22,25:3
When Johnny Comes Marching Home 1943,Mr 5,20:4
Mister Big 1943,Je 14,13:4
Show Business 1944,My 11,25:7
Sensations of 1945 1944,Jl 7,13:2
Patrick the Great 1945,Ap 13,15:2
Bennett, Douglas
Anne of the Indies 1951,O 25,36:3
Bennett, Edna
Big Fight, The 1930,Je 28,9:2
Ladies of the Big House 1932,Ja 1,31:1
Bennett, Enid
Biggest Show on Earth, The 1918,Ap 29,11:1
Vamp, The 1918,Jl 15,9:3
Fuss and Feathers 1918,D 9,11:4
Stepping Out 1919,S 22,8:1
Woman in the Suitcase, The 1920,Ja 12,7:1
Hairpins 1920,Ag 2,12:2
Strangers of the Night 1923,O 8,20:1
Bad Man, The 1923,O 9,17:4
Courtship of Myles Standish, The 1923,D 31,9:3
Sea Hawk, The 1924,Je 3,22:1
Red Lily, The 1924,S 29,10:1
Skippy 1931,Ap 4,23:1
Waterloo Bridge 1931,S 5,7:4
Sooky 1931,D 21,28:4
Intermezzo, A Love Story 1939,O 6,31:1
Strike up the Band 1940,S 30,13:2
Bennett, Fran
Giant 1956,O 11,51:1
Bennett, Gertrude
Merry Widow, The 1925,Ag 27,14:1
Bennett, Howard
Dutchman 1967,F 28,32:1
Bennett, Hugh (Director)
Henry Aldrich for President 1941,O 18,22:2
Bennett, Hywel
Family Way, The 1967,Je 29,32:1
Bennett, J Moy
Unguarded Hour, The 1926,Ja 5,25:2 (In Addenda)
Running Wild 1927,Je 14,33:2
Bennett, Jay (Original Author)
Woman Who Wouldn't Die, The 1965,Je 10,38:1
Bennett, Jill
Moulin Rouge 1953,F 11,33:5
Hell Below Zero 1954,Jl 17,7:3
Lust for Life 1956,S 18,39:1
Nanny, The 1965,N 4,57:2
Inadmissible Evidence 1968,Je 24,44:1
Charge of the Light Brigade, The 1968,O 7,59:1
Bennett, Joan
Power 1928,N 27,34:1
Bulldog Drummond 1929,My 3,23:2
Three Live Ghosts 1929,S 30,23:1
Disraeli 1929,O 3,27:5
Mississippi Gambler, The 1929,O 28,20:1
Puttin' on the Ritz 1930,F 15,15:1
Moby Dick 1930,Ag 15,20:5
Maybe It's Love 1930,O 18,23:2
Scotland Yard 1930,O 20,28:2
Doctors' Wives 1931,Ap 25,23:4
Hush Money 1931,Jl 11,7:6
She Wanted a Millionaire 1932,F 20,11:2
Careless Lady 1932,Ap 18,19:2
Trial of Vivienne Ware, The 1932,Ap 30,19:3
Week Ends Only 1932,Je 18,9:2
Me and my Gal 1932,D 12,18:4
Arizona to Broadway 1933,Jl 22,14:3
Little Women 1933,N 17,22:3
Pursuit of Happiness, The 1934,O 26,25:1
Man Who Reclaimed his Head, The 1935,Ja 9,22:1
Private Worlds 1935,Mr 28,25:2
Mississippi 1935,Ap 18,27:2
Two for Tonight 1935,Ag 31,16:2
She Couldn't Take It 1935,N 7,27:1
Man Who Broke the Bank at Monte Carlo, The 1935,N 15,20:2
13 Hours by Air 1936,Ap 30,17:2
Big Brown Eyes 1936,My 2,11:1
Two in a Crowd 1936,O 5,25:1
Wedding Present 1936,N 19,31:3
Vogues of 1938 1937,Ag 20,21:1
I Met my Love Again 1938,Ja 15,19:1
Texans, The 1938,Jl 28,23:2
Artists and Models Abroad 1938,D 22,25:3
Trade Winds 1939,Ja 13,17:2
Man in the Iron Mask, The 1939,Jl 14,11:1
Housekeeper's Daughter, The 1939,D 2,21:4
Green Hell 1940,Ja 30,15:6
House Across the Bay, The 1940,Mr 22,23:2
Man I Married, The 1940,Ag 3,9:2
Son of Monte Cristo, The 1940,D 5,33:1
Man Hunt 1941,Je 14,20:2
She Knew All the Answers 1941,Je 20,28:4
Wild Geese Calling 1941,Ag 30,10:2
Confirm or Deny 1941,D 19,35:2
Twin Beds 1942,My 1,23:4
Wife Takes a Flyer, The 1942,Je 19,19:1

Bennett, Joan — Cont
Girl Trouble 1942,O 8,31:2
Margin for Error 1943,Ja 25,10:7
Woman in the Window, The 1945,Ja 26,16:4
Nob Hill 1945,Jl 4,10:3
Scarlet Street 1946,F 15,29:2
Colonel Effingham's Raid 1946,Ap 5,21:3
Macomber Affair, The 1947,Ap 21,21:2
Woman on the Beach, The 1947,Je 9,26:6
Secret Beyond the Door 1948,Ja 16,25:4
Hollow Triumph 1948,O 29,29:5
Reckless Moment, The 1949,D 30,13:2
Father of the Bride 1950,My 19,31:2
For Heaven's Sake 1950,D 16,10:5
Father's Little Dividend 1951,Ap 13,18:5
Guy Who Came Back, The 1951,Ag 17,13:2
Highway Dragnet 1954,F 20,8:7
We're no Angels 1955,Jl 8,15:2
There's Always Tomorrow 1956,Ja 21,18:2
Desire in the Dust 1960,O 12,47:2
Bennett, Joseph
Shepherd of the Hills, The 1928,F 20,14:1
Bennett, Katherine
Soul Mates 1926,Ja 4,16:1
Bennett, Lee
Hold 'Em Navy 1937,N 6,14:2
Bennett, Leila
Taxi 1932,Ja 8,27:3
Emma 1932,F 6,14:4
Purchase Price, The 1932,Jl 16,5:5
Doctor X 1932,Ag 4,17:2
Two Against the World 1932,Ag 19,20:6
First Year, The 1932,Ag 22,20:2
Tiger Shark 1932,S 23,22:2
No Other Woman 1933,Ja 30,9:4 (In Addenda)
Study in Scarlet, A 1933,Je 1,15:3
Once to Every Woman 1934,Mr 26,22:3
Housewife 1934,Ag 10,21:2
Dames 1934,Ag 16,20:2
Wagon Wheels 1934,O 4,19:1
Mark of the Vampire 1935,My 3,23:4
Fury 1936,Je 6,21:1
Bennett, Libby
Too Many Girls 1940,N 21,43:1
Bennett, Linda
Seven Little Foys, The 1955,Je 30,18:2
Queen Bee 1955,N 23,18:2
Bennett, Marjorie
June Bride 1948,O 30,10:2
Man Who Cheated Himself, The 1951,F 9,21:2
Limelight 1952,O 24,27:2
Sabrina 1954,S 23,43:2
Young at Heart 1955,Ja 20,35:1
Autumn Leaves 1956,Ag 2,21:2
Rat Race, The 1960,My 26,37:3
Thunder of Drums, A 1961,S 27,35:1
What Ever Happened to Baby Jane? 1962,N 7,48:1
Mary Poppins 1964,S 25,34:1
Family Jewels, The 1965,Ag 12,30:4
Games 1967,S 18,58:2
Bennett, Mickey
Marriage Morals 1923,Ag 14,10:3
Big Brother 1923,D 24,12:1 (In Addenda)
Cohens and the Kellys, The 1926,F 23,26:5
United States Smith 1928,Jl 24,13:3
Ghost Talks, The 1929,F 18,28:1
Dummy, The 1929,Mr 4,20:2
Footlights and Fools 1929,N 9,22:5
Swing High 1930,Je 27,26:3
Father's Son 1931,F 21,15:2
Big Business Girl 1931,Je 12,27:1
Laughter in Hell 1933,Ja 2,29:2
Mayor of Hell, The 1933,Jl 1,16:5
Bennett, Mike
Surfari 1967,Jl 19,26:2
Bennett, Moy
Price of a Party, The 1924,N 26,17:3
Bennett, Raphael
Frame-Up 1937,Ag 9,23:2 (In Addenda)
Female Fugitive 1938,Ap 11,12:3
Adventure in Sahara 1938,D 19,19:2
Romance of the Rio Grande 1940,D 25,33:4
Kansan, The 1943,O 1,15:3
Bennett, Ray
Spoilers, The 1942,My 22,27:2
Canon City 1948,Jl 8,19:2
Northwest Stampede 1948,D 10,34:3
Ma and Pa Kettle 1949,Ag 12,13:2
Apache Drums 1951,My 7,22:2
Redhead From Wyoming, The 1953,Ja 9,17:4
African Manhunt 1957,Ap 20,21:4
Bennett, Richard
Eternal City, The 1924,Ja 21,20:1
Youth for Sale 1924,S 3,17:1
Lying Wives 1925,Je 17,16:2
Home Towners, The 1928,O 24,26:4
Five and Ten 1931,Jl 11,7:6
Bought 1931,Ag 15,18:3
Arrowsmith 1931,D 8,36:4
This Reckless Age 1932,Ja 9,21:1
No Greater Love 1932,My 14,11:5
Madame Racketeer 1932,Jl 23,6:6
Strange Justice 1932,O 20,24:2

Bennett, Richard— Cont
  If I Had a Million 1932,D 3,21:4
  Nana 1934,F 2,20:3
  Magnificent Ambersons, The 1942,Ag 14,13:3
  Journey Into Fear 1943,Mr 19,15:3
  Richard III 1956,Mr 12,1:4
  Happy is the Bride 1959,Je 30,27:2
Bennett, Robert Chalmers (Original Author)
  When G-Men Step In 1938,Mr 14,13:2
Bennett, Robert Russell (Composer)
  Victory at Sea 1954,Jl 14,33:2
Bennett, Seymour (Screenwriter)
  Macomber Affair, The 1947,Ap 21,21:2
Bennett, Spencer G (Director)
  Atomic Submarine, The 1960,Ap 20,45:2
Bennett, Tony
  Oscar, The 1966,Mr 5,16:1
Bennett, Whitman (Director)
  Virtuous Liars 1924,Mr 31,20:1
Bennett, Whitman (Miscellaneous)
  Secrets of Paris 1923,Ja 8,22:1
Bennett, Whitman (Producer)
  Hoosier Schoolmaster, The 1924,Mr 18,25:2
Bennett, Wilda
  What a Life 1939,O 12,33:1
  Those Were the Days 1940,Jl 15,18:4
Benneylon, Yves
  Weekend 1968,S 28,36:1
Bennie, Michael
  Black Rose, The 1950,S 2,11:2
Bennison, Andrew (Director)
  This Sporting Age 1932,O 1,10:4
Bennison, Andrew (Original Author)
  Pot o'Gold 1941,Ap 4,25:2
Bennison, Andrew (Screenwriter)
  Divorce 1923,Je 26,14:2
  Air Circus, The 1928,S 3,14:2
Benny, Jack
  Chasing Rainbows 1930,F 22,13:1
  Transatlantic Merry-Go-Round 1934,N 1,25:2
  Broadway Melody of 1936 1935,S 19,28:1
  It's in the Air 1935,N 8,18:2
  Big Broadcast of 1937, The 1936,O 22,31:1
  College Holiday 1936,D 24,21:2
  Artists and Models 1937,Ag 5,19:2
  Artists and Models Abroad 1938,D 22,25:3
  Man About Town 1939,Je 29,19:1
  Buck Benny Rides Again 1940,Ap 25,28:4
  Love Thy Neighbor 1940,D 18,32:5
  Charley's Aunt 1941,Ag 2,18:2
  To Be or not to Be 1942,Mr 7,13:2
  George Washington Slept Here 1942,O 31,11:1
  Meanest Man in the World, The 1943,F 25,27:3
  Hollywood Canteen 1944,D 16,19:2
  Horn Blows at Midnight, The 1945,Ap 21,18:2
  It's in the Bag 1945,Je 11,12:1
  Guide for the Married Man, A 1967,My 27,16:1
Benny, Jack (Producer)
  Lucky Stiff, The 1949,Ja 31,14:2
Benny, Jack and orchestra
  Manhattan Merry-Go-Round 1937,D 31,9:3
Benoff, Mac (Screenwriter)
  Take It or Leave It 1944,Jl 13,14:2
  Love Happy 1950,Ap 8,9:4
Benois, Robert
  Abysses, Les 1964,N 24,44:1
Benoit, Ludwik
  Eve Wants to Sleep 1961,Je 6,42:2
Benoit, Pierre (Miscellaneous)
  Vautrin, the Thief 1949,N 11,31:2
Benoit, Pierre (Original Author)
  Missing Husbands 1922,My 13,16:1
  Daughter of Israel, A 1928,My 21,25:1
  Surrender 1931,N 28,20:4
  Atlantide, L' 1932,Ag 7,IX,2:1
  Moscow Nights 1938,My 3,19:3
  Siren of Atlantis 1949,Ag 22,13:1
Benoit, Pierre (Screenwriter)
  Colonel Chabert 1947,Je 21,11:2
Benoit-Levy, Jean (Director)
  Maternelle, La 1935,O 15,19:1
  Itto 1936,Ja 29,15:5
  Helene 1938,Ja 22,19:1
  Fire in the Straw 1943,Jl 2,15:2
Benoit-Levy, Jean (Miscellaneous)
  Maternelle, La 1935,O 15,19:1
Benoit-Levy, Jean (Producer)
  Ballet de France 1955,S 26,18:2
Benoit-Levy, Jean (Screenwriter)
  Helene 1938,Ja 22,19:1
  Youth in Revolt 1939,My 16,27:3
  Fire in the Straw 1943,Jl 2,15:2
Benoit-Levy, M (Director)
  Ballerina 1938,N 15,27:1
  Youth in Revolt 1939,My 16,27:3
Benoits
  Ice-Capades 1941,S 25,29:1
Benossi, Memo
  Vecchia Signora, La 1932,D 10,19:3.
Benrath, Martin
  Saboteur, The: Code Name-Mori Turi
    1965,Ag 26,40:2

Benrimo, J H (Original Author)
  Willow Tree, The 1920,F 2,10:1
Benson, Annette
  Shooting Stars 1928,Mr 4,IX,7:7
  Daughter of Israel, A 1928,My 21,25:1
  Shooting Stars 1928,Je 11,27:1
Benson, Ben (Original Author)
  Running Wild 1955,N 12,23:2
Benson, Bernadette
  This Sporting Life 1963,Jl 17,19:2
Benson, E F (Original Author)
  Dead of Night 1946,Je 29,22:6
Benson, Frank
  Old Curiosity Shop, The 1935,D 23,15:5
Benson, Frank
  Hangover Square 1945,F 8,15:2
Benson, George
  Convoy 1941,Ja 17,21:2
  October Man, The 1948,Ap 16,29:2
  Pool of London 1951,N 28,37:2
  Horror of Dracula 1958,My 29,24:4
  They all Died Laughing 1964,Mr 16,37:2
Benson, Hugh (Producer)
  For Those Who Think Young 1964,Jl 9,27:1
Benson, James (Original Author)
  Above Us the Waves 1957,Ap 18,35:2
Benson, Leon (Director)
  Flipper's New Adventure 1964,Ag 27,28:2
Benson, Lucille
  Fugitive Kind, The 1960,Ap 15,13:1
Benson, Martin
  Blind Goddess, The 1949,Je 23,33:3
  Lucky Nick Cain 1951,Ap 23,21:2
  West of Zanzibar 1955,Ja 18,31:2
  23 Paces to Baker Street 1956,My 19,12:6
  King and I, The 1956,Je 29,15:6
  Istanbul 1957,Ja 24,34:1
  Doctor at Large 1957,Jl 29,15:5
  Flesh is Weak, The 1957,N 9,31:2
  Windom's Way 1958,O 1,45:1
  Cosmic Monster, The 1959,Ja 1,38:1
  Two-Headed Spy, The 1959,Mr 3,38:4
  Once More With Feeling 1960,F 12,22:2
  Oscar Wilde 1960,Je 21,28:2
  Satan Never Sleeps 1962,F 22,20:1
  Matter of Who, A 1962,Jl 25,29:2
  Cleopatra 1963,Je 13,29:1
  Shot in the Dark, A 1964,Je 24,28:1
  Goldfinger 1964,D 22,36:1
  Mozambique 1966,F 10,33:1
  Man Could Get Killed, A 1966,My 12,54:2
  Battle Beneath the Earth 1968,S 12,54:3
Benson, Richard (Director)
  Werewolf in a Girls Dormitory 1963,Je 6,39:1
Benson, Richard (Miscellaneous)
  My Heart Is Calling 1935,Ap 15,16:3
Benson, Richard (Screenwriter)
  My Song For You 1935,My 27,20:6
Benson, Roy
  Sweet and Low Down 1944,O 19,19:2
  Billy Rose's Diamond Horseshoe 1945,My 3,37:1
Benson, Sally (Original Author)
  Meet Me in St Louis 1944,N 29,20:2
  Junior Miss 1945,Je 18,15:4
Benson, Sally (Screenwriter)
  Shadow of a Doubt 1943,Ja 13,18:2
  Anna and the King of Siam 1946,Je 21,20:2
  Come to the Stable 1949,Jl 28,19:1
  Conspirator 1950,Ap 28,26:2
  No Man of her Own 1950,My 4,32:3
  Farmer Takes a Wife, The 1953,Je 13,11:2
  Summer Magic 1963,Ag 22,19:2
  Viva Las Vegas 1964,My 21,42:1
  Signpost to Murder 1965,My 20,52:2
  Joy in the Morning 1965,Je 10,38:1
  Singing Nun, The 1966,Mr 18,33:1
Bentham, Josephine (Original Author)
  Janie 1944,Ag 5,16:2
  Janie Gets Married 1946,Je 15,24:2
Benti, Galeazzo
  Angela 1955,Je 4,9:2
  Margaret of Cortona 1957,Ja 21,20:4
Bentine, Fusty
  Raising a Riot 1957,My 8,44:1
Bentley, Beatrice
  Toll of the Sea, The 1922,N 27,18:1
Bentley, Beverley
  Wild 90 1968,Ja 8,33:1
Bentley, Beverly
  Scent of Mystery 1960,F 19,23:1
  Beyond the Law 1968,S 30,60:4
  Beyond the Law 1968,O 24,55:1
Bentley, Bobette
  Courageous Dr Christian, The 1940,Mr 29,25:3
Bentley, Dick
  Gunfighters of Casa Grande 1965,S 2,36:1
Bentley, E C (Original Author)
  Trent's Last Case 1953,N 27,99:9
Bentley, Irene
  My Weakness 1933,S 22,14:1
  Smoky 1934,Ja 1,28:2
  Frontier Marshal 1934,Ja 31,20:3

Bentley, John
  Happiest Days of Your Life, The 1950,S 18,19:2
  Scarlet Spear, The 1954,Ap 10,11:4
  Woman's Angle, The 1954,Ag 27,11:6
  Istanbul 1957,Ja 24,34:1
  Singer not the Song, The 1962,My 3,25:4
Bentley, Thomas (Director)
  Not Quite a Lady 1928,Ag 19,VII,3:7
  Young Woodley 1930,S 27,21:3
  Sleepless Nights 1933,Jl 22,14:2
  Old Curiosity Shop, The 1935,D 23,15:5
  Scotland Yard Mystery, The 1936,Mr 16,21:4
Bentley, Yvette
  Paris Calling 1942,Ja 19,21:2
Bento, Serge
  Landru 1963,Ap 10,31:1
Benton, Anne
  Flaming Star 1960,D 17,19:1
Benton, Curtis
  Fireman, Save My Child 1932,F 18,25:3
Benton, Curtis (Original Author)
  Mighty Lak' a Rose 1923,Mr 20,24:3
Benton, Dean
  Hard Rock Harrigan 1935,Jl 30,16:2
  Thunder Mountain 1935,O 2,27:2
Benton, Garth
  13 Frightened Girls 1963,S 12,32:2
Benton, Robert (Screenwriter)
  Bonnie and Clyde 1967,Ag 14,36:1
Benton, Steve
  Picnic 1956,F 17,13:3
Bentzen, Gudrun
  Sara Laer Sig Folkvett 1938,F 16,17:1
Benucci, Pippo
  Golden Madonna, The 1949,S 5,13:4
Benussi, Femi
  Hawks and the Sparrows, The; Uccellacci e
    Uccellini 1967,Jl 28,15:3
Benvenuti, Jolanda (Miscellaneous)
  Grand Olympics, The 1964,Ap 22,57:2
Benvenuti, Leo (Screenwriter)
  House of Ricordi 1956,Mr 13,32:1
  Guendalina 1958,Je 30,23:2
  Woman in the Painting, The 1959,Ja 15,27:1
  Tailor's Maid, The; (Patri e Figli) 1959,S 2,35:4
  Holiday Island; (Vacanzie a Izchia)
    1959,S 22,46:1
  Girl With a Suitcase 1961,S 12,36:2
  Marriage Italian Style 1964,D 21,42:1
  Bambole; Dolls, The (Monsignor Cupid);
    Monsignor Cupid (The Dolls) 1965,Je 29,26:1
Benyamini, Itzhak
  Clouds Over Israel 1966,My 10,48:6
Benz, Hamilton (Miscellaneous)
  Lost One, The; La Traviata 1948,Mr 30,26:2
Benz, Hamilton (Screenwriter)
  Her Wonderful Lie 1950,Jl 17,15:2
Beradino, John
  Kid From Cleveland, The 1949,S 5,13:2
  Killer is Loose, The 1956,Mr 3,17:2
Beranger, Andre
  Bright Shawl, The 1923,Ap 23,18:3
  Ashes of Vengeance 1923,Ag 7,20:2
  Dulcy 1923,S 17,18:2
  Tiger Rose 1923,D 3,14:1
  Beau Brummell 1924,Mr 31,20:1
  Poisoned Paradise 1924,Ag 11,16:1
  Confessions of a Queen 1925,Mr 24,20:6
  Are Parents People 1925,Je 9,16:3
  Woman's Faith, A 1925,Jl 27,17:3
  Grand Duchess and the Waiter, The
    1926,F 9,22:1
  Miss Brewster's Millions 1926,Mr 8,17:1
  Bat, The 1926,Mr 15,18:3
  So This Is Paris 1926,Ag 16,10:1
  Eagle of the Sea, The 1926,N 17,21:6
  Popular Sin, The 1926,D 20,28:3
  Paradise for Two 1927,Ja 25,18:4
  If I Were Single 1928,Mr 5,21:1
  Strange Cargo 1929,F 18,28:1
  Glad Rag Doll, The 1929,Je 3,27:2
  Boudoir Diplomat, The 1930,D 8,26:1
  Annabelle's Affairs 1931,Je 29,20:3
  Ladies of the Jury 1932,Ap 2,13:2
  Mama Loves Papa 1933,Jl 24,11:2
  Young and Beautiful 1934,S 18,18:4
  Love Before Breakfast 1936,Mr 14,10:1
  Big Noise, The 1936,Jl 4,18:3
  Hot Money 1936,Jl 25,16:2
Beranger, Annie
  Powder my Back 1928,Ag 7,25:4
Beranger, Clara (Original Author)
  Gilded Lily, The 1921,Mr 7,8:1
Beranger, Clara (Screenwriter)
  Miss Lulu Bett 1921,D 25,VI,2:1
  Bought and Paid For 1922,Mr 13,18:2
  Clarence 1922,O 16,20:2
  Grumpy 1923,Mr 26,16:2
  Bedroom Window, The 1924,Je 9,14:3
  Locked Doors 1925,Ja 12,11:2
Beranger, George Andre
  Grounds for Divorce 1925,Je 29,8:2
  Surrender 1931,N 28,20:4

Beranger, George Andre— Cont
Beauty for the Asking 1939,F 10,19:1
Over my Dead Body 1942,D 26,15:2
Road House 1948,N 8,24:2
Beranger, George Andre (Director)
Uncle Sam of Freedom Ridge 1920,S 27,15:2
Beranger, Lee
Five and Ten 1931,Jl 11,7:6
Berankova, Jarmila
Ecstasy of Young Love 1936,Mr 10,27:3
Berardino, John
Kid From Left Field, The 1953,S 26,15:3
Seven Thieves 1960,Mr 12,14:5
Berber, Adi
Carnival Story 1954,Ap 17,8:2
Circus of Love 1958,Ag 16,10:2
Marianne of my Youth; (Marianne de ma
Jeunesse) 1959,Ja 20,43:1
Ben Hur 1959,N 19,50:2
Berbert, Marcel (Producer)
Army Game, The; Tire Au Flanc
1963,Ap 24,40:1
Bercher
Marthe Richard 1944,N 9,23:2
Bercholz, J (Producer)
Man Who Seeks the Truth, The 1941,O 7,26:6
Savage Triangle 1952,S 30,38:2
Bercovici, Eric (Screenwriter)
Day of the Evil Gun 1968,Ap 25,53:2
Bercovici, Konrad (Original Author)
Law of the Lawless, The 1923,Je 19,22:4
Volga Boatman, The 1926,Ap 14,21:1
Revenge 1928,D 10,25:1
Bercovici, Leonardo (Screenwriter)
Racket Busters 1938,Ag 11,13:1
Lost Moment, The 1947,N 22,10:2
Bishop's Wife, The 1947,D 10,44:2
Kiss the Blood off my Hands 1948,O 30,10:2
Monsoon 1953,S 26,15:2
Bercovitch, Reuben (Producer)
What's Up, Tiger Lily? 1966,N 18,33:1
Berczy, Gezo
Paul Street Boys, The 1929,Jl 15,25:1
Berde (Original Author)
Culte de Beaute, Le 1931,Je 8,21:1
Beregi, Oscar
Flaming Forest, The 1926,N 22,28:3
Butterflies in the Rain 1926,D 25,10:5
Moon of Israel 1927,Je 29,29:3
Key Balvany, A 1933,Ap 18,13:6
Kek Balvany, A; Blue Idol, The 1933,Ap 18,13:6
Iza Neni 1934,Je 5,28:6
Rakoczi Indulo 1934,N 21,23:4
Anything Can Happen 1952,Ap 4,21:1
Call Me Madam 1953,Mr 26,37:1
Desert Legion 1953,My 9,13:2
Berendt, Rachel
Paris-Beguin 1932,D 31,10:1
Berengere, Mlle
Sans Famille 1935,Je 4,26:5
Berens, Anje
Having Wonderful Crime 1945,Ap 13,15:2
Berens, Harold
Pure Hell of St Trinian's, The 1961,S 26,31:1
Beres, Ilona
Age of Illusions 1967,Mr 30,55:1
Beresen, Meyer
Alice in Wonderland 1931,D 28,22:1
Beresford, Fred (Screenwriter)
Trifling With Honor 1923,My 30,10:4
Beresford, Harry
Quarterback, The 1926,O 12,30:2
Finn and Hattie 1931,Ja 31,15:1
Charlie Chan Carries On 1931,Mr 21,15:1
Up Pops the Devil 1931,My 16,13:3
Secret Call, The 1931,Jl 13,13:5
Sob Sister 1931,O 3,20:2
Heaven on Earth 1931,D 19,16:4
Mississippi 1931,D 27,VIII,5:4 (In Addenda)
Dance Team 1932,Ja 16,13:1
High Pressure 1932,F 1,22:3
Scandal for Sale 1932,Ap 3,26:2
So Big 1932,Ap 30,19:3
Strange Love of Molly Louvain, The
1932,My 9,19:5
Forgotten Commandments 1932,Je 2,25:2
Doctor X 1932,Ag 4,17:2
Sign of the Cross, The 1932,D 1,25:1
Dinner at Eight 1933,Ag 24,18:1
Night Flight 1933,O 7,18:4
College Coach 1933,N 11,10:4
Friends of Mr Sweeney 1934,Jl 31,20:4
Cleopatra 1934,Ag 17,12:1
Little Minister, The 1934,D 28,25:1
David Copperfield 1935,Ja 19,8:1
I'll Love You Always 1935,Mr 30,11:2
Page Miss Glory 1935,Ag 29,25:2
Anna Karenina 1935,Ag 31,16:2
I Found Stella Parish 1935,N 4,24:4
Seven Keys to Baldpate 1935,D 14,11:2
Follow the Fleet 1936,F 21,21:2
Klondike Annie 1936,Mr 12,18:2
Grand Jury 1936,Ag 1,16:3
In His Steps 1936,O 29,31:1

Go Getter, The 1937,Je 4,27:2
They Won't Forget 1937,Jl 15,16:1
She's no Lady 1937,Ag 12,14:3
Beresford, Miss
Miss Brewster's Millions 1926,Mr 8,17:1
Beresnyef, Nikolai (Director)
Enemies of Progress 1934,Ja 11,19:2
Beret, Dawn
Why Bother to Knock 1965,F 4,24:2
Berezantseva, Tatyana (Director)
Duel, The 1964,S 7,11:2
Berezantseva, Tatyana (Producer)
Duel, The 1964,S 7,11:2
Berezantseva, Tatyana (Screenwriter)
Duel, The 1964,S 7,11:2
Berezin, E
Variety Stars 1955,F 21,16:7
Berezko, G (Director)
If War Comes Tomorrow 1938,Jl 14,17:2
Berezko, G (Screenwriter)
If War Comes Tomorrow 1938,Jl 14,17:2
Berezov, Piotr
Wings of Victory 1941,N 17,15:2
Berezovskaya, N
On his Own 1939,S 13,31:3
Berezowska, Teresa
Kanal 1961,My 10,52:1
BERG
See Also BERGE, BERGH, BURG
Berg, Aimut
Vikings, The 1952,Je 12,35:2
Berg, Cherney (Screenwriter)
Come Spy with Me 1967,F 22,21:1
Berg, Dick (Producer)
Counterpoint 1968,Mr 14,51:2
Berg, Dick Movieland Seals
Big Circus, The 1959,Jl 18,6:1
Berg, Francino
Circle of Love 1965,Mr 25,42:4
Berg, Gertrude
Molly 1951,Mr 8,37:2
Main Street to Broadway 1953,O 14,34:1
Berg, Gertrude (Original Author)
Make a Wish 1937,S 23,33:1
Molly 1951,Mr 8,37:2
Berg, Gertrude (Screenwriter)
Make a Wish 1937,S 23,33:1
Molly 1951,Mr 8,37:2
Berg, Heinrich
Fuerst Woronzeff 1934,N 17,12:2
Berg, Judita (Miscellaneous)
Dybbuk, The 1938,Ja 28,17:2
Berg, Louis Dr (Original Author)
Prison Nurse 1938,Mr 4,17:5
Berg, Nancy
Fail Safe 1964,S 16,36:1
Berg, Stina
For Her Sake 1930,N 11,29:1
Dream Waltz, The 1930,D 27,16:3
BERGE
See Also BERGH, BURG, BERG
Berge, Colette
Abysses, Les 1964,N 24,44:1
Berge, Francine
Abysses, Les 1964,N 24,44:1
Judex 1966,Ap 26,55:1
Benjamin 1968,Mr 26,41:2
Bergen, Arthur
Slums of Berlin 1927,Ja 26,17:1
Bergen, Candice
Group, The 1966,Mr 17,35:1
Sand Pebbles, The 1966,D 21,48:1
Day the Fish Came Out, The 1967,O 3,57:1
Live for Life 1968,O 19,59:1
Magus, The 1968,D 11,57:1
Bergen, Constance
Wives Never Know 1936,O 31,24:2
Turn off the Moon 1937,My 20,17:2
Man Made Monster 1941,Mr 19,25:4
Bergen, Edgar
Goldwyn Follies, The 1938,F 21,15:1
Letter of Introduction 1938,S 1,17:1
You Can't Cheat an Honest Man 1939,F 20,13:2
Charlie McCarthy, Detective 1939,D 25,29:2
Look Who's Laughing 1941,D 25,33:2
Here We Go Again 1942,O 12,12:3
Stage Door Canteen 1943,Je 25,13:2
Song of the Open Road 1944,Je 7,13:3
I Remember Mama 1948,Mr 12,29:2
Captain China 1950,Mr 2,33:2
Don't Make Waves 1967,Je 21,36:2
Bergen, Frances
Titanic 1953,My 28,27:5
Her Twelve Men 1954,Ag 12,23:2
Bergen, Jerry
This Way Please 1937,O 8,27:2
College Swing 1938,Ap 28,27:2
Pirate, The 1948,My 21,19:2
Bergen, Polly
At War With the Army 1951,Ja 25,21:5
That's My Boy 1951,Ag 2,18:1

Bergen, Polly— Cont
Warpath 1951,N 23,32:2
Stooge, The 1953,F 5,19:2
Arena 1953,Jl 23,20:2
Escape from Fort Bravo 1954,Ja 23,11:2
Cape Fear 1962,Ap 19,35:2
Belle Sommers 1962,My 31,23:2
Caretakers, The 1963,Ag 22,19:2
Move Over Darling 1963,D 26,33:1
Kisses for my President 1964,Ag 22,13:1
Guide for the Married Man, A 1967,My 27,16:1
BERGER
See Also BERGERE, BURGER
Berger, Bernard
Lights of Old Broadway 1925,N 2,20:1
Berger, Erna
Marriage of Figaro 1950,N 3,31:2
Don Giovanni 1956,D 27,22:1
Berger, Erno
Ave Maria 1937,O 2,18:1
Berger, Francina
Religieuse, La 1968,S 23,42:3
Berger, Frederick
No Time for Flowers 1952,D 26,20:3
Berger, Fritz
Fidelio 1961,My 13,10:1
Berger, Grete
Bride 68 1930,Ap 15,28:5
Berger, Gustav
My Son 1939,My 10,28:2
God, Man and Devil 1950,Ja 23,16:2
Berger, Harris
Little Tough Guys in Society 1938,N 21,14:4
Newsboys' Home 1939,Ja 23,8:2
Berger, Henning (Original Author)
Sin Flood, The 1922,O 30,11:1
Berger, Kitty
Herzblut 1932,O 3,15:2
Berger, Ludwig (Director)
Cinderella 1926,Ap 5,24:1
Waltz Dream, The 1926,Jl 26,13:2
Woman From Moscow, The 1928,N 5,26:1
Sins of the Fathers 1929,Ja 28,21:1
Meistersinger 1929,D 16,34:2
Vagabond King, The 1930,F 20,22:4
Vagabond King, The 1930,Mr 2,IX,5:1
Burning Heart, The 1930,My 12,27:3
Playboy of Paris 1930,N 1,23:2
Waltz Time in Vienna 1934,N 19,13:2
Three Waltzes 1939,Ap 25,19:2
Thief of Bagdad, The 1940,D 6,28:2
Dream Ballerina 1951,Ap 16,21:2
Berger, Ludwig (Original Author)
Dream Ballerina 1951,Ap 16,21:2
Berger, Ludwig (Producer)
Waltz Time in Vienna 1934,N 19,13:2
Dream Ballerina 1951,Ap 16,21:2
Berger, Maria
Mr Emmanuel 1945,Ja 8,15:2
Berger, Martin (Director)
Rasputin: The Holy Devil 1930,Ag 25,14:2
Verklungene Traume 1930,D 9,31:3
Berger, Martin (Producer)
Rasputin: The Holy Devil 1930,Ag 25,14:2
Berger, Nicole
Game of Love, The 1954,D 15,41:1
Julietta 1957,Je 18,38:2
Premier May 1958,S 17,44:2
He Who Must Die 1958,D 29,21:1
Girls of the Night 1959,Mr 21,13:2
Love Is my Profession 1959,Ap 28,41:1
Chasers, The; Draguers, Les 1960,My 3,43:1
Shoot the Piano Player 1962,Jl 24,19:1
Story of a Three Day Pass, The 1968,Jl 9,31:1
Berger, Richard H (Producer)
Rachel and the Stranger 1948,S 20,21:2
Adventure in Baltimore 1949,Ap 29,27:2
Roughshod 1949,Je 17,27:2
Berger, Senta
Secret Ways, The 1961,My 25,31:1
Good Soldier Schweik, The 1963,Ag 21,38:1
Victors, The 1963,D 20,21:2
Major Dundee 1965,Ap 8,45:1
Cast a Giant Shadow 1966,Mr 31,43:3
Quiller Memorandum, The 1966,D 16,59:1
Bang, Bang, You're Dead 1967,Ja 19,41:2
Poppy is Also a Flower, The 1967,D 14,62:4
Ambushers, The 1967,D 23,29:1
Treasure of San Gennaro 1968,F 27,36:1
Berger, Ted
Where the Boys Are 1961,Ja 20,22:1
Bergerac, Jacques
Girls, Les 1957,O 4,27:2
Gigi 1958,My 16,21:1
Thunder in the Sun 1959,Ap 9,37:2
BERGERE
See Also BURGER, BERGER
Bergere, Ouida
Kick In 1922,D 18,22:2
Bella Donna 1923,Ap 16,20:2
Bergere, Ouida (Screenwriter)
Witness for the Defense, The 1919,S 15,16:3
On With the Dance 1920,F 16,8:1
Three Live Ghosts 1922,Ja 2,20:1

Bergere, Ouida (Screenwriter)— Cont
Man From Home, The 1922,My 1,20:3
To Have and to Hold 1922,N 6,13:1
Rustle of Silk 1923,My 8,22:4
Cheat, The 1923,Ag 27,14:3
Bergere, Roy (Composer)
Three for the Show 1955,F 25,16:1
Bergere, Valerie
It's Love I'm After 1937,N 11,31:2
Bergeron
Abused Confidence 1938,D 1,29:1
S O S Mediterranean 1940,Ja 1,29:2
Pepe le Moko 1941,Mr 4,20:2
Marthe Richard 1944,N 9,23:2
Stormy Waters 1946,Je 17,32:2
Midnight in Paris 1947,O 9,32:3
Bergeron, Rene
Heart of Paris 1939,Ja 13,17:3
Berggren, Thommy
Elvira Madigan 1967,S 30,26:1
Elvira Madigan 1967,O 31,37:2
Berggren, Ulf
Children, The 1949,D 23,17:1
BERGH
See Also BERG, BERGE, BURG
Bergh, Eva
Long Memory, The 1953,Jl 27,15:2
Berghof, Herbert
Five Fingers 1952,F 23,7:5
Diplomatic Courier 1952,Je 14,12:2
Red Planet Mars 1952,Je 16,15:2
Assignment-Paris 1952,O 25,12:6
Fraulein 1958,Je 9,27:2
Cleopatra 1963,Je 13,29:1
Affair of the Skin, An 1963,N 21,43:2
Bergia, Joaquin
Dos Mujeres y un Don Juan 1934,Je 4,12:4
Berglund, Bjoern
Natt, En 1935,Ja 29,24:1
Swedenhielms 1935,S 6,12:3
Loerdagskvaellar 1936,F 13,25:3
Soederkaakar 1936,D 19,16:2
Karl Fredrik Reigns 1938,F 2,15:2
Baldvins Brollop; Baldwin's Wedding
 1938,D 27,13:2
Familjen Andersson; Anderson Family, The
 1939,Ja 24,16:5
Sun Over Klara 1944,My 1,20:8
Berglund, Bullen
Under Falsk Flagg 1937,Ja 20,18:5
Berglund, Erik
For Her Sake 1930,N 11,29:1
Rena Rama Sanningen; Nothing but the Truth
 1939,O 7,11:2
En Enda Natt 1942,D 7,22:2
Interlude 1949,Ja 3,19:2
Katrina 1949,N 18,35:3
Bergman, Hellmuth
Zigeunerweisen; Gypsy Ways 1940,My 11,15:3
Bergman, Henry
Gold Rush, The 1925,Ag 17,10:3
Circus, The 1928,Ja 9,20:1
Modern Times 1936,F 6,23:2
Bergman, Ingmar (Director)
Frustration 1949,Ag 27,7:3
Illicit Interlude 1954,O 27,32:6
Naked Night, The 1956,Ap 10,27:5
Smiles of a Summer Night 1957,D 24,11:1
Seventh Seal 1958,O 14,44:1
Wild Strawberries 1959,Je 23,37:1
Magician, The 1959,Ag 28,27:1
Brink of Life; (Nara Livet) 1959,N 9,36:2
Lesson in Love, A 1960,Mr 15,46:1
Dreams; Kvinnodrom 1960,Je 1,42:1
Virgin Spring, The; Jungfrukallan 1960,N 15,46:1
Secrets of Woman 1961,Jl 12,36:1
Devil's Eye, The 1961,O 31,27:4
Through a Glass Darkly 1962,Mr 14,45:1
Devil's Wanton, The 1962,Jl 5,21:2
Night is my Future 1963,Ja 9,5:6
Winter Light 1963,My 14,32:1
Silence, The 1964,F 4,28:1
All These Women 1964,O 6,35:1
Persona 1966,O 20,52:7
Persona 1967,Mr 7,46:2
Hour of the Wolf 1968,Ap 10,50:2
Shame 1968,D 24,14:1
Bergman, Ingmar (Original Author)
Devil's Eye, The 1960,O 18,47:8
Through a Glass Darkly 1962,Mr 14,45:1
Persona 1966,O 20,52:7
Bergman, Ingmar (Producer)
Devil's Eye, The 1960,O 18,47:8
Silence, The 1964,F 4,28:1
Bergman, Ingmar (Screenwriter)
Torment 1947,Ap 22,34:2
Illicit Interlude 1954,O 27,32:6
Naked Night, The 1956,Ap 10,27:5
Smiles of a Summer Night 1957,D 24,11:1
Seventh Seal 1958,O 14,44:1
Wild Strawberries 1959,Je 23,37:1
Magician, The 1959,Ag 28,27:1
Lesson in Love, A 1960,Mr 15,46:1

Dreams; Kvinnodrom 1960,Je 1,42:1
Secrets of Woman 1961,Jl 12,36:1
Devil's Eye, The 1961,O 31,27:4
Devil's Wanton, The 1962,Jl 5,21:2
Night is my Future 1963,Ja 9,5:6
Winter Light 1963,My 14,32:1
Silence, The 1964,F 4,28:1
All These Women 1964,O 6,35:1
Persona 1967,Mr 7,46:2
Hour of the Wolf 1968,Ap 10,50:2
Shame 1968,D 24,14:1
Bergman, Ingrid
Swedenhielms 1935,S 6,12:3
Paa Solsidan 1936,Ag 26,16:3
Intermezzo 1937,D 25,10:6
Kvinnas Ansikte, En; Woman's Face, A
 1939,S 9,11:2
Intermezzo, A Love Story 1939,O 6,31:1
Rage in Heaven 1941,Mr 21,19:2
Adam Had Four Sons 1941,Mr 28,26:6
Dr Jekyll and Mr Hyde 1941,Ag 13,13:2
Casablanca 1942,N 27,27:1
En Enda Natt 1942,D 7,22:2
For Whom the Bell Tolls 1943,Jl 15,25:2
Gaslight 1944,My 5,17:2
Spellbound 1945,N 2,22:2
Saratoga Trunk 1945,N 22,39:2
Bells of St Mary's, The 1945,D 7,26:2
Notorious 1946,Ag 16,19:2
Arch of Triumph 1948,Ap 21,33:2
Joan of Arc 1948,N 12,30:5
Under Capricorn 1949,S 9,28:3
Surf, The 1949,D 17,15:2
Stromboli 1950,F 16,28:2
Greatest Love, The 1954,Ja 12,19:2
Anastasia 1956,D 14,35:6
Paris Does Strange Things 1957,Mr 30,13:2
Indiscreet 1958,Je 27,18:2
Inn of the Sixth Happiness, The 1958,D 14,2:7
Goodbye Again 1961,Je 30,32:2
Visit, The 1964,O 22,44:1
Yellow Rolls-Royce, The 1965,My 14,42:2
Bergman, Lena
Wild Strawberries 1959,Je 23,37:1
Bergner, Elisabeth
Impetuous Youth 1927,Je 13,17:1
Traeumende Mund, Der 1934,F 5,19:2
Catherine the Great 1934,F 15,15:6
Ariane 1934,Mr 7,23:4
Escape me Never 1935,My 24,24:2
As You Like It 1936,N 6,29:3
Dreaming Lips 1937,My 20,17:1
Stolen Life 1939,Je 15,27:2
Paris Calling 1942,Ja 19,21:2
Bergoe, Aino
Frauenparadies, Das; Woman's Paradise
 1939,Je 24,14:3
Bergryd, Ulla
Bible, The 1966,S 29,60:1
Bergstrom, Torsten
Sunshine Follows Rain 1949,S 29,39:2
Bergunker, Adolph (Director)
Fathers and Sons 1960,D 26,27:2
Bergunker, Adolph (Producer)
Fathers and Sons 1960,D 26,27:2
Bergvall, Sven
Haelsingar 1934,S 25,25:2
Berhard, Raymond
Jeanne Dore 1928,Ja 2,28:3 (In Addenda)
Berisch, Siegfried
Grosse Tenor, Der 1931,My 29,26:5
Blonde Nachtigall, Die 1931,Ag 22,7:5
Beristain, Leopold
Mexico Lindo 1939,F 4,11:1
Beristain, Luis
This Strange Passion 1955,D 5,34:2
Exterminating Angel, The 1967,Ag 22,33:1
Berk, Irma (Original Author)
This Rebel Breed 1960,My 5,41:2
Berke, William (Director)
Falcon in Mexico, The 1944,Ag 5,16:2
Betrayal From the East 1945,Ap 25,27:2
Why Girls Leave Home 1945,Ag 4,7:3
Dick Tracy 1946,Ja 12,10:7
Falcon's Adventure, The 1946,D 14,19:2
Shoot to Kill 1947,My 17,8:5
Jungle Jim 1949,Ja 1,9:2
Zamba 1949,N 7,33:2
Deputy Marshal 1949,N 11,31:3
Mark of the Gorilla 1950,F 17,27:2
Jungle, The 1952,O 2,32:3
Cop Hater 1958,O 2,44:3
Mugger, The 1959,Je 25,20:7
Berke, William (Producer)
Confessions of Boston Blackie 1941,D 8,31:2
Falcon's Alibi, The 1946,Ap 13,23:2
Shoot to Kill 1947,My 17,8:5
Jungle, The 1952,O 2,32:3
Cop Hater 1958,O 2,44:3
Mugger, The 1959,Je 25,20:7
Berke, William (Screenwriter)
Deputy Marshal 1949,N 11,31:3

BERKELEY
See Also BERKLEY
Berkeley, Anthony (Original Author)
Flight From Destiny 1941,Mr 28,26:7
Berkeley, Ballard
East Meets West 1936,O 31,24:2
Saint in London, The 1939,Jl 19,23:3
In Which We Serve 1942,D 24,18:1
Long Dark Hall, The 1951,My 10,38:3
White Fire 1954,S 18,12:4
Berkeley, Bollard
1954,S 18,12:4
Berkeley, Busby
Babes in Arms 1939,O 20,27:2
Berkeley, Busby (Director)
She Had to Say Yes 1933,Jl 29,14:2
Dames 1934,Ag 16,20:2
Gold Diggers of 1935 1935,Mr 15,25:2
Bright Lights 1935,Ag 15,15:2
I Live for Love 1935,O 19,21:2
Stage Struck 1936,S 28,14:4
Go Getter, The 1937,Je 4,27:2
Hollywood Hotel 1938,Ja 13,17:3
Men Are Such Fools 1938,Je 17,25:1
Garden of the Moon 1938,S 24,13:1
Comet over Broadway 1938,D 16,33:3
They Made Me a Criminal 1939,Ja 21,19:2
Fast And Furious 1939,O 12,33:3
Forty Little Mothers 1940,Ap 19,25:2
Strike up the Band 1940,S 30,13:2
Babes on Broadway 1942,Ja 1,37:1
For Me and My Gal 1942,O 22,25:1
Gang's All Here, The 1943,D 23,26:4
Cinderella Jones 1946,Mr 16,9:6
Take Me Out to the Ball Game 1949,Mr 10,35:2
Berkeley, Busby (Miscellaneous)
In Caliente 1935,Je 27,16:1
Gold Diggers of 1937 1936,D 25,19:2
Singing Marine, The 1937,Jl 1,33:2
Varsity Show 1937,S 2,17:2
Gold Diggers in Paris 1938,Je 2,19:2
Girl Crazy 1943,D 3,27:2
Berkeley, Martin (Original Author)
Penalty, The 1941,Ap 10,29:3
Kangaroo 1952,My 17,22:7
Berkeley, Martin (Screenwriter)
Three Men in White 1944,My 26,23:3
Gallant Bess 1946,D 6,27:6
So Dark the Night 1946,D 7,16:2
Green Grass of Wyoming 1948,Je 10,28:3
Sand 1949,Ag 5,23:2
Revenge of the Creature 1955,My 14,10:7
Big Caper, The 1957,Mr 29,16:1
Berkeley, Reginald (Original Author)
French Leave 1931,D 7,16:1
World Moves On, The 1934,Je 30,18:5
Nurse Edith Cavell 1939,S 22,27:4
Berkeley, Reginald (Screenwriter)
Marie Galante 1934,N 21,23:4
Wanted Men 1936,Jl 8,15:2
Berkes, John
Egg and I, The 1947,Ap 25,29:2
Corpse came C O D, The 1947,Ag 19,27:2
Romance on the High Seas 1948,Je 26,10:5
My Dream Is Yours 1949,Ap 16,11:3
Branded 1951,Ja 11,28:5
Ace in the Hole 1951,Je 30,8:6
Journey Into Light 1951,O 5,24:4
Berkey, Ralph (Original Author)
Time Limit 1957,O 24,37:2
BERKLEY
See Also BERKELEY
Berkley, Lynne
Girls' Dormitory 1936,Ag 29,16:2
Berkman, Edward O (Composer)
Murder on Diamond Row 1937,N 12,27:2
Berkman, Edward O (Screenwriter)
Murder on Diamond Row 1937,N 12,27:2
Green Cockatoo, The 1947,Jl 19,10:2
Berkman, Ted (Original Author)
Bedtime for Bonzo 1951,Ap 6,31:4
Cast a Giant Shadow 1966,Mr 31,43:3
Berkman, Ted (Screenwriter)
Fear Strikes Out 1957,Mr 21,37:2
Girl of the Night 1960,N 12,15:1
Berkowitz, Zilla
Dream no More 1950,Ja 6,25:2
Berky, Lila
Az Uj Rokon 1935,Mr 12,25:3
Berky, Lili
Buzavirag 1935,Ja 14,11:3
As Uj Rokon; New Relative, The
 1935,Mr 12,25:3
Zsivany Becsuelet 1935,O 30,16:3
Vasember 1935,D 9,25:3
Kiralyne Huszarja, A 1936,Ja 17,15:3
Harom Sarkany 1936,D 22,32:3
Sziuel Szivert; Heart for Heart 1939,Ja 16,11:3
Eb Ura Fako 1940,Mr 23,16:4
Sut a Nap (Sun Shines, The); Sun Shines, The
 1940,Ap 6,13:3

Berlanga, Luis (Director)
Rocket From Calabuch 1958,O 8,41:1
Not on Your Life; Verdugo, El 1965,Mr 30,52:1
Berlanga, Luis (Original Author)
Rocket From Calabuch 1958,O 8,41:1
Not on Your Life; Verdugo, El 1965,Mr 30,52:1
Berlanga, Luis (Screenwriter)
Not on Your Life; Verdugo, El 1965,Mr 30,52:1
Berle, Milton
New Faces of 1937 1937,Jl 2,25:1
Radio City Revels 1938,Mr 21,18:3
Tall, Dark and Handsome 1941,Ja 24,15:2
Sun Valley Serenade 1941,S 6,20:1
Rise and Shine 1941,D 6,14:3
Gentleman at Heart, A 1942,F 23,25:2
Whispering Ghosts 1942,My 18,19:4
Over my Dead Body 1942,D 26,15:2
Margin for Error 1943,Ja 25;10:7
Always Leave Them Laughing 1949,N 24,48:2
Let's Make Love 1960,S 9,36:1
It's a Mad, Mad, Mad, Mad World
   1963,N 19,47:1
Sound of Laughter, The 1963,D 18,44:2
Loved One, The 1965,O 12,57:1
Oscar, The 1966,Mr 5,16:1
Happening, The 1967,My 18,56:3
Who's Minding the Mint? 1967,D 7,60:3
Where Angels Go-Trouble Follows
   1968,Ap 11,51:1
For Singles Only 1968,Je 6,54:1
Berley, Andre
Passion Of Joan Of Arc, The 1929,Mr 29,21:1
Passion of Jeanne d'Arc, The 1929,Mr 31,VIII,7:1
Si l'Empereur Savait Ca 1931,F 23,20:3
Tu Seras Duchesse 1932,My 7,11:5
Avec l'Assurance 1935,My 4,17:3
Berlicz, Jacques
Human Beast, The 1940,F 20,17:2
Great Temptation, The 1942,Jl 10,13:3
Berlin, Abby (Director)
Mary Ryan, Detective 1949,N 4,33:3
Berlin, Irving
This Is the Army 1943,Jl 29,11:6
Berlin, Irving (Composer)
Puttin' on the Ritz 1930,F 15,15:1
Mammy 1930,Mr 27,24:5
Reaching for the Moon 1930,D 30,24:2
Follow the Fleet 1936,F 21,21:2
On the Avenue 1937,F 5,17:3
Alexander's Ragtime Band 1938,Ag 6,7:2
Carefree 1938,S 23,35:1
Second Fiddle 1939,Jl 1,11:2
Louisiana Purchase 1942,Ja 1,37:1
Holiday Inn 1942,Ag 5,16:1
This Is the Army 1943,Jl 29,11:6
Blue Skies 1946,O 17,28:2
Easter Parade 1948,Jl 1,19:3
Annie Get Your Gun 1950,My 18,37:1
White Christmas 1954,O 15,16:3
Berlin, Irving (Miscellaneous)
Top Hat 1935,Ag 30,12:2
Berlin, Irving (Original Author)
Holiday Inn 1942,Ag 5,16:1
This Is the Army 1943,Jl 29,11:6
Blue Skies 1946,O 17,28:2
Berlin, Patsy
Crime of Dr Crespi, The 1936,Ja 13,14:3
Berlin, Pierre
Stranger, The 1967,D 19,59:1
Berlin Fire Department
When Duty Calls 1929,Ja 1,60:1
Berliner, George
Good Bad Girl, The 1931,My 15,20:6
Berliner, Trude
Because I Loved You 1930,Ja 25,13:2
Tiger von Berlin, Der 1930,S 15,29:3
Maedel von der Reeperbahn, Das 1931,Ja 31,15:1
Rheinlandmaedel, Das 1931,S 18,29:1
Ein Prinz Verliebt Sich 1932,Ap 29,13:4
Die Singende Stadt 1932,My 10,25:4
Stolz der 3 Kompagnie, Der 1932,Jl 21,15:2
Pension Schoeller 1932,S 20,26:3
Week-End Im Paradies 1932,O 24,18:5
Zirkus Leben 1932,D 28,14:7
Hellseher, Der 1933,S 11,20:4
Hochtourist, Der 1934,Ja 13,16:4
Fraeulein-Falsch Verbunden! 1934,Ja 15,12:2
Tausend Fuer Eine Nacht 1934,F 12,19:2
Kaiserwalzer 1934,D 29,11:2
Berlinger, Warren
Teenage Rebel 1956,N 17,17:6
Three Brave Men 1957,Mr 16,13:2
Blue Denim 1959,Jl 31,21:1
Platinum High School 1960,My 26,37:3
Wackiest Ship in the Army, The 1961,F 9,35:1
All Hands on Deck 1961,Ap 1,10:2
Billie 1965,S 16,55:3
Spinout 1966,D 15,60:1
Thunder Valley 1967,S 14,55:1
Thunder Alley 1967,S 14,55:1
Berlioz, Jacques
Crime in the Maginot Line 1939,My 8,21:2
Ruy Blas 1948,O 4,14:2

BERMAN
See Also BURMAN
Berman, E W
Ranson's Folly 1926,My 31,10:2
Berman, Henry (Producer)
Just This Once 1952,Mr 18,22:3
You for Me 1952,S 25,38:3
Men of the Fighting Lady 1954,My 8,15:2
Prisoner of War 1954,My 10,20:2
Bedevilled 1955,Ap 23,23:1
It's a Dog's Life 1955,D 23,14:3
Berman, Monty (Cinematographer)
Edge of the World, The 1938,S 12,13:2
Berman, Monty (Director)
Jack the Ripper 1960,F 18,37:4
Berman, Monty (Producer)
Murder Will Out 1953,Ap 6,24:2
Crawling Eye, The 1959,Ja 1,38:1
Jack the Ripper 1960,F 18,37:4
Home Is the Hero 1961,Ja 26,32:1
No Place Like Homicide 1962,S 13,32:1
Berman, Monty (Screenwriter)
Desert Patrol 1962,Ja 18,23:5
Berman, Pandro S (Producer)
Gay Divorcee, The 1934,N 16,27:1
Little Minister, The 1934,D 28,25:1
Romance in Manhattan 1935,Ja 18,29:2
Roberta 1935,Mr 8,25:2
Laddie 1935,My 6,22:3
Break of Hearts 1935,My 17,24:3
Alice Adams 1935,Ag 16,11:3
Top Hat 1935,Ag 30,12:2
Freckles 1935,O 26,12:2
I Dream too Much 1935,N 29,24:1
In Person 1935,D 13,31:5
Sylvia Scarlett 1936,Ja 10,16:2
Muss 'Em Up 1936,F 3,21:2
Follow the Fleet 1936,F 21,21:2
Mary of Scotland 1936,Jl 31,22:2
Swing Time 1936,Ag 28,21:2
Big Game, The 1936,O 24,23:1
Woman Rebels, A 1936,O 30,27:2
Winterset 1936,D 4,31:1
That Girl From Paris 1937,Ja 1,19:1
Quality Street 1937,Ap 9,19:2
Soldier and the Lady, The 1937,Ap 10,11:1
Shall We Dance 1937,My 14,21:1
Stage Door 1937,O 8,27:2
Damsel in Distress, A 1937,N 25,37:1
Vivacious Lady 1938,Je 3,17:3
Having Wonderful Time 1938,Jl 8,11:2
Mother Carey's Chickens 1938,Ag 5,11:1
Room Service 1938,S 22,27:1
Carefree 1938,S 23,35:1
Flying Irishman, The 1939,Ap 12,27:2
Hunchback of Notre Dame, The 1940,Ja 1,29:2
Ziegfeld Girl 1941,Ap 25,17:2
Love Crazy 1941,Je 6,25:5
Honky Tonk 1941,O 3,27:3
Rio Rita 1942,My 8,27:3
Somewhere I'll Find You 1942,Ag 28,22:4
Slightly Dangerous 1943,Ap 2,17:2
Dragon Seed 1944,Jl 21,16:4
Seventh Cross, The 1944,S 29,18:1
Marriage Is a Private Affair 1944,O 27,17:7
National Velvet 1944,D 15,25:2
Undercurrent 1946,N 29,36:2
Sea of Grass, The 1947,F 28,27:2
Living in a Big Way 1947,O 10,31:4
If Winter Comes 1948,Ja 23,28:4
Three Musketeers, The 1948,O 21,33:2
Bribe, The 1949,F 4,31:2
Madame Bovary 1949,Ag 26,15:2
Doctor and the Girl, The 1949,O 31,20:2
Father of the Bride 1950,My 19,31:2
Soldiers Three 1951,Mr 30,28:5
Father's Little Dividend 1951,Ap 13,18:5
Light Touch, The 1952,Ja 17,23:1
Ivanhoe 1952,Ag 1,8:2
Prisoner of Zenda, The 1952,N 5,36:2
Battle Circus 1953,My 28,27:5
All the Brothers Were Valiant 1953,D 29,19:2
Knights of the Round Table 1954,Ja 8,17:2
Long, Long Trailer, The 1954,F 19,24:3
Blackboard Jungle 1955,Mr 21,21:5
Quentin Durward 1955,N 24,41:1
Bhowani Junction 1956,My 25,26:1
Tea and Sympathy 1956,S 28,24:4
Something of Value 1957,My 11,24:6
Jailhouse Rock 1957,N 14,41:1
Brothers Karamazov, The 1958,F 21,18:2
Reluctant Debutante, The 1958,Ag 15,17:1
All the Fine Young Cannibals 1960,S 23,33:1
Key Witness 1960,N 12,15:1
Butterfield 8 1960,N 17,46:1
Sweet Bird of Youth 1962,Mr 29,28:2
Prize, The 1964,Ja 24,21:1
Patch of Blue, A 1965,D 16,63:1
Berman, Shelley
Best Man, The 1964,Ap 7,29:1
Divorce American Style 1967,Jl 20,30:2

Bermejo, Chiro
Tia Tula, A 1965,Je 3,24:1
Bermudez, Aurora
Corazones en Derrota 1934,O 10,21:4
Bern, Paul (Director)
North Wind's Malice, The 1920,O 18,13:1
Open all Night 1924,S 9,19:1
Worldly Goods 1924,N 3,20:1
Tomorrow's Love 1925,Ja 7,33:5
Dressmaker from Paris, The 1925,Mr 18,19:2
Grounds for Divorce 1925,Je 29,8:2
Flower of the Night 1925,O 19,26:1
Bern, Paul (Screenwriter)
Vanity's Price 1924,O 8,16:2
Beloved Rogue, The 1927,Mr 14,16:1
Berna, Eric (Cinematographer)
This Is China 1937,O 6,29:4
Bernanos, Georges (Original Author)
Diary of a Country Priest 1954,Ap 6,35:2
Mouchette 1968,S 21,26:1
BERNARD
See Also BARNARD, BERNHARD,
   BERNHARDT
Bernard, Alex
Kameradschaft 1932,N 9,28:5
Maternelle, La 1935,O 15,19:1
Bernard, Armand
Miracle of the Wolves, The 1925,F 24,17:3
Miracle des Loups, Le 1930,Jl 28,22:1
Fra Diavolo 1931,N 23,22:1
Monsieur de Pourceaugnac 1932,N 6,IX,4:2
Amphitryon 1937,Mr 24,29:1
Boys' School 1939,Je 6,26:2
Affair Lafont, The; Conflit 1939,O 9,15:2
Noah's Ark 1950,Ag 21,15:1
Hoboes in Paradise 1950,O 9,21:5
Bernard, Barney
Potash and Perlmutter 1923,S 24,5:4
Bernard, Barry
Two Mrs Carrolls, The 1947,Ap 7,20:1
Cry Wolf 1947,Jl 19,10:2
Casbah 1948,My 3,27:4
Woman in White, The 1948,My 8,12:2
Kind Lady 1951,Ag 8,21:2
Titanic 1953,My 28,27:5
Houdini 1953,Jl 3,10:2
Elephant Walk 1954,Ap 22,37:2
Virgin Queen, The 1955,Ag 6,13:2
Bernard, Butch
Seven Year Itch, The 1955,Je 4,9:1
Toy Tiger 1956,Je 30,11:2
All Mine to Give 1959,Ag 4,32:5
Bernard, Carl
Headless Ghost, The 1959,Ap 30,37:2
Bernard, Dick
Bluebeard's Seven Wives 1925,D 28,19:2
Bernard, Guy (Composer)
Paris 1900 1950,O 24,34:6
Bernard, Harry
New Faces of 1937 1937,Jl 2,25:1
Bernard, Ian
Bachelor and the Bobby-Soxer, The
   1947,Jl 25,12:5
Bernard, Ian (Screenwriter)
Synanon 1965,My 6,44:1
Oh Dad, Poor Dad, Mamma's Hung You in the
   Closet and I'm Feeling so Sad 1967,F 16,32:1
Bernard, Ivor
Great Expectations 1947,My 23,31:1
Bernard, Jack (Director)
Unknown Island 1949,Ja 8,11:4
Bernard, Jack (Producer)
Double Trouble 1967,My 25,54:2
Bernard, Jacques
Strange Ones, The 1952,Jl 29,17:3
Caroline Cherie 1954,My 25,23:1
Bernard, Jean-Jacques (Screenwriter)
Katia 1939,D 23,9:2
Bernard, Jeffrey (Producer)
Where Are Your Children? 1944,Ja 17,14:5
Bernard, Joseph
No Other Woman 1933,Ja 30,9:4 (In Addenda)
They Knew What They Wanted 1940,O 11,25:2
House of Dracula 1945,D 22,16:3
Pat and Mike 1952,Je 19,32:6
Murder, Inc 1960,Je 29,26:6
Judgment at Nuremberg 1961,D 20,36:1
Bernard, Josephine
Way Down East 1931,Mr 16,25:1
Bernard, Judd (Producer)
Point Blank 1967,S 19,53:1
Blue 1968,My 11,28:1
Negatives 1968,O 15,40:1
Bernard, Lester
Sweet Rosie O'Grady 1926,D 9,33:1
Flying Romeos 1928,Ap 3,33:2
Bernard, M (Miscellaneous)
Katia 1939,D 23,9:2
Bernard, Napoleon
Golden Mistress, The 1954,O 30,15:6
Bernard, Nicolette
End of the River, The 1948,Je 21,18:2

Bernard, Paul
Pension Mimosas 1936,My 6,27:1
Panic 1947,N 27,50:2
Damned, The; Maudits, Les 1948,Ap 26,27:2
Friend Will come Tonight, A; Ami Viendra Ce
Soir, Un 1948,Jl 12,11:2
Caroline Cherie 1954,My 25,23:1
Dames du Bois de Boulogne, Les; Ladies of the
Park 1964,Ap 4,15:5
Bernard, Raymond (Director)
Miracle of the Wolves, The 1925,F 24,17:3
Chess Player, The 1930,My 19,21:1
Miracle des Loups, Le 1930,Jl 28,22:1
Croix de Bois, Les; Wooden Crosses
1932,Ap 3,VIII,6:4
Miserables, Les 1934,Mr 25,X,4:2
Miserables, Les 1936,O 28,31:2
Mayor's Dilemma, The 1940,Ap 23,19:2
Marthe Richard 1944,N 9,23:2
Miserables, Les 1946,D 26,28:4
Friend Will come Tonight, A; Ami Viendra Ce
Soir, Un 1948,Jl 12,11:2
Fruits of Summer 1956,Jl 18,22:2
Bernard, Raymond (Screenwriter)
Miserables, Les 1936,O 28,31:2
Friend Will come Tonight, A; Ami Viendra Ce
Soir, Un 1948,Jl 12,11:2
Fruits of Summer 1956,Jl 18,22:2
Bernard, Roger
My Wife's Husband 1965,Ja 27,26:1
Bernard, Sam
Wanted by the Police 1938,S 26,13:2
Vicious Circle, The 1948,Jl 22,27:2
When my Baby Smiles at Me 1948,N 24,20:2
Bernard, Tristan (Original Author)
Jeanne Dore 1915,O 21,11:4
Jeanne Dore 1928,Ja 2,28:3 (In Addenda)
Playboy of Paris 1930,N 1,23:2
Slipper Episode, The 1938,My 19,25:2
Bernard, Tristan (Screenwriter)
Slipper Episode, The 1938,My 19,25:2
Bernard-Luc, Jean (Miscellaneous)
Tainted 1950,Ja 21,10:2
Bernard-Luc, Jean (Screenwriter)
Monsieur Vincent 1948,D 21,33:2
Tainted 1950,Ja 21,10:2
Bernardi
Tomorrow Is my Turn 1962,F 2,24:2
Bernardi, Herschel
Green Fields 1937,O 12,31:4
Savage Eye, The 1960,Je 7,27:1
Cold Wind in August, A 1961,Jl 27,23:2
George Raft Story, The 1962,Mr 22,40:1
Irma la Douce 1963,Je 6,39:1
Bernardi, Nerio
Shepherd King, The 1923,D 11,26:2
Delitto di Mastrovanni, Il 1935,Jl 30,16:2
Tempo Massimo 1936,Mr 13,27:2
Fiat Voluntas Dei 1936,Jl 6,11:5
Loyalty of Love 1937,Mr 1,15:1
Avventura di Giacomo Casanova 1938,D 2,27:3
Corsaro Nero, Il; Black Corsair, The
1939,My 8,21:3
Lost One, The; La Traviata 1948,Mr 30,26:2
Heart and Soul 1950,Je 15,41:3
Never Take No for an Answer 1952,Ap 29,32:2
I Cadetti di Guascogna 1952,O 6,22:2
Fanfan the Tulip 1953,My 5,34:2
Theodora, Slave Empress 1955,Ja 12,24:2
Bernardi, Piero di (Screenwriter)
Guendalina 1958,Je 30,23:2
Bernauer, Rudolf (Director)
Hirsekorn Greift Ein 1932,Je 10,22:3
Glueckszylinder, Der 1934,Mr 10,18:4
Bernauer, Rudolf (Original Author)
Garden of Eden, The 1928,Mr 19,26:2
Once a Lady 1931,N 9,22:4
Her Majesty, Love 1931,N 26,37:2
Ihre Majestaet die Liebe 1933,F 7,23:4
Bernauer, Rudolf (Screenwriter)
Forbidden Music 1938,D 27,13:2
Hatter's Castle 1948,Jl 3,8:6
Bernda, Edward (Director)
Blondie Hits the Jackpot 1949,S 9,28:3
Bernds, Edward (Director)
Three Stooges Meet Hercules, The
1962,Ja 27,13:4
Three Stooges in Orbit, The 1962,Jl 12,19:4
Bernds, Edward (Screenwriter)
Tickle Me 1965,Je 24,28:3
Berndt, Gretl
Rheinlandmaedel, Das 1931,S 18,29:1
Berndt, Hilde
Lysistrata 1948,Je 19,19:2
Berndt, Reinhold
Salto Mortale 1931,O 25,VIII,6:1
Kirschen in Nachbars Garten 1937,My 15,23:6
BERNE
See Also BYRNE, BURN
Berne, Josef
Vida Bohemia, La 1939,F 6,8:5
Catskill Honeymoon 1950,Ja 28,10:3

Berne, Josef (Director)
Dawn to Dawn 1933,D 27,23:5
Mirele Efros 1939,O 21,12:2
Berne, Josef (Original Author)
Dawn to Dawn 1933,D 27,23:5
Berne, Josef (Screenwriter)
Mirele Efros 1939,O 21,12:2
Bernede, Arthur (Screenwriter)
Judex 1966,Ap 26,55:1
Berneis, Peter (Screenwriter)
Portrait of Jennie 1949,Mr 30,31:2
Glass Menagerie, The 1950,S 29,31:5
My Man Godfrey 1957,O 12,23:1
Stranger in my Arms 1959,Mr 4,34:2
Escape from East Berlin 1962,D 6,55:3
Berner, Sara
Backlash 1947,My 24,10:5
City Across the River 1949,Ap 8,31:3
Gay Intruders, The 1949,Je 28,33:4
Carrie 1952,Jl 17,20:2
Rear Window 1954,Ag 5,18:2
Spring Reunion 1957,My 6,25:2
Bernerd, Jeffrey
Black Market Babies 1946,Ap 1,23:1
Bernerd, Jeffrey (Producer)
No Greater Sin 1941,Ag 29,18:2
Are These our Parents? 1944,Ag 23,16:2
Allotment Wives 1945,N 22,39:3
Black Gold 1947,S 5,16:4
Blue Grass of Kentucky 1950,Ja 27,29:2
Bernes, Mark
Diary of a Nazi 1943,Mr 25,25:3
Two Soldiers 1944,Jl 27,14:2
Ural Front, The 1945,Je 7,25:3
Turning Point, The 1946,O 28,19:4
Taras Shevchenko 1952,Jl 28,12:6
Maximka 1953,O 12,30:4
Boys From Leningrad, The 1955,My 2,16:5
Frigid Sea, The 1955,N 21,23:4
School of Courage 1957,S 9,21:2
BERNHARD
See Also BERNARD, BARNARD,
BERNHARDT
Bernhard, Curtis (Director)
Kisses for my President 1964,Ag 22,13:1
Bernhard, Curtis (Producer)
Kisses for my President 1964,Ag 22,13:1
Bernhard, Jack (Director)
Decoy 1946,N 2,12:2
Violence 1947,My 10,8:5
Second Face, The 1951,Mr 2,21:3
Bernhard, Jack (Producer)
Decoy 1946,N 2,12:2
Bernhard, Jack (Screenwriter)
West of Carson City 1940,My 7,31:3
Bernhard, Joseph (Producer)
Journey Into Light 1951,O 5,24:4
Japanese War Bride 1952,Ja 30,22:6
Ruby Gentry 1952,D 26,20:2
Moonlighter, The 1953,S 23,37:2
BERNHARDT
See Also BERNARD, BARNARD, BERNHARD
Bernhardt, Curtis
Three Loves 1929,S 9,30:2
Mann der den Mord Beging, Der; Man Who
Committed the Murder, The 1931,F 22,VIII,6:2
Thirteen Men and a Girl 1932,Jl 17,18:2
Die Letze Kompagnie 1932,Ag 26,20:3
Beloved Vagabond, The 1937,F 8,12:5
Crossroads 1939,Mr 14,17:5
My Love Came Back 1940,Jl 13,16:5
Lady With red Hair 1940,D 6,28:2
Conflict 1945,Je 16,10:2
Beau Brummell 1954,O 21,31:5
Bernhardt, Curtis (Director)
Million Dollar Baby 1941,Je 7,20:2
Juke Girl 1942,Je 20,9:2
Happy Go Lucky 1943,Mr 25,25:1
My Reputation 1946,Ja 26,19:2
Devotion 1946,Ap 6,10:5
Stolen Life, A 1946,My 2,27:4
Possessed 1947,My 30,25:2
High Wall 1947,D 26,22:2
Doctor and the Girl, The 1949,O 31,20:2
Payment on Demand 1951,F 16,21:2
Sirocco 1951,Je 14,31:2
Blue Veil, The 1951,O 27,10:5
Merry Widow, The 1952,S 25,38:1
Miss Sadie Thompson 1953,D 24,9:1
Interrupted Melody 1955,My 6,18:1
Gaby 1956,My 10,26:3
Damon and Pythias 1962,S 6,37:2
Bernhardt, Sarah
Jeanne Dore 1915,O 21,11:4
Mothers of France 1917,Mr 12,9:1
Jeanne Dore 1928,Ja 2,28:3 (In Addenda)
Bernheim, Tord
Kalle paa Spaangen 1940,Ja 27,9:3
Sun Over Klara 1944,My 1,20:8
Berni, Mara
Hours of Love, The 1965,S 4,11:5

Bernie, Ben
Shoot the Works 1934,Jl 7,16:5
Stolen Harmony 1935,Ap 20,16:2
Wake up and Live 1937,Ap 24,16:2
Love and Hisses 1938,Ja 1,11:1
Bernie, Thomas S Jr
Ramparts We Watch, The 1940,S 20,27:1
Bernier, George (Director)
Miracle of Saint Therese 1959,F 10,38:4 (In
Addenda)
Bernis, Blanche
Tourmoi, Le 1929,Mr 3,VIII,7:2
BERNS
See Also BYRNES, BURNS
Berns, Larry (Original Author)
Public Pigeon No 1 1957,My 18,23:2
BERNSTEIN
See Also BURNSTINE
Bernstein, Elmer (Composer)
Thoroughly Modern Millie 1967,Mr 23,25:1
Bernstein, Henri (Original Author)
Dreaming Lips 1937,My 20,17:1
Dreaming Lips; (Traumende Mund, The)
1958,N 1,14:3
Bernstein, Henry (Original Author)
Washington Masquerade, The 1932,Jl 22,18:2
Orage 1938,D 12,26:2
Bernstein, Isadore (Original Author)
Proud Heart 1925,N 3,25:4
No Greater Love 1932,My 14,11:5
Bernstein, L (Original Author)
City Streets 1938,Jl 25,18:2
Bernstein, Leonard
Satchmo the Great 1958,Mr 1,12:1
Journey to Jerusalem, A 1968,N 18,59:1
Bernstein, Maurice
Not Wanted 1949,Jl 25,11:4
Bernstein, Richard (Producer)
Why Must I Die? 1960,S 15,45:4
Bernstein, Richard (Screenwriter)
Why Must I Die? 1960,S 15,45:4
Bernstein, Walter (Screenwriter)
Kiss the Blood off my Hands 1948,O 30,10:2
That Kind of Woman 1959,S 12,12:2
Heller in Pink Tights 1960,Mr 17,28:1
Breath of Scandal, A 1960,D 17,19:1
Paris Blues 1961,N 8,41:1
Fail Safe 1964,S 16,36:1
Money Trap, The 1966,My 5,59:1
Bernt, Reinhold
Blue Angel, The 1930,D 6,21:3
Trapeze 1932,My 3,25:2
Rebel, The 1933,Jl 25,17:2
Berntzen, Tutta
Vi Som Gar Koeksvaegen 1933,O 7,18:5
Kaera Slaekten 1934,My 14,20:4
Berog, Jean-Claude
Lost Command 1966,S 15,51:1
Berova, Olinka
Vengance of She, The 1968,My 30,21:4
Berquist, Harold
Guilty as Hell 1932,Ag 6,14:5
Berr, Georges (Original Author)
Million, Le 1931,My 21,33:2
True Confession 1937,D 16,35:2
My Life With Caroline 1941,O 30,27:1
Cross my Heart 1946,D 19,42:3
Berrell, George
City of Masks, The 1920,Jl 12,12:4
Everlasting Whisper, The 1925,O 12,19:3
Berrell, Lloyd
His Majesty O'Keefe 1954,F 6,17:2
Long John Silver 1955,Ap 7,24:1
Berretta, Jane
Mademoiselle 1966,Ag 2,23:1
Berretty, Joka
Scandal in Sorrento 1957,Je 13,37:1
Berri, Claude (Director)
Two of Us, The 1968,F 20,53:1
Berri, Claude (Screenwriter)
Two of Us, The 1968,F 20,53:1
Berri, Robert
Game of Love, The 1954,D 15,41:1
Rouge et Noir 1958,Ap 9,42:1
Night Affair 1961,O 13,27:1
Berriau, Simone
Itto 1936,Ja 29,15:5
Tender Enemy, The 1938,Mr 31,15:2 (In
Addenda)
32 Rue de Montmartre 1944,S 28,26:3
Moulin Rouge 1944,N 23,38:2
Berries, Rockin' The
Go Go Mania 1965,My 20,52:4
Berrington, Jennifer
Father Goose 1964,D 11,55:1
Berrington, Stephanie
Father Goose 1964,D 11,55:1
Berrondo, Paco
Calandria, La 1936,O 12,23:3
BERRY
See Also BARRIE, BARRY

Berry, Aileen
  Soul Fire 1925,My 6,26:3
Berry, Chuck
  Mister Rock and Roll 1957,O 17,42:2
  Jazz on a Summer's Day 1960,Mr 29,46:2
Berry, Donald
  Last Mile, The 1959,F 19,27:1
Berry, Eric
  Edge of the World, The 1938,S 12,13:2
  Red Shoes, The 1948,O 23,9:2
  Miss Robin Hood 1953,Je 27,7:2
  Gilbert and Sullivan 1953,O 28,36:3
Berry, Frank
  Dr Strangelove or: How I Learned to Stop
    Worrying and Love the Bomb 1964,Ja 31,16:1
    (Incorrect in this edition; use 1964,Je 30,24:1
    elsewhere)
Berry, James
  Lady Be Good 1941,S 19,27:1
Berry, John (Director)
  Miss Susie Slagle's 1946,F 7,29:2
  From This Day Forward 1946,Ap 20,16:2
  Cross my Heart 1946,D 19,42:3
  Casbah 1948,My 3,27:4
  Tension 1950,Ja 12,32:4
  He Ran all the Way 1951,Je 21,24:2
  Pantaloons 1956,D 26,34:1
  Tamango 1959,S 17,48:4
Berry, John (Screenwriter)
  Pantaloons 1956,D 26,34:1
  Tamango 1959,S 17,48:4
Berry, Jules
  Crossroads 1939,Mr 14,17:5
  Daybreak 1940,Jl 30,16:2
  32 Rue de Montmartre 1944,S 28,26:3
  Star Without Light; Etoile Sans Lumiere
    1947,Ag 4,14:2
  Devil's Own Envoy, The 1947,Ag 30,8:6
  Symphonie Fantastique, La 1947,D 8,35:2
  Dreams of Love 1954,Je 5,11:2
  Crime of Monsieur Lange, The 1964,Ap 4,15:5
Berry, Julian (Screenwriter)
  Werewolf in a Girls Dormitory 1963,Je 6,39:1
Berry, Mady
  Roi des Resquilleurs, Le 1932,Je 13,19:3
  Maternelle, La 1935,O 15,19:1
  Juif Polonais, Le 1937,S 17,29:3
  Ballerina 1938,N 15,27:1
  Daybreak 1940,Jl 30,16:2
  Personal Column 1941,F 3,13:2
  Ces Dames aux Chapeaux Verts; Ladies in the
    Green Hats, The 1945,Ap 5,26:2
  Twilight 1949,D 30,13:2
  Gates of the Night 1950,Mr 16,40:2
  Ostrich Has two Eggs, The 1960,S 27,40:1
Berry, Nyas
  Lady Be Good 1941,S 19,27:1
  You're my Everything 1949,Jl 23,7:2
Berry, W H
  Student's Romance, The 1936,O 12,23:2
Berry, Walter
  Don Giovanni 1956,D 27,22:1
Berry, Warren
  Lady Be Good 1941,S 19,27:1
  You're my Everything 1949,Jl 23,7:2
Berry Brothers, The
  Panama Hattie 1942,O 2,31:2
Berscholz, J (Producer)
  Nine Bachelors 1942,F 9,19:2
Bersenov, I
  Great Citizen, The 1939,Ja 16,11:2
Bersezio, Vittorio (Original Author)
  His Young Wife 1949,Mr 12,10:2
Bershadsky, Rudolph (Screenwriter)
  In the Rear of the Enemy 1942,O 10,11:2
Berstl, Julius (Original Author)
  Nie Wieder Liebe; No More Love
    1931,O 4,VIII,7:1
BERT
  See Also BURT
Bert, Camille
  David Golder 1932,O 20,24:2
  Frochard et les Deux Orphelines, La
    1934,F 7,16:2
  Itto 1936,Ja 29,15:5
  Lower Depths, The 1937,S 11,20:1
  Heroes of the Marne; (Famille Lefrancois, Le)
    1939,Ap 24,13:2
  Dame de Pique, La 1944,O 19,19:2
Bert, Liliane
  Deadlier Than the Male 1957,O 9,41:1
Bert, Margaret
  Kathleen 1941,D 19,35:3
Bertau, Julien
  Carmen 1946,N 27,20:2
Bertazzolo, Riccardo
  Miracle in Milan 1951,D 18,42:2
Berth, Merlin
  Paisan 1948,Mr 30,26:2
Berthe, Jackie
  Kings Go Forth 1958,Jl 4,15:2

Bertheau, Julien
  Love Is my Profession 1959,Ap 28,41:1
  Possessors, The 1959,Jl 21,24:1
  Madame 1963,Mr 21,8:6
Berthels, Theodor (Screenwriter)
  Skaergaards-Flirt 1936,Ap 8,26:3
  Sun Over Sweden 1938,Ap 9,11:2
Berthier, Jack
  Stolen Affections 1951,Mr 12,20:2
  Master of Ballantrae, The 1953,Ag 6,16:2
Berthomieu (Director)
  Naked Woman, The 1950,Ja 21,10:2
  My First Love 1951,Je 11,20:7
Berthomieu (Screenwriter)
  Resistance; Peleton d'Execution 1946,Jl 5,15:3
Berti, Florella
  Lost in the Dark 1949,My 14,9:2
Berti, Marina
  Earth Cries Out, The; Grido Della Terra, Il
    1949,Ag 31,26:2
  Shamed 1949,O 13,33:3
  Prince of Foxes 1949,D 24,11:2
  Up Front 1951,Mr 26,19:2
  Quo Vadis 1951,N 9,22:2
  Sky Is Red, The 1952,My 27,30:2
  Queen of Sheba, The 1953,N 4,29:3
  Ben Hur 1959,N 19,50:2
  Jessica 1962,Ap 20,20:2
  Damon and Pythias 1962,S 6,37:2
  Cleopatra 1963,Je 13,29:1
  Made in Italy 1967,My 1,44:2
Bertil, Guy
  Ostrich Has two Eggs, The 1960,S 27,40:1
  Green Mare, The; Jument Verte, La
    1961,O 24,41:2
Bertil-Taebe, Sven
  Hugs and Kisses 1968,Ag 19,44:1
Bertin, Francoise
  Guerre est Fini, La; War Is Over, The
    1967,F 2,29:2
Bertin, Pierre
  Queen's Necklace, The 1947,My 17,8:5
  Shop-Girls of Paris; Au Bonheur de Dames
    1947,Je 23,14:4
  Orpheus 1950,N 30,42:2
  Amazing Monsieur Fabre, The 1952,S 9,21:2
  Dr Knock 1955,O 10,31:2
  Babette Goes to War 1960,Je 8,46:1
  Bonnes Femmes, Les 1966,My 13,32:1
Bertin, Yori
  Frantic 1961,Je 12,34:1
  Religieuse, La 1968,S 23,42:3
Bertini, Francesca
  Donna D'una Notte, La 1933,Mr 10,19:4
Bertini, Italo
  Where Words Fail; Donde Mueren las Palabraso
    1948,Ag 19,18:4
Bertl, Maring
  Madame 1963,Mr 21,8:6
Berto, Giuseppe (Original Author)
  Sky Is Red, The 1952,My 27,30:2
  Anna 1953,F 19,20:5
  Eye of the Needle, The 1965,Je 22,25:2
Berto, Giuseppe (Screenwriter)
  Anna 1953,F 19,20:5
Berto, Juliet
  Chinoise, La 1968,Ap 4,58:2
Bertocchi, Antonio
  And There Came a Man 1968,Ap 5,56:4
Bertocchi, Rita
  And There Came a Man 1968,Ap 5,56:4
Bertola, Christian
  They Are not Angels 1948,My 22,8:3
Bertolucci, Bernardo (Director)
  Before the Revolution; Prima della Revolutiona
    1964,S 25,32:1
  Commare Secca, La; Grim Reaper, The
    1966,S 15,51:1
  Partner 1968,S 24,52:2
Bertolucci, Bernardo (Original Author)
  Before the Revolution; Prima della Revolutiona
    1964,S 25,32:1
Bertolucci, Bernardo (Screenwriter)
  Commare Secca, La; Grim Reaper, The
    1966,S 15,51:1
  Partner 1968,S 24,52:2
Bertolucci, Giovanni (Producer)
  Partner 1968,S 24,52:2
Berton, Pierre (Original Author)
  Zaza 1923,S 17,18:2
  Zaza 1939,Ja 5,17:1
Bertone, Alfredo
  White Sister, The 1923,S 6,10:2
  Romola 1924,D 2,13:2
Bertonof, E
  Chalutzim 1934,Ap 2,13:3
Bertoya, Paul
  Hot Rods to Hell 1967,Ag 10,45:5
  Angels From Hell 1968,O 24,55:5
Bertram, Bert
  How to Steal a Million 1966,Jl 15,34:1

Bertram, Frank
  Amateur Gentleman, The 1936,Ap 27,19:2
Bertram, William
  Dramatic Life of Abraham Lincoln, The
    1924,Ja 22,17:3
Bertrand, Jacques-Paul (Producer)
  Triple Cross 1967,Jl 20,20:2
Bertrand, Janette
  Big Red 1962,S 3,11:2
Bertrand, Rafael
  Professionals, The 1966,N 3,45:1
Berubet, Magdeleine
  Miche 1932,D 2,27:4
  Mistigri 1933,Ja 13,19:3
  7 Capital Sins (Gluttony); Gluttony (7 Capital
    Sins) 1963,Ja 17,5:2
Berval
  Dawn Over France 1945,Mr 17,17:2
  Red Angel, The 1950,N 4,13:2
  Light Across the Street, The; Lumiere d'en Face,
    La 1957,Jl 30,20:2
  What Price Murder 1958,N 11,26:1
Berval, M
  Culte de Beaute, Le 1931,Je 8,21:1
Bervil, Andre
  Kreutzer Sonata, The 1938,D 20,30:2
  Devil in the Flesh 1949,My 10,29:2
  Oh, Amelia 1951,D 3,22:2
  Fernandel the Dressmaker 1957,Jl 1,19:2
Berwanger, Jay
  Big Game, The 1936,O 24,23:1
Berwin, Isabel
  Prunelia 1918,Je 3,9:3
Beryll, Eddie
  Open Your Eyes 1919,Je 30,16:3
Berzeil, Wolfe
  Bell, Book and Candle 1958,D 27,2:7
Berzman, Ben (Original Author)
  Never Say Goodbye 1946,N 23,12:2
Berzman, Norma (Original Author)
  Never Say Goodbye 1946,N 23,12:2
Besch, Anthony (Screenwriter)
  Mikado, The 1967,Mr 15,53:1
Besesti, Mario
  Mill on the Po, The 1951,O 23,35:2
  Miss Italy 1952,My 10,16:2
Besier, Rudolf (Original Author)
  Secrets 1924,Mr 25,25:2
  Secrets 1933,Mr 16,21:2
  Barretts of Wimpole Street, The 1934,S 29,12:2
  Barretts of Wimpole Street, The 1957,Ja 18,15:3
Besl, John
  M'liss 1936,Ag 8,5:2
Besnard, Nicole
  Beauty and the Devil 1952,Ag 26,15:2
Besotti, Nino
  Merry Chase, The 1948,S 18,11:4
Besozi, Nino
  Serpente a Sonagli, Il 1936,Ag 17,9:2
Besozzi, Angelo (Director)
  Come le Foglie; Like the Leaves 1938,S 29,31:1
Besozzi, Angelo (Screenwriter)
  Cinderella 1953,My 15,20:2
Besozzi, Mario
  Law Is the Law, The 1959,Mr 11,41:2
Besozzi, Nino
  Tre Anni Senza Donne 1937,My 27,21:4
  Destino di Donna 1937,Je 9,31:6
  Come le Foglie; Like the Leaves 1938,S 29,31:1
  Vivere; To Live 1938,N 15,27:2
  Amore in Quarantena; Love in Quarantine
    1938,D 13,31:2
  Eravamo Sette Sorelle; We Were Seven Sisters
    1939,Mr 3,21:3
  Ho Perduto mio Marito; I Have Lost My
    Husband 1939,O 20,27:4
  Amicizia; Friendship 1940,Mr 1,17:3
  Dama Bianca, La; Lady in White, The
    1940,My 31,15:3
  Rossini 1948,Ja 31,14:2
Bespolyotova, V
  Land, The 1955,Ap 11,29:3
Bess, Big Jeff
  Face in the Crowd, A 1957,My 29,33:1
  Wild River 1960,My 27,22:1
Bessel, Ehmi
  Gruss und Kuss, Veronika 1936,F 24,14:2
Bessell, Ted
  Billie 1965,S 16,55:3
Besser, Joe
  Hot Steel 1940,Je 21,25:3
  Africa Screams 1949,My 5,34:2
  Woman in Hiding 1950,F 23,33:2
  Desert Hawk, The 1950,Ag 26,9:2
  Say One for Me 1959,Je 20,11:2
  Let's Make Love 1960,S 9,36:1
Besserer, Eugenie
  Scarlet Days 1919,N 10,18:2
  Greatest Question, The 1919,D 29,7:2
  Fighting Shepherdess, The 1920,Mr 29,18:1
  Anna Christie 1923,D 10,20:1
  Bread 1924,Jl 21,14:4
  Price She Paid, The 1925,Ja 13,16:1

Besserer, Eugenie— Cont
Confessions of a Queen 1925,Mr 24,20:6
Friendly Enemies 1925,My 5,24:2
Coast of Folly, The 1925,Ag 31,19:3
Circle, The 1925,S 22,22:3
Fire Brigade, The 1926,D 21,20:2
When a Man Loves 1927,F 4,16:6
Captain Salvation 1927,Je 27,25:2
Jazz Singer, The 1927,O 7,24:4
Drums of Love 1928,Ja 25,20:4
Two Lovers 1928,Mr 23,24:4
Yellow Lily, The 1928,My 21,25:1
Lilac Time 1928,Ag 4,7:2
Lady of Chance, A 1929,Ja 14,20:1
Madame X 1929,Ap 25,32:3
Bridge of San Luis Rey, The 1929,My 20,22:6
Thunderbolt 1929,Je 21,17:2
Speedway 1929,S 21,17:1
Illusion 1929,S 28,17:3
Fast Company 1929,O 5,22:5
Seven Faces 1929,N 16,25:2
In Gay Madrid 1930,Je 7,10:4
Besset, Gaby
Magnificent Tramp, The 1962,Ap 25,30:1
Bessie, Alvah (Original Author)
Objective Burma 1945,Ja 27,15:2
Bessie, Alvah (Screenwriter)
Very Thought of You, The 1944,N 18,16:7
Hotel Berlin 1945,Mr 3,11:2
Bessmertnova, Natalia
Bolshoi Ballet 67 1966,S 30,54:1
Bessy, Maurice
Children of Chaos 1950,Ap 20,37:2
Bessy, Maurice (Original Author)
Deadlier Than the Male 1957,O 9,41:1
Best, Edna
Loose Ends 1930,O 18,23:2
Escape 1930,N 1,23:2
Sleeping Partners 1930,D 13,22:2
Calendar, The 1931,N 22,VIII,6:1
Michael and Mary 1932,Mr 5,11:2
Faithful Heart 1933,Ag 15,20:2
Key, The 1934,My 30,14:3
Man Who Knew too Much, The 1935,Mr 23,11:2
Sleeping Partners 1937,Mr 23,IX,6:1
South Riding 1938,Ag 2,15:2
Prison Without Bars 1939,Ap 10,13:2
Intermezzo, A Love Story 1939,O 6,31:1
Swiss Family Robinson 1940,F 9,15:3
Dispatch From Reuters, A 1940,D 12,37:2
Late George Apley, The 1947,Mr 21,29:2
Ghost and Mrs Muir, The 1947,Je 27,17:2
Iron Curtain, The 1948,My 13,31:2
Best, Geoffrey
Born Free 1966,Je 23,29:1
Best, James
Winchester 73 1950,Je 8,38:2
Kansas Raiders 1951,Ja 26,19:2
Target Unknown 1951,Mr 5,24:2
Apache Drums 1951,My 7,22:2
Air Cadet 1951,My 11,32:3
Ma and Pa Kettle at the Fair 1952,Jl 12,16:2
Francis Goes to West Point 1952,Ag 23,10:2
Seven Angry Men 1955,Ap 2,15:2
Gaby 1956,My 10,26:3
Rack, The 1956,N 6,30:1
Left Handed Gun, The 1958,My 8,36:2
Naked and the Dead, The 1958,Ag 7,21:1
Mountain Road, The 1960,Je 30,22:3
Verboten 1960,Jl 12,39:1
Shock Corridor 1963,S 12,32:1
3 on a Couch 1966,Jl 7,30:1
Firecreek 1968,F 22,36:2
Best, Warden Roy
Canon City 1948,Jl 8,19:2
Best, Willie
Little Miss Marker 1934,My 19,18:3
Arizonian, The 1935,Jl 27,16:2
Littlest Rebel, The 1935,D 20,30:1
Murder on a Bridle Path 1936,Ap 11,19:2
Two in Revolt 1936,Ap 25,21:1
Thank You, Jeeves 1936,O 5,25:1
Make Way for a Lady 1936,D 12,15:1
Breezing Home 1937,Mr 20,23:5
Super-Sleuth 1937,Jl 17,18:1
Saturday's Heroes 1937,O 16,22:2
Gold Is Where You Find It 1938,F 14,20:6
Merrily We Live 1938,Mr 18,23:3
Goodbye Broadway 1938,My 14,18:1
Vivacious Lady 1938,Je 3,17:3
Youth Takes a Fling 1938,O 17,12:1
Blondie 1938,D 22,25:4
I Take This Woman 1940,F 16,23:3
Ghost Breakers, The 1940,Jl 4,12:2
Money and the Woman 1940,O 4,29:2
High Sierra 1941,Ja 25,11:2
Road Show 1941,F 19,25:2
Flight From Destiny 1941,Mr 28,26:7
Scattergood Baines 1941,Ap 4,25:2
Lady From Cheyenne, The 1941,Ap 18,18:2
Highway West 1941,Ag 8,13:4
Smiling Ghost, The 1941,S 26,26:5
Nothing but the Truth 1941,O 23,27:1
Body Disappears, The 1942,Ja 31,13:2

Whispering Ghosts 1942,My 18,19:4
Juke Girl 1942,Je 20,9:2
A-Haunting We Will Go 1942,Ag 3,18:4
Busses Roar 1942,S 25,25:4
Hidden Hand, The 1942,N 26,40:4
Cabin in the Sky 1943,My 28,19:3
Kansan, The 1943,O 1,15:3
Thank Your Lucky Stars 1943,O 2,19:2
Home in Indiana 1944,Je 22,23:1
Pillow to Post 1945,My 26,18:2
Hold That Blonde 1945,N 8,17:2
Bride Wore Boots, The 1946,Je 6,16:3
Suddenly It's Spring 1947,F 27,26:2
Red Stallion 1947,N 27,50:3
Bestayeva, Tatiana
Sailor From the Comet, The 1959,Ag 3,21:2
Bester, Rolly
With These Hands 1950,Je 16,28:4
Bestyef, V
Eagle of the Caucasus, The 1932,S 17,18:4
Beswick, Martine
Thunderball 1965,D 22,23:1
Penthouse, The 1967,O 4,38:3
Bethea, David
Green Pastures, The 1936,Jl 17,20:1
Bethea, Jack (Original Author)
Coming Through 1925,F 18,17:3
Bethencourt, Francis
Earth Is Mine, The 1959,Je 27,13:1
Bethman, Sabina
Journey to the Lost City 1960,D 8,43:3
Bethune, Lobert (Director)
Now Cinema! (Malcolm X: Struggle for Freedom);
  Malcolm X: Struggle for Freedom (Now
  Cinema!) 1968,Ap 9,56:1
Bethune, Lobert (Producer)
Now Cinema! (Malcolm X: Struggle for Freedom);
  Malcolm X: Struggle for Freedom (Now
  Cinema!) 1968,Ap 9,56:1
Bethune, Zina
Sunrise at Campobello 1960,S 29,32:1
Betral, Victor
Journey to the Beginning of Time 1967,F 11,20:1
Betrone, Annibale
Duel Without Honor 1953,F 28,8:8
Tormento 1953,Ap 4,9:2
Betschart, Anneliese
It Happened in Broad Daylight 1960,S 30,33:1
Bettac, Ulrich
Eternal Waltz, The; (Ewiger Walzer)
  1959,Jl 9,22:1
Bettarini, Cesare
Marcia Nuziale, La 1936,F 27,23:2
Napoli che mon Muore; Naples That Never Dies
  1940,Mr 4,11:3
Bettauer, Hugo (Original Author)
Streets of Sorrow 1927,Jl 6,23:2
City Without Jews, The 1928,Jl 9,25:1
Bettger, Lyle
No Man of her Own 1950,My 4,32:3
Union Station 1950,O 5,38:3
First Legion, The 1951,Ap 28,9:2
Dear Brat 1951,Jl 5,21:2
Denver and Rio Grande, The 1952,My 17,22:7
Hurricane Smith 1952,O 4,15:2
Great Sioux Uprising, The 1953,Jl 18,6:2
All I Desire 1953,Ag 29,10:1
Forbidden 1954,Ja 23,11:2
Carnival Story 1954,Ap 17,8:2
Sea Chase, The 1955,Je 11,8:7
Lone Ranger, The 1956,F 11,12:1
Gunfight at the O K Corral 1957,My 30,23:2
Johnny Reno 1966,Mr 10,26:3
Fastest Guitar Alive, The 1968,F 15,47:1
Betti, Ugo (Original Author)
Passionate Summer 1957,Jl 22,15:5
Bettinson, Ralph (Miscellaneous)
Mask of the Avenger 1951,Je 27,25:2
Bettinson, Ralph (Screenwriter)
You're in the Army Now 1937,Ap 16,27:2
Rose of the Rio Grande 1938,Jl 9,10:3
Doomed to Die 1940,Jl 30,16:3
1984 1956,O 1,31:1
Bettis, Valerie
Dance Of Life, The 1951,F 28,33:2
Affair in Trinidad 1952,Jl 31,14:2
Let's Do It Again 1953,O 14,34:3
BETTS
See Also BETZ
Betts, Ernest (Miscellaneous)
Forbidden Music 1938,D 27,13:2
Betts, Jack
1+1 1961,N 8,41:1
Betts, William
Sainted Devil, A 1924,N 24,15:3
BETZ
See Also BETTS
Betz, Carl
President's Lady, The 1953,My 22,31:1
Powder River 1953,Jl 4,7:2
Inferno 1953,Ag 12,22:2
Vickie 1953,S 8,26:3
Dangerous Crossing 1953,S 30,37:2

Betz, Carl— Cont
City of Bad Men 1953,O 21,37:6
Spinout 1966,D 15,60:1
Betz, Matthew
Love's Whirlpool 1924,Mr 11,16:2
Those Who Dance 1924,Je 30,16:1
Only Woman, The 1924,N 3,20:1
Siren of Seville, The 1924,N 17,16:1 (In
  Addenda)
Lighthouse by the Sea, The 1924,D 29,11:4
Way of a Girl, The 1925,Mr 30,21:3
Unholy Three, The 1925,Ag 4,14:3
Lights of Old Broadway 1925,N 2,20:1
Little Irish Girl, The 1926,My 11,24:3
Patent Leather Kid, The 1927,Ag 16,31:2
Shepherd of the Hills, The 1928,F 20,14:1
Big City, The 1928,Mr 26,26:2
Telling the World 1928,Jl 16,25:3
Terror, The 1928,Ag 16,25:3
Wedding March, The 1928,O 15,26:1
Sins of the Fathers 1929,Ja 28,21:1
Girls Gone Wild 1929,Ap 22,23:1
Big House, The 1930,Je 25,31:2
Shooting Straight 1930,Jl 28,22:1
See America Thirst 1930,D 12,35:3
Single Sin, The 1931,Mr 17,34:3
Salvation Nell 1931,Jl 6,24:4
Side Show 1931,S 19,10:2
Mystery of the Wax Museum, The
  1933,F 18,13:3
State Trooper 1933,Mr 27,13:6
Tarzan, The Fearless 1933,Ag 12,14:3
I Have Lived 1933,S 6,24:4
House of Rothschild, The 1934,Mr 15,27:2
Florida Special 1936,My 29,15:2
Beucler, Andre (Director)
Adieux les Beaux Jours 1934,Ap 23,20:2
Beughon, Ralph G Lieut (Miscellaneous)
O S S 1946,My 27,15:5
Beutel, Jack
Gone With the Wind 1939,D 20,31:2
Congo Maisie 1940,F 8,18:4
White Witch Doctor 1953,Jl 2,19:3
Jesse James' Women 1954,S 29,23:4
Bevan, A J (Original Author)
Zarak 1956,D 27,22:1
Bevan, Billy
Easy Pickings 1927,Mr 25,25:3
Riley, The Cop 1928,D 4,29:1
Sky Hawk, The 1929,D 12,36:4
Journey's End 1930,Ap 9,25:1
Transatlantic 1931,Jl 31,15:2
Silent Witness, The 1932,F 8,21:1
Sky Devils 1932,Mr 4,17:3
Payment Deferred 1932,N 8,26:3
Cavalcade 1933,Ja 6,23:2
Luxury Liner 1933,F 3,21:3
Looking Forward 1933,My 1,10:2
Study in Scarlet, A 1933,Je 1,15:3
Too Much Harmony 1933,S 23,11:5
Alice in Wonderland 1933,D 23,19:1
Lost Patrol, The 1934,Ap 2,13:2
Caravan 1934,S 28,27:1
Limehouse Blues 1934,D 12,28:2
Mystery Woman 1935,Ja 9,22:2
Black Sheep 1935,Je 28,34:1
Last Outpost, The 1935,O 5,18:2
Tale of Two Cities, A 1935,D 26,21:2
Song and Dance Man 1936,Mr 12,18:2
Dracula's Daughter 1936,My 18,14:2
Piccadilly Jim 1936,Ag 31,19:1
Lloyds of London 1936,N 26,39:1
God's Country and the Woman 1937,Ja 11,15:5
Slave Ship 1937,Je 17,19:2
Another Dawn 1937,Je 18,25:3
Girl of the Golden West, The 1938,Mr 25,15:2
Shadows Over Shanghai 1938,D 1,29:2
Captain Fury 1939,My 26,20:2
We Are not Alone 1939,D 1,27:1
Earl of Chicago, The 1940,Mr 14,29:3
Long Voyage Home, The 1940,O 9,30:2 (In
  Addenda)
Tin Pan Alley 1940,N 22,27:3
Shining Victory 1941,My 31,14:1
Dr Jekyll and Mr Hyde 1941,Ag 13,13:2
Confirm or Deny 1941,D 19,35:2
Man Who Wouldn't Die, The 1942,Ap 28,25:5
Counter-Espionage 1942,S 28,13:2
Picture of Dorian Gray, The 1945,Mr 2,15:2
Terror by Night 1946,F 9,9:2
Cluny Brown 1946,Je 3,27:3
Moss Rose 1947,Jl 3,14:2
Black Arrow, The 1948,O 4,14:2
30 Years of Fun 1963,D 26,33:4
Bevan, Cecil
Gaiety Girls, The 1938,Mr 31,15:1
Blind Goddess, The 1949,Je 23,33:3
Bevan, Donald (Original Author)
Stalag 17 1953,Jl 2,19:2
Bevan, Isla
Sign of the Four, The 1932,Ag 20,7:4
Bevan, William
Swordsman, The 1947,O 17,18:4
It Had to be You 1947,D 8,35:2

Bevan, William— Cont
Fortunes of Captain Blood 1950,Je 10,11:3
Bevani, Alexander
Phantom of the Opera, The 1925,S 7,15:3
Bevans, Clem
Way Down East 1935,O 31,16:2
Rhythm on the Range 1936,Jl 30,22:1
Come and Get It 1936,N 12,31:1
Riding on Air 1937,Je 26,20:2 (In Addenda)
Big City 1937,S 17,29:2
Of Human Hearts 1938,F 18,23:1
Zenobia 1939,My 15,15:2
Thunder Afloat 1939,O 13,27:2
Main Street Lawyer 1939,N 9,27:2
Abe Lincoln in Illinois 1940,F 23,19:2
Young Tom Edison 1940,Mr 15,27:2
Twenty-Mule Team 1940,My 10,26:6
Girl From God's Country 1940,S 9,18:5
She Couldn't Say No 1941,Ja 17,21:3
Sergeant York 1941,Jl 3,15:1
Parson of Panamint, The 1941,Jl 26,18:2
Smiling Ghost, The 1941,S 26,26:5
Captains of the Clouds 1942,F 13,24:2
Saboteur 1942,My 8,27:2
Tombstone, The Town too Tough to Die
  1942,Jl 27,18:2
Forest Rangers, The 1942,O 22,25:2
Human Comedy, The 1943,Mr 3,19:2
Happy Go Lucky 1943,Mr 25,25:1
Woman of the Town, The 1944,Mr 6,17:2
Captain Eddie 1945,Ag 9,24:2
Gallant Bess 1946,D 6,27:6
Wake up and Dream 1947,Ja 24,18:4
Yearling, The 1947,Ja 24,18:2
Mourning Becomes Electra 1947,N 20,38:2
Relentless 1948,Mr 6,17:3
Paleface, The 1948,D 16,41:2
Moonrise 1949,Mr 7,17:2
Portrait of Jennie 1949,Mr 30,31:2
Streets of Laredo 1949,My 12,28:2
Big Jack 1949,My 23,27:4
Deputy Marshal 1949,N 11,31:3
Harvey 1950,D 22,19:1
Hangman's Knot 1952,D 11,45:3
Stranger Wore a Gun, The 1953,Jl 30,20:3
Kentuckian, The 1955,S 2,13:2
Bevans, Philippa
Notorious Landlady, The 1962,Jl 27,15:2
World of Henry Orient, The 1964,Mr 20,27:2
Bever
Back Streets of Paris 1948,O 16,9:2
Beverly, Helen
Green Fields 1937,O 12,31:4
Light Ahead, The 1939,S 23,22:3
Overture to Glory 1940,F 12,14:2
Master Race, The 1944,N 2,22:1
Robe, The 1953,S 17,32:6
Bevilacqua, Amerigo
Gospel According to St Matthew, The
  1966,F 18,23:1
Bevilacqua, Amerigo (Screenwriter)
Eye of the Needle, The 1965,Je 22,25:2
Bevril, Andre
Night Watch, The; Trou, Le 1964,My 27,46:1
Bewes, Rodney
Billy Liar 1963,D 17,49:1
Bey, Erik
Monte Carlo 1930,Ag 28,22:4
Bey, Nora
Clos Pustyni 1933,Ap 21,20:5
Bey, Turhan
Footsteps in the Dark 1941,Mr 15,13:2
Burma Convoy 1941,O 7,26:7
Bombay Clipper 1942,Ja 12,23:3
Drums of the Congo 1942,Jl 20,16:4
Mummy's Tomb, The 1942,O 26,19:2
Destination Unknown 1942,O 29,19:3
Arabian Nights 1942,D 26,15:1
White Savage 1943,Ap 26,15:2
Background to Danger 1943,Jl 3,11:2
Mad Ghoul, The 1943,D 11,11:2
Ali Baba and the Forty Thieves 1944,Mr 16,17:3
Dragon Seed 1944,Jl 21,16:4
Bowery to Broadway 1944,N 30,19:2
Climax, The 1944,D 14,28:5
Frisco Sal 1945,F 17,11:2
Sudan 1945,Ap 19,22:8
Night in Paradise 1946,Je 6,16:3
Adventures of Casanova 1948,Mr 22,18:3
Song of India 1949,Je 10,32:3
Beydts, Louis (Miscellaneous)
Louise 1940,F 3,9:4
BEYER
See Also BAEHR, BAER, BAIR, BEAR, BYER
Beyer, Charles
Unseeing Eyes 1923,O 22,17:1
Man Must Live, A 1925,Ja 29,12:2
Shock Punch, The 1925,My 11,14:3
Unguarded Hour, The 1926,Ja 5,25:2 (In
  Addenda)
Beyer, Frank (Director)
Naked Among the Wolves 1967,Ap 19,54:7

Beyer, Hans-Joachim (Screenwriter)
Our Daily Bread 1950,O 9,21:6
Desires 1954,Jl 2,10:2
Beymer, Richard
So Big 1953,O 22,34:2
Indiscretion of an American Wife 1954,Je 26,7:2
Johnny Tremain 1957,Jl 11,21:1
Diary of Anne Frank, The 1959,Mr 19,40:1
High Time 1960,S 17,15:1
West Side Story 1961,O 19,39:3
Bachelor Flat 1962,Ja 13,14:1
Five Finger Exercise 1962,Ap 20,20:2
Hemingway's Adventures of a Young Man
  1962,Jl 26,17:1
Longest Day, The 1962,O 5,28:1
Stripper, The 1963,Je 20,29:1
Beyots, Louis (Miscellaneous)
Kermesse Heroique, La 1936,S 23,29:1
Beys, Arthur (Screenwriter)
Queen of Spades, The 1949,Jl 1,14:4
Bezaleel, Khalil
In the Heat of the Night 1967,Ag 3,26:1
Bezgin, Boris
Country Bride 1938,Je 4,18:2
Bezyaev, Igor
Mumu 1961,Je 5,37:4
Bezzerides, A I (Miscellaneous)
Action in the North Atlantic 1943,My 22,10:2
Bezzerides, A I (Original Author)
They Drive by Night 1940,Jl 27,17:5
Bezzerides, A I (Screenwriter)
Juke Girl 1942,Je 20,9:2
Northern Pursuit 1943,N 26,29:2
Thieves' Highway 1949,S 24,8:6
Thieves' Highway 1949,S 24,8:6
Sirocco 1951,Je 14,31:2
On Dangerous Ground 1952,F 13,35:2
Holiday for Sinners 1952,S 20,13:2
Beneath the 12-Mile Reef 1953,D 17,52:2
Track of the Cat 1954,D 2,38:2
Bullet for Joey, A 1955,Ap 16,12:1
Angry Hills, The 1959,Jl 16,31:3
Bhaduri, Jaya
Mahanagar; Big City, The 1964,S 28,19:1
Bhagavat
Gyandev of India 1943,Ap 10,12:5
Bi-Brodsky, Yunya
Greater Promise, A 1936,O 8,27:3
Biagi, E (Screenwriter)
Anita Garibaldi 1954,Mr 19,19:4 ·
Biagi, Enzo (Narrator)
Blood on the Balcony 1964,Je 30,22:1
Biagini, Ada
Corsaro Nero, Il; Black Corsair, The
  1939,My 8,21:3
Biagonravov, A I
Oppenheim Family, The 1939,My 24,29:2
Bialis, Rosetta
Americaner Shadchen; American Matchmaker
  1940,My 7,31:3
Bialk, Elisa (Original Author)
Sainted Sisters, The 1948,My 20,35:2
Bialosczynski, Tadeusz
Hearts Aflame 1937,O 14,22:3
Kosciuszki 1938,D 27,13:2
Young Chopin 1952,D 25,34:7 ·
Bianchetti, Suzanne
Madame Sans Gene 1925,Ap 18,19:1
Casanova 1927,Je 23,23:3
Loves of Casanova, The 1929,Ap 30,33:2
Violetera, La 1935,Ja 14,11:3 ·
Bianchi, Daniela
Love Is my Profession 1959,Ap 28,41:1
From Russia with Love 1964,Ap 9,25:1
Weekend, Italian Style 1968,My 23,56:2
Bianchi, Eleanora
Goliath and the Sins of Babylon 1964,Mr 5,36:2
Bianchi, Giorgio
Miracolo Di Sant' Antonio, Il 1932,Ap 18,19:2
Biancini, Ferruccio
Shepherd King, The 1923,D 11,26:2
Bianco, Ernesto
Inheritance, The; Herencia, La 1964,S 16,36:3
Biancoil, Oreste (Screenwriter)
Love and Marriage (One Moment Is Enough); One
  Moment Is Enough (Love and Marriage)
  1966,Ag 5,20:1
Love and Marriage (Saturday, July 18); Saturday,
  July 18 (Love and Marriage) 1966,Ag 5,20:1
Love and Marriage (The Last Resort); Last Resort,
  The (Love and Marriage) 1966,Ag 5,20:1
Love and Marriage (The First Night); First Night,
  The (Love and Marriage) 1966,Ag 5,20:1
Biancoli, Oreste (Director)
Amicizia; Friendship 1940,Mr 1,17:3
Mazura di Papa, La 1940,My 10,26:7
Biancoli, Oreste (Screenwriter)
Match King, The 1932,D 8,25:3
Murders in the Zoo 1933,Ap 3,13:4
Mind Reader, The 1933,Ap 7,22:4
I Cover the Waterfront 1933,My 18,17:3
Gran Varieta 1955,Ap 11,29:5
Marco Polo 1962,S 20,29:2

Bias, Albert
Oppressed, The 1929,Jl 15,25:1
Biasotti, Albert (Miscellaneous)
Via de Oro, La; Gold Route, The
  1932,Ja 3,VIII,6:6
Bibal, Robert (Screenwriter)
Crime in the Maginot Line 1939,My 8,21:2
Bibb, Leon
For Love of Ivy 1968,Jl 18,26:1
Biberman, Abner
Gunga Din 1939,Ja 28,19:2
Rains Came, The 1939,S 9,11:2
Another Thin Man 1939,N 24,29:1
Balalaika 1939,D 15,33:2
His Girl Friday 1940,Ja 12,13:2
Zanzibar 1940,Ap 1,15:3
Enemy Agent 1940,Ap 22,13:3
South of Pago-Pago 1940,Ag 2,12:2
South to Karanga 1940,Ag 9,19:1
Singapore Woman 1941,My 12,13:6
This Woman Is Mine 1941,O 13,21:2
South of Tahiti 1941,N 10,21:3
Whispering Ghosts 1942,My 18,19:4
Broadway 1942,Je 5,23:2
Little Tokyo, USA 1942,Ag 7,13:2
Leopard Man, The 1943,My 20,26:4
Bridge of San Luis Rey, The 1944,Mr 4,11:1
Betrayal From the East 1945,Ap 25,27:2
Salome, Where She Danced 1945,My 3,27:1
Captain Kidd 1945,N 23,26:3
Knock on Wood 1954,Ap 15,34:2
Elephant Walk 1954,Ap 22,37:2
Golden Mistress, The 1954,O 30,15:6
Biberman, Abner (Director)
Running Wild 1955,N 12,23:2
Gun for a Coward 1957,Ja 31,21:1
Biberman, Herbert (Director)
One Way Ticket 1936,Ja 1,35:2
Meet Nero Wolfe 1936,Jl 16,20:1
Master Race, The 1944,N 2,22:1
Salt of the Earth 1954,Mr 15,20:2
Salt of the Earth 1965,N 1,57:1
Biberman, Herbert (Original Author)
King of Chinatown 1939,Mr 16,27:2
Together Again 1944,N 24,19:2
New Orleans 1947,Je 20,25:6
Biberman, Herbert (Screenwriter)
Action in Arabia 1944,F 19,18:7
Master Race, The 1944,N 2,22:1
Bibert, Marcel
Amour Maitre des Choses, L' 1931,Mr 30,25:2
Biberti, Leopold
Last Chance, The 1945,N 28,21:6
Four Days' Leave 1950,Je 9,29:4
Sins of Rose Bernd, The 1959,Ja 24,13:4 (In
  Addenda)
Bibesco, Marthe Princess (Original Author)
Katia 1939,D 23,9:2
Magnificent Sinner 1963,Ap 25,38:1
Bibikov, Maria
Days of Glory 1944,Je 17,10:2
Bibo, Walter (Producer)
Garden of Eden 1957,D 18,45:3
Biby, Edward
Strange Woman, The 1947,F 24,16:4
Bice, Robert
Ghost Ship, The 1943,D 25,19:4
Dragon Seed 1944,Jl 21,16:4
Red Stallion 1947,N 27,50:3
Canon City 1948,Jl 8,19:2
Hiawatha 1952,D 26,20:4
Invasion USA 1953,Ap 30,39:4
Wild One, The 1953,D 31,9:2
Three for the Show 1955,F 25,16:1
Foxfire 1955,Jl 14,19:1
Bices, Robert (Screenwriter)
Screaming Mimi 1958,Je 26,23:3
Bichler, Robert
Four Days' Leave 1950,Je 9,29:4
Bickel, George
Recaptured Love 1930,Ag 9,16:5
Maybe It's Love 1930,O 18,23:2
One Heavenly Night 1931,Ja 10,19:2
Man I Killed, The 1932,Ja 20,17:4
Bickel, Mary (Original Author)
45 Fathers 1937,D 11,22:2
Bicker, George (Original Author)
Fugitive in the Sky 1937,Ja 16,21:1
Bicker, George (Screenwriter)
Fugitive in the Sky 1937,Ja 16,21:1
Bickerton, Derek (Original Author)
Payroll 1963,My 11,15:2
Bickford, Charles
South Sea Rose 1929,D 7,19:3
Dynamite 1929,D 28,11:1
Hell's Heroes 1929,D 28,11:1
Anna Christie 1930,Mr 15,22:5
Passion Flower 1930,D 22,16:2
River's End 1931,Mr 7,17:2
Squaw Man, The 1931,S 19,10:2
Pagan Lady 1931,S 21,20:2
East of Borneo 1931,S 26,25:3
Men in her Life 1931,N 30,16:2

Bickford, Charles— Cont

Panama Flo 1932,Ja 20,17:4
Scandal for Sale 1932,Ap 3,26:2
Thunder Below 1932,Je 20,11:2
Last Man, The 1932,S 17,18:4
Vanity Street 1932,O 15,13:1
No Other Woman 1933,Ja 30,9:4 (In Addenda)
Song of the Eagle 1933,Ap 29,14:3
This Day and Age 1933,S 1,15:4
White Woman 1933,N 18,18:5
White Woman 1933,D 3,IX,9:4 (In Addenda)
Little Miss Marker 1934,My 19,18:3
Wicked Woman, A 1935,Ja 1,24:1
Under Pressure 1935,F 4,11:3
Notorious Gentleman, A 1935,F 16,9:1
Farmer Takes a Wife, The 1935,Ag 9,21:2
Rose of the Rancho 1936,Ja 9,25:2
Pride of the Marines 1936,Ap 27,19:2
Red Wagon 1936,Je 22,22:1
Plainsman, The 1937,Ja 14,16:2
High, Wide and Handsome 1937,Jl 22,15:1
Night Club Scandal 1937,N 12,27:2
Daughter of Shanghai 1937,D 24,21:2
Thunder Trail 1938,F 5,19:3
Gangs of New York 1938,My 28,9:2
Valley of the Giants 1938,S 10,20:2
Storm, The 1938,O 31,12:2
Stand up and Fight 1939,Ja 27,17:2
Romance of the Redwoods 1939,Ap 24,13:2
Street of Missing Men 1939,Je 1,31:3
Our Leading Citizen 1939,Ag 24,17:1
One Hour to Live 1939,N 4,11:3
Mutiny in the Big House 1939,D 11,26:2
Thou Shalt Not Kill 1940,Ja 8,11:2
Of Mice and Men 1940,F 17,9:2
South to Karanga 1940,Ag 9,19:1
Girl From God's Country 1940,S 9,18:5
Burma Convoy 1941,O 7,26:7
Tarzan's New York Adventure 1942,Ag 7,13:2
Mr Lucky 1943,Jl 23,21:2
Song of Bernadette, The 1944,Ja 27,15:2
Wing and a Prayer 1944,Ag 31,14:1
Captain Eddie 1945,Ag 9,24:2
Fallen Angel 1946,F 7,29:4
Farmer's Daughter, The 1947,Mr 26,31:2
Duel in the Sun 1947,My 8,30:2
Woman on the Beach, The 1947,Je 9,26:6
Brute Force 1947,Jl 17,16:2
Babe Ruth Story, The 1948,Jl 29,17:2
Four Faces West 1948,Ag 4,18:3
Johnny Belinda 1948,O 2,11:2
Command Decision 1949,Ja 20,34:2
Roseanna McCoy 1949,O 13,33:2
Whirlpool 1950,Ja 14,9:2
Guilty of Treason 1950,Ap 11,26:2
Riding High 1950,Ap 11,26:2
Branded 1951,Ja 11,28:5
Jim Thorpe - All American 1951,Ag 25,7:2
Elopement 1951,D 21,21:3
Star is Born, A 1954,O 12,23:1
Prince of Players 1955,Ja 12,24:2
Not as a Stranger 1955,Je 29,24:1
Court-Martial of Billy Mitchell, The
 1955,D 23,14:2
Mister Cory 1957,F 23,13:1
Unforgiven, The 1960,Ap 7,46:1
Days of Wine and Roses 1963,Ja 18,7:2
Big Hand for the Little Lady, A 1966,Je 9,54:2

Biddell, Sidney (Original Author)

Submarine Zone; (Escape To Glory)
 1941,Ap 7,13:2
Night Plane From Chungking 1943,My 31,13:2
Dead Reckoning 1947,Ja 23,31:2

Biddell, Sidney (Producer)

Thrill of Brazil, The 1946,S 6,18:3
Dead Reckoning 1947,Ja 23,31:2

Biddle, Cordelia Drexel (Original Author)

Happiest Millionaire, The 1967,D 1,56:1

Biddle, Craig

Three Wise Fools 1923,Jl 23,13:4
Fashion Row 1924,Ja 28,12:1

Bidlake, Richard

Guns at Batasi 1964,N 17,47:1

Bieber, Leo

Take my Life 1949,Ja 19,34:2
Question 7 1961,S 29,30:2

Bieber, Linda

Amazing Mrs Holliday, The 1943,F 22,20:2

Bieber, Nita

Lady Without Passport, A 1950,Ag 4,13:2
Summer Stock 1950,S 1,17:2
Prince Who Was a Thief, The 1951,Jl 4,13:2

Biebrach, Rudolf

Liebe im Ring 1930,Ag 11,13:1

Biebrich, Erica

Klapperstorchverband, Der; Stork Society, The
 1938,O 29,15:3

Biegel, Erwin

Wenn Du eine Schwiegermutter hast; When You
 Have a Mother-in-Law 1938,Ja 29,12:1
Palace Scandal 1949,Je 6,15:5
Berliner, The 1952,O 28,37:1

Biel, Ed

Our Daily Bread 1934,O 3,25:2

Biel, Theodore

Divided Heart, The 1955,Ag 4,16:1

Bielik, Palo

Janosik 1936,D 25,19:3

Bieman, M (Screenwriter)

Secret Agent 1949,F 10,37:3

Bienert, Gerhard

M 1933,Ap 3,13:3
Gruen ist die Heide 1935,O 14,21:2
Musketier Meier III 1938,D 31,7:2
Aufruhr in Damaskus; Tumult in Damascus
 1939,My 6,21:2

Bienvenu, E Mrs

Louisiana Story 1948,S 29,36:2

Bierkowsky, Heinz (Screenwriter)

Togger 1937,Mr 14,XI,4:5 (In Addenda)

Bierry, Etienne

Shameless Old Lady, The 1966,S 27,52:1

Biffie, Baby

Penny Serenade 1941,My 23,25:2

Big Red (horse)

Red Stallion 1947,N 27,50:3

Big Tree, Chief

Iron Horse, The 1924,Ag 29,6:1
Ranson's Folly 1926,My 31,10:2
Hudson's Bay 1941,Ja 10,23:2
Devil's Doorway 1950,N 10,35:1

Big Tree. Chief

Drums Along the Mohawk 1939,N 4,11:2
Western Union 1941,F 7,23:2
She Wore a Yellow Ribbon 1949,N 18,35:2

Bigard, Barney

New Orleans 1947,Je 20,25:6

Bigelow, Joe (Original Author)

Annabel Takes a Tour 1938,D 29,15:3

Bigelow, Joe (Screenwriter)

Woman Chases Man 1937,Je 11,26:2
Wide Open Faces 1938,Ap 15,23:2
Here We Go Again 1942,O 12,12:3

Bigerna, Luigi (Producer)

Island Sinner, The 1960,S 5,11:2

Bigerna, Pietro

Monte Cassino 1948,N 25,47:3

Biggers, Earl Derr (Original Author)

Ruling Passion, The 1922,Ja 23,11:4
Too Much Business 1922,My 1,20:3
Reckless Age, The 1924,Je 10,24:4
Chinese Parrot, The 1928,Ja 2,28:1
Seven Keys to Baldpate 1929,D 26,21:1
Second Story Murder, The 1930,My 3,23:1
Inside the Lines 1930,Jl 5,17:4
Charlie Chan Carries On 1931,Mr 21,15:1
Millionaire, The 1931,Ap 9,30:5
Black Camel, The 1931,Jl 4,11:5
Charlie Chan's Chance 1932,Ja 23,18:4
Charlie Chan's Greatest Case 1933,O 7,18:4
Charlie Chan's Courage 1934,Ag 25,16:6
Charlie Chan in London 1934,S 13,26:1
Charlie Chan in Paris 1935,Ja 22,23:2
Charlie Chan in Egypt 1935,Je 24,12:2
Charlie Chan in Shanghai 1935,O 14,21:1
Seven Keys to Baldpate 1935,D 14,11:2
Charlie Chan's Secret 1936,Ja 18,19:4
Charlie Chan at the Circus 1936,Mr 19,22:4
Charlie Chan at the Race Track 1936,Ag 15,6:2
Charlie Chan at the Olympics 1937,My 24,23:1
Charlie Chan on Broadway 1937,S 20,19:1
Charlie Chan at Monte Carlo 1937,D 18,18:1
Charlie Chan in Honolulu 1938,D 31,7:3
Charlie Chan in Reno 1939,My 31,27:2
Charlie Chan at Treasure Island 1939,S 1,15:5
Charlie Chan in City in Darkness 1939,D 18,29:2
Charlie Chan in Panama 1940,F 23,19:3
Charlie Chan's Murder Cruise 1940,My 3,17:5
One Night in the Tropics 1940,D 20,33:2
Dead Men Tell 1941,Ap 17,29:3
That Way With Women 1947,F 15,20:4

Biggio, Paola

Seduced and Abandoned 1964,Jl 16,23:1

Bignell, John (Miscellaneous)

Ladies Who Do 1963,N 26,52:2

Bigot, Eugene (Miscellaneous)

Louise 1940,F 3,9:4

Bihary, Nandor

Gul Baba 1940,O 26,18:8

Bijuerenda, Frederick

Man of Africa 1956,O 11,51:1

Bikel, Theodore

African Queen, The 1952,F 21,24:3
Never Let Me Go 1953,Je 11,37:2
Melba 1953,Je 25,23:1
Desperate Moment 1953,S 1,19:4
Little Kidnappers, The 1954,S 2,18:1
Chance Meeting 1955,Ap 20,38:1
Vintage, The 1957,My 9,36:5
Pride and the Passion, The 1957,Je 29,10:6
Enemy Below, The 1957,D 26,23:2
Fraulein 1958,Je 9,27:2
Defiant Ones, The 1958,S 25,29:1
I Want to Live 1958,N 19,45:1

Bikel, Theodore— Cont

Woman Obsessed 1959,My 28,34:1
Angry Hills, The 1959,Jl 16,31:3
Blue Angel, The 1959,S 5,11:4
Dog of Flanders, A 1960,Ap 1,37:1
My Fair Lady 1964,O 22,41:1
Sands of the Kalahari 1965,N 25,64:5
Russians are Coming the Russians are Coming,
 The 1966,My 26,55:1
Festival 1967,O 24,53:2
Sweet November 1968,F 9,55:1

Bikel, Theodore (Narrator)

Last Chapter, The 1966,F 22,14:5

Bilancia, Oreste

Avventura di Giacomo Casanova 1938,D 2,27:3
Between Two Worlds 1940,F 9,15:2
Four Steps in the Clouds 1948,N 22,25:2

Bilancioni, Piero

Gold of Naples (The Gambler); Gambler, The
 (Gold of Naples) 1957,F 12,30:1

Bilbrew, A C

Foxes of Harrow, The 1947,S 25,35:4

Bilbrook, Lydia

Mexican Spitfire out West 1940,O 30,29:3
Mexican Spitfire at Sea 1942,Je 26,16:5
Mexican Spitfire's Elephant 1942,S 18,25:2
Pistol Packin' Mama 1943,D 20,27:4
Picture of Dorian Gray, The 1945,Mr 2,15:2
Brighton Strangler, The 1945,My 19,15:2

Bildt, Paul

Slums of Berlin 1927,Ja 26,17:1
Rebel, The 1933,Jl 25,17:2
Schwarzer Jaeger Johanna 1935,Ap 1,17:2
Toerichte Jungfrau, Die 1935,S 9,24:3
Schritt vom Wege, Der; False Step, The
 1939,Ap 29,13:3
Dreyfus Case, The 1940,O 30,29:3
Razzia 1948,Je 14,19:2
Somewhere in Berlin 1949,Ag 16,19:3
Affair Blum, The 1949,O 18,35:2
Our Daily Bread 1950,O 9,21:6

Biler, Bernard

Stranger, The 1967,D 19,59:1

Biliotti, Enzo

One Hundred Days of Napoleon 1936,S 14,25:1
Avventura di Giacomo Casanova 1938,D 2,27:3
Grande Luce, La; Great Light, The
 1940,Mr 15,27:4
Difficult Years 1950,Ag 22,31:2

Bilisci, Tivader

Busuini Nem Jo; Don't Worry 1938,O 29,15:5

Bill, Maude

Sandra 1924,D 22,20:2

Bill, Teddy

Nur am Rhein 1931,S 25,28:7
Die Grosse Attraktion 1933,Jl 24,11:2

Bill, Tony

Come Blow Your Horn 1963,Je 7,37:1
Soldier in the Rain 1963,N 29,67:6 (Incorrect in
 this edition; use 1963,N 28,67:6 elsewhere)
None but the Brave 1965,F 25,24:1
Marriage on the Rocks 1965,S 16,00:0
You're a Big Boy Now 1967,Mr 21,35:3
Never a Dull Moment 1968,Ag 15,46:2
Ice Station Zebra 1968,D 21,49:1

Bill Haley and his Comets

Don't Knock the Rock 1957,F 23,13:1

Billbrew, A C H

Hearts in Dixie 1929,F 28,30:3

Biller, Irene

Man Who Dared, The 1933,S 9,9:3
Lila Akac 1935,My 15,26:3

Billerey, Raoul

Naked Childhood 1968,S 28,36:1

Billi, Minio

If all the Guys in the World 1957,Ap 23,34:1

Billi, Riccardo

I Cadetti di Guascogna 1952,O 6,22:2
My Heart Sings 1954,Mr 5,15:5

Billinger, Richard (Screenwriter)

Mozart Story, The 1948,N 15,21:5

Billings, Elmo

Locked Doors 1925,Ja 12,11:2

Billings, Florence

Little Child Shall Lead Them, A 1922,S 2,10:4
Marriage Morals 1923,Ag 14,10:3
Sinners in Heaven 1924,S 10,21:3
Miss Bluebeard 1925,Ja 28,14:1

Billings, Gary

Raising a Riot 1957,My 8,44:1

Billings, George

Dramatic Life of Abraham Lincoln, The
 1924,Ja 22,17:3
Man Without a Country, The 1925,F 12,16:1
Hands Up 1926,Ja 18,26:2
Woman to Woman 1929,N 12,34:4
As the Earth Turns 1934,Ap 12,27:2
Pursuit of Happiness, The 1934,O 26,25:1
Wicked Woman, A 1935,Ja 1,24:1
Adventures of Tom Sawyer, The 1938,F 18,23:1
Nice Girl 1941,Mr 27,29:6

Billings, Pemberton (Original Author)
High Treason 1929,Ag 25,VIII,4:7 (In Addenda)
Billings, Pemberton (Producer)
High Treason 1929,Ag 25,VIII,4:7 (In Addenda)
Billings, Ted
Bride of Frankenstein, The 1935,My 11,21:2
Billingsley, Barbara
Shadow on the Wall 1950,My 19,31:3
Pretty Baby 1950,S 23,11:2
Three Guys Named Mike 1951,Mr 2,21:2
Tall Target, The 1951,S 28,26:2
Careless Years, The 1957,N 28,57:3
Billingsley, Jennifer
Lady in a Cage 1964,Je 11,27:1
Young Lovers, The 1965,F 18,45:1
Billington, Franceita
Blind Husbands 1919,D 8,20:4
Billington, Kevin (Director)
Interlude 1968,Jl 3,26:1
Billon, Pierre (Director)
Maison dans la Dune, La; House on the Dune,
The 1934,S 16,X,4:1 (In Addenda)
Second Bureau 1936,F 17,21:2
Ruy Blas 1948,O 4,14:2
Eternal Husband, The 1949,Ja 10,19:2
Vautrin, the Thief 1949,N 11,31:2
Billon, Pierre (Screenwriter)
Eternal Husband, The 1949,Ja 10,19:2
Billotti, Enzo
Al Vostri Ordini, Signora; At Your Orders,
Madame 1940,My 25,20:1
Spirit and the Flesh, The 1948,N 1,28:2
Beautiful but Dangerous 1958,F 6,24:1
Billoups, Robert
Wildfire 1925,Je 10,18:2
Billquist, Fritiof
Troette Teodor 1932,Ja 18,18:4
Kustens Glada Kavaljerer; Coast's Happy
Cavaliers, The 1939,My 23,27:2
Bills, Teddy
He Who Must Die 1958,D 29,21:1
Impossible on Saturday 1966,F 17,29:1
Billy, Little
Swing High 1930,Je 27,26:3
Polly of the Circus 1932,Mr 19,11:2
Bilogini, Mauro (Director)
Bell Antonio 1962,Ap 3,43:2
Bilson, George (Original Author)
Talent Scout 1937,Ag 20,21:3
Bilson, George (Screenwriter)
Talent Scout 1937,Ag 20,21:3
Busses Roar 1942,S 25,25:4
Bin
Rango 1931,F 19,20:4
Binarelli, Angelo
Sensualita 1954,Ap 29,40:2
Binder, Steve (Director)
T A M I Show, The 1965,Ja 28,20:1
Binder, Sybilla
Thunder Rock 1944,S 15,16:1
Man From Morocco, The 1946,N 25,38:2
Blanche Fury 1948,N 24,20:2
Broken Journey 1949,My 26,34:3
Against the Wind 1949,Je 27,18:3
Devil's Plot 1953,Je 19,18:1
Bindi, Clara
Most Wonderful Moment, The 1959,Je 1,23:6
Bindon, John
Poor Cow 1968,F 1,28:2
Bing, Herman
Married in Hollywood 1929,S 23,24:3
Show Girl in Hollywood 1930,My 5,27:3
Great Lover, The 1931,Ag 24,13:4
Guardsman, The 1931,S 10,22:4
Jewel Robbery 1932,Jl 23,6:6
Hypnotized 1933,Ja 16,13:3
Great Jasper, The 1933,F 17,5:3
Nuisance, The 1933,My 29,22:2
Dinner at Eight 1933,Ag 24,18:1
Bowery, The 1933,O 5,24:2
My Lips Betray 1933,N 4,18:3
Melody in Spring 1934,Mr 31,8:2
I'll Tell the World 1934,Ap 21,12:2
20th Century 1934,My 4,24:2
Black Cat, The 1934,My 19,18:4
Hide-Out 1934,Ag 25,16:5
Merry Widow, The 1934,O 12,33:1
Crimson Romance 1934,O 13,10:1
Mighty Barnum, The 1934,D 24,17:1
Night is Young, The 1935,Ja 14,11:2
Great Hotel Murder, The 1935,F 28,17:4
Florentine Dagger, The 1935,Ap 27,20:6
Don't Bet on Blondes 1935,Jl 20,16:2
Every Night at Eight 1935,Ag 3,16:2
Fighting Youth 1935,N 2,13:3
Three Kids and a Queen 1935,N 9,19:2
$1,000 a Minute 1935,D 21,11:1
Rose Marie 1936,F 1,9:2
Laughing Irish Eyes 1936,Ap 4,11:2
Great Ziegfeld, The 1936,Ap 9,21:2
Three Wise Guys, The 1936,My 23,12:2
King Steps Out, The 1936,My 29,15:2
Dimples 1936,O 10,21:2

Adventure in Manhattan 1936,O 23,27:5
Come Closer, Folks 1936,N 23,17:3
That Girl From Paris 1937,Ja 1,19:1
Champagne Waltz 1937,F 4,17:2
Maytime 1937,Mr 19,27:1
Beg, Borrow or Steal 1937,D 10,33:2
Every Day's a Holiday 1938,Ja 27,17:2
Paradise for Three 1938,F 16,17:1
Bluebeard's Eighth Wife 1938,Mr 24,21:2
Vacation From Love 1938,N 10,33:2
Great Waltz, The 1938,N 25,19:1
Sweethearts 1938,D 23,16:2
Devil With Hitler, The 1942,O 19,15:2
Where Do We Go From Here? 1945,Je 7,25:2
Bingham, Edfrid (Screenwriter)
Earthbound 1920,Ag 11,9:4
Little Minister, The 1921,D 26,13:3
Law of the Lawless, The 1923,Je 19,22:4
Bini, Alfredo (Producer)
Viaccia, La 1962,S 21,35:1
New Angels, The; I Nuovi Angeli
1965,My 4,49:1
Gospel According to St Matthew, The
1966,F 18,23:1
Mandragola 1966,Je 7,50:2
Hawks and the Sparrows, The; Uccellacci e
Uccellini 1967,Jl 28,15:3
Accattone! 1968,Ap 5,56:1
Biniaris, Gikas
Madame X 1960,O 3,34:5
Binner, Hans
Confess, Dr Corda 1960,O 24,25:5
Binner, Margery
Good Companions, The 1933,O 10,24:1
Binney, Constance
Sporting Life 1918,S 16,9:3
Test of Honor, The 1919,Ap 7,11:5
Stolen Kiss 1920,Ap 5,20:1
Something Different 1921,Ja 30,VI,2:1 (In
Addenda)
Case of Becky, The 1921,O 10,16:1
Binney, Faire
Sporting Life 1918,S 16,9:3
Here Comes the Bride 1919,F 3,13:2
Open Your Eyes 1919,Je 30,16:3
Man's Home, A 1921,D 19,13:1
What Fools Men Are 1922,D 3,VIII,2:2 (In
Addenda)
Second Youth 1924,Ap 22,19:3
Speed Spook, The 1924,O 21,21:3
Binns, Edward
Teresa 1951,Ap 6,31:2
Vice Squad 1953,Ag 26,23:2
Beyond a Reasonable Doubt 1956,S 14,27:2
12 Angry Men 1957,Ap 15,24:1
Portland Expose 1957,S 27,16:6
Compulsion 1959,Ap 2,26:2
Man in the Net, The 1959,Je 11,36:2
North by Northwest 1959,Ag 7,28:1
Desire in the Dust 1960,O 12,47:2
Judgment at Nuremberg 1961,D 20,36:1
Hemingway's Adventures of a Young Man
1962,Jl 26,17:1
Fail Safe 1964,S 16,36:1
Americanization of Emily, The 1964,O 28,51:1
Binyon, Claude (Composer)
Stolen Harmony 1935,Ap 20,16:2
Binyon, Claude (Director)
Saxon Charm, The 1948,S 30,32:3
Family Honeymoon 1949,F 25,28:2
Mother Didn't Tell Me 1950,Mr 4,11:2
Stella 1950,Ag 19,9:2
Aaron Slick From Punkin Crick 1952,Ap 19,18:6
Dreamboat 1952,Jl 26,9:2
Here Come the Girls 1953,D 26,10:1
Binyon, Claude (Original Author)
Daring Young Man, The 1935,Jl 18,15:2
Sing You Sinners 1938,Ag 18,23:1
And the Angels Sing 1944,Jl 13,14:2
Binyon, Claude (Producer)
Suddenly It's Spring 1947,F 27,26:2
Binyon, Claude (Screenwriter)
Gilded Lily, The 1935,F 9,11:2
Mississippi 1935,Ap 18,27:2
Accent on Youth 1935,Ag 12,10:3
Bride Comes Home, The 1935,D 25,30:2
Valiant Is the Word for Carrie 1936,O 8,27:2
I Met Him in Paris 1937,Je 3,29:2
True Confession 1937,D 16,35:2
Sing You Sinners 1938,Ag 18,23:1
Invitation to Happiness 1939,Je 8,31:2
Too Many Husbands 1940,Mr 8,25:2
Arizona 1941,F 7,23:3
You Belong to Me 1941,N 29,14:2
Take a Letter Darling 1942,My 28,13:2
Holiday Inn 1942,Ag 5,16:1
Dixie 1943,Je 24,26:2
This Is the Army 1943,Jl 29,11:6
No Time for Love 1943,D 2,30:1
Incendiary Blonde 1945,Jl 26,13:2
Well Groomed Bride, The 1946,My 11,22:5
Cross my Heart 1946,D 19,42:3
Suddenly It's Spring 1947,F 27,26:2

Binyon, Claude (Screenwriter) — Cont
Saxon Charm, The 1948,S 30,32:3
Mother Didn't Tell Me 1950,Mr 4,11:2
Stella 1950,Ag 19,9:2
My Blue Heaven 1950,S 16,12:6
Emergency Wedding 1950,D 22,19:2
Aaron Slick From Punkin Crick 1952,Ap 19,18:6
Dreamboat 1952,Jl 26,9:2
Down Among the Sheltering Palms
1953,Je 13,11:2
Woman's World 1954,S 29,23:4
Sing Boy Sing 1958,F 22,9:4
Rally Round the Flag Boys! 1958,D 24,2:7
North to Alaska 1960,N 11,36:1
Pepe 1960,D 22,18:1
Satan Never Sleeps 1962,F 22,20:1
Kisses for my President 1964,Ag 22,13:1
Binyon, Conrad
Courage of Lassie 1946,Jl 25,18:5
Biondi, Francesca
Golden Madonna, The 1949,S 5,13:4
Bir, Jacqueline
Depart, Le 1967,S 23,20:3
Birabeau, Andre (Original Author)
Breakfast at Sunrise 1927,N 14,26:1
Biraud, Maurice
Premier May 1958,S 17,44:2
Money, Money, Money 1962,Jl 18,20:1
Paris Pick-Up 1963,Ag 29,36:2
Any Number Can Win 1963,O 9,47:2
Devil and the 10 Commandments, The (Episode
3) 1963,O 15,44:1
Seventh Juror, The 1964,Ja 28,25:1
Taxi for Tobruk 1965,Mr 30,52:1
Cloportes 1966,Ap 19,36:1
BIRCH
See Also BURCH
Birch, Derek
Haunted Strangler, The 1958,Jl 4,15:3
Birch, Frank
When Thief Meets Thief 1937,Je 15,26:2
Victoria the Great 1937,O 29,19:1
Challenge, The 1939,O 2,15:2
Birch, Paul
War of the Worlds, The 1953,Ag 14,10:2
Fastest Gun Alive, The 1956,Jl 13,23:3
Gun for a Coward 1957,Ja 31,21:1
Tattered Dress, The 1957,Mr 15,22:3
Portrait in Black 1960,Jl 28,19:1
Two Rode Together 1961,Jl 27,23:3
Man Who Shot Liberty Valance, The
1962,My 24,29:2
Birch, Wyrley
Air Hawks 1935,Je 4,26:5
Last Days of Pompeii, The 1935,O 17,29:2
Grand Exit 1935,N 4,24:5
Music Goes 'Round, The 1936,F 22,12:1
Mr Deeds Goes to Town 1936,Ap 17,17:2
Trapped by Television 1936,Je 15,24:3
Boomerang 1947,Mr 6,36:2
BIRD
See Also BYRD
Bird, Betty
Waterloo 1929,Ap 16,32:5
Ein Burschenlied aus Heidelberg 1931,S 14,15:3
Opern-Ball, Der; Opera Ball 1931,N 6,28:3
Die Grosse Liebe 1932,F 22,23:2
Ich Will Nicht Wissen Wer Du Bist
1933,F 16,23:2
Walzerparadies 1933,Mr 4,11:3
Die Mutter der Kompagnie 1934,Mr 9,22:3
Feldherrnhuegel, Der 1934,Ap 20,17:2
Was Bin Ich Ohne dich? 1935,D 14,11:2
Salon Dora Green 1937,Jl 26,15:3
Bird, Billie
Mating Season, The 1951,Ap 12,41:2
Darling, How Could You! 1951,N 9,22:4
Just Across the Street 1952,Je 28,12:4
Somebody Loves Me 1952,S 25,38:1
Secret of Deep Harbor 1961,O 26,39:7
Bird, Carol (Original Author)
Bureau of Missing Persons 1933,S 9,9:2
Bird, Charlotte
Mannequinn 1926,Ja 12,27:5
Mantrap 1926,Jl 12,24:4
Padlocked 1926,Ag 2,21:2
Legion of the Condemned, The 1928,Mr 19,26:2
Bird, Chris Willow
Broken Arrow 1950,Jl 21,15:2
Bird, Colin
Ulysses 1967,Mr 14,55:1
Bird, John
30 Is a Dangerous Age, Cynthia 1968,Mr 5,34:1
Bird, Norman
Inspector Calls, An 1954,N 26,24:4
League of Gentlemen, The 1961,Ja 25,30:4
Man in the Moon 1961,Je 13,29:2
Victim 1962,F 6,27:2
Whistle Down the Wind 1962,Ap 23,34:2
Cash on Demand 1962,My 17,31:1
Hill, The 1965,O 4,00:0
Bird, Richard
White Face 1933,D 4,22:3
Mimi 1936,Ja 10,16:3

Bird, Richard — Cont

    Crouching Beast, The 1936,Ag 22,6:1
    Bulldog Drummond at Bay 1937,O 25,23:2
    Invitation to the Waltz 1938,Jl 2,10:3
    Half-Way House 1945,Ag 13,22:4
    Don't Take it to Heart 1948,D 25,10:3

Birdwell, Russell (Director)
    Street Corners 1929,S 2,16:1
    Flying Devils 1933,Ag 26,14:3
    Come on, The 1956,Ap 7,13:1
    Girl in the Kremlin, The 1957,My 22,29:2

Birdwell, Russell J (Original Author)
    Jim Thorpe - All American 1951,Ag 25,7:2

Birell, Tala
    Doomed Battalion, The 1932,Je 11,9:3
    Nagana 1933,F 16,23:2
    Let's Fall in Love 1934,Ja 22,12:3
    Captain Hates the Sea, The 1934,N 29,33:2
    Let's Live Tonight 1935,Mr 18,14:4
    Air Hawks 1935,Je 4,26:5
    Crime and Punishment 1935,N 22,18:2
    Lone Wolf Returns, The 1936,F 4,25:5
    As Good as Married 1937,My 22,19:2
    Bringing Up Baby 1938,Mr 4,17:5
    Invisible Enemy 1938,Ap 30,18:2
    Josette 1938,Je 11,9:1
    Seven Miles From Alcatraz 1942,N 19,31:3
    Song of Bernadette, The 1944,Ja 27,15:2
    Purple Heart, The 1944,Mr 9,15:2
    Woman in Bondage 1944,Mr 27,17:2
    Make Your own Bed 1944,My 27,12:2
    Mrs Parkington 1944,O 13,16:1
    Frozen Ghost, The 1945,Jl 28,7:3
    Dangerous Millions 1947,Mr 15,10:3
    Song of Love 1947,O 10,31:2
    Woman in the Night 1948,Ja 10,16:2

Birgel, Willi
    Untitled-Dance 1937,D 25,10:4
    Zu neven Ufern; To new Shores 1938,Ja 29,12:1

Birgel, Willy
    Fuerst Woronzeff 1934,N 17,12:2
    Maedchen Johanna, Das 1935,O 9,27:2 (In Addenda)
    Einer zu viel an Bord 1936,Ja 25,18:5
    Schlussakkord 1936,S 10,29:4
    Barcarole 1936,O 21,35:3
    Verraeter 1937,Ja 23,13:1
    Verklungene Melodie; Dead Melody 1938,Je 25,7:2
    Blaufuchs; Blue Fox 1939,Mr 4,18:5
    Hotel Sacher 1939,Je 10,14:2
    Gouverneur, Der 1939,S 11,15:2
    Maria Ilona 1940,Ap 20,14:3
    Congo Express 1940,My 11,15:3
    Heidi 1953,D 21,27:2
    Heidi and Peter 1955,D 13,55:2
    Ballerina 1958,My 10,19:2
    Hippodrome 1962,Mr 12,36:1

Birinski, Leo (Original Author)
    Stamboul Quest 1934,Jl 14,16:6
    Gay Desperado, The 1936,O 9,31:4
    Full Confession 1939,S 28,29:4
    Lady Has Plans, The 1942,Mr 5,27:1

Birinski, Leo (Screenwriter)
    Mata Hari 1932,Ja 1,31:1

Birkett, Lord (Producer)
    Persecution and Assassination of Jean-Paul Marat as Performed by the Inmates of the Asylum of Charenton Under the Direction of the Marquis De Sade, The 1967,F 23,41:1

Birkett, Michael (Producer)
    Guest, The 1964,Ja 21,25:2

Birkett, Viva
    Prince of Lovers, The 1927,N 29,31:1

Birkinshaw, Phillip
    Ivory Hunter 1952,Ag 19,19:1

Birl, Lajos (Original Author)
    Eve's Secret 1925,Je 11,14:3

Birman, Seraphima
    Friends 1939,Ja 2,28:3
    Ivan the Terrible, Part I 1947,Mr 10,25:2
    Ivan the Terrible, Part II 1959,N 25,22:4
    Don Quixote 1961,Ja 21,18:1

Birmingham, Alan
    King's Vacation, The 1933,Ja 20,21:2

Birmingham, Allen
    Great Gambini, The 1937,Jl 12,20:4

Biro, Lajos (Miscellaneous)
    Sanders of the River 1935,Je 27,16:1

Biro, Lajos (Original Author)
    Silent Lover, The 1926,N 15,19:1
    Hotel Imperial 1927,Ja 3,16:2
    Heart Thief, The 1927,Ap 27,22:5
    Last Command, The 1928,Ja 23,18:3
    Private Life of Don Juan, The 1934,D 10,16:2
    Dark Journey 1937,Ag 23,22:1
    Divorce of Lady X, The 1938,Ap 1,17:2
    Hotel Imperial 1939,My 11,31:3
    Way of all Flesh, The 1940,Je 6,33:2
    Five Graves to Cairo 1943,My 27,21:2
    Royal Scandal, A 1945,Ap 12,19:2

Biro, Lajos (Screenwriter)
    Adoration 1929,Ja 14,20:1
    Private Life of Henry VIII, The 1933,O 13,25:2

    Catherine the Great 1934,F 15,15:6
    Sanders of the River 1935,Je 27,16:1
    Under the Red Robe 1937,Je 1,27:2
    Divorce of Lady X, The 1938,Ap 1,17:2
    Return of the Scarlet Pimpernel, The 1938,Ap 11,12:2
    Drums 1938,S 30,24:4
    Thief of Bagdad, The 1940,D 6,28:2
    Ideal Husband, An 1948,Ja 15,28:2

Birrie, James
    This Man Is News 1939,Jl 20,16:4

Birsell, Whit
    Double Life, A 1948,F 20,19:1

Birt, Daniel (Director)
    No Room at the Inn 1949,D 26,33:4
    Interrupted Journey 1951,My 29,20:2
    Edge of Divorce 1954,Jl 2,10:1

Bischoff, Sam (Director)
    Last Mile, The 1932,Ag 26,20:3

Bischoff, Samuel (Producer)
    Submarine Zone; (Escape To Glory) 1941,Ap 7,13:2
    They Dare not Love 1941,My 16,21:4
    Texas 1941,O 17,27:3
    You'll Never Get Rich 1941,O 24,27:2
    Two Yanks in Trinidad 1942,Ap 6,19:4
    Night to Remember, A 1943,Ja 1,27:2
    Appointment in Berlin 1943,Jl 17,8:2
    None Shall Escape 1944,Ap 7,23:2
    Carolina Blues 1944,D 8,26:6
    Thousand and one Nights, A 1945,Jl 12,8:2
    Mr District Attorney 1947,F 28,27:3
    Corpse came C O D, The 1947,Ag 19,27:2
    Intrigue 1948,Ap 24,11:2
    Pitfall 1948,Ag 25,31:2
    Outpost in Morocco 1949,Mr 25,28:3
    Mrs Mike 1950,F 9,36:5
    System, The 1953,My 23,19:3
    South Sea Woman 1953,Je 4,33:6
    Bullet for Joey, A 1955,Ap 16,12:1
    Phenix City Story, The 1955,S 3,9:1
    Operation Eichmann 1961,My 4,40:7
    King of the Roaring Twenties 1961,O 5,43:1
    Strangler, The 1964,Je 11,27:4

Bischofvova, Ilse
    Diamonds of the Night 1968,Mr 15,30:1

Biscot
    Heart of a Nation, The 1943,Ap 8,27:2

Biscot, Georges
    Cage aux Rossignols, La; (Cage of Nightingales, A) 1947,Ap 3,31:2

Bishop, Bunny
    Model and the Marriage Broker, The 1952,Ja 12,10:6

Bishop, Detective Sergeant
    Blackmail 1929,O 7,22:1

Bishop, Joey
    Deep Six, The 1958,Ja 16,32:1
    Naked and the Dead, The 1958,Ag 7,21:1
    Onionhead 1958,O 2,44:1
    Ocean's Eleven 1960,Ag 11,19:1
    Pepe 1960,D 22,18:1
    Sergeants 3 1962,F 12,28:2
    Johnny Cool 1963,O 3,31:1
    Texas Across the River 1966,N 24,65:1
    Guide for the Married Man, A 1967,My 27,16:1
    Who's Minding the Mint? 1967,D 7,60:3
    Valley of the Dolls 1967,D 16,51:1

Bishop, John
    Jet Pilot 1957,O 5,8:6

Bishop, Julie
    Nurse's Secret, The 1941,Je 6,25:7
    International Squadron 1941,N 14,28:4
    I Was Framed 1942,Je 12,16:6
    Lady Gangster 1942,Jl 10,13:2
    Busses Roar 1942,S 25,25:4
    Escape From Crime 1942,O 12,12:3
    Hidden Hand, The 1942,N 26,40:4
    Hard Way, The 1943,Mr 13,9:2
    Action in the North Atlantic 1943,My 22,10:2
    Princess O'Rourke 1943,N 6,16:2
    Northern Pursuit 1943,N 26,29:2
    Rhapsody in Blue 1945,Je 28,22:2
    You Came Along 1945,Jl 5,7:2
    Cinderella Jones 1946,Mr 16,9:6
    Murder in the Music Hall 1946,Ap 15,22:2
    Last of the Redmen 1947,Ag 30,8:6
    High Tide 1947,N 8,11:2
    Deputy Marshal 1949,N 11,31:3
    Threat, The 1949,D 2,35:4
    Sands of Iwo Jima 1949,D 31,9:2
    Westward the Women 1952,Ja 1,21:2
    Sabre Jet 1953,N 3,34:1
    High and the Mighty, The 1954,Jl 1,21:2
    Big Land, The 1957,Mr 2,18:2

Bishop, Kenneth J (Producer)
    What Price Vengeance 1937,My 26,30:3

Bishop, Larry
    Wild in the Streets 1968,My 30,21:1
    Savage Seven, The 1968,Ag 22,47:1

Bishop, Piers
    Blues for Lovers 1966,S 8,43:1

Bishop, Richard
    Native Land 1942,My 12,16:3
    Teresa 1951,Ap 6,31:2

Bishop, Robert
    Court Martial 1955,Ag 2,17:1

Bishop, Terry (Director)
    Daybreak in Udi 1950,Je 2,26:2

Bishop, W A Air Marshal
    Captains of the Clouds 1942,F 13,24:2

Bishop, William
    Song of the Thin Man 1947,Ag 29,14:2
    Romance of Rosy Ridge, The 1947,S 12,18:3
    Anna Lucasta 1949,Ag 12,13:2
    Harriet Craig 1950,N 3,31:2
    Killer That Stalked New York, The 1951,Ja 5,17:2
    Frogmen, The 1951,Je 30,8:6
    Texas Rangers, The 1951,Jl 14,7:2
    Basketball Fix, the 1951,S 14,21:2
    Lorna Doone 1951,S 21,19:4
    Raiders, The 1952,D 13,19:2
    Redhead From Wyoming, The 1953,Ja 9,17:4
    Gun Belt 1953,Ag 1,8:2
    Oregon Trail, The 1959,D 10,51:6

Bisoglio, Val
    No Way to Treat a Lady 1968,Mr 21,56:1

Bissell, Richard (Original Author)
    Pajama Game, The 1957,Ag 30,12:2

Bissell, Richard (Screenwriter)
    Pajama Game, The 1957,Ag 30,12:2

Bissell, Whit
    Somewhere in the Night 1946,Je 13,24:2
    Brute Force 1947,Jl 17,16:2
    Senator Was Indiscreet, The 1947,D 27,9:2
    Another Part of the Forest 1948,My 19,30:2
    Canon City 1948,Jl 8,19:2
    That Lady in Ermine 1948,Ag 25,31:2
    Chicken every Sunday 1949,Ja 19,34:2
    He Walked by Night 1949,F 7,15:2
    Anna Lucasta 1949,Ag 12,13:2
    Wyoming Mail 1950,O 23,26:5
    For Heaven's Sake 1950,D 16,10:5
    Great Missouri Raid, The 1951,Ap 9,31:2
    Red Mountain 1952,Ap 26,19:2
    Devil's Canyon 1953,O 3,14:2
    It Should Happen to You 1954,Ja 16,10:5
    Riot in Cell Block 11 1954,F 19,24:5
    Creature from the Black Lagoon 1954,My 1,13:4
    Shanghai Story, The 1954,S 25,10:7
    Atomic Kid, The 1954,D 4,14:2
    Not as a Stranger 1955,Je 29,24:1
    Desperate Hours, The 1955,O 6,25:1
    Shack out on 101 1956,Ja 10,26:2
    At Gunpoint 1956,F 4,24:5
    Dakota Incident 1956,N 10,14:2
    Young Stranger, The 1957,Ap 9,40:1
    Gunfight at the O K Corral 1957,My 30,23:2
    Johnny Tremain 1957,Jl 11,21:1
    I Was a Teenage Frankenstein 1958,Ja 30,19:4
    Defiant Ones, The 1958,S 25,29:1
    Warlock 1959,My 1,34:1
    Never so Few 1960,Ja 22,15:2
    Time Machine, The 1960,Ag 18,19:1
    Birdman of Alcatraz 1962,Jl 19,19:2
    Hud 1963,My 29,36:1
    Seven Days in May 1964,F 20,22:1
    Where Love Has Gone 1964,N 3,26:1
    Hallelujah Trail, The 1965,Jl 2,17:1

Bisset, Donald
    Murder in the Cathedral 1952,Mr 26,35:2
    Battle of the Sexes, The 1960,Ap 19,40:4

Bisset, Jacqueline
    Cul de Sac 1966,N 8,44:2
    Casino Royale 1967,Ap 29,25:1
    Detective, The 1968,My 29,20:3
    Sweet Ride, The 1968,Je 13,57:2
    Bullitt 1968,O 18,41:2

Bisson, Alexandre (Original Author)
    Madame X 1920,S 27,18:1
    Madame X 1929,Ap 25,32:3
    Madame X 1937,O 25,23:1
    Madame X 1960,O 3,34:5
    Madame X 1966,Ap 28,49:1

Biswas, Chabi
    Devi 1962,O 8,19:1
    Music Room, The 1963,O 16,50:6
    Kanchenjungha 1966,Jl 26,27:2

Bit-Rakhman, S A (Screenwriter)
    Arshin Takes a Wife 1950,Jl 31,13:6

Bitenc, Demeter
    Seventh Continent, The 1968,Jl 30,33:2

Bittner, Julius (Miscellaneous)
    Strauss's Great Waltz 1935,Ap 8,23:3

Bityukov, B
    Big Family, A 1955,Je 6,24:1

Bitzer, G W (Cinematographer)
    Greatest Question, The 1919,D 29,7:2

Bixby, Bill
    Ride Beyond Vengance 1966,S 29,60:1
    Doctor, You've Got to be Kidding 1967,My 11,50:1
    Clambake 1967,D 14,62:3
    Speedway 1968,Je 14,43:1

Bixby, Jay Lewis (Original Author)
Fantastic Voyage 1966,S 8,43:1
Bizet, Georges (Composer)
Hers to Hold 1943,Jl 22,15:1
Bizet, Georges (Original Author)
First Opera Film Festival 1948,My 31,12:7
Bizoykishen, Lala
Throw of the Dice 1930,Ja 6,30:5
Bjelic, Severin
Legends of Anika 1956,Ap 19,35:1
Bjelvenstam, Bjors
Smiles of a Summer Night 1957,D 24,11:1
Wild Strawberries 1959,Je 23,37:1
Bjerre, Jens (Cinematographer)
Flame and the Fire 1966,Mr 29,37:1
Bjoerne, Gerda
Frun Tillhanda; Servant Girls 1938,D 30,9:2
Bjork, Anita
Miss Julie 1952,Ap 8,35:2
Night People 1954,Mr 13,11:2
Of Love and Lust (On Payment); On Payment (Of Love and Lust) 1959,My 26,31:2
Secrets of Woman 1961,Jl 12,36:1
Loving Couples 1966,S 20,38:1
Bjorling, Jussi
Fram for Framgang; Head for Success 1938,N 28,11:3
Bjorling, Jussl (Composer)
John Ericsson Victor of Hampton Roads 1938,My 18,17:2
Bjorling, Renee
Lesson in Love, A 1960,Mr 15,46:1
Bjorne, Hugo
Karl Fredrik Reigns 1938,F 2,15:2
Sun Over Sweden 1938,Ap 9,11:2
Frun Tillhanda; Servant Girls 1938,D 30,9:2
Himlaspelet 1944,O 9,17:3
Torment 1947,Ap 22,34:2
Crime and Punishment 1948,Mr 1,17:2
Bjornstrand, Gunnar
Smiles of a Summer Night 1957,D 24,11:1
Seventh Seal 1958,O 14,44:1
Wild Strawberries 1959,Je 23,37:1
Magician, The 1959,Ag 28,27:1
Lesson in Love, A 1960,Mr 15,46:1
Dreams; Kvinnodrom 1960,Je 1,42:1
Secrets of Woman 1961,Jl 12,36:1
Devil's Eye, The 1961,O 31,27:4
Through a Glass Darkly 1962,Mr 14,45:1
Night is my Future 1963,Ja 9,5:6
Winter Light 1963,My 14,32:1
Loving Couples 1966,S 20,38:1
My Sister, My Love 1967,F 20,45:2
Persona 1967,Mr 7,46:2
Hagbard and Signe 1968,My 17,56:1
Here's Your Life 1968,D 20,60:1
Shame 1968,D 24,14:1
Bjoze, Judy
Cyanamide 1954,Mr 26,17:6
Bjuggren, Ingert
Natt, En 1935,Ja 29,24:1
Blacaman
You Can't Cheat an Honest Man 1939,F 20,13:2
Blache, Herbert (Director)
Brat, The 1919,N 3,13:3
Stronger Than Death 1920,Ja 12,7:1
Beggar Maid, The 1921,S 26,18:1
Beggar Maid, The 1921,O 2,VII,3:1
Bashful Suitor, The 1921,D 12,20:2
Blache, Herbert (Miscellaneous)
Young Painter, The 1922,F 26,VI,3:1 (In Addenda)
Black, Alfred (Producer)
Perfect Woman, The 1951,F 17,10:7
Black, Amanda
Mark, The 1961,O 3,46:2
Black, Ben (Composer)
Mister Big 1943,Je 14,13:4
Black, Buck
Which Shall It Be? 1924,Ap 7,15:3
Last Man on Earth, The 1924,D 13,12:4
Senor Daredevil 1926,Ag 17,15:3
Black, Don
Dead March, The 1937,S 20,19:1 (In Addenda)
Black, Dorothy
Captivation 1931,S 28,17:4
Imitation of Life 1934,N 24,19:1
Black, Edward (Producer)
Night Train 1940,D 30,21:1
Girl in the News, The 1941,My 5,13:2
Kipps 1942,My 25,11:2
Young Mr Pitt, The 1943,Mr 11,17:1
Man in Grey, The 1945,N 30,18:6
Man of Evil 1948,Mr 26,26:2
Waterloo Road 1948,D 25,10:3
Man About the House, A 1949,Mr 9,33:2
Bonnie Prince Charlie 1952,Ja 7,14:3
Black, Eunice
Taste of Honey, A 1962,My 1,33:3
Black, G Howe
Wizard of Oz, The 1925,Ap 14,26:1

Black, George (Producer)
Perfect Woman, The 1951,F 17,10:7
Black, George (Screenwriter)
Perfect Woman, The 1951,F 17,10:7
Black, Ian Stuart (Original Author)
In the Wake of a Stranger 1961,Je 22,23:3
Black, Isobel
Kiss of the Vampire 1963,O 10,49:2
Black, John D F (Screenwriter)
Nobody's Perfect 1968,Ap 4,58:3
Black, Karen
You're a Big Boy Now 1967,Mr 21,35:3
Black, Maurice
Carnation Kid, The 1929,F 25,16:1
Street of Chance 1930,F 3,17:1
Framed 1930,Mr 29,23:1
Playing Around 1930,Mr 31,24:3
Runaway Bride 1930,My 17,21:2
Numbered Men 1930,Je 9,23:3
Sea God, The 1930,S 6,9:2
Brothers 1930,N 15,15:3
Little Casear 1931,Ja 10,19:2
Front Page, The 1931,Mr 20,29:1
Smart Money 1931,Je 19,21:1
Sob Sister 1931,O 3,20:2
Women Go on Forever 1931,O 19,28:1
High Pressure 1932,F 1,22:3
Dancers in the Dark 1932,Mr 19,11:2
Strange Love of Molly Louvain, The 1932,My 9,19:5
Scarlet Dawn 1932,N 4,25:4
Grand Slam 1933,F 22,25:2
I Cover the Waterfront 1933,My 18,17:3
Shriek in the Night, A 1933,Jl 24,11:2
Sixteen Fathoms Deep 1934,Ja 19,24:3
Wake up and Dream 1934,O 11,28:3
Three Legionnaires 1937,Jl 10,18:2
Adventure's End 1937,D 20,23:2
Black, Noel (Director)
Pretty Poison 1968,O 25,55:1
Black, Noel (Producer)
Pretty Poison 1968,O 25,55:1
Black, Stephen (Screenwriter)
Girl in the Canal, The 1947,O 9,32:3
Quiet Week-End 1948,Ag 20,13:2
Black, William
Fascinating Youth 1926,My 10,19:1
Blackburn, Clarice
Violators, The 1959,Ag 4,32:5
Pretty Poison 1968,O 25,55:1
Blackburn, Thomas (Original Author)
Short Grass 1951,Ja 13,10:4
Raton Pass 1951,Ap 20,25:1
Cattle Queen of Montana 1955,Ja 26,22:1
Johnny Tremain 1957,Jl 11,21:1
Blackburn, Thomas (Screenwriter)
Colt 45 1950,My 6,8:6
Short Grass 1951,Ja 13,10:4
Raton Pass 1951,Ap 20,25:1
Cavalry Scout 1951,Je 8,32:2
Riding Shotgun 1954,Ap 2,22:2
Davy Crockett, King of the Wild Frontier 1955,My 26,36:1
Blackburn Twins
She's Working her Way Through College 1952,Jl 10,27:2
Blacke, William (Original Author)
Man Who Fights Alone, The 1924,Jl 28,12:2
Blackett, Andrew
Against the Wind 1949,Je 27,18:3
Treasure Island 1950,Ag 16,24:2
Blackford, Mary
Sweetheart of Sigma Chi, The 1933,N 9,27:1
Blackler, Betty
No Room at the Inn 1949,D 26,33:4
Blackley, Douglas
Car 99 1935,F 23,14:7
Love Before Breakfast 1936,Mr 14,10:1
Shoot to Kill 1947,My 17,8:5
Blackman, Don
On the Waterfront 1954,Jl 29,18:1
Santiago 1956,Jl 14,13:2
Blackman, Honor
Quartet (The Alien Corn); Alien Corn, The (Quartet) 1949,Mr 29,30:3
Conspirator 1950,Ap 28,26:2
So Long at the Fair 1951,Ja 22,14:2
A Night to Remember 1958,D 17,2:7
Matter of Who, A 1962,Jl 25,29:2
Goldfinger 1964,D 22,36:1
Secret of my Success, The 1965,N 4,57:2
Life at the Top 1965,D 15,53:1
Moment to Moment 1966,Mr 3,28:1
Shalako 1968,N 6,32:1
Blackman, Joan
Career 1959,O 9,24:1
Great Impostor, The 1961,Mr 30,24:1
Blue Hawaii 1962,F 22,20:2
Kid Galahad 1963,Mr 7,8:5
Twilight of Honor 1963,N 14,41:2
Blackman, John
Visit to a Small Planet 1960,Ap 14,34:1

Blackmer, Sidney
Most Immoral Lady, A 1929,O 21,30:1
Strictly Modern 1930,My 3,23:1
Sweethearts and Wives 1930,Je 28,9:2
Bad Man, The 1930,S 27,21:3
Kismet 1930,O 31,20:1
Mothers Cry 1930,D 6,21:3
Little Casear 1931,Ja 10,19:2
Woman Hungry 1931,Mr 23,24:7
It's a Wise Child 1931,My 16,13:3
Lady Who Dared, The 1931,Je 6,15:5
From Hell to Heaven 1933,Mr 18,9:3
Cocktail Hour 1933,Je 5,18:5
Wrecker, The 1933,Ag 7,18:3
Deluge 1933,O 9,22:3
This Man is Mine 1934,Ap 13,25:1
Down to Their Last Yacht 1934,S 24,14:1
Count of Monte Cristo, The 1934,S 27,25:2
Transatlantic Merry-Go-Round 1934,N 1,25:2
President Vanishes, The 1934,D 8,18:5
Notorious Gentleman, A 1935,F 16,9:1
Little Colonel, The 1935,Mr 22,26:2
Behind the Green Lights 1935,Ap 22,14:2
Great God Gold 1935,My 6,22:3
Woman Trap 1936,Mr 7,11:4
Florida Special 1936,My 29,15:2
Early to Bed 1936,Jl 16,20:2
Missing Girls 1936,O 5,25:1
President's Mystery, The 1936,O 19,22:1
Doctor's Diary, A 1937,F 17,16:4
John Meade's Woman 1937,F 18,19:1
House of Secrets 1937,F 22,13:1
Girl Overboard 1937,Mr 1,15:1
This Is my Affair 1937,My 28,17:1
Shadows of the Orient 1937,O 11,26:6
Wife, Doctor and Nurse 1937,O 11,26:5
Heidi 1937,N 6,14:2
Last Gangster, The 1937,D 10,33:2
Charlie Chan at Monte Carlo 1937,D 18,18:1
Thank You, Mr Moto 1938,Ja 3,16:2
In Old Chicago 1938,Ja 7,15:2
Speed to Burn 1938,S 9,25:1
Straight, Place and Show 1938,O 1,10:2
Suez 1938,O 15,21:2
Sharpshooters 1938,D 5,19:2
While New York Sleeps 1938,D 22,25:3
Trade Winds 1939,Ja 13,17:2
Fast and Loose 1939,Mr 9,18:1
Within the Law 1939,Ap 6,31:2
It's a Wonderful World 1939,My 19,27:2
Hotel for Women 1939,Ag 26,20:2
Maryland 1940,Jl 13,16:5
I Want a Divorce 1940,O 3,31:2
Third Finger, Left Hand 1940,D 12,37:2
Cheers for Miss Bishop 1941,Mr 14,17:2
Great Swindle, The 1941,My 14,25:4
Rookies on Parade 1941,My 22,25:2
Love Crazy 1941,Je 6,25:5
Ellery Queen and the Perfect Crime 1941,Ag 11,17:3
Officer and the Lady, The 1941,Ag 11,17:4
Feminine Touch, The 1941,D 12,35:3
Always in my Heart 1942,Mr 14,19:2
Nazi Agent 1942,Je 13,11:2
Sabotage Squad 1942,Ag 5,16:1
Quiet Please, Murder 1942,D 22,31:1
Murder in Times Square 1943,My 31,13:2
In old Oklahoma 1943,D 6,21:1
Lady and the Monster, The 1944,Ap 8,9:2
Buffalo Bill 1944,Ap 20,22:6
Wilson 1944,Ag 2,18:1
Duel in the Sun 1947,My 8,30:2
My Girl Tisa 1948,F 21,9:2
People Will Talk 1951,Ag 30,20:1
Saturday's Hero 1951,S 12,37:2
San Francisco Story, The 1952,My 10,16:4
Washington Story 1952,Jl 2,22:3
Johnny Dark 1954,Je 26,7:2
High and the Mighty, The 1954,Jl 1,21:2
View From Pompey's Head, The 1955,N 5,22:5
High Society 1956,Ag 10,9:2
Beyond a Reasonable Doubt 1956,S 14,27:2
Tammy and the Bachelor 1957,Je 15,10:7
How to Murder Your Wife 1965,Ja 27,26:1
Joy in the Morning 1965,Je 10,38:1
Covenant with Death, A 1967,F 16,32:3
Rosemary's Baby 1968,Je 13,57:1
Blackmer, Sidney (Narrator)
Farewell to Yesterday 1950,D 1,31:2
Blackmore, Peter (Original Author)
Miranda 1949,Ap 25,20:2
Blackmore, Peter (Screenwriter)
Miranda 1949,Ap 25,20:2
Time, Gentlemen, Please 1953,S 24,39:2
Simon and Laura 1956,Jl 3,17:2
Blackmore, R D (Original Author)
Lorna Doone 1922,D 4,20:2
Blackton, Charles Stuart
Passers By 1920,Je 21,13:1
Blackton, Greg
Fascinating Youth 1926,My 10,19:1

Blackton, J Stuart (Director)
On the Banks of the Wabash 1923,O 23,21:3
Let Not Man Put Asunder 1924,Ja 15,16:1
Between Friends 1924,My 12,14:4
Clean Heart, The 1924,S 15,28:1
Beloved Brute, The 1924,N 10,20:1
Redeeming Sin, The 1925,Ja 20,18:2
Tides of Passion 1925,Ap 20,22:1
Happy Warrior, The 1925,Jl 7,24:2
Blackton, J Stuart (Miscellaneous)
Behold This Woman 1924,Jl 22,9:1
Blackton, J Stuart (Original Author)
Hell-Bent for Heaven 1926,My 4,31:1
Blackton, J Stuart (Producer)
Battle Cry for Peace, The 1915,Ag 7,8:3
Missing 1918,Je 17,11:3
Safe for Democracy 1918,N 4,11:3
Passers By 1920,Je 21,13:1
Blackwell, Carlyle
Restless Sex, The 1920,S 13,12:1
Wrecker, The 1929,Ag 13,23:2
Blackwell, Carlyle Jr
Calling of Dan Matthews, The 1936,Ja 25,18:4
Blackwell, Jim
Love's Wilderness 1924,D 22,20:2
Blackwell, Nell (Original Author)
Man From Yesterday, The 1932,Je 25,18:2
Blackwood, George
I Loved a Woman 1933,S 22,14:2
Son of a Sailor 1933,N 30,38:4
Lady Killer 1934,Ja 1,28:2
Bladick, Clara
Once a Sinner 1931,Ja 17,23:1
Blaess, Regine
Picnic on the Grass 1960,O 12,47:1
Blagovestov, Alexander
And Quiet Flows the Don 1960,My 25,45:2
Blain, Estella
Chasers, The; Draguers, Les 1960,My 3,43:1
Blain, Gerard
Deadlier Than the Male 1957,O 9,41:1
Crime and Punishment 1958,S 16,23:2
Beau Serge, Le 1959,Ag 3,21:1
Cousins, The (Les Cousins) 1959,N 24,44:1
Hatari 1962,Jl 12,19:1
Run With the Devil 1963,Jl 16,25:1
Bonne Soupe, La 1964,Mr 16,37:1
Eye of the Needle, The 1965,Je 22,25:2
Blain, Pierre
Golden Mistress, The 1954,O 30,15:6
Blaine, James
Return of Sophie Lang, The 1936,Jl 24,13:1
Exposed 1938,N 21,14:5
Blaine, Martin
Satan Bug, The 1965,Ap 15,38:1
Blaine, Vivian
He Hired the Boss 1943,Je 4,17:4
Jitterbugs 1943,Je 5,12:2
Greenwich Village 1944,S 28,26:2
Something for the Boys 1944,N 30,19:1
Nob Hill 1945,Jl 4,10:3
State Fair 1945,Ag 31,14:3
Doll Face 1946,Mr 28,35:3
If I'm Lucky 1946,S 20,41:3
Three Little Girls in Blue 1946,S 26,32:3
Skirts Ahoy! 1952,My 29,17:2
Guys and Dolls 1955,N 5,26:1
Public Pigeon No 1 1957,My 18,23:2
Blair
Always Leave Them Laughing 1949,N 24,48:2
Blair, Barbara
Outsider, The 1940,Mr 18,13:2
Frightened Bride, The 1953,Ag 20,18:5
Blair, Bernard
Great Spy Chase, The 1966,O 6,56:4
Blair, Betsy
Guilt of Janet Ames, The 1947,My 23,31:2
Double Life, A 1948,F 20,19:1
Another Part of the Forest 1948,My 19,30:2
Snake Pit, the 1948,N 5,29:2
Mystery Street 1950,Jl 28,12:5
Kind Lady 1951,Ag 8,21:2
Marty 1955,Ap 12,25:3
Lovemaker, The 1958,Mr 11,33:4
Grido, Il 1962,O 23,42:1
Blair, David
Evening With the Royal Ballet, An 1965,D 9,60:1
Romeo and Juliet 1966,O 6,55:1
Blair, Janet
Two Yanks in Trinidad 1942,Ap 6,19:4
Broadway 1942,Je 5,23:2
My Sister Eileen 1942,O 23,15:1
Something to Shout About 1943,Ap 8,27:3
Once Upon a Time 1944,Je 30,17:2
Tonight and Every Night 1945,Mr 9,16:2
Tars and Spars 1946,F 15,29:2
Gallant Journey 1946,O 10,33:2
Fabulous Dorseys, The 1947,My 30,25:3
Fuller Brush Man, The 1948,My 15,18:2
Black Arrow, The 1948,O 4,14:2
Public Pigeon No 1 1957,My 18,23:2
Boys' Night Out 1962,Je 22,15:2
Burn, Witch, Burn 1962,Jl 5,21:2 (In Addenda)

One and Only Genuine Original Family Band,
The 1968,Mr 22,55:1
Blair, Joan
His Woman 1931,D 5,21:2
Murder of Dr Harrigan, The 1936,Ja 21,27:5
Mr District Attorney 1941,Ap 17,29:3
Constant Nymph, The 1943,Jl 24,8:2
Strange Death of Adolf Hitler, The 1943,O 9,11:5
Deadline for Murder 1946,Je 29,22:7
Blair, June
Rabbit Trap, The 1959,O 15,48:1
Blair, Lionel
World of Suzie Wong, The 1960,N 11,36:1
Blair, Milton (Director)
Surfari 1967,Jl 19,26:2
Blair, Nicky
Viva Las Vegas 1964,My 21,42:1
Blaisdell, Anne (Original Author)
Die! Die! My Darling 1965,My 20,52:1
Blaisdell, William
Yankee Clipper, The 1927,My 3,25:1
Blake, Amanda
Duchess of Idaho 1950,Jl 21,15:3
Stars in my Crown 1950,D 22,19:1
Scarlet Angel 1952,Je 21,12:2
Lili 1953,Mr 11,36:7
Sabre Jet 1953,N 3,34:1
Adventures of Haji Baba, The 1954,O 9,8:7
Star is Born, A 1954,O 12,23:1
Glass Slipper, The 1955,Mr 25,19:2
Blake, Angela
I Was a Teenage Frankenstein 1958,Ja 30,19:4
Blake, Anne
Orders to Kill 1958,N 18,41:2
Scream of Fear 1961,Ag 23,29:1
Blake, Arthur
Sherlock Holmes and the Voice Of Terror
1942,S 19,9:2
Port of New York 1950,F 3,29:2
Cyrano De Bergerac 1950,N 17,31:2
Diplomatic Courier 1952,Je 14,12:2
Blake, Ben K (Director)
Two Sisters 1938,D 1,29:3
Blake, Bobby
Andy Hardy's Double Life 1943,Ja 12,23:3
China Girl 1943,Ja 21,27:2
Lost Angel 1944,Ap 10,14:1
Big Noise, The 1944,S 23,16:1
Woman in the Window, The 1945,Ja 26,16:4
Horn Blows at Midnight, The 1945,Ap 21,18:2
Pillow to Post 1945,My 26,18:2
Dakota 1945,D 17,17:2
In old Sacramento 1946,Ap 29,24:4
Humoresque 1946,D 26,28:1
Treasure of Sierra Madre 1948,Ja 24,11:2
Black Rose, The 1950,S 2,11:2
Blake, Charles E (Original Author)
Country Doctor, The 1936,Mr 13,32:2 (Incorrect
in this edition; use 1936,Mr 13,27:2 elsewhere)
Blake, George
Kid Galahad 1937,My 27,21:3
Blake, Gladys
Lucky Night 1939,My 5,29:3
Fast And Furious 1939,O 12,33:3
Young as You Feel 1940,Mr 8,25:3
Andy Hardy Meets Debutante 1940,Ag 2,12:2
Woman of the Year 1942,F 6,23:2
Phantom of the Opera, The 1943,O 15,15:2
Rockin' in The Rockies 1945,Jl 5,7:2
Bewitched 1945,Ag 17,20:3
Blake, Grey
Java Head 1935,Jl 31,21:4
Tawny Pipit 1947,S 8,25:5
Jassy 1948,F 20,19:2
Easy Money (Episode 2) 1949,F 14,15:3
Broken Journey 1949,My 26,34:3
Dancing Years, The 1951,Ja 29,14:4
Blake, Harold
Follow the Sun 1951,Ap 26,34:4
Blake, Larry
Road Back, The 1937,Je 18,25:2
Jury's Secret, The 1938,F 4,17:2
Nurse From Brooklyn 1938,My 13,17:3
They Made Her a Spy 1939,Mr 29,21:4
Smash-Up, The Story of a Woman
1947,Ap 11,31:2
Backlash 1947,My 24,10:5
Second Chance 1947,S 20,12:4
Lucky Stiff, The 1949,Ja 31,14:2
Holiday Affair 1949,N 24,48:2
Sunset Boulevard 1950,Ag 11,15:2
Winning Team, The 1952,Je 21,12:2
High Noon 1952,Jl 25,14:2
Inside Detroit 1956,Ja 28,10:5
Earth vs the Flying Saucers 1956,Ag 2,21:2
Blake, Madge
Between Midnight and Dawn 1950,O 2,19:2
Prowler, The 1951,Jl 2,16:6
Singin' in the Rain 1952,Mr 28,27:2
Long, Long Trailer, The 1954,F 19,24:3
Rhapsody 1954,Mr 12,17:1
Sergeants 3 1962,F 12,28:2

Blake, Marian
Playground, The 1965,O 4,00:0
Blake, Marie
Love Finds Andy Hardy 1938,Jl 22,10:2
Rich Man, Poor Girl 1938,Ag 19,13:3
Dramatic School 1938,D 9,31:2
Calling Dr Kildare 1939,My 12,25:4
Blind Alley 1939,My 23,27:2
Secret of Dr Kildare, The 1939,D 8,33:5
Dr Kildare's Strange Case 1940,Ap 12,19:2
They Knew What They Wanted 1940,O 11,25:2
Dr Kildare's Crisis 1940,D 19,33:1
People vs Dr Kildare, The 1941,My 8,21:1
Remember the Day 1941,D 26,21:2
Dr Kildare's Victory 1942,F 5,25:2
Give Out, Sisters 1942,Ag 28,22:3
Good Morning, Judge 1943,Ap 30,25:4
Between Two Women 1945,Mr 29,18:3
Dark Delusion 1947,Je 26,19:2
Mourning Becomes Electra 1947,N 20,38:2
Innocent Affair, An 1948,S 29,36:2
Blake, Oliver
Wake up and Dream 1947,Ja 24,18:4
Guilty, The 1947,My 19,27:2
Senator Was Indiscreet, The 1947,D 27,9:2
Ma and Pa Kettle Back on the Farm
1951,My 11,32:3
Ma and Pa Kettle at the Fair 1952,Jl 12,16:2
So Big 1953,O 22,34:2
Long, Long Trailer, The 1954,F 19,24:3
Blake, Pamela
This Gun for Hire 1942,My 14,23:2
Maisie Gets her Man 1942,Jl 16,23:2
Slightly Dangerous 1943,Ap 2,17:2
Swing Shift Maisie 1943,S 10,29:2
Swing Fever 1944,Ja 28,14:1
Why Girls Leave Home 1945,Ag 4,7:3
Blake, Richard (Original Author)
Crooked Road, The 1940,Je 11,33:4
Blake, Richard (Screenwriter)
Devil is Driving, The 1937,Jl 16,22:1
Invaders From Mars 1953,My 30,7:1
Blake, Robert
Pork Chop Hill 1959,My 30,9:2
Purple Gang, The 1960,Ja 23,15:5
Town Without Pity 1961,O 11,53:1
Greatest Story Ever Told, The 1965,F 16,40:2
This Property is Condemned 1966,Ag 4,24:1
In Cold Blood 1967,D 15,60:1
Blake, Sam
Kisenga, Man of Africa 1952,Mr 7,18:2
Blake, Tom
Out of the Fog 1919,F 10,11:3
Wildfire 1925,Je 10,18:2
Blake, Whitney
30 1959,N 12,27:1
Blakelock, Alban
Murder in the Cathedral 1952,Mr 26,35:2
Blakely, Colin
Saturday Night and Sunday Morning
1961,Ap 4,44:2
Hellions, The 1962,Mr 15,28:2
This Sporting Life 1963,Jl 17,19:2
Underworld Informers 1965,O 14,53:1
Man for all Seasons, A 1966,D 13,60:1
Spy With a Cold Nose, The 1966,D 20,58:2
Day the Fish Came Out, The 1967,O 3,57:1
Charlie Bubbles 1968,F 12,47:2
Vengance of She, The 1968,My 30,21:4
Blakely, Gene
That Darn Cat 1965,D 3,44:1
Beach Red 1967,Ag 4,18:1
Blakely, Gene (Narrator)
Roosevelt Story, The 1947,Ag 22,11:2
Blakely, James
Broadway Bill 1934,N 30,22:2
Paris in Spring 1935,Jl 13,16:2
Two for Tonight 1935,Ag 31,16:2
She Couldn't Take It 1935,N 7,27:1
Gay Desperado, The 1936,O 9,31:4
Shadow Strikes, The 1937,S 13,17:1
Blakely, Tom (Producer)
Caretaker's Daughter, The 1953,Ag 20,18:5
Man in the Dark 1965,Ja 21,22:1
Blakeney, Olive
Gangway 1937,Ag 21,7:3
That Uncertain Feeling 1941,My 2,25:1
Experiment Perilous 1944,D 30,15:2
Dakota 1945,D 17,17:2
Sentimental Journey 1946,Mr 7,33:2
Strange Woman, The 1947,F 24,16:4
Time Out of Mind 1947,Ap 7,20:1
Sealed Verdict 1948,N 3,36:2
Blakey, Rubie
Miracle in Harlem 1949,O 24,19:4
Blal, Judith
Wanted: Jane Turner 1936,N 30,24:7
BLANC
See Also BLANCK
Blanc, Anne-Marie
Marie-Louise 1945,N 13,24:2

Blanc, Mel
Neptune's Daughter 1949,Je 10,32:2
Kiss Me, Stupid 1964,D 23,22:2
Blanc, Mel (Narrator)
Man Called Flintstone, The 1967,N 25,42:1
Blanc, Sally
Wife Savers 1928,Ja 17,23:2
Blanc-Maeterlinck, Georgette Le
New Enchantment, The 1926,Mr 15,18:3
Blancard, Rene
Cage aux Rossignols, La; (Cage of Nightingales, A) 1947,Ap 3,31:2
Shop-Girls of Paris; Au Bonheur de Dames 1947,Je 23,14:4
Jenny Lamour 1948,Mr 6,17:2
Under the Paris Sky 1952,My 6,35:1
To Catch a Thief 1955,Ag 5,14:2
Diary of a Bad Girl 1958,My 30,13:2
Truth, The 1961,Je 27,23:2
Julie the Redhead 1963,O 15,44:1
Blanch, Anita
Life of Simon Bolivar, The 1943,Je 18,16:5
El Conde de Monte Cristo 1943,N 9,26:2
Blanch, Isabelita
Tu Hijo 1934,D 17,24:3
Blanchar, Dominique
Secret of Mayerling, The 1951,My 8,39:2
Decision Before Dawn 1951,D 22,12:2
Avventura, L' 1961,Ap 5,30:1
Blanchar, Pierre
Marche Nuptiale, La 1929,Mr 3,VIII,7:2
Chess Player, The 1930,My 19,21:1
Atlantide, L' 1932,Ag 7,IX,2:1
Couturiere de Luneville, La 1932,O 14,23:2
Celle Vielle Canaille 1935,Ja 12,12:2
Crime et Chatiment; Crime and Punishment 1935,N 13,25:3
Late Mathias Pascal, The 1937,N 18,27:2
Carnet de Bal, Un 1938,Mr 26,12:1
Volga Boatman, The 1938,Ap 15,23:3
Courier of Lyons, The 1938,Je 3,17:1
Two Women 1940,N 2,19:3
Dame de Pique, La 1944,O 19,19:2
They Are not Angels 1948,My 22,8:3
Symphonie Pastorale 1948,S 14,34:3
Street of Shadows 1948,N 20,9:2
Riff Raff Girls 1962,O 20,13:5
Magnificent Sinner 1963,Ap 25,38:1
Blanchard, Felix (Doc)
Spirit of West Point 1947,O 3,31:2
Blanchard, Mari
On the Riviera 1951,My 24,47:1
No Questions Asked 1951,Ag 10,13:2
Ten Tall Men 1951,O 27,10:5
Veils of Bagdad, The 1953,N 27,99:9
Rails Into Laramie 1954,My 13,34:2
Son of Sinbad 1955,Jl 28,18:2
Return of Jack Slade, The 1955,N 24,41:3
Crooked Web, The 1955,D 10,19:1
Twice Told Tales (Dr Heidegger's Experiment); Dr Heidegger's Experiment (Twice Told Tales) 1964,Mr 28,40:1
Blanchard, Marj
Don't Knock the Twist 1962,Ap 14,14:2
Blanchard, Ralph Lieutenant (Original Author)
Lone Eagle, The 1927,D 20,33:2
Blanche, Francis
Babette Goes to War 1960,Je 8,46:1
Green Mare, The; Jument Verte, La 1961,O 24,41:2
Seventh Juror, The 1964,Ja 28,25:1
Sweet and Sour 1964,D 28,34:2
Thank Heaven for Small Favors 1965,Ja 14,44:2
Male Hunt; Chasse a l'Homme, La 1965,Ap 20,42:1
Great Spy Chase, The 1966,O 6,56:4
Blanche, Kate
Without Limit 1921,Mr 21,11:3
Blanche, Roland
How Not to Rob a Department Store 1965,D 29,23:1
Blancher, Pierre
Cette Vielle Canaille 1935,Ja 12,12:2
Blanchi, Giorgio (Director)
Merry Chase, The 1948,S 18,11:4
Blanchi, Regina
Shoot Loud, Louder... I Don't Understand 1967,S 21,56:4
Blanchi, Tino
Avvocato Difensore, L'; Attorney for the Defense, The 1935,N 13,25:4
Blanchon, J H (Screenwriter)
Boys' School 1939,Je 6,26:2
BLANCK
See Also BLANC
Blanck, Dorothee
Cleo From 5 to 7 1962,S 5,43:4
Blanco, Carlos (Screenwriter)
Mad Queen, The 1950,O 27,24:3
Blanco, Victoria
Corazon Bandolero 1935,Mr 2,18:2
Tesoro de Pancho Villa, El 1936,Ja 27,20:4
Mujeres de Hoy 1936,D 7,27:4

Soy Chato, Pero las Huelo; I Am Snub-nosed but I Can Smell 1939,Jl 22,12:3
Bland, Joyce
Magic Night 1932,N 3,25:3
Dreaming Lips 1937,My 20,17:1
Citadel, The 1938,N 4,27:2
Sixty Glorious Years 1938,N 18,25:2
Spy of Napoleon 1939,Ag 19,18:4
Bland, Trevor
Below the Sea 1933,Je 3,16:4
Paddy the Next Best Thing 1933,Ag 25,12:2
Blandick, Clara
Girl Said No, The 1930,Ap 5,23:3
Sins of the Children 1930,Jl 26,16:4
Romance 1930,Ag 23,7:3
Tom Sawyer 1930,D 20,20:6
Easiest Way, The 1931,F 28,15:2
It's a Wise Child 1931,My 16,13:3
Daybreak 1931,Je 1,15:1
Huckleberry Finn 1931,Ag 8,16:3
Bought 1931,Ag 15,18:3
Murder at Midnight 1931,O 5,17:3
New Adventures of Get-Rich-Quick Wallingford 1931,O 10,20:4
Possessed 1931,N 28,20:4
Expert, The 1932,F 27,22:1
Shopworn 1932,Ap 4,13:6
Wet Parade, The 1932,Ap 22,23:2
Strange Case of Clara Deane, The 1932,My 6,15:3
Two Against the World 1932,Ag 19,20:6
Life Begins 1932,Ag 26,20:3
Three on a Match 1932,O 29,18:4
Bitter Tea of General Yen, The 1933,Ja 12,20:6
Child of Manhattan 1933,F 13,11:4
Mind Reader, The 1933,Ap 7,22:4
Turn Back the Clock 1933,Ag 26,14:2
One Sunday Afternoon 1933,S 2,14:4
Charlie Chan's Greatest Case 1933,O 7,18:4
Ever in my Heart 1933,O 13,25:3
Show-Off, The 1934,Mr 17,11:3
As the Earth Turns 1934,Ap 12,27:2
Sisters Under the Skin 1934,Je 8,18:1
Girl From Missouri, The 1934,Ag 4,14:6
Broadway Bill 1934,N 30,22:2
President Vanishes, The 1934,D 8,18:5
Princess O'Hara 1935,Ap 13,11:3
Hearts Divided 1936,Je 13,13:1
Anthony Adverse 1936,Ag 27,16:1
Case of the Velvet Claws, The 1936,Ag 29,16:3
Gorgeous Hussy, The 1936,S 5,7:1
In His Steps 1936,O 29,31:1
Make Way for a Lady 1936,D 12,15:1
Her Husband's Secretary 1937,Mr 20,23:6
Star Is Born, A 1937,Ap 23,25:1
Wings Over Honolulu 1937,My 29,20:1
Crime Ring 1938,Jl 22,10:3
Huckleberry Finn 1939,Mr 3,21:2
I Was a Convict 1939,Mr 23,27:2
Wizard of Oz, The 1939,Ag 18,16:2
Drums Along the Mohawk 1939,N 4,11:2
Swanee River 1939,D 30,9:2
Anne of Windy Poplars 1940,Ag 13,13:3
Youth Will Be Served 1940,N 15,25:2
Wagons Roll at Night, The 1941,My 10,20:4
Nurse's Secret, The 1941,Je 6,25:7
Private Nurse 1941,Ag 29,13:3
It Started With Eve 1941,O 3,27:1
One Foot in Heaven 1941,N 14,28:3
Can't Help Singing 1944,D 26,22:4
Frontier Gal 1945,D 15,14:2
Pillow of Death 1946,Ja 26,19:3
People Are Funny 1946,Ja 28,15:6
So Goes my Love 1946,My 2,3:7
Stolen Life, A 1946,My 2,27:4
Life With Father 1947,Ag 16,6:6
Bride Goes Wild, The 1948,Je 4,27:2
Love That Brute 1950,My 27,10:6
Blanding, Don (Original Author)
Hawaii Calls 1938,Ap 29,17:2
Blando, Oscar
Under the Sun of Rome 1949,O 6,40:4
Blane, Barbara
Satan Met a Lady 1936,Jl 23,24:2
Blane, Ralph (Composer)
Best Foot Forward 1943,Je 30,25:2
Broadway Rhythm 1944,Ap 14,24:6
Meet Me in St Louis 1944,N 29,20:2
Ziegfeld Follies 1946,Mr 23,8:3
My Blue Heaven 1950,S 16,12:6
Athena 1954,D 22,28:2
Blane, Sally
Fools for Luck 1928,Je 12,33:5
Half Marriage 1929,Ag 19,22:1
Vagabond Lover, The 1929,N 27,30:6
Tanned Legs 1929,D 2,28:2
Little Accident 1930,Ag 4,13:4
Once a Sinner 1931,Ja 17,23:1
Ten Cents a Dance 1931,Mr 7,17:2
Annabelle's Affairs 1931,Je 29,20:3
Women Men Marry 1931,Jl 13,13:5
Star Witness, The 1931,Ag 4,19:5
Star Witness, The 1931,Ag 4,19:5

Blane, Sally — Cont
Spirit of Notre Dame, The 1931,O 16,27:1
Dangerous Affair, A 1931,N 23,22:1
X Marks the Spot 1931,D 7,16:1
Good Sport 1931,D 12,23:3
Cross Examination 1932,F 27,22:1
Disorderly Conduct 1932,Ap 11,19:2
Escapade 1932,My 28,18:2
Phantom Express, The 1932,S 20,26:3
I Am a Fugitive From a Chain Gang 1932,N 11,17:2
Big Pay-Off, The 1933,Ja 17,22:7
Hello, Everybody 1933,Ja 30,9:4
Heritage of the Desert 1933,Mr 11,18:3
Trick for Trick 1933,Je 10,16:4
Advice to the Lovelorn 1933,D 14,28:2
No More Women 1934,My 15,27:4
Half a Sinner 1934,Je 23,16:5
Silver Streak, The 1935,Ja 16,21:1
Angel's Holiday 1937,My 29,20:2
Great Hospital Mystery, The 1937,Jl 16,22:2
One Mile From Heaven 1937,Ag 19,23:1
Story of Alexander Graham Bell, The 1939,Ap 1,17:2
Way Down South 1939,Ag 18,16:4
Charlie Chan at Treasure Island 1939,S 1,15:5
Blaness, Georges
Cloportes 1966,Ap 19,36:1
Blank, Dorothy Ann (Screenwriter)
Snow White and the Seven Dwarfs 1938,Ja 14,21:1 (In Addenda)
Blanke, Henry (Producer)
Gay Sisters, The 1942,Ag 15,14:2
Edge of Darkness 1943,Ap 10,12:4
Constant Nymph, The 1943,Jl 24,8:2
Old Acquaintance 1943,N 3,20:2
Roughly Speaking 1945,F 1,18:4
My Reputation 1946,Ja 26,19:2
Of Human Bondage 1946,Jl 6,11:2
Deception 1946,O 19,15:3
Cry Wolf 1947,Jl 19,10:2
Deep Valley 1947,Ag 23,7:2
Escape me Never 1947,N 8,11:2
Treasure of Sierra Madre 1948,Ja 24,11:2
Winter Meeting 1948,Ap 8,31:2
Woman in White, The 1948,My 8,12:2
June Bride 1948,O 30,10:2
Fountainhead, The 1949,Jl 9,8:5
Beyond the Forest 1949,O 22,11:2
Bright Leaf 1950,Je 17,7:2
Lightning Strikes Twice 1951,Ap 13,18:7
Goodbye, my Fancy 1951,My 30,14:2
Tomorrow Is Another Day 1951,Ag 9,17:5
Come Fill the Cup 1951,N 22,47:2
Room for One More 1952,Ja 16,21:2
Operation Secret 1952,N 6,37:2
Iron Mistress, The 1952,N 20,39:2
She's Back on Broadway 1953,Mr 12,24:2
So This Is Love 1953,Ag 12,22:1
So Big 1953,O 22,34:2
Phantom of the Rue Morgue 1954,Mr 20,10:5
Lucky Me 1954,Ap 10,11:2
King Richard and the Crusaders 1954,Ag 23,20:5
Young at Heart 1955,Ja 20,35:1
McConnell Story, The 1955,S 30,23:1
Sincerely Yours 1955,N 3,37:1
Serenade 1956,Mr 24,21:1 (Incorrect in this edition; use 1956,Mr 23,21:1 elsewhere)
Too Much, Too Soon 1958,My 10,19:2
Nun's Story, The 1959,Je 19,30:1
Miracle, The 1959,N 13,25:4
Cash McCall 1960,Ja 28,26:1
Ice Palace 1960,Je 30,22:1
Sins of Rachel Cade, The 1961,Ap 6,30:3
Hell is for Heroes 1962,Jl 12,19:3
Blanke, Tom
Lunatic at Large, The 1927,F 1,25:1
Blankfort, Henry (Miscellaneous)
Daltons Ride Again, The 1945,D 8,21:2
Blankfort, Henry (Screenwriter)
Tales of Manhattan 1942,S 25,25:1
Open Secret 1948,F 2,15:2
Underworld Story, The 1950,Jl 27,29:4
Blankfort, Michael (Miscellaneous)
New Gulliver, The 1935,N 4,24:4
Blankfort, Michael (Original Author)
Texas 1941,O 17,27:3
Juggler, The 1953,My 6,39:2
Blankfort, Michael (Screenwriter)
Blind Alley 1939,My 23,27:2
Adam Had Four Sons 1941,Mr 28,26:6
Texas 1941,O 17,27:3
Flight Lieutenant 1942,Jl 31,11:1
Live Today for Tomorrow 1948,D 6,29:2
Dark Past, The 1948,D 23,25:2
Broken Arrow 1950,Jl 21,15:2
Halls of Montezuma, The 1951,Ja 6,9:6
My Six Convicts 1952,Mr 28,27:3
Lydia Bailey 1952,My 31,12:5
Juggler, The 1953,My 6,39:2
Tribute to a Bad Man 1956,Mr 31,13:3
Vintage, The 1957,My 9,36:5
Plainsman, The 1966,N 19,26:1

Blano, Peggy Lou
Why Girls Leave Home 1945,Ag 4,7:3
Blareau, Richard (Director)
Ballet de France 1955,S 26,18:2
Blasco, Teresa
Games Men Play, The 1968,Mr 15,30:1
Blasco-Ibanez, Vicente (Original Author)
Four Horsemen of the Apocalypse 1921,Mr 7,8:1
Blood and Sand 1922,Ag 7,14:2
Argentine Love 1924,D 23,16:2
Mare Nostrum 1926,F 16,22:4
Four Horsemen of the Apocalypse, The
1926,S 27,27:3
Temptress, The 1926,O 11,18:1
Blood and Sand 1941,My 23,25:3
4 Horsemen of the Apocalypse, The
1962,Mr 10,10:2
Blasco-Ibanez, Vicente (Screenwriter)
Circe the Enchantress 1924,D 9,23:3
Ibanez's Torrent 1926,F 22,14:1
Blasek, Jiri
Bohemian Rapture 1948,F 16,16:2
Blaselti, Alessandro (Director)
Avventura di Salvator Rosa, Un; Adventure of
Salvator Rosa, An 1940,S 20,27:3
Blaser, Herman (Producer)
Blues for Lovers 1966,S 8,43:1
Blasetti, Alessandro
Bellissima 1953,My 18,26:2
Blasetti, Alessandro (Director)
Terra Madre 1931,O 31,22:2
Gesuzza, La Sposa Garibaldina 1936,N 3,33:4
Piccolo Eroe 1937,Jl 1,33:2
Contessa di Parma, La 1938,F 24,23:2
Four Steps in the Clouds 1948,N 22,25:2
Iron Crown 1949,Je 11,11:2
Fabiola 1951,My 30,14:2
Father's Dilemma 1952,S 23,25:1
Times Gone By (The Trial of Frine); Trial of
Frine, The (Times Gone By) 1953,D 30,16:2
Times Gone By (Less Than a Day); Less Than a
Day (Times Gone By) 1953,D 30,16:2
Times Gone By (The Vise); Vise, The (Times Gone
By) 1953,D 30,16:2
Times Gone By (A Pot-Pourri of Songs);
Pot-Pourri of Songs, A (Times Gone By)
1953,D 30,16:2
Times Gone By (The Idyll); Idyll, The (Times
Gone By) 1953,D 30,16:2
Times Gone By (A Question of Property);
Question of Property, A (Times Gone By)
1953,D 30,16:2
Times Gone By (The Old Book Stand); Old Book
Stand, The (Times Gone By) 1953,D 30,16:2
Too Bad She's Bad 1955,D 26,23:2
Anatomy of Love 1959,S 29,46:2
I Love, You Love 1962,N 10,16:2
Three Fables of Love (The Tortoise and the Hare);
Tortoise and the Hare, The (Three Fables of
Love) 1963,Ag 21,38:1
Very Handy Man, A 1966,D 15,60:1
Blasetti, Alessandro (Miscellaneous)
Three Fables of Love (The Tortoise and the Hare);
Tortoise and the Hare, The (Three Fables of
Love) 1963,Ag 21,38:1
Blasetti, Alessandro (Original Author)
I Love, You Love 1962,N 10,16:2
Blasetti, Alessandro (Screenwriter)
Fabiola 1951,My 30,14:2
Anatomy of Love 1959,S 29,46:2
Blass, Hermann
Dolly Macht Karriere 1931,Jl 18,16:6
Ein Burschenlied aus Heidelberg 1931,S 14,15:3
Kleine Seitensprung, Der 1932,Ja 1,31:1
Zwei Herzen und ein Schlag 1932,S 9,17:5
Koenigin der Unterwelt 1932,D 9,26:5
Es War Einmal ein Walzer 1934,O 15,20:5
Blassi, Silverio
Monte Cassino 1948,N 25,47:3
Blatcher, William
Two Girls Wanted 1927,N 14,26:1
Blatt, Edward A (Director)
Between Two Worlds 1944,My 6,11:2
Escape in the Desert 1945,My 12,10:2
Blatty, William Peter (Original Author)
Man From the Diners' Club, The
1963,Ap 18,39:1
Blatty, William Peter (Screenwriter)
Man From the Diners' Club, The
1963,Ap 18,39:1
Shot in the Dark, A 1964,Je 24,28:1
John Goldfarb, Please Come Home
1965,Mr 25,42:4
Promise her Anything 1966,F 23,46:1
What Did You Do in the War, Daddy?
1966,S 1,28:1
Gunn 1967,Je 29,32:1
Blau, Raphael (Original Author)
Mother is a Freshman 1949,Mr 12,10:2
Bedtime for Bonzo 1951,Ap 6,31:4
Blau, Raphael (Screenwriter)
Fear Strikes Out 1957,Mr 21,37:2
Girl of the Night 1960,N 12,15:1

Blaustein, Julian (Original Author)
Noose Hangs High, The 1948,My 29,8:6
Blaustein, Julian (Producer)
Broken Arrow 1950,Jl 21,15:2
Mister 880 1950,S 30,13:2
Half Angel 1951,Je 16,9:2
Guy Who Came Back, The 1951,Ag 17,13:2
Day the Earth Stood Still, The 1951,S 19,37:1
Outcasts of Poker Flat 1952,My 16,19:3
Don't Bother to Knock 1952,Jl 19,8:2
Desiree 1954,N 18,42:1
Racers, The 1955,F 5,13:2
Storm Center 1956,O 22,25:4
Cowboy 1958,F 20,29:5
Bell, Book and Candle 1958,D 27,2:7
Wreck of the Mary Deare, The 1959,N 7,27:1
Two Loves 1961,Je 22,23:2
4 Horsemen of the Apocalypse, The
1962,Mr 10,10:2
Khartoum 1966,Jl 14,28:1
Blauvelt, Robert T Maj (Miscellaneous)
This Is Your Army 1954,D 15,41:1
Blavette
Amours de Toni, Les 1936,N 5,35:1
Stormy Waters 1946,Je 17,32:2
Nais 1948,Je 16,37:2
Ways of Love (Jofroi); Jofroi (Ways of Love)
1950,D 13,50:2
Picnic on the Grass 1960,O 12,47:1
Toni 1968,S 19,62:2
Blayevitch, F
Gypsies 1936,Jl 30,22:2
Blayne, Andrea
Playground, The 1965,O 4,00:0
Blazejovsky, Antonin
Loves of a Blonde 1966,O 27,55:1
Blazek, Vratislav (Screenwriter)
Lady on the Tracks, The 1968,N 26,39:2
Blazhevich, F L
Heroes of the Sea 1941,Ap 28,21:2
Blazhevitch, F B
Diary of a Revolutionist 1932,Je 10,22:3
Blech, Hans Christian
Affair Blum, The 1949,O 18,35:2
Decision Before Dawn 1951,D 22,12:2
Longest Day, The 1962,O 5,28:1
Visit, The 1964,O 22,44:1
Saboteur, The: Code Name-Mori Turi
1965,Ag 26,40:2
Battle of the Bulge 1965,D 18,36:1
Bledsoe, Jules
Drums of the Congo 1942,Jl 20,16:4
Blees, Robert (Miscellaneous)
Sweater Girl 1942,Jl 13,18:3
Blees, Robert (Original Author)
High School Confidential 1958,My 31,6:6
Blees, Robert (Screenwriter)
Paid in Full 1950,F 16,28:2
All I Desire 1953,Ag 29,10:1
Glass Web, The 1953,N 12,37:5
Playgirl 1954,My 15,13:3
Magnificent Obsession 1954,Ag 5,18:4
Cattle Queen of Montana 1955,Ja 26,22:1
One Desire 1955,S 3,9:1
Slightly Scarlet 1956,Mr 17,13:2
Autumn Leaves 1956,Ag 2,21:2
Black Scorpion, The 1957,O 12,23:2
High School Confidential 1958,My 31,6:6
From the Earth to the Moon 1958,N 27,52:2
Blees, William
Naval Academy 1941,Je 5,27:3
Bleibtreu, Hedwig
Hotel Sacher 1939,Je 10,14:2
Bleibtreu, Hedwig
Ein Maedel der Strasse 1933,Ap 6,22:5
Maedchen Irene, Das 1937,My 22,19:3
Waldrausch; Forest Fever 1940,Ja 20,11:3
Maria Ilona 1940,Ap 20,14:3
Wiener Geschichten; Vienna Tales 1940,S 28,9:3
Third Man, The 1950,F 3,29:2
Bleich, Juda
Victims of Persecution 1933,Je 17,16:6
Cantor's Son, The 1937,D 27,11:1
Bleifer, John
We Americans 1928,Mr 29,25:3
Clear all Wires 1933,Mr 4,11:2
Captured 1933,Ag 18,18:3
Black Fury 1935,Ap 11,27:2
Miserables, Les 1935,Ap 22,14:2
Ladies in Love 1936,O 29,31:1
Charlie Chan at Monte Carlo 1937,D 18,18:1
Thank You, Mr Moto 1938,Ja 3,16:2
Ride a Crooked Mile 1938,D 29,15:2
Pacific Liner 1939,Ja 18,17:3
Mr Moto Takes a Vacation 1939,Je 19,12:6
Full Confession 1939,S 28,29:4
Everything Happens at Night 1939,D 16,12:6
Girl From God's Country 1940,S 9,18:5
Mark of Zorro, The 1940,N 4,23:2
In our Time 1944,F 12,11:2
16 Fathoms Deep 1948,O 7,35:2
Juggler, The 1953,My 6,39:2
Hook, The 1963,F 16,5:6

Bleiman, M (Screenwriter)
Great Citizen, The 1939,Ja 16,11:2
No Greater Love 1944,F 25,23:3
Moscow Skies 1945,Ja 22,22:5
Blensfeld, Paul
Between Worlds 1924,Jl 7,10:4
Bletcher, Billy
Branded Men 1931,D 12,23:3
Diplomaniacs 1933,Ap 29,14:2
Lost City, The 1935,F 21,23:3
High, Wide and Handsome 1937,Jl 22,15:1
Buck Benny Rides Again 1940,Ap 25,28:4
Chatterbox 1943,Jl 2,15:3
Bleudonne, Albert (Original Author)
Forbidden Love 1948,Ag 26,16:4
Blewett, Bill
Girl in the Canal, The 1947,O 9,32:3
Blicher, Steen Steenson (Original Author)
Pastor of Vejlby, The 1931,N 1,VIII,6:1
Blick, Newton
Court Martial 1955,Ag 2,17:1
Third Key, The 1957,Je 3,30:2
Lord Jim 1965,F 26,18:1
Blier, Bernard
Youth in Revolt 1939,My 16,27:3
Daybreak 1940,Jl 30,16:2
Symphonie Fantastique, La 1947,D 8,35:2
Jenny Lamour 1948,Mr 6,17:2
Homme a Hommes D' 1948,Ag 30,14:8
Man to Men 1949,F 21,20:2
Dedee 1949,Ap 9,9:2
Cheat, The 1950,O 2,19:3
Passion for Life 1951,D 21,21:4
Spice of Life, The 1953,D 29,19:3
Bed, The (The Pompadour Bed); Pompadour Bed,
The (The Bed) 1955,Je 8,26:4
There's Always a Price Tag 1958,My 26,25:2
Man in the Raincoat, The 1958,Jl 15,21:2
Crime and Punishment 1958,S 16,23:2
Cat, The 1959,Ap 13,35:1
Possessors, The 1959,Jl 21,24:1
Sans Famille 1959,S 5,11:4
Marie Octobre 1960,Ag 16,25:2
Great War; (Grande Guerra, La) 1961,Ag 31,22:3
Magnificent Tramp, The 1962,Ap 25,30:1
Money, Money, Money 1962,Jl 18,20:1
...And Suddenly It's Murder! 1964,Ja 24,21:1
Seventh Juror, The 1964,Ja 28,25:1
Bonne Soupe, La 1964,Mr 16,37:1
Organizer, The 1964,My 7,31:2
Male Hunt; Chasse a l'Homme, La
1965,Ap 20,42:1
Magnificent Cuckold 1965,Ap 20,42:1
High Infidelity (Modern People); Modern People
(High Infidelity) 1965,Jl 2,17:1
Blin, Roger
Curtain Rises, The 1939,Ap 22,15:2
Passionnelle 1948,Mr 1,17:2
Orpheus 1950,N 30,42:2
Blinikov, S
Alexander Nevsky 1939,Mr 23,27:1
Ural Front, The 1945,Je 7,25:3
Vow, The 1947,Je 23,14:3
Winner, The 1947,D 1,27:2
Inspector General, The 1954,My 3,21:2
Private Ivan 1957,Ap 3,28:2
Blinn, Beatrice
Paid to Dance 1937,D 6,19:1
Golden Boy 1939,S 8,28:2
Street of Missing Women 1940,Ja 8,11:3
Convicted Woman 1940,F 26,11:2
Blinn, Genevieve
Common Clay 1930,Ag 2,16:4
Blinn, Holbrook
Weakness of Men, The 1916,Jl 3,7:4
Rosita 1923,S 4,14:1
Bad Man, The 1923,O 9,17:4
Yolanda 1924,F 20,23:1
Janice Meredith 1924,Ag 6,13:3
Zander the Great 1925,My 4,16:2
New Commandment, The 1925,N 10,25:3
Telephone Girl, The 1927,My 16,24:2
Blinnikoff, A
Girl With the Guitar, The 1960,F 1,22:4
Blinov, Boris
Tchapayef 1935,Ja 15,22:1
Defense of Volotchayevsk, The 1938,Ag 11,13:3
Girl From Leningrad 1941,D 20,25:2
Vanka 1943,Mr 25,25:3
Taxi to Heaven 1944,My 25,16:3
Wait for Me 1945,Mr 19,23:3
Blinova, Maria
Flying Carpet, The 1960,F 28,31:1
Bliss, Anthony (Producer)
Curse of the Werewolf, The 1961,Je 8,40:2
Bliss, Arthur Sir (Composer)
Beggar's Opera, The 1953,Ag 25,18:2
Bliss, Lela
Dark Mirror, The 1946,O 19,15:2
Miracle on 34th Street 1947,Je 5,32:1
Give my Regards to Broadway 1948,Je 23,32:2
Snake Pit, the 1948,N 5,29:2
Intruder in the Dust 1949,N 23,19:1

Bliss, Lela — Cont
  To Please a Lady 1950,O 27,24:3
Blistene, Marcel (Director)
  Star Without Light; Etoile Sans Lumiere
    1947,Ag 4,14:2
  Back Streets of Paris 1948,O 16,9:2
  Fire Under Her Skin 1958,Je 28,13:6
Blistene, Marcel (Original Author)
  Star Without Light; Etoile Sans Lumiere
    1947,Ag 4,14:2
Blistene, Marcel (Screenwriter)
  Fire Under Her Skin 1958,Je 28,13:6
Blistone, John (Director)
  Coming-Out Party 1934,Mr 17,11:3
Blitzstein, Marc (Composer)
  Spanish Earth, The 1937,Ag 21,7:2
  Native Land 1942,My 12,16:3
BLOCH
  See Also BLOCK
Bloch, A
  Othello 1960,My 16,39:1
Bloch, Arthur (Original Author)
  Student Tour 1934,O 31,17:3
Bloch, D (Composer)
  Conquerors of the Arctic 1937,N 22,15:2
Bloch, John W (Screenwriter)
  One Man's Way 1964,Mr 12,40:3
Bloch, Lars
  Wild Eye, The 1968,Ag 22,47:1
Bloch, Noe (Director)
  Casanova 1927,Je 23,23:3
Bloch, Robert (Original Author)
  Psycho 1960,Je 17,37:1
Bloch, Robert (Screenwriter)
  Couch, The 1962,F 22,20:3
  Cabinet of Caligari, The 1962,My 26,13:5
  Strait Jacket 1964,Ja 23,26:1
  Night Walker, The 1965,Ja 21,22:1
  Psycopath, The 1966,S 29,60:1
  Deadly Bees, The 1967,My 20,39:2
  Torture Garden 1968,Jl 20,18:2
Blochman, L G (Original Author)
  Bombay Mail 1934,Ja 6,18:2
  Chinatown Squad 1935,My 30,21:1
  Quiet Please, Murder 1942,D 22,31:1
BLOCK
  See Also BLOCH
Block, Alfred (Original Author)
  It's a Great Life 1930,Ja 18,21:1
Block, Alfred (Screenwriter)
  Way out West 1930,Ag 18,24:1
Block, Bernice (Producer)
  Dino 1957,Je 22,9:2
Block, Bertram (Original Author)
  Oh! What a Nurse! 1926,F 22,14:1
  Dark Victory 1939,Ap 21,27:2
Block, Dorothy
  If I Marry Again 1925,Ja 12,11:2
Block, Frederick (Original Author)
  Patrick the Great 1945,Ap 13,15:2
Block, Irving (Original Author)
  Forbidden Planet 1956,My 4,21:2
  Kronos 1957,My 11,24:6
Block, Jessie
  Kid Millions 1934,N 12,17:2
Block, Kimberly
  Baby, the Rain Must Fall 1965,Ja 14,44:1
Block, Libbie (Original Author)
  Pin Up Girl 1944,My 11,25:6
  Caught 1949,F 18,26:4
Block, Maurice
  Gift of Gab 1934,S 26,17:6
Block, Newton
  Morgan! 1966,Ap 5,42:2
Block, Ralph (Miscellaneous)
  In Caliente 1935,Je 27,16:1
Block, Ralph (Original Author)
  Massacre 1934,Ja 18,19:2
  I am a Thief 1935,Ja 1,24:1
  In Caliente 1935,Je 27,16:1
  It's a Date 1940,Mr 23,16:2
  Patrick the Great 1945,Ap 13,15:2
  Nancy Goes to Rio 1950,Ap 7,22:2
Block, Ralph (Screenwriter)
  I am a Thief 1935,Ja 1,24:1
  Right to Live, The 1935,F 16,9:1
  Melody Lingers on, The 1935,N 7,27:1
  Boulder Dam 1936,Mr 30,17:5
Blocker, Dan
  Lady in Cement 1968,N 21,41:1
Blog, Herman
  Flesh 1932,D 10,19:3
Blomfield, Derek
  Emil 1938,Ap 15,23:2
  Hobson's Choice 1954,Je 15,37:1
  It's Great to be Young 1957,D 26,23:3
  Ship Was Loaded, The 1958,Ja 20,20:1
Blomstedt, George
  Doctor's Women, The 1929,Je 3,27:2
Blomstrand, Ulla
  Flamboyant Sex, The 1963,Ag 13,25:1
Blondel, Jean (Screenwriter)
  Guendalina 1958,Je 30,23:2

Blondell, Gloria
  Daredevil Drivers, The 1938,F 23,27:2
  Accidents Will Happen 1938,Ap 25,19:2
  Four's a Crowd 1938,Ag 12,11:1
  Don't Bother to Knock 1952,Jl 19,8:2
Blondell, Joan
  Office Wife, The 1930,S 27,21:3
  Sinners' Holiday 1930,O 11,21:3
  Illicit 1931,Ja 19,25:1
  Millie 1931,F 7,11:1
  My Past 1931,Mr 12,22:7
  God's Gift to Women 1931,Ap 18,17:3
  Other Men's Women 1931,Ap 20,16:3
  Public Enemy, The 1931,Ap 24,27:1
  Big Business Girl 1931,Je 12,27:1
  Night Nurse 1931,Jl 17,23:4
  Reckless Hour, The 1931,Ag 1,16:4
  Blonde Crazy 1931,D 4,28:2
  Union Depot 1932,Ja 15,24:4
  Greeks Had a Word for Them, The 1932,F 4,25:2
  Crowd Roars, The 1932,Mr 23,25:4
  Crowd Roars, The 1932,Ap 3,VIII,4:4
  Famous Ferguson Case, The 1932,Ap 25,18:6
  Make Me a Star 1932,Jl 1,19:3
  Miss Pinkerton 1932,Jl 9,7:5
  Big City Blues 1932,S 10,18:5
  Three on a Match 1932,O 29,18:4
  Central Park 1932,D 7,29:3
  Lawyer Man 1932,D 27,10:2
  Blondie Johnson 1933,F 27,11:2
  Broadway Bad 1933,Mr 6,16:6
  Gold Diggers of 1933 1933,Je 8,22:3
  Good-Bye Again 1933,S 2,15:2
  Footlight Parade 1933,O 6,21:3
  Havana Widows 1933,N 23,24:3
  Convention City 1933,D 25,28:2
  I've Got Your Number 1934,F 3,9:3
  He Was her Man 1934,My 17,28:2
  Dames 1934,Ag 16,20:2
  Kansas City Princess 1934,N 5,23:1
  Traveling Saleslady 1935,Mr 29,26:2
  Broadway Gondolier 1935,Jl 18,15:2
  We're In the Money 1935,Ag 22,21:4
  Miss Pacific Fleet 1935,D 7,22:2
  Colleen 1936,Mr 9,20:2
  Sons o'Guns 1936,My 14,29:2
  Bullets or Ballots 1936,My 27,27:1
  Stage Struck 1936,S 28,14:4
  Three Men on a Horse 1936,N 26,39:1
  Gold Diggers of 1937 1936,D 25,19:2
  King and the Chorus Girl, The 1937,Mr 29,14:4
  Back in Circulation 1937,O 4,17:1
  Perfect Specimen, The 1937,O 28,29:2
  Stand-In 1937,N 19,27:2
  There's Always a Woman 1938,Ap 29,17:2
  Off the Record 1939,F 18,12:2
  East Side of Heaven 1939,My 5,29:3
  Kid From Kokomo, The 1939,My 20,11:2
  Good Girls Go to Paris 1939,Je 23,23:1
  Amazing Mr Williams, The 1940,Ja 19,15:2
  Two Girls on Broadway 1940,Ap 25,28:4
  I Want a Divorce 1940,O 3,31:2
  Topper Returns 1941,Mr 28,26:6
  Model Wife 1941,Ap 24,25:3
  Lady for a Night 1942,F 12,27:2
  Cry Havoc 1943,N 24,16:2
  Tree Grows in Brooklyn, A 1945,Mr 1,25:5
  Don Juan Quilligan 1945,Jl 30,16:2
  Adventure 1946,F 8,23:2
  Corpse came C O D, The 1947,Ag 19,27:2
  Nightmare Alley 1947,O 10,31:3
  Christmas Eve 1947,N 28,30:2
  For Heaven's Sake 1950,D 16,10:5
  Blue Veil, The 1951,O 27,10:5
  Opposite Sex, The 1956,N 16,23:2
  Lizzie 1957,Ap 5,24:2
  This Could Be the Night 1957,My 15,39:1
  Desk Set 1957,My 16,28:2
  Will Success Spoil Rock Hunter 1957,S 12,37:5
  Angel Baby 1961,O 5,43:1
  Advance to the Rear 1964,Je 11,27:3
  Cincinnati Kid, The 1965,O 28,48:1
  Ride Beyond Vengance 1966,S 29,60:1
  Waterhole #3 1967,O 11,41:4
Blondin, Antoine (Original Author)
  Monkey in Winter 1963,F 1,7:2
Blondin, Antoine (Screenwriter)
  Bed, The (The Pompadour Bed); Pompadour Bed,
    The (The Bed) 1955,Je 8,26:4
BLOOM
  See Also BLUHM, BLUM, BLUME
Bloom, Bill (Producer)
  Man From the Diners' Club, The
    1963,Ap 18,39:1
Bloom, Claire
  Blind Goddess, The 1949,Je 23,33:3
  Limelight 1952,O 24,27:2
  Man Between, The 1953,N 19,41:2
  Innocents in Paris 1955,Mr 5,9:6
  Richard III 1956,Mr 12,1:4
  Alexander the Great 1956,Mr 29,23:1
  Brothers Karamazov, The 1958,F 21,18:2
  Buccaneer, The 1958,D 24,00:0

Bloom, Claire — Cont
  Look Back in Anger 1959,S 16,45:1
  Wonderful World of the Brothers Grimm, The
    1962,Ag 8,35:1
  Chapman Report, The 1962,O 18,49:2
  Haunting, The 1963,S 19,23:1
  Outrage, The 1964,O 8,48:2
  High Infidelity (Sin in the Afternoon); Sin in the
    Afternoon (High Infidelity) 1965,Jl 2,17:1
  Spy Who Came in From the Cold, The
    1965,D 24,24:1
  Charly 1968,S 24,55:1
Bloom, Harold Jack (Original Author)
  Naked Spur, The 1953,Mr 26,37:3
  Land of the Pharaohs 1955,Jl 27,15:2
  Foreign Intrigue 1956,Jl 13,23:2
Bloom, Harold Jack (Screenwriter)
  Arena 1953,Jl 23,20:2
Bloom, Mickey (Composer)
  You're a Sweetheart 1937,D 25,10:5
Bloom, Phyllis
  World Dances 1954,N 8,24:6
Bloom, Rube (Composer)
  Wake up and Dream 1947,Ja 24,18:4
Bloom, William (Original Author)
  Flight Into Nowhere 1938,My 2,13:3
Bloom, William (Producer)
  Inferno 1953,Ag 12,22:2
  Glory Brigade, The 1953,Ag 15,8:4
  On the Threshold of Space 1956,Mr 30,10:5
  I Married a Woman 1958,N 5,42:5
  13 West Street 1962,Je 7,31:2
Bloome, A J (Director)
  Dream of My People, The 1934,F 26,21:4
Bloome, A J (Miscellaneous)
  Dream of My People, The 1934,F 26,21:4
Bloomer, Raymond
  Love Light, The 1921,Ja 10,9:1
  If Winter Comes 1923,S 4,14:1
  Fool, The 1925,Ap 13,24:1
  Sensation Seekers 1927,Mr 16,28:2
Bloomfield, Mike
  Festival 1967,O 24,53:2
Blore, Eric
  Great Gatsby, The 1926,N 22,28:3
  Gay Divorcee, The 1934,N 16,27:1
  Behold My Wife 1935,F 18,19:3
  Folies Bergere 1935,F 25,13:2
  Casino Murder Case, The 1935,Ap 17,26:5
  Diamond Jim 1935,Ag 24,18:2
  Top Hat 1935,Ag 30,12:2
  I Live my Life 1935,O 12,12:2
  To Beat the Band 1935,N 23,23:2
  I Dream too Much 1935,N 29,24:1
  Seven Keys to Baldpate 1935,D 14,11:2
  Two in the Dark 1936,F 1,9:2
  Sons o'Guns 1936,My 14,29:2
  Ex-Mrs Bradford, The 1936,My 28,19:2
  Swing Time 1936,Ag 28,21:2
  Piccadilly Jim 1936,Ag 31,19:1
  Quality Street 1937,Ap 9,19:2
  Soldier and the Lady, The 1937,Ap 10,11:1
  Shall We Dance 1937,My 14,21:1
  It's Love I'm After 1937,N 11,31:2
  Breakfast for Two 1937,N 20,21:2
  Hitting a new High 1937,D 27,11:1
  Joy of Living 1938,My 6,27:1
  Swiss Miss 1938,Je 4,18:2
  $1,000 a Touchdown 1939,O 5,27:2
  Music in My Heart 1940,Ja 4,19:2
  Man Who Wouldn't Talk, The 1940,Ja 12,13:3
  Lone Wolf Strikes, The 1940,F 5,13:2
  'Til We Meet Again 1940,Ap 14,14:2
  Lone Wolf Meets a Lady, The 1940,Je 17,19:2
  Boys From Syracuse, The 1940,Ag 1,25:2
  South of Suez 1940,D 19,33:2
  Lone Wolf Keeps a Date, The 1941,Ja 2,24:3
  Lady Eve, The 1941,F 26,17:1
  Lone Wolf Takes a Chance, The 1941,Ap 7,13:2
  Road to Zanzibar 1941,Ap 10,29:2
  Lady Scarface 1941,Ag 4,16:6
  New York Town 1941,N 13,35:2
  Confirm or Deny 1941,D 19,35:2
  Shanghai Gesture, The 1941,D 26,21:2
  Sullivan's Travels 1942,Ja 29,25:2
  Counter-Espionage 1942,S 28,13:2
  Moon and Sixpence, The 1942,O 28,26:4
  Sky's the Limit, The 1943,S 3,15:2
  Holy Matrimony 1943,S 16,25:2
  San Diego, I Love You 1944,N 10,25:1
  Men in her Diary 1945,S 24,16:5
  Kitty 1946,Ap 1,23:1
  Abie's Irish Rose 1946,D 23,19:4
  Lone Wolf in London, The 1947,N 22,10:3
  Romance on the High Seas 1948,Je 26,10:5
  Love Happy 1950,Ap 8,9:4
  Fancy Pants 1950,Ag 31,21:2
Blore, Eric (Miscellaneous)
  Adventures of Ichabod and Mr Toad, The
    1949,O 10,18:2
Bloss, Schmid
  William Tell 1925,My 20,26:2

Blossom, Henry (Original Author)
Checkers 1919,Ag 25,8:5
Yankee Consul, The 1924,F 11,18:3
Mlle Modiste 1926,Ap 26,25:1
Red Mill, The 1927,F 14,15:1
Blossom, Rose
White Flannels 1927,Mr 22,31:2
Blossom, Winter
Thief of Bagdad, The 1924,Mr 19,19:1
Blot, Florence
Big Chief, The 1960,Ap 27,32:1
Blue, Ben
Follow Your Heart 1936,O 22,31:1
College Holiday 1936,D 24,21:2
Top of the Town 1937,Mr 27,19:2
Turn off the Moon 1937,My 20,17:2
High, Wide and Handsome 1937,Jl 22,15:1
Artists and Models 1937,Ag 5,19:2
Thrill of a Lifetime 1937,D 9,30:2
Big Broadcast of 1938, The 1938,Mr 10,16:2
College Swing 1938,Ap 28,27:2
Cocoanut Grove 1938,Je 16,21:2
Paris Honeymoon 1939,Ja 26,17:1
Panama Hattie 1942,O 2,31:2
For Me and My Gal 1942,O 22,25:1
Thousands Cheer 1943,S 14,27:1
Broadway Rhythm 1944,Ap 14,24:6
Two Girls and a Sailor 1944,Je 15,16:1
Two Sisters From Boston 1946,Je 7,16:2
Easy to Wed 1946,Jl 12,14:2
My Wild Irish Rose 1947,D 25,32:2
One Sunday Afternoon 1948,D 27,16:3
It's a Mad, Mad, Mad, Mad World
1963,N 19,47:1
Russians are Coming the Russians are Coming,
The 1966,My 26,55:1
Guide for the Married Man, A 1967,My 27,16:1
Busy Body, The 1967,Je 8,52:2
Where Were You When the Lights Went Out?
1968,Ag 9,30:2
Blue, James (Director)
Olive Trees of Justice, The 1967,My 5,31:1
Blue, James (Screenwriter)
Olive Trees of Justice, The 1967,My 5,31:1
Blue, Jean
Overlanders, The 1946,D 20,31:2
Blue, Monte
Pettigrew's Girl 1919,Ap 14,11:4
In Mizzoura 1919,O 13,16:3
Everywoman 1919,D 15,20:1
Something to Think About 1920,O 18,13:1
Affairs of Anatol, The 1921,S 12,16:1
Brass 1923,Mr 12,18:1
Main Street 1923,Je 12,22:2
Purple Highway, The 1923,Jl 24,14:3 (In
Addenda)
Lucretia Lombard 1923,D 17,23:1
Marriage Circle, The 1924,F 4,23:3
Mademoiselle Midnight 1924,My 27,14:1
Revelation 1924,Je 24,18:2
Being Respectable 1924,Ag 4,16:3
Lover of Camille, The 1924,N 11,14:1
Black Swan, The 1924,N 25,26:1
Recompense 1925,Ap 20,22:1
Kiss Me Again 1925,Ag 3,10:4
Limited Mail, The 1925,S 1,18:2
Red Hot Tires 1925,O 20,28:1
Hogan's Alley 1925,N 24,28:4
Other Women's Husbands 1926,Ap 27,23:2
Other Men's Wives 1926,My 2,VIII,5:3 (In
Addenda)
So This Is Paris 1926,Ag 16,10:1
Wolf's Clothing 1927,Mr 28,26:4
Brute, The 1927,Ap 21,25:1
White Shadows of the South Seas 1928,Ag 1,13:3
Conquest 1929,F 11,26:3
Skin Deep 1929,S 30,23:1
Show of Shows 1929,N 21,24:5
Tiger Rose 1929,D 25,23:1
Isle of Escape 1930,Mr 31,24:3
Those Who Dance 1930,Jl 7,22:3
Flood, The 1931,Ap 27,25:1
Stoker, The 1932,Jl 16,5:5
Come on Marines 1934,Mr 24,20:3
Last Round-Up, The 1934,My 10,25:2
Wagon Wheels 1934,O 4,19:1
Student Tour 1934,O 31,17:3
Lives of a Bengal Lancer, The 1935,Ja 12,12:2
G Men 1935,My 2,17:1
Treachery Rides the Range 1936,My 30,7:3
Mary of Scotland 1936,Jl 31,22:2
Outcasts of Poker Flat, The 1937,Ap 27,18:3
Souls at Sea 1937,Ag 10,23:2
Thunder Trail 1938,F 5,19:3
Dodge City 1939,Ap 8,19:1
Juarez 1939,Ap 26,27:1
Our Leading Citizen 1939,Ag 24,17:1
Geronimo 1940,F 8,18:3
Mystery Sea Raider 1940,Ag 26,11:4
Little Bit of Heaven, A 1940,N 8,24:2
Across the Pacific 1942,S 5,9:2
Palm Beach Story, The 1942,D 11,33:1
Secret Enemies 1943,Ja 1,27:3

Edge of Darkness 1943,Ap 10,12:4
Northern Pursuit 1943,N 26,29:2
Passage to Marseille 1944,F 17,12:5
Mask of Dimitrios, The 1944,Je 24,16:2
Conspirators, The 1944,O 21,15:2
San Antonio 1945,D 29,19:5
Possessed 1947,My 30,25:2
Life With Father 1947,Ag 16,6:6
Silver River 1948,My 22,8:3
Key Largo 1948,Jl 17,6:6
Two Guys From Texas 1948,Ag 28,8:6
South of St Louis 1949,Mr 7,17:2
Younger Brothers, The 1949,My 28,11:2
This Side of the Law 1950,Jl 7,15:2
Iroquois Trail, The 1950,O 27,24:4
Dallas 1951,Ja 13,10:4
Hangman's Knot 1952,D 11,45:3
Apache 1954,Jl 10,7:2
Blue Ridge Mountain Dancers
Festival 1967,O 24,53:2
Bluemke, Ralph C
Robby 1968,Ag 15,46:3
Bluemke, Ralph C (Director)
Robby 1968,Ag 15,46:3
Bluemke, Ralph C (Producer)
Robby 1968,Ag 15,46:3
Bluemke, Ralph C (Screenwriter)
Robby 1968,Ag 15,46:3
BLUHM
See Also BLUM, BLUME, BLOOM
Bluhm, Walter
Somewhere in Berlin 1949,Ag 16,19:3
BLUM
See Also BLUME, BLOOM, BLUHM
Blum, Edwin (Original Author)
Midnight Story, The 1957,Jl 5,14:2
Blum, Edwin (Screenwriter)
Kidnapped 1938,My 28,9:2
Adventures of Sherlock Holmes, The
1939,S 2,20:1
Young People 1940,Ag 24,16:2
Great American Broadcast, The 1941,My 2,25:2
Boogie Man Will Get You, The 1942,O 12,12:4
Canterville Ghost, The 1944,Jl 29,10:2
Man Alive 1945,N 17,14:5
Down to Earth 1947,S 12,18:2
South Sea Woman 1953,Je 4,33:6
Stalag 17 1953,Jl 2,19:2
Midnight Story, The 1957,Jl 5,14:2
Blum, Sam
Winning of Barbara Worth, The 1926,N 29,16:3
Rio Rita 1929,O 7,22:1
Iron Man 1931,Ap 18,17:3
Night World 1932,My 28,18:2
Blumberg, Lewis (Producer)
Big Boodle, The 1957,Mr 12,38:1
BLUME
See Also BLOOM, BLUHM, BLUM
Blume, Karl
Gruen ist Sie Heide 1935,O 14,21:2
Blumenstock, Mort (Director)
Morals for Women 1931,N 16,23:1
Blumenthal, Dick (Producer)
China 1943,Ap 22,31:2
Lady in the Dark 1944,F 23,17:1
Blumenthal, Oscar (Original Author)
Is Matrimony a Failure 1922,Ap 17,22:3
Blumenthal, Richard (Miscellaneous)
City That Stopped Hitler--Heroic Stalingrad, The
1943,S 6,21:3
Blumenthal-Tamarina, M
Three Women 1936,F 12,25:4
Greater Promise, A 1936,O 8,27:3
Blumgarten, James (Screenwriter)
Mister Rock and Roll 1957,O 17,42:2
Blumner, Rudolf
M 1933,Ap 3,13:3
Blumote, Robert F (Producer)
Yours, Mine and Ours 1968,Ap 25,53:1
Blunt, Gabrielle
Tight Little Island 1949,D 26,33:2
Tony Draws a Horse 1951,My 15,38:6
Clouded Yellow, The 1951,N 13,33:2
Bluthal, John
Knack...and how to get it, The 1965,Je 30,42:1
Help! 1965,Ag 24,25:1
Don't Raise the Bridge, Lower the River
1968,Jl 13,18:1
Bluwal, Marcel (Director)
Paris Pick-Up 1963,Ag 29,36:2
Bluwal, Marcel (Screenwriter)
Paris Pick-Up 1963,Ag 29,36:2
Bly, Nellie
Salvation Hunters, The 1925,F 2,14:1
Blyden, Larry
Bachelor Party, The 1957,Ap 10,37:2
Kiss Them for Me 1957,N 9,31:2
Blye, Margaret
Hombre 1967,Mr 22,41:1
Waterhole #3 1967,O 11,41:4
Blystone, John (Director)
Last Man on Earth, The 1924,D 13,12:4
Dick Turpin 1925,Ja 26,14:1

Blystone, John (Director)— Cont
Lucky Horseshoe, The 1925,Ag 18,14:3
Everlasting Whisper, The 1925,O 12,19:3
Best Bad Man, The 1925,D 2,23:1
My Own Pal 1926,Mr 15,18:3
Ankles Preferred 1927,Ap 18,21:2
Slaves of Beauty 1927,Je 8,23:3
Pajamas 1927,N 7,26:4
Sharp Shooters 1928,Ja 23,18:3
Mother Knows Best 1928,S 17,27:1
Captain Lash 1929,F 4,20:1
Sky Hawk, The 1929,D 12,36:4
So This Is London 1930,My 24,21:2
Tol'able David 1930,N 17,29:1
Mr Lemon of Orange 1931,Mr 28,15:3
Young Sinners 1931,My 9,15:4
Charlie Chan's Chance 1932,Ja 23,18:4
She Wanted a Millionaire 1932,F 20,11:2
Amateur Daddy 1932,Ap 23,11:5
Painted Woman, The 1932,S 16,24:4
Too Busy to Work 1932,D 3,21:4
Hot Pepper 1933,Ja 23,9:2
Shanghai Madness 1933,S 23,11:6
My Lips Betray 1933,N 4,18:3
Change of Heart 1934,My 11,24:2
Hell in the Heavens 1934,D 12,28:2
County Chairman, The 1935,Ja 19,8:1
Bad Boy 1935,O 28,16:3
Gentle Julia 1936,Ap 11,19:1
Little Miss Nobody 1936,Je 6,21:1
Magnificent Brute, The 1936,O 24,23:1
Great Guy 1937,Ja 1,19:2
23 1/2 Hours Leave 1937,My 17,23:2
Woman Chases Man 1937,Je 11,26:2
Music for Madame 1937,O 23,14:1
Swiss Miss 1938,Je 4,18:2
Block-Heads 1938,Ag 30,14:2
Blystone, Stanley
Circus Ace, The 1927,Jl 6,23:2
Young Eagles 1930,Mr 22,22:6
Strange People 1933,Je 17,16:5
Three Musketeers, The 1935,N 1,25:1
Strike Me Pink 1936,Ja 17,15:2
Armored Car 1937,Jl 26,15:2
Boots and Saddles 1937,N 8,19:2
Headin' East 1938,Ja 15,19:2
Blyth, Ann
Chip off the Old Block 1944,Mr 17,14:2
Merry Monahans, The 1944,O 13,16:2
Bowery to Broadway 1944,N 30,19:2
Swell Guy 1947,Ja 27,17:2
Brute Force 1947,Jl 17,16:2
Woman's Vengeance, A 1948,Ja 30,19:2
Killer McCoy 1948,F 12,31:2
Another Part of the Forest 1948,My 19,30:2
Mr Peabody and the Mermaid 1948,Ag 14,6:5
Red Canyon 1949,Ap 28,28:2
Top o' the Morning 1949,S 1,25:2
Once More, my Darling 1949,S 26,17:1
Our Very Own 1950,Jl 28,12:5
Great Caruso, The 1951,My 11,32:2
Thunder on the Hill 1951,O 18,32:3
I'll Never Forget You 1951,D 8,9:2
One Minute to Zero 1952,S 20,13:2
World in His Arms, The 1952,O 10,21:2
All the Brothers Were Valiant 1953,D 29,19:2
Rose Marie 1954,Ap 2,22:2
Student Prince, The 1954,Je 16,18:2
King's Thief, The 1955,Ag 13,7:2
Kismet 1955,D 9,32:2
Slander 1957,Ja 17,34:4
Buster Keaton Story, The 1957,Ap 22,31:6
Helen Morgan Story, The 1957,O 3,33:2
Blyth, Henry (Screenwriter)
Follow a Star 1961,Ap 26,34:1
Coming-Out Party, A 1962,Jl 31,19:2
Crooks Anonymous 1963,O 31,26:3
Blythe, Betty
Nomads of the North 1920,S 27,18:1
Queen of Sheba 1921,Ap 11,9:1
Recoil, The 1924,Je 30,16:1
In Hollywood with Potash and Perlmutter
1924,S 30,27:3
Breath of Scandal, The 1924,N 26,17:3
Folly of Vanity 1925,Ja 28,14:1
Chu Chin Chow 1925,F 11,19:4
Percy 1925,Mr 25,24:2
Million Bid, A 1927,My 31,25:2
Glorious Betsy 1928,Ap 27,16:4
Daughter of Israel, A 1928,My 21,25:1
Pilgrimage 1933,Jl 13,17:5
Only Yesterday 1933,N 10,25:1
Before Midnight 1934,Ja 10,24:3
Ever Since Eve 1934,Mr 28,27:5
Girl of the Limberlost, A 1934,N 9,24:6
Perfect Clue, The 1935,Mr 14,18:1
Yours for the Asking 1936,Ag 20,14:2
Gorgeous Hussy, The 1936,S 5,7:1
Gangster's Boy 1938,N 7,23:6
Honky Tonk 1941,O 3,27:3
Top Sergeant Mulligan 1941,N 12,31:3
Where Are Your Children? 1944,Ja 17,14:5

Blythe, Erik
Invasion USA 1953,Ap 30,39:4
Blythe, Gordon
Condemned to Death 1932,Jl 14,24:2
Blythe, John
This Happy Breed 1947,Ap 14,24:2
Holiday Camp 1948,Ja 24,11:2
Lilli Marlene 1952,Mr 29,19:2
White Fire 1954,S 18,12:4
1954,S 18,12:4
Blythe, Peggy
Constant Nymph, The 1934,Ap 7,19:1
Boa, Bruce
Man in the Moon 1961,Je 13,29:2
Boarang
Wajan 1938,Ap 18,11:1
Boardman, Eleanor
Souls for Sale 1923,Ap 9,14:3
Vanity Fair 1923,My 7,19:3
Three Wise Fools 1923,Jl 23,13:4
Day of Faith, The 1923,N 27,11:2
True as Steel 1924,Je 17,22:4
Wine of Youth 1924,Ag 11,16:1
Sinners in Silk 1924,S 8,15:3
Silent Accuser, The 1924,N 25,26:1
So This Is Marriage 1924,D 23,16:2
Wife of the Centaur, The 1925,Ja 7,33:5
Way of a Girl, The 1925,Mr 30,21:3
Proud Flesh 1925,Ap 14,26:1
Circle, The 1925,S 22,22:3
Exchange of Wives 1925,O 5,25:2
Only Thing, The 1925,N 23,25:4
Memory Lane 1926,F 2,20:4
Auction Block, The 1926,F 15,16:4
Bardelys The Magnificent 1926,N 1,28:1 (In
Addenda)
Tell It to the Marines 1926,D 24,18:2
Crowd, The 1928,F 20,14:1
She Goes to War 1929,Je 10,23:1
Mamba 1930,Mr 11,25:2
Redemption 1930,My 3,23:1
Great Meadow, The 1931,Mr 14,23:2
Flood, The 1931,Ap 27,25:1
Women Love Once 1931,Je 27,20:3
Squaw Man, The 1931,S 19,10:2
Boardman, Nan
Mrs Mike 1950,F 9,36:5
Boardman, True (Original Author)
Hit the Ice 1943,S 23,27:2
Boardman, True (Screenwriter)
Keep 'Em Flying 1941,N 27,29:2
Ride 'Em Cowboy 1942,Mr 5,27:3
Pardon my Sarong 1942,Ag 27,15:1
Between Us Girls 1942,S 25,25:3
Boardman, Virginia True
Third Alarm, The 1923,Ja 10,28:5
Pioneer Trails 1923,N 12,15:3
Home Maker, The 1925,Ag 10,8:2
Lady Lies, The 1929,S 7,15:1
Road to Ruin, The 1934,F 21,23:2
Boasberg, Al (Director)
Myrt and Marge 1934,Ja 17,23:2
Boasberg, Al (Miscellaneous)
Florodora Girl, The 1930,My 31,19:4
Make a Wish 1937,S 23,33:1
Boasberg, Al (Original Author)
Smile, Brother, Smile 1927,Ag 29,21:1
Boasberg, Al (Screenwriter)
Dough Boys 1930,S 30,23:1
Cracked Nuts 1931,Ap 6,24:1
Everything's Rosie 1931,My 22,28:5
Silly Billies 1936,Ap 6,18:1
Boatwright, Helen
Hansel and Gretel 1954,O 11,33:1
Bob (dog)
Eb Ura Fako 1940,Mr 23,16:4
Bob Crosby and orchestra
Presenting Lily Mars 1943,Ap 30,25:3
Bob Lee House and Group
World Dances 1954,N 8,24:6
Bobards, James
Footloose Windows 1926,Je 22,21:2
Bobbie (Monkey)
Hero for a Night, A 1927,D 26,26:6
Bobo, Brunella
Miracle in Milan 1951,D 18,42:2
Bobotchkin, Boris
Tchapayef 1935,Ja 15,22:1
Bobrinskoy, Alexis
I Am a Camera 1955,Ag 9,29:1
Bobronitsky, V (Cinematographer)
Pageant of Russia 1947,Ag 11,17:3
Bobrov, G (Director)
U S S R Today 1953,Ap 20,21:2
Bobrov, I
Paris Commune 1937,Je 2,20:4
Bobrov, Oleg
Hello, Moscow! 1946,Je 15,24:4
Bobrovsky, Anatoli (Director)
Mumu 1961,Je 5,37:4
Bobrovsky, Anatoli (Producer)
Mumu 1961,Je 5,37:4

Boccardo, Delia
Inspector Clouseau 1968,Jl 25,26:1
Wild Eye, The 1968,Ag 22,47:1
Bocci, Gildo
Messalina 1924,Ag 25,16:2
Avvocato Difensore, L'; Attorney for the Defense,
The 1935,N 13,25:4
Boccia, Piero
Awakening, The 1958,Mr 3,24:6
Bocheros, Los
Fiesta 1947,Je 27,17:3
Bochm, Sydney (Screenwriter)
One Foot in Hell 1960,O 20,42:2
Bochner, Lloyd
Drums of Africa 1963,Jl 4,9:1
Night Walker, The 1965,Ja 21,22:1
Sylvia 1965,F 11,45:1
Harlow 1965,My 15,18:1
Point Blank 1967,S 19,53:1
Tony Rome 1967,N 16,58:1
Detective, The 1968,My 29,20:3
Young Runaways, The 1968,S 12,54:3
Horse in the Gray Flannel Suit, The
1968,D 21,49:3
Bochorishvill, Keto
Father of a Soldier 1966,F 21,51:1
BOCK
See Also BACH, BACHE
Bock, Edward (Original Author)
Key Witness 1947,Jl 30,27:6
Bock, Edward (Screenwriter)
Key Witness 1947,Jl 30,27:6
Bocket, Bill
Sous les Toits de Paris; (Under the Roofs of
Paris) 1930,D 16,34:4
Bodamere, Mme de
Rosita 1923,S 4,14:1
Bodansky, Robert (Original Author)
Rogue Song, The 1930,Ja 29,26:4
Bodard, Mag (Producer)
Benjamin 1968,Mr 26,41:2
Young Girls of Rochefort, The 1968,Ap 12,50:1
Viol, Le 1968,S 20,42:1
Boddey, Martin
Valley of the Eagles 1952,Ap 11,19:2
Assassin, The 1953,Ap 18,17:2
Rob Roy 1954,F 4,21:5
How to Murder a Rich Uncle 1957,O 26,19:2
Oscar Wilde 1960,Je 21,28:2
Kitchen, The 1961,N 2,42:1
Boddy, Manchester (Original Author)
Malaya 1950,F 23,33:1
Bode, Heinrich
To Live in Peace 1947,N 25,37:2
Bode-Wab, Steffen
Before Him all Rome Trembled 1947,F 22,16:2
Bodeen, DeWitt (Miscellaneous)
Night Song 1948,Ja 29,27:5
Bodeen, DeWitt (Original Author)
Seventh Victim, The 1943,S 18,11:3
Girl in the Kremlin, The 1957,My 22,29:2
Bodeen, DeWitt (Screenwriter)
Cat People 1942,D 7,22:2
Curse of the Cat People, The 1944,Mr 4,11:1
Yellow Canary, The 1944,Ag 14,24:7
Enchanted Cottage, The 1945,Ap 28,19:2
I Remember Mama 1948,Mr 12,29:2
Mrs Mike 1950,F 9,36:5
Billy Budd 1962,O 31,32:1
Bodegas, Roberto (Screenwriter)
Voyage of Silence 1968,S 12,54:1
BODEN
See Also BOWDEN
Boden, Herman
Siren of Atlantis 1949,Ag 22,13:1
Bodger (dog)
Incredible Journey, The 1963,N 21,43:2
Bodi, Luciano
Romeo and Juliet 1954,D 22,28:1
Bodo, Ban
Za Winy niepopelnione; For Crimes Not Theirs
1939,F 20,13:3
Bodo, Eugene
Kocha, Lubi, Szanuje 1934,N 3,20:4
Pietro Wyzej; Apartment Above 1938,Ja 10,13:4
Neighbors; Shekhonim 1938,D 9,31:3
Bodo, Eugene (Director)
Krolowa Przedmiescia; Queen of the Market
Place 1937,D 29,17:2
Za Winy niepopelnione; For Crimes Not Theirs
1939,F 20,13:3
Bodo, Eugene (Producer)
Ksiazatko; Lottery Prince, The 1937,D 27,11:2
Krolowa Przedmiescia; Queen of the Market
Place 1937,D 29,17:2
Bodogni, Giuseppe (Producer)
Disorder 1964,My 26,44:2
Bodrero, James (Original Author)
White Heat 1934,Je 16,20:2
Three Caballeros, The 1945,F 5,20:1
Bodrero, James (Screenwriter)
Victory Through Air Power 1943,Jl 19,13:1

BOEHM
See Also BOEHME
Boehm, David (Original Author)
Employees' Entrance 1933,Ja 21,10:6
Search for Beauty 1934,F 10,20:2
Midnight Madonna 1937,Jl 17,18:1
Guy Named Joe, A 1943,D 24,17:2
Boehm, David (Screenwriter)
Raven, The 1935,Jl 5,9:2
Florida Special 1936,My 29,15:2
Peck's bad Boy With the Circus 1939,Ja 11,17:4
Powder Town 1942,Je 8,11:2
Knickerbocker Holiday 1944,Ap 20,22:7
Boehm, Karl
4 Horsemen of the Apocalypse, The
1962,Mr 10,10:2
Forever My Love 1962,Mr 28,36:4
Wonderful World of the Brothers Grimm, The
1962,Ag 8,35:1
Cross of the Living 1963,F 5,5:5
Come Fly With Me 1963,My 2,40:2
Golden Plaque, The 1963,Ag 10,8:6
Venetian Affair, The 1967,Ja 19,41:2
Boehm, Karlheinz
Dreimaederlhaus, Das; (House of Three Girls,
The) 1961,N 18,15:1
Boehm, Sydney (Original Author)
Side Street 1950,Mr 24,29:2
Secret of the Incas 1954,My 29,13:3
Boehm, Sydney (Producer)
Woman Obsessed 1959,My 28,34:1
Seven Thieves 1960,Mr 12,14:5
One Foot in Hell 1960,O 20,42:2
Boehm, Sydney (Screenwriter)
High Wall 1947,D 26,22:2
Undercover Man, The 1949,Ap 21,30:2
Side Street 1950,Mr 24,29:2
Mystery Street 1950,Jl 28,12:5
Union Station 1950,O 5,38:3
Branded 1951,Ja 11,28:5
When Worlds Collide 1952,F 7,30:2
Atomic City, The 1952,My 2,21:1
Savage, The 1953,Ja 2,11:1
Second Chance 1953,Jl 23,20:2
Big Heat, The 1953,O 15,43:2
Siege at Red River, The 1954,Ap 3,19:2
Secret of the Incas 1954,My 29,13:3
Raid, The 1954,Ag 21,10:4
Rogue Cop 1954,S 18,12:2
Black Tuesday 1955,Ja 1,16:2
Six Bridges to Cross 1955,Ja 22,8:2
Violent Saturday 1955,My 12,32:2
Tall Men, The 1955,O 12,36:2
Hell on Frisco Bay 1956,Ja 7,21:1
Bottom of the Bottle, The 1956,F 2,19:2
Revolt of Mamie Stover, The 1956,My 12,12:7
Harry Black and the Tiger 1958,S 19,24:4
Nice Little Bank That Should Be Robbed, A
1958,D 11,17:4
Woman Obsessed 1959,My 28,34:1
Seven Thieves 1960,Mr 12,14:5
Shock Treatment 1964,Jl 23,19:1
Sylvia 1965,F 11,45:1
Rough Night in Jericho 1967,N 9,56:4
BOEHME
See Also BOEHM
Boehme, Herbert
Verraeter 1937,Ja 23,13:1
Boel, Lil (Screenwriter)
Face to the Wind 1951,Ja 16,34:2
Boese, Carl (Director)
Bockbierfest 1931,Mr 31,25:3
Ungetreue Eckehart, Der 1932,Ja 23,18:4
Rendez-Vous 1932,Ap 30,19:3
Der Schrecken der Garnison 1932,Je 1,19:5
Dienst Ist Dienst 1932,Je 6,18:5
Keine Feier Ohne Meyer 1932,O 29,18:4
Man Braucht Kein Geld 1932,N 16,15:3
Theodor Koerner 1933,My 6,11:2
Drei Tage Mittelarrest 1933,My 18,17:4
Frechdachs, Der 1934,Ja 6,18:3
Wie Man Maenner Fesselt 1934,My 21,20:3
Roman Einer Nacht 1934,Je 22,24:2
Annemarie, Die Braut der Kompanie
1934,D 8,18:6
Frau wie Du, Eine 1934,D 24,17:3
Im Heidekrug 1934,D 31,9:7
Meine Frau, Die Schuetzenkoenigin
1935,Ja 7,13:3
Kalte Mamsell, Die 1935,Ja 12,12:2
Gretl Zieht das Grosse Los 1935,F 11,14:2
Drei von der Kavallerie 1935,Ap 13,11:4
Unschuld vom Lande, Die 1935,My 13,18:6
Schuechterne Felix, Der 1935,S 7,19:5
Lied vom Glueck, Das; Song of Happiness, The
1935,N 30,12:7
Gruss und Kuss, Veronika 1936,F 24,14:2
Ganzer Kerl, Ein 1936,Ap 25,21:2
Fahrt in Die Jugend, Die 1936,Ag 31,19:2
Drei Blaue Jungs-Ein Blondes Maedel
1936,D 29,16:3
Falscher Fuffziger, Ein 1937,F 13,9:1
Die Herren vom Maxim 1937,Mr 27,19:2

Boese, Carl (Director) — Cont

Fraeulein Frau 1937,Jl 3,18:2
Schwebende Jungfrau, Die 1937,Ag 7,7:2
Herzensclieb; Heart Thief 1938,Jl 2,10:4
Dyplomatyczna Zona 1938,O 24,13:2
Klapperstorchverband, Der; Stork Society, The
  1938,O 29,15:3
Nacht an der Donau, Eine; Night on the Danube,
  A 1938,N 19,9:3
Kleine Suenderin, Die; Little Sinner, The
  1938,D 3,11:3
Dahinten in der Heide; Back in the Country
  1939,Ja 21,19:3
O Schwarzwald, O Heimat; Oh Black Forest, Oh
  Home 1939,Ap 24,13:2
Verliebte Herzen; Hearts in Love 1939,Je 10,14:2
Verkannte Lebemann, Der; Unrecognized Man of
  the World, The 1939,S 16,20:2
Fuenf Millionem suchen einen Erben; Five
  Millions Seek an Heir 1939,O 23,15:3
Drei Vater um Anna; Three Fathers for Anna
  1940,Ja 20,11:3
Gluck auf den Lande; Rural Happiness
  1940,F 10,19:3

Boese, Carl (Miscellaneous)

Liebe Dumme Mama; Stupid Mama
  1935,Mr 2,18:3

Boese, Carl (Producer)

Drei Blaue Jungs-Ein Blondes Maedel
  1936,D 29,16:3

Boesiger, Paul

Taiga 1959,Mr 17,42:4

Boetler, Wade

Man of Action, A 1923,Je 4,13:3
Derelict 1930,N 22,21:3

Boettger, Fritz (Screenwriter)

Beggar Student, The 1958,Ja 25,14:3

Boetticher, Budd (Director)

Bullfighter and the Lady, The 1951,Ap 27,19:2
Red Ball Express 1952,My 30,11:2
Horizons West 1952,N 22,16:5
City Beneath the Sea 1953,Mr 12,24:3
Wings of the Hawk 1953,Ag 27,22:1
Man From the Alamo, The 1953,S 12,13:2
Magnificent Matador, The 1955,My 25,38:1
Killer is Loose, The 1956,Mr 3,17:2
Rise and Fall of Legs' Diamond, The
  1960,F 4,34:1

Boetticher, Budd (Original Author)

Bullfighter and the Lady, The 1951,Ap 27,19:2
Magnificent Matador, The 1955,My 25,38:1

Boetticher, Oscar Jr (Director)

One Mysterious Night 1944,O 21,15:3

Bogaert, Lucienne

Vautrin, the Thief 1949,N 11,31:2
Deadlier Than the Male 1957,O 9,41:1
Inspector Maigret 1958,O 9,47:1
Crime Does Not Pay (The Hugues Case); Hugues
  Case, The (Crime Does Not Pay)
  1962,O 17,35:2
Dames du Bois de Boulogne, Les; Ladies of the
  Park 1964,Ap 4,15:5

Bogarde, Dirk

Quartet (The Alien Corn); Alien Corn, The
  (Quartet) 1949,Mr 29,30:3
Dear Mr Prohack 1950,Jl 15,7:2
Blue Lamp, The 1951,Ja 9,25:1
So Long at the Fair 1951,Ja 22,14:2
Woman in Question, The 1952,F 19,24:2
Stranger in Between, The 1952,Ag 20,21:3
Penny Princess 1953,Mr 25,37:3
Desperate Moment 1953,S 1,19:4
Gentle Gunman, The 1953,O 1,34:3
Sleeping Tiger, The 1954,O 9,8:7
Doctor in the House 1955,F 19,18:3
Simba 1955,O 22,24:2
Doctor at Sea 1956,Mr 1,37:3
Doctor at Large 1957,Jl 29,15:5
Spanish Gardner, The 1957,S 9,21:2
Cast a Dark Shadow 1957,N 28,57:1
Night Ambush 1958,Ap 25,32:4
Tale of Two Cities, A 1958,Ag 5,23:1
Doctor's Dilemma, A 1958,D 18,2:7
Libel 1959,O 24,12:4
Campbell's Kingdom 1960,Ja 11,35:5
Wind Cannot Read, The 1960,Mr 10,36:1
Song Without End 1960,Ag 12,10:2
Angel Wore Red, The 1960,S 29,32:1
Victim 1962,F 6,27:2
Singer not the Song, The 1962,My 3,25:4
Damn the Defiant 1962,S 20,29:2
Password Is Courage, The 1962,D 22,5:2
Mind Benders, The 1963,My 2,40:2
I Could go on Singing 1963,My 16,42:1
Servant, The 1964,Mr 17,30:2
Doctor in Distress 1964,Jl 8,38:2
King and Country 1964,S 24,46:2
Darling 1965,Ag 4,20:1
Agent 8 3/4 1965,O 14,53:1
King and Country 1966,Ja 28,20:4
Modesty Blaise 1966,Ag 11,27:1
Accident 1967,Ap 18,33:1
Our Mother's House 1967,O 10,56:1
Sebastian 1968,Ja 25,33:2

Bogart, Humphrey

Fixer, The 1968,D 9,59:1
Up the River 1930,O 11,21:3
Devil With Women, A 1930,O 20,28:2
Body and Soul 1931,Mr 14,23:2
Bad Sister 1931,Mr 30,25:2
Women of all Nations 1931,My 30,9:2
Holy Terror, A 1931,Jl 20,20:4
Big City Blues 1932,S 10,18:5
Three on a Match 1932,O 29,18:4
Midnight 1934,Mr 10,18:3
Petrified Forest, The 1936,F 7,14:2
Bullets or Ballots 1936,My 27,27:1
China Clipper 1936,Ag 12,14:3
Black Legion 1937,Ja 18,21:1
Great O'Malley, The 1937,Mr 6,10:1
Marked Woman 1937,Ap 12,15:2
Kid Galahad 1937,My 27,21:3
San Quentin 1937,Ag 4,15:2
Dead End 1937,Ag 25,25:1
Stand-In 1937,N 19,27:2
Swing Your Lady 1938,Ja 27,17:2
Crime School 1938,My 61,17:2
Men Are Such Fools 1938,Je 17,25:1
Amazing Dr Clitterhouse, The 1938,Jl 21,14:2
Racket Busters 1938,Ag 11,13:1
Angels With Dirty Faces 1938,N 26,18:1
King of the Underworld 1939,Ja 7,6:2
Oklahoma Kid, The 1939,Mr 11,21:1
You Can't Get Away With Murder
  1939,Mr 25,19:2
Dark Victory 1939,Ap 21,27:2
Roaring Twenties, The 1939,N 11,12:1
Return Of Doctor X, The 1939,N 23,38:5
Invisible Stripes 1940,Ja 13,11:2
It all Came True 1940,Ap 6,13:2
Brother Orchid 1940,Je 8,18:2
They Drive by Night 1940,Jl 27,17:5
High Sierra 1941,Ja 25,11:2
Wagons Roll at Night, The 1941,My 10,20:4
Maltese Falcon, The 1941,O 4,18:2
All Through the Night 1942,Ja 24,13:2
Big Shot, The 1942,Jl 18,8:2
Across the Pacific 1942,S 5,9:2
Casablanca 1942,N 27,27:1
Action in the North Atlantic 1943,My 22,10:2
Thank Your Lucky Stars 1943,O 2,19:2
Sahara 1943,N 12,25:2
Passage to Marseille 1944,F 17,12:5
To Have and Have Not 1944,O 12,24:1
Conflict 1945,Je 16,10:2
Big Sleep, The 1946,Ag 24,6:6
Dead Reckoning 1947,Ja 23,31:2
Two Mrs Carrolls, The 1947,Ap 7,20:1
Dark Passage 1947,S 6,11:2
Treasure of Sierra Madre 1948,Ja 24,11:2
Key Largo 1948,Jl 17,6:6
Knock on any Door 1949,F 23,31:2
Tokyo Joe 1949,O 27,35:2
Chain Lightning 1950,F 20,21:2
In a Lonely Place 1950,My 18,37:2
Enforcer, The 1951,Ja 26,19:2
Sirocco 1951,Je 14,31:2
African Queen, The 1952,F 21,24:3
Deadline U S A 1952,Mr 15,8:2
Battle Circus 1953,My 28,27:5
Beat the Devil 1954,Mr 13,11:2
Caine Mutiny, The 1954,Je 25,17:1
Sabrina 1954,S 23,43:2
Barefoot Contessa, The 1954,S 30,37:1
We're no Angels 1955,Jl 8,15:2
Left Hand of God, The 1955,S 22,34:5
Desperate Hours, The 1955,O 6,25:1
Harder They Fall, The 1956,My 10,26:3

Bogda, Maria

Clos Pustyni 1933,Ap 21,20:5
Mlody Las 1935,D 3,32:7
Pan Redaktor Szaleje; Mr Editor Is Crazy
  1938,Je 14,17:3

Bogdanov, Fyodor

Dom Zhadnosti 1934,Ag 13,9:6
Peter the First 1937,D 25,10:4
Conquests of Peter The Great, The
  1939,Ag 24,17:2
Wings of Victory 1941,N 17,15:2

Bogdanova, Alla

Cranes are Flying, The 1960,Mr 22,31:2

Bogdanova-Chestnokova, G

Tiger Girl 1955,S 5,8:2

Bogdanovich, Peter

Targets 1968,Ag 14,34:1

Bogdanovich, Peter (Director)

Targets 1968,Ag 14,34:1

Bogdanovich, Peter (Original Author)

Targets 1968,Ag 14,34:1

Bogdanovich, Peter (Director)

Targets 1968,Ag 14,34:1

Bogdanovich, Peter (Screenwriter)

Targets 1968,Ag 14,34:1

Bogeaus, Benedict (Producer)

Bridge of San Luis Rey, The 1944,Mr 4,11:1
Dark Waters 1944,N 22,25:2
Captain Kidd 1945,N 23,26:3

Bogeaus, Benedict (Producer) — Cont

Diary of a Chambermaid, The 1946,Je 23,28:2
Mr Ace 1946,S 30,21:3
Macomber Affair, The 1947,Ap 21,21:2
Christmas Eve 1947,N 28,30:2
Miracle Can Happen, A 1948,F 4,28:4
Crooked Way, The 1949,S 5,13:2
Johnny One-Eye 1950,N 17,31:2
My Outlaw Brother 1951,Ag 23,19:2
Count the Hours 1953,Je 24,30:4
Appointment in Honduras 1953,N 19,41:4
Silver Lode 1954,Jl 24,6:6
Passion 1954,D 11,11:1
Cattle Queen of Montana 1955,Ja 26,22:1
Escape to Burma 1955,My 21,11:2
Pearl of the South Pacific 1955,S 17,12:2
Tennessee's Partner 1955,N 5,22:8
Slightly Scarlet 1956,Mr 17,13:2
River's Edge, The 1957,Ap 12,20:2
From the Earth to the Moon 1958,N 27,52:2
Jet Over the Atlantic 1960,Ja 7,24:6
Most Dangerous Man Alive 1961,Jl 5,29:2

Bogert (Screenwriter)

Man With my Face, The 1951,Je 15,27:5

Bogin, Mikhail (Director)

Ballad of Love, A 1966,F 21,51:1

Bogin, Mikhail (Screenwriter)

Ballad of Love, A 1966,F 21,51:1

Bogle, Charles (W C Fields) (Original Author)

Old-Fashioned Way, The 1934,Jl 14,16:5
It's a Gift 1935,Ja 5,20:2
Man on the Flying Trapeze 1935,Ag 3,16:2
You Can't Cheat an Honest Man 1939,F 20,13:2

Bogle, Mary

Its a Boy 1933,Jl 23,IX,2:2 (In Addenda)

Bogner, Norman (Screenwriter)

Privilege 1967,Jl 25,30:2

Bogolepov (Director)

Atoms for Peace 1956,Je 25,19:7

Bogoliubov, Nikolai

Patrioty 1933,S 25,18:5
Peasants 1935,Ag 29,25:2
In the Far East 1937,O 20,27:3
Great Citizen, The 1939,Ja 16,11:2
Lenin in 1918 1939,Je 27,27:2
Fortress on the Volga 1942,D 25,15:3
Vanka 1943,Mr 25,25:3
No Greater Love 1944,F 25,23:3
Moscow Skies 1945,Ja 22,22:5
Vow, The 1947,Je 23,14:3

Bogoliubova, S

Vow, The 1947,Je 23,14:3

Bogomolov, Vladimir (Original Author)

My Name Is Ivan (Ivan's Childhood)
  1963,Je 28,25:4

Bogomolov, Vladimir (Screenwriter)

My Name Is Ivan (Ivan's Childhood)
  1963,Je 28,25:4

Bogoslavsky, A

Sons and Mothers 1967,O 2,58:1

Bogoslavsky, N (Composer)

Two Soldiers 1944,Jl 27,14:2

Bogris, Demetre (Director)

Prosfygopoula; Girl Refugee, The 1938,S 27,25:3

Bogue, M A

Carolina Blues 1944,D 8,26:6

Boguliubov, N

Seven Brave Men 1936,Je 15,24:2

Bohac, Ladislav

Skeleton on Horseback 1940,F 5,13:3

Bohan, Marc

Phaedra 1962,O 19,24:1

Bohaty, Elisabeth

Jonas 1959,Ap 30,37:1

Bohdalova, Jirina

Lady on the Tracks, The 1968,N 26,39:2

Bohdanova, Blanka

Sweet Light in a Dark Room 1966,Je 30,28:1

Bohem, Endre (Original Author)

Lord Jeff 1938,Jl 1,22:2
Four Girls in White 1939,F 23,19:3
Blackmail 1939,S 15,26:3

Bohem, Endre (Producer)

Night Has a Thousand Eyes 1948,O 14,38:3
Alias Nick Beal 1949,Mr 10,35:2

Bohem, Endre (Screenwriter)

House of a Thousand Candles, The
  1936,Ap 2,29:2
Bengazi 1955,O 8,13:4

Bohier, Lalo

Canillita y la Dama, El; Newsie and the Lady,
  The 1939,F 18,12:2

Bohler, Fred

Rough Riders, The 1927,Mr 16,28:2

Bohlin, Allan

Ungkarlspappan 1936,Ja 4,19:1
Under Falsk Flagg 1937,Ja 20,18:5
Familjen Andersson; Anderson Family, The
  1939,Ja 24,16:5

Bohn, Jack

Inside of the Cup, The 1921,Ja 16,VI,2:1 (In
  Addenda)
Story Without a Name, The 1924,O 6,25:1

Bohn, John
Crime of Dr Crespi, The 1936,Ja 13,14:3
Bohn, Walter
Cipher Bureau 1938,D 14,32:6
Bohne, Werner (Cinematographer)
Pori 1930,Je 10,32:2
Bohnen, Michael
Sajenko, The Soviet 1929,Ja 15,22:4
Two Neckties; Zwei Kravatten 1930,N 30,IX,6:5
Viktoria und Ihr Husar 1933,Ap 10,8:3
Wiener Blut 1933,N 13,21:2
Gold 1934,O 22,12:3
Private Life of Louis XIV, The 1936,Ja 9,25:2
August der Starke 1937,Ja 30,21:3
Only for Thee; Solo per To 1938,S 12,13:2
Unsterbliche Herz, Das; Immortal Heart, The
1939,O 21,12:2
Bohnen, Roman
Vogues of 1938 1937,Ag 20,21:1
Of Mice and Men 1940,F 17,9:2
Living Dead, The 1940,D 17,33:2
So Ends our Night 1941,F 28,17:2
They Dare not Love 1941,My 16,21:4
Appointment for Love 1941,N 7,27:1
Bugle Sounds, The 1942,Ap 3,25:2
Grand Central Murder 1942,My 23,8:8
Hard Way, The 1943,Mr 13,9:2
Edge of Darkness 1943,Ap 10,12:4
Mission to Moscow 1943,Ap 30,25:2
Song of Bernadette, The 1944,Ja 27,15:2
Hitler Gang, The 1944,My 8,15:2
Hairy Ape, The 1944,Jl 3,8:3
None but the Lonely Heart 1944,N 18,16:6
Counter-Attack 1945,My 17,15:2
Bell for Adano, A 1945,Jl 6,8:3
Miss Susie Slagle's 1946,F 7,29:2
Hoodlum Saint, The 1946,Je 27,29:1
Strange Love of Martha Ivers, The
1946,Jl 25,18:4
Two Years Before the Mast 1946,S 25,39:2
Mr Ace 1946,S 30,21:3
Best Years of our Lives, The 1946,N 22,27:2
California 1947,Ja 15,31:2
Brute Force 1947,Jl 17,16:2
Song of Love 1947,O 10,31:2
Open Secret 1948,F 2,15:2
Arch of Triumph 1948,Ap 21,33:2
Night Has a Thousand Eyes 1948,O 14,38:3
Joan of Arc 1948,N 12,30:5
Bohnet, Volker
Bridge, The; (Bruecke, Die) 1961,My 2,42:1
Bohr, Carmelina
Asi es la Mujer 1936,O 21,35:3
Bohr, Jose
Ex-Flame 1931,Ja 24,15:1
Hollywood, Ciudad de Ensueno 1934,Ap 4,26:3
Sangre Manda, La 1934,My 15,18:2
Quien Mato a Eva 1934,D 22,21:2
Asi es la Mujer 1936,O 21,35:3
Traidor, El 1938,Ap 9,11:3
Bohr, Jose (Director)
Sangre Manda, La 1934,My 15,18:2
Tu Hijo 1934,D 17,24:3
Quien Mato a Eva 1934,D 22,21:2
Sueno de Amor 1936,Ja 11,9:3
Asi es la Mujer 1936,O 21,35:3
Traidor, El 1938,Ap 9,11:3
Por Mis Pistolas; By My Pistols 1939,Je 10,14:3
Latigo, El; Whip, The 1939,Jl 1,11:3
Herencia Macabra; Macabre Legacy, A
1940,My 4,13:2
Bohr, Jose (Producer)
Sangre Manda, La 1934,My 15,18:2
Traidor, El 1938,Ap 9,11:3
Boi, Aldo
Roof, The 1959,My 13,43:4
BOICE
See Also BOYCE
Boice, Helen
Abilene Town 1946,Mr 4,16:5
Boiduman, Mikhail
In the Far East 1937,O 20,27:3
Boig, Curt
Gypsy Wildcat 1944,O 5,18:6
Boileau, Pierre (Original Author)
Diabolique 1955,N 22,41:1
Demoniaque 1958,Mr 4,34:5
Vertigo 1958,My 29,24:2
Boileau, Pierre (Screenwriter)
Demoniaque 1958,Mr 4,34:5
Bois, Curt
Schlemihl, Der 1932,Ja 17,VIII,6:1
Schlemihl, Der 1934,N 5,23:1
Tovarich 1937,D 31,9:2
Hollywood Hotel 1938,Ja 13,17:3
Romance in the Dark 1938,Mr 21,18:2
Gold Diggers in Paris 1938,Je 2,19:2
Amazing Dr Clitterhouse, The 1938,Jl 21,14:2
Garden of the Moon 1938,S 24,13:1
Great Waltz, The 1938,N 25,19:1
Hotel Imperial 1939,My 11,31:3
He Stayed for Breakfast 1940,Ag 31,16:2
Boom Town 1940,S 6,25:2

Bitter Sweet 1940,N 22,27:1
Lady in Question, The 1940,D 10,33:2
Hullabaloo 1940,D 19,33:1
That Night in Rio 1941,Mr 10,21:2
Hold Back the Dawn 1941,O 2,29:1
Tuttles of Tahiti, The 1942,Ap 30,14:1
Pacific Rendezvous 1942,Jl 8,27:4
Casablanca 1942,N 27,27:1
Destroyer 1943,S 2,15:3
Paris After Dark 1943,O 23,11:1
Princess O'Rourke 1943,N 6,16:2
Desert Song, The 1943,D 18,10:6
Swing Fever 1944,Ja 28,14:1
Cover Girl 1944,Mr 31,26:1
Spanish Main, The 1945,N 7,20:2
Saratoga Trunk 1945,N 22,39:2
Arch of Triumph 1948,Ap 21,33:2
Woman in White, The 1948,My 8,12:2
Caught 1949,F 18,26:4
Kiss in the Dark, A 1949,Mr 26,10:6
Great Sinner, The 1949,Je 30,19:2
Fortunes of Captain Blood 1950,Je 10,11:3
Boisrond, Michel (Director)
Women Are Weak 1959,Je 9,44:2
Come Dance With Me!; Voulez-Vous Danser Avec
Moi 1960,N 8,32:6
Love and the Frenchwoman; (Francaise et
l'Amour, La) 1961,F 28,38:2
Tales of Paris (The Tale of Antonio); Tale of
Antonio, The (Tales of Paris) 1962,Ag 27,18:1
Boisrond, Michel (Screenwriter)
Women Are Weak 1959,Je 9,44:2
Tales of Paris (The Tale of Antonio); Tale of
Antonio, The (Tales of Paris) 1962,Ag 27,18:1
Boissoi, Claude (Director)
Julie the Redhead 1963,O 15,44:1
Boissoi, Claude (Screenwriter)
Julie the Redhead 1963,O 15,44:1
Boissy, Robert (Miscellaneous)
Vie de Boheme, La 1947,N 28,37:4
Boitel, Jeanne
Petits, Les 1936,D 30,17:2
Amphitryon 1937,Mr 24,29:1
Whirlpool; (Remous) 1940,O 8,31:2
Boito, Arrigo (Composer)
Faust and the Devil 1950,My 1,18:2
Boito, Camillo (Original Author)
Senso 1968,Jl 9,31:1
Boize, Sandra
Hysteria 1965,S 9,36:3
Boka, Gilbert
Royal Affairs in Versailles 1957,Mr 9,16:1
Bokanowski, Gilbert (Producer)
Crime Does Not Pay (The Hugues Case); Hugues
Case, The (Crime Does Not Pay)
1962,O 17,35:2
Crime Does Not Pay (The Man on the Avenue);
Man on the Avenue, The (Crime Does Not
Pay) 1962,O 17,35:2
Crime Does Not Pay (The Fenayrou Case);
Fenayrou Case, The (Crime Does Not Pay)
1962,O 17,35:2
Crime Does Not Pay (The Mask); Mask, The
(Crime Does Not Pay) 1962,O 17,35:2
Boky, Colette
Merry Wives of Windsor, The 1966,F 28,21:1
Bolam, James
Kitchen, The 1961,N 2,42:1
Kind of Loving, A 1962,O 2,46:1
Loneliness of the Long Distance Runner, The
1962,O 9,44:1
Murder Most Foul 1965,My 24,36:2
Boland, Bridget (Original Author)
This England 1941,N 18,33:2
Prisoner, The 1955,D 12,37:1
Boland, Bridget (Screenwriter)
Spies of the Air 1940,Jl 4,12:3
Voice in the Night, The 1941,My 23,25:4
Lost People, The 1950,O 2,19:4
Angel Street 1952,N 11,25:2
Prisoner, The 1955,D 12,37:1
War and Peace 1956,Ag 22,26:2
Damon and Pythias 1962,S 6,37:2
Boland, Eddie
Within the Law 1923,Ap 30,11:2
Long Live the King 1923,D 4,24:1
Little Robinson Crusoe 1924,S 3,17:1
Kid Brother, The 1927,Ja 24,14:1
Sunrise 1927,S 24,15:3 (In Addenda)
Miracle Woman, The 1931,Ag 17,18:2
Vanity Street 1932,O 15,13:1
I Have Lived 1933,S 6,24:4
Boland, John (Original Author)
League of Gentlemen, The 1961,Ja 25,30:4
Boland, John J (Director)
Te Quiero con Locura; I'm Crazy About You
1935,N 4,24:6
Boland, Mary
Secrets of a Secretary 1931,Ag 29,16:3
Personal Maid 1931,S 5,7:4
Night of June 13th, The 1932,S 17,18:4
Evenings for Sale 1932,N 12,20:5
If I Had a Million 1932,D 3,21:4

Boland, Mary— Cont
Mama Loves Papa 1933,Jl 24,11:2
Three-Cornered Moon 1933,Ag 12,14:2
Solitaire Man, The 1933,S 23,11:5
Four Frightened People 1934,Ja 27,9:2
Six of a Kind 1934,Mr 10,18:3
Melody in Spring 1934,Mr 31,8:2
Stingaree 1934,My 18,27:1
Here Comes the Groom 1934,Je 16,20:2
Down to Their Last Yacht 1934,S 24,14:1
Pursuit of Happiness, The 1934,O 26,25:1
Ruggles of Red Gap 1935,Mr 7,26:1
People Will Talk 1935,Je 17,20:2
Two for Tonight 1935,Ag 31,16:2
Early to Bed 1936,Jl 16,20:2
Son Comes Home, A 1936,S 5,7:1
Wives Never Know 1936,O 31,24:2
College Holiday 1936,D 24,21:2
Marry the Girl 1937,Jl 31,6:2
Danger-Love at Work 1937,D 11,22:2
there Goes The Groom 1937,D 25,10:6
Little Tough Guys in Society 1938,N 21,14:4
Artists and Models Abroad 1938,D 22,25:3
Magnificent Fraud, The 1939,Jl 20,16:2
Women, The 1939,S 22,27:2
He Married his Wife 1940,Ja 20,11:2
New Moon 1940,Jl 19,22:2
Pride and Prejudice 1940,Ag 9,19:1
Hit Parade of 1941 1940,D 5,33:2
One Night in the Tropics 1940,D 20,33:2
In our Time 1944,F 12,11:2
Nothing but Trouble 1945,Mr 10,14:1
Julia Misbehaves 1948,O 8,30:2
Guilty Bystander 1950,Ap 21,18:2
Bolanos, Alicia
Prisionero 13, El 1934,Ap 30,11:4
Bolchi, S (Screenwriter)
Anita Garibaldi 1954,Mr 19,19:4
Bolden, Harry
Member of the Wedding, The 1952,D 31,10:2
Bolder, Cal
One Spy too Many 1966,D 8,64:1
Bolder, Robert
Strictly Confidential 1919,O 6,15:1
Sea Hawk, The 1924,Je 3,22:1
Captain Blood 1924,S 9,19:1
Vanity's Price 1924,O 8,16:2
Butterflies in the Rain 1926,D 25,10:5
Wise Wife 1927,N 1,21:1 (In Addenda)
Women's Wares 1927,N 15,27:1
Florodora Girl, The 1930,My 31,19:4
Lady of Scandal, The 1930,Je 14,9:4
Grumpy 1930,Ag 2,16.4
BOLES
See Also BOWLES
Boles, Glen
Road to Ruin, The 1934,F 21,23:2
Quitter, The 1934,Mr 14,23:3
Flirtation Walk 1934,N 29,33:1
Babbitt 1934,D 17,24:2
Fighting Youth 1935,N 2,13:3
Boles, Jim
Tattooed Stranger, The 1950,F 10,18:6
Man With my Face, The 1951,Je 15,27:5
Trouble With Angels, The 1966,Ap 7,45:1
Boles, John
So This Is Marriage 1924,D 23,16:2
Shepherd of the Hills, The 1928,F 20,14:1
We Americans 1928,Mr 29,25:3
Fazil 1928,Je 5,21:1
Water Hole, The 1928,S 3,14:2
Man Made Women 1928,S 18,33:2
Romance of the Underworld 1929,Ja 7,36:2
Last Warning, The 1929,Ja 7,36:2
Scandal 1929,Ap 22,23:1
Desert Song, The 1929,My 2,20:6
Rio Rita 1929,O 7,22:1
Song of the West 1930,F 28,20:7
Captain of the Guard 1930,Mr 29,23:1
King of Jazz 1930,My 3,23:1
One Heavenly Night 1931,Ja 10,19:2
Resurrection 1931,Ja 24,15:1
Seed 1931,My 15,20:6
Frankenstein 1931,D 5,21:2
Good Sport 1931,D 12,23:3
Careless Lady 1932,Ap 18,19:2
Back Street 1932,Ag 29,9:2
Six Hours to Live 1932,O 22,18:4
Child of Manhattan 1933,F 13,11:4
My Lips Betray 1933,N 4,18:3
Only Yesterday 1933,N 10,25:1
Beloved 1934,Ja 27,9:3
Bottoms Up 1934,Mr 23,29:2
I Believed in You 1934,Ap 11,25:3
Stand up and Cheer 1934,Ap 20,17:1
Life of Vergie Winters, The 1934,Je 15,26:1
Wild Gold 1934,Jl 24,20:2
Age of Innocence, The 1934,O 19,27:1
White Parade, The 1934,N 10,19:1
Music in the Air 1934,D 14,29:3
Curly Top 1935,Ag 2,22:3
Orchids to You 1935,Ag 10,16:4
Littlest Rebel, The 1935,D 20,30:1
Rose of the Rancho 1936,Ja 9,25:2

Boles, John— Cont

Message to Garcia, A 1936,Ap 10,27:1
Craig's Wife 1936,O 2,29:3
As Good as Married 1937,My 22,19:2
Stella Dallas 1937,Ag 6,21:1
Fight for Your Lady 1937,N 20,21:2
She Married an Artist 1938,F 25,15:2
Romance in the Dark 1938,Mr 21,18:2
Sinners in Paradise 1938,My 20,17:2
Road to Happiness 1942,Mr 27,27:4
Between Us Girls 1942,S 25,25:3
Thousands Cheer 1943,S 14,27:1
Babes in Bagdad 1954,Op 5,21:3

Boleslawski, Richard (Director)

Gay Diplomat, The 1931,O 10,20:4
Rasputin and the Empress 1932,D 24,11:4
Storm at Daybreak 1933,Jl 22,14:2
Beauty for Sale 1933,S 16,9:3
Fugitive Lovers 1934,Ja 13,16:3
Men in White 1934,Je 9,18:2
Operator 13 1934,Je 23,16:5
Painted Veil, The 1934,D 7,29:1
Clive of India 1935,Ja 18,29:1
Miserables, Les 1935,Ap 22,14:2
O'Shaughnessy's Boy 1935,O 5,18:2
Metropolitan 1935,O 18,27:4
Three Godfathers, The 1936,Mr 9,20:2
Theodora Goes Wild 1936,N 13,27:4
Garden of Allah, The 1936,N 20,27:2
Last of Mrs Cheyney, The 1937,F 19,15:1

Boley, May

Dangerous Curves 1929,Jl 15,25:1
Dance of Life, The 1929,Ag 16,18:6
Moby Dick 1930,Ag 15,20:5
Going Wild 1931,Ja 26,21:1
Fighting Caravans 1931,Ja 26,21:1
Woman Commands, A 1932,Ja 28,13:2
Expert, The 1932,F 27,22:1
Advice to the Lovelorn 1933,D 14,28:2
Mighty Barnum, The 1934,D 24,17:1
Informer, The 1935,My 10,25:2
Ready, Willing and Able 1937,Mr 15,27:1
Tovarich 1937,D 31,9:2
Cowboy From Brooklyn 1938,Jl 14,17:1
Prison Farm 1938,Jl 15,13:3
Persons in Hiding 1939,Mr 2,19:2
Death of a Champion 1939,Ag 24,17:3

Bolger, Ray

Great Ziegfeld, The 1936,Ap 9,21:2
Rosalie 1937,D 31,9:2
Sweethearts 1938,D 23,16:2
Wizard of Oz, The 1939,Ag 18,16:2
Sunny 1941,Je 13,22:2
Stage Door Canteen 1943,Je 25,13:2
Harvey Girls, The 1946,Ja 25,26:2
Look for the Silver Lining 1949,Je 24,29:2
Where's Charley? 1952,Je 27,18:3
April in Paris 1952,D 25,34:5
Babes in Toyland 1961,D 15,49:1

Bolin, Shannon

Damn Yankees 1958,S 27,12:7

Bolio, Antonio Mediz (Screenwriter)

Night of the Mayas 1941,Ja 14,16:7

Bolivar, David

Taste of Honey, A 1962,My 1,33:3

Bolkov, B (Director)

One Day With Russians 1961,Mr 13,36:6

Boll, Gertrud

Maedchenraeuber 1936,Ag 15,6:3
Muede Theodor, Der 1936,O 24,23:2

Bolling, Gary

Cool World, The 1964,Ap 21,42:1

Bollmann, Hans Heinz

Lindenwirtin vom Rhein, Die 1931,S 25,28:7
Friederike 1933,F 27,11:3
Bettelstudent, Der 1933,O 14,18:3
Frasquita 1936,Ja 18,19:4

Bologna, Carmine (Producer)

Red Lips 1964,Mr 19,28:2

Bolognesi, Gemma

Streets of Sorrow 1952,N 18,37:4

Bolognesi, Gina

Milizia Territoriale 1936,Ap 6,18:2

Bolognini, Mauro (Director)

Wild Love; (Gli Inamorati) 1961,Ap 6,30:2
From a Roman Balcony 1961,O 16,33:5
Notte Brava, La 1962,Ja 25,25:2
Viaccia, La 1962,S 21,35:1
Bambole; Dolls, The (Monsignor Cupid);
  Monsignor Cupid (The Dolls) 1965,Je 29,26:1
Queens, The (Queen Elena); Queen Elena (The
  Queens) 1968,Mr 11,49:1
Oldest Profession, The (Roman Nights); Roman
  Nights (The Oldest Profession) 1968,N 8,42:1

Bolognini, Mauro (Producer)

Notte Brava, La 1962,Ja 25,25:2

Bolognini, Mauro (Screenwriter)

Wild Love; (GI! Inamorati) 1961,Ap 6,30:2

Bolotova, Zhanna

House I Live in, The 1959,Ap 20,34:2

Bolshakoff, Gregory

Christmas Slippers 1945,D 24,19:2

Bolshakova, Ira

Lonely White Sail 1938,My 7,18:1

Bolshintsov, M (Director)

Law of the Siberian Taiga 1930,Jl 28,22:1

Bolshintsov, M (Screenwriter)

Great Citizen, The 1939,Ja 16,11:2
Moscow Skies 1945,Ja 22,22:5

Bolshoi Ballet

Swan Lake 1960,Ja 26,25:2
Little Humpbacked Horse, The 1962,O 8,19:1

Bolshoi Opera Orchestra

Eugene Onegin 1959,S 14,33:1

Bolsrond, Michel (Director)

Mam'zelle Pigalle 1958,Ap 19,10:4
Parisienne, La 1958,Jl 31,27:1

Bolsrond, Michel (Screenwriter)

Mam'zelle Pigalle 1958,Ap 19,10:4
Parisienne, La 1958,Jl 31,27:1

Bolster, Anita

Saboteur 1942,My 8,27:2
Thin Man Goes Home, The 1945,Ja 26,16:5
My Name is Julia Ross 1945,N 9,16:3
Lost Weekend, The 1945,D 3,17:2
Two Mrs Carrolls, The 1947,Ap 7,20:1
Judge Steps Out, The 1949,Je 3,21:4
You Can't Beat the Irish 1952,My 1,34:4
Botany Bay 1953,O 30,27:2

Bolster, John Cowley

Rising of the Moon, The (The Majesty of the
  Law); Majesty of the Law, The (The Rising of
  the Moon) 1957,Jl 10,23:1

Bolt, Peter (Original Author)

Bride 68 1930,Ap 15,28:5

Bolt, Robert (Original Author)

Man for all Seasons, A 1966,D 13,60:1

Bolt, Robert (Screenwriter)

Lawrence of Arabia 1962,D 17,5:6
Doctor Zhivago 1965,D 23,21:1
Man for all Seasons, A 1966,D 13,60:1

Boltel, Jeanne

Champs-Elysees 1939,F 28,17:2
Inspector Maigret 1958,O 9,47:1

Boltini, Annamaria

Leopard, The 1963,Ag 13,25:1

Boltinoff, Murray (Original Author)

Buy Me That Town 1941,O 23,27:2

Bolton, A J Lieut Comdr (Screenwriter)

Marines Fly High, The 1940,Mr 5,19:2

Bolton, Betty

Jaws of Hell 1931,Ja 5,21:3
Wanted Men 1936,Jl 8,15:2

Bolton, Guy (Miscellaneous)

Ambassador Bill 1931,N 14,15:3

Bolton, Guy (Original Author)

Top Speed 1930,Ag 30,7:4
Transatlantic 1931,Jl 31,15:2
Delicious 1931,D 26,15:5
Girl Crazy 1932,Mr 25,23:3
Ladies Should Listen 1934,Jl 28,16:6
Murder Man, The 1935,Jl 27,16:2
Dark Angel, The 1935,S 6,12:2
Rosalie 1937,D 31,9:2
This'll Make You Whistle 1938,N 1,27:2
Girl Crazy 1943,D 3,27:2
Till the Clouds Roll By 1946,D 6,27:4
Words and Music 1948,D 10,34:2
Anything Goes 1956,Mr 22,38:1

Bolton, Guy (Screenwriter)

Grounds for Divorce 1925,Je 29,8:2
Love Doctor, The 1929,N 9,22:5
Ambassador Bill 1931,N 14,15:3
Morals of Marcus, The 1936,Ja 13,14:2
Mister Hobo 1936,F 8,19:2
Week-End at the Waldorf 1945,O 5,27:2
Anastasia 1956,D 14,35:6
Adorable Julia 1964,Ap 8,33:1

Bolton, Lois

One, Two, Three 1961,D 22,17:1

Bolton, Muriel Roy (Screenwriter)

My Name is Julia Ross 1945,N 9,16:3
Mickey 1948,Jl 19,11:2

Bolton, Whitney (Screenwriter)

Spirit of Culver 1939,Mr 9,18:1

Bolvary, Geza von (Director)

Wrecker, The 1929,Ag 13,23:2
Raub der Mona Lisa, Der; Theft of the Mona Lisa,
  The 1931,S 27,VIII,7:1
Was Frauen Traeumen; What Women Dream
  1933,Jl 2,IX,2:2
Ich Kenn' Dich Nicht und Liebe Dich; I Don't
  Know You, but I Love You 1935,N 18,20:1
Night of the Great Love, The 1937,O 1,19:5
Unwiderst Ehliche, Der; Irresistible Man, The
  1937,D 20,23:3
Abduction, The 1938,Je 11,9:2
Julika, Die 1939,D 23,9:1
Tiszavirag; Flower of the Tisza 1939,D 30,9:3
Spiegel des Lebens, Der; Life's Mirror
  1940,F 17,9:3
Maria Ilona 1940,Ap 20,14:3
Zigeunerweisen; Gypsy Ways 1940,My 11,15:3
Wiener Geschichten; Vienna Tales 1940,S 28,9:3
Opernball; Opera Ball 1940,O 15,29:2

Bolzoni, Adriano (Original Author)

Brief Rapture 1952,F 28,23:2
Cobra, The 1968,Mr 28,52:3

Bolzoni, Adriano (Screenwriter)

Slave, The 1963,My 30,20:1

Bomini, Letizia

Avvocato Difensore, L'; Attorney for the Defense,
  The 1935,N 13,25:4

Bommart, Jean (Original Author)

Continental Express 1942,Ap 7,26:3

Bonacci, Anna (Original Author)

Wife for a Night 1958,Je 12,35:2
Kiss Me, Stupid 1964,D 23,22:2

Bonafield, Jay (Miscellaneous)

Savage Splendor 1949,N 4,37:2
Below the Sahara 1953,S 2,20:1
Mysterians, The 1959,Jl 2,15:2

Bonafield, Jay (Producer)

Tattooed Stranger, The 1950,F 10,18:6
Africa Adventure 1954,S 29,23:4

Bonagura, Gianni

Fiasco in Milan 1963,Ap 11,29:2

Bonaius, James

Prince of Lovers, The 1927,N 29,31:1

Bonaki, Yoichi

Enjo 1964,S 23,54:1

Bonanova, Fortunio

Careless Lady 1932,Ap 18,19:2
Successful Calamity, A 1932,S 23,22:2
Desaparecido, El 1936,Je 2,25:3
Pedoroso Caballero 1936,O 26,20:2
Romance in the Dark 1938,Mr 21,18:2
Tropic Holiday 1938,Je 30,21:2
Inmaculada, La 1939,O 28,11:2
I Was an Adventuress 1940,My 20,13:2
That Night in Rio 1941,Mr 10,21:2
Citizen Kane 1941,My 2,25:1
Blood and Sand 1941,My 23,25:3
Moon Over Miami 1941,Jl 5,14:2
Yank in the R A F, A 1941,S 27,11:3
Mr and Mrs North 1942,Ja 22,13:2
Obliging Young Lady 1942,F 13,24:4
Larceny, Inc 1942,Ap 25,9:1
Sing Your Worries Away 1942,My 15,25:2
Girl Trouble 1942,O 8,31:2
Black Swan, The 1942,D 24,18:3
Five Graves to Cairo 1943,My 27,21:2
For Whom the Bell Tolls 1943,Jl 15,25:2
Ali Baba and the Forty Thieves 1944,Mr 16,17:3
Going my Way 1944,My 3,25:2
Double Indemnity 1944,S 7,21:1
Mrs Parkington 1944,O 13,16:1
Brazil 1944,N 20,25:2
Bell for Adano, A 1945,Jl 6,8:3
Man Alive 1945,N 17,14:5
Monsieur Beaucaire 1946,S 5,23:1
Fiesta 1947,Je 27,17:3
Fugitive, The 1947,D 26,22:2
Romance on the High Seas 1948,Je 26,10:5
Adventures of Don Juan 1948,D 25,10:1
Angel on the Amazon 1948,D 27,16:4
Whirlpool 1950,Ja 14,9:2
Nancy Goes to Rio 1950,Ap 7,22:2
September Affair 1951,F 2,19:2
Thunder Bay 1953,My 21,39:2
Moon Is Blue, The 1953,Jl 9,18:3
Second Chance 1953,Jl 23,20:2
So This Is Love 1953,Ag 12,22:1
Affair to Remember, An 1957,Jl 20,8:5
Thunder in the Sun 1959,Ap 9,37:2

Bonaparte, Napoleon

Scaramouche 1923,O 12,7:2 (Incorrect in this
  edition; use 1927,O 1,7:2 elsewhere)

Bonbon, Jacqueline

Eight and One Half 1963,Je 26,36:1

Boncompain, Claude (Original Author)

Bellman, The 1947,Ap 7,20:5

Bond, Anson (Original Author)

Journey Into Light 1951,O 5,24:4
Japanese War Bride 1952,Ja 30,22:6

Bond, Anson (Producer)

Not Wanted 1949,Jl 25,11:4
Journey Into Light 1951,O 5,24:4
Japanese War Bride 1952,Ja 30,22:6

Bond, Beulah

Rain 1932,O 13,22:3
Southerner, The 1945,Ag 27,22:3

Bond, Brenda

Fool, The 1925,Ap 13,24:1

Bond, David

That Lady in Ermine 1948,Ag 25,31:2
We Were Strangers 1949,Ap 28,28:2
Song of India 1949,Je 10,32:3
Sword of Monte Cristo, The 1951,Ap 23,21:2
Sirocco 1951,Je 14,31:2
Lust for Life 1956,S 18,39:1
Silencers, The 1966,Mr 17,35:1

Bond, Derek

Captive Heart, The 1947,Ap 28,27:2
Nicholas Nickleby 1947,D 1,27:2
Broken Journey 1949,My 26,34:3
Weaker Sex, The 1949,Jl 11,13:2
Christopher Columbus 1949,O 13,33:2

Bond, Derek— Cont

Inheritance, The 1951,F 12,19:2
Scott of the Antarctic 1951,F 26,20:2
Tony Draws a Horse 1951,My 15,38:6
Marry Me 1952,Mr 14,27:3
Hour of 13, The 1952,O 28,37:1
Caretaker's Daughter, The 1953,Ag 20,18:5
Svengali 1955,S 26,18:2
Trouble in Store 1956,Ja 14,13:2
Gideon of Scotland Yard 1959,My 20,38:2

Bond, Diane

In Like Flint 1967,Mr 16,53:2

Bond, Frank

Hogan's Alley 1925,N 24,28:4
Tell It to Sweeney 1927,O 17,20:2

Bond, Fred C

Samurai 1945,Ag 25,7:5

Bond, Gary

Zulu 1964,Jl 8,38:1

Bond, Jack (Director)

Separation 1968,Mr 26,41:2

Bond, Jack (Producer)

Separation 1968,Mr 26,41:2

Bond, Johnny

Gallant Bess 1946,D 6,27:6

Bond, Lillian

Just a Gigolo 1931,Je 13,20:4
Union Depot 1932,Ja 15,24:4
High Pressure 1932,F 1,22:3
Fireman, Save My Child 1932,F 18,25:3
Beauty and the Boss 1932,Ap 2,13:2
It's Tough to be Famous 1932,Ap 9,18:1
Trial of Vivienne Ware, The 1932,Ap 30,19:3
Man About Town 1932,My 28,18:2
Old Dark House, The 1932,O 28,22:4
Hot Saturday 1932,N 5,12:5
Air Mail 1932,N 7,20:3
Hot Pepper 1933,Ja 23,9:2
Pick Up 1933,Mr 25,13:4
When Strangers Marry 1933,My 25,24:3
Double Harness 1933,Jl 21,20:2
Big Brain, The 1933,Ag 5,9:5
Take a Chance 1933,N 27,20:3
Affairs of a Gentleman 1934,Je 23,16:7
China Seas 1935,Ag 10,16:4
Housekeeper's Daughter, The 1939,D 2,21:4
Sued for Libel 1940,Ja 19,15:3
Westerner, The 1940,O 25,25:2
Picture of Dorian Gray, The 1945,Mr 2,15:2
Maze, The 1953,Jl 11,8:2
Man in the Attic 1954,F 6,17:2
Pirates of Tripoli 1955,F 24,21:2

Bond, Raymond

Burning Cross, The 1948,F 20,19:1
Foreign Affair, A 1948,Jl 1,19:3
Canon City 1948,Jl 8,19:2
So Dear to my Heart 1949,Ja 31,14:2
State Department-File 649 1949,F 21,20:2
Special Agent 1949,Ag 22,13:1
Return of the Frontiersman 1950,Je 10,11:3
Outrage 1950,O 16,30:5
Man From Planet X, The 1951,Ap 9,31:2

Bond, Richard

Scoundrel, The 1935,My 3,23:2
Condemned Woman 1938,Ap 22,15:5
Law of the Underworld 1938,Ap 28,27:2
Broadway Musketeers 1938,O 14,27:1
Torchy Blane in Chinatown 1939,F 3,13:2
Here I Am a Stranger 1939,S 30,11:2
Devil's Island 1940,Jl 12,11:4

Bond, Rudy

With These Hands 1950,Je 16,28:4
Streetcar Named Desire, A 1951,S 30,27:1
Miss Sadie Thompson 1953,D 24,9:1
On the Waterfront 1954,Jl 29,18:1
Nightfall 1957,Ja 24,34:1
12 Angry Men 1957,Ap 15,24:1
Middle of the Night 1959,Je 18,36:1
Mountain Road, The 1960,Je 30,22:3

Bond, Sadie

Tiger Makes Out, The 1967,S 19,53:1

Bond, Sheila

Marrying Kind, The 1952,Mr 14,27:1

Bond, Shirley

Virtue 1932,O 25,24:5

Bond, Sidenie

Darling 1965,Ag 4,20:1

Bond, Sudie

Guns of the Trees 1964,F 29,12:2
Andy 1965,Ja 22,21:2

Bond, Tommy

Kid Millions 1934,N 12,17:2
Hideaway 1937,S 25,10:2
City Streets 1938,Jl 25,18:2
Little Bit of Heaven, A 1940,N 8,24:2
Adventure in Washington 1941,Ag 1,11:3
Man From Frisco 1944,Je 16,14:7
Call Me Mister 1951,F 1,21:2

Bond, Ward

Big Trail, The 1930,O 25,20:3
White Eagle 1932,S 24,18:4
Rackety Rax 1932,N 5,12:5
Obey the Law 1933,Mr 13,18:3
When Strangers Marry 1933,My 25,24:3

Wrecker, The 1933,Ag 7,18:3
Frontier Marshal 1934,Ja 31,20:3
Whirlpool 1934,My 5,22:3
Broadway Bill 1934,N 30,22:2
Devil Dogs of the Air 1935,F 7,23:2
Black Fury 1935,Ap 11,27:2
Little Big Shot 1935,O 7,11:2
Muss 'Em Up 1936,F 3,21:2
Leathernecks Have Landed, The 1936,Mr 23,22:5
Pride of the Marines 1936,Ap 27,19:2
Crash Donovan 1936,Ag 10,10:3
Man Who Lived Twice, The 1936,O 12,23:2
Legion of Terror 1936,N 2,24:2
Without Orders 1936,N 4,41:3
Conflict 1937,Ja 18,21:2
You Only Live Once 1937,F 1,15:2
Devil's Playground 1937,F 15,12:5
Night Key 1937,Ap 19,27:2
23 1/2 Hours Leave 1937,My 17,23:2
Fight to the Finish, A 1937,Je 26,20:2 (In Addenda)
Dead End 1937,Ag 25,25:1
Over the Wall 1938,Mr 28,19:2
Mr Moto's Gamble 1938,Ap 8,17:2
Hawaii Calls 1938,Ap 29,17:2
Gun Law 1938,Je 24,15:1
Reformatory 1938,Je 27,13:6
Prison Break 1938,Jl 13,17:4
Professor Beware 1938,Jl 14,17:1
Submarine Patrol 1938,N 19,9:2
Law West of Tombstone, The 1938,N 25,19:1
They Made Me a Criminal 1939,Ja 21,19:2
Made for Each Other 1939,F 17,17:2
Oklahoma Kid, The 1939,Mr 11,21:1
Dodge City 1939,Ap 8,19:1
Return of the Cisco Kid, The 1939,Ap 29,13:2
Kid From Kokomo, The 1939,My 20,11:2
Young Mr Lincoln 1939,Je 3,11:2
Girl From Mexico, The 1939,Je 8,31:4
Waterfront 1939,Jl 17,10:2
Frontier Marshal 1939,Jl 29,18:2
Drums Along the Mohawk 1939,N 4,11:2
Gone With the Wind 1939,D 20,31:2
Cisco Kid and the Lady, The 1939,D 25,29:2
Grapes of Wrath, The 1940,Ja 25,17:2
Little Old New York 1940,F 3,9:2
Mortal Storm, The 1940,Je 21,25:2
Long Voyage Home, The 1940,O 9,30:2 (In Addenda)
Kit Carson 1940,N 15,25:3
Tobacco Road 1941,F 21,16:2
Man Betrayed, A 1941,Mr 27,29:5
Sergeant York 1941,Jl 3,15:1
Manpower 1941,Jl 5,14:2
Shepherd of the Hills, The 1941,Jl 31,13:2
Maltese Falcon, The 1941,O 4,18:2
Swamp Water 1941,N 17,15:2
Wild Bill Hickok Rides 1942,F 7,13:5
Falcon takes Over, The 1942,My 30,9:2
Ten Gentlemen From West Point 1942,Je 5,23:3
Sin Town 1942,O 17,11:2
Gentleman Jim 1942,N 26,40:3
Hello, Frisco, Hello 1943,Mr 25,25:1
Hitler-Dead or Alive 1943,Mr 31,23:3
Slightly Dangerous 1943,Ap 2,17:2
They Came to Blow up America 1943,My 15,13:2
Guy Named Joe, A 1943,D 24,17:2
Sullivans, The 1944,F 10,19:2
Home in Indiana 1944,Je 22,23:1
Tall in the Saddle 1944,D 15,25:3
Dakota 1945,D 17,17:2
They Were Expendable 1945,D 21,25:2
Canyon Passage 1946,Ag 8,18:2
My Darling Clementine 1946,D 4,44:5
It's a Wonderful Life 1946,D 23,19:2
Unconquered 1947,O 11,11:2
Fugitive, The 1947,D 26,22:2
Time of your Life, The 1948,My 27,29:2
Fort Apache 1948,Je 25,26:2
Tap Roots 1948,Ag 26,16:3
Joan of Arc 1948,N 12,30:5
Three Godfathers 1949,Mr 4,25:2
Riding High 1950,Ap 11,26:2
Singing Guns 1950,Je 5,19:3
Wagonmaster 1950,Je 19,17:2
Kiss Tomorrow Goodbye 1950,Ag 5,9:2
Operation Pacific 1951,F 3,10:2
Great Missouri Raid, The 1951,Ap 9,31:2
Only the Valiant 1951,Ap 14,9:6
On Dangerous Ground 1952,F 13,35:2
Quiet Man, The 1952,Ag 22,13:1
Thunderbirds 1953,Mr 12,24:4
Moonlighter, The 1953,S 23,37:2
Blowing Wild 1953,O 8,37:5
Hondo 1953,N 27,99:9
Johnny Guitar 1954,My 28,19:2
Bob Mathias Story, The 1954,O 16,14:6
Long Gray Line, The 1955,F 11,19:2
Mister Roberts 1955,Jl 15,14:1
Searchers, The 1956,My 31,21:4
Pillars of the Sky 1956,O 13,15:2
Dakota Incident 1956,N 10,14:2

Bond, Ward— Cont

Wings of Eagles, The 1957,F 1,28:1
China Doll 1958,D 4,52:1
Rio Bravo 1959,Mr 19,40:2

Bondarchuk, Sergei

Young Guard 1949,D 26,33:6
Dream of a Cossack 1952,F 18,15:2
Taras Shevchenko 1952,Jl 28,12:6
Grasshopper, The 1956,Ap 23,22:1
Othello 1960,My 16,39:1
Fate of Man 1961,Jl 11,28:1
Summer to Remember, A; (Seryozha) 1961,N 7,38:1
War and Peace 1968,Ap 29,50:5

Bondarchuk, Sergei (Director)

Fate of Man 1961,Jl 11,28:1
War and Peace 1967,O 24,27:1
War and Peace 1968,Ap 29,50:5

Bondarchuk, Sergei (Producer)

Fate of Man 1961,Jl 11,28:1

Bondarchuk, Sergei (Screenwriter)

War and Peace 1968,Ap 29,50:5

Bondarev, Yuri (Original Author)

Stillness 1964,Ja 28,25:1 (In Addenda)

Bondi, Beulah

Street Scene 1931,Ag 27,22:5
Arrowsmith 1931,D 8,36:4
Stranger's Return, The 1933,Jl 28,18:2
Christopher Bean 1933,N 25,10:2
Finishing School 1934,Ap 30,11:4
Good Fairy, The 1935,F 1,18:1
Bad Boy 1935,O 28,16:3
Invisible Ray, The 1936,Ja 11,9:3
Trail of the Lonesome Pine, The 1936,F 20,23:5
Moon's our Home, The 1936,My 13,29:2
Case Against Mrs Ames, The 1936,My 28,19:2
Gorgeous Hussy, The 1936,S 5,7:1
Maid of Salem 1937,Mr 4,27:2
Make Way for Tomorrow 1937,My 10,23:1
Buccaneer, The 1938,F 17,17:2
Of Human Hearts 1938,F 18,23:1
Vivacious Lady 1938,Je 3,17:3
Sisters, The 1938,O 15,21:3
On Borrowed Time 1939,Jl 7,13:2
Under-Pup, The 1939,S 5,21:2
Mr Smith Goes to Washington 1939,O 20,27:2
Remember the Night 1940,Ja 18,27:2
Our Town 1940,Je 14,25:3
Penny Serenade 1941,My 23,25:2
Shepherd of the Hills, The 1941,Jl 31,13:2
One Foot in Heaven 1941,N 14,28:3
Tonight We Raid Calais 1943,Ap 15,20:2
Watch on the Rhine 1943,Ag 28,15:1
Our Hearts Were Young and Gay 1944,O 12,24:2
I Love a Soldier 1944,N 2,22:2
Very Thought of You, The 1944,N 18,16:7
And Now Tomorrow 1944,N 23,38:2
Back to Bataan 1945,S 13,26:3
Breakfast in Hollywood 1946,Jl 15,21:1
Sister Kenny 1946,S 30,21:2
It's a Wonderful Life 1946,D 23,19:2
Sainted Sisters, The 1948,My 20,35:2
Snake Pit, the 1948,N 5,29:2
So Dear to my Heart 1949,Ja 31,14:2
Life of Riley, The 1949,Ap 18,18:4
Black Book, The 1949,O 17,18:2
Baron of Arizona, The 1950,Je 23,29:2
Furies, The 1950,Ag 17,23:2
Lone Star 1952,F 2,11:4
Latin Lovers 1953,Ag 13,17:2
Track of the Cat 1954,D 2,38:2
Back From Eternity 1956,S 8,20:6
Unholy Wife, The 1958,Mr 7,17:1
Big Fisherman, The 1959,Ag 6,18:1
Summer Place, A 1959,O 23,24:1
Tammy Tell me True 1961,Jl 27,23:2
Tammy and the Doctor 1963,Je 27,23:2

Bondin, I (Screenwriter)

No Greater Love 1944,F 25,23:3

Bondinella, Giacomo

Escape into Dreams 1950,Ap 13,34:5

Bondire

Living Image, The 1928,Je 4,13:2

Bondireff, A

Hurrah I'm Alive 1930,Je 16,25:3

Bondwin, Billy

Which Shall It Be? 1924,Ap 7,15:3

Bondy, A

Return of Maxim, The 1937,N 2,33:1

Bonell:, Richard

There's Magic in Music 1941,Je 5,27:2

Bonello, Samuel

Strictly Dishonorable 1931,N 11,27:1

Bonerz, Peter

Funnyman 1967,S 25,56:3

Bonerz, Peter (Screenwriter)

Funnyman 1967,S 25,56:3

Bonestall, Chesley (Original Author)

Conquest of Space 1955,My 28,7:6

Bonet, Nai

John Goldfarb, Please Come Home 1965,Mr 25,42:4
Spy With a Cold Nose, The 1966,D 20,58:2

Bonett, Emery (Original Author)
Girl Must Live, A 1942,Mr 24,25:2
Bonfatti, Liliana
Three Girls From Rome 1953,O 14,34:2
Bongini, Rafael
Humming Bird, The 1924,Ja 14,2:1
Sainted Devil, A 1924,N 24,15:3
Amore e Morte; (Love and Death) 1932,O 4,26:4
Bongioanni, Gianni
Wild Eye, The 1968,Ag 22,47:1
Bonham, Frank (Original Author)
Stage to Tucson 1951,My 5,14:2
Bonheur, Gaston (Original Author)
Lady Chatterley's Lover 1959,Jl 11,11:1
Bonheur, Irene
Wicked Duchess, The 1949,N 5,10:5
Bonheur, Stella
Roman Spring of Mrs Stone, The 1961,D 29,11:1
Boni, Carmen
Jolly Peasant, The 1929,Jl 1,31:2
Richiamo del Cuore, Il; Appeal of the Heart, The 1931,Mr 2,19:1
Man to Men 1949,F 21,20:2
Boni, Franca
Summerskin 1962,My 29,22:2
Boni, Louisa
Land of the Pharaohs 1955,Jl 27,15:2
Bonicelli, Vittorio (Screenwriter)
Barbarella 1968,O 12,43:1
Boniface, Symona
Girls' Dormitory 1936,Ag 29,16:2
Bonifas, Paul
Champagne Charlie 1948,Ag 7,8:2
Lisbon Story, The 1951,S 6,39:4
Pardon my French 1952,Mr 31,17:2
Green Glove, The 1952,Ap 24,38:1
Amazing Monsieur Fabre, The 1952,S 9,21:2
Charade 1963,D 6,40:1
Abysses, Les 1964,N 24,44:1
Train, The 1965,Mr 18,25:1
Bonifassy, Luce
10th Victim, The 1965,D 21,46:1
Bonillas, Myrta
Claw, The 1927,My 11,28:3
Gingham Girl, The 1927,Jl 19,27:2
Lummox 1930,Mr 24,25:1
Bonin, Sharon
Nobody Waved Goodbye 1964,S 17,52:1
Boniscolli, Franco
Traviata, La 1968,F 28,43:2
Bonja, H (Screenwriter)
Tkies Khaf; (Vow, The) 1938,S 15,29:3
Bonn, Ferdinand
Strauss, The Waltz King 1929,Jl 22,17:1
Bonn, Walter
International Crime 1938,My 16,14:4
Bonnard, Mario (Director)
Fra Diavolo 1931,N 23,22:1
Sohn der Weissen Berge, Der 1933,O 23,18:3
Marcia Nuziale, La 1936,F 27,23:2
Milizia Territoriale 1936,Ap 6,18:2
Amore che Canta, L' 1937,Mr 31,28:7
Trenta Secondi di Amore 1937,Ap 5,17:3
Albero di Adamo, L'; Adam's Tree 1938,Ja 20,19:2
Kampf ums Matterhorn 1938,Ap 18,11:2
Frenesia; Frenzy 1940,Je 6,33:4
Conte di Brechard, Il; Count of Brechard, The 1940,O 24,31:3
King's Jester, The 1947,Je 26,19:3
Marco Visconti 1947,S 20,12:4
Rossini 1948,Ja 31,14:2
Peddler and the Lady, The 1949,S 30,28:4
Margaret of Cortona 1957,Ja 21,20:4
Last Days of Pompeii, The 1960,Ag 11,19:1
Bonnard, Mario (Producer)
Theatre 1929,Ag 25,VIII,5:1
Bonnard, Mario (Screenwriter)
Rossini 1948,Ja 31,14:2
Margaret of Cortona 1957,Ja 21,20:4
Bonnefoux, Mme
Marriage of Figaro, The 1963,Ap 30,26:1
Bonnell, Lee
Lady Scarface 1941,Ag 4,16:6
Look Who's Laughing 1941,Jl 25,33:2
Army Surgeon 1942,N 5,35:2
Navy Comes Through, The 1942,N 12,30:3
Criminal Court 1946,N 16,15:3
San Quentin 1947,F 10,24:3
Bonnelli, Richard
Enter Madame 1935,Ja 12,12:1
Bonner, Charles (Original Author)
Adam Had Four Sons 1941,Mr 28,26:6
Bonner, Geraldine (Original Author)
Sham 1921,My 6,20:2
Bonner, Isabel
Shrike, The 1955,Jl 8,15:2
Bonner, Marjorie
Reno 1924,Ja 8,27:1
Daughters of Today 1924,Mr 4,17:1
Ancient Highway, The 1925,N 11,27:3

Bonner, Priscilla
Honest Hutch 1920,S 26,VI,2:1 (In Addenda)
Tarnish 1924,O 13,21:1
Charley's Aunt 1925,F 9,15:3
Proud Flesh 1925,Ap 14,26:1
Drusilla With a Million 1925,My 25,21:3
Strong Man, The 1926,S 7,44:2
Long Pants 1927,Mr 29,23:2
Prince of Head-Waiters 1927,Jl 11,23:5
Bonnet, Theodore (Original Author)
Mudlark, The 1950,D 25,25:1
Bonney, John
Paranoiac 1963,My 23,31:2
Bonnon, John
Inspector Clouseau 1968,Jl 25,26:1
Bonnucci, Albert
Neapolitan Carousel 1961,O 12,41:3
Bonomo, Joe
Flaming Frontier, The 1926,Ap 5,24:1
You Never Know Women 1926,Jl 27,15:5
Noah's Ark 1929,Mr 13,28:6
Sign of the Cross, The 1932,D 1,25:1
Bonomyong, Pridi (Producer)
King of the White Elephant, The 1941,Ap 5,12:7
Bonomyong, Pridi (Screenwriter)
King of the White Elephant, The 1941,Ap 5,12:7
Bononova, Fortunio
Where Do We Go From Here? 1945,Je 7,25:2
Bonora, N Maria
Vecchia Signora, La 1932,D 10,19:3
Bonsels, Waldemar (Director)
Adventures of Maya, The 1929,Ap 23,27:1
Bonsels, Waldemar (Original Author)
Adventures of Maya, The 1929,Ap 23,27:1
Bonucci, Alberto
Blood and Roses 1961,O 12,41:4
Love and Larceny 1963,F 2,5:6
Little Nuns, The 1966,Ap 28,49:1
Taming of the Shrew, The 1967,Mr 9,43:1
Bonucci, Alberto (Director)
Of Wayward Love (The Soldier); Soldier, The (Of Wayward Love) 1964,Mr 24,29:1
Of Wayward Love (The Serpent); Serpent, The (Of Wayward Love) 1964,Mr 24,29:1
Of Wayward Love (The Women); Women, The (Of Wayward Love) 1964,Mr 24,29:1
Bonzi, Leonardo
Green Magic 1955,My 17,32:1
Bonzi, Leonardo (Director)
Lost Continent 1957,Mr 12,38:1
Bonzi, Leonardo (Producer)
Lost Continent 1957,Mr 12,38:1
Behind the Great Wall 1959,D 10,51:6
Bonzo
Bedtime for Bonzo 1951,Ap 6,31:4
Boo, Sigrid (Original Author)
Servants' Entrance 1934,S 27,25:2
Boodkin, Celia
Go, Man, Go 1954,Mr 10,29:5
Book-Asta, George
Night Bird, The 1928,O 2,23:5
Hell Harbor 1930,Mr 28,22:6
Booke, Sorrell
Gone are the Days! 1963,S 24,43:2
Black Like Me 1964,My 21,42:1
Fail Safe 1964,S 16,36:1
Joy House 1965,F 18,29:1
Up the Down Staircase 1967,Ag 18,36:2
Bye Bye Braverman 1968,F 22,36:1
Booker, Beulah
Saphead, The 1921,F 14,12:2
Bookholt, Henry
Confessions of Felix Krull, The 1958,Mr 5,38:1
Boolsen, Bjorn
Red Meadows 1950,Ja 19,35:2
Boon, Eric
Champagne Charlie 1948,Ag 7,8:2
Boon, Robert
Tanks are Coming, The 1951,D 6,42:4
Affair in Trinidad 1952,Jl 31,14:2
Last Blitzkrieg, The 1959,Ja 31,13:5
Boone, Bernice (Original Author)
Letter of Introduction 1938,S 1,17:1
Boone, Pat
Bernardine 1957,Jl 25,28:1
April Love 1957,N 28,57:2
Mardi Gras 1958,N 19,45:2
Journey to the Center of the Earth 1959,D 17,51:1
All Hands on Deck 1961,Ap 1,10:2
State Fair 1962,Ap 12,41:4
Yellow Canary, The 1963,My 16,42:1
Main Attraction, The 1963,Je 27,23:3
Goodbye, Charlie 1964,N 19,49:1
Greatest Story Ever Told, The 1965,F 16,40:2
Perils of Pauline, The 1967,Ag 3,26:3
Boone, Richard
Halls of Montezuma, The 1951,Ja 6,9:6
Call Me Mister 1951,F 1,21:2
Desert Fox, The 1951,O 18,32:1
Return of the Texan 1952,F 14,23:1
Smoke Jumpers 1952,Mr 22,9:6
Kangaroo 1952,My 17,22:7

Boone, Richard — Cont
Way of a Gaucho 1952,N 5,36:2
Man on a Tightrope 1953,Je 5,19:1
Vickie 1953,S 8,26:3
Robe, The 1953,S 17,32:6
City of Bad Men 1953,O 21,37:6
Beneath the 12-Mile Reef 1953,D 17,52:2
Siege at Red River, The 1954,Ap 3,19:2
Dragnet 1954,Ag 21,10:2
Raid, The 1954,Ag 21,10:4
Man Without a Star 1955,Mr 25,19:3
Away all Boats 1956,Ag 17,14:2
Lizzie 1957,Ap 5,24:2
Garment Jungle, The 1957,My 16,28:2
Alamo, The 1960,O 27,45:1
Thunder of Drums, A 1961,S 27,35:1
Rio Conchos 1964,O 29,38:1
War Lord, The 1965,N 18,55:2
Hombre 1967,Mr 22,41:1
Boorman, John (Director)
Having a Wild Weekend 1965,Ag 19,35:1
Point Blank 1967,S 19,53:1
Booth, Adrian
Plunders, The 1948,N 1,28:2
Last Bandit, The 1949,Mr 21,19:2
Brimstone 1949,O 7,35:3
Rock Island Trail 1950,Je 5,19:3
Oh! Susanna 1951,Mr 30,28:5
Booth, Anthony
Risk, The 1961,S 25,41:2
Of Human Bondage 1964,S 24,46:2
Booth, Bill
Follow Me, Boys! 1966,D 2,46:1
Booth, Carol
Love-Ins, The 1967,Ag 19,16:1
Booth, Charles G (Original Author)
General Died at Dawn, The 1936,S 3,17:2
Magnificent Fraud, The 1939,Jl 20,16:2
Booth, Charles G (Screenwriter)
House on Ninety-Second Street, The 1945,S 27,24:7
Behind Green Lights 1946,F 16,10:2
Fury at Furnace Creek 1948,Jl 12,11:2
Booth, Edwina
Trader Horn 1931,F 4,21:3
Midnight Patrol, The 1932,My 7,11:5
Booth, Ernest (Original Author)
Ladies of the Mob 1928,Je 18,13:2
Ladies of the Big House 1932,Ja 1,31:1
Women Without Names 1940,My 9,26:4
Booth, Harry (Director)
King's Story, A 1967,My 25,57:2
Booth, Helen
Family Way, The 1967,Je 29,32:1
Booth, James
Trials of Oscar Wilde, The 1960,Je 28,26:1
Hellions, The 1962,Mr 15,28:2
Sparrows Don't Sing 1963,My 7,46:2
Zulu 1964,Jl 8,38:1
Secret of my Success, The 1965,N 4,57:2
90 Degrees in the Shade 1966,N 16,52:1
Robbery 1967,S 28,58:2
Bliss of Mrs Blossom, The 1968,D 12,62:6
Booth, John Hunter (Miscellaneous)
Masquerader, The 1922,Ag 14,12:4
Booth, John Hunter (Screenwriter)
Masquerader, The 1933,S 4,9:5
Booth, Jolyan
Georgy Girl 1966,O 18,48:1
Booth, Karin
Unfinished Dance, The 1947,O 31,29:2
Big City 1948,My 17,23:3
My Foolish Heart 1950,Ja 20,29:2
Cariboo Trail, The 1950,S 1,17:2
Last of the Buccaneers 1950,D 15,43:2
African Manhunt 1957,Ap 20,21:4
Beloved Infidel 1959,N 18,46:1
Booth, Katharine
Holiday Inn 1942,Ag 5,16:1
Swing Shift Maisie 1943,S 10,29:2
Booth, Mary
Girls of the Road 1940,Jl 22,20:2
Booth, Shirley
Come Back, Little Sheba 1952,D 24,13:2 (In Addenda)
Main Street to Broadway 1953,O 14,34:1
About Mrs Leslie 1954,Je 28,16:2
Matchmaker, The 1958,Ag 13,22:1
Hot Spell 1958,S 18,37:2
Booth, Webster
Robber Symphony 1937,Ja 27,17:2
Waltz Time 1946,F 11,25:2
Laughing Lady, The 1950,Ja 23,16:3
Boothby, Valerie
Namensheirat 1933,Ja 9,23:1
Voce del Sangue, La 1933,Ap 17,16:4
Boothe, Clare (Original Author)
Women, The 1939,S 22,27:2
Kiss the Boys Goodbye 1941,Ag 14,21:2
Margin for Error 1943,Ja 25,10:7
Opposite Sex, The 1956,N 16,23:2
Boothroyd, Derrick (Original Author)
Value for Money 1957,Ag 1,20:4

Boothroyd, J B (Screenwriter)
Reluctant Widow, The 1951,S 8,8:6
Borashvill, Mkho
Stepchildren 1962,Jl 2,22:2
Boratto, Caterina
Vivere; To Live 1938,N 15,27:2
Chi e'piu felice di me?; Who Is Happier Than I 1940,F 6,17:5
Peddler and the Lady, The 1949,S 30,28:4
Measure for Measure 1951,D 8,9:2
Eight and One Half 1963,Je 26,36:1
Juliet of the Spirits 1965,N 4,57:1
Tiger and the Pussycat, The 1967,S 21,56:4
Borboni, Paola
Ho Perduto mio Marito; I Have Lost My Husband 1939,O 20,27:4
Lo Smemorato 1940,F 20,17:4
Merry Chase, The 1948,S 18,11:4
Roman Holiday 1953,Ag 28,13:1
His Last Twelve Hours 1953,N 13,24:7
Borchard, Adolphe (Composer)
Story of a Cheat, The 1938,S 27,25:2
Champs-Elysees 1939,F 28,17:2
Ultimatum 1940,F 5,13:2
Nine Bachelors 1942,F 9,19:2
Borchers, Cornell
Big Lift, The 1950,Ap 27,37:2
Divided Heart, The 1955,Ag 4,16:1
Never Say Goodbye 1956,Ap 14,20:1
Istanbul 1957,Ja 24,34:1
Oasis 1960,Jl 7,26:1
Borchert, Ernst
Murderers Among Us 1948,Ag 17,19:6
Borcosque, Carlos (Director)
Dos Noches 1933,Jl 29,14:3
Alas de mi Patria; My Country's Wingo 1940,Je 4,19:4
Borden
Ways of Love (A Day in the Country); Day in the Country, A (Ways of Love) 1950,D 13,50:2
Borden, Cleo Louise
Woman Commands, A 1932,Ja 28,13:2
Borden, Eddie
Battling Butler 1926,Ag 23,9:1
Dove, The 1928,Ja 3,28:2
Rough Romance 1930,Je 16,25:3
Jungle Bride 1933,My 13,16:3
Conflict 1937,Ja 18,21:2
Give Me a Sailor 1938,Ag 11,31:1
Chump at Oxford, A 1940,F 20,17:3
Borden, Ethel (Screenwriter)
Woman I Love, The 1937,Ap 16,27:2
Borden, Eugene
Gentlemen Prefer Blondes 1928,Ja 16,24:1
Hold Your Man 1929,O 14,20:2
Charlie Chan on Broadway 1937,S 20,19:1
Mark of Zorro, The 1940,N 4,23:2
Scotland Yard 1941,Ap 9,33:3
Thrill of Brazil, The 1946,S 6,18:3
So Dark the Night 1946,D 7,16:2
Return of Monte Cristo, The 1947,Ja 3,16:4
Jewels of Brandenburg 1947,My 24,10:5
Saigon 1948,Ap 1,30:5
Last of the Buccaneers 1950,D 15,43:2
American in Paris, An 1951,O 5,24:2
Happy Time, The 1952,O 31,30:2
Far Country, The 1955,F 14,24:2
Perfect Furlough, The 1959,Ja 22,27:4
Borden, Olive
Happy Warrior, The 1925,Jl 7,24:2
Yankee Senor, The 1926,Ja 28,14:4
My Own Pal 1926,Mr 15,18:3
Monkey Talks, The 1927,Ap 5,30:7
Secret Studio, The 1927,Je 15,31:4
Joy Girl, The 1927,S 6,34:3
Pajamas 1927,N 7,26:4
Come to My House 1928,Ja 16,24:1
Sinners in Love 1928,N 19,16:7
Gang War 1928,N 19,16:7
Half Marriage 1929,Ag 19,22:1
Dance Hall 1929,D 16,34:2
Wedding Rings 1930,My 10,25:3
Social Lion, The 1930,Je 14,9:4
Borderie, R (Producer)
Au Grand Balcon 1951,My 5,14:2
Bordey, Pierre
Broken Wings, The 1968,Mr 16,34:1
Bordoff, Trudy
Harvey Middleman, Fireman 1965,Jl 13,39:1
Bordon, Eugene
Dark Waters 1944,N 22,25:2
Bordoni, Irene
Paris 1929,N 8,31:2
Show of Shows 1929,N 21,24:5
Louisiana Purchase 1942,Ja 1,37:1
Bordy, Bella
Piros Bugyellaris; Red Purse 1939,Mr 11,21:2
Uz Bence 1940,Ja 15,11:2
Borei, Fernando
Mujeres que Trabajan; Women Who Work 1940,Ja 1,29:4

Borel, Jacques
Ways of Love (A Day in the Country); Day in the Country, A (Ways of Love) 1950,D 13,50:2
Borel-Clerc (Composer)
Man of the Hour, The 1940,N 21,43:2
Borell, Louis
Head Over Heels in Love 1937,F 13,9:1
Paris After Dark 1943,O 23,11:1
Night of Adventure, A 1944,Je 3,10:4
Borelli, Charles
Regina di Sparta, La 1931,F 23,20:3
Petits, Les 1936,D 30,17:2
Never Take No for an Answer 1952,Ap 29,32:2
Borene, Jackie
Once in a Blue Moon 1936,D 2,35:1
Boreo, Emile
Lady Vanishes, The 1938,D 26,29:1
Carnegie Hall 1947,My 3,10:2
Boretz, Allen (Miscellaneous)
Princess and the Pirate, The 1945,F 10,16:2
Boretz, Allen (Original Author)
Room Service 1938,S 22,27:1
Step Lively 1944,Jl 27,14:1
It Had to be You 1947,D 8,35:2
Girl from Jones Beach, The 1949,Jl 30,9:2
Boretz, Allen (Screenwriter)
It Ain't Hay 1943,Mr 11,17:3
Up in Arms 1944,Mr 3,19:2
Bathing Beauty 1944,Je 28,20:1
Copacabana 1947,Jl 12,7:2
Where There's Life 1947,D 25,32:1
My Girl Tisa 1948,F 21,9:2
Two Guys From Texas 1948,Ag 28,8:6
Borg, Ariane
Charrette Fantome, La 1940,My 28,29:2
Borg, Sven Hugo
Mystery Sea Raider 1940,Ag 26,11:4
Borg, Veda Ann
Three Cheers for Love 1936,Ag 1,16:2
Kid Galahad 1937,My 27,21:3
Singing Marine, The 1937,Jl 1,33:2
San Quentin 1937,Ag 4,15:2
Confession 1937,Ag 19,23:1
It's Love I'm After 1937,N 11,31:2
Submarine D-1 1937,D 30,15:4
She Loved a Fireman 1938,Ja 21,15:3
Over the Wall 1938,Mr 28,19:2
Behind the News 1941,Ja 16,25:3
Penalty, The 1941,Ap 10,29:3
Pittsburgh Kid, The 1941,S 23,27:4
Honky Tonk 1941,O 3,27:3
Corsican Brothers, The 1942,Ja 16,25:4
Two Yanks in Trinidad 1942,Ap 6,19:4
Something to Shout About 1943,Ap 8,27:3
Murder in Times Square 1943,My 31,13:2
Standing Room Only 1944,F 23,17:2
Big Noise, The 1944,S 23,16:1
Irish Eyes Are Smiling 1944,N 8,27:1
Falcon in Hollywood, The 1944,D 9,21:2
Rough, Tough and Ready 1945,Mr 24,22:7
Don Juan Quilligan 1945,Jl 30,16:2
Love, Honor and Goodbye 1945,S 8,12:2
Avalanche 1946,Jl 8,25:2
Bachelor and the Bobby-Soxer, The 1947,Jl 25,12:5
Mother Wore Tights 1947,Ag 21,33:2
Blonde Savage 1947,O 4,9:2
Julia Misbehaves 1948,O 8,30:2
Chicken every Sunday 1949,Ja 19,34:2
One Last Fling 1949,Jl 1,14:6
Aaron Slick From Punkin Crick 1952,Ap 19,18:6
Big Jim McLain 1952,S 18,35:2
Mister Scoutmaster 1953,Ag 29,10:1
Three Sailors and a Girl 1953,N 23,32:2
You're Never too Young 1955,Ag 26,10:2
Guys and Dolls 1955,N 5,26:1
Alamo, The 1960,O 27,45:1
Borgato, Agostino
Kiss in a Taxi, A 1927,Mr 15,29:2
Fashions For Women 1927,Mr 28,26:4
Hula 1927,Ag 29,21:1
Magic Flame, The 1927,S 19,30:3
Coffin Maker, The 1928,O 9,35:1
She Goes to War 1929,Je 10,23:1
Romance of Rio Grande 1929,N 9,22:5
Hot for Paris 1930,Ja 4,21:1
Behind the Makeup 1930,Ja 18,21:1
Redemption 1930,My 3,23:1
Maltese Falcon, The 1931,My 29,26:5
Transgression 1931,Je 15,23:3
Bird of Paradise 1932,S 10,18:5
Borgato, Emilio
Private Life of Helen of Troy, The 1927,D 10,14:7
Borge, Victor
Higher and Higher 1944,Ja 22,8:4
Borges, Graciela
Summerskin 1962,My 29,22:2
Terrace, The 1964,N 25,45:1
Borghese, Viglione
Mill on the Po, The 1951,O 23,35:2
Streets of Sorrow 1952,N 18,37:4

Borghi, Emilia
Before the Revolution; Prima della Revolutiona 1964,S 25,32:1
Borghi, Mario (Producer)
Tombolo 1949,D 31,9:4
Angelo in the Crowd 1952,O 4,15:2
Borgnine, Ernest
Whistle at Eaton Falls, The 1951,O 11,49:2
Mob, The 1951,O 18,32:2
Vikings, The 1958,Je 12,35:2
Stranger Wore a Gun, The 1953,Jl 30,20:3
From Here to Eternity 1953,Ag 6,16:2
Johnny Guitar 1954,My 28,19:2
Demetrius and the Gladiators 1954,Je 19,9:1
Vera Cruz 1954,D 27,22:4
Bad Day at Black Rock 1955,F 2,22:2
Marty 1955,Ap 12,25:3
Run for Cover 1955,Ap 30,10:6
Violent Saturday 1955,My 12,32:2
Square Jungle, The 1955,D 31,17:2
Jubal 1956,Ap 25,39:1
Catered Affair, The 1956,Je 15,32:4
Best Things in Life are Free, The 1956,S 29,12:2
Three Brave Men 1957,Mr 16,13:2
Badlanders, The 1958,S 4,33:1
Torpedo Run 1958,O 25,16:2
Rabbit Trap, The 1959,O 15,48:1
Man on a String 1960,My 21,15:1
Pay or Die 1960,My 27,22:2
Go Naked in the World 1961,Mr 11,15:1
Barabbas 1962,O 11,49:1
McHale's Navy 1964,Jl 11,15:2
Flight of the Phoenix, The 1966,F 1,26:1
Oscar, The 1966,Mr 5,16:1
Dirty Dozen, The 1967,Je 16,36:1
Chuka 1967,N 2,58:3
Legend of Lylah Clare, The 1968,Ag 23,33:1
Split, The 1968,N 5,55:2
Ice Station Zebra 1968,D 21,49:1
Borgstroem, Hilda
Familjen Andersson; Anderson Family, The 1939,Ja 24,16:5
Du Gamla, Du Fria; Thou old, Tho Free 1939,Mr 21,27:2
Borgstrom, Enrico
Gold of Naples (The Gambler); Gambler, The (Gold of Naples) 1957,F 12,30:1
Borgstrom, Hilda
Stroke of Midnight, The 1922,Je 5,16:2
John Ericsson Victor of Hampton Roads 1938,My 18,17:2
Sunshine Follows Rain 1949,S 29,39:2
Each Heart Has Its Own Story 1953,Mr 28,15:2
Night is my Future 1963,Ja 9,5:6
Bori, Diane
Ann Carver's Profession 1933,Je 9,20:2
Borinkov, Gregori
Song Over Moscow 1964,N 23,52:1
Borio, Josephine
Fazil 1928,Je 5,21:1
Borisenko, Don
Nine Hours to Rama 1963,Ap 4,58:2
Genghis Khan 1965,Je 24,28:2
Psycopath, The 1966,S 29,60:1
Boriskin, Pavlik
Fate of Man 1961,Jl 11,28:1
Borisoff, Norman (Screenwriter)
Titan-Story of Michelangelo, The 1950,Ja 23,16:2
Borisoff, S
Flames on the Volga 1929,Ap 2,28:4
Borisoglebskaya, A
Shors 1939,N 21,19:4
Borisov, Alexander
Friends 1939,Ja 2,28:3
Ivan Pavlov 1950,F 13,15:2
Mussorgsky 1951,Ag 20,14:3
Rimsky-Korsakov 1954,Mr 1,16:3
True Friends 1954,N 15,33:2
Flames on the Volga 1958,Ja 27,21:7
Borisova, Yulia
Idiot, The 1960,Jl 22,11:2
Borjavel, Rene (Screenwriter)
Sheep Has Five Legs, The 1955,Ag 10,19:2
Borkon, Jules (Producer)
Crazy in the Noodle 1957,D 15,45:4 (Incorrect in this edition; use 1957,D 17,45:4 elsewhere)
Marriage Came Tumbling Down, The 1968,N 6,32:3
Borkowski, Leopold
Search, The 1948,Mr 24,30:3
Borland, Barlowe
Man Who Fights Alone, The 1924,Jl 28,12:2
Little Minister, The 1934,D 28,25:1
Tale of Two Cities, A 1935,D 26,21:2
Mary of Scotland 1936,Jl 31,22:2
Lloyds of London 1936,N 26,39:1
King of Gamblers 1937,Jl 3,18:1
Easy Living 1937,Jl 8,20:1
Blonde Trouble 1937,Ag 7,7:2
Sophie Lang Goes West 1937,S 30,19:2
Night Club Scandal 1937,N 12,27:2
Dangerous to Know 1938,Mr 11,15:4
Tip-Off Girls 1938,Mr 25,15:3

Borland, Barlowe— Cont
  Hound of the Baskervilles, The 1939,Mr 25,19:2
  Witness Vanishes, The 1939,O 23,15:2
  Tom Brown's School Days 1940,Je 28,22:2
Borland, Carol
  Mark of the Vampire 1935,My 3,23:4
Borne, Hal (Composer)
  Second Chorus 1941,Ja 16,25:2
  Big Store, The 1941,Je 27,14:4
Bornebusch, Arne (Director)
  Skaergaards-Flirt 1936,Ap 8,26:3
  Vaaran Pojke 1936,O 10,21:3
  Sun Over Sweden 1938,Ap 9,11:2
Borodin, Alexander (Composer)
  Kismet 1955,D 9,32:2
Borong, Tor
  Winter Light 1963,My 14,32:1
Boros, Ferike
  Ladies Love Brutes 1930,My 16,20:4
  Born Reckless 1930,Je 7,10:4
  Svengali 1931,My 1,30:3
  Gentleman's Fate 1931,Je 27,20:3
  World and the Flesh, The 1932,My 7,11:5
  Huddle 1932,Je 17,24:1
  Humanity 1933,Ap 22,16:3
  Eight Girls in a Boat 1934,Ja 13,16:3
  Fountain, The 1934,Ag 31,14:1
  Make Way for Tomorrow 1937,My 10,23:1
  Stronger Than Desire 1939,Je 30,17:3
  Bachelor Mother 1939,Je 30,17:2
  Fifth Avenue Girl 1939,Ag 25,12:2
  Dust Be my Destiny 1939,O 7,11:2
  Rio 1939,O 27,27:2
  Light That Failed, The 1939,D 25,19:1
  Three Cheers for the Irish 1940,Mr 9,19:2
  Conga Nights, La 1940,Je 5,33:5
  Girl From God's Country 1940,S 9,18:5
  Argentine Nights 1940,O 11,25:3
  Christmas in July 1940,N 6,35:2
  Sleepers West 1941,Mr 20,25:3
  Caught in the Draft 1941,Je 26,27:3
  Private Nurse 1941,Ag 29,13:3
  Pied Piper, The 1942,Ag 13,15:3
  Once Upon a Honeymoon 1942,N 13,28:1
  Margin for Error 1943,Ja 25,10:7
  Princess O'Rourke 1943,N 6,16:2
  Tree Grows in Brooklyn, A 1945,Mr 1,25:5
  This Love of Ours 1945,N 1,20:2
  Specter of the Rose 1946,S 2,12:4
Boros, Geza
  Sportszerelem; Love of Sport 1938,F 14,20:8
Boroweczyk, Valerian (Director)
  Games of the Angels, The 1967,Ja 16,27:3
Borowsky, Marvin (Original Author)
  Somewhere in the Night 1946,Je 13,24:2
Borowsky, Marvin (Screenwriter)
  Free and Easy 1941,Ap 3,29:4
  Reunion in France 1943,Mr 5,20:3
  Escape in the Desert 1945,My 12,10:2
  Pride of the Marines 1945,Ag 25,7:3
  Big Jack 1949,My 23,27:4
  Gambling House 1951,Mr 19,23:2
Borrah Minnevitch and his Harmonica Rascals
  Hit Parade of 1941 1940,D 5,33:2
Borrah Minnevitch's Harmonica Rascals
  Top Man 1943,O 29,23:2
Borras, Eduardo (Screenwriter)
  Dark River 1956,F 27,19:4
  Rose for Everyone, A 1967,Je 30,30:1
  Games Men Play, The 1968,Mr 15,30:1
Borrell, Louis
  Foreign Correspondent 1940,Ag 28,15:2
Borromei, Charles
  Story of Joseph and his Brethern, The
    1962,D 1,17:1
Borsche, Dieter
  Alles Weg'n Dem Hund 1936,Mr 31,17:3
  Keepers of the Night 1953,Je 9,24:2
  Angelika 1954,S 25,10:7
  Time to Love and a Time to Die, A
    1958,Jl 10,22:1
Borshchagovsky, A (Screenwriter)
  Last Game, The 1964,O 25,41:5 (Incorrect in this
    edition; use 1964,O 26,41:5 elsewhere)
Borsodi, Ursula
  Good Soldier Schweik, The 1963,Ag 21,38:1
Borsody, Eduard von (Director)
  Gruene Hoelle, Die; Green Hell, The
    1939,Ja 21,19:2
  Congo Express 1940,My 11,15:3
  Corinna Darling 1958,Je 14,14:3
Borsten, Orin (Screenwriter)
  Angel Baby 1961,O 5,43:1
Borstwick, Edith
  Thank You 1925,O 6,30:1
Borton, Michael (Original Author)
  Yellow Ticket, The 1931,O 31,22:2
Borunski, Wlodzimierz
  Salto 1966,O 4,50:1
Bory, Jean-Marc
  Lovers, The 1959,O 27,40:2
  Love on a Pillow 1963,D 17,49:1

Boryta, Jaga
  Maryjka 1934,D 3,15:2
Borzaga, Frank (Director)
  Secrets 1924,Mr 25,25:2
  Lady, The 1925,Ja 27,11:2
  Daddy's Gone A-Hunting 1925,F 24,17:3
  Seventh Heaven 1927,My 26,22:1
Borzage, Dan
  Mister Roberts 1955,Jl 15,14:1
  Wings of Eagles, The 1957,F 1,28:1
Borzage, Frank (Director)
  Humoresque 1920,My 31,14:2
  Get-Rich-Quick Wallingford 1921,D 5,20:1
  Back Pay 1922,F 13,10:1
  Pride of Palomar, The 1922,N 20,21:3
  Nth Commandment, The 1923,Ap 10,24:3
  Circle, The 1925,S 22,22:3
  First Year, The 1926,Mr 8,17:1
  They Had to See Paris 1929,O 12,11:1
  Song O' my Heart 1930,Mr 12,32:6
  Liliom 1930,O 4,15:2
  Doctors' Wives 1931,Ap 25,23:4
  Young as You Feel 1931,Ag 8,16:3
  Bad Girl 1931,Ag 15,18:3
  After Tomorrow 1932,Mr 7,13:5
  Young America 1932,My 7,11:5
  Farewell to Arms, A 1932,D 9,26:5
  Secrets 1933,Mr 16,21:2
  Man's Castle 1933,D 30,9:2
  No Greater Glory 1934,My 5,22:2
  Little Man, What Now? 1934,Je 1,29:1
  Flirtation Walk 1934,N 29,33:1
  Living on Velvet 1935,Mr 8,25:4
  Stranded 1935,Je 20,16:2
  Shipmates Forever 1935,O 17,29:3
  Desire 1936,Ap 13,15:1
  Hearts Divided 1936,Je 13,13:1
  Green Light 1937,F 13,9:1
  History Is Made at Night 1937,Mr 29,14:2
  Big City 1937,S 17,29:2
  Mannequin 1938,Ja 21,15:2
  Three Comrades 1938,Je 3,17:1
  Shining Hour, The 1939,Ja 20,15:2
  Disputed Passage 1939,O 26,27:2
  Strange Cargo 1940,Ap 26,25:2
  Mortal Storm, The 1940,Je 21,25:2
  Flight Command 1941,Ja 17,21:2
  Smilin' Through 1941,D 5,29:2
  Vanishing Virginian, The 1942,My 28,13:3
  Seven Sweethearts 1942,N 13,28:1
  Stage Door Canteen 1943,Je 25,13:2
  His Butler's Sister 1943,D 30,13:2
  Till We Meet Again 1944,Ag 30,15:1
  Spanish Main, The 1945,N 7,20:2
  I've Always Loved You 1946,S 7,11:1
  Magnificent Doll 1946,D 9,34:2
  That's my Man 1947,Ap 7,20:2
  Moonrise 1949,Mr 7,17:2
  China Doll 1958,D 4,52:1
  Big Fisherman, The 1959,Ag 6,18:1
Borzage, Frank (Producer)
  Flirtation Walk 1934,N 29,33:1
  Disputed Passage 1939,O 26,27:2
  Till We Meet Again 1944,Ag 30,15:1
  I've Always Loved You 1946,S 7,11:1
  That's my Man 1947,Ap 7,20:2
  China Doll 1958,D 4,52:1
Borzage, Raymond
  Young America 1932,My 7,11:5
  Mayor of Hell, The 1933,Jl 1,16:5
Borzage, Frank (Director)
  River, The; Femme au Corbeau, La
    1930,Ja 5,VIII,5:1
Borzho, V
  Othello 1960,My 16,39:1
Bos, Ery
  Meisterdetektiv, Der 1934,F 13,23:2
  Roman Einer Nacht 1934,Je 22,24:2
  Schuss im Morgengrauen 1934,S 29,12:3
  Liebe in Uniform 1934,O 9,17:2
  Mit dir Durch Dick und Duenn 1934,N 24,19:2
  Lied vom Glueck, Das; Song of Happiness, The
    1935,N 30,12:7
Bosais, Robert (Producer)
  Edward and Caroline 1952,Ap 30,33:3
Bosc, Henri
  Madame Pompadour 1927,Ag 2,19:2
  Douceur D'Aimer, La 1931,D 14,16:3
  Adieux les Beaux Jours 1934,Ap 23,20:2
  Francis the First 1947,N 20,38:4
Boscariol, Angelo
  Bible, The 1966,S 29,60:1
Bose, Gangapado
  Music Room, The 1963,O 16,50:6
Bose, Lucia
  Under the Olive Tree 1951,O 5,24:4
  Rome, 11 O'Clock 1953,Ap 30,39:2
  Three Girls From Rome 1953,O 14,34:2
  Age of Infidelity 1958,Ag 19,23:2
  Of Life and Love 1958,O 7,40:2
  Testament of Orpheus 1962,Ap 10,48:1

Bosek, Pavel
  Report on the Party and the Guests, A
    1968,S 20,37:5
  Report on the Party and the Guests, A
    1968,S 28,37:1
Bosenko
  Vilna Legend, A (American Cast) 1949,S 26,17:1
Bosetti, Giulio
  Made in Italy 1967,My 1,44:2
Boshworth, Hobart
  Stranger's Banquet, The 1923,Ja 1,18:1
Bosic, Andrea
  Greco, El 1967,My 24,52:2
Bosler, Virginia
  Brigadoon 1954,S 17,18:2
  Oklahoma! 1955,O 11,49:1
Bosley, Tom
  World of Henry Orient, The 1964,Mr 20,27:2
  Divorce American Style 1967,Jl 20,30:2
  Secret War of Harry Frigg, The 1968,Mr 5,34:5
  Yours, Mine and Ours 1968,Ap 25,53:1
Bosocki, Madam
  Smiling Irish Eyes 1929,Jl 24,23:2
Bosquet, Jacques (Original Author)
  Blonde or Brunette 1927,Ja 11,18:2
Bossage, Frank (Director)
  Street Angel 1928,Ap 10,33:2
Bosse, Peter
  Schlussakkord 1936,S 10,29:4
  Gaesschen zum Paradies, Das 1937,Ag 21,7:3
Bost, J L (Miscellaneous)
  Chips Are Down, The 1949,F 2,36:1
  Life Begins Tomorrow 1952,N 18,37:2
  Respectful Prostitute, The 1957,Jl 11,21:1
Bost, J L (Screenwriter)
  Heroes and Sinners; (Heros Sont Fatigues, Les)
    1959,My 12,38:2
Bost, Pierre (Miscellaneous)
  Forbidden Games 1952,D 9,43:2
  Eye for an Eye, An 1961,F 10,19:1
Bost, Pierre (Original Author)
  Daughters of Destiny (Jeanne); Jeanne (Daughters
    of Destiny) 1954,Jl 6,19:1
Bost, Pierre (Screenwriter)
  Devil in the Flesh 1949,My 10,29:2
  Walls of Malapaga, The 1950,Mr 21,34:2
  God Needs Men 1951,Mr 27,35:1
  Oh, Amelia 1951,D 3,22:2
  Seven Deadly Sins, The (The Eighth Sin); Eighth
    Sin, The (The Seven Deadly Sins)
    1953,My 12,31:3
  Seven Deadly Sins (Pride); Pride (The Seven
    Deadly Sins) 1953,My 12,31:3
  Seven Deadly Sins, The (Lust); Lust (The Seven
    Deadly Sins) 1953,My 12,31:3
  Daughters of Destiny (Jeanne); Jeanne (Daughters
    of Destiny) 1954,Jl 6,19:1
  Game of Love, The 1954,D 15,41:1
  Proud and the Beautiful, The 1956,My 29,32:2
  Four Bags Full 1957,S 5,32:1
  Gervaise 1957,N 12,46:1
  Rouge et Noir 1958,Ap 9,42:1
  Green Mare, The; Jument Verte, La
    1961,O 24,41:2
  Enough Rope 1966,Jl 15,34:3
Bostock, Evelyn
  Perfect Understanding 1933,F 23,20:2
Bostwick, E F
  Kitty 1929,Je 11,27:2
Bosustow, Stephen (Producer)
  1001 Arabian Nights 1959,D 24,13:6
Boswell, Connie
  Artists and Models 1937,Ag 5,19:2
  Kiss the Boys Goodbye 1941,Ag 14,21:2
  Syncopation 1942,My 29,13:3
Bosworth, Allan R (Original Author)
  Nobody's Perfect 1968,Ap 4,58:3
Bosworth, Hobart
  Oliver Twist 1916,D 11,7:3
  Border Legion, The 1918,Jl 29,9:3
  Behind the Door 1920,Ja 5,15:1
  Below the Surface 1920,Je 7,20:3 (In Addenda)
  Vanity Fair 1923,My 7,19:3
  Eternal Three, The 1923,O 12,7:2 (Incorrect in
    this edition; use 1927,O 1,7:2 elsewhere)
  Common Law, The 1923,O 29,18:1
  In the Palace of the King 1923,D 3,14:1
  Through the Dark 1924,Ja 8,27:1
  Name the Man 1924,F 4,23:3
  Nellie, the Beautiful Cloak Model
    1924,Ap 14,14:1
  Woman on the Jury, The 1924,My 19,14:2
  Captain January 1924,Jl 7,10:4
  Bread 1924,Jl 21,14:4
  Sundown 1924,D 1,17:3
  If I Marry Again 1925,Ja 12,11:2
  Chickie 1925,Ap 27,15:2
  Zander the Great 1925,My 4,16:2
  Half-Way Girl, The 1925,Jl 29,24:4
  Winds of Chance 1925,Ag 17,19:3
  Big Parade, The 1925,N 20,18:1 (In Addenda)
  Steel Preferred 1925,D 22,13:1
  Nervous Wreck, The 1926,O 12,30:2

Three Hours 1927,Mr 8,18:4
Annie Laurie 1927,My 12,24:3
Blood Ship, The 1927,Jl 19,27:2
My Best Girl 1927,N 7,26:4
Chinese Parrot, The 1928,Ja 2,28:1
Smart Set, The 1928,Mr 5,21:1
After the Storm 1928,My 8,25:3
Hangman's House 1928,My 14,25:1
Sawdust Paradise, The 1928,Ag 27,23:1
Woman of Affairs, A 1929,Ja 21,18:4
Eternal Love 1929,My 13,27:2
Show of Shows 1929,N 21,24:5
General Crack 1929,D 4,36:6
Mammy 1930,Mr 27,24:5
Devil's Holiday, The 1930,My 10,25:3
Abraham Lincoln 1930,Ag 26,24:1
Office Wife, The 1930,S 27,21:3
Du Barry, Woman of Passion 1930,N 3,19:3
Just Imagine 1930,N 22,21:3
Sit Tight 1931,F 19,20:4
Dirigible 1931,Ap 6,24:1
Shipmates 1931,My 23,13:4
This Modern Age 1931,S 7,19:3
Fanny Foley Herself 1931,O 26,22:1
Carnival Boat 1932,Mr 21,19:5
Miracle Man, The 1932,Ap 21,25:2
No Greater Love 1932,My 14,11:5
Phantom Express, The 1932,S 20,26:3
Lady for a Day 1933,S 8,22:2
Whom the Gods Destroy 1934,Jl 13,14:2
Music in the Air 1934,D 14,29:3
Keeper of the Bees, The 1935,Ag 17,18:5
Crusades, The 1935,Ag 22,21:3
Steamboat Around the Bend 1935,S 20,17:2
Portia on Trial 1937,D 3,29:2
Bullets for O'Hara 1941,Jl 28,16:4
Law of the Tropics 1941,O 10,26:5
One Foot in Heaven 1941,N 14,28:3
Bullet Scars 1942,Ap 24,21:4
Sin Town 1942,O 17,11:2
Bosworth, Patricia
Nun's Story, The 1959,Je 19,30:1
Boteler, Bruce
Man Next Door, The 1923,My 29,10:3
Boteler, Wade
Twenty-three and a Half Hours' Leave
  1919,O 27,9:3
Old Fashioned Boy, An 1920,N 1,13:2
Going Up 1923,O 10,16:2
Through the Dark 1924,Ja 8,27:1
Capital Punishment 1925,F 5,23:3
Introduce Me 1925,Mr 9,21:1
Winds of Chance 1925,Ag 17,10:3
Seven Keys to Baldpate 1925,N 3,25:4
Last Edition, The 1925,N 11,27:3
That's My Baby 1926,Ap 12,18:4
Hold That Lion 1926,S 6,16:2
Let It Rain 1927,Mr 9,29:1
Soft Cushions 1927,S 12,29:1
High School Hero 1927,O 24,24:3
Let 'Er go, Gallegher 1928,Ja 16,24:1
Sporting Goods 1928,F 13,16:2
Warming Up 1928,Jl 16,25:3
Just Married 1928,Ag 13,23:2
Leatherneck, The 1929,Ap 22,23:1
Close Harmony 1929,Ap 29,29:2
Navy Blues 1930,Ja 11,21:3
Devil's Holiday, The 1930,My 10,25:3
Soldiers and Women 1930,My 12,27:3
College Lovers 1930,N 28,23:1
Beyond Victory 1931,Ap 6,24:1
Kick In 1931,My 25,17:1
Silence 1931,Ag 15,18:3
Penrod and Sam 1931,S 26,25:3
Twenty-Four Hours 1931,O 3,20:2
Bad Company 1931,N 7,16:5
Local Boy Makes Good 1931,N 27,29:3
Man Who Played God, The 1932,F 11,16:1
Painted Woman, The 1932,S 16,24:4
Night Mayor, The 1932,N 25,19:2
Central Park 1932,D 7,29:3
Death Kiss, The 1933,F 5,IX,5:3
She Done Him Wrong 1933,F 10,12:3
Humanity 1933,Ag 22,16:3
Melody in Spring 1934,Mr 31,8:2
Operator 13 1934,Je 23,16:5
Richest Girl in the World, The 1934,S 21,29:2
Belle of the Nineties 1934,S 22,12:2
Black Fury 1935,Ap 11,27:2
Love in Bloom 1935,Ap 20,16:2
Goin' to Town 1935,My 11,21:2
Goose and the Gander, The 1935,S 12,29:2
Three Musketeers, The 1935,N 1,25:1
Exclusive Story 1936,Ja 18,19:2
Whipsaw 1936,Ja 25,18:4
Charlie Chan at the Circus 1936,Mr 19,22:4
President's Mystery, The 1936,O 19,22:1
You Only Live Once 1937,F 1,15:2
Fight to the Finish, A 1937,Je 26,20:2 (In
  Addenda)
Great Hospital Mystery, The 1937,Jl 16,22:2
It Can't Last Forever 1937,Jl 30,22:5
Frame-Up 1937,Ag 9,23:2 (In Addenda)

Valley of the Giants 1938,S 10,20:2
Peck's bad Boy With the Circus 1939,Ja 11,17:4
Oklahoma Kid, The 1939,Mr 11,21:1
Missing Daughters 1939,Je 12,14:5
Everything's on Ice 1939,O 6,31:1
Sabotage 1939,N 16,29:5
Castle on the Hudson 1940,Mr 4,11:2
Three Cheers for the Irish 1940,Mr 9,19:2
Double Alibi 1940,Mr 11,11:2
Hot Steel 1940,Je 21,25:3
Three Faces West 1940,Ag 19,13:2
Howards of Virginia, The 1940,S 27,27:1
Strange Alibi 1941,Ap 28,11:2
It Started With Eve 1941,O 3,27:1
Kathleen 1941,D 19,35:3
Bombay Clipper 1942,Ja 12,23:3
Body Disappears, The 1942,Ja 31,13:2
I Was Framed 1942,Je 12,16:6
Escape From Crime 1942,O 12,12:3
Boteler, Wade (Screenwriter)
That's My Baby 1926,Ap 12,18:4
Botelier, Arcady (Director)
Capitan Aventurero, El; Adventureous Captain,
  The 1939,O 3,19:5
Botiller, Dick
Torrid Zone 1940,My 18,11:3
Wild Bill Hickok Rides 1942,F 7,13:5
Botkin, Perry
Birth of the Blues 1941,D 11,39:1
Botsford, A M (Producer)
Border Flight 1936,Je 22,22:1
Forgotten Faces 1936,Jl 4,18:2
Sudden Death, And 1936,Jl 18,18:2
Return of Sophie Lang, The 1936,Jl 24,13:1
Three Cheers for Love 1936,Ag 1,16:2
Hollywood Boulevard 1936,S 21,26:4
Accusing Finger, The 1936,N 17,35:4
Murder With Pictures 1936,N 21,21:4
Rose Bowl 1936,D 2,35:2
Hideaway Girl 1937,Ja 13,20:4
Botsford, Richard
Satan in Sables 1925,O 15,27:3
Bottar, Frank (Screenwriter)
Young, The Evil and the Savage, The
  1968,Ag 15,46:2
Bottcher, Grit
Great British Train Robbery, The 1967,Ap 6,45:2
Bottome, Phyllis (Original Author)
Private Worlds 1935,Mr 28,25:2
Mortal Storm, The 1940,Je 21,25:2
Danger Signal 1945,N 22,39:2
Bottomley, Roland
Devil, The 1921,Ja 17,9:1
Dawn of a Tomorrow, The 1924,Mr 26,19:2
Enticement 1925,Mr 21,16:3
Boubouca
Madame X 1960,O 3,34:5
Bouchard, Jean
Train, The 1965,Mr 18,25:1
Boucher, Victor
Douceur D'Aimer, La 1931,D 14,16:3
Nine Bachelors 1942,F 9,19:2
Bouchet, Barbara
In Harm's Way 1965,Ap 7,36:1
Agent for H.A.R.M 1966,Ja 6,20:2
Casino Royale 1967,Ap 29,25:1
Danger Route 1968,Je 6,54:2
Bouchey, Willis
Elopement 1951,D 21,21:3
Red Planet Mars 1952,Je 16,15:2
Don't Bother to Knock 1952,Jl 19,8:2
Just for You 1952,O 9,40:6
Million Dollar Mermaid 1952,D 5,35:2
Pickup on South Street 1953,Je 18,38:2
Dangerous Crossing 1953,S 30,37:2
Big Heat, The 1953,O 15,43:2
Suddenly 1954,O 8,27:2
Drum Beat 1954,N 18,42:1
Bridges at Toko-Ri, The 1955,Ja 21,20:2
Long Gray Line, The 1955,F 11,19:2
Big House U S A 1955,Mr 12,11:6
McConnell Story, The 1955,S 30,23:1
Hell on Frisco Bay 1956,Ja 7,21:1
Forever, Darling 1956,F 10,18:1
Johnny Concho 1956,Ag 16,30:1
Pillars of the Sky 1956,O 13,15:2
Sheepman, The 1958,My 8,36:1
Last Hurrah, The 1958,O 24,40:1
Sergeant Rutledge 1960,My 26,37:1
Incident in an Alley 1962,My 17,31:1
Man Who Shot Liberty Valance, The
  1962,My 24,29:2
Where Love Has Gone 1964,N 3,26:1
Bouchier, Chili
Silver King, The 1929,S 2,16:1
Mr Cohen Takes a Walk 1936,F 13,25:2
Murder in Reverse 1947,Ja 11,23:5
Laughing Lady, The 1950,Ja 23,16:3
Mrs Fitzherbert 1950,My 11,37:2
Bouchier, Dorothy
Blue Danube 1934,N 8,27:1

Boucicault, Dion (Original Author)
Bride of the Lake, The 1934,S 11,24:5
Bouicault, Nina
Juggernaut 1937,Jl 15,16:1
Boucot
Culte de Beaute, Le 1931,Je 8,21:1
Three Waltzes 1939,Ap 25,19:2
Boudard, Alphonse (Original Author)
Cloportes 1966,Ap 19,36:1
Boudet, Micheline
Ballerina 1938,N 15,27:1
Eternal Husband, The 1949,Ja 10,19:2
Dream Ballerina 1951,Ap 16,21:2
Would-Be Gentleman, The 1960,Mr 23,31:1
Marriage of Figaro, The 1963,Ap 30,26:1
Boudreaux, Joseph
Louisiana Story 1948,S 29,36:2
Boudroiz, Robert (Director)
Vivre 1928,Ag 12,VII,3:4
Boudwin, Jimmy
One Woman to Another 1927,S 19,30:3
Bouise, Jean
Shameless Old Lady, The 1966,S 27,52:1
Guerre est Fini, La; War Is Over, The
  1967,F 2,29:2
Boulanger, Daniel
Shoot the Piano Player 1962,Jl 24,19:1
King of Hearts 1967,Je 20,34:1
Bride Wore Black, The 1968,Je 26,42:1
Boulanger, Daniel (Screenwriter)
Love Game, The 1960,N 9,44:1
Breathless 1961,F 8,26:1
Joker, The; (Farceur, Le) 1961,Ag 8,32:2
Five Day Lover, The 1961,D 14,55:4
Playtime; Receation, La 1963,Ja 16,5:2
7 Capital Sins (Gluttony); Gluttony (7 Capital
  Sins) 1963,Ja 17,5:2
That Man From Rio 1964,Je 9,30:1
Cartouche 1964,Jl 22,39:1
Backfire 1965,Ap 27,27:1
Up to his Ears 1966,My 18,37:1
King of Hearts 1967,Je 20,34:1
Oldest Profession, The (Mademoiselle Mimi);
  Mademoiselle Mimi (The Oldest Profession)
  1968,N 8,42:1
Bould, Beckett
Lease of Life 1956,F 10,18:1
Boulder, Robert
Dramatic Life of Abraham Lincoln, The
  1924,Ja 22,17:3
Boulle, Pierre (Original Author)
Bridge on the River Kwai 1957,D 19,39:1
Planet of the Apes 1968,F 9,55:2
Boulle, Pierre (Screenwriter)
Bridge on the River Kwai 1957,D 19,39:1
Boulon, Betty
Oytherea 1924,My 26,21:1
Boult, Adrian
Battle for Music 1945,O 15,13:2
Boulter, Rosalyn
Spitfire 1943,Je 14,13:2
For Them that Trespass 1950,S 27,37:2
Boulting, John (Director)
Journey Together 1946,Mr 4,16:5
Seven Days to Noon 1950,D 19,41:3
Young Scarface 1951,N 8,35:2
Magic Box, The 1952,S 24,40:2
Crest of the Wave 1954,N 11,43:2
Private's Progress 1956,Jl 24,19:2
Lucky Jim 1958,S 1,8:6
I'm All Right Jack 1960,Ap 26,40:2
Risk, The 1961,S 25,41:2
Heavens Above! 1963,My 21,28:2
Rotten to the Core 1965,Jl 20,39:2
Family Way, The 1967,Je 29,32:1
Boulting, John (Original Author)
Heavens Above! 1963,My 21,28:2
Boulting, John (Producer)
Pastor Hall 1940,S 21,13:2
Thunder Rock 1944,S 15,16:1
Guinea Pig, The 1949,My 2,20:2
Fame Is the Spur 1949,N 8,34:2
Crest of the Wave 1954,N 11,43:2
Brothers in Law 1957,Ag 20,22:1
Man in a Cocked Hat 1960,Je 15,50:2
French Mistress, A 1960,D 19,34:2
Risk, The 1961,S 25,41:2
Heavens Above! 1963,My 21,28:2
Family Way, The 1967,Je 29,32:1
Boulting, John (Screenwriter)
Private's Progress 1956,Jl 24,19:2
I'm All Right Jack 1960,Ap 26,40:2
Heavens Above! 1963,My 21,28:2
Boulting, Roy
Rotten to the Core 1965,Jl 20,39:2
Boulting, Roy (Director)
Pastor Hall 1940,S 21,13:2
Thunder Rock 1944,S 15,16:1
Burma Victory 1949,Ap 2,12:2
Guinea Pig, The 1949,My 2,20:2
Fame Is the Spur 1949,N 8,34:2
High Treason 1952,My 21,23:3
Sailor of the King 1953,S 3,15:2

Boulting, Roy (Director)— Cont

Crest of the Wave 1954,N 11,43:2
Run for the Sun 1956,Ag 25,7:2
Brothers in Law 1957,Ag 20,22:1
Happy is the Bride 1959,Je 30,27:2
Man in a Cocked Hat 1960,Je 15,50:2
French Mistress, A 1960,D 19,34:2
Risk, The 1961,S 25,41:2
Heavens Above! 1963,My 21,28:2
Family Way, The 1967,Je 29,32:1

Boulting, Roy (Miscellaneous)

Burma Victory 1949,Ap 2,12:2
Risk, The 1961,S 25,41:2

Boulting, Roy (Original Author)

High Treason 1952,My 21,23:3
Rotten to the Core 1965,Jl 20,39:2

Boulting, Roy (Producer)

Seven Days to Noon 1950,D 19,41:3
Young Scarface 1951,N 8,35:2
Crest of the Wave 1954,N 11,43:2
Private's Progress 1956,Jl 24,19:2
Lucky Jim 1958,S 1,8:6
I'm All Right Jack 1960,Ap 26,40:2
French Mistress, A 1960,D 19,34:2
Risk, The 1961,S 25,41:2
Heavens Above! 1963,My 21,28:2
Family Way, The 1967,Je 29,32:1

Boulting, Roy (Screenwriter)

Guinea Pig, The 1949,My 2,20:2
Seven Days to Noon 1950,D 19,41:3
High Treason 1952,My 21,23:3
Crest of the Wave 1954,N 11,43:2
Run for the Sun 1956,Ag 25,7:2
Brothers in Law 1957,Ag 20,22:1
Happy is the Bride 1959,Je 30,27:2
Man in a Cocked Hat 1960,Je 15,50:2
French Mistress, A 1960,D 19,34:2
Rotten to the Core 1965,Jl 20,39:2
Family Way, The 1967,Je 29,32:1

Boulton, Matthew

Woman Alone, The 1937,F 27,9:2
Night Must Fall 1937,Ap 30,17:2
Thirteenth Chair, The 1937,Je 18,25:3
Firefly, The 1937,S 2,17:2
Bulldog Drummond's Peril 1938,Mr 18,23:2
Lord Jeff 1938,Jl 1,22:2
Bulldog Drummond in Africa 1938,Ag 25,15:1
Adventure in Diamonds 1940,Ap 4,27:2
Phantom Raiders 1940,Je 24,19:5
Mystery Sea Raider 1940,Ag 26,11:4
Rage in Heaven 1941,Mr 21,19:2
They Met in Bombay 1941,Jl 4,17:1
Yank on the Burma Road, A 1942,Ja 29,25:3
Counter-Espionage 1942,S 28,13:2
Man in Half Moon Street, The 1945,Ja 20,16:2
Brighton Strangler, The 1945,My 19,15:2
Woman in Green, The 1945,Je 16,10:3
Stallion Road 1947,Ap 5,12:5
Tarzan and the Mermaids 1948,Mr 30,26:4
Woman in White, The 1948,My 8,12:2

Boulven, Gerome

Thirst of Men, The 1952,O 28,37:1

Bouquet, Jean

Boys' School 1939,Je 6,26:2

Bouquet, Michel

This Special Friendship 1967,N 8,56:1
Bride Wore Black, The 1968,Je 26,42:1

Bour, Armand

Femme Nue, La 1933,Ag 25,12:3

Bour, Harry

Sous la Lune du Maroc 1933,Ja 23,9:2

Bourbon, Marie, Princess de

Janice Meredith 1924,Ag 6,13:3

Bourchier, Dorothy

Carnival 1931,N 22,VIII,6:1

Bourday, Simone

Porteuse de Pain, La 1936,Jl 1,29:5
Little Flower of Jesus, The 1938,D 13,31:2
Amore sulle Alpi 1939,O 27,27:3

Bourdelle, Thomy

Sea-Fever 1929,O 28,20:1
Cain 1932,Ja 18,18:4
Milady 1933,S 8,22:3
Quatorez Juillet 1933,O 20,14:2
Fantomas 1934,Mr 13,27:4
Pecheurs d'Islande 1935,S 21,18:2
Maria Chapdelaine 1935,S 25,18:2
Seven Sinners 1936,Ag 22,6:1
Last Will of Dr Mabuse, The 1943,Mr 20,11:1

Bourdet, Edouard (Original Author)

Fric-Frac 1948,My 29,8:6

Bourdet, Simone

Douceur D'Aimer, La 1931,D 14,16:3
Itto 1936,Ja 29,15:5

Bourdin, Lise

Love in the Afternoon 1957,Ag 24,12:1
Last Blitzkrieg, The 1959,Ja 31,13:5

Bourdin, Roger

Barber of Seville 1949,Jl 21,21:2

Bourguignon, Serge (Director)

Sundays and Cybele 1962,N 13,43:3
Reward, The 1965,S 16,55:1

Bourguignon, Serge (Screenwriter)

Sundays and Cybele 1962,N 13,43:3
Reward, The 1965,S 16,55:1

Bourne, Peter

Torn Curtain 1966,Jl 28,23:1

Bourne, Whitney

Crime Without Passion 1934,S 1,16:2
Once in a Blue Moon 1936,D 2,35:1
Head Over Heels in Love 1937,F 13,9:1
Flight From Glory 1937,S 11,20:1
Double Danger 1938,F 10,17:5
Blind Alibi 1938,My 20,17:2
Mad Miss Manton, The 1938,O 21,27:2
Beauty for the Asking 1939,F 10,19:1

Bourneuf, Philip

Big Night, The 1952,Mr 20,37:5
Thunder in the East 1953,F 4,32:2
Beyond a Reasonable Doubt 1956,S 14,27:2
Chamber of Horrors 1966,O 20,52:5

Bourseiller, Antoine

Cleo From 5 to 7 1962,S 5,43:4

Bourvil

Miquette 1951,F 5,18:2
Mr Peek-A-Boo 1951,S 19,37:1
Prize, The 1952,Ap 30,33:2
Four Bags Full 1957,S 5,32:1
Mirror Has two Faces, The 1959,My 27,31:1
Crazy for Love 1960,N 26,13:2
Green Mare, The; Jument Verte, La
  1961,O 24,41:2
Longest Day, The 1962,O 5,28:1
Don't Tempt the Devil 1964,Ap 28,43:1
Thank Heaven for Small Favors 1965,Ja 14,44:2
My Wife's Husband 1965,Ja 27,26:1
Sucker, The 1967,O 9,61:1

Bousquet, Robert

Inside Out 1964,S 25,32:1
Life Upside Down; Inside Out 1965,Ag 18,41:4
Shameless Old Lady, The 1966,S 27,52:1

Bousquets, Joaquin

Almas Encontradas 1933,Je 27,13:5
Tu Hijo 1934,D 17,24:3
Corazon Bandolero 1935,Mr 2,18:2

Boutall, Kathleen

So Well Remembered 1947,N 5,34:3

Boutelje, Phil (Composer)

Romance in the Dark 1938,Mr 21,18:2

Boutelle, Romain

Fire Within, The 1964,F 18,27:1

Bouton, Betty

Don't Ever Marry 1920,Ap 19,13:3

Bouvette, Alain

Gates of Paris 1958,Ja 15,24:1
Me and the Colonel 1958,Ag 27,33:1
Babette Goes to War 1960,Je 8,46:1

Bouvier, Georges

Big Red 1962,S 3,11:2

Bouzauquet

Generals Without Buttons 1938,Mr 8,23:2

Bova, Joseph

Pretty Poison 1968,O 25,55:1

Bover, Jean (Director)

Easiest Profession, The 1960,Mr 26,15:7

Boverid, A

Mystic Mountain, The 1936,Mr 31,17:2

Boverio, Auguste

Call, The 1938,Mr 29,18:3
Crossroads 1939,Mr 14,17:5
Claudine 1940,Ap 1,15:2
Schubert's Serenade 1940,S 3,21:2

Boviello, Mario

Laugh Pagliacci 1948,Ja 31,14:2

Bovio, L (Original Author)

Tormento 1953,Ap 4,9:2

Bovis, Craig

Come Back Baby 1968,Je 14,43:1

Bovo, Brunella

White Sheik, The 1956,Ap 26,37:4
Alone in the Streets 1956,Je 28,33:2

Bovy, Berthe

Man to Men 1949,F 21,20:2
Cupboard was Bare, The; (Armoire Volante, L')
  1952,N 4,33:1

Bovy, Bette

Three Hours 1944,O 30,16:5

Bovykin, Tolya

Maximka 1953,O 12,30:4

BOW

See Also BOWE

Bow, Clara

Down to the Sea in Ships 1923,F 19,10:1
Black Oxen 1924,Ja 7,23:1
Maytime 1924,Je 2,14:3
Poisoned Paradise 1924,Ag 11,16:1
This Woman 1924,O 21,21:3
Capital Punishment 1925,F 5,23:3
Eve's Lover 1925,Jl 27,17:3
Kiss Me Again 1925,Ag 3,10:1
Keeper of the Bees, The 1925,O 28,29:2
Best Bad Man, The 1925,D 2,23:1
Dancing Mothers 1926,F 18,21:1
Runaway, The 1926,Ap 27,23:2
Mantrap 1926,Jl 12,24:4

Bow, Clara— Cont

Plastic Age, The 1926,Jl 19,13:1
Kid Boots 1926,O 11,18:2
It 1927,F 13,VII,7:2 (In Addenda)
Children of Divorce 1927,Ap 26,33:3
Rough House Rosie 1927,My 23,27:2
Wings 1927,Ag 13,10:4
Hula 1927,Ag 29,21:1
Get Your Man 1927,D 5,26:2
Red Hair 1928,Mr 26,26:2
Ladies of the Mob 1928,Je 18,13:2
Fleet's In, The 1928,O 1,23:1
Three Week Ends 1928,D 10,25:1
Wild Party, The 1929,Ap 2,28:4
Dangerous Curves 1929,Jl 15,25:1
Saturday Night Kid, The 1929,N 16,25:2
Paramount on Parade 1930,Ap 21,20:4
True to the Navy 1930,My 24,21:2
Love Among the Millionaires 1930,Jl 5,17:4
Her Wedding Night 1930,S 29,19:1
No Limit 1931,Ja 17,23:1
Kick In 1931,My 25,17:1
Call Her Savage 1932,N 25,19:2
Hoopla 1933,D 1,23:3

BOWDEN

See Also BODEN

Bowdon, Dorris

Young Mr Lincoln 1939,Je 3,11:2
Drums Along the Mohawk 1939,N 4,11:2
Grapes of Wrath, The 1940,Ja 25,17:2
Moon Is Down, The 1943,Mr 27,8:6

BOWE

See Also BOW

Bowe, Hans Dieter (Screenwriter)

Mediterannean Holiday 1964,D 16,51:1

Bowe, Rosemarie

Adventures of Haji Baba, The 1954,O 9,8:7
Golden Mistress, The 1954,O 30,15:6
View From Pompey's Head, The 1955,N 5,22:5

Bowen, Frank C (Screenwriter)

Battles of Coronel and Falkland Islands, The
  1928,F 9,28:4

Bowen, Harry

Harvester, The 1936,Jl 4,18:2

Bowen, Trevor

Darling 1965,Ag 4,20:1

BOWER

See Also BAUER, BAUR

Bower, Dallas (Director)

Alice in Wonderland 1951,Jl 27,15:2

Bower, Pamela (Screenwriter)

Trent's Last Case 1953,N 27,99:9
Laughing Anne 1954,My 8,15:2

Bowers, Cookie

Catskill Honeymoon 1950,Ja 28,10:3

Bowers, Ellene

Violent Saturday 1955,My 12,32:2

Bowers, John

Sis 1919,Mr 3,11:2
Sis Hopkins 1919,Mr 3,11:2
Through the Wrong Door 1919,Jl 21,12:3
Strictly Confidential 1919,O 6,15:1
Godless Men 1921,Ja 31,11:1
Sky Pilot, The 1921,Ap 18,8:1
Bits of Life 1921,O 17,18:1
Silent Call, The 1922,Ja 30,16:2
Lorna Doone 1922,D 4,20:2
Quincy Adams Sawyer 1922,D 18,22:2
Divorce 1923,Je 26,14:2
Richard the Lion-Hearted 1923,O 22,17:1
Barefoot Boy, The 1923,N 11,6:1
When a Man's a Man 1924,F 5,20:1
Code of the Wilderness, The 1924,Jl 1,21:4
So Big 1925,Ja 5,19:1
Confessions of a Queen 1925,Mr 24,20:6
Chickie 1925,Ap 27,15:2
Pals in Paradise 1926,N 24,26:4
Three Hours 1927,Mr 8,18:4
Say It With Songs 1929,Ag 7,29:2
Skin Deep 1929,S 30,23:1

Bowers, Kenny

Best Foot Forward 1943,Je 30,25:2
Broadway Rhythm 1944,Ap 14,24:6
I'll Be Seeing You 1945,Ap 6,20:6

Bowers, Lally

Chalk Garden, The 1964,My 22,42:2

Bowers, William (Miscellaneous)

Higher and Higher 1944,Ja 22,8:4

Bowers, William (Original Author)

Ladies' Man 1947,Ja 13,18:5
Wistful Widow of Wagon Gap, The
  1947,N 21,36:2
Gunfighter, The 1950,Je 24,7:2

Bowers, William (Screenwriter)

My Favorite Spy 1942,My 29,13:4
Seven Days' Leave 1942,D 11,33:2
Night and Day 1946,Jl 26,16:2
Web, The 1947,Je 5,32:1
Something in the Wind 1947,Ag 29,14:3
Black Bart 1948,Mr 4,30:4
River Lady 1948,My 21,19:5
Larceny 1948,S 4,8:6
Gunfighter, The 1950,Je 24,7:2
Cry Danger 1951,F 22,27:3

Bowers, William (Screenwriter)— Cont

Mrs O'Malley and Mr Malone 1951,F 23,33:2
Mob, The 1951,O 18,32:2
Assignment-Paris 1952,O 25,12:6
Split Second 1953,My 13,34:2
She Couldn't Say No 1954,F 27,11:3
Tight Spot 1955,Mr 19,11:7
Five Against the House 1955,Je 11,8:7
Best Things in Life are Free, The 1956,S 29,12:2
My Man Godfrey 1957,O 12,23:1
Sheepman, The 1958,My 8,36:1
Law and Jake Wade, the 1958,Je 7,11:1
Alias Jesse James 1959,My 18,31:2
30 1959,N 12,27:1
Last Time I Saw Archie, The 1961,My 29,9:6
Advance to the Rear 1964,Je 11,27:3
Way...Way Out 1966,O 27,55:1

Bowes, Edward Major (Composer)

Camille 1927,Ap 22,19:1

Bowker, Aldrich

Waterfront 1939,Jl 17,10:2
Angels Wash Their Faces 1939,S 4,16:2
Dress Parade 1939,O 28,11:2
Joe and Ethel Turp Call on the President
    1940,Ja 4,19:2
Abe Lincoln in Illinois 1940,F 23,19:2
Susan and God 1940,Jl 12,11:2
Those Were the Days 1940,Jl 15,18:4
Romance of the Rio Grande 1940,D 25,33:4
Meet John Doe 1941,Mr 13,25:2
Pot o'Gold 1941,Ap 4,25:2
Wagons Roll at Night, The 1941,My 10,20:4
I Was Framed 1942,Je 12,16:6
I Married a Witch 1942,N 20,27:2

Bowklee, Kannikar

Bridge on the River Kwai 1957,D 19,39:1

Bowler, Clive Colin

Small World of Sammy Lee, The 1963,Ag 14,28:1
Girl-Getters, The 1966,Ap 13,37:6

BOWLES

See Also BOLES

Bowles, Paul

8 X 8 1957,Mr 16,13:2

Bowman, Lee

Internes Can't Take Money 1937,My 6,23:2
I Met Him in Paris 1937,Je 3,29:2
Last Train from Madrid, The 1937,Je 19,20:2
Sophie Lang Goes West 1937,S 30,19:2
This Way Please 1937,O 8,27:2
Having Wonderful Time 1938,Jl 8,11:2
Man to Remember, A 1938,N 7,23:2
Tarnished Angel 1938,N 15,27:2
Next Time I Marry 1938,D 2,27:2
Love Affair 1939,Mr 17,25:2
Society Lawyer 1939,Mr 31,19:2
Stronger Than Desire 1939,Je 30,17:3
Miracles for Sale 1939,Ag 10,15:2
Fast And Furious 1939,O 12,33:3
Dancing Co-Ed 1939,N 10,27:3
Great Victor Herbert, The 1939,D 7,35:1
Florian 1940,Je 6,33:2
Gold Rush Maisie 1940,S 2,19:2
Wyoming 1940,O 3,31:4
Third Finger, Left Hand 1940,D 12,37:2
Buck Privates 1941,F 14,15:2
Model Wife 1941,Ap 24,25:3
Washington Melodrama 1941,My 26,15:3
Married Bachelor 1941,O 16,25:3
Design for Scandal 1942,F 6,23:3
Kid Glove Killer 1942,Ap 17,21:4
We Were Dancing 1942,My 1,23:2
Pacific Rendezvous 1942,Jl 8,27:4
Tish 1942,S 18,25:2
Three Hearts for Julia 1943,My 21,22:4
Bataan 1943,Je 4,17:2
Cover Girl 1944,Mr 31,26:1
Impatient Years, The 1944,S 20,20:1
Tonight and Every Night 1945,Mr 9,16:2
She Wouldn't Say Yes 1946,Ja 12,10:7
Walls Came Tumbling Down, The 1946,N 9,13:5
Smash-Up, The Story of a Woman
    1947,Ap 11,31:2
My Dream Is Yours 1949,Ap 16,11:3
There's a Girl in my Heart 1950,Ja 20,29:2
House by the River 1950,My 2,25:2
Youngblood Hawke 1964,N 6,30:1

Bowman, Patricia

Versailles 1929,N 16,25:2

Bowman, Peter (Original Author)

Beach Red 1967,Ag 4,18:1

Bowman, Ralph

Cheers for Miss Bishop 1941,Mr 14,17:2

Bown, John

Master Spy 1964,Ag 20,34:2

Bowsky, Willard (Miscellaneous)

Mr Bug Goes to Town 1942,F 20,21:3

Box, Betty E (Miscellaneous)

Blind Goddess, The 1949,Je 23,33:3

Box, Betty E (Producer)

Miranda 1949,Ap 25,20:2
Here Come the Huggetts 1950,D 25,25:3
Clouded Yellow, The 1951,N 13,33:2
Marry Me 1952,Mr 14,27:3

Assassin, The 1953,Ap 18,17:2
Doctor in the House 1955,F 19,18:3
Doctor at Sea 1956,Mr 1,37:3
Iron Petticoat, The 1957,F 2,12:2
Doctor at Large 1957,Jl 29,15:5
Checkpoint 1957,S 19,25:2
Tale of Two Cities, A 1958,Ag 5,23:1
Campbell's Kingdom 1960,Ja 11,35:5
Wind Cannot Read, The 1960,Mr 10,36:1
Conspiracy of Hearts 1960,Ap 8,24:1
39 Steps, The 1960,O 11,55:2
Upstairs and Downstairs 1960,D 2,53:4
No Love for Johnnie 1961,D 13,55:1
Doctor in Love 1962,Ap 27,27:2
Pair of Briefs, A 1964,F 3,22:2
Young and Willing 1964,F 27,28:1
No, My Darling Daughter 1964,Mr 28,13:5
Doctor in Distress 1964,Jl 8,38:2
Agent 8 3/4 1965,O 14,53:1
Deadlier Than the Male 1967,F 22,21:1
High Commissioner, The 1968,D 12,62:5

Box, Muriel (Director)

Mr Lord Says No! 1952,F 12,22:5
Both Sides of the Law 1954,Ja 12,19:2
Beachcomber, The 1955,Ja 17,27:5
Simon and Laura 1956,Jl 3,17:2
Cash on Delivery 1956,S 1,19:3
Novel Affair, A 1957,Ag 28,22:1
Truth About Women, The 1958,Ag 29,18:2
Rattle of a Simple Man 1964,D 21,42:2

Box, Muriel (Original Author)

Seventh Veil, The 1945,D 26,15:1
Truth About Women, The 1958,Ag 29,18:2

Box, Muriel (Producer)

Smugglers, The 1948,Mr 29,17:1
Dear Murderer 1948,My 8,12:2
Girl in a Million, A 1950,Jl 24,15:2
Truth About Women, The 1958,Ag 29,18:2

Box, Muriel (Screenwriter)

Seventh Veil, The 1945,D 26,15:1
Years Between, The 1947,Mr 10,25:2
Holiday Camp 1948,Ja 24,11:2
Smugglers, The 1948,Mr 29,17:1
Brothers, The 1948,My 5,30:4
Dear Murderer 1948,My 8,12:2
Easy Money (Episode 3) 1949,F 14,15:3
Easy Money (Episode 4) 1949,F 14,15:3
Easy Money (Episode 1) 1949,F 14,15:3
Easy Money (Episode 2) 1949,F 14,15:3
Blind Goddess, The 1949,Je 23,33:3
Daybreak 1949,Jl 4,9:2
Girl in the Painting, The 1949,Ag 22,13:1
Christopher Columbus 1949,O 13,33:2
Facts of Love, The 1949,O 31,20:2
Girl in a Million, A 1950,Jl 24,15:2
Good Time Girl 1950,S 25,18:5
Lost People, The 1950,O 2,19:4
Mr Lord Says No! 1952,F 12,22:5
Both Sides of the Law 1954,Ja 12,19:2
Novel Affair, A 1957,Ag 28,22:1

Box, Sydney (Original Author)

Seventh Veil, The 1945,D 26,15:1

Box, Sydney (Producer)

Seventh Veil, The 1945,D 26,15:1
Years Between, The 1947,Mr 10,25:2
Holiday Camp 1948,Ja 24,11:2
Jassy 1948,F 20,19:2
Smugglers, The 1948,Mr 29,17:1
Brothers, The 1948,My 5,30:4
Dear Murderer 1948,My 8,12:2
Don't Take it to Heart 1948,D 25,10:3
Broken Journey 1949,My 26,34:3
Her Man Gilbey 1949,Je 9,35:2
Daybreak 1949,Jl 4,9:2
Facts of Love, The 1949,O 31,20:2
Girl in a Million, A 1950,Jl 24,15:2
So Long at the Fair 1951,Ja 22,14:2
Prisoner, The 1955,D 12,37:1

Box, Sydney (Screenwriter)

Seventh Veil, The 1945,D 26,15:1
Years Between, The 1947,Mr 10,25:2
Holiday Camp 1948,Ja 24,11:2
Smugglers, The 1948,Mr 29,17:1
Brothers, The 1948,My 5,30:4
Dear Murderer 1948,My 8,12:2
Easy Money (Episode 4) 1949,F 14,15:3
Easy Money (Episode 3) 1949,F 14,15:3
Easy Money (Episode 2) 1949,F 14,15:3
Easy Money (Episode 1) 1949,F 14,15:3
Blind Goddess, The 1949,Je 23,33:3
Daybreak 1949,Jl 4,9:2
Girl in the Painting, The 1949,Ag 22,13:1
Christopher Columbus 1949,O 13,33:2
Facts of Love, The 1949,O 31,20:2
Girl in a Million, A 1950,Jl 24,15:2
Good Time Girl 1950,S 25,18:5
Mr Lord Says No! 1952,F 12,22:5
Both Sides of the Law 1954,Ja 12,19:2
Novel Affair, A 1957,Ag 28,22:1

Boxer, John

October Man, The 1948,Ap 16,29:2
My Brothers Keeper 1949,F 14,15:3
Mister Drake's Duck 1952,Ja 28,15:2

Boxer, John— Cont

Bridge on the River Kwai 1957,D 19,39:1

Boxill, Patrick

Brothers, The 1948,My 5,30:4

Boy, Tommy

Sporting Blood 1931,Ag 15,18:3

Boyanovsky, V

Forty-Nine Days 1964,Ja 27,19:1

BOYCE

See Also BOICE

Boyce, Bruce

Beggar's Opera, The 1953,Ag 25,18:2

Boyce, Donna Jo

Breaking Point, The 1950,O 7,10:6

Boyd, Betty

Green Goddess, The 1930,F 14,20:1
Under a Texas Moon 1930,Ap 4,22:1

Boyd, Dorothy

Constant Nymph, The 1929,Je 10,23:1
Perfect Alibi, The 1931,Ap 20,16:3
Bride of the Lake, The 1934,S 11,24:5

Boyd, Edward (Screenwriter)

Robbery 1967,S 28,58:2

Boyd, Jerold Hayden (Original Author)

Place Called Glory, A 1966,Ag 11,27:4

Boyd, Jerold Hayden (Screenwriter)

Place Called Glory, A 1966,Ag 11,27:4

Boyd, Jimmy

Second Greatest Sex, The 1956,F 11,12:2
Platinum High School 1960,My 26,37:3
High Time 1960,S 17,15:1
Inherit the Wind 1960,O 13,41:1

Boyd, Louis Alex T (Original Author)

You Can't Beat the Irish 1952,My 1,34:4

Boyd, Malcolm Rev

You Are What You Eat 1968,S 25,38:1

Boyd, Marilynn

Temple of Venus, The 1923,N 1,24:3

Boyd, Mildred

Gentlemen Prefer Blondes 1928,Ja 16,24:1
Riley, The Cop 1928,D 4,29:1
Merrily We Go to Hell 1932,Je 11,9:3

Boyd, Stephen

Man Who Never Was, The 1956,Ap 4,24:1
Abandon Ship 1957,Ap 18,35:1
Island in the Sun 1957,Je 13,37:1
Alligator Named Daisy, An 1957,O 7,23:2
Bravados, The 1958,Je 26,23:2
Night Heaven Fell, The 1958,O 22,40:4
Woman Obsessed 1959,My 28,34:1
Best of Everything 1959,O 9,24:2
Ben Hur 1959,N 19,50:2
Big Gamble, The 1961,S 2,19:2
Lisa 1962,My 25,28:1
Jumbo 1962,D 7,49:1
Fall of the Roman Empire, The 1964,Mr 27,14:2
Third Secret, The 1964,Ap 29,27:1
Genghis Khan 1965,Je 24,28:2
Oscar, The 1966,Mr 5,16:1
Fantastic Voyage 1966,S 8,43:1
Bible, The 1966,S 29,60:1
Caper of the Golden Bulls, The 1967,Je 22,46:1
Poppy is Also a Flower, The 1967,D 14,62:4
Assignment K 1968,Jl 20,18:2
Shalako 1968,N 6,32:1

Boyd, Thomas (Original Author)

Blaze O' Glory 1929,D 31,15:1

Boyd, William

Temple of Venus, The 1923,N 1,24:3
Changing Husbands 1924,Je 23,22:4
Tarnish 1924,O 13,21:1
Forty Winks 1925,F 3,24:1
Midshipman, The 1925,O 13,20:1
Road to Yesterday, The 1925,D 1,22:4
Steel Preferred 1925,D 22,13:1
Volga Boatman, The 1926,Ap 14,21:1
Jim, The Conquerer 1926,D 28,17:1
King of Kings, The 1927,Ap 20,29:2
Yankee Clipper, The 1927,My 3,25:1
Two Arabian Knights 1927,O 24,24:3
Dress Parade 1927,O 31,22:1
Night Flyer, The 1928,Mr 13,23:3
Skyscraper 1928,Ap 9,18:2
Cop, The 1928,N 6,35:1
Power 1928,N 27,34:1
Lady of the Pavements 1929,Mr 11,22:2
Leatherneck, The 1929,Ap 22,23:1
His First Command 1929,D 23,18:2
Locked Door, The 1930,Ja 20,21:1
Officer O'Brien 1930,F 24,18:1
Benson Murder Case, The 1930,Ap 12,23:1
Those Who Dance 1930,Jl 7,22:3
Storm, The 1930,Ag 23,7:3
Spoilers, The 1930,S 20,15:4
Derelict 1930,N 22,21:3
Gang Buster, The 1931,Ja 24,15:1
Painted Desert, The 1931,Mr 9,19:1
Beyond Victory 1931,Ap 6,24:1
City Streets 1931,Ap 18,17:3
Gun Smoke 1931,Ap 24,27:1
Murder by the Clock 1931,Jl 18,16:6
Big Gamble, The 1931,S 21,20:2
Road to Reno, The 1931,O 10,20:4
Suicide Fleet 1931,N 23,22:1

Boyd, William— Cont

Sky Devils 1932,Mr 4,17:3
Wiser Sex, The 1932,Mr 12,19:5
Carnival Boat 1932,Mr 21,19:5
State's Attorney 1932,My 6,15:3
Painted Woman, The 1932,S 16,24:4
Madison Square Garden 1932,O 12,26:5
Lucky Devils 1933,F 20,11:5
Oliver Twist 1933,Ap 13,15:3
Emergency Call 1933,Je 24,16:2
Laughing at Life 1933,Jl 15,14:2
Chief, The 1933,D 2,9:4
House on 56th Street, The 1933,D 2,9:3
Cheaters 1934,My 12,12:4
Transatlantic Merry-Go-Round 1934,N 1,25:2
Lost City, The 1935,F 21,23:3
Night Life of the Gods 1935,F 23,14:6
Three on the Trail 1936,My 5,26:5
Hopalong Rides Again 1938,Ja 22,19:1
Partners of the Plains 1938,F 12,20:4
Cassidy of Bar 20 1938,Mr 28,19:2
Heart of Arizona 1938,Ap 16,17:1

Boyer, Charles

Magnificent Lie, The 1931,Jl 25,11:6
Man From Yesterday, The 1932,Je 25,18:2
Red Headed Woman 1932,Jl 1,19:3
Heart Song 1934,Je 6,24:6
Caravan 1934,S 28,27:1
Battle, The 1934,N 23,23:2
Liliom 1935,Mr 18,14:4
Private Worlds 1935,Mr 28,25:2
Break of Hearts 1935,My 17,24:3
Shanghai 1935,Jl 20,16:2
Bonheur, Le 1936,F 28,18:2
Garden of Allah, The 1936,N 20,27:2
History Is Made at Night 1937,Mr 29,14:2
Mayerling 1937,S 14,27:1
Conquest 1937,N 5,19:1
Tovarich 1937,D 31,9:2
Algiers 1938,Jl 15,13:2
Orage 1938,D 12,26:2
Love Affair 1939,Mr 17,25:2
When Tomorrow Comes 1939,Ag 17,16:2
All This and Heaven, Too 1940,Jl 5,10:2
Amoureux, Les 1940,D 9,23:3
Back Street 1941,F 12,25:2
Hold Back the Dawn 1941,O 2,29:1
Appointment for Love 1941,N 7,27:1
Tales of Manhattan 1942,S 25,25:1
Constant Nymph, The 1943,Jl 24,8:2
Flesh and Fantasy 1943,N 18,29:1
Gaslight 1944,My 5,17:2
Together Again 1944,N 24,19:2
Confidential Agent 1945,N 3,11:2
Cluny Brown 1946,Je 3,27:3
Woman's Vengeance, A 1948,Ja 30,19:2
Arch of Triumph 1948,Ap 21,33:2
Thirteenth Letter, The 1951,F 22,27:2
First Legion, The 1951,Ap 28,9:2
Happy Time, The 1952,O 31,30:2
Thunder in the East 1953,F 4,32:2
Earrings of Madame De, The 1954,Jl 20,15:5
Cobweb, The 1955,Ag 6,13:3
Around the World in 80 Days 1956,O 18,37:1
Nana 1957,Ap 13,12:3
Parisienne, La 1958,Jl 31,27:1
Buccaneer, The 1958,D 24,00:0
Paris Hotel 1959,S 12,12:3
Fanny 1961,Jl 7,16:1
4 Horsemen of the Apocalypse, The 1962,Mr 10,10:2
Maxime 1962,O 25,48:3
Love Is a Ball 1963,Ap 25,38:1
Adorable Julia 1964,Ap 8,33:1
Very Special Favor, A 1965,Ag 26,40:3
How to Steal a Million 1966,Jl 15,34:1
Is Paris Burning? 1966,N 11,36:1
Casino Royale 1967,Ap 29,25:1
Barefoot in the Park 1967,My 26,51:1

Boyer, Charles (Narrator)

Heart of a Nation, The 1943,Ap 8,27:2
Battle of the Rails; (Bataille Du Rail) 1949,D 27,27:2

Boyer, Charles (Producer)

Flesh and Fantasy 1943,N 18,29:1

Boyer, Francois

25th Hour, The 1967,F 17,45:1

Boyer, Francois (Miscellaneous)

Monkey in Winter 1963,F 1,7:2

Boyer, Francois (Original Author)

Forbidden Games 1952,D 9,43:2

Boyer, Francois (Screenwriter)

What Price Murder 1958,N 11,26:1
War of the Buttons, The 1963,D 19,40:2
Weekend at Dunkirk 1966,My 19,51:2

Boyer, Jean (Director)

Schubert's Serenade 1940,S 3,21:2
Extenuating Circumstances; Circostances Attenuantes 1946,S 24,41:3
Loves of Casanova 1948,S 18,11:4
Mr Peek-A-Boo 1951,S 19,37:1
Prize, The 1952,Ap 30,33:2
Monte Carlo Baby 1954,My 29,13:4
French Touch, The 1954,S 2,18:2

My Seven Little Sins 1956,My 2,27:1
Senechal the Magnificent 1958,O 14,44:1
Crazy for Love 1960,N 26,13:2

Boyer, Jean (Miscellaneous)

Fernandel the Dressmaker 1957,Jl 1,19:2
Senechal the Magnificent 1958,O 14,44:1

Boyer, Jean (Screenwriter)

Avocate d'Amour 1938,S 8,27:2
Abused Confidence 1938,D 1,29:1
Extenuating Circumstances; Circostances Attenuantes 1946,S 24,41:3
Mr Peek-A-Boo 1951,S 19,37:1
Monte Carlo Baby 1954,My 29,13:4
French Touch, The 1954,S 2,18:2
My Seven Little Sins 1956,My 2,27:1

Boyer, Lucien (Composer)

Queen and the Cardinal, The 1944,Je 1,17:3

Boyer, M (Director)

Fernandel the Dressmaker 1957,Jl 1,19:2

Boyer, Marie France

Bonheur, Le; Happiness 1966,My 24,55:2

Boyl, Catherine

French They Are a Funny Race, The 1957,My 21,41:1

Boylan, Malcolm Stuart (Original Author)

Politics 1931,Ag 1,16:4
Madame Racketeer 1932,Jl 23,6:6
O'Shaughnessy's Boy 1935,O 5,18:2

Boylan, Malcolm Stuart (Screenwriter)

Devil Dogs of the Air 1935,F 7,23:2
Dangerous Waters 1936,Ja 22,15:5
Yank at Oxford, A 1938,F 25,15:1
St Louis Blues 1939,F 9,17:2
Lady's From Kentucky, The 1939,Ap 27,31:1
Mr District Attorney 1941,Ap 17,29:3
Remember Pearl Harbor 1942,Je 4,22:4
Bedside Manner 1945,Je 23,9:6
Unknown, The 1946,Jl 20,10:3
Soldiers Three 1951,Mr 30,28:5

Boyle, Catherine

Intent to Kill 1959,Ap 1,43:2

Boyle, Jack (Original Author)

Through the Dark 1924,Ja 8,27:1
Sporting Chance, The 1925,Je 24,14:3
Meet Boston Blackie 1941,F 26,17:2
One Mysterious Night 1944,O 21,15:3

Boyle, Jack (Screenwriter)

Silent Accuser, The 1924,N 25,26:1

Boyle, John

Lady by Choice 1934,N 17,12:1

Boyle, John W (Producer)

Sweden, Land of the Vikings 1934,Ja 4,17:2

Boyle, Joseph C (Director)

Convoy 1927,My 9,26:4
Broadway Nights 1927,Je 28,29:4
Whip Woman, The 1928,F 13,16:2
Mad Hour, The 1928,Ap 16,20:5

Boyle, Selena

Sullivans, The 1944,F 10,19:2

Boyle, Walden

Burning Cross, The 1948,F 20,19:1

Boyle, Wilfred

Will any Gentleman? 1955,S 28,70:6

Boyne, Eva Leonard

None but the Lonely Heart 1944,N 18,16:6

Boys of the Wiltwyck School

Quiet One, The 1949,F 14,15:2

Boysson, Pascale de

Pot Bouille 1958,O 28,39:1
Moderato Cantabile 1964,Ja 7,24:1
Abysses, Les 1964,N 24,44:1
Shameless Old Lady, The 1966,S 27,52:1

Boytler, Arcady (Director)

Mano in Mano 1933,F 20,11:6
Tesoro de Pancho Villa, El 1936,Ja 27,20:4
Celos 1936,Ap 15,25:2
Mujer del Puerto, La 1936,Ag 24,11:3
Mano a Mano 1938,S 19,16:3
Asi es mi Tierra; Such Is my Country 1939,Mr 18,9:3

Bozan, Olinda

Idolos de la Radio 1935,Jl 2,24:5
Caballo del Pueblo, El 1935,D 16,23:4
Buen Camino, Por 1936,Jl 4,18:3
Doce Mujeres; Twelve Women 1940,Mr 11,11:3
Apuros de Claudina, Los; Claudina's Troubles 1940,Je 8,18:3

Bozan, Sofia

Loco Lindo; Crazy Dandy 1938,Ja 11,27:4

Bozhinova, K

Heroes of Shipka 1956,S 3,10:5

Bozhky, Max

Catskill Honeymoon 1950,Ja 28,10:3

Bozhky, Rose

Catskill Honeymoon 1950,Ja 28,10:3

Bozoky, Istvan

Goose Boy, The 1951,O 13,9:2

Bozyk, Max

Yiddle With his Fiddle 1937,Ja 2,15:1
Purimspieler, Der 1937,D 6,19:2
Dybbuk, The 1938,Ja 28,17:2
Tkies Khaf; (Vow, The) 1938,S 15,29:3
Mamele; Little Mothers 1938,D 26,29:1

My Seven Little Sins 1956,My 2,27:1

Bozyk, Max— Cont

Brivele der Mamen, A; Little Letter to Mother, A 1939,S 15,26:4
God, Man and Devil 1950,Ja 23,16:2

Bozzetto, Bruno (Director)

Two Castles 1967,Ja 16,27:3

Bozzetto, Bruno (Producer)

Life in a Tin 1968,Jl 19,30:1

Bozzi

Amours de Toni, Les 1936,N 5,35:1

Bozzoni, Max

Lover's Return, A; Revenant, Le 1948,Ja 26,15:2

Bozzufi, Marcel

Speaking of Murder 1959,O 12,14:1

Braban, Harvey

Blackmail 1929,O 7,22:1
Should a Doctor Tell 1931,Ag 22,7:5

Brabant, Charles (Director)

Respectful Prostitute, The 1957,Jl 11,21:1
Passionate Summer 1957,Jl 22,15:5

Brabant, Charles (Screenwriter)

Passionate Summer 1957,Jl 22,15:5
No Escape 1959,My 23,18:4

Brabant, M (Director)

No Escape 1959,My 23,18:4

Brabin, Charles (Director)

Six Days 1923,S 24,5:4
So Big 1925,Ja 5,19:1
Twinkletoes 1926,D 27,20:3
Hard-Boiled Haggerty 1927,Ag 23,29:4
Valley of the Giants, The 1927,D 5,26:2
Bridge of San Luis Rey, The 1929,My 20,22:6
Ship From Shanghai, The 1930,Ap 26,11:1
Call of the Flesh 1930,S 13,9:3
Great Meadow, The 1931,Mr 14,23:2
Sporting Blood 1931,Ag 15,18:3
Beast of the City, The 1932,Mr 14,13:3
New Morals for Old 1932,Je 24,15:3
Washington Masquerade, The 1932,Jl 22,18:2
Mask of Fu Manchu, The 1932,D 3,21:4
Secret of Madame Blanche, The 1933,F 4,11:3
Stage Mother 1933,S 30,18:5
Day of Reckoning 1933,N 4,18:2
Wicked Woman, A 1935,Ja 1,24:1

Brabin, Charles J (Director)

Foot Falls 1921,S 9,18:3
Driven 1923,F 12,13:4
Framed 1927,Je 20,25:3

Brabin, Charles J (Screenwriter)

Foot Falls 1921,S 9,18:3

Brabourne, John (Producer)

Harry Black and the Tiger 1958,S 19,24:4
Sink the Bismarck! 1960,F 12,22:3
Damn the Defiant 1962,S 20,29:2
Othello 1966,F 2,24:1
Mikado, The 1967,Mr 15,53:1
Up the Junction 1968,Mr 14,51:1
Romeo and Juliet 1968,O 9,41:1

Braccini, Lola

Voice of Love, The 1950,Ja 7,11:2
Seduced and Abandoned 1964,Jl 16,23:1

Bracena, Catalina

Senor Casada Necesita Marido 1935,F 11,14:3

Bracey, Sidney

Merry Go Round 1923,Jl 2,16:2
Courtship of Myles Standish, The 1923,D 31,9:3
Why Men Leave Home 1924,My 12,14:4
Being Respectable 1924,Ag 4,16:3
So This Is Marriage 1924,D 23,16:2
Her Night of Romance 1925,Ja 13,16:1
Merry Widow, The 1925,Ag 27,14:1
Black Bird, The 1926,F 1,16:1
You Never Know Women 1926,Jl 27,15:5
Painting the Town 1927,Ag 2,19:2
Woman on Trial, The 1927,S 26,27:1
Home James 1928,S 11,31:3
Cameraman, The 1928,S 17,27:1
Man Made Women 1928,S 18,33:2
Win That Girl 1928,O 1,23:1
Wedding March, The 1928,O 15,26:1
Show People 1928,N 12,18:2
Haunted House, The 1928,D 17,23:1
His Captive Woman 1929,Ap 3,26:4
Bishop Murder Case, The 1930,F 1,15:1
Anybody's Woman 1930,Ag 16,8:3
Outside the Law 1930,S 1,16:1
Free Love 1930,D 15,29:1
Ten Cents a Dance 1931,Mr 7,17:2
Parlor, Bedroom and Bath 1931,Ap 4,23:1
Subway Express 1931,My 2,23:4
Deceiver, The 1931,N 23,22:1
Dangerous Affair, A 1931,N 23,22:1
Greeks Had a Word for Them, The 1932,F 4,25:2
No More Orchids 1933,Ja 2,29:2
Corruption 1933,Je 20,22:7
Broken Dreams 1933,N 21,23:3
Ninth Guest, The 1934,Mr 3,8:5
Anna Karenina 1935,Ag 31,16:2
Sutter's Gold 1936,Mr 27,25:2
Baroness and the Butler, The 1938,F 19,19:2
My Bill 1938,Jl 7,22:4
Dawn Patrol 1938,D 24,12:1
On Trial 1939,Ap 5,31:2
Sun Never Sets, The 1939,Je 9,26:2

Bracey, Sidney— Cont
British Intelligence 1940,F 12,14:2
Devil's Island 1940,Jl 12,11:4
My Love Came Back 1940,Jl 13,16:5
Body Disappears, The 1942,Ja 31,13:2
BRACH
See Also BROCK
Brach, Bill
Echoes of Silence 1967,Ap 7,32:2
Brach, Gerard (Screenwriter)
Cul de Sac 1966,N 8,44:2
Two of Us, The 1968,F 20,53:1
Bracher, Egon
Nurse Edith Cavell 1939,S 22,27:4
Brack, Claudia
Come September 1961,S 8,34:1
Brack, Kathleen
Frozen Dead, The 1967,N 16,58:1
Brackebusch, Lotte
Rape on the Moor 1957,N 21,38:1
Bracken, Eddie
Too Many Girls 1940,N 21,43:1
Life With Henry 1941,F 6,25:2
Reaching for the Sun 1941,My 8,21:1
Caught in the Draft 1941,Je 26,27:3
Fleet's In, The 1942,Mr 12,24:2
Sweater Girl 1942,Jl 13,18:3
Star Spangled Rhythm 1942,D 31,20:1
Happy Go Lucky 1943,Mr 25,25:1
Miracle of Morgan's Creek, The 1944,Ja 20,15:2
Hail the Conquering Hero 1944,Ag 10,14:2
Rainbow Island 1944,O 26,19:6
Bring on the Girls 1945,Mr 1,25:5
Out of This World 1945,Je 7,25:2
Duffy's Tavern 1945,S 6,23:3
Hold That Blonde 1945,N 8,17:2
Ladies' Man 1947,Ja 13,18:5
Girl from Jones Beach, The 1949,Jl 30,9:2
Summer Stock 1950,S 1,17:2
Two Tickets to Broadway 1951,N 22,47:2
About Face 1952,My 24,15:3
We're not Married 1952,Jl 12,16:2
Bracken, Jimmy
With Six You Get Egg Roll 1968,O 10,59:6
Brackett, Charles (Original Author)
Tomorrow's Love 1925,Ja 7,33:5
Risky Business 1926,S 8,19:3
Pointed Heels 1929,D 28,11:1
Secrets of a Secretary 1931,Ag 29,16:3
Woman Trap 1936,Mr 7,11:4
To Each his Own 1946,My 24,15:2
Emperor Waltz, The 1948,Je 18,19:2
Niagara 1953,Ja 22,20:3
Brackett, Charles (Producer)
Five Graves to Cairo 1943,My 27,21:2
Uninvited, The 1944,F 21,19:3
Lost Weekend, The 1945,D 3,17:2
To Each his Own 1946,My 24,15:2
Emperor Waltz, The 1948,Je 18,19:2
Foreign Affair, A 1948,Jl 1,19:3
Miss Tatlock's Millions 1948,N 25,47:2
Sunset Boulevard 1950,Ag 11,15:2
Mating Season, The 1951,Ap 12,41:2
Model and the Marriage Broker, The 1952,Ja 12,10:6
Niagara 1953,Ja 22,20:3
Titanic 1953,My 28,27:5
Garden of Evil 1954,Jl 10,17:1
Woman's World 1954,S 29,23:4
Virgin Queen, The 1955,Ag 6,13:2
Girl in the Red Velvet Swing, The 1955,O 20,41:2
D-Day, The Sixth of June 1956,My 30,13:1
King and I, The 1956,Je 29,15:6
Teenage Rebel 1956,N 17,17:6
Wayward Bus, The 1957,Je 6,35:2
Gift of Love, The 1958,F 12,32:2
Ten North Frederick 1958,My 23,29:2
Remarkable Mr Pennypacker, The 1959,F 21,25:2
Blue Denim 1959,Jl 31,21:1
Journey to the Center of the Earth 1959,D 17,51:1
High Time 1960,S 17,15:1
State Fair 1962,Ap 12,41:4
Brackett, Charles (Screenwriter)
Enter Madame 1935,Ja 12,12:1
Rose of the Rancho 1936,Ja 9,25:2
Piccadilly Jim 1936,Ag 31,19:1
Live, Love and Learn 1937,N 19,27:2
Bluebeard's Eighth Wife 1938,Mr 24,21:2
Midnight 1939,Ap 6,31:1
What a Life 1939,O 12,33:1
Ninotchka 1939,N 10,27:2
Arise my Love 1940,O 17,33:2
Hold Back the Dawn 1941,O 2,29:1
Ball of Fire 1942,Ja 16,25:2
Major and the Minor, The 1942,S 17,21:3
Five Graves to Cairo 1943,My 27,21:2
Lost Weekend, The 1945,D 3,17:2
To Each his Own 1946,My 24,15:2
Foreign Affair, A 1948,Jl 1,19:3
Miss Tatlock's Millions 1948,N 25,47:2
Sunset Boulevard 1950,Ag 11,15:2
Mating Season, The 1951,Ap 12,41:2

Model and the Marriage Broker, The 1952,Ja 12,10:6
Titanic 1953,My 28,27:5
Girl in the Red Velvet Swing, The 1955,O 20,41:2
Teenage Rebel 1956,N 17,17:6
Journey to the Center of the Earth 1959,D 17,51:1
Brackett, Leigh (Original Author)
13 West Street 1962,Je 7,31:2
Brackett, Leigh (Screenwriter)
Big Sleep, The 1946,Ag 24,6:6
Rio Bravo 1959,Mr 19,40:2
Gold of the Seven Saints 1961,Ap 6,30:3
Hatari 1962,Jl 12,19:1
Dorado, El 1967,Je 29,32:1
Brackmann, Guenter
Toerichte Jungfrau, Die 1935,S 9,24:3
Bradbury, Frederick (Original Author)
Cradle of Courage, The 1920,S 20,13:1
Bradbury, James Jr
Bits of Life 1921,O 17,18:1
Classmates 1924,D 30,15:3
Let It Rain 1927,Mr 9,29:1
Drop Kick, The 1927,S 20,32:2
She's a Shiek 1927,N 21,20:1
Flying Romeos 1928,Ap 3,33:2
Walking Back 1928,Je 12,33:3
Hell-Ship Bronson 1928,Je 19,31:1
Waterfront 1928,O 22,29:1
In old Arizona 1929,Ja 21,18:4
Alibi 1929,Ap 9,29:1
Rogue Song, The 1930,Ja 29,26:4
Last of the Duanes 1930,S 13,9:3
Cisco Kid, The 1931,O 24,20:3
Bradbury, James Sr
Fascinating Youth 1926,My 10,19:1
Circus Ace, The 1927,Jl 6,23:2
Blood Ship, The 1927,Jl 19,27:2
Leopard Lady, The 1928,F 27,16:2
Skinner's big Idea 1928,Mr 27,30:4
Hot Heels 1928,My 22,19:3
Scarlet Seas 1928,D 31,9:1
Matrimonial Bed, The 1930,Ag 25,14:2
Abraham Lincoln 1930,Ag 26,24:1
Tol'able David 1930,N 17,29:1
Silver Streak, The 1935,Ja 16,21:1
Bradbury, Kitty
Our Hospitality 1923,D 10,20:1
Code of the Wilderness, The 1924,Jl 1,21:4
Bradbury, Ray (Original Author)
It Came From Outer Space 1953,Je 18,38:2
Beast From 20,000 Fathoms, The 1953,Je 25,23:1
Fahrenheit 451 1966,N 15,53:1
Bradbury, Ray (Screenwriter)
Moby Dick 1956,Jl 5,18:1
Braddell, Maurice
Men of Tomorrow 1935,Ap 16,27:2
Things to Come 1936,Ap 18,19:2
Braden, Bernard
Stop Me Before I Kill 1961,Je 22,23:4
Day the Earth Caught Fire, The 1962,Mr 16,25:1
Bradet, Allicia
Bambole; Dolls, The (The Telephone Call); Telephone Call, The (The Dolls) 1965,Je 29,26:1
Bradfield, Louis
Blarney Kiss, The 1933,Ag 19,14:4
Bradford, J S Maj (Original Author)
Dunkirk 1958,S 11,42:2
Bradford, John
365 Nights in Hollywood 1934,N 7,32:1
Life Begins at 40 1935,Ap 5,21:3
Bradford, Lane
Slender Thread, The 1965,D 24,24:2
Bradford, Marshall
I Was a Teenage Frankenstein 1958,Ja 30,19:4
Bradford, Richard
Chase, The 1966,F 19,24:1
Bradford, Roark (Original Author)
Green Pastures, The 1936,Jl 17,20:1
Bradford, Virginia
Wreck of the Hesperus, The 1927,N 28,18:5
Chicago 1927,D 24,9:1
Two Lovers 1928,Mr 23,24:4
Craig's Wife 1928,D 4,29:1
Bradge, Clarence (Director)
Man Power 1927,Jl 26,17:1
Bradin, Jean
Modern du Barry, A 1928,Mr 19,26:2
Moulin Rouge 1929,Ap 30,33:2
At the Edge of the World 1929,Je 18,29:4
Theatre 1929,Ag 25,VIII,5:1
David Golder 1932,O 20,24:2
Bradley, David
Julius Caesar 1952,N 25,33:5
Bradley, David (Director)
Julius Caesar 1952,N 25,33:5
Bradley, F G
Battle for Music 1945,O 15,13:2
Bradley, Grace
Too Much Harmony 1933,S 23,11:5
Way to Love, The 1933,N 11,10:3

Bradley, Grace— Cont
Girl Without a Room 1933,D 7,26:3
Six of a Kind 1934,Mr 10,18:3
Come on Marines 1934,Mr 24,20:3
She Made her Bed 1934,Ap 27,25:1
Cat's Paw, The 1934,Ag 17,12:2
Redhead 1934,N 16,27:1
Gilded Lily, The 1935,F 9,11:2
Stolen Harmony 1935,Ap 20,16:2
Two Fisted 1935,O 5,18:3
Rose of the Rancho 1936,Ja 9,25:2
Dangerous Waters 1936,Ja 22,15:5
Anything Goes 1936,F 6,23:3
13 Hours by Air 1936,Ap 30,17:2
F-Man 1936,My 4,16:1
Three Cheers for Love 1936,Ag 1,16:2
Don't Turn 'em Loose 1936,S 25,20:2
You're in the Army Now 1937,Ap 16,27:2
Wake up and Live 1937,Ap 24,16:2
Roaring Timber 1937,Ag 19,23:1
It's all Yours 1938,Ja 7,15:3
Big Broadcast of 1938, The 1938,Mr 10,16:2
There's Magic in Music 1941,Je 5,27:2
Taxi, Mister 1943,Ap 15,20:2
Bradley, Harry C
Smiling Lieutenant, The 1931,My 23,13:4
Employees' Entrance 1933,Ja 21,10:6
It Happened One Night 1934,F 23,23:2
Heat Lightning 1934,Mr 8,23:2
Caravan 1934,S 28,27:1
Our Daily Bread 1934,O 3,25:2
Last Gentleman, The 1934,O 18,26:5
Private Worlds 1935,Mr 28,25:2
Way Down East 1935,O 31,16:2
$1,000 a Minute 1935,D 21,11:1
Florida Special 1936,My 29,15:2
Come and Get It 1936,N 12,31:1
Gold Diggers of 1937 1936,D 25,19:2
New Faces of 1937 1937,Jl 2,25:1
Jury's Secret, The 1938,F 4,17:2
When Tomorrow Comes 1939,Ag 17,16:2
Our Leading Citizen 1939,Ag 24,17:1
Slightly Tempted 1940,N 1,33:1
Make Your own Bed 1944,My 27,12:2
Bradley, John H
Sands of Iwo Jima 1949,D 31,9:2
Bradley, John J Maj-Gen (Miscellaneous)
Heroes All 1931,N 12,30:2
Bradley, Leslie
Young Mr Pitt, The 1943,Mr 11,17:1
Waterloo Road 1948,D 25,10:3
No Orchids for Miss Blandish 1951,F 23,33:2
Crimson Pirate, The 1952,Ag 28,21:2
Kiss of Fire 1955,S 24,11:2
Seven Cities of Gold 1955,O 8,13:2
Good Morning, Miss Dove 1955,N 24,41:1
Lady Godiva 1955,D 3,13:3
Conqueror, The 1956,Mr 31,13:3
Buccaneer, The 1958,D 24,00:0
Bradley, Lovyss
Outrage 1950,O 16,30:5
Golden Girl 1951,N 21,20:3
Bradley, Malcolm
Sentimental Tommy 1921,My 9,16:2
Bradley, Mary Hastings (Original Author)
I Passed for White 1960,Ag 18,19:3
Bradley, Michael
Promise her Anything 1966,F 23,46:1
Bradley, Samuel R (Director)
False Fronts 1922,Je 5,16:2
Bradley, Truman
Young Doctor Kildare 1938,O 28,27:1
Vacation From Love 1938,N 10,33:2
Spring Madness 1938,D 1,29:3
Hardys Ride High, The 1939,Ap 14,28:2
On Borrowed Time 1939,Jl 7,13:2
Northwest Passage 1940,Mr 8,25:1
Millionaires in Prison 1940,Jl 16,21:3
Dead Men Tell 1941,Ap 17,29:3
Burma Convoy 1941,O 7,26:7
Keep 'Em Flying 1941,N 27,29:2
Bombay Clipper 1942,Ja 12,23:3
Treat 'Em Rough 1942,Ja 19,21:3
Night Before the Divorce, The 1942,Ap 10,21:3
Horn Blows at Midnight, The 1945,Ap 21,18:2
I Wonder Who's Kissing Her Now 1947,Jl 24,27:2
Bradley, Will (Director)
Moonglow 1921,My 9,16:2
Bradley-Smith, Douglas
Dr Crippen 1964,F 15,14:1
Bradna, Olympe
Three Cheers for Love 1936,Ag 1,16:2
College Holiday 1936,D 24,21:2
Last Train from Madrid, The 1937,Je 19,20:2
Souls at Sea 1937,Ag 10,23:2
Stolen Heaven 1938,My 12,27:2
Say It in French 1938,D 1,29:1
Night of Nights, The 1939,D 28,17:1
South of Pago-Pago 1940,Ag 2,12:2
Highway West 1941,Ag 8,13:4
International Squadron 1941,N 14,28:4

Bradshaw, Catherine
Naked Heart, The 1955,Mr 9,22:4
Bradshaw, George (Original Author)
New Faces of 1937 1937,Jl 2,25:1
Second Fiddle 1939,Jl 1,11:2
Bad and the Beautiful, The 1953,Ja 16,19:1
How to Steal a Million 1966,Jl 15,34:1
Bradstreet, Charles
Unfinished Dance, The 1947,O 31,29:2
Abbott and Costello Meet Frankenstein 1948,Jl 29,17:2
Brady, Alice
Bought and Paid For 1916,N 9,11:4
Fear Market, The 1920,Ja 26,16:1
Snow Bride, The 1923,Je 12,22:2
When Ladies Meet 1933,Je 24,16:2
Broadway to Hollywood 1933,S 2,14:4
Beauty for Sale 1933,S 16,9:3
Stage Mother 1933,S 30,18:5
Should Ladies Behave? 1933,D 18,24:3
Miss Fane's Baby is Stolen 1934,Ja 20,12:2
Gay Divorcee, The 1934,N 16,27:1
Gold Diggers of 1935 1935,Mr 15,25:2
Let 'Em Have It 1935,My 30,21:1
Lady Tubbs 1935,Jl 22,20:2
Metropolitan 1935,O 18,27:4
Harvester, The 1936,Jl 4,18:2
My Man Godfrey 1936,S 19,18:1 (Incorrect in this edition; use 1936,S 18,18:1 elsewhere)
Go West, Young Man 1936,N 19,31:3
Three Smart Girls 1937,Ja 25,22:2
Call it a Day 1937,My 7,29:2
Mr Dodd Takes the Air 1937,Ag 12,14:2
100 Men and a Girl 1937,S 18,15:2
Merry-Go-Round of 1938 1937,N 26,27:2
In Old Chicago 1938,Ja 7,15:2
Joy of Living 1938,My 6,27:1
Goodbye Broadway 1938,My 14,18:1
Zenobia 1939,My 15,15:2
Young Mr Lincoln 1939,Je 3,11:2
Brady, Ed
Squaw Man, The 1931,S 19,10:2
Son of Kong 1933,D 30,9:2
Redhead 1934,N 16,27:1
Brady, Edward
To the Last Man 1923,Ag 28,12:1
Price She Paid, The 1925,Ja 13,16:1
Three Faces West 1926,F 16,22:4
Lost at the Front 1927,Je 14,33:2
Clancy's Kosher Wedding 1927,S 7,35:2
Dressed to Kill 1928,Mr 12,26:1
Alibi 1929,Ap 9,29:1
Night Club Lady, The 1932,Ag 27,13:4
Brady, Edwin J
Old Homestead, The 1922,O 9,10:2
Trail of the Lonesome Pine, The 1923,Mr 20,24:3
Broken Wing, The 1923,O 9,17:4
Eternal Struggle, The 1923,O 16,21:3
Fighting American, The 1924,My 13,24:1
Flower of the Night 1925,O 19,26:1
Texan, The 1930,My 17,21:2
Conquering Horde, The 1931,Mr 30,25:2
Brady, Fred
Stage Door Canteen 1943,Je 25,13:2
Swing Shift Maisie 1943,S 10,29:2
3 Is a Family 1944,D 20,20:3
Cat Creeps, The 1946,My 18,12:4
Brady, Fred (Original Author)
Hollywood Story 1951,Je 7,40:6
Taxi 1953,Ja 22,20:3
Never Wave at a Wac 1953,Ap 24,30:2
Brady, Fred (Screenwriter)
Champagne for Caesar 1950,My 12,33:2
Hollywood Story 1951,Je 7,40:6
Brady, Leo (Original Author)
Edge of Doom 1950,Ag 4,13:2
Brady, Leslie
Black Limelight 1939,Je 26,12:2
Brady, Patti
Two Guys From Milwaukee 1946,Jl 27,12:5
Never Say Goodbye 1946,N 23,12:2
Stallion Road 1947,Ap 5,12:5
State of the Union 1948,Ap 23,28:1
Letter to Three Wives, A 1949,Ja 21,24:2
Adventure in Baltimore 1949,Ap 29,27:2
Brady, Philip
Valley of the Giants, The 1927,D 5,26:2
Brady, Ruth
Clock, The 1945,My 4,23:2
Harvey Girls, The 1946,Ja 25,26:2
Arnelo Affair, The 1947,S 13,8:5
Unfinished Dance, The 1947,O 31,29:2
Summer Holiday 1948,Je 12,8:5
Caught 1949,F 18,26:4
Forever, Darling 1956,F 10,18:1
Brady, Scott
Canon City 1948,Jl 8,19:2
He Walked by Night 1949,F 7,15:2
Undertow 1949,D 16,37:2
Port of New York 1950,F 3,29:2
I Was a Shoplifter 1950,Ap 28,26:3
Undercover Girl 1950,N 8,37:2
Kansas Raiders 1951,Ja 26,19:2

Model and the Marriage Broker, The 1952,Ja 12,10:6
Untamed Frontier 1952,Ag 23,10:2
Montana Belle 1952,N 8,9:2
Bloodhounds of Broadway 1952,N 15,15:2
Johnny Guitar 1954,My 28,19:2
White Fire 1954,S 18,12:4
1954,S 18,12:4
Gentlemen Marry Brunettes 1955,O 31,31:5
Maverick Queen, the 1956,Je 4,25:2
John Goldfarb, Please Come Home 1965,Mr 25,42:4
Black Spurs 1965,My 29,17:1
Fort Utah 1967,My 25,54:3
Brady, William
New Faces of 1937 1937,Jl 2,25:1
Brady, William A (Original Author)
Stolen Orders 1918,Je 3,9:3
Brady, William A (Producer)
Bought and Paid For 1916,N 9,11:4
Little Women 1918,N 11,13:3
Bragadin, A (Screenwriter)
Hell Raiders of the Deep 1954,Jl 3,9:2
Bragaglia, Arturo
Documento Fatale, Il 1940,S 26,27:3
Four Steps in the Clouds 1948,N 22,25:2
Miracle in Milan 1951,D 18,42:2
Ring Around the Clock 1953,My 19,36:2
Bragaglia, Carlo Ludovico (Director)
Voice of Love, The 1950,Ja 7,11:2
My Widow and I 1950,Ag 30,27:5
Mighty Crusaders, The 1961,S 23,17:1
Bragaglia, Carlo Ludovico (Original Author)
One Night With You 1949,F 21,20:2
Bragard, Rene (Screenwriter)
Fire Under Her Skin 1958,Je 28,13:6
Bragdon, Cliff
Saint in New York, The 1938,My 26,31:2
Braggiotti, Francesca
Scipio Africanus 1939,S 23,22:2
Braggiotti, Herbert
What a Widow 1930,O 4,15:2
Flying High 1931,D 12,23:3
Bragiel, Krystina
Village, The 1953,S 23,37:2
Braginsky, Emil (Screenwriter)
Mexican, The 1957,Ap 3,28:2
Watch out for the Automobile 1966,My 23,48:1
Braham, Lional
Battle Cry for Peace, The 1915,Ag 7,8:3
Braham, Lionel
Diana the Huntress 1916,Je 19,9:5 (In Addenda)
Skinner's Dress Suit 1926,My 3,27:1
Don Juan 1926,Ag 7,6:1 (In Addenda)
Night Life 1927,D 20,33:2
As You Like It 1936,N 6,29:3
Personal Property 1937,Ap 11,27:2
Wee Willie Winkie 1937,Jl 24,12:1
Christmas Carol, A 1938,D 23,16:2
Little Princess, The 1939,Mr 11,21:1
Macbeth 1950,D 28,22:6
Braham, Philip (Miscellaneous)
Nell Gwyn 1935,Je 20,16:2
Brahim, Mahjoub Ben
Saadia 1954,Mr 20,10:5
Brahimi, Himmoud
Daughter of the Sands 1952,F 18,15:2
Brahm, Hans (Director)
Broken Blossoms 1937,Ja 14,16:3
Brahm, John (Director)
Counsel for Crime 1937,O 9,16:1
Penitentiary 1938,Mr 7,13:2
Girls' School 1938,N 3,27:1
Let Us Live 1939,Mr 30,19:2
Rio 1939,O 27,27:2
Submarine Zone; (Escape To Glory) 1941,Ap 7,13:2
Wild Geese Calling 1941,Ag 30,10:2
Tonight We Raid Calais 1943,Ap 15,20:2
Wintertime 1943,S 30,27:2
Lodger, The 1944,Ja 20,15:3
Hangover Square 1945,F 8,15:2
Guest in the House 1945,F 16,19:2
Locket, The 1947,Mr 20,38:2
Brasher Doubloon, The 1947,My 22,34:5
Singapore 1947,S 17,31:2
Miracle of Our Lady Fatima, The 1952,Ag 21,16:2
Thief of Venice, The 1952,N 28,22:7
Secret Sharer, The 1953,Ja 14,27:2
Diamond Queen, The 1954,Ja 27,24:2
Mad Magician, The 1954,My 20,38:2
Bengazi 1955,O 8,13:4
Golden Plaque, The 1963,Ag 10,8:6
Hot Rods to Hell 1967,Ag 10,45:5
Brahm, Phillip (Composer)
Die Singende Stadt 1932,My 10,25:4
Brahms, Caryl (Original Author)
Gay Lady, The 1951,Ap 16,21:2
Brahms, Caryl (Screenwriter)
One Night With You 1949,F 21,20:2

Braidwood, Jill
Belles of St Trinian's, The 1954,D 23,13:4
Braine, John (Original Author)
Room at the Top 1959,Mr 31,26:1
Life at the Top 1965,D 15,53:1
Brainin, Jerome (Composer)
That's Right, You're Wrong 1939,N 30,25:3
Brainville, Yves
Man Who Knew too Much, The 1956,My 17,37:1
Witches of Salem 1958,D 9,54:2
Crack in the Mirror 1960,My 20,26:1
Braithwaite, E R (Original Author)
To Sir, With Love 1967,Je 15,56:1
Braithwaite, Lilian
Man About the House, A 1949,Mr 9,33:2
Braithwaite, Warwick
Battle for Music 1945,O 15,13:2
Brakhage, Stan (Producer)
Anticipation of the Night 1962,Ag 3,14:2
Brambell, Wilfrid
Small World of Sammy Lee, The 1963,Ag 14,28:1
Three Lives of Thomasina, The 1963,D 12,46:1
Hard Day's Night, A 1964,Ag 12,41:1
Where the Bullets Fly 1967,S 7,50:4
Conqueror Worm, The 1968,Ag 15,46:2
Bramble, A V
Outcast of the Islands 1952,My 16,19:2
Bramble, A V (Director)
Shooting Stars 1928,Je 11,27:1
Bramble, A V (Producer)
Shooting Stars 1928,Mr 4,IX,7:7
Bramhall, Dorothy
Lady Surrenders, A 1947,Je 20,25:6
Weaker Sex, The 1949,Jl 11,13:2
Run for Your Money, A 1950,Ap 10,15:3
Encore (The Ant and the Grasshopper); Ant and the Grasshopper, The (Encore) 1952,Ap 3,45:1
Bramley, Flora
College 1927,S 12,29:1
We Americans 1928,Mr 29,25:3
Flirting Widow, The 1930,Ag 2,16:4
Bramley, Raymond
Scoundrel, The 1935,My 3,23:2
Broken Arrow 1950,Jl 21,15:2
Sun Sets at Dawn, The 1951,Ja 15,13:1
Bramley, William
West Side Story 1961,O 19,39:3
Brampton, Kenneth
Uncivilized 1937,N 17,27:4
Forty Thousand Horsemen 1941,Ag 15,13:2
Brancati, Vitaliano (Original Author)
Difficult Years 1950,Ag 22,31:2
Three Forbidden Stories 1953,N 16,21:4
Bell Antonio 1962,Ap 3,43:2
Brancati, Vitaliano (Screenwriter)
Difficult Years 1950,Ag 22,31:2
Devotion 1953,Ja 31,10:6
Journey to Love 1953,O 9,32:8
His Last Twelve Hours 1953,N 13,24:7
Three Forbidden Stories 1953,N 16,21:4
Brancato, Rosemarie
Bitter Sweet 1940,N 22,27:1
Branch, Houston (Original Author)
Showdown, The 1928,Mr 5,21:1
Alias the Doctor 1932,Mr 3,22:3
Tiger Shark 1932,S 23,22:2
Hard to Handle 1933,F 2,21:5
West of Singapore 1933,Ap 1,18:3
Silk Express, The 1933,Je 28,24:2
Belle of the Yukon 1945,Mr 30,18:4
Wild Harvest 1947,N 13,33:2
River Lady 1948,My 21,19:5
Congo Crossing 1956,Jl 14,13:2
Branch, Houston (Screenwriter)
Don't Get Personal 1936,F 22,12:1
Mr Wong, Detective 1938,N 21,14:4
Mystery Ship 1941,Ag 16,18:3
Pittsburgh Kid, The 1941,S 23,27:4
Woman in Bondage 1944,Mr 27,17:2
Branch, Isabel
Olvidados de Dios, Los; Those Forgotten by God 1940,Ja 15,11:2
Branch, Pamela
Lilies of the Field 1963,O 2,51:1
Branch, Sarah
Hell is a City 1961,Ja 19,26:3
Sword of Sherwood Forest 1961,Ja 26,32:3
Branchi, Daniela
Operation Kid Brother 1967,N 23,58:2
BRAND
See Also BRANT, BRANDT
Brand, Barbara
Seventh Juror, The 1964,Ja 28,25:1
Brand, Christina (Original Author)
Green for Danger 1947,Ag 8,10:2
Brand, Harry (Original Author)
Plastered in Paris 1928,S 24,25:1
Brand, James (Original Author)
Seven Days to Noon 1950,D 19,41:3
Brand, Max (Original Author)
Just Tony 1922,Ag 7,14:2
Best Bad Man, The 1925,D 2,23:1
Cavalier, The 1928,O 31,28:4

Brand, Max (Original Author) — Cont
Holy Terror, A 1931,Jl 20,20:4
Internes Can't Take Money 1937,My 6,23:2
Young Doctor Kildare 1938,O 28,27:1
Calling Dr Kildare 1939,My 12,25:4
Destry Rides Again 1939,N 30,25:1
Secret of Dr Kildare, The 1939,D 19,33:1
Dr Kildare's Strange Case 1940,Ap 12,19:2
Dr Kildare's Crisis 1940,D 19,33:1
People vs Dr Kildare, The 1941,My 8,21:1
Dr Kildare's Victory 1942,F 5,25:2
Powder Town 1942,Je 8,11:2
Desperadoes, The 1943,My 13,17:2
Three Men in White 1944,My 26,23:3
Between Two Women 1945,Mr 29,18:3
Dark Delusion 1947,Je 26,19:2
Singing Guns 1950,Je 5,19:3
My Outlaw Brother 1951,Ag 23,19:2
Brand, Max (Screenwriter)
Uncertain Glory 1944,Ap 8,9:2
Brand, Millen (Screenwriter)
Snake Pit, the 1948,N 5,29:2
Brand, Neville
D O A 1950,My 1,18:2
Halls of Montezuma, The 1951,Ja 6,9:6
Only the Valiant 1951,Ap 14,9:6
Mob, The 1951,O 18,32:2
Red Mountain 1952,Ap 26,19:2
Kansas City Confidential 1952,N 29,11:2
Stalag 17 1953,Jl 2,19:2
Charge at Feather River, The 1953,Jl 16,17:2
Riot in Cell Block 11 1954,F 19,24:5
Return From the Sea 1954,Jl 10,7:3
Prodigal, The 1955,My 14,10:7
Return of Jack Slade, The 1955,N 24,41:3
Raw Edge 1956,Jl 28,10:7
Love Me Tender 1956,N 16,23:1
Way to the Gold, The 1957,My 11,24:6
Tin Star, The 1957,O 24,37:2
Cry Terror 1958,My 15,25:1
Five Gates to Hell 1959,D 10,51:6
Adventures of Huckleberry Fin, The
1960,Ag 4,17:1
Last Sunset, The 1961,Je 15,51:1
George Raft Story, The 1962,Mr 22,40:1
Birdman of Alcatraz 1962,Jl 19,19:2
That Darn Cat 1965,D 3,44:1
Brand, Oscar
8 X 8 1957,Mr 16,13:2
Brand, Roland
Campbell's Kingdom 1960,Ja 11,35:5
Brande, Dorothea (Miscellaneous)
Wake up and Live 1937,Ap 24,16:2
Brander, Allen
Making of O'Malley 1925,Je 22,10:2
Brandes, Aline
Holiday Inn 1942,Ag 5,16:1
Brandet, Alicia
Weekend, Italian Style 1968,My 23,56:2
Brandis, Helmut (Original Author)
Eight Girls in a Boat 1934,Ja 13,16:3
Brando, Jocelyn
Big Heat, The 1953,O 15,43:2
Nightfall 1957,Ja 24,34:1
Explosive Generation, The 1962,F 15,24:2
Ugly American, The 1963,Ap 12,30:2
Bus Riley's Back in Town 1965,Ap 8,45:2
Chase, The 1966,F 19,24:1
Brando, Marlon
Men, The 1950,Jl 21,15:2
Streetcar Named Desire, A 1951,S 30,27:1
Viva Zapata 1952,F 8,19:2
Julius Caesar 1953,Je 5,19:1
Wild One, The 1953,D 31,9:2
On the Waterfront 1954,Jl 29,18:1
Desiree 1954,N 18,42:1
Guys and Dolls 1955,N 5,26:1
Teahouse of the August Moon, The
1956,N 30,19:1
Sayonara 1957,D 6,39:4
Soyonara 1957,D 6,39:4
Young Lions, The 1958,Ap 3,23:1
Fugitive Kind, The 1960,Ap 15,13:1
One Eyed Jacks 1961,Mr 31,21:1
Mutiny on the Bounty 1962,N 9,31:2
Ugly American, The 1963,Ap 12,30:2
Bedtime Story 1964,Je 11,27:1
Saboteur, The: Code Name-Mori Turi
1965,Ag 26,40:2
Chase, The 1966,F 19,24:1
Appaloosa, The 1966,S 15,51:1
Countess from Hong Kong, A 1967,Mr 17,35:1
Reflections in a Golden Eye 1967,O 12,59:1
Candy 1968,D 18,54:2
Brando, Marlon (Director)
One Eyed Jacks 1961,Mr 31,21:1
Brandon, Bill
Black Knight, The 1954,O 29,27:2
Brandon, David
All Hands on Deck 1961,Ap 1,10:2
Marines, Lets Go! 1961,Ag 16,37:2
Brandon, Dickie
Spirit of the U S A, The 1924,My 21,22:3

Brandon, Dorothy (Original Author)
Outsider, The 1931,Je 7,VIII,6:1
Brandon, Harriett
Stage Door 1937,O 8,27:2
Brandon, Henry
Killer at Large 1936,O 26,20:1
Garden of Allah, The 1936,N 20,27:2
Black Legion 1937,Ja 18,21:1
I Promise to Pay 1937,Ap 26,15:2
Conspiracy 1939,Ag 23,19:2
Nurse Edith Cavell 1939,S 22,27:4
Ski Patrol 1940,My 21,29:4
Dark Streets of Cairo 1940,D 2,19:3
Son of Monte Cristo, The 1940,D 5,33:1
Underground 1941,Je 23,13:2
Edge of Darkness 1943,Ap 10,12:4
Canon City 1948,Jl 8,19:2
Old Los Angeles 1948,Jl 12,11:2
Fighting O'Flynn, The 1949,F 28,16:2
Cattle Drive 1951,Ag 9,17:5
Scarlet Angel 1952,Je 21,12:2
Hurricane Smith 1952,O 4,15:2
Pony Express 1953,Je 6,8:6
Scared Stiff 1953,Jl 3,10:2
Vera Cruz 1954,D 27,22:4
Searchers, The 1956,My 31,21:4
Auntie Mame 1958,D 5,39:1
Buccaneer, The 1958,D 24,00:0
Big Fisherman, The 1959,Ag 6,18:1
Two Rode Together 1961,Jl 27,23:3
Brandon, Mary
Bashful Suitor, The 1921,D 12,20:2
Brandon, Michael
Arnelo Affair, The 1947,S 13,8:5
Gunfighter, The 1950,Je 24,7:2
Brandon-Thomas, Amy
Mystery at the Villa Rose 1930,Je 2,25:4
Brandowska-Turska, Ewa
Halka 1938,Ja 17,11:3
BRANDT
See Also BRANT, BRAND
Brandt, Bernard (Producer)
Decoy 1946,N 2,12:2
Story of the Pope, The 1946,D 20,31:3
Brandt, Bert Jr
Flying Classroom, The 1958,Je 28,13:7
Brandt, Else-Marie
Inga 1968,N 21,41:2
Brandt, Frances
Mr Belvedere Rings the Bell 1951,Ag 2,18:1
Drums of Tahiti 1954,Ap 24,14:5
Brandt, Harry (Miscellaneous)
Roosevelt Story, The 1947,Ag 22,11:2
Brandt, Henry (Director)
Masters of the Congo Jungle 1960,My 5,41:2
Brandt, Ivan
Forever Yours 1937,Je 7,22:2
Fugitive, The 1940,Jl 23,22:2
It Happened to One Man 1941,F 24,11:6
Brandt, J Dr (Original Author)
Gitta Entdeckt Ihr Herz 1932,S 30,17:3
Madame Spy 1934,F 10,20:1
Brandt, J Dr (Screenwriter)
Youth Astray 1928,My 29,17:2
Brandt, Janet
Cold Wind in August, A 1961,Jl 27,23:2
Brandt, Jerrold T (Producer)
Scattergood Baines 1941,Ap 4,25:2
At Swords Point 1952,Ap 10,37:1
Brandt, Lou (Director)
Stop! Look! and Laugh! 1961,F 9,36:1
Brandt, Louis
Mirele Efros 1939,O 21,12:2
Brandt, Martin
Devil at 4 O'Clock, The 1961,O 19,39:3
Judgment at Nuremberg 1961,D 20,36:1
Brandt, Rainer
Judge and the Sinner, The 1964,Je 6,14:2
Branion, Antonio
Cabiria 1921,Jl 4,10:2
Branker, Roy (Composer)
See my Lawyer 1945,My 4,23:4
Brannan, Carol
Adventure in Baltimore 1949,Ap 29,27:2
Branner, Per-Axel (Director)
Pettersson & Bendel 1934,F 22,25:2
Ungdom Av I Dag 1936,Je 23,27:7
Brannigan, Owen
Gilbert and Sullivan 1953,O 28,36:3
Brannigan, Paddy
Treasure Island 1950,Ag 16,24:2
Brannon, Carol
Cynthia 1947,S 19,27:2
Take Care of my Little Girl 1951,Jl 19,20:2
Brannum, Tom
John Paul Jones 1959,Je 17,39:1
Bransten, Richard (Original Author)
San Diego, I Love You 1944,N 10,25:1
Margie 1946,O 17,28:3
Trouble With Women, The 1947,Jl 14,14:4
BRANT
See Also BRAND, BRANDT

Brant, Lynton
Our Daily Bread 1934,O 3,25:2
Frontier Town 1938,Mr 12,13:3
Brant, Neil (Original Author)
International House 1933,My 27,11:5
Brantford, Albert
This Freedom 1923,N 28,15:1
Brantford, Mickey
This Freedom 1923,N 28,15:1
Mare Nostrum 1926,F 16,22:4
Suspense 1930,N 8,21:3
Mr Cohen Takes a Walk 1936,F 13,25:2
Last Journey, The 1936,Je 8,22:4
Branzilla, Franco
Piccolo Eroe 1937,Jl 1,33:2
Bras, Jean Pierre
Lovers of Teruel, The 1962,D 15,5:1
Brascia, John
White Christmas 1954,O 15,16:3
Meet Me in Las Vegas 1956,Mr 14,39:2
Ambushers, The 1967,D 23,29:1
Brasfield, Rod
Face in the Crowd, A 1957,My 29,33:1
Brash, Henry (Producer)
Her Sister's Secret 1947,Ja 23,31:3
Brasini, Armando (Producer)
Theodora 1921,O 15,16:2
Brasini, Piero
First Opera Film Festival 1948,My 31,12:7
Braskins, Leonard (Screenwriter)
Call of the Wild 1935,Ag 15,15:2
Brasno, George
Charlie Chan at the Circus 1936,Mr 19,22:4
Brasno, Olive
Charlie Chan at the Circus 1936,Mr 19,22:4
Brasscur, Pierre
Lovers of Verona, The 1951,Mr 12,20:2
Brasselle, Keefe
River Gang 1945,O 6,9:7
Not Wanted 1949,Jl 25,11:4
Dial 1119 1950,D 4,32:6
Place in the Sun, A 1951,Ag 29,20:1
Unknown Man, The 1951,N 17,9:5
It's a big Country 1952,Ja 9,25:2
Skirts Ahoy! 1952,My 29,17:2
Eddie Cantor Story, The 1953,D 26,10:2
Three Young Texans 1954,Ap 7,8:2
Mad at the World 1955,My 14,10:8
Brassens, Georges
Gates of Paris 1958,Ja 15,24:1
Brasseur, Claude
Rue de Paris 1960,D 23,14:3
7 Capital Sins (Envy); Envy (7 Capital Sins)
1963,Ja 17,5:2
Elusive Corporal, The 1963,F 19,5:1
Band of Outsiders 1964,S 19,19:1
Sweet and Sour 1964,D 28,34:2
Banana Peel; Peau de Banane 1965,Ja 19,29:1
Band of Outsiders; Bande a Part 1966,Mr 16,48:3
Brasseur, Pierre
Mademoiselle ma Mere 1939,S 19,29:2
Port of Shadows 1939,O 30,13:2
Last Desire 1939,D 22,15:2
Claudine 1940,Ap 1,15:2
Jericho 1946,D 16,31:2
Enfants du Paradis, Les 1947,F 20,32:2
Gates of the Night 1950,Mr 16,40:2
Noah's Ark 1950,Ag 21,15:1
Skipper Next to God 1953,Ja 13,24:2
Dirty Hands 1954,My 11,25:5
Plaisir, Le (The House of Madame Tellier); House
of Madame Tellier (Le Plaisir)
1954,My 20,38:1
Gates of Paris 1958,Ja 15,24:1
Possessors, The 1959,Jl 21,24:1
Sans Famille 1959,S 5,11:4
Oasis 1960,Jl 7,26:1
Where the Hot Wind Blows 1960,N 12,15:1
Carthage in Flames 1961,Ja 26,32:3
Bell Antonio 1962,Ap 3,43:2
Crime Does Not Pay (The Fenayrou Case);
Fenayrou Case, The (Crime Does Not Pay)
1962,O 17,35:2
Candide 1962,N 20,39:1
Don't Tempt the Devil 1964,Ap 28,43:1
Cloportes 1966,Ap 19,36:1
Very Handy Man, A 1966,D 15,60:1
Vie de Chateau, La 1967,Mr 21,35:1
King of Hearts 1967,Je 20,34:1
Birds in Peru 1968,N 7,51:2
Brassler, Robert (Producer)
Brasher Doubloon, The 1947,My 22,34:5
Brastoff, Sascha S/Sgt
Winged Victory 1944,D 21,16:2
Bratersky, Nikolai
Signal, The 1943,Mr 25,25:3
Rainbow, The 1944,O 23,14:3
Bratt, Anatol (Original Author)
How to Seduce a Playboy 1968,My 16,53:2
BRAUER
See Also BROWER

Brauer, Peter Paul (Director)
Meadehen von Gestern Nacht, Das; Girl of Last
Night, The 1938,Je 18,18:2
Jugend von Heute; Youth of Today
1938,N 5,15:3

Brault, Michel (Director)
Adolescents, The (Genevieve); Genevieve (The
Adolescents) 1967,Ap 14,33:1

Brault, Michel (Director)
Moontrap, The; Pour la Suite du Monde
1964,N 11,38:1

Brault, Michel (Screenwriter)
Moontrap, The; Pour la Suite du Monde
1964,N 11,38:1

BRAUN
See Also BROWN, BROWNE

Braun, Alfred (Director)
Girls Behind Bars 1950,My 10,41:2

Braun, Carl Johannes (Screenwriter)
City of Secrets 1963,Jl 27,10:2

Braun, Curt J (Screenwriter)
Last Waltz, The 1958,Ap 12,13:1
Corinna Darling 1958,Je 14,14:3
Gypsy Baron, The 1959,N 14,13:1

Braun, Hans
St Matthew Passion 1952,Ja 29,17:4

Braun, Harold Dr (Director)
Keepers of the Night 1953,Je 9,24:2
Glass Tower, The; (Glaserne Turm, Der)
1959,Ag 27,24:4

Braun, Harold Dr (Screenwriter)
Secrets of a Soul 1950,S 16,12:6
Keepers of the Night 1953,Je 9,24:2

Braun, Hermann
Jugend von Heute; Youth of Today
1938,N 5,15:3
Jugend; Youth 1939,D 9,18:2
D III 88, Die neue deutsche Luftwaffe greift an; D
III 88, The New German Air Force Attacks
1940,F 17,9:3

Braun, Judith
Red Ball Express 1952,My 30,11:2
Horizons West 1952,N 22,16:5

Braun, K
Drei Maeoerl um Schubert 1937,Je 5,21:2

Braun, L (Director)
Maximka 1953,O 12,30:4

Braun, Pinkos
Aren't We Wonderful? 1959,O 16,27:1

Braun, V (Director)
Heroes of the Sea 1941,Ap 28,11:2
Blue Cliff, The 1943,Mr 25,25:3
Malva 1957,D 23,18:2

Braun, Zev (Producer)
Goldstein 1965,My 8,19:7

Braunberger, Pierre (Director)
Bullfight 1956,Jl 4,15:2

Braunberger, Pierre (Original Author)
Paris 1900 1950,O 24,34:6
Bullfight 1956,Jl 4,15:2

Braunberger, Pierre (Producer)
Shoot the Piano Player 1962,Jl 24,19:1
My Life to Live 1963,S 24,43:2
Winner, The 1965,Jl 1,34:1

Brauner, Arthur (Producer)
Confess, Dr Corda 1960,O 24,25:5
Corrupt Ones, The 1967,F 23,41:3

Braus, Mortimer (Original Author)
Women in Prison 1938,Mr 1,19:3
Three Loves Has Nancy 1938,S 2,21:2
Twice Blessed 1945,Jl 7,7:5
Let's Make It Legal 1951,N 7,35:3

Braus, Mortimer (Screenwriter)
Hannibal 1960,Ag 4,17:1

Brausewetter, Hans
Jolly Peasant, The 1929,Jl 1,31:2
Oberkellner, Der 1929,Jl 1,31:2
Ein Burschenlied aus Heidelberg 1931,S 14,15:3
Liebe Ist Liebe 1932,Je 2,25:2
Barberina, Die Taenzerin Von Sans-Souci
1932,O 26,15:4
Ich Geh' aus und Du Bleibst da 1932,N 21,21:1
Drunter und Drueber 1932,D 19,19:5
Hertha's Erwachen 1933,Mr 14,18:3 (Incorrect in
this edition; use 1933,Mr 14,19:2 elsewhere)
Abel Mit Der Mundharmonika 1934,S 1,16:3
Freundin Eines Grossen Mannes, Die
1934,S 11,24:5
Gretl Zieht das Grosse Los 1935,F 11,14:2
Unbekannte Gast, Der; Unknown Guest, The
1935,Je 1,18:3
Frischer Wind aus Kanada 1935,S 21,18:2
Vier Musketiere, Die; Four Musketeers, The
1935,N 9,19:3
Wenn der Hahn Kraeht 1936,N 14,23:3
Raub der Sabinerinnen, Der 1937,Ja 16,21:1
Zwischen den Eltern; Between the Parents
1938,Jl 30,10:3
Klapperstorchverband, Der; Stork Society, The
1938,O 29,15:3
Gluck auf den Lande; Rural Happiness
1940,F 10,19:3
Paradies der Junggesellen; Bachelors' Paradise

1940,Ap 13,21:3
Fledermaus, Die; Bat, The 1948,Mr 15,26:2

Braut, Frigga
Lindenwirtin vom Rhein, Die 1931,S 25,28:7
Herzblut 1932,O 3,15:2

Bravo, Antonio
Ay Jalisco no te Rajes 1943,Ap 24,17:3
Passion Island 1943,My 1,11:2
Virgin of Guadalupe, The 1943,My 15,13:3
Miserables, Los 1944,O 24,17:2
St Francis of Assisi 1947,Ap 5,12:5
Exterminating Angel, The 1967,Ag 22,33:1

Bravo, Jamie
Love Has Many Faces 1965,F 25,24:1

Bravos, Peter
Flight of the Phoenix, The 1966,F 1,26:1

Brawner, Hilda
1+1 1961,N 8,41:1

Bray, David K
Bird of Paradise 1951,Mr 15,37:2

Bray, Richard
Terror in the City 1966,N 9,43:4

Bray, Robert
Return of the Badmen 1948,Ag 5,16:2
Blood on the Moon 1948,N 12,30:5
Strange Bargain 1949,S 30,28:3
Bus Stop 1956,S 1,19:2
Wayward Bus, The 1957,Je 6,35:2
Never Love a Stranger 1958,N 22,27:4
Never so Few 1960,Ja 22,15:2

Bray, Yvonne de
Eternal Return, The; Eternel Retour, L'
1948,Ja 5,15:2
Gigi 1950,Ja 31,20:2
Storm Within, The; (Parents Terribles, Les)
1950,Ap 24,21:2
Pit of Loneliness 1954,Ap 9,19:2

Bray (Producer)
Col Heeza Liar's Treasure Island 1923,F 5,18:2

Brayton, Margaret
Frontier Marshal 1939,Jl 29,18:2
Quiet Please, Murder 1942,D 22,31:1
Goddess, The 1958,Je 25,24:1

Brazaglia, Arturo
Tears of Blood 1952,Ja 19,13:2

Brazeale, Hal
Death of a Champion 1939,Ag 24,17:3

Brazee, Laurie (Screenwriter)
And So They Were Married 1936,My 14,29:3
Outer Gate, The 1937,N 22,15:2

Brazell, Wolfe
Atlantis the Lost Continent 1961,My 27,12:1

Brazier, Edward
Dark Odyssey 1961,Je 26,22:2

Brazil, Thomas Lieut
Three Stripes in the Sun 1955,N 24,41:2

Brazybulski, N (Director)
Spelnione Marzenia; Fulfilled Dreams
1939,D 14,35:3

Brazzi, Lydia
Christmas That Almost Wasn't 1966,N 24,65:2
After the Fox 1966,D 24,11:1

Brazzi, Oscar (Producer)
China Is Near 1968,Ja 9,37:1

Brazzi, Rossano
King's Jester, The 1947,Je 26,19:3
Great Dawn, The 1947,Ag 28,28:3
Story of Tosca, The 1947,D 19,34:2
Foria 1948,Ja 21,30:2
Furia 1948,Ja 21,30:2
Merry Chase, The 1948,S 18,11:4
Little Women 1949,Mr 11,33:2
Bullet for Stefano 1950,O 26,38:7
Malia 1952,F 2,11:4
Volcano 1953,Jl 21,19:2
Three Coins in the Fountain 1954,My 21,18:2
Barefoot Contessa, The 1954,S 30,37:1
Angela 1955,Je 4,9:2
Summertime 1955,Je 22,25:1
Story of Esther Costello, The 1957,N 6,43:1
Legend of the Lost 1957,D 23,18:2
South Pacific 1958,Mr 20,33:1
Ten Commandments, The 1958,Ap 7,26:1
Certain Smile, A 1958,Ag 1,13:2
Flesh and Desire 1958,N 27,52:4
Count Your Blessings 1959,Ap 24,23:1
Light in the Piazza 1962,F 8,25:1
Rome Adventure 1962,Mr 16,25:1
Siege of Syracuse, The 1962,Ag 9,17:8
Three Fables of Love (The Tortoise and the Hare);
Tortoise and the Hare, The (Three Fables of
Love) 1963,Ag 21,38:1
Dark Purpose 1964,F 6,36:4
Battle of the Villa Fiorita, The 1965,My 27,28:1
Engagement Italiano 1966,Je 21,35:1
Christmas That Almost Wasn't 1966,N 24,65:2
Woman Times Seven 1967,Je 28,38:1
Bobo, The 1967,S 29,53:1

Brazzi, Rossano (Director)
Christmas That Almost Wasn't 1966,N 24,65:2

Brazzou, Anna
Bed of Grass 1957,D 28,9:2

Brdeca, Jiri (Original Author)
Lemonade Joe 1967,N 21,53:1

Brdeca, Jiri (Screenwriter)
Lemonade Joe 1967,N 21,53:1

Brdecka, Jiri (Original Author)
Emperor and the Golem, The 1955,Ja 10,27:4

Brdecka, Jiri (Screenwriter)
Emperor and the Golem, The 1955,Ja 10,27:4

Breakston, George
No Greater Glory 1934,My 5,22:2
Mrs Wiggs of the Cabbage Patch 1934,O 29,14:2
Dark Angel, The 1935,S 6,12:2
Return of Peter Grimm, The 1935,O 4,25:2
Second Wife 1936,Ag 29,16:3
Love Finds Andy Hardy 1938,Jl 22,10:2
Jesse James 1939,Ja 14,13:1
Andy Hardy Gets Spring Fever 1939,Jl 19,23:2
Judge Hardy and Son 1940,Ja 18,27:3 (In
Addenda)
Andy Hardy Meets Debutante 1940,Ag 2,12:2
Andy Hardy's Private Secretary 1941,Mr 7,17:2
Courtship of Andy Hardy, The 1942,Ap 10,21:2

Breakston, George (Director)
Scarlet Spear, The 1954,Ap 10,11:4
Boy Cried Murder, The 1966,Ap 14,42:3

Breakston, George (Original Author)
Scarlet Spear, The 1954,Ap 10,11:4

Breakston, George (Producer)
Urubu 1948,O 21,33:3
Tokyo File 212 1951,Je 1,20:7

Breakston, George (Screenwriter)
Urubu 1948,O 21,33:3

Breakstone, George
Swanee River 1939,D 30,9:2

Breal, P A (Screenwriter)
Deadlier Than the Male 1957,O 9,41:1

Breamer, Sylvia
Missing 1918,Je 17,11:3
We Can't Have Everything 1918,Jl 15,9:3
My Lady's Garter 1920,Mr 15,13:2
Devil, The 1921,Ja 17,9:1
Doubling for Romeo 1921,O 24,13:1
Man Unconquerable, The 1922,Jl 17,16:3
Girl of the Golden West, The 1923,My 21,12:2
Barefoot Boy, The 1923,N 11,6:1
Flaming Youth 1923,N 26,15:6
Her Temporary Husband 1924,Ja 1,20:1
Lilies of the Field 1924,Mr 17,9:1
Woman on the Jury, The 1924,My 19,14:2
Up in Mabel's Room 1926,Je 29,21:2

Breasted, Charles (Screenwriter)
Human Adventure, The 1935,O 30,16:3

Breasted, James Henry (Producer)
Human Adventure, The 1935,O 30,16:3

Brecher, Egon
As the Earth Turns 1934,Ap 12,27:2
No Greater Glory 1934,My 5,22:2
Black Cat, The 1934,My 19,18:4
Many Happy Returns 1934,Je 9,18:2
Now and Forever 1934,O 13,10:1
Black Fury 1935,Ap 11,27:2
Florentine Dagger, The 1935,Ap 27,20:6
Charlie Chan's Secret 1936,Ja 18,19:4
Boulder Dam 1936,Mr 30,17:5
Till We Meet Again 1936,My 9,11:2
Sins of Man 1936,Je 19,17:2
White Angel, The 1936,Je 25,24:1
Ladies in Love 1936,O 29,31:1
Black Legion 1937,Ja 18,21:1
Stolen Holiday 1937,F 1,15:3
I Met Him in Paris 1937,Je 3,29:2
Love Under Fire 1937,Ag 28,8:2
Thin Ice 1937,S 4,8:2
Heidi 1937,N 6,14:2
Spy Ring, The 1938,Ja 15,19:1
Invisible Enemy 1938,Ap 30,18:2
You and Me 1938,Je 2,19:1
Three Musketeers, The 1939,F 18,12:2
Juarez 1939,Ap 26,27:1
Angels Wash Their Faces 1939,S 4,16:2
I Was an Adventuress 1940,My 20,13:2
Four Sons 1940,Je 8,18:4
Devil's Island 1940,Jl 12,11:4
Man I Married, The 1940,Ag 3,9:2
They Dare not Love 1941,My 16,21:4
Underground 1941,Je 23,13:2
Manpower 1941,Jl 5,14:2
Hairy Ape, The 1944,Jl 3,8:3
Royal Scandal, A 1945,Ap 12,19:2
O S S 1946,My 27,15:5
So Dark the Night 1946,D 7,16:2

Brecher, Irving (Director)
Life of Riley, The 1949,Ap 18,18:4
Somebody Loves Me 1952,S 25,38:1
Sail a Crooked Ship 1962,F 3,12:6

Brecher, Irving (Miscellaneous)
Fools for Scandal 1938,Mr 25,15:3

Brecher, Irving (Producer)
Life of Riley, The 1949,Ap 18,18:4

Brecher, Irving (Screenwriter)
New Faces of 1937 1937,Jl 2,25:1
At the Circus 1939,N 17,17:2
Go West 1941,F 21,16:2

Brecher, Irving (Screenwriter) — Cont
Shadow of the Thin Man 1941,N 21,23:2
Best Foot Forward 1943,Je 30,25:2
Du Barry Was a Lady 1943,Ag 20,13:1
Meet Me in St Louis 1944,N 29,20:2
Yolanda and the Thief 1945,N 23,26:2
Summer Holiday 1948,Je 12,8:5
Life of Riley, The 1949,Ap 18,18:4
Somebody Loves Me 1952,S 25,38:1
Cry for Happy 1961,Mr 4,16:1
Bye Bye Birdie 1963,Ap 5,27:3

Brecht, Bertolt (Original Author)
Dreigroschenoper, Die; Beggar's Opera, The 1931,My 18,21:2
Hangmen Also Die 1943,Ap 16,24:2
Threepenny Opera, The 1960,Jl 11,24:4
Shameless old Lady, The 1966,S 19,57:1
Shameless Old Lady, The 1966,S 27,52:1

Brecht, Bertolt (Screenwriter)
Kuhle Wampe 1933,Ap 24,11:4
Hangmen Also Die 1943,Ap 16,24:2

Breck, Peter
Portrait of a Mobster 1961,Ap 20,30:4
Lad: A Dog 1963,My 2,40:2
Shock Corridor 1963,S 12,32:1

Breckenridge, Betty
Tom, Dick and Harry 1941,Jl 18,22:2

Brecker, Fred
Folly of Vanity 1925,Ja 28,14:1

Breckner, Gary
Love and Hisses 1938,Ja 1,11:1
Rebecca of Sunnybrook Farm 1938,Mr 26,12:1
Thanks For Everything 1938,D 10,13:2

Bredin, Patricia
Bridal Path, The 1959,D 21,34:2
Left, Right and Centre 1961,F 10,19:1
Secret of Monte Cristo, The 1962,My 3,25:4

Breeden, John
William Fox Movietone Follies of 1929 1929,My 27,22:1
Salute 1929,O 5,22:5
Shannons of Broadway, The 1929,D 21,17:1
Beloved Bachelor, The 1931,O 17,20:1
Madame Racketeer 1932,Jl 23,6:6

Breen, Bobby
Let's Sing Again 1936,My 9,11:2
Rainbow on the River 1936,D 18,31:4
Make a Wish 1937,S 23,33:1
Hawaii Calls 1938,Ap 29,17:2
Breaking the Ice 1938,S 23,35:3
Fisherman's Wharf 1939,F 24,15:2
Way Down South 1939,Ag 18,16:4
Johnny Doughboy 1943,My 6,25:3

Breen, Edmund
Return of the Scarlet Pimpernel, The 1938,Ap 11,12:2
Man With 100 Faces 1938,N 1,27:2

Breen, George
Jigsaw 1949,My 30,9:4

Breen, Joe Jr (Screenwriter)
Breakthrough 1950,N 18,10:2
Prodigal, The 1955,My 14,10:7

Breen, Julian (Original Author)
Love on the Run 1936,N 28,13:3

Breen, Margaret
Heads Up 1930,O 13,31:1

Breen, Richard (Director)
Stopover Tokyo 1957,D 27,23:4

Breen, Richard (Original Author)
Appointment With Danger 1951,My 10,38:2
Niagara 1953,Ja 22,20:3

Breen, Richard (Screenwriter)
Foreign Affair, A 1948,Jl 1,19:3
Isn't It Romantic? 1948,O 7,35:2
Miss Tatlock's Millions 1948,N 25,47:2
Top o' the Morning 1949,S 1,25:2
Mating Season, The 1951,Ap 12,41:2
Model and the Marriage Broker, The 1952,Ja 12,10:6
O Henry's Full House (The Gift of the Magi); Gift of the Magi, The (O Henry's Full House) 1952,O 17,33:1
O Henry's Full House (The Last Leaf 1952,O 17,33:1
O Henry's Full House (The Clarion Call); Clarion Call, The (O Henry's Full House) 1952,O 17,33:1
O Henry's Full House (The Cop and the Anthem); Cop and the Anthem, The (O Henry's Full House) 1952,O 17,33:1
Titanic 1953,My 28,27:5
Dragnet 1954,Ag 21,10:2
Pete Kelly's Blues 1955,Ag 19,10:1
Seven Cities of Gold 1955,O 8,13:2
Stopover Tokyo 1957,D 27,23:4
F B I Story, The 1959,S 25,23:1
Wake Me When It's Over 1960,Ap 9,17:2
State Fair 1962,Ap 12,41:4
PT 109 1963,Je 27,23:1
Mary, Mary 1963,O 25,38:2
Captain Newman, MD 1964,F 21,36:1
Do Not Disturb 1965,D 25,17:2
Man Could Get Killed, A 1966,My 12,54:2
Tony Rome 1967,N 16,58:1

Breen, Thomas E
B F's Daughter 1948,Mr 25,35:2
Luxury Liner 1948,S 10,19:2
Battleground 1949,N 12,8:4
River, The 1951,S 11,33:2

Breese, Edmund
Marriage Morals 1923,Ag 14,10:3
Speed Spook, The 1924,O 21,21:3
Wildfire 1925,Je 10,18:2
Womanhandled 1926,Ja 5,25:2
Brown Derby, The 1926,Je 14,24:1
Paradise for Two 1927,Ja 25,18:4
Home Made 1927,D 13,33:2
Finders-Keepers 1928,Mr 5,21:3
Burning Daylight 1928,Ap 23,20:2
Perfect Crime, The 1928,Ag 6,15:2
On Trial 1928,N 15,26:5
Haunted House, The 1928,D 17,23:1
Conquest 1929,F 11,26:3
Sonny Boy 1929,Mr 9,24:3
Girls Gone Wild 1929,Ap 22,23:1
Hottentot, The 1929,S 7,15:1
Hold Everything 1930,Ap 23,24:1
All Quiet on The Western Front 1930,Ap 30,29:1
Czar of Broadway, The 1930,Je 30,22:6
Top Speed 1930,Ag 30,7:4
Kismet 1930,O 31,20:1
Tol'able David 1930,N 17,29:1
Millie 1931,F 7,11:1
Bright Lights 1931,F 10,24:4
Last Parade, The 1931,Mr 2,19:1
Painted Desert, The 1931,Mr 9,19:1
Young Sinners 1931,My 9,15:4
Good Bad Girl, The 1931,My 15,20:6
She-Wolf 1931,My 28,30:6
Public Defender, The 1931,Ag 1,16:4
Platinum Blonde 1931,O 31,22:2
Morals for Women 1931,N 16,23:1
Mata Hari 1932,Ja 1,31:1
Hatchet Man, The 1932,F 4,25:2
Cross Examination 1932,F 27,22:1
Fame Street 1932,Ap 2,13:2
Cabin in the Cotton 1932,S 30,17:3
Match King, The 1932,D 8,25:3
Madame Butterfly 1932,D 26,26:2
Billion Dollar Scandal, The 1933,Ja 9,23:1
International House 1933,My 27,11:5
Duck Soup 1933,N 23,24:2
Beloved 1934,Ja 27,9:3
Come on Marines 1934,Mr 24,20:3
Dancing Man 1934,Jl 16,11:3
Broadway Bill 1934,N 30,22:2

Breese, Edmund (Original Author)
Man's Home, A 1921,D 19,13:1

Breffort, Alexandre (Original Author)
Irma la Douce 1963,Je 6,39:1

Brega, Mario
For a Few Dollars More 1967,Jl 4,23:1
Minute to Pray, A Second to Die, A 1968,My 23,56:2

Bregman, Judith (Miscellaneous)
Symmetry 1967,Ja 21,35:1

Bregovska, Zorka
Ljubav I Strast 1932,D 16,25:5

Brehat, Georges
Not Guilty 1948,Ap 23,28:2
Farewell to Arms, A 1958,Ja 25,14:1
Quiet American, The 1958,F 6,24:1

Breil, Paulette
Doulos-The Finger Man 1964,Mr 3,31:1

Brejchova, Hana
Loves of a Blonde 1966,S 13,51:2

Brem, Beppo
Musketier Meier III 1938,D 31,7:2
Arme Millionar, Der; Poor Millionaire, The 1939,D 30,9:2
Drei Vater um Anna; Three Fathers for Anna 1940,Ja 20,11:3
Tonio Kroger 1968,Ja 16,24:1

Breman, Lennie
Inspector General, The 1949,D 31,9:2
M 1951,Je 11,20:7

Bremer, Lucille
Meet Me in St Louis 1944,N 29,20:2
Yolanda and the Thief 1945,N 23,26:2
Ziegfeld Follies 1946,Mr 23,8:3
Till the Clouds Roll By 1946,D 6,27:4
Dark Delusion 1947,Je 26,19:2
Adventures of Casanova 1948,Mr 22,18:3
Ruthless 1948,S 4,8:7

Bren, J Robert (Original Author)
Looking for Trouble 1934,Ap 12,27:2
Band Plays on, The 1934,D 22,21:2
High Tension 1936,Jl 11,11:4
Bad Guy 1937,Ag 26,25:2
Argentine Nights 1940,O 11,25:3
In old California 1942,Je 18,25:3
El Paso 1949,Mr 24,35:2
Siege at Red River, The 1954,Ap 3,19:2
Naked Alibi 1954,O 2,21:2

Bren, J Robert (Producer)
First Yank into Tokyo 1945,O 25,18:2

Bren, J Robert (Screenwriter)
Without Orders 1936,N 4,41:3
Man Who Found Himself, The 1937,Ap 9,19:3
China Passage 1937,Ap 16,27:2
Behind the Headlines 1937,Je 1,27:2
Hideaway 1937,S 25,10:2
Double Danger 1938,F 10,17:5
Crime Ring 1938,Jl 22,10:3
Parents on Trial 1939,S 18,15:5
American Empire 1943,Ja 14,25:4
First Yank into Tokyo 1945,O 25,18:2
Great Sioux Uprising, The 1953,Jl 18,6:2

Bren, Milton H (Director)
3 for Bedroom C 1952,Je 27,18:3

Bren, Milton H (Producer)
Merrily We Live 1938,Mr 18,23:3
There Goes my Heart 1938,O 14,27:1
Topper Takes a Trip 1938,D 30,11:2
Remember? 1939,D 15,33:4
Wyoming 1940,O 3,31:4
Barnacle Bill 1941,Jl 25,12:4
Borderline 1950,Mr 6,17:2

Bren, Milton H (Screenwriter)
3 for Bedroom C 1952,Je 27,18:3

Brenda, Baby
Kathleen 1938,Ja 24,17:1

Brenda and Cobina
Time Out for Rhythm 1941,Jl 10,16:3

Brendel, El
You Never Know Women 1926,Jl 27,15:5
Campus Flirt, The 1926,S 22,31:1
Wings 1927,Ag 13,10:4
Cock Eyed World, The 1929,Ag 5,25:2
Sunny Side Up 1929,O 4,24:5
Frozen Justice 1929,O 26,15:1
Hot for Paris 1930,Ja 4,21:1
Happy Days 1930,F 14,20:1
Her Golden Calf 1930,My 5,27:3
New Movietone Follies of 1930, The 1930,Je 21,20:5
Big Trail, The 1930,O 25,20:3
Just Imagine 1930,N 22,21:3
Mr Lemon of Orange 1931,Mr 28,15:3
Six Cylinder Love 1931,My 16,31:3
Women of all Nations 1931,My 30,9:2
Spider, The 1931,S 5,7:4
Delicious 1931,D 26,15:5
Disorderly Conduct 1932,Ap 11,19:2
Handle with Care 1932,D 24,11:4
Hot Pepper 1933,Ja 23,9:2
My Lips Betray 1933,N 4,18:3
God's Country and the Woman 1937,Ja 11,15:5
Holy Terror, The 1937,Ja 30,21:2
Blonde Trouble 1937,Ag 7,7:2
Happy Landing 1938,Ja 22,19:1
Little Miss Broadway 1938,Jl 23,10:4
Valley of the Giants 1938,S 10,20:2
Risky Business 1939,Mr 23,27:2
If I Had my Way 1940,My 6,13:2
Captain Caution 1940,O 21,21:3
Gallant Sons 1940,D 12,37:2
Beautiful Blonde From Bashful Bend, The 1949,My 28,11:2

Brendl, Jola
Fuerst Sepp'l 1937,Jl 17,18:1

Breneman, Tom
Breakfast in Hollywood 1946,Jl 15,21:1

Brenlin, George
Cimarron 1961,F 17,12:2

Brenn, Doris
Beloved Brat 1938,My 2,13:2

Brennan, Dennis
Rising of the Moon, The (1921); 1921 (The Rising of the Moon) 1957,Jl 10,23:1
Broth of a Boy 1959,D 28,18:1

Brennan, Frederick Hazlitt (Miscellaneous)
College Swing 1938,Ap 28,27:2

Brennan, Frederick Hazlitt (Original Author)
Strong Boy 1929,Ap 1,22:1
One Night at Susie's 1930,N 24,26:5
Sporting Blood 1931,Ag 15,18:3
Shanghai Madness 1933,S 23,11:6
St Louis Kid, The 1934,N 1,25:2
Miss Pacific Fleet 1935,D 7,22:2
Little Miss Nobody 1936,Je 6,21:1
Big Broadcast of 1938, The 1938,Mr 10,16:2
Greenwich Village 1944,S 28,26:2
Follow the Sun 1951,Ap 26,34:4
Girl in Every Port, A 1952,F 14,23:1

Brennan, Frederick Hazlitt (Screenwriter)
Wives Never Know 1936,O 31,24:2
St Louis Blues 1939,F 9,17:2
Sailor's Lady 1940,Je 29,12:2
Untamed 1940,Jl 25,14:3
Guy Named Joe, A 1943,D 24,17:2
Adventure 1946,F 8,23:2
Killer McCoy 1948,F 12,31:2
Follow the Sun 1951,Ap 26,34:4
Thunder in the East 1953,F 4,32:2
Devil's Canyon 1953,O 3,14:2

Brennan, Jay (Screenwriter)
Expensive Husbands 1938,Ja 8,19:3

Brennan, Jay Kern (Composer)
Young and Beautiful 1934,S 18,18:4
Brennan, John
Where the Boys Are 1961,Ja 20,22:1
Brennan, Kevin
Massacre Hill 1950,D 14,51:3
Brennan, Michael
Operation Disaster 1951,Ja 15,13:1
Circle of Danger 1951,Jl 12,21:6
Clouded Yellow, The 1951,N 13,33:2
Ivanhoe 1952,Ag 1,8:2
Trouble in Store 1956,Ja 14,13:2
Day They Robbed the Bank of England, The
1960,S 5,11:2
Brennan, Ruth
Oh! Susanna 1951,Mr 30,28:5
Brennan, Walter
Law and Order 1932,F 29,21:3
Half a Sinner 1934,Je 23,16:5
Wedding Night, The 1935,Mr 16,19:1
Lady Tubbs 1935,Jl 22,20:2
Man on the Flying Trapeze 1935,Ag 3,16:2
Barbary Coast 1935,O 14,21:1
Seven Keys to Baldpate 1935,D 14,11:2
Three Godfathers, The 1936,Mr 9,20:2
These Three 1936,Mr 19,22:4
Moon's our Home, The 1936,My 13,29:2
Fury 1936,Je 6,21:1
Come and Get It 1936,N 12,31:1
Banjo on My Knee 1936,D 12,15:1
When Love Is Young 1937,Ap 17,15:1
Wild and Woolly 1937,S 6,20:1
Buccaneer, The 1938,F 17,17:2
Adventures of Tom Sawyer, The 1938,F 18,23:1
Texans, The 1938,Jl 28,23:2
Mother Carey's Chickens 1938,Ag 5,11:1
Cowboy and the Lady, The 1938,N 25,19:3
Kentucky 1938,D 24,12:1
Story of Vernon and Irene Castle, The
1939,Mr 31,19:2
They Shall Have Music 1939,Jl 26,17:2
Stanley and Livingstone 1939,Ag 5,18:2
Joe and Ethel Turp Call on the President
1940,Ja 4,19:2
Northwest Passage 1940,Mr 8,25:1
Maryland 1940,Jl 13,16:5
Westerner, The 1940,O 25,25:2
Meet John Doe 1941,Mr 13,25:2
Nice Girl 1941,Mr 27,29:6
Sergeant York 1941,Jl 3,15:1
This Woman Is Mine 1941,O 13,21:2
Swamp Water 1941,N 17,15:2
Rise and Shine 1941,D 6,14:3
Pride of the Yankees, The 1942,Jl 16,23:1
Stand by for Action 1943,Mr 12,12:2
Slightly Dangerous 1943,Ap 2,17:2
Hangmen Also Die 1943,Ap 16,24:2
North Star, The 1943,N 5,23:1
Home in Indiana 1944,Je 22,23:1
To Have and Have Not 1944,O 12,24:1
Princess and the Pirate, The 1945,F 10,16:2
Dakota 1945,D 17,17:2
Stolen Life, A 1946,My 2,27:4
Nobody Lives Forever 1946,N 2,12:2
My Darling Clementine 1946,D 4,44:5
Scudda-Hoo! Scudda-Hay! 1948,Ap 15,31:1
Red River 1948,O 1,31:2
Blood on the Moon 1948,N 12,30:5
Green Promise, The 1949,Je 24,29:2
Task Force 1949,O 1,8:6
Brimstone 1949,O 7,35:3
Ticket to Tomahawk, A 1950,My 20,8:6
Singing Guns 1950,Je 5,19:3
Curtain Call at Cactus Creek 1950,S 22,35:4
Surrender 1950,O 9,21:5
Along the Great Divide 1951,My 17,38:3
Best of the Badmen 1951,Ag 10,13:2
Return of the Texan 1952,F 14,23:1
Lure of the Wilderness 1952,O 4,15:2
Four Guns to the Border 1954,N 6,15:3
Bad Day at Black Rock 1955,F 2,22:2
Far Country, The 1955,F 14,24:2
At Gunpoint 1956,F 4,24:5
Proud Ones, The 1956,Ag 11,10:2
Way to the Gold, The 1957,My 11,24:6
Tammy and the Bachelor 1957,Je 15,10:7
God Is my Partner 1958,Je 5,39:2
Rio Bravo 1959,Mr 19,40:2
Those Calloways 1965,Ap 15,38:2
Oscar, The 1966,Mr 5,16:1
Gnome-Mobile, The 1967,Jl 20,30:2
Who's Minding the Mint? 1967,D 7,60:3
One and Only Genuine Original Family Band,
The 1968,Mr 22,55:1
Brenner, Alfred (Screenwriter)
Key Witness 1960,N 12,15:1
Brenon, Donald
Our Neighbors-The Carters 1940,F 15,15:2
Brenon, Herbert (Director)
Daughter of the Gods, A 1916,O 18,9:1
Twelve:Ten 1919,D 22,18:3
Stage Romance A 1922,Mr 26,VI,2:1 (In
Addenda)

Rustle of Silk, The 1923,My 8,22:4
Spanish Dancer, The 1923,O 8,20:1
Side Show of Life, The 1924,Jl 22,9:1
Alaskan, The 1924,S 15,28:1
Peter Pan 1924,D 29,11:4
Little French Girl, The 1925,Je 1,10:3
Street of Forgotten Men, The 1925,Jl 21,26:2
Kiss for Cinderella, A 1925,D 26,11:2
Song and Dance Man, The 1926,F 1,16:1
Dancing Mothers 1926,F 18,21:1
God Gave Me Twenty Cents 1926,N 20,3:2
Great Gatsby, The 1926,N 22,28:3
Telephone Girl, The 1927,My 16,24:2
Sorrell and Son 1927,N 14,26:1
Laugh, Clown, Laugh 1928,My 28,23:2
Laugh, Clown, Laugh! 1928,Je 3,VIII,5:1
Rescue, The 1929,Ja 14,20:1
Case of Sergeant Grischa, The 1930,Mr 8,21:1
Lummox 1930,Mr 24,25:1
Beau Ideal 1931,Ja 19,25:1
Transgression 1931,Je 15,23:3
Girl of the Rio 1932,Ja 9,21:1
Wine, Women and Song 1934,Mr 21,24:3
Housemaster 1939,Ap 10,13:2
Brenon, Herbert (Producer)
Fall of the Romanoffs, The 1917,S 7,9:2
Fall of the Romanoffs, The 1917,S 24,11:2
Passion Flower, The 1921,Ap 4,18:1
Sign on the Door, The 1921,Jl 18,16:4 (In
Addenda)
Brenon, Juliet
Street of Forgotten Men, The 1925,Jl 21,26:2
Brenst, George
So Big 1932,Ap 30,19:3
Brent, Earl (Composer)
Kathleen 1941,D 19,35:3
Thousands Cheer 1943,S 14,27:1
Call Me Mister 1951,F 1,21:2
Brent, Eve
Tarzan's Fight for Life 1958,Ag 16,10:2
Guide for the Married Man, A 1967,My 27,16:1
Brent, Evelyn
Other Man's Wife, The 1919,Je 9,16:3
Smooth as Satin 1925,Je 23,24:3
Love 'Em and Leave 'Em 1926,D 8,24:3
Love's Greatest Mistake 1927,F 21,14:2
Blind Alleys 1927,Mr 1,31:1
Underworld 1927,Ag 22,21:3
Women's Wares 1927,N 15,27:1
Last Command, The 1928,Ja 23,18:3
Beau Sabreur 1928,Ja 23,18:3
Showdown, The 1928,Mr 5,21:1
Night of Mystery, A 1928,Ap 16,20:5
His Tiger Lady 1928,My 28,23:2
Tiger Lady, The 1928,Je 3,VIII,5:1
Drag Net, The 1928,Je 4,13:2
Mating Call, The 1928,O 8,14:2
Interference 1928,N 17,23:1
Broadway 1929,My 28,36:2
Woman Trap 1929,Ag 31,13:4
Why Bring That Up? 1929,O 5,22:5
Slightly Scarlet 1930,Mr 1,23:1
Framed 1930,Mr 29,23:1
Nuits de Chicago; Underworld
1930,Ap 20,VIII,6:5
Silver Horde, The 1930,O 25,20:6
Madonna of the Streets 1930,N 29,21:4
Traveling Husbands 1931,Ag 8,16:3
Mad Parade, The 1931,S 19,10:2
Pagan Lady 1931,S 21,20:2
High Pressure 1932,F 1,22:3
Attorney for the Defense 1932,My 28,18:2
Crusader, The 1932,O 8,15:4
World Gone Mad, The 1933,Ap 15,16:3
Home on the Range 1935,F 13,24:4
President's Mystery, The 1936,O 19,22:1
Night Club Scandal 1937,N 12,27:2
Daughter of Shanghai 1937,D 24,21:2
Tip-Off Girls 1938,Mr 25,15:3
Mr Wong, Detective 1938,N 21,14:4
Law West of Tombstone, The 1938,N 25,19:1
Mad Empress, The 1940,F 15,15:1
Seventh Victim, The 1943,S 18,11:3
Brent, George
Once a Sinner 1931,Ja 17,23:1
Charlie Chan Carries On 1931,Mr 21,15:1
Homicide Squad 1931,O 19,28:1
Rich are Always With Us, The 1932,My 16,19:5
Week-End Marriage 1932,Je 4,9:2
Miss Pinkerton 1932,Jl 9,7:5
Purchase Price, The 1932,Jl 16,5:5
Crash, The 1932,S 9,17:5
They Call It Sin 1932,O 21,25:4
Luxury Liner 1933,F 3,21:3
42d Street 1933,Mr 10,19:3
Keyhold, The 1933,Mr 31,23:3
Lilly Turner 1933,Je 15,21:2
Baby Face 1933,Je 24,16:2
Female 1933,N 4,18:3
From Headquarters 1933,N 17,22:4
Stamboul Quest 1934,Jl 14,16:6
Housewife 1934,Ag 10,21:2
Desirable 1934,S 15,20:5

Brent, George — Cont
Painted Veil, The 1934,D 7,29:1
Right to Live, The 1935,F 16,9:1
Living on Velvet 1935,Mr 8,25:4
Stranded 1935,Je 20,16:2
Front Page Woman 1935,Jl 12,15:1
Goose and the Gander, The 1935,S 12,29:2
Special Agent 1935,S 19,28:1
In Person 1935,D 13,31:5
Snowed Under 1936,Mr 30,17:5
Golden Arrow, The 1936,My 4,16:1
Case Against Mrs Ames, The 1936,My 28,19:2
Give Me your Heart 1936,S 17,18:2
More Than a Secretary 1936,D 11,35:2
God's Country and the Woman 1937,Ja 11,15:5
Mountain Justice 1937,My 13,31:2
Go Getter, The 1937,Je 4,27:2
Submarine D-1 1937,D 30,15:4
Gold Is Where You Find It 1938,F 14,20:6
Jezebel 1938,Mr 11,15:2
Racket Busters 1938,Ag 11,13:1
Secrets of an Actress 1938,O 8,10:2
Wings of the Navy 1939,F 4,11:1
Dark Victory 1939,Ap 21,27:2
Old Maid, The 1939,Ag 12,16:2
Rains Came, The 1939,S 9,11:2
Fighting 69th, The 1940,Ja 27,9:2
Adventure in Diamonds 1940,Ap 4,27:2
'Til We Meet Again 1940,Ap 14,14:2
Man Who Talked too Much, The 1940,Je 29,12:2
South of Suez 1940,D 19,33:2
Honeymoon for Three 1941,F 8,19:2
Great Lie, The 1941,Ap 12,19:2
They Dare not Love 1941,My 16,21:4
International Lady 1941,N 11,29:2
Twin Beds 1942,My 1,23:4
In This our Life 1942,My 9,10:2
Gay Sisters, The 1942,Ag 15,14:2
You Can't Escape Forever 1942,O 17,11:1
Silver Queen 1943,Ja 11,18:4
Experiment Perilous 1944,D 30,15:2
Affairs of Susan, The 1945,Mr 29,18:2
My Reputation 1946,Ja 26,19:2
Spiral Staircase, The 1946,F 7,29:3
Tomorrow Is Forever 1946,F 22,21:2
Lover Come Back 1946,Je 20,20:3
Temptation 1946,D 25,33:6
Slave Girl 1947,Jl 18,21:3
Corpse came C O D, The 1947,Ag 19,27:2
Christmas Eve 1947,N 28,30:2
Luxury Liner 1948,S 10,19:2
Angel on the Amazon 1948,D 27,16:4
Red Canyon 1949,Ap 28,28:2
Illegal Entry 1949,Je 11,11:2
Kid From Cleveland, The 1949,S 5,13:2
Bride for Sale 1949,N 21,29:4 (In Addenda)
Montana Belle 1952,N 8,9:2
Brent, John
Greenwich Village Story 1963,Jl 12,14:3
Brent, Milarde (Screenwriter)
Four Faces West 1948,Ag 4,18:3
Brent, Romney
East Meets West 1936,O 31,24:2
Head Over Heels in Love 1937,F 13,9:1
Dreaming Lips 1937,My 20,17:1
Under the Red Robe 1937,Je 1,27:2
Dinner at the Ritz 1937,D 4,21:1
School for Husbands 1939,F 7,16:2
Fugitive, The 1940,Jl 23,22:2
Let George Do It 1940,O 14,25:5
Adventures of Don Juan 1948,D 25,10:1
Dream Ballerina 1951,Ap 16,21:2
Virgin Queen, The 1955,Ag 6,13:2
Don't Go Near the Water 1957,N 15,37:1
Screaming Mimi 1958,Je 26,23:3
Brent, Romney (Narrator)
Days of our Years 1951,D 6,42:2
Brent, Romney (Screenwriter)
Dinner at the Ritz 1937,D 4,21:1
Days of our Years 1951,D 6,42:2
Brent, William (Screenwriter)
Four Faces West 1948,Ag 4,18:3
Brentano, Lowell (Miscellaneous)
I'm no Angel 1933,O 14,18:2
Brentano, Lowell (Original Author)
Spider, The 1931,S 5,7:4
Melody Lingers on, The 1935,N 7,27:1
Crime Nobody Saw, The 1937,Ap 5,17:2
Spider, The 1946,Je 21,20:3
Breon, Edmund
Dawn Patrol, The 1930,Jl 11,22:1
Love Habit, The 1931,F 2,23:1
Born to Love 1931,Ap 25,23:4
Chances 1931,Je 12,27:1
I Like Your Nerve 1931,S 12,15:4
Waltz Time 1933,S 29,24:2
No Funny Business 1934,Mr 9,22:4
Private Life of Don Juan, The 1934,D 10,16:2
Scarlet Pimpernel, The 1935,F 8,27:2
Strangers on a Honeymoon 1937,Mr 13,23:2
Yank at Oxford, A 1938,F 25,15:1
Goodbye Mr Chips 1939,My 16,27:2
Outsider, The 1940,Mr 18,13:2
It Happened to One Man 1941,F 24,11:6

Breon, Edmund— Cont
She Shall Have Music 1942,O 31,11:2
Gaslight 1944,My 5,17:2
Hour Before the Dawn, The 1944,My 11,25:6
Casanova Brown 1944,S 15,16:1
Man in Half Moon Street, The 1945,Ja 20,16:2
Woman in the Window, The 1945,Ja 26,16:4
Devotion 1946,Ap 6,10:5
Dressed to Kill 1946,My 25,12:4
Imperfect Lady, The 1947,My 22,34:5
Forever Amber 1947,O 23,31:2
Hills of Home 1948,N 26,32:2
Enchantment 1948,D 27,16:2
Challenge to Lassie 1950,Ap 7,22:3

Bresig, Paula
Hirsekorn Greift Ein 1932,Je 10,22:3

Breslau, Joan
Amateur Daddy 1932,Ap 23,11:5
In Person 1935,D 13,31:5

Bresler, Jerry (Producer)
Main Street After Dark 1945,Ja 13,15:4
Bewitched 1945,Ag 17,20:3
Web, The 1947,Je 5,32:1
Arnelo Affair, The 1947,S 13,8:5
Singapore 1947,S 17,31:2
Another Part of the Forest 1948,My 19,30:2
Live Today for Tomorrow 1948,D 6,29:2
Abandoned Woman 1949,O 27,35:3
Flying Missile, The 1950,D 25,25:1
Mob, The 1951,O 18,32:2
Vikings, The 1958,Je 12,35:2
Assignment-Paris 1952,O 25,12:6
Lizzie 1957,Ap 5,24:2
Spring Reunion 1957,My 6,25:2·
Gidget Goes Hawaiian 1961,Ag 10,17:4
Diamond Head 1963,F 21,5:2
Gidget Goes to Rome 1963,S 12,32:2
Love Has Many Faces 1965,F 25,24:1
Major Dundee 1965,Ap 8,45:1
Casino Royale 1967,Ap 29,25:1

Breslin, Howard (Original Author)
Bad Day at Black Rock 1955,F 2,22:2
Platinum High School 1960,My 26,37:3

Breslin, John
Shake Hands With the Devil 1959,Je 25,20:7

Breslin, Patricia
Go, Man, Go 1954,Mr 10,29:5
Andy Hardy Comes Home 1958,D 24,00:0
Homicidal 1961,Jl 27,23:4
I Saw What You Did 1965,Jl 22,24:2

Breslow, Lou (Miscellaneous)
Little Egypt 1951,Ag 30,20:3

Breslow, Lou (Original Author)
Charlie Chan at the Race Track 1936,Ag 15,6:2
Holy Terror, The 1937,Ja 30,21:2
Dangerously Yours 1937,O 18,14:2
Hollywood Cavalcade 1939,O 14,13:2
A-Haunting We Will Go 1942,Ag 3,18:4
Second Chance 1947,S 20,12:4
My Favorite Spy 1951,Je 29,19:3
Crooked Web, The 1955,D 10,19:1

Breslow, Lou (Screenwriter)
Silk Hat Kid 1935,Ag 7,22:5
Paddy O'Day 1936,F 8,19:2
Little Miss Nobody 1936,Je 6,21:1
High Tension 1936,Jl 11,11:4
36 Hours to Live 1936,Ag 15,6:3
Fifteen Maiden Lane 1936,O 17,21:3
Time for Romance 1937,Mr 13,23:2
Sing and Be Happy 1937,Je 19,20:2
One Mile From Heaven 1937,Ag 19,23:1
Big Town Girl 1937,D 13,23:4
International Settlement 1938,F 12,20:3
Battle of Broadway 1938,Ap 25,19:2
Mr Moto Takes a Chance 1938,Je 13,15:4
City Streets 1938,Jl 25,18:2
Five of a Kind 1938,O 31,12:2
Up the River 1938,D 3,11:2
It Could Happen to You 1939,Je 9,26:3
Pack·up Your Troubles 1939,O 27,27:2
20,000 Men a Year 1939,O 28,11:2
Shooting High 1940,Ap 12,19:2
Sleepers West 1941,Mr 20,25:3
Great Guns 1941,O 3,27:2
Whispering Ghosts 1942,My 18,19:4
A-Haunting We Will Go 1942,Ag 3,18:4
Something to Shout About 1943,Ap 8,27:3
Follow the Boys 1944,Ap 26,24:6
Murder, He Says 1945,Je 25,20:3
Abbott and Costello in Hollywood
  1945,N 23,26:2
Merton of the Movies 1947,N 7,20:3
Miracle Can Happen, A 1948,F 4,28:4
Innocent Affair, An 1948,S 29,36:2
And Baby Makes Three 1949,D 23,17:3
Never a Dull Moment 1950,N 22,20:2
Bedtime for Bonzo 1951,Ap 6,31:4
Steel Town 1952,My 10,16:4
Crooked Web, The 1955,D 10,19:1

Bressart, Felix
Drei von ver Tankstelle, Die 1931,Je 20,20:4
Wahre Jakob, Der 1931,Ag 7,20:2
Alte Lied, Das 1931,S 11,24:2
Nie Wieder Liebe; No More Love

  1931,O 4,VIII,7:1
Eine Freundin so Goldig wie Du 1931,O 24,20:3
Nie Wieder Liebe 1932,Ja 16,13:1
Der Schrecken der Garnison 1932,Je 1,19:5
Hirsekorn Greift Ein 1932,Je 10,22:3
Der Herr Buerovorsteher 1932,Je 17,24:1
Holzapfel Weiss Alles 1933,Ja 7,11:3
Drei Tage Mittelarrest 1933,My 18,17:4
Sohn der Weissen Berge, Der 1933,O 23,18:3
Glueckszylinder, Der 1934,Mr 10,18:4
Und Wer Kuesst Mich? 1935,Ja 28,10:5
Bridal Suite 1939,My 26,20:2
Ninotchka 1939,N 10,27:2
Swanee River 1939,D 30,9:2
Shop Around the Corner, The 1940,Ja 26,13:2
It all Came True 1940,Ap 6,13:2
Edison the Man 1940,Je 7,27:2
Escape 1940,N 1,33:1
Bitter Sweet 1940,N 22,27:1
Third Finger, Left Hand 1940,D 12,37:2
Comrade X 1940,D 26,23:1
Ziegfeld Girl 1941,Ap 25,17:2
Blossoms in the Dust 1941,Je 27,14:4
Married Bachelor 1941,O 16,25:3
Kathleen 1941,D 19,35:3
Mr and Mrs North 1942,Ja 22,13:2
To Be or not to Be 1942,Mr 7,13:2
Crossroads 1942,Jl 27,18:2
Iceland 1942,O 15,27:1
Three Hearts for Julia 1943,My 21,22:4
Above Suspicion 1943,Ag 6,10:3
Song of Russia 1944,F 11,17:2
Greenwich Village 1944,S 28,26:2
Seventh Cross, The '1944,S 29,18:1
Without Love 1945,Mr 23,13:1
Thrill of Brazil, The 1946,S 6,18:3
I've Always Loved You 1946,S 7,11:1
Her Sister's Secret 1947,Ja 23,31:3
Song Is Born, A 1948,O 20,37:2
Portrait of Jennie 1949,Mr 30,31:2
Take one False Step 1949,Je 23,33:2

Bresslaw, Bernard
Too Many Crooks 1959,Ap 25,14:2
Morgan! 1966,Ap 5,42:2

Bresson, Carl
Knowing Men 1930,Mr 9,IX,6:1

Bresson, Christian de
Question 7 1961,S 29,30:2

Bresson, Robert (Director)
Angels of the Streets 1950,Ja 17,24:2
Diary of a Country Priest 1954,Ap 6,35:2
Man Escaped, A 1957,Ag 27,33:2
Pickpocket 1963,My 22,36:2
Dames du Bois de Boulogne, Les; Ladies of the
  Park 1964,Ap 4,15:5
Trial of Joan of Arc, The 1965,F 12,19:1
Balthazar 1966,S 16,31:2
Mouchette 1968,S 21,26:1

Bresson, Robert (Screenwriter)
Angels of the Streets 1950,Ja 17,24:2
Diary of a Country Priest 1954,Ap 6,35:2
Man Escaped, A 1957,Ag 27,33:2
Pickpocket 1963,My 22,36:2
Dames du Bois de Boulogne, Les; Ladies of the
  Park 1964,Ap 4,15:5
Trial of Joan of Arc, The 1965,F 12,19:1
Mouchette 1968,S 21,26:1

Brest, George
Assignment in Brittany 1943,Ap 22,31:2

Bret, Tom (Miscellaneous)
Reported Missing 1922,Ap 24,18:3

Bretano, Faustino
Cancion del Dia, La 1933,Ag 26,14:3

Bretherton, Howard (Director)
Hills of Kentucky 1927,Mr 2,29:3
Silver Slave, The 1928,Ja 3,28:2
Caught in the Fog 1928,D 4,29:1
Redeeming Sin, The 1929,F 16,14:6
Argyle Case, The 1929,Ag 31,13:4
Second Choice 1930,Ja 4,21:4
Isle of Escape 1930,Mr 31,24:3
Match King, The 1932,D 8,25:3
Ladies They Talk About 1933,F 25,20:4
Return of the Terror 1934,Jl 11,20:2
Cantante de Napoles, El; Singer of Naples, The
  1935,F 25,13:4
Leathernecks Have Landed, The 1936,Mr 23,22:5
Three on the Trail 1936,My 5,26:5
King of the Royal Mounted 1936,S 29,35:2
Secret Valley 1937,Ja 25,22:2
It Happened Out West 1937,Je 7,22:3
Wanted by the Police 1938,S 26,13:2

Bretherton, Vivien R (Original Author)
Love Finds Andy Hardy 1938,Jl 22,10:2

Breton, Auguste la (Original Author)
Razzi 1957,N 19,39:4
Sinners of Paris 1959,Ap 24,23:1

Breton, Auguste le
Razzi 1957,N 19,39:4

Breton, Auguste le (Narrator)
Razzi 1957,N 19,39:4

Breton, auguste le (Original Author)
Rififi 1956,Je 6,37:1

Breton, Auguste le (Screenwriter)
Rififi 1956,Je 6,37:1
Riff Raff Girls 1962,O 20,13:5

Breton, Marie Claude
Anatomy of a Marriage; My Days With Jean
  Marc; My Nights With Francoise
  1964,O 27,42:2

Bretonniers, Jean
Green Glove, The 1952,Ap 24,38:1
Mam'zelle Pigalle 1958,Ap 19,10:4

Brett, Allan
So Ends our Night 1941,F 28,17:2

Brett, Ingrid
Devil's Own, The 1967,Mr 16,53:2
Jokers, The 1967,My 16,50:1
Inadmissible Evidence 1968,Je 24,44:1

Brett, Jeremy
War and Peace 1956,Ag 22,26:2
My Fair Lady 1964,O 22,41:1
Model Murder Case, The 1964,N 25,45:1

Breuer, Bessie (Original Author)
In Name Only 1939,Ag 4,11:3

Breuer, Siegfried
Wiener Geschichten; Vienna Tales 1940,S 28,9:3
Fledermaus, Die; Bat, The 1948,Mr 15,26:2
Operetta 1949,Je 6,15:4
Third Man, The 1950,F 3,29:2
Last Waltz, The 1958,Ap 12,13:1

Breville, Madeline
Fra Diavolo 1931,N 23,22:1

Brewer, Betty
Rangers of Fortune 1940,S 19,27:2
Roundup, The 1941,Mr 13,25:4
Las Vegas Nights 1941,Mr 20,25:2
Wild Bill Hickok Rides 1942,F 7,13:5
Juke Girl 1942,Je 20,9:2
My Kingdom for a Cook 1943,O 15,15:3

Brewer, George Emerson Jr (Original Author)
Dark Victory 1939,Ap 21,27:2

Brewer, Jameson (Screenwriter)
Okinawa 1952,Ap 24,38:3
Swingin' Along 1962,Ag 27,18:1
Incredible Mr Limpet, The 1964,Mr 26,40:4

Brewer, Monte (Sonny)
Mr Dynamite 1941,Mr 13,25:2

Brewer, Teresa
Those Redheads From Seattle 1953,O 1,34:2

Brewster, Carol
Barkleys of Broadway, The 1949,My 5,34:2
Cat-Women of the Moon 1954,Mr 20,10:7

Brewster, Diane
Black Patch 1958,Ap 24,38:1
Torpedo Run 1958,O 25,16:2
Young Philadelphians, The 1959,My 22,32:1
Man in the Net, The 1959,Je 11,36:2

Brewster, June
Melody Cruise 1933,Je 23,15:2
Bombshell 1933,O 21,11:2
Private Scandal 1934,Je 15,26:2
Case Against Mrs Ames, The 1936,My 28,19:2
Spendthrift 1936,Jl 23,24:1

Brewster, Margaret
My Cousin Rachel 1952,D 26,20:2
Second Chance 1953,Jl 23,20:2

Brewster, Rickie
Little Fugitive 1953,O 7,35:1

Brewster Twins
Wake up and Live 1937,Ap 24,16:2
Wife, Doctor and Nurse 1937,O 11,26:5
Love and Hisses 1938,Ja 1,11:1
Hold That Co-ed 1938,S 24,13:1

Brey, Claire du
Sea Hawk, The 1924,Je 3,22:1

Briac, Jean de
Duchess of Buffalo, The 1926,Ag 9,10:3

Brialy, Jean-Claude
Beau Serge, Le 1959,Ag 3,21:1
Cousins, The (Les Cousins) 1959,N 24,44:1
Notte Brava, La 1962,Ja 25,25:2
Paris Belongs to Us 1962,N 6,38:1
Burning Court, The 1963,Ag 1,17:2
Devil and the 10 Commandments, The (Episode
  7) 1963,O 15,44:1
Two Are Guilty 1964,F 29,12:1
Bonne Soupe, La 1964,Mr 16,37:1
Woman Is a Woman, A 1964,S 19,19:1
Chateau en Suede; Castle in Switzerland
  1964,O 14,51:1
Circle of Love 1965,Mr 25,42:4
Male Hunt; Chasse a l'Homme, La
  1965,Ap 20,42:1
How Not to Rob a Department Store
  1965,D 29,23:1
Male Companion 1966,F 15,33:2
Mandragola 1966,Je 7,50:2
King of Hearts 1967,Je 20,34:1
Tonio Kroger 1968,Ja 16,24:1
Bride Wore Black, The 1968,Je 26,42:1
Oldest Profession, The (Mademoiselle Mimi);
  Mademoiselle Mimi (The Oldest Profession)
  1968,N 8,42:1

BRIAN
See Also BRYAN
Brian, David
Flamingo Road 1949,My 7,10:2
Beyond the Forest 1949,O 22,11:2
Intruder in the Dust 1949,N 23,19:1
Damned Don't Cry, The 1950,Ap 8,9:2
Great Jewel Robber, The 1950,Ag 4,13:2
Breakthrough 1950,N 18,10:2
Inside Straight 1951,Mr 16,34:2
Inside the Walls of Folsom Prison 1951,My 28,17:4
Fort Worth 1951,Jl 13,12:7
ThIs Woman is Dangerous 1952,F 28,23:2
Springfield Rifle 1952,O 23,40:2
Million Dollar Mermaid 1952,D 5,35:2
High and the Mighty, The 1954,Jl 1,21:2
Dawn at Socorro 1954,Ag 28,8:2
Timberjack 1955,Mr 10,33:3
Rabbit Trap, The 1959,O 15,48:1
Pocketful of Miracles 1961,D 19,39:1
Rare Breed, The 1966,Ap 14,42:3
Brian, Eddie
What a Life 1939,O 12,33:1
East Side Kids 1940,F 19,21:6
Brian, Mary
Peter Pan 1924,D 29,11:4
Air Mail, The 1925,Mr 17,18:1
Little French Girl, The 1925,Je 1,10:3
Street of Forgotten Men, The 1925,Jl 21,26:2
Regular Fellow, A 1925,O 5,25:2
Enchanted Hill, The 1925,D 29,19:2 (In Addenda)
Behind the Front 1926,F 10,16:2
Brown of Harvard 1926,My 3,27:1
Beau Geste 1926,Ag 26,17:3
Prince of Tempters, The 1926,O 18,18:1
Knockout Reilly 1927,Ap 18,21:2
Running Wild 1927,Je 14,33:2
Man Power 1927,Jl 26,17:1
Shanghai Bound 1927,N 7,26:4
Two Flaming Youths 1928,Ja 2,28:1
Partners in Crime 1928,Ap 30,18:3
Big Killing, The 1928,Jl 2,11:2
Forgotten Faces 1928,Ag 6,15:2
Harold Teen 1928,Ag 14,15:4
Varsity 1928,O 29,29:1
Some One to Love 1928,D 4,29:1
Man I Love, The 1929,My 28,36:2
River of Romance, The 1929,Jl 29,23:3
Marriage Playground, The 1929,D 14,22:4
Kibitzer, The 1929,D 21,17:1
Virginian, The 1929,D 23,18:2
Burning Up 1930,F 8,12:5
Only the Brave 1930,Mr 8,21:1
Light of Western Stars, The 1930,Ap 26,11:1
Social Lion, The 1930,Je 14,9:4
Only Saps Work 1930,D 13,22:2
Royal Family of Broadway, The 1930,D 23,25:1
Front Page, The 1931,Mr 20,29:1
Gun Smoke 1931,Ap 24,27:1
Run Around, The 1931,Ag 10,18:3
Homicide Squad 1931,O 19,28:1
It's Tough to be Famous 1932,Ap 9,18:1
Blessed Event 1932,S 3,16:2
Hard to Handle 1933,F 2,21:5
Girl Missing 1933,Ap 1,18:2
World Gone Mad, The 1933,Ap 15,16:3
Song of the Eagle 1933,Ap 29,14:3
Moonlight and Pretzels 1933,Ag 23,21:2
Shadows of Sing Sing 1934,F 21,23:2
Ever Since Eve 1934,Mr 28,27:5
Private Scandal 1934,Je 15,26:2
College Rhythm 1934,N 24,19:1
Charlie Chan in Paris 1935,Ja 22,23:2
Man on the Flying Trapeze 1935,Ag 3,16:2
Spendthrift 1936,Jl 23,24:1
Killer at Large 1936,O 26,20:1
Calaboose 1943,Jl 30,19:2
Brian Sisters
Sally, Irene and Mary 1938,F 26,9:2
Kentucky Moonshine 1938,My 21,9:2
Bribiesca, Antonio
Garden of Evil 1954,Jl 10,17:1
Rosanna 1956,My 17,37:2
Brice, Betty
Beau Brummell 1924,Mr 31,20:1
Brice, Fannie
My Man 1928,D 22,14:3
Night Club 1929,Ag 12,22:2
Be Yourself 1930,Mr 7,20:5
Great Ziegfeld, The 1936,Ap 9,21:2
Everybody Sing 1938,Mr 11,15:3
Ziegfeld Follies 1946,Mr 23,8:3
Brice, Lew
Partners Again, With Potash and Perlmutter 1926,F 15,16:4
Two Seconds 1932,My 19,25:3
Brice, Monte (Director)
Casey at the Bat 1927,Ap 4,30:5
Moonlight and Pretzels 1933,Ag 23,21:2
Take a Chance 1933,N 27,20:3

Brice, Monte (Original Author)
Fireman, Save My Child 1927,O 10,24:1
We're in the Air Now 1927,D 31,31:1
Moonlight and Pretzels 1933,Ag 23,21:2
Merry-Go-Round of 1938 1937,N 26,27:2
Pot o'Gold 1941,Ap 4,25:2
Fleet's In, The 1942,Mr 12,24:2
Brice, Monte (Screenwriter)
Tell It to Sweeney 1927,O 17,20:2
Merry-Go-Round of 1938 1937,N 26,27:2
You're a Sweetheart 1937,D 25,10:5
Sing Your Worries Away 1942,My 15,25:2
Mexican Spitfire Sees a Ghost 1942,Jl 31,11:2
Radio Stars on Parade 1945,S 22,14:2
Variety Girl 1947,O 16,34:4
Brice, Monty (Original Author)
Hands Up 1926,Ja 18,26:2
Brice, Pierre
Cossacks, The 1960,S 6,41:4
Cheaters, The; (Tricheurs, Les) 1961,Je 5,37:4
Pharaohs' Woman, The 1962,Ap 19,35:2
Samson and the Slave Queen 1964,Mr 5,36:2
Place Called Glory, A 1966,Ag 11,27:4
Brick, Ben
Itto 1936,Ja 29,15:5
Bricken, Jules (Producer)
Train, The 1965,Mr 18,25:1
Bricker, George (Original Author)
Pay-Off, The 1935,N 13,25:3
Law in her Hands, The 1936,Je 6,21:2
Mr Moto in Danger Island 1938,Mr 20,13:3
Accidents Will Happen 1938,Ap 25,19:2
They Made Her a Spy 1939,Mr 29,21:4
Murder by Invitation 1941,Jl 23,15:4
Dancing Masters, The 1943,D 2,30:2
Loophole 1954,Mr 13,11:3
Bricker, George (Screenwriter)
Pay-Off, The 1935,N 13,25:3
Broadway Hostess 1935,D 16,23:3
Fish 1936,Ja 25,18:5
Freshman Love 1936,Ja 25,18:5
Law in her Hands, The 1936,Je 6,21:2
Big Noise, The 1936,Jl 4,18:3
Melody for Two 1937,My 21,19:5
Sh! The Octopus 1937,D 24,21:2
Kid Comes Back, The 1938,F 7,10:2
Over the Wall 1938,Mr 28,19:2
Torchy Blane in Panama 1938,Ap 18,11:1
Accidents Will Happen 1938,Ap 25,19:2
King of the Underworld 1939,Ja 7,6:2
Torchy Blane in Chinatown 1939,F 3,13:2
Missing Daughters 1939,Je 12,14:5
Murder by Invitation 1941,Jl 23,15:4
Frisco Lil 1942,F 12,27:2
North to the Klondike 1942,Mr 12,24:3
Little Tokyo, USA 1942,Ag 7,13:2
Mark of the Whistler, The 1944,N 11,19:2
Pillow of Death 1946,Ja 26,19:3
House of Horrors 1946,F 23,20:3
She Wolf of London 1946,Ap 6,10:6
Inside Job 1946,Je 15,24:3
If I'm Lucky 1946,S 20,41:3
Big Fix, The 1947,My 3,10:3
Corpse came C O D, The 1947,Ag 19,27:2
Alimony 1949,Jl 22,16:3
Mary Ryan, Detective 1949,N 4,33:3
Bodyhold 1949,D 12,29:4
Beauty on Parade 1950,Ag 18,17:2
Al Jennings of Oklahoma 1951,My 18,34:6
Man in the Dark 1953,Ap 9,31:5
Cry Vengence 1955,F 19,18:3
Brickhill, Paul (Original Author)
Reach for the Sky 1957,My 1,40:1
Bricklayers, The
Something to Shout About 1943,Ap 8,27:3
Bricusse, Leslie (Composer)
Stop the World-I Want to Get Off 1966,My 12,54:2
Bricusse, Leslie (Original Author)
Stop the World-I Want to Get Off 1966,My 12,54:2
Bricusse, Leslie (Screenwriter)
Swingin' Maiden, The 1964,Ja 1,16:2
Doctor Dolittle 1967,D 20,55:1
Brideston, Guillermo
Games Men Play, The 1968,Mr 15,30:1
Bridge, Alan
Lawless Nineties, The 1936,Je 29,11:1
Woman Chases Man 1937,Je 11,26:2
Partners of the Plains 1938,F 12,20:4
Crime School 1938,My 11,17:2
Highway Patrol 1938,Ag 4,15:2
Adventure in Sahara 1938,D 19,19:2
Romance of the Redwoods 1939,Ap 24,13:2
Christmas in July 1940,N 6,35:2
Lady From Cheyenne, The 1941,Ap 18,18:2
Little Foxes, The 1941,Ag 22,19:2
Sullivan's Travels 1942,Ja 29,25:2
Miracle of Morgan's Creek, The 1944,Ja 20,15:2
Hail the Conquering Hero 1944,Ag 10,14:2
Thunderhead 1945,Mr 16,21:2
Falcon's Alibi, The 1946,Ap 13,23:2
Cross my Heart 1946,D 19,42:3

Bridge, Alan— Cont
Black Gold 1947,S 5,16:4
Silver River 1948,My 22,8:3
Unfaithfully Yours 1948,N 6,9:2
Beautiful Blonde From Bashful Bend, The 1949,My 28,11:2
Mad Wednesday 1951,Ja 25,21:5
Oh! Susanna 1951,Mr 30,28:5
We're not Married 1952,Jl 12,16:2
Bridgers, Aaron
Paris Blues 1961,N 8,41:1
Bridgers, Ann Preston (Original Author)
Coquette 1929,Ap 6,14:4 (In Addenda)
Bridges, Al
Good Fairy, The 1935,F 1,18:1
Public Enemy's Wife 1936,Jl 9,17:2
Bridges, Beau
Force of Evil 1948,D 27,16:2
No Minor Vices 1949,F 26,11:2
Red Pony, The 1949,Mr 9,33:2
Zamba 1949,N 7,33:2
Incident, The 1967,N 6,65:1
For Love of Ivy 1968,Jl 18,26:1
Bridges, Darlene
Prince of Peace, The 1951,Mr 24,8:3
Bridges, James (Screenwriter)
Appaloosa, The 1966,S 15,51:1
Bridges, Lloyd
Lone Wolf Takes a Chance, The 1941,Ap 7,13:2
Harmon of Michigan 1941,O 2,29:2
Canal Zone 1942,Mr 30,21:2
Atlantic Convoy 1942,Jl 6,18:5
Flight Lieutenant 1942,Jl 31,11:1
Sahara 1943,N 12,25:2
Heat's on, The 1943,N 26,29:2
Master Race, The 1944,N 2,22:1
Strange Confession 1945,N 8,17:3
Walk in the Sun, A 1946,Ja 12,10:6
Miss Susie Slagle's 1946,F 7,29:2
Abilene Town 1946,Mr 4,16:5
Canyon Passage 1946,Ag 8,18:2
Ramrod 1947,Je 30,25:6
Trouble With Women, The 1947,Jl 14,14:4
16 Fathoms Deep 1948,O 7,35:2
Moonrise 1949,Mr 7,17:2
Red Canyon 1949,Ap 28,28:2
Home of the Brave 1949,My 13,29:1
Calamity Jane and Sam Bass 1949,Jl 18,14:2
Trapped 1949,N 26,10:6
Colt 45 1950,My 6,8:6
Rocketship X-M 1950,My 27,10:6
White Tower, The 1950,Jl 3,9:2
Try and Get Me 1951,My 7,22:2
Three Steps North 1951,Je 29,14:2
Little Big Horn 1951,Jl 27,15:2
Whistle at Eaton Falls, The 1951,O 11,49:2
High Noon 1952,Jl 25,14:2
Plymouth Adventure 1952,N 14,20:3
Tall Texan, The 1953,Ap 13,32:4
Kid From Left Field, The 1953,S 26,15:3
City of Bad Men 1953,O 21,37:6
Wetbacks 1956,My 5,13:2
Rainmaker, The 1956,D 13,51:1
Goddess, The 1958,Je 25,24:1
Around the World Under the Sea 1966,Jl 21,20:2
Attack on the Iron Coast 1968,Je 6,54:2
Bridges, Tom (Original Author)
Gang's All Here, The 1943,D 23,26:4
Bridie, James (Miscellaneous)
Storm in a Teacup 1938,Mr 22,18:4
Paradine Case, The 1948,Ja 9,26:2
Bridie, James (Original Author)
Folly to be Wise 1953,D 28,17:2
Bridie, James (Screenwriter)
Under Capricorn 1949,S 9,28:3
Bridou, Lucienne
Funny Thing Happened on the Way to the Forum, A 1966,O 17,48:1
Brien, Louise
British Intelligence 1940,F 12,14:2
Brier, Margot
Illiac Passion, The 1968,Ap 19,40:1
Briers, Richard
Matter of Who, A 1962,Jl 25,29:2
Fathom 1967,D 14,62:1
Bries, Rob de
Ciske 1963,Ag 3,8:2
Briesc, Gerd
U-Boat 9 1929,Ja 22,23:1
Briese, Gaston
Der Schrecken der Garnison 1932,Je 1,19:5
Briese, Naemi
Frustration 1949,Ag 27,7:3
Brieux, Eugene (Screenwriter)
Marriage Forbidden 1938,Jl 16,7:2
Brigante, Luis
Guns of the Trees 1964,F 29,12:2
Briggs, Charles
Merrill's Marauders 1962,Je 14,23:4
13 Frightened Girls 1963,S 12,32:2
Captain Newman, MD 1964,F 21,36:1
Briggs, Donald
Love Before Breakfast 1936,Mr 14,10:1
Man of the People 1937,F 23,25:4

Briggs, Donald— Cont

Captains Courageous 1937,My 12,27:1
They Won't Forget 1937,Jl 15,16:1
Fit for a King 1937,O 15,18:5
Daredevil Drivers, The 1938,F 23,27:2
Love, Honor and Behave 1938,Mr 21,18:2
Beloved Brat 1938,My 2,13:2
Crime School 1938,My 11,17:2
Men Are Such Fools 1938,Je 17,25:1
Cowboy From Brooklyn 1938,Jl 14,17:1
Wings of the Navy 1939,F 4,11:1
Hardys Ride High, The 1939,Ap 14,28:2
Ex-Champ 1939,My 12,25:3
Forgotten Woman, The 1939,Ag 4,11:2
Unexpected Father 1939,Ag 11,12:2
Outside the Three-Mile Limit 1940,Ap 8,15:2
Hot Steel 1940,Je 21,25:3
Men Against the Sky 1940,S 12,31:2

Briggs, Harlan

Dodsworth 1936,S 24,29:1
Mad Holiday 1936,N 26,39:2
Family Affair, A 1937,Ap 20,29:2
Riding on Air 1937,Je 26,20:2 (In Addenda)
Easy Living 1937,Jl 8,20:1
Exclusive 1937,Jl 22,15:1
Live, Love and Learn 1937,N 19,27:2
Beg, Borrow or Steal 1937,D 10,33:2
One Wild Night 1938,Je 3,17:2
Having Wonderful Time 1938,Jl 8,11:2
Meet the Girls 1938,S 3,16:6
Missing Guest, The 1938,S 7,30:7
Man to Remember, A 1938,N 7,23:2
Calling Dr Kildare 1939,My 12,25:4
Tell no Tales 1939,Je 2,27:3
Maisie 1939,Je 23,23:1
Flight at Midnight 1939,S 7,29:2
Man Who Wouldn't Talk, The 1940,Ja 12,13:3
Abe Lincoln in Illinois 1940,F 23,19:2
Young as You Feel 1940,Mr 8,25:3
My Little Chickadee 1940,Mr 16,8:2
Charlie Chan's Murder Cruise 1940,My 3,17:5
Bank Dick, The 1940,D 13,29:2
One Foot in Heaven 1941,N 14,28:3
Among the Living 1941,D 13,25:2
Vanishing Virginian, The 1942,My 28,13:3
Cynthia 1947,S 19,27:2
Double Life, A 1948,F 20,19:1
Carrie 1952,Jl 17,20:2

Briggs, Jack

Joan of Paris 1942,Ja 26,18:2
Mexican Spitfire's Elephant 1942,S 18,25:2
Army Surgeon 1942,N 5,35:2
Ladies' Day 1943,Mr 26,14:3
My Forbidden Past 1951,Ap 26,34:2

Briggs, Johnny

Leather Boys, The 1965,N 9,50:1

Briggs, Julie

Nobody Waved Goodbye 1964,S 17,52:1

Briggs, Matt

Advice to the Lovelorn 1933,D 14,28:2
Hips, Hips, Hooray 1934,F 24,18:3
Meanest Man in the World, The 1943,F 25,27:3
Ox-Bow Incident, The 1943,My 10,15:2 (In
    Addenda)
Coney Island 1943,Je 17,17:2
Dancing Masters, The 1943,D 2,30:2
Buffalo Bill 1944,Ap 20,22:6
Roger Touhy, Gangster 1944,Je 5,14:7
Babe Ruth Story, The 1948,Jl 29,17:2

Briggs (Producer)

S'prise Party 'n Ever'thing, A 1919,Ap 7,11:5
Saturday 1919,O 13,16:3

Brigham, Constance

Hansel and Gretel 1954,O 11,33:1

Brighouse, Harold (Original Author)

Children of Jazz 1923,Jl 9,8:4
Hobson's Choice 1954,Je 15,37:1

Bright, John (Miscellaneous)

Open Secret 1948,F 2,15:2

Bright, John (Original Author)

Public Enemy, The 1931,Ap 24,27:1
Smart Money 1931,Je 19,21:1
Blonde Crazy 1931,D 4,28:2
John Meade's Woman 1937,F 18,19:1
San Quentin 1937,Ag 4,15:2
Kid From Cleveland, The 1949,S 5,13:2

Bright, John (Screenwriter)

Three on a Match 1932,O 29,18:4
Accusing Finger, The 1936,N 17,35:4
Back Door to Heaven 1939,Ap 20,21:2
Glamour for Sale 1940,N 5,33:2
Broadway 1942,Je 5,23:2
Sherlock Holmes and the Voice Of Terror
    1942,S 19,9:2
We Accuse 1945,Je 4,22:4
I Walk Alone 1948,Ja 22,36:3
Close-Up 1948,Ap 5,24:2
Kid From Cleveland, The 1949,S 5,13:2
Brave Bulls, The 1951,Ap 19,39:2

Bright, Richard

Odds Against Tomorrow 1959,O 16,27:1

Brightman, Homer (Original Author)

Saludos Amigos 1943,F 13,8:2
Three Caballeros, The 1945,F 5,20:1

Brightman, Homer (Screenwriter)

Adventures of Ichabod and Mr Toad, The
    1949,O 10,18:2

Brignone, Ellia

Violent Summer 1961,My 20,12:1

Brignone, Guido (Director)

Maciste in Hell 1931,Je 29,20:3
Rubacuori 1932,Mr 5,11:2
Dopo una Notte d'Amore; After a Night of Love
    1935,O 29,16:5
Lorenzino de Medici 1936,Ap 14,19:3
Passaporto Rosso 1936,S 2,18:2
Loyalty of Love 1937,Mr 1,15:1
Amore e Denaro 1937,Mr 13,23:3
Voce Lontana, La 1937,Ap 24,16:3
Amore e Dolore 1937,My 13,31:4
Tre Anni Senza Donne 1937,My 27,21:4
Destino di Donna 1937,Je 9,31:6
Maestrina, La; Little School Mistress, The
    1938,Ap 29,17:2
Antenato, L'; Ancestor, The 1938,O 22,14:3
Vivere; To Live 1938,N 15,27:2
Wally, La 1939,Ja 2,28:3
Per Vomini Soli; For Men Only 1939,Ap 21,27:4
Chi e'piu felice di me?; Who Is Happier Than I
    1940,F 6,17:5
Dead Woman's Kiss, A 1951,O 6,16:4
Tears of Blood 1952,Ja 19,13:2
Count of St Elmo, The 1953,Mr 14,13:2
Genoese Dragnet 1954,F 12,20:5
Sword and the Cross, The 1960,Jl 7,26:1

Brignone, Guido (Producer)

Sign of the Gladiator 1959,D 3,46:1

Brignone, Guido (Screenwriter)

Genoese Dragnet 1954,F 12,20:5
Sign of the Gladiator 1959,D 3,46:1
Sword and the Cross, The 1960,Jl 7,26:1

Brignone, Lilla

Serpente a Sonagli, Il 1936,Ag 17,9:2
Eclipse 1962,D 21,5:1

Brignone, Mercedes

Rubacuori 1932,Mr 5,11:2

Brilant, Arthur M (Original Author)

Strange Case of Clara Deane, The
    1932,My 6,15:3

Briley, John

Situation Hopeless-But not Serious
    1965,O 14,53:1

Briley, John (Screenwriter)

Invasion Quartet 1961,D 11,41:2
Children of the Damned 1964,Ja 30,24:2

Brill, Michael

Barretts of Wimpole Street, The 1957,Ja 18,15:3

Brill, Patti

Music in Manhattan 1944,O 7,11:2

Brillant, Irene

Coiffeur Pour Dames 1932,O 31,18:4
Queen and the Cardinal, The 1944,Je 1,17:3

Brillas, Marilde

Cruz Diablo 1935,Ap 6,10:1

Brilliant, Alfredda (Original Author)

Proud Valley 1941,My 17,19:2

Brilling, N

Othello 1960,My 16,39:1

Brilmayer, Robert (Original Author)

Pot o'Gold 1941,Ap 4,25:2

Brimmell, Max

Haunted Strangler, The 1958,Jl 4,15:3

Brinckerhoff, Burt

Goddess, The 1958,Je 25,24:1
Greatest Story Ever Told, The 1965,F 16,40:2

Brind, Tessa

Youth Runs Wild 1944,S 2,17:2

Brindeau, Jeanne

Michael Strogoff 1926,D 6,28:3
End of the World, The 1934,Ap 18,23:3
Dark Eyes 1938,Ap 19,24:5

Brindley, Madge

Hobson's Choice 1954,Je 15,37:1

Brinegar, Paul

Larceny 1948,S 4,8:6
Captive City, The 1952,Mr 27,34:2
Human Desire 1954,Ag 7,7:2

Bring, Lou (Composer)

You're a Sweetheart 1937,D 25,10:5

Bringuer, Paul (Original Author)

Au Nom de la Loi; In the Name of the Law
    1932,My 1,VIII,4:1 (In Addenda)

Brinig, Myron (Original Author)

Sisters, The 1938,O 15,21:3

Brink, Carol (Original Author)

All I Desire 1953,Ag 29,10:1

Brink, Elga

Quo Vadis 1925,F 16,24:1
Bride 68 1930,Ap 15,28:5
Der Herr Finanzdirektor 1932,Je 25,18:2
Pension Schoeller 1932,S 20,26:3
Goethe's Jugendgeliebte 1932,D 26,26:2
Feldherrnhuegel, Der 1934,Ap 20,17:2
Spiel mit dem Feuer 1934,N 26,12:2
Choral von Leuthen, Der 1935,Ja 21,19:4
Heimatland; Homeland 1939,O 28,11:2

Brinkley, Neil

Great White Way, The 1924,Ja 4,10:1

Brinkley, William (Original Author)

Don't Go Near the Water 1957,N 15,37:1

Brinkman, Dolores

Mysterious Island, The 1929,D 21,17:1

Brinley, Charles

It Happened in Hollywood 1937,O 2,18:1

Brinley, Madge

Spider and the Fly, The 1952,Jl 29,17:3

Brinquier, Paul (Miscellaneous)

Volga Boatman, The 1938,Ap 15,23:3

Brion, Francoise

Tales of Paris (The Tale of Francoise); Tale of
    Francoise, The (Tales of Paris) 1962,Ag 27,18:1
Magnificent Sinner 1963,Ap 25,38:1
French Game 1963,S 21,13:5
Sweet and Sour 1964,D 28,34:2

Briones, Luis

Torero! 1957,My 22,29:2

Brionne, Trude

Bockbierfest 1931,Mr 31,25:3
Waltz Time in Vienna 1934,N 19,13:2
Und Wer Kuesst Mich? 1935,Ja 28,10:5

Briquet, Sacha

Elusive Corporal, The 1963,F 19,5:1
Landru 1963,Ap 10,31:1
Bonnes Femmes, Les 1966,My 13,32:1

Brisbane, Arthur

Great White Way, The 1924,Ja 4,10:1

Brisbane, William

Shall We Dance 1937,My 14,21:1
You Can't Beat Love 1937,Je 25,25:3
Meet the Missus 1937,Jl 2,25:2
there Goes The Groom 1937,D 25,10:6
She's Got Everything 1938,Ja 14,21:3

Briskin, Mort (Producer)

Jackie Robinson Story, The 1950,My 17,36:1
Quicksand 1950,Je 16,28:4
Second Woman, The 1951,F 2,19:2
Magic Face, The 1951,O 1,19:2
No Time for Flowers 1952,D 26,20:3

Briskin, Mort (Screenwriter)

Magic Face, The 1951,O 1,19:2

Briskin, Samuel J (Producer)

Strategic Air Command 1955,Ap 21,33:1
Joker Is Wild, The 1957,S 27,16:6

Brissac, Virginia

Murder by an Aristocrat 1936,Je 13,13:2
Big Noise, The 1936,Jl 4,18:3
White Bondage 1937,Ag 6,21:3
Torchy Blane, The Adventurous Blonde
    1937,D 18,18:1
Secrets of a Nurse 1938,D 12,26:2
Jesse James 1939,Ja 14,13:1
Woman Doctor 1939,Mr 24,27:3
Dark Victory 1939,Ap 21,27:2
Forgotten Woman, The 1939,Ag 4,11:2
Parents on Trial 1939,S 18,15:5
Remember the Night 1940,Ja 18,27:2
Little Old New York 1940,F 3,9:2
Black Friday 1940,Mr 22,23:3
It's a Date 1940,Mr 23,16:2
Alias the Deacon 1940,My 14,27:5
Ghost Breakers, The 1940,Jl 4,12:2
Wagons Westward 1940,Jl 8,13:2
Hired Wife 1940,S 14,11:2
Strike up the Band 1940,S 30,13:2
Always a Bride 1940,N 21,43:3
Great Lie, The 1941,Ap 12,19:2
Washington Melodrama 1941,My 26,15:3
Nurse's Secret, The 1941,Je 6,25:7
Bad Men of Missouri 1941,Ag 16,18:2
Dressed to Kill 1941,Ag 22,19:3
Little Foxes, The 1941,Ag 22,19:2
Appointment for Love 1941,N 7,27:1
One Foot in Heaven 1941,N 14,28:3
Lady Gangster 1942,Jl 10,13:2
Big Shot, The 1942,Jl 18,8:2
Mummy's Tomb, The 1942,O 26,19:2
Phantom Lady 1944,F 18,15:2
Why Girls Leave Home 1945,Ag 4,7:3
Bewitched 1945,Ag 17,20:3
Daltons Ride Again, The 1945,D 8,21:2
Renegades 1946,Jl 11,18:2
Captain from Castile 1947,D 26,22:4
Mating of Millie, The 1948,Mr 13,12:2
Summer Holiday 1948,Je 12,8:5
Old Los Angeles 1948,Jl 12,11:2
Live Today for Tomorrow 1948,D 6,29:2
Last Bandit, The 1949,Mr 21,19:2
Cheaper by the Dozen 1950,Ap 1,12:2
Edge of Doom 1950,Ag 4,13:2
Harriet Craig 1950,N 3,31:2
Operation Pacific 1951,F 3,10:2
Two of a Kind 1951,Je 30,8:6
Executive Suite 1954,My 7,19:1
About Mrs Leslie 1954,Je 28,16:2

Brisson, Carl

Ring, The 1927,D 25,VIII,7:7 (In Addenda)
Manxman, The 1929,D 17,28:7
Murder at the Vanities 1934,My 21,20:2
All the King's Horses 1935,Mr 9,19:1

Brisson, Frederick (Producer)
Never Wave at a Wac 1953,Ap 24,30:2
Five Finger Exercise 1962,Ap 20,20:2
Under the Yum Yum Tree 1963,N 21,43:2

Bristow, Gwen (Original Author)
Tomorrow Is Forever 1946,F 22,21:2
Jubilee Trail 1954,My 1,13:3

Bristow, Jimmy
Lady's From Kentucky, The 1939,Ap 27,31:1

British Royal Air Force, Members of
Lion Has Wings, The 1940,Ja 22,11:2

Britneva, Maria
Suddenly, Last Summer 1959,D 23,22:1

Britt, Leo
Take my Life 1949,Ja 19,34:2
Magnetic Monster, The 1953,My 14,32:5
Elephant Walk 1954,Ap 22,37:2
Dial M for Murder 1954,My 29,13:2

Britt, May
Affairs of a Model 1952,Ag 7,12:8
Lupa, La 1954,F 18,36:2
Illicit Interlude 1954,O 27,32:6
Young Lions, The 1958,Ap 3,23:1
Hunters, The 1958,Ag 27,33:1
Blue Angel, The 1959,S 5,11:4
Murder, Inc 1960,Je 29,26:6
Matter of Morals, A 1961,Je 1,31:1
Secrets of Woman 1961,Jl 12,36:1

Brittain, Donald (Director)
Memorandum 1967,S 26,54:4

Brittain, Donald (Screenwriter)
Memorandum 1967,S 26,54:4

Britton, Barbara
Wake Island 1942,S 2,19:2
So Proudly We Hail 1943,S 10,29:1
Story of Dr Wassell, The 1944,Je 7,13:2
Till We Meet Again 1944,Ag 30,15:1
Great John L, The 1945,Jl 9,14:6
Captain Kidd 1945,N 23,26:3
Virginian, The 1946,Ap 18,22:2
Return of Monte Cristo, The 1947,Ja 3,16:4
Gunfighters 1947,Jl 25,12:5
Albuquerque 1948,Mr 1,17:2
I Shot Jesse James 1949,Ap 2,12:2
Champagne for Caesar 1950,My 12,33:2
Raiders, The 1952,D 13,19:2
Bwana Devil 1953,F 19,20:5
Spoilers, The 1955,D 24,10:2

Britton, Florence
Devil to Pay, The 1930,D 19,30:1
Confessions of a Co-Ed 1931,Je 20,20:4
Compromised 1931,N 7,16:5
Arrowsmith 1931,D 8,36:4
Merrily We Go to Hell 1932,Je 11,9:3
King of the Jungle 1933,F 25,20:3
Brief Moment 1933,S 30,18:5

Britton, Jocelyn
Sapphire 1959,N 3,27:1

Britton, Keith
Storm Fear 1955,D 17,19:2

Britton, Kenneth
Romance on the High Seas 1948,Je 26,10:5
Lady Takes a Sailor, The 1949,D 17,15:2

Britton, Milt and His Band
Riding High 1943,D 23,26:4

Britton, Pamela
Anchors Aweigh 1945,Jl 20,15:2
Letter for Evie, A 1946,Je 28,17:4
Key to the City 1950,F 2,31:2
D O A 1950,My 1,18:2
Watch the Birdie 1950,D 12,46:4

Britton, Tony
Operation Amsterdam 1960,Jl 7,26:1
Risk, The 1961,S 25,41:2
Portrait of a Sinner 1961,D 7,52:1

Brittor, Florence
Strange Case of Clara Deane, The
1932,My 6,15:3

Brive, Pierre (Screenwriter)
Eternal Husband, The 1949,Ja 10,19:2

Brix, Herman
Student Tour 1934,O 31,17:3
New Adventures of Tarzan, The 1935,O 15,19:3
Danger Patrol 1937,N 19,27:3
Maria Ilona 1940,Ap 20,14:3

Brixton, Lew
Gay Desperado, The 1936,O 9,31:4

BROAD
See Also BROD

Broad, Kid
Great White Way, The 1924,Ja 4,10:1

Broadhurst, George (Original Author)
Bought and Paid For 1916,N 9,11:4
What Happened to Jones 1920,Ag 9,6:3
Bought and Paid For 1922,Mr 13,18:2
Wildfire 1925,Je 10,18:2
What Happened to Jones 1926,F 9,22:1
Today 1930,N 17,29:1

Broadhurst, Thomas W (Original Author)
Damaged Love 1931,Ja 19,25:1

Broadley, Colin
Abandon Ship 1957,Ap 18,35:1

Broadley, Edward
Jury's Secret, The 1938,F 4,17:2
Women Are Like That 1938,Ap 11,12:2

Broadney, Oscar (Screenwriter)
Little Egypt 1951,Ag 30,20:3

Broadniewicz, Pan
Wrzos; Heather 1938,N 7,23:4

Broberg, Lily
Eric Soya's 17 1967;Ja 25,37:1

Broca, Philippe de (Director)
Love Game, The 1960,N 9,44:1
Joker, The; (Farceur, Le) 1961,Ag 8,32:2
Five Day Lover, The 1961,D 14,55:4
7 Capital Sins (Gluttony); Gluttony (7 Capital
Sins) 1963,Ja 17,5:2
That Man From Rio 1964,Je 9,30:1
Cartouche 1964,Jl 22,39:1
Male Companion 1966,F 15,33:2
Up to his Ears 1966,My 18,37:1
King of Hearts 1967,Je 20,34:1
Oldest Profession, The (Mademoiselle Mimi);
Mademoiselle Mimi (The Oldest Profession)
1968,N 8,42:1

Broca, Philippe de (Producer)
King of Hearts 1967,Je 20,34:1
Voyage of Silence 1968,S 12,54:1

Broca, Philippe de (Screenwriter)
Love Game, The 1960,N 9,44:1
Joker, The; (Farceur, Le) 1961,Ag 8,32:2
Five Day Lover, The 1961,D 14,55:4
That Man From Rio 1964,Je 9,30:1
Cartouche 1964,Jl 22,39:1

Brocceli, Albert R (Producer)
Paratrooper 1953,D 31,9:3

Brocco, Peter
Gallant Blade 1948,O 13,31:3
Black Hand 1950,Mr 13,15:2
House by the River 1950,My 2,25:2
Breaking Point, The 1950,O 7,10:6
Tall Target, The 1951,S 28,26:2
Prisoner of Zenda, The 1952,N 5,36:2
Rogue Cop 1954,S 18,12:2
Spartacus 1960,O 7,28:1
Balcony, The 1963,Mr 22,7:1

Broccoli, Albert R (Producer)
Hell Below Zero 1954,Jl 17,7:3
Black Knight, The 1954,O 29,27:2
Prize of Gold, A 1955,O 15,19:2
Cockleshell Heroes, The 1956,Je 4,25:2
Zarak 1956,D 27,22:1
Fire Down Below 1957,Ag 9,11:2
Man Inside, The 1959,F 5,24:7
Dr No 1963,My 30,20:1
Call Me Bwana 1963,Jl 4,9:1
From Russia with Love 1964,Ap 9,25:1
Goldfinger 1964,D 22,36:1
You Only Live Twice 1967,Je 14,40:1
Chitty Chitty Bang Bang 1968,D 19,64:4

Brochard, Jean
Jericho 1946,D 16,31:2
Angel and Sinner 1947,F 24,16:5
Lover's Return, A; Revenant, Le 1948,Ja 26,15:2
Corbeau, Le; Raven, The 1948,F 24,21:1
Who Killed Santa Claus? 1948,Ap 21,33:2
God Needs Men 1951,Mr 27,35:1
Simple Case of Money, A 1952,F 2,11:2
Under the Paris Sky 1952,My 6,35:1
Ramuntcho 1953,Mr 2,19:2
Dr Knock 1955,O 10,31:2
Diabolique 1955,N 22,41:1
Vitelloni 1956,O 24,43:1
Pot Bouille 1958,O 28,39:1
Law Is the Law, The 1959,Mr 11,41:2
Sinners of Paris 1959,Ap 24,23:1
Virtuous Bigamist, The 1959,My 28,34:3

Brocher, Egon
Here's to Romance 1935,O 3,29:2

BROCK
See Also BRACH

Brock, Baby
Woman on Trial, The 1927,S 26,27:1

Brock, Dorothy
Lilies of the Field 1924,Mr 17,19:1
Christine of the Hungry Heart 1924,D 8,13:3
So Big 1925,Ja 5,19:1
Just a Woman 1925,My 26,24:2

Brock, Lou (Original Author)
Down to Their Last Yacht 1934,S 24,14:1
Top of the Town 1937,Mr 27,19:2

Brock, Lou (Screenwriter)
Enchanted Forest, The 1945,D 17,17:2

Brock, Louis (Original Author)
Flying Down to Rio 1933,D 22,25:2

Brock, Stanley
Black Like Me 1964,My 21,42:1

Brockman, James (Composer)
New Movietone Follies of 1930, The
1930,Je 21,20:5

Brockner, Gary
Star Dust 1940,My 4,13:1

Brocks, Phyllis
In Old Chicago 1938,Ja 7,15:2

Brockwell, Gladys
Oliver Twist 1922,O 30,11:1
Penrod and Sam 1923,Je 25,16:5
Hunchback of Notre Dame, The 1923,S 3,9:3
Darling of New York, The 1924,Ja 18,20:1
So Big 1925,Ja 5,19:1
Chickie 1925,Ap 27,15:2
Splendid Road, The 1926,Je 13,31:1
Twinkletoes 1926,D 27,20:3
Long Pants 1927,Mr 29,23:2
Seventh Heaven 1927,My 26,22:1
Satin Woman, The 1927,Ag 10,21:4
Man, Woman and Sin 1927,D 5,26:2
Lights of New York 1928,Jl 9,25:1
Home Towners, The 1928,O 24,26:4
Woman Disputed, The 1928,N 10,20:8
Drake Case, The 1929,S 16,30:1

BROD
See Also BROAD

Brod, Max (Original Author)
That Murder in Berlin 1929,Mr 12,26:2

Brodax, Al (Producer)
Yellow Submarine 1968,N 14,56:1

Brodax, Al (Screenwriter)
Yellow Submarine 1968,N 14,56:1

Brode, Robert Stephen (Screenwriter)
Dick Tracy's Dilemma 1947,Jl 14,14:5

Brodel, Joan
Camille 1937,Ja 23,13:1
Winter Carnival 1939,Jl 28,14:2
Military Academy 1940,Ag 5,10:4

Brodelet, Esther
Young as You Feel 1940,Mr 8,25:3

Broderick, Helen
Fifty Million Frenchmen 1931,Mr 26,31:2
Top Hat 1935,Ag 30,12:2
To Beat the Band 1935,N 23,23:2
Love on a Bet 1936,Mr 5,25:2
Murder on a Bridle Path 1936,Ap 11,19:2
Swing Time 1936,Ag 28,21:2
We're on the Jury 1937,F 10,18:5
Meet the Missus 1937,Jl 2,25:2
Life of the Party, The 1937,O 4,17:1
She's Got Everything 1938,Ja 14,21:3
Radio City Revels 1938,Mr 21,18:3
Rage of Paris 1938,Jl 2,10:2
Road to Reno, The 1938,O 3,11:2
Service de Luxe 1938,O 24,13:2
Stand up and Fight 1939,Ja 27,17:2
Naughty but Nice 1939,Je 23,23:2
Honeymoon in Bali 1939,S 21,21:1
No, No, Nanette 1940,D 20,33:1
Virginia 1941,Ja 29,21:2
Nice Girl 1941,Mr 27,29:6
Father takes a Wife 1941,S 5,19:3
Stage Door Canteen 1943,Je 25,13:2
Chip off the Old Block 1944,Mr 17,14:2
Her Primitive Man 1944,Ap 1,11:1
3 Is a Family 1944,D 20,20:3
Love, Honor and Goodbye 1945,S 8,12:2
Because of Him 1946,Ja 25,26:6

Broderick, James
Girl of the Night 1960,N 12,15:1
Group, The 1966,Mr 17,35:1

BRODIE
See Also BRODY

Brodie, Buster
All Abroad 1927,Ap 19,24:4

Brodie, Don
Kennel Murder Case, The 1933,O 30,14:2
Strike Me Pink 1936,Ja 17,15:2
Girl from Scotland Yard, The 1937,My 31,11:2
Lady in the Morgue, The 1938,My 9,13:3
Give Me a Sailor 1938,Ag 11,31:1
Last Express, The 1938,O 11,24:4
Gracie Allen Murder Case, The 1939,Je 8,31:3
Exile Express 1939,Ag 16,21:3
Music in My Heart 1940,Ja 4,19:2
Second Chorus 1941,Ja 16,25:2
Street Corner 1948,D 4,9:4

Brodie, Kevin
Night of the Grizzly, The 1966,Je 23,29:1
Eight on the Lam 1967,Ap 27,52:1

Brodie, Steve
This Man's Navy 1945,Ap 16,18:6
Walk in the Sun, A 1946,Ja 12,10:6
Badman's Territory 1946,My 31,27:2
Young Widow 1946,Jl 29,12:8
Criminal Court 1946,N 16,15:3
Falcon's Adventure, The 1946,D 14,19:2
Trail Street 1947,Ap 10,35:2
Crossfire 1947,Jl 23,19:2
Out of the Past 1947,N 26,18:2
Return of the Badmen 1948,Ag 5,16:2
Home of the Brave 1949,My 13,29:1
Massacre River 1949,Jl 15,17:2
Winchester 73 1950,Je 8,38:2
Kiss Tomorrow Goodbye 1950,Ag 5,9:2
Admiral Was a Lady, The 1950,O 13,23:3
Steel Helmet, The 1951,Ja 25,21:5
Only the Valiant 1951,Ap 14,9:6

Brodie, Steve— Cont
Sword of Monte Cristo, The 1951,Ap 23,21:2
Fighting Coast Guard 1951,My 12,14:6
M 1951,Je 11,20:7
3 for Bedroom C 1952,Je 27,18:3
Lady in the Iron Mask 1952,Jl 5,7:2
Beast From 20,000 Fathoms, The 1953,Je 25,23:1
Charge at Feather River, The 1953,Jl 16,17:2
Donovan's Brain 1954,Ja 21,28:2
Far Country, The 1955,F 14,24:2
Girl Named Tamiku, A 1963,Mr 15,8:2
Of Love and Desire 1963,S 12,32:1
Brodin, Helena
Guilt 1967,N 21,53:1
Brodkin, Herbert (Producer)
Sebastian 1968,Ja 25,33:2
Brodney, Oscar (Original Author)
Yes Sir, That's my Baby 1949,N 11,31:2
Frenchie 1951,F 12,19:2
Double Crossbones 1951,Ap 27,19:2
Little Egypt 1951,Ag 30,20:3
Francis Goes to West Point 1952,Ag 23,10:2
Sign of the Pagan 1955,F 14,24:2
Lady Godiva 1955,D 3,13:3
Brodney, Oscar (Producer)
All Hands on Deck 1961,Ap 1,10:2
Right Approach, The 1961,My 18,41:1
Brodney, Oscar (Screenwriter)
When Johnny Comes Marching Home
 1943,Mr 5,20:4
She Wrote the Book 1946,Je 20,20:3
If You Knew Susie 1948,F 23,19:2
Are You With It? 1948,Ap 15,31:2
For the Love of Mary 1948,S 23,37:2
Mexican Hayride 1949,Ja 12,33:3
Arctic Manhunt 1949,Ag 19,12:5
Yes Sir, That's my Baby 1949,N 11,31:2
South Sea Sinner 1950,Ja 16,18:4
Comanche Territory 1950,Ap 8,9:3
Harvey 1950,D 22,19:1
Frenchie 1951,F 12,19:2
Double Crossbones 1951,Ap 27,19:2
Francis Goes to the Races 1951,Jl 25,19:2
Scarlet Angel 1952,Je 21,12:2
Francis Goes to West Point 1952,Ag 23,10:2
Walking my Baby Back Home 1954,Ja 16,10:5
Glenn Miller Story, The 1954,F 11,33:2
Black Shield of Falworth, The 1954,O 7,16:2
Sign of the Pagan 1955,F 14,24:2
Purple Mask, The 1955,Je 16,35:7
Lady Godiva 1955,D 3,13:3
Spoilers, The 1955,D 24,10:2
Tammy and the Bachelor 1957,Je 15,10:7
Tammy Tell me True 1961,Jl 27,23:2
Tammy and the Doctor 1963,Je 27,23:2
Brass Bottle, The 1964,My 21,42:1
I'd Rather Be Rich 1964,S 3,24:2
Brodniewicz, Franciszek
Prokurator 1934,My 22,28:4
Sluby Ulanskie; Love in the Army 1935,F 22,27:3
Milosc Wszystko Zwycieza 1936,Ja 28,15:3
Tredowata 1936,D 31,21:2
Wrzos; Heather 1938,N 7,23:4
Brodo, E
Clos Pustyni 1933,Ap 21,20:5
Brodo, E (Director)
Clos Pustyni 1933,Ap 21,20:5
Brodrick, Malcolm
Man on Fire 1957,Ag 23,10:1
That Night 1957,O 15,39:3
Brodski, Iona
Son of the Land, A 1931,My 23,13:4
Brodsky, Benjamin (Original Author)
Trip Thru China 1917,My 22,11:3
Brodsky, Nicholas (Composer)
Gitta Entdeckt Ihr Herz 1932,S 30,17:3
Toast of New Orleans, The 1950,S 30,13:3
Rich, Young and Pretty 1951,Jl 26,17:3
Latin Lovers 1953,Ag 13,17:2
Meet Me in Las Vegas 1956,Mr 14,39:2
Opposite Sex, The 1956,N 16,23:2
Ten Thousand Bedrooms 1957,Ap 4,37:1
Brodsky, Vlastimil
Transport From Paradise 1967,F 8,22:1
Closely Watched Trains 1967,O 16,59:2
Capricious Summer 1968,S 18,50:2
Capricious Summer 1968,S 25,38:2
BRODY
See Also BRODIE
Brody, Alexander (Original Author)
Surrender 1927,O 11,27:1
Brody, Ann
Sainted Devil, A 1924,N 24,15:3
Manicure Girl, The 1925,Je 15,10:1
Clancy's Kosher Wedding 1927,S 7,35:2
Alias the Lone Wolf 1927,S 20,32:2
My Man 1928,D 22,14:3
Case of Lena Smith, The 1929,Ja 15,22:4
Wolf Song 1929,F 25,16:1
So This Is College 1929,N 9,22:5
Playing Around 1930,Mr 31,24:3
Fall Guy, The 1930,My 27,27:2
Heart of New York, The 1932,Mr 2,15:3
Lawyer Man 1932,D 27,10:2

High Gear 1933,Ap 15,16:2
Brody, Estelle
Kitty 1929,Je 11,27:2
Fanny Hawthorn 1929,N 11,20:2
Lilli Marlene 1952,Mr 29,19:2
Safari 1956,Je 21,35:2
Brody, Lewis
Between Worlds 1924,Jl 7,10:4
Brody, Marvin
Guide for the Married Man, A 1967,My 27,16:1
Brody, Merrill (Producer)
Blast of Silence 1961,D 30,12:1
Terror in the City 1966,N 9,43:4
Brody, Todd
Cuban Rebel Girls 1959,D 26,7:3
Brodyadnsky, Boris (Original Author)
Children of the New Day 1930,Je 30,22:6
Brodyansky, Boris (Director)
Krasnaya Derevnya 1935,My 2,17:1
Brodzisz, Adam
Dziesieciu z Pawiaka 1932,Ap 21,25:2
Clos Pustyni 1933,Ap 21,20:5
Mlody Las 1935,D 3,32:7
Pan Redaktor Szaleje; Mr Editor Is Crazy
 1938,Je 14,17:3
Brogan, Annie
Playboy of the Western World, The
 1963,Mr 19,8:2
Brogan, Harry
Shake Hands With the Devil 1959,Je 25,20:7
Broth of a Boy 1959,D 28,18:1
Poacher's Daughter, The 1960,F 16,31:2
Night Fighters, The 1960,D 15,59:1
Home Is the Hero 1961,Ja 26,32:1
Broggi, Isidora (Producer)
Crazy Desire 1964,Jl 3,13:2
Fascist, The 1965,Je 18,28:3
Broggi, Isidoro (Producer)
Hours of Love, The 1965,S 4,11:5
Brogle, Peter
Signs of Life; Lebenszeichent 1968,S 26,60:1
Broidy, William F (Producer)
Las Vegas Shakedown 1955,Je 18,14:2
Legion of the Doomed 1959,Mr 12,27:5
Brok, B (Original Author)
First Start, The 1953,F 2,17:3
Brokaw, Charles
Fascinating Youth 1926,My 10,19:1
I Cover the War 1937,Ag 2,10:2
Outer Gate, The 1937,N 22,15:2
Idol of the Crowd 1937,D 4,21:1
Murder in the Air 1940,Jl 4,12:2
Brokenshire, Norman (Narrator)
Soviet Russia Through the Eyes of an American
 1935,S 28,12:2
Brolin, James
Von Ryan's Express 1965,Je 24,28:1
Bromberg, J Edward
Under Two Flags 1936,My 1,19:1
Sins of Man 1936,Je 19,17:2
Crime of Dr Forbes, The 1936,Jl 6,11:4
Girls' Dormitory 1936,Ag 29,16:2
Star for a Night 1936,S 5,7:2
Ladies in Love 1936,O 29,31:1
Reunion 1936,N 27,27:1
Stowaway 1936,D 19,16:1
Seventh Heaven 1937,Mr 26,25:1
That I May Live 1937,My 10,23:2
Charlie Chan on Broadway 1937,S 20,19:1
Second Honeymoon 1937,N 13,11:2
Baroness and the Butler, The 1938,F 19,19:2
Rebecca of Sunnybrook Farm 1938,Mr 26,12:1
Four Men and a Prayer 1938,My 7,18:1
One Wild Night 1938,Je 3,17:2
Mr Moto Takes a Chance 1938,Je 13,15:4
I'll Give a Million 1938,Jl 16,7:2
Suez 1938,O 15,21:2
Jesse James 1939,Ja 14,13:1
Wife, Husband and Friend 1939,F 25,19:2
Hollywood Cavalcade 1939,O 14,13:2
Three Sons 1939,N 24,29:3
Strange Cargo 1940,Ap 26,25:2
Return of Frank James, The 1940,Ag 10,16:4
Mark of Zorro, The 1940,N 4,23:2
Dance Hall 1941,Jl 19,16:2
Pacific Blackout 1942,Ja 15,25:2
Invisible Agent 1942,Ag 6,23:2
Life Begins at Eight-Thirty 1942,D 10,35:2
Tennessee Johnson 1943,Ja 13,18:2
Reunion in France 1943,Mr 5,20:3
Lady of Burlesque 1943,My 14,17:2
Phantom of the Opera, The 1943,O 15,15:2
Son of Dracula 1943,N 6,16:4
Voice in the Wind 1944,Mr 16,17:2
Chip off the Old Block 1944,Mr 17,14:2
Salome, Where She Danced 1945,My 3,27:1
Pillow of Death 1946,Ja 26,19:3
Tangier 1946,Je 7,II,16:4
Cloak and Dagger 1946,O 5,13:2
Walls Came Tumbling Down, The 1946,N 9,13:5
Arch of Triumph 1948,Ap 21,33:2
Song Is Born, A 1948,O 20,37:2
I Shot Jesse James 1949,Ap 2,12:2

Bromberg, J Edward— Cont
Guilty Bystander 1950,Ap 21,18:2
Bromberger, Herve (Director)
Three Fables of Love (The Fox and the Crow)
 1963,Ag 21,38:1
Bromberger, Herve (Miscellaneous)
Three Fables of Love (The Fox and the Crow)
 1963,Ag 21,38:1
Three Fables of Love (Two Pigeons)
 1963,Ag 21,38:1
Bromfield, John
Harpoon 1948,D 9,48:8
Rope of Sand 1949,Ag 4,19:2
Paid in Full 1950,F 16,28:2
Furies, The 1950,Ag 17,23:2
Flat Top 1952,D 6,17:2
Easy to Love 1953,N 27,99:9
Ring of Fear 1954,Jl 29,18:3
Black Dakotas, The 1954,O 2,21:2
Revenge of the Creature 1955,My 14,10:7
Three bad Sisters 1956,F 13,24:1
Bromfield, Louis (Original Author)
One Heavenly Night 1931,Ja 10,19:2
Twenty-Four Hours 1931,O 3,20:2
Night after Night 1932,O 31,18:4
Modern Hero, A 1934,Ap 20,17:1
Life of Vergie Winters, The 1934,Je 15,26:1
Rains Came, The 1939,S 9,11:2
It all Came True 1940,Ap 6,13:2
Brigham Young - Frontiersman 1940,S 21,13:2
Johnny Come Lately 1943,S 24,26:1
Mrs Parkington 1944,O 13,16:1
Rains of Ranchipur, The 1955,D 16,38:2
Bromiley, Dorothy
Girls of Pleasure Island, The 1953,My 16,10:1
It's Great to be Young 1957,D 26,23:3
Bromilow, Peter
Camelot 1967,O 26,54:1
Bromley, Haworth (Screenwriter)
Pastor Hall 1940,S 21,13:2
What's Cookin' 1942,F 26,15:5
Bromley, Sheila
West of Shanghai 1937,O 29,19:2
Idol of the Crowd 1937,D 4,21:1
Missing Witness 1937,D 10,33:3
Making the Headlines 1938,Ap 1,17:2
King of the Newsboys 1938,Ap 2,18:2
Accidents Will Happen 1938,Ap 25,19:2
Reformatory 1938,Je 27,13:6
Mystery House 1938,Je 29,15:5
Girls on Probation 1938,O 21,27:3
Women in the Wind 1939,Ap 13,27:2
Waterfront 1939,Jl 17,10:2
Thou Shalt Not Kill 1940,Ja 8,11:2
Calling Philo Vance 1940,F 9,15:3
Fugitive From Justice, A 1940,Jl 8,13:3
Time to Kill 1942,D 25,15:4
Hotel 1967,Ja 20,27:1
Bromley, Sydney
Saint Joan 1957,Je 27,21:1
Smashing Time 1967,D 21,44:1
Bromly, Alan (Director)
Angel Who Pawned her Harp, The
 1956,F 29,35:2
Bron, Eleanor
Help! 1965,Ag 24,25:1
Alfie 1966,Ag 25,42:1
Two for the Road 1967,Ap 28,36:2
Bedazzled 1967,D 11,65:2
Bronder, Lucia (Original Author)
Rockabye 1932,D 5,21:2
Bronecki, S
Dybbuk, The 1938,Ja 28,17:2
Broniewska, M
Border Street 1950,Ap 26,35:2
Bronska-Pampuch, Wanda
Artists Under the Big Top Perplexed
 1968,S 27,34:1
Bronson, Betty
Peter Pan 1924,D 29,11:4
Are Parents People 1925,Je 9,16:3
Not so Long Ago 1925,Jl 28,24:4
Golden Princess 1925,S 7,15:3
Kiss for Cinderella, A 1925,D 26,11:2
Ben Hur 1925,D 31,10:5 (In Addenda)
Paradise 1926,O 4,20:2
Everybody's Acting 1926,N 8,19:2
Paradise for Two 1927,Ja 25,18:4
Ritzy 1927,Je 20,25:3
Singing Fool, The 1928,S 20,33:2
Bellamy Trial, The 1929,Ja 24,30:5
Sonny Boy 1929,Mr 9,24:3
Locked Door, The 1930,Ja 20,21:1
Lover Come Back 1931,Je 5,26:5
Ben Hur 1931,D 4,28:2
Midnight Patrol, The 1932,My 7,11:5
Naked Kiss, The 1964,O 29,38:1
Bronson, Charles
Drum Beat 1954,N 18,42:1
Big House U S A 1955,Mr 12,11:6
Target Zero 1955,N 16,43:2
Jubal 1956,Ap 25,39:1
Run of the Arrow 1957,Ag 3,8:6
Never so Few 1960,Ja 22,15:2

Bronson, Charles— Cont
Magnificent Seven, The 1960,N 24,48:3
Master of the World 1961,S 16,9:1
Thunder of Drums, A 1961,S 27,35:1
X-15 1962,Ap 5,30:2
Kid Galahad 1963,Mr 7,8:5
Great Escape, The 1963,Ag 8,19:1
4 for Texas 1963,D 26,33:3
Sandpiper, The 1965,Jl 16,14:1
Battle of the Bulge 1965,D 18,36:1
This Property is Condemned 1966,Ag 4,24:1
Dirty Dozen, The 1967,Je 16,36:1
Guns for San Sebastian 1968,Mr 21,57:2
Villa Rides 1968,Jl 18,26:3
Bronson, Harry
Crooked Way, The 1949,S 5,13:2
Johnny One-Eye 1950,N 17,31:2
Thief, The 1952,O 16,37:1
Bronson, Lillian
Enter Arsene Lupin 1944,D 2,17:6
Molly and Me 1945,My 26,18:2
Sentimental Journey 1946,Mr 7,33:2
Shocking Miss Pilgrim, The 1947,F 12,34:2
Hucksters, The 1947,Jl 18,21:2
Family Honeymoon 1949,F 25,28:2
In the Good Old Summertime 1949,Ag 5,23:2
Next Voice You Hear, The 1950,Je 30,18:2
Excuse my Dust 1951,Je 28,21:2
No Room for the Groom 1952,Je 14,12:2
Affair With a Stranger 1953,Jl 11,8:2
So This Is Love 1953,Ag 12,22:1
Spencer's Mountain 1963,My 17,26:6
Bronsten, N A (Producer)
Give Us This Day 1949,D 21,41:2
Silent Dust 1949,D 30,13:2
Hidden Room, The 1950,Ja 9,19:2
Valley of the Eagles 1952,Ap 11,19:2
Bronston, Samuel (Producer)
Jack London 1944,Mr 3,19:3
John Paul Jones 1959,Je 17,39:1
King of Kings 1961,O 12,41:2
Cid, El 1961,D 15,49:1
55 Days at Peking 1963,My 30,20:1
Fall of the Roman Empire, The 1964,Mr 27,14:2
Circus World 1964,Je 26,34:2
Bronte, Charlotte (Original Author)
Jane Eyre 1922,Ja 29,VI,2:1 (In Addenda)
Jane Eyre 1944,F 4,12:5
Bronte, Emily (Original Author)
Wuthering Heights 1939,Ap 14,28:2
Bronte, Peter
Green Hell 1940,Ja 30,15:6
Brook, Cecil
Caravan 1949,Ap 21,30:4
Brook, Charles
Paradise 1926,O 4,20:2
Brook, Claudio
Young One, The 1961,Ja 19,26:1
Viva Maria 1965,D 20,48:2
Simon of the Desert 1966,S 21,42:2
Upper Hand, The 1967,Jl 29,29:3
Exterminating Angel, The 1967,Ag 22,33:1
Brook, Clive
Woman to Woman 1924,Ap 1,19:3
Recoil, The 1924,Je 30,16:1
Christine of the Hungry Heart 1924,D 8,13:3
Enticement 1925,Mr 21,16:3
Declassee 1925,Mr 23,14:2
Playing With Souls 1925,Ap 20,18:1 (Incorrect in this edition; use 1925,Ap 28,18:1 elsewhere)
If Marriage Fails 1925,Je 2,16:3
Home Maker, The 1925,Ag 10,8:2
Compromise 1925,O 27,23:3
Seven Sinners 1925,D 8,28:5
You Never Know Women 1926,Jl 27,15:5
For Alimony Only 1926,S 21,33:1
Popular Sin, The 1926,D 20,28:3
Afraid to Love 1927,Ap 12,25:3
Barbed Wire 1927,Ag 8,10:3
Underworld 1927,Ag 22,21:3
Hula 1927,Ag 29,21:1
French Dressing 1927,D 13,33:2
Devil Dancer, The 1927,D 19,30:1
Yellow Lily, The 1928,My 21,25:1
Forgotten Faces 1928,Ag 6,15:2
Perfect Crime, The 1928,Ag 6,15:2
Interference 1928,N 17,23:1
Dangerous Woman, A 1929,My 20,22:6
Four Feathers, The 1929,Je 13,35:4
Charming Sinners 1929,Jl 8,17:3
Return of Sherlock Holmes, The 1929,O 19,22:6
Laughing Lady, The 1930,Ja 4,21:1
Slightly Scarlet 1930,Mr 1,23:1
Paramount on Parade 1930,Ap 21,20:4
Sweethearts and Wives 1930,Je 28,9:2
Anybody's Woman 1930,Ag 16,8:3
Scandal Sheet 1931,F 9,25:3
East Lynne 1931,F 21,15:2
Tarnished Lady 1931,Ap 30,29:3
Lawyer's Secret, The 1931,My 30,9:2
Silence 1931,Ag 15,18:3
Twenty-Four Hours 1931,O 3,20:2
Husband's Holiday 1931,D 25,29:2
Shanghai Express 1932,F 18,25:3

Man From Yesterday, The 1932,Je 25,18:2
Night of June 13th, The 1932,S 17,18:4
Sherlock Holmes 1932,N 12,20:5
Cavalcade 1933,Ja 6,23:2
Midnight Club 1933,Jl 29,14:2
If I Were Free 1934,Ja 5,25:2
Gallant Lady 1934,Ja 22,12:3
Where Sinners Meet 1934,My 25,25:2
Let's Try Again 1934,Je 22,24:1
Dictator, The 1935,Mr 24,VIII,3:6 (In Addenda)
Loves of a Dictator 1935,Je 1,18:2
Love in Exile 1936,D 10,35:3
Ware Case, The 1939,Jl 22,12:2
Convoy 1941,Ja 17,21:2
Voice in the Night, The 1941,My 23,25:4
On Approval 1945,Ja 29,17:1
List of Adrian Messenger, The 1963,My 30,20:1
Brook, Clive (Director)
On Approval 1945,Ja 29,17:1
Brook, Clive (Producer)
On Approval 1945,Ja 29,17:1
Brook, Clive (Screenwriter)
On Approval 1945,Ja 29,17:1
Brook, Faith
Jungle Book 1942,Ap 6,19:1
Across the Bridge 1957,O 30,24:1
Chase a Crooked Shadow 1958,Mr 25,28:4
39 Steps, The 1960,O 11,55:2
To Sir, With Love 1967,Je 15,56:1
Brook, Fay
Separation 1968,Mr 26,41:2
Brook, Helene
Woman Hater, The 1925,Jl 13,20:2
Brook, James Ten
If Winter Comes 1923,S 4,14:1
Brook, Lesley
Dead Men Tell no Tales 1939,Jl 24,9:2
Brook, Lyndon
Purple Plain, The 1955,Ap 11,29:1
Reach for the Sky 1957,My 1,40:1
Spanish Gardner, The 1957,S 9,21:2
Song Without End 1960,Ag 12,10:2
Surprise Package 1960,O 15,26:2
Brook, Olive
This Freedom 1923,N 28,15:1
Why Girls Go Back Home 1926,My 18,28:2
Brook, Patrick
Johnny Doughboy 1943,My 6,25:3
Brook, Peter (Director)
Beggar's Opera, The 1953,Ag 25,18:2
Lord of the Flies 1963,Ag 20,37:1
Moderato Cantabile 1964,Ja 7,24:1
Persecution and Assassination of Jean-Paul Marat as Performed by the Inmates of the Asylum of Charenton Under the Direction of the Marquis De Sade, The 1967,F 23,41:1
London Scene, The (The Benefit of the Doubt); Benefit of the Doubt, The (The London Scene) 1967,S 27,39:1
Tell Me Lies 1968,F 13,46:3
Brook, Peter (Producer)
Tell Me Lies 1968,F 13,46:3
Brook, Peter (Screenwriter)
Lord of the Flies 1963,Ag 20,37:1
Persecution and Assassination of Jean-Paul Marat as Performed by the Inmates of the Asylum of Charenton Under the Direction of the Marquis De Sade, The 1967,F 23,41:1
Brook-Jones, Elwin
Odd Man Out 1947,Ap 24,30:2
Brook-Jones, Elwyn
Good Time Girl 1950,S 25,18:5
Lucky Nick Cain 1951,Ap 23,21:2
Wonder Boy 1951,D 26,19:5
Beau Brummell 1954,O 21,31:5
Pure Hell of St Trinian's, The 1961,S 26,31:1
Brooke, Claude
Pied Piper Malone 1924,Ja 28,12:1
Classmates 1924,D 30,15:3
Brooke, Clifford
Woman's Face, A 1941,My 16,21:2
Wilson 1944,Ag 2,18:1
Suspect, The 1945,F 1,18:5
Hangover Square 1945,F 8,15:2
Molly and Me 1945,My 26,18:2
Three Strangers 1946,F 23,20:2
Black Beauty 1946,Ag 30,13:2
Woman in White, The 1948,My 8,12:2
First Legion, The 1951,Ap 28,9:2
Brooke, Clifton
Sea Hawk, The 1940,Ag 10,16:2
Brooke, Eleanor (Original Author)
That Certain Felling 1956,Je 21,35:2
Brooke, Harold (Original Author)
Pair of Briefs, A 1964,F 3,22:2
Brooke, Hillary
Sherlock Holmes and the Voice Of Terror 1942,S 19,9:2
Counter-Espionage 1942,S 28,13:2
Sherlock Holmes Faces Death 1943,O 8,15:3
Jane Eyre 1944,F 4,12:5
Standing Room Only 1944,F 23,17:2
Ministry of Fear 1945,F 8,15:2

Brooke, Hillary— Cont
Crime Doctor's Courage, The 1945,Mr 3,11:3
Enchanted Cottage, The 1945,Ap 28,19:2
Woman in Green, The 1945,Je 16,10:3
Up Goes Maisie 1946,Ja 25,26:7
Road to Utopia 1946,F 28,20:2
Earl Carroll Sketchbook 1946,Ag 30,13:2
Monsieur Beaucaire 1946,S 5,23:1
Strange Woman, The 1947,F 24,16:4
Fuller Brush Man, The 1948,My 15,18:2
Africa Screams 1949,My 5,34:2
Alimony 1949,Jl 22,16:3
Bodyhold 1949,D 12,29:4
Beauty on Parade 1950,Ag 18,17:2
Admiral Was a Lady, The 1950,O 13,23:3
Vendetta 1950,D 26,19:1
Confidence Girl 1952,Je 21,12:2
Never Wave at a Wac 1953,Ap 24,30:2
Invaders From Mars 1953,My 30,7:1
Maze, The 1953,Jl 11,8:2
Bengazi 1955,O 8,13:4
Man Who Knew too Much, The 1956,My 17,37:1
Brooke, Hugh (Screenwriter)
ThIs is my Love 1954,D 25,7:3
Brooke, Michael
Bulldog Drummond's Peril 1938,Mr 18,23:2
Bulldog Drummond in Africa 1938,Ag 25,15:1
Dawn Patrol 1938,D 24,12:1
Magnet, The 1951,F 27,22:6
Third Key, The 1957,Je 3,30:2
Brooke, Peter R (Screenwriter)
Basketball Fix, the 1951,S 14,21:2
Brooke, Ralph
Shot in the Dark, A 1935,My 22,23:2
Thin Man Goes Home, The 1945,Ja 26,16:5
Mystery Submarine 1951,F 2,19:2
Charge at Feather River, The 1953,Jl 16,17:2
Third Voice, The 1960,Mr 7,24:5
Brooke, Sybil
Moonlight Sonata 1938,My 10,17:2
Brooke, Tyler
Rich but Honest 1927,My 18,29:3
Fazil 1928,Je 5,21:1
Dynamite 1929,D 28,11:1
Divorcee, The 1930,My 10,25:3
Monte Carlo 1930,Ag 28,22:4
Playboy of Paris 1930,N 1,23:2
Magnificent Lie, The 1931,Jl 25,11:6
Dangerous Affair, A 1931,N 23,22:1
Love Me Tonight 1932,Ag 19,20:6
Hallelujah, I'm a Bum 1933,F 9,15:2
Child of Manhattan 1933,F 13,11:4
Morning Glory 1933,Ag 18,18:2
Blind Date 1934,S 1,16:3
To Mary-With Love 1936,Ag 27,16:1
You Can't Have Everything 1937,Ag 4,15:2
In Old Chicago 1938,Ja 7,15:2
Little Old New York 1940,F 3,9:2
Tin Pan Alley 1940,N 22,27:3
Brooke, Van Dyke
Passionate Pilgrim, The 1921,Ja 3,20:2
Midnight Bell, A 1921,Ag 8,12:2
Brooke, Walter
Bullet Scars 1942,Ap 24,21:4
Conquest of Space 1955,My 28,7:6
Graduate, The 1967,D 22,44:4
Sergeant Ryker 1968,Mr 21,56:2
Brookes, Olwen
Inspector Calls, An 1954,N 26,24:4
Brooks, Alan
Red Dice 1926,Ap 16,20:3
Young April 1926,Ag 31,15:3
Pals in Paradise 1926,N 24,26:4
King of Kings, The 1927,Ap 20,29:2
Shanghaied 1927,S 13,36:2
South Sea Love 1928,F 7,30:3
Hole in the Wall, The 1929,Ap 15,22:6
Enemies of the Law 1931,Jl 13,13:5
League of Frightened Men, The 1937,Jl 2,25:1
Brooks, Bobby
Crazy House 1943,D 16,33:3
Brooks, Clarence
Arrowsmith 1931,D 8,36:4
Spirit of Youth 1938,F 28,19:1
Brooks, Cyrus (Screenwriter)
Emil 1938,Ap 15,23:2
Brooks, George S (Original Author)
Big News 1929,O 7,22:1
Brooks, Geraldine
Possessed 1947,My 30,25:2
Cry Wolf 1947,Jl 19,10:2
Live Today for Tomorrow 1948,D 6,29:2
Younger Brothers, The 1949,My 28,11:2
Reckless Moment, The 1949,D 30,13:2
Challenge to Lassie 1950,Ap 7,22:3
Green Glove, The 1952,Ap 24,38:1
Streets of Sorrow 1952,N 18,37:4
Volcano 1953,Jl 21,19:2
Johnny Tiger 1966,Je 16,53:4
Brooks, Hadda
In a Lonely Place 1950,My 18,37:2
Brooks, Harvey (Composer)
I'm no Angel 1933,O 14,18:2

Brooks, Hazel
Body and Soul 1947,N 10,21:2
Sleep, My Love 1948,F 19,29:4
Basketball Fix, the 1951,S 14,21:2
Brooks, Howard
Man in the Iron Mask, The 1939,Jl 14,11:1
Brooks, Jack (Composer)
Here Come the Co-Eds 1945,F 19,21:1
Naughty Nineties, The 1945,Je 21,16:2
Night in Paradise 1946,Je 6,16:3
Black Angel 1946,S 26,32:4
Artists and Models 1955,D 22,20:1
Brooks, Jean
Leopard Man, The 1943,My 20,26:4
Falcon in Danger, The 1943,Jl 23,21:2
Seventh Victim, The 1943,S 18,11:3
Night of Adventure, A 1944,Je 3,10:4
Youth Runs Wild 1944,S 2,17:2
Falcon in Hollywood, The 1944,D 9,21:2
Two O'Clock Courage 1945,Ap 14,13:3
Falcon's Alibi, The 1946,Ap 13,23:2
Brooks, Jeremy (Screenwriter)
Our Mother's House 1967,O 10,56:1
Brooks, Jess
Drums of the Congo 1942,Jl 20,16:4
Jungle Siren 1942,O 10,11:3
Brooks, Leslie
You Were Never Lovelier 1942,D 4,31:1
What's Buzzin Cousin 1943,Jl 23,21:4
Two Senoritas From Chicago 1943,Ag 6,10:4
Cover Girl 1944,Mr 31,26:1
Tonight and Every Night 1945,Mr 9,16:2
Corpse came C O D, The 1947,Ag 19,27:2
Romance on the High Seas 1948,Je 26,10:5
Hollow Triumph 1948,O 29,29:5
Brooks, Lola
On the Beach 1959,D 18,34:1
Sundowners, The 1960,D 9,39:1
Brooks, Louise
American Venus, The 1926,Ja 26,25:2
Social Celebrity, A 1926,Ap 19,24:3
It's the old Army Game 1926,Jl 5,6:4
Show-Off, The 1926,Ag 23,9:1
Love 'Em and Leave 'Em 1926,D 8,24:3
Girl from Coney Island or Just Another Blonde
  1926,D 13,27:1
Evening Clothes 1927,Mr 21,10:4
Rolled Stockings 1927,Jl 19,27:2
City Gone Wild, The 1927,D 6,27:1
We're in the Air Now 1927,D 31,31:1
Girl in Every Port, A 1928,F 20,14:1
Beggars of Life 1928,S 24,25:1
Pandora's Box 1929,D 2,28:2
Pays to Advertise, It 1931,F 21,15:2
It Pays to Advertise 1931,F 21,15:2
God's Gift to Women 1931,Ap 18,17:3
Public Enemy, The 1931,Ap 24,27:1
Brooks, Margaret
Our Mother's House 1967,O 10,56:1
Brooks, Marjorie
Evergreen 1935,Ja 11,29:1
This'll Make You Whistle 1938,N 1,27:2
She Shall Have Music 1942,O 31,11:2
Brooks, Matt (Miscellaneous)
Duffy's Tavern 1945,S 6,23:3
Brooks, Matt (Original Author)
Radio City Revels 1938,Mr 21,18:3
Ship Ahoy 1942,Je 26,16:5
Swing Fever 1944,Ja 28,14:1
Brooks, Matt (Screenwriter)
Radio City Revels 1938,Mr 21,18:3
Brooks, Mel (Director)
Producers, The 1968,Mr 19,38:1
Brooks, Mel (Screenwriter)
New Faces 1954,F 20,8:7
Producers, The 1968,Mr 19,38:1
Brooks, Norman
Best Things in Life are Free, The 1956,S 29,12:2
Brooks, Norman (Original Author)
Attack! 1956,S 20,29:4
Brooks, Paul
Falcon's Alibi, The 1946,Ap 13,23:2
Brooks, Pauline
Student Tour 1934,O 31,17:3
Make a Million 1935,N 9,19:3
Brooks, Peter
Hud 1963,My 29,36:1
Gidget Goes to Rome 1963,S 12,32:2
Brooks, Phyllis
McFadden's Flats 1935,Mr 13,16:2
To Beat the Band 1935,N 23,23:2
You Can't Have Everything 1937,Ag 4,15:2
Dangerously Yours 1937,O 18,14:2
City Girl 1938,F 4,17:3
Rebecca of Sunnybrook Farm 1938,Mr 26,12:1
Walking Down Broadway 1938,Ap 1,17:3
Little Miss Broadway 1938,Jl 23,10:4
Straight, Place and Show 1938,O 1,10:2
Up the River 1938,D 3,11:2
Charlie Chan in Honolulu 1938,D 31,7:3
Charlie Chan in Reno 1939,My 31,27:2
Slightly Honorable 1940,My 17,23:4
Shanghai Gesture, The 1941,D 26,21:2

Lady in the Dark 1944,F 23,17:1
Unseen, The 1945,My 14,20:5
Brooks, Rand
Dramatic School 1938,D 9,31:2
Old Maid, The 1939,Ag 12,16:2
Babes in Arms 1939,O 20,27:2
Gone With the Wind 1939,D 20,31:2
And One Was Beautiful 1940,Ap 11,32:4
Florian 1940,Je 6,33:2
Son of Monte Cristo, The 1940,D 5,33:1
Life With Henry 1941,F 6,25:2
Lady Scarface 1941,Ag 4,16:6
Lady in the Dark 1944,F 23,17:1
Riding High 1950,Ap 11,26:2
Brooks, Ray
Knack...and how to get it, The 1965,Je 30,42:1
Brooks, Richard (Director)
Crisis 1950,Jl 4,10:2
Light Touch, The 1952,Ja 17,23:1
Deadline U S A 1952,Mr 15,8:2
Battle Circus 1953,My 28,27:5
Take the High Ground 1953,N 20,19:2
Flame and the Flesh 1954,My 3,21:2
Last Time I saw Paris, The 1954,N 19,20:2
Blackboard Jungle 1955,Mr 21,21:5
Last Hunt, The 1956,Mr 1,37:2
Catered Affair, The 1956,Je 15,32:4
Something of Value 1957,My 11,24:6
Brothers Karamazov, The 1958,F 21,18:2
Elmer Gantry 1960,Jl 8,16:1
Sweet Bird of Youth 1962,Mr 29,28:2
Lord Jim 1965,F 26,18:1
Professionals, The 1966,N 3,45:1
In Cold Blood 1967,D 15,60:1
Brooks, Richard (Miscellaneous)
Sin Town 1942,O 17,11:2
Brooks, Richard (Original Author)
Crossfire 1947,Jl 23,19:2
Brooks, Richard (Producer)
Lord Jim 1965,F 26,18:1
In Cold Blood 1967,D 15,60:1
Brooks, Richard (Screenwriter)
White Savage 1943,Ap 26,15:2
Cobra Woman 1944,My 18,17:2
Swell Guy 1947,Ja 27,17:2
Brute Force 1947,Jl 17,16:2
To the Victor 1948,Ap 17,11:2
Key Largo 1948,Jl 17,6:6
Any Number Can Play 1949,Jl 1,14:4
Crisis 1950,Jl 4,10:2
Mystery Street 1950,Jl 28,12:5
Storm Warning 1951,Mr 3,8:2
Light Touch, The 1952,Ja 17,23:1
Deadline U S A 1952,Mr 15,8:2
Battle Circus 1953,My 28,27:5
Last Time I saw Paris, The 1954,N 19,20:2
Blackboard Jungle 1955,Mr 21,21:5
Last Hunt, The 1956,Mr 1,37:2
Something of Value 1957,My 11,24:6
Brothers Karamazov, The 1958,F 21,18:2
Cat on a Hot Tin Roof 1958,S 19,24:1
Elmer Gantry 1960,Jl 8,16:1
Sweet Bird of Youth 1962,Mr 29,28:2
Lord Jim 1965,F 26,18:1
Professionals, The 1966,N 3,45:1
In Cold Blood 1967,D 15,60:1
Brooks, Robert
Hearts in Dixie 1929,F 28,30:3
Brooks, Thor (Director)
Legion of the Doomed 1959,Mr 12,27:5
Brooks, Victor
Brides of Dracula, The 1960,S 6,41:4
Eyes of Annie Jones, The 1964,My 14,39:1
Brooks, William
Michigan Kid 1947,F 22,16:3
I'll Be Yours 1947,F 22,16:2
Song of Scheherazade 1947,F 27,26:2
Broony, Edward S
Yes or No 1920,Jl 5,12:4
Brophy, Edward
Those Three French Girls 1930,O 11,21:3
Remote Control 1930,D 8,26:1
Parlor, Bedroom and Bath 1931,Ap 4,23:1
Champ, The 1931,N 10,29:4
Dangerous Affair, A 1931,N 23,22:1
Freaks 1932,Jl 9,7:5
Speak Easily 1932,Ag 19,20:6
Flesh 1932,D 10,19:3
What! No Beer? 1933,F 11,11:3
Broadway to Hollywood 1933,S 2,14:4
Thin Man, The 1934,Je 30,18:5
Paris Interlude 1934,Jl 28,16:5
Hide-Out 1934,Ag 25,16:5
Death on the Diamond 1934,S 24,14:1
Evelyn Prentice 1934,N 10,19:1
I'll Fix It 1934,N 12,17:3
Whole Town's Talking, The 1935,Mr 1,16:2
Shadow of Doubt 1935,Mr 11,15:1
Naughty Marietta 1935,Mr 23,11:2
People Will Talk 1935,Je 17,20:2
Mad Love 1935,Ag 5,20:2
China Seas 1935,Ag 10,16:4
Remember Last Night? 1935,N 21,27:2

Brophy, Edward— Cont
Show Them no Mercy 1935,D 9,25:2
$1,000 a Minute 1935,D 21,11:1
Strike Me Pink 1936,Ja 17,15:2
Woman Trap 1936,Mr 7,11:4
Case Against Mrs Ames, The 1936,My 28,19:2
Spendthrift 1936,Jl 23,24:1
Kelly the Second 1936,O 3,21:2
Wedding Present 1936,N 19,31:3
Great Guy 1937,Ja 1,19:2
Hideaway Girl 1937,Ja 13,20:4
Soldier and the Lady, The 1937,Ap 10,11:1
Hit Parade, The 1937,My 31,11:2
Oh, Doctor 1937,Je 19,20:3
Great Gambini, The 1937,Jl 12,20:4
Varsity Show 1937,S 2,17:2
Girl Said No, The 1937,O 18,14:1
Trapped by G-Men 1937,N 4,29:1
Blossoms On Broadway 1937,D 3,29:2
Slight Case of Murder, A 1938,F 28,19:1
Gold Diggers in Paris 1938,Je 2,19:2
Come on Leathernecks 1938,S 15,29:3
Gambling Ship 1939,Ja 21,19:2
You Can't Cheat an Honest Man 1939,F 20,13:2
Kid From Kokomo, The 1939,My 20,11:2
Kid Nightingale 1939,D 8,33:6
Big Guy, The 1940,Ja 1,29:2
Calling Philo Vance 1940,F 9,15:3
Alias the Deacon 1940,My 14,27:5
Dance, Girl, Dance 1940,O 11,25:2
Great Profile, The 1940,O 18,25:1
Sleepers West 1941,Mr 20,25:3
Bride Came C O D, The 1941,Jl 26,18:2
Buy Me That Town 1941,O 23,27:2
Nine Loves Are not Enough 1941,O 30,27:2
All Through the Night 1942,Ja 24,13:2
Larceny, Inc 1942,Ap 25,9:1
Destroyer 1943,S 2,15:3
Cover Girl 1944,Mr 31,26:1
It Happened Tomorrow 1944,My 29,18:2
Night of Adventure, A 1944,Je 3,10:4
Thin Man Goes Home, The 1945,Ja 26,16:5
Wonder Man 1945,Je 9,17:2
It Happened on Fifth Avenue 1947,Je 11,33:2
Last Hurrah, The 1958,O 24,40:1
Last Gangster, The 1937,D 10,33:2
Hold That Kiss 1938,Je 11,9:1
Passport Husband 1938,Ag 5,11:2
Vacation From Love 1938,N 10,33:2
Society Lawyer 1939,Mr 31,19:2
Golden Boy 1939,S 8,28:2
Amazing Mr Williams, The 1940,Ja 19,15:2
Golden Gloves 1940,Ag 21,23:6
Broadway 1942,Je 5,23:2
Air Force 1943,F 4,29:1
See my Lawyer 1945,My 4,23:4
Falcon in San Francisco, The 1945,Jl 21,7:2
Falcon's Adventure, The 1946,D 14,19:2
Brophy, John (Original Author)
Immortal Sergeant 1943,F 4,29:2
Fixed Bayonets 1951,N 21,20:2
Turn the Key Softly 1954,F 4,21:6
Day They Robbed the Bank of England, The
  1960,S 5,11:2
Brophy, Sallie
Storm Center 1956,O 22,25:4
Brosio, Valentino (Director)
Spirit and the Flesh, The 1948,N 1,28:2
Brosset, Colette
Belle Americaine, La 1961,D 18,42:1
Counterfeit Constable, The 1966,N 22,32:2
Brosset, Yvonne
Lesson in Love, A 1960,Mr 15,46:1
Brost, Gudrun
Himlaspelet 1944,O 9,17:3
Virgin Spring, The; Jungfrukallan 1960,N 15,46:1
Hour of the Wolf 1968,Ap 10,50:2
Brostrom, Gunnel
Of Love and Lust (Doll's House, A); Doll's House,
  A (Of Love and Lust) 1959,My 26,31:2
Wild Strawberries 1959,Je 23,37:1
Brothers, Four Step
Shine on Harvest Moon 1944,Mr 11,10:2
Brothers, Hakim (Producer)
Human Beast, The 1940,F 20,17:2
Baker's Wife, The 1940,F 27,17:2
Brothers, King (Producer)
Suspense 1946,Jl 5,15:3
Brothers Williamson (Producer)
Submarine Eye, The 1917,My 28,11:2
Brouchard
Scandals of Clochemerle, The 1950,Mr 28,28:2
Brouer, Jerry
Sergeant, The 1968,D 26,53:5
Brough, Antonia
Farmer's Wife, The 1930,Ja 7,28:3
Murder in the Old Red Barn 1936,Ag 19,18:3
Broun, Heywood Hale
It Should Happen to You 1954,Ja 16,10:5
Brouner, Ella
Mirele Efros 1939,O 21,12:2
Brounon, Aggelon
Dr Epameinondas 1938,Ap 5,19:6

Brousse, Liliane
Paranoiac 1963,My 23,31:2
Maniac 1963,O 31,26:3
Browallius, Carl
Sun Over Sweden 1938,Ap 9,11:2
BROWER
See Also BRAUER
Brower, Otto (Director)
Light of Western Stars, The 1930,Ap 26,11:1
Sante Fe Trail, The 1930,O 18,23:2
Fighting Caravans 1931,Ja 26,21:1
Headline Shooters 1933,O 23,18:3
Sins of Man 1936,Je 19,17:2
Speed to Burn 1938,S 9,25:1
Stop, Look and Love 1939,S 8,28:5
Gay Caballero, The 1940,O 25,25:3
Youth Will Be Served 1940,N 15,25:2
Little Tokyo, USA 1942,Ag 7,13:2
Dixie Dugan 1943,Ap 9,25:5
Behind Green Lights 1946,F 16,10:2
Brower, Robert
Lottery Man, The 1919,N 17,20:1
Hawthorne of the U.S.A. 1919,N 17,20:1
Long Live the King 1923,D 4,24:1
Fifth Avenue Models 1925,My 4,16:2
Last Trail, The 1927,Ja 26,17:1
Gay Defender, The 1927,D 26,26:6
Beggars of Life 1928,S 24,25:1
Brower, Tom
Lawless Nineties, The 1936,Je 29,11:1
Love Begins at 20 1936,S 19,20:1
Browles, Frank
Beloved Brute, The 1924,N 10,20:1
BROWN
See Also BRAUN, BROWNE
Brown, A J
Lord Jim 1965,F 26,18:1
Brown, Ada
Stormy Weather 1943,Jl 22,15:1
Brown, Al
Cuban Rebel Girls 1959,D 26,7:3
Brown, Alan (Producer)
Truth About Spring, The 1965,Je 17,27:2
Brown, Alfred
Seventh Voyage of Sinbad 1958,D 24,00:0
Brown, Anne
Rhapsody in Blue 1945,Je 28,22:2
Brown, Barbara
Wife Takes a Flyer, The 1942,Je 19,19:1
You Were Never Lovelier 1942,D 4,31:1
Reveille With Beverly 1943,Ap 24,17:2
Top Man 1943,O 29,23:2
Janie 1944,Ag 5,16:2
Doughgirls, The 1944,Ag 31,14:1
Pillow to Post 1945,My 26,18:2
Mildred Pierce 1945,S 29,12:2
Too Young to Know 1945,D 8,21:2
Janie Gets Married 1946,Je 15,24:2
White Tie and Tails 1946,N 8,28:2
Beast With Five Fingers, The 1946,D 26,28:3
That Way With Women 1947,F 15,20:4
Love and Learn 1947,My 3,10:3
High Barbaree 1947,Je 6,27:2
That Hagen Girl 1947,O 25,13:2
Wallflower 1948,Je 12,8:5
Yes Sir, That's my Baby 1949,N 11,31:2
Born Yesterday 1950,D 27,30:2
Ma and Pa Kettle Back on the Farm
1951,My 11,32:3
Jack and the Beanstalk 1952,Ap 8,35:3
You for Me 1952,S 25,38:3
Annapolis Story, An 1955,Ap 9,8:2
My Sister Eileen 1955,S 23,21:1
Sincerely Yours 1955,N 3,37:1
Brown, Barry
Flesh 1968,S 27,36:1
Brown, Bert C (Original Author)
Southside 1-1000 1950,N 3,31:2
Brown, Beth (Original Author)
Applause 1929,O 8,24:5
Brown, Beverly C
Panic in the Streets 1950,Ag 5,9:2
Brown, Bill
It Happened in Athens 1962,N 15,46:2
Brown, Boots
Tomorrow the World 1944,D 22,12:4
Brown, Boyce
Birthright 1952,F 15,17:2
Brown, Bruce (Cinematographer)
Endless Summer, The 1966,Je 16,53:2
Brown, Bruce (Producer)
Endless Summer, The 1966,Je 16,53:2
Brown, Bruce (Screenwriter)
Endless Summer, The 1966,Je 16,53:2
Brown, Carl (Screenwriter)
Calling of Dan Matthews, The 1936,Ja 25,18:4
Brown, Carlos
No Exit 1962,D 6,55:2
Brown, Carol
Fistful of Dollars, A 1967,F 2,29:1
Brown, Charles
Dance of Life, The 1929,Ag 16,18:6

Brown, Charles D
Dangerous Curves 1929,Jl 15,25:1
Secret Call, The 1931,Jl 13,13:5
Murder by the Clock 1931,Jl 18,16:6
Touchdown 1931,N 16,23:1
Woman I Stole, The 1933,Je 28,24:3
Gold Diggers of 1937 1936,D 25,19:2
Thoroughbreds Don't Cry 1937,N 26,27:4
Mr Moto in Danger Island 1938,Mr 20,13:3
Mr Moto's Gamble 1938,Ap 8,17:2
Island in the Sky 1938,My 14,18:1
Shopworn Angel, The 1938,Jl 8,11:2
Algiers 1938,Jl 15,13:2
Crowd Roars, The 1938,Ag 5,11:1
Speed to Burn 1938,S 9,25:1
Five of a Kind 1938,O 31,12:2
Exposed 1938,N 21,14:5
Up the River 1938,D 3,11:2
Duke of West Point, The 1938,D 16,33:2
Disbarred 1939,Ja 19,17:2
Ice Follies of 1939 1939,Mr 17,25:2
Charlie Chan in Reno 1939,My 31,27:2
Smashing the Money Ring 1939,N 17,17:2
Kid Nightingale 1939,D 8,33:6
He Married his Wife 1940,Ja 20,11:2
Grapes of Wrath, The 1940,Ja 25,17:2
Brother Orchid 1940,Je 8,18:2
Sailor's Lady 1940,Je 29,12:2
Pier 13 1940,Ag 9,19:3
Santa Fe Trail 1940,D 21,21:2
Tall, Dark and Handsome 1941,Ja 24,15:2
Reaching for the Sun 1941,My 8,21:1
International Lady 1941,N 11,29:2
Fingers at the Window 1942,Ap 23,27:3
Lady Takes a Chance, A 1943,S 16,25:2
Jam Session 1944,My 3,25:3
Secret Command 1944,Je 14,16:2
Having Wonderful Crime 1945,Ap 13,15:2
Night Editor 1946,Mr 30,11:2
Strange Love of Martha Ivers, The
1946,Jl 25,18:4
Big Sleep, The 1946,Ag 24,6:6
Killers, The 1946,Ag 29,24:2
Wake up and Dream 1947,Ja 24,18:4
Smash-Up, The Story of a Woman
1947,Ap 11,31:2
Merton of the Movies 1947,N 7,20:3
Senator Was Indiscreet, The 1947,D 27,9:2
Miracle Can Happen, A 1948,F 4,28:4
Follow Me Quietly 1949,Jl 8,14:5
Sealed Cargo 1951,My 24,47:1
Brown, Clarence (Director)
Great Redeemer, The 1920,O 25,18:1
Last of the Mohicans, The 1921,Ja 3,20:2
Acquittal, The 1923,D 12,24:5
Signal Tower, The 1924,Jl 21,14:4
Smouldering Fires 1925,Mr 31,17:4
Goose Woman, The 1925,Ag 4,14:3
Eagle, The 1925,N 9,25:1
Kiki 1926,Ap 6,26:4
Flesh and the Devil 1927,Ja 10,20:2
Trail of '98, The 1928,Mr 21,30:3
Woman of Affairs, A 1929,Ja 21,18:4
Navy Blues 1930,Ja 11,21:3
Anna Christie 1930,Mr 15,22:5
Romance 1930,Ag 23,7:3
Inspiration 1931,F 9,25:3
Free Soul, A 1931,Je 3,29:2
Possessed 1931,N 28,20:4
Emma 1932,F 6,14:4
Letty Lynton 1932,Ap 30,19:3
Son-Daughter, The 1933,Ja 2,29:2
Looking Forward 1933,My 1,10:2
Night Flight 1933,O 7,18:4
Sadie McKee 1934,My 18,18:3 (Incorrect in this
edition; use 1934,My 19,18:3 elsewhere)
Chained 1934,S 1,16:2
Anna Karenina 1935,Ag 31,16:2
Ah, Wilderness! 1935,D 25,30:2
Wife vs Secretary 1936,F 29,11:1
Gorgeous Hussy, The 1936,S 5,7:1
Conquest 1937,N 5,19:1
Of Human Hearts 1938,F 18,23:1
Idiot's Delight 1939,F 3,13:1
Rains Came, The 1939,S 9,11:2
Edison the Man 1940,Je 7,27:2
Come Live With Me 1941,F 28,17:3
They Met in Bombay 1941,Jl 4,17:1
Human Comedy, The 1943,Mr 3,19:2
White Cliffs of Dover, The 1944,My 12,15:2
National Velvet 1944,D 15,25:2
Yearling, The 1947,Ja 24,18:2
Song of Love 1947,O 10,31:2
Intruder in the Dust 1949,N 23,19:1
To Please a Lady 1950,O 27,24:3
Angels in the Outfield 1951,O 18,32:1
It's a big Country 1952,Ja 9,25:2
When in Rome 1952,My 12,21:2
Plymouth Adventure 1952,N 14,20:3
Brown, Clarence (Producer)
Come Live With Me 1941,F 28,17:3
Human Comedy, The 1943,Mr 3,19:2
Song of Love 1947,O 10,31:2

Brown, Clarence (Producer)— Cont
Intruder in the Dust 1949,N 23,19:1
To Please a Lady 1950,O 27,24:3
Angels in the Outfield 1951,O 18,32:1
When in Rome 1952,My 12,21:2
Never Let Me Go 1953,Je 11,37:2
Brown, Courtney
Flipper's New Adventure 1964,Ag 27,28:2
Brown, De Sylva (Original Author)
Indiscreet 1931,My 7,21:4
Brown, Dolores
Cimarron 1931,Ja 27,20:5
Brown, Don (Cinematographer)
Surfari 1967,Jl 19,26:2
Brown, Don (Miscellaneous)
Perfect Clue, The 1935,Mr 14,18:1
Brown, Don (Producer)
Surfari 1967,Jl 19,26:2
Brown, Dorothy
Girl from Havana, The 1929,S 2,16:1
Brown, Edwin
Jenny, Be Good 1920,Je 28,13:2
Brown, Eleanor
Two Women; (Ciociara, La) 1961,My 9,43:2
Sailor From Gibraltar, The 1967,Ap 25,38:2
Tiger and the Pussycat, The 1967,S 21,56:4
Young, The Evil and the Savage, The
1968,Ag 15,46:2
Brown, Elmer
Counsellor-At-Law 1933,D 8,31:2
Brown, Everett
Nagana 1933,F 16,23:2
Brown, Floyce
Elmer and Elsie 1934,Ag 4,14:5
Brown, Forman (Composer)
I Am Suzanne 1934,Ja 19,24:3
Knickerbocker Holiday 1944,Ap 20,22:7
Brown, Frederic (Original Author)
Crack-Up 1946,S 7,11:1
Screaming Mimi 1958,Je 26,23:3
Brown, Gary
Secret Life of an American Wife, The
1968,Je 26,42:2
Brown, George
It's a Pleasure 1945,My 4,23:3
Brown, George (Producer)
Land of Fury 1955,My 3,37:4
Murder at the Gallop 1963,Je 25,23:2
Brown, George Carleton (Original Author)
Gambling Ship 1939,Ja 21,19:2
Thou Shalt Not Kill 1940,Ja 8,11:2
Man From Frisco 1944,Je 16,14:7
Half Angel 1951,Je 16,9:2
Brown, George Carleton (Screenwriter)
Chatterbox 1943,Jl 2,15:3
Atlantic City 1944,Ag 14,11:4
Here Comes Trouble 1948,Ap 15,31:4
McHale's Navy 1964,Jl 11,15:2
Brown, George H (Original Author)
Hotel Sahara 1952,Ja 1,21:4
Brown, George H (Producer)
Sleeping Car to Trieste 1949,Ap 18,18:6
Amazing Mr Beecham, The 1949,D 26,33:4
Hotel Sahara 1952,Ja 1,21:4
Desperate Moment 1953,S 1,19:4
Rooney 1958,Je 6,29:2
Dangerous Exile 1958,O 11,18:3
Boy Who Stole a Million, The 1960,D 22,18:3
Double Bunk 1961,N 17,41:3
Ladies Who Do 1963,N 26,52:2
Guns at Batasi 1964,N 17,47:1
Brown, George H (Screenwriter)
Hotel Sahara 1952,Ja 1,21:4
Desperate Moment 1953,S 1,19:4
Brown, George N (Producer)
Murder She Said 1962,Ja 8,27:2
Brown, George Stanford
Comedians, The 1967,N 1,37:1
Dayton's Devils 1968,O 3,56:4
Brown, Georgia
Study in Terror, A 1966,N 3,45:3
Fixer, The 1968,D 9,59:1
Brown, Gilbert (Screenwriter)
Boy of the Streets 1938,Ja 24,17:1
Little Tough Guy 1938,Ag 18,23:3
Brown, Hal
Open Your Eyes 1919,Je 30,16:3
Democracy, The Vision Restored 1920,Ag 25,6:4
Brown, Harry
Marine Raiders 1944,Jl 1,10:7
Brown, Harry (Director)
Squealer, The 1930,S 8,17:1
Brown, Harry (Original Author)
Walk in the Sun, A 1946,Ja 12,10:6
Sands of Iwo Jima 1949,D 31,9:2
Apache Drums 1951,My 7,22:2
Eight Iron Men 1953,Ja 2,11:1
Dorado, El 1967,Je 29,32:1
Brown, Harry (Screenwriter)
Other Love, The 1947,My 15,32:4
Arch of Triumph 1948,Ap 21,33:2
Wake of the Red Witch 1949,Ja 10,19:2
Sands of Iwo Jima 1949,D 31,9:2
Man on the Eiffel Tower, The 1950,Ja 30,12:2

Brown, Harry (Screenwriter)— Cont
Kiss Tomorrow Goodbye 1950,Ag 5,9:2
Only the Valiant 1951,Ap 14,9:6
Place in the Sun, A 1951,Ag 29,20:1
Bugles in the Afternoon 1952,Mr 5,32:2
Sniper, The 1952,My 10,16:3
Eight Iron Men 1953,Ja 2,11:1
All the Brothers Were Valiant 1953,D 29,19:2
Many Rivers to Cross 1955,F 24,21:2
Virgin Queen, The 1955,Ag 6,13:2
D-Day, The Sixth of June 1956,My 30,13:1
Between Heaven and Hell 1956,O 12,33:2
Deep Six, The 1958,Ja 16,32:1
Ocean's Eleven 1960,Ag 11,19:1

Brown, Harry D
Wanderer of the Wasteland 1945,S 29,12:2

Brown, Harry Joe (Director)
Parade of the West 1930,Mr 3,18:4
Woman of Experience, A 1931,Jl 9,26:5
Madison Square Garden 1932,O 12,26:5
Billion Dollar Scandal, The 1933,Ja 9,23:1
I Love That Man 1933,Jl 10,11:7
Sitting Pretty 1933,D 2,9:3
Knickerbocker Holiday 1944,Ap 20,22:7

Brown, Harry Joe (Producer)
Young People 1940,Ag 24,16:2
Moon Over Miami 1941,Jl 5,14:2
Wild Geese Calling 1941,Ag 30,10:2
Desperadoes, The 1943,My 13,17:2
Knickerbocker Holiday 1944,Ap 20,22:7
Gunfighters 1947,Jl 25,12:5
Spirit of West Point 1947,O 3,31:2
Nevadan, The 1950,Ja 13,19:4
Fortunes of Captain Blood 1950,Je 10,11:3
Santa Fe 1951,My 4,31:2
Stage to Tucson 1951,My 5,14:2
Hangman's Knot 1952,D 11,45:3
Stranger Wore a Gun, The 1953,Jl 30,20:3
Three Hours to Kill 1954,S 4,6:4
Screaming Mimi 1958,Je 26,23:3

Brown, Harry Joe Jr (Original Author)
Duffy 1968,S 17,50:3

Brown, Helen
Big Brown Eyes 1936,My 2,11:1
To Mary-With Love 1936,Ag 27,16:1
Hidden Power 1939,Jl 26,17:3
Mr District Attorney 1941,Ap 17,29:3
Tampico 1944,Je 2,21:2
Walls of Jericho, The 1948,Ag 5,16:2
Arctic Manhunt 1949,Ag 19,12:5
Holiday Affair 1949,N 24,48:2
Shadow on the Wall 1950,My 19,31:3
Molly 1951,Mr 8,37:2
Shane 1953,Ap 24,30:3

Brown, Helen Gurley (Original Author)
Sex and the Single Girl 1964,D 26,9:2

Brown, Himan (Producer)
That Night 1957,O 15,39:3
Violators, The 1959,Ag 4,32:5

Brown, Hugh (Producer)
Three Violent People 1957,F 11,34:2

Brown, Jackie
Adventures of Mark Twain, The 1944,My 4,25:5

Brown, Jacques
Always a Bride 1954,My 28,19:2

Brown, James
Forest Rangers, The 1942,O 22,25:2
Air Force 1943,F 4,29:1
Corvette K-225 1943,O 21,30:1
Going my Way 1944,My 3,25:2
Our Hearts Were Young and Gay 1944,O 12,24:2
Objective Burma 1945,Ja 27,15:2
Our Hearts Were Growing Up 1946,Ag 12,17:2
Big Fix, The 1947,My 3,10:3
Fabulous Texan, The 1947,D 26,22:5
Younger Brothers, The 1949,My 28,11:2
Anna Lucasta 1949,Ag 12,13:2
Brimstone 1949,O 7,35:3
Yes Sir, That's my Baby 1949,N 11,31:2
Sands of Iwo Jima 1949,D 31,9:2
Montana 1950,F 4,9:2
Chain Lightning 1950,F 20,21:2
Groom Wore Spurs, The 1951,Mr 14,41:2
Wild Blue Yonder, The 1952,Ja 2,20:1
Pride of St Louis, The 1952,My 3,17:5
Springfield Rifle 1952,O 23,40:2
Charge at Feather River, The 1953,Jl 16,17:2
Thunder Over the Plains 1953,D 10,64:4
Star is Born, A 1954,O 12,23:1
20,000 Eyes 1961,Je 19,30:1
Targets 1968,Ag 14,34:1

Brown, James (Original Author)
Magic Garden, The 1952,F 6,24:2

Brown, James and the Famous Flames
Ski Party 1965,O 23,17:3

Brown, Janet
Folly to be Wise 1953,D 28,17:2

Brown, Jim
Rio Conchos 1964,O 29,38:1
Dirty Dozen, The 1967,Je 16,36:1
Dark of the Sun 1968,Jl 4,13:1
Split, The 1968,N 5,55:2
Ice Station Zebra 1968,D 21,49:1

Brown, Joe
Dressed to Kill 1928,Mr 12,26:1
Me, Gangster 1928,O 22,29:1
In old Arizona 1929,Ja 21,18:4
Ghost Talks, The 1929,F 18,28:1
Cock Eyed World, The 1929,Ag 5,25:2
Sunny Side Up 1929,O 4,24:5
Born Reckless 1930,Je 7,10:4
Rackety Rax 1932,N 5,12:5

Brown, Joe David (Original Author)
Stars in my Crown 1950,D 22,19:1
Kings Go Forth 1958,Jl 4,15:2

Brown, Joe E
Crooks Can't Win 1928,My 29,17:2
Hit of the Show 1928,Jl 9,25:1
Take Me Home 1928,O 23,33:1
Circus Kid, The 1928,D 17,23:1
On With the Show 1929,My 29,28:6
Sally 1929,D 24,14:4
Song of the West 1930,F 28,20:7
Hold Everything 1930,Ap 23,24:1
Top Speed 1930,Ag 30,7:4
Maybe It's Love 1930,O 18,23:2
Lottery Bride, The 1930,N 29,21:4
Going Wild 1931,Ja 26,21:1
Sit Tight 1931,F 19,20:4
Broad Minded 1931,Jl 6,24:4
Local Boy Makes Good 1931,N 27,29:3
Fireman, Save My Child 1932,F 18,25:3
Tenderfoot, The 1932,My 23,18:4
You Said a Mouthful 1932,N 18,23:2
Elmer the Great 1933,My 26,24:2
Son of a Sailor 1933,N 30,38:4
Circus Clown, The 1934,Je 30,18:6
6-Day Bike Rider 1934,N 3,20:3
Alibi Ike 1935,Jl 17,22:1
Bright Lights 1935,Ag 15,15:2
Midsummer Night's Dream, A 1935,O 10,31:1
Sons o'Guns 1936,My 14,29:2
Earthworm Tractors 1936,Jl 25,16:1
Polo Joe 1936,N 5,35:1
When's Your Birthday? 1937,Mr 19,27:2
Riding on Air 1937,Je 26,20:2 (In Addenda)
Fit for a King 1937,O 15,18:5
Wide Open Faces 1938,Ap 15,23:2
Gladiator, The 1938,Ag 29,10:2
Flirting With Fate 1938,D 15,35:3
$1,000 a Touchdown 1939,O 5,27:2
Beware, Spooks 1939,N 3,17:4
So You Won't Talk 1940,O 17,33:2
Chatterbox 1943,Jl 2,15:3
Pin Up Girl 1944,My 11,25:6
Hollywood Canteen 1944,D 16,19:2
Show Boat 1951,Jl 20,14:1
Around the World in 80 Days 1956,O 18,37:1
Some Like It Hot 1959,Mr 30,23:1
It's a Mad, Mad, Mad, Mad World 1963,N 19,47:1

Brown, Joe Jr
High School 1940,Ja 5,15:5
Conga Nights, La 1940,Je 5,33:5
Youth Will Be Served 1940,N 15,25:2
Naval Academy 1941,Je 5,27:3
Juke Box Jenny 1942,Ap 17,21:3
Ten Gentlemen From West Point 1942,Je 5,23:3
Wild Blue Yonder, The 1952,Ja 2,20:1
Fugitive Kind, The 1960,Ap 15,13:1

Brown, John
Horn Blows at Midnight, The 1945,Ap 21,18:2
Life of Riley, The 1949,Ap 18,18:4
Strangers on a Train 1951,Jl 4,13:2
Day the Earth Stood Still, The 1951,S 19,37:1
Hans Christian Andersen 1952,N 26,20:2
Wild One, The 1953,D 31,9:2

Brown, John Mack
Fair Co-ed, The 1927,O 24,24:3
Divine Woman, The 1928,Ja 16,24:1
Soft Living 1928,F 27,16:2
Play Girl, The 1928,Ap 23,20:2
Our Dancing Daughters 1928,O 8,14:2
Lady of Chance, A 1929,Ja 14,20:1
Woman of Affairs, A 1929,Ja 21,18:4
Coquette 1929,Ap 6,14:4 (In Addenda)
Valiant, The 1929,My 13,27:2
Single Standard, The 1929,Jl 29,23:3
Jazz Heaven 1929,O 30,29:2
Undertow 1930,Mr 1,23:1
Montana Moon 1930,Ap 14,24:2
Billy the Kid 1930,O 18,23:2
Great Meadow, The 1931,Mr 14,23:2
Secret Six, The 1931,My 2,23:4
Last Flight, The 1931,Ag 20,17:4
70,000 Witnesses 1932,S 3,16:2
Saturday's Millions 1933,O 14,18:3
Female 1933,N 4,18:3
Son of a Sailor 1933,N 30,38:4
Belle of the Nineties 1934,S 22,12:2
Wells Fargo 1937,D 30,15:2
Chip of the Flying U 1940,Ja 22,11:3
West of Carson City 1940,My 7,31:3
Ride 'Em Cowboy 1942,Mr 5,27:3
Stampede 1949,S 16,36:2
Short Grass 1951,Ja 13,10:4

Brown, John Mason (Screenwriter)
Paris 1900 1950,O 24,34:6

Brown, John Moulder
Uncle, The 1966,Jl 19,34:1

Brown, John R Cpl
D I, The 1957,Je 6,35:2

Brown, Johnny
Man Called Adam, A 1966,Ag 4,24:2

Brown, Josephine
Strange Cargo 1929,F 18,28:1
Man Inside, The 1959,F 5,24:7

Brown, Karl (Director)
Stark Love 1927,F 28,22:3
His Dog 1927,Ag 16,31:2
In His Steps 1936,O 29,31:1
Federal Bullets 1937,D 27,11:1
Port of Missing Girls, The 1938,Ap 4,12:5

Brown, Karl (Original Author)
Port of Missing Girls, The 1938,Ap 4,12:5
Gangster's Boy 1938,N 7,23:6
My Son Is Guilty 1940,Ja 15,11:2
Before I Hang 1940,O 3,31:3
Chicago Kid, The 1945,F 12,24:3

Brown, Karl (Screenwriter)
Cheerful Fraud, The 1926,D 28,17:1
Stark Love 1927,F 28,22:3
In His Steps 1936,O 29,31:1
Federal Bullets 1937,D 27,11:1
Gangster's Boy 1938,N 7,23:6
Woman Is the Judge, A 1939,S 28,29:5
Man With Nine Lives, The 1940,Ap 29,12:3
Gangs of Chicago 1940,Je 13,29:2
Military Academy 1940,Ag 5,10:4
Mr District Attorney 1941,Ap 17,29:3
Rookies on Parade 1941,My 22,25:2
I Was a Prisoner on Devil's Island 1941,Jl 28,16:4
Hitler-Dead or Alive 1943,Mr 31,23:3

Brown, Kelly
Daddy Long Legs 1955,My 6,17:5
Oklahoma! 1955,O 11,49:1
Girl Most Likely, The 1958,O 9,47:1

Brown, Kenneth
In the Navy 1941,Je 12,29:2

Brown, Kenneth H (Original Author)
Brig, The 1964,S 21,37:4

Brown, Kurt J (Screenwriter)
Grapes are Ripe, The 1953,O 15,43:2

Brown, Lawrence
Dark Sands 1938,Ag 17,23:4

Brown, Les and his orchestra
Seven Days' Leave 1942,D 11,33:2

Brown, Les Jr
Wild Wild Winter 1966,Ja 6,20:2

Brown, Lew
Crime and Punishment, U S A 1959,Je 17,39:3

Brown, Lew (Composer)
Hold Everything 1930,Ap 23,24:1
Stand up and Cheer 1934,Ap 20,17:1
Music Goes 'Round, The 1936,F 22,12:1
New Faces of 1937 1937,Jl 2,25:1
Vogues of 1938 1937,Ag 20,21:1
Hold That Co-ed 1938,S 24,13:1
Straight, Place and Show 1938,O 1,10:2
Thousands Cheer 1943,S 14,27:1
I Dood It 1943,N 11,29:1
George White's Scandals 1945,O 11,26:2

Brown, Lew (Miscellaneous)
Strike Me Pink 1936,Ja 17,15:2
Straight, Place and Show 1938,O 1,10:2

Brown, Lewis Allen (Original Author)
Naughty but Nice 1927,Jl 5,19:2

Brown, Louis P
World Dances 1954,N 8,24:6

Brown, Lowell
Day Mars Invaded Earth, The 1964,Ap 2,28:3

Brown, Lucile
Last of the Duanes 1930,S 13,9:3
Young as You Feel 1931,Ag 8,16:3
Girls About Town 1931,N 2,27:1
Devil's Brother, The 1933,Je 10,16:4
Double Harness 1933,Jl 21,20:2
No Sad Songs for Me 1950,Ap 28,26:2

Brown, Marguerite
Ramparts We Watch, The 1940,S 20,27:1

Brown, Marjorie (Original Author)
Nell Gwyn 1926,Ja 19,13:1

Brown, Martin (Original Author)
Exciters, The 1923,Je 4,13:3
Lady, The 1925,Ja 27,11:2
Soul Fire 1925,My 6,26:3
Cobra 1925,D 7,19:1
Paris 1929,N 8,31:2
Mad Genius, The 1931,O 24,20:3
Secret of Madame Blanche, The 1933,F 4,11:3

Brown, Martin (Screenwriter)
Java Head 1935,Jl 31,21:4

Brown, Melville (Director)
Her big Night 1926,O 13,21:1
Taxi, Taxi 1927,F 15,23:1
Fast and Furious 1927,Jl 4,20:3
13 Washington Square 1928,Ja 30,18:1
Buck Privates 1928,Ja 30,18:1

Brown, Melville (Director) — Cont
Geraldine 1929,Mr 4,20:2
Jazz Heaven 1929,O 30,29:2
Love Doctor, The 1929,N 9,22:5
Dance Hall 1929,D 16,34:2
Lovin' the Ladies 1930,Mr 22,22:6
She's my Weakness 1930,Je 21,20:5
Behind Office Doors 1931,Mr 21,15:1
White Shoulders 1931,Je 5,26:5
Fanny Foley Herself 1931,O 26,22:1
Redhead 1934,N 16,27:1
Nut Farm, The 1935,Ap 8,23:3

Brown, Mende (Producer)
That Night 1957,O 15,39:3

Brown, Naaman
White Witch Doctor 1953,Jl 2,19:3

Brown, Nacio Herb (Composer)
Broadway Melody, The 1929,F 9,15:3
Hold Your Man 1933,Jl 1,16:6
Stage Mother 1933,S 30,18:5
Going Hollywood 1933,D 23,19:2
Sadie McKee 1934,My 18,18:3 (Incorrect in this
 edition; use 1934,My 19,18:3 elsewhere)
Hollywood Party 1934,My 26,12:2
Student Tour 1934,O 31,17:3
Broadway Melody of 1936 1935,S 19,28:1
Night at the Opera, A 1935,D 7,22:1
Broadway Melody of 1938 1937,S 3,12:1
Thoroughbreds Don't Cry 1937,N 26,27:4
Babes in Arms 1939,O 20,27:2
Ziegfeld Girl 1941,Ap 25,17:2
Wintertime 1943,S 30,27:2
Greenwich Village 1944,S 28,26:2
On an Island With You 1948,Jl 30,13:2
Pagan Love Song 1950,D 26,19:1

Brown, Nacio Herb (Miscellaneous)
Devil is a Sissy, The 1936,O 17,21:2
After the Thin Man 1936,D 25,19:2

Brown, Pamela
One of our Aircraft Is Missing 1942,N 2,17:2
I Know Where I'm Going 1947,Ag 20,25:2
Tales of Hoffmann 1951,Ap 5,34:2
Alice in Wonderland 1951,Jl 27,15:2
Personal Affair 1954,O 23,13:2
Richard III 1956,Mr 12,1:4
Lust for Life 1956,S 18,39:1
Scapegoat, The 1959,Ag 7,28:1
Cleopatra 1963,Je 13,29:1
Becket 1964,Mr 12,40:2
Secret Ceremony 1968,O 24,55:1

Brown, Peter
Darby's Rangers 1958,F 13,23:2
Onionhead 1958,O 2,44:1
Merrill's Marauders 1962,Je 14,23:4
Summer Magic 1963,Ag 22,19:2
Tiger Walks, A 1964,Ag 27,28:2
Kitten With a Whip 1964,N 5,50:4
Ride the Wild Surf 1964,D 24,8:4

Brown, Phil
I Wanted Wings 1941,Mr 27,29:4
H M Pulham, Esq 1941,D 19,35:1
Calling Dr Gillespie 1942,Jl 9,17:4
Pierre of the Plains 1942,Jl 30,17:3
Weird Woman 1944,Ap 1,11:1
Impatient Years, The 1944,S 20,20:1
Jungle Captive 1945,Jl 7,7:5
Over 21 1945,Ag 17,20:2
Without Reservations 1946,Je 8,17:2
Killers, The 1946,Ag 29,24:2
Johnny O'Clock 1947,Mr 27,39:2
If You Knew Susie 1948,F 23,19:2
Luck of the Irish, The 1948,S 16,34:1
Moonrise 1949,Mr 7,17:2
Hidden Room, The 1950,Ja 9,19:2
Green Scarf, The 1955,Ja 15,10:2
Camp on Blood Island, The 1958,S 18,37:2
Bedford Incident, The 1965,N 3,43:1
Boy Cried Murder, The 1966,Ap 14,42:3

Brown, Raymond
My Woman 1933,O 16,20:3
Dr Socrates 1935,O 3,29:2
Story of Louis Pasteur, The 1936,F 10,15:1
Magnificent Brute, The 1936,O 24,23:1
Holy Terror, The 1937,Ja 30,21:2
We Have our Moments 1937,Ap 30,17:3
Back in Circulation 1937,O 4,17:1
King of the Underworld 1939,Ja 7,6:2

Brown, Robert
Time, Gentlemen, Please 1953,S 24,39:2
Shake Hands With the Devil 1959,Je 25,20:7
Campbell's Kingdom 1960,Ja 11,35:5
300 Spartans, The 1962,S 20,29:2
Billy Budd 1962,O 31,32:1
Operation Crossbow 1965,Ap 2,29:1
One Million Years BC 1967,F 22,21:1

Brown, Robin
Raising a Riot 1957,My 8,44:1

Brown, Rowland (Director)
Quick Millions 1931,Ap 18,17:3
Hell's Highway 1932,S 26,18:2
Blood Money 1933,N 16,30:5

Brown, Rowland (Original Author)
Doorway to Hell, The 1930,N 1,23:2
Blood Money 1933,N 16,30:5

Brown, Rowland (Screenwriter)
Hell's Highway 1932,S 26,18:2
Johnny Apollo 1940,Ap 13,21:2

Brown, Russ
Moulin Rouge 1934,F 8,14:4
Love Captive, The 1934,Je 8,18:1
Let's Talk It Over 1934,Je 16,20:2
South Pacific 1958,Mr 20,33:1
Anatomy of a Murder 1959,Jl 3,10:1
It Happened to Jane 1959,Ag 6,18:3
Advise and Consent 1962,Je 7,31:2

Brown, Stanley
Adventure in Sahara 1938,D 19,19:2
Blondie Meets the Boss 1939,Ap 27,31:1
Blind Alley 1939,My 23,27:2
Good Girls Go to Paris 1939,Je 23,23:1
Man With Nine Lives, The 1940,Ap 29,12:3
Island Of Doomed Men 1940,Je 10,21:2
Face Behind the Mask, The 1941,F 7,23:2
Harmon of Michigan 1941,O 2,29:2
Canal Zone 1942,Mr 30,21:2
Atlantic Convoy 1942,Jl 6,18:5
You Were Never Lovelier 1942,D 4,31:1
Tarzan Triumphs 1943,F 5,16:3
Two Senoritas From Chicago 1943,Ag 6,10:4

Brown, Steve
I Remember Mama 1948,Mr 12,29:2

Brown, Strelsa
Quo Vadis 1951,N 9,22:2

Brown, Tally
Illiac Passion, The 1968,Ap 19,40:1

Brown, Thomas
Central Airport 1933,My 4,20:5

Brown, Toch
Wind Across the Everglades 1958,S 12,21:1

Brown, Tom
Hoosier Schoolmaster, The 1924,Mr 18,25:2
Lady Lies, The 1929,S 7,15:1
Queen High 1930,Ag 9,16:5
Famous Ferguson Case, The 1932,Ap 25,18:6
Tom Brown of Culver 1932,Jl 30,16:5
Hell's Highway 1932,S 26,18:2
Laughter in Hell 1933,Ja 2,29:2
Destination Unknown 1933,Ap 8,16:2
Three-Cornered Moon 1933,Ag 12,14:2
This Side of Heaven 1934,F 10,21:2
Witching Hour, The 1934,Ap 28,11:3
Judge Priest 1934,O 12,33:1
Anne of Green Gables 1934,D 22,21:1
Black Sheep 1935,Je 28,34:1
Annapolis Farewell 1935,Ag 24,18:2
Freckles 1935,O 26,12:2
Gentle Julia 1936,Ap 11,19:1
Sudden Death, And 1936,Jl 18,18:2
I'd Give my Life 1936,Ag 17,9:1
Rose Bowl 1936,D 2,35:2
Her Husband Lies 1937,Mr 18,20:1
Maytime 1937,Mr 19,27:1
That Man's Here Again 1937,My 6,23:3
Navy Blue and Gold 1937,D 24,21:2
In Old Chicago 1938,Ja 7,15:2
Merrily We Live 1938,Mr 18,23:3
Goodbye Broadway 1938,My 14,18:1
Storm, The 1938,O 31,12:2
Swing That Cheer 1938,N 11,31:2
Duke of West Point, The 1938,D 16,33:2
Sergeant Madden 1939,Mr 24,27:2
Big Town Czar 1939,My 4,27:3
Ex-Champ 1939,My 12,25:3
These Glamour Girls 1939,Ag 31,14:2
Sandy Is a Lady 1940,Je 28,22:2
House on Ninety-Second Street, The
 1945,S 27,24:7
Buck Privates Come Home 1947,Ap 12,11:3
Ringside 1949,S 17,10:8

Brown, Troy
Nothing Sacred 1937,N 26,27:2

Brown, Vanessa
I've Always Loved You 1946,S 7,11:1
Margie 1946,O 17,28:3
Late George Apley, The 1947,Mr 21,29:2
Ghost and Mrs Muir, The 1947,Je 27,17:2
Mother Wore Tights 1947,Ag 21,33:2
Foxes of Harrow, The 1947,S 25,35:4
Big Jack 1949,My 23,27:4
Heiress, The 1949,O 7,35:2
Tarzan and the Slave Girl 1950,Je 24,7:3
Three Husbands 1951,Mr 9,30:2
Basketball Fix, the 1951,S 14,21:2
Fighter, The 1952,My 31,12:6
Bad and the Beautiful, The 1953,Ja 16,19:1
Rosie 1968,F 8,36:1

Brown, Vera (Original Author)
Redhead 1934,N 16,27:1

Brown, Virginia
Old Fashioned Boy, An 1920,N 1,13:2

Brown, Wally
Around the World 1943,N 25,39:2
Seven Days Ashore 1944,Ap 26,24:7
Step Lively 1944,Jl 27,14:1
Zombies on Broadway 1945,Ap 27,23:2
Radio Stars on Parade 1945,S 22,14:2
From This Day Forward 1946,Ap 20,16:2
Notorious 1946,Ag 16,19:2
As Young as You Feel 1951,Ag 3,10:6
High and the Mighty, The 1954,Jl 1,21:2
Untamed Youth 1957,My 11,24:6
Absent-Minded Professor, The 1961,Mr 16,44:2

Brown, Wenzell (Original Author)
Violators, The 1959,Ag 4,32:5

Brown, Will C (Original Author)
Man of the West 1958,O 2,44:3

Brown, William
Last Outpost, The 1935,O 5,18:2

Brown, William H (Producer)
Ski Champs 1951,D 15,11:2

Brown (Composer)
Sunny Side Up 1929,O 4,24:5
Just Imagine 1930,N 22,21:3

Brown (Miscellaneous)
Just Imagine 1930,N 22,21:3

Brown (Original Author)
Sunny Side Up 1929,O 4,24:5
Follow Thru 1930,S 13,9:3

Brown Eyes (cow)
Go West 1925,O 26,25:2

Brown, George H (Producer)
Kill or Cure 1962,N 13,43:4

BROWNE
See Also BROWN, BRAUN

Browne, Alfred
Greatest Love, The 1954,Ja 12,19:2

Browne, Arthur Jr (Screenwriter)
Clambake 1967,D 14,62:3

Browne, Barton (Original Author)
Garden of the Moon 1938,S 24,13:1

Browne, Cicely
Drums of Tahiti 1954,Ap 24,14:5

Browne, Coral
Amateur Gentleman, The 1936,Ap 27,19:2
We're Going to Be Rich 1938,Jl 4,10:2
Black Limelight 1939,Je 26,12:2
Let George Do It 1940,O 14,25:5
Piccadilly Incident 1948,Ag 5,16:2
Kathy's Love Affair 1952,Jl 3,16:2
Auntie Mame 1958,D 5,39:1
Roman Spring of Mrs Stone, The 1961,D 29,11:1
Dr Crippen 1964,F 15,14:1
Night of the Generals, The 1967,F 3,38:1
Killing of Sister George, The 1968,D 17,58:4

Browne, Earle
Mr Robinson Crusoe 1932,S 22,25:4

Browne, Eleanor (Original Author)
Cross Country Romance 1940,Jl 19,22:3

Browne, Graham
Moonlight Sonata 1938,My 10,17:2

Browne, Howard (Screenwriter)
Portrait of a Mobster 1961,Ap 20,30:4
St Valentine's Day Massacre, The 1967,Jl 27,29:2

Browne, Irene
Letter, The 1929,Mr 8,30:1
Cavalcade 1933,Ja 6,23:2
Christopher Strong 1933,Mr 10,19:2
Peg o'my Heart 1933,My 20,11:4
Berkeley Square 1933,S 14,26:2
My Lips Betray 1933,N 4,18:3
Amateur Gentleman, The 1936,Ap 27,19:2
Pygmalion 1938,D 8,34:2
Prime Minister, The 1942,F 4,23:2
Meet Me at Dawn 1948,My 18,26:2
Red Shoes, The 1948,O 23,9:2
Quartet (The Alien Corn); Alien Corn, The
 (Quartet) 1949,Mr 29,30:3
Madeleine 1950,S 1,17:2
I'll Never Forget You 1951,D 8,9:2
All at Sea 1957,D 23,18:2
Rooney 1958,Je 6,29:2

Browne, J C (Original Author)
Nut Farm, The 1935,Ap 8,23:3

Browne, J Edwin
Scaramouche 1923,O 12,7:2 (Incorrect in this
 edition; use 1927,O 1,7:2 elsewhere)

Browne, Kathie
Brass Bottle, The 1964,My 21,42:1

Browne, Michael
Sunday Punch 1942,My 11,19:2
Spirit of West Point 1947,O 3,31:2

Browne, Paddy
Blackout 1940,D 2,19:2

Browne, Porter Emerson (Original Author)
Seventh Day, The 1922,Mr 13,18:2
Bad Man, The 1923,O 9,17:4
Bad Man, The 1930,S 27,21:3
Trumpet Blows, The 1934,Ap 14,18:2
West of Shanghai 1937,O 29,19:2
Bad Man, The 1941,Ap 4,25:1

Browne, Porter Emerson (Screenwriter)
Fighting Roosevelts, The 1919,Ja 20,13:2

Browne, Roscoe Lee
Connection, The 1962,O 4,44:1
Black Like Me 1964,My 21,42:1
Terror in the City 1966,N 9,43:4
Comedians, The 1967,N 1,37:1
Up Tight 1968,D 19,62:1
Browne, W Graham
Lady is Willing, The 1934,Ag 11,16:5
Browne, Walter (Original Author)
Everywoman 1919,D 15,20:1
Browne, Wynyard (Screenwriter)
Hobson's Choice 1954,Je 15,37:1
Brownell, J C (Original Author)
Bad Company 1925,Mr 16,16:1
Brownie (Dog)
Little Johnny Jones 1923,Ag 13,16:1
Browning, Alan
Guns at Batasi 1964,N 17,47:1
Browning, Ivan
Mr Peabody and the Mermaid 1948,Ag 14,6:5
Sunrise at Campobello 1960,S 29,32:1
Browning, Jill
Utah 1945,Mr 12,22:7
Browning, Natalie
Wandering Jew, The 1933,O 21,11:2
Browning, Ricou
Creature Walks among Us, The 1956,Ap 27,21:6
Browning, Ricou (Original Author)
Flipper 1963,S 19,23:1
Browning, Tod (Director)
Virgin of Stamboul, The 1920,Mr 28,V,9:1
Drifting 1923,Ag 20,4:2
Day of Faith, The 1923,N 27,11:2
Unholy Three, The 1925,Ag 4,14:3
Mystic, The 1925,Ag 31,19:3
Outside the Law 1926,My 12,31:1
Show, The 1927,Mr 14,16:1
Unknown, The 1927,Je 13,17:1
London After Midnight 1927,D 31,31:1
Big City, The 1928,Mr 26,26:2
West of Zanzibar 1928,D 31,9:1
Where East Is East 1929,My 27,22:1
Outside the Law 1930,S 1,16:1
Dracula 1931,F 13,21:3
Iron Man 1931,Ap 18,17:3
Freaks 1932,Jl 9,7:5
Fast Workers 1933,Mr 20,18:2
Mark of the Vampire 1935,My 3,23:4
Devil Doll, The 1936,Ag 8,5:2
Miracles for Sale 1939,Ag 10,15:2
Browning, Tod (Original Author)
Black Bird, The 1926,F 1,16:1
Road to Mandalay, The 1926,Je 29,21:2
Unknown, The 1927,Je 13,17:1
Inside Job 1946,Je 15,24:3
Browning, Tod (Screenwriter)
Mystic, The 1925,Ag 31,19:3
Outside the Law 1926,My 12,31:1
London After Midnight 1927,D 31,31:1
Outside the Law 1930,S 1,16:1
Devil Doll, The 1936,Ag 8,5:2
Brownise, Francis
Terror Trail 1933,F 11,11:3
Brownlee, Frank
Brass Buttons 1919,Ap 7,11:5
Riders of the Dawn 1920,My 3,18:1
Shore Acres 1920,My 17,19:3
Desert Flower, The 1925,Je 1,10:3
Social Highwayman, The 1926,Je 15,23:3
Sawdust Paradise, The 1928,Ag 27,23:1
Beggars of Life 1928,S 24,25:1
Brownlow, Kevin (Director)
It Happened Here 1966,Ag 9,29:2
Brownlow, Kevin (Producer)
It Happened Here 1966,Ag 9,29:2
Brownlow, Kevin (Screenwriter)
It Happened Here 1966,Ag 9,29:2
Brownstone, Mina (Screenwriter)
Tomorrow's a Wonderful Day 1949,Ap 11,29:4
Brox Sisters
Hollywood Revue, The 1929,Ag 15,20:5
King of Jazz 1930,My 3,23:1
Broyer, Eve
Women Without Names 1951,Ag 7,22:2
Broza, Irene
My Father's House 1947,S 26,28:3
Bru, Myriam
Morena Clara 1938,Je 18,18:3
House of Ricordi 1956,Mr 13,32:1
Of Life and Love 1958,O 7,40:2
Holiday Island; (Vacanzie a Izchia)
1959,S 22,46:1
Bruar, Paul
Valentino 1951,Ap 20,25:1
Brubaker, Robert
Seconds 1966,O 6,56:1
Bruce, Alan
You Can't Beat Love 1937,Je 25,25:3
Meet the Missus 1937,Jl 2,25:2
Super-Sleuth 1937,Jl 17,18:1
Saturday's Heroes 1937,O 16,22:2
Music for Madame 1937,O 23,14:1
She's Got Everything 1938,Ja 14,21:3

Mr Doodle Kicks Off 1938,S 28,29:4
Bruce, Amelia
Games Men Play, The 1968,Mr 15,30:1
Bruce, Betty
Gypsy 1962,N 2,24:1
Island of Love 1963,Je 13,30:4
Bruce, Brenda
Piccadilly Incident 1948,Ag 5,16:2
My Brothers Keeper 1949,F 14,15:3
While the Sun Shines 1950,Jl 1,9:2
Marry Me 1952,Mr 14,27:3
Final Test, The 1954,Ja 26,21:5
Law and Disorder 1958,Ag 6,20:1
Nightmare 1964,Je 18,29:2
Uncle, The 1966,Jl 19,34:1
Bruce, Carol
This Woman Is Mine 1941,O 13,21:2
Keep 'Em Flying 1941,N 27,29:2
Bruce, Clifford
Devil May Care 1929,D 23,18:2
Bruce, David
Man Who Talked too Much, The 1940,Je 29,12:2
Sea Hawk, The 1940,Ag 10,16:2
Dispatch From Reuters, A 1940,D 12,37:2
Santa Fe Trail 1940,D 21,21:2
Sea Wolf, The 1941,Mr 26,27:3
Flight From Destiny 1941,Mr 28,26:7
Singapore Woman 1941,My 12,13:6
Sergeant York 1941,Jl 3,15:1
Smiling Ghost, The 1941,S 26,26:5
Body Disappears, The 1942,Ja 31,13:2
Flying Tigers 1942,O 23,25:2
Corvette K-225 1943,O 21,30:1
Mad Ghoul, The 1943,D 11,11:2
Gung Ho! 1944,Ja 26,23:2
Calling Dr Death 1944,F 12,11:3
Ladies Courageous 1944,Mr 16,17:2
Christmas Holiday 1944,Je 29,16:1
Can't Help Singing 1944,D 26,22:4
Salome, Where She Danced 1945,My 3,27:1
Lady on a Train 1945,S 15,21:2
That Night With You 1945,N 9,16:2
Bruce, Edgar
Storm in a Teacup 1938,Mr 22,18:4
Bruce, George (Original Author)
Navy Blue and Gold 1937,D 24,21:2
Crowd Roars, The 1938,Ag 5,11:1
Killer McCoy 1948,F 12,31:2
Lorna Doone 1951,S 21,19:4
Brigand, The 1952,Jl 26,9:2
Bruce, George (Screenwriter)
She's no Lady 1937,Ag 12,14:3
Navy Blue and Gold 1937,D 24,21:2
Crowd Roars, The 1938,Ag 5,11:1
Duke of West Point, The 1938,D 16,33:2
King of the Turf 1939,My 8,21:2
Man in the Iron Mask, The 1939,Jl 14,11:1
South of Pago-Pago 1940,Ag 2,12:2
Kit Carson 1940,N 15,25:3
Son of Monte Cristo, The 1940,D 5,33:1
Corsican Brothers, The 1942,Ja 16,25:4
Gentleman After Dark, A 1942,Ap 17,21:2
Miss Annie Rooney 1942,Je 8,11:1
Stand by for Action 1943,Mr 12,12:2
Salute to the Marines 1943,Ag 30,11:3
Keep Your Powder Dry 1945,Mr 12,22:6
Two Years Before the Mast 1946,S 25,39:2
Return of Monte Cristo, The 1947,Ja 3,16:4
Fiesta 1947,Je 27,17:3
Killer McCoy 1948,F 12,31:2
Walk a Crooked Mile 1948,O 13,31:2
Valentino 1951,Ap 20,25:1
Kansas City Confidential 1952,N 29,11:2
Solomon and Sheba 1959,D 26,7:2
Bruce, Jay
Cougar, the King Killer 1933,My 22,18:6
Bruce, Jean (Original Author)
OSS 117-Mission for a Killer 1966,O 13,50:3
Viscount, The 1967,My 11,50:1
Bruce, Kate
Romance of Happy Valley, A 1919,Ja 27,11:4
Girl Who Stayed Home, The 1919,Mr 24,11:3
Scarlet Days 1919,N 10,18:2
Experience 1921,Ag 8,12:2
White Rose, The 1923,My 23,18:3
I Want my Man 1925,Ap 6,17:3
Secret Studio, The 1927,Je 15,31:4
Way Down East 1931,Mr 16,25:1
Bruce, Lenny
Lenny Bruce 1967,Mr 20,26:4
Bruce, Nicholas
Black Magic 1949,N 9,37:2
Conspirator 1950,Ap 28,26:2
To Paris With Love 1955,Mr 29,33:4
Othello 1955,S 13,27:1
Bruce, Nigel
I Was a Spy 1934,Ja 15,12:2
Coming-Out Party 1934,Mr 17,11:3
Stand up and Cheer 1934,Ap 20,17:1
Murder in Trinidad 1934,My 16,22:2
Channel Crossing 1934,My 24,28:3
Lady is Willing, The 1934,Ag 11,16:5
Treasure Island 1934,Ag 18,5:5

Scarlet Pimpernel, The 1935,F 8,27:2
Becky Sharp 1935,Je 14,27:2
She 1935,Jl 26,18:2
Jalna 1935,S 14,8:4
Man Who Broke the Bank at Monte Carlo, The
1935,N 15,20:2
Trail of the Lonesome Pine, The 1936,F 20,23:5
Under Two Flags 1936,My 1,19:1
White Angel, The 1936,Je 25,24:1
Follow Your Heart 1936,O 22,31:1
Man I Marry, The 1936,O 31,24:3
Charge of the Light Brigade, The 1936,N 2,24:1
Last of Mrs Cheyney, The 1937,F 19,15:1
Thunder in the City 1937,Ap 23,25:2
Baroness and the Butler, The 1938,F 19,19:2
Kidnapped 1938,My 28,9:2
Suez 1938,O 15,21:2
Hound of the Baskervilles, The 1939,Mr 25,19:2
Adventures of Sherlock Holmes, The
1939,S 2,20:1
Rains Came, The 1939,S 9,11:2
Blue Bird, The 1940,Ja 20,11:2
Rebecca 1940,Mr 29,25:2
Adventure in Diamonds 1940,Ap 4,27:2
Lillian Russell 1940,My 18,11:2
Susan and God 1940,Jl 12,11:2
Dispatch From Reuters, A 1940,D 12,37:2
Hudson's Bay 1941,Ja 10,23:2
Play Girl 1941,Ja 30,19:3
Free and Easy 1941,Ap 3,29:4
This Woman Is Mine 1941,O 13,21:2
Chocolate Soldier, The 1941,N 1,20:2
Suspicion 1941,N 21,23:2
Roxie Hart 1942,F 20,21:1
This Above All 1942,My 13,14:3
Eagle Squadron 1942,Jl 3,12:5
Sherlock Holmes and the Voice Of Terror
1942,S 19,9:2
Journey for Margaret 1942,D 18,36:7
Sherlock Holmes and the Secret Weapon
1943,Ja 5,15:2
Lassie Come Home 1943,O 8,15:4
Sherlock Holmes Faces Death 1943,O 8,15:3
Spider Woman 1944,Ja 17,14:5
Scarlet Claw, The 1944,My 19,12:1
Pearl of Death 1944,Ag 26,15:2
Frenchman's Creek 1944,S 21,26:2
Gypsy Wildcat 1944,O 5,18:6
House of Fear, The 1945,Mr 19,23:3
Corn is Green, The 1945,Mr 30,18:2
Son of Lassie 1945,Je 11,12:1
Woman in Green, The 1945,Je 16,10:3
Pursuit to Algiers 1945,O 27,12:2
Terror by Night 1946,F 9,9:2
Dressed to Kill 1946,My 25,12:4
Two Mrs Carrolls, The 1947,Ap 7,20:1
Exile, The 1947,D 26,22:4
Julia Misbehaves 1948,O 8,30:2
Vendetta 1950,D 26,19:1
Hong Kong 1952,Ap 5,20:3
Limelight 1952,O 24,27:2
Bwana Devil 1953,F 19,20:5
World for Ransom 1954,Je 5,11:2
Bruce, Robert
Risk, The 1961,S 25,41:2
Nothing but the Best 1964,Jl 14,28:1
Bruce, Robert C (Director)
Wanderer and the Whozitt, The 1918,D 16,13:3
River Gray and the River Green, The
1919,Ja 6,11:3
Restless Three, The 1919,F 10,11:3
And Women Must Weep 1922,F 20,7:1
Bruce, Robert C (Original Author)
My Country 1922,Je 12,16:2
Nights of Many Shadows 1922,Jl 17,16:3
Split Outfit, The 1922,D 4,20:2
Bruce, Robert C (Producer)
'Tis tough To Be Tender 1918,S 16,9:3
Wee Bit Odd, A 1918,N 25,11:3
Wolf of the Tetons, The 1919,Ap 21,13:4
Frozen Thrills 1919,N 17,20:1
Bruce, Rodman
Untamed Fury 1947,Ap 26,10:6
Bruce, Sally Jane
Night of the Hunter, The 1955,S 30,23:1
Bruce, Toni Edgar
Battle of Gallipoli, The 1931,D 7,16:1
Blame the Woman 1932,O 25,24:5
Broken Melody, The 1934,O 31,17:3
Spitfire 1943,Je 14,13:2
Bruce, Virginia
Love Parade, The 1929,N 20,32:6
Slightly Scarlet 1930,Mr 1,23:1
Safety in Numbers 1930,My 31,19:4
Miracle Man, The 1932,Ap 21,25:2
Sky Bride 1932,Ap 23,11:5
Winner Take All 1932,Je 18,9:2
Downstairs 1932,O 8,15:4
Kongo 1932,N 17,22:5
Mighty Barnum, The 1934,D 24,17:1
Society Doctor 1935,F 4,11:3
Shadow of Doubt 1935,Mr 11,15:1
Times Square Lady 1935,Mr 15,25:3

Bruce, Virginia— Cont

Let 'Em Have It 1935,My 30,21:1
Escapade 1935,Jl 6,16:2
Murder Man, The 1935,Jl 27,16:2
Metropolitan 1935,O 18,27:4
Garden Murder Case, The 1936,Mr 2,13:2
Great Ziegfeld, The 1936,Ap 9,21:2
Born to Dance 1936,D 5,16:1
Women of Glamour 1937,Mr 6,10:1
When Love Is Young 1937,Ap 17,15:1
Between Two Women 1937,Ag 6,21:1
Wife, Doctor and Nurse 1937,O 11,26:5
Bad Man of Brimstone, The 1938,F 4,17:2
Arsene Lupin Returns 1938,Mr 9,21:1
First 100 Years, The 1938,My 13,17:2
Yellow Jack 1938,My 20,17:2
Woman Against Woman 1938,Ag 23,20:6
There Goes my Heart 1938,O 14,27:1
There's That Woman Again 1939,Ja 6,25:4
Let Freedom Ring 1939,Mr 10,19:2
Society Lawyer 1939,Mr 31,19:2
Stronger Than Desire 1939,Je 30,17:3
Flight Angels 1940,My 27,23:2
Man Who Talked too Much, The 1940,Je 29,12:2
Hired Wife 1940,S 14,11:2
Invisible Woman, The 1941,Ja 9,27:2
Adventure in Washington 1941,Ag 1,11:3
Butch Minds the Baby 1942,My 1,23:3
Pardon my Sarong 1942,Ag 27,15:1
Action in Arabia 1944,F 19,18:7
Brazil 1944,N 20,25:2
Love, Honor and Goodbye 1945,S 8,12:2
Night Has a Thousand Eyes 1948,O 14,38:3
State Department-File 649 1949,F 21,20:2
Strangers When we Meet 1960,Je 30,22:2

Bruce, William

All the King's Men 1949,N 9,37:2

Bruce (Producer)

Men I Have Met 1919,Je 2,20:4
Sundown 1919,Je 23,10:3
Chilkat Cubs 1919,D 29,7:2
Wanderlust 1920,Ja 26,16:1

Bruchard, Marcel

Winner, The 1965,Jl 1,34:1

Bruck, Anne

Sunderin 1954,D 24,7:2

Bruckberger, R L (Screenwriter)

Angels of the Streets 1950,Ja 17,24:2

Bruckman, Clyde (Director)

General, The 1927,F 8,21:1
Everything's Rosie 1931,My 22,28:5
Movie Crazy 1932,S 15,19:3
Man on the Flying Trapeze 1935,Ag 3,16:2

Bruckman, Clyde (Original Author)

Professor Beware 1938,Jl 14,17:1

Bruckman, Clyde (Screenwriter)

Sherlock Jr 1924,My 26,21:1
Navigator, The 1924,O 13,21:1
General, The 1927,F 8,21:1
Feet First 1930,O 31,20:1
Swingtime Johnny 1943,D 17,23:3
She Gets her Man 1945,F 9,20:5

Brudern, Gerd

Angelika 1954,S 25,10:7
Glass Tower, The; (Glaserne Turm, Der) 1959,Ag 27,24:4

Brueck, Betty

Jesse James' Women 1954,S 29,23:4

Bruel, Birgit

Weekend 1964,Ap 27,24:1

Bruggeman, George

I'm no Angel 1933,O 14,18:2

Brugman, Walter

Explosion 1927,D 13,33:2

Bruguera, Jose

Adventures of Scaramouche, The 1964,N 23,34:1
(Incorrect in this edition; use 1964,N 21,34:1 elsewhere)

Bruhl, Heidi

Captain Sindbad 1963,Jl 4,9:1

Bruhl, Linda

Papa's Delicate Condition 1963,Mr 7,8:5

Bruhn, Erik

Hans Christian Andersen 1952,N 26,20:2

Bruian, Lex de

Chinoise, La 1968,Ap 4,58:2

Brule, Claude (Miscellaneous)

Tales of Paris (The Tale of Francoise); Tale of Francoise, The (Tales of Paris) 1962,Ag 27,18:1

Brule, Claude (Screenwriter)

Liaisons Dangereuses, Les 1961,D 19,39:1
Up From the Beach 1965,Je 10,38:1
Champagne Murders, The 1968,Ap 25,53:1
Barbarella 1968,O 12,43:1

Brulier, Nigel de

Salome 1923,Ja 1,18:1
Rupert of Hentzau 1923,Jl 9,8:4
Hunchback of Notre Dame, The 1923,S 3,9:3
Regular Fellow, A 1925,O 5,25:2
Greater Glory, The 1926,My 4,31:1
Four Horsemen of the Apocalypse, The 1926,S 27,27:3

Brum, Mark (Miscellaneous)

Harvest 1939,O 3,19:4

Bruman, Ernst

Skaergaards-Flirt 1936,Ap 8,26:3

Brumbach Circus

Man on a Tightrope 1953,Je 5,19:1

Brummer, Richard Serly (Miscellaneous)

Jazz Dance 1954,S 21,24:1

Brunchugin, Eugeny (Director)

Ukrainian Festival 1965,N 1,57:1

Brundage, Mathilde

Strangers of the Night 1923,O 8,20:1
Fashion Row 1924,Ja 28,12:1
Charmer, The 1925,Ap 6,17:3
Seven Sinners 1925,D 8,28:5
Love Me and the World Is Mine 1928,F 6,12:3
That's my Daddy 1928,F 13,16:2

Brunder, Lena

Night Games 1966,D 20,58:1

Brundy, Blanchette

Bernadette of Lourdes 1962,Ja 30,20:2

Brune, Gabrielle

At Dawn We Die 1943,My 8,19:2
Titfield Thunderbolt, The 1953,O 6,34:2
White Fire 1954,S 18,12:4
1954,S 18,12:4
Touch and go 1956,Mr 20,13:2

Bruneel, Bernard

Condemned to Death 1932,Jl 14,24:2

Brunel, Adrian (Director)

Lion Has Wings, The 1940,Ja 22,11:2

Brunel, Adrian (Screenwriter)

Return of the Scarlet Pimpernel, The 1938,Ap 11,12:2

Bruner, Calven

Private Hell 36 1954,S 4,6:4

Brunet, Genevieve

French They Are a Funny Race, The 1957,My 21,41:1

Brunette, Fritzi

Woman Thou Gavest Me, The 1919,Je 9,16:3
Man From Lost River, The 1922,Ja 16,18:3

Brunetti, Argentina

California 1947,Ja 15,31:2
High Tide 1947,N 8,11:2
Man-Eater of Kumaon 1948,Jl 2,24:2
Lawless, The 1950,Je 23,29:2
Broken Arrow 1950,Jl 21,15:2
Force of Arms 1951,Ag 14,20:2
When in Rome 1952,My 12,21:2
My Cousin Rachel 1952,D 26,20:2
Caddy, The 1953,S 18,16:6
King of the Khyber Rifles 1953,D 23,21:1
Rains of Ranchipur, The 1955,D 16,38:2
Anything Goes 1956,Mr 22,38:1
Midnight Story, The 1957,Jl 5,14:2
George Raft Story, The 1962,Mr 22,40:1
Appaloosa, The 1966,S 15,51:1

Bruni, Sandro

Little Nuns, The 1966,Ap 28,49:1

Brunies, David

Lord of the Flies 1963,Ag 20,37:1

Brunil, Jean

Prenez Garde a la Peinture 1935,Ag 17,18:6

Brunius, Anne-Maris

Ungdom Av I Dag 1936,Je 23,27:7

Brunius, Britta

Frun Tillhanda; Servant Girls 1938,D 30,9:2
Vi paa Solglantan; We at Solglantan 1940,O 9,30:3
Children, The 1949,D 23,17:1

Brunius, Jacques

Sea Devils 1953,Jl 31,11:5
Golden Mask, The 1954,Mr 20,10:5
Always a Bride 1954,My 28,19:2
To Paris With Love 1955,Mr 29,33:4
Orders to Kill 1958,N 18,41:2
Age d'Or, L'; Golden Age, The 1964,S 22,44:1

Brunius, John

Roeda Dagen 1932,My 21,9:2

Brunius, John (Director)

En Glad Gutt 1933,N 24,25:7

Brunius, Pauline

Charlotte Loewenskoeld 1932,F 22,23:2
Karl Fredrik Reigns 1938,F 2,15:2

Brunn, Frederic

Woman in Bondage 1944,Mr 27,17:2

Brunn, Frederick

Passage to Marseille 1944,F 17,12:5

Brunneau, Helen

Hunchback of Notre Dame, The 1923,S 3,9:3

Brunngraber, Rudolf (Screenwriter)

Trial, The 1952,Mr 15,8:2
April 1, 2000 1954,F 17,27:2

Bruno, Cinzia

Mafioso 1964,Jl 1,42:1

Bruno, F

Merlusse 1938,Mr 17,17:2

Bruno, Frank

Treachery Rides the Range 1936,My 30,7:3
Mr Wong, Detective 1938,N 21,14:4
Tall, Dark and Handsome 1941,Ja 24,15:2

Bruno, Nando

Open City; Citta Aperta 1946,F 26,21:2
Life Begins Anew; Vita Ricomincia, La 1947,Ap 7,20:5
To Live in Peace 1947,N 25,37:2
Angelina 1948,Ap 6,27:2
Lost Youth 1949,O 27,35:4
Ring Around the Clock 1953,My 19,36:2
Journey to Love 1953,O 9,32:8
Hello Elephant 1954,S 10,18:5
Time Out for Love 1963,Ap 23,31:2

Bruno, Pierrette

Letters From my Windmill (The Secret of Master Cornille); Secret of Master Cornille, The (Letters From my Windmill) 1955,D 19,33:1
Wild Oat, The 1956,Je 28,33:2

Brunot, Andre

Curtain Rises, The 1939,Ap 22,15:2
Hotel du Nord 1940,D 30,21:2
Personal Column 1941,F 3,13:2
Portrait of Innocence 1948,Je 9,35:2
Virtuous Scoundrel, The 1957,O 23,37:1
Rouge et Noir 1958,Ap 9,42:1
Picnic on the Grass 1960,O 12,47:1

Brunoy, Blanchette

Youth in Revolt 1939,My 16,27:3
Human Beast, The 1940,F 20,17:2
Claudine 1940,Ap 1,15:2
Two Women 1940,N 2,19:3
It Happened at the Inn; Goupi Mains Rouge 1945,D 22,16:2
Shop-Girls of Paris; Au Bonheur de Dames 1947,Je 23,14:4
Marie du Port 1951,Jl 24,21:2
Sextette (Part 4-Snow Queen); Snow Queen (Sextette) 1953,Mr 2,19:2
French Touch, The 1954,S 2,18:2
Bonne Soupe, La 1964,Mr 16,37:1

Bruns, George (Composer)

Babes in Toyland 1961,D 15,49:1

Brunskill, John

Long John Silver 1955,Ap 7,24:1

Brunskill, Muriel

Gilbert and Sullivan 1953,O 28,36:3

Brunskog, Bengt

Loving Couples 1966,S 20,38:1

Brusarosco, Ferruccio (Producer)

Little Nuns, The 1966,Ap 28,49:1

Brusati, Franco (Director)

Disorder 1964,My 26,44:2

Brusati, Franco (Original Author)

Anna 1953,F 19,20:5
Run With the Devil 1963,Jl 16,25:1

Brusati, Franco (Screenwriter)

Anna 1953,F 19,20:5
Ulysses 1955,Ag 18,17:2
Wife for a Night 1958,Je 12,35:2
Run With the Devil 1963,Jl 16,25:1
Disorder 1964,My 26,44:2
Romeo and Juliet 1968,O 9,41:1

Brush, Katherine (Original Author)

Drop Kick, The 1927,S 20,32:2
Night Club 1929,Ag 12,22:2
Footlights and Fools 1929,N 9,22:5
Young Man of Manhattan 1930,Ap 19,15:1
Red Headed Woman 1932,Jl 1,19:3
Lady of Secrets 1936,F 22,12:1
Mannequin 1938,Ja 21,15:2
Listen, Darling 1938,N 24,37:2
Honeymoon in Bali 1939,S 21,21:1
Andy Hardy's Private Secretary 1941,Mr 7,17:2

Brusse, Kees

Ciske 1963,Ag 3,8:2

Bruun, Lauridas (Original Author)

Midnight Sun, The 1926,Ap 24,20:4

Bruyere, Gaby

Plaisir, Le (The Mask); Mask, The (Le Plaisir) 1954,My 20,38:1

Bruzzolari, Mario

Stella del Mare; Star of the Sea 1940,My 3,17:6

Bry, Henry

Personal Column 1941,F 3,13:2

BRYAN

See Also BRIAN

Bryan, Alfred (Composer)

Oh, You Beautiful Doll 1949,N 12,8:4

Bryan, C D B (Screenwriter)

Face of War, The 1963,N 1,30:2
Face of War, The 1963,N 1,30:2

Bryan, Dora

Fallen Idol, The 1949,N 16,39:2
No Room at the Inn 1949,D 26,33:4
Interrupted Journey 1951,My 29,20:2
Circle of Danger 1951,Jl 12,21:6
High Treason 1952,My 21,23:3
Glory at Sea 1953,Mr 11,36:7
Miss Robin Hood 1953,Je 27,7:2
Time, Gentlemen, Please 1953,S 24,39:2
Both Sides of the Law 1954,Ja 12,19:2
Intruder, The 1955,Ja 26,22:1
Cockleshell Heroes, The 1956,Je 4,25:2
Green Man, The 1957,My 23,40:1
Carry on Sergeant 1959,O 28,40:5

Bryan, Dora— Cont
    Taste of Honey, A 1962,My 1,33:3
Bryan, George (Narrator)
    Will It Happen Again 1948,My 17,23:4
    Lost Continent 1957,Mr 12,38:1
Bryan, Grace Lovell (Original Author)
    You Never Can Tell 1920,O 4,14:3
Bryan, Jane
    Case of the Black Cat, The 1936,D 26,15:4
    Marked Woman 1937,Ap 12,15:2
    Kid Galahad 1937,My 27,21:3
    Confession 1937,Ag 19,23:1
    Slight Case of Murder, A 1938,F 28,19:1
    Sisters, The 1938,O 15,21:3
    Girls on Probation 1938,O 21,27:3
    Brother Rat 1938,N 5,15:2
    Each Dawn I Die 1939,Jl 22,12:2
    Old Maid, The 1939,Ag 12,16:2
    These Glamour Girls 1939,Ag 31,14:2
    We are not Alone 1939,D 1,27:1
    Invisible Stripes 1940,Ja 13,11:2
    Brother Rat and a Baby 1940,Ja 27,9:4
Bryan, John (Miscellaneous)
    Great Expectations 1947,My 23,31:1
Bryan, John (Producer)
    Promoter, The 1952,O 29,36:2
    Man With a Million 1954,Je 29,21:2
    Purple Plain, The 1955,Ap 11,29:1
    Spanish Gardner, The 1957,S 9,21:2
    Windom's Way 1958,O 1,45:1
    Horse's Mouth, The 1958,N 12,41:1
    Tamahine 1964,Jl 16,23:1
    After the Fox 1966,D 24,11:1
    Touchables, The 1968,N 21,41:1
Bryan, John (Screenwriter)
    Spanish Gardner, The 1957,S 9,21:2
Bryan, Michael (Original Author)
    Intent to Kill 1959,Ap 1,43:2
Bryan, Paul
    Easy to Love 1953,N 27,99:9
Bryan, Peter (Screenwriter)
    Hounds of the Baskervilles, The 1959,Jl 4,9:4
    Brides of Dracula, The 1960,S 6,41:4
Bryant, Betty
    Forty Thousand Horsemen 1941,Ag 15,13:2
Bryant, Charles
    Eye for Eye 1918,D 23,9:1
    Out of the Fog 1919,F 10,11:3
    Brat, The 1919,N 3,13:3
    Stronger Than Death 1920,Ja 12,7:1
    Heart of a Child, The 1920,Ap 12,13:1
Bryant, Charles (Director)
    Stronger Than Death 1920,Ja 12,7:1
    Doll's House, A 1922,F 13,10:1
    Salome 1923,Ja 1,18:1
Bryant, John
    From Here to Eternity 1953,Ag 6,16:2
    Strangers When we Meet 1960,Je 30,22:2
Bryant, Joyce
    East Side Kids 1940,F 19,21:6
Bryant, Kay
    Wild Party, The 1929,Ap 2,28:4
Bryant, Marie
    They Live by Night 1949,N 4,33:2
    Wabash Avenue 1950,Ap 29,8:3
Bryant, Michael
    Mind Benders, The 1963,My 2,40:2
    Walk in the Shadow 1966,S 12,52:5
Bryant, Nana
    Feather in her Hat, A 1935,O 25,24:5
    One Way Ticket 1936,Ja 1,35:2
    Lone Wolf Returns, The 1936,F 4,25:5
    Lady of Secrets 1936,F 22,12:1
    You may Be Next 1936,F 24,14:1
    King Steps Out, The 1936,My 29,15:2
    Meet Nero Wolfe 1936,Jl 16,20:1
    Man Who Lived Twice, The 1936,O 12,23:2
    Theodora Goes Wild 1936,N 13,27:4
    Pennies From Heaven 1936,D 10,35:2
    League of Frightened Men, The 1937,Jl 2,25:1
    Devil is Driving, The 1937,Jl 16,22:1
    Counsel for Crime 1937,O 9,16:1
    Man-Proof 1938,Ja 14,21:1
    Adventures of Tom Sawyer, The 1938,F 18,23:1
    Mad About Music 1938,Mr 12,13:2
    Sinners in Paradise 1938,My 20,17:2
    Give Me a Sailor 1938,Ag 11,31:1
    Always in Trouble 1938,N 3,27:1
    Out West With the Hardys 1938,D 9,31:2
    Peck's bad Boy With the Circus 1939,Ja 11,17:4
    Street of Missing Men 1939,Je 1,31:3
    Parents on Trial 1939,S 18,15:5
    Espionage Agent 1939,S 23,22:2
    Brother Rat and a Baby 1940,Ja 27,9:4
    Our Neighbors-The Carters 1940,F 15,15:2
    If I Had my Way 1940,My 6,13:2
    Little Bit of Heaven, A 1940,N 8,24:2
    Nice Girl 1941,Mr 27,29:6
    Reluctant Dragon, The 1941,Jl 25,12:2
    One Foot in Heaven 1941,N 14,28:3
    Corsican Brothers, The 1942,Ja 16,25:4
    Calling Dr Gillespie 1942,Jl 9,17:4
    Get Help to Love 1942,O 19,15:3
    Thunder Birds 1942,O 29,19:2

Hangmen Also Die 1943,Ap 16,24:2
Song of Bernadette, The 1944,Ja 27,15:2
Adventures of Mark Twain, The 1944,My 4,25:5
Take It or Leave It 1944,Jl 13,14:2
Brewster's Millions 1945,Ap 27,23:2
Black Market Babies 1946,Ap 1,23:1
Runaround, The 1946,Je 7,16:3
Perfect Marriage, The 1947,Ja 16,30:3
Big Fix, The 1947,My 3,10:3
Unsuspected, The 1947,O 4,9:2
Her Husband's Affairs 1947,N 14,29:2
State Department-File 649 1949,F 21,20:2
Lady Gambles, The 1949,My 21,9:2
Harvey 1950,D 22,19:1
Follow the Sun 1951,Ap 26,34:4
Bright Victory 1951,Ag 1,19:2
About Mrs Leslie 1954,Je 28,16:2
Outcast, The 1954,Jl 3,9:2
Private War of Major Benson, The
    1955,Ag 3,27:2
Bryant, Samuel W (Miscellaneous)
    Golden Twenties, The 1950,Ap 10,15:2
Bryant, Theona
    Last Time I Saw Archie, The 1961,My 29,9:6
Bryant, Walter
    Respectful Prostitute, The 1957,Jl 11,21:1
Bryar, Claudia
    I Was a Teenage Frankenstein 1958,Ja 30,19:4
Bryar, Paul
    Tenth Avenue Kid 1938,S 2,21:3
    Paris Calling 1942,Ja 19,21:2
    Jungle Siren 1942,O 10,11:3
    Walk a Crooked Mile 1948,O 13,31:2
    Mary Ryan, Detective 1949,N 4,33:3
    Under my Skin 1950,Mr 18,9:2
    Cavalry Scout 1951,Je 8,32:2
    Dangerous When Wet 1953,Je 19,18:1
    Mad at the World 1955,My 14,10:8
    Inside Detroit 1956,Ja 28,10:5
    Killer is Loose, The 1956,Mr 3,17:2
    Saintly Sinners 1962,Mr 29,28:2
Bryce, Alex (Director)
    Macushla 1940,Ja 6,9:2
    Song of the Road 1940,My 6,13:2
Bryce, Alex (Original Author)
    Macushla 1940,Ja 6,9:2
Bryden, Sonja
    Letters From an Unknown Woman
    1948,Ap 29,20:6
Bryden, William
    Mask, The 1961,O 28,12:4
Bryne, Eddie
    Jack the Ripper 1960,F 18,37:4
Bryning, John
    Rembrandt 1936,D 3,31:1
Brynner, Yul
    Port of New York 1950,F 3,29:2
    King and I, The 1956,Je 29,15:6
    Ten Commandments, The 1956,N 9,35:2
    Anastasia 1956,D 14,35:6
    Brothers Karamazov, The 1958,F 21,18:2
    Buccaneer, The 1958,D 24,00:0
    Journey, The 1959,F 20,19:1
    Sound and the Fury, The 1959,Mr 28,11:1
    Solomon and Sheba 1959,D 26,7:2
    Once More With Feeling 1960,F 12,22:2
    Surprise Package 1960,O 15,26:2
    Magnificent Seven, The 1960,N 24,48:3
    Testament of Orpheus 1962,Ap 10,48:1
    Escape from Zahrain 1962,Jl 12,19:3
    Taras Bulba 1962,D 26,5:2
    King of the Sun 1963,D 26,33:4
    Flight From Ashiya 1964,Ap 23,34:1
    Invitation to a Gunfighter 1964,O 28,51:3
    Saboteur, The: Code Name-Mori Turi
    1965,Ag 26,40:2
    Cast a Giant Shadow 1966,Mr 31,43:3
    Return of the Seven 1966,O 20,52:5
    Triple Cross 1967,Jl 20,20:2
    Long Duel, The 1967,N 2,58:3
    Poppy is Also a Flower, The 1967,D 14,62:4
    Double Man, The 1968,My 2,57:1
    Villa Rides 1968,Jl 18,26:3
Brynych, Zbynek (Director)
    Transport From Paradise 1967,F 8,22:1
    Transport From Paradise 1967,Je 19,41:1
    Fifth Horseman is Fear, The 1968,My 7,52:1
Brynych, Zbynek (Screenwriter)
    Transport From Paradise 1967,F 8,22:1
    Fifth Horseman is Fear, The 1968,My 7,52:1
Bryson, Arthur
    Wildfire 1925,Je 10,18:2
Bryson, Betty
    Shine on Harvest Moon 1944,Mr 11,10:2
Bryson, Ceil
    8 X 8 1957,Mr 16,13:2
Bryson, Tom
    Woman in Green, The 1945,Je 16,10:3
Bryson, Winifred
    Hunchback of Notre Dame, The 1923,S 3,9:3
    Pleasure Mad 1924,Ja 7,23:1

Bryson, Winifred— Cont
    Broken Barriers 1924,Ag 4,16:3
    Flirting With Love 1924,S 1,9:1
    Awful Truth, The 1925,Jl 2,12:4
    Adoration 1929,Ja 14,20:1
Brzezinska, Hanna
    Wrzos; Heather 1938,N 7,23:4
Brzobohaty, Radoslav
    Lady on the Tracks, The 1968,N 26,39:2
Buades, Michael
    Birds in Peru 1968,N 7,51:2
Buazzelli, Tino
    Count of St Elmo, The 1953,Mr 14,13:2
    Margaret of Cortona 1957,Ja 21,20:4
Bubbell, Edward (Director)
    Hollywood Speaks 1932,Ag 12,18:2
Bubnov, V
    Signal, The 1943,Mr 25,25:3
    Heroes Are Made 1944,Mr 11,10:2
Buccella, Maria Grazia
    Love and Marriage (The First Night); First Night,
    The (Love and Marriage) 1966,Ag 5,20:1
    After the Fox 1966,D 24,11:1
    Villa Rides 1968,Jl 18,26:3
Buccola, Guy
    Street Girl 1929,Jl 31,17:3
BUCH
    See Also BUSCH, BUSH
Buch, Fritz Peter (Director)
    Koenigin der Liebe 1936,My 4,16:2
    Waldwinter 1936,N 14,23:3
    Katzensteg 1938,Ja 22,19:2
    Freiheit und Liebe, Um; For Freedom and Love
    1938,F 5,19:3
Buchan, John (Original Author)
    Thirty-Nine Steps, The 1935,S 14,8:4
    39 Steps, The 1960,O 11,55:2
Buchanan, C S
    Birthright 1952,F 15,17:2
Buchanan, Claud
    Fascinating Youth 1926,My 10,19:1
    Running Wild 1927,Je 14,33:2
Buchanan, Edgar
    My Son Is Guilty 1940,Ja 15,11:2
    Too Many Husbands 1940,Mr 8,25:2
    Tear Gas Squad 1940,My 31,15:3
    Arizona 1941,F 7,23:3
    Submarine Zone; (Escape To Glory)
    1941,Ap 7,13:2
    Penny Serenade 1941,My 23,25:2
    Texas 1941,O 17,27:3
    You Belong to Me 1941,N 29,14:2
    Tombstone, The Town too Tough to Die
    1942,Jl 27,18:2
    Talk of the Town, The 1942,Ag 28,22:3
    Desperadoes, The 1943,My 13,17:2
    Destroyer 1943,S 2,15:3
    Buffalo Bill 1944,Ap 20,22:6
    Bride by Mistake 1944,S 16,20:2
    Impatient Years, The 1944,S 20,20:1
    Fighting Guardsman, The 1945,O 6,9:6
    Abilene Town 1946,Mr 4,16:5
    Bandit of Sherwood Forest, The 1946,Mr 23,8:4
    Perilous Holiday 1946,Je 1,10:4
    Renegades 1946,Jl 11,18:2
    If I'm Lucky 1946,S 20,41:3
    Walls Came Tumbling Down, The 1946,N 9,13:5
    Sea of Grass, The 1947,F 28,27:2
    Framed 1947,My 26,24:2
    Swordsman, The 1947,O 17,18:4
    Black Arrow, The 1948,O 4,14:2
    Man From Colorado 1948,Ja 21,24:3
    Red Canyon 1949,Ap 28,28:2
    Any Number Can Play 1949,Jl 1,14:4
    Lust for Gold 1949,Jl 4,9:2
    Cargo to Capetown 1950,Mr 31,36:3
    Cheaper by the Dozen 1950,Ap 1,12:2
    Big Hangover, The 1950,My 26,20:3
    Devil's Doorway 1950,N 10,35:1
    Rawhide 1951,Mr 26,19:2
    Great Missouri Raid, The 1951,Ap 9,31:2
    Big Trees, The 1952,F 6,24:2
    Shane 1953,Ap 24,30:3
    She Couldn't Say No 1954,F 27,11:3
    Make Haste to Live 1954,Mr 26,16:2
    Human Desire 1954,Ag 7,7:2
    Dawn at Socorro 1954,Ag 28,8:2
    Day of the Badman 1958,Ja 30,19:2
    Sheepman, The 1958,My 8,36:1
    It Started With a Kiss 1959,Ag 20,14:2
    Edge of Eternity 1960,F 25,34:2
    Cimarron 1961,F 17,12:2
    Tammy Tell me True 1961,Jl 27,23:2
    Comancheros, The 1961,N 2,42:1
    Ride the High Country 1962,Je 21,26:2
    Ticklish Affair, A 1963,Ag 22,19:2
    McLintock 1963,N 14,41:3
    Move Over Darling 1963,D 26,33:1
    Rounders, The 1965,Ap 29,40:2
    Welcome to Hard Times 1967,My 2,56:1
Buchanan, Elsa
    Charlie Chan in London 1934,S 13,26:1
    Here's to Romance 1935,O 3,29:2
    Peter Ibbetson 1935,N 8,18:2

Buchanan, Elsa— Cont
Lloyds of London 1936,N 26,39:1
Call it a Day 1937,My 7,29:2
Buchanan, Jack
Paris 1929,N 8,31:2
Monte Carlo 1930,Ag 28,22:4
Good Night, Vienna 1932,My 1,VIII,5:4
Magic Night 1932,N 3,25:3
Brewster's Millions 1935,Ap 8,23:3
This'll Make You Whistle 1938,N 1,27:2
Break the News 1941,Ja 2,24:2
Larceny Street 1941,Ja 6,11:2
When Knights Were Bold 1942,Mr 31,29:2
Band Wagon, The 1953,Jl 10,10:2
French They Are a Funny Race, The
  1957,My 21,41:1
Buchanan, James D (Original Author)
Happening, The 1967,My 18,56:3
Buchanan, James D (Screenwriter)
Happening, The 1967,My 18,56:3
Buchanan, Jane
World of Henry Orient, The 1964,Mr 20,27:2
Buchanan, Larry (Director)
Free, White and 21 1963,Je 20,29:3
Buchanan, Larry (Screenwriter)
Free, White and 21 1963,Je 20,29:3
Buchanan, Meg
Brave Don't Cry, The 1952,N 6,37:2
High and Dry 1954,Ag 31,25:5
Buchanan, Nigel
Woman in the Hall, The 1949,Ja 24,16:2
Buchanan, Sidney (Screenwriter)
She Married her Boss 1935,S 27,25:3
Buchanan, Thompson (Original Author)
Easy to Love 1934,Ja 15,12:2
Buchanan, Thompson (Screenwriter)
Jes' Call Me Jim 1920,My 24,20:3
Buchbinder, Bernhard (Screenwriter)
Versuchen Sie Meine Schwester 1931,Je 20,20:4
Buchel, Brian
Bulldog Drummond at Bay 1937,O 25,23:2
Buchenan, Elsa
Invisible Enemy 1938,Ap 30,18:2
Buchholz, Horst
Montpi 1959,Ap 21,40:1
Sky Without Stars 1959,My 30,9:2
Tiger Bay 1959,D 15,50:1
Magnificent Seven, The 1960,N 24,48:3
Fanny 1961,Jl 7,16:1
One, Two, Three 1961,D 22,17:1
Nine Hours to Rama 1963,Ap 4,58:2
Empty Canvas, The 1964,My 16,21:1 (Incorrect
  in this edition; use 1964,My 16,12:1 elsewhere)
That Man in Istanbul 1966,My 19,51:2
Marco the Magnificent 1966,D 15,60:1
Buchhorn, Josef (Original Author)
Student Sein 1931,My 4,15:3
Buchi, Ella
Faust 1963,Ap 16,31:1
Buchinsky, Charles
U S S Teakettle 1951,F 24,11:2
My Six Convicts 1952,Mr 28,27:3
Bloodhounds of Broadway 1952,N 15,15:2
Miss Sadie Thompson 1953,D 24,9:1
Crime Wave 1954,Ja 13,26:2
Riding Shotgun 1954,Ap 2,22:2
Apache 1954,Jl 10,7:2
Buchma, A
Jimmie Higgins 1933,F 22,25:3
Polish Terror, The 1933,Mr 13,18:3
Buchma, A (Director)
Land, The 1955,Ap 11,29:3
Buchma, Alexei
Ivan the Terrible, Part I 1947,Mr 10,25:2
Ivan the Terrible, Part II 1959,N 25,22:4
Buchma, Ambros
Secret Agent 1949,F 10,37:3
Buchman, Harold (Original Author)
Case of the Missing Man, The 1935,N 23,23:2
Don't Gamble With Love 1936,Mr 2,13:3
Shall We Dance 1937,My 14,21:1
Devil is Driving, The 1937,Jl 16,22:1
It Can't Last Forever 1937,Jl 30,22:5
Buchman, Harold (Screenwriter)
Case of the Missing Man, The 1935,N 23,23:2
Don't Gamble With Love 1936,Mr 2,13:3
Trapped by Television 1936,Je 15,24:3
Come Closer, Folks 1936,N 23,17:3
It Can't Last Forever 1937,Jl 30,22:5
Counsel for Crime 1937,O 9,16:1
Forgotten Woman, The 1939,Ag 4,11:2
Double Alibi 1940,Mr 11,11:2
Romance of the Rio Grande 1940,D 25,33:4
Gentleman at Heart, A 1942,F 23,25:2
It Happened in Flatbush 1942,Jl 3,12:8
Dixie Dugan 1943,Ap 9,25:5
Paris After Dark 1943,O 23,11:1
Take It or Leave It 1944,Jl 13,14:2
Snafu 1945,D 26,15:2
Cynthia 1947,S 19,27:2
Operation Snafu 1965,My 22,18:1
Buchman, Sidney (Original Author)
Matinee Ladies 1927,Ap 13,29:4
Music Goes 'Round, The 1936,F 22,12:1

Buchman, Sidney (Producer)
Song to Remember, A 1945,Ja 26,16:4
Over 21 1945,Ag 17,20:2
Jolson Sings Again 1949,Ag 18,16:6
Group, The 1966,Mr 17,35:1
Buchman, Sidney (Screenwriter)
I'll Love You Always 1935,Mr 30,11:2
Love Me Forever 1935,Je 28,24:1
King Steps Out, The 1936,My 29,15:2
Adventure in Manhattan 1936,O 23,27:5
Theodora Goes Wild 1936,N 13,27:4
Holiday 1938,Je 24,15:1
Mr Smith Goes to Washington 1939,O 20,27:2
Howards of Virginia, The 1940,S 27,27:1
Here Comes Mr Jordan 1941,Ag 8,13:2
Talk of the Town, The 1942,Ag 28,22:3
Song to Remember, A 1945,Ja 26,16:4
Over 21 1945,Ag 17,20:2
Buchman, sidney (Screenwriter)
Jolson Sings Again 1949,Ag 18,16:6
Buchman, Sidney (Screenwriter)
Saturday's Hero 1951,S 12,37:2
Mark, The 1961,O 3,46:2
Cleopatra 1963,Je 13,29:1
Group, The 1966,Mr 17,35:1
BUCHNER
See Also BUCKNER
Buchner, Georg (Original Author)
Wozzeck 1962,Mr 3,13:1
Bucholtz, Gerhard T (Screenwriter)
No Way Back 1955,My 19,25:5
Buchowetzki, Dimitri (Director)
All for a Woman 1921,D 5,20:1
Othello 1923,F 26,15:1
Mad Love 1923,Mr 5,15:3
Peter the Great 1923,Je 25,16:5
Men 1924,My 5,18:3
Lily of the Dust 1924,Ag 25,16:2
Swan, The 1925,Mr 2,14:1
Graustark 1925,S 8,29:1
Crown of Lies 1926,Mr 30,20:6
Midnight Sun, The 1926,Ap 24,20:4
Valencia 1926,D 27,20:3
Buchowetzki, Dimitri (Screenwriter)
Men 1924,My 5,18:3
Buchs, Jose (Director)
Dos Mujeres y un Don Juan 1934,Je 4,12:4
Buchsbaum, Max
Question 7 1961,S 29,30:2
Buchwald, Art (Original Author)
Surprise Package 1960,O 15,26:2
Buck
Country Beyond, The 1936,Ap 30,17:3
Buck, Charles Neville (Original Author)
Runaway, The 1926,Ap 27,23:2
Buck, David
Deadfall 1968,S 12,54:1
Buck, Donald
Little Men 1935,F 18,19:3
Buck, Frank
Bring 'Em Back Alive 1932,Je 18,9:2
Africa Screams 1949,My 5,34:2
Buck, Frank (Director)
Fang and Claw 1935,D 28,10:5
Buck, Frank (Miscellaneous)
Frank Buck's Jungle Cavalcade 1941,Jl 4,17:1
Buck, Frank (Narrator)
Fang and Claw 1935,D 28,10:5
Jacare 1942,D 28,23:2
Buck, Frank (Producer)
Jacare 1942,D 28,23:2
Buck, Jules (Cinematographer)
Report From the Aleutians 1943,Jl 31,8:2
Buck, Jules (Producer)
Fixed Bayonets 1951,N 21,20:2
Treasure of the Golden Condor 1953,My 23,19:2
Day They Robbed the Bank of England, The
  1960,S 5,11:2
Operation Snatch 1962,S 25,31:4
Buck, Nell Roy
Peter Ibbetson; (Forever) 1921,O 17,18:1
Buck, Pearl S (Original Author)
Good Earth, The 1937,F 3,27:1
Dragon Seed 1944,Jl 21,16:4
China Sky 1945,My 25,22:3
Satan Never Sleeps 1962,F 22,20:1
Buck, Pearl S (Screenwriter)
Guide, The 1965,F 10,44:2
Buck and Bubbles
Varsity Show 1937,S 2,17:2
Atlantic City 1944,Ag 14,11:4
Song Is Born, A 1948,O 20,37:2
Buckhoj, Per
Red Meadows 1950,Ja 19,35:2
Buckingham, Tom (Director)
Tony Runs Wild 1926,Ap 28,28:3
Cock of the Air 1932,Ja 25,20:3
Buckingham, Tom (Original Author)
Officer O'Brien 1930,F 24,18:1
Destination Unknown 1933,Ap 8,16:2
Buckingham, Tom (Screenwriter)
Painted Desert, The 1931,Mr 9,19:1
Secret Bride, The 1935,F 2,10:1

Buckingham, Tom (Screenwriter)— Cont
Stage Struck 1936,S 28,14:4
Buckingham, Yvonne
Sapphire 1959,N 3,27:1
Buckinsky, Charles
Vera Cruz 1954,D 27,22:4
Buckland, Veda
Texan, The 1930,My 17,21:2
This mad World 1930,Jl 21,20:3
Right to Love, The 1931,Ja 2,25:1
Sinners in the Sun 1932,My 14,11:5
Doctor Bull 1933,O 6,21:2
Buckland, Vera
Mystery of Edwin Drood, The 1935,Mr 21,27:1
Buckle, Ken
Treasure Island 1950,Ag 16,24:2
Buckler, Hugh
Crash Donovan 1936,Ag 10,10:3
Last of the Mohicans, The 1936,S 3,17:3
Jungle Princess 1936,D 24,21:3
Lost Horizon 1937,Mr 4,27:1
Buckler, John
David Copperfield 1935,Ja 19,8:1
Unguarded Hour, The 1936,Ap 4,11:1
Tarzan Escapes 1936,N 20,27:2
Buckles, Ann
Crowning Experience, The 1960,O 24,25:3
Buckley, Buz
Fabulous Dorseys, The 1947,My 30,25:3
Buckley, Harold (Original Author)
Road Gang 1936,F 24,14:1
Sinners in Paradise 1938,My 20,17:2
Nick Carter, Master Detective 1939,D 14,35:2
Buckley, Harold (Screenwriter)
Public Enemy's Wife 1936,Jl 9,17:2
Idol of the Crowd 1937,D 4,21:1
Black Doll, The 1938,F 7,10:2
Sinners in Paradise 1938,My 20,17:2
Buckley, Kay
Stage to Tucson 1951,My 5,14:2
Millionaire for Christy, A 1951,O 5,24:3
Buckley, Keith
King and Country 1966,Ja 28,20:4
Buckley, Kenneth
Stolen Life 1939,Je 15,27:2
This Man Is News 1939,Jl 20,16:4
Buckmaster, Maurice
Odette 1951,Mr 28,33:2
Bucknall, Nathalie (Original Author)
Four Girls in White 1939,F 23,19:3
BUCKNER
See Also BUCHNER
Buckner, Robert (Original Author)
Espionage Agent 1939,S 23,22:2
Primrose Path 1940,Mr 23,16:2
Yankee Doodle Dandy 1942,My 30,9:1
Rogues' Regiment 1948,D 20,31:2
When in Rome 1952,My 12,21:2
Safari 1956,Je 21,35:2
Buckner, Robert (Producer)
Gentleman Jim 1942,N 26,40:3
Mission to Moscow 1943,Ap 30,25:2
Desert Song, The 1943,D 18,10:6
Uncertain Glory 1944,Ap 8,9:2
God is my Co-Pilot 1945,Mr 24,22:6
Confidential Agent 1945,N 3,11:2
San Antonio 1945,D 29,19:5
Devotion 1946,Ap 6,10:5
Cheyenne 1947,Je 7,9:2
Life With Father 1947,Ag 16,6:6
Rogues' Regiment 1948,D 20,31:2
Sword in the Desert 1949,Ag 25,20:2
Deported 1950,N 2,39:3
Bright Victory 1951,Ag 1,19:2
From Hell to Texas 1958,Je 5,39:2
Buckner, Robert (Screenwriter)
Gold Is Where You Find It 1938,F 14,20:6
Love, Honor and Behave 1938,Mr 21,18:2
Comet over Broadway 1938,D 16,33:3
Oklahoma Kid, The 1939,Mr 11,21:1
You Can't Get Away With Murder
  1939,Mr 25,19:2
Dodge City 1939,Ap 8,19:1
Angels Wash Their Faces 1939,S 4,16:2
Virginia City 1940,Mr 23,16:3
My Love Came Back 1940,Jl 13,16:5
Knute Rockne-All American 1940,O 19,21:2
Santa Fe Trail 1940,D 21,21:2
Dive Bomber 1941,Ag 30,10:2
Yankee Doodle Dandy 1942,My 30,9:1
Confidential Agent 1945,N 3,11:2
Rogues' Regiment 1948,D 20,31:2
Sword in the Desert 1949,Ag 25,20:2
Deported 1950,N 2,39:3
Bright Victory 1951,Ag 1,19:2
To Paris With Love 1955,Mr 29,33:4
Prize of Gold, A 1955,O 15,19:2
Love Me Tender 1956,N 16,23:1
Triple Deception 1957,O 7,23:2
From Hell to Texas 1958,Je 5,39:2
Buckstone, Roland
Enemy to the King, An 1916,N 27,9:1

Bucquet, Harold S (Director)
Young Doctor Kildare 1938,O 28,27:1
Calling Dr Kildare 1939,My 12,25:4
On Borrowed Time 1939,Jl 7,13:2
Secret of Dr Kildare, The 1939,D 8,33:5
Dr Kildare's Strange Case 1940,Ap 12,19:2
We Who Are Young 1940,S 13,27:2
Dr Kildare Goes Home 1940,S 19,27:4
Dr Kildare's Crisis 1940,D 19,33:1
Penalty, The 1941,Ap 10,29:3
People vs Dr Kildare, The 1941,My 8,21:1
Kathleen 1941,D 19,35:3
Calling Dr Gillespie 1942,Jl 9,17:4
War Against Mrs Hadley, The 1942,N 26,40:2
Adventures of Tartu, The 1943,S 24,26:1
Dragon Seed 1944,Jl 21,16:4
Without Love 1945,Mr 23,13:1

Buczkowski, Leonard (Director)
First Start, The 1953,F 2,17:3
Adventure in Warsaw 1955,O 24,22:2

Bud, Peter
African Queen, The 1952,F 21,24:3

Budarov, G
Professor Mamlock 1938,N 8,26:2

Buday, B (Miscellaneous)
Thank You, Madame 1937,Ap 27,18:2

Budberg, Moura (Miscellaneous)
Sea Gull, The 1968,D 24,14:1

Budberg, Moura (Screenwriter)
Sea Gull, The 1968,D 24,14:1

Budd, Norman
Turnabout 1940,Jl 27,17:6
Red Menace, The 1949,Je 27,18:2
Surrender 1950,O 9,21:5
Atomic City, The 1952,My 2,21:1

Buddy
Sandy Is a Lady 1940,Je 28,22:2

Buddy (dog)
Devil's Circus, The 1926,Mr 29,24:3

Buder, Ernst Erich (Miscellaneous)
Student Sein 1931,My 4,15:3

Budington, Clarence (Original Author)
Contraband 1925,Mr 24,20:6

Budinova, Slavka
Fifth Horseman is Fear, The 1968,My 7,52:1
Girl With Three Camels, The 1968,Ag 13,45:2

Budjuhn, Horst (Screenwriter)
White Horse Inn, The 1957,D 4,50:3

BUEHLER
See Also BUHLER

Buehler, Betty
Mob, The 1951,O 18,32:2

Buenaventura, Angel
Walls of Hell, The 1965,N 18,55:3

Buendia, Manuel
Madres del Mundo 1936,Ag 17,9:3
Tras la Reja 1937,Ja 11,15:7
No te Enganes, Corazon; Don't Fool Thyself,
Heart 1937,D 14,33:6
Infidelidad 1939,My 8,21:3
China Hilaria, La 1939,Ag 12,16:3

Bueno, J Louis (Producer)
Muertos Hablan, Los; Dead Speak, The
1935,N 25,22:2

Bueno, Jose Luis (Producer)
Ave sin Rumbo; Wandering Bird 1938,Ja 24,17:2
Noches de Gloria; Glorious Nights
1938,Ap 23,19:3
Padre de Mas de Cuatro; Father of More Than
Four 1939,Ap 24,13:3
Luces de Barriada; Neighborhood Lights
1940,S 2,19:2

Bueno, Salvador (Producer)
Nostradamus 1937,S 6,20:1
Senor Alcalde, El; Mayor, The 1939,My 20,11:2

Buetel, Jack
Outlaw, The 1947,S 12,18:4
Best of the Badmen 1951,Ag 10,13:2
Half Breed, The 1952,Jl 5,7:2

Buetner, H H
Eine Tuer geht Auf 1933,F 6,11:5
Selige Exzellenz, Die 1937,Je 15,26:2

Buferd, Marilyn
Beauties of the Night 1954,Mr 23,23:5
Wayward Wife, The 1955,Ap 11,29:3
Adorable Creatures 1956,Ja 11,36:2

Buffington, Adele (Miscellaneous)
Beauty for the Asking 1939,F 10,19:1

Buffington, Adele (Original Author)
Cheaters 1934,My 12,12:4
Hell Cat, The 1934,Jl 7,16:5
Prison Nurse 1938,Mr 4,17:5

Buffington, Adele (Screenwriter)
Keeper of the Bees, The 1935,Ag 17,18:5
Powdersmoke Range 1936,Mr 9,20:2
Tenth Avenue Kid 1938,S 2,21:3

Buffington, Sam
They Came to Cordura 1959,O 22,47:2

Buffum, Ray (Original Author)
Playgirl 1954,My 15,13:3
Black Dakotas, The 1954,O 2,21:2
So This Is Paris 1955,F 12,11:1

Buffum, Ray (Screenwriter)
Girls in the Night 1953,Ja 16,19:3
Black Dakotas, The 1954,O 2,21:2

Buggs, Donald
Made for Each Other 1939,F 17,17:2

Bugler, Bror
Sun Over Klara 1944,My 1,20:8

Bugler, Bror (Director)
Each Heart Has Its Own Story 1953,Mr 28,15:2

Bugler, Bror (Screenwriter)
Each Heart Has Its Own Story 1953,Mr 28,15:2

Buhary, Joseph
Eb Ura Fako 1940,Mr 23,16:4

BUHLER
See Also BUEHLER

Buhler, Kitty (Screenwriter)
China Doll 1958,D 4,52:1

Buhr, Arturo Garcia
Asi es la Vida; Such Is Life 1940,Ag 6,15:1

Buhr, Gerard
One Step to Eternity 1955,O 3,22:2
Me and the Colonel 1958,Ag 27,33:1
Michael Strogoff 1960,My 21,15:1
Lovers on a Tightrope 1962,O 25,48:3

Buiera, Sam
Rat Race, The 1960,My 26,37:3

Bujold, Genevieve
Guerre est Fini, La; War Is Over, The
1967,F 2,29:2
Adolescents, The (Genevieve); Genevieve (The
Adolescents) 1967,Ap 14,33:1
King of Hearts 1967,Je 20,34:1
Thief of Paris, The 1967,Ag 24,43:2
Isabel 1968,Jl 24,47:1

Buka, Donald
Watch on the Rhine 1943,Ag 28,15:1
Street with no Name, The 1948,Jl 15,26:6
Between Midnight and Dawn 1950,O 2,19:2
Vendetta 1950,D 26,19:1
New Mexico 1951,Jl 14,7:2
Operation Eichmann 1961,My 4,40:7

Bukofzer, Frederick (Producer)
Snow Was Black, The 1956,O 16,36:5

Bukovsky, Anatoly (Director)
Ukrainian Festival 1965,N 1,57:1

Bulatch, T
Dom Zhadnosti 1934,Ag 13,9:6

Bulgakov, Leo
This Land Is Mine 1943,My 28,19:1
For Whom the Bell Tolls 1943,Jl 15,25:2
Song of Russia 1944,F 11,17:2

Bulgakov, Leo (Director)
I'll Love You Always 1935,Mr 30,11:2
Marusia 1938,D 12,26:2

Bulganov, Ivan
Country Doctor, The 1953,F 16,16:2

Buli, Peter
Beau Brummell 1954,O 21,31:5

Bulifant, Joyce
Happiest Millionaire, The 1967,D 1,56:1

Bull, Charles Edward
Iron Horse, The 1924,Ag 29,6:1

Bull, Donald (Screenwriter)
Dear Mr Prohack 1950,Jl 15,7:2

Bull, Peter
As You Like It 1936,N 6,29:3
Dreaming Lips 1937,My 20,17:1
Ware Case, The 1939,Jl 22,12:2
Saraband 1949,Je 13,16:3
Lucky Nick Cain 1951,Ap 23,21:2
Oliver Twist 1951,Jl 31,17:2
Lavender Hill Mob, The 1951,O 16,35:2
Tom Thumb 1958,D 24,00:0
Scapegoat, The 1959,Ag 7,28:1
Three Worlds of Gulliver, The 1960,D 17,19:3
Goodbye Again 1961,Je 30,32:2
Call Me Genius 1961,O 17,47:1
Tom Jones 1963,O 8,48:1
Old Dark House, The 1963,O 31,26:3
Dr Strangelove or: How I Learned to Stop
Worrying and Love the Bomb 1964,Ja 31,16:1
(Incorrect in this edition; use 1964,Ja 30,24:1
elsewhere)
2nd Best Secret Agent in the Whole Wide World,
The 1966,Ap 28,49:1
Doctor Dolittle 1967,D 20,55:1

Bull, Richard
Satan Bug, The 1965,Ap 15,38:1
Hour of the Gun 1967,N 2,58:4
Secret Life of an American Wife, The
1968,Je 26,42:2

Bulla, Elma
Liebling von Wien, Der 1933,Je 10,16:5

Bullman, Gertrude
Mamele; Little Mothers 1938,D 26,29:1

Bulloch, Sally
Pure Hell of St Trinian's, The 1961,S 26,31:1

Bullock, Boris
Forgotten Commandments 1932,Je 2,25:2

Bullock, Harvey (Original Author)
Man Called Flintstone, The 1967,N 25,42:1

Bullock, Harvey (Screenwriter)
Girl Happy 1965,My 27,28:1
Who's Minding the Mint? 1967,D 7,60:3
With Six You Get Egg Roll 1968,O 10,59:6

Bullock, Walter (Composer)
New Faces of 1937 1937,Jl 2,25:1
Happy Landing 1938,Ja 22,19:1
Sally, Irene and Mary 1938,F 26,9:2
Little Miss Broadway 1938,Jl 23,10:4
Just Around the Corner 1938,D 3,11:2
Three Musketeers, The 1939,F 18,12:2
Wife, Husband and Friend 1939,F 25,19:2
Hit Parade of 1941 1940,D 5,33:2

Bullock, Walter (Miscellaneous)
Sing, Baby, Sing 1936,S 12,20:1
Blue Bird, The 1940,Ja 20,11:2

Bullock, Walter (Original Author)
Gay Caballero, The 1940,O 25,25:3

Bullock, Walter (Screenwriter)
Moon Over her Shoulder 1941,N 5,31:2
Springtime in the Rockies 1942,N 12,30:2
Gang's All Here, The 1943,D 23,26:4
Greenwich Village 1944,S 28,26:2
Repeat Performance 1947,Jl 2,19:2
Adventures of Casanova 1948,Mr 22,18:3
Golden Girl 1951,N 21,20:3
O Henry's Full House (The Gift of the Magi); Gift
of the Magi, The (O Henry's Full House)
1952,O 17,33:1
O Henry's Full House (The Clarion Call); Clarion
Call, The (O Henry's Full House)
1952,O 17,33:1
O Henry's Full House (The Last Leaf
1952,O 17,33:1
O Henry's Full House (The Cop and the Anthem);
Cop and the Anthem, The (O Henry's Full
House) 1952,O 17,33:1
Farmer Takes a Wife, The 1953,Je 13,11:2

Bulman, Gertrude
Youth of Russia, The 1934,N 10,19:3
Brivele der Mamen, A; Little Letter to Mother, A
1939,S 15,26:4

Buloff, Joseph
Let's Make Music 1941,Ja 23,19:2
Carnegie Hall 1947,My 3,10:2
To the Victor 1948,Ap 17,11:2
Loves of Carmen, The 1948,S 3,16:2
Kiss in the Dark, A 1949,Mr 26,10:6
Vilna Legend, A (American Cast) 1949,S 26,17:1
Somebody up There Likes Me 1956,Jl 6,16:1
Silk Stockings 1957,Jl 19,11:1

Bulwer-Lytton, Edward (Original Author)
In the Name of Love 1925,Ag 27,14:1

Bulwer-Lytton, Edward Sir (Original Author)
Cardinal Richelieu 1935,Ap 19,24:2

Buma, A M
Nazar Stodolya 1937,Ag 7,7:2

Bumpa, Bob
Ace in the Hole 1951,Je 30,8:6

Bunce, Alan
Last Mile, The 1959,F 19,27:1
Sunrise at Campobello 1960,S 29,32:1

Bunce, Alan (Miscellaneous)
Unknown Soldier Speaks, The 1934,My 26,12:3

Bundy, A Frank (Producer)
Easy Money (Episode 3) 1949,F 14,15:3
Easy Money (Episode 4) 1949,F 14,15:3
Easy Money (Episode 1) 1949,F 14,15:3
Easy Money (Episode 2) 1949,F 14,15:3
Christopher Columbus 1949,O 13,33:2

Bundy, Brooke
Firecreek 1968,F 22,36:2
Young Runaways, The 1968,S 12,54:3

Bunimovich, Theodore (Cinematographer)
August 14; One Day in the USSR
1948,Ag 16,12:2

Bunin, Lou (Producer)
Alice in Wonderland 1951,Jl 27,15:2

Bunin's Puppets
Ziegfeld Follies 1946,Mr 23,8:3

Bunke, Ralph
Scrambled Wives 1921,My 23,16:3

Bunker, Ralph
Hucksters, The 1947,Jl 18,21:2

Bunkley, Billy
Mad Doctor of Market Street, The 1942,Ja 5,21:5

Bunn, Erale D
Last Parade, The 1931,Mr 2,19:1

Bunnage, Avis
Expresso Bongo 1960,Ap 13,44:1
Saturday Night and Sunday Morning
1961,Ap 4,44:2
Loneliness of the Long Distance Runner, The
1962,O 9,44:1
Sparrows Don't Sing 1963,My 7,46:2
L-Shaped Room, The 1963,My 28,32:1
Rotten to the Core 1965,Jl 20,39:2
Whisperers, The 1967,Ag 1,24:1

Bunny, George
Lost World, The 1925,F 9,15:3
Enticement 1925,Mr 21,16:3
Lights of Old Broadway 1925,N 2,20:1
Man and the Moment, The 1929,Ag 5,25:2

Bunny, George— Cont
　Locked Door, The　1930,Ja 20,21:1
Bunston, Henry
　I Like Your Nerve　1931,S 12,15:4
Bunston, Herbert
　Last of Mrs Cheyney, The　1929,Ag 12,22:2
　Lady of Scandal, The　1930,Je 14,9:4
　Dracula　1931,F 13,21:3
　Always Good-Bye　1931,My 23,13:4
　Once a Lady　1931,N 9,22:4
　Charlie Chan's Chance　1932,Ja 23,18:4
　File No 113　1932,F 20,11:2
　Long Lost Father　1934,F 19,18:2
　Dr Monica　1934,Je 21,28:2
　Richest Girl in the World, The　1934,S 21,29:2
　Little Minister, The　1934,D 28,25:1
　Clive of India　1935,Ja 18,29:1
　After Office Hours　1935,Mr 9,19:1
　Cardinal Richelieu　1935,Ap 19,24:2
　Shot in the Dark, A　1935,My 22,23:2
Bunuel, Luis (Director)
　Young and the Damned, The　1952,Mr 25,23:2
　Mexican Bus ride　1954,Jl 21,18:3
　Adventures of Robinson Crusoe, The
　　1954,Ag 6,10:5
　This Strange Passion　1955,D 5,34:2
　Young One, The　1961,Ja 19,26:1
　Viridiana　1962,Mr 20,43:4
　Diary of a Chambermaid; Journal d'une Femme de
　　Chambre, Le　1964,S 22,44:1
　Age d'Or, L'; Golden Age, The　1964,S 22,44:1
　Simon of the Desert　1966,S 21,42:2
　Exterminating Angel, The　1967,Ag 22,33:1
　Belle de Jour　1968,Ap 11,51:1
　Nazarin　1968,Je 21,48:1
Bunuel, Luis (Original Author)
　Exterminating Angel, The　1967,Ag 22,33:1
Bunuel, Luis (Producer)
　Age d'Or, L'; Golden Age, The　1964,S 22,44:1
Bunuel, Luis (Screenwriter)
　Young and the Damned, The　1952,Mr 25,23:2
　Adventures of Robinson Crusoe, The
　　1954,Ag 6,10:5
　This Strange Passion　1955,D 5,34:2
　Young One, The　1961,Ja 19,26:1
　Viridiana　1962,My 20,43:4
　Diary of a Chambermaid; Journal d'une Femme de
　　Chambre, Le　1964,S 22,44:1
　Age d'Or, L'; Golden Age, The　1964,S 22,44:1
　Exterminating Angel, The　1967,Ag 22,33:1
　Belle de Jour　1968,Ap 11,51:1
　Nazarin　1968,Je 21,48:1
Bunzi, Josef
　Holzapfel Weiss Alles　1933,Ja 7,11:3
Buono, Victor
　What Ever Happened to Baby Jane?
　　1962,N 7,48:1
　4 for Texas　1963,D 26,33:3
　Strangler, The　1964,Je 11,27:4
　Robin and the 7 Hoods　1964,Ag 6,20:1
　Greatest Story Ever Told, The　1965,F 16,40:2
　Hush...Hush, Sweet Charlotte　1965,Mr 4,36:1
　Young Dillinger　1965,My 13,32:3
　Silencers, The　1966,Mr 17,35:1
　Who's Minding the Mint?　1967,D 7,60:3
Bupp, Sonny
　Swing Your Lady　1938,Ja 27,17:2
　Three Faces West　1940,Ag 19,13:2
　Father's Son　1941,F 13,25:3
　Citizen Kane　1941,My 2,25:1
Bupp, Tommy
　Girl of the Limberlost, A　1934,N 9,24:6
　It's a Gift　1935,Ja 5,20:2
　Little Men　1935,F 18,19:3
　Pepper　1936,Ag 24,11:2
　Piccadilly Jim　1936,Ag 31,19:1
　Conflict　1937,Ja 18,21:2
　High, Wide and Handsome　1937,Jl 22,15:1
　Love Is on the Air　1937,N 12,27:3
　Swing Your Lady　1938,Ja 27,17:2
　Over the Wall　1938,Mr 28,19:2
　Blind Alibi　1938,My 20,17:2
　Devil's Party, The　1938,My 31,8:3
　Reformatory　1938,Je 27,13:6
　Fisherman's Wharf　1939,F 24,15:2
　Indianapolis Speedway　1939,Jl 15,8:2
　Naval Academy　1941,Je 5,27:3
Buquet, Jean
　Three Waltzes　1939,Ap 25,19:2
　Portrait of Innocence　1948,Je 9,35:2
Buranelli, Prosper (Narrator)
　Search for Paradise　1957,S 25,25:2
Buranelli, Prosper (Screenwriter)
　Seven Wonders of the World　1956,Ap 11,29:1
　Search for Paradise　1957,S 25,25:2
Burani, Michelette
　Aloma of the South Seas　1926,My 17,19:1
　Enter Madame　1935,Ja 12,12:1
　Gilded Lily, The　1935,F 9,11:2
　Give Us This Night　1936,Ap 6,18:1
　Everybody Sing　1938,Mr 11,15:3
　Fools for Scandal　1938,Mr 25,15:3

Burbridge, Ben (Producer)
　Gorilla Hunt, The　1926,D 14,25:3
Burbridge, Betty (Original Author)
　Utah　1945,Mr 12,22:7
Burbridge, Betty (Screenwriter)
　Redhead　1934,N 16,27:1
　Under Western Stars　1938,Je 25,7:3
　Santa Fe Stampede　1939,Ap 26,27:3
BURCH
　See Also BIRCH
Burch, John
　Great Expectations　1947,My 23,31:1
Burchardt, Elsa
　Eva and the Grasshopper　1928,N 19,16:7
Burchett, Kevin
　Boy, Did I Get a Wrong Number!　1966,Je 9,54:2
　Yours, Mine and Ours　1968,Ap 25,53:1
BURD
　See BYRD, BIRD
Burden, Hugh
　One of our Aircraft Is Missing　1942,N 2,17:2
　Way Ahead, The　1945,Je 4,22:3
　Sleeping Car to Trieste　1949,Ap 18,18:6
　Fame Is the Spur　1949,N 8,34:2
　Malta Story　1954,Jl 17,7:2
　No Love for Johnnie　1961,D 13,55:1
　Funeral in Berlin　1966,D 23,17:1
Burden, William Douglas (Producer)
　Silent Enemy, The　1930,My 20,32:3
Burdette, Elsa
　Street of Sin, The　1928,My 28,23:2
Burdette, Jack
Burdette, Trevor
　Westerner, The　1940,O 25,25:2
Burdick, Eugene (Original Author)
　Ugly American, The　1963,Ap 12,30:2
　Fail Safe　1964,S 16,36:1
Burdick, Hal (Original Author)
　Night Editor　1946,Mr 30,11:2
Burdick, Rose
　Butterflies in the Rain　1926,D 25,10:5
　Kiss in a Taxi, A　1927,Mr 15,29:2
Burdon, Albert
　It's a Boy　1934,Je 8,18:2
Burenkov, Eugenie
　Miles of Fire　1958,N 10,36:6 (In Addenda)
　Sun Shines for All　1961,Jl 10,25:3
　Apartment in Moscow　1962,My 28,25:5
Burfield, Joan
　No More Ladies　1935,Je 22,18:5
Burford, John
　Gallant Bess　1946,D 6,27:6
Burford, Roger (Miscellaneous)
　Dance Band　1936,Ja 4,19:2
　April Romance　1937,Ja 27,17:4
Burford, Roger (Screenwriter)
　Dance Band　1936,Ja 4,19:2
　Abdul the Damned　1936,My 11,16:2
　Red Wagon　1936,Je 22,22:1
　April Romance　1937,Ja 27,17:4
　Dr Syn　1937,N 15,15:1
　Three on a Week-End　1938,Je 2,19:3
　Clown Must Laugh, A　1938,O 12,35:2
　Molly and Me　1945,My 26,18:2
BURG
　See Also BERG, BERGE, BERGH
Burg, Eugen
　Wrath of the Seas, The　1929,Ag 19,22:1
Burge, Stuart
　Malta Story　1954,Jl 17,7:2
Burge, Stuart (Director)
　Othello　1966,F 2,24:1
　Mikado, The　1967,Mr 15,53:1
BURGER
　See Also BERGER, BERGERE
Burger, Hans (Director)
　Seeds of Freedom　1943,Ag 25,17:2
Burger, Hans (Miscellaneous)
　Crisis　1939,Mr 13,12:2
Burger, Paul (Original Author)
　Fifteen Maiden Lane　1936,O 17,21:3
　Charlie Chan at the Olympics　1937,My 24,23:1
Burger, Paul (Screenwriter)
　Little Miss Nobody　1936,Je 6,21:1
Burgess, Alan (Original Author)
　Inn of the Sixth Happiness, The　1958,D 14,2:7
Burgess, Betty
　Coronado　1935,D 19,33:4
Burgess, Dorothy
　In old Arizona　1929,Ja 21,18:4
　Pleasure Crazed　1929,Jl 15,25:1
　Swing High　1930,Je 27,26:3
　Recaptured Love　1930,Ag 9,16:5
　Taxi　1932,Ja 8,27:3
　Play Girl　1932,Mr 19,11:2
　Stoker, The　1932,Jl 16,5:5
　Ladies They Talk About　1933,F 25,20:4
　What Price Decency?　1933,Mr 2,20:6
　Strictly Personal　1933,Mr 20,18:2
　Hold Your Man　1933,Jl 1,16:6
　It's Great to be Alive　1933,Jl 8,14:6
　I Love That Man　1933,Jl 10,11:7
　From Headquarters　1933,N 17,22:4

Burgess, Dorothy— Cont
　Miss Fane's Baby is Stolen　1934,Ja 20,12:2
　Fashions of 1934　1934,Ja 20,12:2
　Orient Express　1934,F 28,23:2
　Modern Hero, A　1934,Ap 20,17:1
　Affairs of a Gentleman　1934,Je 23,16:7
　Black Moon　1934,Je 28,26:2
　Circus Clown, The　1934,Je 30,18:6
　Hat, Coat and Glove　1934,Jl 27,21:2
　Friends of Mr Sweeney　1934,Jl 31,20:4
　Gambling　1934,D 4,22:3
　I Want a Divorce　1940,O 3,31:2
　Lady for a Night　1942,F 12,27:2
Burgess, Gelett (Original Author)
　Countess Charming　1917,S 17,11:3
　Cave Man, The　1926,Mr 1,17:1
　Two in the Dark　1936,F 1,9:2
Burgess, Grover
　Naked City, The　1948,Mr 5,17:2
Burgess, Harry
　Murder by the Clock　1931,Jl 18,16:6
Burgess, Helen
　Plainsman, The　1937,Ja 14,16:2
　Doctor's Diary, A　1937,F 17,16:4
　King of Gamblers　1937,Jl 3,18:1
Burgess, Maynard
　Forest Ring, The　1930,Ap 26,11:1
Burghardt, George
　Richthofen: The Red Knight of the Air
　　1929,S 2,16:1
Burghart, Sheila
　Guide, The　1965,F 10,44:2
BURGHER
　See BERGER, BERGERE, BURGER
Burgmer, Elly
　Razzia　1948,Je 14,19:2
　Marriage in the Shadows　1948,S 17,28:3
Burgoyne, Ollie
　Laughter　1930,N 15,15:3
Burh, A Garcia
　Dancing, El　1935,Ja 28,10:6
Burian, E F (Composer)
　Journey to the Beginning of Time　1967,F 11,20:1
Burian, Vlasta
　Versuchen Sie Meine Schwester　1931,Je 20,20:4
　Der Falsche Feldmarschall　1932,Je 30,26:2
　Adjutant Seiner Hoheit, Der　1934,O 22,12:3
　Inspector General, The　1937,N 25,37:1
Buris, Helen
　One Woman's Story　1949,My 18,33:2
Burke, Albert
　Surrender　1931,N 28,20:4
Burke, Alfred
　Touch and go　1956,Mr 20,13:2
　Man Upstairs, The　1959,Ag 11,23:2
　Angry Silence, The　1960,D 13,25:2
　Children of the Damned　1964,Ja 30,24:2
　Nanny, The　1965,N 4,57:2
Burke, Billie
　Gloria's Romance　1916,My 23,9:2
　Peggy　1916,Je 17,20:1
　Let's Get a Divorce　1918,Ap 29,11:1
　In Pursuit of Polly　1918,S 2,7:1
　Make-Believe Wife, The　1918,N 18,13:3
　Good Gracious, Annabelle　1919,Mr 31,11:3
　Misleading Widow, The　1919,S 1,5:6
　Bill of Divorcement, A　1932,O 3,15:2
　Christopher Strong　1933,Mr 10,19:2
　Dinner at Eight　1933,Ag 24,18:1
　Only Yesterday　1933,N 10,25:1
　Finishing School　1934,Ap 30,11:4
　Where Sinners Meet　1934,My 25,25:2
　We're Rich Again　1934,S 1,16:3
　Forsaking all Others　1934,D 21,18:1
　Society Doctor　1935,F 4,11:3
　After Office Hours　1935,Mr 9,19:1
　Becky Sharp　1935,Je 14,27:2
　Doubting Thomas　1935,Jl 11,24:2
　Feather in her Hat, A　1935,O 25,24:5
　She Couldn't Take It　1935,N 7,27:1
　Splendor　1935,N 23,23:2
　My American Wife　1936,Ag 21,12:3
　Piccadilly Jim　1936,Ag 31,19:1
　Craig's Wife　1936,O 2,29:3
　Parnell　1937,Je 4,27:2
　Topper　1937,Ag 20,21:2
　Bride Wore Red, The　1937,O 15,18:4
　Navy Blue and Gold　1937,D 24,21:2
　Everybody Sing　1938,Mr 11,15:3
　Merrily We Live　1938,Mr 18,23:3
　Young in Heart, The　1938,N 4,27:2
　Topper Takes a Trip　1938,D 30,11:2
　Zenobia　1939,My 15,15:2
　Bridal Suite　1939,My 26,20:2
　Wizard of Oz, The　1939,Ag 18,16:2
　Eternally Yours　1939,O 7,11:2
　Remember?　1939,D 15,33:4
　And One Was Beautiful　1940,Ap 11,32:4
　Irene　1940,My 24,23:3
　Dulcy　1940,N 28,28:2
　Hullabaloo　1940,D 19,33:1
　Topper Returns　1941,Mr 28,26:6
　One Night in Lisbon　1941,Je 12,29:3
　Man Who Came to Dinner, The　1942,Ja 2,25:2

Burke, Billie— Cont

What's Cookin' 1942,F 26,15:5
In This our Life 1942,My 9,10:2
They all Kissed the Bride 1942,Jl 31,11:1
Girl Trouble 1942,O 8,31:2
Hi Diddle Diddle 1943,S 24,26:2
Cheaters, The 1945,Jl 21,7:2
Breakfast in Hollywood 1946,Jl 15,21:1
Bachelor's Daughters, The 1946,O 7,23:2
Barkleys of Broadway, The 1949,My 5,34:2
And Baby Makes Three 1949,D 23,17:3
Father of the Bride 1950,My 19,31:2
Three Husbands 1951,Mr 9,30:2
Father's Little Dividend 1951,Ap 13,18:5
Small Town Girl 1953,My 7,37:2
Young Philadelphians, The 1959,My 22,32:1
Sergeant Rutledge 1960,My 26,37:1
Pepe 1960,D 22,18:1

Burke, Brian
Lady in the Morgue, The 1938,My 9,13:3

Burke, Edwin (Director)
Now I'll Tell 1934,My 26,12:2

Burke, Edwin (Miscellaneous)
Mr Lemon of Orange 1931,Mr 28,15:3

Burke, Edwin (Original Author)
Woman Trap 1929,Ag 31,13:4
Girl from Havana, The 1929,S 2,16:1
Happy Days 1930,F 14,20:1
Bright Eyes 1934,D 21,31:1
This Thing Called Love 1941,F 14,15:2

Burke, Edwin (Screenwriter)
One More Spring 1935,F 22,27:1
Farmer Takes a Wife, The 1935,Ag 9,21:2
Littlest Rebel, The 1935,D 20,30:1

Burke, Frankie
Outside the Law 1930,S 1,16:1
Angels With Dirty Faces 1938,N 26,18:1
Women in the Wind 1939,Ap 13,27:2
Hell's Kitchen 1939,Jl 3,10:5
Prison Camp 1940,Ag 3,9:3
Ghost Creeps, The 1940,Ag 19,13:3
Quarterback, The 1940,O 17,33:3

Burke, Georgia
Anna Lucasta 1959,Ja 15,27:1
Cool World, The 1964,Ap 21,42:1

Burke, James
Lady's Profession, A 1933,Mr 25,13:3
Girl in 419 1933,My 20,11:5
Six of a Kind 1934,Mr 10,18:3
Wharf Angel 1934,Ap 21,12:1
Little Miss Marker 1934,My 19,18:3
Lady by Choice 1934,N 17,12:1
It's a Gift 1935,Ja 5,20:2
Ruggles of Red Gap 1935,Mr 7,26:1
Broadway Gondolier 1935,Jl 18,15:2
Call of the Wild 1935,Ag 15,15:2
Here Comes Cookie 1935,O 12,12:2
Make a Million 1935,N 9,19:3
Case of the Missing Man, The 1935,N 23,23:2
So Red the Rose 1935,N 28,39:1
Coronado 1935,D 19,33:4
Song and Dance Man 1936,Mr 12,18:2
Leathernecks Have Landed, The 1936,Mr 23,22:5
Dancing Feet 1936,Mr 28,11:2
Forgotten Faces 1936,Jl 4,18:2
Rhythm on the Range 1936,Jl 30,22:1
36 Hours to Live 1936,Ag 15,6:3
Old Hutch 1936,D 7,27:4
Great Guy 1937,Ja 1,19:2
Champagne Waltz 1937,F 4,17:2
High, Wide and Handsome 1937,Jl 22,15:1
Dead End 1937,Ag 25,25:1
Perfect Specimen, The 1937,O 28,29:2
Flight Into Nowhere 1938,My 2,13:3
Joy of Living 1938,My 6,27:1
Affairs of Annabel, The 1938,O 13,29:2
Mad Miss Manton, The 1938,O 21,27:2
Men With Wings 1938,O 27,27:2
Dawn Patrol 1938,D 24,12:1
Saint Strikes Back, The 1939,Mr 9,18:2
I'm From Missouri 1939,Mr 23,27:1
Within the Law 1939,Ap 6,31:2
On Borrowed Time 1939,Jl 7,13:2
Beau Geste 1939,Ag 3,15:2
Fast And Furious 1939,O 12,33:3
At the Circus 1939,N 17,17:2
Cisco Kid and the Lady, The 1939,D 25,29:2
Double Alibi 1940,Mr 11,11:2
Saint Takes Over, The 1940,My 28,29:3
No Time for Comedy 1940,S 7,9:2
Golden Fleecing, The 1940,N 7,33:4
Ellery Queen, Master Detective 1940,D 19,33:1
Ellery Queen's Penthouse Mystery 1941,Mr 7,17:2
Pot o'Gold 1941,Ap 4,25:2
Reaching for the Sun 1941,My 8,21:1
Million Dollar Baby 1941,Je 7,20:2
Ellery Queen and the Perfect Crime 1941,Ag 11,17:3
Maltese Falcon, The 1941,O 4,18:2
Ellery Queen and the Murder Ring 1941,O 21,29:4
All Through the Night 1942,Ja 24,13:2
It Happened in Flatbush 1942,Jl 3,12:8

Enemy Agents meet Ellery Queen 1942,Ag 22,16:2
Army Surgeon 1942,N 5,35:2
Night to Remember, A 1943,Ja 1,27:2
Horn Blows at Midnight, The 1945,Ap 21,18:2
Shady Lady 1945,O 11,26:2
Two Years Before the Mast 1946,S 25,39:2
California 1947,Ja 15,31:2
Easy Come, Easy Go 1947,F 6,29:2
Blaze of Noon 1947,Mr 5,31:2
Down to Earth 1947,S 12,18:2
Nightmare Alley 1947,O 10,31:3
Body and Soul 1947,N 10,21:2
June Bride 1948,O 30,10:2
Copper Canyon 1950,N 16,39:2
Raton Pass 1951,Ap 20,25:1
Lone Star 1952,F 2,11:4
Lucky Me 1954,Ap 10,11:2

Burke, Joe
His Children's Children 1923,N 5,15:1
West of the Water Tower 1923,D 31,9:3
Pied Piper Malone 1924,Ja 28,12:1
Too Many Kisses 1925,Mr 3,20:1
Fascinating Youth 1926,My 10,19:1
Hangman's House 1928,My 14,25:1

Burke, Johnny
Good-Bye Kiss, The 1928,N 12,18:2
Little Men 1940,D 9,23:2

Burke, Johnny (Composer)
Double or Nothing 1937,S 2,17:3
Doctor Rhythm 1938,My 19,25:2
Sing You Sinners 1938,Ag 18,23:1
East Side of Heaven 1939,My 5,29:3
Road to Singapore 1940,Mr 14,29:2
Love Thy Neighbor 1940,D 18,32:5
Road to Zanzibar 1941,Ap 10,29:2
Playmates 1941,D 26,21:3
My Favorite Spy 1942,My 29,13:4
Road to Morocco 1942,N 12,30:1
Dixie 1943,Je 24,26:2
Lady in the Dark 1944,F 23,17:1
Going my Way 1944,My 3,25:2
And the Angels Sing 1944,Jl 13,14:2
Belle of the Yukon 1945,Mr 30,18:4
Duffy's Tavern 1945,S 6,23:3
Road to Utopia 1946,F 28,20:2
Road to Rio 1948,F 19,29:3
Vagabond King, The 1956,S 13,39:6

Burke, Johnny (Miscellaneous)
Pennies From Heaven 1936,D 10,35:2
If I Had my Way 1940,My 6,13:2

Burke, Kathleen
Island of Lost Souls 1933,Ja 13,19:2
Murders in the Zoo 1933,Ap 3,13:4
Mad Game, The 1933,N 13,21:1
Good Dame 1934,Mr 17,11:4
Bulldog Drummond Strikes Back 1934,Ag 16,20:2
Lives of a Bengal Lancer, The 1935,Ja 12,12:2
Last Outpost, The 1935,O 5,18:2
Craig's Wife 1936,O 2,29:3
Boy of the Streets 1938,Ja 24,17:1
Rascals 1938,My 27,12:2

Burke, Marcella (Original Author)
Mad About Music 1938,Mr 12,13:2
Toy Tiger 1956,Je 30,11:2

Burke, Marie
Little Miss Rebellion 1920,S 20,13:1
Heart Raider, The 1923,Je 6,24:5
Little Old New York 1923,Ag 2,10:3
Three Miles Out 1924,Ja 1,20:1
After the Ball 1933,Mr 20,18:3
Madness of the Heart 1950,O 12,43:2
Odette 1951,Mr 28,33:2
Constant Husband, The 1957,Jl 26,10:3
Snorkel, The 1958,S 18,37:2
Rattle of a Simple Man 1964,D 21,42:2

Burke, Orrin
Here's to Romance 1935,O 3,29:2
Show Them no Mercy 1935,D 9,25:2
Nobody's Baby 1937,My 20,17:3

Burke, Patricia
Lisbon Story, The 1951,S 6,39:4
Day the Fish Came Out, The 1967,O 3,57:1

Burke, Paul
South Sea Woman 1953,Je 4,33:6
Valley of the Dolls 1967,D 16,51:1
Thomas Crown Affair, The 1968,Je 27,48:2

Burke, Richard (Original Author)
Dressed to Kill 1941,Ag 22,19:3

Burke, Robert Easton
Red Badge of Courage, The 1951,O 19,22:2

Burke, Samson
Three Stooges Meet Hercules, The 1962,Ja 27,13:4

Burke, Sonny (Composer)
Lady and the Tramp 1955,Je 24,17:1

Burke, Thomas (Original Author)
Broken Blossoms 1919,My 14,15:5
Twinkletoes 1926,D 27,20:3
Broken Blossoms 1937,Ja 14,16:3

Burke, Tom
Kathleen 1938,Ja 24,17:1
Father O'Flynn 1938,D 26,29:2

Burke, Walter
All the King's Men 1949,N 9,37:2
Mystery Street 1950,Jl 28,12:5
M 1951,Je 11,20:7
Guy Who Came Back, The 1951,Ag 17,13:2
Wreck of the Mary Deare, The 1959,N 7,27:1
Let no Man Write my Epitaph 1960,N 11,36:2
Jack the Giant Killer 1962,Jl 26,17:1
President's Analyst, The 1967,D 22,44:4

Burke, William
Nous, La Liberte, A 1932,My 18,25:2

Burkett, James S (Producer)
16 Fathoms Deep 1948,O 7,35:2

Burkhanov, Shukur
Sword and the Dragon, The 1960,N 17,46:3

Burkhart, Harry
Are We Civilized? 1934,Je 14,28:5

Burkhart, Monte
Flaming Star 1960,D 17,19:1

Burlaiev, Kolya
My Name Is Ivan (Ivan's Childhood) 1963,Je 28,25:4

Burlo, Josephine
Cossacks, The 1928,Je 25,27:1

Burls, Helen
Quiet Week-End 1948,Ag 20,13:2

BURMAN
See Also BERMAN

Burman, Ann (Producer)
Flamboyant Sex, The 1963,Ag 13,25:1

Burman, Ben Lucien (Original Author)
Heaven on Earth 1931,D 19,16:4
Mississippi 1931,D 27,VIII,5:4 (In Addenda)
Steamboat Around the Bend 1935,S 20,17:2

Burman, Ian
Mister Moses 1965,My 13,32:1

BURN
See Also BYRNE, BERNE

Burn, Jonathan
Persecution and Assassination of Jean-Paul Marat as Performed by the Inmates of the Asylum of Charenton Under the Direction of the Marquis De Sade, The 1967,F 23,41:1

Burnaby, Anne (Screenwriter)
Landfall 1953,My 11,25:2
Weak and the Wicked, The 1954,Ag 21,10:3
Yellow Balloon, The 1954,O 13,28:2

Burnbay, Davy
Are You a Mason? 1934,O 30,23:5

Burne, Bob
Tropic Holiday 1938,Je 30,21:2

Burne, Nancy
Norah O'Neale 1934,O 25,26:3

Burne, Robert
Heaven on Earth 1931,D 19,16:4

Burnell, Janet
Troopship 1938,Ap 26,18:2
Henry V 1946,Je 18,30:2

Burness, William
Little Colonel, The 1935,Mr 22,26:2

Burnet, Dana (Original Author)
Mr Billings Spends his Dime 1923,Mr 5,15:3
Wandering Daughters 1923,Jl 2,16:2
Marriage Clause, The 1926,S 28,30:2
Four Walls 1928,Ag 20,21:3
Shopworn Angel, The 1929,Ja 1,60:1
High Society Blues 1930,Ap 19,15:1
Stolen Heaven 1931,F 14,11:4
Straight Is the Way 1934,Ag 29,13:2
Follow Your Heart 1936,O 22,31:1
Shopworn Angel, The 1938,Jl 8,11:2

Burnet, Dana (Screenwriter)
Great Commandment, The 1942,O 17,11:1

Burnett, Carol
Who's Been Sleeping in My Bed? 1963,D 26,33:2

Burnett, Don
Tea and Sympathy 1956,S 28,24:4
Untamed Youth 1957,My 11,24:6
Damon and Pythias 1962,S 6,37:2

Burnett, Frances Hodgson (Original Author)
Little Lord Fauntleroy 1914,Je 23,11:3
Louisiana 1919,Jl 21,12:3
Little Lord Fauntleroy 1921,S 16,17:3
Little Lord Fauntleroy 1936,Ap 3,27:1
Little Princess, The 1939,Mr 11,21:1

Burnett, Louise
Pan-Americana 1945,Mr 23,13:2

Burnett, Mrs (Original Author)
Little Princess, The 1917,N 12,11:3

Burnett, Murray (Original Author)
Casablanca 1942,N 27,27:1

Burnett, W R (Miscellaneous)
Action in the North Atlantic 1943,My 22,10:2

Burnett, W R (Original Author)
Little Casear 1931,Ja 10,19:2
Iron Man 1931,Ap 18,17:3
Beast of the City, The 1932,Mr 14,13:3
Dark Hazard 1934,F 23,23:3
Whole Town's Talking, The 1935,Mr 1,16:2
Dr Socrates 1935,O 3,29:2
36 Hours to Live 1936,Ag 15,6:3
King of the Underworld 1939,Ja 7,6:2

Burnett, W R (Original Author)— Cont
Dark Command 1940,My 11,15:2
High Sierra 1941,Ja 25,11:2
Dance Hall 1941,Jl 19,16:2
Crash Dive 1943,Ap 29,25:2
Yellow Sky 1949,F 2,36:1
Asphalt Jungle, The 1950,Je 9,29:3
Arrowhead 1953,S 16,38:6
Badlanders, The 1958,S 4,33:1
Burnett, W R (Screenwriter)
Finger Points, The 1931,Mr 28,15:3
Some Blondes Are Dangerous 1937,N 3,29:3
High Sierra 1941,Ja 25,11:2
Get-Away, The 1941,Jl 17,23:4
This Gun for Hire 1942,My 14,23:2
Wake Island 1942,S 2,19:2
Background to Danger 1943,Jl 3,11:2
San Antonio 1945,D 29,19:5
Nobody Lives Forever 1946,N 2,12:2
Belle Star's Daughter 1949,Ja 10,19:2
Vendetta 1950,D 26,19:1
Racket, The 1951,D 13,44:2
Illegal 1955,O 29,12:6
I Died a Thousand Times 1955,N 10,45:2
September Storm 1960,O 29,26:7
Sergeants 3 1962,F 12,28:2
Great Escape, The 1963,Ag 8,19:1
Burnett, William R (Original Author)
Law and Order 1932,F 29,21:3
Iron Man 1951,Ag 20,14:2
Burnette, Smiley
Border Patrolman 1936,Je 29,11:2
Boots and Saddles 1937,N 8,19:2
Manhattan Merry-Go-Round 1937,D 31,9:3
Stadium Murders, The 1938,Ap 9,11:2
Under Western Stars 1938,Je 25,7:3
Burney, Myno
Four Bags Full 1957,S 5,32:1
Burnford, Paul (Miscellaneous)
Time in the Sun 1940,O 1,29:2
Burnford, Sheila (Original Author)
Incredible Journey, The 1963,N 21,43:2
Burnham, Beatrice
Riders of the Purple Sage 1925,Ap 15,16:1
Siege 1925,Je 16,24:1
Burnham, Edward
To Sir, With Love 1967,Je 15,56:1
Burnham, Jeremy
Bonjour Tristesse 1958,Ja 16,32:1
Law and Disorder 1958,Ag 6,20:1
I Could go on Singing 1963,My 16,42:1
Burnham, Nicholas
Uncle Sam of Freedom Ridge 1920,S 27,15:2
Burnham, Terry
Imitation of Life 1959,Ap 18,18:1
Boy, Did I Get a Wrong Number! 1966,Je 9,54:2
Burnhett, Mr
Sign of the Four, The 1932,Ag 20,7:4
Burnier, Robert
Miche 1932,D 2,27:4
Chasseur de Chez Maxim's, Le 1935,F 4,11:4
Criez-Le sur les Toits; Shout it From the
Housetops 1935,Je 22,18:5
Belle Americaine, La 1961,D 18,42:1
Landru 1963,Ap 10,31:1
BURNS
See Also BRYNES, BERNS
Burns, Bart
Fear Strikes Out 1957,Mr 21,37:2
Seven Days in May 1964,F 20,22:1
Burns, Bernard K (Original Author)
Woman on the Jury, The 1924,My 19,14:2
Burns, Bob
Rhythm on the Range 1936,Jl 30,22:1
Big Broadcast of 1937, The 1936,O 22,31:1
Waikiki Wedding 1937,Mr 25,29:1
Mountain Music 1937,Je 24,30:3
Wells Fargo 1937,D 30,15:2
Wells Fargo 1938,Ja 16,X,5:1 (In Addenda)
Radio City Revels 1938,Mr 21,18:3
Arkansas Traveler, The 1938,N 17,29:2
I'm From Missouri 1939,Mr 23,27:1
Our Leading Citizen 1939,Ag 24,17:1
Alias the Deacon 1940,My 14,27:5
Comin' Round the Mountain 1940,S 26,27:3
Belle of the Yukon 1945,Mr 30,18:4
Burns, Bobby
William Fox Movietone Follies of 1929
1929,My 27,22:1
Cock Eyed World, The 1929,Ag 5,25:2
Burns, David
Strangers on a Honeymoon 1937,Mr 13,23:2
Crime Over London 1938,Jl 28,23:2
Saint in London, The 1939,Jl 19,23:3
Sidewalks of London 1940,F 15,15:1
Larceny Street 1941,Ja 6,11:2
Girl Must Live, A 1942,Mr 24,25:2
Knock on Wood 1954,Ap 15,34:2
Deep in my Heart 1954,D 10,35:2
It's Always Fair Weather 1955,S 16,19:1
Let's Make Love 1960,S 9,36:1
Tiger Makes Out, The 1967,S 19,53:1

Burns, Eddie
Dramatic Life of Abraham Lincoln, The
1924,Ja 22,17:3
Burns, Edmund
Manicure Girl, The 1925,Je 15,10:1
Hell's Highroad 1925,Ag 26,14:2
Simon the Jester 1925,N 19,22:1
Chinese Parrot, The 1928,Ja 2,28:1
She Goes to War 1929,Je 10,23:1
Hard to Get 1929,S 28,17:3
Tanned Legs 1929,D 2,28:2
Western Limited 1932,D 12,18:4
Death Kiss, The 1933,F 5,IX,5:3
Dangerously Yours 1933,F 23,20:3
Burns, Edward
To Please one Woman 1920,D 20,11:2
Ruling Passion, The 1922,Ja 23,11:4
Scars of Jealousy 1923,My 7,19:3
Country Kid, The 1923,O 30,16:1
Humming Bird, The 1924,Ja 14,2:1
Broadway After Dark 1924,My 20,15:2
Guilty One, The 1924,Je 17,22:4
Burns, Fred
Rio Rita 1929,O 7,22:1
Parade of the West 1930,Mr 3,18:4
Trail of the Lonesome Pine, The 1936,F 20,23:5
Burns, George
International House 1933,My 27,11:5
College Humor 1933,Je 23,15:4
Six of a Kind 1934,Mr 10,18:3
We're not Dressing 1934,Ap 26,27:2
Many Happy Returns 1934,Je 9,18:2
Love in Bloom 1935,Ap 20,16:2
Big Broadcast of 1936, The 1935,S 16,15:2
Here Comes Cookie 1935,O 12,12:2
Big Broadcast of 1937, The 1936,O 22,31:1
College Holiday 1936,D 24,21:2
Damsel in Distress, A 1937,N 25,37:1
College Swing 1938,Ap 28,27:2
Honolulu 1939,F 23,19:2
Burns, George (Composer)
Sleeping Beauty 1959,F 18,36:1
Burns, Harry
Love in the Rough 1930,S 27,21:3
Hot Money 1936,Jl 25,16:2
Kid Nightingale 1939,D 8,33:6
Lady Scarface 1941,Ag 4,16:6
Tortilla Flat 1942,My 22,27:1
Burns, Harry A Commander USN (Original Author)
Men of the Fighting Lady 1954,My 8,15:2
Burns, Jack
Night They Raided Minsky's, The
1968,D 23,43:1
Burns, Larry
Count Five and Die 1958,My 15,25:1
Burns, Marion
Me and my Gal 1932,D 12,18:4
Devil Tiger 1934,F 9,23:2
Born to be Bad 1934,My 31,22:6
Burns, Michael
Mr Hobbs Takes a Vacation 1962,Je 16,11:2
Burns, Neal
Mary's Ankle 1920,Mr 1,16:2
Sob Sister 1931,O 3,20:2
Burns, Paul
Return of the Cisco Kid, The 1939,Ap 29,13:2
Rose of Washington Square 1939,My 6,21:2
Chad Hanna 1940,D 26,23:1
Belle Starr 1941,N 1,20:2
Swamp Water 1941,N 17,15:2
Meanest Man in the World, The 1943,F 25,27:3
Relentless 1948,Mr 6,17:3
Hollow Triumph 1948,O 29,29:5
Burns, Paul E
Hell Harbor 1930,Mr 28,22:6
Jesse James 1939,Ja 14,13:1
Seventeen 1940,F 29,15:2
Mummy's Tomb, The 1942,O 26,19:2
Dragon Seed 1944,Jl 21,16:4
Barbary Coast Gent 1944,S 29,18:2
Night Editor 1946,Mr 30,11:2
Framed 1947,My 26,24:2
Johnny Allegro 1949,My 31,19:2
Look for the Silver Lining 1949,Je 24,29:2
Lust for Gold 1949,Jl 4,9:2
Arctic Manhunt 1949,Ag 19,12:5
Woman on Pier 13, The 1950,Je 16,28:4
Frenchie 1951,F 12,19:2
Storm Warning 1951,Mr 3,8:2
Son of Paleface 1952,O 2,32:3
Burns, Robert
Quick Millions 1931,Ap 18,17:3
Fast Workers 1933,Mr 20,18:2
Burns, Robert E (Original Author)
I Am a Fugitive From a Chain Gang
1932,N 11,17:2
Burns, Ronnie
Bernardine 1957,Jl 25,28:1
Burns, Tito
Don't Look Back 1967,S 7,50:2
Burns, Tommy
Rugged O'Riordans, The 1950,Ja 6,25:2
Legendary Champions, The 1968,O 29,54:1

Burns, Walter Noble (Original Author)
Billy the Kid 1930,O 18,23:2
Robin Hood of El Dorado, The 1936,Mr 14,10:1
Billy the Kid 1941,Je 20,28:2
Burnsby, Anne (Screenwriter)
Young Wives' Tale 1952,N 4,33:1
Burnside, Henrietta
Ladies Should Listen 1934,Jl 28,16:6
Burnside, Norman (Original Author)
Dr Ehrlich's Magic Bullet 1940,F 24,9:2
Burnside, Norman (Screenwriter)
Dr Ehrlich's Magic Bullet 1940,F 24,9:2
Burnside, R H (Director)
Manhattan 1924,O 29,18:1
Burnside, R H (Miscellaneous)
Smiling Faces 1932,Ag 31,12:3
BURNSTINE
See Also BERNSTEIN
Burnstine, Norman (Screenwriter)
Sins of the Fathers 1929,Ja 28,21:1
Arson Racket Squad 1938,Je 18,18:2
Burr, Ann
Night Unto Night 1949,Je 11,11:2
Follow the Sun 1951,Ap 26,34:4
Burr, Jane (Original Author)
Arnelo Affair, The 1947,S 13,8:5
Burr, Raymond
San Quentin 1947,F 10,24:3
Sleep, My Love 1948,F 19,29:4
Raw Deal 1948,Jl 9,11:4
Pitfall 1948,Ag 25,31:2
Ruthless 1948,S 4,8:7
Walk a Crooked Mile 1948,O 13,31:2
Adventures of Don Juan 1948,D 25,10:1
Bride of Vengeance 1949,Ap 7,38:2
Abandoned Woman 1949,O 27,35:3
Black Magic 1949,N 9,37:2
Red Light 1950,Ja 16,18:4
Key to the City 1950,F 2,31:2
Borderline 1950,Mr 6,17:2
Love Happy 1950,Ap 8,9:4
M 1951,Je 11,20:7
Place in the Sun, A 1951,Ag 29,20:1
Meet Danny Wilson 1952,Mr 27,34:4
Mara Maru 1952,Ap 24,38:1
Horizons West 1952,N 22,16:5
Blue Gardenia, The 1953,Ap 28,31:1
Casanova's Big Night 1954,Ap 19,19:1
Gorilla at Large 1954,Je 12,13:2
Rear Window 1954,Ag 5,18:2
Khyber Patrol 1954,S 20,19:2
Passion 1954,D 11,11:1
You're Never too Young 1955,Ag 26,10:2
Godzilla, King of the Monsters 1956,Ap 28,11:1
Great Day in the Morning 1956,My 19,12:6
Cry in the Night, A 1956,S 1,19:4
Crime of Passion 1957,Ja 10,25:1
Desire in the Dust 1960,O 12,47:2
P J 1968,Mr 7,52:3
Burrell, George
Sea Hunt, The 1926,Ja 16,8:5
Sea Beast, The 1926,Ja 16,8:5
Burrell, Sheila
Paranoiac 1963,My 23,31:2
Burress, Jimmy
Green Pastures, The 1936,Jl 17,20:1
Burress, William
Heartsease 1919,Ag 25,8:5
Lord and Lady Algy 1919,S 29,16:1
Paid in Advance 1919,D 1,9:3
Local Boy Makes Good 1931,N 27,29:3
Blonde Crazy 1931,D 4,28:2
Strange Love of Molly Louvain, The
1932,My 9,19:5
Love Is a Racket 1932,Je 11,9:3
You Said a Mouthful 1932,N 18,23:2
They Just Had to Get Married 1933,F 13,11:4
World Changes, The 1933,O 27,22:3
Broadway Thru a Keyhole 1933,N 2,18:3
Fashions of 1934 1934,Ja 20,12:2
Babes in Toyland 1934,D 13,28:2
Grand Old Girl 1935,F 26,16:4
Dr Socrates 1935,O 3,29:2
Burri, Emil Dr (Screenwriter)
Stefanie 1959,Je 18,36:1
BURROUGHS
See Also BURROWS
Burroughs, Clark
Smart Money 1931,Je 19,21:1
Burroughs, Edgar Rice (Miscellaneous)
Tarzan and the Amazons 1945,Ap 30,13:4
Tarzan and the Mermaids 1948,Mr 30,26:4
Burroughs, Edgar Rice (Original Author)
Tarzan, The Ape Man 1932,Mr 28,11:2
Tarzan, The Fearless 1933,Ag 12,14:3
Tarzan and his Mate 1934,Ap 21,12:1
New Adventures of Tarzan, The 1935,O 15,19:3
Tarzan Escapes 1936,N 20,27:2
Tarzan's Revenge 1938,Ja 10,13:3
Tarzan Finds a Son 1939,Je 15,27:2
Tarzan's Secret Treasure 1941,D 25,33:1
Tarzan's New York Adventure 1942,Ag 7,13:2
Tarzan Triumphs 1943,F 5,16:3

Burroughs, Edgar Rice (Original Author)— Cont
Tarzan's Desert Mystery 1943,D 27,23:3
Tarzan and the Leopard Woman 1946,F 11,25:2
Tarzan and the Huntress 1947,Ap 7,20:4
Tarzan's Magic Fountain 1949,F 7,15:2
Tarzan and the Slave Girl 1950,Je 24,7:3
Tarzan and the Lost Safari 1957,Ap 13,12:3
Tarzan's Fight for Life 1958,Ag 16,10:2
Tarzan the Magnificent 1960,Jl 21,17:1
Tarzan and the Valley of Gold 1967,Mr 30,55:1

Burroughs, Henry
Our Daily Bread 1934,O 3,25:2

Burroughs, William S
Chappaqua 1967,N 6,65:2

BURROWS
See Also BURROUGHS

Burrows, Abe (Miscellaneous)
Duffy's Tavern 1945,S 6,23:3

Burrows, Abe (Original Author)
Guys and Dolls 1955,N 5,26:1
Can-Can 1960,Mr 10,36:1

Burrows, Abe (Screenwriter)
Solid Gold Cadillac, The 1956,O 25,40:3

Burrows, John H (Producer)
Al Capone 1959,Mr 26,27:1

Burrows, Ken (Producer)
Murder a la Mod 1968,My 2,57:1

Burrud, Billy
Three Kids and a Queen 1935,N 9,19:2
His Night Out 1935,N 16,19:2
Pride of the Marines 1936,Ap 27,19:2
Magnificent Brute, The 1936,O 24,23:1
Girl Overboard 1937,Mr 1,15:1
Captains Courageous 1937,My 12,27:1
Man in Blue, The 1937,Ag 30,25:2
It Happened in Hollywood 1937,O 2,18:1
Idol of the Crowd 1937,D 4,21:1

Burston, Janet
Blondie Goes Latin 1941,F 26,17:3

Burston, Louis (Miscellaneous)
Forget Me Not 1922,Jl 24,10:2

Burstyn, Artkino (Miscellaneous)
Guerrilla Brigade 1942,Ap 14,17:2

Burstyn, Joseph (Miscellaneous)
Eternal Mask, The 1937,Ja 13,20:3
Guerrilla Brigade 1942,Ap 14,17:2

Burstyn, Joseph (Producer)
Russian Story, The 1943,Je 9,17:2

BURT
See Also BERT

Burt, Benny
Pick a Star 1937,My 28,17:2
Cry Danger 1951,F 22,27:3
M 1951,Je 11,20:7
Steel Trap, The 1952,N 13,35:2

Burt, Frank (Screenwriter)
Barbary Pirate 1949,O 28,29:3
Chinatown at Midnight 1949,N 18,35:3
Fortunes of Captain Blood 1950,Je 10,11:3
Groom Wore Spurs, The 1951,Mr 14,41:2
Stage to Tucson 1951,My 5,14:2
Man From Laramie, The 1955,S 1,20:2

Burt, Frederick
Shadow of the Law 1930,Je 7,10:4
Eyes of the World 1930,Ag 15,20:5
Royal Bed, The 1931,Ja 31,15:1
Up for Murder 1931,My 30,9:2
Cisco Kid, The 1931,O 24,20:3

Burt, Katherine Newlin (Original Author)
Snowblind 1921,My 23,16:3
Body and Soul 1927,N 8,33:1

Burt, Katherine Newlin (Screenwriter)
Man From Lost River, The 1922,Ja 16,18:3
Way of a Girl, The 1925,Mr 30,21:3

Burt, Kendal (Original Author)
One That Got Away, The 1958,Ap 23,40:2

Burt, Margaret
Night of Mystery, A 1928,Ap 16,20:5

Burt, Olivier
Othello 1960,My 16,39:1

Burt, William P
Leopard Lady, The 1928,F 27,16:2
Danger Lights 1930,D 15,29:1

Burtis, Eric
East Side Kids 1940,F 19,21:6

Burtis, James
Ladies in Love 1930,Je 14,9:4
Lawless Woman, The 1931,Je 8,21:1
Strangers of the Evening 1932,Je 4,9:2
Trick for Trick 1933,Je 10,16:4
One Sunday Afternoon 1933,S 2,14:4
Hips, Hips, Hooray 1934,F 24,18:3
20th Century 1934,My 4,24:2
Young and Beautiful 1934,S 18,18:4
Case of the Howling Dog, The 1934,O 18,26:5
Wings in the Dark 1935,F 2,10:1
Mr Dynamite 1935,My 25,12:1
Keeper of the Bees, The 1935,Ag 17,18:5
$1,000 a Minute 1935,D 21,11:1

Burtis, Marilyn
Last Time I Saw Archie, The 1961,My 29,9:6

Burtis, Thomson (Original Author)
Madison Square Garden 1932,O 12,26:5
Soldiers of the Storm 1933,My 17,15:3

In old Oklahoma 1943,D 6,21:1
Crosswinds 1951,D 7,35:4

Burton, Basil
Murder in the Cathedral 1952,Mr 26,35:2

Burton, Charles (Producer)
Time of Their Lives, The 1946,N 28,40:2

Burton, Clarence
Forbidden Fruit 1921,Ja 24,16:2
Miss Lulu Bett 1921,D 25,VI,2:1
Man Unconquerable, The 1922,Jl 17,16:3
Ten Commandments, The 1923,D 22,8:1
Bluff 1924,Ap 28,18:2
Coming of Amos, The 1925,S 8,29:1
Road to Yesterday, The 1925,D 1,22:4
Three Faces West 1926,F 16,22:4
Red Dice 1926,Ap 16,20:3
Nervous Wreck, The 1926,O 12,30:2
Rubber Tires 1927,Mr 9,29:1
King of Kings, The 1927,Ap 20,29:2
Yankee Clipper, The 1927,My 3,25:1
Fighting Eagle, The 1927,Ag 15,22:5
Angel of Broadway 1927,N 1,21:1 (In Addenda)
Chicago 1927,D 24,9:1
Stand and Deliver 1928,Ap 2,25:1
Submarine 1928,Ag 31,23:3
Unholy Three, The 1930,Jl 5,17:4
Only Saps Work 1930,D 13,22:2
Sign of the Cross, The 1932,D 1,25:1

Burton, David
Free and Easy 1930,Ap 19,15:1

Burton, David (Director)
Bishop Murder Case, The 1930,F 1,15:1
Fighting Caravans 1931,Ja 26,21:1
Confessions of a Co-Ed 1931,Je 20,20:4
Dancers in the Dark 1932,Mr 19,11:2
Brief Moment 1933,S 30,18:5
Let's Fall in Love 1934,Ja 22,12:3
Sisters Under the Skin 1934,Je 8,18:1
Princess O'Hara 1935,Ap 13,11:3
Melody Lingers on, The 1935,N 7,27:1
Make Way for a Lady 1936,D 12,15:1
Man Who Wouldn't Talk, The 1940,Ja 12,13:3
Private Nurse 1941,Ag 29,13:3

Burton, David (Miscellaneous)
Lady by Choice 1934,N 17,12:1

Burton, Floyd Lieut
Unidentified Flying Objects 1956,Je 13,46:2

Burton, Frederick
Anne of Green Gables 1919,D 22,18:3
Yes or No 1920,Jl 5,12:4
Heliotrope 1920,N 29,20:3
Bits of Life 1921,O 17,18:1
Fighting Blade, The 1923,O 15,15:4
Rejected Woman, The 1924,My 5,18:3
Running Wild 1927,Je 14,33:2
Big Trail, The 1930,O 25,20:3
Sweepstakes 1931,Je 25,23:5
American Tragedy, An 1931,Ag 6,22:5
Woman From Monte Carlo, The 1931,D 31,17:6
Wet Parade, The 1932,Ap 22,23:2
State's Attorney 1932,My 6,15:3
Okay America 1932,S 10,18:5
One Way Passage 1932,O 14,23:2
Too Busy to Work 1932,D 3,21:4
No Other Woman 1933,Ja 30,9:4 (In Addenda)
Broadway Bad 1933,Mr 6,16:6
Working Man, The 1933,Ap 21,20:3
Counsellor-At-Law 1933,D 8,31:2
Belle of the Nineties 1934,S 22,12:2
Flirtation Walk 1934,N 29,33:1
Transient Lady 1935,Mr 11,15:1
McFadden's Flats 1935,Mr 13,16:2
Shipmates Forever 1935,O 17,29:3
Voice of Bugle Ann, The 1936,F 27,23:1
Theodora Goes Wild 1936,N 13,27:4
Man in Blue, The 1937,Ag 30,25:2
Saint in New York, The 1938,My 26,31:2
Kentucky 1938,D 24,12:1
Confessions of a Nazi Spy 1939,Ap 29,13:2
Man From Dakota, The 1940,F 22,29:2
Washington Melodrama 1941,My 26,15:3
Babes on Broadway 1942,Ja 1,37:1

Burton, George
Ruggles of Red Gap 1935,Mr 7,26:1
Bill and Coo 1948,Mr 29,17:4

Burton, Humphrey
Interlude 1968,Jl 3,26:1

Burton, Jeff
Planet of the Apes 1968,F 9,55:2

Burton, John
Lloyds of London 1936,N 26,39:1
Beloved Enemy 1936,D 26,15:2
Lord Jeff 1938,Jl 1,22:2
Storm Over Bengal 1938,D 8,34:4
Sun Never Sets, The 1939,Je 9,26:2
Black Swan, The 1942,D 24,18:3
Black Beauty 1946,Ag 30,13:2
Fan, The 1949,Ap 2,12:2
House on Telegraph Hill, The 1951,My 14,29:1
David and Bathsheba 1951,Ag 15,23:2

Burton, Julian
Young Lions, The 1958,Ap 3,23:1

Burton, Lee
Calling of Dan Matthews, The 1936,Ja 25,18:4

Burton, Leonard M (Producer)
Satan in High Heels 1962,Mr 24,15:6

Burton, Martin
Ladies' Man 1931,My 1,30:3
When Ladies Meet 1933,Je 24,16:2

Burton, Peter
Wooden Horse, The 1951,Ag 29,20:2
Three Cases of Murder (Lord Mountdrago); Lord
Mountdrago (Three Cases of Murder)
1955,Mr 16,39:4
Third Key, The 1957,Je 3,30:2

Burton, Richard
Dolwyn 1949,Ag 30,18:4
Her Panelled Door 1951,Ag 28,18:2
My Cousin Rachel 1952,D 26,20:2
Desert Rats, The 1953,My 9,13:2
Robe, The 1953,S 17,32:6
Prince of Players 1955,Ja 12,24:2
Rains of Ranchipur, The 1955,D 16,38:2
Alexander the Great 1956,Mr 29,23:1
Sea Wife 1957,S 5,45:2
Look Back in Anger 1959,S 16,45:1
Bramble Bush, The 1960,F 25,34:2
Ice Palace 1960,Je 30,22:1
Midsummer Night's Dream, A 1961,D 19,39:1
Longest Day, The 1962,O 5,28:1
Cleopatra 1963,Je 13,29:1
V I P's, The 1963,S 20,29:1
Becket 1964,Mr 12,40:2
Night of the Iguana, The 1964,Jl 1,42:1
Hamlet 1964,S 24,46:1
Sandpiper, The 1965,Jl 16,14:1
Spy Who Came in From the Cold, The
1965,D 24,24:1
Who's Afraid of Virginia Wooll? 1966,Je 30,28:1
Who's Afraid of Virginia Woolf? 1966,Jl 10,II,1:5
Taming of the Shrew, The 1967,Mr 9,43:1
Comedians, The 1967,N 1,37:1
Doctor Faustus 1968,F 7,38:1
Boom! 1968,My 27,56:1
Candy 1968,D 18,54:2

Burton, Richard (Director)
Doctor Faustus 1968,F 7,38:1

Burton, Richard (Producer)
Taming of the Shrew, The 1967,Mr 9,43:1
Doctor Faustus 1968,F 7,38:1

Burton, Robert
Above and Beyond 1953,Ja 31,10:6
Inferno 1953,Ag 12,22:2
Latin Lovers 1953,Ag 13,17:2
Big Heat, The 1953,O 15,43:2
All the Brothers Were Valiant 1953,D 29,19:2
Siege at Red River, The 1954,Ap 3,19:2
Broken Lance 1954,Jl 30,9:1
Man Called Peter, A 1955,Ap 1,22:1
Ransom 1956,Ja 25,28:3
Jubal 1956,Ap 25,39:1
Rack, The 1956,N 6,30:1
I Was a Teenage Frankenstein 1958,Ja 30,19:4
Compulsion 1959,Ap 2,26:2
Private's Affair, A 1959,Ag 15,8:7
Story of Page One, The 1960,Ja 14,28:1
Gallant Hours, The 1960,Je 23,19:4
Young Savages, The 1961,My 25,31:1
Jumbo 1962,D 7,49:1

Burton, Tom
Ghost Ship, The 1943,D 25,19:4

Burton, Val (Composer)
Girl Without a Room 1933,D 7,26:3
Cockeyed Cavaliers 1934,Jl 25,22:2
Down to Their Last Yacht 1934,S 24,14:1

Burton, Val (Original Author)
Lord Jeff 1938,Jl 1,22:2
Hullabaloo 1940,D 19,33:1

Burton, Val (Screenwriter)
Henry Aldrich for President 1941,O 18,22:2
Time of Their Lives, The 1946,N 28,40:2
Bedtime for Bonzo 1951,Ap 6,31:4

Burton, William A (Original Author)
Easy Pickings 1927,Mr 25,25:3

Burtt, Robert M (Original Author)
Sky Parade, The 1936,Ap 20,17:1

Burtwell, Frederick
Rembrandt 1936,D 3,31:1
Dr Syn 1937,N 15,15:1
Laburnum Grove 1941,D 2,29:2
Silver Fleet, The 1945,Mr 24,22:6
Inheritance, The 1951,F 12,19:2

Burwell, Faith
New Faces 1954,F 20,8:7
One Potato, Two Potato 1964,Jl 30,16:1

Burzynski, Zenon
Guests are Coming; Jada Goscie Jada
1967,Ja 13,15:1

Bus-Fekete, Ladislaus (Original Author)
Ladies in Love 1936,O 29,31:1
Baroness and the Butler, The 1938,F 19,19:2
Lydia 1941,S 19,27:1
Appointment for Love 1941,N 7,27:1
Reunion in France 1943,Mr 5,20:3
Heaven Can Wait 1943,Ag 12,15:1

Bus-Fekete, Ladislaus (Original Author)— Cont
Perfect Strangers 1950,Mr 11,8:2
Girl Next Door, The 1953,S 5,7:4
Embezzled Heaven 1959,Ap 24,23:1
Bus-Fekete, Ladislaus (Screenwriter)
Casbah 1948,My 3,27:4
Busatt, Ivan
Overture to Glory 1940,F 12,14:2
BUSCH
See Also BUCH, BUSH
Busch, Ernst
Dreigroschenoper, Die; Beggar's Opera, The
1931,My 18,21:2
Niemandsland; No Man's Land
1932,Ja 24,VIII,5:1
Kameradschaft 1932,N 9,28:5
Kuhle Wampe 1933,Ap 24,11:4
Hell on Earth 1934,Ja 29,10:2
Kampf, Der 1936,S 11,29:3
Gilgi Eine Von Uns 1937,Jl 10,18:2
Threepenny Opera, The 1960,Jl 11,24:4
Busch, Mae
Devil's Pass Key, The 1920,Ag 9,6:3
Brothers Under the Skin 1922,N 13,12:1
Christian, The 1923,F 12,13:4
Souls for Sale 1923,Ap 9,14:3
Name the Man 1924,F 4,23:3
Nellie, the Beautiful Cloak Model
1924,Ap 14,14:1
Shooting of Dan McGrew, The 1924,Je 9,14:3
Bread 1924,Jl 21,14:4
Broken Barriers 1924,Ag 4,16:3
Married Flirts 1924,N 19,19:3
Flaming Love 1925,Ja 19,14:1
Unholy Three, The 1925,Ag 4,14:3
Time, the Comedian 1925,D 14,18:2
San Francisco Nights 1928,Ja 31,29:1
Fazil 1928,Je 5,21:1
While the City Sleeps 1928,O 22,29:1
Alibi 1929,Ap 9,29:1
Man's Man, A 1929,Je 3,27:2
Wicked 1931,S 19,10:2
Man Called Back, The 1932,Jl 30,16:5
Blondie Johnson 1933,F 27,11:2
Sucker Money 1933,Ap 7,22:5
Cheating Blondes 1933,My 20,11:4
Lilly Turner 1933,Je 15,21:2
Dance, Girl, Dance 1933,O 25,23:3
Sons of the Desert 1934,Ja 12,29:3
Beloved 1934,Ja 27,9:3
I Like It That Way 1934,Ap 18,23:3
Bohemian Girl, The 1936,F 17,21:1
Daughter of Shanghai 1937,D 24,21:2
Prison Farm 1938,Jl 15,13:3
Women Without Names 1940,My 9,26:4
Busch, Niven (Original Author)
College Coach 1933,N 11,10:4
In Old Chicago 1938,Ja 7,15:2
Belle Starr 1941,N 1,20:2
Till the End of Time 1946,Jl 24,24:1
Duel in the Sun 1947,My 8,30:2
Capture, The 1950,My 20,8:6
Furies, The 1950,Ag 17,23:2
Distant Drums 1951,D 26,19:3
Man From the Alamo, The 1953,S 12,13:2
Moonlighter, The 1953,S 23,37:2
Busch, Niven (Producer)
Capture, The 1950,My 20,8:6
Busch, Niven (Screenwriter)
Babbitt 1934,D 17,24:2
Off the Record 1939,F 18,12:2
Angels Wash Their Faces 1939,S 4,16:2
Westerner, The 1940,O 25,25:2
Postman Always Rings Twice, The
1946,My 3,15:3
Pursued 1947,Mr 8,10:2
Moss Rose 1947,Jl 3,14:2
Distant Drums 1951,D 26,19:3
Moonlighter, The 1953,S 23,37:2
Treasure of Pancho Villa, The 1955,N 25,38:2
Busch, Paul
China Gate 1957,My 23,40:2
Buschbeck, Grandolf
Lysistrata 1948,Je 19,19:2
BUSH
See Also BUCH, BUSCH
Bush, Jack (Miscellaneous)
If Moscow Strikes 1952,Ap 30,33:4
Bush, James
Great Jasper, The 1933,F 17,5:3
One Man's Journey 1933,S 1,15:2
Eight Girls in a Boat 1934,Ja 13,16:3
Beggars in Ermine 1934,Ap 25,25:3
Young and Beautiful 1934,S 18,18:4
Crimson Romance 1934,O 13,10:1
Shot in the Dark, A 1935,My 22,23:2
Arizonian, The 1935,Jl 27,16:2
Return of Peter Grimm, The 1935,O 4,25:2
Harmony Lane 1935,O 24,19:4
Freckles 1935,O 26,12:2
Ceiling Zero 1936,Ja 20,22:2
O'Malley of the Mounted 1936,Ap 6,18:1
M'liss 1936,Ag 8,5:2

Good Old Soak 1937,Ap 20,25:3
I Cover the War 1937,Ag 2,10:2
Outlaws of the Orient 1937,S 25,10:2
Sky Giant 1938,Jl 20,22:2
Come on Leathernecks 1938,S 15,29:3
You Can't Cheat an Honest Man 1939,F 20,13:2
Family Next Door, The 1939,Ap 28,31:2
They Asked for It 1939,Je 30,17:4
Joe and Ethel Turp Call on the President
1940,Ja 4,19:2
Beyond Tomorrow 1940,S 27,27:1
A-Haunting We Will Go 1942,Ag 3,18:4
He Hired the Boss 1943,Je 4,17:4
Shine on Harvest Moon 1944,Mr 11,10:2
Big Noise, The 1944,S 23,16:1
Beginning or the End, The 1947,F 21,15:1
Man From Colorado 1949,Ja 21,24:3
Bush, Kenneth R
Drivin' Fool, The 1923,O 29,18:1
Bush, Paul H (Producer)
Cruz Diablo 1935,Ap 6,10:1
Bush, Pauline
Enemy Sex, The 1924,Jl 1,21:4
Bush, Vannevar (Original Author)
If Moscow Strikes 1952,Ap 30,33:4
Bushell, Anthony
Disraeli 1929,O 3,27:5
Show of Shows 1929,N 21,24:5
Lovin' the Ladies 1930,Mr 22,22:6
Journey's End 1930,Ap 9,25:1
Flirting Widow, The 1930,Ag 2,16:4
Three Faces East 1930,S 6,9:2
Royal Bed, The 1931,Ja 31,15:1
Born to Love 1931,Ap 25,23:4
Chances 1931,Je 12,27:1
Five Star Final 1931,S 11,24:2
Expensive Women 1931,N 14,15:3
Woman Commands, A 1932,Ja 28,13:2
Escapade 1932,My 28,18:2
I Was a Spy 1934,Ja 15,12:2
Ghoul, The 1934,Ja 27,9:2
Channel Crossing 1934,My 24,28:3
Woman in Command, The 1934,My 29,22:2
Scarlet Pimpernel, The 1935,F 8,27:2
Red Wagon 1936,Je 22,22:1
Dark Journey 1937,Ag 23,22:1
Return of the Scarlet Pimpernel, The
1938,Ap 11,12:2
Troopship 1938,Ap 26,18:2
Lion Has Wings, The 1940,Ja 22,11:2
Miniver Story, The 1950,O 27,24:2
Long Dark Hall, The 1951,My 10,38:3
Angel With the Trumpet 1951,D 21,21:5
Small Back Room, The 1952,F 2,11:3
High Treason 1952,My 21,23:3
Passionate Sentry, The 1953,N 12,37:5
Paratrooper 1953,D 31,9:3
Black Knight, The 1954,O 29,27:2
Purple Plain, The 1955,Ap 11,29:1
Pursuit of the Graf Spee 1957,D 27,33:2
A Night to Remember 1958,D 17,2:7
Wind Cannot Read, The 1960,Mr 10,36:1
Bushell, Anthony (Director)
Long Dark Hall, The 1951,My 10,38:3
Angel With the Trumpet 1951,D 21,21:5
Bushell, David
Cry From the Streets, A 1959,F 24,32:2
Bushelman, John (Director)
Sniper's Ridge 1961,Ag 24,25:3
Bushelman, John (Producer)
Sniper's Ridge 1961,Ag 24,25:3
Bushkin, Joe
Rat Race, The 1960,My 26,37:3
Bushman, Francis X
Romeo and Juliet 1916,O 23,10:3
Masked Bride, The 1925,N 30,17:1
Ben Hur 1925,D 31,10:5
Marriage Clause, The 1926,S 28,30:2
Lady in Ermine, The 1927,Ja 3,16:2
Thirteenth Juror, The 1927,N 22,20:1
Grip of the Yukon, The 1928,Jl 10,17:3
Once a Gentleman 1930,O 4,15:2
Ben Hur 1931,D 4,28:2
Hollywood Boulevard 1936,S 21,26:4
David and Bathsheba 1951,Ag 15,23:2
Sabrina 1954,S 23,43:2
Story of Mankind, The 1957,N 9,31:2
Bushman, Francis X Jr
Brown of Harvard 1926,My 3,27:1
Understanding Heart, The 1927,My 10,24:5
Four Sons 1928,F 14,27:1
Girl Said No, The 1930,Ap 5,23:3
Sins of the Children 1930,Jl 26,16:4
Way out West 1930,Ag 18,24:1
Viva Villa! 1934,Ap 11,25:2
Bushman, Lenore
Just a Gigolo 1931,Je 13,20:4
Bushman, Ralph E
It's a Great Life 1920,Ag 30,12:3
Our Hospitality 1923,D 10,20:1
Bushuyev, C
We Are From Kronstadt 1936,My 2,11:1

Busley, Jessie
Personal Maid 1931,S 5,7:4
Brother Rat 1938,N 5,15:2
King of the Underworld 1939,Ja 7,6:2
Brother Rat and a Baby 1940,Ja 27,9:4
It all Came True 1940,Ap 6,13:2
Submarine Zone; (Escape To Glory)
1941,Ap 7,13:2
Busquets, Joaquin
Sangre Manda, La 1934,My 15,18:2
Enemigos 1934,Ag 18,5:6
Tierra, Amor y Dolor 1935,Ag 10,16:5
Mujer del Puerto, La 1936,Ag 24,11:3
El Misterio del Rostro Palido 1937,Ja 4,20:5
Gran Cruz, La; Heavy Cross, The 1937,D 7,31:6
Bussa, Livio
Monte Cassino 1948,N 25,47:3
Bussieres, Raymond
They Are not Angels 1948,My 22,8:3
Portrait of Innocence 1948,Je 9,35:2
Gates of the Night 1950,Mr 16,40:2
Children of Chaos 1950,Ap 20,37:2
Alice in Wonderland 1951,Jl 27,15:2
Ma Pomme 1951,O 15,22:2
Casque D'Or 1952,Ag 19,19:1
Justice Is Done 1953,Mr 3,23:2
Beauties of the Night 1954,Mr 23,23:5
Gates of Paris 1958,Ja 15,24:1
Mam'zelle Pigalle 1958,Ap 19,10:4
Sans Famille 1959,S 5,11:4
Paris Hotel 1959,S 12,12:3
Fanny 1961,Jl 7,16:1
Wonders of Aladdin, The 1961,D 23,16:1
Paris When it Sizzles 1964,Ap 9,25:3
Up From the Beach 1965,Je 10,38:1
Bussola, Raffaello Rossi
Marriage Italian Style 1964,D 21,42:1
Bussonet, Roger
Barber of Seville 1949,Jl 21,21:2
Bustamente, Alfonso Rivas (Director)
Rancho Grande 1938,D 2,27:2
Bustamente, Alfonso Rivas (Producer)
Rancho Grande 1938,D 2,27:2
Bustamente, Maria
Yanco 1964,Je 18,29:2
Buster, Robert
Prison Farm 1938,Jl 15,13:3
Bustillo-Oro, Juan (Director)
Monjes, Des 1935,Ja 21,19:3
Busto, Paco
Buen Camino, Por 1936,Jl 4,18:3
Doce Mujeres; Twelve Women 1940,Mr 11,11:3
Apuros de Claudina, Los; Claudina's Troubles
1940,Je 8,18:3
Buszynski, G
Young Chopin 1952,D 25,34:7
But, Igor
Lonely White Sail 1938,My 7,18:1
Butch
Sandy Is a Lady 1940,Je 28,22:2
Butch and Buddy
Spring Parade 1940,O 4,29:2
Little Bit of Heaven, A 1940,N 8,24:2
Never Give a Sucker an Even Break
1941,O 27,21:2
Johnny Doughboy 1943,My 6,25:3
Butchart, Anne
Forbidden Street, The 1949,My 14,9:2
Brave Don't Cry, The 1952,N 6,37:2
Butcher, Cyril
Night Birds 1931,Ja 3,21:2
Butcher, Edward (Producer)
County Chairman, The 1935,Ja 19,8:1
Our Little Girl 1935,Je 7,24:4
Old Kentucky, In 1935,N 29,24:1
Butcher, Ernest
Years Between, The 1947,Mr 10,25:2
Butchma, Ambrosi
Taras Family, The 1946,D 9,34:4
Bute, Mary Ellen (Director)
Passages From James Joyce's Finnegans Wake
1967,O 10,56:1
Bute, Mary Ellen (Producer)
Passages From James Joyce's Finnegans Wake
1967,O 10,56:1
Bute, Mary Ellen (Screenwriter)
Passages From James Joyce's Finnegans Wake
1967,O 10,56:1
Butenina, Ludmilla
Day the War Ended, The 1961,Ja 30,17:2
Buti, Carlo
I due Gemelli; Twins, The 1938,Ag 15,11:2
Per Vomini Soli; For Men Only 1939,Ap 21,27:4
Butland, D S M, William
Q Ships 1928,S 17,27:1
Butler, Carolyn
Dream Girl 1948,Je 17,29:2
Butler, Carolyn (Screenwriter)
Hostages 1943,O 11,23:2
Butler, Crilly
That's my Boy 1932,N 21,21:1

Butler, David
Greatest Thing in Life, The 1918,D 23,9:1
Upstairs and Down 1919,Je 16,11:2
Nugget Nell 1919,Jl 28,8:5
Sky Pilot, The 1921,Ap 18,8:1
Village Blacksmith, The 1922,N 3,17:5
Poor Men's Wives 1923,Ja 29,11:1
Temple of Venus, The 1923,N 1,24:3
In Hollywood with Potash and Perlmutter 1924,S 30,27:3
Narrow Street, The 1925,Ja 5,19:1
Code of the West 1925,Ap 13,24:1
Private Affairs 1925,Jl 15,22:3
Tracked in the Snow Country 1925,Jl 20,19:2
His Majesty Bunker Bean 1925,S 15,12:1
Man on the Box, The 1925,S 28,24:1
Plastic Age, The 1926,Jl 19,13:1
Oh Baby! 1926,Ag 11,25:2
Quarterback, The 1926,O 12,30:2
Nobody's Widow 1927,Ja 13,29:1
Seventh Heaven 1927,My 26,22:1
Rush Hour, The 1928,Ja 31,29:1
Salute 1929,O 5,22:5

Butler, David (Director)
High School Hero 1927,O 24,24:3
News Parade, The 1928,My 29,17:2
Win That Girl 1928,O 1,23:1
Prep and Pep 1928,D 24,11:1
William Fox Movietone Follies of 1929 1929,My 27,22:1
Sunny Side Up 1929,O 4,24:5
High Society Blues 1930,Ap 19,15:1
Just Imagine 1930,N 22,21:3
Connecticut Yankee, A 1931,Ap 13,17:1
Delicious 1931,D 26,15:5
Business and Pleasure 1932,F 13,23:4
Down to Earth 1932,S 2,19:2
Handle with Care 1932,D 24,11:4
Hold Me Tight 1933,My 22,18:6
My Weakness 1933,S 22,14:1
Bottoms Up 1934,Mr 23,29:2
Handy Andy 1934,Ag 4,14:5
Have a Heart 1934,O 20,20:2
Bright Eyes 1934,D 21,31:1
Little Colonel, The 1935,Mr 22,26:2
Doubting Thomas 1935,Jl 11,24:2
Littlest Rebel, The 1935,D 20,30:1
Captain January 1936,Ap 25,21:1
White Fang 1936,Jl 18,18:2
Pigskin Parade 1936,N 14,23:3
Ali Baba Goes to Town 1937,O 23,14:1
You're a Sweetheart 1937,D 25,10:5
Kentucky Moonshine 1938,My 21,9:2
Straight, Place and Show 1938,O 1,10:2
Kentucky 1938,D 24,12:1
East Side of Heaven 1939,My 5,29:3
That's Right, You're Wrong 1939,N 30,25:3
If I Had my Way 1940,My 6,13:2
You'll Find Out 1940,N 15,25:2
Caught in the Draft 1941,Je 26,27:3
Playmates 1941,D 26,21:3
Road to Morocco 1942,N 12,30:1
They Got Me Covered 1943,Mr 5,20:2
Thank Your Lucky Stars 1943,O 2,19:2
Shine on Harvest Moon 1944,Mr 11,10:2
Princess and the Pirate, The 1945,F 10,16:2
San Antonio 1945,D 29,19:5
Two Guys From Milwaukee 1946,Jl 27,12:5
Time, The Place And The Girl, The 1946,D 27,14:3
Two Guys From Texas 1948,Ag 28,8:6
John Loves Mary 1949,F 5,11:2
Look for the Silver Lining 1949,Je 24,29:2
It's a Great Feeling 1949,Ag 13,6:6
Story of Seabiscuit, The 1949,N 12,8:4
Daughter of Rosie O'Grady, The 1950,Mr 31,36:2
Tea for Two 1950,S 2,11:2
Lullaby of Broadway 1951,Mr 27,35:2
Painting the Clouds With Sunshine 1951,S 1,9:6
Where's Charley? 1952,Je 27,18:3
April in Paris 1952,D 25,34:5
By the Light of the Silvery Moon 1953,Mr 27,28:2
Calamity Jane 1953,N 5,40:2
Command, The 1954,Ja 16,10:5
King Richard and the Crusaders 1954,Ag 23,20:5
Girl He Left Behind, The 1956,O 27,17:1
Right Approach, The 1961,My 18,41:1
C'mon Let's Live a Little 1967,My 4,34:1

Butler, David (Original Author)
Handle with Care 1932,D 24,11:4
Bottoms Up 1934,Mr 23,29:2
Have a Heart 1934,O 20,20:2
Bright Eyes 1934,D 21,31:1
East Side of Heaven 1939,My 5,29:3
That's Right, You're Wrong 1939,N 30,25:3
You'll Find Out 1940,N 15,25:2

Butler, David (Producer)
That's Right, You're Wrong 1939,N 30,25:3
If I Had my Way 1940,My 6,13:2
You'll Find Out 1940,N 15,25:2
Playmates 1941,D 26,21:3

Butler, David (Screenwriter)
High School Hero 1927,O 24,24:3

Butler, Ellis Parker (Original Author)
Jack-Knife Man, The 1920,Ag 2,12:2

Butler, Ewan Col (Original Author)
Dunkirk 1958,S 11,42:2

Butler, Frank
Tailor Made Man, A 1922,O 16,20:2
Satan in Sables 1925,O 15,27:3
Compromise 1925,O 27,23:3

Butler, Frank (Original Author)
White Woman 1933,N 18,18:5
Vagabond Lady 1935,Je 15,20:2
Waikiki Wedding 1937,Mr 25,29:1
Tropic Holiday 1938,Je 30,21:2
Island of Lost Men 1939,Ag 17,16:3
Welcome Stranger 1947,Ag 7,15:2
Road to Bali 1953,Ja 30,25:1

Butler, Frank (Screenwriter)
Montana Moon 1930,Ap 14,24:2
Prosperity 1932,N 26,11:4
Babes in Toyland 1934,D 13,28:2
Coronado 1935,D 19,33:4
Strike Me Pink 1936,Ja 17,15:2
Milky Way, The 1936,Mr 26,27:2
Princess Comes Across, The 1936,Je 4,27:2
Champagne Waltz 1937,F 4,17:2
Waikiki Wedding 1937,Mr 25,29:1
Tropic Holiday 1938,Je 30,21:2
Give Me a Sailor 1938,Ag 11,31:1
Paris Honeymoon 1939,Ja 26,17:1
Never Say Die 1939,Mr 9,18:1
Star Maker, The 1939,Ag 31,14:2
Road to Singapore 1940,Mr 14,29:2
Untamed 1940,Jl 25,14:3
Rangers of Fortune 1940,S 19,27:2
I Want a Divorce 1940,O 3,31:2
Road to Zanzibar 1941,Ap 10,29:2
Aloma of the South Seas 1941,Ag 28,23:4
My Favorite Blonde 1942,Ap 2,27:2
Beyond the Blue Horizon 1942,Je 25,27:2
Wake Island 1942,S 2,19:2
Road to Morocco 1942,N 12,30:1
China 1943,Ap 22,31:2
Hostages 1943,O 11,23:2
Going my Way 1944,My 3,25:2
Medal for Benny, A 1945,My 24,15:2
Incendiary Blonde 1945,Jl 26,13:2
Kid From Brooklyn, The 1946,Ap 19,25:2
California 1947,Ja 15,31:2
Perils of Pauline, The 1947,Jl 10,17:2
Golden Earrings 1947,D 4,41:3
Whispering Smith 1949,F 15,28:2
Road to Bali 1953,Ja 30,25:1
Strange Lady in Town 1955,My 21,11:1
Miracle, The 1959,N 13,25:4

Butler, Frank E
Bluebeard's 8th Wife 1923,Ag 7,20:2

Butler, Fred J
Bluff 1924,Ap 28,18:2
Welcome Stranger 1924,O 14,21:5

Butler, George
Clouds Over Europe 1939,Je 16,27:2

Butler, Gerald (Original Author)
Kiss the Blood off my Hands 1948,O 30,10:2
On Dangerous Ground 1952,F 13,35:2

Butler, H E (Producer)
World Struggle for Oil, The 1924,Ap 22,19:3

Butler, Hugo (Original Author)
Edison the Man 1940,Je 7,27:2
Woman of Distinction, A 1950,Mr 17,28:2

Butler, Hugo (Screenwriter)
Big City 1937,S 17,29:2
Christmas Carol, A 1938,D 23,16:2
Huckleberry Finn 1939,Mr 3,21:2
Society Lawyer 1939,Mr 31,19:2
Young Tom Edison 1940,Mr 15,27:2
Wyoming 1940,O 3,31:4
Barnacle Bill 1941,Jl 25,12:4
Yank on the Burma Road, A 1942,Ja 29,25:3
Lassie Come Home 1943,O 8,15:4
Southerner, The 1945,Ag 27,22:3
Miss Susie Slagle's 1946,F 7,29:2
From This Day Forward 1946,Ap 20,16:2
Roughshod 1949,Je 17,27:2
Eye Witness 1950,Ag 28,13:2
He Ran all the Way 1951,Je 21,24:2
Prowler, The 1951,Jl 2,16:6
Sodom and Gomorrah 1963,Ja 24,5:3
Eva 1965,Je 5,21:2
Legend of Lylah Clare, The 1968,Ag 23,33:1

Butler, Jimmy
Only Yesterday 1933,N 10,25:1
No Greater Glory 1934,My 5,22:2
Mrs Wiggs of the Cabbage Patch 1934,O 29,14:2
I'll Fix It 1934,N 12,17:3
Romance in Manhattan 1935,Ja 18,29:2
When a Man's a Man 1935,F 22,27:2
Laddie 1935,My 6,22:3
Dark Angel, The 1935,S 6,12:2
Stella Dallas 1937,Ag 6,21:1
Wells Fargo 1937,D 30,15:2
Boys Town 1938,S 9,25:1

Butler, Jimmy— Cont
Winter Carnival 1939,Jl 28,14:2
Nurse Edith Cavell 1939,S 22,27:4
Escape, The 1939,N 3,17:4
Military Academy 1940,Ag 5,10:4
Naval Academy 1941,Je 5,27:3

Butler, John
Make Way for a Lady 1936,D 12,15:1
Some Blondes Are Dangerous 1937,N 3,29:3
Expensive Husbands 1938,Ja 8,19:3
Accidents Will Happen 1938,Ap 25,19:2
Exposed 1938,N 21,14:5
We Who Are Young 1940,S 13,27:2
Yellow Cab Man, The 1950,Mr 27,19:2
Branded 1951,Ja 11,28:5

Butler, John K (Screenwriter)
Utah 1945,Mr 12,22:7
My Pal Trigger 1946,Ag 17,16:3
Outcast, The 1954,Jl 3,9:2

Butler, Lois
Mickey 1948,Jl 19,11:2
High Lonesome 1950,D 8,40:4

Butler, Mary Ellen
Samurai 1945,Ag 25,7:5

Butler, Michael
Seven Sweethearts 1942,N 13,28:1

Butler, Rachel (Original Author)
Mamma's Affair 1921,Ja 24,16:2

Butler, Rosita
Cradle Song 1933,N 20,18:2

Butler, Samuel (Original Author)
Way of all Flesh, The 1927,Jl 3,VII,3:1

Butrym, S
Young Chopin 1952,D 25,34:7

Butt, Lawson
Earthbound 1920,Ag 11,9:4
Ten Commandments, The 1923,D 22,8:1
Dante's Inferno 1924,S 30,27:3
Barriers Burned Away 1925,Mr 12,17:2
Any Woman 1925,My 27,26:2
Beloved Rogue, The 1927,Mr 14,16:1

Butterfield, Alfred (Producer)
Fifty Years Before your Eyes 1950,Je 30,18:2
(Incorrect in this edition; use 1950,Je 28,32:3 elsewhere)

Butterfield, Alfred (Screenwriter)
Fifty Years Before your Eyes 1950,Je 30,18:2
(Incorrect in this edition; use 1950,Je 28,32:3 elsewhere)
Secrets of the Reef 1956,Jl 24,19:2

Butterfield, Allyn (Miscellaneous)
Leopard Men of Africa, The 1940,Jl 29,10:6

Butterfield, Herbert
House on Telegraph Hill, The 1951,My 14,29:1

Butterfield, Paul
You Are What You Eat 1968,S 25,38:1

Butterfield, Paul, Blues Band
Festival 1967,O 24,53:2

Butterfield, Roger (Original Author)
Pride of the Marines 1945,Ag 25,7:3

Butterworth, Charles
Life of the Party, The 1930,N 10,16:2
Illicit 1931,Ja 19,25:1
Bargain, The 1931,S 5,7:4
Side Show 1931,S 19,10:2
Mad Genius, The 1931,O 24,20:3
Manhattan Parade 1931,D 25,29:2
Beauty and the Boss 1932,Ap 2,13:2
Love Me Tonight 1932,Ag 19,20:6
Nuisance, The 1933,My 29,22:2
Penthouse 1933,S 9,9:2
My Weakness 1933,S 22,14:1
Cat and the Fiddle, The 1934,F 17,20:2
Hollywood Party 1934,My 26,12:2
Bulldog Drummond Strikes Back 1934,Ag 16,20:2
Student Tour 1934,O 31,17:3
Forsaking all Others 1934,D 21,18:1
Night is Young, The 1935,Ja 14,11:2
Orchids to You 1935,Ag 10,16:4
Magnificent Obsession 1935,D 31,11:2
Moon's our Home, The 1936,My 13,29:2
Half Angel 1936,My 30,7:3
We Went to College 1936,Jl 27,20:2
Rainbow on the River 1936,D 18,31:4
Swing High, Swing Low 1937,Ap 15,19:1
Every Day's a Holiday 1938,Ja 27,17:2
Thanks for the Memory 1938,D 8,34:3
Let Freedom Ring 1939,Mr 10,19:2
Boys From Syracuse, The 1940,Ag 1,25:2
Second Chorus 1941,Ja 16,25:2
Road Show 1941,F 19,25:2
Sis Hopkins 1941,My 1,27:5
What's Cookin' 1942,F 26,15:5
Night in New Orleans 1942,Jl 2,25:2
Give Out, Sisters 1942,Ag 28,22:3
This Is the Army 1943,Jl 29,11:6
Follow the Boys 1944,Ap 26,24:6
Bermuda Mystery 1944,My 13,17:1

Butterworth, Donna
Family Jewels, The 1965,Ag 12,30:4
Paradise, Hawaiian Style 1966,Je 16,15:3

Butterworth, Ernest
Soul of Youth, The 1920,Ag 16,8:2
Deadwood Coach, The 1925,Ja 21,19:3

Butterworth, Joe
Penrod and Sam 1923,Je 25,16:5
Narrow Street, The 1925,Ja 5,19:1
Little Annie Rooney 1925,O 19,26:1
Born to the West 1926,Je 30,18:1 (In Addenda)

Butterworth, Peter
Mister Drake's Duck 1952,Ja 28,15:2
Penny Princess 1953,Mr 25,37:3
Tom Thumb 1958,D 24,00:0

Butti, Jeannette
Souvenir 1950,O 3,34:4

Buttolph, Dave (Composer)
Bill and Coo 1948,Mr 29,17:4

Buttons, Red
Winged Victory 1944,D 21,16:2
Sayonara 1957,D 6,39:4
Imitation General 1958,Ag 21,22:2
Big Circus, The 1959,Jl 18,6:1
Hatari 1962,Jl 12,19:1
Five Weeks in a Balloon 1962,Ag 27,18:1
Longest Day, The 1962,O 5,28:1
Gay Purr--ee 1962,D 6,55:3
Ticklish Affair, A 1963,Ag 22,19:2
Your Cheatin' Heart 1965,My 20,52:2
Up From the Beach 1965,Je 10,38:1
Harlow 1965,Jl 22,24:1
Stagecoach 1966,Je 16,53:1

Buttram, Pat
Roustabout 1964,N 11,38:1

Butts, Billy
Two-Gun Man, The 1926,Jl 13,19:3
Canadian, The 1926,N 30,27:1
Alias Jimmy Valentine 1928,N 16,28:6
Young Sinners 1931,My 9,15:4
Are These our Children 1931,N 14,15:3
Lady and Gent 1932,Jl 16,5:5
Night of June 13th, The 1932,S 17,18:4

Butumkin, Gregory
Rasputin, The Holy Sinner 1929,Ja 15,22:4

Bux, Juan
Aventura Peligrosa, Una; Dangerous Adventure,
The 1940,My 20,13:2

Buziak, David (Director)
My Wild Irish Rose 1947,D 25,32:2

Buzzanca, Lando
Divorce-Italian Style 1962,S 18,34:1
Seduces and Abandoned 1964,Jl 16,23:1
Love and Marriage (The First Night); First Night,
The (Love and Marriage) 1966,Ag 5,20:1
After the Fox 1966,D 24,11:1
Made in Italy 1967,My 1,44:2
Rose for Everyone, A 1967,Je 30,30:1
Sucker, The 1967,O 9,61:1

Buzzell, Eddie
Little Johnny Jones 1930,F 1,15:1

Buzzell, Edward (Director)
Virtue 1932,O 25,24:5
Child of Manhattan 1933,F 13,11:4
Ann Carver's Profession 1933,Je 9,20:2
Love, Honor and Oh, Baby! 1933,O 28,20:3
Cross Country Cruise 1934,Ja 20,12:3
Human Side, The 1934,S 15,20:3
Transient Lady 1935,Mr 11,15:1
Girl Friend, The 1935,S 28,12:2
Luckiest Girl in the World, The 1936,D 5,16:3
As Good as Married 1937,My 22,19:2
Paradise for Three 1938,F 16,17:1
Fast Company 1938,Jl 6,21:2
Honolulu 1939,F 23,19:2
At the Circus 1939,N 17,17:2
Go West 1941,F 21,16:2
Get-Away, The 1941,Jl 17,23:4
Married Bachelor 1941,O 16,25:3
Ship Ahoy 1942,Je 26,16:5
Youngest Profession, The 1943,Je 25,13:3
Best Foot Forward 1943,Je 30,25:2
Keep Your Powder Dry 1945,Mr 12,22:6
Easy to Wed 1946,Jl 12,14:2
Three Wise Fools 1946,S 27,19:2
Song of the Thin Man 1947,Ag 29,14:2
Neptune's Daughter 1949,Je 10,32:2
Woman of Distinction, A 1950,Mr 17,28:2
Emergency Wedding 1950,D 22,19:2
Ain't Misbehavin' 1955,Jl 2,13:2

Buzzell, Edward (Screenwriter)
Ain't Misbehavin' 1955,Jl 2,13:2

Buzzelli, Tino
After the Fox 1966,D 24,11:1

Byalik, Boris (Screenwriter)
Gordeyev Family, The 1961,O 16,33:6

Byelokurov, Victor
Military Secret 1945,Ag 2,16:2

Byelov, Anton
Winner, The 1947,D 1,27:2

BYER
See Also BAEHR, BAER, BAIR, BEAR, BEYER

Byer, Charles
New York 1927,Ja 31,13:1
Cabaret 1927,My 2,26:4
Shanghai Bound 1927,N 7,26:4
Alex The Great 1928,My 1,33:3
Clothes Make the Woman 1928,Je 5,21:1

Red Hot Speed 1929,F 5,26:3
Romance of Rio Grande 1929,N 9,22:5

Bygraves, Max
Tom Brown's School Days 1952,Ja 8,23:5
Cry From the Streets, A 1959,F 24,32:2

Byington, Spring
Little Women 1933,N 17,22:3
Werewolf of London, The 1935,My 10,25:2
Love Me Forever 1935,Je 28,24:1
Orchids to You 1935,Ag 10,16:4
Way Down East 1935,O 31,16:2
Mutiny on the Bounty 1935,N 9,19:2
Great Impersonation, The 1935,D 14,11:1
Broadway Hostess 1935,D 16,23:3
Ah, Wilderness! 1935,D 25,30:2
Voice of Bugle Ann, The 1936,F 27,23:1
Every Saturday Night 1936,Mr 14,10:2
Educating Father 1936,Je 20,22:2
Dodsworth 1936,S 24,29:1
Stage Struck 1936,S 28,14:4
Charge of the Light Brigade, The 1936,N 2,24:1
Girl on the Front Page, The 1936,N 7,15:2
Theodora Goes Wild 1936,N 13,27:4
Off to the Races 1937,F 6,15:2
Green Light 1937,F 13,9:1
Penrod and Sam 1937,Mr 29,14:3
Family Affair, A 1937,Ap 20,29:2
Big Business 1937,Je 1,27:2
Road Back, The 1937,Je 18,25:2
Hot Water 1937,N 5,19:4
Buccaneer, The 1938,F 17,17:2
Adventures of Tom Sawyer, The 1938,F 18,23:1
Jezebel 1938,Mr 11,15:2
Penrod and his Twin Brother 1938,Ap 18,11:1
Trip to Paris, A 1938,Je 10,18:2
You Can't Take It With You 1938,S 2,21:2
Safety in Numbers 1938,S 6,17:2
Story of Alexander Graham Bell, The
1939,Ap 1,17:2
Child Is Born, A 1940,Ja 11,19:2
Blue Bird, The 1940,Ja 20,11:2
Young as You Feel 1940,Mr 8,25:3
My Love Came Back 1940,Jl 13,16:5
Lucky Partners 1940,S 6,25:2
Meet John Doe 1941,Mr 13,25:2
Devil and Miss Jones, The 1941,My 16,21:2
Ellery Queen and the Perfect Crime
1941,Ag 11,17:3
When Ladies Meet 1941,S 5,19:2
Roxie Hart 1942,F 20,21:1
Rings on her Fingers 1942,Ap 24,21:4
Vanishing Virginian, The 1942,My 28,13:3
War Against Mrs Hadley, The 1942,N 26,40:2
Presenting Lily Mars 1943,Ap 30,25:3
Heaven Can Wait 1943,Ag 12,15:1
Heavenly Body, The 1944,Mr 24,17:3
I'll Be Seeing You 1945,Ap 6,20:6
Salty O'Rourke 1945,Ap 26,26:2
Enchanted Cottage, The 1945,Ap 28,19:2
Thrill of a Romance 1945,My 25,22:2
Captain Eddie 1945,Ag 9,24:2
Dragonwyck 1946,Ap 11,35:2
Letter for Evie, A 1946,Je 28,17:4
My Brother Talks to Horses 1947,Je 19,27:4
Singapore 1947,S 17,31:2
Cynthia 1947,S 19,27:2
Living in a Big Way 1947,O 10,31:4
It Had to be You 1947,D 8,35:2
B F's Daughter 1948,Mr 25,35:2
In the Good Old Summertime 1949,Ag 5,23:2
Please Believe Me 1950,Je 12,19:4
Skipper Surprised his Wife, The 1950,Je 30,18:2
Walk Softly Stranger 1950,O 16,30:5
Louisa 1950,O 25,45:2
Devil's Doorway 1950,N 10,35:1
Angels in the Outfield 1951,O 18,32:1
No Room for the Groom 1952,Je 14,12:2
Because You're Mine 1952,S 26,18:2
Please Don't Eat the Daisies 1960,Ap 1,37:1

Bykov, Leonid
Tiger Girl 1955,S 5,8:2
House on the Front Line, The 1963,S 2,18:1

Bykov, Roland
Overcoat, The 1965,Mr 2,31:2
Meet Me in Moscow 1966,My 3,51:1
Marriage of Baezaminov, The 1966,Je 11,20:2

Byles, Louis
Crowning Experience, The 1960,O 24,25:3

Bynan, Brandon
Youth Takes a Fling 1938,O 17,12:1

Byng, Douglas
Hotel Paradiso 1966,O 15,34:2

Byorninon, O
Optimistic Tragedy, The 1964,F 24,20:2

Byram, Ronald
Out of the Shadow 1919,Ja 13,9:3

BYRD
See Also BIRD, BURD

Byrd, Ralph
Criminals of the Air 1937,O 28,29:2
Paid to Dance 1937,D 6,19:1
Army Girl 1938,Ag 12,11:1

Byrd, Ralph— Cont
S O S Tidal Wave 1939,Je 22,19:3
Mickey, the Kid 1939,Jl 6,27:1
Howards of Virginia, The 1940,S 27,27:1
Golden Fleecing, The 1940,N 7,33:4
Dark Streets of Cairo 1940,D 2,19:3
Son of Monte Cristo, The 1940,D 5,33:1
Penalty, The 1941,Ap 10,29:3
Yank in the R A F, A 1941,S 27,11:3
Jungle Book 1942,Ap 6,19:1
Moontide 1942,Ap 30,41:1
Ten Gentlemen From West Point 1942,Je 5,23:3
Manila Calling 1942,S 28,13:1
Time to Kill 1942,D 25,15:4
They Came to Blow up America
1943,My 15,13:2
Guadalcanal Diary 1943,N 18,29:1
Stallion Road 1947,Ap 5,12:5
Dick Tracy's Dilemma 1947,Jl 14,14:5
Dick Tracy and Gruesome 1947,S 27,11:2
Canon City 1948,Jl 8,19:2
Redhead and the Cowboy, The 1951,Je 6,37:2

Byrd, William
Betrayal, The 1948,Je 26,10:5

BYRNE
See Also BERNE, BURN

Byrne, Betsy
Love's Greatest Mistake 1927,F 21,14:2

Byrne, Cecily
Loyalties 1934,O 26,25:1

Byrne, Donn
Hangman's House Smiling Faces
1928,My 14,25:1

Byrne, Donn (Original Author)
Stranger's Banquet, The 1923,Ja 1,18:1
His Captive Woman 1929,Ap 3,26:4
Wings of the Morning 1937,Mr 12,19:1
Irish and Proud of It 1938,O 31,12:3

Byrne, Eddie
Captain Boycott 1947,D 6,11:2
Saints and Sinners 1949,S 12,17:2
Time, Gentlemen, Please 1953,S 24,39:2
Gentle Gunman, The 1953,O 1,34:3
Tonight's the Night 1954,D 23,13:4
Three Cases of Murder (In the Picture); In the
Picture (Three Cases of Murder)
1955,Mr 16,39:4
Trouble in the Glen 1955,Ap 11,29:2
Divided Heart, The 1955,Ag 4,16:1
Abandon Ship 1957,Ap 18,35:1
Admirable Crichton, The 1957,D 15,45:4
(Incorrect in this edition; use 1957,D 17,45:4
elsewhere)
Rooney 1958,Je 6,29:2
Dunkirk 1958,S 11,42:2
Mark, The 1961,O 3,46:2
Johnny Nobody 1965,N 24,35:1

Byrne, Eddie (Narrator)
Annapurna 1953,D 14,45:4

Byrne, John (Screenwriter)
Guerrilla Girl 1953,Jl 7,23:7

Byrne, Mary
They Got Me Covered 1943,Mr 5,20:2

Byrne, Muriel St Claire (Original Author)
Haunted Honeymoon 1940,O 31,28:2

Byrne, Rosalind
Fast Set, The 1924,N 18,22:1

Byrne-Grant, Helena
Dark Angel, The 1935,S 6,12:2

BYRNES
See Also BERNS, BURNS

Byrnes, Edward
Darby's Rangers 1958,F 13,23:2
Marjorie Morningstar 1958,Ap 25,32:2
Up Periscope 1959,Mr 5,35:4
Yellowstone Kelly 1959,N 12,27:1
Mutiny on the Bounty 1962,N 9,31:2
Secret Invasion, The 1964,S 17,52:5
Secret Invasion, The 1964,S 17,52:6
Any Gun Can Play 1968,S 14,34:2
Payment in Blood 1968,D 5,59:1

Byron, A S
Big Shot, The 1932,Ja 2,14:2
You Said a Mouthful 1932,N 18,23:2
One Sunday Afternoon 1933,S 2,14:4
Two for Tonight 1935,Ag 31,16:2
Bride Comes Home, The 1935,D 25,30:2

Byron, Arthur
Fast Life 1932,D 24,11:4
Mummy, The 1933,Ja 7,11:2
20,000 Years in Sing Sing 1933,Ja 10,26:2
Tonight Is Ours 1933,Ja 21,10:6
Gabriel Over the White House 1933,Ap 1,18:2
Silk Express, The 1933,Je 28,24:2
Mayor of Hell, The 1933,Jl 1,16:5
Private Detective 62 1933,Jl 7,20:2
College Coach 1933,N 11,10:4
House of Rothschild, The 1934,Mr 15,27:2
Stand up and Cheer 1934,Ap 20,17:1
Fog over Frisco 1934,Je 7,26:2
Man With two Faces, The 1934,Jl 12,20:2
Notorious Sophie Lang, The 1934,Jl 21,14:2
Marie Galante 1934,N 21,23:4
President Vanishes, The 1934,D 8,18:5
Secret Bride, The 1935,F 2,10:1
Whole Town's Talking, The 1935,Mr 1,16:2

Byron, Arthur— Cont
Shadow of Doubt 1935,Mr 11,15:1
Casino Murder Case, The 1935,Ap 17,26:5
Murder in the Fleet 1935,Je 3,22:2
Oil for the Lamps of China 1935,Je 6,25:2
Prisoner of Shark Island, The 1936,F 13,25:2

Byron, Brook
Auntie Mame 1958,D 5,39:1

Byron, Delma
Dimples 1936,O 10,21:2

Byron, Eva
Kreutzer Sonata, The 1928,S 10,29:3

Byron, George
Gold Dust Gertie 1931,My 30,9:2
Sob Sister 1931,O 3,20:2
Deceiver, The 1931,N 23,22:1
Chatterbox 1943,Jl 2,15:3

Byron, Jack
Fighting American, The 1924,My 13,24:1
Air Mail, The 1925,Mr 17,18:1
Four Walls 1928,Ag 20,21:3
Spite Marriage 1929,Mr 25,32:2
Lord Byron of Broadway 1930,Mr 8,21:1
Social Lion, The 1930,Je 14,9:4

Byron, Jean
Magnetic Monster, The 1953,My 14,32:5
Wall of Noise 1963,S 5,27:1

Byron, Katherine
Othello 1960,My 16,39:1

Byron, Katheryn
Mummy, The 1933,Ja 7,11:2

Byron, Kathleen
Silver Fleet, The 1945,Mr 24,22:6
Stairway to Heaven 1946,D 26,28:1
Black Narcissus 1947,Ag 14,29:2
Madness of the Heart 1950,O 12,43:2
Prelude to Fame 1950,N 10,35:3
Reluctant Widow, The 1951,S 8,8:6
I'll Never Forget You 1951,D 8,9:2
Tom Brown's School Days 1952,Ja 8,23:5
Small Back Room, The 1952,F 2,11:3
Young Bess 1953,My 22,31:1
Hand in Hand 1961,F 7,41:3
Burn, Witch, Burn 1962,Jl 5,21:2 (In Addenda)

Byron, Marion
Steamboat Bill, Jr 1928,My 15,17:3
Plastered in Paris 1928,S 24,25:1
His Captive Woman 1929,Ap 3,26:4
So Long Letty 1930,F 8,12:5
Song of the West 1930,F 28,20:7
Playing Around 1930,Mr 31,24:3
Golden Dawn 1930,Jl 26,16:4
Matrimonial Bed, The 1930,Ag 25,14:2
Girls Demand Excitement 1931,F 7,11:1
Children of Dreams 1931,Jl 20,20:4
Heart of New York, The 1932,Mr 2,15:3
Tenderfoot, The 1932,My 23,18:4
Love Me Tonight 1932,Ag 19,20:6
Gift of Gab 1934,S 26,17:6
Five of a Kind 1938,O 31,12:2

Byron, Richard
Are These our Parents? 1944,Ag 23,16:2

Byron, Roy
Palm Beach Girl, The 1926,Je 22,21:2

Byron, Walter
Awakening, The 1928,D 31,9:1
Sacred Flame, The 1929,N 23,18:5
Not Damaged 1930,Je 9,23:3
Dancers, The 1930,N 15,15:3
Reckless Hour, The 1931,Ag 1,16:4
Last Flight, The 1931,Ag 20,17:4
Yellow Ticket, The 1931,O 31,22:2
Leftover Ladies 1931,N 9,22:4
Menace, The 1932,Ja 30,13:2
Three Wise Girls 1932,F 6,14:4
Sinners in the Sun 1932,My 14,11:5
Society Girl 1932,Je 10,22:3
Week Ends Only 1932,Je 18,9:2
This Sporting Age 1932,O 1,10:4
Crusader, The 1932,O 8,15:4
Grand Slam 1933,F 22,25:2
What Price Decency? 1933,Mr 2,20:6
Charlie Chan's Greatest Case 1933,O 7,18:4
Man of Two Worlds 1934,Ja 12,29:2
Once to Every Woman 1934,Mr 26,22:3
British Agent 1934,S 20,20:1
Folies Bergere 1935,F 25,13:2
Don't Bet on Blondes 1935,Jl 20,16:2
Mary of Scotland 1936,Jl 31,22:2
Back in Circulation 1937,O 4,17:1
Trade Winds 1939,Ja 13,17:2

Bystritskaya, Ellina
And Quiet Flows the Don 1960,My 25,45:2

C

Caan, James
Lady in a Cage 1964,Je 11,27:1
Red Line 7000 1965,D 9,60:4
Dorado, El 1967,Je 29,32:1
Games 1967,S 18,58:2
Countdown 1968,My 2,57:3

Cabal, Robert
Mara Maru 1952,Ap 24,38:1
Hell's Island 1955,My 7,10:2

Caballero, Oscar
Terrace, The 1964,N 25,45:1

Cabanne, Christy (Director)
Youth for Sale 1924,S 3,17:1
Midshipman, The 1925,O 13,20:1
Masked Bride, The 1925,N 30,17:1
Hotel Continental 1932,Mr 21,19:5
Midnight Patrol, The 1932,My 7,11:5
Red-Haired Alibi 1932,O 24,18:5
Western Limited 1932,D 12,18:4
Daring Daughters 1933,Mr 25,13:4
World Gone Mad, The 1933,Ap 15,16:3
Midshipman Jack 1933,N 20,18:2
Girl of the Limberlost, A 1934,N 9,24:6
Behind the Green Lights 1935,Ap 22,14:2
Keeper of the Bees, The 1935,Ag 17,18:5
Last Outlaw, The 1936,Je 15,24:1
We Who Are About to Die 1937,Ja 2,15:1
Criminal Lawyer 1937,Ja 27,17:3
Don't Tell the Wife 1937,F 19,15:2
Outcasts of Poker Flat, The 1937,Ap 27,18:3
You Can't Beat Love 1937,Je 25,25:3
Annapolis Salute 1937,O 2,18:1
Westland Case, The 1937,O 23,14:2
Alas sobre el Chaco; Wings Over the Chaco
  1939,Mr 28,20:2
Mutiny on the Blackhawk 1939,Ag 2,17:2
Tropic Fury 1939,S 8,28:4
Legion of Lost Flyers 1939,O 30,13:3
Alias the Deacon 1940,My 14,27:5
Hot Steel 1940,Je 21,25:3
Black Diamonds 1940,S 10,26:6
Mummy's Hand, The 1940,S 20,27:2
Devil's Pipeline, The 1940,N 11,22:4
Scattergood Baines 1941,Ap 4,25:2
Drums of the Congo 1942,Jl 20,16:4

Cabanne, Christy (Original Author)
Annapolis Salute 1937,O 2,18:1

Cabeen, Boyd
Gentlemen Marry Brunettes 1955,O 31,31:5

Cabellos, Carlos
Tesoro de Pancho Villa, El 1936,Ja 27,20:4

Cable, Boyd (Miscellaneous)
Somme, The 1928,N 27,34:1

Cabo, Louise
Risky Business 1926,S 8,19:3

Cabot, Bruce
Roadhouse Murder 1932,Ap 29,13:4
Great Jasper, The 1933,F 17,5:3
Lucky Devils 1933,F 20,11:5
King Kong 1933,Mr 3,12:1
Disgraced 1933,Jl 15,14:2
Flying Devils 1933,Ag 26,14:3
Ann Vickers 1933,S 29,24:1
Midshipman Jack 1933,N 20,18:2
Shadows of Sing Sing 1934,F 21,23:2
Finishing School 1934,Ap 30,11:4
Murder on the Blackboard 1934,Je 20,24:2
His Greatest Gamble 1934,Jl 18,20:2
Their big Moment 1934,S 6,22:4
Redhead 1934,N 16,27:1
Let 'Em Have It 1935,My 30,21:1
Show Them no Mercy 1935,D 9,25:2
Don't Gamble With Love 1936,Mr 2,13:3
Robin Hood of El Dorado, The 1936,Mr 14,10:1
Three Wise Guys, The 1936,My 23,12:2
Fury 1936,Je 6,21:1
Last of the Mohicans, The 1936,S 3,17:3
Don't Turn 'em Loose 1936,S 25,20:2
Big Game, The 1936,O 24,23:1
Legion of Terror 1936,N 2,24:2
Sinner Take All 1937,F 3,27:1
Bad Guy 1937,Ag 26,25:2
Love Takes Flight 1937,S 27,24:3
Bad Man of Brimstone, The 1938,F 4,17:2
Sinners in Paradise 1938,My 20,17:2
Smashing the Rackets 1938,Ag 9,22:5
Tenth Avenue Kid 1938,S 2,21:3
Homicide Bureau 1939,F 2,17:2
Dodge City 1939,Ap 8,19:1
Mickey, the Kid 1939,Jl 6,27:1
My Son Is Guilty 1940,Ja 15,11:2
Susan and God 1940,Jl 12,11:2
Captain Caution 1940,O 21,21:3
Girls Under 21 1940,N 11,22:4
Flame of New Orleans, The 1941,Ap 26,20:2
Wild Bill Hickok Rides 1942,F 7,13:5
Pierre of the Plains 1942,Jl 30,17:3
Silver Queen 1943,Ja 11,18:4
Desert Song, The 1943,D 18,10:6
Salty O'Rourke 1945,Ap 26,26:2
Fallen Angel 1946,F 7,29:4
Smoky 1946,Je 27,29:1
Avalanche 1946,Jl 8,25:2
Angel and the Badman 1947,Mr 3,28:4
Gunfighters 1947,Jl 25,12:5
Sorrowful Jones 1949,Je 6,15:2
Rock Island Trail 1950,Je 5,19:3
Fancy Pants 1950,Ag 31,21:2
Best of the Badmen 1951,Ag 10,13:2

Cabot, Bruce— Cont
Quiet American, The 1958,F 6,24:1
Sheriff of Fractured Jaw, The 1959,Mr 14,27:4
John Paul Jones 1959,Je 17,39:1
Goliath and the Barbarians 1960,Ja 7,24:6
Comancheros, The 1961,N 2,42:1
Hatari 1962,Jl 12,19:1
McLintock 1963,N 14,41:3
Law of the Lawless 1964,Ag 27,28:2
In Harm's Way 1965,Ap 7,36:1
Black Spurs 1965,My 29,17:1
Cat Ballou 1965,Je 25,36:1
War Wagon, The 1967,Ag 3,26:3
Green Berets, The 1968,Je 20,49:1

Cabot, Elliott
Puritan Passions 1923,O 15,15:4

Cabot, Sebastian
Wonder Boy 1951,D 26,19:5
Ivanhoe 1952,Ag 1,8:2
Babes in Bagdad 1954,Ap 5,21:3
Always a Bride 1954,My 28,19:2
Romeo and Juliet 1954,D 22,28:1
Kismet 1955,D 9,32:2
Dragoon Wells Massacre 1957,My 6,25:2
Johnny Tremain 1957,Jl 11,21:1
Black Patch 1958,Ag 24,38:1
In Love and War 1958,N 1,14:2
Say One for Me 1959,Je 20,11:2
Angry Hills, The 1959,Jl 16,31:3
Seven Thieves 1960,Mr 12,14:5
Time Machine, The 1960,Ag 18,19:1
Twice Told Tales (Dr Heidegger's Experiment); Dr
  Heidegger's Experiment (Twice Told Tales)
  1964,Mr 28,40:1
Family Jewels, The 1965,Ag 12,30:4

Cabot, Susan
Enforcer, The 1951,Ja 26,19:2
Tomahawk 1951,F 19,19:2
Flame of Araby 1951,D 20,41:7
Battle at Apache Pass, The 1952,My 10,16:4
Duel at Silver Creek 1952,Ag 2,7:6
Son of Ali Baba 1952,Ag 16,7:4

Cabre, Mario
Pandora and the Flying Dutchman 1951,D 7,35:2

Cabrini, Carlo
Fiances, The 1964,Ja 29,23:1

Cacoyannis, Miahael (Producer)
Day the Fish Came Out, The 1967,O 3,57:1

Cacoyannis, Michael (Director)
Windfall in Athens 1956,O 1,31:1
Stella 1957,Je 11,40:1
Girl in Black, A 1957,S 17,39:2
Electra 1962,D 18,5:2
Wastrel, The 1963,N 5,24:1
Zorba, The Greek 1964,D 18,25:1
Day the Fish Came Out, The 1967,O 3,57:1

Cacoyannis, Michael (Original Author)
Windfall in Athens 1956,O 1,31:1

Cacoyannis, Michael (Producer)
Electra 1962,D 18,5:2
Zorba, The Greek 1964,D 18,25:1

Cacoyannis, Michael (Screenwriter)
Windfall in Athens 1956,O 1,31:1
Stella 1957,Je 11,40:1
Girl in Black, A 1957,S 17,39:2
Electra 1962,D 18,5:2
Wastrel, The 1963,N 5,24:1
Zorba, The Greek 1964,D 18,25:1
Day the Fish Came Out, The 1967,O 3,57:1

Cade, Jerry (Original Author)
Island in the Sky 1938,My 14,18:1

Cadeac, Paul (Producer)
OSS 117-Mission for a Killer 1966,O 13,50:3
Two of Us, The 1968,F 20,53:1

Cadell, Jean
Fires of Fate 1933,Ap 3,13:4
Little Friend 1934,O 20,20:2
David Copperfield 1935,Ja 19,8:1
Love From a Stranger 1937,Ap 19,27:2
Pygmalion 1938,D 8,34:2
Mozart 1940,O 4,29:2
Quiet Wedding 1941,D 29,27:4
Young Mr Pitt, The 1943,Mr 11,17:1
I Know Where I'm Going 1947,Ag 20,25:2
Jassy 1948,F 20,19:2
Tight Little Island 1949,D 26,33:2
If This Be Sin 1950,Jl 1,9:2
Madeleine 1950,S 1,17:2
No Place for Jennifer 1951,Jl 17,31:2
Reluctant Widow, The 1951,S 8,8:6
Obsessed 1952,F 6,24:2
Marry Me 1952,Mr 14,27:3
Little Hut, The 1957,My 4,25:1

Cadeo, Guiseppe
Organizer, The 1964,My 7,31:2

Caderon, Pedro A (Producer)
St Francis of Assisi 1947,Ap 5,12:5

Cadet, Rivers
Louise 1940,F 3,9:4
Open Road, The 1940,O 5,20:2

Cadet Corps of the Virginia Military Institute
Mardi Gras 1958,N 19,45:2

Cadile, Angela
Divorce-Italian Style 1962,S 18,34:1
Cadillac, Rita
Any Number Can Win 1963,O 9,47:2
Cadle, C Ernest Dr (Narrator)
Wild Men of Kalihari 1930,N 25,30:6
Cadman, Charles Wakefield (Composer)
Captain of the Guard 1930,Mr 29,23:1
Go West 1941,F 21,16:2
Cadman, Charles Wakefield (Miscellaneous)
Drums of Love 1928,Ja 25,20:4
Cadoni, Fernanda
Cinderella 1953,My 15,20:2
Cady, Frank
Great Rupert, The 1950,Ap 14,27:2
Ace in the Hole 1951,Je 30,8:6
Dear Brat 1951,Jl 5,21:2
When Worlds Collide 1952,F 7,30:2
Atomic City, The 1952,My 2,21:1
Rear Window 1954,Ag 5,18:2
Indian Fighter, The 1955,D 22,20:1
Bad Seed, The 1956,S 13,39:6
Girl Most Likely, The 1958,O 9,47:1
Cady, Jerry (Original Author)
Play Girl 1941,Ja 30,19:3
Obliging Young Lady 1942,F 13,24:4
Man Alive 1945,N 17,14:5
Cry Danger 1951,F 22,27:3
Cady, Jerry (Screenwriter)
Great Hospital Mystery, The 1937,Jl 16,22:2
Charlie Chan on Broadway 1937,S 20,19:1
Charlie Chan at Monte Carlo 1937,D 18,18:1
Mr Moto's Gamble 1938,Ap 8,17:2
One Wild Night 1938,Je 3,17:2
Time Out for Murder 1938,O 7,21:2
Five came Back 1939,Jl 5,20:2
Full Confession 1939,S 28,29:4
Sued for Libel 1940,Ja 19,15:3
Marines Fly High, The 1940,Mr 5,19:2
You Can't Fool Your Wife 1940,My 24,23:4
Cross Country Romance 1940,Jl 19,22:3
Anne of Windy Poplars 1940,Ag 23,13:3
Play Girl 1941,Ja 30,19:3
Saint in Palm Springs, The 1941,Ja 31,15:5
What's Cookin' 1942,F 26,15:5
Mexican Spitfire at Sea 1942,Je 26,16:5
Silver Skates 1943,Mr 19,15:3
Guadalcanal Diary 1943,N 18,29:1
Purple Heart, The 1944,Mr 9,15:2
Roger Touhy, Gangster 1944,Je 5,14:7
Wing and a Prayer 1944,Ag 31,14:1
Forever Amber 1947,O 23,31:2
Thunder in the Valley 1947,N 28,30:1
Call Northside 777 1948,F 19,29:2
Sand 1949,Ag 5,23:2
Caesar, Arthur (Miscellaneous)
Transient Lady 1935,Mr 11,15:1
Loves of Edgar Allan Poe, The 1942,S 21,19:2
Caesar, Arthur (Original Author)
Napoleon's Barber 1928,N 26,30:2
Side Show 1931,S 19,10:2
Fireman, Save My Child 1932,F 18,25:3
Chief, The 1933,D 2,9:4
Manhattan Melodrama 1934,My 5,22:2
Star Maker, The 1939,Ag 31,14:2
Pistol Packin' Mama 1943,D 20,27:4
Atlantic City 1944,Ag 14,11:4
Caesar, Arthur (Screenwriter)
McFadden's Flats 1935,Mr 13,16:2
Alias Mary Dow 1935,Je 29,16:2
Star Maker, The 1939,Ag 31,14:2
Little Men 1940,D 9,23:2
Adventure in Washington 1941,Ag 1,11:3
Anne of the Indies 1951,O 25,36:3
Caesar, Irving (Composer)
George White's Scandals 1934,Mr 16,24:2
Hit the Deck 1955,Mr 4,17:1
Caesar, Irving (Miscellaneous)
Curly Top 1935,Ag 2,22:3
Stowaway 1936,D 19,16:1
No, No, Nanette 1940,D 20,33:1
Caesar, Irving (Original Author)
Straight, Place and Show 1938,O 1,10:2
Caesar, Sid
Tars and Spars 1946,F 15,29:2
Guilt of Janet Ames, The 1947,My 23,31:2
It's a Mad, Mad, Mad, Mad World 1963,N 19,47:1
Guide for the Married Man, A 1967,My 27,16:1
Busy Body, The 1967,Je 8,52:2
Caffrey, Sean
Time Lost and Time Remembered 1966,Ag 30,35:2
Cagarp, Carl-Henry (Producer)
Magician, The 1959,Ag 28,27:1
Cagney, James
Sinners' Holiday 1930,O 11,21:3
Doorway to Hell, The 1930,N 1,23:2
Millionaire, The 1931,Ap 9,30:5
Other Men's Women 1931,Ap 20,16:3
Public Enemy, The 1931,Ap 24,27:1
Smart Money 1931,Je 19,21:1
Blonde Crazy 1931,D 4,28:2

Taxi 1932,Ja 8,27:3
Crowd Roars, The 1932,Mr 23,25:4
Crowd Roars, The 1932,Ap 3,VIII,4:4
Winner Take All 1932,Je 18,9:2
Hard to Handle 1933,F 2,21:5
Picture Snatcher 1933,My 19,20:3
Mayor of Hell, The 1933,Jl 1,16:5
Footlight Parade 1933,O 6,21:3
Lady Killer 1934,Ja 1,28:2
Jimmy the Gent 1934,Mr 26,22:3
He Was her Man 1934,My 17,28:2
Here Comes the Navy 1934,Jl 21,14:2
St Louis Kid, The 1934,N 1,25:2
Devil Dogs of the Air 1935,F 7,23:2
G Men 1935,My 2,17:1
Irish in US, The 1935,Ag 1,15:1
Midsummer Night's Dream, A 1935,O 10,31:1
Frisco Kid 1935,N 25,22:1
Ceiling Zero 1936,Ja 20,22:2
Great Guy 1937,Ja 1,19:2
Something to Sing About 1937,S 21,29:4
Boy Meets Girl 1938,Ag 27,7:2
Angels With Dirty Faces 1938,N 26,18:1
Oklahoma Kid, The 1939,Mr 11,21:1
Each Dawn I Die 1939,Jl 22,12:2
Roaring Twenties, The 1939,N 11,12:1
Fighting 69th, The 1940,Ja 27,9:2
Torrid Zone 1940,My 18,11:3
City for Conquest 1940,S 28,9:2
Strawberry Blonde 1941,F 22,11:2
Bride Came C O D, The 1941,Jl 26,18:2
Captains of the Clouds 1942,F 13,24:2
Yankee Doodle Dandy 1942,My 30,9:1
Johnny Come Lately 1943,S 24,26:1
Blood on the Sun 1945,Je 29,12:2
13 Rue Madeleine 1947,Ja 16,30:2
Time of your Life, The 1948,My 27,29:2
White Heat 1949,S 3,7:2
Kiss Tomorrow Goodbye 1950,Ag 5,9:2
West Point Story, The 1950,D 23,11:3
Come Fill the Cup 1951,N 22,47:2
Starlift 1951,D 15,11:2
What Price Glory 1952,Ag 23,10:2
Lion Is in the Streets, A 1953,S 24,39:2
Run for Cover 1955,Ap 30,10:6
Love Me or Leave Me 1955,My 27,14:1
Seven Little Foys, The 1955,Je 30,18:2
Mister Roberts 1955,Jl 15,14:1
Tribute to a Bad Man 1956,Mr 31,13:3
These Wilder Years 1956,Ag 18,11:2
Man of a Thousand Faces 1957,Ag 14,21:1
Never Steal Anything Small 1959,F 12,23:1
Shake Hands With the Devil 1959,Je 25,20:7
Gallant Hours, The 1960,Je 23,19:4
One, Two, Three 1961,D 22,17:1
Cagney, Jean
Queen of the Mob 1940,Jl 1,23:2
Golden Gloves 1940,Ag 21,23:6
Rhythm on the River 1940,Ag 29,23:2
Cagney, Jeanne
Yankee Doodle Dandy 1942,My 30,9:1
Time of your Life, The 1948,My 27,29:2
Quicksand 1950,Je 16,28:4
Don't Bother to Knock 1952,Jl 19,8:2
Lion Is in the Streets, A 1953,S 24,39:2
Man of a Thousand Faces 1957,Ag 14,21:1
Cagney, William
Ace of Aces 1933,N 11,10:4
Palooka 1934,F 28,23:2
Stolen Harmony 1935,Ap 20,16:2
Cagney, William (Producer)
Johnny Come Lately 1943,S 24,26:1
Blood on the Sun 1945,Je 29,12:2
Time of your Life, The 1948,My 27,29:2
Kiss Tomorrow Goodbye 1950,Ag 5,9:2
Cahan, Oscar
Mystery of the Hooded Horsemen, The 1937,Ag 13,13:2
Cahill, Barry
Sweet Bird of Youth 1962,Mr 29,28:2
Cahill, Drew
Sad Sack, The 1957,N 28,57:1
Cahill, Lily
My Sin 1931,S 11,24:2
CAHN
See Also KAHN
Cahn, Edward L (Director)
Law and Order 1932,F 29,21:3
Radio Patrol 1932,Jl 14,24:2
Afraid to Talk 1932,D 19,19:5
Laughter in Hell 1933,Ja 2,29:2
Emergency Call 1933,Je 24,16:2
Bad Guy 1937,Ag 26,25:2
Main Street After Dark 1945,Ja 13,15:4
Dangerous Partners 1945,N 2,22:4
Operation Bottleneck 1961,S 7,40:2
Secret of Deep Harbor 1961,O 26,39:7
Incident in an Alley 1962,My 17,31:1
Cahn, Sammy (Composer)
Rookies on Parade 1941,My 22,25:2
Time Out for Rhythm 1941,Jl 10,16:3
Heat's on, The 1943,N 26,29:2
Knickerbocker Holiday 1944,Ap 20,22:7

Cahn, Sammy (Composer) — Cont
Step Lively 1944,Jl 27,14:1
Carolina Blues 1944,D 8,26:6
Tonight and Every Night 1945,Mr 9,16:2
Anchors Aweigh 1945,Jl 20,15:2
Tars and Spars 1946,F 15,29:2
Kid From Brooklyn, The 1946,Ap 19,25:2
Earl Carroll Sketchbook 1946,Ag 30,13:2
It Happened in Brooklyn 1947,Mr 14,28:5
It's a Great Feeling 1949,Ag 13,6:6
Always Leave Them Laughing 1949,N 24,48:2
Toast of New Orleans, The 1950,S 30,13:3
Court Jester, The 1956,F 2,19:1
Meet Me in Las Vegas 1956,Mr 14,39:2
Anything Goes 1956,Mr 22,38:1
Pardners 1956,Jl 26,20:2
Opposite Sex, The 1956,N 16,23:2
Ten Thousand Bedrooms 1957,Ap 4,37:1
Rock-a-Bye Baby 1958,Jl 24,18:1
Cahn, Sammy (Miscellaneous)
Manhattan Merry-Go-Round 1937,D 31,9:3
Rich, Young and Pretty 1951,Jl 26,17:3
Cahn, Sammy (Original Author)
Rookies on Parade 1941,My 22,25:2
Two Tickets to Broadway 1951,N 22,47:2
Cahn, Sammy (Producer)
Three Sailors and a Girl 1953,N 23,32:2
Caho, Mari Loli
Tia Tula, A 1965,Je 3,24:1
Cahoon, Wyn
Murder in Greenwich Village 1937,O 30,22:2
Women in Prison 1938,Mr 1,19:3
Who Killed Gail Preston? 1938,My 6,27:2
Caillaux, Roland
Itto 1936,Ja 29,15:5
Caillava, Raymond (Screenwriter)
Diary of a Bad Girl 1958,My 30,13:2
Caillavet, G A De (Original Author)
Royal Affair, A; (Roi, Le) 1950,Mr 9,25:2
Caillavet, G M (Original Author)
Miquette 1951,F 5,18:2
Caillou, Alan
Clarence, the Cross-Eyed Lion 1965,Ag 5,15:3
Caillou, Alan (Original Author)
Rampage 1963,O 17,39:2
Caillou, Alan (Screenwriter)
Clarence, the Cross-Eyed Lion 1965,Ag 5,15:3
Cailloux
Miserables, Les 1936,O 28,31:2
CAIN
See Also CAINE, KANE, CANE
Cain, Charles
My Favorite Blonde 1942,Ap 2,27:2
Cain, James M (Miscellaneous)
Algiers 1938,Jl 15,13:2
Cain, James M (Original Author)
She Made her Bed 1934,Ap 27,25:1
Wife, Husband and Friend 1939,F 25,19:2
When Tomorrow Comes 1939,Ag 17,16:2
Money and the Woman 1940,O 4,29:2
Double Indemnity 1944,S 7,21:1
Mildred Pierce 1945,S 29,12:2
Postman Always Rings Twice, The 1946,My 3,15:3
Everybody Does It 1949,O 26,32:2
Slightly Scarlet 1956,Mr 17,13:2
Serenade 1956,Mr 24,21:1 (Incorrect in this edition; use 1956,Mr 23,21:1 elsewhere)
Cain, James M (Screenwriter)
Stand up and Fight 1939,Ja 27,17:2
Gypsy Wildcat 1944,O 5,18:6
Cain, Robert
In Mizzoura 1919,O 13,16:3
Male and Female 1919,N 24,13:1
Man-Woman-Marriage 1921,Mr 28,11:4
Crossroads of New York, The 1922,My 22,18:4
Impossible Mrs Bellew, The 1922,O 23,10:1
Drums of Fate 1923,Ja 15,18:3
Children of Jazz 1923,Jl 9,8:4
Three Weeks 1924,Ap 1,19:3
Golden Bed, The 1925,Ja 20,18:2
Wings of Youth 1925,Ap 20,18:1 (Incorrect in this edition; use 1925,Ap 28,18:1 elsewhere)
Everlasting Whisper, The 1925,O 12,19:3
Dancers of Paris, The 1926,Mr 29,24:3
Wilderness Woman, The 1926,My 10,19:1
CAINE
See Also KANE, CANE, CAIN
Caine, Derwent Hall
Deemster, The 1917,Ap 16,9:2
Caine, Georgia
Good Intentions 1930,Jl 26,16:4
Cradle Song 1933,N 20,18:2
I Am Suzanne 1934,Ja 19,24:3
Once to Every Woman 1934,Mr 26,22:3
Call it Luck 1934,Jl 10,24:5
Count of Monte Cristo, The 1934,S 27,25:2
Hooray for Love 1935,Jl 13,16:2
One Rainy Afternoon 1936,My 14,29:2
White Angel, The 1936,Je 25,24:1
Sing Me a Love Song 1936,D 26,15:2
It's Love I'm After 1937,N 11,31:2
Women Are Like That 1938,Ap 11,12:2
Dodge City 1939,Ap 8,19:1

Caine, Georgia— Cont
  Juarez 1939,Ap 26,27:1
  Honeymoon in Bali 1939,S 21,21:1
  Remember the Night 1940,Ja 18,27:2
  Lone Wolf Meets a Lady, The 1940,Je 17,19:2
  Christmas in July 1940,N 6,35:2
  Nurse's Secret, The 1941,Je 6,25:7
  Wife Takes a Flyer, The 1942,Je 19,19:1
  Miracle of Morgan's Creek, The 1944,Ja 20,15:2
  Hail the Conquering Hero 1944,Ag 10,14:2
  Give my Regards to Broadway 1948,Je 23,32:2
  Beautiful Blonde From Bashful Bend, The
    1949,My 28,11:2
  Mad Wednesday 1951,Ja 25,21:5
Caine, Hall (Original Author)
  Eternal City, The 1915,Ap 13,11:2
  Deemster, The 1917,Ap 16,9:2
  Manx-Man, The 1917,Ag 20,12:4
  Woman Thou Gavest Me, The 1919,Je 9,16:3
  Christian, The 1923,F 12,13:4
  Eternal City, The 1924,Ja 21,20:1
  Name the Man 1924,F 4,23:3
  Barbed Wire 1927,Ag 8,10:3
  Manxman, The 1929,D 17,28:7
Caine, Henry
  Dreyfus Case, The 1931,Ag 31,11:5
  Ghost Train, The 1933,F 18,13:3
Caine, Howard
  Pay or Die 1960,My 27,22:2
  Man From the Diners' Club, The
    1963,Ap 18,39:1
  Alvarez Kelly 1966,N 17,55:2
Caine, Michael
  How to Murder a Rich Uncle 1957,O 26,19:2
  Zulu 1964,Jl 8,38:1
  Ipcress File, The 1965,Ag 3,35:1
  Wrong Box 1966,Jl 20,46:1
  Alfie 1966,Ag 25,42:1
  Gambit 1966,D 22,40:2
  Funeral in Berlin 1966,D 23,17:1
  Hurry Sundown 1967,Mr 24,22:1
  Woman Times Seven 1967,Je 28,38:1
  London Scene, The (Tonite Let's All Make Love
    in London 1967,S 27,39:1
  Billion Dollar Brain 1967,D 23,29:1
  Deadfall 1968,S 12,54:1
  Magus, The 1968,D 11,57:1
Caine, Stanley
  Billion Dollar Brain 1967,D 23,29:1
Caiocci, Pier Luigi
  Bebo's Girl 1964,N 12,40:1
Cairncross, James
  Tom Jones 1963,O 8,48:1
Cairney, John
  A Night to Remember 1958,D 17,2:7
  Victim 1962,F 6,27:2
  Cleopatra 1963,Je 13,29:1
Cairns, Dorothy (Screenwriter)
  Sin Takes a Holliday 1930,N 28,23:1
Cairolt
  I Love, You Love 1962,N 10,16:2
Caithness, Wilfred
  Brandy for the Parson 1952,Ag 18,13:4
Caits, Joe
  Hollywood Cowboy 1937,Jl 24,12:1
  Reformatory 1938,Je 27,13:6
Caivino, Italo (Original Author)
  Of Wayward Love (The Soldier); Soldier, The (Of
    Wayward Love) 1964,Mr 24,29:1
  Of Wayward Love (The Women); Women, The
    (Of Wayward Love) 1964,Mr 24,29:1
  Of Wayward Love (The Serpent); Serpent, The (Of
    Wayward Love) 1964,Mr 24,29:1
Cajano, Carlo (Producer)
  See Naples and Die 1959,Ag 31,16:2
Calamal, Clara
  Merry Chase, The 1948,S 18,11:4
  White Nights 1961,My 29,9:6
Calaman
  Generals Without Buttons 1938,Mr 8,23:2
Calano, Carlo (Producer)
  Nights of Lucretia Borgia, The 1960,O 6,51:4
Calano, Mario (Screenwriter)
  Nights of Lucretia Borgia, The 1960,O 6,51:4
Calaveras Trio
  Three Caballeros, The 1945,F 5,20:1
Calazza, Alfred
  Good Morning, Miss Dove 1955,N 24,41:1
Caldara, Orme
  Spreading Dawn, The 1917,O 22,13:2
Calder, Alexander
  8 X 8 1957,Mr 16,13:2
Calder, Alexander (Miscellaneous)
  Dreams that Money can Buy 1948,Ap 24,11:2
Calder, King
  Rains of Ranchipur, The 1955,D 16,38:2
  Timetable 1956,Mr 17,13:2
Calderon, Pedro A (Producer)
  Loyola, The Soldier Saint 1952,Ap 25,19:2
Calderwood, Diana
  Kipps 1942,My 25,11:2
  Curtain Up 1953,F 2,17:3

Caldicot, Richard
  Horse's Mouth, The 1958,N 12,41:1
Caldwell, Anne (Composer)
  Dixiana 1930,S 5,21:1
  Half Shot at Sunrise 1930,O 11,21:3
Caldwell, Anne (Original Author)
  Marry Me 1925,Jl 13,20:2
  Dixiana 1930,S 5,21:1
Caldwell, Betty
  Miracle Can Happen, A 1948,F 4,28:4
Caldwell, Bobbie
  West Point of the Air 1935,Ap 6,10:1
Caldwell, Erskine (Miscellaneous)
  Volcano 1953,Jl 21,19:2
Caldwell, Erskine (Original Author)
  Tobacco Road 1941,F 21,16:2
  God's Little Acre 1958,Ag 14,23:2
  Claudelle Inglish 1961,S 21,40:2
Caldwell, H H (Miscellaneous)
  Singed 1927,Jl 12,29:3
Caldwell, Orville
  French Doll, The 1923,S 5,15:3
  Sackcloth and Scarlet 1925,Mr 25,24:2
  Judgment of the Hills 1927,Ag 2,19:2
  Harvester, The 1927,N 7,33:1
  Patsy, The 1928,Ap 23,20:2
  Just Around the Corner 1938,D 3,11:2
  Last Warning, The 1938,D 8,34:4
Caldwell, Peter
  One Foot in Heaven 1941,N 14,28:3
Cale, Gene
  Happy Go Lucky 1943,Mr 25,25:1
Calef, Henri (Director)
  Jericho 1946,D 16,31:2
  Wench, The 1949,Mr 14,15:5
Calef, Noel (Original Author)
  Stranger on the Prowl 1953,N 10,38:1
  Tiger Bay 1959,D 15,50:1
  Frantic 1961,Je 12,34:1
Calef, Noel (Producer)
  Stranger on the Prowl 1953,N 10,38:1
Calfa, Don
  No More Excuses 1968,My 22,53:1
Calhern, Louis
  Stolen Heaven 1931,F 14,11:4
  Road to Singapore, The 1931,O 1,25:2
  Blonde Crazy 1931,D 4,28:2
  Okay America 1932,S 10,18:5
  They Call It Sin 1932,O 21,25:4
  Night after Night 1932,O 31,18:4
  Afraid to Talk 1932,D 19,19:5
  Frisco Jenny 1933,Ja 7,11:2
  20,000 Years in Sing Sing 1933,Ja 10,26:2
  Woman Accused, The 1933,Mr 13,18:2
  Strictly Personal 1933,Mr 20,18:2
  World Gone Mad, The 1933,Ap 15,16:3
  Diplomaniacs 1933,Ap 29,14:2
  Duck Soup 1933,N 23,24:2
  Man With two Faces, The 1934,Jl 12,20:2
  Affairs of Cellini, The 1934,S 6,22:3
  Count of Monte Cristo, The 1934,S 27,25:2
  Sweet Adeline 1935,Ja 7,13:2
  Arizonian, The 1935,Jl 27,16:2
  Last Days of Pompeii, The 1935,O 17,29:2
  Gorgeous Hussy, The 1936,S 5,7:1
  Her Husband Lies 1937,Mr 18,20:1
  Life of Emile Zola, The 1937,Ag 12,14:2
  Fast Company 1938,Jl 6,21:2
  Juarez 1939,Ap 26,27:1
  Fifth Avenue Girl 1939,Ag 25,12:2
  Charlie McCarthy, Detective 1939,D 25,29:2
  I Take This Woman 1940,F 16,23:3
  Dr Ehrlich's Magic Bullet 1940,F 24,9:2
  Heaven Can Wait 1943,Ag 12,15:1
  Up in Arms 1944,Mr 3,19:2
  Bridge of San Luis Rey, The 1944,Mr 4,11:1
  Notorious 1946,Ag 16,19:2
  Arch of Triumph 1948,Ap 21,33:2
  Red Pony, The 1949,Mr 9,33:2
  Red Danube, The 1949,D 9,37:3
  Nancy Goes to Rio 1950,Ap 7,22:2
  Annie Get Your Gun 1950,My 18,37:1
  Asphalt Jungle, The 1950,Je 9,29:3
  Life of her Own, A 1950,O 12,43:2
  Devil's Doorway 1950,N 10,35:1
  Two Weeks With Love 1950,N 24,31:2
  Magnificent Yankee, The 1951,Ja 19,21:2
  Man With a Cloak, The 1951,N 28,37:2
  Invitation 1952,Ja 30,22:6
  Washington Story 1952,Jl 2,22:3
  We're not Married 1952,Jl 12,16:2
  Prisoner of Zenda, The 1952,N 5,36:2
  Julius Caesar 1953,Je 5,19:1
  Latin Lovers 1953,Ag 13,17:2
  Main Street to Broadway 1953,O 14,34:1
  Rhapsody 1954,Mr 12,17:1
  Executive Suite 1954,My 7,19:1
  Men of the Fighting Lady 1954,My 8,15:2
  Student Prince, The 1954,Je 16,18:2
  Betrayed 1954,S 9,36:1
  Athena 1954,D 22,28:2
  Blackboard Jungle 1955,Mr 21,21:5
  Prodigal, The 1955,My 14,10:7

Calhern, Louis— Cont
  Forever, Darling 1956,F 10,18:1
  High Society 1956,Ag 10,9:2
Calhoun, Alice
  Masters of Men 1923,My 15,22:1
  Man Next Door, The 1923,My 29,10:3
  Pioneer Trails 1923,N 12,15:3
  Man From Brodney's, The 1923,D 18,16:3
  Flowing Gold 1924,Mr 10,18:2
  Between Friends 1924,My 12,14:4
  Code of the Wilderness, The 1924,Jl 1,21:4
  Pampered Youth 1925,F 10,20:1
  Happy Warrior, The 1925,Jl 7,24:2
  Man on the Box, The 1925,S 28,24:1
  Everlasting Whisper, The 1925,O 12,19:3
Calhoun, Kathleen
  Man on the Box, The 1925,S 28,24:1
Calhoun, Rory
  Red House, The 1947,Mr 17,27:2
  Adventure Island 1947,O 20,29:2
  That Hagen Girl 1947,O 25,13:2
  Miraculous Journey 1948,S 20,21:2
  Massacre River 1949,Jl 15,17:2
  Sand 1949,Ag 5,23:2
  Ticket to Tomahawk, A 1950,My 20,8:6
  Return of the Frontiersman 1950,Je 10,11:3
  Rogue River 1951,F 16,21:4
  I'd Climb the Highest Mountain 1951,My 10,38:1
  Meet Me After the Show 1951,Ag 16,23:2
  With a Song in my Heart 1952,Ap 5,20:2
  Way of a Gaucho 1952,N 5,36:2
  Powder River 1953,Jl 4,7:2
  How to Marry a Millionaire 1953,N 11,37:1
  River of no Return 1954,My 1,13:2
  Dawn at Socorro 1954,Ag 28,8:2
  Four Guns to the Border 1954,N 6,15:3
  Bullet is Waiting, A 1954,N 12,17:2
  Ain't Misbehavin' 1955,Jl 2,13:2
  Treasure of Pancho Villa, The 1955,N 25,38:2
  Spoilers, The 1955,D 24,10:2
  Raw Edge 1956,Jl 28,10:7
  Flight to Hong Kong 1957,Ja 3,28:2
  Big Caper, The 1957,Mr 29,16:1
  Colossus of Rhodes, The 1961,D 14,55:6
  Secret of Monte Cristo, The 1962,My 3,25:4
  Marco Polo 1962,S 20,29:2
  Requiem for a Heavyweight 1962,O 17,35:1
  Black Spurs 1965,My 29,17:1
  Dayton's Devils 1968,O 3,56:4
Cali, Giulio
  Mill on the Po, The 1951,O 23,35:2
Califano, Mario
  Pirates of Capri, The 1949,D 26,33:5
Californian Collegians
  Top of the Town 1937,Mr 27,19:2
Caligola (dog)
  Man Who Wagged his Tail, The 1961,S 19,39:1
Calindri, Ernesto
  Mademoiselle Gobette 1955,F 5,13:3
  Most Wonderful Moment, The 1959,Je 1,23:6
  Eye of the Needle, The 1965,Je 22,25:2
Calkins, John
  Sullivans, The 1944,F 10,19:2
  Life With Father 1947,Ag 16,6:6
  Boy With Green Hair, The 1949,Ja 13,26:2
Call, Giulio
  Overcoat, The 1953,O 13,34:1
Call, John
  Hangman's Knot 1952,D 11,45:3
  Santa Claus Conquers the Martians
    1964,D 17,50:2
Call, John W
  Soak the Rich 1936,F 5,14:2
Callahan, Andrew J
  Redskin 1929,Ja 28,21:1
Callahan, George (Original Author)
  Step by Step 1946,Ag 24,6:7
Callahan, George (Screenwriter)
  Babe Ruth Story, The 1948,Jl 29,17:2
  Red Light 1950,Ja 16,18:4
  Lucky Nick Cain 1951,Ap 23,21:2
Callahan, Margaret
  Seven Keys to Baldpate 1935,D 14,11:2
  Muss 'Em Up 1936,F 3,21:2
  Special Investigator 1936,Ap 25,21:1
  Last Outlaw, The 1936,Je 15,24:1
Callahan, Mushy
  Madison Square Garden 1932,O 12,26:5
Callahan, Viola
  Luckiest Girl in the World, The 1936,D 5,16:3
Callahan, William
  Chicken every Sunday 1949,Ja 19,34:2
Callam, D
  Little Lord Fauntleroy 1914,Je 23,11:3
Callamand, Lucien
  Passion for Life 1951,D 21,21:4
  Pardon my French 1952,Mr 31,17:2
Callan, Michael
  They Came to Cordura 1959,O 22,47:2
  Flying Fontaines, The 1959,D 24,13:6
  Pepe 1960,D 22,18:1
  Gidget Goes Hawaiian 1961,Ag 10,17:4
  Mysterious Island 1961,D 21,30:6
  Bon Voyage! 1962,My 18,34:2

Callan, Michael— Cont
13 West Street 1962,Je 7,31:2
Interns, The 1962,Ag 9,17:5
Victors, The 1963,D 20,21:2
New Interns, The 1964,Ag 20,34:2
Cat Ballou 1965,Je 25,36:1
Callas, Charlie
Big Mouth, The 1967,Jl 13,30:2
CALLAWAY
See Also CALLOWAY
Callaway, Cheryl
Bridges at Toko-Ri, The 1955,Ja 21,20:2
Cry Vengence 1955,F 19,18:3
Calle, Jose
Susana Tiene un Secreto 1935,Je 5,22:2
Vida Hija del Panal, La; Warden's Daughter, The 1940,Ja 6,9:2
Calle, Pepe
Nobleza Baturra; Rustic Chivalry 1938,Mr 28,19:3
Morena Clara 1938,Je 18,18:3
Rumbo al Cairo; Bound for Cairo 1940,Je 8,18:3
Callegari, G P (Miscellaneous)
Stromboli 1950,F 16,28:2
Callegari, Gian Paola (Screenwriter)
Minotaur, The 1961,N 8,41:1
Head of a Tyrant 1962,Je 7,31:2
Callegari, Gian Paolo (Original Author)
300 Spartans, The 1962,S 20,29:2
Callegari, Gian Paolo (Screenwriter)
Warrior and the Slave, The 1960,Mr 10,36:2
Calleia, Joseph
His Woman 1931,D 5,21:2
Public Hero No 1 1935,Je 8,12:2
Riffraff 1936,Ja 13,14:2
Exclusive Story 1936,Ja 18,19:2
His Brother's Wife 1936,Ag 15,6:2
Sworn Enemy 1936,S 12,20:1
After the Thin Man 1936,D 25,19:2
Sinner Take All 1937,F 3,27:1
Man of the People 1937,F 23,25:4
Bad Man of Brimstone, The 1938,F 4,17:2
Algiers 1938,Jl 15,13:2
Four's a Crowd 1938,Ag 12,11:1
Juarez 1939,Ap 26,27:1
Gorilla, The 1939,My 28,6:2
Five came Back 1939,Jl 5,20:2
Golden Boy 1939,S 8,28:2
Full Confession 1939,S 28,29:4
My Little Chickadee 1940,Mr 16,8:2
Wyoming 1940,O 3,31:4
Monster and the Girl, The 1941,Mr 20,25:3
Jungle Book 1942,Ap 6,19:1
Glass Key, The 1942,O 16,23:1
For Whom the Bell Tolls 1943,Jl 15,25:2
Cross of Lorraine, The 1943,D 3,27:4
Conspirators, The 1944,O 21,15:2
Gilda 1946,Mr 15,27:2
Deadline at Dawn 1946,Ap 4,33:2
Beginning or the End, The 1947,F 21,15:1
Lured 1947,Ag 29,14:4
Noose Hangs High, The 1948,My 29,8:6
Four Faces West 1948,Ag 4,18:3
Captain Carey U S A 1950,Mr 30,40:5
Vendetta 1950,D 26,19:1
Branded 1951,Ja 11,28:5
Valentino 1951,Ap 20,25:1
Light Touch, The 1952,Ja 17,23:1
When in Rome 1952,My 12,21:2
Underwater! 1955,F 10,27:2
Treasure of Pancho Villa, The 1955,N 25,38:2
Littlest Outlaw, The 1955,D 27,31:1
Hot Blood 1956,Mr 24,14:2
Serenade 1956,Mr 24,21:1 (Incorrect in this edition; use 1956,Mr 23,21:1 elsewhere)
Wild Is the Wind 1957,D 12,35:1
Touch of Evil 1958,My 22,25:2
Light in the Forest, The 1958,Jl 11,15:2
Cry Tough 1959,S 17,48:4
Calleia, Joseph (Screenwriter)
Robin Hood of El Dorado, The 1936,Mr 14,10:1
Callejo, Cecilia
Dramatic School 1938,D 9,31:2
Renegade Ranger, The 1939,F 17,17:3
It's a Wonderful World 1939,My 19,27:2
Passport to Alcatraz 1940,Je 15,12:2
Falcon in Mexico, The 1944,Ag 5,16:2
Callejo, Maria Luz
Mama 1933,Jl 8,14:6
Callendar, Red
New Orleans 1947,Je 20,25:6
Callender, Romaine
And So They Were Married 1936,My 14,29:3
High Tension 1936,Jl 11,11:4
36 Hours to Live 1936,Ag 15,6:3
Pepper 1936,Ag 24,11:2
45 Fathers 1937,D 11,22:2
One Wild Night 1938,Je 3,17:2

Sharpshooters 1938,D 5,19:2
Wuthering Heights 1939,Ap 14,28:2
It's a Date 1940,Mr 23,16:2
Wife Takes a Flyer, The 1942,Je 19,19:1
Two Senoritas From Chicago 1943,Ag 6,10:4
Callers, Joseph
Tough Guy 1936,Mr 14,10:1
Calles, Guillermo
Tesoro de Pancho Villa, El 1936,Ja 27,20:4
Maria Elena 1936,F 18,27:1
My Outlaw Brother 1951,Ag 23,19:2
Calles, Guillermo (Director)
Vuelo de la Muerte, El 1935,Ap 16,27:3
Héroe de Nacozari, El 1935,S 23,20:4
Virgen de la Sierra, La 1939,Mr 6,11:3
Calles, William
Last Frontier, The 1955,D 8,45:1
Calley, John (Producer)
Loved One, The 1965,O 12,57:1
Don't Make Waves 1967,Je 21,36:2
Eye of the Devil 1967,D 7,60:1
Calliga, George
Bedroom Window, The 1924,Je 9,14:3
Callix, Genevieve
Moulin Rouge 1944,N 23,38:2
CALLOWAY
See Also CALLAWAY
Calloway, Cab
St Louis Blues 1958,Ap 12,13:1
Cincinnati Kid, The 1965,O 28,48:1
Calloway, Cab and His Band
Singing Kid, The 1936,Ag 4,11:1
Manhattan Merry-Go-Round 1937,D 31,9:3
Stormy Weather 1943,Jl 22,15:1
Sensations of 1945 1944,Jl 7,13:2
Calnan, Matilda
Made in Paris 1966,F 17,29:1
Calo, Carla
Bebo's Girl 1964,N 12,40:1
Eye of the Needle, The 1965,Je 22,25:2
Calo, Romano
Last Chance, The 1945,N 28,21:6
Calogerikou, Christina
Stella 1957,Je 11,40:1
Caloni, Livia
Legittima Difesa; Self Defense 1940,Ap 6,13:3
Calthrop, Donald
Shooting Stars 1928,Mr 4,IX,7:7
Shooting Stars 1928,Je 11,27:1
Blackmail 1929,O 7,22:1
Atlantic 1930,Ja 26,VIII,6:2
Atlantic 1930,O 6,21:1
Loose Ends 1930,O 18,23:2
Murder 1930,O 25,20:6
Two Worlds 1930,N 22,21:3
Almost a Honeymoon 1931,Ja 10,19:2
Love Storm 1931,O 19,28:1
Money for Nothing 1932,F 21,VIII,5:2 (In Addenda)
Rome Express 1932,D 18,X,6:5
Ghost Train, The 1933,F 18,13:3
Rome Express 1933,F 27,11:2
Fires of Fate 1933,Ap 3,13:4
F P 1 1933,S 16,9:3
I Was a Spy 1934,Ja 15,12:2
Orders Is Orders 1934,My 7,20:2
Friday the 13th 1934,My 15,18:1
Sorrell and Son 1934,My 29,22:1
Clairvoyant, The 1935,Je 8,12:2
Scrooge 1935,D 14,11:1
Man Who Lived Again, The 1936,D 16,35:4
Broken Blossoms 1937,Ja 14,16:3
Fire Over England 1937,Mr 5,16:2
Love From a Stranger 1937,Ap 19,27:2
Dreaming Lips 1937,My 20,17:1
Let George Do It 1940,O 14,25:5
Major Barbara 1941,My 15,27:1
Calton, John (Screenwriter)
Invisible Ray, The 1936,Ja 11,9:3
Caltzman, Harry (Producer)
Dr No 1963,My 30,20:1
Calve, Jean-Francois
Bride Is Much too Beautiful, The 1958,Ja 21,35:1
Girl in the Bikini, The 1958,O 25,16:3
Calvelli, Joseph (Screenwriter)
My Six Loves 1963,Ap 4,58:4
Calvert, C S (Director)
Prince of Lovers, The 1927,N 29,31:1
Calvert, Catherine
Fires of Faith 1919,My 6,16:2
Career of Catherine Bush, The 1919,Ag 4,8:3
Calvert, E H
Silent Partner, The 1923,Ag 20,4:2
Bluff 1924,Ap 28,18:2
Why Men Leave Home 1924,My 12,14:4
Only Woman, The 1924,N 3,20:1
Inez From Hollywood 1924,D 16,28:1
East of Suez 1925,Ja 26,22:1
Sally 1925,Mr 16,16:1
Talker, The 1925,My 12,26:2
Girl From Montmarte, The 1926,F 25,26:2
Rookies 1927,Ap 25,20:4
First Auto, The 1927,Je 28,28:4

Calvert, E H— Cont
Let 'Er go, Gallegher 1928,Ja 16,24:1
Legion of the Condemned, The 1928,Mr 19,26:2
Why Sailors Go Wrong 1928,Ap 9,18:2
Moran of the Marines 1928,O 15,16:1
Prep and Pep 1928,D 24,11:1
Canary Murder Case, The 1929,Mr 11,22:2
Studio Murder Mystery, The 1929,Je 10,23:1
Thunderbolt 1929,Je 21,17:2
Greene Murder Case, The 1929,Ag 10,11:3
Virginian, The 1929,D 23,18:2
Mighty, The 1929,D 30,16:4
Behind the Makeup 1930,Ja 18,21:1
Benson Murder Case, The 1930,Ap 12,23:1
Social Lion, The 1930,My 14,9:4
Border Legion, The 1930,Je 30,22:6
Man From Wyoming, A 1930,Jl 12,16:4
Half Shot at Sunrise 1930,O 11,21:3
Widow From Chicago, The 1930,D 20,20:6
Beyond Victory 1931,Ap 6,24:1
Here Comes the Groom 1934,Je 16,20:2
Calvert, Eddie
Beyond Mombasa 1957,My 31,14:2
Calvert, John
Mark of the Whistler, The 1944,N 11,19:2
Calvert, Phyllis
Let George Do It 1940,O 14,25:5
Kipps 1942,My 25,11:2
Young Mr Pitt, The 1943,Mr 11,17:1
Fanny by Gaslight 1944,Jl 16,II,3:4
Man in Grey, The 1945,N 30,18:6
Madonna of the Seven Moons 1946,My 23,18:4
They Were Sisters 1946,Jl 24,24:2
Time Out of Mind 1947,Ap 7,20:1
Magic Bow, The 1947,Jl 7,13:2
Man of Evil 1948,Mr 26,26:2
My Own True Love 1949,F 3,27:3
Broken Journey 1949,My 26,34:3
Golden Madonna, The 1949,S 5,13:4
Appointment With Danger 1951,My 10,38:2
Her Panelled Door 1951,Ag 28,18:2
Kisenga, Man of Africa 1952,Mr 7,18:2
Story of Mandy, The 1953,F 24,21:3
Mr Denning Drives North 1953,S 2,20:1
Project M 7 1953,N 27,22:5
Indiscreet 1958,Je 27,18:2
Oscar Wilde 1960,Je 21,28:2
Battle of the Villa Fiorita, The 1965,My 27,28:1
Calvert, Robert
Dutchman 1967,F 28,32:1
Calvet, Corinne
Rope of Sand 1949,Ag 4,19:2
When Willie Comes Marching Home 1950,F 18,9:2
My Friend Irma Goes West 1950,Ag 3,20:2
Quebec 1951,Mr 16,34:2
On the Riviera 1951,My 24,47:1
Peking Express 1951,Jl 19,20:2
Sailor Beware 1952,F 1,17:1
What Price Glory 1952,Ag 23,10:2
Thunder in the East 1953,F 4,32:2
Powder River 1953,Jl 4,7:2
Flight to Tangier 1953,N 26,50:4
So This Is Paris 1955,F 12,11:1
Far Country, The 1955,F 14,24:2
One Step to Eternity 1955,O 3,22:2
Sins of Casanova 1957,O 7,23:2
Bluebeard's Ten Honeymoons 1960,N 8,32:6
Hemingway's Adventures of a Young Man 1962,Jl 26,17:1
Calvin, Henry
Toby Tyler 1960,Ap 20,45:2
Sign of Zorro, The 1961,S 5,37:6
Babes in Toyland 1961,D 15,49:1
Calvin, William
Soldiers and Women 1930,My 12,27:3
Calvo, Armando
Goyescas 1944,My 29,18:3
Calvo, Eva
Life in the Balance, A 1955,Jl 14,19:1
Calvo, Jose
Fistful of Dollars, A 1967,F 2,29:1
Calvo, Juan
Goyescas 1944,My 29,18:3
Don Quixote 1949,My 13,29:3
Marcelino 1956,O 23,39:1
Rocket From Calabuch 1958,O 8,41:1
Calvo, Maria
Primavera en Otono 1933,My 18,17:3
Granaderos del Amor 1934,S 4,23:4
Forgive Me, Son 1937,O 23,14:2
Perfidia; Perfidy 1940,F 17,9:3
Calvo, Pablito
Marcelino 1956,O 23,39:1
Pepote 1958,D 2,46:1
Man Who Wagged his Tail, The 1961,S 19,39:1
Calvo, Rafael
Marcelino 1956,O 23,39:1
Fedra, the Devil's Daughter 1957,O 26,19:2
Warrior and the Slave, The 1960,Mr 10,36:2
Calzavara, Flavio (Director)
Piccoli Avventurieri; Little Adventures 1940,Ap 26,25:2
Carmela 1949,My 14,9:2

Cama, Charles
Lady and the Monster, The 1944,Ap 8,9:2
Camacho, Chuca
Mexico Lindo 1939,F 4,11:1
Camardiel, Roberto
Backfire 1965,Ap 27,27:1
Camarillo, Dolares
Caballo a Caballo; Horse for Horse
  1940,F 10,19:2
Que Lindo es Michoacan 1944,Ap 22,8:7
Camarillo, Lolita
Enemigos 1934,Ag 18,5:6
Rayo, El 1935,O 19,21:3
Huapango 1938,Je 11,9:1
Cobarde, El; Coward, The 1939,Mr 27,11:2
Creo en Dios 1943,Jl 17,8:3
Camax, Valentine
Mr Hulot's Holiday 1954,Je 17,36:2
Cambanelis, J (Original Author)
Stella 1957,Je 11,40:1
Cambi, Flora
Miracle in Milan 1951,D 18,42:2
Cambo
Ramuntcho 1953,Mr 2,19:2
Cambo, Paul
Heroes of the Marne; (Famille Lefrancois, Le)
  1939,Ap 24,13:2
Devil Is an Empress, The 1939,D 4,18:4
Cambre, Del
Tundra 1936,D 3,31:2
Cambridge, Godfrey
Last Angry Man, The 1959,O 23,24:1
Gone are the Days! 1963,S 24,43:2
Troublemaker, The 1964,Je 23,25:1
Busy Body, The 1967,Je 8,52:2
President's Analyst, The 1967,D 22,44:4
Biggest Bundle of Them All, The 1968,Ja 18,46:1
Bye Bye Braverman 1968,F 22,36:1
Camby, William
Green Pastures, The 1936,Jl 17,20:1
Camden, Joan
Captive City, The 1952,Mr 27,34:2
Strange Lady in Town 1955,My 21,11:1
Catered Affair, The 1956,Je 15,32:4
Gunfight at the O K Corral 1957,My 30,23:2
Cameo (the wonder dog)
Days of Thrills and Laughter 1961,Mr 22,37:1
Camere, Manuel
Tiger Love 1924,Je 16,18:3
Camerini, Augusto (Screenwriter)
Miller's Beautiful Wife, The 1957,Je 12,40:2
Camerini, Mario (Director)
Figaro E La Sua Gran Giornata 1933,O 28,20:4
Cappello a Tre Punte, Il 1936,S 28,14:5
Daro Un Milione 1937,Mr 29,14:3
Grande Appello, Il; Last Roll-Call, The
  1939,Ap 11,18:6
Signor Max, Il; Mr Max 1939,O 6,31:4
But It's Nothing Serious 1939,O 10,27:2
Documento Fatale, Il 1940,S 26,27:3
Woman Trouble 1949,My 26,34:2
Ulysses 1955,Ag 18,17:2
Miller's Beautiful Wife, The 1957,Je 12,40:2
Awakening, The 1958,Mr 3,24:6
Wife for a Night 1958,Je 12,35:2
Holiday Island; (Vacanzie a Izchia)
  1959,S 22,46:1
Run With the Devil 1963,Jl 16,25:1
...And Suddenly It's Murder! 1964,Ja 24,21:1
Camerini, Mario (Original Author)
Awakening, The 1958,Mr 3,24:6
Run With the Devil 1963,Jl 16,25:1
Camerini, Mario (Producer)
Spirit and the Flesh, The 1948,N 1,28:2
Camerini, Mario (Screenwriter)
Spirit and the Flesh, The 1948,N 1,28:2
Ulysses 1955,Ag 18,17:2
War and Peace 1956,Ag 22,26:2
Miller's Beautiful Wife, The 1957,Je 12,40:2
Awakening, The 1958,Mr 3,24:6
Wife for a Night 1958,Je 12,35:2
Holiday Island; (Vacanzie a Izchia)
  1959,S 22,46:1
Run With the Devil 1963,Jl 16,25:1
Cameron, Ann (Original Author)
Mr Skitch 1933,D 23,19:1
Cameron, Carol
Woman in the Window, The 1945,Ja 26,16:4
Cameron, David
Suddenly, Last Summer 1959,D 23,22:1
Cameron, Earl
Pool of London 1951,N 28,37:2
Hundred Hour Hunt 1953,Je 17,32:2
Heart of the Matter, The 1954,N 19,20:2
Simba 1955,O 22,24:2
Safari 1956,Je 21,35:2
Sapphire 1959,N 3,27:1
Flame in the Streets 1962,S 13,32:1
Guns at Batasi 1964,N 17,47:1
Battle Beneath the Earth 1968,S 12,54:3
Cameron, Gene
Circe the Enchantress 1924,D 9,23:3
Excuse Me 1925,Ja 27,11:2

Gay Retreat, The 1927,O 10,24:1
Cameron, George (Original Author)
Million Bid, A 1927,My 31,25:2
Cameron, Herbert
Scotland Yard Mystery, The 1936,Mr 16,21:4
Spitfire 1943,Je 14,13:2
Cameron, Hope
Chapman Report, The 1962,O 18,49:2
Cameron, Hugh
Cappy Ricks 1921,Ag 22,13:6
Homeward Bound 1923,Jl 31,12:4
Pied Piper Malone 1924,Ja 28,12:1
Man Who Found Himself, The 1925,Ag 24,17:3
For the Love of Mike 1927,Ag 24,27:5
One Heavenly Night 1931,Ja 10,19:2
One Third of a Nation 1939,F 11,13:2
Back Door to Heaven 1939,Ap 20,21:2
Cameron, Isla
Innocents, The 1961,D 26,15:2
Cameron, Jack
Applause 1929,O 8,24:5
Cameron, James (Director)
Eyewitness..North Vietnam 1966,N 23,29:1
Cameron, James (Narrator)
Eyewitness..North Vietnam 1966,N 23,29:1
Cameron, James (Producer)
Eyewitness..North Vietnam 1966,N 23,29:1
Cameron, James (Screenwriter)
Eyewitness..North Vietnam 1966,N 23,29:1
Cameron, John
Beggar's Opera, The 1953,Ag 25,18:2
Cameron, Marlene
Happy Time, The 1952,O 31,30:2
Cameron, Mary Lady (Original Author)
Many Happy Returns 1934,Je 9,18:2
Cameron, Rod
Quarterback, The 1940,O 17,33:3
Christmas in July 1940,N 6,35:2
Monster and the Girl, The 1941,Mr 20,25:3
Henry Aldrich for President 1941,O 18,22:2
Night of January 16th, The 1941,D 19,35:1
No Hands on the Clock 1941,D 22,24:6
Remarkable Andrew, The 1942,Mr 6,17:2
True to the Army 1942,Je 15,15:4
Priorities on Parade 1942,Jl 23,19:2
Forest Rangers, The 1942,O 22,25:2
Kansan, The 1943,O 1,15:3
No Time for Love 1943,D 2,30:1
Riding High 1943,D 23,26:4
Gung Ho! 1944,Ja 26,23:2
Salome, Where She Danced 1945,My 3,27:1
Frontier Gal 1945,D 15,14:2
Runaround, The 1946,Je 7,16:3
Pirates of Monterey 1947,D 17,41:4
River Lady 1948,My 21,19:5
Plunders, The 1948,N 1,28:2
Belle Star's Daughter 1949,Ja 10,19:2
Stampede 1949,S 16,36:2
Brimstone 1949,O 7,35:3
Dakota Lil 1950,Mr 3,21:5
Short Grass 1951,Ja 13,10:4
Oh! Susanna 1951,Mr 30,28:5
Stage to Tucson 1951,My 5,14:2
Cavalry Scout 1951,Je 8,32:2
Woman of the North Country 1952,Ag 30,6:2
Jungle, The 1952,O 2,32:3
Commandos Strike at Dawn 1954,Ja 14,25:1
Southwest Passage 1954,S 11,11:2
Hell's Outpost 1955,F 26,13:3
Cameron, Rudolph
For the Love of Mike 1927,Ag 24,27:5
Coney Island 1928,F 14,27:1 (In Addenda)
Queen High 1930,Ag 9,16:5
Cameron, William (Director)
Always Good-Bye 1931,My 23,13:4
Camiel, Eric (Director)
Riff '65 1966,N 25,49:1
Camilla
Cairo Road 1952,N 1,17:2
Camilli, Bernardo
Regina di Sparta, La 1931,F 23,20:3
Cammage, Maurice (Director)
Bouquets From Nicholas 1939,Mr 2,19:1
Cammarata, Pietro
Salvatore Giuliano 1964,S 18,28:1
Cammell, David (Miscellaneous)
Touchables, The 1968,N 21,41:1
Cammell, Donald (Miscellaneous)
Touchables, The 1968,N 21,41:1
Cammell, Donald (Original Author)
Duffy 1968,S 17,50:3
Cammell, Donald (Screenwriter)
Duffy 1968,S 17,50:3
Cammerer, Roland (Producer)
Helga 1968,O 5,40:1
Camoletti, Marc (Original Author)
Boeing Boeing 1965,D 24,24:4
Camp, Hamilton
Perils of Pauline, The 1967,Ag 3,26:3
Camp, Robin
Mrs Mike 1950,F 9,36:5
Outrage 1950,O 16,30:5
My Cousin Rachel 1952,D 26,20:2

Camp, Shep
Song of the Flame 1930,My 7,24:5
Camp, Wadsworth (Original Author)
Signal Tower, The 1924,Jl 21,14:4
Campa, Pia
Tears of Blood 1952,Ja 19,13:2
Campagna, Rita
Redhead 1934,N 16,27:1
Campana, Nina
Petrified Forest, The 1936,F 7,14:2
Call of the Yukon 1938,My 6,27:1
Arizona 1941,F 7,23:3
Tortilla Flat 1942,My 22,27:1
Campanari, Giuseppe
Webb Singing Pictures 1917,Ja 15,7:1
Campanella, Frank
Somebody up There Likes Me 1956,Jl 6,16:1
Stage Struck 1958,Ap 23,40:1
What's so bad About Feeling Good?
  1968,My 25,27:1
Campanella, Joseph
Young Lovers, The 1965,F 11,45:1
St Valentine's Day Massacre, The 1967,Jl 27,29:2
Campanile, Pasquale Festa (Director)
White Voices; Voci Blanche 1965,Ap 13,32:2
Girl and the General, The 1967,D 7,60:1
Campanile, Pasquale Festa (Original Author)
Girl and the General, The 1967,D 7,60:1
Campanile, Pasquale Festa (Screenwriter)
Poor but Beautiful 1958,Je 11,39:4
Wild Love; (Gli Inamorati) 1961,Ap 6,30:2
Rocco and his Brothers 1961,Je 28,40:2
Viaccia, La 1962,S 21,35:1
Four Days of Naples, The 1963,Mr 20,5:1
Leopard, The 1963,Ag 13,25:1
White Voices; Voci Blanche 1965,Ap 13,32:2
Campanini, Carlo
Anything for a Song 1947,Ag 5,26:2
Schoolgirl Diary 1947,O 18,9:2
Lady is Fickle, The 1948,F 7,10:4
His Young Wife 1949,Mr 12,10:2
Bandit, The 1949,Je 7,26:3
Voice of Love, The 1950,Ja 7,11:2
Mad About Opera 1950,Ap 6,33:2
Escape into Dreams 1950,Ap 13,34:5
Bullet for Stefano 1950,O 26,38:7
I Cadetti di Guascogna 1952,O 6,22:2
O K Nero 1953,Je 20,8:6
My Heart Sings 1954,Mr 5,15:5
Sins of Casanova 1957,O 7,23:2
Ten Commandments, The 1958,Ap 7,26:1
Pepote 1958,D 2,46:1
Campano, Nina
South of Pago-Pago 1940,Ag 2,12:2
Campardo, Adelino
Seduced and Abandoned 1964,Jl 16,23:1
Campaux, Francois (Original Author)
Blue Veil, The 1947,O 2,32:6
Blue Veil, The 1951,O 27,10:5
Campaux, Francois (Screenwriter)
Blue Veil, The 1947,O 2,32:6
Campbell, Alan (Miscellaneous)
Moon's our Home, The 1936,My 13,29:2
Little Foxes, The 1941,Ag 22,19:2
Campbell, Alan (Original Author)
Forever and a Day 1943,Mr 13,9:2
Campbell, Alan (Screenwriter)
Suzy 1936,Jl 25,16:1
Lady, Be Careful 1936,O 10,21:1
Star Is Born, A 1937,Ap 23,25:1
Woman Chases Man 1937,Je 11,26:2
Sweethearts 1938,D 23,16:2
Trade Winds 1939,Ja 13,17:2
Week End for Three 1941,O 24,27:4
Tales of Manhattan 1942,S 25,25:1
Woman on the Run 1950,N 30,24:2
Star is Born, A 1954,O 12,23:1
Campbell, Alexander
Jigsaw 1949,My 30,9:4
Lost Boundaries 1949,Jl 1,14:4
Campbell, Alice (Original Author)
Juggernaut 1937,Jl 15,16:1
Campbell, B H (Original Author)
Rio Bravo 1959,Mr 19,40:2
Campbell, Beatrice
Meet Me at Dawn 1948,My 18,26:2
My Brother Jonathan 1949,Je 29,34:4
Silent Dust 1949,D 30,13:2
Last Holiday 1950,N 14,39:4
Mudlark, The 1950,D 25,25:1
No Place for Jennifer 1951,Jl 17,31:2
Laughter in Paradise 1951,N 12,21:2
I'll Never Forget You 1951,D 8,9:2
Master of Ballantrae, The 1953,Ag 6,16:2
Cockleshell Heroes, The 1956,Je 4,25:2
Campbell, Betty
Hound of the Baskervilles, The 1922,S 11,20:2
Campbell, Beverly
D O A 1950,My 1,18:2
Campbell, Bill
Breakthrough 1950,N 18,10:2
Operation Pacific 1951,F 3,10:2

Campbell, Carole Ann
I'll Cry Tomorrow 1956,Ja 13,18:1
Campbell, Colin
White Monkey, The 1925,Je 9,16:3
Road to Singapore, The 1931,O 1,25:2
Gay Diplomat, The 1931,O 10,20:4
Deceiver, The 1931,N 23,22:1
Alice in Wonderland 1933,D 23,19:1
Eight Girls in a Boat 1934,Ja 13,16:3
Life Begins at Eight-Thirty 1942,D 10,35:2
Lodger, The 1944,Ja 20,15:3
Two Mrs Carrolls, The 1947,Ap 7,20:1
Lost World, The 1960,Jl 14,23:1
Leather Boys, The 1965,N 9,50:1
Campbell, Colin (Director)
Where Lights Are Low 1921,Ag 1,8:3 (Incorrect
in this edition; use 1921,Ag 1,6:4 elsewhere)
Campbell, Colin (Miscellaneous)
Adventures of Ichabod and Mr Toad, The
1949,O 10,18:2
Campbell, Daphne
Overlanders, The 1946,D 20,31:2
Campbell, Diana
No Resting Place 1952,My 5,18:5
Campbell, Douglas
Oedipus Rex 1957,Ja 8,26:1
Campbell, E Murray (Original Author)
Last Outlaw, The 1936,Je 15,24:1
Campbell, Elizabeth
Bridal Path, The 1959,D 21,34:2
Campbell, Eric
30 Years of Fun 1963,D 26,33:4
Campbell, Evelyn (Original Author)
Love's Wilderness 1924,D 22,20:2
Irresistible Lover, The 1927,O 19,24:4
Campbell, Evelyn (Screenwriter)
Western Limited 1932,D 12,18:4
Campbell, George (Original Author)
Voice in the Night, The 1941,My 23,25:4
Cry for Happy 1961,Mr 4,16:1
Campbell, Harry
Sky Giant 1938,Jl 20,22:2
Campbell, Huntley
Simba 1955,O 22,24:2
Campbell, Jo Ann
Hey, Lets Twist 1962,F 8,25:1
Campbell, Joan
Sullivans, The 1944,F 10,19:2
Campbell, John
Sweet and Low Down 1944,O 19,19:2
Campbell, John W Jr (Original Author)
Thing, The 1951,My 3,34:4
Campbell, Judy
Convoy 1941,Ja 17,21:2
Green for Danger 1947,Ag 8,10:2
Bonnie Prince Charlie 1952,Ja 7,14:3
Campbell, Kane (Original Author)
Enchanted April 1935,Mr 9,19:1
Campbell, Keith (Screenwriter)
Snowbound 1949,F 21,20:2
Campbell, Kippy
Wrong Man, The 1956,D 24,8:1
Campbell, Louise
Bulldog Drummond Comes Back 1937,S 4,8:3
Night Club Scandal 1937,N 12,27:2
Bulldog Drummond's Revenge 1937,D 17,33:2
Scandal Street 1938,F 5,19:2 (In Addenda)
Bulldog Drummond's Peril 1938,Mr 18,23:2
Men With Wings 1938,O 27,27:2
Star Maker, The 1939,Ag 31,14:2
Anne of Windy Poplars 1940,Ag 23,13:3
Campbell, Margaret
Fast Worker, The 1924,N 12,13:1
Home Maker, The 1925,Ag 10,8:2
Campbell, Marguerite
Hello, Everybody 1933,Ja 30,9:4
Campbell, Maurice (Director)
Exciters, The 1923,Je 4,13:3
Campbell, Ned
Native Son 1951,Je 18,19:2
Campbell, Norma Arden
Bachelor Party, The 1957,Ap 10,37:2
Campbell, Patrick (Screenwriter)
Horse's Mouth, The 1959,Ja 20,33:4
Lucky Jim 1958,S 1,8:6
Model Murder Case, The 1964,N 25,45:1
Campbell, Patrick Mrs
Dancers, The 1930,N 15,15:3
Riptide 1934,Mr 31,8:2
One More River 1934,Ag 10,21:1
Outcast Lady 1934,N 3,20:3
Crime and Punishment 1935,N 22,18:2
Campbell, Paul
Gallant Blade 1948,O 13,31:3
Golden Coach, The 1954,Ja 22,30:2
Campbell, R Wright
Young Racers, The 1963,O 10,49:3
Campbell, R Wright (Original Author)
Gun for a Coward 1957,Ja 31,21:1
Campbell, R Wright (Screenwriter)
Man of a Thousand Faces 1957,Ag 14,21:1
Quantez 1957,S 7,12:7
Night Fighters, The 1960,D 15,59:1

Young Racers, The 1963,O 10,49:3
Secret Invasion, The 1964,S 17,52:6
Masque of the Red Death, The 1964,S 17,52:6
Secret Invasion, The 1964,S 17,52:5
Hells Angels on Wheels 1967,Jl 29,29:3
Campbell, Raymond
Paisan 1948,Mr 30,26:2
Campbell, Tim
George Washington Carver 1940,Ap 17,26:4
Campbell, Virginia
Unconquered 1947,O 11,11:2
That Lady in Ermine 1948,Ag 25,31:2
Campbell, Webster
In the Next Room 1930,Ap 7,21:1
Campbell, William
Breaking Point, The 1950,O 7,10:6
Inside the Walls of Folsom Prison
1951,My 28,17:4
People Against O'Hara, The 1951,S 6,39:3
Holiday for Sinners 1952,S 20,13:2
Battle Circus 1953,My 28,27:5
Escape from Fort Bravo 1954,Ja 23,11:2
High and the Mighty, The 1954,Jl 1,21:2
Battle Cry 1955,F 3,18:1
Man Without a Star 1955,Mr 25,19:3
Running Wild 1955,N 12,23:2
Backlash 1956,Ap 21,11:2
Love Me Tender 1956,N 16,23:1
Eighteen and Anxious 1957,D 14,16:6
Naked and the Dead, The 1958,Ag 7,21:1
Sheriff of Fractured Jaw, The 1959,Mr 14,27:4
Young Racers, The 1963,O 10,49:3
Dementia 13 1963,O 24,37:1
Secret Invasion, The 1964,S 17,52:6
Secret Invasion, The 1964,S 17,52:5
Hush...Hush, Sweet Charlotte 1965,Mr 4,36:1
Campbell, William (Director)
Tray Full of Trouble, A 1920,N 22,13:3
Campeau, Frank
Jordan Is a Hard Road 1915,N 15,11:1
Cheating Cheaters 1919,Ja 27,11:4
Knickerbocker Buckaroo, The 1919,My 26,19:4
Life of the Party, The 1920,N 22,13:3
Just Tony 1922,Ag 7,14:2
Skin Deep 1922,O 23,10:1
Isle of Lost Ships, The 1923,My 14,18:2
Alaskan, The 1924,S 15,28:1
Coming Through 1925,F 18,17:3
Golden Cocoon, The 1925,D 15,14:5
Sea Horses 1926,F 23,26:5
Let It Rain 1927,Mr 9,29:1
First Auto, The 1927,Je 28,28:4
Gamblers, The 1929,Ag 24,11:5
Abraham Lincoln 1930,Ag 26,24:1
Last of the Duanes 1930,S 13,9:3
Lightnin' 1930,N 29,21:4
Fighting Caravans 1931,Ja 26,21:1
Soldiers Plaything, A 1931,My 2,23:4
Captain Thunder 1931,My 11,15:4
Girl of the Rio 1932,Ja 9,21:1
White Eagle 1932,S 24,18:4
Smoky 1934,Ja 1,28:2
Campeau, George
Nurse's Secret, The 1941,Je 6,25:7
Campi, Maria
Shoe-Shine 1947,Ag 27,19:2
Campillo, Anita
Cruz y la Espada, La 1934,F 5,19:3
Cuesta Abajo 1934,Ag 15,13:5
Buenaventura, La 1934,S 15,20:3
Tres Amores 1934,N 5,23:1
Hombre Peligroso, Un; Dangerous Man, A
1935,O 14,21:2
Vida Bohemia, La 1939,F 6,8:5
Virgen de la Sierra, La 1939,Mr 6,11:3
India Bonita, La; Pretty Indian Girl, The
1939,Ap 15,15:2
Hotel de los Chiflados, El 1939,Ag 28,17:2
Campion
Parisian, The 1931,Ag 22,7:5
Campion, Anne
Damned, The; Maudits, Les 1948,Ap 26,27:2
Campion, Cyril (Screenwriter)
Juggernaut 1937,Jl 15,16:1
Campion, Gerald
Pickwick Papers, The 1954,Ap 5,21:2
School for Scoundrels 1960,Jl 12,39:1
Campion, Leo
Crazy in the Noodle 1957,D 15,45:4 (Incorrect in
this edition; use 1957,D 17,45:4 elsewhere)
Campion, Nardi R (Original Author)
Long Gray Line, The 1955,F 11,19:2
Campo, Cesar Del
Exterminating Angel, The 1967,Ag 22,33:1
Campo, Pepe del
Ahora Seremos Felices; Now We Shall Be Happy
1940,Mr 16,8:2
Cancion del Regreso, La; Home-Coming Song
1940,Je 22,18:4
Campo, Pupi
Hole in the Head, A 1959,Jl 16,31:2

Campoamor, Alfonso
Corazones en Derrota 1934,O 10,21:4
Campoamor, Arturo
Prisionero 13, El 1934,Ap 30,11:4
Pulpo Humano, El 1935,My 6,22:4
Campogalliani, Carlo (Director)
Grande Luce, La; Great Light, The
1940,Mr 15,27:4
Goliath and the Barbarians 1960,Ja 7,24:6
Son of Samson 1962,S 27,33:4
Campogalliani, Carlo (Screenwriter)
Goliath and the Barbarians 1960,Ja 7,24:6
Campora, Giuseppe
Aida 1954,N 12,17:1
Campos, Batista
Tropics 1968,S 24,52:1
Campos, Chela
Passion Island 1943,My 1,11:2
Campos, Graciele
Tropics 1968,S 24,52:1
Campos, Lidia
Way of a Gaucho 1952,N 5,36:2
Campos, Rafael
Blackboard Jungle 1955,Mr 21,21:5
Trial 1955,O 14,21:2
This Could Be the Night 1957,My 15,39:1
Light in the Forest, The 1958,Jl 11,15:2
Tonka 1959,Mr 26,27:1
Lady in a Cage 1964,Je 11,27:1
Agent for H.A.R.M 1966,Ja 6,20:2
Appaloosa, The 1966,S 15,51:1
Mister Buddwing 1966,O 12,36:1
Campuzano, Aurora
Nostradamus 1937,S 6,20:1
Camus, Albert (Original Author)
Stranger, The 1967,D 19,59:1
Camus, Marcel (Director)
Black Orpheus 1959,D 22,41:1
Dragon Sky 1964,Ag 25,28:2
Camus, Marcel (Screenwriter)
Dragon Sky 1964,Ag 25,28:2
Canaday, Bill (Screenwriter)
Ipcress File, The 1965,Ag 3,35:1
Canale, Gianna Maria
Rigoletto 1949,N 10,41:4
Go for Broke 1951,My 25,31:2
Dead Woman's Kiss, A 1951,O 6,16:4
Man From Cairo, The 1953,D 17,52:4
Theodora, Slave Empress 1955,Ja 12,24:2
See Naples and Die 1959,Ag 31,16:2
Warrior and the Slave, The 1960,Mr 10,36:2
Sword and the Cross, The 1960,Jl 7,26:1
Queen of the Pirates 1961,Jl 27,23:4
Mighty Crusaders, The 1961,S 23,17:1
Slave, The 1963,My 30,20:1
Adventures of Scaramouche, The 1964,N 23,34:1
(Incorrect in this edition; use 1964,N 21,34:1
elsewhere)
Canales, Ricardo
Song of Dolores 1951,Je 16,9:2
Canales, Susana
John Paul Jones 1959,Je 17,39:1
Canali, Anna Maria
House of Ricordi 1956,Mr 13,32:1
Canary, David
Hombre 1967,Mr 22,41:1
St Valentine's Day Massacre, The 1967,Jl 27,29:2
Canas, Gonzalo
Adventures of Scaramouche, The 1964,N 23,34:1
(Incorrect in this edition; use 1964,N 21,34:1
elsewhere)
Cancellieri, Alba
Juliet of the Spirits 1965,N 4,57:1
Cancellieri, E (Director)
First Opera Film Festival 1948,My 31,12:7
Cancio, Raul
Fedra, the Devil's Daughter 1957,O 26,19:2
Cancura, Vladislav (Original Author)
Capricious Summer 1968,S 18,50:2
Candiani, Carla
Story of Tosca, The 1947,D 19,34:2
Loves of Don Juan, The 1948,S 2,18:4
Candido, Candy
Something to Sing About 1937,S 21,29:4
Cowboy From Brooklyn 1938,Jl 14,17:1
Great Rupert, The 1950,Ap 14,27:2
Candler, Chick
Captain Eddie 1945,Ag 9,24:2
Candoli Brothers
Bell, Book and Candle 1958,D 27,2:7
Candons, Richard (Original Author)
Happy Thieves, The 1962,F 5,19:4
Candy and Coco
Sadie McKee 1934,My 18,18:3 (Incorrect in this
edition; use 1934,My 19,18:3 elsewhere)
CANE
See Also CAIN, CAINE, KANE
Cane, Charles
Mayor of Hell, The 1933,Jl 1,16:5
All Through the Night 1942,Ja 24,13:2
Man in the Trunk, The 1942,O 23,25:1
Hello, Frisco, Hello 1943,Mr 25,25:1
Hairy Ape, The 1944,Jl 3,8:3

Cane, Charles— Cont
Don Juan Quilligan 1945,Jl 30,16:2
Dead Reckoning 1947,Ja 23,31:2
Guilt of Janet Ames, The 1947,My 23,31:2
Dark Past, The 1948,D 23,25:2
Prison Warden 1949,O 21,31:2
Southside 1-1000 1950,N 3,31:2
Belle le Grand 1951,My 18,34:6
Native Son 1951,Je 18,19:2
Scandal Sheet 1952,Ja 17,23:1
Lone Star 1952,F 2,11:4
Models, Inc 1952,My 26,18:4
Ruby Gentry 1952,D 26,20:2

Cane, Georgia
Hurry, Charlie, Hurry 1941,N 12,31:3

Canedo, Roberto
Hidden River 1950,D 1,31:2

Canel, Leon (Producer)
Sans Famille 1959,S 5,11:4

Canete, Maria
Mad Queen, The 1950,O 27,24:3

Canfield, Alyce (Original Author)
Models, Inc 1952,My 26,18:4

Canfield, Dorothy (Original Author)
Home Maker, The 1925,Ag 10,8:2

Canfield, Mark (Original Author)
Desired Woman, The 1927,Ag 30,21:3
Maybe It's Love 1930,O 18,23:2

Canfield, Mark (Screenwriter)
My Man 1928,D 22,14:3
Crack in the Mirror 1960,My 20,26:1

Canfield, Mary Grace
Pollyanna 1960,My 20,26:1

Caniglia, Maria
Manon Lescaut 1941,Ap 14,23:5
Tosca 1958,O 24,40:3

Canino, Ernestina
Romance Tropical 1934,O 15,20:5

Canino, Raquel
Romance Tropical 1934,O 15,20:5

Cannan, Denis
Beggar's Opera, The 1953,Ag 25,18:2

Cannan, Denis (Screenwriter)
Beggar's Opera, The 1953,Ag 25,18:2
Why Bother to Knock 1965,F 4,24:2
Boy Ten Feet Tall, A 1965,My 13,32:2
Amorous Adventures of Moll Flanders, The
1965,My 27,28:1
High Wind in Jamaica, A 1965,Je 17,27:2

Cannan, Louis (Screenwriter)
Tell Me Lies 1968,F 13,46:3

Canning, Victor (Original Author)
Spy Hunt 1950,S 8,25:2
Golden Salamander 1951,Mr 24,8:3
Assassin, The 1953,Ap 18,17:2
House of the Seven Hawks, The 1959,D 17,51:2
Masquerade 1965,Ap 29,40:2

Canning, Victor (Screenwriter)
Golden Salamander 1951,Mr 24,8:3
Assassin, The 1953,Ap 18,17:2

Cannon, Diane
This Rebel Breed 1960,My 5,41:2

Cannon, Esma
I Met a Murderer 1939,O 2,15:2
Years Between, The 1947,Mr 10,25:2
Holiday Camp 1948,Ja 24,11:2
Jassy 1948,F 20,19:2
Don't Take it to Heart 1948,D 25,10:3
Last Holiday 1950,N 14,39:4
Guilt is my Shadow 1954,Mr 25,36:4
Panic in the Parlor 1957,D 18,45:1

Cannon, Glenn
Mad Dog Coll 1961,My 13,10:1

Cannon, J D
American Dream, An 1966,S 1,28:2
Cool Hand Luke 1967,N 2,58:1

Cannon, Maureen
Gals, Inc 1943,Ag 13,13:4

Cannon, Maurice
Trilby 1923,Jl 30,11:4
Shadows of Paris 1924,F 18,13:1
Side Show of Life, The 1924,Jl 22,9:1
Alaskan, The 1924,S 15,28:1
Love's Wilderness 1924,D 22,20:2
Little French Girl, The 1925,Je 1,10:3
Forbidden Hours 1928,Jl 23,11:2
Roots of Heaven, The 1958,O 16,46:1

Cannon, Norman
Disraeli 1929,O 3,27:5

Cannon, Pomeray
Four Horsemen of the Apocalypse, The
1926,S 27,27:3

Cannon, Raymond
Nugget Nell 1919,Jl 28,8:5
Nobody Home 1919,Ag 25,8:5

Cannon, Raymond (Director)
Why Leave Home 1929,S 16,30:1
Outer Gate, The 1937,N 22,15:2
Swing It, Sailor 1937,D 13,23:5
Samurai 1945,Ag 25,7:5

Cannon, Reymond (Screenwriter)
Samurai 1945,Ag 25,7:5

Cano, Antonio
Belles and Ballets 1960,N 15,45:3

Cano, Juan
Roots, The (The Cows); Cows, The (The Roots)
1957,S 3,23:2

Canova, Judy
Artists and Models 1937,Ag 5,19:2
Thrill of a Lifetime 1937,D 9,30:2
Sis Hopkins 1941,My 1,27:5
True to the Army 1942,Je 15,15:4
Chatterbox 1943,Jl 2,15:3
Adventures of Huckleberry Fin, The
1960,Ag 4,17:1

Canova Family
In Caliente 1935,Je 27,16:1
Broadway Gondolier 1935,Jl 18,15:2

Canran, Denis (Screenwriter)
Tamahine 1964,Jl 16,23:1

Cansino, Enrique
My Outlaw Brother 1951,Ag 23,19:2

Cansino, Vernon
Song of my Heart 1948,Mr 5,17:3

Cantinflas
Ni Sangre, Ni Arena; Neither Blood nor Sand
1941,Je 15,IX,3:4 (In Addenda)
Romeo and Juliet 1944,Je 17,10:3
Around the World in 80 Days 1956,O 18,37:1
Pepe 1960,D 22,18:1

Cantini, Guido (Original Author)
Streets of Sorrow 1952,N 18,37:4

Cantini, Guido (Screenwriter)
Manon Lescaut 1941,Ap 14,23:5
Eternal Melodies 1948,F 14,17:3
Two Orphans, The 1950,O 19,40:6

Cantonwine, Howard
Merry-Go-Round of 1938 1937,N 26,27:2

CANTOR
See Also KANTER, KANTOR

Cantor, Charles
Duffy's Tavern 1945,S 6,23:3
Stop, You're Killing Me 1952,D 11,45:3

Cantor, D A
Laughter Through Tears 1933,N 13,21:2

Cantor, Eddie
Kid Boots 1926,O 11,18:2
Special Delivery 1927,Ap 26,33:3
Whoopee 1930,O 1,26:3
Palmy Days 1931,S 24,21:2
Kid From Spain, The 1932,N 18,23:2
Roman Scandals 1933,D 25,28:2
Kid Millions 1934,N 12,17:2
Strike Me Pink 1936,Ja 17,15:2
Ali Baba Goes to Town 1937,O 23,14:1
Forty Little Mothers 1940,Ap 19,25:2
Thank Your Lucky Stars 1943,O 2,19:2
Show Business 1944,My 11,25:7
Hollywood Canteen 1944,D 16,19:2
If You Knew Susie 1948,F 23,19:2

Cantor, Eddie (Miscellaneous)
Special Delivery 1927,Ap 26,33:3
Mr Lemon of Orange 1931,Mr 28,15:3
Palmy Days 1931,S 24,21:2

Cantor, Eddie (Original Author)
Caught Short 1930,Je 21,20:5

Cantor, Eddie (Producer)
Show Business 1944,My 11,25:7
If You Knew Susie 1948,F 23,19:2

Cantor, Eddie (Screenwriter)
Palmy Days 1931,S 24,21:2

Cantor, Sam
Going Wild 1931,Ja 26,21:1

Cantu, Guillermo
Por Mis Pistolas; By My Pistols 1939,Je 10,14:3

Canty, Marietta
Lady is Willing, The 1942,Ap 24,21:2
Spoilers, The 1942,My 22,27:2
Magnificent Dope, The 1942,Jl 3,12:5
Three Hearts for Julia 1943,My 21,22:4
Lady in the Dark 1944,F 23,17:1
Sunday Dinner for a Soldier 1945,Ja 25,16:2
Searching Wind, The 1946,Je 27,29:1
Mother is a Freshman 1949,Mr 12,10:2
Dear Wife 1950,F 2,31:2
Father of the Bride 1950,My 19,31:2
Bright Leaf 1950,Je 17,7:2
Father's Little Dividend 1951,Ap 13,18:5
Valentino 1951,Ap 20,25:1
Belle le Grand 1951,My 18,34:6
Man Called Peter, A 1955,Ap 1,22:1
Rebel without a Cause 1955,O 27,28:3

Canutt, Edwaard Tap
State Fair 1962,Ap 12,41:4

Canutt, Yakima
Rocky Mountain 1950,N 4,13:2

Canzi, Anna
Fiances, The 1964,Ja 29,23:1

Canzoneri, Tony
Ringside 1949,S 17,10:8

Caortos, Julius
111-es Szobaban; In Room 111 1938,Ap 2,18:2

Capa, Robert
Temptation 1946,D 25,33:6

Capacchione, Frank (Miscellaneous)
Mau Mau 1955,Jl 14,19:1

Capacci, Aldo
Angelo in the Crowd 1952,O 4,15:2

Capanna, Vittorio
Loves of Don Juan, The 1948,S 2,18:4

Caparros, Ernesto (Director)
Serpiente Roja, La; Red Serpent, The
1937,S 27,24:3

Capek, Karel (Original Author)
Skeleton on Horseback 1940,F 5,13:3
Krakatit 1951,Ap 30,16:2

Capell, Peter
Walk East on Beacon 1952,My 29,17:2
Paths of Glory 1957,D 26,23:2
For the First Time 1959,Ag 15,8:7
I Aim at the Stars 1960,O 20,42:2
Big Show, The 1961,My 11,42:4
One, Two, Three 1961,D 22,17:1

Capell, Peter (Narrator)
Titan-Story of Michelangelo, The 1950,Ja 23,16:2

Capellani, Albert (Director)
Eye for Eye 1918,D 23,9:1
Out of the Fog 1919,F 10,11:3
Red Lantern, The 1919,My 5,11:1
Inside of the Cup, The 1921,Ja 16,VI,2:1 (In
Addenda)
Sisters 1922,Ap 4,15:3

Capellani, Roger (Director)
Avec l'Assurance 1935,My 4,17:3

Capernaros, Vrassidas (Narrator)
Shrine of Victory 1943,Ag 20,13:2

Capitani, Tonino
Delitto di Mastrovanni, Il 1935,Jl 30,16:2

Caplan, Marcos
Ultimo Encventro, El; Last Meeting, The
1939,Ag 26,20:3
Senderos de Fe; Paths of Faith 1940,Mr 2,9:5

Caplat, Moran
Challenge, The 1939,O 2,15:2

Capodaglio, Wand
Tears of Blood 1952,Ja 19,13:2

Capolicchio, Lino
Taming of the Shrew, The 1967,Mr 9,43:1

Caporilli, Raffaele
Professor, My Son 1949,Ap 18,18:4

Capote, Truman (Miscellaneous)
Indiscretion of an American Wife 1954,Je 26,7:2

Capote, Truman (Original Author)
Breakfast at Tiffany's 1961,O 6,28:1
In Cold Blood 1967,D 15,60:1

Capote, Truman (Screenwriter)
Beat the Devil 1954,Mr 13,11:2
Innocents, The 1961,D 26,15:2

Capozzi, Alberto
Marco Visconti 1947,S 20,12:4

Capp, Al
That Certain Felling 1956,Je 21,35:2

Capp, Al (Miscellaneous)
Li'l Abner 1959,D 12,19:2

Cappy Barra Boys
Rockin' in the Rockies 1945,Jl 5,7:2
Radio Stars on Parade 1945,S 22,14:2

Capra, Frank (Director)
Long Pants 1927,Mr 29,23:2
For the Love of Mike 1927,Ag 24,27:5
Submarine 1928,Ag 31,23:3
Younger Generation, The 1929,Mr 11,22:2
Donovan Affair, The 1929,Ap 29,29:2
Flight 1929,S 14,17:1
Ladies of Leisure 1930,My 24,21:2
Rain or Shine 1930,Ag 8,11:1
Dirigible 1931,Ap 6,24:1
Miracle Woman, The 1931,Ag 17,18:2
Platinum Blonde 1931,O 31,22:2
Forbidden 1932,Ja 11,28:5
American Madness 1932,Ag 6,14:5
Bitter Tea of General Yen, The 1933,Ja 12,20:6
Lady for a Day 1933,S 8,22:2
It Happened One Night 1934,F 23,23:2
Broadway Bill 1934,N 30,22:2
Mr Deeds Goes to Town 1936,Ap 17,17:2
Lost Horizon 1937,Mr 4,27:1
You Can't Take It With You 1938,S 2,21:2
Mr Smith Goes to Washington 1939,O 20,27:2
Meet John Doe 1941,Mr 13,25:2
Tunisian Victory 1944,Mr 24,17:2
Arsenic and old Lace 1944,S 2,17:2
It's a Wonderful Life 1946,D 23,19:2
State of the Union 1948,Ap 23,28:1
Riding High 1950,Ap 11,26:2
Here Comes the Groom 1951,S 21,19:2
Pocketful of Miracles 1961,D 19,39:1
Rendezvous in Space 1964,S 10,27:1

Capra, Frank (Original Author)
Strong Man, The 1926,S 7,44:2
Westward the Women 1952,Ja 1,21:2

Capra, Frank (Producer)
Lost Horizon 1937,Mr 4,27:1
You Can't Take It With You 1938,S 2,21:2
Mr Smith Goes to Washington 1939,O 20,27:2

Capra, Frank (Producer)— Cont
  Meet John Doe 1941,Mr 13,25:2
  Prelude to War 1943,My 14,16:1
  Battle of Russia, The 1943,N 15,23:3
  Tunisian Victory 1944,Mr 24,17:2
  It's a Wonderful Life 1946,D 23,19:2
  State of the Union 1948,Ap 23,28:1
  Riding High 1950,Ap 11,26:2
  Here Comes the Groom 1951,S 21,19:2
  Pocketful of Miracles 1961,D 19,39:1
Capra, Frank (Screenwriter)
  His First Flame 1927,My 2,26:4
  Forbidden 1932,Ja 11,28:5
  It's a Wonderful Life 1946,D 23,19:2
Capri, Alaine
  Good Morning and Goodbye! 1968,F 20,53:1
Capri, Anna
  Kisses for my President 1964,Ag 22,13:1
Capri, Olga
  Terra Madre 1931,O 31,22:2
  Bertoldo, Bertoldino, Cacasenno 1937,D 22,32:3
Caprice, June
  Caprice of the Mountains 1916,Jl 10,9:5
Caprille, Anna
  Anatomy of a Marriage; My Days With Jean
    Marc; My Nights With Francoise
    1964,O 27,42:2
Caprioli, Vittorio
  Where the Hot Wind Blows 1960,N 12,15:1
  General Della Rovere 1960,N 22,41:1
  Zazie 1961,N 21,45:5
  White Voices; Voci Blanche 1965,Ap 13,32:2
Capua, Vincenza
  Love in old Naples 1940,Ja 26,13:3
Capuano, L (Director)
  What Price Innocence? 1953,My 2,13:3
Capuano, L (Original Author)
  Malia 1952,F 2,11:4
  What Price Innocence? 1953,My 2,13:3
Capuano, L (Screenwriter)
  What Price Innocence? 1953,My 2,13:3
Capuano, Sam
  Hoodlum Priest, The 1961,Ap 3,28:5
Capucine
  Song Without End 1960,Ag 12,10:2
  North to Alaska 1960,N 11,36:1
  Walk on the Wild Side 1962,F 22,20:1
  Lion, The 1962,D 22,5:2
  Pink Panther, The 1964,Ap 24,25:1
  Seventh Dawn, The 1964,S 3,24:1
  What's New Pussycat? 1965,Je 23,49:1
  Honey Pot, The 1967,My 23,52:1
  Queens, The (Queen Marta); Queen Marta (The
    Queens) 1968,Mr 11,49:1
Car, Nat
  Proud Heart 1925,N 3,25:4
Caraballo, Jose
  Contra la Corriente 1936,Mr 10,27:3
Caralis, Costa
  Stella 1957,Je 11,40:1
Carasa, Angel
  Ay Jalisco no te Rajes 1943,Ap 24,17:3
Carato, Vincent
  Hell in the Heavens 1934,D 12,28:2
Caravaca
  Silk, Blood and Sun 1943,Ja 30,10:6
Carb, David (Original Author)
  Chatterbox 1936,F 15,18:6
Carbajal, Tony
  Of Love and Desire 1963,S 12,32:1
Carballeira, Enriqueta
  Tia Tula, A 1965,Je 3,24:1
Carballido, Emilio (Screenwriter)
  Macario 1961,S 28,48:6
Carbonari, Virgilio
  Boheme, La 1965,O 20,51:2
Carbone, Anthony
  Pit and the Pendulum, The 1961,Ag 24,25:3
Carbonnaux, Norbert (Director)
  Candide 1962,N 20,39:1
Carbonnaux, Norbert (Screenwriter)
  Candide 1962,N 20,39:1
Carby, Fanny
  Sparrows Don't Sing 1963,My 7,46:2
  Family Way, The 1967,Je 29,32:1
Carco, Francis
  Marked Girls 1949,Je 25,8:7
Carco, Francis (Original Author)
  Shadows of Paris 1924,F 18,13:1
Card, Kathryn
  Kiss and Tell 1945,O 26,16:2
  It Shouldn't Happen to a Dog 1946,S 7,11:2
  Born to Kill 1947,My 1,34:2
  Hucksters, The 1947,Jl 18,21:2
  That Hagen Girl 1947,O 25,13:2
  Three Daring Daughters 1948,F 13,26:3
  Sainted Sisters, The 1948,My 20,35:2
  Dark Past, The 1948,D 23,25:2
  Skipper Surprised his Wife, The 1950,Je 30,18:2
  Harriet Craig 1950,N 3,31:2
  Model and the Marriage Broker, The
    1952,Ja 12,10:6
  Paula 1952,Jl 16,21:2
  Home Before Dark 1958,N 7,23:1

  Unsinkable Molly Brown, The 1964,Jl 17,15:1
Cardel, Silvia
  Cementario de las Aquilas, El; Eagles' Cementery,
    The 1939,S 2,20:1
Cardenas, Elsa
  Giant 1956,O 11,51:1
  Brave One, The 1957,Mr 22,26:1
  Of Love and Desire 1963,S 12,32:1
  Fun in Acapulco 1964,F 20,22:4
  Taggart 1964,D 25,24:4
Cardew, Valerie
  Woman's Vengeance, A 1948,Ja 30,19:2
  Thunder on the Hill 1951,O 18,32:3
Cardi, Denise
  Daughter of the Sands 1952,F 18,15:2
Cardi, Pat
  ...And Now Miguel 1966,S 8,43:1
  Let's Kill Uncle 1966,N 19,26:1
Cardiff, Jack (Cinematographer)
  Girl on a Motorcycle, The 1968,N 28,66:5
Cardiff, Jack (Director)
  Intent to Kill 1959,Ap 1,43:2
  Scent of Mystery 1960,F 19,23:1
  Sons and Lovers 1960,Ag 3,35:1
  My Geisha 1962,Je 14,23:2
  Long Ships, The 1964,Je 25,25:1
  Young Cassidy 1965,Mr 23,35:1
  Liquidator, The 1966,O 29,34:1
  Dark of the Sun 1968,Jl 4,13:1
  Girl on a Motorcycle, The 1968,N 28,66:5
Cardiff, Jack (Miscellaneous)
  Girl on a Motorcycle, The 1968,N 28,66:5
Cardinal, Marie
  Mouchette 1968,S 21,26:1
Cardinale, Claudia
  Big Deal on Madonna Street, The 1960,N 23,20:1
  Upstairs and Downstairs 1960,D 2,53:4
  Rocco and his Brothers 1961,Je 28,40:2
  Girl With a Suitcase 1961,S 12,36:2
  Bell Antonio 1962,Ap 3,43:2
  Viaccia, La 1962,S 21,35:1
  Fiasco in Milan 1963,Ap 11,29:2
  Eight and One Half 1963,Je 26,36:1
  Leopard, The 1963,Ag 13,25:1
  Pink Panther, The 1964,Ap 24,25:1
  Circus World 1964,Je 26,34:2
  Cartouche 1964,Jl 22,39:1
  Bebo's Girl 1964,N 12,40:1
  Magnificent Cuckold 1965,Ap 20,42:1
  Facts of Murder, The 1965,Jl 1,34:1
  Vaghe Stelle dell'Orsa; Of These Thousand
    Pleasures 1965,S 4,11:4
  Time of Indifference 1965,O 13,50:1
  Sandra 1966,Ja 17,32:1
  Blindfold 1966,My 26,55:2
  Lost Command 1966,S 15,51:1
  Time of Indifference 1966,O 13,50:1
  Professionals, The 1966,N 3,45:1
  Don't Make Waves 1967,Je 21,36:2
  Rose for Everyone, A 1967,Je 30,30:1
  Queens, The (Queen Armenia); Queen Armenia
    (The Queens) 1968,Mr 11,49:1
  Hell With Heroes, The 1968,S 3,54:2
Cardona, Rene
  Obre las Olas 1934,Mr 17,11:4
  Sobre Las Olas 1934,Mr 17,11:4
  Calvario de una Esposa, El 1936,S 26,11:2
  Asi es la Mujer 1936,O 21,35:3
  Alla en el Rancho Grande 1936,N 23,17:3
  El Misterio del Rostro Palido 1937,Ja 4,20:5
  Silencio Sublime 1937,Ja 16,21:2
  Liaga, La; Torment, The 1937,O 4,17:2
  Baul Macabro, El; Macabre Trunk, The
    1937,N 30,26:3
  Gran Cruz, La; Heavy Cross, The 1937,D 7,31:6
  Don Juan Tenorio 1937,D 28,29:3
  Cuna Vacia, La; Empty Cradle, The
    1938,Mr 21,18:3
  Traidor, El 1938,Ap 9,11:3
  Mano a Mano 1938,S 19,16:3
  Rancho Grande 1938,D 2,27:2
  Alla en el Tropico; Down in the Tropics
    1943,My 8,19:3
  El Conde de Monte Cristo 1943,N 9,26:2
Cardona, Rene (Director)
  Don Juan Tenorio 1937,D 28,29:3
  Tierra Brava 1938,O 29,15:6
  Alarma 1939,Ja 23,8:2
  Alla en el Rancho Chico; Out on the Little Ranch
    1939,F 25,19:3
  Cobarde, El; Coward, The 1939,Mr 27,11:2
  Estrellita; Starlet 1939,Ap 12,27:3
  Reina del Rio, La; Queen of the River, The
    1940,F 24,9:3
Cardwell, Barry
  Sand Castle, The 1961,Ag 16,37:2
Cardwell, James
  Sullivans, The 1944,F 10,19:2
  Sweet and Low Down 1944,O 19,19:2
  Walk in the Sun, A 1946,Ja 12,10:6
  Harpoon 1948,D 9,48:8
  He Walked by Night 1949,F 7,15:2
  Tokyo Joe 1949,O 27,35:2

Cardwell, James— Cont
  And Baby Makes Three 1949,D 23,17:3
Cardwell, Laurie
  Sand Castle, The 1961,Ag 16,37:2
Cardy, Raymond
  Nous, La Liberte, A 1932,My 18,25:2
Careili, Enzo (Producer)
  Overcoat, The 1953,O 13,34:1
Carel, Roger
  Two of Us, The 1968,F 20,53:1
Carell, Lianella
  Bicycle Thief, The 1949,D 13,44:2
  Genoese Dragnet 1954,F 12,20:5
Carelton, Claire
  It's a Great Feeling 1949,Ag 13,6:6
Carena, Anna
  Mill on the Po, The 1951,O 23,35:2
  Miracle in Milan 1951,D 18,42:2
  Overcoat, The 1953,O 13,34:1
Carere, Christine
  Certain Smile, A 1958,Ag 1,13:2
  Mardi Gras 1958,N 19,45:2
  Private's Affair, A 1959,Ag 15,8:7
Carette
  Grand Illusion 1938,S 13,28:2
  Heart of Paris 1939,Ja 13,17:3
  Curtain Rises, The 1939,Ap 22,15:2
  Human Beast, The 1940,F 20,17:2
  32 Rue de Montmartre 1944,S 28,26:3
  Gates of the Night 1950,Mr 16,40:2
  Rules of the Game, The 1950,Ap 10,15:3
  Marie du Port 1951,Jl 24,21:2
  Oh, Amelia 1951,D 3,22:2
  Red Inn, The 1954,Je 8,25:2
  Mirror Has two Faces, The 1959,My 27,31:1
  Rules of the Game, The 1961,Ja 19,26:1
  Green Mare, The; Jument Verte, La
    1961,O 24,41:2
Carette, Jean
  Adieu les Beaux Jours 1934,Ap 23,20:2
Carette, Julien
  Sylvie and the Phantom 1950,O 16,30:5
  Riptide 1951,Ap 7,9:2
  His Last Twelve Hours 1953,N -13,24:7
  Crime and Punishment 1958,S 16,23:2
  Paris Hotel 1959,S 12,12:3
  Magnificent Tramp, The 1962,Ap 25,30:1
Carew, Helen
  Boomerang 1947,Mr 6,36:2
Carew, James
  Twelve:Ten 1919,D 22,18:3
  You Made Me Love You 1934,My 30,14:3
  Dark Sands 1938,Ag 17,23:4
Carewe, Andrew
  Breath of the Gods, The 1920,Jl 26,9:5
Carewe, Arthur Edmund
  Ghost Breaker, The 1922,S 11,20:2
  Daddy 1923,Ap 16,20:2
  Trilby 1923,Jl 30,11:4
  Song of Love, The 1924,F 25,13:1
  Price of a Party, The 1924,N 26,17:3
  Sandra 1924,D 22,20:2
  Boomerang, The 1925,Jl 1,16:1
  Phantom of the Opera, The 1925,S 7,15:3
  Only Thing, The 1925,N 23,25:4
  Ibanez's Torrent 1926,F 22,14:1
  Diplomacy 1926,S 13,18:1
  Silent Lover, The 1926,N 15,19:1
  Claw, The 1927,My 11,28:3
  Cat and the Canary, The 1927,S 10,9:4
  Man's Past, A 1927,O 4,34:2
  Uncle Tom's Cabin 1927,N 5,16:2
  Matrimonial Bed, The 1930,Ag 25,14:2
  God's Gift to Women 1931,Ap 18,17:3
  Gay Diplomat, The 1931,O 10,20:4
  Doctor X 1932,Ag 4,17:2
  Mystery of the Wax Museum, The
    1933,F 18,13:3
  Charlie Chan's Secret 1936,Ja 18,19:4
Carewe, Edwin (Director)
  Isobel, or the Trail's End 1920,D 20,11:2
  Silver Wings 1922,My 18,14:4
  Mighty Lak' a Rose 1923,Mr 20,24:3
  Girl of the Golden West, The 1923,My 21,12:2
  Bad Man, The 1923,O 9,17:4
  Lady Who Lied 1925,Jl 7,24:2
  Joanna 1925,D 15,14:5
  Resurrection 1927,My 17,27:2
  Ramona 1928,My 15,17:3
  Revenge 1928,D 10,25:1
  Evangeline 1929,Jl 29,23:3
  Spoilers, The 1930,S 20,15:4
  Resurrection 1931,Ja 24,15:1
  Are We Civilized? 1934,Je 14,28:5
Carewe, Edwin (Producer)
  Are We Civilized? 1935,N 18,19:6
Carewe, Ora
  Too Many Millions 1918,D 9,11:4
Carewe, Rita
  Joanna 1925,D 15,14:5
  Revenge 1928,D 10,25:1

CAREY
See Also CARY
Carey, Ernestine Gilbreth (Original Author)
Cheaper by the Dozen 1950,Ap 1,12:2
Belles on Their Toes 1952,My 3,17:5
Carey, Harry
Man to Man 1922,Mr 28,17:4
Roaring Rails 1924,O 15,27:3
Silent Sanderson 1925,Je 11,14:3
Texas Trail, The 1925,Jl 9,14:2
Little Journey, A 1927,Ja 4,21:1
Slide, Kelly, Slide 1927,Mr 23,19:2
Trail of '98, The 1928,Mr 21,30:3
Trader Horn 1931,F 4,21:3
Bad Company 1931,N 7,16:5
Law and Order 1932,F 29,21:3
Barbary Coast 1935,O 14,21:1
Prisoner of Shark Island, The 1936,F 13,25:2
Powdersmoke Range 1936,Mr 9,20:2
Sutter's Gold 1936,Mr 27,25:2
Little Miss Nobody 1936,Je 6,21:1
Last Outlaw, The 1936,Je 15,24:1
Valiant Is the Word for Carrie 1936,O 8,27:2
Accusing Finger, The 1936,N 17,35:4
Kid Galahad 1937,My 27,21:3
Border Cafe 1937,Je 8,30:2
Born Reckless 1937,Jl 30,22:6
Souls at Sea 1937,Ag 10,23:2
Annapolis Salute 1937,O 2,18:1
Danger Patrol 1937,N 19,27:3
Port of Missing Girls, The 1938,Ap 4,12:5
You and Me 1938,Je 2,19:1
Sky Giant 1938,Jl 20,22:2
Gateway 1938,Ag 8,9:2
King of Alcatraz 1938,O 7,21:2
Law West of Tombstone, The 1938,N 25,19:1
Street of Missing Men 1939,Je 1,31:3
Mr Smith Goes to Washington 1939,O 20,27:2
My Son Is Guilty 1940,Ja 15,11:2
Outside the Three-Mile Limit 1940,Ap 8,15:2
Beyond Tomorrow 1940,S 27,27:1
They Knew What They Wanted 1940,O 11,25:2
Shepherd of the Hills, The 1941,Jl 31,13:2
Parachute Battalion 1941,Ag 29,13:2
Among the Living 1941,D 13,25:2
Spoilers, The 1942,My 22,27:2
Air Force 1943,F 4,29:1
Happy Land 1943,D 9,33:3
Great Moment, The 1944,N 13,15:2
Sea of Grass, The 1947,F 28,27:2
Angel and the Badman 1947,Mr 3,28:4
Duel in the Sun 1947,My 8,30:2
Red River 1948,O 1,31:2
So Dear to my Heart 1949,Ja 31,14:2
House of Bamboo 1955,Jl 2,13:2
Bandolero 1968,Jl 18,26:2
Carey, Harry Jr
Pursued 1947,Mr 8,10:2
Red River 1948,O 1,31:2
Three Godfathers 1949,Mr 4,25:2
Moonrise 1949,Mr 7,17:2
She Wore a Yellow Ribbon 1949,N 18,35:2
Wagonmaster 1950,Je 19,17:2
Copper Canyon 1950,N 16,39:2
Rio Grande 1950,N 20,21:2
Warpath 1951,N 23,32:2
Wild Blue Yonder, The 1952,Ja 2,20:1
Island in the Sky 1953,S 10,22:2
Beneath the 12-Mile Reef 1953,D 17,52:2
Long Gray Line, The 1955,F 11,19:2
Mister Roberts 1955,Jl 15,14:1
Searchers, The 1956,My 31,21:4
Great Locomotive Chase, The 1956,Je 27,35:1
River's Edge, The 1957,Ap 12,20:2
Kiss Them for Me 1957,N 9,31:2
From Hell to Texas 1958,Je 5,39:2
Rio Bravo 1959,Mr 19,40:2
Great Impostor, The 1961,Mr 30,24:1
Alvarez Kelly 1966,N 17,55:2
Carey, Joyce
In Which We Serve 1942,D 24,18:1
Blithe Spirit 1945,O 4,27:2
Johnny in the Clouds 1945,N 16,16:2
Brief Encounter 1946,Ag 26,21:2
October Man, The 1948,Ap 16,29:2
Dulcimer Street 1948,N 8,24:2
Amazing Mr Beecham, The 1949,D 26,33:4
Astonished Heart, The 1950,F 15,23:2
Happy Go Lovely 1951,Jl 26,17:2
Cry, the Beloved Country 1952,Ja 24,23:2
Greyfriars' Bobby 1961,O 12,41:4
Portrait of a Sinner 1961,D 7,52:1
Eyes of Annie Jones, The 1964,My 14,39:1
Carey, Leonard
Laughter 1930,N 15,15:3
Honor Among Lovers 1931,F 28,15:2
This Reckless Age 1932,Ja 9,21:1
Nice Women 1932,F 20,11:2
Merrily We Go to Hell 1932,Je 11,9:3
Infernal Machine 1933,Ap 8,16:3
Avenger, The 1933,O 3,28:3
Bombshell 1933,O 21,11:2
Worst Woman in Paris, The 1933,N 25,10:3

Double Door 1934,My 5,22:3
His Greatest Gamble 1934,Jl 18,20:2
Age of Innocence, The 1934,O 19,27:1
I Sell Anything 1934,D 27,25:2
Little Minister, The 1934,D 28,25:1
Hold 'Em Yale 1935,Ap 27,20:6
Our Little Girl 1935,Je 7,24:4
Bunker Bean 1936,Je 27,21:2
Last of Mrs Cheyney, The 1937,F 19,15:1
Hitting a new High 1937,D 27,11:1
Lone Wolf Spy Hunt, The 1939,Mr 6,11:3
Zero Hour, The 1939,Jl 5,20:3
Rebecca 1940,Mr 29,25:2
Private Affairs 1940,Jl 5,10:3
Hired Wife 1940,S 14,11:2
Private Nurse 1941,Ag 29,13:3
Moon Over her Shoulder 1941,N 5,31:2
Give Out, Sisters 1942,Ag 28,22:3
Slightly French 1949,My 27,25:3
Kind Lady 1951,Ag 8,21:2
Snows of Kilimanjaro, The 1952,S 19,19:2
Thunder in the East 1953,F 4,32:2
Carey, Lynn
Lord Love a Duck 1966,F 22,14:6
Carey, Macdonald
Take a Letter Darling 1942,My 28,13:2
Dr Broadway 1942,Je 25,27:3
Wake Island 1942,S 2,19:2
Star Spangled Rhythm 1942,D 31,20:1
Shadow of a Doubt 1943,Ja 13,18:2
Suddenly It's Spring 1947,F 27,26:2
Hazard 1948,Je 3,19:2
Dream Girl 1948,Je 17,29:2
Bride of Vengeance 1949,Ap 7,38:2
Streets of Laredo 1949,My 12,28:2
Great Gatsby, The 1949,Jl 14,20:5
South Sea Sinner 1950,Ja 16,18:4
Comanche Territory 1950,Ap 8,9:3
Lawless, The 1950,Je 23,29:2
Copper Canyon 1950,N 16,39:2
Mystery Submarine 1951,F 2,19:2
Great Missouri Raid, The 1951,Ap 9,31:2
Excuse my Dust 1951,Je 28,21:2
Meet Me After the Show 1951,Ag 16,23:2
Let's Make It Legal 1951,N 7,35:3
My Wife's Best Friend 1952,O 11,17:2
Count the Hours 1953,Je 24,30:4
Fire over Africa 1954,N 22,29:5
John Paul Jones 1959,Je 17,39:1
Blue Denim 1959,Jl 31,21:1
Tammy and the Doctor 1963,Je 27,23:2
These Are the Damned 1965,Jl 8,35:1
Carey, Michele
Dorado, El 1967,Je 29,32:1
Sweet Ride, The 1968,Je 13,57:2
Carey, Olive
On Dangerous Ground 1952,F 13,35:2
Bride Comes to Yellow Sky, The 1953,Ja 14,27:2
Affair With a Stranger 1953,Jl 11,8:2
Rogue Cop 1954,S 18,12:2
I Died a Thousand Times 1955,N 10,45:2
Searchers, The 1956,My 31,21:4
Gunfight at the O K Corral 1957,My 30,23:2
Night Passage 1957,Jl 25,28:1
Run of the Arrow 1957,Ag 3,8:6
Carey, Philip
Operation Pacific 1951,F 3,10:2
I Was a Communist for the F B I 1951,My 3,34:4
Inside the Walls of Folsom Prison 1951,My 28,17:4
Tanks are Coming, The 1951,D 6,42:4
ThIs Woman is Dangerous 1952,F 28,23:2
Springfield Rifle 1952,O 23,40:2
Calamity Jane 1953,N 5,40:2
Pushover 1954,Jl 31,6:3
Long Gray Line, The 1955,F 11,19:2
Mister Roberts 1955,Jl 15,14:1
Three Stripes in the Sun 1955,N 24,41:2
Port Afrique 1956,N 3,27:5
Screaming Mimi 1958,Je 26,23:3
Tonka 1959,Mr 26,27:1
Trunk, The 1962,N 1,34:3
Dead Ringer 1964,F 20,22:3
FBI Code 98 1964,Ap 9,25:6
Carey, Timothy
Bloodhounds of Broadway 1952,N 15,15:2
White Witch Doctor 1953,Jl 2,19:3
East of Eden 1955,Mr 10,33:1
Finger Man 1955,Jl 16,12:4
Killing, The 1956,My 21,20:1
Francis in the Haunted House 1956,Jl 21,9:2
Last Wagon, The 1956,S 22,20:2
Paths of Glory 1957,D 26,23:2
One Eyed Jacks 1961,Mr 31,21:1
Second Time Around, The 1961,D 23,16:1
Convicts 4 1962,O 4,44:2
Waterhole #3 1967,O 11,41:4
Head 1968,N 7,51:1
Carfrae, Elizabeth
Forest Ring, The 1930,Ap 26,11:1
Cargiff, Jack (Director)
Lion, The 1962,D 22,5:2

Cargill, Patrick
Help! 1965,Ag 24,25:1
Countess from Hong Kong, A 1967,Mr 17,35:1
Inspector Clouseau 1968,Jl 25,26:1
Hammerhead 1968,S 12,54:3
Cargill, Peter
Alligator Named Daisy, An 1957,O 7,23:2
Carideo, Frank
Spirit of Notre Dame, The 1931,O 16,27:1
Carillo, Leo
Tight Shoes 1941,Je 19,25:2
Men of Texas 1942,Jl 13,18:3 (In Addenda)
Pancho Villa Returns 1950,O 24,34:6
Carillo, Mario
Song of Love, The 1924,F 25,13:1
His Hour 1924,O 7,26:1
Declassee 1925,Mr 23,14:2
Eve's Secret 1925,Je 11,14:3
Lost-a Wife 1925,Je 22,10:2
Only Thing, The 1925,N 23,25:4
Dance Madness 1926,Ja 25,21:2
Ibanez's Torrent 1926,F 22,14:1
Girl From Montmarte, The 1926,F 25,26:2
Barrier, The 1926,Mr 22,16:1
Diplomacy 1926,S 13,18:1
Venus of Venice 1927,My 3,25:1
Time to Love 1927,Je 23,23:3
Private Life of Helen of Troy, The 1927,D 10,14:7
His Tiger Lady 1928,My 28,23:2
Hot News 1928,Jl 23,11:2
Just Married 1928,Ag 13,23:2
Carini, Luigi
Pierpin, La Figlia Ritrovata 1936,Mr 27,25:3
Loyalty of Love 1937,Mr 1,15:1
Carioca Boys
Road to Rio 1948,F 19,29:3
Cariroli, Zulema Haydee
Ley que Olvidaron, La; Law They Forgot, The 1940,Ja 13,11:3
Carisson, Elsa
Of Love and Lust (On Payment); On Payment (Of Love and Lust) 1959,My 26,31:2
Carjol, M
Crainquebille 1934,D 10,16:3
CARL
See Also CARLE, KARL
Carl, Joe
Tel Aviv Taxi 1956,D 31,10:7
Carl, M Roger
Jade Casket, The 1929,Je 24,27:1
Carl, Raymond
Mr Hulot's Holiday 1954,Je 17,36:2
Carl, Renee
Miserables, Les 1926,Jl 9,17:1
Miserables, Les 1927,Ag 23,29:4
Carl, Rudolph
Polenblut; Polish Blood 1935,N 16,19:3
Frasquita 1936,Ja 18,19:4
Tanzmusik 1936,My 26,27:2
Fahrt in Die Jugend, Die 1936,Ag 31,19:2
Postillon of Lonjumeau, The 1937,N 20,21:3
Liebe im Dreiviertel Takt; Love in Waltz Time 1938,S 24,13:1
Teufelskerl, Ein; Devil of a Fellow, A 1938,O 1,10:3
Wir Sind vom K u K Infantrie-Regiment 1938,N 19,9:2
Carlaon, Vicki
Violated 1953,D 12,23:8
Carlberg, Hilbur
Witch Woman, The 1929,Ap 8,32:1
CARLE
See Also CARL, KARL
Carle, Frankie
My Dream Is Yours 1949,Ap 16,11:3
Carle, Naida
Wild Bill Hickok 1923,N 21,22:1
Carle, Richard
Zander the Great 1925,My 4,16:2
Coming of Amos, The 1925,S 8,29:1
Understanding Heart, The 1927,My 10,24:5
Soft Cushions 1927,S 12,29:1
Fleet's In, The 1928,O 1,23:1
While the City Sleeps 1928,O 22,29:1
Madame X 1929,Ap 25,32:3
His Glorious Night 1929,O 5,22:5
Grand Parade, The 1930,F 1,15:1
Fireman, Save My Child 1932,F 18,25:3
One Hour with You 1932,Mr 24,17:5
Night of June 13th, The 1932,S 17,18:4
Private Jones 1933,Mr 25,13:3
Diplomaniacs 1933,Ap 29,14:2
Morning Glory 1933,Ag 18,18:2
George White's Scandals 1934,Mr 16,24:2
Sing and Like It 1934,Ap 14,18:2
Witching Hour, The 1934,Ap 28,11:3
Last Round-Up, The 1934,My 10,25:2
Hollywood Party 1934,My 26,12:2
Affairs of a Gentleman 1934,Je 23,16:7
Old-Fashioned Way, The 1934,Jl 14,16:5
Caravan 1934,S 28,27:1
Wake up and Dream 1934,O 11,28:3

Carle, Richard— Cont

When a Man's a Man 1935,F 22,27:2
Night Life of the Gods 1935,F 23,14:6
Ghost Walks, The 1935,Mr 30,11:2
Love in Bloom 1935,Ap 20,16:2
Gay Deception, The 1935,O 11,31:1
Bride Comes Home, The 1935,D 25,30:2
Dangerous 1935,D 27,14:1
Anything Goes 1936,F 6,23:3
Trail of the Lonesome Pine, The 1936,F 20,23:5
Let's Sing Again 1936,My 9,11:2
One Rainy Afternoon 1936,My 14,29:2
Case Against Mrs Ames, The 1936,My 28,19:2
Spendthrift 1936,Jl 23,24:1
Man I Marry, The 1936,O 31,24:3
Outcast 1937,Mr 3,27:2
Top of the Town 1937,Mr 27,19:2
Racketeers in Exile 1937,Ap 12,15:3
Man in Blue, The 1937,Ag 30,25:2
45 Fathers 1937,D 11,22:2
True Confession 1937,D 16,35:2
I'll Take Romance 1937,D 17,33:2
It's all Yours 1938,Ja 7,15:3
Persons in Hiding 1939,Mr 2,19:2
It's a Wonderful World 1939,My 19,27:2
Undercover Doctor 1939,Je 1,31:2
Maisie 1939,Je 23,23:1
Ninotchka 1939,N 10,27:2
Remember? 1939,D 15,33:4
Parole Fixer 1940,Ap 18,28:5
Comin' Round the Mountain 1940,S 26,27:3
Golden Fleecing, The 1940,N 7,33:4
Seven Sinners 1940,N 18,23:2
One Night in the Tropics 1940,D 20,33:2
That Uncertain Feeling 1941,My 2,25:1
Devil and Miss Jones, The 1941,My 16,21:2
Million Dollar Baby 1941,Je 7,20:2
Moonlight in Hamaii 1941,O 10,26:6
Buy Me That Town 1941,O 23,27:2
New Wine 1942,F 2,11:2
Carlebach, Julius
8 X 8 1957,Mr 16,13:2
CARLETON
See Also CARLTON
Carleton, Claire
Crooked Road, The 1940,Je 11,33:4
Night of Adventure, A 1944,Je 3,10:4
My Pal, Wolf 1944,O 9,17:2
Double Life, A 1948,F 20,19:1
Bad Men of Tombstone 1949,Mr 5,10:2
Red Light 1950,Ja 16,18:4
Born Yesterday 1950,D 27,30:2
Death of a Salesman 1951,D 21,21:3
Witness to Murder 1954,Ap 16,16:4
Buster Keaton Story, The 1957,Ap 22,31:6
Careless Years, The 1957,N 28,57:3
Carleton, George
Just off Broadway 1942,Ag 29,18:4
Great Gildersleeve, The 1942,D 18,36:8
Over my Dead Body 1942,D 26,15:2
And Now Tomorrow 1944,N 23,38:2
Carleton, George de
New Klondike, The 1926,Mr 22,16:1
Carleton, Jane
Spy Ring, The 1938,Ja 15,19:1
Carleton, Marjorie (Original Author)
Cry Wolf 1947,Jl 19,10:2
Carleton, Robert
Barretts of Wimpole Street, The 1934,S 29,12:2
Carleton, Will (Original Author)
Over the Hill to the Poor House 1920,S 18,16:2
Over the Hill 1931,N 21,20:4
Carleton, William
Inside of the Cup, The 1921,Ja 16,VI,2:1 (In
   Addenda)
Law and the Woman, The 1922,Ja 22,VI,3:1 (In
   Addenda)
Zandunga, La 1938,My 14,18:2
Miserables, Los 1944,O 24,17:2
Loyola, The Soldier Saint 1952,Ap 25,19:2
Naked Jungle, The 1954,Ap 3,19:2
On the Threshold of Space 1956,Mr 30,10:5
Carleton, William P
Perfect Clue, The 1935,Mr 14,18:1
Bohemian Girl, The 1936,F 17,21:1
Border Patrolman 1936,Je 29,11:2
Carleton, William T
Gloria's Romance 1916,My 23,9:2
Homeward Bound 1923,Jl 31,12:4
Carletti, Louise
Portrait of Innocence 1948,Je 9,35:2
Carlier, Gerard (Screenwriter)
Three Feet in a Bed 1957,My 18,23:2
Fernandel the Dressmaker 1957,Jl 1,19:2
Carlin, George
With Six You Get Egg Roll 1968,O 10,59:6
Carlin, Jean
Are These our Parents? 1944,Ag 23,16:2
Carlin, Lynn
Faces 1968,S 23,42:4
Faces 1968,N 25,54:2
Carlin, Thomas
Young Don't Cry, The 1957,Jl 27,10:7

Carling, Foster (Composer)
Hit Parade of 1947 1947,My 5,32:8
Carlini, Paolo
Roman Holiday 1953,Ag 28,13:1
Gioconda, La 1958,O 13,33:4
It Started in Naples 1960,S 3,7:6
Carlino, Antonio
Shoe-Shine 1947,Ag 27,19:2
Carlino, Lewis John (Screenwriter)
Seconds 1966,O 6,56:1
Fox, The 1968,F 8,36:1
CARLISLE
See Also CARLYLE
Carlisle, Alexandra
Half a Sinner 1934,Je 23,16:5
Carlisle, Helen Grace (Original Author)
Mothers Cry 1930,D 6,21:3
Live, Love and Learn 1937,N 19,27:2
Carlisle, Kitty
Murder at the Vanities 1934,My 21,20:2
She Loves Me Not 1934,S 8,18:5
Here is my Heart 1934,D 22,21:1
Night at the Opera, A 1935,D 7,22:1
Carlisle, Mary
This Reckless Age 1932,Ja 9,21:1
Hotel Continental 1932,Mr 21,19:5
Night Court 1932,My 27,27:5
Down to Earth 1932,S 2,19:2
Her mad Night 1932,N 15,24:5
Men Must Fight 1933,Mr 11,18:3
College Humor 1933,Je 23,15:4
Saturday's Millions 1933,O 14,18:3
Sweetheart of Sigma Chi, The 1933,N 9,27:1
Should Ladies Behave? 1933,D 18,24:3
This Side of Heaven 1934,F 10,21:2
Palooka 1934,F 28,23:2
Once to Every Woman 1934,Mr 26,22:3
Handy Andy 1934,Ag 4,14:5
Million Dollar Ransom 1934,S 19,15:2
Kentucky Kernels 1935,Ja 5,20:2
Grand Old Girl 1935,F 26,16:4
Great Hotel Murder, The 1935,F 28,17:4
It's in the Air 1935,N 8,18:2
Lady, Be Careful 1936,O 10,21:1
Love in Exile 1936,D 10,35:3
Double or Nothing 1937,S 2,17:3
Hold 'Em Navy 1937,N 6,14:2
Tip-Off Girls 1938,Mr 25,15:3
Doctor Rhythm 1938,My 19,25:2
Hunted Men 1938,My 21,9:2
Touchdown Army 1938,O 28,27:2
Illegal Traffic 1938,N 17,29:3
Say It in French 1938,D 1,29:1
Hawaiian Nights 1939,S 29,19:4
Beware, Spooks 1939,N 3,17:4
Dance, Girl, Dance 1940,O 11,25:2
Carlisle, Rita
Brothers 1930,N 15,15:3
Waterloo Bridge 1931,S 5,7:4
Vampire Bat, The 1933,Ja 23,9:1
Carlisle, Robert (Director)
Sofi 1968,Mr 28,52:3
Carlisle, Robert (Producer)
Sofi 1968,Mr 28,52:3
Carlisle, Tyrell
Murder at Midnight 1931,O 5,17:3
Carll, Laura
Cossacks, The 1960,S 6,41:4
Carlo, Yvonne de
Law of the Lawless 1964,Ag 27,28:2
Carlos
Llorona, La 1935,Jl 20,16:2
Carlot, Marie
Midnight in Paris 1947,O 9,32:3
Carlquist, Margit
Smiles of a Summer Night 1957,D 24,11:1
Carlsen, Carla
Glueckliche Reise 1936,Ja 20,22:3
Carlsen, Henning (Director)
Hunger 1966,S 14,53:2
Hunger 1968,Ag 13,45:2
Carlsen, Henning (Screenwriter)
Hunger 1968,Ag 13,45:2
Carlsen, John
Bambole; Dolls, The (The Soup); Soup, The (The
   Dolls) 1965,Je 29,26:1
Carlsen, Traute
Heidi and Peter 1955,D 13,55:2
Carlson, Astrid
Soederkaakar 1936,D 19,16:2
Carlson, June
Every Saturday Night 1936,Mr 14,10:2
Educating Father 1936,Je 20,22:2
Off to the Races 1937,F 6,15:2
Big Business 1937,Je 1,27:2
Hot Water 1937,N 5,19:4
Trip to Paris, A 1938,Je 10,18:2
Safety in Numbers 1938,S 6,17:2
Young as You Feel 1940,Mr 8,25:3
Mom and Dad 1957,Ja 31,21:1
Carlson, Mats
Paisan 1948,Mr 30,26:2

Carlson, Philip
Secret Cinema, The 1968,My 2,57:1
Carlson, Richard
Young in Heart, The 1938,N 4,27:2
Duke of West Point, The 1938,D 16,33:2
Winter Carnival 1939,Jl 28,14:2
These Glamour Girls 1939,Ag 31,14:2
Dancing Co-Ed 1939,N 10,27:3
Little Accident 1939,N 24,29:3
Ghost Breakers 1940,Jl 4,12:2
Beyond Tomorrow 1940,S 27,27:1
Howards of Virginia, The 1940,S 27,27:1
Too Many Girls 1940,N 21,43:1
No, No, Nanette 1940,D 20,33:1
Back Street 1941,F 12,25:2
Hold That Ghost 1941,Ag 8,13:3
Little Foxes, The 1941,Ag 22,19:2
West Point Widow 1941,S 11,21:5
White Cargo 1942,N 27,27:2
Presenting Lily Mars 1943,Ap 30,25:3
Man From Down Under, The 1943,S 27,23:2
So Well Remembered 1947,N 5,34:3
King Solomon's Mines 1950,N 10,35:1
Valentino 1951,Ap 20,25:1
Try and Get Me 1951,My 7,22:2
Millionaire for Christy, A 1951,O 5,24:3
Blue Veil, The 1951,O 27,10:5
Retreat Hell! 1952,F 20,26:2
Flat Top 1952,D 6,17:2
Magnetic Monster, The 1953,My 14,32:5
It Came From Outer Space 1953,Je 18,38:2
Maze, The 1953,Jl 11,8:2
All I Desire 1953,Ag 29,10:1
Riders to the Stars 1954,Mr 20,10:7
Creature from the Black Lagoon 1954,My 1,13:4
Bengazi 1955,O 8,13:4
Three for Jamie Dawn 1956,Jl 7,11:3
Helen Morgan Story, The 1957,O 3,33:2
Kid Rodelo 1966,F 23,46:1
Power, The 1968,Mr 7,52:2
Carlson, Richard (Director)
Riders to the Stars 1954,Mr 20,10:7
Four Guns to the Border 1954,N 6,15:3
Appointment With a Shadow 1959,Ja 8,24:2
Kid Rodelo 1966,F 23,46:1
Carlson, Steve
Deadlier Than the Male 1967,F 22,21:1
Young Warriors, The 1968,F 8,36:1
Nobody's Perfect 1968,Ap 4,58:3
Carlssen, Carla
Frau Lehmann's Toechter 1933,O 27,22:3
Carlsson, Alice
Tjocka Slaekten; Near Relatives 1935,My 20,20:5
Carlsson, Elsa
Pettersson & Bendel 1934,F 22,25:2
Familjen Andersson; Anderson Family, The
   1939,Ja 24,16:5
Carlsson, Karin
Under Falsk Flagg 1937,Ja 20,18:5
Carlsson, Sickan
Kaera Slaekten 1934,My 14,20:4
Sangen Till Henne; Song to Her, The
   1935,F 22,27:3
Klart till Drabbning; Cleared for Action
   1937,D 10,33:3
Rena Rama Sanningen; Nothing but the Truth
   1939,O 7,11:2
Carlsson, Sven-Eric
Med Folket Foer Fosterlandet 1939,F 21,14:2
Carlsten, Dora
Kaera Slaekten 1934,My 14,20:4
Karl Fredrik Reigns 1938,F 2,15:2
Carlsten, Rune
Lasse-Maja 1943,Mr 22,15:4
CARLTON
See Also CARLETON
Carlton, George de
American Venus, The 1926,Ja 26,25:2
Carlton, Rex (Producer)
Guilty Bystander 1950,Ap 21,18:2
Carlton, Sue
Models, Inc 1952,My 26,18:4
Carlton, William P
Society Exile, A 1919,Ag 18,9:2
Carlucci, Adele
Passa L'Amore 1933,N 25,10:3
CARLYLE
See Also CARLISLE
Carlyle, Aileen
Too Young to Marry 1931,My 4,15:3
Miracle Woman, The 1931,Ag 17,18:2
Play Girl 1932,Mr 19,11:2
Stranger's Return, The 1933,Jl 28,18:2
Country Doctor, The 1936,Mr 13,32:2 (Incorrect
   in this edition; use 1936,Mr 13,27:2 elsewhere)
Carlyle, David
Cain and Mabel 1936,O 19,22:1
Smart Blonde 1937,Ja 9,21:1
Kid Comes Back, The 1938,F 7,10:2
Carlyle, Grace
Fast Set, The 1924,N 18,22:1
Notorious Lady, The 1927,Ap 11,18:3

Carlyle, Helen
Forgotten Commandments 1932,Je 2,25:2

Carlyle, Jack
Billy the Kid 1930,O 18,23:2
Carnival Boat 1932,Mr 21,19:5
Last Man, The 1932,S 17,18:4

Carlyle, Richard
Copperhead, The 1920,F 9,10:3
Inside of the Cup, The 1921,Ja 16,VI,2:1 (In Addenda)
Hearts in Dixie 1929,F 28,30:3
Playing Around 1930,Mr 31,24:3
Guilty 1930,Ap 7,21:1
Girl of the Golden West, The 1930,O 27,17:1
Kismet 1930,O 31,20:1
Tol'able David 1930,N 17,29:1
Sons of Steel 1935,Ap 15,16:3
Target Unknown 1951,Mr 5,24:2
Iron Mistress 1952,N 20,39:2
Torpedo Run 1958,O 25,16:2
Gallant Hours, The 1960,Je 23,19:4

Carlyle, Sidney
Humoresque 1920,My 31,14:2

Carmagnole, Dancers
Orphans of the Storm 1922,Ja 29,VI,2:1 (In Addenda)

Carmassi, Maria Grazia
Climax, The 1967,S 12,55:1

Carme, Pamela
Almost a Honeymoon 1931,Ja 10,19:2
Girl Was Young, The 1938,F 11,27:2

Carmel, Jean
Babette Goes to War 1960,Je 8,46:1

Carmel, Roger C
Goodbye, Charlie 1964,N 19,49:1
Silencers, The 1966,Mr 17,35:1
Alvarez Kelly 1966,N 17,55:2
Gambit 1966,D 22,40:2
Venetian Affair, The 1967,Ja 19,41:2

Carmelita
Por Mis Pistolas; By My Pistols 1939,Je 10,14:3

Carmen
Last of the Secret Agents, The? 1966,Je 23,29:1

Carmen, Herlinda del
Chuka 1967,N 2,58:3

Carmen, Jeanne
Untamed Youth 1957,My 11,24:6
Portland Expose 1957,S 27,16:6

Carmen, Jewel
Nobody 1921,Jl 25,8:3
Bat, The 1926,Mr 15,18:3

Carmen, Mary del
Rumbo al Cairo; Bound for Cairo 1940,Je 8,18:3

Carmet, Jean
Dr Knock 1955,O 10,31:2
Belle Americaine, La 1961,D 18,42:1
Elusive Corporal, The 1963,F 19,5:1
Any Number Can Win 1963,O 9,47:2
Devil and the 10 Commandments, The (Episode 7) 1963,O 15,44:1

Carmi, Vera
Anything for a Song 1947,Ag 5,26:2
His Young Wife 1949,Mr 12,10:2
Escape into Dreams 1950,Ap 13,34:5
Island of Procida, The 1952,Mr 15,8:2
Journey to Love 1953,O 9,32:8

Carmichael, H Kenn (Screenwriter)
Mark of the Hawk, The 1958,Mr 6,32:1

Carmichael, Hoagy
To Have and Have Not 1944,O 12,24:1
Johnny Angel 1945,D 28,12:2
Canyon Passage 1946,Ag 8,18:2
Best Years of our Lives, The 1946,N 22,27:2
Night Song 1948,Ja 29,27:5
Young Man With a Horn 1950,F 10,18:4
Johnny Holiday 1950,My 17,36:1
Las Vegas Story, The 1952,Ja 31,37:6
Belles on Their Toes 1952,My 3,17:5
Timberjack 1955,Mr 10,33:3

Carmichael, Hoagy (Composer)
Anything Goes 1936,F 6,23:3
Every Day's a Holiday 1938,Ja 27,17:2
College Swing 1938,Ap 28,27:2
Sing You Sinners 1938,Ag 18,23:1
Road Show 1941,F 19,25:2
Mr Bug Goes to Town 1942,F 20,21:3
Three for the Show 1955,F 25,16:1
Timberjack 1955,Mr 10,33:3

Carmichael, Ian
Betrayed 1954,S 9,36:1
Storm over the Nile 1956,Je 9,14:2
Simon and Laura 1956,Jl 3,17:2
Private's Progress 1956,Jl 24,19:2
Brothers in Law 1957,Ag 20,22:1
Colditz Story, The 1957,O 25,23:2
Lucky Jim 1958,S 1,8:6
Happy is the Bride 1959,Je 30,27:2
I'm All Right Jack 1960,Ap 26,40:2
School for Scoundrels 1960,Jl 12,39:1
Left, Right and Centre 1961,F 10,19:1
Double Bunk 1961,N 17,41:3
Heavens Above! 1963,My 21,28:2
Hide and Seek 1964,Mr 12,40:3

Smashing Time 1967,D 21,44:1

Carminati, Tullio
Bat, The 1926,Mr 15,18:3
Duchess of Buffalo, The 1926,Ag 9,10:3
Honeymoon Hate 1927,D 31,31:1
Three Sinners 1928,Ap 23,20:2
Gallant Lady 1934,Ja 22,12:3
Moulin Rouge 1934,F 8,14:4
One Night of Love 1934,S 7,25:3
Let's Live Tonight 1935,Mr 18,14:4
Paris in Spring 1935,Jl 13,16:2
Marcia Nuziale, La 1936,F 27,23:2
Girl in the Street 1938,My 26,31:2
Suicide Legion 1940,My 6,13:3
Safari 1940,Je 20,29:2
Golden Madonna, The 1949,S 5,13:4
Beauty and the Devil 1952,Ag 26,15:2
Secret Conclave, The 1953,My 16,10:1
Roman Holiday 1953,Ag 28,13:1
Breath of Scandal, A 1960,D 17,19:1
Cid, El 1961,D 15,49:1
Swordsman of Siena 1962,D 6,55:3
Cardinal, The 1963,D 13,41:1

Carmine, Giullano (Screenwriter)
Mighty Ursus, The 1962,Jl 26,17:1

Carmona, Gabriel
Pandora and the Flying Dutchman 1951,D 7,35:2

Carnabuci, Piero
Scipio Africanus 1939,S 23,22:2

Carnahan, Suzanne
Santa Fe Trail 1940,D 21,21:2

Carnall, Suzi
Studs Lonigan 1960,D 15,59:1
Explosive Generation, The 1962,F 15,24:2

Carne, Judy
Pair of Briefs, A 1964,F 3,22:2

Carne, Marcel (Director)
Bizarre, Bizarre 1939,Mr 21,27:2
Port of Shadows 1939,O 30,13:2
Daybreak 1940,Jl 30,16:2
Hotel du Nord 1940,D 30,21:2
Enfants du Paradis, Les 1947,F 20,32:2
Devil's Own Envoy, The 1947,Ag 30,8:6
Gates of the Night 1950,Mr 16,40:2
Marie du Port 1951,Jl 24,21:2
Adulteress, The 1958,Ja 14,42:1
Cheaters, The; (Tricheurs, Les) 1961,Je 5,37:4

Carne, Marcel (Producer)
Gates of the Night 1950,Mr 16,40:2
Marie du Port 1951,Jl 24,21:2

Carne, Marcel (Screenwriter)
Adulteress, The 1958,Ja 14,42:1
Cheaters, The; (Tricheurs, Les) 1961,Je 5,37:4

Carnell, Cliff
Too Late Blues 1962,Mr 1,27:4

Carnell, Jonas (Screenwriter)
Puss and Kram 1967,S 25,56:1

Carnera, Primo
Prizefighter and the Lady, The 1933,N 11,11:3
Iron Crown 1949,Je 11,11:2
Prince Valiant 1954,Ap 7,40:2
Casanova's Big Night 1954,Ap 19,19:1
Kid for two Farthings, A 1956,Ap 18,25:1
Hercules Unchained 1960,Jl 14,23:1

Carnero, Irena
Przysieglas 1932,My 16,19:5

CARNEY
See Also KEARNEY

Carney, Alan
Mr Lucky 1943,Jl 23,21:2
Around the World 1943,N 25,39:2
Seven Days Ashore 1944,Ap 26,24:7
Step Lively 1944,Jl 27,14:1
Zombies on Broadway 1945,Ap 27,23:2
Radio Stars on Parade 1945,S 22,14:2
Pretender, The 1947,Ag 12,26:2
Li'l Abner 1959,D 12,19:2
It's a Mad, Mad, Mad, Mad World 1963,N 19,47:1

Carney, Art
Guide for the Married Man, A 1967,My 27,16:1

Carney, George
Dreaming Lips 1937,My 20,17:1
Forbidden Music 1938,D 27,13:2
Convoy 1941,Ja 17,21:2
Stars Look Down, The 1941,Jl 24,15:2
Lady in Distress 1942,F 16,21:2
In Which We Serve 1942,D 24,18:1
Love on the Dole 1945,O 13,11:2
I Know Where I'm Going 1947,Ag 20,25:2
Tawny Pipit 1947,S 8,25:5
Agitator, The 1949,Ag 19,12:5
Good Time Girl 1950,S 25,18:5
Little Ballerina, The 1951,F 28,33:2

Carney, James
Sez O'Reilly to MacNab 1938,F 19,19:4
Haunted Honeymoon 1940,O 31,28:2

Carney, Otis (Screenwriter)
Cinerama Holiday 1955,F 9,31:1

Carnii, Luigi
Lancieri di Savoia 1938,Mr 8,23:2

Carnovsky, Morris
Life of Emile Zola, The 1937,Ag 12,14:2
Tovarich 1937,D 31,9:2
Edge of Darkness 1943,Ap 10,12:4
Address Unknown 1944,Ap 17,20:1
Master Race, The 1944,N 2,22:1
Rhapsody in Blue 1945,Je 28,22:2
Our Vines Have Tender Grapes 1945,S 7,21:2
Cornered 1945,D 26,15:1
Miss Susie Slagle's 1946,F 7,29:2
Dead Reckoning 1947,Ja 23,31:2
Dishonored Lady 1947,My 24,10:5
Saigon 1948,Ap 1,30:5
Man-Eater of Kumaon 1948,Jl 2,24:2
Siren of Atlantis 1949,Ag 22,13:1
Thieves' Highway 1949,S 24,8:6
Gun Crazy 1950,Ag 25,17:5
Cyrano De Bergerac 1950,N 17,31:2
Second Woman, The 1951,F 2,19:2
View From the Bridge, A 1962,Ja 23,36:1

Carns, Roscoe
Moran of the Marines 1928,O 15,16:1

Caro, Julia Delgado
Age of Infidelity 1958,Ag 19,23:2

Caro, Nidia
Heroina 1965,N 11,58:2

CAROL
See Also CARROLL

Carol, Cindy
Gidget Goes to Rome 1963,S 12,32:2
Dear Brigitte 1965,Ja 28,20:1

Carol, Joan
One Mile From Heaven 1937,Ag 19,23:1
Lancer Spy 1937,N 4,29:1
Mr Moto's Last Warning 1939,Ja 27,17:3
Barricade 1939,D 9,18:2
Champagne Charlie 1948,Ag 7,8:2

Carol, John
Silver Fleet, The 1945,Mr 24,22:6
It Always Rains on Sunday 1949,F 14,15:5
Pink String and Sealing Wax 1950,O 4,38:2
Spider and the Fly, The 1952,Jl 29,17:3

Carol, Martine
Voyage Surprise 1948,F 14,17:3
Lovers of Verona, The 1951,Mr 12,20:2
Sextette (Part 6-Ski Champ); Ski Champ (Sextette) 1953,Mr 2,19:2
Beauties of the Night 1954,Mr 23,23:5
Caroline Cherie 1954,My 25,23:1
Daughters of Destiny (Lysistrata); Lysistrata (Daughters of Destiny) 1954,Jl 6,19:1
Bed, The (The Pompadour Bed); Pompadour Bed, The (The Bed) 1955,Je 8,26:4
Adorable Creatures 1956,Ja 11,36:2
Sins of the Borgias 1956,My 5,21:1
Around the World in 80 Days 1956,O 18,37:1
Nana 1957,Ap 13,12:3
French They Are a Funny Race, The 1957,My 21,41:1
Action of the Tiger 1957,N 14,41:1
Foxiest Girl in Paris 1958,S 20,10:6
Second to Hell 1959,Jl 18,6:3
Defend my Love; (Difendo il Mio Amore) 1959,O 8,48:7
Love and the Frenchwoman; (Francaise et l'Amour, La) 1961,F 28,38:2
Money, Money, Money 1962,Jl 18,20:1
Lola Montes 1968,S 23,42:6

Carol, Sue
Slaves of Beauty 1927,Je 8,23:3
Soft Cushions 1927,S 12,29:1
Cohens and the Kellys In Paris, The 1928,F 6,12:3
Skyscraper 1928,Ap 9,18:2
Walking Back 1928,Je 12,33:3
Beau Broadway 1928,Jl 30,21:2
Air Circus, The 1928,S 3,14:2
Win That Girl 1928,O 1,23:1
Captain Swagger 1928,D 24,17:7
Girls Gone Wild 1929,Ap 22,23:1
William Fox Movietone Follies of 1929 1929,My 27,22:1
Why Leave Home 1929,S 16,30:1
Her Golden Calf 1930,My 5,27:3
She's my Weakness 1930,Je 21,20:5
Dancing Sweeties 1930,Ag 16,8:3

Carole, Joseph (Screenwriter)
My Son Is Guilty 1940,Ja 15,11:2
Convicted Woman 1940,F 26,11:2
Men Without Souls 1940,My 13,21:2

Carolilla, Juan
Stowaway Girl 1957,N 6,43:3

Caron, Irma
Romance of Hine-Moa, The 1929,O 1,29:1

Caron, Leonard
Thomas Crown Affair, The 1968,Je 27,48:2

Caron, Leslie
American in Paris, An 1951,O 5,24:2
Man With a Cloak, The 1951,N 28,37:2
Glory Alley 1952,Jl 30,20:8
Story of Three Loves, The (Mademoiselle); Mademoiselle (The Story of Three Loves) 1953,Mr 6,29:2

Caron, Leslie— Cont

Lili 1953,Mr 11,36:7
Glass Slipper, The 1955,Mr 25,19:2
Daddy Long Legs 1955,My 6,17:5
Gaby 1956,My 10,26:3
Gigi 1958,My 16,21:1
Doctor's Dilemma, A 1958,D 18,2:7
Man Who Understood, The 1959,O 3,14:7
Subterraneans, The 1960,Jl 7,26:1
Fanny 1961,Jl 7,16:1
Guns of Darkness 1962,Ag 18,10:1
L-Shaped Room, The 1963,My 28,32:1
Three Fables of Love (Two Pigeons); Two Pigeons
  (Three Fables of Love) 1963,Ag 21,38:1
Father Goose 1964,D 11,55:1
Very Special Favor, A 1965,Ag 26,40:3
Promise her Anything 1966,F 23,46:1
Is Paris Burning? 1966,N 11,36:1

Caron, Patricia

Fourflusher, The 1928,Ja 16,24:1
Home Towners, The 1928,O 24,26:4
Dance Hall 1929,D 16,34:2
Girls About Town 1931,N 2,27:1

Caron, Sandra

Don't Raise the Bridge, Lower the River
  1968,Jl 13,18:1

Carotenuto, Mario

Scandal in Sorrento 1957,Je 13,37:1
Poor but Beautiful 1958,Je 11,39:4
Love and Larceny 1963,F 2,5:6

Carotenuto, Memmo

Bread, Love and Dreams 1954,S 21,24:1
Too Bad She's Bad 1955,D 26,23:2
Bigamist, The 1958,My 12,25:1
Most Wonderful Moment, The 1959,Je 1,23:6
Big Deal on Madonna Street, The 1960,N 23,20:1
World in my Pocket, The 1962,My 10,30:2
Lazarillo 1963,Ap 5,27:6

Carothers, A J (Screenwriter)

Miracle of the White Stallions 1963,My 23,31:2
Emil and the Detectives 1964,D 24,8:3
Happiest Millionaire, The 1967,D 1,56:1
Never a Dull Moment 1968,Ag 15,46:2

Carpegna, Alfredo

Wayward Wife, The 1955,Ap 11,29:3

Carpenter, Betty

Iron Trail, The 1921,O 31,19:3
Cardigan 1922,F 20,7:1

Carpenter, Carleton

Lost Boundaries 1949,Jl 1,14:4
Three Little Words 1950,Ag 10,21:2
Summer Stock 1950,S 1,17:2
Two Weeks With Love 1950,N 24,31:2
Vengeance Valley 1951,F 16,21:2
Whistle at Eaton Falls, The 1951,O 11,49:2
Take the High Ground 1953,N 20,19:2
Up Periscope 1959,Mr 5,35:4

Carpenter, Constance

Two Worlds 1930,N 22,21:3

Carpenter, Edward Childs (Original Author)

Three Men and a Girl 1919,Mr 31,11:3
Love Mart, The 1927,D 26,16:6
Bachelor Father, The 1931,F 2,23:1
Whistling in the Dark 1933,F 5,IX,5:1
Perfect Gentleman, The 1935,D 19,33:4
Whistling in the Dark 1941,Ag 28,23:2
Major and the Minor, The 1942,S 17,21:3

Carpenter, Francis

Jack and the Beanstalk 1917,Jl 31,7:2

Carpenter, Grant (Screenwriter)

Pride of Palomar, The 1922,N 20,21:3

Carpenter, Jean

Boy of Flanders, A 1924,Ap 15,24:1

Carpenter, Jeanne

Ashes of Vengeance 1923,Ag 7,20:2

Carpenter, Margaret (Original Author)

Experiment Perilous 1944,D 30,15:2

Carpenter, Paul

Night People 1954,Mr 13,11:2
Unholy Four, The 1954,N 20,10:2
Chance Meeting 1955,Ap 20,38:1
Iron Petticoat, The 1957,F 2,12:2
Intent to Kill 1959,Ap 1,43:2
Murder Reported 1960,Jl 12,39:1
Call Me Bwana 1963,Jl 4,9:1
Dr Crippen 1964,F 15,14:1

Carpenter, Richard

Damn the Defiant 1962,S 20,29:2

Carpentier, Emmy

Der Falsche Feldmarschall 1932,Je 30,26:2

Carpentier, Georges

Wonder Man, The 1920,My 30,6:4
Pathetic Symphony 1928,D 16,IX,8:2
Show of Shows 1929,N 21,24:5
Hold Everything 1930,Ap 23,24:1

Carpentier, Luigi (Producer)

Matchless 1967,N 11,26:3

Carpentier, Marcel

He 1933,D 27,23:6
Crise est Finie, La 1935,Mr 14,18:1
Kermesse Heroique, La 1936,S 23,29:1
Katia 1939,D 23,9:2

Carpentieri, Luigi (Producer)

Marco Polo 1962,S 20,29:2
Story of Joseph and his Brethern, The
  1962,D 1,17:1
Love and Marriage (The Last Resort); Last Resort,
  The (Love and Marriage) 1966,Ag 5,20:1
Love and Marriage (Saturday, July 18); Saturday,
  July 18 (Love and Marriage) 1966,Ag 5,20:1
Love and Marriage (One Moment Is Enough); One
  Moment Is Enough (Love and Marriage)
  1966,Ag 5,20:1
Love and Marriage (The First Night); First Night,
  The (Love and Marriage) 1966,Ag 5,20:1
Hills Run Red, The 1967,N 11,26:3
Navajo Joe 1967,D 7,60:2

Carpi, Tito (Original Author)

Payment in Blood 1968,D 5,59:1

Carpi, Tito (Screenwriter)

Payment in Blood 1968,D 5,59:1

CARR

See Also KARR

Carr, (Fatty)

Little Johnny Jones 1923,Ag 13,16:1

Carr, Albert H Z (Original Author)

Women Are Like That 1938,Ap 11,12:2

Carr, Alexander

Potash and Perlmutter 1923,S 24,5:4
In Hollywood with Potash and Perlmutter
  1924,S 30,27:3
Partners Again, With Potash and Perlmutter
  1926,F 15,16:4
No Greater Love 1932,My 14,11:5
Uptown New York 1932,D 10,19:3
Hypnotized 1933,Ja 16,13:3
Death Kiss, The 1933,F 5,IX,5:3
Out all Night 1933,Ap 8,16:2
Christmas in July 1940,N 6,35:2

Carr, Betty

Seven Brides for Seven Brothers 1954,Jl 23,8:3

Carr, Bridget

That Midnight Kiss 1949,S 23,28:2
Please Believe Me 1950,Je 12,19:4
Mark of the Renegade 1951,S 7,24:2

Carr, Cameron

W Plan, The 1931,Mr 23,24:7

Carr, Charmian

Sound of Music, The 1965,Mr 3,34:1

Carr, Cliff

Adventures of Casanova 1948,Mr 22,18:3

Carr, Estelle

Passage West 1951,Ag 31,12:2

Carr, George

Middle Watch, The 1930,D 20,20:6

Carr, Georgia

Will Success Spoil Rock Hunter 1957,S 12,37:5

Carr, Geraldine

Sniper, The 1952,My 10,16:3

Carr, Harry (Original Author)

Paid to Love 1927,Jl 25,25:3

Carr, Hilliard

Big Shot, The 1932,Ja 2,14:2

Carr, Jack

Personal Secretary 1938,O 5,20:2
Way Down South 1939,Ag 18,16:4
One Hour to Live 1939,N 4,11:3
Safari 1940,Je 20,29:2
East of the River 1940,O 28,21:2
Flight for Freedom 1943,Ap 16,24:2
My Six Convicts 1952,Mr 28,27:3

Carr, James (Producer)

Antarctic Crossing 1959,My 11,30:1

Carr, Jane

Triumph of Sherlock Holmes, The
  1935,My 27,20:6

Carr, Jimmie

Night Club 1929,Ag 12,22:2

Carr, Joan

Stolen Heaven 1931,F 14,11:4
Devotion 1931,O 3,20:2
Orders Is Orders 1934,My 7,20:2

Carr, Joe

Hue and Cry 1951,Ja 9,25:2
Galloping Major, The 1951,D 17,27:2

Carr, John Dickson (Original Author)

Man With a Cloak, The 1951,N 28,37:2
Dangerous Crossing 1953,S 30,37:2
Burning Court, The 1963,Ag 1,17:2

Carr, Lovella

Over the Hill to the Poor House 1920,S 18,16:2

Carr, Marian

San Quentin 1947,F 10,24:3
World for Ransom 1954,Je 5,11:2
Ring of Fear 1954,Jl 29,18:3
Harder They Fall, The 1956,My 10,26:3
Nightmare 1956,My 12,12:7

Carr, Mary

Mrs Wiggs of the Cabbage Patch 1919,F 17,11:3
Over the Hill to the Poor House 1920,S 18,16:2
Thunderclap 1921,Jl 31,22:4
Silver Wings 1922,My 18,14:4
On the Banks of the Wabash 1923,O 23,21:3
Painted People 1924,Ja 29,16:1
Why Men Leave Home 1924,My 12,14:4

Carr, Mary— Cont

Woman on the Jury, The 1924,My 19,14:2
Spirit of the U S A, The 1924,My 21,22:3
For Sale 1924,Jl 14,11:5
Three Women 1924,O 6,25:1
East of Broadway 1924,N 12,13:1
Capital Punishment 1925,F 5,23:3
Parasite, The 1925,F 16,24:1
Wizard of Oz, The 1925,Ap 14,26:1
Drusilla With a Million 1925,My 25,21:3
Slave of Fashion, A 1925,Jl 21,26:2
Go Straight 1925,O 6,30:1
Hogan's Alley 1925,N 24,28:4
Red Kimono, The 1926,F 3,23:1
Blonde or Brunette 1927,Ja 11,18:2
Fourth Commandment, The 1927,Ap 6,25:1
Special Delivery 1927,Ap 26,33:3
Jesse James 1927,O 17,20:2
On Your Toes 1928,Ja 9,20:1
Dame Care 1928,My 20,VIII,8:3
Lights of New York 1928,Jl 9,25:1
Sailor's Holiday 1929,O 21,30:1
Second Wife 1930,F 10,20:4
Ladies in Love 1930,Je 14,9:4
Kept Husbands 1931,Mr 24,31:2
Beyond Victory 1931,Ap 6,24:1
Honeymoon Lane 1931,Ag 1,16:4
Pack up Your Troubles 1932,O 1,10:4
Police Call 1933,Ag 22,20:3
Change of Heart 1934,My 11,24:2
World Accuses, The 1935,Mr 21,27:2
East Side of Heaven 1939,My 5,29:3
Friendly Persuasion 1956,N 2,30:1

Carr, May Beth

Madonna of the Streets 1924,O 28,23:4

Carr, Nat

Kosher Kitty Kelly 1926,S 28,30:2
Her big Night 1926,O 13,21:1
Private Izzy Murphy 1926,N 10,25:1
Love Thrill, The 1927,My 10,24:5
Jazz Singer, The 1927,O 7,24:4
Fifty Million Frenchmen 1931,Mr 26,31:2
Next Time We Love 1936,Ja 31,16:2
Torchy Gets her Man 1938,N 18,25:3

Carr, Paul

Young Don't Cry, The 1957,Jl 27,10:7

Carr, Percy

One Exciting Night 1922,O 24,17:3

Carr, Richard (Miscellaneous)

Too Late Blues 1962,Mr 1,27:4

Carr, Richard (Screenwriter)

Hell is for Heroes 1962,Jl 12,19:3

Carr, Roy

Passport to Pimlico 1949,O 27,35:2
Galloping Major, The 1951,D 17,27:2

Carr, Stephen

Little Old New York 1923,Ag 2,10:3
North of 36 1924,D 8,13:3
Life of Riley, The 1927,S 5,13:2
Hell's Angels 1930,Ag 16,8:3

Carr, Tex Chimpanzees

Big Circus, The 1959,Jl 18,6:1

Carr, Thomas (Director)

Three for Jamie Dawn 1956,Jl 7,11:3
Dino 1957,Je 22,9:2

Carr, Trem (Producer)

Conflict 1937,Ja 18,21:2
Spy Ring, The 1938,Ja 15,19:1

Carra, Rattatila

Von Ryan's Express 1965,Je 24,28:1

Carradine, John

Prisoner of Shark Island, The 1936,F 13,25:2
Under Two Flags 1936,My 1,19:1
White Fang 1936,Jl 18,18:2
Mary of Scotland 1936,Jl 31,22:2
Ramona 1936,O 7,32:4
Dimples 1936,O 10,21:2
Daniel Boone 1936,O 24,23:2
Garden of Allah, The 1936,N 20,27:2
Winterset 1936,D 4,31:1
Nancy Steele is Missing 1937,Mr 8,22:1
Captains Courageous 1937,My 12,27:1
This Is my Affair 1937,My 28,17:1
Love Under Fire 1937,Ag 28,8:2
Ali Baba Goes to Town 1937,O 23,14:1
Hurricane, The 1937,N 10,31:2
Last Gangster, The 1937,D 10,33:2
Danger-Love at Work 1937,D 11,22:2
Thank You, Mr Moto 1938,Ja 3,16:2
International Settlement 1938,F 12,20:3
Of Human Hearts 1938,F 18,23:1
Four Men and a Prayer 1938,My 7,18:1
Kentucky Moonshine 1938,My 21,9:2
Kidnapped 1938,My 28,9:2
I'll Give a Million 1938,Jl 16,7:2
Alexander's Ragtime Band 1938,Ag 6,7:2
Gateway 1938,Ag 8,9:2
Submarine Patrol 1938,N 19,9:2
Jesse James 1939,Ja 14,13:1
Mr Moto's Last Warning 1939,Ja 27,17:3
Three Musketeers, The 1939,F 18,12:2
Stagecoach 1939,Mr 3,21:1
Hound of the Baskervilles, The 1939,Mr 25,19:2
Captain Fury 1939,My 26,20:2

Carradine, John— Cont
Five came Back 1939,Jl 5,20:2
Frontier Marshal 1939,Jl 29,18:2
Drums Along the Mohawk 1939,N 4,11:2
Grapes of Wrath, The 1940,Ja 25,17:2
Return of Frank James, The 1940,Ag 10,16:4
Brigham Young - Frontiersman 1940,S 21,13:2
Chad Hanna 1940,D 26,23:1
Western Union 1941,F 7,23:2
Blood and Sand 1941,My 23,25:3
Man Hunt 1941,Je 14,20:2
Swamp Water 1941,N 17,15:2
Son of Fury 1942,Ja 30,23:2
Whispering Ghosts 1942,My 18,19:4
Reunion in France 1943,Mr 5,20:3
Captive Wild Woman 1943,Je 7,9:4
Hitler's Madman 1943,Ag 28,15:1
Adventures of Mark Twain, The 1944,My 4,25:5
Invisible Man's Revenge, The 1944,Je 10,12:2
Mummy's Ghost, The 1944,Jl 1,10:7
Barbary Coast Gent 1944,S 29,18:2
House of Frankenstein 1944,D 16,19:3
It's in the Bag 1945,Je 11,12:1
Captain Kidd 1945,N 23,26:3
House of Dracula 1945,D 22,16:3
Fallen Angel 1946,F 7,29:4
Private Affairs of Bel Ami, The 1947,Je 16,25:4
C-Man 1949,My 28,11:4
Casanova's Big Night 1954,Ap 19,19:1
Johnny Guitar 1954,My 28,19:2
Egyptian, The 1954,Ag 25,23:1
Kentuckian, The 1955,S 2,13:2
Desert Sands 1955,N 19,22:7
Court Jester, The 1956,F 2,19:1
Around the World in 80 Days 1956,O 18,37:1
Ten Commandments, The 1956,N 9,35:2
True Story of Jesse James, The 1957,Mr 23,17:2
Story of Mankind, The 1957,N 9,31:2
Proud Rebel, The 1958,Jl 2,23:4
Last Hurrah, The 1958,O 24,40:1
Oregon Trail, The 1959,D 10,51:6
Tarzan the Magnificent 1960,Jl 21,17:1
Adventures of Huckleberry Fin, The
  1960,Ag 4,17:1
Man Who Shot Liberty Valance, The
  1962,My 24,29:2
Patsy, The 1964,Ag 13,24:2
Cheyenne Autumn 1964,D 24,8:1
Munster, Go Home 1966,Je 16,53:4
Carrado, Gina
Flaming Youth 1923,N 26,15:6
Reckless Age, The 1924,Je 10,24:4
Carraro, Tino
Hell Raiders of the Deep 1954,Jl 3,9:2
Constantine and the Cross 1963,Mr 14,8:2
Carrasco, Ricardo Pfc
Cease Fire! 1953,N 25,17:1
Carre, Albert Z (Original Author)
Johnny Nobody 1965,N 24,35:1
Carre, Leon (Producer)
Diary of a Country Priest 1954,Ap 6,35:2
Carrel, Anton
Kampf ums Matterhorn 1938,Ap 18,11:2
Carrel, Dany
Passionate Summer 1957,Jl 22,15:5
Gates of Paris 1958,Ja 15,24:1
Pot Bouille 1958,O 28,39:1
Chasers, The; Draguers, Les 1960,My 3,43:1
Enemy General, The 1960,O 20,42:2
Carrell, Annette
Martin Luther 1953,S 10,22:1
Carrell, Lianella
Gold of Naples (The Racketeer); Racketeer, The
  (Gold of Naples) 1957,F 12,30:1
Carrell, Moon
Dracula 1931,F 13,21:3
Carreras, Michael (Director)
Passport to China 1961,Mr 23,28:1
House of Fright 1961,Ag 24,25:4
Maniac 1963,O 31,26:3
Lost Continent, The 1968,Je 20,50:2
Carreras, Michael (Producer)
Blackout 1954,My 22,8:2
Unholy Four, The 1954,N 20,10:2
Snorkel, The 1958,S 18,37:2
Second to Hell 1959,Jl 18,6:3
Mummy, The 1959,D 17,51:4
Yesterday's Enemy 1960,Mr 4,19:1
Hell is a City 1961,Ja 19,26:3
Passport to China 1961,Mr 23,28:1
Cash on Demand 1962,My 17,31:1
She 1965,S 2,36:1
One Million Years BC 1967,F 22,21:1
Lost Continent, The 1968,Je 20,50:2
Carreras, Michael (Screenwriter)
Unholy Four, The 1954,N 20,10:2
One Million Years BC 1967,F 22,21:1
Carrere, Christine
Pantaloons 1956,D 26,34:1
Carrere, Marlena
Day the Fish Came Out, The 1967,O 3,57:1
Carretero, J M (Original Author)
Venenosa, La 1928,D 16,IX,8:2

Carrez, Florence
Trial of Joan of Arc, The 1965,F 12,19:1
Carrick, Herbert
Magic Night 1932,N 3,25:3
Carrickson, S B
Irish Luck 1925,N 24,28:4
Carrie, Marie-Claire
Belles and Ballets 1960,N 15,45:3
Carrier, Albert
Desert Sands 1955,N 19,22:7
Tender is the Night 1962,Ja 20,13:2
Do Not Disturb 1965,D 25,17:2
Thoroughly Modern Millie 1967,Mr 23,25:1
Secret Life of an American Wife, The
  1968,Je 26,42:2
Carrier, Rick (Cinematographer)
Strangers in the City 1962,Jl 17,19:2
Carrier, Rick (Director)
Strangers in the City 1962,Jl 17,19:2
Carrier, Rick (Producer)
Strangers in the City 1962,Jl 17,19:2
Carrier, Rick (Screenwriter)
Strangers in the City 1962,Jl 17,19:2
Carrier, Suzy
Clandestine 1948,My 24,23:2
Carriere, Anna Marie
My Wife's Husband 1965,Ja 27,26:1
Carriere, Jean-Claude (Miscellaneous)
Yo Yo 1967,Mr 1,50:1
Carriere, Jean-Claude (Screenwriter)
Suitor, The; Soupirant, Le 1963,S 18,35:1
Diary of a Chambermaid; Journal d'une Femme de
  Chambre, Le 1964,S 22,44:1
Viva Maria 1965,D 20,48:2
Hôtel Paradiso 1966,O 15,34:2
Yo Yo 1967,Mr 1,50:1
Thief of Paris, The 1967,Ag 24,43:2
Belle de Jour 1968,Ap 11,51:1
Carriere, Matthieu
Young Torless 1967,S 25,56:2
Tonio Kroger 1968,Ja 16,24:1
Young Torless 1968,Jl 23,27:2
Carrigan, Thomas J
Checkers 1919,Ag 25,8:5
Making of O'Malley 1925,Je 22,10:2
Carrigan, Tom
Big Broadcast, The 1932,O 15,13:1
Carrik, E
Conquests of Peter The Great, The
  1939,Ag 24,17:2
Carril, Hugo del
Vida es un Tango, La; Life is a Tango
  1939,Jl 8,20:5
Madreselva; Honeysuckle 1939,Ag 19,18:4
Gente Bien 1939,O 9,15:2
Vida de Carlos Gardel, A 1940,Ja 6,9:2
Carrillo, Cely
Rampage 1963,O 17,39:2
Carrillo, Leo
Hell Bound 1931,My 9,15:4
Homicide Squad 1931,O 19,28:1
Guilty Generation, The 1931,N 21,20:4
Girl of the Rio 1932,Ja 9,21:1
Broken Wing, The 1932,Mr 26,17:2
Deception 1933,Ja 10,26:2
Parachute Jumper 1933,Ja 26,12:2
Racetrack 1933,Mr 6,16:6
Obey the Law 1933,Mr 13,18:3
Moonlight and Pretzels 1933,Ag 23,21:2
Four Frightened People 1934,Ja 27,9:2
Viva Villa! 1934,Ap 11,25:2
Manhattan Melodrama 1934,My 5,22:2
Gay Bride, The 1934,D 19,27:2
Band Plays on, The 1934,D 22,21:2
Winning Ticket, The 1935,F 11,14:2
In Caliente 1935,Je 27,16:1
Love Me Forever 1935,Je 28,24:1
If You Could Only Cook 1935,D 26,21:4
It Had to Happen 1936,F 15,18:6
Moonlight Murder 1936,Mr 28,11:2
Gay Desperado, The 1936,O 9,31:4
History Is Made at Night 1937,Mr 29,14:2
I Promise to Pay 1937,Ap 26,15:2
52d Street 1937,N 15,15:1
Barrier, The 1937,N 27,21:2
Manhattan Merry-Go-Round 1937,D 31,9:3
Girl of the Golden West, The 1938,Mr 25,15:2
Blockade 1938,Je 17,25:1
City Streets 1938,Jl 25,18:2
too Hot To Handle 1938,S 30,24:2
Flirting With Fate 1938,D 15,35:3
Fisherman's Wharf 1939,F 24,15:2
Society Lawyer 1939,Mr 31,19:2
Girl and the Gambler, The 1939,Je 28,17:3
Rio 1939,O 27,27:2
Twenty-Mule Team 1940,My 10,26:6
Lillian Russell 1940,My 18,11:2
Wyoming 1940,O 3,31:4
Captain Caution 1940,O 21,21:3
One Night in the Tropics 1940,D 20,33:2
Horror Island 1941,Mr 31,11:3
Barnacle Bill 1941,Jl 25,12:4
Kid From Kansas, The 1941,D 2,29:4

Carrillo, Leo— Cont
What's Cookin' 1942,F 26,15:5
Sin Town 1942,O 17,11:2
American Empire 1943,Ja 14,25:4
Frontier Badmen 1943,Ag 14,12:8
Crazy House 1943,D 16,33:3
Ghost Catchers 1944,My 31,22:3
Gypsy Wildcat 1944,O 5,18:6
Bowery to Broadway 1944,N 30,19:2
Crime Incorporated 1945,Je 23,9:7
Mexicana 1945,N 17,14:6
Fugitive, The 1947,D 26,22:2
Carrington, Tom
Air Mail 1932,N 7,20:3
Carrington, C B (Original Author)
Home Made 1927,D 13,33:2
Carrington, Evelyn C
In Search of a Sinner 1920,Mr 8,9:5
In Search of a Sinner 1920,Mr 8,9:6
After Tonight 1933,N 3,23:2
Carrington, Helen
Queen High 1930,Ag 9,16:5
Heads Up 1930,O 13,31:1
Carrington, Jack
Crime Doctor's Courage, The 1945,Mr 3,11:3
Carrington, Jane Howard (Screenwriter)
Kaleidoscope 1966,S 23,45:1
Wait Until Dark 1967,O 27,48:1
Carrington, Robert (Screenwriter)
Kaleidoscope 1966,S 23,45:1
Wait Until Dark 1967,O 27,48:1
CARROLL
See Also CAROL
Carroll, Arlene
Night Life of the Gods 1935,F 23,14:6
Carroll, Barbara
Last Days of Pompeii, The 1960,Ag 11,19:1
Carroll, Beeson
Mister Buddwing 1966,O 12,36:1
Carroll, Bob Jr (Original Author)
Yours, Mine and Ours 1968,Ap 25,53:1
Carroll, Diahann
Carmen Jones 1954,O 29,27:2
Porgy and Bess 1959,Je 25,20:3
Goodbye Again 1961,Je 30,32:2
Paris Blues 1961,N 8,41:1
Hurry Sundown 1967,Mr 24,22:1
Split, The 1968,N 5,55:2
Carroll, Earl
Night at Earl Carroll's, A 1941,Ja 23,19:1
Carroll, Earl (Original Author)
Murder at the Vanities 1934,My 21,20:2
Carroll, Earl (Producer)
Night at Earl Carroll's, A 1941,Ja 23,19:1
Carroll, Georgia
Navy Blues 1941,S 20,11:2
Around the World 1943,N 25,39:2
Carolina Blues 1944,D 8,26:6
Carroll, Gladys Hasty (Original Author)
As the Earth Turns 1934,Ap 12,27:2
Carroll, Gordon (Producer)
Cool Hand Luke 1967,N 2,58:1
Carroll, Harry (Composer)
Ziegfeld Girl 1941,Ap 25,17:2
Carroll, Helena (Narrator)
Spell of Ireland, The 1954,My 11,25:5
Carroll, Janice
Shane 1953,Ap 24,30:3
How to be Very, Very Popular 1955,Jl 23,10:1
Carroll, Jean
Legend of Lylah Clare, The 1968,Ag 23,33:1
Carroll, Joan
Primrose Path 1940,Mr 23,16:2
Anne of Windy Poplars 1940,Ag 23,13:3
Obliging Young Lady 1942,F 13,24:4
Meet Me in St Louis 1944,N 29,20:2
Tomorrow the World 1944,D 22,12:4
Bells of St Mary's, The 1945,D 7,26:2
Carroll, John
Muss 'Em Up 1936,F 3,21:2
Murder on a Bridle Path 1936,Ap 11,19:2
We Who Are About to Die 1937,Ja 2,15:1
Rose of the Rio Grande 1938,Jl 9,10:3
Only Angels Have Wings 1939,My 12,25:2
Congo Maisie 1940,F 8,18:4
Phantom Raiders 1940,Je 24,19:5
Susan and God 1940,Jl 12,11:2
Hired Wife 1940,S 14,11:2
Go West 1941,F 21,16:2
Sunny 1941,Je 13,22:2
Lady Be Good 1941,S 19,27:1
This Woman Is Mine 1941,O 13,21:2
Rio Rita 1942,My 8,27:3
Pierre of the Plains 1942,Jl 30,17:3
Flying Tigers 1942,O 23,25:2
Hit Parade of 1943 1943,Ap 16,24:3
Youngest Profession, The 1943,Je 25,13:3
Bedside Manner 1945,Je 23,9:6
Letter for Evie, A 1946,Je 28,17:4
Fiesta 1947,Je 27,17:3
Wyoming 1947,Jl 25,12:5
Fabulous Texan, The 1947,D 26,22:5
Flame, The 1948,F 20,19:2
I, Jane Doe 1948,Jl 5,8:4

Carroll, John— Cont
Old Los Angeles 1948,Jl 12,11:2
Surrender 1950,O 9,21:5
Belle le Grand 1951,My 18,34:6
Farmer Takes a Wife, The 1953,Je 13,11:2
Carroll, June
New Faces 1954,F 20,8:7
Carroll, Leo G
Sadie McKee 1934,My 18,18:3 (Incorrect in this edition; use 1934,My 19,18:3 elsewhere)
Barretts of Wimpole Street, The 1934,S 29,12:2
Outcast Lady 1934,N 3,20:3
Clive of India 1935,Ja 18,29:1
Right to Live, The 1935,F 16,9:1
Murder on a Honeymoon 1935,Mr 4,12:2
Casino Murder Case, The 1935,Ap 17,26:5
London by Night 1937,Ag 13,13:1
Christmas Carol, A 1938,D 23,16:2
Bulldog Drummond's Secret Police 1939,Mr 30,19:3
Wuthering Heights 1939,Ap 14,28:2
Private Lives of Elizabeth and Essex, The 1939,D 2,21:2
Tower of London 1939,D 12,37:2
Charlie Chan in City in Darkness 1939,D 18,29:2
Rebecca 1940,Mr 29,25:2
Charlie Chan's Murder Cruise 1940,My 3,17:5
Scotland Yard 1941,Ap 9,33:3
This Woman Is Mine 1941,O 13,21:2
Suspicion 1941,N 21,23:2
Bahama Passage 1942,F 19,23:2
House on Ninety-Second Street, The 1945,S 27,24:7
Spellbound 1945,N 2,22:2
Time Out of Mind 1947,Ap 7,20:1
Song of Love 1947,O 10,31:2
Forever Amber 1947,O 23,31:2
Paradine Case, The 1948,Ja 9,26:2
So Evil my Love 1948,Jl 22,27:2
Enchantment 1948,D 27,16:2
Father of the Bride 1950,My 19,31:2
First Legion, The 1951,Ap 28,9:2
Strangers on a Train 1951,Jl 4,13:2
Desert Fox, The 1951,O 18,32:1
Snows of Kilimanjaro, The 1952,S 19,19:2
Bad and the Beautiful, The 1953,Ja 16,19:1
Young Bess 1953,My 22,31:1
Treasure of the Golden Condor 1953,My 23,19:2
We're no Angels 1955,Jl 8,15:2
Swan, The 1956,Ap 27,21:5
North by Northwest 1959,Ag 7,28:1
Parent Trap, The 1961,Je 22,23:1
1 ‖ 1 1961,N 8,41:1
Prize, The 1964,Ja 24,21:1
One Spy too Many 1966,D 8,64:1.
Carroll, Lewis (Original Author)
Alice in Wonderland 1921,Mr 22,15:3
Alice in Wonderland 1931,D 28,22:1
Alice in Wonderland 1933,D 23,19:1
Alice in Wonderland 1951,Jl 27,15:2
Alice in Wonderland 1951,Jl 30,12:4
Carroll, Lucia
Manpower 1941,Jl 5,14:2
Wild Bill Hickok Rides 1942,F 7,13:5
Carroll, Madeleine
First Born, The 1929,Ja 13,VIII,5:2 (In Addenda)
Atlantic 1930,Ja 26,VIII,6:2
Young Woodley 1930,S 27,21:3
Atlantic 1930,O 6,21:1
Escape 1930,N 1,23:2
W Plan, The 1931,Mr 23,24:7
French Leave 1931,D 7,16:1
I Was a Spy 1934,Ja 15,12:2
World Moves On, The 1934,Je 30,18:5
Dictator, The 1935,Mr 24,VIII,3:6 (In Addenda)
Loves of a Dictator 1935,Je 1,18:2
Thirty-Nine Steps, The 1935,S 14,8:4
Case Against Mrs Ames, The 1936,My 28,19:2
Secret Agent 1936,Je 13,13:1
General Died at Dawn, The 1936,S 3,17:2
Lloyds of London 1936,N 26,39:1
On the Avenue 1937,F 5,17:3
Prisoner of Zenda, The 1937,S 3,12:1
It's all Yours 1938,Ja 7,15:3
Blockade 1938,Je 17,25:1
Cafe Society 1939,F 23,19:2
Honeymoon in Bali 1939,S 21,21:1
My Son, My Son! 1940,My 10,26:6
Safari 1940,Je 20,29:2
North West Mounted Police 1940,N 7,33:2
Virginia 1941,Ja 29,21:2
One Night in Lisbon 1941,Je 12,29:3
Bahama Passage 1942,F 19,23:2
My Favorite Blonde 1942,Ap 2,27:2
Innocent Affair, An 1948,S 29,36:2
Fan, The 1949,Ap 2,12:2
Carroll, Mary
Woman Obsessed 1959,My 28,34:1
Carroll, Moon
Last of Mrs Cheyney, The 1929,Ag 12,22:2
Lady of Sandcal, The 1930,Je 14,9:4
Carroll, Nancy
Ladies Must Dress 1927,D 31,31:1
Abie's Irish Rose 1928,Ap 20,26:7

Easy Come, Easy Go 1928,My 8,25:3
Chicken a la King 1928,Je 11,27:1
Water Hole, The 1928,S 3,14:2
Manhattan Cocktail 1928,N 26,30:2
Shopworn Angel, The 1929,Ja 1,60:1
Wolf of Wall Street, The 1929,Ja 28,21:1
Close Harmony 1929,Ap 29,29:2
Dance of Life, The 1929,Ag 16,18:6
Illusion 1929,S 28,17:3
Sweetie 1929,O 26,15:1
Dangerous Paradise 1930,F 16,III,8:1
Dangerous Paradise 1930,Mr 2,IX,5:1
Honey 1930,Mr 29,23:1
Paramount on Parade 1930,Ap 21,20:4
Devil's Holiday, The 1930,My 10,25:3
Follow Thru 1930,S 19,9:3
Laughter 1930,N 15,15:3
Stolen Heaven 1931,F 14,11:4
Night Angel, The 1931,Je 11,28:4
Personal Maid 1931,S 5,7:4
Man I Killed, The 1932,Ja 20,17:4
Wayward 1932,F 15,13:1
Scarlet Dawn 1932,N 4,25:4
Hot Saturday 1932,N 5,12:5
Under-Cover Man 1932,D 5,21:2
Child of Manhattan 1933,F 13,11:4
Woman Accused, The 1933,Mr 13,18:2
Kiss Before the Mirror, The 1933,My 15,16:2
I Love That Man 1933,Jl 10,11:7
Transatlantic Merry-Go-Round 1934,N 1,25:2
I'll Love You Always 1935,Mr 30,11:2
There Goes my Heart 1938,O 14,27:1
That Certain Age 1938,N 5,15:2
Carroll, Pat
With Six You Get Egg Roll 1968,O 10,59:6
Carroll, Paul Vincent (Miscellaneous)
Against the Wind 1949,Je 27,18:3
Carroll, Paul Vincent (Original Author)
Saints and Sinners 1949,S 12,17:2
Carroll, Paul Vincent (Screenwriter)
Saints and Sinners 1949,S 12,17:2
Carroll, Richard (Original Author)
Five came Back 1939,Jl 5,20:2
You Can't Fool Your Wife 1940,My 24,23:4
Flight Lieutenant 1942,Jl 31,11:1
Carroll, Richard (Screenwriter)
Ape, The 1940,N 28,28:3
Two Yanks in Trinidad 1942,Ap 6,19:4
Carroll, Robert
Walk East on Beacon 1952,My 29,17:2
Carroll, Sidney (Miscellaneous)
Gods of Bali 1952,O 13,26:3
Carroll, Sidney (Original Author)
Gambit 1966,D 22,40:2
Carroll, Sidney (Screenwriter)
Three Cases of Murder (You Killed Elizabeth); You Killed Elizabeth (Three Cases of Murder) 1955,Mr 16,39:4
Three Cases of Murder (Lord Mountdrago); Lord Mountdrago (Three Cases of Murder) 1955,Mr 16,39:4
Three Cases of Murder (In the Picture); In the Picture (Three Cases of Murder) 1955,Mr 16,39:4
Hustler, The 1961,S 27,35:1
Big Hand for the Little Lady, A 1966,Je 9,54:2
Carroll, Taylor
Fighting American, The 1924,My 13,24:1
Carroll, Terry
Personal Maid 1931,S 5,7:4
Carroll, Vinnette
One Potato, Two Potato 1964,Jl 30,16:1
Up the Down Staircase 1967,Ag 18,36:2
Carroll, Virginia
Toast of New York, The 1937,Jl 23,16:2
Waterloo Bridge 1940,My 17,23:2
Bigger Than Life 1956,Ag 3,11:2
Carroll, William A
Bill Henry 1919,Ag 18,9:2
Sporting Youth 1924,Ap 2,16:1
Wanderer of the Wasteland, The 1924,Jl 8,14:2
K-The Unknown 1924,N 18,22:1
Unknown, The 1924,N 18,22:1
North of 36 1924,D 8,13:3
I'll Show You the Town 1925,Je 8,19:1
Ancient Highway, The 1925,N 11,27:3
Born to the West 1926,Je 30,18:1 (In Addenda)
Carroll, Zelma (Original Author)
Lost City, The 1935,F 21,23:3
Carroll Brothers, The
Don't Knock the Twist 1962,Ap 14,14:2
Carruth, Milton (Director)
Breezing Home 1937,Mr 20,23:5
Man in Blue, The 1937,Ag 30,25:2
Reported Missing 1937,S 3,12:2
Some Blondes Are Dangerous 1937,N 3,29:3
Carruthers, Benito
Shadows 1961,Mr 22,37:1
Guns of the Trees 1964,F 29,12:2
Goldstein 1965,My 8,19:7
High Wind in Jamaica, A 1965,Je 17,27:2
Lost Continent, The 1968,Je 20,50:2

Carruthers, Steve (Original Author)
Angela 1955,Je 4,9:2
Carson, Bob
Greatest Show on Earth, The 1952,Ja 11,17:2
Carson, Charles
Dreyfus Case, The 1931,Ag 31,11:5
There Goes the Bride 1933,Mr 4,11:3
Broken Melody, The 1934,O 31,17:3
Men of Tomorrow 1935,Ap 16,27:2
Sanders of the River 1935,Je 27,16:1
Scrooge 1935,D 14,11:1
Abdul the Damned 1936,My 11,16:2
Secret Agent 1936,Je 13,13:1
I Stand Condemned 1936,Jl 2,27:2
April Romance 1937,Ja 27,17:4
Beloved Vagabond, The 1937,F 8,12:5
Fire Over England 1937,Mr 5,16:2
Talk of the Devil 1937,My 15,23:5
Dreaming Lips 1937,My 20,17:1
Forever Yours 1937,Je 7,22:2
Victoria the Great 1937,O 29,19:1
We're Going to Be Rich 1938,Jl 4,10:2
Sixty Glorious Years 1938,N 18,25:2
Wings and the Woman 1942,O 8,31:1
Courageous Mr Penn 1943,D 23,26:5
Battle for Music 1945,O 15,13:2
Pink String and Sealing Wax 1950,O 4,38:2
Cry, the Beloved Country 1952,Ja 24,23:2
Beau Brummell 1954,O 21,31:5
Reach for the Sky 1957,My 1,40:1
Touch of Larceny, A 1960,Mr 17,28:1
Carson, Frances
Java Head 1935,Jl 31,21:4
Two Faced Woman 1942,Ja 1,37:2
Saboteur 1942,My 8,27:2
Carson, Fred
Charge at Feather River, The 1953,Jl 16,17:2
Wall of Noise 1963,S 5,27:1
Carson, Jack
Music for Madame 1937,O 23,14:1
Stand-In 1937,N 19,27:2
Crashing Hollywood 1938,Ja 8,19:2
She's Got Everything 1938,Ja 14,21:3
Law of the Underworld 1938,Ap 28,27:2
Saint in New York, The 1938,My 26,31:2
Vivacious Lady 1938,Je 3,17:3
Go Chase Yourself 1938,Je 15,27:1
Having Wonderful Time 1938,Jl 8,11:2
Carefree 1938,S 23,35:1
Mr Doodle Kicks Off 1938,S 28,29:4
Legion of Lost Flyers 1939,O 30,13:3
Escape, The 1939,N 3,17:4
Destry Rides Again 1939,N 30,25:1
Honeymoon's Over, The 1939,D 15,33:3
I Take This Woman 1940,F 16,23:3
Young as You Feel 1940,Mr 8,25:3
Shooting High 1940,Ap 12,19:2
Enemy Agent 1940,Ap 22,13:3
Alias the Deacon 1940,My 14,27:5
Typhoon 1940,My 23,28:4
Girl in 313 1940,Je 14,25:3
Queen of the Mob 1940,Jl 1,23:2
Lucky Partners 1940,S 6,25:2
Love Thy Neighbor 1940,D 18,32:5
Mr and Mrs Smith 1941,F 21,16:3
Strawberry Blonde 1941,F 22,11:2
Love Crazy 1941,Je 6,25:5
Bride Came C O D, The 1941,Jl 26,18:2
Navy Blues 1941,S 20,11:2
Blues in the Night 1941,D 12,35:2
Male Animal, The 1942,Mr 28,11:1
Larceny, Inc 1942,Ap 25,9:1
Wings for the Eagle 1942,Ag 1,14:2
Gentleman Jim 1942,N 26,40:3
Hard Way, The 1943,Mr 13,9:2
Thank Your Lucky Stars 1943,O 2,19:2
Princess O'Rourke 1943,N 6,16:2
Shine on Harvest Moon 1944,Mr 11,10:2
Make Your own Bed 1944,My 27,12:2
Doughgirls, The 1944,Ag 31,14:1
Arsenic and old Lace 1944,S 2,17:2
Hollywood Canteen 1944,D 16,19:2
Roughly Speaking 1945,F 1,18:4
Mildred Pierce 1945,S 29,12:2
One More Tomorrow 1946,My 25,12:2
Two Guys From Milwaukee 1946,Jl 27,12:5
Time, The Place And The Girl, The 1946,D 27,14:3
Love and Learn 1947,My 3,10:3
April Showers 1948,Mr 27,10:2
Romance on the High Seas 1948,Je 26,10:5
Two Guys From Texas 1948,Ag 28,8:6
John Loves Mary 1949,F 5,11:2
My Dream Is Yours 1949,Ap 16,11:3
It's a Great Feeling 1949,Ag 13,6:6
Bright Leaf 1950,Je 17,7:2
Good Humor Man, The 1950,Jl 14,17:2
Groom Wore Spurs, The 1951,Mr 14,41:2
Mr Universe 1951,Mr 23,16:2
Dangerous When Wet 1953,Je 19,18:1
Red Garters 1954,Mr 27,13:5
Star is Born, A 1954,O 12,23:1
Phffft 1954,N 11,43:2

Carson, Jack— Cont
Ain't Misbehavin' 1955,Jl 2,13:2
Bottom of the Bottle, The 1956,F 2,19:2
Tattered Dress, The 1957,Mr 15,22:3
Tarnished Angels, The 1958,Ja 7,31:1
Cat on a Hot Tin Roof 1958,S 19,24:1
Rally Round the Flag Boys! 1958,D 24,2:7
Bramble Bush, The 1960,F 25,34:2
King of the Roaring Twenties 1961,O 5,43:1
Carson, James B
Crime School 1938,My 11,17:2
Secrets of an Actress 1938,O 8,10:2
Girl Downstairs, The 1939,Ja 26,17:1
Carson, Jean
Phenix City Story, The 1955,S 3,9:1
Sanctuary 1961,F 22,31:1
Carson, Jeannie
Mad Little Island 1958,D 31,12:1
Carson, Joan
Alligator Named Daisy, An 1957,O 7,23:2
Carson, John
Quentin Durward 1955,N 24,41:1
Master Spy 1964,Ag 20,34:2
Carson, Peggy
Gorilla Man, The 1943,Ja 15,21:4
Carson, Rachel L (Original Author)
Sea Around Us, The 1953,Jl 8,24:4
Carson, Renee
Picture of Dorian Gray, The 1945,Mr 2,15:2
House on Ninety-Second Street, The
  1945,S 27,24:7
Deadline for Murder 1946,Je 29,22:7
Carson, Robert
For Men Only 1952,Ja 16,21:2
Carson, Robert (Original Author)
Star Is Born, A 1937,Ap 23,25:1
Last Gangster, The 1937,D 10,33:2
Across the Pacific 1942,S 5,9:2
Bedside Manner 1945,Je 23,9:6
Perilous Holiday 1946,Je 1,10:4
You Gotta Stay Happy 1948,N 5,29:2
Once More, my Darling 1949,S 26,17:1
Reformer and the Redhead, The 1950,Ap 10,15:2
Groom Wore Spurs, The 1951,Mr 14,41:2
Star is Born, A 1954,O 12,23:1
Ain't Misbehavin' 1955,Jl 2,13:2
Carson, Robert (Screenwriter)
Star Is Born, A 1937,Ap 23,25:1
Men With Wings 1938,O 27,27:2
Beau Geste 1939,Ag 3,15:2
Light That Failed, The 1939,D 25,19:1
Western Union 1941,F 7,23:2
Desperadoes, The 1943,My 13,17:2
Once More, my Darling 1949,S 26,17:1
Groom Wore Spurs, The 1951,Mr 14,41:2
Just for You 1952,O 9,40:6
Star is Born, A 1954,O 12,23:1
Bundle of Joy 1956,D 20,36:1
Action of the Tiger 1957,N 14,41:1
Carson, Sue
Best of Everything 1959,O 9,24:2
Carstairs, John Paddy (Director)
Saint in London, The 1939,Jl 19,23:3
Sleeping Car to Trieste 1949,Ap 18,18:6
Amazing Mr Beecham, The 1949,D 26,33:4
Tony Draws a Horse 1951,My 15,38:6
Trouble in Store 1956,Ja 14,13:2
Week-End With Lulu, A 1962,My 24,29:2
Carstairs, John Paddy (Screenwriter)
You Can't Beat the Irish 1952,My 1,34:4
Trouble in Store 1956,Ja 14,13:2
Carstairs, Maxwell
Track of Thunder 1968,F 1,28:4
Carsten, Peter
Devil Strikes at Night, The 1959,Ja 30,31:3
Quiller Memorandum, The 1966,D 16,59:1
Dark of the Sun 1968,Jl 4,13:1
Carstens, Lina
Zerbrochene Krug, Der; Broken Jugi, The
  1938,Ja 15,19:2
Last Illusion, The 1951,Mr 8,37:2
Cartellieri, Carmen
Hands of Orlac, The 1928,Je 5,21:1
CARTER
See Also CARTIER
Carter, Ann
North Star, The 1943,N 5,23:1
Curse of the Cat People, The 1944,Mr 4,11:1
Two Mrs Carrolls, The 1947,Ap 7,20:1
Fabulous Dorseys, The 1947,My 30,25:3
Song of Love 1947,O 10,31:2
Ruthless 1948,S 4,8:7
Blondie Hits the Jackpot 1949,S 9,28:3
Member of the Wedding, The 1952,D 31,10:2
Commandos Strike at Dawn 1954,Ja 14,25:1
Carter, Arthur (Original Author)
Operation Mad Ball 1957,N 21,38:1
Carter, Arthur (Screenwriter)
Operation Mad Ball 1957,N 21,38:1
Carter, Audrey (Original Author)
Notorious Affair, A 1930,Ap 26,11:1
Carter, Ben
Little Old New York 1940,F 3,9:2
Maryland 1940,Jl 13,16:5

South to Karanga 1940,Ag 9,19:1
Tin Pan Alley 1940,N 22,27:3
Chad Hanna 1940,D 26,23:1
Sleepers West 1941,Mr 20,25:3
Ride on Vaquero 1941,Ap 19,20:2
Dressed to Kill 1941,Ag 22,19:3
Crash Dive 1943,Ap 29,25:2
Bowery to Broadway 1944,N 30,19:2
Lady on a Train 1945,S 15,21:2
Harvey Girls, The 1946,Ja 25,26:2
Night Without Sleep 1952,S 27,13:2
Carter, Benny and his band
Thousands Cheer 1943,S 14,27:1
Carter, Betty
Inside the Lines 1930,Jl 5,17:4
Carter, Bill
My Kingdom for a Cook 1943,O 15,15:3
Carter, Boake (Narrator)
Dead March, The 1937,S 20,19:1 (In Addenda)
Carter, Calvert
Slave of Desire 1923,D 11,26:2
Carter, Cathy
It Happened on Fifth Avenue 1947,Je 11,33:2
Carter, Desmond (Composer)
Dance Band 1936,Ja 4,19:2
Carter, Desmond (Miscellaneous)
Dance Band 1936,Ja 4,19:2
Carter, Dorothy Elizabeth (Original Author)
Remodeling her Husband 1920,Je 7,20:3 (In
  Addenda)
Carter, Everett (Composer)
See my Lawyer 1945,My 4,23:4
Carter, Gloria
Our Neighbors-The Carters 1940,F 15,15:2
Carter, Harrison (Original Author)
Frozen Ghost, The 1945,Jl 28,7:3
Carter, Harry
Smoky 1946,Je 27,29:1
Yellow Sky 1949,F 2,36:1
Ticket to Tomahawk, A 1950,My 20,8:6
Broken Arrow 1950,Jl 21,15:2
Two Flags West 1950,O 13,23:2
Golden Girl 1951,N 21,20:3
Lure of the Wilderness 1952,O 4,15:2
Titanic 1953,My 28,27:5
Pickup on South Street 1953,Je 18,38:2
Dangerous Crossing 1953,S 30,37:2
How to Marry a Millionaire 1953,N 11,37:1
Hell and High Water 1954,F 2,20:6
Compulsion 1959,Ap 2,26:2
Carter, Helena
Time Out of Mind 1947,Ap 7,20:1
Something in the Wind 1947,Ag 29,14:3
Intrigue 1948,Ap 24,11:2
River Lady 1948,My 21,19:5
Fighting O'Flynn, The 1949,F 28,16:2
South Sea Sinner 1950,Ja 16,18:4
Kiss Tomorrow Goodbye 1950,Ag 5,9:2
Double Crossbones 1951,Ap 27,19:2
Fort Worth 1951,Jl 13,12:7
Bugles in the Afternoon 1952,Mr 5,32:2
Golden Hawk, The 1952,O 18,16:4
Invaders From Mars 1953,My 30,7:1
Carter, Jack
Miracle in Harlem 1949,O 24,19:4
Horizontal Lieutenant, The 1962,My 12,15:3
Carter, Janis
Cadet Girl 1941,D 11,39:1
Secret Agent of Japan 1942,Mr 23,19:3
Who Is Hope Schuyler 1942,My 22,27:1
I Married an Angel 1942,Jl 10,13:2
Just off Broadway 1942,Ag 29,18:4
Girl Trouble 1942,O 8,31:2
Thunder Birds 1942,O 29,19:2
One Mysterious Night 1944,O 21,15:3
Mark of the Whistler, The 1944,N 11,19:2
Fighting Guardsman, The 1945,O 6,9:6
Night Editor 1946,Mr 30,11:2
Framed 1947,My 26,24:2
Slightly French 1949,My 27,25:3
And Baby Makes Three 1949,D 23,17:3
Woman of Distinction, A 1950,Mr 17,28:2
Woman on Pier 13, The 1950,Je 16,28:4
Her Wonderful Lie 1950,Jl 17,15:2
My Forbidden Past 1951,Ap 26,34:2
Santa Fe 1951,My 4,31:2
Flying Leathernecks 1951,S 20,37:1
Half Breed, The 1952,Jl 5,7:2
Carter, Lavada
Miracle in Harlem 1949,O 24,19:4
Carter, Leslie Mrs
Heart of Maryland, The 1915,Mr 21,II,12:4
Carter, Leslie Mrs (Original Author)
Lady With red Hair 1940,D 6,28:2
Carter, Lincoln J (Original Author)
Fast Mail, The 1922,Jl 10,9:5
Carter, Louise
Man I Killed, The 1932,Ja 20,17:4
Week-End Marriage 1932,Je 4,9:2
Last Mile, The 1932,Ag 26,20:3
Blondie of the Follies 1932,S 2,19:2
Tess of the Storm Country 1932,N 19,20:2
Madame Butterfly 1932,D 26,26:2

Carter, Louise— Cont
Jennie Gerhardt 1933,Je 9,20:2
Pilgrimage 1933,Jl 13,17:5
Beloved 1934,Ja 27,9:3
You're Telling Me 1934,Ap 7,19:1
Mystery of Edwin Drood, The 1935,Mr 21,27:1
Rose of the Rancho 1936,Ja 9,25:2
Paddy O'Day 1936,F 8,19:2
Carter, Lynn
Port of New York 1950,F 3,29:2
Carter, Monte
Vice Squad, The 1931,Je 6,15:5
Redhead 1934,N 16,27:1
Make a Million 1935,N 9,19:3
Carter, Ray (Composer)
Christmas That Almost Wasn't 1966,N 24,65:2
Carter, Richard
Tony Runs Wild 1926,Ap 28,28:3
Carter, Richard (Original Author)
Slaughter on Tenth Avenue 1957,N 6,43:1
Carter, Waverly (Original Author)
Notorious Affair, A 1930,Ap 26,11:1
Carter, William
I've Always Loved You 1946,S 7,11:1
Carter, Winifred (Original Author)
Mrs Fitzherbert 1950,My 11,37:2
CARTIER
See Also CARTER
Cartier, Henri (Director)
Return to Life 1938,Ag 4,15:1
Cartier, Jacques
King of Jazz 1930,My 3,23:1
Cartier, Max
Rocco and his Brothers 1961,Je 28,40:2
Cartier, Rudolph (Original Author)
Man From Morocco, The 1946,N 25,38:2
Cartier, Rudolph (Screenwriter)
Corridor of Mirrors 1949,Mr 23,35:3
Cartledge, Bill
Red Stallion 1947,N 27,50:3
Carton, Kenneth
In Which We Serve 1942,D 24,18:1
Carton, Pauline
Living Dead Man, The 1927,Mr 7,16:3
Parisian, The 1931,Ag 22,7:5
Meet Miss Mozart 1937,N 27,21:3
Pearls of the Crown, The 1938,Ap 12,26:2
Story of a Cheat, The 1938,S 27,25:2
Forty Little Mothers 1938,D 23,16:3
Indiscretions 1939,My 1,21:1
Affair Lafont, The; Conflit 1939,O 9,15:2
Louise 1940,F 3,9:4
Private Life of an Actor; En Scene 1948,S 7,21:3
Miquette 1951,F 5,18:2
Prize, The 1952,Ap 30,33:2
Cupboard was Bare, The; (Armoire Volante, L')
  1952,N 4,33:1
Fruits of Summer 1956,Jl 18,22:2
Virtuous Scoundrel, The 1957,O 23,37:1
Cartwright, Angela
Lad: A Dog 1963,My 2,40:2
Sound of Music, The 1965,Mr 3,34:1
Cartwright, Peggy
Iron Horse, The 1924,Ag 29,6:1
Magic Night 1932,N 3,25:3
Cartwright, Veronica
Childrens Hour, The 1962,Mr 15,28:2
Birds, The 1963,Ap 1,5:5 (Incorrect in this
  edition; use 1963,Ap 1,54:1 elsewhere)
One Man's Way 1964,Mr 12,40:3
Carty, Sheila
Against the Wind 1949,Je 27,18:3
Carty, Tom
Sunrise at Campobello 1960,S 29,32:1
Caruso, Anthony
Tall, Dark and Handsome 1941,Ja 24,15:2
Always in my Heart 1942,Mr 14,19:2
Sunday Punch 1942,My 11,19:2
And Now Tomorrow 1944,N 23,38:2
Objective Burma 1945,Ja 27,15:2
Crime Doctor's Courage, The 1945,Mr 3,11:3
Pride of the Marines 1945,Ag 25,7:3
That Night With You 1945,N 9,16:2
Tarzan and the Leopard Woman 1946,F 11,25:2
Wild Harvest 1947,N 13,33:2
To the Victor 1948,Ap 17,11:2
Bride of Vengeance 1949,Ap 7,38:2
Undercover Man, The 1949,Ap 21,30:2
Song of India 1949,Je 10,32:3
Scene of the Crime 1949,Jl 29,12:2
Anna Lucasta 1949,Ag 12,13:2
Threat, The 1949,D 2,35:4
Asphalt Jungle, The 1950,Je 9,29:3
Tarzan and the Slave Girl 1950,Je 24,7:3
Boots Malone 1952,Mr 13,26:2
Iron Mistress, The 1952,N 20,39:2
Desert Legion 1953,My 9,13:2
Saskatchewan 1954,N 11,26:2
Phantom of the Rue Morgue 1954,Mr 20,10:5
Drum Beat 1954,N 18,42:1
Passion 1954,D 11,11:1
Cattle Queen of Montana 1955,Ja 26,22:1
Magnificent Matador, The 1955,My 25,38:1
Tennessee's Partner 1955,N 5,22:8

Caruso, Anthony— Cont

Hell on Frisco Bay 1956,Ja 7,21:1
Big Land, The 1957,Mr 2,18:2
Baby Face Nelson 1957,D 12,35:1
Badlanders, The 1958,S 4,33:1
Never Steal Anything Small 1959,F 12,23:1
Legion of the Doomed 1959,Mr 12,27:5
Most Dangerous Man Alive 1961,Jl 5,29:2
Where Love Has Gone 1964,N 3,26:1

Caruso, Dorothy (Original Author)
Great Caruso, The 1951,My 11,32:2

Caruso, Enrico
Webb Singing Pictures 1917,Ja 15,7:1
My Cousin 1918,N 25,11:3
Cantante de Napoles, El; Singer of Naples, The
 1935,F 25,13:4

Caruso, Enrico Jr
Buenaventura, La 1934,S 15,20:3

Caruso, Margherita
Gospel According to St Matthew, The
 1966,F 18,23:1

Caruso, Nicholas
In Gay Madrid 1930,Je 7,10:4

Caruth, Burr
Double Door 1934,My 5,22:3
Pursuit of Happiness, The 1934,O 26,25:1
Harvester, The 1936,Jl 4,18:2
Under Western Stars 1938,Je 25,7:3
Invitation to Happiness 1939,Je 8,31:2

Carvajal, Emperatriz
Nuestra Tierra de Paz; Our Land of Peace
 1940,Je 1,12:3

Carvajat, Tony
Treasure of Pancho Villa, The 1955,N 25,38:2

Carver, Catherine
Beware of Widows 1927,My 24,23:4

Carver, Cynthia May
Second Greatest Sex, The 1956,F 11,12:2

Carver, George Washington Dr
George Washington Carver 1940,Ap 17,26:4

Carver, H P (Director)
Silent Enemy, The 1930,My 20,32:3

Carver, Kathryn
Service for Ladies 1927,Ag 15,22:5
Serenade 1927,D 19,30:1
His Private Life 1928,N 12,18:2
Outcast 1928,N 26,30:2

Carver, Louise
Fortune Hunter, The 1928,Ja 10,28:4
Man From Blankley's, The 1930,Mr 29,23:1
Big Trail, The 1930,O 25,20:3
Side Show 1931,S 19,10:2
Hallelujah, I'm a Bum 1933,F 9,15:2

Carver, Lynne
Maytime 1937,Mr 19,27:1
Bride Wore Red, The 1937,O 15,18:4
Madame X 1937,O 25,23:1
Everybody Sing 1938,Mr 11,15:3
Young Doctor Kildare 1938,O 28,27:1
Christmas Carol, A 1938,D 23,16:2
Huckleberry Finn 1939,Mr 3,21:2
Within the Law 1939,Ap 6,31:2
Calling Dr Kildare 1939,My 12,25:4
Broadway Melody of 1940 1940,Mr 29,25:3
Sporting Blood 1940,Jl 22,20:2
Bitter Sweet 1940,N 22,27:1
Dulcy 1940,N 28,28:2
Tennessee Johnson 1943,Ja 13,18:2

Carver, Tina
Hell on Frisco Bay 1956,Ja 7,21:1
Inside Detroit 1956,Ja 28,10:5

Carvi, Gino
Eye of the Needle, The 1965,Je 22,25:2

Carvill, Henry
If I Were King 1920,Ag 10,10:3
Disraeli 1929,O 3,27:5

Carwardine, Richard
Doctor Faustus 1968,F 7,38:1

Carwood, Roberto (Producer)
China Hilaria, La 1939,Ag 12,16:3

CARY
See Also CAREY

Cary, Falkland L (Original Author)
Panic in the Parlor 1957,D 18,45:1

Cary, Falkland L (Screenwriter)
Panic in the Parlor 1957,D 18,45:1

Cary, Joyce (Original Author)
Kisenga, Man of Africa 1952,Mr 7,18:2
Horse's Mouth, The 1958,N 12,41:1

Cary, Lucian (Original Author)
White Flannels 1927,Mr 22,31:2
Duke Steps Out, The 1929,Ap 15,22:6
Saturday's Millions 1933,O 14,18:3

Casa, Jose
Wild Oat, The 1956,Je 28,33:2

Casa, Lisa Della
Don Giovanni 1956,D 27,22:1

Casa, R
Avocate d'Amour 1938,S 8,27:2

Casadessus
Rothchild 1938,O 12,35:2

Casadesus, Gisele
Loves of Casanova 1948,S 18,11:4
Eternal Husband, The 1949,Ja 10,19:2

Vautrin, the Thief 1949,N 11,31:2
Between Eleven and Midnight 1950,F 23,33:3

Casadesus, Mathilde
Gervaise 1957,N 12,46:1
Love Is my Profession 1959,Ap 28,41:1

Casado, J J Martinez
Almas Encontradas 1933,Je 27,13:5
Corazon Bandolero 1935,Mr 2,18:2
Rayo, El 1935,O 19,21:3
Maria Elena 1936,F 18,27:1
Malditas Sean las Mujeres 1936,Ag 29,16:3
Irma la Mala 1936,O 6,28:7
Mujeres de Hoy 1936,D 7,27:4
Obligation to Assassinate, The 1937,O 19,29:6
Forgive Me, Son 1937,O 23,14:2
Eterna Martir 1938,Ja 3,16:3
Mujer Mexicana, La; Mexican Woman, The
 1938,Ap 18,11:2
Alma Jarocha 1938,Ap 30,18:2
Huapango 1938,Je 11,9:1
Guadalupe la Chinaca 1938,S 12,13:3
Asi es mi Tierra; Such Is my Country
 1939,Mr 18,9:3
Tia de las Muchachas, La; Girls' Aunt, The
 1939,O 30,13:3
Ahora Seremos Felices; Now We Shall Be Happy
 1940,Mr 16,8:2

Casagrande, Natilde
Fiat Voluntas Dei 1936,Jl 6,11:5

Casajuana, Maria
Girl in Every Port, A 1928,F 20,14:1

Casaleggio, Mario
Signor Max, Il; Mr Max 1939,O 6,31:4

Casanas, Marta
Heroina 1965,N 11,58:2

Casani, Santos
Spies of the Air 1940,Jl 4,12:3

Casanova, Fernando
This Strange Passion 1955,D 5,34:2

Casaravilla, Carlos
Age of Infidelity 1958,Ag 19,23:2
Lazarillo 1963,Ap 5,27:6

Casares, Maria
Wench, The 1949,Mr 14,15:5
Orpheus 1950,N 30,42:2
Testament of Orpheus 1962,Ap 10,48:1
Dames du Bois de Boulogne, Les; Ladies of the
 Park 1964,Ap 4,15:5

Casarvitla, Carlos
Ceremony, The 1964,My 14,39:1

Casas, Antonio
Goyescas 1944,My 29,18:3

Casati, Alberto (Producer)
Fuga, La 1966,Mr 22,33:1

Case, Gerald
In Which We Serve 1942,D 24,18:1
Henry V 1946,Je 18,30:2
Dancing Years, The 1951,Ja 29,14:4
Murder on Monday 1953,O 7,35:2

Case, Kathleen
Human Desire 1954,Ag 7,7:2
Running Wild 1955,N 12,23:2
Second Greatest Sex, The 1956,F 11,12:2

Caselotti, Luisa
Sei tu l'Amore 1930,N 18,28:4

Casero, Luis
Tras la Reja 1937,Ja 11,15:7

Casetelnuovo, Nino
Umbrellas of Cherbourg, The; Parpapluis de
 Cherbourg, Les 1964,D 17,50:1

Casey, Dolores
Doctor Rhythm 1938,My 19,25:2

Casey, Rosemary (Original Author)
Fools for Scandal 1938,Mr 25,15:3

Casey, Stuart
Age of Indiscretion 1935,My 18,21:2
Captain Blood 1935,D 27,14:1

Casey, Sue
Camelot 1967,O 26,54:1

Cash, Johnny
Festival 1967,O 24,53:2

Cashier, Isidore
Broken Hearts 1926,Mr 3,26:1
Green Fields 1937,O 12,31:4
Light Ahead, The 1939,S 23,22:3

Casile, Genevieve
7 Capital Sins (Envy); Envy (7 Capital Sins)
 1963,Ja 17,5:2

Casilio, Maria Pia
Bread, Love and Dreams 1954,S 21,24:1
Umberto D 1955,N 8,37:1
Neapolitan Carousel 1961,O 12,41:3

Casino, Del
Citizen Saint 1948,My 28,28:2

Caslans, Raymond (Miscellaneous)
My Wife's Husband 1965,Ja 27,26:1

Caslar, Dan (Composer)
Amore che Canta, L' 1937,Mr 31,28:7

Casne, Francis (Producer)
Tales of Paris (The Tale of Ella); Tale of Ella, The
 (Tales of Paris) 1962,Ag 27,18:1

Casolaro, S V (Director)
Parlami d'Amore Mariu 1934,O 20,20:3

Cason, John
Ringside 1949,S 17,10:8
Traveling Saleswoman 1950,Ja 6,25:3
From Here to Eternity 1953,Ag 6,16:2
Saskatchewan 1954,Mr 11,26:2

Caspary, Vera (Original Author)
Night of June 13th, The 1932,S 17,18:4
Such Women Are Dangerous 1934,Je 9,18:3
Private Scandal 1934,Je 15,26:2
Easy Living 1937,Jl 8,20:1
Scandal Street 1938,F 5,19:2 (In Addenda)
Service de Luxe 1938,O 24,13:2
Laura 1944,O 12,24:1
Bedelia 1947,F 8,10:2
Three Husbands 1951,Mr 9,30:2
Blue Gardenia, The 1953,Ap 28,31:1
Girls, Les 1957,O 4,27:2
Bachelor in Paradise 1961,N 17,41:2

Caspary, Vera (Screenwriter)
I'll Love You Always 1935,Mr 30,11:2
Lady From Louisiana 1941,My 15,27:2
Claudia and David 1946,Ag 15,19:2
Bedelia 1947,F 8,10:2
Letter to Three Wives, A 1949,Ja 21,24:2
Three Husbands 1951,Mr 9,30:2
I Can Get It for You Wholesale 1951,Ap 5,34:4

Casper, Robert
Studs Lonigan 1960,D 15,59:1

Caspersen, Karen
David Copperfield 1923,N 6,23:3

Cass, Henry (Director)
Facts of Love, The 1949,O 31,20:2
Last Holiday 1950,N 14,39:4
No Place for Jennifer 1951,Jl 17,31:2
Young Wives' Tale 1952,N 4,33:1
Castle in the Air 1953,Ja 5,19:2

Cass, Henry (Screenwriter)
Glass Mountain, The 1950,My 18,37:3

Cass, Lou
You Belong to Me 1934,S 13,26:1

Cass, Maurice
Two for Tonight 1935,Ag 31,16:2
Whispering Smith Speaks 1936,F 17,21:1
Charlie Chan at the Opera 1936,D 5,16:2
Champagne Waltz 1937,F 4,17:2
She Had to Eat 1937,Jl 24,12:1
Thin Ice 1937,S 4,8:2
Life Begins In College 1937,O 9,16:1
Wife, Doctor and Nurse 1937,O 11,26:5
Ali Baba Goes to Town 1937,O 23,14:1
Danger-Love at Work 1937,D 11,22:2
Big Town Girl 1937,D 13,23:4
Baroness and the Butler, The 1938,F 19,19:2
Making the Headlines 1938,Ap 1,17:2
Lone Wolf in Paris, The 1938,My 23,21:2
Gangs of New York 1938,My 28,9:2
Gold Diggers in Paris 1938,Je 2,19:2
When Were You Born? 1938,Je 9,27:2
Breaking the Ice 1938,S 23,35:3
Exposed 1938,N 21,14:5
Second Fiddle 1939,Jl 1,11:2
Charley's Aunt 1941,Ag 2,18:2
Angel on my Shoulder 1946,O 21,27:2
Song of my Heart 1948,Mr 5,17:3
Once More, my Darling 1949,S 26,17:1

Cass, Peggy
Marrying Kind, The 1952,Mr 14,27:1
Auntie Mame 1958,D 5,39:1
Gidget Goes Hawaiian 1961,Ag 10,17:4

Cass County Boys
Sioux City Sue 1947,Jl 23,19:3

Cassanto, Aurino
Black Orpheus 1959,D 22,41:1

Cassares, Maria
Enfants du Paradis, Les 1947,F 20,32:2

Cassavetes, John
Night Holds Terror, The 1955,S 15,39:2
Crime in the Streets 1956,My 24,27:4
Edge of the City 1957,Ja 30,33:2
Saddle the Wind 1958,Mr 21,17:1
Virgin Island 1960,Mr 24,39:5
Killers, The 1964,Jl 18,10:4
Dirty Dozen, The 1967,Je 16,36:1
Devil's Angels 1967,O 5,46:1
Rosemary's Baby 1968,Je 13,57:1

Cassavetes, John (Director)
Shadows 1961,Mr 22,37:1
Too Late Blues 1962,Mr 1,27:4
Child Is Waiting, A 1963,F 14,5:6
Faces 1968,S 23,42:4
Faces 1968,N 25,54:2

Cassavetes, John (Producer)
Too Late Blues 1962,Mr 1,27:4

Cassavetes, John (Screenwriter)
Too Late Blues 1962,Mr 1,27:4
Faces 1968,S 23,42:4
Faces 1968,N 25,54:2

CASSEL
See Also CASTLE, CASSELL

Cassel, Jean-Pierre
Love Game, The 1960,N 9,44:1
Joker, The; (Farceur, Le) 1961,Ag 8,32:2
Five Day Lover, The 1961,D 14,55:4
Candide 1962,N 20,39:1
Elusive Corporal, The 1963,F 19,5:1
Cyrano and D'Artagnan 1964,S 26,16:1
Those Magnificent Men in Their Flying Machines
  (Or How I Flew From London to Paris in 25
  Hours and 11 Minutes) 1965,Je 17,27:1
High Infidelity (The Victim); Victim, The (High
  Infidelity) 1965,Jl 2,17:1
Male Companion 1966,F 15,33:2
Is Paris Burning? 1966,N 11,36:1
Killing Game, The 1968,Ag 27,36:1
Cassel, Seymour
Too Late Blues 1962,Mr 1,27:4
Faces 1968,S 23,42:4
Cassel, Seymour
Faces 1968,N 25,54:2
CASSELL
See Also CASTLE, CASSEL
Cassell, Cindy
Emil and the Detectives 1964,D 24,8:3
Cassell, Malcolm
Room for One More 1952,Ja 16,21:2
Cassell, Wally
Story of G I Joe 1945,O 6,9:6
Gallant Bess 1946,D 6,27:6
Guilty, The 1947,My 19,27:2
Ramrod 1947,Je 30,25:6
Saigon 1948,Ap 1,30:5
We Were Strangers 1949,Ap 28,28:2
Arctic Manhunt 1949,Ag 19,12:5
White Heat 1949,S 3,7:2
Sands of Iwo Jima 1949,D 31,9:2
Quicksand 1950,Je 16,28:4
Highway 301 1950,D 9,13:2
Oh! Susanna 1951,Mr 30,28:5
Little Big Horn 1951,Jl 27,15:2
Wild Blue Yonder, The 1952,Ja 2,20:1
Thunderbirds 1953,Mr 12,24:4
City That Never Sleeps 1953,Ag 8,14:2
Island in the Sky 1953,S 10,22:2
Princess of the Nile 1954,Je 12,13:2
Timberjack 1955,Mr 10,33:3
Come on, The 1956,Ap 7,13:1
Until They Sail 1957,O 9,41:2
Cassella, Alberto (Original Author)
Death Takes a Holiday 1934,F 24,18:4
Cassellano, Renato (Original Author)
Kiss the Other Sheik 1968,Jl 30,33:1
Cassellano, Renato (Screenwriter)
Kiss the Other Sheik 1968,Jl 30,33:1
Casshyap, J S
Nine Hours to Rama 1963,Ap 4,58:2
Cassidy, Diane
Invitation 1952,Ja 30,22:6
Lovely to Look At 1952,My 30,11:2
Everything I Have is Yours 1952,O 30,40:5
Cassidy, Edward
Frontier Town 1938,Mr 12,13:3
Rawhide 1938,Ap 25,19:2
Cassidy, Ellen
Other Man's Wife, The 1919,Je 9,16:3
Checkers 1919,Ag 25,8:5
Cassidy, Jack
Look in any Window 1962,Mr 22,40:1
FBI Code 98 1964,Ap 9,25:6
Cassidy, James F
Santa Fe Stampede 1939,Ap 26,27:3
Cassidy, Maureen
Careless Years, The 1957,N 28,57:3
Cassidy, Morley F (Original Author)
On Such a Night 1937,S 17,29:2
Cassinelli, Antonio
Aida 1954,N 12,17:1
Cassinelli, Dolores
Lafayette, We Come 1918,N 4,11:3
Peter Ibbetson; (Forever) 1921,O 17,18:1
Secrets of Paris 1923,Ja 8,22:1
Dangerous Money 1924,O 14,21:5
Unguarded Hour, The 1926,Ja 5,25:2 (In
  Addenda)
Cassity, Ellen
Passers By 1920,Je 21,13:1
Cassola, Carlo (Original Author)
Bebo's Girl 1964,N 12,40:1
Casson, Ann
Escape 1930,N 1,23:2
Casson, Lewis
Escape 1930,N 1,23:2
Victoria the Great 1937,O 29,19:1
South Riding 1938,Ag 2,15:2
Sixty Glorious Years 1938,N 18,25:2
Cassot, Marc
If all the Guys in the World 1957,Ap 23,34:1
Demoniaque 1958,Mr 4,34:5
Passion of Slow Fire, The 1962,O 12,26:1
Other One, The 1967,S 29,53:1
Cassuto, Emanuele (Producer)
Night, The; Notte, La 1962,F 20,29:4

Castaine, Robert B
Atlantic City 1944,Ag 14,11:4
Castaldo, Ernest
Householder, The 1963,O 22,43:2
Castaneda, Luis Acedes
Mexican Bus ride 1954,Jl 21,18:3
Nazarin 1968,Je 21,48:1
Castanier, Jean (Original Author)
Crime of Monsieur Lange, The 1964,Ap 4,15:5
Castegren, Hilda
Haelsingar 1934,S 25,25:2
Casteinuovo, Nino
Cavern, The 1965,D 25,17:2
Castel, Don
Stampede 1949,S 16,36:2
Castel, Lou
Fist in his Pocket 1968,My 28,40:1
Casteliano, Franco (Screenwriter)
Crazy Desire 1964,Jl 3,13:2
Castellani, Bruto
Quo Vadis 1925,F 16,24:1
Castellani, Renato (Director)
Professor, My Son 1949,Ap 18,18:4
It's Forever Springtime 1951,D 29,7:7
Two Cents Worth of Hope 1952,D 16,44:2
Romeo and Juliet 1954,D 22,28:1
Castellani, Renato (Original Author)
Under the Sun of Rome 1949,O 6,40:4
Two Cents Worth of Hope 1952,D 16,44:2
Castellani, Renato (Screenwriter)
Under the Sun of Rome 1949,O 6,40:4
It's Forever Springtime 1951,D 29,7:7
Malia 1952,F 2,11:4
Two Cents Worth of Hope 1952,D 16,44:2
Marriage Italian Style 1964,D 21,42:1
Castellano, Franco (Screenwriter)
Little Nuns, The 1966,Ap 28,49:1
Castellano (Original Author)
Hours of Love, The 1965,S 4,11:5
Castellano (Screenwriter)
Hours of Love, The 1965,S 4,11:5
Castellari, Enzo G (Director)
Any Gun Can Play 1968,S 14,34:2
Castelli, C (Miscellaneous)
This Wine of Love 1948,Ap 19,27:2
Castelli, C (Screenwriter)
This Wine of Love 1948,Ap 19,27:2
Aida 1954,N 12,17:1
Castelli, Philippe
Elusive Corporal, The 1963,F 19,5:1
Castello, Don
New Adventures of Tarzan, The 1935,O 15,19:3
Castello, William
Man on a Tightrope 1953,Je 5,19:1
Castellot, Florencio
Silk, Blood and Sun 1943,Ja 30,10:6
Marvels of the Bull Ring 1943,Jl 3,11:3
Castellvi, Jose (Director)
Mercedes 1935,My 14,17:5
Castelnuovo, Nino
Everybody go Home!; Tutti a Casa 1962,N 6,38:1
Eye of the Needle, The 1965,Je 22,25:2
Facts of Murder, The 1965,Jl 1,34:1
Reward, The 1965,S 16,55:1
Young World, A 1966,My 17,52:1
Creatures, Les 1966,S 16,31:2
Castelot, Jacques
Passionnelle 1948,Mr 1,17:2
Paris Waltz, The 1950,Ag 23,35:2
Topaze 1952,O 28,37:1
Justice Is Done 1953,Mr 3,23:2
Dirty Hands 1954,My 11,25:5
Nana 1957,Ap 13,12:3
Folies Bergere 1958,My 28,37:2
Forbidden Fruit 1959,F 23,19:1
Lafayette 1963,Ap 11,29:1
Castenada, Movita
El Escandalo 1934,S 22,12:3
Diablo Del Mar, El 1936,Ap 1,29:2
Hurricane, The 1937,N 10,31:2
Red Light 1950,Ja 16,18:4
Wagonmaster 1950,Je 19,17:2
Furies, The 1950,Ag 17,23:2
Castiglioni, Iphigenie
Story of Louis Pasteur, The 1936,F 10,15:1
Funny Face 1957,Mr 29,16:1
Rome Adventure 1962,Mr 16,25:1
Castil-Blaise (Composer)
Barber of Seville 1949,Jl 21,21:2
Castillo, Gloria
Night of the Hunter, The 1955,S 30,23:1
Castillo, Miguel
Kid Rodelo 1966,F 23,46:1
Castillon, Chuy
Pan-Americana 1945,Mr 23,13:2
CASTLE
See Also CASSEL, CASSELL
Castle, Dolores
Cry of the City 1948,S 30,32:4
Castle, Don
Love Finds Andy Hardy 1938,Jl 22,10:2
Rich Man, Poor Girl 1938,Ag 19,13:3
Out West With the Hardys 1938,D 9,31:2

Castle, Don— Cont
These Glamour Girls 1939,Ag 31,14:2
I Take This Woman 1940,F 16,23:3
Power Dive 1941,My 29,15:4
World Premiere 1941,Ag 21,15:2
Tombstone, The Town too Tough to Die
  1942,Jl 27,18:2
Guilty, The 1947,My 19,27:2
Invisible Wall, The 1947,N 1,11:2
High Tide 1947,N 8,11:2
Roses Are Red 1947,N 15,11:2
Big Land, The 1957,Mr 2,18:2
Gunfight at the O K Corral 1957,My 30,23:2
Castle, Egerton (Director)
Young April 1926,Ag 31,15:3
Castle, Egerton (Original Author)
Sweet Kitty Bellairs 1930,S 6,9:2
Castle, Gabe
Sniper's Ridge 1961,Ag 24,25:3
Castle, Hubert
Sensations of 1945 1944,Jl 7,13:2
Castle, Irene
Firing Line, The 1919,Jl 7,18:5
Slim Shoulders 1922,S 4,14:4
Castle, Irene (Original Author)
Story of Vernon and Irene Castle, The
  1939,Mr 31,19:2
Castle, Joan
Mr Lemon of Orange 1931,Mr 28,15:3
Young Sinners 1931,My 9,15:4
Castle, John
Lion in Winter, The 1968,O 31,54:1
Castle, John (Original Author)
Password Is Courage, The 1962,D 22,5:2
Castle, Mary
Eight Iron Men 1953,Ja 2,11:1
White Fire 1954,S 18,12:4
1954,S 18,12:4
Jailbreakers, The 1961,Ja 5,27:2
Castle, Maxine
Monkey Business 1931,O 8,22:6
Castle, Nick (Composer)
Hold That Co-ed 1938,S 24,13:1
Rookies on Parade 1941,My 22,25:2
Castle, Nick (Miscellaneous)
Life Begins In College 1937,O 9,16:1
Just Around the Corner 1938,D 3,11:2
Everything Happens at Night 1939,D 16,12:6
Swanee River 1939,D 30,9:2
Castle, Peggie
Buccaneer's Girl 1950,Mr 27,19:2
Payment on Demand 1951,F 16,21:2
Air Cadet 1951,My 11,32:3
Prince Who Was a Thief, The 1951,Jl 4,13:2
Invasion USA 1953,Ap 30,39:4
I, The Jury 1953,Ag 22,8:2
99 River Street 1953,O 3,14:2
Long Wait, The 1954,Jl 3,9:2
Jesse James' Women 1954,S 29,23:4
Finger Man 1955,Jl 16,12:4
Target Zero 1955,N 16,43:2
Miracle in the Rain 1956,Ap 2,18:1
Beginning of the End 1957,Jl 4,16:1
Seven Hills of Rome 1958,Ja 28,24:2 (Incorrect
  in this edition; use 1958,Ja 31,24:2 elsewhere)
Castle, Richard
Six Bridges to Cross 1955,Ja 22,8:2
To Hell and Back 1955,S 23,21:2
Castle, Robert
Single Standard, The 1929,Jl 29,23:3
Castle, William (Director)
Whistler, The 1944,Ap 29,12:2
Mark of the Whistler, The 1944,N 11,19:2
Johnny Stool Pigeon 1949,S 23,28:3
Undertow 1949,D 16,37:2
Fat Man, The 1951,My 25,31:2
Hollywood Story 1951,Je 7,40:6
Fort Ti 1953,My 30,7:1
Drums of Tahiti 1954,Ap 24,14:5
Saracen Blade, The 1954,My 15,13:4
Americano, The 1955,Ja 20,35:1
New Orleans Uncensored 1955,Ap 30,10:8
Macabre 1958,Jl 24,18:1
House on Haunted Hill 1959,Mr 12,27:5
Tingler, The 1960,Mr 10,36:2
13 Ghosts 1960,Ag 6,9:2
Homicidal 1961,Jl 27,23:4
Mr Sardonicus 1961,O 19,39:3
Zotz! 1962,O 4,44:3
13 Frightened Girls 1963,S 12,32:2
Old Dark House, The 1963,O 31,26:3
Strait Jacket 1964,Ja 23,26:1
Night Walker, The 1965,Ja 21,22:1
I Saw What You Did 1965,Jl 22,24:2
Let's Kill Uncle 1966,N 19,26:1
Busy Body, The 1967,Je 8,52:2
Castle, William (Original Author)
North to the Klondike 1942,Mr 12,24:3
Castle, William (Producer)
Macabre 1958,Jl 24,18:1
House on Haunted Hill 1959,Mr 12,27:5
Tingler, The 1960,Mr 10,36:2
13 Ghosts 1960,Ag 6,9:2
Homicidal 1961,Jl 27,23:4

Castle, William (Producer)— Cont

Mr Sardonicus 1961,O 19,39:3
Zotz! 1962,O 4,44:3
13 Frightened Girls 1963,S 12,32:2
Old Dark House, The 1963,O 31,26:3
Strait Jacket 1964,Ja 23,26:1
Night Walker, The 1965,Ja 21,22:1
I Saw What You Did 1965,Jl 22,24:2
Let's Kill Uncle 1966,N 19,26:1
Busy Body, The 1967,Je 8,52:2
Rosemary's Baby 1968,Je 13,57:1

Castlerosse, Lord (Miscellaneous)
Young Mr Pitt, The 1943,Mr 11,17:1

Castlerosse, Lord (Original Author)
Wings and the Woman 1942,O 8,31:1

Castleton, Barbara
Silver King, The 1919,Ja 13,9:3
Man Who Turned White, The 1919,Je 2,20:4
False Fronts 1922,Je 5,16:2

Castleton, Paul A (Original Author)
Bandit of Sherwood Forest, The 1946,Mr 23,8:4

Castleton, Paul A (Screenwriter)
Bandit of Sherwood Forest, The 1946,Mr 23,8:4

Castor, Chris
No Place for Jennifer 1951,Jl 17,31:2

Castrito, A
Podoroso Caballero 1936,O 26,20:2

Castro, Juanita
Baul Macabro, El; Macabre Trunk, The 1937,N 30,26:3

Castro, Luis (El Soldado)
Torero! 1957,My 22,29:2

Castro, Rosita
El Escandalo 1934,S 22,12:3

Castronova, Tom
Mad Dog Coll 1961,My 13,10:1

Catalano
Pearls of the Crown, The 1938,Ap 12,26:2

Catalano, Clare (Miscellaneous)
Mill on the Po, The 1951,O 23,35:2

Catalano, Rolando
Village, The 1953,S 23,37:2

Cataldo, Gaspare (Screenwriter)
Before Him all Rome Trembled 1947,F 22,16:2
Duel Without Honor 1953,F 28,8:8
Genoese Dragnet 1954,F 12,20:5

Catalina
Julieta Compra un Hijo; Julieta Buys a Baby 1935,Mr 25,12:3

Catania, Antonio
White Line, The 1952,D 6,17:2

Catarino, Don
India Bonita, La; Pretty Indian Girl, The 1939,Ap 15,15:2
Por Mis Pistolas; By My Pistols 1939,Je 10,14:3

Cate, Gertrudten
Last Chance, The 1945,N 28,21:6

Catelain, Jacques
New Enchantment, The 1926,Mr 15,18:3
Living Image, The 1928,Je 4,13:2
Apaches of Paris 1928,D 11,35:3
Bonheur, Le 1936,F 28,18:2
Entente Cordiale 1939,D 26,23:2
Stolen Affections 1951,Mr 12,20:2

Cates, Gilbert (Director)
Rings Around the World 1967,D 7,60:3

Cates, Gilbert (Producer)
Rings Around the World 1967,D 7,60:3

Cates, Warren
Major Dundee 1965,Ap 8,45:1

Cathcart, Countess (Miscellaneous)
Woman Tempted, The 1928,Ap 24,29:3

Cathcart-Borer, Mary (Screenwriter)
Little Ballerina, The 1951,F 28,33:2

Cathcart-Jones, Owen
Captains of the Clouds 1942,F 13,24:2

Cather, Willa (Original Author)
Lost Lady, A 1925,Ja 19,14:1
Lost Lady, A 1934,O 4,19:1

Catherine the Great (Original Author)
Scralet Empress, The 1934,S 15,20:2

Cathrey, George
Eternally Yours 1939,O 7,11:2
Raffles 1940,Ja 13,11:2

Catineau, Patrice
Gervaise 1957,N 12,46:1

Catlett, Walter
Second Youth 1924,Ap 22,19:3
Summer Bachelors 1926,D 20,28:3
Why Leave Home 1929,S 16,30:1
Married in Hollywood 1929,S 23,24:3
Happy Days 1930,F 14,20:1
Let's Go Places 1930,Mr 1,23:1
Florodora Girl, The 1930,My 31,19:4
Front Page, The 1931,Mr 20,29:1
Platinum Blonde 1931,O 31,22:2
Maker of Men 1931,D 19,16:4
Cock of the Air 1932,Ja 25,20:3
Expert, The 1932,F 27,22:1
It's Tough to be Famous 1932,Ap 9,18:1
Back Street 1932,Ag 29,9:2
Big City Blues 1932,S 10,18:5
Okay America 1932,S 10,18:5
Rain 1932,O 13,22:3

Rockabye 1932,D 5,21:2
Sport Parade, The 1932,D 17,22:3
Private Jones 1933,Mr 25,13:3
Mama Loves Papa 1933,Jl 24,11:2
Only Yesterday 1933,N 10,25:1
Unknown Blonde 1934,Ap 24,27:2
Captain Hates the Sea, The 1934,N 29,33:2
Every Night at Eight 1935,Ag 3,16:2
Tale of Two Cities, A 1935,D 26,21:2
Mr Deeds Goes to Town 1936,Ap 17,17:2
We Went to College 1936,Jl 27,20:2
Cain and Mabel 1936,O 19,22:1
Follow Your Heart 1936,O 22,31:1
Banjo on My Knee 1936,D 12,15:1
Sing Me a Love Song 1936,D 26,15:2
On the Avenue 1937,F 5,17:3
Love Is News 1937,Mr 6,10:1
Wake up and Live 1937,Ap 24,16:2
Love Under Fire 1937,Ag 28,8:2
Varsity Show 1937,S 2,17:2
Danger-Love at Work 1937,D 11,22:2
Every Day's a Holiday 1938,Ja 27,17:2
Bringing Up Baby 1938,Mr 4,17:5
Zaza 1939,Ja 5,17:1
Going Places 1939,Ja 7 6:1
Exile Express 1939,Ag 16,21:3
Kid Nightingale 1939,D 8,33:6
Pop Always Pays 1940,Ag 30,16:6
Spring Parade 1940,O 4,29:2
Quarterback, The 1940,O 17,33:3
Honeymoon for Three 1941,F 8,19:2
You're the One 1941,F 20,23:2
Horror Island 1941,Mr 31,11:3
Million Dollar Baby 1941,Je 7,20:2
Manpower 1941,Jl 5,14:2
Bad Men of Missouri 1941,Ag 16,18:2
Unfinished Business 1941,S 2,20:2
It Started With Eve 1941,O 3,27:1
My Gal Sal 1942,My 1,23:1
Yankee Doodle Dandy 1942,My 30,9:1
Maisie Gets her Man 1942,Jl 16,23:2
Give Out, Sisters 1942,Ag 28,22:3
Between Us Girls 1942,S 25,25:3
Star Spangled Rhythm 1942,D 31,20:1
They Got Me Covered 1943,Mr 5,20:2
Hit Parade of 1943 1943,Ap 16,24:3
Cowboy in Manhattan 1943,My 28,19:2
Fired Wife 1943,O 1,15:2
His Butler's Sister 1943,D 30,13:2
Up in Arms 1944,Mr 3,19:2
Her Primitive Man 1944,Ap 1,11:1
Ghost Catchers 1944,My 31,22:3
3 Is a Family 1944,D 20,20:3
Lake Placid Serenade 1944,D 25,15:6
I'll Be Yours 1947,F 22,16:2
Are You With It? 1948,Ap 15,31:2
Boy With Green Hair, The 1949,Ja 13,26:2
Look for the Silver Lining 1949,Je 24,29:2
Dancing in the Dark 1949,D 3,8:6
Inspector General, The 1949,D 31,9:2
Here Comes the Groom 1951,S 21,19:2
Friendly Persuasion 1956,N 2,30:1

Catron & Popp
Song of the Open Road 1944,Je 7,13:3

Catselli, Aleka
Electra 1962,D 18,5:2

Cattell, Irene
Another Language 1933,Ag 5,9:5

Cattle, Harry
Me, Gangster 1928,O 22,29:1

Catto, Max (Original Author)
Prize of Gold, A 1955,O 15,19:2
Fire Down Below 1957,Ag 9,11:2
Seven Thieves 1960,Mr 12,14:5
Devil at 4 O'Clock, The 1961,O 19,39:3
Mister Moses 1965,My 13,32:1

Catto, Max (Screenwriter)
West of Zanzibar 1955,Ja 18,31:2

Cau, Jean (Screenwriter)
Game is Over, The 1967,Ja 10,34:1

Caudani, M (Screenwriter)
Bandit, The 1949,Je 7,26:3

Cauldwell, Brendan
Playboy of the Western World, The 1963,Mr 19,8:2

Cauley, Bernard
Top o' the Morning 1949,S 1,25:2

Caulfield, Betty
Bigger Than Life 1956,Ag 3,11:2

Caulfield, Joan
Miss Susie Slagle's 1946,F 7,29:2
Monsieur Beaucaire 1946,S 5,23:1
Blue Skies 1946,O 17,28:2
Dear Ruth 1947,Je 11,33:3
Welcome Stranger 1947,Ag 7,15:2
Unsuspected, The 1947,O 4,9:2
Sainted Sisters, The 1948,My 20,35:2
Larceny 1948,S 4,8:6
Dear Wife 1950,F 2,31:2
Petty Girl, The 1950,Ag 18,17:2
Lady Says No, The 1952,Ja 7,14:3
Rains of Ranchipur, The 1955,D 16,38:2

Caupolican, Chief
Whoopee 1930,O 1,26:3

Caussimon, Roger
Red Inn, The 1954,Je 8,25:2
French-Cancan 1956,Ap 17,26:2
House on the Waterfront, The 1959,F 21,25:2

Cauterio, Robert
Farewell to Arms, A 1932,D 9,26:5

Cauvin, Andre (Director)
Black Shadows 1949,N 7,33:2

Cauvin, Andre (Producer)
Black Shadows 1949,N 7,33:2

Cauvin, M (Cinematographer)
Black Shadows 1949,N 7,33:2

Cavagna, Cesare (Screenwriter)
Beautiful but Dangerous 1958,F 6,24:1

Cavalcanti, Alberto (Director)
Sea-Fever 1929,O 28,20:1

Cavalcanti, Alberto (Producer)
Shrine of Victory 1943,Ag 20,13:2

Cavalcanti, Alfredo (Director)
48 Hours 1944,Je 26,21:2
Dead of Night 1946,Je 29,22:6
Nicholas Nickleby 1947,D 1,27:2
Champagne Charlie 1948,Ag 7,8:2
For Them that Trespass 1950,S 27,37:2

Cavalcanti, M A (Original Author)
Petite Lillie 1927,D 4,X,11:4 (In Addenda)

Cavalier, Cino
White Line, The 1952,D 6,17:2

Cavalier, d'Alain (Miscellaneous)
Vie de Chateau, La 1967,Mr 21,35:1

Cavalier, Gianni
White Line, The 1952,D 6,17:2

Cavalier, Marjorie
Eight Girls in a Boat 1934,Ja 13,16:3

Cavalier, Nita
Cross Examination 1932,F 27,22:1

Cavaliere, Nicholas (Cinematographer)
Fang and Claw 1935,D 28,10:5
If Moscow Strikes 1952,Ap 30,33:4

Cavalieri, Gino
To Live in Peace 1947,N 25,37:2

Cavalieri, Lina
Manon Lescaut 1914,Je 14,15:1
Eternal Temptress, The 1917,D 10,15:4
Woman of Impulse, A 1918,O 21,15:1

Cavallaro, Carmen
Billy Rose's Diamond Horseshoe 1945,My 3,37:1

Cavallaro, Carmen and Orchestra
Hollywood Canteen 1944,D 16,19:2
Time, The Place And The Girl, The 1946,D 27,14:3

Cavan, Barbara
His Excellency 1956,F 2,19:3

CAVANAGH
See Also CAVANAUGH, KAVANAGH, KAVANAUGH

Cavanagh, James P (Screenwriter)
Murder at the Gallop 1963,Je 25,23:2

Cavanagh, Paul
Woman in the Night, A 1929,Mr 11,22:2
Grumpy 1930,Ag 2,16:4
Storm, The 1930,Ag 23,7:3
Devil to Pay, The 1930,D 19,30:1
Unfaithful 1931,Mr 7,17:2
Born to Love 1931,Ap 25,23:4
Always Good-Bye 1931,My 23,13:4
Transgression 1931,Je 15,23:3
Squaw Man, The 1931,S 19,10:2
Heartbreak 1931,O 17,20:1
Devil's Lottery 1932,Ap 2,13:2
Crash, The 1932,S 9,17:5
Bill of Divorcement, A 1932,O 3,15:2
Tonight Is Ours 1933,Ja 21,10:6
Kennel Murder Case, The 1933,O 30,14:2
Sin of Nora Moran, The 1933,D 13,29:3
Tarzan and his Mate 1934,Ap 21,12:1
Shoot the Works 1934,Jl 7,16:5
Notorious Sophie Lang, The 1934,Jl 21,14:2
Menace 1934,N 22,27:2
Goin' to Town 1935,My 11,21:2
Splendor 1935,N 23,23:2
Champagne Charlie 1936,My 7,21:2
Crime Over London 1938,Jl 28,23:2
Within the Law 1939,Ap 6,31:2
Under-Pup, The 1939,S 5,21:2
Reno 1939,D 21,29:2
I Take This Woman 1940,F 16,23:3
Case of the Black Parrot, The 1941,Ja 10,23:3
Maisie Was a Lady 1941,F 13,25:2
Captains of the Clouds 1942,F 13,24:2
Strange Case of Dr Rx 1942,Mr 28,11:2
Eagle Squadron 1942,Jl 3,12:5
Pacific Rendezvous 1942,Jl 8,27:4
Gorilla Man, The 1943,Ja 15,21:4
Hard Way, The 1943,Mr 13,9:2
Scarlet Claw, The 1944,My 19,12:1
Maisie Goes to Reno 1944,S 29,18:1
Marriage Is a Private Affair 1944,O 27,17:7
Man in Half Moon Street, The 1945,Ja 20,16:2
House of Fear, The 1945,Mr 19,23:3
Woman in Green, The 1945,Je 16,10:3

Cavanagh, Paul— Cont

Night in Paradise 1946,Je 6,16:3
Night and Day 1946,Jl 26,16:2
Verdict, The 1946,D 13,29:4
Humoresque 1946,D 26,28:1
Dishonored Lady 1947,My 24,10:5
Ivy 1947,Je 26,19:1
Secret Beyond the Door 1948,Ja 16,25:4
Babe Ruth Story, The 1948,Jl 29,17:2
Black Arrow, The 1948,O 4,14:2
You Gotta Stay Happy 1948,N 5,29:2
Iroquois Trail, The 1950,O 27,24:4
Hollywood Story 1951,Je 7,40:6
Strange Door, The 1951,D 10,34:6
Golden Hawk, The 1952,O 18,16:4
Mississippi Gambler, The 1953,Ja 30,25:1
House of Wax 1953,Ap 11,15:2
Casanova's Big Night 1954,Ap 19,19:1
Magnificent Obsession 1954,Ag 5,18:4
Khyber Patrol 1954,S 20,19:2
Purple Mask, The 1955,Je 16,35:7
King's Thief, The 1955,Ag 13,7:2
Francis in the Haunted House 1956,Jl 21,9:2

CAVANAUGH

See Also CAVANAGH, KAVANAGH,
KAVANAUGH

Cavanaugh, Florence E (Original Author)
Iron Major, The 1943,N 1,12:5

Cavanaugh, Helene
Ranger of the big Trees, The 1925,Jl 28,24:4

Cavanaugh, Hobart
San Francisco Nights 1928,Ja 31,29:1
I Cover the Waterfront 1933,My 18,17:3
Lilly Turner 1933,Je 15,21:2
Private Detective 62 1933,Jl 7,20:2
No Marriage Ties 1933,Ag 4,18:2
Mary Stevens, M D 1933,Ag 5,9:6
Good-Bye Again 1933,S 2,15:2
Devil's Mate 1933,S 23,11:7
My Woman 1933,O 16,20:3
Broadway Thru a Keyhole 1933,N 2,18:3
From Headquarters 1933,N 17,22:4
Convention City 1933,D 25,28:2
Easy to Love 1934,Ja 15,12:2
Fashions of 1934 1934,Ja 20,12:2
Hi, Nellie! 1934,F 1,15:5
I've Got Your Number 1934,F 3,9:3
Mandalay 1934,F 15,15:6
Dark Hazard 1934,F 23,23:3
Jimmy the Gent 1934,Mr 26,22:3
Modern Hero, A 1934,Ap 20,17:1
Now I'll Tell 1934,My 26,12:2
Key, The 1934,My 30,14:3
Housewife 1934,Ag 10,21:2
Lost Lady, A 1934,O 4,19:1
Madame Du Barry 1934,O 25,26:2
St Louis Kid, The 1934,N 1,25:2
Kansas City Princess 1934,N 5,23:1
Firebird, The 1934,N 15,25:2
I Sell Anything 1934,D 27,25:2
I am a Thief 1935,Ja 1,24:1
Bordertown 1935,Ja 24,22:5
Wings in the Dark 1935,F 2,10:1
While the Patient Slept 1935,Mr 2,18:2
Broadway Gondolier 1935,Jl 18,15:2
Don't Bet on Blondes 1935,Jl 20,16:2
Page Miss Glory 1935,Ag 29,25:2
Dr Socrates 1935,O 3,29:2
Midsummer Night's Dream, A 1935,O 10,31:1
I Live for Love 1935,O 19,21:2
Captain Blood 1935,D 27,14:1
Lady Consents, The 1936,F 6,23:4
Wife vs Secretary 1936,F 29,11:1
Colleen 1936,Mr 9,20:2
Golden Arrow, The 1936,My 4,16:1
Love Begins at 20 1936,S 19,20:1
Stage Struck 1936,S 28,14:4
Cain and Mabel 1936,O 19,22:1
Here Comes Carter 1936,N 14,23:3
Sing Me a Love Song 1936,D 26,15:2
Three Smart Girls 1937,Ja 25,22:2
Mysterious Crossing 1937,F 2,20:5
Girl Overboard 1937,Mr 1,15:1
Night Key 1937,Ap 19,27:2
Reported Missing 1937,S 3,12:2
Cowboy From Brooklyn 1938,Jl 14,17:1
Rose of Washington Square 1939,My 6,21:2
Zenobia 1939,My 15,15:2
Tell no Tales 1939,Je 2,27:3
Career 1939,Jl 28,14:2
That's Right, You're Wrong 1939,N 30,25:3
Honeymoon's Over, The 1939,D 15,33:3
Reno 1939,D 21,29:2
Child Is Born, A 1940,Ja 11,19:2
Shooting High 1940,Ap 12,19:2
Angel From Texas, An 1940,My 10,26:7
You Can't Fool Your Wife 1940,My 24,23:4
Hired Wife 1940,S 14,11:2
Public Deb No 1 1940,S 18,19:2
Great Plane Robbery, The 1940,N 15,25:2
Santa Fe Trail 1940,D 21,21:2
Meet the Chump 1941,F 27,23:4
I Wanted Wings 1941,Mr 27,29:4
Horror Island 1941,Mr 31,11:3

My Favorite Spy 1942,My 29,13:4
Jackass Mail 1942,Jl 2,25:2
Magnificent Dope, The 1942,Jl 3,12:5
Whistling in Dixie 1942,D 31,20:4
Meanest Man in the World, The 1943,F 25,27:3
Stand by for Action 1943,Mr 12,12:2
Man From Down Under, The 1943,S 27,23:2
Kansan, The 1943,O 1,15:3
Sweet Rosie O'Grady 1943,O 21,30:2
Jack London 1944,Mr 3,19:3
Kismet 1944,Ag 23,16:1
Don Juan Quilligan 1945,Jl 30,16:2
Cinderella Jones 1946,Mr 16,9:6
Spider Woman Strikes Back, The 1946,Mr 23,8:3
Black Angel 1946,S 26,32:4
Margie 1946,O 17,28:3
Up in Central Park 1948,My 27,29:3
Letter to Three Wives, A 1949,Ja 21,24:2
Stella 1950,Ag 19,9:2

Cavanaugh, W M
Snow Bride, The 1923,Je 12,22:2

Cavanaugh Page Trio
Big City 1948,My 17,23:3

Cavanna, Elise
Love 'Em and Leave 'Em 1926,D 8,24:3

Cavara, Paolo (Director)
Women of the World 1963,Jl 3,14:1
Malamondo 1964,N 19,49:1
Wild Eye, The 1968,Ag 22,47:1

Cavara, Paolo (Screenwriter)
Wild Eye, The 1968,Ag 22,47:1

Cavell, Butch
Man From the Alamo, The 1953,S 12,13:2

Cavell, Lionella
Always Victorious 1960,Ap 7,46:1

Cavell, Marc
Thunder in the East 1953,F 4,32:2
Diane 1956,Ja 13,18:1
Purple Gang, The 1960,Ja 23,15:5
Hemingway's Adventures of a Young Man
 1962,Jl 26,17:1
Wild Angels, The 1966,D 22,40:4
Love-Ins, The 1967,Ag 19,16:1
Devil's Angels 1967,O 5,46:1
Cool Hand Luke 1967,N 2,58:1

Cavell, Maurice
Citizen Saint 1948,My 28,28:2
Up Front 1951,Mr 26,19:2

Caven, Taylor (Original Author)
China Passage 1937,Ap 16,27:2

Caven, Taylor (Screenwriter)
Untamed Fury 1947,Ap 26,10:6

Cavender, Glenn
General, The 1927,F 8,21:1

Cavendish, David
Random Harvest 1942,D 18,36:6

Cavenna, Alice
I Met my Love Again 1938,Ja 15,19:1

Cavens, Albert
Cyrano De Bergerac 1950,N 17,31:2

Cavens, Fred
Three Must-Get-Theres, The 1922,Ag 28,14:1
Man in the Iron Mask, The 1939,Jl 14,11:1

Cavett, Frank (Original Author)
Vanity Street 1932,O 15,13:1
Forsaking all Others 1934,D 21,18:1
Second Chorus 1941,Ja 16,25:2
Smash-Up, The Story of a Woman
 1947,Ap 11,31:2
Across the Wide Missouri 1951,N 7,35:4
Greatest Show on Earth, The 1952,Ja 11,17:2

Cavett, Frank (Screenwriter)
Rulers of the Sea 1939,N 9,27:1
Tom Brown's School Days 1940,Je 28,22:2
Second Chorus 1941,Ja 16,25:2
Syncopation 1942,My 29,13:3
Going my Way 1944,My 3,25:2
Corn is Green, The 1945,Mr 30,18:2

Caviglia, Orestes
Palermo 1938,O 22,14:2
Viento Norte; North Wind 1939,S 16,20:3
Huella; Trial 1940,O 22,27:3

Caviglia, Orestes (Director)
Matrero, El; Outlaw, The 1940,Mr 18,13:2
Con las Alas Rotas; With Broken Rings
 1940,Mr 23,00:0

Cavin, Alin
Are We Civilized? 1934,Je 14,28:5

Cavin, Jess
Ramona 1928,My 15,17:3
Revenge 1928,D 10,25:1

Cavvadia, Tasso
Stella 1957,Je 11,40:1

Cawthorn, Joseph
Secret Studio, The 1927,Je 15,31:4
Two Girls Wanted 1927,N 14,26:1
Very Confidential 1927,N 29,31:1
Silk Legs 1927,D 26,26:6
At Yale 1928,Jl 30,21:2
Street Girl 1929,Jl 31,17:3
Jazz Heaven 1929,O 30,29:2
Taming of the Shrew, The 1929,N 30,23:1
Dance Hall 1929,D 16,34:2

Cawthorn, Joseph— Cont

Dixiana 1930,S 5,21:1
Princess and the Plumber, The 1930,D 23,25:1
Kiki 1931,Mr 6,16:1
Tailor-Made Man, A 1931,Ap 25,23:4
Run Around, The 1931,Ag 10,18:3
Peach O'Reno 1931,D 24,20:8
White Zombie 1932,Jl 29,18:2
Love Me Tonight 1932,Ag 19,20:6
They Call It Sin 1932,O 21,25:4
Whistling in the Dark 1933,F 5,IX,5:1
Grand Slam 1933,F 22,25:2
Blondie Johnson 1933,F 27,11:2
Made on Broadway 1933,Jl 8,14:5
Best of Enemies 1933,Jl 17,19:5
Broken Dreams 1933,N 21,23:3
Cat and the Fiddle, The 1934,F 17,20:2
Lazy River 1934,Ap 4,26:2
20 Million Sweethearts 1934,Ap 27,25:1
Glamour 1934,My 12,12:3
Housewife 1934,Ag 10,21:2
Human Side, The 1934,S 15,20:3
Young and Beautiful 1934,S 18,18:4
Last Gentleman, The 1934,O 18,26:5
Music in the Air 1934,D 14,29:3
Sweet Adeline 1935,Ja 7,13:2
Maybe It's Love 1935,F 11,14:2
Sweet Music 1935,F 21,23:2
Gold Diggers of 1935 1935,Mr 15,25:2
Naughty Marietta 1935,Mr 23,11:2
Bright Lights 1935,Ag 15,15:2
Page Miss Glory 1935,Ag 29,25:2
Harmony Lane 1935,O 24,19:4
Fish 1936,Ja 25,18:5
Freshman Love 1936,Ja 25,18:5
Brides are Like That 1936,Mr 23,22:5
Great Ziegfeld, The 1936,Ap 9,21:2
One Rainy Afternoon 1936,My 14,29:2
Hot Money 1936,Jl 25,16:2
Crime Over London 1938,Jl 28,23:2
Lillian Russell 1940,My 18,11:2
So Ends our Night 1941,F 28,17:2

Cawthorne, Peter
His Glorious Night 1929,O 5,22:5
Those Three French Girls 1930,O 11,21:3
Just Smith 1934,Ap 23,20:2
Crouching Beast, The 1936,Ag 22,6:1

Cayatte, Andre (Director)
Shop-Girls of Paris; Au Bonheur de Dames
 1947,Je 23,14:4
Lovers of Verona, The 1951,Mr 12,20:2
Justice Is Done 1953,Mr 3,23:2
We Are all Murderers 1957,Ja 9,27:2
Mirror Has two Faces, The 1959,My 27,31:1
Eye for an Eye, An 1961,F 10,19:1
Two Are Guilty 1964,F 29,12:1
Anatomy of a Marriage; My Days With Jean
 Marc; My Nights With Francoise
 1964,O 27,42:2

Cayatte, Andre (Miscellaneous)
Tomorrow Is my Turn 1962,F 2,24:2

Cayatte, Andre (Original Author)
Lovers of Verona, The 1951,Mr 12,20:2
Justice Is Done 1953,Mr 3,23:2
Anatomy of a Marriage; My Days With Jean
 Marc; My Nights With Francoise
 1964,O 27,42:2

Cayatte, Andre (Producer)
Eye for an Eye, An 1961,F 10,19:1

Cayatte, Andre (Screenwriter)
Stormy Waters 1946,Je 17,32:2
Shop-Girls of Paris; Au Bonheur de Dames
 1947,Je 23,14:4
We Are all Murderers 1957,Ja 9,27:2
Mirror Has two Faces, The 1959,My 27,31:1
Eye for an Eye, An 1961,F 10,19:1
Tomorrow Is my Turn 1962,F 2,24:2
Two Are Guilty 1964,F 29,12:1
Anatomy of a Marriage; My Days With Jean
 Marc; My Nights With Francoise
 1964,O 27,42:2

Caylor, Rose (Original Author)
Fingers at the Window 1942,Ap 23,27:3

Caylor, Rose (Screenwriter)
Fingers at the Window 1942,Ap 23,27:3

Cayrol, Jean (Screenwriter)
Muriel 1963,O 31,26:1

Cayton, William (Producer)
Journey to the Beginning of Time 1967,F 11,20:1
Legendary Champions, The 1968,O 29,54:1

Cazabon, John
Curtain Up 1953,F 2,17:3

Cazenave, Jean
Belles and Ballets 1960,N 15,45:3

Cazenuve, Paul
French Doll, The 1923,S 5,15:3

Cebotari, Maria
Only for Thee; Solo per To 1938,S 12,13:2
Ueber Alles die Treue 1939,F 13,13:3
Life of Giuseppe Verdi 1940,Ap 3,19:2
Dream of Butterfly, The 1941,F 13,25:2

Ceccacci, Tina
Miracolo Di Sant' Antonio, Il 1932,Ap 18,19:2

Ceccaldi, Daniel
Light Across the Street, The; Lumiere d'en Face, La 1957,Jl 30,20:2
Soft Skin, The; Peau Douce, La 1964,O 13,49:2
How Not to Rob a Department Store 1965,D 29,23:1
Cecchi, Emilio (Original Author)
Professor, My Son 1949,Ap 18,18:4
Cecchi, Emilio (Screenwriter)
Under the Sun of Rome 1949,O 6,40:4
Cecchi, Suso (Screenwriter)
Flesh will Surrender 1950,O 26,38:7
Cecchini, Giorgio (Producer)
Mondo Pazzo 1965,Ap 1,30:3
Cecconi, Aldo
Tramplers, The 1966,D 8,64:1
Ceccu, Peppedu
Bandits of Orgosolo 1964,Ap 14,32:1
Cecil, Edward
Phantom of the Opera, The 1925,S 7,15:3
What Happened to Jones 1926,F 9,22:1
Crown of Lies 1926,Mr 30,20:6
Resurrection 1931,Ja 24,15:1
Cecil, Henry (Original Author)
Brothers in Law 1957,Ag 20,22:1
Cecil, Mary
Women, The 1939,S 22,27:2
Cecil, Nora
Prunella 1918,Je 3,9:3
Deadwood Coach, The 1925,Ja 21,19:3
His Majesty Bunker Bean 1925,S 15,12:1
Devil Dancer, The 1927,D 19,30:1
Fortune Hunter, The 1928,Ja 10,28:4
Cavalier, The 1928,O 31,28:4
Seven Days' Leave 1930,Ja 25,13:2
Little Accident 1930,Ag 4,13:4
Only Saps Work 1930,D 13,22:2
Street Scene 1931,Ag 27,22:5
Caught Plastered 1931,S 12,15:4
Peg o'my Heart 1933,My 20,11:4
Doctor Bull 1933,O 6,21:2
Design for Living 1933,N 23,24:2
Once to Every Woman 1934,Mr 26,22:3
You're Telling Me 1934,Ap 7,19:1
Old-Fashioned Way, The 1934,Jl 14,16:5
Car 99 1935,F 23,14:7
Dancing Pirate 1936,Je 18,19:1
Easy Living 1937,Jl 8,20:1
King of Alcatraz 1938,O 7,21:2
What a Life 1939,O 12,33:1
Mourning Becomes Electra 1947,N 20,38:2
Cedar, Ralph (Director)
Wife Savers 1928,Ja 17,23:2
Cedar, Ralph (Miscellaneous)
Perfect Clue, The 1935,Mr 14,18:1
Cederborg, Artur
Vaermlaenningarna 1932,N 18,23:2
Sara Laer Sig Folkvett 1938,F 16,17:1
Cederlund, Gosta
Vaaran Pojke 1936,O 10,21:3
Med Folket Foer Fosterlandet 1939,F 21,14:2
Vi Tvaa; We Two 1939,D 2,21:3
Hennes Lilla Majestat; Her Little Majesty 1940,Ap 20,14:2
Torment 1947,Ap 22,34:2
Cederstrand, Soelve (Director)
Tjocka Slaekten; Near Relatives 1935,My 20,20:5
Cederstrand, Torleif
491 1967,D 21,45:1
Ceeley, Leonard
Moonlight Murder 1936,Mr 28,11:2
Day at the Races, A 1937,Je 18,25:2
Cegani, Elisa
Contessa di Parma, La 1938,F 24,23:2
Lancieri di Savoia 1938,Mr 8,23:2
But It's Nothing Serious 1939,O 10,27:2
Iron Crown 1949,Je 11,11:2
Fabiola 1951,My 30,14:2
Times Gone By (The Vise); Vise, The (Times Gone By) 1953,D 30,16:2
House of Ricordi 1956,Mr 13,32:1
Nana 1957,Ap 13,12:3
Anatomy of Love 1959,S 29,46:2
Constantine and the Cross 1963,Mr 14,8:2
Celano, Guido
Deported 1950,N 2,39:3
Never Take No for an Answer 1952,Ap 29,32:2
Thief of Venice, The 1952,N 28,22:7
Man From Cairo, The 1953,D 17,52:4
Seven Hills of Rome 1958,Ja 28,24:2 (Incorrect in this edition; use 1958,Ja 31,24:2 elsewhere)
This Angry Age 1958,Je 26,23:3
Cele, Willard
Magic Garden, The 1952,F 6,24:2
Celeridge, Ishel
Laburnum Grove 1941,D 2,29:2
Celestin, Jack (Original Author)
Silent Witness, The 1932,F 8,21:1
Celi, Adolfo
Escape into Dreams 1950,Ap 13,34:5
That Man From Rio 1964,Je 9,30:1
Von Ryan's Express 1965,Je 24,28:1
Thunderball 1965,D 22,23:1

Male Companion 1966,F 15,33:2
Grand-Prix 1966,D 22,40:1
Honey Pot, The 1967,My 23,52:1
Greco, El 1967,My 24,52:2
King of Hearts 1967,Je 20,34:1
Bobo, The 1967,S 29,53:1
Operation Kid Brother 1967,N 23,58:2
Grand Slam 1968,F 21,60:4
And There Came a Man 1968,Ap 5,56:4
Danger Diabolik 1968,D 12,62:6
Celia, Ettore
It Happened in Broad Daylight 1960,S 30,33:1
Celis, Jose Luis (Screenwriter)
Cucaracha, La 1961,N 2,42:1
Cella, Ettore
Portrait of a Woman 1946,Ap 22,26:2
Celleis, Joseph
Caddy, The 1953,S 18,16:6
Celli, Adolfo
Guaglio 1949,My 19,35:2
Celli, Teresa
Border Incident 1949,N 21,29:2
Black Hand 1950,Mr 13,15:2
Asphalt Jungle, The 1950,Je 9,29:3
Crisis 1950,Jl 4,10:2
Right Cross 1950,N 16,39:2
Cellier, Antoinette
Great Barrier, The 1937,F 5,17:5
Silent Barriers 1937,Mr 26,25:1
Ourselves Alone 1937,Jl 31,6:2
Tenth Man, The 1937,N 15,15:2
River of Unrest 1937,N 27,21:2
End of the River, The 1948,Je 21,18:2
Cellier, Frank
Woman in Command, The 1934,My 29,22:2
Loves of a Dictator 1935,Je 1,18:2
Thirty-Nine Steps, The 1935,S 14,8:4
Mister Hobo 1936,F 8,19:2
Rhodes 1936,F 29,11:1
Passing of the Third Floor Back, The 1936,Ap 29,19:2
Nine Days a Queen 1936,O 3,21:1
Man Who Lived Again, The 1936,D 16,35:4
You're in the Army Now 1937,Ap 16,27:2
Non-Stop New York 1937,N 29,19:2
Sixty Glorious Years 1938,N 18,25:2
Ware Case, The 1939,Jl 22,12:2
Queen of Crime 1941,F 19,25:2
Quiet Wedding 1941,D 29,27:4
Ships With Wings 1942,My 25,11:2
Love on the Dole 1945,O 13,11:2
Magic Bow, The 1947,Jl 7,13:2
Easy Money (Episode 4) 1949,F 14,15:3
Blind Goddess, The 1949,Je 23,33:3
Cellier, Peter
Morgan! 1966,Ap 5,42:2
Cellini, Gianna
Pierpin, La Figlia Ritrovata 1936,Mr 27,25:3
Cendrars, Blaise (Original Author)
Sutter's Gold 1936,Mr 27,25:2
Cennamo, Pasquale
Gold of Naples (The Racketeer); Racketeer, The (Gold of Naples) 1957,F 12,30:1
Yesterday, Today and Tomorrow (Part 1-Adelina Naples); Adelina Naples (Yesterday, Today and Tomorrow) 1964,Mr 18,46:1
Centa, Antonio
Contessa di Parma, La 1938,F 24,23:2
Lotte nell Ombra; Battles in the Shadow 1939,Mr 21,27:3
Sotto la Croce del Sud; Under the Southern Cross 1939,Ap 10,13:4
Squadrone Bianco, Lo; White Squadrone, The 1939,D 1,27:2
Moglie in Pericolo, Una; Wife in Danger, A 1940,Je 7,27:3
Glass Mountain, The 1950,My 18,37:3
Fugitive Lady 1951,Ag 25,7:2
Scarred 1951,O 27,10:5
Man With the Grey Glove, The 1953,Ja 3,11:2
Secret Conclave, The 1953,My 16,10:1
Wages of Fear, The 1955,F 17,23:1
Central Documentary Studios (Cinematographer)
Whale Hunt, The 1952,N 24,19:2
Ceram, C W (Original Author)
Valley of the Kings 1954,Jl 22,15:2
Cerato, Clorindo
Sensualita 1954,Ap 29,40:2
Cerchio, Fernando (Director)
Mistress of the Mountains 1954,My 27,34:5
Head of a Tyrant 1962,Je 7,31:2
Cerchio, Fernando (Screenwriter)
Cinderella 1953,My 15,20:2
Head of a Tyrant 1962,Je 7,31:2
Cerlesi, Ennio
Armata Azzurra, La; Blue Fleet, The 1937,D 13,23:4
Dottor Antonio, Il 1939,D 7,35:1
Cernitz, Arthur W
Balalaika 1939,D 15,33:2
Cerny, Frantisek
Emperor and the Golem, The 1955,Ja 10,27:4

Cerretani, Guido
Gospel According to St Matthew, The 1966,F 18,23:1
Certain, Solange
Every Second Counts 1957,O 15,39:4
Cerusico, Enzo
Hercules, Samson and Ulysses 1965,N 4,57:2
Cerval, Claude
Cousins, The (Les Cousins) 1959,N 24,44:1
Love Game, The 1960,N 9,44:1
Crime Does Not Pay (The Hugues Case); Hugues Case, The (Crime Does Not Pay) 1962,O 17,35:2
Two Are Guilty 1964,F 29,12:1
Cervantes, Miguel de (Original Author)
Don Quixote 1961,Ja 21,18:1
Cervantes (Original Author)
Don Quixote 1915,D 20,11:1
Don Quichotte 1933,Ap 23,X,4:1
Don Quixote 1934,D 24,17:1
Don Quixote 1949,My 13,29:3
Cervi, Antonio (Director)
Moment of Truth, The 1965,Ag 10,18:1
Cervi, Antonio (Producer)
Red Desert 1965,F 9,43:1
Cervi, Gino
Matrimonio Ideale, Un 1939,D 15,33:3
Avventura di Salvator Rosa, Un; Adventure of Salvator Rosa, An 1940,S 20,27:3
Revenge 1947,N 28,37:4
Furia 1948,Ja 21,30:2
Foria 1948,Ja 21,30:2
Eternal Melodies 1948,F 14,17:3
Anna Karenina 1948,Ap 28,32:2
Spirit and the Flesh, The 1948,N 1,28:2
Four Steps in the Clouds 1948,N 22,25:2
His Young Wife 1949,Mr 12,10:2
Iron Crown 1949,Je 11,11:2
My Widow and I 1950,Ag 30,27:5
Fabiola 1951,My 30,14:2
Women Without Names 1951,Ag 7,22:2
Malia 1952,F 2,11:4
Miserables, Les 1952,Mr 25,23:2
Cliff of Sin, The 1952,N 22,16:5
Little World of Don Camillo, The 1953,Ja 14,27:1
Strange Deception 1953,My 27,28:2
O K Nero 1953,Je 20,8:6
Queen of Sheba, The 1953,N 4,29:3
Three Forbidden Stories 1953,N 16,21:4
Indiscretion of an American Wife 1954,Je 26,7:2
Return of Don Camillo, The 1956,Mr 27,41:1
Wife for a Night 1958,Je 12,35:2
Naked Maja, The 1959,Je 11,36:2
Sans Famille 1959,S 5,11:4
Big Chief, The 1960,Ap 27,32:1
Wild Love; (Gli Inamorati) 1961,Ap 6,30:2
Revolt of the Slaves, The 1961,N 8,41:1
Becket 1964,Mr 12,40:2
Cesana, Renzo
Stromboli 1950,F 16,28:2
Lady Without Passport, A 1950,Ag 4,13:2
Try and Get Me 1951,My 7,22:2
Mark of the Renegade 1951,S 7,24:2
Naked Maja, The 1959,Je 11,36:2
For the First Time 1959,Ag 15,8:7
Fast and Sexy 1960,O 6,51:4
Francis of Assisi 1961,Jl 29,8:2
Cesana, Renzo (Miscellaneous)
Stromboli 1950,F 16,28:2
Cesderus, Mathilde
Five Miles to Midnight 1963,Mr 21,8:6
Ceseri, Lugi
But It's Nothing Serious 1939,O 10,27:2
Ceseri, Ugo
Passaporto Rosso 1936,S 2,18:2
Conte di Brechard, Il; Count of Brechard, The 1940,O 24,31:3
Cesini, Giordano
White Line, The 1952,D 6,17:2
Cesoron, Gilbert (Screenwriter)
Bernadette of Lourdes 1962,Ja 30,20:2
Cessarskaya, Emma
Cossacks of the Don 1932,Mr 19,11:2
Cevenini, Leo (Producer)
Psycosissimo 1962,S 8,16:2
Cevenini, Leo (Screenwriter)
Dead Woman's Kiss, A 1951,O 6,16:4
Cey, Jacques
To Paris With Love 1955,Mr 29,33:4
Circle of Deception 1961,F 18,12:2
Cezar, George
Crooked Web, The 1955,D 10,19:1
Chaban, A I
Prisoners 1937,F 20,9:2
Chaber, M E (Original Author)
Man Inside, The 1959,F 5,24:7
Chabrol, Claude (Director)
Cousins, The (Les Cousins) 1959,N 24,44:1
Leda 1961,Jl 19,33:1
7 Capital Sins (Greed); Greed (7 Capital Sins) 1963,Ja 17,5:2
Landru 1963,Ap 10,31:1

Chabrol, Claude (Director)— Cont
Third Lover, The 1963,Je 25,23:3
Six in Paris 1965,S 16,54:2
Bonnes Femmes, Les 1966,My 13,32:1
Champagne Murders, The 1968,Ap 25,53:1
Biches, Les 1968,S 27,34:1
Chabrol, Claude (Producer)
Beau Serge, Le 1959,Ag 3,21:1
Cousins, The (Les Cousins) 1959,N 24,44:1
Love Game, The 1960,N 9,44:1
Chabrol, Claude (Screenwriter)
Beau Serge, Le 1959,Ag 3,21:1
Cousins, The (Les Cousins) 1959,N 24,44:1
Third Lover, The 1963,Je 25,23:3
Biches, Les 1968,S 27,34:1
Chabrun, Raymonde
Mouchette 1968,S 21,26:1
Chabukiani, Eteri
Ballet of Othello, The 1964,My 4,35:1
Chabukiani, V
Stars of the Russian Ballet (The Flames of Paris);
   Flames of Paris, The (Stars of the Russian
   Ballet) 1954,S 6,9:2
Ballet of Othello, The 1964,My 4,35:1
Chabukiani, V (Director)
Ballet Tales 1956,O 25,40:5
Ballet of Othello, The 1964,My 4,35:1
Chacon, Juan
Salt of the Earth 1954,Mr 15,20:2
Salt of the Earth 1965,N 1,57:1
Chacour, Miguel
Echoes of Silence 1967,Ap 7,32:2
Chadarain, Lesma
Cinderella 1961,D 19,39:1
Chadimova, Karla
Devil's Trap, The 1964,Ag 14,16:1
Sweet Light in a Dark Room 1966,Je 30,28:1
Seventh Continent, The 1968,Jl 30,33:2
Chadwell, Wallace
Adam Had Four Sons 1941,Mr 28,26:6
Bringing Up Father 1946,N 22,27:3
Chadwick, Clive
Woman Hater, The 1925,Jl 13,20:2
Chadwick, Cyril
Thirty Days 1922,D 11,22:1
Christian, The 1923,F 12,13:4
Brass 1923,Mr 12,18:1
Rustle of Silk, The 1923,My 8,22:4
Slander the Woman 1923,My 28,18:2
Don't Marry for Money 1923,Ag 21,17:3
Happiness 1924,Mr 11,16:2
Iron Horse, The 1924,Ag 29,6:1
Man Who Came Back, The 1924,S 1,9:1
Peter Pan 1924,D 29,11:4
Forty Winks 1925,F 3,24:1
His Supreme Moment 1925,Ap 13,24:1
Thank You 1925,O 6,30:1
Best Bad Man, The 1925,D 2,23:1
Hold That Lion 1926,S 6,16:2
Gigolo 1926,O 5,27:1
Is Zat So? 1927,My 17,27:2
Actress, The 1928,Jl 9,25:1
Excess Baggage 1928,S 24,25:1
Mating Call, The 1928,O 8,14:2
Black Watch, The 1929,My 23,26:3
Last of Mrs Cheyney, The 1929,Ag 12,22:2
Temple Tower 1930,My 10,25:3
Lady of Scandal, The 1930,Je 14,9:4
Chadwick, E R
Daybreak in Udi 1950,Je 2,26:2
Chadwick, Helene
Heartsease 1919,Ag 25,8:5
Scratch my Back 1920,Je 5,19:3
Cupid, the Cowpuncher 1920,Jl 26,9:5
Godless Men 1921,Ja 31,11:1
Old Nest, The 1921,Je 29,10:3
Dangerous Curve Ahead 1921,O 3,16:2
Glorious Fool, The 1922,Mr 20,10:3
Yellow Men and Gold 1922,My 29,14:1
Dust Flower, The 1922,Jl 3,8:6
Sin Flood, The 1922,O 30,11:1
Brothers Under the Skin 1922,N 13,12:1
Gimme 1923,Ja 15,18:3
Reno 1924,Ja 8,27:1
Why Men Leave Home 1924,My 12,14:4
Black Swan, The 1924,N 25,26:1
Golden Cocoon, The 1925,D 15,14:5
Father and Son 1929,Je 4,29:3
Hell Bound 1931,My 9,15:4
Chadwick, Les
Ferry Cross the Mersey 1965,F 20,16:2
Chaffers, Edward
Malta Story 1954,Jl 17,7:2
Chaffey, Don (Director)
Flesh is Weak, The 1957,N 9,31:2
Man Upstairs, The 1959,Ag 11,23:2
Breakout 1960,My 19,44:3
Question of Adultery, A 1961,Jl 6,18:2
Nearly a Nasty Accident 1962,Je 28,21:2
Matter of Who, A 1962,Jl 25,29:2
Jason and the Argonauts 1963,Ag 8,19:1
Three Lives of Thomasina, The 1963,D 12,46:1
They all Died Laughing 1964,Mr 16,37:2
Crooked Road, The 1965,F 4,24:2

One Million Years BC 1967,F 22,21:1
Chaflan
Ay Jalisco no te Rajes 1943,Ap 24,17:3
Passion Island 1943,My 1,11:2
Alla en el Tropico; Down in the Tropics
   1943,My 8,19:3
Guadalajara 1943,Je 12,9:3
Chaitin, Norman C (Director)
Small Hours, The 1962,Ag 14,34:1
Chaitin, Norman C (Producer)
Small Hours, The 1962,Ag 14,34:1
Chaitin, Norman C (Screenwriter)
Small Hours, The 1962,Ag 14,34:1
Chaizel
Men in White 1934,Je 9,18:2
Chakhava, F
Dragonfly, The 1955,Je 27,18:2
Chakiris, George
West Side Story 1961,O 19,39:3
Diamond Head 1963,F 21,5:2
King of the Sun 1963,D 26,33:4
Flight From Ashiya 1964,Ap 23,34:1
633 Squadron 1964,Je 25,25:1
Bebo's Girl 1964,N 12,40:1
Is Paris Burning? 1966,N 11,36:1
Young Girls of Rochefort, The 1968,Ap 12,50:1
Chakolouny
Michael Strogoff 1926,D 6,28:3
Chakrabandhu, M R B
Bridge on the River Kwai 1957,D 19,39:1
Chakrabority, Tulshi
Pather Panchali 1958,S 23,37:2
Chakravarty, Alok
World of Apu; Apur Sansar 1960,O 5,45:1
Chakravarty, Sincouri
Throw of the Dice 1930,Ja 6,30:5
Chakravaryl, Khagesh
Devi 1962,O 8,19:1
Chalais, Francois (Screenwriter)
Inside a Girls' Dormitory 1956,F 6,27:7
Chalco, Enrique
Way of a Gaucho 1952,N 5,36:2
Chaldecott, Denis
Dark Angel, The 1935,S 6,12:2
Chaldecott, Fay
David Copperfield 1935,Ja 19,8:1
Dark Angel, The 1935,S 6,12:2
Tale of Two Cities, A 1935,D 26,21:2
Chalet, Rich
Impossible Years, The 1968,D 6,54:1
Chaliapin, Feodor
Don Quichotte 1933,Ap 23,X,4:1
Don Quixote 1934,D 24,17:1
For Whom the Bell Tolls 1943,Jl 15,25:2
Three Russian Girls 1944,F 5,13:2
Song of Russia 1944,F 11,17:2
Chaliapin, Feodor Jr
Exile Express 1939,Ag 16,21:3
Chalis, George
Kameradschaft 1932,N 9,28:5
Challapin, Feodor
Sodom and Gomorrah 1963,Ja 24,5:3
Challee, William
Days of Glory 1944,Je 17,10:2
None but the Lonely Heart 1944,N 18,16:6
Black Book, The 1949,O 17,18:2
Port of New York 1950,F 3,29:2
Outrage 1950,O 16,30:5
Chicago Syndicate 1955,Je 21,37:1
Challenger, Percy
Sky Hawk, The 1929,D 12,36:4
Challis, Barbara
Cynthia 1947,S 19,27:2
Chalmers, Thomas
Puritan Passions 1923,O 15,15:4
Blind Alleys 1927,Mr 1,31:1
All the Way Home 1963,O 30,46:1
Outrage, The 1964,O 8,48:2
Chalmers, Thomas (Miscellaneous)
World in Flames, The 1940,O 24,31:2
Chalmers, Thomas (Narrator)
River, The 1938,F 5,19:2 (In Addenda)
Chalzel, Leo
Come on Marines 1934,Mr 24,20:3
Chamales, Tom T (Original Author)
Never so Few 1960,Ja 22,15:2
Go Naked in the World 1961,Mr 11,15:1
Chamarat, Georges
Carnival of Sinners 1947,Ap 8,34:2
Shop-Girls of Paris; Au Bonheur de Dames
   1947,Je 23,14:4
Three Sinners 1952,Jl 8,23:2
French Touch, The 1954,S 2,18:2
Diabolique 1955,N 22,41:1
Adorable Creatures 1956,Ja 11,36:2
Wild Oat, The 1956,Je 28,33:2
Julietta 1957,Je 18,38:2
Fernandel the Dressmaker 1957,Jl 1,19:2
Premier May 1958,S 17,44:2
Senechal the Magnificent 1958,O 14,44:1
Mirror Has two Faces, The 1959,My 27,31:1
Would-Be Gentleman, The 1960,Mr 23,31:1
Big Chief, The 1960,Ap 27,32:1

Chamarat, Georges— Cont
Thief of Baghdad, The 1961,Ag 17,18:2
Tomorrow Is my Turn 1962,F 2,24:2
Marriage of Figaro, The 1963,Ap 30,26:1
Up From the Beach 1965,Je 10,38:1
Chambati, Omar
Born Free 1966,Je 23,29:1
CHAMBERLAIN
See Also CHAMBERLIN
Chamberlain, Cyril
Blue Murder at St Trinian's 1958,My 27,27:1
Carry on Nurse 1960,S 10,11:1
Pure Hell of St Trinian's, The 1961,S 26,31:1
Chamberlain, George Agnew (Original Author)
Home in Indiana 1944,Je 22,23:1
Red House, The 1947,Mr 17,27:2
Scudda-Hoo! Scudda-Hay! 1948,Ap 15,31:1
April Love 1957,N 28,57:2
Chamberlain, Richard
Thunder of Drums, A 1961,S 27,35:1
Twilight of Honor 1963,N 14,41:2
Joy in the Morning 1965,Je 10,38:1
Petulia 1968,Je 11,54:4 —
Chamberlain, William (Original Author)
Imitation General 1958,Ag 21,22:2
CHAMBERLIN
See Also CHAMBERLAIN
Chamberlin, Howland
Web, The 1947,Je 5,32:1
Song Is Born, A 1948,O 20,37:2
Force of Evil 1948,D 27,16:2
And Baby Makes Three 1949,D 23,17:3
Francis 1950,Mr 16,40:2
House by the River 1950,My 2,25:2
Edge of Doom 1950,Ag 4,13:2
Mister 880 1950,S 30,13:2
Surrender 1950,O 9,21:5
Pickup 1951,Ag 31,12:2
Racket, The 1951,D 13,44:2
Big Night, The 1952,Mr 20,37:5
Chambers, Barbara (Screenwriter)
New York 1927,Ja 31,13:1
Chambers, C Haddon (Original Author)
Passers By 1920,Je 21,13:1
Chambers, Everett
Too Late Blues 1962,Mr 1,27:4
Chambers, Margaret
Woman to Woman 1929,N 12,34:4
Chambers, Marie
That Royle Girl 1926,Ja 4,33:1
Chambers, Ralph
Pajama Game, The 1957,Ag 30,12:2
Chambers, Richard
Too Late Blues 1962,Mr 1,27:4
Chambers, Robert W (Miscellaneous)
America 1924,F 22,20:1
Chambers, Robert W (Original Author)
Girl Philippa, The 1917,Ja 1,10:2
Danger Mark, The 1918,Jl 8,9:4
Firing Line, The 1919,Jl 7,18:5
Restless Sex, The 1920,S 13,12:1
Cardigan 1922,F 20,7:1
Common Law, The 1923,O 29,18:1
Between Friends 1924,My 12,14:4
Common Law, The 1931,Jl 20,20:4
Operator 13 1934,Je 23,16:5
Chambers, Robert W (Screenwriter)
America 1924,F 22,20:1
Chambers, Shirley
Half-Naked Truth, The 1932,D 31,10:1
Melody Cruise 1933,Je 23,15:2
Chambers, Wheaton
This Land Is Mine 1943,My 28,19:1
Falcon out West, The 1944,Mr 18,18:2
Tall in the Saddle 1944,D 15,25:3
Not Wanted 1949,Jl 25,11:4
Prowler, The 1951,Jl 2,16:6
Chambers, Whitman (Original Author)
Sinner Take All 1937,F 3,27:1
Come on, The 1956,Ap 7,13:1
Chambers, Whitman (Screenwriter)
Manhandled 1949,My 26,34:2
Special Agent 1949,Ag 22,13:1
Come on, The 1956,Ap 7,13:1
Chambois
Thirst of Men, The 1952,O 28,37:1
Chambreuil
Idiot, The 1948,F 5,26:2
Chambrun, Countess de (Original Author)
Playing With Souls 1925,Ap 20,18:1 (Incorrect in
   this edition; use 1925,Ap 28,18:1 elsewhere)
Champagne, Jacques
Quebec 1951,Mr 16,34:2
Champion, Gower
Till the Clouds Roll By 1946,D 6,27:4
Mr Music 1950,D 21,34:3
Show Boat 1951,Jl 20,14:1
Lovely to Look At 1952,My 30,11:2
Everything I Have is Yours 1952,O 30,40:5
Jupiter's Darling 1955,F 18,18:4
Three for the Show 1955,F 25,16:1
Champion, Gower (Director)
My Six Loves 1963,Ap 4,58:4

Champion, Jean
Muriel 1963,O 31,26:1
Champion, John C (Original Author)
Attack on the Iron Coast 1968,Je 6,54:2
Champion, John C (Producer)
Zero Hour 1957,N 14,41:1
Attack on the Iron Coast 1968,Je 6,54:2
Champion, John C (Screenwriter)
Stampede 1949,S 16,36:2
Zero Hour 1957,N 14,41:1
Champion, Marge
Mr Music 1950,D 21,34:3
Show Boat 1951,Jl 20,14:1
Lovely to Look At 1952,My 30,11:2
Everything I Have is Yours 1952,O 30,40:5
Jupiter's Darling 1955,F 18,18:4
Three for the Show 1955,F 25,16:1
Party, The 1968,Ap 5,56:2
Swimmer, The 1968,My 16,53:1
Champion (horse)
Sioux City Sue 1947,Jl 23,19:3
Champlim, Irene
Guerrilla Girl 1953,Jl 7,23:7
Champreux, Jacques (Screenwriter)
Judex 1966,Ap 26,55:1
Chan, Frances
Samurai 1945,Ag 25,7:5
Chan, George
Blood Alley 1955,O 6,25:3
Chan, Jacqueline
World of Suzie Wong, The 1960,N 11,36:1
Cleopatra 1963,Je 13,29:1
Chan, Luke
Mysterious Mr Wong, The 1935,Mr 7,26:1
West of Shanghai 1937,O 29,19:2
Samurai 1945,Ag 25,7:5
Chan, Oie
Daughter of the Dragon 1931,Ag 22,7:5
Chan-Fei, Kao
Fight to the Last 1938,D 22,25:3
Chance, Naomi
Trials of Oscar Wilde, The 1960,Je 28,26:1
Chancel, Jules (Original Author)
Love Parade, The 1929,N 20,32:6
Chancellor, John (Original Author)
King of the Damned 1936,F 1,9:2
Chandeau, Robert
Picnic on the Grass 1960,O 12,47:1
Chandlee, Harry (Miscellaneous)
Adventures of Mark Twain, The 1944,My 4,25:5
Chandlee, Harry (Original Author)
Platinum Blonde 1931,O 31,22:2
Chandlee, Harry (Screenwriter)
It Happened Out West 1937,Je 7,22:3
Our Town 1940,Je 14,25:3
Sergeant York 1941,Jl 3,15:1
3 Is a Family 1944,D 20,20:3
Tarzan's Magic Fountain 1949,F 7,15:2
Chandler, Anna
Big Broadcast, The 1932,O 15,13:1
Chandler, Chick
Melody Cruise 1933,Je 23,15:2
Blood Money 1933,N 16,30:5
Murder on a Honeymoon 1935,Mr 4,12:2
Alias Mary Dow 1935,Je 29,16:2
Star for a Night 1936,S 5,7:2
Woman Wise 1937,Ja 23,13:1
Off to the Races 1937,F 6,15:2
Time Out for Romance 1937,Mr 13,23:2
Sing and Be Happy 1937,Je 19,20:2
Born Reckless 1937,Jl 30,22:6
One Mile From Heaven 1937,Ag 19,23:1
Portia on Trial 1937,D 3,29:2
Love and Hisses 1938,Ja 1,11:1
City Girl 1938,F 4,17:3
Mr Moto Takes a Chance 1938,Je 13,15:4
Alexander's Ragtime Band 1938,Ag 6,7:2
Speed to Burn 1938,S 9,25:1
Time Out for Murder 1938,O 7,21:2
While New York Sleeps 1938,D 22,25:3
Hotel for Women 1939,Ag 26,20:2
Hollywood Cavalcade 1939,O 14,13:2
Missing Evidence 1939,N 17,17:3
Swanee River 1939,D 30,9:2
Honeymoon Deferred 1940,F 16,23:4
Free, Blonde and 21 1940,Ap 5,25:2
Tom Brown's School Days 1940,Je 28,22:2
Pier 13 1940,Ag 9,19:3
People vs Dr Kildare, The 1941,My 8,21:1
Bride Came C O D, The 1941,Jl 26,18:2
Cadet Girl 1941,D 11,39:1
Gentleman at Heart, A 1942,F 23,25:2
Big Shot, The 1942,Jl 18,8:2
Springtime in the Rockies 1942,N 12,30:2
Action in the North Atlantic 1943,My 22,10:2
He Hired the Boss 1943,Je 4,17:4
Hi Diddle Diddle 1943,S 24,26:2
Maisie Goes to Reno 1944,S 29,18:1
Irish Eyes Are Smiling 1944,N 8,27:1
Chicago Kid, The 1945,F 12,24:3
Do You Love Me 1946,My 25,12:2
Mother Wore Tights 1947,Ag 21,33:2
Family Honeymoon 1949,F 25,28:2

Great Rupert, The 1950,Ap 14,27:2
Curtain Call at Cactus Creek 1950,S 22,35:4
Aaron Slick From Punkin Crick 1952,Ap 19,18:6
Chandler, Colin
Love on the Dole 1945,O 13,11:2
Chandler, David (Screenwriter)
Apache Drums 1951,My 7,22:2
Chandler, Eddie
Dixiana 1930,S 5,21:1
Carnival Boat 1932,Mr 21,19:5
State Trooper 1933,Mr 27,13:6
Car 99 1935,F 23,14:7
She Loved a Fireman 1938,Ja 21,15:3
Gold Is Where You Find It 1938,F 14,20:6
Over the Wall 1938,Mr 28,19:2
Penrod and his Twin Brother 1938,Ap 18,11:1
Roaring Twenties, The 1939,N 11,12:1
Double Alibi 1940,Mr 11,11:2
Fugitive From Justice, A 1940,Jl 8,13:3
Chandler, Gene
Don't Knock the Twist 1962,Ap 14,14:2
Chandler, George
Light of Western Stars, The 1930,Ap 26,11:1
In Gay Madrid 1930,Je 7,10:4
Only Saps Work 1930,D 13,22:2
Man of the World 1931,Mr 21,15:1
Doctors' Wives 1931,Ap 25,23:4
Too Many Cooks 1931,Ag 17,18:2
Blessed Event 1932,S 3,16:2
Me and my Gal 1932,D 12,18:4
Hi, Nellie! 1934,F 1,15:5
Country Doctor, The 1936,Mr 13,32:2 (Incorrect
  in this edition; use 1936,Mr 13,27:2 elsewhere)
Fury 1936,Je 6,21:1
Libeled Lady 1936,O 31,24:2
Three Men on a Horse 1936,N 26,39:1
Woman Chases Man 1937,Je 11,26:2
Nothing Sacred 1937,N 26,27:2
Big Town Girl 1937,D 13,23:4
Secrets of a Nurse 1938,D 12,26:2
Jesse James 1939,Ja 14,13:1
King of the Turf 1939,My 8,21:2
Second Fiddle 1939,Jl 1,11:2
I Stole a Million 1939,Ag 7,11:2
Calling All Marines 1939,O 26,27:2
Thou Shalt Not Kill 1940,Ja 8,11:2
Return of Frank James, The 1940,Ag 10,16:4
Arizona 1941,F 7,23:3
Western Union 1941,F 7,23:2
Reaching for the Sun 1941,My 8,21:1
Roxie Hart 1942,F 20,21:1
Great Man's Lady, The 1942,Ap 30,14:3
Buffalo Bill 1944,Ap 20,22:6
It Happened Tomorrow 1944,My 29,18:2
Since You Went Away 1944,Jl 21,16:2
This Man's Navy 1945,Ap 16,18:6
Strange Confession 1945,N 8,17:3
Lover Come Back 1946,Je 20,20:3
Dead Reckoning 1947,Ja 23,31:2
Hollow Triumph 1948,O 29,29:5
Perfect Strangers 1950,Mr 11,8:2
Singing Guns 1950,Je 5,19:3
Pretty Baby 1950,S 23,11:2
Kansas Raiders 1951,Ja 26,19:2
Across the Wide Missouri 1951,N 7,35:4
My Man and I 1952,S 6,12:6
Hans Christian Andersen 1952,N 26,20:2
High and the Mighty, The 1954,Jl 1,21:2
Spring Reunion 1957,My 6,25:2
Dead Ringer 1964,F 20,22:3
Chandler, Harry (Screenwriter)
Jolson Story, The 1946,O 11,28:2
Chandler, Helen
Music Master, The 1927,Ja 17,12:4 (In Addenda)
Joy Girl, The 1927,S 6,34:3
Mother's Boy 1929,My 8,34:6
Salute 1929,O 5,22:5
Sky Hawk, The 1929,D 12,36:4
Rough Romance 1930,Je 16,25:3
Outward Bound 1930,S 18,28:3
Mothers Cry 1930,D 6,21:3
Dracula 1931,F 13,21:3
Daybreak 1931,Je 1,15:1
Salvation Nell 1931,Jl 6,24:4
Last Flight, The 1931,Ag 20,17:4
Fanny Foley Herself 1931,O 26,22:1
House Divided, A 1932,Ja 9,21:1
Vanity Street 1932,O 15,13:1
Christopher Strong 1933,Mr 10,19:2
Alimony Madness 1933,My 5,18:1
Good-Bye Again 1933,S 2,15:2
Worst Woman in Paris, The 1933,N 25,10:3
Long Lost Father 1934,F 19,18:2
Midnight Alibi 1934,Jl 4,18:3
Unfinished Symphony 1935,Ja 14,11:2
Chandler, James
Sweet Bird of Youth 1962,Mr 29,28:2
Jumbo 1962,D 7,49:1
Chandler, Jeff
Johnny O'Clock 1947,Mr 27,39:2
Invisible Wall, The 1947,N 1,11:2
Roses Are Red 1947,N 15,11:2
Sword in the Desert 1949,Ag 25,20:2

Chandler, Jeff— Cont
Abandoned Woman 1949,O 27,35:3
Broken Arrow 1950,Jl 21,15:2
Two Flags West 1950,O 13,23:2
Deported 1950,N 2,39:3
Bird of Paradise 1951,Mr 15,37:2
Smuggler's Island 1951,My 24,47:2
Iron Man 1951,Ag 20,14:2
Flame of Araby 1951,D 20,41:7
Battle at Apache Pass, The 1952,My 10,16:4
Red Ball Express 1952,My 30,11:2
Because of You 1952,D 4,47:3
Great Sioux Uprising, The 1953,Jl 18,6:2
Yankee Pasha 1954,Ap 19,19:2
Sign of the Pagan 1955,F 14,24:2
Foxfire 1955,Jl 14,19:1
Female on the Beach 1955,Ag 20,20:2
Spoilers, The 1955,D 24,10:2
Toy Tiger 1956,Je 30,11:2
Away all Boats 1956,Ag 17,14:2
Pillars of the Sky 1956,O 13,15:2
Tattered Dress, The 1957,Mr 15,22:3
Jeanne Eagels 1957,Ag 31,19:1
Man With a Shadow 1958,Ja 23,24:3
Lady Takes a Flyer, The 1958,Ja 30,19:2
Raw Wind in Eden 1958,S 20,10:6
Stranger in my Arms 1959,Mr 4,34:2
Thunder in the Sun 1959,Ap 9,37:2
Second to Hell 1959,Jl 18,6:3
Return to Peyton Place 1961,My 6,26:1
Mad Dog Coll 1961,My 13,10:1
Merrill's Marauders 1962,Je 14,23:4
Chandler, Jeffrey
High Wind in Jamaica, A 1965,Je 17,27:2
Chandler, Joan
Humoresque 1946,D 26,28:1
Street with no Name, The 1948,Jl 15,26:6
Rope 1948,Ag 27,12:4
Chandler, John (Screenwriter)
Pacific Adventure 1947,N 26,18:2
Chandler, John Davis
Young Savages, The 1961,My 25,31:1
Once a Thief 1965,S 9,36:1
Chandler, Lane
Love and Learn 1928,F 20,14:1
Legion of the Condemned, The 1928,Mr 19,26:2
Red Hair 1928,Mr 26,26:2
Big Killing, The 1928,Jl 2,11:2
First Kiss, The 1928,Ag 20,21:3
Studio Murder Mystery, The 1929,Je 10,23:1
Single Standard, The 1929,Jl 29,23:3
Forward Pass, The 1929,N 29,25:1
Devil's Brother, The 1933,Je 10,16:4
Corruption 1933,Je 20,22:7
Lawless Nineties, The 1936,Je 29,11:1
Sea Racketeers 1937,O 4,17:2
She Loved a Fireman 1938,Ja 21,15:3
Heroes of the Alamo 1938,Ap 2,18:2
Heart of Arizona 1938,Ap 16,17:1
Campus Confessions 1938,S 23,35:1
Great Plane Robbery, The 1940,N 15,25:2
Vigilantes Return, The 1947,Jl 1,30:2
Song of my Heart 1948,Mr 5,17:3
Northwest Stampede 1948,D 10,34:3
Samson and Delilah 1949,D 22,29:2
Lion and the Horse, The 1952,My 19,12:2
Charge at Feather River, The 1953,Jl 16,17:2
Thunder Over the Plains 1953,D 10,64:4
Chandler, Mimi
And the Angels Sing 1944,Jl 13,14:2
Chandler, Perdita
Great Jewel Robber, The 1950,Ag 4,13:2
Glass Menagerie, The 1950,S 29,31:5
Scandal at Scourie 1953,Je 16,24:2
Jet Pilot 1957,O 5,8:6
Chandler, Raymond (Original Author)
Falcon takes Over, The 1942,My 30,9:2
Time to Kill 1942,D 25,15:4
Murder, my Sweet 1945,Mr 9,16:2
Big Sleep, The 1946,Ag 24,6:6
Lady in the Lake 1947,Ja 24,18:3
Brasher Doubloon, The 1947,My 22,34:5
Chandler, Raymond (Screenwriter)
Double Indemnity 1944,S 7,21:1
And Now Tomorrow 1944,N 23,38:2
Unseen, The 1945,My 14,20:5
Blue Dahlia, The 1946,My 9,27:3
Strangers on a Train 1951,Jl 4,13:2
Chandler, Tanis
Lured 1947,Ag 29,14:4
Spirit of West Point 1947,O 3,31:2
16 Fathoms Deep 1948,O 7,35:2
Chandos, John
Invaders, The 1942,Mr 6,17:1
Next of Kin 1943,My 6,25:2
Long Memory, The 1953,Jl 27,15:2
Ship That Died of Shame, The 1956,Ag 21,33:2
Green Man, The 1957,My 23,40:1
Pursuit of the Graf Spee 1957,D 27,33:2
Little Ones, The 1965,S 16,55:2
Chandra
Crazy House 1943,D 16,33:3

Chandra Kaly and his Dancers
Time, The Place And The Girl, The 1946,D 27,14:3
Chane, Lon
Frontier Badmen 1943,Ag 14,12:8
Chanel, Lorraine
Magnificent Matador, The 1955,My 25,38:1
CHANEY
See Also CHENEY
Chaney, Creighton
Bird of Paradise 1932,S 10,18:5
Lucky Devils 1933,F 20,11:5
Sixteen Fathoms Deep 1934,Ja 19,24:3
Life of Vergie Winters, The 1934,Je 15,26:1
Chaney, Lon
Miracle Man, The 1919,Ag 27,9:5
Paid in Advance 1919,D 1,9:3
Victory 1919,D 28,4:4
Treasure Island 1920,Ap 12,13:1
Nomads of the North 1920,S 27,18:1
Penalty, The 1920,N 15,12:2
Bits of Life 1921,O 17,18:1
Oliver Twist 1922,O 30,11:1
Blind Bargain, A 1922,D 4,20:2
Quincy Adams Sawyer 1922,D 18,22:2
Hunchback of Notre Dame, The 1923,S 3,9:3
He Who Gets Slapped 1924,N 10,20:1
Monster, The 1925,F 16,24:1
Unholy Three, The 1925,Ag 4,14:3
Phantom of the Opera, The 1925,S 7,15:3
Tower of Lies, The 1925,S 28,24:1
Black Bird, The 1926,F 1,16:1
Outside the Law 1926,My 12,31:1
Road to Mandalay, The 1926,Je 29,21:2
Tell It to the Marines 1926,D 24,18:2
Mr Wu 1927,My 16,24:2
Unknown, The 1927,Je 13,17:1
Mockery 1927,Ag 22,21:3
London After Midnight 1927,D 31,31:1
Big City, The 1928,Mr 26,26:2
Laugh, Clown, Laugh 1928,My 28,23:2
Laugh, Clown, Laugh! 1928,Je 3,VIII,5:1
While the City Sleeps 1928,O 22,29:1
West of Zanzibar 1928,D 31,9:1
Where East Is East 1929,My 27,22:1
Thunder 1929,Jl 8,17:3
Phantom of the Opera 1930,F 10,20:4
Unholy Three, The 1930,Jl 5,17:4
Chaney, Lon Jr
Accent on Youth 1935,Ag 12,10:3
Angel's Holiday 1937,My 29,20:2
Wild and Woolly 1937,S 6,20:1
Mr Moto's Gamble 1938,Ap 8,17:2
Passport Husband 1938,Ag 5,11:2
Jesse James 1939,Ja 14,13:1
Union Pacific 1939,My 11,31:2
Frontier Marshal 1939,Jl 29,18:2
Charlie Chan in City in Darkness 1939,D 18,29:2
Of Mice and Men 1940,F 17,9:2
One Million BC 1940,Ap 27,9:2
North West Mounted Police 1940,N 7,33:2
Man Made Monster 1941,Mr 19,25:4
Billy the Kid 1941,Je 20,28:2
Badlands of Dakota 1941,S 9,27:6
Wolf Man, The 1941,D 22,24:5
North to the Klondike 1942,Mr 12,24:3
Ghost of Frankenstein, The 1942,Ap 4,19:2
Eyes of the Underworld 1942,O 5,15:2
Mummy's Tomb, The 1942,O 26,19:2
Frankenstein Meets the Wolf Man 1943,Mr 6,8:3
Son of Dracula 1943,N 6,16:4
Crazy House 1943,D 16,33:3
Calling Dr Death 1944,F 12,11:3
Weird Woman 1944,Ap 1,11:1
Cobra Woman 1944,My 18,17:2
Ghost Catchers 1944,My 31,22:3
Mummy's Ghost, The 1944,Jl 1,10:7
Dead Man's Eyes 1944,O 7,11:2
House of Frankenstein 1944,D 16,19:3
Here Come the Co-Eds 1945,F 19,21:1
Mummy's Curse, The 1945,Mr 31,16:1
Frozen Ghost, The 1945,Jl 28,7:3
Strange Confession 1945,N 8,17:3
Daltons Ride Again, The 1945,D 8,21:2
House of Dracula 1945,D 22,16:3
Pillow of Death 1946,Ja 26,19:3
My Favorite Brunette 1947,Mr 20,38:2
Albuquerque 1948,Mr 1,17:2
Abbott and Costello Meet Frankenstein 1948,Jl 29,17:2
16 Fathoms Deep 1948,O 7,35:2
There's a Girl in my Heart 1950,Ja 20,29:2
Captain China 1950,Mr 2,33:2
Once a Thief 1951,Ja 19,21:3
Inside Straight 1951,Mr 16,34:2
Only the Valiant 1951,Ap 14,9:6
Behave Yourself 1951,N 8,35:2
Flame of Araby 1951,D 20,41:7
Thief of Damascus 1952,My 8,37:2
High Noon 1952,Jl 25,14:2
Springfield Rifle 1952,O 23,40:2
Black Castle, The 1952,D 26,20:4
Lion Is in the Streets, A 1953,S 24,39:2

Jivaro 1954,F 13,11:5
Casanova's Big Night 1954,Ap 19,19:1
Passion 1954,D 11,11:1
Big House U S A 1955,Mr 12,11:6
Not as a Stranger 1955,Je 29,24:1
I Died a Thousand Times 1955,N 10,45:2
Indian Fighter, The 1955,D 22,20:1
Pardners 1956,Jl 26,20:2
Rebellion in Cuba 1961,Jl 1,9:1
Haunted Palace, The 1964,Ja 30,24:1
Law of the Lawless 1964,Ag 27,28:2
Black Spurs 1965,My 29,17:1
Johnny Reno 1966,Mr 10,26:3
Welcome to Hard Times 1967,My 2,56:1
Chang, Anna
Hatchet Man, The 1932,F 4,25:2
Chang, Danny
Hong Kong 1952,Ap 5,20:3
China Doll 1958,D 4,52:1
Chang, H H Dr
So Proudly We Hail 1943,S 10,29:1
Chang, Jane
Operation Bottleneck 1961,S 7,40:2
Chang, Kev
Purple Heart, The 1944,Mr 9,15:2
Chang, King Hou
Son of the Gods 1930,Ja 31,24:1
Chang, S K (Producer)
Sable Cicada 1939,Ja 14,13:1
Chang, Tisa
Ambush Bay 1966,S 15,51:4
Chang, W T
Blood Alley 1955,O 6,25:3
Chanler, William C (Producer)
Silent Enemy, The 1930,My 20,32:3
Channing, Carol
Thoroughly Modern Millie 1967,Mr 23,25:1
Channing, Ruth
Vanity Street 1932,O 15,13:1
Broadway to Hollywood 1933,S 2,14:4
Lazy River 1934,Ap 4,26:2
Merry Widow, The 1934,O 12,33:1
Chanslor, Marjorie (Original Author)
Girl on the Front Page, The 1936,N 7,15:2
Chanslor, Roy (Original Author)
Final Edition, The 1932,F 22,23:2
Hi, Nellie! 1934,F 1,15:5
Murder in the Clouds 1934,D 26,18:1
Bengal Tiger 1936,Jl 30,22:1
Girl on the Front Page, The 1936,N 7,15:2
Love Is on the Air 1937,N 12,27:3
One Hour to Live 1939,N 4,11:3
Honeymoon Deferred 1940,F 16,23:4
You Can't Escape Forever 1942,O 17,11:1
Hazard 1948,Je 3,19:2
House Across the Street 1949,S 2,14:4
Johnny Guitar 1954,My 28,19:2
Cat Ballou 1965,Je 25,36:1
Chanslor, Roy (Screenwriter)
Murder in the Clouds 1934,D 26,18:1
Front Page Woman 1935,Jl 12,15:1
Man Hunt 1936,Ja 30,14:2
Times Square Playboy 1936,My 2,11:2
Murder by an Aristocrat 1936,Je 13,13:2
Bengal Tiger 1936,Jl 30,22:1
Here Comes Carter 1936,N 14,23:3
Nurse From Brooklyn 1938,My 13,17:3
Goodbye Broadway 1938,My 14,18:1
Devil's Party, The 1938,My 31,8:3
Road to Reno, The 1938,O 3,11:2
Honeymoon Deferred 1940,F 16,23:4
Washington Melodrama 1941,My 26,15:3
Burma Convoy 1941,O 7,26:7
Flying Cadets 1941,O 14,29:2
Bombay Clipper 1942,Ja 12,23:3
Treat 'Em Rough 1942,Ja 19,21:3
Drums of the Congo 1942,Jl 20,16:4
Navy Comes Through, The 1942,N 12,30:3
Tarzan Triumphs 1943,F 5,16:3
Secret Command 1944,Je 14,16:2
Destiny 1945,F 3,16:5
House of Fear, The 1945,Mr 19,23:3
Daltons Ride Again, The 1945,D 8,21:2
Perilous Holiday 1946,Je 1,10:4
Black Angel 1946,S 26,32:4
Michigan Kid 1947,F 22,16:3
Vigilantes Return, The 1947,Jl 1,30:2
Hazard 1948,Je 3,19:2
Chantal, Marcelle
Au Nom de la Loi; In the Name of the Law 1932,My 1,VIII,4:1 (In Addenda)
Ordonnance, L'; Orderly, The 1935,Jl 1,22:3
Rasputin 1939,O 17,31:4
Great Temptation, The 1942,Jl 10,13:3
Chantal, Monique
On the Riviera 1951,My 24,47:1
Chantel, Vivane
Purple Noon 1961,S 1,12:1
Chantler, David T (Screenwriter)
Cash on Demand 1962,My 17,31:1
Follow the Boys 1963,F 28,8:2
She 1965,S 2,36:1

Chapeland, Claudy
Return of Don Camillo, The 1956,Mr 27,41:1
Chapelle, Pola
Windflowers 1968,F 23,43:1
Chaperot, Georges (Director)
Little Flower of Jesus, The 1938,D 13,31:2
Chaperot, Georges (Original Author)
Cage aux Rossignols, La; (Cage of Nightingales, A) 1947,Ap 3,31:2
Chapin, Alice
Manhattan 1924,O 29,18:1
Argentine Love 1924,D 23,16:2
Crowded Hour, The 1925,Ap 27,15:2
Chapin, Anne Morrison (Original Author)
This Man is Mine 1934,Ap 13,25:1
Love Takes Flight 1937,S 27,24:3
Chapin, Anne Morrison (Screenwriter)
Romance in the Dark 1938,Mr 21,18:2
Listen, Darling 1938,N 24,37:2
Sailor Takes a Wife, The 1946,Mr 1,17:2
Secret Heart, The 1946,D 26,28:2
High Barbaree 1947,Je 6,27:2
Big City 1948,My 17,23:3
Chapin, Benjamin
Lincoln Cycle (My Mother; My Father; Myself; The Call to Arms) 1917,My 28,11:2
Chapin, Benjamin (Producer)
Lincoln Cycle (My Mother; My Father; Myself; The Call to Arms) 1917,My 28,11:2
Chapin, Billy
Affair With a Stranger 1953,Jl 11,8:2
Kid From Left Field, The 1953,S 26,15:3
Naked Alibi 1954,O 2,21:2
Man Called Peter, A 1955,Ap 1,22:1
Night of the Hunter, The 1955,S 30,23:1
Chapin, Frederic (Original Author)
Night Bride, The 1927,Mr 30,22:6
Chapin, Harry (Director)
Legendary Champions, The 1968,O 29,54:1
Chapin, Harry (Screenwriter)
Legendary Champions, The 1968,O 29,54:1
Chapin, Jack
Lady, Be Careful 1936,O 10,21:1
Thanks for the Memory 1938,D 8,34:3
Some Like It Hot 1939,My 25,31:2
Disputed Passage 1939,O 26,27:2
Geronimo 1940,F 8,18:3
North West Mounted Police 1940,N 7,33:2
Chapin, Jacques
Beggars of Life 1928,S 24,25:1
Chapin, Ken
Something Wild 1961,D 24,30:6
Chapin, Michael
Strange Bargain 1949,S 30,28:3
Chapin, Robert (Screenwriter)
Hot Water 1937,N 5,19:4
Walking Down Broadway 1938,Ap 1,17:3
Passport Husband 1938,Ag 5,11:2
Safety in Numbers 1938,S 6,17:2
Always in Trouble 1938,N 3,27:1
Chapin, Tom
Lord of the Flies 1963,Ag 20,37:1
Chaplain, Prescott (Original Author)
Woman of the North Country 1952,Ag 30,6:2
Chapligin, N
Lenin in October 1938,Ap 2,18:1
Vow, The 1947,Je 23,14:3
Admiral Nakhimov 1948,N 25,47:4
Chaplin, Alice
Icebound 1924,Mr 3,22:3 (In Addenda)
Chaplin, Charles
Police 1916,My 22,20:4
Dog's Life, A 1918,Ap 15,13:3
Bond, The 1918,S 30,7:1
Shoulder Arms 1918,O 21,15:1
Night in the Show, A 1919,F 24,11:3
Bank, The 1919,Mr 17,13:2
His Prehistoric Past 1919,Mr 31,11:3
Police 1919,Ap 14,11:4
Adventurer, The 1919,Ap 21,13:4
Cure, The 1919,My 12,11:4
Sunnyside 1919,Je 16,11:2
Easy Street 1919,Je 23,10:3
Day's Pleasure, A 1919,D 8,20:4
Adventurer, The 1920,Ag 16,8:2
Kid, The 1921,Ja 22,9:2
Kid, The 1921,F 7,8:2
Idle Class, The 1921,S 26,18:1
Pay Day 1922,Ap 3,18:2
Pilgrim, The 1923,F 26,15:1
Gold Rush, The 1925,Ag 17,10:3
Count, The 1927,F 6,VII,7:3 (In Addenda)
Easy Street 1927,F 6,VII,7:3 (In Addenda)
His Prehistoric Past 1927,Ag 17,27:5
Circus, The 1928,Ja 9,20:1
Floorwalker, The 1929,Mr 12,26:2
Rink, The 1929,My 27,22:1
Bank, The 1929,S 2,16:1
City Lights 1931,F 7,11:1
Modern Times 1936,F 6,23:2
Great Dictator, The 1940,O 16,29:1
Gold Rush, The 1942,Ap 20,17:1
Limelight 1952,O 24,27:2

Chaplin, Charles— Cont
When Comedy Was King 1960,Mr 30,42:1
Days of Thrills and Laughter 1961,Mr 22,37:1
30 Years of Fun 1963,D 26,33:4
Monsieur Verdoux 1964,Jl 4,8:2
Countess from Hong Kong, A 1967,Mr 17,35:1
Show People 1967,O 2,58:2
Chaplin, Charles (Composer)
Modern Times 1936,F 6,23:2
Chaplin, Charles (Director)
Pilgrim, The 1923,F 26,15:1
Woman of Paris, A 1923,O 2,7:2
Gold Rush, The 1925,Ag 17,10:3
Circus, The 1928,Ja 9,20:1
City Lights 1931,F 7,11:1
Modern Times 1936,F 6,23:2
Great Dictator, The 1940,O 16,29:1
Limelight 1952,O 24,27:2
Countess from Hong Kong, A 1967,Mr 17,35:1
Chaplin, Charles (Original Author)
Great Dictator, The 1940,O 16,29:1
Chaplin, Charles (Producer)
Modern Times 1936,F 6,23:2
Great Dictator, The 1940,O 16,29:1
Limelight 1952,O 24,27:2
Chaplin, Charles (Screenwriter)
Pay Day 1922,Ap 3,18:2
Shoulder Arms 1922,Jl 17,16:3
Pilgrim, The 1923,F 26,15:1
Woman of Paris, A 1923,O 2,7:2
Gold Rush, The 1925,Ag 17,10:3
Circus, The 1928,Ja 9,20:1
City Lights 1931,F 7,11:1
Modern Times 1936,F 6,23:2
Limelight 1952,O 24,27:2
Countess from Hong Kong, A 1967,Mr 17,35:1
Chaplin, Charles Jr
Limelight 1952,O 24,27:2
High School Confidential 1958,My 31,6:6
Chaplin, Geraldine
Doctor Zhivago 1965,D 23,21:1
Chaplin, Prescott (Screenwriter)
Never Give a Sucker an Even Break
1941,O 27,21:2
Chaplin, Saul (Composer)
Rookies on Parade 1941,My 22,25:2
Time Out for Rhythm 1941,Jl 10,16:3
Chaplin, Saul (Miscellaneous)
Manhattan Merry-Go-Round 1937,D 31,9:3
Chaplin, Saul (Original Author)
Rookies on Parade 1941,My 22,25:2
Chaplin, Saul (Producer)
Star! 1968,O 23,36:2
Chaplin, Sidney
Submarine Pirate, A 1915,N 15,11:1
Submarine Pirate, The 1919,Je 9,16:3
Pilgrim, The 1923,F 26,15:1
Her Temporary Husband 1924,Ja 1,20:1
Perfect Flapper, The 1924,Je 23,22:4
Charley's Aunt 1925,F 9,15:3
Man on the Box, The 1925,S 28,24:1
Oh! What a Nurse! 1926,F 22,14:1
Better 'Ole, The 1926,O 8,23:2
Missing Link, The 1927,My 7,15:2
Fortune Hunter, The 1928,Ja 10,28:4
30 Years of Fun 1963,D 26,33:4
Chaplin, Sydney
Limelight 1952,O 24,27:2
Land of the Pharaohs 1955,Jl 27,15:2
Pillars of the Sky 1956,O 13,15:2
Four Girls in Town 1957,Ja 17,34:5
Quantez 1957,S 7,12:7
Countess from Hong Kong, A 1967,Mr 17,35:1
Chapman, Ben
Creature from the Black Lagoon 1954,My 1,13:4
Chapman, Ben (Original Author)
Six Lessons From Madame La Zonga
1941,F 19,25:2
Dangerous Game, A 1941,Mr 4,20:3
Chapman, Ben (Screenwriter)
Devil's Pipeline, The 1940,N 11,22:4
Six Lessons From Madame La Zonga
1941,F 19,25:2
Dangerous Game, A 1941,Mr 4,20:3
Chapman, Bob
For Men Only 1952,Ja 16,21:2
Chapman, Don
State Trooper 1933,Mr 27,13:6
Chapman, Edward
Juno and the Paycock 1930,Je 30,22:6
Murder 1930,O 25,20:6
Skin Game, The 1931,Je 20,20:4
Things to Come 1936,Ap 18,19:2
Rembrandt 1936,D 3,31:1
April Romance 1937,Ja 27,17:4
Man Who Could Work Miracles, The
1937,F 22,13:1
Citadel, The 1938,N 4,27:2
Secret Four, The 1940,Ap 22,13:2
Convoy 1941,Ja 17,21:2
Proud Valley 1941,My 17,19:2
Ships With Wings 1942,My 25,11:2
Wings and the Woman 1942,O 8,31:1
Jeannie 1943,S 13,14:2

October Man, The 1948,Ap 16,29:2
Mr Perrin and Mr Traill 1949,Ja 17,15:2
It Always Rains on Sunday 1949,F 14,15:5
Madeleine 1950,S 1,17:2
History of Mr Polly, The 1951,O 25,36:3
Man on the Run 1952,F 27,22:5
Spider and the Fly, The 1952,Jl 29,17:3
Promoter, The 1952,O 29,36:2
Story of Mandy, The 1953,F 24,21:3
Folly to be Wise 1953,D 28,17:2
His Excellency 1956,F 2,19:3
Bhowani Junction 1956,My 25,26:1
Lisbon 1956,Ag 30,19:2
Doctor at Large 1957,Jl 29,15:5
Oscar Wilde 1960,Je 21,28:2
School for Scoundrels 1960,Jl 12,39:1
Chapman, Edythe
Everywoman 1919,D 15,20:1
Huckleberry Finn 1920,F 23,11:2
Bunty Pulls the Strings 1921,Ja 9,VI,2:1 (In
Addenda)
Girl I Loved, The 1923,My 14,18:2
Divorce 1923,Je 26,14:2
Broken Barriers 1924,Ag 4,16:3
Worldly Goods 1924,N 3,20:1
Learning to Love 1925,F 23,24:1
Daddy's Gone A-Hunting 1925,F 24,17:3
Lightnin 1925,Jl 22,14:4
In the Name of Love 1925,Ag 27,14:1
Classified 1925,N 2,20:1
Soul Mates 1926,Ja 4,16:1
Three Faces West 1926,F 16,22:4
Runaway, The 1926,Ap 27,23:2
One Minute to Play 1926,S 6,16:2
Naughty but Nice 1927,Jl 5,19:2
American Beauty 1927,O 11,27:1
Crystal Cup, The 1927,O 25,33:3
Man Crazy 1927,D 19,30:1
Shepherd of the Hills, The 1928,F 20,14:1
Count of Ten, The 1928,Mr 13,23:3
Love Hungry 1928,Ap 16,20:5
Happiness Ahead 1928,Je 19,31:1
Three Week Ends 1928,D 10,25:1
Synthetic Sin 1929,Ja 7,36:2
Idle Rich, The 1929,Je 17,29:1
Twin Beds 1929,Jl 15,25:1
Navy Blues 1930,Ja 11,21:3
Double Cross Roads 1930,Ap 29,31:1
Chapman, Helen
Last Angry Man, The 1959,O 23,24:1
Chapman, Janet
Broadway Musketeers 1938,O 14,27:1
Heart of the North 1938,D 21,29:2
On Trial 1939,Ap 5,31:2
Presenting Lily Mars 1943,Ap 30,25:3
Chapman, John T (Screenwriter)
Satan in High Heels 1962,Mr 24,15:6
Chapman, Lonny
Young at Heart 1955,Ja 20,35:1
East of Eden 1955,Mr 10,33:1
Baby Doll 1956,D 19,40:2
Chapman, Marcia
Girl from Havana, The 1929,S 2,16:1
Chapman, Marguerite
Charlie Chan At the Wax Museum 1940,S 28,9:3
Girl, a Guy and a Gob, A 1941,Ap 24,25:3
Navy Blues 1941,S 20,11:2
Body Disappears, The 1942,Ja 31,13:2
Parachute Nurse 1942,Jl 27,18:2
Murder in Times Square 1943,My 31,13:2
Appointment in Berlin 1943,Jl 17,8:2
Destroyer 1943,S 2,15:3
My Kingdom for a Cook 1943,O 15,15:3
Counter-Attack 1945,My 17,15:2
Pardon my Past 1946,Ja 28,15:5
Walls Came Tumbling Down, The 1946,N 9,13:5
Mr District Attorney 1947,F 28,27:3
Relentless 1948,Mr 6,17:3
Gallant Blade 1948,O 13,31:3
Green Promise, The 1949,Je 24,29:2
Kansas Raiders 1951,Ja 26,19:2
Bloodhounds of Broadway 1952,N 15,15:2
Seven Year Itch, The 1955,Je 4,9:1
Amazing Transparent Man, The 1961,Mr 30,24:2
Chapman, Marion
Little Ballerina, The 1951,F 28,33:2
Chapman, Nolia
Satan in High Heels 1962,Mr 24,15:6
Chapman, Robert (Original Author)
Murder Reported 1960,Jl 12,39:1
Billy Budd 1962,O 31,32:1
Chapman, Tedwell (Screenwriter)
Abroad with two Yanks 1944,O 26,19:7
Chapman, Vern
Luck of Ginger Coffey, The 1964,S 22,44:1
Chapman, William
There's Magic in Music 1941,Je 5,27:2
Chapsal, Madeleine (Miscellaneous)
To Die in Madrid 1965,S 16,00:0
Witness, The 1967,N 7,47:1
Charbert, Philip
This Woman Is Mine 1941,O 13,21:2

Charell, Erik (Director)
Congress Dances, The 1931,N 22,VIII,6:6
Congress Dances 1932,My 12,23:2
Caravan 1934,S 28,27:1
Charell, Erik (Original Author)
What a Woman 1943,D 3,27:2
White Horse Inn, The 1957,D 4,50:3
Charell, Erik (Producer)
White Horse Inn, The 1957,D 4,50:3
Charell, Erik (Screenwriter)
Casbah 1948,My 3,27:4
White Horse Inn, The 1957,D 4,50:3
Charifal, Zharira
Judith 1966,Ja 21,22:1
Charioteers, The
Road Show 1941,F 19,25:2
Charisse, Andre
Man in a Cocked Hat 1960,Je 15,50:2
Charisse, Cyd
Harvey Girls, The 1946,Ja 25,26:2
Ziegfeld Follies 1946,Mr 23,8:3
Three Wise Fools 1946,S 27,19:2
Till the Clouds Roll By 1946,D 6,27:4
Fiesta 1947,Je 27,17:3
Unfinished Dance, The 1947,O 31,29:2
On an Island With You 1948,Jl 30,13:2
Words and Music 1948,D 10,34:2
East Side, West Side 1949,D 23,17:2
Tension 1950,Ja 12,32:4
Mark of the Renegade 1951,S 7,24:2
Singin' in the Rain 1952,Mr 28,27:2
Wild North, The 1952,My 12,21:2
Sombrero 1953,Ap 23,37:2
Band Wagon, The 1953,Jl 10,10:2
Brigadoon 1954,S 17,18:2
Deep in my Heart 1954,D 10,35:2
It's Always Fair Weather 1955,S 16,19:1
Meet Me in Las Vegas 1956,Mr 14,39:2
Silk Stockings 1957,Jl 19,11:1
Twilight for the Gods 1958,Ag 7,21:1
Party Girl 1958,O 29,30:1
Five Golden Hours 1961,O 19,39:3
Black Tights 1962,F 21,54:2
Two Weeks in Another Town 1962,Ag 18,10:1
Charland, Ainse
Keeper of the Bees, The 1925,O 28,29:2
Charland, Aime
Boy of Flanders, A 1924,Ap 15,24:1
Charlemagne, Jaime
Terror in the City 1966,N 9,43:4
Charles, Hughie (Composer)
Mister Big 1943,Je 14,13:4
Charles, II King (Miscellaneous)
Nell Gwyn 1935,Je 20,16:2
Charles, Lewis
Panic in the Streets 1950,Ag 5,9:2
Rose Tattoo, The 1955,D 13,55:1
Monkey on my Back 1957,My 30,23:2
Sweet Smell of Success 1957,Je 28,29:2
Party Girl 1958,O 29,30:1
Al Capone 1959,Mr 26,27:1
Birdman of Alcatraz 1962,Jl 19,19:2
Who's Got the Action? 1962,D 26,5:4
Soldier in the Rain 1963,N 29,67:6 (Incorrect in
this edition; use 1963,N 28,67:6 elsewhere)
House is not a Home, A 1964,S 2,33:1
Charles, Mole (Screenwriter)
Bad Sister 1948,Je 11,27:3
Charles, Ray
Blues for Lovers 1966,S 8,43:1
Charles, Ray, Orchestra
Blues for Lovers 1966,S 8,43:1
Charles, Rosalind
Love Parade, The 1929,N 20,32:6
Charles, Theresa (Original Author)
Her Panelled Door 1951,Ag 28,18:2
Charles, Zachary A
Flying Missile, The 1950,D 25,25:1
Gambling House 1951,Mr 19,23:2
Charles-Tacchelia, Jean (Screenwriter)
Law Is the Law, The 1959,Nr 11,41:2
Charles-Williams, Liz (Screenwriter)
Deadlier Than the Male 1967,F 22,21:1
Charleson, Mary
Upstairs and Down 1919,Je 16,11:2
Charlesworth, John
Christmas Carol, A 1951,N 29,41:2
Tom Brown's School Days 1952,Ja 8,23:5
Horse's Mouth, The 1954,Ja 20,33:4
Blonde Sinner 1957,Ja 24,34:1
Man Upstairs, The 1959,Ag 11,23:2
Charlia, Georges
Equipage, L' 1928,My 20,VIII,5:7
Legion of Honor, The 1928,Jl 20,8:4
Soul of France, The 1929,O 12,11:1
Sea-Fever 1929,O 28,20:1
Charlita
Brimstone 1949,O 7,35:3
Brave Bulls, The 1951,Ap 19,39:2
Come Fill the Cup 1951,N 22,47:2
Ride Vaquero 1953,Jl 16,17:2
Green Fire 1954,D 25,7:1

Charlo
Puerto Nuevo; New Port 1937,F 20,9:3

Charlot, Andre
Falcon's Brother, The 1942,O 3,9:5
Falcon Strikes Back, The 1943,Ap 2,17:4
Constant Nymph, The 1943,Jl 24,8:2
Man From Down Under, The 1943,S 27,23:2
Action in Arabia 1944,F 19,18:7
Summer Storm 1944,O 23,14:3
Delightfully Dangerous 1945,Je 9,17:3
This Love of Ours 1945,N 1,20:2
Temptation 1946,D 25,33:6

Charlot, Andre (Director)
Elstree Calling 1930,Mr 9,IX,6:1

Charmarat, Georges
Man to Men 1949,F 21,20:2
Dirty Hands 1954,My 11,25:5
Girls of the Night 1959,Mr 21,13:2

Charney, Kim
Suddenly 1954,O 8,27:2
Bottom of the Bottle, The 1956,F 2,19:2

Charnovolenko, G
Frigid Sea, The 1955,N 21,23:4

Charon, Andre
Emma 1932,F 6,14:4

Charon, Jacques
Paris Waltz, The 1950,Ag 23,35:2
Would-Be Gentleman, The 1960,Mr 23,31:1
In the French Style 1963,S 19,23:1
Cartouche 1964,Jl 22,39:1

Charon, Jacques (Director)
Flea in her Ear, A 1968,N 28,66:1

Charpenay, Huguette
Devil's Daughter 1949,F 26,11:2

Charpentier, Gustave (Producer)
Louise 1940,F 3,9:4

Charpentier, Gustave (Screenwriter)
Louise 1940,F 3,9:4

Charpin
Marius 1933,Ap 14,22:5
Barbier de Seville, Le 1936,S 23,29:2
They Were Five 1938,Je 1,19:5
Baker's Wife, The 1940,F 27,17:2
Mayor's Dilemma, The 1940,Ap 23,19:2
They Met on Skis 1940,D 23,23:2
Pepe le Moko 1941,Mr 4,20:2
Barge-Keeper's Daughter, The 1945,S 6,23:3
Well-Digger's Daughter, The 1946,S 30,21:4
Blue Veil, The 1947,O 2,32:6
Fanny 1948,F 13,26:2
Cesar 1948,O 28,36:2
Ignace 1950,S 19,39:4

Charrat, Janine
Ballerina 1938,N 15,27:1

Charret, Henri
Devil's Daughter 1949,F 26,11:2
Royal Affair, A; (Roi, Le) 1950,Mr 9,25:2

Charrier, Jacques
Chasers, The; Draguers, Les 1960,My 3,43:1
Babette Goes to War 1960,Je 8,46:1
Cheaters, The; (Tricheurs, Les) 1961,Je 5,37:4
Belle Americaine, La 1961,D 18,42:1
7 Capital Sins (Greed); Greed (7 Capital Sins) 1963,Ja 17,5:2
Third Lover, The 1963,Je 25,23:3
Anatomy of a Marriage; My Days With Jean Marc; My Nights With Francoise 1964,O 27,42:2
Oldest Profession, The (Anticipation) 1968,N 8,42:1

Charsky, Boris
Red Dance, The 1928,Je 26,29:1
Captain Lash 1929,F 4,20:1

Charter, Don (Director)
Greyfriars' Bobby 1961,O 12,41:4

Charteris, Leslie (Original Author)
Saint in New York, The 1938,My 26,31:2
Saint Strikes Back, The 1939,Mr 9,18:2
Saint in London, The 1939,Jl 19,23:3
Saint's Double Trouble, The 1940,F 13,27:2
Saint Takes Over, The 1940,My 28,29:3
Saint in Palm Springs, The 1941,Ja 31,15:5
Saint's Vacation, The 1941,Je 13,22:2
Lady on a Train 1945,S 15,21:2

Charteris, Leslie (Screenwriter)
River Gang 1945,O 6,9:7
Two Smart People 1947,F 15,20:4

Charters, Spencer
Little Old New York 1923,Ag 2,10:3
Janice Meredith 1924,Ag 6,13:3
Whoopee 1930,O 1,26:3
Bat Whispers, The 1931,Ja 16,27:1
Lonely Wives 1931,Mr 16,25:1
Front Page, The 1931,Mr 20,29:1
Traveling Husbands 1931,Ag 8,16:3
Palmy Days 1931,S 24,21:2
Tenderfoot, The 1932,My 23,18:4
Jewel Robbery 1932,Jl 23,6:6
Central Park 1932,D 7,29:3
Match King, The 1932,D 8,25:3
20,000 Years in Sing Sing 1933,Ja 10,26:2
Broadway Bad 1933,Mr 6,16:6
So This Is Africa! 1933,Ap 24,11:3

Kennell Murder Case, The 1933,O 30,14:2
Female 1933,N 4,18:3
Hips, Hips, Hooray 1934,F 24,18:3
Half a Sinner 1934,Je 23,16:5
Blind Date 1934,S 1,16:3
Wake up and Dream 1934,O 11,28:3
Pursuit of Happiness, The 1934,O 26,25:1
St Louis Kid, The 1934,N 1,25:2
Firebird, The 1934,N 15,25:2
It's a Gift 1935,Ja 5,20:2
Murder on a Honeymoon 1935,Mr 4,12:2
Ghost Walks, The 1935,Mr 30,11:2
Nut Farm, The 1935,Ap 8,23:3
Raven, The 1935,Jl 5,9:2
Don't Bet on Blondes 1935,Jl 20,16:2
Goose and the Gander, The 1935,S 12,29:2
In Person 1935,D 13,31:5
$1,000 a Minute 1935,D 21,11:1
Whispering Smith Speaks 1936,F 17,21:1
Don't Get Personal 1936,F 22,12:1
Farmer in the Dell, The 1936,Mr 7,11:4
Colleen 1936,Mr 9,20:2
Murder on a Bridle Path 1936,Ap 11,19:2
Mr Deeds Goes to Town 1936,Ap 17,17:2
Moon's our Home, The 1936,My 13,29:2
Harvester, The 1936,Jl 4,18:2
Mine With the Iron Door, The 1936,Jl 11,11:3
Spendthrift 1936,Jl 23,24:1
Libeled Lady 1936,O 31,24:2
Banjo on My Knee 1936,D 12,15:1
Lady From Nowhere 1936,D 21,19:2
Fugitive in the Sky 1937,Ja 16,21:1
Pick a Star 1937,My 28,17:2
Fifty Roads to Town 1937,Je 5,21:1
Mountain Music 1937,Je 24,30:3
Back in Circulation 1937,O 4,17:1
Hurricane, The 1937,N 10,31:2
Big Town Girl 1937,D 13,23:4
Wells Fargo 1937,D 30,15:2
In Old Chicago 1938,Ja 7,15:2
Lady Behave 1938,Ja 28,17:3
Joy of Living 1938,My 6,27:1
Crime School 1938,My 11,17:2
One Wild Night 1938,Je 3,17:2
Three Blind Mice 1938,Je 18,18:2
Professor Beware 1938,Jl 14,17:1
Texans, The 1938,Jl 28,23:2
Breaking the Ice 1938,S 23,35:3
Road to Reno, The 1938,O 3,11:2
Five of a Kind 1938,O 31,12:2
Topper Takes a Trip 1938,D 30,11:2
Jesse James 1939,Ja 14,13:1
I'm From Missouri 1939,Mr 23,27:1
Woman Doctor 1939,Mr 24,27:3
They Made Her a Spy 1939,Mr 29,21:4
Flying Irishman, The 1939,Ap 12,27:2
Young Mr Lincoln 1939,Je 3,11:2
They Asked for It 1939,Je 30,17:4
Second Fiddle 1939,Jl 1,11:2
In Name Only 1939,Ag 4,11:3
Unexpected Father 1939,Ag 11,12:2
Exile Express 1939,Ag 16,21:3
Drums Along the Mohawk 1939,N 4,11:2
Hunchback of Notre Dame, The 1940,Ja 1,29:2
Remember the Night 1940,Ja 18,27:2
He Married his Wife 1940,Ja 20,11:2
Alias the Deacon 1940,My 14,27:5
Our Town 1940,Je 14,25:3
Maryland 1940,Jl 13,16:5
Three Faces West 1940,Ag 19,13:2
Girl From God's Country 1940,S 9,18:5
Golden Fleecing, The 1940,N 7,33:4
Santa Fe Trail 1940,D 21,21:2
She Couldn't Say No 1941,Ja 17,21:3
Tobacco Road 1941,F 21,16:2
So Ends our Night 1941,F 28,17:2
Lady From Cheyenne 1941,Ap 18,18:2
Moon Over Miami 1941,Jl 5,14:2
Man at Large 1941,O 11,21:4
Look Who's Laughing 1941,D 25,33:2
Pacific Blackout 1942,Ja 15,25:2
Remarkable Andrew, The 1942,Mr 6,17:2
Night Before the Divorce, The 1942,Ap 10,21:3
Juke Girl 1942,Je 20,9:2

Chartoff, Robert (Producer)
Point Blank 1967,S 19,53:1
Split, The 1968,N 5,55:2

Chartrand, Lois
Great Missouri Raid, The 1951,Ap 9,31:2
Place in the Sun, A 1951,Ag 29,20:1

Charvey, Marcel
Claudine 1940,Ap 1,15:2
Desperate Decision 1954,N 9,31:5

Chase, Alden
Right to Romance, The 1933,D 15,28:2
Madame Spy 1934,F 10,20:1
Carolina 1934,F 16,17:2
Little Colonel, The 1935,Mr 22,26:2
Fighting Youth 1935,N 2,13:3
Millions in the Air 1935,D 12,33:4
Forty Naughty Girls 1937,S 18,15:3
Heart of Arizona 1938,Ap 16,17:1
Under Western Stars 1938,Je 25,7:3

Chase, Alden— Cont
East Side Kids 1940,F 19,21:6
Ghost Creeps, The 1940,Ag 19,13:3

Chase, Barrie
Mardi Gras 1958,N 19,45:2
George Raft Story, The 1962,Mr 22,40:1
Cape Fear 1962,Ap 19,35:2
It's a Mad, Mad, Mad, Mad World 1963,N 19,47:1

Chase, Borden (Original Author)
Under Pressure 1935,F 4,11:3
Devil's Party, The 1938,My 31,8:3
Dr Broadway 1942,Je 25,27:3
Navy Comes Through, The 1942,N 12,30:3
Fighting Seabees, The 1944,Mr 20,14:2
This Man's Navy 1945,Ap 16,18:6
I've Always Loved You 1946,S 7,11:1
Red River 1948,O 1,31:2
Man From Colorado 1949,Ja 21,24:3
Lone Star 1952,F 2,11:4
Vera Cruz 1954,D 27,22:4
Gunfighters of Casa Grande 1965,S 2,36:1

Chase, Borden (Screenwriter)
Under Pressure 1935,F 4,11:3
Destroyer 1943,S 2,15:3
Fighting Seabees, The 1944,Mr 20,14:2
This Man's Navy 1945,Ap 16,18:6
Flame of Barbary Coast 1945,My 28,22:2
I've Always Loved You 1946,S 7,11:1
Tycoon 1947,D 26,22:6
Red River 1948,O 1,31:2
Montana 1950,F 4,9:2
Winchester 73 1950,Je 8,38:2
Great Jewel Robber, The 1950,Ag 4,13:2
Iron Man 1951,Ag 20,14:2
Lone Star 1952,F 2,11:4
Bend of the River 1952,Ap 10,37:1
World in His Arms, The 1952,O 10,21:2
Sea Devils 1953,Jl 31,11:5
His Majesty O'Keefe 1954,F 6,17:2
Far Country, The 1955,F 14,24:2
Man Without a Star 1955,Mr 25,19:3
Backlash 1956,Ap 21,11:2
Night Passage 1957,Jl 25,28:1
Gunfighters of Casa Grande 1965,S 2,36:1

Chase, Charlie
Sons of the Desert 1934,Ja 12,29:3
Kelly the Second 1936,O 3,21:2
When Comedy Was King 1960,Mr 30,42:1
Days of Thrills and Laughter 1961,Mr 22,37:1
Laurel and Hardy's Laughing 20's 1965,N 18,55:2
Further Perils of Laurel and Hardy, The 1968,Ap 1,56:6

Chase, Charlie (Miscellaneous)
Fight Pest, The 1929,D 17,28:7

Chase, Chaz
Start Cheering 1938,Mr 17,17:3
Man on the Eiffel Tower, The 1950,Ja 30,12:2
I Love, You Love 1962,N 10,16:2

Chase, Clarence
Man From Colorado 1949,Ja 21,24:3

Chase, Colin
Iron Horse, The 1924,Ag 29,6:1
Big News 1929,O 7,22:1
Renegades 1930,N 8,21:3

Chase, Duane
Sound of Music, The 1965,Mr 3,34:1

Chase, Frank
Red Ball Express 1952,My 30,11:2
Saskatchewan 1954,Mr 11,26:2
Man Without a Star 1955,Mr 25,19:3

Chase, Ilka
Why Leave Home 1929,S 16,30:1
Paris Bound 1929,S 21,17:1
South Sea Rose 1929,D 7,19:3
Let's Go Places 1930,Mr 1,23:1
Florodora Girl, The 1930,My 31,19:4
On Your Back 1930,S 15,29:3
Fast and Loose 1930,D 1,21:1
Free Love 1930,D 15,29:1
Once a Sinner 1931,Ja 17,23:1
Gay Diplomat, The 1931,O 10,20:4
Animal Kingdom, The 1932,D 30,14:2
Soak the Rich 1936,F 5,14:2
Lady Consents, The 1936,F 6,23:4
Stronger Than Desire 1939,Je 30,17:3
Now, Voyager 1942,O 23,25:3
No Time for Love 1943,D 2,30:1
Miss Tatlock's Millions 1948,N 25,47:2
It Should Happen to You 1954,Ja 16,10:5
Johnny Dark 1954,Je 26,7:2
Big Knife, The 1955,N 9,41:2
Ocean's Eleven 1960,Ag 11,19:1

Chase, James Hadley (Miscellaneous)
Night of the Generals, The 1967,F 3,38:1

Chase, James Hadley (Original Author)
No Orchids for Miss Blandish 1951,F 23,33:2
Lucky Nick Cain 1951,Ap 23,21:2
There's Always a Price Tag 1958,My 26,25:2
Man in the Raincoat, The 1958,Jl 15,21:2
What Price Murder 1958,N 11,26:1
Young Girls Beware 1959,Ag 22,8:2
World in my Pocket, The 1962,My 10,30:2
Eva 1965,Je 5,21:2

Chase, Mary C (Original Author)
Harvey 1950,D 22,19:1
Bernardine 1957,Jl 25,28:1
Chase, Mary C (Screenwriter)
Harvey 1950,D 22,19:1
Chase, Patricia (Original Author)
Gunfighters of Casa Grande 1965,S 2,36:1
Chase, Patricia (Screenwriter)
Gunfighters of Casa Grande 1965,S 2,36:1
Chase, Stanley (Producer)
Hell With Heroes, The 1968,S 3,54:2
Chase, Stephen
Bad Boy 1949,Mr 23,35:2
Belle le Grand 1951,My 18,34:6
Cavalry Scout 1951,Je 8,32:2
My Favorite Spy 1951,D 26,19:3
When Worlds Collide 1952,F 7,30:2
No Room for the Groom 1952,Je 14,12:2
Stop, You're Killing Me 1952,D 11,45:3
Hiawatha 1952,D 26,20:4
Great Sioux Uprising, The 1953,Jl 18,6:2
Buccaneer, The 1958,D 24,00:0
Appointment With a Shadow 1959,Ja 8,24:2
Chasen, Dave
Rain or Shine 1930,Ag 8,11:1
Millions in the Air 1935,D 12,33:4
Chatburn, Jean
No More Ladies 1935,Je 22,18:5
Great Ziegfeld, The 1936,Ap 9,21:2
Bad Guy 1937,Ag 26,25:2
Dramatic School 1938,D 9,31:2
Chater, Geoffrey
Cosmic Monster, The 1959,Ja 1,38:1
Chatterjee, Anil
Devi 1962,O 8,19:1
Two Daughters (The Postman); Postman, The
(Two Daughters) 1963,My 1,35:1
Mahanagar; Big City, The 1964,S 28,19:1
Kanchenjungha 1966,Jl 26,27:2
Big City, The; Mahanager 1967,Je 30,30:1
Chatterjee, Haran
Mahanagar; Big City, The 1964,S 28,19:1
Chatterjee, Soumitra
World of Apu; Apur Sansar 1960,O 5,45:1
Devi 1962,O 8,19:1
Two Daughters (The Conclusion); Conclusion, The
(Two Daughters) 1963,My 1,35:1
Charulata 1965,S 11,16:1
Chatterton, Ruth
Sins of the Fathers 1929,Ja 28,21:1
Doctor's Secret, The 1929,F 4,20:1
Dummy, The 1929,Mr 4,20:2
Madame X 1929,Ap 25,32:3
Charming Sinners 1929,Jl 8,17:3
Laughing Lady, The 1930,Ja 4,21:1
Sarah and Son 1930,Mr 13,22:4
Paramount on Parade 1930,Ap 21,20:4
Lady of Scandal, The 1930,Je 14,9:4
Anybody's Woman 1930,Ag 16,8:3
Right to Love, The 1931,Ja 2,25:1
Unfaithful 1931,Mr 7,17:2
Magnificent Lie, The 1931,Jl 25,11:6
Once a Lady 1931,N 9,22:4
Tomorrow and Tomorrow 1932,Ja 30,13:2
Rich are Always With Us, The 1932,My 16,19:5
Crash, The 1932,S 9,17:5
Frisco Jenny 1933,Ja 7,11:2
Lilly Turner 1933,Je 15,21:2
Female 1933,N 4,18:3
Journal of a Crime 1934,Ap 28,11:3
Lady of Secrets 1936,F 22,12:1
Girls' Dormitory 1936,Ag 29,16:2
Dodsworth 1936,S 24,29:1
Rat, The 1938,F 28,19:1
Chatterton, Thomas
Fight to the Finish, A 1937,Je 26,20:2 (In
Addenda)
Chatterton, Tom
Under Western Stars 1938,Je 25,7:3
Smash-Up, The Story of a Woman
1947,Ap 11,31:2
Chatterton, Vivienne
Dinner at the Ritz 1937,D 4,21:1
Chatto, Tom
Oscar Wilde 1960,Je 21,28:2
Chattopadaya, Harlendernath
Householder, The 1963,O 22,43:2
Chau, Vo Doan
Quiet American, The 1958,F 6,24:1
Chauffard, Jacquest-Rene
Blood and Roses 1961,O 12,41:4
Chaumette, Francois
Night Affair 1961,O 13,27:1
Chautard, Emile
Bardelys The Magnificent 1926,N 1,28:1 (In
Addenda)
Flaming Forest, The 1926,N 22,28:3
Blonde or Brunette 1927,Ja 11,18:2
Seventh Heaven 1927,My 26,22:1
Love Mart, The 1927,D 26,16:6
We're in the Air Now 1927,D 31,31:1
His Tiger Lady 1928,My 28,23:2
Lilac Time 1928,Ag 4,7:2

Out of the Ruins 1928,Ag 20,21:3
Caught in the Fog 1928,D 4,29:1
Adoration 1929,Ja 14,20:1
Marianne 1929,O 19,22:6
Man From Wyoming, A 1930,Jl 12,16:4
Enigmatique Monsieur Parkes, L' 1930,S 2,19:3
Road to Reno, The 1931,O 10,20:4
Cock of the Air 1932,Ja 25,20:3
Shanghai Express 1932,F 18,25:3
Man From Yesterday, The 1932,Je 25,18:2
Design for Living 1933,N 23,24:2
Man of Two Worlds 1934,Ja 12,29:2
Chautard, Emile (Director)
Under the Greenwood Tree 1918,D 9,11:4
Out of the Shadow 1919,Ja 13,9:3
Marriage Price, The 1919,Mr 17,13:2
Black Panther's Cub, The 1921,My 30,12:5
Chauvel, Charles (Director)
Uncivilized 1937,N 17,27:4
Forty Thousand Horsemen 1941,Ag 15,13:2
Rugged O'Riordans, The 1950,Ja 6,25:2
Rats of Tobruk, The 1951,My 24,47:3
Jedda the Uncivilized 1957,F 28,18:7
Chauvel, Charles (Original Author)
Uncivilized 1937,N 17,27:4
Jedda the Uncivilized 1957,F 28,18:7
Chauvel, Charles (Producer)
Forty Thousand Horsemen 1941,Ag 15,13:2
Rugged O'Riordans, The 1950,Ja 6,25:2
Rats of Tobruk, The 1951,My 24,47:3
Jedda the Uncivilized 1957,F 28,18:7
Chauvel, Charles (Screenwriter)
Forty Thousand Horsemen 1941,Ag 15,13:2
Rugged O'Riordans, The 1950,Ja 6,25:2
Chauvel, Elsa (Original Author)
Jedda the Uncivilized 1957,F 28,18:7
Chauvel, Elsa (Screenwriter)
Rugged O'Riordans, The 1950,Ja 6,25:2
Chauvin, Lilyan
Perfect Furlough, The 1959,Ja 22,27:4
Chauvire, Yvette
Ballerina 1938,N 15,27:1
Neapolitan Carousel 1961,O 12,41:3
Chaux, Robert
Merlusse 1938,Mr 17,17:2
Chavance, Louis (Miscellaneous)
Lover's Return, A; Revenant, Le 1948,Ja 26,15:2
Corbeau, Le; Raven, The 1948,F 24,21:1
Chavance, Louis (Original Author)
Thirteenth Letter, The 1951,F 22,27:2
Chavance, Louis (Screenwriter)
Corbeau, Le; Raven, The 1948,F 24,21:1
Marie du Port 1951,Jl 24,21:2
Chavane, Francois (Producer)
Back to the Wall; (Dos au Mur) 1959,S 8,43:2
Chavchavadze, T
Keto and Kote 1954,Ap 5,21:4
Chavdar, E
Cossack Beyond the Danube, A 1954,F 8,18:5
Chave, Kotti
Ungdom Av I Dag 1936,Je 23,27:7
Sara Laer Sig Folkvett 1938,F 16,17:1
John Ericsson Victor of Hampton Roads
1938,My 18,17:2
Med Folket Foer Fosterlandet 1939,F 21,14:2
Chavers, Rudolph
Gambling Ship 1939,Ja 21,19:2
Chavez, Jose
Adventures of Robinson Crusoe, The
1954,Ag 6,10:5
Professionals, The 1966,N 3,45:1
Guns for San Sebastian 1968,Mr 21,57:2
Chavez, Velazquez (Original Author)
Wave, The 1937,Ap 21,18:1
Chayefsky, Paddy (Original Author)
As Young as You Feel 1951,Ag 3,10:6
Marty 1955,Ap 12,25:3
Catered Affair, The 1956,Je 15,32:4
Bachelor Party, The 1957,Ap 10,37:2
Goddess, The 1958,Je 25,24:1
Middle of the Night 1959,Je 18,36:1
Chayefsky, Paddy (Screenwriter)
Marty 1955,Ap 12,25:3
Bachelor Party, The 1957,Ap 10,37:2
Middle of the Night 1959,Je 18,36:1
Americanization of Emily, The 1964,O 28,51:1
Cheaney, Loia
Footloose Heiress 1937,O 9,16:2
Women Are Like That 1938,Ap 11,12:2
Beloved Brat 1938,My 2,13:2
Torchy Gets her Man 1938,N 18,25:3
Cheavens, Martha (Original Author)
Penny Serenade 1941,My 23,25:2
Sunday Dinner for a Soldier 1945,Ja 25,16:2
Cheban, A I
Lower Depths, The 1947,D 1,27:2
Chebat, Georges
Son of the Sahara, A 1924,My 27,14:1
Checchi, Andrea
Schoolgirl Diary 1947,O 18,9:2
Tragic Hunt 1948,O 22,30:2
Earth Cries Out, The; Grido Della Terra, Il
1949,Ag 31,26:2

Checchi, Andrea— Cont
Walls of Malapaga, The 1950,Mr 21,34:2
Tears of Blood 1952,Ja 19,13:2
Paolo and Francesca 1953,F 14,8:3
Times Gone By (Less Than a (Day)
1953,D 30,16:2
House of Ricordi 1956,Mr 13,32:1
Black Sunday 1961,Mr 9,23:1
Italiano Brava Gente 1966,F 4,20:1
Checco, Al
Hotel 1967,Ja 20,27:1
Chechotkina, Natasha
Summer to Remember, A; (Seryozha)
1961,N 7,38:1
Chechova, Olga
Eternal Mask, The 1937,Ja 13,20:3
Checker, Chubby
Twist Around the Clock 1962,Ja 27,13:4
Don't Knock the Twist 1962,Ap 14,14:2
Chee-Ak
Igloo 1932,Jl 21,15:2
Checka
Silent Enemy, The 1930,My 20,32:3
Cheetah (Monkey)
Tarzan Escapes 1936,N 20,27:2
Cheetham, Robert
Born Free 1966,Je 23,29:1
Cheever, John (Original Author)
Swimmer, The 1968,My 16,53:1
Chefe, Jack
It's a Pleasure 1945,My 4,23:3
Cheff, Andre
Red Inn, The 1954,Je 8,25:2
Cheirel, Micheline
Kermesse Heroique, La 1936,S 23,29:1
They Were Five 1938,Je 1,19:5
Hold Back the Dawn 1941,O 2,29:1
Ces Dames aux Chapeaux Verts; Ladies in the
Green Hats, The 1945,Ap 5,26:2
Cornered 1945,D 26,15:1
So Dark the Night 1946,D 7,16:2
Jewels of Brandenburg 1947,My 24,10:5
Chejnacka, Jadwige
First Start, The 1953,F 2,17:3
Chekan, S
Devotion 1955,Ag 1,15:2
Wrestler and the Clown, The 1959,Ja 1,38:1
Chekayevski, A
Lonely White Sail 1938,My 7,18:1
Chekhikvadze, R
Dragonfly, The 1955,Je 27,18:2
Chekhov, Anton (Original Author)
Summer Storm 1944,O 23,14:3
Jubilee 1945,F 22,31:3
Marriage 1945,F 22,31:3
Anna Cross, The 1954,O 25,30:7
Safety Match, The 1955,Mr 28,24:5
Ladies 1955,Je 27,18:2
Grasshopper, The 1956,Ap 23,22:1
Lady With the Dog, The 1962,N 7,48:1
Steppe, The 1963,O 1,33:1
Duel, The 1964,S 7,11:2
House With an Attic 1964,D 21,42:5
Sea Gull, The 1968,D 24,14:1
Chekhov, Michael
Song of Russia 1944,F 11,17:2
In our Time 1944,F 12,11:2
Spellbound 1945,N 2,22:2
Specter of the Rose 1946,S 2,12:4
Cross my Heart 1946,D 19,42:3
Abie's Irish Rose 1946,D 23,19:4
Invitation 1952,Ja 30,22:6
Holiday for Sinners 1952,S 20,13:2
Rhapsody 1954,Mr 12,17:1
Chekin, P
Tsar's Bride, The 1966,Mr 12,13:2
Chekmarov, V
Lust for Gold 1958,Jl 24,18:1
Chekoerski, V
Hamlet 1966,Mr 16,48:1
Chekova, Olga
Moulin Rouge 1929,Ap 30,33:2
Pawns of Passion 1929,My 27,22:1
His Late Excellency 1929,Je 11,27:2
City of Temptation 1929,S 2,16:1
Chelieu, Arman (Director)
Toast to Love 1951,N 7,35:5
Chelieu, Arman (Screenwriter)
Toast to Love 1951,N 7,35:5
Chelimsky, Kathy
Two for the Road 1967,Ap 28,36:2
Chelimsky, Thomas
Charade 1963,D 6,40:1
Chellini, Amelia
Passa L'Amore 1933,N 25,10:3
Fiat Voluntas Dei 1936,Jl 6,11:5
Eravamo Sette Vedove; We Were Seven Widows
1940,F 16,23:4
Chemodurov, A
Dream of a Cossack 1952,F 18,15:2
Vasili's Return 1953,S 28,21:4
Chen, Lin
Satan Never Sleeps 1962,F 22,20:1

Chen, Lo (Director)
Shepherd Girl, The 1965,S 2,36:3
Chen, Silan
South Sea Sinner 1950,Ja 16,18:4
Chenal, Pierre (Director)
Crime et Chatiment; Crime and Punishment
  1935,N 13,25:3
Late Mathias Pascal, The 1937,N 18,27:2
Alibi, L' 1939,Ap 10,13:3
Sirocco 1946,Ag 12,17:3
Devil and the Angel, The 1949,D 3,8:6
Scandals of Clochemerle, The 1950,Mr 28,28:2
Native Son 1951,Je 18,19:2
Sinners of Paris 1959,Ap 24,23:1
Chenal, Pierre (Screenwriter)
Devil and the Angel, The 1949,D 3,8:6
Native Son 1951,Je 18,19:2
Sinners of Paris 1959,Ap 24,23:1
Chendru
Flute and the Arrow, The 1960,O 11,55:1
CHENEY
See Also CHANEY
Cheney, J Benton (Screenwriter)
Rockin' in The Rockies 1945,Jl 5,7:2
Cheng, Y C (Director)
Fight to the Last 1938,D 22,25:3
Chepurnov, Kyril
Fortress on the Volga 1942,D 25,15:3
Cher
Good Times 1967,Ag 3,26:4
Cheredniachenko, Irina
Winner, The 1947,D 1,27:2
Cherkasova, Olga
Flying Carpet, The 1960,F 28,31:1
Cherkassov, Nikolai
Baltic Deputy 1937,S 4,8:2
Peter the First 1937,D 25,10:4
Ski Battalion 1938,Mr 14,13:1
Friends 1939,Ja 2,28:3
Untitled-Capt Grant's Children 1939,Ja 12,23:3
Captain Grant's Children 1939,Ja 12,23:3
Man With the Gun, The 1939,Ja 30,9:3
Alexander Nevsky 1939,Mr 23,27:1
Lenin in 1918 1939,Je 27,27:2
Conquests of Peter The Great, The
  1939,Ag 24,17:2
General Suvorov 1941,S 20,11:2
Ivan the Terrible, Part I 1947,Mr 10,25:2
In the Name of Life 1947,O 20,29:2
Spring 1948,Mr 15,26:2
First Front, The 1949,N 14,19:2
Ivan Pavlov 1950,F 13,15:2
Mussorgsky 1951,Ag 20,14:3
Rimsky-Korsakov 1954,Mr 1,16:3
Ivan the Terrible, Part II 1959,N 25,22:4
Don Quixote 1961,Ja 21,18:1
Cherkose, Eddie (Composer)
Under Western Stars 1938,Je 25,7:3
Rose of the Rio Grande 1938,Jl 9,10:3
Rookies on Parade 1941,My 22,25:2
Crazy House 1943,D 16,33:3
Cherkose, Eddie (Miscellaneous)
New Faces of 1937 1937,Jl 2,25:1
Music for Madame 1937,O 23,14:1
Cherkovalenko, G
Paris Commune 1937,Je 2,20:4
Cherney, Linda
Screaming Mimi 1958,Je 26,23:3
Cherniavsky, Josef (Miscellaneous)
We Americans 1928,Mr 29,25:3
Show Boat 1929,Ap 18,32:3
Chernov, M
Road to Life 1956,Je 11,26:6
Chernova, Tamara
Horsemen, The 1951,Ja 29,14:5
Chernovolenko, G
Skanderbeg 1954,Jl 5,6:4
Chernus, Sonia (Original Author)
Big Fix, The 1947,My 3,10:3
Cheron, Andre
Marriage Clause, The 1926,S 28,30:2
Evening Clothes 1927,Mr 21,10:4
Magic Flame, The 1927,S 19,30:3
Rose of the Golden West 1927,S 26,27:1
4 Devils 1928,O 4,26:3
His Private Life 1928,N 12,18:2
True Heaven 1929,F 11,26:3
They Had to See Paris 1929,O 12,11:1
Enigmatique Monsieur Parkes, L' 1930,S 2,19:3
Sea Legs 1930,N 11,29:1
Man of the World 1931,Mr 21,15:1
I Like Your Nerve 1931,S 12,15:4
Black Cat, The 1934,My 19,18:4
Girl From 10th Avenue, The 1935,My 27,20:6
Artists and Models Abroad 1938,D 22,25:3
Cherrill, Virginia
Girls Demand Excitement 1931,F 7,11:1
City Lights 1931,F 7,11:1
Brat, The 1931,Ag 24,13:4
Delicious 1931,D 26,15:5
Fast Workers 1933,Mr 20,18:2
Nuisance, The 1933,My 29,22:2
Charlie Chan's Greatest Case 1933,O 7,18:4

White Heat 1934,Je 16,20:2
Cherrington, Ruth
Caught in the Fog 1928,D 4,29:1
Lone Wolf's Daughter, The 1929,Mr 4,20:2
Cherry, Helen
Adam and Evelyn 1950,My 12,33:4
Last Holiday 1950,N 14,39:4
Operation Disaster 1951,Ja 15,13:1
Her Panelled Door 1951,Ag 28,18:2
Young Wives' Tale 1952,N 4,33:1
Castle in the Air 1953,Ja 5,19:2
Three Cases of Murder (Lord Mountdrago); Lord
  Mountdrago (Three Cases of Murder)
  1955,Mr 16,39:4
His Excellency 1956,F 2,19:3
Naked Edge 1961,Jl 1,9:1
Flipper's New Adventure 1964,Ag 27,28:2
Cherry, Robert
Vicious Circle, The 1948,Jl 22,27:2
Traveling Saleswoman 1950,Ja 6,25:3
Cherryman, Rex
Madame Peacock 1920,O 25,18:1
Chertok, Jack (Producer)
Kid Glove Killer 1942,Ap 17,21:4
Eyes in the Night 1942,O 16,23:1
Northern Pursuit 1943,N 26,29:2
Conspirators, The 1944,O 21,15:2
Corn is Green, The 1945,Mr 30,18:2
Strange Woman, The 1947,F 24,16:4
Dishonored Lady 1947,My 24,10:5
Cherviakof, Evgeny (Director)
Prisoners 1937,F 20,9:2
Chesebro, George
Sky Spider, The 1931,Ag 31,11:5
Lawless Nineties, The 1936,Je 29,11:1
Cheshire, Harry
If I'm Lucky 1946,S 20,41:3
Invisible Wall, The 1947,N 1,11:2
16 Fathoms Deep 1948,O 7,35:2
Moonrise 1949,Mr 7,17:2
Sand 1949,Ag 5,23:2
Brimstone 1949,O 7,35:3
No Sad Songs for Me 1950,Ap 28,26:2
Woman on Pier 13, The 1950,Je 16,28:4
Phone Call From a Stranger 1952,F 2,11:2
Sniper, The 1952,My 10,16:3
Dangerous Mission 1954,Mr 6,13:5
Chesnakov, Alex
Man in a Cocked Hat 1960,Je 15,50:2
Chesnakov, Lexis
Never Let Me Go 1953,Je 11,37:2
Chesney, Arthur
French Leave 1931,D 7,16:1
Fires of Fate 1933,Ap 3,13:4
Girl in the Street 1938,My 26,31:2
Chessnokov, V
Professor Mamlock 1938,N 8,26:2
Chester, Alfred
Miracle in Harlem 1949,Q 24,19:4
Chester, Alma
Beloved Bachelor, The 1931,O 17,20:1
Dude Ranger, The 1934,O 2,18:5
Chester, Betty
Co-Optimists, The 1930,F 5,27:2
Be Mine Tonight 1933,Ap 14,22:5
Chester, C L (Producer)
Kaieteur, The Perfect Cataract 1918,Ap 22,9:1
Training Eve 1919,N 17,20:1
Chester, George Randolph (Original Author)
My Man 1924,F 11,18:3
Soft Cushions 1927,S 12,29:1
New Adventures of Get-Rich-Quick Wallingford
  1931,O 10,20:4
Chester, George Randolph (Producer)
Black Beauty 1921,F 21,16:1
Chester, George Randolph Mrs (Producer)
Black Beauty 1921,F 21,16:1
Chester, Hal (Producer)
Beast From 20,000 Fathoms, The 1953,Je 25,23:1
Chester, Hal E (Original Author)
Joe Palooka, Champ 1946,Ap 6,10:6
Crashout 1955,Jl 9,9:2
Chester, Hal E (Producer)
Joe Palooka, Champ 1946,Ap 6,10:6
Underworld Story, The 1950,Jl 27,29:4
Models, Inc 1952,My 26,18:4
Crashout 1955,Jl 9,9:2
Bold and the Brave, The 1956,My 26,15:2
School for Scoundrels 1960,Jl 12,39:1
Hide and Seek 1964,Mr 12,40:3
Secret War of Harry Frigg, The 1968,Mr 5,34:5
Double Man, The 1968,My 2,57:1
Chester, Hal E (Screenwriter)
School for Scoundrels 1960,Jl 12,39:1
Chester, Hally
Little Tough Guy 1938,Ag 18,23:3
Juvenile Court 1938,S 12,13:2
Little Tough Guys in Society 1938,N 21,14:4
Newsboys' Home 1939,Ja 23,8:2
Ghost Creeps, The 1940,Ag 19,13:3
Chester (Producer)
Mountaineering Memory, A 1918,My 13,11:3
Coorial on the Orinoco, A 1918,My 20,11:3

Chester (Producer) — Cont
Untitled-Travel, Patamona 1918,My 27,11:3
Zuni Kicking Race, A 1918,Je 24,9:1
Dam Catastrophe, A 1918,Jl 1,9:3
Unblazed Trail, The 1918,Jl 15,9:3
Pin Feather Picitaninnies 1918,Ag 19,7:1
Finest on Four Feet 1918,S 16,9:3
Ballahooing on the Anarika 1919,Mr 17,13:2
Wasmanipae Week-End, A 1919,Ap 7,11:5
Up in the Air After Alligators 1919,Ap 14,11:4
Cameraing Through Africa 1919,Ap 21,13:4
Mr Outing Floats a Dream 1919,My 5,11:1
Itasca Makes Her Bow 1919,My 19,20:5
Wrangling Dudes 1919,Je 9,16:3
Mr Outing Climbs Aboard 1919,Je 30,16:3
Getting the Cassiar's Goat 1919,Jl 7,18:5
Haitian Night Tale 1919,Jl 21,12:3
Put Your Cares on Ice 1919,Jl 28,8:5
Japanese Study, A 1919,Ag 11,9:1
Untitled-Travel, South America 1920,F 23,11:2
Some Speed to Surago 1920,Mr 8,9:5
Some Speed to Surago 1920,Mr 8,9:6
Pigs and Kava 1920,My 24,20:3
Some More Samoa 1920,Jl 26,9:5
Lovely Maoriland 1920,N 1,13:2
Tray Full of Trouble, A 1920,N 22,13:3
Lost a Yodel 1920,D 27,11:3
Last Hope, The 1921,O 3,16:2
Cheta (Chimp)
Tarzan's Fight for Life 1958,Ag 16,10:2
Cheta (Chimpanzee)
Tarzan and the Huntress 1947,Ap 7,20:4
Chetham-Strode, Warren (Original Author)
Edge of Divorce 1954,Jl 2,10:1
Chetham-Strode, Warren (Screenwriter)
Abdul the Damned 1936,My 11,16:2
Odette 1951,Mr 28,33:2
Edge of Divorce 1954,Jl 2,10:1
Chetvrikov, Victor
Lullaby, The 1961,My 15,35:2
Chevalier, Louise
Up From the Beach 1965,Je 10,38:1
Chevalier, Maurice
Innocents of Paris 1929,Ap 27,16:5
Chason de Paris, La; Innocents of Paris
  1929,Ag 25,VIII,5:1
Love Parade, The 1929,N 20,32:6
Love Parade, The 1930,Mr 23,IX,6:1
Paramount on Parade 1930,Ap 21,20:4
Big Pond, The 1930,My 19,21:1
Playboy of Paris 1930,N 1,23:2
Petit Cafe, Le 1931,Ja 25,VIII,5:6 (In Addenda)
Smiling Lieutenant, The 1931,My 23,13:4
One Hour with You 1932,Mr 24,17:5
Love Me Tonight 1932,Ag 19,20:6
Bedtime Story, A 1933,Ap 20,20:3
Way to Love, The 1933,N 11,10:3
Way to Love, The 1933,N 20,18:2
Merry Widow, The 1934,O 12,33:1
Folies Bergere 1935,F 25,13:2
Homme des Folies Bergere, L' 1936,Ap 18,19:3
Beloved Vagabond, The 1937,F 8,12:5
With a Smile 1939,F 6,8:4
Man of the Hour, The 1940,N 21,43:2
Break the News 1941,Ja 2,24:2
Personal Column 1941,F 3,13:2
Man About Town 1947,O 22,37:1
Royal Affair, A; (Roi, Le) 1950,Mr 9,25:2
Ma Pomme 1951,O 15,22:2
My Seven Little Sins 1956,My 2,27:1
Love in the Afternoon 1957,Ag 24,12:1
Gigi 1958,My 16,21:1
Count Your Blessings 1959,Ap 24,23:1
Can-Can 1960,Mr 10,36:1
Breath of Scandal, A 1960,D 17,19:1
Pepe 1960,D 22,18:1
Fanny 1961,Jl 7,16:1
Jessica 1962,Ap 20,20:2
In Search of the Castaways 1962,D 22,5:2
I'd Rather Be Rich 1964,S 3,24:2
Monkeys Go Home 1967,Mr 30,55:1
Chevalier, Maurice (Narrator)
Black Tights 1962,F 21,54:2
Chevallier, Gabriel (Original Author)
Scandals of Clochemerle, The 1950,Mr 28,28:2
Easiest Profession, The 1960,Mr 26,15:7
Chevallier, Gabriel (Screenwriter)
Scandals of Clochemerle, The 1950,Mr 28,28:2
Easiest Profession, The 1960,Mr 26,15:7
Chevance, Zanine
Loves of a Greek in Paris 1960,Ag 15,19:7
Chevane, Francois (Miscellaneous)
Back to the Wall; (Dos au Mur) 1959,S 8,43:2
Chevane, Francois (Screenwriter)
Back to the Wall; (Dos au Mur) 1959,S 8,43:2
Chevie, Edmond (Producer)
Eighteen and Anxious 1957,D 14,16:6
Chevigny, Hector (Screenwriter)
You Can't Escape Forever 1942,O 17,11:1
Chevillat, Dick (Miscellaneous)
She Gets her Man 1945,F 9,20:5
Chevrement, Sexto
Romance Tropical 1934,O 15,20:5

Chevret, Lita
Kept Husbands 1931,Mr 24,31:2
Girl Crazy 1932,Mr 25,23:3
Ladies of the Jury 1932,Ap 2,13:2
Symphony of Six Million 1932,Ap 15,23:1
Daring Daughters 1933,Mr 25,13:4
Goldie Gets Along 1933,Je 3,16:4

Chevrier, Jean
Paris Frills 1946,N 25,38:3
Souvenir 1950,O 3,34:4
Of Love and Bandits 1953,Ja 17,12:4
Doctors, The 1956,Ag 7,19:2

Chevron, John
Goliath and the Sins of Babylon 1964,Mr 5,36:2

Chew, Frank
Shanghai Bound 1927,N 7,26:4
Chinatown Nights 1929,Ap 1,22:1

Chew, Richard (Miscellaneous)
Have You Heard of the San Francisco Mime
Troup? 1968,Je 28,37:1

Cheyko, George (Producer)
Don't Tempt the Devil 1964,Ap 28,43:1

Cheyney, Peter (Original Author)
Diplomatic Courier 1952,Je 14,12:2

Chi, Greta
Fathom 1967,D 14,62:1

Chi, Lo
Empress Wu 1965,Mr 16,42:2

Chi, Penn
Seven Hills of Rome 1958,Ja 28,24:2 (Incorrect
in this edition; use 1958,Ja 31,24:2 elsewhere)

Chi-ching, Yang
Last Woman of Shang, The 1964,D 15,56:2
Love Eterne, The; Liang Shan Po and Chu
Ying-lai 1965,Ja 16,14:1
Lady General, The 1965,F 12,19:1
Shepherd Girl, The 1965,S 2,36:3

Chiaki, Minoru
Rasho-Mon 1951,D 27,18:3
Magnificent Seven, The 1956,N 20,46:2
Hidden Fortress The 1962,Ja 24,24:2
Lower Depths, The 1962,F 10,12:5
Idiot, The 1963,My 1,35:1

Chiantoni, Renato
Barefoot Contessa, The 1954,S 30,37:1

Chiari, Vito
Peddlin' in Society 1950,F 23,33:3

Chiari, Walter
I Cadetti di Guascogna 1952,O 6,22:2
Bellissima 1953,My 18,26:2
O K Nero 1953,Je 20,8:6
Lucky Five, The 1953,N 27,22:5
Moment of Truth, The 1954,Ap 27,36:2
Nana 1957,Ap 13,12:3
Little Hut, The 1957,My 4,25:1
Bonjour Tristesse 1958,Ja 16,32:1
Premier May 1958,S 17,44:2
Of Life and Love 1958,O 7,40:2
Pepote 1958,D 2,46:1
Day in Court, A 1963,My 11,15:2
Falstaff; Chimes at Midnight 1967,Mr 18,19:2
Made in Italy 1967,My 1,44:2
Sucker, The 1967,O 9,61:1

Chiarini, Luigi (Screenwriter)
Indiscretion of an American Wife 1954,Je 26,7:2

Chiatsintova, S
Vow, The 1947,Je 23,14:3

Chiaureli, M (Director)
They Wanted Peace 1940,Ja 8,11:3
Vow, The 1947,Je 23,14:3
Fall of Berlin 1952,Je 9,19:2

Chiaureli, M (Original Author)
They Wanted Peace 1940,Ja 8,11:3

Chiaureli, M (Screenwriter)
Vow, The 1947,Je 23,14:3
Fall of Berlin 1952,Je 9,19:2

Chiba, Sachiko
Kimiko 1937,Ap 13,31:3

Chiba, Yasuki (Director)
Different Sons 1964,F 13,25:1
Honolulu-Tokyo-Hong Kong 1964,S 2,33:3

Chibbius, Nikolai
Road Home, The 1947,My 2,28:3

Chicarell, Lokelani S
Hawaii 1966,O 11,54:1

Chichay
No Man is an Island 1962,O 11,49:2

Chichester, Emily
Nugget Nell 1919,Jl 28,8:5
Nobody Home 1919,Ag 25,8:5
School for Wives 1925,Ap 1,21:3

Chichinadze, D
Dragonfly, The 1955,Je 27,18:2

Chief Big Tree
Susannah of the Mounties 1939,Je 24,13:2

Chieh, Jen
Love Eterne, The; Liang Shan Po and Chu
Ying-lai 1965,Ja 16,14:1

Chiffre, Yvan
Anatomy of a Marriage; My Days With Jean
Marc; My Nights With Francoise
1964,O 27,42:2

Chih-chiang, Hsu (Cinematographer)
China 1965,My 26,41:1

Chikamatsu, Monzaemon (Screenwriter)
Prodigal Son 1964,Ja 30,24:3 (Incorrect in this
edition; use 1964,Ja 31,16:1 elsewhere)

Chikhladze, M
They Wanted Peace 1940,Ja 8,11:3

Chikvindize, Nani
Stepchildren 1962,Jl 2,22:2

Chikvinidze, K
Magdana's Donkey 1958,Ja 27,21:7

Child, Jeremy
Privilege 1967,Jl 25,30:2

Child, Richard Washburn (Original Author)
Hellotrope 1920,N 29,20:3
Forgotten Faces 1928,Ag 6,15:2
Forgotten Faces 1936,Jl 4,18:2
Gentleman After Dark, A 1942,Ap 17,21:2
Tokyo File 212 1951,Je 1,20:7

Childers, Naomi
Lord and Lady Algy 1919,S 29,16:1
Earthbound 1920,Ag 11,9:4
Success 1923,Jl 10,22:5
Virtuous Liars 1924,Mr 31,20:1
White Heat 1934,Je 16,20:2

Childress, Alvin
Anna Lucasta 1959,Ja 15,27:1
Man in the Net, The 1959,Je 11,36:2

Childs, Gilbert
Co-Optimists, The 1930,F 5,27:2

Childs, Herbert (Original Author)
Way of a Gaucho 1952,N 5,36:2

Chiles, George
King of Jazz 1930,My 3,23:1

Chiles, Linden
Rage to Live, A 1965,O 21,97:1
Counterpoint 1968,Mr 14,51:2

Chili, G W (Director)
Ten Commandments, The 1958,Ap 7,26:1

Chilikin, Andrei
Chuk and Gek 1953,D 21,27:4

Chilton & Thomas
Love and Hisses 1938,Ja 1,11:1

Chimpanzee
Jungle Siren 1942,O 10,11:3
Tarzan and the Lost Safari 1957,Ap 13,12:3

Chin, To (Screenwriter)
Yang Kwei Fei 1956,S 11,41:2

Chin, Tsai
Face of Fu Manchu, The 1965,N 11,58:3
You Only Live Twice 1967,Je 14,40:1
Vengeance of Fu Manchu, The 1968,F 15,47:1

Chinacos, Trovadores
Gay Desperado, The 1936,O 9,31:4

Ching, Bo
Petticoat Fever 1936,Mr 21,13:2

Ching, William
Something in the Wind 1947,Ag 29,14:3
Wistful Widow of Wagon Gap, The
1947,N 21,36:2
D O A 1950,My 1,18:2
In a Lonely Place 1950,My 18,37:2
Surrender 1950,O 9,21:5
Oh! Susanna 1951,Mr 30,28:5
Belle le Grand 1951,My 18,34:6
Wild Blue Yonder, The 1952,Ja 2,20:1
Pat and Mike 1952,Je 19,32:6
Never Wave at a Wac 1953,Ap 24,30:2
Scared Stiff 1953,Jl 3,10:2
Moonlighter, The 1953,S 23,37:2

Ching, William Brooks
Magnificent Matador, The 1955,My 25,38:1

Chinh, Kieu
Yank in Vietnam, A 1964,F 6,36:4

Chinita
Hit Parade of 1943 1943,Ap 16,24:3

Chinn, Anthony
Satan Never Sleeps 1962,F 22,20:1

Chinpae, Paul
Sand Pebbles, The 1966,D 21,48:1

Chio, Princess
Nine Bachelors 1942,F 9,19:2

Chiocto
Flor Sylvestre 1945,Ja 16,17:2

Chiola, Sebastian
Matrero, El; Outlaw, The 1940,Mr 18,13:2
Loco Serenata, El; Crazy Musician, The
1940,Ap 22,13:2

Chionette, Carlo
Red Desert 1965,F 9,43:1

Chippman, Jan
Illiac Passion, The 1968,Ap 19,40:1

Chirello, George
Macbeth 1950,D 28,22:6

Chirkov, Boris
Youth of Maxim, The 1935,Ap 20,16:1
Return of Maxim, The 1937,N 2,33:1
Great Citizen, The 1939,Ja 16,11:2
Man With the Gun, The 1939,Ja 30,9:3
New Horizons 1939,My 12,25:3
New Teacher, The 1941,Ap 7,13:3
Great Glinka, The 1947,D 22,30:2
Miners of the Don 1951,N 12,21:2

Chirkov, Boris— Cont
True Friends 1954,N 15,33:2

Chirskov, Boris (Screenwriter)
Wings of Victory 1941,N 17,15:2
Zoya 1945,Ap 16,18:6
Turning Point, The 1946,O 28,19:4
Sisters 1959,My 25,33:2

Chisholm, Robert
Lottery Bride, The 1930,N 29,21:4
Father O'Flynn 1938,D 26,29:2

Chissell, Noble (Kid)
Ex-Champ 1939,My 12,25:3
Home in Indiana 1944,Je 22,23:1

Chistiakov, A
Men on Wings 1935,Je 11,24:5
Return of Maxim, The 1937,N 2,33:1
New Horizons 1939,My 12,25:3

Chitnis, Leela
Guide, The 1965,F 10,44:2

Chittell, Christopher
To Sir, With Love 1967,Je 15,56:1

Chitty, Erik
Day They Robbed the Bank of England, The
1960,S 5,11:2

Chiurazzi, Gaetano
Under the Sun of Rome 1949,O 6,40:4

Chiyaki
Three Stripes in the Sun 1955,N 24,41:2

Chjrkov, Boris
Dream of a Cossack 1952,F 18,15:2

Chkeidze, N
They Wanted Peace 1940,Ja 8,11:3

Chkeidze, Reza (Director)
Magdana's Donkey 1958,Ja 27,21:7
Father of a Soldier 1966,F 21,51:1

Chlud, Lola
Heilige und Ihr Narr, Die; Saint and Her Fool,
The 1935,N 29,24:2
Abduction, The 1938,Je 11,9:2

Chmara, Gregor
Rasputin 1929,O 21,30:1
Strange Case of District Attorney M, The
1930,Mr 17,20:3
Schwartze Husar, Der 1932,D 23,20:1

Chmielewski, Tadeusz (Director)
Eve Wants to Sleep 1961,Je 6,42:2

Chmielewski, Tadeusz (Screenwriter)
Eve Wants to Sleep 1961,Je 6,42:2

Chmielewski, Zygmunt
Maryjka 1934,D 3,15:2

Cho-Cho, Lim
Song of China 1936,N 10,31:3

Chobur, V
Red Tanks 1942,Je 6,9:2

Chodorov, Edward (Original Author)
Madame Du Barry 1934,O 25,26:2
Those Endearing Young Charms 1945,Je 20,26:5
Kind Lady 1951,Ag 8,21:2

Chodorov, Edward (Producer)
Rich Man, Poor Girl 1938,Ag 19,13:3
Woman Against Woman 1938,Ag 23,20:6
Spring Madness 1938,D 1,29:3
Tell no Tales 1939,Je 2,27:3
Man From Dakota, The 1940,F 22,29:2
Road House 1948,N 8,24:2

Chodorov, Edward (Screenwriter)
Yellow Jack 1938,My 20,17:2
Woman Against Woman 1938,Ag 23,20:6
Spring Madness 1938,D 1,29:3
Undercurrent 1946,N 29,36:2
Hucksters, The 1947,Jl 18,21:2
Road House 1948,N 8,24:2
Kind Lady 1951,Ag 8,21:2

Chodorov, Jerome (Original Author)
Murder in the Big House 1942,My 8,27:3
My Sister Eileen 1942,O 23,15:1
Junior Miss 1945,Je 18,15:4
My Sister Eileen 1955,S 23,21:1
Happy Anniversary 1959,N 11,41:1

CHodorov, Jerome (Screenwriter)
Case of the Lucky Legs, The 1935,N 1,25:1
Dancing Feet 1936,Mr 28,11:2

Chodorov, Jerome (Screenwriter)
Devil's Playground 1937,F 15,12:5
Reported Missing 1937,S 3,12:2
Rich Man, Poor Girl 1938,Ag 19,13:3
Conspiracy 1939,Ag 23,19:2
Mad Empress, The 1940,F 15,15:1
Two Girls on Broadway 1940,Ap 25,28:4
Dulcy 1940,N 28,28:2
Louisiana Purchase 1942,Ja 1,37:1
My Sister Eileen 1942,O 23,15:1
Those Endearing Young Charms 1945,Je 20,26:5
Man From Texas 1948,Ag 12,16:5
Happy Anniversary 1959,N 11,41:1

Chollet, Nicole
Naked Autumn 1963,N 15,25:3

Chometre, Henri (Director)
Prenez Garde a la Peinture 1935,Ag 17,18:6

Chong, Peter
Mission to Moscow 1943,Ap 30,25:2
Purple Heart, The 1944,Mr 9,15:2
To the Ends of the Earth 1948,F 13,26:2
Intrigue 1948,Ap 24,11:2

Chong, Peter— Cont
Peking Express 1951,Jl 19,20:2
South Sea Woman 1953,Je 4,33:6
Miss Sadie Thompson 1953,Je 24,9:1
Tribute to a Bad Man 1956,Mr 31,13:3
Chong, Wong Show
Lady From Shanghai, The 1948,Je 10,28:2
Chopin (Composer)
Ballerina 1938,N 15,27:1
Chopnacka, Jadwiga
Treasure, The 1951,Mr 29,24:4
Chopra, Ram
Doctor Faustus 1968,F 7,38:1
Chordes, Ray (Screenwriter)
It's a big Country 1952,Ja 9,25:2
Choreau, Etchika
Paris in the Month of August 1968,Ag 26,46:4
Choree, Sonny
Her Jungle Love 1938,Ap 14,27:2
Chorie, Marie
White Fang 1936,Jl 18,18:2
Chorniuk, Peter
Marusia 1938,D 12,26:2
Chorny
Last Game, The 1964,O 25,41:5 (Incorrect in this
edition; use 1964,O 26,41:5 elsewhere)
Chorus, of the Opera Comique, Paris
Barber of Seville 1949,Jl 21,21:2
**Chorus of the Welsh Presbyterian Church of Los
/Angeles**
How Green Was my Valley 1941,O 29,27:2
Chotin, Andre E (Director)
Clandestine 1948,My 24,23:2
Choudhuri, Indranath
Kanchenjungha 1966,Jl 26,27:2
Choudhury, Arpen
Devi 1962,O 8,19:1
Choukhrai, Grigory (Director)
There Was an old Couple 1967,My 22,53:1
Choureau, Etchika
Fruits of Summer 1956,Jl 18,22:2
Darby's Rangers 1958,F 13,23:2
Lafayette Escadrille 1958,Ap 19,10:4
Choux, Jean (Director)
Jean de la Lune 1932,Mr 12,19:5
Maternite 1937,Je 8,30:2
Choux, Jean (Screenwriter)
Maternite 1937,Je 8,30:2
Chow, Chin Kuang
China Sky 1945,My 25,22:3
Chow, David
Samurai 1945,Ag 25,7:5
Chow, Michael
Marco Polo 1962,S 20,29:2
Chowdhury, Nihma Roy
Kanchenjungha 1966,Jl 26,27:2
Choy, Ah Chong
Beachcomber, The 1955,Ja 17,27:5
Chrichton, Charles (Director)
Girl in the Canal, The 1947,O 9,32:3
Boy Who Stole a Million, The 1960,D 22,18:3
Chris
Weddings and Babies 1960,O 6,51:3
Chris, Marilyn
Love With the Proper Stranger 1963,D 26,33:1
Chrisander, Nils Olaf (Director)
Heart Thief, The 1927,Ap 27,22:5
Fighting Love 1927,My 23,27:2
Christaldi, Franco (Miscellaneous)
China Is Near 1968,Ja 9,37:1
CHRISTENSEN
See Also CHRISTIANSEN
Christensen, Benjamin
Chained 1926,D 15,30:4
Christensen, Benjamin (Director)
Mockery 1927,Ag 22,21:3
Haunted House, The 1928,D 17,23:1
Witchcraft Through the Ages 1929,My 28,36:2
Christensen, Benjamin (Screenwriter)
Mockery 1927,Ag 22,21:3
Christensen, Bent (Producer)
Weekend 1964,Ap 27,24:1
Christensen, Carol
Big Show, The 1961,My 11,42:4
Three Stooges in Orbit, The 1962,Jl 12,19:4
Swingin' Along 1962,Ag 27,18:1
Christensen, Charles (Original Author)
His Night Out 1935,N 16,19:2
Christensen, Emil Hass
Ordet 1957,D 16,33:6
Christensen, Hass
Young Have no Time, The 1959,N 23,41:2
Christensson, Irma
One Summer of Happiness 1955,Mr 22,35:2
Devil's Wanton, The 1962,Jl 5,21:2
Christian, Helen
Back Door to Heaven 1939,Ap 20,21:2
Christian, John
Flesh 1968,S 27,36:1
Christian, John (Director)
Guerrilla Girl 1953,Jl 7,23:7
Christian, John (Producer)
Guerrilla Girl 1953,Jl 7,23:7

Christian, Linda
Holiday in Mexico 1946,Ag 16,19:3
Green Dolphin Street 1947,O 16,34:2
Tarzan and the Mermaids 1948,Mr 30,26:4
Happy Time, The 1952,O 31,30:2
Battle Zone 1952,N 1,17:2
Athena 1954,D 22,28:2
House of the Seven Hawks, The 1959,D 17,51:2
V I P's, The 1963,S 20,29:1
Moment of Truth, The 1965,Ag 10,18:1
How to Seduce a Playboy 1968,My 16,53:2
Christian, Paul
Bagdad 1949,D 24,11:4
Thief of Venice, The 1952,N 28,22:7
No Time for Flowers 1952,D 26,20:3
Beast From 20,000 Fathoms, The 1953,Je 25,23:1
Journey to the Lost City 1960,D 8,43:3
Christian, Susanne
Paths of Glory 1957,D 26,23:2
Christian, Tony
Target Unknown 1951,Mr 5,24:2
Tanks are Coming, The 1951,D 6,42:4
Christian-Jacque (Director)
Man to Men 1949,F 21,20:2
Madame 1963,Mr 21,8:6
Christian-Jacque (Screenwriter)
Madame 1963,Mr 21,8:6
Christian-Jaque (Director)
Francis the First 1947,N 20,38:4
Symphonie Fantastique, La 1947,D 8,35:2
Fanfan the Tulip 1953,My 5,34:2
Sins of the Borgias 1956,Mr 5,21:1
Foxiest Girl in Paris 1958,S 20,10:6
Law Is the Law, The 1959,Mr 11,41:2
Babette Goes to War 1960,Je 8,46:1
Love and the Frenchwoman; (Francaise et
l'Amour, La) 1961,F 28,38:2
Don't Tempt the Devil 1964,Ap 28,43:1
Christian-Jaque (Producer)
Fanfan the Tulip 1953,My 5,34:2
Foxiest Girl in Paris 1958,S 20,10:6
Christian-Jaque (Screenwriter)
Man to Men 1949,F 21,20:2
Fanfan the Tulip 1953,My 5,34:2
Sins of the Borgias 1956,Mr 5,21:1
Christianis, The
Sensations of 1945 1944,Jl 7,13:2
Carolina Blues 1944,D 8,26:6
Christians, Mady
Waltz Dream, The 1926,Jl 26,13:2
Slums of Berlin 1927,Ja 26,17:1
Because I Loved You 1930,Ja 25,13:2
Burning Heart, The 1930,My 12,27:3
Leutnant Warst Du Einst bei den Husaren
1932,Mr 14,13:3
Schwartze Husar, Der 1932,D 23,20:1
Friederike 1933,F 27,11:3
Die Frau von der Man Spricht 1933,Ap 22,16:4
Das Schicksal der Renate Langen 1933,N 4,18:4
Heart Song 1934,Je 6,24:6
Wicked Woman, A 1935,Ja 1,24:1
Escapade 1935,Jl 6,16:2
Come and Get It 1936,N 12,31:1
Seventh Heaven 1937,Mr 26,25:1
Woman I Love, The 1937,Ap 16,27:2
Salon Dora Green 1937,Jl 26,15:3
Heidi 1937,N 6,14:2
Address Unknown 1944,Ap 17,20:1
Tender Comrade 1944,Je 2,21:2
All my Sons 1948,Mr 29,17:3
Letters From an Unknown Woman
1948,Ap 29,20:6
Christians, Margarete
Audrey 1916,Mr 27,9:2
CHRISTIANSEN
See Also CHRISTENSEN
Christiansen, Arthur
Day the Earth Caught Fire, The 1962,Mr 16,25:1
Christiansen, Cay
Girls are Willing, The 1959,My 11,30:1
Christiansen, Elsa
As Good as Married 1937,My 22,19:2
Christiansen, Rasmus
David Copperfield 1923,N 6,23:3
Christianson, Benjamin (Director)
Devil's Circus, The 1926,Mr 29,24:3
Haunted House, The 1928,D 23,VIII,7:1
Christianson, Benjamin (Screenwriter)
Devil's Circus, The 1926,Mr 29,24:3
CHRISTIE
See Also CHRISTY
Christie, Agatha (Original Author)
Love From a Stranger 1937,Ap 19,27:2
And Then There Were None 1945,N 1,20:2
Love From a Stranger 1947,N 28,30:1
Witness for the Prosecution 1958,F 7,16:1
Murder She Said 1962,Ja 8,27:2
Murder at the Gallop 1963,Je 25,23:2
Murder Most Foul 1965,My 24,36:2
Ten Little Indians 1966,F 10,33:1
Alphabet Murders, The 1966,Jl 12,36:2

Christie, Al (Director)
Charley's Aunt 1930,D 26,18:4
Christie, Audrey
Keeper of the Flame 1943,Mr 19,15:2
Deadline U S A 1952,Mr 15,8:2
Carousel 1956,F 17,13:1
Splendor in the Grass 1961,O 11,53:1
Unsinkable Molly Brown, The 1964,Jl 17,15:1
Harlow 1965,My 15,18:1
Frankie and Johnny 1966,Jl 21,20:2
Ballad of Josie, The 1968,Mr 14,51:2
Christie, Campbell (Miscellaneous)
Third Key, The 1957,Je 3,30:2
Christie, Campbell (Original Author)
Court Martial 1955,Ag 2,17:1
His Excellency 1956,F 2,19:3
Christie, Campbell (Screenwriter)
Jassy 1948,F 20,19:2
Christie, Dorothy (Miscellaneous)
Third Key, The 1957,Je 3,30:2
Christie, Dorothy (Original Author)
Court Martial 1955,Ag 2,17:1
His Excellency 1956,F 2,19:3
Christie, Dorothy (Screenwriter)
Jassy 1948,F 20,19:2
Christie, Gay
Traum vom Rhein, Der 1935,D 9,25:2
Christie, Howard (Producer)
Abbott and Costello Meet the Invisible Man
1951,Ap 13,18:6
Comin' Round the Mountain 1951,Jl 27,15:2
Against all Flags 1952,D 25,34:6
Lone Hand 1953,Je 27,7:2
Yankee Pasha 1954,Ap 19,19:2
Purple Mask, The 1955,Je 16,35:7
Toy Tiger 1956,Je 30,11:2
Congo Crossing 1956,Jl 14,13:2
I've Lived Before 1956,Ag 4,13:1
Away all Boats 1956,Ag 17,14:2
Nobody's Perfect 1968,Ap 4,58:3
Christie, Ivan
Son of the Gods 1930,Ja 31,24:1
Christie, Julie
Crooks Anonymous 1963,O 31,26:3
Billy Liar 1963,D 17,49:1
Young Cassidy 1965,Mr 23,35:1
Darling 1965,Ag 4,20:1
Doctor Zhivago 1965,D 23,21:1
Fahrenheit 451 1966,N 15,53:1
London Scene, The (Tonite Let's All Make Love
in London 1967,S 27,39:1
Far From the Madding Crowd 1967,O 19,59:1
Petulia 1968,Je 11,54:4
Christie, Robert
Incredible Journey, The 1963,N 21,43:2
Christine, Virginia
Truck Busters 1943,Ja 29,23:5
Mummy's Curse, The 1945,Mr 31,16:1
Killers, The 1946,Ag 29,24:2
Gangster, The 1947,O 31,29:3
Invisible Wall, The 1947,N 1,11:2
Woman in the Night 1948,Ja 10,16:2
Cyrano De Bergerac 1950,N 17,31:2
Never Wave at a Wac 1953,Ap 24,30:2
Not as a Stranger 1955,Je 29,24:1
Killer is Loose, The 1956,Mr 3,17:2
Nightmare 1956,My 12,12:7
Three Brave Men 1957,Mr 16,13:2
Careless Years, The 1957,N 28,57:3
Judgment at Nuremberg 1961,D 20,36:1
Incident in an Alley 1962,My 17,31:1
Prize, The 1964,Ja 24,21:1
One Man's Way 1964,Mr 12,40:3
Christine (Original Author)
Culte de Beaute, Le 1931,Je 8,21:1
Christofarides, Pericles
Madame X 1960,O 3,34:5
Fortune Teller, The 1961,My 22,37:5
Christophe, Francoise
Possessors, The 1959,Jl 21,24:1
King of Hearts 1967,Je 20,34:1
Christopher, Jordan
Return of the Seven 1966,O 20,52:5
Christopher, Kay
Dick Tracy's Dilemma 1947,Jl 14,14:5
Christopher, Robert
Bedevilled 1955,Ap 23,23:1
Buster Keaton Story, The 1957,Ap 22,31:6
Hell's Five Hours 1957,Jl 24,18:1
Hell's Five Hours 1958,Jl 24,18:1
CHRISTY
See Also CHRISTIE
Christy, Ann
Speedy 1928,Ap 7,20:4
Water Hole, The 1928,S 3,14:2
Christy, Bill
Song of the Open Road 1944,Je 7,13:3
Christy, Dorothy
So This Is London 1930,My 24,21:2
Playboy of Paris 1930,N 1,23:2
Extravagance 1930,D 9,31:3
She Got What She Wanted 1930,D 29,18:1
Parlor, Bedroom and Bath 1931,Ap 4,23:1

Christy, Dorothy— Cont

Gold Dust Gertie 1931,My 30,9:2
Big Business Girl 1931,Je 12,27:1
Union Depot 1932,Ja 15,24:4
Devil and the Deep 1932,Ag 20,7:4
Lawyer Man 1932,D 27,10:2
Second Hand Wife 1933,Ja 14,8:4
Sons of the Desert 1934,Ja 12,29:3
Servants' Entrance 1934,S 27,25:2
6-Day Bike Rider 1934,N 3,20:3
Bright Eyes 1934,D 21,31:1
Daring Young Man, The 1935,Jl 18,15:2
Woman Against Woman 1938,Ag 23,20:6
East Side of Heaven 1939,My 5,29:3
So Big 1953,O 22,34:2

Christy, Eileen

Dream of Jeanie, I 1952,Je 26,26:2
Thunderbirds 1953,Mr 12,24:4

Christy, Howard (Director)

Sing Sinner Sing 1933,Ag 15,20:2

Christy, Ken

Harmon of Michigan 1941,O 2,29:2
Burma Convoy 1941,O 7,26:7
He Hired the Boss 1943,Je 4,17:4
Gildersleeve's Bad Day 1943,Je 11,23:1
Scudda-Hoo! Scudda-Hay! 1948,Ap 15,31:1
Cheaper by the Dozen 1950,Ap 1,12:2
No Way Out 1950,Ag 17,23:1
My Sister Eileen 1955,S 23,21:1
Inside Detroit 1956,Ja 28,10:5
Blackjack Ketchum Desperado 1956,Ap 5,26:2

Christy, Suzanne

Little Flower of Jesus, The 1938,D 13,31:2

Chronopoulou, Mary

Red Lanterns 1965,Ap 1,30:1
Naked Brigade, The 1965,Je 17,27:2
Fear, The 1967,O 10,56:3

Chroscicki, Enrico (Producer)

Magnificent Cuckold 1965,Ap 20,42:1

Chroscicki, Henryk (Producer)

Conjugal Bed, The 1963,S 17,30:1

Chrystal, Belle

Friday the 13th 1934,My 15,18:1
Edge of the World, The 1938,S 12,13:2

Chrystall, Belle

Criminal at Large 1933,D 20,27:2
Scotland Yard Mystery, The 1936,Mr 16,21:4

Chuan, Chu Shao

This Angry Age 1958,Je 26,23:3

Chuan, King

Sons of Good Earth 1967,S 16,37:5

Chuan, Yen

Empress Wu 1965,Mr 16,42:2

Chuchunov, Yura

Chuk and Gek 1953,D 21,27:4

Chuckles, The

Girl Can't Help It, The 1957,F 9,12:7

Chudakov, V

Pugachev 1938,Jl 4,10:2

Chugunov

On his Own 1939,S 13,31:3

Chukhrai, Grigori

Clear Skies 1963,N 27,30:1

Chukhrai, Grigori (Director)

Forty-First, The 1957,Je 15,10:7
Ballad of a Soldier 1960,D 27,22:1

Chukhrai, Grigori (Producer)

Forty-First, The 1957,Je 15,10:7

Chukhrai, Grigori (Screenwriter)

Ballad of a Soldier 1960,D 27,22:1

Chukova, K

Heroes of Shipka 1956,S 3,10:5

Chulyukin, Yuri (Screenwriter)

Ballad of Love, A 1966,F 21,51:1

Chuman, Howard

Three Came Home 1950,F 21,22:5
Halls of Montezuma, The 1951,Ja 6,9:6
Mara Maru 1952,Ap 24,38:1

Chun, William

Steel Helmet, The 1951,Ja 25,21:5
Mission Over Korea 1953,S 19,7:2

Chun, Yen

Grand Substitution, The 1965,N 25,64:5

Chun, Yen (Director)

Grand Substitution, The 1965,N 25,64:5

Chun-li, Chen

Song of China 1936,N 10,31:3

Chung, Frances

Woman in the Night 1948,Ja 10,16:2

Chung, Kei

House on Telegraph Hill, The 1951,My 14,29:1
Love Is a Many-Splendored Thing 1955,Ag 19,10:1

Chung, Paul Chang

Empress Wu 1965,Mr 16,42:2

Chung-wen, Chang

Empress Wu 1965,Mr 16,42:2

Church, Berton

So This Is Africa! 1933,Ap 24,11:3

Church, Clair (Screenwriter)

$1,000 a Minute 1935,D 21,11:1

Church, Esme

Autumn Crocus 1934,O 25,26:2

Church, Sandra

Ugly American, The 1963,Ap 12,30:2

Church, Stanley Mayor

Great Jewel Robber, The 1950,Ag 4,13:2

Churchill, Berton

Tongues of Flame 1924,D 16,28:1
Nothing but the Truth 1929,Ap 22,23:1
Secrets of a Secretary 1931,Ag 29,16:3
Husband's Holiday 1931,D 25,29:2
Taxi 1932,Ja 8,27:3
Impatient Maiden, The 1932,Mr 4,17:3
Scandal for Sale 1932,Ap 3,26:2
Rich are Always With Us, The 1932,My 16,19:5
Two Seconds 1932,My 19,25:3
Dark Horse, The 1932,Je 9,27:3
Week Ends Only 1932,Je 18,9:2
American Madness 1932,Ag 6,14:5
Okay America 1932,S 10,18:5
Cabin in the Cotton 1932,S 30,17:3
I Am a Fugitive From a Chain Gang 1932,N 11,17:2
False Faces 1932,N 25,19:2
Afraid to Talk 1932,D 19,19:5
Laughter in Hell 1933,Ja 2,29:2
Billion Dollar Scandal, The 1933,Ja 9,23:1
Employees' Entrance 1933,Ja 21,10:6
From Hell to Heaven 1933,Mr 18,9:3
Private Jones 1933,Mr 25,13:3
Elmer the Great 1933,My 26,24:2
Little Giant, The 1933,My 27,11:5
Heroes for Sale 1933,Jl 22,14:3
Big Brain, The 1933,Ag 5,9:5
Her First Mate 1933,S 2,14:5
Avenger, The 1933,O 3,28:3
Doctor Bull 1933,O 6,21:2
Only Yesterday 1933,N 10,25:1
College Coach 1933,N 11,10:4
Master of Men 1933,N 29,23:4
Frontier Marshal 1934,Ja 31,20:3
Hi, Nellie! 1934,F 1,15:5
Half a Sinner 1934,Je 23,16:5
Friends of Mr Sweeney 1934,Jl 31,20:4
Dames 1934,Ag 16,20:2
Judge Priest 1934,O 12,33:1
Kid Millions 1934,N 12,17:2
Redhead 1934,N 16,27:1
Menace 1934,N 22,27:2
Babbitt 1934,D 17,24:2
County Chairman, The 1935,Ja 19,8:1
Sing Sing Nights 1935,Ja 26,13:2
Night at the Ritz, A 1935,My 16,20:2
Vagabond Lady 1935,Je 15,20:2
Page Miss Glory 1935,Ag 29,25:2
Steamboat Around the Bend 1935,S 20,17:2
I Live for Love 1935,O 19,21:2
Rainmakers, The 1935,N 2,13:2
Coronado 1935,D 19,33:4
You may Be Next 1936,F 24,14:1
Colleen 1936,Mr 9,20:2
Parole 1936,Je 27,21:1
Bunker Bean 1936,Je 27,21:2
Dimples 1936,O 10,21:2
Under Your Spell 1936,N 7,15:2
Parnell 1937,Je 4,27:2
Sing and Be Happy 1937,Je 19,20:2
You Can't Beat Love 1937,Je 25,25:3
Singing Marine, The 1937,Jl 1,33:2
Wild and Woolly 1937,S 6,20:1
In Old Chicago 1938,Ja 7,15:2
Wide Open Faces 1938,Ap 15,23:2
Four Men and à Prayer 1938,My 7,18:1
Kentucky Moonshine 1938,My 21,9:2
Cowboy and the Lady, The 1938,N 25,19:3
Sweethearts 1938,D 23,16:2
Stagecoach 1939,Mr 3,21:1
Daughters Courageous 1939,Je 24,14:2
Angels Wash Their Faces 1939,S 4,16:2
On Your Toes 1939,O 21,12:2
Brother Rat and a Baby 1940,Ja 27,9:4
Saturday's Children 1940,My 4,13:1
Twenty-Mule Team 1940,My 10,26:6
Way of all Flesh, The 1940,Je 6,33:2
Cross Country Romance 1940,Jl 19,22:3
Turnabout 1940,Jl 27,17:6
Public Deb No 1 1940,S 18,19:2

Churchill, Bonnie Jean

Give Me a Sailor 1938,Ag 11,31:1

Churchill, Diana

School for Husbands 1939,F 7,16:2
Housemaster 1939,Ap 10,13:2
Scott of the Antarctic 1951,F 26,20:2
History of Mr Polly, The 1951,O 25,36:3

Churchill, Donald

Victim 1962,F 6,27:2

Churchill, Douglas W (Original Author)

Platinum Blonde 1931,O 31,22:2

Churchill, Edward (Screenwriter)

Power Dive 1941,My 29,15:4

Churchill, Frank (Composer)

Snow White and the Seven Dwarfs 1938,Ja 14,21:1 (In Addenda)
Breaking the Ice 1938,S 23,35:3
Reluctant Dragon, The 1941,Jl 25,12:2

Churchill, Frank (Composer)— Cont

Dumbo 1941,O 24,27:2
Bambi 1942,Ag 14,13:1

Churchill, Marguerite

Valiant, The 1929,My 13,27:2
Pleasure Crazed 1929,Jl 15,25:1
They Had to See Paris 1929,O 12,11:1
Seven Faces 1929,N 16,25:2
Born Reckless 1930,Je 7,10:4
Good Intentions 1930,Jl 26,16:4
Big Trail, The 1930,O 25,20:3
Girls Demand Excitement 1931,F 7,11:1
Charlie Chan Carries On 1931,Mr 21,15:1
Quick Millions 1931,Ap 18,17:3
Riders of the Purple Sage 1931,S 26,25:3
Ambassador Bill 1931,N 14,15:3
Forgotten Commandments 1932,Je 2,25:2
Girl Without a Room 1933,D 7,26:3
Man Hunt 1936,Ja 30,14:2
Walking Dead, The 1936,Mr 2,13:2
Dracula's Daughter 1936,My 18,14:2
Murder by an Aristocrat 1936,Je 13,13:2
Final Hour, The 1936,Ag 1,16:3
Legion of Terror 1936,N 2,24:2

Churchill, Sarah

All Over the Town 1949,My 26,34:4
Royal Wedding 1951,Mr 9,30:2

Churchill, Savannah

Miracle in Harlem 1949,O 24,19:4

Churchill, Winston

Finest Hours, The 1964,N 11,38:1
Liberation of Europe, The 1968,S 29,IV,7:1

Churchill, Winston (Original Author)

Inside of the Cup, The 1921,Ja 16,VI,2:1 (In Addenda)

Churchman, Ybanne

Othello 1960,My 16,39:1

Chursina, Lea

When the Trees Were Tall 1965,F 22,14:1

Churskov, B (Screenwriter)

Dream of a Cossack 1952,F 18,15:2

Chuvelev, I

Peasants 1935,Ag 29,25:2
Ski Battalion 1938,Mr 14,13:1
Untitled-Capt Grant's Children 1939,Ja 12,23:3
On his Own 1939,S 13,31:3

Chwalibog, Maria

Joan of the Angels? 1962,My 8,43:6

Chytilova, Vera (Director)

Daisies 1967,Je 19,41:1
Daisies 1967,O 26,54:2

Chytilova, Vera (Original Author)

Daisies 1967,O 26,54:2

Chytilova, Vera (Screenwriter)

Daisies 1967,O 26,54:2

Cialente, Renato

Amo Te Sola 1936,Jl 20,11:2
Albero di Adamo, L'; Adam's Tree 1938,Ja 20,19:2
Maestrina, La; Little School Mistress, The 1938,Ap 29,17:2
Lotte nell Ombra; Battles in the Shadow 1939,Mr 21,27:3

Ciampi, Yves (Director)

Heroes and Sinners; (Heros Sont Fatigues, Les) 1959,My 12,38:2

Ciampi, Yves (Screenwriter)

Perfectionist, The 1952,My 2,21:3
Heroes and Sinners; (Heros Sont Fatigues, Les) 1959,My 12,38:2

Ciangottini, Valeria

Dolce Vita, La 1961,Ap 20,30:1

Ciangottini, Valerie

From a Roman Balcony 1961,O 16,33:5
Family Diary 1963,N 12,48:1

Ciannelli, Eduardo

Reunion in Vienna 1933,Ap 29,14:2
Scoundrel, The 1935,My 3,23:2
Winterset 1936,D 4,31:1
Criminal Lawyer 1937,Ja 27,17:3
Marked Woman 1937,Ap 12,15:2
Girl From Scotland Yard, The 1937,My 31,11:2
League of Frightened Men, The 1937,Jl 2,25:1
Super-Sleuth 1937,Jl 17,18:1
On Such a Night 1937,S 17,29:2
Hitting a new High 1937,D 27,11:1
Law of the Underworld 1938,Ap 28,27:2
Blind Alibi 1938,My 20,17:2
Gunga Din 1939,Ja 28,19:2
Risky Business 1939,Mr 23,27:2
Society Lawyer 1939,Mr 31,19:2
Bulldog Drummond's Bride 1939,Jl 13,17:2
Angels Wash Their Faces 1939,S 4,16:2
Zanzibar 1940,Ap 1,15:3
Outside the Three-Mile Limit 1940,Ap 8,15:2
Strange Cargo 1940,Ap 26,25:2
Foreign Correspondent 1940,Ag 28,15:2
Mummy's Hand, The 1940,S 20,27:2
Kitty Foyle 1941,Ja 9,27:2
Ellery Queen's Penthouse Mystery 1941,Mr 7,17:2
They Met in Bombay 1941,Jl 4,17:1
I Was a Prisoner on Devil's Island 1941,Jl 28,16:4

Ciannelli, Eduardo— Cont

Paris Calling 1942,Ja 19,21:2
Dr Broadway 1942,Je 25,27:3
You Can't Escape Forever 1942,O 17,11:1
Cairo 1942,N 6,27:2
They Got Me Covered 1943,Mr 5,20:2
Flight for Freedom 1943,Ap 16,24:2
Constant Nymph, The 1943,Jl 24,8:2
Passage to Marseille 1944,F 17,12:5
Mask of Dimitrios, The 1944,Je 24,16:2
Storm Over Lisbon 1944,S 11,14:1
Conspirators, The 1944,O 21,15:2
Dillinger 1945,Ap 26,26:2
Bell for Adano, A 1945,Jl 6,8:3
Incendiary Blonde 1945,Jl 26,13:2
Joe Palooka, Champ 1946,Ap 6,10:6
Wife of Monte Cristo, The 1946,Ap 8,31:2
Heartbeat 1946,My 11,22:4
Perilous Holiday 1946,Je 1,10:4
California 1947,Ja 15,31:2
Lost Moment, The 1947,N 22,10:2
Miracle Can Happen, A 1948,F 4,28:4
To the Victor 1948,Ap 17,11:2
Rapture 1950,D 14,51:3
Fugitive Lady 1951,Ag 25,7:2
People Against O'Hara, The 1951,S 6,39:3
Volcano 1953,Jl 21,19:2
Stranger's Hand, The 1955,F 16,24:5
Mambo 1955,Mr 31,23:3
Helen of Troy 1956,Ja 27,21:4
Attila 1958,My 19,19:4
Houseboat 1958,N 14,24:1

Ciannelli, Lewis E (Director)

O K Nero 1953,Je 20,8:6

Cianni, Eloisia

It Happened in the Park 1957,Ag 13,23:2

Cianquerotti, Alejandro

Bohemios 1935,S 16,15:3

Cibardo, Giuseppe

Path of Hope, The (Il Cammino Della Speranza) 1952,Ag 5,15:5

Cibrian, Jose

Games Men Play, The 1968,Mr 15,30:1

Cichportiche, Marlene

Eye for an Eye, An 1961,F 10,19:1

Cidor, King (Director)

Hallelujah 1929,Ag 21,33:1

Ciecierski, Jan

Ashes and Diamonds 1961,My 30,8:1

Ciepielewska, Anna

Joan of the Angels? 1962,My 8,43:6
Passenger 1964,S 21,37:3

Ciermont, Robert

Corbeau, Le; Raven, The 1948,F 24,21:1

Cifariello, Antonio

Scandal in Sorrento 1957,Je 13,37:1
Awakening, The 1958,Mr 3,24:6
Holiday Island; (Vacanzie a Izchia) 1959,S 22,46:1
Jessica 1962,Ap 20,20:2
In Search of the Castaways 1962,D 22,5:2

Cigoli, Emilio

Shoe-Shine 1947,Ag 27,19:2
Most Wonderful Moment, The 1959,Je 1,23:6

Cilento, Diane

Angel Who Pawned her Harp, The 1956,F 29,35:2
Admirable Crichton, The 1957,D 15,45:4 (Incorrect in this edition; use 1957,D 17,45:4 elsewhere)
Truth About Women, The 1958,Ag 29,18:2
Stop Me Before I Kill 1961,Je 22,23:4
Naked Edge 1961,Jl 1,9:1
I Thank a Fool 1962,S 15,15:1
Tom Jones 1963,O 8,48:1
Third Secret, The 1964,Ap 29,27:1
Rattle of a Simple Man 1964,D 21,42:2
Agony and the Ecstacy, The 1965,O 9,5:6
Hombre 1967,Mr 22,41:1
Negatives 1968,O 15,40:1

Cimara, Luigi

Re Burlone, Il 1936,Mr 28,11:3
Loyalty of Love 1937,Mr 1,15:1
Destino, Il 1938,F 8,17:3
Anything for a Song 1947,Ag 5,26:2

Cintron, Conchita

Marvels of the Bull Ring 1943,Jl 3,11:3

Ciolli, Augusta

Marty 1955,Ap 12,25:3

Ciotti, Mirella

Path of Hope, The (Il Cammino Della Speranza) 1952,Ag 5,15:5

Cipen, Tubby

Along Came Sally 1934,Je 16,20:3

Ciral, Karen

Good Morning and Goodbye! 1968,F 20,53:1

Cirelli, Antonio

Guaglio 1949,My 19,35:2

Cirillo, Carmela

Two Cents Worth of Hope 1952,D 16,44:2

Cirino, Giulio

Giovanni De Medici, The Leader 1940,Ja 5,15:4

Cirino, Natale

Genoese Dragnet 1954,F 12,20:5
Of Life and Love 1958,O 7,40:2

Cisar, George

Johnny Holiday 1950,My 17,36:1

Cisney, Marcella

Hard, Fast and Beautiful 1951,Jl 2,16:6

Cisney, Michael

And Baby Makes Three 1949,D 23,17:3

Citroen, Andre (Miscellaneous)

Croisiere Jaune, La; Yellow Journey, The 1934,My 6,IX,4:5 (In Addenda)

Citti, Franco

Accattone 1966,S 17,20:2
Accattone! 1968,Ap 5,56:1

Ciuffini, Sabatino (Screenwriter)

Tartars, The 1962,Je 21,26:2

Ciuffre, Aldo

Love and Marriage (The Last Resort); Last Resort, The (Love and Marriage) 1966,Ag 5,20:1

Civallero, Carlo (Producer)

Devotion 1953,Ja 31,10:6
His Last Twelve Hours 1953,N 13,24:7
Times Gone By (The Old Book Stand) 1953,D 30,16:2
Times Gone By (The Trial of Frine) 1953,D 30,16:2
Times Gone By (The Vise) 1953,D 30,16:2
Times Gone By (A Question of Property) 1953,D 30,16:2
Times Gone By (Less Than a Day) 1953,D 30,16:2
Times Gone By (The Idyll) 1953,D 30,16:2
Times Gone By (A Pot-Pourri of Songs) 1953,D 30,16:2
Woman in the Painting, The 1959,Ja 15,27:1

Claar, Ivana

Dama Bianca, La; Lady in White, The 1940,My 31,15:3

Claesson, Ake

Miss Julie 1952,Ap 8,35:2

CLAIR

See Also CLAIRE, CLARE

Clair, Denise

Moment of Truth, The 1954,Ap 27,36:2
Grisbi 1959,Jl 13,23:1

Clair, Ethlyne

Second Choice 1930,Ja 4,21:1

Clair, Rene (Director)

Sous les Toits de Paris; (Under the Roofs of Paris) 1930,D 16,34:4
Million, Le 1931,My 21,33:2
Million, The 1931,Jl 19,VIII,2:5
Million, The 1931,Jl 19,VIII,4:3
Horse Ate the Hat, The 1931,S 1,30:6
A Nous la Liberte 1932,Ja 10,VIII,5:1
A Nous, la Liberte 1932,F 14,VIII,6:1
Nous, La Liberte, A 1932,My 18,25:2
July 14th 1933,Mr 19,IX,4:1 (In Addenda)
Quatorez Juillet 1933,O 20,14:2
Dernier Milliardaire, Le 1935,O 30,16:2
Ghost Goes West, The 1935,D 18,33:8
Ghost Goes West, The 1936,Ja 11,9:2
Break the News 1941,Ja 2,24:2
Flame of New Orleans, The 1941,Ap 26,20:2
I Married a Witch 1942,N 20,27:2
Forever and a Day 1943,Mr 13,9:2
It Happened Tomorrow 1944,My 29,18:2
And Then There Were None 1945,N 1,20:2
Man About Town 1947,O 22,37:1
Beauty and the Devil 1952,Ag 26,15:2
Beauties of the Night 1954,Mr 23,23:5
Grand Maneuver, The 1956,O 2,39:1
Gates of Paris 1958,Ja 15,24:1
Love and the Frenchwoman; (Francaise et l'Amour, La) 1961,F 28,38:2
Three Fables of Love (Two Pigeons); Two Pigeons (Three Fables of Love) 1963,Ag 21,38:1

Clair, Rene (Miscellaneous)

Beauty and the Devil 1952,Ag 26,15:2
Three Fables of Love (Two Pigeons); Two Pigeons (Three Fables of Love) 1963,Ag 21,38:1

Clair, Rene (Original Author)

Man About Town 1947,O 22,37:1

Clair, Rene (Producer)

Break the News 1941,Ja 2,24:2
Forever and a Day 1943,Mr 13,9:2
And Then There Were None 1945,N 1,20:2
Man About Town 1947,O 22,37:1

Clair, Rene (Screenwriter)

Nous, La Liberte, A 1932,My 18,25:2
It Happened Tomorrow 1944,My 29,18:2
Beauty and the Devil 1952,Ag 26,15:2
Beauties of the Night 1954,Mr 23,23:5
Grand Maneuver, The 1956,O 2,39:1
Gates of Paris 1958,Ja 15,24:1
Love and the Frenchwoman; (Francaise et l'Amour, La) 1961,F 28,38:2

CLAIRE

See Also CLAIR, CLARE

Claire, Bernice

No, No, Nanette 1930,Ja 4,21:1
Song of the Flame 1930,My 7,24:5

Claire, Bernice— Cont

Numbered Men 1930,Je 9,23:3
Top Speed 1930,Ag 30,7:4
Kiss Me Again 1931,Ja 8,21:4

Claire, Gertrude

Stepping Out 1919,S 22,8:1
Widow by Proxy 1919,S 22,8:1
Cradle of Courage, The 1920,S 20,13:1
Hail the Woman 1922,Ja 16,18:3
Daughters of Today 1924,Mr 4,17:1
Wine of Youth 1924,Ag 11,16:1
Goose Hangs High, The 1925,Mr 10,19:3
His Majesty Bunker Bean 1925,S 15,12:1
Tumbleweeds 1925,D 21,27:2
Little Irish Girl, The 1926,My 11,24:3
We're all Gamblers 1927,O 12,30:6

Claire, Ina

Polly With a Past 1921,Ja 10,9:1
Royal Family of Broadway, The 1930,D 23,25:1
Rebound 1931,Ag 29,16:3
Greeks Had a Word for Them, The 1932,F 4,25:2
Ninotchka 1939,N 10,27:2
Stage Door Canteen 1943,Je 25,13:2
Claudia 1943,N 5,23:2

Claire, Marion

Make a Wish 1937,S 23,33:1

Claire, Mavis

Battle for Music 1945,O 15,13:2

Claire, Willis

Fugitive From Justice, A 1940,Jl 8,13:3

Clairond, Aime

Loves of Casanova 1948,S 18,11:4

Clama, Renee

Man they Couldn't Arrest, The 1933,Mr 14,19:3

Clampi, Yves (Director)

Perfectionist, The 1952,My 2,21:3

Clancy, Jacques

Friend Will come Tonight, A; Ami Viendra Ce Soir, Un 1948,Jl 12,11:2
Caroline Cherie 1954,My 25,23:1
Love Is my Profession 1959,Ap 28,41:1

Clancy, Kitty

Midnight Madonna 1937,Jl 17,18:1

Clannelli (Screenwriter)

O K Nero 1953,Je 20,8:6

Clanton, Hampton

Cool World, The 1964,Ap 21,42:1

Clanton, Jimmy

Teenage Millionaire 1962,Ja 12,29:2

Clanton, Ralph

Cyrano De Bergerac 1950,N 17,31:2
Johnny Tremain 1957,Jl 11,21:1

Clapham, Leonard

To the Last Man 1923,Ag 28,12:1
Our Hospitality 1923,D 10,20:1
Call of the Canyon, The 1923,D 17,23:1
Heritage of the Desert, The 1924,Ja 24,15:1

CLARE

See Also CLAIR, CLAIRE

Clare, Colleen

We're on the Jury 1937,F 10,18:5
Last of Mrs Cheyney, The 1937,F 19,15:1

Clare, Diane

Reluctant Debutante, The 1958,Ag 15,17:1
Desert Attack 1961,Mr 23,28:1
Whistle Down the Wind 1962,Ap 23,34:2
Vulture, The 1967,My 20,39:2

Clare, Mary

Prince of Lovers, The 1927,N 29,31:1
Constant Nymph, The 1934,Ap 7,19:1
Power 1934,O 5,29:3
Clairvoyant, The 1935,Je 8,12:2
Mister Hobo 1936,F 8,19:2
Passing of the Third Floor Back, The 1936,Ap 29,19:2
Rat, The 1938,F 28,19:1
Citadel, The 1938,N 4,27:2
Lady Vanishes, The 1938,D 26,29:1
Climbing High 1939,Je 5,20:3
Challenge, The 1939,O 2,15:2
Mill On the Floss, The 1939,N 15,19:3
Fugitive, The 1940,Jl 23,22:2
Girl Must Live, A 1942,Mr 24,25:2
Next of Kin 1943,My 6,25:2
Patient Vanishes, The 1947,My 23,31:2
My Brother Jonathan 1949,Je 29,34:4
Mrs Fitzherbert 1950,My 11,37:2
Black Rose, The 1950,S 2,11:2
Oliver Twist 1951,Jl 31,17:2
Moulin Rouge 1953,F 11,33:5
Penny Princess 1953,Mr 25,37:3
Beggar's Opera, The 1953,Ag 25,18:2
Mambo 1955,Mr 31,23:3

Clare, Phyllis

Roadhouse Murder 1932,Ap 29,13:4
Along Came Sally 1934,Je 16,20:3
Clive of India 1935,Ja 18,29:1
His Brother's Wife 1936,Ag 15,6:2
Convicted 1938,Ag 22,9:3

Clare, Sidney (Composer)

Jimmy and Sally 1933,D 16,12:3
Call it Luck 1934,Jl 10,24:5
Transatlantic Merry-Go-Round 1934,N 1,25:2
365 Nights in Hollywood 1934,N 7,32:1

Clare, Sidney (Composer) — Cont
Bright Eyes 1934,D 21,31:1
Song and Dance Man 1936,Mr 12,18:2
Crime of Dr Forbes, The 1936,Jl 6,11:4
Holy Terror, The 1937,Ja 30,21:2
Sing and Be Happy 1937,Je 19,20:2
She Had to Eat 1937,Jl 24,12:1
Big Town Girl 1937,D 13,23:4
Battle of Broadway 1938,Ap 25,19:2
Rascals 1938,My 27,12:2
Hold That Co-ed 1938,S 24,13:1
Rookies on Parade 1941,My 22,25:2
Lullaby of Broadway 1951,Mr 27,35:2
Clare, Sidney (Miscellaneous)
She Learned About Sailors 1934,Jl 30,9:4
Black Sheep 1935,Je 28,34:1
Paddy O'Day 1936,F 8,19:2
Little Miss Nobody 1936,Je 6,21:1
Clarence, O B
Man From Chicago, The 1931,Ja 16,27:1
Magic Night 1932,N 3,25:3
Perfect Understanding 1933,F 23,20:2
Friday the 13th 1934,My 15,18:1
Heart Song 1934,Je 6,24:6
Scarlet Pimpernel, The 1935,F 8,27:2
Seven Sinners 1936,Ag 22,6:1
East Meets West 1936,O 31,24:2
Return of the Scarlet Pimpernel, The 1938,Ap 11,12:2
Pygmalion 1938,D 8,34:2
Courageous Mr Penn 1943,D 23,26:5
On Approval 1945,Ja 29,17:1
Great Expectations 1947,My 23,31:1
Meet Me at Dawn 1948,My 18,26:2
Place of One's Own, A 1949,F 8,30:2
Inheritance, The 1951,F 12,19:2
Clarenden, Jean
Mourning Becomes Electra 1947,N 20,38:2
Clarieux
Battle of the Rails; (Bataille Du Rail) 1949,D 27,27:2
Clarieux, Jean
Bernadette of Lourdes 1962,Ja 30,20:2
Clarin, Hans
Spessart Inn, The 1961,F 18,12:3
Clariond, Aime
Sans Famille 1935,Je 4,26:5
Prince Jean, Le 1936,D 12,15:2
Lucrezia Borgia 1937,O 13,27:2
Lie of Nina Petrovna, The 1938,Mr 30,19:2
Boys' School 1939,Je 6,26:2
Katia 1939,D 23,9:2
Entente Cordiale 1939,D 26,23:2
Mayerling to Sarajevo 1940,O 30,27:6
32 Rue de Montmartre 1944,S 28,26:3
Colonel Chabert 1947,Je 21,11:2
Blue Veil, The 1947,O 2,32:6
Midnight in Paris 1947,O 9,32:3
Mlle Desiree 1948,N 19,35:2
Monsieur Vincent 1948,D 21,33:2
Wicked Duchess, The 1949,N 5,10:5
My First Love 1951,Je 11,20:7
Deadlier Than the Male 1957,O 9,41:1
Possessors, The 1959,Jl 21,24:1
Mistress for the Summer, A 1964,Mr 28,13:5
CLARK
See Also CLARKE
Clark
Lost in the Arctic 1928,Jl 26,25:3
Clark, Alan R (Original Author)
High Wall 1947,D 26,22:2
Clark, Andrew
Sporting Chance, The 1925,Je 24,14:3
Clark, Andy
Beggars of Life 1928,S 24,25:1
Hit the Deck 1930,Ja 15,28:6
Clark, Barry
Flower Thief, The 1962,Jl 14,11:5
Clark, Bobby
Ransom 1956,Ja 25,28:3
Happy Road, The 1957,Je 21,20:2
Clark, Bridgetta
Greater Glory, The 1926,My 4,31:1
Clark, Bridggetta
Four Horsemen of the Apocalypse, The 1926,S 27,27:3
Clark, Buddy
Seven Days' Leave 1942,D 11,33:2
Subterraneans, The 1960,Jl 7,26:1
Clark, Charles Dow
Confidence Man, The 1924,Ap 15,24:1
Old Home Week 1925,My 25,21:3
Bat Whispers, The 1931,Ja 16,27:1
Ladies of the Jury 1932,Ap 2,13:2
Half-Naked Truth, The 1932,D 31,10:1
Clark, Cheryl
Oh Men! Oh Women! 1957,F 22,25:2
Clark, Cliff
Mr Moto's Gamble 1938,Ap 8,17:2
Patient in Room 18, The 1938,Ap 22,15:6
Time Out for Murder 1938,O 7,21:2
While New York Sleeps 1938,D 22,25:3
Kentucky 1938,D 24,12:1
Honolulu 1939,F 23,19:2

Within the Law 1939,Ap 6,31:2
It's a Wonderful World 1939,My 19,27:2
Young Mr Lincoln 1939,Je 3,11:2
Miracles for Sale 1939,Ag 10,15:2
Fast And Furious 1939,O 12,33:3
Missing Evidence 1939,N 17,17:3
Grapes of Wrath, The 1940,Ja 25,17:2
Honeymoon Deferred 1940,F 16,23:4
Three Cheers for the Irish 1940,Mr 9,19:2
Double Alibi 1940,Mr 11,11:2
Cross Country Romance 1940,Jl 19,22:3
Stranger on the Third Floor 1940,S 2,19:2
Black Diamonds 1940,S 10,26:6
Strange Alibi 1941,Ap 28,11:2
Wagons Roll at Night, The 1941,My 10,20:4
Washington Melodrama 1941,My 26,15:3
Manpower 1941,Jl 5,14:2
Law of the Tropics 1941,O 10,26:5
Nine Loves Are not Enough 1941,O 30,27:2
Babes on Broadway 1942,Ja 1,37:1
Jail House Blues 1942,F 6,23:2
Kid Glove Killer 1942,Ap 17,21:4
Fingers at the Window 1942,Ap 23,27:3
Who Is Hope Schuyler 1942,My 22,27:1
Falcon's Brother, The 1942,O 3,9:5
Mummy's Tomb, The 1942,O 26,19:2
Army Surgeon 1942,N 5,35:2
Secret Enemies 1943,Ja 1,27:3
Ladies' Day 1943,Mr 26,14:3
Falcon Strikes Back, The 1943,Ap 2,17:4
Falcon in Danger, The 1943,Jl 23,21:2
Falcon out West, The 1944,Mr 18,18:2
Corpse came C O D, The 1947,Ag 19,27:2
Bury Me Dead 1947,O 25,13:3
Deep Waters 1948,Jl 23,12:4
Home of the Brave 1949,My 13,29:1
Stratton Story, The 1949,My 13,29:1
Gunfighter, The 1950,Je 24,7:2
Men, The 1950,Jl 21,15:2
Second Woman, The 1951,F 2,19:2
Operation Pacific 1951,F 3,10:2
Try and Get Me 1951,My 7,22:2
Cavalry Scout 1951,Je 8,32:2
Sniper, The 1952,My 10,16:3
Clark, Colbert (Original Author)
Marines are Coming, The 1935,F 23,14:7
Clark, Colbert (Producer)
Atlantic Convoy 1942,Jl 6,18:5
Murder in Times Square 1943,My 31,13:2
Rockin' in The Rockies 1945,Jl 5,7:2
Clark, Dane
Destination Tokyo 1944,Ja 1,9:2
Destination Tokyo 1944,Ja 9,II,3:1
Very Thought of You, The 1944,N 18,16:7
Hollywood Canteen 1944,D 16,19:2
God is my Co-Pilot 1945,Mr 24,22:6
Pride of the Marines 1945,Ag 25,7:3
Stolen Life, A 1946,My 2,27:4
Her Kind of Man 1946,My 4,10:6
That Way With Women 1947,F 15,20:4
Deep Valley 1947,Ag 23,7:2
Whiplash 1948,D 27,16:3
Moonrise 1949,Mr 7,17:2
Backfire 1950,Ja 27,29:2
Barricade 1950,Mr 25,8:6
Without Honor 1950,Jl 3,9:2
Never Trust a Gambler 1951,Jl 20,14:2
Go, Man, Go 1954,Mr 10,29:5
Blackout 1954,My 22,8:2
Port of Hell 1954,D 18,12:2
Massacre 1956,Je 2,13:5
Clark, Dave
Having a Wild Weekend 1965,Ag 19,35:1
Clark, Davison
Dishonored 1931,Mr 6,16:1
Vice Squad, The 1931,Je 6,15:5
This is the Night 1932,Ap 16,11:2
We Live Again 1934,N 2,27:2
Miserables, Les 1935,Ap 22,14:2
Return of Frank James, The 1940,Ag 10,16:4
North West Mounted Police 1940,N 7,33:2
Four Faces West 1948,Ag 4,18:3
Sand 1949,Ag 5,23:2
Clark, Dick
Young Doctors, The 1961,Ag 24,25:2
Clark, Dick (Producer)
Psych-Out 1968,Mr 28,52:1
Savage Seven, The 1968,Ag 22,47:1
Clark, Don (Screenwriter)
I Married Adventure 1940,S 24,26:5
Clark, Dort
In Harm's Way 1965,Ap 7,36:1
Clark, Downing
America 1924,F 22,20:1
Clark, Ed
Bedtime for Bonzo 1951,Ap 6,31:4
Clark, Edward
Amazon Quest 1949,My 14,9:3
Petty Girl, The 1950,Ag 18,17:2
Branded 1951,Ja 11,28:5
Clark, Edward (Original Author)
De Luxe Annie 1918,My 20,9:7

Clark, Edward (Screenwriter)
Marriage by Contract 1928,N 13,37:1
Clark, Ernest
Beau Brummell 1954,O 21,31:5
1984 1956,O 1,31:1
Baby and the Battleship, The 1957,O 1,37:2
Time Without Pity 1957,N 23,11:2
Tale of Two Cities, A 1958,Ag 5,23:1
Sink the Bismarck! 1960,F 12,22:3
Touch of Larceny, A 1960,Mr 17,28:1
Nothing but the Best 1964,Jl 14,28:1
Arabesque 1966,My 6,54:1
Salt and Pepper 1968,S 19,62:3
Clark, Estelle
Sinners in Silk 1924,S 8,15:3
So This Is Marriage 1924,D 23,16:2
Denial, The 1925,Mr 10,19:3
Merry Widow, The 1925,Ag 27,14:1
His Secretary 1925,D 21,27:2
Tillie the Toiler 1927,Je 7,27:4
Clark, Frank
Hell's Angels 1930,Ag 16,8:3
Cross Examination 1932,F 27,22:1
Lost Squadron, The 1932,Mr 11,15:4
Call Me Mister 1951,F 1,21:2
Clark, Frank Howard (Original Author)
Traveling Saleslady 1935,Mr 29,26:2
Clark, Frank Howard (Screenwriter)
O'Malley of the Mounted 1936,Ap 6,18:1
Two in Revolt 1936,Ap 25,21:1
Clark, Fred
Unsuspected, The 1947,O 4,9:2
Ride the Pink Horse 1947,O 9,32:3
Hazard 1948,Je 3,19:2
Fury at Furnace Creek 1948,Jl 12,11:2
Mr Peabody and the Mermaid 1948,Ag 14,6:5
Two Guys From Texas 1948,Ag 28,8:6
Cry of the City 1948,S 30,32:4
Alias Nick Beal 1949,Mr 10,35:2
Flamingo Road 1949,My 7,10:2
Younger Brothers, The 1949,My 28,11:2
White Heat 1949,S 3,7:2
Lady Takes a Sailor, The 1949,D 17,15:2
Return of the Frontiersman 1950,Je 10,11:3
Eagle and the Hawk, The 1950,Jl 6,31:2
Sunset Boulevard 1950,Ag 11,15:2
Jackpot, The 1950,N 23,55:2
Mrs O'Malley and Mr Malone 1951,F 23,33:2
Lemon Drop Kid, The 1951,Mr 22,41:2
Hollywood Story 1951,Je 7,40:6
Meet Me After the Show 1951,Ag 16,23:2
Place in the Sun, A 1951,Ag 29,20:1
3 for Bedroom C 1952,Je 27,18:3
Dreamboat 1952,Jl 26,9:2
Stars Are Singing, The 1953,Mr 12,24:2
Caddy, The 1953,S 18,16:6
How to Marry a Millionaire 1953,N 11,37:1
Here Come the Girls 1953,D 26,10:i
Living It Up 1954,Jl 24,6:6
Daddy Long Legs 1955,My 6,17:5
How to be Very, Very Popular 1955,Jl 23,10:1
Court-Martial of Billy Mitchell, The 1955,D 23,14:2
Miracle in the Rain 1956,Ap 2,18:1
Birds and the Bees, The 1956,Ap 23,22:1
Back From Eternity 1956,S 8,20:6
Solid Gold Cadillac, The 1956,O 25,40:3
Joe Butterfly 1957,My 30,23:2
Don't Go Near the Water 1957,N 15,37:1
Mardi Gras 1958,N 19,45:2
Auntie Mame 1958,D 5,39:1
Mating Game, The 1959,Ap 30,37:1
It Started With a Kiss 1959,Ag 20,14:2
Visit to a Small Planet 1960,Ap 14,34:1
Bells Are Ringing 1960,Je 24,31:2
Boys' Night Out 1962,Je 22,15:2
Hemingway's Adventures of a Young Man 1962,Jl 26,17:1
Zotz! 1962,O 4,44:3
Move Over Darling 1963,D 26,33:1
John Goldfarb, Please Come Home 1965,Mr 25,42:4
Sergeant Deadhead 1965,O 23,17:3
When the Boys Meet the Girls 1966,Ja 20,29:1
Dr Goldfoot and the Bikini Machine 1966,F 17,29:3
Horse in the Gray Flannel Suit, The 1968,D 21,49:3
Clark, Freddy
Treasure Island 1950,Ag 16,24:2
Clark, George Dow
Okay America 1932,S 10,18:5
Clark, Gordon
Song of my Heart 1948,Mr 5,17:3
Clark, Griff
You're not so Tough 1940,Jl 9,25:3
Clark, Gwen
Girl in a Million, A 1950,Jl 24,15:2
Clark, Harry
Ice-Capades 1941,S 25,29:1
Taxi 1953,Ja 22,20:3

Clark, Harry (Original Author)
  Smiling Faces 1932,Ag 31,12:3
Clark, Harvey
  In the Palace of the King 1923,D 3,14:1
  Secrets 1924,Mr 25,25:2
  Man Who Came Back, The 1924,S 1,9:1
  He Who Gets Slapped 1924,N 10,20:1
  Roughneck, The 1924,D 3,14:1
  Man Without a Country, The 1925,F 12,16:1
  Midnight Lovers 1926,O 26,23:1
  Camille 1927,Ap 22,19:1
  Understanding Heart, The 1927,My 10,24:5
  Magic Flame, The 1927,S 19,30:3
  Rose of the Golden West 1927,S 26,27:1
  In old Kentucky 1927,N 21,20:1
  Get Your Man 1927,D 5,26:2
  Ladies' Night in a Turkish Bath 1928,Ap 9,18:2
  Night Bird, The 1928,O 2,23:5
  Seven Keys to Baldpate 1929,D 26,21:1
  What a Man 1930,Jl 21,20:3
  Anybody's Woman 1930,Ag 16,8:3
  Going Wild 1931,Ja 26,21:1
  Millie 1931,F 7,11:1
  Cracked Nuts 1931,Ap 6,24:1
  Deceiver, The 1931,N 23,22:1
  Big Shot, The 1932,Ja 2,14:2
  Red Headed Woman 1932,Jl 1,19:3
  Down to Earth 1932,S 2,19:2
  Strictly Personal 1933,Mr 20,18:2
  West of Singapore 1933,Ap 1,18:3
  Shriek in the Night, A 1933,Jl 24,11:2
  Alice in Wonderland 1933,D 23,19:1
  Charlie Chan's Courage 1934,Ag 25,16:6
  Peck's bad Boy 1934,O 6,20:1
  Dance Charlie Dance 1937,Ag 26,25:2
  It's Love I'm After 1937,N 11,31:2
  Partners of the Plains 1938,F 12,20:4
  Mother Carey's Chickens 1938,Ag 5,11:1
Clark, Herbert
  Big News 1929,O 7,22:1
  Bride of the Regiment 1930,My 22,32:6
  In Gay Madrid 1930,Je 7,10:4
Clark, Jack
  Wells Fargo 1937,D 30,15:2
Clark, James B (Director)
  Dog of Flanders, A 1960,Ap 1,37:1
  One Foot in Hell 1960,O 20,42:2
  Big Show, The 1961,My 11,42:4
  Misty 1961,Jl 18,33:2
  Drums of Africa 1963,Jl 4,9:1
  Flipper 1963,S 19,23:1
  Island of the Blue Dolphins 1964,Jl 4,8:2
  ...And Now Miguel 1966,S 8,43:1
Clark, James B (Producer)
  Big Show, The 1961,My 11,42:4
Clark, James L
  Explorers of the World 1931,D 18,29:3
Clark, Jameson
  Tight Little Island 1949,D 26,33:2
  Brave Don't Cry, The 1952,N 6,37:2
  Scotch on the Rocks 1954,Je 14,18:2
  High and Dry 1954,Ag 31,25:5
  Little Kidnappers, The 1954,S 2,18:1
  Wee Geordie 1956,O 8,31:1
  Key, The 1958,Jl 2,23:3
  Battle of the Sexes, The 1960,Ap 19,40:4
  39 Steps, The 1960,O 11,55:2
  Pair of Briefs, A 1964,F 3,22:2
Clark, Jimmy
  Eve of St Mark, The 1944,My 31,22:2
  Mom and Dad 1957,Ja 31,21:1
Clark, John J
  Pajamas 1927,N 7,26:4
Clark, Johnny
  Locket, The 1947,Mr 20,38:2
Clark, Judy
  Minstrel Man 1944,Jl 17,18:5
  Uncle Harry 1945,Ag 24,14:5
  Crooked Web, The 1955,D 10,19:1
Clark, Ken
  On the Threshold of Space 1956,Mr 30,10:5
  Proud Ones, The 1956,Ag 11,10:2
  Last Wagon, The 1956,S 22,20:2
  Between Heaven and Hell 1956,O 12,33:2
  Love Me Tender 1956,N 16,23:1
  South Pacific 1958,Mr 20,33:1
Clark, Kendall
  Shrike, The 1955,Jl 8,15:2
Clark, Lawrence (Original Author)
  All the King's Horses 1935,Mr 9,19:1
Clark, Les
  When Willie Comes Marching Home
    1950,F 18,9:2
Clark, Mamo
  Hurricane, The 1937,N 10,31:2
  Hawaii Calls 1938,Ap 29,17:2
  Booloo 1938,Jl 30,10:2
  Mutiny on the Blackhawk 1939,Ag 2,17:2
  One Million BC 1940,Ap 27,9:2
  Girl From God's Country 1940,S 9,18:5
Clark, Marguerite
  Still Waters 1915,N 8,13:5
  Prince and the Pauper, The 1915,N 29,11:3

Molly Make Believe 1916,Ap 17,9:3
  Silk and Satins 1916,Je 12,9:3 (In Addenda)
  Little Lady Eileen 1916,Ag 14,7:6
  Miss George Washington 1916,N 20,11:1 (In Addenda)
  Snow White 1916,D 25,7:1
  Prunelia 1918,Je 3,9:3
  Out of a Clear Sky 1918,S 23,7:1
  Mrs Wiggs of the Cabbage Patch 1919,F 17,11:3
  Three Men and a Girl 1919,Mr 31,11:3
  Come out of the Kitchen 1919,My 12,11:4
  Widow by Proxy 1919,S 22,8:1
  Scrambled Wives 1921,My 23,16:3
Clark, Marilyn
  Too Late Blues 1962,Mr 1,27:4
  Horror of Party Beach, The 1964,Ap 30,30:1
Clark, Matt
  In the Heat of the Night 1967,Ag 3,26:1
Clark, Maurice (Miscellaneous)
  Three Russian Girls 1944,F 5,13:2
Clark, Miles Jr
  Bwana Devil 1953,F 19,20:5
Clark, Neville
  Barretts of Wimpole Street, The 1934,S 29,12:2
  Clive of India 1935,Ja 18,29:1
Clark, Pat
  Cass Timberlane 1947,N 7,20:2
Clark, Paul
  Boy Meets Girl 1938,Ag 27,7:2
Clark, Petula
  Gay Intruders, The 1946,Mr 18,24:2
  Murder in Reverse 1947,Ja 11,23:5
  I Know Where I'm Going 1947,Ag 20,25:2
  Easy Money (Episode 1) 1949,F 14,15:3
  Here Come the Huggetts 1950,D 25,25:3
  White Corridors 1952,Jl 16,21:1
  Promoter, The 1952,O 29,36:2
  Runaway Bus, The 1954,O 25,30:7
  Finian's Rainbow 1968,O 10,59:5
Clark, Polly
  Man Upstairs, The 1959,Ag 11,23:2
Clark, Roger
  You Belong to Me 1941,N 29,14:2
  Two Yanks in Trinidad 1942,Ap 6,19:4
  Lady is Willing, The 1942,Ap 24,21:2
  Wife Takes a Flyer, The 1942,Je 19,19:1
  They all Kissed the Bride 1942,Jl 31,11:1
  Pin Up Girl 1944,My 11,25:6
  Eve of St Mark, The 1944,My 31,22:2
  Something for the Boys 1944,N 30,19:1
  Angel Baby 1961,O 5,43:1
Clark, Russ
  Sinners in the Sun 1932,My 14,11:5
  Men Without Names 1935,Je 29,16:2
  Mr Moto's Gamble 1938,Ap 8,17:2
  Dance Hall 1941,Jl 19,16:2
  Date With the Falcon, A 1941,N 25,33:2
  Sing Your Worries Away 1942,My 15,25:2
  Ladies' Day 1943,Mr 26,14:3
Clark, Sanders
  Miserables, Les 1952,Ag 15,11:2
Clark, Sheila
  Show Boat 1951,Jl 20,14:1
  Round Trip 1967,Jl 20,30:2
Clark, Stephen
  Man Trailer, The 1934,My 23,22:3
Clark, Steven
  For Men Only 1952,Ja 16,21:2
Clark, Susan
  Banning 1967,D 14,62:2
  Madigan 1968,Mr 30,22:2
  Coogan's Bluff 1968,O 3,56:1
Clark, Trilby
  Lover of Camille, The 1924,N 11,14:1
  Silent Sanderson 1925,Je 11,14:3
Clark, W H
  As You Like It 1936,N 6,29:3
Clark, Wallis
  Hell's House 1932,F 12,24:5
  Final Edition, The 1932,F 22,23:2
  Alias the Doctor 1932,Mr 3,22:3
  Shopworn 1932,Ap 4,13:6
  Attorney for the Defense 1932,My 28,18:2
  Okay America 1932,S 10,18:5
  My Pal the King 1932,O 4,26:4
  Night Mayor, The 1932,N 25,19:2
  Luxury Liner 1933,F 3,21:3
  They Just Had to Get Married 1933,F 13,11:4
  World Gone Mad, The 1933,Ap 15,16:3
  Working Man, The 1933,Ap 21,20:3
  Kiss Before the Mirror, The 1933,My 15,16:2
  Double Harness 1933,Jl 21,20:2
  Lady for a Day 1933,S 8,22:2
  Bureau of Missing Persons 1933,S 9,9:2
  World Changes, The 1933,O 27,22:3
  Massacre 1934,Ja 18,19:2
  It Happened One Night 1934,F 23,23:2
  Life of Vergie Winters, The 1934,Je 15,26:1
  I'll Fix It 1934,N 12,17:3
  It Happened in New York 1935,Ap 6,10:1
  Chinatown Squad 1935,My 30,21:1
  Mutiny on the Bounty 1935,N 9,19:2
  Unguarded Hour, The 1936,Ap 4,11:1

Clark, Wallis— Cont
  Parole 1936,Je 27,21:1
  Missing Girls 1936,O 5,25:1
  Come Closer, Folks 1936,N 23,17:3
  Great Guy 1937,Ja 1,19:2
  Last of Mrs Cheyney, The 1937,F 19,15:1
  I Promise to Pay 1937,Ap 26,15:2
  Big Business 1937,Je 1,27:2
  She Had to Eat 1937,Jl 24,12:1
  Main Street Lawyer 1939,N 9,27:2
  Allegheny Uprising 1939,N 10,27:3
  Big Guy, The 1940,Ja 1,29:2
  Penny Serenade 1941,My 23,25:2
  Murder by Invitation 1941,Jl 23,15:4
  Remarkable Andrew, The 1942,Mr 6,17:2
  Gentleman Jim 1942,N 26,40:3
  Uncertain Glory 1944,Ap 8,9:2
Clark, Walter Van Tilburg (Original Author)
  Ox-Bow Incident, The 1943,My 10,15:2 (In Addenda)
  Track of the Cat 1954,D 2,38:2
CLARKE
  See Also CLARK
Clarke, Angela
  Undercover Man, The 1949,Ap 21,30:2
  Mrs Mike 1950,F 9,36:5
  Captain Carey U S A 1950,Mr 30,40:5
  Gunfighter, The 1950,Je 24,7:2
  Outrage 1950,O 16,30:5
  Undercover Girl 1950,N 8,37:2
  Great Caruso, The 1951,My 11,32:2
  Darling, How Could You! 1951,N 9,22:4
  It's a big Country 1952,Ja 9,25:2
  Miracle of Our Lady Fatima, The
    1952,Ag 21,16:2
  House of Wax 1953,Ap 11,15:2
  Houdini 1953,Jl 3,10:2
  Beneath the 12-Mile Reef 1953,D 17,52:2
  Seven Little Foys, The 1955,Je 30,18:2
  Silencers, The 1966,Mr 17,35:1
  Blindfold 1966,My 26,55:2
Clarke, Arthur C (Screenwriter)
  2001 A Space Odyssey 1968,Ap 4,58:1
Clarke, Betty Ross
  If I Were King 1920,Ag 10,10:3
  Age for Love, The 1931,N 13,27:2
  Murders in the Rue Morgue 1932,F 11,16:1
  Judge Hardy's Children 1938,Ap 8,17:2
  Love Finds Andy Hardy 1938,Jl 22,10:2
  Woman Against Woman 1938,Ag 23,20:6
  too Hot To Handle 1938,S 30,24:2
Clarke, Burke
  Wayward 1932,F 15,13:1
Clarke, David
  Long Night, The 1947,S 17,31:2
  Killer McCoy 1948,F 12,31:2
  Boy With Green Hair, The 1949,Ja 13,26:2
  Man From Colorado 1949,Ja 21,24:3
  Set-Up, The 1949,Mr 30,31:2
  Red Canyon 1949,Ap 28,28:2
  Thieves' Highway 1949,S 24,8:6
  Abandoned Woman 1949,O 27,35:3
  Intruder in the Dust 1949,N 23,19:1
  Gunfighter, The 1950,Je 24,7:2
  House on Telegraph Hill, The 1951,My 14,29:1
  Narrow Margin, The 1952,My 5,18:7
  Edge of the City 1957,Ja 30,33:2
  Great St Louis Bank Robbery, The 1960,F 4,34:1
Clarke, Donald Henderson (Original Author)
  Born Reckless 1930,Je 7,10:4
  Millie 1931,F 7,11:1
  Impatient Maiden, The 1932,Mr 4,17:3
  Housekeeper's Daughter, The 1939,D 2,21:4
Clarke, Donald Henderson (Screenwriter)
  Ghost Ship, The 1943,D 25,19:4
Clarke, Dort
  Bells Are Ringing 1960,Je 24,31:2
Clarke, Downing
  Monsieur Beaucaire 1924,Ag 12,12:1 (In Addenda)
Clarke, E E B (Screenwriter)
  Passport to Pimlico 1949,O 27,35:2
Clarke, Fred
  Fuzzy Pink Nightgown, The 1957,O 31,41:1
Clarke, Frederick
  Ever Since Eve 1937,Je 25,25:2
  Blossoms On Broadway 1937,D 3,29:2
Clarke, Gage
  Nightmare 1956,My 12,12:7
  Bad Seed, The 1956,S 13,39:6
  Fury at Showdown 1957,Ap 20,21:3
  Brothers Karamazov, The 1958,F 21,18:2
  I Want to Live 1958,N 19,45:1
  Pollyanna 1960,My 20,26:1
Clarke, Gary
  Missle to the Moon 1958,N 17,37:2
  Wild Wild Winter 1966,Ja 6,20:2
Clarke, Gordon B
  Hustler, The 1961,S 27,35:1
Clarke, Jacqueline
  Blithe Spirit 1945,O 4,27:2
  Escape 1948,Ag 16,12:2

Clarke, Jean
Goodbye Again 1961,Je 30,32:2
Clarke, John
Operation Bottleneck 1961,S 7,40:2
Satan Bug, The 1965,Ap 15,38:1
Clarke, John S Jr (Producer)
Matto Grosso 1933,Ja 14,8:5
Clarke, Kenneth B (Original Author)
Rough Romance 1930,Je 16,25:3
Clarke, Lydia
Atomic City, The 1952,My 2,21:1
Clarke, Mae
Big Time 1929,S 9,30:2
Nix on Dames 1929,N 23,18:5
Fall Guy, The 1930,My 27,27:2
Dancers, The 1930,N 15,15:3
Front Page, The 1931,Mr 20,29:1
Public Enemy, The 1931,Ap 24,27:1
Good Bad Girl, The 1931,My 15,20:6
Waterloo Bridge 1931,S 5,7:4
Frankenstein 1931,D 5,21:2
Reckless Living 1931,D 5,21:2
Three Wise Girls 1932,F 6,14:4
Final Edition, The 1932,F 22,23:2
Impatient Maiden, The 1932,Mr 4,17:3
Night World 1932,My 28,18:2
Fast Workers 1933,Mr 20,18:2
Parole Girl 1933,Ap 10,8:2
Turn Back the Clock 1933,Ag 26,14:2
Penthouse 1933,S 9,9:2
Lady Killer 1934,Ja 1,28:2
Nana 1934,F 2,20:3
This Side of Heaven 1934,F 10,21:2
Let's Talk It Over 1934,Je 16,20:2
Man With two Faces, The 1934,Jl 12,20:2
Daring Young Man, The 1935,Jl 18,15:2
Silk Hat Kid 1935,Ag 7,22:5
House of a Thousand Candles, The
1936,Ap 2,29:2
Great Guy 1937,Ja 1,19:2
Trouble in Morocco 1937,Mr 15,27:1
Outlaws of the Orient 1937,S 25,10:2
Women in War 1940,My 30,21:2
Flying Tigers 1942,O 23,25:2
Because of You 1952,D 4,47:3
Women's Prison 1955,F 3,18:5
Not as a Stranger 1955,Je 29,24:1
Clarke, Margaret
Frenzy 1946,Jl 20,10:3
Clarke, Paul
Cry Tough 1959,S 17,48:4
Clarke, Redfield
$20 a Week 1924,Je 10,24:4
Clarke, Richard
Charlie Chan in City in Darkness 1939,D 18,29:2
Swanee River 1939,D 30,9:2
Man Who Wouldn't Talk, The 1940,Ja 12,13:3
Clarke, Robert
Falcon in Hollywood, The 1944,D 9,21:2
Radio Stars on Parade 1945,S 22,14:2
Wanderer of the Wasteland 1945,S 29,12:2
Game of Death, A 1945,N 24,22:4
San Quentin 1947,F 10,24:3
Outrage 1950,O 16,30:5
Man From Planet X, The 1951,Ap 9,31:2
Hard, Fast and Beautiful 1951,Jl 2,16:6
Clarke, Shirley (Director)
Connection, The 1962,O 4,44:1
Cool World, The 1964,Ap 21,42:1
Portrait of Jason 1967,S 30,26:1
Portrait of Jason 1967,O 3,57:1
Clarke, Shirley (Producer)
Connection, The 1962,O 4,44:1
Portrait of Jason 1967,S 30,26:1
Portrait of Jason 1967,O 3,57:1
Clarke, Shirley (Screenwriter)
Cool World, The 1964,Ap 21,42:1
Clarke, T E B (Screenwriter)
Johnny Frenchman 1946,O 21,27:3
Against the Wind 1949,Je 27,18:3
Hue and Cry 1951,Ja 9,25:2
Blue Lamp, The 1951,Ja 9,25:1
Magnet, The 1951,F 27,22:6
Lavender Hill Mob, The 1951,O 16,35:2
Encore (The Ant and the Grasshopper); Ant and
the Grasshopper, The (Encore) 1952,Ap 3,45:1
Encore (Gigolo and Gigolette); Gigolo and
Gigolette (Encore) 1952,Ap 3,45:1
Encore (Winter Cruise); Winter Cruise (Encore)
1952,Ap 3,45:1
Train of Events 1952,My 26,18:4
Titfield Thunderbolt, The 1953,O 6,34:2
All at Sea 1957,D 23,18:2
Tale of Two Cities, A 1958,Ag 5,23:1
Law and Disorder 1958,Ag 6,20:1
Gideon of Scotland Yard 1959,My 20,38:2
Sons and Lovers 1960,Ag 3,35:1
Man Could Get Killed, A 1966,My 12,54:2
Clarke, Wescott
Trial of Mary Dugan, The 1929,Mr 29,21:1
Clarke-Smith, D A
Atlantic 1930,O 6,21:1
Michael and Mary 1932,Mr 5,11:2

Waltz Time 1933,S 29,24:2
Good Companions, The 1933,O 10,24:1
Criminal at Large 1933,D 20,27:2
Ghoul, The 1934,Ja 27,9:2
Friday the 13th 1934,My 15,18:1
Quo Vadis 1951,N 9,22:2
Sword and the Rose, The 1953,Ag 20,18:3
Baby and the Battleship, The 1957,O 1,37:2
Clarlond, Alme
Eternal Husband, The 1949,Ja 10,19:2
Clary, Charles
Connecticut Yankee in King Arthur's Court, A
1921,Mr 15,14:3
In the Palace of the King 1923,D 3,14:1
Empty Hands 1924,Ag 18,8:2
Breath of Scandal, The 1924,N 26,17:3
Golden Bed, The 1925,Ja 20,18:2
Auction Block, The 1926,F 15,16:4
Red Dice 1926,Ap 16,20:3
Beverly of Graustark 1926,Ap 19,24:3
When a Man Loves 1927,F 4,16:6
See You in Jail 1927,Ap 4,30:5
Smile, Brother, Smile 1927,Ag 29,21:1
Sailor's Holiday 1929,O 21,30:1
Clary, Robert
New Faces 1954,F 20,8:7
New Kind of Love, A 1963,O 31,26:2
Clasis, Charlotte
Prenez Garde a la Peinture 1935,Ag 17,18:6
Twilight 1949,D 30,13:2
Clasis, Germaine
Human Beast, The 1940,F 20,17:2
Class, Buck
In Love and War 1958,N 1,14:2
Blue Denim 1959,Jl 31,21:1
Beloved Infidel 1959,N 18,46:1
Claty, Charles
Seven Days 1925,Ag 31,19:3
Claude, Felix
Devil's Daughter 1949,F 26,11:2
Claude, Pierre
Without Pity; (Senza Pieta) 1950,Mr 16,40:4
Claude, Toby
Lost-a Wife 1925,Je 22,10:2
For Alimony Only 1926,S 21,33:1
Claude-Poirier, Maria
Naked Autumn 1963,N 15,25:3
Claudio, Jean
Crossroads 1939,Mr 14,17:5
Boys' School 1939,Je 6,26:2
Rasputin 1939,O 17,31:4
Dangerous Exile 1958,O 11,18:3
Picnic on the Grass 1960,O 12,47:1
Claudius, Marie-Luise
August der Starke 1937,Ja 30,21:3
Claudius, Marieluise
Krach um Iolanthe 1935,My 11,21:3
Alte und der Junge Koenig, Der 1935,D 10,31:2
Verlorene Tal, Das 1936,My 30,7:3
Zwei lustige Abenteurer; Two Merry Adventures
1938,Ja 1,11:2
Abduction, The 1938,Je 11,9:2
Peer Gynt 1939,N 11,12:2
Claudon, Paul (Producer)
Suitor, The; Soupirant, Le 1963,S 18,35:1
Yo Yo 1967,Mr 1,50:1
CLAUSEN
See Also CLAWSON
Clausen, Carl (Original Author)
Killer at Large 1936,O 26,20:1
Clausen, Claus
Comrades of 1918 1931,F 20,18:5
Skandal Um Eva 1931,Ap 21,35:2
Unsere Fahne Flattert Uns Voran 1934,Jl 7,16:6
Alte und der Junge Koenig, Der 1935,D 10,31:2
Devil Makes Three, The 1952,Ag 30,6:2
Clauson, Bill
Wistful Widow of Wagon Gap, The
1947,N 21,36:2
Claussen, Aase
Ungkarlspappan 1936,Ja 4,19:1
Claussen, Joy
Troublemaker, The 1964,Je 23,25:1
Claveau, Andre
French-Cancan 1956,Ap 17,26:2
Clavel, Maurice (Original Author)
Pantaloons 1956,D 26,34:1
Mistress for the Summer, A 1964,Mr 28,13:5
Clavel, Maurice (Screenwriter)
Pantaloons 1956,D 26,34:1
Passionate Summer 1957,Jl 22,15:5
Mistress for the Summer, A 1964,Mr 28,13:5
Clavell, James (Director)
Five Gates to Hell 1959,D 10,51:6
Walk Like a Dragon 1960,S 16,24:1
To Sir, With Love 1967,Je 15,56:1
Clavell, James (Original Author)
King Rat 1965,O 28,48:1
Clavell, James (Producer)
Five Gates to Hell 1959,D 10,51:6
Walk Like a Dragon 1960,S 16,24:1
To Sir, With Love 1967,Je 15,56:1

Clavell, James (Screenwriter)
Fly, The 1958,Ag 30,6:6
Watusi 1959,Jl 2,15:2
Five Gates to Hell 1959,D 10,51:6
Walk Like a Dragon 1960,S 16,24:1
Great Escape, The 1963,Ag 8,19:1
633 Squadron 1964,Je 25,25:1
Satan Bug, The 1965,Ap 15,38:1
To Sir, With Love 1967,Je 15,56:1
Clavering, Eric
Invaders, The 1942,Mr 6,17:1
Tower of Terror 1942,Je 29,11:4
Patient Vanishes, The 1947,My 23,31:2
Incredible Journey, The 1963,N 21,43:2
CLAWSON
See Also CLAUSEN
Clawson, Howard (Original Author)
Leatherneck, The 1929,Ap 22,23:1
Claxton, Oliver (Original Author)
Lucky Night 1939,My 5,29:3
Claxton, William F (Director)
Young Jesse James 1960,Ag 25,25:1
Desire in the Dust 1960,O 12,47:2
Claxton, William F (Producer)
Desire in the Dust 1960,O 12,47:2
Clay, Cassius
Requiem for a Heavyweight 1962,O 17,35:1
Clay, Philippe
French-Cancan 1956,Ap 17,26:2
Hunchback of Notre Dame, The 1957,D 12,35:1
Foxiest Girl in Paris 1958,S 20,10:6
Bell, Book and Candle 1958,D 27,2:7
Claydon, George
Berserk! 1968,Ja 11,42:2
Clayton, Arthur
Whip, The 1928,S 17,28:2
Three Live Ghosts 1929,S 30,23:1
Road to Singapore, The 1931,O 1,25:2
White Heat 1934,Je 16,20:2
Crimson Romance 1934,O 13,10:1
Clayton, Bob
Bellboy, The 1960,Jl 21,17:1
Clayton, Eddie
Mad Hour, The 1928,Ap 16,20:5
Lady Be Good 1928,My 28,23:2
College Coquette, The 1929,Ag 26,17:1
Pick Up 1933,Mr 25,13:4
Clayton, Edward
Guilty 1930,Ap 7,21:1
Clayton, Ethel
Pettigrew's Girl 1919,Ap 14,11:4
Woman Next Door, The 1919,My 19,20:5
Men, Women and Money 1919,Je 16,11:2
Sporting Chance, A 1919,Jl 14,12:2
Sham 1921,My 6,20:2
Beyond 1921,S 5,12:4
Wings of Youth 1925,Ap 20,18:1 (Incorrect in
this edition; use 1925,Ap 28,18:1 elsewhere)
Lightnin 1925,Jl 22,14:4
Risky Business 1926,S 8,19:3
Mother Machree 1928,Mr 6,20:3
Hit the Deck 1930,Ja 15,28:6
Hotel Continental 1932,Mr 21,19:5
Clayton, Gilbert
Below the Line 1925,S 21,12:4
Partners Again, With Potash and Perlmutter
1926,F 15,16:4
Clayton, Jack (Director)
Bespoke Overcoat, The 1956,O 8,31:1
Room at the Top 1959,Mr 31,26:1
Innocents, The 1961,D 26,15:2
Pumpkin Eater, The 1964,N 10,58:1
Our Mother's House 1967,O 10,56:1
Clayton, Jack (Producer)
Panic in the Parlor 1957,D 18,45:1
Innocents, The 1961,D 26,15:2
Our Mother's House 1967,O 10,56:1
Clayton, Jan
Flight Angels 1940,My 27,23:2
This Man's Navy 1945,Ap 16,18:6
Clayton, Lou
Roadhouse Nights 1930,F 22,13:1
Clayton, Marguerite
Inside of the Cup, The 1921,Ja 16,VI,2:1 (In
Addenda)
Dawn of a Tomorrow, The 1924,Mr 26,19:2
Palm Beach Girl, The 1926,Je 22,21:2
Clayton, Marion
All Quiet on The Western Front 1930,Ap 30,29:1
Barretts of Wimpole Street, The 1934,S 29,12:2
Magnificent Obsession 1935,D 31,11:2
Clayton, Powell
Trail of the Lonesome Pine, The 1936,F 20,23:5
Clayton, Richard
Our Neighbors-The Carters 1940,F 15,15:2
Clayworth, June
Good Fairy, The 1935,F 1,18:1
Transient Lady 1935,Mr 11,15:1
Lady Tubbs 1935,Jl 22,20:2
Two-Fisted Gentleman 1936,Ag 24,11:2
Married Before Breakfast 1937,Jl 23,16:2
Between Two Women 1937,Ag 6,21:1
Live, Love and Learn 1937,N 19,27:2

Clayworth, June— Cont
Truth About Murder, The 1946,Jl 27,12:6
Criminal Court 1946,N 16,15:3
Dick Tracy and Gruesome 1947,S 27,11:2
White Tower, The 1950,Jl 3,9:2
At Swords Point 1952,Ap 10,37:1
Dream Wife 1953,Jl 30,20:1
Marriage-Go-Round 1961,Ja 7,12:2
Cleary, Jon (Original Author)
Sundowners, The 1960,D 9,39:1
High Commissioner, The 1968,D 12,62:5
Cleary, Jon (Screenwriter)
Green Helmet, The 1961,Jl 20,32:2
Cleary, Leo
You Can't Fool Your Wife 1940,My 24,23:4
Red Menace, The 1949,Je 27,18:2
Johnny Holiday 1950,My 17,36:1
Pride of St Louis, The 1952,My 3,17:5
Cleave, Arthur
Better 'Ole, The 1919,F 24,11:3
Clecchi, Andrea
Manon Lescaut 1941,Ap 14,23:5
Clech, Yvonne
Zazie 1961,N 21,45:5
Fire Within, The 1964,F 18,27:1
Inside Out 1964,S 25,32:1
Cleckler, Robert
Show Them no Mercy 1935,D 9,25:2
Cleckley, Hervey M Dr (Original Author)
Three Faces of Eve, The 1957,S 27,16:6
Cleef, Lee Van
Kansas City Confidential 1952,N 29,11:2
Cleese, John
Interlude 1968,Jl 3,26:1
Clegg, Tom
Moby Dick 1956,Jl 5,18:1
Clein, John (Producer)
Mill On the Floss, The 1939,N 15,19:3
Room 43 1959,D 3,46:1
Dr Crippen 1964,F 15,14:1
Cleland, John (Original Author)
Fanny Hill 1965,D 2,48:1
Clemenceau, Georges (Original Author)
Veil of Happiness, The 1928,My 1,33:3
Clemens, Brian (Screenwriter)
Telltale Heart, The 1963,My 16,42:1
Station Six-Sahara 1964,N 12,40:2
Corrupt Ones, The 1967,F 23,41:3
Clemens, Gertrude
War Is a Racket 1934,D 10,16:2
Clemens, LeRoy
Aloma of the South Seas 1926,My 17,19:1
Clemens, LeRoy (Original Author)
Alias the Deacon 1927,Je 21,29:2
Love, Live and Laugh 1929,N 2,14:6
Half a Sinner 1934,Je 23,16:5
Alias the Deacon 1940,My 14,27:5
Clemens, Samuel (Mark Twain) (Original Author)
Prince and the Pauper, The 1915,N 29,11:3
Huckleberry Finn 1920,F 23,11:2
Connecticut Yankee in King Arthur's Court, A 1921,Mr 15,14:3
Connecticut Yankee at the Court of King Arthur, A 1936,My 4,16:1
Clemens, William (Director)
Man Hunt 1936,Ja 30,14:2
Law in her Hands, The 1936,Je 6,21:2
Case of the Velvet Claws, The 1936,Ag 29,16:3
Here Comes Carter 1936,N 14,23:3
Talent Scout 1937,Ag 20,21:3
Footloose Heiress 1937,O 9,16:2
Missing Witness 1937,D 10,33:3
Torchy Blane in Panama 1938,Ap 18,11:1
Accidents Will Happen 1938,Ap 25,19:2
Dress Parade 1939,O 28,11:2
Calling Philo Vance 1940,F 9,15:3
King of the Lumberjacks 1940,Ap 15,21:3
Devil's Island 1940,Jl 12,11:4
She Couldn't Say No 1941,Ja 17,21:3
Night of January 16th, The 1941,D 19,35:1
Night in New Orleans 1942,Jl 2,25:2
Sweater Girl 1942,Jl 13,18:3
Falcon in Danger, The 1943,Jl 23,21:2
Falcon out West, The 1944,Mr 18,18:2
Clement, Andree
Symphonie Pastorale 1948,S 14,34:3
Back Streets of Paris 1948,O 16,9:2
Devil's Daughter 1949,F 26,11:2
Just a big Simple Girl; Une Grande Fille Toute Simple 1949,O 28,29:2
God Needs Men 1951,Mr 27,35:1
Thirst of Men, The 1952,O 28,37:1
Daughters of Destiny (Jeanne); Jeanne (Daughters of Destiny) 1954,Jl 6,19:1
Clement, Charles (Miscellaneous)
Girl From Leningrad 1941,D 20,25:2
Guerrilla Brigade 1942,Ap 14,17:2
Rainbow, The 1944,O 23,14:3
Hello, Moscow! 1946,Je 15,24:4
Ivan the Terrible, Part I 1947,Mr 10,25:2
Clement, Clay
Washington Merry-Go-Round 1932,O 24,18:5
Evenings for Sale 1932,N 12,20:5
Second Hand Wife 1933,Ja 14,8:4

Tonight Is Ours 1933,Ja 21,10:6
Past of Mary Holmes, The 1933,My 1,10:3
Hold Me Tight 1933,My 22,18:6
Bureau of Missing Persons 1933,S 9,9:2
World Changes, The 1933,O 27,22:3
Son of a Sailor 1933,N 30,38:4
Journal of a Crime 1934,Ap 28,11:3
Personality Kid, The 1934,Ag 1,14:2
I Sell Anything 1934,D 27,25:2
Sweet Music 1935,F 21,23:2
Chinatown Squad 1935,My 30,21:1
Don't Bet on Blondes 1935,Jl 20,16:2
Whipsaw 1936,Ja 25,18:4
Leathernecks Have Landed, The 1936,Mr 23,22:5
Let's Sing Again 1936,My 9,11:2
Nobody's Fool 1936,Je 4,27:2
Bad Guy 1937,Ag 26,25:2
Rosalie 1937,D 31,9:2
Trip to Paris, A 1938,Je 10,18:2
Arson Racket Squad 1938,Je 18,18:2
Disbarred 1939,Ja 19,17:2
Off the Record 1939,F 18,12:2
Each Dawn I Die 1939,Jl 22,12:2
Passport to Alcatraz 1940,Je 15,12:2
I'm Still Alive 1940,O 11,25:4
Clement, Dick (Screenwriter)
Jokers, The 1967,My 16,50:1
Clement, Dora
Private Worlds 1935,Mr 28,25:2
I Married a Doctor 1936,Ap 20,17:1
Forgotten Faces 1936,Jl 4,18:2
Nobody's Baby 1937,My 20,17:3
Hawaii Calls 1938,Ap 29,17:2
Under Western Stars 1938,Je 25,7:3
Hold That Co-ed 1938,S 24,13:1
Buck Privates 1941,F 14,15:2
Lady Eve, The 1941,F 26,17:1
Clement, Rene (Director)
Mr Orchid; Pere Tranquille, Le 1948,Mr 29,17:3
Damned, The; Maudits, Les 1948,Ap 26,27:2
Battle of the Rails; (Bataille Du Rail) 1949,D 27,27:2
Walls of Malapaga, The 1950,Mr 21,34:2
Forbidden Games 1952,D 9,43:2
Gervaise 1957,N 12,46:1
This Angry Age 1958,Je 26,23:3
Purple Noon 1961,S 1,12:1
Day and the Hour, The 1964,F 20,22:2
Joy House 1965,F 18,29:1
Knave of Hearts; Lovers, Happy Lovers 1965,S 9,36:1
Clement, Rene (Miscellaneous)
Forbidden Games 1952,D 9,43:2
Lovers, Happy Lovers 1954,O 1,19:2
Clement, Rene (Producer)
Battle of the Rails; (Bataille Du Rail) 1949,D 27,27:2
Clement, Rene (Screenwriter)
Damned, The; Maudits, Les 1948,Ap 26,27:2
Lovers, Happy Lovers 1954,O 1,19:2
This Angry Age 1958,Je 26,23:3
Purple Noon 1961,S 1,12:1
Day and the Hour, The 1964,F 20,22:2
Joy House 1965,F 18,29:1
Clemente, Steve
Rainbow Trail, The 1925,Je 3,26:4
Clementelli, Silvio (Producer)
Poor but Beautiful 1958,Je 11,39:4
Defend my Love; (Difendo il Mio Amore) 1959,O 8,48:7
Clementi, Pierre
Leopard, The 1963,Ag 13,25:1
How Not to Rob a Department Store 1965,D 29,23:1
Benjamin 1968,Mr 26,41:2
Belle de Jour 1968,Ap 11,51:1
Partner 1968,S 24,52:2
Clemento, Steve
Temptress, The 1926,O 11,18:1
Most Dangerous Game, The 1932,N 21,21:1
King Kong 1933,Mr 3,12:1
It Happened Out West 1937,Je 7,22:3
Clements, Albert
Island of Allah 1956,Je 27,35:1
Clements, Calvin (Screenwriter)
Firecreek 1968,F 22,36:2
Clements, Charles (Miscellaneous)
Wandering Jew, The 1949,Mr 11,33:2
Clements, Colin (Original Author)
Call of the West 1930,My 27,27:2
Notorious Gentleman, A 1935,F 16,9:1
Clements, Dudley
Outcasts of Poker Flat, The 1937,Ap 27,18:3
You Can't Buy Luck 1937,My 14,21:2
New Faces of 1937 1937,Jl 2,25:1
Toast of New York, The 1937,Jl 23,16:2
Big Shot, The 1937,Ag 13,13:1
Hideaway 1937,S 25,10:2
Clements, Hal
Seventeen 1940,F 29,15:2
Clements, John
Rembrandt 1936,D 3,31:1
Knight Without Armor 1937,Jl 9,18:1

Clements, John— Cont
South Riding 1938,Ag 2,15:2
Four Feathers 1939,Ag 4,11:1
Convoy 1941,Ja 17,21:2
This England 1941,N 18,33:2
Ships With Wings 1942,My 25,11:2
At Dawn We Die 1943,My 8,19:2
They Came to a City 1945,F 19,21:3
Train of Events 1952,My 26,18:4
Mind Benders, The 1963,My 2,40:2
Clements, Stanley
Tall, Dark and Handsome 1941,Ja 24,15:2
More the Merrier, The 1943,My 14,17:1
Sweet Rosie O'Grady 1943,O 21,30:2
Going my Way 1944,My 3,25:2
Salty O'Rourke 1945,Ap 26,26:2
See my Lawyer 1945,My 4,23:4
Hazard 1948,Je 3,19:2
Canon City 1948,Jl 8,19:2
Bad Boy 1949,Mr 23,35:2
Johnny Holiday 1950,My 17,36:1
Boots Malone 1952,My 13,26:2
Off Limits 1953,Mr 30,25:5
Mad at the World 1955,My 14,10:8
Nice Little Bank That Should Be Robbed, A 1958,D 11,17:4
Sniper's Ridge 1961,Ag 24,25:3
Saintly Sinners 1962,Mr 29,28:2
Tammy and the Doctor 1963,Je 27,23:2
Clemons, Larry (Screenwriter)
Reluctant Dragon, The 1941,Jl 25,12:2
Clemons, Mary Ellen
Night of the Hunter, The 1955,S 30,23:1
Clerget, Paul
Woman 1918,O 28,11:1
My Lady's Garter 1920,Mr 15,13:2
Clerk, Clive
Send Me no Flowers 1964,N 13,30:1
Clermont, Robert
Man and his Wife, A 1939,Mr 28,20:1
Clesha, I (Screenwriter)
Concentration Camp 1939,Mr 20,13:2
Cleve, Heinz von
Waltz Time in Vienna 1934,N 19,13:2
Ball im Metropol 1938,Mr 5,11:3
Biberpelz, Der; Beaver Coat, The 1939,S 9,11:3
Cleveland, George
Keeper of the Bees, The 1935,Ag 17,18:5
Make a Million 1935,N 9,19:3
Don't Get Personal 1936,F 22,12:1
Revolt of the Zombies 1936,Je 5,17:2
Adventure's End 1937,D 20,23:2
Port of Missing Girls, The 1938,Ap 4,12:5
Rose of the Rio Grande 1938,Jl 9,10:3
Streets of New York 1939,My 1,21:1
Mutiny in the Big House 1939,D 11,26:2
Girl, a Guy and a Gob, A 1941,Ap 24,25:3
Man at Large 1941,O 11,21:4
All That Money Can Buy 1941,O 17,27:2
Look Who's Laughing 1941,D 25,33:2
Playmates 1941,D 26,21:3
Call out the Marines 1942,Ja 26,18:3
Obliging Young Lady 1942,F 13,24:4
Valley of the Sun 1942,Mr 19,29:2
Spoilers, The 1942,My 22,27:2
My Favorite Spy 1942,My 29,13:4
Falcon takes Over, The 1942,My 30,9:2
Powder Town 1942,Je 8,11:2
Big Street, The 1942,Ag 14,13:1
Mexican Spitfire's Elephant 1942,S 18,25:2
Army Surgeon 1942,N 5,35:2
Seven Miles From Alcatraz 1942,N 19,31:3
Ladies' Day 1943,Mr 26,14:3
Cowboy in Manhattan 1943,My 28,19:2
Johnny Come Lately 1943,S 24,26:1
Woman of the Town, The 1944,Mr 6,17:2
It Happened Tomorrow 1944,My 29,18:2
My Pal, Wolf 1944,O 9,17:2
Abroad With two Yanks 1944,O 26,19:7
Can't Help Singing 1944,D 26,22:4
It's in the Bag 1945,Je 11,12:1
Dakota 1945,D 17,17:2
She Wouldn't Say Yes 1946,Ja 12,10:7
Pillow of Death 1946,Ja 26,19:3
Little Giant 1946,My 9,27:5
Runaround, The 1946,Je 7,16:3
Courage of Lassie 1946,Jl 25,18:5
Step by Step 1946,Ag 24,6:7
Wake up and Dream 1947,Ja 24,18:4
Easy Come, Easy Go 1947,F 6,29:2
Show-Off, The 1947,Mr 20,38:2
I Wonder Who's Kissing Her Now 1947,Jl 24,27:2
Mother Wore Tights 1947,Ag 21,33:2
Wistful Widow of Wagon Gap, The 1947,N 21,36:2
My Wild Irish Rose 1947,D 25,32:2
Albuquerque 1948,Mr 1,17:2
Fury at Furnace Creek 1948,Jl 12,11:2
Date with Judy, A 1948,Ag 7,8:2
Miraculous Journey 1948,S 20,21:2
Plunders, The 1948,N 1,28:2
Please Believe Me 1950,Je 12,19:4
Frenchie 1951,F 12,19:2

Cleveland, George— Cont
Carson City 1952,Je 14,12:2
Affair With a Stranger 1953,Jl 11,8:2
Walking my Baby Back Home 1954,Ja 16,10:5
Cleveland, John (Original Author)
Mayor of Forty-Fourth Street, The
1942,Je 11,27:4
Cleveland, John (Screenwriter)
New Faces 1954,F 20,8:7
Cleveland Indians Baseball team
Kid From Cleveland, The 1949,S 5,13:2
Clevers, Lynne
Kermesse Heroique, La 1936,S 23,29:1
Whirlpool; (Remous) 1940,O 8,31:2
Cleves, Claudie
Rothchild 1938,O 12,35:2
Clewes, Howard (Miscellaneous)
Up From the Beach 1965,Je 10,38:1
Clewes, Howard (Original Author)
Long Memory, The 1953,Jl 27,15:2
Clewes, Howard (Screenwriter)
One That Got Away, The 1958,Ap 23,40:2
Day They Robbed the Bank of England, The
1960,S 5,11:2
Clewes, Lorraine
Prison Without Bars 1939,Ap 10,13:2
Clifden, James (Screenwriter)
So Goes my Love 1946,My 2,3:7
Cliff, John
Milkman, The 1951,Ja 1,13:6
Demetrius and the Gladiators 1954,Je 19,9:1
Finger Man 1955,Jl 16,12:4
Midnight Story, The 1957,Jl 5,14:2
I Was a Teenage Frankenstein 1958,Ja 30,19:4
Cliff, Laddie
Co-Optimists, The 1930,F 5,27:2
Cliffe, Fred E (Composer)
Let George Do It 1940,O 14,25:5
It's in the Air 1940,D 10,33:2
Cliffe, H Cooper
His Children's Children 1923,N 5,15:1
Monsieur Beaucaire 1924,Ag 12,12:1 (In
Addenda)
Clifford, Bill (Director)
Birthright 1952,F 15,17:2
Clifford, Charles L (Original Author)
Army Girl 1938,Ag 12,11:1
Real Glory, The 1939,S 15,26:2
Clifford, Francis (Original Author)
Guns of Darkness 1962,Ag 18,10:1
Naked Runner, The 1967,Jl 20,30:2
Clifford, Frank (Screenwriter)
Christina 1951,Ja 15,13:1
Clifford, Jack
Skippy 1931,Ap 4,23:1
One Sunday Afternoon 1933,S 2,14:4
One Way Ticket 1936,Ja 1,35:2
Dimples 1936,O 10,21:2
High, Wide and Handsome 1937,Jl 22,15:1
Rockin' in The Rockies 1945,Jl 5,7:2
Clifford, Jill
No Highway in the Sky 1951,S 22,8:6
Knights of the Round Table 1954,Ja 8,17:2
Clifford, Kathleen
When Clouds Roll by 1919,D 29,7:2
Richard the Lion-Hearted 1923,O 22,17:1
Excess Baggage 1928,S 24,25:1
Clifford, Peggy Ann
Kind Hearts and Coronets 1950,Je 15,41:2
Clifford, Ruth
Dangerous Age, The 1923,Ja 29,11:1
Daughters of the Rich 1923,Je 18,13:5
Ponjola 1923,N 19,19:3
Dramatic Life of Abraham Lincoln, The
1924,Ja 22,17:3
Tornado, The 1924,D 15,14:1
As Man Desires 1925,F 10,20:1
Love Hour, The 1925,S 2,21:3
Only Yesterday 1933,N 10,25:1
Elmer and Elsie 1934,Ag 4,14:5
To Mary-With Love 1936,Ag 27,16:1
Not Wanted 1949,Jl 25,11:4
Slattery's Hurricane 1949,Ag 13,6:6
Wagonmaster 1950,Je 19,17:2
Man in the Gray Flannel Suit, The
1956,Ap 13,21:1
Clifford, Tommy
Song O' my Heart 1930,Mr 12,32:6
Shepper - Newfounder, The 1930,D 25,31:5
Clifford, W K Mrs (Original Author)
Eve's Lover 1925,Jl 27,17:3
Clifford, William
Ashes of Vengeance 1923,Ag 7,20:2
Clifford, William H (Original Author)
See You in Jail 1927,Ap 4,30:5
Clift, Denison (Director)
Paradise 1929,N 4,28:1
Clift, Denison (Original Author)
Yankee Clipper, The 1927,My 3,25:1
Woman Disputed, The 1928,N 10,20:8
Scotland Yard 1930,O 20,28:2
Man About Town 1932,My 28,18:2
Scotland Yard 1941,Ap 9,33:3

Clift, Montgomery
Search, The 1948,Mr 24,30:3
Red River 1948,O 1,31:2
Heiress, The 1949,O 7,35:2
Big Lift, The 1950,Ap 27,37:2
Place in the Sun, A 1951,Ag 29,20:1
I Confess 1953,Mr 23,28:2
From Here to Eternity 1953,Ag 6,16:2
Indiscretion of an American Wife 1954,Je 26,7:2
Raintree County 1957,D 21,22:1
Young Lions, The 1958,Ap 3,23:1
Lonelyhearts 1959,Mr 5,35:3
Suddenly, Last Summer 1959,D 23,22:1
Wild River 1960,My 27,22:1
Misfits, The 1961,F 2,24:2
Judgment at Nuremberg 1961,D 20,36:1
Freud 1962,D 13,37:1
Defector, The 1966,N 17,55:1
Clifton, Elmer
Fall of Babylon, The 1919,Jl 22,10:2
Birth of a Nation, The 1930,D 22,16:2
Clifton, Elmer (Director)
Boots 1919,Mr 10,9:3
Peppy Polly 1919,Ap 7,11:5
Nugget Nell 1919,Jl 28,8:5
Nobody Home 1919,Au 25,8:5
Turning the Tables 1919,N 3,13:3
Mary Ellen Comes to Town 1920,Mr 22,12:1
Down to the Sea in Ships 1923,F 19,10:1
Wreck of the Hesperus, The 1927,N 28,18:5
Let 'Er go, Gallegher 1928,Ja 16,24:1
Crusade Against Rackets 1937,Jl 26,15:3
Isle of Destiny 1940,Ap 8,15:2
Swamp Woman 1941,D 27,15:2
Not Wanted 1949,Jl 25,11:4
Clifton, Elmer (Screenwriter)
Teen Age 1944,Je 19,17:1
Clifton, Franklin M (Screenwriter)
Jesse James 1927,O 17,20:2
Clifton, Herbert
She's Got Everything 1938,Ja 14,21:3
Clifton-Taylor, Alec (Miscellaneous)
Palaces of a Queen 1967,Je 27,32:1
Climati, Antonio (Cinematographer)
Mondo Cane; Dog's World, A 1963,Ap 4,58:1 (In
Addenda)
Women of the World 1963,Jl 3,14:1
Africa Addio 1967,Mr 13,47:3
Climenhaga, Joel
One-Way Ticket to Hell 1955,D 8,45:1
Clinch, William J Capt (Composer)
I Wanted Wings 1941,Mr 27,29:4
CLINE
See Also KLEIN, KLINE, CLYNE
Cline, Brady
Fourth Commandment, The 1927,Ap 6,25:1
Hooray for Love 1935,Jl 13,16:2
Cline, Edward F (Director)
Circus Days 1923,Ag 6,14:2
When a Man's a Man 1924,F 5,20:1
Captain January 1924,Jl 7,10:4
Old Clothes 1925,N 9,25:1
Let It Rain 1927,Mr 9,29:1
Soft Cushions 1927,S 12,29:1
Forward Pass, The 1929,N 29,25:1
In the Next Room 1930,Ap 7,21:1
Leathernecking 1930,S 13,9:3
Widow From Chicago, The 1930,D 20,20:6
Hook, Line and Sinker 1930,D 25,31:5
Cracked Nuts 1931,Ap 6,24:1
Naughty Flirt, The 1931,Ap 13,17:1
Girl Habit, The 1931,Jl 4,11:5
Million Dollar Legs 1932,Jl 9,7:5
Parole Girl 1933,Ap 10,8:2
Dude Ranger, The 1934,O 2,18:5
Peck's bad Boy 1934,O 6,20:1
When a Man's a Man 1935,F 22,27:2
F-Man 1936,My 4,16:1
On Again-Off Again 1937,S 18,15:3
Forty Naughty Girls 1937,S 18,15:3
Hawaii Calls 1938,Ap 29,17:2
Go Chase Yourself 1938,Je 15,27:1
Breaking the Ice 1938,S 23,35:3
Peck's bad Boy With the Circus 1939,Ja 11,17:4
My Little Chickadee 1940,Mr 16,8:2
Bank Dick, The 1940,D 13,29:2
Meet the Chump 1941,F 27,23:4
Never Give a Sucker an Even Break
1941,O 27,21:2
What's Cookin' 1942,F 26,15:5
Private Buckaroo 1942,Je 25,27:4
Give Out, Sisters 1942,Ag 28,22:3
He's my Guy 1943,Mr 12,12:3
Crazy House 1943,D 16,33:3
Swingtime Johnny 1943,D 17,23:3
Ghost Catchers 1944,My 31,22:3
See my Lawyer 1945,My 4,23:4
Bringing Up Father 1946,N 22,27:3
Cline, Edward F (Original Author)
Bringing Up Father 1946,N 22,27:3
Cline, George
Janice Meredith 1924,Ag 6,13:3

Cline, Robert
Temple of Venus, The 1923,N 1,24:3
Clinton, Vivien
Cry, the Beloved Country 1952,Ja 24,23:2
Clive, Colin
Journey's End 1930,Ap 9,25:1
Frankenstein 1931,D 5,21:2
Lily Christine 1932,My 29,VIII,4:4 (In Addenda)
Christopher Strong 1933,Mr 10,19:2
Looking Forward 1933,My 1,10:2
Key, The 1934,My 30,14:3
One More River 1934,Ag 10,21:1
Clive of India 1935,Ja 18,29:1
Right to Live, The 1935,F 16,9:1
Bride of Frankenstein, The 1935,My 11,21:2
Girl From 10th Avenue, The 1935,My 27,20:6
Mad Love 1935,Ag 5,20:2
Man Who Broke the Bank at Monte Carlo, The
1935,N 15,20:2
History Is Made at Night 1937,Mr 29,14:2
Woman I Love, The 1937,Ap 16,27:2
Clive, E E
Invisible Man, The 1933,N 18,18:4
One More River 1934,Ag 10,21:1
Bulldog Drummond Strikes Back 1934,Ag 16,20:2
Charlie Chan in London 1934,S 13,26:1
Mystery of Edwin Drood, The 1935,Mr 21,27:1
Bride of Frankenstein, The 1935,My 11,21:2
Stars Over Broadway 1935,N 14,17:3
Tale of Two Cities, A 1935,D 26,21:2
Captain Blood 1935,D 27,14:1
Little Lord Fauntleroy 1936,Ap 3,27:1
Unguarded Hour, The 1936,Ap 4,11:1
Golden Arrow, The 1936,My 4,16:1
Dracula's Daughter 1936,My 18,14:2
Trouble for Two 1936,My 30,7:2
Ticket to Paradise 1936,Ag 8,5:3
Piccadilly Jim 1936,Ag 31,19:1
Cain and Mabel 1936,O 19,22:1
Libeled Lady 1936,O 31,24:2
Charge of the Light Brigade, The 1936,N 2,24:1
Tarzan Escapes 1936,N 20,27:2
Lloyds of London 1936,N 26,39:1
Camille 1937,Ja 23,13:1
On the Avenue 1937,F 5,17:3
Maid of Salem 1937,Mr 4,27:2
Ready, Willing and Able 1937,Mr 15,27:1
Personal Property 1937,Ap 11,27:2
Night Must Fall 1937,Ap 30,17:2
Emperor's Candlesticks, The 1937,Jl 9,18:1
Love Under Fire 1937,Ag 28,8:2
Bulldog Drummond Comes Back 1937,S 4,8:3
It's Love I'm After 1937,N 11,31:2
Live, Love and Learn 1937,N 19,27:2
Beg, Borrow or Steal 1937,D 10,33:2
Danger-Love at Work 1937,D 11,22:2
Bulldog Drummond's Revenge 1937,D 17,33:2
Arsene Lupin Returns 1938,Mr 9,21:1
Bulldog Drummond's Peril 1938,Mr 18,23:2
First 100 Years, The 1938,My 13,17:2
Kidnapped 1938,My 28,9:2
Gateway 1938,Ag 8,9:2
Bulldog Drummond in Africa 1938,Ag 25,15:1
Submarine Patrol 1938,N 19,9:2
Last Warning, The 1938,D 8,34:4
Arrest Bulldog Drummond 1939,Ja 12,23:2
Little Princess, The 1939,Mr 11,21:1
I'm From Missouri 1939,Mr 23,27:1
Hound of the Baskervilles, The 1939,Mr 25,19:2
Bulldog Drummond's Secret Police
1939,Mr 30,19:3
Rose of Washington Square 1939,My 6,21:2
Man About Town 1939,Je 29,19:1
Bachelor Mother 1939,Je 30,17:2
Bulldog Drummond's Bride 1939,Jl 13,17:2
Adventures of Sherlock Holmes, The
1939,S 2,20:1
Honeymoon's Over, The 1939,D 15,33:3
Raffles 1940,Ja 13,11:2
Congo Maisie 1940,F 8,18:4
Earl of Chicago, The 1940,Mr 14,29:3
Pride and Prejudice 1940,Ag 9,19:1
Foreign Correspondent 1940,Ag 28,15:2
Clive, Henry
Fighting Odds 1917,O 1,14:2
Obey the Law 1933,Mr 13,18:3
Clive, Iris
Cat Creeps, The 1946,My 18,12:4
Cloche, Maurice (Director)
Ces Dames aux Chapeaux Verts; Ladies in the
Green Hats, The 1945,Ap 5,26:2
Monsieur Vincent 1948,D 21,33:2
Never Take No for an Answer 1952,Ap 29,32:2
Girls of the Night 1959,Mr 21,13:2
Viscount, The 1967,My 11,50:1
Cloche, Maurice (Screenwriter)
Ces Dames aux Chapeaux Verts; Ladies in the
Green Hats, The 1945,Ap 5,26:2
Girls of the Night 1959,Mr 21,13:2
Cloete, Stuart (Original Author)
Fiercest Heart, The 1961,Ag 3,13:5

Clogg, Si
Our Daily Bread 1934,O 3,25:2
Clonbough, G Butler
Till I Come Back to You 1918,Ag 26,9:1
Cloninger, Ralph
Monte Cristo 1922,Ag 15,20:3
Clooney, Rosemary
Stars Are Singing, The 1953,Mr 12,24:2
Here Come the Girls 1953,D 26,10:1
Red Garters 1954,Mr 27,13:5
White Christmas 1954,O 15,16:3
Deep in my Heart 1954,D 10,35:2
Clore, Leon (Producer)
Virgin Island 1960,Mr 24,39:5
Morgan! 1966,Ap 5,42:2
Clori, Enrico
Sotto la Croce del Sud; Under the Southern Cross
1939,Ap 10,13:4
Clork, Harry (Miscellaneous)
Diamond Jim 1935,Ag 24,18:2
King Solomon of Broadway 1935,O 19,12:2
New Faces of 1937 1937,Jl 2,25:1
Reluctant Dragon, The 1941,Jl 25,12:2
Clork, Harry (Original Author)
Milky Way, The 1936,Mr 26,27:2
See my Lawyer 1945,My 4,23:4
Kid From Brooklyn, The 1946,Ap 19,25:2
Clork, Harry (Screenwriter)
Princess O'Hara 1935,Ap 13,11:3
Mr Dynamite 1935,My 25,12:1
His Night Out 1935,N 16,19:2
Remember Last Night? 1935,N 21,27:2
Absolute Quiet 1936,My 2,11:1
Flying Hostess 1936,D 14,29:4
When's Your Birthday? 1937,Mr 19,27:2
Oh, Doctor 1937,Je 19,20:3
Flirting With Fate 1938,D 15,35:3
And One Was Beautiful 1940,Ap 11,32:4
Conga Nights, La 1940,Je 5,33:5
Moon Over Burma 1940,D 12,37:4
Las Vegas Nights 1941,Mr 20,25:2
Whistling in the Dark 1941,Ag 28,23:2
Born to Sing 1942,F 19,23:2
Ship Ahoy 1942,Je 26,16:5
Broadway Rhythm 1944,Ap 14,24:6
Thrill of Brazil, The 1946,S 6,18:3
Mighty McGurk, The 1947,Ap 4,19:4
Sainted Sisters, The 1948,My 20,35:2
Tea for Two 1950,S 2,11:2
Painting the Clouds With Sunshine 1951,S 1,9:6
Closas, Alberto
Age of Infidelity 1958,Ag 19,23:2
Close, Iva
Jolly Peasant, The 1929,Jl 1,31:2
Close, Pat
Sunrise at Campobello 1960,S 29,32:1
Close, William
Voice of the Hurricane 1964,Je 3,36:4
Closson, Herman (Screenwriter)
We Lived Through Buchenwald 1947,Jl 24,27:3
Clothier, William C (Cinematographer)
Memphis Belle, The 1944,Ap 14,1:2
Cloud, Blue
Sante Fe Trail, The 1930,O 18,23:2
Cloud, Thunder Chief
Geronimo 1940,F 8,18:3
Cloud, Walter
Run, Appaloosa, Run! 1966,Jl 14,28:1
Clouse, Russel (Original Author)
Tall Story 1960,Ap 7,46:1
Clouston, J Storer (Original Author)
Lunatic at Large, The 1927,F 1,25:1
U-Boat 29 1939,O 6,31:3
Cloutier, Suzanne
Temptation 1946,D 25,33:6
Doctor in the House 1955,F 19,18:3
Othello 1955,S 13,27:1
Romanoff and Juliet 1961,Je 9,26:1
Clouzot, Henri-Georges (Director)
Murderer Lives at Number 21, The
1947,Ag 18,12:3
Corbeau, Le; Raven, The 1948,F 24,21:1
Jenny Lamour 1948,Mr 6,17:2
Manon 1950,D 26,19:1
Miquette 1951,F 5,18:2
Wages of Fear, The 1955,F 17,23:1
Diabolique 1955,N 22,41:1
Mystery of Picasso, The 1957,O 8,41:2
Truth, The 1961,Je 27,23:2
Clouzot, Henri-Georges (Miscellaneous)
Corbeau, Le; Raven, The 1948,F 24,21:1
Strangers in the House 1949,O 13,33:3
Clouzot, Henri-Georges (Producer)
Diabolique 1955,N 22,41:1
Mystery of Picasso, The 1957,O 8,41:2
Clouzot, Henri-Georges (Screenwriter)
Barge-Keeper's Daughter, The 1945,S 6,23:3
Murderer Lives at Number 21, The
1947,Ag 18,12:3
Corbeau, Le; Raven, The 1948,F 24,21:1
Jenny Lamour 1948,Mr 6,17:2
Strangers in the House 1949,O 13,33:3
Manon 1950,D 26,19:1

Miquette 1951,F 5,18:2
Wages of Fear, The 1955,F 17,23:1
Diabolique 1955,N 22,41:1
If all the Guys in the World 1957,Ap 23,34:1
Truth, The 1961,Je 27,23:2
Clouzot, Jean (Miscellaneous)
Proud and the Beautiful, The 1956,My 29,32:2
Clouzot, Vera
Wages of Fear, The 1955,F 17,23:1
Diabolique 1955,N 22,41:1
Clovelly, Cecil
Forest Ring, The 1930,Ap 26,11:1
So Young, So Bad 1950,Jl 24,15:2
Clowes, St John L (Director)
No Orchids for Miss Blandish 1951,F 23,33:2
Clowes, St John L (Original Author)
Dear Murderer 1948,My 8,12:2
Clowes, St John L (Producer)
No Orchids for Miss Blandish 1951,F 23,33:2
Clowes, St John L (Screenwriter)
Battle for Music 1945,O 15,13:2
No Orchids for Miss Blandish 1951,F 23,33:2
Clsar, George
Nightfall 1957,Ja 24,34:1
Clugston, D N
In the Palace of the King 1923,D 3,14:1
Clugston, H M
Navigator, The 1924,O 13,21:1
Clugston, Kaiharine (Original Author)
Last Gentleman, The 1934,O 18,26:5
Clum, Woodworth (Original Author)
Walk the Proud Land 1956,S 8,20:6 (In
Addenda)
Clune, Peter
Blast of Silence 1961,D 30,12:1
Clunes, Alec
Melba 1953,Je 25,23:1
Quentin Durward 1955,N 24,41:1
Richard III 1956,Mr 12,1:4
Cluny, Genevieve
Cousins, The (Les Cousins) 1959,N 24,44:1
Love Game, The 1960,N 9,44:1
Joker, The; (Farceur, Le) 1961,Ag 8,32:2
Cluny, Genevieve (Miscellaneous)
Love Game, The 1960,N 9,44:1
Cluradei, Giacomo
Mill on the Po, The 1951,O 23,35:2
Clurman, Harold (Director)
Deadline at Dawn 1946,Ap 4,33:2
Clustam, G H (Composer)
Mimi 1936,Ja 10,16:3
Clute, Chester
Exclusive 1937,Jl 22,15:1
Dance Charlie Dance 1937,Ag 26,25:2
Great Garrick, The 1937,O 25,23:1
Rascals 1938,My 27,12:2
Service de Luxe 1938,O 24,13:2
Touchdown Army 1938,O 28,27:2
Annabel Takes a Tour 1938,D 29,15:3
Dancing Co-Ed 1939,N 10,27:3
Doctor Takes a Wife, The 1940,Je 15,12:2
Millionaires in Prison 1940,Jl 16,21:3
Hired Wife 1940,S 14,11:2
Dance, Girl, Dance 1940,O 11,25:2
Too Many Girls 1940,N 21,43:1
Love Thy Neighbor 1940,D 18,32:5
She Couldn't Say No 1941,Ja 17,21:3
My Favorite Spy 1942,My 29,13:4
Yankee Doodle Dandy 1942,My 30,9:1
Wife Takes a Flyer, The 1942,Je 19,19:1
Just off Broadway 1942,Ag 29,18:4
Chatterbox 1943,Jl 2,15:3
Crazy House 1943,D 16,33:3
Rationing 1944,Ap 10,14:2
Arsenic and old Lace 1944,S 2,17:2
San Diego, I Love You 1944,N 10,25:1
Mildred Pierce 1945,S 29,12:2
Guest Wife 1945,O 18,21:2
She Went to the Races 1946,F 1,29:2
Cinderella Jones 1946,Mr 16,9:6
Angel on my Shoulder 1946,O 21,27:2
Hit Parade of 1947 1947,My 5,32:8
Something in the Wind 1947,Ag 29,14:3
Mary Ryan, Detective 1949,N 4,33:3
Clute, Sidney
Crime and Punishment, U S A 1959,Je 17,39:3
Cry of Battle 1963,O 12,27:2
Clutsam, G H (Composer)
Kiss the Boys Goodbye 1941,Ag 14,21:2
Clutsam, G H (Miscellaneous)
April Romance 1937,Ja 27,17:4
Clutsam, G H (Screenwriter)
April Romance 1937,Ja 27,17:4
Cluytens, Andre (Composer)
Barber of Seville 1949,Jl 21,21:2
Clyde, Andy
Good-Bye Kiss, The 1928,N 12,18:2
Million Dollar Legs 1932,Jl 9,7:5
Little Minister, The 1934,D 28,25:1
McFadden's Flats 1935,Mr 13,16:2
Annie Oakley 1935,D 24,10:5
Yellow Dust 1936,F 24,14:1
Two in a Crowd 1936,O 5,25:1

Clyde, Andy— Cont
Barrier, The 1937,N 27,21:2
It's a Wonderful World 1939,My 19,27:2
Bad Lands 1939,Ag 9,15:2
Abe Lincoln in Illinois 1940,F 23,19:2
Cherokee Strip 1940,N 4,23:2
Green Years, The 1946,Ap 5,21:2
Plainsman and the Lady, The 1946,N 4,33:1
When Comedy Was King 1960,Mr 30,42:1
Sound of Laughter, The 1963,D 18,44:2
30 Years of Fun 1963,D 26,33:4
Clyde, David
Cardinal Richelieu 1935,Ap 19,24:2
Hard Rock Harrigan 1935,Jl 30,16:2
Man on the Flying Trapeze 1935,Ag 3,16:2
Suzy 1936,Jl 25,16:1
Another Dawn 1937,Je 18,25:3
Fury and the Woman 1937,Je 22,26:2
Love Under Fire 1937,Ag 28,8:2
Arrest Bulldog Drummond 1939,Ja 12,23:2
Bulldog Drummond's Secret Police
1939,Mr 30,19:3
Death of a Champion 1939,Ag 24,17:3
Rulers of the Sea 1939,N 9,27:1
Adventure in Diamonds 1940,Ap 4,27:2
Smilin' Through 1941,D 5,29:2
Feminine Touch, The 1941,D 12,35:3
H M Pulham, Esq 1941,D 19,35:1
Gay Sisters, The 1942,Ag 15,14:2
Now, Voyager 1942,O 23,25:3
Nightmare 1942,D 4,31:2
Lodger, The 1944,Ja 20,15:3
Scarlet Claw, The 1944,My 19,12:1
House of Fear, The 1945,Mr 19,23:3
Molly and Me 1945,My 26,18:2
Clyde, June
Tanned Legs 1929,D 2,28:2
Hit the Deck 1930,Ja 15,28:6
Cuckoos, The 1930,Ap 26,11:1
Midnight Mystery 1930,Je 2,25:4
Men Are Like That 1931,Ag 17,18:2
Mad Parade, The 1931,S 19,10:2
Morals for Women 1931,N 16,23:1
Branded Men 1931,D 12,23:3
Secret Witness, The 1931,D 21,28:4
File No 113 1932,F 20,11:2
Cohens and Kellys in Hollywood, The
1932,Ap 22,23:2
Radio Patrol 1932,Jl 14,24:2
Back Street 1932,Ag 29,9:2
All American, The 1932,O 22,18:4
Tess of the Storm Country 1932,N 19,20:2
Hold Me Tight 1933,My 22,18:6
Study in Scarlet, A 1933,Je 1,15:3
Only Yesterday 1933,N 10,25:1
Hollywood Party 1934,My 26,12:2
Dance Band 1936,Ja 4,19:2
Forbidden Music 1938,D 27,13:2
School for Husbands 1939,F 7,16:2
Unfinished Business 1941,S 2,20:2
She Shall Have Music 1942,O 31,11:2
Hi 'Ya Chum 1943,F 26,17:4
Night Without Stars 1953,Jl 14,19:4
Clyde, Thomas (Producer)
Malaga 1962,F 22,20:3
Guns of Darkness 1962,Ag 18,10:1
Clyde Valley Stompers
Dream Maker, The 1964,Ap 23,34:1
Clymer, John B (Original Author)
Emergency Call 1933,Je 24,16:2
CLYNE
See Also CLINE, KLEIN, KLINE
Clyne, Fiona
High and Dry 1954,Ag 31,25:5
Bridal Path, The 1959,D 21,34:2
Coad, Joyce
Society Scandal, A 1924,Mr 10,18:2
Devil's Circus, The 1926,Mr 29,24:3
Scarlet Letter, The 1926,Ag 10,19:2
Mother 1927,My 4,29:2
Drums of Love 1928,Ja 25,20:4
Devotion 1931,O 3,20:2
X Marks the Spot 1931,D 7,16:1
Captured 1933,Ag 18,18:3
Coad, Joyce Marie
One Woman to Another 1927,S 19,30:3
Coakley, Marion
Enchanted Cottage, The 1924,Ap 14,14:1
Coates, Albert
Two Girls and a Sailor 1944,Je 15,16:1
Coates, Albert (Miscellaneous)
Clown Must Laugh, A 1938,O 12,35:2
Coates, Edith
Beggar's Opera, The 1953,Ag 25,18:2
Coates, Phyllis
I Was a Teenage Frankenstein 1958,Ja 30,19:4
Cobb, Edmund
I'm From the City 1938,Ag 19,13:4
I Was a Prisoner on Devil's Island
1941,Jl 28,16:4
Texas 1941,O 17,27:3
River of no Return 1954,My 1,13:2

Cobb, Elisabeth (Original Author)
She Was a Lady 1934,Ag 22,21:2
Cobb, Humphrey (Original Author)
Paths of Glory 1957,D 26,23:2
Cobb, Humphrey (Screenwriter)
San Quentin 1937,Ag 4,15:2
Cobb, Irvin S
Great White Way, The 1924,Ja 4,10:1
Steamboat Around the Bend 1935,S 20,17:2
Everybody's Old Man 1936,Mr 26,27:2
Pepper 1936,Ag 24,11:2
Hawaii Calls 1938,Ap 29,17:2
Young in Heart, The 1938,N 4,27:2
Arkansas Traveler, The 1938,N 17,29:2
Cobb, Irvin S (Miscellaneous)
Peck's bad Boy 1921,Ap 25,9:2
Cobb, Irvin S (Original Author)
Face in the Dark, The 1918,Ap 15,13:3
Life of the Party, The 1920,N 22,13:3
Boys Will Be Boys 1921,My 6,20:2 (Incorrect in
this edition; use 1921,My 16,20:2 elsewhere)
Woman Accused 1933,Mr 13,18:2
Judge Priest 1934,O 12,33:1
Our Leading Citizen 1939,Ag 24,17:1
Sun Shines Bright, The 1954,Mr 17,25:2
Cobb, Lee J
Golden Boy 1939,S 8,28:2
This Thing Called Love 1941,F 14,15:2
Men of Boys Town 1941,Ap 11,24:6
Paris Calling 1942,Ja 19,21:2
Moon Is Down, The 1943,Mr 27,8:6
Tonight We Raid Calais 1943,Ap 15,20:2
Song of Bernadette, The 1944,Ja 27,15:2
Winged Victory 1944,D 21,16:2
Anna and the King of Siam 1946,Je 21,20:2
Boomerang 1947,Mr 6,36:2
Johnny O'Clock 1947,Mr 27,39:2
Captain from Castile 1947,D 26,22:4
Call Northside 777 1948,F 19,29:2
Miracle of the Bells, The 1948,Mr 17,30:1
Luck of the Irish, The 1948,S 16,34:1
Dark Past, The 1948,D 23,25:2
Thieves' Highway 1949,S 24,8:6
Man Who Cheated Himself, The 1951,F 9,21:2
Sirocco 1951,Je 14,31:2
Fighter, The 1952,My 31,12:6
Tall Texan, The 1953,Ap 13,32:4
Yankee Pasha 1954,Ap 19,19:2
Gorilla at Large 1954,Je 12,13:2
On the Waterfront 1954,Jl 29,18:1
Racers, The 1955,F 5,13:2
Left Hand of God, The 1955,S 22,34:5
Man in the Gray Flannel Suit, The
1956,Ap 13,21:1
12 Angry Men 1957,Ap 15,24:1
Garment Jungle, The 1957,My 16,28:2
Three Faces of Eve, The 1957,S 27,16:6
Brothers Karamazov, The 1958,F 21,18:2
Man of the West 1958,O 2,44:3
Party Girl 1958,O 29,30:1
Trap, The 1959,Ja 29,18:4
Green Mansions 1959,Mr 20,26:1
But Not for Me 1959,O 3,14:6
Exodus 1960,D 16,44:1
4 Horsemen of the Apocalypse, The
1962,Mr 10,10:2
How the West Was Won 1963,Ap 1,54:1
Come Blow Your Horn 1963,Je 7,37:1
Our Man Flint 1966,Ja 26,23:4
In Like Flint 1967,Mr 16,53:2
Coogan's Bluff 1968,O 3,56:1
Cobb, Ty
Ninth Inning, The 1942,Ja 8,30:3
Cobb (Original Author)
Fighting Odds 1917,O 1,14:2
Cobelli, Giancario
Taming of the Shrew, The 1967,Mr 9,43:1
Cobham, Alan Sir (Cinematographer)
With Cobham to the Cape 1927,Je 13,17:1
Cobo, Alejandro
Dama de las Camelias, La 1944,S 26,16:1
Cobo, Roberto
Young and the Damned, The 1952,Mr 25,23:2
Mexican Bus ride 1954,Jl 21,18:3
Cobos, German
Taxi for Tobruk 1965,Mr 30,52:1
Coburn, Charles
Boss Tweed 1933,S 1,15:4
Of Human Hearts 1938,F 18,23:1
Yellow Jack 1938,My 20,17:2
Vivacious Lady 1938,Je 3,17:3
Lord Jeff 1938,Jl 1,22:2
Idiot's Delight 1939,F 3,13:1
Made for Each Other 1939,F 17,17:2
Story of Alexander Graham Bell, The
1939,Ap 1,17:2
Bachelor Mother 1939,Je 30,17:2
In Name Only 1939,Ag 4,11:3
Stanley and Livingstone 1939,Ag 5,18:2
Road to Singapore 1940,Mr 14,29:2
Florian 1940,Je 6,33:2
Edison the Man 1940,Je 7,27:2
Three Faces West 1940,Ag 19,13:2

Lady Eve, The 1941,F 26,17:1
Devil and Miss Jones, The 1941,My 16,21:2
Our Wife 1941,S 18,31:1
Unexpected Uncle 1941,S 25,29:1
H M Pulham, Esq 1941,D 19,35:1
Kings Row 1942,F 3,23:2
In This our Life 1942,My 9,10:2
George Washington Slept Here 1942,O 31,11:1
More the Merrier, The 1943,My 14,17:1
Constant Nymph, The 1943,Jl 24,8:2
Heaven Can Wait 1943,Ag 12,15:1
My Kingdom for a Cook 1943,O 15,15:3
Princess O'Rourke 1943,N 6,16:2
Knickerbocker Holiday 1944,Ap 20,22:7
Wilson 1944,Ag 2,18:1
Impatient Years, The 1944,S 20,20:1
Together Again 1944,N 24,19:2
Royal Scandal, A 1945,Ap 12,19:2
Rhapsody in Blue 1945,Je 28,22:2
Over 21 1945,Ag 17,20:2
Shady Lady 1945,O 11,26:2
Green Years, The 1946,Ag 5,21:2
Colonel Effingham's Raid 1946,Ap 5,21:3
Lured 1947,Ag 29,14:4
Paradine Case, The 1948,Ja 9,26:2
B F's Daughter 1948,Mr 25,35:2
Green Grass of Wyoming 1948,Je 10,28:3
Impact 1949,Mr 21,19:2
Everybody Does It 1949,O 26,32:2
Doctor and the Girl, The 1949,O 31,20:2
Yes Sir, That's my Baby 1949,N 11,31:2
Peggy 1950,Jl 21,15:4
Louisa 1950,O 25,45:2
Mr Music 1950,D 21,34:3
Has Anybody Seen My Gal 1952,Jl 5,7:2
Monkey Business 1952,S 6,12:6
Trouble Along the Way 1953,My 7,37:2
Gentlemen Prefer Blondes 1953,Jl 16,17:2
Long Wait, The 1954,Jl 3,9:2
How to be Very, Very Popular 1955,Jl 23,10:1
Power and The Prize, The 1956,S 27,42:1
Around the World in 80 Days 1956,O 18,37:1
How to Murder a Rich Uncle 1957,O 26,19:2
Story of Mankind, The 1957,N 9,31:2
Remarkable Mr Pennypacker, The 1959,F 21,25:2
Stranger in my Arms 1959,Mr 4,34:2
John Paul Jones 1959,Je 17,39:1
Pepe 1960,D 22,18:1
Coburn, Dorothy
Laurel and Hardy's Laughing 20's 1965,N 18,55:2
Coburn, Frank
Operation Disaster 1951,Ja 15,13:1
Coburn, Helen
Skyscraper Souls 1932,Ag 5,11:2
Coburn; James
Magnificent Seven, The 1960,N 24,48:3
Hell is for Heroes 1962,Jl 12,19:3
Great Escape, The 1963,Ag 8,19:1
Charade 1963,D 6,40:1
Man From Galveston, The 1964,Ja 23,26:3
Americanization of Emily, The 1964,O 28,51:1
Major Dundee 1965,Ap 8,45:1
High Wind in Jamaica, A 1965,Je 17,27:2
Loved One, The 1965,O 12,57:1
Our Man Flint 1966,Ja 26,23:4
What Did You Do in the War, Daddy?
1966,S 1,28:1
Dead Heat on a Merry-Go-Round
1966,O 13,50:1
In Like Flint 1967,Mr 16,53:2
President's Analyst, The 1967,D 22,44:4
Duffy 1968,S 17,50:3
Candy 1968,D 18,54:2
Coby, Fred
White Heat 1949,S 3,7:2
Coca, Imogene
Under the Yum Yum Tree 1963,N 21,43:2
Sound of Laughter, The 1963,D 18,44:2
Cocchi, Umberto
Terra Madre 1931,O 31,22:2
Coccia, Aurelio
Humming Bird, The 1924,Ja 14,2:1
Argentine Love 1924,D 23,16:2
Aloma of the South Seas 1926,My 17,19:1
Cochetti, Ranieri (Screenwriter)
Theodora, Slave Empress 1955,Ja 12,24:2
COCHRAN
See Also COCHRANE
Cochran, Dorcas (Original Author)
Frisco Lil 1942,F 12,27:2
Cochran, Dorcas (Screenwriter)
Juke Box Jenny 1942,Ap 17,21:3
Wife of Monte Cristo, The 1946,Ap 8,31:2
Cochran, Eddie
Girl Can't Help It, The 1957,F 9,12:7
Untamed Youth 1957,My 11,24:6
Cochran, Rice E (Original Author)
Mister Scoutmaster 1953,Ag 29,10:1
Cochran, Robert
Sanders of the River 1935,Je 27,16:1
Scrooge 1935,D 14,11:1
I Stand Condemned 1936,Jl 2,27:2
Man Who Could Work Miracles, The

Cochran, Robert — Cont
1937,F 22,13:1
Troopship 1938,Ap 26,18:2
Cochran, Steve
Wonder Man 1945,Je 9,17:2
Kid From Brooklyn, The 1946,Ap 19,25:2
Chase, The 1946,N 18,31:2
Best Years of our Lives, The 1946,N 22,27:2
Copacabana 1947,Jl 12,7:2
Song Is Born, A 1948,O 20,37:2
White Heat 1949,S 3,7:2
Damned Don't Cry, The 1950,Ap 8,9:2
Highway 301 1950,D 9,13:2
Dallas 1951,Ja 13,10:4
Storm Warning 1951,Mr 3,8:2
Raton Pass 1951,Ap 20,25:1
Inside the Walls of Folsom Prison
1951,My 28,17:4
Tomorrow Is Another Day 1951,Ag 9,17:5
Jim Thorpe - All American 1951,Ag 25,7:2
Tanks are Coming, The 1951,D 6,42:4
Lion and the Horse, The 1952,My 19,12:2
Operation Secret 1952,N 6,37:2
She's Back on Broadway 1953,Mr 12,24:2
Desert Song, The 1953,My 21,39:2
Carnival Story 1954,Ap 17,8:2
Slander 1957,Ja 17,34:4
Beat Generation, The 1959,O 22,47:4
Deadly Companions, The 1962,Ap 12,41:7
Grido, Il 1962,O 23,42:1
Of Love and Desire 1963,S 12,32:1
Mozambique 1966,F 10,33:1
COCHRANE
See Also COCHRAN
Cochrane, Frank
Yellow Mask, The 1930,D 8,26:1
Chu Chin Chow 1934,S 22,12:2
Bulldog Drummond at Bay 1937,O 25,23:2
Tenth Man, The 1937,N 15,15:2
Dark Sands 1938,Ag 17,23:4
Cochrane, Nick
Priorities on Parade 1942,Jl 23,19:2
Cockerell, Alston
Hold 'Em Navy 1937,N 6,14:2
Cockrell, Francis (Original Author)
Walking on Air 1936,S 12,20:2
Professor Beware 1938,Jl 14,17:1
Dark Waters 1944,N 22,25:2
On the Threshold of Space 1956,Mr 30,10:5
Cockrell, Francis (Screenwriter)
Lady in a Jam 1942,S 11,25:2
Rhubarb 1951,Ag 31,12:2
Inferno 1953,Ag 12,22:2
Raid, The 1954,Ag 21,10:4
Cockrell, Gary
Tarzan the Magnificent 1960,Jl 21,17:1
Lolita 1962,Je 14,23:2
War Lover, The 1963,Mr 7,8:5
Tiara Tahiti 1963,N 6,32:1
Man in the Middle 1964,Mr 5,36:1
Americanization of Emily, The 1964,O 28,51:1
Bedford Incident, The 1965,N 3,43:1
Cockrell, Marian (Original Author)
Professor Beware 1938,Jl 14,17:1
Dark Waters 1944,N 22,25:2
Cockrell, Marian (Screenwriter)
Dark Waters 1944,N 22,25:2
Cocteau, Jean
Strange Ones, The 1952,Jl 29,17:3
Testament of Orpheus 1962,Ap 10,48:1
Cocteau, Jean (Director)
Sang d'un Poete, Le 1933,N 3,23:3
Beauty and the Beast 1947,D 24,12:2
Eagle with Two Heads 1948,D 30,24:2
Storm Within, The; (Parents Terribles, Les)
1950,Ap 24,21:2
Orpheus 1950,N 30,42:2
Testament of Orpheus 1962,Ap 10,48:1
Cocteau, Jean (Miscellaneous)
Eternal Return, The; Eternel Retour, L'
1948,Ja 5,15:2
Days of our Years 1951,D 6,42:2
Dames du Bois de Boulogne, Les; Ladies of the
Park 1964,Ap 4,15:5
Cocteau, Jean (Original Author)
Strange Ones, The 1952,Jl 29,17:3
Intimate Relations 1954,F 22,15:4
Cocteau, Jean (Screenwriter)
Beauty and the Beast 1947,D 24,12:2
Eternal Return, The; Eternel Retour, L'
1948,Ja 5,15:2
Ruy Blas 1948,O 4,14:2
Eagle with Two Heads 1948,D 30,24:2
Storm Within, The; (Parents Terribles, Les)
1950,Ap 24,21:2
Orpheus 1950,N 30,42:2
Daughter of the Sands 1952,F 18,15:2
Strange Ones, The 1952,Jl 29,17:3
Testament of Orpheus 1962,Ap 10,48:1
Coddard, Charles W (Original Author)
Misleading Lady, The 1932,Ap 9,18:1
Codee, Ann
Under the Pampas Moon 1935,My 31,11:1
Expensive Husbands 1938,Ja 8,19:3

Codee, Ann— Cont

Come Live With Me 1941,F 28,17:3
Tonight We Raid Calais 1943,Ap 15,20:2
Paris After Dark 1943,O 23,11:1
Hangover Square 1945,F 8,15:2
This Love of Ours 1945,N 1,20:2
Holiday in Mexico 1946,Ag 16,19:3
So Dark the Night 1946,D 7,16:2
Other Love, The 1947,My 15,32:4
Unfinished Dance, The 1947,O 31,29:2
That Midnight Kiss 1949,S 23,28:2
Under my Skin 1950,Mr 18,9:2
On the Riviera 1951,My 24,47:1
Mr Imperium 1951,O 15,22:2
Dangerous When Wet 1953,Je 19,18:1
Kiss Me Kate 1953,N 6,23:2
Interrupted Melody 1955,My 6,18:1
Daddy Long Legs 1955,My 6,17:5
Kings Go Forth 1958,Jl 4,15:2

Coder, Ann

War of the Worlds, The 1953,Ag 14,10:2

Codrick, Thomas H (Miscellaneous)

Bambi 1942,Ag 14,13:1

Cody, Iron Eyes

Senator Was Indiscreet, The 1947,D 27,9:2
Paleface, The 1948,D 16,41:2
Massacre River 1949,Jl 15,17:2
Sand 1949,Ag 5,23:2
Red Mountain 1952,Ap 26,19:2
Son of Paleface 1952,O 2,32:3
Sitting Bull 1954,N 26,24:4
Gun for a Coward 1957,Ja 31,21:1

Cody, J W

Massacre River 1949,Jl 15,17:2

Cody, Joseph

Sand 1949,Ag 5,23:2

Cody, Lew

Don't Change Your Husband 1919,F 3,13:2
Life Line, The 1919,S 29,16:1
Secrets of Paris 1923,Ja 8,22:1
Souls for Sale 1923,Ap 9,14:3
Within the Law 1923,Ap 30,11:2
Rupert of Hentzau 1923,Jl 9,8:4
Lawful Larceny 1923,Jl 24,14:3 (In Addenda)
Reno 1924,Ja 8,27:1
Nellie, the Beautiful Cloak Model
   1924,Ap 14,14:1
Woman on the Jury, The 1924,My 19,14:2
Shooting of Dan McGrew, The 1924,Je 9,14:3
Revelation 1924,Je 24,18:2
Three Women 1924,O 6,25:1
Husbands and Lovers 1924,D 9,23:3
So This Is Marriage 1924,D 23,16:2
Man and Maid 1925,Ap 7,17:3
Sporting Venus, The 1925,My 11,14:3
Slave of Fashion, A 1925,Jl 21,26:2
Exchange of Wives 1925,O 5,25:2
Time, the Comedian 1925,D 14,18:2
His Secretary 1925,D 21,27:2
Adam and Evil 1927,Ag 10,21:4
Tea For Three 1927,O 31,22:1
Beau Broadway 1928,Jl 30,21:2
What a Widow 1930,O 4,15:2
Dishonored 1931,Mr 6,16:1
Divorce Among Friends 1931,Ap 2,30:4
Three Rogues 1931,Ap 4,23:1
Beyond Victory 1931,Ap 6,24:1
Three Girls Lost 1931,My 2,23:4
Sweepstakes 1931,Je 25,23:5
Woman of Experience, A 1931,Jl 9,26:5
Common Law, The 1931,Jl 20,20:4
Sporting Blood 1931,Ag 15,18:3
X Marks the Spot 1931,D 7,16:1
File No 113 1932,F 20,11:2
Tenderfoot, The 1932,My 23,18:4
70,000 Witnesses 1932,S 3,16:2
Crusader, The 1932,O 8,15:4
Madison Square Garden 1932,O 12,26:5
Under-Cover Man 1932,D 5,21:2
I Love That Man 1933,Jl 10,11:7
Sitting Pretty 1933,D 2,9:3
Wine, Women and Song 1934,Mr 21,24:3
Private Scandal 1934,Je 15,26:2
Shoot the Works 1934,Jl 7,16:5
Show People 1967,O 2,58:2

Coe, Barry

On the Threshold of Space 1956,Mr 30,10:5
Peyton Place 1957,D 13,35:1
Bravados, The 1958,Je 26,23:2
Private's Affair, A 1959,Ag 15,8:7
But Not for Me 1959,O 3,14:6
One Foot in Hell 1960,O 20,42:2
Wizard of Baghdad, The 1961,Mr 4,16:1
300 Spartans, The 1962,S 20,29:2

Coe, Charles Francis (Original Author)

River Pirate, The 1928,S 17,27:1
Me, Gangster 1928,O 22,29:1
Nancy Steele is Missing 1937,Mr 8,22:1

Coe, Fred (Director)

Thousand Clowns, A 1965,D 14,54:2

Coe, Fred (Producer)

Left Handed Gun, The 1958,My 8,36:2
Miracle Worker, The 1962,My 24,29:2
Thousand Clowns, A 1965,D 14,54:2

Coe, Fred (Screenwriter)

This Property is Condemned 1966,Ag 4,24:1

Coe, Peter

Gung Ho! 1944,Ja 26,23:2
Gypsy Wildcat 1944,O 5,18:6
House of Frankenstein 1944,D 16,19:3
Mummy's Curse, The 1945,Mr 31,16:1
Sword in the Desert 1949,Ag 25,20:2
Sands of Iwo Jima 1949,D 31,9:2
Rocky Mountain 1950,N 4,13:2
Road to Bali 1953,Ja 30,25:1

Coe, Rose

Melody Lane 1929,Jl 16,23:5

Coedel, Lucien

Resistance; Peleton d'Execution 1946,Jl 5,15:3
Carmen 1946,N 27,20:2
Bellman, The 1947,Ap 7,20:5
Idiot, The 1948,F 5,26:2
Portrait of Innocence 1948,Je 9,35:2
Strangers in the House 1949,O 13,33:3
Counter Investigation 1949,D 30,13:2

COEN

See Also COHAN, COHEN, KOHN

Coen, Franklin (Original Author)

Johnny Dark 1954,Je 26,7:2
Train, The 1965,Mr 18,25:1

Coen, Franklin (Screenwriter)

Till We Meet Again 1936,My 9,11:2
We're on the Jury 1937,F 10,18:5
Exposed 1938,N 21,14:5
Glory Brigade, The 1953,Ag 15,8:4
Four Guns to the Border 1954,N 6,15:3
Chief Crazy Horse 1955,Ap 28,25:1
This Island Earth 1955,Je 11,8:7
Kiss of Fire 1955,S 24,11:2
Night of the Quarter Moon 1959,Mr 5,35:5
Train, The 1965,Mr 18,25:1
Alvarez Kelly 1966,N 17,55:2

Coen, Guido (Producer)

Murder Reported 1960,Jl 12,39:1

Coen, Massimo

Hotel Sahara 1952,Ja 1,21:4

Coen, Massino

Snowbound 1949,F 21,20:2

COFFEE

See Also COFFEY

Coffee, Lenore

Angel of Broadway 1927,N 1,21:1 (In Addenda)

Coffee, Lenore (Original Author)

Lonesome Ladies 1927,Ag 2,19:2
Age of Indiscretion 1935,My 18,21:2
Good Girls Go to Paris 1939,Je 23,23:1
Guilt of Janet Ames, The 1947,My 23,31:2
Another Time Another Place 1958,My 3,10:4

Coffee, Lenore (Screenwriter)

For Alimony Only 1926,S 21,33:1
Night of Love, The 1927,Ja 25,18:4
Evelyn Prentice 1934,N 10,19:1
Vanessa: Her Love Story 1935,Ap 13,11:3
Suzy 1936,Jl 25,16:1
Four Daughters 1938,Ag 19,13:3
My Son, My Son! 1940,My 10,26:6
Way of all Flesh, The 1940,Je 6,33:2
Great Lie, The 1941,Ap 12,19:2
Gay Sisters, The 1942,Ag 15,14:2
Old Acquaintance 1943,N 3,20:2
Till We Meet Again 1944,Ag 30,15:1
Marriage Is a Private Affair 1944,O 27,17:7
Tomorrow Is Forever 1946,F 22,21:2
Beyond the Forest 1949,O 22,11:2
Lightning Strikes Twice 1951,Ap 13,18:7
Sudden Fear 1952,Ag 8,9:2
Young at Heart 1955,Ja 20,35:1
End of the Affair, The 1955,Ap 29,28:2
Footsteps of the Fog 1955,S 15,39:2
Cash McCall 1960,Ja 28,26:1

COFFEY

See Also COFFEE

Coffey, Denise

Waltz of the Toreadors 1962,Ag 14,34:1
Georgy Girl 1966,O 18,48:1

Coffin, Bettina

I, A Man 1967,Ag 25,28:1

Coffin, Haskell

With These Hands 1950,Je 16,28:4

Coffin, Tris

Good Neighbor Sam 1964,Jl 23,19:1

Coffin, Tristram

No Greater Sin 1941,Ag 29,18:2
Blackmail 1947,Ag 5,26:3
Outrage 1950,O 16,30:5
Undercover Girl 1950,N 8,37:2
Short Grass 1951,Ja 13,10:4

Coffinet, Anne Marie

Any Number Can Win 1963,O 9,47:2

Coffman, Hal

Great White Way, The 1924,Ja 4,10:1

Coffyn, Frank

Deadwood Coach, The 1925,Ja 21,19:3
Ranson's Folly 1926,My 31,10:2

Coffyn, Pauline

Passers By 1920,Je 21,13:1

COGAN

See Also KOGAN

Cogan, Nathan

Tel Aviv Taxi 1956,D 31,10:7

Cogan, Shaye

Comin' Round the Mountain 1951,Jl 27,15:2
Jack and the Beanstalk 1952,Ap 8,35:3

Coggio, Roger

Immortal Story, The 1968,S 19,62:2

Coghill, Nevill (Director)

Doctor Faustus 1968,F 7,38:1

Coghill, Nevill (Screenwriter)

Doctor Faustus 1968,F 7,38:1

Coghlan, Frank Jr

Mike 1926,Ja 11,33:1
Rubber Tires 1927,Mr 9,29:1
Slide, Kelly, Slide 1927,Mr 23,19:2
Yankee Clipper, The 1927,My 3,25:1
Let 'Er go, Gallegher 1928,Ja 16,24:1
Girl Said No, The 1930,Ap 5,23:3
Pays to Advertise, It 1931,F 21,15:2
It Pays to Advertise 1931,F 21,15:2
River's End 1931,Mr 7,17:2
Penrod and Sam 1931,S 26,25:3
Union Depot 1932,Ja 15,24:4
Hell's House 1932,F 12,24:5
Racetrack 1933,Mr 6,16:6
Charlie Chan at the Race Track 1936,Ag 15,6:2
Make Way for a Lady 1936,D 12,15:1
Service de Luxe 1938,O 24,13:2
Meet Doctor Christian 1939,D 1,27:2

Coghlan, Phyllis

Right to Live, The 1935,F 16,9:1
Parnell 1937,Je 4,27:2

Coghlan, Rose

Secrets of Paris 1923,Ja 8,22:1
Under the Red Robe 1923,N 13,25:3
Hot Saturday 1932,N 5,12:5

Cogley, Nick

Toby's Bow 1919,D 15,20:1
Jes' Call Me Jim 1920,My 24,20:3
Old Nest, The 1921,Je 29,10:3
In old Kentucky 1927,N 21,20:1
Abie's Irish Rose 1928,Ap 20,26:7
Cohens and Kellys in Africa, The 1930,D 20,20:6

Coguelin, Jean

David Golder 1932,O 20,24:2

COHAN

See Also COHEN, KOHN, COEN

Cohan, George M

Broadway Jones 1917,Mr 26,11:4
Hit-the Trail Holliday 1918,Je 10,9:3
Phantom President, The 1932,O 1,10:4
Gambling 1934,D 4,22:3

Cohan, George M (Composer)

Yankee Doodle Dandy 1942,My 30,9:1

Cohan, George M (Original Author)

Prince There Was 1921,N 14,18:1
Get-Rich-Quick Wallingford 1921,D 5,20:1
Little Johnny Jones 1923,Ag 13,16:1
Seven Keys to Baldpate 1925,N 3,25:4
Song and Dance Man, The 1926,F 1,16:1
Home Towners, The 1928,O 24,26:4
Fast Company 1929,O 5,22:5
Seven Keys to Baldpate 1929,D 26,21:1
Miracle Man, The 1932,Ap 21,25:2
Elmer the Great 1933,My 26,24:2
Gambling 1934,D 4,22:3
Seven Keys to Baldpate 1935,D 14,11:2
Song and Dance Man 1936,Mr 12,18:2
Times Square Playboy 1936,My 2,11:2
Ladies Must Live 1940,S 6,25:3
Little Nellie Kelly 1940,D 25,33:2
Yankee Doodle Dandy 1942,My 30,9:1

Cohan, George M (Producer)

Little Nellie Kelly 1940,D 25,33:2

Cohan, Helen

Lightnin' 1930,N 29,21:4

Cohan, Morrie

Iron Man 1931,Ap 18,17:3
I'm no Angel 1933,O 14,18:2
Belle of the Nineties 1934,S 22,12:2

COHEN

See Also KOHN, COEN, COHAN

Cohen, Alain

Two of Us, The 1968,F 20,53:1

Cohen, Albert J (Original Author)

I Sell Anything 1934,D 27,25:2
Times Square Lady 1935,Mr 15,25:3
Night at the Ritz, A 1935,My 16,20:2
King Solomon of Broadway 1935,O 19,12:2
Moonlight Murder 1936,Mr 28,11:2
Invisible Enemy 1938,Ap 30,18:2

Cohen, Albert J (Producer)

Walls Came Tumbling Down, The 1946,N 9,13:5
Unknown Island 1949,Ja 8,11:4
Prehistoric Women 1950,D 29,15:5
Horizons West 1952,N 22,16:5
Because of You 1952,D 4,47:3
Girls in the Night 1953,Ja 16,19:3
City Beneath the Sea 1953,Mr 12,24:3
Great Sioux Uprising, The 1953,Jl 18,6:2
Glass Web, The 1953,N 12,37:5

Cohen, Albert J (Producer) — Cont
Veils of Bagdad, The 1953,N 27,99:9
Playgirl 1954,My 15,13:3
Tanganyika 1954,Je 19,9:2
So This Is Paris 1955,F 12,11:1
Sign of the Pagan 1955,F 14,24:2
Second Greatest Sex, The 1956,F 11,12:2
Never Say Goodbye 1956,Ap 14,20:1
Istanbul 1957,Ja 24,34:1
Naked Brigade, The 1965,Je 17,27:2

Cohen, Albert J (Screenwriter)
Night at the Ritz, A 1935,My 16,20:2
King Solomon of Broadway 1935,O 19,12:2
Invisible Enemy 1938,Ap 30,18:2
Let's Live a Little 1948,D 10,34:2
Naked Brigade, The 1965,Je 17,27:2

Cohen, Bennett (Original Author)
Renegade Ranger, The 1939,F 17,17:3

Cohen, Bennett R (Original Author)
Female Fugitive 1938,Ap 11,12:3

Cohen, Bennett R (Screenwriter)
Female Fugitive 1938,Ap 11,12:3

Cohen, Bergstein
Tel Aviv Taxi 1956,D 31,10:7

Cohen, Emanuel (Producer)
Go West, Young Man 1936,N 19,31:3
Pennies From Heaven 1936,D 10,35:2
Outcast 1937,Mr 3,27:2
Girl From Scotland Yard, The 1937,My 31,11:2
Midnight Madonna 1937,Jl 17,18:1
On Such a Night 1937,S 17,29:2
Every Day's a Holiday 1938,Ja 27,17:2
Doctor Rhythm 1938,My 19,25:2
Appointment in Tokyo 1945,D 8,21:3

Cohen, Herbert (Producer)
I Was a Teenage Frankenstein 1958,Ja 30,19:4

Cohen, Herman (Original Author)
Berserk! 1968,Ja 11,42:2

Cohen, Herman (Producer)
Konga 1961,S 16,9:1
Black Zoo 1963,My 16,42:1
Study in Terror, A 1966,N 3,45:3
Berserk! 1968,Ja 11,42:2

Cohen, Herman (Screenwriter)
Headless Ghost, The 1959,Ap 30,37:2
Konga 1961,S 16,9:1
Black Zoo 1963,My 16,42:1
Berserk! 1968,Ja 11,42:2

Cohen, Larry (Screenwriter)
Return of the Seven 1966,O 20,52:5

Cohen, Lester (Original Author)
Nagana 1933,F 16,23:2
Sweepings 1933,Mr 24,22:3
Break of Hearts 1935,My 17,24:3
Three Sons 1939,N 24,29:3

Cohen, Martin (Producer)
Catskill Honeymoon 1950,Ja 28,10:3

Cohen, Mr (Producer)
Horrors of the Black Museum 1959,Ap 30,37:2

Cohen, Octavus Roy (Original Author)
Red Dice 1926,Ap 16,20:3
Why Bring That Up? 1929,O 5,22:5
Social Lion, The 1930,Je 14,9:4
Big Gamble, The 1931,S 21,20:2
Transient Lady 1935,Mr 11,15:1
They Met in a Taxi 1936,S 7,20:5
Outer Gate, The 1937,N 22,15:2
I Love You Again 1940,Ag 16,11:2
Pittsburgh Kid, The 1941,S 23,27:4

Cohen, Ronald M (Original Author)
Blue 1968,My 11,28:1

Cohen, Ronald M (Screenwriter)
Blue 1968,My 11,28:1

Cohen, Ronnie
My Father's House 1947,S 26,28:3

Cohen, Sammy
Skyrocket, The 1926,Ja 26,25:2
What Price Glory 1926,N 24,26:4
Cradle Snatchers 1927,My 31,25:2
Gay Retreat, The 1927,O 10,24:1
Why Sailors Go Wrong 1928,Ap 9,18:2
Plastered in Paris 1928,S 24,25:1
Sailor's Luck 1933,Mr 17,21:2
Arizona to Broadway 1933,Jl 22,14:3
45 Fathers 1937,D 11,22:2
Battle of Broadway 1938,Ap 25,19:2
Fighting 69th, The 1940,Ja 27,9:2

Cohen, Sanford
Edge, The 1968,Mr 28,52:1

Cohen, Sol (Miscellaneous)
Drums of Love 1928,Ja 25,20:4

Cohen (Original Author)
Tundra 1936,D 3,31:2

Cohn, Alfred A (Original Author)
Frisco Sally Levy 1927,Ap 13,29:4
Son of a Sailor 1933,N 30,38:4

Cohn, Alfred A (Screenwriter)
Carnation Kid, The 1929,F 25,16:1
Feet First 1930,O 31,20:1

Cohn, Art (Miscellaneous)
Stromboli 1950,F 16,28:2

Cohn, Art (Original Author)
Smoke Jumpers 1952,Mr 22,9:6
Carbine Williams 1952,My 8,37:2

Ten Thousand Bedrooms 1957,Ap 4,37:1
Joker Is Wild, The 1957,S 27,16:6

Cohn, Art (Producer)
Sky Above, The-Mud Below, The 1962,Je 20,40:1
Paris Secret 1965,S 4,11:5
Woman Times Seven 1967,Je 28,38:1

Cohn, Art (Screenwriter)
Set-Up, The 1949,Mr 30,31:2
Illegal Entry 1949,Je 11,11:2
Tomorrow Is Another Day 1951,Ag 9,17:5
Tall Target, The 1951,S 28,26:2
Carbine Williams 1952,My 8,37:2
Glory Alley 1952,Jl 30,20:8
Men of the Fighting Lady 1954,My 8,15:2
Seven Hills of Rome 1958,Ja 28,24:2 (Incorrect in this edition; use 1958,Ja 31,24:2 elsewhere)

Cohn, Ben (Screenwriter)
Border Patrolman 1936,Je 29,11:2

Cohn, Harry (Miscellaneous)
Broadway Melody of 1936 1935,S 19,28:1

Cohn, Harry (Producer)
Father and Son 1929,Je 4,29:3

Cohn, Ralph (Producer)
Girls Under 21 1940,N 11,22:4
Lone Wolf Keeps a Date, The 1941,Ja 2,24:3
Phantom Submarine, The 1941,F 12,25:3
Meet Boston Blackie 1941,F 26,17:2
Enemy Agents meet Ellery Queen 1942,Ag 22,16:2
Crime Doctor 1943,Jl 5,11:4
Sleep, My Love 1948,F 19,29:4

Cohn, Robert (Producer)
Killer That Stalked New York, The 1951,Ja 5,17:2
Mission Over Korea 1953,S 19,7:2
Interns, The 1962,Ag 9,17:5
New Interns, The 1964,Ag 20,34:2

Cohn-Seat, Gilbert (Producer)
Lady Chatterley's Lover 1959,Jl 11,11:1

Cohoon, Ronald
Incredible Journey, The 1963,N 21,43:2

Coke, Eddie
It Happened Tomorrow 1944,My 29,18:2

Coke, Peter
Smiling Along 1939,F 20,13:2
I Met a Murderer 1939,O 2,15:2
Ship Was Loaded, The 1958,Ja 20,20:1

Coker, John
Reach for Glory 1963,S 10,46:1

Colbert, Claudette
For the Love of Mike 1927,Ag 24,27:5
Hole in the Wall, The 1929,Ap 15,22:6
Lady Lies, The 1929,S 7,15:1
Young Man of Manhattan 1930,Ap 19,15:1
Big Pond, The 1930,My 19,21:1
Manslaughter 1930,Jl 24,26:4
Enigmatique Monsieur Parkes, L' 1930,S 2,19:3
Honor Among Lovers 1931,F 28,15:2
Smiling Lieutenant, The 1931,My 23,13:4
Secrets of a Secretary 1931,Ag 29,16:3
His Woman 1931,D 5,21:2
Wiser Sex, The 1932,Mr 12,19:5
Misleading Lady, The 1932,Ap 9,18:1
Man From Yesterday, The 1932,Je 25,18:2
Phantom President, The 1932,O 1,10:4
Sign of the Cross, The 1932,D 1,25:1
Tonight Is Ours 1933,Ja 21,10:6
I Cover the Waterfront 1933,My 18,17:3
Three-Cornered Moon 1933,Ag 12,14:2
Torch Singer 1933,O 7,18:5
Four Frightened People 1934,Ja 27,9:2
It Happened One Night 1934,F 23,23:2
Cleopatra 1934,Ag 17,12:1
Imitation of Life 1934,N 24,19:1
Gilded Lily, The 1935,F 9,11:2
Private Worlds 1935,Mr 28,25:2
She Married her Boss 1935,S 27,25:3
Bride Comes Home, The 1935,D 25,30:2
Under Two Flags 1936,My 1,19:1
Maid of Salem 1937,Mr 4,27:2
I Met Him in Paris 1937,Je 3,29:2
Tovarich 1937,D 31,9:2
Bluebeard's Eighth Wife 1938,Mr 24,21:2
Zaza 1939,Ja 5,17:1
Midnight 1939,Ap 6,31:1
It's a Wonderful World 1939,My 19,27:2
Drums Along the Mohawk 1939,N 4,11:2
Boom Town 1940,S 6,25:2
Arise my Love 1940,O 17,33:2
Skylark 1941,N 20,39:2
Remember the Day 1941,D 26,21:2
Palm Beach Story, The 1942,D 11,33:1
So Proudly We Hail 1943,S 10,29:1
No Time for Love 1943,D 2,30:1
Since You Went Away 1944,Jl 21,16:2
Practically Yours 1945,Mr 29,18:2
Guest Wife 1945,O 18,21:2
Tomorrow Is Forever 1946,F 22,21:2
Without Reservations 1946,Je 8,17:2
Secret Heart, The 1946,D 26,28:2
Egg and I, The 1947,Ap 25,29:2
Sleep, My Love 1948,F 19,29:4
Family Honeymoon 1949,F 25,28:2

Colbert, Claudette — Cont
Bride for Sale 1949,N 21,29:4 (In Addenda)
Three Came Home 1950,F 21,22:5
Secret Fury, The 1950,Je 22,34:2
Thunder on the Hill 1951,O 18,32:3
Let's Make It Legal 1951,N 7,35:3
Outpost in Malaya 1952,N 27,49:2
Daughters of Destiny (Elizabeth) 1954,Jl 6,19:1
Royal Affairs in Versailles 1957,Mr 9,16:1
Parrish 1961,My 5,22:1

Colbert, Stanley (Producer)
Private Property 1960,Ap 25,40:2
Explosive Generation, The 1962,F 15,24:2

Colby, Anita
Mary of Scotland 1936,Jl 31,22:2
Walking on Air 1936,S 12,20:2
Cover Girl 1944,Mr 31,26:1
Brute Force 1947,Jl 17,16:2

Colcord, Mabel
Little Women 1933,N 17,22:3
David Copperfield 1935,Ja 19,8:1
Law in her Hands, The 1936,Je 6,21:2
Great O'Malley, The 1937,Mr 6,10:1
Cowboy and the Lady, The 1938,N 25,19:3

Coldeway, Anthony (Original Author)
Torchy Blane in Panama 1938,Ap 18,11:1
Pacific Liner 1939,Ja 18,17:3
Devil's Island 1940,Jl 12,11:4
Busses Roar 1942,S 25,25:4

Coldeway, Anthony (Screenwriter)
Gentleman of Leisure, A 1923,Jl 16,14:2
Rejuvenation of Aunt Mary, The 1927,Jl 27,27:4
White Bondage 1937,Ag 6,21:3
Over the Goal 1937,O 16,22:2
Accidents Will Happen 1938,Ap 25,19:2
When Were You Born? 1938,Je 9,27:2
Smashing the Money Ring 1939,N 17,17:2
Nurse's Secret, The 1941,Je 6,25:7
Lady Gangster 1942,Jl 10,13:2
Busses Roar 1942,S 25,25:4
Hidden Hand, The 1942,N 26,40:4
Gorilla Man, The 1943,Ja 15,21:4

Cole, Buddy
Johnny Holiday 1950,My 17,36:1

Cole, Burt (Original Author)
Bobo, The 1967,S 29,53:1

Cole, Corinne
Swinger, The 1966,D 15,60:1
Party, The 1968,Ap 5,56:2

Cole, David
Christopher Columbus 1949,O 13,33:2
Voice of the Hurricane 1964,Je 3,36:4

Cole, Elizabeth
Hawaii 1966,O 11,54:1

Cole, Francis Mrs (Narrator)
Eleanor Roosevelt Story, The 1965,N 9,50:1

Cole, George
My Brothers Keeper 1949,F 14,15:3
Quartet (The Kite); Kite, The (Quartet) 1949,Mr 29,30:3
Operation Disaster 1951,Ja 15,13:1
Laughter in Paradise 1951,N 12,21:2
Christmas Carol, A 1951,N 29,41:2
Mr Lord Says No! 1952,F 12,22:5
Spider and the Fly, The 1952,Jl 29,17:3
Mr Potts Goes to Moscow 1953,S 3,15:2
Passionate Sentry, The 1953,N 12,37:5
Tonight's the Night 1954,D 23,13:4
Belles of St Trinian's, The 1954,D 23,13:4
Adventures of Sadie, The 1955,My 18,35:2
Will any Gentleman? 1955,S 28,70:6
Prize of Gold, A 1955,O 15,19:2
Quentin Durward 1955,N 24,41:1
Green Man, The 1957,My 23,40:1
Constant Husband, The 1957,Jl 26,10:3
Blue Murder at St Trinian's 1958,My 27,27:1
Too Many Crooks 1959,Ap 25,14:2
Bridal Path, The 1959,D 21,34:2
Pure Hell of St Trinian's, The 1961,S 26,31:1
Cleopatra 1963,Je 13,29:1
One Way Pendulum 1965,Mr 3,34:3

Cole, Jack
Designing Woman 1957,My 17,20:2

Cole, Jack and Co
Moon Over Miami 1941,Jl 5,14:2

Cole, Lester (Miscellaneous)
Men in her Diary 1945,S 24,16:5

Cole, Lester (Original Author)
Jury's Secret, The 1938,F 4,17:2
Crime of Dr Hallet, The 1938,Mr 24,21:3
I Stole a Million 1939,Ag 7,11:2
Among the Living 1941,D 13,25:2

Cole, Lester (Screenwriter)
Under Pressure 1935,F 4,11:3
President's Mystery, The 1936,O 19,22:1
Follow Your Heart 1936,O 22,31:1
Man in Blue, The 1937,Ag 30,25:2
Jury's Secret, The 1938,F 4,17:2
Crime of Dr Hallet, The 1938,Mr 24,21:3
Sinners in Paradise 1938,My 20,17:2
Secrets of a Nurse 1938,D 12,26:2
Winter Carnival 1939,Jl 28,14:2
Big Guy, The 1940,Ja 1,29:2
Invisible Man Returns, The 1940,Ja 16,19:2

Cole, Lester (Screenwriter)— Cont

House of the Seven Gables, The 1940,Ap 15,21:3
Footsteps in the Dark 1941,Mr 15,13:2
Among the Living 1941,D 13,25:2
Pacific Blackout 1942,Ja 15,25:2
Night Plane From Chungking 1943,My 31,13:2
None Shall Escape 1944,Ap 7,23:2
Objective Burma 1945,Ja 27,15:2
Blood on the Sun 1945,Je 29,12:2
Fiesta 1947,Je 27,17:3
Romance of Rosy Ridge, The 1947,S 12,18:3
High Wall 1947,D 26,22:2

Cole, Michael
Chuka 1967,N 2,58:3

Cole, Nat (King)
Blue Gardenia, The 1953,Ap 28,31:1
Small Town Girl 1953,My 7,37:2
Istanbul 1957,Ja 24,34:1
China Gate 1957,My 23,40:2
St Louis Blues 1958,Ap 12,13:1
Night of the Quarter Moon 1959,Mr 5,35:5
Cat Ballou 1965,Je 25,36:1

Cole, Nat (King) Composer
See my Lawyer 1945,My 4,23:4

Cole, Royal K (Original Author)
Alimony 1949,Jl 22,16:3

Cole, Royal K (Screenwriter)
Blackmail 1947,Ag 5,26:3

Cole, Sidney (Miscellaneous)
One Day in Soviet Russia 1941,O 27,21:2

Cole, Sidney (Producer)
Angel Who Pawned her Harp, The 1956,F 29,35:2 *
Kitchen, The 1961,N 2,42:1

Cole, Sidney (Screenwriter)
They Came to a City 1945,F 19,21:3
Angel Who Pawned her Harp, The 1956,F 29,35:2
Kitchen, The 1961,N 2,42:1

Colebrook, Edward
Destination Unknown 1942,O 29,19:3

Coleburn, Catherine
Society Scandal, A 1924,Mr 10,18:2

Colella, Alfredo
Favorita, La 1953,O 30,27:4

COLEMAN
See Also COLMAN

Coleman, Brian
Lady in Distress 1942,F 16,21:2
Jassy 1948,F 20,19:2
Sword and the Rose, The 1953,Ag 20,18:3

Coleman, Bruce
In Gay Madrid 1930,Je 7,10:4

Coleman, C C Jr (Director)
Legion of Terror 1936,N 2,24:2
Parole Racket 1937,Mr 8,22:1
Fight to the Finish, A 1937,Je 26,20:2 (In Addenda)
Criminals of the Air 1937,O 28,29:2
Paid to Dance 1937,D 6,19:1
Shadow, The 1937,D 17,33:3
When G-Men Step In 1938,Mr 14,13:2
Highway Patrol 1938,Ag 4,15:2
Homicide Bureau 1939,F 2,17:2
Missing Daughters 1939,Je 12,14:5

Coleman, Caryl (Original Author)
Black Gold 1947,S 5,16:4

Coleman, Charles
That's my Daddy 1928,F 13,16:2
Good Morning, Judge 1928,Je 26,29:1
Beyond Victory 1931,Ap 6,24:1
Bachelor Apartment 1931,My 16,13:3
Heart of New York, The 1932,Mr 2,15:3
Play Girl 1932,Mr 19,11:2
Merrily We Go to Hell 1932,Je 11,9:3
Winner Take All 1932,Je 18,9:2
Jewel Robbery 1932,Jl 23,6:6
Sailor Be Good 1933,F 27,11:2
Diplomaniacs 1933,Ap 29,14:2
Gallant Lady 1934,Ja 22,12:3
Housewife 1934,Ag 10,21:2
Million Dollar Ransom 1934,S 19,15:2
Down to Their Last Yacht 1934,S 24,14:1
Becky Sharp 1935,Je 14,27:2
Goose and the Gander, The 1935,S 12,29:2
Colleen 1936,Mr 9,20:2
Everybody's Old Man 1936,Mr 26,27:2
Poor Little Rich Girl, The 1936,Je 26,16:1
Walking on Air 1936,S 12,20:2
Lloyds of London 1936,N 26,39:1
There Goes my Girl 1937,Je 12,8:2
Fight for Your Lady 1937,N 20,21:2
Rage of Paris 1938,Jl 2,10:2
Alexander's Ragtime Band 1938,Ag 6,7:2
Gateway 1938,Ag 9,2:2
That Certain Age 1938,N 5,15:2
You Can't Cheat an Honest Man 1939,F 20,13:2
First Love 1939,N 9,27:3
Mexican Spitfire 1940,Ja 10,16:4
Mexican Spitfire out West 1940,O 30,29:3
Free and Easy 1941,Ap 3,29:4
It Started With Eve 1941,O 3,27:1
Design for Scandal 1942,F 6,23:3
Twin Beds 1942,My 1,23:4

Almost Married 1942,Je 5,23:2
Arabian Nights 1942,D 26,15:1
It Comes up Love 1943,Ja 22,25:3
Pittsburgh 1943,F 25,27:2
Whistler, The 1944,Ap 29,12:2
Stork Club, The 1945,D 20,18:2
Runaround, The 1946,Je 7,16:3
Never Say Goodbye 1946,N 23,12:2
Imperfect Lady, The 1947,My 22,34:5

Coleman, Claudia
Warrior's Husband, The 1933,My 12,20:4
I Cover the Waterfront 1933,My 18,17:3
Big Hearted Herbert 1934,N 14,23:2
Let's Live Tonight 1935,Mr 18,14:4
Frisco Kid 1935,N 25,22:1
King of Burlesque 1936,Ja 16,25:2
Country Beyond, The 1936,Ap 30,17:3
Little Miss Nobody 1936,Je 6,21:1
Under Your Spell 1936,N 7,15:2
Lady From Nowhere 1936,D 21,19:2
Test Pilot 1938,Ap 16,17:1
Penrod and his Twin Brother 1938,Ap 18,11:1
Keep Smiling 1938,Ag 10,15:2

Coleman, Dabney
Slender Thread, The 1965,D 24,24:2
This Property is Condemned 1966,Ag 4,24:1

Coleman, Emil
Nob Hill 1945,Jl 4,10:3

Coleman, Herbert (Director)
Battle at Bloody Beach, The 1961,Ag 17,18:2

Coleman, Leo
Medium, The 1951,S 6,39:2

Coleman, Lonnie (Original Author)
Hot Spell 1958,S 18,37:2

Coleman, Mabel
Snob, The 1924,D 15,14:1
Corporal Kate 1926,D 15,30:4
King of Kings, The 1927,Ap 20,29:2

Coleman, Major
Romance of Rio Grande 1929,N 9,22:5

Coleman, Nancy
Kings Row 1942,F 3,23:2
Dangerously They Live 1942,Ap 11,9:2
Gay Sisters, The 1942,Ag 15,14:2
Desperate Journey 1942,S 26,11:2
Edge of Darkness 1943,Ap 10,12:4
In our Time 1944,F 12,11:2
Devotion 1946,Ap 6,10:5
Her Sister's Secret 1947,Ja 23,31:3
Violence 1947,My 10,8:5
Mourning Becomes Electra 1947,N 20,38:2

Coleman, Ornette
Chappaqua 1967,N 6,65:2

Coleman, Patricia (Screenwriter)
Above Suspicion 1943,Ag 6,10:3

Coleman, Rosmary
Powers Girl, The 1943,Mr 26,14:2 (In Addenda)

Coleman, Ruth
Doctor's Diary, A 1937,F 17,16:4
Crime Nobody Saw, The 1937,Ap 5,17:2
Headin' East 1938,Ja 15,19:2

Coleman, Vincent
Partners of the Night 1920,Mr 1,16:2
Purple Highway, The 1923,Jl 24,14:3 (In Addenda)

Coleman, Wilson
Dr Syn 1937,N 15,15:4

Coleridge, Ethel
Fallen Idol, The 1949,N 16,39:2

Coleridge, Sylvia
I Met a Murderer 1939,O 2,15:2

Coles, Mildred
Ladies Must Live 1940,S 6,25:3
Play Girl 1941,Ja 30,19:3
Lady Scarface 1941,Ag 4,16:6
Hurry, Charlie, Hurry 1941,N 12,31:3

Colette (Original Author)
Gigi 1950,Ja 31,20:2
Minne 1951,Ap 17,35:2
Seven Deadly Sins, The (Envy); Envy (The Seven Deadly Sins) 1953,My 12,31:3
Game of Love, The 1954,D 15,41:1
Mitsou 1958,Ap 15,42:5
Gigi 1958,My 16,21:1

Colette (Screenwriter)
Pit of Loneliness 1954,Ap 9,19:2

Coletti, Duilio (Director)
Pierpin, La Figlia Ritrovata 1936,Mr 27,25:3
Earth Cries Out, The; Grido Della Terra, Il 1949,Ag 31,26:2
Merchant of Slaves 1949,O 27,35:4
Heart and Soul 1950,Je 15,41:3
Miss Italy 1952,My 10,16:2
Lure of the Sira 1953,D 26,10:7
Hell Raiders of the Deep 1954,Jl 3,9:2
House of Intrigue, The 1960,Mr 10,36:3
Under ten Flags 1960,S 16,24:1

Coletti, Duilio (Producer)
House of Intrigue, The 1960,Mr 10,36:3

Coletti, Duilio (Screenwriter)
Hell Raiders of the Deep 1954,Jl 3,9:2
House of Intrigue, The 1960,Mr 10,36:3
Under ten Flags 1960,S 16,24:1

COLEY
See Also COLLEY

Coley, Thomas
Dr Cyclops 1940,Ap 11,32:3

Colgan, Michael
Donovan's Brain 1954,Ja 21,28:2

Colin, Georges
End of the World, The 1934,Ap 18,23:3
Open Road, The 1940,O 5,20:2
Vautrin, the Thief 1949,N 11,31:2

Colin, Jean
Hate Ship, The 1930,N 15,15:3
Mikado, The 1939,Je 2,27:2
Last Holiday 1950,N 14,39:4
Scotch on the Rocks 1954,Je 14,18:2

Collagare, G (Screenwriter)
Ring Around the Clock 1953,My 19,36:2

Collande, Gisela
Rape on the Moor 1957,N 21,38:1

Collande, Volker
Thunder, Lightening and Sunshine 1937,N 13,11:2
Liebe im Gleitflug; Love in Stunt Flying 1938,Je 18,18:3
Kleine Suenderin, Die; Little Sinner, The 1938,D 3,11:3
Ihr Erstes Erlebnis; Her First Experience 1940,Je 8,18:3

Colleano, Bonar
Johnny in the Clouds 1945,N 16,16:2
Wanted for Murder 1946,D 12,38:4
Stairway to Heaven 1946,D 26,28:1
One Night With You 1949,F 21,20:2
Sleeping Car to Trieste 1949,Ap 18,18:6
Give Us This Day 1949,D 21,41:2
Good Time Girl 1950,S 25,18:5
Pool of London 1951,N 28,37:2
Eight Iron Men 1953,Ja 2,11:1
Tale of Five Women, A 1953,Ja 16,19:2
Flame and the Flesh 1954,My 3,21:2
Joe Macbeth 1956,Ap 7,13:1
Zarak 1956,D 27,22:1
Fire Down Below 1957,Ag 9,11:2
Man Inside, The 1959,F 5,24:7

Colleano, Bonar Jr
While the Sun Shines 1950,Jl 1,9:2

Colleran, Bill (Director)
Windjammer 1958,Ap 10,32:2

Collet, Pierre
Mademoiselle 1966,Ag 2,23:1

COLLEY
See Also COLEY

Colley, James
Ashes of Vengeance 1923,Ag 7,20:2

Colley, Kenneth
Jokers, The 1967,My 16,50:1

Colli, Tonino Delli (Cinematographer)
World by Night 1962,Ja 11,26:1

COLLIER
See Also COLLYER

Collier, Antoinette
Randolph Family 1945,Mr 13,19:4

Collier, Buster Jr
Sporting Chance 1931,N 28,20:4

Collier, Constance
Macbeth 1916,Je 5,9:1
Bohemian Girl, The 1923,F 5,18:2
Shadow of Doubt 1935,Mr 11,15:1
Professional Soldier 1936,Ja 30,14:2
Girls' Dormitory 1936,Ag 29,16:2
Thunder in the City 1937,Ap 23,25:2
Wee Willie Winkie 1937,Jl 24,12:1
Stage Door 1937,O 8,27:2
Damsel in Distress, A 1937,N 25,37:1
Zaza 1939,Ja 5,17:1
Susan and God 1940,Jl 12,11:2
Kitty 1946,Ap 1,23:1
Dark Corner, The 1946,My 9,27:3
Monsieur Beaucaire 1946,S 5,23:1
Perils of Pauline, The 1947,Jl 10,17:2
Ideal Husband, An 1948,Ja 15,28:2
Rope 1948,Ag 27,12:4
Whirlpool 1950,Ja 14,9:2

Collier, Constance (Original Author)
Rat, The 1938,F 28,19:1

Collier, Constance (Screenwriter)
Peter Ibbetson 1935,N 8,18:2

Collier, Don
Safe at Home 1962,Ap 14,14:1

Collier, Frank
Quiet Week-End 1948,Ag 20,13:2

Collier, John (Screenwriter)
Sylvia Scarlett 1936,Ja 10,16:2
Elephant Boy 1937,Ap 6,20:2
Her Cardboard Lover 1942,Jl 17,19:2
Deception 1946,O 19,15:3
Roseanna McCoy 1949,O 13,33:2
Story of Three Loves, The (Equilibrium); Equilibrium (The Story of Three Loves) 1953,Mr 6,29:2
Story of Three Loves, The (Mademoiselle); Mademoiselle (The Story of Three Loves) 1953,Mr 6,29:2

Collier, John (Screenwriter) — Cont
Story of Three Loves, The (The Jealous Lover);
  Jealous Lover, The (The Story of Three Loves)
  1953,Mr 6,29:2
Story of Three Loves, The 1953,Mr 6,29:2
Equilibrium 1953,Mr 6,29:2
I Am a Camera 1955,Ag 9,29:1
War Lord, The 1965,N 18,55:2
Collier, Kathryn
Bill of Divorcement, A 1940,Jl 12,11:2
Collier, Lois
Ladies Courageous 1944,Mr 16,17:2
Weird Woman 1944,Ap 1,11:1
Cobra Woman 1944,My 18,17:2
Jungle Woman 1944,Jl 15,19:6
Naughty Nineties, The 1945,Je 21,16:2
Cat Creeps, The 1946,My 18,12:4
Night in Casablanca, A 1946,Ag 12,17:2
Slave Girl 1947,Jl 18,21:3
Collier, Sherlee
Enchantment 1948,D 27,16:2
Kind Lady 1951,Ag 8,21:2
Collier, Shirlee
Two Tickets to London 1943,Jl 3,11:2
Collier, Terence
Lost Patrol, The 1929,D 16,34:2
Collier, William Jr
Bugle Call, The 1916,My 1,9:1
Cardigan 1922,F 20,7:1
Secrets of Paris 1923,Ja 8,22:1
Enemies of Women 1923,Ap 1,5:4
Pleasure Mad 1924,Ja 7,23:1
Sea Hawk, The 1924,Je 3,22:1
Wine of Youth 1924,Ag 11,16:1
Lighthouse by the Sea, The 1924,D 29,11:4
Devil's Cargo, The 1925,F 3,24:1
Playing With Souls 1925,Ap 20,18:1 (Incorrect in
  this edition; use 1925,Ap 28,18:1 elsewhere)
Eve's Secret 1925,Je 11,14:3
Wanderer, The 1925,Ag 20,22:1
Rainmaker, The 1926,My 18,28:2
God Gave Me Twenty Cents 1926,N 20,3:2
Girl from Coney Island or Just Another Blonde
  1926,D 13,27:1
Convoy 1927,My 9,26:4
Dearie 1927,Jl 4,20:3
Desired Woman, The 1927,Ag 30,21:3
College Widow, The 1927,N 7,26:4
Night of Mystery, A 1928,Ap 16,20:5
Lion and the Mouse, The 1928,Je 16,11:4
Women They Talk About 1928,O 15,16:1
Donovan Affair, The 1929,Ap 29,29:2
College Coquette, The 1929,Ag 26,17:1
Show of Shows 1929,N 21,24:5
Lummox 1930,Mr 24,25:1
New Movietone Follies of 1930, The
  1930,Je 21,20:5
Rain or Shine 1930,Ag 8,11:1
Little Caesar 1931,Ja 10,19:2
Reducing 1931,Ja 17,23:1
Cimarron 1931,Ja 27,20:5
Street Scene 1931,Ag 27,22:5
Big Gamble, The 1931,S 21,20:2
Secret Witness, The 1931,D 21,28:4
File No 113 1932,F 20,11:2
Dancers in the Dark 1932,Mr 19,11:2
Phantom Express, The 1932,S 20,26:3
Story of Temple Drake, The 1933,My 6,11:2
All of Me 1934,F 5,19:2
People's Enemy, The 1935,Ap 30,13:7
Collier, William Sr
Plain Jane 1916,Ag 28,7:5
Servant Question, The 1920,Je 21,13:1
Happy Days 1930,F 14,20:1
Free and Easy 1930,Ap 19,15:1
High Society Blues 1930,Ap 19,15:1
She's my Weakness 1930,Je 21,20:5
Up the River 1930,O 11,21:3
Mr Lemon of Orange 1931,Mr 28,15:3
Six Cylinder Love 1931,My 16,31:3
Annabelle's Affairs 1931,Je 29,20:3
Brat, The 1931,Ag 24,13:4
Stepping Sisters 1932,Ja 9,21:1
After Tomorrow 1932,Mr 7,13:5
Washington Masquerade, The 1932,Jl 22,18:2
Madison Square Garden 1932,O 12,26:5
Hot Saturday 1932,N 5,12:5
Cheaters 1934,My 12,12:4
Murder Man, The 1935,Jl 27,16:2
Annapolis Farewell 1935,Ag 24,18:2
Bride Comes Home, The 1935,D 25,30:2
Love on a Bet 1936,Mr 5,25:2
Give Us This Night 1936,Ap 6,18:1
Valiant Is the Word for Carrie 1936,O 8,27:2
Cain and Mabel 1936,O 19,22:1
Josette 1938,Je 11,9:1
Say It in French 1938,D 1,29:1
Thanks for the Memory 1938,D 8,34:3
Persons in Hiding 1939,Mr 2,19:2
Invitation to Happiness 1939,Je 8,31:2
Disputed Passage 1939,O 26,27:2
There's Magic in Music 1941,Je 5,27:2

Collier, William Sr (Original Author)
Hottentot, The 1923,F 19,10:1
Hottentot, The 1929,S 7,15:1
Going Places 1939,Ja 7,6:1
Colligan, William (Miscellaneous)
Ecstasy 1940,D 25,33:2
Collin, George
Noah's Ark 1950,Ag 21,15:1
Collin, John
Devil's Own, The 1967,Mr 16,53:2
Colline, Paul
Trois Mousquetaires, Les 1933,My 1,10:2
Milady 1933,S 8,22:3
Collinge, Patricia
Little Foxes, The 1941,Ag 22,19:2
Shadow of a Doubt 1943,Ja 13,18:2
Tender Comrade 1944,Je 2,21:2
Casanova Brown 1944,S 15,16:1
Teresa 1951,Ap 6,31:2
Washington Story 1952,Jl 2,22:3
Nun's Story, The 1959,Je 19,30:1
Collings, Anne
Mask, The 1961,O 28,12:4
Collings, Pierre (Original Author)
Story of Louis Pasteur, The 1936,F 10,15:1
Collings, Pierre (Screenwriter)
Story of Louis Pasteur, The 1936,F 10,15:1
Collingwood, Peter
Up the Creek 1958,N 11,26:2
Collino, Frederico
Sono Stato Io; It Was I 1940,My 10,26:7
Collins, Alan
Young, The Evil and the Savage, The
  1968,Ag 15,46:2
Collins, Anthony (Miscellaneous)
Victoria the Great 1937,O 29,19:1
Collins, Arthur Greville (Director)
Widow From Monte Carlo, The 1936,Ja 23,25:2
Nobody's Fool 1936,Je 4,27:2
Thank You, Jeeves 1936,O 5,25:1
Collins, C Pat
Racket, The 1928,Jl 9,25:1
Collins, Charles
Smiling Faces 1932,Ag 31,12:3
Dancing Pirate 1936,Je 18,19:1
Collins, Charlie
Steel Trap, The 1952,N 13,35:2
Collins, Chick
Million Dollar Legs 1932,Jl 9,7:5
Quiet Please, Murder 1942,D 22,31:1
Collins, Cora Sue
Strange Case of Clara Deane, The
  1932,My 6,15:3
Jennie Gerhardt 1933,Je 9,20:2
Torch Singer 1933,O 7,18:5
As the Earth Turns 1934,Ap 12,27:2
Black Moon 1934,Je 28,26:2
Evelyn Prentice 1934,N 10,19:1
Little Men 1935,F 18,19:3
World Accuses, The 1935,Mr 21,27:2
Public Hero No 1 1935,Je 8,12:2
Anna Karenina 1935,Ag 31,16:2
Dark Angel, The 1935,S 6,12:2
Harmony Lane 1935,O 24,19:4
Magnificent Obsession 1935,D 31,11:2
Harvester, The 1936,Jl 4,18:2
Adventures of Tom Sawyer, The 1938,F 18,23:1
Stop, Look and Love 1939,S 8,28:5
Blood and Sand 1941,My 23,25:3
Get Help to Love 1942,O 19,15:3
Johnny Doughboy 1943,My 6,25:3
Roughly Speaking 1945,F 1,18:4
Collins, Dale (Original Author)
Sal of Singapore 1929,Ja 29,27:1
His Woman 1931,D 5,21:2
Collins, Eddie
In Old Chicago 1938,Ja 7,15:2
Sally, Irene and Mary 1938,F 26,9:2
Penrod and his Twin Brother 1938,Ap 18,11:1
Kentucky Moonshine 1938,My 21,9:2
Alexander's Ragtime Band 1938,Ag 6,7:2
Always in Trouble 1938,N 3,27:1
Up the River 1938,D 3,11:2
Charlie Chan in Honolulu 1938,D 31,7:3
Charlie Chan in Reno 1939,My 31,27:2
Young Mr Lincoln 1939,Je 3,11:2
News Is Made at Night 1939,Jl 13,17:2
Stop, Look and Love 1939,S 8,28:5
Quick Millions 1939,S 22,27:5
Hollywood Cavalcade 1939,O 14,13:2
Drums Along the Mohawk 1939,N 4,11:2
Blue Bird, The 1940,Ja 20,11:2
Return of Frank James, The 1940,Ag 10,16:4
Collins, Frank J (Original Author)
Mouthpiece, The 1932,Ap 21,25:2
Man Who Talked too Much, The 1940,Je 29,12:2
Illegal 1955,O 29,12:6
Collins, Freeman C Sgt (Cinematographer)
Report from the Aleutians 1943,Jl 31,8:2
Collins, Gene
Pride of the Yankees, The 1942,Jl 16,23:1
Fighting Father Dunne 1948,Je 25,26:2
Happy Time, The 1952,O 31,30:2

Collins, George Pat
Be Yourself 1930,Mr 7,20:5
All Quiet on The Western Front 1930,Ap 30,29:1
Manslaughter 1930,Jl 24,26:4
Only Saps Work 1930,D 13,22:2
Vice Squad, The 1931,Je 6,15:5
Central Park 1932,D 7,29:3
20,000 Years in Sing Sing 1933,Ja 10,26:2
Parachute Jumper 1933,Ja 26,12:2
Girl Missing 1933,Ap 1,18:2
Picture Snatcher 1933,My 19,20:3
Silk Express, The 1933,Je 28,24:2
Big Shakedown, The 1934,F 12,19:2
Crime Doctor, The 1934,My 11,24:3
Personality Kid, The 1934,Ag 1,14:2
West Point of the Air 1935,Ap 6,10:1
Black Fury 1935,Ap 11,27:2
Mr Dynamite 1935,My 25,12:1
White Heat 1949,S 3,7:2
Woman on Pier 13, The 1950,Je 16,28:4
Collins, Hal (Screenwriter)
Love-Ins, The 1967,Ag 19,16:1
For Singles Only 1968,Je 6,54:1
Collins, Harry (Original Author)
Fashions of 1934 1934,Ja 20,12:2
Collins, Jackie
All at Sea 1957,D 23,18:2
Safecracker, The 1958,Mr 6,32:1
Collins, Joan
I Believe in You 1953,My 5,34:3
Decameron Nights 1953,N 17,38:2
Turn the Key Softly 1954,F 4,21:6
Adventures of Sadie, The 1955,My 18,35:2
Land of the Pharaohs 1955,Jl 27,15:2
Virgin Queen, The 1955,Ag 6,13:2
Girl in the Red Velvet Swing, The
  1955,O 20,41:2
Opposite Sex, The 1956,N 16,23:2
Wayward Bus, The 1957,Je 6,35:2
Island in the Sun 1957,Je 13,37:1
Sea Wife 1957,D 5,45:2
Stopover Tokyo 1957,D 27,23:4
Bravados, The 1958,Je 26,23:2
Rally Round the Flag Boys! 1958,D 24,2:7
Seven Thieves 1960,Mr 12,14:5
Esther and the King 1960,N 19,13:4
Road to Hong Kong, The 1962,Je 28,21:1
Collins, Judy
Inheritance, The 1964,N 9,42:2
Festival 1967,O 24,53:2
Collins, Kathleen
Black Cyclone 1925,My 19,24:2
Collins, Larry (Original Author)
Is Paris Burning? 1966,N 11,36:1
Collins, Leroy
Betrayal, The 1948,Je 26,10:5
Collins, Lewis D (Director)
Sing Sing Nights 1935,Ja 26,13:2
Make a Million 1935,N 9,19:3
Down Under the Sea 1936,Ag 10,10:2
Fury and the Woman 1937,Je 22,26:2
Trapped by G-Men 1937,N 4,29:1
Under Suspicion 1937,D 20,23:2 (In Addenda)
Making the Headlines 1938,Ap 1,17:2
Flight Into Nowhere 1938,My 2,13:3
Reformatory 1938,Je 27,13:6
Crime Takes a Holiday 1938,N 28,11:2
Hidden Power 1939,Jl 26,17:3
Fugitive at Large 1939,N 13,15:2
Outside the Three-Mile Limit 1940,Ap 8,15:2
Passport to Alcatraz 1940,Je 15,12:2
Prison Camp 1940,Ag 3,9:3
Great Plane Robbery, The 1940,N 15,25:2
Great Swindle, The 1941,My 14,25:4
Collins, Lewis D (Producer)
Devil's Pit, The 1929,O 14,20:2
Collins, Mae
Red Hot Romance 1922,Ja 23,11:4
Collins, Monte
Long Live the King 1923,D 4,24:1
Our Hospitality 1923,D 10,20:1
Boy of Flanders, A 1924,Ap 15,24:1
Men 1924,My 5,18:3
Tiger Love 1924,Je 16,18:3
Desert Flower, The 1925,Je 1,10:3
Tumbleweeds 1925,D 21,27:2
Loves of Ricardo, The 1926,Ag 16,10:1
Buck Benny Rides Again 1940,Ap 25,28:4
Collins, Monte Jr
Why Bring That Up? 1929,O 5,22:5
Collins, Monty F
Hollywood Round-Up 1938,Mr 5,11:2
Kathleen 1941,D 19,35:3
Collins, Monty F (Miscellaneous)
Shady Lady 1945,O 11,26:2
Collins, Monty F (Original Author)
Green Promise, The 1949,Je 24,29:2
Collins, Monty F (Producer)
Green Promise, The 1949,Je 24,29:2
Collins, Monty F (Screenwriter)
Tangier 1946,Je 7,II,16:4
Green Promise, The 1949,Je 24,29:2

Collins, Norman (Original Author)
Dulcimer Street 1948,N 8,24:2
Invasion Quartet 1961,D 11,41:2
Collins, Pat
Divorce American Style 1967,Jl 20,30:2
Collins, Ray
Citizen Kane 1941,My 2,25:1
Big Street, The 1942,Ag 14,13:1
Magnificent Ambersons, The 1942,Ag 14,13:3
Navy Comes Through, The 1942,N 12,30:3
Human Comedy, The 1943,Mr 3,19:2
Slightly Dangerous 1943,Ap 2,17:2
Crime Doctor 1943,Jl 5,11:4
Salute to the Marines 1943,Ag 30,11:3
See Here Private Hargrove 1944,Mr 22,17:2
Whistling in Brooklyn 1944,Mr 24,17:3
Hitler Gang, The 1944,My 8,15:2
Eve of St Mark, The 1944,My 31,22:2
Barbary Coast Gent 1944,S 29,18:2
Seventh Cross, The 1944,S 29,18:1
Can't Help Singing 1944,D 26,22:4
Roughly Speaking 1945,F 1,18:4
Hidden Eye, The 1945,Ag 31,14:3
Leave Her to Heaven 1945,D 26,15:1
Up Goes Maisie 1946,Ja 25,26:7
Miss Susie Slagle's 1946,F 7,29:2
Badman's Territory 1946,My 31,27:2
Night in Paradise 1946,Je 6,16:3
Boy's Ranch 1946,Ag 9,12:2
Crack-Up 1946,S 7,11:1
Two Years Before the Mast 1946,S 25,39:2
Three Wise Fools 1946,S 27,19:2
Best Years of our Lives, The 1946,N 22,27:2
Return of Monte Cristo, The 1947,Ja 3,16:4
Bachelor and the Bobby-Soxer, The
1947,Jl 25,12:5
Swordsman, The 1947,O 17,18:4
Red Stallion 1947,N 27,50:3
Senator Was Indiscreet, The 1947,D 27,9:2
Double Life, A 1948,F 20,19:1
Homecoming 1948,Ap 30,28:4
Good Sam 1948,S 17,28:2
For the Love of Mary 1948,S 23,37:2
Command Decision 1949,Ja 20,34:2
Man From Colorado 1949,Ja 21,24:3
It Happens Every Spring 1949,Je 11,11:2
Fountainhead, The 1949,Jl 9,8:5
Red Stallion in the Rockies 1949,Ag 26,15:2
Heiress, The 1949,O 7,35:2
Paid in Full 1950,F 16,28:2
Francis 1950,Mr 16,40:2
Reformer and the Redhead, The 1950,Ap 10,15:2
Kill the Umpire 1950,My 29,10:6
Summer Stock 1950,S 1,17:2
Vengeance Valley 1951,F 16,21:2
U S S Teakettle 1951,F 24,11:2
Ma and Pa Kettle Back on the Farm
1951,My 11,32:3
Racket, The 1951,D 13,44:2
I Want You 1951,D 24,9:1
Invitation 1952,Ja 30,22:6
Young Man With Ideas 1952,Je 7,22:6
Dreamboat 1952,Jl 26,9:2
Desert Song, The 1953,My 21,39:2
Kid From Left Field, The 1953,S 26,15:3
Bad for Each Other 1953,D 24,9:3
Commandos Strike at Dawn 1954,Ja 14,25:1
Rose Marie 1954,Ap 2,22:2
Athena 1954,D 22,28:2
Desperate Hours, The 1955,O 6,25:1
Never Say Goodbye 1956,Ap 14,20:1
Solid Gold Cadillac, The 1956,O 25,40:3
Touch of Evil 1958,My 22,25:2
Collins, Reg
Kangaroo 1952,My 17,22:7
Collins, Richard (Original Author)
Thousands Cheer 1943,S 14,27:1
Little Giant 1946,My 9,27:5
Riot in Cell Block 11 1954,F 19,24:5
Collins, Richard (Screenwriter)
Rulers of the Sea 1939,N 9,27:1
One Crowded Night 1940,Ag 27,17:2
Lady Scarface 1941,Ag 4,16:6
Thousands Cheer 1943,S 14,27:1
Song of Russia 1944,F 11,17:2
Adventures of Haji Baba, The 1954,O 9,8:7
Bob Mathias Story, The 1954,O 16,14:6
Kiss of Fire 1955,S 24,11:2
Spanish Affair 1958,F 6,24:1
Badlanders, The 1958,S 4,33:1
Edge of Eternity 1960,F 25,34:2
Pay or Die 1960,My 27,22:2
Collins, Rufus
Brig, The 1964,S 21,37:4
Collins, Russell
Close-Up 1948,Ap 5,24:2
Niagara 1953,Ja 22,20:3
Destination Gobi 1953,My 30,7:1
Miss Sadie Thompson 1953,D 24,9:1
Monte Carlo Baby 1954,My 29,13:4
Bad Day at Black Rock 1955,F 2,22:2
Soldier of Fortune 1955,My 28,7:4
Last Frontier, The 1955,D 8,45:1

Raintree County 1957,D 21,22:1
Enemy Below, The 1957,D 26,23:2
Matchmaker, The 1958,Ag 13,22:1
Fail Safe 1964,S 16,36:1
Collins, Ted
Hello, Everybody 1933,Ja 30,9:4
Collins, Tom
Fast and Loose 1939,Mr 9,18:1
Tell no Tales 1939,Je 2,27:3
These Glamour Girls 1939,Ag 31,14:2
Dr Kildare's Strange Case 1940,Ap 12,19:2
Collins, Wilkie (Original Author)
Woman in White, The 1948,My 8,12:2
Collins, Winnie
Yellow Mask, The 1930,D 8,26:1
Collinson, Peter (Director)
Penthouse, The 1967,O 4,38:3
Up the Junction 1968,Mr 14,51:1
Long Day's Dying, The 1968,My 29,20:1
Collinson, Peter (Producer)
Long Day's Dying, The 1968,My 29,20:1
Collinson, Peter (Screenwriter)
Penthouse, The 1967,O 4,38:3
Collison, Wilson (Original Author)
Getting Gertie's Garter 1927,F 9,17:3
Expensive Women 1931,N 14,15:3
Three Wise Girls 1932,F 6,14:4
Crusader, The 1932,O 8,15:4
Red-Haired Alibi 1932,O 24,18:5
Red Dust 1932,N 5,12:5
Sing Sinner Sing 1933,Ag 15,20:2
There's Always a Woman 1938,Ap 29,17:2
Mad Miss Manton, The 1938,O 21,27:2
There's That Woman Again 1939,Ja 6,25:4
Maisie 1939,Je 23,23:1
Congo Maisie 1940,F 8,18:4
Gold Rush Maisie 1940,S 2,19:2
Moon Over Burma 1940,D 12,37:4
Swing Shift Maisie 1943,S 10,29:2
Up in Mabel's Room 1944,Ap 22,8:6
Maisie Goes to Reno 1944,S 29,18:1
Up Goes Maisie 1946,Ja 25,26:7
Getting Gertie's Garter 1946,F 4,21:2
Mogambo 1953,O 2,18:1
Collomb, Jean
Live for Life 1967,D 19,59:1
Collum, John
Tom Brown's School Days 1940,Je 28,22:2
COLLYER
See Also COLLIER
Collyer, June
East Side, West Side 1927,O 18,33:2
Four Sons 1928,F 14,27:1
Hangman's House 1928,My 14,25:1
Me, Gangster 1928,O 22,29:1
Not Quite Decent 1929,My 6,30:4
River of Romance, The 1929,Jl 29,23:3
Illusion 1929,S 28,17:3
Love Doctor, The 1929,N 9,22:5
Man From Wyoming, A 1930,Jl 12,16:4
Sweet Kitty Bellairs 1930,S 6,9:2
Extravagance 1930,D 9,31:3
Charley's Aunt 1930,D 26,18:4
Kiss Me Again 1931,Ja 8,21:4
Damaged Love 1931,Ja 19,25:1
Dude Ranch 1931,Ap 25,23:4
Honeymoon Lane 1931,Ag 1,16:4
Brat, The 1931,Ag 24,13:4
Alexander Hamilton 1931,S 17,21:4
Before Midnight 1934,Ja 10,24:3
Cheaters 1934,My 12,12:4
Ghost Walks, The 1935,Mr 30,11:2
COLMAN
See Also COLEMAN
Colman, Booth
Big Sky, The 1952,Ag 20,21:1
Colman, Bruce
Confessions of a Co-Ed 1931,Je 20,20:4
Colman, Ronald
White Sister, The 1923,S 6,10:2
$20 a Week 1924,Je 10,24:4
Tarnish 1924,O 13,21:1
Romola 1924,D 2,13:2
Her Night of Romance 1925,Ja 13,16:1
Thief in Paradise, A 1925,Ja 26,14:1
His Supreme Moment 1925,Ap 13,21:1
Sporting Venus, The 1925,My 11,14:3
Dark Angel, The 1925,O 12,19:3
Stella Dallas 1925,N 17,30:2
Lady Windemere's Fan 1925,D 28,19:2
Kiki 1926,Ap 6,26:4
Beau Geste 1926,Ag 26,17:3
Winning of Barbara Worth, The 1926,N 29,16:3
Night of Love, The 1927,Ja 25,18:4
Magic Flame, The 1927,S 19,30:3
Two Lovers 1928,Mr 23,24:4
White Sister, The 1928,My 21,25:1
Rescue, The 1929,Ja 14,20:1
Bulldog Drummond 1929,My 3,23:2
Condemned 1929,N 4,28:1
Raffles 1930,Jl 25,20:4
Handsome Gigolo, Poor Gigolo 1930,Ag 3,4:1
Devil to Pay, The 1930,D 19,30:1

Colman, Ronald — Cont
Unholy Garden, The 1931,O 29,27:1
Arrowsmith 1931,D 8,36:4
Cynara 1932,D 26,26:2
Masquerader, The 1933,S 4,9:5
Bulldog Drummond Strikes Back 1934,Ag 16,20:2
Clive of India 1935,Ja 18,29:1
Man Who Broke the Bank at Monte Carlo, The
1935,N 15,20:2
Tale of Two Cities, A 1935,D 26,21:2
Under Two Flags 1936,My 1,19:1
Lost Horizon 1937,Mr 4,27:1
Prisoner of Zenda, The 1937,S 3,12:1
If I Were King 1938,S 29,31:1
Light That Failed, The 1939,D 25,19:1
Lucky Partners 1940,S 6,25:2
My Life With Caroline 1941,O 30,27:1
Talk of the Town, The 1942,Ag 28,22:3
Random Harvest 1942,D 18,36:6
Kismet 1944,Ag 23,16:1
Late George Apley, The 1947,Mr 21,29:2
Double Life, A 1948,F 20,19:1
Champagne for Caesar 1950,My 12,33:2
Around the World in 80 Days 1956,O 18,37:1
Story of Mankind, The 1957,N 9,31:2
Colmans, David
Wetbacks 1956,My 5,13:2
Colmans, Edward
Sirocco 1951,Je 14,31:2
Thief of Damascus 1952,My 8,37:2
Iron Mistress, The 1952,N 20,39:2
Secret of the Incas 1954,My 29,13:3
Third Voice, The 1960,Mr 7,24:5
Colmes, Walter (Director)
Burning Cross, The 1948,F 20,19:1
Colmes, Walter (Producer)
Burning Cross, The 1948,F 20,19:1
Kid From Cleveland, The 1949,S 5,13:2
Colombier, Pierre (Director)
Roi des Resquilleurs, Le 1932,Je 13,19:3
Charlemagne 1935,Ag 24,18:3
King, The 1941,O 23,29:3
Ignace 1950,S 19,39:4
Colombo, Enzo
Fiat Voluntas Dei 1936,Jl 6,11:5
Colombo, Eugenio
Fiat Voluntas Dei 1936,Jl 6,11:5
Colombo, Harry (Producer)
Fistful of Dollars, A 1967,F 2,29:1
Grand Slam 1968,F 21,60:4
Colombo, Luigi
Sei tu l'Amore 1930,N 18,28:4
Colome, Antonio
Crisis Mundial; World Crisis 1937,F 15,12:6
Colomer, Antonita
Mercedes 1935,My 14,17:5
Colon, Louis
Way Out 1967,O 26,54:3
Colon, Miriam
Crowded Paradise 1956,Je 22,15:1
One Eyed Jacks 1961,Mr 31,21:1
Harbor Lights 1964,F 13,25:3
Appaloosa, The 1966,S 15,51:1
Colone, Pierre
Enemy to the King, An 1916,N 27,9:1
Colonello, Vittorina
Trovatore, Il 1950,F 9,36:7
Colonna, G A (Original Author)
Pirates of Capri, The 1949,D 26,33:5
Colonna, Golfiero (Producer)
Last Paradise, The 1958,Mr 1,12:1
Colonna, Jerry
52d Street 1937,N 15,15:1
Rosalie 1937,D 31,9:2
College Swing 1938,Ap 28,27:2
Valley of the Giants 1938,S 10,20:2
Naughty but Nice 1939,Je 23,23:2
Road to Singapore 1940,Mr 14,29:2
Comin' Round the Mountain 1940,S 26,27:3
You're the One 1941,F 20,23:2
Sis Hopkins 1941,My 1,27:5
Ice-Capades 1941,S 25,29:1
True to the Army 1942,Je 15,15:4
Priorities on Parade 1942,Jl 23,19:2
Star Spangled Rhythm 1942,D 31,20:1
Atlantic City 1944,Ag 14,11:4
It's in the Bag 1945,Je 11,12:1
Road to Rio 1948,F 19,29:3
Meet Me in Las Vegas 1956,Mr 14,39:2
Andy Hardy Comes Home 1958,D 24,00:0
Colpet, Max (Original Author)
Once a Thief 1951,Ja 19,21:3
Colpeyn, Louisa
Passion of Slow Fire, The 1962,O 12,26:1
Band of Outsiders 1964,S 19,19:1
Colpi, Henri (Director)
Long Absence, The 1962,N 16,23:2
Colscicchi, L (Miscellaneous)
Tre Anni Senza Donne 1937,My 27,21:4
Colt, Bobby
Catskill Honeymoon 1950,Ja 28,10:3
Colt, John Drew
Double Life, A 1948,F 20,19:1

Colt, Steve
Fear and Desire 1953,Ap 1,35:2
Colterell, Geoffrey (Screenwriter)
Tiara Tahiti 1963,N 6,32:1
Colton, John (Original Author)
Drifting 1923,Ag 20,4:2
Shanghai Lady 1929,N 11,20:2
Shanghai Gesture, The 1941,D 26,21:2
Colton, John (Screenwriter)
Exciters, The 1923,Je 4,13:3
Wild Orchids 1929,Ap 1,22:1
Werewolf of London, The 1935,My 10,25:2
Colton, Scott
Murder in Greenwich Village 1937,O 30,22:2
Women in Prison 1938,Mr 1,19:3
Colton, Trax
Marriage-Go-Round 1961,Ja 7,12:2
It Happened in Athens 1962,N 15,46:2
Colum, Padraic (Screenwriter)
Hansel and Gretel 1954,O 11,33:1
Columbo, Russ
Wolf Song 1929,F 25,16:1
Broadway Thru a Keyhole 1933,N 2,18:3
Wake up and Dream 1934,O 11,28:3
Coluzzi, Chicco
Path of Hope, The (Il Cammino Della Speranza)
1952,Ag 5,15:5
Coluzzi, Luciana
Path of Hope, The (Il Cammino Della Speranza)
1952,Ag 5,15:5
Colvin, Gilly
Nix on Dames 1929,N 23,18:5
Colvin, William
My Own Pal 1926,Mr 15,18:3
Cohens and the Kelleys In Scotland, The
1930,Mr 10,24:1
Girl Without a Room 1933,D 7,26:3
Colwell, Robert T (Original Author)
Strictly Dynamite 1934,Jl 4,18:2
Comadore, Joe
Tanganyika 1954,Je 19,9:2
Shrike, The 1955,Jl 8,15:2
Comandini, Adele (Original Author)
Hell Bound 1931,My 9,15:4
Beyond Tomorrow 1940,S 27,27:1
Mating of Millie, The 1948,Mr 13,12:2
Flame of the Islands 1956,F 25,12:4
Comandini, Adele (Screenwriter)
Girl of the Limberlost, A 1934,N 9,24:6
Country Beyond, The 1936,Ap 30,17:3
Three Smart Girls 1937,Ja 25,22:2
Road.to Reno, The 1938,O 3,11:2
Beyond Tomorrow 1940,S 27,27:1
Always in my Heart 1942,Mr 14,19:2
Christmas in Connecticut 1945,Jl 28,7:2
Danger Signal 1945,N 22,39:2
Comanez, Jacques (Original Author)
Three Hours 1944,O 30,16:5
Combe, Boyce
Daddies 1924,F 11,18:3
Combell, Minna
After Tomorrow 1932,Mr 7,13:5
Comber, Jeanette
Pancho Villa Returns 1950,O 24,34:6
Comber, Tully
Song of the Road 1940,My 6,13:2
Combo, Clyde
Overlanders, The 1946,D 20,31:2
Bush Christmas 1947,N 27,50:4
Kangaroo 1952,My 17,22:7
Combs, Jackie
Lovey Mary 1926,Je 21,17:2
Sweet Rosie O'Grady 1926,Jl 9,33:1
Comden, Betty (Original Author)
On the Town 1949,D 9,37:2
Singin' in the Rain 1952,Mr 28,27:2
Band Wagon, The 1953,Jl 10,10:2
It's Always Fair Weather 1955,S 16,19:1
Bells Are Ringing 1960,Je 24,31:2
Comden, Betty (Screenwriter)
Good News 1947,D 5,33:2
Barkleys of Broadway, The 1949,My 5,34:2
On the Town 1949,D 9,37:2
Singin' in the Rain 1952,Mr 28,27:2
Band Wagon, The 1953,Jl 10,10:2
It's Always Fair Weather 1955,S 16,19:1
Auntie Mame 1958,D 5,39:1
Bells Are Ringing 1960,Je 24,31:2
What a Way to Go! 1964,My 15,44:1
Comegys, Kathleen
Mr Belvedere Rings the Bell 1951,Ag 2,18:1
Miracle Worker, The 1962,My 24,29:2
Comencini, Luigi (Director)
Guaglio 1949,My 19,35:2
Behind Closed Shutters 1952,Je 10,22:7
Heidi 1953,D 21,27:2
Bread, Love and Dreams 1954,S 21,24:1
Frisky 1955,O 25,37:3
Everybody go Home!; Tutti a Casa 1962,N 6,38:1
Bebo's Girl 1964,N 12,40:1
Bambole; Dolls, The (Treatise on Eugenics);
  Treatise on Eugenics (The Dolls)
  1965,Je 29,26:1

Comencini, Luigi (Original Author)
Frisky 1955,O 25,37:3
Comencini, Luigi (Screenwriter)
Bread, Love and Dreams 1954,S 21,24:1
Everybody go Home!; Tutti a Casa 1962,N 6,38:1
Coment, Mathilda
Escapade 1935,Jl 6,16:2
Comer, Anjanette
Quick, Before it Melts 1965,Ap 1,30:2
Loved One, The 1965,O 12,57:1
Appaloosa, The 1966,S 15,51:1
Banning 1967,D 14,62:2
Guns for San Sebastian 1968,Mr 21,57:2
Comer, John
I'm All Right Jack 1960,Ap 26,40:2
Family Way, The 1967,Je 29,32:1
Comerate, Sheridan
3:10 to Yuma 1957,Ag 29,22:1
Operation Mad Ball 1957,N 21,38:1
Story of Page One, The 1960,Ja 14,28:1
Ice Palace 1960,Je 30,22:1
Comfort, Lance (Director)
Squadron Leader X 1943,Jl 23,21:2
Courageous Mr Penn 1943,D 23,26:5
Bedelia 1947,F 8,10:2
Hatter's Castle 1948,Jl 3,8:6
Temptation Harbor 1949,My 11,34:7
Silent Dust 1949,D 30,13:2
Portrait of Clare 1951,D 26,19:6
Eight O'Clock Walk 1955,Ap 30,10:6
Man in the Dark 1965,Ja 21,22:1
Comi, Paul
In Love and War 1958,N 1,14:2
Pork Chop Hill 1959,My 30,9:2
Outsider, The 1962,F 8,25:1
Cape Fear 1962,Ap 19,35:2
Blindfold 1966,My 26,55:2
Cominetti, Edino (Director)
Via de Oro, La; Gold Route, The
  1932,Ja 3,VIII,6:6
Comingore, Dorothy
Citizen Kane 1941,My 2,25:1
Hairy Ape, The 1944,Jl 3,8:3
Any Number Can Play 1949,Jl 1,14:4
Big Night, The 1952,Mr 20,37:5
Cominquez, Columba
Hidden River 1950,D 1,31:2
Comisky, Pat
Harder They Fall, The 1956,My 10,26:3
Commings, Hugh (Screenwriter)
Earthworm Tractors 1936,Jl 25,16:1
Como, Perry
Something for the Boys 1944,N 30,19:1
Doll Face 1946,Mr 28,35:3
If I'm Lucky 1946,S 20,41:3
Words and Music 1948,D 10,34:2
Comolli, Jean-Louis
Alphaville 1965,O 26,49:1
Comont, Mathilde
Rosita 1923,S 4,14:1
If Marriage Fails 1925,Je 2,16:3
Enchanted Hill, The 1925,D 29,19:2 (In
  Addenda)
Sea Beast, The 1926,Ja 16,8:5
Boheme, La 1926,F 25,26:2
Girl From Montmarte, The 1926,F 25,26:2
Puppets 1926,Je 21,17:2
Loves of Carmen 1927,S 27,31:1
Streets of Shanghai 1928,F 21,19:3
Ramona 1928,My 15,17:3
Romance 1930,Ag 23,7:3
Call of the Flesh 1930,S 13,9:3
Lash, The 1931,Ja 1,31:3
Lady Who Dared, The 1931,Je 6,15:5
Cuban Love Song, The 1931,D 5,21:2
Here's to Romance 1935,O 3,29:2
Ceiling Zero 1936,Ja 20,22:2
Poor Little Rich Girl, The 1936,Je 26,16:1
Anthony Adverse 1936,Ag 27,16:1
Comont, Nattie
His Hour 1924,O 7,26:1
Comont, Nellie Mme
Mademoiselle Midnight 1924,My 27,14:1
Comp, Rosella
Seven Hills of Rome 1958,Ja 28,24:2 (Incorrect
  in this edition; use 1958,Ja 31,24:2 elsewhere)
Compana, Nina
It Happened Out West 1937,Je 7,22:3
Companeez, Jacques (Original Author)
Tempest in the Flesh 1957,Ja 19,12:2
Folies Bergere 1958,My 28,37:2
Companeez, Jacques (Screenwriter)
Lower Depths, The 1937,S 11,20:1
Personal Column 1941,F 3,13:2
It Happened in Gibraltar 1943,N 16,27:1
Sirocco 1946,Ag 12,17:3
Postmaster's Daughter, The 1946,Ag 19,17:6
Confessions of a Rogue 1948,Mr 30,26:3
Damned, The; Maudits, Les 1948,Ap 26,27:2
Friend Will come Tonight, A; Ami Viendra Ce
  Soir, Un 1948,Jl 12,11:2
Counter Investigation 1949,D 30,13:2
Casque D'Or 1952,Ag 19,19:1

Companeez, Jacques (Screenwriter)— Cont
Tale of Five Women, A 1953,Ja 16,19:2
Naughty Martine 1953,Ap 13,32:4
Companions of the Night 1954,N 25,44:2
Adorable Creatures 1956,Ja 11,36:2
Sorciere, La 1956,D 28,17:2
Forbidden Fruit 1959,F 23,19:1
Companeez, Joseph (Screenwriter)
Lover's Net 1957,Jl 23,23:1
Companeez, Nina (Screenwriter)
Benjamin 1968,Mr 26,41:2
Companeez (Screenwriter)
Betrayal 1939,S 16,20:2
Compbell, Patrick (Screenwriter)
Law and Disorder 1958,Ag 6,20:1
Compson, Betty
Miracle Man, The 1919,Ag 27,9:5
Prisoners of Love 1921,Ja 17,9:1
At the End of the World 1921,Ag 15,14:3
Ladies Must Live 1921,N 21,20:1
Little Minister, The 1921,D 26,13:3
Law and the Woman, The 1922,Ja 22,VI,3:1 (In
  Addenda)
Green Temptation, The 1922,Mr 20,10:3
To Have and to Hold 1922,N 6,13:1
Kick In 1922,D 18,22:2
Rustle of Silk, The 1923,My 8,22:4
Woman With Four Faces, The 1923,Je 18,13:5
Hollywood 1923,Jl 30,11:4
Stranger, The 1924,F 5,20:1
Woman to Woman 1924,Ap 1,19:3
Miami 1924,Je 3,22:2
Enemy Sex, The 1924,Jl 1,21:4
Female, The 1924,S 2,19:2
Garden of Weeds, The 1924,N 4,24:1
Fast Set, The 1924,N 18,22:1
Locked Doors 1925,Ja 12,11:2
New Lives for Old 1925,F 25,16:7
Eve's Secret 1925,Je 11,14:3
Paths to Paradise 1925,Je 30,14:3
Paths to Paradise 1925,Jl 5,VII,2:1
Pony Express, The 1925,S 14,16:1
Cheating Cheaters 1927,D 6,27:1
Love Me and the World Is Mine 1928,F 6,12:3
Big City, The 1928,Mr 26,26:2
Docks of New York, The 1928,S 17,28:2
Barker, The 1928,D 6,35:1
Scarlet Seas 1928,D 31,9:1
Weary River 1929,Ja 25,20:6
On With the Show 1929,My 29,28:6
Time, The Place and the Girl, The 1929,Jl 8,17:3
Street Girl 1929,Jl 31,17:3
Great Gabbo, The 1929,S 13,33:1
Skin Deep 1929,S 30,23:1
Woman to Woman 1929,N 12,34:4
Show of Shows 1929,N 21,24:5
Blaze O' Glory 1929,D 31,15:1
Case of Sergeant Grischa, The 1930,Mr 8,21:1
Isle of Escape 1930,Mr 31,24:3
Midnight Mystery 1930,Je 2,25:4
Czar of Broadway, The 1930,Je 30,22:6
Inside the Lines 1930,Jl 5,17:4
Those Who Dance 1930,Jl 7,22:3
Spoilers, The 1930,S 20,15:4
Boudoir Diplomat, The 1930,D 8,26:1
She Got What She Wanted 1930,D 29,18:1
Virtuous Husband 1931,My 8,30:2
Gay Diplomat, The 1931,O 10,20:4
Silver Lining, The 1932,My 30,16:5
West of Singapore 1933,Ap 1,18:3
Destination Unknown 1933,Ap 8,16:2
Laughing Irish Eyes 1936,Ap 4,11:2
Hollywood Boulevard 1936,S 21,26:4
Killer at Large 1936,O 26,20:1
Federal Bullets 1937,D 27,11:1
Port of Missing Girls, The 1938,Ap 4,12:5
Torchy Blane in Panama 1938,Ap 18,11:1
News Is Made at Night 1939,Jl 13,17:2
Mr and Mrs Smith 1941,F 21,16:3
Invisible Ghost, The 1941,My 8,21:2
Second Chance 1947,S 20,12:4
Here Comes Trouble 1948,Ap 15,31:4
Compton, Fay
This Freedom 1923,N 28,15:1
Fashions in Love 1929,Jl 1,31:2
Love Storm 1931,O 19,28:1
Battle of Gallipoli, The 1931,D 7,16:1
Autumn Crocus 1934,O 25,26:2
Strauss's Great Waltz 1935,Ap 8,23:3
Mill On the Floss, The 1939,N 15,19:3
Prime Minister, The 1942,F 4,23:2
Odd Man Out 1947,Ap 24,30:2
Dulcimer Street 1948,N 8,24:2
Forbidden Street, The 1949,My 14,9:2
Laughter in Paradise 1951,N 12,21:2
Lady Possessed 1952,F 15,17:2
Othello 1955,S 13,27:1
Story of Esther Costello, The 1957,N 6,43:1
Haunting, The 1963,S 19,23:1
Compton, Forrest
Outsider, The 1962,F 8,25:1
Compton, Francis
Soak the Rich 1936,F 5,14:2
Rage in Heaven 1941,Mr 21,19:2

Compton, Francis — Cont
Witness for the Prosecution 1958,F 7,16:1
Compton, John
Mildred Pierce 1945,S 29,12:2
Glass Menagerie, The 1950,S 29,31:5
Oh! Susanna 1951,Mr 30,28:5
Compton, Joyce
What Fools Men 1925,S 29,31:3
Syncopating Sue 1926,N 2,35:1
Ankles Preferred 1927,Ap 18,21:2
Soft Living 1928,F 27,16:2
Wild Party, The 1929,Ap 2,28:4
Dangerous Curves 1929,Jl 15,25:1
Salute 1929,O 5,22:5
Sky Hawk, The 1929,D 12,36:4
High Society Blues 1930,Ap 19,15:1
Wild Company 1930,Jl 19,7:5
Lightnin' 1930,N 29,21:4
Three Rogues 1931,Ap 4,23:1
Three Girls Lost 1931,My 2,23:4
Up Pops the Devil 1931,My 16,13:3
Women of all Nations 1931,My 30,9:2
Annabelle's Affairs 1931,Je 29,20:3
Good Sport 1931,D 12,23:3
Under Eighteen 1931,D 26,15:5
Lena Rivers 1932,My 21,9:2
Lady and Gent 1932,Jl 16,5:5
False Faces 1932,N 25,19:2
Afraid to Talk 1932,D 19,19:5
Sing Sinner Sing 1933,Ag 15,20:2
Only Yesterday 1933,N 10,25:1
Affairs of a Gentleman 1934,Je 23,16:7
White Parade, The 1934,N 10,19:1
Go Into Your Dance 1935,My 4,17:2
Let 'Em Have It 1935,My 30,21:1
Trapped by Television 1936,Je 15,24:3
Harvester, The 1936,Jl 4,18:2
Star for a Night 1936,S 5,7:2
Murder With Pictures 1936,N 21,21:4
Top of the Town 1937,Mr 27,19:2
China Passage 1937,Ap 16,27:2
Pick a Star 1937,My 28,17:2
Wings Over Honolulu 1937,My 29,20:1
Toast of New York, The 1937,Jl 23,16:2
Sea Racketeers 1937,O 4,17:2
Awful Truth, The 1937,N 5,19:3
Women Are Like That 1938,Ap 11,12:2
Spring Madness 1938,D 1,29:3
Last Warning, The 1938,D 8,34:4
Artists and Models Abroad 1938,D 22,25:3
Going Places 1939,Ja 7,6:1
Flying Irishman, The 1939,Ap 12,27:2
Rose of Washington Square 1939,My 6,21:2
Hotel for Women 1939,Ag 26,20:2
Balalaika 1939,D 15,33:2
Reno 1939,D 21,29:2
Honeymoon Deferred 1940,F 16,23:4
Turnabout 1940,Jl 27,17:6
City for Conquest 1940,S 28,9:2
Sky Murder 1940,N 14,28:3
Let's Make Music 1941,Ja 23,19:2
Manpower 1941,Jl 5,14:2
Moon Over her Shoulder 1941,N 5,31:2
Blues in the Night 1941,D 12,35:2
Bedtime Story 1942,Mr 20,25:4
Silver Skates 1943,Mr 19,15:3
Christmas in Connecticut 1945,Jl 28,7:2
Danger Signal 1945,N 22,39:2
Southern Yankee, A 1948,N 25,47:2
Jet Pilot 1957,O 5,8:6
Compton, Juliette
Nell Gwyn 1926,Jl 19,13:1
Woman Tempted, The 1928,Ap 24,29:3
Triumph of the Scarlet Pimpernel, The
1929,Jl 8,17:3
Woman to Woman 1929,N 12,34:4
Ladies of Leisure 1930,My 24,21:2
Anybody's Woman 1930,Ag 16,8:3
Morocco 1930,N 17,29:1
Unfaithful 1931,Mr 7,17:2
Kick In 1931,My 25,17:1
Women Love Once 1931,Je 27,20:3
Compromised 1931,N 7,16:5
Rich Man's Folly 1931,N 27,29:3
Husband's Holiday 1931,D 25,29:2
No One Man 1932,Ja 23,18:4
Strangers in Love 1932,Mr 5,11:2
Westward Passage 1932,Je 4,9:2
Man Called Back, The 1932,Jl 30,16:5
Devil and the Deep 1932,Ag 20,7:4
Match King, The 1932,D 8,25:3
Peg o'my Heart 1933,My 20,11:4
Masquerader, The 1933,S 4,9:5
Berkeley Square 1933,S 14,26:2
Grand Canary 1934,Jl 20,11:1
Count of Monte Cristo, The 1934,S 27,25:2
Behold My Wife 1935,F 18,19:3
Irene 1940,My 24,23:3
That Hamilton Woman 1941,Ap 4,25:1
Compton, Madge
Randolph Family 1945,Mr 13,19:4
Compton, Viola
Good Companions, The 1933,O 10,24:1
Last Journey, The 1936,Je 8,22:4

Comstock, F Roy (Miscellaneous)
Hearts of the World 1918,Ap 5,13:1
Comstock, Howard Warren (Original Author)
Stepping Sisters 1932,Ja 9,21:1
Doctor X 1932,Ag 4,17:2
Comstock & Gest (Producer)
Thief of Bagdad, The 1924,Mr 19,19:1
Conan, Zolla
Her Bodyguard 1933,Ag 7,18:2
Concello, Antoinette
Greatest Show on Earth, The 1952,Ja 11,17:2
Concepcion, M
Mask of the Himalayas 1953,Ag 12,22:3
Conchita
Three on the Trail 1936,My 5,26:5
Conchon, Georges (Screenwriter)
Stranger, The 1967,D 19,59:1
Conde, Carlos
Raton Pass 1951,Ap 20,25:1
My Man and I 1952,S 6,12:6
Conde, Carmen
Asi es la Mujer 1936,O 21,35:3
Adios, Nicanor 1938,Mr 14,13:2
Conde, Ritz
Ride the Pink Horse 1947,O 9,32:3
Condi, Harry
Beiden Seehunde, Die 1935,Mr 9,19:2
Condit, Steve
To Kill a Mockingbird 1963,F 15,10:2
Condon, Charles R (Original Author)
Daredevil Drivers, The 1938,F 23,27:2
Condon, Frank (Original Author)
Hollywood 1923,Jl 30,11:4
Rubber Tires 1927,My 9,29:1
Condon, Frank (Screenwriter)
Waking up the Town 1925,Mr 31,17:4
Condon, Richard (Original Author)
Manchurian Candidate, The 1962,O 25,48:3
Condon, Robert
Home in Indiana 1944,Je 22,23:1
Condos, Nick
Dancing Feet 1936,Mr 28,11:2
Condos and Brandow
She's Back on Broadway 1953,Mr 12,24:2
Condos Brothers
Wake up and Live 1937,Ap 24,16:2
Happy Landing 1938,Ja 22,19:1
In the Navy 1941,Je 12,29:2
Moon Over Miami 1941,Jl 5,14:2
Pin Up Girl 1944,My 11,25:6
Song of the Open Road 1944,Je 7,13:3
Time, The Place And The Girl, The
1946,D 27,14:3
Conesa, Marie
Webb Singing Pictures 1917,Ja 15,7:1
Conesa, Matilde
Don Quixote 1949,My 13,29:3
Conforti, Donna
Santa Claus Conquers the Martians
1964,D 17,50:2
Conforti, Gino
How Sweet It Is 1968,Ag 22,47:1
Congdon, James
Left Handed Gun, The 1958,My 8,36:2
Group, The 1966,Mr 17,35:1
Conklin, Charles
Day of Faith, The 1923,N 27,11:2
Find Your Man 1924,S 23,26:1
Below the Line 1925,S 21,12:4
Red Hot Tires 1925,O 20,28:1
Seven Sinners 1925,D 8,28:5
Conklin, Chester
Greed 1924,D 5,28:1
Where Was I 1925,Ag 19,14:4
Masked Bride, The 1925,N 30,17:1
Woman of the World, A 1925,D 14,18:2
Behind the Front 1926,F 10,16:2
Social Celebrity, A 1926,Ap 19,24:3
Wilderness Woman, The 1926,My 10,19:1
Say It Again 1926,Je 7,23:2
Duchess of Buffalo, The 1926,Ag 9,10:3
Nervous Wreck, The 1926,O 12,30:2
Midnight Lovers 1926,O 26,23:1
We're in the Navy Now 1926,N 8,19:2
McFadden's Flats 1927,F 13,VII,7:2 (In
Addenda)
Kiss in a Taxi, A 1927,Mr 15,29:2
Cabaret 1927,My 2,26:4
Rubber Heels 1927,Je 28,29:4
Tell It to Sweeney 1927,O 17,20:2
Two Flaming Youths 1928,Ja 2,28:1
Gentlemen Prefer Blondes 1928,Ja 16,24:1
Big Noise, The 1928,My 7,29:1
Fools for Luck 1928,Je 12,33:5
Varsity 1928,O 29,29:1
Haunted House, The 1928,D 17,23:1
Haunted House, The 1928,D 23,VIII,7:1
Marquis Preferred 1929,Ja 21,18:4
Studio Murder Mystery, The 1929,Je 10,23:1
Show of Shows 1929,N 21,24:5
Virginian, The 1929,D 23,18:2
Swing High 1930,Je 27,26:3
Her Majesty, Love 1931,N 26,37:2

Conklin, Chester — Cont
Hallelujah, I'm a Bum 1933,F 9,15:2
Modern Times 1936,F 6,23:2
Preview Murder Mystery, The 1936,Mr 21,13:2
Every Day's a Holiday 1938,Ja 27,17:2
Hollywood Cavalcade 1939,O 14,13:2
Great Dictator, The 1940,O 16,29:1
Harmon of Michigan 1941,O 2,29:2
Knickerbocker Holiday 1944,Ap 20,22:7
Hail the Conquering Hero 1944,Ag 10,14:2
Sunday Dinner for a Soldier 1945,Ja 25,16:2
Perils of Pauline, The 1947,Jl 10,17:2
Beautiful Blonde From Bashful Bend, The
1949,My 28,11:2
When Comedy Was King 1960,Mr 30,42:1
Conklin, Frank
Federal Man-Hunt 1939,F 2,17:3
Conklin, Hal (Original Author)
Spieler, The 1929,F 25,16:1
Big Shot, The 1932,Ja 2,14:2
Silver Lining, The 1932,My 30,16:5
Conklin, Heinie
Clash of the Wolves, The 1925,N 18,27:4
Night Cry, The 1926,Ap 7,26:6
Beware of Widows 1927,My 24,23:4
Silk Stockings 1927,N 29,31:1
Feel my Pulse 1928,F 27,16:2
Beau Broadway 1928,Jl 30,21:2
Air Circus, The 1928,S 3,14:2
All Quiet on The Western Front 1930,Ap 30,29:1
Hollywood Cavalcade 1939,O 14,13:2
Perils of Pauline, The 1947,Jl 10,17:2
Conklin, Peggy
President Vanishes, The 1934,D 8,18:5
One Way Ticket 1936,Ja 1,35:2
Devil is a Sissy, The 1936,O 17,21:2
Having Wonderful Time 1938,Jl 8,11:2
Conklin, Russ
Siren of Atlantis 1949,Ag 22,13:1
Conklin, Thomas
Caught Short 1930,Je 21,20:5
Conklin, William
Hay Foot, Straw Foot 1919,Je 23,10:3
Red Hot Dollars 1919,D 29,7:2
Woman in the Suitcase, The 1920,Ja 12,7:1
Hairpins 1920,Ag 2,12:2
Darling of New York, The 1924,Ja 18,20:1
Goldfish, The 1924,My 20,15:2
Man Without a Country, The 1925,F 12,16:1
Fifth Avenue Models 1925,My 4,16:2
Winds of Chance 1925,Ag 17,10:3
Sweet Rosie O'Grady 1926,D 9,33:1
Rose of the Golden West 1927,S 26,27:1
Divine Lady, The 1929,Mr 23,22:4
Conlan, Frank
Scoundrel, The 1935,My 3,23:2
Chad Hanna 1940,D 26,23:1
Billy the Kid 1941,Je 20,28:2
Lydia 1941,S 19,27:1
All That Money Can Buy 1941,O 17,27:2
Crystal Ball, The 1943,F 19,22:2
Black Book, The 1949,O 17,18:2
Perfect Strangers 1950,Mr 11,8:2
Conlan, Jocko
Safe at Home 1941,N 26,31:2
CONLEY
See Also CONNELLY, CONNOLLY
Conley, Darlene
Faces 1968,S 23,42:4
Conley, Onest
Grand Old Girl 1935,F 26,16:4
Conlin, J
Remarkable Andrew, The 1942,Mr 6,17:2
Conlin, Jimmy
Sudden Death, And 1936,Jl 18,18:2
Second Chorus 1941,Ja 16,25:2
Palm Beach Story, The 1942,D 11,33:1
Taxi, Mister 1943,Ap 15,20:2
Hitler's Madman 1943,Ag 28,15:1
Hail the Conquering Hero 1944,Ag 10,14:2
Dick Tracy's Dilemma 1947,Jl 14,14:5
Mourning Becomes Electra 1947,N 20,38:2
Great Rupert, The 1950,Ap 14,27:2
Mad Wednesday 1951,Ja 25,21:5
Anatomy of a Murder 1959,Jl 3,10:1
Conlin, Joe
Thief, The 1952,O 16,37:1
Conlin, Richard (Original Author)
Angels in the Outfield 1951,O 18,32:1
Conlin, Terence
Laburnum Grove 1941,D 2,29:2
Conlin, Terry
Patient Vanishes, The 1947,My 23,31:2
Conlon, Francis
New Toys 1925,F 17,18:1
Conlon, James
Bride Comes Home, The 1935,D 25,30:2
Man Who Found Himself, The 1937,Ap 9,19:3
Torchy Blane, The Adventurous Blonde
1937,D 18,18:1
Crashing Hollywood 1938,Ja 8,19:2
Torchy Blane in Panama 1938,Ap 18,11:1
Broadway Musketeers 1938,O 14,27:1
Calling Philo Vance 1940,F 9,15:3

Conlon, Tommy
Young America 1932,My 7,11:5
Rebecca of Sunnybrook Farm 1932,Jl 30,16:5
Sign of the Cross, The 1932,D 1,25:1
No Man of her Own 1932,D 31,10:1
Laughter in Hell 1933,Ja 2,29:2
Only Yesterday 1933,N 10,25:1
Conn, Billy
Pittsburgh Kid, The 1941,S 23,27:4
Conn, Harry W (Miscellaneous)
Transatlantic Merry-Go-Round 1934,N 1,25:2
Conn, Jacob Captain (Original Author)
Found Alive 1934,F 12,19:2
Conn, Maurice H (Original Author)
Zamba 1949,N 7,33:2
Conn, Maurice H (Producer)
Zamba 1949,N 7,33:2
Conne, E R (Producer)
King's People, The 1937,My 12,27:1
Connel, Maureen
Rising of the Moon, The (A Minute's Wait);
Minute's Wait, A (The Rising of the Moon)
1957,Jl 10,23:1
Connel, Paul
You Can't Beat the Irish 1952,My 1,34:4
Connell, Barbara (Miscellaneous)
Time for Burning, A 1967,F 24,26:2
Connell, Del (Original Author)
Three Caballeros, The 1945,F 5,20:1
Connell, Howard
Little Kidnappers, The 1954,S 2,18:1
Fuss Over Feathers 1954,D 27,22:6
Connell, Jane
Ladybug, Ladybug 1963,D 24,9:1
Connell, John
Fail Safe 1964,S 16,36:1
Connell, Maureen
Lucky Jim 1958,S 1,8:6
Man Upstairs, The 1959,Ag 11,23:2
Connell, Miranda
Admirable Crichton, The 1957,D 15,45:4
(Incorrect in this edition; use 1957,D 17,45:4
elsewhere)
Connell, Richard (Original Author)
East of Broadway 1924,N 12,13:1
Bright Lights 1925,N 18,27:4
Seven Faces 1929,N 16,25:2
Most Dangerous Game, The 1932,N 21,21:1
F-Man 1936,My 4,16:1
Brother Orchid 1940,Je 8,18:2
Meet John Doe 1941,Mr 13,25:2
Game of Death, A 1945,N 24,22:4
Run for the Sun 1956,Ag 25,7:2
Connell, Richard (Screenwriter)
Milky Way, The 1936,Mr 26,27:2
Our Relations 1936,N 11,55:1
Doctor Rhythm 1938,My 19,25:2
Hired Wife 1940,S 14,11:2
Nice Girl 1941,Mr 27,29:6
Rio Rita 1942,My 8,27:3
Presenting Lily Mars 1943,Ap 30,25:3
Two Girls and a Sailor 1944,Je 15,16:1
Thrill of a Romance 1945,My 25,22:2
Her Highness and the Bellboy 1945,S 28,16:2
Kid From Brooklyn, The 1946,Ap 19,25:2
Luxury Liner 1948,S 10,19:2
Connell, Robert (Original Author)
Not Damaged 1930,Je 9,23:3
Connell, W Merle (Cinematographer)
World Dances 1954,N 8,24:6
Connell, W Merle (Director)
Flesh Merchant, The 1956,My 19,12:6
Connell, W Merle (Producer)
Flesh Merchant, The 1956,My 19,12:6
CONNELLY
See Also CONLEY, CONNOLLY
Connelly, Bobby
Youthful Affair, A 1918,Ap 15,13:3
Unpardonable Sin, The 1919,My 3,11:3
Humoresque 1920,My 31,14:2
Connelly, Bobby (Miscellaneous)
Ready, Willing and Able 1937,Mr 15,27:1
Connelly, Edward
Willow Tree, The 1920,F 2,10:1
Shore Acres 1920,My 17,19:3
Conquering Power, The 1921,Jl 10,VI,2:1 (In
Addenda)
Red Hot Romance 1922,Ja 23,11:4
Turn to the Right 1922,Ja 24,11:1
Trifling Women 1922,O 4,23:4
Where the Pavement Ends 1923,Ap 2,22:1
Scaramouche 1923,O 12,7:2 (Incorrect in this
edition; use 1927,O 1,7:2 elsewhere)
Slave of Desire 1923,D 11,26:2
Goldfish, The 1924,My 20,15:2
Revelation 1924,Je 24,18:2
Sinners in Silk 1924,S 8,15:3
So This Is Marriage 1924,D 23,16:2
Denial, The 1925,Mr 10,19:3
Unholy Three, The 1925,Ag 4,14:3
Sun Up 1925,Ag 18,14:3
Only Thing, The 1925,N 23,25:4
Ibanez's Torrent 1926,F 22,14:1

Bardelys The Magnificent 1926,N 1,28:1 (In
Addenda)
Show, The 1927,Mr 14,16:1
Lovers 1927,Ap 19,24:4
Student Prince, The 1927,S 22,33:2
Across to Singapore 1928,Ap 30,18:3
Forbidden Hours 1928,Jl 23,11:2
Mysterious Lady, The 1928,Ag 6,15:2
Connelly, Erwin
Sherlock Jr 1924,My 26,21:1
Seven Chances 1925,Mr 17,18:1
Beggar on Horseback 1925,Je 6,9:2
Crown of Lies 1926,Mr 30,20:6
Kiki 1926,Ap 6,26:4
Son of the Sheik, The 1926,Jl 26,13:2
Winning of Barbara Worth, The 1926,N 29,16:3
Fire Brigade, The 1926,D 21,20:2
Rubber Tires 1927,Mr 9,29:1
Cheating Cheaters 1927,D 6,27:1
Connelly, Jane
Sherlock Jr 1924,My 26,21:1
Connelly, Joe (Original Author)
Private War of Major Benson, The
1955,Ag 3,27:2
Connelly, Joe (Producer)
Munster, Go Home 1966,Je 16,53:4
Connelly, Joe (Screenwriter)
Munster, Go Home 1966,Je 16,53:4
Connelly, Marc
Spirit of St Louis, The 1957,F 22,25:1
Connelly, Marc (Director)
Green Pastures, The 1936,Jl 17,20:1
Connelly, Marc (Miscellaneous)
Impostor, The 1944,Mr 27,17:2
Fabiola 1951,My 30,14:2
Crowded Paradise 1956,Je 22,15:1
Connelly, Marc (Original Author)
Dulcy 1923,S 17,18:2
To the Ladies 1923,N 26,15:6
Merton of the Movies 1924,S 8,15:3
Beggar on Horseback 1925,Je 6,9:2
Not so Dumb 1930,F 8,12:5
Make Me a Star 1932,Jl 1,19:3
Elmer and Elsie 1934,Ag 4,14:5
Farmer Takes a Wife, The 1935,Ag 9,21:2
Green Pastures, The 1936,Jl 17,20:1
Dulcy 1940,N 28,28:2
Merton of the Movies 1947,N 7,20:3
Farmer Takes a Wife, The 1953,Je 13,11:2
Connelly, Marc (Screenwriter)
Green Pastures, The 1936,Jl 17,20:1
Captains Courageous 1937,My 12,27:1
I Married a Witch 1942,N 20,27:2
Reunion in France 1943,Mr 5,20:3
Connelly, Mate
Tall Story 1960,Ap 7,46:1
Connelly, One-Eye
Barker, The 1928,D 6,35:1
Connelly, Paul
Top o' the Morning 1949,S 1,25:2
CONNER
See Also CONNOR
Conner, Nadine
Of Men and Music 1951,F 15,27:2
Conner, Reardon (Original Author)
Shake Hands With the Devil 1959,Je 25,20:7
Conner, Tami
Peyton Place 1957,D 13,35:1
Conners, Barry (Original Author)
Patsy, The 1928,Ap 23,20:2
Me and my Gal 1932,D 12,18:4
Brides are Like That 1936,Mr 23,22:5
Pier 13 1940,Ag 9,19:3
Always a Bride 1940,N 21,43:3
Connery, Neil
Operation Kid Brother 1967,N 23,58:2
Connery, Sean
Another Time Another Place 1958,My 3,10:4
Darby O'Gill and the Little People 1959,Jl 1,26:1
Tarzan's Greatest Adventure 1959,Jl 9,22:1
Longest Day, The 1962,O 5,28:1
Dr No 1963,My 30,20:1
From Russia with Love 1964,Ap 9,25:1
Marnie 1964,Je 23,19:1
Woman of Straw 1964,O 1,30:6
Goldfinger 1964,D 22,36:1
Operation Snafu 1965,My 22,18:1
Hill, The 1965,O 4,00:0
Thunderball 1965,D 22,23:1
Fine Madness, A 1966,Je 30,28:2
You Only Live Twice 1967,Je 14,40:1
Shalako 1968,N 6,32:1
CONNOLLY
See Also CONLEY, CONNELLY
Connolly, Bobby (Director)
Expensive Husbands 1938,Ja 8,19:3
Patient in Room 18, The 1938,Ap 22,15:6
Connolly, Bobby (Miscellaneous)
Go Into Your Dance 1935,My 4,17:2
Singing Kid, The 1936,Ap 4,11:1
Cain and Mabel 1936,O 19,22:1

Connolly, Mike (Original Author)
I'll Cry Tomorrow 1956,Ja 13,18:1
Connolly, Myles (Original Author)
Face in the Sky 1933,F 20,11:5
Right to Romance, The 1933,D 15,28:2
It Happened in Hollywood 1937,O 2,18:1
House Across the Bay, The 1940,Mr 22,23:2
Maisie Was a Lady 1941,F 13,25:2
Tarzan's New York Adventure 1942,Ag 7,13:2
Hans Christian Andersen 1952,N 26,20:2
Connolly, Myles (Screenwriter)
Wives Under Suspicion 1938,Jl 1,22:3
Youth Takes a Fling 1938,O 17,12:1
Tarzan's Secret Treasure 1941,D 25,33:1
Tarzan's New York Adventure 1942,Ag 7,13:2
Between Us Girls 1942,S 25,25:3
Music for Millions 1944,D 22,12:4
Two Sisters From Boston 1946,Je 7,16:2
Till the Clouds Roll By 1946,D 6,27:4
Unfinished Dance, The 1947,O 31,29:2
State of the Union 1948,Ap 23,28:1
Here Comes the Groom 1951,S 21,19:2
My Son John 1952,Ap 9,27:1
Connolly, Norma
Wrong Man, The 1956,D 24,8:1
Connolly, Randolph
Dark Angel, The 1935,S 6,12:2
Connolly, Walter
Washington Merry-Go-Round 1932,O 24,18:5
Man Against Woman 1932,D 17,22:3
No More Orchids 1933,Ja 2,29:2
Bitter Tea of General Yen, The 1933,Ja 12,20:6
Paddy the Next Best Thing 1933,Ag 25,12:2
Lady for a Day 1933,S 8,22:2
Master of Men 1933,N 29,23:4
Man's Castle 1933,D 30,9:2
Eight Girls in a Boat 1934,Ja 13,16:3
It Happened One Night 1934,F 23,23:2
Once to Every Woman 1934,Mr 26,22:3
20th Century 1934,My 4,24:2
Whom the Gods Destroy 1934,Jl 13,14:2
Servants' Entrance 1934,S 27,25:2
Lady by Choice 1934,N 17,12:1
Captain Hates the Sea, The 1934,N 29,33:2
Broadway Bill 1934,N 30,22:2
She Couldn't Take It 1935,N 7,27:1
So Red the Rose 1935,N 28,39:1
One Way Ticket 1936,Ja 1,35:2
Soak the Rich 1936,F 5,14:2
Music Goes 'Round, The 1936,F 22,12:1
King Steps Out, The 1936,My 29,15:2
Libeled Lady 1936,O 31,24:2
Good Earth, The 1937,F 3,27:1
Nancy Steele is Missing 1937,Mr 8,22:1
League of Frightened Men, The 1937,Jl 2,25:1
Nothing Sacred 1937,N 26,27:2
First Lady 1937,D 23,25:1
Penitentiary 1938,Mr 7,13:2
Start Cheering 1938,Mr 17,17:3
Four's a Crowd 1938,Ag 12,11:1
too Hot To Handle 1938,S 30,24:2
Girl Downstairs, The 1939,Ja 26,17:1
Huckleberry Finn 1939,Mr 3,21:2
Bridal Suite 1939,My 26,20:2
Good Girls Go to Paris 1939,Je 23,23:1
Fifth Avenue Girl 1939,Ag 25,12:2
Those High Grey Walls 1939,O 19,27:2
Great Victor Herbert, The 1939,D 7,35:1
CONNOR
See Also CONNER
Connor, Allen
Kiss Before the Mirror, The 1933,My 15,16:2
Connor, Edgar
Hallelujah, I'm a Bum 1933,F 9,15:2
Connor, Edric
Cry, the Beloved Country 1952,Ja 24,23:2
West of Zanzibar 1955,Ja 18,31:2
Moby Dick 1956,Jl 5,18:1
Fire Down Below 1957,Ag 9,11:2
Roots of Heaven, The 1958,O 16,46:1
Only When I Larf 1968,O 24,55:3
Connor, Francis
Mister Roberts 1955,Jl 15,14:1
Connor, Kaye
There's Magic in Music 1941,Je 5,27:2
Connor, Kenneth
Ladykillers 1956,F 21,37:2
Carry on Sergeant 1959,O 28,40:5
Carry on Nurse 1960,S 10,11:1
Nearly a Nasty Accident 1962,Je 28,21:2
No Place Like Homicide 1962,S 13,32:1
Carry on Cleo 1965,O 23,17:2
Connor, Mary
Irish Destiny 1927,Mr 29,23:2 (In Addenda)
Connor, Ralph (Original Author)
Sky Pilot, The 1921,Ap 18,8:1
Connor, Whitfield
Tap Roots 1948,Ag 26,16:3
Scarlet Angel 1952,Je 21,12:2
President's Lady, The 1953,My 22,31:1
City of Bad Men 1953,O 21,37:6
Saracen Blade, The 1954,My 15,13:4
Butterfield 8 1960,N 17,46:1

Connors, Chuck
Pat and Mike 1952,Je 19,32:6
Trouble Along the Way 1953,My 7,37:2
South Sea Woman 1953,Je 4,33:6
Naked Alibi 1954,O 2,21:2
Human Jungle, The 1954,N 26,24:6
Target Zero 1955,N 16,43:2
Good Morning, Miss Dove 1955,N 24,41:1
Three Stripes in the Sun 1955,N 24,41:2
Designing Woman 1957,My 17,20:2
Old Yeller 1957,D 26,23:4
Lady Takes a Flyer, The 1958,Ja 30,19:2
Flipper 1963,S 19,23:1
Move Over Darling 1963,D 26,33:1
Synanon 1965,My 6,44:1
Ride Beyond Vengance 1966,S 29,60:1
Connors, Floraine
Unstrap Me 1968,N 21,41:2
Connors, Joan
Dime With a Halo 1963,Je 27,23:3
Connors, Michael
Good Neighbor Sam 1964,Jl 23,19:1
Where Love Has Gone 1964,N 3,26:1
Harlow 1965,Jl 22,24:1
Situation Hopeless-But not Serious 1965,O 14,53:1
Stagecoach 1966,Je 16,53:1
Kiss the Girls and Make Them Die 1967,Ja 26,25:1
Connors, Tom
Native Land 1942,My 12,16:3
Connors, Touch
Sudden Fear 1952,Ag 8,9:2
Conocchi, Mario
Juliet of the Spirits 1965,N 4,57:1
Conovan, King
Man From Texas 1948,Ag 12,16:5
Conover, Theresa Maxwell
When Knighthood Was in Flower 1922,S 15,17:2 (In Addenda)
Yolanda 1924,F 20,23:1
I Want my Man 1925,Ap 6,17:3
Queen High 1930,Ag 9,16:5
Kid From Spain, The 1932,N 18,23:2
Silver Dollar 1932,D 23,20:1
Brief Moment 1933,S 30,18:5
Gallant Lady 1934,Ja 22,12:3
Half a Sinner 1934,Je 23,16:5
Night Life of the Gods 1935,F 23,14:6
Mississippi 1935,Ap 18,27:2
Peter Ibbetson 1935,N 8,18:2
Free and Easy 1941,Ap 3,29:4
Conrad, Allan
Barretts of Wimpole Street, The 1934,S 29,12:2
Conrad, Bart
Mister Buddwing 1966,O 12,36:1
Conrad, Bill (Narrator)
Cowboy, The 1954,Ag 3,14:2
Conrad, Charles J
Hell's Five Hours 1957,Jl 24,18:1
Hell's Five Hours 1958,Jl 24,18:1
Conrad, Con (Composer)
New Movietone Follies of 1930, The 1930,Je 21,20:5
Wine, Women and Song 1934,Mr 21,24:3
Gift of Gab 1934,S 26,17:6
Gay Divorcee, The 1934,N 16,27:1
Reckless 1935,Ap 20,16:1
Here's to Romance 1935,O 3,29:2
King Solomon of Broadway 1935,O 19,12:2
Great Ziegfeld, The 1936,Ap 9,21:2
Conrad, Con (Miscellaneous)
I'd Give my Life 1936,Ag 17,9:1
Margie 1946,O 17,28:3
Conrad, Eddie
Blaze O' Glory 1929,D 31,15:1
I Live for Love 1935,O 19,21:2
Stars Over Broadway 1935,N 14,17:3
Hot Money 1936,Jl 25,16:2
Happy Landing 1938,Ja 22,19:1
Always Goodbye 1938,Je 25,7:2
Gateway 1938,Ag 8,9:2
Just Around the Corner 1938,D 3,11:2
Topper Takes a Trip 1938,D 30,11:2
I Was an Adventuress 1940,My 20,13:2
Foreign Correspondent 1940,Ag 28,15:2
Lucky Partners 1940,S 6,25:2
Down Argentine Way 1940,O 18,25:1
Chad Hanna 1940,D 26,23:1
Behind the News 1941,Ja 16,25:3
You're the One 1941,F 20,23:2
That Night in Rio 1941,Mr 10,21:2
West Point Widow 1941,S 11,21:5
Hurry, Charlie, Hurry 1941,N 12,31:3
Conrad, Eugene (Screenwriter)
Fall In 1943,My 15,13:3
Chip off the Old Block 1944,Mr 17,14:2
Love and Learn 1947,My 3,10:3
Conrad, George
Fixed Bayonets 1951,N 21,20:2
Conrad, Jack
Surrender 1931,N 28,20:4
Brasher Doubloon, The 1947,My 22,34:5

Conrad, Jan
Mouse on the Moon, The 1963,Je 18,32:1
Conrad, Jess
Konga 1961,S 16,9:1
Conrad, Joseph (Original Author)
Victory 1919,D 28,4:4
Lord Jim 1925,N 16,19:4
Road to Romance, The 1927,O 10,24:1
Rescue, The 1929,Ja 14,20:1
Dangerous Paradise 1930,F 16,III,8:1
Dangerous Paradise 1930,Mr 2,IX,5:1
Woman Alone, The 1937,F 27,9:2
Razumov 1937,Mr 9,27:2
Victory 1940,D 23,23:2
Outcast of the Islands 1952,My 16,19:2
Secret Sharer, The 1953,Ja 14,27:2
Laughing Anne 1954,My 8,15:2
Lord Jim 1965,F 26,18:1
Conrad, Michael
Requiem for a Heavyweight 1962,O 17,35:1
Conrad, Mikel
Untamed Fury 1947,Ap 26,10:6
Man From Colorado 1949,Ja 21,24:3
Take one False Step 1949,Je 23,33:2
Sand 1949,Ag 5,23:2
Arctic Manhunt 1949,Ag 19,12:5
Flying Saucer, The 1950,Ja 5,28:3
Francis 1950,Mr 16,40:2
Conrad, Mikel (Director)
Flying Saucer, The 1950,Ja 5,28:3
Conrad, Mikel (Original Author)
Flying Saucer, The 1950,Ja 5,28:3
Conrad, Mikel (Producer)
Flying Saucer, The 1950,Ja 5,28:3
Conrad, Robert
Palm Springs Weekend 1963,N 6,32:1
Young Dillinger 1965,My 13,32:3
Conrad, Walter
Full of Life 1957,F 13,38:1
Conrad, William
Killers, The 1946,Ag 29,24:2
Body and Soul 1947,N 10,21:2
To the Victor 1948,Ap 17,11:2
Arch of Triumph 1948,Ap 21,33:2
Four Faces West 1948,Ag 4,18:3
Sorry, Wrong Number 1948,S 2,18:2
Any Number Can Play 1949,Jl 1,14:4
East Side, West Side 1949,D 23,17:2
Tension 1950,Ja 12,32:4
One Way Street 1950,My 12,33:3
Dial 1119 1950,D 4,32:6
Milkman, The 1951,Ja 1,13:6
Cry Danger 1951,F 22,27:3
Sword of Monte Cristo, The 1951,Ap 23,21:2
Racket, The 1951,D 13,44:2
Lone Star 1952,F 2,11:4
Naked Jungle, The 1954,Ap 3,19:2
Conqueror, The 1956,Mr 31,13:3
Johnny Concho 1956,Ag 16,30:1
Ride Back, The 1957,Ap 30,24:1
30 1959,N 12,27:1
Conrad, William (Director)
Man From Galveston, The 1964,Ja 23,26:3
Two on a Guillotine 1965,Ja 14,44:3
My Blood Runs Cold 1965,Mr 25,42:4
Brainstorm 1965,Je 10,38:1
Conrad, William (Narrator)
Naked Sea, The 1955,D 21,37:1
Conrad, William (Producer)
Ride Back, The 1957,Ap 30,24:1
Two on a Guillotine 1965,Ja 14,44:3
My Blood Runs Cold 1965,Mr 25,42:4
Brainstorm 1965,Je 10,38:1
American Dream, An 1966,S 1,28:2
Covenant with Death, A 1967,F 16,32:3
First to Fight 1967,Mr 30,55:1
Cool Ones, The 1967,My 11,50:1
Countdown 1968,My 2,57:3
Conrad (Composer)
William Fox Movietone Follies of 1929 1929,My 27,22:1
Conrad (Miscellaneous)
I Like It That Way 1934,Ap 18,23:3
Conradi, Kurt
Great British Train Robbery, The 1967,Ap 6,45:2
Conradi, Marion
Because I Loved You 1930,Ja 25,13:2
Conried, Hans
Dramatic School 1938,D 9,31:2
It's a Wonderful World 1939,My 19,27:2
Dulcy 1940,N 28,28:2
Week End for Three 1941,O 24,27:4
Falcon takes Over, The 1942,My 30,9:2
Wife Takes a Flyer, The 1942,Je 19,19:1
Nightmare 1942,D 4,31:2
Hitler's Children 1943,F 25,27:1
Journey Into Fear 1943,Mr 19,15:3
Lady Takes a Chance, A 1943,S 16,25:2
Crazy House 1943,D 16,33:3
His Butler's Sister 1943,D 30,13:2
Passage to Marseille 1944,F 17,12:5
Senator Was Indiscreet, The 1947,D 27,9:2
My Friend Irma 1949,S 29,39:2

Conried, Hans— Cont
Nancy Goes to Rio 1950,Ap 7,22:2
Summer Stock 1950,S 1,17:2
Rich, Young and Pretty 1951,Jl 26,17:3
Behave Yourself 1951,N 8,35:2
Too Young to Kiss 1951,N 23,32:2
3 for Bedroom C 1952,Je 27,18:3
Big Jim McLain 1952,S 18,35:2
World in His Arms, The 1952,O 10,21:2
5,000 Fingers of Dr T, The 1953,Je 20,8:6
Davy Crockett, King of the Wild Frontier 1955,My 26,36:1
Birds and the Bees, The 1956,Ap 23,22:1
Bus Stop 1956,S 1,19:2
Jet Pilot 1957,O 5,8:6
Big Beat, The 1958,Je 26,23:4
Rock-a-Bye Baby 1958,Jl 24,18:1
My Six Loves 1963,Ap 4,58:4
Patsy, The 1964,Ag 13,24:2
Conried, Hans (Narrator)
Design for Death 1948,Je 11,27:2
Conroy, Allen
New Faces 1954,F 20,8:7
Conroy, Cindy
Come September 1961,S 8,34:1
Conroy, Frank
Royal Family of Broadway, The 1930,D 23,25:1
Bad Company 1931,N 7,16:5
Possessed 1931,N 28,20:4
Hell Divers 1931,D 23,27:3
Manhattan Parade 1931,D 25,29:2
Disorderly Conduct 1932,Ap 11,19:2
Grand Hotel 1932,Ap 13,23:2
Ann Carver's Profession 1933,Je 9,20:2
Midnight Mary 1933,Jl 15,14:2
Night Flight 1933,O 7,18:4
Kennell Murder Case, The 1933,O 30,14:2
Ace of Aces 1933,N 11,10:4
Frontier Marshal 1934,Ja 31,20:3
Cat and the Fiddle, The 1934,F 17,20:2
Little Miss Marker 1934,My 19,18:3
White Parade, The 1934,N 10,19:1
Little Minister, The 1934,D 28,25:1
West Point of the Air 1935,Ap 6,10:1
Charlie Chan in Egypt 1935,Je 24,12:2
Call of the Wild 1935,Ag 15,15:2
I Live my Life 1935,O 12,12:2
Last Days of Pompeii, The 1935,O 17,29:2
Show Them no Mercy 1935,D 9,25:2
Nobody's Fool 1936,Je 4,27:2
White Angel, The 1936,Je 25,24:1
Meet Nero Wolfe 1936,Jl 16,20:1
Gorgeous Hussy, The 1936,S 5,7:1
Charlie Chan at the Opera 1936,D 5,16:2
Stolen Holiday 1937,F 1,15:3
Love Is News 1937,Mr 6,10:1
Nancy Steele is Missing 1937,Mr 8,22:1
That I May Live 1937,My 10,23:2
This Is my Affair 1937,My 28,17:1
Big Business 1937,Je 1,27:2
Emperor's Candlesticks, The 1937,Jl 9,18:1
Music for Madame 1937,O 23,14:1
Last Gangster, The 1937,D 10,33:2
Wells Fargo 1937,D 30,15:2
This Woman Is Mine 1941,O 13,21:2
Adventures of Martin Eden 1942,Mr 16,19:2
Crossroads 1942,Jl 27,18:2
Loves of Edgar Allan Poe, The 1942,S 21,19:2
Crash Dive 1943,Ap 29,25:2
Ox-Bow Incident, The 1943,My 10,15:2 (In Addenda)
Lady of Burlesque 1943,My 14,17:2
That Hagen Girl 1947,O 25,13:2
Naked City, The 1948,Mr 5,17:2
All my Sons 1948,Mr 29,17:3
For the Love of Mary 1948,S 23,37:2
Sealed Verdict 1948,N 3,36:2
Snake Pit, the 1948,N 5,29:2
Rogues' Regiment 1948,D 20,31:2
Threat, The 1949,D 2,35:4
Lightning Strikes Twice 1951,Ap 13,18:7
Day the Earth Stood Still, The 1951,S 19,37:1
Last Mile, The 1959,F 19,27:1
Young Philadelphians, The 1959,My 22,32:1
Bramble Bush, The 1960,F 25,34:2
Conroy, Martin
Crime Doctor, The 1934,My 11,24:3
Conroy, Michael
Fugitive From Justice, A 1940,Jl 8,13:3
Conroy, Sue
Girl Habit, The 1931,Jl 4,11:5
Conroy, Thomas (Producer)
Best of Cinerama, The 1963,D 26,33:2
Conselman, William (Miscellaneous)
Handy Andy 1934,Ag 4,14:5
Conselman, William (Original Author)
Ella Cinders 1926,Je 7,23:2
Gay Retreat, The 1927,O 10,24:1
Pajamas 1927,N 7,26:4
Arizona to Broadway 1933,Jl 22,14:3
That's Right, You're Wrong 1939,N 30,25:3
Conselman, William (Screenwriter)
High School Hero 1927,O 24,24:3
Why Sailors Go Wrong 1928,Ap 9,18:2

Conselman, William (Screenwriter)— Cont
365 Nights in Hollywood 1934,N 7,32:1
Little Colonel, The 1935,Mr 22,26:2
Doubting Thomas 1935,Jl 11,24:2
Private Number 1936,Je 12,19:1
Pigskin Parade 1936,N 14,23:3
Stowaway 1936,D 19,16:1
On the Avenue 1937,F 5,17:3
That I May Live 1937,My 10,23:2
Fifty Roads to Town 1937,Je 5,21:1
Great Hospital Mystery, The 1937,Jl 16,22:2
Smiling Along 1939,F 20,13:2
East Side of Heaven 1939,My 5,29:3
That's Right, You're Wrong 1939,N 30,25:3
If I Had my Way 1940,My 6,13:2
Considine, Bob (Original Author)
Babe Ruth Story, The 1948,Jl 29,17:2
Hoodlum Empire 1952,Mr 6,25:6
Considine, Bob (Screenwriter)
Babe Ruth Story, The 1948,Jl 29,17:2
Hoodlum Empire 1952,Mr 6,25:6
Considine, John
Greatest Story Ever Told, The 1965,F 16,40:2
Considine, John W Jr (Director)
Disorderly Conduct 1932,Ap 11,19:2
Considine, John W Jr (Original Author)
Puttin' on the Ritz 1930,F 15,15:1
Considine, John W Jr (Producer)
Evelyn Prentice 1934,N 10,19:1
Gay Bride, The 1934,D 19,27:2
Sequoia 1935,F 23,14:6
Mad Love 1935,Ag 5,20:2
Broadway Melody of 1936 1935,S 19,28:1
Voice of Bugle Ann, The 1936,F 27,23:1
Robin Hood of El Dorado, The 1936,Mr 14,10:1
Absolute Quiet 1936,My 2,11:1
Personal Property 1937,Ap 11,27:2
Emperor's Candlesticks, The 1937,Jl 9,18:1
Of Human Hearts 1938,F 18,23:1
Arsene Lupin Returns 1938,Mr 9,21:1
Hold That Kiss 1938,Je 11,9:1
Boys Town 1938,S 9,25:1
Vacation From Love 1938,N 10,33:2
Society Lawyer 1939,Mr 31,19:2
Stronger Than Desire 1939,Je 30,17:3
Blackmail 1939,S 15,26:3
Young Tom Edison 1940,Mr 15,27:2
Edison the Man 1940,Je 7,27:2
Third Finger, Left Hand 1940,D 12,37:2
Men of Boys Town 1941,Ap 11,24:6
Design for Scandal 1942,F 6,23:3
Johnny Eager 1942,F 20,21:2
Jackass Mail 1942,Jl 2,25:2
Yank at Eton, A 1942,O 16,23:1
Three Hearts for Julia 1943,My 21,22:4
Salute to the Marines 1943,Ag 30,11:3
Considine, Mildred (Original Author)
Let's Be Fashionable 1920,Je 14,13:2
Considine, Robert (Original Author)
Thirty Seconds Over Tokyo 1944,N 16,19:1
Beginning or the End, The 1947,F 21,15:1
Considine, Tim
Clown, The 1953,Ja 29,25:1
Executive Suite 1954,My 7,19:1
Her Twelve Men 1954,Ag 12,23:2
Unchained 1955,Ja 28,15:2
Private War of Major Benson, The
1955,Ag 3,27:2
Shaggy Dog, The 1959,Mr 20,26:2
Sunrise at Campobello 1960,S 29,32:1
Constad, Ira
Island of Allah 1956,Je 27,35:1
Constanduros, Denis (Original Author)
Facts of Love, The 1949,O 31,20:2
Constanduros, Denis (Screenwriter)
Here Come the Huggetts 1950,D 25,25:3
Constanduros, Mabel
Gay Intruders, The 1946,Mr 18,24:2
Bad Sister 1948,Je 11,27:3
Easy Money (Episode 1) 1949,F 14,15:3
Constanduros, Mabel (Original Author)
Facts of Love, The 1949,O 31,20:2
Constanduros, Mabel (Screenwriter)
Here Come the Huggetts 1950,D 25,25:3
Constant, Yvonne
Gigot 1962,S 28,26:1
Monkeys Go Home 1967,Mr 30,55:1
Constantaras, Lambros
Anna of Rhodes 1950,Mr 23,34:2
Constantin, Giorgio
Favorita, La 1953,O 30,27:4
Constantin, Michel
Night Watch, The; Trou, Le 1964,My 27,46:1
Constantin, Milo
Black Oxen 1924,Ja 7,23:1
Constantine
Specter of the Rose 1946,S 2,12:4
Constantine, Eddie
Folies Bergere 1958,My 28,37:2
Room 43 1959,D 3,46:1
S O S Pacific 1960,O 13,41:3
Riff Raff Girls 1962,O 20,13:5
7 Capital Sins (Laziness) 1963,Ja 17,5:2
Alphaville 1965,S 8,51:1

Alphaville 1965,O 26,49:1
Constantine, Michael
Cyanamide 1954,Mr 26,17:6
Last Mile, The 1959,F 19,27:1
Hustler, The 1961,S 27,35:1
Island of Love 1963,Je 13,30:4
Quick, Before it Melts 1965,Ap 1,30:2
Beau Geste 1966,S 8,43:1
Hawaii 1966,O 11,54:1
Constantineau, Rene
Quebec 1951,Mr 16,34:2
Constantini, Giorgio
Loves of Don Juan, The 1948,S 2,18:4
Constantini, Nino
6 1/2 x 11 1929,Ag 13,23:2
Ramuntcho 1953,Mr 2,19:2
Constantino, Alexandro
Black Orpheus 1959,D 22,41:1
Consuella, Senorita
Temple of Venus, The 1923,N 1,24:3
Contant, Andree
Golden Mistress, The 1954,O 30,15:6
Conte, John
Our Neighbors-The Carters 1940,F 15,15:2
Thousands Cheer 1943,S 14,27:1
Lost in a Harem 1944,N 9,23:2
Man With the Golden Arm, The 1955,D 16,38:2
Conte, Louise
Oh, Amelia 1951,D 3,22:2
Conte, Richard
Guadalcanal Diary 1943,N 18,29:1
Purple Heart, The 1944,Mr 9,15:2
Bell for Adano, A 1945,Jl 6,8:3
Captain Eddie 1945,Ag 9,24:2
Walk in the Sun, A 1946,Ja 12,10:6
Somewhere in the Night 1946,Je 13,24:2
Spider, The 1946,Je 21,20:3
13 Rue Madeleine 1947,Ja 16,30:2
Other Love, The 1947,My 15,32:4
Call Northside 777 1948,F 19,29:2
Cry of the City 1948,S 30,32:4
Big Jack 1949,My 23,27:4
House of Strangers 1949,Jl 2,8:2
Thieves' Highway 1949,S 24,8:6
Whirlpool 1950,Ja 14,9:2
Sleeping City, The 1950,S 21,20:2
Under the Gun 1951,F 23,33:2
Hollywood Story 1951,Je 7,40:6
Fighter, The 1952,My 31,12:6
Raiders, The 1952,D 13,19:2
Blue Gardenia, The 1953,Ap 28,31:1
Desert Legion 1953,My 9,13:2
Highway Dragnet 1954,F 20,8:7
New York Confidential 1955,F 19,18:1
Big Combo, The 1955,Mr 26,13:2
Bengazi 1955,O 8,13:4
Target Zero 1955,N 16,43:2
I'll Cry Tomorrow 1956,Ja 13,18:1
Full of Life 1957,F 13,38:1
This Angry Age 1958,Je 26,23:3
They Came to Cordura 1959,O 22,47:2
Ocean's Eleven 1960,Ag 11,19:1
Pepe 1960,D 22,18:1
Who's Been Sleeping in My Bed? 1963,D 26,33:2
Eyes of Annie Jones, The 1964,My 14,39:1
Circus World 1964,Je 26,34:2
Greatest Story Ever Told, The 1965,F 16,40:2
Synanon 1965,My 6,44:1
Assault on a Queen 1966,Jl 28,23:3
Tony Rome 1967,N 16,58:1
Lady in Cement 1968,N 21,41:1
Contet, Henri (Composer)
Star Without Light; Etoile Sans Lumiere
1947,Ag 4,14:2
Conti, Albert
Merry Widow, The 1925,Ag 27,14:1
Eagle, The 1925,N 9,25:1
Old Loves and New 1926,Ap 20,24:7
Blonde Saint, The 1926,N 23,27:1
Camille 1927,Ap 22,19:1
Devil Dancer, The 1927,D 19,30:1
Chinese Parrot, The 1928,Ja 2,28:1
Love Me and the World Is Mine 1928,F 6,12:3
Legion of the Condemned, The 1928,Mr 19,26:2
Alex The Great 1928,My 1,33:3
Magnificent Flirt, The 1928,Je 25,27:1
Plastered in Paris 1928,S 24,25:1
Stocks and Blondes 1928,O 23,33:1
Dry Martini 1928,N 5,26:5 (In Addenda)
Captain Lash 1929,F 4,20:1
Lady of the Pavements 1929,Mr 11,22:2
Saturday's Children 1929,Ap 29,29:2
Jazz Heaven 1929,O 30,29:2
Such Men Are Dangerous 1930,Mr 8,21:1
One Romantic Night 1930,My 31,19:4
Monte Carlo 1930,Ag 28,22:4
Sea Legs 1930,N 11,29:1
Morocco 1930,N 17,29:1
Gang Buster, The 1931,Ja 24,15:1
Strangers May Kiss 1931,Ap 13,17:1
Just a Gigolo 1931,Je 13,20:4
This Modern Age 1931,S 7,19:3
Lady With a Past 1932,F 22,23:2

Conti, Albert— Cont
Shopworn 1932,Ap 4,13:6
As You Desire Me 1932,Je 3,23:4
Doomed Battalion, The 1932,Je 11,9:3
Night Club Lady, The 1932,Ag 27,13:4
Topaze 1933,F 10,12:2
Beloved 1934,Ja 27,9:3
Elmer and Elsie 1934,Ag 4,14:5
Night is Young, The 1935,Ja 14,11:2
Here's to Romance 1935,O 3,29:2
Fatal Lady 1936,Jl 11,11:3
Hollywood Boulevard 1936,S 21,26:4
One in a Million 1937,Ja 1,19:3
Dangerously Yours 1937,O 18,14:2
Always Goodbye 1938,Je 25,7:2
Gateway 1938,Ag 8,9:2
Suez 1938,O 15,21:2
Conti, Carla (Miscellaneous)
Fuga, La 1966,Mr 22,33:1
Conti, Gabriella
Mafioso 1964,Jl 1,42:1
Conti, Joe
East of the River 1940,O 28,21:2
Conti, Witold
Clos Pustyni 1933,Ap 21,20:5
Ulan I Dziewczyna 1933,O 9,22:3
Sluby Ulanskie; Love in the Army 1935,F 22,27:3
Continenza, Age (Screenwriter)
O K Nero 1953,Je 20,8:6
Continenza, Alessandro (Screenwriter)
Too Bad She's Bad 1955,D 26,23:2
Miller's Beautiful Wife, The 1957,Je 12,40:2
Mighty Crusaders, The 1961,S 23,17:1
Minotaur, The 1961,N 8,41:1
Love and Larceny 1963,F 2,5:6
Day in Court, A 1963,My 11,15:2
Contino, Dick
Big Night, The 1960,F 18,37:4
Contreras, Alberto
Bodas de Sangre; Bloody Wedding
1939,N 13,15:3
Contreras, Miguel (Director)
Tribu 1935,Je 10,14:7
Contreras, Miguel (Producer)
Tribu 1935,Je 10,14:7
Contreras, Rosa
Cadetes de San Martin 1939,Jl 3,10:6
Contreras, Rosita
Viento Norte; North Wind 1939,S 16,20:3
Convent Garden Orchestra
Royal Ballet, The (Ondine); Ondine (The Royal
Ballet) 1960,O 5,45:2
Converse, Frank
Hurry Sundown 1967,Mr 24,22:1
Hour of the Gun 1967,N 2,58:4
Converse, Peggy
Miss Sadie Thompson 1953,D 24,9:1
Converse, Roger
Calling Dr Kildare 1939,My 12,25:4
Converse, Thelma Mrs
Society Scandal, A 1924,Mr 10,18:2
Conversi, Luciano
Bible, The 1966,S 29,60:1
Conversi, Spartico
Woman 1950,F 9,36:6
Convy, Bert
Susan Slade 1961,N 11,14:6
Act One 1963,D 27,17:2
Conway, Bert
Native Land 1942,My 12,16:3
Open Secret 1948,F 2,15:2
Man From Texas 1948,Ag 12,16:5
You Gotta Stay Happy 1948,N 5,29:2
Trapped 1949,N 26,10:6
Conway, Curt
Singapore 1947,S 17,31:2
Gentleman's Agreement 1947,N 12,36:2
Casbah 1948,My 3,27:4
Raw Deal 1948,Jl 9,11:4
Lady Gambles, The 1949,My 21,9:2
Goddess, The 1958,Je 25,24:1
Wind Across the Everglades 1958,S 12,21:1
Hud 1963,My 29,36:1
Conway, Cyril
Spring in Park Lane 1949,S 21,38:2
High Treason 1952,My 21,23:3
Conway, Gary
I Was a Teenage Frankenstein 1958,Ja 30,19:4
Conway, Harold
Battle in Outer Space 1960,Jl 9,10:5
Conway, Jack (Director)
Lucretia Lombard 1923,D 17,23:1
Only Thing, The 1925,N 23,25:4
Soul Mates 1926,Ja 4,16:1
Brown of Harvard 1926,My 3,27:1
Understanding Heart, The 1927,My 10,24:5
Twelve Miles Out 1927,Jl 26,17:1
Smart Set, The 1928,Mr 5,21:1
Bringing Up Father 1928,Mr 19,26:2
While the City Sleeps 1928,O 22,29:1
Alias Jimmy Valentine 1928,N 16,28:6
Untamed 1929,N 30,23:1
Easiest Way, The 1931,F 28,15:2
Just a Gigolo 1931,Je 13,20:4

Conway, Jack (Director) — Cont

Arsene Lupin 1932,F 27,22:1
But the Flesh Is Weak 1932,Ap 16,11:2
Red Headed Woman 1932,Jl 1,19:3
Hell Below 1933,Ap 26,13:2
Nuisance, The 1933,My 29,22:2
Solitaire Man, The 1933,S 23,11:5
Viva Villa! 1934,Ap 11,25:2
Girl From Missouri, The 1934,Ag 4,14:6
Gay Bride, The 1934,D 19,27:2
Tale of Two Cities, A 1935,D 26,21:2
Libeled Lady 1936,O 31,24:2
Saratoga 1937,Jl 23,16:3
Yank at Oxford, A 1938,F 25,15:1
too Hot To Handle 1938,S 30,24:2
Let Freedom Ring 1939,Mr 10,19:2
Lady of the Tropics 1939,S 8,28:3
Boom Town 1940,S 6,25:2
Love Crazy 1941,Je 6,25:5
Honky Tonk 1941,O 3,27:3
Crossroads 1942,Jl 27,18:2
Assignment in Brittany 1943,Ap 22,31:2
Dragon Seed 1944,Jl 21,16:4
High Barbaree 1947,Je 6,27:2
Hucksters, The 1947,Jl 18,21:2
Julia Misbehaves 1948,O 8,30:2

Conway, Jack (Producer)
Our Modern Maidens 1929,S 7,15:1

Conway, Jan
Gidget Goes Hawaiian 1961,Ag 10,17:4

Conway, John (Director)
Roughneck, The 1924,D 3,14:1

Conway, Julie
Around the World 1943,N 25,39:2

Conway, Morgan
Looking for Trouble 1934,Ap 12,27:2
Nurse From Brooklyn 1938,My 13,17:3
Sinners in Paradise 1938,My 20,17:2
Crime Ring 1938,Jl 22,10:3
Off the Record 1939,F 18,12:2
Blackwell's Island 1939,Mr 2,19:1
Kid From Kokomo, The 1939,My 20,11:2
Charlie Chan in Reno 1939,My 31,27:2
Grand Jury Secrets 1939,Je 29,19:2
Spellbinder, The 1939,Ag 24,17:3
Sued for Libel 1940,Ja 19,15:3
Three Cheers for the Irish 1940,Mr 9,19:2
Saint Takes Over, The 1940,My 28,29:3
Brother Orchid 1940,Je 8,18:2
Fugitive From Justice, A 1940,Jl 8,13:3
Millionaires in Prison 1940,Jl 16,21:3
Sing Your Worries Away 1942,My 15,25:2
Jack London 1944,Mr 3,19:3
Dick Tracy 1946,Ja 12,10:7
Badman's Territory 1946,My 31,27:2
Truth About Murder, The 1946,Jl 27,12:6
Dick Tracy vs Cueball 1946,N 23,12:2

Conway, Pat
Invitation 1952,Ja 30,22:6
Above and Beyond 1953,Ja 31,10:6
Annapolis Story, An 1955,Ap 9,8:2
Flight to Hong Kong 1957,Ja 3,28:2

Conway, Philip (Screenwriter)
Fury and the Woman 1937,Je 22,26:2

Conway, Richard S (Screenwriter)
Once a Thief 1951,Ja 19,21:3

Conway, Robert
Four Sons 1940,Je 8,18:4
Down Argentine Way 1940,O 18,25:1
Youth Will Be Served 1940,N 15,25:2
Moon Over Miami 1941,Jl 5,14:2

Conway, Russ
Larceny 1948,S 4,8:6
Trapped 1949,N 26,10:6
Tomahawk 1951,F 19,19:2
My Six Convicts 1952,Mr 28,27:3
Outcasts of Poker Flat 1952,My 16,19:3
Love Me Tender 1956,N 16,23:1
Midnight Story, The 1957,Jl 5,14:2
Portland Expose 1957,S 27,16:6
Fort Dobbs 1958,Ap 19,10:4
Dream Maker, The 1964,Ap 23,34:1
Our Man Flint 1966,Ja 26,23:4

Conway, Shirl
You Can't Fool an Irishman 1950,D 7,45:4

Conway, Tim
McHale's Navy 1964,Jl 11,15:2

Conway, Tom
Sky Murder 1940,N 14,28:3
Trial of Mary Dugan, The 1941,Mr 6,25:4
Free and Easy 1941,Ap 3,29:4
Bad Man, The 1941,Ap 4,25:1
People vs Dr Kildare, The 1941,My 8,21:1
Lady Be Good 1941,S 19,27:1
Tarzan's Secret Treasure 1941,D 25,33:1
Mr and Mrs North 1942,Ja 22,13:2
Rio Rita 1942,My 8,27:3
Grand Central Murder 1942,My 23,8:8
Falcon's Brother, The 1942,O 3,9:5
Cat People 1942,D 7,22:2
Falcon Strikes Back, The 1943,Ap 2,17:4
I Walked With a Zombie 1943,Ap 22,31:5
Falcon in Danger, The 1943,Jl 23,21:2
Seventh Victim, The 1943,S 18,11:3

Falcon out West, The 1944,Mr 18,18:2
Night of Adventure, A 1944,Je 3,10:4
Falcon in Mexico, The 1944,Ag 5,16:2
Falcon in Hollywood, The 1944,D 9,21:2
Two O'Clock Courage 1945,Ap 14,13:3
Falcon in San Francisco, The 1945,Jl 21,7:2
Whistle Stop 1946,Mr 18,24:2
Falcon's Alibi, The 1946,Ap 13,23:2
Criminal Court 1946,N 16,15:3
Falcon's Adventure, The 1946,D 14,19:2
Lost Honeymoon 1947,Je 20,25:6
Repeat Performance 1947,Jl 2,19:2
One Touch of Venus 1948,O 29,29:5
Painting the Clouds With Sunshine 1951,S 1,9:6
Confidence Girl 1952,Je 21,12:2
Death of a Scoundrel 1956,N 6,30:1

Conwell, Carolyn
Torn Curtain 1966,Jl 28,23:1

Conwell, Mary
Untamed Fury 1947,Ap 26,10:6

Conyngham, Fred
Crouching Beast, The 1936,Ag 22,6:1

Coody, Millard
Prince of Peace, The 1951,Mr 24,8:3

Coogan, Jackie
Kid, The 1921,Ja 22,9:2
Kid, The 1921,F 7,8:2
Peck's bad Boy 1921,Ap 25,9:2
Oliver Twist 1922,O 30,11:1
Daddy 1923,Ap 16,20:2
Circus Days 1923,Ag 6,14:2
Long Live the King 1923,D 4,24:1
Boy of Flanders, A 1924,Ap 15,24:1
Little Robinson Crusoe 1924,S 3,17:1
Old Clothes 1925,N 9,25:1
Tom Sawyer 1930,D 20,20:6
Huckleberry Finn 1931,Ag 8,16:3
Home on the Range 1935,F 13,24:4
College Swing 1938,Ap 28,27:2
Outlaw Woman 1952,Ap 5,20:3
Buster Keaton Story, The 1957,Ap 22,31:6
Joker Is Wild, The 1957,S 27,16:6
Eighteen and Anxious 1957,D 14,16:6
High School Confidential 1958,My 31,6:6
Lonelyhearts 1959,Mr 5,35:3
Beat Generation, The 1959,O 22,47:4
John Goldfarb, Please Come Home
    1965,Mr 25,42:4
Shakiest Gun in the West, The 1968,Jl 11,30:1

Coogan, Richard
Three Hours to Kill 1954,S 4,6:4
Revolt of Mamie Stover, The 1956,My 12,12:7

Coogan, Robert
Skippy 1931,Ap 4,23:1
Sooky 1931,D 21,28:4
Miracle Man, The 1932,Ap 21,25:2
Sky Bride 1932,Ap 23,11:5
Johnny Doughboy 1943,My 6,25:3

COOK
See Also COOKE

Cook, Albert Bernard
Cease Fire! 1953,N 25,17:1

Cook, Billy
Sons of the Legion 1938,S 30,24:3
Men With Wings 1938,O 27,27:2
Invitation to Happiness 1939,Je 8,31:2
Disputed Passage 1939,O 26,27:2
Blue Bird, The 1940,Ja 20,11:2
Naval Academy 1941,Je 5,27:3

Cook, Carole
Palm Springs Weekend 1963,N 6,32:1
Incredible Mr Limpet, The 1964,Mr 26,40:4

Cook, Christopher
Prince of Players 1955,Ja 12,24:2
Swan, The 1956,Ap 27,21:5

Cook, Clyde
Eskimo, The 1922,O 23,10:1
He Who Gets Slapped 1924,N 10,20:1
So This Is Marriage 1924,D 23,16:2
Winning of Barbara Worth, The 1926,N 29,16:3
White Gold 1927,Ap 11,18:3
Brute, The 1927,Ap 21,25:1
Climbers, The 1927,My 4,29:2
Barbed Wire 1927,Ag 8,10:3
Good Time Charley 1927,N 21,20:1
Beware of Married Men 1928,Ap 10,33:2
Docks of New York, The 1928,S 17,28:2
Captain Lash 1929,F 4,20:1
Spieler, The 1929,F 25,16:1
Strong Boy 1929,Ap 1,22:1
Dangerous Woman, A 1929,My 20,22:6
Jazz Heaven 1929,O 30,29:2
Taming of the Shrew, The 1929,N 30,23:1
Officer O'Brien 1930,F 24,18:1
Women Everywhere 1930,Je 23,15:1
Dawn Patrol 1930,Jl 11,22:1
Sunny 1930,D 27,16:3
Daybreak 1931,Je 1,15:1
Never the Twain Shall Meet 1931,Je 6,15:5
Secret Witness, The 1931,D 21,28:4
Blondie of the Follies 1932,S 2,19:2
West of Singapore 1933,Ap 1,18:3
Oliver Twist 1933,Ap 13,15:3

Cook, Clyde — Cont

Barbary Coast 1935,O 14,21:1
White Angel, The 1936,Je 25,24:1
Wee Willie Winkie 1937,Jl 24,12:1
Love Under Fire 1937,Ag 28,8:2
Kidnapped 1938,My 28,9:2
Storm Over Bengal 1938,D 8,34:4
Arrest Bulldog Drummond 1939,Ja 12,23:2
Little Princess, The 1939,Mr 11,21:1
Bulldog Drummond's Secret Police
    1939,Mr 30,19:3
Sea Hawk, The 1940,Ag 10,16:2
Ladies in Retirement 1941,N 7,27:1
White Cargo 1942,N 27,27:2
Mysterious Doctor, The 1943,My 20,26:4
Man From Down Under, The 1943,S 27,23:2

Cook, Clyde (Miscellaneous)
Huntsman, The 1920,N 8,20:2

Cook, David
King and Country 1966,Ja 28,20:4

Cook, Don
Safe in Hell 1931,D 19,16:4

Cook, Donald
Unfaithful 1931,Mr 7,17:2
Public Enemy, The 1931,Ap 24,27:1
Party Husband 1931,My 16,13:3
Side Show 1931,S 19,10:2
Mad Genius, The 1931,O 24,20:3
Man Who Played God, The 1932,F 11,16:1
Heart of New York, The 1932,Mr 2,15:3
Trial of Vivienne Ware, The 1932,Ap 30,19:3
Conquerors, The 1932,N 21,21:1
Frisco Jenny 1933,Ja 7,11:2
Private Jones 1933,Mr 25,13:3
Circus Queen Murder, The 1933,My 9,20:5
Kiss Before the Mirror, The 1933,My 15,16:2
Jennie Gerhardt 1933,Je 9,20:2
Baby Face 1933,Je 24,16:2
Woman I Stole, The 1933,Je 28,24:3
Brief Moment 1933,S 30,18:5
World Changes, The 1933,O 27,22:3
Long Lost Father 1934,F 19,18:2
Ninth Guest, The 1934,Mr 3,8:5
Viva Villa! 1934,Ap 11,25:2
Whirlpool 1934,My 5,22:3
Night is Young, The 1935,Ja 14,11:2
Behind the Evidence 1935,Ja 26,13:2
Casino Murder Case, The 1935,Ap 17,26:5
Gigolette 1935,My 13,18:6
Murder in the Fleet 1935,Je 3,22:2
Calling of Dan Matthews, The 1936,Ja 25,18:4
Show Boat 1936,My 15,29:4
Murder in the Blue Room 1944,O 28,12:2
Bowery to Broadway 1944,N 30,19:2
Here Come the Co-Eds 1945,F 19,21:1
Patrick the Great 1945,Ap 13,15:2
Our Very Own 1950,Jl 28,12:5

Cook, Edwin
Born Losers, The 1967,Ag 19,16:2

Cook, Elisha Jr
Two in a Crowd 1936,O 5,25:1
Pigskin Parade 1936,N 14,23:3
Love Is News 1937,Mr 6,10:1
Breezing Home 1937,Mr 20,23:5
They Won't Forget 1937,Jl 15,16:1
Devil is Driving, The 1937,Jl 16,22:1
Life Begins In College 1937,O 9,16:1
Wife, Doctor and Nurse 1937,O 11,26:5
My Lucky Star 1938,S 10,20:2
Submarine Patrol 1938,N 19,9:2
Newsboys' Home 1939,Ja 23,8:2
Grand Jury Secrets 1939,Je 29,19:2
He Married his Wife 1940,Ja 20,11:2
Stranger on the Third Floor 1940,S 2,19:2
Public Deb No 1 1940,S 18,19:2
Tin Pan Alley 1940,N 22,27:3
Love Crazy 1941,Je 6,25:5
Maltese Falcon, The 1941,O 4,18:2
Man at Large 1941,O 11,21:4
I Wake up Screaming 1942,Ja 17,13:2
Gentleman at Heart, A 1942,F 23,25:2
A-Haunting We Will Go 1942,Ag 3,18:4
Manila Calling 1942,S 28,13:1
Phantom Lady 1944,F 18,15:2
Up in Arms 1944,Mr 3,19:2
Dark Waters 1944,N 22,25:2
Dillinger 1945,Ap 26,26:2
Why Girls Leave Home 1945,Ag 4,7:3
Cinderella Jones 1946,Mr 16,9:6
Joe Palooka, Champ 1946,Ap 6,10:6
Falcon's Alibi, The 1946,Ap 13,23:2
Big Sleep, The 1946,Ag 24,6:6
Two Smart People 1947,F 15,20:4
Born to Kill 1947,My 1,34:2
Long Night, The 1947,S 17,31:2
Gangster, The 1947,O 31,29:3
Great Gatsby, The 1949,Jl 14,20:5
Behave Yourself 1951,N 8,35:2
Don't Bother to Knock 1952,Jl 19,8:2
Shane 1953,Ap 24,30:3
I, The Jury 1953,Ag 22,8:2
Thunder Over the Plains 1953,D 10,64:4
Drum Beat 1954,N 18,42:1
Timberjack 1955,Mr 10,33:3

Cook, Elisha Jr — Cont
Indian Fighter, The 1955,D 22,20:1
Killing, The 1956,My 21,20:1
Chicago Confidential 1957,Ag 31,19:1
House on Haunted Hill 1959,Mr 12,27:5
Platinum High School 1960,My 26,37:3
College Confidential 1960,Ag 22,23:1
One Eyed Jacks 1961,Mr 31,21:1
Johnny Cool 1963,O 3,31:1
Haunted Palace, The 1964,Ja 30,24:1
Welcome to Hard Times 1967,My 2,56:1
Cook, Fielder (Director)
Patterns 1956,Mr 28,26:1
Home Is the Hero 1961,Ja 26,32:1
Big Hand for the Little Lady, A 1966,Je 9,54:2
How to Save a Marriage - And Ruin Your Life
1968,Ja 19,30:1
Prudence and the Pill 1968,My 24,37:1
Cook, Fielder (Producer)
Big Hand for the Little Lady, A 1966,Je 9,54:2
Cook, George
Mikado, The 1967,Mr 15,53:1
Cook, J C (Miscellaneous)
Ravaged Earth 1942,N 27,27:3
Cook, Joe
Rain or Shine 1930,Ag 8,11:1
Sound of Laughter, The 1963,D 18,44:2
Cook, Marianne
Four Girls in Town 1957,Ja 17,34:5
Devil's General, The 1957,Ap 16,38:2
Fledermaus, Die 1964,F 8,15:2
Cook, Mary Lou
Ride 'Em Cowboy 1942,Mr 5,27:3
Cook, Peter
Wrong Box 1966,Jl 20,46:1
Bedazzled 1967,D 11,65:2
Dandy in Aspic, A 1968,Ap 3,40:1
Cook, Peter (Original Author)
Bedazzled 1967,D 11,65:2
Cook, Peter (Screenwriter)
Bedazzled 1967,D 11,65:2
Cook, Rowenna
Kit Carson 1940,N 15,25:3
Cook, Tommy
Wanderer of the Wasteland 1945,S 29,12:2
Tarzan and the Leopard Woman 1946,F 11,25:2
Humoresque 1946,D 26,28:1
Homestretch, The 1947,Ap 24,30:2
Cry of the City 1948,S 30,32:4
Bad Boy 1949,Mr 23,35:2
Kid From Cleveland, The 1949,S 5,13:2
Panic in the Streets 1950,Ag 5,9:2
American Guerrilla in the Philippines
1950,N 8,37:2
Night Passage 1957,Jl 25,28:1
Missle to the Moon 1958,N 17,37:2
Cook, Vera
Brides of Dracula, The 1960,S 6,41:4
Cook, Warren
My Lady's Garter 1920,Mr 15,13:2
Lady Rose's Daughter 1920,Ag 30,12:3
Silent Command, The 1923,S 5,15:3
Wild, Wild Susan 1925,Ag 5,12:4
Knockout, The 1925,O 27,23:3
Lunatic at Large, The 1927,F 1,25:1
Cook, Whitfield (Miscellaneous)
Strangers on a Train 1951,Jl 4,13:2
Cook, Whitfield (Screenwriter)
Sailor Takes a Wife, The 1946,Mr 1,17:2
Secret Heart, The 1946,D 26,28:2
High Barbaree 1947,Je 6,27:2
Big City 1948,My 17,23:3
Stage Fright 1950,F 24,27:2
Cook, Will (Original Author)
Two Rode Together 1961,Jl 27,23:3
Tramplers, The 1966,D 8,64:1
Cook, William Wallace (Screenwriter)
Speed Spook, The 1924,O 21,21:3
Cook and Brown
52d Street 1937,N 15,15:1
COOKE
See Also COOK
Cooke, Al
Legionnaires in Paris 1927,D 26,26:6
Cooke, Beach
Classmates 1924,D 30,15:3
Cooke, Frank
Three Must-Get-Theres, The 1922,Ag 28,14:1
Cooke, Ray
Mammy 1930,Mr 27,24:5
True to the Navy 1930,My 24,21:2
Girls Demand Excitement 1931,F 7,11:1
Taxi 1932,Ja 8,27:3
Good-Bye Again 1933,S 2,15:2
Now I'll Tell 1934,My 26,12:2
Cooke, Victor Ray
King of the Newsboys 1938,Ap 2,18:2
Cooke, Warren
Shore Leave 1925,S 14,16:1
Cooksey, Curtis
Silver Horde, The 1920,My 10,18:2
Misleading Lady, The 1932,Ap 9,18:1
Scaramouche 1952,My 9,20:2
Girl in White, The 1952,My 31,12:5

Young Man With Ideas 1952,Je 7,22:6
Because You're Mine 1952,S 26,18:2
Storm Center 1956,O 22,25:4
Death of a Scoundrel 1956,N 6,30:1
Cookson, Catherine (Original Author)
Rooney 1958,Je 6,29:2
Cookson, Georgina
Your Past Is Showing 1958,Jl 1,36:2
Woman Who Wouldn't Die, The 1965,Je 10,38:1
Cookson, Peter
Swingtime Johnny 1943,D 17,23:3
Cooley, Ballam
Wedding Rings 1930,My 10,25:3
Cooley, Charles
Lemon Drop Kid, The 1951,Mr 22,41:2
Son of Paleface 1952,O 2,32:3
Cooley, Frank
First Year, The 1926,Mr 8,17:1
Honor Bound 1928,Ap 30,18:3
Cooley, Hallam
Girl Dodger, The 1919,F 24,11:3
Girl From Outside, The 1919,N 10,18:2
Old Fashioned Boy, An 1920,N 1,13:2
Ten-Dollar Raise, The 1921,Je 13,16:1
What Do Men Want? 1921,N 14,18:1
One Week of Love 1923,Ja 8,22:1
Going Up 1923,O 10,16:2
Sporting Youth 1924,Ap 2,16:1
Monster, The 1925,F 16,24:1
Stop Flirting 1925,Je 18,16:3
Seven Days 1925,Ag 31,19:3
Forever After 1926,N 9,31:1
Ladies at Play 1926,N 16,25:3
Wedding Bills 1927,Je 29,29:3
Naughty but Nice 1927,Jl 5,19:2
Ladies Must Dress 1927,D 31,31:1
Her Wild Oat 1928,F 6,12:3
Paris Bound 1929,S 21,17:1
Tonight at Twelve 1929,S 23,24:3
So Long Letty 1930,F 8,12:5
Back Pay 1930,My 31,19:4
Holiday 1930,Jl 3,25:4
Sporting Blood 1931,Ag 15,18:3
Too Many Cooks 1931,Ag 17,18:2
Frisco Jenny 1933,Ja 7,11:2
Cooley, Isabelle
Anna Lucasta 1959,Ja 15,27:1
Cleopatra 1963,Je 13,29:1
Cooley, James
Song of Love, The 1924,F 25,13:1
Cooley, Marjorie
Girls of the Road 1940,Jl 22,20:2
Great Commandment, The 1942,O 17,11:1
Cooley, Spade
Rockin' in The Rockies 1945,Jl 5,7:2
Cooley, Spade and his Boys
Chatterbox 1943,Jl 2,15:3
Cooley, Willard
Fog Bound 1923,My 29,10:3
Wanderer of the Wasteland, The 1924,Jl 8,14:2
Enchanted Hill, The 1925,D 29,19:2 (In
Addenda)
Cooley, William
Flipper's New Adventure 1964,Ag 27,28:2
Coolidge, Philip
Boomerang 1947,Mr 6,36:2
Slander 1957,Ja 17,34:4
I Want to Live 1958,N 19,45:1
Mating Game, The 1959,Ap 30,37:1
North by Northwest 1959,Ag 7,28:1
Tingler, The 1960,Mr 10,36:2
Inherit the Wind 1960,O 13,41:1
Hamlet 1964,S 24,46:1
Russians are Coming the Russians are Coming,
The 1966,My 26,55:1
Never a Dull Moment 1968,Ag 15,46:2
Coolidge String Quartet
Adventure in Music 1944,Mr 6,17:3
Coombe, Carol
Ghost Train, The 1933,F 18,13:3
Coomes, Carol
It's a Wonderful Life 1946,D 23,19:2
COON
See Also KUHN
Coon, Gene L (Screenwriter)
Girl in the Kremlin, The 1957,My 22,29:2
Man With a Shadow 1958,Ja 23,24:3
Killers, The 1964,Jl 18,10:4
First to Fight 1967,Mr 30,55:1
Coonan, Dorothy
Wild Boys of the Road 1933,S 22,14:1
Coonan, Sheila
Cyanamide 1954,Mr 26,17:6
Cooney, Ray (Screenwriter)
No Place Like Homicide 1962,S 13,32:1
Cooney, Terrence (Producer)
Justice and Caryl Chessman 1960,Mr 3,24:5
Coop, Franco
Terra Madre 1931,O 31,22:2
Passa L'Amore 1933,N 25,10:3
I Tre Innamorati 1937,Je 17,19:2
Scipio Africanus 1939,S 23,22:2
Golden Madonna, The 1949,S 5,13:4

Coop, Franco — Cont
Mademoiselle Gobette 1955,F 5,13:3
Cooper, Anthony Kemble
Adventures of Sherlock Holmes, The
1939,S 2,20:1
I Was an Adventuress 1940,My 20,13:2
Cooper, Ashley
Paradise 1926,O 4,20:2
Cooper, B (Screenwriter)
Lady in Distress 1942,F 16,21:2
Cooper, Ben
Thunderbirds 1953,Mr 12,24:4
Johnny Guitar 1954,My 28,19:2
Outcast, The 1954,Jl 3,9:2
Hell's Outpost 1955,F 26,13:3
Eternal Sea, The 1955,Je 10,16:2
Rose Tattoo, The 1955,D 13,55:1
Cooper, Betty
Hidden Room, The 1950,Ja 9,19:2
Cooper, Betty Jane
Collegiate 1936,Ja 23,25:2
Cooper, Bigelow
Exciters, The 1923,Je 4,13:3
Bad Company 1925,Mr 16,16:1
Cooper, Bobby
Little Men 1940,D 9,23:2
My Reputation 1946,Ja 26,19:2
Cooper, Charles
Wrong Man, The 1956,D 24,8:1
Cooper, Clancy
Native Land 1942,My 12,16:3
Flight Lieutenant 1942,Jl 31,11:1
Whistler, The 1944,Ap 29,12:2
Enchanted Forest, The 1945,D 17,17:2
Sainted Sisters, The 1948,My 20,35:2
Lulu Belle 1948,Je 21,18:3
Man From Texas 1948,Ag 12,16:5
Mr Belvedere Goes to College 1949,Ap 16,11:2
Mary Ryan, Detective 1949,N 4,33:3
Great Rupert, The 1950,Ap 14,27:2
Distant Drums 1951,D 26,19:3
Wild North, The 1952,My 12,21:2
All the Brothers Were Valiant 1953,D 29,19:2
Incident in an Alley 1962,My 17,31:1
Cooper, Clarence
Quiet One, The 1949,F 14,15:2
Cooper, Claude
Struggle, The 1931,D 11,35:1
Cooper, Courtney Riley (Screenwriter)
White Desert, The 1925,Jl 8,12:4
Weary River 1929,Ja 25,20:6
Cooper, Dennis (Screenwriter)
City Across the River 1949,Ap 8,31:3
Cooper, Dorothy (Original Author)
Rich, Young and Pretty 1951,Jl 26,17:3
Small Town Girl 1953,My 7,37:2
Cooper, Dorothy (Screenwriter)
On an Island With You 1948,Jl 30,13:2
Date with Judy, A 1948,Ag 7,8:2
Duchess of Idaho 1950,Jl 21,15:3
Rich, Young and Pretty 1951,Jl 26,17:3
Small Town Girl 1953,My 7,37:2
Cooper, Ed
Enter Arsene Lupin 1944,D 2,17:6
Cooper, Edna Mae
Folly of Vanity 1925,Ja 28,14:1
Grounds for Divorce 1925,Je 29,8:2
Cooper, Edward
Working Man, The 1933,Ap 21,20:3
Diplomaniacs 1933,Ap 29,14:2
Female 1933,N 4,18:3
Clive of India 1935,Ja 18,29:1
Perfect Gentleman, The 1935,D 19,33:4
To Mary-With Love 1936,Ag 27,16:1
On the Avenue 1937,F 5,17:3
Rascals 1938,My 27,12:2
Wife, Husband and Friend 1939,F 25,19:2
Cooper, Edwin
Guilt of Janet Ames, The 1947,My 23,31:2
Cooper, Elizabeth (Original Author)
Drusilla With a Million 1925,My 25,21:3
Cooper, Eon
Flight Nurse 1954,Ja 30,9:6
Cooper, Frederick
Dark Sands 1938,Ag 17,23:4
Great Mr Handel, The 1943,S 10,29:3
Thunder Rock 1944,S 15,16:1
Henry V 1946,Je 18,30:2
Cooper, Gary
Winning of Barbara Worth, The 1926,N 29,16:3
Children of Divorce 1927,Ap 26,33:3
Wings 1927,Ag 13,10:4
Beau Sabreur 1928,Ja 23,18:3
Legion of the Condemned, The 1928,Mr 19,26:2
Doomsday 1928,Ap 2,25:1
Lilac Time 1928,Ag 4,7:2
First Kiss, The 1928,Ag 20,21:3
Shopworn Angel, The 1929,Ja 1,60:1
Wolf Song 1929,F 25,16:1
Betrayal 1929,My 6,30:4
Virginian, The 1929,D 23,18:2
Seven Days' Leave 1930,Ja 25,13:2
Only the Brave 1930,Mr 8,21:1
Texan, The 1930,My 17,21:2

Cooper, Gary— Cont
Man From Wyoming, A 1930,Jl 12,16:4
Spoilers, The 1930,S 20,15:4
Morocco 1930,N 17,29:1
Fighting Caravans 1931,Ja 26,21:1
City Streets 1931,Ap 18,17:3
I Take This Woman 1931,Je 13,20:4
His Woman 1931,D 5,21:2
Devil and the Deep 1932,Ag 20,7:4
If I Had a Million 1932,D 3,21:4
Farewell to Arms, A 1932,D 9,26:5
Today We Live 1933,Ap 15,16:2
One Sunday Afternoon 1933,S 2,14:4
Design for Living 1933,N 23,24:2
Alice in Wonderland 1933,D 23,19:1
Operator 13 1934,Je 23,16:5
Now and Forever 1934,O 13,10:1
Lives of a Bengal Lancer, The 1935,Ja 12,12:2
Wedding Night, The 1935,Mr 16,19:1
Peter Ibbetson 1935,N 8,18:2
Desire 1936,Ap 13,15:1
Mr Deeds Goes to Town 1936,Ap 17,17:2
General Died at Dawn, The 1936,S 3,17:2
Plainsman, The 1937,Ja 14,16:2
Souls at Sea 1937,Ag 10,23:2
Bluebeard's Eighth Wife 1938,Mr 24,21:2
Cowboy and the Lady, The 1938,N 25,19:3
Beau Geste 1939,Ag 3,15:2
Real Glory, The 1939,S 15,26:2
Westerner, The 1940,O 25,25:2
North West Mounted Police 1940,N 7,33:2
Meet John Doe 1941,Mr 13,25:2
Sergeant York 1941,Jl 3,15:1
Ball of Fire 1942,Ja 16,25:2
Pride of the Yankees, The 1942,Jl 16,23:1
For Whom the Bell Tolls 1943,Jl 15,25:2
Story of Dr Wassell, The 1944,Je 7,13:2
Casanova Brown 1944,S 15,16:1
Along Came Jones 1945,Jl 19,8:7
Saratoga Trunk 1945,N 22,39:2
Cloak and Dagger 1946,O 5,13:2
Unconquered 1947,O 11,11:2
Good Sam 1948,S 17,28:2
Fountainhead, The 1949,Jl 9,8:5
Task Force 1949,O 1,8:6
Bright Leaf 1950,Je 17,7:2
Dallas 1951,Ja 13,10:4
U S S Teakettle 1951,F 24,11:2
Starlift 1951,D 15,11:2
Distant Drums 1951,D 26,19:3
It's a big Country 1952,Ja 9,25:2
High Noon 1952,Jl 25,14:2
Springfield Rifle 1952,O 23,40:2
Return to Paradise 1953,S 11,24:2
Blowing Wild 1953,O 8,37:5
Garden of Evil 1954,Jl 10,17:1
Vera Cruz 1954,D 27,22:4
Court-Martial of Billy Mitchell, The
  1955,D 23,14:2
Friendly Persuasion 1956,N 2,30:1
Love in the Afternoon 1957,Ag 24,12:1
Ten North Frederick 1958,My 23,29:2
Man of the West 1958,O 2,44:3
Hanging Tree, The 1959,F 12,23:1
They Came to Cordura 1959,O 22,47:2
Wreck of the Mary Deare, The 1959,N 7,27:1
Naked Edge 1961,Jl 1,9:1
Adventures of Marco Polo, The 1965,Ap 8,17:2
Cooper, Gary (Producer)
Along Came Jones 1945,Jl 19,8:7
Cooper, George
Turn to the Right 1922,Ja 24,11:1
Nth Commandment, The 1923,Ap 10,24:3
Shriek of Araby, The 1923,Je 11,16:2
Eternal Three, The 1923,O 12,7:2 (Incorrect in
  this edition; use 1927,O 1,7:2 elsewhere)
Her Temporary Husband 1924,Ja 1,20:1
Through the Dark 1924,Ja 8,27:1
Devil's Cargo, The 1925,F 3,24:1
Great Divide, The 1925,F 11,19:4
Smouldering Fires 1925,Mr 31,17:4
Just a Woman 1925,My 26,24:2
Goose Woman, The 1925,Ag 4,14:3
Barrier, The 1926,Mr 22,16:1
Red Dice 1926,Ap 16,20:3
Unknown Soldier, The 1926,My 31,10:2
Tin Hats 1926,N 29,16:3
Lovelorn, The 1927,D 19,30:1
Rose-Marie 1928,F 13,16:2
Trail of '98, The 1928,Mr 21,30:3
Lilac Time 1928,Ag 4,7:2
Barker, The 1928,D 6,35:1
Unholy Night, The 1929,O 12,11:1
Sailor's Holiday 1929,O 21,30:1
Under a Texas Moon 1930,Ap 4,22:1
Numbered Men 1930,Je 9,23:3
Shooting Straight 1930,Jl 28,22:1
Girl of the Golden West, The 1930,O 27,17:1
Renegades 1930,N 8,21:3
Paid 1931,Ja 3,21:2
Gentleman's Fate 1931,Je 27,20:3
Laughing Sinners 1931,Jl 4,11:5
Sky Devils 1932,Mr 4,17:3
Uptown New York 1932,D 10,19:3

Soldiers of the Storm 1933,My 17,15:3
Big Shakedown, The 1934,F 12,19:2
Personality Kid, The 1934,Ag 1,14:2
Broadway Bill 1934,N 30,22:2
Murder in the Clouds 1934,D 26,18:1
Doubting Thomas 1935,Jl 11,24:2
Missing Girls 1936,O 5,25:1
Adventure in Manhattan 1936,O 23,27:5
Step Lively, Jeeves 1937,Ap 2,19:6
That I May Live 1937,My 10,23:2
Think Fast, Mr Moto 1937,Ag 16,15:3
Portia on Trial 1937,D 3,29:2
Missing Guest, The 1938,S 7,30:7
Crossfire 1947,Jl 23,19:2
Blood on the Moon 1948,N 12,30:5
Roughshod 1949,Je 17,27:2
Zamba 1949,N 7,33:2
Eight Iron Men 1953,Ja 2,11:1
Men of the Fighting Lady 1954,My 8,15:2
Cooper, George A
Hell is a City 1961,Ja 19,26:3
Tom Jones 1963,O 8,48:1
Nightmare 1964,Je 18,29:2
Life at the Top 1965,D 15,53:1
Strange Affair, The 1968,Jl 25,26:2
Cooper, Gerald
Men of Tomorrow 1935,Ap 16,27:2
Cooper, Gladys
Bohemian Girl, The 1923,F 5,18:2
Iron Duke, The 1935,Ja 25,27:2
Rebecca 1940,Mr 29,25:2
Kitty Foyle 1941,Ja 9,27:2
That Hamilton Woman 1941,Ap 4,25:1
Black Cat, The 1941,Ap 26,20:3
This Above All 1942,My 13,14:3
Eagle Squadron 1942,Jl 3,12:5
Now, Voyager 1942,O 23,25:3
Forever and a Day 1943,Mr 13,9:2
Mr Lucky 1943,Jl 23,21:2
Princess O'Rourke 1943,N 6,16:2
Song of Bernadette, The 1944,Ja 27,15:2
White Cliffs of Dover, The 1944,My 12,15:2
Mrs Parkington 1944,O 13,16:1
Valley of Decision, The 1945,My 4,23:2
Love Letters 1945,Ag 27,22:3
Green Years, The 1946,Ap 5,21:2
Cockeyed Miracle, The 1946,O 25,28:1
Green Dolphin Street 1947,O 16,34:2
Beware of Pity 1947,N 1,11:2
Bishop's Wife, The 1947,D 10,44:2
Homecoming 1948,Ap 30,28:4
Pirate, The 1948,My 21,19:2
Madame Bovary 1949,Ag 26,15:2
Thunder on the Hill 1951,O 18,32:3
At Swords Point 1952,Ap 10,37:1
Man Who Loved Redheads, The 1955,Jl 26,29:2
Separate Tables 1958,D 19,2:7
List of Adrian Messenger, The 1963,My 30,20:1
My Fair Lady 1964,O 22,41:1
Happiest Millionaire, The 1967,D 1,56:1
Cooper, Harry
Thomas Crown Affair, The 1968,Je 27,48:2
Cooper, Horace
Where's Charley? 1952,Je 27,18:3
Cooper, Inez
Mr and Mrs North 1942,Ja 22,13:2
I Married an Angel 1942,Jl 10,13:2
Stand by for Action 1943,Mr 12,12:2
Barkleys of Broadway, The 1949,My 5,34:2
Cooper, Irving H (Screenwriter)
Jet Over the Atlantic 1960,Ja 7,24:6
Cooper, J Gordon (Director)
Broadway Gold 1923,Jl 31,12:4
Cooper, Jack
Three Live Ghosts 1929,S 30,23:1
Cooper, Jack (Original Author)
Criminals of the Air 1937,O 28,29:2
Cooper, Jackie
Skippy 1931,Ap 4,23:1
Donovan's Kid 1931,My 22,28:5
Champ, The 1931,N 10,29:4
Sooky 1931,D 21,28:4
When a Feller Needs a Friend 1932,My 14,11:5
Divorce in the Family 1932,O 31,18:4
Broadway to Hollywood 1933,S 2,14:4
Bowery, The 1933,O 5,24:2
Treasure Island 1934,Ag 18,5:5
Peck's bad Boy 1934,O 6,20:1
O'Shaughnessy's Boy 1935,O 5,18:2
Tough Guy 1936,Mr 14,10:1
Devil is a Sissy, The 1936,O 17,21:2
Boy of the Streets 1938,Ja 24,17:1
White Banners 1938,Je 23,27:1
That Certain Age 1938,N 5,15:2
Gangster's Boy 1938,N 7,23:6
Newsboys' Home 1939,Ja 23,8:2
Spirit of Culver 1939,Mr 9,18:1
Streets of New York 1939,My 1,21:1
Two Bright Boys 1939,S 22,27:3
What a Life 1939,O 12,33:1
Big Guy, The 1940,Ja 1,29:2
Seventeen 1940,F 29,15:2
Return of Frank James, The 1940,Ag 10,16:4

Cooper, Jackie— Cont
Gallant Sons 1940,D 12,37:2
Life With Henry 1941,F 6,25:2
Ziegfeld Girl 1941,Ap 25,17:2
Syncopation 1942,My 29,13:3
Men of Texas 1942,Jl 13,18:3 (In Addenda)
Navy Comes Through, The 1942,N 12,30:3
Where Are Your Children? 1944,Ja 17,14:5
Everything's Ducky 1961,D 21,30:6
Cooper, James Fenimore (Original Author)
Last of the Mohicans, The 1921,Ja 3,20:2
Last of the Mohicans, The 1936,S 3,17:3
Last of the Redmen 1947,Ag 30,8:6
Iroquois Trail, The 1950,O 27,24:4
Cooper, Jeanne
Redhead From Wyoming, The 1953,Ja 9,17:4
Man From the Alamo, The 1953,S 12,13:2
Five Steps to Danger 1957,Ja 31,21:1
Let no Man Write my Epitaph 1960,N 11,36:2
House of Women 1962,Ap 12,41:6
Intruder, The 1962,My 15,48:1
Black Zoo 1963,My 16,42:1
Cooper, Jeff
Born Losers, The 1967,Ag 19,16:2
Impossible Years, The 1968,D 6,54:1
Cooper, Jerry
Hollywood Hotel 1938,Ja 13,17:3
Cooper, Joe (Composer)
Golden Girl 1951,N 21,20:3
Cooper, John C (Screenwriter)
Haunted Strangler, The 1958,Jl 4,15:3
Cooper, Lillian
White Angel, The 1936,Je 25,24:1
Cooper, Lillian Kemble
Gone With the Wind 1939,D 20,31:2
So Big 1953,O 22,34:2
King's Thief, The 1955,Ag 13,7:2
Cooper, Mae
Sally, Irene and Mary 1925,D 7,19:1
Cooper, Marian C (Producer)
She 1935,Jl 26,18:2
Fugitive, The 1947,D 26,22:2
Cooper, Marie Louise
These Three 1936,Mr 19,22:4
Cooper, Marion
Birth of a Nation, The 1930,D 22,16:2
Cooper, Maxine
Autumn Leaves 1956,Ag 2,21:2
Cooper, Melville
Private Life of Don Juan, The 1934,D 10,16:2
Scarlet Pimpernel, The 1935,F 8,27:2
Gorgeous Hussy, The 1936,S 5,7:1
Last of Mrs Cheyney, The 1937,F 19,15:1
Thin Ice 1937,S 4,8:2
Great Garrick, The 1937,O 25,23:1
Tovarich 1937,D 31,9:2
Women Are Like That 1938,Ap 11,12:2
Adventures of Robin Hood, The 1938,My 13,17:2
Gold Diggers in Paris 1938,Je 2,19:2
Four's a Crowd 1938,Ag 12,11:1
Garden of the Moon 1938,S 24,13:1
Hard to Get 1938,N 14,15:2
Dramatic School 1938,D 9,31:2
Comet over Broadway 1938,D 16,33:3
Dawn Patrol 1938,D 24,12:1
I'm From Missouri 1939,Mr 23,27:1
Blind Alley 1939,My 23,27:2
Sun Never Sets, The 1939,Je 9,26:2
Two Bright Boys 1939,S 22,27:3
Too Many Husbands 1940,Mr 8,25:2
Rebecca 1940,Mr 29,25:2
Pride and Prejudice 1940,Ag 9,19:1
Lady Eve, The 1941,F 26,17:1
Submarine Zone; (Escape To Glory)
  1941,Ap 7,13:2
Scotland Yard 1941,Ap 9,33:3
Flame of New Orleans, The 1941,Ap 26,20:2
You Belong to Me 1941,N 29,14:2
This Above All 1942,My 13,14:3
Life Begins at Eight-Thirty 1942,D 10,35:2
Random Harvest 1942,D 18,36:6
Immortal Sergeant 1943,F 4,29:2
Hit Parade of 1943 1943,Ap 16,24:3
Holy Matrimony 1943,S 16,25:2
My Kingdom for a Cook 1943,O 15,15:3
Heartbeat 1946,My 11,22:4
13 Rue Madeleine 1947,Ja 16,30:2
Imperfect Lady, The 1947,My 22,34:5
Enchantment 1948,D 27,16:2
Red Danube, The 1949,D 9,37:3
And Baby Makes Three 1949,D 23,17:3
Love Happy 1950,Ap 8,9:4
Father of the Bride 1950,My 19,31:2
Underworld Story, The 1950,Jl 27,29:4
Petty Girl, The 1950,Ag 18,17:2
Let's Dance 1950,N 30,42:2
It Should Happen to You 1954,Ja 16,10:5
Moonfleet 1955,Je 25,9:2
King's Thief, The 1955,Ag 13,7:2
Diane 1956,Ja 13,18:1
Around the World in 80 Days 1956,O 18,37:1
Bundle of Joy 1956,D 20,36:1
Story of Mankind, The 1957,N 9,31:2
From the Earth to the Moon 1958,N 27,52:2

Cooper, Merian C (Cinematographer)
Gow, The Head Hunter 1928,D 25,31:3
Cooper, Merian C (Director)
King Kong 1933,Mr 3,12:1
Cooper, Merian C (Miscellaneous)
Lost Empire 1929,Ja 22,23:1
Cooper, Merian C (Original Author)
King Kong 1933,Mr 3,12:1
Cooper, Merian C (Producer)
Grass 1925,Mr 31,17:4
Chang 1927,Ap 30,25:3 (In Addenda)
Four Feathers, The 1929,Je 13,35:4
Last Days of Pompeii, The 1935,O 17,29:2
Toy Wife, The 1938,Je 24,15:1
Fort Apache 1948,Je 25,26:2
Three Godfathers 1949,Mr 4,25:2
Mighty Joe Young 1949,Jl 28,19:3
Rio Grande 1950,N 20,21:2
Quiet Man, The 1952,Ag 22,13:1
ThIs is Cinerama 1952,O 1,1:7
Sun Shines Bright, The 1954,Mr 17,25:2
Searchers, The 1956,My 31,21:4
Best of Cinerama, The 1963,D 26,33:2
Cooper, Miriam
Mother and the Law, The 1919,Ag 19,10:1
Evangeline 1919,Ag 20,12:3
Oath, The 1921,Ap 11,9:1
Birth of a Nation, The 1921,My 2,12:1
Kindred of the Dust 1922,Ag 28,14:1
Birth of a Nation, The 1922,D 5,24:3
Daughters of the Rich 1923,Je 18,13:5
Broken Wing, The 1923,O 9,17:4
Cooper, Mort
Safe at Home 1941,N 26,31:2
Cooper, Olive (Miscellaneous)
Follow Your Heart 1936,O 22,31:1
Cooper, Olive (Original Author)
Cocoanut Grove 1938,Je 16,21:2
Cooper, Olive (Screenwriter)
Dancing Feet 1936,Mr 28,11:2
Laughing Irish Eyes 1936,Ap 4,11:2
Lady Behave 1938,Ja 28,17:3
Cocoanut Grove 1938,Je 16,21:2
Annabel Takes a Tour 1938,D 29,15:3
Ice-Capades 1941,S 25,29:1
Sioux City Sue 1947,Jl 23,19:3
Cooper, Phillip
Cuban Love Song, The 1931,D 5,21:2
Viva Villa! 1934,Ap 11,25:2
Under the Pampas Moon 1935,My 31,11:1
Come and Get It 1936,N 12,31:1
Cooper, Ralph
White Hunter 1936,N 26,39:2
Cooper, Richard
Mystery at the Villa Rose 1930,Je 2,25:4
Shipyard Sally 1940,Ja 18,27:3
Cooper, Rosemary
Spirit of the U S A, The 1924,My 21,22:3
Dressmaker from Paris, The 1925,Mr 18,19:2
White Flannels 1927,Mr 22,31:2
Climbers, The 1927,My 4,29:2
Drums of Love 1928,Ja 25,20:4
Cooper, Sally
Kind Lady 1951,Ag 8,21:2
Cooper, Stuart
I'll Never Forget What's 'Isname
1968,Ap 15,51:1
Cooper, Ted
20,000 Leagues Under the Sea 1954,D 24,7:2
Cooper, Terence
Casino Royale 1967,Ap 29,25:1
Cooper, Tom
Dawn Over Ireland 1938,F 19,19:2
Cooper, Tom (Director)
Dawn Over Ireland 1938,F 19,19:2
Cooper, Tom (Original Author)
Dawn Over Ireland 1938,F 19,19:2
Cooper, Tom (Screenwriter)
Dawn Over Ireland 1938,F 19,19:2
Cooper, Violet
Cardinal Richelieu 1935,Ap 19,24:2
Cooper, Violet Kemble
Fountain, The 1934,Ag 31,14:1
Invisible Ray, The 1936,Ja 11,9:3
Romeo and Juliet 1936,Ag 21,12:2
Cooper, Willis (Original Author)
Mr Moto Takes a Chance 1938,Je 13,15:4
Cooper, Willis (Screenwriter)
Thank You, Mr Moto 1938,Ja 3,16:2
Son of Frankenstein 1939,Ja 30,9:2
Cooper, Wyatt (Screenwriter)
Chapman Report, The 1962,O 18,49:2
Coote, Richard
V I P's, The 1963,S 20,29:1
Coote, Robert
Yank at Oxford, A 1938,F 25,15:1
Girl Downstairs, The 1939,Ja 26,17:1
Mr Moto's Last Warning 1939,Ja 27,17:3
Gunga Din 1939,Ja 28,19:2
Bad Lands 1939,Ag 9,15:2
Nurse Edith Cavell 1939,S 22,27:4
Vigil in the Night 1940,Mr 9,19:2
You Can't Fool Your Wife 1940,My 24,23:4

Stairway to Heaven 1946,D 26,28:1
Ghost and Mrs Muir, The 1947,Je 27,17:2
Forever Amber 1947,O 23,31:2
Exile, The 1947,D 26,22:4
Berlin Express 1948,My 21,19:3
Three Musketeers, The 1948,O 21,33:2
Red Danube, The 1949,D 9,37:3
Soldiers Three 1951,Mr 30,28:5
Scaramouche 1952,My 9,20:2
Merry Widow, The 1952,S 25,38:1
Prisoner of Zenda, The 1952,N 5,36:2
Commandos Strike at Dawn 1954,Ja 14,25:1
Othello 1955,S 13,27:1
Swan, The 1956,Ap 27,21:5
Constant Husband, The 1957,Jl 26,10:3
Merry Andrews 1958,Mr 21,17:1
Horse's Mouth, The 1958,N 12,41:1
League of Gentlemen, The 1961,Ja 25,30:4
Man Could Get Killed, A 1966,My 12,54:2
Swinger, The 1966,D 15,60:1
Cool Ones, The 1967,My 11,50:1
Prudence and the Pill 1968,My 24,37:1
Coover, Rex
Smiling Faces 1932,Ag 31,12:3
Cope, Kenneth
Dunkirk 1958,S 11,42:2
Genghis Khan 1965,Je 24,28:2
Copeau, Jacques
Razumov 1937,Mr 9,27:2
Courier of Lyons, The 1938,Je 3,17:1
Affair Lafont, The; Conflit 1939,O 9,15:2
Copeland, Jack L (Director)
Hell's Five Hours 1957,Jl 24,18:1
Hell's Five Hours 1958,Jl 24,18:1
Copeland, Jack L (Original Author)
Hell's Five Hours 1958,Jl 24,18:1
Copeland, Jack L (Producer)
Hell's Five Hours 1957,Jl 24,18:1
Hell's Five Hours 1958,Jl 24,18:1
Copeland, Jack L (Screenwriter)
Hell's Five Hours 1957,Jl 24,18:1
Copeland, James
High and Dry 1954,Ag 31,25:5
Innocents in Paris 1955,Mr 5,9:6
Copeland, Joan
Goddess, The 1958,Je 25,24:1
Middle of the Night 1959,Je 18,36:1
Copeland, Nick
Deceiver, The 1931,N 23,22:1
Legion of Terror 1936,N 2,24:2
Main Event, The 1938,Je 20,11:3
Copelands, The
Sensations of 1945 1944,Jl 7,13:2
Copelin, Campbell
Kiss the Blood off my Hands 1948,O 30,10:2
Copland, Aaron (Composer)
Our Town 1940,Je 14,25:3
Copland, Aaron (Miscellaneous)
Fiesta 1947,Je 27,17:3
Coplen, Elbert Jr
Bachelor Mother 1939,Je 30,17:2
Coplen, Yorke (Producer)
Urubu 1948,O 21,33:3
Copley, Gerald L C (Screenwriter)
Born Free 1966,Je 23,29:1
Copley, Peter
Golden Salamander 1951,Mr 24,8:3
Promoter, The 1952,O 29,36:2
Sword and the Rose, The 1953,Ag 20,18:3
Foreign Intrigue 1956,Jl 13,23:2
Time Without Pity 1957,N 23,11:2
Victim 1962,F 6,27:2
King and Country 1964,S 24,46:2
King and Country 1966,Ja 28,20:4
Coppa, Joe
Keeper of the Bees, The 1925,O 28,29:2
Coppel, Alec (Original Author)
Hidden Room, The 1950,Ja 9,19:2
Mr Denning Drives North 1953,S 2,20:1
Captain's Paradise, The 1953,S 29,25:5
Gazebo, The 1960,Ja 16,14:4
Moment to Moment 1966,Mr 3,28:1
Bliss of Mrs Blossom, The 1968,D 12,62:6
Coppel, Alec (Screenwriter)
Pacific Adventure 1947,N 26,18:2
Hidden Room, The 1950,Ja 9,19:2
No Highway in the Sky 1951,S 22,8:6
Mr Denning Drives North 1953,S 2,20:1
Captain's Paradise, The 1953,S 29,25:5
Hell Below Zero 1954,Jl 17,7:3
Black Knight, The 1954,O 29,27:2
Vertigo 1958,My 29,24:2
Appointment With a Shadow 1959,Ja 8,24:2
Swordsman of Siena 1962,D 6,55:3
Bliss of Mrs Blossom, The 1968,D 12,62:6
Coppel, Myra (Original Author)
Gazebo, The 1960,Ja 16,14:4
Coppin, Grace
Lost Boundaries 1949,Jl 1,14:4
So Young, So Bad 1950,Jl 24,15:2
Coppley, Lewis (Screenwriter)
Operation Eichmann 1961,My 4,40:7

Coppola, Francis Ford (Director)
Dementia 13 1963,O 24,37:1
You're a Big Boy Now 1967,Mr 21,35:3
Finian's Rainbow 1968,O 10,59:5
Coppola, Francis Ford (Screenwriter)
Dementia 13 1963,O 24,37:1
This Property is Condemned 1966,Ag 4,24:1
Is Paris Burning? 1966,N 11,36:1
You're a Big Boy Now 1967,Mr 21,35:3
Coquelin, Jean
Pearls of the Crown, The 1938,Ap 12,26:2
End of a Day, The 1939,S 12,28:4
Carnival of Sinners 1947,Ap 8,34:2
Coquelin, Jean-Paul
Night Watch, The; Trou, Le 1964,My 27,46:1
Coquillon, John (Cinematographer)
Zanzabuku 1956,Ag 16,30:3
Coral, Tito
Marie Galante 1934,N 21,23:4
Goin' to Town 1935,My 11,21:2
Coray, Isabelle
Head of a Tyrant 1962,Je 7,31:2
Corbaley, Kate (Screenwriter)
Silent Sanderson 1925,Je 11,14:3
Fire Brigade, The 1926,D 21,20:2
Corbella, Vincenzo
Night, The; Notte, La 1962,F 20,29:4
Corbett, Ben
Racketeers of the Range 1939,Je 8,31:4
Corbett, Carol
Thomas Crown Affair, The 1968,Je 27,48:2
Corbett, Frank
Forest Ring, The 1930,Ap 26,11:1
Corbett, Glenn
Fireball, The 1950,N 10,35:4
Man on a String 1960,My 21,15:1
Mountain Road, The 1960,Je 30,22:3
All the Young Men 1960,Ag 27,8:6
Homicidal 1961,Jl 27,23:4
Shenandoah 1965,Jl 29,18:3
Corbett, Harry H
In the Wake of a Stranger 1961,Je 22,23:3
Ladies Who Do 1963,N 26,52:2
Rattle of a Simple Man 1964,D 21,42:2
Boy Ten Feet Tall, A 1965,My 13,32:2
Corbett, James J
Happy Days 1930,F 14,20:1
Legendary Champions, The 1968,O 29,54:1
Corbett, James J (Miscellaneous)
Gentleman Jim 1942,N 26,40:3
Corbett, Jean
Young Stranger, The 1957,Ap 9,40:1
Corbett, Jim (Original Author)
Man-Eater of Kumaon 1948,Jl 2,24:2
Corbett, Leonora
Constant Nymph, The 1934,Ap 7,19:1
Friday the 13th 1934,My 15,18:1
Troopship 1938,Ap 26,18:2
Corbett, Ronald
Mad Little Island 1958,D 31,12:1
Corbett, William D
Uncle Sam of Freedom Ridge 1920,S 27,15:2
Corbin, Virginia Lee
Wine of Youth 1924,Ag 11,16:1
Sinners in Silk 1924,S 8,15:3
Broken Laws 1925,Ja 21,19:3
Hands Up 1926,Ja 18,26:2
Ladies at Play 1926,N 16,25:3
Loose Ankles 1926,N 21,VIII,7:3 (In Addenda)
Perfect Sap, The 1927,Ja 11,18:2
Footlights and Fools 1929,N 9,22:5
Morals for Women 1931,N 16,23:1
X Marks the Spot 1931,D 7,16:1
Corbucci, Bruno (Screenwriter)
Slave, The 1963,My 30,20:1
Corbucci, Sergio (Director)
Island Sinner, The 1960,S 5,11:2
Slave, The 1963,My 30,20:1
Duel of the Titans 1963,Ag 8,19:1
Navajo Joe 1967,D 7,60:2
Corbucci, Sergio (Miscellaneous)
Island Sinner, The 1960,S 5,11:2
Corbucci, Sergio (Screenwriter)
Last Days of Pompeii, The 1960,Ag 11,19:1
Duel of the Titans 1963,Ag 8,19:1
Corby, Ellen
I Remember Mama 1948,Mr 12,29:2
Dark Past, The 1948,D 23,25:2
Little Women 1949,Mr 11,33:2
Captain China 1950,Mr 2,33:2
Caged 1950,My 20,8:6
Gunfighter, The 1950,Je 24,7:2
Edge of Doom 1950,Ag 4,13:2
Harriet Craig 1950,N 3,31:2
Mating Season, The 1951,Ap 12,41:2
Goodbye, my Fancy 1951,My 30,14:2
On Moonlight Bay 1951,Jl 27,15:2
Angels in the Outfield 1951,O 18,32:1
Big Trees, The 1952,F 6,24:2
Shane 1953,Ap 24,30:3
Lion Is in the Streets, A 1953,S 24,39:2
Monsoon 1953,S 26,15:2
About Mrs Leslie 1954,Je 28,16:2

Corby, Ellen— Cont
Sabrina 1954,S 23,43:2
Illegal 1955,O 29,12:6
Slightly Scarlet 1956,Mr 17,13:2
Seventh Sin, The 1957,Je 29,10:6
Macabre 1958,Jl 24,18:1
Saintly Sinners 1962,N 29,28:2
Caretakers, The 1963,Ag 22,19:2
Strangler, The 1964,Je 11,27:4
Family Jewels, The 1965,Ag 12,30:4
Glass Bottom Boat, The 1966,Je 10,54:1
Night of the Grizzly, The 1966,Je 23,29:1
Corcoran, Ann
Escape From Crime 1942,O 12,12:3
Take It or Leave It 1944,Jl 13,14:2
Corcoran, Brian
Babes in Toyland 1961,D 15,49:1
Corcoran, Donna
Angels in the Outfield 1951,O 18,32:1
Young Man With Ideas 1952,Je 7,22:6
Don't Bother to Knock 1952,Jl 19,8:2
Million Dollar Mermaid 1952,D 5,35:2
Scandal at Scourie 1953,Je 16,24:2
Dangerous When Wet 1953,Je 19,18:1
Violent Saturday 1955,My 12,32:2
Moonfleet 1955,Je 25,9:2
Corcoran, George
Not Damaged 1930,Je 9,23:3
Shepper - Newfounder, The 1930,D 25,31:5
Corcoran, Kevin
Violent Saturday 1955,My 12,32:2
Old Yeller 1957,D 26,23:4
Shaggy Dog, The 1959,Mr 20,26:2
Rabbit Trap, The 1959,O 15,48:1
Toby Tyler 1960,Ap 20,45:2
Pollyanna 1960,My 20,26:1
Swiss Family Robinson 1960,D 24,8:4
Babes in Toyland 1961,D 15,49:1
Bon Voyage! 1962,My 18,34:2
Savage Sam 1963,Ag 1,17:3
Tiger Walks, A 1964,Ag 27,28:2
Corcoran, Michael
Pool of London 1951,N 28,37:2
Touch and go 1956,Mr 20,13:2
Smallest Show on Earth, The 1957,N 23,11:2
Corcoran, Noreen
I Love Melvin 1953,Ap 10,18:4
Young Bess 1953,My 22,31:1
So This Is Love 1953,Ag 12,22:1
Tanganyika 1954,Je 19,9:2
Violent Saturday 1955,My 12,32:2
Corcoran, William (Original Author)
Trail Street 1947,Ap 10,35:2
Cord, Alex
Synanon 1965,My 6,44:1
Stagecoach 1966,Je 16,53:1
Minute to Pray, A Second to Die, A
1968,My 23,56:2
Corda, Luciana (Screenwriter)
Fast and Sexy 1960,O 6,51:4
Corda, Maria
Madame Wants no Children 1927,Je 21,23:3
Moon of Israel 1927,Je 29,29:3
Guardsman, The 1927,S 7,35:2
Private Life of Helen of Troy, The
1927,D 10,14:7
Modern du Barry, A 1928,Mr 19,26:2
Tesha 1928,S 16,IX,5:7 (In Addenda)
Woman in the Night, A 1929,Mr 11,22:2
Corday, Andree
Big Pond, The 1930,My 19,21:1
Corday, Claudia
Dr Coppelius 1968,D 26,56:1
Corday, Mara
Dawn at Socorro 1954,Ag 28,8:2
So This Is Paris 1955,F 12,11:1
Man Without a Star 1955,Mr 25,19:3
Foxfire 1955,Jl 14,19:1
Raw Edge 1956,Jl 28,10:7
Black Scorpion, The 1957,O 12,23:2
Corday, Marcelle
Lost-a Wife 1925,Je 22,10:2
We Moderns 1925,D 8,28:5
Splendid Crime, The 1925,D 17,27:1
Scarlet Letter, The 1926,Ag 10,19:2
Into her Kingdom 1926,Ag 10,19:2
Jim, The Conquerer 1926,D 28,17:1
When a Man Loves 1927,F 4,16:6
Quality Street 1927,N 2,24:5
Dry Martini 1928,N 5,26:5 (In Addenda)
They Had to See Paris 1929,O 12,11:1
Trespasser, The 1929,N 2,14:6
Midnight Mystery 1930,Je 2,25:4
This Modern Age 1931,S 7,19:3
Whistling in the Dark 1933,F 5,IX,5:1
Barbarian, The 1933,My 13,16:2
World Moves On, The 1934,Je 30,18:5
Hands Across the Table 1935,N 2,13:2
Peter Ibbetson 1935,N 8,18:2
Great Ziegfeld, The 1936,Ap 9,21:2
Dead End 1937,Ag 25,25:1
Happy Landing 1938,Ja 22,19:1
Always Goodbye 1938,Je 25,7:2
Suez 1938,O 15,21:2

Swamp Fire 1946,Ag 26,21:4
Corday, Paula
Sword of Monte Cristo, The 1951,Ap 23,21:2
Too Young to Kiss 1951,N 23,32:2
You for Me 1952,S 25,38:3
Because You're Mine 1952,S 26,18:2
Black Castle, The 1952,D 26,20:4
French Line, The 1954,My 15,13:2
Corday, Rita
Falcon Strikes Back, The 1943,Ap 2,17:4
Falcon in Hollywood, The 1944,D 9,21:2
Body Snatcher, The 1945,My 26,18:3
Falcon in San Francisco, The 1945,Jl 21,7:2
West of the Pecos 1945,Ag 11,14:6
Falcon's Alibi, The 1946,Ap 13,23:2
Truth About Murder, The 1946,Jl 27,12:6
Dick Tracy vs Cueball 1946,N 23,12:2
Cordell, Cathleen
Angel Street 1952,N 11,25:2
Cordell, Frank
Sundowners, The 1950,My 5,17:2
High Lonesome 1950,D 8,40:4
Cordell, Ricky
Singing Nun, The 1966,Mr 18,33:1
Cordell, Shane
Fiend Without a Face 1958,Jl 4,15:3
Corden, Henry
Secret Life of Walter Mitty, The 1947,Ag 15,12:2
Abbott and Costello in the Foreign Legion
1950,Ag 14,14:4
Behave Yourself 1951,N 8,35:2
Carbine Williams 1952,My 8,37:2
Hiawatha 1952,D 26,20:4
King Richard and the Crusaders 1954,Ag 23,20:5
Corder, Collett
Der Herr Finanzdirektor 1932,Je 25,18:2
Cordier, Jean
Winner's Circle, The 1957,My 6,25:2
Cordier, Stephane (Narrator)
Rubens 1949,Ap 30,9:2
Cording, Harry
Knockout, The 1925,O 27,23:3
Patriot, The 1928,Ag 18,7:2 (In Addenda)
Rescue, The 1929,Ja 14,20:1
Sins of the Fathers 1929,Ja 28,21:1
Christina 1929,Ap 1,22:1
Squall, The 1929,My 10,32:5
Captain of the Guard 1930,Mr 29,23:1
Bride of the Regiment 1930,My 22,32:6
Rough Romance 1930,Je 16,25:3
Conquering Horde, The 1931,Mr 30,25:2
Honor of the Family 1931,O 17,20:1
File No 113 1932,F 20,11:2
World and the Flesh, The 1932,My 7,11:5
Forgotten Commandments 1932,Je 2,25:2
Cabin in the Cotton 1932,S 30,17:3
Captain Blood 1935,D 27,14:1
Road Gang 1936,F 24,14:1
Sutter's Gold 1936,Mr 27,25:2
White Angel, The 1936,Je 25,24:1
Daniel Boone 1936,O 24,23:2
Prince and the Pauper, The 1937,My 6,23:1
Crime School 1938,My 11,17:2
Adventures of Robin Hood, The 1938,My 13,17:2
Valley of the Giants 1938,S 10,20:2
Painted Desert 1938,S 14,26:5
Each Dawn I Die 1939,Jl 22,12:2
Passport to Alcatraz 1940,Je 15,12:2
Great Plane Robbery, The 1940,N 15,25:2
Lady From Cheyenne, The 1941,Ap 18,18:2
Mutiny in the Arctic 1941,My 3,20:5
Arabian Nights 1942,D 26,15:1
Sherlock Holmes and the Secret Weapon
1943,Ja 5,15:2
Ali Baba and the Forty Thieves 1944,Mr 16,17:3
Gypsy Wildcat 1944,O 5,18:6
Mrs Parkington 1944,O 13,16:1
House of Fear, The 1945,Mr 19,23:3
Sudan 1945,Ap 19,22:8
Dressed to Kill 1946,My 25,12:4
Woman's Vengeance, A 1948,Ja 30,19:2
That Lady in Ermine 1948,Ag 25,31:2
Fighting O'Flynn, The 1949,F 28,16:2
Fortunes of Captain Blood 1950,Je 10,11:3
Last of the Buccaneers 1950,D 15,43:2
Mask of the Avenger 1951,Je 27,25:2
Big Trees, The 1952,F 6,24:2
Against all Flags 1952,D 25,34:6
Cordoba, Irma
Noches de Buenos Aires 1935,D 10,31:3
Noches de Buenos Aires; Buenos Aires Nights
1935,D 12,33:4
Caballo del Pueblo, El 1935,D 16,23:4
Que Tiempos Aquellos; Those Were the Days
1938,Mr 7,13:2
Fuera de la Ley; Outside the Law
1940,My 13,21:2
Cordon, Maude Turner
Careless Lady 1932,Ap 18,19:2
Cordoue, Michele
Desperate Decision 1954,N 9,31:5
Proud and the Beautiful, The 1956,My 29,32:2
Young Girls Beware 1959,Ag 22,8:2

Cordova, Fred
House of Dracula 1945,D 22,16:3
Cordy, Raymond
A Nous la Liberte 1932,Ja 10,VIII,5:1
Quatorez Juillet 1933,O 20,14:2
Dernier Milliardaire, Le 1935,O 30,16:2
Mysteres de Paris, Les 1937,Ja 30,21:2
Slipper Episode, The 1938,My 19,25:2
They Were Five 1938,Je 1,19:5
She Returned at Dawn; Retour a l'Aube
1947,Ag 1,21:5
Man About Town 1947,O 22,37:1
Ignace 1950,S 19,39:4
Beauty and the Devil 1952,Ag 26,15:2
Beauties of the Night 1954,Mr 23,23:5
Grand Maneuver, The 1956,O 2,39:1
Girl in the Bikini, The 1958,O 25,16:3
Corell, Matilde
Pecados de Amor 1934,Ap 24,27:2
Rapsodia Mexicana 1938,N 26,18:2
Muerto Murio, El; Dead Man Died, The
1939,Jl 29,18:3
Corelli, Aldo
Tosca 1958,O 24,40:3
Corelli, Franco
Tosca 1958,O 24,40:3
Corelli, Lia
Bitter Rice 1950,S 19,39:2
Corelli, Marie (Original Author)
Sorrows of Satan, The 1926,O 13,21:1
COREY
See Also CORY
Corey, George (Screenwriter)
Mr Winkle Goes to War 1944,Ag 3,16:1
Corey, Isabelle
And God Created Woman 1957,O 22,41:1
Holiday Island; (Vacanzie a Izchia)
1959,S 22,46:1
From a Roman Balcony 1961,O 16,33:5
Last of the Vikings 1962,S 27,33:4
Corey, Jeff
Man Who Wouldn't Die, The 1942,Ap 28,25:5
My Friend Flicka 1943,My 27,21:4
Somewhere in the Night 1946,Je 13,24:2
Killers, The 1946,Ag 29,24:2
Brute Force 1947,Jl 17,16:2
Canon City 1948,Jl 8,19:2
Joan of Arc 1948,N 12,30:5
Wake of the Red Witch 1949,Ja 10,19:2
City Across the River 1949,Ap 8,31:3
Home of the Brave 1949,My 13,29:1
Roughshod 1949,Je 17,27:2
Follow Me Quietly 1949,Jl 8,14:5
Bagdad 1949,D 24,11:4
Nevadan, The 1950,Ja 13,19:4
Outriders, The 1950,Mr 9,25:2
Singing Guns 1950,Je 5,19:3
Rock Island Trail 1950,Je 5,19:3
Bright Leaf 1950,Je 17,7:2
Next Voice You Hear, The 1950,Je 30,18:2
Fourteen Hours 1951,Mr 7,43:2
Rawhide 1951,Mr 26,19:2
Only the Valiant 1951,Ap 14,9:6
Prince Who Was a Thief, The 1951,Jl 4,13:2
Never Trust a Gambler 1951,Jl 20,14:2
Red Mountain 1952,Ap 26,19:2
Balcony, The 1963,Mr 22,7:1
Yellow Canary, The 1963,My 16,42:1
Lady in a Cage 1964,Je 11,27:1
Once a Thief 1965,S 9,36:1
Mickey One 1965,S 9,36:1
Cincinnati Kid, The 1965,O 28,48:1
Seconds 1966,O 6,56:1
In Cold Blood 1967,D 15,60:1
Boston Strangler, The 1968,O 17,52:1
Corey, Jeff (Narrator)
Black Shadows 1949,N 7,33:2
Corey, Jim
Terror Trail 1933,F 11,11:3
Trail of the Lonesome Pine, The 1936,F 20,23:5
Corey, Jonathan
Thelma Jordon 1950,Ja 19,35:2
Corey, Joseph
Gaby 1956,My 10,26:3
Delicate Delinquent, The 1957,Jl 4,16:1
Corey, Milton R Sr
Rawhide 1951,Mr 26,19:2
Corey, Robin
Thelma Jordon 1950,Ja 19,35:2
Corey, Wendell
Desert Fury 1947,S 25,35:4
I Walk Alone 1948,Ja 22,36:3
Man-Eater of Kumaon 1948,Jl 2,24:2
Sorry, Wrong Number 1948,S 2,18:2
Accused, The 1949,Ja 13,26:2
Any Number Can Play 1949,Jl 1,14:4
Holiday Affair 1949,N 24,48:2
Thelma Jordon 1950,Ja 19,35:2
No Sad Songs for Me 1950,Ap 28,26:2
Furies, The 1950,Ag 17,23:2
Harriet Craig 1950,N 3,31:2
Great Missouri Raid, The 1951,Ap 9,31:2
Rich, Young and Pretty 1951,Jl 26,17:3

Corey, Wendell— Cont

Wild Blue Yonder, The 1952,Ja 2,20:1
Carbine Williams 1952,My 8,37:2
Wild North, The 1952,My 12,21:2
My Man and I 1952,S 6,12:6
Hell's Half Acre 1954,F 27,11:3
Laughing Anne 1954,My 8,15:2
Rear Window 1954,Ag 5,18:2
Big Knife, The 1955,N 9,41:2
Killer is Loose, The 1956,Mr 3,17:2
Bold and the Brave, The 1956,My 26,15:2
Rack, The 1956,N 6,30:1
Rainmaker, The 1956,D 13,51:1
Loving You 1957,Jl 18,19:2
Light in the Forest, The 1958,Jl 11,15:2
Alias Jesse James 1959,My 18,31:2
Agent for H.A.R.M 1966,Ja 6,20:2
Picture Mommy Dead 1966,N 3,45:4

Corfield, John (Producer)
Blackout 1940,D 2,19:2
Angel Street 1952,N 11,25:2

Corio, Ann
Swamp Woman 1941,D 27,15:2
Jungle Siren 1942,O 10,11:3
Sarong Girl 1943,Je 18,16:6

Corio, Rafael
Ladies Should Listen 1934,Jl 28,16:6
Farmer in the Dell, The 1936,Mr 7,11:4
His Brother's Wife 1936,Ag 15,6:2
Sophie Lang Goes West 1937,S 30,19:2

Corky
When's Your Birthday? 1937,Mr 19,27:2

Corley, Cynthia
Senator Was Indiscreet, The 1947,D 27,9:2
Mr Peabody and the Mermaid 1948,Ag 14,6:5

Corliss, Allene (Original Author)
I Met my Love Again 1938,Ja 15,19:1

Corliss, Tom
Alice in Wonderland 1931,D 28,22:1

Cormack, Bartlett (Original Author)
This Day and Age 1933,S 1,15:4
Racket, The 1951,D 13,44:2

Cormack, Bartlett (Screenwriter)
Phantom of Crestwood, The 1932,O 17,18:3
Doubting Thomas 1935,Jl 11,24:2
Orchids to You 1935,Ag 10,16:4
Fury 1936,Je 6,21:1
Beachcomber, The 1938,D 26,29:3
Unholy Partners 1941,D 29,21:4

Cormack, Bob (Director)
Make Mine Music 1946,Ap 22,26:2

Cormack, George
Smallest Show on Earth, The 1957,N 23,11:2

Corman, Gene (Producer)
Intruder, The 1962,My 15,48:1
Secret Invasion, The 1964,S 17,52:6
Secret Invasion, The 1964,S 17,52:5
Ski Party 1965,O 23,17:3
Tobruk 1967,F 9,33:2

Corman, Roger (Director)
House of Usher, The 1960,S 15,45:4
Atlas 1961,Ag 10,17:4
Pit and the Pendulum, The 1961,Ag 24,25:3
Intruder, The 1962,My 15,48:1
Premature Burial, The 1962,My 24,29:2
Tales of Terror 1962,Jl 5,21:2 (In Addenda)
Raven, The 1963,Ja 26,5:8
Young Racers, The 1963,O 10,49:3
X - The Man With X-Ray Eyes 1963,O 24,37:1
Haunted Palace, The 1964,Ja 30,24:1
Secret Invasion, The 1964,S 17,52:6
Secret Invasion, The 1964,S 17,52:5
Tomb of Ligeia 1965,My 6,44:1
Wild Angels, The 1966,D 22,40:4
St Valentine's Day Massacre, The 1967,Jl 27,29:2
Trip, The 1967,Ag 24,43:1

Corman, Roger (Original Author)
Highway Dragnet 1954,F 20,8:7

Corman, Roger (Producer)
House of Usher, The 1960,S 15,45:4
Atlas 1961,Ag 10,17:4
Pit and the Pendulum, The 1961,Ag 24,25:3
Intruder, The 1962,My 15,48:1
Premature Burial, The 1962,My 24,29:2
Tales of Terror 1962,Jl 5,21:2 (In Addenda)
Young Racers, The 1963,O 10,49:3
X - The Man With X-Ray Eyes 1963,O 24,37:1
Dementia 13 1963,O 24,37:1
Haunted Palace, The 1964,Ja 30,24:1
Tomb of Ligeia 1965,My 6,44:1
Wild Angels, The 1966,D 22,40:4
St Valentine's Day Massacre, The 1967,Jl 27,29:2
Trip, The 1967,Ag 24,43:1

Cormand, Evelyn
Don Juan 1956,Mr 6,26:2

Cormon, Eugene (Original Author)
Frochard et les Deux Orphelines, La
1934,F 7,16:2

Cornall, Jack (Original Author)
Appointment in Honduras 1953,N 19,41:4

Corncob
Way Down East 1935,O 31,16:2

Cornelius, Henry (Director)
Passport to Pimlico 1949,O 27,35:2
Galloping Major, The 1951,D 17,27:2
Genevieve 1954,F 16,30:2
I Am a Camera 1955,Ag 9,29:1
Next to no Time 1960,My 28,13:2

Cornelius, Henry (Producer)
Genevieve 1954,F 16,30:2

Cornelius, Henry (Screenwriter)
It Always Rains on Sunday 1949,F 14,15:5
Galloping Major, The 1951,D 17,27:2
Next to no Time 1960,My 28,13:2

Cornell, Connie
Unfinished Dance, The 1947,O 31,29:2

Cornell, Dale
Address Unknown 1944,Ap 17,20:1

Cornell, Dolores
Native Land 1942,My 12,16:3

Cornell, Jane
Constant Nymph, The 1934,Ap 7,19:1

Cornell, John (Director)
Hugs and Kisses 1968,Ag 19,44:1

Cornell, John (Screenwriter)
Hugs and Kisses 1968,Ag 19,44:1

Cornell, Jonas (Director)
Puss and Kram 1967,S 25,56:1

Cornell, Katharine
Stage Door Canteen 1943,Je 25,13:2

Cornell, Katharine (Narrator)
Unconquered, The; (Helen Keller in Her Story)
1954,Je 16,37:1

Cornell, Lillian
Buck Benny Rides Again 1940,Ap 25,28:4
Rhythm on the River 1940,Ag 29,23:2
Quarterback, The 1940,O 17,33:3
Night at Earl Carroll's, A 1941,Ja 23,19:1
You're the One 1941,F 20,23:2
Las Vegas Nights 1941,Mr 20,25:2
Gals, Inc 1943,Ag 13,13:4

Cornell, Melva
William Fox Movietone Follies of 1929
1929,My 27,22:1

Cornell, Steve
Courtship of Andy Hardy, The 1942,Ap 10,21:2

Corner, James
Winter Carnival 1939,Jl 28,14:2
What a Life 1939,O 12,33:1

Corner, Sally
Once More, my Darling 1949,S 26,17:1
Two Flags West 1950,O 13,23:2
Man Called Peter, A 1955,Ap 1,22:1

Cornfield, Hubert (Director)
Third Voice, The 1960,Mr 7,24:5
Pressure Point 1962,O 11,49:3

Cornfield, Hubert (Producer)
Third Voice, The 1960,Mr 7,24:5

Cornfield, Hubert (Screenwriter)
Third Voice, The 1960,Mr 7,24:5
Pressure Point 1962,O 11,49:3

Corniglion-Moliner, Edward (Producer)
Hatred 1941,Ja 27,11:2

Cornsweet, Harold (Producer)
Clouds Over Israel 1966,My 10,48:6

Cornthwaite, Robert
Thing, The 1951,My 3,34:4
Something to Live For 1952,Mr 8,11:2
Monkey Business 1952,S 6,12:6
War of the Worlds, The 1953,Ag 14,10:2
Purple Mask, The 1955,Je 16,35:7
Leather Saint, The 1956,Je 16,12:2
Second to Hell 1959,Jl 18,6:3

Cornwall, Anne
Dulcy 1923,S 17,18:2
Roughneck, The 1924,D 3,14:1
Introduce Me 1925,Mr 9,21:1
Rainbow Trail, The 1925,Je 3,26:4
Splendid Crime, The 1925,D 17,27:1
Flaming Frontier, The 1926,Ap 5,24:1
College 1927,S 12,29:1

Corog, Laslo (Original Author)
She Wouldn't Say Yes 1946,Ja 12,10:7

Corona, Isabela
Night of the Mayas 1941,Ja 14,16:7
Passion Island 1943,My 1,11:2
Creo en Dios 1943,Jl 17,8:3

Coroner, Clet (Original Author)
Backfire 1965,Ap 27,27:1

Corps de Ballet
Royal Ballet, The (Ondine); Ondine (The Royal
Ballet) 1960,O 5,45:2

Corra, Bruna
Age of Infidelity 1958,Ag 19,23:2

Corradi, Nelly
Signora di Tutti, La 1936,Mr 26,27:3
Alpine Love 1936,Je 8,22:5
Luci Sommerse 1936,Je 22,22:2
Terra di Nessuno; Nobody's Land 1940,O 25,25:4
Barber of Seville, The 1947,My 6,35:2
Lucia di Lammermoor 1947,N 1,11:3
Lost One, The; La Traviata 1948,Mr 30,26:2
This Wine of Love 1948,Ap 19,27:2
Faust and the Devil 1950,My 1,18:2
Measure for Measure 1951,D 8,9:2

Corradi, Nelly— Cont

Forza del Destino, La 1952,O 17,33:1
Count of St Elmo, The 1953,Mr 14,13:2

Corrado, Gino
Men 1924,My 5,18:3
Desert Flower, The 1925,Je 1,10:3
Boheme, La 1926,F 25,26:2
Amateur Gentleman, The 1926,Ag 17,15:3
White Black Sheep, The 1926,D 21,20:2
Women's Wares 1927,N 15,27:1
Iron Mask, The 1929,F 22,18:6
One Woman Idea, The 1929,Je 10,23:1
Last Parade, The 1931,Mr 2,19:1
Obey the Law 1933,Mr 13,18:3
Top Hat 1935,Ag 30,12:2
Magnificent Obsession 1935,D 31,11:2
Daughter of Shanghai 1937,D 24,21:2
Doctor Rhythm 1938,My 19,25:2
Rose of the Rio Grande 1938,Jl 9,10:3
Two Sisters From Boston 1946,Je 7,16:2

Correll, Charles J
Check and Double Check 1930,N 1,23:1 (In
Addenda)

Correll, Mady
Midnight Madonna 1937,Jl 17,18:1
Invisible Enemy 1938,Ap 30,18:2
Girl, a Guy and a Gob, A 1941,Ap 24,25:3

Correll, Matilde
Senor Alcalde, El; Mayor, The 1939,My 20,11:2

Corri, Adrienne
River, The 1951,S 11,33:2
Little Kidnappers, The 1954,S 2,18:1
Lease of Life 1956,F 10,18:1
Make Me an Offer 1956,F 29,35:2
3 Men in a Boat 1959,Jl 29,33:2
Telltale Heart, The 1963,My 16,42:1
Corridors of Blood 1963,Je 6,39:1
Sword of Lancelot 1963,O 10,49:2
Doctor Zhivago 1965,D 23,21:1
Study in Terror, A 1966,N 3,45:3
Africa-Texas Style! 1967,Jl 13,30:2

Corrigan, D'Arcy
Merry Widow, The 1925,Ag 27,14:1
Napoleon's Barber 1928,N 26,30:2
Last Warning, The 1929,Ja 7,36:2
Man From Blankley's, The 1930,Mr 29,23:1
Murders in the Rue Morgue 1932,F 11,16:1
Informer, The 1935,My 10,25:2
Mary of Scotland 1936,Jl 31,22:2
Christmas Carol, A 1938,D 23,16:2
Great Commandment, The 1942,O 17,11:1

Corrigan, Douglas
Flying Irishman, The 1939,Ap 12,27:2

Corrigan, E
Partners of the Night 1920,Mr 1,16:2

Corrigan, Emmet
Dirigible 1931,Ap 6,24:1

Corrigan, Emmett
Lion and the Mouse, The 1928,Je 16,11:4
Soldiers and Women 1930,My 12,27:3
American Tragedy, An 1931,Ag 6,22:5
Corsair 1931,N 19,27:5
Beast of the City, The 1932,Mr 14,13:3
World and the Flesh, The 1932,My 7,11:5
Night Mayor, The 1932,N 25,19:2
Man Against Woman 1932,D 17,22:3
Silver Dollar 1932,D 23,20:1
Bitter Tea of General Yen, The 1933,Ja 12,20:6

Corrigan, James
Divorce 1923,Je 26,14:2
Slave of Fashion, A 1925,Jl 21,26:2
Auction Block, The 1926,F 15,16:4

Corrigan, Lloyd
Splendid Crime, The 1925,D 17,27:1
Young Tom Edison 1940,Mr 15,27:2
Two Girls on Broadway 1940,Ap 25,28:4
Ghost Breakers, The 1940,Jl 4,12:2
Sporting Blood 1940,Jl 22,20:2
Return of Frank James, The 1940,Ag 10,16:4
Public Deb No 1 1940,S 18,19:2
Captain Caution 1940,O 21,21:3
Dark Streets of Cairo 1940,D 2,19:3
Lady in Question, The 1940,D 10,33:2
Men of Boys Town 1941,Ap 11,24:6
Girl, a Guy and a Gob, A 1941,Ap 24,25:3
Confessions of Boston Blackie 1941,D 8,31:2
Kathleen 1941,D 19,35:3
Bombay Clipper 1942,Ja 12,23:3
Treat 'Em Rough 1942,Ja 19,21:3
North to the Klondike 1942,Mr 12,24:3
Great Man's Lady, The 1942,Ap 30,14:3
Mystery of Marie Roget, The 1942,My 5,17:3
Wife Takes a Flyer, The 1942,Je 19,19:1
Maisie Gets her Man 1942,Jl 16,23:2
Eyes of the Underworld 1942,O 5,15:2
Great Commandment, The 1942,O 17,11:1
Tennessee Johnson 1943,Ja 13,18:2
Lucky Jordan 1943,Ja 25,10:8
Hitler's Children 1943,F 25,27:1
Captive Wild Woman 1943,Je 7,9:4
Stage Door Canteen 1943,Je 25,13:2
Since You Went Away 1944,Jl 21,16:2
Lake Placid Serenade 1944,D 25,15:6
Thin Man Goes Home, The 1945,Ja 26,16:5

Corrigan, Lloyd— Cont

Bring on the Girls 1945,Mr 1,25:5
Crime Doctor's Courage, The 1945,Mr 3,11:3
Fighting Guardsman, The 1945,O 6,9:6
Bandit of Sherwood Forest, The 1946,Mr 23,8:4
She Wolf of London 1946,Ap 6,10:6
Lady Luck 1946,O 31,22:3
Chase, The 1946,N 18,31:2
Two Smart People 1947,F 15,20:4
Blaze of Noon 1947,Mr 5,31:2
Stallion Road 1947,Ap 5,12:5
Adventures of Casanova 1948,Mr 22,18:3
Big Clock, The 1948,Ap 22,34:2
Bride Goes Wild, The 1948,Je 4,27:2
Date with Judy, A 1948,Ag 7,8:2
Girl from Jones Beach, The 1949,Jl 30,9:2
Blondie Hits the Jackpot 1949,S 9,28:3
Dancing in the Dark 1949,D 3,8:6
And Baby Makes Three 1949,D 23,17:3
When Willie Comes Marching Home
 1950,F 18,9:2
My Friend Irma Goes West 1950,Ag 3,20:2
Cyrano De Bergerac 1950,N 17,31:2
Last Outpost, The 1951,Je 22,16:3
Son of Paleface 1952,O 2,32:3
Stars Are Singing, The 1953,Mr 12,24:2
Return From the Sea 1954,Jl 10,7:3
Manchurian Candidate, The 1962,O 25,48:3
It's a Mad, Mad, Mad, Mad World
 1963,N 19,47:1

Corrigan, Lloyd (Director)

Follow Thru 1930,S 13,9:3
Daughter of the Dragon 1931,Ag 22,7:5
Beloved Bachelor, The 1931,O 17,20:1
No One Man 1932,Ja 23,18:4
Broken Wing, The 1932,Mr 26,17:2
Murder on a Honeymoon 1935,Mr 4,12:2
Dancing Pirate 1936,Je 18,19:1
Night Key 1937,Ap 19,27:2
Lady Behave 1938,Ja 28,17:3

Corrigan, Lloyd (Original Author)

What a Night! 1928,D 24,11:1
Campus Confessions 1938,S 23,35:1
Touchdown Army 1938,O 28,27:2

Corrigan, Lloyd (Screenwriter)

Wedding Bills 1927,Je 29,29:3
Swim, Girl, Swim 1927,S 5,13:2
Sweetie 1929,O 26,15:1
Hold 'Em Navy 1937,N 6,14:2
Campus Confessions 1938,S 23,35:1
Touchdown Army 1938,O 28,27:2

Corrigan, Ray

Call the Mesquiteers 1938,Mr 19,11:2
Santa Fe Stampede 1939,Ap 26,27:3
Zamba 1949,N 7,33:2

Corrigan, Tom

You Can't Fool Your Wife 1923,Ap 24,25:3

Corsaro, Franco

Heavenly Body, The 1944,Mr 24,17:3
Dangerous Millions 1947,Mr 15,10:3
Black Magic 1949,N 9,37:2
Pay or Die 1960,My 27,22:2

Corsaro, Frank

Rachel Rachel 1968,Ag 27,36:1

Corseaut, Aneta

Blob, The 1958,N 7,23:1

Corsi, J (Screenwriter)

Ring Around the Clock 1953,My 19,36:2

Corsini, Ignacio

Idolos de la Radio 1935,Jl 2,24:5

Corsini, Silvana

Accattone! 1968,Ap 5,56:1

Corso, Robert

Strangers in the City 1962,Jl 17,19:2

Corson, William

There Goes my Girl 1937,Je 12,8:2
New Faces of 1937 1937,Jl 2,25:1
Super-Sleuth 1937,Jl 18,18:1
Hideaway 1937,S 25,10:2
Stage Door 1937,O 8,27:2
Sky Giant 1938,Jl 20,22:2

Cort, Van (Original Author)

Mail Order Bride 1964,Je 11,27:3

Cortazar, Ernesto

Adios, Nicanor 1938,Mr 14,13:2
Silk, Blood and Sun 1943,Ja 30,10:6

Cortazar, Ernesto (Composer)

Reina del Rio, La; Queen of the River, The
 1940,F 24,9:3
Silk, Blood and Sun 1943,Ja 30,10:6
Tierra de Pasiones 1944,N 7,24:3

Cortazar, Ernesto (Original Author)

Silk, Blood and Sun 1943,Ja 30,10:6
Guadalajara 1943,Je 12,9:3

Cortazar, Ernesto (Producer)

Reina del Rio, La; Queen of the River, The
 1940,F 24,9:3

Cortazar, Ernesto (Screenwriter)

Que Lindo es Michoacan 1944,Ap 22,8:7

Corte, Bianca della

Schoolgirl Diary 1947,O 18,9:2

Cortes, Armand

Palm Beach Girl, The 1926,Je 22,21:2
Music Master, The 1927,Ja 17,12:4 (In Addenda)

Bluebeard's Eighth Wife 1938,Mr 24,21:2

Cortes, Aurora

Suprema Ley; Supreme Law 1938,Ja 15,19:2

Cortes, Fernando

Dona Francisquita 1935,Ap 27,20:6
Incertidumbre 1936,S 21,26:5
Ultima Melodia, La; Last Melody, The
 1939,Ag 5,18:3

Cortes, Mapy

Paraiso Recobrado, El 1936,Ap 27,19:3
Ahora Seremos Felices; Now We Shall Be Happy
 1940,Mr 16,8:2
Seven Days' Leave 1942,D 11,33:2
El Conde de Monte Cristo 1943,N 9,26:2

Cortes, Margarita

Maria Candelaria 1944,S 12,23:7
Miserables, Los 1944,O 24,17:2

Cortes, Mary

Dos Mujeres y un Don Juan 1934,Je 4,12:4

Cortesa, Margarita

Padre Mercader; Merchant Father 1939,Jl 15,8:3
Tierra de Pasiones 1944,N 7,24:3

Cortese, Leonardo

Cavalleria Rusticana 1947,D 20,21:2
Black Magic 1949,N 9,37:2
Verginita 1953,Ap 18,17:2

Cortese, Valentina

Wandering Jew, The 1949,Mr 11,33:2
Thieves' Highway 1949,S 24,8:6
Malaya 1950,F 23,33:1
Glass Mountain, The 1950,My 18,37:3
Bullet for Stefano 1950,O 26,38:7
House on Telegraph Hill, The 1951,My 14,29:1
Women Without Names 1951,Ag 7,22:2
Miserables, Les 1952,Mr 25,23:2
Barefoot Contessa, The 1954,S 30,37:1
Angels of Darkness 1956,N 22,51:1
Ten Commandments, The 1958,Ag 7,26:1
Rocket From Calabuch 1958,O 8,41:1
Barabbas 1962,O 11,49:1
Visit, The 1964,O 22,44:1
Juliet of the Spirits 1965,N 4,57:1
Legend of Lylah Clare, The 1968,Ag 23,33:1

Cortesi, Giulio

Loves of Ricardo, The 1926,Ag 16,10:1

Cortesi, Giulio Mrs

Loves of Ricardo, The 1926,Ag 16,10:1

Cortesina, Elena

Eavesdropper, The 1966,S 15,51:1

Cortez, Armand

Wages of Virtue 1924,N 24,15:3
Crowded Hour, The 1925,Ap 27,15:2
Rubber Heels 1927,Je 28,29:4

Cortez, Bella

Tartars, The 1962,Je 21,26:2

Cortez, Espanita

Amazing Monsieur Fabre, The 1952,S 9,21:2
Girl in the Bikini, The 1958,O 25,16:3
Female, The 1960,Ap 28,29:1

Cortez, Ricardo

Sixty Cents an Hour 1923,My 15,22:1
Children of Jazz 1923,Jl 9,8:4
Call of the Canyon, The 1923,D 17,23:1
Society Scandal, A 1924,Mr 10,18:2
Bedroom Window, The 1924,Je 9,14:3
Feet of Clay 1924,S 22,16:1
City That Never Sleeps, The 1924,S 29,10:1
This Woman 1924,O 21,21:3
Argentine Love 1924,D 23,16:2
Swan, The 1925,Mr 2,14:1
Not so Long Ago 1925,Jl 28,24:4
In the Name of Love 1925,Ag 27,14:1
Pony Express, The 1925,S 14,16:1
Ibanez's Torrent 1926,F 22,14:1
Volcano 1926,My 24,24:3
Sorrows of Satan, The 1926,O 13,21:1
Eagle of the Sea, The 1926,N 17,21:6
New York 1927,Ja 31,13:1
Mockery 1927,Ag 22,21:3
Private Life of Helen of Troy, The
 1927,D 10,14:7
Ladies of the Night Club 1928,Jl 17,15:3
Excess Baggage 1928,S 24,25:1
Younger Generation, The 1929,Mr 11,22:2
Lost Zeppelin, The 1930,F 3,17:1
Montana Moon 1930,Ap 14,24:2
Her Man 1930,O 4,15:2
Illicit 1931,Ja 19,25:1
Ten Cents a Dance 1931,Mr 7,17:2
Behind Office Doors 1931,Mr 21,15:1
Maltese Falcon, The 1931,My 29,26:5
White Shoulders 1931,Je 5,26:5
Big Business Girl 1931,Je 12,27:1
Transgression 1931,Je 15,23:3
Bad Company 1931,N 7,16:5
Reckless Living 1931,D 5,21:2
Men of Chance 1931,D 28,22:1
No One Man 1932,Ja 23,18:4
Symphony of Six Million 1932,Ap 15,23:1
Is my Face red 1932,Je 11,9:3
Thirteen Women 1932,O 15,13:1
Phantom of Crestwood, The 1932,O 17,18:3
Flesh 1932,D 10,19:3

Cortez, Ricardo— Cont

Broadway Bad 1933,Mr 6,16:6
Midnight Mary 1933,Jl 15,14:2
Torch Singer 1933,O 7,18:5
House on 56th Street, The 1933,D 2,9:3
Big Shakedown, The 1934,F 12,19:2
Mandalay 1934,F 15,15:6
Wonder Bar 1934,Mr 1,23:2
Man With two Faces, The 1934,Jl 12,20:2
Hat, Coat and Glove 1934,Jl 27,21:2
Lost Lady, A 1934,O 4,19:1
Firebird, The 1934,N 15,25:2
I am a Thief 1935,Ja 1,24:1
White Cockatoo, The 1935,Ja 16,21:1
Shadow of Doubt 1935,Mr 11,15:1
Special Agent 1935,S 19,28:1
Frisco Kid 1935,N 25,22:1
Murder of Dr Harrigan, The 1936,Ja 21,27:5
Man Hunt 1936,Ja 30,14:2
Walking Dead, The 1936,Mr 2,13:2
Case of the Black Cat, The 1936,D 26,15:4
Her Husband Lies 1937,Mr 18,20:1
Talk of the Devil 1937,My 15,23:5
West of Shanghai 1937,O 29,19:2
City Girl 1938,F 4,17:3
Mr Moto's Last Warning 1939,Ja 27,17:3
Charlie Chan in Reno 1939,My 31,27:2
Romance of the Rio Grande 1940,D 25,33:4
World Premiere 1941,Ag 21,15:2
Who Is Hope Schuyler 1942,My 22,27:1
Make Your own Bed 1944,My 27,12:2
Locket, The 1947,Mr 20,38:2
Blackmail 1947,Ag 5,26:3
Last Hurrah, The 1958,O 24,40:1

Cortez, Ricardo (Director)

Escape, The 1939,N 3,17:4
City of Chance 1940,Ja 22,11:3
Free, Blonde and 21 1940,Ap 5,25:2
Girl in 313 1940,Je 14,25:3

Corthell, Herbert

Second Youth 1924,Ap 22,19:3
Classmates 1924,D 30,15:3
Saturday's Millions 1933,O 14,18:3
Let's Talk It Over 1934,Je 16,20:2
Story of Louis Pasteur, The 1936,F 10,15:1
Dancing Feet 1936,Mr 28,11:2
Man in Blue, The 1937,Ag 30,25:2
Renfrew of the Royal Mounted 1937,N 3,29:4

Cortini, Generoso

Marriage Italian Style 1964,D 21,42:1

Cortman, Bob

Trail of the Lonesome Pine, The 1936,F 20,23:5

Corvelatti, Pietro

Grido, Il 1962,O 23,42:1

Corwin, Norman (Narrator)

People's Avengers 1944,Je 15,16:3

Corwin, Norman (Original Author)

Forever and a Day 1943,Mr 13,9:2
Once Upon a Time 1944,Je 30,17:2

Corwin, Norman (Screenwriter)

Blue Veil, The 1951,O 27,10:5
Lust for Life 1956,S 18,39:1
Naked Maja, The 1959,Je 11,36:2
Story of Ruth, The 1960,Je 18,12:3
Madison Avenue 1962,Mr 29,28:2

CORY

See Also COREY

Cory, Desmond (Original Author)

Deadfall 1968,S 12,54:1

Cory, John

Return of Monte Cristo, The 1947,Ja 3,16:4

Cosart, Ernest

Top of the Town 1937,Mr 27,19:2

Cosbey, Jackie

Carolina 1934,F 16,17:2

Cosbey, Ronald

Man From Yesterday, The 1932,Je 25,18:2
Broadway Bad 1933,Mr 6,16:6
Sutter's Gold 1936,Mr 27,25:2

Cosbey, Ronnie

East Lynne 1931,F 21,15:2
Iron Master, The 1933,F 4,11:3
King of the Jungle 1933,F 25,20:3
Carolina 1934,F 16,17:2
Now I'll Tell 1934,My 26,12:2
Circus Clown, The 1934,Je 30,18:6
Housewife 1934,Ag 10,21:2
West Point of the Air 1935,Ap 6,10:1
Oil for the Lamps of China 1935,Je 6,25:2
Next Time We Love 1936,Ja 31,16:2
Birth of the Blues 1941,D 11,39:1

Cosby, Vivian (Original Author)

Mind Reader, The 1933,Ap 7,22:4
Trick for Trick 1933,Je 10,16:4

Cosci, Elio

Richiamo del Cuore, Il; Appeal of the Heart, The
 1931,Mr 2,19:1

Cosgrave, Jack

Percy 1925,Mr 25,24:2

Cosgrave, Luke

Light That Failed, The 1923,N 27,11:2
Flaming Barriers 1924,Ja 29,16:1
Merton of the Movies 1924,S 8,15:3
Contraband 1925,Mr 24,20:6

Cosgrave, Luke— Cont

Welcome Home 1925,My 18,12:1
Gentlemen Prefer Blondes 1928,Ja 16,24:1
Mating Call, The 1928,O 8,14:2
Red Mark, The 1928,O 30,27:3
Lightnin' 1930,N 29,21:4
Squaw Man, The 1931,S 19,10:2
Sinners in the Sun 1932,My 14,11:5
Comin' Round the Mountain 1940,S 26,27:3

Cosgriff, Robert James (Original Author)

Roaring Timber 1937,Ag 19,23:1
Naval Academy 1941,Je 5,27:3

Cosgriff, Robert James (Screenwriter)

Roaring Timber 1937,Ag 19,23:1

Cosgrove, Douglas

Hush Money 1931,Jl 11,7:6
She Wanted a Millionaire 1932,F 20,11:2
Too Busy to Work 1932,D 3,21:4
Man Who Dared, The 1933,S 9,9:3
Lady Killer 1934,Ja 1,28:2
Fog over Frisco 1934,Je 7,26:2
Dancing Man 1934,Jl 16,11:3

Cosgrove, Jack (Miscellaneous)

Gone With the Wind 1939,D 20,31:2

Cosima, Renee

Strange Ones, The 1952,Jl 29,17:3

Cosini, Nelo (Director)

Escuadron Azul, El; Blue Squadron, The
1938,Je 4,18:3

Coslow, Sam (Composer)

College Humor 1933,Je 23,15:4
Too Much Harmony 1933,S 23,11:5
Many Happy Returns 1934,Je 9,18:2
You Belong to Me 1934,S 13,26:1
Belle of the Nineties 1934,S 22,12:2
Limehouse Blues 1934,D 12,28:2
Gilded Lily, The 1935,F 9,11:2
Ruggles of Red Gap 1935,Mr 7,26:1
All the King's Horses 1935,Mr 9,19:1
Hands Across the Table 1935,N 2,13:2
Millions in the Air 1935,D 12,33:4
Coronado 1935,D 19,33:4
It's Love Again 1936,My 23,12:1
Champagne Waltz 1937,F 4,17:2
Swing High, Swing Low 1937,Ap 15,19:1
Turn off the Moon 1937,My 20,17:2
Mountain Music 1937,Je 24,30:3
Double or Nothing 1937,S 2,17:3
Thrill of a Lifetime 1937,D 9,30:2
Alligator Named Daisy, An 1957,O 7,23:2

Coslow, Sam (Miscellaneous)

Eight Girls in a Boat 1934,Ja 13,16:3

Coslow, Sam (Original Author)

Out of This World 1945,Je 7,25:2

Coslow, Sam (Producer)

Copacabana 1947,Jl 12,7:2

Cosme, Eusebia

Pawnbroker, The 1965,Ap 21,51:1

Cosne, Francis (Miscellaneous)

Tales of Paris (The Tale of Sophie); Tale of Sophie,
The (Tales of Paris) 1962,Ag 27,18:1
Tales of Paris (The Tale of Francoise); Tale of
Francoise, The (Tales of Paris) 1962,Ag 27,18:1

Cosne, Francis (Producer)

Storm Within, The; (Parents Terribles, Les)
1950,Ap 24,21:2
Sins of the Borgias 1956,Mr 5,21:1
Parisienne, La 1958,Jl 31,27:1
Love on a Pillow 1963,D 17,49:1

Cosne, Francis (Screenwriter)

Tales of Paris (The Tale of Antonio); Tale of
Antonio, The (Tales of Paris) 1962,Ag 27,18:1

Coss, Joaquin

Obre las Olas 1934,Mr 17,11:4
Sobre Las Olas 1934,Mr 17,11:4
Tiburon 1934,Ap 18,23:3
Pecados de Amor 1934,Ap 24,27:2
Prisionero 13, El 1934,Ap 30,11:4
Que Hago con la Criatura? 1936,Mr 17,25:6
Desheredados, Los 1936,Mr 23,22:6
Newspaper Boys, The 1937,N 6,14:3
Rapsodia Mexicana 1938,N 26,18:2
Ojos Tapatios 1939,F 13,13:3
Su Gran Aventura; His Great Adventure
1939,Ap 3,11:6
Odio; Hate 1940,Ap 6,13:2
Vivire Otra Vez; I Shall Live Again
1940,O 23,27:2

Cossa, Enzo (Producer)

Hell Raiders of the Deep 1954,Jl 3,9:2

Cossar, John

Hunchback of Notre Dame, The 1923,S 3,9:3

Cossart, Ernest

Scoundrel, The 1935,My 3,23:2
Accent on Youth 1935,Ag 12,10:3
Two for Tonight 1935,Ag 31,16:2
Great Ziegfeld, The 1936,Ap 9,21:2
Desire 1936,Ap 13,15:1
My American Wife 1936,Ag 21,12:3
Murder With Pictures 1936,N 21,21:4
Three Smart Girls 1937,Ja 25,22:2
Champagne Waltz 1937,F 4,17:2
As Good as Married 1937,My 22,19:2
Angel 1937,N 4,29:1

Letter of Introduction 1938,S 1,17:1
Zaza 1939,Ja 5,17:1
Never Say Die 1939,Mr 9,18:1
Three Smart Girls Grow Up 1939,Mr 18,9:2
Magnificent Fraud, The 1939,Jl 20,16:2
Lady of the Tropics 1939,S 8,28:3
Tower of London 1939,D 12,37:2
Light That Failed, The 1939,D 25,19:1
Tom Brown's School Days 1940,Je 28,22:2
Bill of Divorcement, A 1940,Jl 12,11:2
Kitty Foyle 1941,Ja 9,27:2
Charley's Aunt 1941,Ag 2,18:2
One Foot in Heaven 1941,N 14,28:3
Skylark 1941,N 20,39:2
Kings Row 1942,F 3,23:2
Knickerbocker Holiday 1944,Ap 20,22:7
Tonight and Every Night 1945,Mr 9,16:2
Love Letters 1945,Ag 27,22:3
Cluny Brown 1946,Je 3,27:3
Jolson Story, The 1946,O 11,28:2
Love From a Stranger 1947,N 28,30:1
John Loves Mary 1949,F 5,11:2

Cossery, Albert (Screenwriter)

Marriage Came Tumbling Down, The
1968,N 6,32:3

Cossini

Maternite 1937,Je 8,30:2

Cossins, James

How I Won the War 1967,N 9,56:1
Anniversary, The 1968,Mr 21,57:2

Cosslett, Frances

Life at the Top 1965,D 15,53:1

Cossu, Michele

Bandits of Orgosolo 1964,Ap 14,32:1

Cossy, Hans

Great British Train Robbery, The 1967,Ap 6,45:2

Costa, B (Screenwriter)

Ring Around the Clock 1953,My 19,36:2

Costa, Mario (Director)

Barber of Seville, The 1947,My 6,35:2
This Wine of Love 1948,Ap 19,27:2
Mad About Opera 1950,Ap 6,33:2
Love of a Clown (Pagliacci) 1950,Ap 17,18:5
Queen of the Pirates 1961,Jl 27,23:4

Costa, Mario (Miscellaneous)

This Wine of Love 1948,Ap 19,27:2

Costa, Mario (Screenwriter)

This Wine of Love 1948,Ap 19,27:2
Mad About Opera 1950,Ap 6,33:2

Costa, Mary

Big Caper, The 1957,Mr 29,16:1

Costa, Miss

Jeanne Dore 1928,Ja 2,28:3 (In Addenda)

Costa, Philip

Pagan Love Song 1950,D 26,19:1

Costa, Romolo

Loyalty of Love 1937,Mr 1,15:1
Avventura di Giacomo Casanova 1938,D 2,27:3

Costa, Sam

Pickwick Papers, The 1954,Ap 5,21:2

Costain, Thomas B (Original Author)

Black Rose, The 1950,S 2,11:2
Silver Chalice, The 1954,D 27,22:5

Coste, Pierre

Passion for Life 1951,D 21,21:4

Costello, Anthony

Blue 1968,My 11,28:1

Costello, Delmar

Four Frightened People 1934,Ja 27,9:2

Costello, Diosa

Bullfighters, The 1945,My 12,10:3
Miss Sadie Thompson 1953,D 24,9:1

Costello, Dolores

Lawful Larceny 1923,Jl 24,14:3 (In Addenda)
Mannequinn 1926,Ja 12,27:5
Sea Hunt, The 1926,Ja 16,8:5
Sea Beast, The 1926,Ja 16,8:5
Bride of the Storm 1926,Ap 5,24:1
Little Irish Girl, The 1926,My 11,24:3
When a Man Loves 1927,F 4,16:6
Third Degree, The 1927,F 15,23:1
Million Bid, A 1927,My 31,25:2
Old San Francisco 1927,Je 23,23:3
College Widow, The 1927,N 7,26:4
Tenderloin 1928,Mr 15,28:3
Glorious Betsy 1928,Ap 27,16:4
Redeeming Sin, The 1929,F 16,14:6
Noah's Ark 1929,Mr 13,28:6
Glad Rag Doll, The 1929,Je 3,27:2
Madonna of Avenue A 1929,Ag 12,22:2
Show of Shows 1929,N 21,24:5
Hearts in Exile 1929,N 29,25:1
Second Choice 1930,Ja 4,21:1
Expensive Women 1931,N 14,15:3
Beloved Brat 1938,My 2,13:2
Breaking the Ice 1938,S 23,35:3
King of the Turf 1939,My 8,21:2
Magnificent Ambersons, The 1942,Ag 14,13:3
This Is the Army 1943,Jl 29,11:6

Costello, Don

Another Thin Man 1939,N 24,29:1
Joe and Ethel Turp Call on the President
1940,Ja 4,19:2

Costello, Don— Cont

One Crowded Night 1940,Ag 27,17:2
Sleepers West 1941,Mr 20,25:3
Ride on Vaquero 1941,Ap 19,20:2
I'll Wait for You 1941,Je 2,13:6
Here Comes Mr Jordan 1941,Ag 8,13:2
Whistling in the Dark 1941,Ag 28,23:2
Unholy Partners 1941,D 29,21:4
Johnny Eager 1942,F 20,21:2
Joe Smith, American 1942,Ap 2,27:4
A-Haunting We Will Go 1942,Ag 3,18:4
Just off Broadway 1942,Ag 29,18:4
Night to Remember, A 1943,Ja 1,27:2
Truck Busters 1943,Ja 29,23:5
Air Raid Wardens 1943,Ap 5,15:5
Crime Doctor 1943,Jl 5,11:4
Lady Takes a Chance, A 1943,S 16,25:2
Whistler, The 1944,Ap 29,12:2
Blue Dahlia, The 1946,My 9,27:3

Costello, Grace

Johnny Doughboy 1943,My 6,25:3

Costello, Helene

Man on the Box, The 1925,S 28,24:1
Bobbed Hair 1925,N 4,17:4
Wet Paint 1926,My 17,19:1
Don Juan 1926,Ag 7,6:1 (In Addenda)
Good Time Charley 1927,N 21,20:1
In old Kentucky 1927,N 21,20:1
Fortune Hunter, The 1928,Ja 10,28:4
Lights of New York 1928,Jl 9,25:1
Midnight Taxi, The 1928,O 29,29:1
Circus Kid, The 1928,D 17,23:1
Show of Shows 1929,N 21,24:5

Costello, John

Top o' the Morning 1949,S 1,25:2
Virgin Queen, The 1955,Ag 6,13:2

Costello, Lou

One Night in the Tropics 1940,D 20,33:2
Buck Privates 1941,F 14,15:2
In the Navy 1941,Je 12,29:2
Hold That Ghost 1941,Ag 8,13:3
Keep 'Em Flying 1941,N 27,29:2
Ride 'Em Cowboy 1942,Mr 5,27:3
Rio Rita 1942,My 8,27:3
Pardon my Sarong 1942,Ag 27,15:1
Who Done It 1942,D 3,35:2
It Ain't Hay 1943,My 11,17:3
Hit the Ice 1943,S 23,27:2
In Society 1944,Ag 17,20:2
Lost in a Harem 1944,N 9,23:2
Here Come the Co-Eds 1945,F 19,21:1
Naughty Nineties, The 1945,Je 21,16:2
Abbott and Costello in Hollywood
1945,N 23,26:2
Little Giant 1946,My 9,27:5
Time of Their Lives, The 1946,N 28,40:2
Buck Privates Come Home 1947,Ap 12,11:3
Wistful Widow of Wagon Gap, The
1947,N 21,36:2
Noose Hangs High, The 1948,My 29,8:6
Abbott and Costello Meet Frankenstein
1948,Jl 29,17:2
Mexican Hayride 1949,Ja 12,33:3
Africa Screams 1949,My 5,34:2
Abbott and Costello Meet the Killer Boris Karloff
1949,S 19,18:3
Abbott and Costello in the Foreign Legion
1950,Ag 14,14:4
Abbott and Costello Meet the Invisible Man
1951,Ap 13,18:6
Comin' Round the Mountain 1951,Jl 27,15:2
Jack and the Beanstalk 1952,Ap 8,35:3
Dance With Me Henry 1956,D 24,8:2

Costello, Maurice

Glimpses of the Moon 1923,Ap 3,23:4
Fog Bound 1923,My 29,10:3
Let Not Man Put Asunder 1924,Ja 15,16:1
Virtuous Liars 1924,Mr 31,20:1
Story Without a Name, The 1924,O 6,25:1
Camille 1927,Ap 22,19:1
Hollywood Boulevard 1936,S 21,26:4
Little Bit of Heaven, A 1940,N 8,24:2
Lady From Louisiana 1941,My 15,27:2

Costello, Pat

Mexican Hayride 1949,Ja 12,33:3

Costello, Tom

Man of the World 1931,Mr 21,15:1

Costello, Ward

Gallant Hours, The 1960,Je 23,19:4

Costello, William

Port of Missing Girls, The 1938,Ap 4,12:5
Wanted by the Police 1938,S 26,13:2
Balalaika 1939,D 15,33:2

COSTER

See Also KOSTER

Coster, Charles de (Original Author)

Hochzeitstreise, Die; Wedding Journey, The
1939,My 13,11:5

Coster, Henry (Director)

Story of Ruth, The 1960,Je 18,12:3

Coster, Nicholas

My Blood Runs Cold 1965,Mr 25,42:4

Costes, Mary
Nuit est a Nous, La; (Night is Ours, The) 1931,F 21,15:2
Costillo, Carmen
Loves of Carmen 1927,S 27,31:1
Costl, Maria
Barefoot Battalion 1954,My 29,13:4
Costo, Putro
Regina di Sparta, La 1931,F 23,20:3
Cota, David
Voice in the Wind 1944,Mr 16,17:2
Two Smart People 1947,F 15,20:4
Cotes, Peter
Pastor Hall 1940,S 21,13:2
Cotet, Jean (Director)
Beau Serge, Le 1959,Ag 3,21:1
Cotler, Gordon (Original Author)
Horizontal Lieutenant, The 1962,My 12,15:3
Arabesque 1966,My 6,54:1
Cotlow, Lewis (Director)
Primitive Paradise 1961,My 27,12:1
Cotlow, Lewis (Miscellaneous)
Savage Splendor 1949,N 4,37:2
Cotlow, Lewis (Producer)
Zanzabuku 1956,Ag 16,30:3
Primitive Paradise 1961,My 27,12:1
Cotsworth, Staats
Peyton Place 1957,D 13,35:1
Cott, Jonathan
Night Into Morning 1951,Je 11,20:7
Lone Star 1952,F 2,11:4
Scaramouche 1952,My 9,20:2
Clown, The 1953,Ja 29,25:1
Above and Beyond 1953,Ja 31,10:6
Battle Circus 1953,My 28,27:5
Dream Wife 1953,Jl 30,20:1
All the Brothers Were Valiant 1953,D 29,19:2
Cottafari, Vittorio (Director)
Warrior and the Slave, The 1960,Mr 10,36:2
Cottafavi, Vittorio (Director)
Goliath and the Dragon 1961,Ja 5,27:2
Legions of the Nile 1961,Mr 4,16:1
Cotten, Joseph
Citizen Kane 1941,My 2,25:1
Lydia 1941,S 19,27:1
Magnificent Ambersons, The 1942,Ag 14,13:3
Shadow of a Doubt 1943,Ja 13,18:2
Journey Into Fear 1943,Mr 19,15:3
Hers to Hold 1943,Jl 22,15:1
Gaslight 1944,My 5,17:2
Since You Went Away 1944,Jl 21,16:2
I'll Be Seeing You 1945,Ap 6,20:6
Love Letters 1945,Ag 27,22:3
Farmer's Daughter, The 1947,Mr 26,31:2
Duel in the Sun 1947,My 8,30:2
Duel in the Sun 1947,My 8,30:2
Portrait of Jennie 1949,Mr 30,31:2
Under Capricorn 1949,S 9,28:3
Beyond the Forest 1949,O 22,11:2
Third Man, The 1950,F 3,29:2
Two Flags West 1950,O 13,23:2
Walk Softly Stranger 1950,O 16,30:5
September Affair 1951,F 2,19:2
Half Angel 1951,Je 16,9:2
Peking Express 1951,Jl 19,20:2
Man With a Cloak, The 1951,N 28,37:2
Untamed Frontier 1952,Ag 23,10:2
Steel Trap, The 1952,N 13,35:2
Niagara 1953,Ja 22,20:3
Blueprint for Murder, A 1953,Jl 25,8:2
Bottom of the Bottle, The 1956,F 2,19:2
Killer is Loose, The 1956,Mr 3,17:2
From the Earth to the Moon 1958,N 27,52:2
Angel Wore Red, The 1960,S 29,32:1
Last Sunset, The 1961,Je 15,51:1
Hush...Hush, Sweet Charlotte 1965,Mr 4,36:1
Oscar, The 1966,Mr 5,16:1
Money Trap, The 1966,My 5,59:1
Tramplers, The 1966,D 8,64:1
Jack of Diamonds 1967,N 11,26:3
Petulia 1968,Je 11,54:4
Cotten, Joseph (Screenwriter)
Journey Into Fear 1943,Mr 19,15:3
Cotton, Billy
Old Nest, The 1921,Je 29,10:3
Cotton, Carolina
World Dances 1954,N 8,24:6
Cotton, Diana
Little Friend 1934,O 20,20:2
Cotton, Larry
Pot o'Gold 1941,Ap 4,25:2
Cotton, Lucy
Devil, The 1921,Ja 17,9:1
Cottrell, Dorothy (Original Author)
Wild Innocence 1938,N 11,31:2
Cottrell, William
Man on the Eiffel Tower, The 1950,Ja 30,12:2
Strange Door, The 1951,D 10,34:6
Julius Caesar 1953,Je 5,19:1
Three Caballeros, The 1945,F 5,20:1
Cottrell, William (Screenwriter)
Pinocchio 1940,F 8,18:3
Reluctant Dragon, The 1941,Jl 25,12:2

Victory Through Air Power 1943,Jl 19,13:1
Cotts, Campbell
Dear Mr Prohack 1950,Jl 15,7:2
Last Holiday 1950,N 14,39:4
Encore (The Ant and the Grasshopper); Ant and the Grasshopper, The (Encore) 1952,Ap 3,45:1
3 Men in a Boat 1959,Jl 29,33:2
Couch, Robert
Hallelujah 1929,Ag 21,33:1
Couchy, Daniel
I Spit on Your Grave 1963,Je 29,13:5
Couderc, Pierre (Original Author)
Captain Thunder 1931,My 11,15:4
Couffer, Jack (Director)
Nikki, Wild Dog of the North 1961,S 5,37:6
Couffer, Jack C (Cinematographer)
Living Desert, The 1953,N 10,38:1
Coughlan, Eileen
Dark Waters 1944,N 22,25:2
Coughlan, Gene
Unidentified Flying Objects 1956,Je 13,46:2
Coughlin, Kevin
Storm Center 1956,O 22,25:4
Defiant Ones, The 1958,S 25,29:1
Happy Anniversary 1959,N 11,41:1
Wild in the Streets 1968,My 30,21:1
Young Runaways, The 1968,S 12,54:3
Coulan, Francis X
Bought and Paid For 1916,N 9,11:4
Coulcouris, George
Outcast of the Islands 1952,My 16,19:2
Coulouris, George
Christopher Bean 1933,N 25,10:2
All This and Heaven, Too 1940,Jl 5,10:2
Lady in Question, The 1940,D 10,33:2
Citizen Kane 1941,My 2,25:1
Assignment in Brittany 1943,Ap 22,31:2
This Land Is Mine 1943,My 28,19:1
For Whom the Bell Tolls 1943,Jl 15,25:2
Watch on the Rhine 1943,Ag 28,15:1
Between Two Worlds 1944,My 6,11:2
Mr Skeffington 1944,My 26,23:2
Master Race, The 1944,N 2,22:1
None but the Lonely Heart 1944,N 18,16:6
None but the Lonely Heart 1944,D 3,II,1:8
Song to Remember, A 1945,Ja 26,16:4
Hotel Berlin 1945,Mr 3,11:2
Lady on a Train 1945,S 15,21:2
Confidential Agent 1945,N 3,11:2
Nobody Lives Forever 1946,N 2,12:2
Verdict, The 1946,D 13,29:4
California 1947,Ja 15,31:2
Mr District Attorney 1947,F 28,27:3
Where There's Life 1947,D 25,32:1
Sleep, My Love 1948,F 19,29:4
Beyond Glory 1948,Ag 4,18:2
Joan of Arc 1948,N 12,30:5
Southern Yankee, A 1948,N 25,47:2
Island Rescue 1952,Jl 1,19:4
Assassin, The 1953,Ap 18,17:2
Duel in the Jungle 1954,Ag 9,13:2
Runaway Bus, The 1954,O 25,30:7
Heart of the Matter, The 1954,N 19,20:2
Doctor in the House 1955,F 19,18:3
Doctor at Sea 1956,Mr 1,37:3
Tarzan and the Lost Safari 1957,Ap 13,12:3
Doctor at Large 1957,Jl 29,15:5
I Accuse! 1958,Mr 6,32:1
Law and Disorder 1958,Ag 6,20:1
Conspiracy of Hearts 1960,Ap 8,24:1
Surprise Package 1960,O 15,26:2
Bluebeard's Ten Honeymoons 1960,N 8,32:6
Boy Who Stole a Million, The 1960,D 22,18:3
Crooked Road, The 1965,F 4,24:2
Arabesque 1966,My 6,54:1
Coulson, Frank
Never Take No for an Answer 1952,Ap 29,32:2
Coulson, Roy
Scaramouche 1923,O 12,7:2 (Incorrect in this edition; use 1927,O 1,7:2 elsewhere)
Don Q, Son of Zorro 1925,Je 16,24:1
Temptress, The 1926,O 11,18:1
Flaming Forest, The 1926,N 22,28:3
Coulter, Frazier
Heart Raider, The 1923,Je 6,24:5
Prince of Tempters, The 1926,O 18,18:1
Council, Elizabeth
I Passed for White 1960,Ag 18,19:3
Counsell, John
Return of the Scarlet Pimpernel, The 1938,Ap 11,12:2
Counselman, William N (Screenwriter)
Paid to Love 1927,Jl 25,25:3
Couper, Barbara
Dolwyn 1949,Ag 30,18:4
Happy Go Lovely 1951,Jl 26,17:2
Coupland, Diana
Millionairess, The 1961,F 10,19:1
Family Way, The 1967,Je 29,32:1
Courant, Kurt (Cinematographer)
Three Loves 1929,S 9,30:2

Courau, Madeleine (Screenwriter)
Your Shadow Is Mine 1963,My 15,32:1
Courau, Pierre (Producer)
Your Shadow Is Mine 1963,My 15,32:1
Courcel, Nicole
Marie du Port 1951,Jl 24,21:2
Mama, Papa, the Maid and I 1956,Ag 28,31:1
Sorciere, La 1956,D 28,17:2
Case of Dr Laurent, The 1958,Je 26,23:2
Tomorrow Is my Turn 1962,F 2,24:2
Sundays and Cybele 1962,N 13,43:3
Stop Train 349 1964,N 12,40:2
Court, Hazel
Holiday Camp 1948,Ja 24,11:2
Dear Murderer 1948,My 8,12:2
Meet Me at Dawn 1948,My 18,26:2
Showtime 1948,My 20,35:3
Bond Street 1950,Mr 30,40:6
Curse of Frankenstein, The 1957,Ag 8,15:5
Premature Burial, The 1962,My 24,29:2
Raven, The 1963,Ja 26,5:8
Masque of the Red Death, The 1964,S 17,52:6
Court, John (Producer)
Don't Look Back 1967,S 7,50:2
Courtal, Suzanne
Forbidden Games 1952,D 9,43:2
Courtenay, Margaret
Touch and go 1956,Mr 20,13:2
Courtenay, Tom
Loneliness of the Long Distance Runner, The 1962,O 9,44:1
King and Country 1964,S 24,46:2
Operation Crossbow 1965,Ap 2,29:1
King Rat 1965,O 28,48:1
Doctor Zhivago 1965,D 23,21:1
King and Country 1966,Ja 28,20:4
Night of the Generals, The 1967,F 3,38:1
Day the Fish Came Out, The 1967,O 3,57:1
Dandy in Aspic, A 1968,Ap 3,40:1
Courtenay, William
Evidence 1929,O 5,22:5
Show of Shows 1929,N 21,24:5
Sacred Flame, The 1929,N 23,18:5
Three Faces East 1930,S 6,9:2
Way of all Men, The 1930,S 20,15:4
Courtin, Jacques
Private Life of an Actor; En Scene 1948,S 7,21:3
Courtland, Jerome
Together Again 1944,N 24,19:2
Kiss and Tell 1945,O 26,16:2
Man From Colorado 1949,Ja 21,24:3
Tokyo Joe 1949,O 27,35:2
Battleground 1949,N 12,8:4
Woman of Distinction, A 1950,Mr 17,28:2
Santa Fe 1951,My 4,31:2
Texas Rangers, The 1951,Jl 14,7:2
Take the High Ground 1953,N 20,19:2
Tonka 1959,Mr 26,27:1
Black Spurs 1965,My 29,17:1
Courtleigh, Stephen
Yellowback 1957,Ap 5,24:2
Courtleigh, William
Eyes of Youth 1919,D 1,9:3
Madame X 1920,S 27,18:1
Courtneidge, Cicely
Ghost Train, The 1933,F 18,13:3
Night and Day 1933,My 29,22:2
Woman in Command, The 1934,My 29,22:2
Along Came Sally 1934,Je 16,20:3
Perfect Gentleman, The 1935,D 19,33:4
L-Shaped Room, The 1963,My 28,32:1
Wrong Box 1966,Jl 20,46:1
Courtney, Bob
Summer Love 1958,Je 26,23:4
After You, Comrade 1967,Ap 11,54:1
Courtney, Chuck
Long Gray Line, The 1955,F 11,19:2
Courtney, Daphne
They Are not Angels 1948,My 22,8:3
Courtney, Inez
Song of the Flame 1930,My 7,24:5
Not Damaged 1930,Je 9,23:3
Sunny 1930,D 27,16:3
Bright Lights 1931,F 10,24:4
Hot Heiress, The 1931,Mr 14,23:2
Big City Blues 1932,S 10,18:5
Cheating Blondes 1933,My 20,11:4
Broadway Bill 1934,N 30,22:2
Break of Hearts 1935,My 17,24:3
Raven, The 1935,Jl 5,9:2
Girl Friend, The 1935,S 28,12:2
Millions in the Air 1935,D 12,33:4
Magnificent Obsession 1935,D 31,11:2
Let's Sing Again 1936,My 9,11:2
Suzy 1936,Jl 25,16:1
Wedding Present 1936,N 19,31:3
Hit Parade, The 1937,My 31,11:2
Armored Car 1937,Jl 26,15:2
Hurricane, The 1937,N 10,31:2
Thirteenth Man, The 1938,Ja 1,11:2
Having Wonderful Time 1938,Jl 8,11:2
Shop Around the Corner, The 1940,Ja 26,13:2

Courtney, Inez— Cont
Crime Ring 1938,Jl 22,10:3
Five of a Kind 1938,O 31,12:2
Beauty for the Asking 1939,F 10,19:1
Blondie Meets the Boss 1939,Ap 27,31:1
Missing Evidence 1939,N 17,17:3
Farmer's Daughter, The 1940,F 16,23:4
Turnabout 1940,Jl 27,17:6

Courtney, Tom
Billy Liar 1963,D 17,49:1

Courtot, Marguerite
Unbeliever, The 1918,F 12,9:2
Cradle Buster, The 1922,My 22,18:4
Down to the Sea in Ships 1923,F 19,10:1
Steadfast Heart, The 1923,D 25,26:1

Courtright, Jennie Lee
Bill Henry 1919,Ag 18,9:2

Courtwright, William
Peaceful Valley 1920,O 11,19:3
Girl I Loved, The 1923,My 14,18:2
Man of Action, A 1923,Je 4,13:3
Are Parents People 1925,Je 9,16:3
Trouble With Wives, The 1925,Ag 5,12:4
Thank You 1925,O 6,30:1
Grand Duchess and the Waiter, The
    1926,F 9,22:1
Two-Gun Man, The 1926,Jl 13,19:3
For Wives Only 1926,D 1,24:5
Jesse James 1927,O 17,20:2

Courvitch, Rolla
Life of Emile Zola, The 1937,Ag 12,14:2

Cousins, Margaret (Original Author)
Lucy Gallant 1955,O 21,30:1

Coussoneau, Maurice
Naked Childhood 1968,S 28,36:1

Cousteau, Jacques-Yves
World Without Sun 1964,D 23,22:1

Cousteau, Jacques-Yves (Director)
World Without Sun 1964,D 23,22:1

Cousteau, Jacques-Yves (Miscellaneous)
Silent World, The 1956,S 25,30:1
World Without Sun 1964,D 23,22:1

Cousteau, Jacques-Yves (Narrator)
Silent World, The 1956,S 25,30:1

Cousteau, Jacques-Yves Mrs
World Without Sun 1964,D 23,22:1

Coutard, Raoul (Cinematographer)
Married Woman, The; Femme Mariee, La
    1965,Ag 17,39:1

Couteaux, Andre (Original Author)
Male Companion 1966,F 15,33:2

Coutts, John E (Producer)
Sawing a Lady in Half 1922,My 15,20:3

Coutu, Jean
Nikki, Wild Dog of the North 1961,S 5,37:6

Couzy, Jean (Miscellaneous)
Annapurna 1953,D 14,45:4

Cova, Amelia
Force of Arms 1951,Ag 14,20:2

Cover, Franklin B
Mirage 1965,My 27,28:1

Covey, Annabelle
Belles of St Trinian's, The 1954,D 23,13:4

Covington, Bruce
Fighting Coward, The 1924,Mr 17,19:1
Love's Wilderness 1924,D 22,20:2
Wife of the Centaur, The 1925,Ja 7,33:5
Phantom of the Opera, The 1925,S 7,15:3
On the Border 1930,F 3,17:1
Under a Texas Moon 1930,Ap 4,22:1
Dixiana 1930,S 5,21:1
Mississippi 1935,Ap 18,27:2

Covington, Z Wall
To the Ladies 1923,N 26,15:6
Goose Hangs High, The 1925,Mr 10,19:3

Covington, Z Wall (Screenwriter)
Faith Healer, The 1921,Mr 14,9:2

Cow, Peter
Secret Invasion, The 1964,S 17,52:5

COWAN
See Also COWEN

Cowan, Ashley
Mutiny on the Bounty 1962,N 9,31:2

Cowan, Douglas
Thirty Seconds Over Tokyo 1944,N 16,19:1

Cowan, Jerome
Beloved Enemy 1936,D 26,15:2
You Only Live Once 1937,F 1,15:2
Shall We Dance 1937,My 14,21:1
New Faces of 1937 1937,Jl 2,25:1
Vogues of 1938 1937,Ag 20,21:1
Hurricane, The 1937,N 10,31:2
Goldwyn Follies, The 1938,F 21,15:1
There's Always a Woman 1938,Ap 29,17:2
St Louis Blues 1939,F 9,17:2
Saint Strikes Back, The 1939,Mr 9,18:2
East Side of Heaven 1939,My 5,29:3
Gracie Allen Murder Case, The 1939,Je 8,31:3
Old Maid, The 1939,Ag 12,16:2
Exile Express 1939,Ag 16,21:3
Great Victor Herbert, The 1939,D 7,35:1
Castle on the Hudson 1940,Mr 4,11:2
Torrid Zone 1940,My 18,11:3
City for Conquest 1940,S 28,9:2

Quarterback, The 1940,O 17,33:3
Meet the Wildcat 1940,O 23,27:2
Victory 1940,D 23,23:2
Melody Ranch 1940,D 26,23:3
High Sierra 1941,Ja 25,11:2
Roundup, The 1941,Mr 13,25:4
Great Lie, The 1941,Ap 12,19:2
Singapore Woman 1941,My 12,13:6
Affectionally Yours 1941,My 24,18:2
Kiss the Boys Goodbye 1941,Ag 14,21:2
Maltese Falcon, The 1941,O 4,18:2
One Foot in Heaven 1941,N 14,28:3
Mr and Mrs North 1942,Ja 22,13:2
Frisco Lil 1942,F 12,27:2
Gentleman at Heart, A 1942,F 23,25:2
Bugle Sounds, The 1942,Ap 3,25:2
Moontide 1942,Ap 30,14:1
Street Of Chance 1942,N 19,31:3
Who Done It 1942,D 3,35:2
Ladies' Day 1943,Mr 26,14:3
Mission to Moscow 1943,Ap 30,25:2
Song of Bernadette, The 1944,Ja 27,15:2
Mr Skeffington 1944,My 26,23:2
Minstrel Man 1944,Jl 17,18:5
Guest in the House 1945,F 16,19:2
Crime Doctor's Courage, The 1945,Mr 3,11:3
Jungle Captive 1945,Jl 7,7:5
My Reputation 1946,Ja 26,19:2
Getting Gertie's Garter 1946,F 4,21:2
Deadline at Dawn 1946,Ap 4,33:2
Murder in the Music Hall 1946,Ap 15,22:2
Kid From Brooklyn, The 1946,Ap 19,25:2
Night in Paradise 1946,Je 6,16:3
Deadline for Murder 1946,Je 29,22:7
Claudia and David 1946,Ag 15,19:2
Mr Ace 1946,S 30,21:3
Perfect Marriage, The 1947,Ja 16,30:3
Miracle on 34th Street 1947,Je 5,32:1
Unfaithful, The 1947,Je 28,10:2
Riff-Raff 1947,Je 30,25:7
Cry Wolf 1947,Jl 19,10:2
Wallflower 1948,Je 12,8:5
Night Has a Thousand Eyes 1948,O 14,38:3
June Bride 1948,O 30,10:2
Fountainhead, The 1949,Jl 9,8:5
Scene of the Crime 1949,Jl 29,12:2
Girl from Jones Beach, The 1949,Jl 30,9:2
Blondie Hits the Jackpot 1949,S 9,28:3
Always Leave Them Laughing 1949,N 24,48:2
Young Man With a Horn 1950,F 10,18:4
Fuller Brush Girl, The 1950,O 6,23:2
West Point Story, The 1950,D 23,11:3
Dallas 1951,Ja 13,10:4
Fat Man, The 1951,My 25,31:2
Criminal Lawyer 1951,Ag 24,11:4
System, The 1953,My 23,19:3
Private Property 1960,Ap 25,40:2
All in a Nights Work 1961,Mr 23,28:1
Pocketful of Miracles 1961,D 19,39:1
Black Zoo 1963,My 16,42:1
John Goldfarb, Please Come Home
    1965,Mr 25,42:4

Cowan, Lester (Producer)
You Can't Cheat an Honest Man 1939,F 20,13:2
My Little Chickadee 1940,Mr 16,8:2
Ladies in Retirement 1941,N 7,27:1
Tomorrow the World 1944,D 22,12:4
Story of G I Joe 1945,O 6,9:6
One Touch of Venus 1948,O 29,29:5
Love Happy 1950,Ap 8,9:4

Cowan, Lynn
Compromise 1925,O 27,23:3
Social Highwayman, The 1926,Je 15,23:3

Cowan, Maurice (Miscellaneous)
Wanted for Murder 1946,D 12,38:4
Meet Me at Dawn 1948,My 18,26:2

Cowan, Maurice (Producer)
Murder on Monday 1953,O 7,35:2
Turn the Key Softly 1954,F 4,21:6
Trouble in Store 1956,Ja 14,13:2
Operation Amsterdam 1960,Jl 7,26:1

Cowan, Maurice (Screenwriter)
Yank in London, A 1946,Ap 20,16:3
Turn the Key Softly 1954,F 4,21:6
Trouble in Store 1956,Ja 14,13:2

Cowan, Sada (Screenwriter)
Why Change Your Wife 1920,Ap 26,18:1
Fool's Paradise 1921,D 10,11:4
Rustle of Silk, The 1923,My 8,22:4
Silent Partner, The 1923,Ag 20,4:2
Fashion Row 1924,Ja 28,12:1
Trouble with Wives, The 1925,Ag 5,12:4
Stand and Deliver 1928,Ap 2,25:1
Stop, Look and Love 1939,S 8,28:5

Cowan, Verlie
Betrayal, The 1948,Je 26,10:5

Cowan, Will (Director)
Big Beat, The 1958,Je 26,23:4
Thing That Couldn't Die, The 1958,Je 28,13:7

Cowan, William (Director)
Ned McCobb's Daughter 1929,F 18,28:1
Half Marriage 1929,Ag 19,22:1
Kongo 1932,N 17,22:5

Cowan, William (Director)— Cont
Oliver Twist 1933,Ap 13,15:3

Cowan, William (Original Author)
They Gave Him a Gun 1937,My 14,21:1
Blind Alibi 1938,My 20,17:2
Good Girls Go to Paris 1939,Je 23,23:1

Cowan, William (Producer)
Dead Man's Eyes 1944,O 7,11:2
Big Beat, The 1958,Je 26,23:4
Thing That Couldn't Die, The 1958,Je 28,13:7

Coward, Noel
Scoundrel, The 1935,My 3,23:2
In Which We Serve 1942,D 24,18:1
Astonished Heart, The 1950,F 15,23:2
Around the World in 80 Days 1956,O 18,37:1
Our Man in Havana 1960,Ja 28,26:1
Surprise Package 1960,O 15,26:2
Paris When it Sizzles 1964,Ap 9,25:3
Bunny Lake is Missing 1965,O 4,00:0
Boom! 1968,My 27,56:1

Coward, Noel (Composer)
Bitter Sweet 1933,Ag 24,18:2
Bitter Sweet 1940,N 22,27:1
In Which We Serve 1942,D 24,18:1

Coward, Noel (Director)
In Which We Serve 1942,D 24,18:1

Coward, Noel (Original Author)
Private Lives 1931,D 19,16:4
Cavalcade 1933,Ja 6,23:2
Tonight Is Ours 1933,Ja 21,10:6
Bitter Sweet 1933,Ag 24,18:2
Design for Living 1933,N 23,24:2
Bitter Sweet 1940,N 22,27:1
We Were Dancing 1942,My 1,23:2
Blithe Spirit 1945,O 4,27:2
Brief Encounter 1946,Ag 26,21:2
This Happy Breed 1947,Ap 14,24:2
Tonight at 8:30 (Ways and Means); Ways and
    Means (Tonight at 8:30) 1953,My 26,33:2
Tonight at 8:30 (Fumed Oak); Fumed Oak
    (Tonight at 8:30) 1953,My 26,33:2
Matter of Innocence, A 1968,F 22,36:1

Coward, Noel (Producer)
In Which We Serve 1942,D 24,18:1
Blithe Spirit 1945,O 4,27:2
Brief Encounter 1946,Ag 26,21:2
This Happy Breed 1947,Ap 14,24:2

Coward, Noel (Screenwriter)
In Which We Serve 1942,D 24,18:1
Brief Encounter 1946,Ag 26,21:2
Astonished Heart, The 1950,F 15,23:2

Cowden, Jack (Original Author)
Flipper 1963,S 19,23:1

Cowdron, Robert
Saturday Night and Sunday Morning
    1961,Ap 4,44:2

COWEN
See Also COWAN

Cowis, Denis
Talk of the Devil 1937,My 15,23:5

Cowl, Darry
Please Mr Balzac 1957,N 18,37:2
Lovers and Thieves 1958,Ag 5,23:2
Paris Hotel 1959,S 12,12:3
Dog, a Mouse and a Sputnik, A; Pied, a Cheval et
    un Sputnik, A 1960,N 1,46:2
Magnificent Tramp, The 1962,Ap 25,30:1
Up to his Ears 1966,My 18,37:1

Cowl, George
Secrets 1924,Mr 25,25:2

Cowl, Jane
Spreading Dawn, The 1917,O 22,13:2
Once More, my Darling 1949,S 26,17:1
No Man of her Own 1950,My 4,32:3
Secret Fury, The 1950,Je 22,34:2
Payment on Demand 1951,F 16,21:2

Cowl, Jane (Original Author)
Lilac Time 1928,Ag 4,7:2
Smilin' Through 1932,O 15,13:1
Smilin' Through 1941,D 5,29:2

Cowles, Jules
Ne'er Do-Well, The 1923,My 1,24:3
Lost World, The 1925,F 9,15:3
Seven Chances 1925,Mr 17,18:1
Lord Jim 1925,N 16,19:4
Scarlet Letter, The 1926,Ag 10,19:2
Road to Romance, The 1927,O 10,24:1
Bringing Up Father 1928,Mr 19,26:2
Sal of Singapore 1929,Ja 29,27:1
Leatherneck, The 1929,Ap 22,23:1
Heaven on Earth 1931,D 19,16:4
Pursuit of Happiness, The 1934,O 26,25:1
Mississippi 1935,Ap 18,27:2
Barbary Coast 1935,O 14,21:1

Cowles, Virginia Spencer (Original Author)
Ladies Courageous 1944,Mr 16,17:2

Cowley, John
Underworld Informers 1965,O 14,53:1

Cowling, Bruce
Till the Clouds Roll By 1946,D 6,27:4
Song of the Thin Man 1947,Ag 29,14:2
Stratton Story, The 1949,My 13,29:1
Battleground 1949,N 12,8:4
Ambush 1950,Ja 19,35:2

Cowling, Bruce— Cont
Lady Without Passport, A 1950,Ag 4,13:2
Devil's Doorway 1950,N 10,35:1
Cause for Alarm 1951,Mr 30,28:5
Battle at Apache Pass, The 1952,My 10,16:4
To Hell and Back 1955,S 23,21:2
COX
See Also COXE
Cox, Bobby
Little Men 1935,F 18,19:3
Cox, Freddie
Lovey Mary 1926,Je 21,17:2
Cox, John
Car 99 1935,F 23,14:7
Cox, Marilyn
Cool World, The 1964,Ap 21,42:1
Cox, Morgan B (Screenwriter)
Frontier Badmen 1943,Ag 14,12:8
Cox, Vivian A (Producer)
Prisoner, The 1955,D 12,37:1
Tears for Simon 1957,Ap 18,35:2
Triple Deception 1957,O 7,23:2
Cox, Vivian A (Screenwriter)
Swingin' Maiden, The 1964,Ja 1,16:2
Cox, Wally
State Fair 1962,Ap 12,41:4
Spencer's Mountain 1963,My 17,26:6
Fate Is the Hunter 1964,D 10,61:1
Yellow Rolls-Royce, The 1965,My 14,42:2
Saboteur: The Code Name-Mori Turi
 1965,Ag 26,40:2
Bedford Incident, The 1965,N 3,43:1
Guide for the Married Man, A 1967,My 27,16:1
One and Only Genuine Original Family Band,
 The 1968,Mr 22,55:1
Cox, William R (Original Author)
Tanganyika 1954,Je 19,9:2
Cox, William R (Screenwriter)
Veils of Bagdad, The 1953,N 27,99:9
COXE
See Also COX
Coxe, George Harmon (Original Author)
Murder With Pictures 1936,N 21,21:4
Hidden Eye, The 1945,Ag 31,14:3
Coxe, George Harmon (Screenwriter)
Arsene Lupin Returns 1938,Mr 9,21:1
Hidden Eye, The 1945,Ag 31,14:3
Coxe, Louis O (Original Author)
Billy Budd 1962,O 31,32:1
Coxen, Edward
Our Hospitality 1923,D 10,20:1
Singer Jim McKee 1924,Mr 24,13:1
Man Without a Country, The 1925,F 12,16:1
Coxhead, Elizabeth (Original Author)
Cry From the Streets, A 1959,F 24,32:2
Coy, Johnny
Bring on the Girls 1945,Mr 1,25:5
That's the Spirit 1945,Je 2,11:2
Duffy's Tavern 1945,S 6,23:3
Earl Carroll Sketchbook 1946,Ag 30,13:2
Ladies' Man 1947,Ja 13,18:5
Top Banana 1954,F 20,8:6
Coy, Walter
Barricade 1950,Mr 25,8:6
Colt 45 1950,My 6,8:6
Lusty Men, The 1952,O 25,12:6
Flat Top 1952,D 6,17:2
So Big 1953,O 22,34:2
Running Wild 1955,N 12,23:2
On the Threshold of Space 1956,Mr 30,10:5
Coyle, John T (Producer)
Great Commandment, The 1942,O 17,11:1
Coyne, Jeanne
Kiss Me Kate 1953,N 6,23:2
Cozzens, James Gould (Original Author)
Doctor Bull 1933,O 6,21:2
By Love Possessed 1961,Jl 20,32:2
Cpervinsky, Mikhail (Screenwriter)
Song Over Moscow 1964,N 23,52:1
Crabb, James
Hue and Cry 1951,Ja 9,25:2
Crabbe, Larry (Buster)
King of the Jungle 1933,F 25,20:3
Tarzan, The Fearless 1933,Ag 12,14:3
Sweetheart of Sigma Chi, The 1933,N 9,27:1
Search for Beauty 1934,F 10,20:2
You're Telling Me 1934,Ap 7,19:1
We're Rich Again 1934,S 1,16:3
Hold 'Em Yale 1935,Ap 27,20:6
Lady, Be Careful 1936,O 10,21:1
Rose Bowl 1936,D 2,35:2
King of Gamblers 1937,Jl 3,18:1
Sophie Lang Goes West 1937,S 30,19:2
Thrill of a Lifetime 1937,D 9,30:2
Daughter of Shanghai 1937,D 24,21:2
Tip-Off Girls 1938,Mr 25,15:3
Hunted Men 1938,My 21,9:2
Mars Attacks the World 1938,N 8,26:3
Illegal Traffic 1938,N 17,29:3
Sailor's Lady 1940,Je 29,12:2
Jungle Siren 1942,O 10,11:3
Swamp Fire 1946,Ag 26,21:4
Last of the Redmen 1947,Ag 30,8:6

Crabtree, Arthur (Director)
Madonna of the Seven Moons 1946,My 23,18:4
They Were Sisters 1946,Jl 24,24:2
Dear Murderer 1948,My 8,12:2
Quartet (The Kite); Kite, The (Quartet)
 1949,Mr 29,30:3
Caravan 1949,Ap 21,30:4
Lilli Marlene 1952,Mr 29,19:2
Fiend Without a Face 1958,Jl 4,15:3
Crabtree, Arthur (Screenwriter)
Horrors of the Black Museum 1959,Ap 30,37:2
Crabtree, Paul (Screenwriter)
Johnny Tiger 1966,Je 16,53:4
Crabtrey, Herman Corp (Cinematographer)
Report From the Aleutians 1943,Jl 31,8:2
Cracker
Big Country, The 1958,O 2,44:1
Craddock, Andrew (Screenwriter)
Fort Utah 1967,My 25,54:3
Craddock, Claudia
Lady's Profession, A 1933,Mr 25,13:3
Crady, Billy Jr (Original Author)
Red Ball Express 1952,My 30,11:2
CRAFT
See Also KRAFT
Craft, William James (Director)
Painting the Town 1927,Ag 2,19:2
Hero for a Night, A 1927,D 26,26:6
Hot Heels 1928,My 22,19:3
How to Handle Women 1928,Je 18,13:2
Cohens and the Kellys In Atlantic City, The
 1929,Mr 18,30:6
Skinner Steps Out 1929,D 7,19:3
Cohens and the Kelleys In Scotland, The
 1930,Mr 10,24:1
Dames Ahoy 1930,Mr 29,23:1
See America Thirst 1930,D 12,35:3
Honeymoon Lane 1931,Ag 1,16:4
Run Around, The 1931,Ag 10,18:3
Craft, William James (Screenwriter)
Hot Heels 1928,My 22,19:3
Crafts, Griffin
I Passed for White 1960,Ag 18,19:3
Crago, Bill
Air Force 1943,F 4,29:1
Craig, Alec
Mary of Scotland 1936,Jl 31,22:2
Winterset 1936,D 4,31:1
That Girl From Paris 1937,Ja 1,19:1
China Passage 1937,Ap 16,27:2
Woman I Love, The 1937,Ap 16,27:2
There Goes my Girl 1937,Je 12,8:2
Super-Sleuth 1937,Jl 17,18:1
Hideaway 1937,S 25,10:2
Crashing Hollywood 1938,Ja 8,19:2
Wise Girl 1938,Ja 10,13:3
She's Got Everything 1938,Ja 14,21:3
Vivacious Lady 1938,Je 3,17:3
Abe Lincoln in Illinois 1940,F 23,19:2
Phantom Raiders 1940,Je 24,19:5
Tom Brown's School Days 1940,Je 28,22:2
Golden Gloves 1940,Ag 21,23:6
Stranger on the Third Floor 1940,S 2,19:2
Shining Victory 1941,My 31,14:1
Date With the Falcon, A 1941,N 25,33:2
Night Before the Divorce, The 1942,Ap 10,21:3
Cat People 1942,D 7,22:2
Tennessee Johnson 1943,Ja 13,18:2
Appointment in Berlin 1943,Jl 17,8:2
Holy Matrimony 1943,S 16,25:2
Lassie Come Home 1943,Ag 8,15:4
Northern Pursuit 1943,N 26,29:2
Spider Woman 1944,Ja 17,14:5
Calling Dr Death 1944,F 12,11:3
Kitty 1946,Ap 1,23:1
Craig, Blanche
Peter Ibbetson 1935,N 8,18:2
Craig, Carolyn
Fury at Showdown 1957,Ap 20,21:3
Portland Expose 1957,S 27,16:6
House on Haunted Hill 1959,Mr 12,27:5
Studs Lonigan 1960,D 15,59:1
Craig, Catherine
Doomed to Die 1940,Jl 30,16:3
Louisiana Purchase 1942,Ja 1,37:1
Parachute Nurse 1942,Jl 27,18:2
You Were Never Lovelier 1942,D 4,31:1
Lady in the Dark 1944,F 23,17:1
Here Come the Waves 1944,D 28,25:2
Perfect Marriage, The 1947,Ja 16,30:3
Pretender, The 1947,Ag 12,26:2
Albuquerque 1948,Mr 1,17:2
El Paso 1949,Mr 24,35:2
Craig, Charles
Sporting Life 1918,S 16,9:3
My Lady's Garter 1920,Mr 15,13:2
Craig, Charles G Mrs
Barriers Burned Away 1925,Mr 12,17:2
Craig, Charles Mrs
Name the Man 1924,F 4,23:3
Craig, Davina
Are You a Mason? 1934,O 30,23:5
Girl in the Street 1938,My 26,31:2

Craig, Davina— Cont
Suicide Legion 1940,My 6,13:3
Craig, Dean (Screenwriter)
Hills Run Red, The 1967,N 11,26:3
Matchless 1967,N 11,26:3
Navajo Joe 1967,D 7,60:2
Craig, Edith
Harmony Lane 1935,O 24,19:4
Behind the Headlines 1937,Je 1,27:2
Smashing the Rackets 1938,Ag 9,22:5
Craig, Edward (Composer)
Kukan 1941,Je 24,17:2
Craig, Gordon Sir (Producer)
Collision 1932,F 21,VIII,5:2 (In Addenda)
Royal Tour of Queen Elizabeth and Philip, The
 1954,Je 22,24:2
Craig, Hal
Love and Learn 1928,F 20,14:1
Craig, Harry A L (Screenwriter)
Anzio 1968,Jl 25,26:1
Craig, Helen
Snake Pit, the 1948,N 5,29:2
They Live by Night 1949,N 4,33:2
Craig, James
Thunder Trail 1938,F 5,19:3
Zanzibar 1940,Ap 1,15:3
South to Karanga 1940,Ag 9,19:1
Seven Sinners 1940,N 18,23:2
Kitty Foyle 1941,Ja 9,27:2
Unexpected Uncle 1941,S 25,29:1
All That Money Can Buy 1941,O 17,27:2
Valley of the Sun 1942,Mr 19,29:2
Friendly Enemies 1942,Je 22,19:1
Seven Miles From Alcatraz 1942,N 19,31:3
Human Comedy, The 1943,Mr 3,19:2
Swing Shift Maisie 1943,S 10,29:2
Heavenly Body, The 1944,Mr 24,17:3
Lost Angel 1944,Ap 10,14:1
Kismet 1944,Ag 23,16:1
Marriage Is a Private Affair 1944,O 27,17:7
Gentle Annie 1945,My 5,11:5
Our Vines Have Tender Grapes 1945,S 7,21:2
Dangerous Partners 1945,N 2,22:4
She Went to the Races 1946,F 1,29:2
Boy's Ranch 1946,Ag 9,12:2
Dark Delusion 1947,Je 26,19:2
Man From Texas 1948,Ag 12,16:5
Northwest Stampede 1948,D 10,34:3
Side Street 1950,Mr 24,29:2
Lady Without Passport, A 1950,Ag 4,13:2
Hurricane Smith 1952,O 4,15:2
While the City Sleeps 1956,My 17,37:1
Massacre 1956,Je 2,13:5
Fort Utah 1967,My 25,54:3
Craig, John
Silence 1931,Ag 15,18:3
Shock Corridor 1963,S 12,32:1
One and Only Genuine Original Family Band,
 The 1968,Mr 22,55:1
Craig, May
Quiet Man, The 1952,Ag 22,13:1
Rising of the Moon, The (A Minute's Wait);
 Minute's Wait, A (The Rising of the Moon)
 1957,Jl 10,23:1
Girl With Green Eyes 1964,Ag 11,37:2
Craig, Michael
Blonde Sinner 1957,Ja 24,34:1
Triple Deception 1957,O 7,23:2
Elephant Gun 1959,Je 20,11:2
Sapphire 1959,N 3,27:1
Campbell's Kingdom 1960,Ja 11,35:5
Upstairs and Downstairs 1960,D 2,53:4
Angry Silence, The 1960,D 13,25:2
Trouble in the Sky 1961,Jl 13,26:3
Mysterious Island 1961,D 21,30:6
Desert Patrol 1962,Ja 18,23:5
Doctor in Love 1962,Ap 27,27:2
Payroll 1963,My 11,15:2
Stolen Hours 1963,O 17,39:1
Swingin' Maiden, The 1964,Ja 1,16:2
Pair of Briefs, A 1964,F 3,22:2
No, My Darling Daughter 1964,Mr 28,13:5
Life at the Top 1965,D 15,53:1
Sandra 1966,Ja 17,32:1
Modesty Blaise 1966,Ag 11,27:1
Walk in the Shadow 1966,S 12,52:5
Star! 1968,O 23,36:2
Craig, Michael (Original Author)
Angry Silence, The 1960,D 13,25:2
Craig, Neil
Queen of Sheba 1921,Ap 11,9:1
Dramatic Life of Abraham Lincoln, The
 1924,Ja 22,17:3
Boy of Flanders, A 1924,Ap 15,24:1
Calling Dr Kildare 1939,My 12,25:4
Secret of Dr Kildare, The 1939,D 8,33:5
Dr Kildare's Strange Case 1940,Ap 12,19:2
People vs Dr Kildare, The 1941,My 8,21:1
Dr Kildare's Wedding Day 1941,S 18,31:1
Dr Kildare's Victory 1942,F 5,25:2
Calling Dr Gillespie 1942,Jl 19,17:2
Three Men in White 1944,My 26,23:3
Between Two Women 1945,Mr 29,18:3
Dark Delusion 1947,Je 26,19:2

Craig, Robert
New Klondike, The 1926,Mr 22,16:1
Craig, Robert W
Quarterback, The 1926,O 12,30:2
Craig, Wendy
Mind Benders, The 1963,My 2,40:2
Servant, The 1964,Mr 17,30:2
Nanny, The 1965,N 4,57:2
I'll Never Forget What's 'Isname 1968,Ap 15,51:1
Craig, Yvonne
Gene Krupa Story, The 1959,D 26,7:1
High Time 1960,S 17,15:1
By Love Possessed 1961,Jl 20,32:2
Seven Women From Hell 1962,F 1,22:2
It Happened at the World's Fair 1963,My 30,20:1
Kissin' Cousins 1964,Ap 2,28:3
Quick, Before it Melts 1965,Ap 1,30:2
Ski Party 1965,O 23,17:3
One Spy too Many 1966,D 8,64:1
In Like Flint 1967,Mr 16,53:2
Craigie, Jill (Screenwriter)
Man With a Million 1954,Je 29,21:2
Windom's Way 1958,O 1,45:1
CRAIN
See Also CRANE
Crain, Jeanne
Home in Indiana 1944,Je 22,23:1
Winged Victory 1944,D 21,16:2
State Fair 1945,Ag 31,14:3
Leave Her to Heaven 1945,D 26,15:1
Centennial Summer 1946,Jl 18,20:2
Margie 1946,O 17,28:3
You Were Meant for Me 1948,Ja 29,27:5
Apartment for Peggy 1948,O 16,9:2
Letter to Three Wives, A 1949,Ja 21,24:2
Fan, The 1949,Ap 2,12:2
Pinky 1949,S 30,28:2
Cheaper by the Dozen 1950,Ap 1,12:2
Take Care of my Little Girl 1951,Jl 19,20:2
People Will Talk 1951,Ag 30,20:1
Model and the Marriage Broker, The 1952,Ja 12,10:6
Belles on Their Toes 1952,My 3,17:5
O Henry's Full House (The Gift of the Magi); Gift of the Magi, The (O Henry's Full House) 1952,O 17,33:1
Vickie 1953,S 8,26:3
Dangerous Crossing 1953,S 30,37:2
City of Bad Men 1953,O 21,37:6
Duel in the Jungle 1954,Ag 9,13:2
Man Without a Star 1955,Mr 25,19:3
Gentlemen Marry Brunettes 1955,O 31,31:5
Second Greatest Sex, The 1956,F 11,12:2
Fastest Gun Alive, The 1956,Jl 13,23:3
Tattered Dress, The 1957,Mr 15,22:3
Joker Is Wild, The 1957,S 27,16:6
Madison Avenue 1962,Mr 29,28:2
Hot Rods to Hell 1967,Ag 10,45:2
Cram, Frank
Dark Sands 1938,Ag 17,23:4
Cram, Mildred (Original Author)
Subway Sadie 1926,S 13,18:1
Behind the Makeup 1930,Ja 18,21:1
This Modern Age 1931,S 7,19:3
Amateur Daddy 1932,Ap 23,11:5
Sinners in the Sun 1932,My 14,11:5
Faithless 1932,N 19,20:2
Stars Over Broadway 1935,N 14,17:3
Wings Over Honolulu 1937,My 29,20:1
Love Affair 1939,Mr 17,25:2
Beyond Tomorrow 1940,S 27,27:1
Cramer, Marc
Canterville Ghost, The 1944,Jl 29,16:2
Bride by Mistake 1944,S 16,20:2
Pan-Americana 1945,Mr 23,13:2
Those Endearing Young Charms 1945,Je 20,26:5
Isle of the Dead 1945,S 8,12:2
First Yank into Tokyo 1945,O 25,18:2
Cramer, Marguerite
Wild Party, The 1929,Ap 2,28:4
Cramer, Michael
Babette Goes to War 1960,Je 8,46:1
Cramer, Richard
Captain of the Guard 1930,Mr 29,23:1
Sweet Mamma 1930,Jl 12,16:4
American Tragedy, An 1931,Ag 6,22:5
Strange Love of Molly Louvain, The 1932,My 9,19:5
Tenderfoot, The 1932,My 23,18:4
Pack up Your Troubles 1932,O 1,10:4
O'Malley of the Mounted 1936,Ap 6,18:1
Woman Chases Man 1937,Je 11,26:2
Crusade Against Rackets 1937,Jl 26,15:3
Cramer, Susanne
Every Second Counts 1957,O 15,39:4
Tempestous Love 1958,N 22,27:4
Holiday Island; (Vacanzie a Izchia) 1959,S 22,46:1
Bedtime Story 1964,Je 11,27:1
Cramer, Wright
Before I Hang 1940,O 3,31:3

Crandall, Edward
Glorifying the American Girl 1930,Ja 11,21:3
Over the Hill 1931,N 21,20:4
Dance Team 1932,Ja 16,13:1
Crandall, Robert H (Cinematographer)
Living Desert, The 1953,N 10,38:1
CRANE
See Also CRAIN
Crane, Bob
Wicked Dreams of Paula Schultz, The 1968,Ja 4,28:1
Crane, Fred
Gone With the Wind 1939,D 20,31:2
Crane, Gardner Mrs
Meet John Doe 1941,Mr 13,25:2
Crane, George (Director)
Hollywood, Ciudad de Ensueno 1934,Ap 4,26:3
Crane, Harry (Miscellaneous)
Two Sisters From Boston 1946,Je 7,16:2
Song of the Thin Man 1947,Ag 29,14:2
Great Rupert, The 1950,Ap 14,27:2
Crane, Harry (Screenwriter)
Air Raid Wardens 1943,Ap 5,15:5
Lost in a Harem 1944,N 9,23:2
Harvey Girls, The 1946,Ja 25,26:2
Crane, Helen
Hole in the Wall, The 1929,Ap 15,22:6
Crane, James
Drake Case, The 1929,S 16,30:1
One Night at Susie's 1930,N 24,26:5
Dude Ranch 1931,Ap 25,23:4
Two Kinds of Women 1932,Ja 16,13:1
Lady and Gent 1932,Jl 16,5:5
Crane, Jimmy
Dick Tracy vs Cueball 1946,N 23,12:2
Crane, Les
American Dream, An 1966,S 1,28:2
Crane, Lloyd
Girl From Scotland Yard, The 1937,My 31,11:2
Crane, Mack (Original Author)
Bombshell 1933,O 21,11:2
Crane, Madge
Bachelor's Daughters, The 1946,O 7,23:2
Crane, Maes
Mummy, The 1933,Ja 7,11:2
Crane, Norma
Tea and Sympathy 1956,S 28,24:4
All in a Nights Work 1961,Mr 23,28:1
Penelope 1966,N 11,36:6
Crane, Phyllis
So This Is College 1929,N 9,22:5
Forward Pass, The 1929,N 29,25:1
Girl Said No, The 1930,Ap 5,23:3
College Lovers 1930,N 28,23:1
Ten Cents a Dance 1931,Mr 7,17:2
Crane, Richard
Susan and God 1940,Jl 12,11:2
Happy Land 1943,D 9,33:3
None Shall Escape 1944,Ap 7,23:2
Wing and a Prayer 1944,Ag 31,14:1
Captain Eddie 1945,Ag 9,24:2
Behind Green Lights 1946,F 16,10:2
Angel on the Amazon 1948,D 27,16:4
Lady Without Passport, A 1950,Ag 4,13:2
Bailout at 43,000 1957,Je 8,13:2
Surf Party 1964,Mr 12,40:4
Crane, Stephen
Cry of the Werewolf, The 1944,Ag 12,16:5
Crime Doctor's Courage, The 1945,Mr 3,11:3
Tonight and Every Night 1945,Mr 9,16:2
Crane, Stephen (Original Author)
Red Badge of Courage, The 1951,O 19,22:2
Bride Comes to Yellow Sky, The 1953,Ja 14,27:2
Crane, Violet
Unholy Three, The 1925,Ag 4,14:3
Crane, Ward
Famous Mrs Fair, The 1923,Ap 23,18:3
Within the Law 1923,Ap 30,11:2
Pleasure Mad 1924,Ja 7,23:1
Sherlock Jr 1924,My 26,21:1
Bread 1924,Jl 21,14:4
Empty Hands 1924,Ag 18,8:2
Price of Pleasure, The 1925,My 26,24:2
Crimson Runner, The 1925,My 27,26:2
How Baxter Buttered In 1925,Je 23,24:3
Mad Whirl, The 1925,Jl 1,16:1
Classified 1925,N 2,20:1
Flaming Frontier, The 1926,Ap 5,24:1
Blind Goddess 1926,Ap 6,26:4 (In Addenda)
Risky Business 1926,S 8,19:3
Upstage 1926,N 15,19:1
Lady in Ermine, The 1927,Ja 3,16:2
Rush Hour, The 1928,Ja 31,29:1
Crane, William H
Saphead, The 1921,F 14,12:2
Three Wise Fools 1923,Jl 23,13:4
True as Steel 1924,Je 17,22:4
Cranof, Alexander
Crown of Thorns 1934,Mr 28,27:6
Cranville, Sydney
Mikado, The 1939,Je 2,27:2

Crara, Mildred (Original Author)
Affair to Remember, An 1957,Jl 20,8:5
Crauchet, Paul
Guerre est Fini, La; War Is Over, The 1967,F 2,29:2
Zita 1968,Ag 12,40:2
Cravat, Nick
Flame and the Arrow, The 1950,Jl 8,7:2
Crimson Pirate, The 1952,Ag 28,21:2
Veils of Bagdad, The 1953,N 27,99:9
Davy Crockett, King of the Wild Frontier 1955,My 26,36:1
Run Silent, Run Deep 1958,Mr 28,29:1
Cravat, Noel
Walls Came Tumbling Down, The 1946,N 9,13:5
Iron Curtain, The 1948,My 13,31:2
South Sea Woman 1953,Je 4,33:6
5,000 Fingers of Dr T, The 1953,Je 20,8:6
Cravath, Jeff
Fighting Youth 1935,N 2,13:3
Craven, Eddie
Gilded Lily, The 1935,F 9,11:2
Invisible Menace, The 1938,F 14,20:6
Craven, Frank
State Fair 1933,Ja 27,13:2
He Was her Man 1934,My 17,28:2
Let's Talk It Over 1934,Je 16,20:2
Car 99 1935,F 23,14:7
Vagabond Lady 1935,Je 15,20:2
Barbary Coast 1935,O 14,21:1
Small Town Girl 1936,Ap 11,19:1
Harvester, The 1936,Jl 4,18:2
Penrod and Sam 1937,Mr 29,14:3
Blossoms On Broadway 1937,D 3,29:2
You're Only Young Once 1938,Ja 3,16:2
Penrod and his Twin Brother 1938,Ap 18,11:1
Miracles for Sale 1939,Ag 10,15:2
Our Neighbors-The Carters 1940,F 15,15:2
Our Town 1940,Je 14,25:3
City for Conquest 1940,S 28,9:2
Lady From Cheyenne, The 1941,Ap 18,18:2
In This our Life 1942,My 9,10:2
Girl Trouble 1942,O 8,31:2
Keeper of the Flame 1943,Mr 19,15:2
Son of Dracula 1943,N 6,16:4
Jack London 1944,Mr 3,19:3
Destiny 1945,F 3,16:5
Colonel Effingham's Raid 1946,Ap 5,21:3
Craven, Frank (Original Author)
New Brooms 1925,N 4,17:4
First Year, The 1926,Mr 8,17:1
Too Many Cooks 1931,Ag 17,18:2
First Year, The 1932,Ag 22,20:2
Her First Mate 1933,S 2,14:5
Sons of the Desert 1934,Ja 12,29:3
Craven, Frank (Screenwriter)
Annapolis Farewell 1935,Ag 24,18:2
Our Town 1940,Je 14,25:3
Craven, Hazel
Lord Byron of Broadway 1930,Mr 8,21:1
Craven, James
Pearls of the Crown, The 1938,Ap 12,26:2
Yank in the R A F, A 1941,S 27,11:3
Fighting O'Flynn, The 1949,F 28,16:2
Craven, John
Pittsburgh 1943,F 25,27:2
Human Comedy, The 1943,Mr 3,19:2
Purple Heart, The 1944,Mr 9,15:2
Meet The People 1944,S 8,16:2
Swell Guy 1947,Ja 27,17:2
Count the Hours 1953,Je 24,30:4
Cravina, Cesare
Merry Go Round 1923,Jl 2,16:2
Crawford, Andrew
Brothers, The 1948,My 5,30:4
Dear Murderer 1948,My 8,12:2
Dulcimer Street 1948,N 8,24:2
Broken Journey 1949,My 26,34:3
Operation Disaster 1951,Ja 15,13:1
Gay Lady, The 1951,Ap 16,21:2
Crawford, Anne
They Were Sisters 1946,Jl 24,24:2
Bedelia 1947,F 8,10:2
Caravan 1949,Ap 21,30:4
Blind Goddess, The 1949,Je 23,33:3
Master of Bankdam 1949,O 17,18:2
Mr Know-All 1950,O 11,42:1
It's Hard to be Good 1950,D 25,25:3
Tony Draws a Horse 1951,My 15,38:6
Thunder on the Hill 1951,O 18,32:3
Knights of the Round Table 1954,Ja 8,17:2
Both Sides of the Law 1954,Ja 12,19:2
Crawford, Broderick
Woman Chases Man 1937,Je 11,26:2
Submarine D-1 1937,D 30,15:4
Start Cheering 1938,Mr 17,17:3
Ambush 1939,F 9,17:2
Undercover Doctor 1939,Je 1,31:2
Beau Geste 1939,Ag 3,15:2
Real Glory, The 1939,S 15,26:2
Eternally Yours 1939,O 7,11:2
Slightly Honorable 1940,My 17,23:4
When the Daltons Rode 1940,Ag 23,13:3

Crawford, Broderick — Cont

Seven Sinners 1940,N 18,23:2
Trail of the Vigilantes 1940,D 7,13:2
Texas Rangers Ride Again 1941,Ja 9,27:4
Black Cat, The 1941,Ap 26,20:3
Tight Shoes 1941,Je 19,25:2
Badlands of Dakota 1941,S 9,27:6
South of Tahiti 1941,N 10,21:3
North to the Klondike 1942,Mr 12,24:3
Larceny, Inc 1942,Ap 25,9:1
Butch Minds the Baby 1942,My 1,23:3
Broadway 1942,Je 5,23:2
Men of Texas 1942,Jl 13,18:3 (In Addenda)
Sin Town 1942,O 17,11:2
Runaround, The 1946,Je 7,16:3
Black Angel 1946,S 26,32:4
Slave Girl 1947,Jl 18,21:3
Flame, The 1948,F 20,19:2
Time of your Life, The 1948,My 27,29:2
Sealed Verdict 1948,N 3,36:2
Bad Men of Tombstone 1949,Mr 5,10:2
Kiss in the Dark, A 1949,Mr 26,10:6
Night Unto Night 1949,Je 11,11:2
Anna Lucasta 1949,Ag 12,13:2
All the King's Men 1949,N 9,37:2
Cargo to Capetown 1950,Mr 31,36:3
Born Yesterday 1950,D 27,30:2
Mob, The 1951,O 18,32:2
Scandal Sheet 1952,Ja 17,23:1
Lone Star 1952,F 2,11:4
Stop, You're Killing Me 1952,D 11,45:3
Night People 1954,Mr 13,11:2
Human Desire 1954,Ag 7,7:2
Down Three Dark Streets 1954,S 4,6:4
New York Confidential 1955,F 19,18:1
Big House U S A 1955,Mr 12,11:6
Not as a Stranger 1955,Je 29,24:1
Fastest Gun Alive, The 1956,Jl 13,23:3
Between Heaven and Hell 1956,O 12,33:2
Decks Ran Red, The 1958,O 11,18:2
Goliath and the Dragon 1961,Ja 5,27:2
Convicts 4 1962,O 4,44:2
Castilian, The 1963,O 3,31:1
House is not a Home, A 1964,S 2,33:1
Bidone, Il 1964,N 20,42:1
Up From the Beach 1965,Je 10,38:1
Kid Rodelo 1966,F 23,46:1
Oscar, The 1966,Mr 5,16:1
Vulture, The 1967,My 20,39:2

Crawford, Carita
Girl Said No, The 1937,O 18,14:1

Crawford, Earl
Arizona 1941,F 7,23:3

Crawford, F Marion (Original Author)
White Sister, The 1923,S 6,10:2
In the Palace of the King 1923,D 3,14:1
White Sister, The 1928,My 21,25:1
Son of India 1931,Jl 25,11:6
White Sister, The 1933,Mr 18,9:3

Crawford, Gwen
Here Come the Waves 1944,D 28,25:2

Crawford, Howard Marion
Hasty Heart, The 1950,Ja 21,10:5
Man in the White Suit, The 1952,Ap 1,35:2
Where's Charley? 1952,Je 27,18:3
West of Zanzibar 1955,Ja 18,31:2
His Excellency 1956,F 2,19:3
Reach for the Sky 1957,My 1,40:1
Silken Affair, The 1957,O 31,41:1
Othello 1960,My 16,39:1
Face of Fu Manchu, The 1965,N 11,58:3
Vengeance of Fu Manchu, The 1968,F 15,47:1

Crawford, Jimmy
Play it Cool 1963,Jl 18,15:3

Crawford, Joan
Old Clothes 1925,N 9,25:1
Sally, Irene and Mary 1925,D 7,19:1
Tramp, Tramp, Tramp 1926,My 24,24:3
Paris 1926,Je 1,29:3
Taxi Dancer, The 1927,Mr 8,18:4
Understanding Heart, The 1927,My 10,24:5
Unknown, The 1927,Je 13,17:1
Twelve Miles Out 1927,Jl 26,17:1
Spring Fever 1927,O 18,33:2
West Point 1928,Ja 2,28:1
Rose-Marie 1928,F 13,16:2
Across to Singapore 1928,Ap 30,18:3
Four Walls 1928,Ag 20,21:3
Our Dancing Daughters 1928,O 8,14:2
Dream of Love 1928,D 24,11:1
Duke Steps Out, The 1929,Ap 15,22:6
Hollywood Revue, The 1929,Ag 15,20:5
Our Modern Maidens 1929,S 7,15:1
Untamed 1929,N 30,23:1
Montana Moon 1930,Ap 14,24:2
Our Blushing Brides 1930,Ag 2,16:4
Paid 1931,Ja 3,21:2
Dance, Fools, Dance 1931,Mr 21,15:1
Laughing Sinners 1931,Jl 4,11:5
This Modern Age 1931,S 7,19:3
Possessed 1931,N 28,20:4
Pente, La; Dance Fools Dance 1932,Ja 10,VIII,5:1
Grand Hotel 1932,Ap 13,23:2

Letty Lynton 1932,Ap 30,19:3
Rain 1932,O 13,22:3
Today We Live 1933,Ap 15,16:2
Grand Hotel 1933,Je 4,IX,2:1 (In Addenda)
Dancing Lady 1933,D 1,23:2
Sadie McKee 1934,My 18,18:3 (Incorrect in this edition; use 1934,My 19,18:3 elsewhere)
Chained 1934,S 1,16:2
Forsaking all Others 1934,D 21,18:1
No More Ladies 1935,Je 22,18:5
I Live my Life 1935,O 12,12:2
Gorgeous Hussy, The 1936,S 5,7:1
Love on the Run 1936,N 28,13:3
Last of Mrs Cheyney, The 1937,F 19,15:1
Bride Wore Red, The 1937,O 15,18:4
Mannequin 1938,Ja 21,15:2
Shining Hour, The 1939,Ja 20,15:2
Ice Follies of 1939 1939,Mr 17,25:2
Women, The 1939,S 22,27:2
Strange Cargo 1940,Ap 26,25:2
Susan and God 1940,Jl 12,11:2
Woman's Face, A 1941,My 16,21:2
When Ladies Meet 1941,S 5,19:2
They all Kissed the Bride 1942,Jl 31,11:1
Reunion in France 1943,Mr 5,20:3
Above Suspicion 1943,Ag 6,10:3
Hollywood Canteen 1944,D 16,19:2
Mildred Pierce 1945,S 29,12:2
Humoresque 1946,D 26,28:1
Possessed 1947,My 30,25:2
Daisy Kenyon 1947,D 25,32:1
Flamingo Road 1949,My 7,10:2
Damned Don't Cry, The 1950,Ap 8,9:2
Harriet Craig 1950,N 3,31:2
Goodbye, my Fancy 1951,My 30,14:2
This Woman is Dangerous 1952,F 28,23:2
Sudden Fear 1952,Ag 8,9:2
Torch Song 1953,O 13,34:2
Johnny Guitar 1954,My 28,19:2
Female on the Beach 1955,Ag 20,20:2
Queen Bee 1955,N 23,18:2
Autumn Leaves 1956,Ag 2,21:2
Story of Esther Costello, The 1957,N 6,43:1
Best of Everything 1959,O 9,24:2
What Ever Happened to Baby Jane? 1962,N 7,48:1
Caretakers, The 1963,Ag 22,19:2
Strait Jacket 1964,Ja 23,26:1
I Saw What You Did 1965,Jl 22,24:2
Berserk! 1968,Ja 11,42:2

Crawford, Joanna
Dear Heart 1965,Mr 8,33:1

Crawford, John
Cyrano De Bergerac 1950,N 17,31:2
Raton Pass 1951,Ap 20,25:1
Key, The 1958,Jl 2,23:3
Orders to Kill 1958,N 18,41:2
John Paul Jones 1959,Je 17,39:1
Solomon and Sheba 1959,D 26,7:2
Hell is a City 1961,Ja 19,26:3
300 Spartans, The 1962,S 20,29:2
Americanization of Emily, The 1964,O 28,51:1
Duel at Diablo 1966,Je 16,53:1

Crawford, John Robert
Red Line 7000 1965,D 9,60:4

Crawford, Junia
Doctor at Large 1957,Jl 29,15:5
Touch of Larceny, A 1960,Mr 17,28:1

Crawford, Kathryn
King of Jazz 1930,My 3,23:1
Safety in Numbers 1930,My 31,19:4
Flying High 1931,D 12,23:3
Emma 1932,F 6,14:4
New Morals for Old 1932,Je 24,15:3

Crawford, Leslie
Hide and Seek 1964,Mr 12,40:3

Crawford, Lester
Fifty Million Frenchmen 1931,Mr 26,31:2
My Woman 1933,O 16,20:3

Crawford, M D C (Screenwriter)
Knockout, The 1925,O 27,23:3

Crawford, Michael
War Lover, The 1963,Mr 7,8:5
Knack...and how to get it, The 1965,Je 30,42:1
Funny Thing Happened on the Way to the Forum, A 1966,O 17,48:1
Jokers, The 1967,My 16,50:1
How I Won the War 1967,N 9,56:1

Crawford, Oliver (Original Author)
Man From the Alamo, The 1953,S 12,13:2

Crawford, Richard
Night Bride, The 1927,Mr 30,22:6

Crawford, Robert
Great Impostor, The 1961,Mr 30,24:1
Hawaii 1966,O 11,54:1

Crawford, Robert Jr
Wonderful World of the Brothers Grimm, The (The Singing Bone); Singing Bone, The (The Wonderful World of the Brothers Grimm) 1962,Ag 8,35:1

Crawford, Sam
College 1927,S 12,29:1

Crawford, Stuart
Mr and Mrs North 1942,Ja 22,13:2
Yank on the Burma Road, A 1942,Ja 29,25:3
Ship Ahoy 1942,Je 26,16:5

Crawford, William
Synanon 1965,My 6,44:1

Craydon, Letty
Kangaroo 1952,My 17,22:7

Cream, Patrick
Seven Hills of Rome 1958,Ja 28,24:2 (Incorrect in this edition; use 1958,Ja 31,24:2 elsewhere)
Naked Maja, The 1959,Je 11,36:2

Creedon, Richard (Screenwriter)
Snow White and the Seven Dwarfs 1938,Ja 14,21:1 (In Addenda)

Creehan, Joe
Outlaws of the Orient 1937,S 25,10:2

Creehan, Joseph
Woman Against Woman 1938,Ag 23,20:6

Creelman, James Ashmore (Miscellaneous)
Red Peacock, The 1922,Ap 3,18:2

Creelman, James Ashmore (Original Author)
Fine Manners 1926,Ag 30,10:3
Circus Kid, The 1928,D 17,23:1
Last Performance, The 1929,N 4,28:1
Vagabond Lover, The 1929,N 27,30:6
Half Shot at Sunrise 1930,O 11,21:3
Danger Lights 1930,D 15,29:1
Dancers in the Dark 1932,Mr 19,11:2
These Thirty Years 1934,My 24,28:3
Last Days of Pompeii, The 1935,O 17,29:2

Creelman, James Ashmore (Screenwriter)
Smilin' Through 1922,Ap 17,22:3
Puritan Passions 1923,O 15,15:4
Gang War 1928,N 19,16:7

Cregan, N R
Alice in Wonderland 1931,D 28,22:1

Cregar, Laird
Hudson's Bay 1941,Ja 10,23:2
Blood and Sand 1941,My 23,25:3
Charley's Aunt 1941,Ag 2,18:2
I Wake up Screaming 1942,Ja 17,13:2
Joan of Paris 1942,Ja 26,18:2
Rings on her Fingers 1942,Ap 24,21:4
This Gun for Hire 1942,My 14,23:2
Ten Gentlemen From West Point 1942,Je 5,23:3
Black Swan, The 1942,D 24,18:3
Hello, Frisco, Hello 1943,Mr 25,25:1
Heaven Can Wait 1943,Ag 12,15:1
Holy Matrimony 1943,S 16,25:2
Lodger, The 1944,Ja 20,15:3
Hangover Square 1945,F 8,15:2

Cregar, Lawrence
Undercover Girl 1950,N 8,37:2
Johnny One-Eye 1950,N 17,31:2

Crehan, Joseph
Stolen Heaven 1931,F 14,11:4
Before Midnight 1934,Ja 10,24:3
Hell Cat, The 1934,Jl 7,16:5
Traveling Saleslady 1935,Mr 29,26:2
Black Fury 1935,Ap 11,27:2
Go Into Your Dance 1935,My 4,17:2
Oil for the Lamps of China 1935,Je 6,25:2
Stranded 1935,Je 20,16:2
Front Page Woman 1935,Jl 12,15:1
Alibi Ike 1935,Jl 17,22:1
Bright Lights 1935,Ag 15,15:2
Page Miss Glory 1935,Ag 29,25:2
Special Agent 1935,S 19,28:1
Shipmates Forever 1935,O 17,29:3
Case of the Lucky Legs, The 1935,N 1,25:1
Pay-Off, The 1935,N 13,25:3
Frisco Kid 1935,N 25,22:1
Man of Iron 1935,D 7,22:2
Murder of Dr Harrigan, The 1936,Ja 21,27:5
Road Gang 1936,F 24,14:1
Singing Kid, The 1936,Ap 4,11:1
Bullets or Ballots 1936,My 27,27:1
Law in her Hands, The 1936,Je 6,21:2
Murder by an Aristocrat 1936,Je 13,13:2
Bengal Tiger 1936,Jl 30,22:1
Jailbreak 1936,Ag 6,22:1
China Clipper 1936,Ag 12,14:3
Anthony Adverse 1936,Ag 27,16:1
Gold Diggers of 1937 1936,D 25,19:2
Smart Blonde 1937,Ja 9,21:1
God's Country and the Woman 1937,Ja 11,15:5
Midnight Court 1937,Mr 4,27:3
Her Husband's Secretary 1937,Mr 20,23:6
Kid Galahad 1937,My 27,21:3
There Goes my Girl 1937,Je 12,8:2
Midnight Madonna 1937,Jl 17,18:1
Born Reckless 1937,Jl 30,22:6
Talent Scout 1937,Ag 20,21:3
Happy Landing 1938,Ja 22,19:1
Kid Comes Back, The 1938,F 7,10:2
Alexander's Ragtime Band 1938,Ag 6,7:2
Four's a Crowd 1938,Ag 12,11:1
Arkansas Traveler, The 1938,N 17,29:2
Crime Takes a Holiday 1938,N 28,11:2
You Can't Get Away With Murder 1939,Mr 25,19:2
Society Lawyer 1939,Mr 31,19:2

Crehan, Joseph— Cont

Tell no Tales 1939,Je 2,27:3
Maisie 1939,Je 23,23:1
Stanley and Livingstone 1939,Ag 5,18:2
Behind Prison Gates 1939,Ag 21,9:3
Babes in Arms 1939,O 20,27:2
Roaring Twenties, The 1939,N 11,12:1
Return Of Doctor X, The 1939,N 23,38:5
Music in My Heart 1940,Ja 4,19:2
Geronimo 1940,F 8,18:3
Brother Orchid 1940,Je 8,18:2
Secret Seven, The 1940,Ag 12,11:6
Case of the Black Parrot, The 1941,Ja 10,23:3
Andy Hardy's Private Secretary 1941,Mr 7,17:2
Scattergood Baines 1941,Ap 4,25:2
Washington Melodrama 1941,My 26,15:3
Love Crazy 1941,Je 6,25:5
Manpower 1941,Jl 5,14:2
Texas 1941,O 17,27:3
Nine Loves Are not Enough 1941,O 30,27:2
Treat 'Em Rough 1942,Ja 19,21:3
Courtship of Andy Hardy, The 1942,Ap 10,21:2
Larceny, Inc 1942,Ap 25,9:1
Murder in the Big House 1942,My 8,27:3
Phantom Lady 1944,F 18,15:2
Shine on Harvest Moon 1944,Mr 11,10:2
One Mysterious Night 1944,O 21,15:3
Chicago Kid, The 1945,F 12,24:3
Dick Tracy 1946,Ja 12,10:7
Deadline at Dawn 1946,Ap 4,33:2
O S S 1946,My 27,15:5
Dick Tracy vs Cueball 1946,N 23,12:2
Falcon's Adventure, The 1946,D 14,19:2
April Showers 1948,Mr 27,10:2
Silver River 1948,My 22,8:3
Street Corner 1948,D 4,9:4
Last Bandit, The 1949,Mr 21,19:2
Amazon Quest 1949,My 14,9:3
Ringside 1949,S 17,10:8

Creighton, Patsy

Mating of Millie, The 1948,Mr 13,12:2
Adventure in Baltimore 1949,Ap 29,27:2

Creighton, Sally

Thing, The 1951,My 3,34:4

Creighton, Walter (Screenwriter)

Beloved Vagabond, The 1937,F 8,12:5

Creley, Jack

Dr Strangelove or: How I Learned to Stop
Worrying and Love the Bomb 1964,Ja 31,16:1
(Incorrect in this edition; use 1964,Ja 30,24:1
elsewhere)

Cremer, Bruno

Is Paris Burning? 1966,N 11,36:1
Stranger, The 1967,D 19,59:1
Viol, Le 1968,S 20,42:1

Cremieux

Nine Bachelors 1942,F 9,19:2

Cremieux, Andre

Francois Villon 1950,Jl 3,9:2

Cremieux, Henri

Stormy Waters 1946,Je 17,32:2
Orpheus 1950,N 30,42:2
Mr Peek-A-Boo 1951,S 19,37:1
Holiday for Henrietta 1955,Ja 25,21:1
Easiest Profession, The 1960,Mr 26,15:7
Nude in a White Car 1960,O 27,47:2

Cremieux, Henry

Paris Incident 1954,Ag 18,20:2

Cremillon, Jean (Director)

Stormy Waters 1946,Je 17,32:2

Crenna, Richard

Pride of St Louis, The 1952,My 3,17:5
It Grows on Trees 1952,N 29,11:2
John Goldfarb, Please Come Home
1965,Mr 25,42:4
Made in Paris 1966,F 17,29:1
Sand Pebbles, The 1966,D 21,48:1
Wait Until Dark 1967,O 27,48:1
Star! 1968,O 23,36:2

Crenshaw, Hugh

Free, White and 21 1963,Je 20,29:3

Creona, D

Cossacks in Exile 1939,Ja 28,19:2

Crescenzi, Gianluigi

Bible, The 1966,S 29,60:1

Crespo, Jose

Revenge 1928,D 10,25:1
Dos Noches 1933,Jl 29,14:3
Ciudad de Carton, La 1934,F 28,23:3
Tres Amores 1934,N 5,23:1
Senor Casada Necesita Marido 1935,F 11,14:3
Angelita 1935,S 11,19:5
Ultima Cita, La 1936,Ja 22,15:6
Rascals 1938,My 27,12:2
Vida Bohemia, La 1939,F 6,8:5
Alas sobre el Chaco; Wings Over the Chaco
1939,Mr 28,20:2

Cressan, Alex

Tamango 1959,S 17,48:4

Cresse, R W (Miscellaneous)

Ecco 1965,N 5,28:1

Cresson, James

Greenwich Village Story 1963,Jl 12,14:3

Cressov, Pierre

Marco Polo 1962,S 20,29:2

Cressoy, Pierre

Caroline Cherie 1954,My 25,23:1
Hell Raiders of the Deep 1954,Jl 3,9:2
Companions of the Night 1954,N 25,44:2
Life and Music of Giuseppe Verdi, The
1957,My 2,26:2

Cresswell, John (Screenwriter)

Woman in Question, The 1952,F 19,24:2
So Little Time 1953,Jl 28,23:2
Port Afrique 1956,N 3,27:5
Blonde Sinner 1957,Ja 24,34:1
Cast a Dark Shadow 1957,N 28,57:1

Creste

Vagabond King, The 1956,S 13,39:6

Creswell, Peter (Original Author)

Showtime 1948,My 20,35:3

Creti, Vasco

Terra Madre 1931,O 31,22:2
Fiat Voluntas Dei 1936,Jl 6,11:5

Creville, Vanda

Million, Le 1931,My 21,33:2

Crewdson, Robert

One That Got Away, The 1958,Ap 23,40:2
Psycopath, The 1966,S 29,60:1

CREWS

See Also CRUZ, KRUSE

Crews, Jerry

Sunrise at Campobello 1960,S 29,32:1

Crews, Laura Hope

Charming Sinners 1929,Jl 8,17:3
New Morals for Old 1932,Je 24,15:3
Out all Night 1933,Ap 8,16:2
Silver Cord, The 1933,My 5,18:1
I Loved You Wednesday 1933,Je 16,20:2
Ever in my Heart 1933,O 13,25:3
Blind Adventure 1933,O 31,24:3
If I Were Free 1934,Ja 5,25:2
Age of Innocence, The 1934,O 19,27:1
Behold My Wife 1935,F 18,19:3
Escapade 1935,Jl 6,16:2
Melody Lingers on, The 1935,N 7,27:1
Camille 1937,Ja 23,13:1
Road Back, The 1937,Je 18,25:2
Confession 1937,Ag 19,23:1
Angel 1937,N 4,29:1
Doctor Rhythm 1938,My 19,25:2
Sisters, The 1938,O 15,21:3
Thanks for the Memory 1938,D 8,34:3
Idiot's Delight 1939,F 3,13:1
Star Maker, The 1939,Ag 31,14:2
Rains Came, The 1939,S 9,11:2
Remember? 1939,D 15,33:4
Gone With the Wind 1939,D 20,31:2
Reno 1939,D 21,29:2
Blue Bird, The 1940,Ja 20,11:2
Lady With red Hair 1940,D 6,28:2
Flame of New Orleans, The 1941,Ap 26,20:2
One Foot in Heaven 1941,N 14,28:3

Crews, Tania

Unsinkable Molly Brown, The 1964,Jl 17,15:1

Crhova, Jitka

Daisies 1967,O 26,54:2

Cribbins, Bernard

World of Suzie Wong, The 1960,N 11,36:1
Two-Way Stretch 1961,Ja 24,20:3
Wrong Arm of the Law, The 1963,Ap 3,39:1
Mouse on the Moon, The 1963,Je 18,32:1
She 1965,S 2,36:1
Counterfeit Constable, The 1966,N 22,32:2
Don't Raise the Bridge, Lower the River
1968,Jl 13,18:1

Crichton, Charles (Director)

Dead of Night 1946,Je 29,22:6
Against the Wind 1949,Je 27,18:3
Hue and Cry 1951,Ja 9,25:2
Another Shore 1951,F 12,19:3
Lavender Hill Mob, The 1951,O 16,35:2
Stranger in Between, The 1952,Ag 20,21:3
Titfield Thunderbolt, The 1953,O 6,34:2
Divided Heart, The 1955,Ag 4,16:1
Law and Disorder 1958,Ag 6,20:1
Battle of the Sexes, The 1960,Ap 19,40:4
Third Secret, The 1964,Ap 29,27:1
He Who Rides a Tiger 1968,S 10,39:1

Crichton, Charles (Screenwriter)

Boy Who Stole a Million, The 1960,D 22,18:3

Crichton, Kyle (Original Author)

Happiest Millionaire, The 1967,D 1,56:1

Crichton, Robert (Original Author)

Great Impostor, The 1961,Mr 30,24:1

Criddle, Tom

Midsummer Night's Dream, A 1961,D 19,39:1

Crider, Dorothy (Original Author)

Wild and Wonderful 1964,Je 11,27:4

Crimmins, Dan

Midnight Express, The 1924,N 19,19:3
Not so Long Ago 1925,Jl 28,24:4
White Zombie 1932,Jl 29,18:2
Vagabond Lady 1935,Je 15,20:2

Criner, Lawrence

Black Moon 1934,Je 28,26:2
Miracle in Harlem 1949,O 24,19:4

Crino, Isa

Lilies of the Field 1963,O 2,51:1

Crinoline Choir, The

Day at the Races, A 1937,Je 18,25:2

Cripps, Kernan

Alibi 1929,Ap 9,29:1
Mary Burns, Fugitive 1935,N 16,19:2
Mary Ryan, Detective 1949,N 4,33:3

Crisa, Erno

White Line, The 1952,D 6,17:2
Half a Century of Songs 1954,O 30,15:6
Cavalcade of Song 1954,D 27,22:8
Pantaloons 1956,D 26,34:1
Gold of Naples (Theresa); Theresa (Gold of
Naples) 1957,F 12,30:1
Lady Chatterley's Lover 1959,Jl 11,11:1
Cossacks, The 1960,S 6,41:4
Purple Noon 1961,S 1,12:1
Goliath and the Sins of Babylon 1964,Mr 5,36:2

Crisham, Walter

No Orchids for Miss Blandish 1951,F 23,33:2
Moulin Rouge 1953,F 11,33:5
Beachcomber, The 1955,Ja 17,27:5

Crisler, Ben (Miscellaneous)

Pasha's Wives, The 1942,Ap 6,19:2

Crisler, Herb (Cinematographer)

White Wilderness 1958,Ag 13,22:1

Crisler, Lois (Cinematographer)

White Wilderness 1958,Ag 13,22:1

Crisman, Nino

Angela 1955,Je 4,9:2
Greco, El 1967,My 24,52:2

Crisp, Donald

Broken Blossoms 1919,My 14,15:5
Bonnie Brier Bush, The 1921,N 28,16:1
Don Q, Son of Zorro 1925,Je 16,24:1
Black Pirate, The 1926,Mr 9,21:4
River Pirate, The 1928,S 17,27:1
Viking, The 1928,N 29,32:4
Pagan, The 1929,My 14,29:1
Return of Sherlock Holmes, The 1929,O 19,22:6
Scotland Yard 1930,O 20,28:2
Birth of a Nation, The 1930,D 22,16:2
Svengali 1931,My 1,30:3
Kick In 1931,My 25,17:1
Passport to Hell, A 1932,Ag 27,13:4
Red Dust 1932,N 5,12:5
Broadway Bad 1933,Mr 6,16:6
Crime Doctor, The 1934,My 11,24:3
Key, The 1934,My 30,14:3
Life of Vergie Winters, The 1934,Je 15,26:1
What Every Woman Knows 1934,O 27,20:2
Little Minister, The 1934,D 28,25:1
Vanessa: Her Love Story 1935,Ap 13,11:3
Laddie 1935,My 6,22:3
Oil for the Lamps of China 1935,Je 6,25:2
Mutiny on the Bounty 1935,N 9,19:2
White Angel, The 1936,Je 25,24:1
Mary of Scotland 1936,Jl 31,22:2
Woman Rebels, A 1936,O 30,27:2
Charge of the Light Brigade, The 1936,N 2,24:1
Beloved Enemy 1936,D 26,15:2
Great O'Malley, The 1937,Mr 6,10:1
Parnell 1937,Je 4,27:2
Life of Emile Zola, The 1937,Ag 12,14:2
Confession 1937,Ag 19,23:1
That Certain Woman 1937,S 16,29:1
Jezebel 1938,Mr 11,15:2
Beloved Brat 1938,My 2,13:2
Amazing Dr Clitterhouse, The 1938,Jl 21,14:2
Valley of the Giants 1938,S 10,20:2
Sisters, The 1938,O 15,21:3
Comet over Broadway 1938,D 16,33:3
Dawn Patrol 1938,D 24,12:1
Oklahoma Kid, The 1939,Mr 11,21:1
Wuthering Heights 1939,Ap 14,28:2
Juarez 1939,Ap 26,27:1
Daughters Courageous 1939,Je 24,14:2
Old Maid, The 1939,Ag 12,16:2
Private Lives of Elizabeth and Essex, The
1939,D 2,21:2
Dr Ehrlich's Magic Bullet 1940,F 24,9:2
Brother Orchid 1940,Je 8,18:2
Sea Hawk, The 1940,Ag 10,16:2
City for Conquest 1940,S 28,9:2
Knute Rockne-All American 1940,O 19,21:2
Shining Victory 1941,My 31,14:1
Dr Jekyll and Mr Hyde 1941,Ag 13,13:2
How Green Was my Valley 1941,O 29,27:2
Gay Sisters, The 1942,Ag 15,14:2
Forever and a Day 1943,Mr 13,9:2
Lassie Come Home 1943,O 8,15:4
Uninvited, The 1944,F 21,19:3
Adventures of Mark Twain, The 1944,My 4,25:5
National Velvet 1944,D 15,25:2
Valley of Decision, The 1945,My 4,23:2
Son of Lassie 1945,Je 11,12:1
Ramrod 1947,Je 30,25:6
Hills of Home 1948,N 26,32:2
Whispering Smith 1949,F 15,28:2

Crisp, Donald— Cont

Challenge to Lassie 1950,Ap 7,22:3
Bright Leaf 1950,Je 17,7:2
Prince Valiant 1954,Ap 7,40:2
Long Gray Line, The 1955,F 11,19:2
Man From Laramie, The 1955,S 1,20:2
Saddle the Wind 1958,Mr 21,17:1
Last Hurrah, The 1958,O 24,40:1
Dog of Flanders, A 1960,Ap 1,37:1
Pollyanna 1960,My 20,26:1
Greyfriars' Bobby 1961,O 12,41:4
Spencer's Mountain 1963,My 17,26:6

Crisp, Donald (Director)

Why Smith Left Home 1919,O 13,16:3
Bonnie Brier Bush, The 1921,N 28,16:1
Ponjola 1923,N 19,19:3
Navigator, The 1924,O 13,21:1
Don Q, Son of Zorro 1925,Je 16,24:1
Young April 1926,Ag 31,15:3
Nobody's Widow 1927,Ja 13,29:1
Man Bait 1927,Ja 19,21:1
Vanity 1927,Je 15,31:4
Fighting Eagle, The 1927,Ag 15,22:5
Dress Parade 1927,O 31,22:1
Stand and Deliver 1928,Ap 2,25:1
Runaway Bride 1930,My 17,21:2

Crisp, Donald (Narrator)

Battle of Midway, The 1942,S 15,19:3

Crisp, Marie

Moonlight Follies 1921,S 19,12:1

Crisp, Tracey

Casino Royale 1967,Ap 29,25:1

Crispin, Jeanine

Second Bureau 1936,F 17,21:2
Grandeur et Decadence 1937,My 31,11:3
Constant Nymph, The 1943,Jl 24,8:2
Postmaster's Daughter, The 1946,Ag 19,17:6
They Are not Angels 1948,My 22,8:3
Au Grand Balcon 1951,My 5,14:2
Lady Chatterley's Lover 1959,Jl 11,11:1

Crispo, Vittoria

Bread, Love and Dreams 1954,S 21,24:1

Cristal, Linda

Perfect Furlough, The 1959,Ja 22,27:4
Cry Tough 1959,S 17,48:4
Alamo, The 1960,O 27,45:1
Legions of the Nile 1961,Mr 4,16:1
Two Rode Together 1961,Jl 27,23:3
Pharaohs' Woman, The 1962,Ap 19,35:2

Cristaldi, Franco (Director)

China Is Near 1968,Ja 9,37:1

Cristaldi, Franco (Producer)

White Nights 1961,My 29,9:6
Divorce-Italian Style 1962,S 18,34:1
Fiasco in Milan 1963,Ap 11,29:2
Organizer, The 1964,My 7,31:2
Seduced and Abandoned 1964,Jl 16,23:1
Bebo's Girl 1964,N 12,40:1
Time of Indifference 1965,O 13,50:1
Sandra 1966,Ja 17,32:1
Lady Killer From Rome, The 1966,Je 9,54:3
Time of Indifference 1966,O 13,50:1
Rose for Everyone, A 1967,Je 30,30:1

Cristallini, Giorgio (Screenwriter)

Legions of the Nile 1961,Mr 4,16:1

Cristians, Corky

Unstrap Me 1968,N 21,41:2

Cristillo, Sebastian (Producer)

Wave, A Wac and a Marine, A 1944,Ag 14,11:4

Cristina, Olinto

Between Two Worlds 1940,F 9,15:2

Crittenden, Dwight

Veiled Adventure, The 1919,Jl 7,18:5
Old Nest, The 1921,Je 29,10:3
Pioneer Trails 1923,N 12,15:3
Fast Worker, The 1924,N 12,13:1

Crizer, Thomas (Screenwriter)

Rubber Heels 1927,Je 28,29:4
Sporting Goods 1928,F 13,16:2
Take Me Home 1928,O 23,33:1

Croccolo, Carlo

I Cadetti di Guascogna 1952,O 6,22:2
Count of St Elmo, The 1953,Mr 14,13:2
Gran Varieta 1955,Ap 11,29:5
Five Day Lover, The 1961,D 14,55:4
Jessica 1962,Ap 20,20:2
Reluctant Saint, The 1962,D 4,47:2

Crocker, Harry

Tillie the Toiler 1927,Je 7,27:4
Circus, The 1928,Ja 9,20:1
South Sea Love 1928,F 7,30:3
Gentleman Jim 1942,N 26,40:3
Great John L, The 1945,Jl 9,14:6

Crocker, John

Invasion Quartet 1961,D 11,41:2

Crocker-King, C H

One Exciting Night 1922,O 24,17:3

Crockett, Charles

Sundown 1924,D 1,17:3
Daddy's Gone A-Hunting 1925,F 24,17:3
Dressmaker from Paris, The 1925,Mr 18,19:2
Winds of Chance 1925,Ag 17,10:3
Vanishing American, The 1925,O 16,18:2
Into her Kingdom 1926,Ag 10,19:2

Abraham Lincoln 1930,Ag 26,24:1
Ex-Flame 1931,Ja 24,15:1
Guilty Hands 1931,Ag 29,16:3

Crockett, Dick

This Man's Navy 1945,Ap 16,18:6
Wabash Avenue 1950,Ap 29,8:3
Operation Mad Ball 1957,N 21,38:1
Perfect Furlough, The 1959,Ja 22,27:4
Operation Petticoat 1959,D 6,38:1
High Time 1960,S 17,15:1
Gunn 1967,Je 29,32:1

Crockett, Lucy Herndon (Original Author)

Proud and Profane, The 1956,Je 14,41:2

Crockett, Lute

Colt 45 1950,My 6,8:6

Crockett, Luther

Kill the Umpire 1950,My 29,10:6
Golden Girl 1951,N 21,20:3
Scandal Sheet 1952,Ja 17,23:1

Croft, Douglas

Remember the Day 1941,D 26,21:2
Yankee Doodle Dandy 1942,My 30,9:1
Pride of the Yankees, The 1942,Jl 16,23:1
George Washington Slept Here 1942,O 31,11:1
Presenting Lily Mars 1943,Ap 30,25:3
Killer McCoy 1948,Jl 12,31:2

Croft, Leila

Stop the World-I Want to Get Off 1966,My 12,54:2

Croft, Mary Jane

Kathy O' 1958,S 25,29:2

Croft, Peter

King of the Damned 1936,F 1,9:2
Yank at Oxford, A 1938,F 25,15:1

Croft, Valerie

Stop the World-I Want to Get Off 1966,My 12,54:2

Crohem, Daniel

Paris Belongs to Us 1962,N 6,38:1

Croisset, Francis de (Original Author)

Afraid to Love 1927,Ap 12,25:3
Nouveau Messieurs, Les; New Gentlemen, The 1929,D 15,X,6:5
Arsene Lupin 1932,F 27,22:1
Ciboulette 1934,Ja 7,X,4:2
Head Over Heels in Love 1937,F 13,9:1
Amoureux, Les 1940,D 9,23:3
Woman's Face, A 1941,My 16,21:2

Croker-King, Charles

White Angel, The 1936,Je 25,24:1
Crime of Dr Forbes, The 1936,Jl 6,11:4
Lloyds of London 1936,N 26,39:1

Crolla, Henri (Composer)

World Without Sun 1964,D 23,22:1

Crommelynck, Pietrangeli Ferrand (Original Author)

Magnificent Cuckold 1965,Ap 20,42:1

Cromwell, Helen

Silver Cord, The 1933,My 5,18:1

Cromwell, John

Dummy, The 1929,Mr 4,20:2
Top Secret Affair 1957,Ja 31,21:1

Cromwell, John (Director)

Close Harmony 1929,Ap 29,29:2
Dance of Life, The 1929,Ag 16,18:6
Mighty, The 1929,D 30,16:4
Street of Chance 1930,F 3,17:1
Texan, The 1930,My 17,21:2
Tom Sawyer 1930,D 20,20:6
Scandal Sheet 1931,F 9,25:3
Unfaithful 1931,Mr 7,17:2
Vice Squad, The 1931,Je 6,15:5
Rich Man's Folly 1931,N 27,29:3
World and the Flesh, The 1932,My 7,11:5
Sweepings 1933,Mr 24,22:3
Silver Cord, The 1933,My 5,18:1
Double Harness 1933,Jl 21,20:2
Ann Vickers 1933,S 29,24:1
Spitfire 1934,Mr 9,22:3
This Man is Mine 1934,Ap 13,25:1
Of Human Bondage 1934,Je 29,17:1
Fountain, The 1934,Ag 31,14:1
Jalna 1935,S 14,8:4
I Dream too Much 1935,N 29,24:1
Little Lord Fauntleroy 1936,Ap 3,27:1
To Mary-With Love 1936,Ag 27,16:1
Banjo on My Knee 1936,D 12,15:1
Prisoner of Zenda, The 1937,S 3,12:1
Algiers 1938,Jl 15,13:2
Made for Each Other 1939,F 17,17:2
In Name Only 1939,Ag 4,11:3
Abe Lincoln in Illinois 1940,F 23,19:2
Victory 1940,D 23,23:2
So Ends our Night 1941,F 28,17:2
Son of Fury 1942,Ja 30,23:2
Since You Went Away 1944,Jl 21,16:2
Enchanted Cottage, The 1945,Ap 28,19:2
Anna and the King of Siam 1946,Je 21,20:2
Dead Reckoning 1947,Ja 23,31:2
Night Song 1948,Ja 29,27:5
Caged 1950,My 20,8:6
Company She Keeps, The 1951,Ja 29,14:4
Racket, The 1951,D 13,44:2
Goddess, The 1958,Je 25,24:1

Cromwell, John (Director)— Cont

Matter of Morals, A 1961,Je 1,31:1

Cromwell, Richard

Tol'able David 1930,N 17,29:1
Fifty Fathoms Deep 1931,S 19,10:2
Maker of Men 1931,D 19,16:4
Emma 1932,F 6,14:4
Strange Love of Molly Louvain, The 1932,My 9,19:5
Tom Brown of Culver 1932,Jl 30,16:5
Age of Consent, The 1932,S 3,16:2
That's my Boy 1932,N 21,21:1
This Day and Age 1933,S 1,15:4
Hoopla 1933,D 1,23:3
Carolina 1934,F 16,17:2
Lives of a Bengal Lancer, The 1935,Ja 12,12:2
McFadden's Flats 1935,Mr 13,16:2
Life Begins at 40 1935,Ap 5,21:3
Annapolis Farewell 1935,Ag 24,18:2
Poppy 1936,Je 18,19:1
Road Back, The 1937,Je 18,25:2
Jezebel 1938,Mr 11,15:2
Come on Leathernecks 1938,S 15,29:3
Storm Over Bengal 1938,D 8,34:4
Young Mr Lincoln 1939,Je 3,11:2
Torpedoed 1939,S 26,20:5
Enemy Agent 1940,Ap 22,13:3
Parachute Battalion 1941,Ag 29,13:2

Crone, George J (Director)

Introduce Me 1925,Mr 9,21:1
Blaze O' Glory 1929,D 31,15:1
Reno 1930,N 4,36:1

Crone, George J (Screenwriter)

That's My Baby 1926,Ap 12,18:4

Cronin, A J (Original Author)

Once to Every Woman 1934,Mr 26,22:3
Grand Canary 1934,Jl 20,11:1
Citadel, The 1938,N 4,27:2
Vigil in the Night 1940,Mr 9,19:2
Shining Victory 1941,My 31,14:1
Stars Look Down, The 1941,Jl 24,15:2
Keys of the Kingdom, The 1944,D 30,15:2
Green Years, The 1946,Ap 5,21:2
Hatter's Castle 1948,Jl 3,8:6
Spanish Gardner, The 1957,S 9,21:2

Cronin, John

Twist Around the Clock 1962,Ja 27,13:4

Cronjager, Henry (Cinematographer)

Love Light, The 1921,Ja 10,9:1

Cronley, Ed

Crime Incorporated 1945,Je 23,9:7

Cronyn, Hume

Shadow of a Doubt 1943,Ja 13,18:2
Phantom of the Opera, The 1943,O 15,15:2
Cross of Lorraine, The 1943,D 3,27:4
Lifeboat 1944,Ja 13,17:1
Seventh Cross, The 1944,S 29,18:1
Main Street After Dark 1945,Ja 13,15:4
Sailor Takes a Wife, The 1946,Mr 1,17:2
Ziegfeld Follies 1946,Mr 23,8:3
Green Years, The 1946,Ap 5,21:2
Postman Always Rings Twice, The 1946,My 3,15:3
Letter for Evie, A 1946,Je 28,17:4
Beginning or the End, The 1947,F 21,15:1
Brute Force 1947,Jl 17,16:2
Bride Goes Wild, The 1948,Je 4,27:2
Top o' the Morning 1949,S 1,25:2
People Will Talk 1951,Ag 30,20:1
Crowded Paradise 1956,Je 22,15:1
Sunrise at Campobello 1960,S 29,32:1
Cleopatra 1963,Je 13,29:1
Hamlet 1964,S 24,46:1

Cronyn, Hume (Miscellaneous)

Under Capricorn 1949,S 9,28:3

Cronyn, Hume (Screenwriter)

Rope 1948,Ag 27,12:4

Cropeza, Andre

Third Voice, The 1960,Mr 7,24:5

Crore, Peter

Escape 1948,Ag 16,12:2

Crosbie, Martin

Young Cassidy 1965,Mr 23,35:1

Crosby, Bing

Big Broadcast, The 1932,O 15,13:1
College Humor 1933,Je 23,15:4
Too Much Harmony 1933,S 23,11:5
Going Hollywood 1933,D 23,19:2
We're not Dressing 1934,Ap 26,27:2
She Loves Me Not 1934,S 8,18:5
Here is my Heart 1934,D 22,21:1
Mississippi 1935,Ap 18,27:2
Two for Tonight 1935,Ag 31,16:2
Anything Goes 1936,F 6,23:3
Rhythm on the Range 1936,Jl 30,22:1
Pennies From Heaven 1936,D 10,35:2
Waikiki Wedding 1937,Mr 25,29:1
Double or Nothing 1937,S 2,17:3
Doctor Rhythm 1938,My 19,25:2
Sing You Sinners 1938,Ag 18,23:1
Paris Honeymoon 1939,Ja 26,17:1
East Side of Heaven 1939,My 5,29:3
Star Maker, The 1939,Ag 31,14:2
Road to Singapore 1940,Mr 14,29:2

Crosby, Bing— Cont

If I Had my Way 1940,My 6,13:2
Rhythm on the River 1940,Ag 29,23:2
Road to Zanzibar 1941,Ap 10,29:2
Birth of the Blues 1941,D 11,39:1
Holiday Inn 1942,Ag 5,16:1
Road to Morocco 1942,N 12,30:1
Star Spangled Rhythm 1942,D 31,20:1
Dixie 1943,Je 24,26:2
Going my Way 1944,My 3,25:2
Here Come the Waves 1944,D 28,25:2
Duffy's Tavern 1945,S 6,23:3
Bells of St Mary's, The 1945,D 7,26:2
Road to Utopia 1946,F 28,20:2
Blue Skies 1946,O 17,28:2
Welcome Stranger 1947,Ag 7,15:2
Road to Rio 1948,F 19,29:3
Emperor Waltz, The 1948,Je 18,19:2
Connecticut Yankee in King Arthur's Court, A
  1949,Ap 8,31:2
Top o' the Morning 1949,S 1,25:2
Riding High 1950,Ap 11,26:2
Mr Music 1950,D 21,34:3
Here Comes the Groom 1951,S 21,19:2
Just for You 1952,O 9,40:6
Road to Bali 1953,Ja 30,25:1
Little Boy Lost 1953,S 22,38:2
White Christmas 1954,O 15,16:3
Country Girl, The 1954,D 16,51:2
Anything Goes 1956,Mr 22,38:1
High Society 1956,Ag 10,9:2
Man on Fire 1957,Ag 23,10:1
Say One for Me 1959,Je 20,11:2
Let's Make Love 1960,S 9,36:1
High Time 1960,S 17,15:1
Pepe 1960,D 22,18:1
Road to Hong Kong, The 1962,Je 28,21:1
Sound of Laughter, The 1963,D 18,44:2
Robin and the 7 Hoods 1964,Ag 6,20:1
Stagecoach 1966,Je 16,53:1

Crosby, Bing (Narrator)

Adventures of Ichabod and Mr Toad, The
  1949,O 10,18:2
Cinerama's Russian Adventure 1966,Ap 14,42:1

Crosby, Bob

Let's Make Music 1941,Ja 23,19:2
Sis Hopkins 1941,My 1,27:5
Rookies on Parade 1941,My 22,25:2
Reveille With Beverly 1943,Ap 24,17:2
See Here Private Hargrove 1944,Mr 22,17:2
Two Tickets to Broadway 1951,N 22,47:2
Five Pennies, The 1959,Je 19,30:1

Crosby, Bob (Composer)

Let's Make Music 1941,Ja 23,19:2

Crosby, Bob and his orchestra

Thousands Cheer 1943,S 14,27:1

Crosby, Cathy

College Confidential 1960,Ag 22,23:1

Crosby, Dennis

Duffy's Tavern 1945,S 6,23:3
Sergeants 3 1962,F 12,28:2

Crosby, Floyd (Cinematographer)

River, The 1938,F 5,19:2 (In Addenda)

Crosby, Floyd D (Producer)

Matto Grosso 1933,Ja 14,8:5

Crosby, Gary

Star Spangled Rhythm 1942,D 31,20:1
Duffy's Tavern 1945,S 6,23:3
Mardi Gras 1958,N 19,45:2
Holiday for Lovers 1959,Jl 25,10:2
Private's Affair, A 1959,Ag 15,8:7
Right Approach, The 1961,My 18,41:1
Battle at Bloody Beach, The 1961,Ag 17,18:2
Two Tickets to Paris 1962,N 29,46:5
Girl Happy 1965,My 27,28:1

Crosby, Jack

Black Is White 1920,Mr 8,9:6

Crosby, Juliette

Charming Sinners 1929,Jl 8,17:3
Paris Bound 1929,S 21,17:1

Crosby, Lin

Duffy's Tavern 1945,S 6,23:3

Crosby, Lindsay

Sergeants 3 1962,F 12,28:2
Glory Stompers, The 1968,Mr 28,52:4

Crosby, Lou

Days of Glory 1944,Je 17,10:2

Crosby, Marshall

Overlanders, The 1946,D 20,31:2
Pacific Adventure 1947,N 26,18:2

Crosby, Percy (Miscellaneous)

Skippy 1931,Ap 4,23:1

Crosby, Percy (Original Author)

Sooky 1931,D 21,28:4

Crosby, Phillip

Duffy's Tavern 1945,S 6,23:3
Sergeants 3 1962,F 12,28:2

Crosby, Ronnie

Ever in my Heart 1933,O 13,25:3
Little Men 1935,F 18,19:3

Crosby, Wade

Ride a Crooked Mile 1938,D 29,15:2
Arizona 1941,F 7,23:3
Paleface, The 1948,D 16,41:2

Black Book, The 1949,O 17,18:2
Invasion USA 1953,Ap 30,39:4

Croset, Paule

Exile, The 1947,D 26,22:4

Crosland, Alan (Director)

Enemies of Women 1923,Ap 1,5:4
Under the Red Robe 1923,N 13,25:3
Three Weeks 1924,Ap 1,19:3
Miami 1924,Ja 3,22:2
Unguarded Women 1924,Je 24,18:2
Sinners in Heaven 1924,S 10,21:3
Contraband 1925,Mr 24,20:6
Compromise 1925,O 27,23:3
Bobbed Hair 1925,N 4,17:4
Don Juan 1926,Ag 7,6:1 (In Addenda)
When a Man Loves 1927,F 4,16:6
Beloved Rogue, The 1927,Mr 14,16:1
Old San Francisco 1927,Je 23,23:3
Jazz Singer, The 1927,O 7,24:4
Glorious Betsy 1928,Ap 27,16:4
Scarlet Lady, The 1928,Ag 15,19:4
On With the Show 1929,My 29,28:6
General Crack 1929,D 4,36:6
Furies, The 1930,Ap 19,15:1
Song of the Flame 1930,My 7,24:5
Big Boy 1930,S 13,9:3
Viennese Nights 1930,N 27,32:5
Captain Thunder 1931,My 11,15:4
Children of Dreams 1931,Jl 20,20:4
Silver Lining, The 1932,My 30,16:5
Week Ends Only 1932,Je 18,9:2
Hello Sister! 1933,My 6,11:2
Massacre 1934,Ja 18,19:2
Midnight Alibi 1934,Jl 4,18:3
Personality Kid, The 1934,Ag 1,14:2
Case of the Howling Dog, The 1934,O 18,26:5
White Cockatoo, The 1935,Ja 16,21:1
It Happened in New York 1935,Ap 6,10:1
Mr Dynamite 1935,My 25,12:1
Lady Tubbs 1935,Jl 22,20:2
King Solomon of Broadway 1935,O 19,12:2
Great Impersonation, The 1935,D 14,11:1

Crosland, Alan Jr

Three Weeks 1924,Ap 1,19:3

Crosman, Henrietta

How Molly Made Good 1915,O 20,5:5
Royal Family of Broadway, The 1930,D 23,25:1
Pilgrimage 1933,Jl 13,17:5
Carolina 1934,F 16,17:2
Such Women Are Dangerous 1934,Je 9,18:3
Menace 1934,N 22,27:2
Right to Live, The 1935,F 16,9:1
Dark Angel, The 1935,S 6,12:2
Charlie Chan's Secret 1936,Ja 18,19:4
Moon's our Home, The 1936,My 13,29:2
Follow Your Heart 1936,O 22,31:1
Personal Property 1937,Ap 11,27:2

Cross, Alexander

China Clipper 1936,Ag 12,14:3
I Met Him in Paris 1937,Je 3,29:2

Cross, Alfred

Smart Woman 1931,O 12,28:2

Cross, Beverley (Screenwriter)

Jason and the Argonauts 1963,Ag 8,19:1
Long Ships, The 1964,Je 25,25:1
Genghis Khan 1965,Je 24,28:2

Cross, Beverly (Screenwriter)

Half a Sixpence 1968,F 21,60:3

Cross, David

Night Holds Terror, The 1955,S 15,39:2
Decks Ran Red, The 1958,O 11,18:2

Cross, Dennis

Crime of Passion 1957,Ja 10,25:1

Cross, Edwin

Found Alive 1934,F 12,19:2

Cross, George

Smallest Show on Earth, The 1957,N 23,11:2

Cross, Gerald

Murder She Said 1962,Ja 8,27:2
Murder Ahoy 1964,S 23,55:3

Cross, Henry (Screenwriter)

Teenage Millionaire 1962,Ja 12,29:2
Night Train to Paris 1964,D 3,58:2

Cross, Hugh

Seven Days to Noon 1950,D 19,41:3
Svengali 1955,S 26,18:2

Cross, Jack J (Producer)

Crack-Up 1946,S 7,11:1

Cross, James

Ship Ahoy 1942,Je 26,16:5

Cross, Jimmy

Amazing Colossal Man, The 1957,O 26,19:2

Cross, Joan

Beggar's Opera, The 1953,Ag 25,18:2

Cross, Rhoda M

Give and Take 1928,D 27,27:1

Cross, Ruth (Original Author)

Golden Cocoon, The 1925,D 15,14:5

Crosse, Rupert

Shadows 1961,Mr 22,37:1

Crossland, Marjorie

Louisa 1950,O 25,45:2
Take Care of my Little Girl 1951,Jl 19,20:2

Crossland, Marjorie— Cont

I Want You 1951,D 24,9:1
Captive City, The 1952,Mr 27,34:2

Crossley, Syd

Unknown Soldier, The 1926,My 31,10:2
Gorilla, The 1927,N 21,20:1
We're Going to Be Rich 1938,Jl 4,10:2

Crossman, Melville (Original Author)

Life of the Party, The 1930,N 10,16:2
Thanks a Million 1935,N 14,17:1
Yank in the R A F, A 1941,S 27,11:3
Thunder Birds 1942,O 29,19:2
China Girl 1943,Ja 21,27:2
Purple Heart, The 1944,Mr 9,15:2

Crossman, Melville (Screenwriter)

Tenderloin 1928,Mr 15,28:3

Crosson, Robert

White Christmas 1954,O 15,16:3

Crother, Rachel (Original Author)

Old Lady 31 1920,My 24,20:3

Crothers, Rachel (Original Author)

Wine of Youth 1924,Ag 11,16:1
Little Journey, A 1927,Ja 4,21:1
When Ladies Meet 1933,Je 24,16:2
As Husbands Go 1934,Ja 26,20:3
Splendor 1935,N 23,23:2
Mother Carey's Chickens 1938,Ag 5,11:1
Susan and God 1940,Jl 12,11:2
When Ladies Meet 1941,S 5,19:2

Crothers, Rachel (Screenwriter)

Splendor 1935,N 23,23:2

Crotsel, Max

Dog of Flanders, A 1960,Ap 1,37:1

Croucher, Roger

Genghis Khan 1965,Je 24,28:2

Crousat, Henri (Original Author)

Temptation 1962,N 10,16:2

Crouse, Russel (Miscellaneous)

Anything Goes 1936,F 6,23:3
Big Broadcast of 1938, The 1938,Mr 10,16:2
Anything Goes 1956,Mr 22,38:1

Crouse, Russel (Original Author)

Artists and Models Abroad 1938,D 22,25:3
Life With Father 1947,Ag 16,6:6
State of the Union 1948,Ap 23,28:1
Call Me Madam 1953,Mr 26,37:1
Sound of Music, The 1965,Mr 3,34:1

Crouse, Russel (Screenwriter)

Mountain Music 1937,Je 24,30:3
Artists and Models Abroad 1938,D 22,25:3
Great Victor Herbert, The 1939,D 7,35:1

Crouzat, Henri (Screenwriter)

Temptation 1962,N 10,16:2

Crouzet, Roger

Letters From my Windmill (The Secret of Master
  Cornille); Secret of Master Cornille, The (Letters
  From my Windmill) 1955,D 19,33:1

Crovblier, Claude (Screenwriter)

Chateau en Suede; Castle in Switzerland
  1964,O 14,51:1

Crowden, Graham

Morgan! 1966,Ap 5,42:2

Crowdson, Michael

Prelude to Fame 1950,N 10,35:3

Crowe, Eileen

Plough and the Stars, The 1937,Ja 29,15:1
Hungry Hill 1947,O 11,11:2
Top o' the Morning 1949,S 1,25:2
Quiet Man, The 1952,Ag 22,13:1
Rising of the Moon, The (1921) 1957,Jl 10,23:1
Night Fighters, The 1960,D 15,59:1
Home Is the Hero 1961,Ja 26,32:1
Girl With Green Eyes 1964,Ag 11,37:2

Crowe, H P Lt Col U S M C

Sands of Iwo Jima 1949,D 31,9:2

Crowell, Arthur

For Wives Only 1926,D 1,24:5

Crowell, Josephine

Greatest Question, The 1919,D 29,7:2
Bunty Pulls the Strings 1921,Ja 9,VI,2:1 (In
  Addenda)
Birth of a Nation, The 1922,D 5,24:3
Rupert of Hentzau 1923,Jl 9,8:4
Ashes of Vengeance 1923,Ag 7,20:2
Flowing Gold 1924,Mr 10,18:2
Hot Water 1924,O 27,27:1
Sporting Venus, The 1925,My 11,14:3
Welcome Home 1925,My 18,12:1
Merry Widow, The 1925,Ag 27,14:1
New Brooms 1925,N 4,17:4
Splendid Crime 1925,D 17,27:1
Mantrap 1926,Jl 12,24:4
Fighting Love 1927,My 23,27:2
Man Who Laughs, The 1928,Ap 28,12:3
Laurel and Hardy's Laughing 20's 1965,N 18,55:2

Crowell, William

Revolt of the Zombies 1936,Je 5,17:2

Crowley, Dave
Fugitive, The 1940,Jl 23,22:2
Crowley, Ginger
She's Working her Way Through College 1952,Jl 10,27:2
Crowley, Jim
Spirit of Notre Dame, The 1931,O 16,27:1
Crowley, Kathleen
Farmer Takes a Wife, The 1953,Je 13,11:2
Sabre Jet 1953,N 3,34:1
FBI Code 98 1964,Ap 9,25:6
Crowley, Matt
Mob, The 1951,O 18,32:2
Somebody up There Likes Me 1956,Jl 6,16:1
Crowley, Pat
Forever Female 1954,Ja 13,26:2
Money From Home 1954,F 27,11:3
Red Garters 1954,Mr 27,13:5
Square Jungle, The 1955,D 31,17:2
There's Always Tomorrow 1956,Ja 21,18:2
Walk the Proud Land 1956,S 8,20:6 (In Addenda)
Hollywood or Bust 1956,D 24,8:1
Key Witness 1960,N 12,15:1
Croy, Homer (Original Author)
They Had to See Paris 1929,O 12,11:1
Down to Earth 1932,S 2,19:2
Cohens and Kellys in Trouble, The 1933,Ap 17,16:4
Lady Tubbs 1935,Jl 22,20:2
I'm From Missouri 1939,Mr 23,27:1
Family Honeymoon 1949,F 25,28:2
Croy, Homer (Screenwriter)
Harvester, The 1936,Jl 4,18:2
Croydon, Joan
Bad Seed, The 1956,S 13,39:6
Croydon, John (Producer)
White Corridors 1952,Jl 16,21:1
Tarzan and the Lost Safari 1957,Ap 13,12:3
Haunted Strangler, The 1958,Jl 15,13:3
Fiend Without a Face 1958,Jl 4,15:3
Corridors of Blood 1963,Je 6,39:1
Crozier, Helen
Foxes of Harrow, The 1947,S 25,35:4
Cruger, Franz
Germany Year Zero 1949,S 20,35:2
Cruger, Paul A (Original Author)
Easy Pickings 1927,Mr 25,25:3
Cruickshank, Andrew
Eye Witness 1950,Ag 28,13:2
Reluctant Widow, The 1951,S 8,8:6
Richard III 1956,Mr 12,1:4
John and Julie 1957,My 7,40:1
39 Steps, The 1960,O 11,55:2
Question of Adultery, A 1961,Jl 6,18:2
Greyfriars' Bobby 1961,O 12,41:4
Cid, El 1961,D 15,49:1
Come Fly With Me 1963,My 2,40:2
Murder Most Foul 1965,My 24,36:2
Cruikshank, Laurence (Director)
Wild Angels, The 1966,D 22,40:4
Cruikshank, Laurence (Producer)
Wild Angels, The 1966,D 22,40:4
Crump, Owen (Director)
Cease Fire! 1953,N 25,17:1
Couch, The 1962,F 22,20:3
Crump, Owen (Original Author)
Cease Fire! 1953,N 25,17:1
Amazon Trader, The 1956,N 17,17:6
Couch, The 1962,F 22,20:3
Crump, Owen (Producer)
Silver River 1948,My 22,8:3
Night Unto Night 1949,Je 11,11:2
Couch, The 1962,F 22,20:3
Gunn 1967,Je 29,32:1
Crump, Owen (Screenwriter)
Manhunt in the Jungle 1958,Ap 12,13:1
Crutcher, Gary (Screenwriter)
Name of the Game Is Kill, The 1968,Je 6,54:1
Crutcher, Robert Riley (Screenwriter)
Girl Trouble 1942,O 8,31:2
Key to the City 1950,F 2,31:2
Crutchfield, Les (Original Author)
Tarzan's Greatest Adventure 1959,Jl 9,22:1
Crutchley, Rosalie
Take my Life 1949,Ja 19,34:2
Give Us This Day 1949,Jl 21,41:2
Prelude to Fame 1950,N 10,35:3
Quo Vadis 1951,N 9,22:2
Sword and the Rose, The 1953,Ag 20,18:3
Flame and the Flesh 1954,My 3,21:2
Malta Story 1954,Jl 17,7:2
Make Me an Offer 1956,F 29,35:2
Spanish Gardner, The 1957,S 9,21:2
Tale of Two Cities, A 1958,Ag 5,23:1
Nun's Story, The 1959,Je 19,30:1
Sons and Lovers 1960,Ag 3,35:1
No Love for Johnnie 1961,D 13,55:1
Freud 1962,D 13,37:1
Haunting, The 1963,S 19,23:1
Model Murder Case, The 1964,N 25,45:1

Crute, Dally
His Children's Children 1923,N 5,15:1
Cruthers, Scat Man
Walking my Baby Back Home 1954,Ja 16,10:5
Lady in a Cage 1964,Je 11,27:1
CRUZ
See Also CREWS, KRUSE
Cruz, Angelo
Typhoon 1940,My 23,28:4
Cruz, Vera
Warrior and the Slave, The 1960,Mr 10,36:2
Bike Boy 1967,O 6,31:2
Cruze, Fannie (Director)
Mannequinn 1926,Ja 12,27:5
Cruze, James (Director)
Roaring Road, The 1919,Ap 14,11:4
You're Fired 1919,Je 16,11:2
Love Burglar, The 1919,Jl 28,8:5
Lottery Man, The 1919,O 6,15:1
Lottery Man, The 1919,N 17,20:1
What Happened to Jones 1920,Ag 9,6:3
One Glorious Day 1922,Ja 30,16:2
Is Matrimony a Failure 1922,Ap 17,22:3
Dictator, The 1922,Jl 3,8:6
Old Homestead, The 1922,O 9,10:2
Thirty Days 1922,D 11,22:1
Ruggles of Red Gap 1923,S 10,15:4
To the Ladies 1923,N 26,15:6
Fighting Coward, The 1924,Mr 17,19:1
Enemy Sex, The 1924,Jl 1,21:4
Merton of the Movies 1924,S 8,15:3
City That Never Sleeps, The 1924,S 29,10:1
Garden of Weeds, The 1924,N 4,24:1
Welcome Home 1925,My 18,12:1
Beggar on Horseback 1925,Je 6,9:2
Marry Me 1925,Jl 13,20:2
Pony Express, The 1925,S 14,16:1
Old Ironsides 1926,D 7,21:2
We're all Gamblers 1927,O 12,30:6
Night Flyer, The 1928,Mr 13,23:3
Excess Baggage 1928,S 24,25:1
Mating Call, The 1928,O 8,14:2
Red Mark, The 1928,O 30,27:3
Duke Steps Out, The 1929,Ap 15,22:6
Man's Man, A 1929,Je 3,27:2
Great Gabbo, The 1929,S 13,33:1
Big Fight, The 1930,Je 28,9:2
Once a Gentleman 1930,O 4,15:2
She Got What She Wanted 1930,D 29,18:1
Salvation Nell 1931,Jl 6,24:4
Washington Merry-Go-Round 1932,O 24,18:5
If I Had a Million 1932,D 3,21:4
Sailor Be Good 1933,F 27,11:2
Racetrack 1933,Mr 6,16:6
I Cover the Waterfront 1933,My 18,17:3
Mr Skitch 1933,D 23,19:1
David Harum 1934,Mr 2,23:2
Their big Moment 1934,S 6,22:4
Helldorado 1935,Ja 7,13:2
Two Fisted 1935,O 5,18:3
Sutter's Gold 1936,Mr 27,25:2
Prison Nurse 1938,Mr 4,17:5
Gangs of New York 1938,My 28,9:2
Come on Leathernecks 1938,S 15,29:3
Cruze, James (Miscellaneous)
Hawthorne of the U.S.A. 1919,N 17,20:1
Cruze, James (Producer)
City Gone Wild, The 1927,D 6,27:1
Costello Case, The 1930,N 4,36:1
Cruze, James (Screenwriter)
Waking up the Town 1925,Mr 31,17:4
Crydon, John (Producer)
High Wind in Jamaica, A 1965,Je 17,27:2
Crystal
Queen, The 1968,Je 18,37:1
Csalazar, Abel
Virgin of Guadalupe, The 1943,My 15,13:3
Csepreghy, Jeno (Director)
Busuini Nem Jo; Don't Worry 1938,O 29,15:5
Uz Bence 1940,Ja 15,11:2
Csepreghy, Jeno (Miscellaneous)
Szegeny Gazdagok; Poor Plutocrats 1939,D 4,18:4
Csikos, Rozsi
Filleres Gyoers 1933,Mr 27,13:7
Rosen aus dem Sueden; Roses from the South 1935,Ap 23,24:5
Zsivany Becsuelet 1935,O 30,16:3
Csortos, Gyula
Egy ej Velencebzn 1935,D 27,14:2
Csak Egy Ejszakara 1936,Mr 16,21:5
Az Ember Neha Teved; Man Sometimes Errs 1938,Mr 28,19:3
Csortos, Julius
Az uj Foeldesur 1936,S 22,30:5
Legy Jo Mindhalalig 1936,O 26,20:2
Sarga Csiko 1937,Ja 29,15:2
Szerelemboel Noesueltem; I Married for Love 1938,F 7,10:3
Sziuel Sizivert; Heart for Heart 1939,Ja 16,11:3
Eb Ura Fako 1940,Mr 23,16:4

Cuadros, Maria
Pearl, The 1948,F 18,36:4
Cube, J V (Original Author)
Be Mine Tonight 1933,Ap 14,22:5
Cube, J V (Screenwriter)
Lied fur Dich, Ein; Song for You, A 1933,Jl 2,IX,2:2
Mayerling 1937,S 14,27:1
Cucciola
Greatest Show on Earth, The 1952,Ja 11,17:2
Cucciolla, Riccardo
Italiano Brava Gente 1966,F 4,20:1
Grand Slam 1968,F 21,60:4
Cudart, Felix
Hoboes in Paradise 1950,O 9,21:5
Cudot, Jacques Dr (Miscellaneous)
Annapurna 1953,D 14,45:4
Cuevas, Consuelo
Dos Mujeres y un Don Juan 1934,Je 4,12:4
Cugat, Xavier
Holiday in Mexico 1946,Ag 16,19:3
This Time for Keeps 1947,D 5,33:4
On an Island With You 1948,Jl 30,13:2
Date with Judy, A 1948,Ag 7,8:2
Luxury Liner 1948,S 10,19:2
Neptune's Daughter 1949,Je 10,32:2
Chicago Syndicate 1955,Je 21,37:1
Cugat, Xavier and his orchestra
You Were Never Lovelier 1942,D 4,31:1
Stage Door Canteen 1943,Je 25,13:2
Heat's on, The 1943,N 26,29:2
Two Girls and a Sailor 1944,Je 15,16:1
Bathing Beauty 1944,Je 28,20:1
Week-End at the Waldorf 1945,O 5,27:2
No Leave, No Love 1946,O 18,29:2
Cukor, George (Director)
Virtuous Sin 1930,N 2,VIII,5:2 (In Addenda)
Royal Family of Broadway, The 1930,D 23,25:1
Tarnished Lady 1931,Ap 30,29:3
Girls About Town 1931,N 2,27:1
What Price Hollywood 1932,Jl 16,5:5
Bill of Divorcement, A 1932,O 3,15:2
Rockabye 1932,D 5,21:2
Our Betters 1933,F 24,13:2
Dinner at Eight 1933,Ag 24,18:1
Little Women 1933,N 17,22:3
David Copperfield 1935,Ja 19,8:1
Sylvia Scarlett 1936,Ja 10,16:2
Romeo and Juliet 1936,Ag 21,12:2
Camille 1937,Ja 23,13:1
Holiday 1938,Je 24,15:1
Zaza 1939,Ja 5,17:1
Women, The 1939,S 22,27:2
Susan and God 1940,Jl 12,11:2
Philadelphia Story, The 1940,D 27,22:2
Woman's Face, A 1941,My 16,21:2
Two Faced Woman 1942,Ja 1,37:2
Her Cardboard Lover 1942,Jl 17,19:2
Keeper of the Flame 1943,Mr 19,15:2
Gaslight 1944,My 5,17:2
Winged Victory 1944,D 21,16:2
Double Life, A 1948,F 20,19:1
Edward my Son 1949,Je 3,21:2
Adam's Rib 1949,D 26,33:2
Life of her Own, A 1950,O 12,43:2
Born Yesterday 1950,D 27,30:2
Model and the Marriage Broker, The 1952,Ja 12,10:6
Marrying Kind, The 1952,Mr 14,27:1
Pat and Mike 1952,Je 19,32:6
Actress, The 1953,O 13,34:1
It Should Happen to You 1954,Ja 16,10:5
Star is Born, A 1954,O 12,23:1
Bhowani Junction 1956,My 25,26:1
Girls, Les 1957,O 4,27:2
Wild Is the Wind 1957,D 12,35:1
Heller in Pink Tights 1960,Mr 17,28:1
Song Without End 1960,Ag 12,10:2
Let's Make Love 1960,S 9,36:1
Chapman Report, The 1962,O 18,49:2
My Fair Lady 1964,O 22,41:1
Culder, Mary
Man Next Door, The 1923,My 29,10:3
Culhane, James (Miscellaneous)
Mr Bug Goes to Town 1942,F 20,21:3
Culkin, Candace
Up the Down Staircase 1967,Ag 18,36:2
Cull, Howard
Music Master, The 1927,Ja 17,12:4 (In Addenda)
Cullen, James F
Summer Bachelors 1926,D 20,28:3
Cullen, Nan
Luck of the Irish, The 1937,Ja 16,21:1
Cullen, R J (Screenwriter)
Escape me Never 1935,My 24,24:2
As You Like It 1936,N 6,29:3
Culley, Frederick
Private Life of Henry VIII, The 1933,O 13,25:2
Talk of the Devil 1937,My 15,23:5
Knight Without Armor 1937,Jl 9,18:1
Rat, The 1938,F 28,19:1
Drums 1938,S 30,24:4
Four Feathers 1939,Ag 4,11:1

Culley, Frederick— Cont

Young Mr Pitt, The 1943,Mr 11,17:1

Culloz, Albert

Amazing Monsieur Fabre, The 1952,S 9,21:2

Culloz, Catherine

Amazing Monsieur Fabre, The 1952,S 9,21:2

Cullum, Charles

Perfect Understanding 1933,F 23,20:2

Legend of William Tell, The 1935,O 2,27:1

Amazing Mr Beecham, The 1949,D 26,33:4

Cullum, John

All the Way Home 1963,O 30,46:1

Hamlet 1964,S 24,46:1

Hawaii 1966,O 11,54:1

Cullz, Albert

Pardon my French 1952,Mr 31,17:2

Culp, Robert

PT 109 1963,Je 27,23:1

Sunday in New York 1964,F 12,30:2

Rhino! 1964,Ag 27,28:2

Culton, Eric

Pirates of Capri, The 1949,D 26,33:5

Culver, Robert

Holly and the Ivy, The 1954,F 5,16:1

Culver, Roland

There Goes the Bride 1933,Mr 4,11:3

Accused 1936,D 17,35:1

Gaiety Girls, The 1938,Mr 31,15:1

French Without Tears 1940,Ap 29,12:2

Night Train 1940,D 30,21:1

This England 1941,N 18,33:2

Quiet Wedding 1941,D 29,27:4

Avengers, The 1942,N 25,18:2

Spitfire 1943,Je 14,13:2

On Approval 1945,Ja 29,17:1

Randolph Family 1945,Mr 13,19:4

Life and Death of Colonel Blimp, The 1945,Mr 30,18:2

Vacation From Marriage 1946,Mr 15,27:2

To Each his Own 1946,My 24,15:2

Dead of Night 1946,Je 29,22:6

Wanted for Murder 1946,D 12,38:4

Down to Earth 1947,S 12,18:2

Singapore 1947,S 17,31:2

Emperor Waltz, The 1948,Je 18,19:2

Isn't It Romantic? 1948,O 7,35:2

Her Man Gilbey 1949,Je 9,35:2

Great Lover, The 1949,N 24,48:2

Sanitorium 1950,O 11,42:1

Hotel Sahara 1952,Ja 1,21:4

Obsessed 1952,F 6,24:2

Encore (The Ant and the Grasshopper); Ant and the Grasshopper, The (Encore) 1952,Ap 3,45:1

Hour of 13, The 1952,O 28,37:1

Folly to be Wise 1953,D 28,17:2

Betrayed 1954,S 9,36:1

Man Who Loved Redheads, The 1955,Jl 26,29:2

Teckman Mystery, The 1955,Ag 22,18:2

Touch and go 1956,Mr 20,13:2

Safari 1956,Je 21,35:2

Ship That Died of Shame, The 1956,Ag 21,33:2

Alligator Named Daisy, An 1957,O 7,23:2

Bonjour Tristesse 1958,Ja 16,32:1

Truth About Women, The 1958,Ag 29,18:2

Mad Little Island 1958,D 31,12:1

Circle, The 1959,Ap 16,29:2

Next to no Time 1960,My 28,13:2

Term of Trial 1963,Ja 31,5:2

Pair of Briefs, A 1964,F 3,22:2

Yellow Rolls-Royce, The 1965,My 14,42:2

Thunderball 1965,D 22,23:1

Man Could Get Killed, A 1966,My 12,54:2

Cumberland, John

Baby Mine 1917,S 24,11:2

Cumming, Dorothy

Cheat, The 1923,Ag 27,14:3

Twenty-One 1924,F 18,13:1

Nellie, the Beautiful Cloak Model 1924,Ap 14,14:1

Manicure Girl, The 1925,Je 15,10:1

Coast of Folly, The 1925,Ag 31,19:3

New Commandment, The 1925,N 10,25:3

Dancing Mothers 1926,F 18,21:1

Mlle Modiste 1926,Ap 26,25:1

For Wives Only 1926,D 1,24:5

Butterflies in the Rain 1926,D 25,10:5

King of Kings, The 1927,Ap 20,29:2

In old Kentucky 1927,N 21,20:1

Lovelorn, The 1927,D 19,30:1

Divine Woman, The 1928,Ja 16,24:1

Forbidden Hours 1928,Jl 23,11:2

Our Dancing Daughters 1928,O 8,14:2

Wind, The 1928,N 5,26:1

Divine Lady, The 1929,Mr 23,22:4

Kitty 1929,Je 11,27:2

Applause 1929,O 8,24:5

CUMMINGS

See Also CUMMINS

Cummings, Billy

Sullivans, The 1944,F 10,19:2

Sunday Dinner for a Soldier 1945,Ja 25,16:2

Circumstantial Evidence 1945,Ap 21,18:3

Fighting Father Dunne 1948,Je 25,26:2

Cummings, Constance

Criminal Code, The 1931,Ja 5,21:3

Last Parade, The 1931,Mr 2,19:1

Lover Come Back 1931,Je 5,26:5

Traveling Husbands 1931,Ag 8,16:3

Guilty Generation, The 1931,N 21,20:4

Behind the Mask 1932,My 2,13:2

Attorney for the Defense 1932,My 28,18:2

American Madness 1932,Ag 6,14:5

Movie Crazy 1932,S 15,19:3

Last Man, The 1932,S 17,18:4

Washington Merry-Go-Round 1932,O 24,18:5

Night after Night 1932,O 31,18:4

Billion Dollar Scandal, The 1933,Ja 9,23:1

Mind Reader, The 1933,Ap 7,22:4

Broadway Thru a Keyhole 1933,N 2,18:3

Charming Deceiver, The 1933,D 9,18:3

Looking for Trouble 1934,Ap 12,27:2

This Man is Mine 1934,Ap 13,25:1

Glamour 1934,My 12,12:3

Channel Crossing 1934,My 24,28:3

Remember Last Night? 1935,N 21,27:2

Seven Sinners 1936,Ag 22,6:1

Strangers on a Honeymoon 1937,Mr 13,23:2

Haunted Honeymoon 1940,O 31,28:2

This England 1941,N 18,33:2

Somewhere in France 1943,Jl 12,11:2

Blithe Spirit 1945,O 4,27:2

Man in the Dinghy 1951,N 1,34:2

John and Julie 1957,My 7,40:1

Battle of the Sexes, The 1960,Ap 19,40:4

In the Cool of the Day 1963,My 30,20:1

Boy Ten Feet Tall, A 1965,My 13,32:2

Cummings, Dwight (Screenwriter)

Smoky 1946,Je 27,29:1

Cummings, Hugh

Men Are Like That 1931,Ag 17,18:2

Cummings, Hugh (Screenwriter)

Polo Joe 1936,N 5,35:1

Penrod and Sam 1937,Mr 29,14:3

Penrod and his Twin Brother 1938,Ap 18,11:1

Cummings, Irving

Men, Women and Money 1919,Je 16,11:2

Everywoman 1919,D 15,20:1

Saphead, The 1921,F 14,12:2

As Man Desires 1925,F 10,20:1

Cummings, Irving (Director)

As Man Desires 1925,F 10,20:1

Desert Flower, The 1925,Je 1,10:3

One Year to Live 1925,Jl 6,12:2

Infatuation 1926,Ja 4,16:1

Bertha, The Sewing Machine Girl 1927,Ja 4,21:1

Brute, The 1927,Ap 21,25:1

Dressed to Kill 1928,Mr 12,26:1

Romance of the Underworld 1929,Ja 7,36:2

In old Arizona 1929,Ja 21,18:4

Not Quite Decent 1929,My 6,30:4

Cameo Kirby 1930,F 8,12:5

Devil With Women, A 1930,O 20,28:2

Holy Terror, A 1931,Jl 20,20:4

Cisco Kid, The 1931,O 24,20:3

Attorney for the Defense 1932,My 28,18:2

Night Club Lady, The 1932,Ag 27,13:4

Man Against Woman 1932,D 17,22:3

Woman I Stole, The 1933,Je 28,24:3

Mad Game, The 1933,N 13,21:1

I Believed in You 1934,Ap 11,25:3

Grand Canary 1934,Jl 20,11:1

White Parade, The 1934,N 10,19:1

Curly Top 1935,Ag 2,22:3

Poor Little Rich Girl, The 1936,Je 26,16:1

Girls' Dormitory 1936,Ag 29,16:2

White Hunter 1936,N 26,39:2

Vogues of 1938 1937,Ag 20,21:1

Merry-Go-Round of 1938 1937,N 26,27:2

Little Miss Broadway 1938,Jl 23,10:4

Just Around the Corner 1938,D 3,11:2

Story of Alexander Graham Bell, The 1939,Ap 1,17:2

Hollywood Cavalcade 1939,O 14,13:2

Everything Happens at Night 1939,D 16,12:6

Lillian Russell 1940,My 18,11:2

Down Argentine Way 1940,O 18,25:1

That Night in Rio 1941,Mr 10,21:2

Belle Starr 1941,N 1,20:2

Louisiana Purchase 1942,Ja 1,37:1

My Gal Sal 1942,My 1,23:1

Springtime in the Rockies 1942,N 12,30:2

Sweet Rosie O'Grady 1943,O 21,30:2

What a Woman 1943,D 3,27:2

Impatient Years, The 1944,S 20,20:1

Dolly Sisters, The 1945,N 15,24:6

Double Dynamite 1951,D 26,19:4

Cummings, Irving (Producer)

Impatient Years, The 1944,S 20,20:1

Cummings, Irving Jr (Original Author)

Jewels of Brandenburg 1947,My 24,10:5

Cummings, Irving Jr (Producer)

Sign of the Ram, The 1948,Mr 4,30:2

Double Dynamite 1951,D 26,19:4

Girl in Every Port, A 1952,F 14,23:1

Cummings, Irving Jr (Screenwriter)

He Hired the Boss 1943,Je 4,17:4

Deadline for Murder 1946,Je 29,22:7

Dangerous Millions 1947,Mr 15,10:3

Cummings, Jack (Producer)

Winning Ticket, The 1935,F 11,14:2

Born to Dance 1936,D 5,16:1

Broadway Melody of 1938 1937,S 3,12:1

Yellow Jack 1938,My 20,17:2

Listen, Darling 1938,N 24,37:2

Honolulu 1939,F 23,19:2

Broadway Melody of 1940 1940,Mr 29,25:3

Two Girls on Broadway 1940,Ap 25,28:4

Go West 1941,F 21,16:2

Ship Ahoy 1942,Je 26,16:5

I Dood It 1943,N 11,29:1

Broadway Rhythm 1944,Ap 14,24:6

Bathing Beauty 1944,Je 28,20:1

Easy to Wed 1946,Jl 12,14:2

It Happened in Brooklyn 1947,Mr 14,28:5

Fiesta 1947,Je 27,17:3

Romance of Rosy Ridge, The 1947,S 12,18:3

Stratton Story, The 1949,My 13,29:1

Neptune's Daughter 1949,Je 10,32:2

Three Little Words 1950,Ag 10,21:2

Two Weeks With Love 1950,N 24,31:2

Excuse my Dust 1951,Je 28,21:2

Texas Carnival 1951,O 13,9:1

Lovely to Look At 1952,My 30,11:2

Sombrero 1953,Ap 23,37:2

Kiss Me Kate 1953,N 6,23:2

Seven Brides for Seven Brothers 1954,Jl 23,8:3

Last Time I saw Paris, The 1954,N 19,20:2

Many Rivers to Cross 1955,F 24,21:2

Interrupted Melody 1955,My 6,18:1

Teahouse of the August Moon, The 1956,N 30,19:1

Blue Angel, The 1959,S 5,11:4

Can-Can 1960,Mr 10,36:1

Second Time Around, The 1961,D 23,16:1

Bachelor Flat 1962,Ja 13,14:1

Viva Las Vegas 1964,My 21,42:1

Cummings, Margery (Composer)

Ship Ahoy 1942,Je 26,16:5

Cummings, Peggy

Ship Was Loaded, The 1958,Ja 20,20:1

Captain's Table, The 1960,S 27,40:1

Cummings, Richard

Thank You 1925,O 6,30:1

Social Lion, The 1930,Je 14,9:4

Cummings, Robert

So Red the Rose 1935,N 28,39:1

Millions in the Air 1935,D 12,33:4

Border Flight 1936,Je 22,22:1

Forgotten Faces 1936,Jl 4,18:2

Three Cheers for Love 1936,Ag 1,16:2

Hollywood Boulevard 1936,S 21,26:4

Accusing Finger, The 1936,N 17,35:4

Hideaway Girl 1937,Ja 13,20:4

Last Train from Madrid, The 1937,Je 19,20:2

Souls at Sea 1937,Ag 10,23:2

Sophie Lang Goes West 1937,S 30,19:2

Wells Fargo 1937,D 30,15:2

College Swing 1938,Ap 28,27:2

You and Me 1938,Je 2,19:1

Texans, The 1938,Jl 28,23:2

Touchdown Army 1938,O 28,27:2

I Stand Accused 1939,Ja 5,17:1

Three Smart Girls Grow Up 1939,Mr 18,9:2

Under-Pup, The 1939,S 5,21:2

Rio 1939,O 27,27:2

Everything Happens at Night 1939,D 16,12:6

Charlie McCarthy, Detective 1939,D 25,29:2

And One Was Beautiful 1940,Ap 11,32:4

Private Affairs 1940,Jl 5,10:3

Spring Parade 1940,O 4,29:2

One Night in the Tropics 1940,D 20,33:2

Free and Easy 1941,Ap 3,29:4

Devil and Miss Jones, The 1941,My 16,21:2

Moon Over Miami 1941,Jl 5,14:2

It Started With Eve 1941,O 3,27:1

Kings Row 1942,F 3,23:2

Saboteur 1942,My 8,27:2

Between Us Girls 1942,S 25,25:3

Forever and a Day 1943,Mr 13,9:2

Princess O'Rourke 1943,N 6,16:2

Flesh and Fantasy 1943,N 18,29:1

You Came Along 1945,Jl 5,7:2

Bride Wore Boots, The 1946,Je 6,16:3

Chase, The 1946,N 18,31:2

Heaven Only Knows 1947,N 14,29:3

Lost Moment, The 1947,N 22,10:2

Sleep, My Love 1948,F 19,29:4

Let's Live a Little 1948,D 10,34:2

Accused, The 1949,Ja 13,26:2

Black Book, The 1949,O 17,18:2

Paid in Full 1950,F 16,28:2

Petty Girl, The 1950,Ag 18,17:2

For Heaven's Sake 1950,D 16,10:5

Lucky Me 1954,Ap 10,11:2

Dial M for Murder 1954,My 29,13:2

How to be Very, Very Popular 1955,Jl 23,10:1

My Geisha 1962,Je 14,23:2

Cummings, Robert— Cont
Beach Party 1963,S 26,40:2
What a Way to Go! 1964,My 15,44:1
Carpetbaggers, The 1964,Jl 2,24:4
Promise her Anything 1966,F 23,46:1
Stagecoach 1966,Je 16,53:1
Cummings, Robert (Producer)
Let's Live a Little 1948,D 10,34:2
Cummings, Susan
Verboten 1960,Jl 12,39:1
Cummings, Vicki
I Can Get It for You Wholesale 1951,Ap 5,34:4
Cummings (Director)
Just a Woman 1925,My 26,24:2
CUMMINS
See Also CUMMINGS
Cummins, Dwight (Screenwriter)
Thunderhead 1945,Mr 16,21:2
Cummins, Peggy
Late George Apley, The 1947,Mr 21,29:2
Moss Rose 1947,Jl 3,14:2
Green Grass of Wyoming 1948,Je 10,28:3
Escape 1948,Ag 16,12:2
Her Man Gilbey 1949,Je 9,35:2
If This Be Sin 1950,Jl 1,9:2
Gun Crazy 1950,Ag 25,17:5
Operation X 1950,D 11,31:2
Passionate Sentry, The 1953,N 12,37:5
Both Sides of the Law 1954,Ja 12,19:2
Always a Bride 1954,My 28,19:2
Cash on Delivery 1956,S 1,19:3
Cummins, Samuel (Director)
War Is a Racket 1934,D 10,16:2
Cummins, Samuel (Miscellaneous)
Forgotten Men 1933,My 15,16:2
Man of Courage 1934,N 14,23:2
Cummins, Samuel (Original Author)
Ecstasy 1940,D 25,33:2
Cummins, Samuel (Producer)
War Is a Racket 1934,D 10,16:2
Why This War? 1939,O 9,15:2
Cumo, Pablo
Where Words Fail; Donde Mueren las Palabraso
1948,Ag 19,18:4
Cunard, Basil
Guinea Pig, The 1949,My 2,20:2
Cunard, Grace
Last Man on Earth, The 1924,D 13,12:4
Untamed 1929,N 30,23:1
Resurrection 1931,Ja 24,15:1
Ladies They Talk About 1933,F 25,20:4
Cunha, Richard (Director)
Frankenstein's Daughter 1958,N 17,37:2
Missle to the Moon 1958,N 17,37:2
Cunning, Patrick
Very Confidential 1927,N 29,31:1
Cunningham, Ann (Screenwriter)
Sequoia 1935,F 23,14:6
Cunningham, Anne
This Sporting Life 1963,Jl 17,19:2
Cunningham, Bill (Original Author)
Consolation Marriage 1931,O 30,26:4
Cunningham, Cecil
Their own Desire 1930,Ja 25,13:2
Anybody's Woman 1930,Ag 16,8:3
Playboy of Paris 1930,N 1,23:2
Susan Lenox; Her Fall and Rise 1931,O 17,20:1
Safe in Hell 1931,D 19,16:4
Impatient Maiden, The 1932,Mr 4,17:3
Love Is a Racket 1932,Je 11,9:3
Love Me Tonight 1932,Ag 19,20:6
Ladies They Talk About 1933,F 25,20:4
From Hell to Heaven 1933,Mr 18,9:3
Life of Vergie Winters, The 1934,Je 15,26:1
We Live Again 1934,N 2,27:2
Come and Get It 1936,N 12,31:1
Swing High, Swing Low 1937,Ap 15,19:1
King of Gamblers 1937,Jl 3,18:1
Artists and Models 1937,Ag 5,19:2
This Way Please 1937,O 8,27:2
Awful Truth, The 1937,N 5,19:3
Night Club Scandal 1937,N 12,27:2
Daughter of Shanghai 1937,D 24,21:2
Scandal Street 1938,F 5,19:2 (In Addenda)
College Swing 1938,Ap 28,27:2
Four Men and a Prayer 1938,My 7,18:1
Kentucky Moonshine 1938,My 21,9:2
Wives Under Suspicion 1938,Jl 1,22:3
Girls' School 1938,N 3,27:1
Family Next Door, The 1939,Ap 28,31:2
It's a Wonderful World 1939,My 19,27:2
Winter Carnival 1939,Jl 28,14:2
Lady of the Tropics 1939,S 8,28:3
New Moon 1940,Jl 19,22:2
Great Profile, The 1940,O 18,25:1
Kitty Foyle 1941,Ja 9,27:2
Back Street 1941,F 12,25:2
Blossoms in the Dust 1941,Je 27,14:4
Hurry, Charlie, Hurry 1941,N 12,31:3
Wife Takes a Flyer, The 1942,Je 19,19:1
Hidden Hand, The 1942,N 26,40:4
In old Oklahoma 1943,D 6,21:1
Cyanamide 1954,Mr 26,17:6

Cunningham, Dan
Richard III 1956,Mr 12,1:4
Cunningham, E V (Miscellaneous)
Penelope 1966,N 11,36:6
Cunningham, Jack
Quare Fellow 1963,F 20,6:1
Cunningham, Jack (Original Author)
Professor Beware 1938,Jl 14,17:1
Painted Desert 1938,S 14,26:5
Arkansas Traveler, The 1938,N 17,29:2
Cunningham, Jack (Screenwriter)
Beyond the Rocks 1922,My 8,14:3
Ghost Breaker, The 1922,S 11,20:2
Tiger's Claw, The 1923,Mr 19,22:2
Heart Raider, The 1923,Je 6,24:5
Gentleman of Leisure, A 1923,Jl 16,14:2
It's a Gift 1935,Ja 5,20:2
Mississippi 1935,Ap 18,27:2
Union Pacific 1939,My 11,31:2
Cunningham, James
Condemned to Death 1932,Jl 14,24:2
Cunningham, Joe
Hot Money 1936,Jl 25,16:2
Fugitive in the Sky 1937,Ja 16,21:1
Kid Galahad 1937,My 27,21:3
Torchy Blane in Panama 1938,Ap 18,11:1
Four's a Crowd 1938,Ag 12,11:1
Torchy Gets her Man 1938,N 18,25:3
Going Places 1939,Ja 7,6:1
Blackwell's Island 1939,Mr 2,19:1
It's in the Air 1940,D 10,33:2
Tom, Dick and Harry 1941,Jl 18,22:2
I Live on Danger 1942,Ag 22,16:2
Cunningham, John M (Original Author)
Stranger Wore a Gun, The 1953,Jl 30,20:3
Day of the Badman 1958,Ja 30,19:2
Cunningham, June
Smallest Show on Earth, The 1957,N 23,11:2
Horrors of the Black Museum 1959,Ap 30,37:2
Cunningham, L V (Original Author)
Sylvia 1965,F 11,45:1
Cunningham, Margo
Taste of Honey, A 1962,My 1,33:3
Cunningham, Robert
I, The Jury 1953,Ag 22,8:2
It Started With a Kiss 1959,Ag 20,14:2
Cunningham, Sarah
Black Like Me 1964,My 21,42:1
Cunningham, Zamaä
Dream Girl 1948,Je 17,29:2
Key to the City 1950,F 2,31:2
Here Come the Girls 1953,D 26,10:1
Baby, the Rain Must Fall 1965,Ja 14,44:1
Cuny, Alain
Devil's Own Envoy, The 1947,Ag 30,8:6
Strange Deception 1953,My 27,28:2
Anita Garibaldi 1954,Mr 19,19:4
Hunchback of Notre Dame, The 1957,D 12,35:1
Lovers, The 1959,O 27,40:2
Dolce Vita, La 1961,Ap 20,30:1
Banana Peel; Peau de Banane 1965,Ja 19,29:1
Cuny, Louis (Director)
Belles and Ballets 1960,N 15,45:3
Cuny, Louis (Producer)
Belles and Ballets 1960,N 15,45:3
Cupane, Franca
Gospel According to St Matthew, The
1966,F 18,23:1
Cupito, Suzanne
Gypsy 1962,N 2,24:1
Yours, Mine and Ours 1968,Ap 25,53:1
Curacao, Harcourt
Stowaway Girl 1957,N 6,43:3
Curci, Elvira
Case Against Mrs Ames, The 1936,My 28,19:2
Always in my Heart 1942,Mr 14,19:2
Song of my Heart 1948,My 5,17:3
Raton Pass 1951,Ap 20,25:1
Curci, Gennaro
Melody Lingers on, The 1935,N 7,27:1
I'll Take Romance 1937,D 17,33:2
Manhattan Merry-Go-Round 1937,D 31,9:3
Midnight 1939,Ap 6,31:1
Juarez 1939,Ap 26,27:1
Curcio, Armando (Original Author)
Tarantella Napoletana 1954,Ap 19,19:3
Curetti, Silvia
White Line, The 1952,D 6,17:2
Curie, Eve (Original Author)
Madame Curie 1943,D 17,23:1
Curik, Jan (Director)
Wandering 1967,Je 19,41:1
Curioni, Federico (Miscellaneous)
Scipio Africanus 1939,S 23,22:2
Curioni, Federico (Producer)
Two Orphans, The 1950,O 19,40:6
Curlay, Leo
Johnny Holiday 1950,My 17,36:1
Curley, Miss
Girl Philippa, The 1917,Ja 1,10:2
Curley, Pauline
Turn in the Road, The 1919,Mr 30,IV,6:1
Power 1928,N 27,34:1

Curly Joe
Three Stooges Go Around the World in a Daze,
The 1963,D 19,40:2
Curnow, Graham
Horrors of the Black Museum 1959,Ap 30,37:2
Curradine, John
Miserables, Les 1935,Ap 22,14:2
Curram, Roland
Dunkirk 1958,S 11,42:2
Curram, Ronald
Darling 1965,Ag 4,20:1
Curran, Charles (Original Author)
No Marriage Ties 1933,Ag 4,18:2
Curran, Chris
Ulysses 1967,Mr 14,55:1
Curran, Paul
Nothing but the Best 1964,Jl 14,28:1
CURRIE
See Also CURRY
Currie, Clive
Magic Night 1932,N 3,25:3
Currie, Finlay
Rome Express 1933,F 27,11:2
Good Companions, The 1933,O 10,24:1
Criminal at Large 1933,D 20,27:2
Orders Is Orders 1934,My 7,20:2
Princess Charming 1935,Je 22,18:5
Edge of the World, The 1938,S 12,13:2
Invaders, The 1942,Mr 6,17:1
Avengers, The 1942,N 25,18:2
Thunder Rock 1944,S 15,16:1
Great Expectations 1947,My 23,31:1
I Know Where I'm Going 1947,Ag 20,25:2
Brothers, The 1948,My 5,30:4
Mr Perrin and Mr Traill 1949,Ja 17,15:2
Sleeping Car to Trieste 1949,Ap 18,18:6
My Brother Jonathan 1949,Je 29,34:4
Treasure Island 1950,Ag 16,24:2
Black Rose, The 1950,S 2,11:2
Sanitorium 1950,O 11,42:1
Operation X 1950,D 11,31:2
Mudlark, The 1950,D 25,25:1
People Will Talk 1951,Ag 30,20:1
History of Mr Polly, The 1951,O 25,36:3
Quo Vadis 1951,N 9,22:2
Bonnie Prince Charlie 1952,Ja 7,14:3
Kangaroo 1952,My 17,22:7
Walk East on Beacon 1952,My 29,17:2
Ivanhoe 1952,Ag 1,8:2
Stars and Stripes Forever 1952,D 23,17:2
Treasure of the Golden Condor 1953,My 23,19:2
Rob Roy 1954,F 4,21:5
Footsteps of the Fog 1955,S 15,39:2
Make Me an Offer 1956,F 29,35:2
Around the World in 80 Days 1956,O 18,37:1
Zarak 1956,D 27,22:1
Abandon Ship 1957,Ap 18,35:1
Little Hut, The 1957,My 4,25:1
Saint Joan 1957,Je 27,21:1
Naked Earth 1958,Ag 29,18:1
Dangerous Exile 1958,O 11,18:3
Tempest 1959,Mr 27,19:2
Ben Hur 1959,N 19,50:2
Solomon and Sheba 1959,D 26,7:2
Campbell's Kingdom 1960,Ja 11,35:5
Kidnapped 1960,My 19,44:3
Adventures of Huckleberry Fin, The
1960,Ag 4,17:1
Angel Wore Red, The 1960,S 29,32:1
Hand in Hand 1961,F 7,41:3
Francis of Assisi 1961,Jl 29,8:2
Five Golden Hours 1961,O 19,39:3
Lisa 1962,My 25,28:1
Story of Joseph and his Brethern, The
1962,D 1,17:1
Corridors of Blood 1963,Je 6,39:1
Three Lives of Thomasina, The 1963,D 12,46:1
Billy Liar 1963,D 17,49:1
Fall of the Roman Empire, The 1964,Mr 27,14:2
Bunny Lake is Missing 1965,O 4,00:0
Currie, George
It's the old Army Game 1926,Jl 5,6:4
Currie, Louise
Backlash 1947,My 24,10:5
Second Chance 1947,S 20,12:4
Crimson Key, The 1947,O 18,9:2
And Baby Makes Three 1949,D 23,17:3
Currie, Michael
Troublemaker, The 1964,Je 23,25:1
Currier, Art
That's my Daddy 1928,F 13,16:2
Currier, Frank
Her Kingdom of Dreams 1919,S 22,8:1
Should a Woman Tell? 1920,Ja 5,15:1
Rookie's Return, The 1920,D 27,11:3
Without Limit 1921,Mr 21,11:3
Children of Jazz 1923,Jl 9,8:4
Stephen Steps Out 1923,N 19,19:3
Darling of New York, The 1924,Ja 18,20:1
Sea Hawk, The 1924,Je 3,22:1
Revelation 1924,Je 24,18:2
Being Respectable 1924,Ag 4,16:3
Red Lily, The 1924,S 29,10:1

Currier, Frank— Cont

Too Many Kisses 1925,Mr 3,20:1
Graustark 1925,S 8,29:1
Lights of Old Broadway 1925,N 2.20:1
Ben Hur 1925,D 31,10:5 (In Addenda)
Boheme, La 1926,F 25,26:2
First Year, The 1926,Mr 8,17:1
Men of Steel 1926,Jl 12,24:4
Tell It to the Marines 1926,D 24,18:2
Rookies 1927,Ap 25,20:4
Annie Laurie 1927,My 12,24:3
Callahans and the Murphys, The 1927,Jl 12,29:3
Enemy, The 1927,D 28,26:6
Across to Singapore 1928,Ap 30,18:3
Easy Come, Easy Go 1928,My 8,25:3
Telling the World 1928,Jl 16,25:3
Ben Hur 1931,D 4,28:2

Currier, Mary

Everything's on Ice 1939,O 6,31:1
Great Victor Herbert, The 1939,D 7,35:1
That Uncertain Feeling 1941,My 2,25:1
Adventure in Washington 1941,Ag 1,11:3
Falcon in Mexico, The 1944,Ag 5,16:2
Dark Delusion 1947,Je 26,19:2
Magic Town 1947,O 8,29:2
Body and Soul 1947,N 10,21:2

Currin, Brenda C

In Cold Blood 1967,D 15,60:1

CURRY

See Also CURRIE

Curry, John

Day of Faith, The 1923,N 27,11:2

Curry, Nathan

Tarzan and his Mate 1934,Ap 21,12:1
Congo Maisie 1940,F 8,18:4

CURTIS

See Also CURTISS

Curtis, Alan

Walking on Air 1936,S 12,20:2
Mannequin 1938,Ja 21,15:2
Yellow Jack 1938,My 20,17:2
Shopworn Angel, The 1938,Jl 8,11:2
Duke of West Point, The 1938,D 16,33:2
Sergeant Madden 1939,Mr 24,27:2
Good Girls Go to Paris 1939,Je 23,23:1
Hollywood Cavalcade 1939,O 14,13:2
Four Sons 1940,Je 8,18:4
High Sierra 1941,Ja 25,11:2
Buck Privates 1941,F 14,15:2
New Wine 1942,F 2,11:2
Remember Pearl Harbor 1942,Je 4,22:4
Two Tickets to London 1943,Jl 3,11:2
Hitler's Madman 1943,Ag 28,15:1
Gung Ho! 1944,Ja 26,23:2
Phantom Lady 1944,F 18,15:2
Invisible Man's Revenge, The 1944,Je 10,12:2
Destiny 1945,F 3,16:5
Frisco Sal 1945,F 17,11:2
See my Lawyer 1945,My 4,23:4
Naughty Nineties, The 1945,Je 21,16:2
Shady Lady 1945,O 11,26:2
Daltons Ride Again, The 1945,D 8,21:2
Inside Job 1946,Je 15,24:3
Pirates of Capri, The 1949,D 26,33:5

Curtis, Alice F (Original Author)

Man Who Found Himself, The 1937,Ap 9,19:3

Curtis, Anthony

City Across the River 1949,Ap 8,31:3
Lady Gambles, The 1949,My 21,9:2
Johnny Stool Pigeon 1949,S 23,28:3
Francis 1950,Mr 16,40:2
I Was a Shoplifter 1950,Ap 28,26:3
Winchester 73 1950,Je 8,38:2
Sierra 1950,S 15,31:2

Curtis, Barry

Marrying Kind, The 1952,Mr 14,27:1
One Desire 1955,S 3,9:1
3:10 to Yuma 1957,Ag 29,22:1

Curtis, Beatrice

Paid to Dance 1937,D 6,19:1

Curtis, Billy

Saboteur 1942,My 8,27:2
Wings for the Eagle 1942,Ag 1,14:2
Three Wise Fools 1946,S 27,19:2
April Showers 1948,Mr 27,10:2
Incredible Shrinking Man, The 1957,F 23,13:1

Curtis, Dick

Shooting Straight 1930,Jl 28,22:1
Paid to Dance 1937,D 6,19:1
Shadow, The 1937,D 17,33:3
Women in Prison 1938,Mr 1,19:3
Penitentiary 1938,Mr 7,13:2
Rawhide 1938,Ap 25,19:2
Main Event, The 1938,Je 20,11:3
Adventure in Sahara 1938,D 19,19:2
Behind Prison Gates 1939,Ag 21,9:3
My Son Is Guilty 1940,Ja 15,11:2
Men Without Souls 1940,My 13,21:2
Roundup, The 1941,Mr 13,25:4
Billy the Kid 1941,Je 20,28:2
I Was a Prisoner on Devil's Island
    1941,Jl 28,16:4
Mystery Ship 1941,Ag 16,18:3
Two Yanks in Trinidad 1942,Ap 6,19:4

Jackass Mail 1942,Jl 2,25:2
Salute to the Marines 1943,Ag 30,11:3
Abilene Town 1946,Mr 4,16:5
Wyoming 1947,Jl 25,12:5

Curtis, Donald

Salute to the Marines 1943,Ag 30,11:3
Swing Shift Maisie 1943,S 10,29:2
Cross of Lorraine, The 1943,D 3,27:4
See Here Private Hargrove 1944,Mr 22,17:2
Thirty Seconds Over Tokyo 1944,N 16,19:1
This Man's Navy 1945,Ap 16,18:6
Thrill of a Romance 1945,My 25,22:2
Son of Lassie 1945,Je 11,12:1
Spellbound 1945,N 2,22:2
They Were Expendable 1945,D 21,25:2
Bad Bascomb 1946,My 23,18:4
Letter for Evie, A 1946,Je 28,17:4
White Tie and Tails 1946,N 8,28:2
Gallant Bess 1946,D 6,27:6
Night Song 1948,Ja 29,27:5
Fuller Brush Man, The 1948,My 15,18:2
Stampede 1949,S 16,36:2
Phffft 1954,N 11,43:2
Flame of the Islands 1956,F 25,12:4
All That Heaven Allows 1956,F 29,35:1
Earth vs the Flying Saucers 1956,Ag 2,21:2
Ten Commandments, The 1956,N 9,35:2

Curtis, Elaine

China Doll 1958,D 4,52:1

Curtis, Jack

Masters of Men 1923,My 15,22:1
Spoilers, The 1923,Ag 6,14:2
Day of Faith, The 1923,N 27,11:2
Captain Blood 1924,S 9,19:1
Free and Equal 1925,Ap 20,22:1
Baree, Son of Kazan 1925,My 19,24:2
Scarlet Seas 1928,D 31,9:1
Mammy 1930,Mr 27,24:5
Under a Texas Moon 1930,Ap 4,22:1
Hold Everything 1930,Ap 23,24:1
Moby Dick 1930,Ag 15,20:5

Curtis, Jackie

Flesh 1968,S 27,36:1

Curtis, James (Screenwriter)

Missing Ten Days 1941,Ap 21,15:5 (In Addenda)

Curtis, Keene

Macbeth 1950,D 28,22:6

Curtis, Ken

Mister Roberts 1955,Jl 15,14:1
Searchers, The 1956,My 31,21:4
Wings of Eagles, The 1957,F 1,28:1
Last Hurrah, The 1958,O 24,40:1
Cheyenne Autumn 1964,D 24,8:1

Curtis, Lucille

Invitation 1952,Ja 30,22:6
Third Voice, The 1960,Mr 7,24:5

Curtis, Lucinda

Nothing but the Best 1964,Jl 14,28:1

Curtis, Michael (Director)

Adventures of Huckleberry Fin, The
    1960,Ag 4,17:1

Curtis, Nat (Screenwriter)

Jack and the Beanstalk 1952,Ap 8,35:3

Curtis, Nathaniel (Miscellaneous)

Blood on the Sun 1945,Je 29,12:2

Curtis, Nathaniel (Screenwriter)

Harvey Girls, The 1946,Ja 25,26:2
Time of your Life, The 1948,My 27,29:2
Please Believe Me 1950,Je 12,19:4

Curtis, Peter (Original Author)

Guilt is my Shadow 1954,Mr 25,36:4
Devil's Own, The 1967,Mr 16,53:2

Curtis, Tony

Kansas Raiders 1951,Ja 26,19:2
Prince Who Was a Thief, The 1951,Jl 4,13:2
Flesh and Fury 1952,Mr 28,27:4
Vikings, The 1952,Je 12,35:2
No Room for the Groom 1952,Je 14,12:2
Son of Ali Baba 1952,Ag 16,7:4
Houdini 1953,Jl 3,10:2
Forbidden 1954,Ja 23,11:2
Beachhead 1954,Ap 17,8:2
Johnny Dark 1954,Je 26,7:2
Black Shield of Falworth, The 1954,O 7,16:2
Six Bridges to Cross 1955,Ja 22,8:2
So This Is Paris 1955,F 12,11:1
Purple Mask, The 1955,Je 16,35:7
Square Jungle, The 1955,D 31,17:2
Trapeze 1956,Je 5,39:2
Rawhide Years, The 1956,Je 16,12:2
Mister Cory 1957,F 23,13:1
Sweet Smell of Success 1957,Je 28,29:2
Midnight Story, The 1957,Jl 5,14:2
Kings Go Forth 1958,Jl 4,15:2
Defiant Ones, The 1958,S 25,29:1
Perfect Furlough, The 1959,Ja 22,27:4
Some Like It Hot 1959,Mr 30,23:1
Operation Petticoat 1959,D 6,38:1
Who Was That Lady? 1960,Ap 16,10:1
Rat Race, The 1960,My 26,37:3
Spartacus 1960,O 7,28:1
Great Impostor, The 1961,Mr 30,24:1
Outsider, The 1962,F 8,25:1

Curtis, Tony— Cont

Taras Bulba 1962,D 26,5:2
40 Pounds of Trouble 1963,Ja 24,5:2
List of Adrian Messenger, The 1963,My 30,20:1
Captain Newman, MD 1964,F 21,36:1
Wild and Wonderful 1964,Je 11,27:4
Goodbye, Charlie 1964,N 19,49:1
Sex and the Single Girl 1964,D 26,9:2
Great Race, The 1965,S 16,00:0
Boeing Boeing 1965,D 24,24:4
Not With my Wife, You Don't! 1966,N 3,45:2
Arrivederci, Baby! 1966,D 29,22:1
Don't Make Waves 1967,Je 21,36:2
Boston Strangler, The 1968,O 17,52:1

Curtis, Willa Pearl

Native Son 1951,Je 18,19:2
Queen Bee 1955,N 23,18:2

CURTISS

See Also CURTIS

Curtiss, Ursula (Original Author)

I Saw What You Did 1965,Jl 22,24:2

Curtiz, Gabor

Girl in the Kremlin, The 1957,My 22,29:2

Curtiz, Gabriel

Juggler, The 1953,My 6,39:2
Death of a Scoundrel 1956,N 6,30:1

Curtiz, Michael (Director)

Third Degree, The 1927,F 15,23:1
Million Bid, A 1927,My 31,25:2
Moon of Israel 1927,Je 29,29:3
Desired Woman, The 1927,Ag 30,21:3
Good Time Charley 1927,N 21,20:1
Tenderloin 1928,Mr 15,28:3
Noah's Ark 1929,Mr 13,28:6
Glad Rag Doll, The 1929,Je 3,27:2
Madonna of Avenue A 1929,Ag 12,22:2
Gamblers, The 1929,Ag 24,11:5
Hearts in Exile 1929,N 29,25:1
Mammy 1930,Mr 27,24:5
Under a Texas Moon 1930,Ap 4,22:1
Matrimonial Bed, The 1930,Ag 25,14:2
Bright Lights 1931,F 10,24:4
River's End 1931,Mr 7,17:2
God's Gift to Women 1931,Ap 18,17:3
Soldiers Plaything, A 1931,My 2,23:4
Mad Genius, The 1931,O 24,20:3
Woman From Monte Carlo, The 1931,D 31,17:6
Strange Love of Molly Louvain, The
    1932,My 9,19:5
Doctor X 1932,Ag 4,17:2
Cabin in the Cotton 1932,S 30,17:3
20,000 Years in Sing Sing 1933,Ja 10,26:2
Mystery of the Wax Museum, The
    1933,F 18,13:3
Keyhole, The 1933,Mr 31,23:3
Private Detective 62 1933,Jl 7,20:2
Good-Bye Again 1933,S 2,15:2
Kennel Murder Case, The 1933,O 30,14:2
Female 1933,N 4,18:3
Mandalay 1934,F 15,15:6
Jimmy the Gent 1934,Mr 26,22:3
Key, The 1934,My 30,14:3
British Agent 1934,S 20,20:1
Case of the Curious Bride, The 1935,Ap 5,21:3
Black Fury 1935,Ap 11,27:2
Front Page Woman 1935,Jl 12,15:1
Little Big Shot 1935,O 7,11:2
Captain Blood 1935,D 27,14:1
Walking Dead, The 1936,Mr 2,13:2
Charge of the Light Brigade, The 1936,N 2,24:1
Stolen Holiday 1937,F 1,15:3
Mountain Justice 1937,My 13,31:2
Kid Galahad 1937,My 27,21:3
Perfect Specimen, The 1937,O 28,29:2
Gold Is Where You Find It 1938,F 14,20:6
Adventures of Robin Hood, The 1938,My 13,17:2
Four's a Crowd 1938,Ag 12,11:1
Four Daughters 1938,Ag 19,13:3
Angels With Dirty Faces 1938,N 26,18:1
Dodge City 1939,Ap 8,19:1
Daughters Courageous 1939,Je 24,14:2
Private Lives of Elizabeth and Essex, The
    1939,D 2,21:2
Four Wives 1939,D 23,9:1
Virginia City 1940,Mr 23,16:3
Sea Hawk, The 1940,Ag 10,16:2
Santa Fe Trail 1940,D 21,21:2
Sea Wolf, The 1941,Mr 26,27:3
Dive Bomber 1941,Ag 30,10:2
Captains of the Clouds 1942,F 13,24:2
Yankee Doodle Dandy 1942,My 30,9:1
Casablanca 1942,N 27,27:1
Mission to Moscow 1943,Ap 30,25:2
This Is the Army 1943,Jl 29,11:6
Passage to Marseille 1944,F 17,12:5
Janie 1944,Ag 5,16:2
Roughly Speaking 1945,F 1,18:4
Mildred Pierce 1945,S 29,12:2
Night and Day 1946,Jl 26,16:2
Life With Father 1947,Ag 16,6:6
Unsuspected, The 1947,O 4,9:2
Romance on the High Seas 1948,Je 26,10:5
My Dream Is Yours 1949,Ap 16,11:3
Flamingo Road 1949,My 7,10:2

Curtiz, Michael (Director) — Cont
Lady Takes a Sailor, The 1949,D 17,15:2
Young Man With a Horn 1950,F 10,18:4
Bright Leaf 1950,Je 17,7:2
Breaking Point, The 1950,O 7,10:6
Force of Arms 1951,Ag 14,20:2
Jim Thorpe - All American 1951,Ag 25,7:2
I'll See You in my Dreams 1951,D 7,35:1
Story of Will Rogers, The 1952,Jl 18,10:5
Jazz Singer, The 1953,Ja 14,27:3
Trouble Along the Way 1953,My 7,37:2
Egyptian, The 1954,Ag 25,23:1
White Christmas 1954,O 15,16:3
We're no Angels 1955,Jl 8,15:2
Vagabond King, The 1956,S 13,39:6
Best Things in Life are Free, The 1956,S 29,12:2
Helen Morgan Story, The 1957,O 3,33:2
Proud Rebel, The 1958,Jl 2,23:4
King Creole 1958,Jl 4,15:2
Man in the Net, The 1959,Je 11,36:2
Breath of Scandal, A 1960,D 17,19:1
Francis of Assisi 1961,Jl 29,8:2
Comancheros, The 1961,N 2,42:1

Curtiz, Michael (Producer)
Unsuspected, The 1947,O 4,9:2

Curtright, Jorja
Whistle Stop 1946,Mr 18,24:2
Heaven Only Knows 1947,N 14,29:3
M 1951,Je 11,20:7
Love Is a Many-Splendored Thing 1955,Ag 19,10:1
Revolt of Mamie Stover, The 1956,My 12,12:7

Curwen, Patric
Ringer, The 1932,Je 2,25:2
Loyalties 1934,O 26,25:1
Don't Take it to Heart 1948,D 25,10:3

Curwood, James Oliver (Original Author)
Paid in Advance 1919,D 1,9:3
Rivers End, The 1920,F 23,11:2
Nomads of the North 1920,S 27,18:1
Isobel, or the Trail's End 1920,D 20,11:2
Northern Trail, The 1921,Jl 4,10:2
Golden Snare, The 1921,Jl 11,9:3
Alaskan, The 1924,S 15,28:1
Baree, Son of Kazan 1925,My 19,24:2
Steele of the Royal Mounted 1925,Je 18,16:3
Ancient Highway, The 1925,N 11,27:3
Flaming Forest, The 1926,N 22,28:3
Back to God's Country 1927,O 24,24:3
River's End 1931,Mr 7,17:2
Country Beyond, The 1936,Ap 30,17:3
God's Country and the Woman 1937,Ja 11,15:5
Call of the Yukon 1938,My 6,27:1
River's End 1940,Ag 26,11:4
Nikki, Wild Dog of the North 1961,S 5,37:6

Curzon, Charlotte
Jokers, The 1967,My 16,50:1

Curzon, George
Woman in Chains 1932,N 21,21:1
After the Ball 1933,Mr 20,18:3
Man Who Knew too Much, The 1935,Mr 23,11:2
Java Head 1935,Jl 31,21:4
Scotland Yard Mystery, The 1936,Mr 16,21:4
White Angel, The 1936,Je 25,24:1
Girl Was Young, The 1938,F 11,27:2
Clouds Over Europe 1939,Je 16,27:2
Jamaica Inn 1939,O 12,33:1
Inheritance, The 1951,F 12,19:2

Cusack, Cyril
Odd Man Out 1947,Ap 24,30:2
Escape 1948,Ag 16,12:2
All Over the Town 1949,My 26,34:4
Blue Lagoon, The 1949,O 3,13:2
Soldiers Three 1951,Mr 30,28:5
Blue Veil, The 1951,O 27,10:5
Wild Heart, The 1952,My 29,17:2
Saadia 1954,Mr 20,10:5
Fighting Pimpernel, The 1954,Ap 19,19:1
Man Who Never Was, The 1956,Ap 4,24:1
Rising of the Moon, The (The Majesty of the Law) 1957,Jl 10,23:1
Spanish Gardner, The 1957,S 9,21:2
Night Ambush 1958,Ap 25,32:4
Gideon of Scotland Yard 1959,My 20,38:2
Shake Hands With the Devil 1959,Je 25,20:7
Night Fighters, The 1960,D 15,59:1
Waltz of the Toreadors 1962,Ag 14,34:1
I Thank a Fool 1962,S 15,15:1
Johnny Nobody 1965,N 24,35:1
Spy Who Came in From the Cold, The 1965,D 24,24:1
Where the Spies Are 1966,Ja 27,29:1
Time Lost and Time Remembered 1966,Ag 30,35:2
Fahrenheit 451 1966,N 15,53:1
Taming of the Shrew, The 1967,Mr 9,43:1
Oedipus the King 1968,S 19,62:2

Cusack, Noel
Convicted 1938,Ag 22,9:3

Cusanelli, Joseph
Hoodlum Priest, The 1961,Ap 3,28:5

Cusanelli, Peter
Bell for Adano, A 1945,Jl 6,8:3

Cushing, Catherine Chisholm (Screenwriter)
Prince and the Pauper, The 1937,My 6,23:1

Cushing, Peter
Chump at Oxford, A 1940,F 20,17:3
Vigil in the Night 1940,Mr 9,19:2
Hamlet 1948,S 30,32:2
Black Knight, The 1954,O 29,27:2
End of the Affair, The 1955,Ap 29,28:2
Alexander the Great 1956,Mr 29,23:1
Curse of Frankenstein, The 1957,Ag 8,15:5
Time Without Pity 1957,N 23,11:2
Horror of Dracula 1958,My 29,24:4
John Paul Jones 1959,Je 17,39:1
Hounds of the Baskervilles, The 1959,Jl 4,9:4
Mummy, The 1959,D 17,51:4
Brides of Dracula, The 1960,S 6,41:4
Sword of Sherwood Forest 1961,Ja 26,32:3
Naked Edge 1961,Jl 1,9:1
Trouble in the Sky 1961,Jl 13,26:3
Risk, The 1961,S 25,41:2
Cash on Demand 1962,My 17,31:1
Evil of Frankenstein, The 1964,Je 18,29:2
She 1965,S 2,36:1
Torture Garden 1968,Jl 20,18:2
Corruption 1968,D 5,59:1

Cushing, Tom (Original Author)
Laugh, Clown, Laugh 1928,My 28,23:2
Laugh, Clown, Laugh! 1928,Je 3,VIII,5:1
South Sea Rose 1929,D 7,19:3

Cushing, Winnifred
Little Fugitive 1953,O 7,35:1

Cushman, Clarissa Fairchild (Original Author)
Young Widow 1946,Jl 29,12:8

Cushman, Dan (Original Author)
Timberjack 1955,Mr 10,33:3

Cushman, Nancy
Swimmer, The 1968,My 16,53:1

Cusick, Peter (Producer)
Long Dark Hall, The 1951,My 10,38:3
Pardon my French 1952,Mr 31,17:2

Cusin, Georges
Pot Bouille 1958,O 28,39:1
Virtuous Bigamist, The 1959,My 28,34:3

Cusmic, Mario
Messalina 1924,Ag 25,16:2

Custis, Micky
Fires on the Plain 1963,S 25,39:1

Custodio, Ana Maria
Su Ultimo Amor 1933,Ag 19,14:5

Cuthbertson, Allan
Court Martial 1955,Ag 2,17:1
Novel Affair, A 1957,Ag 28,22:1
Law and Disorder 1958,Ag 6,20:1
Room at the Top 1959,Mr 31,26:1
Killers of Kilimanjaro 1960,Ap 7,46:1
Tunes of Glory 1960,D 21,38:2
On the Double 1961,My 20,12:1
Guns of Navarone, The 1961,Je 23,19:1
Term of Trial 1963,Ja 31,5:2
Running Man, The 1963,O 3,31:1
Seventh Dawn, The 1964,S 3,24:1
Operation Crossbow 1965,Ap 2,29:1
Life at the Top 1965,D 15,53:1

Cutler, Bunty
New Moon 1940,Jl 19,22:2

Cutler, Kate
I Stand Condemned 1936,Jl 2,27:2
Pygmalion 1938,D 8,34:2
When Knights Were Bold 1942,Mr 31,29:2

Cutler, Vic
Walk in the Sun, A 1946,Ja 12,10:6
Canyon Passage 1946,Ag 8,18:2
Man From Texas 1948,Ag 12,16:5

Cutter, Murray (Miscellaneous)
Girl of the Golden West, The 1938,Mr 25,15:2

Cutting, Catherine Chisholm (Original Author)
Topsy and Eva 1927,Ag 8,10:3

Cutting, Richard
Chicago Syndicate 1955,Je 21,37:1
South Pacific 1958,Mr 20,33:1

Cutts, Graham (Director)
Sign of the Four, The 1932,Ag 20,7:4

Cutts, Patricia
Man Who Loved Redheads, The 1955,Jl 26,29:2
Merry Andrews 1958,Mr 21,17:1
Tingler, The 1960,Mr 10,36:2

Cuveller, Marcel
Doulos-The Finger Man 1964,Mr 3,31:1

Cuvivier, Julien (Director)
Poil de Carotte 1933,My 26,24:2

Cvetic, Matt (Original Author)
I Was a Communist for the F B I 1951,My 3,34:4

Cwai, Victor
Magic Garden, The 1952,F 6,24:2

Cwiklinska, M
Dodek na Froncie 1936,Mr 30,17:6
Tredowata 1936,D 31,21:2
Dzien Upragniony; Anticipated Day, The 1939,Mr 13,12:3

Cybulski, Mieczyslaw
Przysieglas 1932,My 16,19:5
Mlody Las 1935,D 3,32:7
Hearts Aflame 1937,O 14,22:3
Rena 1939,Ja 27,17:3

Cybulski, Zbigniew
Eighth Day of the Week, The 1959,Mr 24,45:2
Ashes and Diamonds 1961,My 30,8:1
Love at Twenty 1963,F 7,5:6
Poupee, La 1963,Ag 28,39:1
To Love; Att Alska 1964,S 23,45:3 (Incorrect in this edition; use 1964,S 23,54:1 elsewhere)
Salto 1966,O 4,50:1

Cyliakus, Marie
Strange Ones, The 1952,Jl 29,17:3

Cyne, Aminta
Song of India 1949,Je 10,32:3

Cynt, Greta
Dear Murderer 1948,My 8,12:2

Czarniak, Henry
Birds in Peru 1968,N 7,51:2

Czeike, Peter
No Time for Flowers 1952,D 26,20:3
Desires 1954,Jl 2,10:2

Czekalski, A (Screenwriter)
Eve Wants to Sleep 1961,Je 6,42:2

Czepa, Friedl
Thank You, Madame 1937,Ap 27,18:2
Episode 1937,My 17,23:2
Fasching in Wien 1939,Mr 18,9:2
Blumen aus Nizza; Flowers From Nice 1939,Ap 1,17:3
Unsterblicher Walzer; Immortal Waltz 1939,N 18,22:6
Alle stehen Kopf; General Confusion 1940,Je 22,18:4

Cziffra, Geza (Director)
Mindent a Noert! 1934,O 17,26:3
Egy ej Velencebzn 1935,D 23,11:2
Szent Peter Esernyoeje 1936,Ja 8,22:2

Czinner, Paul (Director)
Husbands or Lovers 1927,N 22,32:2
Traeumende Mund, Der 1934,F 5,19:2
Catherine the Great 1934,F 15,15:6
Ariane 1934,Mr 7,23:4
Escape me Never 1935,My 24,24:2
As You Like It 1936,N 6,29:3
Dreaming Lips 1937,My 20,17:1
Stolen Life 1939,Je 15,27:2
Bolshoi Ballet, The 1957,D 18,45:1
Royal Ballet, The (The Firebird) 1960,O 5,45:2
Royal Ballet, The (Ondine) 1960,O 5,45:2
Royal Ballet, The (Swan Lake Act II) 1960,O 5,45:2
Rosenkavalier, Der 1962,O 10,57:1
Romeo and Juliet 1966,O 6,55:1

Czinner, Paul (Miscellaneous)
Don Giovanni 1956,D 27,22:1

Czinner, Paul (Producer)
As You Like It 1936,N 6,29:3
Dreaming Lips 1937,My 20,17:1
Stolen Life 1939,Je 15,27:2
Bolshoi Ballet, The 1957,D 18,45:1
Royal Ballet, The (The Firebird) 1960,O 5,45:2
Royal Ballet, The (Ondine) 1960,O 5,45:2
Royal Ballet, The (Swan Lake Act II) 1960,O 5,45:2
Rosenkavalier, Der 1962,O 10,57:1
Romeo and Juliet 1966,O 6,55:1

Czinner, Paul (Screenwriter)
Dreaming Lips; (Traumende Mund, The) 1958,N 1,14:3

Czortos, Gyula
Rakoczi Indulo 1934,N 21,23:4

D

Da Cilva, Henry
Brazil 1944,N 20,25:2

da Costa, Therenzena Prates
Amazon Trader, The 1956,N 17,17:6

da Silva, Adhemar
Black Orpheus 1959,D 22,41:1

da Silva, Howard
Abe Lincoln in Illinois 1940,F 23,19:2
I'm Still Alive 1940,O 11,25:4
Sea Wolf, The 1941,Mr 26,27:3
Strange Alibi 1941,Ap 28,11:2
Sergeant York 1941,Jl 3,15:1
Bad Men of Missouri 1941,Ag 16,18:2
Nine Loves Are not Enough 1941,O 30,27:2
Blues in the Night 1941,D 12,35:2
Wild Bill Hickok Rides 1942,F 7,13:5
Bullet Scars 1942,Ap 24,21:4
Native Land 1942,My 12,16:3
Juke Girl 1942,Je 20,9:2
Big Shot, The 1942,Jl 18,8:2
Reunion in France 1943,Mr 5,20:3
Keeper of the Flame 1943,Mr 19,15:2
Tonight We Raid Calais 1943,Ap 15,20:2
Duffy's Tavern 1945,S 6,23:3
Lost Weekend, The 1945,D 3,17:2

da Silva, Howard — Cont
Blue Dahlia, The 1946,My 9,27:3
Two Years Before the Mast 1946,S 25,39:2
Blaze of Noon 1947,Mr 5,31:2
Unconquered 1947,O 11,11:2
Great Gatsby, The 1949,Jl 14,20:5
They Live by Night 1949,N 4,33:2
Border Incident 1949,N 21,29:2
Underworld Story, The 1950,Jl 27,29:4
Wyoming Mail 1950,O 23,26:5
Tripoli 1950,N 10,35:2
Fourteen Hours 1951,Mr 7,43:2
Three Husbands 1951,Mr 9,30:2
M 1951,Je 11,20:7
David and Lisa 1962,D 27,5:5
Outrage, The 1964,O 8,48:2
Nevada Smith 1966,Je 24,28:1 (Incorrect in this
  edition; use 1966,Je 30,28:1 elsewhere)

Da Silva, Maria Luisa
My Seven Little Sins 1956,My 2,27:1

Da Silveira, Walter
Given Word, The 1964,Mr 25,47:1

Daay, Alfred (Director)
Nem Elhetek Muzsikaszo Nelkuel 1936,F 21,21:2

Dabit, Eugene (Original Author)
Hotel du Nord 1940,D 30,21:2

Dable, Frances
Constant Nymph, The 1929,Je 10,23:1

Dabney, Augusta
That Night 1957,O 15,39:3

Dabney, Virginia
Prison Farm 1938,Jl 15,13:3
King of Alcatraz 1938,O 7,21:2
Disbarred 1939,Ja 19,17:2
Magnificent Fraud, The 1939,Jl 20,16:2
Women Without Names 1940,My 9,26:4

Dac, Pierre
Belle Americaine, La 1961,D 18,42:1

Dacic, Jolanda
Kaya 1968,S 25,39:1

DaCosta, Morton (Director)
Auntie Mame 1958,D 5,39:1
Music Man, The 1962,Ag 24,14:1
Island of Love 1963,Je 13,30:4

DaCosta, Morton (Producer)
Music Man, The 1962,Ag 24,14:1
Island of Love 1963,Je 13,30:4

Dacqmine, Jacques
Queen's Necklace, The 1947,My 17,8:5
Back Streets of Paris 1948,O 16,9:2
Secret of Mayerling, The 1951,My 8,39:2
Caroline Cherie 1954,My 25,23:1
Leda 1961,Jl 19,33:1

Dada, Jorge M (Director)
Tras la Reja 1937,Ja 11,15:7
Ojos Tapatios 1939,F 13,13:3

Dada, Jorge M (Producer)
Virgen de la Sierra, La 1939,Mr 6,11:3
Infidelidad 1939,My 8,21:3

Dada, Jorge M (Screenwriter)
Tras la Reja 1937,Ja 11,15:7

Dadaras, D (Director)
Shepherd's Daughter, The 1956,My 14,23:3

Daddio, Anthony
Synanon 1965,My 6,44:1

Dade, Frances
He Knew Women 1930,Ap 23,24:1
Raffles 1930,Jl 25,20:4
Grumpy 1930,Ag 2,16:4
Dracula 1931,F 13,21:3
Seed 1931,My 15,20:6
She-Wolf 1931,My 28,30:6
Daughter of the Dragon 1931,Ag 22,7:5

Dae, Frank
In Old Chicago 1938,Ja 7,15:2
Stanley and Livingstone 1939,Ag 5,18:2

Daele, Van
Mystere de la Chambre Jaune, Le
  1931,My 26,33:2

Daems, Marie
Maid in Paris 1957,Jl 13,11:1
Journey, The 1959,F 20,19:1

Dagan, Gavriel
They Were Ten; (Heym Hayu Assara)
  1961,Ap 18,44:2

Dagan, Gavriel (Screenwriter)
They Were Ten; (Heym Hayu Assara)
  1961,Ap 18,44:2

Daghofer, Fritz
Foresterchristl, Die 1931,Ap 27,25:1

Dagmarov, M
Golden Key, The 1939,D 21,29:3

Dagna, Jeanette
Cock Eyed World, The 1929,Ag 5,25:2

D'Agostini, Bruno (Original Author)
Singing Taxi Driver 1953,My 16,10:1

Dagover, Lil
Between Worlds 1924,Jl 7,10:4
Beyond the Wall 1927,F 3,18:5
Tartuffe 1927,Jl 25,25:3
Love Makes Us Blind 1927,Ag 23,29:4
At the Grey House 1927,N 8,33:1
Discord 1928,F 7,30:3
Two Brothers, The 1928,Ag 21,27:4

Hungarian Rhapsody 1929,Ag 5,25:2
Hungarian Nights 1930,Je 10,32:2
White Devil, The 1931,Ag 28,20:1
Alte Lied, Das 1931,S 11,24:2
Elisabeth von Oesterreich 1931,D 11,35:1
Woman From Monte Carlo, The 1931,D 31,17:6
Congress Dances 1932,My 12,23:2
Fall des Oberst Redl, Der 1932,Ag 18,23:3
Barberina, Die Taenzerin Von Sans-Souci
  1932,O 26,15:4
Madame Blaubart 1933,My 11,14:2
Storch Hat Uns Getraut, Der 1933,D 1,23:2
Johannisnact 1935,F 25,13:4
Fluechtling aus Chicago, Der 1936,Mr 16,21:4
Hoehere Befehl, Der 1936,Mr 31,17:3
Eine Frau die Weiss Was sie Will 1936,Jl 18,18:3
Schlussakkord 1936,S 10,29:4
August der Starke 1937,Ja 30,21:3
Kreutzer Sonata 1937,Mr 14,XI,4:6 (In Addenda)
Maedchen Irene, Das 1937,My 22,19:3
Kreutzer Sonata, The 1938,My 28,9:3
Dreikland; Triad 1938,Jl 23,10:5
Streitum den Knaben Jo; Strife Over the Boy Jo
  1938,D 10,13:2
Fridericus 1939,F 25,19:2

DaGradi, Don (Miscellaneous)
Fun and Fancy Free 1947,S 29,17:2 (In
  Addenda)

DaGradi, Don (Screenwriter)
Mary Poppins 1964,S 25,34:1
Blackbeard's Ghost 1968,Ap 11,51:3

D'Aguiar, A (Producer)
Forbidden Fruit 1959,F 23,19:1

d'Agular, Thelma
Chase a Crooked Shadow 1958,Mr 25,28:4

D'Agular (Producer)
Ignace 1950,S 19,39:4

Dahike, Paul
Secrets of a Soul 1950,S 16,12:6
Confessions of Felix Krull, The 1958,Mr 5,38:1
Third Sex, The 1959,Mr 26,27:1
Head, The 1963,Je 20,29:1

Dahl, Arlene
My Wild Irish Rose 1947,D 25,32:2
Bride Goes Wild, The 1948,Je 4,27:2
Southern Yankee, A 1948,N 25,47:2
Scene of the Crime 1949,Jl 29,12:2
Black Book, The 1949,O 17,18:2
Ambush 1950,Ja 19,35:2
Outriders, The 1950,Mr 9,25:2
Three Little Words 1950,Ag 10,21:2
Watch the Birdie 1950,D 12,46:4
Inside Straight 1951,Mr 16,34:2
No Questions Asked 1951,Ag 10,13:2
Desert Legion 1953,My 9,13:2
Sangaree 1953,Je 5,19:1
Here Come the Girls 1953,D 26,10:1
Diamond Queen, The 1954,Ja 27,24:2
Woman's World 1954,S 29,23:4
Bengal Brigade 1954,N 13,13:2
Slightly Scarlet 1956,Mr 17,13:2
Journey to the Center of the Earth
  1959,D 17,51:1
Kisses for my President 1964,Ag 22,13:1

Dahl, Roald (Screenwriter)
You Only Live Twice 1967,Je 14,40:1
Chitty Chitty Bang Bang 1968,D 19,64:4

Dahlbeck, Eva
Village, The 1953,S 23,37:2
Smiles of a Summer Night 1957,D 24,11:1
Brink of Life; (Nara Livet) 1959,N 9,36:2
Lesson in Love, A 1960,Mr 15,46:1
Dreams; Kvinnodrom 1960,Je 1,42:1
Matter of Morals, A 1961,Je 1,31:1
Secrets of Woman 1961,Jl 12,36:1
Counterfeit Traitor, The 1962,Ap 18,28:1
All These Women 1964,O 6,35:1
Creatures, Les 1966,S 16,31:2
Loving Couples 1966,S 20,38:1
Hagbard and Signe 1968,My 17,56:1

Dahlberg, Gilda
Eight and One Half 1963,Je 26,36:1

Dahlen, Armin
Divided Heart, The 1955,Ag 4,16:1
Rape on the Moor 1957,N 21,38:1

Dahlgren, Nils
Torment 1947,Ap 22,34:2
I Am With You 1949,Mr 1,30:5

Dahlin, Hans (Director)
Unmarried Mothers 1956,F 23,32:5

Dahlin, Mlle
Mystere de la Villa Rose, Le 1932,Ja 11,28:5

Dahlke, Paul
Verraeter 1937,Ja 23,13:1
Kleine Suenderin, Die; Little Sinner, The
  1938,D 3,11:3
Befreite Hande; Freed Hans 1940,My 25,20:1
Long Is the Road 1948,N 12,30:5
Flying Classroom, The 1958,Je 28,13:7
Situation Hopeless-But not Serious
  1965,O 14,53:1

Dahlquist, Ake (Director)
Vi Som Gar Koeksvaegen 1933,O 7,18:5

Dai, Lin
Last Woman of Shang, The 1964,D 15,56:2

Daiban, Max
Boudu Saved From Drowning; Boudu Sauve Des
  Eaux 1967,F 24,26:2

DAILEY
See Also DALEY, DALY, DAILY

Dailey, Dan
Mortal Storm, The 1940,Je 21,25:2
Dulcy 1940,N 28,28:2
Hullabaloo 1940,D 19,33:1
Ziegfeld Girl 1941,Ap 25,17:2
Washington Melodrama 1941,My 26,15:3
Get-Away, The 1941,Jl 17,23:4
Lady Be Good 1941,S 19,27:1
Moon Over her Shoulder 1941,N 5,31:2
Sunday Punch 1942,My 11,19:2
Give Out, Sisters 1942,Ag 28,22:3
Panama Hattie 1942,O 2,31:2
Mother Wore Tights 1947,Ag 21,33:2
You Were Meant for Me 1948,Ja 29,27:5
Give my Regards to Broadway 1948,Je 23,32:2
When my Baby Smiles at Me 1948,N 24,20:2
Chicken every Sunday 1949,Ja 19,34:2
You're my Everything 1949,Jl 23,7:2
When Willie Comes Marching Home
  1950,F 18,9:2
Ticket to Tomahawk, A 1950,My 20,8:6
My Blue Heaven 1950,S 16,12:6
Call Me Mister 1951,F 1,21:2
I Can Get It for You Wholesale 1951,Ap 5,34:4
Pride of St Louis, The 1952,My 3,17:5
What Price Glory 1952,Ag 23,10:2
Taxi 1953,Ja 22,20:3
Girl Next Door, The 1953,S 5,7:4
Kid From Left Field, The 1953,S 26,15:3
There's no Business Like Show Business
  1954,D 17,37:3
It's Always Fair Weather 1955,S 16,19:1
Meet Me in Las Vegas 1956,Mr 14,39:2
Best Things in Life are Free, The 1956,S 29,12:2
Wings of Eagles, The 1957,F 1,28:1
Oh Men! Oh Women! 1957,F 22,25:2
Wayward Bus, The 1957,Je 6,35:2
Pepe 1960,D 22,18:1
Hemingway's Adventures of a Young Man
  1962,Jl 26,17:1

Dailey, E V Rev (Miscellaneous)
Citizen Saint 1948,My 28,28:2

Dailey, E V Rev (Narrator)
Citizen Saint 1948,My 28,28:2

Dailey, Irene
No Way to Treat a Lady 1968,Mr 21,56:1

Dailey, John Hammond
Counsellor-At-Law 1933,D 8,31:2

Dailo, Marcel
Song Without End 1960,Ag 12,10:2

DAILY
See Also DAILEY, DALEY, DALY

Daily, Margaret
Devotion 1931,O 3,20:2

Dainton, Noel
Murder in the Old Red Barn 1936,Ag 19,18:3

Dainton, Patricia
Dancing Years, The 1951,Ja 29,14:4
Castle in the Air 1953,Ja 5,19:2
Novel Affair, A 1957,Ag 28,22:1

Daisy (Dog)
Blondie 1938,D 22,25:4
Blondie Meets the Boss 1939,Ap 27,31:1
Blondie Goes Latin 1941,F 26,17:3
Red Stallion 1947,N 27,50:3

Daix, Didier
Belle Americaine, La 1961,D 18,42:1

Daix, Didier (Original Author)
How to Murder a Rich Uncle 1957,O 26,19:2

Daix, Hubert
Criez-Le sur les Toits; Shout it From the
  Housetops 1935,Je 22,18:5

Daix, Jacqueline
Tender Enemy, The 1938,Mr 31,15:2 (In
  Addenda)

Dajbukat, Ilona
Kiralyne Huszarja, A 1936,Ja 17,15:3

Dajevskis, Evalds (Miscellaneous)
Hansel and Gretel 1954,O 11,33:1

Dakin, Gay Ellen
Broadway Limited 1941,Je 16,11:6

Dakin, Phillip
Wake up and Dream 1934,O 11,28:3

Dakotas, The
Go Go Mania 1965,My 20,52:4

Dakovsky, D
Heroes of Shipka 1956,S 3,10:5

dal Monte, Toti
Carnevale di Venezia, Il; Carnival of Venice, The
  1940,O 11,25:2
King's Jester, The 1947,Je 26,19:3

D'Alba, Rossana
Miracolo Di Sant' Antonio, Il 1932,Ap 18,19:2

Dalban
Toni 1968,S 19,62:2
Dalban, Max
Panic 1947,N 27,50:2
Scandals of Clochemerle, The 1950,Mr 28,28:2
Dalban, Robert
Resistance; Peleton d'Execution 1946,Jl 5,15:3
Walls of Malapaga, The 1950,Mr 21,34:2
Moment of Truth, The 1954,Ap 27,36:2
Daughters of Destiny (Jeanne) 1954,Jl 6,19:1
Marie Octobre 1960,Ag 16,25:2
Paris Pick-Up 1963,Ag 29,36:2
Love on a Pillow 1963,D 17,49:1
Seventh Juror, The 1964,Ja 28,25:1
Fantomas 1966,Ap 6,36:2
Great Spy Chase, The 1966,O 6,56:4
Dalbert, Suzanne
Accused, The 1949,Ja 13,26:2
Mark of the Gorilla 1950,F 17,27:2
Breakthrough 1950,N 18,10:2
Target Unknown 1951,Mr 5,24:2
D'Albie, Julian
So Well Remembered 1947,N 5,34:3
Edward my Son 1949,Je 3,21:2
Gay Adventure, The 1954,S 16,35:7
Dalbon
Strollers, The 1952,Jl 22,22:7
D'Albrook, Sidney
King of Kings, The 1927,Ap 20,29:2
Chicago 1927,D 24,9:1
Matinee Idol, The 1928,Ap 24,29:3
Party Girl 1930,Ja 2,28:2
Bat Whispers, The 1931,Ja 16,27:1
Dalby, Amy
Wicked Lady, The 1946,D 23,19:5
Man Upstairs, The 1959,Ag 11,23:2
Spy With a Cold Nose, The 1966,D 20,58:2
Dalby, Edmund
Man With 100 Faces 1938,N 1,27:2
Dale, Alan
Don't Knock the Rock 1957,F 23,13:1
Dale, Anne
Fool, The 1925,Ap 13,24:1
Dale, Charles
Manhattan Parade 1931,D 25,29:2
Heart of New York, The 1932,Mr 2,15:3
Two Tickets to Broadway 1951,N 22,47:2
Dale, Dana
Ladies Must Live 1940,S 6,25:3
Dale, Dick and the Del-Tones
Beach Party 1963,S 26,40:2
Dale, Esther
Crime Without Passion 1934,S 1,16:2
Wedding Night, The 1935,Mr 16,19:1
Private Worlds 1935,Mr 28,25:2
Curly Top 1935,Ag 2,22:3
I Dream too Much 1935,N 29,24:1
Old Kentucky, In 1935,N 29,24:1
Great Impersonation, The 1935,D 14,11:1
Lady of Secrets 1936,F 22,12:1
Timothy's Quest 1936,F 29,11:2
Farmer in the Dell, The 1936,Mr 7,11:4
Case Against Mrs Ames, The 1936,My 28,19:2
Fury 1936,Je 6,21:1
Hollywood Boulevard 1936,S 21,26:4
Magnificent Brute, The 1936,O 24,23:1
Outcast 1937,Mr 3,27:2
Easy Living 1937,Jl 8,20:1
Dead End 1937,Ag 25,25:1
Awful Truth, The 1937,N 5,19:3
Condemned Woman 1938,Ag 22,15:5
Stolen Heaven 1938,My 12,27:2
Prison Farm 1938,Jl 15,13:3
Marriage Forbidden 1938,Jl 16,7:2
Girls on Probation 1938,O 21,27:3
Made for Each Other 1939,F 17,17:2
Broadway Serenade 1939,Ap 7,25:2
Big Town Czar 1939,My 4,27:3
Tell no Tales 1939,Je 2,27:3
Six Thousand Enemies 1939,Je 9,26:2
Blackmail 1939,S 15,26:3
Women, The 1939,S 22,27:2
Convicted Woman 1940,F 26,11:2
And One Was Beautiful 1940,Ap 11,32:4
Women Without Names 1940,My 9,26:4
Mortal Storm, The 1940,Je 21,25:2
Untamed 1940,Jl 25,14:3
Arise my Love 1940,O 17,33:2
Back Street 1941,F 12,25:2
Mr and Mrs Smith 1941,F 21,16:3
There's Magic in Music 1941,Je 5,27:2
Aloma of the South Seas 1941,Ag 28,23:4
Unfinished Business 1941,S 2,20:2
Dangerously They Live 1942,Ap 11,9:2
Ten Gentlemen From West Point 1942,Je 5,23:3
Amazing Mrs Holliday, The 1943,F 22,20:2
Murder in Times Square 1943,My 31,13:2
Old Acquaintance 1943,N 3,20:2
North Star, The 1943,N 5,23:1
Bedside Manner 1945,Je 23,9:6
My Reputation 1946,Ja 26,19:2
Stolen Life, A 1946,My 2,27:4
Smoky 1946,Je 27,29:1

Margie 1946,O 17,28:3
Egg and I, The 1947,Ap 25,29:2
Unfinished Dance, The 1947,O 31,29:2
Song Is Born, A 1948,O 20,37:2
Ma and Pa Kettle 1949,Ag 12,13:2
Holiday Affair 1949,N 24,48:2
Surrender 1950,O 9,21:5
Walk Softly Stranger 1950,O 16,30:5
Too Young to Kiss 1951,N 23,32:2
Ma and Pa Kettle at the Fair 1952,Jl 12,16:2
Monkey Business 1952,S 6,12:6
Oklahoman, The 1957,My 15,39:1
Dale, Grover
Unsinkable Molly Brown, The 1964,Jl 17,15:1
Half a Sixpence 1968,F 21,60:3
Young Girls of Rochefort, The 1968,Ap 12,50:1
Dale, Highland
Black Beauty 1946,Ag 30,13:2
Dale, James
Victoria the Great 1937,O 29,19:1
Dale, Jean
Missing Witness 1937,D 10,33:3
Dale, Jim
Carry on Cleo 1965,O 23,17:2
Dale, Joan
Alice in Wonderland 1951,Jl 27,15:2
Dale, Lilia
Manon Lescaut 1941,Ap 14,23:5
Dale, Margaret
Disraeli 1921,Ag 22,13:6
One Exciting Night 1922,O 24,17:3
Second Youth 1924,Ap 22,19:3
Man With two Faces, The 1934,Jl 12,20:2
Dale, Marjorie
Dead Men Tell no Tales 1939,Jl 24,9:2
Dale, Rudy
Lemonade Joe 1967,N 21,53:1
Dale, Virginia
No Time to Marry 1938,F 23,27:2
Start Cheering 1938,Mr 17,17:3
Idiot's Delight 1939,F 3,13:1
Death of a Champion 1939,Ag 24,17:3
Parole Fixer 1940,Ap 18,28:5
Buck Benny Rides Again 1940,Ap 25,28:4
Quarterback, The 1940,O 17,33:3
Love Thy Neighbor 1940,D 18,32:5
Las Vegas Nights 1941,Mr 20,25:2
Kiss the Boys Goodbye 1941,Ag 14,21:2
World Premiere 1941,Ag 21,15:2
Holiday Inn 1942,Ag 5,16:1
Daleky, N (Screenwriter)
Bountiful Summer 1951,D 24,9:1
Dales, Arthur (Screenwriter)
Sheriff of Fractured Jaw, The 1959,Mr 14,27:4
DALEY
See Also DALY, DAILY, DAILEY
Daley, Cass
Fleet's In, The 1942,Mr 12,24:2
Star Spangled Rhythm 1942,D 31,20:1
Crazy House 1943,D 16,33:3
Riding High 1943,D 23,26:4
Out of This World 1945,Je 7,25:2
Duffy's Tavern 1945,S 6,23:3
Ladies' Man 1947,Ja 13,18:5
Here Comes the Groom 1951,S 21,19:2
Red Garters 1954,Mr 27,13:5
Daley, Jack
Sap From Syracuse, The 1930,Jl 26,16:4
O'Shaughnessy's Boy 1935,O 5,18:2
Goodbye Broadway 1938,My 14,18:1
Mutiny in the Big House 1939,D 11,26:2
Daley, Jacqueline
Treasure of Sierra Madre 1948,Ja 24,11:2
Daley, Jeff
Enemy Below, The 1957,D 26,23:2
Daley, Jerome
Girl Habit, The 1931,Jl 4,11:5
Daley, Ray
Thin Red Line, The 1964,O 29,38:1
D'Algy, Antonio
Rejected Woman, The 1924,My 5,18:3
Sainted Devil, A 1924,N 24,15:3
D'Algy, Helena
Let Not Man Put Asunder 1924,Ja 15,16:1
Sainted Devil, A 1924,N 24,15:3
Don Juan 1926,Ag 7,6:1 (In Addenda)
D'Algy, Tony
Figaro 1929,N 25,22:1
Toda una Vida 1933,O 23,18:3
Dali, Salvador (Screenwriter)
Age d'Or, L'; Golden Age, The 1964,S 22,44:1
Dalibert, A
Dr Knock 1955,O 10,31:2
Dalio, Marcel
Grand Illusion 1938,S 13,28:2
Curtain Rises, The 1939,Ap 22,15:2
Affair Lafont, The; Conflict 1939,O 9,15:2
Kiss of Fire 1940,N 20,27:4
Pepe le Moko 1941,Mr 4,20:2
Unholy Partners 1941,D 29,21:4
Pasha's Wives, The 1942,Ap 6,19:2
Flight Lieutenant 1942,Jl 31,11:1
Pied Piper, The 1942,Ag 13,15:3

Dalio, Marcel — Cont
Casablanca 1942,N 27,27:1
Tonight We Raid Calais 1943,Ap 15,20:2
Constant Nymph, The 1943,Jl 24,8:2
Paris After Dark 1943,O 23,11:1
Desert Song, The 1943,D 18,10:6
Song of Bernadette, The 1944,Ja 27,15:2
Action in Arabia 1944,F 19,18:7
Pin Up Girl 1944,My 11,25:6
Wilson 1944,Ag 2,18:1
To Have and Have Not 1944,O 12,24:1
Marthe Richard 1944,N 9,23:2
Bell for Adano, A 1945,Jl 6,8:3
Sirocco 1946,Ag 12,17:3
Damned, The; Maudits, Les 1948,Ap 26,27:2
Snowbound 1949,F 21,20:2
Dedee 1949,Ap 9,9:2
Temptation Harbor 1949,My 11,34:7
Rules of the Game, The 1950,Ap 10,15:3
Lovers of Verona, The 1951,Mr 12,20:2
On the Riviera 1951,My 24,47:1
Rich, Young and Pretty 1951,Jl 26,17:3
Snows of Kilimanjaro, The 1952,S 19,19:2
Happy Time, The 1952,O 31,30:2
Gentlemen Prefer Blondes 1953,Jl 16,17:2
Flight to Tangier 1953,N 26,50:4
Lucky Me 1954,Ap 10,11:2
Sabrina 1954,S 23,43:2
Anything Goes 1956,Mr 22,38:1
Miracle in the Rain 1956,Ap 2,18:1
Ten Thousand Bedrooms 1957,Ap 4,37:1
Tip on a Dead Jockey 1957,S 7,12:7
Razzi 1957,N 19,39:4
Lafayette Escadrille 1958,Ap 19,10:4
Man Who Understood, The 1959,O 3,14:7
Pillow Talk 1959,O 7,47:2
Can-Can 1960,Mr 10,36:1
Rules of the Game, The 1961,Ja 19,26:1
Jessica 1962,Ap 20,20:2
Wild and Wonderful 1964,Je 11,27:4
Cartouche 1964,Jl 22,39:1
Male Companion 1966,F 15,33:2
Made in Paris 1966,F 17,29:1
Lady L 1966,My 19,51:1
How to Steal a Million 1966,Jl 15,34:1
25th Hour, The 1967,F 17,45:1
Tender Scoundrel 1967,N 16,58:2
How Sweet It Is 1968,Ag 22,47:1
Dalkhart, Elynore (Original Author)
Great God Gold 1935,My 6,22:3
DALL
See Also DAHL, DOLL
Dall, Fabienne
Doulos-The Finger Man 1964,Mr 3,31:1
Dall, John
Corn is Green, The 1945,Mr 30,18:2
Something in the Wind 1947,Ag 29,14:3
Another Part of the Forest 1948,My 19,30:2
Rope 1948,Ag 27,12:4
Gun Crazy 1950,Ag 25,17:5
Man Who Cheated Himself, The 1951,F 9,21:2
Spartacus 1960,O 7,28:1
Atlantis the Lost Continent 1961,My 27,12:1
Dall, Yiannis (Director)
Moussitsa 1960,O 31,25:2
Dall, Yiannis (Screenwriter)
Moussitsa 1960,O 31,25:2
Dallan
Amours de Toni, Les 1936,N 5,35:1
Dallanidis, Yannis (Director)
Stefania 1968,N 29,56:1
Dallanidis, Yannis (Screenwriter)
Stefania 1968,N 29,56:1
Dallas, Jan
Eight and One Half 1963,Je 26,36:1
Dallas, Jimmy
Stand up and Cheer 1934,Ap 20,17:1
Dallas, Julian
This Was a Woman 1949,Ja 5,22:2
Mrs Fitzherbert 1950,My 11,37:2
Reluctant Widow, The 1951,S 8,8:6
Dallesandro, Joe
Flesh 1968,S 27,36:1
Dallimore, Maurice
Collector, The 1965,Je 18,28:1
Dallinger, Nat (Original Author)
Shakedown 1950,S 4,11:2
Dallo, Marcel
Shanghai Gesture, The 1941,D 26,21:2
Conspirators, The 1944,O 21,15:2
Lovely to Look At 1952,My 30,11:2
Merry Widow, The 1952,S 25,38:1
Captain Black Jack 1952,O 22,31:3
China Gate 1957,My 23,40:2
Lover's Net 1957,Jl 23,23:1
Perfect Furlough, The 1959,Ja 22,27:4
Donovan's Reef 1963,Jl 25,14:1
D'Alma, Rubi
Signor Max, Il; Mr Max 1939,O 6,31:4
Dalmas, Herbert (Original Author)
Adventures of Don Juan 1948,D 25,10:1
Dalmas, Herbert (Screenwriter)
Address Unknown 1944,Ap 17,20:1
American Romance, An 1944,N 24,19:1

Dalmas, Herbert (Screenwriter)— Cont
Last of the Redmen 1947,Ag 30,8:6
Star of India 1956,Ap 28,11:1
Dalmatoff, Michael
Once in a Blue Moon 1936,D 2,35:1
Song of Russia 1944,F 11,17:2
Irish Eyes Are Smiling 1944,N 8,27:1
Dalmayne, Malcolm
Mine Own Executioner 1949,Ja 19,34:2
D'Almeida, Elaine
Belle Americaine, La 1961,D 18,42:1
Dalpas, Lon (Screenwriter)
Youth of Athens 1949,O 31,20:4
Dalquist, Valdemar
Troette Teodor 1932,Ja 18,18:4
Dalrymple, Ian (Director)
Storm in a Teacup 1938,Mr 22,18:4
Dalrymple, Ian (Producer)
Before the Raid 1944,F 26,10:3
Coastal Command 1944,Ap 19,26:1
Woman in the Hall, The 1949,Ja 24,16:2
Wooden Horse, The 1951,Ag 29,20:2
Heart of the Matter, The 1954,N 19,20:2
Three Cases of Murder (In the Picture)
1955,Mr 16,39:4
Three Cases of Murder (You Killed Elizabeth)
1955,Mr 16,39:4
Three Cases of Murder (Lord Mountdrago)
1955,Mr 16,39:4
Raising a Riot 1957,My 8,44:1
Admirable Crichton, The 1957,D 15,45:4
(Incorrect in this edition; use 1957,D 17,45:4
elsewhere)
Cry From the Streets, A 1959,F 24,32:2
Dalrymple, Ian (Screenwriter)
South Riding 1938,Ag 2,15:2
Citadel, The 1938,N 4,27:2
Clouds Over Europe 1939,Je 16,27:2
Lion Has Wings, The 1940,Ja 22,11:2
Lady in Distress 1942,F 16,21:2
Woman in the Hall, The 1949,Ja 24,16:2
Dear Mr Prohack 1950,Jl 15,7:2
Heart of the Matter, The 1954,N 19,20:2
Three Cases of Murder (Lord Mountdrago)
1955,Mr 16,39:4
Three Cases of Murder (In the Picture)
1955,Mr 16,39:4
Three Cases of Murder (You Killed Elizabeth)
1955,Mr 16,39:4
Raising a Riot 1957,My 8,44:1
Dalrymple, Jean (Original Author)
It Happened in New York 1935,Ap 6,10:1
Dalrymple, Leona (Original Author)
Dangerous Number 1937,Mr 12,19:2
Dalschaft, Maly
Caught in Berlin's Underworld 1930,F 10,20:4
Dalsheim, Friedrich (Cinematographer)
Bride of Palo 1934,My 27,X,4:2 (In Addenda)
Dalsheim, Friedrich (Miscellaneous)
Wedding of Palo, The 1937,Mr 2,17:1
Wajan 1938,Ap 18,11:1
Dalthoff, Alfred
Marriage of Figaro 1950,N 3,31:2
Dalton, Abby
Stakeout on Dope Street 1958,Ap 24,38:1
Plainsman, The 1966,N 19,26:1
Dalton, Audrey
My Cousin Rachel 1952,D 26,20:2
Girls of Pleasure Island, The 1953,My 16,10:1
Titanic 1953,My 28,27:5
Casanova's Big Night 1954,Ap 19,19:1
Drum Beat 1954,N 18,42:1
Prodigal, The 1955,My 14,10:7
Separate Tables 1958,D 19,2:7
Mr Sardonicus 1961,O 19,39:3
Dalton, Charles
Fighting Odds 1917,O 1,14:2
Dalton, Dorothy
Black Is White 1920,Mr 8,9:6
Fool's Paradise 1921,D 10,11:4
Moran of the Lady Letty 1922,F 6,9:1
Crimson Challenge, The 1922,Ap 10,18:2
On the High Seas 1922,O 8,VI,3:1 (In Addenda)
Fog Bound 1923,My 29,10:3
Law of the Lawless, The 1923,Je 19,22:4
Moral Sinner, The 1924,Ap 7,15:3
Lone Wolf, The 1924,My 7,19:4
Dalton, Emmett (Original Author)
When the Daltons Rode 1940,Ag 23,13:3
Dalton, Irene
Children of Jazz 1923,Jl 9,8:4
Bluebeard's 8th Wife 1923,Ag 7,20:2
Dalton, Timothy
Lion in Winter, The 1968,O 31,54:1
D'Alvarez, Margarita
Pandora and the Flying Dutchman 1951,D 7,35:2
D'Alvarez, Marguerite
Till We Meet Again 1944,Ag 30,15:1
Dalvos, George
World Dances 1954,N 8,24:6
DALY
See Also DAILY, DAILEY, DALEY

Daly, Jack
Kathleen 1938,Ja 24,17:1
Once a Thief 1951,Ja 19,21:3
Pickup 1951,Ag 31,12:2
Daly, James
Court-Martial of Billy Mitchell, The
1955,D 23,14:2
Young Stranger, The 1957,Ap 9,40:1
I Aim at the Stars 1960,O 20,42:2
Planet of the Apes 1968,F 9,55:2
Daly, Jane
West of Zanzibar 1928,D 31,9:1
Mysterious Island, The 1929,D 21,17:1
Daly, Jonathan
Young Warriors, The 1968,F 8,36:1
Daly, Marcella
Folly of Vanity 1925,Ja 28,14:1
Silk Stockings 1927,N 29,31:1
Two Lovers 1928,Mr 23,24:4
Daly, Mark
Wings of the Morning 1937,Mr 12,19:1
Break the News 1941,Ja 2,24:2
Daly, Ray
Five Pennies, The 1959,Je 19,30:1
Daly, Tom
Spider Woman Strikes Back, The 1946,Mr 23,8:3
Third Voice, The 1960,Mr 7,24:5
Daly, Tom (Producer)
Royal Journey 1952,F 29,19:2
Daly, William
Air Mail 1932,N 7,20:3
Daly, William (Miscellaneous)
Champagne Waltz 1937,F 4,17:2
Dalya, Jacqueline
One Million BC 1940,Ap 27,9:2
Gay Caballero, The 1940,O 25,25:3
Lady From Louisiana 1941,My 15,27:2
Voice in the Wind 1944,Mr 16,17:2
Bathing Beauty 1944,Je 28,20:1
Adventures of Casanova 1948,Mr 22,18:3
Wabash Avenue 1950,Ap 29,8:3
Damari, Shoshana
Hill 24 Doesn't Answer 1955,N 3,37:1
d'Amboise, Jacques
Seven Brides for Seven Brothers 1954,Jl 23,8:3
Carousel 1956,F 17,13:1
Best Things in Life are Free, The 1956,S 29,12:2
Midsummer Night's Dream, A 1967,Ap 18,32:1
D'Ambricourt, Adrienne
Wages of Virtue 1924,N 24,15:3
Trial of Mary Dugan, The 1929,Mr 29,21:1
Bad One, The 1930,Je 13,28:3
Enigmatique Monsieur Parkes, L' 1930,S 2,19:3
What a Widow 1930,O 4,15:2
Svengali 1931,My 1,30:3
Transgression 1931,Je 15,23:3
This Modern Age 1931,S 7,19:3
Men in her Life 1931,N 30,16:2
Design for Living 1933,N 23,24:2
Gallant Lady 1934,Ja 22,12:3
Cat and the Fiddle, The 1934,F 17,20:2
It Happened in New York 1935,Ap 6,10:1
Goin' to Town 1935,My 11,21:2
Peter Ibbetson 1935,N 8,18:2
Bulldog Drummond's Bride 1939,Jl 13,17:2
Pack up Your Troubles 1939,O 27,27:2
Charlie Chan in City in Darkness 1939,D 18,29:2
Saratoga Trunk 1945,N 22,39:2
Dame, Beverly
Medium, The 1951,S 6,39:2
Damerel, Donna
Myrt and Marge 1934,Ja 17,23:2
Damerell, Stanley (Composer)
Charming Deceiver, The 1933,D 9,18:3
Damert, Lilo (Original Author)
Cross of Lorraine, The 1943,D 3,27:4
Damia
Pearls of the Crown, The 1938,Ap 12,26:2
Damiana, Damiano (Screenwriter)
Head of a Tyrant 1962,Je 7,31:2
Damiani, Damiano (Director)
Empty Canvas, The 1964,My 16,21:1 (Incorrect
in this edition; use 1964,My 16,12:1 elsewhere)
Damiani, Damiano (Screenwriter)
Arturo Island 1962,D 22,5:2
Empty Canvas, The 1964,My 16,21:1 (Incorrect
in this edition; use 1964,My 16,12:1 elsewhere)
Damianos, Alexis
Fear, The 1967,O 10,56:3
D'Amico, Angelo
Shoe-Shine 1947,Ag 27,19:2
D'Amico, Masolino (Screenwriter)
Romeo and Juliet 1968,O 9,41:1
D'Amico, Suso Cecchi (Miscellaneous)
Three Fables of Love (The Tortoise and the Hare);
Tortoise and the Hare, The (Three Fables of
Love) 1963,Ag 21,38:1
D'Amico, Suso Cecchi (Original Author)
Professor, My Son 1949,Ap 18,18:4
Guaglio 1949,My 19,35:2
Walls of Malapaga, The 1950,Mr 21,34:2
Hello Elephant 1954,S 10,18:5
Rocco and his Brothers 1961,Je 28,40:2

D'Amico, Suso Cecchi (Screenwriter)
To Live in Peace 1947,N 25,37:2
Angelina 1948,Ap 6,27:2
Guaglio 1949,My 19,35:2
It's Forever Springtime 1951,D 29,7:7
Bellissima 1953,My 18,26:2
His Last Twelve Hours 1953,N 13,24:7
Too Bad She's Bad 1955,D 26,23:2
Anatomy of Love 1959,S 29,46:2
It Started in Naples 1960,S 3,7:6
Big Deal on Madonna Street, The 1960,N 23,20:1
Violent Summer 1961,My 20,12:1
White Nights 1961,My 29,9:6
Rocco and his Brothers 1961,Je 28,40:2
Boccaccio '70 (The Job); Job, The (Boccaccio '70)
1962,Je 27,40:1
Best of Enemies, The 1962,Ag 7,35:2
Leopard, The 1963,Ag 13,25:1
Salvatore Giuliano 1964,S 18,28:1
Sandra 1966,Ja 17,32:1
Taming of the Shrew, The 1967,Mr 9,43:1
Shoot Loud, Louder... I Don't Understand
1967,S 21,56:4
Stranger, The 1967,D 19,59:1
Queens, The (Queen Armenia); Queen Armenia
(The Queens) 1968,Mr 11,49:1
Senso 1968,Jl 9,31:1
Damita, Lily
Forbidden Love 1929,Ja 14,20:1
Rescue, The 1929,Ja 14,20:1
Bridge of San Luis Rey, The 1929,My 20,22:6
Scandal In Paris, A 1929,Je 10,23:1
Cock Eyed World, The 1929,Ag 5,25:2
Dancer of Barcelona, The 1929,N 25,22:1
Fighting Caravans 1931,Ja 26,21:1
Woman Between, The 1931,O 24,20:3
Friends and Lovers 1931,N 7,16:5
This is the Night 1932,Ap 16,11:2
Match King, The 1932,D 8,25:3
Goldie Gets Along 1933,Je 3,16:4
Brewster's Millions 1935,Ap 8,23:3
Frisco Kid 1935,N 25,22:1
Damle (Director)
Gyandev of India 1943,Ap 10,12:5
Damler, John
Atomic City, The 1952,My 2,21:1
Damman, Gerhart
Wenn Herzen Sich Finden 1934,N 12,17:3
Dammann, Anna
Reise Nach Tilsit, Die; Trip to Tilsit, The
1940,F 10,19:2
Johannis fever; St Johns' Fire 1940,Ap 6,13:2
Damon, Mark
Inside Detroit 1956,Ja 28,10:5
Between Heaven and Hell 1956,O 12,33:2
This Rebel Breed 1960,My 5,41:2
House of Usher, The 1960,S 15,45:4
Young Racers, The 1963,O 10,49:3
Anzio 1968,Jl 25,26:1
Young, The Evil and the Savage, The
1968,Ag 15,46:2
Damon, Peter
Fall of the Roman Empire, The 1964,Mr 27,14:2
Damonde, Renee
All Quiet on The Western Front 1930,Ap 30,29:1
Damone, Vic
Rich, Young and Pretty 1951,Jl 26,17:3
Deep in my Heart 1954,D 10,35:2
Athena 1954,D 22,28:2
Hit the Deck 1955,Mr 4,17:1
Kismet 1955,D 9,32:2
Hell to Eternity 1960,O 13,41:1
Damore, James
Hail the Conquering Hero 1944,Ag 10,14:2
Damores, P
Morgane, the Enchantress 1929,Je 21,17:2
Damper, Fritz
Doppelbraeutigam, Der; Double Fiance, The
1935,Mr 23,11:3
Dampier, Claude
She Shall Have Music 1942,O 31,11:2
Don't Take it to Heart 1948,D 25,10:3
Damrosch, Walter
Star Maker, The 1939,Ag 31,14:2
Carnegie Hall 1947,My 3,10:2
DAN
See Also DANN
Dan, Kacuo (Original Author)
Magic Boy 1963,D 23,18:2
Dan, Reiko
Sanjuro 1963,My 8,34:2
When a Woman Ascends the Stairs
1963,Je 26,36:4
My Hobo 1963,Jl 24,27:3
Naked General, The 1964,D 16,51:2
Red Beard 1968,D 20,60:4
Dana, Bill
Busy Body, The 1967,Je 8,52:2
Dana, Dick
Top Banana 1954,F 20,8:6
Dana, Leora
3:10 to Yuma 1957,Ag 29,22:1
Kings Go Forth 1958,Jl 4,15:2

Dana, Leora— Cont
Some Came Running 1959,Ja 23,17:1
Pollyanna 1960,My 20,26:1
Gathering of Eagles, A 1963,Jl 11,21:2

Dana, Mark
Thunder Over the Plains 1953,D 10,64:4
Big Fisherman, The 1959,Ag 6,18:1
Tarzan Goes to India 1962,S 6,37:2

Dana, Muriel Frances
Fast Worker, The 1924,N 12,13:1
Compromise 1925,O 27,23:3
Mike 1926,Ja 11,33:1

Dana, Richard Henry Jr (Original Author)
Two Years Before the Mast 1946,S 25,39:2

Dana, Vic
Don't Knock the Twist 1962,Ap 14,14:2

Dana, Viola
Willow Tree, The 1920,F 2,10:1
Revelation 1924,Je 24,18:2
Merton of the Movies 1924,S 8,15:3
Open all Night 1924,S 9,19:1
Forty Winks 1925,F 3,24:1
As Man Desires 1925,F 10,20:1
Winds of Chance 1925,Ag 17,10:3
Bigger Than Barnum's 1926,Jl 13,19:3
Kosher Kitty Kelly 1926,S 28,30:2
Ice Flood, The 1926,O 19,26:2
Silent Lover, The 1926,N 15,19:1
Show of Shows 1929,N 21,24:5

Danaroff, Alex
Anything Can Happen 1952,Ap 4,21:1

Danby, Frank (Original Author)
Heart of a Child, The 1920,Ap 12,13:1

Dance, Patsy
Householder, The 1963,O 22,43:2

Dance, Reginald
Dreyfus Case, The 1931,Ag 31,11:5

Dancers and Corps de Ballet of the Bolshoi Theatre
Ballet of Romeo and Juliet, The 1956,Ap 3,31:2

Danciger, George (Producer)
Sins of the Borgias 1956,Mr 5,21:1

Danciger, Georges (Producer)
Eagle with Two Heads 1948,D 30,24:2
Rue de Paris 1960,D 23,14:3
Five Day Lover, The 1961,D 14,55:4
That Man From Rio 1964,Je 9,30:1
Up to his Ears 1966,My 18,37:1
Live for Life 1967,D 19,59:1

Dancigers, Oscar (Producer)
Pearl, The 1948,F 18,36:4
Young and the Damned, The 1952,Mr 25,23:2
Adventures of Robinson Crusoe, The
   1954,Ag 6,10:5
This Strange Passion 1955,D 5,34:2
Viva Maria 1965,D 20,48:2

D'Ancora, Maurizio
Miracolo Di Sant' Antonio, Il 1932,Ap 18,19:2
Vecchia Signora, La 1932,D 10,19:3
Figaro E La Sua Gran Giornata 1933,O 28,20:4
Al Buio Insieme 1937,Ag 6,21:3
Antenato, L'; Ancestor, The 1938,O 22,14:3
Documento Fatale, Il 1940,S 26,27:3
Terra di Nessuno; Nobody's Land 1940,O 25,25:4

D'Ancora, Monte
Milizia Territoriale 1936,Ap 6,18:2

Dandau, Nick
Skyrocket, The 1926,Ja 26,25:2

Danderas, P (Producer)
Shepherd's Daughter, The 1956,My 14,23:3

D'Andrea, Diletta
Hours of Love, The 1965,S 4,11:5

D'Andrea, Tom
This Is the Army 1943,Jl 29,11:6
Pride of the Marines 1945,Ag 25,7:3
Night and Day 1946,Jl 26,16:2
Two Guys From Milwaukee 1946,Jl 27,12:5
Never Say Goodbye 1946,N 23,12:2
Humoresque 1946,D 26,28:1
Love and Learn 1947,My 3,10:3
Dark Passage 1947,S 6,11:2
To the Victor 1948,Ap 17,11:2
Silver River 1948,My 22,8:3
Fighter Squadron 1948,N 20,9:2
Tension 1950,Ja 12,32:4
Kill the Umpire 1950,My 29,10:6
Next Voice You Hear, The 1950,Je 30,18:2
Little Egypt 1951,Ag 30,20:3

Dandridge, Dorothy
Lady From Louisiana 1941,My 15,27:2
Sun Valley Serenade 1941,S 6,20:1
Bahama Passage 1942,F 19,23:2
Drums of the Congo 1942,Jl 20,16:4
Hit Parade of 1943 1943,Ap 16,24:3
Bright Road 1953,Ap 29,33:5
Carmen Jones 1954,O 29,27:2
Island in the Sun 1957,Je 13,37:1
Decks Ran Red, The 1958,O 11,18:2
Porgy and Bess 1959,Je 25,20:3
Tamango 1959,S 17,48:4
Malaga 1962,F 22,20:3

Dandridge, Robert
Father's Son 1931,F 21,15:2
Penrod and Sam 1931,S 26,25:3

Dandridge, Ruby
Tish 1942,S 18,25:2
Cabin in the Sky 1943,My 28,19:3
Dead Reckoning 1947,Ja 23,31:2
Arnelo Affair, The 1947,S 13,8:5
My Wild Irish Rose 1947,D 25,32:2
Tap Roots 1948,Ag 26,16:3
Hole in the Head, A 1959,Jl 16,31:2

D'Androa, Carole
West Side Story 1961,O 19,39:3

Dandy
Miquette 1951,F 5,18:2

DANE
See Also DEAN, DEANE, DEHN

Dane, Clemence (Miscellaneous)
Bride of Vengeance 1949,Ap 7,38:2

Dane, Clemence (Original Author)
Murder 1930,O 25,20:6
Bill of Divorcement, A 1932,O 3,15:2
Bill of Divorcement, A 1940,Jl 12,11:2

Dane, Clemence (Screenwriter)
Anna Karenina 1935,Ag 31,16:2
Amateur Gentleman, The 1936,Ap 27,19:2
Fire Over England 1937,Mr 5,16:2
Sidewalks of London 1940,F 15,15:1
Vacation From Marriage 1946,Mr 15,27:2
Bonnie Prince Charlie 1952,Ja 7,14:3

Dane, Constance
House is not a Home, A 1964,S 2,33:1

Dane, Faith
Gypsy 1962,N 2,24:1

Dane, Frank
Hoosier Schoolmaster, The 1924,Mr 18,25:2

Dane, Karl
Everlasting Whisper, The 1925,O 12,19:3
Lights of Old Broadway 1925,N 2,20:1
Big Parade, The 1925,N 20,18:1 (In Addenda)
His Secretary 1925,D 21,27:2
Son of the Sheik, The 1926,Jl 26,13:2
Scarlet Letter, The 1926,Ag 10,19:2
Bardelys The Magnificent 1926,N 1,28:1 (In
   Addenda)
Red Mill, The 1927,F 14,15:1
Slide, Kelly, Slide 1927,Mr 23,19:2
Rookies 1927,Ap 25,20:4
Enemy, The 1927,D 28,26:6
Baby Mine 1928,Ja 9,20:1
Trail of '98, The 1928,Mr 21,30:3
Circus Rookies 1928,My 14,25:1
Alias Jimmy Valentine 1928,N 16,28:6
Duke Steps Out, The 1929,Ap 15,22:6
Speedway 1929,S 21,17:1
Navy Blues 1930,Ja 11,21:3
Montana Moon 1930,Ap 14,24:2
Free and Easy 1930,Ap 19,15:1
Big House, The 1930,Je 25,31:2
Billy the Kid 1930,O 18,23:2
Show People 1967,O 2,58:2

Dane, Michael (Screenwriter)
Moonspinners, The 1964,N 4,47:1

Dane, Pat
Are You With It? 1948,Ap 15,31:2

Dane, Patricia
Life Begins for Andy Hardy 1941,Ag 22,19:4
Johnny Eager 1942,F 20,21:2
Rio Rita 1942,My 8,27:3
Grand Central Murder 1942,My 23,8:8
Somewhere I'll Find You 1942,Ag 28,22:4
I Dood It 1943,N 11,29:1

Dane, Peter
Al Capone 1959,Mr 26,27:1

Daneel, Sylvia
Seven Women From Hell 1962,F 1,22:2

Danegger, J
Einmal Moecht' Ich Keine Sorgen Haben
   1933,My 25,24:4

Danegger, Mathilde
Marie-Louise 1945,N 13,24:2

Danegger, Theodor
Ehestreik 1935,Ag 31,16:3
Royal Waltz, The 1936,Ap 10,27:1
Weiberregiment 1936,S 14,25:2
Drei Vater um Anna; Three Fathers for Anna
   1940,Ja 20,11:3

Danelia, Georgy (Director)
Summer to Remember, A; (Seryozha)
   1961,N 7,38:1
Meet Me in Moscow 1966,My 3,51:1

Danelia, Georgy (Screenwriter)
Summer to Remember, A; (Seryozha)
   1961,N 7,38:1

Daneman, Paul
Time Without Pity 1957,N 23,11:2
Zulu 1964,Jl 8,38:1

Danet, Jean
Diary of a Country Priest 1954,Ap 6,35:2
Hunchback of Notre Dame, The 1957,D 12,35:1

Danfield, Sidney (Director)
Bring on the Girls 1945,Mr 1,25:5

Danforth, William
Girl Said No, The 1937,O 18,14:1

D'Angelo, Salvo (Producer)
Beauty and the Devil 1952,Ag 26,15:2
Father's Dilemma 1952,S 23,25:1
Terra Trema, La 1965,O 13,39:1

Dani, Sandro
Giovanni De Medici, The Leader 1940,Ja 5,15:4

Dani, Vera
Cieca di Sorrento, La 1936,Ag 3,11:3

Daniel, Ann
Island of the Blue Dolphins 1964,Jl 4,8:2

Daniel, Eliot (Composer)
Make Mine Music 1946,Ap 22,26:2
Golden Girl 1951,N 21,20:3

Daniel, Eliot (Miscellaneous)
Melody Time 1948,My 28,28:2

Daniel, Elsa
Casa del Angel, La 1960,Ag 30,25:1
Hand in the Trap 1963,Jl 2,16:2
Games Men Play, The 1968,Mr 15,30:1

Daniel, Jennifer
Kiss of the Vampire 1963,O 10,49:2

Daniel, Roger
Boy Slaves 1939,F 9,17:3
King of the Turf 1939,My 8,21:2

Daniel, Viora
Life of the Party, The 1920,N 22,13:3

Daniel, William
Two for the Road 1967,Ap 28,36:2

Daniel-Norman, Jacques (Director)
Red Angel, The 1950,N 4,13:2

Danielewski, Tad (Director)
No Exit 1962,D 6,55:2
Guide, The 1965,F 10,44:2

Danielewski, Tad (Producer)
Guide, The 1965,F 10,44:2

Danielewski, Tad (Screenwriter)
Guide, The 1965,F 10,44:2

Daniell, Athalie
Model and the Marriage Broker, The
   1952,Ja 12,10:6

Daniell, Bruna
Streets of Sorrow 1952,N 18,37:4

Daniell, Henry
Jealousy 1929,S 14,17:1
Unguarded Hour, The 1936,Ap 4,11:1
Under Cover of Night 1937,Ja 20,18:4
Camille 1937,Ja 23,13:1
Thirteenth Chair, The 1937,Je 18,25:3
Firefly, The 1937,S 2,17:2
Madame X 1937,O 25,23:1
Marie Antoinette 1938,Ag 17,23:2
We Are not Alone 1939,D 1,27:1
Private Lives of Elizabeth and Essex, The
   1939,D 2,21:2
All This and Heaven, Too 1940,Jl 5,10:2
Sea Hawk, The 1940,Ag 10,16:2
Great Dictator, The 1940,O 16,29:1
Philadelphia Story, The 1940,D 27,22:2
Woman's Face, A 1941,My 16,21:2
Dressed to Kill 1941,Ag 22,19:3
Feminine Touch, The 1941,D 12,35:3
Sherlock Holmes and the Voice Of Terror
   1942,S 19,9:2
Nightmare 1942,D 4,31:2
Reunion in France 1943,Mr 5,20:3
Mission to Moscow 1943,Ap 30,25:2
Watch on the Rhine 1943,Ag 28,15:1
Jane Eyre 1944,F 4,12:5
Suspect, The 1945,F 1,18:5
Hotel Berlin 1945,Mr 3,11:2
Body Snatcher, The 1945,My 26,18:3
Woman in Green, The 1945,Je 16,10:3
Captain Kidd 1945,N 23,26:3
Bandit of Sherwood Forest, The 1946,Mr 23,8:4
Song of Love 1947,O 10,31:2
Exile, The 1947,D 26,22:4
Wake of the Red Witch 1949,Ja 10,19:2
Siren of Atlantis 1949,Ag 22,13:1
Buccaneer's Girl 1950,Mr 27,19:2
Egyptian, The 1954,Ag 25,23:1
Diane 1956,Ja 13,18:1
Man in the Gray Flannel Suit, The
   1956,Ap 13,21:1
Lust for Life 1956,S 18,39:1
Mister Cory 1957,F 23,13:1
Sun Also Rises, The 1957,Ag 24,12:2
Girls, Les 1957,O 4,27:2
Story of Mankind, The 1957,N 9,31:2
Witness for the Prosecution 1958,F 7,16:1
From the Earth to the Moon 1958,N 27,52:2
Comancheros, The 1961,N 2,42:1
Madison Avenue 1962,Mr 29,28:2
Notorious Landlady, The 1962,Jl 27,15:2
Five Weeks in a Balloon 1962,Ag 27,18:1
Chapman Report, The 1962,O 18,49:2

Daniels, Bebe
Everywoman 1919,D 15,20:1
Why Change Your Wife 1920,Ap 26,18:1
Dancin' Fool, The 1920,My 3,18:1
You Never Can Tell 1920,O 4,14:3
Affairs of Anatol, The 1921,S 12,16:1
North of the Rio Grande 1922,My 15,20:3
Pink Gods 1922,S 25,10:2

Daniels, Bebe— Cont

Glimpses of the Moon 1923,Ap 3,23:4
Exciters, The 1923,Je 4,13:3
His Children's Children 1923,N 5,15:1
Heritage of the Desert, The 1924,Ja 24,15:1
Unguarded Women 1924,Je 24,18:2
Monsieur Beaucaire 1924,Ag 12,12:1 (In Addenda)
Sinners in Heaven 1924,S 10,21:3
Dangerous Money 1924,O 14,21:5
Argentine Love 1924,D 23,16:2
Miss Bluebeard 1925,Ja 28,14:1
Crowded Hour, The 1925,Ap 27,15:2
Manicure Girl, The 1925,Je 15,10:1
Wild, Wild Susan 1925,Ag 5,12:4
Lovers in Quarantine 1925,O 13,20:1
Splendid Crime, The 1925,D 17,27:1
Miss Brewster's Millions 1926,Mr 8,17:1
Volcano 1926,My 24,24:3
Palm Beach Girl, The 1926,Je 22,21:2
Campus Flirt, The 1926,S 22,31:1
Stranded in Paris 1926,D 13,27:1
Kiss in a Taxi, A 1927,Mr 15,29:2
Senorita 1927,My 9,26:4
Swim, Girl, Swim 1927,S 5,13:2
She's a Shiek 1927,N 21,20:1
Feel my Pulse 1928,F 27,16:2
Fifty-Fifty Girl, The 1928,My 14,25:1
Hot News 1928,Jl 23,11:2
Take Me Home 1928,O 23,33:1
What a Night! 1928,D 24,11:1
Rio Rita 1929,O 7,22:1
Love Comes Along 1930,F 1,15:1
Alias French Gertie 1930,Ap 14,24:2
Lawful Larceny 1930,Jl 12,16:4
Dixiana 1930,S 5,21:1
Reaching for the Moon 1930,D 30,24:2
My Past 1931,Mr 12,22:7
Maltese Falcon, The 1931,My 29,26:5
Honor of the Family 1931,O 17,20:1
Silver Dollar 1932,D 23,20:1
42d Street 1933,Mr 10,19:3
Cocktail Hour 1933,Je 5,18:5
Counsellor-At-Law 1933,D 8,31:2
Daniels, Billy
Hold 'Em Navy 1937,N 6,14:2
Frenchman's Creek 1944,S 21,26:2
Masquerade in Mexico 1945,N 29,27:2
Beat Generation, The 1959,O 22,47:4
Daniels, Billy (Miscellaneous)
Road to Rio 1948,F 19,29:3
Daniels, Danny
Woman of Straw 1964,O 1,30:6
Daniels, Hank
Meet Me in St Louis 1944,N 29,20:2
Chicago Kid, The 1945,F 12,24:3
Green Years, The 1946,Ap 5,21:2
In old Sacramento 1946,Ap 29,24:4
Burning Cross, The 1948,F 20,19:1
Daniels, Harold
Hollywood Cowboy 1937,Jl 24,12:1
Daniels, Harold (Director)
Prince of Peace, The 1951,Mr 24,8:3
Daniels, Henry H Jr
Bewitched 1945,Ag 17,20:3
Daniels, Keith
House of a Thousand Candles, The 1936,Ap 2,29:2
Sky Parade, The 1936,Ap 20,17:1
Yours for the Asking 1936,Ag 20,14:2
Daniels, Lisa
Man in the Attic 1954,F 6,17:2
Gambler From Natchez, The 1954,Ag 14,8:2
Glass Slipper, The 1955,Mr 25,19:2
Virgin Queen, The 1955,Ag 6,13:2
Daniels, Mark
Joe Smith, American 1942,Ap 2,27:4
Fingers at the Window 1942,Ap 23,27:3
Grand Central Murder 1942,My 23,8:8
Vanishing Virginian, The 1942,My 28,13:3
War Against Mrs Hadley, The 1942,N 26,40:2
Whistling in Dixie 1942,D 31,20:4
Winged Victory 1944,D 21,16:2
Bury Me Dead 1947,O 25,13:3
Life of Riley, The 1949,Ap 18,18:4
Daniels, Mickey
Magnificent Obsession 1935,D 31,11:2
Daniels, Richard
Girl Shy 1924,Ap 21,21:4
Daniels, Viola
South Sea Woman 1953,Je 4,33:6
Daniels, Walter
Dove, The 1928,Ja 3,28:2
Daniels, William
Family Honeymoon 1949,F 25,28:2
Ladybug, Ladybug 1963,D 24,9:1
Thousand Clowns, A 1965,D 14,54:2
Graduate, The 1967,D 22,44:4
Daniels, William H (Producer)
Marriage on the Rocks 1965,S 16,00:0
Danielson, Cliff
Seven Sweethearts 1942,N 13,28:1

Daniely, Lisa
Lilli Marlene 1952,Mr 29,19:2
Circle, The 1959,Ap 16,29:2
Danilevski, G P (Original Author)
Betrayal 1939,S 16,20:2
Danilova, A
Frigid Sea, The 1955,N 21,23:4
Danilova, A S
Alexander Nevsky 1939,Mr 23,27:1
Daninos, Pierre (Original Author)
French They Are a Funny Race, The 1957,My 21,41:1
Danischewsky, Monja (Producer)
Galloping Major, The 1951,D 17,27:2
Battle of the Sexes, The 1960,Ap 19,40:4
Danischewsky, Monja (Screenwriter)
Shrine of Victory 1943,Ag 20,13:2
Galloping Major, The 1951,D 17,27:2
Mad Little Island 1958,D 31,12:1
Battle of the Sexes, The 1960,Ap 19,40:4
Topkapi 1964,S 18,25:1
Mister Moses 1965,My 13,32:1
DANN
See Also DAN
Dann, Asher
September Storm 1960,O 29,26:7
Dann, Judy
Destination Gobi 1953,My 30,7:1
Spiral Road, The 1962,Ag 4,11:2
War Is Hell 1964,Ja 23,26:1
Kill a Dragon 1967,D 7,60:2
Dann, Peter
Zwischen den Eltern; Between the Parents 1938,Jl 30,10:3
Dann, Roger
Porteuse de Pain, La 1936,Jl 1,29:5
I, Jane Doe 1948,Jl 5,8:4
I Confess 1953,Mr 23,28:2
Dannemann, Karl
Krach um Iolanthe 1935,My 11,21:3
Dannhoff, Erika
Rebel, The 1933,Jl 25,17:2
Tannenberg 1934,Ap 3,26:6
Waldrausch; Forest Fever 1940,Ja 20,11:3
D'Anniable, Albert (Screenwriter)
Jazz on a Summer's Day 1960,Mr 29,46:2
D'Annunzio, Gabriele (Original Author)
Cabiria 1921,Jl 4,10:2
Ship, The 1927,O 19,24:4
Cabiria 1929,My 14,29:1
Flesh will Surrender 1950,O 26,38:7
D'Annunzio, Gabriele (Screenwriter)
Cabiria 1914,Je 2,11:5
D'Annunzio, Lola
Wrong Man, The 1956,D 24,8:1
Dano, Royal
Undercover Girl 1950,N 8,37:2
Under the Gun 1951,F 23,33:2
Red Badge of Courage, The 1951,O 19,22:2
Bend of the River 1952,Ap 10,37:1
Johnny Guitar 1954,My 28,19:2
Far Country, The 1955,F 14,24:2
Trouble With Harry, The 1955,O 18,46:2
Tribute to a Bad Man 1956,Mr 31,13:3
Moby Dick 1956,Jl 5,18:1
Santiago 1956,Jl 14,13:2
Crime of Passion 1957,Ja 10,25:1
Trooper Hook 1957,Jl 13,11:2
Saddle the Wind 1958,Mr 21,17:1
Man of the West 1958,O 2,44:3
Never Steal Anything Small 1959,F 12,23:1
These Thousand Hills 1959,My 7,36:1
Hound-Dog Man 1960,Ap 28,29:1
Adventures of Huckleberry Fin, The 1960,Ag 4,17:1
Cimarron 1961,F 17,12:2
King of Kings 1961,O 12,41:2
Savage Sam 1963,Ag 1,17:3
Welcome to Hard Times 1967,My 2,56:1
Last Challenge, The 1967,D 28,25:1
If He Hollers, Let Him Go 1968,O 10,59:7
Danova, Cesare
Genoese Dragnet 1954,F 12,20:5
Don Juan 1956,Mr 6,26:2
Man Who Understood Women, The 1959,O 3,14:7
Tender is the Night 1962,Ja 20,13:2
Cleopatra 1963,Je 13,29:1
Gidget Goes to Rome 1963,S 12,32:2
Viva Las Vegas 1964,My 21,42:1
Boy, Did I Get a Wrong Number! 1966,Je 9,54:2
Chamber of Horrors 1966,O 20,52:5
Danska, Herbert (Director)
Sweet Love, Bitter 1967,Ja 31,50:1
Danska, Herbert (Screenwriter)
Sweet Love, Bitter 1967,Ja 31,50:1
Dantan, Andre A (Cinematographer)
Farrebique 1948,F 24,21:2
Dante
Golden Coach, The 1954,Ja 22,30:2
Dante, Anthony
Walk in the Sun, A 1946,Ja 12,10:6

Dante, Michael
Seven Thieves 1960,Mr 12,14:5
Kid Galahad 1963,Mr 7,8:5
Naked Kiss, The 1964,O 29,38:1
Harlow 1965,My 15,18:1
Dante, the Magician
A-Haunting We Will Go 1942,Ag 3,18:4
Dantes, Claude
Blood and Black Lace 1965,N 11,58:3
Dantes, Henri
Circus World 1964,Je 26,34:2
Dantes, Suzanne
Extenuating Circumstances; Circostances Attenuantes 1946,S 24,41:3
Dantine, Helmut
Mrs Miniver 1942,Je 5,23:1
Casablanca 1942,N 27,27:1
Edge of Darkness 1943,Ap 10,12:4
Mission to Moscow 1943,Ap 30,25:2
Northern Pursuit 1943,N 26,29:2
Passage to Marseille 1944,F 17,12:5
Hollywood Canteen 1944,D 16,19:2
Hotel Berlin 1945,Mr 3,11:2
Escape in the Desert 1945,My 12,10:2
Whispering City 1948,My 10,25:5
Call Me Madam 1953,Mr 26,37:1
Guerrilla Girl 1953,Jl 7,23:7
Alexander the Great 1956,Mr 29,23:1
War and Peace 1956,Ag 22,26:2
Story of Mankind, The 1957,N 9,31:2
Fraulein 1958,Je 9,27:2
Tempest 1959,Mr 27,19:2
Operation Crossbow 1965,Ap 2,29:1
Danton, Donna
Hurry Sundown 1967,Mr 24,22:1
Danton, June
One Man's Way 1964,Mr 12,40:3
Danton, Ray
Chief Crazy Horse 1955,Ap 28,25:1
Spoilers, The 1955,D 24,10:2
I'll Cry Tomorrow 1956,Ja 13,18:1
Too Much, Too Soon 1958,My 10,19:2
Onionhead 1958,O 2,44:1
Beat Generation, The 1959,O 22,47:4
Yellowstone Kelly 1959,N 12,27:1
Rise and Fall of Legs' Diamond, The 1960,F 4,34:1
Ice Palace 1960,Je 30,22:1
Portrait of a Mobster 1961,Ap 20,30:4
Fever in the Blood 1961,Ap 20,30:4
Majority of One, A 1962,Ja 12,29:2
Longest Day, The 1962,O 5,28:1
Chapman Report, The 1962,O 18,49:2
FBI Code 98 1964,Ap 9,25:6
D'Antoni, Philip (Producer)
Bullitt 1968,O 18,41:2
D'Antonio, Carmen
Long Voyage Home, The 1940,O 9,30:2 (In Addenda)
Arabian Nights 1942,D 26,15:1
Coney Island 1943,Je 17,17:2
Cobra Woman 1944,My 18,17:2
Golden Girl 1951,N 21,20:3
Salome 1953,Mr 25,37:1
World for Ransom 1954,Je 5,11:2
Cheyenne Autumn 1964,D 24,8:1
Dantzer, Marc
Sous la Lune du Maroc 1933,Ja 23,9:2
Danziger, Edward J (Producer)
Jigsaw 1949,My 30,9:4
So Young, So Bad 1950,Jl 24,15:2
Babes in Bagdad 1954,Ap 5,21:3
Satellite in the Sky 1956,S 4,32:7
Telltale Heart, The 1963,My 16,42:1
Danziger, Harry Lee (Producer)
Jigsaw 1949,My 30,9:4
So Young, So Bad 1950,Jl 24,15:2
Babes in Bagdad 1954,Ap 5,21:3
Satellite in the Sky 1956,S 4,32:7
Telltale Heart, The 1963,My 16,42:1
Danziger, Isaac
My Father's House 1947,S 26,28:3
Dapcevic, Milena
Legends of Anika 1956,Ap 19,35:1
Dapp, Ronnie
Kisses for my President 1964,Ag 22,13:1
Dapporto, Carlo
Mademoiselle Gobette 1955,F 5,13:3
DaPron, Louis
Three Cheers for Love 1936,Ag 1,16:2
College Holiday 1936,D 24,21:2
Hideaway Girl 1937,Ja 13,20:4
He's my Guy 1943,Mr 12,12:3
Dixie 1943,Je 24,26:2
Daquin, Louis (Director)
Portrait of Innocence 1948,Je 9,35:2
Dar, Bella
Racers, The 1955,F 5,13:2
D'Arbanville, Patti
Flesh 1968,S 27,36:1
Darbon, Emile (Producer)
Riptide 1951,Ap 7,9:2

Darbon, Francois
Elusive Corporal, The 1963,F 19,5:1
Darby, Ken (Composer)
Golden Girl 1951,N 21,20:3
Darby, Ken (Miscellaneous)
Melody Time 1948,My 28,28:2
Darby, Kim
Bus Riley's Back in Town 1965,Ap 8,45:2
Darby, Nettie Bell
Greatest Love of All, The 1924,N 11,14:1
Darc, Mireille
Male Hunt; Chasse a l'Homme, La 1965,Ap 20,42:1
Great Spy Chase, The 1966,O 6,56:4
Galia 1966,D 20,50:4
Weekend 1968,S 28,36:1
Darcante, Jean
Room Upstairs, The 1948,S 4,8:6
Darcel, Denise
Battleground 1949,N 12,8:4
Tarzan and the Slave Girl 1950,Je 24,7:3
Westward the Women 1952,Ja 1,21:2
Young Man With Ideas 1952,Je 7,22:6
Dangerous When Wet 1953,Je 19,18:1
Vera Cruz 1954,D 27,22:4
Seven Women From Hell 1962,F 1,22:2
Darcey, Janine
Curtain Rises, The 1939,Ap 22,15:2
Entente Cordiale 1939,D 26,23:2
French Without Tears 1940,Ap 29,12:2
Children of Chaos 1950,Ap 20,37:2
Rififi 1956,Je 6,37:1
Darcey-Roche, Clara
Miserables, Les 1927,Ag 23,29:4
Darche, Locelyne
Julie the Redhead 1963,O 15,44:1
Darclea, Edy
Shepherd King, The 1923,D 11,26:2
D'Arcy, Alex
Man on a Tightrope 1953,Je 5,19:1
Vickie 1953,S 8,26:3
How to Marry a Millionaire 1953,N 11,37:1
Soldier of Fortune 1955,My 28,7:4
Fanny Hill 1965,D 2,48:1
D'Arcy, Alexander
Paradise 1929,N 4,28:1
Kermesse Heroique, La 1936,S 23,29:1
Stolen Holiday 1937,F 1,15:3
Awful Truth, The 1937,N 5,19:3
She Married an Artist 1938,F 25,15:2
Topper Takes a Trip 1938,D 30,11:2
Good Girls Go to Paris 1939,Je 23,23:1
Fifth Avenue Girl 1939,Ag 25,12:2
Three Sons 1939,N 24,29:3
City of Chance 1940,Ja 22,11:3
D'Arcy, Gene
Miami Story, The 1954,My 15,13:2
Darcy, Georgine
Rear Window 1954,Ag 5,18:2
Don't Knock the Twist 1962,Ap 14,14:2
Darcy, Rene
Children of Chaos 1950,Ap 20,37:2
D'Arcy, Roy
Graustark 1925,S 8,29:1
Masked Bride, The 1925,N 30,17:1
Boheme, La 1926,F 25,26:2
Beverly of Graustark 1926,Ap 19,24:3
Temptress, The 1926,O 11,18:1
Bardelys The Magnificent 1926,N 1,28:1 (In Addenda)
Valencia 1926,D 27,20:3
Frisco Sally Levy 1927,Ap 13,29:4
Lovers 1927,Ap 19,24:4
Adam and Evil 1927,Ag 10,21:4
Road to Romance, The 1927,O 10,24:1
Actress, The 1928,Jl 9,25:1
Forbidden Hours 1928,Jl 23,11:2
Beware of Blondes 1928,Ag 21,27:4
Last Warning, The 1929,Ja 7,36:2
Girls Gone Wild 1929,Ap 22,23:1
Black Watch, The 1929,My 23,26:3
File No 113 1932,F 20,11:2
Sherlock Holmes 1932,N 12,20:5
Orient Express 1934,F 28,23:2
Revolt of the Zombies 1936,Je 5,17:2
Hollywood Boulevard 1936,S 21,26:4
Darcy, Sheila
Wells Fargo 1937,D 30,15:2
Union Pacific 1939,My 11,31:2
D'Arcy, Yvonne
Friends and Lovers 1931,N 7,16:5
Dard, Frederic (Miscellaneous)
Back to the Wall; (Dos au Mur) 1959,S 8,43:2
Dard, Frederic (Original Author)
Back to the Wall; (Dos au Mur) 1959,S 8,43:2
Paris Pick-Up 1963,Ag 29,36:2
Dard, Frederic (Screenwriter)
Back to the Wall; (Dos au Mur) 1959,S 8,43:2
Port of Desire 1960,N 3,49:2
Paris Pick-Up 1963,Ag 29,36:2
Darden, Michael
Miracle Worker, The 1962,My 24,29:2

Darden, Severn
Goldstein 1965,My 8,19:7
Dead Heat on a Merry-Go-Round 1966,O 13,50:1
Luv 1967,Jl 27,29:1
President's Analyst, The 1967,D 22,44:4
Dare, Carla
Citizen Saint 1948,My 28,28:2
Dare, Daniel (Director)
Main Event, The 1938,Je 20,11:3
Dare, Daniel (Miscellaneous)
52d Street 1937,N 15,15:1
Dare, Daniel (Producer)
Our Hearts Were Growing Up 1946,Ag 12,17:2
Ladies' Man 1947,Ja 13,18:5
My Favorite Brunette 1947,Mr 20,38:2
Variety Girl 1947,O 16,34:4
Road to Rio 1948,F 19,29:3
Isn't It Romantic? 1948,O 7,35:2
Dare, Dorothy
Happiness Ahead 1934,O 11,28:2
St Louis Kid, The 1934,N 1,25:2
Sweet Adeline 1935,Ja 7,13:2
Maybe It's Love 1935,F 11,14:2
Gold Diggers of 1935 1935,Mr 15,25:2
In Caliente 1935,Je 27,16:1
Front Page Woman 1935,Jl 12,15:1
Dare, Irene
Everything's on Ice 1939,O 6,31:1
Silver Skates 1943,Mr 19,15:3
Dare, Phillip
Clive of India 1935,Ja 18,29:1
Folies Bergere 1935,F 25,13:2
Dare, Phyllis
Common Law, The 1923,O 29,18:1
Dare, Richard
World Dances 1954,N 8,24:6
Darellada, Juan (Director)
Incertidumbre 1936,S 21,26:5
Darene, Robert (Director)
Bernadette of Lourdes 1962,Ja 30,20:2
Darieuil, Colette
He 1933,D 27,23:6
End of the World, The 1934,Ap 18,23:3
Ne Sirj Edesanyam 1936,N 24,35:4
Mad Emperor, The 1941,Mr 10,21:3
Thirteen Days of Love 1942,N 6,27:3
Heart of a Nation, The 1943,Ap 8,27:2
Sextette (Part I-The Gun); Gun, The (Sextette) 1953,Mr 2,19:2
Darfier, Gene
Faces 1968,S 23,42:4
Dargomijsky (Miscellaneous)
Don Quixote 1934,D 24,17:1
Dargy, Teddy
Petits, Les 1936,D 30,17:2
Darien, Frank
Cimarron 1931,Ja 27,20:5
June Moon 1931,Mr 14,23:2
Big Business Girl 1931,Je 12,27:1
Bad Girl 1931,Ag 15,18:3
Big Shot, The 1932,Ja 2,14:2
Miracle Man, The 1932,Ap 21,25:2
Okay America 1932,S 10,18:5
Prosperity 1932,N 26,11:4
Hello, Everybody 1933,Ja 30,9:4
Journal of a Crime 1934,Ap 28,11:3
Marie Galante 1934,N 21,23:4
Behind the Evidence 1935,Ja 26,13:2
Perfect Clue, The 1935,Mr 14,18:1
Little Colonel, The 1935,Mr 22,26:2
Here Comes Cookie 1935,O 12,12:2
Trapped by G-Men 1937,N 4,29:1
Prison Break 1938,Jl 13,17:4
Sabotage 1939,N 16,29:5
Grapes of Wrath, The 1940,Ja 25,17:2
Arizona 1941,F 7,23:3
Hello, Frisco, Hello 1943,Mr 25,25:1
Bad Bascomb 1946,My 23,18:4
Woman on the Beach, The 1947,Je 9,26:6
Flying Saucer, The 1950,Ja 5,28:3
Darien, George (Original Author)
Thief of Paris, The 1967,Ag 24,43:2
Darin, Bobby
Pepe 1960,D 22,18:1
Come September 1961,S 8,34:1
Too Late Blues 1962,Mr 1,27:4
State Fair 1962,Ap 12,41:4
Hell is for Heroes 1962,Jl 12,19:3
Pressure Point 1962,O 11,49:3
If a Man Answers 1962,N 22,43:1
Captain Newman, MD 1964,F 21,36:1
That Funny Feeling 1965,O 21,57:2
Dark, Christopher
Suddenly 1954,O 8,27:2
Johnny Concho 1956,Ag 16,30:1
Private Navy of Sgt O'Farrell, The 1968,My 9,54:1
Dark, John (Producer)
Half a Sixpence 1968,F 21,60:3
Dark, Michael
Flaming Youth 1923,N 26,15:6
Beau Brummell 1924,Mr 31,20:1

Dark, Michael— Cont
Broadway After Dark 1924,My 20,15:2
Regular Fellow, A 1925,O 5,25:2
Dove, The 1928,Ja 3,28:2
Darling, Anne
Bride of Frankenstein, The 1935,My 11,21:2
Darling, Candy
Flesh 1968,S 27,36:1
Darling, Ida
Ruling Passion, The 1922,Ja 23,11:4
Heart of a Siren, The 1925,Ap 8,24:3
Irene 1926,Mr 1,17:1
Stranded in Paris 1926,D 13,27:1
Singed 1927,Jl 12,29:3
Lummox 1930,Mr 24,25:1
Darling, Joan
Troublemaker, The 1964,Je 23,25:1
Darling, Miss
Witches of Salem 1958,D 9,54:2
Darling, Romere
Mrs Mike 1950,F 9,36:5
Darling, W Scott (Miscellaneous)
Weird Woman 1944,Ap 1,11:1
Stampede 1949,S 16,36:2
Darling, W Scott (Original Author)
Scarlet Seas 1928,D 31,9:1
Murder at Midnight 1931,O 5,17:3
Atlantic Flight 1937,N 1,24:5
He Married his Wife 1940,Ja 20,11:2
Cobra Woman 1944,My 18,17:2
Meet Me After the Show 1951,Ag 16,23:2
Darling, W Scott (Screenwriter)
Charlie Chan at the Opera 1936,D 5,16:2
Atlantic Flight 1937,N 1,24:5
Adventure's End 1937,D 20,23:2
Boy of the Streets 1938,Ja 24,17:1
Mister Wong in Chinatown 1939,Jl 31,9:2 (In Addenda)
Body Disappears, The 1942,Ja 31,13:2
Ghost of Frankenstein, The 1942,Ap 4,19:2
Sin Town 1942,O 17,11:2
Sherlock Holmes and the Secret Weapon 1943,Ja 5,15:2
Jitterbugs 1943,Je 5,12:2
Dancing Masters, The 1943,D 2,30:2
Bermuda Mystery 1944,My 13,17:1
Big Noise, The 1944,S 23,16:1
Bullfighters, The 1945,My 12,10:3
Caribbean Mystery, The 1945,Ag 20,22:4
Behind Green Lights 1946,F 16,10:2
Spider, The 1946,Je 21,20:3
Blue Grass of Kentucky 1950,Ja 27,29:2
Prince of Peace, The 1951,Mr 24,8:3
Darly, Yvette
Amour Maitre des Choses, L' 1931,Mr 30,25:2
Darmond, Grace
Below the Surface 1920,Je 7,20:3 (In Addenda)
Marriage Clause, The 1926,S 28,30:2
Darmour, Larry (Producer)
Perfect Clue, The 1935,Mr 14,18:1
Great Plane Robbery, The 1940,N 15,25:2
Great Swindle, The 1941,My 14,25:4
Ellery Queen and the Murder Ring 1941,O 21,29:4
Darnay
Paris Incident 1954,Ag 18,20:2
Darnborough, Antony (Director)
Astonished Heart, The 1950,F 15,23:2
So Long at the Fair 1951,Ja 22,14:2
Darnborough, Antony (Producer)
My Brothers Keeper 1949,F 14,15:3
Quartet (The Colonel's Lady); Colonel's Lady, The (Quartet) 1949,Mr 29,30:3
Quartet (The Alien Corn); Alien Corn, The (Quartet) 1949,Mr 29,30:3
Quartet (The Kite); Kite, The (Quartet) 1949,Mr 29,30:3
Quartet (The Facts of Life); Facts of Life, The (Quartet) 1949,Mr 29,30:3
Once Upon a Dream 1949,Jl 15,17:2
Girl in the Painting, The 1949,Ag 22,13:1
Astonished Heart, The 1950,F 15,23:2
Trio 1950,O 11,42:1
Encore (The Ant and the Grasshopper); Ant and the Grasshopper, The (Encore) 1952,Ap 3,45:1
Encore (Winter Cruise); Winter Cruise (Encore) 1952,Ap 3,45:1
Encore (Gigolo and Gigolette); Gigolo and Gigolette (Encore) 1952,Ap 3,45:1
Project M 7 1953,N 27,22:5
Personal Affair 1954,O 23,13:2
To Paris With Love 1955,Mr 29,33:4
Baby and the Battleship, The 1957,O 1,37:2
Darnell, Linda
Hotel for Women 1939,Ag 26,20:2
Daytime Wife 1939,N 24,29:1
Star Dust 1940,My 4,13:1
Brigham Young - Frontiersman 1940,S 21,13:2
Mark of Zorro, The 1940,N 4,23:2
Chad Hanna 1940,D 26,23:1
Blood and Sand 1941,My 23,25:3
Rise and Shine 1941,D 6,14:3
Loves of Edgar Allan Poe, The 1942,S 21,19:2
Buffalo Bill 1944,Ap 20,22:6

Darnell, Linda— Cont

It Happened Tomorrow 1944,My 29,18:2
Sweet and Low Down 1944,O 19,19:2
Summer Storm 1944,O 23,14:3
Hangover Square 1945,F 8,15:2
Great John L, The 1945,Jl 9,14:6
Fallen Angel 1946,F 7,29:4
Anna and the King of Siam 1946,Je 21,20:2
Centennial Summer 1946,Jl 18,20:2
My Darling Clementine 1946,D 4,44:5
Forever Amber 1947,O 23,31:2
Walls of Jericho, The 1948,Ag 5,16:2
Unfaithfully Yours 1948,N 6,9:2
Letter to Three Wives, A 1949,Ja 21,24:2
Slattery's Hurricane 1949,Ag 13,6:6
Everybody Does It 1949,O 26,32:2
No Way Out 1950,Ag 17,23:1
Two Flags West 1950,O 13,23:2
Thirteenth Letter, The 1951,F 22,27:2
Guy Who Came Back, The 1951,Ag 17,13:2
Night Without Sleep 1952,S 27,13:2
Blackbeard the Pirate 1952,D 26,20:3
Second Chance 1953,Jl 23,20:2
This is my Love 1954,D 25,7:3
Dakota Incident 1956,N 10,14:2
Angels of Darkness 1956,N 22,51:1
Zero Hour 1957,N 14,41:1
Black Spurs 1965,My 29,17:1

Darnton, Charles (Screenwriter)
Folly of Vanity 1925,Ja 28,14:1

Daroy, Jacques (Director)
Generals Without Buttons 1938,Mr 8,23:2
Rumors 1949,Mr 19,10:7

D'Arpe, Gustavo
Seduced and Abandoned 1964,Jl 16,23:1

Darr, Captain
Tanga Tika 1953,O 6,34:4

Darr, Kathlyn
City That Never Sleeps, The 1924,S 29,10:1

Darr, Molly
Julius Caesar 1952,N 25,33:5

Darr, Vondell
City That Never Sleeps, The 1924,S 29,10:1
Pony Express, The 1925,S 14,16:1
On Trial 1928,N 15,26:5
Dummy, The 1929,Mr 4,20:2

Darr, Vondell (Original Author)
City That Never Sleeps, The 1924,S 29,10:1

D'Arrast, H D'Abbadie (Director)
Service for Ladies 1927,Ag 15,22:5
Gentleman of Paris, A 1927,O 3,20:1
Serenade 1927,D 19,30:1
Magnificent Flirt, The 1928,Je 25,27:1
Laughter 1930,N 15,15:3
Topaze 1933,F 10,12:2

D'Arrast, H D'Abbadie (Original Author)
Laughter 1930,N 15,15:3

Darraux, Christian (Cinematographer)
Survival 1967 1968,Je 12,40:2

Darrell, Steve
Fugitive From Justice, A 1940,Jl 8,13:3
I'll Wait for You 1941,Je 2,13:6
Song of my Heart 1948,Mr 5,17:3
Abandoned Woman 1949,O 27,35:3
Thunder Over the Plains 1953,D 10,64:4
Dangerous Mission 1954,Mr 6,13:5
Tall Men, The 1955,O 12,36:2

Darren, James
Operation Mad Ball 1957,N 21,38:1
Gidget 1959,Ap 23,27:4
Gene Krupa Story, The 1959,D 26,7:1
All the Young Men 1960,Ag 27,8:6
Let no Man Write my Epitaph 1960,N 11,36:2
Guns of Navarone, The 1961,Je 23,19:1
Gidget Goes Hawaiian 1961,Ag 10,17:4
Diamond Head 1963,F 21,5:2
Gidget Goes to Rome 1963,S 12,32:2
For Those Who Think Young 1964,Jl 9,27:1
Lively Set, The 1964,O 15,54:1

Darrid, Bill
That Night 1957,O 15,39:3

Darrieu, Gerard
Elusive Corporal, The 1963,F 19,5:1

Darrieux, Danielle
Bal, Le 1932,S 28,22:5
Crise est Finie, La 1935,Mr 14,18:1
Mayerling 1937,S 14,27:1
Club De Femmes 1937,O 20,27:2
Meet Miss Mozart 1937,N 27,21:3
Rage of Paris 1938,Jl 2,10:2
Avocate d'Amour 1938,S 8,27:2
Abused Confidence 1938,N 1,29:1
Mademoiselle ma Mere 1939,S 19,29:2
Katia 1939,D 23,9:2
I Give my Life 1941,S 1,18:4
Her First Affair; (Children of Paradise)
  1947,F 20,32:3
She Returned at Dawn; Retour a l'Aube
  1947,Ag 1,21:5
Ruy Blas 1948,O 4,14:2
Rich, Young and Pretty 1951,Jl 26,17:3
Oh, Amelia 1951,D 3,22:2
Five Fingers 1952,F 23,7:5
Ronde, La 1954,Mr 17,27:2

Plaisir, Le (The House of Madame Tellier); House
  of Madame Tellier (Le Plaisir)
  1954,My 20,38:1
Earrings of Madame De, The 1954,Jl 20,15:5
One Step to Eternity 1955,O 3,22:2
Adorable Creatures 1956,Ja 11,36:2
Alexander the Great 1956,Mr 29,23:1
Rouge et Noir 1958,Ap 9,42:1
Pot Bouille 1958,O 28,39:1
Lady Chatterley's Lover 1959,Jl 11,11:1
Marie Octobre 1960,Ag 16,25:2
Night Affair 1961,O 13,27:1
Loss of Innocence 1961,N 22,27:1
Crime Does Not Pay (The Man on the Avenue);
  Man on the Avenue, The (Crime Does Not
  Pay) 1962,O 17,35:2
Landru 1963,Ap 10,31:1
Devil and the 10 Commandments, The (Episode
  6) 1963,O 15,44:1
Friend of the Family 1965,N 18,55:3
Young Girls of Rochefort, The 1968,Ap 12,50:1
24 Hours in a Woman's Life 1968,S 25,39:1
Birds in Peru 1968,N 7,51:2

Darrieux, Olivier
Panic 1947,N 27,50:2

Darrin, Diana
Amazing Colossal Man, The 1957,O 26,19:2

Darrin, Sonia
Big Sleep, The 1946,Ag 24,6:6
Bury Me Dead 1947,O 25,13:3
Caught 1949,F 18,26:4

Darro, Frankie
Signal Tower, The 1924,Jl 21,14:4
Roaring Rails 1924,O 15,27:3
So Big 1925,Ja 5,19:1
Confessions of a Queen 1925,Mr 24,20:6
Mike 1926,Ja 11,33:1
Memory Lane 1926,F 2,20:4
Kiki 1926,Ap 6,26:4
Long Pants 1927,Mr 29,23:2
Judgment of the Hills 1927,Ag 2,19:2
Circus Kid, The 1928,D 17,23:1
Rainbow Man, The 1929,Ap 17,30:6
Blaze O' Glory 1929,D 31,15:1
Mad Genius, The 1931,O 24,20:3
Way Back Home 1932,Ja 16,13:1
Amateur Daddy 1932,Ap 23,11:5
Mayor of Hell, The 1933,Jl 1,16:5
Laughing at Life 1933,Jl 15,14:2
Tugboat Annie 1933,Ag 12,14:2
Wild Boys of the Road 1933,S 22,14:1
No Greater Glory 1934,My 5,22:2
Broadway Bill 1934,N 30,22:2
Little Men 1935,F 18,19:3
Red Hot Tires 1935,Mr 1,16:3
Stranded 1935,Je 20,16:2
Three Kids and a Queen 1935,N 9,19:2
Pay-Off, The 1935,N 13,25:3
Ex-Mrs Bradford, The 1936,My 28,19:2
Charlie Chan at the Race Track 1936,Ag 15,6:2
Saratoga 1937,Jl 23,16:3
Thoroughbreds Don't Cry 1937,N 26,27:4
Reformatory 1938,Je 27,13:6
Juvenile Court 1938,S 12,13:2
Wanted by the Police 1938,S 26,13:2
That's my Man 1947,Ap 7,20:2
Riding High 1950,Ap 11,26:2
Wyoming Mail 1950,O 23,26:5
Across the Wide Missouri 1951,N 7,35:4

Darrow, Barbara
French Line, The 1954,My 15,13:2
Tall Story 1960,Ap 7,46:1

Darrow, Clarence (Miscellaneous)
Mystery of Life, The 1931,Jl 6,24:4

Darrow, John
High School Hero 1927,O 24,24:3
Racket, The 1928,Jl 9,25:1
Prep and Pep 1928,D 24,11:1
Girls Gone Wild 1929,Ap 22,23:1
Argyle Case, The 1929,Ag 31,13:4
Hell's Angels 1930,Ag 16,8:3
Ten Nights in a Barroom 1931,F 28,15:2
Everything's Rosie 1931,My 22,28:5
Bargain, The 1931,S 5,7:4
Fanny Foley Herself 1931,O 26,22:1
Midnight Lady, The 1932,Jl 1,19:3
All American, The 1932,O 22,18:4
Strange People 1933,Je 17,16:5
Midshipman Jack 1933,N 20,18:2
I Give my Love 1934,Jl 17,24:2
Flirtation Walk 1934,N 29,33:1
Notorious Gentleman, A 1935,F 16,9:1
Crime Over London 1938,Jl 28,23:2

D'Artega, Alfonso
Carnegie Hall 1947,My 3,10:2

Darteuil, Pierre
Call, The 1938,Mr 29,18:3

Darthez, Robert
Culte de Beaute, Le 1931,Je 8,21:1

Dartnell, Stephen
Oscar Wilde 1960,Je 21,28:2

Darvas, Charles
Fashions For Women 1927,Mr 28,26:4
Dove, The 1928,Ja 3,28:2

Darvas, Lili
Affairs of Maupassant, The 1938,F 12,20:2
Meet Me in Las Vegas 1956,Mr 14,39:2
Cimarron 1961,F 17,12:2

Darvel, Christine
Cross of the Living 1963,F 5,5:5

Darvell, Evelyn
Madonna of the Seven Moons 1946,My 23,18:4

Darvi, Bella
Hell and High Water 1954,F 2,20:6
Egyptian, The 1954,Ag 25,23:1
Sinners of Paris 1959,Ap 24,23:1

Darwell, Jane
Tom Sawyer 1930,D 20,20:6
Huckleberry Finn 1931,Ag 8,16:3
Ladies of the Big House 1932,Ja 1,31:1
Back Street 1932,Ag 29,9:2
Hot Saturday 1932,N 5,12:5
Air Hostess 1933,Ja 23,9:2
Child of Manhattan 1933,F 13,11:4
Bondage 1933,Ap 24,11:3
One Sunday Afternoon 1933,S 2,14:4
Before Dawn 1933,O 17,26:2
Only Yesterday 1933,N 10,25:1
Design for Living 1933,N 23,24:2
Heat Lightning 1934,Mr 8,23:2
Once to Every Woman 1934,Mr 26,22:3
Change of Heart 1934,My 11,24:2
Let's Talk It Over 1934,Je 16,20:2
Blind Date 1934,S 1,16:3
Happiness Ahead 1934,O 11,28:2
White Parade, The 1934,N 10,19:1
Bright Eyes 1934,D 21,31:1
One More Spring 1935,F 22,27:1
McFadden's Flats 1935,Mr 13,16:2
Life Begins at 40 1935,Ap 5,21:3
Curly Top 1935,Ag 2,22:3
We're Only Human 1936,Ja 18,19:2
Paddy O'Day 1936,F 8,19:2
Country Doctor, The 1936,Mr 13,32:2 (Incorrect
  in this edition; use 1936,Mr 13,27:2 elsewhere)
Captain January 1936,Ap 25,21:1
Little Miss Nobody 1936,Je 6,21:1
Private Number 1936,Je 12,19:1
Poor Little Rich Girl, The 1936,Je 26,16:1
White Fang 1936,Jl 18,18:2
Star for a Night 1936,S 5,7:2
Craig's Wife 1936,O 2,29:3
Ramona 1936,O 7,32:4
Love Is News 1937,Mr 6,10:1
Nancy Steele is Missing 1937,Mr 8,22:1
Fifty Roads to Town 1937,Je 5,21:1
Slave Ship 1937,Je 17,19:2
Singing Marine, The 1937,Jl 1,33:2
Great Hospital Mystery, The 1937,Jl 16,22:2
Wife, Doctor and Nurse 1937,O 11,26:5
Dangerously Yours 1937,O 18,14:2
Battle of Broadway 1938,Ap 25,19:2
Three Blind Mice 1938,Je 18,18:2
Little Miss Broadway 1938,Jl 23,10:4
Time Out for Murder 1938,O 7,21:2
Five of a Kind 1938,O 31,12:2
Up the River 1938,D 3,11:2
Jesse James 1939,Ja 14,13:1
Grand Jury Secrets 1939,Je 29,19:2
Zero Hour, The 1939,Jl 5,20:3
Unexpected Father 1939,Ag 11,12:2
Rains Came, The 1939,S 9,11:2
20,000 Men a Year 1939,O 28,11:2
Gone With the Wind 1939,D 20,31:2
Grapes of Wrath, The 1940,Ja 25,17:2
Untamed 1940,Jl 25,14:3
Brigham Young - Frontiersman 1940,S 21,13:2
Youth Will Be Served 1940,N 15,25:2
Chad Hanna 1940,D 26,23:1
Private Nurse 1941,Ag 29,13:3
All That Money Can Buy 1941,O 17,27:2
All Through the Night 1942,Ja 24,13:2
It Happened in Flatbush 1942,Jl 3,12:8
Men of Texas 1942,Jl 13,18:3 (In Addenda)
Loves of Edgar Allan Poe, The 1942,S 21,19:2
Great Gildersleeve, The 1942,D 18,36:8
Ox-Bow Incident, The 1943,My 10,15:2 (In
  Addenda)
Gildersleeve's Bad Day 1943,Je 11,23:1
Stage Door Canteen 1943,Je 25,13:2
Government Girl 1944,Ja 7,13:2
Tender Comrade 1944,Je 2,21:2
Impatient Years, The 1944,S 20,20:1
Music in Manhattan 1944,O 7,11:2
Sunday Dinner for a Soldier 1945,Ja 25,16:2
Yank in London, A 1946,Ap 20,16:3
Three Wise Fools 1946,S 27,19:2
My Darling Clementine 1946,D 4,44:5
Red Stallion 1947,N 27,50:3
Three Godfathers 1949,Mr 4,25:2
Red Canyon 1949,Ap 28,28:2
Daughter of Rosie O'Grady, The
  1950,Mr 31,36:2
Caged 1950,My 20,8:6

Darwell, Jane — Cont
Wagonmaster 1950,Je 19,17:2
Surrender 1950,O 9,21:5
Second Face, The 1951,Mr 2,21:3
Three Husbands 1951,Mr 9,30:2
Lemon Drop Kid, The 1951,Mr 22,41:2
Excuse my Dust 1951,Je 28,21:2
We're not Married 1952,Jl 12,16:2
Affair With a Stranger 1953,Jl 11,8:2
Bigamist, The 1953,D 26,10:4
Hit the Deck 1955,Mr 4,17:1
There's Always Tomorrow 1956,Ja 21,18:2
Last Hurrah, The 1958,O 24,40:1
Mary Poppins 1964,S 25,34:1

Darwell, Jane (Narrator)
Battle of Midway, The 1942,S 15,19:3

Dary, Rene
Moulin Rouge 1944,N 23,38:2
Postmaster's Daughter, The 1946,Ag 19,17:6
Grisbi 1959,Jl 13,23:1
Sins of Youth 1960,D 24,8:2

Daryl, Lauria
Pardon my French 1952,Mr 31,17:2

Daryll, Natalie
Girl in the Kremlin, The 1957,My 22,29:2

Das, Eddie
Man-Eater of Kumaon 1948,Jl 2,24:2

Das Bolas, Xan
Backfire 1965,Ap 27,27:1

das Gupta, Aparna
Two Daughters (The Conclusion); Conclusion, The (Two Daughters) 1963,My 1,35:1

Das Gupta, Bandana
Mark, The 1961,O 3,46:2

D'Ashelbe (Original Author)
Pepe le Moko 1941,Mr 4,20:2

Dashiell, Williard
Cheat, The 1931,D 12,23:3
War Is a Racket 1934,D 10,16:2

Dassas, Stella
Hiroshima, Mon Amour 1960,My 17,43:1

Dassin, Jules
Never on Sunday 1960,O 19,54:1
Phaedra 1962,O 19,24:1

Dassin, Jules (Director)
Nazi Agent 1942,Je 13,11:2
Reunion in France 1943,Mr 5,20:3
Canterville Ghost, The 1944,Jl 29,16:2
Letter for Evie, A 1946,Je 28,17:4
Two Smart People 1947,F 15,20:4
Brute Force 1947,Jl 17,16:2
Naked City, The 1948,Mr 5,17:2
Thieves' Highway 1949,S 24,8:6
Night and the City 1950,Je 10,11:2
Rififi 1956,Je 6,37:1
He Who Must Die 1958,D 29,21:1
Never on Sunday 1960,O 19,54:1
Where the Hot Wind Blows 1960,N 12,15:1
Phaedra 1962,O 19,24:1
Topkapi 1964,S 18,25:1
10:30 PM Summer 1966,O 20,52:1
Survival 1967 1968,Je 12,40:2
Up Tight 1968,D 19,62:1

Dassin, Jules (Producer)
Phaedra 1962,O 19,24:1
Topkapi 1964,S 18,25:1
10:30 PM Summer 1966,O 20,52:1
Survival 1967 1968,Je 12,40:2
Up Tight 1968,D 19,62:1

Dassin, Jules (Screenwriter)
Rififi 1956,Je 6,37:1
He Who Must Die 1958,D 29,21:1
Never on Sunday 1960,O 19,54:1
Where the Hot Wind Blows 1960,N 12,15:1
Phaedra 1962,O 19,24:1
10:30 PM Summer 1966,O 20,52:1
Up Tight 1968,D 19,62:1

Dassonville, Helene
Loves of Casanova 1948,S 18,11:4

D'Assunta, Rocco
O K Nero 1953,Je 20,8:6
Seduced and Abandoned 1964,Jl 16,23:1

Daste, Edouard
Grand Illusion 1938,S 13,28:2

Daste, Jean
Zero de Conduite 1947,Je 23,14:5
Atalante, L' 1947,Je 23,14:5
Muriel 1963,O 31,26:1
Guerre est Fini, La; War Is Over, The 1967,F 2,29:2
Boudu Saved From Drowning; Boudu Sauve Des Eaux 1967,F 24,26:2

Daste, Marie-Helene
Katia 1939,D 23,9:2
Who Killed Santa Claus? 1948,Ap 21,33:2
Angels of the Streets 1950,Ja 17,24:2
End of Desire 1962,Jl 10,29:2

Datlowe, Samuel (Screenwriter)
Monkey Into Man 1941,My 31,14:1

D'Attino, Giacomo
White Sister, The 1923,S 6,10:2

Datzig, Elfriede
Anton der Letzte; Anthony the Last 1940,Mr 30,11:2

Daubigny, Lise
Abysses, Les 1964,N 24,44:1

Daubigny, Robert Ciroz (Producer)
Lovers on a Tightrope 1962,O 25,48:3

d'Auburn, Dennis
Unfaithful 1931,Mr 7,17:2
Body and Soul 1931,Mr 14,23:2

Daudert, Charlotte
Frasquita 1936,Ja 18,19:4
Alte Kameraden 1936,Ap 27,19:3
Dell Etappenhase 1938,Ja 1,11:3
Liebesbriefe aus dem Engadin; Love Letters From the Engadine 1938,D 24,12:2
Kluge Schwiegermutter, Die; Wise Mother-in-Law, The 1939,O 9,15:3

Daudet, Alphonse (Original Author)
Confessions of a Queen 1925,Mr 24,20:6
Letters From my Windmill (The Three Low Masses); Three Low Masses, The (Letters From my Windmill) 1955,D 19,33:1
Letters From my Windmill (The Secret of Master Cornille); Secret of Master Cornille, The (Letters From my Windmill) 1955,D 19,33:1
Letters From my Windmill (The Elixir of Father Gaucher); Elixir of Father Gaucher, The (Letters From my Windmill) 1955,D 19,33:1

Daudet, Jeanette
Lily of the Dust 1924,Ag 25,16:2

DAUGHERTY
See Also DOHERTY, DOUGHERTY

Daugherty, Herschel (Director)
Light in the Forest, The 1958,Jl 11,15:2

Dauman, Alain (Producer)
Muriel 1963,O 31,26:1

Dauman, Anatole
Muriel 1963,O 31,26:1

Dauman, Anatole (Producer)
Chronicle of a Summer; Chronique d'un Ete 1965,My 7,34:1
Mouchette 1968,S 21,26:1

Daumerey, Carey
Young April 1926,Ag 31,15:3

Daumery, Carrie
Grand Canary 1934,Jl 20,11:1

Daumery, Carry
Last Warning, The 1929,Ja 7,36:2

d'Aumery, Mme
Forbidden Paradise 1924,N 17,16:1

Daumery, Mme
Cameo Kirby 1930,F 8,12:5

Daumier, Sophie
Sweet and Sour 1964,D 28,34:2
How Not to Rob a Department Store 1965,D 29,23:1

Dauphin, Claude
Slipper Episode, The 1938,My 19,25:2
Curtain Rises, The 1939,Ap 22,15:2
Affair Lafont, The; Conflit 1939,O 9,15:2
Her Man Gilbey 1949,Je 9,35:2
Twilight 1949,D 30,13:2
Deported 1950,N 2,39:3
Affaire, L' 1950,N 13,23:2
Casque D'Or 1952,Ag 19,19:1
April in Paris 1952,D 25,34:5
Naughty Martine 1953,Ap 13,32:4
Little Boy Lost 1953,S 22,38:2
Phantom of the Rue Morgue 1954,Mr 20,10:5
Plaisir, Le (The Mask); Mask, The (Le Plaisir) 1954,My 20,38:1
Innocents in Paris 1955,Mr 5,9:6
Quiet American, The 1958,F 6,24:1
Stop Me Before I Kill 1961,Je 22,23:4
Devil and the 10 Commandments, The (Episode 4) 1963,O 15,44:1
Tiara Tahiti 1963,N 6,32:1
Bonne Soupe, La 1964,Mr 16,37:1
Visit, The 1964,O 22,44:1
Symphony for a Massacre 1965,My 28,40:1
Lady L 1966,My 19,51:1
Is Paris Burning? 1966,N 11,36:1
Grand-Prix 1966,D 22,40:1
Two for the Road 1967,Ap 28,36:2
Other One, The 1967,S 29,53:1
Barbarella 1968,O 12,43:1

Dauran
Jenny Lamour 1948,Mr 6,17:2
Battle of the Rails; (Bataille Du Rail) 1949,D 27,27:2

Daurat, Charles
Youth in Revolt 1939,My 16,27:3

D'Auray, Jacques
Claw, The 1927,My 11,28:3

d'Auril, Yola
Shanghai Lady 1929,N 11,20:2

Daushvili, K
Friends 1939,Ja 2,28:3

Daussmond, Betty
Indiscretions 1939,My 1,21:1

D'Autheville, Francis (Original Author)
Saadia 1954,Mr 20,10:5

Dauvia, Charlotte
Song of the Street 1939,S 5,21:2

Dauvray, Marise
J'Accuse 1920,My 23,VI,2:2
I Accuse; (J'Accuse) 1921,O 10,16:1

Davalos, Ellen
Interns, The 1962,Ag 9,17:5

Davalos, Richard
East of Eden 1955,Mr 10,33:1
All the Young Men 1960,Ag 27,8:6
Cabinet of Caligari, The 1962,My 26,13:5
Cool Hand Luke 1967,N 2,58:1

Davanzati, D Forges (Producer)
Heart and Soul 1950,Je 15,41:3

Davanzati, Fiore
Heart and Soul 1950,Je 15,41:3

Daven, Andre (Producer)
Razumov 1937,Mr 9,27:2
Tonight We Raid Calais 1943,Ap 15,20:2
Paris After Dark 1943,O 23,11:1
Home in Indiana 1944,Je 22,23:1
Nob Hill 1945,Jl 4,10:3
Gates of Paris 1958,Ja 15,24:1

Davenport, Adele
Lost Honeymoon 1947,Je 20,25:6

Davenport, Bromley
Captivation 1931,S 28,17:4
Bride of the Lake, The 1934,S 11,24:5
To the Victor 1938,Ap 13,21:2
Jamaica Inn 1939,O 12,33:1
Young Mr Pitt, The 1943,Mr 11,17:1

Davenport, Danny
Big Lift, The 1950,Ap 27,37:2
I'll Get by 1950,N 2,39:3

Davenport, David
Carry on Cleo 1965,O 23,17:2

Davenport, Doris
Kid Millions 1934,N 12,17:2
Westerner, The 1940,O 25,25:2
Behind the News 1941,Ja 16,25:3

Davenport, Gail (Original Author)
Rockin' in The Rockies 1945,Jl 5,7:2

Davenport, Gwen (Original Author)
Sitting Pretty 1948,Mr 11,35:2

Davenport, Harris
Rear Window 1954,Ag 5,18:2

Davenport, Harry
My Sin 1931,S 11,24:2
His Woman 1931,D 5,21:2
Scoundrel, The 1935,My 3,23:2
Three Men on a Horse 1936,N 26,39:1
Case of the Black Cat, The 1936,D 26,15:4
Under Cover of Night 1937,Ja 20,18:4
Her Husband's Secretary 1937,Mr 20,23:6
As Good as Married 1937,My 22,19:2
Fly Away Baby 1937,Jl 9,18:2
They Won't Forget 1937,Jl 15,16:1
Armored Car 1937,Jl 26,15:2
White Bondage 1937,Ag 6,21:3
Mr Dodd Takes the Air 1937,Ag 12,14:2
Life of Emile Zola, The 1937,Ag 12,14:2
Fit for a King 1937,O 15,18:5
Perfect Specimen, The 1937,O 28,29:2
First Lady 1937,D 23,25:1
Wells Fargo 1937,D 30,15:2
Gold Is Where You Find It 1938,F 14,20:6
First 100 Years, The 1938,My 13,17:2
Rage of Paris 1938,Jl 2,10:2
You Can't Take It With You 1938,S 2,21:2
Cowboy and the Lady, The 1938,N 25,19:3
Made for Each Other 1939,F 17,17:2
Story of Alexander Graham Bell, The 1939,Ap 1,17:2
Juarez 1939,Ap 26,27:1
Exile Express 1939,Ag 16,21:3
Death of a Champion 1939,Ag 24,17:3
Gone With the Wind 1939,D 20,31:2
Hunchback of Notre Dame, The 1940,Ja 1,29:2
Dr Ehrlich's Magic Bullet 1940,F 24,9:2
Too Many Husbands 1940,Mr 8,25:2
All This and Heaven, Too 1940,Jl 5,10:2
Foreign Correspondent 1940,Ag 28,15:2
Lucky Partners 1940,S 6,25:2
I Want a Divorce 1940,O 3,31:2
I Wanted Wings 1941,Mr 27,29:4
That Uncertain Feeling 1941,My 2,25:1
Bride Came C O D, The 1941,Jl 26,18:2
One Foot in Heaven 1941,N 14,28:3
Son of Fury 1942,Ja 30,23:2
Kings Row 1942,F 3,23:2
Larceny, Inc 1942,Ap 25,9:1
Ten Gentlemen From West Point 1942,Je 5,23:3
Tales of Manhattan 1942,S 25,25:1
Amazing Mrs Holliday, The 1943,F 22,20:2
Ox-Bow Incident, The 1943,My 10,15:2 (In Addenda)
We've Never Been Licked 1943,Ag 19,23:1
Princess O'Rourke 1943,N 6,16:2
Government Girl 1943,Ja 7,13:2
Jack London 1944,Mr 3,19:3
Kismet 1944,Ag 23,16:1
Impatient Years, The 1944,S 20,20:1
Meet Me in St Louis 1944,N 29,20:2
Music for Millions 1944,D 22,12:4
Thin Man Goes Home, The 1945,Ja 26,16:5

Davenport, Harry— Cont

This Love of Ours 1945,N 1,20:2
Too Young to Know 1945,D 8,21:2
Enchanted Forest, The 1945,D 17,17:2
She Wouldn't Say Yes 1946,Ja 12,10:7
Pardon my Past 1946,Ja 28,15:5
Adventure 1946,F 8,23:2
Courage of Lassie 1946,Jl 25,18:5
Claudia and David 1946,Ag 15,19:2
Three Wise Fools 1946,S 27,19:2
Lady Luck 1946,O 31,22:3
Farmer's Daughter, The 1947,Mr 26,31:2
Stallion Road 1947,Ap 5,12:5
Bachelor and the Bobby-Soxer, The
  1947,Jl 25,12:5
That Hagen Girl 1947,O 25,13:2
Fabulous Texan, The 1947,D 26,22:5
Three Daring Daughters 1948,F 13,26:3
Man From Texas 1948,Ag 12,16:5
That Lady in Ermine 1948,Ag 25,31:2
For the Love of Mary 1948,S 23,37:2
Decision of Christopher Blake, The
  1948,D 11,12:2
Down to the Sea in Ships 1949,F 23,31:2
Little Women 1949,Mr 11,33:2
That Forsyte Woman 1949,N 11,31:2

Davenport, Marcia (Original Author)

Valley of Decision, The 1945,My 4,23:2
East Side, West Side 1949,D 23,17:2

Davenport, Milla

In Mizzoura 1919,O 13,16:3
Forbidden Woman, The 1920,F 23,11:2
Man From Lost River, The 1922,Ja 16,18:3
Dulcy 1923,S 17,18:2
Shooting of Dan McGrew, The 1924,Je 9,14:3
Red Lily, The 1924,S 29,10:1
Dangerous Innocence 1925,Je 8,19:1
Merrily We Go to Hell 1932,Je 11,9:3
In Love With Life 1934,My 12,12:3
Wedding Night, The 1935,Mr 16,19:1
Here Comes Cookie 1935,O 12,12:2

Davenport, Nigel

High Wind in Jamaica, A 1965,Je 17,27:2
Sands of the Kalahari 1965,N 25,64:5
Life at the Top 1965,D 15,53:1
Where the Spies Are 1966,Ja 27,29:1
Man for all Seasons, A 1966,D 13,60:1
Sebastian 1968,Ja 25,33:2
Strange Affair, The 1968,Jl 25,26:2

Daver, Emmet (Screenwriter)

Williamsburg: The Story of a Patriot
  1957,Ap 1,22:2

D'Aversa, Alberto (Director)

Voice in Your Heart, A 1952,F 23,7:5

D'Aversa, Alberto (Original Author)

Voice in Your Heart, A 1952,F 23,7:5

D'Aversa, Alberto (Screenwriter)

Voice in Your Heart, A 1952,F 23,7:5

DAVES

See Also DAVIES, DAVIS

Daves, Delbert (Director)

Battle of the Villa Fiorita, The 1965,My 27,28:1

Daves, Delbert (Producer)

Battle of the Villa Fiorita, The 1965,My 27,28:1

Daves, Delbert (Screenwriter)

Battle of the Villa Fiorita, The 1965,My 27,28:1

Daves, Delmer

Bishop Murder Case, The 1930,F 1,15:1

Daves, Delmer (Director)

Destination Tokyo 1944,Ja 1,9:2
Very Thought of You, The 1944,N 18,16:7
Hollywood Canteen 1944,D 16,19:2
Pride of the Marines 1945,Ag 25,7:3
Red House, The 1947,Mr 17,27:2
Dark Passage 1947,S 6,11:2
To the Victor 1948,Ap 17,11:2
Kiss in the Dark, A 1949,Mr 26,10:6
Task Force 1949,O 1,8:6
Broken Arrow 1950,Jl 21,15:2
Return of the Texan 1952,F 14,23:1
Treasure of the Golden Condor 1953,My 23,19:2
Never Let Me Go 1953,Je 11,37:2
Demetrius and the Gladiators 1954,Je 19,9:1
Drum Beat 1954,N 18,42:1
Jubal 1956,Ap 25,39:1
Last Wagon, The 1956,S 22,20:2
3:10 to Yuma 1957,Ag 29,22:1
Cowboy 1958,F 20,29:5
Kings Go Forth 1958,Jl 4,15:2
Badlanders, The 1958,S 4,33:1
Hanging Tree, The 1959,F 12,23:1
Summer Place, A 1959,O 23,24:1
Parrish 1961,My 5,22:1
Susan Slade 1961,N 11,14:6
Rome Adventure 1962,Mr 16,25:1
Spencer's Mountain 1963,My 17,26:6
Youngblood Hawke 1964,N 6,30:1

Daves, Delmer (Original Author)

Divorce in the Family 1932,O 31,18:4
Dames 1934,Ag 16,20:2
Shipmates Forever 1935,O 17,29:3
Farmer's Daughter, The 1940,F 16,23:4
Drum Beat 1954,N 18,42:1

Rome Adventure 1962,Mr 16,25:1

Daves, Delmer (Producer)

Bird of Paradise 1951,Mr 15,37:2
Summer Place, A 1959,O 23,24:1
Parrish 1961,My 5,22:1
Susan Slade 1961,N 11,14:6
Youngblood Hawke 1964,N 6,30:1

Daves, Delmer (Screenwriter)

Flirtation Walk 1934,N 29,33:1
Stranded 1935,Je 20,16:2
Page Miss Glory 1935,Ag 29,25:2
Shipmates Forever 1935,O 17,29:3
Petrified Forest, The 1936,F 7,14:2
Go Getter, The 1937,Je 4,27:2
Singing Marine, The 1937,Jl 1,33:2
She Married an Artist 1938,F 25,15:2
Professor Beware 1938,Jl 14,17:1
Love Affair 1939,Mr 17,25:2
$1,000 a Touchdown 1939,O 5,27:2
Safari 1940,Je 20,29:2
Unexpected Uncle 1941,S 25,29:1
Night of January 16th, The 1941,D 19,35:1
You Were Never Lovelier 1942,D 4,31:1
Stage Door Canteen 1943,Je 25,13:2
Destination Tokyo 1944,Ja 1,9:2
Very Thought of You, The 1944,N 18,16:7
Hollywood Canteen 1944,D 16,19:2
Red House, The 1947,Mr 17,27:2
Dark Passage 1947,S 6,11:2
Task Force 1949,O 1,8:6
Bird of Paradise 1951,Mr 15,37:2
Treasure of the Golden Condor 1953,My 23,19:2
White Feather 1955,F 17,23:1
Jubal 1956,Ap 25,39:1
Last Wagon, The 1956,S 22,20:2
Affair to Remember, An 1957,Jl 20,8:5
Summer Place, A 1959,O 23,24:1
Susan Slade 1961,N 11,14:6
Spencer's Mountain 1963,My 17,26:6

Davet, Michel (Original Author)

Love Story 1949,Je 27,18:4

David, Charles (Director)

Mam'zelle Nitouche 1933,N 20,18:3
Lady on a Train 1945,S 15,21:2
River Gang 1945,O 6,9:7

David, Charles (Producer)

River Gang 1945,O 6,9:7

David, Constantin (Director)

Herzblut 1932,O 3,15:2

David, Constantin J (Director)

Berlin After Dark 1929,My 28,36:2

David, Constantin J (Producer)

Alimony 1949,Jl 22,16:3

David, Ingold

Eric Soya's 17 1967,Ja 25,37:1

David, Liliane

Breathless 1961,F 8,26:1

David, Mack (Composer)

Pot o'Gold 1941,Ap 4,25:2
Cinderella 1950,F 23,33:1

David, Mario

Love Game, The 1960,N 9,44:1
Leda 1961,Jl 19,33:1
Elusive Corporal, The 1963,F 19,5:1
Landru 1963,Ap 10,31:1
Bonnes Femmes, Les 1966,My 13,32:1

David, Michael

Inn of the Sixth Happiness, The 1958,D 14,2:7
Let's Make Love 1960,S 9,36:1
Snow White and the Three Stooges 1961,Jl 1,9:1
Fiercest Heart, The 1961,Ag 3,13:5
Moonspinners, The 1964,N 4,47:1

David, Saul (Producer)

Von Ryan's Express 1965,Je 24,28:1
Our Man Flint 1966,Ja 26,23:4
Fantastic Voyage 1966,S 8,43:1

David, Thayer

Time to Love and a Time to Die, A
  1958,Jl 10,22:1
Journey to the Center of the Earth
  1959,D 17,51:1
Story of Ruth, The 1960,Je 18,12:3

David, Zorro

Reflections in a Golden Eye 1967,O 12,59:1

Davidge, Margaret

Clairvoyant, The 1935,Je 8,12:2

Davidik, Filip

Janosik 1936,D 25,19:3

Davidof, R

Chalutzim 1934,Ap 2,13:3

Davidov, Vassili

Cossacks of the Kuban 1950,O 30,22:4

Davidovich, Raquel

Ljubav I Strast 1932,D 16,25:5

DAVIDSON

See Also DAVISON, DAVISSON

Davidson, Bert

Walk a Crooked Mile 1948,O 13,31:2
Right Cross 1950,N 16,39:2

Davidson, Cliff

Code of the Wilderness, The 1924,Jl 1,21:4

Davidson, Dore

Humoresque 1920,My 31,14:2
Success 1923,Jl 10,22:5
Great White Way, The 1924,Ja 4,10:1
Welcome Stranger 1924,O 14,21:5
That Royle Girl 1926,Ja 4,33:1
East Side, West Side 1927,O 18,33:2

Davidson, John

Under Two Flags 1922,S 25,10:2
His Children's Children 1923,N 5,15:1
Monsieur Beaucaire 1924,Ag 12,12:1 (In
  Addenda)
Rescue, The 1929,Ja 14,20:1
Queen of the Night Clubs 1929,Mr 18,30:6
Time, The Place and the Girl, The 1929,Jl 8,17:3
Skin Deep 1929,S 30,23:1
Life of the Party, The 1930,N 10,16:2
Arsene Lupin 1932,F 27,22:1
Six Hours to Live 1932,O 22,18:4
Dinner at Eight 1933,Ag 24,18:1
Mad Game, The 1933,N 13,21:1
Bombay Mail 1934,Ja 6,18:2
Hold That Girl 1934,Mr 24,20:3
Murder in Trinidad 1934,My 16,22:2
Shot in the Dark, A 1935,My 22,23:2
Last Days of Pompeii, The 1935,O 17,29:2
Tale of Two Cities, A 1935,D 26,21:2
Mr Moto's Last Warning 1939,Ja 27,17:3
Mr Moto Takes a Vacation 1939,Je 19,12:6
Where Do We Go From Here? 1945,Je 7,25:2
Daisy Kenyon 1947,D 25,32:1
Slattery's Hurricane 1949,Ag 13,6:6
Happiest Millionaire, The 1967,D 1,56:1
One and Only Genuine Original Family Band,
  The 1968,Mr 22,55:1

Davidson, Lawford

Miami 1924,Je 3,22:2
Wildfire 1925,Je 10,18:2
Bright Lights 1925,N 18,27:4
Tony Runs Wild 1926,Ap 28,28:3
Little Journey, A 1927,Ja 4,21:1
Patent Leather Kid, The 1927,Ag 16,31:2
Burning Daylight 1928,Ap 23,20:2
Insidious Dr Fu Manchu, The 1929,Jl 22,17:1
Love Doctor, The 1929,N 9,22:5
Her Private Affair 1930,Ja 11,21:3
Vagabond King, The 1930,F 20,22:4
Ladies Love Brutes 1930,My 16,20:4

Davidson, Lenny

Having a Wild Weekend 1965,Ag 19,35:1

Davidson, Max

Darling of New York, The 1924,Ja 18,20:1
Old Clothes 1925,N 9,25:1
Hogan's Alley 1925,N 24,28:4
Hotel Imperial 1927,Ja 3,16:2
So This Is College 1929,N 9,22:5
Girl Said No, The 1937,O 18,14:1
Great Commandment, The 1942,O 17,11:1
Laurel and Hardy's Laughing 20's 1965,N 18,55:2

Davidson, Michael (Original Author)

Artists and Models 1955,D 22,20:1

Davidson, Ronald (Narrator)

Zanzabuku 1956,Ag 16,30:3

Davidson, Tito (Director)

Murio el Sargento Laprida; Sergeant Laprida Died
  1939,Mr 20,13:2

Davidson, William

Nobody 1921,Jl 25,8:3
Last Trail, The 1927,Ja 26,17:1
Cradle Snatchers 1927,My 31,25:2
Good Morning, Judge 1928,Je 26,29:1
Queen of the Night Clubs 1929,Mr 18,30:6
Blaze O' Glory 1929,D 31,15:1
Silver Horde, The 1930,O 25,20:6
Playboy of Paris 1930,N 1,23:2
Scarlet Pages 1930,D 6,21:3
Hook, Line and Sinker 1930,D 25,31:5
Sunny 1930,D 27,16:3
Menace, The 1932,Ja 30,13:2
Billion Dollar Scandal, The 1933,Ja 9,23:1
Hello, Everybody 1933,Ja 30,9:4
Dangerously Yours 1933,F 23,20:3
I'm no Angel 1933,O 14,18:2
Lady Killer 1934,Ja 1,28:2
Fog over Frisco 1934,Je 7,26:2
Friends of Mr Sweeney 1934,Jl 31,20:4
Dragon Murder Case, The 1934,Ag 23,13:3
St Louis Kid, The 1934,N 1,25:2
Man Who Reclaimed his Head, The
  1935,Ja 9,22:1
Bordertown 1935,Ja 24,22:5
Secret Bride, The 1935,F 2,10:1
Devil Dogs of the Air 1935,F 7,23:2
Go Into Your Dance 1935,My 4,17:2
Night at the Ritz, A 1935,My 16,20:2
Oil for the Lamps of China 1935,Je 6,25:2
Special Agent 1935,S 19,28:1
Show Them no Mercy 1935,D 9,25:2
Dangerous 1935,D 27,14:1
Road Gang 1936,F 24,14:1
Singing Kid, The 1936,Ap 4,11:1
Murder by an Aristocrat 1936,Je 13,13:2
Big Noise, The 1936,Jl 4,18:3

Davidson, William— Cont

Gold Diggers of 1937 1936,D 25,19:2
Midnight Court 1937,Mr 4,27:3
Let Them Live 1937,Je 8,30:3
Ever Since Eve 1937,Je 25,25:2
Something to Sing About 1937,S 21,29:4
Hollywood Hotel 1938,Ja 13,17:3
Blockade 1938,Je 17,25:1
Cowboy From Brooklyn 1938,Jl 14,17:1
They Made Me a Criminal 1939,Ja 21,19:2
Tail Spin 1939,F 11,13:2
Off the Record 1939,F 18,12:2
On Trial 1939,Ap 5,31:2
Naughty but Nice 1939,Je 23,23:2
Indianapolis Speedway 1939,Jl 15,8:2
Each Dawn I Die 1939,Jl 22,12:2
Dust Be my Destiny 1939,O 7,11:2
Smashing the Money Ring 1939,N 17,17:2
Three Cheers for the Irish 1940,Mr 9,19:2
Lillian Russell 1940,My 18,11:2
Florian 1940,Je 6,33:2
Girl in 313 1940,Je 14,25:3
Hired Wife 1940,S 14,11:2
Man Made Monster 1941,Mr 19,25:4
Hold That Ghost 1941,Ag 8,13:3
Keep 'Em Flying 1941,N 27,29:2
Juke Girl 1942,Je 20,9:2
Over my Dead Body 1942,D 26,15:2
Truck Busters 1943,Ja 29,23:5
Hers to Hold 1943,Jl 22,15:1
Calaboose 1943,Jl 30,19:2
Shine on Harvest Moon 1944,Mr 11,10:2
My Wild Irish Rose 1947,D 25,32:2

Davidson, William B

White Raven, The 1917,Ja 15,7:2
Partners of the Night 1920,Mr 1,16:2
Recompense 1925,Ap 20,22:1
Gentleman of Paris, A 1927,O 3,20:1
Carnation Kid, The 1929,F 25,16:1
Woman Trap 1929,Ag 31,13:4
Man From Wyoming, A 1930,Jl 12,16:4
For the Defense 1930,Jl 19,7:5
Hell's Angels 1930,Ag 16,8:3
Vice Squad, The 1931,Je 6,15:5
Secret Call, The 1931,Jl 13,13:5
Sky Devils 1932,Mr 4,17:3
Guilty as Hell 1932,Ag 6,14:5
Her mad Night 1932,N 15,24:5
Animal Kingdom, The 1932,D 30,14:2
Meet the Baron 1933,O 28,20:3
Sweet Music 1935,F 21,23:2
Marked Woman 1937,Ap 12,15:2
Road Back, The 1937,Je 18,25:2
Easy Living 1937,Jl 8,20:1
It Happened in Hollywood 1937,O 2,18:1
Mr Doodle Kicks Off 1938,S 28,29:4
Hidden Power 1939,Jl 26,17:3
Honeymoon in Bali 1939,S 21,21:1
Sailor's Lady 1940,Je 29,12:2
Tin Pan Alley 1940,N 22,27:3
Male Animal, The 1942,Mr 28,11:1
In This our Life 1942,My 9,10:2
In Society 1944,Ag 17,20:2
See my Lawyer 1945,My 4,23:4
Plainsman and the Lady, The 1946,N 4,33:1
That's my Man 1947,Ap 7,20:2
Dick Tracy's Dilemma 1947,Jl 14,14:5
That Hagen Girl 1947,O 25,13:2

DAVIES
See Also DAVES, DAVIS

Davies, Albert
Nine Days a Queen 1936,O 3,21:1

Davies, Alex
We're Going to Be Rich 1938,Jl 4,10:2

Davies, Betty Ann
Escape 1948,Ag 16,12:2
It Always Rains on Sunday 1949,F 14,15:5
One Woman's Story 1949,My 18,33:2
Sanitorium 1950,O 11,42:1
History of Mr Polly, The 1951,O 25,36:3
Outcast of the Islands 1952,My 16,19:2
Tonight at 8:30 (Fumed Oak); Fumed Oak
  (Tonight at 8:30) 1953,My 26,33:2
Blackout 1954,My 22,8:2
Belles of St Trinian's, The 1954,D 23,13:4

Davies, Brian
Bedford Incident, The 1965,N 3,43:1

Davies, David
Treasure Island 1950,Ag 16,24:2

Davies, Dilys
Citadel, The 1938,N 4,27:2
Proud Valley 1941,My 17,19:2

Davies, Edna
Loose Ends 1930,O 18,23:2

Davies, Edward
Magnet, The 1951,F 27,22:6

Davies, Griffith
Sparrows Don't Sing 1963,My 7,46:2

Davies, Howard
Code 7...Victim 5 1965,My 20,52:1

Davies, Hubert Henry (Original Author)
Strictly Modern 1930,My 3,23:1
Girl From 10th Avenue, The 1935,My 27,20:6

Davies, Hunter (Original Author)
Here We Go Around the Mulberry Bush
  1968,Mr 5,34:5

Davies, Hunter (Screenwriter)
Here We Go Around the Mulberry Bush
  1968,Mr 5,34:5

Davies, Jack (Miscellaneous)
Dance Band 1936,Ja 4,19:2

Davies, Jack (Original Author)
Mr Potts Goes to Moscow 1953,S 3,15:2

Davies, Jack (Screenwriter)
Dance Band 1936,Ja 4,19:2
Mimi 1936,Ja 10,16:3
Laughter in Paradise 1951,N 12,21:2
Curtain Up 1953,F 2,17:3
Mr Potts Goes to Moscow 1953,S 3,15:2
Tonight's the Night 1954,D 23,13:4
Doctor at Sea 1956,Mr 1,37:3
Alligator Named Daisy, An 1957,O 7,23:2
Follow a Star 1961,Ap 26,34:1
Nearly a Nasty Accident 1962,Je 28,21:2
Coming-Out Party, A 1962,Jl 31,19:2
Crooks Anonymous 1963,O 31,26:3
Those Magnificent Men in Their Flying Machines
  (Or How I Flew From London to Paris in 25
  Hours and 11 Minutes) 1965,Je 17,27:1
Cavern, The 1965,D 25,17:2

Davies, John Howard
Rocking Horse Winner, The 1950,Je 9,29:2
Oliver Twist 1951,Jl 31,17:2
Tom Brown's School Days 1952,Ja 8,23:5

Davies, Joseph E Ambassador (Original Author)
Mission to Moscow 1943,Ap 30,25:2

Davies, Lloyd G
Red Menace, The 1949,Je 27,18:2

Davies, Marianne
Sez O'Reilly to MacNab 1938,F 19,19:4

Davies, Marion
Cecilia of the Pink Roses 1918,Je 3,9:3
Restless Sex, The 1920,S 13,12:1
Buried Treasure 1921,F 14,12:2
Beauty's Worth 1922,Mr 27,12:1
When Knighthood Was in Flower 1922,S 15,17:2
  (In Addenda)
Little Old New York 1923,Ag 2,10:3
Yolanda 1924,F 20,23:1
Janice Meredith 1924,Ag 6,13:3
Zander the Great 1925,My 4,16:2
Lights of Old Broadway 1925,N 2,20:1
Beverly of Graustark 1926,Ap 19,24:3
Red Mill, The 1927,F 14,15:1
Tillie the Toiler 1927,Je 7,27:4
Fair Co-ed, The 1927,O 24,24:3
Quality Street 1927,N 2,24:5
Patsy, The 1928,Ap 23,20:2
Cardboard Lover, The 1928,S 3,14:2
Show People 1928,N 12,18:2
Hollywood Revue, The 1929,Ag 15,20:5
Marianne 1929,O 19,22:6
Not so Dumb 1930,F 8,12:5
Floradora Girl, The 1930,My 31,19:4
Bachelor Father, The 1931,F 2,23:1
It's a Wise Child 1931,My 16,13:3
Five and Ten 1931,Jl 11,7:6
Polly of the Circus 1932,Mr 19,11:2
Blondie of the Follies 1932,S 2,19:2
Peg o'my Heart 1933,My 20,11:4
Going Hollywood 1933,D 23,19:2
Operator 13 1934,Je 23,16:5
Page Miss Glory 1935,Ag 29,25:2
Hearts Divided 1936,Je 13,13:1
Cain and Mabel 1936,O 19,22:1
Ever Since Eve 1937,Je 25,25:2
Show People 1967,O 2,58:2

Davies, Marion Hall
Ring, The 1927,D 25,VIII,7:7 (In Addenda)

Davies, Muggins
Sunny 1941,Je 13,22:2

Davies, Rhys Lieut Col (Original Author)
Safecracker, The 1958,Mr 6,32:1

Davies, Richard
Unfinished Business 1941,S 2,20:2
Mad Doctor of Market Street, The 1942,Ja 5,21:5
Private Buckaroo 1942,Je 25,27:4
Eagle Squadron 1942,Jl 3,12:5
Give Out, Sisters 1942,Ag 28,22:3
When Johnny Comes Marching Home
  1943,Mr 5,20:4
Falcon in Danger, The 1943,Jl 23,21:2
Jungle Woman 1944,Jl 15,19:6

Davies, Rupert
Key, The 1958,Jl 2,23:3
Sapphire 1959,N 3,27:1
Spy Who Came in From the Cold, The
  1965,D 24,24:1
Uncle, The 1966,Jl 19,34:1
Conqueror Worm, The 1968,Ag 15,46:2

Davies, Valentine (Director)
Benny Goodman Story 1956,F 22,22:1

Davies, Valentine (Original Author)
Syncopation 1942,My 29,13:3
Miracle on 34th Street 1947,Je 5,32:1
It Started With a Kiss 1959,Ag 20,14:2

Davies, Valentine (Screenwriter)
Three Little Girls in Blue 1946,S 26,32:3
You Were Meant for Me 1948,Ja 29,27:5
Chicken every Sunday 1949,Ja 19,34:2
It Happens Every Spring 1949,Je 11,11:2
On the Riviera 1951,My 24,47:1
Sailor of the King 1953,S 3,15:2
Glenn Miller Story, the 1954,F 11,33:2
Bridges at Toko-Ri, The 1955,Ja 21,20:2
Strategic Air Command 1955,Ap 21,33:1
Benny Goodman Story 1956,F 22,22:1
Bachelor in Paradise 1961,N 17,41:2

Davinci, Elena
Girl in the Kremlin, The 1957,My 22,29:2

Davion, Alex
Song Without End 1960,Ag 12,10:2
Rattle of a Simple Man 1964,D 21,42:2
Man in the Dark 1965,Ja 21,22:1
Valley of the Dolls 1967,D 16,51:1

DAVIS
See Also DAVES, DAVIES

Davis, A Anthony (Screenwriter)
Toast to Love 1951,N 7,35:5

Davis, Aaron (Original Author)
Her Golden Calf 1930,My 5,27:3

Davis, Alan
Magnificent Obsession 1935,D 31,11:2
Penrod and Sam 1937,Mr 29,14:3
Barrier, The 1937,N 27,21:2
Over the Wall 1938,Mr 28,19:2
Wings of the Navy 1939,F 4,11:1
Big Guy, The 1940,Ja 1,29:2

Davis, Alfred (Original Author)
Till We Meet Again 1936,My 9,11:2

Davis, Ann B
Pepe 1960,D 22,18:1
Lover Come Back 1962,F 9,21:1

Davis, Benny (Composer)
Tin Pan Alley 1940,N 22,27:3

Davis, Benny (Miscellaneous)
Margie 1946,O 17,28:3

Davis, Bette
Bad Sister 1931,Mr 30,25:2
Seed 1931,My 15,20:6
Waterloo Bridge 1931,S 5,7:4
Way Back Home 1932,Ja 16,13:1
Menace, The 1932,Ja 30,13:2
Man Who Played God, The 1932,F 11,16:1
Hell's House 1932,F 12,24:5
So Big 1932,Ap 30,19:3
Rich are Always With Us, The 1932,My 16,19:5
Dark Horse, The 1932,Je 9,27:3
Cabin in the Cotton 1932,S 30,17:3
Three on a Match 1932,O 29,18:4
20,000 Years in Sing Sing 1933,Ja 10,26:2
Parachute Jumper 1933,Ja 26,12:2
Working Man, The 1933,Ap 21,20:3
Ex-Lady 1933,My 15,16:2
Bureau of Missing Persons 1933,S 9,9:2
Fashions of 1934 1934,Ja 20,12:2
Big Shakedown, The 1934,F 12,19:2
Jimmy the Gent 1934,Mr 26,22:3
Fog over Frisco 1934,Je 7,26:2
Of Human Bondage 1934,Je 29,17:1
Housewife 1934,Ag 10,21:2
Bordertown 1935,Ja 24,22:5
Girl From 10th Avenue, The 1935,My 27,20:6
Front Page Woman 1935,Jl 12,15:1
Special Agent 1935,S 19,28:1
Dangerous 1935,D 27,14:1
Petrified Forest, The 1936,F 7,14:2
Golden Arrow, The 1936,My 4,16:1
Satan Met a Lady 1936,Jl 23,24:2
Marked Woman 1937,Ap 12,15:2
Kid Galahad 1937,My 27,21:3
That Certain Woman 1937,S 16,29:1
It's Love I'm After 1937,N 11,31:2
Jezebel 1938,Mr 11,15:2
Sisters, The 1938,O 15,21:3
Dark Victory 1939,Ap 21,27:2
Juarez 1939,Ap 26,27:1
Old Maid, The 1939,Ag 12,16:2
Private Lives of Elizabeth and Essex, The
  1939,D 2,21:2
All This and Heaven, Too 1940,Jl 5,10:2
Letter, The 1940,N 23,12:6
Great Lie, The 1941,Ap 12,19:2
Bride Came C O D, The 1941,Jl 26,18:2
Little Foxes, The 1941,Ag 22,19:2
Man Who Came to Dinner, The 1942,Ja 2,25:2
In This our Life 1942,My 9,10:2
Now, Voyager 1942,O 23,25:3
Watch on the Rhine 1943,Ag 28,15:1
Thank Your Lucky Stars 1943,O 2,19:2
Old Acquaintance 1943,N 3,20:2
Mr Skeffington 1944,My 26,23:2
Hollywood Canteen 1944,D 16,19:2
Corn is Green, The 1945,Mr 30,18:2
Stolen Life, A 1946,My 2,27:4
Deception 1946,O 19,15:3
Winter Meeting 1948,Ap 8,31:2
June Bride 1948,O 30,10:2
Beyond the Forest 1949,O 22,11:2

Davis, Bette— Cont

All About Eve 1950,O 14,13:2
Payment on Demand 1951,F 16,21:2
Another Man's Poison 1952,Ja 7,14:3
Phone Call From a Stranger 1952,F 2,11:2
Star, The 1953,Ja 29,25:1
Virgin Queen, The 1955,Ag 6,13:2
Catered Affair, The 1956,Je 15,32:4
Storm Center 1956,O 22,25:4
John Paul Jones 1959,Je 17,39:1
Scapegoat, The 1959,Ag 7,28:1
Pocketful of Miracles 1961,D 19,39:1
What Ever Happened to Baby Jane?
1962,N 7,48:1
Dead Ringer 1964,F 20,22:3
Empty Canvas, The 1964,My 16,21:1 (Incorrect
in this edition; use 1964,My 16,12:1 elsewhere)
Where Love Has Gone 1964,N 3,26:1
Hush...Hush, Sweet Charlotte 1965,Mr 4,36:1
Of Human Bondage 1965,S 15,41:1
Nanny, The 1965,N 4,57:2
Anniversary, The 1968,Mr 21,57:2

Davis, Billie

Go Go Mania 1965,My 20,52:4

Davis, Boyd

Smiling Faces 1932,Ag 31,12:3
You'll Never Get Rich 1941,O 24,27:2
Terror by Night 1946,F 9,9:2
Unknown, The 1946,Jl 20,10:3
Foreign Affair, A 1948,Jl 1,19:3
Ma and Pa Kettle 1949,Ag 12,13:2

Davis, Charles

Desert Rats, The 1953,My 9,13:2
Student Prince, The 1954,Je 16,18:2
Five Steps to Danger 1957,Ja 31,21:1
Oh Men! Oh Women! 1957,F 22,25:2
Young Stranger, The 1957,Ap 9,40:1

Davis, Clifford

Last Mile, The 1959,F 19,27:1
Invitation to a Gunfighter 1964,O 28,51:3

Davis, Clyde Brion (Original Author)

Adventure 1946,F 8,23:2

Davis, Curt

Safe at Home 1941,N 26,31:2

Davis, Desmond (Director)

Girl With Green Eyes 1964,Ag 11,37:2
Uncle, The 1966,Jl 19,34:1
Time Lost and Time Remembered
1966,Ag 30,35:2
Smashing Time 1967,D 21,44:1

Davis, Desmond (Screenwriter)

Inspector Calls, An 1954,N 26,24:4
Uncle, The 1966,Jl 19,34:1
Time Lost and Time Remembered
1966,Ag 30,35:2

Davis, Dix

Our Town 1940,Je 14,25:3

Davis, Don

San Diego, I Love You 1944,N 10,25:1

Davis, Donald

Oedipus Rex 1957,Ja 8,26:1
Joy in the Morning 1965,Je 10,38:1

Davis, Donald (Miscellaneous)

Good Earth, The 1937,F 3,27:1

Davis, Donald (Original Author)

Damaged Lives 1937,Je 14,26:2

Davis, Dorothy Patrick

View From Pompey's Head, The 1955,N 5,22:5

Davis, Dorrance (Original Author)

Virtuous Husband 1931,My 8,30:2

Davis, Eddie (Miscellaneous)

Duffy's Tavern 1945,S 6,23:3

Davis, Eddie (Screenwriter)

Radio City Revels 1938,Mr 21,18:3

Davis, Edward

Sea Hawk, The 1924,Je 3,22:1
Only Woman, The 1924,N 3,20:1
Price She Paid, The 1925,Ja 13,16:1
Contraband 1925,Mr 24,20:6
Charmer, The 1925,Ap 6,17:3
Best People 1925,O 21,21:3
Joanna 1925,D 15,14:5
Tramp, Tramp, Tramp 1926,My 24,24:3
Splendid Road, The 1926,Je 13,31:1
Amateur Gentleman, The 1926,Ag 17,15:3
Butterflies in the Rain 1926,D 25,10:5
Life of Riley, The 1927,S 5,13:2
Love in the Rough 1930,S 27,21:3
Hello, Everybody 1933,Ja 30,9:4

Davis, Eileen

Dawn Over Ireland 1938,F 19,19:2

Davis, Elaine

Atomic Kid, The 1954,D 4,14:2
Last Time I Saw Archie, The 1961,My 29,9:6

Davis, Elmer (Original Author)

I'll Show You the Town 1925,Je 8,19:1
Friends of Mr Sweeney 1934,Jl 31,20:4
My American Wife 1936,Ag 21,12:3

Davis, Fitzroy (Screenwriter)

Heat's on, The 1943,N 26,29:2

Davis, Forrest (Original Author)

Smashing the Rackets 1938,Ag 9,22:5

Davis, Frank (Miscellaneous)

Jim Thorpe - All American 1951,Ag 25,7:2

Davis, Frank (Original Author)

Train, The 1965,Mr 18,25:1

Davis, Frank (Producer)

Petticoat Fever 1936,Mr 21,13:2
Devil is a Sissy, The 1936,O 17,21:2
Lord Jeff 1938,Jl 1,22:2
Chaser, The 1938,Ag 2,15:3
It's a Wonderful World 1939,My 19,27:2

Davis, Frank (Screenwriter)

Dance, Girl, Dance 1940,O 11,25:2
Remember the Day 1941,D 26,21:2
Are Husbands Necessary? 1942,Jl 9,17:2
Tree Grows in Brooklyn, A 1945,Mr 1,25:5
Woman on the Beach, The 1947,Je 9,26:6
Fighting Father Dunne 1948,Je 25,26:2
Ten Tall Men 1951,O 27,10:5
Story of Will Rogers, The 1952,Jl 18,10:5
Springfield Rifle 1952,O 23,40:2
Jazz Singer, The 1953,Ja 14,27:3
Indian Fighter, The 1955,D 22,20:1
Night of the Quarter Moon 1959,Mr 5,35:5
Train, The 1965,Mr 18,25:1

Davis, Frederick C (Original Author)

Double Alibi 1940,Mr 11,11:2

Davis, George

Sherlock Jr 1924,My 26,21:1
He Who Gets Slapped 1924,N 10,20:1
Magic Flame, The 1927,S 19,30:3
Circus, The 1928,Ja 9,20:1
4 Devils 1928,O 4,26:3
Awakening, The 1928,D 31,9:1
Broadway 1929,My 28,36:2
Kiss, The 1929,N 16,25:2
Devil May Care 1929,D 23,18:2
Not so Dumb 1930,F 8,12:5
Laugh and get Rich 1931,Mr 28,15:3
Strangers May Kiss 1931,Ap 13,17:1
Private Lives 1931,D 19,16:4
Arsene Lupin 1932,F 27,22:1
Man From Yesterday, The 1932,Je 25,18:2
Love Me Tonight 1932,Ag 19,20:6
Under-Cover Man 1932,D 5,21:2
Good Fairy, The 1935,F 1,18:1
History Is Made at Night 1937,Mr 29,14:2
I Met Him in Paris 1937,Je 3,29:2
Thin Ice 1937,S 4,8:2
Charlie Chan at Monte Carlo 1937,D 18,18:1
Baroness and the Butler, The 1938,F 19,19:2
Hunted Men 1938,My 21,9:2
Always Goodbye 1938,Je 25,7:2
Bulldog Drummond's Bride 1939,Jl 13,17:2
Everything Happens at Night 1939,D 16,12:6
Charlie Chan in City in Darkness 1939,D 18,29:2
Chad Hanna 1940,D 26,23:1
Lady Says No, The 1952,Ja 7,14:3

Davis, Gilbert

Reserved for Ladies 1932,My 21,9:2
Condemned to Death 1932,Jl 14,24:2
Sign of the Four, The 1932,Ag 20,7:4
Amateur Gentleman, The 1936,Ap 27,19:2
Frieda 1947,Ag 15,12:3
Against the Wind 1949,Je 27,18:3

Davis, Glenn

Spirit of West Point 1947,O 3,31:2

Davis, Gwen (Original Author)

What a Way to Go! 1964,My 15,44:1

Davis, Harry

America America 1963,D 16,44:1
Fortune Cookie, The 1966,O 20,52:1
Waterhole #3 1967,O 11,41:4

Davis, Hassoldt, Capt (Director)

Sorcerers' Village 1958,Jl 3,22:6

Davis, Irving Kay (Original Author)

Woman Between, The 1931,O 24,20:3

Davis, J Edward

Woman on the Jury, The 1924,My 19,14:2
Madonna of the Streets 1930,N 29,21:4

Davis, J Gunnis

Winds of Chance 1925,Ag 17,10:3
Lucky Horseshoe, The 1925,Ag 18,14:3
Lord Jim 1925,N 16,19:4
Notorious Lady, The 1927,Ap 11,18:3
East Lynne 1931,F 21,15:2
Charlie Chan Carries On 1931,Mr 21,15:1
One More River 1934,Ag 10,21:1
Bride of Frankenstein, The 1935,My 11,21:2

Davis, Jack

Up Goes Maisie 1946,Ja 25,26:7

Davis, Jean

Othello 1955,S 13,27:1

Davis, Jerry (Screenwriter)

Duchess of Idaho 1950,Jl 21,15:3
Pagan Love Song 1950,D 26,19:1
Kind Lady 1951,Ag 8,21:2
Devil Makes Three, The 1952,Ag 30,6:2
Pardners 1956,Jl 26,20:2

Davis, Jim

Gallant Bess 1946,D 6,27:6
Beginning or the End, The 1947,F 21,15:1
Romance of Rosy Ridge, The 1947,S 12,18:3
Fabulous Texan, The 1947,D 26,22:5

Davis, Jim— Cont

Winter Meeting 1948,Ap 8,31:2
Hellfire 1949,My 30,9:4
Red Stallion in the Rockies 1949,Ag 26,15:2
Brimstone 1949,O 7,35:3
Yes Sir, That's my Baby 1949,N 11,31:2
California Passage 1950,D 16,10:5
Oh! Susanna 1951,Mr 30,28:5
Cavalry Scout 1951,Je 8,32:2
Little Big Horn 1951,Jl 27,15:2
Big Sky, The 1952,Ag 20,21:1
Woman of the North Country 1952,Ag 30,6:2
Jubilee Trail 1954,My 1,13:3
Outcast, The 1954,Jl 3,9:2
Hell's Outpost 1955,F 26,13:3
Timberjack 1955,Mr 10,33:3
Bottom of the Bottle, The 1956,F 2,19:2
Maverick Queen, the 1956,Je 4,25:2
Alias Jesse James 1959,My 18,31:2
Fort Utah 1967,My 25,54:3

Davis, Jimmy

Any Number Can Win 1963,O 9,47:2

Davis, Jimmy (Composer)

Two Tickets to London 1943,Jl 3,11:2

Davis, Joan

Millions in the Air 1935,D 12,33:4
Holy Terror, The 1937,Ja 30,21:2
On the Avenue 1937,F 5,17:3
Time Out for Romance 1937,Mr 13,23:2
Wake up and Live 1937,Ap 24,16:2
Angel's Holiday 1937,My 29,20:2
Sing and Be Happy 1937,Je 19,20:2
Great Hospital Mystery, The 1937,Jl 16,22:2
Thin Ice 1937,S 4,8:2
Life Begins In College 1937,O 9,16:1
Love and Hisses 1938,Ja 1,11:1
Sally, Irene and Mary 1938,F 26,9:2
Josette 1938,Je 11,9:1
My Lucky Star 1938,S 10,20:2
Hold That Co-ed 1938,S 24,13:1
Just Around the Corner 1938,D 3,11:2
Tail Spin 1939,F 11,13:2
Daytime Wife 1939,N 24,29:1
Free, Blonde and 21 1940,Ap 5,25:2
Sailor's Lady 1940,Je 29,12:2
Hold That Ghost 1941,Ag 8,13:3
Sun Valley Serenade 1941,S 6,20:1
He's my Guy 1943,Mr 12,12:3
Two Senoritas From Chicago 1943,Ag 6,10:4
Around the World 1943,N 25,39:2
Show Business 1944,My 11,25:7
She Gets her Man 1945,F 9,20:5
George White's Scandals 1945,O 11,26:2
She Wrote the Book 1946,Je 20,20:3
If You Knew Susie 1948,F 23,19:2
Traveling Saleswoman 1950,Ja 6,25:3
Love That Brute 1950,My 27,10:6
Groom Wore Spurs, The 1951,Mr 14,41:2

Davis, Joel

Curse of the Cat People, The 1944,Mr 4,11:1

Davis, John

Lawless, The 1950,Je 23,29:2

Davis, John (Producer)

Model Murder Case, The 1964,N 25,45:1

Davis, Johnnie

Varsity Show 1937,S 2,17:2
Over the Goal 1937,O 16,22:2
Hollywood Hotel 1938,Ja 13,17:3
Men Are Such Fools 1938,Je 17,25:1
Cowboy From Brooklyn 1938,Jl 14,17:1
Brother Rat 1938,N 5,15:2
Child Is Born, A 1940,Ja 11,19:2

Davis, Johnny Scat

Sarong Girl 1943,Je 18,16:6
Knickerbocker Holiday 1944,Ap 20,22:7

Davis, Julian

Nude Restaurant, The 1967,N 14,52:1

Davis, Karl

Salome 1953,Mr 25,37:1
Demetrius and the Gladiators 1954,Je 19,9:1
Timberjack 1955,Mr 10,33:3

Davis, Leonard (Producer)

Uncle, The 1966,Jl 19,34:1

Davis, Lisa

Virgin Queen, The 1955,Ag 6,13:2

Davis, Luther (Original Author)

Mayor of Forty-Fourth Street, The
1942,Je 11,27:4
Kiss Them for Me 1957,N 9,31:2

Davis, Luther (Producer)

Lady in a Cage 1964,Je 11,27:1

Davis, Luther (Screenwriter)

Hucksters, The 1947,Jl 18,21:2
B F's Daughter 1948,Mr 25,35:2
Black Hand 1950,Mr 13,15:2
Lion Is in the Streets, A 1953,S 24,39:2
New Faces 1954,F 20,8:7
Kismet 1955,D 9,32:2
Gift of Love, The 1958,F 12,32:2
Holiday for Lovers 1959,Jl 25,10:2
Wonders of Aladdin, The 1961,D 23,16:1
Lady in a Cage 1964,Je 11,27:1

Davis, Madelyn (Original Author)
Yours, Mine and Ours 1968,Ap 25,53:1
Davis, Marvin
Sullivans, The 1944,F 10,19:2
Tomorrow the World 1944,D 22,12:4
Scandal In Paris, A 1946,S 16,9:7
Davis, Maureen
To Paris With Love 1955,Mr 29,33:4
Third Key, The 1957,Je 3,30:2
Davis, Mike Lieut Col
Three Stripes in the Sun 1955,N 24,41:2
Davis, Mildred
Safety Last. 1923,Ap 2,22:1
Davis, Nancy
Doctor and the Girl, The 1949,O 31,20:2
East Side, West Side 1949,D 23,17:2
Shadow on the Wall 1950,My 19,31:3
Next Voice You Hear, The 1950,Je 30,18:2
Night Into Morning 1951,Je 11,20:7
It's a big Country 1952,Ja 9,25:2
Shadow in the Sky 1952,Jl 19,8:2
Donovan's Brain 1954,Ja 21,28:2
Davis, Norman Dancers
I Love, You Love 1962,N 10,16:2
Davis, Ossie
No Way Out 1950,Ag 17,23:1
Gone are the Days! 1963,S 24,43:2
Cardinal, The 1963,D 13,41:1
Shock Treatment 1964,Jl 23,19:1
Hill, The 1965,O 4,00:0
Man Called Adam, A 1966,Ag 4,24:2
Scalphunters, The 1968,Ap 3,40:1
Davis, Ossie (Original Author)
Gone are the Days! 1963,S 24,43:2
Davis, Ossie (Screenwriter)
Gone are the Days! 1963,S 24,43:2
Davis, Owen (Miscellaneous)
Frozen Justice 1929,O 26,15:1
Good Earth, The 1937,F 3,27:1
Davis, Owen (Original Author)
Eternal Grind, The 1916,Ap 10,11:3
Nellie, the Beautiful Cloak Model
1924,Ap 14,14:3
Broadway After Dark 1924,My 20,15:2
Lighthouse by the Sea, The 1924,D 29,11:4
Up the Ladder 1925,My 12,26:2
Nervous Wreck, The 1926,O 12,30:2
Forever After 1926,N 9,31:1
Blind Alleys 1927,Mr 1,31:1
Cabaret 1927,My 2,26:4
Beware of Widows 1927,My 24,23:4
Easy Come, Easy Go 1928,My 8,25:3
Haunted House, The 1928,D 17,23:1
Haunted House, The 1928,D 23,VIII,7:1
Donovan Affair, The 1929,Ap 29,29:2
Tonight at Twelve 1929,S 23,24:3
Ninth Guest, The 1934,Mr 3,8:5
Jezebel 1938,Mr 11,15:2
Mr and Mrs North 1942,Ja 22,13:2
Up in Arms 1944,Mr 3,19:2
Great Gatsby, The 1949,Jl 14,20:5
Davis, Owen (Screenwriter)
Icebound 1924,Mr 3,22:3 (In Addenda)
How Baxter Buttered In 1925,Je 23,24:3
Davis, Owen Jr
They Had to See Paris 1929,O 12,11:1
All Quiet on The Western Front 1930,Ap 30,29:1
Good Intentions 1930,Jl 26,16:4
Murder on a Bridle Path 1936,Ap 11,19:2
Special Investigator 1936,Ap 25,21:1
Bunker Bean 1936,Je 27,21:2
Grand Jury 1936,Ag 1,16:3
Plot Thickens, The 1936,D 9,35:2
Woman I Love, The 1937,Ap 16,27:2
Touchdown Army 1938,O 28,27:2
These Glamour Girls 1939,Ag 31,14:2
Thou Shalt Not Kill 1940,Ja 8,11:2
Davis, Pat Lieutenant
Eternally Yours 1939,O 7,11:2
Davis, Richard (Producer)
Midsummer Night's Dream, A 1967,Ap 18,32:1
Davis, Richard Harding (Original Author)
Soldiers of Fortune 1919,N 24,13:1
Dictator, The 1922,Jl 3,8:6
Stephen Steps Out 1923,N 19,19:3
Love and Glory 1924,Ag 5,10:2
Race, The 1924,S 30,27:3
Ranson's Folly 1926,My 31,10:2
Let 'Er go, Gallegher 1928,Ja 16,24:1
It's a Dog's Life 1955,D 23,14:3
Davis, Robert
Confessions of a Nazi Spy 1939,Ap 29,13:2
Davis, Robert H (Original Author)
Confidence Man, The 1924,Ap 15,24:1
Miracle Man, The 1932,Ap 21,25:2
Davis, Robert O
Espionage Agent 1939,S 23,22:2
Four Sons 1940,Je 8,18:4
Great Dictator, The 1940,O 16,29:1
Arise my Love 1940,O 17,33:2
Meet the Wildcat 1940,O 23,27:2
Desperate Journey 1942,S 26,11:2
Sherlock Holmes and the Secret Weapon

1943,Ja 5,15:2
Watch on the Rhine 1943,Ag 28,15:1
Davis, Roger
Social Celebrity, A 1926,Ap 19,24:3
Davis, Ronnie (Director)
Have You Heard of the San Francisco Mime
Troup? 1968,Je 28,37:1
Davis, Roy
Letter, The 1940,N 23,12:6
Davis, Rufe
Mountain Music 1937,Je 24,30:3
This Way Please 1937,O 8,27:2
Blossoms On Broadway 1937,D 3,29:2
Big Broadcast of 1938, The 1938,Mr 10,16:2
Doctor Rhythm 1938,My 19,25:2
Cocoanut Grove 1938,Je 16,21:2
Ambush 1939,F 9,17:2
Some Like It Hot 1939,My 25,31:2
Radio Stars on Parade 1945,S 22,14:2
Davis, Ruth Staudinger (Cinematographer)
Sorcerers' Village 1958,Jl 3,22:6
Davis, Sammy
Man Called Adam, A 1966,Ag 4,24:2
Davis, Sammy Jr
Benny Goodman Story 1956,F 22,22:1
Anna Lucasta 1959,Ja 15,27:1
Porgy and Bess 1959,Je 25,20:3
Ocean's Eleven 1960,Ag 11,19:1
Pepe 1960,D 22,18:1
Sergeants 3 1962,F 12,28:2
Johnny Cool 1963,O 3,31:1
Robin and the 7 Hoods 1964,Ag 6,20:1
Salt and Pepper 1968,S 19,62:3
Davis, Spencer Group
Go Go Mania 1965,My 20,52:4
Davis, Stanley (Screenwriter)
Murder in the Blue Room 1944,O 28,12:2
See my Lawyer 1945,My 4,23:4
Davis, Stringer
Happiest Days of Your Life, The 1950,S 18,19:2
Curtain Up 1953,F 2,17:3
Smallest Show on Earth, The 1957,N 23,11:2
Murder She Said 1962,Ja 8,27:2
Murder at the Gallop 1963,Je 25,23:2
Murder Ahoy 1964,S 23,55:3
Murder Most Foul 1965,My 24,36:2
Davis, Tim
Gambling Ship 1939,Ja 21,19:2
Our Town 1940,Je 14,25:3
Davis, Tyrell
Mother's Boy 1929,My 8,34:6
Let Us Be Gay 1930,Jl 12,16:4
Rain or Shine 1930,Ag 8,11:1
Love in the Rough 1930,S 27,21:3
Paid 1931,Ja 3,21:2
God's Gift to Women 1931,Ap 18,17:3
Magnificent Lie, The 1931,Jl 25,11:6
Road to Singapore, The 1931,O 1,25:2
Dangerously Yours 1933,F 23,20:3
Our Betters 1933,F 24,13:2
Peg o'my Heart 1933,My 20,11:4
Blind Adventure 1933,O 31,24:3
Dinner at the Ritz 1937,D 4,21:1
Davis, Virginia
Street Scene 1931,Ag 27,22:5
Davis, William
Arabian Nights 1942,D 26,15:1
Bodyhold 1949,D 12,29:4
Samson and Delilah 1949,D 22,29:2
Asphalt Jungle, The 1950,Je 9,29:3
Abbott and Costello in the Foreign Legion
1950,Ag 14,14:4
Son of Paleface 1952,O 2,32:3
To Catch a Thief 1955,Ag 5,14:2
Davis, Wray (Producer)
Yank in Vietnam, A 1964,F 6,36:4
Davis Jr, Sammy
Convicts 4 1962,O 4,44:2
DAVISON
See Also DAVIDSON, DAVISSON
Davison, Davey
Strangler, The 1964,Je 11,27:4
Marriage on the Rocks 1965,S 16,00:0
Davison, Grace
Wives of Men 1918,Ag 26,9:1 (In Addenda)
Davison, John Porter
Girl-Getters, The 1966,Ap 13,37:6
DAVISSON
See Also DAVIDSON, DAVISON
Davisson, Richard (Miscellaneous)
Symmetry 1967,Ja 21,35:1
Davitt, Hal (Original Author)
Captain Thunder 1931,My 11,15:4
Davitt, Theodora
Buccaneer, The 1958,D 24,00:0
Davlon, Alexander
Paranoiac 1963,My 23,31:2
Davo, Jose Marco
Marcelino 1956,O 23,39:1
Night Heaven Fell, The 1958,O 22,40:4
Davoil, Mos
Seven Hills of Rome 1958,Ja 28,24:2 (Incorrect
in this edition; use 1958,Ja 31,24:2 elsewhere)

Davoli, Ninetto
Hawks and the Sparrows, The 1966,S 17,28:2
Hawks and the Sparrows, The; Uccellacci e
Uccellini 1967,Jl 28,15:3
Davor, Alexis
End of St Petersberg, The 1928,My 31,21:2 (In
Addenda)
Davrath, Netania
Journey to Jerusalem, A 1968,N 18,59:1
Davray, Dominique
Casque D'Or 1952,Ag 19,19:1
Big Chief, The 1960,Ap 27,32:1
Cleo From 5 to 7 1962,S 5,43:4
Any Number Can Win 1963,O 9,47:2
Davri, Serge
Shoot the Piano Player 1962,Jl 24,19:1
Army Game, The; Tire Au Flanc
1963,Ap 24,40:1
d'Avril, Yola
Orchids and Ermine 1927,Ap 19,24:4
Hard-Boiled Haggerty 1927,Ag 23,29:4
American Beauty 1927,O 11,27:1
Valley of the Giants, The 1927,D 5,26:2
Lady Be Good 1928,My 28,23:2
She Goes to War 1929,Je 10,23:1
Hot for Paris 1930,Ja 4,21:1
All Quiet on The Western Front 1930,Ap 30,29:1
Bad One, The 1930,Je 13,28:3
New Movietone Follies of 1930, The
1930,Je 21,20:5
Those Three French Girls 1930,O 11,21:3
Truth About Youth, The 1930,D 13,22:2
Right of Way, The 1931,Mr 24,31:2
God's Gift to Women 1931,Ap 18,17:3
Svengali 1931,My 1,30:3
Just a Gigolo 1931,Je 13,20:4
Women Go on Forever 1931,O 19,28:1
Cock of the Air 1932,Ja 25,20:3
Sky Devils 1932,Mr 4,17:3
Passport to Hell, A 1932,Ag 27,13:4
Scarlet Dawn 1932,N 4,25:4
Glamour 1934,My 12,12:3
Little Boy Lost 1953,S 22,38:2
Davy, Hope
Sorrell and Son 1934,My 29,22:1
Davy, Jean
Champs-Elysees 1939,F 28,17:2
Naked Woman, The 1950,Ja 21,10:2
Sinners, The 1950,N 11,11:2
Davy, Peter
Lord of the Flies 1963,Ag 20,37:1
Davydov, Vladien
Sisters 1959,My 25,33:2
Daw, Evelyn
Something to Sing About 1937,S 21,29:4
Daw, Marjorie
Knickerbocker Buckaroo, The 1919,My 26,19:4
Rivers End, The 1920,F 23,11:2
Don't Ever Marry 1920,Ap 19,13:3
Great Redeemer, The 1920,O 25,18:1
Dinty 1920,N 22,13:3
Bob Hampton of Placer 1921,My 2,12:1
Penrod 1922,F 20,7:1
Pride of Palomar, The 1922,N 20,21:3
Wandering Daughters 1923,Jl 2,16:2
Rupert of Hentzau 1923,Jl 9,8:4
Going Up 1923,O 10,16:2
Barefoot Boy, The 1923,N 11,6:1
Dangerous Maid, The 1923,D 11,26:2
Call of the Canyon, The 1923,D 17,23:1
Revelation 1924,Je 24,18:2
Topsy and Eva 1927,Ag 8,10:3
Prince of Lovers, The 1927,N 29,31:1
Home Made 1927,D 13,33:2
Dawe, Rex
Wherever She Goes 1953,Ja 28,24:4
Dawkins, Paul
Far From the Madding Crowd 1967,O 19,59:1
Dawley, Herbert M (Producer)
Ghost of Slumber Mountain, The 1918,N 18,13:3
Ghost of Slumber Mountain, The
1919,Ap 14,11:4
Dawley, Herbert M (Screenwriter)
Almanac 1921,My 9,16:2
Tooth Carpenter, The 1921,My 30,12:5
Dawley, J Searle (Director)
Virgin Paradise, A 1921,Ag 4,18:3
Little Child Shall Lead Them, A 1922,S 2,10:4
Dawn, Hazel
Under Cover 1916,Jl 24,7:4
Margie 1946,O 17,28:3
Dawn, Isabel (Miscellaneous)
Up in Mabel's Room 1944,Ap 22,8:6
Dawn, Isabel (Original Author)
Don't Bet on Blondes 1935,Jl 20,16:2
Ice-Capades 1941,S 25,29:1
French Line, The 1954,My 15,13:2
Dawn, Isabel (Screenwriter)
Don't Bet on Blondes 1935,Jl 20,16:2
Moon's our Home, The 1936,My 13,29:2
Wings Over Honolulu 1937,My 29,20:1
Girl of the Golden West, The 1938,Mr 25,15:2
Behind the News 1941,Ja 16,25:3

Dawn, Isabel (Screenwriter)— Cont
Man Betrayed, A 1941,Mr 27,29:5
Lady for a Night 1942,F 12,27:2
Remember Pearl Harbor 1942,Je 4,22:4
Dawn, Lili
Violated 1953,D 12,23:8
Dawn, Marpessa
Black Orpheus 1959,D 22,41:1
Dawn, Norman (Director)
Tundra 1936,D 3,31:2
Dawson, Anthony
Long Dark Hall, The 1951,My 10,38:3
Wooden Horse, The 1951,Ag 29,20:2
Valley of the Eagles 1952,Ap 11,19:2
Dial M for Murder 1954,My 29,13:2
Haunted Strangler, The 1958,Jl 4,15:3
Tiger Bay 1959,D 15,50:1
Midnight Lace 1960,O 14,27:1
Dr No 1963,My 30,20:1
Dawson, Anthony (Director)
Wild, Wild Planet 1967,Ag 10,45:5
Young, The Evil and the Savage, The 1968,Ag 15,46:2
Dawson, Anthony (Original Author)
Snorkel, The 1958,S 18,37:2
Dawson, Anthony (Screenwriter)
Young, The Evil and the Savage, The 1968,Ag 15,46:2
Dawson, Billy
Ladies Must Live 1940,S 6,25:3
Dispatch From Reuters, A 1940,D 12,37:2
Father's Son 1941,F 13,25:3
Adventure in Washington 1941,Ag 1,11:3
Major and the Minor, The 1942,S 17,21:3
Dawson, Coningsby (Original Author)
Coast of Folly, The 1925,Ag 31,19:3
Girl From Scotland Yard, The 1937,My 31,11:2
Dawson, Doris
Kentucky Courage 1928,My 14,25:1
Naughty Baby 1929,F 5,26:3
Hot Stuff 1929,My 13,27:2
Broadway Scandals 1929,O 29,35:1
Silver Streak, The 1935,Ja 16,21:1
Dawson, Frank
Double Door 1934,My 5,22:3
Broadway Hostess 1935,D 16,23:3
Ladies in Love 1936,O 29,31:1
Four Men and a Prayer 1938,My 7,18:1
I'll Give a Million 1938,Jl 16,7:2
Cafe Society 1939,F 23,19:2
Adventures of Sherlock Holmes, The 1939,S 2,20:1
Blue Bird, The 1940,Ja 20,11:2
Scotland Yard 1941,Ap 9,33:3
Crash Dive 1943,Ap 29,25:2
What a Woman 1943,D 3,27:2
Woman in the Window, The 1945,Ja 26,16:4
Dawson, Hal K
Another Language 1933,Ag 5,9:5
Firebird, The 1934,N 15,25:2
Dr Socrates 1935,O 3,29:2
Public Enemy's Wife 1936,Jl 9,17:2
My American Wife 1936,Ag 21,12:3
Libeled Lady 1936,O 31,24:2
We're on the Jury 1937,F 10,18:5
Cafe Metropole 1937,Ap 29,17:1
On Again-Off Again 1937,S 18,15:3
Wife, Doctor and Nurse 1937,O 11,26:5
Second Honeymoon 1937,N 13,11:2
Wells Fargo 1937,D 30,15:2
Love and Hisses 1938,Ja 1,11:1
Keep Smiling 1938,Ag 10,15:2
Just Around the Corner 1938,D 3,11:2
Rose of Washington Square 1939,My 6,21:2
Great Victor Herbert, The 1939,D 7,35:1
Star Dust 1940,My 4,13:1
Doctor Takes a Wife, The 1940,Je 15,12:2
We Who Are Young 1940,S 13,27:2
Great Profile, The 1940,O 18,25:1
Tin Pan Alley 1940,N 22,27:3
Washington Melodrama 1941,My 26,15:3
Week-End in Havana 1941,N 8,11:2
Song of the Islands 1942,Mr 12,24:4
Magnificent Dope, The 1942,Jl 3,12:5
Life Begins at Eight-Thirty 1942,D 10,35:2
Coney Island 1943,Je 17,17:2
Guest Wife 1945,O 18,21:2
Shocking Miss Pilgrim, The 1947,F 12,34:2
Fabulous Dorseys, The 1947,My 30,25:3
You Gotta Stay Happy 1948,N 5,29:2
Chicken every Sunday 1949,Ja 19,34:2
Wabash Avenue 1950,Ap 29,8:3
Captive City, The 1952,Mr 27,34:2
Park Row 1952,D 22,20:2
Three for the Show 1955,F 25,16:1
Dawson, Ian
Hue and Cry 1951,Ja 9,25:2
Dawson, Ivo
Hate Ship, The 1930,N 15,15:3
Dawson, Nora (Original Author)
Children on Trial 1947,N 10,21:3
Dax, Jean
Last Flight, The 1929,Je 17,29:1
Congress Dances 1932,My 12,23:2

Charlemagne 1935,Ag 24,18:3
Mayerling 1937,S 14,27:1
Slipper Episode, The 1938,My 19,25:2
Glory of Faith, The 1938,N 24,37:2
Dax, Micheline
Pantaloons 1956,D 26,34:1
Tender Scoundrel 1967,N 16,58:2
Daxely
Letters From my Windmill (The Three Low Masses); Three Low Masses, The (Letters From my Windmill) 1955,D 19,33:1
Day, Alice
Temple of Venus, The 1923,N 1,24:3
Secrets 1924,Mr 25,25:2
See You in Jail 1927,Ap 4,30:5
Gorilla, The 1927,N 21,20:1
Night Life 1927,D 20,33:2
Smart Set, The 1928,Mr 5,21:1
Red Hot Speed 1929,F 5,26:3
Drag 1929,Je 21,17:2
Skin Deep 1929,S 30,23:1
Is Everybody Happy? 1929,N 2,14:6
Little Johnny Jones 1930,F 1,15:1
In the Next Room 1930,Ap 7,21:1
Ladies in Love 1930,Je 14,9:4
Viennese Nights 1930,N 27,32:5
Day, Annette
Double Trouble 1967,My 25,54:2
Day, Clarence Jr (Original Author)
Life With Father 1947,Ag 16,6:6
Day, Dennis
Buck Benny Rides Again 1940,Ap 25,28:4
Powers Girl, The 1943,Mr 26,14:2 (In Addenda)
Music in Manhattan 1944,O 7,11:2
I'll Get by 1950,N 2,39:3
Golden Girl 1951,N 21,20:3
Girl Next Door, The 1953,S 5,7:4
Day, Diana
Belles of St Trinian's, The 1954,D 23,13:4
Day, Doris
Thou Shalt Not Kill 1940,Ja 8,11:2
Romance on the High Seas 1948,Je 26,10:5
My Dream Is Yours 1949,Ap 16,11:3
It's a Great Feeling 1949,Ag 13,6:6
Young Man With a Horn 1950,F 10,18:4
Tea for Two 1950,S 2,11:2
West Point Story, The 1950,D 23,11:3
Storm Warning 1951,Mr 3,8:2
Lullaby of Broadway 1951,Mr 27,35:2
On Moonlight Bay 1951,Jl 27,15:2
I'll See You in my Dreams 1951,D 7,35:1
Starlift 1951,D 15,11:2
Winning Team, The 1952,Je 21,12:2
April in Paris 1952,D 25,34:5
By the Light of the Silvery Moon 1953,Mr 27,28:2
Calamity Jane 1953,N 5,40:2
Lucky Me 1954,Ap 10,11:2
Young at Heart 1955,Ja 20,35:1
Love Me or Leave Me 1955,My 27,14:1
Man Who Knew too Much, The 1956,My 17,37:1
Julie 1956,N 22,51:1
Pajama Game, The 1957,Ag 30,12:2
Teacher's Pet 1958,Mr 20,33:1
Tunnel of Love 1958,N 22,27:4
It Happened to Jane 1959,Ag 6,18:3
Pillow Talk 1959,O 7,47:2
Please Don't Eat the Daisies 1960,Ap 1,37:1
Midnight Lace 1960,O 14,27:1
Lover Come Back 1962,F 9,21:1
That Touch of Mink 1962,Je 15,16:2
Jumbo 1962,D 7,49:1
Thrill of it All, The 1963,Ag 2,15:3
Move Over Darling 1963,D 26,33:1
Send Me no Flowers 1964,N 13,30:1
Do Not Disturb 1965,D 25,17:2
Glass Bottom Boat, The 1966,Je 10,54:1
Caprice 1967,Je 8,52:2
Ballad of Josie, The 1968,Mr 14,51:2
Where Were You When the Lights Went Out? 1968,Ag 9,30:2
With Six You Get Egg Roll 1968,O 10,59:6
Day, Dorothy (Original Author)
Woman Hater, The 1925,Jl 13,20:2
Day, Dwane
That Certain Woman 1937,S 16,29:1
Day, Edith
Romance of the Air, A 1918,N 11,13:3
Day, Edmund (Original Author)
Roundup, The 1941,Mr 13,25:4
Day, Esther Lynd (Original Author)
Beggars in Ermine 1934,Ap 25,25:3
Day, Frances
Girl From Maxim's, The 1936,S 16,29:1
Day, Gloria
Charlie Chan at the Race Track 1936,Ag 15,6:2
Day, Holman (Original Author)
Clothes Make the Pirate 1925,N 30,17:1
Day, Jill
Always a Bride 1954,My 28,19:2
Day, John
Champion 1949,Ap 11,29:2
Abbott and Costello Meet the Invisible Man

Day, John— Cont
1951,Ap 13,18:6
Yankee Pasha 1954,Ap 19,19:2
Square Jungle, The 1955,D 31,17:2
Badlanders, The 1958,S 4,33:1
Day, Josette
Barbier de Seville, Le 1936,S 23,29:2
Lucrezia Borgia 1937,O 13,27:2
Club De Femmes 1937,O 20,27:2
Man of the Hour, The 1940,N 21,43:2
Mad Emperor, The 1941,Mr 10,21:3
Barge-Keeper's Daughter, The 1945,S 6,23:3
Well-Digger's Daughter, The 1946,S 30,21:4
Beauty and the Beast 1947,D 24,12:2
Storm Within, The; (Parents Terribles, Les) 1950,Ap 24,21:2
Four Days' Leave 1950,Je 9,29:4
Stolen Affections 1951,Mr 12,20:2
Day, Laraine
Sergeant Madden 1939,Mr 24,27:2
Calling Dr Kildare 1939,My 12,25:4
Tarzan Finds a Son 1939,Je 15,27:2
Secret of Dr Kildare, The 1939,D 8,33:5
I Take This Woman 1940,F 16,23:3
And One Was Beautiful 1940,Ap 11,32:4
Dr Kildare's Strange Case 1940,Ap 12,19:2
My Son, My Son! 1940,My 10,26:6
Foreign Correspondent 1940,Ag 28,15:2
Dr Kildare Goes Home 1940,S 19,27:4
Dr Kildare's Crisis 1940,D 19,33:1
Trial of Mary Dugan, The 1941,Mr 6,25:4
Bad Man, The 1941,Ap 4,25:1
People vs Dr Kildare, The 1941,My 8,21:1
Dr Kildare's Wedding Day 1941,S 18,31:1
Kathleen 1941,D 19,35:3
Unholy Partners 1941,D 29,21:4
Yank on the Burma Road, A 1942,Ja 29,25:3
Fingers at the Window 1942,Ap 23,27:3
Journey for Margaret 1942,D 18,36:7
Mr Lucky 1943,Jl 23,21:2
Story of Dr Wassell, The 1944,Je 7,13:2
Bride by Mistake 1944,S 16,20:2
Keep Your Powder Dry 1945,Mr 12,22:6
Those Endearing Young Charms 1945,Je 20,26:5
Locket, The 1947,Mr 20,38:2
Tycoon 1947,D 26,22:6
My Dear Secretary 1949,F 14,15:4
Woman on Pier 13, The 1950,Je 16,28:4
Without Honor 1950,Jl 3,9:2
High and the Mighty, The 1954,Jl 1,21:2
Toy Tiger 1956,Je 30,11:2
Three for Jamie Dawn 1956,Jl 7,11:3
Third Voice, The 1960,Mr 7,24:5
Day, Lillian (Original Author)
Our Wife 1941,S 18,31:1
Youngest Profession, The 1943,Je 25,13:3
Day, Marceline
Barrier, The 1926,Mr 22,16:1
Splendid Road, The 1926,Je 13,31:1
Beloved Rogue, The 1927,Mr 14,16:1
Rookies 1927,Ap 25,20:4
Captain Salvation 1927,Je 27,25:2
Road to Romance, The 1927,O 10,24:1
London After Midnight 1927,D 31,31:1
Big City, The 1928,Mr 26,26:2
Certain Young Man, A 1928,Je 11,27:1
Cameraman, The 1928,S 17,27:1
Restless Youth 1929,Ja 1,60:1
Jazz Age, The 1929,Ja 7,36:2
Wild Party, The 1929,Ap 2,28:4
One Woman Idea, The 1929,Je 10,23:1
Temple Tower 1930,My 10,25:3
Sunny Skies 1930,My 17,21:2
Mad Parade, The 1931,S 19,10:2
Crusader, The 1932,O 8,15:4
Damaged Lives 1937,Je 14,26:2
Day, Olga
Casanova 1927,Je 23,23:3
Loves of Casanova, The 1929,Ap 30,33:2
Day, Richard (Producer)
Never Love a Stranger 1958,N 22,27:4
Day, Richard (Screenwriter)
Never Love a Stranger 1958,N 22,27:4
Day, Robert (Director)
Green Man, The 1957,My 23,40:1
Haunted Strangler, The 1958,Jl 4,15:3
Tarzan the Magnificent 1960,Jl 21,17:1
Two-Way Stretch 1961,Ja 24,20:3
Call Me Genius 1961,O 17,47:1
Operation Snatch 1962,S 25,31:4
Corridors of Blood 1963,Je 6,39:1
She 1965,S 2,36:1
Tarzan and the Valley of Gold 1967,Mr 30,55:1
Day, Robert (Screenwriter)
Tarzan the Magnificent 1960,Jl 21,17:1
Day, Shannon
Marriage Morals 1923,Ag 14,10:3
So This Is Marriage 1924,D 23,16:2
Vanishing American, The 1925,O 16,18:2
Barrier, The 1926,Mr 22,16:1
Day, Tom
Red Raiders, The 1927,S 28,28:3

Day, Vera
Kid for two Farthings, A 1956,Ap 18,25:1
Prince and the Showgirl 1957,Je 14,22:2
Haunted Strangler, The 1958,Jl 4,15:3
Up the Creek 1958,N 11,26:2
Too Many Crooks 1959,Ap 25,14:2
Trunk, The 1962,N 1,34:3
Day, Yvonne
Don Juan 1926,Ag 7,6:1 (In Addenda)
Day-Helveg, Anne (Original Author)
Liane, Jungle Goddess 1959,F 23,19:1
Dayde, Bernard
Portrait of Innocence 1948,Je 9,35:2
Daye, Harold
Verboten 1960,Jl 12,39:1
Dayka, Margit
Piri Mindont Tud 1933,Ja 26,12:3
Rakoczi Indulo 1934,N 21,23:4
Torockoi Menyasszony; Torockoi Bride 1938,Mr 5,11:2
Az Ember Neha Teved; Man Sometimes Errs 1938,Mr 28,19:3
Falu Rossza, A; Village Rogue, The 1938,Ap 18,11:2
Harapos Ferj; Biting Husbank 1939,Ja 28,19:2
Borcsa Amerikaben; Barbara in America 1939,F 11,13:2
Ele serelt Ember; Changed Man 1939,F 25,19:3
Janos Vitez; John, The Hero 1939,Ap 8,19:2
Vadroza; Wild Rose 1940,Ja 29,11:6
Dayle, Lucien
Adieux les Beaux Jours 1934,Ap 23,20:2
Abused Confidence 1938,D 1,29:1
Dayton, Charles
Bride of Vengeance 1949,Ap 7,38:2
Sunset Boulevard 1950,Ag 11,15:2
Union Station 1950,O 5,38:3
Place in the Sun, A 1951,Ag 29,20:1
Dayton, Dan
At War With the Army 1951,Ja 25,21:5
No Questions Asked 1951,Ag 10,13:2
Turning Point, The 1952,N 15,15:2
Guys and Dolls 1955,N 5,26:1
Dayton, Katharine (Original Author)
First Lady 1937,D 23,25:1
Dayton, Lewis
Slander the Woman 1923,My 28,18:2
What Fools Men 1925,S 29,31:3
Dazey, Charles T (Original Author)
In old Kentucky 1927,N 21,20:1
Old Kentucky, In 1935,N 29,24:1
Dazey, Frank (Miscellaneous)
Klondike Annie 1936,Mr 12,18:2
Dazey, Frank (Original Author)
Poor Men's Wives 1923,Ja 29,11:1
Devil Is Driving, The 1932,D 16,25:5
Dazey, Frank (Screenwriter)
Rich Men's Wives 1922,Ag 21,6:2
When a Man's a Man 1935,F 22,27:2
Dazey, Frank Mitchell (Original Author)
Helldorado 1935,Ja 7,13:2
13 Hours by Air 1936,Ap 30,17:2
Nobody's Fool 1936,Je 4,27:2
De Alaracon, Petro A (Screenwriter)
Nail, The 1949,Jl 1,14:6
De Alba, Felipe
Adventures of Robinson Crusoe, The 1954,Ag 6,10:5
de Almeyda, Jose
Gay Adventure, The 1954,S 16,35:7
De Amicis, Edmondo (Original Author)
Carmela 1949,My 14,9:2
Heart and Soul 1950,Je 15,41:3
de Anda, Raul
Tesoro de Pancho Villa, El 1936,Ja 27,20:4
de Anda, Raul (Producer)
Hidden River 1950,D 1,31:2
De Angelis, Mario
Variety Lights; Luci del Varieta 1965,My 7,34:1
de Antonio, Emile (Director)
Rush to Judgement 1967,Je 3,18:1
de Antonio, Emile (Producer)
Point of Order 1964,Ja 15,27:2
Rush to Judgement 1967,Je 3,18:1
de Bancelli, J (Screenwriter)
One Step to Eternity 1955,O 3,22:2
de Banos, Ramon (Cinematographer)
Fury Over Spain 1937,Jl 21,19:2
De Banzie, Brenda
Long Dark Hall, The 1951,My 10,38:3
I Believe in You 1953,My 5,34:3
Hobson's Choice 1954,Je 15,37:1
Purple Plain, The 1955,Ap 11,29:1
Doctor at Sea 1956,Mr 1,37:3
Kid for two Farthings, A 1956,Ap 18,25:1
Man Who Knew too Much, The 1956,My 17,37:1
Triple Deception 1957,O 7,23:2
Too Many Crooks 1959,Ap 25,14:2
Room 43 1959,D 3,46:1
Entertainer, The 1960,O 4,49:2
39 Steps, The 1960,O 11,55:2
Come September 1961,S 8,34:1
Mark, The 1961,O 3,46:2

Flame in the Streets 1962,S 13,32:1
Pair of Briefs, A 1964,F 3,22:2
Pink Panther, The 1964,Ap 24,25:1
Matter of Innocence, A 1968,F 22,36:1
De Barr, Estelle
Loves of Ricardo, The 1926,Ag 16,10:1
de Baumont, Leprince Mme (Original Author)
Beauty and the Beast 1947,D 24,12:2
de Beauregard, Georges (Producer)
Lola 1962,O 15,32:2
Third Lover, The 1963,Je 25,23:3
Doulos-The Finger Man 1964,Mr 3,31:1
Woman Is a Woman, A 1964,S 19,19:1
Contempt 1964,D 19,25:2
Petit Soldat, Le 1967,Ap 21,48:1
Made in U S A 1967,S 28,58:2
Carabiniers, Les 1967,S 28,58:3
Religieuse, La 1968,S 23,42:3
De Beck, Billy
Great White Way, The 1924,Ja 4,10:1
De Becker, Marie
Mrs Miniver 1942,Je 5,23:1
Random Harvest 1942,D 18,36:6
Devotion 1946,Ap 6,10:5
De Benedetti, Aldo (Original Author)
My Seven Little Sins 1956,My 2,27:1
De Benedetti, Aldo (Screenwriter)
Life Begins Anew; Vita Ricomincia, La 1947,Ap 7,20:5
Voice of Love, The 1950,Ja 7,11:2
My Widow and I 1950,Ag 30,27:5
Tormento 1953,Ap 4,9:2
Singing Taxi Driver 1953,My 16,10:1
Mademoiselle Gobette 1955,F 5,13:3
Virtuous Bigamist, The 1959,My 28,34:3
De Benning, Jeff
How to Succeed in Business Without Really Trying 1967,Mr 10,30:1
De Berg, Marina
Pit of Loneliness 1954,Ap 9,19:2
De Bergh, Joanne
Call Northside 777 1948,F 19,29:2
Doctor and the Girl, The 1949,O 31,20:2
De Bernardi, Piero (Screenwriter)
Woman in the Painting, The 1959,Ja 15,27:1
Holiday Island; (Vacanzie a Izchia) 1959,S 22,46:1
Girl With a Suitcase 1961,S 12,36:2
Marriage Italian Style 1964,D 21,42:1
Bambole; Dolls, The (Monsignor Cupid); Monsignor Cupid (The Dolls) 1965,Je 29,26:1
De Blasi, Virgilio (Producer)
Warrior and the Slave, The 1960,Mr 10,36:2
De Blasio, G (Producer)
Young, The Evil and the Savage, The 1968,Ag 15,46:2
De Bolt, Birdie
Hawaii Calls 1938,Ap 29,17:2
de Bordes, Armand
White Cockatoo, The 1935,Ja 16,21:1
De Briac, Jean
Love Light, The 1921,Ja 10,9:1
Divine Woman, The 1928,Ja 16,24:1
Wise Girl 1938,Ja 10,13:3
Swiss Miss 1938,Je 4,18:2
De Briac twins
Daddies 1924,F 11,18:3
De Bruce, Robert
Scotland Yard 1941,Ap 9,33:3
de Brulier, Nigel
Four Horsemen of the Apocalypse 1921,Mr 7,8:1
Without Benefit of Clergy 1921,Je 20,17:2
Three Musketeers, The 1921,Ag 29,14:4
Wild Oranges 1924,Mr 3,22:3
Three Weeks 1924,Ap 1,19:3
Boy of Flanders, A 1924,Ap 15,24:1
Mademoiselle Midnight 1924,My 27,14:1
Ben Hur 1925,D 31,10:5
Don Juan 1926,Ag 7,6:1 (In Addenda)
Beloved Rogue, The 1927,Mr 14,16:1
Wings 1927,Ag 13,10:4
Soft Cushions 1927,S 12,29:1
Surrender 1927,O 11,27:1
Gaucho, The 1927,N 22,32:2
Two Lovers 1928,Mr 23,24:4
Loves of an Actress 1928,Jl 30,21:2
Me, Gangster 1928,O 22,29:1
Iron Mask, The 1929,F 22,18:6
Noah's Ark 1929,Mr 13,28:6
Thru Different Eyes 1929,Ap 15,22:6
Wheel of Life, The 1929,Je 24,27:1
Green Goddess, The 1930,F 14,20:1
Moby Dick 1930,Ag 15,20:5
Son of India 1931,Jl 25,11:6
Ben Hur 1931,D 4,28:2
Miss Pinkerton 1932,Jl 9,7:5

de Brulier, Nigel — Cont
I'm no Angel 1933,O 14,18:2
Charlie Chan in Egypt 1935,Je 24,12:2
Three Musketeers, The 1935,N 1,25:1
Mary of Scotland 1936,Jl 31,22:2
Down Under the Sea 1936,Ag 10,10:2
Hound of the Baskervilles, The 1939,Mr 25,19:2
Mad Empress, The 1940,F 15,15:1
Viva Cisco Kid 1940,Mr 22,23:4
One Million BC 1940,Ap 27,9:2
Tonight We Raid Calais 1943,Ap 15,20:2
de Cabo, Rosita
Incertidumbre 1936,S 21,26:5
De Caillavet (Original Author)
King, The 1941,O 23,29:3
de Campo, Giuseppe
Arab, The 1924,Jl 14,11:5
De Canlo, Tommy
Little Fugitive 1953,O 7,35:1
de Carco, Francis (Director)
Marked Girls 1949,Je 25,8:7
de Carco, Francis (Original Author)
Marked Girls 1949,Je 25,8:7
De Carlo, Yvonne
Salome, Where She Danced 1945,My 3,27:1
Frontier Gal 1945,D 15,14:2
Song of Scheherazade 1947,F 27,26:2
Brute Force 1947,Jl 17,16:2
Slave Girl 1947,Jl 18,21:3
Black Bart 1948,Mr 4,30:4
Casbah 1948,My 3,27:4
River Lady 1948,My 21,19:5
Criss Cross 1949,Mr 12,10:2
Calamity Jane and Sam Bass 1949,Jl 18,14:2
Buccaneer's Girl 1950,Mr 27,19:2
Desert Hawk, The 1950,Ag 26,9:2
Tomahawk 1951,F 19,19:2
Hotel Sahara 1952,Ja 1,21:4
San Francisco Story, The 1952,My 10,16:4
Scarlet Angel 1952,Je 21,12:2
Hurricane Smith 1952,O 4,15:2
Sombrero 1953,Ap 23,37:2
Sea Devils 1953,Jl 31,11:5
Captain's Paradise, The 1953,S 29,25:5
Passion 1954,D 11,11:1
Tonight's the Night 1954,D 23,13:4
Flame of the Islands 1956,F 25,12:4
Raw Edge 1956,Jl 28,10:7
Death of a Scoundrel 1956,N 6,30:1
Ten Commandments, The 1956,N 9,35:2
Band of Angels 1957,Jl 11,21:1
McLintock 1963,N 14,41:3
Global Affair, A 1964,My 7,31:2
Munster, Go Home 1966,Je 16,53:4
Power, The 1968,Mr 7,52:2
De Carmine, Renato
Mistress of the Mountains 1954,My 27,34:5
de Casalis, Jeanne
Nell Gwyn 1935,Je 20,16:2
Jamaica Inn 1939,O 12,33:1
Gay Intruders, The 1946,Mr 18,24:2
De Castro, Babette
Helen Morgan Story, The 1957,O 3,33:2
De Castro, Cherl
Helen Morgan Story, The 1957,O 3,33:2
de Castro, Elsa
Nar Rosorna Sla Ut 1931,F 10,24:4
De Castro, Peggy
Helen Morgan Story, The 1957,O 3,33:2
de Chabaneix, Marie France
Adolescents, The (Marie-France and Veronica); Marie-France and Veronica (The Adolescents) 1967,Ap 14,33:1
De Chalonge, Christian (Director)
Voyage of Silence 1968,S 12,54:1
De Chalonge, Christian (Screenwriter)
Voyage of Silence 1968,S 12,54:1
de Chalus, Pauline
Mill On the Floss, The 1939,N 15,19:3
de Chauveron, Andrea
Would-Be Gentleman, The 1960,Mr 23,31:1
De Cicco, Pat
Night Life of the Gods 1935,F 23,14:6
de Codecido, Francisco Bonmati (Screenwriter)
Loyola, The Soldier Saint 1952,Ap 25,19:2
de Combray, Richard
Tender is the Night 1962,Ja 20,13:2
De Concini, Ennio (Miscellaneous)
See Naples and Die 1959,Ag 31,16:2
De Concini, Ennio (Original Author)
Run With the Devil 1963,Jl 16,25:1
Italiano Brava Gente 1966,F 4,20:1
Treasure of San Gennaro 1968,F 27,36:1
Weekend, Italian Style 1968,My 23,56:2
De Concini, Ennio (Screenwriter)
Sensualita 1954,Ap 29,40:2
Hell Raiders of the Deep 1954,Jl 3,9:2
Mambo 1955,Mr 31,23:3
Ulysses 1955,Ag 18,17:2
War and Peace 1956,Ag 22,26:2
Miller's Beautiful Wife, The 1957,Je 12,40:2
Attila 1958,My 19,19:4
Hercules 1959,Jl 23,32:2
See Naples and Die 1959,Ag 31,16:2

De Concini, Ennio (Screenwriter) — Cont

Warrior and the Slave, The 1960,Mr 10,36:2
House of Intrigue, The 1960,Mr 10,36:3
Always Victorious 1960,Ap 7,46:1
Giant of Marathon, The 1960,My 26,37:3
Hercules Unchained 1960,Jl 14,23:1
Last Days of Pompeii, The 1960,Ag 11,19:1
Carthage in Flames 1961,Ja 26,32:3
Legions of the Nile 1961,Mr 4,16:1
Black Sunday 1961,Mr 9,23:1
Warrior Empress, The 1961,Ag 10,17:4
Colossus of Rhodes, The 1961,D 14,55:6
Divorce-Italian Style 1962,S 18,34:1
Grido, Il 1962,O 23,42:1
Nude Odyssey 1962,O 27,14:6
Constantine and the Cross 1963,Mr 14,8:2
Madame 1963,Mr 21,8:6
Run With the Devil 1963,Jl 16,25:1
My Son, The Hero 1963,S 19,23:1
Facts of Murder, The 1965,Jl 1,34:1
Italiano Brava Gente 1966,F 4,20:1
Love and Marriage (Saturday, July 18); Saturday,
   July 18 (Love and Marriage) 1966,Ag 5,20:1
Love and Marriage (The First Night); First Night,
   The (Love and Marriage) 1966,Ag 5,20:1
Love and Marriage (The Last Resort); Last Resort,
   The (Love and Marriage) 1966,Ag 5,20:1
Love and Marriage (One Moment Is Enough); One
   Moment Is Enough (Love and Marriage)
   1966,Ag 5,20:1
Rose for Everyone, A 1967,Je 30,30:1
Treasure of San Gennaro 1968,F 27,36:1

De Conde, Syn
Girl Who Stayed Home, The 1919,Mr 24,11:3

De Cordoba, Arturo
Celos 1936,Ap 15,25:2
Cielito Lindo 1936,N 9,22:5
Esos Hombres 1937,Ag 21,7:3
Ave sin Rumbo; Wandering Bird 1938,Ja 24,17:2
Zandunga, La 1938,My 14,18:2
Hombres de Mar; Men of the Sea 1938,N 7,23:6
Casa del Ogro, La; House of the Ogre, The
   1939,F 13,13:2
Mientras Mexico Duerme; While Mexico Sleeps
   1940,F 12,14:3
Odio; Hate 1940,Ap 6,13:2
Bestia Negra, La; Black Beast, The 1940,Je 3,11:2
Night of the Mayas 1941,Ja 14,16:7
For Whom the Bell Tolls 1943,Jl 15,25:2
Hostages 1943,O 11,23:2
El Conde de Monte Cristo 1943,N 9,26:2
Frenchman's Creek 1944,S 21,26:2
Medal for Benny, A 1945,My 24,15:2
Incendiary Blonde 1945,Jl 26,13:2
Duffy's Tavern 1945,S 6,23:3
Masquerade in Mexico 1945,N 29,27:2
New Orleans 1947,Je 20,25:6
Adventures of Casanova 1948,Mr 22,18:3
This Strange Passion 1955,D 5,34:2

De Cordoba, Pedro
New Moon, The 1919,My 12,11:4
World and his Wife, The 1920,Jl 19,16:3
When Knighthood Was in Flower 1922,S 15,17:2
   (In Addenda)
Enemies of Women 1923,Ap 1,5:4
Purple Highway, The 1923,Jl 24,14:3 (In
   Addenda)
Bandolero, The 1924,O 27,27:1
New Commandment, The 1925,N 10,25:3
Crusades, The 1935,Ag 22,21:3
Captain Blood 1935,D 27,14:1
Rose of the Rancho 1936,Ja 9,25:2
Professional Soldier 1936,Ja 30,14:2
Moonlight Murder 1936,Mr 28,11:2
Trouble for Two 1936,My 30,7:2
Devil Doll, The 1936,Ag 8,5:2
His Brother's Wife 1936,Ag 15,6:2
Anthony Adverse 1936,Ag 27,16:1
Ramona 1936,O 7,32:4
Maid of Salem 1937,Mr 4,27:2
International Settlement 1938,F 12,20:3
Marriage Forbidden 1938,Jl 16,7:2
Keep Smiling 1938,Ag 10,15:2
Heart of the North 1938,D 21,29:2
Juarez 1939,Ap 26,27:1
Man of Conquest 1939,Ap 28,31:2
Charlie Chan in City in Darkness 1939,D 18,29:2
Light That Failed, The 1939,D 25,19:1
My Favorite Wife 1940,My 31,15:2
Earthbound 1940,Je 7,27:4
Ghost Breakers, The 1940,Jl 4,12:2
Devil's Island 1940,Jl 12,11:4
South of Pago-Pago 1940,Ag 2,12:2
Sea Hawk, The 1940,Ag 10,16:2
Before I Hang 1940,O 3,31:3
Mark of Zorro, The 1940,N 4,23:2
Romance of the Rio Grande 1940,D 25,33:4
Phantom Submarine, The 1941,F 12,25:3
Blood and Sand 1941,My 23,25:3
Aloma of the South Seas 1941,Ag 28,23:4

Corsican Brothers, The 1942,Ja 16,25:4
Son of Fury 1942,Ja 30,23:2
Saboteur 1942,My 8,27:2
Tarzan Triumphs 1943,F 5,16:3
Background to Danger 1943,Jl 3,11:2
For Whom the Bell Tolls 1943,Jl 15,25:2
Song of Bernadette, The 1944,Ja 27,15:2
Uncertain Glory 1944,Ap 8,9:2
Falcon in Mexico, The 1944,Ag 5,16:2
San Antonio 1945,D 29,19:5
Swamp Fire 1946,Ag 26,21:4
Scandal In Paris, A 1946,S 16,9:7
Beast With Five Fingers, The 1946,D 26,28:3
Carnival in Costa Rica 1947,Mr 29,21:2
Time of your Life, The 1948,My 27,29:2
Mexican Hayride 1949,Ja 12,33:3
Comanche Territory 1950,Ap 8,9:3

De Cordoba, Pedro (Miscellaneous)
First World War, The 1934,N 8,27:1

de Cordoba, Pedro (Narrator)
Through the Centuries 1933,D 2,9:8 (In
   Addenda)

de Cordova, Frederick (Director)
Too Young to Know 1945,D 8,21:2
Her Kind of Man 1946,My 4,10:6
That Way With Women 1947,F 15,20:4
Love and Learn 1947,My 3,10:3
Always Together 1947,D 11,46:1
Wallflower 1948,Je 12,8:5
For the Love of Mary 1948,S 23,37:2
Illegal Entry 1949,Je 11,11:2
Buccaneer's Girl 1950,Mr 27,19:2
Peggy 1950,Jl 21,15:4
Desert Hawk, The 1950,Ag 26,9:2
Bedtime for Bonzo 1951,Ap 6,31:4
Little Egypt 1951,Ag 30,20:3
I'll Take Sweden 1965,Ag 12,30:4
Frankie and Johnny 1966,Jl 21,20:2

de Cordova, Joseph
Badjao 1962,S 21,35:1
No Man is an Island 1962,O 11,49:2

de Cordova, Leander (Director)
Polly With a Past 1921,Ja 10,9:1

De Corsia, Ted
Naked City, The 1948,Mr 5,17:2
Lady From Shanghai, The 1948,Je 10,28:2
Life of Riley, The 1949,Ap 18,18:4
Neptune's Daughter 1949,Je 10,32:2
It Happens Every Spring 1949,Je 11,11:2
Outriders, The 1950,Mr 9,25:2
Cargo to Capetown 1950,Mr 31,36:3
Three Secrets 1950,O 21,10:6
Enforcer, The 1951,Ja 26,19:2
Vengeance Valley 1951,F 16,21:2
Inside the Walls of Folsom Prison
   1951,My 28,17:4
New Mexico 1951,Jl 14,7:2
Place in the Sun, A 1951,Ag 29,20:1
Turning Point, The 1952,N 15,15:2
Savage, The 1953,Ja 2,11:1
Man in the Dark 1953,Ap 9,31:5
Ride Vaquero 1953,Jl 16,17:2
Crime Wave 1954,Ja 13,26:2
20,000 Leagues Under the Sea 1954,D 24,7:2
Big Combo, The 1955,Mr 26,13:2
Kismet 1955,D 9,32:2
Man With the Gun 1955,D 23,14:2
Steel Jungle, The 1956,Mr 10,9:5
Slightly Scarlet 1956,Mr 17,13:2
Conqueror, The 1956,Mr 31,13:3
Killing, The 1956,My 21,20:1
Dance With Me Henry 1956,D 24,8:2
Gunfight at the O K Corral 1957,My 30,23:2
Midnight Story, The 1957,Jl 5,14:2
Joker Is Wild, The 1957,S 27,16:6
Baby Face Nelson 1957,D 12,35:1
Buccaneer, The 1958,D 24,00:0

De Costa, Leon (Original Author)
San Francisco Nights 1928,Ja 31,29:1

De Costa, Leon (Screenwriter)
Kosher Kitty Kelly 1926,S 28,30:2

De Courville, Albert (Director)
There Goes the Bride 1933,Mr 4,11:3
Seven Sinners 1936,Ag 22,6:1
Strangers on a Honeymoon 1937,Mr 13,23:2
Man With 100 Faces 1938,N 1,27:2

de Cruciati, Fernando
Cieca di Sorrento, La 1936,Ag 3,11:3

de Cuevas, Marquis Grand Ballet
Neapolitan Carousel 1961,O 12,41:3

de Diestro, Alfredo
Juarez y Maximiliano 1935,F 16,9:2

De Domenicis, Mario
Sei tu l'Amore 1930,N 18,28:4

De Fas, Boris
Tempest 1928,My 18,27:3
Woman Disputed, The 1928,N 10,20:8
Madonna of the Sleeping Cars, The
   1929,O 14,20:2
Bride 68 1930,Ap 15,28:5
Volga, Volga 1933,D 15,28:3

de Felice, Alfredo
Messalina 1924,Ag 25,16:2

De Felice, Ermelinda
Ape Woman, The 1964,S 23,55:1

de Felice, Lionello (Director)
Constantine and the Cross 1963,Mr 14,8:2

de Felice, Lionello (Screenwriter)
Constantine and the Cross 1963,Mr 14,8:2

De Feo, Francesco (Screenwriter)
Sign of the Gladiator 1959,D 3,46:1
Warrior and the Slave, The 1960,Mr 10,36:2
Sword and the Cross, The 1960,Jl 7,26:1

de Feo, Sandro (Original Author)
Three Forbidden Stories 1953,N 16,21:4

de Feo, Sandro (Screenwriter)
Greatest Love, The 1954,Ja 12,19:2
Wayward Wife, The 1955,Ap 11,29:3

de Fernandez, Emilio (Screenwriter)
Maria Candelaria 1944,S 12,23:7

De Filippo, Eduardo
Cappello a Tre Punte, Il 1936,S 28,14:5
Commedia Fra I Pazzi, Una 1937,Jl 8,20:2
Sono Stato Io; It Was I 1940,My 10,26:7
Life Begins Anew; Vita Ricomincia, La
   1947,Ap 7,20:5
Scarred 1951,O 27,10:5
Three Girls From Rome 1953,O 14,34:2
Lucky Five, The 1953,N 27,22:5
Side Street Story 1954,Je 24,30:4
It Happened in the Park 1957,Ag 13,23:2
Raw Wind in Eden 1958,S 20,10:6
Everybody go Home!; Tutti a Casa 1962,N 6,38:1
Shoot Loud, Louder... I Don't Understand
   1967,S 21,56:4

De Filippo, Eduardo (Director)
Side Street Story 1954,Je 24,30:4
Shoot Loud, Louder... I Don't Understand
   1967,S 21,56:4

De Filippo, Eduardo (Original Author)
Side Street Story 1954,Je 24,30:4
Marriage Italian Style 1964,D 21,42:1
Shoot Loud, Louder... I Don't Understand
   1967,S 21,56:4

De Filippo, Eduardo (Producer)
Side Street Story 1954,Je 24,30:4

De Filippo, Eduardo (Screenwriter)
Scarred 1951,O 27,10:5
Side Street Story 1954,Je 24,30:4
Yesterday, Today and Tomorrow (Part 1-Adelina
   Naples); Adelina Naples (Yesterday, Today and
   Tomorrow) 1964,Mr 18,46:1
Yesterday, Today, and Tomorrow (Part III-Mara
   Rome); Mara Rome (Yesterday, Today and
   Tomorrow) 1964,Mr 18,46:1
Yesterday, Today and Tomorrow (Part II-Anna
   Milan); Anna Milan (Yesterday, Today and
   Tomorrow) 1964,Mr 18,46:1
Marriage Italian Style 1964,D 21,42:1
Shoot Loud, Louder... I Don't Understand
   1967,S 21,56:4

De Filippo, Peppino
Cappello a Tre Punte, Il 1936,S 28,14:5
Commedia Fra I Pazzi, Una 1937,Jl 8,20:2
Sono Stato Io; It Was I 1940,My 10,26:7
Peddler and the Lady, The 1949,S 30,28:4
Escape into Dreams 1950,Ap 13,34:5
Holiday Island; (Vacanzie a Izchia)
   1959,S 22,46:1
Fast and Sexy 1960,O 6,51:4
Boccaccio '70 (The Tempation of Dr Antonio);
   Temptation of Dr Antonio, The (Boccaccio '70)
   1962,Je 27,40:1
Love and Larceny 1963,F 2,5:6
Day in Court, A 1963,My 11,15:2
Variety Lights; Luci del Varieta 1965,My 7,34:1

De Filippo, Titina
Sono Stato Io; It Was I 1940,My 10,26:7
Scarred 1951,O 27,10:5
Lucky Five, The 1953,N 27,22:5
Side Street Story 1954,Je 24,30:4
Flesh and Desire 1958,N 27,52:4

De Filippo, Titina (Screenwriter)
Two Cents Worth of Hope 1952,D 16,44:2

de Filmorin, Louise (Miscellaneous)
Immortal Story, The 1968,S 19,62:2

de Flers, R (Original Author)
Miquette 1951,F 5,18:2

De Flers (Original Author)
King, The 1941,O 23,29:3

de Floer, Eleonor
Med Folket Foer Fosterlandet 1939,F 21,14:2

De Foe, Annette
One Clear Call 1922,Je 19,10:3

De Foranda, Pituka
Passion Island 1943,My 1,11:2

de Foronda, Pituka
Marvels of the Bull Ring 1943,Jl 3,11:3

de Fuentes, Fernando (Director)
Prisionero 13, El 1934,Ap 30,11:4
Tigre de Yautepec, El 1934,O 20,20:3
Compadre Mendoza, El 1934,N 19,13:2
Cruz Diablo 1935,Ap 6,10:1
Fantasma del Convento, El; Fantasy of the

de Fuentes, Fernando (Director) — Cont
Monastery 1935,Ap 22,14:3
Familia Dressel, La 1936,My 4,16:2
Calandria, La 1936,O 12,23:3
Alla en el Rancho Grande 1936,N 23,17:3
Rancho Grande 1938,D 2,27:2
Creo en Dios 1943,Jl 17,8:3
Asi Se Quiere En Jalisco 1943,Ag 7,6:2
de Fuentes, Fernando (Producer)
Rancho Grande 1938,D 2,27:2
Asi Se Quiere En Jalisco 1943,Ag 7,6:2
de Fuentes, Fernando (Screenwriter)
Creo en Dios 1943,Jl 17,8:3
de Garde, Adele
Within the Law 1917,Ap 30,11:3
De Gastayne, Marco (Director)
Rothchild 1938,O 12,35:2
de Giorgi, Elsa
Loyalty of Love 1937,Mr 1,15:1
Destino di Donna 1937,Je 9,31:6
Signora Paradiso 1937,Jl 22,15:2
de Goldschmidt, Gilbert (Producer)
Girl With the Golden Eyes, The 1962,Ag 21,36:2
Three Fables of Love (Two Pigeons); Two Pigeons
(Three Fables of Love) 1963,Ag 21,38:1
Three Fables of Love (The Tortoise and the Hare);
Tortoise and the Hare, The (Three Fables of
Love) 1963,Ag 21,38:1
Three Fables of Love (The Fox and the Crow);
Fox and the Crow, The (Three Fables of Love)
1963,Ag 21,38:1
de Gonzague-Frick, L
Zero de Conduite 1947,Je 23,14:5
De Gorter, Fred (Screenwriter)
Dayton's Devils 1968,O 3,56:4
De Grandcourt, Charles (Original Author)
Earl of Chicago, The 1940,Mr 14,29:3
De Grandcourt, Charles (Screenwriter)
Victoria the Great 1937,O 29,19:1
De Grasse, Joseph (Director)
Nineteen and Phyllis 1920,D 27,11:3
Old Swimmin' Hole, The 1921,F 28,16:2
Tailor Made Man, A 1922,O 16,20:2
Flowing Gold 1924,Mr 10,18:2
De Greeff, Peter
Champagne Charlie 1948,Ag 7,8:2
de Gresac, Fred (Original Author)
Afraid to Love 1927,Ap 12,25:3
Escape from Devil's Island 1935,N 25,22:2
Sweethearts 1938,D 23,16:2
De Grey, Sidney
My Man 1924,F 11,18:3
Wine of Youth 1924,Ag 11,16:1
Steele of the Royal Mounted 1925,Je 18,16:3
Just Imagine 1930,N 22,21:3
de Grunwald, Anatole (Original Author)
Courageous Mr Penn 1943,D 23,26:5
Innocents in Paris 1955,Mr 5,9:6
de Grunwald, Anatole (Producer)
Johnny in the Clouds 1945,N 16,16:2
Adventure for Two 1945,D 14,24:5
Queen of Spades, The 1949,Jl 1,14:4
Dolwyn 1949,Ag 30,18:4
Bond Street 1950,Mr 30,40:6
Winslow Boy, The 1950,Je 7,34:4
While the Sun Shines 1950,Jl 1,9:2
Holly and the Ivy, The 1954,F 5,16:1
Gay Adventure, The 1954,S 16,35:7
Innocents in Paris 1955,Mr 5,9:6
Doctor's Dilemma, A 1958,D 18,2:7
Libel 1959,O 24,12:4
I Thank a Fool 1962,S 15,15:1
Come Fly With Me 1963,My 2,40:2
V I P's, The 1963,S 20,29:1
Yellow Rolls-Royce, The 1965,My 14,42:2
de Grunwald, Anatole (Screenwriter)
Quiet Wedding 1941,D 29,27:4
Mister V 1942,F 13,24:4
Avengers, The 1942,N 25,18:2
At Dawn We Die 1943,My 8,19:2
Spitfire 1943,Je 14,13:2
Jeannie 1943,S 13,14:2
Adventure for Two 1945,D 14,24:5
Her Man Gilbey 1949,Je 9,35:2
Bond Street 1950,Mr 30,40:6
Winslow Boy, The 1950,Je 7,34:4
While the Sun Shines 1950,Jl 1,9:2
Murder on Monday 1953,O 7,35:2
Holly and the Ivy, The 1954,F 5,16:1
Doctor's Dilemma, A 1958,D 18,2:7
Libel 1959,O 24,12:4
de Grunwald, Antole (Screenwriter)
Voice in the Night, The 1941,My 23,25:4
de Grunwald, Dimitri (Producer)
Trial and Error 1962,N 17,17:2
Shalako 1968,N 6,32:1
de Hartog, Jan (Miscellaneous)
Skipper Next to God 1953,Ja 13,24:2
de Hartog, Jan (Original Author)
Four Poster, The 1952,O 16,37:1
Skipper Next to God 1953,Ja 13,24:2
Key, The 1958,Jl 2,23:3
Lisa 1962,My 25,28:1

Spiral Road, The 1962,Ag 4,11:2
de Hartog, Jan (Screenwriter)
Skipper Next to God 1953,Ja 13,24:2
De Havilland, Olivia
Alibi Ike 1935,Jl 17,22:1
Irish in US, The 1935,Ag 1,15:1
Midsummer Night's Dream, A 1935,O 10,31:1
Captain Blood 1935,D 27,14:1
Anthony Adverse 1936,Ag 27,16:1
Charge of the Light Brigade, The 1936,N 2,24:1
Call it a Day 1937,My 7,29:2
Great Garrick, The 1937,O 25,23:1
It's Love I'm After 1937,N 11,31:2
Gold Is Where You Find It 1938,F 14,20:6
Adventures of Robin Hood, The 1938,My 13,17:2
Four's a Crowd 1938,Ag 12,11:1
Hard To Get 1938,N 14,15:2
Wings of the Navy 1939,F 4,11:1
Dodge City 1939,Ap 8,19:1
Private Lives of Elizabeth and Essex, The
1939,D 2,21:2
Gone With the Wind 1939,D 20,31:2
Raffles 1940,Ja 13,11:2
My Love Came Back 1940,Jl 13,16:5
Santa Fe Trail 1940,D 21,21:2
Strawberry Blonde 1941,F 22,11:2
Hold Back the Dawn 1941,O 2,29:1
They Died With Their Boots On 1941,N 21,23:3
Male Animal, The 1942,Mr 28,11:1
In This our Life 1942,My 9,10:2
Thank Your Lucky Stars 1943,O 2,19:2
Princess O'Rourke 1943,N 6,16:2
Government Girl 1944,Ja 7,13:2
Devotion 1946,Ap 6,10:5
Well Groomed Bride, The 1946,My 11,22:5
To Each his Own 1946,My 24,15:2
Dark Mirror, The 1946,O 19,15:2
Snake Pit, the 1948,N 5,29:2
Heiress, The 1949,O 7,35:2
My Cousin Rachel 1952,D 26,20:2
That Lady 1955,Je 11,8:7
Not as a Stranger 1955,Je 29,24:1
Ambassador's Daughter, The 1956,Ag 30,19:1
Proud Rebel, The 1958,Jl 2,23:4
Libel 1959,O 24,12:4
Light in the Piazza 1962,F 8,25:1
Lady in a Cage 1964,Je 11,27:1
Hush...Hush, Sweet Charlotte 1965,Mr 4,36:1
de Hedemann, Baroness
Her Love Story 1924,O 7,26:1
de Herrera, Nana
Red Angel, The 1950,N 4,13:2
De Hoyas, Kitty
Heroina 1965,N 11,58:2
De Hoyos, Jorge Martinez
Magnificent Seven, The 1960,N 24,48:3
Guns for San Sebastian 1968,Mr 21,57:2
de Juan, Manuel
Fedra, the Devil's Daughter 1957,O 26,19:2
de Kay, Furland (Miscellaneous)
Lost Boundaries 1949,Jl 1,14:4
de Keczer, Irma
Second Youth 1924,Ap 22,19:3
De Keyser, David
Having a Wild Weekend 1965,Ag 19,35:1
Separation 1968,Mr 26,41:2
De Kirby, Annette
Mother Knows Best 1928,S 17,27:1
De Kirby, Ivor
Mother Knows Best 1928,S 17,27:1
De Knight, Fannie Belle
Hallelujah 1929,Ag 21,33:1
De Kova, Frank
Viva Zapata 1952,F 8,19:2
Big Sky, The 1952,Ag 20,21:1
Split Second 1953,My 13,34:2
Desert Song, The 1953,My 21,39:2
Arrowhead 1953,S 16,38:6
King of the Khyber Rifles 1953,D 23,21:1
All the Brothers Were Valiant 1953,D 29,19:2
Drum Beat 1954,N 18,42:1
Passion 1954,D 11,11:1
Strange Lady in Town 1955,My 21,11:1
Man From Laramie, The 1955,S 1,20:2
Shack out on 101 1956,Ja 10,26:2
Santiago 1956,Jl 14,13:2
Ten Commandments, The 1956,N 9,35:2
Cowboy 1958,F 20,29:5
Brothers Karamazov, The 1958,F 21,18:2
Appointment With a Shadow 1959,Ja 8,24:2
Atlantis the Lost Continent 1961,My 27,12:1
Greatest Story Ever Told, The 1965,F 16,40:2
De Koven, Roger
Up Front 1951,Mr 26,19:2
de Kowa, Viktor
Wahre Jakob, Der 1931,Ag 7,20:2
Stolz der 3 Kompagnie, Der 1932,Jl 21,15:2
Tannenberg 1934,Ap 3,26:6
Lockvogel 1935,Ja 5,20:3
Finanzen des Grossherzogs, Die; Grand Duke's
Finances, The 1935,Ap 6,10:3

de Kowa, Viktor — Cont
Schloss im Sueden, Das 1936,F 24,14:2
Madonna, Wo Bist Du? 1936,Mr 21,13:3
Pappi 1936,My 16,11:3
Ein Lied Geht um die Welt 1936,S 25,20:3
Zwei im Sonnenschein 1937,Jl 31,6:2
Herzensclieb; Heart Thief 1938,Jl 2,10:4
Mit versiegelter Order; Under Sealed Orders
1938,Jl 30,10:2
Joseph Schmidt Story, The 1951,Mr 5,24:2
Devil's General, The 1957,Ap 16,38:2
de Kruif, Paul (Original Author)
Yellow Jack 1938,My 20,17:2
Fight for Life, The 1940,Mr 7,19:2
De Kuh, Arthur
Baby Face 1933,Je 24,16:2
De La Berg, Guy
Obession 1968,Ag 29,46:3
De La Cruz, Joe
Devil With Women, A 1930,O 20,28:2
Four Frightened People 1934,Ja 27,9:2
de la Cruz, Jose
Black Scorpion, The 1957,O 12,23:2
De La Cruz, Juan
Roots, The (The Cows); Cows, The (The Roots)
1957,S 3,23:2
De La Cruze, Jimmy
Flight 1929,S 14,17:1
de la Falaise, Henry (Director)
Legong 1935,O 2,27:1
Kliou, The Killer 1937,Ag 16,15:1
de la Falaise, Henry (Original Author)
Legong 1935,O 2,27:1
de la Falaise, Henry (Producer)
Kliou, The Killer 1937,Ag 16,15:1
de la Fourcharliere, Georges (Original Author)
Scarlet Street 1946,F 15,29:2
de la Grandiere, Georges (Producer)
Every Second Counts 1957,O 15,39:4
Bernadette of Lourdes 1962,Ja 30,20:2
de la Motte, Marguerite
Mark of Zorro, The 1920,N 29,20:3
Three Musketeers, The 1921,Ag 29,14:4
Famous Mrs Fair, The 1923,Ap 23,18:3
Scars of Jealousy 1923,My 7,19:3
Man of Action, A 1923,Je 4,13:3
Wandering Daughters 1923,Jl 2,16:2
Richard the Lion-Hearted 1923,O 22,17:1
When a Man's a Man 1924,F 5,20:1
Behold This Woman 1924,Jl 22,9:1
Clean Heart, The 1924,S 15,28:1
Beloved Brute, The 1924,N 10,20:1
East of Broadway 1924,N 12,13:1
Cheaper to Marry 1925,F 2,14:1
Red Dice 1926,Ap 16,20:3
Unknown Soldier, The 1926,My 31,10:2
Pals in Paradise 1926,N 24,26:4
Iron Mask, The 1929,F 22,18:6
de la Muir, Jean (Director)
Parisian, The 1931,Ag 22,7:5
de la Patelliere, Denys (Director)
Possessors, The 1959,Jl 21,24:1
Ostrich Has two Eggs, The 1960,S 27,40:1
Rue de Paris 1960,D 23,14:3
Taxi for Tobruk 1965,Mr 30,52:1
Marco the Magnificent 1966,D 15,60:1
Upper Hand, The 1967,Jl 29,29:3
de la Patelliere, Denys (Original Author)
Marco the Magnificent 1966,D 15,60:1
de la Patelliere, Denys (Producer)
Taxi for Tobruk 1965,Mr 30,52:1
de la Patelliere, Denys (Screenwriter)
Possessors, The 1959,Jl 21,24:1
Ostrich Has two Eggs, The 1960,S 27,40:1
Rue de Paris 1960,D 23,14:3
Marco the Magnificent 1966,D 15,60:1
Upper Hand, The 1967,Jl 29,29:3
de la Roche, Mazo (Original Author)
Jalna 1935,S 14,8:4
de la Salle, Pierre (Original Author)
Duffy 1968,S 17,50:3
De La Terre, Raf
Golden Coach, The 1954,Ja 22,30:2
de la Torre, Enrique (Screenwriter)
Heroina 1965,N 11,58:2
de Lacy, Philippe
Peter Pan 1924,D 29,11:4
Is Zat So? 1927,My 17,27:2
Student Prince, The 1927,S 22,33:2
Mother Machree 1928,Mr 6,20:3
4 Devils 1928,O 4,26:3
Napoleon's Barber 1928,N 26,30:2
Redeeming Sin, The 1929,F 16,14:6
Marriage Playground, The 1929,D 14,22:4
Sarah and Son 1930,Mr 13,22:4
One Romantic Night 1930,My 31,19:4

de Lacy, Philippe (Director)
Cinerama Holiday 1955,F 9,31:1
de Lacy, Phillipe
Shooting of Dan McGrew, The 1924,Je 9,14:3
Love 1927,N 30,22:4
Four Feathers, The 1929,Je 13,35:4
de Laisky, Gertrud
Die Blonde Christl 1934,F 23,23:3
De Lamater, Eleanor (Original Author)
Hot Water 1937,N 5,19:4
de Lamberdesque, Cardinal
Age d'Or, L'; Golden Age, The 1964,S 22,44:1
De Landa, Juan
Se ha Fugado un Preso 1935,My 21,22:3
King's Jester, The 1947,Je 26,19:3
Brief Rapture 1952,F 28,23:2
Devotion 1953,Ja 31,10:6
de Lange, Eddie
Half Shot at Sunrise 1930,O 11,21:3
De Lange, Edgar (Composer)
If I'm Lucky 1946,S 20,41:3
De Lange, Sann
After You, Comrade 1967,Ap 11,54:1
de LaParrent, H
Four Bags Full 1957,S 5,32:1
Gervaise 1957,N 12,46:1
de Lappe, Gemze
King and I, The 1956,Je 29,15:6
De Laurentis, Dino (Director)
Side Street Story 1954,Je 24,30:4
De Laurentis, Dino (Producer)
Woman Trouble 1949,My 26,34:2
Bitter Rice 1950,S 19,39:2
Lure of the Sira 1953,D 26,10:7
Side Street Story 1954,Je 24,30:4
Mambo 1955,Mr 31,23:3
Strada, La 1956,Jl 17,19:2
War and Peace 1956,Ag 22,26:2
Miller's Beautiful Wife, The 1957,Je 12,40:2
Cabiria 1957,O 29,34:2
This Angry Age 1958,Je 26,23:3
Tempest 1959,Mr 27,19:2
Five Branded Women 1960,Je 2,27:2
Under ten Flags 1960,S 16,24:1
Great War; (Grande Guerra, La) 1961,Ag 31,22:3
Best of Enemies, The 1962,Ag 7,35:2
Barabbas 1962,O 11,49:1
Everybody go Home!; Tutti a Casa 1962,N 6,38:1
I Love, You Love 1962,N 10,16:2
To Bed...Or not to Bed 1963,D 23,18:2
...And Suddenly It's Murder! 1964,Ja 24,21:1
Mafioso 1964,Jl 1,42:1
Bible, The 1966,S 29,60:1
Kiss the Girls and Make Them Die 1967,Ja 26,25:1
Stranger, The 1967,D 19,59:1
Anzio 1968,Jl 25,26:1
Violent Four, The 1968,Ag 15,46:2
Barbarella 1968,O 12,43:1
Danger Diabolik 1968,D 12,62:6
De Laurentis, Luigi (Producer)
Hell Raiders of the Deep 1954,Jl 3,9:2
de Lavallade, Carmen
Lydia Bailey 1952,My 31,12:5
Demetrius and the Gladiators 1954,Je 19,9:1
De Leo, Alfred
Ring Around the Clock 1953,My 19,36:2
De Leon, Don Pedro
Dancer of Barcelona, The 1929,N 25,22:1
De Leon, Galvan
South Pacific 1958,Mr 20,33:1
De Leon, Gerardo (Director)
Terror is a Man 1960,Jl 14,23:1
Walls of Hell, The 1965,N 18,55:3
De Leon, Jack (Original Author)
Silent Witness, The 1932,F 8,21:1
de Leon, Jacques
Doulos-The Finger Man 1964,Mr 3,31:1
de Leon, Luis Perez
Heroes del Barrio, Los 1936,D 28,12:4
de Leon, Luisito Perez
Heroes del Barrio, Los 1936,D 28,12:4
de Leon, Manuel (Producer)
Badjao 1962,S 21,35:1
De Leon, Raoul
Third Voice, The 1960,Mr 7,24:5
Advise and Consent 1962,Je 7,31:2
Pleasure Seekers, The 1964,D 26,9:1
De Leon, Walter (Original Author)
Upstage 1926,N 15,19:1
De Leza, Marisa
Alexander the Great 1956,Mr 29,23:1
de Libero, Libero (Screenwriter)
Under the Olive Tree 1951,O 5,24:4
de Liguoro, Eugenio
Fast Set, The 1924,N 18,22:1
de Liguoro, Rina
Messalina 1924,Ag 25,16:2
Mystic Mirror, The 1928,O 1,23:1
Loves of Casanova, The 1929,Ap 30,33:2
Romance 1930,Ag 23,7:3

de Limur, Count
Arab, The 1924,Jl 14,11:5
de Limur, Jean (Director)
Letter, The 1929,Mr 8,30:1
Jealousy 1929,S 14,17:1
Slipper Episode, The 1938,My 19,25:2
De Linsky, Anna
Death Takes a Holiday 1934,F 24,18:4
De Lirio, Carmen
Backfire 1965,Ap 27,27:1
De Little, Johnny
Dream Maker, The 1964,Ap 23,34:1
De Lorde, Andre (Original Author)
Diary of a Chambermaid, The 1946,Je 23,28:2
de Lorenzo, Candida
Romance Tropical 1934,O 15,20:5
de Lorez, Claire
Queen of Sheba 1921,Ap 11,9:1
Beau Brummell 1924,Mr 31,20:1
Three Weeks 1924,Ap 1,19:3
So This Is Marriage 1924,D 23,16:2
My Wife and I 1925,My 20,26:2
Last Flight, The 1929,Je 17,29:1
Morgane, the Enchantress 1929,Je 21,17:2
De Los Arcos, Luis (Screenwriter)
Castilian, The 1963,O 3,31:1
de los Rios, Fernando (Miscellaneous)
Spain in Flames 1937,Ja 30,21:2
De Luca, Dino
Hey, Lets Twist 1962,F 8,25:1
De Luca, Lorella
Poor but Beautiful 1958,Je 11,39:4
Tailor's Maid, The; (Patri e Figli) 1959,S 2,35:4
De Lucio, Carmen
Morena Clara 1938,Je 18,18:3
Mad Queen, The 1950,O 27,24:3
De Luise, Dom
Glass Bottom Boat, The 1966,Je 10,54:1
Busy Body, The 1967,Je 8,52:2
What's so bad About Feeling Good? 1968,My 25,27:1
De Lullo, Giorgio
Professor, My Son 1949,Ap 18,18:4
Heart and Soul 1950,Je 15,41:3
de Luna, Alvaro
That Man in Istanbul 1966,My 19,51:2
De Lungo, Tony
Constant Nymph, The 1934,Ap 7,19:1
de Maigret, Liev
One Rainy Afternoon 1936,My 14,29:2
de Maigret, Live
China Seas 1935,Ag 10,16:4
de Malet, Hubert
Honorable Catherine, The 1948,Ag 23,13:3
de Malgret, Vanni
Arturo Island 1962,D 22,5:2
de Mandiargues, Andre Pieyre (Original Author)
Girl on a Motorcycle, The 1968,N 28,66:5
de March, Alme
Doulos-The Finger Man 1964,Mr 3,31:1
De Marco, Tony
Gang's All Here, The 1943,D 23,26:4
De Marco Sisters
Skirts Ahoy! 1952,My 29,17:2
de Marguenat, Jean (Director)
Miche 1932,D 2,27:4
Prince Jean, Le 1936,D 12,15:2
De Maris, Merrill (Screenwriter)
Snow White and the Seven Dwarfs 1938,Ja 14,21:1 (In Addenda)
De Marney, Derrick
Things to Come 1936,Ap 18,19:2
Victoria the Great 1937,O 29,19:1
Girl Was Young, The 1938,F 11,27:2
Pearls of the Crown, The 1938,Ap 12,26:2
Sixty Glorious Years 1938,N 18,25:2
Forbidden Music 1938,D 27,13:2
Lion Has Wings, The 1940,Ja 22,11:2
Suicide Squadron 1942,My 14,23:2
Spitfire 1943,Je 14,13:2
Frenzy 1946,Jl 20,10:3
Sleeping Car to Trieste 1949,Ap 18,18:6
Inheritance, The 1951,F 12,19:2
De Marney, Derrick (Producer)
Frenzy 1946,Jl 20,10:3
de Marney, Terence
Silver Chalice, The 1954,D 27,22:5
Target Zero 1955,N 16,43:2
Desert Sands 1955,N 19,22:7
Wreck of the Mary Deare, The 1959,N 7,27:1
Strange Affair, The 1968,Jl 25,26:2
de Marney, Terence (Screenwriter)
Wanted for Murder 1946,D 12,38:4
de Marney, Terrence
On the Double 1961,My 20,12:1
Separation 1968,Mr 26,41:2
De Martino, Ferruccio (Producer)
Aida 1954,N 12,17:1
De Masure, Louis (Producer)
Dog, a Mouse and a Sputnik, A; Pied, a Cheval et un Sputnik, A 1960,N 1,46:2

De Mattlazzis
Lullaby of Broadway 1951,Mr 27,35:2
De Mello, Susan
Open the Door and See all the People 1964,Ap 2,28:1
De Mendelssohn, P (Original Author)
Marianne of my Youth; (Marianne de ma Jeunesse) 1959,Ja 20,43:1
de Mendoza, Alberto
Adventures of Scaramouche, The 1964,N 23,34:1 (Incorrect in this edition; use 1964,N 21,34:1 elsewhere)
De Mendoza, Carlo
Dancer of Barcelona, The 1929,N 25,22:1
de Metz, Danielle
Jessica 1962,Ap 20,20:2
de Metz, Deanielle
Gidget Goes to Rome 1963,S 12,32:2
De Meulan
Face to the Wind 1951,Ja 16,34:2
De Mille, Cecil B (Director)
Ten Commandments, The 1956,N 9,35:2
De Mitri, Leonardo (Director)
Angelo in the Crowd 1952,O 4,15:2
Verginita 1953,Ap 18,17:2
De Mitri, Leonardo (Original Author)
Verginita 1953,Ap 18,17:2
De Mitri, Leonardo (Screenwriter)
Verginita 1953,Ap 18,17:2
De Montez, Rico
Brazil 1944,N 20,25:2
de Moraes, Vinicius (Original Author)
Black Orpheus 1959,D 22,41:1
de Murat, Ulysses Petit (Screenwriter)
Where Words Fail; Donde Mueren las Palabraso 1948,Ag 19,18:4
de Musset, Alfred (Original Author)
Rules of the Game, The 1961,Ja 19,26:1
de Neel, Germaine
Coming-Out Party 1934,Mr 17,11:3
de Nesi, Germaine
Buenaventura, La 1934,S 15,20:3
De Nicola, Francesco
Shoe-Shine 1947,Ag 27,19:2
De Niro, Robert
Greetings 1968,D 16,61:2
de Novara, Medea
Noche del Pecado, La 1933,D 26,19:4
Juarez y Maximiliano 1935,F 16,9:2
de Noyelle, Francis (Miscellaneous)
Annapurna 1953,D 14,45:4
de Nubila, Italia
Immortal Sergeant 1943,F 4,29:2
de Oliveira, Lourdes
Black Orpheus 1959,D 22,41:1
De Oliveira, Ubiracy
That Man From Rio 1964,Je 9,30:1
de Orduna, Juan (Director)
Mad Queen, The 1950,O 27,24:3
de Palma, Brian (Director)
Murder a la Mod 1968,My 2,57:1
Greetings 1968,D 16,61:2
de Palma, Brian (Miscellaneous)
Murder a la Mod 1968,My 2,57:1
de Palma, Brian (Screenwriter)
Murder a la Mod 1968,My 2,57:1
Greetings 1968,D 16,61:2
De Palma, Walter
Hollywood Cowboy 1937,Jl 24,12:1
De Pascale, Ugo
Roman Holiday 1953,Ag 28,13:1
de Pasquale, Frederic
Viol, Le 1968,S 20,42:1
De Pedrelli, Sylvio
Stolen Affections 1951,Mr 12,20:2
de Peyret-Chappuis, Charles (Screenwriter)
Vierge Folle, La 1938,D 30,11:3
Twilight 1949,D 30,13:2
de Phillips, Aicia
St Francis of Assisi 1947,Ap 5,12:5
de Pina, Albert (Screenwriter)
Joe Palooka, Champ 1946,Ap 6,10:6
De Pitra, D'Ariette (Screenwriter)
Crazy for Love 1960,N 26,13:2
de Poligny, Serge (Director)
As du Turf, Les; Acres of Turf 1935,My 11,21:3
Claudine 1940,Ap 1,15:2
Thirst of Men, The 1952,O 28,37:1
de Poligny, Serge (Screenwriter)
Thirst of Men, The 1952,O 28,37:1
De Poliolo, Dorothy
Avventura, L' 1961,Ap 5,30:1
de Pomes, Felix
Toda una Vida 1933,O 23,18:3
Dona Francisquita 1935,Ap 27,20:6
de Pomes, Isabel
Marcelino 1956,O 23,39:1
Man Who Wagged his Tail, The 1961,S 19,39:1
de Portago, Marquis
Sanders of the River 1935,Je 27,16:1

de Prorok, Byron Khun Count (Producer)
Lost Gods 1930,Jl 7,22:3
De Putti, Lya
Heart Thief, The 1927,Ap 27,22:5
Buck Privates 1928,Ja 30,18:1
Scarlet Lady, The 1928,Ag 15,19:4
Jealousy 1928,D 4,29:1
de Rahm, Whitney
White Heat 1934,Je 16,20:2
De Ramey, Pierre
Time to Love 1927,Je 23,23:3
Sinners in the Sun 1932,My 14,11:5
de Rasi, Ena
Passion of St Francis, The 1932,D 17,22:3
de Re, Michel
Sundays and Cybele 1962,N 13,43:3
Poupee, La 1963,Ag 28,39:1
Paris in the Month of August 1968,Ag 26,46:4
de Remer, Ruby
Fires of Faith 1919,My 6,16:2
Gorgeous Hussy, The 1936,S 5,7:1
de Remer, Rubye
Passionate Pilgrim, The 1921,Ja 3,20:2
Don't Marry for Money 1923,Ag 21,17:3
De Renz, Claudio
Sailor From Gibraltar, The 1967,Ap 25,38:2
de Ribon, Roberto (Director)
Man of the Sea 1948,Ja 24,11:2
De Rieux, Max
Cross of the Living 1963,F 5,5:5
De Riso, Arpad (Screenwriter)
Gioconda, La 1958,O 13,33:4
De Rita, Joe
Doughgirls, The 1944,Ag 31,14:1
Bravados, The 1958,Je 26,23:2
De Rita, Massimo (Screenwriter)
Violent Four, The 1968,Ag 15,46:2
de River, Jacqueline
Courageous Dr Christian, The 1940,Mr 29,25:3
De Robertis, Francesco (Director)
Angelo 1951,Mr 26,19:4
De Robertis, Francesco (Screenwriter)
Angelo 1951,Mr 26,19:4
de Roche, Charles
Shadows of Paris 1924,F 18,13:1
White Moth, The 1924,Je 16,18:3
Love and Glory 1924,Ag 5,10:2
Madame Sans Gene 1925,Ap 18,19:1
de Rochemont, Louis (Director)
Ramparts We Watch, The 1940,S 20,27:1
We Are the Marines 1942,D 14,19:2
de Rochemont, Louis (Miscellaneous)
First World War, The 1934,N 8,27:1
de Rochemont, Louis (Producer)
Ramparts We Watch, The 1940,S 20,27:1
We Are the Marines 1942,D 14,19:2
House on Ninety-Second Street, The
1945,S 27,24:7
13 Rue Madeleine 1947,Ja 16,30:2
Boomerang 1947,Mr 6,36:2
Lost Boundaries 1949,Jl 1,14:4
Whistle at Eaton Falls, The 1951,O 11,49:2
Walk East on Beacon 1952,My 29,17:2
Martin Luther 1953,S 10,22:1
Cinerama Holiday 1955,F 9,31:1
Man on a String 1960,My 21,15:1
Roman Spring of Mrs Stone, The 1961,D 29,11:1
de Rochemont, Louis (Screenwriter)
Cinerama Holiday 1955,F 9,31:1
de Rochemont, Louis 3d (Director)
Windjammer 1958,Ap 10,32:2
de Rochemont, Louis 3d (Producer)
Windjammer 1958,Ap 10,32:2
de Rochemont, Richard (Producer)
Story of the Vatican, The 1941,S 20,11:3
Golden Twenties, The 1950,Ap 10,15:2
If Moscow Strikes 1952,Ap 30,33:4
De Rodrigo, Solar (Original Author)
Dancer of Barcelona, The 1929,N 25,22:1
De Rolf, Paul
Seven Little Foys, The 1955,Je 30,18:2
De Rosa, A
Sainted Devil, A 1924,N 24,15:3
de Rothschild, Philippe (Original Author)
Lady Chatterley's Lover 1959,Jl 11,11:1
de Rouen, Reed
You Can't Fool an Irishman 1950,D 7,45:4
Sheriff of Fractured Jaw, The 1959,Mr 14,27:4
de Rouen, Reed (Original Author)
Miss Robin Hood 1953,Je 27,7:2
de Rouves, Nicole
Abused Confidence 1938,D 1,29:1
de Ruelle, Emile (Miscellaneous)
Flame of Love, The 1930,N 3,19:3
de Ruiz, Nick
Mademoiselle Midnight 1924,My 27,14:1
Forbidden Paradise 1924,N 17,16:1
Unknown, The 1927,Je 13,17:1
Rio Rita 1929,O 7,22:1
de Sa, Alfredo
Brazil 1944,N 20,25:2

De Sabata, Eliana (Screenwriter)
Love and Marriage (Saturday, July 18); Saturday,
July 18 (Love and Marriage) 1966,Ag 5,20:1
Love and Marriage (The Last Resort); Last Resort,
The (Love and Marriage) 1966,Ag 5,20:1
Love and Marriage (One Moment Is Enough); One
Moment Is Enough (Love and Marriage)
1966,Ag 5,20:1
Love and Marriage (The First Night); First Night,
The (Love and Marriage) 1966,Ag 5,20:1
de Sade, Marquis (Original Author)
Vice and Virtue 1965,Mr 18,25:1
de Sainte-Colombe, Paul (Screenwriter)
Outpost in Morocco 1949,Mr 25,28:3
De Santis, Giuseppe (Director)
Tragic Hunt 1948,O 22,30:2
Bitter Rice 1950,S 19,39:2
Under the Olive Tree 1951,O 5,24:4
Rome, 11 O'Clock 1953,Ap 30,39:2
Italiano Brava Gente 1966,F 4,20:1
De Santis, Giuseppe (Original Author)
Tragic Hunt 1948,O 22,30:2
Bitter Rice 1950,S 19,39:2
Under the Olive Tree 1951,O 5,24:4
Italiano Brava Gente 1966,F 4,20:1
De Santis, Giuseppe (Screenwriter)
Tragic Hunt 1948,O 22,30:2
Outcry 1949,Mr 14,15:5
Bitter Rice 1950,S 19,39:2
Under the Olive Tree 1951,O 5,24:4
Rome, 11 O'Clock 1953,Ap 30,39:2
Italiano Brava Gente 1966,F 4,20:1
De Santis, Joe
Slattery's Hurricane 1949,Ag 13,6:6
Man With a Cloak, The 1951,N 28,37:2
Deadline U S A 1952,Mr 15,8:2
Last Hunt, The 1956,Mr 1,37:2
Full of Life 1957,F 13,38:1
Dino 1957,Je 22,9:2
Unholy Wife, The 1958,Mr 7,17:1
Al Capone 1959,Mr 26,27:1
Cry Tough 1959,S 17,48:4
Cold Wind in August, A 1961,Jl 27,23:2
George Raft Story, The 1962,Mr 22,40:1
...And Now Miguel 1966,S 8,43:1
Professionals, The 1966,N 3,45:1
Venetian Affair, The 1967,Ja 19,41:2
Blue 1968,My 11,28:1
De Santis, Joe (Narrator)
Titan-Story of Michelangelo, The 1950,Ja 23,16:2
de Santis, Nanda
Mafia; (In Nome Della Legge) 1950,Mr 2,33:2
de Sarigny, Peter (Original Author)
Never Let Go 1963,Je 15,10:2
de Sarigny, Peter (Producer)
Malta Story 1954,Jl 17,7:2
Simba 1955,O 22,24:2
Waltz of the Toreadors 1962,Ag 14,34:1
Never Let Go 1963,Je 15,10:2
De Sarro, Raoul (Screenwriter)
Anthony of Padua 1952,Mr 29,19:2
Queen of Sheba, The 1953,N 4,29:3
De Sates, Francis
Majority of One, A 1962,Ja 12,29:2
de Sax, Guillaume
Carnival of Sinners 1947,Ap 8,34:2
de Saxe, Guillaume
Three Waltzes 1939,Ap 25,19:2
Clandestine 1948,My 24,23:2
De Selfa, Erin
Caravan 1949,Ap 21,30:4
de Sentmenat, Ramon
Incertidumbre 1936,S 21,26:5
de Sequeiros, Adela
Prisionero 13, El 1934,Ap 30,11:4
De Seta, Vittorio (Director)
Bandits of Orgosolo 1964,Ap 14,32:1
De Seta, Vittorio (Screenwriter)
Bandits of Orgosolo 1964,Ap 14,32:1
de Seversky, Alexander P Major (Miscellaneous)
Victory Through Air Power 1943,Jl 19,13:1
de Seversky, Alexander P Major (Original Author)
Victory Through Air Power 1943,Jl 19,13:1
De Shannon, Jackie
Surf Party 1964,Mr 12,40:4
C'mon Let's Live a Little 1967,My 4,34:1
de Shishmareff, Kyrill (Original Author)
Expensive Husbands 1938,Ja 8,19:3
De Sica, Vittorio
Passa L'Amore 1933,N 25,10:3
Tempo Massimo 1936,Mr 13,27:2
Canzione del Sole, La 1936,My 6,27:2
Amo Te Sola 1936,Jl 20,11:2
Mazurka di Papa, La 1940,My 10,26:7
Due Madri, Le; Two Mothers, The
1940,My 17,23:3
Manon Lescaut 1941,Ap 14,23:5
Lost in the Dark 1949,My 14,9:2
Peddlin' in Society 1950,F 23,33:3
Escape into Dreams 1950,Ap 13,34:5
Heart and Soul 1950,Je 15,41:3
My Widow and I 1950,Ag 30,27:5

De Sica, Vittorio— Cont
Doctor, Beware 1951,Ap 30,16:3
Miracle in Milan 1951,D 18,42:2
Tomorrow is too Late 1952,Ap 14,22:2
Times Gone By (The Trial of Frine); Trial of
Frine, The (Times Gone By) 1953,D 30,16:2
Earrings of Madame De, The 1954,Jl 20,15:5
Hello Elephant 1954,S 10,18:5
Bread, Love and Dreams 1954,S 21,24:1
Gran Varieta 1955,Ap 11,29:5
Bed, The (The Divorce); Divorce, The (The Bed)
1955,Je 8,26:4
Frisky 1955,O 25,37:3
Too Bad She's Bad 1955,D 26,23:2
Gold of Naples (The Gambler); Gambler, The
(Gold of Naples) 1957,F 12,30:1
Miller's Beautiful Wife, The 1957,Je 12,40:2
Scandal in Sorrento 1957,Je 13,37:1
It Happened in the Park 1957,Ag 13,23:2
Farewell to Arms, A 1958,Ja 25,14:1
Monte Carlo Story, The 1958,F 13,23:2
Bigamist, The 1958,My 12,25:1
Tailor's Maid, The; (Patri e Figli) 1959,S 2,35:4
Holiday Island; (Vacanzie a Izchia)
1959,S 22,46:1
Anatomy of Love 1959,S 29,46:2
Always Victorious 1960,Ap 7,46:1
It Started in Naples 1960,S 3,7:6
Angel Wore Red, The 1960,S 29,32:1
Fast and Sexy 1960,O 6,51:4
General Della Rovere 1960,N 22,41:1
Millionairess, The 1961,F 10,19:1
Wonders of Aladdin, The 1961,D 23,16:1
Lafayette 1963,Ap 11,29:1
Amorous Adventures of Moll Flanders, The
1965,My 27,28:1
Biggest Bundle of Them All, The 1968,Ja 18,46:1
Shoes of the Fisherman, The 1968,N 15,40:3
De Sica, Vittorio (Director)
Shoe-Shine 1947,Ag 27,19:2
Bicycle Thief, The 1949,D 13,44:2
Doctor, Beware 1951,Ap 30,16:3
Indiscretion of an American Wife 1954,Je 26,7:2
Umberto D 1955,N 8,37:1
Gold of Naples (The Gambler); Gambler, The
(Gold of Naples) 1957,F 12,30:1
Gold of Naples (Theresa); Theresa (Gold of
Naples) 1957,F 12,30:1
Gold of Naples (The Racketeer); Racketeer, The
(Gold of Naples) 1957,F 12,30:1
Gold of Naples (Pizza on Credit); Pizza on Credit
(Gold of Naples) 1957,F 12,30:1
Roof, The 1959,My 13,43:4
Two Women; (Ciociara, La) 1961,My 9,43:2
Boccaccio '70 (The Raffle); Raffle, The (Boccaccio
'70) 1962,Je 27,40:1
Condemned of Altona, The 1963,O 31,26:1
Yesterday, Today, and Tomorrow (Part III-Mara
Rome); Mara Rome (Yesterday, Today and
Tomorrow) 1964,Mr 18,46:1
Yesterday, Today and Tomorrow (Part 1-Adelina
Naples); Adelina Naples (Yesterday, Today and
Tomorrow) 1964,Mr 18,46:1
Yesterday, Today and Tomorrow (Part II-Anna
Milan); Anna Milan (Yesterday, Today and
Tomorrow) 1964,Mr 18,46:1
Marriage Italian Style 1964,D 21,42:1
Young World, A 1966,My 17,52:1
After the Fox 1966,D 24,11:1
Woman Times Seven 1967,Je 28,38:1
De Sica, Vittorio (Miscellaneous)
Fast and Sexy 1960,O 6,51:4
De Sica, Vittorio (Original Author)
Escape into Dreams 1950,Ap 13,34:5
De Sica, Vittorio (Producer)
Indiscretion of an American Wife 1954,Je 26,7:2
Roof, The 1959,My 13,43:4
De Sica, Vittorio (Screenwriter)
Doctor, Beware 1951,Ap 30,16:3
Umberto D 1955,N 8,37:1
Gold of Naples (The Racketeer); Racketeer, The
(Gold of Naples) 1957,F 12,30:1
Gold of Naples (Theresa); Theresa (Gold of
Naples) 1957,F 12,30:1
Gold of Naples (The Gambler); Gambler, The
(Gold of Naples) 1957,F 12,30:1
Gold of Naples (Pizza on Credit); Pizza on Credit
(Gold of Naples) 1957,F 12,30:1
De Silva, Aura
Sutter's Gold 1936,Mr 27,25:2
De Silva, Enrico
Shoe-Shine 1947,Ag 27,19:2
de Silva, Fred
Sea Hawk, The 1924,Je 3,22:1
Rainbow Trail, The 1925,Je 3,26:4
de Silva, Nancy
Forest Ring, The 1930,Ap 26,11:1
de Sousa, Henrique
Voyage of Silence 1968,S 12,54:1
De Souza, Edward
Phantom of the Opera, The 1962,Ag 23,25:2
Kiss of the Vampire 1963,O 10,49:2

de Souza, Waldetar
Black Orpheus 1959,D 22,41:1

de Stephanie, Joseph
Twelve Crowded Hours 1939,F 24,15:2

De Sylva, B G (Composer)
Sunny Side Up 1929,O 4,24:5
Just Imagine 1930,N 22,21:3
My Weakness 1933,S 22,14:1
Love Affair 1939,Mr 17,25:2
If You Knew Susie 1948,F 23,19:2
Lullaby of Broadway 1951,Mr 27,35:2

De Sylva, B G (Miscellaneous)
Just Imagine 1930,N 22,21:3

De Sylva, B G (Original Author)
Sunny Side Up 1929,O 4,24:5
Follow Thru 1930,S 13,9:3
My Weakness 1933,S 22,14:1
Bottoms Up 1934,Mr 23,29:2
Have a Heart 1934,O 20,20:2
Born to Dance 1936,D 5,16:1
Louisiana Purchase 1942,Ja 1,37:1
Panama Hattie 1942,O 2,31:2
Du Barry Was a Lady 1943,Ag 20,13:1

De Sylva, B G (Producer)
Under the Pampas Moon 1935,My 31,11:1
Doubting Thomas 1935,Jl 11,24:2
Rage of Paris 1938,Jl 2,10:2
Bachelor Mother 1939,Je 30,17:2
Caught in the Draft 1941,Je 26,27:3
Aloma of the South Seas 1941,Ag 28,23:4
Birth of the Blues 1941,D 11,39:1
Louisiana Purchase 1942,Ja 1,37:1
For Whom the Bell Tolls 1943,Jl 15,25:2
Lady in the Dark 1944,F 23,17:1
Stork Club, The 1945,D 20,18:2

De Sylva, B G (Screenwriter)
Stork Club, The 1945,D 20,18:2

De Sylva, Brown, Henderson (Composer)
Bill and Coo 1948,Mr 29,17:4

De Taranto, Vito
Barber of Seville, The 1947,My 6,35:2
Forza del Destino, La 1952,O 17,33:1
Cinderella 1953,My 15,20:2
Tosca 1958,O 24,40:3

de Tillere, Christian
Army Game, The; Tire Au Flanc
1963,Ap 24,40:1

de Tolignac, Maston (Screenwriter)
Hearts of the World 1918,Ap 5,13:1

de Toth, Andre (Director)
None Shall Escape 1944,Ap 7,23:2
Dark Waters 1944,N 22,25:2
Other Love, The 1947,My 15,32:4
Ramrod 1947,Je 30,25:6
Pitfall 1948,Ag 25,31:2
Slattery's Hurricane 1949,Ag 13,6:6
Carson City 1952,Je 14,12:2
Springfield Rifle 1952,O 23,40:2
House of Wax 1953,Ap 11,15:2
Stranger Wore a Gun, The 1953,Jl 30,20:3
Thunder Over the Plains 1953,D 10,64:4
Crime Wave 1954,Ja 13,26:2
Riding Shotgun 1954,Ap 2,22:2
Tanganyika 1954,Je 19,9:2
Indian Fighter, The 1955,D 22,20:1
Monkey on my Back 1957,My 30,23:2
Two-Headed Spy, The 1959,Mr 3,38:4
Man on a String 1960,My 21,15:1
Morgan the Pirate 1961,Jl 20,32:2

de Toth, Andre (Original Author)
Gunfighter, The 1950,Je 24,7:2

de Toth, Andre (Producer)
Billion Dollar Brain 1967,D 23,29:1

De Toth, Andre (Screenwriter)
Paper Lion 1968,O 24,54:1

De Triana, Rosita
Strangers in the City 1962,Jl 17,19:2

de Unamuno, Miguel (Original Author)
Tia Tula, A 1965,Je 3,24:1

de Valdes, Francois B (Miscellaneous)
Rumba 1935,F 25,13:2

de Valdez, Carlos
Little Man, What Now? 1934,Je 1,29:1
Robin Hood of El Dorado, The 1936,Mr 14,10:1
Langer Spy 1937,N 4,29:1
Romance in the Dark 1938,Mr 21,18:2
Blockade 1938,Je 17,25:1
Suez 1938,O 15,21:2
British Intelligence 1940,F 12,14:2

De Valesco, Mercedes
Behind That Curtain 1929,Jl 1,31:2

de Vargas, Valentin
Touch of Evil 1958,My 22,25:2
Hatari 1962,Jl 12,19:1

De Varney, E J
Gambling 1934,D 4,22:3

De Vaull, Billie
Lights of Old Broadway 1925,N 2,20:1

De Vaux, Renee
Rhodes 1936,F 29,11:1

De Vega, Jose
West Side Story 1961,O 19,39:3

de Vesa, Leonardo
His Tiger Lady 1928,My 28,23:2

de Vilbiss, Robert
Reno 1924,Ja 8,27:1

De Villalonga, Jose Louis
Hired Killer, The 1967,Mr 2,30:3

de Villalonga, Jose Luis
Lovers, The 1959,O 27,40:2
Cleo From 5 to 7 1962,S 5,43:4
Any Number Can Win 1963,O 9,47:2
Naked Autumn 1963,N 15,25:3
Don't Tempt the Devil 1964,Ap 28,43:1
Darling 1965,Ag 4,20:1
Juliet of the Spirits 1965,N 4,57:1

de Vilmorin, Louise (Original Author)
Earrings of Madame De, The 1954,Jl 20,15:5
Julietta 1957,Je 18,38:2

de Vilmorin, Louise (Screenwriter)
Love and the Frenchwoman; (Francaise et
l'Amour, La) 1961,F 28,38:2

De Viovanni, Augusto
Dottor Antonio, Il 1939,D 7,35:1

de Vogt, Carl
Waterloo 1929,Ap 16,32:5
Lumpenball 1931,Ap 27,25:1
Wenn am Sonntagabend die Dorfmusik Spielt
1935,D 9,25:3

de Vogth, Hans Otto
Moritz Macht Sein Glueck 1932,D 24,11:4

De Vol (Composer)
Glass Bottom Boat, The 1966,Je 10,54:1

De Vonde, Chester (Original Author)
West of Zanzibar 1928,D 31,9:1
Kongo 1932,N 17,22:5

De Vorska, Jesse
Last Parade, The 1931,Mr 2,19:1
Women of all Nations 1931,My 30,9:2
Transatlantic 1931,Jl 31,15:2
Spider, The 1931,S 5,7:4
Blessed Event 1932,S 3,16:2

De Voto, Bernard (Original Author)
Across the Wide Missouri 1951,N 7,35:4

De Vries, Henri
Cleopatra 1917,O 15,11:2
White Cargo 1930,F 24,18:1

De Vries, Peter (Original Author)
Tunnel of Love 1958,N 22,27:4

De Warfaz, George
Captivation 1931,S 28,17:4
French Leave 1931,D 7,16:1
Sleeping Car to Trieste 1949,Ap 18,18:6
Beau Brummell 1954,O 21,31:5

de Wilde, Brandon
Member of the Wedding, The 1952,D 31,10:2
Shane 1953,Ap 24,30:3
Night Passage 1957,Jl 25,28:1
Blue Denim 1959,Jl 31,21:1
All Fall Down 1962,Ap 12,41:3
Hud 1963,My 29,36:1
In Harm's Way 1965,Ap 7,36:1
Those Calloways 1965,Ap 15,38:2

de Winton, Albert
Love Parade, The 1929,N 20,32:6

de Wit, Jacqueline
Dragon Seed 1944,Jl 21,16:4
Men in her Diary 1945,S 24,16:5
That Night With You 1945,N 9,16:2
Saratoga Trunk 1945,N 22,39:2
Little Giant 1946,My 9,27:5
She Wrote the Book 1946,Je 20,20:3
Something in the Wind 1947,Ag 29,14:3
Snake Pit, the 1948,N 5,29:2
It's a Great Feeling 1949,Ag 13,6:6
Chinatown at Midnight 1949,N 18,35:3
Damned Don't Cry, The 1950,Ap 8,9:2
Great Jewel Robber, The 1950,Ag 4,13:2
First Legion, The 1951,Ap 28,9:2
Carrie 1952,Jl 17,20:2
She's Back on Broadway 1953,Mr 12,24:2
All That Heaven Allows 1956,F 29,35:1
Tea and Sympathy 1956,S 28,24:4
Twice Told Tales (The House of the Seven
Gables); House of the Seven Gables, The (Twice
Told Tales) 1964,My 28,40:1
Harper 1966,Mr 31,43:1

De Witt, Jennings
Deadwood Coach, The 1925,Ja 21,19:3

de Wohl, Louis (Original Author)
Crime Over London 1938,Jl 28,23:2
Francis of Assisi 1961,Jl 29,8:2

De Wolf, Francis
Under Capricorn 1949,S 9,28:3
Treasure Island 1950,Ag 16,24:2
Gay Lady, The 1951,Ap 16,21:2
Christmas Carol, A 1951,N 29,41:2
Tom Brown's School Days 1952,Ja 8,23:5
Ivanhoe 1952,Ag 1,8:2
Miss Robin Hood 1953,Je 27,7:2
Diamond Wizard, The 1954,Jl 17,7:4
Little Kidnappers, The 1954,S 2,18:1
Naked Heart, The 1955,Mr 9,22:4

De Wolf, Francis — Cont
Moby Dick 1956,Jl 5,18:1
Wee Geordie 1956,O 8,31:1
Saint Joan 1957,Je 27,21:1
Smallest Show on Earth, The 1957,N 23,11:2
Roots of Heaven, The 1958,O 16,46:1
Hounds of the Baskervilles, The 1959,Jl 4,9:4
House of Fright 1961,Ag 24,25:4
From Russia with Love 1964,Ap 9,25:1
2nd Best Secret Agent in the Whole Wide World,
The 1966,Ap 28,49:1

De Wolf, Karen (Miscellaneous)
Notorious Gentleman, A 1935,F 16,9:1

De Wolf, Karen (Original Author)
Go West, Young Lady 1941,N 24,11:6
Return of October, The 1949,F 23,31:2

De Wolf, Karen (Screenwriter)
Hot Water 1937,N 5,19:4
Walking Down Broadway 1938,Ap 1,17:3
Passport Husband 1938,Ag 5,11:2
Safety in Numbers 1938,S 6,17:2
Always in Trouble 1938,N 3,27:1
Blondie Goes Latin 1941,F 26,17:3
Go West, Young Lady 1941,N 24,11:6
Getting Gertie's Garter 1946,F 4,21:2
Cockeyed Miracle, The 1946,O 25,28:1
Bury Me Dead 1947,O 25,13:3
Adventures of Casanova 1948,Mr 22,18:3
Slightly French 1949,My 27,25:3
Johnny Allegro 1949,My 31,19:2
Holiday in Havana 1949,O 14,33:5
Count the Hours 1953,Je 24,30:4
Appointment in Honduras 1953,N 19,41:4
Silver Lode 1954,Jl 24,6:6

De Wolfe, Billy
Dixie 1943,Je 24,26:2
Duffy's Tavern 1945,S 6,23:3
Miss Susie Slagle's 1946,F 7,29:2
Our Hearts Were Growing Up 1946,Ag 12,17:2
Blue Skies 1946,O 17,28:2
Dear Ruth 1947,Je 11,33:3
Perils of Pauline, The 1947,Jl 10,17:2
Isn't It Romantic? 1948,O 7,35:2
Dear Wife 1950,F 2,31:2
Tea for Two 1950,S 2,11:2
Lullaby of Broadway 1951,Mr 27,35:2
Dear Brat 1951,Jl 5,21:2
Call Me Madam 1953,Mr 26,37:1
Billie 1965,S 16,55:3

de Wolfe, Elsie
Democracy, The Vision Restored 1920,Ag 25,6:4

De Wolfe, Marie
Kingdom of Youth, The 1918,O 7,11:3

De Wood, Lorraine
Bullfighters, The 1945,My 12,10:3

de Xandovai, Guerrero
Carmen 1928,My 7,29:1

de Zarate, Ortiz
Romeo and Juliet 1944,Je 17,10:3

Dea, Marie
Personal Column 1941,F 3,13:2
Devil's Own Envoy, The 1947,Ag 30,8:6
Foolish Husbands 1948,O 11,27:2
Orpheus 1950,N 30,42:2
Caroline Cherie 1954,My 25,23:1
Two Are Guilty 1964,F 29,12:1

Deacon, Michael
Kind of Loving, A 1962,O 2,46:1

Deacon, Richard
Desiree 1954,N 18,42:1
My Sister Eileen 1955,S 23,21:1
Good Morning, Miss Dove 1955,N 24,41:1
Hot Blood 1956,Mr 24,14:2
Francis in the Haunted House 1956,Jl 21,9:2
Power and The Prize, the 1956,S 27,42:1
Solid Gold Cadillac, The 1956,O 25,40:3
Spring Reunion 1957,My 6,25:2
Nice Little Bank That Should Be Robbed, A
1958,D 11,17:4
Remarkable Mr Pennypacker, The 1959,F 21,25:2
Young Philadelphians, The 1959,My 22,32:1
Dear Heart 1965,Mr 8,33:1
John Goldfarb, Please Come Home
1965,Mr 25,42:4
That Darn Cat 1965,D 3,44:1
Gnome-Mobile, The 1967,Jl 20,30:2
Enter Laughing 1967,Ag 1,24:1
One and Only Genuine Original Family Band,
The 1968,Mr 22,55:1

Deagneaux
Battle of the Rails; (Bataille Du Rail)
1949,D 27,27:2

DEAL
See Also DIAL, DIEHL

Deal, Borden (Original Author)
Wild River 1960,My 27,22:1

DEAN
See Also DEANE, DEHN, DANE

Dean, Barbara
Peter Ibbetson; (Forever) 1921,O 17,18:1

Dean, Barney
Thanks for the Memory 1938,D 8,34:3

Dean, Barney (Miscellaneous)
Duffy's Tavern 1945,S 6,23:3
Dean, Barry
Whistle Down the Wind 1962,Ap 23,34:2
Dean, Basil (Director)
Constant Nymph, The 1929,Je 10,23:1
Return of Sherlock Holmes, The 1929,O 19,22:6
Escape 1930,N 1,23:2
Perfect Alibi, The 1931,Ap 20,16:3
Woman in Chains 1932,N 21,21:1
Constant Nymph, The 1934,Ap 7,19:1
Autumn Crocus 1934,O 25,26:2
Loyalties 1934,O 26,25:1
21 Days Together 1940,My 23,28:4
Mozart 1940,O 4,29:2
Dean, Basil (Original Author)
Constant Nymph, The 1943,Jl 24,8:2
Dean, Basil (Producer)
Perfect Alibi, The 1931,Ap 20,16:3
Mozart 1940,O 4,29:2
Laburnum Grove 1941,D 2,29:2
Dean, Basil (Screenwriter)
Constant Nymph, The 1934,Ap 7,19:1
21 Days Together 1940,My 23,28:4
Dean, Dinky
Pilgrim, The 1923,F 26,15:1
Dean, Don
Native Son 1951,Je 18,19:2
Dean, Isabel
One Woman's Story 1949,My 18,33:2
Gilbert and Sullivan 1953,O 28,36:3
Woman's Angle, The 1954,Ag 27,11:6
Virgin Island 1960,Mr 24,39:5
Light in the Piazza 1962,F 8,25:1
High Wind in Jamaica, A 1965,Je 17,27:2
Man Could Get Killed, A 1966,My 12,54:2
Inadmissible Evidence 1968,Je 24,44:1
Dean, James
East of Eden 1955,Mr 10,33:1
Rebel without a Cause 1955,O 27,28:3
Giant 1956,O 11,51:1
Dean, Jean
Pirate, The 1948,My 21,19:2
Dean, Jo Ann
Silver Skates 1943,Mr 19,15:3
Dean, Joel
Blondie Meets the Boss 1939,Ap 27,31:1
Dean, Julia
How Molly Made Good 1915,O 20,5:5
Curse of the Cat People, The 1944,Mr 4,11:1
Experiment Perilous 1944,D 30,15:2
O S S 1946,My 27,15:5
Magic Town 1947,O 8,29:2
Nightmare Alley 1947,O 10,31:3
Emperor Waltz, The 1948,Je 18,19:2
Girl's School 1950,F 3,29:2
People Will Talk 1951,Ag 30,20:1
Elopement 1951,D 21,21:3
Dean, Man Mountain
Reckless 1935,Ap 20,16:1
Gladiator, The 1938,Ag 29,10:2
Surprise Package 1960,O 15,26:2
Dean, Margia
Ringside 1949,S 17,10:8
Baron of Arizona, The 1950,Je 23,29:2
Sins of Jezebel 1954,Ja 9,12:2
Villa 1958,D 24,00:0
Big Show, The 1961,My 11,42:4
Seven Women From Hell 1962,F 1,22:2
Dean, Priscilla
Two-Soul Woman, The 1918,Ap 29,11:1
Paid in Advance 1919,D 1,9:3
Virgin of Stamboul, The 1920,Mr 28,V,9:1
Wild Honey 1922,F 28,17:4
Under Two Flags 1922,S 25,10:2
Drifting 1923,Ag 20,4:2
Siren of Seville, The 1924,N 17,16:1 (In Addenda)
Cafe in Cairo, A 1925,Mr 18,19:2
Crimson Runner, The 1925,My 27,26:2
Outside the Law 1926,My 12,31:1
Dean, Quentin
In the Heat of the Night 1967,Ag 3,26:1
Young Runaways, The 1968,S 12,54:3
Dean, William A
Panic in the Streets 1950,Ag 5,9:2
DEANE
See Also DEHN, DANE, DEAN
Deane, Philip (Narrator)
Mr Kennedy, Mr Reagan and the Big, Beautiful, Beleaguered American Dream 1967,N 23,58:1
Deane, Richard
Nurse Edith Cavell 1939,S 22,27:4
Swamp Woman 1941,D 27,15:2
Deane, Shirley
King of Burlesque 1936,Ja 16,25:2
Charlie Chan at the Circus 1936,Mr 19,22:4
Educating Father 1936,Je 20,22:2
Girls' Dormitory 1936,Ag 29,16:2
One in a Million 1937,Ja 1,19:3
Off to the Races 1937,F 6,15:2
Nancy Steele is Missing 1937,Mr 8,22:1
Big Business 1937,Je 1,27:2

Hot Water 1937,N 5,19:4
Trip to Paris, A 1938,Je 10,18:2
Safety in Numbers 1938,S 6,17:2
Deane, Sidney
America 1924,F 22,20:1
Deane, Verna
Lady Lies, The 1929,S 7,15:1
Deans, Marjorie (Screenwriter)
Tenth Man, The 1937,N 15,15:2
Dear, Elizabeth
Loss of Innocence 1961,N 22,27:1
Battle of the Villa Fiorita, The 1965,My 27,28:1
Dear, Michael
Oliver Twist 1951,Jl 31,17:2
Dearden, Basil (Director)
They Came to a City 1945,F 19,21:3
Half-Way House 1945,Ag 13,22:4
Dead of Night 1946,Je 29,22:6
Captive Heart, The 1947,Ap 28,27:2
Frieda 1947,Ag 15,12:3
Saraband 1949,Je 13,16:3
Blue Lamp, The 1951,Ja 9,25:1
Pool of London 1951,N 28,37:2
Case of Gold 1952,Ja 19,13:3
Cage of Gold 1952,Ja 19,13:3
I Believe in You 1953,My 5,34:3
Gentle Gunman, The 1953,O 1,34:3
Ship That Died of Shame, The 1956,Ag 21,33:2
Out of the Clouds 1957,Ag 1,20:4
Smallest Show on Earth, The 1957,N 23,11:2
Sapphire 1959,N 3,27:1
Man in the Moon 1961,Je 13,29:2
Victim 1962,F 6,27:2
Mind Benders, The 1963,My 2,40:2
Woman of Straw 1964,O 1,30:6
Masquerade 1965,Ap 29,40:2
Khartoum 1966,Jl 14,28:1
Walk in the Shadow 1966,S 12,52:5
Only When I Larf 1968,O 24,55:3
Dearden, Basil (Producer)
I Believe in You 1953,My 5,34:3
Gentle Gunman, The 1953,O 1,34:3
Ship That Died of Shame, The 1956,Ag 21,33:2
Out of the Clouds 1957,Ag 1,20:4
Mad Little Island 1958,D 31,12:1
Victim 1962,F 6,27:2
Masquerade 1965,Ap 29,40:2
Dearden, Basil (Screenwriter)
They Came to a City 1945,F 19,21:3
Train of Events 1952,My 26,18:4
I Believe in You 1953,My 5,34:3
Ship That Died of Shame, The 1956,Ag 21,33:2
Dearden, Harold (Original Author)
Interference 1928,N 17,23:1
Dearholt (Original Author)
Tundra 1936,D 3,31:2
Dearing, Dorothy
Up the River 1938,D 3,11:2
Wife, Husband and Friend 1939,F 25,19:2
Blue Bird, The 1940,Ja 20,11:2
Free, Blonde and 21 1940,Ap 5,25:2
Girl in 313 1940,Je 14,25:3
Great Profile, The 1940,O 18,25:1
Dearing, Edgar
Jazz Age, The 1929,Ja 7,36:2
Free and Easy 1930,Ap 19,15:1
Man From Wyoming, A 1930,Jl 12,16:4
Abraham Lincoln 1930,Ag 26,24:1
Rainmakers, The 1935,N 2,13:2
Sky Parade, The 1936,Ap 20,17:1
Swing Time 1936,Ag 28,21:2
They Gave Him a Gun 1937,My 14,21:1
Married Before Breakfast 1937,Jl 23,16:2
Big City 1937,S 17,29:2
It Happened in Hollywood 1937,O 2,18:1
Thanks For Everything 1938,D 10,13:2
Honolulu 1939,F 23,19:2
Nick Carter, Master Detective 1939,D 14,35:2
Sailor's Lady 1940,Je 29,12:2
Cross Country Romance 1940,Jl 19,22:3
When the Daltons Rode 1940,Ag 23,13:3
No Time for Comedy 1940,S 7,9:2
Little Bit of Heaven, A 1940,N 8,24:2
Caught in the Draft 1941,Je 26,27:3
Wings for the Eagle 1942,Ag 1,14:3
Star Spangled Rhythm 1942,D 31,20:1
It Came From Outer Space 1953,Je 18,38:2
Pollyanna 1960,My 20,26:1
Dearing, R E (Producer)
Madonna of the Seven Moons 1946,My 23,18:4
Dearly, Max
Madame Borary 1934,N 19,13:2
Dernier Milliardaire, Le 1935,O 30,16:2
Miserables, Les 1936,O 28,31:2
Claudine 1940,Ap 1,15:2
They Met on Skis 1940,D 23,23:2
Nine Bachelors 1942,F 9,19:2
Dearman, Glyn
Christmas Carol, A 1951,N 29,41:2
Tom Brown's School Days 1952,Ja 8,23:5
Four Sided Triangle 1953,My 16,10:1

Dearman, Jennifer
Four Sided Triangle 1953,My 16,10:1
Dearth, John
Circle of Deception 1961,F 18,12:2
Dease, John
Pacific Adventure 1947,N 26,18:2
Deatsch, David (Producer)
Nothing but the Best 1964,Jl 14,28:1
Debain, Henri
Maternelle, La 1935,O 15,19:1
Debar, Andree
Seven Deadly Sins, The (Envy); Envy (The Seven Deadly Sins) 1953,My 12,31:3
House on the Waterfront, The 1959,F 21,25:2
DeBecker, Harold
Sherlock Holmes and the Secret Weapon 1943,Ja 5,15:2
Lodger, The 1944,Ja 20,15:3
Debelka, Frantisek
Firemen's Ball, The 1968,S 30,60:1
Debene, Floren
Nobleza Gaucha; Gaucho Chivalry 1938,Ap 2,18:2
DeBenning, Burr
Beach Red 1967,Ag 4,18:1
Sweet November 1968,F 9,55:1
DeBlasio, Edward (Original Author)
Legend of Lylah Clare, The 1968,Ag 23,33:1
Debonairs, The
Priorities on Parade 1942,Jl 23,19:2
Debord, Michel
Masculine Feminine 1966,S 19,57:1
Debrai, Eddy
Crossroads 1939,Mr 14,17:5
DeBrey, Claire
Man and his Money, A 1919,Ap 14,11:4
Juke Box Jenny 1942,Ap 17,21:3
Debroy, Helen
Life and Death of Colonel Blimp, The 1945,Mr 30,18:2
Debucourt, Jean
Mistigri 1933,Ja 13,19:3
Agonie des Aigles, L' 1934,D 1,8:5
Prince Jean, Le 1936,D 12,15:2
Mayerling 1937,S 14,27:1
Life and Loves of Beethoven, The 1937,N 22,15:1
Mayerling to Sarajevo 1940,O 30,27:6
Idiot, The 1948,F 5,26:2
Not Guilty 1948,Ap 23,28:2
Monsieur Vincent 1948,D 21,33:2
Eagle with Two Heads 1948,D 30,24:2
Man to Men 1949,F 21,20:2
Woman Who Dared, The 1949,Mr 19,10:7
Devil in the Flesh 1949,My 10,29:2
Love Story 1949,Je 27,18:4
Tainted 1950,Ja 21,10:2
Secret of Mayerling, The 1951,My 8,39:2
Justice Is Done 1953,Mr 3,23:2
Seven Deadly Sins (Pride); Pride (The Seven Deadly Sins) 1953,My 12,31:3
Golden Coach, The 1954,Ja 22,30:2
Desperate Decision 1954,N 9,31:5
Doctors, The 1956,Ag 7,19:2
Nana 1957,Ap 13,12:3
Light Across the Street, The; Lumiere d'en Face, La 1957,Jl 30,20:2
Inspector Maigret 1958,O 9,47:1
Witches of Salem 1958,D 9,54:2
Miracle of Saint Therese 1959,F 10,38:4 (In Addenda)
Debully, Jean-Claude
S O S Mediterranean 1940,Ja 1,29:2
Decae, Henri (Cinematographer)
Circle of Love 1965,Mr 25,42:4
Bonnes Femmes, Les 1966,My 13,32:1
Decaitre, Marie
Olive Trees of Justice, The 1967,My 5,31:1
DeCamp, Rosemary
Cheers for Miss Bishop 1941,Mr 14,17:2
Hold Back the Dawn 1941,O 2,29:1
Jungle Book 1942,Ap 6,19:1
Yankee Doodle Dandy 1942,My 30,9:1
Eyes in the Night 1942,O 16,23:1
This Is the Army 1943,Jl 29,11:6
Merry Monahans, The 1944,O 13,16:2
Bowery to Broadway 1944,N 30,19:2
Practically Yours 1945,Mr 29,18:2
Rhapsody in Blue 1945,Je 28,22:2
Blood on the Sun 1945,Je 29,12:2
Pride of the Marines 1945,Ag 25,7:3
Danger Signal 1945,N 22,39:2
Too Young to Know 1945,D 8,21:2
From This Day Forward 1946,Ap 20,16:2
Two Guys From Milwaukee 1946,Jl 27,12:5
Nora Prentiss 1947,F 22,16:2
Life of Riley, The 1949,Ag 18,18:4
Night Unto Night 1949,Je 11,11:2
Look for the Silver Lining 1949,Je 24,29:2
Story of Seabiscuit, The 1949,N 12,8:4
Big Hangover, The 1950,My 26,20:3
Night Into Morning 1951,Je 11,20:7
On Moonlight Bay 1951,Jl 27,15:2

DeCamp, Rosemary— Cont

Scandal Sheet 1952,Ja 17,23:1
By the Light of the Silvery Moon
  1953,Mr 27,28:2
So This Is Love 1953,Ag 12,22:1
Main Street to Broadway 1953,O 14,34:1
Commandos Strike at Dawn 1954,Ja 14,25:1
Many Rivers to Cross 1955,F 24,21:2
Strategic Air Command 1955,Ap 21,33:1
13 Ghosts 1960,Ag 6,9:2

DeCamp, Victor
Harmony Lane 1935,O 24,19:4

DeCarlo, Vinnie
Harder They Fall, The 1956,My 10,26:3

Decaux, Annie
Belle Americaine, La 1961,D 18,42:1

Decaux, Lucile (Miscellaneous)
Katia 1939,D 23,9:2

Decazes, Pierre
Shameless Old Lady, The 1966,S 27,52:1

Dechamps, Charles
Indiscretions 1939,My 1,21:1
Oh, Amelia 1951,D 3,22:2

Decharme, Paul-Edmond (Producer)
Manon 1950,D 26,19:1
Miquette 1951,F 5,18:2
Bay of the Angels; Baie des Anges, La
  1964,N 24,44:1
Banana Peel; Peau de Banane 1965,Ja 19,29:1
Backfire 1965,Ap 27,27:1
Tender Scoundrel 1967,N 16,58:2

Decker, Diana
Meet Me at Dawn 1948,My 18,26:2
Lovers, Happy Lovers 1954,O 1,19:2
Will any Gentleman? 1955,S 28,70:6
Lolita 1962,Je 14,23:2

Decker, Gene
Foreign Intrigue 1956,Jl 13,23:2

Decker, Karen
Imitation of Life 1959,Ap 18,18:1

Decker, Marge (Screenwriter)
To Please a Lady 1950,O 27,24:3

Deckers, Eugene
Sleeping Car to Trieste 1949,Ap 18,18:6
Mrs Fitzherbert 1950,My 11,37:2
Madeleine 1950,S 1,17:2
So Long at the Fair 1951,Ja 22,14:2
Golden Salamander 1951,Mr 24,8:3
Tony Draws a Horse 1951,My 15,38:6
Hotel Sahara 1952,Ja 1,21:4
Night Without Stars 1953,Jl 14,19:4
Port Afrique 1956,N 3,27:5
Flame Over India 1960,Ap 30,14:1

DeClercq, Kuulei
Hurricane, The 1937,N 10,31:2

Decoin, Henri (Director)
Abused Confidence 1938,D 1,29:1
Mademoiselle ma Mere 1939,S 19,29:2
Her First Affair; (Children of Paradise)
  1947,F 20,32:3
She Returned at Dawn; Retour a l'Aube
  1947,Ag 1,21:5
Not Guilty 1948,Ap 23,28:2
Monelle 1950,F 3,29:2
Between Eleven and Midnight 1950,F 23,33:3
Au Grand Balcon 1951,My 5,14:2
Lovers of Toledo, The 1954,Ap 10,11:3
Paris Incident 1954,Ag 18,20:2
Bed, The (The Billet); Billet, The (The Bed)
  1955,Je 8,26:4
One Step to Eternity 1955,O 3,22:2
Inside a Girls' Dormitory 1956,F 6,27:7
Razzi 1957,N 19,39:4
Folies Bergere 1958,My 28,37:2
Cat, The 1959,Ap 13,35:1
Love and the Frenchwoman; (Francaise et
  l'Amour, La) 1961,F 28,38:2

Decoin, Henri (Original Author)
Folies Bergere 1958,My 28,37:2

Decoin, Henri (Producer)
Not Guilty 1948,Ap 23,28:2
Devil's Daughter 1949,F 26,11:2

Decoin, Henri (Screenwriter)
Soir de Rafle, Un 1931,O 16,27:1
Abused Confidence 1938,D 1,29:1
Her First Affair; (Children of Paradise)
  1947,F 20,32:3
Devil's Daughter 1949,F 26,11:2
Between Eleven and Midnight 1950,F 23,33:3
One Step to Eternity 1955,O 3,22:2
Inside a Girls' Dormitory 1956,F 6,27:7
Razzi 1957,N 19,39:4
Cat, The 1959,Ap 13,35:1

Decombie, Guy
Francois Villon 1950,Jl 3,9:2
Jour de Fete 1952,F 20,26:4
Inspector Maigret 1958,O 9,47:1
400 Blows, The; (Les Quatre Cents Coups)
  1959,N 17,41:1
Cousins, The (Les Cousins) 1959,N 24,44:1

Decroux, Etienne
Enfants du Paradis, Les 1947,F 20,32:2
Voyage Surprise 1948,F 14,17:3

Decsey, Ernst (Original Author)
King Steps Out, The 1936,My 29,15:2

Dediseff, L
Storm Over Asla 1930,S 8,17:1

Dee, Ann
Thoroughly Modern Millie 1967,Mr 23,25:1

Dee, Blanche
Hallelujah the Hills 1963,D 17,49:1

Dee, Frances
Playboy of Paris 1930,N 1,23:2
June Moon 1931,Mr 14,23:2
American Tragedy, An 1931,Ag 6,22:5
Rich Man's Folly 1931,N 27,29:3
This Reckless Age 1932,Ja 9,21:1
Nice Women 1932,F 20,11:2
Strange Case of Clara Deane, The
  1932,My 6,15:3
Love Is a Racket 1932,Je 11,9:3
Night of June 13th, The 1932,S 17,18:4
If I Had a Million 1932,D 3,21:4
King of the Jungle 1933,F 25,20:3
Crime of the Century, The 1933,Mr 13,18:2
Silver Cord, The 1933,My 5,18:1
One Man's Journey 1933,S 1,15:2
Headline Shooters 1933,O 23,18:3
Blood Money 1933,N 16,30:5
Little Women 1933,N 17,22:3
Coming-Out Party 1934,Mr 17,11:3
Finishing School 1934,Ap 30,11:4
Of Human Bondage 1934,Je 29,17:1
Becky Sharp 1935,Je 14,27:2
Gay Deception, The 1935,O 11,31:1
Half Angel 1936,My 30,7:3
Souls at Sea 1937,Ag 10,23:2
Wells Fargo 1937,D 30,15:2
Wells Fargo 1938,Ja 16,X,5:1 (In Addenda)
If I Were King 1938,S 29,31:1
So Ends our Night 1941,F 28,17:2
Man Betrayed, A 1941,Mr 27,29:5
I Walked With a Zombie 1943,Ap 22,31:5
Happy Land 1943,D 9,33:3
Patrick the Great 1945,Ap 13,15:2
Private Affairs of Bel Ami, The 1947,Je 16,25:4
Four Faces West 1948,Ag 4,18:3
Payment on Demand 1951,F 16,21:2
Because of You 1952,D 4,47:3
Mister Scoutmaster 1953,Ag 29,10:1

Dee, Joey
Hey, Lets Twist 1962,F 8,25:1
Two Tickets to Paris 1962,N 29,46:5

Dee, Ruby
Jackie Robinson Story, The 1950,My 17,36:1
No Way Out 1950,Ag 17,23:1
Tall Target, The 1951,S 28,26:2
Go, Man, Go 1954,Mr 10,29:5
Edge of the City 1957,Ja 30,33:2
St Louis Blues 1958,Ap 12,13:1
Virgin Island 1960,Mr 24,39:5
Take a Giant Step 1961,Mr 6,28:2
Raisin in the Sun, A 1961,Mr 30,24:1
Balcony, The 1963,Mr 22,7:1
Gone are the Days! 1963,S 24,43:2
Incident, The 1967,N 6,65:1
Up Tight 1968,D 19,62:1

Dee, Ruby (Screenwriter)
Up Tight 1968,D 19,62:1

Dee, Sandra
Until They Sail 1957,O 9,41:2
Reluctant Debutante, The 1958,Ag 15,17:1
Stranger in my Arms 1959,Mr 4,34:2
Imitation of Life 1959,Ap 18,18:1
Gidget 1959,Ap 23,27:4
Summer Place, A 1959,O 23,24:1
Portrait in Black 1960,Jl 28,19:1
Romanoff and Juliet 1961,Je 9,26:1
Tammy Tell me True 1961,Jl 27,23:2
Come September 1961,S 8,34:1
If a Man Answers 1962,N 22,43:1
Tammy and the Doctor 1963,Je 27,23:2
Take Her, She's Mine 1963,N 14,41:1
I'd Rather Be Rich 1964,S 3,24:2
That Funny Feeling 1965,O 21,57:2
Man Could Get Killed, A 1966,My 12,54:2
Doctor, You've Got to be Kidding
  1967,My 11,50:1
Rosie 1968,F 8,36:1

Dee, Sandra (Narrator)
Snow Queen, The 1960,Ap 14,34:1

Deel, Kale
Time Limit 1957,O 24,37:2

Deeley, Ben
Victory 1919,D 28,4:4
Acquittal, The 1923,D 12,24:5

Deeley, Michael (Producer)
One Way Pendulum 1965,Mr 3,34:3
Robbery 1967,S 28,58:2

Deem, Lola
Pirate, The 1948,My 21,19:2

Deeming, Marianne
Across the Bridge 1957,O 30,24:1
Victors, The 1963,D 20,21:2

Deene, Carol
Dream Maker, The 1964,Ap 23,34:1

Deeping, Warwick (Original Author)
Sorrell and Son 1927,N 14,26:1
Doomsday 1928,Ap 2,25:1
Kitty 1929,Je 11,27:2
Sorrell and Son 1934,My 29,22:1

Deer, Don (Original Author)
Hoodlum Priest, The 1961,Ap 3,28:5

Deer, Don (Screenwriter)
Hoodlum Priest, The 1961,Ap 3,28:5

Deer, Louis
Unseeing Eyes 1923,O 22,17:1

Deering, Elizabeth
Faces 1968,S 23,42:4

Deering, John
Forgotten Commandments 1932,Je 2,25:2

Deering, Marda
Night Life of the Gods 1935,F 23,14:6

Deering, Olive
Samson and Delilah 1949,D 22,29:2
Caged 1950,My 20,8:6
Ten Commandments, The 1956,N 9,35:2

Deering, Patricia
Lady Lies, The 1929,S 7,15:1

Deering, Rex
Life at the Top 1965,D 15,53:1

Deery, Jack
Disraeli 1929,O 3,27:5

Defoe, Daniel (Original Author)
Adventures of Robinson Crusoe, The
  1954,Ag 6,10:5
Robinson Crusoe on Mars 1964,Ag 27,28:2
Amorous Adventures of Moll Flanders, The
  1965,My 27,28:1

Defore, Don
Male Animal, The 1942,Mr 28,11:1

DeFore, Don
Wings for the Eagle 1942,Ag 1,14:2

Defore, Don
You Can't Escape Forever 1942,O 17,11:1
Human Comedy, The 1943,Mr 3,19:2
Guy Named Joe, A 1943,D 24,17:2
Thirty Seconds Over Tokyo 1944,N 16,19:1
Affairs of Susan, The 1945,Mr 29,18:2
You Came Along 1945,Jl 5,7:2
Stork Club, The 1945,D 20,18:2
Without Reservations 1946,Je 8,17:2
It Happened on Fifth Avenue 1947,Je 11,33:2
Ramrod 1947,Je 30,25:6
Romance on the High Seas 1948,Je 26,10:5
One Sunday Afternoon 1948,D 27,16:3
Too Late for Tears 1949,Ag 15,12:3
My Friend Irma 1949,S 29,39:2
Dark City 1950,O 19,40:5
Southside 1-1000 1950,N 3,31:2
Guy Who Came Back, The 1951,Ag 17,13:2
Girl in Every Port, A 1952,F 14,23:1
No Room for the Groom 1952,Je 14,12:2
She's Working her Way Through College
  1952,Jl 10,27:2
Jumping Jacks 1952,Jl 24,30:2
Battle Hymn 1957,F 16,14:1
Time to Love and a Time to Die, A
  1958,Jl 10,22:1
Facts of Life, The 1961,F 11,27:1

Defoucault, Gilberte
Pardon my French 1952,Mr 31,17:2

Dega, Igor
My Wild Irish Rose 1947,D 25,32:2

Degan, Werner
We Lived Through Buchenwald 1947,Jl 24,27:3

Degas, Brian (Screenwriter)
Barbarella 1968,O 12,43:1
Danger Diabolik 1968,D 12,62:6

DeGaw, Boyce (Original Author)
Don't Bet on Blondes 1935,Jl 20,16:2
Ice-Capades 1941,S 25,29:1

DeGaw, Boyce (Screenwriter)
Don't Bet on Blondes 1935,Jl 20,16:2
Moon's our Home, The 1936,My 13,29:2
Wings Over Honolulu 1937,My 29,20:1
Girl of the Golden West, The 1938,Mr 25,15:2
Behind the News 1941,Ja 16,25:3
Lady for a Night 1942,F 12,27:2

Degermark, Pia
Elvira Madigan 1967,S 30,26:1
Elvira Madigan 1967,O 31,37:2

Deghy, Guy
Mr Emmanuel 1945,Ja 8,15:2
Surprise Package 1960,O 15,26:2
Matter of Who, A 1962,Jl 25,29:2
Dark of the Sun 1968,Jl 4,13:1
Duffy 1968,S 17,50:3

Degischer, Vilma
Embezzled Heaven 1959,Ap 24,23:1

DeGradi, Don (Screenwriter)
Lt Robin Crusoe, USN 1966,Jl 14,28:1

DeGrasse, Sam
Sis 1919,Mr 3,11:2
Sis Hopkins 1919,Mr 3,11:2
Heart o' the Hills 1919,D 1,9:3
Blind Husbands 1919,D 8,20:4

DeGrasse, Sam— Cont
Devil's Pass Key, The 1920,Ag 9,6:3
Robin Hood 1922,O 31,15:4 (In Addenda)
Circus Days 1923,Ag 6,14:2
Spoilers, The 1923,Ag 6,14:2
In the Palace of the King 1923,D 3,14:1
Tiger Rose 1923,D 3,14:1
Courtship of Myles Standish, The 1923,D 31,9:3
Painted People 1924,Ja 29,16:1
Sun Up 1925,Ag 18,14:3
Mike 1926,Ja 11,33:1
When a Man Loves 1927,F 4,16:6
King of Kings, The 1927,Ap 20,29:2
Captain Salvation 1927,Je 27,25:2
Fighting Eagle, The 1927,Ag 15,22:5
Wreck of the Hesperus, The 1927,N 28,18:5
Man Who Laughs, The 1928,Ap 28,12:3
Honor Bound 1928,Ap 30,18:3
Racket, The 1928,Jl 9,25:1
Our Dancing Daughters 1928,O 8,14:2
Last Performance, The 1929,N 4,28:1
Wall Street 1929,N 25,22:1
Captain of the Guard 1930,Mr 29,23:1

DeHaven, Carter
Close to Nature 1919,Ag 18,9:2
Why Divorce? 1919,O 13,16:3
Beating Cheaters 1920,Je 14,13:2
Twin Beds 1920,N 1,13:2
Ringer for Dad, A 1923,Mr 5,15:3
Great Dictator, The 1940,O 16,29:1
30 Years of Fun 1963,D 26,33:4

DeHaven, Carter (Producer)
Dead Heat on a Merry-Go-Round 1966,O 13,50:1

DeHaven, Carter Jr
Courage 1930,My 23,21:1

DeHaven, Carter Mrs
Close to Nature 1919,Ag 18,9:2
Why Divorce? 1919,O 13,16:3
Twin Beds 1920,N 1,13:2
Ringer for Dad, A 1923,Mr 5,15:3

DeHaven, Gloria
Susan and God 1940,Jl 12,11:2
Penalty, The 1941,Ap 10,29:3
Best Foot Forward 1943,Je 30,25:2
Thousands Cheer 1943,S 14,27:1
Broadway Rhythm 1944,Ap 14,24:6
Two Girls and a Sailor 1944,Je 15,16:1
Step Lively 1944,Jl 27,14:1
Thin Man Goes Home, The 1945,Ja 26,16:5
Between Two Women 1945,Mr 29,18:3
Summer Holiday 1948,Je 12,8:5
Scene of the Crime 1949,Jl 29,12:2
Doctor and the Girl, The 1949,O 31,20:2
Yes Sir, That's my Baby 1949,N 11,31:2
Yellow Cab Man, The 1950,Mr 27,19:2
Three Little Words 1950,Ag 10,21:2
Summer Stock 1950,S 1,17:2
I'll Get by 1950,N 2,39:3
Two Tickets to Broadway 1951,N 22,47:2
Down Among the Sheltering Palms 1953,Je 13,11:2
So This Is Paris 1955,F 12,11:1

DeHaven, Robert
Gallant Journey 1946,O 10,33:2

Dehelly, Paula
Angels of the Streets 1950,Ja 17,24:2
Up From the Beach 1965,Je 10,38:1

Dehelly, Suzanne
Crise est Finie, La 1935,Mr 14,18:1
Her First Affair; (Children of Paradise) 1947,F 20,32:3
Au Grand Balcon 1951,My 5,14:2
Prize, The 1952,Ap 30,33:2
Night is my Kingdom, The 1953,S 30,37:1
Pit of Loneliness 1954,Ap 9,19:2

Deher, Paul (Original Author)
Seven Days to Noon 1950,D 19,41:3

Dehl, Gladys
Smiling Along 1939,F 20,13:2

DEHN
See Also DANE, DEAN, DEANE

Dehn, Dorothy
So This Is College 1929,N 9,22:5

Dehn, Paul (Screenwriter)
Orders to Kill 1958,N 18,41:2
Goldfinger 1964,D 22,36:1
Spy Who Came in From the Cold, The 1965,D 24,24:1
Night of the Generals, The 1967,F 3,38:1
Taming of the Shrew, The 1967,Mr 9,43:1

Dehner, John
Blonde Savage 1947,O 4,9:2
Barbary Pirate 1949,O 28,29:3
Mary Ryan, Detective 1949,N 4,33:3
Bodyhold 1949,D 12,29:4
Last of the Buccaneers 1950,D 15,43:2
Texas Rangers, The 1951,Jl 14,7:2
Lorna Doone 1951,S 21,19:4
Ten Tall Men 1951,O 27,10:5
Scaramouche 1952,My 9,20:2
California Conquest 1952,Je 7,22:6
Plymouth Adventure 1952,N 14,20:3
Man on a Tightrope 1953,Je 5,19:1

Powder River 1953,Jl 4,7:2
Gun Belt 1953,Ag 1,8:2
Apache 1954,Jl 10,7:2
Southwest Passage 1954,S 11,11:2
Prodigal, The 1955,My 14,10:7
King's Thief, The 1955,Ag 13,7:2
Carousel 1956,F 17,13:1
Fastest Gun Alive, The 1956,Jl 13,23:3
Trooper Hook 1957,Jl 13,11:2
Left Handed Gun, The 1958,My 8,36:2
Man of the West 1958,O 2,44:3
Canadians, The 1961,Je 1,31:1
Sign of Zorro, The 1961,S 5,37:6
Chapman Report, The 1962,O 18,49:2

Dehner, John (Narrator)
Cowboy, The 1954,Ag 3,14:2

Dei, Diana
I Cadetti di Guascogna 1952,O 6,22:2

Deiderfield, R F (Original Author)
All Over the Town 1949,My 26,34:4

Deighton, Len (Original Author)
Ipcress File, The 1965,Ag 3,35:1
Funeral in Berlin 1966,D 23,17:1
Billion Dollar Brain 1967,D 23,29:1
Only When I Larf 1968,O 24,55:3

Deighton, Len (Producer)
Only When I Larf 1968,O 24,55:3

Dein, Dr (Director)
Shack out on 101 1956,Ja 10,26:2

Dein, Edward (Miscellaneous)
Leopard Man, The 1943,My 20,26:4

Dein, Edward (Original Author)
Pistol Packin' Mama 1943,D 20,27:4
Gallant Blade 1948,O 13,31:3

Dein, Edward (Screenwriter)
Falcon Strikes Back, The 1943,Ap 2,17:4
Gals, Inc 1943,Ag 13,13:4
Pistol Packin' Mama 1943,D 20,27:4
Calling Dr Death 1944,F 12,11:3
Jungle Woman 1944,Jl 15,19:6
Soul of a Monster, The 1944,S 9,12:4
Fighting Guardsman, The 1945,O 6,9:6
Cat Creeps, The 1946,My 18,12:4
Shack out on 101 1956,Ja 10,26:2

Dein, Mildred (Screenwriter)
Shack out on 101 1956,Ja 10,26:2

Deischsit, Maly
Meine Frau, Die Hochstaplerin 1932,F 6,14:4

Deishaft, Maly
Verklungene Traume 1930,D 9,31:3

Deitz, Susi
Girls Behind Bars 1950,My 10,41:2

deKerekjarto, Duci
Rich, Young and Pretty 1951,Jl 26,17:3

Dekker, Albert
Great Garrick, The 1937,O 25,23:1
She Married an Artist 1938,F 25,15:2
Lone Wolf in Paris, The 1938,My 23,21:2
Marie Antoinette 1938,Ag 17,23:2
Hotel Imperial 1939,My 11,31:3
Man in the Iron Mask, The 1939,Jl 14,11:1
Beau Geste 1939,Ag 3,15:2
Dr Cyclops 1940,Ap 11,32:3
Strange Cargo 1940,Ap 26,25:2
Rangers of Fortune 1940,S 19,27:2
Seven Sinners 1940,N 18,23:2
You're the One 1941,F 20,23:2
Reaching for the Sun 1941,My 8,21:1
Honky Tonk 1941,O 3,27:3
Buy Me That Town 1941,O 23,27:2
Among the Living 1941,D 13,25:2
Lady Has Plans, The 1942,Mr 5,27:1
In old California 1942,Je 18,25:3
Night in New Orleans 1942,Jl 2,25:2
Wake Island 1942,S 2,19:2
Great Commandment, The 1942,O 17,11:1
Forest Rangers, The 1942,O 22,25:2
Once Upon a Honeymoon 1942,N 13,28:1
Kansan, The 1943,O 1,15:3
In old Oklahoma 1943,D 6,21:1
Woman of the Town, The 1944,Mr 6,17:2
Experiment Perilous 1944,D 30,15:2
Salome, Where She Danced 1945,My 3,27:1
Incendiary Blonde 1945,Jl 26,13:2
Hold That Blonde 1945,N 8,17:2
Suspense 1946,Jl 5,15:3
Killers, The 1946,Ag 29,24:2
Two Years Before the Mast 1946,S 25,39:2
California 1947,Ja 15,31:2
Slave Girl 1947,Jl 18,21:3
Wyoming 1947,Jl 25,12:5
Pretender, The 1947,Ag 12,26:2
Cass Timberlane 1947,N 7,20:2
Gentleman's Agreement 1947,N 12,36:2
Fabulous Texan, The 1947,D 26,22:5
Lulu Belle 1948,Je 21,18:3
Fury at Furnace Creek 1948,Jl 12,11:2
Tarzan's Magic Fountain 1949,F 7,15:2
Bride of Vengeance 1949,Ap 7,38:2
Kid From Texas, The 1950,Je 2,26:2
Furies, The 1950,Ag 17,23:2
As Young as You Feel 1951,Ag 3,10:6
Wait Till the Sun Shines, Nellie 1952,Je 28,12:2

Dekker, Albert— Cont
Silver Chalice, The 1954,D 27,22:5
East of Eden 1955,Mr 10,33:1
Illegal 1955,O 29,12:6
Sound and the Fury, The 1959,Mr 28,11:1
These Thousand Hills 1959,My 7,36:1
Middle of the Night 1959,Je 18,36:1
Wonderful Country, The 1959,N 5,39:7
Suddenly, Last Summer 1959,D 23,22:1
Come Spy with Me 1967,F 22,21:1

Dekker, Albert (Narrator)
Leonardo Da Vinci 1952,N 21,21:5

Dekobra, Maurice (Original Author)
Madonna of the Sleeping Cars, The 1929,O 14,20:2
Friends and Lovers 1931,N 7,16:5
Secret Document-Vienna 1954,Mr 29,22:4

Dekock, Alain
Cartouche 1964,Jl 22,39:1

Dekock, Marc
Big Chief, The 1960,Ap 27,32:1

Dekormos, Wera
Run With the Devil 1963,Jl 16,25:1

del Campo, Enrique
El Escandalo 1934,S 22,12:3
Fantasma del Convento, El; Fantasy of the Monastery 1935,Ap 22,14:3

Del Carril, Hugo
Dark River 1956,F 27,19:4

Del Carril, Hugo (Director)
Dark River 1956,F 27,19:4

Del Carril, Hugo (Producer)
Dark River 1956,F 27,19:4

del Duca, Cino (Producer)
Avventura, L' 1961,Ap 5,30:1

Del Ducca, Robert (Miscellaneous)
Ernst Thaelmann: Fighter Against Fascism 1934,S 20,20:3

Del Fabro, Iolanda
Voice in Your Heart, A 1952,F 23,7:5

Del Gado, Ramon
Sword of the Avenger 1948,Ag 26,16:4

Del Giudice, Filippo (Producer)
Hungry Hill 1947,O 11,11:2

Del Grosso, Domigio (Original Author)
300 Spartans, The 1962,S 20,29:2

Del Grosso, Remigio (Screenwriter)
Pharaohs' Woman, The 1962,Ap 19,35:2

Del Guercio, Ann
Bachelor Flat 1962,Ja 13,14:1

Del Guidice, Filippo (Miscellaneous)
Hamlet 1948,S 30,32:2

del Lago, Alicia
Roots, The (The Filly); Filly, The (The Roots) 1957,S 3,23:2
Bravados, The 1958,Je 26,23:2

Del Mar, Xenia
It Happened in Athens 1962,N 15,46:2

Del Monaco, Mario
Man With the Grey Glove, The 1953,Ja 3,11:2
Young Caruso, The 1953,O 13,34:4
Cavalleria Rusticana 1953,D 28,17:2
House of Ricordi 1956,Mr 13,32:1
Beautiful but Dangerous 1958,F 6,24:1

del Moral, Jorge
Vuelo de la Muerte, El 1935,Ap 16,27:3

Del Poggio, Carla
Tragic Hunt 1948,O 22,30:2
Bandit, The 1949,Je 7,26:3
Lost Youth 1949,O 27,35:4
Without Pity; (Senza Pieta) 1950,Mr 16,40:4
Mill on the Po, The 1951,O 23,35:2
Rome, 11 O'Clock 1953,Ap 30,39:2
Variety Lights; Luci del Varieta 1965,My 7,34:1

Del Poze, Angel
Place Called Glory, A 1966,Ag 11,27:4

Del Rey, Geraldo
Given Word, The 1964,Mr 25,47:1

Del Rey, Philar
Kid From Texas, The 1950,Je 2,26:2

Del Rey, Pilar
...And Now Miguel 1966,S 8,43:1

Del Rio, Ascension Trio
Three Caballeros, The 1945,F 5,20:1

Del Rio, Diana
Remember Pearl Harbor 1942,Je 4,22:4

Del Rio, Dolores
Joanna 1925,D 15,14:5
What Price Glory 1926,N 24,26:4
Resurrection 1927,My 17,27:2
Loves of Carmen 1927,S 27,31:1
Gateway of the Moon, The 1928,Ja 9,20:1
Trail of '98, The 1928,Mr 21,30:3
Ramona 1928,My 15,17:3
Red Dance, The 1928,Je 26,29:1
Revenge 1928,D 10,25:1
Evangeline 1929,Jl 29,23:3
Bad One, The 1930,Je 13,28:3
Girl of the Rio 1932,Ja 9,21:1
Bird of Paradise 1932,S 10,18:5
Flying Down to Rio 1933,D 22,25:2
Wonder Bar 1934,Mr 1,23:2
Madame Du Barry 1934,O 25,26:2
In Caliente 1935,Je 27,16:1

Del Rio, Dolores— Cont
I Live for Love 1935,O 19,21:2
Accused 1936,D 17,35:1
Devil's Playground 1937,F 15,12:5
Lancer Spy 1937,N 4,29:1
International Settlement 1938,F 12,20:3
Man From Dakota, The 1940,F 22,29:2
Journey Into Fear 1943,Mr 19,15:3
Maria Candelaria 1944,S 12,23:7
Flor Sylvestre 1945,Ja 16,17:2
Fugitive, The 1947,D 26,22:2
Flaming Star 1960,D 17,19:1
Cucaracha, La 1961,N 2,42:1
Cheyenne Autumn 1964,D 24,8:1
More Than a Miracle 1967,N 2,58:2

Del Rio, Evelyn
Bank Dick, The 1940,D 13,29:2
Aloma of the South Seas 1941,Ag 28,23:4

del Rio, Grazia
Rubacuori 1932,Mr 5,11:2

Del Rio, Jack
Between Midnight and Dawn 1950,O 2,19:2

Del Rio, Teresa
Alexander the Great 1956,Mr 29,23:1

Del Ruth, Hampton (Director)
First Auto, The 1927,Je 28,28:4

Del Ruth, Roy (Director)
Footloose Widows 1926,Je 22,21:2
Wolf's Clothing 1927,Mr 28,26:4
If I Were Single 1928,Mr 5,21:1
Terror, The 1928,Ag 16,25:3
Conquest 1929,F 11,26:3
Desert Song, The 1929,My 2,20:6
Gold Diggers of Broadway, The 1929,Ag 31,13:4
Aviator, The 1930,Ja 11,21:3
Hold Everything 1930,Ap 23,24:1
Second Story Murder, The 1930,My 3,23:1
Three Faces East 1930,S 6,9:2
Life of the Party, The 1930,N 10,16:2
My Past 1931,Mr 12,22:7
Divorce Among Friends 1931,Ap 2,30:4
Maltese Falcon, The 1931,My 29,26:5
Side Show 1931,S 19,10:2
Blonde Crazy 1931,D 4,28:2
Taxi 1932,Ja 8,27:3
Beauty and the Boss 1932,Ap 2,13:2
Winner Take All 1932,Je 18,9:2
Blessed Event 1932,S 3,16:2
Employees' Entrance 1933,Ja 21,10:6
Mind Reader, The 1933,Ap 7,22:4
Little Giant, The 1933,My 27,11:5
Captured 1933,Ag 18,18:3
Bureau of Missing Persons 1933,S 9,9:2
Lady Killer 1934,Ja 1,28:2
Upper World 1934,My 25,25:4
Bulldog Drummond Strikes Back 1934,Ag 16,20:2
Kid Millions 1934,N 12,17:2
Folies Bergere 1935,F 25,13:2
Broadway Melody of 1936 1935,S 19,28:1
Thanks a Million 1935,N 14,17:1
Homme des Folies Bergere, L' 1936,Ap 18,19:3
Private Number 1936,Je 12,19:1
Born to Dance 1936,D 5,16:1
On the Avenue 1937,F 5,17:3
Broadway Melody of 1938 1937,S 3,12:1
Happy Landing 1938,Ja 22,19:1
My Lucky Star 1938,S 10,20:2
Tail Spin 1939,F 11,13:2
Star Maker, The 1939,Ag 31,14:2
Here I Am a Stranger 1939,S 30,11:2
He Married his Wife 1940,Ja 20,11:2
Topper Returns 1941,Mr 28,26:6
Chocolate Soldier, The 1941,N 1,20:2
Maisie Gets her Man 1942,Jl 16,23:2
Du Barry Was a Lady 1943,Ag 20,13:1
Broadway Rhythm 1944,Ap 14,24:6
Barbary Coast Gent 1944,S 29,18:2
It Happened on Fifth Avenue 1947,Je 11,33:2
Babe Ruth Story, The 1948,Jl 29,17:2
Always Leave Them Laughing 1949,N 24,48:2
Red Light 1950,Ja 16,18:4
West Point Story, The 1950,D 23,11:3
On Moonlight Bay 1951,Jl 27,15:2
Starlift 1951,D 15,11:2
About Face 1952,My 24,15:3
Stop, You're Killing Me 1952,D 11,45:3
Phantom of the Rue Morgue 1954,Mr 20,10:5

Del Ruth, Roy (Producer)
It Happened on Fifth Avenue 1947,Je 11,33:2
Babe Ruth Story, The 1948,Jl 29,17:2
Red Light 1950,Ja 16,18:4

Del Signore, Gino
Cinderella 1953,My 15,20:2

Del Sordo, Alfonso
Two Cents Worth of Hope 1952,D 16,44:2

Del Val, Jean
Sainted Devil, A 1924,N 24,15:3
Sea Legs 1930,N 11,29:1
Women Men Marry 1931,Jl 13,13:5
Magnificent Lie, The 1931,Jl 25,11:6
Passionate Plumber, The 1932,Mr 12,19:5
Flying Deuces, The 1939,N 24,29:2

Mystery Sea Raider 1940,Ag 26,11:4
Secret Agent of Japan 1942,Mr 23,19:3
For Whom the Bell Tolls 1943,Jl 15,25:2
Paris After Dark 1943,O 23,11:1
Molly and Me 1945,My 26,18:2
Spider, The 1946,Je 21,20:3
So Dark the Night 1946,D 7,16:2
Return of Monte Cristo, The 1947,Ja 3,16:4
Last of the Buccaneers 1950,D 15,43:2
Hitch-Hiker, The 1953,Ap 30,39:3
Little Boy Lost 1953,S 22,38:2
Funny Face 1957,Mr 29,16:1
Fantastic Voyage 1966,S 8,43:1

Del Valle, Raul
Dark River 1956,F 27,19:4

Del Vando, Amapola
Cowboy 1958,F 20,29:5

del Vando, Poppy A
Golden Hawk, The 1952,O 18,16:4

Delac, Charles (Producer)
David Golder 1932,O 20,24:2

DeLacey, Jack
Making of O'Malley 1925,Je 22,10:2

Delafield, E M (Miscellaneous)
Moonlight Sonata 1938,My 10,17:2

Delahere, Michael
Alphaville 1965,O 26,49:1

Delahaye, Agnes (Producer)
End of Desire 1962,Jl 10,29:2
Pickpocket 1963,My 22,36:2
Trial of Joan of Arc, The 1965,F 12,19:1

Delaine, Heather
Hue and Cry 1951,Ja 9,25:2

Delair, Suzy
Murderer Lives at Number 21, The 1947,Ag 18,12:3
Vie de Boheme, La 1947,N 28,37:4
Jenny Lamour 1948,Mr 6,17:2
Confessions of a Rogue 1948,Mr 30,26:3
Lady Paname 1951,Mr 20,35:4
Utopia 1954,D 15,41:1
Fernandel the Dressmaker 1957,Jl 1,19:2
Gervaise 1957,N 12,46:1
Rocco and his Brothers 1961,Je 28,40:2
Is Paris Burning? 1966,N 11,36:1

DeLaira, Diane
Human Desire 1954,Ag 7,7:2

Delaitre, Marcel
That They May Live 1939,N 7,31:2
Heritage 1940,N 5,33:2
Corbeau, Le; Raven, The 1948,F 24,21:1
Mr Orchid; Pere Tranquille, Le 1948,Mr 29,17:3
Royal Affair, A; (Roi, Le) 1950,Mr 9,25:2

Delamare, Gil
One Step to Eternity 1955,O 3,22:2

Delamare, Jean-Philippe
Man Escaped, A 1957,Ag 27,33:2

Delamare, Lise
Pension Mimosas 1936,My 6,27:1
Marseillaise 1939,N 6,20:2
Symphonie Fantastique, La 1947,D 8,35:2
Mlle Desiree 1948,N 19,35:2
Monsieur Vincent 1948,D 21,33:2
Wicked Duchess, The 1949,N 5,10:5
Grand Maneuver, The 1956,O 2,39:1
Foxiest Girl in Paris 1958,S 20,10:6
Bernadette of Lourdes 1962,Ja 30,20:2
Bernadette of Lourdes 1962,Ja 30,20:2

Delamater, Eleanor (Original Author)
Big Business 1937,Je 1,27:2

Delancy, Henriette
Daughter of Israel, A 1928,My 21,25:1

DELANEY
See Also DELANY

Delaney, Charles
Those Who Dance 1924,Je 30,16:1
Frisco Sally Levy 1927,Ap 13,29:4
Main Event, The 1927,O 31,22:1
Thirteenth Hour, The 1927,N 28,18:5
Lovelorn, The 1927,D 19,30:1
Cohens and the Kellys In Paris, The 1928,F 6,12:3
After the Storm 1928,My 8,25:3
Air Circus, The 1928,S 3,14:2
Home James 1928,S 11,31:3
Show Girl 1928,N 5,26:1
Hard to Get 1929,S 28,17:3
Girl From Woolworth's, The 1929,D 21,17:1
Man Hunter, The 1930,Ap 5,23:3
Millie 1931,F 7,11:1
Elmer the Great 1933,My 26,24:2
Corruption 1933,Je 20,22:7
Kansas Raiders 1951,Ja 26,19:2

Delaney, Iris
This Freedom 1923,N 28,15:1

Delaney, Jere
Lights of New York 1928,Jl 9,25:1

Delaney, Jerry
Regular Girl, A 1919,N 11,13:3

Delaney, Joan
President's Analyst, The 1967,D 22,44:4

Delaney, M (Director)
Moment of Truth, The 1954,Ap 27,36:2

Delaney, Maureen
Odd Man Out 1947,Ap 24,30:2
Captain Boycott 1947,D 6,11:2
Under Capricorn 1949,S 9,28:3
Saints and Sinners 1949,S 12,17:2
Holly and the Ivy, The 1954,F 5,16:1
Third Key, The 1957,Je 3,30:2
Doctor's Dilemma, A 1958,D 18,2:7

Delaney, Pauline
Rooney 1958,Je 6,29:2
Nothing but the Best 1964,Jl 14,28:1
Young Cassidy 1965,Mr 23,35:1

Delaney, Shelagh (Original Author)
Taste of Honey, A 1962,My 1,33:3
Charlie Bubbles 1968,F 12,47:2

Delaney, Shelagh (Screenwriter)
Taste of Honey, A 1962,My 1,33:3
Charlie Bubbles 1968,F 12,47:2

Delaney, Trevor
Cul de Sac 1966,N 8,44:2

Delanne, Lena
Shameless Old Lady, The 1966,S 27,52:1

Delannoy, Henrietta
Ingenu Libertin, L' 1929,Ag 25,VIII,5:1

Delannoy, Henriette
Java, Une 1928,Jl 15,VIII,3:4 (In Addenda)

Delannoy, Jean (Director)
Resistance; Peleton d'Execution 1946,Jl 5,15:3
Eternal Return, The; Eternel Retour, L' 1948,Ja 5,15:2
Blind Desire 1948,Je 10,28:4
Symphonie Pastorale 1948,S 14,34:3
Chips Are Down, The 1949,F 2,36:1
Souvenir 1950,O 3,34:4
God Needs Men 1951,Mr 27,35:1
Savage Triangle 1952,S 30,38:2
Daughters of Destiny (Jeanne); Jeanne (Daughters of Destiny) 1954,Jl 6,19:1
Hunchback of Notre Dame, The 1957,D 12,35:1
Inspector Maigret 1958,O 9,47:1
Love and the Frenchwoman; (Francaise et l'Amour, La) 1961,F 28,38:2
This Special Friendship 1967,N 8,56:1

Delannoy, Jean (Miscellaneous)
Chips Are Down, The 1949,F 2,36:1

Delannoy, Jean (Original Author)
Secret of Mayerling, The 1951,My 8,39:2

Delannoy, Jean (Screenwriter)
Blind Desire 1948,Je 10,28:4
Symphonie Pastorale 1948,S 14,34:3
Moment of Truth, The 1954,Ap 27,36:2
Bed, The (The Pompadour Bed); Pompadour Bed, The (The Bed) 1955,Je 8,26:4
Inspector Maigret 1958,O 9,47:1

Delannoy, M (Director)
Secret of Mayerling, The 1951,My 8,39:2
Bed, The (The Pompadour Bed); Pompadour Bed, The (The Bed) 1955,Je 8,26:4

Delano, Clothilde
Scaramouche 1923,O 12,7:2 (Incorrect in this edition; use 1927,O 1,7:2 elsewhere)

Delano, Edith Barnard (Original Author)
White Pearl, The 1915,O 11,9:5

DELANY
See Also DELANEY

Delaro, Mattie
Mind-the-Paint Girl, The 1919,N 24,13:1
Janice Meredith 1924,Ag 6,13:3

Delaroche, Christine
Young World, A 1966,My 17,52:1
Defector, The 1966,N 17,55:1

Delaroche, Gerard
Lola 1962,O 15,32:2

DeLavallade, Carmen
Odds Against Tomorrow 1959,O 16,27:1

Delavanti, Cyril
Oh Dad, Poor Dad, Mamma's Hung You in the Closet and I'm Feeling so Sad 1967,F 16,32:1

Delavaud, Monique
Sextette (Part 3-The Key to Sin); Key to Sin, The (Sextette) 1953,Mr 2,19:2

Delbat, Germaine
Four Bags Full 1957,S 5,32:1
Gigot 1962,S 28,26:1
Up From the Beach 1965,Je 10,38:1

Delbene, Floren
Ayudame a Vivir; Help Me to Live 1938,My 7,18:2
Ultimo Encventro, El; Last Meeting, The 1939,Ag 26,20:3
Besos Brujos; Bewitching Kisses 1939,O 21,12:3
Senderos de Fe; Paths of Faith 1940,Mr 2,9:5

Delbo, Jean-Jacques
Confessions of a Rogue 1948,Mr 30,26:3
Sextette (Part I-The Gun); Gun, The (Sextette) 1953,Mr 2,19:2
Big Chief, The 1960,Ap 27,32:1
Bernadette of Lourdes 1962,Ja 30,20:2

Delbo, Marion
Club De Femmes 1937,O 20,27:2

Delcambre, Alfred
You're Telling Me 1934,Ap 7,19:1
Wharf Angel 1934,Ap 21,12:1
Wagon Wheels 1934,O 4,19:1
Car 99 1935,F 23,14:7
So Red the Rose 1935,N 28,39:1
Delcassan
Jour de Fete 1952,F 20,26:4
Delderfield, R F (Original Author)
Carry on Sergeant 1959,O 28,40:5
Operation Snafu 1965,My 22,18:1
Delderfield, R F (Screenwriter)
Value for Money 1957,Ag 1,20:4
DeLeon, Walter (Original Author)
You're Telling Me 1934,Ap 7,19:1
DeLeon, Walter (Screenwriter)
College Rhythm 1934,N 24,19:1
Ruggles of Red Gap 1935,Mr 7,26:1
Big Broadcast of 1936, The 1935,S 16,15:2
Strike Me Pink 1936,Ja 17,15:2
Collegiate 1936,Ja 23,25:2
Princess Comes Across, The 1936,Je 4,27:2
Rhythm on the Range 1936,Jl 30,22:1
Big Broadcast of 1937, The 1936,O 22,31:1
Waikiki Wedding 1937,Mr 25,29:1
Artists and Models 1937,Ag 5,19:2
Big Broadcast of 1938, The 1938,Mr 10,16:2
College Swing 1938,Ap 28,27:2
Union Pacific 1939,My 11,31:2
Cat and the Canary, The 1939,N 23,38:5
Man Who Talked too Much, The 1940,Je 29,12:2
Ghost Breakers, The 1940,Jl 4,12:2
Tugboat Annie Sails Again 1940,N 9,20:2
Pot o'Gold 1941,Ap 4,25:2
Birth of the Blues 1941,D 11,39:1
Fleet's In, The 1942,Mr 12,24:2
Happy Go Lucky 1943,Mr 25,25:1
Riding High 1943,D 23,26:4
Rainbow Island 1944,O 26,19:6
Out of This World 1945,Je 7,25:2
Delightfully Dangerous 1945,Je 9,17:3
Hold That Blonde 1945,N 8,17:2
Little Giant 1946,My 9,27:5
Time of Their Lives, The 1946,N 28,40:2
Scared Stiff 1953,Jl 3,10:2
Delerue, Georges (Composer)
Joker, The; (Farceur, Le) 1961,Ag 8,32:2
Delessert, Jacquine (Original Author)
Of Love and Desire 1963,S 12,32:1
Delevanti, Cyril
Devotion 1931,O 3,20:2
Night Monster 1942,N 30,18:5
Night of the Iguana, The 1964,Jl 1,42:1
Mary Poppins 1964,S 25,34:1
Greatest Story Ever Told, The 1965,F 16,40:2
DeLey, Yvan
Mr Emmanuel 1945,Ja 8,15:2
Delf, Harry (Original Author)
Stop, Look and Love 1939,S 8,28:5
Delgado, Camilo
Strangers in the City 1962,Jl 17,19:2
Delgado, Henry
Third Voice, The 1960,Mr 7,24:5
Delgado, Lucy
Quien Mato a Eva 1934,D 22,21:2
Maria Elena 1936,F 18,27:1
Luna Criolla; Creole Moon 1940,Ap 8,15:3
Delgado, Miguel
Enemigos 1934,Ag 18,5:6
Quien Mato a Eva 1934,D 22,21:2
Delgado, Miguel (Director)
Romeo and Juliet 1944,Je 17,10:3
Delgado, Roger
Stowaway Girl 1957,N 6,43:3
Road to Hong Kong, The 1962,Je 28,21:1
Agent 8 3/4 1965,O 14,53:1
Delgrange, Elaine
Face to the Wind 1951,Ja 16,34:2
Delhort, Adria
Tigre de Yautepec, El 1934,O 20,20:3
Sor Juana Ines de la Cruz 1936,Je 6,21:2
Calandria, La 1936,O 12,23:3
Silencio Sublime 1937,Ja 16,21:2
Liaga, La; Torment, The 1937,O 4,17:2
Casa del Ogro, La; House of the Ogre, The 1939,F 13,13:2
Cobarde, El; Coward, The 1939,Mr 27,11:2
Bestia Negra, La; Black Beast, The 1940,Je 3,11:2
Delhumeau, Jean-Paul
Man Escaped, A 1957,Ag 27,33:2
Deli, David (Screenwriter)
Baltic Deputy 1937,S 4,8:2
Delia-Col
Marthe Richard 1944,N 9,23:2
Deligne, Michel (Original Author)
Three Hours 1944,O 30,16:5
Delille
Maternelle, La 1935,O 15,19:1
Dell, Claudia
Sweet Kitty Bellairs 1930,S 6,9:2
Big Boy 1930,S 13,9:3
Sit Tight 1931,F 19,20:4
Fifty Million Frenchmen 1931,Mr 26,31:2

Bachelor Apartment 1931,My 16,13:3
Confessions of a Co-Ed 1931,Je 20,20:4
Leftover Ladies 1931,N 9,22:4
Sporting Chance 1931,N 28,20:4
Scandal for Sale 1932,Ap 3,26:2
Midnight Lady, The 1932,Jl 1,19:3
Cleopatra 1934,Ag 17,12:1
Lost City, The 1935,F 21,23:3
Algiers 1938,Jl 15,13:2
Dell, Dorothy
Wharf Angel 1934,Ap 21,12:1
Little Miss Marker 1934,My 19,18:3
Shoot the Works 1934,Jl 7,16:5
Dell, Edith (Screenwriter)
Satellite in the Sky 1956,S 4,32:7
Dell, Ethel M (Original Author)
Top of the World, The 1925,F 17,18:1
High Treason 1937,Ja 27,17:3
Dell, Floyd (Original Author)
Casanova Brown 1944,S 15,16:1
Dell, Gabriel
Dead End 1937,Ag 25,25:1
Crime School 1938,My 11,17:2
Little Tough Guy 1938,Ag 18,23:3
Angels With Dirty Faces 1938,N 26,18:1
They Made Me a Criminal 1939,Ja 21,19:2
Hell's Kitchen 1939,Jl 3,10:5
Angels Wash Their Faces 1939,S 4,16:2
Dress Parade 1939,O 28,11:2
You're not so Tough 1940,Jl 9,25:3
Give Us Wings 1940,N 21,43:3
Hit the Road 1941,Jl 3,15:3
Mob Town 1941,N 20,39:3
Mr Wise Guy 1942,Mr 5,27:2
Dell, Jeffrey (Director)
Don't Take it to Heart 1948,D 25,10:3
It's Hard to be Good 1950,D 25,25:3
Dark Man, The 1952,My 26,18:4
Man in a Cocked Hat 1960,Je 15,50:2
Dell, Jeffrey (Miscellaneous)
Sanders of the River 1935,Je 27,16:1
Queen of Crime 1941,F 19,25:2
Risk, The 1961,S 25,41:2
Dell, Jeffrey (Original Author)
Payment Deferred 1932,N 8,26:3
Spies of the Air 1940,Jl 4,12:3
Footsteps in the Dark 1941,Mr 15,13:2
Rotten to the Core 1965,Jl 20,39:2
Dell, Jeffrey (Screenwriter)
Sanders of the River 1935,Je 27,16:1
Queen of Crime 1941,F 19,25:2
Voice in the Night, The 1941,My 23,25:4
Saint's Vacation, The 1941,Je 13,22:2
Thunder Rock 1944,S 15,16:1
Don't Take it to Heart 1948,D 25,10:3
It's Hard to be Good 1950,D 25,25:3
Brothers in Law 1957,Ag 20,22:1
Happy is the Bride 1959,Je 30,27:2
Man in a Cocked Hat 1960,Je 15,50:2
French Mistress, A 1960,D 19,34:2
As the Sea Rages 1961,My 18,41:1
Rotten to the Core 1965,Jl 20,39:2
Family Way, The 1967,Je 29,32:1
Dell, Myrna
Step by Step 1946,Ag 24,6:7
Nocturne 1946,N 11,42:2
Falcon's Adventure, The 1946,D 14,19:2
Locket, The 1947,Mr 20,38:2
Fighting Father Dunne 1948,Je 25,26:2
Judge Steps Out, The 1949,Je 3,21:4
Roughshod 1949,Je 17,27:2
Lust for Gold 1949,Jl 4,9:2
Girl from Jones Beach, The 1949,Jl 30,9:2
Furies, The 1950,Ag 17,23:2
Never Trust a Gambler 1951,Jl 20,14:2
Dell, Sylvia
Two Sisters 1938,D 1,29:3
Della Noce, Luisa
Railroad Man, The; Ferroviere, Il 1965,O 25,46:2
Juliet of the Spirits 1965,N 4,57:1
All the Other Girls Do! 1967,My 30,12:1
della Post, Carlo
Guaglio 1949,My 19,35:2
Delly, Ferenc
As Uj Rokon; New Relative, The 1935,Mr 12,25:3
Az Uj Rokon 1935,Mr 12,25:3
Nem Elhetek Muzsikaszo Nelkuel 1936,F 21,21:2
Sportszerelem; Love of Sport 1938,F 14,20:8
Delmar, Kenny
Strangers in the City 1962,Jl 17,19:2
Delmar, Tom
Bad Man, The 1923,O 9,17:4
Rainbow Trail, The 1925,Je 3,26:4
Delmar, Vina (Original Author)
Dance Hall 1929,D 16,34:2
Playing Around 1930,Mr 31,24:3
Soldiers Plaything, A 1931,My 2,23:4
Bad Girl 1931,Ag 15,18:3
Uptown New York 1932,D 10,19:3
Woman Accused, The 1933,Mr 13,18:2
Pick Up 1933,Mr 25,13:4
Chance at Heaven 1933,D 26,19:3

Delmar, Vina (Original Author)— Cont
Sadie McKee 1934,My 18,18:3 (Incorrect in this edition; use 1934,My 19,18:3 elsewhere)
Bad Boy 1935,O 28,16:3
Hands Across the Table 1935,N 2,13:2
King of Burlesque 1936,Ja 16,25:2
Great Man's Lady, The 1942,Ap 30,14:3
Cynthia 1947,S 19,27:2
About Mrs Leslie 1954,Je 28,16:2
Delmar, Vina (Screenwriter)
Make Way for Tomorrow 1937,My 10,23:1
Awful Truth, The 1937,N 5,19:3
Delmare, Fred
Naked Among the Wolves 1967,Ap 19,54:7
Delmas, Suzanne
Rasputin 1929,O 21,30:1
Delmatoff, Michael
Shanghai Gesture, The 1941,D 26,21:2
Delmer, Paul (Cinematographer)
Caravan to Russia 1959,O 26,34:4
Delmer, Paul (Director)
Caravan to Russia 1959,O 26,34:4
Delmer, Paul (Producer)
Caravan to Russia 1959,O 26,34:4
Delmont, Edouard
Amours de Toni, Les 1936,N 5,35:1
Heroes of the Marne; (Famille Lefrancois, Le) 1939,Ap 24,13:2
Heartbeat 1939,S 5,21:3
Harvest 1939,O 30,16:5
Port of Shadows 1939,O 30,13:2
Three Hours 1944,O 30,16:5
Wench, The 1949,Mr 14,15:5
Passion for Life 1951,D 21,21:4
Sheep Has Five Legs, The 1955,Ag 10,19:2
Letters From my Windmill (The Secret of Master Cornille); Secret of Master Cornille, The (Letters From my Windmill) 1955,D 19,33:1
Return of Don Camillo, The 1956,Mr 27,41:1
Toni 1968,S 19,62:2
Delney, Pauline
Quare Fellow 1963,F 20,6:1
Delon, Alain
Women Are Weak 1959,Je 9,44:2
Rocco and his Brothers 1961,Je 28,40:2
Purple Noon 1961,S 1,12:1
Eclipse 1962,D 21,5:1
Leopard, The 1963,Ag 13,25:1
Any Number Can Win 1963,O 9,47:2
Devil and the 10 Commandments, The (Episode 6) 1963,O 15,44:1
Joy House 1965,F 18,29:1
Yellow Rolls-Royce, The 1965,My 14,42:2
Once a Thief 1965,S 9,36:1
Lost Command 1966,S 15,51:1
Is Paris Burning? 1966,N 11,36:1
Texas Across the River 1966,N 24,65:1
Girl on a Motorcycle, The 1968,N 28,66:5
Delorez, Claire
Siren of Seville, The 1924,N 17,16:1 (In Addenda)
Delorme, Daniele
Gigi 1950,Ja 31,20:2
Miquette 1951,F 5,18:2
Minne 1951,Ap 17,35:2
Pit of Loneliness 1954,Ap 9,19:2
Desperate Decision 1954,N 9,31:5
House of Ricordi 1956,Mr 13,32:1
Royal Affairs in Versailles 1957,Mr 9,16:1
Deadlier Than the Male 1957,O 9,41:1
Mitsou 1958,Ap 15,42:5
Seventh Juror, The 1964,Ja 28,25:1
Delorme, Daniele (Producer)
War of the Buttons, The 1963,D 19,40:2
Delouche, Dominique (Director)
24 Hours in a Woman's Life 1968,S 25,39:1
Delouche, Dominique (Screenwriter)
24 Hours in a Woman's Life 1968,S 25,39:1
Delphin
Kermesse Heroique, La 1936,S 23,29:1
Devil Is an Empress, The 1939,D 4,18:4
Zero de Conduite 1947,Je 23,14:5
Delroy, Irene
Life of the Party, The 1930,N 10,16:2
Divorce Among Friends 1931,Ap 2,30:4
Delschaft, Maly
Last Laugh, The 1925,Ja 28,14:1
Dienst Ist Dienst 1932,Je 6,18:5
Keine Feier Ohne Meyer 1932,O 29,18:4
Heimat am Rhein 1934,D 11,29:4
Delsoi, Gerald
Children of the Damned 1964,Ja 30,24:2
Delta Rhythm Boys
Follow the Boys 1944,Ap 26,24:6
Delteil, Joseph (Director)
Passion of Jeanne d'Arc, The 1929,Mr 31,VIII,7:1
Delteil, Joseph (Original Author)
Passion of Joan of Arc, The 1929,Ja 20,VIII,7:5
Passion of Jeanne d'Arc, The 1929,Mr 31,VIII,7:1
Delteil, Joseph (Screenwriter)
Passion of Joan of Arc, The 1928,Ap 1,IX,5:5 (In Addenda)
Passion Of Joan Of Arc, The 1929,Mr 29,21:1

Deltgen, Rene
Einer zu viel an Bord 1936,Ja 25,18:5
Kleine Suenderin, Die; Little Sinner, The
   1938,D 3,11:3
Gruene Hoelle, Die; Green Hell, The
   1939,Ja 21,19:2
Congo Express 1940,My 11,15:3
Mozart Story, The 1948,N 15,21:5
Keepers of the Night 1953,Je 9,24:2
Desires 1954,Jl 2,10:2
No Way Back 1955,My 19,25:5

Delubac, Jacqueline
Pearls of the Crown, The 1938,Ap 12,26:2
Story of a Cheat, The 1938,S 27,25:2
Champs-Elysees 1939,F 28,17:2
Indiscretions 1939,My 1,21:1
Last Desire 1939,D 22,15:2
Man Who Seeks the Truth, The 1941,O 7,26:6
Volpone 1947,D 27,9:3
My First Love 1951,Je 11,20:7

DeLuce, Virginia
New Faces 1954,F 20,8:7

Delutri, Gabe
Jailbreakers, The 1961,Ja 5,27:2

Delvaux, Andre
Man With the Shaven Head, The 1966,S 21,42:2

Delvaux, Andre (Director)
Man With the Shaven Head, The 1966,S 21,42:2

Delve, Suzanne
Si l'Empereur Savait Ca 1931,F 23,20:3

Delvincourt, C (Miscellaneous)
Yellow Cruise, The 1936,N 18,31:3

Delysia, Alice
Evensong 1934,N 17,12:1

DeMain, Gordon
Marriage Playground, The 1929,D 14,22:4
Young Eagles 1930,Mr 22,22:6
Behind the Evidence 1935,Ja 26,13:2
International Lady 1941,N 11,29:2

Demange, Paul
Back Streets of Paris 1948,O 16,9:2
Gigi 1950,Ja 31,20:2
Scandals of Clochemerle, The 1950,Mr 28,28:2
Red Angel, The 1950,N 4,13:2
Premier May 1958,S 17,44:2

DeMarco, Tony and Sally
Greenwich Village 1944,S 28,26:2

DeMarcos, The
In Caliente 1935,Je 27,16:1
Crazy House 1943,D 16,33:3

Demare
Boliche 1935,My 28,30:2

Demarest, Drew
Broadway Melody, The 1929,F 9,15:3
Lord Byron of Broadway 1930,Mr 8,21:1
Today 1930,N 17,29:1
Jury's Secret, The 1938,F 4,17:2
Spoilers, The 1942,My 22,27:2

Demarest, Rube
Gracie Allen Murder Case, The 1939,Je 8,31:3
Girl, a Guy and a Gob, A 1941,Ap 24,25:3

Demarest, William
Don't Tell the Wife 1927,F 22,23:2
Matinee Ladies 1927,Ap 13,29:4
Million Bid, A 1927,My 31,25:2
Old San Francisco 1927,Je 23,23:3
First Auto, The 1927,Je 28,28:4
Jazz Singer, The 1927,O 7,24:4
Sharp Shooters 1928,Ja 23,18:3
Girl in Every Port, A 1928,F 20,14:1
Escape, The 1928,My 7,29:1
Butter and Egg Man, The 1928,Ag 28,27:4
Fog over Frisco 1934,Je 7,26:2
Many Happy Returns 1934,Je 9,18:2
Bright Lights 1935,Ag 15,15:2
Diamond Jim 1935,Ag 24,18:2
Hands Across the Table 1935,N 2,13:2
Wedding Present 1936,N 19,31:3
Love on the Run 1936,N 28,13:3
Charlie Chan at the Opera 1936,D 5,16:2
Don't Tell the Wife 1937,F 19,15:2
Time Out for Romance 1937,Mr 13,23:2
Hit Parade, The 1937,My 31,11:2
Oh, Doctor 1937,Je 19,20:3
Easy Living 1937,Jl 8,20:1
Great Gambini, The 1937,Jl 12,20:4
Great Hospital Mystery, The 1937,Jl 16,22:2
Blonde Trouble 1937,Ag 7,7:2
Big City 1937,S 17,29:2
Rebecca of Sunnybrook Farm 1938,Mr 26,12:1
One Wild Night 1938,Je 3,17:2
Josette 1938,Je 11,9:1
While New York Sleeps 1938,D 22,25:3
Peck's bad Boy With the Circus 1939,Ja 11,17:4
Great Man Votes, The 1939,Ja 20,15:2
King of the Turf 1939,My 8,21:2
Gracie Allen Murder Case, The 1939,Je 8,31:3
Miracles for Sale 1939,Ag 10,15:2
Mr Smith Goes to Washington 1939,O 20,27:2
Farmer's Daughter, The 1940,F 16,23:4
Great McGinty, The 1940,Ag 15,23:1
Comin' Round the Mountain 1940,S 26,27:3
Christmas in July 1940,N 6,35:2

Golden Fleecing, The 1940,N 7,33:4
Tin Pan Alley 1940,N 22,27:3
Little Men 1940,D 9,23:2
Lady Eve, The 1941,F 26,17:1
Ride on Vaquero 1941,Ap 19,20:2
Devil and Miss Jones, The 1941,My 16,21:2
Rookies on Parade 1941,My 22,25:2
Dressed to Kill 1941,Ag 22,19:3
All Through the Night 1942,Ja 24,13:2
Sullivan's Travels 1942,Ja 29,25:2
My Favorite Spy 1942,My 29,13:4
True to the Army 1942,Je 15,15:4
Pardon my Sarong 1942,Ag 27,15:1
Life Begins at Eight-Thirty 1942,D 10,35:2
Palm Beach Story, The 1942,D 11,33:1
Johnny Doughboy 1943,My 6,25:3
Stage Door Canteen 1943,Je 25,13:2
True to Life 1943,O 14,26:1
Miracle of Morgan's Creek, The 1944,Ja 20,15:2
Once Upon a Time 1944,Je 30,17:2
Hail the Conquering Hero 1944,Ag 10,14:2
Great Moment, The 1944,N 13,15:2
Salty O'Rourke 1945,Ap 26,26:2
Along Came Jones 1945,Jl 19,8:7
Duffy's Tavern 1945,S 6,23:3
Pardon my Past 1946,Ja 28,15:5
Our Hearts Were Growing Up 1946,Ag 12,17:2
Jolson Story, The 1946,O 11,28:2
Perils of Pauline, The 1947,Jl 10,17:2
Variety Girl 1947,O 16,34:4
Miracle Can Happen, A 1948,F 4,28:4
Sainted Sisters, The 1948,My 20,35:2
Night Has a Thousand Eyes 1948,O 14,38:3
Whispering Smith 1949,F 15,28:2
Sorrowful Jones 1949,Je 6,15:2
Jolson Sings Again 1949,Ag 18,16:6
Red, Hot and Blue 1949,O 20,39:2
When Willie Comes Marching Home
   1950,F 18,9:2
Riding High 1950,Ap 11,26:2
He's a Cockeyed Wonder 1950,O 20,32:4
Never a Dull Moment 1950,N 22,20:2
First Legion, The 1951,Ap 28,9:2
Excuse my Dust 1951,Je 28,21:2
Behave Yourself 1951,N 8,35:2
What Price Glory 1952,Ag 23,10:2
Lady Wants Mink, The 1953,Ap 6,24:2
Dangerous When Wet 1953,Je 19,18:1
Here Come the Girls 1953,D 26,10:1
Escape from Fort Bravo 1954,Ja 23,11:2
Jupiter's Darling 1955,F 18,18:4
Far Horizons, The 1955,My 21,11:1
Private War of Major Benson, The
   1955,Ag 3,27:2
Lucy Gallant 1955,O 21,30:1
Sincerely Yours 1955,N 3,37:1
Hell on Frisco Bay 1956,Ja 7,21:1
Rawhide Years, The 1956,Je 16,12:2
Mountain, The 1956,N 15,44:6
Pepe 1960,D 22,18:1
King of the Roaring Twenties 1961,O 5,43:1
Son of Flubber 1963,F 9,5:2
It's a Mad, Mad, Mad, Mad World
   1963,N 19,47:1
Viva Las Vegas 1964,My 21,42:1
That Darn Cat 1965,D 3,44:1

Demaret, James
Follow the Sun 1951,Ap 26,34:4

DeMario, Donna
Apache Rose 1947,Jl 23,19:3

DeMartino, Alberto (Director)
Operation Kid Brother 1967,N 23,58:2

Demartino, Inigo (Screenwriter)
Enamorada 1949,D 3,8:6

Demasin, Larry
Island of the Blue Dolphins 1964,Jl 4,8:2

Demazis, Orane
Marius 1933,Ap 14,22:5
Heartbeat 1939,S 5,21:3
Harvest 1939,O 3,19:4
Fire in the Straw 1943,Jl 2,15:2
Miserables, Les 1946,D 26,28:4
Fanny 1948,F 13,26:2
Cesar 1948,O 28,36:2
Wench, The 1949,Mr 14,15:5

Dembl, T (Screenwriter)
Eye of the Needle, The 1965,Je 22,25:2

Demel, Paul
State Secret 1950,O 5,38:2
Hue and Cry 1951,Ja 9,25:2
His Excellency 1956,F 2,19:3

Demetrio, Anna
Too Much Harmony 1933,S 23,11:5
McFadden's Flats 1935,Mr 13,16:2
Next Time We Love 1936,Ja 31,16:2
Texans, The 1938,Jl 28,23:2
Big Store, The 1941,Je 27,14:4
Dragon Seed 1944,Jl 21,16:4
Carnival in Costa Rica 1947,Mr 29,21:2
September Affair 1951,F 2,19:2
Force of Arms 1951,Ag 14,20:2

Demetrious, Theodore
Electra 1962,D 18,5:2

Demetros, Pete
Three Stripes in the Sun 1955,N 24,41:2

Demick, Irina
Visit, The 1964,O 22,44:1
Up From the Beach 1965,Je 10,38:1
Those Magnificent Men in Their Flying Machines
   (Or How I Flew From London to Paris in 25
   Hours and 11 Minutes) 1965,Je 17,27:1
Male Companion 1966,F 15,33:2
Cloportes 1966,Ap 19,36:1
Prudence and the Pill 1968,My 24,37:1

DeMille, Cecil B
Star Spangled Rhythm 1942,D 31,20:1
Sunset Boulevard 1950,Ag 11,15:2

DeMille, Cecil B (Director)
Old Wives for New 1918,My 20,9:7
We Can't Have Everything 1918,Jl 15,9:3
Till I Come Back to You 1918,Ag 26,9:1
Squaw Man, The 1918,D 30,7:3
Don't Change Your Husband 1919,F 3,13:2
For Better, For Worse 1919,Ap 28,13:2
Affairs of Anatol, The 1921,S 12,16:1
Fool's Paradise 1921,D 10,11:4
Triumph 1924,Ap 21,21:4
Feet of Clay 1924,S 22,16:1
Golden Bed, The 1925,Ja 20,18:2
Volga Boatman, The 1926,Ap 14,21:1
King of Kings, The 1927,Ap 20,29:2
Godless Girl, The 1929,Ap 1,22:1
Dynamite 1929,D 28,11:1
Madam Satan 1930,O 6,21:1
Squaw Man, The 1931,S 19,10:2
Sign of the Cross, The 1932,D 1,25:1
This Day and Age 1933,S 1,15:4
Four Frightened People 1934,Ja 27,9:2
Cleopatra 1934,Ag 17,12:1
Crusades, The 1935,Ag 22,21:3
Plainsman, The 1937,Ja 14,16:2
Buccaneer, The 1938,F 17,17:2
Union Pacific 1939,My 11,31:2
North West Mounted Police 1940,N 7,33:2
Reap the Wild Wind 1942,Mr 27,27:2
Story of Dr Wassell, The 1944,Je 7,13:2
Unconquered 1947,O 11,11:2
Samson and Delilah 1949,D 22,29:2
Greatest Show on Earth, The 1952,Ja 11,17:2

DeMille, Cecil B (Miscellaneous)
Land of Liberty 1939,Je 16,27:3
Land of Liberty 1941,Ja 30,19:2
Buccaneer, The 1958,D 24,00:0

DeMille, Cecil B (Producer)
Joan, the Woman 1916,D 25,7:1
Male and Female 1919,N 24,13:1
Why Change Your Wife 1920,Ap 26,18:1
Something to Think About 1920,O 18,13:1
Forbidden Fruit 1921,Ja 24,16:2
Manslaughter 1922,S 18,14:2
Plainsman, The 1937,Ja 14,16:2
Buccaneer, The 1938,F 17,17:2
Union Pacific 1939,My 11,31:2
North West Mounted Police 1940,N 7,33:2
Reap the Wild Wind 1942,Mr 27,27:2
Story of Dr Wassell, The 1944,Je 7,13:2
Unconquered 1947,O 11,11:2
Samson and Delilah 1949,D 22,29:2
Greatest Show on Earth, The 1952,Ja 11,17:2
Ten Commandments, The 1956,N 9,35:2

DeMille, Henry C (Original Author)
Men and Women 1925,Mr 30,21:3

DeMille, Henry C (Screenwriter)
Forty Winks 1925,F 3,24:1

DeMille, Katherine
Viva Villa! 1934,Ap 11,25:2
Trumpet Blows, The 1934,Ap 14,18:2
Belle of the Nineties 1934,S 22,12:2
All the King's Horses 1935,Mr 9,19:1
Call of the Wild 1935,Ag 15,15:2
Crusades, The 1935,Ag 22,21:3
Sky Parade, The 1936,Ap 20,17:1
Ramona 1936,O 7,32:4
Banjo on My Knee 1936,D 12,15:1
Charlie Chan at the Olympics 1937,My 24,23:1
Love Under Fire 1937,Ag 28,8:2
Under Suspicion 1937,D 20,23:2 (In Addenda)
Blockade 1938,Je 17,25:1
Isle of Destiny 1940,Ap 8,15:2
Dark Streets of Cairo 1940,D 2,19:3
Ellery Queen, Master Detective 1940,D 19,33:1
Aloma of the South Seas 1941,Ag 28,23:4
Black Gold 1947,S 5,16:4
Unconquered 1947,O 11,11:2

DeMille, William (Director)
Conrad in Quest of his Youth 1920,N 8,20:2
Midsummer Madness 1920,D 6,19:1
Lost Romance, The 1921,My 9,16:2
Bought and Paid For 1922,Mr 13,18:2
Clarence 1922,O 16,20:2
World's Applause 1923,F 4,VII,3:2 (In Addenda)
Grumpy 1923,Mr 26,16:2
Only 38 1923,Je 11,16:2
Don't Call it Love 1923,D 25,26:1

DeMille, William (Director) — Cont
Icebound 1924,Mr 3,22:3 (In Addenda)
Bedroom Window, The 1924,Je 9,14:3
Fast Set, The 1924,N 18,22:1
Locked Doors 1925,Ja 12,11:2
Men and Women 1925,Mr 30,21:3
Lost-a Wife 1925,Je 22,10:2
New Brooms 1925,N 4,17:4
Splendid Crime, The 1925,D 17,27:1
Runaway, The 1926,Ap 27,23:2
For Alimony Only 1926,S 21,33:1
Craig's Wife 1928,D 4,29:1
Doctor's Secret, The 1929,F 4,20:1
Idle Rich, The 1929,Je 17,29:1
Passion Flower 1930,D 22,16:2
Two Kinds of Women 1932,Ja 16,13:1
DeMille, William (Original Author)
Why Change Your Wife 1920,Ap 26,18:1
Classmates 1924,D 30,15:3
Splendid Crime, The 1925,D 17,27:1
Telephone Girl, The 1927,My 16,24:2
Forest Ring, The 1930,Ap 26,11:1
Secret Call, The 1931,Jl 13,13:5
DeMille, William (Producer)
Miss Lulu Bett 1921,D 25,VI,2:1
DeMille, William (Screenwriter)
Captain Fury 1939,My 26,20:2
Deming, Walter
Passionate Youth 1925,Je 30,14:3
Demion, Irinia
Longest Day, The 1962,O 5,28:1
Demko, Iren
Vasember 1935,D 9,25:3
Demming, Richard (Original Author)
Arrivederci, Baby! 1966,D 29,22:1
DeMond, Albert (Original Author)
Sphinx, The 1933,Jl 6,26:5
Outside the Three-Mile Limit 1940,Ap 8,15:2
Shock 1946,Mr 9,10:2
Red Menace, The 1949,Je 27,18:2
DeMond, Albert (Screenwriter)
Perfect Clue, The 1935,Mr 14,18:1
Torchy Gets her Man 1938,N 18,25:3
Women in the Wind 1939,Ap 13,27:2
Outside the Three-Mile Limit 1940,Ap 8,15:2
Passport to Alcatraz 1940,Je 15,12:2
Prison Camp 1940,Ag 3,9:3
Great Plane Robbery, The 1940,N 15,25:2
Great Swindle, The 1941,My 14,25:4
Red Menace, The 1949,Je 27,18:2
Demongeot, Catherine
Zazie 1961,N 21,45:5
Demongeot, Mylene
Bonjour Tristesse 1958,Ja 16,32:1
What Price Murder 1958,N 11,26:1
Witches of Salem 1958,D 9,54:2
Women Are Weak 1959,Je 9,44:2
Giant of Marathon, The 1960,My 26,37:3
Under ten Flags 1960,S 16,24:1
Upstairs and Downstairs 1960,D 2,53:4
Notte Brava, La 1962,Ja 25,25:2
Singer not the Song, The 1962,My 3,25:4
Doctor in Distress 1964,Jl 8,38:2
Fantomas 1966,Ap 6,36:2
OSS 117-Mission for a Killer 1966,O 13,50:3
Private Navy of Sgt O'Farrell, The
1968,My 9,54:1
Demorget, Robert
Children of Chaos 1950,Ap 20,37:2
Dempsey, Clifford
Ghost Talks, The 1929,F 18,28:1
Valiant, The 1929,My 13,27:2
Salute 1929,O 5,22:5
Only Saps Work 1930,D 13,22:2
Everything's Rosie 1931,My 22,28:5
Too Many Cooks 1931,Ag 17,18:2
Sob Sister 1931,O 3,20:2
Guilty as Hell 1932,Ag 6,14:5
Dempsey, Jack
Prizefighter and the Lady, The 1933,N 11,11:3
Off Limits 1953,Mr 30,25:5
Requiem for a Heavyweight 1962,O 17,35:1
Legendary Champions, The 1968,O 29,54:1
Dempsey, Martin
Ulysses 1967,Mr 14,55:1
Dempsey, Thomas
Elmer and Elsie 1934,Ag 4,14:5
Dempster, Carol
Girl Who Stayed Home, The 1919,Mr 24,11:3
Scarlet Days 1919,N 10,18:2
Love Flower, The 1920,Ag 23,9:2
Sherlock Holmes 1922,My 8,14:3
One Exciting Night 1922,O 24,17:3
White Rose, The 1923,My 23,18:3
America 1924,F 22,20:1
Isn't Life Wonderful? 1924,D 1,17:3
That Royle Girl 1926,Ja 4,33:1
Sorrows of Satan, The 1926,O 13,21:1
Dempster, Hugh
Student's Romance, The 1936,O 12,23:2
April Romance 1937,Ja 27,17:4
Waltz Time 1946,F 11,25:2
Anna Karenina 1948,Ap 28,32:2
Fan, The 1949,Ap 2,12:2

Happy Go Lovely 1951,Jl 26,17:2
Babes in Bagdad 1954,Ap 5,21:3
Demura, Ryuzo
Geisha Boy, The 1958,D 24,00:0
Demy, Jacques (Composer)
Umbrellas of Cherbourg, The; Parpapluis de
Cherbourg, Les 1964,D 17,50:1
Demy, Jacques (Director)
Lola 1962,O 15,32:2
7 Capital Sins (Lust); Lust (7 Capital Sins)
1963,Ja 17,5:2
Bay of the Angels; Baie des Anges, La
1964,N 24,44:1
Umbrellas of Cherbourg, The; Parpapluis de
Cherbourg, Les 1964,D 17,50:1
Young Girls of Rochefort, The 1968,Ap 12,50:1
Demy, Jacques (Screenwriter)
Lola 1962,O 15,32:2
7 Capital Sins (Lust); Lust (7 Capital Sins)
1963,Ja 17,5:2
Bay of the Angels; Baie des Anges, La
1964,N 24,44:1
Umbrellas of Cherbourg, The; Parpapluis de
Cherbourg, Les 1964,D 17,50:1
Young Girls of Rochefort, The 1968,Ap 12,50:1
Demyanenko, Aleksandr
Grown-Up Children 1963,Ap 15,36:5
Peace to Him Who Enters 1963,N 25,23:5
Demyanov, Andryusha
Gift for Music 1957,Jl 15,15:2
DeMyest, E G (Director)
We Lived Through Buchenwald 1947,Jl 24,27:3
den Berg, Han Bentz
Last Blitzkrieg, The 1959,Ja 31,13:5
Dena Picture (Miscellaneous)
Five Pennies, The 1959,Je 19,30:1
Dench, Judi
Study in Terror, A 1966,N 3,45:3
He Who Rides a Tiger 1968,S 10,39:1
Dench and Stewart
Ice-Capades 1941,S 25,29:1
Denes, George
Jo as a Haznal; Father Knows Best 1935,F 5,22:4
Naszut Felaron 1937,F 13,9:2
Denes, Miklos
Baratsagos Arcot Kerek; Keep Smiling
1936,O 5,25:2
Denetdeel, Bahe
Untamed 1940,Jl 25,14:3
Deneuve, Catherine
Tales of Paris (The Tale of Sophie); Tale of Sophie,
The (Tales of Paris) 1962,Ag 27,18:1
Umbrellas of Cherbourg, The; Parpapluis de
Cherbourg, Les 1964,D 17,50:1
Vice and Virtue 1965,Mr 18,25:1
Male Hunt; Chasse a l'Homme, La
1965,Ap 20,42:1
Repulsion 1965,O 4,7:6
Male Companion 1966,F 15,33:2
Creatures, Les 1966,S 16,31:2
Vie de Chateau, La 1967,Mr 21,35:1
Benjamin 1968,Mr 26,41:2
Belle de Jour 1968,Ap 11,51:1
Young Girls of Rochefort, The 1968,Ap 12,50:1
Denevi, Marco (Original Author)
Secret Ceremony 1968,O 24,55:1
Dengate, Dennis
Rogues' Regiment 1948,D 20,31:2
Denham, Maurice
Jassy 1948,F 20,19:2
Smugglers, The 1948,Mr 29,17:1
End of the River, The 1948,Je 21,18:2
Escape 1948,Ag 16,12:2
Dulcimer Street 1948,N 8,24:2
Blanche Fury 1948,N 24,20:2
Take my Life 1949,Ja 19,34:2
Easy Money (Episode 1) 1949,F 14,15:3
Blind Goddess, The 1949,Je 23,33:3
Once Upon a Dream 1949,Jl 15,17:2
Blue Lagoon, The 1949,O 3,13:2
Madness of the Heart 1950,O 12,43:2
Spider and the Fly, The 1952,Jl 29,17:3
Landfall 1953,My 11,25:2
Project M 7 1953,N 27,22:5
Man With a Million 1954,Je 29,21:2
Purple Plain, The 1955,Ap 11,29:1
Eight O'Clock Walk 1955,Ap 30,10:6
Court Martial 1955,Ag 2,17:1
Doctor at Sea 1956,Mr 1,37:3
23 Paces to Baker Street 1956,My 19,12:6
Simon and Laura 1956,Jl 3,17:2
Checkpoint 1957,S 19,25:2
All at Sea 1957,D 23,18:2
Our Man in Havana 1960,Ja 28,26:1
Sink the Bismarck! 1960,F 12,22:3
Captain's Table, The 1960,S 27,40:1
Two-Way Stretch 1961,Ja 24,20:3
Mark, The 1961,O 3,46:2
Loss of Innocence 1961,N 22,27:1
Invasion Quartet 1961,D 11,41:2
Damn the Defiant 1962,S 20,29:2
Paranoiac 1963,My 23,31:2
Seventh Dawn, The 1964,S 3,24:1

Denham, Maurice — Cont
Operation Crossbow 1965,Ap 2,29:1
Hysteria 1965,S 9,36:3
Nanny, The 1965,N 4,57:2
Alphabet Murders, The 1966,Jl 12,36:2
Uncle, The 1966,Jl 19,34:1
After the Fox 1966,D 24,11:1
Long Duel, The 1967,N 2,58:3
Attack on the Iron Coast 1968,Je 6,54:2
Danger Route 1968,Je 6,54:2
Negatives 1968,O 15,40:1
Denham, Reginald (Director)
Crimson Circle, The 1936,D 28,12:3
Queen of Crime 1941,F 19,25:2
Fast and Sexy 1960,O 6,51:4
Denham, Reginald (Original Author)
Ladies in Retirement 1941,N 7,27:1
Wallflower 1948,Je 12,8:5
Denham, Reginald (Screenwriter)
Ladies in Retirement 1941,N 7,27:1
Denhez, Christian
Gervaise 1957,N 12,46:1
Deni, Vernon
Business and Pleasure 1932,F 13,23:4
Deniaud, Yves
Blind Desire 1948,Je 10,28:4
Simple Case of Money, A 1952,F 2,11:2
Dr Knock 1955,O 10,31:2
DENIS
See Also DENNIS
Denis, Armand (Director)
Wild Cargo 1934,Mr 30,27:2
Frank Buck's Jungle Cavalcade 1941,Jl 4,17:1
Below the Sahara 1953,S 2,20:1
Denis, Armand (Miscellaneous)
Dark Rapture 1938,O 10,14:3
Dangerous Journey 1944,O 2,22:2
Among the Headhunters 1958,S 20,10:6
Denis, Armand (Producer)
Goona Goona 1932,S 17,18:4
Dark Rapture 1938,O 10,14:3
Savage Splendor 1949,N 4,37:2
Below the Sahara 1953,S 2,20:1
Denis, Maria
Re Burlone, Il 1936,Mr 28,11:3
Fiat Voluntas Dei 1936,Jl 6,11:5
Lacrime e Sorrisi 1936,D 17,35:2
Amore in Quarantena; Love in Quarantine
1938,D 13,31:2
Zio d'America, Lo; Uncle From America, The
1939,S 15,26:5
Ultima Nemica, L'; Last Enemy, The
1940,Ap 18,28:5
Documento Fatale, Il 1940,S 26,27:3
Cuore Napoletano; Neapolitan Heart
1940,O 8,31:2
Vie de Boheme, La 1947,N 28,37:4
Two Orphans, The 1950,O 19,40:6
Malia 1952,F 2,11:4
Denis, Michaela (Miscellaneous)
Among the Headhunters 1958,S 20,10:6
Denise, Patricia
Marjorie Morningstar 1958,Ap 25,32:2
Denison, Edward
Town That Forgot God, The 1922,N 1,16:3
Denison, Leslie
Submarine Zone; (Escape To Glory)
1941,Ap 7,13:2
Secret Agent of Japan 1942,Mr 23,19:3
Bombs Over Burma 1942,Ag 10,15:2
Five Graves to Cairo 1943,My 27,21:2
Murder in Times Square 1943,My 31,13:2
Frenchman's Creek 1944,S 21,26:2
Hangover Square 1945,F 8,15:2
Bandit of Sherwood Forest, The 1946,Mr 23,8:4
Black Arrow, The 1948,O 4,14:2
Fighting O'Flynn, The 1949,F 28,16:2
Denison, Michael
Hungry Hill 1947,O 11,11:2
Blind Goddess, The 1949,Je 23,33:3
My Brother Jonathan 1949,Je 29,34:4
Glass Mountain, The 1950,My 18,37:3
Franchise Affair, The 1952,Je 6,19:2
Importance of Being Earnest, The 1952,D 23,17:2
Landfall 1953,My 11,25:2
Frightened Bride, The 1953,Ag 20,18:5
Angels One Five 1954,Ap 30,28:2
Truth About Women, The 1958,Ag 29,18:2
Denison, Muriel (Original Author)
Susannah of the Mounties 1939,Je 24,13:2
Denk, Paula
Peter, Paul und Nanette 1940,My 25,20:1
Denker, Henry
Time Limit 1957,O 24,37:2
Denker, Henry (Screenwriter)
Time Limit 1957,O 24,37:2
Hook, The 1963,F 16,5:6
Twilight of Honor 1963,N 14,41:2
Denn, Paul (Screenwriter)
Deadly Affair, The 1967,Ja 27,31:1
Denne, Carole
State Department-File 649 1949,F 21,20:2

Dennen, Barry
Secret Cinema, The 1968,My 2,57:1
Denner, Charles
Landru 1963,Ap 10,31:1
Inside Out 1964,S 25,32:1
Life Upside Down; Inside Out 1965,Ag 18,41:4
Sleeping Car Murder, The 1966,Mr 8,45:1
Thief of Paris, The 1967,Ag 24,43:2
Two of Us, The 1968,F 20,53:1
Bride Wore Black, The 1968,Je 26,42:1
Denner, John
Youngblood Hawke 1964,N 6,30:1
D'Ennery, Adolf (Original Author)
Frochard et les Deux Orphelines, La 1934,F 7,16:2
D'Ennery, Guy
Lights of New York 1928,Jl 9,25:1
Anna Karenina 1935,Ag 31,16:2
Edison the Man 1940,Je 7,27:2
Mark of Zorro, The 1940,N 4,23:2
Dennett, Jill
Tenderfoot, The 1932,My 23,18:4
Picture Snatcher 1933,My 19,20:3
Devil is a Woman, The 1935,My 4,17:2
Denni, Lucien (Composer)
In the Navy 1941,Je 12,29:2
Denning, Richard
Hold 'Em Navy 1937,N 6,14:2
Her Jungle Love 1938,Ap 14,27:2
Campus Confessions 1938,S 23,35:1
Illegal Traffic 1938,N 17,29:3
King of Chinatown 1939,Mr 16,27:2
Some Like It Hot 1939,My 25,31:2
Geronimo 1940,F 8,18:3
Our Neighbors-The Carters 1940,F 15,15:2
Farmer's Daughter, The 1940,F 16,23:4
Seventeen 1940,F 29,15:2
Parole Fixer 1940,Ap 18,28:5
Queen of the Mob 1940,Jl 1,23:2
Those Were the Days 1940,Jl 15,18:4
Golden Gloves 1940,Ag 21,23:6
North West Mounted Police 1940,N 7,33:2
Love Thy Neighbor 1940,D 18,32:5
Adam Had Four Sons 1941,Mr 28,26:6
West Point Widow 1941,S 11,21:5
Beyond the Blue Horizon 1942,Je 25,27:2
Glass Key, The 1942,O 16,23:1
Quiet Please, Murder 1942,D 22,31:1
Black Beauty 1946,Ag 30,13:2
Unknown Island 1949,Ja 8,11:4
No Man of her Own 1950,My 4,32:3
Okinawa 1952,Ap 24,38:3
Scarlet Angel 1952,Je 21,12:2
Hangman's Knot 1952,D 11,45:3
Glass Web, The 1953,N 12,37:5
Jivaro 1954,F 13,11:5
Creature from the Black Lagoon 1954,My 1,13:4
Magnificent Matador, The 1955,My 25,38:1
Crooked Web, The 1955,D 10,19:1
Affair to Remember, An 1957,Jl 20,8:5
Black Scorpion, The 1957,O 12,23:2
Lady Takes a Flyer, The 1958,Ja 30,19:2
Twice Told Tales (The House of the Seven Gables); House of the Seven Gables, The (Twice Told Tales) 1964,My 28,40:1
DENNIS
See Also DENIS
Dennis, Beverly
Take Care of my Little Girl 1951,Jl 19,20:2
Westward the Women 1952,Ja 1,21:2
Dennis, Danny
Blackboard Jungle 1955,Mr 21,21:5
Dennis, Eddie
All Abroad 1927,Ap 19,24:4
Dennis, Eugene (Miscellaneous)
Hell's Holiday 1933,Jl 15,14:3
Dennis, Harold J (Producer)
Cinerama's Russian Adventure 1966,Ap 14,42:1
Dennis, Jack (Miscellaneous)
Victory Through Air Power 1943,Jl 19,13:1
Dennis, John
From Here to Eternity 1953,Ag 6,16:2
Naked Street, The 1955,O 1,11:2
Target Zero 1955,N 16,43:2
Too Much, Too Soon 1958,My 10,19:2
Mister Buddwing 1966,O 12,36:1
Dennis, John (Screenwriter)
By Love Possessed 1961,Jl 20,32:2
Dennis, Mark
Secret Beyond the Door 1948,Ja 16,25:4
Dennis, Nick
Sirocco 1951,Je 14,31:2
Streetcar Named Desire, A 1951,S 30,27:1
Ten Tall Men 1951,O 27,10:5
Anything Can Happen 1952,Ap 4,21:1
Iron Mistress, The 1952,N 20,39:2
Eight Iron Men 1953,Ja 2,11:1
Man in the Dark 1953,Ap 9,31:5
Glory Brigade, The 1953,Ag 15,8:4
East of Eden 1955,Mr 10,33:1
Big Knife, The 1955,N 9,41:2
Hot Blood 1956,Mr 24,14:2
Slaughter on Tenth Avenue 1957,N 6,43:1

Spartacus 1960,O 7,28:1
Too Late Blues 1962,Mr 1,27:4
Birdman of Alcatraz 1962,Jl 19,19:2
4 for Texas 1963,D 26,33:3
Dennis, Patrick (Original Author)
Auntie Mame 1958,D 5,39:1
Dennis, Sandy
Splendor in the Grass 1961,O 11,53:1
Who's Afraid of Virginia Woolf? 1966,Je 30,28:1
Who's Afraid of Virginia Woolf? 1966,Jl 10,II,1:5
Up the Down Staircase 1967,Ag 18,36:2
Fox, The 1968,F 8,36:1
Sweet November 1968,F 9,55:1
Dennis, Winifred
1 ■ 1 1961,N 8,41:1
Dennison, Eva
His Glorious Night 1929,O 5,22:5
Squaw Man, The 1931,S 19,10:2
Passport to Hell, A 1932,Ag 27,13:4
Dennison, Jo-Carroll
Winged Victory 1944,D 21,16:2
Jolson Story, The 1946,O 11,28:2
Pickup 1951,Ag 31,12:2
Millionaire for Christy, A 1951,O 5,24:3
Dennison, Leslie
Counter-Espionage 1942,S 28,13:2
Return of the Vampire, The 1944,Ja 29,10:1
Dennsy, Renee
Prenez Garde a la Peinture 1935,Ag 17,18:6
Denny, Barry
Loves of Edgar Allan Poe, The 1942,S 21,19:2
Denny, Malcolm
Sporting Youth 1924,Ap 2,16:1
Any Woman 1925,My 27,26:2
Blonde Saint, The 1926,N 23,27:1
Denny, Reginald
Iron Trail, The 1921,O 31,19:3
Abysmal Brute, The 1923,Ap 18,24:5
Sporting Youth 1924,Ap 2,16:1
Reckless Age, The 1924,Je 10,24:4
Fast Worker, The 1924,N 12,13:1
Oh, Doctor! 1925,F 23,24:1
I'll Show You the Town 1925,Je 8,19:1
Where Was I 1925,Ag 19,14:4
California Straight Ahead 1926,Ja 12,27:5
What Happened to Jones 1926,F 9,22:1
Skinner's Dress Suit 1926,My 3,27:1
Rolling Home 1926,Je 8,22:1
Take It From Me 1926,N 2,35:1
Cheerful Fraud, The 1926,D 28,17:1
Fast and Furious 1927,Jl 4,20:3
Out all Night 1927,S 27,31:1
On Your Toes 1928,Ja 9,20:1
That's my Daddy 1928,F 13,16:2
Good Morning, Judge 1928,Je 26,29:1
Night Bird, The 1928,O 2,23:5
Red Hot Speed 1929,F 5,26:3
Clear the Decks 1929,Ap 1,22:1
What a Man 1930,Jl 21,20:3
Madam Satan 1930,O 6,21:1
Those Three French Girls 1930,O 11,21:3
Lady's Morals, A 1930,N 8,21:3
Kiki 1931,Mr 6,16:1
Parlor, Bedroom and Bath 1931,Ap 4,23:1
Private Lives 1931,D 19,16:4
Strange Justice 1932,O 20,24:2
Iron Master, The 1933,F 4,11:3
Barbarian, The 1933,My 13,16:2
Only Yesterday 1933,N 10,25:1
Lost Patrol, The 1934,Ap 2,13:2
Of Human Bondage 1934,Je 29,17:1
World Moves On, The 1934,Je 30,18:5
Dancing Man 1934,Jl 16,11:3
One More River 1934,Ag 10,21:1
We're Rich Again 1934,S 1,16:3
Richest Girl in the World, The 1934,S 21,29:2
Little Minister, The 1934,D 28,25:1
Vagabond Lady 1935,Je 15,20:2
No More Ladies 1935,Je 22,18:5
Anna Karenina 1935,Ag 31,16:2
Here's to Romance 1935,O 3,29:2
Remember Last Night? 1935,N 21,27:2
Preview Murder Mystery, The 1936,Mr 21,13:2
Romeo and Juliet 1936,Ag 21,12:2
Two in a Crowd 1936,O 5,25:1
More Than a Secretary 1936,D 11,35:2
Women of Glamour 1937,Mr 6,10:1
Great Gambini, The 1937,Jl 12,20:4
Bulldog Drummond Comes Back 1937,S 4,8:3
Beg, Borrow or Steal 1937,D 10,33:2
Bulldog Drummond's Revenge 1937,D 17,33:2
Bulldog Drummond's Peril 1938,Mr 18,23:2
Four Men and a Prayer 1938,My 7,18:1
Blockade 1938,Je 17,25:1
Bulldog Drummond in Africa 1938,Ag 25,15:1
Arrest Bulldog Drummond 1939,Ja 12,23:2
Bulldog Drummond's Secret Police 1939,Mr 30,19:3
Bulldog Drummond's Bride 1939,Jl 13,17:2
Rebecca 1940,Mr 29,25:2
Spring Parade 1940,O 4,29:2
Seven Sinners 1940,N 18,23:2
One Night in Lisbon 1941,Je 12,29:3

Denny, Reginald— Cont
Appointment for Love 1941,N 7,27:1
International Squadron 1941,N 14,28:4
Captains of the Clouds 1942,F 13,24:2
Sherlock Holmes and the Voice Of Terror 1942,S 19,9:2
Eyes in the Night 1942,O 16,23:1
Thunder Birds 1942,O 29,19:2
Over my Dead Body 1942,D 26,15:2
Song of the Open Road 1944,Je 7,13:3
Love Letters 1945,Ag 27,22:3
Tangier 1946,Je 7,II,16:4
My Favorite Brunette 1947,Mr 20,38:2
Locket, The 1947,Mr 20,38:2
Macomber Affair, The 1947,Ap 21,21:2
Secret Life of Walter Mitty, The 1947,Ag 15,12:2
Escape me Never 1947,N 8,11:2
Christmas Eve 1947,N 28,30:2
Mr Blandings Builds his Dream House 1948,Mr 26,26:2
Iroquois Trail, The 1950,O 27,24:4
World for Ransom 1954,Je 5,11:2
Around the World in 80 Days 1956,O 18,37:1
Cat Ballou 1965,Je 25,36:1
Denny, Reginald (Original Author)
Fast and Furious 1927,Jl 4,20:3
Denny, Reginald (Screenwriter)
That's my Daddy 1928,F 13,16:2
Denovitch, Abe
Lady by Choice 1934,N 17,12:1
Denovitz, Barry
World Dances 1954,N 8,24:6
D'Enrico, Corrado (Director)
Tutta la Vita in una Notte; All of Life in one Night 1940,My 2,29:6
Dent, David (Producer)
Intimate Relations 1954,F 22,15:4
Dent, Vernon
Extra Girl, The 1924,Ja 21,20:1
His First Flame 1927,My 2,26:4
Million Dollar Legs 1932,Jl 9,7:5
Shadow, The 1937,D 17,33:3
Thanks for the Memory 1938,D 8,34:3
Beasts of Berlin 1939,N 20,15:6
Rockin' in The Rockies 1945,Jl 5,7:2
When Comedy Was King 1960,Mr 30,42:1
30 Years of Fun 1963,D 26,33:4
Denton, Arthur
Hue and Cry 1951,Ja 9,25:2
Denton, Coby
Wild Angels, The 1966,D 22,40:4
Denton, Crahan
Great St Louis Bank Robbery, The 1960,F 4,34:1
Young One, The 1961,Ja 26,16:1
Parent Trap, The 1961,Je 22,23:1
Birdman of Alcatraz 1962,Jl 19,19:2
To Kill a Mockingbird 1963,F 15,10:2
Hud 1963,My 29,36:1
Captain Newman, MD 1964,F 21,36:1
Bus Riley's Back in Town 1965,Ap 8,45:2
Denton, Geoffrey
Adam and Evalyn 1950,My 12,33:4
Denton, Jack
Little Lord Fauntleroy 1914,Je 23,11:3
Denton, Paul
Catered Affair, The 1956,Je 15,32:4
Dents, Patricia
Knock on Wood 1954,Ap 15,34:2
DeNuccio, Jerome
No Time for Love 1943,D 2,30:1
Denver, Bob
Private's Affair, A 1959,Ag 15,8:7
For Those Who Think Young 1964,Jl 9,27:1
Who's Minding the Mint? 1967,D 7,60:3
Sweet Ride, The 1968,Je 13,57:2
Denver, Maryesther
Fortune Cookie, The 1966,O 20,52:1
DePaul, Gene (Composer)
In the Navy 1941,Je 12,29:2
Two Tickets to London 1943,Jl 3,11:2
I Dood It 1943,N 11,29:1
Crazy House 1943,D 16,33:3
Broadway Rhythm 1944,Ap 14,24:6
Date with Judy, A 1948,Ag 7,8:2
Adventures of Ichabod and Mr Toad, The 1949,O 10,18:2
Seven Brides for Seven Brothers 1954,Jl 23,8:3
Li'l Abner 1959,D 12,19:2
Depew, Joseph
Steadfast Heart, The 1923,D 25,26:1
Icebound 1924,Mr 3,22:3 (In Addenda)
Swan, The 1925,Mr 2,14:1
Queen of the Night Clubs 1929,Mr 18,30:6
Deplanque, Pierrette
Naked Childhood 1968,S 28,36:1
Depp, Harry
Inez From Hollywood 1924,D 16,28:1
Deppe, Hans
Eine Tuer geht Auf 1933,F 6,11:5
Stern von Valencia, Der 1934,Ap 21,12:2
Schimmelreiter, Der; Rider of the White Horse, The 1935,F 25,13:3
Berliner, The 1952,O 28,37:1

Deppe, Hans (Director)
Schloss Hubertus 1935,F 9,11:3
Schimmelreiter, Der; Rider of the White Horse, The 1935,F 25,13:3
Ferien vom Ich 1935,Ap 1,17:2
Herr Kobin Geht auf Abenteuer; Mr Kobin Seeks Adventure 1935,N 26,28:2
Heilige und Ihr Narr, Die; Saint and Her Fool, The 1935,N 29,24:2
Mutige Seefahrer, Der 1936,N 21,21:5
Jaeger von Fall, Der 1937,Ap 24,16:4
Pretty Miss Schragg 1937,S 25,10:2
Silence of the Forest, The; Schweigen im Walde, Das 1937,D 6,19:2
Gewitter im Mai; Storms in May 1938,Mr 5,11:3
Zweimal zwei im Himmelbett; Twice Two in a Four-Post Bed 1939,F 5,19:3
Kluge Schwiegermutter, Die; Wise Mother-in-Law, The 1939,O 9,15:3
Ekel, Das; Grouch, The 1939,D 4,18:4
Drei um Christine, Die; Three After Christine, The 1940,My 4,13:2

Deprends, Jeffrey (Original Author)
Slander the Woman 1923,My 28,18:2

Derame, Margaret
State Fair 1962,Ap 12,41:4

D'Erano, Giovanni (Original Author)
300 Spartans, The 1962,S 20,29:2

DeRavenne, Charles
Love and Glory 1924,Ag 5,10:2
House of a Thousand Candles, The 1936,Ap 2,29:2

Deray, Jacques (Director)
Symphony for a Massacre 1965,My 28,40:1

Deray, Jacques (Screenwriter)
Symphony for a Massacre 1965,My 28,40:1

Derba, Mimi
Martin Garatuza 1935,S 30,13:1
Sor Juana Ines de la Cruz 1936,Je 6,21:2
Abnegacion 1938,My 31,8:3
Flor Sylvestre 1945,Ja 16,17:2

Derberg, Susan
American Dream, An 1966,S 1,28:2

Derbysheva, L (Director)
World Dances, The 1958,Je 5,39:2

Dercvschikova, Elena
Stone Flower 1946,D 30,15:2

Dere, Ann
Streetcar Named Desire, A 1951,S 30,27:1

Dereal, colette
Little Boy Lost 1953,S 22,38:2

Dereal, Colette
Happy Road, The 1957,Je 21,20:2

Derean, Rosine
Frochard et les Deux Orphelines, La 1934,F 7,16:2
Luc Aux Dames 1936,Ja 15,14:4
Story of a Cheat, The 1938,S 27,25:2
Sacrifice d'Honneur 1938,D 2,27:2

Derede, Julian (Producer)
Visit, The 1964,O 22,44:1

Derek, John
Knock on any Door 1949,F 23,31:2
All the King's Men 1949,N 9,37:2
Mask of the Avenger 1951,Je 27,25:2
Saturday's Hero 1951,S 12,37:2
Scandal Sheet 1952,Ja 17,23:1
Thunderbirds 1953,Mr 12,24:4
Mission Over Korea 1953,S 19,7:2
Outcast, The 1954,Jl 3,9:2
Adventures of Haji Baba, The 1954,O 9,8:7
Prince of Players 1955,Ja 12,24:2
Annapolis Story, An 1955,Ap 9,8:2
Run for Cover 1955,Ap 30,10:6
Leather Saint, The 1956,Je 16,12:2
Ten Commandments, The 1956,N 9,35:2
Fury at Showdown 1957,Ap 20,21:3
Omar Khayyam 1957,Ag 24,12:4
Flesh is Weak, The 1957,N 9,31:2
Prisoner of the Volga 1960,Je 2,27:2
Exodus 1960,D 16,44:1

Dereon, Rosine
Sous la Lune du Maroc 1933,Ja 23,9:2

Deresford, Evelyn
Prisoner of Zenda, The 1937,S 3,12:1

Derigney, Louise
My Lady's Garter 1920,Mr 15,13:2

Derjavin, Mikhail
Days and Nights 1946,Ap 29,24:4

Derlan, Guy
Man and his Wife, A 1939,Mr 28,20:1

Dermastro, Luigi
Guaglio 1949,My 19,35:2

Dermery, A (Original Author)
Two Orphans, The 1950,O 19,40:6

Dermit, Edouard
Orpheus 1950,N 30,42:2
Strange Ones, The 1952,Jl 29,17:3
Testament of Orpheus 1962,Ap 10,48:1

Dermota, Anton
Don Giovanni 1956,D 27,22:1

Dermoz, Germaine
Bal, Le 1932,S 28,22:5
Porteuse de Pain, La 1936,Jl 1,29:5
Moscow Nights 1938,My 3,19:3
Heroes of the Marne; (Famille Lefrancois, Le) 1939,Ap 24,13:2
Monsieur Vincent 1948,D 21,33:2
Prize, The 1952,Ap 30,33:2

Dern, Bruce
Wild River 1960,My 27,22:1
Hush...Hush, Sweet Charlotte 1965,Mr 4,36:1
Wild Angels, The 1966,D 22,40:4
St Valentine's Day Massacre, The 1967,Jl 27,29:2
Waterhole #3 1967,O 11,41:4
Psych-Out 1968,Mr 28,52:1
Will Penny 1968,Ap 11,51:2

Derocles, Georges (Producer)
Olive Trees of Justice, The 1967,My 5,31:1

Derode, Julien (Producer)
Symphony for a Massacre 1965,My 28,40:1
Male Companion 1966,F 15,33:2
Sleeping Car Murder, The 1966,Mr 8,45:1

Derosa, Frank
Young, The Evil and the Savage, The 1968,Ag 15,46:2

Derr, Albert (Original Author)
For Singles Only 1968,Je 6,54:1

Derr, Bruce
Trip, The 1967,Ag 24,43:1

Derr, Richard
Man at Large 1941,O 11,21:4
Gentleman at Heart, A 1942,F 23,25:2
Man Who Wouldn't Die, The 1942,Ap 28,25:5
Ten Gentlemen From West Point 1942,Je 5,23:3
Just off Broadway 1942,Ag 29,18:4
Secret Heart, The 1946,D 26,28:2
Bride Goes Wild, The 1948,Je 4,27:2
Luxury Liner 1948,S 10,19:2
Joan of Arc 1948,N 12,30:5
Guilty of Treason 1950,Ap 11,26:2
When Worlds Collide 1952,F 7,30:2
Something to Live For 1952,Mr 8,11:2
Commandos Strike at Dawn 1954,Ja 14,25:1
Terror is a Man 1960,Jl 14,23:1

Derrico, Corrado (Director)
Stella del Mare; Star of the Sea 1940,My 3,17:6

Derrien, Marcelle
Man About Town 1947,O 22,37:1

Derringer, Paul
Safe at Home 1941,N 26,31:2

Dervis, Charles
Red Mark, The 1928,O 30,27:3

Derwent, Clarence
Night Angel, The 1931,Je 11,28:4
Story of Vernon and Irene Castle, The 1939,Mr 31,19:2
Stanley and Livingstone 1939,Ag 5,18:2
British Intelligence 1940,F 12,14:2
Uncle Vanya 1958,Ap 29,26:2

Derzhavin, Mikhail
Turning Point, The 1946,O 28,19:4

Des Autels, Van
Crooked Web, The 1955,D 10,19:1

des Ligneris, Francoise (Original Author)
Psyche 39 1964,Ap 30,30:1

Des Vailleres, Jean (Screenwriter)
My Seven Little Sins 1956,My 2,27:1

Des Vallieres, Jean (Screenwriter)
My Seven Little Sins 1956,My 2,27:1

Desai, V
Gyandev of India 1943,Ap 10,12:5

Desailly, Jean
Symphonie Pastorale 1948,S 14,34:3
Just a big Simple Girl; Une Grande Fille Toute Simple 1949,O 28,29:2
Sylvie and the Phantom 1950,O 16,30:5
Oh, Amelia 1951,D 3,22:2
Grand Maneuver, The 1956,O 2,39:1
Inspector Maigret 1958,O 9,47:1
Possessors, The 1959,Jl 21,24:1
Passion of Slow Fire, The 1962,O 12,26:1
Doulos-The Finger Man 1964,Mr 3,31:1
Soft Skin, The; Peau Douce, La 1964,O 13,49:2

Desailly, Paul
7 Capital Sins (Lust); Lust (7 Capital Sins) 1963,Ja 17,5:2

DeSanotis, Gino (Screenwriter)
White Warrior, The 1961,F 11,27:2

Descaut, France
Amazing Monsieur Fabre, The 1952,S 9,21:2

Descaut, Frances
Miracle of Saint Therese 1959,F 10,38:4 (In Addenda)

Deschamps, Bernard (Director)
He 1933,D 27,23:6

Deschamps, Charles
Postmaster's Daughter, The 1946,Ag 19,17:6
Lovers of Verona, The 1951,Mr 12,20:2
Game of Love, The 1954,D 15,41:1
Virtuous Bigamist, The 1959,My 28,34:3

Deschamps, Claude
Fire Within, The 1964,F 18,27:1

Deschamps, Hubert
Zazie 1961,N 21,45:5
Fire Within, The 1964,F 18,27:1

Descher, Sandy
It Grows on Trees 1952,N 29,11:2
Them 1954,Je 17,36:2
Last Time I saw Paris, The 1954,N 19,20:2
Prodigal, The 1955,My 14,10:7
Bottom of the Bottle, The 1956,F 2,19:2
Man in the Gray Flannel Suit, The 1956,Ap 13,21:1
Opposite Sex, The 1956,N 16,23:2

Descrieres, George
Would-Be Gentleman, The 1960,Mr 23,31:1

Descrieres, Georges
Lovers on a Tightrope 1962,O 25,48:3
Marriage of Figaro, The 1963,Ap 30,26:1
Two for the Road 1967,Ap 28,36:2
Flea in her Ear, A 1968,N 28,66:1

DeSegurola, Andre
Bringing Up Father 1928,Mr 19,26:2
Glorious Betsy 1928,Ap 27,16:4
Red Dance, The 1928,Je 26,29:1
Cardboard Lover, The 1928,S 3,14:2
My Man 1928,D 22,14:3
General Crack 1929,D 4,36:6
Song O' my Heart 1930,Mr 12,32:6
Mama 1933,Jl 8,14:6
Su Ultimo Amor 1933,Ag 19,14:5
El Principe Gondolero 1933,S 11,20:4
Cascarrabias 1933,O 30,14:2
Ciudad de Carton, La 1934,F 28,23:3
Granaderos del Amor 1934,S 4,23:4
One Night of Love 1934,S 7,25:3
Dos Mas Uno Dos 1934,O 27,20:3

DeSimone
Bambole; Dolls, The (The Soup); Soup, The (The Dolls) 1965,Je 29,26:1

DeSimone, Pat
Dino 1957,Je 22,9:2

Desjardins, Maxime
J'Accuse 1920,My 23,VI,2:2
I Accuse; (J'Accuse) 1921,O 10,16:1
Legion of Honor, The 1928,Jl 20,8:4
Soul of France, The 1929,O 12,11:1
Mystere de la Chambre Jaune, Le 1931,My 26,33:2

Deslys, Kay
Tarnish 1924,O 13,21:1
Case of Lena Smith, The 1929,Ja 15,22:4
Friends and Lovers 1931,N 7,16:5

Desmarets, Jacqueline
Her First Affair; (Children of Paradise) 1947,F 20,32:3

Desmarets, Sophia
Sextette (Part 2-Female Affair); Female Affair (Sextette) 1953,Mr 2,19:2

Desmarets, Sophie
Royal Affair, A; (Roi, Le) 1950,Mr 9,25:2
Ma Pomme 1951,O 15,22:2
Sweet and Sour 1964,D 28,34:2

Desmond, Brian (Director)
River of Unrest 1937,N 27,21:2
Malta Story 1954,Jl 17,7:2

Desmond, Cleo
Spirit of Youth 1938,F 28,19:1

Desmond, Dagmar
Man and Maid 1925,Ap 7,17:3

Desmond, Danny
Walk in the Sun, A 1946,Ja 12,10:6

Desmond, Florence
Mr Skitch 1933,D 23,19:1
Accused 1936,D 17,35:1
Three Came Home 1950,F 21,22:5

Desmond, James (Cinematographer)
Monterey Pop 1968,D 27,44:1

Desmond, Johnny
China Doll 1958,D 4,52:1

Desmond, Marc
Name of the Game Is Kill, The 1968,Je 6,54:1

Desmond, Rosbert
Cockleshell Heroes, The 1956,Je 4,25:2

Desmond, Stanley
Major and the Minor, The 1942,S 17,21:3

Desmond, William
Pretender, The 1918,O 21,15:1
Twin Beds 1920,N 1,13:2
Fightin' Mad 1921,N 21,20:1
Extra Girl, The 1924,Ja 21,20:1
Powdersmoke Range 1936,Mr 9,20:2
Hollywood Boulevard 1936,S 21,26:4
Little Bit of Heaven, A 1940,N 8,24:2

Desmond-Hurst, Brian (Producer)
Tom Brown's School Days 1952,Ja 8,23:5

Desmonde, Jerry
Trouble in Store 1956,Ja 14,13:2
Angel Who Pawned her Harp, The 1956,F 29,35:2
Follow a Star 1961,Ap 26,34:1
Stolen Hours 1963,O 17,39:1

Desners, Suzanne
drame De Shanghai; Shanghai Drama, The 1945,Ja 11,19:2

Desni, Tamara
Der Schrecken der Garnison 1932,Je 1,19:5
Jack Ahoy 1935,F 9,11:2
Fire Over England 1937,Mr 5,16:2
Murder on Diamond Row 1937,N 12,27:2
Desni, Xenia
Waltz Dream, The 1926,Jl 26,13:2
Oberkellner, Der 1929,Jl 1,31:2
Desny, Ivan
Madeleine 1950,S 1,17:2
No Way Back 1955,My 19,25:5
Anastasia 1956,D 14,35:6
Respectful Prostitute, The 1957,Jl 11,21:1
Ballerina 1958,My 10,19:2
Tempestous Love 1958,N 22,27:4
Mirror Has two Faces, The 1959,My 27,31:1
Song Without End 1960,Ag 12,10:2
Bon Voyage! 1962,My 18,34:2
End of Desire 1962,Jl 10,29:2
Golden Plaque, The 1963,Ag 10,8:6
Guns for San Sebastian 1968,Mr 21,57:2
Lola Montes 1968,S 23,42:6
DeSouza, Herbert
Booloo 1938,Jl 30,10:2
Despax, Olivier
Dark of the Sun 1968,Jl 4,13:1
Despeaux, Jean
Murderer Lives at Number 21, The
1947,Ag 18,12:3
Despres, Suzanne
Maria Chapdelaine 1935,S 25,18:2
Flight Into Darkness (L'Equipage)
1938,O 17,12:1
Louise 1940,F 3,9:4
Dessau, Benie
Weekend 1964,Ap 27,24:1
Dessau, Paul (Composer)
Trapeze 1932,My 3,25:2
Ich Glaub' nie Mehr an Eine Frau
1933,O 13,25:4
Ski Chase, The 1938,Mr 26,12:1
Dest, Jo
Damned, The; Maudits, Les 1948,Ap 26,27:2
Wages of Fear, The 1955,F 17,23:1
Destailles, Pierre
Under the Paris Sky 1952,My 6,35:1
Destain, Robert
My Seven Little Sins 1956,My 2,27:1
Fernandel the Dressmaker 1957,Jl 1,19:2
Belle Americaine, La 1961,D 18,42:1
Deste, Luli
Thunder in the City 1937,Ap 23,25:2
Thank You, Madame 1937,Ap 27,18:2
She Married an Artist 1938,F 25,15:2
Ski Patrol 1940,My 21,29:4
South to Karanga 1940,Ag 9,19:1
Case of the Black Parrot, The 1941,Ja 10,23:3
d'Estee, Mimi
Whispering City 1948,My 10,25:5
Destefani, A (Screenwriter)
Man of the Sea 1948,Ja 24,11:2
Desval, Rodolfo
Cancion del Regreso, La; Home-Coming Song
1940,Je 22,18:4
Desvallieres, Maurice (Original Author)
Hotel Paradiso 1966,O 15,34:2
Desy, Johanne (Miscellaneous)
Take it All; A Tout Prendre 1966,Ap 26,55:1
Desy, Victor
Take it All; A Tout Prendre 1966,Ap 26,55:1
Desy, Victor (Miscellaneous)
Take it All; A Tout Prendre 1966,Ap 26,55:1
DeSylva, B G (Producer)
Little Colonel, The 1935,Mr 22,26:2
DeToth, Andre (Screenwriter)
Morgan the Pirate 1961,Jl 20,32:2
Detto, Loredana
Sound of Trumpets, The 1963,O 23,36:1
Detzer, Karl (Original Author)
Car 99 1935,F 23,14:7
Detzer, Karl (Screenwriter)
Car 99 1935,F 23,14:7
Crash Donovan 1936,Ag 10,10:3
Deuel, Peter
Hell With Heroes, The 1968,S 3,54:2
Deuesa, Jaime
Hombre Peligroso, Un; Dangerous Man, A
1935,O 14,21:2
Deurell, Carl
En Saga 1938,Ja 8,19:2
Deutchman, Clara
Mirele Efros 1939,O 21,12:2
Deutsch, Adolph (Composer)
Valley of the Giants 1938,S 10,20:2
Deutsch, Armand (Producer)
Ambush 1950,Ja 19,35:2
Right Cross 1950,N 16,39:2
Magnificent Yankee, The 1951,Ja 19,21:2
Three Guys Named Mike 1951,Mr 2,21:2
Kind Lady 1951,Ag 8,21:2
Carbine Williams 1952,My 8,37:2
Girl in White, The 1952,My 31,12:5
Green Fire 1954,D 25,7:1

Slander 1957,Ja 17,34:4
Saddle the Wind 1958,Mr 21,17:1
Deutsch, David (Producer)
Chance Meeting 1960,O 27,45:2
Play it Cool 1963,Jl 18,15:3
Having a Wild Weekend 1965,Ag 19,35:1
Interlude 1968,Jl 3,26:1
Deutsch, Ernst
Nurse Edith Cavell 1939,S 22,27:4
Man I Married, The 1940,Ag 3,9:2
So Ends our Night 1941,F 28,17:2
Third Man, The 1950,F 3,29:2
Deutsch, Helen (Composer)
Glass Slipper, The 1955,Mr 25,19:2
Deutsch, Helen (Miscellaneous)
Glass Slipper, The 1955,Mr 25,19:2
Deutsch, Helen (Screenwriter)
Seventh Cross, The 1944,S 29,18:1
National Velvet 1944,D 15,25:2
Golden Earrings 1947,D 4,41:3
Loves of Carmen, The 1948,S 3,16:2
King Solomon's Mines 1950,N 10,35:1
Kim 1950,D 8,40:4
It's a big Country 1952,Ja 9,25:2
Plymouth Adventure 1952,N 14,20:3
Lili 1953,Mr 11,36:7
Flame and the Flesh 1954,My 3,21:2
Glass Slipper, The 1955,Mr 25,19:2
I'll Cry Tomorrow 1956,Ja 13,18:1
Forever, Darling 1956,F 10,18:1
Unsinkable Molly Brown, The 1964,Jl 17,15:1
Valley of the Dolls 1967,D 16,51:1
Deval, Jacques (Director)
Club De Femmes 1937,O 20,27:2
Deval, Jacques (Original Author)
Journal of a Crime 1934,Ap 28,11:3
Marie Galante 1934,N 21,23:4
Tovarich 1937,D 31,9:2
Say It in French 1938,D 1,29:1
Her Cardboard Lover 1942,Jl 17,19:2
Seven Days Ashore 1944,Ap 26,24:7
Miss Tatlock's Millions 1948,N 25,47:2
Deval, Jacques (Screenwriter)
Cafe Metropole 1937,Ap 29,17:1
Club De Femmes 1937,O 20,27:2
Balalaika 1939,D 15,33:2
New Moon 1940,Jl 19,22:2
Her Cardboard Lover 1942,Jl 17,19:2
Deval, Marguerite
Man of the Hour, The 1940,N 21,43:2
Nine Bachelors 1942,F 9,19:2
Marked Girls 1949,Je 25,8:7
Spice of Life, The 1953,D 29,19:3
Devan, Billy
When Comedy Was King 1960,Mr 30,42:1
Devenish, Ross (Director)
Goal 1967,Ja 19,26:1
Deveny, Laci
Legy Jo Mindhalalig 1936,O 26,20:2
Devere, Arthur
Kermesse Heroique, La 1936,S 23,29:1
End of a Day, The 1939,S 12,28:4
It Happened at the Inn; Goupi Mains Rouge
1945,D 22,16:2
Devere, Harry
Hunchback of Notre Dame, The 1923,S 3,9:3
Devereaux, Ed
Password Is Courage, The 1962,D 22,5:2
Wrong Arm of the Law, The 1963,Ap 3,39:1
Devereux, Marie
Mark, The 1961,O 3,46:2
Deverill, John
Monte Carlo Madness 1932,Je 4,9:2
Devesa, Jaime
Tango en Broadway, El 1934,D 29,11:3
Devhrys, Rachel
Morgane, the Enchantress 1929,Je 21,17:2
Devi, Bopha Princess
Dragon Sky 1964,Ag 25,28:2
Devi, Chunibala
Pather Panchali 1958,S 23,37:2
Devi, Kamala
Harry Black and the Tiger 1958,S 19,24:4
Brass Bottle, The 1964,My 21,42:1
Devi, Pagma
Music Room, The 1963,O 16,50:6
Devi, Reva
Pather Panchali 1958,S 23,37:2
Devi, Seeta
Light of Asia, The 1928,My 12,8:4
Shiraz 1928,O 7,IX,7:7
Shiraz 1929,Mr 19,37:2
Throw of the Dice 1930,Ja 6,30:5
Devierine, Maurice
Tender Enemy, The 1938,Mr 31,15:2 (In
Addenda)
Devigny, Andre (Original Author)
Man Escaped, A 1957,Ag 27,33:2
Devil Tiger, The
Devil Tiger 1934,F 9,23:2
Devilbliss, Robert
Old Nest, The 1921,Je 29,10:3

Deviliers, Renee
French Touch, The 1954,S 2,18:2
Deville, Michel (Director)
Benjamin 1968,Mr 26,41:2
Devillers, Renee
Douceur D'Aimer, La 1931,D 14,16:3
That They May Live 1939,N 7,31:2
Man of the Hour, The 1940,N 21,43:2
Heart of a Nation, The 1943,Ap 8,27:2
Monelle 1950,F 3,29:2
Perfectionist, The 1952,My 2,21:3
Game of Love, The 1954,D 15,41:1
Devin, Marilyn
First to Fight 1967,Mr 30,55:1
Devine, Andy
We Americans 1928,Mr 29,25:3
Red Lips 1928,O 16,29:2 (In Addenda)
Naughty Baby 1929,F 5,26:3
Hot Stuff 1929,My 13,27:2
Spirit of Notre Dame, The 1931,O 16,27:1
Three Wise Girls 1932,F 6,14:4
Law and Order 1932,F 29,21:3
Impatient Maiden, The 1932,Mr 4,17:3
Man Wanted 1932,Ap 16,11:2
Man From Yesterday, The 1932,Je 25,18:2
Radio Patrol 1932,Jl 14,24:2
Tom Brown of Culver 1932,Jl 30,16:5
All American, The 1932,O 22,18:4
Cohens and Kellys in Trouble, The
1933,Ap 17,16:4
Song of the Eagle 1933,Ap 29,14:3
Big Cage, The 1933,My 9,20:5
Midnight Mary 1933,Jl 15,14:2
Doctor Bull 1933,O 6,21:2
Saturday's Millions 1933,O 14,18:3
Chance at Heaven 1933,D 26,19:3
Stingaree 1934,My 18,27:1
Upper World 1934,My 25,25:4
Let's Talk It Over 1934,Je 16,20:2
Million Dollar Ransom 1934,S 19,15:2
Gift of Gab 1934,S 26,17:6
Wake up and Dream 1934,O 11,28:3
President Vanishes, The 1934,D 8,18:5
Hell in the Heavens 1934,D 12,28:2
Hold 'Em Yale 1935,Ap 27,20:6
Chinatown Squad 1935,My 30,21:1
Farmer Takes a Wife, The 1935,Ag 9,21:2
Way Down East 1935,O 31,16:2
Fighting Youth 1935,N 2,13:3
Coronado 1935,D 19,33:4
Small Town Girl 1936,Ap 11,19:1
Romeo and Juliet 1936,Ag 21,12:2
Big Game, The 1936,O 24,23:1
Flying Hostess 1936,D 14,29:4
Mysterious Crossing 1937,F 2,20:5
Star Is Born, A 1937,Ap 23,25:1
Road Back, The 1937,Je 18,25:2
Double or Nothing 1937,S 2,17:3
You're a Sweetheart 1937,D 25,10:5
In Old Chicago 1938,Ja 7,15:2
Doctor Rhythm 1938,My 19,25:2
Yellow Jack 1938,My 20,17:2
Personal Secretary 1938,O 5,20:2
Men With Wings 1938,O 27,27:2
Storm, The 1938,O 31,12:2
Swing That Cheer 1938,N 11,31:2
Stagecoach 1939,Mr 3,21:1
Spirit of Culver 1939,Mr 9,18:1
Never Say Die 1939,Mr 9,18:1
Mutiny on the Blackhawk 1939,Ag 2,17:2
Tropic Fury 1939,S 8,28:4
Legion of Lost Flyers 1939,O 30,13:3
Little Old New York 1940,F 3,9:2
Geronimo 1940,F 8,18:3
Buck Benny Rides Again 1940,Ap 25,28:4
Torrid Zone 1940,My 18,11:3
Hot Steel 1940,Je 21,25:3
When the Daltons Rode 1940,Ag 23,13:3
Black Diamonds 1940,S 10,26:6
Devil's Pipeline, The 1940,N 11,22:4
Trail of the Vigilantes 1940,D 7,13:2
Flame of New Orleans, The 1941,Ap 26,20:2
Mutiny in the Arctic 1941,My 3,20:5
Badlands of Dakota 1941,S 27:6
South of Tahiti 1941,N 10,21:3
Kid From Kansas, The 1941,D 2,29:4
North to the Klondike 1942,Mr 12,24:3
Between Us Girls 1942,S 25,25:3
Sin Town 1942,O 17,11:2
Frontier Badmen 1943,Ag 14,12:8
Corvette K-225 1943,O 21,30:1
Crazy House 1943,D 16,33:3
Ali Baba and the Forty Thieves 1944,Mr 16,17:3
Ghost Catchers 1944,My 31,22:3
Bowery to Broadway 1944,N 30,19:2
Frisco Sal 1945,F 17,11:2
Sudan 1945,Ap 19,22:8
That's the Spirit 1945,Je 2,11:2
Frontier Gal 1945,D 15,14:2
Canyon Passage 1946,Ag 18:2
Michigan Kid 1947,F 22,16:3
Vigilantes Return, The 1947,Jl 1,30:2
Slave Girl 1947,Jl 18,21:3

Devine, Andy— Cont
Fabulous Texan, The 1947,D 26,22:5
Old Los Angeles 1948,Jl 12,11:2
Last Bandit, The 1949,Mr 21,19:2
Traveling Saleswoman 1950,Ja 6,25:3
Never a Dull Moment 1950,N 22,20:2
New Mexico 1951,Jl 14,7:2
Montana Belle 1952,N 8,9:2
Island in the Sky 1953,S 10,22:2
Pete Kelly's Blues 1955,Ag 19,10:1
Around the World in 80 Days 1956,O 18,37:1
Adventures of Huckleberry Fin, The
  1960,Ag 4,17:1
Two Rode Together 1961,Jl 27,23:3
Man Who Shot Liberty Valance, The
  1962,My 24,29:2
It's a Mad, Mad, Mad, Mad World
  1963,N 19,47:1
Ballad of Josie, The 1968,Mr 14,51:2

Devine, Dennis
Canyon Passage 1946,Ag 8,18:2
Lafayette Escadrille 1958,Ap 19,10:4

Devine, George
Continental Express 1942,Ap 7,26:3
Promoter, The 1952,O 29,36:2
Beggar's Opera, The 1953,Ag 25,18:2
Time Without Pity 1957,N 23,11:2
Tom Jones 1963,O 8,48:1

Devine, Jerry
Potash and Perlmutter 1923,S 24,5:4
Steadfast Heart, The 1923,D 25,26:1
Tongues of Flame 1924,D 16,28:1
Mad Game, The 1933,N 13,21:1

Devine, John
Over the Hill to the Poor House 1920,S 18,16:2

Devine, Tad
Canyon Passage 1946,Ag 8,18:2

Devirys, Rachel
Crainquebille 1934,D 10,16:3
Gervaise 1957,N 12,46:1

Devis, Pamela
Perfect Woman, The 1951,F 17,10:7

Devlin, Donald
Swell Guy 1947,Ja 27,17:2

Devlin, Harry (Producer)
Spell of Ireland, The 1954,My 11,25:5

Devlin, J G
Darby O'Gill and the Little People 1959,Jl 1,26:1
I Thank a Fool 1962,S 15,15:1

Devlin, Joe
Oklahoma Kid, The 1939,Mr 11,21:1
Fugitive From Justice, A 1940,Jl 8,13:3
Devil With Hitler, The 1942,O 19,15:2
They Got Me Covered 1943,Mr 5,20:2
Taxi, Mister 1943,Ap 15,20:2
That Nazty Nuisance 1943,My 29,10:3
Criminal Court 1946,N 16,15:3
Bringing Up Father 1946,N 22,27:3
San Quentin 1947,F 10,24:3
That Way With Women 1947,F 15,20:4
Body and Soul 1947,N 10,21:2

Devlin, William
Mutiny of the Elsinore, The 1939,F 16,17:2
I Met a Murderer 1939,O 2,15:2
Mill On the Floss, The 1939,N 15,19:3
Treasure Island 1950,Ag 16,24:2
Oscar Wilde 1960,Je 21,28:2
Jokers, The 1967,My 16,50:1
Shuttered Room, The 1968,F 15,47:1

DeVol, Frank
Parent Trap, The 1961,Je 22,23:1
Big Mouth, The 1967,Jl 13,30:2

Devon, Laura
Goodbye, Charlie 1964,N 19,49:1
Red Line 7000 1965,D 9,60:4
Chamber of Horrors 1966,O 20,52:5
Covenant with Death, A 1967,F 16,32:3
Gunn 1967,Je 29,32:1

Devon, Richard
Comancheros, The 1961,N 2,42:1
Silencers, The 1966,Mr 17,35:1

Devore, Dorothy
Narrow Street, The 1925,Ja 5,19:1
How Baxter Buttered In 1925,Je 23,24:3
His Majesty Bunker Bean 1925,S 15,12:1
Social Highwayman, The 1926,Je 15,23:3
Senor Daredevil 1926,Ag 17,15:3

Devrient, Babette
Thank You, Madame 1937,Ap 27,18:2

Devry, Elaine
Man Trap 1961,N 30,40:4
Diary of a Madman 1963,Je 6,39:1

Dew, Eddie
Military Academy 1940,Ag 5,10:4
Army Surgeon 1942,N 5,35:2
Ladies' Day 1943,Mr 26,14:3

Dewey, Arthur
America 1924,F 22,20:1

Dewey, Jane
Wells Fargo 1937,D 30,15:2

Dewhurst, Colleen
Nun's Story, The 1959,Je 19,30:1
Man on a String 1960,My 21,15:1
Fine Madness, A 1966,Je 30,28:2

Dewhurst, William
Woman Alone, The 1937,F 27,9:2
Bulldog Drummond at Bay 1937,O 25,23:2
Victoria the Great 1937,O 29,19:1
Non-Stop New York 1937,N 29,19:2
Dinner at the Ritz 1937,D 4,21:1
Sailing Along 1938,Ap 16,17:1
21 Days Together 1940,My 23,28:4

DeWitt, George
Hole in the Head, A 1959,Jl 16,31:2

DeWitt, Jack (Original Author)
International Lady 1941,N 11,29:2
Canadian Pacific 1949,My 20,32:4
Women's Prison 1955,F 3,18:5

DeWitt, Jack (Screenwriter)
Bomba, the Jungle Boy 1949,Ap 16,11:4
Canadian Pacific 1949,My 20,32:4
Gun Belt 1953,Ag 1,8:2
Khyber Patrol 1954,S 20,19:2
Sitting Bull 1954,N 26,24:4
Women's Prison 1955,F 3,18:5
Portland Expose 1957,S 27,16:6
Purple Gang, The 1960,Ja 23,15:5
Jack of Diamonds 1967,N 11,26:3

Dewlen, Al (Original Author)
Twilight of Honor 1963,N 14,41:2
Ride Beyond Vengance 1966,S 29,60:1

DeWolfe, Ronald
Interlude 1949,Ja 3,19:2

Dexter, Alan
It Came From Outer Space 1953,Je 18,38:2
Forbidden 1954,Ja 23,11:2
Time Limit 1957,O 24,37:2
Enemy Below, The 1957,D 26,23:2

Dexter, Anthony
Valentino 1951,Ap 20,25:1
Brigand, The 1952,Jl 26,9:2
Thoroughly Modern Millie 1967,Mr 23,25:1

Dexter, Aubrey
Angel Street 1952,N 11,25:2
Prince and the Showgirl 1957,Je 14,22:2

Dexter, Brad
Asphalt Jungle, The 1950,Je 9,29:3
Las Vegas Story, The 1952,Ja 31,37:6
Macao 1952,My 1,34:2
99 River Street 1953,O 3,14:2
Untamed 1955,Mr 12,11:6
House of Bamboo 1955,Jl 2,13:2
Bottom of the Bottle, The 1956,F 2,19:2
Between Heaven and Hell 1956,O 12,33:2
Oklahoman, The 1957,My 15,39:1
Run Silent, Run Deep 1958,Mr 28,29:1
Last Train from Gun Hill 1959,Jl 30,31:2
Magnificent Seven, The 1960,N 24,48:3
George Raft Story, The 1962,Mr 22,40:1
X-15 1962,Ap 5,30:2
Taras Bulba 1962,D 26,5:2
Johnny Cool 1963,O 3,31:1
King of the Sun 1963,D 26,33:4
Invitation to a Gunfighter 1964,O 28,51:3
None but the Brave 1965,F 25,24:1
Bus Riley's Back in Town 1965,Ap 8,45:2
Von Ryan's Express 1965,Je 24,28:1
Blindfold 1966,My 26,55:2

Dexter, Brad (Producer)
Naked Runner, The 1967,Jl 20,30:2

Dexter, Elliott
Heart of Nora Flynn, The 1916,Ap 24,11:2
Rise of Jennie Cushing, The 1917,N 12,11:3
We Can't Have Everything 1918,Jl 15,9:3
Squaw Man, The 1918,D 30,7:3
Don't Change Your Husband 1919,F 3,13:2
For Better, For Worse 1919,Ap 28,13:2
Behold my Wife 1920,O 11,19:3
Something to Think About 1920,O 18,13:1
Affairs of Anatol, The 1921,S 12,16:1
Peter Ibbetson; (Forever) 1921,O 17,18:1
Don't Tell Everything 1921,D 12,20:2
Grand Larceny 1922,F 27,13:4
Only 38 1923,Je 11,16:2
Broadway Gold 1923,Jl 31,12:4
Common Law, The 1923,O 29,18:1
Flaming Youth 1923,N 26,15:6
Fast Set, The 1924,N 18,22:1
Capital Punishment 1925,F 5,23:3

Dexter, John (Director)
Othello 1966,F 2,24:1

Dexter, Maury (Director)
Harbor Lights 1964,F 13,25:3
Surf Party 1964,Mr 12,40:4
Day Mars Invaded Earth, The 1964,Ap 2,28:3
Naked Brigade, The 1965,Je 17,27:2
Maryjane 1968,Mr 14,51:4
Mini-Skirt Mob, The 1968,O 24,55:5
Born Wild 1968,D 12,62:6

Dexter, Maury (Producer)
Third Voice, The 1960,Mr 7,24:5
Yellow Canary, The 1963,My 16,42:1
Harbor Lights 1964,F 13,25:3
Surf Party 1964,Mr 12,40:4
Day Mars Invaded Earth, The 1964,Ap 2,28:3
Maryjane 1968,Mr 14,51:4
Mini-Skirt Mob, The 1968,O 24,55:5

Dexter, Maury (Producer)— Cont
Born Wild 1968,D 12,62:6

Dexter, Rosemarie
Casanova 1965,Jl 21,43:1
All the Other Girls Do! 1967,My 30,12:1
For a Few Dollars More 1967,Jl 4,23:1

Dexter, William
Knack...and how to get it, The 1965,Je 30,42:1

Deyers, Lien
Spione; Spies 1928,My 20,VIII,8:5
Spies 1929,Mr 5,29:1
Rosenmontag 1931,Mr 28,15:3
Hampelmann, Der 1931,S 8,38:7
Alte Lied, Das 1931,S 11,24:2
Sein Scheidungsgrund 1932,F 20,11:2
Ein Prinz Verliebt Sich 1932,Ap 29,13:4
Drunter und Drueber 1932,D 19,19:5
Lachende Erben 1933,N 18,18:6
Melodie der Liebe 1934,S 17,20:3
Gold 1934,O 22,12:3
Doppelbraeutigam, Der; Double Fiance, The
  1935,Mr 23,11:3
Die vom Niederrhein; Lower Rhine Folks
  1935,My 20,20:6
Ich Sing Mich in Dein Herz Hinein
  1935,Je 3,22:3
Vetter aus Dingsda, Der 1936,F 1,9:3
Karneval und Liebe 1936,Ap 4,11:2
Ganzer Kerl, Ein 1936,Ap 25,21:2
Fahrt ins Gruene, Die 1936,My 23,12:2
Ist Mein Mann Nicht Fabelhaft 1936,D 8,31:3
Punks Kommt aus Amerika 1937,Je 12,8:2
Selige Exzellenz, Die 1937,Je 15,26:2

Deyl, Rudolf
Ecstasy of Young Love 1936,Mr 10,27:3

DeYoung, Frances
Betrayal, The 1948,Je 26,10:5

Dhawan, Krishna
Guide, The 1965,F 10,44:2

d'Hee, Louis (Screenwriter)
Angel and Sinner 1947,F 24,16:5

Dhepley, Ruth
When Knighthood Was in Flower 1922,S 15,17:2
  (In Addenda)

Dheran, Bernard
Doctors, The 1956,Ag 7,19:2
Holiday Island; (Vacanzie a Izchia)
  1959,S 22,46:1
Belle Americaine, La 1961,D 18,42:1
Story of Monte Cristo, The 1962,N 7,48:1

Dhery, Robert
Belle Americaine, La 1961,D 18,42:1
Counterfeit Constable, The 1966,N 22,32:2

Dhery, Robert (Director)
Belle Americaine, La 1961,D 18,42:1
Counterfeit Constable, The 1966,N 22,32:2

Dhery, Robert (Screenwriter)
Belle Americaine, La 1961,D 18,42:1
Counterfeit Constable, The 1966,N 22,32:2

Dhiegh, Khigh
Manchurian Candidate, The 1962,O 25,48:3
13 Frightened Girls 1963,S 12,32:2
Seconds 1966,O 6,56:1

Dhlamini, Max
Cry, the Beloved Country 1952,Ja 24,23:2

Dhlamini, Ribbon
Cry, the Beloved Country 1952,Ja 24,23:2

Dhome, Sylvain (Director)
7 Capital Sins (Anger); Anger (7Capital Sins)
  1963,Ja 17,5:2

Dhome, Sylvain (Screenwriter)
Olive Trees of Justice, The 1967,My 5,31:1

di Benedetta, Marie
Greatest Love of All, The 1924,N 11,14:1

Di Capua, Vincenza
Marriage Italian Style 1964,D 21,42:1

di Ciagomo, Salvatore (Original Author)
Scarred 1951,O 27,10:5

Di Cicco, Pat (Producer)
Avalanche 1946,Jl 8,25:2

di Claudio, Naudio
Rome, 11 O'Clock 1953,Ap 30,39:2

di Donato, Pietro (Miscellaneous)
Open City; Citta Aperta 1946,F 26,21:2

di Donato, Pietro (Original Author)
Give Us This Day 1949,D 21,41:2

Di Fiori, Maria
Roof, The 1959,My 13,43:4

Di Gatano, Adam
Night and Day 1946,Jl 26,16:2

Di Gatano, Jayne
Night and Day 1946,Jl 26,16:2

Di Giovanni, Augusto
Marco Visconti 1947,S 20,12:4

di Lanti, Stella
Only Woman, The 1924,N 3,20:1
Don Q, Son of Zorro 1925,Je 16,24:1

di Lelio, Loretta
Lucia di Lammermoor 1947,N 1,11:3
This Wine of Love 1948,Ap 19,27:2

Di Leo, Anna
Journey to Love 1953,O 9,32:8

Di Leo, Fernando (Screenwriter)
Navajo Joe 1967,D 7,60:2
Di Leo, Lia
Moment of Truth, The 1954,Ap 27,36:2
Di Lorenzo, Edward (Screenwriter)
Place Called Glory, A 1966,Ag 11,27:4
di Luca, Dino
Richiamo del Cuore, Il; Appeal of the Heart, The 1931,Mr 2,19:1
Cieca di Sorrento, La 1936,Ag 3,11:3
Manon Lescaut 1941,Ap 14,23:5
Spirit and the Flesh, The 1948,N 1,28:2
Di Maggio, Carlo
Dolce Vita, La 1961,Ap 20,30:1
Di Maio, Gaspere (Original Author)
Tormento 1953,Ap 4,9:2
Di Maria, Nino (Original Author)
Path of Hope, The (Il Cammino Della Speranza) 1952,Ag 5,15:5
di Nardo, Maurizio
Young Caruso, The 1953,O 13,34:4
Times Gone By (The Idyll); Idyll, The (Times Gone By) 1953,D 30,16:2
di Palma, Dario (Cinematographer)
Almost a Man 1966,S 23,43:1
Di Paolella (Screenwriter)
Gran Varieta 1955,Ap 11,29:5
Di Paolo, Dante
Story of Joseph and his Brethren, The 1962,D 1,17:1
Blood and Black Lace 1965,N 11,58:3
Di Porto, Settimo
Gospel According to St Matthew, The 1966,F 18,23:1
di Reda, Joe
Gaby 1956,My 10,26:3
Time Limit 1957,O 24,37:2
Enemy Below, The 1957,D 26,23:2
In Love and War 1958,N 1,14:2
Big Fisherman, The 1959,Ag 6,18:1
Flight From Ashiya 1964,Ap 23,34:1
di Reda, Joseph
Sand Pebbles, The 1966,D 21,48:1
Di Rocco, Rossano
Gospel According to St Matthew, The 1966,F 18,23:1
Bible, The 1966,S 29,60:1
Di Rollo, Maria
Roof, The 1959,My 13,43:4
Di Savola, Lionello Pio
Made in Italy 1967,My 1,44:2
Di Stefano Brothers
Difficult Years 1950,Ag 22,31:2
DIAL
See Also DEAL, DIEHL
Dial, Patterson
Happiness 1924,Mr 11,16:2
Secrets 1924,Mr 25,25:2
Married Flirts 1924,N 19,19:3
Diamand-Berger, Henri (Director)
Amazing Monsieur Fabre, The 1952,S 9,21:2
Diamant, Catherine
Religieuse, La 1968,S 23,42:3
Diamant-Berger, Henri (Director)
Milady 1923,Ja 22,10:1
Vierge Folle, La 1938,D 30,11:3
Diamant-Berger, Henri (Producer)
Belle Americaine, La 1961,D 18,42:1
Thank Heaven for Small Favors 1965,Ja 14,44:2
Diamantidou, Despo
Never on Sunday 1960,O 19,54:1
Red Lanterns 1965,Ap 1,30:1
Diamond, Arnold
Othello 1960,My 16,39:1
Hand in Hand 1961,F 7,41:3
Diamond, Bobby
Young Man With Ideas 1952,Je 7,22:6
Diamond, David (Composer)
Strange Victory 1948,S 27,27:2
Diamond, David (Original Author)
Swing It, Sailor 1937,D 13,23:5
Diamond, David (Producer)
I Was an American Spy 1951,Jl 4,13:2
Bullet for Joey, A 1955,Ap 16,12:1
Phenix City Story, The 1955,S 3,9:1
Operation Eichmann 1961,My 4,40:7
King of the Roaring Twenties 1961,O 5,43:1
Strangler, The 1964,Je 11,27:4
Diamond, David (Screenwriter)
Torchy Blane, The Adventurous Blonde 1937,D 18,18:1
Diamond, Don
Borderline 1950,Mr 6,17:2
Diamond, I A L (Original Author)
It's a Great Feeling 1949,Ag 13,6:6
Diamond, I A L (Screenwriter)
Murder in the Blue Room 1944,O 28,12:2
Two Guys From Milwaukee 1946,Jl 27,12:5
Never Say Goodbye 1946,N 23,12:2
Love and Learn 1947,My 3,10:3
Always Together 1947,D 11,46:1
Two Guys From Texas 1948,Ag 28,8:6

Girl from Jones Beach, The 1949,Jl 30,9:2
Let's Make It Legal 1951,N 7,35:3
Monkey Business 1952,S 6,12:6
Something for the Birds 1952,N 15,15:2
That Certain Felling 1956,Je 21,35:2
Love in the Afternoon 1957,Ag 24,12:1
Merry Andrews 1958,Mr 21,17:1
Some Like It Hot 1959,Mr 30,23:1
Apartment, The 1960,Je 16,37:2
One, Two, Three 1961,D 22,17:1
Irma la Douce 1963,Je 6,39:1
Kiss Me, Stupid 1964,D 23,22:2
Fortune Cookie, The 1966,O 20,52:1
Diamond, Jack
Taxi 1953,Ja 22,20:3
Diamond Brothers
He's my Guy 1943,Mr 12,12:3
Diana, Clara
Amore e Morte; (Love and Death) 1932,O 4,26:4
Diana, Laure
Cheat, The 1950,O 2,19:3
Diancoll, O (Screenwriter)
Bandit, The 1949,Je 7,26:3
Dias, Selma Vaz
One of our Aircraft Is Missing 1942,N 2,17:2
Diaz, Antonio
Padre Mercader; Merchant Father 1939,Jl 15,8:3
Diaz, Luz
Heroe de Nacozari, El 1935,S 23,20:4
Diaz, Manolito
Song of Dolores 1951,Je 16,9:2
Diaz, Manuel
Juarez 1939,Ap 26,27:1
Diaz, Paulino Rodrigo (Screenwriter)
Castilian, The 1963,O 3,31:1
Diaz, Ponciana
Torero! 1957,My 22,29:2
Diaz, Ramon Perez
Madrina del Diablo, La; Devil's Godmother, The 1938,F 21,15:2
Diaz, Rosita
Se ha Fugado un Preso 1935,My 21,22:3
Susana Tiene un Secreto 1935,Je 5,22:2
Hombre que se Reia del Amor, El 1935,Jl 18,15:3
Angelita 1935,S 11,19:5
Rosa de Francia 1935,O 28,16:3
Vida Bohemia, La 1939,F 6,8:5
Diaz, Tony
Marvels of the Bull Ring 1943,Jl 3,11:3
Dama de las Camelias, La 1944,S 26,16:1
Dibbs, Kem
Paths of Glory 1957,D 26,23:2
Party Girl 1958,O 29,30:1
Dibner, Martin (Original Author)
Deep Six, The 1958,Ja 16,32:1
Diccioni, Franca
Island Sinner, The 1960,S 5,11:2
Dicenta, Mauel
Morena Clara 1938,Je 18,18:3
Dick, Douglas
Searching Wind, The 1946,Je 27,29:1
Saigon 1948,Ap 1,30:5
Casbah 1948,My 3,27:4
Rope 1948,Ag 27,12:4
Accused, The 1949,Ja 13,26:2
Home of the Brave 1949,My 13,29:1
Red Badge of Courage, The 1951,O 19,22:2
Something to Live For 1952,Mr 8,11:2
Iron Mistress, The 1952,N 20,39:2
So This Is Love 1953,Ag 12,22:1
Gambler From Natchez, The 1954,Ag 14,8:2
North to Alaska 1960,N 11,36:1
Flaming Star 1960,D 17,19:1
Dick, R A (Original Author)
Ghost and Mrs Muir, The 1947,Je 27,17:2
Dickason, Deane H (Producer)
Virgins of Bali 1932,D 12,18:4
Dickens, Charles (Original Author)
Oliver Twist 1916,D 11,7:3
Our Mutual Friend 1921,N 29,20:3
Oliver Twist 1922,O 30,11:1
Rich Man's Folly 1931,N 27,29:3
Oliver Twist 1933,Ap 13,15:3
David Copperfield 1935,Ja 19,8:1
Mystery of Edwin Drood, The 1935,Mr 21,27:1
Scrooge 1935,D 14,11:1
Old Curiosity Shop, The 1935,D 23,15:5
Tale of Two Cities, A 1935,D 26,21:2
Christmas Carol, A 1938,D 23,16:2
Great Expectations 1947,My 23,31:1
Nicholas Nickleby 1947,D 1,27:2
Oliver Twist 1951,Jl 31,17:2
Christmas Carol, A 1951,N 29,41:2
Pickwick Papers, The 1954,Ap 5,21:2
Tale of Two Cities, A 1958,Ag 5,23:1
Oliver! 1968,D 11,57:1
Dickens, Richard
Two Tickets to Paris 1962,N 29,46:5
Dickens, Robert
It's Great to be Young 1957,D 26,23:3
Dickerson, Dudley
Green Pastures, The 1936,Jl 17,20:1
Some Like It Hot 1939,My 25,31:2

Dickerson, Milton
Hallelujah 1929,Ag 21,33:1
Dickert, Lois (Miscellaneous)
Ladybug, Ladybug 1963,D 24,9:1
DICKEY
See Also DICKIE
Dickey, Bill
Pride of the Yankees, The 1942,Jl 16,23:1
Stratton Story, The 1949,My 13,29:1
Dickey, Paul (Original Author)
Ghost Breaker, The 1922,S 11,20:2
Broken Wing, The 1923,O 9,17:4
Broken Wing, The 1932,Mr 26,17:2
Misleading Lady, The 1932,Ap 9,18:1
Crashing Hollywood 1938,Ja 8,19:2
Ghost Breakers, The 1940,Jl 4,12:2
Scared Stiff 1953,Jl 3,10:2
Dickey, Paul (Screenwriter)
Fog Bound 1923,My 29,10:3
DICKIE
See Also DICKEY
Dickie, Olga
Horror of Dracula 1958,My 29,24:4
Dickins, Ann
She Didn't Say No 1963,Jl 30,18:1
Dickins, Stafford (Screenwriter)
Dead Men Tell no Tales 1939,Jl 24,9:2
Dickinson, Angie
China Gate 1957,My 23,40:2
Cry Terror 1958,My 15,25:1
Rio Bravo 1959,Mr 19,40:2
Bramble Bush, The 1960,F 25,34:2
Ocean's Eleven 1960,Ag 11,19:1
Sins of Rachel Cade, The 1961,Ap 6,30:3
Fever in the Blood 1961,Ap 20,30:4
Rome Adventure 1962,Mr 16,25:1
Jessica 1962,Ap 20,20:2
Captain Newman, MD 1964,F 21,36:1
Killers, The 1964,Jl 18,10:4
Art of Love, The 1965,Jl 1,34:1
Chase, The 1966,F 19,24:1
Cast a Giant Shadow 1966,Mr 31,43:3
Point Blank 1967,S 19,53:1
Poppy is Also a Flower, The 1967,D 14,62:4
Last Challenge, The 1967,D 28,25:1
Dickinson, Thorold (Director)
Prime Minister, The 1942,F 4,23:2
Next of Kin 1943,My 6,25:2
Queen of Spades, The 1949,Jl 1,14:4
Kisenga, Man of Africa 1952,Mr 7,18:2
Angel Street 1952,N 11,25:2
Hill 24 Doesn't Answer 1955,N 3,37:1
Dickinson, Thorold (Producer)
Hill 24 Doesn't Answer 1955,N 3,37:1
Dickinson, Thorold (Screenwriter)
Next of Kin 1943,My 6,25:2
Kisenga, Man of Africa 1952,Mr 7,18:2
Dicks, Ted
30 Is a Dangerous Age, Cynthia 1968,Mr 5,34:1
DICKSON
See Also DIXON
Dickson, Dick
House of Dracula 1945,D 22,16:3
Dickson, Dick (Producer)
American Empire 1943,Ja 14,25:4
Dickson, Dorothy
Channel Crossing 1934,My 24,28:3
Dickson, Gloria
They Won't Forget 1937,Jl 15,16:1
Gold Diggers in Paris 1938,Je 2,19:2
Racket Busters 1938,Ag 11,13:1
Secrets of an Actress 1938,O 8,10:2
Heart of the North 1938,D 21,29:2
They Made Me a Criminal 1939,Ja 21,19:2
Waterfront 1939,Jl 17,10:2
On Your Toes 1939,O 21,12:2
Tear Gas Squad 1940,My 31,15:3
I Want a Divorce 1940,O 3,31:2
This Thing Called Love 1941,F 14,15:2
Lady of Burlesque 1943,My 14,17:2
Dickson, Helen
Late George Apley, The 1947,Mr 21,29:2
Dickson, Lamont
Almost a Honeymoon 1931,Ja 10,19:2
Dickson, Lydia
Don't Marry 1928,My 21,25:1
Dickson, Paul (Director)
Satellite in the Sky 1956,S 4,32:7
Dickson, Thomas J Lieut Col (Miscellaneous)
War's End 1934,My 19,18:5
Dicky, Alexei
First Front, The 1949,N 14,19:2
DiCola, Baldi Schwarze-Emanuele (Cinematographer)
Ecco 1965,N 5,28:1
Didelot, Francis (Original Author)
Seventh Juror, The 1964,Ja 23,25:1
Diderot, Denis (Original Author)
Dames du Bois de Boulogne, Les; Ladies of the Park 1964,Ap 4,15:5
Religieuse, La 1968,S 23,42:3
Didier, Cecile
Night is my Kingdom, The 1953,S 30,37:1

Didier, Jean
Dame de Pique, La 1944,O 19,19:2
Damned, The; Maudits, Les 1948,Ap 26,27:2
Dido, Michael
Ride a Crooked Mile 1938,D 29,15:2
Diecerle, William (Director)
Boots Malone 1952,Mr 13,26:2
Diega, Igor
Bachelor's Daughters, The 1946,O 7,23:2
Diegel, Don (Director)
No Time for Flowers 1952,D 26,20:3
Diegelmann, Wilhelm
Hungarian Nights 1930,Je 10,32:2
Blue Angel, The 1930,D 6,21:3
Wahre Jakob, Der 1931,Ag 7,20:2
Goethe's Jugendgeliebte 1932,D 26,26:2
Schimmelreiter, Der; Rider of the White Horse,
The 1935,F 25,13:3
Diego, Emilio
Pleasure Seekers, The 1964,D 26,9:1
DIEHL
See Also DIAL, DEAL
Diehl, Karl Ludwig
Rosenmontag 1931,Mr 28,15:3
Liebeswalzer 1931,My 4,15:3
Koenigin der Unterwelt 1932,D 9,26:5
Zirkus Leben 1932,D 28,14:7
Ein Maedel der Strasse 1933,Ap 6,22:5
Freundin Eines Grossen Mannes, Die
1934,S 11,24:5
Schuss im Morgengrauen 1934,S 29,12:3
Mann Will Nach Deutschland, Ein
1934,N 13,22:4
Aschermittwoch; Ash Wednesday
1935,Mr 11,15:2
Spy 77 1936,F 10,15:1
Hoehere Befehl, Der 1936,Mr 31,17:3
Ein Liebesroman im Hause Habsburg
1936,O 12,23:2
Die Ganze Welt Dreht Sich um Liebe
1936,N 27,27:2
Idealer Gatte, Ein 1937,Ja 11,15:7
Episode 1937,My 17,23:2
Seine Tochter Ist der Peter; His Daughter is Peter
1938,Mr 28,19:3
Es geht um mein Leben; My Life Is at Stake
1938,Ap 11,12:3
Schritt vom Wege, Der; False Step, The
1939,Ap 29,13:3
Ein Hoffnungsloser Fall 1939,S 18,15:5
Devil's General, The 1957,Ap 16,38:2
Story of Vickie, The 1958,Ja 30,19:2
City of Secrets 1963,Jl 27,10:2
Diehl Brothers (Producer)
Seven Ravens, The 1953,Ap 3,20:6
Dienar, Baruch (Director)
They Were Ten; (Heym Hayu Assara)
1961,Ap 18,44:2
Dienar, Baruch (Producer)
They Were Ten; (Heym Hayu Assara)
1961,Ap 18,44:2
Dienar, Baruch (Screenwriter)
They Were Ten; (Heym Hayu Assara)
1961,Ap 18,44:2
Diener, Arpad
I Aim at the Stars 1960,O 20,42:2
Dierkes, John
Macbeth 1950,D 28,22:6
Red Badge of Courage, The 1951,O 19,22:2
Shane 1953,Ap 24,30:3
Moonlighter, The 1953,S 23,37:2
Naked Jungle, The 1954,Ap 3,19:2
Prince Valiant 1954,Ap 7,40:2
Jubal 1956,Ap 25,39:1
Buccaneer, The 1958,D 24,00:0
Alamo, The 1960,O 27,45:1
Comancheros, The 1961,N 2,42:1
Premature Burial, The 1962,My 24,29:2
Haunted Palace, The 1964,Ja 30,24:1
Dierkop, Charles
Pawnbroker, The 1965,Ap 21,51:1
Diesel, Gustav
That Murder in Berlin 1929,Mr 12,26:2
Prisoners of the Mountain 1930,Ja 12,VIII,5:5 (In
Addenda)
White Hell of Pitz Palu, The 1930,S 27,21:3
Living Corpse, The 1931,Ja 4,27:2
Mother Love 1931,F 16,17:1
Comrades of 1918 1931,F 20,18:5
Leutnant Warst Du Einst bei den Husaren
1932,Mr 14,13:3
Teilnehmer Antwortet Nicht 1932,N 30,23:6
Roman Einer Nacht 1934,Je 22,24:2
Alles um Eine Frau 1935,D 21,11:1
Gilgi Eine Von Uns 1937,Jl 10,18:2
Tiger von Eschnapur, Der 1938,Ap 30,18:2
Indian Tomb, The; Tiger von Eschnapur, Der
1938,My 14,18:2
Gruene Hoelle, Die; Green Hell, The
1939,Ja 21,19:2
Wiesse Majestat, Die; White Majesty
1939,My 27,13:3
Amore sulle Alpi 1939,O 27,27:3

Schatten der Vergangeheit; Shadows of the Past
1940,Ap 20,14:2
Diesem, Linda
No More Excuses 1968,My 22,53:1
Diessle, Dorothea
Moritz Macht Sein Glueck 1932,D 24,11:4
Diestro, Alfredo de
Prisionero 13, El 1934,Ap 30,11:4
Oro y Plata 1934,Ag 29,13:2
Compadre Mendoza, El 1934,N 19,13:2
Nada Mas Que Una Mujer 1934,N 26,12:2
Chucho el Roto 1935,Mr 30,11:3
Tribu 1935,Je 10,14:7
Llorona, La 1935,Jl 20,16:2
Sor Juana Ines de la Cruz 1936,Je 6,21:2
Silencio Sublime 1937,Ja 16,21:2
Pasado Acusa, El; Accusing Past, The
1938,O 15,21:4
Sonadores de la Gloria; Dreamers of Glory
1938,D 10,13:3
Alarma 1939,Ja 23,8:2
Casa del Ogro, La; House of the Ogre, The
1939,F 13,13:2
Su Gran Aventura; His Great Adventure
1939,Ap 3,11:6
Padre de Mas de Cuatro; Father of More Than
Four 1939,Ap 24,13:3
Diestro-Alfredo de (Director)
Nobleza Ranchero; Rural Chivalry
1939,F 20,13:3
Dieterle, Eugene
Three Way Works, The 1926,Mr 19,25:1
Backstairs 1926,Je 4,26:2
Dieterle, Wilhelm (Director)
Adorable 1933,My 19,20:2
Dieterle, William
Faust 1926,D 7,21:2
Dame Care 1928,My 20,VIII,8:3
Russia-1908 1929,Ja 7,36:2
Behind the Altar 1929,Ja 29,27:1
At the Edge of the World 1929,Je 18,29:4
Weavers, The 1929,O 7,22:1
Those Who Dance; Tanz Geht Weiter, Der
1930,D 7,IX,6:4
Tanz Geht Weiter, Der 1931,Ja 6,25:1
Behind the Altar 1929,Ja 29,27:1
Those Who Dance; Tanz Geht Weiter, Der
1930,D 7,IX,6:4
Last Flight, The 1931,Ag 20,17:4
Her Majesty, Love 1931,N 26,37:2
Man Wanted 1932,Ap 16,11:2
Jewel Robbery 1932,Jl 23,6:6
Crash, The 1932,S 9,17:5
Six Hours to Live 1932,O 22,18:4
Scarlet Dawn 1932,N 4,25:4
Lawyer Man 1932,D 27,10:2
Grand Slam 1933,F 22,25:2
Devil's in Love, The 1933,Jl 28,18:2
From Headquarters 1933,N 17,22:4
Fashions of 1934 1934,Ja 20,12:2
Fog over Frisco 1934,Je 7,26:2
Madame Du Barry 1934,O 25,26:2
Firebird, The 1934,N 15,25:2
Secret Bride, The 1935,F 2,10:1
Dr Socrates 1935,O 3,29:2
Midsummer Night's Dream, A 1935,O 10,31:1
Story of Louis Pasteur, The 1936,F 10,15:1
White Angel, The 1936,Je 25,24:1
Satan Met a Lady 1936,Jl 23,24:2
Great O'Malley, The 1937,Mr 6,10:1
Another Dawn 1937,Je 18,25:3
Life of Emile Zola, The 1937,Ag 12,14:2
Blockade 1938,Je 17,25:1
Juarez 1939,Ap 26,27:1
Hunchback of Notre Dame, The 1940,Ja 1,29:2
Dr Ehrlich's Magic Bullet 1940,F 24,9:2
Dispatch From Reuters, A 1940,D 12,37:2
All That Money Can Buy 1941,O 17,27:2
Syncopation 1942,My 29,13:3
Tennessee Johnson 1943,Ja 13,18:2
Kismet 1944,Ag 23,16:1
I'll Be Seeing You 1945,Ap 6,20:6
Love Letters 1945,Ag 27,22:3
This Love of Ours 1945,N 1,20:2
Searching Wind, The 1946,Je 27,29:1
Accused, The 1949,Ja 13,26:2
Portrait of Jennie 1949,Mr 30,31:2
Rope of Sand 1949,Ag 4,19:2
Paid in Full 1950,F 16,28:2
Dark City 1950,O 19,40:5
September Affair 1951,F 2,19:2
Peking Express 1951,Jl 19,20:2
Red Mountain 1952,Ap 26,19:2
Turning Point, The 1952,N 15,15:2
Salome 1953,Mr 25,37:1
Volcano 1953,Jl 21,19:2
Elephant Walk 1954,Ap 22,37:2
Omar Khayyam 1957,Ag 24,12:4
Dieterle, William (Producer)
All That Money Can Buy 1941,O 17,27:2
Syncopation 1942,My 29,13:3
Volcano 1953,Jl 21,19:2

Dietgen, Rene
Maedchen Johanna, Das 1935,O 9,27:2 (In
Addenda)
Dietrich, Marlene
Manon Lescaut 1926,N 30,27:1
Three Loves 1929,S 9,30:2
Morocco 1930,N 17,29:1
Blue Angel, The 1930,D 6,21:3
Dishonored 1931,Mr 6,16:1
Shanghai Express 1932,F 18,25:3
I Kiss Your Hand, Madame 1932,Ag 29,9:2
Blonde Venus 1932,S 24,18:4
Song of Songs 1933,Jl 20,22:2
Scralet Empress, The 1934,S 15,20:2
Devil is a Woman, The 1935,My 4,17:2
Desire 1936,Ap 13,15:1
Garden of Allah, The 1936,N 20,27:2
Knight Without Armor 1937,Jl 9,18:1
Angel 1937,N 4,29:1
Destry Rides Again 1939,N 30,25:1
Seven Sinners 1940,N 18,23:2
Flame of New Orleans, The 1941,Ap 26,20:2
Manpower 1941,Jl 5,14:2
Lady is Willing, The 1942,Ap 24,21:2
Spoilers, The 1942,My 22,27:2
Pittsburgh 1943,F 25,27:2
Follow the Boys 1944,Ap 26,24:6
Kismet 1944,Ag 23,16:1
Golden Earrings 1947,D 4,41:3
Foreign Affair, A 1948,Jl 1,19:3
Room Upstairs, The 1948,S 4,8:6
Stage Fright 1950,F 24,27:2
No Highway in the Sky 1951,S 22,8:6
Rancho Notorious 1952,My 15,39:5
Around the World in 80 Days 1956,O 18,37:1
Witness for the Prosecution 1958,F 7,16:1
Monte Carlo Story, The 1958,F 13,23:2
Judgment at Nuremberg 1961,D 20,36:1
Dietrich, Marlene (Narrator)
Black Fox 1963,Ap 30,26:1
Dietrich, Ralph (Original Author)
Mystery Submarine 1951,F 2,19:2
Dietrich, Ralph (Producer)
Gay Caballero, The 1940,O 25,25:3
Man at Large 1941,O 11,21:4
Night Before the Divorce, The 1942,Ap 10,21:3
Quiet Please, Murder 1942,D 22,31:1
Margin for Error 1943,Ja 25,10:7
My Friend Flicka 1943,My 27,21:4
Undertow 1949,D 16,37:2
Peggy 1950,Jl 21,15:4
Spy Hunt 1950,S 8,25:2
Mystery Submarine 1951,F 2,19:2
Under the Gun 1951,F 23,33:2
Dietrich, Ruth
Father takes a Wife 1941,S 5,19:3
Dietz, Alfred
Young Torless 1967,S 25,56:2
Young Torless 1968,Jl 23,27:2
Dietz, Fritz
O Alte Burschenherrlichkeit 1932,Je 18,9:2
Dietz, Howard (Composer)
Band Wagon, The 1953,Jl 10,10:2
Torch Song 1953,O 13,34:2
Dietz, Howard (Miscellaneous)
Under Your Spell 1936,N 7,15:2
Dietz, Howard (Original Author)
Hollywood Party 1934,My 26,12:2
Dietz, Howard (Producer)
Hollywood Party 1934,My 26,12:2
Dietz, Jack (Producer)
Beast From 20,000 Fathoms, The 1953,Je 25,23:1
Black Scorpion, The 1957,O 12,23:2
Dietz, Lilliane
Canzione del Sole, La 1936,My 6,27:2
Verlorene Tal, Das 1936,My 30,7:3
Dietze, Otti
Kyritz-Pyritz 1932,Ag 9,20:5
Dieudonne, Albert
Napoleon 1927,Je 5,VII,5:6 (In Addenda)
Napoleon 1928,Mr 4,IX,6:3
Napoleon 1929,F 12,23:1
Dieudonne, Helene
Belle Americaine, La 1961,D 18,42:1
Diffring, Anton
State Secret 1950,O 5,38:2
Hotel Sahara 1952,Ja 1,21:4
Betrayed 1954,S 9,36:1
I Am a Camera 1955,Ag 9,29:1
Triple Deception 1957,O 7,23:2
Circus of Horrors 1960,S 1,31:1
Question of Adultery, A 1961,Jl 6,18:2
Heroes of Telemark, The 1966,Mr 10,26:1
Fahrenheit 451 1966,N 15,53:1
Counterpoint 1968,Mr 14,51:2
Double Man, The 1968,My 2,57:1
Digby, Bob
Tiger Makes Out, The 1967,S 19,53:1
Digdy, Thomas (Miscellaneous)
Jumping Jack, The; Hampelmann, Der
1931,My 24,VIII,4:1

Digges, Dudley
Condemned 1929,N 4,28:1
Outward Bound 1930,S 18,28:3
Maltese Falcon, The 1931,My 29,26:5
Alexander Hamilton 1931,S 17,21:4
Devotion 1931,O 3,20:2
Ruling Voice, The 1931,N 5,29:3
Hatchet Man, The 1932,F 4,25:2
Strange Case of Clara Deane, The 1932,My 6,15:3
Roar of the Dragon 1932,Jl 25,11:2
First Year, The 1932,Ag 22,20:2
Tess of the Storm Country 1932,N 19,20:2
King's Vacation, The 1933,Ja 20,21:2
Silk Express, The 1933,Je 28,24:2
Mayor of Hell, The 1933,Jl 1,16:5
Narrow Corner, The 1933,Jl 14,15:3
Emperor Jones, The 1933,S 20,26:2
Before Dawn 1933,O 17,26:2
Invisible Man, The 1933,N 18,18:4
Massacre 1934,Ja 18,19:2
World Moves On, The 1934,Je 30,18:5
Caravan 1934,S 28,27:1
What Every Woman Knows 1934,O 27,20:2
I am a Thief 1935,Ja 1,24:1
Notorious Gentleman, A 1935,F 16,9:1
China Seas 1935,Ag 10,16:4
Mutiny on the Bounty 1935,N 9,19:2
Voice of Bugle Ann, The 1936,F 27,23:1
Unguarded Hour, The 1936,Ap 4,11:1
General Died at Dawn, The 1936,S 3,17:2
Valiant Is the Word for Carrie 1936,O 8,27:2
Love Is News 1937,Mr 6,10:1
Light That Failed, The 1939,D 25,19:1
Raffles 1940,Ja 13,11:2
Fight for Life, The 1940,Mr 7,19:2
Son of Fury 1942,Ja 30,23:2
Searching Wind, The 1946,Je 27,29:1
Diggins, Peggy
Navy Blues 1941,S 20,11:2
Lady Gangster 1942,Jl 10,13:2
Truck Busters 1943,Ja 29,23:5
Diggs, John
Corvette K-225 1943,O 21,30:1
Dighton, John (Original Author)
Happiest Days of Your Life, The 1950,S 18,19:2
Dighton, John (Screenwriter)
Let George Do It 1940,O 14,25:5
Three Cockeyed Sailors 1942,Ja 26,18:3
Next of Kin 1943,My 6,25:2
Somewhere in France 1943,Jl 12,11:2
Nicholas Nickleby 1947,D 1,27:2
Champagne Charlie 1948,Ag 7,8:2
Saraband 1949,Je 13,16:3
Kind Hearts and Coronets 1950,Je 15,41:2
Man in the White Suit, The 1952,Ap 1,35:2
Roman Holiday 1953,Ag 28,13:1
Passionate Sentry, The 1953,N 12,37:5
Folly to be Wise 1953,D 28,17:2
Swan, The 1956,Ap 27,21:5
Barretts of Wimpole Street, The 1957,Ja 18,15:3
Devil's Disciple, The 1959,Ag 21,12:1
Season of Passion 1962,F 5,19:4
Dignam, Basil
His Excellency 1956,F 2,19:3
Touch and go 1956,Mr 20,13:2
Brothers in Law 1957,Ag 20,22:1
Risk, The 1961,S 25,41:2
Walk in the Shadow 1966,S 12,52:5
Dignam, Mark
Murder in the Cathedral 1952,Mr 26,35:2
High and Dry 1954,Ag 31,25:5
Beau Brummell 1954,O 21,31:5
Court Martial 1955,Ag 2,17:1
Prisoner, The 1955,D 12,37:1
Sink the Bismarck! 1960,F 12,22:3
Sword of Lancelot 1963,O 10,49:2
They all Died Laughing 1964,Mr 16,37:2
Dijon, Alan
Dolce Vita, La 1961,Ap 20,30:1
Dikki, Alexi
Admiral Nakhimov 1948,N 25,47:4
Dilian, Irasena
Schoolgirl Diary 1947,O 18,9:2
Doctor, Beware 1951,Ap 30,16:3
Women Without Names 1951,Ag 7,22:2
Diligent, Raya
Zero de Conduite 1947,Je 23,14:5
Dill, Robert (Cinematographer)
Hunters of the Deep 1954,D 17,37:4
Dillane, Michael
Man of Aran 1934,O 19,27:1
Dillaway, Donald
Min and Bill 1930,N 24,26:5
Body and Soul 1931,Mr 14,23:2
Mr Lemon of Orange 1931,Mr 28,15:3
Young as You Feel 1931,Ag 8,16:3
Skyline 1931,O 5,17:3
Platinum Blonde 1931,O 31,22:2
She Wanted a Millionaire 1932,F 20,11:2
Cross Examination 1932,F 27,22:1
Pack up Your Troubles 1932,O 1,10:4
Night Mayor, The 1932,N 25,19:2

Men Must Fight 1933,Mr 11,18:3
Mind Reader, The 1933,Ap 7,22:4
Little Giant, The 1933,My 27,11:5
Sing Sinner Sing 1933,Ag 15,20:2
Cipher Bureau 1938,D 14,32:6
I'm Still Alive 1940,O 11,25:4
Juke Box Jenny 1942,Ap 17,21:3
Magnificent Ambersons, The 1942,Ag 14,13:3
Over my Dead Body 1942,D 26,15:2
Amazon Quest 1949,My 14,9:3
Sealed Cargo 1951,My 24,47:1
Diller, Marie
Sainted Devil, A 1924,N 24,15:3
Diller, Phyllis
Over the Hill to the Poor House 1920,S 18,16:2
Boy, Did I Get a Wrong Number! 1966,Je 9,54:2
Eight on the Lam 1967,Ap 27,52:1
Private Navy of Sgt O'Farrell, The 1968,My 9,54:1
Dilling, Mildred
Adventure in Music 1944,Mr 6,17:3
Dillion, John Webb
Air Mail, The 1925,Mr 17,18:1
Vanishing American, The 1925,O 16,18:2
Cross Examination 1932,F 27,22:1
Dillman, Bradford
Certain Smile, A 1958,Ag 1,13:2
In Love and War 1958,N 1,14:2
Compulsion 1959,Ap 2,26:2
Crack in the Mirror 1960,My 20,26:1
Circle of Deception 1961,F 18,12:2
Sanctuary 1961,F 22,31:1
Francis of Assisi 1961,Jl 29,8:2
Rage to Live, A 1965,O 21,57:1
Plainsman, The 1966,N 19,26:1
Sergeant Ryker 1968,Mr 21,56:2
Jigsaw 1968,Je 6,54:2
Dillon, Andrew
Little Old New York 1923,Ag 2,10:3
Dillon, Edward
Skyrocket, The 1926,Ja 26,25:2
Lilac Time 1928,Ag 4,7:2
Broadway Melody, The 1929,F 9,15:3
Hot for Paris 1930,Ja 4,21:1
Caught Short 1930,Je 21,20:5
Sob Sister 1931,O 3,20:2
Trial of Vivienne Ware, The 1932,Ap 30,19:3
Sherlock Holmes 1932,N 12,20:5
Dillon, Edward (Director)
Broadway Gold 1923,Jl 31,12:4
Dillon, John
In old Arizona 1929,Ja 21,18:4
Cisco Kid, The 1931,O 24,20:3
Dillon, John Francis (Director)
Suds 1920,Je 28,13:2
Flaming Youth 1923,N 26,15:6
Lilies of the Field 1924,Mr 17,19:1
Perfect Flapper, The 1924,Je 23,22:4
Flirting With Love 1924,S 1,9:1
If I Marry Again 1925,Ja 12,11:2
If I Marry Again 1925,Ja 12,11:2
Chickie 1925,Ap 27,15:2
Half-Way Girl, The 1925,Jl 29,24:4
We Moderns 1925,D 8,28:5
Midnight Lovers 1926,O 26,23:1
Prince of Head-Waiters 1927,Jl 11,23:5
Smile, Brother, Smile 1927,Ag 29,21:1
Crystal Cup, The 1927,O 25,33:3
Man Crazy 1927,D 19,30:1
Heart of a Follies Girl, The 1928,Mr 12,26:1
Out of the Ruins 1928,Ag 20,21:3
Scarlet Seas 1928,D 31,9:1
Careers 1929,Je 10,23:1
Fast Life 1929,Ag 17,5:3
Sally 1929,D 24,14:4
Bride of the Regiment 1930,My 22,32:6
Girl of the Golden West, The 1930,O 27,17:1
Kismet 1930,O 31,20:1
One Night at Susie's 1930,N 24,26:5
Finger Points, The 1931,Mr 28,15:3
Reckless Hour, The 1931,Ag 1,16:4
Pagan Lady 1931,S 21,20:2
Cohens and Kellys in Hollywood, The 1932,Ap 22,23:2
Behind the Mask 1932,My 2,13:2
Man About Town 1932,My 28,18:2
Call Her Savage 1932,N 25,19:2
Humanity 1933,Ap 22,16:3
Big Shakedown, The 1934,F 12,19:2
Dillon, John Webb
Devil's Cargo, The 1925,F 3,24:1
Wolf's Clothing 1927,Mr 28,26:4
Dillon, Josephine
Lady and the Monster, The 1944,Ap 8,9:2
Dillon, Robert (Original Author)
Lost City, The 1935,F 21,23:3
Orchids to You 1935,Ag 10,16:4
Dillon, Robert (Producer)
Muscle Beach Party 1964,My 28,40:1
Dillon, Robert (Screenwriter)
Safe at Home 1962,Ap 14,14:1
13 Frightened Girls 1963,S 12,32:2
X - The Man With X-Ray Eyes 1963,O 24,37:1

Dillon, Robert (Screenwriter) — Cont
Old Dark House, The 1963,O 31,26:3
Muscle Beach Party 1964,My 28,40:1
Bikini Beach 1964,S 17,52:6
Dillon, Robert A (Screenwriter)
Crusade Against Rackets 1937,Jl 26,15:3
Dillon, Thomas P
Black Beauty 1946,Ag 30,13:2
Woman on the Run 1950,N 30,24:2
Dillon, Tom
Whistling in Brooklyn 1944,Mr 24,17:3
My Girl Tisa 1948,F 21,9:2
Saints and Sinners 1949,S 12,17:2
Night Tide 1963,Je 7,37:1
Dilloway, Donald
Cimarron 1931,Ja 27,20:5
Men in her Life 1931,N 30,16:2
Lady With a Past 1932,F 22,23:2
Strange Love of Molly Louvain, The 1932,My 9,19:5
Attorney for the Defense 1932,My 28,18:2
Miss Pinkerton 1932,Jl 9,7:5
Animal Kingdom, The 1932,D 30,14:2
Circus Clown, The 1934,Je 30,18:6
Dills, William
Chechahcos, The 1924,My 19,14:2
Dilson, Clyde
Men Without Names 1935,Je 29,16:2
King Solomon of Broadway 1935,O 19,12:2
You may Be Next 1936,F 24,14:1
13 Hours by Air 1936,Ap 30,17:2
Florida Special 1936,My 29,15:2
There Goes my Girl 1937,Je 12,8:2
Under Suspicion 1937,D 20,23:2 (In Addenda)
Secrets of a Nurse 1938,D 12,26:2
Dilson, John
Every Night at Eight 1935,Ag 3,16:2
Women in the Wind 1939,Ap 13,27:2
Fixer Dugan 1939,My 6,21:2
Racketeers of the Range 1939,Je 8,31:4
Woman Is the Judge, A 1939,S 28,29:5
Man With Nine Lives, The 1940,Ap 29,12:3
Girls Under 21 1940,N 11,22:4
Father's Son 1941,F 13,25:3
Man Made Monster 1941,Mr 19,25:4
Naval Academy 1941,Je 5,27:3
You Can't Escape Forever 1942,O 17,11:1
Diltz, Charles (Miscellaneous)
Scorched Earth 1942,S 12,9:2
DiMaggio, Joe
Untitled-Baseball Technique 1941,Ja 17,11:3
Ninth Inning, The 1942,Ja 8,30:3
Dime, James
Stand and Deliver 1928,Ap 2,25:1
Dimech, John
Killers of Kilimanjaro 1960,Ap 7,46:1
DiMeo, Luisa
Seven Hills of Rome 1958,Ja 28,24:2 (Incorrect in this edition; use 1958,Ja 31,24:2 elsewhere)
Dimitri
Naked Heart, The 1955,Mr 9,22:4
Dimitrieff, D
Hurrah I'm Alive 1930,Je 16,25:3
Secrets of the Orient 1932,Ja 4,27:3
Dimitriou, Theodore
Aunt From Chicago, The 1960,Je 6,33:6
Dimopoulos, Dino (Director)
Horse and Carriage 1958,Je 30,23:3
Astero 1960,Ap 25,32:2
House on Stournara Street, The 1960,O 17,33:4
Dimov
Steppe, The 1963,O 1,33:1
Dimsdale, Howard (Original Author)
Love Laughs at Andy Hardy 1947,Ja 8,28:2
Traveling Saleswoman 1950,Ja 6,25:3
Curtain Call at Cactus Creek 1950,S 22,35:4
Dimsdale, Howard (Screenwriter)
Somewhere in the Night 1946,Je 13,24:2
Traveling Saleswoman 1950,Ja 6,25:3
Lady Without Passport, A 1950,Ag 4,13:2
Curtain Call at Cactus Creek 1950,S 22,35:4
Dimsdales, Young
Eight on the Lam 1967,Ap 27,52:1
Din, Jalal (Original Author)
Maya 1966,Je 23,29:4
Dina, Wissia
They Met on Skis 1940,D 23,23:2
Dinan, Albert
Loves of Casanova 1948,S 18,11:4
Four in a Jeep 1951,Je 12,35:2
Magnificent Tramp, The 1962,Ap 25,30:1
Gigot 1962,S 28,26:1
Dinay, Monette
Four Bags Full 1957,S 5,32:1
Dineff, Dimitri
My Life to Live 1963,S 24,43:2
Dinehart, Alan
Brat, The 1931,Ag 24,13:4
Wicked 1931,S 19,10:2
Girls About Town 1931,N 2,27:1
Good Sport 1931,D 12,23:3
Disorderly Conduct 1932,Ap 11,19:2
Trial of Vivienne Ware, The 1932,Ap 30,19:3
Street of Women 1932,My 30,16:5

Dinehart, Alan— Cont

Bachelor's Affairs 1932,Je 25,18:2
Okay America 1932,S 10,18:5
Washington Merry-Go-Round 1932,O 24,18:5
Rackety Rax 1932,N 5,12:5
Devil Is Driving, The 1932,D 16,25:5
Lawyer Man 1932,D 27,10:2
Sweepings 1933,Mr 24,22:3
Supernatural 1933,Ap 22,16:3
Study in Scarlet, A 1933,Je 1,15:3
No Marriage Ties 1933,Ag 4,18:2
Her Bodyguard 1933,Ag 7,18:2
I Have Lived 1933,S 6,24:4
Bureau of Missing Persons 1933,S 9,9:2
Dance, Girl, Dance 1933,O 25,23:3
World Changes, The 1933,O 27,22:3
Sin of Nora Moran, The 1933,D 13,29:3
Cross Country Cruise 1934,Ja 20,12:3
Jimmy the Gent 1934,Mr 26,22:3
Love Captive, The 1934,Je 8,18:1
Baby, Take a Bow 1934,Je 30,18:6
Cat's Paw, The 1934,Ag 17,12:2
Dante's Inferno 1935,Ag 1,15:1
Pay-Off, The 1935,N 13,25:3
Thanks a Million 1935,N 14,17:1
Old Kentucky, In 1935,N 29,24:1
Your Uncle Dudley 1935,D 12,33:4
Everybody's Old Man 1936,Mr 26,27:2
Country Beyond, The 1936,Ap 30,17:3
Human Cargo 1936,My 16,11:2
Parole 1936,Je 27,21:1
Crime of Dr Forbes, The 1936,Jl 6,11:4
Charlie Chan at the Race Track 1936,Ag 15,6:2
Star for a Night 1936,S 5,7:2
King of the Royal Mounted 1936,S 29,35:2
Reunion 1936,N 27,27:1
Born to Dance 1936,D 5,16:1
Woman Wise 1937,Ja 23,13:1
Step Lively, Jeeves 1937,Ap 2,19:6
This Is my Affair 1937,My 28,17:1
Fifty Roads to Town 1937,Je 5,21:1
Dangerously Yours 1937,O 18,14:2
Ali Baba Goes to Town 1937,O 23,14:1
Danger-Love at Work 1937,D 11,22:2
Big Town Girl 1937,D 13,23:4
Rebecca of Sunnybrook Farm 1938,Mr 26,12:1
First 100 Years, The 1938,My 13,17:2
Up the River 1938,D 3,11:2
Fast and Loose 1939,Mr 9,18:1
King of the Turf 1939,My 8,21:2
Second Fiddle 1939,Jl 1,11:2
Hotel for Women 1939,Ag 26,20:2
Two Bright Boys 1939,S 22,27:3
Everything Happens at Night 1939,D 16,12:6
Slightly Honorable 1940,My 17,23:4
Girl Trouble 1942,O 8,31:2
Sweet Rosie O'Grady 1943,O 21,30:2
Heat's on, The 1943,N 26,29:2
What a Woman 1943,D 3,27:2
Seven Days Ashore 1944,Ap 26,24:7
Whistler, The 1944,Ap 29,12:2
Minstrel Man 1944,Jl 17,18:5
Wave, A Wac and a Marine, A 1944,Ag 14,11:4

Dinehart, Alan 3d
Careless Years, The 1957,N 28,57:3

Dinelli, Mel (Miscellaneous)
Reckless Moment, The 1949,D 30,13:2

Dinelli, Mel (Original Author)
Beware my Lovely 1952,S 13,10:5

Dinelli, Mel (Screenwriter)
Spiral Staircase, The 1946,F 7,29:3
Window, The 1949,Ag 8,10:5
House by the River 1950,My 2,25:2
Cause for Alarm 1951,Mr 30,28:5
Beware my Lovely 1952,S 13,10:5
Jeopardy 1953,Mr 31,36:2
Lizzie 1957,Ap 5,24:2

Dinelli, Minni
Serpente a Sonagli, Il 1936,Ag 17,9:2

Dinensen, Marie
David Copperfield 1923,N 6,23:3

Dinensen, Robert
Tatjana 1927,My 18,29:3

Dinensen, Robert (Director)
Tatjana 1927,My 18,29:3

D'Ines, Denis
Heroes of the Marne; (Famille Lefrancois, Le) 1939,Ap 24,13:2
Rasputin 1939,O 17,31:4
Angel and Sinner 1947,F 24,16:5
Man to Men 1949,F 21,20:2

Dinesen, Isak (Original Author)
Immortal Story, The 1968,S 19,62:2

Dingle, Charles
One Third of a Nation 1939,F 11,13:2
Little Foxes, The 1941,Ag 22,19:2
Unholy Partners 1941,D 29,21:4
Johnny Eager 1942,F 20,21:2
Calling Dr Gillespie 1942,Jl 9,17:4
Are Husbands Necessary? 1942,Jl 9,17:2
Talk of the Town, The 1942,Ag 28,22:3
Somewhere I'll Find You 1942,Ag 28,22:4
George Washington Slept Here 1942,O 31,11:1
Tennessee Johnson 1943,Ja 13,18:2

Edge of Darkness 1943,Ap 10,12:4
Lady of Burlesque 1943,My 14,17:2
Song of Bernadette, The 1944,Ja 27,15:2
Home in Indiana 1944,Je 22,23:1
Together Again 1944,N 24,19:2
Here Come the Co-Eds 1945,F 19,21:1
Medal for Benny, A 1945,My 24,15:2
Guest Wife 1945,O 18,21:2
Cinderella Jones 1946,Mr 16,9:6
Wife of Monte Cristo, The 1946,Ap 8,31:2
Centennial Summer 1946,Jl 18,20:2
Three Wise Fools 1946,S 27,19:2
Sister Kenny 1946,S 30,21:2
Beast With Five Fingers, The 1946,D 26,28:3
My Favorite Brunette 1947,Mr 20,38:2
Duel in the Sun 1947,My 8,30:2
Welcome Stranger 1947,Ag 7,15:2
Romance of Rosy Ridge, The 1947,S 12,18:3
If You Knew Susie 1948,F 23,19:2
State of the Union 1948,Ap 23,28:1
Southern Yankee, A 1948,N 25,47:2
Big Jack 1949,My 23,27:4
Call Me Madam 1953,Mr 26,37:1
Never Wave at a Wac 1953,Ap 24,30:2
Court-Martial of Billy Mitchell, The 1955,D 23,14:2

Dinneen, Joseph F (Original Author)
Let Us Live 1939,Mr 30,19:2
Six Bridges to Cross 1955,Ja 22,8:2

Dinnen, Janice
Cinerama-South Seas Adventure 1958,Jl 16,26:1

Dinner, William (Original Author)
Obsessed 1952,F 6,24:2

Dino, Abidine (Director)
Goal 1967,Ja 19,26:1

Dion, Hector
Courtship of Myles Standish, The 1923,D 31,9:3

Dione, Rose
Woman and the Puppet 1920,Ap 5,20:1
Suds 1920,Je 28,13:2
Little Lord Fauntleroy 1921,S 16,17:3
Salome 1923,Ja 1,18:1
Drifting 1923,Ag 20,4:2
French Doll, The 1923,S 5,15:3
Shadows of Paris 1924,F 18,13:1
Lover of Camille, The 1924,N 11,14:1
Inez From Hollywood 1924,D 16,28:1
Fifth Avenue Models 1925,My 4,16:2
Mlle Modiste 1926,Ap 26,25:1
Paris 1926,Je 1,29:3
Duchess of Buffalo, The 1926,Ag 9,10:3
When a Man Loves 1927,F 4,16:6
Beloved Rogue, The 1927,Mr. 14,16:1
Camille 1927,Ap 22,19:1
Old San Francisco 1927,Je 23,23:3
Bringing Up Father 1928,Mr 19,26:2
Mad Hour, The 1928,Ap 16,20:5
His Tiger Lady 1928,My 28,23:2
Out of the Ruins 1928,Ag 20,21:3
Red Mark, The 1928,O 30,27:3
Naughty Baby 1929,F 5,26:3
Hearts in Exile 1929,N 29,25:1
Women Everywhere 1930,Je 23,15:1
Salvation Nell 1931,Jl 6,24:4
Freaks 1932,Jl 9,7:5

Dionne, Annette
Reunion 1936,N 27,27:1

Dionne, Cecile
Reunion 1936,N 27,27:1

Dionne, Emilie
Reunion 1936,N 27,27:1

Dionne, Marie
Reunion 1936,N 27,27:1

Dionne, Yvonne
Reunion 1936,N 27,27:1

Dionne Quintuplets
Five of a Kind 1938,O 31,12:2

Dionnet, Philippe
Yo Yo 1967,Mr 1,50:1

Diosdado, Enrique
Song of Dolores 1951,Je 16,9:2
Fedra, the Devil's Daughter 1957,O 26,19:2

Dirgley, John
Return Of Doctor X, The 1939,N 23,38:5

Dirnbach, Zora (Screenwriter)
Ninth Circle, The 1961,S 15,30:3

Dirrane, Maggie
Man of Aran 1934,O 19,27:1

Disney, Doris Miles (Original Author)
Stella 1950,Ag 19,9:2
Fugitive Lady 1951,Ag 25,7:2

Disney, Walt (Producer)
Snow White and the Seven Dwarfs 1938,Ja 14,21:1 (In Addenda)
Fantasia 1940,N 14,28:2
Reluctant Dragon, The 1941,Jl 25,12:2
Three Caballeros, The 1945,F 5,20:1
Fun and Fancy Free 1947,S 29,17:2 (In Addenda)
Melody Time 1948,My 28,28:2
Alice in Wonderland 1951,Jl 30,12:4
Men Against the Arctic 1956,Je 27,35:1
Snow White and the Seven Dwarfs

Disney, Walt (Producer)— Cont

1958,Mr 2,II,1:8 (In Addenda)
White Wilderness 1958,Ag 13,22:1
Sleeping Beauty 1959,F 18,36:1
Kidnapped 1960,My 19,44:3
Absent-Minded Professor, The 1961,Mr 16,44:2
Parent Trap, The 1961,Je 22,23:1
Greyfriars' Bobby 1961,O 12,41:4
Moon Pilot 1962,Ap 6,30:2
Big Red 1962,S 3,11:2
Almost Angels 1962,N 1,34:2
Legend of Lobo, The 1962,N 10,16:2
In Search of the Castaways 1962,D 22,5:2
Son of Flubber 1963,F 9,5:2
Savage Sam 1963,Ag 1,17:3
Tiger Walks, A 1964,Ag 27,28:2
Mary Poppins 1964,S 25,34:1
Moonspinners, The 1964,N 4,47:1
Winnie the Pooh and the Honey Tree 1966,Ap 7,45:1
Follow Me, Boys! 1966,D 2,46:1
Happiest Millionaire, The 1967,D 1,56:1

Disney, Walt Studio Staff
Reluctant Dragon, The 1941,Jl 25,12:2

Disreali
Spy With a Cold Nose, The 1966,D 20,58:2

Distal, Sacha
Bonne Soupe, La 1964,Mr 16,37:1

Ditlovich, S
Diary of a Nazi 1943,Mr 25,25:3

Ditmar (Original Author)
Untitled-Nature 1918,Je 3,9:3

Ditmars, Raymond L Dr (Producer)
Like a Beaver 1931,F 10,24:4

Ditmars (Producer)
Four Seasons, The 1921,O 2,VII,3:1

Ditrichstein, Leo
How Molly Made Good 1915,O 20,5:5

Ditrichstein, Leo (Original Author)
Great Lover, The 1931,Ag 24,13:4

Dits, Hans Emil (Original Author)
Confession of Ina Kahn, The 1958,Ja 1,31:4

Diukeznov, Ivan
Country Bride 1938,Je 4,18:2

Divine, David (Original Author)
Boy on a Dolphin 1957,Ap 20,21:2

Divine, David (Screenwriter)
Dunkirk 1958,S 11,42:2

Divivier, Julien (Director)
Panic 1947,N 27,50:2
Return of Don Camillo, The 1956,Mr 27,41:1
Man in the Raincoat, The 1958,Jl 15,21:2

Divivier, Julien (Screenwriter)
Return of Don Camillo, The 1956,Mr 27,41:1

Divorsky, Jesse
Wine, Women and Song 1934,Mr 21,24:3

Dix, Beulah Marie (Miscellaneous)
Fires of Faith 1919,My 6,16:2

Dix, Beulah Marie (Original Author)
Road to Yesterday, The 1925,D 1,22:4
Life of Jimmy Dolan, The 1933,Je 14,22:3
Ever in my Heart 1933,O 13,25:3
They Made Me a Criminal 1939,Ja 21,19:2
Sweater Girl 1942,Jl 13,18:3

Dix, Beulah Marie (Screenwriter)
Woman Thou Gavest Me, The 1919,Je 9,16:3
In Mizzoura 1919,O 13,16:3
Easy Road, The 1921,F 20,VI,2:2 (In Addenda)
Fool's Paradise 1921,D 10,11:4
Crimson Challenge, The 1922,Ap 10,18:2
Borderland 1922,Jl 24,10:2
Children of Jazz 1923,Jl 9,8:4
Fighting Blade, The 1923,O 15,15:4
Midnight Mystery 1930,Je 2,25:4

Dix, Dorothy
First Mrs Fraser, The 1932,My 29,VIII,4:5 (In Addenda)

Dix, Marion (Original Author)
Climbing High 1939,Je 5,20:3

Dix, Marion (Screenwriter)
Two Against the World 1932,Ag 19,20:6
It's Love Again 1936,My 23,12:1
Forbidden Music 1938,D 27,13:2

Dix, Richard
Dangerous Curve Ahead 1921,O 3,16:2
Glorious Fool, The 1922,Mr 20,10:3
Yellow Men and Gold 1922,My 29,14:1
Wall Flower, The 1922,Je 26,16:2
Fools First 1922,Jl 31,12:3
Sin Flood, The 1922,O 30,11:1
Christian, The 1923,F 12,13:4
Souls for Sale 1923,Ap 9,14:3
To the Last Man 1923,Ag 28,12:1
Call of the Canyon, The 1923,D 17,23:1
Stranger, The 1924,F 5,20:1
Icebound 1924,Mr 3,22:3 (In Addenda)
Unguarded Women 1924,Je 24,18:2
Sinners in Heaven 1924,S 10,21:3
Manhattan 1924,O 29,18:1
Man Must Live, A 1925,Ja 29,12:2
Too Many Kisses 1925,Mr 3,20:1
Men and Women 1925,Mr 30,21:3
Shock Punch, The 1925,My 11,14:3
Lady Who Lied, The 1925,Jl 7,24:2

Dix, Richard— Cont

Lucky Devil, The 1925,Jl 8,12:4
Vanishing American, The 1925,O 16,18:2
Womanhandled 1926,Ja 5,25:2
Let's Get Married 1926,Mr 2,22:1
Say It Again 1926,Je 7,23:2
Quarterback, The 1926,O 12,30:2
Paradise for Two 1927,Ja 25,18:4
Knockout Reilly 1927,Ap 18,21:2
Man Power 1927,Jl 26,17:1
Shanghai Bound 1927,N 7,26:4
Gay Defender, The 1927,D 26,26:6
Sporting Goods 1928,F 13,16:2
Easy Come, Easy Go 1928,My 8,25:3
Warming Up 1928,Jl 16,25:3
Moran of the Marines 1928,O 15,16:1
Redskin 1929,Ja 28,21:1
Nothing but the Truth 1929,Ap 22,23:1
Wheel of Life, The 1929,Je 24,27:1
Love Doctor, The 1929,N 9,22:5
Seven Keys to Baldpate 1929,D 26,21:1
Lovin' the Ladies 1930,Mr 22,22:6
Shooting Straight 1930,Jl 28,22:1
Cimarron 1931,Ja 27,20:5
Donovan's Kid 1931,My 22,28:5
Public Defender, The 1931,Ag 1,16:4
Secret Service 1931,D 14,16:3
Lost Squadron, The 1932,Mr 11,15:4
Roar of the Dragon 1932,Jl 25,11:2
Hell's Highway 1932,S 26,18:2
Conquerors, The 1932,N 21,21:1
Great Jasper, The 1933,F 17,5:3
No Marriage Ties 1933,Ag 4,18:2
Day of Reckoning 1933,N 4,18:2
Ace of Aces 1933,N 11,10:4
Stingaree 1934,My 18,27:1
His Greatest Gamble 1934,Jl 18,20:2
West of the Pecos 1934,D 29,11:2
Arizonian, The 1935,Jl 27,16:2
Transatlantic Tunnel 1935,O 28,16:2
Yellow Dust 1936,F 24,14:1
Special Investigator 1936,Ap 25,21:1
Devil's Squadron 1936,My 11,16:2
Devil's Playground 1937,F 15,12:5
Devil is Driving, The 1937,Jl 16,22:1
It Happened in Hollywood 1937,O 2,18:1
Blind Alibi 1938,My 20,17:2
Sky Giant 1938,Jl 20,22:2
Twelve Crowded Hours 1939,F 24,15:2
Man of Conquest 1939,Ap 28,31:2
Here I Am a Stranger 1939,S 30,11:2
Reno 1939,D 21,29:2
Men Against the Sky 1940,S 12,31:2
Cherokee Strip 1940,N 4,23:2
Roundup, The 1941,Mr 13,25:4
Badlands of Dakota 1941,S 9,27:6
Tombstone, The Town too Tough to Die
  1942,Jl 27,18:2
Eyes of the Underworld 1942,O 5,15:2
American Empire 1943,Ja 14,25:4
Kansan, The 1943,O 1,15:3
Top Man 1943,O 29,23:2
Ghost Ship, The 1943,D 25,19:4
Whistler, The 1944,Ap 29,12:2
Mark of the Whistler, The 1944,N 11,19:2

Dix, Robert
Forbidden Planet 1956,My 4,21:2
Young Jesse James 1960,Ag 25,25:1

Dix, Rollo
Bulldog Drummond in Africa 1938,Ag 25,15:1

Dix, Tommy
Best Foot Forward 1943,Je 30,25:2

Dix, William
Nanny, The 1965,N 4,57:2
Doctor Dolittle 1967,D 20,55:1

DIXON
See Also DICKSON

Dixon, Campbell (Original Author)
Secret Agent 1936,Je 13,13:1

Dixon, Conway
Broken Melody, The 1934,O 31,17:3
Triumph of Sherlock Holmes, The
  1935,My 27,20:6
Mutiny of the Elsinore, The 1939,F 16,17:2

Dixon, Deirdre
Royal Ballet, The (Swan Lake Act II); Swan Lake
  Act II (The Royal Ballet) 1960,O 5,45:2

Dixon, Florence
Independence B'Gosh 1918,D 2,11:3

Dixon, Glenn
Untamed Youth 1957,My 11,24:6

Dixon, Ivan
Something of Value 1957,My 11,24:6
Porgy and Bess 1959,Je 25,20:3
Raisin in the Sun, A 1961,Mr 30,24:1
Nothing but a Man 1964,S 21,37:2
Patch of Blue, A 1965,D 16,63:1

Dixon, Jean
Lady Lies, The 1929,S 7,15:1
Kiss Before the Mirror, The 1933,My 15,16:2
Sadie McKee 1934,My 18,18:3 (Incorrect in this
  edition; use 1934,My 19,18:3 elsewhere)
I'll Love You Always 1935,Mr 30,11:2
Mr Dynamite 1935,My 25,12:1

She Married her Boss 1935,S 27,25:3
To Mary-With Love 1936,Ag 27,16:1
My Man Godfrey 1936,S 19,18:1 (Incorrect in
  this edition; use 1936,S 18,18:1 elsewhere)
Magnificent Brute, The 1936,O 24,23:1
You Only Live Once 1937,F 1,15:2
Swing High, Swing Low 1937,Ap 15,19:1
Joy of Living 1938,My 6,27:1
Holiday 1938,Je 24,15:1

Dixon, Lee
Gold Diggers of 1937 1936,D 25,19:2
Ready, Willing and Able 1937,Mr 15,27:1
Singing Marine, The 1937,Jl 1,33:2
Varsity Show 1937,S 2,17:2
Angel and the Badman 1947,Mr 3,28:4

Dixon, Marion
Courtship of Myles Standish, The 1923,D 31,9:3

Dixon, Mort (Composer)
Key, The 1934,My 30,14:3
Housewife 1934,Ag 10,21:2
Dames 1934,Ag 16,20:2
Happiness Ahead 1934,O 11,28:2
Flirtation Walk 1934,N 29,33:1
Sweet Music 1935,F 21,23:2
I Live for Love 1935,O 19,21:2
Broadway Hostess 1935,D 16,23:3

Dixon, Mort (Miscellaneous)
In Caliente 1935,Je 27,16:1
Bright Lights 1935,Ag 15,15:2

Dixon, Ralph (Miscellaneous)
I Married Adventure 1940,S 24,26:5

Dixon, Thomas (Original Author)
Birth of a Nation, The 1915,Mr 4,9:4
Fall of a Nation, The 1916,Je 7,11:1
Birth of a Nation, The 1921,My 2,12:1
Birth of a Nation, The 1922,D 5,24:3

Djevanshirov, L
Arshin Takes a Wife 1950,Jl 31,13:6

Djurberg, Bengt
Vi Som Gar Koeksvaegen 1933,O 7,18:5
Familjen Som Var En Karusel 1937,My 22,19:3
Skicka Hem Nr 7; Send Home No 7
  1939,My 9,29:2

Djurdievic, Milan
Steppe, The 1963,O 1,33:1

Dmitri (Composer)
Red Tanks 1942,Je 6,9:2

Dmitrief, A (Director)
Rivals 1933,Ap 5,22:6

Dmitriev, I
Behind the Show Window 1957,Ap 17,37:1
Hamlet 1964,S 15,32:1
Hamlet 1966,Mr 16,48:1

Dmitriev, Igor
And Quiet Flows the Don 1960,My 25,45:2

Dmitriev, Ivan
My Daughter 1960,N 28,40:2

Dmitriev, Viktor
New Number Comes to Moscow, A
  1959,Jl 6,23:1

Dmitrievskaya, Lisa
Four Hearts 1946,F 25,21:5

Dmochowski, Boris
Zygmunt Kolosowski 1947,N 13,13:3

Dmochowski, Boris (Director)
Zygmunt Kolosowski 1947,N 13,13:3

Dmokhovskaya, Anna
Country Bride 1938,Je 4,18:2

Dmokhovsky, Dmitri
Fortress on the Volga 1942,D 25,15:3

Dmytryk, Edward (Director)
Golden Gloves 1940,Ag 21,23:6
Mystery Sea Raider 1940,Ag 26,11:4
Devil Commands, The 1941,F 14,15:3
Confessions of Boston Blackie 1941,D 8,31:2
Counter-Espionage 1942,S 28,13:2
Seven Miles From Alcatraz 1942,N 19,31:3
Hitler's Children 1943,F 25,27:1
Falcon Strikes Back, The 1943,Ap 2,17:4
Captive Wild Woman 1943,Je 7,9:4
Behind the Rising Sun 1943,O 14,26:2
Tender Comrade 1944,Je 2,21:2
Murder, my Sweet 1945,Mr 9,16:2
Back to Bataan 1945,S 13,26:3
Cornered 1945,D 26,15:1
Till the End of Time 1946,Jl 24,24:1
Crossfire 1947,Jl 23,19:2
So Well Remembered 1947,N 5,34:3
Give Us This Day 1949,D 21,41:2
Hidden Room, The 1950,Ja 9,19:2
Mutiny 1952,Mr 20,37:5
Sniper, The 1952,My 10,16:3
Eight Iron Men 1953,Ja 2,11:1
Juggler, The 1953,My 6,39:2
Caine Mutiny, The 1954,Je 25,17:1
Broken Lance 1954,Jl 30,9:1
End of the Affair, The 1955,Ap 29,28:2
Soldier of Fortune 1955,My 28,7:4
Left Hand of God, The 1955,S 22,34:5
Mountain, The 1956,N 15,44:6
Young Lions, The 1958,Ap 3,23:1
Warlock 1959,My 1,34:1
Blue Angel, The 1959,S 5,11:4

Dmytryk, Edward (Director)— Cont

Walk on the Wild Side 1962,F 22,20:1
Reluctant Saint, The 1962,D 4,47:2
Carpetbaggers, The 1964,Jl 2,24:4
Where Love Has Gone 1964,N 3,26:1
Mirage 1965,My 27,28:1
Alvarez Kelly 1966,N 17,55:2
Anzio 1968,Jl 25,26:1
Shalako 1968,N 6,32:1

Dmytryk, Edward (Producer)
Mountain, The 1956,N 15,44:6
Warlock 1959,My 1,34:1
Reluctant Saint, The 1962,D 4,47:2

Dneprov, S I
Oppenheim Family, The 1939,My 24,29:2

Do Vries, Harry
Two Brothers, The 1928,Ag 21,27:4

Doanne, Andre
Entente Cordiale 1939,D 26,23:2

Dobbins, Barbara
French Line, The 1954,My 15,13:2

Dobbs, George
Footlight Serenade 1942,S 10,30:3
Gang's All Here, The 1943,D 23,26:4

Dobert (Producer)
Minne 1951,Ap 17,35:2

Dobie, Alan
Long Day's Dying, The 1968,My 29,20:1

Dobina, Z V
Lenin in 1918 1939,Je 27,27:2

Dobkin, Larry
Not Wanted 1949,Jl 25,11:4
Twelve O'Clock High 1950,Ja 28,10:2
Frenchie 1951,F 12,19:2
Five Fingers 1952,F 23,7:5
Above and Beyond 1953,Ja 31,10:6
Kiss of Fire 1955,S 24,11:2
Ten Commandments, The 1956,N 9,35:2
Sweet Smell of Success 1957,Je 28,29:2
Portland Expose 1957,S 27,16:6
Defiant Ones, The 1958,S 25,29:1
Cabinet of Caligari, The 1962,My 26,13:5

Dobkin, Larry (Narrator)
Cowboy, The 1954,Ag 3,14:2

Doblin, Alfred (Original Author)
Berlin-Alexanderplatz 1933,My 11,14:1

Doblin, Hugo
Strange Case of Captain Ramper, The
  1928,Je 4,13:2

Dobos, Annie
Budai Cukraszda 1936,Ja 2,21:5
Tommy 1937,O 16,22:3
Pesti Mese; Tales of Budapest 1938,Ja 3,16:3

Dobronravof, B G
Prisoners 1937,F 20,9:2

Dobronravov, V
Frontier 1935,D 28,10:5

Dobronravova, E
Big Family, A 1955,Je 6,24:1

Dobrovolski, V
Peter the First 1937,D 25,10:4
Conquests of Peter The Great, The
  1939,Ag 24,17:2
Ural Front, The 1945,Je 7,25:3
Secret Agent 1949,F 10,37:3
Bountiful Summer 1951,D 24,9:1

Dobrzhanskaya, Lubov
Uncommon Thief, An 1967,D 1,56:2

Dobson, James
Tanks are Coming, The 1951,D 6,42:4
For Men Only 1952,Ja 16,21:2
Okinawa 1952,Ap 24,38:3
Come Fly With Me 1963,My 2,40:2
Track of Thunder 1968,F 1,28:4

Dobtcheff, Vernon
Taming of the Shrew, The 1967,Mr 9,43:1

Dobuzinsky, Valeric
Moderato Cantabile 1964,Ja 7,24:1

Dockson, Evllyn
Let's Face It 1943,Ag 5,18:1

Dockstader, George
Jackie Robinson Story, The 1950,My 17,36:1
Private Hell 36 1954,S 4,6:4

Doctorow, E L (Original Author)
Welcome to Hard Times 1967,My 2,56:1

Dodd, Bo
Intruder, The 1962,My 15,48:1

Dodd, Claire
Secret Call, The 1931,Jl 13,13:5
Girls About Town 1931,N 2,27:1
Under Eighteen 1931,D 26,15:5
Two Kinds of Women 1932,Ja 16,13:1
Alias the Doctor 1932,Mr 3,22:3
Broken Wing, The 1932,Mr 26,17:2
Man Wanted 1932,Ap 16,11:2
This is the Night 1932,Ap 16,11:2
Guilty as Hell 1932,Ag 6,14:5
Crooner 1932,Ag 20,7:4
Match King, The 1932,D 8,25:3
Lawyer Man 1932,D 27,10:2
Parachute Jumper 1933,Ja 26,12:2
Hard to Handle 1933,F 2,21:5
Blondie Johnson 1933,F 27,11:2
Ex-Lady 1933,My 15,16:2

Dodd, Claire— Cont
Elmer the Great 1933,My 26,24:2
Ann Carver's Profession 1933,Je 9,20:2
Footlight Parade 1933,O 6,21:3
My Woman 1933,O 16,20:3
Massacre 1934,Ja 18,19:2
Gambling Lady 1934,Ap 5,25:2
Journal of a Crime 1934,Ap 28,11:3
Personality Kid, The 1934,Ag 1,14:2
Babbitt 1934,D 17,24:2
I Sell Anything 1934,D 27,25:2
Roberta 1935,Mr 8,25:2
Case of the Curious Bride, The 1935,Ap 5,21:3
Glass Key, The 1935,Je 15,20:2
Don't Bet on Blondes 1935,Jl 20,16:2
Goose and the Gander, The 1935,S 12,29:2
Pay-Off, The 1935,N 13,25:3
Singing Kid, The 1936,Ap 4,11:1
Murder by an Aristocrat 1936,Je 13,13:2
Case of the Velvet Claws, The 1936,Ag 29,16:3
Romance in the Dark 1938,Mr 21,18:2
Fast Company 1938,Jl 6,21:2
Three Loves Has Nancy 1938,S 2,21:2
Charlie Chan in Honolulu 1938,D 31,7:3
Woman Doctor 1939,Mr 24,27:3
If I Had my Way 1940,My 6,13:2
Slightly Honorable 1940,My 17,23:4
Black Cat, The 1941,Ap 26,20:3
In the Navy 1941,Je 12,29:2
Mad Doctor of Market Street, The 1942,Ja 5,21:5
Dodd, James
Those Were the Days 1940,Jl 15,18:4
Flying Tigers 1942,O 23,25:2
Song of my Heart 1948,Mr 5,17:3
You Gotta Stay Happy 1948,N 5,29:2
Singing Guns 1950,Je 5,19:3
Second Woman, The 1951,F 2,19:2
Winning Team, The 1952,Je 21,12:2
Dodd, Lee Wilson (Original Author)
His Majesty Bunker Bean 1925,S 15,12:1
Bunker Bean 1936,Je 27,21:2
Dodd, Neal Rev
Only Woman, The 1924,N 3,20:1
Merrily We Go to Hell 1932,Je 11,9:3
You Belong to Me 1934,S 13,26:1
Dodge, David (Original Author)
Plunder of the Sun 1953,Ag 27,22:1
To Catch a Thief 1955,Ag 5,14:2
Dodge, Frank
East Side, West Side 1927,O 18,33:2
Dodge, Henry Irving (Original Author)
Skinner's Dress Suit 1917,F 19,9:3
Skinner's Dress Suit 1926,My 3,27:1
Thirteenth Juror, The 1927,N 22,20:1
Skinner's big Idea 1928,Mr 27,30:4
Skinner Steps Out 1929,D 7,19:3
Dodson, Jon
St Louis Blues 1939,F 9,17:2
Dodson, Kenneth (Original Author)
Away all Boats 1956,Ag 17,14:2
Dodsworth, John
Bwana Devil 1953,F 19,20:5
Maze, The 1953,Jl 11,8:2
Doeblin, Alfred (Original Author)
Berlin-Alexanderplatz 1931,N 15,VIII,6:1
Doeblin, Hugo
Horst Wessel; Hans Westmar 1934,F 4,IX,4:4
Doederlein, Fred
Purpur und Waschblau 1932,Jl 11,11:4
Drei Tage Mittelarrest 1933,My 18,17:4
Gordian, Der Tyrann 1937,Je 21,15:3
Rote Orchideen; Red Orchids 1939,Ap 15,15:2
Kamera den auf See; Comrades at Sea 1939,Ap 22,15:3
Doeinitz, Marc
Roots of Heaven, The 1958,O 16,46:1
Doelle, Franz (Composer)
Amphitryon 1937,Mr 24,29:1
Aus den Wolken Kommt das Glueck; Luck Comes From the Clouds 1938,Ap 16,17:2
Doelnitz, Marc
Zazie 1961,N 21,45:5
Doermer, Christian
Love at Twenty 1963,F 7,5:6
Joanna 1968,N 25,54:1
Doff, Red (Producer)
Andy Hardy Comes Home 1958,D 24,00:0
Platinum High School 1960,My 26,37:3
Everything's Ducky 1961,D 21,30:6
Doggett, Norma
Seven Brides for Seven Brothers 1954,Jl 23,8:3
Doheny, Lawrence F (Director)
Teenage Millionaire 1962,Ja 12,29:2
DOHERTY
See Also DAUGHERTY, DOUGHERTY
Doherty, Edward J (Original Author)
Under Pressure 1935,F 4,11:3
Sullivans, The 1944,F 10,19:2
Doherty, Ethel (Miscellaneous)
Ten Modern Commandments 1927,Jl 11,23:4
Doherty, Ethel (Original Author)
Sailor Be Good 1933,F 27,11:2

Doherty, Ethel (Screenwriter)
Home on the Range 1935,F 13,24:4
Dohm, Will
Kreuzer Emden 1932,S 8,17:2
Barcarole 1936,O 21,35:3
Liebe auf Umwegen; Love by Indirection 1937,D 18,18:2
Krach und Glueckum Kuennemann; Row and Joy About Kuennemann 1938,S 17,20:3
Nanu, Sie Kennen Korff noch Nicht?; So, You Don't Know Korff Yet? 1939,My 22,15:3
Opernball; Opera Ball 1940,O 15,29:2
Fledermaus, Die; Bat, The 1948,Mr 15,26:2
Dohnanyi, Ernest
Hello Budapest 1935,N 14,17:4
Dojdev, Pavlik
University of Life 1941,F 26,17:1
Dol, Mona
Cheat, The 1950,O 2,19:3
Riptide 1951,Ap 7,9:2
Fire Within, The 1964,F 18,27:1
DOLAN
See Also DOLIN
Dolan, Bobby Jr
Good Sam 1948,S 17,28:2
Dolan, Frank
Charly 1968,S 24,55:1
Dolan, Frank (Original Author)
Man of the People 1937,F 23,25:4
Dolan, Frank (Screenwriter)
Man of the People 1937,F 23,25:4
Street of Missing Men 1939,Je 1,31:3
Dolan, Joann
Eve of St Mark, The 1944,My 31,22:2
Dolan, Michael
Saints and Sinners 1949,S 12,17:2
Christmas Carol, A 1951,N 29,41:2
You Can't Beat the Irish 1952,My 1,34:4
Dolan, Robert Emmett (Producer)
White Christmas 1954,O 15,16:3
Anything Goes 1956,Mr 22,38:1
Dolbert, Claude (Producer)
Barber of Seville 1949,Jl 21,21:2
Gigi 1950,Ja 31,20:2
Red Angel, The 1950,N 4,13:2
Dolby, Amy
Secret of my Success, The 1965,N 4,57:2
Dole, Adrienne
Alias the Doctor 1932,Mr 3,22:3
Doleman, Guy
Kangaroo 1952,My 17,22:7
His Majesty O'Keefe 1954,F 6,17:2
On the Beach 1959,D 18,34:1
Ipcress File, The 1965,Ag 3,35:1
Thunderball 1965,D 22,23:1
Girl-Getters, The 1966,Ap 13,37:6
Idol, The 1966,Ag 11,27:1
Funeral in Berlin 1966,D 23,17:1
Deadly Bees, The 1967,My 20,39:2
Billion Dollar Brain 1967,D 23,29:1
Dolenz, George
Fired Wife 1943,O 1,15:2
Strange Death of Adolf Hitler, The 1943,O 9,11:5
In Society 1944,Ag 17,20:2
Bowery to Broadway 1944,N 30,19:2
Enter Arsene Lupin 1944,D 2,17:6
Climax, The 1944,D 14,28:5
Night in Paradise 1946,Je 6,16:3
Song of Scheherazade 1947,F 27,26:2
Vendetta 1950,D 26,19:1
My Cousin Rachel 1952,D 26,20:2
Scared Stiff 1953,Jl 3,10:2
Wings of the Hawk 1953,Ag 27,22:1
Last Time I saw Paris, The 1954,N 19,20:2
Racers, The 1955,F 5,13:2
Sign of the Pagan 1955,F 14,24:2
Bullet for Joey, A 1955,Ap 16,12:1
Purple Mask, The 1955,Je 16,35:7
Sad Sack, The 1957,N 28,57:1
4 Horsemen of the Apocalypse, The 1962,Mr 10,10:2
Look in any Window 1962,Mr 22,40:1
Dolenz, Micky
Head 1968,N 7,51:1
Doler, Mikhail
Horizon, The Wandering Jew 1933,My 12,20:4
Dolfi, Fioretta
Lady is Fickle, The 1948,F 7,10:4
Dolgopolov, M (Screenwriter)
Springtime on the Volga 1961,D 25,27:4
Dolgoruki, Igor
Days of Glory 1944,Je 17,10:2
Dolgov, G
Guerrilla Brigade 1942,Ap 14,17:2
Dolgy, Wolf (Screenwriter)
Dimka 1964,Mr 21,13:5
Doli, Dora
Lovemaker, The 1958,Mr 11,33:4
Dolidze, S (Director)
Dragonfly, The 1955,Je 27,18:2
DOLIN
See Also DOLAN

Dolin, Anton (Miscellaneous)
Invitation to the Waltz 1938,Jl 2,10:3
Dolin, B (Director)
New Number Comes to Moscow, A 1959,Jl 6,23:1
Cinerama's Russian Adventure 1966,Ap 14,42:1
Dolin, B (Screenwriter)
New Number Comes to Moscow, A 1959,Jl 6,23:1
Dolinin, Andrei
Thirteen, The 1937,Je 19,20:2
Dolinski, Voytek
Village, The 1953,S 23,37:2
Blue Angel, The 1959,S 5,11:4
d'Olivo, Erminio
Loyalty of Love 1937,Mr 1,15:1
DOLL
See Also DAHL, DALL
Doll, Dora
Pardon my French 1952,Mr 31,17:2
Savage Triangle 1952,S 30,38:2
Young Lions, The 1958,Ap 3,23:1
Grisbi 1959,Jl 13,23:1
Any Number Can Win 1963,O 9,47:2
Doll, Robert M
Greatest Love of All, The 1924,N 11,14:1
Doller, M (Director)
General Suvorov 1941,S 20,11:2
Dolman, Richard
Good Companions, The 1933,O 10,24:1
Man Who Changed his Name, The 1934,O 17,26:2
Dolmatovsky, E (Narrator)
Great is my Country 1959,Jl 1,26:1
Dolya, E
Mass Struggle 1934,S 17,20:3
Dolys, Jane
Little Flower of Jesus, The 1938,D 13,31:2
Domasheva, Marta
Baltic Deputy 1937,S 4,8:2
Domasin, Larry
Dime With a Halo 1963,Je 27,23:3
Fun in Acapulco 1964,F 20,22:4
Domb, Adam
Without a Home 1939,Ap 1,17:3
Domergue, Faith
Young Widow 1946,Jl 29,12:8
Vendetta 1950,D 26,19:1
Where Danger Lives 1951,Ja 1,13:6
Duel at Silver Creek 1952,Ag 2,7:6
Great Sioux Uprising, The 1953,Jl 18,6:2
This is my Love 1954,D 25,7:3
This Island Earth 1955,Je 11,8:7
Track of Thunder 1968,F 1,28:4
Domgraf-Fassbender, Willi
Theodor Koerner 1933,My 6,11:2
Verkaufte Braut, Die 1934,Ap 27,25:2
Aufforderung zum Tanz; Invitation to the Dance 1935,N 23,23:3
Marriage of Figaro 1950,N 3,31:2
Domin, Friedrich
Lied der Wuste, Das; Desert Song 1940,F 3,9:3
Marianne of my Youth; (Marianne de ma Jeunesse) 1959,Ja 20,43:1
Dominguez, Abel (Composer)
Tierra de Pasiones 1944,N 7,24:3
Dominguez, Adriano
Marcelino 1956,O 23,39:1
Night Heaven Fell, The 1958,O 22,40:4
Dominguez, Bobby
Green Fire 1954,D 25,7:1
Dominguez, Columba
Devotion 1953,Ja 31,10:6
Important Man, The; El Mayordoma 1962,Je 26,25:2
Dominguez, Ernesto (Composer)
Tierra de Pasiones 1944,N 7,24:3
Dominguez, Frances
Ace in the Hole 1951,Je 30,8:6
Dominguez, Francisco (Composer)
Maria Candelaria 1944,S 12,23:7
Dominguez, Joe
Geronimo 1940,F 8,18:3
Streets of Laredo 1949,My 12,28:2
Green Fire 1954,D 25,7:1
Ride Back, The 1957,Ap 30,24:1
Dominguez, Jose
One Way Street 1950,My 12,33:3
Dallas 1951,Ja 13,10:4
Dominguez Brothers
Tropic Holiday 1938,Je 30,21:2
Dominguin
Testament of Orpheus 1962,Ap 10,48:1
Dominguin, Luis Miguel
Around the World in 80 Days 1956,O 18,37:1
Dominiak, Franciszek
Dziesieciu z Pawiaka 1932,Ap 21,25:2
Dominiani, Maria
Eravamo Sette Vedove; We Were Seven Widows 1940,F 16,23:4
Dominici, Arturo
Hercules 1959,Jl 23,32:2
Goliath and the Barbarians 1960,Ja 7,24:6

Dominici, Arturo — Cont
Black Sunday 1961,Mr 9,23:1
Thief of Baghdad, The 1961,Ag 17,18:2
Dominici, Mario
William Fox Movietone Follies of 1929
1929,My 27,22:1
Domino, Fats
Girl Can't Help It, The 1957,F 9,12:7
Domnick, Ottomar Dr (Director)
Jonas 1959,Ap 30,37:1
Domnick, Ottomar Dr (Producer)
Jonas 1959,Ap 30,37:1
Domnick, Ottomar Dr (Screenwriter)
Jonas 1959,Ap 30,37:1
don Eugenio, Prince
Dolce Vita, La 1961,Ap 20,30:1
Donadio, Giulio
Passaporto Rosso 1936,S 2,18:2
Donadio, Guido
Manon Lescaut 1941,Ap 14,23:5
Donadio, Guilio
Between Two Worlds 1940,F 9,15:2
Donahue, Frank
Frogmen, The 1951,Je 30,8:6
Donahue, Frank (Screenwriter)
Espionage Agent 1939,S 23,22:2
Donahue, Jean
Down to Earth 1947,S 12,18:2
Donahue, Joe
Sunny 1930,D 27,16:3
Party Husband 1931,My 16,13:3
Reckless Hour, The 1931,Ag 1,16:4
Expensive Women 1931,N 14,15:3
Donahue, Mary Eleanor
Mister Big 1943,Je 14,13:4
Unfinished Dance, The 1947,O 31,29:2
Three Daring Daughters 1948,F 13,26:3
Donahue, Stephen J Mgr
Pope Speaks, The 1933,Ap 17,13:3 (In Addenda)
Donahue, Troy
This Happy Feeling 1958,Je 19,28:2
Summer Love 1958,Je 26,23:4
Voice in the Mirror 1958,Ag 14,23:2
Perfect Furlough, The 1959,Ja 22,27:4
Imitation of Life 1959,Ap 18,18:1
Summer Place, A 1959,O 23,24:1
Crowded Sky, The 1961,F 11,27:2
Parrish 1961,My 5,22:1
Susan Slade 1961,N 11,14:6
Rome Adventure 1962,Mr 16,25:1
Palm Springs Weekend 1963,N 6,32:1
Distant Trumpet, A 1964,My 28,40:1
My Blood Runs Cold 1965,Mr 25,42:4
Come Spy with Me 1967,F 22,21:1
Those Fantastic Flying Fools 1967,O 19,59:2
Donahue, Vincent
Beyond Glory 1948,Ag 4,18:2
Donald, James
In Which We Serve 1942,D 24,18:1
Way Ahead, The 1945,Je 4,22:3
Broken Journey 1949,My 26,34:3
Edward my Son 1949,Je 3,21:2
Gay Lady, The 1951,Ap 16,21:2
Case of Gold 1952,Ja 19,13:3
Cage of Gold 1952,Ja 19,13:3
Vikings, The 1952,Je 12,35:2
White Corridors 1952,Jl 16,21:1
Brandy for the Parson 1952,Ag 18,13:4
Glory at Sea 1953,Mr 11,36:7
Project M 7 1953,N 27,22:5
Pickwick Papers, The 1954,Ap 5,21:2
Beau Brummell 1954,O 21,31:5
Lust for Life 1956,S 18,39:1
Bridge on the River Kwai 1957,D 19,39:1
Third Man on the Mountain 1959,N 12,27:1
Great Escape, The 1963,Ag 8,19:1
King Rat 1965,O 28,48:1
Cast a Giant Shadow 1966,Mr 31,43:3
Jokers, The 1967,My 16,50:1
Five Million Years to Earth 1968,My 30,21:4
Donaldson, Arthur
When Knighthood Was in Flower 1922,S 15,17:2
(In Addenda)
Yolanda 1924,F 20,23:1
America 1924,F 22,20:1
Bandolero, The 1924,O 27,27:1
Swan, The 1925,Mr 2,14:1
School for Wives 1925,Ap 1,21:3
Love 'Em and Leave 'Em 1926,D 8,24:3
Donaldson, Gil
Dallas 1951,Ja 13,10:4
Donaldson, Ted
Once Upon a Time 1944,Je 30,17:2
Mr Winkle Goes to War 1944,Ag 3,16:1
Tree Grows in Brooklyn, A 1945,Mr 1,25:5
Red Stallion 1947,N 27,50:3
Decision of Christopher Blake, The
1948,D 11,12:2
Green Promise, The 1949,Je 24,29:2
Phone Call From a Stranger 1952,F 2,11:2
Donaldson, Walter (Composer)
Hollywood Party 1934,My 26,12:2
Operator 13 1934,Je 23,16:5
Kid Millions 1934,N 12,17:2

Great Ziegfeld, The 1936,Ap 9,21:2
Good Old Soak 1937,Ap 20,25:3
That's Right, You're Wrong 1939,N 30,25:3
Panama Hattie 1942,O 2,31:2
Donaldson, Walter (Miscellaneous)
Kid Millions 1934,N 12,17:2
Suzy 1936,Jl 25,16:1
After the Thin Man 1936,D 25,19:2
Saratoga 1937,Jl 23,16:3
Broadway Serenade 1939,Ap 7,25:2
Donat, Agi
Tokaji Rapszodia 1938,N 7,23:5
Megvedten Egy Asszony; I Defended a Woman
1939,O 14,13:3
Donat, John
This Land Is Mine 1943,My 28,19:1
Donat, Robert
Private Life of Henry VIII, The 1933,O 13,25:2
For Love or Money 1934,Jl 26,14:2
Count of Monte Cristo, The 1934,S 27,25:2
Men of Tomorrow 1935,Ap 16,27:2
Thirty-Nine Steps, The 1935,S 14,8:4
Ghost Goes West, The 1935,D 18,33:8
Ghost Goes West, The 1936,Ja 11,9:2
Knight Without Armor 1937,Jl 9,18:1
Citadel, The 1938,N 4,27:2
Goodbye Mr Chips 1939,My 16,27:2
Young Mr Pitt, The 1943,Mr 11,17:1
Adventures of Tartu, The 1943,S 24,26:1
Vacation From Marriage 1946,Mr 15,27:2
Captain Boycott 1947,D 6,11:2
Winslow Boy, The 1950,Je 7,34:4
Magic Box, The 1952,S 24,40:2
Lease of Life 1956,F 10,18:1
Inn of the Sixth Happiness, The 1958,D 14,2:7
Donath, Addison
Renegades 1946,Jl 11,18:2
Donath, Louis
Enemy Agents meet Ellery Queen
1942,Ag 22,16:2
Master Race, The 1944,N 2,22:1
Donath, Ludwig
Strange Death of Adolf Hitler, The 1943,O 9,11:5
Hitler Gang, The 1944,My 8,15:2
Counter-Attack 1945,My 17,15:2
Jolson Story, The 1946,O 11,28:2
Return of Monte Cristo, The 1947,Ja 3,16:4
To the Ends of the Earth 1948,F 13,26:2
Sealed Verdict 1948,N 3,36:2
Fighting O'Flynn, The 1949,F 28,16:2
Great Sinner, The 1949,Je 30,19:2
Jolson Sings Again 1949,Ag 18,16:6
There's a Girl in my Heart 1950,Ja 20,29:2
Killer That Stalked New York, The
1951,Ja 5,17:2
Mystery Submarine 1951,F 2,19:2
Great Caruso, The 1951,My 11,32:2
Sirocco 1951,Je 14,31:2
Journey Into Light 1951,O 5,24:4
Veils of Bagdad, The 1953,N 27,99:9
Sins of Jezebel 1954,Ja 9,12:2
Donati, Donate
It's Forever Springtime 1951,D 29,7:7
Donati, Ermanno (Producer)
Marco Polo 1962,S 20,29:2
Son of Samson 1962,S 27,33:4
Love and Marriage (The Last Resort); Last Resort,
The (Love and Marriage) 1966,Ag 5,20:1
Love and Marriage (Saturday, July 18); Saturday,
July 18 (Love and Marriage) 1966,Ag 5,20:1
Love and Marriage (The First Night); First Night,
The (Love and Marriage) 1966,Ag 5,20:1
Love and Marriage (One Moment Is Enough); One
Moment Is Enough (Love and Marriage)
1966,Ag 5,20:1
Hills Run Red, The 1967,N 11,26:3
Matchless 1967,N 11,26:3
Navajo Joe 1967,D 7,60:2
Donati, Maria
Life Begins Anew; Vita Ricomincia, La
1947,Ap 7,20:5
Angelina 1948,Ap 6,27:2
Tears of Blood 1952,Ja 19,13:2
Donati, Sergio (Screenwriter)
Big Gundown, The 1968,Ag 23,33:1
Donatov, A (Screenwriter)
Tsar's Bride, The 1966,Mr 12,13:2
Donavan, Hobart (Screenwriter)
Escape to Burma 1955,My 21,11:2
Donde, Manuel
Treasure of Sierra Madre 1948,Ja 24,11:2
Garden of Evil 1954,Jl 10,17:1
Mexican Bus ride 1954,Jl 21,18:3
This Strange Passion 1955,D 5,34:2
Last Frontier, The 1955,D 8,45:1
Dondini, Ada
Amo Te Sola 1936,Jl 20,11:2
Zio d'America, Lo; Uncle From America, The
1939,S 15,26:5
Schoolgirl Diary 1947,O 18,9:2
I Cadetti di Guascogna 1952,O 6,22:2

Donea, Stanley (Director)
Singin' in the Rain 1952,Mr 28,27:2
Donegan, Dorothy
Sensations of 1945 1944,Jl 7,13:2
Donehue, Vincent J (Director)
Lonelyhearts 1959,Mr 5,35:3
Sunrise at Campobello 1960,S 29,32:1
Donen, Stanley (Director)
On the Town 1949,D 9,37:2
Royal Wedding 1951,Mr 9,30:2
Love Is Better Than Ever 1952,Mr 4,23:2
Seven Brides for Seven Brothers 1954,Jl 23,8:3
Deep in my Heart 1954,D 10,35:2
It's Always Fair Weather 1955,S 16,19:1
Funny Face 1957,Mr 29,16:1
Pajama Game, The 1957,Ag 30,12:2
Kiss Them for Me 1957,N 9,31:2
Indiscreet 1958,Je 27,18:2
Damn Yankees 1958,S 27,12:7
Once More With Feeling 1960,F 12,22:2
Surprise Package 1960,O 15,26:2
Grass is Greener, The 1960,D 24,8:2
Charade 1963,D 6,40:1
Arabesque 1966,My 6,54:1
Two for the Road 1967,Ap 28,36:2
Bedazzled 1967,D 11,65:2
Donen, Stanley (Original Author)
Take Me Out to the Ball Game 1949,Mr 10,35:2
Donen, Stanley (Producer)
Pajama Game, The 1957,Ag 30,12:2
Indiscreet 1958,Je 27,18:2
Damn Yankees 1958,S 27,12:7
Once More With Feeling 1960,F 12,22:2
Surprise Package 1960,O 15,26:2
Grass is Greener, The 1960,D 24,8:2
Charade 1963,D 6,40:1
Arabesque 1966,My 6,54:1
Two for the Road 1967,Ap 28,36:2
Bedazzled 1967,D 11,65:2
Dongen, Fritz van
Indian Tomb, The; Tiger von Eschnapur, Der
1938,My 14,18:2
Verwehte Spuren; Covered Tracks
1939,O 14,13:3
Reise Nach Tilsit, Die; Trip to Tilsit, The
1940,F 10,19:2
Walzerlange; Waltz Melodies 1940,Ap 27,9:3
Doniger, Walter (Director)
Duffy of San Quentin 1954,F 10,38:5
Steel Jungle, The 1956,Mr 10,9:5
House of Women 1962,Ap 12,41:6
Safe at Home 1962,Ap 14,14:1
Doniger, Walter (Original Author)
Rope of Sand 1949,Ag 4,19:2
Doniger, Walter (Producer)
Duffy of San Quentin 1954,F 10,38:5
Doniger, Walter (Screenwriter)
Rope of Sand 1949,Ag 4,19:2
Tokyo Joe 1949,O 27,35:2
Along the Great Divide 1951,My 17,38:3
Cease Fire! 1953,N 25,17:1
Duffy of San Quetin 1954,F 10,38:5
Alaska Seas 1954,Mr 6,13:5
Steel Jungle, The 1956,Mr 10,9:5
Doniol-Valcroze, Jacques (Director)
French Game 1963,S 21,13:5
Viol, Le 1968,S 20,42:1
Doniol-Valcroze, Jacques (Screenwriter)
French Game 1963,S 21,13:5
Viol, Le 1968,S 20,42:1
Donion, Patricia Dolores
Nude Odyssey 1962,O 27,14:6
Donizetti, Gaetano (Composer)
Andy Hardy's Private Secretary 1941,Mr 7,17:2
This Wine of Love 1948,Ap 19,27:2
Donizetti, Gaetano (Original Author)
Lucia di Lammermoor 1947,N 1,11:3
First Opera Film Festival 1948,My 31,12:7
DONLAN
See Also DONLON
Donlan, James
Bishop Murder Case, The 1930,F 1,15:1
Remote Control 1930,D 8,26:1
Good Bad Girl, The 1931,My 15,20:6
Final Edition, The 1932,F 22,23:2
Back Street 1932,Ag 29,9:2
They Just Had to Get Married 1933,F 13,11:4
Avenger, The 1933,O 3,28:3
Hi, Nellie! 1934,F 1,15:5
Cat's Paw, The 1934,Ag 17,12:2
Belle of the Nineties 1934,S 22,12:2
Under Pressure 1935,F 4,11:3
Whole Town's Talking, The 1935,Mr 1,16:2
Traveling Saleslady 1935,Mr 29,26:2
Daring Young Man, The 1935,Jl 18,15:2
Murder on a Bridle Path 1936,Ap 11,19:2
Crash Donovan 1936,Ag 10,10:3
Plot Thickens, The 1936,D 9,35:2
It Happened in Hollywood 1937,O 2,18:1
Donlan, Yolande
Mister Drake's Duck 1952,Ja 28,15:2
Penny Princess 1953,Mr 25,37:3
Tarzan and the Lost Safari 1957,Ap 13,12:3

Donlan, Yolande— Cont

Expresso Bongo 1960,Ap 13,44:1
Donlevy, Brian
Mother's Boy 1929,My 8,34:6
Barbary Coast 1935,O 14,21:1
Mary Burns, Fugitive 1935,N 16,19:2
Strike Me Pink 1936,Ja 17,15:2
13 Hours by Air 1936,Ap 30,17:2
Human Cargo 1936,My 16,11:2
Half Angel 1936,My 30,7:3
High Tension 1936,Jl 11,11:4
36 Hours to Live 1936,Ag 15,6:3
Crack-Up 1937,Ja 4,20:4
This Is my Affair 1937,My 28,17:1
Born Reckless 1937,Jl 30,22:6
In Old Chicago 1938,Ja 7,15:2
Battle of Broadway 1938,Ap 25,19:2
We're Going to Be Rich 1938,Jl 4,10:2
Sharpshooters 1938,D 5,19:2
Jesse James 1939,Ja 14,13:1
Union Pacific 1939,My 11,31:2
Beau Geste 1939,Ag 3,15:2
Behind Prison Gates 1939,Ag 21,9:3
Allegheny Uprising 1939,N 10,27:3
Destry Rides Again 1939,N 30,25:1
Great McGinty, The 1940,Ag 15,23:1
When the Daltons Rode 1940,Ag 23,13:3
Brigham Young - Frontiersman 1940,S 21,13:2
I Wanted Wings 1941,Mr 27,29:4
Billy the Kid 1941,Je 20,28:2
Hold Back the Dawn 1941,O 2,29:1
South of Tahiti 1941,N 10,21:3
Birth of the Blues 1941,D 11,39:1
Remarkable Andrew, The 1942,Mr 6,17:2
Two Yanks in Trinidad 1942,Ap 6,19:4
Gentleman After Dark, A 1942,Ap 17,21:2
Great Man's Lady, The 1942,Ap 30,14:3
Wake Island 1942,S 2,19:2
Glass Key, The 1942,O 16,23:1
Nightmare 1942,D 4,31:2
Stand by for Action 1943,Mr 12,12:2
Hangmen Also Die 1943,Ap 16,24:2
Miracle of Morgan's Creek, The 1944,Ja 20,15:2
American Romance, An 1944,N 24,19:1
Duffy's Tavern 1945,S 6,23:3
Virginian, The 1946,Ap 18,22:2
Canyon Passage 1946,Ag 8,18:2
Our Hearts Were Growing Up 1946,Ag 12,17:2
Two Years Before the Mast 1946,S 25,39:2
Beginning or the End, The 1947,F 21,15:1
Song of Scheherazade 1947,F 27,26:2
Trouble With Women, The 1947,Jl 14,14:4
Kiss of Death 1947,Ag 28,28:2
Heaven Only Knows 1947,N 14,29:3
Killer McCoy 1948,F 12,31:2
Southern Yankee, A 1948,N 25,47:2
Command Decision 1949,Ja 20,34:2
Lucky Stiff, The 1949,Ja 31,14:2
Impact 1949,Mr 21,19:2
Shakedown 1950,S 4,11:2
Kansas Raiders 1951,Ja 26,19:2
Fighting Coast Guard 1951,My 12,14:6
Hoodlum Empire 1952,Mr 6,25:6
Big Combo, The 1955,Mr 26,13:2
Cry in the Night, A 1956,S 1,19:4
Cowboy 1958,F 20,29:5
Never so Few 1960,Ja 22,15:2
Pigeon That Took Rome, The 1962,Ag 23,25:1
How to Stuff a Wild Bikini 1967,Ja 12,48:1
Donlevy, Brian (Narrator)
City That Stopped Hitler--Heroic Stalingrad, The 1943,S 6,21:3
Donley, Robert Morris (Screenwriter)
Andy Hardy Comes Home 1958,D 24,00:0
Donley, Robert P
Strange Victory 1948,S 27,27:2
Donlin, Mike
Woman Proof 1923,O 30,16:1
Unknown Purple, The 1924,Mr 24,13:1
Oh, Doctor! 1925,F 23,24:1
Fifth Avenue Models 1925,My 4,16:2
Sea Hunt, The 1926,Ja 16,8:5
Sea Beast, The 1926,Ja 16,8:5
Ella Cinders 1926,Je 7,23:2
Slide, Kelly, Slide 1927,Mr 23,19:2
Warming Up 1928,Jl 16,25:3
Beggars of Life 1928,S 24,25:1
Riley, The Cop 1928,D 4,29:1
Thunderbolt 1929,Je 21,17:2
Born Reckless 1930,Je 7,10:4
Iron Man 1931,Ap 18,17:3
Tip Off, The 1931,O 26,22:1
Air Hostess 1933,Ja 23,9:2
High Gear 1933,Ap 15,16:2
DONLON
See Also DONLAN
Donlon, Dolores
Long Wait, The 1954,Jl 3,9:2
Flight to Hong Kong 1957,Ja 3,28:2
Donlon, James
Beau Bandit 1930,Je 14,9:4
Half-Naked Truth, The 1932,D 31,10:1
Death Kiss, The 1933,F 5,IX,5:3
Now I'll Tell 1934,My 26,12:2

Donmullahy, Don (Original Author)
Bowery Blitzkrieg 1941,O 1,24:5
Donn-Bryne, Dorothea (Original Author)
Enter Madame 1935,Ja 12,12:1
Donn-Byrne, Archibald (Original Author)
Enter Madame 1935,Ja 12,12:1
Donnay, Maurice (Original Author)
Barge-Keeper's Daughter, The 1945,S 6,23:3
Donne, Carole
Miraculous Journey 1948,S 20,21:2
Amazon Quest 1949,My 14,9:3
Not Wanted 1949,Jl 25,11:4
Donnell, Jeff
Boogie Man Will Get You, The 1942,O 12,12:4
My Sister Eileen 1942,O 23,15:1
Night to Remember, A 1943,Ja 1,27:2
What's Buzzin Cousin 1943,Jl 23,21:4
Carolina Blues 1944,D 8,26:6
3 Is a Family 1944,D 20,20:3
Over 21 1945,Ag 17,20:2
Tars and Spars 1946,F 15,29:2
Night Editor 1946,Mr 30,11:2
Unknown, The 1946,Jl 20,10:3
Mr District Attorney 1947,F 28,27:3
Roughshod 1949,Je 17,27:2
Easy Living 1949,O 13,33:3
In a Lonely Place 1950,My 18,37:2
Fuller Brush Girl, The 1950,O 6,23:2
Walk Softly Stranger 1950,O 16,30:5
Three Guys Named Mike 1951,Mr 2,21:2
Thief of Damascus 1952,My 8,37:2
Because You're Mine 1952,S 26,18:2
Blue Gardenia, The 1953,Ap 28,31:1
So This Is Love 1953,Ag 12,22:1
Flight Nurse 1954,Ja 30,9:6
Sweet Smell of Success 1957,Je 28,29:2
My Man Godfrey 1957,O 12,23:1
Gidget Goes Hawaiian 1961,Ag 10,17:4
Swingin' Maiden, The 1964,Ja 1,16:2
Donnelly, Bill
Flying Missile, The 1950,D 25,25:1
Donnelly, Donal
Rising of the Moon, The (The Majesty of the Law); Majesty of the Law, The (The Rising of the Moon) 1957,Jl 10,23:1
I'm All Right Jack 1960,Ap 26,40:2
Young Cassidy 1965,Mr 23,35:1
Knack...and how to get it, The 1965,Je 30,42:1
Donnelly, Donald
Rising of the Moon, The (1921); 1921 (The Rising of the Moon) 1957,Jl 10,23:1
Donnelly, Dorothy (Original Author)
Poppy 1936,Je 18,19:1
Donnelly, Leo
Roadhouse Nights 1930,F 22,13:1
Donnelly, Ruth
Rubber Heels 1927,Je 28,29:4
Transatlantic 1931,Jl 31,15:2
Spider, The 1931,S 5,7:4
Wicked 1931,S 19,10:2
Rainbow Trail, The 1932,Ja 30,13:2
Make Me a Star 1932,Jl 1,19:3
Jewel Robbery 1932,Jl 23,6:6
Blessed Event 1932,S 3,16:2
Employees' Entrance 1933,Ja 21,10:6
Hard to Handle 1933,F 2,21:5
Ladies They Talk About 1933,F 25,20:4
Lilly Turner 1933,Je 15,21:2
Private Detective 62 1933,Jl 7,20:2
Sing Sinner Sing 1933,Ag 15,20:2
Good-Bye Again 1933,S 2,15:2
Bureau of Missing Persons 1933,S 9,9:2
Footlight Parade 1933,O 6,21:3
Ever in my Heart 1933,O 13,25:3
Female 1933,N 4,18:3
Havana Widows 1933,N 23,24:3
Convention City 1933,D 25,28:2
Mandalay 1934,F 15,15:6
Wonder Bar 1934,Mr 1,23:2
Heat Lightning 1934,Mr 8,23:2
Housewife 1934,Ag 10,21:2
Romance in the Rain 1934,S 8,18:5
Happiness Ahead 1934,O 11,28:2
White Cockatoo, The 1935,Ja 16,21:1
Maybe It's Love 1935,F 11,14:2
Traveling Saleslady 1935,Mr 29,26:2
Alibi Ike 1935,Jl 17,22:1
Red Salute 1935,S 30,13:1
Metropolitan 1935,O 18,27:4
Hands Across the Table 1935,N 2,13:2
Song and Dance Man 1936,Mr 12,18:2
Mr Deeds Goes to Town 1936,Ap 17,17:2
13 Hours by Air 1936,Ap 30,17:2
Fatal Lady 1936,Jl 11,11:3
Cain and Mabel 1936,O 19,22:1
More Than a Secretary 1936,D 11,35:2
Roaring Timber 1937,Ag 19,23:1
Portia on Trial 1937,D 3,29:2
Slight Case of Murder, A 1938,F 28,19:1
Army Girl 1938,Ag 12,11:1
Meet the Girls 1938,S 3,16:6
Personal Secretary 1938,O 5,20:2
Affairs of Annabel, The 1938,O 13,29:2

Donnelly, Ruth— Cont

Annabel Takes a Tour 1938,D 29,15:3
Family Next Door, The 1939,Ap 28,31:2
Mr Smith Goes to Washington 1939,O 20,27:2
Amazing Mr Williams, The 1940,Ja 19,15:2
My Little Chickadee 1940,Mr 16,8:2
Roundup, The 1941,Mr 13,25:4
Model Wife 1941,Ap 24,25:3
You Belong to Me 1941,N 29,14:2
Rise and Shine 1941,D 6,14:3
Johnny Doughboy 1943,My 6,25:3
This Is the Army 1943,Jl 29,11:6
Thank Your Lucky Stars 1943,O 2,19:2
Pillow to Post 1945,My 26,18:2
Bells of St Mary's, The 1945,D 7,26:2
Cinderella Jones 1946,Mr 16,9:6
In old Sacramento 1946,Ap 29,24:4
Cross my Heart 1946,D 19,42:3
Fabulous Texan, The 1947,D 26,22:5
Fighting Father Dunne 1948,Je 25,26:2
Snake Pit, the 1948,N 5,29:2
Where the Sidewalk Ends 1950,Jl 8,7:4
I'd Climb the Highest Mountain 1951,My 10,38:1
Secret of Convict Lake, The 1951,Ag 4,7:2
Wild Blue Yonder, The 1952,Ja 2,20:1
Spoilers, The 1955,D 24,10:2
Autumn Leaves 1956,Ag 2,21:2
Way to the Gold, The 1957,My 11,24:6
Donner, Clive (Director)
Guest, The 1964,Ja 21,25:2
Nothing but the Best 1964,Jl 14,28:1
What's New Pussycat? 1965,Je 23,49:1
Luv 1967,Jl 27,29:1
Here We Go Around the Mulberry Bush 1968,Mr 5,34:5
Donner, Clive (Producer)
Here We Go Around the Mulberry Bush 1968,Mr 5,34:5
Donner, Jorn (Director)
To Love; Att Alska 1964,S 23,45:3 (Incorrect in this edition; use 1964,S 23,54:1 elsewhere)
Donner, Jorn (Screenwriter)
To Love; Att Alska 1964,S 23,45:3 (Incorrect in this edition; use 1964,S 23,54:1 elsewhere)
Donner, Judith
Seance on a Wet Afternoon 1964,N 6,30:1
Donner, Richard (Director)
X-15 1962,Ap 5,30:2
Salt and Pepper 1968,S 19,62:3
Donner, Robert
Cool Hand Luke 1967,N 2,58:1
Donnini, Giulio
Island of Procida, The 1952,Mr 15,8:2
O K Nero 1953,Je 20,8:6
Greco, El 1967,My 24,52:2
Donnio, M
Don Quixote 1934,D 24,17:1
Petits, Les 1936,D 30,17:2
Donoghue, Steve
Wings of the Morning 1937,Mr 12,19:1
Donohue, Elinor
Love Is Better Than Ever 1952,Mr 4,23:2
Donohue, Jack
Smiling Along 1939,F 20,13:2
Donohue, Jack (Director)
Close-Up 1948,Ap 5,24:2
Yellow Cab Man, The 1950,Mr 27,19:2
Watch the Birdie 1950,D 12,46:4
Lucky Me 1954,Ap 10,11:2
Babes in Toyland 1961,D 15,49:1
Marriage on the Rocks 1965,S 16,00:0
Assault on a Queen 1966,Jl 28,23:3
Donohue, Jack (Miscellaneous)
Close-Up 1948,Ap 5,24:2
Donohue, Jack (Original Author)
Sons o'Guns 1936,My 14,29:2
Donohue, Joseph
$20 a Week 1924,Je 10,24:4
Donovan
Don't Look Back 1967,S 7,50:2
Festival 1967,O 24,53:2
Donovan, Arthur
Pittsburgh Kid, The 1941,S 23,27:4
Donovan, Gloria
I've Always Loved You 1946,S 7,11:1
Donovan, King
Cargo to Capetown 1950,Mr 31,36:3
One Way Street 1950,My 12,33:3
Sun Sets at Dawn, The 1951,Ja 15,13:1
Enforcer, The 1951,Ja 26,19:2
Redhead and the Cowboy, The 1951,Je 6,37:2
Angels in the Outfield 1951,O 18,32:1
Merry Widow, The 1952,S 25,38:1
Mississippi Gambler, The 1953,Ja 30,25:1
Magnetic Monster, The 1953,My 14,32:5
Beast From 20,000 Fathoms, The 1953,Je 25,23:1
Easy to Love 1953,N 27,99:9
Forever Female 1954,Ja 13,26:2
Birds and the Bees, The 1956,Ap 23,22:1
Cowboy 1958,F 20,29:5
Defiant Ones, The 1958,S 25,29:1
Perfect Furlough, The 1959,Ja 22,27:4

Donovan, Robert J (Original Author)
PT 109 1963,Je 27,23:1
Donovan, Wilfred
Society Scandal, A 1924,Mr 10,18:2
Donovan, William
Son of the Sheik, The 1926,Jl 26,13:2
Donskola, I (Screenwriter)
Sons and Mothers 1967,O 2,58:1
Donskoy, M (Director)
Pesnya O Stchasti 1935,Ap 8,23:4
University of Life 1941,F 26,17:1
Signal, The 1943,Mr 25,25:3
Donskoy, Mark (Director)
Childhood of Maxim Gorky 1938,S 28,29:3
On his Own 1939,S 13,31:3
Heroes Are Made 1944,Mr 11,10:2
Rainbow, The 1944,O 23,14:3
Taras Family, The 1946,D 9,34:4
Village Teacher 1948,Jl 5,8:4
1905 1956,Jl 9,27:2
Gordeyev Family, The 1961,O 16,33:6
Sons and Mothers 1967,O 2,58:1
Donskoy, Mark (Producer)
Village Teacher 1948,Jl 5,8:4
Donskoy, Mark (Screenwriter)
Heroes Are Made 1944,Mr 11,10:2
Taras Family, The 1946,D 9,34:4
1905 1956,Jl 9,27:2
Gordeyev Family, The 1961,O 16,33:6
Dooley, Billy
Call of the Yukon 1938,My 6,27:1
Dooley, John
Yolanda 1924,F 20,23:1
East Side, West Side 1927,O 18,33:2
Dooley, Johnny
When Knighthood Was in Flower 1922,S 15,17:2
(In Addenda)
Dooley, Ray
Honeymoon Lane 1931,Ag 1,16:4
Doonan, Patric
Blue Lamp, The 1951,Ja 9,25:1
Lavender Hill Mob, The 1951,O 16,35:2
Man in the White Suit, The 1952,Ap 1,35:2
High Treason 1952,My 21,23:3
Glory at Sea 1953,Mr 11,36:7
Project M 7 1953,N 27,22:5
Paratrooper 1953,D 31,9:3
Crest of the Wave 1954,N 11,43:2
John and Julie 1957,My 7,40:1
Door, Lester
Hollywood Cowboy 1937,Jl 24,12:1
Dopagne, Jacques (Screenwriter)
I Spit on Your Grave 1963,Je 29,13:5
Doph, Josephine
Our Modern Maidens 1929,S 7,15:1
Dor, Christiane
Poil de Carotte 1933,My 26,24:2
Man and his Wife, A 1939,Mr 28,20:1
Dor, Jacqueline
Scandals of Clochemerle, The 1950,Mr 28,28:2
Dor, Karin
You Only Live Twice 1967,Je 14,40:1
d'Or, Tarquini
Congress Dances 1932,My 12,23:2
D'Ora, Daisy
Hungarian Nights 1930,Je 10,32:2
Nur am Rhein 1931,S 25,28:7
Dora, Josefine
Vienna Burgtheater 1937,O 27,47:1
Dora, Josephine
Goethe's Jugendgeliebte 1932,D 26,26:2
Brave Suender, Der 1933,Mr 29,13:2
Endstation 1937,Jl 17,18:1
Doraine, Lucy
Queen of Sin and the Spectacle of Sodom and
Gomorrah 1923,Mr 27,24:3 (In Addenda)
Doran, Ann
Let's Sing Again 1936,My 9,11:2
Missing Girls 1936,O 5,25:1
Women in Prison 1938,Mr 1,19:3
Penitentiary 1938,Mr 7,13:2
Highway Patrol 1938,Ag 4,15:2
You Can't Take It With You 1938,S 2,21:2
Blondie 1938,D 22,25:4
Blind Alley 1939,My 23,27:2
Girls of the Road 1940,Jl 22,20:2
Ellery Queen's Penthouse Mystery
1941,Mr 7,17:2
Meet John Doe 1941,Mr 13,25:2
Penny Serenade 1941,My 23,25:2
Kid From Kansas, The 1941,D 2,29:4
Mr Wise Guy 1942,Mr 5,27:2
Air Force 1943,F 4,29:1
Hard Way, The 1943,Mr 13,9:2
I Love a Soldier 1944,N 2,22:2
Here Come the Waves 1944,D 28,25:2
Roughly Speaking 1945,F 1,18:4
Pride of the Marines 1945,Ag 25,7:3
Strange Love of Martha Ivers, The
1946,Jl 25,18:4
Perfect Marriage, The 1947,Ja 16,30:3
My Favorite Brunette 1947,Mr 20,38:2
Fear in the Night 1947,Ap 19,11:3

Second Chance 1947,S 20,12:4
Magic Town 1947,O 8,29:2
Crimson Key, The 1947,O 18,9:2
Pitfall 1948,Ag 25,31:2
Snake Pit, the 1948,N 5,29:2
No Minor Vices 1949,F 26,11:2
One Last Fling 1949,Jl 1,14:6
Kid From Cleveland, The 1949,S 5,13:2
Holiday in Havana 1949,O 14,33:5
No Sad Songs for Me 1950,Ap 28,26:2
Never a Dull Moment 1950,N 22,20:2
Tomahawk 1951,F 19,19:2
Gambling House 1951,Mr 19,23:2
Love Is Better Than Ever 1952,Mr 4,23:2
So This Is Love 1953,Ag 12,22:1
Eddie Cantor Story, The 1953,D 26,10:2
High and the Mighty, The 1954,Jl 1,21:2
Bob Mathias Story, The 1954,O 16,14:6
Rebel without a Cause 1955,O 27,28:3
Voice in the Mirror 1958,Ag 14,23:2
Brass Bottle, The 1964,My 21,42:1
Where Love Has Gone 1964,N 3,26:1
Kitten With a Whip 1964,N 5,50:4
Not With my Wife, You Don't! 1966,N 3,45:2
Doran, James (Screenwriter)
Ipcress File, The 1965,Ag 3,35:1
Doran, Mary
Broadway Melody, The 1929,F 9,15:3
Lucky Boy 1929,F 25,16:1
Their own Desire 1930,Ja 25,13:2
New York Nights 1930,F 1,15:1
Divorcee, The 1930,My 10,25:3
Sins of the Children 1930,Jl 26,16:4
Remote Control 1930,D 8,26:1
Criminal Code, The 1931,Ja 5,21:3
Iron Man 1931,Ap 18,17:3
Party Husband 1931,My 16,13:3
Fifty Fathoms Deep 1931,S 19,10:2
Under Eighteen 1931,D 26,15:5
Union Depot 1932,Ja 15,24:4
Final Edition, The 1932,F 22,23:2
Beauty and the Boss 1932,Ap 2,13:2
Strange Love of Molly Louvain, The
1932,My 9,19:5
Silver Lining, The 1932,My 30,16:5
Miss Pinkerton 1932,Jl 9,7:5
Love Me Tonight 1932,Ag 19,20:6
Grand Slam 1933,F 22,25:2
Saturday's Millions 1933,O 14,18:3
Sing Sing Nights 1935,Ja 26,13:2
Border Patrolman 1936,Je 29,11:2
Dorat, Charles
Golem, The 1937,Mr 22,27:2
They Were Five 1938,Je 1,19:5
Panic 1947,N 27,50:2
Dorat, Charles (Original Author)
Deadlier Than the Male 1957,O 9,41:1
D'Ordan, Cot
Stolen Life 1939,Je 15,27:2
DORE
See Also DORR
Dore, Adrienne
Wild Party, The 1929,Ap 2,28:4
Pointed Heels 1929,D 28,11:1
Union Depot 1932,Ja 15,24:4
Expert, The 1932,F 27,22:1
Play Girl 1932,Mr 19,11:2
Famous Ferguson Case, The 1932,Ap 25,18:6
Rich are Always With Us, The 1932,My 16,19:5
Two Seconds 1932,My 19,25:3
Street of Women 1932,My 30,16:5
Love, Honor and Oh, Baby! 1933,O 28,20:3
Dorene Sisters
He's my Guy 1943,Mr 12,12:3
Dorff, Marta
Miss Julie 1952,Ap 8,35:2
Dorfmann, Annie (Producer)
Gervaise 1957,N 12,46:1
Dorfmann, Robert (Producer)
Forbidden Games 1952,D 9,43:2
Justice Is Done 1953,Mr 3,23:2
Grisbi 1959,Jl 13,23:1
Young Girls Beware 1959,Ag 22,8:2
Cheaters, The; (Tricheurs, Les) 1961,Je 5,37:4
My Wife's Husband 1965,Ja 27,26:1
Sucker, The 1967,O 9,61:1
d'Orgaz, Elena
Tu Hijo 1934,D 17,24:3
Hoy Comienza la Vida 1936,Je 27,21:2
Perjura 1939,Ja 16,11:2
Casa del Ogro, La; House of the Ogre, The
1939,F 13,13:2
St Francis of Assisi 1947,Ap 5,12:5
Dorgeles, Raymond (Original Author)
Croix de Bois, Les; Wooden Crosses
1932,Ap 3,VIII,6:4
Dori, Sandro
Kiss the Girls and Make Them Die
1967,Ja 26,25:1
Doria, Annette
Heritage 1940,N 5,33:2

Doria, Bianca
Anna 1953,F 19,20:5
Dorian, Angela
Chuka 1967,N 2,58:3
Rosemary's Baby 1968,Je 13,57:1
Dorian, Elsa
No Exit 1962,D 6,55:2
Dorian, Ernest
Enemy Agents meet Ellery Queen
1942,Ag 22,16:2
Reunion in France 1943,Mr 5,20:3
Moon Is Down, The 1943,Mr 27,8:6
Night Plane From Chungking 1943,My 31,13:2
Isle of the Dead 1945,S 8,12:2
Dorian, Marion
Volpone 1947,D 27,9:3
Dorio, Lucian (Producer)
Island of Procida, The 1952,Mr 15,8:2
Doris, Pierre
Julie the Redhead 1963,O 15,44:1
Story of a Three Day Pass, The 1968,Jl 9,31:1
Dorival
Dawn Over France 1945,Mr 17,17:2
Dorlan, Marion
Queen's Necklace, The 1947,My 17,8:5
Dorle, Enzo
Head of a Tyrant 1962,Je 7,31:2
Dorleac, Francoise
Girl With the Golden Eyes, The 1962,Ag 21,36:2
That Man From Rio 1964,Je 9,30:1
Soft Skin, The; Peau Douce, La 1964,O 13,49:2
Male Hunt; Chasse a l'Homme, La
1965,Ap 20,42:1
Genghis Khan 1965,Je 24,28:2
Where the Spies Are 1966,Ja 27,29:1
Cul de Sac 1966,N 8,44:2
Billion Dollar Brain 1967,D 23,29:1
Young Girls of Rochefort, The 1968,Ap 12,50:1
Dorliak, D
Paris Commune 1937,Je 2,20:4
Dorman, Shirley
Honeymoon Hate 1927,D 31,31:1
One Woman Idea, The 1929,Je 10,23:1
Dorman, V (Director)
Springtime on the Volga 1961,D 25,27:4
Dorn, Blake
Gangway 1937,Ag 21,7:3
Dorn, Dolores
Phantom of the Rue Morgue 1954,Mr 20,10:5
Underworld, U S A 1961,My 13,10:1
13 West Street 1962,Je 7,31:2
Dorn, Doris (Screenwriter)
Roaring Rails 1924,O 15,27:3
Dorn, Philip
Enemy Agent 1940,Ap 22,13:3
Ski Patrol 1940,My 21,29:4
Diamond Frontiers 1940,O 4,29:2
Escape 1940,N 1,33:1
Ziegfeld Girl 1941,Ap 25,17:2
Underground 1941,Je 23,13:2
Tarzan's Secret Treasure 1941,D 25,33:1
Calling Dr Gillespie 1942,Jl 9,17:4
Random Harvest 1942,D 18,36:6
Reunion in France 1943,Mr 5,20:3
Chetniks 1943,Mr 19,15:3
Paris After Dark 1943,O 23,11:1
Passage to Marseille 1944,F 17,12:5
Escape in the Desert 1945,My 12,10:2
I've Always Loved You 1946,S 7,11:1
I Remember Mama 1948,Mr 12,29:2
Fighting Kentuckian, The 1949,S 19,18:3
Spy Hunt 1950,S 8,25:2
Sealed Cargo 1951,My 24,47:1
Dorn-Heft, Dolores
Uncle Vanya 1958,Ap 29,26:2
Dorna, Mary
Trial of Mary Dugan, The 1929,Mr 29,21:1
Dorne, Mary
Trial of Mary Dugan, The 1929,Mr 29,21:1
Dorne, Sandra
Happy Go Lovely 1951,Jl 26,17:2
Clouded Yellow, The 1951,N 13,33:2
Yellow Balloon, The 1953,N 13,28:2
Iron Petticoat, The 1957,F 2,12:2
Orders to Kill 1958,N 18,41:2
Secret Door, The 1964,Je 4,28:1
Dorning, Robert
Die! Die! My Darling 1965,My 20,52:1
Cul de Sac 1966,N 8,44:2
Dorny, Therese
Douceur D'Aimer, La 1931,D 14,16:3
Cognasse 1935,Ap 15,16:4
Dr Knock 1937,My 1,16:4
Abused Confidence 1938,D 1,29:1
Katia 1939,D 23,9:2
Voyage Surprise 1948,F 14,17:3
Devil's Daughter 1949,F 26,11:2
Faust and the Devil 1950,My 1,18:2
Diabolique 1955,N 22,41:1
Doro, Marie
White Pearl, The 1915,O 11,9:5
Heart of Nora Flynn, The 1916,Ap 24,11:2
Oliver Twist 1916,D 11,7:3

Doro, Marie— Cont
Lost and Won 1917,Ja 22,9:1
Twelve:Ten 1919,D 22,18:3

Doro, Mino
Musica in Piazza 1936,My 7,21:3
Destino di Donna 1937,Je 9,31:6
Piccolo Eroe 1937,Jl 1,33:2
Signora Paradiso 1937,Jl 22,15:2
Dottor Antonio, Il 1939,D 7,35:1
Tutta la Vita in una Notte; All of Life in one
   Night 1940,My 2,29:6
Bandit, The 1949,Je 7,26:3
What Price Innocence? 1953,My 2,13:3
Two Weeks in Another Town 1962,Ag 18,10:1

Doro, Peggy
Three Steps North 1951,Je 29,14:2

Dorofeyev, V
Secret Brigade 1951,Mr 19,23:2
Bride with a Dowry 1954,Ag 23,20:5
Mexican, The 1957,Ap 3,28:2
Captain's Daughter, The 1959,N 23,41:3

Dorokhin, Nikolai
Last Night, The 1937,Ap 28,18:3
In the Far East 1937,O 20,27:3
Defense of Volotchayevsk, The 1938,Ag 11,13:3
Last Hill, The 1945,Je 26,13:2

Doronin, I
Petersburg Nights 1934,S 10,20:4
Concentration Camp 1939,Mr 20,13:2

Doronin, Mikhail
Horizon, The Wandering Jew 1933,My 12,20:4
Nightingale 1936,N 4,41:2

Doronin, Mikhail (Director)
Last Insult, The 1932,O 24,18:5

Doronin, V
Miners of the Don 1951,N 12,21:2

Doronne, Dina
Clouds Over Israel 1966,My 10,48:6

Doroshina, N
Apartment in Moscow 1962,My 28,25:5

Doroshkin, N
University of Life 1941,F 26,17:1

Doroshow, Jack
Queen, The 1968,Je 18,37:1

Doroshow, Jack (Narrator)
Queen, The 1968,Je 18,37:1

DORR
See Also DORE

Dorr, Lester
Riders of the Purple Sage 1931,S 26,25:3
Criminals of the Air 1937,O 28,29:2
Main Event, The 1938,Je 20,11:3

Dorraine, Lucy
Adoration 1929,Ja 14,20:1
Christina 1929,Ap 1,22:1

Dorrell, Artie
Body and Soul 1947,N 10,21:2

Dorrell, Don
That Darn Cat 1965,D 3,44:1

Dorris, Anita
Student Sein 1931,My 4,15:3
Theaternaechte von Berlin 1932,Ja 11,28:5

Dors, Diana
Good Time Girl 1950,S 25,18:5
Here Come the Huggetts 1950,D 25,25:3
Weak and the Wicked, The 1954,Ag 21,10:3
Kid for two Farthings, A 1956,Ap 18,25:1
Blonde Sinner 1957,Ja 24,34:1
Value for Money 1957,Ag 1,20:4
Alligator Named Daisy, An 1957,O 7,23:2
Unholy Wife, The 1958,Mr 7,17:1
I Married a Woman 1958,N 5,42:5
Room 43 1959,D 3,46:1
Scent of Mystery 1960,F 19,23:1
On the Double 1961,My 20,12:1
King of the Roaring Twenties 1961,O 5,43:1
Counterfeit Constable, The 1966,N 22,32:2
Berserk! 1968,Ja 11,42:2
Danger Route 1968,Je 6,54:2
Hammerhead 1968,S 12,54:3

D'Orsay, Fifi
They Had to See Paris 1929,O 12,11:1
Hot for Paris 1930,Ja 4,21:1
Women Everywhere 1930,Je 23,15:1
On the Level 1930,Jl 5,17:4
Those Three French Girls 1930,O 11,21:3
Mr Lemon of Orange 1931,Mr 28,15:3
Women of all Nations 1931,My 30,9:2
Young as You Feel 1931,Ag 8,16:3
Life of Jimmy Dolan, The 1933,Je 14,22:3
Going Hollywood 1933,D 23,19:2
Wonder Bar 1934,Mr 1,23:2
Three Legionnaires 1937,Jl 10,18:2
Gangster, The 1947,O 31,29:3
What a Way to Go! 1964,My 15,44:1

D'Orsay, Lawrence
His Children's Children 1923,N 5,15:1
Side Show of Life, The 1924,Jl 22,9:1
Sorrows of Satan, The 1926,O 13,21:1

Dorsch, Kaethe
Drei Tage Liebe; Three Days of Love
   1931,Mr 15,IX,6:1
Lindenwirtin vom Rhein, Die 1931,S 25,28:7
Frau Ohne Bedeutung, Ein 1938,Ap 16,17:2

Mutterliebe; Mother Love 1940,Mr 16,8:3
Singing Angels 1952,Ja 16,21:2

Dorsey, Jimmy
Fabulous Dorseys, The 1947,My 30,25:3

Dorsey, Jimmy and his band
Fleet's In, The 1942,Mr 12,24:2
Four Jills in a Jeep 1944,Ap 6,27:2

Dorsey, Tommy
Fabulous Dorseys, The 1947,My 30,25:3
Song Is Born, A 1948,O 20,37:2

Dorsey, Tommy and his orchestra
Ship Ahoy 1942,Je 26,16:5
Presenting Lily Mars 1943,Ap 30,25:3
Du Barry Was a Lady 1943,Ag 20,13:1
Girl Crazy 1943,D 3,27:2
Broadway Rhythm 1944,Ap 14,24:6

D'Orsi, Umberto
Successo, Il 1965,Ap 29,40:2
Hours of Love, The 1965,S 4,11:5
Little Nuns, The 1966,Ap 28,49:1
Love and Marriage (The First Night); First Night,
   The (Love and Marriage) 1966,Ag 5,20:1

Dortman, Irvin S (Producer)
Sound of Laughter, The 1963,D 18,44:2

Dortmann, Annie (Producer)
End of Desire 1962,Jl 10,29:2

Dortort, David (Screenwriter)
Lusty Men, The 1952,O 25,12:6
Cry in the Night, A 1956,S 1,19:4
Big Land, The 1957,Mr 2,18:2

Dorval, Mareal Mlle
Son of the Sahara, A 1924,My 27,14:1

Dorville
Don Quichotte 1933,Ap 23,X,4:1
Entente Cordiale 1939,D 26,23:2
Mayor's Dilemma, The 1940,Ap 23,19:2
drame De Shanghai; Shanghai Drama, The
   1945,Ja 11,19:2
Extenuating Circumstances; Circostances
   Attenuantes 1946,S 24,41:3

Dorville, Henry
Sans Famille 1935,Je 4,26:5

Dorville, M
Courier of Lyons, The 1938,Je 3,17:1

Dory, Leon
Depart, Le 1967,S 23,20:3

Doryon, Avraham
Dream no More 1950,Ja 6,25:2

Dorziat, Gabrielle
Mayerling 1937,S 14,27:1
Lie of Nina Petrovna, The 1938,Mr 30,19:2
Forty Little Mothers 1938,D 23,16:3
Vierge Folle, La 1938,D 30,11:3
End of a Day, The 1939,S 12,28:4
Mayerling to Sarajevo 1940,O 30,27:6
Hatred 1941,Ja 27,11:2
Man Who Seeks the Truth, The 1941,O 7,26:6
32 Rue de Montmartre 1944,S 28,26:3
drame De Shanghai; Shanghai Drama, The
   1945,Ja 11,19:2
Paris Frills 1946,N 25,38:3
Her First Affair; (Children of Paradise)
   1947,F 20,32:3
Ruy Blas 1948,O 4,14:2
Monsieur Vincent 1948,D 21,33:2
Just a big Simple Girl; Une Grande Fille Toute
   Simple 1949,O 28,29:2
Storm Within, The; (Parents Terribles, Les)
   1950,Ap 24,21:2
Manon 1950,D 26,19:1
Dream Ballerina 1951,Ap 16,21:2
Tomorrow is too Late 1952,Ap 14,22:2
French Way, The 1952,S 6,12:6
So Little Time 1953,Jl 28,23:2
Little Boy Lost 1953,S 22,38:2
Act of Love 1954,F 12,20:5
Mitsou 1958,Ap 15,42:5
Gigot 1962,S 28,26:1
Monkey in Winter 1963,F 1,7:2

Dos Passos, John (Miscellaneous)
Wave, The 1937,Ap 21,18:1

dos Santos, Jorge
Black Orpheus 1959,D 22,41:1

Dos Santos, Manuel
Torero! 1957,My 22,29:2

Dossena, Anna Maria
Eravamo Sette Vedove; We Were Seven Widows
   1940,F 16,23:4

Dossett, Chappell
Madame X 1929,Ap 25,32:3
Insidious Dr Fu Manchu, The 1929,Jl 22,17:1

Dostal, Karel
Bohemian Rapture 1948,F 16,16:2

Dostoevski, Feodor (Original Author)
Crime and Punishment 1927,Jl 13,21:2
Murderer Dimitri Karamasoff, The
   1931,Mr 1,VIII,6:7 (In Addenda)
Karamazof 1931,S 21,20:2
Petersburg Nights 1934,S 10,20:4
Crime and Punishment 1935,N 22,18:2
Idiot, The 1948,F 5,26:2
Crime and Punishment 1948,Mr 1,17:2
Eternal Husband, The 1949,Ja 10,19:2

Dostoevski, Feodor (Original Author)— Cont
Brothers Karamazov, The 1958,F 21,18:2
Crime and Punishment 1958,S 16,23:2
Crime and Punishment, U S A 1959,Je 17,39:3
Idiot, The 1960,Jl 22,11:2
White Nights 1961,My 29,9:6
Idiot, The 1963,My 1,35:1
Partner 1968,S 24,52:2

Dotrice, Karen
Three Lives of Thomasina, The 1963,D 12,46:1
Mary Poppins 1964,S 25,34:1
Gnome-Mobile, The 1967,Jl 20,30:2

Dotrice, Roy
Heroes of Telemark, The 1966,Mr 10,26:1

Dottesio, Attilo
Gioconda, La 1958,O 13,33:4

Doty, Douglas (Original Author)
Laughter 1930,N 15,15:3
Gallant Lady 1934,Ja 22,12:3
Always Goodbye 1938,Je 25,7:2

Doty, Douglas (Screenwriter)
King on Main Street, The 1925,O 26,25:2
Young April 1926,Ag 31,15:3

Doubleday, Kay
Mad Dog Coll 1961,My 13,10:1
Across the River 1965,Ap 27,27:1

Doucet, Catharine
As Husbands Go 1934,Ja 26,20:3
Little Man, What Now? 1934,Je 1,29:1
Servants' Entrance 1934,S 27,25:2
Wake up and Dream 1934,O 11,28:3
Age of Indiscretion 1935,My 18,21:2
Accent on Youth 1935,Ag 12,10:3
Millions in the Air 1935,D 12,33:4
These Three 1936,Mr 19,22:4
Golden Arrow, The 1936,My 4,16:1
Poppy 1936,Je 18,19:1
Longest Night, The 1936,O 17,21:2
Luckiest Girl in the World, The 1936,D 5,16:3
When You're in Love 1937,F 19,15:2
Man of the People 1937,F 23,25:4
Oh, Doctor 1937,Je 19,20:3
It Started With Eve 1941,O 3,27:1
Nothing but the Truth 1941,O 23,27:1
Family Honeymoon 1949,F 25,28:2

Doucet, Paul
Little French Girl, The 1925,Je 1,10:3

Doucette, John
Burning Cross, The 1948,F 20,19:1
Canon City 1948,Jl 8,19:2
Fighting O'Flynn, The 1949,F 28,16:2
Criss Cross 1949,Mr 12,10:2
Crooked Way, The 1949,S 5,13:2
Black Book, The 1949,O 17,18:2
Breaking Point, The 1950,O 7,10:6
Iroquois Trail, The 1950,O 27,24:4
Cavalry Scout 1951,Je 8,32:2
Strangers on a Train 1951,Jl 4,13:2
San Francisco Story, The 1952,My 10,16:4
Beachhead 1954,Ap 17,8:2
Return From the Sea 1954,Jl 10,7:3
Last Time I saw Paris, The 1954,N 19,20:2
Cry Vengence 1955,F 19,18:3
House of Bamboo 1955,Jl 2,13:2
Seven Cities of Gold 1955,O 8,13:2
Maverick Queen, the 1956,Je 4,23:2
Fastest Gun Alive, The 1956,Jl 13,23:3
Dakota Incident 1956,N 10,14:2
Cleopatra 1963,Je 13,29:1
Sons of Katie Elder, The 1965,Ag 26,40:3
Nevada Smith 1966,Je 24,28:1 (Incorrect in this
   edition; use 1966,Je 30,28:1 elsewhere)

Douchet, Jean (Director)
Six in Paris 1965,S 16,54:2

Douchey, Willis
Spoilers, The 1955,D 24,10:2

Doucoure, Marguerite
Cage aux Rossignols, La; (Cage of Nightingales,
   A) 1947,Ap 3,31:2

Doud, Gil (Original Author)
Port of Hell 1954,D 18,12:2
Hell to Eternity 1960,O 13,41:1

Doud, Gil (Screenwriter)
Thunder Bay 1953,My 21,39:2
Forbidden 1954,Ja 23,11:2
Saskatchewan 1954,Mr 11,26:2
Port of Hell 1954,D 18,12:2
To Hell and Back 1955,S 23,21:2
Walk the Proud Land 1956,S 8,20:6 (In
   Addenda)

Doudauz, Solo
Dead March, The 1937,S 20,19:1 (In Addenda)

Douday, Salo
House on Ninety-Second Street, The
   1945,S 27,24:7

Doude, Van
Happy Road, The 1957,Je 21,20:2
Love in the Afternoon 1957,Ag 24,12:1
Pot Bouille 1958,O 28,39:1
Breathless 1961,F 8,26:1
Passion of Slow Fire, The 1962,O 12,26:1

Douenias, Clement (Miscellaneous)
Crossroads 1939,Mr 14,17:5

Dougan, Vikki
Tunnel of Love 1958,N 22,27:4
DOUGHERTY
See Also DAUGHERTY, DOHERTY
Dougherty, Jack
Special Delivery 1927,Ap 26,33:3
Dougherty, Richard (Original Author)
Madigan 1968,Mr 30,22:2
Doughty, Yvonne
Wild One, The 1953,D 31,9:2
DOUGLAS
See Also DOUGLASS
Douglas, Angela
Dream Maker, The 1964,Ap 23,34:1
Douglas, Burt
High School Confidential 1958,My 31,6:6
Law and Jake Wade, the 1958,Je 7,11:1
Douglas, Byron
Silent Command, The 1923,S 5,15:3
Perfect Sap, The 1927,Ja 11,18:2
Drake Case, The 1929,S 16,30:1
Douglas, Carol
Strangers When we Meet 1960,Je 30,22:2
Douglas, Chet
Cry for Happy 1961,Mr 4,16:1
Douglas, Chloe
Give Us This Night 1936,Ap 6,18:1
Douglas, Colin
Crawling Eye, The 1959,Ja 1,38:1
Douglas, Dan
Dead Men Tell 1941,Ap 17,29:3
Douglas, Diana
Sign of the Ram, The 1948,Mr 4,30:2
House of Strangers 1949,Jl 2,8:2
Whistle at Eaton Falls, The 1951,O 11,49:2
Mask of the Himalayas 1953,Ag 12,22:3
Monsoon 1953,S 26,15:2
Indian Fighter, The 1955,D 22,20:1
Douglas, Don
Great Gabbo, The 1929,S 13,33:1
Men in White 1934,Je 9,18:2
Headin' East 1938,Ja 15,19:2
Fast Company 1938,Jl 6,21:2
Crowd Roars, The 1938,Ag 5,11:1
Smashing the Rackets 1938,Ag 9,22:5
Convicted 1938,Ag 22,9:3
Gladiator, The 1938,Ag 29,10:2
Wings of the Navy 1939,F 4,11:1
Within the Law 1939,Ap 6,31:2
Zero Hour, The 1939,Jl 5,20:3
Dress Parade 1939,O 28,11:2
Fugitive at Large 1939,N 13,15:2
Sabotage 1939,N 16,29:5
Calling Philo Vance 1940,F 9,15:3
Fugitive From Justice, A 1940,Jl 8,13:3
I Love You Again 1940,Ag 16,11:2
Flight Command 1941,Ja 17,21:2
Cheers for Miss Bishop 1941,Mr 14,17:2
Sleepers West 1941,Mr 20,25:3
Great Swindle, The 1941,My 14,25:4
Get-Away, The 1941,Jl 17,23:4
Whistling in the Dark 1941,Ag 28,23:2
Night of January 16th, The 1941,D 19,35:1
Juke Box Jenny 1942,Ap 17,21:3
Little Tokyo, USA 1942,Ag 7,13:2
Tales of Manhattan 1942,S 25,25:1
Crystal Ball, The 1943,F 19,22:2
Meanest Man in the World, The 1943,F 25,27:3
He's my Guy 1943,Mr 12,12:3
More the Merrier, The 1943,My 14,17:1
Action in the North Atlantic 1943,My 22,10:2
Appointment in Berlin 1943,Jl 17,8:2
Wintertime 1943,S 30,27:2
Behind the Rising Sun 1943,O 14,26:2
Falcon out West, The 1944,Mr 18,18:2
Show Business 1944,My 11,25:7
Heavenly Days 1944,O 21,15:2
Tall in the Saddle 1944,D 15,25:3
Murder, my Sweet 1945,Mr 9,16:2
Royal Scandal, A 1945,Ap 12,19:2
Tarzan and the Amazons 1945,Ap 30,13:4
Truth About Murder, The 1946,Jl 27,12:6
Career 1959,O 9,24:1
Lover Come Back 1962,F 9,21:1
Frankie and Johnny 1966,Jl 21,20:2
Douglas, Earl
Las Vegas Nights 1941,Mr 20,25:2
Douglas, George
Let Us Live 1939,Mr 30,19:2
City of Chance 1940,Ja 22,11:3
Douglas, Gilbert
Dulcy 1923,S 17,18:2
Douglas, Gordon (Director)
Zenobia 1939,My 15,15:2
Saps at Sea 1940,Ap 29,12:2
Broadway Limited 1941,Je 16,11:6
Devil With Hitler, The 1942,O 19,15:2
Great Gildersleeve, The 1942,D 18,36:8
Gildersleeve's Bad Day 1943,Je 11,23:1
Night of Adventure, A 1944,Je 3,10:4
Falcon in Hollywood, The 1944,D 9,21:2
Zombies on Broadway 1945,Ap 27,23:2
First Yank into Tokyo 1945,O 25,18:2

Dick Tracy vs Cueball 1946,N 23,12:2
San Quentin 1947,F 10,24:3
If You Knew Susie 1948,F 23,19:2
Black Arrow, The 1948,O 4,14:2
Walk a Crooked Mile 1948,O 13,31:2
Nevadan, The 1950,Ja 13,19:4
Fortunes of Captain Blood 1950,Je 10,11:3
Kiss Tomorrow Goodbye 1950,Ag 5,9:2
Between Midnight and Dawn 1950,O 2,19:2
Great Missouri Raid, The 1951,Ap 9,31:2
Only the Valiant 1951,Ap 14,9:6
I Was a Communist for the F B I 1951,My 3,34:4
Come Fill the Cup 1951,N 22,47:2
Mara Maru 1952,Ap 24,38:1
Iron Mistress, The 1952,N 20,39:2
She's Back on Broadway 1953,Mr 12,24:2
Charge at Feather River, The 1953,Jl 16,17:2
So This Is Love 1953,Ag 12,22:1
Them 1954,Je 17,36:2
Young at Heart 1955,Ja 20,35:1
McConnell Story, The 1955,S 30,23:1
Sincerely Yours 1955,N 3,37:1
Santiago 1956,Jl 14,13:2
Big Land, The 1957,Mr 2,18:2
Bombers B-52 1957,N 23,11:2
Fort Dobbs 1958,Ap 19,10:4
Up Periscope 1959,Mr 5,35:4
Yellowstone Kelly 1959,N 12,27:1
Gold of the Seven Saints 1961,Ap 6,30:3
Sins of Rachel Cade, The 1961,Ap 6,30:3
Claudelle Inglish 1961,S 21,40:2
Follow That Dream 1962,Ag 9,17:7
Call Me Bwana 1963,Jl 4,9:1
Robin and the 7 Hoods 1964,Ag 6,20:1
Rio Conchos 1964,O 29,38:1
Sylvia 1965,F 11,45:1
Harlow 1965,Jl 22,24:1
Stagecoach 1966,Je 16,53:1
Way...Way Out 1966,O 27,55:1
In Like Flint 1967,Mr 16,53:2
Chuka 1967,N 2,58:3
Tony Rome 1967,N 16,58:1
Detective, The 1968,My 29,20:3
Lady in Cement 1968,N 21,41:1
Douglas, Gordon (Screenwriter)
Kelly the Second 1936,O 3,21:2
Housekeeper's Daughter, The 1939,D 2,21:4
Topper Returns 1941,Mr 28,26:6
Douglas, Howard
Treasure Island 1950,Ag 16,24:2
Douglas, Hugh
Nur am Rhein 1931,S 25,28:7
Hell on Earth 1934,Ja 29,10:2
Douglas, James
Time Limit 1957,O 24,37:2
G I Blues 1960,N 5,28:1
Thunder of Drums, A 1961,S 27,35:1
Sweet Bird of Youth 1962,Mr 29,28:2
Douglas, Katya
Kill or Cure 1962,N 13,43:4
Murder at the Gallop 1963,Je 25,23:2
Douglas, Keith
Nurse's Secret, The 1941,Je 6,25:7
Bride Came C O D, The 1941,Jl 26,18:2
Douglas, Kent
Paid 1931,Ja 3,21:2
Daybreak 1931,Je 1,15:1
Five and Ten 1931,Jl 11,7:6
Waterloo Bridge 1931,S 5,7:4
House Divided, A 1932,Ja 9,21:1
Douglas, Kirk
Strange Love of Martha Ivers, The
1946,Jl 25,18:4
Mourning Becomes Electra 1947,N 20,38:2
Out of the Past 1947,N 26,18:2
I Walk Alone 1948,Ja 22,36:3
Walls of Jericho, The 1948,Ag 5,16:2
Letter to Three Wives, A 1949,Ja 21,24:2
My Dear Secretary 1949,F 14,15:4
Champion 1949,Ap 11,29:2
Young Man With a Horn 1950,F 10,18:4
Glass Menagerie, The 1950,S 29,31:5
Along the Great Divide 1951,My 17,38:3
Ace in the Hole 1951,Je 30,8:6
Detective Story 1951,N 7,35:2
Big Trees, The 1952,F 6,24:2
Vikings, The 1952,Je 12,35:2
Big Sky, The 1952,Ag 20,21:1
Bad and the Beautiful, The 1953,Ja 16,19:1
Story of Three Loves, The (Equilibrium);
Equilibrium (The Story of Three Loves)
1953,Mr 6,29:2
Equilibrium 1953,Mr 6,29:2
Juggler, The 1953,My 6,39:2
Act of Love 1954,F 12,20:5
20,000 Leagues Under the Sea 1954,D 24,7:2
Racers, The 1955,F 5,13:2
Man Without a Star 1955,Mr 25,19:3
Ulysses 1955,Ag 18,17:2
Indian Fighter, The 1955,D 22,20:1
Lust for Life 1956,S 18,39:1
Top Secret Affair 1957,Ja 31,21:1
Gunfight at the O K Corral 1957,My 30,23:2

Douglas, Kirk— Cont
Paths of Glory 1957,D 26,23:2
Last Train from Gun Hill 1959,Jl 30,31:2
Devil's Disciple, The 1959,Ag 21,12:1
Strangers When we Meet 1960,Je 30,22:2
Spartacus 1960,O 7,28:1
Last Sunset, The 1961,Je 15,51:1
Town Without Pity 1961,O 11,53:1
Lonely are the Brave 1962,Je 28,21:2
Two Weeks in Another Town 1962,Ag 18,10:1
Hook, The 1963,F 16,5:6
List of Adrian Messenger, The 1963,My 30,20:1
For Love or Money 1963,Ag 8,19:1
Seven Days in May 1964,F 20,22:1
In Harm's Way 1965,Ap 7,36:1
Heroes of Telemark, The 1966,Mr 10,26:1
Cast a Giant Shadow 1966,Mr 31,43:3
Is Paris Burning? 1966,N 11,36:1
Way West, The 1967,My 25,54:1
War Wagon, The 1967,Ag 3,26:3
Lovely Way to Die, A 1968,Jl 13,18:1
Douglas, Laurie
When Love Is Young 1937,Ap 17,15:1
Holiday Inn 1942,Ag 5,16:1
Douglas, Lloyd C (Original Author)
Magnificent Obsession 1935,D 31,11:2
Green Light 1937,F 13,9:1
White Banners 1938,Je 23,27:1
Disputed Passage 1939,O 26,27:2
Robe, The 1953,S 17,32:6
Magnificent Obsession 1954,Ag 5,18:4
Big Fisherman, The 1959,Ag 6,18:1
Douglas, Louis
Niemandsland; No Man's Land
1932,Ja 24,VIII,5:1
Hell on Earth 1934,Ja 29,10:2
Douglas, Marion
Shepherd of the Hills, The 1928,F 20,14:1
Douglas, Melvyn
Tonight or Never 1931,D 18,29:2
Prestige 1932,F 5,25:2
Wiser Sex, The 1932,Mr 12,19:5
Broken Wing, The 1932,Mr 26,17:2
As You Desire Me 1932,Je 3,23:4
Old Dark House, The 1932,O 28,22:4
Vampire Bat, The 1933,Ja 23,9:1
Nagana 1933,F 16,23:2
Counsellor-At-Law 1933,D 8,31:2
People's Enemy, The 1935,Ap 30,13:7
She Married her Boss 1935,S 27,25:3
Mary Burns, Fugitive 1935,N 16,19:2
Annie Oakley 1935,D 24,10:5
Lone Wolf Returns, The 1936,F 4,25:5
And So They Were Married 1936,My 14,29:3
Gorgeous Hussy, The 1936,S 5,7:1
Theodora Goes Wild 1936,N 23,17:4
Women of Glamour 1937,Mr 6,10:1
Captains Courageous 1937,My 12,27:1
I Met Him in Paris 1937,Je 3,29:2
Angel 1937,N 4,29:1
I'll Take Romance 1937,D 17,33:2
Arsene Lupin Returns 1938,Mr 9,21:1
There's Always a Woman 1938,Ap 29,17:2
Toy Wife, The 1938,Je 24,15:1
Fast Company 1938,Jl 6,21:2
That Certain Age 1938,N 5,15:2
There's That Woman Again 1939,Ja 6,25:4
Shining Hour, The 1939,Ja 20,15:2
Tell no Tales 1939,Je 2,27:3
Good Girls Go to Paris 1939,Je 23,23:1
Ninotchka 1939,N 10,27:2
Amazing Mr Williams, The 1940,Ja 19,15:2
Too Many Husbands 1940,Mr 8,25:2
He Stayed for Breakfast 1940,Ag 31,16:2
Third Finger, Left Hand 1940,D 12,37:2
This Thing Called Love 1941,F 14,15:2
That Uncertain Feeling 1941,My 2,25:1
Woman's Face, A 1941,My 16,21:2
Our Wife 1941,S 18,31:1
Two Faced Woman 1942,Ja 1,37:2
We Were Dancing 1942,My 1,23:2
They all Kissed the Bride 1942,Jl 31,11:1
Three Hearts for Julia 1943,My 21,22:4
Sea of Grass, The 1947,F 28,27:2
Guilt of Janet Ames, The 1947,My 23,31:2
Mr Blandings Builds his Dream House
1948,Mr 26,26:2
My Own True Love 1949,F 3,27:3
Great Sinner, The 1949,Je 30,19:2
My Forbidden Past 1951,Ap 26,34:2
Billy Budd 1962,O 31,32:1
Hud 1963,My 29,36:1
Advance to the Rear 1964,Je 11,27:3
Americanization of Emily, The 1964,O 28,51:1
Rapture 1965,Ag 24,25:3
Hotel 1967,Ja 20,27:1
Douglas, Milton
Viennese Nights 1930,N 27,32:5
Douglas, Nathan E (Screenwriter)
Defiant Ones, The 1958,S 25,29:1
Inherit the Wind 1960,O 13,41:1
Douglas, Pam
Surfari 1967,Jl 19,26:2

Douglas, Paul
Letter to Three Wives, A 1949,Ja 21,24:2
It Happens Every Spring 1949,Je 11,11:2
Everybody Does It 1949,O 26,32:2
Big Lift, The 1950,Ap 27,37:2
Love That Brute 1950,My 27,10:6
Panic in the Streets 1950,Ag 5,9:2
Fourteen Hours 1951,Mr 7,43:2
Guy Who Came Back, The 1951,Ag 17,13:2
Angels in the Outfield 1951,O 18,32:1
When in Rome 1952,My 12,21:2
Clash by Night 1952,Je 19,32:6
We're not Married 1952,Jl 12,16:2
Never Wave at a Wac 1953,Ap 24,30:2
Forever Female 1954,Ja 13,26:2
Executive Suite 1954,My 7,19:1
High and Dry 1954,Ag 31,25:5
Green Fire 1954,D 25,7:1
Joe Macbeth 1956,Ap 7,13:1
Leather Saint, The 1956,Je 16,12:2
Solid Gold Cadillac, The 1956,O 25,40:3
This Could Be the Night 1957,My 15,39:1
Beau James 1957,Je 27,21:1
Mating Game, The 1959,Ap 30,37:1

Douglas, Robert
Blarney Kiss, The 1933,Ag 19,14:4
Girl in the Street 1938,My 26,31:2
Challenge, The 1939,O 2,15:2
Lion Has Wings, The 1940,Ja 22,11:2
Chinese Den 1941,Mr 26,27:3
Decision of Christopher Blake, The
1948,D 11,12:2
Adventures of Don Juan 1948,D 25,10:1
Fountainhead, The 1949,Jl 9,8:5
Lady Takes a Sailor, The 1949,D 17,15:2
Barricade 1950,Mr 25,8:6
Buccaneer's Girl 1950,Mr 27,19:2
This Side of the Law 1950,Jl 7,15:2
Flame and the Arrow, The 1950,Jl 8,7:2
Spy Hunt 1950,S 8,25:2
Kim 1950,D 8,40:4
Mystery Submarine 1951,F 2,19:2
Target Unknown 1951,Mr 5,24:2
Thunder on the Hill 1951,O 18,32:3
At Swords Point 1952,Ap 10,37:1
Ivanhoe 1952,Ag 1,8:2
Prisoner of Zenda, The 1952,N 5,36:2
Desert Rats, The 1953,My 9,13:2
Fair Wind to Java 1953,Ag 28,13:3
Flight to Tangier 1953,N 26,50:4
Saskatchewan 1954,Mr 11,26:2
King Richard and the Crusaders 1954,Ag 23,20:5
Scarlet Coat, The 1955,Jl 30,14:2
Virgin Queen, The 1955,Ag 6,13:2
Good Morning, Miss Dove 1955,N 24,41:1
Helen of Troy 1956,Ja 27,21:4
Young Philadelphians, The 1959,My 22,32:1

Douglas, Robert (Director)
Night Train to Paris 1964,D 3,58:2

Douglas, Sharon
Gentleman After Dark, A 1942,Ap 17,21:2
Our Hearts Were Growing Up 1946,Ag 12,17:2

Douglas, Susan
Private Affairs of Bel Ami, The 1947,Je 16,25:4
Lost Boundaries 1949,Jl 1,14:4
Five 1951,Ap 26,34:2

Douglas, Tom
Foot Falls 1921,S 9,18:3
Road to Reno, The 1931,O 10,20:4
Man I Killed, The 1932,Ja 20,17:4
Sky Bride 1932,Ap 23,11:5
West of Singapore 1933,Ap 1,18:3

Douglas, Wallace
Spies of the Air 1940,Jl 4,12:3
Break the News 1941,Ja 2,24:2
Chinese Den 1941,Mr 26,27:3

Douglas, Warren
Northern Pursuit 1943,N 26,29:2
Destination Tokyo 1944,Ja 1,9:2
God is my Co-Pilot 1945,Mr 24,22:6
Pride of the Marines 1945,Ag 25,7:3
Man I Love, The 1947,Ja 25,12:2
Task Force 1949,O 1,8:6
Cry Vengence 1955,F 19,18:3
Helen Morgan Story, The 1957,O 3,33:2

Douglas, Warren (Original Author)
Return of Jack Slade, The 1955,N 24,41:3

Douglas, Warren (Screenwriter)
Torpedo Valley 1952,D 20,15:3
Jack Slade 1953,O 29,42:6
Loophole 1954,Mr 13,11:3
Cry Vengence 1955,F 19,18:3
Finger Man 1955,Jl 16,12:4
Come on, The 1956,Ap 7,13:1
Dragoon Wells Massacre 1957,My 6,25:2
Night of the Grizzly, The 1966,Je 23,29:1

DOUGLASS
See Also DOUGLAS

Douglass, Amy
Unsinkable Molly Brown, The 1964,Jl 17,15:1

Douking, Georges
Mademoiselle 1966,Ag 2,23:1

Doumel
Cesar 1948,O 28,36:2
Ignace 1950,S 19,39:4

Dounsky, Yuli (Screenwriter)
There Was an old Couple 1967,My 22,53:1

Douvan-Torzow, J N
Taras Bulba 1927,D 28,26:6

Dovas, Robert
Cool Hand Luke 1967,N 2,58:1

Dove, Billie
Wanderer of the Wasteland, The 1924,Jl 8,14:2
Roughneck, The 1924,D 3,14:1
Folly of Vanity 1925,Ja 28,14:1
Air Mail, The 1925,Mr 17,18:1
Light of the Western Stars, The 1925,Je 24,14:3
Wild Horse Mesa 1925,Ag 10,8:2
Lucky Horseshoe, The 1925,Ag 18,14:3
Ancient Highway, The 1925,N 11,27:3
Black Pirate, The 1926,Mr 9,21:4
Marriage Clause, The 1926,S 28,30:2
Kid Boots 1926,O 11,18:2
Affair of the Follies, An 1927,F 28,22:3
Sensation Seekers 1927,Mr 16,28:2
Tender Hour, The 1927,Je 7,27:4
Stolen Bride, The 1927,Ag 10,21:4
American Beauty 1927,O 11,27:1
Love Mart, The 1927,D 26,16:6
Heart of a Follies Girl, The 1928,Mr 12,26:1
Yellow Lily, The 1928,My 21,25:1
Night Watch, The 1928,O 8,14:2
Careers 1929,Je 10,23:1
Man and the Moment, The 1929,Ag 5,25:2
Notorious Affair, A 1930,Ap 26,11:1
Sweethearts and Wives 1930,Je 28,9:2
One Night at Susie's 1930,N 24,26:5
Lady Who Dared, The 1931,Je 6,15:5
Age for Love, The 1931,N 13,27:2
Cock of the Air 1932,Ja 25,20:3
Blondie of the Follies 1932,S 2,19:2

Dovells, The
Don't Knock the Twist 1962,Ap 14,14:2

Dover, Nancy
Scandal 1929,Ap 22,23:1
Dynamite 1929,D 28,11:1
Cimarron 1931,Ja 27,20:5
Big Business Girl 1931,Je 12,27:1

Dover, Nita
Queen of Sheba, The 1953,N 4,29:3

Dover, Nyta
Women Without Names 1951,Ag 7,22:2

Dover, William B (Original Author)
You Said a Mouthful 1932,N 18,23:2

Dovima
Funny Face 1957,Mr 29,16:1

Dovjenko, Alexander (Director)
Soil 1930,O 21,34:4
Frontier 1935,D 28,10:5

Dovorska, Jess
Unknown Soldier, The 1926,My 31,10:2

Dovzhenko, A (Director)
Poem of the Sea 1959,D 21,34:4

Dovzhenko, Alexander (Director)
Ivan 1933,F 27,11:3
Shors 1939,N 21,19:4

Dovzhenko, Alexander (Original Author)
Life in Bloom 1949,My 9,20:4

Dovzhenko, Alexander (Producer)
Arsenal 1929,N 11,20:2
Ukraine in Flames 1944,Ap 3,18:2
Life in Bloom 1949,My 9,20:4

Dovzhenko, Alexander (Screenwriter)
Shors 1939,N 21,19:4
Ukraine in Flames 1944,Ap 3,18:2
Poem of the Sea 1959,D 21,34:4

Dovzhenko, Alexander Mrs (Miscellaneous)
Poem of the Sea 1959,D 21,34:4

Dow, Mary E
Sea Horses 1926,F 23,26:5

Dow, Peggy
Undertow 1949,D 16,37:2
Woman in Hiding 1950,F 23,33:2
Shakedown 1950,S 4,11:2
Sleeping City, The 1950,S 21,20:2
Harvey 1950,D 22,19:1
Bright Victory 1951,Ag 1,19:2
I Want You 1951,D 24,9:1

Dowd, Francine
Night Angel, The 1931,Je 11,28:4

Dowd, John
Illiac Passion, The 1968,Ap 19,40:1

Dowding, Liana
Babes in Toyland 1961,D 15,49:1

Dowell, Anthony
Romeo and Juliet 1966,O 6,55:1

Dowell, George B (Original Author)
Goin' to Town 1935,My 11,21:2
Klondike Annie 1936,Mr 12,18:2

Dowell, Robin
Prelude to Fame 1950,N 10,35:3
Tom Brown's School Days 1952,Ja 8,23:5

Dowling, Allan (Screenwriter)
Hunters of the Deep 1954,D 17,37:4

Dowling, Catherine
Down Argentine Way 1940,O 18,25:1

Dowling, Constance
Up in Arms 1944,Mr 3,19:2
Knickerbocker Holiday 1944,Ap 20,22:7
Well Groomed Bride, The 1946,My 11,22:5
Black Angel 1946,S 26,32:4
Flame, The 1948,F 20,19:2
Mad About Opera 1950,Ap 6,33:2
Her Wonderful Lie 1950,Jl 17,15:2
Voice in Your Heart, A 1952,F 23,7:5
Miss Italy 1952,My 10,16:2
Duel Without Honor 1953,F 28,8:8
Gog 1954,Ag 14,8:2

Dowling, Doris
Lost Weekend, The 1945,D 3,17:2
Blue Dahlia, The 1946,My 9,27:3
Crimson Key, The 1947,O 18,9:2
Bitter Rice 1950,S 19,39:2
Othello 1955,S 13,27:1

Dowling, Eddie
Rainbow Man, The 1929,Ap 17,30:6
Blaze O' Glory 1929,D 31,15:1
Honeymoon Lane 1931,Ag 1,16:4

Dowling, Eddie (Screenwriter)
Rainbow Man, The 1929,Ap 17,30:6

Dowling, Joan
No Room at the Inn 1949,D 26,33:4
Bond Street 1950,Mr 30,40:6
Hue and Cry 1951,Ja 9,25:2
Pool of London 1951,N 28,37:2
Murder Without Crime 1951,D 26,19:6
Train of Events 1952,My 26,18:4
Landfall 1953,My 11,25:2

Dowling, Joseph
Little Lord Fauntleroy 1921,S 16,17:3
Tiger Rose 1923,D 3,14:1
Courtship of Myles Standish, The 1923,D 31,9:3
Women Who Give 1924,Je 3,22:1
Tess of the D'Urbervilles 1924,Jl 28,12:2
New Lives for Old 1925,F 25,16:7
Confessions of a Queen 1925,Mr 24,20:6
Free and Equal 1925,Ap 20,22:1
Golden Princess 1925,S 7,15:3
Flower of the Night 1925,O 19,26:1
Lord Jim 1925,N 16,19:4
Little Irish Girl, The 1926,My 11,24:3
Why Girls Go Back Home 1926,My 18,28:2
Rainmaker, The 1926,My 18,28:2
Two-Gun Man, The 1926,Jl 13,19:3

Dowling, Thomas
Down Argentine Way 1940,O 18,25:1

Down, John
Trail of '98, The 1928,Mr 21,30:3

Downes, Donald (Original Author)
Pigeon That Took Rome, The 1962,Ag 23,25:1

Downes, Donald C (Original Author)
Orders to Kill 1958,N 18,41:2

Downes, Olin
Carnegie Hall 1947,My 3,10:2

Downes, Olin (Narrator)
First Opera Film Festival 1948,My 31,12:7

Downes, Terry
Study in Terror, A 1966,N 3,45:3
Fearless Vampire Killers, The, or Pardon Me but
Your Teeth are in my Neck 1967,N 14,52:1

Downey, Elsie
Chafed Elbows 1967,Ja 5,30:1

Downey, Kenneth
Dulcimer Street 1948,N 8,24:2
Happiest Days of Your Life, The 1950,S 18,19:2

Downey, Morton
Syncopation 1929,Ap 8,32:1
Mother's Boy 1929,My 8,34:6
Lucky in Love 1929,D 14,22:4
Devil's Holiday, The 1930,My 10,25:3
Ghost Catchers 1944,My 31,22:3

Downey, Robert
No More Excuses 1968,My 22,53:1

Downey, Robert (Director)
Chafed Elbows 1967,Ja 5,30:1
No More Excuses 1968,My 22,53:1

Downey, Robert (Producer)
Chafed Elbows 1967,Ja 5,30:1

Downey, Robert (Screenwriter)
Chafed Elbows 1967,Ja 5,30:1
No More Excuses 1968,My 22,53:1

Downing, Joseph
Case of the Lucky Legs, The 1935,N 1,25:1
Slight Case of Murder, A 1938,F 28,19:1
Wide Open Faces 1938,Ap 15,23:2
Devil's Party, The 1938,My 31,8:3
Racket Busters 1938,Ag 11,13:1
Angels With Dirty Faces 1938,N 26,18:1
You Can't Get Away With Murder
1939,Mr 25,19:2
Each Dawn I Die 1939,Jl 22,12:2
Forgotten Woman, The 1939,Ag 4,11:2
Missing Evidence 1939,N 17,17:3
Smashing the Money Ring 1939,N 17,17:2
Invisible Stripes 1940,Ja 13,11:2
Sandy Is a Lady 1940,Je 28,22:2
Secret Seven, The 1940,Ag 12,11:6

Downing, Joseph— Cont
Strange Alibi 1941,Ap 28,11:2
Belle Starr 1941,N 1,20:2
Unholy Partners 1941,D 29,21:4
Johnny Eager 1942,F 20,21:2
Larceny, Inc 1942,Ap 25,9:1
My Gal Sal 1942,My 1,23:1
Big Shot, The 1942,Jl 18,8:2
You Can't Escape Forever 1942,O 17,11:1
Slaughter on Tenth Avenue 1957,N 6,43:1
Downing, Rex
Wuthering Heights 1939,Ap 14,28:2
Nurse Edith Cavell 1939,S 22,27:4
Escape, The 1939,N 3,17:4
Adventure in Diamonds 1940,Ap 4,27:2
Blood and Sand 1941,My 23,25:3
Mayor of Forty-Fourth Street, The
   1942,Je 11,27:4
Downing, Vernon
Barretts of Wimpole Street, The 1934,S 29,12:2
Clive of India 1935,Ja 18,29:1
Miserables, Les 1935,Ap 22,14:2
Mutiny on the Bounty 1935,N 9,19:2
Sherlock Holmes Faces Death 1943,O 8,15:3
Spider Woman 1944,Ja 17,14:5
Downing, Virginia
Butterfield 8 1960,N 17,46:1
Downing, Wilfred
It's Great to be Young 1957,D 26,23:3
She Didn't Say No 1963,Jl 30,18:1
Downs, Bill (Narrator)
Ukraine in Flames 1944,Ap 3,18:2
Downs, Cathy
Dark Corner, The 1946,My 9,27:3
My Darling Clementine 1946,D 4,44:5
Noose Hangs High, The 1948,My 29,8:6
Massacre River 1949,Jl 15,17:2
Sundowners, The 1950,My 5,17:2
Short Grass 1951,Ja 13,10:4
Amazing Colossal Man, The 1957,O 26,19:2
Missle to the Moon 1958,N 17,37:2
Downs, Johnny
So Red the Rose 1935,N 28,39:1
Coronado 1935,D 19,33:4
Everybody's Old Man 1936,Mr 26,27:2
Pigskin Parade 1936,N 14,23:3
College Holiday 1936,D 24,21:2
Turn off the Moon 1937,My 20,17:2
Blonde Trouble 1937,Ag 7,7:2
Thrill of a Lifetime 1937,D 9,30:2
Hunted Men 1938,My 21,9:2
Algiers 1938,Jl 15,13:2
Hold That Co-ed 1938,S 24,13:1
Parents on Trial 1939,S 18,15:5
Hawaiian Nights 1939,S 29,19:4
Child Is Born, A 1940,Ja 11,19:2
Slightly Tempted 1940,N 1,33:1
Honeymoon for Three 1941,F 8,19:2
Adam Had Four Sons 1941,Mr 28,26:6
Moonlight in Hamaii 1941,O 10,26:6
Dowst, Henry Payson (Original Author)
Dancin' Fool, The 1920,My 3,18:1
Doyan, Jacqueline
Very Private Affair, A 1962,S 29,15:1
Doyle, Adalyn
Advice to the Lovelorn 1933,D 14,28:2
Finishing School 1934,Ap 30,11:4
Doyle, Arthur Conan Sir (Miscellaneous)
Pursuit to Algiers 1945,O 27,12:2
Study in Terror, A 1966,N 3,45:3
Doyle, Arthur Conan Sir (Original Author)
Sherlock Holmes 1922,My 8,14:3
Lost World, The 1925,F 9,15:3
Fighting Eagle, The 1927,Ag 15,22:5
Return of Sherlock Holmes, The 1929,O 19,22:6
Sherlock Holmes's Fatal Hour 1931,Jl 13,13:5
Speckled Band, The 1931,N 7,16:5
Missing Rembrandt, The 1932,Mr 26,17:2
Sign of the Four, The 1932,Ag 20,7:4
Sherlock Holmes 1932,N 12,20:5
Fires of Fate 1933,Ap 3,13:4
Study in Scarlet, A 1933,Je 1,15:3
Triumph of Sherlock Holmes, The
   1935,My 27,20:6
Hound of the Baskervilles, The 1939,Mr 25,19:2
Sherlock Holmes and the Secret Weapon
   1943,Ja 5,15:2
Sherlock Holmes Faces Death 1943,O 8,15:3
Spider Woman 1944,Ja 17,14:5
Scarlet Claw, The 1944,My 19,12:1
Pearl of Death 1944,Ag 26,15:2
House of Fear, The 1945,Mr 19,23:3
Woman in Green, The 1945,Je 16,10:3
Dressed to Kill 1946,My 25,12:4
Hounds of the Baskervilles, The 1959,Jl 4,9:4
Lost World, The 1960,Jl 14,23:1
Doyle, Buddy
Great Ziegfeld, The 1936,Ap 9,21:2
Doyle, David
Act One 1963,D 27,17:2
No Way to Treat a Lady 1968,Mr 21,56:1
Paper Lion 1968,O 24,54:1

Doyle, Desmond
Romeo and Juliet 1966,O 6,55:1
Doyle, Dierdre
Promoter, The 1952,O 29,36:2
Doyle, Jack
Navy Spy 1937,Mr 22,27:3
Doyle, James D
Backbone 1923,Ap 30,11:2
Doyle, John T
Mother's Boy 1929,My 8,34:6
His Woman 1931,D 5,21:2
Gambling 1934,D 4,22:3
Doyle, Laird (Original Author)
Jimmy the Gent 1934,Mr 26,22:3
Dangerous 1935,D 27,14:1
Another Dawn 1937,Je 18,25:3
Singapore Woman 1941,My 12,13:6
Doyle, Laird (Screenwriter)
Bordertown 1935,Ja 24,22:5
Oil for the Lamps of China 1935,Je 6,25:2
Front Page Woman 1935,Jl 12,15:1
Special Agent 1935,S 19,28:1
Dangerous 1935,D 27,14:1
Hearts Divided 1936,Je 13,13:1
Cain and Mabel 1936,O 19,22:1
Three Men on a Horse 1936,N 26,39:1
Prince and the Pauper, The 1937,My 6,23:1
Another Dawn 1937,Je 18,25:3
Northwest Outpost 1947,Ag 8,10:2
Doyle, Mary
Beloved Brat 1938,My 2,13:2
Doyle, Maxine
Key, The 1934,My 30,14:3
Student Tour 1934,O 31,17:3
6-Day Bike Rider 1934,N 3,20:3
Babbitt 1934,D 17,24:2
Doyle, Mimi
Mister Roberts 1955,Jl 15,14:1
Doyle, Tony
Ulysses 1967,Mr 14,55:1
D'Oyly Carte Opera Company (Miscellaneous)
Mikado, The 1939,Je 2,27:2
Mikado, The 1967,Mr 15,53:1
Dozier, Robert (Original Author)
Young Stranger, The 1957,Ap 9,40:1
I Could go on Singing 1963,My 16,42:1
Dozier, Robert (Screenwriter)
Cardinal, The 1963,D 13,41:1
Dozier, William (Producer)
Harriet Craig 1950,N 3,31:2
Two of a Kind 1951,Je 30,8:6
Batman 1966,Ag 25,42:4
Drabios, Edvard
Nine Lives 1959,Ja 6,28:1
Drach, Vania
Seventh Continent, The 1968,Jl 30,33:2
Drache, Heinz
Rest Is Silence, The 1960,Ag 2,22:6
Drady, Alan (Original Author)
Bride Wore Crutches, The 1941,My 26,15:3
Dragic, Nedejko (Producer)
Diogenes Perhaps 1968,Ja 20,21:3
Dragman, Ervina
Ninth Circle, The 1961,S 15,30:3
Dragonette, Jessica (Miscellaneous)
Gulliver's Travels 1939,D 21,29:1
Dragoslav, Radolcic
Last Bridge, The 1957,Ag 21,22:2
Drain, Emile
Madame Sans Gene 1925,Ap 18,19:1
Violetera, La 1935,Ja 14,11:3
Pearls of the Crown, The 1938,Ap 12,26:2
Champs-Elysees 1939,F 28,17:2
Panic 1947,N 27,50:2
Drainie, John
Incredible Journey, The 1963,N 21,43:2
Drainie, John (Narrator)
Stratford Adventure, The 1954,Ag 3,14:2
Drake, Alfred
Tars and Spars 1946,F 15,29:2
Hamlet 1964,S 24,46:1
Strange Victory 1948,S 27,27:2
Drake, Betsy
Every Girl Should be Married 1948,D 24,14:2
Dancing in the Dark 1949,D 3,8:6
Pretty Baby 1950,S 23,11:2
Second Woman, The 1951,F 2,19:2
Room for One More 1952,Ja 16,21:2
Will Success Spoil Rock Hunter 1957,S 12,37:5
Intent to Kill 1959,Ap 1,43:2
Next to no Time 1960,My 28,13:2
Clarence, the Cross-Eyed Lion 1965,Ag 5,15:3
Drake, Carolle
Band of Angels 1957,Jl 11,21:1
Drake, Charles
Career 1939,Jl 28,14:2
Nine Loves Are not Enough 1941,O 30,27:2
Man Who Came to Dinner, The 1942,Ja 2,25:2
Busses Roar 1942,S 25,25:4
Now, Voyager 1942,O 23,25:3
Air Force 1943,F 4,29:1
Mr Skeffington 1944,My 26,23:2
Conflict 1945,Je 16,10:2

Drake, Charles— Cont
You Came Along 1945,Jl 5,7:2
Whistle Stop 1946,Mr 18,24:2
Night in Casablanca, A 1946,Ag 12,17:2
Pretender, The 1947,Ag 12,26:2
Tarzan's Magic Fountain 1949,F 7,15:2
Comanche Territory 1950,Ap 8,9:3
I Was a Shoplifter 1950,Ap 28,26:3
Winchester 73 1950,Je 8,38:2
Peggy 1950,Jl 21,15:4
Harvey 1950,D 22,19:1
Air Cadet 1951,My 11,32:3
Little Egypt 1951,Ag 30,20:3
Red Ball Express 1952,My 30,11:2
It Came From Outer Space 1953,Je 18,38:2
Lone Hand 1953,Je 27,7:2
Glenn Miller Story, the 1954,F 11,33:2
Female on the Beach 1955,Ag 20,20:2
To Hell and Back 1955,S 23,21:2
All That Heaven Allows 1956,F 29,35:1
Walk the Proud Land 1956,S 8,20:6 (In
   Addenda)
Jeanne Eagels 1957,Ag 31,19:1
Until They Sail 1957,O 9,41:2
Tammy Tell me True 1961,Jl 27,23:2
Back Street 1961,O 13,27:1
Lively Set, The 1964,O 15,54:1
Dear Heart 1965,Mr 8,33:1
Valley of the Dolls 1967,D 16,51:1
Swimmer, The 1968,My 16,53:1
Drake, Charles Francis (Miscellaneous)
Democracy Crucified 1939,My 28,6:3
Drake, Charles Francis (Narrator)
Russia Marches On 1938,F 9,16:1
Drake, Charles Francis (Producer)
Russia Marches On 1938,F 9,16:1
Drake, Chris
Walk in the Sun, A 1946,Ja 12,10:6
For Men Only 1952,Ja 16,21:2
Them 1954,Je 17,36:2
Drake, Claudia
Enemy of Women 1944,S 12,23:6
Bedside Manner 1945,Je 23,9:6
Why Girls Leave Home 1945,Ag 4,7:3
Drake, Dona
Aloma of the South Seas 1941,Ag 28,23:4
Louisiana Purchase 1942,Ja 1,37:1
Road to Morocco 1942,N 12,30:1
Star Spangled Rhythm 1942,D 31,20:1
Let's Face It 1943,Ag 5,18:1
Without Reservations 1946,Je 8,17:2
Dangerous Millions 1947,Mr 15,10:3
Another Part of the Forest 1948,My 19,30:2
Girl from Jones Beach, The 1949,Jl 30,9:2
Fortunes of Captain Blood 1950,Je 10,11:3
Valentino 1951,Ap 20,25:1
Princess of the Nile 1954,Je 12,13:2
Drake, Ellis
Sez O'Reilly to MacNab 1938,F 19,19:4
Drake, Fabia
All Over the Town 1949,My 26,34:4
White Corridors 1952,Jl 16,21:1
Drake, Frances
Bolero 1934,F 17,20:3
Trumpet Blows, The 1934,Ap 14,18:2
Ladies Should Listen 1934,Jl 28,16:6
Forsaking all Others 1934,D 21,18:1
Transient Lady 1935,Mr 11,15:1
Miserables, Les 1935,Ap 22,14:2
Mad Love 1935,Ag 5,20:2
Invisible Ray, The 1936,Ja 11,9:3
Preview Murder Mystery, The 1936,Mr 21,13:2
Florida Special 1936,My 29,15:2
Sudden Death, And 1936,Jl 18,18:2
I'd Give my Life 1936,Ag 17,9:1
Love Under Fire 1937,Ag 28,8:2
She Married an Artist 1938,F 25,15:2
There's Always a Woman 1938,Ap 29,17:2
Lone Wolf in Paris, The 1938,My 23,21:2
It's a Wonderful World 1939,My 19,27:2
I Take This Woman 1940,F 16,23:3
Drake, Josephine
Song and Dance Man, The 1926,F 1,16:1
Social Celebrity, A 1926,Ap 19,24:3
Palm Beach Girl, The 1926,Je 22,21:2
Drake, Ken
Crime and Punishment, U S A 1959,Je 17,39:3
Drake, Lisa
Rat Race, The 1960,My 26,37:3
Drake, Melissa
Conjugal Bed, The 1963,S 17,30:1
Drake, Milton (Composer)
Awful Truth, The 1937,N 5,19:3
Everything's on Ice 1939,O 6,31:1
Big Store, The 1941,Je 27,14:4
Drake, Oliver (Original Author)
Gun Law 1938,Je 24,15:1
Dragoon Wells Massacre 1957,My 6,25:2
Drake, Oliver (Screenwriter)
Boots and Saddles 1937,N 8,19:2
Gun Law 1938,Je 24,15:1
Painted Desert 1938,S 14,26:5
Racketeers of the Range 1939,Je 8,31:4

Drake, Pauline
Jam Session 1944,My 3,25:3
Drake, Peggy
Tuttles of Tahiti, The 1942,Ap 30,14:1
Drake, Roger
Hurricane, The 1937,N 10,31:2
Drake, Tom
Two Girls and a Sailor 1944,Je 15,16:1
Maisie Goes to Reno 1944,S 29,18:1
Mrs Parkington 1944,O 13,16:1
Marriage Is a Private Affair 1944,O 27,17:7
Meet Me in St Louis 1944,N 29,20:2
This Man's Navy 1945,Ap 16,18:6
Green Years, The 1946,Ap 5,21:2
Courage of Lassie 1946,Jl 25,18:5
Beginning or the End, The 1947,F 21,15:1
I'll Be Yours 1947,F 22,16:2
Cass Timberlane 1947,N 7,20:2
Hills of Home 1948,N 26,32:2
Words and Music 1948,D 10,34:2
Mr Belvedere Goes to College 1949,Ap 16,11:2
Scene of the Crime 1949,Jl 29,12:2
Great Rupert, The 1950,Ap 14,27:2
Never Trust a Gambler 1951,Jl 20,14:2
Sangaree 1953,Je 5,19:1
Raintree County 1957,D 21,22:1
Warlock 1959,My 1,34:1
Bramble Bush, The 1960,F 25,34:2
Sandpiper, The 1965,Jl 16,14:1
Johnny Reno 1966,Mr 10,26:3
Drake, William A (Original Author)
Strange Justice 1932,O 20,24:2
Drake, William A (Screenwriter)
Three Musketeers, The 1939,F 18,12:2
Adventures of Sherlock Holmes, The
1939,S 2,20:1
Drakulic, Nikola (Director)
Gods of Bali 1952,O 13,26:3
Drakulic, Nikola (Producer)
Gods of Bali 1952,O 13,26:3
Drane, Richard
Eternal Sea, The 1955,Je 10,16:2
Dranem
Il est Charmant; He is Charming
1932,Mr 27,VIII,6:2
Il est Charmant 1932,Ap 9,18:1
Miche 1932,D 2,27:4
Soir de Reveillon 1935,Ja 19,8:2
Dranovskayr, Lydia
Train Goes East, The 1949,S 5,13:3
Draper, Billy
Navajo 1952,F 21,24:4
Draper, David
Don't Make Waves 1967,Je 21,36:2
Draper, Fred
Faces 1968,S 23,42:4
Faces 1968,N 25,54:2
Draper, Golda (Original Author)
Night Waitress 1936,D 18,31:5
Draper, Natalie
Forever Amber 1947,O 23,31:2
Draper, Paul
Colleen 1936,Mr 9,20:2
Time of your Life, The 1948,My 27,29:2
Draper, Peter (Screenwriter)
Girl-Getters, The 1966,Ap 13,37:6
I'll Never Forget What's 'Isname
1968,Ap 15,51:1
Drapinska, Barbara
Last Stop, The 1949,Mr 22,31:2
Drapkin, Z (Director)
Red Tanks 1942,Je 6,9:2
Drapkin, Z (Screenwriter)
Red Tanks 1942,Je 6,9:2
Dratler, Jay (Original Author)
Girls Under 21 1940,N 11,22:4
Meet Boston Blackie 1941,F 26,17:2
Confessions of Boston Blackie 1941,D 8,31:2
It Comes up Love 1943,Ja 22,25:3
Pitfall 1948,Ag 25,31:2
Las Vegas Story, The 1952,Ja 31,37:6
We're not Married 1952,Jl 12,16:2
Dratler, Jay (Screenwriter)
Conga Nights, La 1940,Je 5,33:5
Girls Under 21 1940,N 11,22:4
Meet Boston Blackie 1941,F 26,17:2
Wife Takes a Flyer, The 1942,Je 19,19:1
Get Help to Love 1942,O 19,15:3
Higher and Higher 1944,Ja 22,8:4
Laura 1944,O 12,24:1
It's in the Bag 1945,Je 11,12:1
Dark Corner, The 1946,My 9,27:3
Call Northside 777 1948,F 19,29:2
That Wonderful Urge 1948,D 22,29:6
Impact 1949,Mr 21,19:2
I Aim at the Stars 1960,O 20,42:2
Drawbell, J W (Original Author)
Lady Surrenders, A 1947,Je 20,25:6
Dray, Douglas
Body and Soul 1931,Mr 14,23:2
Drayton, Alfred
Friday the 13th 1934,My 15,18:1
It's a Boy 1934,Je 8,18:2

Jack Ahoy 1935,F 9,11:2
Loves of a Dictator 1935,Je 1,18:2
First a Girl 1936,Ja 4,19:1
Crimson Circle, The 1936,D 28,12:3
Half-Way House 1945,Ag 13,22:4
Nicholas Nickleby 1947,D 1,27:2
Don't Take it to Heart 1948,D 25,10:3
Drayton, Noel
Under my Skin 1950,Mr 18,9:2
Plymouth Adventure 1952,N 14,20:3
Elephant Walk 1954,Ap 22,37:2
Virgin Queen, The 1955,Ag 6,13:2
Court Jester, The 1956,F 2,19:1
Drchalova, Jana
Capricious Summer 1968,S 18,50:2
Capricious Summer 1968,S 25,38:2
Drean
As du Turf, Les; Acres of Turf 1935,My 11,21:3
Porteuse de Pain, La 1936,Jl 1,29:5
Dreelen, John Van
Enemy General, The 1960,O 20,42:2
Dreher, Carl (Original Author)
Crime of Dr Hallet, The 1938,Mr 24,21:3
Dreifuss, Arthur (Director)
Sarong Girl 1943,Je 18,16:6
There's a Girl in my Heart 1950,Ja 20,29:2
Last Blitzkrieg, The 1959,Ja 31,13:5
Quare Fellow 1963,F 20,6:1
Love-Ins, The 1967,Ag 19,16:1
For Singles Only 1968,Je 6,54:1
Young Runaways, The 1968,S 12,54:3
Dreifuss, Arthur (Producer)
There's a Girl in my Heart 1950,Ja 20,29:2
Dreifuss, Arthur (Screenwriter)
Quare Fellow 1963,F 20,6:1
Love-Ins, The 1967,Ag 19,16:1
For Singles Only 1968,Je 6,54:1
Dreiser, Theodore (Miscellaneous)
Strange Case of Tom Mooney, The
1933,Jl 24,11:2
Dreiser, Theodore (Original Author)
American Tragedy, An 1931,Ag 6,22:5
Jennie Gerhardt 1933,Je 9,20:2
Prince Who Was a Thief, The 1951,Jl 4,13:2
Place in the Sun, A 1951,Ag 29,20:1
Carrie 1952,Jl 17,20:2
Dresdel, Sonia
This Was a Woman 1949,Ja 5,22:2
Fallen Idol, The 1949,N 16,39:2
Clouded Yellow, The 1951,N 13,33:2
Trials of Oscar Wilde, The 1960,Je 28,26:1
Dresden, Albert
Cock Eyed World, The 1929,Ag 5,25:2
Dresher, Beatrice A (Original Author)
Passion 1954,D 11,11:1
Dresher, Beatrice A (Screenwriter)
Passion 1954,D 11,11:1
Dresser, Louise
Prodigal Daughters 1923,Ap 17,26:3
Ruggles of Red Gap 1923,S 10,15:4
Woman Proof 1923,O 30,16:1
To the Ladies 1923,N 26,15:6
City That Never Sleeps, The 1924,S 29,10:1
Enticement 1925,Mr 21,16:3
Percy 1925,Mr 25,24:2
Goose Woman, The 1925,Ag 4,14:3
Eagle, The 1925,N 9,25:1
Blind Goddess 1926,Ap 6,26:4 (In Addenda)
Padlocked 1926,Ag 2,21:2
Everybody's Acting 1926,N 8,19:2
Third Degree, The 1927,F 15,23:1
White Flannels 1927,Mr 22,31:2
Mr Wu 1927,My 16,24:2
Garden of Eden, The 1928,Mr 19,26:2
Air Circus, The 1928,S 3,14:2
Ship Comes in, A 1928,S 4,21:2
Mother Knows Best 1928,S 17,27:1
Not Quite Decent 1929,My 6,30:4
Madonna of Avenue A 1929,Ag 12,22:2
Mammy 1930,Mr 27,24:5
This mad World 1930,Jl 21,20:3
Lightnin' 1930,N 29,21:4
Stepping Sisters 1932,Ja 9,21:1
State Fair 1933,Ja 27,13:2
Song of the Eagle 1933,Ap 29,14:3
Doctor Bull 1933,O 6,21:2
Cradle Song 1933,N 20,18:2
David Harum 1934,Mr 2,23:2
World Moves On, The 1934,Je 30,18:5
Scralet Empress, The 1934,S 15,20:2
Servants' Entrance 1934,S 27,25:2
Girl of the Limberlost, A 1934,N 9,24:6
County Chairman, The 1935,Ja 19,8:1
Maid of Salem 1937,Mr 4,27:2
Dresser, Paul (Composer)
My Gal Sal 1942,My 1,23:1
Dressler, Marie
Agonies of Agnes, The 1918,F 19,9:2
Callahans and the Murphys, The 1927,Jl 12,29:3
Joy Girl, The 1927,S 6,34:3
Breakfast at Sunrise 1927,N 14,26:1
Bringing Up Father 1928,Mr 19,26:2
Patsy, The 1928,Ap 23,20:2

Dressler, Marie— Cont
Divine Lady, The 1929,Mr 23,22:4
Hollywood Revue, The 1929,Ag 15,20:5
Vagabond Lover, The 1929,N 27,30:6
Chasing Rainbows 1930,F 22,13:1
Anna Christie 1930,Mr 15,22:5
Girl Said No, The 1930,Ap 5,23:3
One Romantic Night 1930,My 31,19:4
Caught Short 1930,Je 21,20:5
Let Us Be Gay 1930,Jl 12,16:4
Min and Bill 1930,N 24,26:5
Reducing 1931,Ja 17,23:1
Politics 1931,Ag 1,16:4
Emma 1932,F 6,14:4
Prosperity 1932,N 26,11:4
Tugboat Annie 1933,Ag 12,14:2
Dinner at Eight 1933,Ag 24,18:1
Christopher Bean 1933,N 25,10:2
Dreville, Jean (Director)
Man and his Wife, A 1939,Mr 28,20:1
Devil Is an Empress, The 1939,D 4,18:4
Cage aux Rossignols, La; (Cage of Nightingales,
A) 1947,Ap 3,31:2
Tainted 1950,Ja 21,10:2
Seven Deadly Sins, The (Sloth); Sloth (The Seven
Deadly Sins) 1953,My 12,31:3
Spice of Life, The 1953,D 29,19:3
Dog, a Mouse and a Sputnik, A; Pied, a Cheval et
un Sputnik, A 1960,N 1,46:2
Lafayette 1963,Ap 11,29:1
Dreville, Jean (Producer)
Kreutzer Sonata, The 1938,D 20,30:2
Drew, Ann
Red Raiders, The 1927,S 28,28:3
Drew, Barbara
Some Like It Hot 1959,Mr 30,23:1
Drew, Ellen
Sing You Sinners 1938,Ag 18,23:1
If I Were King 1938,S 29,31:1
Lady's From Kentucky, The 1939,Ap 27,31:1
Gracie Allen Murder Case, The 1939,Je 8,31:3
Geronimo 1940,F 8,18:3
Buck Benny Rides Again 1940,Ap 25,28:4
French Without Tears 1940,Ap 29,12:2
Women Without Names 1940,My 9,26:4
Christmas in July 1940,N 6,35:2
Texas Rangers Ride Again 1941,Ja 9,27:4
Mad Doctor, The 1941,F 27,23:4
Monster and the Girl, The 1941,Mr 20,25:3
Reaching for the Sun 1941,My 8,21:1
Parson of Panamint, The 1941,Jl 26,18:2
Our Wife 1941,S 18,31:1
Night of January 16th, The 1941,D 19,35:1
Remarkable Andrew, The 1942,Mr 6,17:2
My Favorite Spy 1942,My 29,13:4
Night Plane From Chungking 1943,My 31,13:2
Impostor, The 1944,Mr 27,17:2
China Sky 1945,My 25,22:3
Isle of the Dead 1945,S 8,12:2
Man Alive 1945,N 17,14:5
Johnny O'Clock 1947,Mr 27,39:2
Swordsman, The 1947,O 17,18:4
Man From Colorado 1949,Ja 21,24:3
Crooked Way, The 1949,S 5,13:2
Davy Crockett, Indian Scout 1950,Mr 17,28:3
Cargo to Capetown 1950,Mr 31,36:3
Baron of Arizona, The 1950,Je 23,29:2
Stars in my Crown 1950,D 22,19:1
Great Missouri Raid, The 1951,Ap 9,31:2
Drew, George
Lady's From Kentucky, The 1939,Ap 27,31:1
Drew, Jerry
Power 1928,N 27,34:1
Drew, Lowell
Miserables, Les 1935,Ap 22,14:2
Drew, Norma
What a Man 1930,Jl 21,20:3
Drew, Paula
Vigilantes Return, The 1947,Jl 1,30:2
Drew, Roland
Ramona 1928,My 15,17:3
Evangeline 1929,Jl 29,23:3
Racketeer, The 1930,Ja 6,30:8
Ex-Flame 1931,Ja 24,15:1
Great Gambini, The 1937,Jl 12,20:4
Some Blondes Are Dangerous 1937,N 3,29:3
Lady in the Morgue, The 1938,My 9,13:3
Last Warning, The 1938,D 8,34:4
Beasts of Berlin 1939,N 20,15:6
Saint Takes Over, The 1940,My 28,29:3
Underground 1941,Je 23,13:2
Bullets for O'Hara 1941,Jl 28,16:4
Smiling Ghost, The 1941,S 26,26:5
Dangerously They Live 1942,Ap 11,9:2
Bullet Scars 1942,Ap 24,21:4
Murder in the Big House 1942,My 8,27:3
I Was Framed 1942,Je 12,16:6
Lady Gangster 1942,Jl 10,13:2
Spy Ship 1942,Jl 11,8:2
Big Shot, The 1942,Jl 18,8:2
Across the Pacific 1942,S 5,9:2
Hidden Hand, The 1942,N 26,40:4
Secret Enemies 1943,Ja 1,27:3
Bermuda Mystery 1944,My 13,17:1

Drew, Roland— Cont
Two O'Clock Courage 1945,Ap 14,13:3
Drew, Sidney
Youthful Affair, A 1918,Ap 15,13:3
Romance and Rings 1919,Ja 6,11:3
Once a Mason 1919,Mr 10,9:3
Amateur Liar, The 1919,Mr 31,11:3
Harold, the Last of the Saxons 1919,My 12,11:4
Drew, Sidney Mrs
Youthful Affair, A 1918,Ap 15,13:3
Romance and Rings 1919,Ja 6,11:3
Once a Mason 1919,Mr 10,9:3
Amateur Liar, The 1919,Mr 31,11:3
Harold, the Last of the Saxons 1919,My 12,11:4
Bunkered 1919,Jl 14,12:2
Drew, Sidney Mrs (Producer)
Bunkered 1919,Jl 14,12:2
Drewett, Pauline
Belles of St Trinian's, The 1954,D 23,13:4
Drews, Berta
Unsere Fahne Flattert Uns Voran 1934,Jl 7,16:6
Urlaub auf Ehrenwort; Furlough on Word of
Honor 1938,Mr 28,19:2
Girls Behind Bars 1950,My 10,41:2
It Happened in Broad Daylight 1960,S 30,33:1
Drexel, Nancy
Escape, The 1928,My 7,29:1
4 Devils 1928,O 4,26:3
Riley, The Cop 1928,D 4,29:1
Prep and Pep 1928,D 24,11:1
Hollywood, Ciudad de Ensueno 1934,Ap 4,26:3
Dreyer, Carl (Director)
Chained 1926,D 15,30:4
Passion of Joan of Arc, The 1928,Ap 1,IX,5:5 (In
Addenda)
Passion of Joan of Arc, The 1929,Ja 20,VIII,7:5
Passion Of Joan Of Arc, The 1929,Mr 29,21:1
Passion of Jeanne d'Arc, The 1929,Mr 31,VIII,7:1
Witch Woman, The 1929,Ap 8,32:1
Vampire 1932,Jl 31,IX,3:4
Day of Wrath 1948,Ap 26,27:2
Ordet 1957,D 16,33:6
Gertrud 1966,Je 3,33:1
Dreyer, Carl (Producer)
Passion of Joan of Arc, The 1928,Ag 12,VII,3:4
Day of Wrath 1948,Ap 26,27:2
Dreyer, Carl (Screenwriter)
Day of Wrath 1948,Ap 26,27:2
Ordet 1957,D 16,33:6
Gertrud 1966,Je 3,33:1
Dreyer, Dave (Composer)
Sing and Like It 1934,Ap 14,18:2
Silly Billies 1936,Ap 6,18:1
On Again-Off Again 1937,S 18,15:3
Hold That Ghost 1941,Ag 8,13:3
Dreyfuss, Michael
Patterns 1956,Mr 28,26:1
Dreyfuss, Richard
Young Runaways, The 1968,S 12,54:3
Dria, Paola
Lotte nell Ombra; Battles in the Shadow
1939,Mr 21,27:3
Drigo, Riccardo (Composer)
Let Freedom Ring 1939,Mr 10,19:2
Drinkwater, John (Miscellaneous)
April Romance 1937,Ja 27,17:4
Clown Must Laugh, A 1938,O 12,35:2
Mill On the Floss, The 1939,N 15,19:3
Drinkwater, John (Screenwriter)
April Romance 1937,Ja 27,17:4
King's People, The 1937,My 12,27:1
Driscoll, Bobby
Sullivans, The 1944,F 10,19:2
Sunday Dinner for a Soldier 1945,Ja 25,16:2
Big Bonanza, The 1945,F 26,14:5
From This Day Forward 1946,Ap 20,16:2
So Goes my Love 1946,My 2,3:7
O S S 1946,My 27,15:5
Song of the South 1946,N 28,40:2
If You Knew Susie 1948,F 23,19:2
So Dear to my Heart 1949,Ja 31,14:2
Window, The 1949,Ag 8,10:5
Treasure Island 1950,Ag 16,24:2
Happy Time, The 1952,O 31,30:2
Scarlet Coat, The 1955,Jl 30,14:2
Driscoll, Mike
Rulers of the Sea 1939,N 9,27:1
Driscoll, Patricia
Wackiest Ship in the Army, The 1961,F 9,36:1
Driskill, William (Screenwriter)
Ada 1961,Ag 26,15:1
Dritsa, K (Screenwriter)
Take Me Away, My Love 1962,Jl 30,15:5
Driver, Edgar
Suicide Legion 1940,My 6,13:3
Driver, Teddy
Cheaper by the Dozen 1950,Ap 1,12:2
Drobysheva, Nina
Clear Skies 1963,N 27,30:1
Drohan, Benny
Winter Carnival 1939,Jl 28,14:2
Drohocka, H
Last Stop, The 1949,Mr 22,31:2

Drollet, David
Versailles 1929,N 16,25:2
Dromgold, George
Waking up the Town 1925,Mr 31,17:4
Dromgold, George (Original Author)
Big Shot, The 1932,Ja 2,14:2
Dromm, Andrea
Russians are Coming the Russians are Coming,
The 1966,My 26,55:1
Come Spy with Me 1967,F 22,21:1
Drouot, Claire
Bonheur, Le; Happiness 1966,My 24,55:2
Drouot, Jean-Claude
Bonheur, Le; Happiness 1966,My 24,55:2
Drouot, Olivier
Bonheur, Le; Happiness 1966,My 24,55:2
Drouot, Sandrine
Bonheur, Le; Happiness 1966,My 24,55:2
Drpbazynski, Romuald (Director)
Guests are Coming; Jada Goscie Jada
1967,Ja 13,15:1
Dru, Joanne
Abie's Irish Rose 1946,D 23,19:4
Red River 1948,O 1,31:2
All the King's Men 1949,N 9,37:2
She Wore a Yellow Ribbon 1949,N 18,35:2
Wagonmaster 1950,Je 19,17:2
711 Ocean Drive 1950,Jl 20,21:2
Vengeance Valley 1951,F 16,21:2
Mr Belvedere Rings the Bell 1951,Ag 2,18:1
Return of the Texan 1952,F 14,23:1
Pride of St Louis, The 1952,My 3,17:5
Thunder Bay 1953,My 21,39:2
Forbidden 1954,Ja 23,11:2
Duffy of San Quentin 1954,F 10,38:5
Siege at Red River, The 1954,Ap 3,19:2
Southwest Passage 1954,S 11,11:2
Three Ring Circus 1954,D 25,7:2
Warriors, The 1955,S 10,11:2
Sincerely Yours 1955,N 3,37:1
Hell on Frisco Bay 1956,Ja 7,21:1
Light in the Forest, The 1958,Jl 11,15:2
September Storm 1960,O 29,26:7
Sylvia 1965,F 11,45:1
Druce, Hubert
Return of Sherlock Holmes, The 1929,O 19,22:6
Laughing Lady, The 1930,Ja 4,21:1
Night Angel, The 1931,Je 11,28:4
Drucker, Rolf
Gloria 1932,O 28,22:4
Das Schicksal der Renate Langen 1933,N 4,18:4
Drummond, Reginald
Treasure Island 1950,Ag 16,24:2
Druon, Maurice (Original Author)
Possessors, The 1959,Jl 21,24:1
Drury, Allen (Original Author)
Advise and Consent 1962,Je 7,31:2
Drury, James
Forbidden Planet 1956,My 4,21:2
Last Wagon, The 1956,S 22,20:2
Love Me Tender 1956,N 16,23:1
Bernardine 1957,Jl 25,28:1
Toby Tyler 1960,Ap 20,45:2
Pollyanna 1960,My 20,26:1
Ride the High Country 1962,Je 21,26:2
Young Warriors, The 1968,F 8,36:1
Drury, Norma
Stage Door 1937,O 8,27:2
That Hamilton Woman 1941,Ap 4,25:1
Mystery of Marie Roget, The 1942,My 5,17:3
Drury, Sarah
Happy is the Bride 1959,Je 30,27:2
Drusovich, Erika
Landstreicher, Die; Hoboes, The 1938,N 26,18:1
Drute, Dena
Green Fields 1937,O 12,31:4
Drutman, Irving (Composer)
Bachelor's Daughters, The 1946,O 7,23:2
Druzhnikov, Vladimir
Stone Flower 1946,D 30,15:2
Symphony of Life 1948,D 28,19:7
Secret Brigade 1951,Mr 19,23:2
Miners of the Don 1951,N 12,21:2
Attack From the Sea 1954,Ap 19,19:4
Grasshopper, The 1956,Ap 23,22:1
Duel, The 1964,S 7,11:2
Drvota, Mojmir (Screenwriter)
Distant Journey 1950,Ag 28,13:3
Dryden, Norman
Tell-Tale Heart, The 1934,Je 15,26:3
Dryden, Wheeler
Limelight 1952,O 24,27:2
Dryer, Bernard V (Original Author)
Port Afrique 1956,N 3,27:5
Dryhurst, Edward (Screenwriter)
Frightened Lady 1941,N 10,21:3
Man From Morocco, The 1946,N 25,38:2
Agitator, The 1949,Ag 19,12:5
Master of Bankdam 1949,O 17,18:2
Dryhurst, Howard (Producer)
Castle in the Air 1953,Ja 5,19:2

Dryhurst, Howard (Screenwriter)
Castle in the Air 1953,Ja 5,19:2
Drysdale, Tim
Wherever She Goes 1953,Ja 28,24:4
Du Bois, Gladys
Dance of Life, The 1929,Ag 16,18:6
Du Bois, Gladys (Composer)
I'm no Angel 1933,O 14,18:2
Du Bois, Jeanette
Man Called Adam, A 1966,Ag 4,24:2
du Bois, Raoul Pene (Miscellaneous)
Lady in the Dark 1944,F 23,17:1
Du Bois, Val
Lieutenant Craig-Missing 1951,My 19,9:4
Du Count, George
Gay Desperado, The 1936,O 9,31:4
Du Crow, Tote
Pride of Palomar, The 1922,N 20,21:3
Thief of Bagdad, The 1924,Mr 19,19:1
Little Robinson Crusoe 1924,S 3,17:1
Don Q, Son of Zorro 1925,Je 16,24:1
du Maurier, Daphne (Original Author)
Jamaica Inn 1939,O 12,33:1
Rebecca 1940,Mr 29,25:2
Frenchman's Creek 1944,S 21,26:2
Years Between, The 1947,Mr 10,25:2
Hungry Hill 1947,O 11,11:2
My Cousin Rachel 1952,D 26,20:2
Scapegoat, The 1959,Ag 7,28:1
Birds, The 1963,Ap 1,5:5 (Incorrect in this
edition; use 1963,Ap 1,54:1 elsewhere)
du Maurier, Daphne (Screenwriter)
Hungry Hill 1947,O 11,11:2
du Maurier, George (Original Author)
Peter Ibbetson; (Forever) 1921,O 17,18:1
Trilby 1923,Jl 30,11:4
Svengali 1931,My 1,30:3
Peter Ibbetson 1935,N 8,18:2
Svengali 1955,S 26,18:2
du Maurier, Gerald
Escape 1930,N 1,23:2
I Was a Spy 1934,Ja 15,12:2
Catherine the Great 1934,F 15,15:6
Power 1934,O 5,29:3
Scotland Yard Mystery, The 1936,Mr 16,21:4
Dancers, The 1925,Ja 26,22:1
Dancers, The 1930,N 15,15:3
Du Pont, Miss
Broken Wing, The 1923,O 9,17:4
Common Law, The 1923,O 29,18:1
Man From Brodney's, The 1923,D 18,16:3
Sinners in Silk 1924,S 8,15:3
Mantrap 1926,Jl 12,24:4
Du Veron
Zero de Conduite 1947,Je 23,14:5
Duane, Jack
Redskin 1929,Ja 28,21:1
Duane, Jed
Cyanamide 1954,Mr 26,17:6
Duane, Michael
Swordsman, The 1947,O 17,18:4
Gallant Blade 1948,O 13,31:3
Duart, Carl
Smiling Faces 1932,Ag 31,12:3
Duarte, Anselmo (Director)
Given Word, The 1964,Mr 25,47:1
Duarte, Anselmo (Screenwriter)
Given Word, The 1964,Mr 25,47:1
Dubbini, Agnese
Angelina 1948,Ap 6,27:2
Dubbins, Don
From Here to Eternity 1953,Ag 6,16:2
Tribute to a Bad Man 1956,Mr 31,13:3
These Wilder Years 1956,Ag 18,11:2
D I, The 1957,Je 6,35:2
From the Earth to the Moon 1958,N 27,52:2
Prize, The 1964,Ja 24,21:1
Duberg, Axel
Magician, The 1959,Ag 28,27:1
Virgin Spring, The; Jungfrukallan 1960,N 15,46:1
Devil's Eye, The 1961,O 31,27:4
Dubin, Al
42d Street 1933,Mr 10,19:3
Dubin, Al (Composer)
42d Street 1933,Mr 10,19:3
Gold Diggers of 1933 1933,Je 8,22:3
Footlight Parade 1933,O 6,21:3
Roman Scandals 1933,D 25,28:2
Moulin Rouge 1934,F 8,14:4
Wonder Bar 1934,Mr 1,23:2
20 Million Sweethearts 1934,Ap 27,25:1
Sweet Music 1935,F 21,23:2
Gold Diggers of 1935 1935,Mr 15,25:2
Go Into Your Dance 1935,My 4,17:2
Shipmates Forever 1935,O 17,29:3
Stars Over Broadway 1935,N 14,17:3
Colleen 1936,Mr 9,20:2
Sons o'Guns 1936,My 14,29:2
Hearts Divided 1936,Je 13,13:1
Marked Woman 1937,Ap 12,15:2
Melody for Two 1937,My 21,19:5
Singing Marine, The 1937,Jl 1,33:2
Mr Dodd Takes the Air 1937,Ag 12,14:2

Dubin, Al (Composer) — Cont
Gold Diggers in Paris 1938,Je 2,19:2
Garden of the Moon 1938,S 24,13:1
Stage Door Canteen 1943,Je 25,13:2
Lullaby of Broadway 1951,Mr 27,35:2
Dubin, Al (Miscellaneous)
In Caliente 1935,Je 27,16:1
Broadway Gondolier 1935,Jl 18,15:2
Cain and Mabel 1936,O 19,22:1
Gold Diggers of 1937 1936,O 25,19:2
Sing Me a Love Song 1936,D 26,15:2
Dubin, Charles (Director)
Mister Rock and Roll 1957,O 17,42:2
Dubin, Sidney
711 Ocean Drive 1950,Jl 20,21:2
Dubin (Composer)
Dames 1934,Ag 16,20:2
Dubinsky, Yudel
Shir Hashirim 1935,O 11,31:1
Americaner Shadchen; American Matchmaker
1940,My 7,31:3
Dubner, Mirtha
Terrace, The 1964,N 25,45:1
Dubois, Andre
Mr Hulot's Holiday 1954,Je 17,36:2
Dubois, Colette
Little Flower of Jesus, The 1938,D 13,31:2
Dubois, Diane
Amazing Mrs Holliday, The 1943,F 22,20:2
Dubois, Helen
Icebound 1924,Mr 3,22:3 (In Addenda)
Dubois, Marie
Jules and Jim 1962,Ap 24,32:1
Shoot the Piano Player 1962,Jl 24,19:1
Circle of Love 1965,Mr 25,42:4
Male Hunt; Chasse a l'Homme, La
1965,Ap 20,42:1
Thief of Paris, The 1967,Ag 24,43:2
Marriage Came Tumbling Down, The
1968,N 6,32:3
Dubois, Roger
Tainted 1950,Ja 21,10:2
DuBois, William (Original Author)
Pagan Lady 1931,S 21,20:2
I Loved You Wednesday 1933,Je 16,20:2
Dubont, Paulette
7 Capital Sins (Envy); Envy (7 Capital Sins)
1963,Ja 17,5:2
Dubosc
Dark Eyes 1938,Ap 19,24:5
Dubosc, Andre
Mistigri 1933,Ja 13,19:3
Mayerling 1937,S 14,27:1
Dubosc, Gaston
Serment, Le 1934,Mr 14,23:2
Pearls of the Crown, The 1938,Ap 12,26:2
Mayerling to Sarajevo 1940,O 30,27:6
King, The 1941,O 23,29:3
Dubost, Paulette
Ordonnance, L'; Orderly, The 1935,Jl 1,22:3
Bonheur, Le 1936,F 28,18:2
Lie of Nina Petrovna, The 1938,Mr 30,19:2
Song of the Street 1939,S 5,21:2
Hotel du Nord 1940,D 30,21:2
Rules of the Game, The 1950,Ap 10,15:3
Four in a Jeep 1951,Je 12,35:2
Plaisir, Le (The House of Madame Tellier); House
of Madame Tellier (Le Plaisir)
1954,My 20,38:1
Holiday for Henrietta 1955,Ja 25,21:1
Sheep Has Five Legs, The 1955,Ag 10,19:2
Inspector Maigret 1958,O 9,47:1
Sans Famille 1959,S 5,11:4
Picnic on the Grass 1960,O 12,47:1
Rules of the Game, The 1961,Ja 19,26:1
Playtime; Receation, La 1963,Ja 16,5:2
Viva Maria 1965,D 20,48:2
Dubov, Paul
Bombay Clipper 1942,Ja 12,23:3
Cyrano De Bergerac 1950,N 17,31:2
I, The Jury 1953,Ag 22,8:2
Mad at the World 1955,My 14,10:8
China Gate 1957,My 23,40:2
Verboten 1960,Jl 12,39:1
Underworld, U S A 1961,My 13,10:1
Dubov, Paul (Narrator)
Suicide Attack 1951,Jl 14,7:2
Dubov, Paul (Original Author)
With Six You Get Egg Roll 1968,O 10,59:6
Dubov, Paul (Screenwriter)
With Six You Get Egg Roll 1968,O 10,59:6
DuBray, Claire
Heart of a Child, The 1920,Ap 12,13:1
Drusilla With a Million 1925,My 25,21:3
Infatuation 1926,Ja 4,16:1
Devil Dancer, The 1927,D 19,30:1
Shadows of Sing Sing 1934,F 21,23:2
Devil Doll, The 1936,Ag 8,5:2
Ramona 1936,O 7,32:4
Jesse James 1939,Ja 14,13:1
Story of Alexander Graham Bell, The
1939,Ap 1,17:2
Blue Bird, The 1940,Ja 20,11:2
Charlie Chan's Murder Cruise 1940,My 3,17:5

Private Nurse 1941,Ag 29,13:3
DuBrey, Claire
Ponjola 1923,N 19,19:3
Gabriel Over the White House 1933,Ap 1,18:2
Sin of Nora Moran, The 1933,D 13,29:3
Nothing Sacred 1937,N 26,27:2
Baroness and the Butler, The 1938,F 19,19:2
Song to Remember, A 1945,Ja 26,16:4
Dakota 1945,D 17,17:2
Dubrou, John
Merlusse 1938,Mr 17,17:2
Duby, Jacques
Adulteress, The 1958,Ja 14,42:1
Man in the Raincoat, The 1958,Jl 15,21:2
Pot Bouille 1958,O 28,39:1
Oldest Profession, The (Paris Today); Paris Today
(The Oldest Profession) 1968,N 8,42:1
Duby, Satya Dev
Guide, The 1965,F 10,44:2
Duc, Helene
Picnic on the Grass 1960,O 12,47:1
Male Hunt; Chasse a l'Homme, La
1965,Ap 20,42:1
Ducaux, Annie
Agonie des Aigles, L' 1934,D 1,8:5
Life and Loves of Beethoven, The
1937,N 22,15:1
Vierge Folle, La 1938,D 30,11:3
Affair Lafont, The; Conflit 1939,O 9,15:2
Two Women 1940,N 2,19:3
Forbidden Love 1948,Ag 26,16:4
Royal Affair, A; (Roi, Le) 1950,Mr 9,25:2
Dreams of Love 1954,Je 5,11:2
Possessors, The 1959,Jl 21,24:1
Duchamp, Marcel
8 X 8 1957,Mr 16,13:2
Duchamp, Marcel (Miscellaneous)
Dreams that Money can Buy 1948,Ap 24,11:2
Ducharme, Camille
Thirteenth Letter, The 1951,F 22,27:2
Duchaussoy, Michel
Killing Game, The 1968,Ag 27,36:1
Duchesne, Louis (Director)
Sins of Youth 1960,D 24,8:2
Duchesne, Raphael (Composer)
Thrill of Brazil, The 1946,S 6,18:3
Duchesne, Roger
Golem, The 1937,Mr 22,27:2
Affair Lafont, The; Conflit 1939,O 9,15:2
It Happened in Gibraltar 1943,N 16,27:1
Savage Brigade 1948,D 3,33:4
Duchin, Eddie
Hit Parade, The 1937,My 31,11:2
Duchin, Eddie Orchestra
Coronado 1935,D 19,33:4
Duchin, Peter
World of Henry Orient, The 1964,Mr 20,27:2
Duckse, Maria Esther
Terrace, The 1964,N 25,45:1
Ducount, George
White Fang 1936,Jl 18,18:2
Ducouret, Marguerite
Culte de Beaute, Le 1931,Je 8,21:1
Kermesse Heroique, La 1936,S 23,29:1
Dr Knock 1937,My 1,16:4
Dudan, Pierre
Roots of Heaven, The 1958,O 16,46:1
Dudarova, Ludmilla
Father's Dilemma 1952,S 23,25:1
Dude
Big Country, The 1958,O 2,44:1
Dudgeon, Elspeth
Vanessa: Her Love Story 1935,Ap 13,11:3
Becky Sharp 1935,Je 14,27:2
Give Me your Heart 1936,S 17,18:2
Prince and the Pauper, The 1937,My 6,23:1
Sh! The Octopus 1937,D 24,21:2
Mystery House 1938,Je 29,15:5
Bulldog Drummond's Secret Police
1939,Mr 30,19:3
Lust for Gold 1949,Jl 4,9:2
Dudgeon, John
Old Dark House, The 1932,O 28,22:4
Dudicourt, Marc
King of Hearts 1967,Je 20,34:1
Dudinskaya, Natalia
Stars of the Russian Ballet (Swan Lake); Swan
Lake (Stars of the Russian Ballet) 1954,S 6,9:2
Sleeping Beauty, The 1966,My 4,50:1
Dudko, Appolonari (Screenwriter)
Sleeping Beauty, The 1966,My 4,50:1
Sleeping Beauty, The 1966,My 4,50:1
Dudley
Beachcomber, The 1938,D 26,29:3
Dudley, Carl (Director)
Cinerama-South Seas Adventure 1958,Jl 16,26:1
Dudley, Carl (Producer)
Cinerama-South Seas Adventure 1958,Jl 16,26:1
Dudley, Doris
Woman Rebels, A 1936,O 30,27:2
Moon and Sixpence, The 1942,O 28,26:4
Secret Fury, The 1950,Je 22,34:2

Dudley, E Lawrence (Original Author)
Voltaire 1933,Ag 23,21:2
Dudley, Florence
Broadway 1929,My 28,36:2
Party Girl 1930,Ja 2,28:2
Pick Up 1933,Mr 25,13:4
Dudley, Janet
Slender Thread, The 1965,D 24,24:2
Dudley, Lesley
John and Julie 1957,My 7,40:1
Dudley, Paul (Screenwriter)
Monkey on my Back 1957,My 30,23:2
Solomon and Sheba 1959,D 26,7:2
Dudley, Robert
Sixty Cents an Hour 1923,My 15,22:1
Day of Faith, The 1923,N 27,11:2
Marriage Clause, The 1926,S 28,30:2
Night Flyer, The 1928,Mr 13,23:3
Skinner's big Idea 1928,Mr 27,30:4
Fools for Luck 1928,Je 12,33:5
Big News 1929,O 7,22:1
Three Wise Girls 1932,F 6,14:4
Toast of New York, The 1937,Jl 23,16:2
Palm Beach Story, The 1942,D 11,33:1
It Happened Tomorrow 1944,My 29,18:2
Magic Town 1947,O 8,29:2
Portrait of Jennie 1949,Mr 30,31:2
Dudley, Susan
Tony Draws a Horse 1951,My 15,38:6
Dudley-Ward, Penelope
Escape me Never 1935,My 24,24:2
I Stand Condemned 1936,Jl 2,27:2
Major Barbara 1941,My 15,27:1
Dudnikov, D
New Horizons 1939,My 12,25:3
Red Tanks 1942,Je 6,9:2
Dudow, S T (Director)
Kuhle Wampe 1933,Ap 24,11:4
Dudow, Slaten (Director)
Our Daily Bread 1950,O 9,21:6
Dudow, Slaten (Screenwriter)
Our Daily Bread 1950,O 9,21:6
Dudrumet, Jean-Charles (Director)
Lovers on a Tightrope 1962,O 25,48:3
Dudrumet, Jean-Charles (Screenwriter)
Lovers on a Tightrope 1962,O 25,48:3
Due, Jacqueline
Three Feet in a Bed 1957,My 18,23:2
Duering, Carl
Arabesque 1966,My 6,54:1
Duffy 1968,S 17,50:3
Dueringer, Annemarie
Eternal Waltz, The; (Ewiger Walzer)
1959,Jl 9,22:1
City of Secrets 1963,Jl 27,10:2
You Are the World for Me 1964,D 26,9:4
Duerrenmatt, Friedrich (Original Author)
It Happened in Broad Daylight 1960,S 30,33:1
Duerrenmatt, Friedrich (Screenwriter)
It Happened in Broad Daylight 1960,S 30,33:1
Duff, Amanda
Mr Moto in Danger Island 1938,Mr 20,13:3
Just Around the Corner 1938,D 3,11:2
Hotel for Women 1939,Ag 26,20:2
Escape, The 1939,N 3,17:4
City of Chance 1940,Ja 22,11:3
Devil Commands, The 1941,F 14,15:3
Duff, Harry
Tom Brown's School Days 1940,Je 28,22:2
Duff, Howard
Brute Force 1947,Jl 17,16:2
Naked City, The 1948,Mr 5,17:2
All my Sons 1948,Mr 29,17:3
Red Canyon 1949,Ap 28,28:2
Illegal Entry 1949,Je 11,11:2
Calamity Jane and Sam Bass 1949,Jl 18,14:2
Johnny Stool Pigeon 1949,S 23,28:3
Woman in Hiding 1950,F 23,33:2
Shakedown 1950,S 4,11:2
Spy Hunt 1950,S 8,25:2
Steel Town 1952,My 10,16:4
Models, Inc 1952,My 26,18:4
Tanganyika 1954,Je 19,9:2
Women's Prison 1955,F 3,18:5
Flame of the Islands 1956,F 25,12:4
Blackjack Ketchum Desperado 1956,Ap 5,26:2
While the City Sleeps 1956,My 17,37:1
Boys' Night Out 1962,Je 22,15:2
Duff, Warren (Miscellaneous)
In Caliente 1935,Je 27,16:1
Duff, Warren (Original Author)
X Marks the Spot 1931,D 7,16:1
Fashions of 1934 1934,Ja 20,12:2
Sweet Music 1935,F 21,23:2
In Caliente 1935,Je 27,16:1
Frisco Kid 1935,N 25,22:1
Stolen Holiday 1937,F 1,15:3
Varsity Show 1937,S 2,17:2
Marine Raiders 1944,Jl 1,10:7
Appointment With Danger 1951,My 10,38:2
Duff, Warren (Producer)
Experiment Perilous 1944,D 30,15:2
Lady Luck 1946,O 31,22:3

Duff, Warren (Producer)— Cont

Honeymoon 1947,My 19,27:2
Out of the Past 1947,N 26,18:2
Gambling House 1951,Mr 19,23:2
Sealed Cargo 1951,My 24,47:1
Duff, Warren (Screenwriter)
St Louis Kid, The 1934,N 1,25:2
Broadway Gondolier 1935,Jl 18,15:2
Frisco Kid 1935,N 25,22:1
Singing Kid, The 1936,Ap 4,11:1
Gold Diggers of 1937 1936,D 25,19:2
Ready, Willing and Able 1937,Mr 15,27:1
Varsity Show 1937,S 2,17:2
Back in Circulation 1937,O 4,17:1
Submarine D-1 1937,D 30,15:4
Gold Is Where You Find It 1938,F 14,20:6
Gold Diggers in Paris 1938,Je 2,19:2
Angels With Dirty Faces 1938,N 26,18:1
Oklahoma Kid, The 1939,Mr 11,21:1
Each Dawn I Die 1939,Jl 22,12:2
Espionage Agent 1939,S 23,22:2
Invisible Stripes 1940,Ja 13,11:2
'Til We Meet Again 1940,Ap 14,14:2
Lady From Cheyenne, The 1941,Ap 18,18:2
Fallen Sparrow, The 1943,Ag 20,13:1
Iron Major, The 1943,N 1,12:5
No Time for Love 1943,D 2,30:1
Step Lively 1944,Jl 27,14:1
Experiment Perilous 1944,D 30,15:2
Chicago Deadline 1949,N 3,37:2
Dangerous Profession, A 1949,D 12,29:4
Turning Point, The 1952,N 15,15:2
Make Haste to Live 1954,Mr 26,16:2
Duffell, Bee
Fahrenheit 451 1966,N 15,53:1
Duffield, Brainard
Jigsaw 1949,My 30,9:4
Macbeth 1950,D 28,22:6
Duffy, Albert (Original Author)
Hunted Men 1938,My 21,9:2
Gay Caballero, The 1940,O 25,25:3
Duffy, Albert (Screenwriter)
Blind Alley 1939,My 23,27:2
Coast Guard 1939,Ag 28,17:2
Beware, Spooks 1939,N 3,17:4
Lone Wolf Strikes, The 1940,F 5,13:2
I Married Adventure 1940,S 24,26:5
Gay Caballero, The 1940,O 25,25:3
Reveille With Beverly 1943,Ap 24,17:2
Dark Past, The 1948,D 23,25:2
Three Stripes in the Sun 1955,N 24,41:2
Duffy, Brian (Producer)
Only When I Larf 1968,O 24,55:3
Duffy, Clinton T (Original Author)
Duffy of San Quentin 1954,F 10,38:5
Duffy, Gerard
Men of Ireland 1938,S 30,24:2
Duffy, Jack
Stop Flirting 1925,Je 18,16:3
Harold Teen 1928,Ag 14,15:4
Sally 1929,D 24,14:4
Heaven on Earth 1931,D 19,16:4
Alice in Wonderland 1933,D 23,19:1
Duffy, James
Our Hospitality 1923,D 10,20:1
Duffy, John (Director)
Men of Ireland 1938,S 30,24:2
Duffy, John (Screenwriter)
Men of Ireland 1938,S 30,24:2
Duffy, Mark
Brig, The 1964,S 21,37:4
Duffy, William (Screenwriter)
Round Trip 1967,Jl 20,30:2
Dufilho, Jacques
Saadia 1954,Mr 20,10:5
Happy Road, The 1957,Je 21,20:2
Poupee, La 1963,Ag 28,39:1
Julie the Redhead 1963,O 15,44:1
War of the Buttons, The 1963,D 19,40:2
Sweet and Sour 1964,D 28,34:2
Lady L 1966,My 19,51:1
Benjamin 1968,Mr 26,41:2
Duflos, Henriette
Mystere de la Chambre Jaune, Le
1931,My 26,33:2
Duflos, Huguette
Pearls of the Crown, The 1938,Ap 12,26:2
Dufour, Giovani
Flight Into France 1949,Jl 22,16:2
Dufour, Val
Lonely Night, The 1954,Mr 29,22:2
Dufresne, Henry
32 Rue de Montmartre 1944,S 28,26:3
DUGAN
See Also DUGGAN
Dugan, Harry (Cinematographer)
Spell of Ireland, The 1954,My 11,25:5
Dugan, Harry (Director)
Hills of Ireland, The 1951,My 22,38:2
Spell of Ireland, The 1954,My 11,25:5
Dugan, Harry (Screenwriter)
Hills of Ireland, The 1951,My 22,38:2
Spell of Ireland, The 1954,My 11,25:5

Dugan, Irvin
Reflections in a Golden Eye 1967,O 12,59:1
Dugan, James
Warming Up 1928,Jl 16,25:3
Dugan, James (Miscellaneous)
Silent World, The 1956,S 25,30:1
Dugan, Mary
River, The 1928,D 24,11:1
Dugan, Michael
Yes Sir, That's my Baby 1949,N 11,31:2
She Wore a Yellow Ribbon 1949,N 18,35:2
Dugan, Thomas J (Original Author)
Pick a Star 1937,My 28,17:2
Dugan, Thomas J (Screenwriter)
Pick a Star 1937,My 28,17:2
Dugan, Tom
Sharp Shooters 1928,Ja 23,18:3
Soft Living 1928,F 27,16:2
Dressed to Kill 1928,Mr 12,26:1
Lights of New York 1928,Jl 9,25:1
Melody of Love 1928,O 22,29:1
Midnight Taxi, The 1928,O 29,29:1
Sonny Boy 1929,Mr 9,24:3
Drag 1929,Je 21,17:2
Drake Case, The 1929,S 16,30:1
Hearts in Exile 1929,N 29,25:1
Bright Lights 1931,F 10,24:4
Hot Heiress, The 1931,Mr 14,23:2
Woman Hungry 1931,Mr 23,24:7
Star Witness, The 1931,Ag 4,19:5
Doctor X 1932,Ag 4,17:2
Blessed Event 1932,S 3,16:2
Big City Blues 1932,S 10,18:5
Grand Slam 1933,F 22,25:2
Trick for Trick 1933,Je 10,16:4
Don't Bet on Love 1933,Jl 31,16:2
Sweetheart of Sigma Chi, The 1933,N 9,27:1
Palooka 1934,F 28,23:2
No More Women 1934,Mr 15,27:4
President Vanishes, The 1934,D 8,18:5
Princess O'Hara 1935,Ap 13,11:3
Case of the Missing Man, The 1935,N 23,23:2
Calling of Dan Matthews, The 1936,Ja 25,18:4
Wife vs Secretary 1936,F 29,11:1
Pennies From Heaven 1936,D 10,35:2
Nobody's Baby 1937,My 20,17:3
Pick a Star 1937,My 28,17:2
She Had to Eat 1937,Jl 24,12:1
True Confession 1937,D 16,35:2
Four Daughters 1938,Ag 19,13:3
There's That Woman Again 1939,Ja 6,25:4
Lone Wolf Spy Hunt, The 1939,Mr 6,11:3
I'm From Missouri 1939,Mr 23,27:1
$1,000 a Touchdown 1939,O 5,27:2
Missing Evidence 1939,N 17,17:3
Housekeeper's Daughter, The 1939,D 2,21:4
Fighting 69th, The 1940,Ja 27,9:2
Farmer's Daughter, The 1940,F 16,23:4
Too Many Husbands 1940,Mr 8,25:2
Isle of Destiny 1940,Ap 8,15:2
Star Dust 1940,My 4,13:1
Ghost Breakers, The 1940,Jl 4,12:2
Cross Country Romance 1940,Jl 19,22:3
So You Won't Talk 1940,O 17,33:2
Little Bit of Heaven, A 1940,N 8,24:2
You're the One 1941,F 20,23:2
Ellery Queen's Penthouse Mystery
1941,Mr 7,17:2
Monster and the Girl, The 1941,Mr 20,25:3
Tight Shoes 1941,Je 19,25:2
Ellery Queen and the Murder Ring
1941,O 21,29:4
To Be or not to Be 1942,Mr 7,13:2
Bugle Sounds, The 1942,Ap 3,25:2
Moontide 1942,Ap 30,14:1
Bataan 1943,Je 4,17:2
Swingtime Johnny 1943,D 17,23:3
Up in Arms 1944,Mr 3,19:2
Earl Carroll Vanities 1945,Ap 2,15:6
Bringing Up Father 1946,N 22,27:3
Fabulous Dorseys, The 1947,My 30,25:3
Good News 1947,D 5,33:2
Take Me Out to the Ball Game 1949,Mr 10,35:2
Lemon Drop Kid, The 1951,Mr 22,41:2
Further Perils of Laurel and Hardy, The
1968,Ap 1,56:6
Dugan, Vicki
Great Man, The 1957,Ja 2,28:2
Dugan, Val
Heart of a Salome, The 1927,Je 6,27:2
Dugan, William Francis
Hit of the Show 1928,Jl 9,25:1
Duganne, Phyllis (Original Author)
Nice Girl 1941,Mr 27,29:6
Dugay, Yvette
Ali Baba and the Forty Thieves 1944,Mr 16,17:3
People Against O'Hara, The 1951,S 6,39:3
Hiawatha 1952,D 26,20:4
Cattle Queen of Montana 1955,Ja 26,22:1
Duges, A (Director)
Great Test, The 1928,Ap 27,8:2
Legion of Honor, The 1928,Jl 20,8:4
Soul of France, The 1929,O 12,11:1

DUGGAN
See Also DUGAN
Duggan, Andrew
Three Brave Men 1957,Mr 16,13:2
Bravados, The 1958,Je 26,23:2
House of Women 1962,Ap 12,41:6
Chapman Report, The 1962,O 18,49:2
Palm Springs Weekend 1963,N 6,32:1
Seven Days in May 1964,F 20,22:1
Incredible Mr Limpet, The 1964,Mr 26,40:4
FBI Code 98 1964,Ap 9,25:6
In Like Flint 1967,Mr 16,53:2
Secret War of Harry Frigg, The 1968,Mr 5,34:5
Duggan, Gerry
L-Shaped Room, The 1963,My 28,32:1
Duggan, Jan
Old-Fashioned Way, The 1934,Jl 14,16:5
Wagon Wheels 1934,O 4,19:1
County Chairman, The 1935,Ja 19,8:1
Mountain Music 1937,Je 24,30:3
Damsel in Distress, A 1937,N 25,37:1
Scandal Street 1938,F 5,19:2 (In Addenda)
One Wild Night 1938,Je 3,17:2
Thanks For Everything 1938,D 10,13:2
Story of Alexander Graham Bell, The
1939,Ap 1,17:2
Meanest Man in the World, The 1943,F 25,27:3
Duggan, Pat (Producer)
Just for You 1952,O 9,40:6
Forever Female 1954,Ja 13,26:2
Red Garters 1954,Mr 27,13:5
We're no Angels 1955,Jl 8,15:2
Vagabond King, The 1956,S 13,39:6
Duggan, Tom
You Can't Fool an Irishman 1950,D 7,45:4
Andy Hardy Comes Home 1958,D 24,00:0
But Not for Me 1959,O 3,14:6
Duhamel, Marcel
Bizarre, Bizarre 1939,Mr 21,27:2
Stormy Waters 1946,Je 17,32:2
Duhart, Simone
Game of Love, The 1954,D 15,41:1
Duhour, Clement
Lovers and Thieves 1958,Ag 5,23:2
Dukas, James
Great St Louis Bank Robbery, The 1960,F 4,34:1
Duke, Ivy
Decameron Nights 1928,My 29,17:2
Duke, John
Never Steal Anything Small 1959,F 12,23:1
Duke, Patty
Goddess, The 1958,Je 25,24:1
Happy Anniversary 1959,N 11,41:1
Miracle Worker, The 1962,My 24,29:2
Billie 1965,S 16,55:3
Valley of the Dolls 1967,D 16,51:1
Duke, Vernon (Composer)
Cabin in the Sky 1943,My 28,19:3
I Dood It 1943,N 11,29:1
Dukes, Ashley (Screenwriter)
Abdul the Damned 1936,My 11,16:2
Dukinsky, Ivan (Director)
New China, The 1952,Mr 10,18:4
Dulay, Arthur
Mrs Fitzherbert 1950,My 11,37:2
Dulier, Suzanne
Dia que me Quieras, El; Day You Love Me, The
1935,Ag 27,23:3
Dull, Orville O (Producer)
When Ladies Meet 1941,S 5,19:2
We Were Dancing 1942,My 1,23:2
Tish 1942,S 18,25:2
Stand by for Action 1943,Mr 12,12:2
Man From Down Under, The 1943,S 27,23:2
Rationing 1944,Ap 10,14:2
Barbary Coast Gent 1944,S 29,18:2
Bad Bascomb 1946,My 23,18:4
Secret Land, The 1948,D 2,39:2
Dullac, Paul
Harvest 1939,O 3,19:4
Marseillaise 1939,N 6,20:2
Dullea, Keir
Hoodlum Priest, The 1961,Ap 3,28:5
David and Lisa 1962,D 27,5:5
Mail Order Bride 1964,Je 11,27:3
Thin Red Line, The 1964,O 29,38:1
Bunny Lake is Missing 1965,O 4,00:0
Madame X 1966,Ap 28,49:1
Fox, The 1968,F 8,36:1
2001 A Space Odyssey 1968,Ap 4,58:1
Dullin, Charles
Miracle of the Wolves, The 1925,F 24,17:3
Chess Player, The 1930,My 19,21:1
Miracle des Loups, Le 1930,Jl 28,22:1
Miserables, Les 1936,O 28,31:2
Courier of Lyons, The 1938,Je 3,17:1
Miserables, Les 1946,D 26,28:4
Volpone 1947,Je 27,9:3
Jenny Lamour 1948,Mr 6,17:2
Chips Are Down, The 1949,F 2,36:1
Dumarcay, Philippe (Screenwriter)
Girl With the Golden Eyes, The 1962,Ag 21,36:2

Dumas, Alexandre (Original Author)
Three Musketeers, The 1921,Ag 29,14:4
Monte Cristo 1922,Ag 15,20:3
Milady 1923,Ja 22,10:1
Edmund Kean, Prince Among Lovers
  1927,Je 1,25:2
Iron Mask, The 1929,F 22,18:6
Collier de la Reine, Le (Queen's Necklace, The)
  1931,F 9,25:3
Count of Monte Cristo, The 1934,S 27,25:2
Dame aux Camelias, La 1935,Mr 21,27:1
Three Musketeers, The 1935,N 1,25:1
Camille 1937,Ja 23,13:1
Three Musketeers, The 1939,F 18,12:2
Man in the Iron Mask, The 1939,Jl 14,11:1
Corsican Brothers, The 1942,Ja 16,25:4
El Conde de Monte Cristo 1943,N 9,26:2
Dama de las Camelias, La 1944,S 26,16:1
Fighting Guardsman, The 1945,O 6,9:6
Three Musketeers, The 1948,O 21,33:2
Black Magic 1949,N 9,37:2
Story of Monte Cristo, The 1962,N 7,48:1
Dumas, Alexandre fils (Original Author)
Camille 1927,Ap 22,19:1
Dumas, Andre
Rise of Louis XIV, The 1967,S 26,54:2
Dumas, Eugene
Luc Aux Dames 1936,Ja 15,14:4
Dumas, Frederic
Silent World, The 1956,S 25,30:1
Dumas, Jean
Our Hospitality 1923,D 10,20:1
Last Man on Earth, The 1924,D 13,12:4
Dumas, Roger
Bride Is Much too Beautiful, The 1958,Ja 21,35:1
Rue de Paris 1960,D 23,14:3
Cross of the Living 1963,F 5,5:5
Dumas, Roland
Way of a Gaucho 1952,N 5,36:2
Dumbar, Helen
Fighting Coward, The 1924,Mr 17,19:1
Dumbrille, Douglas
His Woman 1931,D 5,21:2
Wiser Sex, The 1932,Mr 12,19:5
Blondie of the Follies 1932,S 2,19:2
That's my Boy 1932,N 21,21:1
Laughter in Hell 1933,Ja 2,29:2
King of the Jungle 1933,F 25,20:3
Elmer the Great 1933,My 26,24:2
Baby Face 1933,Je 24,16:2
Voltaire 1933,Ag 23,21:2
Man Who Dared, The 1933,S 9,9:3
World Changes, The 1933,O 27,22:3
Female 1933,N 4,18:3
Way to Love, The 1933,N 11,10:3
Lady Killer 1934,Ja 1,28:2
Massacre 1934,Ja 18,19:2
Hi, Nellie! 1934,F 1,15:5
Journal of a Crime 1934,Ap 28,11:3
Fog over Frisco 1934,Je 7,26:2
Operator 13 1934,Je 23,16:5
Broadway Bill 1934,N 30,22:2
Lives of a Bengal Lancer, The 1935,Ja 12,12:2
Secret Bride, The 1935,F 2,10:1
Naughty Marietta 1935,Mr 23,11:2
Cardinal Richelieu 1935,Ap 19,24:2
Air Hawks 1935,Je 4,26:5
Love Me Forever 1935,Je 28,24:1
Peter Ibbetson 1935,N 8,18:2
Crime and Punishment 1935,N 22,18:2
Calling of Dan Matthews, The 1936,Ja 25,18:4
Lone Wolf Returns, The 1936,F 4,25:5
Music Goes 'Round, The 1936,F 22,12:1
You may Be Next 1936,F 24,14:1
Mr Deeds Goes to Town 1936,Ap 17,17:2
Witness Chair, The 1936,Ap 18,19:2
Princess Comes Across, The 1936,Je 4,27:2
M'liss 1936,Ag 8,5:2
Counterfeit Lady 1937,Ja 11,15:6
Day at the Races, A 1937,Je 18,25:2
Emperor's Candlesticks, The 1937,Jl 9,18:1
Firefly, The 1937,S 2,17:2
Ali Baba Goes to Town 1937,O 23,14:1
Buccaneer, The 1938,F 17,17:2
Mr Moto in Danger Island 1938,Mr 20,13:3
Stolen Heaven 1938,My 12,27:2
Fast Company 1938,Jl 6,21:2
Crime Takes a Holiday 1938,N 28,11:2
Sharpshooters 1938,D 5,19:2
Storm Over Bengal 1938,D 8,34:4
Kentucky 1938,D 24,12:1
Three Musketeers, The 1939,F 18,12:2
Captain Fury 1939,My 26,20:2
Tell no Tales 1939,Je 2,27:3
Charlie Chan at Treasure Island 1939,S 1,15:5
Thunder Afloat 1939,O 13,27:2
Charlie Chan in City in Darkness 1939,D 18,29:2
Slightly Honorable 1940,My 17,23:4
South of Pago-Pago 1940,Ag 2,12:2
Michael Shayne, Private Detective
  1940,D 19,33:2
Roundup, The 1941,Mr 13,25:4
Washington Melodrama 1941,My 26,15:3

Big Store, The 1941,Je 27,14:4
Ellery Queen and the Perfect Crime
  1941,Ag 11,17:3
Ride 'Em Cowboy 1942,Mr 5,27:3
Gentleman After Dark, A 1942,Ap 17,21:2
Ten Gentlemen From West Point 1942,Je 5,23:3
I Married an Angel 1942,Jl 10,13:2
Stand by for Action 1943,Mr 12,12:2
Du Barry Was a Lady 1943,Ag 20,13:1
Uncertain Glory 1944,Ap 8,9:2
Gypsy Wildcat 1944,O 5,18:6
Lost in a Harem 1944,N 9,23:2
Medal for Benny, A 1945,My 24,15:2
Frozen Ghost, The 1945,Jl 28,7:3
Daltons Ride Again, The 1945,D 8,21:2
Pardon my Past 1946,Ja 28,15:5
Road to Utopia 1946,F 28,20:2
Cat Creeps, The 1946,My 18,12:4
Night in Paradise 1946,Je 6,16:3
Catman of Paris, The 1946,Jl 13,12:2
Monsieur Beaucaire 1946,S 5,23:1
Dishonored Lady 1947,My 24,10:5
Blonde Savage 1947,O 4,9:2
Christmas Eve 1947,N 28,30:2
Fabulous Texan, The 1947,D 26,22:5
Alimony 1949,Jl 22,16:3
Buccaneer's Girl 1950,Mr 27,19:2
Riding High 1950,Ap 11,26:2
Her Wonderful Lie 1950,Jl 17,15:2
Abbott and Costello in the Foreign Legion
  1950,Ag 14,14:4
Rapture 1950,D 14,51:3
Millionaire for Christy, A 1951,O 5,24:3
Son of Paleface 1952,O 2,32:3
Plunder of the Sun 1953,Ag 27,22:1
World for Ransom 1954,Je 5,11:2
Jupiter's Darling 1955,F 18,18:4
Ten Commandments, The 1956,N 9,35:2
Buccaneer, The 1958,D 24,00:0
Dumcke, Ernst
Feldherrnhuegel, Der 1934,Ap 20,17:2
Schoen Ist Es Verliebt zu Sein 1936,Ap 7,31:2
Wenn Du eine Schwiegermutter hast; When You
  Have a Mother-in-Law 1938,Ja 29,12:1
Gross Reinemachen; General Housecleaning
  1938,Je 23,27:2
Herbst-Monoever; Fall Manoeuvres
  1939,Mr 18,9:3
Henker Fraven und Soldaten; Hangmen, Women
  and Soldiers 1940,Ja 13,11:3
Dumesnil, Jacques
Lucrezia Borgia 1937,O 13,27:2
Two Women 1940,N 2,19:3
She Returned at Dawn; Retour a l'Aube
  1947,Ag 1,21:5
Forbidden Love 1948,Ag 26,16:4
Rumors 1949,Mr 19,10:7
Anna 1953,F 19,20:5
Ulysses 1955,Ag 18,17:2
Please Mr Balzac 1957,N 18,37:2
Dumke, Ralph
All the King's Men 1949,N 9,37:2
Mystery Street 1950,Jl 28,12:5
Breaking Point, The 1950,O 7,10:6
Where Danger Lives 1951,Ja 1,13:6
Law and the Lady, The 1951,Ag 16,23:2
Mob, The 1951,O 18,32:2
Boots Malone 1952,Mr 13,26:2
Carbine Williams 1952,My 8,37:2
San Francisco Story, The 1952,My 10,16:4
Mississippi Gambler, The 1953,Ja 30,25:1
Lili 1953,Mr 11,36:7
President's Lady, The 1953,My 22,31:1
Alaska Seas 1954,Mr 6,13:5
Rails Into Laramie 1954,My 13,34:2
Forever, Darling 1956,F 10,18:1
Francis in the Haunted House 1956,Jl 21,9:2
Solid Gold Cadillac, The 1956,O 25,40:3
Buster Keaton Story, The 1957,Ap 22,31:6
Dumo, Evelyn
Love Light, The 1921,Ja 10,9:1
Dumont, Danielle
Hunchback of Notre Dame, The 1957,D 12,35:1
Pot Bouille 1958,O 28,39:1
Dumont, Ghislaine
Picnic on the Grass 1960,O 12,47:1
Dumont, J M
City of Masks, The 1920,Jl 12,12:4
Dumont, Margaret
Cocoanuts, The 1929,My 25,17:3
Animal Crackers 1930,Ag 29,20:3
Girl Habit, The 1931,Jl 4,11:5
Duck Soup 1933,N 23,24:2
Night at the Opera, A 1935,D 7,22:1
Anything Goes 1936,F 6,23:3
Song and Dance Man 1936,Mr 12,18:2
Day at the Races, A 1937,Je 18,25:2
Life of the Party, The 1937,O 4,17:1
Wise Girl 1938,Ja 10,13:3
At the Circus 1939,N 17,17:2
Big Store, The 1941,Je 27,14:4
Never Give a Sucker an Even Break
  1941,O 27,21:2

Dumont, Margaret— Cont
Born to Sing 1942,F 19,23:2
Sing Your Worries Away 1942,My 15,25:2
Dancing Masters, The 1943,D 2,30:2
Up in Arms 1944,Mr 3,19:2
Seven Days Ashore 1944,Ap 26,24:7
Horn Blows at Midnight, The 1945,Ap 21,18:2
Billy Rose's Diamond Horseshoe 1945,My 3,37:1
Little Giant 1946,My 9,27:5
Stop, You're Killing Me 1952,D 11,45:3
Zotz! 1962,O 4,44:3
What a Way to Go! 1964,My 15,44:1
Dumont, Montague
Midnight Romance, A 1919,Mr 10,9:3
Duna, Steffi
Man of Two Worlds 1934,Ja 12,29:2
Dancing Pirate 1936,Je 18,19:1
Anthony Adverse 1936,Ag 27,16:1
Rascals 1938,My 27,12:2
Clown Must Laugh, A 1938,O 12,35:2
Flirting With Fate 1938,D 15,35:3
Girl and the Gambler, The 1939,Je 28,17:3
Magnificent Fraud, The 1939,Jl 20,16:2
Way Down South 1939,Ag 18,16:4
Beasts of Berlin 1939,N 20,15:6
Waterloo Bridge 1940,My 17,23:2
Phantom Raiders 1940,Je 24,19:5
Great McGinty, The 1940,Ag 15,23:1
River's End 1940,Ag 26,11:4
Dunagan, Donnie
Mother Carey's Chickens 1938,Ag 5,11:1
Son of Frankenstein 1939,Ja 30,9:2
Forgotten Woman, The 1939,Ag 4,11:2
Tower of London 1939,D 12,37:2
Dunaway, Faye
Happening, The 1967,My 18,56:3
Bonnie and Clyde 1967,Ag 14,36:1
Thomas Crown Affair, The 1968,Je 27,48:2
Dunayevsky, Isaac (Composer)
Moscow Laughs 1935,Mr 25,12:2
Beethoven Concerto 1937,Mr 24,29:1
Country Bride 1938,Je 4,18:2
Volga-Volga 1941,My 17,19:2
Spring 1948,Mr 15,26:2
Cossacks of the Kuban 1950,O 30,22:4
Dunaysky, Anton
Heroes Are Made 1944,Mr 11,10:2
Rainbow, The 1944,O 23,14:3
Dunbar, Charles
What! No Beer? 1933,F 11,11:3
Dunbar, Dixie
George White's Scandals 1934,Mr 16,24:2
King of Burlesque 1936,Ja 16,25:2
Professional Soldier 1936,Ja 30,14:2
Educating Father 1936,Je 20,22:2
Girls' Dormitory 1936,Ag 29,16:2
Sing, Baby, Sing 1936,S 12,20:1
Pigskin Parade 1936,N 14,23:3
One in a Million 1937,Ja 1,19:3
Sing and Be Happy 1937,Je 19,20:2
Life Begins In College 1937,O 9,16:1
Rebecca of Sunnybrook Farm 1938,Mr 26,12:1
Walking Down Broadway 1938,Ap 1,17:3
Alexander's Ragtime Band 1938,Ag 6,7:2
Dunbar, Dorothy
Amateur Gentleman, The 1926,Ag 17,15:3
Dunbar, Helen
Behold my Wife 1920,O 11,19:3
Thirty Days 1922,D 11,22:1
Cheat, The 1923,Ag 27,14:3
Call of the Canyon, The 1923,D 17,23:1
Three Weeks 1924,Ap 1,19:3
Changing Husbands 1924,Je 23,22:4
This Woman 1924,O 21,21:3
New Lives for Old 1925,F 25,16:7
Siege 1925,Je 16,24:1
Woman Hater, The 1925,Jl 13,20:2
His Majesty Bunker Bean 1925,S 15,12:1
Compromise 1925,O 27,23:3
Rose of the World 1925,N 10,25:3
Fine Manners 1926,Ag 30,10:3
Sweet Rosie O'Grady 1926,D 9,33:1
Stranded in Paris 1926,D 13,27:1
Dunbar, Robert (Producer)
Man Upstairs, The 1959,Ag 11,23:2
Duncan, Angus
High Time 1960,S 17,15:1
Duncan, Anna
Dinner at Eight 1933,Ag 24,18:1
Black Cat, The 1934,My 19,18:4
Duncan, Archie
Brave Don't Cry, The 1952,N 6,37:2
Both Sides of the Law 1954,Ja 12,19:2
Rob Roy 1954,F 4,21:5
Trouble in the Glen 1955,Ap 11,29:2
Saint Joan 1957,Je 27,21:1
John Paul Jones 1959,Je 17,39:1
Sword of Lancelot 1963,O 10,49:2
Duncan, Arletta
Back Street 1932,Ag 29,9:2
Unknown Blonde 1934,Ap 24,27:2
Menace 1934,N 22,27:2
Marriage Forbidden 1938,Jl 16,7:2

Duncan, Bud
Haunted Ship, The 1928,Ja 23,18:3
Duncan, Charles
Little Tough Guys in Society 1938,N 21,14:4
Newsboys' Home 1939,Ja 23,8:2
Duncan, David (Original Author)
Jivaro 1954,F 13,11:5
Duncan, David (Screenwriter)
Sangaree 1953,Je 5,19:1
Black Scorpion, The 1957,O 12,23:2
Thing That Couldn't Die, The 1958,Je 28,13:7
Time Machine, The 1960,Ag 18,19:1
Duncan, Fiona
To Sir, With Love 1967,Je 15,56:1
Duncan, John
Teen Age 1944,Je 19,17:1
Street Corner 1948,D 4,9:4
Duncan, Kenneth
Mars Attacks the World 1938,N 8,26:3
Storm Over Lisbon 1944,S 11,14:1
Chicago Kid, The 1945,F 12,24:3
Davy Crockett, Indian Scout 1950,Mr 17,28:3
Duncan, Mary
Very Confidential 1927,N 29,31:1
Soft Living 1928,F 27,16:2
4 Devils 1928,O 4,26:3
Thru Different Eyes 1929,Ap 15,22:6
Romance of Rio Grande 1929,N 9,22:5
River, The; Femme au Corbeau, La
1930,Ja 5,VIII,5:1
Kismet 1930,O 31,20:1
Boudoir Diplomat, The 1930,D 8,26:1
Men Call it Love 1931,Je 20,20:4
Five and Ten 1931,Jl 11,7:6
Age for Love, The 1931,N 13,27:2
State's Attorney 1932,My 6,15:3
Thirteen Women 1932,O 15,13:1
Phantom of Crestwood, The 1932,O 17,18:3
Morning Glory 1933,Ag 18,18:2
Duncan, Rita
Invisible Wall, The 1947,N 1,11:2
Duncan, Robert
Uncle, The 1966,Jl 19,34:1
Duncan, Ronald (Screenwriter)
Girl on a Motorcycle, The 1968,N 28,66:5
Duncan, Rosetta
Topsy and Eva 1927,Ag 8,10:3
It's a Great Life 1930,Ja 18,21:1
Duncan, Sam (Original Author)
Suez 1938,O 15,21:2
Circumstantial Evidence 1945,Ap 21,18:3
Duncan, Sam (Screenwriter)
White Fang 1936,Jl 18,18:2
White Hunter 1936,N 26,39:2
Duncan, Taylor
Below the Line 1925,S 21,12:4
Tumbleweeds 1925,D 21,27:2
Ranson's Folly 1926,My 31,10:2
Duncan, Ted Captain
Buck Privates 1928,Ja 30,18:1
Duncan, Todd
Syncopation 1942,My 29,13:3
Unchained 1955,Ja 28,15:2
Duncan, Tom
Star Witness, The 1931,Ag 4,19:5
Duncan, Vernon B
Betrayal, The 1948,Je 26,10:5
Duncan, Vivian
Topsy and Eva 1927,Ag 8,10:3
It's a Great Life 1930,Ja 18,21:1
Duncan, William
Three on the Trail 1936,My 5,26:5
Hopalong Rides Again 1938,Ja 22,19:1
Farmer's Daughter, The 1940,F 16,23:4
Texas Rangers Ride Again 1941,Ja 9,27:4
Dundas, David
Prudence and the Pill 1968,My 24,37:1
Dundas, Stella
Illiac Passion, The 1968,Ap 19,40:1
Dundee, Jimmie
Hail the Conquering Hero 1944,Ag 10,14:2
At War With the Army 1951,Ja 25,21:5
Dunham, George
Sand Castle, The 1961,Ag 16,37:2
Dunham, Joanna
Greatest Story Ever Told, The 1965,F 16,40:2
Dunham, Katherine
Star Spangled Rhythm 1942,D 31,20:1
Casbah 1948,My 3,27:4
Mambo 1955,Mr 31,23:3
Dunham, Katherine and her Dancers
Casbah 1948,My 3,27:4
Dunham, Katherine, and her Troupe
Stormy Weather 1943,Jl 22,15:1
Dunham, Phil
Navy Spy 1937,Mr 22,27:3
Our Leading Citizen 1939,Ag 24,17:1
Dunham, Philip
Dangerous Maid, The 1923,D 11,26:2
Dunhill, Steve
Rocky Mountain 1950,N 4,13:2
Dallas 1951,Ja 13,10:4

Dunkin, Claude
Red Planet Mars 1952,Je 16,15:2
Dunkinson, Harry
Last Man on Earth, The 1924,D 13,12:4
Smile, Brother, Smile 1927,Ag 29,21:1
Amateur Daddy 1932,Ap 23,11:5
Design for Living 1933,N 23,24:2
Dunlap, Scott R (Director)
Silent Sanderson 1925,Je 11,14:3
Texas Trail, The 1925,Jl 9,14:2
Dunlap, Scott R (Producer)
Atlantic Flight 1937,N 1,24:5
Federal Bullets 1937,D 27,11:1
Thirteenth Man, The 1938,Ja 1,11:2
Mr Wong, Detective 1938,N 21,14:4
Mutiny in the Big House 1939,D 11,26:2
Road to Happiness 1942,Mr 27,27:4
Short Grass 1951,Ja 13,10:4
Return From the Sea 1954,Jl 10,7:3
Dunleavy, James
Way Out 1967,O 26,54:3
Dunleavy, Terry
Return to Paradise 1953,S 11,24:2
DunLevy, Brian
School for Wives 1925,Ap 1,21:3
Dunmar, David
North of 36 1924,D 8,13:3
DUNN
See Also DUNNE
Dunn, Bobbie
Parade of the West 1930,Mr 3,18:4
Dunn, Caesar (Original Author)
Fourflusher, The 1928,Ja 16,24:1
Dunn, Cathy
Lovers and Lollipops 1956,Ap 19,35:1
Dunn, Eddie
Fleet's In, The 1928,O 1,23:1
True to the Navy 1930,My 24,21:2
Gang Buster, The 1931,Ja 24,15:1
Preview Murder Mystery, The 1936,Mr 21,13:2
Rascals 1938,My 27,12:2
Give Me a Sailor 1938,Ag 11,31:1
Tail Spin 1939,F 11,13:2
Let Freedom Ring 1939,Mr 10,19:2
Great Dictator, The 1940,O 16,29:1
Great Profile, The 1940,O 18,25:1
Mexican Spitfire out West 1940,O 30,29:3
Saint in Palm Springs, The 1941,Ja 31,15:5
Date With the Falcon, A 1941,N 25,33:2
Mexican Spitfire at Sea 1942,Je 26,16:5
Falcon's Brother, The 1942,O 3,9:5
Hello, Frisco, Hello 1943,Mr 25,25:1
Falcon in Danger, The 1943,Jl 23,21:2
Dead Man's Eyes 1944,O 7,11:2
Mother is a Freshman 1949,Mr 12,10:2
I Shot Jesse James 1949,Ap 2,12:2
Dunn, Emma
Old Lady 31 1920,My 24,20:3
Pied Piper Malone 1924,Ja 28,12:1
Side Street 1929,S 9,30:2
Texan, The 1930,My 17,21:2
Manslaughter 1930,Jl 24,26:4
Bad Sister 1931,Mr 30,25:2
Too Young to Marry 1931,My 4,15:3
Prodigal, The 1931,Je 27,20:3
This Modern Age 1931,S 7,19:3
Compromised 1931,N 7,16:5
Bad Company 1931,N 7,16:5
Morals for Women 1931,N 16,23:1
Guilty Generation, The 1931,N 21,20:4
Under Eighteen 1931,D 26,15:5
Man I Killed, The 1932,Ja 20,17:4
Hell's House 1932,F 12,24:5
It's Tough to be Famous 1932,Ap 9,18:1
Cohens and Kellys in Hollywood, The
1932,Ap 22,23:2
Wet Parade, The 1932,Ap 22,23:2
Letty Lynton 1932,Ap 30,19:3
Blessed Event 1932,S 3,16:2
Hard to Handle 1933,F 2,21:5
Grand Slam 1933,F 22,25:2
Private Jones 1933,Mr 25,13:3
Elmer the Great 1933,My 26,24:2
It's Great to be Alive 1933,Jl 8,14:6
Dark Hazard 1934,F 23,23:3
Quitter, The 1934,Mr 14,23:3
Dr Monica 1934,Je 21,28:2
George White's 1935 Scandals 1935,Ap 29,12:3
Glass Key, The 1935,Je 15,20:2
Keeper of the Bees, The 1935,Ag 17,18:5
Little Big Shot 1935,O 7,11:2
Seven Keys to Baldpate 1935,D 14,11:2
Mr Deeds Goes to Town 1936,Ap 17,17:2
Harvester, The 1936,Jl 4,18:2
Second Wife 1936,Ag 29,16:3
When You're in Love 1937,F 19,15:2
Emperor's Candlesticks, The 1937,Jl 9,18:1
Varsity Show 1937,S 2,17:2
Hideaway 1937,S 25,10:2
Madame X 1937,O 25,23:1
Lord Jeff 1938,Jl 1,22:2
Cowboy From Brooklyn 1938,Jl 14,17:1
Three Loves Has Nancy 1938,S 2,21:2

Dunn, Emma— Cont
Young Doctor Kildare 1938,O 28,27:1
Cowboy and the Lady, The 1938,N 25,19:3
Thanks for the Memory 1938,D 8,34:3
Duke of West Point, The 1938,D 16,33:2
Son of Frankenstein 1939,Ja 30,9:2
Calling Dr Kildare 1939,My 12,25:4
Each Dawn I Die 1939,Jl 22,12:2
Secret of Dr Kildare, The 1939,D 8,33:5
Dr Kildare's Strange Case 1940,Ap 12,19:2
You Can't Fool Your Wife 1940,My 24,23:4
One Crowded Night 1940,Ag 27,17:2
Dr Kildare Goes Home 1940,S 19,27:4
Great Dictator, The 1940,O 16,29:1
Mr and Mrs Smith 1941,F 21,16:3
Scattergood Baines 1941,Ap 4,25:2
Penalty, The 1941,Ap 10,29:3
Dr Kildare's Wedding Day 1941,S 18,31:1
Ladies in Retirement 1941,N 7,27:1
Rise and Shine 1941,D 6,14:3
Babes on Broadway 1942,Ja 1,37:1
Talk of the Town, The 1942,Ag 28,22:3
I Married a Witch 1942,N 20,27:2
When Johnny Comes Marching Home
1943,Mr 5,20:4
Bridge of San Luis Rey, The 1944,Mr 4,11:1
It Happened Tomorrow 1944,My 29,18:2
Are These our Parents? 1944,Ag 23,16:2
Hoodlum Saint, The 1946,Je 27,29:1
Life With Father 1947,Ag 16,6:6
Mourning Becomes Electra 1947,N 20,38:2
Woman in White, The 1948,My 8,12:2
Dunn, Frank
Cardinal Richelieu 1935,Ap 19,24:2
Dunn, Geoffrey
Quo Vadis 1951,N 9,22:2
Dunn, George
How to Marry a Millionaire 1953,N 11,37:1
Long, Hot Summer, The 1958,Ap 4,16:1
Operation Petticoat 1959,D 6,38:1
Baby, the Rain Must Fall 1965,Ja 14,44:1
Dunn, H Alan (Original Author)
Young Tom Edison 1940,Mr 15,27:2
Dunn, J Malcolm
Sap From Syracuse, The 1930,Jl 26,16:4
Dunn, J Norton
Margin for Error 1943,Ja 25,10:7
Dunn, James
Bad Girl 1931,Ag 15,18:3
Sob Sister 1931,O 3,20:2
Over the Hill 1931,N 21,20:4
Dance Team 1932,Ja 16,13:1
Society Girl 1932,Je 10,22:3
Handle with Care 1932,D 24,11:4
Sailor's Luck 1933,Mr 17,21:2
Hello Sister! 1933,My 6,11:2
Girl in 419 1933,My 20,11:5
Hold Me Tight 1933,My 22,18:6
Arizona to Broadway 1933,Jl 22,14:3
Take a Chance 1933,N 27,20:3
Jimmy and Sally 1933,D 16,12:3
Hold That Girl 1934,Mr 24,20:3
Stand up and Cheer 1934,Ap 20,17:1
Change of Heart 1934,My 11,24:2
Baby, Take a Bow 1934,Je 30,18:6
Have a Heart 1934,O 20,20:2
365 Nights in Hollywood 1934,N 7,32:1
Bright Eyes 1934,D 21,31:1
George White's 1935 Scandals 1935,Ap 29,12:3
Daring Young Man, The 1935,Jl 18,15:2
Bad Boy 1935,O 28,16:3
Pay-Off, The 1935,N 13,25:3
Don't Get Personal 1936,F 22,12:1
Two-Fisted Gentleman 1936,Ag 24,11:2
Come Closer, Folks 1936,N 23,17:3
Mysterious Crossing 1937,F 2,20:5
We Have our Moments 1937,Ap 30,17:3
Shadows Over Shanghai 1938,D 1,29:2
Government Girl 1944,Ja 7,13:2
Tree Grows in Brooklyn, A 1945,Mr 1,25:5
Caribbean Mystery, The 1945,Ag 20,22:4
That Brennan Girl 1946,D 9,34:3
Killer McCoy 1948,F 12,31:2
Bramble Bush, The 1960,F 25,34:2
Hemingway's Adventures of a Young Man
1962,Jl 26,17:1
Oscar, The 1966,Mr 5,16:1
Dunn, Josephine
Fascinating Youth 1926,My 10,19:1
Love's Greatest Mistake 1927,F 21,14:2
Swim, Girl, Swim 1927,S 5,13:2
Fireman, Save My Child 1927,O 10,24:1
She's a Shiek 1927,N 21,20:1
Get Your Man 1927,D 5,26:2
We Americans 1928,Mr 29,25:3
Singing Fool, The 1928,S 20,33:2
Excess Baggage 1928,S 24,25:1
Man's Man, A 1929,Je 3,27:2
Melody Lane 1929,Jl 16,23:5
Big Time 1929,S 9,30:2
Most Immoral Lady, A 1929,O 21,30:1
Safety in Numbers 1930,My 31,19:4
Madonna of the Streets 1930,N 29,21:4
Two Kinds of Women 1932,Ja 16,13:1

Dunn, Josephine— Cont
One Hour with You 1932,Mr 24,17:5
Big City Blues 1932,S 10,18:5
Dunn, Kathy
13 Frightened Girls 1963,S 12,32:2
Dunn, Louise
Saturday Night and Sunday Morning
1961,Ap 4,44:2
Dunn, Maxwell (Miscellaneous)
Rugged O'Riordans, The 1950,Ja 6,25:2
Dunn, Michael
Junior Miss 1945,Je 18,15:4
Shock 1946,Mr 9,10:2
Doll Face 1946,Mr 28,35:3
Mother Wore Tights 1947,Ag 21,33:2
Ship of Fools 1965,Jl 29,18:1
You're a Big Boy Now 1967,Mr 21,35:3
No Way to Treat a Lady 1968,Mr 21,56:1
Madigan 1968,Mr 30,22:2
Boom! 1968,My 27,56:1
Dunn, Nell (Miscellaneous)
Up the Junction 1968,Mr 14,51:1
Dunn, Nell (Original Author)
Poor Cow 1968,F 1,28:2
Dunn, Nell (Screenwriter)
Poor Cow 1968,F 1,28:2
Dunn, Patricia
Kismet 1955,D 9,32:2
Dunn, Ralph
Tenth Avenue Kid 1938,S 2,21:3
Tail Spin 1939,F 11,13:2
Return of the Cisco Kid, The 1939,Ap 29,13:2
Lady From Cheyenne, The 1941,Ap 18,18:2
Moontide 1942,Ap 30,14:1
Laura 1944,O 12,24:1
Circumstantial Evidence 1945,Ap 21,18:3
Babe Ruth Story, The 1948,Jl 29,17:2
Singing Guns 1950,Je 5,19:3
Crowded Paradise 1956,Je 22,15:1
Pajama Game, The 1957,Ag 30,12:2
Black Like Me 1964,My 21,42:1
Dunn, Richard
Angels One Five 1954,Ap 30,28:2
Dunn, Robert A Rev
Lost Boundaries 1949,Jl 1,14:4
Whistle at Eaton Falls, The 1951,O 11,49:2
Walk East on Beacon 1952,My 29,17:2
Dunn, Violet
Doctors' Wives 1931,Ap 25,23:4
Black Camel, The 1931,Jl 4,11:5
Dunn, William
Redeeming Sin, The 1925,Ja 20,18:2
Devil's Island 1926,Ag 2,21:2
Nagana 1933,F 16,23:2
Dunn, Winifred (Original Author)
Sparrows 1926,S 20,21:3
DUNNE
See Also DUNN
Dunne, Burt (Producer)
Night of the Grizzly, The 1966,Je 23,29:1
Dunne, Eithne
No Resting Place 1952,My 5,18:5
Eight O'Clock Walk 1955,Ap 30,10:6
Dementia 13 1963,O 24,37:1
Dunne, Elizabeth
Stage Door 1937,O 8,27:2
Naughty but Nice 1939,Je 23,23:2
Cat People 1942,D 7,22:2
Double Life, A 1948,F 20,19:1
Dunne, Finley Peter (Miscellaneous)
Magnificent Obsession 1935,D 31,11:2
Dunne, Finley Peter Jr (Original Author)
We Went to College 1936,Jl 27,20:2
Breezing Home 1937,Mr 20,23:5
Dunne, Irene
Leathernecking 1930,S 13,9:3
Cimarron 1931,Ja 27,20:5
Bachelor Apartment 1931,My 16,13:3
Great Lover, The 1931,Ag 24,13:4
Consolation Marriage 1931,O 30,26:4
Symphony of Six Million 1932,Ap 15,23:1
Back Street 1932,Ag 29,9:2
Thirteen Women 1932,O 15,13:1
No Other Woman 1933,Ja 30,9:4 (In Addenda)
Secret of Madame Blanche, The 1933,F 4,11:3
Silver Cord, The 1933,My 5,18:1
Ann Vickers 1933,S 29,24:1
If I Were Free 1934,Ja 5,25:2
This Man is Mine 1934,Ap 13,25:1
Stingaree 1934,My 18,27:1
Age of Innocence, The 1934,O 19,27:1
Sweet Adeline 1935,Ja 7,13:2
Roberta 1935,Mr 8,25:2
Magnificent Obsession 1935,D 31,11:2
Show Boat 1936,My 15,29:4
Theodora Goes Wild 1936,N 13,27:4
High, Wide and Handsome 1937,Jl 22,15:1
Awful Truth, The 1937,N 5,19:3
Joy of Living 1938,My 6,27:1
Love Affair 1939,Mr 17,25:2
Invitation to Happiness 1939,Je 8,31:2
When Tomorrow Comes 1939,Ag 17,16:2
My Favorite Wife 1940,My 31,15:2
Penny Serenade 1941,My 23,25:2

Unfinished Business 1941,S 2,20:2
Lady in a Jam 1942,S 11,25:2
Guy Named Joe, A 1943,D 24,17:2
Guy Named Joe, A 1944,Ja 9,II,3:1
White Cliffs of Dover, The 1944,My 12,15:2
Together Again 1944,N 24,19:2
Over 21 1945,Ag 17,20:2
Anna and the King of Siam 1946,Je 21,20:2
Life With Father 1947,Ag 16,6:6
I Remember Mama 1948,Mr 12,29:2
Never a Dull Moment 1950,N 22,20:2
Mudlark, The 1950,D 25,25:1
It Grows on Trees 1952,N 29,11:2
Dunne, John
Pacific Adventure 1947,N 26,18:2
Dunne, Philip (Director)
Prince of Players 1955,Ja 12,24:2
View From Pompey's Head, The 1955,N 5,22:5
Hilda Crane 1956,My 3,35:2
Three Brave Men 1957,Mr 16,13:2
Ten North Frederick 1958,My 23,29:2
In Love and War 1958,N 1,14:2
Blue Denim 1959,Jl 31,21:1
Wild in the Country 1961,Je 10,12:2
Lisa 1962,My 25,28:1
Blindfold 1966,My 26,55:2
Dunne, Philip (Original Author)
Breezing Home 1937,Mr 20,23:5
Demetrius and the Gladiators 1954,Je 19,9:1
Dunne, Philip (Producer)
Way of a Gaucho 1952,N 5,36:2
Prince of Players 1955,Ja 12,24:2
View From Pompey's Head, The 1955,N 5,22:5
Dunne, Philip (Screenwriter)
Student Tour 1934,O 31,17:3
Melody Lingers on, The 1935,N 7,27:1
Last of the Mohicans, The 1936,S 3,17:3
Lancer Spy 1937,N 4,29:1
Suez 1938,O 15,21:2
Stanley and Livingstone 1939,Ag 5,18:2
Rains Came, The 1939,S 9,11:2
Swanee River 1939,D 30,9:2
Johnny Apollo 1940,Ap 13,21:2
How Green Was my Valley 1941,O 29,27:2
Son of Fury 1942,Ja 30,23:2
Late George Apley, The 1947,Mr 21,29:2
Ghost and Mrs Muir, The 1947,Je 27,17:2
Forever Amber 1947,O 23,31:2
Escape 1948,Ag 16,12:2
Luck of the Irish, The 1948,S 16,34:1
Pinky 1949,S 30,28:2
David and Bathsheba 1951,Ag 15,23:2
Anne of the Indies 1951,O 25,36:3
Lydia Bailey 1952,My 31,12:5
Way of a Gaucho 1952,N 5,36:2
Robe, The 1953,S 17,32:6
Egyptian, The 1954,Ag 25,23:1
View From Pompey's Head, The 1955,N 5,22:5
Hilda Crane 1956,My 3,35:2
Three Brave Men 1957,Mr 16,13:2
Ten North Frederick 1958,My 23,29:2
Blue Denim 1959,Jl 31,21:1
Agony and the Ecstacy, The 1965,O 9,5:6
Blindfold 1966,My 26,55:2
Dunne, Stephen
Dark Past, The 1948,D 23,25:2
Lady Possessed 1952,F 15,17:2
Above and Beyond 1953,Ja 31,10:6
Dunne, Steve
Ten Thousand Bedrooms 1957,Ap 4,37:1
I Married a Woman 1958,N 5,42:5
Home Before Dark 1958,N 7,23:1
Explosive Generation, The 1962,F 15,24:2
Dunne, Tom
Ireland's Border Line 1939,O 13,27:3
Dunning, Alfred (Original Author)
Dance Little Lady 1955,D 26,23:3
Dunning, Decla (Original Author)
Stranger, The 1946,Jl 11,18:2
Dunning, Decla (Screenwriter)
Hairy Ape, The 1944,Jl 3,8:3
Tars and Spars 1946,F 15,29:2
I, Jane Doe 1948,Jl 5,8:4
Dunning, Don
Union Station 1950,O 5,38:3
Submarine Command 1952,Ja 19,13:2
Dunning, George (Director)
Yellow Submarine 1968,N 14,56:1
Dunning, Philip (Original Author)
Broadway 1929,My 28,36:2
Lilly Turner 1933,Je 15,21:2
Page Miss Glory 1935,Ag 29,25:2
Remember the Day 1941,D 26,21:2
Broadway 1942,Je 5,23:2
Dunning, Ruth
Woman in the Hall, The 1949,Ja 24,16:2
Intimate Relations 1954,F 22,15:4
Dunnock, Mildred
Corn is Green, The 1945,Mr 30,18:2
Kiss of Death 1947,Ag 28,28:2
Death of a Salesman 1951,D 21,21:3
I Want You 1951,D 24,9:1
Viva Zapata 1952,F 8,19:2

Dunnock, Mildred— Cont
Girl in White, The 1952,My 31,12:5
Jazz Singer, The 1953,Ja 14,27:3
Bad for Each Other 1953,D 24,9:3
Hansel and Gretel 1954,O 11,33:1
Trouble With Harry, The 1955,O 18,46:2
Love Me Tender 1956,N 16,23:1
Baby Doll 1956,D 19,40:2
Peyton Place 1957,D 13,35:1
Nun's Story, The 1959,Je 19,30:1
Story of Page One, The 1960,Ja 14,28:1
Butterfield 8 1960,N 17,46:1
Something Wild 1961,D 24,30:6
Sweet Bird of Youth 1962,Mr 29,28:2
Behold a Pale Horse 1964,Ag 14,16:1
Youngblood Hawke 1964,N 6,30:1
7 Women 1966,My 5,59:1
Dunot, Jean
Prize, The 1952,Ap 30,33:2
Four Bags Full 1957,S 5,32:1
Sins of Youth 1960,D 24,8:2
Dunsany, Lord (Original Author)
It Happened Tomorrow 1944,My 29,18:2
Dunskus, Erich
Gluck auf den Lande; Rural Happiness
1940,F 10,19:3
Girls Behind Bars 1950,My 10,41:2
Dunsmuir, John
Enemies of the Law 1931,Jl 13,13:5
Dunstan, Cliff
Room Service 1938,S 22,27:1
Dunstead, Shirley
Wild Boys of the Road 1933,S 22,14:1
Dunton, John
America 1924,F 22,20:1
Dunton, Mary (Miscellaneous)
We Lived Through Buchenwald 1947,Jl 24,27:3
Dunton, Ray
George Raft Story, The 1962,Mr 22,40:1
Duntz, G
Day the War Ended, The 1961,Ja 30,17:2
Duperey, Anny
Two or Three Things I Know About Her
1968,S 26,60:1
Duperoux, Annie
Lola 1962,O 15,32:2
Dupont, E A (Director)
Variety 1926,Je 28,15:5
Love Me and the World Is Mine 1928,F 6,12:3
Affairs of Hannerl 1928,F 12,VIII,7:2 (In
Addenda)
Moulin Rouge 1929,Ap 30,33:2
Piccadilly 1929,Jl 15,25:1
Atlantic 1930,O 6,21:1
Two Worlds 1930,N 22,21:3
Love Storm 1931,O 19,28:1
Trapeze 1932,My 3,25:2
Forgotten Faces 1936,Jl 4,18:2
Son Comes Home, A 1936,S 5,7:1
On Such a Night 1937,S 17,29:2
Hell's Kitchen 1939,Jl 3,10:5
Screen, The 1951,Ap 23,21:2
Dupont, E A (Original Author)
Salto Mortale 1931,O 25,VIII,6:1
Dupont, E A (Producer)
Atlantic 1930,Ja 26,VIII,6:2
Dupont, E A (Screenwriter)
Screen, The 1951,Ap 23,21:2
Dupont, Gretl
Days of Glory 1944,Je 17,10:2
Street Corner 1948,D 4,9:4
Dupont, Jacques (Director)
Congolaise 1950,My 22,17:4
Heartbreak Ridge 1955,My 5,41:2
Dupont, Jean
32 Rue de Montmartre 1944,S 28,26:3
Duport, Catherine
Masculine Feminine 1966,S 19,57:1
Depart, Le 1967,S 23,20:3
Dupray, Gaston
Amour Maitre des Choses, L' 1931,Mr 30,25:2
Story of a Cheat, The 1938,S 27,25:2
Dupre, Vanda
Girl in the Kremlin, The 1957,My 22,29:2
Dupree, Minnie
Night Club 1929,Ag 12,22:2
Young in Heart, The 1938,N 4,27:2
Anne of Windy Poplars 1940,Ag 23,13:3
Dupree, Roland
Miss Annie Rooney 1942,Je 8,11:1
Maisie Goes to Reno 1944,S 29,18:1
Dupreyon, Rene
Love Has Many Faces 1965,F 25,24:1
Duprez, Fred
Dance Band 1936,Ja 4,19:2
Head Over Heels in Love 1937,F 13,9:1
Kathleen 1938,Ja 24,17:1
Pearls of the Crown, The 1938,Ap 12,26:2
Duprez, Hatton
Dulcimer Street 1948,N 8,24:2
Duprez, John
Four Feathers 1939,Ag 4,11:1

Duprez, June
Crimson Circle, The 1936,D 28,12:3
U-Boat 29 1939,O 6,31:3
Lion Has Wings, The 1940,Ja 22,11:2
Thief of Bagdad, The 1940,D 6,28:2
Little Tokyo, USA 1942,Ag 7,13:2
None but the Lonely Heart 1944,N 18,16:6
None but the Lonely Heart 1944,D 3,II,1:8
Brighton Strangler, The 1945,My 19,15:2
And Then There Were None 1945,N 1,20:2
That Brennan Girl 1946,D 9,34:3
Calcutta 1947,Ap 24,30:2
1 ■ 1 1961,N 8,41:1

Dupuis, Claudine
Jenny Lamour 1948,Mr 6,17:2
Francois Villon 1950,Jl 3,9:2
Seven Deadly Sins, The (Gluttony); Gluttony (The Seven Deadly Sins) 1953,My 12,31:3

Dupuis, Paul
Johnny Frenchman 1946,O 21,27:3
Bad Sister 1948,Je 11,27:3
Sleeping Car to Trieste 1949,Ap 18,18:6
Against the Wind 1949,Je 27,18:3
Passport to Pimlico 1949,O 27,35:2
Madness of the Heart 1950,O 12,43:2
Reluctant Widow, The 1951,S 8,8:6

Dupuy, Rene
Fire Within, The 1964,F 18,27:1

Dupuy-Mazuel, Henri (Original Author)
Miracle of the Wolves, The 1925,F 24,17:3
Chess Player, The 1930,My 19,21:1
Devil Is an Empress, The 1939,D 4,18:4

Dupuy-Mazuel, Henri (Screenwriter)
Queen and the Cardinal, The 1944,Je 1,17:3

Dur, Poldy
Margin for Error 1943,Ja 25,10:7
They Came to Blow up America 1943,My 15,13:2
Hitler Gang, The 1944,My 8,15:2

Duran, Elsie Mrs
Tundra 1936,D 3,31:2

Duran, Larry
One Eyed Jacks 1961,Mr 31,21:1

Duran, Laurence
Hawaii Calls 1938,Ap 29,17:2

Duran, Michel (Miscellaneous)
Her First Affair; (Children of Paradise) 1947,F 20,32:3
Shop-Girls of Paris; Au Bonheur de Dames 1947,Je 23,14:4

Duran, Michel (Original Author)
He Stayed for Breakfast 1940,Ag 31,16:2
Male Hunt; Chasse a l'Homme, La 1965,Ap 20,42:1

Duran, Michel (Screenwriter)
Heartbeat 1946,My 11,22:4
Fric-Frac 1948,My 29,8:6

Duran, Nellie
South of Pago-Pago 1940,Ag 2,12:2

Duran, Rafael
Nail, The 1949,Jl 1,14:6
Loyola, The Soldier Saint 1952,Ap 25,19:2

Duran, Ruben
Hawaii Calls 1938,Ap 29,17:2

Duran, Tommy
Seven Little Foys, The 1955,Je 30,18:2

Durand, David
Innocents of Paris 1929,Ap 27,16:5
Song of Love, The 1929,N 14,24:3
Ladies Love Brutes 1930,My 16,20:4
Bad Sister 1931,Mr 30,25:2
Rich Man's Folly 1931,N 27,29:3
Silver Dollar 1932,D 23,20:1
Jennie Gerhardt 1933,Je 9,20:2
Life of Jimmy Dolan, The 1933,Je 14,22:3
Cradle Song 1933,N 20,18:2
Viva Villa! 1934,Ap 11,25:2
As the Earth Turns 1934,Ap 12,27:2
Wednesday's Child 1934,D 15,9:3
Band Plays on, The 1934,D 22,21:2
Little Men 1935,F 18,19:3
Streets of New York 1939,My 1,21:1
Golden Gloves 1940,Ag 21,23:6
Naval Academy 1941,Je 5,27:3

Durand, Edward
King on Main Street, The 1925,O 26,25:2

Durant
Stand up and Cheer 1934,Ap 20,17:1

Durant, Eddie Rhumba Orchestra
Time Out for Rhythm 1941,Jl 10,16:3

Durant, Edouard
Lone Wolf, The 1924,My 7,19:4

Durant, Harry (Original Author)
Heart Raider, The 1923,Je 6,24:5

Durant, Henry
What Price Decency? 1933,Mr 2,20:6

Durant, Jack
She Learned About Sailors 1934,Jl 30,9:4
365 Nights in Hollywood 1934,N 7,32:1
Singing Kid, The 1936,Ap 4,11:1
Journey Into Fear 1943,Mr 19,15:3

Durant, Marjorie
Friendly Persuasion 1956,N 2,30:1
Summer Love 1958,Je 26,23:4

Durant, Tim
Red Badge of Courage, The 1951,O 19,22:2

Durant, V
What Price Decency? 1933,Mr 2,20:6

Durante, Checco
Woman Trouble 1949,My 26,34:2
Variety Lights; Luci del Varieta 1965,My 7,34:1

Durante, Jimmy
Roadhouse Nights 1930,F 22,13:1
Roadhouse Nights 1930,Mr 2,IX,5:1
New Adventures of Get-Rich-Quick Wallingford 1931,O 10,20:4
Cuban Love Song, The 1931,D 5,21:2
Passionate Plumber, The 1932,Mr 12,19:5
Wet Parade, The 1932,Ap 22,23:2
Speak Easily 1932,Ag 19,20:6
Blondie of the Follies 1932,S 2,19:2
Phantom President, The 1932,O 1,10:4
What! No Beer? 1933,F 11,11:3
Hell Below 1933,Ap 26,13:2
Meet the Baron 1933,O 28,20:3
Palooka 1934,F 28,23:2
George White's Scandals 1934,Mr 16,24:2
Hollywood Party 1934,My 26,12:2
Strictly Dynamite 1934,Jl 4,18:2
Student Tour 1934,O 31,17:3
Carnival 1935,F 16,9:1
Sally, Irene and Mary 1938,F 26,9:2
Start Cheering 1938,Mr 17,17:3
Little Miss Broadway 1938,Jl 23,10:4
Forbidden Music 1938,D 27,13:2
Melody Ranch 1940,D 26,23:3
You're in the Army Now 1941,D 26,21:4
Man Who Came to Dinner, The 1942,Ja 2,25:2
Two Girls and a Sailor 1944,Je 15,16:1
Music for Millions 1944,D 22,12:4
Two Sisters From Boston 1946,Je 7,16:2
It Happened in Brooklyn 1947,Mr 14,28:5
This Time for Keeps 1947,D 5,33:4
On an Island With You 1948,Jl 30,13:2
Great Rupert, The 1950,Ap 14,27:2
Milkman, The 1951,Ja 1,13:6
Pepe 1960,D 22,18:1
Jumbo 1962,D 7,49:1
It's a Mad, Mad, Mad, Mad World 1963,N 19,47:1

Durante, Jimmy (Composer)
Strictly Dynamite 1934,Jl 4,18:2

Duranti, Doris
Sotto la Croce del Sud; Under the Southern Cross 1939,Ap 10,13:4
King's Jester, The 1947,Je 26,19:3
Cavalleria Rusticana 1947,D 20,21:2
Carmela 1949,My 14,9:2
Moment of Truth, The 1954,Ap 27,36:2

Durar, Larry
Good Times 1967,Ag 3,26:4

Duras, Marguerite (Original Author)
Hiroshima, Mon Amour 1960,My 17,43:1
Moderato Cantabile 1964,Ja 7,24:1
10:30 PM Summer 1966,O 20,52:1
Sailor From Gibraltar, The 1967,Ap 25,38:2

Duras, Marguerite (Screenwriter)
Hiroshima, Mon Amour 1960,My 17,43:1
Long Absence, The 1962,N 16,23:2
Moderato Cantabile 1964,Ja 7,24:1
10:30 PM Summer 1966,O 20,52:1

Durasov, L
Man of Music 1953,My 11,25:2

Durat, M (Screenwriter)
Deadlier Than the Male 1957,O 9,41:1

Durbin, Deanna
Three Smart Girls 1937,Ja 25,22:2
100 Men and a Girl 1937,S 18,15:2
Mad About Music 1938,Mr 12,13:2
That Certain Age 1938,N 5,15:2
Three Smart Girls Grow Up 1939,Mr 18,9:2
First Love 1939,N 9,27:3
It's a Date 1940,Mr 23,16:2
Spring Parade 1940,O 4,29:2
Nice Girl 1941,Mr 27,29:6
It Started With Eve 1941,O 3,27:1
Amazing Mrs Holliday, The 1943,F 22,20:2
Hers to Hold 1943,Jl 22,15:1
His Butler's Sister 1943,D 30,13:2
Christmas Holiday 1944,Je 29,16:1
Can't Help Singing 1944,D 26,22:4
Lady on a Train 1945,S 15,21:2
Because of Him 1946,Ja 25,26:6
I'll Be Yours 1947,F 22,16:2
Something in the Wind 1947,Ag 29,14:3
Up in Central Park 1948,My 27,29:3
For the Love of Mary 1948,S 23,37:2

Durbridge, Francis (Original Author)
Teckman Mystery, The 1955,Ag 22,18:2

Durbridge, Francis (Screenwriter)
Teckman Mystery, The 1955,Ag 22,18:2
Circle, The 1959,Ap 16,29:2

Durden-Smith, Richard
Doctor Faustus 1968,F 7,38:1

Durdey, Robert
Big Noise, The 1944,S 23,16:1

Duren, Ernest van
Manege 1928,Mr 11,VIII,7:6 (In Addenda)

Durgel, Rosa Elena
Exterminating Angel, The 1967,Ag 22,33:1

Durgeon, Augusta
Ramparts We Watch, The 1940,S 20,27:1

Durham, Lowell
Magnificent Obsession 1935,D 31,11:2

Durieux, Tilla
Last Bridge, The 1957,Ag 21,22:2

Duringer, Annemarie
Count Five and Die 1958,My 15,25:1
Devil Strikes at Night, The 1959,Ja 30,31:3

Durkee, William (Original Author)
Unholy Wife, The 1958,Mr 7,17:1

Durkin, Grace
Man Who Played God, The 1932,F 11,16:1
Cleopatra 1934,Ag 17,12:1
Thirteenth Man, The 1938,Ja 1,11:2

Durkin, James
Shadow of the Law 1930,Je 7,10:4
Recaptured Love 1930,Ag 9,16:5
Sante Fe Trail, The 1930,O 18,23:2
Derelict 1930,N 22,21:3
Tom Sawyer 1930,D 20,20:6
Conquering Horde, The 1931,Mr 30,25:2
Gun Smoke 1931,Ap 24,27:1
Vice Squad, The 1931,Je 6,15:5
Huckleberry Finn 1931,Ag 8,16:3
Hell's House 1932,F 12,24:5
Nice Women 1932,F 20,11:2
Big Cage, The 1933,My 9,20:5
Secret of the Blue Room, The 1933,S 13,22:1
Heat Lightning 1934,Mr 8,23:2
Little Men 1935,F 18,19:3

Durkin, Trent
Big Hearted Herbert 1934,N 14,23:2

Durlam, Arthur G (Screenwriter)
Swamp Woman 1941,D 27,15:2

Durland, Edward
Potash and Perlmutter 1923,S 24,5:4

Durling, E V (Miscellaneous)
Reported Missing 1922,Ap 24,18:3

Durning, Bernard J (Director)
Fast Mail, The 1922,Jl 10,9:5
Eleventh Hour, The 1923,Ag 28,12:1

Durning, Charles
Harvey Middleman, Fireman 1965,Jl 13,39:1

d'Uro, Mizzo
Dopo una Notte d'Amore; After a Night of Love 1935,O 29,16:5

Durocher, Leo
Safe at Home 1941,N 26,31:2
Main Street to Broadway 1953,O 14,34:1

Durousseau, Antoine
Porgy and Bess 1959,Je 25,20:3

Durrance, Dick (Cinematographer)
Ski Champs 1951,D 15,11:2

Durrance, Dick (Director)
Ski Champs 1951,D 15,11:2

Durrant, Theo (Original Author)
Macabre 1958,Jl 24,18:1

Durrell, Lawrence (Original Author)
Judith 1966,Ja 21,22:1

Durrenmatt, Friedrich (Original Author)
Visit, The 1964,O 22,44:1

Durst, Edward L
Days of Glory 1944,Je 17,10:2

Duryea, Dan
Little Foxes, The 1941,Ag 22,19:2
Ball of Fire 1942,Ja 16,25:2
Pride of the Yankees, The 1942,Jl 16,23:1
Sahara 1943,N 12,25:2
Man From Frisco 1944,Je 16,14:7
Mrs Parkington 1944,O 13,16:1
None but the Lonely Heart 1944,N 18,16:6
Main Street After Dark 1945,Ja 13,15:4
Great Flamario, The 1945,Ja 15,15:5
Woman in the Window, The 1945,Ja 26,16:4
Ministry of Fear 1945,F 8,15:2
Valley of Decision, The 1945,My 4,23:2
Along Came Jones 1945,Jl 19,8:7
Lady on a Train 1945,S 15,21:2
Scarlet Street 1946,F 15,29:2
Black Angel 1946,S 26,32:4
White Tie and Tails 1946,N 8,28:2
Black Bart 1948,Mr 4,30:4
Another Part of the Forest 1948,My 19,30:2
River Lady 1948,My 21,19:5
Larceny 1948,S 4,8:6
Criss Cross 1949,Mr 12,10:2
Manhandled 1949,My 26,34:2
Too Late for Tears 1949,Ag 15,12:3
Johnny Stool Pigeon 1949,S 23,28:3
One Way Street 1950,My 12,33:3
Winchester 73 1950,Je 8,38:2
Underworld Story, The 1950,Jl 27,29:4
Al Jennings of Oklahoma 1951,My 18,34:6
Thunder Bay 1953,My 21,39:2

Duryea, Dan— Cont
Rails Into Laramie 1954,My 13,34:2
World for Ransom 1954,Je 5,11:2
Silver Lode 1954,Jl 24,6:6
ThIs is my Love 1954,D 25,7:3
Foxfire 1955,Jl 14,19:1
Storm Fear 1955,D 17,19:2
Battle Hymn 1957,F 16,14:1
Night Passage 1957,Jl 25,28:1
Slaughter on Tenth Avenue 1957,N 6,43:1
Kathy O' 1958,S 25,29:2
Platinum High School 1960,My 26,37:3
6 Black Horses 1962,Ap 25,30:1
He Rides Tall 1957,N 27,28:1
Taggart 1964,D 25,24:4
Flight of the Phoenix, The 1966,F 1,26:1
Hills Run Red, The 1967,N 11,26:3

Duryea, George
Godless Girl, The 1929,Ap 1,22:1
Honky Tonk 1929,Je 5,32:3
Thunder 1929,Jl 8,17:3
Beau Bandit 1930,Je 14,9:4
Tol'able David 1930,N 17,29:1

Duse, Carlo
Coraggio Della Gioventu Mussoliniana, Il 1936,F 5,14:2
Grande Luce, La; Great Light, The 1940,Mr 15,27:4
Before Him all Rome Trembled 1947,F 22,16:2

Duse, Eleanora
Madre 1927,S 21,26:2

Duse, Margadonna (Screenwriter)
Secret Conclave, The 1953,My 16,10:1

Duse, Vittorio
Tragic Hunt 1948,O 22,30:2
Outcry 1949,Mr 14,15:5
Island Sinner, The 1960,S 5,11:2

DuSoe, Robert C (Original Author)
Twenty-Mule Team 1940,My 10,26:6

d'Usseau, Arnaud (Original Author)
Tomorrow the World 1944,D 22,12:4

d'Usseau, Arnaud (Screenwriter)
One Crowded Night 1940,Ag 27,17:2
Lady Scarface 1941,Ag 4,16:6
Man Who Wouldn't Die, The 1942,Ap 28,25:5
Who Is Hope Schuyler 1942,My 22,27:1
Just off Broadway 1942,Ag 29,18:4

d'Usseau, Leon (Original Author)
Wine, Women and Song 1934,Mr 21,24:3

d'Usseau, Leon (Screenwriter)
Lost City, The 1935,F 21,23:3

Dust, Red
Stars Are Singing, The 1953,Mr 12,24:2

Duszynski, Jerzy
Treasure, The 1951,Mr 29,24:4

Dutertre, Armand
Garden of Allah, The 1927,S 3,13:5

Dutilho, Jacques
Zazie 1961,N 21,45:5

Dutt, Dilip
Guide, The 1965,F 10,44:2

Dutt, Sunil
Handful of Grain, A 1959,Jl 4,9:4

Dutt, Uptal
Shakespeare Wallah 1966,Mr 23,40:2

Duvail, Robert
Countdown 1968,My 2,57:3

Duval, Emma
Que Lindo es Michoacan 1944,Ap 22,8:7

Duval, Franca
Tosca 1958,O 24,40:3

Duval, Jacqueline
Rhapsody 1954,Mr 12,17:1

Duval, Jacques-Henri
Voyage Surprise 1948,F 14,17:3
Francois Villon 1950,Jl 3,9:2

Duval, Joan
Kings Row 1942,F 3,23:2

Duval, John (Director)
Diablo Del Mar, El 1936,Ap 1,29:2

Duval, Juan
Neptune's Daughter 1949,Je 10,32:2

Duval, Leonie
Schuechterne Felix, Der 1935,S 7,19:5
Wackere Schustermeister, Der 1936,Jl 7,22:4

Duval, Nikki
Quebec 1951,Mr 16,34:2

Duval, Paulette
Nero 1922,My 26,17:2
Monsieur Beaucaire 1924,Ag 12,12:1 (In Addenda)
He Who Gets Slapped 1924,N 10,20:1
Lady, The 1925,Ja 27,11:2
Cheaper to Marry 1925,F 2,14:1
Man and Maid 1925,Ap 7,17:3
Time, the Comedian 1925,D 14,18:2
Skyrocket, The 1926,Ja 26,25:2
Beverly of Graustark 1926,Ap 19,24:3
Beware of Widows 1927,My 24,23:4
Twelve Miles Out 1927,Jl 26,17:1
Alias the Lone Wolf 1927,S 20,32:2
Breakfast at Sunrise 1927,N 14,26:1
Divine Woman, The 1928,Ja 16,24:1

Duval, Veronique
Adolescents, The (Marie-France and Veronica); Marie-France and Veronica (The Adolescents) 1967,Ap 14,33:1

Duvall, Robert
To Kill a Mockingbird 1963,F 15,10:2
Captain Newman, MD 1964,F 21,36:1
Chase, The 1966,F 19,24:1
Bullitt 1968,O 18,41:2

Duvalleix, Christian
King, The 1941,O 23,29:3
Prize, The 1952,Ap 30,33:2
Crazy in the Noodle 1957,D 15,45:4 (Incorrect in this edition; use 1957,D 17,45:4 elsewhere)
Paris When it Sizzles 1964,Ap 9,25:3

Duvalles
Paris-Mediterranee 1932,Mr 27,VIII,6:2
On Demande un Compaznon 1933,Je 5,18:5
Burning Court, The 1963,Ag 1,17:2

Duvalles and Roberts, Helene
King, The 1941,O 23,29:3

Duveen, Lorna
Knockout, The 1925,O 27,23:3
Unguarded Hour, The 1926,Ja 5,25:2 (In Addenda)

Duverger, Pierre
Gervaise 1957,N 12,46:1

Duvernois, Henri (Miscellaneous)
Song of the Street 1939,S 5,21:2

Duvernoy, Georges (Screenwriter)
Itto 1936,Ja 29,15:5

Duvivier, Albert (Director)
Female, The 1960,Ap 28,29:1

Duvivier, Julien (Composer)
Man in the Raincoat, The 1958,Jl 15,21:2

Duvivier, Julien (Director)
David Golder 1932,O 20,24:2
Sous la Lune du Maroc 1933,Ja 23,9:2
Maria Chapdelaine 1935,S 25,18:2
Golem, The 1937,Mr 22,27:2
Carnet de Bal, Un 1938,Mr 26,12:1
They Were Five 1938,Je 1,19:5
Great Waltz, The 1938,N 25,19:1
Escape From Yesterday 1939,My 3,27:2
Charrette Fantome, La 1940,My 28,29:2
Man of the Hour, The 1940,N 21,43:2
Pepe le Moko 1941,Mr 4,20:2
Lydia 1941,S 19,27:1
Tales of Manhattan 1942,S 25,25:1
Heart of a Nation, The 1943,Ap 8,27:2
Flesh and Fantasy 1943,N 18,29:1
Impostor, The 1944,Mr 27,17:2
Anna Karenina 1948,Ap 28,32:2
Sinners, The 1950,N 11,11:2
Under the Paris Sky 1952,My 6,35:1
Captain Black Jack 1952,O 22,31:3
Holiday for Henrietta 1955,Ja 25,21:1
Pot Bouille 1958,O 28,39:1
Marianne of my Youth; (Marianne de ma Jeunesse) 1959,Ja 20,43:1
Marie Octobre 1960,Ag 16,25:2
Burning Court, The 1963,Ag 1,17:2
Devil and the 10 Commandments, The (Episode 7) 1963,O 15,44:1
Devil and the 10 Commandments, The (Episode 4) 1963,O 15,44:1
Devil and the 10 Commandments, The (Episode 6) 1963,O 15,44:1
Devil and the 10 Commandments, The (Episode 5) 1963,O 15,44:1
Devil and the 10 Commandments, The (Episode 3) 1963,O 15,44:1
Devil and the 10 Commandments, The (Episode 2) 1963,O 15,44:1
Devil and the 10 Commandments, The (Episode 1) 1963,O 15,44:1

Duvivier, Julien (Miscellaneous)
Man in the Raincoat, The 1958,Jl 15,21:2

Duvivier, Julien (Original Author)
They Were Five 1938,Je 1,19:5
Lydia 1941,S 19,27:1
Deadlier Than the Male 1957,O 9,41:1
Paris When it Sizzles 1964,Ap 9,25:3

Duvivier, Julien (Producer)
Flesh and Fantasy 1943,N 18,29:1
Impostor, The 1944,Mr 27,17:2
Captain Black Jack 1952,O 22,31:3

Duvivier, Julien (Screenwriter)
Paquebot Tenacity 1934,Ag 12,IX,2:1
Carnet de Bal, Un 1938,Mr 26,12:1
End of a Day, The 1939,S 12,28:4
Charrette Fantome, La 1940,My 28,29:2
Man of the Hour, The 1940,N 21,43:2
Heart of a Nation, The 1943,Ap 8,27:2
Impostor, The 1944,Mr 27,17:2
Panic 1947,N 27,50:2
Anna Karenina 1948,Ap 28,32:2
Sinners, The 1950,N 11,11:2
Under the Paris Sky 1952,My 6,35:1
Captain Black Jack 1952,O 22,31:3
Little World of Don Camillo, The 1953,Ja 14,27:1
Holiday for Henrietta 1955,Ja 25,21:1

Duvivier, Julien (Screenwriter)— Cont
Man in the Raincoat, The 1958,Jl 15,21:2
Marianne of my Youth; (Marianne de ma Jeunesse) 1959,Ja 20,43:1
Female, The 1960,Ap 28,29:1
Marie Octobre 1960,Ag 16,25:2
Burning Court, The 1963,Ag 1,17:2

Duvivier, M (Director)
End of a Day, The 1939,S 12,28:4
Little World of Don Camillo, The 1953,Ja 14,27:1
Deadlier Than the Male 1957,O 9,41:1

Duvivier, M (Screenwriter)
Escape From Yesterday 1939,My 3,27:2
Deadlier Than the Male 1957,O 9,41:1

Dux, Eckart
Merry Wives of Windsor, The 1952,S 22,19:2

Dux, Pierre
Queen's Necklace, The 1947,My 17,8:5
She Returned at Dawn; Retour a l'Aube 1947,Ag 1,21:5
Paris Waltz, The 1950,Ag 23,35:2
Grand Maneuver, The 1956,O 2,39:1
Girl on the Third Floor, The; (Sophie et le Crime) 1958,O 11,47:1 (Incorrect in this edition; use 1958,O 11,18:4 elsewhere)
Goodbye Again 1961,Je 30,32:2
Day and the Hour, The 1964,F 20,22:2
Friend of the Family 1965,N 18,55:3
Is Paris Burning? 1966,N 11,36:1

Duxbury, Elspeth
Make Mine Mink 1960,D 20,43:4

Duyen, Ky
What Price Murder 1958,N 11,26:1

Duzer, Winifred Van (Original Author)
Pasado Acusa, El; Accusing Past, The 1938,O 15,21:4

Dvchinikov, V (Composer)
Violin and Roller 1962,Ag 20,18:2

Dvne, Aminta
Molly and Me 1945,My 26,18:2

Dvoinikova, Gertruda
My Daughter 1960,N 28,40:2

Dvorak, Ann
Sky Devils 1932,Mr 4,17:3
Crowd Roars, The 1932,Mr 23,25:4
Crowd Roars, The 1932,Ap 3,VIII,4:4
Strange Love of Molly Louvain, The 1932,My 9,19:5
Scarface, The Shame of the Nation 1932,My 20,22:3
Love Is a Racket 1932,Je 11,9:3
Stranger in Town 1932,Jl 8,22:5
Crooner 1932,Ag 20,7:4
Three on a Match 1932,O 29,18:4
Way to Love, The 1933,N 11,10:3
College Coach 1933,N 11,10:4
Massacre 1934,Ja 18,19:2
Heat Lightning 1934,Mr 8,23:2
Midnight Alibi 1934,Jl 4,18:3
Friends of Mr Sweeney 1934,Jl 31,20:4
Housewife 1934,Ag 10,21:2
Side Streets 1934,Ag 15,13:5
Gentlemen are Born 1934,N 22,27:2
Murder in the Clouds 1934,D 26,18:1
I Sell Anything 1934,D 27,25:2
Sweet Music 1935,F 21,23:2
G Men 1935,My 2,17:1
Bright Lights 1935,Ag 15,15:2
Dr Socrates 1935,O 3,29:2
Thanks a Million 1935,N 14,17:1
We Who Are About to Die 1937,Ja 2,15:1
Midnight Court 1937,Mr 4,27:3
She's no Lady 1937,Ag 12,14:3
Manhattan Merry-Go-Round 1937,D 31,9:3
Merrily We Live 1938,Mr 18,23:3
Gangs of New York 1938,My 28,9:2
Blind Alley 1939,My 23,27:2
Stronger Than Desire 1939,Je 30,17:3
Street of Missing Women 1940,Ja 8,11:2
Girls of the Road 1940,Jl 22,20:2
Squadron Leader X 1943,Jl 23,21:2
Flame of Barbary Coast 1945,My 28,22:2
Masquerade in Mexico 1945,N 29,27:2
Abilene Town 1946,Mr 4,16:5
Bachelor's Daughters, The 1946,O 7,23:2
Private Affairs of Bel Ami, The 1947,Je 16,25:4
Long Night, The 1947,S 17,31:2
Walls of Jericho, The 1948,Ag 5,16:2
Our Very Own 1950,Jl 28,12:5
Life of her Own, A 1950,O 12,43:2
Mrs O'Malley and Mr Malone 1951,F 23,33:2
I Was an American Spy 1951,Jl 4,13:2
Secret of Convict Lake, The 1951,Ag 4,7:2

Dvorak, F A (Screenwriter)
Devil's Trap, The 1964,Ag 14,16:1

Dvornik, Boris
Ninth Circle, The 1961,S 15,30:3

Dwain, Harold (Screenwriter)
Free, White and 21 1963,Je 20,29:3

Dwan, Allan (Director)
Cheating Cheaters 1919,Ja 27,11:4
Sahara 1919,Je 30,16:3
Robin Hood 1922,O 31,15:4 (In Addenda)

Dwan, Allan (Director) — Cont

Glimpses of the Moon 1923,Ap 3,23:4
Lawful Larceny 1923,Jl 24,14:3 (In Addenda)
Zaza 1923,S 17,18:2
Big Brother 1923,D 24,12:1 (In Addenda)
Society Scandal, A 1924,Mr 10,18:2
Manhandled 1924,Jl 29,9:2
Her Love Story 1924,O 7,26:1
Wages of Virtue 1924,N 24,15:3
Argentine Love 1924,D 23,16:2
Night Life of New York 1925,Jl 14,14:1
Coast of Folly, The 1925,Ag 31,19:3
Stage Struck 1925,N 16,19:4
Sea Horses 1926,F 23,26:5
Padlocked 1926,Ag 2,21:2
Summer Bachelors 1926,D 20,28:3
Joy Girl, The 1927,S 6,34:3
East Side, West Side 1927,O 18,33:2
French Dressing 1927,D 13,33:2
Big Noise, The 1928,My 7,29:1
Iron Mask, The 1929,F 22,18:6
Frozen Justice 1929,O 26,15:1
South Sea Rose 1929,D 7,19:3
What a Widow 1930,O 4,15:2
Man to Man 1931,Ja 3,21:2
Chances 1931,Je 12,27:1
Wicked 1931,S 19,10:2
Black Sheep 1935,Je 28,34:1
Song and Dance Man 1936,Mr 12,18:2
Human Cargo 1936,My 16,11:2
High Tension 1936,Jl 11,11:4
Fifteen Maiden Lane 1936,O 17,21:3
Woman Wise 1937,Ja 23,13:1
That I May Live 1937,My 10,23:2
One Mile From Heaven 1937,Ag 19,23:1
Heidi 1937,N 6,14:2
Rebecca of Sunnybrook Farm 1938,Mr 26,12:1
Josette 1938,Je 11,9:1
Suez 1938,O 15,21:2
Three Musketeers, The 1939,F 18,12:2
Gorilla, The 1939,My 28,6:2
Frontier Marshal 1939,Jl 29,18:2
Sailor's Lady 1940,Je 29,12:2
Young People 1940,Ag 24,16:2
Trail of the Vigilantes 1940,D 7,13:2
Rise and Shine 1941,D 6,14:3
Look Who's Laughing 1941,D 25,33:2
Friendly Enemies 1942,Je 22,19:1
Here We Go Again 1942,O 12,12:3
Around the World 1943,N 25,39:2
Up in Mabel's Room 1944,Ap 22,8:6
Abroad With two Yanks 1944,O 26,19:7
Brewster's Millions 1945,Ap 27,23:2
Getting Gertie's Garter 1946,F 4,21:2
Rendezvous With Annie 1946,S 23,29:3
Northwest Outpost 1947,Ag 8,10:2
Sands of Iwo Jima 1949,D 31,9:2
Surrender 1950,O 9,21:5
Belle le Grand 1951,My 18,34:6
Wild Blue Yonder, The 1952,Ja 2,20:1
Dream of Jeanie, I 1952,Je 26,26:2
Montana Belle 1952,N 8,9:2
Flight Nurse 1954,Ja 30,9:6
Silver Lode 1954,Jl 24,6:6
Passion 1954,D 11,11:1
Cattle Queen of Montana 1955,Ja 26,22:1
Escape to Burma 1955,My 21,11:2
Pearl of the South Pacific 1955,S 17,12:2
Tennessee's Partner 1955,N 5,22:8
Slightly Scarlet 1956,Mr 17,13:2
River's Edge, The 1957,Ap 12,20:2
Most Dangerous Man Alive 1961,Jl 5,29:2

Dwan, Allan (Miscellaneous)
Tin Gods 1926,S 20,21:3

Dwan, Allan (Original Author)
Music Master, The 1927,Ja 17,12:4 (In Addenda)

Dwan, Allan (Producer)
Soldiers of Fortune 1919,N 24,13:1
Look Who's Laughing 1941,D 25,33:2
Here We Go Again 1942,O 12,12:3
Around the World 1943,N 25,39:2

Dwan, Allan (Screenwriter)
Black Sheep 1935,Je 28,34:1
Getting Gertie's Garter 1946,F 4,21:2

Dwan, Dorothy
Sinners in Silk 1924,S 8,15:3
Parasite, The 1925,F 16,24:1
Wizard of Oz, The 1925,Ap 14,26:1
Hills of Kentucky 1927,Mr 2,29:3

Dwire, Earl
Tundra 1936,D 3,31:2
Mystery of the Hooded Horsemen, The
  1937,Ag 13,13:2
Accidents Will Happen 1938,Ap 25,19:2
Under Western Stars 1938,Je 25,7:3
On Trial 1939,Ap 5,31:2

Dworkin, Ida
My Son 1939,My 10,28:2

Dworshak, Lois
Ice-Capades 1941,S 25,29:1

Dwyer, Hilary
Conqueror Worm, The 1968,Ag 15,46:2

Dwyer, James Frances (Original Author)
Bride of the Storm 1926,Ap 5,24:1

Dwyer, John
Over the Hill to the Poor House 1920,S 18,16:2

Dwyer, Leslie
Way Ahead, The 1945,Je 4,22:3
Piccadilly Incident 1948,Ag 5,16:2
Temptation Harbor 1949,My 11,34:7
Bond Street 1950,Mr 30,40:6
Little Ballerina, The 1951,F 28,33:2
Laughter in Paradise 1951,N 12,21:2
Wall of Death 1952,My 19,12:4
Hour of 13, The 1952,O 28,37:1
Double Confession 1953,My 1,17:2
Act of Love 1954,F 12,20:5
Midnight Episode 1955,My 19,25:5
39 Steps, The 1960,O 11,55:2

Dwyer, Marlo
Crossfire 1947,Jl 23,19:2
Walk Softly Stranger 1950,O 16,30:5
Short Grass 1951,Ja 13,10:4
Sniper, The 1952,My 10,16:3
Dangerous Mission 1954,Mr 6,13:5

Dwyer, P
Uncivilized 1937,N 17,27:4

Dwyer, Ruth
Reckless Age, The 1924,Je 10,24:4
Seven Chances 1925,Mr 17,18:1
Brown Derby, The 1926,Je 14,24:1
Hero for a Night, A 1927,D 26,26:6
Sailors' Wives 1928,F 28,18:4
Alex The Great 1928,My 1,33:3

Dwyer, William
Charly 1968,S 24,55:1

Dwyre, Roger (Miscellaneous)
Survival 1967 1968,Je 12,40:2

Dyakonov, N (Screenwriter)
Bride with a Dowry 1954,Ag 23,20:5

Dyall, Franklin
Atlantic 1930,Ja 26,VIII,6:2
Atlantic 1930,O 6,21:1
Ringer, The 1932,Je 2,25:2
Private Life of Henry VIII, The 1933,O 13,25:2
Iron Duke, The 1935,Ja 25,27:2
Bonnie Prince Charlie 1952,Ja 7,14:3

Dyall, Valentine
Yellow Canary, The 1944,Ap 14,24:7
Life and Death of Colonel Blimp, The
  1945,Mr 30,18:2
Henry V 1946,Je 18,30:2
Frenzy 1946,Jl 20,10:3
Brief Encounter 1946,Ag 26,21:2
I Know Where I'm Going 1947,Ag 20,25:2
My Brothers Keeper 1949,F 14,15:3
Corridor of Mirrors 1949,Mr 23,35:3
Ivanhoe 1952,Ag 1,8:2
Horror Hotel 1963,Je 20,29:1
Haunting, The 1963,S 19,23:1

Dyall, Valentine (Narrator)
Tsar to Lenin 1966,My 27,33:3

Dyanananda
Light of Asia, The 1928,My 12,8:4

Dyar, Ralph E (Original Author)
Voice in the Dark, A 1921,Je 6,16:4

D''i'd, Didier
Private Life of an Actor; En Scene 1948,S 7,21:3
Red Inn, The 1954,Je 8,25:2

d'Yd, Jean
Passion Of Joan Of Arc, The 1929,Mr 29,21:1
Passion of Jeanne d'Arc, The 1929,Mr 31,VIII,7:1
Rothchild 1938,O 12,35:2
Entente Cordiale 1939,D 26,23:2
S O S Mediterranean 1940,Ja 1,29:2
Eternal Return, The; Eternel Retour, L'
  1948,Ja 5,15:2
Room Upstairs, The 1948,S 4,8:6

Dyer, Charles
Rattle of a Simple Man 1964,D 21,42:2
Knack...and how to get it, The 1965,Je 30,42:1
Rattle of a Simple Man 1964,D 21,42:2

Dyer, Charles (Screenwriter)
Rattle of a Simple Man 1964,D 21,42:2

Dyer, George (Original Author)
Fog over Frisco 1934,Je 7,26:2
Spy Ship 1942,Jl 11,8:2

Dyer, Raymond
Loneliness of the Long Distance Runner, The
  1962,O 9,44:1

Dyer, William
Silent Call, The 1922,Ja 30,16:2
Pioneer Trails 1923,N 12,15:3
Wild Bill Hickok 1923,N 21,22:1
Singer Jim McKee 1924,Mr 24,13:1

Dygat, Stanislaw (Original Author)
Partings 1962,N 28,44:1

Dygat, Stanislaw (Screenwriter)
Partings 1962,N 28,44:1

Dyke, Dick Van
Chitty Chitty Bang Bang 1968,D 19,64:4

Dyke, Willard Van (Cinematographer)
River, The 1938,F 5,19:2 (In Addenda)

Dykes, Jimmy
Stratton Story, The 1949,My 13,29:1

Dykes, John B (Composer)
Two Tickets to London 1943,Jl 3,11:2

Dykki, A
1812 1944,S 11,14:1

Dyks, A
Victors and the Vanquished, The 1950,My 1,18:2

Dylan, Bob
Don't Look Back 1967,S 7,50:2
Festival 1967,O 24,53:2

Dymow, Ossip
Overture to Glory 1940,F 12,14:2

Dymow, Ossip (Original Author)
Overture to Glory 1940,F 12,14:2

Dymow, Ossip (Screenwriter)
Sins of Man 1936,Je 19,17:2
Mirele Efros 1939,O 21,12:2

Dymsza, Adolf
Kazdemu Wolno Kochac 1933,My 24,24:3
Parada Rezerwistow 1934,My 1,26:6
Dodek na Froncie 1936,Mr 30,17:6
Treasure, The 1951,Mr 29,24:4

Dynam, Jacques
Ma Pomme 1951,O 15,22:2
Night is my Kingdom, The 1953,S 30,37:1
Fantomas 1966,Ap 6,36:2

Dyne, Aminta
Hour Before the Dawn, The 1944,My 11,25:6
Kiss the Blood off my Hands 1948,O 30,10:2

Dyne, Michael
Hangover Square 1945,F 8,15:2
Kitty 1946,Ap 1,23:1
Cluny Brown 1946,Je 3,27:3
Moss Rose 1947,Jl 3,14:2

Dyneley, Peter
Beau Brummell 1954,O 21,31:5
Chance Meeting 1955,Ap 20,38:1
Call Me Bwana 1963,Jl 4,9:1

Dyott, George M (Miscellaneous)
Savage Gold 1933,Jl 25,17:2

Dyott, George M (Narrator)
Hunting Tigers in India 1929,D 10,36:4

Dyott, George M (Original Author)
Manhunt in the Jungle 1958,Ap 12,13:1

Dyrenforth, Harold
Carnegie Hall 1947,My 3,10:2
Crooked Web, The 1955,D 10,19:1

Dyrenforth, James
Fiend Without a Face 1958,Jl 4,15:3
A Night to Remember 1958,D 17,2:7
Man in a Cocked Hat 1960,Je 15,50:2

Dyson, Katherine
Mikado, The 1967,Mr 15,53:1

Dzhafafarof, Mikhail
Road to Life 1932,Ja 28,24:2

Dzhandarbekov, Kurmanbek
Amangeldy 1939,Je 16,27:4

Dzhandarbekova, Shara
Amangeldy 1939,Je 16,27:4

Dzhaparidze, M
Keto and Kote 1954,Ap 5,21:4

Dziewonski, Edward
Eroica (First Episode) 1966,F 2,24:1

Dzigan, E (Director)
Woman's World 1933,Ja 23,9:2
We Are From Kronstadt 1936,My 2,11:1
Moscow Music Hall 1946,S 9,20:1

Dzigan, E (Producer)
If War Comes Tomorrow 1938,Jl 14,17:2

Dzigan, E (Screenwriter)
If War Comes Tomorrow 1938,Jl 14,17:2

Dzigan, Sz
Without a Home 1939,Ap 1,17:3

E

E-Hsin, Chen (Screenwriter)
Grand Substitution, The 1965,N 25,64:5

Eaden, Margaret
Town Like Alice, A 1958,S 22,27:1

Eady, David (Director)
Three Cases of Murder (In the Picture); In the
  Picture (Three Cases of Murder)
  1955,Mr 16,39:4
Three Cases of Murder (Lord Mountdrago); Lord
  Mountdrago (Three Cases of Murder)
  1955,Mr 16,39:4
Three Cases of Murder (You Killed Elizabeth);
  You Killed Elizabeth (Three Cases of Murder)
  1955,Mr 16,39:4
In the Wake of a Stranger 1961,Je 22,23:3

EAGAN
See Also EGAN

Eagan, Alberta Stedman (Original Author)
They Call It Sin 1932,O 21,25:4

Eagan, Jack
Mad Hour, The 1928,Ap 16,20:5
Harold Teen 1928,Ag 14,15:4

Eagels, Jeanne
Man, Woman and Sin 1927,D 5,26:2
Letter, The 1929,Mr 8,30:1

Eagels, Jeanne— Cont
Jealousy 1929,S 14,17:1
Eagle, Arnold
8 X 8 1957,Mr 16,13:2
Eagle, Arnold (Cinematographer)
8 X 8 1957,Mr 16,13:2
Eagle, Dan Red
Unseeing Eyes 1923,O 22,17:1
Eagle, Frances Red
Unseeing Eyes 1923,O 22,17:1
Eagle, James
Crooks Can't Win 1928,My 29,17:2
Eagle, James C
She Done Him Wrong 1933,F 10,12:3
Eagle, John War
Tomahawk 1951,F 19,19:2
Great Sioux Uprising, The 1953,Jl 18,6:2
Man From Laramie, The 1955,S 1,20:2
Eagle, S P (Producer)
Tales of Manhattan 1942,S 25,25:1
Stranger, The 1946,Jl 11,18:2
We Were Strangers 1949,Ap 28,28:2
Prowler, The 1951,Jl 2,16:6
African Queen, The 1952,F 21,24:3
Melba 1953,Je 25,23:1
Eagle Eye
Shooting of Dan McGrew, The 1924,Je 9,14:3
Eagle Wing, Chief
Ranson's Folly 1926,My 31,10:2
Eagles, James
You Said a Mouthful 1932,N 18,23:2
Story of Temple Drake, The 1933,My 6,11:2
Charlie Chan in Egypt 1935,Je 24,12:2
Eagles, James C
From Hell to Heaven 1933,Mr 18,9:3
Eaker, Ira C (Producer)
Thunderbolt 1945,O 27,12:5
Eames, Claire
Swan, The 1925,Mr 2,14:1
New Commandment, The 1925,N 10,25:3
EARL
See Also EARLE
Earl, Elizabeth
River's End 1940,Ag 26,11:4
Letter, The 1940,N 23,12:6
Earl, Jane
Irma la Douce 1963,Je 6,39:1
Earl, Kenneth (Original Author)
Love on a Bet 1936,Mr 5,25:2
Star Dust 1940,My 4,13:1
Bride Came C O D, The 1941,Jl 26,18:2
Footlight Serenade 1942,S 10,30:3
Bathing Beauty 1944,Je 28,20:1
Carolina Blues 1944,D 8,26:6
Whiplash 1948,D 27,16:3
Big Trees, The 1952,F 6,24:2
Earl, Kenneth (Screenwriter)
White Hunter 1936,N 26,39:2
She Knew All the Answers 1941,Je 20,28:4
Twin Beds 1942,My 1,23:4
Seven Days' Leave 1942,D 11,33:2
Earl, Ruth
Irma la Douce 1963,Je 6,39:1
Earl, Wally
Anna Lucasta 1959,Ja 15,27:1
EARLE
See Also EARL
Earle, Craig E Dr
Start Cheering 1938,Mr 17,17:3
Earle, Dorothy
Out all Night 1927,S 27,31:1
Earle, Edward
False Fronts 1922,Je 5,16:2
Man Who Played God, The 1922,O 2,21:2
Lady Who Lied, The 1925,Jl 7,24:2
Irene 1926,Mr 1,17:1
Greater Glory, The 1926,My 4,31:1
Splendid Road, The 1926,Je 13,31:1
Spring Fever 1927,O 18,33:2
Wind, The 1928,N 5,26:1
Spite Marriage 1929,Mr 25,32:2
Smiling Irish Eyes 1929,Jl 24,23:2
Hottentot, The 1929,S 7,15:1
Woman of Experience, A 1931,Jl 9,26:5
Alimony Madness 1933,My 5,18:1
Little Miss Marker 1934,My 19,18:3
Magnificent Obsession 1935,D 31,11:2
Frame-Up 1937,Ag 9,23:2 (In Addenda)
When G-Men Step In 1938,Mr 14,13:2
Her Jungle Love 1938,Ap 14,27:2
Give Me a Sailor 1938,Ag 11,31:1
East Side of Heaven 1939,My 5,29:3
Sued for Libel 1940,Ja 19,15:3
Seventeen 1940,F 29,15:2
Scattergood Baines 1941,Ap 4,25:2
Dancing Masters, The 1943,D 2,30:2
Harvey Girls, The 1946,Ja 25,26:2
Beginning or the End, The 1947,F 21,15:1
Ride the Pink Horse 1947,O 9,32:3
Command Decision 1949,Ja 20,34:2
That Midnight Kiss 1949,S 23,28:2
Stranger Wore a Gun, The 1953,Jl 30,20:3

Earle, Eyvind (Miscellaneous)
Sleeping Beauty 1959,F 18,36:1
Earle, Josephine
Woman to Woman 1924,Ap 1,19:3
Earles, Daisy
Freaks 1932,Jl 9,7:5
Earles, Harry
Unholy Three, The 1925,Ag 4,14:3
That's My Baby 1926,Ap 12,18:4
Unholy Three, The 1930,Jl 5,17:4
Freaks 1932,Jl 9,7:5
Early, Dory
Music Goes 'Round, The 1936,F 22,12:1
Early, Margaret
Stage Door 1937,O 8,27:2
Jezebel 1938,Mr 11,15:2
Young in Heart, The 1938,N 4,27:2
Swing That Cheer 1938,N 11,31:2
Judge Hardy and Son 1940,Ja 18,27:3 (In Addenda)
Forty Little Mothers 1940,Ap 19,25:2
Strike up the Band 1940,S 30,13:2
Andy Hardy's Private Secretary 1941,Mr 7,17:2
To the Shores of Tripoli 1942,Mr 26,27:2
Stage Door Canteen 1943,Je 25,13:2
3 Is a Family 1944,D 20,20:3
Earnshaw, Harry A (Original Author)
Chandu the Magician 1932,O 1,10:4
Easdale, Brian (Composer)
Red Shoes, The 1948,O 23,9:2
Eason, B Reeves (Director)
Alimony Madness 1933,My 5,18:1
Kid Comes Back, The 1938,F 7,10:2
Daredevil Drivers, The 1938,F 23,27:2
Call of the Yukon 1938,My 6,27:1
Murder in the Big House 1942,My 8,27:3
Spy Ship 1942,Jl 11,8:2
Truck Busters 1943,Ja 29,23:5
East, Carlos
Blue 1968,My 11,28:1
East, Henry
On Moonlight Bay 1951,Jl 27,15:2
East, John
Little Lord Fauntleroy 1914,Je 23,11:3
East, Leonard
Michigan Kid 1947,F 22,16:3
Eastham, Richard
There's no Business Like Show Business 1954,D 17,37:3
Man on Fire 1957,Ag 23,10:1
Toby Tyler 1960,Ap 20,45:2
That Darn Cat 1965,D 3,44:1
Not With my Wife, You Don't! 1966,N 3,45:2
Murderers' Row 1966,D 22,40:3
Eastman, Marilyn
Night of the Living Dead 1968,D 5,59:2
Eastman, Max (Miscellaneous)
Tsar to Lenim 1937,Mr 9,27:2
Easton, Jay
Man Made Women 1928,S 18,33:2
Easton, Lorraine
Temple of Venus, The 1923,N 1,24:3
Easton, Phillip
Farewell to Love 1933,N 25,10:2
Easton, Robert
Somebody up There Likes Me 1956,Jl 6,16:1
War Lover, The 1963,Mr 7,8:5
Easton, Sidney
His Woman 1931,D 5,21:2
Wayward 1932,F 15,13:1
Eastwood, Clint
Fistful of Dollars, A 1967,F 2,29:1
For a Few Dollars More 1967,Jl 4,23:1
Good, The Bad and the Ugly, The 1968,Ja 25,33:1
Hang 'Em High 1968,Ag 8,27:3
Coogan's Bluff 1968,O 3,56:1
Eastwood, James (Original Author)
Beyond Mombasa 1957,My 31,14:2
Eaton, Charles
Peter Ibbetson; (Forever) 1921,O 17,18:1
Prodigal Judge, The 1922,F 5,VI,3:1 (In Addenda)
Ghost Talks, The 1929,F 18,28:1
Eaton, Evelynne
Where Are Your Children? 1944,Ja 17,14:5
Why Girls Leave Home 1945,Ag 4,7:3
Allotment Wives 1945,N 22,39:3
Finger Man 1955,Jl 16,12:4
Eaton, Jack (Producer)
Spirit of the Red Cross, The 1918,Ap 21,IV,11:8
Leading a Dog's Life 1921,F 7,8:2
Happy Duffer, The 1921,Mr 7,8:1
Fish and Totem 1921,My 30,12:5
Speed 1921,O 24,13:1
Eaton, Jay
Lady Be Good 1928,My 28,23:2
Naughty Baby 1929,F 5,26:3
Cocktail Hour 1933,Je 5,18:5
Affairs of Cellini, The 1934,S 6,22:3
Eaton, Marjorie
Witness for the Prosecution 1958,F 7,16:1
Night Tide 1963,Je 7,37:1

Eaton, Marjorie— Cont
Mary Poppins 1964,S 25,34:1
Eaton, Mary
His Children's Children 1923,N 5,15:1
Cocoanuts, The 1929,My 25,17:3
Glorifying the American Girl 1930,Ja 11,21:3
Eaton, Shirley
Doctor at Large 1957,Jl 29,15:5
Panic in the Parlor 1957,D 18,45:1
Your Past Is Showing 1958,Jl 1,36:2
3 Men in a Boat 1959,Jl 29,33:2
Carry on Sergeant 1959,O 28,40:5
Carry on Nurse 1960,S 10,11:1
In the Wake of a Stranger 1961,Je 22,23:3
Week-End With Lulu, A 1962,My 24,29:2
Nearly a Nasty Accident 1962,Je 28,21:2
No Place Like Homicide 1962,S 13,32:1
Rhino! 1964,Ag 27,28:2
Goldfinger 1964,D 22,36:1
Naked Brigade, The 1965,Je 17,27:2
Ten Little Indians 1966,F 10,33:1
Around the World Under the Sea 1966,Jl 21,20:2
Eight on the Lam 1967,Ap 27,52:1
Ebara, Tatsuyoshi
Rebellion 1967,S 25,56:4
Rebellion 1968,O 26,27:4
Ebbecke, Berthold
Maedchenraeuber 1936,Ag 15,6:3
Bettelstudent, Der 1936,D 28,12:3
Trouble Back Stairs; Krach im Hinterhaus 1937,D 4,21:1
Ebberling, June
Black Fury 1935,Ap 11,27:2
Ebbesen, Dagmar
Roeda Dagen 1932,My 21,9:2
Tjocka Slaekten; Near Relatives 1935,My 20,20:5
Larsson I Andra Giftet 1935,O 19,21:3
Loerdagskvaellar 1936,F 13,25:3
Skaergaards-Flirt 1936,Ap 8,26:3
Soederkaakar 1936,D 19,16:2
Old Gods Still Live, The 1937,N 5,19:4
Karl Fredrik Reigns 1938,F 2,15:2
Baldvins Brollop; Baldwin's Wedding 1938,D 27,13:2
Frun Tillhanda; Servant Girls 1938,D 30,9:2
Du Gamla, Du Fria; Thou old, Tho Free 1939,Mr 21,27:2
Skicka Hem Nr 7; Send Home No 7 1939,My 9,29:2
Kvinnorna Kring Larsson; Women Around Larsson, The 1940,My 18,11:3
Vi paa Solglantan; We at Solglantan 1940,O 9,30:3
Each Heart Has Its Own Story 1953,Mr 28,15:2
Lesson in Love, A 1960,Mr 15,46:1
Ebbesen, Elsa
Winter Light 1963,My 14,32:1
Ebbins, Milton (Producer)
Salt and Pepper 1968,S 19,62:3
Ebele, Ed
Wedding Night, The 1935,Mr 16,19:1
Ebelsbacher, Oscar
Mr Emmanuel 1945,Ja 8,15:2
Eben, Al
Brasher Doubloon, The 1947,My 22,34:5
City Across the River 1949,Ap 8,31:3
Sirocco 1951,Je 14,31:2
Eberhardt, Mignon G (Original Author)
Great Hospital Mystery, The 1937,Jl 16,22:2
Eberhart, Billie Jean
Street Corner 1948,D 4,9:4
Eberhart, Mignon G (Original Author)
White Cockatoo, The 1935,Ja 16,21:1
While the Patient Slept 1935,Mr 2,18:2
Murder of Dr Harrigan, The 1936,Ja 21,27:5
Murder by an Aristocrat 1936,Je 13,13:2
Patient in Room 18, The 1938,Ap 22,15:6
Mystery House 1938,Je 29,15:5
Eberle, Ray
Mister Big 1943,Je 14,13:4
Eberle, Ray and his orchestra
This is the Life 1944,Ap 28,23:3
Eberly, Bob
I Dood It 1943,N 11,29:1
Ebermayer, Erich (Screenwriter)
Deadly Decision 1958,Ap 29,26:2
Ebert, Arno
Confession of Ina Kahn, The 1958,Ja 1,31:4
Ebert, Michael
Hamlet 1964,S 24,46:1
Ebert, Walter (Original Author)
Man Between, The 1953,N 19,41:2
Eberts, John
Last Man, The 1932,S 17,18:4
Dancing Pirate 1936,Je 18,19:1
Ebeson, William R
Best Man, The 1964,Ap 7,29:1
Ebgelmann, Andrew
Abenteurer von Paris, Der 1937,My 29,20:3
Ebinger, Blandine
Sein Scheidungsgrund 1932,F 20,11:2
Gitta Entdeckt Ihr Herz 1932,S 30,17:3
Frischer Wind aus Kanada 1935,S 21,18:2
Biberpelz, Der; Beaver Coat, The 1939,S 9,11:3

Ebinger, Blandine— Cont
Fraulein 1958,Je 9,27:2
Ebsen, Buddy
Broadway Melody of 1936 1935,S 19,28:1
Captain January 1936,Ap 25,21:1
Born to Dance 1936,D 5,16:1
Banjo on My Knee 1936,D 12,15:1
Broadway Melody of 1938 1937,S 3,12:1
Girl of the Golden West, The 1938,Mr 25,15:2
Yellow Jack 1938,My 20,17:2
My Lucky Star 1938,S 10,20:2
Four Girls in White 1939,F 23,19:3
Parachute Battalion 1941,Ag 29,13:2
Sing Your Worries Away 1942,My 15,25:2
Night People 1954,Mr 13,11:2
Red Garters 1954,Mr 27,13:5
Davy Crockett, King of the Wild Frontier
1955,My 26,36:1
Attack! 1956,S 20,29:4
Between Heaven and Hell 1956,O 12,33:2
Breakfast at Tiffany's 1961,O 6,28:1
Interns, The 1962,Ag 9,17:5
Mail Order Bride 1964,Je 11,27:3
One and Only Genuine, Original Family Band,
The 1968,Mr 22,55:1
Eburne, Maude
Bat Whispers, The 1931,Ja 16,27:1
Lonely Wives 1931,Mr 16,25:1
Indiscreet 1931,My 7,21:4
Man in Possession, The 1931,Jl 18,16:6
Bought 1931,Ag 15,18:3
Guardsman, The 1931,S 10,22:4
Her Majesty, Love 1931,N 26,37:2
Blonde Crazy 1931,D 4,28:2
Under Eighteen 1931,D 26,15:5
Woman From Monte Carlo, The 1931,D 31,17:6
This Reckless Age 1932,Ja 9,21:1
Panama Flo 1932,Ja 20,17:4
Passionate Plumber, The 1932,Mr 12,19:5
Polly of the Circus 1932,Mr 19,11:2
Trial of Vivienne Ware, The 1932,Ap 30,19:3
Stranger in Town 1932,Jl 8,22:5
First Year, The 1932,Ag 22,20:2
Vampire Bat, The 1933,Ja 23,9:1
Ladies They Talk About 1933,F 25,20:4
Warrior's Husband, The 1933,My 12,20:4
Shanghai Madness 1933,S 23,11:6
My Lips Betray 1933,N 4,18:3
Lazy River 1934,Ap 4,26:2
Here Comes the Navy 1934,Jl 21,14:2
Maybe It's Love 1935,F 11,14:2
Ruggles of Red Gap 1935,Mr 7,26:1
Don't Bet on Blondes 1935,Jl 20,16:2
Man Hunt 1936,Ja 30,14:2
Valiant Is the Word for Carrie 1936,O 8,27:2
Champagne Waltz 1937,F 4,17:2
When's Your Birthday? 1937,Mr 19,27:2
Hollywood Cowboy 1937,Jl 24,12:1
Live, Love and Learn 1937,N 19,27:2
Fight for Your Lady 1937,N 20,21:2
Exile Express 1939,Ag 16,21:3
Sabotage 1939,N 16,29:5
Meet Doctor Christian 1939,D 1,27:2
Courageous Dr Christian, The 1940,Mr 29,25:3
West Point Widow 1941,S 11,21:5
You Belong to Me 1941,N 29,14:2
Among the Living 1941,D 13,25:2
To Be or not to Be 1942,Mr 7,13:2
Almost Married 1942,Je 5,23:2
Boogie Man Will Get You, The 1942,O 12,12:4
Bowery to Broadway 1944,N 30,19:2
Suspect, The 1945,F 1,18:5
Princess and the Pirate, The 1945,F 10,16:2
Mother Wore Tights 1947,Ag 21,33:2
Plunders, The 1948,N 1,28:2
Prince of Peace, The 1951,Mr 24,8:3
Eby, Lois (Original Author)
Larceny 1948,S 4,8:6
Eby-Rock, Helyn
Ann Vickers 1933,S 29,24:1
Eccles, Jane
Look Back in Anger 1959,S 16,45:1
Eccles, Jeremy
Doctor Faustus 1968,F 7,38:1
Echard, Margaret (Original Author)
Lightning Strikes Twice 1951,Ap 13,18:7
Echegaray, Alfredo (Screenwriter)
Mad Queen, The 1950,O 27,24:3
Echeverria, Racquel
Waikiki Wedding 1937,Mr 25,29:1
Eck, N (Director)
Path to Life, The 1931,Jl 9,VIII,4:3
Eckard, Max
Wozzeck 1962,Mr 3,13:1
Faust 1963,Ap 16,31:1
Eckart, Phillip
Albert Schweitzer 1957,Ja 21,20:2
Eckert, Robert
Tod Ueber Schanghai 1933,D 16,12:4
Eckhardt, Fritz
Almost Angels 1962,N 1,34:2
Eckhardt, Oliver
Last Trail, The 1927,Ja 26,17:1
Cavalier, The 1928,O 31,28:4

Eckhausen, Sylvia
Ordet 1957,D 16,33:6
Eckhoff, Julius
Liebe in Uniform 1934,O 9,17:2
Eckles, Amy
No More Excuses 1968,My 22,53:1
Eckles, Lew
House on Ninety-Second Street, The
1945,S 27,24:7
Eckstine, Billy
Skirts Ahoy! 1952,My 29,17:2
Eckstine, Ronnie
Love-Ins, The 1967,Ag 19,16:1
Ed, Carl (Original Author)
Harold Teen 1928,Ag 14,15:4
Eddie, Bonnie Kay
Winning Team, The 1952,Je 21,12:2
Eddington, Paul
Devil's Bride, The 1968,D 19,60:1
Eddison, Robert
Angel Who Pawned her Harp, The
1956,F 29,35:2
Eddy, Benny Kay
Atomic City, The 1952,My 2,21:1
Eddy, Duane
Thunder of Drums, A 1961,S 27,35:1
Savage Seven, The 1968,Ag 22,47:1
Eddy, Helen Jerome
Turn in the Road, The 1919,Mr 30,IV,6:1
Pollyanna 1920,Ja 19,16:3
First Born, The 1921,Ja 31,11:1
Ten-Dollar Raise, The 1921,Je 13,16:1
Flirt, The 1922,D 31,VII,2:2 (In Addenda)
Country Kid, The 1923,O 30,16:1
To the Ladies 1923,N 26,15:6
Marry Me 1925,Jl 13,20:2
Dark Angel, The 1925,O 12,19:3
Padlocked 1926,Ag 2,21:2
Camille 1927,Ap 22,19:1
Quality Street 1927,N 2,24:5
13 Washington Square 1928,Ja 30,18:1
Chicago After Midnight 1928,Mr 6,20:3
Two Lovers 1928,Mr 23,24:4
War Nurse 1930,O 24,31:1
Reaching for the Moon 1930,D 30,24:2
Girls Demand Excitement 1931,F 7,11:1
Great Meadow, The 1931,Mr 14,23:2
Skippy 1931,Ap 4,23:1
Sooky 1931,D 21,28:4
Mata Hari 1932,Ja 1,31:1
No Greater Love 1932,My 14,11:5
Make Me a Star 1932,Jl 1,19:3
Night of June 13th, The 1932,S 17,18:4
Madame Butterfly 1932,D 26,26:2
Frisco Jenny 1933,Ja 7,11:2
Bitter Tea of General Yen, The 1933,Ja 12,20:6
Strictly Personal 1933,Mr 20,18:2
Masquerader, The 1933,S 4,9:5
Torch Singer 1933,O 7,18:5
Broadway Thru a Keyhole 1933,N 2,18:3
Riptide 1934,Mr 31,8:2
Unknown Blonde 1934,Ap 24,27:2
Girl of the Limberlost, A 1934,N 9,24:6
Helldorado 1935,Ja 7,13:2
Shot in the Dark, A 1935,My 22,23:2
Girl From 10th Avenue, The 1935,My 27,20:6
Keeper of the Bees, The 1935,Ag 17,18:5
Klondike Annie 1936,Mr 12,18:2
Country Doctor, The 1936,Mr 13,32:2 (Incorrect
in this edition; use 1936,Mr 13,27:2 elsewhere)
Winterset 1936,D 4,31:1
Stowaway 1936,D 19,16:1
City Streets 1938,Jl 25,18:2
Strike up the Band 1940,S 30,13:2
Eddy, Lorraine
Gentleman of Paris, A 1927,O 3,20:1
Carnation Kid, The 1929,F 25,16:1
Charming Sinners 1929,Jl 8,17:3
Eddy, Nelson
Student Tour 1934,O 31,17:3
Naughty Marietta 1935,Mr 23,11:2
Rose Marie 1936,F 1,9:2
Maytime 1937,Mr 19,27:1
Rosalie 1937,D 31,9:2
Girl of the Golden West, The 1938,Mr 25,15:2
Sweethearts 1938,D 23,16:2
Let Freedom Ring 1939,Mr 10,19:2
Balalaika 1939,D 15,33:2
New Moon 1940,Jl 19,22:2
Bitter Sweet 1940,N 22,27:1
Chocolate Soldier, The 1941,N 1,20:2
I Married an Angel 1942,Jl 10,13:2
Phantom of the Opera, The 1943,O 15,15:2
Knickerbocker Holiday 1944,Ap 20,22:7
Northwest Outpost 1947,Ag 8,10:2
Edel, Alfred
Artists Under the Big Top Perplexed
1968,S 27,34:1
Edelman, Herbert
In Like Flint 1967,Mr 16,53:2
Barefoot in the Park 1967,My 26,51:1
Odd Couple, The 1968,My 3,42:1
I Love You Alice B Toklas! 1968,O 8,40:1

Edelman, Lou (Original Author)
Flirtation Walk 1934,N 29,33:1
Edelman, Louis F (Producer)
You Were Never Lovelier 1942,D 4,31:1
Once Upon a Time 1944,Je 30,17:2
Hotel Berlin 1945,Mr 3,11:2
White Heat 1949,S 3,7:2
West Point Story, The 1950,D 23,11:3
Operation Pacific 1951,F 3,10:2
I'll See You in my Dreams 1951,D 7,35:1
Big Trees, The 1952,F 6,24:2
Springfield Rifle 1952,O 23,40:2
Stop, You're Killing Me 1952,D 11,45:3
Edelmann, Heinz (Miscellaneous)
Yellow Submarine 1968,N 14,56:1
Edelmann, Otto
Don Giovanni 1956,D 27,22:1
Rosenkavalier, Der 1962,O 10,57:1
Eden, Alice
Career 1939,Jl 28,14:2
Eden, Barbara
Private's Affair, A 1959,Ag 15,8:7
Flaming Star 1960,D 17,19:1
All Hands on Deck 1961,Ap 1,10:2
Voyage to the Bottom of the Sea 1961,Jl 20,32:2
Wonderful World of the Brothers Grimm, The
1962,Ag 8,35:1
Swingin' Along 1962,Ag 27,18:1
Five Weeks in a Balloon 1962,Ag 27,18:1
Yellow Canary, The 1963,My 16,42:1
Brass Bottle, The 1964,My 21,42:1
7 Faces of Dr Lao 1964,Jl 23,19:1
New Interns, The 1964,Ag 20,34:2
Ride the Wild Surf 1964,D 24,8:4
Eden, Chana
Wind Across the Everglades 1958,S 12,21:1
Eden, Elana
Story of Ruth, The 1960,Je 18,12:3
Eden, John (Screenwriter)
Kiss of the Vampire 1963,O 10,49:2
Eden, Mark
Heavens Above! 1963,My 21,28:2
L-Shaped Room, The 1963,My 28,32:1
Seance on a Wet Afternoon 1964,N 6,30:1
Man in the Dark 1965,Ja 21,22:1
Pleasure Girls, The 1966,Ap 21,43:1
Attack on the Iron Coast 1968,Je 6,54:2
Eden, Michael
Come September 1961,S 8,34:1
Eden, Rob (Original Author)
Dancing Feet 1936,Mr 28,11:2
Edenkoben, Richard S (Director)
Toerichte Jungfrau, Die 1935,S 9,24:3
Edens, Olive (Original Author)
House Divided, A 1932,Ja 9,21:1
Edens, Roger (Composer)
Love Finds Andy Hardy 1938,Jl 22,10:2
Strike up the Band 1940,S 30,13:2
Go West 1941,F 21,16:2
Ziegfeld Girl 1941,Ap 25,17:2
Lady Be Good 1941,S 19,27:1
Kathleen 1941,D 19,35:3
Babes on Broadway 1942,Ja 1,37:1
Panama Hattie 1942,O 2,31:2
Presenting Lily Mars 1943,Ap 30,25:3
Funny Face 1957,Mr 29,16:1
Edens, Roger (Miscellaneous)
Everybody Sing 1938,Mr 11,15:3
On the Town 1949,D 9,37:2
Edens, Roger (Producer)
Deep in my Heart 1954,D 10,35:2
Funny Face 1957,Mr 29,16:1
Eder, Boris
Tiger Girl 1955,S 5,8:2
Ederle, Gertrude
Swim, Girl, Swim 1927,S 5,13:2
Edeson, Arthur (Cinematographer)
Robin Hood 1922,O 31,15:4 (In Addenda)
Edeson, Robert
How Molly Made Good 1915,O 20,5:5
Prisoner of Zenda, The 1922,Ag 1,14:3
Spoilers, The 1923,Ag 6,14:2
Silent Partner, The 1923,Ag 20,4:2
To the Last Man 1923,Ag 28,12:1
Don't Call it Love 1923,D 25,26:1
Thy Name Is Woman 1924,Mr 4,17:1
Triumph 1924,Ap 21,21:4
Men 1924,My 5,18:3
Mademoiselle Midnight 1924,My 27,14:1
Bedroom Window, The 1924,Je 9,14:3
Feet of Clay 1924,S 22,16:1
Welcome Stranger 1924,O 14,21:5
Locked Doors 1925,Ja 12,11:2
Golden Bed, The 1925,Ja 20,18:2
Men and Women 1925,Mr 30,21:3
Hell's Highroad 1925,Ag 26,14:2
Go Straight 1925,O 6,30:1
Volga Boatman, The 1926,Ap 14,21:1
Night Bride, The 1927,Mr 30,22:6
King of Kings, The 1927,Ap 20,29:2
Heart Thief, The 1927,Ap 27,22:5
His Dog 1927,Ag 16,31:2
Chicago 1927,D 24,9:1

Edeson, Robert— Cont
Walking Back 1928,Je 12,33:3
Beware of Blondes 1928,Ag 21,27:4
Ship Comes in, A 1928,S 4,21:2
Tenth Avenue 1928,O 9,35:1
Home Towners, The 1928,O 24,26:4
Marriage by Contract 1928,N 13,37:1
Little Wildcat, The 1929,Ja 21,18:4
Doctor's Secret, The 1929,F 4,20:1
Marianne 1929,O 19,22:6
Romance of Rio Grande 1929,N 9,22:5
Dynamite 1929,D 28,11:1
Little Johnny Jones 1930,F 1,15:1
Cameo Kirby 1930,F 8,12:5
Swing High 1930,Je 27,26:3
Way of all Men, The 1930,S 20,15:4
Danger Lights 1930,D 15,29:1
Lash, The 1931,Ja 1,31:3
Edgar, Hindle
Private Life of Don Juan, The 1934,D 10,16:2
Strauss's Great Waltz 1935,Ap 8,23:3
Edgely, George
Free, White and 21 1963,Je 20,29:3
Edginton, May (Original Author)
Secrets 1924,Mr 25,25:2
Triumph 1924,Ap 21,21:4
Joy Girl, The 1927,S 6,34:3
Secrets 1933,Mr 16,21:2
Edgren, Gustaf (Director)
Troette Teodor 1932,Ja 18,18:4
Roeda Dagen 1932,My 21,9:2
Vaermlaenningarna 1932,N 18,23:2
Karl Fredrik Reigns 1938,F 2,15:2
John Ericsson Victor of Hampton Roads
 1938,My 18,17:2
Sunshine Follows Rain 1949,S 29,39:2
Katrina 1949,N 18,35:3
Edgren, Gustaf (Screenwriter)
Sunshine Follows Rain 1949,S 29,39:2
Edgren, Gustav (Screenwriter)
Katrina 1949,N 18,35:3
Edgren, Linnea
Vaermlaenningarna 1932,N 18,23:2
Edhofer, Walter
Liebeskommando 1932,Ap 27,13:6
Edin, Ulla
Swedish Wedding Night 1965,N 15,48:1
Edington, A C (Original Author)
Marines Fly High, The 1940,Mr 5,19:2
Edington, Harry (Producer)
Green Hell 1940,Ja 30,15:6
Edington, John P
Madame X 1929,Ap 25,32:3
Edington, May (Original Author)
Lying Lips 1921,Mr 7,8:1
His Supreme Moment 1925,Ap 13,24:1
Three Hours 1927,Mr 8,18:4
Adventure in Manhattan 1936,O 23,27:5
Edmiston, Alan
Double Life, A 1948,F 20,19:1
Edmiston, James (Screenwriter)
Dangerous Mission 1954,Mr 6,13:5
Edmond, Elsie
Royal Family of Broadway, The 1930,D 23,25:1
EDMONDS
See Also EDMUNDS
Edmonds, Ann
Nurse's Secret, The 1941,Je 6,25:7
Edmonds, Dale
Paisan 1948,Mr 30,26:2
Edmonds, Don
Gidget Goes Hawaiian 1961,Ag 10,17:4
Wild Wild Winter 1966,Ja 6,20:2
Edmonds, Walter D (Original Author)
Farmer Takes a Wife, The 1935,Ag 9,21:2
Drums Along the Mohawk 1939,N 4,11:2
Chad Hanna 1940,D 26,23:1
Farmer Takes a Wife, The 1953,Je 13,11:2
Edmund, Marie
Cuban Rebel Girls 1959,D 26,7:3
Edmund, Terence
Murder Ahoy 1964,S 23,55:3
EDMUNDS
See Also EDMONDS
Edmunds, Robert (Miscellaneous)
My Heart Is Calling 1935,Ap 15,16:3
My Song For You 1935,My 27,20:6
Princess Charming 1935,Je 22,18:5
Edmunds, William
Idiot's Delight 1939,F 3,13:1
Fixer Dugan 1939,My 6,21:2
Rains Came, The 1939,S 9,11:2
Nurse Edith Cavell 1939,S 22,27:4
Everything Happens at Night 1939,D 16,12:6
He Married his Wife 1940,Ja 20,11:2
Geronimo 1940,F 8,18:3
Mortal Storm, The 1940,Je 21,25:2
Girls Under 21 1940,N 11,22:4
Mr and Mrs Smith 1941,F 21,16:3
Man at Large 1941,O 11,21:4
Paris Calling 1942,Ja 19,21:2
Wife Takes a Flyer, The 1942,Je 19,19:1
Big Shot, The 1942,Jl 18,8:2
Pied Piper, The 1942,Ag 13,15:3

Berlin Correspondent 1942,S 4,19:2
Assignment in Brittany 1943,Ap 22,31:2
One Body too Many 1944,N 25,21:2
Climax, The 1944,D 14,28:5
House of Frankenstein 1944,D 16,19:3
Bell for Adano, A 1945,Jl 6,8:3
Anna and the King of Siam 1946,Je 21,20:2
Nobody Lives Forever 1946,N 2,12:2
It's a Wonderful Life 1946,D 23,19:2
Beast With Five Fingers, The 1946,D 26,28:3
Man I Love, The 1947,Ja 25,12:2
Lost Moment, The 1947,N 22,10:2
Ringside 1949,S 17,10:8
Lawless, The 1950,Je 23,29:2
Edmundson, Al
Merry Go Round 1923,Jl 2,16:2
Edouarde, Carl
Soul Fire 1925,My 6,26:3
Edquist, Dagmar (Original Author)
Night is my Future 1963,Ja 9,5:6
Edredge, John
Whispering Smith 1949,F 15,28:2
Edsen, Vilma
Broadway Melody of 1936 1935,S 19,28:1
Edson, Arthur (Cinematographer)
Thief of Bagdad, The 1924,Mr 19,19:1
Edthofer, Anton
Burning Heart, The 1930,My 12,27:3
Traeumende Mund, Der 1934,F 5,19:2
Eine Frau die Weiss Was sie Will 1936,Jl 18,18:3
Pompadour, Die 1939,F 27,11:3
Edwall, Allan
Virgin Spring, The; Jungfrukallan 1960,N 15,46:1
Devil's Eye, The 1961,O 31,27:4
Winter Light 1963,My 14,32:1
All These Women 1964,O 6,35:1
Edward, Dennis
Prince and the Showgirl 1957,Je 14,22:2
Edward, Jose (Director)
Tosca, La 1921,N 21,20:1
Edward, Nils
Husbands or Lovers 1927,N 22,32:2
Edward, Sarah
Young People 1940,Ag 24,16:2
Edwardes, Olga
Christmas Carol, A 1951,N 29,41:2
Edwards, Aaron
Are We Civilized? 1934,Je 14,28:5
Edwards, Alan
Virgin Paradise, A 1921,Ag 4,18:3
Clear all Wires 1933,Mr 4,11:2
White Sister, The 1933,Mr 18,9:3
Stage Mother 1933,S 30,18:5
Frontier Marshal 1934,Ja 31,20:3
Show-Off, The 1934,Mr 17,11:3
Hold That Girl 1934,Mr 24,20:3
If You Could Only Cook 1935,D 26,21:4
Forgotten Faces 1936,Jl 4,18:2
Make Way for a Lady 1936,D 12,15:1
Forty Naughty Girls 1937,S 18,15:3
Mr District Attorney 1941,Ap 17,29:3
Mr Ace 1946,S 30,21:3
Edwards, Anne (Screenwriter)
Question of Adultery, A 1961,Jl 6,18:2
Edwards, Bill
Hail the Conquering Hero 1944,Ag 10,14:2
Our Hearts Were Young and Gay 1944,O 12,24:2
Miss Susie Slagle's 1946,F 7,29:2
Virginian, The 1946,Ap 18,22:2
Our Hearts Were Growing Up 1946,Ag 12,17:2
First Legion, The 1951,Ap 28,9:2
War Lover, The 1963,Mr 7,8:5
Edwards, Blake (Director)
Mister Cory 1957,F 23,13:1
This Happy Feeling 1958,Je 19,28:2
Perfect Furlough, The 1959,Ja 22,27:4
Operation Petticoat 1959,D 6,38:1
High Time 1960,S 17,15:1
Breakfast at Tiffany's 1961,O 6,28:1
Experiment in Terror 1962,Ap 14,14:1
Days of Wine and Roses 1963,Ja 18,7:2
Pink Panther, The 1964,Ap 24,25:1
Shot in the Dark, A 1964,Je 24,28:1
Great Race, The 1965,S 16,00:0
What Did You Do in the War, Daddy?
 1966,S 1,28:1
Gunn 1967,Je 29,32:1
Party, The 1968,Ap 5,56:2
Edwards, Blake (Miscellaneous)
Inspector Clouseau 1968,Jl 25,26:1
Edwards, Blake (Original Author)
Atomic Kid, The 1954,D 4,14:2
Couch, The 1962,F 22,20:3
Great Race, The 1965,S 16,00:0
What Did You Do in the War, Daddy?
 1966,S 1,28:1
Gunn 1967,Je 29,32:1
Party, The 1968,Ap 5,56:2
Edwards, Blake (Producer)
Experiment in Terror 1962,Ap 14,14:1
Shot in the Dark, A 1964,Je 24,28:1
What Did You Do in the War, Daddy?
 1966,S 1,28:1

Edwards, Blake (Producer)— Cont
Party, The 1968,Ap 5,56:2
Edwards, Blake (Screenwriter)
Stampede 1949,S 16,36:2
Drive a Crooked Road 1954,Ap 3,19:3
My Sister Eileen 1955,S 23,21:1
Mister Cory 1957,F 23,13:1
Operation Mad Ball 1957,N 21,38:1
This Happy Feeling 1958,Je 19,28:2
Notorious Landlady, The 1962,Jl 27,15:2
Soldier in the Rain 1963,N 29,67:6 (Incorrect in
 this edition; use 1963,N 28,67:6 elsewhere)
Pink Panther, The 1964,Ap 24,25:1
Shot in the Dark, A 1964,Je 24,28:1
Gunn 1967,Je 29,32:1
Party, The 1968,Ap 5,56:2
Edwards, Bruce
Marry the Boss's Daughter 1941,D 4,33:4
Hitler-Dead or Alive 1943,Mr 31,23:3
Fallen Sparrow, The 1943,Ag 20,13:1
Iron Major, The 1943,N 1,12:5
Bride by Mistake 1944,S 16,20:2
My Pal, Wolf 1944,O 9,17:2
Betrayal From the East 1945,Ap 25,27:2
West of the Pecos 1945,Ag 11,14:6
So Goes my Love 1946,My 2,3:7
Cool World, The 1964,Ap 21,42:1
Edwards, Cliff
Marianne 1929,O 19,22:6
So This Is College 1929,N 9,22:5
Lord Byron of Broadway 1930,Mr 8,21:1
Montana Moon 1930,Ap 14,24:2
Way out West 1930,Ag 18,24:1
Good News 1930,S 6,9:2
Dough Boys 1930,S 30,23:1
Those Three French Girls 1930,O 11,21:3
Dance, Fools, Dance 1931,Mr 21,15:1
Parlor, Bedroom and Bath 1931,Ap 4,23:1
Shipmates 1931,My 23,13:4
Prodigal, The 1931,Je 27,20:3
Laughing Sinners 1931,Jl 4,11:5
Great Lover, The 1931,Ag 24,13:4
Sin of Madelon Claudet, The 1931,O 31,22:2
Hell Divers 1931,D 23,27:3
Love Starved 1932,Ap 15,23:1
Fast Life 1932,D 24,11:4
Flying Devils 1933,Ag 26,14:3
Take a Chance 1933,N 27,20:3
George White's Scandals 1934,Mr 16,24:2
George White's 1935 Scandals 1935,Ap 29,12:3
Red Salute 1935,S 30,13:1
Man I Marry, The 1936,O 31,24:3
They Gave Him a Gun 1937,My 14,21:1
Saratoga 1937,Jl 23,16:3
Between Two Women 1937,Ag 6,21:1
Bad Guy 1937,Ag 26,25:2
Bad Man of Brimstone, The 1938,F 4,17:2
Girl of the Golden West, The 1938,Mr 25,15:2
Maisie 1939,Je 23,23:1
Gone With the Wind 1939,D 20,31:2
His Girl Friday 1940,Ja 12,13:2
Millionaires in Prison 1940,Jl 16,21:3
Flowing Gold 1940,S 2,19:3
She Couldn't Say No 1941,Ja 17,21:3
Monster and the Girl, The 1941,Mr 20,25:3
Power Dive 1941,My 29,15:4
International Squadron 1941,N 14,28:4
Seven Miles From Alcatraz 1942,N 19,31:3
American Empire 1943,Ja 14,25:4
Falcon Strikes Back, The 1943,Ap 2,17:4
Edwards, Edgar
His Brother's Wife 1936,Ag 15,6:2
Convicted 1938,Ag 22,9:3
Wings of the Navy 1939,F 4,11:1
One Million BC 1940,Ap 27,9:2
Broadway Limited 1941,Je 16,11:6
Convicted 1938,Ag 22,9:3
Edwards, Edith
Three Loves 1929,S 9,30:2
Edwards, Elaine
Purple Gang, The 1960,Ja 23,15:5
Pamela, Pamela You Are.... 1968,D 21,49:4
Edwards, Frank
Modigliani of Montparnasse 1961,Mr 1,27:3
Edwards, George (Original Author)
Games 1967,S 18,58:2
Edwards, George (Producer)
Games 1967,S 18,58:2
Edwards, Glynn
Zulu 1964,Jl 8,38:1
Edwards, Gus
Hollywood Revue, The 1929,Ag 15,20:5
Edwards, Gus (Miscellaneous)
Star Maker, The 1939,Ag 31,14:2
Edwards, Harry
Little Lord Fauntleroy 1914,Je 23,11:3
Edwards, Harry (Director)
Tramp, Tramp, Tramp 1926,My 24,24:3
His First Flame 1927,My 2,26:4
Edwards, Henry
Magic Bow, The 1947,Jl 7,13:2
Take my Life 1949,Ja 19,34:2
Dear Mr Prohack 1950,Jl 15,7:2
Madeleine 1950,S 1,17:2

Edwards, Henry — Cont
Verger, The 1950,O 11,42:1
Oliver Twist 1951,Jl 31,17:2
Man Who Changed his Name, The 1934,O 17,26:2
Are You a Mason? 1934,O 30,23:5
Scrooge 1935,D 14,11:1
High Treason 1937,Ja 27,17:3
Juggernaut 1937,Jl 15,16:1

Edwards, Herbert T (Producer)
Kukan 1941,Je 24,17:2
Pledge to Bataan 1943,Jl 2,15:2

Edwards, Hilton
Quare Fellow 1963,F 20,6:1

Edwards, Hugh
Lord of the Flies 1963,Ag 20,37:1

Edwards, J Gordon (Director)
Salome 1918,O 7,11:3
Last of the Duanes, The 1919,S 15,16:3
If I Were King 1920,Ag 10,10:3
Queen of Sheba 1921,Ap 11,9:1
Nero 1922,My 26,17:2
Silent Command, The 1923,S 5,15:3
Shepherd King, The 1923,D 11,26:2

Edwards, J Gordon Jr
Plastic Age, The 1926,Jl 19,13:1

Edwards, Jack
So This Is Marriage 1924,D 23,16:2
East Side Kids 1940,F 19,21:6
Ghost Creeps, The 1940,Ag 19,13:3

Edwards, Jack Jr
Cross of Lorraine, The 1943,D 3,27:4

Edwards, James
Set-Up, The 1949,Mr 30,31:2
Home of the Brave 1949,My 13,29:1
Steel Helmet, The 1951,Ja 25,21:5
Bright Victory 1951,Ag 1,19:2
Member of the Wedding, The 1952,D 31,10:2
Joe Louis Story, The 1953,N 4,29:4
Innocents in Paris 1955,Mr 5,9:6
Seven Angry Men 1955,Ap 2,15:2
Phenix City Story, The 1955,S 3,9:1
Killing, The 1956,My 21,20:1
Battle Hymn 1957,F 16,14:1
Men in War 1957,Mr 20,32:4
African Manhunt 1957,Ap 20,21:4
Alligator Named Daisy, An 1957,O 7,23:2
Fraulein 1958,Je 9,27:2
Tarzan's Fight for Life 1958,Ag 16,10:2
Anna Lucasta 1959,Ja 15,27:1
Night of the Quarter Moon 1959,Mr 5,35:5
Pork Chop Hill 1959,My 30,9:2
3 Men in a Boat 1959,Jl 29,33:2
Nearly a Nasty Accident 1962,Je 28,21:2
Manchurian Candidate, The 1962,O 25,48:3
Sandpiper, The 1965,Jl 16,14:1

Edwards, Joan
Hit Parade of 1947 1947,My 5,32:8

Edwards, Leslie
Royal Ballet, The (Ondine); Ondine (The Royal Ballet) 1960,O 5,45:2
Royal Ballet, The (Swan Lake Act II); Swan Lake Act II (The Royal Ballet) 1960,O 5,45:2
Romeo and Juliet 1966,O 6,55:1

Edwards, Mary Ann
Giant 1956,O 11,51:1

Edwards, Mattie
Give Us This Night 1936,Ap 6,18:1

Edwards, Maudie
Pink String and Sealing Wax 1950,O 4,38:2
Only Two Can Play 1962,Mr 21,33:2

Edwards, Meredith
Run for Your Money, A 1950,Ap 10,15:3
Blue Lamp, The 1951,Ja 9,25:1
Magnet, The 1951,F 27,22:6
Wall of Death 1952,My 19,12:4
Ivory Hunter 1952,Ag 19,19:1
Glory at Sea 1953,Mr 11,36:7
Cruel Sea, The 1953,Ag 11,18:5
Midnight Episode 1955,My 19,25:5
Third Key, The 1957,Je 3,30:2
Law and Disorder 1958,Ag 6,20:1
Dunkirk 1958,S 11,42:2
Tiger Bay 1959,D 15,50:1

Edwards, Meredith (Narrator)
Conquest of Everest, The 1953,D 10,64:4

Edwards, Milton
Othello 1955,S 13,27:1

Edwards, Neely
I'll Show You the Town 1925,Je 8,19:1
Footloose Windows 1926,Je 22,21:2
Excess Baggage 1928,S 24,25:1
Show Boat 1929,Ap 18,32:3
Gold Diggers of Broadway, The 1929,Ag 31,13:4
Dynamite 1929,D 28,11:1
Diplomaniacs 1933,Ap 29,14:2
Love, Honor and Oh, Baby! 1933,O 28,20:3

Edwards, Paul Jr
No Man is an Island 1962,O 11,49:2
Walls of Hell, The 1965,N 18,55:3

Edwards, Penny
That Hagen Girl 1947,O 25,13:2
Two Guys From Texas 1948,Ag 28,8:6
Wild Blue Yonder, The 1952,Ja 2,20:1

Pony Soldier 1952,D 20,15:2
Powder River 1953,Jl 4,7:2

Edwards, Peter
Run for Your Money, A 1950,Ap 10,15:3

Edwards, Ralph
George Washington Carver 1940,Ap 17,26:4
Radio Stars on Parade 1945,S 22,14:2

Edwards, Ronnie Claire
All the Way Home 1963,O 30,46:1

Edwards, Rowland G (Original Author)
Man From Yesterday, The 1932,Je 25,18:2

Edwards, Sam
East Side Kids 1940,F 19,21:6
Street with no Name, The 1948,Jl 15,26:6
Twelve O'Clock High 1950,Ja 28,10:2
Sun Sets at Dawn, The 1951,Ja 15,13:1

Edwards, Sarah
Glorifying the American Girl 1930,Ja 11,21:3
Ruggles of Red Gap 1935,Mr 7,26:1
World Accuses, The 1935,Mr 21,27:2
Dark Angel, The 1935,S 6,12:2
Golden Arrow, The 1936,My 4,16:1
Earthworm Tractors 1936,Jl 25,16:1
We're on the Jury 1937,F 10,18:5
It's Love I'm After 1937,N 11,31:2
Women Are Like That 1938,Ap 11,12:2
Touchdown Army 1938,O 28,27:2
Meet Doctor Christian 1939,D 1,27:2
Strike up the Band 1940,S 30,13:2
Meet John Doe 1941,Mr 13,25:2
Mr District Attorney 1941,Ap 17,29:3
Calaboose 1943,Jl 30,19:2
Where Are Your Children? 1944,Ja 17,14:5
Storm Over Lisbon 1944,S 11,14:1
Saratoga Trunk 1945,N 22,39:2
It's a Wonderful Life 1946,D 23,19:2
Bishop's Wife, The 1947,D 10,44:2
Petty Girl, The 1950,Ag 18,17:2
Glass Menagerie, The 1950,S 29,31:5

Edwards, Saundra
Parrish 1961,My 5,22:1

Edwards, Snitz
City of Masks, The 1920,Jl 12,12:4
Ladies Must Live 1921,N 21,20:1
Ghost Breaker, The 1922,S 11,20:2
Rosita 1923,S 4,14:1
Hill Billy, The 1924,Mr 12,19:4
Thief of Bagdad, The 1924,Mr 19,19:1
Tiger Love 1924,Je 16,18:3
Tarnish 1924,O 13,21:1
Tornado, The 1924,D 15,14:1
Inez From Hollywood 1924,D 16,28:1
Seven Chances 1925,Mr 17,18:1
Phantom of the Opera, The 1925,S 7,15:3
Battling Butler 1926,Ag 23,9:1
Red Mill, The 1927,F 14,15:1
College 1927,S 12,29:1
Dangerous Woman, A 1929,My 20,22:6
Mysterious Island, The 1929,D 21,17:1
Phantom of the Opera 1930,F 10,20:4
Sit Tight 1931,F 19,20:4
Right of Way, The 1931,Mr 24,31:2

Edwards, Vince
Mr Universe 1951,Mr 23,16:2
Sailor Beware 1952,F 1,17:1
Rogue Cop 1954,S 18,12:2
Night Holds Terror, The 1955,S 15,39:2
Serenade 1956,Mr 24,21:1 (Incorrect in this edition; use 1956,Mr 23,21:1 elsewhere)
Killing, The 1956,My 21,20:1
Too Late Blues 1962,Mr 1,27:4
Victors, The 1963,D 20,21:2
Devil's Brigade, The 1968,My 23,56:2
Hammerhead 1968,S 12,54:3

Edwards, Virginia
Silver Dollar 1932,D 23,20:1

Edwards, Walter (Director)
Veiled Adventure, The 1919,Jl 7,18:5

Edwin, J H
Ireland's Border Line 1939,O 13,27:3

Edwin, Lee (Screenwriter)
Flying Fontaines, The 1959,D 24,13:6

Edwin, Stuart
Dude Ranch 1931,Ap 25,23:4

Efendiev, I
Arshin Takes a Wife 1950,Jl 31,13:6

Efendiev, I (Director)
Arshin Takes a Wife 1950,Jl 31,13:6

Effernelli, Enrico
His Young Wife 1949,Mr 12,10:2

Effimov, Yuri (Composer)
Cinerama's Russian Adventure 1966,Ap 14,42:1

Effinlon, Anne
Youth of Athens 1949,O 31,20:4

Efrikian, Laura
Crime Does Not Pay (The Mask); Mask, The (Crime Does Not Pay) 1962,O 17,35:2

Efrom, Marshall
Funnyman 1967,S 25,56:3

Efron, N E
Lenin in 1918 1939,Je 27,27:2

Efthimiou, Christos
Madame X 1960,O 3,34:5

EGAN
See Also EAGAN

Egan, Beresford
Silver Fleet, The 1945,Mr 24,22:6
Frenzy 1946,Jl 20,10:3

Egan, Jack
Potters, The 1927,Ja 18,23:1
Cabaret 1927,My 2,26:4
Big Noise, The 1928,My 7,29:1
Broadway Scandals 1929,O 29,35:1

Egan, Jenny
Pollyanna 1960,My 20,26:1

Egan, Richard
Damned Don't Cry, The 1950,Ap 8,9:2
Wyoming Mail 1950,O 23,26:5
Undercover Girl 1950,N 8,37:2
Highway 301 1950,D 9,13:2
Kansas Raiders 1951,Ja 26,19:2
Up Front 1951,Mr 26,19:2
Hollywood Story 1951,Je 7,40:6
Bright Victory 1951,Ag 1,19:2
Flame of Araby 1951,D 20,41:7
Devil Makes Three, The 1952,Ag 30,6:2
One Minute to Zero 1952,S 20,13:2
Blackbeard the Pirate 1952,D 26,20:3
Split Second 1953,My 13,34:2
Glory Brigade, The 1953,Ag 15,8:4
Kid From Left Field, The 1953,S 26,15:3
Wicked Woman 1954,Mr 27,13:6
Demetrius and the Gladiators 1954,Je 19,9:1
Gog 1954,Ag 14,8:2
Khyber Patrol 1954,S 20,19:2
Underwater! 1955,F 10,27:2
Untamed 1955,Mr 12,11:6
Violent Saturday 1955,My 12,32:2
Seven Cities of Gold 1955,O 8,13:2
View From Pompey's Head, The 1955,N 5,22:5
Revolt of Mamie Stover, The 1956,My 12,12:7
Love Me Tender 1956,N 16,23:1
Slaughter on Tenth Avenue 1957,N 6,43:1
Voice in the Mirror 1958,Ag 14,23:2
Hunters, The 1958,Ag 27,33:1
These Thousand Hills 1959,My 7,36:1
Summer Place, A 1959,O 23,24:1
Pollyanna 1960,My 20,26:1
Esther and the King 1960,N 19,13:4
300 Spartans, The 1962,S 20,29:2

Egawa, Ureo
Escapde in Japan 1957,D 24,11:1

Egen, Austin (Composer)
Kyritz-Pyritz 1932,Ag 9,20:5

Eger, J C (Screenwriter)
One Step to Eternity 1955,O 3,22:2

Eger, Raymond (Producer)
Lovers of Toledo, The 1954,Ap 10,11:3
One Step to Eternity 1955,O 3,22:2
Inside a Girls' Dormitory 1956,F 6,27:7
Please Mr Balzac 1957,M 18,37:2
Blood and Roses 1961,O 12,41:4
Champagne Murders, The 1968,Ap 25,53:1

Egert, K
Red and White 1932,N 29,23:5

Eggar, Samantha
Dr Crippen 1964,F 15,14:1
Young and Willing 1964,F 27,28:1
Psyche 39 1964,Ap 30,30:1
Doctor in Distress 1964,Jl 8,38:2
Collector, The 1965,Je 18,28:1
Return From the Ashes 1965,N 17,53:1
Walk, Don't Run 1966,Ag 25,42:3
Doctor Dolittle 1967,D 20,55:1

Eggenton, Joseph
Doctor Takes a Wife, The 1940,Je 15,12:2
You'll Find Out 1940,N 15,25:2

Egger, Jack
Stella Dallas 1937,Ag 6,21:1

Egger, Jose
For a Few Dollars More 1967,Jl 4,23:1

Egger, Josef
Fledermaus, Die; Bat, The 1943,Mr 15,26:2
Marika 1953,F 18,27:2

Eggers, Fred (Screenwriter)
Port of Hell 1954,D 18,12:2
Legion of the Doomed 1959,Mr 12,27:5
Return of Mr Moto 1965,D 2,48:1

Eggers, Lillian
Powers Girl, The 1943,Mr 26,14:2 (In Addenda)

Eggert, Alnut
Question 7 1961,S 29,30:2

Eggert, E W
Aelita: The Revolt of the Robots 1929,Mr 26,34:1

Eggert, E W (Director)
Aelita: The Revolt of the Robots 1929,Mr 26,34:1

Eggert, K V
Gobsek 1937,Jl 16,22:1

Eggert, Konstantin (Director)
Gobsek 1937,Jl 16,22:1

Eggerth, Marta
Traum von Schoenbrunn 1933,Je 1,15:4
Blaue Vom Himmel, Das 1934,S 8,18:6
Es War Einmal ein Walzer 1934,O 15,20:5
Kaiserwalzer 1934,D 29,11:2
Unfinished Symphony 1935,Ja 14,11:2
My Heart Is Calling 1935,Ap 15,16:3
Csardasfuerstin 1935,Ap 25,18:3
Ein Lied, Ein Kuss, Ein Maeder 1936,D 12,29:4
World's in Love, The 1937,My 19,27:2
Schloss im Flandern, Das 1937,Ag 7,7:3
Casta Oiva 1937,O 5,29:2
Charm of la Boheme, The 1938,Mr 19,11:2
Ihr Groesster Erfolg; Her Greatest Success
1939,F 12,20:4
Blonde Carmen, Die 1939,O 7,11:3
Walzerlange; Waltz Melodies 1940,Ap 27,9:3
For Me and My Gal 1942,O 22,25:1
Presenting Lily Mars 1943,Ap 30,25:3
Her Wonderful Lie 1950,Jl 17,15:2
Eggleston, Edward (Original Author)
Hoosier Schoolmaster, The 1924,Mr 18,25:2
Eglevsky, Andre
Limelight 1952,O 24,27:2
Egorova, Elena
Cain and Artem 1930,Je 7,10:4
Egorova, G
Paris Commune 1937,Je 2,20:4
Egri, Istvan
Treasured Earth 1950,D 14,51:3
Egry, Maria
Az uj Foeldesur 1936,S 22,30:5
Erik/a/Buzakalasz; Wheat Ripens, The
1939,S 11,15:2
Fehervari Huszarok; Hussars of Fehervari
1939,S 16,20:3
Varju a Toronyoran; Crow on the Tower
1939,N 18,22:6
Pentek Rezi; Friday Rose 1939,D 23,9:2
Egyed, Zoltan (Original Author)
Dramatic School 1938,D 9,31:2
Eheling, Monica
Wild Strawberries 1959,Je 23,37:1
Ehlers, Gerd
Naked Among the Wolves 1967,Ap 19,54:7
Ehlers, Walter D
Long Gray Line, The 1955,F 11,19:2
Ehmann, Karl
Mein Liebster Ist ein Jaegersmann 1936,S 15,37:6
April 1, 2000 1954,F 17,27:2
Ehmig, George
Panic in the Streets 1950,Ag 5,9:2
Ehre, Ida
Seven Journeys 1951,Mr 12,20:2
Ehrenburg, Ilya (Original Author)
Love of Jeanne Ney, The 1928,Ja 15,VIII,7:5
Ehrhard-Hardt, Carl
Rosen aus dem Sueden; Roses from the South
1935,Ap 23,24:5
Ehrhardt, Bess
Ice Follies of 1939 1939,Mr 17,25:2
Ehrhardt, Hermann
Dell Etappenhase 1938,Ja 1,11:3
Ehrhart, Eddie
Gunfighter, The 1950,Je 24,7:2
Ehrie, Kurt
Queen of Sin and the Spectacle of Sodom and
Gomorrah 1923,Mr 27,24:3 (In Addenda)
EHRLICH
See Also ERLICH
Ehrlich, Henry (Producer)
Adventures of Robinson Crusoe, The
1954,Ag 6,10:5
Ehrlich, Karl (Producer)
Good Soldier Schweik, The 1963,Ag 21,38:1
Ehrlich, Max
Wien Du Stadt der Lieder; (Vienna City of Song)
1931,Mr 20,29:1
Susanne Macht Ordnung 1931,O 12,28:2
Die vom Rummelplatz 1932,Ja 2,14:2
Tanzhusar, Der 1933,Ap 10,8:4
Hochtourist, Der 1934,Ja 13,16:4
Schlemihl, Der 1934,N 5,23:1
Ehrlich, Max (Original Author)
Glass Web, The 1953,N 12,37:5
Naked Edge 1961,Jl 1,9:1
Ehrlich, Peter
Emil and the Detectives 1964,D 24,8:3
Ehser, Else
Girls Behind Bars 1950,My 10,41:2
Glass Tower, The; (Glaserne Turm, Der)
1959,Ag 27,24:4
Eibenschuetz, Lia
Korvettenkapitaen, Der 1933,Mr 20,18:3
Eichberg, Richard (Director)
Monna Vanna 1923,S 25,8:2
Whirl of Life, The 1929,Mr 25,32:2
Wasted Love 1929,D 30,16:4
Why Cry at Parting 1930,F 4,28:3
Night Birds 1931,Ja 3,21:2
Draufganger, Der; Daredevil, The
1932,Ja 17,VIII,6:1
Koenigin der Unterwelt 1932,D 9,26:5

Es geht um mein Leben; My Life Is at Stake
1938,Ap 11,12:3
Tiger von Eschnapur, Der 1938,Ap 30,18:2
Indian Tomb, The; Tiger von Eschnapur, Der
1938,My 14,18:2
Eichberg, Richard (Producer)
Song 1928,Ag 22,24:2
Koenigin der Unterwelt 1932,D 9,26:5
Eichberger, Willy
Inge und die Millionen 1934,Ap 13,25:1
Kaiserwalzer 1934,D 29,11:2
Liebelei 1936,F 28,18:2
Vienna Burgtheater 1937,O 27,47:1
Postillon of Lonjumeau, The 1937,N 20,21:3
Prater, Wiener 1938,D 3,11:3
Wiener Prater 1938,D 3,11:3
Alles Fuer Veronika 1939,F 4,11:2
Pompadour, Die 1939,F 27,11:3
Favorit der Kaiserin, Der; Favorite of the Empress,
The 1939,D 25,29:3
Eichbichler, Thea
Zwischen Himmel und Erde; Between Heaven and
Earth 1935,Ja 21,19:3
Eichheim, Josef
Klein Dorrit 1935,O 19,21:2
Klosterjaeger, Der 1936,Ja 3,13:7
Frauen vom Tannhof, Die 1936,F 18,27:1
Gordian, Der Tyrann 1937,Je 21,15:3
Drama on the Threshing Floor 1937,O 30,22:3
Lachdoktor, Der; Laugh Doctor, The
1938,Mr 12,13:4
Lachende Dritte, Der 1938,Ap 9,11:2
Gross Reinemachen; General Housecleaning
1938,Je 23,27:2
Kampf mit dem Drachen, Der; Fight With the
Dragon, The 1939,N 6,20:3
Eichlerowna, Irene
Krawa Roza; Red Rose 1938,O 13,29:2
Eichnor, Edna
Roughneck, The 1924,D 3,14:1
Eidsaa, Alma
Disputed Passage 1939,O 26,27:2
Eiger, W (Composer)
Beyond Endurance 1946,My 20,18:8
Eileen, Sister (Original Author)
Journey's End, The 1921,Jl 18,16:3
Eilers, Kurt
Last ten Days, The 1956,Ap 12,26:1
Eilers, Sally
Good-Bye Kiss, The 1928,N 12,18:2
Sailor's Holiday 1929,O 21,30:1
Long, Long Trail, The 1929,N 4,28:1
Show of Shows 1929,N 21,24:5
She Couldn't Say No 1930,F 16,III,8:1
Let Us Be Gay 1930,Jl 12,16:4
Dough Boys 1930,S 30,23:1
Reducing 1931,Ja 17,23:1
Parlor, Bedroom and Bath 1931,Ap 4,23:1
Quick Millions 1931,Ap 18,17:3
Black Camel, The 1931,Jl 4,11:5
Holy Terror, A 1931,Jl 20,20:4
Bad Girl 1931,Ag 15,18:3
Over the Hill 1931,N 21,20:4
Dance Team 1932,Ja 16,13:1
Disorderly Conduct 1932,Ap 11,19:2
Hat Check Girl 1932,O 8,15:4
Second Hand Wife 1933,Ja 14,8:4
State Fair 1933,Ja 27,13:2
Sailor's Luck 1933,Mr 17,21:2
Central Airport 1933,My 4,20:5
Hold Me Tight 1933,My 22,18:6
Made on Broadway 1933,Jl 8,14:5
Walls of Gold 1933,O 21,11:3
She Made her Bed 1934,Ap 27,25:1
Carnival 1935,F 16,9:1
Alias Mary Dow 1935,Je 29,16:2
Remember Last Night? 1935,N 21,27:2
Strike Me Pink 1936,Ja 17,15:2
Don't Get Personal 1936,F 22,12:1
Florida Special 1936,My 29,15:2
Without Orders 1936,N 4,41:3
We Have our Moments 1937,Ap 30,17:3
Talk of the Devil 1937,My 15,23:5
Danger Patrol 1937,N 19,27:3
Lady Behave 1938,Ja 28,17:3
Condemned Woman 1938,Ap 22,15:5
Nurse From Brooklyn 1938,My 13,17:3
Tarnished Angel 1938,N 15,27:2
They Made Her a Spy 1939,Mr 29,21:4
Full Confession 1939,S 28,29:4
I Was a Prisoner on Devil's Island
1941,Jl 28,16:4
Wave, A Wac and a Marine, A 1944,Ag 14,11:4
Stage to Tucson 1951,My 5,14:2
Eilum, Joan
South Riding 1938,Ag 2,15:2
Eimberg, Hal (Screenwriter)
In Like Flint 1967,Mr 16,53:2
Einhorn, Carl
Brig, The 1964,S 21,37:4
Einstein, Arik
Sallah 1965,O 13,39:1

Einstein, Carl (Screenwriter)
Amours de Toni, Les 1936,N 5,35:1
Toni 1968,S 19,62:2
Einstein, Charles (Original Author)
While the City Sleeps 1956,My 17,37:1
Eis, Egon (Original Author)
Prison Without Bars 1939,Ap 10,13:2
Eis, Egon (Screenwriter)
Tiger von Berlin, Der 1930,S 15,29:3
Eis, O (Original Author)
Prison Without Bars 1939,Ap 10,13:2
Eisen, A
Flames on the Volga 1958,Ja 27,21:7
Eisenstein, Sergei M (Director)
Ten Days That Shook the World 1928,N 3,24:3
Old and New 1930,My 3,23:1
Thunder Over Mexico 1933,S 25,18:4
Thunder Over Mexico 1939,F 13,13:3
Alexander Nevsky 1939,Mr 23,27:1
Time in the Sun 1940,O 1,29:2
Ivan the Terrible, Part I 1947,Mr 10,25:2
Ivan the Terrible, Part II 1959,N 25,22:4
Eisenstein, Sergei M (Miscellaneous)
Eisenstein in Mexico 1933,N 1,25:5
Eisenstein, Sergei M (Original Author)
Alexander Nevsky 1939,Mr 23,27:1
Eisenstein, Sergei M (Producer)
Seeds of Freedom 1943,Ag 25,17:2
Eisenstein, Sergei M (Screenwriter)
Ivan the Terrible, Part I 1947,Mr 10,25:2
Ivan the Terrible, Part II 1959,N 25,22:4
Eisentein, Sergei (Miscellaneous)
Strike 1968,Mr 15,30:1
Eiser, Frank B (Original Author)
Farmer Takes a Wife, The 1935,Ag 9,21:2
Eisholtz, Peter
Truxa 1937,Jl 26,15:2
Eisimont, Victor (Director)
Girl From Leningrad 1941,D 20,25:2
Once There Was a Girl 1945,D 24,19:2
Eisinger, Jo (Original Author)
Just off Broadway 1942,Ag 29,18:4
Walls Came Tumbling Down, The 1946,N 9,13:5
Crime of Passion 1957,Ja 10,25:1
Eisinger, Jo (Screenwriter)
Spider, The 1946,Je 21,20:3
Night and the City 1950,Je 10,11:2
Sleeping City, The 1950,S 21,20:2
System, The 1953,My 23,19:3
Bedevilled 1955,Ap 23,23:1
Crime of Passion 1957,Ja 10,25:1
House of the Seven Hawks, The 1959,D 17,51:2
As the Sea Rages 1961,My 18,41:1
Poppy is Also a Flower, The 1967,D 14,62:4
Eisler, Hanns (Composer)
Abdul the Damned 1936,My 11,16:2
400,000,000, The 1939,Mr 8,19:2
Forgotten Village, The 1941,N 19,26:3
Eisler, Hanns (Miscellaneous)
Clown Must Laugh, A 1938,O 12,35:2
Eisler, Hanns (Screenwriter)
Fidelio 1961,My 13,10:1
Eisley, Anthony
Naked Kiss, The 1964,O 29,38:1
Eismont, V (Director)
Apartment in Moscow 1962,My 28,25:5
Eisner, Maria
Lindenwirtin vom Rhein, Die 1931,S 25,28:7
Das Lockende Ziel 1933,Je 19,18:2
Eisteddfod Chorus of Blaendy
Proud Valley 1941,My 17,19:2
Eitz, Theodor von
Locked Doors 1925,Ja 12,11:2
Ek, Anders
Naked Night, The 1956,Ap 10,27:5
Seventh Seal 1958,O 14,44:1
Ekaterinsky, M
New Teacher, The 1941,Ap 7,13:3
Ekberg, Anita
Blood Alley 1955,O 6,25:3
Artists and Models 1955,D 22,20:1
War and Peace 1956,Ag 22,26:2
Back From Eternity 1956,S 8,20:6
Hollywood or Bust 1956,D 24,8:1
Zarak 1956,D 27,22:1
Paris Holiday 1958,My 10,19:2
Screaming Mimi 1958,Je 26,23:3
Man Inside, The 1959,F 5,24:7
Sign of the Gladiator 1959,D 3,46:1
Dolce Vita, La 1961,Ap 20,30:1
Boccaccio '70 (The Temptation of Dr Antonio);
Temptation of Dr Antonio, The (Boccaccio '70)
1962,Je 27,40:1
Call Me Bwana 1963,Jl 4,9:1
4 for Texas 1963,D 26,33:3
Alphabet Murders, The 1966,Jl 12,36:2
Way...Way Out 1966,O 27,55:1
Woman Times Seven 1967,Je 28,38:1
Cobra, The 1968,Mr 28,52:3
Ekborg, Lars
Magician, The 1959,Ag 28,27:1
Swedish Wedding Night 1965,N 15,48:1

Ekelund, Allan (Producer)
Wild Strawberries 1959,Je 23,37:1
Ekelund, Karin
Haelsingar 1934,S 25,25:2
Flickorna Fran Gamla Stan 1934,D 27,25:4
Skaergaards-Flirt 1936,Ap 8,26:3
Vaaran Pojke 1936,O 10,21:3
Familjen Som Var En Karusel 1937,My 22,19:3
Old Gods Still Live, The 1937,N 5,19:4
Berslagsfolk 1938,Mr 12,13:3
Du Gamla, Du Fria; Thou old, Tho Free
1939,Mr 21,27:2
Kustens Glada Kavaljerer; Coast's Happy
Cavaliers, The 1939,My 23,27:2
Ekerot, Bengt
Interlude 1949,Ja 3,19:2
Seventh Seal 1958,O 14,44:1
Magician, The 1959,Ag 28,27:1
Ekezian, Harry
Island of Lost Souls 1933,Ja 13,19:2
Alice in Wonderland 1933,D 23,19:1
Man on the Flying Trapeze 1935,Ag 3,16:2
Ekk, Nikolai
Nightingale 1936,N 4,41:2
Ekk, Nikolai (Director)
Road to Life 1932,Ja 28,24:2
Nightingale 1936,N 4,41:2
Ekk, Nikolai (Original Author)
Nightingale 1936,N 4,41:2
Ekk, Nikolai (Screenwriter)
Road to Life 1932,Ja 28,24:2
Ekland, Britt
After the Fox 1966,D 24,11:1
Bobo, The 1967,S 29,53:1
Double Man, The 1968,My 2,57:1
Night They Raided Minsky's, The
1968,D 23,43:1
Ekloff, Frank
Dawn to Dawn 1933,D 27,23:5
Eklund, Bengt
Doll, The 1964,Ja 14,27:1
Eklund, Ernst
Sangen Till Henne; Song to Her, The
1935,F 22,27:3
Under Falsk Flagg 1937,Ja 20,18:5
Froeken Blir Piga 1937,Je 12,8:3
Ekman, Goesta
Faust 1926,D 7,21:2
Heart of a Clown 1928,Ja 17,23:2
Discord 1928,F 7,30:3
Husband by Proxy, A 1928,Je 11,27:1
Last Night, The 1930,Ja 27,18:4
For Her Sake 1930,N 11,29:1
Brokiga Blad 1931,N 30,16:2
Charles XII 1933,Mr 31,23:3
Kaera Slaekten 1934,My 14,20:4
Swedenhielms 1935,S 6,12:3
Intermezzo 1937,D 25,10:6
Ekman, Hans
John Ericsson Victor of Hampton Roads
1938,My 18,17:2
Ekman, Hasse
Med Folket Foer Fosterlandet 1939,F 21,14:2
Interlude 1949,Ja 3,19:2
Naked Night, The 1956,Ap 10,27:5
Devil's Wanton, The 1962,Jl 5,21:2
Ekman, Hasse (Director)
Interlude 1949,Ja 3,19:2
Ekman, Hasse (Screenwriter)
Interlude 1949,Ja 3,19:2
Ekman, John
Baldvins Brollop; Baldwin's Wedding
1938,D 27,13:2
Lasse-Maja 1943,Mr 22,15:4
Ekmanner, Agneta
Puss and Kram 1967,S 25,56:1
Hugs and Kisses 1968,Ag 19,44:1
Ekstam, Nils
Vaaran Pojke 1936,O 10,21:3
Sun Over Klara 1944,My 1,20:8
Ekstrom, Maria
Katrina 1949,N 18,35:3
Ekstrom, Marta
John Ericsson Victor of Hampton Roads
1938,My 18,17:2
Ekstrom, Per Olof (Original Author)
One Summer of Happiness 1955,Mr 22,35:2
El, Sam
Dragon Sky 1964,Ag 25,28:2
El Atrache, Farid
Little Miss Devil 1951,D 8,9:2
el Aziz, Abd
Stampede 1930,Ap 28,24:5
El Chafian
Zandunga, La 1938,My 14,18:2
Tierra Brava 1938,O 29,15:6
Bajo el Cielo de Mexico; Beneath the Sky of
Mexico 1938,D 31,7:3
El Chicote
Juntos pero no Revueltos; United but not Mixed
1939,O 23,15:3

El Kader, Fawzia
Battle of Algiers, The 1967,S 21,56:1
el Laberinto, Paco
Pride and the Passion, The 1957,Je 29,10:6
Elaine, Sybil
People's Enemy, The 1935,Ap 30,13:7
Elam, Jack
Sundowners, The 1950,My 5,17:2
One Way Street 1950,My 12,33:3
American Guerrilla in the Philippines
1950,N 8,37:2
High Lonesome 1950,D 8,40:4
Bird of Paradise 1951,Mr 15,37:2
Rawhide 1951,Mr 26,19:2
Rancho Notorious 1952,My 15,39:5
My Man and I 1952,S 6,12:6
Lure of the Wilderness 1952,O 4,15:2
Kansas City Confidential 1952,N 29,11:2
Count the Hours 1953,Je 24,30:4
Ride Vaquero 1953,Jl 16,17:2
Gun Belt 1953,Ag 1,8:2
Moonlighter, The 1953,S 23,37:2
Appointment in Honduras 1953,N 19,41:4
Vera Cruz 1954,D 27,22:4
Cattle Queen of Montana 1955,Ja 26,22:1
Far Country, The 1955,F 14,24:2
Moonfleet 1955,Je 25,9:2
Man From Laramie, The 1955,S 1,20:2
Kismet 1955,D 9,32:2
Artists and Models 1955,D 22,20:1
Jubal 1956,Ap 25,39:1
Dragoon Wells Massacre 1957,My 6,25:2
Gunfight at the O K Corral 1957,My 30,23:2
Night Passage 1957,Jl 25,28:1
Baby Face Nelson 1957,D 12,35:1
Last Sunset, The 1961,Je 15,51:1
Comancheros, The 1961,N 2,42:1
Pocketful of Miracles 1961,D 19,39:1
Night of the Grizzly, The 1966,Je 23,29:1
Last Challenge, The 1967,D 28,25:1
Firecreek 1968,F 22,36:2
Never a Dull Moment 1968,Ag 15,46:2
Elambert, Paulette
Sans Famille 1935,Je 4,26:5
Maternelle, La 1935,O 15,19:1
Crime et Chatiment; Crime and Punishment
1935,N 13,25:3
Man of the Hour, The 1940,N 21,43:2
Elan, Joan
Girls of Pleasure Island, The 1953,My 16,10:1
King's Thief, The 1955,Ag 13,7:2
Darby's Rangers 1958,F 13,23:2
Elanskaya, Klavdia
House I Live in, The 1959,Ap 20,34:2
Elanskya, E
Mistress, The 1954,My 31,9:2
Elbaum, Ruth
Mirele Efros 1939,O 21,12:2
Elberhardt, William
Footloose Heiress 1937,O 9,16:2
Elbeze, Max
Gervaise 1957,N 12,46:1
Elbozhenko
Last Game, The 1964,O 25,41:5 (Incorrect in this
edition; use 1964,O 26,41:5 elsewhere)
Elder, John (Screenwriter)
Curse of the Werewolf, The 1961,Je 8,40:2
Phantom of the Opera, The 1962,Ag 23,25:2
Evil of Frankenstein, The 1964,Je 18,29:2
Elder, Ruth
Moran of the Marines 1928,O 15,16:1
Eldredge, Florence
Thirteen Women 1932,O 15,13:1
Eldredge, George
Jam Session 1944,My 3,25:3
Just Across the Street 1952,Je 28,12:4
Pickup on South Street 1953,Je 18,38:2
It Came From Outer Space 1953,Je 18,38:2
Mom and Dad 1957,Ja 31,21:1
Third Voice, The 1960,Mr 7,24:5
Eldredge, John
Man With two Faces, The 1934,Jl 12,20:2
Flirtation Walk 1934,N 29,33:1
White Cockatoo, The 1935,Ja 16,21:1
Woman in Red, The 1935,Mr 23,11:3
Girl From 10th Avenue, The 1935,My 27,20:6
Oil for the Lamps of China 1935,Je 6,25:2
Goose and the Gander, The 1935,S 12,29:2
Dr Socrates 1935,O 3,29:2
Man of Iron 1935,D 7,22:2
Dangerous 1935,D 27,14:1
Snowed Under 1936,Mr 30,17:5
Murder by an Aristocrat 1936,Je 13,13:2
His Brother's Wife 1936,Ag 15,6:2
Follow Your Heart 1936,O 22,31:1
Holy Terror, The 1937,Ja 30,21:2
Mysterious Crossing 1937,F 2,20:5
Charlie Chan at the Olympics 1937,My 24,23:1
Go Getter, The 1937,Je 4,27:2
Mr Dodd Takes the Air 1937,Ag 12,14:2
One Mile From Heaven 1937,Ag 19,23:1
Sh! The Octopus 1937,D 24,21:2
Women Are Like That 1938,Ap 11,12:2

Eldredge, John — Cont
King of the Underworld 1939,Ja 7,6:2
Undercover Doctor 1939,Je 1,31:2
Dr Kildare's Strange Case 1940,Ap 12,19:2
Devil's Pipeline, The 1940,N 11,22:4
Always a Bride 1940,N 21,43:3
Flight From Destiny 1941,Mr 28,26:7
Horror Island 1941,Mr 31,11:3
Black Cat, The 1941,Ap 26,20:3
Blossoms in the Dust 1941,Je 27,14:4
Mad Doctor of Market Street, The 1942,Ja 5,21:5
Bermuda Mystery 1944,My 13,17:1
Circumstantial Evidence 1945,Ap 21,18:3
Up Goes Maisie 1946,Ja 25,26:7
Backlash 1947,My 24,10:5
Second Chance 1947,S 20,12:4
Top o' the Morning 1949,S 1,25:2
Champagne for Caesar 1950,My 12,33:2
Eldrett, Freddie
Reach for Glory 1963,S 10,46:1
Eldridge, Florence
Studio Murder Mystery, The 1929,Je 10,23:1
Charming Sinners 1929,Jl 8,17:3
Greene Murder Case, The 1929,Ag 10,11:3
Divorcee, The 1930,My 10,25:3
Matrimonial Bed, The 1930,Ag 25,14:2
Great Jasper, The 1933,F 17,5:3
Dangerously Yours 1933,F 23,20:3
Story of Temple Drake, The 1933,My 6,11:2
Modern Hero, A 1934,Ap 20,17:1
Miserables, Les 1935,Ap 22,14:2
Mary of Scotland 1936,Jl 31,22:2
Another Part of the Forest 1948,My 19,30:2
Live Today for Tomorrow 1948,D 6,29:2
Christopher Columbus 1949,O 13,33:2
Inherit the Wind 1960,O 13,41:1
Eldridge, John
Murder of Dr Harrigan, The 1936,Ja 21,27:5
Blind Alley 1939,My 23,27:2
Eldridge, John (Director)
Brandy for the Parson 1952,Ag 18,13:4
Scotch on the Rocks 1954,Je 14,18:2
Fuss Over Feathers 1954,D 27,22:6
Eldridge, John (Screenwriter)
Pool of London 1951,N 28,37:2
Scotch on the Rocks 1954,Je 14,18:2
Out of the Clouds 1957,Ag 1,20:4
Smallest Show on Earth, The 1957,N 23,11:2
Boy Who Stole a Million, The 1960,D 22,18:3
Electric Flag
You Are What You Eat 1968,S 25,38:1
Eles, Sandor
Naked Edge 1961,Jl 1,9:1
Evil of Frankenstein, The 1964,Je 18,29:2
Elesinger, Tess (Screenwriter)
Are Husbands Necessary? 1942,Jl 9,17:2
Elfstrom, John
One Summer of Happiness 1955,Mr 22,35:2
Lesson in Love, A 1960,Mr 15,46:1
Elfusio, Maud
Flamboyant Sex, The 1963,Ag 13,25:1
Elg, Taina
Prodigal, The 1955,My 14,10:7
Diane 1956,Ja 13,18:1
Gaby 1956,My 10,26:3
Girls, Les 1957,O 4,27:2
Imitation General 1958,Ag 21,22:2
Watusi 1959,Jl 2,15:2
39 Steps, The 1960,O 11,55:2
Elgar, Avril
Room at the Top 1959,Mr 31,26:1
Ladies Who Do 1963,N 26,52:2
Elgen, Jack
Hoodlum Priest, The 1961,Ap 3,28:5
Elgen, Madge
Kyritz-Pyritz 1932,Ag 9,20:5
Elhardt, Kaye
Psychomania 1964,F 15,14:3
Elias, Cyrus
Francis of Assisi 1961,Jl 29,8:2
Elias, Francisco (Director)
Boliche 1935,My 28,30:2
Mi Madrecita; My Little Mother 1940,S 24,26:6
Elias, Francisco (Producer)
Boliche 1935,My 28,30:2
Elias, Michael
Brig, The 1964,S 21,37:4
Elias, Miriam
Broken Hearts 1926,Mr 3,26:1
Eliazaroff, E
His Hour 1924,O 7,26:1
Elick, E H
Walleyed Nippon 1963,S 3,36:1
Elinor, Peggy
Sinners in Silk 1924,S 8,15:3
Elinson, Irving (Miscellaneous)
Lemon Drop Kid, The 1951,Mr 22,41:2
Elinson, Irving (Screenwriter)
Belle of New York, The 1952,Mr 6,25:6
By the Light of the Silvery Moon
1953,Mr 27,28:2
Lucky Me 1954,Ap 10,11:2

Eliopoulos, Dinos
House on Stournara Street, The 1960,O 17,33:4
ELIOT
See Also ELLIOT, ELLIOTT
Eliot, George (Original Author)
Romola 1924,D 2,13:2
Mill On the Floss, The 1939,N 15,19:3
Eliot, Jamor George Fielding (Original Author)
Federal Bullets 1937,D 27,11:1
Eliot, T S
Murder in the Cathedral 1952,Mr 26,35:2
Eliot, T S (Screenwriter)
Murder in the Cathedral 1952,Mr 26,35:2
Elis, Edward
Thin Man, The 1934,Je 30,18:5
Eliscu, Edward (Composer)
Flying Down to Rio 1933,D 22,25:2
Stingaree 1934,My 18,27:1
Heat's on, The 1943,N 26,29:2
Eliscu, Edward (Miscellaneous)
Diplomaniacs 1933,Ap 29,14:2
Paddy O'Day 1936,F 8,19:2
Eliscu, Edward (Screenwriter)
Silk Hat Kid 1935,Ag 7,22:5
Paddy O'Day 1936,F 8,19:2
Every Saturday Night 1936,Mr 14,10:2
Little Miss Nobody 1936,Je 6,21:1
High Tension 1936,Jl 11,11:4
Little Tough Guys in Society 1938,N 21,14:4
Charlie McCarthy, Detective 1939,D 25,29:2
Sis Hopkins 1941,My 1,27:5
Something to Shout About 1943,Ap 8,27:3
Three Husbands 1951,Mr 9,30:2
Alice in Wonderland 1951,Jl 27,15:2
Eliscu, Fernanda
Winterset 1936,D 4,31:1
Elizabeth (Original Author)
Mr Skeffington 1944,My 26,23:2
Elizondo, Salvador (Producer)
Rosanna 1956,My 17,37:2
Elkas, Edward
West of the Water Tower 1923,D 31,9:3
Elkins, Michael (Screenwriter)
Esther and the King 1960,N 19,13:4
Elkins, Saul (Original Author)
Crime of Dr Forbes, The 1936,Jl 6,11:4
Charlie Chan at the Race Track 1936,Ag 15,6:2
Off the Record 1939,F 18,12:2
Elkins, Saul (Producer)
One Last Fling 1949,Jl 1,14:6
House Across the Street 1949,S 2,14:4
Barricade 1950,Mr 25,8:6
Colt 45 1950,My 6,8:6
Return of the Frontiersman 1950,Je 10,11:3
This Side of the Law 1950,Jl 7,15:2
Sugarfoot 1951,F 12,19:4
Raton Pass 1951,Ap 20,25:1
Elkins, Saul (Screenwriter)
Crime of Dr Forbes, The 1936,Jl 6,11:4
Under Your Spell 1936,N 7,15:2
Women in Prison 1938,Mr 1,19:3
Elkus, Edward
Sainted Devil, A 1924,N 24,15:3
Ellen, Jack
Headless Ghost, The 1959,Ap 30,37:2
Ellenstein, Robert
Rogue Cop 1954,S 18,12:2
Illegal 1955,O 29,12:6
3:10 to Yuma 1957,Ag 29,22:1
Too Much, Too Soon 1958,My 10,19:2
North by Northwest 1959,Ag 7,28:1
Gazebo, The 1960,Ja 16,14:4
Pay or Die 1960,My 27,22:2
Deathwatch 1967,Je 28,38:1
Ellerbe, Harry
Misleading Lady, The 1932,Ap 9,18:1
Murder on a Honeymoon 1935,Mr 4,12:2
So Red the Rose 1935,N 28,39:1
Magnetic Monster, The 1953,My 14,32:5
Desk Set 1957,My 16,28:2
Man Who Understood, The 1959,O 3,14:7
House of Usher, The 1960,S 15,45:4
Haunted Palace, The 1964,Ja 30,24:1
Ellers, Sally
Dry Martini 1928,N 5,26:5 (In Addenda)
Ellie, Diane
Laughter 1930,N 15,15:3
Ellin, Stanley (Original Author)
Big Night, The 1952,Mr 20,37:5
Leda 1961,Jl 19,33:1
Nothing but the Best 1964,Jl 14,28:1
Ellin, Stanley (Screenwriter)
Big Night, The 1952,Mr 20,37:5
Elling, Alwin (Director)
Befehl Ist Befehl 1936,N 28,13:3
Kein Wort von Liebe; Not a Word About Love 1938,S 10,20:3
Seefahrt die Ist Lustig, Eine; Merry Sea Trip, A 1938,O 22,14:2
Kleines Bezirksgericht; Little Country Court 1939,F 18,12:4
Hummel-Hummel 1939,Mr 11,21:2
Lustige Witwenball, Der; Merry Widows' Ball,

The 1939,My 1,21:2
Ellington, Duke
Hit Parade, The 1937,My 31,11:2
Reveille With Beverly 1943,Ap 24,17:2
Anatomy of a Murder 1959,Jl 3,10:1
Ellington, Duke (Composer)
Hit Parade, The 1937,My 31,11:2
New Faces of 1937 1937,Jl 2,25:1
Ellington, E A (Original Author)
Irish Eyes Are Smiling 1944,N 8,27:1
Gilda 1946,Mr 15,27:2
ELLIOT
See Also ELIOT, ELLIOTT
Elliot, Arthur (Screenwriter)
Mediterannean Holiday 1964,D 16,51:1
Elliot, Biff
I, The Jury 1953,Ag 22,8:2
House of Bamboo 1955,Jl 2,13:2
Good Morning, Miss Dove 1955,N 24,41:1
Enemy Below, The 1957,D 26,23:2
Pork Chop Hill 1959,My 30,9:2
Story of Page One, The 1960,Ja 14,28:1
Elliot, Laura
Special Agent 1949,Ag 22,13:1
Thelma Jordon 1950,Ja 19,35:2
Girl's School 1950,F 3,29:2
Paid in Full 1950,F 16,28:2
Strangers on a Train 1951,Jl 4,13:2
When Worlds Collide 1952,F 7,30:2
Denver and Rio Grande, The 1952,My 17,22:7
French Line, The 1954,My 15,13:2
About Mrs Leslie 1954,Je 28,16:2
Elliot, Rita
Robby 1968,Ag 15,46:3
ELLIOTT
See Also ELIOT, ELLIOT
Elliott, Clinton (Composer)
Secrets of the Reef 1956,Jl 24,19:2
Elliott, Clyde E (Cinematographer)
Booloo 1938,Jl 30,10:2
Elliott, Clyde E (Director)
Western Ways 1922,Ja 30,16:2
Lamp Lighter, The 1922,Ap 3,18:2
My Rural Relations 1922,D 24,VII,2:2 (In Addenda)
Bring 'Em Back Alive 1932,Je 18,9:2
Devil Tiger 1934,F 9,23:2
Frank Buck's Jungle Cavalcade 1941,Jl 4,17:1
Elliott, Clyde E (Miscellaneous)
Winter's Tale, A 1922,Ja 23,11:4
Elliott, Clyde E (Original Author)
Booloo 1938,Jl 30,10:2
Elliott, Del
Desert Song, The 1929,My 2,20:6
Elliott, Denholm
Dear Mr Prohack 1950,Jl 15,7:2
Breaking Through the Sound Barrier 1952,N 7,19:1
Cruel Sea, The 1953,Ag 11,18:5
Holly and the Ivy, The 1954,F 5,16:1
Heart of the Matter, The 1954,N 19,20:2
Man Who Loved Redheads, The 1955,Jl 26,29:2
Night my Number Came up, The 1955,D 20,39:5
Lease of Life 1956,F 10,18:1
Scent of Mystery 1960,F 19,23:1
Nothing but the Best 1964,Jl 14,28:1
Station Six-Sahara 1964,N 12,40:2
King Rat 1965,O 28,48:1
Alfie 1966,Ag 25,42:1
Spy With a Cold Nose, The 1966,D 20,58:2
Night They Raided Minsky's, The 1968,D 23,43:1
Sea Gull, The 1968,D 24,14:1
Elliott, Dick
It Happened in New York 1935,Ap 6,10:1
China Passage 1937,Ap 16,27:2
Outcasts of Poker Flat, The 1937,Ap 27,18:3
Under Western Stars 1938,Je 25,7:3
Mr Smith Goes to Washington 1939,O 20,27:2
Flight Angels 1940,My 27,23:2
Behind the News 1941,Ja 16,25:3
Pittsburgh Kid, The 1941,S 23,27:4
Top Sergeant Mulligan 1941,N 12,31:3
Wintertime 1943,S 30,27:2
Christmas in Connecticut 1945,Jl 28,7:2
Night Unto Night 1949,Je 11,11:2
Blue Grass of Kentucky 1950,Ja 27,29:2
Rock Island Trail 1950,Je 5,19:3
Park Row 1952,D 22,20:2
Witness to Murder 1954,Ap 16,16:4
Elliott, Duncan
Triumph over Violence 1968,Jl 10,27:3
Elliott, Duncan (Narrator)
Kamikaze 1962,O 3,44:4
Elliott, Edythe
Show Them no Mercy 1935,D 9,25:2
I Married a Doctor 1936,Ap 20,17:1
Double Danger 1938,F 10,17:5

Elliott, Edythe— Cont
Fixer Dugan 1939,My 6,21:2
Dick Tracy 1946,Ja 12,10:7
That Brennan Girl 1946,D 9,34:3
Elliott, Eileen
Dr Coppelius 1968,D 26,56:1
Elliott, Frank
Impossible Mrs Bellew, The 1922,O 23,10:1
Ruggles of Red Gap 1923,S 10,15:4
Red Lights 1923,S 10,15:4
Secrets 1924,Mr 25,25:2
Goldfish, The 1924,My 20,15:2
For Sale 1924,Jl 14,11:5
Sinners in Silk 1924,S 8,15:3
This Woman 1924,O 21,21:3
Love's Wilderness 1924,D 22,20:2
Dark Angel, The 1925,O 12,19:3
Fourth Commandment, The 1927,Ap 6,25:1
Playboy of Paris 1930,N 1,23:2
Doctor Rhythm 1938,My 19,25:2
Life With Father 1947,Ag 16,6:6
Fan, The 1949,Ap 2,12:2
Elliott, Gerald (Miscellaneous)
Inspector Hornleigh 1939,Je 15,27:3
Elliott, Gerald (Screenwriter)
Great Mr Handel, The 1943,S 10,29:3
Elliott, Gordon
Private Life of Helen of Troy, The 1927,D 10,14:7
Restless Youth 1929,Ja 1,60:1
Broadway Scandals 1929,O 29,35:1
Devil Dogs of the Air 1935,F 7,23:2
Traveling Saleslady 1935,Mr 29,26:2
Girl From 10th Avenue, The 1935,My 27,20:6
Goose and the Gander, The 1935,S 12,29:2
Murder of Dr Harrigan, The 1936,Ja 21,27:5
Murder by an Aristocrat 1936,Je 13,13:2
Case of the Velvet Claws, The 1936,Ag 29,16:3
Polo Joe 1936,N 5,35:1
Case of the Black Cat, The 1936,D 26,15:4
Fugitive in the Sky 1937,Ja 16,21:1
Midnight Court 1937,Mr 4,27:3
Melody for Two 1937,My 21,19:5
Love Takes Flight 1937,S 27,24:3
Wife, Doctor and Nurse 1937,O 11,26:5
Boots and Saddles 1937,N 8,19:2
Boy of the Streets 1938,Ja 24,17:1
Lady in the Morgue, The 1938,My 9,13:3
Devil's Party, The 1938,My 31,8:3
Elliott, Jack (Composer)
Apache Rose 1947,Jl 23,19:3
Elliott, James S (Producer)
It Happened in Athens 1962,N 15,46:2
Elliott, John
Spoilers, The 1923,Ag 6,14:2
What Happened to Jones 1926,F 9,22:1
For the Defense 1930,Jl 19,7:5
Conquering Horde, The 1931,Mr 30,25:2
Week Ends Only 1932,Je 18,9:2
Call Her Savage 1932,N 25,19:2
Red Hot Tires 1935,Mr 1,16:3
Headin' East 1938,Ja 15,19:2
Heart of Arizona 1938,Ap 16,17:1
Jesse James 1939,Ja 14,13:1
Elliott, Leonard
Overture to Glory 1940,F 12,14:2
Buck Privates 1941,F 14,15:2
It Started With Eve 1941,O 3,27:1
Weddings and Babies 1960,O 6,51:3
Elliott, Lillian
Proud Flesh 1925,Ap 14,26:1
Old Clothes 1925,N 9,25:1
Sally, Irene and Mary 1925,D 7,19:1
Partners Again, With Potash and Perlmutter 1926,F 15,16:4
Ankles Preferred 1927,Ap 18,21:2
Her Wedding Night 1930,S 29,19:1
Liliom 1930,O 4,15:2
Single Sin, The 1931,Mr 17,34:3
Man I Killed, The 1932,Ja 20,17:4
Polly of the Circus 1932,Mr 19,11:2
Trumpet Blows, The 1934,Ap 14,18:2
Jury's Secret, The 1938,F 4,17:2
Wanted by the Police 1938,S 26,13:2
Road to Happiness 1942,Mr 27,27:4
Laurel and Hardy's Laughing 20's 1965,N 18,55:2
Elliott, Mary
Thousands Cheer 1943,S 14,27:1
Elliott, Maxine
Fighting Odds 1917,O 1,14:2
Elliott, Peter
Battle Beneath the Earth 1968,S 12,54:3
Elliott, Richard
Gift of Gab 1934,S 26,17:6
My Favorite Blonde 1942,Ap 2,27:2
Elliott, Richard Karl Sgt
Cease Fire! 1953,N 25,17:1
Elliott, Robert
Checkers 1919,Ag 25,8:5
Virgin Paradise, A 1921,Ag 4,18:3
Lights of New York 1928,Jl 9,25:1
Romance of the Underworld 1929,Ja 7,36:2
Lone Wolf's Daughter, The 1929,Mr 4,20:2
Thunderbolt 1929,Je 21,17:2

Elliott, Robert— Cont

Hide Out 1930,Ap 12,23:1
Divorcee, The 1930,My 10,25:3
Sweet Mamma 1930,Jl 12,16:4
Doorway to Hell, The 1930,N 1,23:2
Finger Points, The 1931,Mr 28,15:3
Captain Thunder 1931,My 11,15:4
Maltese Falcon, The 1931,My 29,26:5
Star Witness, The 1931,Ag 4,19:5
Five Star Final 1931,S 11,24:2
Murder at Midnight 1931,O 5,17:3
Midnight Patrol, The 1932,My 7,11:5
White Eagle 1932,S 24,18:4
Madison Square Garden 1932,O 12,26:5
Phantom of Crestwood, The 1932,O 17,18:3
Crime of the Century, The 1933,Mr 13,18:2
Lady Killer 1934,Ja 1,28:2
Gambling Lady 1934,Ap 5,25:2
Transatlantic Merry-Go-Round 1934,N 1,25:2
Times Square Lady 1935,Mr 15,25:3
World Accuses, The 1935,Mr 21,27:2
Trade Winds 1939,Ja 13,17:2
Saint Strikes Back, The 1939,Mr 9,18:2
Mickey, the Kid 1939,Jl 6,27:1
I Stole a Million 1939,Ag 7,11:2
Roaring Twenties, The 1939,N 11,12:1

Elliott, Rose
Woman on the Run 1950,N 30,24:2

Elliott, Ross
Angel on the Amazon 1948,D 27,16:4
Chinatown at Midnight 1949,N 18,35:3
I Can Get It for You Wholesale 1951,Ap 5,34:4
Beast From 20,000 Fathoms, The 1953,Je 25,23:1
Women's Prison 1955,F 3,18:5
D-Day, The Sixth of June 1956,My 30,13:1
African Manhunt 1957,Ap 20,21:4

Elliott, Scott
Kiss and Tell 1945,O 26,16:2
Song of my Heart 1948,Mr 5,17:3
French Line, The 1954,My 15,13:2

Elliott, Stephen
Three Hours to Kill 1954,S 4,6:4

Elliott, Tom
Win That Girl 1928,O 1,23:1

Elliott, William
Hearts of the World 1918,Ap 5,13:1
In old Sacramento 1946,Ap 29,24:4
Plainsman and the Lady, The 1946,N 4,33:1
Wyoming 1947,Jl 25,12:5
Fabulous Texan, The 1947,D 26,22:5
Old Los Angeles 1948,Jl 12,11:2
Last Bandit, The 1949,Mr 21,19:2
Hellfire 1949,My 30,9:4

Ellis, Andersen (Screenwriter)
Mortal Storm, The 1940,Je 21,25:2

Ellis, Antony (Original Author)
Ride Back, The 1957,Ap 30,24:1

Ellis, Bobby
Babe Ruth Story, The 1948,Jl 29,17:2
El Paso 1949,Mr 24,35:2

Ellis, Dellie
Girls Under 21 1940,N 11,22:4

Ellis, Desmond Walter
Ship Was Loaded, The 1958,Ja 20,20:1

Ellis, Diane
Leatherneck, The 1929,Ap 22,23:1

Ellis, Dick
Juvenile Court 1938,S 12,13:2

Ellis, Dione
Is Zat So? 1927,My 17,27:2
Cradle Snatchers 1927,My 31,25:2

Ellis, Edith (Original Author)
Idle Rich, The 1929,Je 17,29:1
Affairs of a Gentleman 1934,Je 23,16:7

Ellis, Edward
I Am a Fugitive From a Chain Gang 1932,N 11,17:2
Strictly Personal 1933,Mr 20,18:2
Girl Missing 1933,Ap 1,18:2
After Tonight 1933,N 3,23:2
From Headquarters 1933,N 17,22:4
Hi, Nellie! 1934,F 1,15:5
Ninth Guest, The 1934,Mr 3,8:5
Trumpet Blows, The 1934,Ap 14,18:2
Last Gentleman, The 1934,O 18,26:5
President Vanishes, The 1934,D 8,18:5
Transient Lady 1935,Mr 11,15:1
Return of Peter Grimm, The 1935,O 4,25:2
Lady Consents, The 1936,F 6,23:4
Chatterbox 1936,F 15,18:6
Fury 1936,Je 6,21:1
Texas Rangers, The 1936,S 24,29:1
Winterset 1936,D 4,31:1
Maid of Salem 1937,Mr 4,27:2
Let Them Live 1937,Je 8,30:3
Midnight Madonna 1937,Jl 17,18:1
Man in Blue, The 1937,Ag 30,25:2
Little Miss Broadway 1938,Jl 23,10:4
Man to Remember, A 1938,N 7,23:2
Man of Conquest 1939,Ap 28,31:2
Career 1939,Jl 28,14:2
Main Street Lawyer 1939,N 9,27:2
Three Sons 1939,N 24,29:3
Man Betrayed, A 1941,Mr 27,29:5

Ellis, Edward (Original Author)
Affairs of a Gentleman 1934,Je 23,16:7

Ellis, Elaine
Home Maker, The 1925,Ag 10,8:2

Ellis, Evelyn
Lady From Shanghai, The 1948,Je 10,28:2
Joe Louis Story, The 1953,N 4,29:4
Interrupted Melody 1955,My 6,18:1

Ellis, George
Dragnet 1954,Ag 21,10:2

Ellis, Jacqueline
Traitors, The 1963,Je 27,23:4

Ellis, John
Beasts of Berlin 1939,N 20,15:6
Ski Patrol 1940,My 21,29:4

Ellis, Juney
Jubal 1956,Ap 25,39:1
Last Wagon, The 1956,S 22,20:2
Blue Denim 1959,Jl 31,21:1

Ellis, Kenneth M (Original Author)
Trial of Vivienne Ware, The 1932,Ap 30,19:3

Ellis, Lillian
Strauss, The Waltz King 1929,Jl 22,17:1
Kyritz-Pyritz 1932,Ag 9,20:5
Schoen Ist die Manoeverzeit 1932,Ag 19,20:6
Die Frau von der Man Spricht 1933,Ap 22,16:4

Ellis, Mary
Bella Donna 1935,F 26,16:4
All the King's Horses 1935,Mr 9,19:1
Paris in Spring 1935,Jl 13,16:2
Fatal Lady 1936,Jl 11,11:3
Three Worlds of Gulliver, The 1960,D 17,19:3

Ellis, Mary Jo
Make Way for a Lady 1936,D 12,15:1
Pirate, The 1948,My 21,19:2

Ellis, Maurice
Lost Boundaries 1949,Jl 1,14:4

Ellis, Mirko
Daughters of Destiny (Elizabeth); Elizabeth (Daughters of Destiny) 1954,Jl 6,19:1

Ellis, Patricia
Three on a Match 1932,O 29,18:4
Central Park 1932,D 7,29:3
King's Vacation, The 1933,Ja 20,21:2
Picture Snatcher 1933,My 19,20:3
Elmer the Great 1933,My 26,24:2
Narrow Corner, The 1933,Jl 14,15:3
World Changes, The 1933,O 27,22:3
Convention City 1933,D 25,28:2
Easy to Love 1934,Ja 15,12:2
Here Comes the Groom 1934,Je 16,20:2
Affairs of a Gentleman 1934,Je 23,16:7
Circus Clown, The 1934,Je 30,18:6
St Louis Kid, The 1934,N 1,25:2
Big Hearted Herbert 1934,N 14,23:2
While the Patient Slept 1935,Mr 2,18:2
Hold 'Em Yale 1935,Ap 27,20:6
Night at the Ritz, A 1935,My 16,20:2
Stranded 1935,Je 20,16:2
Bright Lights 1935,Ag 15,15:2
Case of the Lucky Legs, The 1935,N 1,25:1
Pay-Off, The 1935,N 13,25:3
Fish 1936,Ja 25,18:5
Freshman Love 1936,Ja 25,18:5
Boulder Dam 1936,Mr 30,17:5
Snowed Under 1936,Mr 30,17:5
Love Begins at 20 1936,S 19,20:1
Sing Me a Love Song 1936,D 26,15:2
Step Lively, Jeeves 1937,Ap 2,19:6
Melody for Two 1937,My 21,19:5
Gaiety Girls, The 1938,Mr 31,15:1
Lady in the Morgue, The 1938,My 9,13:3
Block-Heads 1938,Ag 30,14:2
Back Door to Heaven 1939,Ap 20,21:2
Fugitive at Large 1939,N 13,15:2

Ellis, Patti Marie
Bright Road 1953,Ap 29,33:5

Ellis, Paul
Dancers of Paris, The 1926,Mr 29,24:3
Three Hours 1927,Mr 8,18:4
Bridge of San Luis Rey, The 1929,My 20,22:6
Common Law, The 1931,Jl 20,20:4
No Man of her Own 1932,D 31,10:1
Hombre Peligroso, Un; Dangerous Man, A 1935,O 14,21:2
No Mataras; Thou Shalt not Kill 1935,N 11,20:2
Ultima Cita, La 1936,Ja 22,15:6
House of a Thousand Candles, The 1936,Ap 2,29:2
Sonadores de la Gloria; Dreamers of Glory 1938,D 10,13:3
Di que me Quieres; Say That You Love Me 1939,Ap 24,13:2
Papa Soltero; Bachelor Father 1939,N 6,20:3

Ellis, Peter
Lord Jeff 1938,Jl 1,22:2

Ellis, Robert
Upstairs and Down 1919,Je 16,11:2
Louisiana 1919,Jl 21,12:3
Ladies Must Live 1921,N 21,20:1
Wild Honey 1922,F 28,17:4
For Sale 1924,Jl 14,11:5
Capital Punishment 1925,F 5,23:3

Ellis, Robert— Cont

Cafe in Cairo, A 1925,Mr 18,19:2
Girl From Montmarte, The 1926,F 25,26:2
Varsity 1928,O 29,29:1
Restless Youth 1929,Ja 1,60:1
Broadway 1929,My 28,36:2
Tonight at Twelve 1929,S 23,24:3
Night Parade 1929,N 11,20:2
Undertow 1930,Mr 1,23:1
Last Parade, The 1931,Mr 2,19:1
Good Bad Girl, The 1931,My 15,20:6
Murder at Midnight 1931,O 5,17:3
American Madness 1932,Ag 6,14:5
Last Man, The 1932,S 17,18:4
White Eagle 1932,S 24,18:4
Soldiers of the Storm 1933,My 17,15:3
Sphinx, The 1933,Jl 6,26:5
Police Call 1933,Ag 22,20:3
I've Got Your Number 1934,F 3,9:3
Madame Spy 1934,F 10,20:1
Dancing Man 1934,Jl 16,11:3
Girl of the Limberlost, A 1934,N 9,24:6
April Showers 1948,Mr 27,10:2
Green Promise, The 1949,Je 24,29:2
Walk Softly Stranger 1950,O 16,30:5
Call Me Mister 1951,F 1,21:2
Retreat Hell! 1952,F 20,26:2
McConnell Story, The 1955,S 30,23:1
Gidget 1959,Ap 23,27:4

Ellis, Robert (Original Author)
Dance, Girl, Dance 1933,O 25,23:3
Quitter, The 1934,Mr 14,23:3
In Love With Life 1934,My 12,12:3
Off to the Races 1937,F 6,15:2
Charlie Chan on Broadway 1937,S 20,19:1
Charlie Chan at Monte Carlo 1937,D 18,18:1
I'll Get by 1950,N 2,39:3

Ellis, Robert (Screenwriter)
Charlie Chan in Egypt 1935,Je 24,12:2
Charlie Chan's Secret 1936,Ja 18,19:4
Charlie Chan at the Circus 1936,Mr 19,22:4
Charlie Chan at the Race Track 1936,Ag 15,6:2
Off to the Races 1937,F 6,15:2
Charlie Chan at the Olympics 1937,My 24,23:1
Big Business 1937,Je 1,27:2
Born Reckless 1937,Jl 30,22:6
Big Town Girl 1937,D 13,23:4
Rascals 1938,My 27,12:2
Trip to Paris, A 1938,Je 10,18:2
Speed to Burn 1938,S 9,25:1
Sharpshooters 1938,D 5,19:2
Susannah of the Mounties 1939,Je 24,13:2
Escape, The 1939,N 3,17:4
Charlie Chan in City in Darkness 1939,D 18,29:2
Man Who Wouldn't Talk, The 1940,Ja 12,13:3
Star Dust 1940,My 4,13:1
Lucky Cisco Kid 1940,Je 24,19:5
Tin Pan Alley 1940,N 22,27:3
Great American Broadcast, The 1941,My 2,25:2
Sun Valley Serenade 1941,S 6,20:1
Song of the Islands 1942,Mr 12,24:4
Footlight Serenade 1942,S 10,30:3
Iceland 1942,O 15,27:1
Hello, Frisco, Hello 1943,Mr 25,25:1
Four Jills in a Jeep 1944,Ap 6,27:2
Pin Up Girl 1944,My 11,25:6
Something for the Boys 1944,N 30,19:1
Do You Love Me 1946,My 25,12:2
If I'm Lucky 1946,S 20,41:3
Three Little Girls in Blue 1946,S 26,32:3

Ellis, Walter (Original Author)
Almost a Honeymoon 1931,Ja 10,19:2

Ellis, Ward
Second Greatest Sex, The 1956,F 11,12:2

Ellison, Ben (Composer)
I'm no Angel 1933,O 14,18:2

Ellison, Connie
Secret Cinema, The 1968,My 2,57:1

Ellison, Curley
Betrayal, The 1948,Je 26,10:5

Ellison, H C (Miscellaneous)
Mr Bug Goes to Town 1942,F 20,21:3

Ellison, Harlan (Screenwriter)
Oscar, The 1966,Mr 5,16:1

Ellison, James
Play Girl 1932,Mr 19,11:2
Winning Ticket, The 1935,F 11,14:2
Reckless 1935,Ap 20,16:1
Leathernecks Have Landed, The 1936,Mr 23,22:5
Three on the Trail 1936,My 5,26:5
Plainsman, The 1937,Ja 14,16:2
23 1/2 Hours Leave 1937,My 17,23:2
Annapolis Salute 1937,O 2,18:1
Barrier, The 1937,N 27,21:2
Vivacious Lady 1938,Je 3,17:3
Mother Carey's Chickens 1938,Ag 5,11:1
Next Time I Marry 1938,D 2,27:2
Zenobia 1939,My 15,15:2
Fifth Avenue Girl 1939,Ag 25,12:2
Hotel for Women 1939,Ag 26,20:2
You Can't Fool Your Wife 1940,My 24,23:4
Anne of Windy Poplars 1940,Ag 23,13:3
Play Girl 1941,Ja 30,19:3
Charley's Aunt 1941,Ag 2,18:2

Ellison, James — Cont
Ice-Capades 1941,S 25,29:1
Army Surgeon 1942,N 5,35:2
Dixie Dugan 1943,Ap 9,25:5
I Walked With a Zombie 1943,Ap 22,31:5
Gang's All Here, The 1943,D 23,26:4

Ellopoulos, Dinos
Castle in Greece 1960,D 12,38:2

Elloy, Max
Father's Dilemma 1952,S 23,25:1
Babette Goes to War 1960,Je 8,46:1

Ellsberg, Edward Commander (Original Author)
Hell Below 1933,Ap 26,13:2

Ellsler, Effie
Honeymoon Hate 1927,D 31,31:1
Actress, The 1928,Jl 9,25:1
Woman Trap 1929,Ag 31,13:4
Song O' my Heart 1930,Mr 12,32:6
Lady of Scandal, The 1930,Je 14,9:4
Front Page, The 1931,Mr 20,29:1
Up Pops the Devil 1931,My 16,13:3
Daddy Long Legs 1931,Je 6,15:5
Second Hand Wife 1933,Ja 14,8:4
Girl in 419 1933,My 20,11:5
Doctor Bull 1933,O 6,21:2
Chief, The 1933,D 2,9:4
Hold That Girl 1934,Mr 24,20:3
Whole Town's Talking, The 1935,Mr 1,16:2
Black Fury 1935,Ap 11,27:2

Ellsworth, Buzz Corp (Cinematographer)
Report From the Aleutians 1943,Jl 31,8:2

Ellsworth, Heinz
Flower Thief, The 1962,Jl 14,11:5

Ellsworth, Robert
King of Kings, The 1927,Ap 20,29:2

Ellyn, Jean
C-Man 1949,My 28,11:4

Ellys, France
Ballerina 1938,N 15,27:1
Three Waltzes 1939,Ap 25,19:2
Sextette (Part 5-Seducer's Fate); Seducer's Fate (Sextette) 1953,Mr 2,19:2

Elm-Tornquist, Gunilla
To Bed...Or not to Bed 1963,D 23,18:2

Elma, Ismeil
Fedra, the Devil's Daughter 1957,O 26,19:2

Elman, Irving (Miscellaneous)
No Greater Love 1944,F 25,23:3

Elman, Irving (Original Author)
Backlash 1947,My 24,10:5
Crimson Key, The 1947,O 18,9:2

Elman, Irving (Screenwriter)
Backlash 1947,My 24,10:5
Jewels of Brandenburg 1947,My 24,10:5
Crimson Key, The 1947,O 18,9:2
Roses Are Red 1947,N 15,11:2

Elman, Ziggy
Benny Goodman Story 1956,F 22,22:1

Elmer, Clarence
Joy Girl, The 1927,S 6,34:3

Elmer, William
Condemned 1929,N 4,28:1

Elmes, Guy (Original Author)
Outpost in Malaya 1952,N 27,49:2

Elmes, Guy (Screenwriter)
Outpost in Malaya 1952,N 27,49:2
Stranger's Hand, The 1955,F 16,24:5
Across the Bridge 1957,O 30,24:1
Elephant Gun 1959,Je 20,11:2
Greco, El 1967,My 24,52:2

Elmo, Cloe
First Opera Film Festival 1948,My 31,12:7

Elphinstone, Derek
Four Feathers 1939,Ag 4,11:1
In Which We Serve 1942,D 24,18:1

Elredge, John
Stampede 1949,S 16,36:2

Elridge, John (Screenwriter)
Operation Amsterdam 1960,Jl 7,26:1

Elser, Frank B (Original Author)
Farmer Takes a Wife, The 1953,Je 13,11:2

Elsie
Little Men 1940,D 9,23:2

Elsinger, Irene
Foresterchristl, Die 1931,Ap 27,25:1

Elsinger, Jo (Screenwriter)
Gilda 1946,Mr 15,27:2
Big Boodle, The 1957,Mr 12,38:1
Oscar Wilde 1960,Je 21,28:2

Elsley, Fred
Young Philadelphians, The 1959,My 22,32:1

Elsom, Isobel
Ladies in Retirement 1941,N 7,27:1
Eagle Squadron 1942,Jl 3,12:5
Seven Sweethearts 1942,N 13,28:1
War Against Mrs Hadley, The 1942,N 26,40:2
You Were Never Lovelier 1942,D 4,31:1
First Comes Courage 1943,S 3,15:3
My Kingdom for a Cook 1943,O 15,15:3
Between Two Worlds 1944,My 6,11:2
Casanova Brown 1944,S 15,16:1
Unseen, The 1945,My 14,20:5
Two Sisters From Boston 1946,Je 7,16:2
Of Human Bondage 1946,Jl 6,11:2

Two Mrs Carrolls, The 1947,Ap 7,20:1
Ivy 1947,Je 26,19:1
Ghost and Mrs Muir, The 1947,Je 27,17:2
Escape me Never 1947,N 8,11:2
Love From a Stranger 1947,N 28,30:1
Her Wonderful Lie 1950,Jl 17,15:2
Desiree 1954,N 18,42:1
Deep in my Heart 1954,D 10,35:2
King's Thief, The 1955,Ag 13,7:2
Love Is a Many-Splendored Thing 1955,Ag 19,10:1
23 Paces to Baker Street 1956,My 19,12:6
Lust for Life 1956,S 18,39:1
Rock-a-Bye Baby 1958,Jl 24,18:1
Young Philadelphians, The 1959,My 22,32:1
Miracle, The 1959,N 13,25:4
Second Time Around, The 1961,D 23,16:1
Who's Minding the Store? 1963,N 29,67:6
My Fair Lady 1964,O 22,41:1
Pleasure Seekers, The 1964,D 26,9:1

Elson, Bob (Narrator)
Ninth Inning, The 1942,Ja 8,30:3

Elson, Isabel
Dance Magic 1927,Jl 13,21:2

Elster, Else
Blonde Nachtigall, Die 1931,Ag 22,7:5
Purpur und Waschblau 1932,Jl 11,11:4
Week-End Im Paradies 1932,O 24,18:5
Friederike 1933,F 27,11:3
Viktoria und Ihr Husar 1933,Ap 10,8:3
Liebling von Wien, Der 1933,Je 10,16:5
Frau Lehmann's Toechter 1933,O 27,22:3
Tod Ueber Schanghai 1933,D 16,12:4
Frechdachs, Der 1934,Ja 6,18:3
Tante Gusti Kommandiert 1934,My 4,24:4
Hochzeit am Wolfgangsee 1934,N 17,12:2
Drei Kaiserjaeger 1935,Mr 16,19:1
Drei von der Kavallerie 1935,Ap 13,11:4
Wenn am Sonntagabend die Dorfmusik Spielt 1935,D 9,25:3
Wackere Schustermeister, Der 1936,Jl 7,22:4
Drei Maeoerl um Schubert 1937,Je 5,21:2
Trouble Back Stairs; Krach im Hinterhaus 1937,D 4,21:1
Veilchen vom Potsdamer Platz, La; Violet of Potsdam Square, The 1939,Ap 8,19:3

Elston, Allan Vaughn (Original Author)
Isle of Destiny 1940,Ap 8,15:2

Elter, Anielka
Last Moment, The 1928,Mr 12,26:1
Fantomas 1934,Mr 13,27:4

Elter, Marco (Director)
Measure for Measure 1951,D 8,9:2

Elther, Don (Screenwriter)
Sofi 1968,Mr 28,52:3

Eltinge, Julian
How Molly Made Good 1915,O 20,5:5
Countess Charming 1917,S 17,11:3
If I Had my Way 1940,My 6,13:2

Elton, Edmund
Stella Dallas 1937,Ag 6,21:1
Thou Shalt Not Kill 1940,Ja 8,11:2
Abe Lincoln in Illinois 1940,F 23,19:2

Eltz, Theodore von
No Other Woman 1933,Ja 30,9:4 (In Addenda)

Elumuze, Fanny
Daybreak in Udi 1950,Je 2,26:2

Elvenspoeck, Hans
Bridge, The; (Bruecke, Die) 1961,My 2,42:1

Elvey, Maurice (Director)
Resident Patient, The 1922,Ap 24,18:3
Hound of the Baskervilles, The 1922,S 11,20:2
Folly of Vanity 1925,Ja 28,14:1
Woman Tempted, The 1928,Ap 24,29:3
Palais de Danse 1928,Ag 19,VII,3:7
Fanny Hawthorn 1929,N 11,20:2
Jaws of Hell 1931,Ja 5,21:3
Monastery Garden 1932,My 1,VIII,5:4
Woman in Command, The 1934,My 29,22:2
Bride of the Lake, The 1934,S 11,24:5
Wandering Jew, The 1935,Ja 14,11:3
In a Monastery Garden 1935,Mr 13,16:2
Phantom Fiend 1935,Ap 22,14:2
My Song For You 1935,Mr 27,20:6
Clairvoyant, The 1935,Je 8,12:2
Princess Charming 1935,Je 22,18:5
Transatlantic Tunnel 1935,O 28,16:2
Spy of Napoleon 1939,Ag 19,18:4
Gay Intruders, The 1946,Mr 18,24:2
Beware of Pity 1947,N 1,11:2
Obsessed 1952,F 6,24:2

Elvey, Maurice (Miscellaneous)
High Treason 1929,Ag 25,VIII,4:7 (In Addenda)

Elvey, Maurice (Producer)
Beware of Pity 1947,N 1,11:2

Elvidge, June
Quincy Adams Sawyer 1922,D 18,22:2
Eleventh Hour, The 1923,Ag 28,12:1
Painted People 1924,Ja 29,16:1

Elvin, June
Wonder Boy 1951,D 26,19:5

Elvin, Violetta
Melba 1953,Je 25,23:1

Elvira, Gonzalo (Screenwriter)
Tierra de Pasiones 1944,N 7,24:3

Elvira (Producer)
Adelita, La 1938,O 12,35:2

Elwen, Lottie
C-Man 1949,My 28,11:4

Elwes, Mark
Billion Dollar Brain 1967,D 23,29:1

Elwin, Roger
Lord of the Flies 1963,Ag 20,37:1

Ely, David (Original Author)
Seconds 1966,O 6,56:1

Ely, Ron
South Pacific 1958,Mr 20,33:1
Remarkable Mr Pennypacker, The 1959,F 21,25:2

Elzer, Karl
Luther 1929,Je 24,27:1
Das Lockende Ziel 1933,Je 19,18:2

Elzy, Ruby
Emperor Jones, The 1933,S 20,26:2
Birth of the Blues 1941,D 11,39:1

Emanuel, Benjamin
Paisan 1948,Mr 30,26:2

Emanuel, Elzie
Intruder in the Dust 1949,N 23,19:1
White Witch Doctor 1953,Jl 2,19:3

Emelyanov, Victor
Problem Child 1955,Ja 24,20:5
Immortal Garrison, The 1957,Mr 4,30:2
School of Courage 1957,S 9,21:2

Emer, Michel (Composer)
Man of the Hour, The 1940,N 21,43:2

Emerald, Charles
Betrayal, The 1929,Ap 29,29:2
Lost Patrol, The 1929,D 16,34:2

Emeri, Renate
Backfire 1965,Ap 27,27:1

Emerson, Allen
Thomas Crown Affair, The 1968,Je 27,48:2

Emerson, Dorothy (Miscellaneous)
Little Minister, The 1934,D 28,25:1

Emerson, Edmund
Big Trail, The 1930,O 25,20:3

Emerson, Faye
Bad Men of Missouri 1941,Ag 16,18:2
Nine Loves Are not Enough 1941,O 30,27:2
Wild Bill Hickok Rides 1942,F 7,13:5
Murder in the Big House 1942,My 8,27:3
Juke Girl 1942,Je 20,9:2
Lady Gangster 1942,Jl 10,13:2
Secret Enemies 1943,Ja 1,27:3
Air Force 1943,F 4,29:1
Hard Way, The 1943,Mr 13,9:2
Desert Song, The 1943,D 18,10:6
Destination Tokyo 1944,Ja 1,9:2
Uncertain Glory 1944,Ap 8,9:2
Between Two Worlds 1944,My 6,11:2
Mask of Dimitrios, The 1944,Je 24,16:2
Very Thought of You, The 1944,N 18,16:7
Hollywood Canteen 1944,D 16,19:2
Hotel Berlin 1945,Mr 3,11:2
Danger Signal 1945,N 22,39:2
Her Kind of Man 1946,My 4,10:6
Nobody Lives Forever 1946,N 2,12:2
Guilty Bystander 1950,Ap 21,18:2
Main Street to Broadway 1953,O 14,34:1

Emerson, Hope
Smiling Faces 1932,Ag 31,12:3
Cry of the City 1948,S 30,32:4
That Wonderful Urge 1948,D 22,29:6
House of Strangers 1949,Jl 2,8:2
Thieves' Highway 1949,S 24,8:6
Roseanna McCoy 1949,O 13,33:2
Dancing in the Dark 1949,D 3,8:6
Adam's Rib 1949,D 26,33:2
Caged 1950,My 20,8:6
Copper Canyon 1950,N 16,39:2
Double Crossbones 1951,Ap 27,19:2
Belle le Grand 1951,My 18,34:6
Westward the Women 1952,Ja 1,21:2
Lady Wants Mink, The 1953,Ap 6,24:2
Casanova's Big Night 1954,Ap 19,19:1
Untamed 1955,Mr 12,11:6
All Mine to Give 1959,Ag 4,32:5

Emerson, John (Director)
Macbeth 1916,Je 5,9:1
Come On In 1918,S 23,7:1
Come On In 1918,S 23,7:1
Mamma's Affair 1921,Ja 24,16:2

Emerson, John (Miscellaneous)
Woman's Place 1921,O 23,VI,4:1 (In Addenda)

Emerson, John (Original Author)
Temperamental Wife, A 1919,S 15,16:3
Struggle, The 1931,D 11,35:1
Girl From Missouri, The 1934,Ag 4,14:6

Emerson, John (Producer)
Temperamental Wife, A 1919,S 15,16:3
Virtuous Vamp, A 1919,N 17,20:1
In Search of a Sinner 1920,Mr 8,9:5
In Search of a Sinner 1920,Mr 8,9:6
San Francisco 1936,Je 27,21:1

Emerson, John (Screenwriter)
Let's Get a Divorce 1918,Ap 29,11:1
Come on In 1918,S 23,7:1
Come On In 1918,S 23,7:1
Isle of Conquest, The 1919,O 27,9:3
Red Hot Romance 1922,Ja 23,11:4
Learning to Love 1925,F 23,24:1
Emerson, Ralph
Enemy, The 1927,D 28,26:6
West Point 1928,Ja 2,28:1
Marriage by Contract 1928,N 13,37:1
Dance Hall 1929,D 16,34:2
Emerton, Roy
Sign of the Four, The 1932,Ag 20,7:4
Triumph of Sherlock Holmes, The
1935,My 27,20:6
Java Head 1935,Jl 31,21:4
Nine Days a Queen 1936,O 3,21:1
Silent Barriers 1937,Mr 26,25:1
Dr Syn 1937,N 15,15:1
Drums 1938,S 30,24:4
Haunted Honeymoon 1940,O 31,28:2
Thief of Bagdad, The 1940,D 6,28:2
Frightened Lady 1941,N 10,21:3
Young Mr Pitt, The 1943,Mr 11,17:1
Henry V 1946,Je 18,30:2
Emery, Gilbert
Behind That Curtain 1929,Jl 1,31:2
Sky Hawk, The 1929,D 12,36:4
Sarah and Son 1930,Mr 13,22:4
Let Us Be Gay 1930,Jl 12,16:4
Lady's Morals, A 1930,N 8,21:3
Royal Bed, The 1931,Ja 31,15:1
Scandal Sheet 1931,F 9,25:3
Ladies' Man 1931,My 1,30:3
Party Husband 1931,My 16,13:3
Ruling Voice, The 1931,N 5,29:3
Rich Man's Folly 1931,N 27,29:3
Man Called Back, The 1932,Jl 30,16:5
Farewell to Arms, A 1932,D 9,26:5
All of Me 1934,F 5,19:2
House of Rothschild, The 1934,Mr 15,27:2
Coming-Out Party 1934,Mr 17,11:3
Where Sinners Meet 1934,My 25,25:2
Whom the Gods Destroy 1934,Jl 13,14:2
Grand Canary 1934,Jl 20,11:1
One More River 1934,Ag 10,21:1
Now and Forever 1934,O 13,10:1
Man Who Reclaimed his Head, The
1935,Ja 9,22:1
Clive of India 1935,Ja 18,29:1
Night Life of the Gods 1935,F 23,14:6
Let's Live Tonight 1935,Mr 18,14:4
Goin' to Town 1935,My 11,21:2
Harmony Lane 1935,O 24,19:4
Peter Ibbetson 1935,N 8,18:2
Magnificent Obsession 1935,D 31,11:2
Wife vs Secretary 1936,F 29,11:1
Dracula's Daughter 1936,My 18,14:2
Bullets or Ballots 1936,My 27,27:1
Girl on the Front Page, The 1936,N 7,15:2
Souls at Sea 1937,Ag 10,23:2
Life of Emile Zola, The 1937,Ag 12,14:2
Double or Nothing 1937,S 2,17:3
Making the Headlines 1938,Ap 1,17:2
Lord Jeff 1938,Jl 1,22:2
Man to Remember, A 1938,N 7,23:2
Storm Over Bengal 1938,D 8,34:4
Saint Strikes Back, The 1939,Mr 9,18:2
Lady's From Kentucky, The 1939,Ap 27,31:1
Nurse Edith Cavell 1939,S 22,27:4
Raffles 1940,Ja 13,11:2
House of the Seven Gables, The 1940,Ap 15,21:3
Anne of Windy Poplars 1940,Ag 23,13:3
Rage in Heaven 1941,Mr 21,19:2
That Hamilton Woman 1941,Ap 4,25:1
Scotland Yard 1941,Ap 9,33:3
Singapore Woman 1941,My 12,13:6
Woman's Face, A 1941,My 16,21:2
New Wine 1942,F 2,11:2
Remarkable Andrew, The 1942,Mr 6,17:2
Loves of Edgar Allan Poe, The 1942,S 21,19:2
Return of the Vampire, The 1944,Ja 29,10:1
Between Two Worlds 1944,My 6,11:2
Brighton Strangler, The 1945,My 19,15:2
Emery, Gilbert (Original Author)
Tarnish 1924,O 13,21:1
Gallant Lady 1934,Ja 22,12:3
Always Goodbye 1938,Je 25,7:2
Swell Guy 1947,Ja 27,17:2
Emery, John
Road Back, The 1937,Je 18,25:2
Here Comes Mr Jordan 1941,Ag 8,13:2
Corsican Brothers, The 1942,Ja 16,25:4
Two Yanks in Trinidad 1942,Ap 6,19:4
Ship Ahoy 1942,Je 26,16:5
Eyes in the Night 1942,O 16,23:1
George Washington Slept Here 1942,O 31,11:1
Assignment in Brittany 1943,Ap 22,31:2
Blood on the Sun 1945,Je 29,12:2
Spellbound 1945,N 2,22:2
Spanish Main, The 1945,N 7,20:2
Voice of the Turtle, The 1947,D 26,22:4

Woman in White, The 1948,My 8,12:2
Joan of Arc 1948,N 12,30:5
Gay Intruders, The 1949,Je 28,33:4
Dakota Lil 1950,Mr 3,21:5
Rocketship X-M 1950,My 27,10:6
Frenchie 1951,F 12,19:2
Double Crossbones 1951,Ap 27,19:2
Mad Magician, The 1954,My 20,38:2
Forever, Darling 1956,F 10,18:1
Girl Can't Help It, The 1957,F 9,12:7
Kronos 1957,My 11,24:6
Ten North Frederick 1958,My 23,29:2
Youngblood Hawke 1964,N 6,30:1
Emery, Katherine
Eyes in the Night 1942,O 16,23:1
Isle of the Dead 1945,S 8,12:2
Walls Came Tumbling Down, The 1946,N 9,13:5
Locket, The 1947,Mr 20,38:2
Private Affairs of Bel Ami, The 1947,Je 16,25:4
Chicken every Sunday 1949,Ja 19,34:2
Strange Bargain 1949,S 30,28:3
Untamed Frontier 1952,Ag 23,10:2
Hiawatha 1952,D 26,20:4
Maze, The 1953,Jl 11,8:2
Emery, Luciano (Director)
Three Girls From Rome 1953,O 14,34:2
Emery, Polly
Peg of Old Drury 1936,Ap 13,15:1
Emhardt, Robert
Iron Mistress, The 1952,N 20,39:2
3:10 to Yuma 1957,Ag 29,22:1
Badlanders, The 1958,S 4,33:1
Wake Me When It's Over 1960,Ap 9,17:2
Underworld, U S A 1961,My 13,10:1
Intruder, The 1962,My 15,48:1
Kid Galahad 1963,Mr 7,8:5
Group, The 1966,Mr 17,35:1
Emile, Mme
Zero de Conduite 1947,Je 23,14:5
Emilfork, Daniel
Poupee, La 1963,Ag 28,39:1
Lady L 1966,My 19,51:1
Emmanuel, Dharma
Outcast of the Islands 1952,My 16,19:2
Emmanuel, Ivor
Zulu 1964,Jl 8,38:1
Emmanuel, Jacques
Amazing Monsieur Fabre, The 1952,S 9,21:2
Emmanuel, Jacques (Screenwriter)
Parisienne, La 1958,Jl 31,27:1
Law Is the Law, The 1959,Mr 11,41:2
Babette Goes to War 1960,Je 8,46:1
Emmanuel, Takis
Electra 1962,D 18,5:2
Zorba, The Greek 1964,D 18,25:1
Emmanuelli, Gilda
Pure Hell of St Trinian's, The 1961,S 26,31:1
Emmer, Luciano (Director)
Leonardo Da Vinci 1952,N 21,21:5
Picasso 1955,D 23,14:4
Bigamist, The 1958,My 12,25:1
Most Wonderful Moment, The 1959,Je 1,23:6
Emmer, Luciano (Miscellaneous)
Pictura 1952,Ap 8,35:3
Emmet, Katherine
Night Angel, The 1931,Je 11,28:4
Emmett, E V H (Miscellaneous)
On Approval 1945,Ja 29,17:1
Emmett, E V H (Narrator)
Among the Headhunters 1958,S 20,10:6
Emmett, Fern
Vampire Bat, The 1933,Ja 23,9:1
Hello, Everybody 1933,Ja 30,9:4
Harvester, The 1936,Jl 4,18:2
Hunted Men 1938,My 21,9:2
Made for Each Other 1939,F 17,17:2
Star Dust 1940,My 4,13:1
Scattergood Baines 1941,Ap 4,25:2
Love Crazy 1941,Je 6,25:5
San Diego, I Love You 1944,N 10,25:1
Together Again 1944,N 24,19:2
Song to Remember, A 1945,Ja 26,16:4
Pillow of Death 1946,Ja 26,19:3
Emmett, Jay
Jungle Bride 1933,My 13,16:3
Emmett, Katherine
Hole in the Wall, The 1929,Ap 15,22:6
Emmons, Della Gould (Original Author)
Far Horizons, The 1955,My 21,11:1
Emmons, Louise
Heaven on Earth 1931,D 19,16:4
Emmy, Cousin
Festival 1967,O 24,53:2
Emney, Fred
Brewster's Millions 1935,Ap 8,23:3
Emo, E W (Director)
Hampelmann, Der 1931,S 8,38:7
Der Storch Streikt 1932,My 2,13:2
Heute Nacht-Eventuell 1933,Je 24,16:3
Fraeulein-Falsch Verbunden! 1934,Ja 15,12:2
Marion, Das Gehoert Sich Nicht 1934,D 15,9:4
Jungfrau Gegen Moench; Maiden vs Monk
1935,Mr 16,19:2

Emo, E W (Director)— Cont
Himmel auf Erden, Der 1935,D 26,21:4
Drei Maeoerl um Schubert 1937,Je 5,21:2
Endstation 1937,Jl 17,18:1
Schabernack 1937,Ag 14,16:5
Fiakerlied, Das; (Cabbie's Song, The)
1937,S 6,20:2
Familie Schimek 1939,S 2,20:2
Unsterblicher Walzer; Immortal Waltz
1939,N 18,22:6
Anton der Letzte; Anthony the Last
1940,Mr 30,11:2
Emo, E W (Producer)
Anton der Letzte; Anthony the Last
1940,Mr 30,11:2
Emory, Richard
Battle Zone 1952,N 1,17:2
Crooked Web, The 1955,D 10,19:1
Empey, Arthur Guy
Over the Top 1918,Ap 1,9:3 (In Addenda)
Empey, Arthur Guy (Original Author)
Over the Top 1918,Ap 1,9:3 (In Addenda)
Bigger Than Barnum's 1926,Jl 13,19:3
Empey, Arthur Guy (Screenwriter)
Troopers Three 1930,F 17,17:6
Emrich, Serge
Man to Men 1949,F 21,20:2
Emrifork, Daniel
Chateau en Suede; Castle in Switzerland
1964,O 14,51:1
Enav, Haim
Hill 24 Doesn't Answer 1955,N 3,37:1
Encinas, Lalo
Call of the Wild 1935,Ag 15,15:2
Hurry, Charlie, Hurry 1941,N 12,31:3
Enciso, Luis (Screenwriter)
Tia Tula, A 1965,Je 3,24:1
Endang, Oudy Rachmat
Seventh Continent, The 1968,Jl 30,33:2
Enderle, Liselotte (Screenwriter)
Spessart Inn, The 1961,F 18,12:3
Enders, Robert J (Producer)
Thunder of Drums, A 1961,S 27,35:1
Endfield, Cy (Director)
Underworld Story, The 1950,Jl 27,29:4
Try and Get Me 1951,My 7,22:2
Mysterious Island 1961,D 21,30:6
Hide and Seek 1964,Mr 12,40:3
Zulu 1964,Jl 8,38:1
Sands of the Kalahari 1965,N 25,64:5
Endfield, Cy (Producer)
Zulu 1964,Jl 8,38:1
Sands of the Kalahari 1965,N 25,64:5
Endfield, Cy (Screenwriter)
Zulu 1964,Jl 8,38:1
Sands of the Kalahari 1965,N 25,64:5
Endo, Tatsuo
Majin 1968,Ag 10,15:5
Endo, Teppet
Golden Demon 1956,Ja 31,34:3
Endore, Guy (Original Author)
Rumba 1935,F 25,13:2
Mark of the Vampire 1935,My 3,23:4
Song of Russia 1944,F 11,17:2
Whirlpool 1950,Ja 14,9:2
Tomorrow Is Another Day 1951,Ag 9,17:5
Curse of the Werewolf, The 1961,Je 8,40:2
Endore, Guy (Screenwriter)
Mark of the Vampire 1935,My 3,23:4
Mad Love 1935,Ag 5,20:2
Devil Doll, The 1936,Ag 8,5:2
League of Frightened Men, The 1937,Jl 2,25:1
Lady From Louisiana 1941,My 15,27:2
Story of G I Joe 1945,O 6,9:6
Vicious Circle, The 1948,Jl 22,27:2
Johnny Allegro 1949,My 31,19:2
He Ran all the Way 1951,Je 21,24:2
Tomorrow Is Another Day 1951,Ag 9,17:5
Enevoldsen, Bob
Subterraneans, The 1960,Jl 7,26:1
Enfield, Hugh
I'll Tell the World 1934,Ap 21,12:2
Paris in Spring 1935,Jl 13,16:2
Enfield, Richard (Producer)
Oregon Trail, The 1959,D 10,51:6
ENGEL
See Also ENGLE
Engel, Alexander
Eines Prinzen Junge Liebe 1934,Mr 24,20:4
Einer zu viel an Bord 1936,Ja 25,18:5
Merry Wives of Windsor, The 1952,S 22,19:2
Engel, Bill
Our Daily Bread 1934,O 3,25:2
Engel, Erich (Director)
Wer Nimmt die Liebe Ernst; Who Takes Love
Seriously 1931,D 27,VIII,7:1
Fuenf von der Jazzband; Five of the Jazzband
1932,My 15,VIII,4:4 (In Addenda)
Inge und die Millionen 1934,Ap 13,25:1
Pechmarie 1935,Ap 22,14:3
Wer Nimmt die Liebe Ernst? 1936,F 10,15:2
Madchenjahre einer Konigin; Girlhood of a
Queen 1936,Ap 26,IX,4:4 (In Addenda)
Thunder, Lightening and Sunshine

Engel, Erich (Director) — Cont
1937,N 13,11:2
Maulkorb, Der 1938,Ap 9,11:3
Hohe Schule; College 1939,Ap 8,19:3
Hotel Sacher 1939,Je 10,14:2
Ein Hoffnungsloser Fall 1939,S 18,15:5
Affair Blum, The 1949,O 18,35:2
Grapes are Ripe, The 1953,O 15,43:2

Engel, Erich (Miscellaneous)
Murderer Dimitri Karamasoff, The
1931,Mr 1,VIII,6:7 (In Addenda)

Engel, Fred (Producer)
Duel at Diablo 1966,Je 16,53:1
Will Penny 1968,Ap 11,51:2

Engel, Harry
Great British Train Robbery, The 1967,Ap 6,45:2

Engel, Joseph (Producer)
Silk Hat Kid 1935,Ag 7,22:5

Engel, Lehman (Composer)
Strange Victory 1948,S 27,27:2

Engel, Morris (Director)
Little Fugitive 1953,O 7,35:1
Lovers and Lollipops 1956,Ap 19,35:1
Weddings and Babies 1960,O 6,51:3

Engel, Morris (Original Author)
Lovers and Lollipops 1956,Ap 19,35:1
Weddings and Babies 1960,O 6,51:3

Engel, Morris (Producer)
Little Fugitive 1953,O 7,35:1
Lovers and Lollipops 1956,Ap 19,35:1
Weddings and Babies 1960,O 6,51:3

Engel, Morris (Screenwriter)
Little Fugitive 1953,O 7,35:1

Engel, Olga
Congress Dances 1932,My 12,23:2

Engel, Roy
Flying Saucer, The 1950,Ja 5,28:3
Outrage 1950,O 16,30:5
Rogue River 1951,F 16,21:4
Man From Planet X, The 1951,Ap 9,31:2
M 1951,Je 11,20:7
Vickie 1953,S 8,26:3

Engel, Samuel G (Original Author)
Big Shakedown, The 1934,F 12,19:2
Johnny Apollo 1940,Ap 13,21:2

Engel, Samuel G (Producer)
Crack-Up 1937,Ja 4,20:4
We're Going to Be Rich 1938,Jl 4,10:2
Gateway 1938,Ag 8,9:2
My Darling Clementine 1946,D 4,44:5
Sitting Pretty 1948,Mr 11,35:2
Street with no Name, The 1948,Jl 15,26:6
Deep Waters 1948,Jl 23,12:4
Mr Belvedere Goes to College 1949,Ap 16,11:2
Come to the Stable 1949,Jl 28,19:1
Night and the City 1950,Je 10,11:2
Jackpot, The 1950,N 23,55:2
Rawhide 1951,Mr 26,19:2
Follow the Sun 1951,Ap 26,34:4
Frogmen, The 1951,Je 30,8:6
Smoke Jumpers 1952,Mr 22,9:6
Belles on Their Toes 1952,My 3,17:5
Something for the Birds 1952,N 15,15:2
Pony Soldier 1952,D 20,15:2
Taxi 1953,Ja 22,20:3
Man Called Peter, A 1955,Ap 1,22:1
Daddy Long Legs 1955,My 6,17:5
Good Morning, Miss Dove 1955,N 24,41:1
Boy on a Dolphin 1957,Ap 20,21:2
Bernardine 1957,Jl 25,28:1
Story of Ruth, The 1960,Je 18,12:3

Engel, Samuel G (Screenwriter)
Sins of Man 1936,Je 19,17:2
She Had to Eat 1937,Jl 24,12:1
Viva Cisco Kid 1940,Mr 22,23:4
Earthbound 1940,Je 7,27:4
Romance of the Rio Grande 1940,D 25,33:4
Scotland Yard 1941,Ap 9,33:3
Ride on Vaquero 1941,Ap 19,20:2
Private Nurse 1941,Ag 29,13:3
My Darling Clementine 1946,D 4,44:5

Engel-Berger, Willy (Miscellaneous)
Maedel von der Reeperbahn, Das 1931,Ja 31,15:1

Engelke, Lucie
Bockbierfest 1931,Mr 31,25:3

Engelman, Andrews
Love in Morocco 1933,Mr 20,18:3

Engels, Erich (Director)
Wenn Herzen Sich Finden 1934,N 12,17:3
Kirschen in Nachbars Garten 1937,My 15,23:6
Nacht mit dem Kaiser, Die 1937,Ag 14,16:5
Graue Dame, Die; Gray Lady, The
1938,D 17,10:4
Peter, Paul und Nanette 1940,My 25,20:1

Engels, Wera
Great Jasper, The 1933,F 17,5:3
Great Impersonation, The 1935,D 14,11:1

Engels, Werner
Brand in der Oper 1932,Jl 11,11:4

Enget, Roy
Well, The 1951,S 27,37:2

Engfeldt, Aake
Kryss med Albertina, Paa; Cruise in the Albertina,
A 1940,Mr 25,11:3

Engl, Olga
Emil und die Detektive 1931,D 21,28:4
Rebel, The 1933,Jl 25,17:2

England, Paul
Charlie Chan in London 1934,S 13,26:1
Knock on Wood 1954,Ap 15,34:2

England, Paul (Screenwriter)
She Shall Have Music 1942,O 31,11:2

England, Sue
This Love of Ours 1945,N 1,20:2
City Across the River 1949,Ap 8,31:3
Funny Face 1957,Mr 29,16:1

Englander, Alec
Enchanted Cottage, The 1945,Ap 28,19:2

Englander, Otto (Miscellaneous)
Massacre River 1949,Jl 15,17:2

Englander, Otto (Screenwriter)
Snow White and the Seven Dwarfs
1938,Ja 14,21:1 (In Addenda)
Pinocchio 1940,F 8,18:3
Diamond Queen, The 1954,Ja 27,24:2

ENGLE
See Also ENGEL

Engle, Billy
It's a Gift 1935,Ja 5,20:2
Our Neighbors-The Carters 1940,F 15,15:2

Engle, Darleen
South Pacific 1958,Mr 20,33:1

Engleman
Pearls of the Crown, The 1938,Ap 12,26:2

Engleman, Andre von
Mare Nostrum 1926,F 16,22:4

Engleman, Andrews
Wanted Men 1936,Jl 8,15:2
Crouching Beast, The 1936,Ag 22,6:1

Englisch, Lucie
Rheinlandmaedel, Das 1931,S 18,29:1
Zwei Menschen 1931,D 23,27:3
Ungetreue Eckehart, Der 1932,Ja 23,18:4
Mein Leopold 1932,Ap 1,17:4
Reserve Hat Ruh 1932,Ap 11,19:2
Rendez-Vous 1932,Ap 30,19:3
Graefin von Monte Christo, Die; Countess of
Monte Christo, The 1932,My 15,VIII,4:2 (In
Addenda)
Der Schrecken der Garnison 1932,Je 1,19:5
Dienst Ist Dienst 1932,Je 6,18:5
Hurra! Ein Junge! 1932,Je 21,19:6
Schubert's Fruehlingstraum 1932,Je 22,19:4
Keine Feier Ohne Meyer 1932,O 29,18:4
Drei Tage Mittelarrest 1933,My 18,17:4
Das Lockende Ziel 1933,Je 19,18:2
Annemarie, Die Braut der Kompanie
1934,D 8,18:6
Heimat am Rhein 1934,D 11,29:4
Meine Frau, Die Schuetzenkoenigin
1935,Ja 7,13:3
Kalte Mamsell, Die 1935,Ja 12,12:2
Gretl Zieht das Grosse Los 1935,F 11,14:2
Unschuld vom Lande, Die 1935,My 13,18:6
Unbekannte Gast, Der; Unknown Guest, The
1935,Je 1,18:3
Mutige Seefahrer, Der 1936,N 21,21:5
Falscher Fuffziger, Ein 1937,F 13,9:1
Postillon of Lonjumeau, The 1937,N 20,21:3
Lachende Dritte, Der 1938,Ap 9,11:2
Landstreicher, Die; Hoboes, The 1938,N 26,18:1
Kleines Bezirksgericht; Little Country Court
1939,F 18,12:4
Dingehort mein Herz; My Heart Belongs to Thee
1939,Mr 25,19:2
Solo per Danne 1939,My 30,13:3
Kampf mit dem Drachen, Der; Fight With the
Dragon, The 1939,N 6,20:3
Our Little Wife 1940,Ja 27,9:2
Walzerlange; Waltz Melodies 1940,Ap 27,9:3

English, Harold D Cpl
Cease Fire! 1953,N 25,17:1

English, John (Director)
Call the Mesquiteers 1938,Mr 19,11:2
Utah 1945,Mr 12,22:7
Murder in the Music Hall 1946,Ap 15,22:2

English, Maria
Shield for Murder 1954,Ag 28,8:3
Desert Sands 1955,N 19,22:7
Three bad Sisters 1956,F 13,24:1

English, Richard (Original Author)
Cadet Girl 1941,D 11,39:1
Brazil 1944,N 20,25:2
Copper Canyon 1950,N 16,39:2
Big Jim McLain 1952,S 18,35:2

English, Richard (Screenwriter)
Sweet and Low Down 1944,O 19,19:2
Thousand and one Nights, A 1945,Jl 12,8:2
Fabulous Dorseys, The 1947,My 30,25:3
Lust for Gold 1949,Jl 4,9:2
711 Ocean Drive 1950,Jl 20,21:2
Flying Missile, The 1950,D 25,25:1
Beyond Mombasa 1957,My 31,14:2

English, Robert
This Freedom 1923,N 28,15:1

Englund, George (Director)
Ugly American, The 1963,Ap 12,30:2
Signpost to Murder 1965,My 20,52:2

Englund, George (Producer)
World, The Flesh and the Devil, The
1959,My 21,35:1
Ugly American, The 1963,Ap 12,30:2
Dark of the Sun 1968,Jl 4,13:1
Shoes of the Fisherman, The 1968,N 15,40:3

Englund, Jan
Bait 1954,F 24,21:3

Englund, Ken (Original Author)
Wicked Dreams of Paula Schultz, The
1968,Ja 4,28:1

Englund, Ken (Screenwriter)
Big Broadcast of 1938, The 1938,Mr 10,16:2
Artists and Models Abroad 1938,D 22,25:3
There's That Woman Again 1939,Ja 6,25:4
Good Girls Go to Paris 1939,Je 23,23:1
Slightly Honorable 1940,My 17,23:4
Doctor Takes a Wife, The 1940,Je 15,12:2
No, No, Nanette 1940,D 20,33:1
This Thing Called Love 1941,F 14,15:2
Nothing but the Truth 1941,O 23,27:1
Rings on her Fingers 1942,Ap 24,21:4
Springtime in the Rockies 1942,N 12,30:2
Sweet Rosie O'Grady 1943,O 21,30:2
Here Come the Waves 1944,D 28,25:2
Unseen, The 1945,My 14,20:5
Secret Life of Walter Mitty, The 1947,Ag 15,12:2
Good Sam 1948,S 17,28:2
Millionaire for Christy, A 1951,O 5,24:3
Androcles and the Lion 1953,Ja 15,23:2
Never Wave at a Wac 1953,Ap 24,30:2
Vagabond King, The 1956,S 13,39:6

Englund, Patricia
Stage Struck 1958,Ap 23,40:1

Engstrand, Stuart (Original Author)
Beyond the Forest 1949,O 22,11:2

Engstroe, Alexandra
Rendez-Vous 1932,Ap 30,19:3

Engstroem, Alexa
Brand in der Oper 1932,Jl 11,11:4

Engstroem, Avon
Unschuld vom Lande, Die 1935,My 13,18:6

Enhart, Vicente
Luna Criolla; Creole Moon 1940,Ap 8,15:3

Ennis, Patrick
Ireland, A Nation 1914,S 24,11:6

Ennis, Skinnay
College Swing 1938,Ap 28,27:2

Eno, E W (Director)
Unbekannte Gast, Der; Unknown Guest, The
1935,Je 1,18:3

Eno, E W (Miscellaneous)
Und Wer Kuesst Mich? 1935,Ja 28,10:5

Enoch, Russell
Intimate Relations 1954,F 22,15:4

Enomoto, Kenichi
Men Who Tread on the Tiger's Tail, The
1960,Ja 11,35:7

Enrico, Robert (Director)
Zita 1968,Ag 12,40:2

Enrico, Robert (Screenwriter)
Zita 1968,Ag 12,40:2

Enright, Commissioner (Original Author)
Into the Net 1924,Ag 23,10:2

Enright, Florence
Nice Women 1932,F 20,11:2
Gift of Gab 1934,S 26,17:6

Enright, Ray (Director)
Tracked by the Police 1927,Ap 27,22:5
Girl From Chicago, The 1927,D 20,33:2
Skin Deep 1929,S 30,23:1
Song of the West 1930,F 28,20:7
Golden Dawn 1930,Jl 26,16:4
Dancing Sweeties 1930,Ag 16,8:3
Scarlet Pages 1930,D 6,21:3
Play Girl 1932,Mr 19,11:2
Tenderfoot, The 1932,My 23,18:4
Blondie Johnson 1933,F 27,11:2
Silk Express, The 1933,Je 28,24:2
Tomorrow at Seven 1933,Jl 3,14:6
Havana Widows 1933,N 23,24:3
I've Got Your Number 1934,F 3,9:3
20 Million Sweethearts 1934,Ap 27,25:1
Circus Clown, The 1934,Je 30,18:6
Dames 1934,Ag 16,20:2
St Louis Kid, The 1934,N 1,25:2
While the Patient Slept 1935,Mr 2,18:2
Traveling Saleslady 1935,Mr 29,26:2
Alibi Ike 1935,Jl 17,22:1
Miss Pacific Fleet 1935,D 7,22:2
Snowed Under 1936,Mr 30,17:5
Earthworm Tractors 1936,Jl 25,16:1
China Clipper 1936,Ag 12,14:3
Sing Me a Love Song 1936,D 26,15:2
Ready, Willing and Able 1937,Mr 15,27:1
Slim 1937,Je 24,30:2
Singing Marine, The 1937,Jl 1,33:2
Back in Circulation 1937,O 4,17:1
Swing Your Lady 1938,Ja 27,17:2
Gold Diggers in Paris 1938,Je 2,19:2

Enright, Ray (Director) — Cont

Hard To Get 1938,N 14,15:2
Going Places 1939,Ja 7,6:1
Naughty but Nice 1939,Je 23,23:2
Angels Wash Their Faces 1939,S 4,16:2
On Your Toes 1939,O 21,12:2
Brother Rat and a Baby 1940,Ja 27,9:4
Angel From Texas, An 1940,My 10,26:7
River's End 1940,Ag 26,11:4
Wagons Roll at Night, The 1941,My 10,20:4
Bad Men of Missouri 1941,Ag 16,18:2
Law of the Tropics 1941,O 10,26:5
Wild Bill Hickok Rides 1942,F 7,13:5
Spoilers, The 1942,My 22,27:2
Men of Texas 1942,Jl 13,18:3 (In Addenda)
Sin Town 1942,O 17,11:2
Iron Major, The 1943,N 1,12:5
Gung Ho! 1944,Ja 26,23:2
China Sky 1945,My 25,22:3
Man Alive 1945,N 17,14:5
Trail Street 1947,Ap 10,35:2
Albuquerque 1948,Mr 1,17:2
Return of the Badmen 1948,Ag 5,16:2
South of St Louis 1949,Mr 7,17:2
Montana 1950,F 4,9:2
Kansas Raiders 1951,Ja 26,19:2
Man From Cairo, The 1953,D 17,52:4

Enright, Ray (Original Author)
Side Show 1931,S 19,10:2
Fireman, Save My Child 1932,F 18,25:3

Ensescalle, Bob Jr (Screenwriter)
Stranger Returns, The 1968,S 12,54:3

Enstedt, Howard
Rolling Home 1926,Je 8,22:1

Enters, Angna (Miscellaneous)
Lost Angel 1944,Ap 10,14:1

Entratter, Jack
Pepe 1960,D 22,18:1

Entwhistle, Harold
Our Betters 1933,F 24,13:2

Entwistle, Peg
Thirteen Women 1932,O 15,13:1

Enyeart, Stacy (Producer)
Robby 1968,Ag 15,46:3

Enzo, Currell (Screenwriter)
Steppe, The 1963,O 1,33:1

Eogolyubov, N I
Oppenheim Family, The 1939,My 24,29:2

Eon, Andre Mouezy (Director)
Sans Famille 1935,Je 4,26:5

Eori, Elisabeth
Piri Mindont Tud 1933,Ja 26,12:3

Epailly, Jules
Honor Among Lovers 1931,F 28,15:2

Ephron, Henry (Director)
Sing Boy Sing 1958,F 22,9:4

Ephron, Henry (Original Author)
3 Is a Family 1944,D 20,20:3
Take Her, She's Mine 1963,N 14,41:1

Ephron, Henry (Producer)
Carousel 1956,F 17,13:1
23 Paces to Baker Street 1956,My 19,12:6
Best Things in Life are Free, The 1956,S 29,12:2
Desk Set 1957,My 16,28:2
Sing Boy Sing 1958,F 22,9:4
Certain Smile, A 1958,Ag 1,13:2

Ephron, Henry (Screenwriter)
Bride by Mistake 1944,S 16,20:2
Always Together 1947,D 11,46:1
Wallflower 1948,Je 12,8:5
John Loves Mary 1949,F 5,11:2
Look for the Silver Lining 1949,Je 24,29:2
Jackpot, The 1950,N 23,55:2
On the Riviera 1951,My 24,47:1
Belles on Their Toes 1952,My 3,17:5
What Price Glory 1952,Ag 23,10:2
There's no Business Like Show Business
  1954,D 17,37:3
Daddy Long Legs 1955,My 6,17:5
Carousel 1956,F 17,13:1
Desk Set 1957,My 16,28:2
Captain Newman, MD 1964,F 21,36:1

Ephron, Phoebe (Original Author)
3 Is a Family 1944,D 20,20:3
Take Her, She's Mine 1963,N 14,41:1

Ephron, Phoebe (Screenwriter)
Bride by Mistake 1944,S 16,20:2
Always Together 1947,D 11,46:1
Wallflower 1948,Je 12,8:5
John Loves Mary 1949,F 5,11:2
Look for the Silver Lining 1949,Je 24,29:2
Jackpot, The 1950,N 23,55:2
On the Riviera 1951,My 24,47:1
Belles on Their Toes 1952,My 3,17:5
What Price Glory 1952,Ag 23,10:2
There's no Business Like Show Business
  1954,D 17,37:3
Daddy Long Legs 1955,My 6,17:5
Carousel 1956,F 17,13:1
Best Things in Life are Free, The 1956,S 29,12:2
Desk Set 1957,My 16,28:2
Captain Newman, MD 1964,F 21,36:1

Epifantsev, Georgi
Gordeyev Family, The 1961,O 16,33:6

Eppel, I J (Director)
Irish Destiny 1927,Mr 29,23:2 (In Addenda)

Eppel, I J (Screenwriter)
Irish Destiny 1927,Mr 29,23:2 (In Addenda)

Eppler, Dieter
Head, The 1963,Je 20,29:1

Epstein, Brian (Producer)
Ferry Cross the Mersey 1965,F 20,16:2

Epstein, Claire
Dream no More 1950,Ja 6,25:2

Epstein, David (Screenwriter)
Of Men and Music 1951,F 15,27:2

Epstein, Israela
My Father's House 1947,S 26,28:3

Epstein, Jean (Director)
6 1/2 x 11 1929,Ag 13,23:2
Homme a l'Hispano, L'; Man in the Hispano-Suiza,
  The 1933,Je 11,IX,2:5

Epstein, Jerome (Producer)
Countess from Hong Kong, A 1967,Mr 17,35:1

Epstein, Julius J (Miscellaneous)
Honeymoon for Three 1941,F 8,19:2
One More Tomorrow 1946,My 25,12:2

Epstein, Julius J (Original Author)
Living on Velvet 1935,Mr 8,25:4
I Live for Love 1935,O 19,21:2
Chicken every Sunday 1949,Ja 19,34:2

Epstein, Julius J (Producer)
Mr Skeffington 1944,My 26,23:2
Take a Giant Step 1961,Mr 6,28:2
Any Wednesday 1966,O 14,50:1

Epstein, Julius J (Screenwriter)
Living on Velvet 1935,Mr 8,25:4
In Caliente 1935,Je 27,16:1
Little Big Shot 1935,O 7,11:2
I Live for Love 1935,O 19,21:2
Stars Over Broadway 1935,N 14,17:3
Sons o'Guns 1936,My 14,29:2
Confession 1937,Ag 19,23:1
Four Daughters 1938,Ag 19,13:3
Secrets of an Actress 1938,O 8,10:2
Daughters Courageous 1939,Je 24,14:2
Four Wives 1939,D 23,9:1
Saturday's Children 1940,My 4,13:1
No Time for Comedy 1940,S 7,9:2
Strawberry Blonde 1941,F 22,11:2
Bride Came C O D, The 1941,Jl 26,18:2
Man Who Came to Dinner, The 1942,Ja 2,25:2
Male Animal, The 1942,Mr 28,11:1
Casablanca 1942,N 27,27:1
Mr Skeffington 1944,My 26,23:2
Arsenic and old Lace 1944,S 2,17:2
Romance on the High Seas 1948,Je 26,10:5
My Foolish Heart 1950,Ja 20,29:2
Take Care of my Little Girl 1951,Jl 19,20:2
Forever Female 1954,Ja 13,26:2
Last Time I saw Paris, The 1954,N 19,20:2
Young at Heart 1955,Ja 20,35:1
Tender Trap, The 1955,N 11,29:6
Kiss Them for Me 1957,N 9,31:2
Tall Story 1960,Ap 7,46:1
Take a Giant Step 1961,Mr 6,28:2
Fanny 1961,Jl 7,16:1
Light in the Piazza 1962,F 8,25:1
Send Me no Flowers 1964,N 13,30:1
Return From the Ashes 1965,N 17,53:1
Any Wednesday 1966,O 14,50:1

Epstein, Marie (Director)
Maternelle, La 1935,O 15,19:1
Itto 1936,Ja 29,15:5

Epstein, Marie (Miscellaneous)
Maternelle, La 1935,O 15,19:1

Epstein, Marie (Screenwriter)
Helene 1938,Ja 22,19:1
Ballerina 1938,N 15,27:1
Youth in Revolt 1939,My 16,27:3

Epstein, Mel (Producer)
Hazard 1948,Je 3,19:2
Copper Canyon 1950,N 16,39:2
Branded 1951,Ja 11,28:5
Molly 1951,Mr 8,37:2
Dear Brat 1951,Jl 5,21:2
Savage, The 1953,Ja 2,11:1
Alaska Seas 1954,Mr 6,13:5
Secret of the Incas 1954,My 29,13:3

Epstein, Nina Alicia
Silencio Sublime 1937,Ja 16,21:2

Epstein, Philip G (Miscellaneous)
Honeymoon for Three 1941,F 8,19:2
One More Tomorrow 1946,My 25,12:2

Epstein, Philip G (Original Author)
Gift of Gab 1934,S 26,17:6
Chicken every Sunday 1949,Ja 19,34:2

Epstein, Philip G (Producer)
Mr Skeffington 1944,My 26,23:2

Epstein, Philip G (Screenwriter)
Love on a Bet 1936,Mr 5,25:2
Bride Walks Out, The 1936,Jl 10,15:1
Grand Jury 1936,Ag 1,16:3
New Faces of 1937 1937,Jl 2,25:1
Mad Miss Manton, The 1938,O 21,27:2

Epstein, Philip G (Screenwriter) — Cont

There's That Woman Again 1939,Ja 6,25:4
Daughters Courageous 1939,Je 24,14:2
Four Wives 1939,D 23,9:1
Saturday's Children 1940,My 4,13:1
No Time for Comedy 1940,S 7,9:2
Strawberry Blonde 1941,F 22,11:2
Bride Came C O D, The 1941,Jl 26,18:2
Man Who Came to Dinner, The 1942,Ja 2,25:2
Male Animal, The 1942,Mr 28,11:1
Casablanca 1942,N 27,27:1
Mr Skeffington 1944,My 26,23:2
Arsenic and old Lace 1944,S 2,17:2
Romance on the High Seas 1948,Je 26,10:5
My Foolish Heart 1950,Ja 20,29:2
Take Care of my Little Girl 1951,Jl 19,20:2
Forever Female 1954,Ja 13,26:2
Last Time I saw Paris, The 1954,N 19,20:2

Equiluz, Kurt
Rosenkavalier, Der 1962,O 10,57:1

Eraehel, Clement
Daybreak in Udi 1950,Je 2,26:2

Erard, Charles Captain (Narrator)
World Tours of the Prince of Wales, The
  1930,F 3,17:1

Erard, Jean (Producer)
Noah's Ark 1950,Ag 21,15:1

Eras, Eva
Gibt nur eine Liebe, Es 1937,Ja 23,23:2

Erbeya, Blanca
Padre Mercader; Merchant Father 1939,Jl 15,8:3

Erbeya, Margot
Pulpo Humano, El 1935,My 6,22:4

Ercolani, Renato
Rosenkavalier, Der 1962,O 10,57:1

Ercoll, Luciano (Producer)
Pistol for Ringo, A 1966,N 3,45:4

Ercy, Elizabeth
Phaedra 1962,O 19,24:1

Erdelyi, Dani
Father 1967,S 29,53:1

Erdelyi, Mici
Pesti Szerelem 1934,My 10,25:3
Huszarszerelem 1935,Ap 23,24:5
Koeszoenoem Hogy Elgazolt 1935,My 7,28:2
Edes Mostoha 1935,N 21,27:2
Okos Mama, Az 1936,Ap 13,15:2
Naszut Felaron 1937,F 13,9:2
Tisztelet a Kivetelnek 1937,Je 14,26:3
Szerelemboel Noesueltem; I Married for Love
  1938,F 7,10:3
Edes a Bosszu; Sweet Revenge 1938,S 10,20:3
Rad Bizom a Felesegem; I Entrust my Wife to
  You 1939,My 6,21:3
Pillanatnyi Pezzavar; Temporarily Broke
  1939,My 20,11:3
Erik/a/Buzakalasz; Wheat Ripens, The
  1939,S 11,15:2
Pentek Rezi; Friday Rose 1939,D 23,9:2

Erdman, N (Screenwriter)
Hello, Moscow! 1946,Je 15,24:4
Horsemen, The 1951,Ja 29,14:5
Safety Match, The 1955,Mr 28,24:5

Erdman, Richard
Janie 1944,Ag 5,16:2
Very Thought of You, The 1944,N 18,16:7
Objective Burma 1945,Ja 27,15:2
Danger Signal 1945,N 22,39:2
Too Young to Know 1945,D 8,21:2
Janie Gets Married 1946,Je 15,24:2
Nobody Lives Forever 1946,N 2,12:2
That Way With Women 1947,F 15,20:4
Wild Harvest 1947,N 13,33:2
Time of your Life, The 1948,My 27,29:2
Four Days' Leave 1950,Je 9,29:4
Men, The 1950,Jl 21,15:2
Admiral Was a Lady, The 1950,O 13,23:3
Cry Danger 1951,F 22,27:3
U S S Teakettle 1951,F 24,11:2
Wild Blue Yonder, The 1952,Ja 2,20:1
San Francisco Story, The 1952,My 10,16:4
Jumping Jacks 1952,Jl 24,30:2
Stooge, The 1953,F 5,19:2
Blue Gardenia, The 1953,Ap 28,31:1
Stalag 17 1953,Jl 2,19:2
Mission Over Korea 1953,S 19,7:2
Francis in the Navy 1955,Ag 6,13:4
Bengazi 1955,O 8,13:4
Anything Goes 1956,Mr 22,38:1
Power and the Prize, the 1956,S 27,42:1
Saddle the Wind 1958,Mr 21,17:1
Brass Bottle, The 1964,My 21,42:1

Erenberg, V
Hamlet 1964,S 15,32:1

Ergas, Moris (Producer)
Steppe, The 1963,O 1,33:1
Kapo 1964,Je 2,33:3
Love a la Carte 1965,Ja 12,31:1
Vista, La; Visit, The 1966,Ag 10,32:1

Erhardt, Hermann
Ehestreik 1935,Ag 31,16:3
Klosterjaeger, Der 1936,Ja 3,13:7
Weiberregiment 1936,S 14,25:2
Silence of the Forest, The; Schweigen im Walde,

Erhardt, Hermann— Cont
  Das 1937,D 6,19:2
Erhardt, Kurt
  Affair Blum, The 1949,O 18,35:2
Erhart, Thomas
  Goldstein 1965,My 8,19:7
Eri, Chiemi
  Country Doctor, The 1963,Ag 14,28:1
ERICKSON
  See Also ERICSON, ERICSSON, ERIKSEN
Erickson, A F (Director)
  Rough Romance 1930,Je 16,25:3
  This Sporting Age 1932,O 1,10:4
Erickson, Carl (Miscellaneous)
  Stranded 1935,Je 20,16:2
Erickson, Carl (Original Author)
  Stranger in Town 1932,Jl 8,22:5
  Girl Missing 1933,Ap 1,18:2
  Sweet Music 1935,F 21,23:2
Erickson, Carl (Screenwriter)
  Black Fury 1935,Ap 11,27:2
Erickson, Dell
  Blue Angel, The 1959,S 5,11:4
  Take a Giant Step 1961,Mr 6,28:2
Erickson, Knute
  Monster, The 1925,F 16,24:1
  Waterfront 1928,O 22,29:1
  Scarlet Seas 1928,D 31,9:1
  Squall, The 1929,My 10,32:5
  Twin Beds 1929,Jl 15,25:1
  Illusion 1929,S 28,17:3
  Spoilers, The 1930,S 20,15:4
  Bitter Tea of General Yen, The 1933,Ja 12,20:6
Erickson, Lee
  Seven Little Foys, The 1955,Je 30,18:2
  Kentuckian, The 1955,S 2,13:2
  Long, Hot Summer, The 1958,Ap 4,16:1
Erickson, Leif
  College Holiday 1936,D 24,21:2
  Waikiki Wedding 1937,Mr 25,29:1
  Conquest 1937,N 5,19:1
  Thrill of a Lifetime 1937,D 9,30:2
  Big Broadcast of 1938, The 1938,Mr 10,16:2
  Ride a Crooked Mile 1938,D 29,15:2
  One Third of a Nation 1939,F 11,13:2
  Nothing but the Truth 1941,O 23,27:1
  H M Pulham, Esq 1941,D 19,35:1
  Fleet's In, The 1942,Mr 12,24:2
  Eagle Squadron 1942,Jl 3,12:5
  Are Husbands Necessary? 1942,Jl 9,17:2
  Pardon my Sarong 1942,Ag 27,15:1
  Night Monster 1942,N 30,18:5
  Arabian Nights 1942,D 26,15:1
  Blonde Savage 1947,O 4,9:2
  Gangster, The 1947,O 31,29:3
  Sorry, Wrong Number 1948,S 2,18:2
  Snake Pit, the 1948,N 5,29:2
  Joan of Arc 1948,N 12,30:5
  Miss Tatlock's Millions 1948,N 25,47:2
  Lady Gambles, The 1949,My 21,9:2
  Gay Intruders, The 1949,Je 28,33:4
  Johnny Stool Pigeon 1949,S 23,28:3
  Mother Didn't Tell Me 1950,Mr 4,11:2
  Love That Brute 1950,My 27,10:6
  Stella 1950,Ag 19,9:2
  Three Secrets 1950,O 21,10:6
  Dallas 1951,Ja 13,10:4
  Show Boat 1951,Jl 20,14:1
  Tall Target, The 1951,S 28,26:2
  Sailor Beware 1952,F 1,17:1
  With a Song in my Heart 1952,Ap 5,20:2
  Carbine Williams 1952,My 8,37:2
  My Wife's Best Friend 1952,O 11,17:2
  Never Wave at a Wac 1953,Ap 24,30:2
  Trouble Along the Way 1953,My 7,37:2
  Invaders From Mars 1953,My 30,7:1
  On the Waterfront 1954,Jl 29,18:1
  Fastest Gun Alive, The 1956,Jl 13,23:3
  Tea and Sympathy 1956,S 28,24:4
  Istanbul 1957,Ja 24,34:1
  Vintage, The 1957,My 9,36:5
  Kiss Them for Me 1957,N 9,31:2
  Twilight for the Gods 1958,Ag 7,21:1
  Gathering of Eagles, A 1963,Jl 11,21:2
  Hot Horse 1963,Jl 25,14:2
  Strait Jacket 1964,Ja 23,26:1
  Carpetbaggers, The 1964,Jl 2,24:4
  Roustabout 1964,N 11,38:1
  Mirage 1965,My 27,28:1
  I Saw What You Did 1965,Jl 22,24:2
Erickson, Leif (Miscellaneous)
  Crisis 1939,Mr 13,12:2
Erickson, Louise
  Three Husbands 1951,Mr 9,30:2
Erickson, Paul
  White Fire 1954,S 18,12:4
    1954,S 18,12:4
Erickson, Paul (Screenwriter)
  White Fire 1954,S 18,12:4
ERICSON
  See Also ERICKSON, ERICSSON, ERIKSEN
Ericson, Annalisa
  Vaermlaenningarna 1932,N 18,23:2
  Skanor-Falsterbo 1939,Ap 17,13:2

Folket Pa Hogbogarden; People of the Hogbo
    Farm, The 1940,F 24,9:3
  Illicit Interlude 1954,O 27,32:6
Ericson, Helen
  Wife, Husband and Friend 1939,F 25,19:2
  Escape, The 1939,N 3,17:4
  Blue Bird, The 1940,Ja 20,11:2
  Young as You Feel 1940,Mr 8,25:3
  Free, Blonde and 21 1940,Ap 5,25:2
Ericson, John
  Teresa 1951,Ap 6,31:2
  Rhapsody 1954,Mr 12,17:1
  Student Prince, The 1954,Je 16,18:2
  Green Fire 1954,D 25,7:1
  Bad Day at Black Rock 1955,F 2,22:2
  Return of Jack Slade, The 1955,N 24,41:3
  Day of the Badman 1958,Ja 30,19:2
  Under ten Flags 1960,S 16,24:1
  Pretty Boy Floyd 1960,N 3,49:2
  7 Faces of Dr Lao 1964,Jl 23,19:1
Ericson, Nils
  Under Falsk Flagg 1937,Ja 20,18:5
  Sun Over Sweden 1938,Ap 9,11:2
Ericson, Walter (Original Author)
  Mirage 1965,My 27,28:1
Ericson-Hannes, Greta
  Sun Over Sweden 1938,Ap 9,11:2
ERICSSON
  See Also ERICKSON, ERICSON, ERIKSEN
Ericsson, John
  Children, The 1949,D 23,17:1
Erictson, Bengt (Screenwriter)
  Vicious Breed, The 1958,My 23,29:2
ERIKSEN
  See Also ERICKSON, ERICSON, ERICSSON
Eriksen, Dan (Director)
  Midsummer Night's Dream, A 1967,Ap 18,32:1
Eriksen, Edel
  Boer Boerson Jr 1939,N 4,11:3
Eriksson, Georg (Producer)
  Obession 1968,Ag 29,46:3
Eriksson, Gerd
  Unmarried Mothers 1956,F 23,32:5
Erkelenz, Peter
  Blonde Crazy 1931,D 4,28:2
  Eine Tuer geht Auf 1933,F 6,11:5
  Stern von Valencia, Der 1934,Ap 21,12:2
Erksine, John (Miscellaneous)
  Story of a Cheat, The 1938,S 27,25:2
Erlandsen, Edmund
  Last ten Days, The 1956,Ap 12,26:1
  Song Without End 1960,Ag 12,10:2
Erlanger, Philippe (Screenwriter)
  Rise of Louis XIV, The 1967,S 26,54:2
Erlanger (Director)
  Life and Works of Richard Wagner, The
    1913,N 21,9:4
Erler, Tino
  Last Chance, The 1945,N 28,21:6
ERLICH
  See Also EHRLICH
Erlich, A (Screenwriter)
  Russian Ballerina 1947,S 11,31:2
Ermakovitch, N M
  Prisoners 1937,F 20,9:2
Ermelli, Claudio
  Roman Holiday 1953,Ag 28,13:1
  It Started in Naples 1960,S 3,7:6
Ermler, Frederick (Director)
  Pozor 1933,Mr 11,18:4
  Peasants 1935,Ag 29,25:2
  Great Citizen, The 1939,Ja 16,11:2
  No Greater Love 1944,F 25,23:3
  Turning Point, The 1946,O 28,19:4
Ermler, Frederick (Miscellaneous)
  Spring Song 1942,S 12,9:2
  Taxi to Heaven 1944,My 25,16:3
Ermler, Frederick (Producer)
  Lad From our Town 1943,O 7,26:2
  We Will Come Back 1943,O 15,15:2
  No Greater Love 1944,F 25,23:3
Ermler, Frederick (Screenwriter)
  Fragment of an Empire, A 1930,Ja 27,18:4
  Great Citizen, The 1939,Ja 16,11:2
Ermler, M (Director)
  Fragment of an Empire, A 1930,Ja 27,18:4
Ermolieff, Joseph N (Director)
  Taras Bulba 1927,D 28,26:6
Ermolieff, Joseph N (Original Author)
  Outpost in Morocco 1949,Mr 25,28:3
Ermolieff, Joseph N (Producer)
  Outpost in Morocco 1949,Mr 25,28:3
Ernart, Egi
  Topkapi 1964,S 18,25:1
Erneberg, V
  Hamlet 1966,Mr 16,48:1
Ernest, George
  Star Witness, The 1931,Ag 4,19:5
  Fireman, Save My Child 1932,F 18,25:3
  Handle with Care 1932,D 24,11:4
  Human Side, The 1934,S 15,20:3
  Little Men 1935,F 18,19:3
  Mystery of Edwin Drood, The 1935,Mr 21,27:1

Ernest, George— Cont
  Trail of the Lonesome Pine, The 1936,F 20,23:5
  Every Saturday Night 1936,Mr 14,10:2
  Educating Father 1936,Je 20,22:2
  Reunion 1936,N 27,27:1
  Off to the Races 1937,F 6,15:2
  Big Business 1937,Je 1,27:2
  Wife, Doctor and Nurse 1937,O 11,26:5
  Hot Water 1937,N 5,19:4
  Lady Behave 1938,Ja 28,17:3
  Trip to Paris, A 1938,Je 10,18:2
  Safety in Numbers 1938,S 6,17:2
  20,000 Men a Year 1939,O 28,11:2
  Young as You Feel 1940,Mr 8,25:3
  Four Sons 1940,Je 8,18:4
  Golden Gloves 1940,Ag 21,23:6
Ernest, Harry
  New Adventures of Tarzan, The 1935,O 15,19:3
Ernest, Rolf
  No Greater Glory 1934,My 5,22:2
Ernestos, The
  Minstrel Man 1944,Jl 17,18:5
Ernst, Dorothea
  8 X 8 1957,Mr 16,13:2
Ernst, Jessie (Screenwriter)
  That Night in Rio 1941,Mr 10,21:2
Ernst, Leila
  Life With Henry 1941,F 6,25:2
Ernst, Max
  8 X 8 1957,Mr 16,13:2
  Age d'Or, L'; Golden Age, The 1964,S 22,44:1
Ernst, Max (Miscellaneous)
  Dreams that Money can Buy 1948,Ap 24,11:2
Ernster, Deszo
  Don Giovanni 1956,D 27,22:1
Eroman, Richard
  Happy Time, The 1952,O 31,30:2
Eross, Tamas
  Age of Illusions 1967,Mr 30,55:1
Errol, Leon
  Yolanda 1924,F 20,23:1
  Sally 1925,Mr 16,16:1
  Clothes Make the Pirate 1925,N 30,17:1
  Lunatic at Large, The 1927,F 1,25:1
  Paramount on Parade 1930,Ap 21,20:4
  Only Saps Work 1930,D 13,22:2
  One Heavenly Night 1931,Ja 10,19:2
  Finn and Hattie 1931,Ja 31,15:1
  Her Majesty, Love 1931,N 26,37:2
  Alice in Wonderland 1933,D 23,19:1
  We're not Dressing 1934,Ap 26,27:2
  Notorious Sophie Lang, The 1934,Jl 21,14:2
  Captain Hates the Sea, The 1934,N 29,33:2
  Princess O'Hara 1935,Ap 13,11:3
  Coronado 1935,D 19,33:4
  Make a Wish 1937,S 23,33:1
  Girl From Mexico, The 1939,Je 8,31:4
  Career 1939,Jl 28,14:2
  Dancing Co-Ed 1939,N 10,27:3
  Mexican Spitfire 1940,Ja 10,16:4
  Pop Always Pays 1940,Ag 30,16:6
  Mexican Spitfire out West 1940,O 30,29:3
  Golden Fleecing, The 1940,N 7,33:4
  Six Lessons From Madame La Zonga
    1941,F 19,25:2
  Moonlight in Hawaii 1941,O 10,26:6
  Never Give a Sucker an Even Break
    1941,O 27,21:2
  Hurry, Charlie, Hurry 1941,N 12,31:3
  Mexican Spitfire at Sea 1942,Je 26,16:5
  Mexican Spitfire Sees a Ghost 1942,Jl 31,11:2
  Mexican Spitfire's Elephant 1942,S 18,25:2
  Cowboy in Manhattan 1943,My 28,19:2
  Gals, Inc 1943,Ag 13,13:4
  Higher and Higher 1944,Ja 22,8:4
  Invisible Man's Revenge, The 1944,Je 10,12:2
  She Gets her Man 1945,F 9,20:5
  Joe Palooka, Champ 1946,Ap 6,10:6
  Noose Hangs High, The 1948,My 29,8:6
Ershov, P (Original Author)
  Magic Horse, The 1949,Je 20,14:7
Ershov, V I
  Alexander Nevsky 1939,Mr 23,27:1
  Conquests of Peter The Great, The
    1939,Ag 24,17:2
Erskine, Chester (Director)
  Midnight 1934,Mr 10,18:3
  Egg and I, The 1947,Ap 25,29:2
  Take one False Step 1949,Je 23,33:2
  Girl in Every Port, A 1952,F 14,23:1
  Androcles and the Lion 1953,Ja 15,23:2
Erskine, Chester (Original Author)
  Master of Men 1933,N 29,23:4
  Sailor Takes a Wife, The 1946,Mr 1,17:2
  Split Second 1953,My 13,34:2
Erskine, Chester (Producer)
  Egg and I, The 1947,Ap 25,29:2
  All my Sons 1948,Mr 29,17:3
  Take one False Step 1949,Je 23,33:2
  Witness to Murder 1954,Ap 16,16:4
  Wonderful Country, The 1959,N 5,39:7
Erskine, Chester (Screenwriter)
  Sailor Takes a Wife, The 1946,Mr 1,17:2
  Egg and I, The 1947,Ap 25,29:2

Erskine, Chester (Screenwriter) — Cont
All my Sons 1948,Mr 29,17:3
Take one False Step 1949,Je 23,33:2
Girl in Every Port, A 1952,F 14,23:1
Belle of New York, The 1952,Mr 6,25:6
Androcles and the Lion 1953,Ja 15,23:2
Witness to Murder 1954,Ap 16,16:4
Erskine, Eileen
This Happy Breed 1947,Ap 14,24:2
Great Expectations 1947,My 23,31:1
Hills of Home 1948,N 26,32:2
Lady Possessed 1952,F 15,17:2
Erskine, Elizabeth
You Can't Beat the Irish 1952,My 1,34:4
Erskine, John (Miscellaneous)
Baker's Wife, The 1940,F 27,17:2
Erskine, John (Original Author)
Private Life of Helen of Troy, The
  1927,D 10,14:7
Lady Surrenders, A 1930,O 4,15:2
President's Mystery, The 1936,O 19,22:1
Diane 1956,Ja 13,18:1
Erskine, Laurie York (Original Author)
Confidence Man, The 1924,Ap 15,24:1
Renfrew of the Royal Mounted 1937,N 3,29:4
Erskine, Marilyn
Westward the Women 1952,Ja 1,21:2
Just This Once 1952,Mr 18,22:3
Girl in White, The 1952,My 31,12:5
Above and Beyond 1953,Ja 31,10:6
Eddie Cantor Story, The 1953,D 26,10:2
Erskine-Lindop, Audrey (Screenwriter)
Portrait of a Sinner 1961,D 7,52:1
Erskine-Lindop, John (Miscellaneous)
I Thank a Fool 1962,S 15,15:1
Erstich, Tony
Land of Fury 1955,My 3,37:4
Ertaud, Jacques
Man Escaped, A 1957,Ag 27,33:2
Ertz, Susan (Original Author)
In the Cool of the Day 1963,My 30,20:1
ERVIN
See Also IRVIN, IRVINE
Ervin, Jacques
Katia 1939,D 23,9:2
Ervine, St John (Original Author)
First Mrs Fraser, The 1932,My 29,VIII,4:5 (In
  Addenda)
Erway, Ben
Tampico 1944,Je 2,21:2
Lulu Belle 1948,Je 21,18:3
Sand 1949,Ag 5,23:2
Erwin, Jacques
Sous la Lune du Maroc 1933,Ja 23,9:2
Kreutzer Sonata, The 1938,D 20,30:2
Chips Are Down, The 1949,F 2,36:1
Erwin, Stuart
Speakeasy 1929,Mr 11,22:2
Dangerous Curves 1929,Jl 15,25:1
Cock Eyed World, The 1929,Ag 5,25:2
Sweetie 1929,O 26,15:1
This Thing Called Love 1929,D 14,22:4
Men Without Women 1930,F 1,15:1
Young Eagles 1930,Mr 22,22:6
Dangerous Nan McGrew 1930,Je 21,20:5
Playboy of Paris 1930,N 1,23:2
Only Saps Work 1930,D 13,22:2
No Limit 1931,Ja 17,23:1
Up Pops the Devil 1931,My 16,13:3
Magnificent Lie, The 1931,Jl 25,11:6
Two Kinds of Women 1932,Ja 16,13:1
Strangers in Love 1932,Mr 5,11:2
Misleading Lady, The 1932,Ap 9,18:1
Make Me a Star 1932,Jl 1,19:3
Big Broadcast, The 1932,O 15,13:1
Face in the Sky 1933,F 20,11:5
Crime of the Century, The 1933,Mr 13,18:2
International House 1933,My 27,11:5
Hold Your Man 1933,Jl 1,16:6
Stranger's Return, The 1933,Jl 28,18:2
Before Dawn 1933,O 17,26:2
Day of Reckoning 1933,N 4,18:2
Going Hollywood 1933,D 23,19:2
Palooka 1934,F 28,23:2
Viva Villa! 1934,Ap 11,25:2
Chained 1934,S 1,16:2
Have a Heart 1934,O 20,20:2
Band Plays on, The 1934,D 22,21:2
After Office Hours 1935,Mr 9,19:1
Exclusive Story 1936,Ja 18,19:2
Ceiling Zero 1936,Ja 20,22:2
Absolute Quiet 1936,My 2,11:1
Pigskin Parade 1936,N 14,23:3
Slim 1937,Je 24,30:2
Dance Charlie Dance 1937,Ag 26,25:2
Second Honeymoon 1937,N 13,11:2
I'll Take Romance 1937,D 17,33:2
Three Blind Mice 1938,Je 18,18:2
Passport Husband 1938,Ag 5,11:2
Back Door to Heaven 1939,Ap 20,21:2
It Could Happen to You 1939,Je 9,26:3
Hollywood Cavalcade 1939,O 14,13:2
Honeymoon's Over, The 1939,D 15,33:3
Our Town 1940,Je 14,25:3

When the Daltons Rode 1940,Ag 23,13:3
Little Bit of Heaven, A 1940,N 8,24:2
Bride Came C O D, The 1941,Jl 26,18:2
Adventures of Martin Eden 1942,Mr 16,19:2
Drums of the Congo 1942,Jl 20,16:4
He Hired the Boss 1943,Je 4,17:4
Pillow to Post 1945,My 26,18:2
Heaven Only Knows 1947,N 14,29:3
When Comedy Was King 1960,Mr 30,42:1
Misadventure of Merlin Jones, The
  1964,Mr 26,40:4
Erzinkyan, M (Original Author)
Heart Sings, The 1958,Ag 18,15:2
Erzsi, Somogy
Csokolj Meg Edes 1932,N 25,19:2
Esam, John
Chappaqua 1967,N 6,65:2
Escalante, Henry
Captain Carey U S A 1950,Mr 30,40:5
Creature from the Black Lagoon 1954,My 1,13:4
Escalmel, E R (Screenwriter)
Rothchild 1938,O 12,35:2
Escande, Maurice
Trois Mousquetaires, Les 1933,My 1,10:2
Lucrezia Borgia 1937,O 13,27:2
Queen's Necklace, The 1947,My 17,8:5
Man to Men 1949,F 21,20:2
Escane, Stanley
Hue and Cry 1951,Ja 9,25:2
I Believe in You 1953,My 5,34:3
Eschasserlaux, Bernard (Original Author)
Sundays and Cybele 1962,N 13,43:3
Escobedo, Josefina
Martin Garatuza 1935,S 30,13:1
Hoy Comienza la Vida 1936,Je 27,21:2
Supremo Sacrificio; Supreme Sacrifice
  1938,N 29,27:2
Cobarde, El; Coward, The 1939,Mr 27,11:2
Escoffier
Moscow Nights 1938,My 3,19:3
Escoffier, Aul
Crise est Finie, La 1935,Mr 14,18:1
Escolano, Angel (Producer)
Falstaff; Chimes at Midnight 1967,Mr 18,19:2
Escudero, Antonio
Tarantos, Los 1964,Je 30,22:1
Escudero, Vincente
Here's to Romance 1935,O 3,29:2
Escudero, Vincente (Miscellaneous)
Goyescas 1944,My 29,18:3
Esdale, Charles
Soul Fire 1925,My 6,26:3
Summer Bachelors 1926,D 20,28:3
Esdra, Micaela
Adolescents, The (Flammetta); Flammetta (The
  Adolescents) 1967,Ap 14,33:1
Esipova, Raissa
We Are From Kronstadt 1936,My 2,11:1
Eskay, Alexander (Screenwriter)
Cross of Lorraine, The 1943,D 3,27:4
Esler, Lemist (Screenwriter)
Whistle at Eaton Falls, The 1951,O 11,49:2
Esmelton, Fred
Avalanche, The 1919,Je 30,16:3
Dulcy 1923,S 17,18:2
Lady of the Night 1925,Mr 2,14:1
Smooth as Satin 1925,Je 23,24:3
Red Hot Tires 1925,O 20,28:1
California Straight Ahead 1926,Ja 12,27:5
Kid Boots 1926,O 11,18:2
Shield of Honor 1927,D 13,33:2
Gay Defender, The 1927,D 26,26:6
Chinese Parrot, The 1928,Ja 2,28:1
Two Lovers 1928,Mr 23,24:4
Michigan Kid, The 1928,Jl 2,11:2
Born to Love 1931,Ap 25,23:4
Esmond, Annie
Reserved for Ladies 1932,My 21,9:2
Private Life of Don Juan, The 1934,D 10,16:2
Iron Duke, The 1935,Ja 25,27:2
Men of Tomorrow 1935,Ap 16,27:2
Thunder in the City 1937,Ap 23,25:2
Bulldog Drummond at Bay 1937,O 25,23:2
Stolen Life 1939,Je 15,27:2
Esmond, Carl
Evensong 1934,N 17,12:1
April Romance 1937,Ja 27,17:4
Invitation to the Waltz 1938,Jl 2,10:3
Dawn Patrol 1938,D 24,12:1
Thunder Afloat 1939,O 13,27:2
Pacific Rendezvous 1942,Jl 8,27:4
Panama Hattie 1942,O 2,31:2
Navy Comes Through, The 1942,N 12,30:3
Seven Sweethearts 1942,N 13,28:1
Margin for Error 1943,Ja 25,10:7
First Comes Courage 1943,S 3,15:3
Address Unknown 1944,Ap 17,20:1
Story of Dr Wassell, The 1944,Je 7,13:2
Master Race, The 1944,N 2,22:1
Experiment Perilous 1944,D 30,15:2
Ministry of Fear 1945,F 8,15:2
Without Love 1945,Mr 23,13:1
Her Highness and the Bellboy 1945,S 28,16:2

Esmond, Carl — Cont
This Love of Ours 1945,N 1,20:2
Lover Come Back 1946,Je 20,20:3
Catman of Paris, The 1946,Jl 13,12:2
Smash-Up, The Story of a Woman
  1947,Ap 11,31:2
Slave Girl 1947,Jl 18,21:3
Walk a Crooked Mile 1948,O 13,31:2
Desert Hawk, The 1950,Ag 26,9:2
Mystery Submarine 1951,F 2,19:2
World in His Arms, The 1952,O 10,21:2
From the Earth to the Moon 1958,N 27,52:2
Thunder in the Sun 1959,Ap 9,37:2
Agent for H.A.R.M 1966,Ja 6,20:2
Esmond, Charles
Little Men 1940,D 9,23:2
Sergeant York 1941,Jl 3,15:1
Esmond, H V (Original Author)
Under the Greenwood Tree 1918,D 9,11:4
Esmond, Jill
Skin Game, The 1931,Je 20,20:4
Once a Lady 1931,N 9,22:4
Ladies of the Jury 1932,Ap 2,13:2
State's Attorney 1932,My 6,15:3
Is my Face red 1932,Je 11,9:3
Thirteen Women 1932,O 15,13:1
F P 1 1933,S 16,9:3
No Funny Business 1934,Mr 9,22:4
This Above All 1942,My 13,14:3
Eagle Squadron 1942,Jl 3,12:5
Pied Piper, The 1942,Ag 13,15:3
Random Harvest 1942,D 18,36:6
Journey for Margaret 1942,D 18,36:7
White Cliffs of Dover, The 1944,My 12,15:2
Casanova Brown 1944,S 15,16:1
My Pal, Wolf 1944,O 9,17:2
Bandit of Sherwood Forest, The 1946,Mr 23,8:4
Bedelia 1947,F 8,10:2
Escape 1948,Ag 16,12:2
Night People 1954,Mr 13,11:2
Man Called Peter, A 1955,Ap 1,22:1
Esmonds, Elsie
Camille 1937,Ja 23,13:1
Espantaleon, Juan
Don Quixote 1949,My 13,29:3
Nail, The 1949,Jl 1,14:6
Mad Queen, The 1950,O 27,24:3
Espe, Walter Maria (Original Author)
Crime of the Century, The 1933,Mr 13,18:2
Espejo, Fernando (Screenwriter)
Roots, The (The Filly); Filly, The (The Roots)
  1957,S 3,23:2
Roots, The (The One-Eyed Boy); One-Eyed Boy,
  The (The Roots) 1957,S 3,23:2
Roots, The (The Cows); Cows, The (The Roots)
  1957,S 3,23:2
Roots, The (Our Lady); Our Lady (The Roots)
  1957,S 3,23:2
Esperon, Manuel (Composer)
Silk, Blood and Sun 1943,Ja 30,10:6
Ay Jalisco no te Rajes 1943,Ap 24,17:3
Tierra de Pasiones 1944,N 7,24:3
Three Caballeros, The 1945,F 5,20:1
Esphagen, Claes
Swedish Wedding Night 1965,N 15,48:1
Espinosa
Frenzy 1946,Jl 20,10:3
Espinosa, Robert
Cargo to Capetown 1950,Mr 31,36:3
One Way Street 1950,My 12,33:3
Espiritu, Roque
Bataan 1943,Je 4,17:2
Esposito, Emilio
Bebo's Girl 1964,N 12,40:1
Esposito, Giani
French-Cancan 1956,Ap 17,26:2
Paris Belongs to Us 1962,N 6,38:1
Cross of the Living 1963,F 5,5:5
Anatomy of a Marriage; My Days With Jean
  Marc; My Nights With Françoise
  1964,O 27,42:2
Esquires, The Four
Top of the Town 1937,Mr 27,19:2
Essel, Franz
Deadly Decision 1958,Ap 29,26:2
Essen, Robert
Wrong Man, The 1956,D 24,8:1
Essen, Viola
Specter of the Rose 1946,S 2,12:4
Esser, Karl Wright
Great Lover, The 1949,N 24,48:2
Esser, Paul
Merry Wives of Windsor, The 1952,S 22,19:2
Third Sex, The 1959,Mr 26,27:1
Essex, David
Eve of St Mark, The 1944,My 31,22:2
Essex, Harry (Director)
I, The Jury 1953,Ag 22,8:2
Mad at the World 1955,My 14,10:8
Essex, Harry (Miscellaneous)
He Walked by Night 1949,F 7,15:2
Essex, Harry (Original Author)
Man Made Monster 1941,Mr 19,25:4
Mad at the World 1955,My 14,10:8

Essex, Harry (Screenwriter)
Wyoming Mail 1950,O 23,26:5
Undercover Girl 1950,N 8,37:2
Killer That Stalked New York, The
1951,Ja 5,17:2
Fat Man, The 1951,My 25,31:2
Las Vegas Story, The 1952,Ja 31,37:6
Models, Inc 1952,My 26,18:4
Kansas City Confidential 1952,N 29,11:2
It Came From Outer Space 1953,Je 18,38:2
I, The Jury 1953,Ag 22,8:2
Creature from the Black Lagoon 1954,My 1,13:4
Southwest Passage 1954,S 11,11:2
Raw Edge 1956,Jl 28,10:7
Sons of Katie Elder, The 1965,Ag 26,40:3
Essipova, R D
Oppenheim Family, The 1939,My 24,29:2
Essler, Fred
Where Do We Go From Here? 1945,Je 7,25:2
Saratoga Trunk 1945,N 22,39:2
White Tower, The 1950,Jl 3,9:2
Admiral Was a Lady, The 1950,O 13,23:3
Unsinkable Molly Brown, The 1964,Jl 17,15:1
Estabrook, Howard (Miscellaneous)
Wells Fargo 1937,D 30,15:2
Dakota 1945,D 17,17:2
Estabrook, Howard (Original Author)
Conquerors, The 1932,N 21,21:1
Heavenly Days 1944,O 21,15:2
Estabrook, Howard (Screenwriter)
David Copperfield 1935,Ja 19,8:1
Orchids to You 1935,Ag 10,16:4
Way Down East 1935,O 31,16:2
International Lady 1941,N 11,29:2
Corsican Brothers, The 1942,Ja 16,25:4
New Wine 1942,F 2,11:2
Human Comedy, The 1943,Mr 3,19:2
Bridge of San Luis Rey, The 1944,Mr 4,11:1
Heavenly Days 1944,O 21,15:2
Virginian, The 1946,Ap 18,22:2
Lone Star 1952,F 2,11:4
Passion 1954,D 11,11:1
Cattle Queen of Montana 1955,Ja 26,22:1
Big Fisherman, The 1959,Ag 6,18:1
Esterhazy, Agnes
Streets of Sorrow 1927,Jl 6,23:2
Wrath of the Seas, The 1929,Ag 19,22:1
Spy of Madame de Pompadour, The
1929,S 10,27:1
Esterhazy, Ilona
Buzavirag 1935,Ja 14,11:3
Lila Akac 1935,My 15,26:3
Esterhuizen, Wilhelm
After You, Comrade 1967,Ap 11,54:1
Estes, Fred
Little Men 1940,D 9,23:2
Estrabau, Carmen
Corazon Bandolero 1935,Mr 2,18:2
Estrabeau, Carmen
Donovan's Reef 1963,Jl 25,14:1
Estrabrook, Howard (Director)
Heavenly Days 1944,O 21,15:2
Estrada, Carlos
Tia Tula, A 1965,Je 3,24:1
Estridge, Robin (Screenwriter)
Chance Meeting 1955,Ap 20,38:1
Simba 1955,O 22,24:2
Above Us the Waves 1957,Ap 18,35:2
Checkpoint 1957,S 19,25:2
Dangerous Exile 1958,O 11,18:3
Campbell's Kingdom 1960,Ja 11,35:5
Escape from Zahrain 1962,Jl 12,19:3
Drums of Africa 1963,Jl 4,9:1
Boy Cried Murder, The 1966,Ap 14,42:3
Eye of the Devil 1967,D 7,60:1
Esway, Alexander (Director)
Children of Chance 1931,Ja 24,15:1
Man Who Seeks the Truth, The 1941,O 7,26:6
Barge-Keeper's Daughter, The 1945,S 6,23:3
They Are not Angels 1948,My 22,8:3
Esway, Alexander (Producer)
Thunder in the City 1937,Ap 23,25:2
Eszterggalyos, Cecilla
Age of Illusions 1967,Mr 30,55:1
Eszterhazy, Andrea Count
Roman Holiday 1953,Ag 28,13:1
Etaix, Pierre
Pickpocket 1963,My 22,36:2
Suitor, The; Soupirant, Le 1963,S 18,35:1
Yo Yo 1967,Mr 1,50:1
Etaix, Pierre (Director)
Suitor, The; Soupirant, Le 1963,S 18,35:1
Yo Yo 1967,Mr 1,50:1
Etaix, Pierre (Miscellaneous)
Yo Yo 1967,Mr 1,50:1
Etaix, Pierre (Screenwriter)
Suitor, The; Soupirant, Le 1963,S 18,35:1
Yo Yo 1967,Mr 1,50:1
Etchepare, Pierre
Tu Seras Duchesse 1932,My 7,11:5
Etcheverry, Michel
Sorciere, La 1956,D 28,17:2
Tomorrow Is my Turn 1962,F 2,24:2

Julie the Redhead 1963,O 15,44:1
Ethelyn, Rae
Time, the Comedian 1925,D 14,18:2
Ethier, Alphonse
Moral Sinner, The 1924,Ap 7,15:3
Lone Wolf, The 1924,My 7,19:4
Alaskan, The 1924,S 15,28:1
Contraband 1925,Mr 24,20:6
Fighting Eagle, The 1927,Ag 15,22:5
Alias the Lone Wolf 1927,S 20,32:2
In old Arizona 1929,Ja 21,18:4
Donovan Affair, The 1929,Ap 29,29:2
Honor of the Family 1931,O 17,20:1
Law and Order 1932,F 29,21:3
Rebecca of Sunnybrook Farm 1932,Jl 30,16:5
Match King, The 1932,D 8,25:3
Ex-Lady 1933,My 15,16:2
Baby Face 1933,Je 24,16:2
No More Women 1934,Mr 15,27:4
British Agent 1934,S 20,20:1
Baroness and the Butler, The 1938,F 19,19:2
Ethridge, Ella
Anna Karenina 1935,Ag 31,16:2
Ethridge, Samuel
Old-Fashioned Way, The 1934,Jl 14,16:5
Etievant, Jean
Diary of a Country Priest 1954,Ap 6,35:2
Etievant, Yvette
Prize, The 1952,Ap 30,33:2
We Are all Murderers 1957,Ja 9,27:2
Crime and Punishment 1958,S 16,23:2
War of the Buttons, The 1963,D 19,40:2
Guerre est Fini, La; War Is Over, The
1967,F 2,29:2
Etlinger, Karl
Melodie der Liebe 1934,S 17,20:3
Ettel, Friedrich
Lachende Erben 1933,N 18,18:6
Etter, Marco (Director)
Alpine Love 1936,Je 8,22:5
Etting, Ruth
Roman Scandals 1933,D 25,28:2
Hips, Hips, Hooray 1934,F 24,18:3
Gift of Gab 1934,S 26,17:6
Ettinger, Edward (Screenwriter)
Man Who Wouldn't Talk, The 1940,Ja 12,13:3
Ettinger, Norman
Mask, The 1961,O 28,12:4
Nobody Waved Goodbye 1964,S 17,52:1
Ettlinger, Don (Original Author)
Sally, Irene and Mary 1938,F 26,9:2
My Lucky Star 1938,S 10,20:2
Hold That Co-ed 1938,S 24,13:1
Ettlinger, Don (Screenwriter)
Life Begins In College 1937,O 9,16:1
Rebecca of Sunnybrook Farm 1938,Mr 26,12:1
Hold That Co-ed 1938,S 24,13:1
Shipyard Sally 1940,Ja 18,27:3
I Was an Adventuress 1940,My 20,13:2
Young People 1940,Ag 24,16:2
Great American Broadcast, The 1941,My 2,25:2
Guilty Bystander 1950,Ap 21,18:2
Ettlinger, Karl
That Murder in Berlin 1929,Mr 12,26:2
Zwei Hertzen in Drei-Viertel Takt
1930,O 13,31:1
Olympia 1930,D 7,IX,6:4
Skandal Um Eva 1931,Ap 21,35:2
Liebeswalzer 1931,My 4,15:3
Bomben auf Monte Carlo; Bombardment of Monte
Carlo, The 1931,S 27,VIII,7:1
Ettori, Claudye
Boom! 1968,My 27,56:1
Etush, V
Gadfly, The 1956,S 17,22:2
Eugene, Billy
Denial, The 1925,Mr 10,19:3
Son of his Father, A 1925,S 29,31:3
Big Shot, The 1932,Ja 2,14:2
Eugene, William
Women Who Give 1924,Je 3,22:1
Shooting of Dan McGrew, The 1924,Je 9,14:3
Captain Blood 1924,S 9,19:1
Girl From Montmarte, The 1926,F 25,26:2
Eugene, William (Screenwriter)
Women Who Give 1924,Je 3,22:1
Eugenia, Maria
Littlest Outlaw, The 1955,D 27,31:1
Eugeniou, George
Kitchen, The 1961,N 2,42:1
Eugens, Arthur Fritz
Maria, Die Magd 1937,My 22,19:2
Dr Engel, Child Specialist 1937,S 20,19:2
Eunson, Dale (Original Author)
Guest in the House 1945,F 16,19:2
How to Marry a Millionaire 1953,N 11,37:1
All Mine to Give 1959,Ag 4,32:5
Eunson, Dale (Screenwriter)
Star, The 1953,Ja 29,25:1
Sabre Jet 1953,N 3,34:1
Eighteen and Anxious 1957,D 14,16:6
All Mine to Give 1959,Ag 4,32:5
Gidget Goes to Rome 1963,S 12,32:2

Eunson, Katherine (Screenwriter)
Eighteen and Anxious 1957,D 14,16:6
All Mine to Give 1959,Ag 4,32:5
Gidget Goes to Rome 1963,S 12,32:2
Euridice, Maria
Tropics 1968,S 24,52:1
Eurneaux, Yvonne
Repulsion 1965,O 4,7:6
Eustace, Fred
Little Lord Fauntleroy 1914,Je 23,11:3
Eustace, Harry
War Is a Racket 1934,D 10,16:2
Eustace, Harry (Cinematographer)
Through Darkest Africa 1927,Mr 22,31:2
Eustrel, Antony
Under the Red Robe 1937,Je 1,27:2
Revenge of General Ling, The 1938,F 21,15:1
Adventures of Tartu, The 1943,S 24,26:1
Silver Fleet, The 1945,Mr 24,22:6
Caesar and Cleopatra 1946,S 6,18:2
Story of Robin Hood, The 1952,Je 27,18:3
Devil's Plot 1953,Je 19,18:1
King Richard and the Crusaders 1954,Ag 23,20:5
Unsinkable Molly Brown, The 1964,Jl 17,15:1
Games 1967,S 18,58:2
Eva, Evi
Carnival Crime, The 1929,Jl 8,17:3
Theatre 1929,Ag 25,VIII,5:1
Eva, Fenyvessi
Hyppolit, A Lakaj 1933,Ja 4,22:6
Evald, Johanna
Fight for Matterhorn, The 1929,Jl 29,23:3
Evangelista, Lucia
Traviata, La 1953,D 28,17:2
Evangelisti, Franco (Screenwriter)
Difficult Years 1950,Ag 22,31:2
Evanoff, Linda
Flower Thief, The 1962,Jl 14,11:5
Evans, Adoree
Marines, Lets Go! 1961,Ag 16,37:2
Evans, Barry
Here We Go Around the Mulberry Bush
1968,Mr 5,34:5
Evans, Bob
Kid Galahad 1937,My 27,21:3
Flame of New Orleans, The 1941,Ap 26,20:2
Evans, Brandon
Emperor Jones, The 1933,S 20,26:2
Evans, Brooks
Let's Face It 1943,Ag 5,18:1
Evans, Bruce
Back Door to Heaven 1939,Ap 20,21:2
Evans, Cecile
Worldly Goods 1924,N 3,20:1
Goose Hangs High, The 1925,Mr 10,19:3
Talker, The 1925,My 12,26:2
Evans, Charles
Disraeli 1929,O 3,27:5
Man Who Played God, The 1932,F 11,16:1
Expert, The 1932,F 27,22:1
King's Vacation, The 1933,Ja 20,21:2
Working Man, The 1933,Ap 21,20:3
Peck's bad Boy 1934,O 6,20:1
Clive of India 1935,Ja 18,29:1
Cardinal Richelieu 1935,Ap 19,24:2
Over 21 1945,Ag 17,20:2
Black Beauty 1946,Ag 30,13:2
Dark Mirror, The 1946,O 19,15:2
It Had to be You 1947,D 8,35:2
Beyond Glory 1948,Ag 4,18:2
Ruthless 1948,S 4,8:7
Isn't It Romantic? 1948,O 7,35:2
Walk a Crooked Mile 1948,O 13,31:2
Sealed Verdict 1948,N 3,36:2
Crooked Way, The 1949,S 5,13:2
Woman of Distinction, A 1950,Mr 17,28:2
Reformer and the Redhead, The 1950,Ap 10,15:2
Colt 45 1950,My 6,8:6
My Friend Irma Goes West 1950,Ag 3,20:2
Furies, The 1950,Ag 17,23:2
Harriet Craig 1950,N 3,31:2
Flying Missile, The 1950,D 25,25:1
Stage to Tucson 1951,My 5,14:2
Last Outpost, The 1951,Je 22,16:3
Desert Fox, The 1951,O 18,32:1
Sangaree 1953,Je 5,19:1
Demetrius and the Gladiators 1954,Je 19,9:1
Evans, Clem
Kansan, The 1943,O 1,15:3
Evans, Clifford
Ourselves Alone 1937,Jl 31,6:2
Tenth Man, The 1937,N 15,15:2
River of Unrest 1937,N 27,21:2
Mutiny of the Elsinore, The 1939,F 16,17:2
Proud Valley 1941,My 17,19:2
Voice in the Night, The 1941,My 23,25:4
Somewhere in France 1943,Jl 12,11:2
Courageous Mr Penn 1943,D 23,26:5
Love on the Dole 1945,O 13,11:2
S O S Pacific 1960,O 13,41:3
Curse of the Werewolf, The 1961,Je 8,40:2
Kiss of the Vampire 1963,O 10,49:2
Long Ships, The 1964,Je 25,25:1

Evans, Clifford (Screenwriter)
Run for Your Money, A 1950,Ap 10,15:3
Evans, Dale
Girl Trouble 1942,O 8,31:2
In old Oklahoma 1943,D 6,21:1
Utah 1945,Mr 12,22:7
My Pal Trigger 1946,Ag 17,16:3
Apache Rose 1947,Jl 23,19:3
Evans, David (Original Author)
Girl in the Painting, The 1949,Ag 22,13:1
Evans, David (Screenwriter)
Irish and Proud of It 1938,O 31,12:3
Macushla 1940,Ja 6,9:2
Obsessed 1952,F 6,24:2
Evans, Dillon
Hamlet 1964,S 24,46:1
Evans, Doug
Crimson Key, The 1947,O 18,9:2
Evans, Douglas
No Sad Songs for Me 1950,Ap 28,26:2
Champagne for Caesar 1950,My 12,33:2
Eddie Cantor Story, The 1953,D 26,10:2
Evans, Edith
Queen of Spades, The 1949,Jl 1,14:4
Dolwyn 1949,Ag 30,18:4
Importance of Being Earnest, The 1952,D 23,17:2
Nun's Story, The 1959,Je 19,30:1
Look Back in Anger 1959,S 16,45:1
Tom Jones 1963,O 8,48:1
Chalk Garden, The 1964,My 22,42:2
Young Cassidy 1965,Mr 23,35:1
Whisperers, The 1967,Ag 1,24:1
Fitzwilly 1967,D 21,45:1
Prudence and the Pill 1968,My 24,37:1
Evans, Edward
Angel Who Pawned her Harp, The 1956,F 29,35:2
Evans, Estelle
Quiet One, The 1949,F 14,15:2
To Kill a Mockingbird 1963,F 15,10:2
Evans, Evan (Original Author)
Branded 1951,Ja 11,28:5
Evans, Evan S
How Green Was my Valley 1941,O 29,27:2
Evans, Evans
All Fall Down 1962,Ap 12,41:3
Bonnie and Clyde 1967,Ag 14,36:1
Evans, Eynon
Sheriff of Fractured Jaw, The 1959,Mr 14,27:4
Evans, Frank
Running Wild 1927,Je 14,33:2
Evans, Gene
It Happens Every Spring 1949,Je 11,11:2
Wyoming Mail 1950,O 23,26:5
Steel Helmet, The 1951,Ja 25,21:5
Sugarfoot 1951,F 12,19:4
Ace in the Hole 1951,Je 30,8:6
I Was an American Spy 1951,Jl 4,13:2
Force of Arms 1951,Ag 14,20:2
Fixed Bayonets 1951,N 21,20:2
Mutiny 1952,Mr 20,37:5
Park Row 1952,D 22,20:2
Thunderbirds 1953,Mr 12,24:4
Donovan's Brain 1954,Ja 21,28:2
Hell and High Water 1954,F 2,20:6
Long Wait, The 1954,Jl 3,9:2
Cattle Queen of Montana 1955,Ja 26,22:1
Crashout 1955,Jl 9,9:2
Helen Morgan Story, The 1957,O 3,33:2
Sad Sack, The 1957,N 28,57:1
Bravados, The 1958,Je 26,23:2
Operation Petticoat 1959,D 6,38:1
Gold of the Seven Saints 1961,Ap 6,30:3
Shock Corridor 1963,S 12,32:1
Nevada Smith 1966,Je 24,28:1 (Incorrect in this
edition; use 1966,Je 30,28:1 elsewhere)
Evans, Haydn Roth (Original Author)
Pot o'Gold 1941,Ap 4,25:2
Evans, Helena Phillips
Elmer and Elsie 1934,Ag 4,14:5
I'll Fix It 1934,N 12,17:3
My Bill 1938,Jl 7,22:4
Six Thousand Enemies 1939,Je 9,26:2
Evans, Herbert
Secrets 1933,Mr 16,21:2
Reunion in Vienna 1933,Ap 29,14:2
Brief Moment 1933,S 30,18:5
Glass Key, The 1935,Je 15,20:2
Sudden Death, And 1936,Jl 18,18:2
Dawn Patrol 1938,D 24,12:1
Susannah of the Mounties 1939,Je 24,13:2
Man About Town 1939,Je 29,19:1
Rains Came, The 1939,S 9,11:2
Blue Bird, The 1940,Ja 20,11:2
Man Hunt 1941,Je 14,20:2
Her Primitive Man 1944,Ap 1,11:1
Abroad With two Yanks 1944,O 26,19:7
Pardon my Past 1946,Ja 28,15:5
Evans, Jacqueline
Adventures of Casanova 1948,Mr 22,18:3
Evans, Jean
Mile-a-Minute Kendall 1918,My 6,11:3

Evans, Jean (Original Author)
Hot Blood 1956,Mr 24,14:2
Evans, Jill
Facts of Love, The 1949,O 31,20:2
Evans, Joan
Roseanna McCoy 1949,O 13,33:2
Our Very Own 1950,Jl 28,12:5
Edge of Doom 1950,Ag 4,13:2
Skirts Ahoy! 1952,My 29,17:2
It Grows on Trees 1952,N 29,11:2
Flying Fontaines, The 1959,D 24,13:6
Evans, John
Outcast, The 1954,Jl 3,9:2
Evans, Julius (Screenwriter)
Sword of the Avenger 1948,Ag 26,16:4
Evans, Karin
Trial of Donald Westhof, The 1928,F 18,11:2
Thirteen Men and a Girl 1931,Ag 17,18:2
Die Letze Kompagnie 1932,Ag 26,20:3
Mein Leben fuer Maria Isabell; My Life for Maria
Isabell 1935,N 5,33:5
Affair Blum, The 1949,O 18,35:2
Evans, Kendall
Hold 'Em Yale 1935,Ap 27,20:6
Evans, Larry (Original Author)
Judgment of the Hills 1927,Ag 2,19:2
Evans, Linda
Those Calloways 1965,Ap 15,38:2
Evans, Lyn
Years Between, The 1947,Mr 10,25:2
Smugglers, The 1948,Mr 29,17:1
Quartet (The Colonel's Lady); Colonel's Lady, The
(Quartet) 1949,Mr 29,30:3
Blue Lagoon, The 1949,O 3,13:2
Kind Hearts and Coronets 1950,Je 15,41:2
Evans, Madge
Classmates 1924,D 30,15:3
Son of India 1931,Jl 25,11:6
Sporting Blood 1931,Ag 15,18:3
Guilty Hands 1931,Ag 29,16:3
Heartbreak 1931,O 17,20:1
Greeks Had a Word for Them, The 1932,F 4,25:2
Lovers Courageous 1932,F 20,11:2
Huddle 1932,Je 17,24:1
Fast Life 1932,D 24,11:4
Hallelujah, I'm a Bum 1933,F 9,15:2
Hell Below 1933,Ap 26,13:2
Nuisance, The 1933,My 29,22:2
Mayor of Hell, The 1933,Jl 1,16:5
Made on Broadway 1933,Jl 8,14:5
Dinner at Eight 1933,Ag 24,18:1
Broadway to Hollywood 1933,S 2,14:4
Beauty for Sale 1933,S 16,9:3
Day of Reckoning 1933,N 4,18:2
Fugitive Lovers 1934,Ja 13,16:3
Show-Off, The 1934,Mr 17,11:3
Stand up and Cheer 1934,Ap 20,17:1
Grand Canary 1934,Jl 20,11:1
Paris Interlude 1934,Jl 28,16:5
Death on the Diamond 1934,S 24,14:1
What Every Woman Knows 1934,O 27,20:2
Helldorado 1935,Ja 7,13:2
David Copperfield 1935,Ja 19,8:1
Age of Indiscretion 1935,My 18,21:2
Men Without Names 1935,Je 29,16:2
Transatlantic Tunnel 1935,O 28,16:2
Exclusive Story 1936,Ja 18,19:2
Moonlight Murder 1936,Mr 28,11:2
Piccadilly Jim 1936,Ag 31,19:1
Pennies From Heaven 1936,D 10,35:2
Espionage 1937,Mr 9,27:3
Thirteenth Chair, The 1937,Je 18,25:3
Sinners in Paradise 1938,My 20,17:2
Army Girl 1938,Ag 12,11:1
Evans, Marguerite
Stage Struck 1925,N 16,19:4
Evans, Maurice
White Cargo 1930,F 24,18:1
Should a Doctor Tell 1931,Ag 22,7:5
Heart Song 1934,Je 6,24:6
Scrooge 1935,D 14,11:1
Kind Lady 1951,Ag 8,21:2
Androcles and the Lion 1953,Ja 15,23:2
Gilbert and Sullivan 1953,O 28,36:3
War Lord, The 1965,N 18,55:2
Jack of Diamonds 1967,N 11,26:3
Planet of the Apes 1968,F 9,55:2
Rosemary's Baby 1968,Je 13,57:1
Evans, Max (Original Author)
Rounders, The 1965,Ap 29,40:2
Evans, Michael
Bye Bye Birdie 1963,Ap 5,27:3
Love-Ins, The 1967,Ag 19,16:1
Evans, Monica
Odd Couple, The 1968,My 3,42:1
Evans, Muriel
Pack up Your Troubles 1932,O 1,10:4
Fast Workers 1933,Mr 20,18:2
Prizefighter and the Lady, The 1933,N 11,11:3
Heat Lightning 1934,Mr 8,23:2
Manhattan Melodrama 1934,My 5,22:2
Hide-Out 1934,Ag 25,16:5
Have a Heart 1934,O 20,20:2

Evans, Muriel— Cont
Mr Deeds Goes to Town 1936,Ap 17,17:2
Three on the Trail 1936,My 5,26:5
Two-Fisted Gentleman 1936,Ag 24,11:2
Missing Girls 1936,O 5,25:1
House of Secrets 1937,F 22,13:1
Evans, Myddleton
This Freedom 1923,N 28,15:1
Evans, Nancy
Life With Father 1947,Ag 16,6:6
Evans, Peggy
Blue Lamp, The 1951,Ja 9,25:1
Evans, Perry
Great Commandment, The 1942,O 17,11:1
Evans, Ray
Sunset Boulevard 1950,Ag 11,15:2
Evans, Ray (Composer)
Private's Affair, A 1959,Ag 15,8:7
Evans, Rex
Along Came Sally 1934,Je 16,20:3
Zaza 1939,Ja 5,17:1
Adventure in Diamonds 1940,Ap 4,27:2
Philadelphia Story, The 1940,D 27,22:2
Shanghai Gesture, The 1941,D 26,21:2
Frankenstein Meets the Wolf Man 1943,Mr 6,8:3
Higher and Higher 1944,Ja 22,8:4
Brighton Strangler, The 1945,My 19,15:2
Till the Clouds Roll By 1946,D 6,27:4
Dangerous Millions 1947,Mr 15,10:3
It Should Happen to You 1954,Ja 16,10:5
Birds and the Bees, The 1956,Ap 23,22:1
Merry Andrews 1958,Mr 21,17:1
Matchmaker, The 1958,Ag 13,22:1
On the Double 1961,My 20,12:1
Evans, Richard
Synanon 1965,My 6,44:1
Return of Mr Moto 1965,D 2,48:1
Evans, Robert
Best of Everything 1959,O 9,24:2
Evans, Robert J
Man of a Thousand Faces 1957,Ag 14,21:1
Sun Also Rises, The 1957,Ag 24,12:2
Evans, Rose (Screenwriter)
Fan, The 1949,Ap 2,12:2
Evans, Rudolph
Kisenga, Man of Africa 1952,Mr 7,18:2
Evans, Russell
Detective Story 1951,N 7,35:2
Glory Brigade, The 1953,Ag 15,8:4
Band of Angels 1957,Jl 11,21:1
Evans, Tolchard (Composer)
Charming Deceiver, The 1933,D 9,18:3
Evans, Vincent (Screenwriter)
Chain Lightning 1950,F 20,21:2
Battle Hymn 1957,F 16,14:1
Evans, Wilbur
Man With a Million 1954,Je 29,21:2
Evanson, Edith
Life With Henry 1941,F 6,25:2
Woman of the Year 1942,F 6,23:2
Orchestra Wives 1942,S 24,23:2
Reunion in France 1943,Mr 5,20:3
Singapore 1947,S 17,31:2
I Remember Mama 1948,Mr 12,29:2
Rope 1948,Ag 27,12:4
You Gotta Stay Happy 1948,N 5,29:2
Damned Don't Cry, The 1950,Ap 8,9:2
Magnificent Yankee, The 1951,Ja 19,21:2
Day the Earth Stood Still, The 1951,S 19,37:1
Shane 1953,Ap 24,30:3
Down Among the Sheltering Palms 1953,Je 13,11:2
Desiree 1954,N 18,42:1
Leather Saint, The 1956,Je 16,12:2
Toby Tyler 1960,Ap 20,45:2
Twice Told Tales (Rappaccini's Daughter);
Rappaccini's Daughter (Twice Told Tales)
1964,Mr 28,40:1
Evarts, Hal G (Original Author)
Silent Call, The 1922,Ja 30,16:2
Tumbleweeds 1925,D 21,27:2
Sante Fe Trail, The 1930,O 18,23:2
Evarts, Hal G (Screenwriter)
Big Trail, The 1930,O 25,20:3
Evashevski, Forest
Harmon of Michigan 1941,O 2,29:2
Evelyn, Baby
Greatest Love of All, The 1924,N 11,14:1
Evelyn, Judith
Thirteenth Letter, The 1951,F 22,27:2
Rear Window 1954,Ag 5,18:2
Egyptian, The 1954,Ag 25,23:1
Female on the Beach 1955,Ag 20,20:2
Hilda Crane 1956,My 3,35:2
Brothers Karamazov, The 1958,F 21,18:2
Twilight for the Gods 1958,Ag 7,21:1
Tingler, The 1960,Mr 10,36:2
Everest, Barbara
There Goes the Bride 1933,Mr 4,11:3
Phantom Fiend 1935,Ap 22,14:2
Scrooge 1935,D 14,11:1
Passing of the Third Floor Back, The 1936,Ap 29,19:2
When Thief Meets Thief 1937,Je 15,26:2

Everest, Barbara— Cont

Mission to Moscow 1943,Ap 30,25:2
Phantom of the Opera, The 1943,O 15,15:2
Jane Eyre 1944,F 4,12:5
Uninvited, The 1944,F 21,19:3
Gaslight 1944,My 5,17:2
Valley of Decision, The 1945,My 4,23:2
Wanted for Murder 1946,D 12,38:4
Patient Vanishes, The 1947,My 23,31:2
Frieda 1947,Ag 15,12:3
Madeleine 1950,S 1,17:2
Tony Draws a Horse 1951,My 15,38:6
Commandos Strike at Dawn 1954,Ja 14,25:1
Safecracker, The 1958,Mr 6,32:1

Everett, Chad

Claudelle Inglish 1961,S 21,40:2
Chapman Report, The 1962,O 18,49:2
Get Yourself a College Girl 1965,Ap 29,40:2
Made in Paris 1966,F 17,29:1
Singing Nun, The 1966,Mr 18,33:1
Johnny Tiger 1966,Je 16,53:4
First to Fight 1967,Mr 30,55:1
Last Challenge, The 1967,D 28,25:1
Impossible Years, The 1968,D 6,54:1

Everett, Peter (Original Author)

Negatives 1968,O 15,40:1

Everett, Peter (Screenwriter)

Negatives 1968,O 15,40:1

Everett, Timmy

Music Man, The 1962,Ag 24,14:1

Everitt, J T (Screenwriter)

We Are the Marines 1942,D 14,19:2

Evers, Ann

Forgotten Faces 1936,Jl 4,18:2
Son Comes Home, A 1936,S 5,7:1
Frontier Town 1938,Mr 12,13:3
Mad Miss Manton, The 1938,O 21,27:2
Beauty for the Asking 1939,F 10,19:1

Evers, Gayle

Bill of Divorcement, A 1932,O 3,15:2

Evers, Herb

Pretty Boy Floyd 1960,N 3,49:2

Evers, Jason

P J 1968,Mr 7,52:3

Evers, Juanita

Farmer Takes a Wife, The 1953,Je 13,11:2

Evers, King

Daddies 1924,F 11,18:3

Everth, Francis

Prince and the Pauper, The 1922,Ag 14,12:4

Everton, Paul

Conquest of Canaan, The 1921,Jl 11,9:3
That Royle Girl 1926,Ja 4,33:1
They Won't Forget 1937,Jl 15,16:1
Life of Emile Zola, The 1937,Ag 12,14:2
Great Garrick, The 1937,O 25,23:1
Merrily We Live 1938,Mr 18,23:3
Beloved Brat 1938,My 2,13:2
Gun Law 1938,Je 24,15:1
Reformatory 1938,Je 27,13:6
Touchdown Army 1938,O 28,27:2
Topper Takes a Trip 1938,D 30,11:2
Stand up and Fight 1939,Ja 27,17:2
Maisie 1939,Je 23,23:1
Mexican Spitfire out West 1940,O 30,29:3
Leave Her to Heaven 1945,D 26,15:1

Everts, Heidi

Ciske 1963,Ag 3,8:2

Eville, William

Virtuous Vamp, A 1919,N 17,20:1

Evrard, Jane

Collier de la Reine, Le (Queen's Necklace, The)
1931,F 9,25:3

Evstratova, V

Mistress, The 1954,My 31,9:2

Ewart, John

Rugged O'Riordans, The 1950,Ja 6,25:2

Ewell, Tom

Adam's Rib 1949,D 26,33:2
Life of her Own, A 1950,O 12,43:2
American Guerrilla in the Philippines
1950,N 8,37:2
Mr Music 1950,D 21,34:3
Up Front 1951,Mr 26,19:2
Seven Year Itch, The 1955,Je 4,9:1
Lieutenant Wore Skirts, The 1956,Ja 12,22:1
Girl Can't Help It, The 1957,F 9,12:7
Tender is the Night 1962,Ja 20,13:2
State Fair 1962,Ap 12,41:4

Ewens, James (Original Author)

Emergency Call 1933,Je 24,16:2

Ewers, Hans Heinz (Original Author)

Alraune 1928,My 20,VIII,8:4
Horst Wessel; Hans Westmar 1934,F 4,IX,4:4

Ewert, Renate

I Spit on Your Grave 1963,Je 29,13:5

Ewing, Montague (Composer)

Charming Deceiver, The 1933,D 9,18:3

Exton, Clive (Screenwriter)

Night Must Fall 1964,Mr 19,28:1

Eybner, Richard

Mozart Story, The 1948,N 15,21:5

Eyck, Peter Van

Station Six-Sahara 1964,N 12,40:2

Eyer, Richard

Desperate Hours, The 1955,O 6,25:1
Sincerely Yours 1955,N 3,37:1
Friendly Persuasion 1956,N 2,30:1
Slander 1957,Ja 17,34:4
Bailout at 43,000 1957,Je 8,13:2
Fort Dobbs 1958,Ap 19,10:4
Seventh Voyage of Sinbad 1958,D 24,00:0
Hell to Eternity 1960,O 13,41:1

Eyer, Robert

Khovanschina 1960,S 23,33:1
Back Street 1961,O 13,27:1

Eyfel, Eveline

Bonjour Tristesse 1958,Ja 16,32:1

Eymond, Louis

Open Road, The 1940,O 5,20:2
Resistance; Peleton d'Execution 1946,Jl 5,15:3

Eyre, Laurence (Original Author)

Lights of Old Broadway 1925,N 2,20:1
Volcano 1926,My 24,24:3

Eyser, Jacques

Would-Be Gentleman, The 1960,Mr 23,31:1

Eysoldt, Gertrude

Keepers of the Night 1953,Je 9,24:2

Eyssen, John Van

One That Got Away, The 1958,Ap 23,40:2
Chance Meeting 1960,O 27,45:2

Eythe, William

Ox-Bow Incident, The 1943,My 10,15:2 (In
Addenda)
Song of Bernadette, The 1944,Ja 27,15:2
Eve of St Mark, The 1944,My 31,22:2
Wilson 1944,Ag 2,18:1
Wing and a Prayer 1944,Ag 31,14:1
Royal Scandal, A 1945,Ap 12,19:2
House on Ninety-Second Street, The
1945,S 27,24:7
Colonel Effingham's Raid 1946,Ap 5,21:3
Centennial Summer 1946,Jl 18,20:2
Meet Me at Dawn 1948,My 18,26:2
Special Agent 1949,Ag 22,13:1

Eyton, Frank (Composer)

My Song For You 1935,My 27,20:6

Eyton, Frank (Miscellaneous)

Heart Song 1934,Je 6,24:6

F

Fabares, Shelley

Never Say Goodbye 1956,Ap 14,20:1
Summer Love 1958,Je 26,23:4
Ride the Wild Surf 1964,D 24,8:4
Girl Happy 1965,My 27,28:1
Hold On! 1966,Je 23,29:4
Spinout 1966,D 15,60:1
Clambake 1967,D 14,62:3

Fabbri, Diego (Screenwriter)

Fear No Evil 1949,Mr 31,31:2
Verginita 1953,Ap 18,17:2
His Last Twelve Hours 1953,N 13,24:7
Ten Commandments, The 1958,Ap 7,26:1
General Della Rovere 1960,N 22,41:1
Your Shadow Is Mine 1963,My 15,32:1
Magnificent Cuckold 1965,Ap 20,42:1

Fabbri, Jacques

Seven Deadly Sins, The (Lust); Lust (The Seven
Deadly Sins) 1953,My 12,31:3
Grand Maneuver, The 1956,O 2,39:1
Belle Americaine, La 1961,D 18,42:1

Fabeni, Enno

Under the Sun of Rome 1949,O 6,40:4

Faber, Ann

Happy Time, The 1952,O 31,30:2

Faber, Erich (Original Author)

Gitta Entdeckt Ihr Herz 1932,S 30,17:3

Faber, Erwin

At the Edge of the World 1929,Je 18,29:4
Bride 68 1930,Ap 15,28:5

Faber, Juliette

Vierge Folle, La 1938,D 30,11:3
Shop-Girls of Paris; Au Bonheur de Dames
1947,Je 23,14:4
Strangers in the House 1949,O 13,33:3
We Are all Murderers 1957,Ja 9,27:2

Faber, Leslie

White Cargo 1930,F 24,18:1

Faber, Robert (Original Author)

Zombies on Broadway 1945,Ap 27,23:2

Faber, Robert (Producer)

Snow Queen, The 1960,Ap 14,34:1

Fabert, Henri

Battle, The 1934,N 23,23:2

Fabert, Maxime

Femme Nue, La 1933,Ag 25,12:3

Fabian

Hound-Dog Man 1960,Ap 28,29:1
High Time 1960,S 17,15:1
North to Alaska 1960,N 11,36:1
Love in a Goldfish Bowl 1961,Jl 13,26:3
Mr Hobbs Takes a Vacation 1962,Je 16,11:2

Fabian— Cont

Five Weeks in a Balloon 1962,Ag 27,18:1
Longest Day, The 1962,O 5,28:1
Ride the Wild Surf 1964,D 24,8:4
Dear Brigitte 1965,Ja 28,20:1
Ten Little Indians 1966,F 10,33:1
Fireball 500 1966,N 24,65:4
Thunder Valley 1967,S 14,55:1
Thunder Alley 1967,S 14,55:1

Fabian, Francoise

Fernandel the Dressmaker 1957,Jl 1,19:2
Mam'zelle Pigalle 1958,Ap 19,10:4
Thief of Paris, The 1967,Ag 24,43:2

Fabian, John

Cockleshell Heroes, The 1956,Je 4,25:2
Town Like Alice, A 1958,S 22,27:1

Fabian, Olga

Voice in the Wind 1944,Mr 16,17:2
Ship of Fools 1965,Jl 29,18:1

Fabian, Warner (Original Author)

Flaming Youth 1923,N 26,15:6
Summer Bachelors 1926,D 20,28:3
Sailors' Wives 1928,F 28,18:4
Wild Party, The 1929,Ap 2,28:4
Men in her Life 1931,N 30,16:2
Week Ends Only 1932,Je 18,9:2

Fabianova, Vkasta

Bohemian Rapture 1948,F 16,16:2
Krakatit 1951,Ap 30,16:2

Fabiole, Luce

Two of Us, The 1968,F 20,53:1

Fabisiak, Kazimierz

Joan of the Angels? 1962,My 8,43:6

Fabray, Nanette

Private Lives of Elizabeth and Essex, The
1939,D 2,21:2
Child Is Born, A 1940,Ja 11,19:2
Band Wagon, The 1953,Jl 10,10:2

Fabre, Fernand

Appassionata 1929,Jl 8,17:3
Collier de la Reine, Le (Queen's Necklace, The)
1931,F 9,25:3
Chance, La 1932,My 28,18:2
Madame Borary 1934,N 19,13:2
Heroes of the Marne; (Famille Lefrancois, Le)
1939,Ap 24,13:2
Crime in the Maginot Line 1939,My 8,21:2
Man of the Hour, The 1940,N 21,43:2
Queen and the Cardinal, The 1944,Je 1,17:3
Colonel Chabert 1947,Je 21,11:2
Chips Are Down, The 1949,F 2,36:1
Sword and the Rose, The 1953,Ag 20,18:3
Rise of Louis XIV, The 1967,S 26,54:2

Fabre, Maurice (Screenwriter)

Backfire 1965,Ap 27,27:1

Fabre, Saturnin

Paris-Beguin 1932,D 31,10:1
Petits, Les 1936,D 30,17:2
Generals Without Buttons 1938,Mr 8,23:2
Mayor's Dilemma, The 1940,Ap 23,19:2
Pepe le Moko 1941,Mr 4,20:2
Nine Bachelors 1942,F 9,19:2
Pasha's Wives, The 1942,Ap 6,19:2
Friend Will come Tonight, A; Ami Viendra Ce
Soir, Un 1948,Jl 12,11:2
Gates of the Night 1950,Mr 16,40:2
Scandals of Clochemerle, The 1950,Mr 28,28:2
Ignace 1950,S 19,39:4
Miquette 1951,F 5,18:2
French Way, The 1952,S 6,12:6
Holiday for Henrietta 1955,Ja 25,21:1

Fabregas, Virginia

Sangre Manda, La 1934,My 15,18:2
Abnegacion 1938,My 31,8:3

Fabri, Zoltan (Director)

Merry Go-Round 1958,Ap 3,23:3

Fabri, Zoltan (Screenwriter)

Merry Go-Round 1958,Ap 3,23:3

Fabricus, Hintz

Glass Tower, The; (Glaserne Turm, Der)
1959,Ag 27,24:4

Fabrizi, Aldo

Open City; Citta Aperta 1946,F 26,21:2
To Live in Peace 1947,N 25,37:2
Professor, My Son 1949,Ap 18,18:4
Peddler and the Lady, The 1949,S 30,28:4
Tombolo 1949,D 31,9:4
Escape into Dreams 1950,Ap 13,34:5
Flesh will Surrender 1950,O 26,38:7
Three Steps North 1951,Je 29,14:2
Anthony of Padua 1952,Mr 29,19:2
Father's Dilemma 1952,S 23,25:1
Flowers of St Francis 1952,O 7,26:2
Lucky Five, The 1953,N 27,22:5
Times Gone By (The Old Book Stand); Old Book
Stand, The (Times Gone By) 1953,D 30,16:2
Premier May 1958,S 17,44:2
Of Life and Love 1958,O 7,40:2
Angel Wore Red, The 1960,S 29,32:1
Teacher and the Miracle, The 1961,Ap 24,36:4
Wonders of Aladdin, The 1961,D 23,16:1
Three Bites of the Apple 1967,My 25,54:2

Fabrizi, Aldo (Director)
Of Life and Love 1958,O 7,40:2
Teacher and the Miracle, The 1961,Ap 24,36:4
Fabrizi, Aldo (Original Author)
Escape into Dreams 1950,Ap 13,34:5
Fabrizi, Aldo (Producer)
Teacher and the Miracle, The 1961,Ap 24,36:4
Fabrizi, Aldo (Screenwriter)
To Live in Peace 1947,N 25,37:2
Flesh will Surrender 1950,O 26,38:7
Teacher and the Miracle, The 1961,Ap 24,36:4
Fabrizi, Franco
Vitelloni 1956,O 24,43:1
Woman of Rome 1956,N 6,30:1
No Sun in Venice 1958,Je 10,40:2
Rocket From Calabuch 1958,O 8,41:1
Nights of Lucretia Borgia, The 1960,O 6,51:4
Run With the Devil 1963,Jl 16,25:1
Wastrel, The 1963,N 5,24:1
Bidone, Il 1964,N 20,42:1
Facts of Murder, The 1965,Jl 1,34:1
Birds, the Bees and the Italians, The
  1967,Ag 8,33:2
Fadden, Tom
I Stole a Million 1939,Ag 7,11:2
Destry Rides Again 1939,N 30,25:1
Congo Maisie 1940,F 8,18:4
Zanzibar 1940,Ap 1,15:3
Shepherd of the Hills, The 1941,Jl 31,13:2
Night Before the Divorce, The 1942,Ap 10,21:3
Wings for the Eagle 1942,Ag 1,14:2
Edge of Darkness 1943,Ap 10,12:4
Northern Pursuit 1943,N 26,29:2
Hairy Ape, The 1944,Jl 3,8:3
Tomorrow the World 1944,D 22,12:4
That Hagen Girl 1947,O 25,13:2
State of the Union 1948,Ap 23,28:1
Singing Guns 1950,Je 5,19:3
Toby Tyler 1960,Ap 20,45:2
Fadeyechev, Nicolai
Swan Lake 1960,Ja 26,25:2
Fadeyev, Alexander (Original Author)
Young Guard 1949,D 26,33:6
Fadeyeva, Elena
Sons and Mothers 1967,O 2,58:1
Fadiman, William (Producer)
Last Frontier, The 1955,D 8,45:1
Jubal 1956,Ap 25,39:1
Rampage 1963,O 17,39:2
Fadl, Achmed Sheik
Stampede 1930,Ap 28,24:5
Faeti, Guiseppe
Prince of Foxes 1949,D 24,11:2
Fafino
I Love, You Love 1962,N 10,16:2
Fagan, Charles
Luck of the Irish, The 1937,Ja 16,21:1
Fagan, James Bernard (Original Author)
Lottery Man, The 1919,N 17,20:1
Wheel of Life, The 1929,Je 24,27:1
Forgotten Commandments 1932,Je 2,25:2
Bella Donna 1935,F 26,16:4
Temptation 1946,D 25,33:6
Fagan, Myron C (Original Author)
Smart Woman 1931,O 12,28:2
Fagan, William
Rembrandt 1936,D 3,31:1
Faget, Huguette
Antoine and Antoinette 1948,Ap 16,29:2
Last Stop, The 1949,Mr 22,31:2
Fagioli, Giovanni
Theodora, Slave Empress 1955,Ja 12,24:2
Fagstad, Elnar
Vi Som Gar Koeksvaegen 1933,O 7,18:5
Faherty, William Barby (Original Author)
Guns for San Sebastian 1968,Mr 21,57:2
FAHEY
See Also FAHY
Fahey, Myrna
Story of Page One, The 1960,Ja 14,28:1
House of Usher, The 1960,S 15,45:4
Fahrson, Honor
It Happened Here 1966,Ag 9,29:2
FAHY
See Also FAHEY
Fahy, Douglas
What a Life 1939,O 12,33:1
FAIN
See Also FINE
Fain, Matty
Law in her Hands, The 1936,Je 6,21:2
Border Flight 1936,Je 22,22:1
Lady From Nowhere 1936,D 21,19:2
Great Guy 1937,Ja 1,19:2
House of Secrets 1937,F 22,13:1
Shadows of the Orient 1937,O 11,26:6
Federal Bullets 1937,D 27,11:1
Thirteenth Man, The 1938,Ja 1,11:2
Port of Missing Girls, The 1938,Ap 4,12:5
Wanted by the Police 1938,S 26,13:2
Personal Secretary 1938,O 5,20:2
Get-Away, The 1941,Jl 17,23:4
Frisco Lil 1942,F 12,27:2

Fain, Sammy
Dames 1934,Ag 16,20:2
Fain, Sammy (Composer)
Moonlight and Pretzels 1933,Ag 23,21:2
Footlight Parade 1933,O 6,21:3
Strictly Dynamite 1934,Jl 4,18:2
Dames 1934,Ag 16,20:2
Happiness Ahead 1934,O 11,28:2
Gentlemen are Born 1934,N 22,27:2
Sweet Music 1935,F 21,23:2
Goin' to Town 1935,My 11,21:2
New Faces of 1937 1937,Jl 2,25:1
Vogues of 1938 1937,Ag 20,21:1
I Dood It 1943,N 11,29:1
See my Lawyer 1945,My 4,23:4
George White's Scandals 1945,O 11,26:2
Two Sisters From Boston 1946,Je 7,16:2
Call Me Mister 1951,F 1,21:2
Jazz Singer, The 1953,Ja 14,27:3
Mardi Gras 1958,N 19,45:2
Fainsilber, Samson
Trois Mousquetaires, Les 1933,My 1,10:2
Milady 1933,S 8,22:3
Serment, Le 1934,Mr 14,23:2
Thirteen Days of Love 1942,N 6,27:3
Queen and the Cardinal, The 1944,Je 1,17:3
Clandestine 1948,My 24,23:2
Fair, Elinor
Driven 1923,F 12,13:4
Wife Who Wasn't Wanted, The 1925,S 9,23:1
Volga Boatman, The 1926,Ap 14,21:1
Jim, The Conqueror 1926,D 28,17:1
Yankee Clipper, The 1927,My 3,25:1
Let 'Er go, Gallegher 1928,Ja 16,24:1
Fair, Florence
Moral Sinner, The 1924,Ap 7,15:3
Firebird, The 1934,N 15,25:2
I am a Thief 1935,Ja 1,24:1
Florentine Dagger, The 1935,Ap 27,20:6
Oil for the Lamps of China 1935,Je 6,25:2
Man of Iron 1935,D 7,22:2
Fish 1936,Ja 25,18:5
Freshman Love 1936,Ja 25,18:5
Murder by an Aristocrat 1936,Je 13,13:2
Second Wife 1936,Ag 29,16:3
Fair, Jody
High School Confidential 1958,My 31,6:6
Fair, Michael
Drifter, The 1967,My 25,54:1
Fairbanks, Douglas
Habit of Happiness, The 1916,Mr 13,5:5
Good Bad Man, The 1916,Ap 22,9:1
Reggie Mixes In 1916,My 29,9:2
Flirting With Fate 1916,Je 26,11:3
Half Breed, The 1916,Jl 10,9:5
Manhattan Madness 1916,S 11,11:4 (Incorrect in
  this edition; use 1916,S 11,7:4 elsewhere)
American Aristocracy 1916,N 6,9:2
Matrimaniac, The 1916,D 4,11:3
Americano, The 1916,D 25,7:1
In Again, Out Again 1917,Ap 23,7:5
Man From Painted Post, The 1917,O 1,14:2
Reaching for the Moon 1917,N 19,9:4
Mr Fix-It 1918,Ap 22,9:1
Say, Young Fellow 1918,Je 17,11:3
Bound in Morocco 1918,Jl 29,9:3
He Comes Up Smiling 1918,S 9,9:1
Arizona 1918,D 16,13:3
Knickerbocker Buckaroo, The 1919,My 26,19:4
When Clouds Roll by 1919,D 29,7:2
Mollycoddle, The 1920,Je 14,13:2
Mark of Zorro, The 1920,N 29,20:3
Three Musketeers, The 1921,Ag 29,14:4
Robin Hood 1922,O 31,15:4 (In Addenda)
Thief of Bagdad, The 1924,Mr 19,19:1
Don Q, Son of Zorro 1925,Je 16,24:1
Black Pirate, The 1926,Mr 9,21:4
Gaucho, The 1927,N 22,32:2
Iron Mask, The 1929,F 22,18:6
Taming of the Shrew, The 1929,N 30,23:1
Reaching for the Moon 1930,D 30,24:2
Mr Robinson Crusoe 1932,S 22,25:4
Private Life of Don Juan, The 1934,D 10,16:2
Days of Thrills and Laughter 1961,Mr 22,37:1
Fairbanks, Douglas (Miscellaneous)
Around the World in Eighty Minutes with Douglas
  Fairbanks 1931,N 20,28:3
Fairbanks, Douglas Jr
Stephen Steps Out 1923,N 19,19:3
Air Mail, The 1925,Mr 17,18:1
Wild Horse Mesa 1925,Ag 10,8:2
Stella Dallas 1925,N 17,30:2
American Venus, The 1926,Ja 26,25:2
Padlocked 1926,Ag 2,21:2
Man Bait 1927,Ja 19,21:1
Is Zat So? 1927,My 17,27:2
Texas Steer, A 1928,Ja 2,28:1
Barker, The 1928,D 6,35:1
Jazz Age, The 1929,Ja 7,36:2
Woman of Affairs, A 1929,Ja 21,18:4
Fast Life 1929,Ag 17,5:3
Our Modern Maidens 1929,S 7,15:1

Fairbanks, Douglas Jr— Cont
Careless Age, The 1929,S 21,17:1
Show of Shows 1929,N 21,24:5
Forward Pass, The 1929,N 29,25:1
Party Girl 1930,Ja 2,28:2
Dawn Patrol, The 1930,Jl 11,22:1
Little Accident 1930,Ag 4,13:4
Outward Bound 1930,S 18,28:3
Way of all Men, The 1930,S 20,15:4
One Night at Susie's 1930,N 24,26:5
Little Casear 1931,Ja 10,19:2
Chances 1931,Je 12,27:1
I Like Your Nerve 1931,S 12,15:4
Union Depot 1932,Ja 15,24:4
It's Tough to be Famous 1932,Ap 9,18:1
Love Is a Racket 1932,Je 11,9:3
Scarlet Dawn 1932,N 4,25:4
Parachute Jumper 1933,Ja 26,12:2
Life of Jimmy Dolan, The 1933,Je 14,22:3
Narrow Corner, The 1933,Jl 14,15:3
Captured 1933,Ag 18,18:3
Morning Glory 1933,Ag 18,18:2
Catherine the Great 1934,F 15,15:6
Success at any Price 1934,My 4,24:2
Mimi 1936,Ja 10,16:3
Amateur Gentleman, The 1936,Ap 27,19:2
Accused 1936,D 17,35:1
When Thief Meets Thief 1937,Je 15,26:2
Prisoner of Zenda, The 1937,S 3,12:1
Joy of Living 1938,My 6,27:1
Rage of Paris 1938,Jl 2,10:2
Having Wonderful Time 1938,Jl 8,11:2
Young in Heart, The 1938,N 4,27:2
Gunga Din 1939,Ja 28,19:2
Sun Never Sets, The 1939,Je 9,26:2
Rulers of the Sea 1939,N 9,27:1
Green Hell 1940,Ja 30,15:6
Safari 1940,Je 20,29:2
Angels Over Broadway 1940,N 18,23:2
Corsican Brothers, The 1942,Ja 16,25:4
Sinbad the Sailor 1947,Ja 23,31:2
Exile, The 1947,D 26,22:4
That Lady in Ermine 1948,Ag 25,31:2
Fighting O'Flynn, The 1949,F 28,16:2
State Secret 1950,O 5,38:2
Mister Drake's Duck 1952,Ja 28,15:2
Fairbanks, Douglas Jr (Producer)
Angels Over Broadway 1940,N 18,23:2
Exile, The 1947,D 26,22:4
Chase a Crooked Shadow 1958,Mr 25,28:4
Fairbanks, Douglas Jr (Screenwriter)
Exile, The 1947,D 26,22:4
Fighting O'Flynn, The 1949,F 28,16:2
Fairbanks, Flobelle
Climbers, The 1927,My 4,29:2
Fairbanks, Lucille
Flight Angels 1940,My 27,23:2
Fugitive From Justice, A 1940,Jl 8,13:3
Strawberry Blonde 1941,F 22,11:2
Fairbanks Twins
Mirror, The 1923,Ja 15,18:3
On With the Show 1929,My 29,28:6
Fairbrother, Sydney
Nell Gwyn 1926,Jl 19,13:1
Chu Chin Chow 1934,S 22,12:2
Brewster's Millions 1935,Ap 8,23:3
Last Journey, The 1936,Je 8,22:4
Dreaming Lips 1937,My 20,17:1
King Solomon's Mines 1937,Jl 3,18:1
Gaiety Girls, The 1938,Mr 31,15:1
Fairchild, Edgar (Composer)
Here Come the Co-Eds 1945,F 19,21:1
Naughty Nineties, The 1945,Je 21,16:2
Black Angel 1946,S 26,32:4
Fairchild, William (Director)
John and Julie 1957,My 7,40:1
Fairchild, William (Original Author)
Do Not Disturb 1965,D 25,17:2
Fairchild, William (Screenwriter)
Operation Disaster 1951,Ja 15,13:1
Outcast of the Islands 1952,My 16,19:2
Glory at Sea 1953,Mr 11,36:7
Project M 7 1953,N 27,22:5
Malta Story 1954,Jl 17,7:2
Front Page Story 1955,Ap 19,28:1
Land of Fury 1955,My 3,37:4
John and Julie 1957,My 7,40:1
Value for Money 1957,Ap 1,20:4
Star! 1968,O 23,36:2
Faire, Virginia Brown
Without Benefit of Clergy 1921,Je 20,17:2
Monte Cristo 1922,Ag 15,20:3
Welcome Stranger 1924,O 14,21:5
Peter Pan 1924,D 29,11:4
Recompense 1925,Ap 20,22:1
Friendly Enemies 1925,My 5,24:2
Proud Heart 1926,N 3,25:4
Temptress, The 1926,O 11,18:1
White Flannels 1927,Mr 22,31:2
Tracked by the Police 1927,Ap 27,22:5
Donovan Affair, The 1929,Ap 29,29:2
Fairfax, Beatrice (Original Author)
Lovelorn, The 1927,D 19,30:1

Fairfax, Betty
Black Arrow, The 1948,O 4,14:2
Fairfax, James
Mrs Mike 1950,F 9,36:5
Fairfax, Marion (Screenwriter)
Don't Ever Marry 1920,Ap 19,13:3
Through the Back Door 1921,My 6,20:2
(Incorrect in this edition; use 1921,My 16,20:2 elsewhere)
Eternal Flame, The 1922,S 18,14:2
Talker, The 1925,My 12,26:2
Fairfax, Thur
Rose of the Golden West 1927,S 26,27:1
Fairlie, Gerald (Miscellaneous)
Jack Ahoy 1935,F 9,11:2
Born for Glory 1935,O 21,22:4
Fairlie, Gerald (Original Author)
Charlie Chan in Shanghai 1935,O 14,21:1
Fairlie, Gerald (Screenwriter)
Alias Bulldog Drummond 1935,S 10,26:2
Charlie Chan in Shanghai 1935,O 14,21:1
Conspirator 1950,Ap 28,26:2
Fairman, Austin
British Intelligence 1940,F 12,14:2
Fairweather, Helen
Private Life of Helen of Troy, The 1927,D 10,14:7
Faison, Ellen
Round Trip 1967,Jl 20,30:2
Fait, A
Golden Taiga 1935,Ag 2,22:3
Thirteen, The 1937,Je 19,20:2
Boule de Suif 1958,My 5,24:1
Faith, Adam
Never Let Go 1963,Je 15,10:2
Faith, Jordana
Casa del Angel, La 1960,Ag 30,25:1
Faithful, Marianne
I'll Never Forget What's 'Isname 1968,Ap 15,51:1
Girl on a Motorcycle, The 1968,N 28,66:5
Faivre, Paul
Francis the First 1947,N 20,38:4
Thirst of Men, The 1952,O 28,37:1
Demoniaque 1958,Mr 4,34:5
Fajardo, Eduardo
Mad Queen, The 1950,O 27,24:3
Fakiel, D
Yiddle With his Fiddle 1937,Ja 2,15:1
Falana, Lola
Man Called Adam, A 1966,Ag 4,24:2
Falavigna, Louis
Gigot 1962,S 28,26:1
Falck, Ake (Director)
Swedish Wedding Night 1965,N 15,48:1
Falck, Edward (Composer)
Blue Bird, The 1918,Ap 1,9:3
Falck, Ragnar
Children, The 1949,D 23,17:1
Falckenberg, Gina
Zigeunerbaron 1935,S 14,8:5
Boccaccio 1937,F 27,9:3
Lachende Dritte, Der 1938,Ap 9,11:2
Winter Stuerme; Winter Storms 1938,O 1,10:2
Julika, Die 1939,D 23,9:1
Falco, Albert
Silent World, The 1956,S 25,30:1
Falco, Andre
World Without Sun 1964,D 23,22:1
Falco, Claudette
Loves of Casanova 1948,S 18,11:4
Falcon, Ada
Idolos de la Radio 1935,Jl 2,24:5
Falcon, Rafael
Zandunga, La 1938,My 14,18:2
Cancion del Alma; Song of the Soul 1938,O 11,20:4
Tierra Brava 1938,O 29,15:6
Bajo el Cielo de Mexico; Beneath the Sky of Mexico 1938,D 31,7:3
Hotel de los Chiflados, El 1939,Ag 28,17:2
Juntos pero no Revueltos; United but not Mixed 1939,O 23,15:3
Reina del Rio, La; Queen of the River, The 1940,F 24,9:3
FALCONER
See Also FAULKNER
Falconer, Alun (Original Author)
Man Upstairs, The 1959,Ag 11,23:2
Falconer, Alun (Screenwriter)
Man Upstairs, The 1959,Ag 11,23:2
Never Let Go 1963,Je 15,10:2
Underworld Informers 1965,O 14,53:1
Falconer, Sheila
Half a Sixpence 1968,F 21,60:3
Falconetti, Maria
Passion of Joan of Arc, The 1928,Ap 1,IX,5:5 (In Addenda)
Passion of Joan of Arc, The 1928,Ag 12,VII,3:4
Passion of Joan of Arc, The 1929,Ja 20,VIII,7:5
Passion Of Joan Of Arc, The 1929,Mr 29,21:1
Passion of Jeanne d'Arc, The 1929,Mr 31,VIII,7:1

Falconi, Armando
Rubacuori 1932,Mr 5,11:2
Passa L'Amore 1933,N 25,10:3
Re Burlone, Il 1936,Mr 28,11:3
Zio d'America, Lo; Uncle From America, The 1939,S 15,26:5
Documento Fatale, Il 1940,S 26,27:3
Rossini 1948,Ja 31,14:2
Spirit and the Flesh, The 1948,N 1,28:2
Falconi, Arturo
Vecchia Signora, La 1932,D 10,19:3
Cappello a Tre Punte, Il 1936,S 28,14:5
Falconi, Dino (Director)
Loves of Don Juan, The 1948,S 2,18:4
Falconi, Dino (Screenwriter)
Gran Varieta 1955,Ap 11,29:5
Faleron, Jean
Paris 1926,Je 1,29:3
Fales, Dean (Original Author)
College Humor 1933,Je 23,15:4
Falgar, Erika
O Schwarzwald, O Heimat; Oh Black Forest, Oh Home 1939,Ap 24,13:2
Falk, Henri (Original Author)
Blonde or Brunette 1927,Ja 11,18:2
Falk, Lauritz
Foreign Intrigue 1956,Jl 13,23:2
To Bed...Or not to Bed 1963,D 23,18:2
Falk, Norbert (Screenwriter)
Casanova 1927,Je 23,23:3
Falk, Norman (Original Author)
Congress Dances 1932,My 12,23:2
Falk, Peter
Wind Across the Everglades 1958,S 12,21:1
Murder, Inc 1960,Je 29,26:6
Pocketful of Miracles 1961,D 19,39:1
Pressure Point 1962,O 11,49:3
Balcony, The 1963,Mr 22,7:1
It's a Mad, Mad, Mad, Mad World 1963,N 19,47:1
Robin and the 7 Hoods 1964,Ag 6,20:1
Great Race, The 1965,S 16,00:0
Italiano Brava Gente 1966,F 4,20:1
Penelope 1966,N 11,36:6
Luv 1967,Jl 27,29:1
Anzio 1968,Jl 25,26:1
Falk, Rossella
Eight and One Half 1963,Je 26,36:1
Modesty Blaise 1966,Ag 11,27:1
Made in Italy 1967,My 1,44:2
Legend of Lylah Clare, The 1968,Ag 23,33:1
Falkberget, Johan (Original Author)
Boer Boerson Jr 1939,N 4,11:3
Falke, Evelyn
Man From Down Under, The 1943,S 27,23:2
Falkenberg, Gina
Page vom Dalmasse-Hotel, Der 1935,Mr 25,12:3
Ferien vom Ich 1935,Ap 1,17:2
Liebesleute 1936,O 3,21:2
Women Without Names 1951,Ag 7,22:2
Falkenburg, Jinx
Sing for Your Supper 1941,D 1,15:5
Two Senoritas From Chicago 1943,Ag 6,10:4
Cover Girl 1944,Mr 31,26:1
Falkenstein, Fritz (Original Author)
Rheinlandmaedel, Das 1931,S 18,29:1
Breaking the Ice 1938,S 23,35:3
Falkenstein, Fritz (Screenwriter)
Perfect Specimen, The 1937,O 28,29:2
Falkenstein, Julius
Waltz Dream, The 1926,Jl 26,13:2
Meistersinger 1929,D 16,34:2
Voruntersuchung; Inquest 1931,My 24,VIII,4:1
Wahre Jakob, Der 1931,Ag 7,20:2
Nur am Rhein 1931,S 25,28:7
Secrets of the Orient 1932,Ja 4,27:3
Nie Wieder Liebe 1932,Ja 16,13:1
Sein Scheidungsgrund 1932,F 20,11:2
Stuerme der Leidenschaft 1932,Mr 16,17:3
Die Csikos Baroness 1932,Mr 28,11:2
Ein Ausgekochter Junge 1932,My 3,25:5
Liebe Ist Liebe 1932,Je 2,25:2
Brand in der Oper 1932,Jl 11,11:4
Week-End Im Paradies 1932,O 24,18:5
Mensch Ohne Namen 1932,N 7,20:3
Drunter und Drueber 1932,D 19,19:5
Holzapfel Weiss Alles 1933,Ja 7,11:3
Die Lustigen Musikanten 1933,My 27,11:6
Ich und die Kaiserin 1933,My 28,IX,2:5 (In Addenda)
Lachende Erben 1933,N 18,18:6
Luegen auf Ruegen 1934,Ja 1,28:2
Heart Song 1934,Je 6,24:6
Wenn Herzen Sich Finden 1934,N 12,17:3
Marion, Das Gehoert Sich Nicht 1934,D 15,9:4
Kalte Mamsell, Die 1935,Ja 12,12:2
Falkenv
Ferien vom Ich 1935,Ap 1,17:2
Falkind, Alexandre Michel (Producer)
Trial, The 1963,F 21,5:1
Falkner, J Meade (Original Author)
Moonfleet 1955,Je 25,9:2

Falkner Orchestra
Johnny Doughboy 1943,My 6,25:3
Fall, Assane
Roots of Heaven, The 1958,O 16,46:1
Fall, Richard (Composer)
Sehnsucht 202; Longing 202 1932,N 13,IX,4:2
Fallada, Hans (Original Author)
Little Man, What Now? 1934,Je 1,29:1
Fallec, Gerard
Deadlier Than the Male 1957,O 9,41:1
Fallet, Rene (Original Author)
Fanfan the Tulip 1953,My 5,34:2
Paris in the Month of August 1968,Ag 26,46:4
Fallon, Charles
Man Who Broke the Bank at Monte Carlo, The 1935,N 15,20:2
Next Time We Love 1936,Ja 31,16:2
Fallon, Gabriel
Men of Ireland 1938,S 30,24:2
Fallon, Thomas F (Original Author)
Last Warning, The 1929,Ja 7,36:2
Fallows, Ruth
Emergency Call 1933,Je 24,16:2
Advice to the Lovelorn 1933,D 14,28:2
Falvre, Paul
Passionate Summer 1957,Jl 22,15:5
Famery, Jacques
My First Love 1951,Je 11,20:7
Fancher, Hampton
Parrish 1961,My 5,22:1
Rome Adventure 1962,Mr 16,25:1
Fanchon (Producer)
Turn off the Moon 1937,My 20,17:2
Thrill of a Lifetime 1937,D 9,30:2
Fancioli, Armando
Pharaohs' Woman, The 1962,Ap 19,35:2
Fanck, Arnold Dr (Director)
Peaks of Destiny 1927,N 29,31:1
White Hell of Pitz Palu, The 1930,S 27,21:3
Weisse Rausch, Der; White Ecstasy, The 1932,Ja 24,VIII,5:1
Avalanche 1932,Mr 26,17:2
Ski Chase, The 1938,Mr 26,12:1
Fanck, Arnold Dr (Miscellaneous)
Sturme Uber dem Mont Blanc; Storms on Mont Blanc 1931,Mr 1,VIII,6:6 (In Addenda)
Fanck, Arnold Dr (Original Author)
S O S Iceberg 1933,S 25,18:4
Fanck, Arnold Dr (Screenwriter)
Peaks of Destiny 1927,N 29,31:1
Slalom 1936,D 16,35:3
Fanery, Jacques
Sextette (Part I-The Gun); Gun, The (Sextette) 1953,Mr 2,19:2
Fang, Charles
Backbone 1923,Ap 30,11:2
Ragged Edge, The 1923,Je 5,24:5
Fanning, Frank
Dance Hall 1941,Jl 19,16:2
Fano, Jacques (Screenwriter)
Bed, The (Riviera Express); Riviera Express (The Bed) 1955,Je 8,26:4
Bed, The (The Billet); Billet, The (The Bed) 1955,Je 8,26:4
Fant, Curt-Henrik
Devil's Wanton, The 1962,Jl 5,21:2
Fant, George
Katrina 1949,N 18,35:3
Blood and Fire 1950,Je 24,7:4
Of Love and Lust (Doll's House, A); Doll's House, A (Of Love and Lust) 1959,My 26,31:2
Time of Desire 1959,N 21,26:5
Fant, Kenne (Director)
Wonderful Adventures of Nils, The 1962,S 14,37:1
Fant, Kenne (Producer)
Wonderful Adventures of Nils, The 1962,S 14,37:1
Fant, Roy
Desire Under the Elms 1958,Mr 13,24:2
Pretty Boy Floyd 1960,N 3,49:2
Fantauzzi, John
Up the Down Staircase 1967,Ag 18,36:2
Fante, John (Original Author)
East of the River 1940,O 28,21:2
Golden Fleecing, The 1940,N 7,33:4
Youth Runs Wild 1944,S 2,17:2
Full of Life 1957,F 13,38:1
Fante, John (Screenwriter)
Youth Runs Wild 1944,S 2,17:2
My Man and I 1952,S 6,12:6
Full of Life 1957,F 13,38:1
Jeanne Eagels 1957,Ag 31,19:1
Walk on the Wild Side 1962,F 22,20:1
Reluctant Saint, The 1962,D 4,47:2
My Six Loves 1963,Ap 4,58:4
Maya 1966,Je 23,29:4
Fantoni, Barry
Strange Affair, The 1968,Jl 25,26:2
Fantoni, Cesare
Loves of Don Juan, The 1948,S 2,18:4

Fantoni, Sergio
Giant of Marathon, The 1960,My 26,37:3
Esther and the King 1960,N 19,13:4
Prize, The 1964,Ja 24,21:1
Von Ryan's Express 1965,Je 24,28:1
High Infidelity (The Victim); Victim, The (High Infidelity) 1965,Jl 2,17:1
Do Not Disturb 1965,D 25,17:2
What Did You Do in the War, Daddy? 1966,S 1,28:1
Farago, Alexander (Original Author)
Top Hat 1935,Ag 30,12:2
Farago, Sandor (Original Author)
Marry the Boss's Daughter 1941,D 4,33:4
Faragoh, Francis Edwards (Screenwriter)
Becky Sharp 1935,Je 14,27:2
Return of Peter Grimm, The 1935,O 4,25:2
Dancing Pirate 1936,Je 18,19:1
My Friend Flicka 1943,My 27,21:4
Renegades 1946,Jl 11,18:2
Easy Come, Easy Go 1947,F 6,29:2
Farah, Jameel
Blackboard Jungle 1955,Mr 21,21:5
Faralla, William D (Director)
Two Before Zero 1962,N 1,34:1
Farbar, Buzz
Wild 90 1968,Ja 8,33:1
Beyond the Law 1968,S 30,60:4
Beyond the Law 1968,O 24,55:1
Farbar, Buzz (Producer)
Beyond the Law 1968,S 30,60:4
Beyond the Law 1968,O 24,55:1
Farber, Arlene Sue
Teenage Mother 1968,S 19,62:4
Farber, Jerry
Macbeth 1950,D 28,22:6
Farebrother, Violet
Mystery at the Villa Rose 1930,Je 2,25:4
Mr Cohen Takes a Walk 1936,F 13,25:2
Farel, Catherine
Personal Column 1941,F 3,13:2
Farentino, James
Psychomania 1964,F 15,14:3
War Lord, The 1965,N 18,55:2
Pad, The (And How to Use It) 1966,Ag 18,27:2
Banning 1967,D 14,62:2
Rosie 1968,F 8,36:1
Farere, Claude
Vitelloni 1956,O 24,43:1
Fares, Oreste
Passaporto Rosso 1936,S 2,18:2
Manon Lescaut 1941,Ap 14,23:5
Farfan, Robert
Alias the Doctor 1932,Mr 3,22:3
Farguette, Gabriel
Glory of Faith, The 1938,N 24,37:2
Farina
Life of Jimmy Dolan, The 1933,Je 14,22:3
Mayor of Hell, The 1933,Jl 1,16:5
Reckless 1935,Ap 20,16:1
Farina, Dick
Festival 1967,O 24,53:2
Farina, Mimi
Festival 1967,O 24,53:2
Farinon, Gabriella
Blood and Roses 1961,O 12,41:4
FARIS
See Also FERRIS
Faris, Franco
Regina di Sparta, La 1931,F 23,20:3
Faris, William (Miscellaneous)
Ravaged Earth 1942,N 27,27:3
Farjat, Jose
Torero! 1957,My 22,29:2
Farjeon, Herbert
April in Paris 1952,D 25,34:5
Farjeon, J Jefferson (Original Author)
Last Journey, The 1936,Je 8,22:4
Farkas, Karl (Original Author)
Wonder Bar 1934,Mr 1,23:2
Farkas, Nicholas (Director)
Battle, The 1934,N 23,23:2
I Give my Life 1941,S 1,18:4
Farkas, Nicholas (Producer)
Mad Emperor, The 1941,Mr 10,21:3
Farkas, Zoltan (Director)
Sportszerelem; Love of Sport 1938,F 14,20:8
Farkash, Hans
Cinerama-South Seas Adventure 1958,Jl 16,26:1
Farley, Dot
Crossroads of New York, The 1922,My 22,18:4
Acquittal, The 1923,D 12,24:5
Boy of Mine 1923,D 24,12:1 (In Addenda)
Enemy Sex, The 1924,Jl 1,21:4
Signal Tower, The 1924,Jl 21,14:4
Vanity's Price 1924,O 8,16:2
So Big 1925,Ja 5,19:1
Woman of the World, A 1925,D 14,18:2
Memory Lane 1926,F 2,20:4
Grand Duchess and the Waiter, The 1926,F 9,22:1
Little Irish Girl, The 1926,My 11,24:3
Money Talks 1926,My 11,24:3

Young April 1926,Ag 31,15:3
Nobody's Widow 1927,Ja 13,29:1
All Aboard 1927,Ap 19,24:4
His First Flame 1927,My 2,26:4
Climbers, The 1927,My 4,29:2
Lady Be Good 1928,My 28,23:2
Marquis Preferred 1929,Ja 21,18:4
Little Accident 1930,Ag 4,13:4
Road to Paradise, The 1931,Ja 20,21:3
Road to Reno, The 1938,O 3,11:2
Farley, Duke
Misty 1961,Jl 18,33:2
Farley, Edward
Music Goes 'Round, The 1936,F 22,12:1
Farley, James
Nugget Nell 1919,Jl 28,8:5
Woman With Four Faces, The 1923,Je 18,13:5
Wild Bill Hickok 1923,N 21,22:1
Son of his Father, A 1925,S 29,31:3
General, The 1927,F 8,21:1
Mad Hour, The 1928,Ap 16,20:5
Grip of the Yukon, The 1928,Jl 10,17:3
Voice of the City, The 1929,Ap 29,29:2
Dance of Life, The 1929,Ag 16,18:6
Danger Lights 1930,D 15,29:1
Fighting Caravans 1931,Ja 26,21:1
Three Rogues 1931,Ap 4,23:1
Scandal for Sale 1932,Ap 3,26:2
Captain January 1936,Ap 25,21:1
Dancing Pirate 1936,Je 18,19:1
East Side Kids 1940,F 19,21:6
Farley, James (Original Author)
City That Never Sleeps, The 1924,S 29,10:1
Farley, Morgan
Greene Murder Case, The 1929,Ag 10,11:3
Half Marriage 1929,Ag 19,22:1
Love Doctor, The 1929,N 9,22:5
Mighty, The 1929,D 30,16:4
Slightly Scarlet 1930,Mr 1,23:1
Only the Brave 1930,Mr 8,21:1
Devil's Holiday, The 1930,My 10,25:3
Man From Wyoming, A 1930,Jl 12,16:4
Beloved 1934,Ja 27,9:3
Gentleman's Agreement 1947,N 12,36:2
Open Secret 1948,F 2,15:2
Hollow Triumph 1948,O 29,29:5
Top o' the Morning 1949,S 1,25:2
Abbott and Costello Meet the Killer Boris Karloff 1949,S 19,18:3
Barricade 1950,Mr 25,8:6
Macbeth 1950,D 28,22:6
Man Who Cheated Himself, The 1951,F 9,21:2
Double Crossbones 1951,Ap 27,19:2
Sealed Cargo 1951,My 24,47:1
Goodbye, my Fancy 1951,My 30,14:2
Strange Door, The 1951,D 10,34:6
Wild North, The 1952,My 12,21:2
Julius Caesar 1953,Je 5,19:1
Jivaro 1954,F 13,11:5
Farley, Patricia
King of the Jungle 1933,F 25,20:3
Farmaniantz, Georgi
Ballet of Romeo and Juliet, The 1956,Ap 3,31:2
Farmer, Art
Subterraneans, The 1960,Jl 7,26:1
Farmer, Frances
Border Flight 1936,Je 22,22:1
Rhythm on the Range 1936,Jl 30,22:1
Come and Get It 1936,N 12,31:1
Exclusive 1937,Jl 22,15:1
Toast of New York, The 1937,Jl 23,16:2
Ebb Tide 1937,N 18,27:2
Ride a Crooked Mile 1938,D 29,15:2
South of Pago-Pago 1940,Ag 2,12:2
Flowing Gold 1940,S 2,19:3
World Premiere 1941,Ag 21,15:2
Badlands of Dakota 1941,S 9,27:6
Among the Living 1941,D 13,25:2
Son of Fury 1942,Ja 30,23:2
Farmer, Michael
Perfect Understanding 1933,F 23,20:2
Farmer, Mimsy
Spencer's Mountain 1963,My 17,26:6
Bus Riley's Back in Town 1965,Ap 8,45:2
Hot Rods to Hell 1967,Ag 10,45:5
Devil's Angels 1967,O 5,46:1
Farmer, Virginia
Hangmen Also Die 1943,Ap 16,24:2
Lady in the Dark 1944,F 23,17:1
To Each his Own 1946,My 24,15:2
Bury Me Dead 1947,O 25,13:3
Another Part of the Forest 1948,My 19,30:2
Captain Carey U S A 1950,Mr 30,40:5
Men, The 1950,Jl 21,15:2
Born to be Bad 1950,S 29,31:5
Cyrano De Bergerac 1950,N 17,31:2
Darling, How Could You! 1951,N 9,22:4
Farner, Ellen
Umbrellas of Cherbourg, The; Parapluis de Cherbourg, Les 1964,D 17,50:1
Farnese, Alberto
Gold of Naples (Pizza on Credit); Pizza on Credit (Gold of Naples) 1957,F 12,30:1

Farnese, Andrea
Body Is a Shell, The 1957,S 9,21:2
Farnese, Tatiana
Schoolgirl Diary 1947,O 18,9:2
Farney, Milton
Untamed 1929,N 30,23:1
FARNHAM
See Also FARNUM
Farnham, Joseph W (Miscellaneous)
Country Flapper, The 1922,Jl 31,12:3
Farnham, Joseph W (Screenwriter)
Wonder Man, The 1920,My 30,6:4
Farnham, Matcel Howe (Original Author)
Wayward 1932,F 15,13:1
Farnol, Jeffrey (Original Author)
Manhattan 1924,O 29,18:1
Amateur Gentleman, The 1926,Ag 17,15:3
Amateur Gentleman, The 1936,Ap 27,19:2
FARNUM
See Also FARNHAM
Farnum, Dorothy (Screenwriter)
Unknown Soldier, The 1926,My 31,10:2
Call of the Flesh 1930,S 13,9:3
Lady's Morals, A 1930,N 8,21:3
Evensong 1934,N 17,12:1
Farnum, Dustin
Gentlemen from Indiana, The 1915,N 29,11:3
David Garrick 1916,My 1,9:1
Spy, The 1917,Ag 28,7:6
My Man 1924,F 11,18:3
Flaming Frontier, The 1926,Ap 5,24:1
Cheers for Miss Bishop 1941,Mr 14,17:2
Farnum, Franklyn
Three Rogues 1931,Ap 4,23:1
Leftover Ladies 1931,N 9,22:4
Powdersmoke Range 1936,Mr 9,20:2
Farnum, William
Conqueror, The 1917,S 11,11:3
Miserables, Les 1917,D 5,13:2
Man Hunter, The 1919,Mr 3,11:2
Last of the Duanes, The 1919,S 15,16:3
If I Were King 1920,Ag 10,10:3
Stage Romance A 1922,Mr 26,VI,2:1 (In Addenda)
Man Who Fights Alone, The 1924,Jl 28,12:2
If I Were King 1930,Mr 2,IX,5:1
Du Barry, Woman of Passion 1930,N 3,19:3
Ten Nights in a Barroom 1931,F 28,15:2
Painted Desert, The 1931,Mr 9,19:1
Connecticut Yankee, A 1931,Ap 13,17:1
Mr Robinson Crusoe 1932,S 22,25:4
Supernatural 1933,Ap 22,16:3
Are We Civilized? 1934,Je 14,28:5
Count of Monte Cristo, The 1934,S 27,25:2
Silver Streak, The 1935,Ja 16,21:1
Crusades, The 1935,Ag 22,21:3
Powdersmoke Range 1936,Mr 9,20:2
Connecticut Yankee at the Court of King Arthur, A 1936,My 4,16:1
Maid of Salem 1937,Mr 4,27:2
If I Were King 1938,S 29,31:1
Santa Fe Stampede 1939,Ap 26,27:3
Convicted Woman 1940,F 26,11:2
Kit Carson 1940,N 15,25:3
Woman's Face, A 1941,My 16,21:2
Corsican Brothers, The 1942,Ja 16,25:4
Spoilers, The 1942,My 22,27:2
Men of Texas 1942,Jl 13,18:3 (In Addenda)
Tennessee Johnson 1943,Ja 13,18:2
American Empire 1943,Ja 14,25:4
Frontier Badmen 1943,Ag 14,12:8
Captain Kidd 1945,N 23,26:3
Perils of Pauline, The 1947,Jl 10,17:2
Bride of Vengeance 1949,Ap 7,38:2
Samson and Delilah 1949,D 22,29:2
Lone Star 1952,F 2,11:4
Jack and the Beanstalk 1952,Ap 8,35:3
Faro, Ninnette
Once a Sinner 1931,Ja 17,23:1
Farquharson, Robert
Captivation 1931,S 28,17:4
Man they Couldn't Arrest, The 1933,Mr 14,19:3
Farr, Audrey
Not Wanted 1949,Jl 25,11:4
Farr, Derek
Voice in the Night, The 1941,My 23,25:4
Quiet Wedding 1941,D 29,27:4
Wanted for Murder 1946,D 12,38:4
Quiet Week-End 1948,Ag 20,13:2
Silent Dust 1949,D 30,13:2
Conspiracy in Teheran 1950,Mr 11,8:3
Bond Street 1950,Mr 30,40:6
Murder Without Crime 1951,D 26,19:6
Man on the Run 1952,F 27,22:5
Young Wives' Tale 1952,N 4,33:1
Double Confession 1953,My 1,17:2
Front Page Story 1955,Ap 19,28:1
Eight O'Clock Walk 1955,Ap 30,10:6
Doctor at Large 1957,Jl 29,15:5
Value for Money 1957,Ag 1,20:4
Truth About Women, The 1958,Ag 29,18:2
Circle, The 1959,Ap 16,29:2

Farr, Felicia
Timetable 1956,Mr 17,13:2
Jubal 1956,Ap 25,39:1
First Texan, The 1956,Je 23,20:2
Last Wagon, The 1956,S 22,20:2
3:10 to Yuma 1957,Ag 29,22:1
Onionhead 1958,O 2,44:1
Kiss Me, Stupid 1964,D 23,22:2
Venetian Affair, The 1967,Ja 19,41:2
Farr, Jamie
Greatest Story Ever Told, The 1965,F 16,40:2
Farr, Patricia
Secret Call, The 1931,Jl 13,13:5
Helldorado 1935,Ja 7,13:2
Orchids to You 1935,Ag 10,16:4
Criminals of the Air 1937,O 28,29:2
Lady Behave 1938,Ja 28,17:3
Trade Winds 1939,Ja 13,17:2
Mr and Mrs Smith 1941,F 21,16:3
West Point Widow 1941,S 11,21:5
Farr, Randy
Big House U S A 1955,Mr 12,11:6
Farra, Anita
Bertoldo, Bertoldino, Cacasenno 1937,D 22,32:3
Farragoh, Edward James (Original Author)
Lady From Louisiana 1941,My 15,27:2
Farragoh, Francis (Original Author)
Lady From Louisiana 1941,My 15,27:2
Farrar, David
48 Hours 1944,Je 26,21:2
Black Narcissus 1947,Ag 14,29:2
Frieda 1947,Ag 15,12:3
Mr Perrin and Mr Traill 1949,Ja 17,15:2
Lisbon Story, The 1951,S 6,39:4
Case of Gold 1952,Ja 19,13:3
Cage of Gold 1952,Ja 19,13:3
Small Back Room, The 1952,F 2,11:3
Obsessed 1952,F 6,24:2
Wild Heart, The 1952,My 29,17:2
Night Without Stars 1953,Jl 14,19:4
Duel in the Jungle 1954,Ag 9,13:2
Black Shield of Falworth, The 1954,O 7,16:2
Escape to Burma 1955,My 21,11:2
Sea Chase, The 1955,Je 11,8:7
Pearl of the South Pacific 1955,S 17,12:2
Tears for Simon 1957,Ap 18,35:2
I Accuse! 1958,Mr 6,32:1
John Paul Jones 1959,Je 17,39:1
Watusi 1959,Jl 2,15:2
Solomon and Sheba 1959,D 26,7:2
300 Spartans, The 1962,S 20,29:2
Farrar, Geraldine
Carmen 1915,N 1,11:1
Temptation 1916,Ja 3,22:4
Maria Rosa 1916,My 8,7:2
Joan, the Woman 1916,D 25,7:1
Joan the Woman 1917,F 25,III,2:3 (In Addenda)
Woman God Forgot, The 1917,O 29,11:2
Devil-Stone, The 1917,D 17,11:4
Turn of the Wheel 1918,S 2,7:1
Hell Cat, The 1918,N 25,11:3
Shadows 1919,F 10,11:3
Stronger Vow, The 1919,Ap 28,13:2
World and Its Woman, The 1919,S 8,16:1
Flame of the Desert 1919,O 27,9:3
Woman and the Puppet 1920,Ap 5,20:1
Farrar, Gwen
She Shall Have Music 1942,O 31,11:2
Farrar, Jane
Phantom of the Opera, The 1943,O 15,15:2
Climax, The 1944,D 14,28:5
Farrel, Claude
Secret of Mayerling, The 1951,My 8,39:2
Woman's Angle, The 1954,Ag 27,11:6
Farrell, Charles
Wings of Youth 1925,Ap 20,18:1 (Incorrect in this edition; use 1925,Ap 28,18:1 elsewhere)
Love Hour, The 1925,S 2,21:3
Clash of the Wolves, The 1925,N 18,27:4
Old Ironsides 1926,D 7,21:2
Rough Riders, The 1927,Mr 16,28:2
Seventh Heaven 1927,My 26,22:1
Street Angel 1928,Ap 10,33:2
Fazil 1928,Je 5,21:1
Red Dance, The 1928,Je 26,29:1
River, The 1928,D 24,11:1
Lucky Star 1929,Jl 22,17:1
Sunny Side Up 1929,O 4,24:5
River, The; Femme au Corbeau, La 1930,Ja 5,VIII,5:1
Happy Days 1930,F 14,20:1
High Society Blues 1930,Ap 19,15:1
Liliom 1930,O 4,15:2
Princess and the Plumber, The 1930,D 23,25:1
Man Who Came Back, The 1931,Ja 3,21:2
Body and Soul 1931,Mr 14,23:2
Merely Mary Ann 1931,S 12,15:4
Heartbreak 1931,O 17,20:1
Delicious 1931,D 26,15:5
After Tomorrow 1932,Mr 7,13:5
First Year, The 1932,Ag 22,20:2
Tess of the Storm Country 1932,N 19,20:2
Aggie Appleby, Maker of Men 1933,O 20,14:2

Girl Without a Room 1933,D 7,26:3
Big Shakedown, The 1934,F 12,19:2
Change of Heart 1934,My 11,24:2
Fighting Youth 1935,N 2,13:3
Trouble Ahead 1936,S 21,26:5
Moonlight Sonata 1937,Je 6,XI,4:4 (In Addenda)
Moonlight Sonata 1938,My 10,17:2
Just Around the Corner 1938,D 3,11:2
Tail Spin 1939,F 11,13:2
Convoy 1941,Ja 17,21:2
Night and the City 1950,Je 10,11:2
Farrell, Glenda
Little Casear 1931,Ja 10,19:2
Scandal for Sale 1932,Ap 3,26:2
Life Begins 1932,Ag 26,20:3
Three on a Match 1932,O 29,18:4
I Am a Fugitive From a Chain Gang 1932,N 11,17:2
Match King, The 1932,D 8,25:3
Mystery of the Wax Museum, The 1933,F 18,13:3
Grand Slam 1933,F 22,25:2
Keyhold, The 1933,Mr 31,23:3
Girl Missing 1933,Ap 1,18:2
Central Airport 1933,My 4,20:5
Gambling Ship 1933,Jl 13,17:5
Mary Stevens, M D 1933,Ag 5,9:6
Lady for a Day 1933,S 8,22:2
Bureau of Missing Persons 1933,S 9,9:2
Havana Widows 1933,N 23,24:3
Man's Castle 1933,D 30,9:2
Hi, Nellie! 1934,F 1,15:5
I've Got Your Number 1934,F 3,9:3
Big Shakedown, The 1934,F 12,19:2
Dark Hazard 1934,F 23,23:3
Heat Lightning 1934,Mr 8,23:2
Personality Kid, The 1934,Ag 1,14:2
Kansas City Princess 1934,N 5,23:1
Secret Bride, The 1935,F 2,10:1
Gold Diggers of 1935 1935,Mr 15,25:2
Traveling Saleslady 1935,Mr 29,26:2
Go Into Your Dance 1935,My 4,17:2
In Caliente 1935,Je 27,16:1
We're In the Money 1935,Ag 22,21:4
Little Big Shot 1935,O 7,11:2
Miss Pacific Fleet 1935,D 7,22:2
Snowed Under 1936,Mr 30,17:5
Nobody's Fool 1936,Je 4,27:2
Law in her Hands, The 1936,Je 6,21:2
High Tension 1936,Jl 11,11:4
Here Comes Carter 1936,N 14,23:3
Gold Diggers of 1937 1936,D 25,19:2
Smart Blonde 1937,Ja 9,21:1
Fly Away Baby 1937,Jl 9,18:2
Dance Charlie Dance 1937,Ag 26,25:2
Breakfast for Two 1937,N 20,21:2
Torchy Blane, The Adventurous Blonde 1937,D 18,18:1
Hollywood Hotel 1938,Ja 13,17:3
Stolen Heaven 1938,My 12,27:2
Prison Break 1938,Jl 13,17:4
Road to Reno, The 1938,O 3,11:2
Torchy Gets her Man 1938,N 18,25:3
Exposed 1938,N 21,14:5
Torchy Blane in Chinatown 1939,F 3,13:2
Johnny Eager 1942,F 20,21:2
Twin Beds 1942,My 1,23:4
Talk of the Town, The 1942,Ag 28,22:3
Lulu Belle 1948,Je 21,18:3
Girls in the Night 1953,Ja 16,19:3
Secret of the Incas 1954,My 29,13:3
Susan Slept Here 1954,Jl 30,9:1
Girl in the Red Velvet Swing, The 1955,O 20,41:2
Middle of the Night 1959,Je 18,36:1
Kissin' Cousins 1964,Ap 2,28:3
Disorderly Orderly, The 1964,D 24,8:3
Farrell, Henry (Original Author)
What Ever Happened to Baby Jane? 1962,N 7,48:1
Hush...Hush, Sweet Charlotte 1965,Mr 4,36:1
Farrell, Henry (Screenwriter)
Hush...Hush, Sweet Charlotte 1965,Mr 4,36:1
Farrell, James T (Miscellaneous)
Studs Lonigan 1960,D 15,59:1
Farrell, John
Portrait of Jennie 1949,Mr 30,31:2
Farrell, Leslie
Move Over Darling 1963,D 26,33:1
Farrell, Major
Girl From Scotland Yard, The 1937,My 31,11:2
Farrell, Paul
Rising of the Moon, The (The Majesty of the Law); Majesty of the Law, The (The Rising of the Moon) 1957,Jl 10,23:1
Rising of the Moon, The (A Minute's Wait); Minute's Wait, A (The Rising of the Moon) 1957,Jl 10,23:1
Becket 1964,Mr 12,40:2
Farrell, Pauline
World Dances 1954,N 8,24:6

Farrell, Sharon
Lovely Way to Die, A 1968,Jl 13,18:1
Farrell, Suzanne
Midsummer Night's Dream, A 1967,Ap 18,32:1
Farrell, Tommy
Duchess of Idaho 1950,Jl 21,15:3
At War With the Army 1951,Ja 25,21:5
Yank in Korea, A 1951,Ap 2,29:2
Meet Danny Wilson 1952,Mr 27,34:4
Farrere, Claude (Original Author)
Woman From Monte Carlo, The 1931,D 31,17:6
Battle, The 1934,N 23,23:2
Sacrifice d'Honneur 1938,D 2,27:2
Farringdon, Kenneth
One Way Pendulum 1965,Mr 3,34:3
Farrington, Adele
Black Beauty 1921,F 21,16:1
Man Next Door, The 1923,My 29,10:3
Gentleman of Leisure, A 1923,Jl 16,14:2
Farrington, Betty
Fall of Eve, The 1929,Je 18,29:4
Anybody's War 1930,Jl 11,22:1
Our Neighbors-The Carters 1940,F 15,15:2
Farrington, Frank
Courtship of Myles Standish, The 1923,D 31,9:3
Man Who Fights Alone, The 1924,Jl 28,12:2
Farron, Julia
Royal Ballet, The (Ondine); Ondine (The Royal Ballet) 1960,O 5,45:2
Romeo and Juliet 1966,O 6,55:1
Farrow, John (Director)
West of Shanghai 1937,O 29,19:2
She Loved a Fireman 1938,Ja 21,15:3
Invisible Menace, The 1938,F 14,20:6
My Bill 1938,Jl 7,22:4
Broadway Musketeers 1938,O 14,27:1
Saint Strikes Back, The 1939,Mr 9,18:2
Women in the Wind 1939,Ap 13,27:2
Five came Back 1939,Jl 5,20:2
Full Confession 1939,S 28,29:4
Reno 1939,D 21,29:2
Married and in Love 1940,F 2,13:2
Bill of Divorcement, A 1940,Jl 12,11:2
Wake Island 1942,S 2,19:2
China 1943,Ap 22,31:2
Hitler Gang, The 1944,My 8,15:2
You Came Along 1945,Jl 5,7:2
Two Years Before the Mast 1946,S 25,39:2
California 1947,Ja 15,31:2
Easy Come, Easy Go 1947,F 6,29:2
Blaze of Noon 1947,Mr 5,31:2
Calcutta 1947,Ap 24,30:2
Big Clock, The 1948,Ap 22,34:2
Beyond Glory 1948,Ag 4,18:2
Night Has a Thousand Eyes 1948,O 14,38:3
Alias Nick Beal 1949,Mr 10,35:2
Red, Hot and Blue 1949,O 20,39:2
Copper Canyon 1950,N 16,39:2
Where Danger Lives 1951,Ja 1,13:6
His Kind of Woman 1951,Ag 30,20:2
Submarine Command 1952,Ja 19,13:2
Ride Vaquero 1953,Jl 16,17:2
Plunder of the Sun 1953,Ag 27,22:1
Botany Bay 1953,O 30,27:2
Hondo 1953,N 27,99:9
Commandos Strike at Dawn 1954,Ja 14,25:1
Bullet is Waiting, A 1954,N 12,17:2
Sea Chase, The 1955,Je 11,8:7
Back From Eternity 1956,S 8,20:6
Unholy Wife, The 1958,Mr 7,17:1
John Paul Jones 1959,Je 17,39:1
Farrow, John (Original Author)
Bad One, The 1930,Je 13,28:3
Woman of Experience, A 1931,Jl 9,26:5
Last of the Pagans 1936,Ja 9,25:2
Farrow, John (Producer)
Where Danger Lives 1951,Ja 1,13:6
Sea Chase, The 1955,Je 11,8:7
Back From Eternity 1956,S 8,20:6
Unholy Wife, The 1958,Mr 7,17:1
Farrow, John (Screenwriter)
Last of the Pagans 1936,Ja 9,25:2
Red, Hot and Blue 1949,O 20,39:2
John Paul Jones 1959,Je 17,39:1
Farrow, Mia
Guns at Batasi 1964,N 17,47:1
Dandy in Aspic, A 1968,Ap 3,40:1
Rosemary's Baby 1968,Je 13,57:1
Secret Ceremony 1968,O 24,55:1
Farry, S P
My Hustler 1967,Jl 11,29:2
Farwell, Frances
Friendly Persuasion 1956,N 2,30:1
Faryll, Carla
Body Is a Shell, The 1957,S 9,21:2
Fasken, Ruth (Original Author)
Youth Will Be Served 1940,N 15,25:2
Fassett, Jay
My Sin 1931,S 11,24:2
Cheat, The 1931,D 12,23:3
Fassett, Julia
One Third of a Nation 1939,F 11,13:2

Fast, Howard (Narrator)
Zoya 1945,Ap 16,18:6
Fast, Howard (Original Author)
Rachel and the Stranger 1948,S 20,21:2
Spartacus 1960,O 7,28:1
Man in the Middle 1964,Mr 5,36:1
Jigsaw 1968,Je 6,54:2
Fatehlal (Director)
Gyandev of India 1943,Ap 10,12:5
Fatigati, Giuseppe (Director)
Laugh Pagliacci 1948,Ja 31,14:2
Fatima
Moonlighting Wives 1968,My 9,54:4
Fauche, Miriam
Fourflusher, The 1928,Ja 16,24:1
Fauchois, Rene
Champs-Elysees 1939,F 28,17:2
Fauchois, Rene (Original Author)
Boudu Saved From Drowning; Boudu Sauve Des
Eaux 1967,F 24,26:2
Fauchois, Rene (Screenwriter)
Dreams of Love 1954,Je 5,11:2
Faulds, Andrew
Crawling Eye, The 1959,Ja 1,38:1
Cleopatra 1963,Je 13,29:1
Fauley, Wilbur Finley (Original Author)
Jenny, Be Good 1920,Je 28,13:2
Faulk, John Henry
Best Man, The 1964,Ap 7,29:1
FAULKNER
See Also FALCONER
Faulkner, Edward
Tickle Me 1965,Je 24,28:3
Faulkner, Keith
Scotch on the Rocks 1954,Je 14,18:2
Tunes of Glory 1960,D 21,38:2
Faulkner, Norbert (Screenwriter)
Lady With red Hair 1940,D 6,28:2
Faulkner, Ralph
Three Musketeers, The 1935,N 1,25:1
Prisoner of Zenda, The 1937,S 3,12:1
Faulkner, Trader
Murder Game, The 1966,Mr 31,43:2
Faulkner, Virginia (Original Author)
Bridal Suite 1939,My 26,20:2
Faulkner, William (Original Author)
Today We Live 1933,Ap 15,16:2
Story of Temple Drake, The 1933,My 6,11:2
Road to Glory, The 1936,Ag 6,22:1
Slave Ship 1937,Je 17,19:2
Intruder in the Dust 1949,N 23,19:1
Land of the Pharaohs 1955,Jl 27,15:2
Tarnished Angels, The 1958,Ja 7,31:1
Long, Hot Summer, The 1958,Ap 4,16:1
Sound and the Fury, The 1959,Mr 28,11:1
Sanctuary 1961,F 22,31:1
Faulkner, William (Screenwriter)
Road to Glory, The 1936,Ag 6,22:1
To Have and Have Not 1944,O 12,24:1
Big Sleep, The 1946,Ag 24,6:6
Faure, Renee
Bellman, The 1947,Ap 7,20:5
Great Dawn, The 1947,Ag 28,28:3
Who Killed Santa Claus? 1948,Ap 21,33:2
Angels of the Streets 1950,Ja 17,24:2
Francois Villon 1950,Jl 3,9:2
Adorable Creatures 1956,Ja 11,36:2
Faurez, Jean (Director)
Counter Investigation 1949,D 30,13:2
Fauslino, Pedro
Badjao 1962,S 21,35:1
Faussek, N
Professor Mamlock 1938,N 8,26:2
Faust, Edward
Enemy Sex, The 1924,Jl 1,21:4
New Lives for Old 1925,F 25,16:7
Fashions For Women 1927,Mr 28,26:4
Gentlemen Prefer Blondes 1928,Ja 16,24:1
Faust, Louis R
Plunders, The 1948,N 1,28:2
Last Bandit, The 1949,Mr 21,19:2
Hellfire 1949,My 30,9:4
Faust, Martin
Silent Command, The 1923,S 5,15:3
Under the Red Robe 1923,N 13,25:3
Yolanda 1924,F 20,23:1
I Am the Man 1925,Mr 6,23:1
Hell Bound 1931,My 9,15:4
Faust, Victoria
Lady of Burlesque 1943,My 14,17:2
Faustinelli, Mario (Screenwriter)
World of Topo Gigio 1965,N 27,34:1
Faustman, Erik
Katrina 1949,N 18,35:3
Faustman, Hampe
Crime and Punishment 1948,Mr 1,17:2
Matter of Morals, A 1961,Je 1,31:1
Faustman, Hampe (Director)
Crime and Punishment 1948,Mr 1,17:2
Fausto, Antonio R
Cancion del Alma; Song of the Soul
1938,O 11,20:4
Cada Loco con su Tema; Every Madman to his

Specialty 1939,Ap 29,13:3
Faut, Paul
Peasant's Wedding, The 1939,Ap 19,20:5
Favalelli, Max
Belle Americaine, La 1961,D 18,42:1
Favart, Robert
Sextette (Part 3-The Key to Sin); Key to Sin, The
(Sextette) 1953,Mr 2,19:2
Gentlemen Marry Brunettes 1955,O 31,31:5
Favel, Paul
My Life to Live 1963,S 24,43:2
Faversham, Alec
Gay Intruders, The 1946,Mr 18,24:2
Faversham, Philip
Captured 1933,Ag 18,18:3
World Changes, The 1933,O 27,22:3
House on 56th Street, The 1933,D 2,9:3
Big Shakedown, The 1934,F 12,19:2
Jimmy the Gent 1934,Mr 26,22:3
Gambling Lady 1934,Ap 5,25:2
Faversham, William
Silver King, The 1919,Ja 13,9:3
Man Who Lost Himself, The 1920,My 31,14:2
Sin That Was His, The 1920,D 6,19:1
Mystery Woman 1935,Ja 9,22:2
Becky Sharp 1935,Je 14,27:2
Favier, Yves (Screenwriter)
Wild Oat, The 1956,Je 28,33:2
Favieres, Guy
It Happened at the Inn; Goupi Mains Rouge
1945,D 22,16:2
Panic 1947,N 27,50:2
Favieres, Henry
Madame Sans Gene 1925,Ap 18,19:1
Favio, Leonardo
Hand in the Trap 1963,Jl 2,16:2
Terrace, The 1964,N 25,45:1
Favor, Toni
Eve of St Mark, The 1944,My 31,22:2
Favrel-Chantal, Marcelle
Collier de la Reine, Le (Queen's Necklace, The)
1931,F 9,25:3
Fawcett, Charles
When in Rome 1952,My 12,21:2
Boy on a Dolphin 1957,Ap 20,21:2
Heaven on Earth 1960,O 11,55:3
300 Spartans, The 1962,S 20,29:2
Fawcett, George
Panthea 1917,Ja 8,9:2
Hearts of the World 1918,Ap 5,13:1
Great Love, The 1918,Ag 12,7:1
Hope Chest, The 1919,Ja 6,11:3
Romance of Happy Valley, A 1919,Ja 27,11:4
Girl Who Stayed Home, The 1919,Mr 24,11:3
I'll Get Him yet 1919,My 19,20:5
Hearts of the World 1919,Ag 12,7:6
Nobody Home 1919,Ag 25,8:5
Turning the Tables 1919,N 3,13:3
Scarlet Days 1919,N 10,18:2
Greatest Question, The 1919,D 29,7:2
Two Weeks 1920,Ja 26,16:1
Branded Woman, The 1920,S 6,10:5
Little Miss Rebellion 1920,S 20,13:1
Sentimental Tommy 1921,My 9,16:2
Peter Ibbetson; (Forever) 1921,O 17,18:1
Old Homestead, The 1922,O 9,10:2
Ebb Tide 1922,N 20,21:3
Drums of Fate 1923,Ja 15,18:3
Mr Billings Spends his Dime 1923,Mr 5,15:3
Only 38 1923,Je 11,16:2
Woman With Four Faces, The 1923,Je 18,13:5
His Children's Children 1923,N 5,15:1
West of the Water Tower 1923,D 31,9:3
Pied Piper Malone 1924,Ja 28,12:1
Triumph 1924,Ap 21,21:4
Bedroom Window, The 1924,Je 9,14:3
Tess of the D'Urbervilles 1924,Jl 28,12:2
Broken Barriers 1924,Ag 4,16:3
Her Love Story 1924,O 7,26:1
Lost Lady, A 1925,Ja 19,14:1
Sporting Venus, The 1925,My 11,14:3
Up the Ladder 1925,My 12,26:2
Price of Pleasure, The 1925,My 26,24:2
Sporting Chance, The 1925,Je 24,14:3
Mad Whirl, The 1925,Jl 1,16:1
Home Maker, The 1925,Ag 10,8:2
Merry Widow, The 1925,Ag 27,14:1
Souls for Sables 1925,S 15,12:1 (Incorrect in this
edition; use 1925,S 15,29:1 elsewhere)
Circle, The 1925,S 22,22:3
Go Straight 1925,O 6,30:1
Thank You 1925,O 30,30:1
Joanna 1925,D 15,14:5
Flaming Frontier, The 1926,Ap 5,24:1
Men of Steel 1926,Jl 12,24:4
Son of the Sheik, The 1926,Jl 26,13:2
Flesh and the Devil 1927,Ja 10,20:2
See You in Jail 1927,Ap 4,30:5
Tillie the Toiler 1927,Je 7,27:4
Captain Salvation 1927,Je 27,25:2
Painting the Town 1927,Ag 2,19:2
Hard-Boiled Haggerty 1927,Ag 23,29:4
Spring Fever 1927,O 18,33:2

Fawcett, George — Cont
Love 1927,N 30,22:4
Valley of the Giants, The 1927,D 5,26:2
Private Life of Helen of Troy, The
1927,D 10,14:7
Enemy, The 1927,D 28,26:6
Tempest 1928,My 18,27:3
Wedding March, The 1928,O 15,26:1
Little Wildcat, The 1929,Ja 21,18:4
Lady of the Pavements 1929,Mr 11,22:2
His Captive Woman 1929,Ap 3,26:4
Innocents of Paris 1929,Ap 27,16:5
Four Feathers, The 1929,Je 13,35:4
Wonder of Women 1929,Jl 22,17:1
Gamblers, The 1929,Ag 24,11:5
Hearts in Exile 1929,N 29,25:1
Hot for Paris 1930,Ja 4,21:1
Great Divide, The 1930,F 17,17:6
Ladies of Leisure 1930,My 24,21:2
Bad One, The 1930,Je 13,28:3
Swing High 1930,Je 27,26:3
Wild Company 1930,Jl 19,7:5
Once a Gentleman 1930,O 4,15:2
Woman of Experience, A 1931,Jl 9,26:5
Personal Maid 1931,S 5,7:4
Fawcett, George Mrs
Innocents of Paris 1929,Ap 27,16:5
River of Romance, The 1929,Jl 29,23:3
Fawcett, William
Barbary Pirate 1949,O 28,29:3
Lion and the Horse, The 1952,My 19,12:2
No Time for Sergeants 1958,My 30,13:2
Saintly Sinners 1962,Mr 29,28:2
Fax, Jesslyn
Rear Window 1954,Ag 5,18:2
How to be Very, Very Popular 1955,Jl 23,10:1
Affair to Remember, An 1957,Jl 20,8:5
Family Jewels, The 1965,Ag 12,30:4
FAY
See Also FAYE
Fay, Ann
Vanity Street 1932,O 15,13:1
Fay, Bela
Szent Peter Esernyoeje 1936,Ja 8,22:2
Szerelmi Almok 1937,Ja 5,19:2
Fay, Frank
Show of Shows 1929,N 21,24:5
Under a Texas Moon 1930,Ap 4,22:1
Matrimonial Bed, The 1930,Ag 25,14:2
Bright Lights 1931,F 10,24:4
God's Gift to Women 1931,Ap 18,17:3
Stars Over Broadway 1935,N 14,17:3
Nothing Sacred 1937,N 26,27:2
I Want a Divorce 1940,O 3,31:2
They Knew What They Wanted 1940,O 11,25:2
Fay, Gaby
I Married a Doctor 1936,Ap 20,17:1
Fay, Hugh
Little Annie Rooney 1925,O 19,26:1
Fay, Jimmy
Princess O'Hara 1935,Ap 13,11:3
Million Dollar Baby 1935,My 6,22:3
Fay, Mary (Original Author)
Girl Next Door, The 1953,S 5,7:4
Embezzled Heaven 1959,Ap 24,23:1
Fay, Vivian
Day at the Races, A 1937,Je 18,25:2
Dance, Girl, Dance 1940,O 11,25:2
Fay, W G
Blarney Kiss, The 1933,Ag 19,14:4
Storm in a Teacup 1938,Mr 22,18:4
Odd Man Out 1947,Ap 24,30:2
Patient Vanishes, The 1947,My 23,31:2
Oliver Twist 1951,Jl 31,17:2
Fay, William (Original Author)
Guy Who Came Back, The 1951,Ag 17,13:2
Fay, William (Screenwriter)
Kid Galahad 1963,Mr 7,8:5
FAYE
See Also FAY
Faye, Abdoulaye
Winner, The 1965,Jl 1,34:1
Faye, Alice
George White's Scandals 1934,Mr 16,24:2
Now I'll Tell 1934,My 26,12:2
She Learned About Sailors 1934,Jl 30,9:4
365 Nights in Hollywood 1934,N 7,32:1
George White's 1935 Scandals 1935,Ap 29,12:3
Every Night at Eight 1935,Ag 3,16:2
King of Burlesque 1936,Ja 16,25:2
Poor Little Rich Girl, The 1936,Je 26,16:1
Sing, Baby, Sing 1936,S 12,20:1
Stowaway 1936,D 19,16:1
On the Avenue 1937,F 5,17:3
Wake up and Live 1937,Ap 24,16:2
You Can't Have Everything 1937,Ag 4,15:2
You're a Sweetheart 1937,D 25,10:5
In Old Chicago 1938,Ja 7,15:2
Sally, Irene and Mary 1938,F 26,9:2
Alexander's Ragtime Band 1938,Ag 6,7:2
Tail Spin 1939,F 11,13:2
Rose of Washington Square 1939,My 6,21:2
Hollywood Cavalcade 1939,O 14,13:2
Barricade 1939,D 9,18:2

Faye, Alice— Cont

Little Old New York 1940,F 3,9:2
Lillian Russell 1940,My 18,11:2
Tin Pan Alley 1940,N 22,27:3
That Night in Rio 1941,Mr 10,21:2
Great American Broadcast, The 1941,My 2,25:2
Week-End in Havana 1941,N 8,11:2
Hello, Frisco, Hello 1943,Mr 25,25:1
Gang's All Here, The 1943,D 23,26:4
Four Jills in a Jeep 1944,Ap 6,27:2
Fallen Angel 1946,F 7,29:4
State Fair 1962,Ap 12,41:4

Faye, Herbie
Top Banana 1954,F 20,8:6
Shrike, The 1955,Jl 8,15:2
Harder They Fall, The 1956,My 10,26:3
Requiem for a Heavyweight 1962,O 17,35:1
Thoroughly Modern Millie 1967,Mr 23,25:1

Faye, Janina
Story of Esther Costello, The 1957,N 6,43:1
Horror of Dracula 1958,My 29,24:4
Day of the Triffids 1963,My 11,15:2

Faye, Joey
Close-Up 1948,Ap 5,24:2
Top Banana 1954,F 20,8:6
Tender Trap, The 1955,N 11,29:6
That Touch of Mink 1962,Je 15,16:2

Faye, Julia
Stepping Out 1919,S 22,8:1
Life of the Party, The 1920,N 22,13:3
Ten Commandments, The 1923,D 22,8:1
Don't Call it Love 1923,D 25,26:1
Triumph 1924,Ap 21,21:4
Changing Husbands 1924,Je 23,22:4
Feet of Clay 1924,S 22,16:1
Golden Bed, The 1925,Ja 20,18:2
Hell's Highroad 1925,Ag 26,14:2
Road to Yesterday, The 1925,D 1,22:4
Volga Boatman, The 1926,Ap 14,21:1
Corporal Kate 1926,D 15,30:4
King of Kings, The 1927,Ap 20,29:2
Yankee Clipper, The 1927,My 3,25:1
Fighting Eagle, The 1927,Ag 15,22:5
His Dog 1927,Ag 16,31:2
Main Event, The 1927,O 31,22:1
Chicago 1927,D 24,9:1
Dynamite 1929,D 28,11:1
Not so Dumb 1930,F 8,12:5
Squaw Man, The 1931,S 19,10:2
Till We Meet Again 1936,My 9,11:2
California 1947,Ja 15,31:2
Connecticut Yankee in King Arthur's Court, A 1949,Ap 8,31:2
Samson and Delilah 1949,D 22,29:2
Greatest Show on Earth, The 1952,Ja 11,17:2
Ten Commandments, The 1956,N 9,35:2

Faye, Randall (Miscellaneous)
Return of the Vampire, The 1944,Ja 29,10:1

Faye, Randall (Original Author)
She Learned About Sailors 1934,Jl 30,9:4

Faye, Randall (Screenwriter)
Sharp Shooters 1928,Ja 23,18:3
Murder in the Old Red Barn 1936,Ag 19,18:3

Faylen, Frank
Bullets or Ballots 1936,My 27,27:1
Border Flight 1936,Je 22,22:1
Kid Galahad 1937,My 27,21:3
They Won't Forget 1937,Jl 15,16:1
Dance Charlie Dance 1937,Ag 26,25:2
Headin' East 1938,Ja 15,19:2
Invisible Menace, The 1938,F 14,20:6
Waterfront 1939,Jl 17,10:2
Nick Carter, Master Detective 1939,D 14,35:2
Reno 1939,D 21,29:2
Grapes of Wrath, The 1940,Ja 25,17:2
Married and in Love 1940,F 2,13:2
Curtain Call 1940,Ap 19,25:2
No Time for Comedy 1940,S 7,9:2
Come Live With Me 1941,F 28,17:3
Tanks a Million 1941,O 9,27:2
Top Sergeant Mulligan 1941,N 12,31:3
No Hands on the Clock 1941,D 22,24:6
Silver Skates 1943,Mr 19,15:3
Taxi, Mister 1943,Ap 15,20:2
Good Morning, Judge 1943,Ap 30,25:4
Fall In 1943,My 15,13:3
That Nazty Nuisance 1943,My 29,10:3
Address Unknown 1944,Ap 17,20:1
And the Angels Sing 1944,Jl 13,14:2
Canterville Ghost, The 1944,Jl 29,16:2
Lost Weekend, The 1945,D 3,17:2
Blue Dahlia, The 1946,My 9,27:3
To Each his Own 1946,My 24,15:2
Our Hearts Were Growing Up 1946,Ag 12,17:2
Blue Skies 1946,O 17,28:2
It's a Wonderful Life 1946,D 23,19:2
California 1947,Ja 15,31:2
Easy Come, Easy Go 1947,F 6,29:2
Suddenly It's Spring 1947,F 27,26:2
Perils of Pauline, The 1947,Jl 10,17:2
Trouble With Women, The 1947,Jl 14,14:4
Welcome Stranger 1947,Ag 7,15:2
Variety Girl 1947,O 16,34:4
Road to Rio 1948,F 19,29:3

Hazard 1948,Je 3,19:2
Race Street 1948,Ag 23,13:3
Blood on the Moon 1948,N 12,30:5
Whispering Smith 1949,F 15,28:2
Nevadan, The 1950,Ja 13,19:4
Francis 1950,Mr 16,40:2
Eagle and the Hawk, The 1950,Jl 6,31:2
Copper Canyon 1950,N 16,39:2
Fourteen Hours 1951,Mr 7,43:2
Passage West 1951,Ag 31,12:2
Detective Story 1951,N 7,35:2
Sniper, The 1952,My 10,16:3
Lusty Men, The 1952,O 25,12:6
Hangman's Knot 1952,D 11,45:3
99 River Street 1953,O 3,14:2
Riot in Cell Block 11 1954,F 19,24:5
Red Garters 1954,Mr 27,13:5
McConnell Story, The 1955,S 30,23:1
Three Brave Men 1957,Mr 16,13:2
Gunfight at the O K Corral 1957,My 30,23:2
Dino 1957,Je 22,9:2
Monkey's Uncle, The 1965,Ag 19,35:4
When the Boys Meet the Girls 1966,Ja 20,29:1
Funny Girl 1968,S 20,42:1

Fazan, Eleanor
Inadmissible Evidence 1968,Je 24,44:1

Fazekas, Mihaly (Original Author)
Goose Boy, The 1951,O 13,9:2

Fazenda, Louise
Beautiful and Damned, The 1922,D 11,22:1
Quincy Adams Sawyer 1922,D 18,22:2
Main Street 1923,Je 12,22:2
Spoilers, The 1923,Ag 6,14:2
Dramatic Life of Abraham Lincoln, The 1924,Ja 22,17:3
True as Steel 1924,Je 17,22:4
Being Respectable 1924,Ag 4,16:3
This Woman 1924,O 21,21:3
Lighthouse by the Sea, The 1924,D 29,11:4
Cheaper to Marry 1925,F 2,14:1
Declassee 1925,Mr 23,14:2
Night Club, The 1925,My 5,24:2
Price of Pleasure, The 1925,My 26,24:2
Grounds for Divorce 1925,Je 29,8:2
Love Hour, The 1925,S 2,21:3
Compromise 1925,O 27,23:3
Bobbed Hair 1925,N 4,17:4
Hogan's Alley 1925,N 24,28:4
Bat, The 1926,Mr 15,18:3
Footloose Windows 1926,Je 22,21:2
Ladies at Play 1926,N 16,25:3
Loose Ankles 1926,N 21,VIII,7:3 (In Addenda)
Red Mill, The 1927,F 14,15:1
Cradle Snatchers 1927,My 31,25:2
Texas Steer, A 1928,Ja 2,28:1
Terror, The 1928,Ag 16,25:3
Heart to Heart 1928,S 10,29:2
Outcast 1928,N 26,30:2
Riley, The Cop 1928,D 4,29:1
Noah's Ark 1929,Mr 13,28:6
Desert Song, The 1929,My 2,20:6
Hot Stuff 1929,My 13,27:2
On With the Show 1929,My 29,28:6
Hard to Get 1929,S 28,17:3
Show of Shows 1929,N 21,24:5
No, No, Nanette 1930,Ja 4,21:1
Wide Open 1930,Mr 22,22:6
High Society Blues 1930,Ap 19,15:1
Bride of the Regiment 1930,My 22,32:6
Rain or Shine 1930,Ag 8,11:1
Leathernecking 1930,S 13,9:3
Viennese Nights 1930,N 27,32:5
Gun Smoke 1931,Ap 24,27:1
Newly Rich 1931,Jl 3,22:1
Mad Parade, The 1931,S 19,10:2
Cuban Love Song, The 1931,D 5,21:2
Once in a Lifetime 1932,O 29,18:4
Alice in Wonderland 1933,D 23,19:1
Wonder Bar 1934,Mr 1,23:2
Caravan 1934,S 28,27:1
Winning Ticket, The 1935,F 11,14:2
Casino Murder Case, The 1935,Ap 17,26:5
Broadway Gondolier 1935,Jl 18,15:2
Bad Boy 1935,O 28,16:3
Colleen 1936,Mr 9,20:2
I Married a Doctor 1936,Ap 20,17:1
Ready, Willing and Able 1937,Mr 15,27:1
Road Back, The 1937,Je 18,25:2
Ever Since Eve 1937,Je 25,25:2
Merry-Go-Round of 1938 1937,N 26,27:2
First Lady 1937,D 23,25:1
Swing Your Lady 1938,Ja 27,17:2
Old Maid, The 1939,Ag 12,16:2

Fazio, Salvatore
Seduced and Abandoned 1964,Jl 16,23:1

Fealy, Margaret
Love Parade, The 1929,N 20,32:6
Cross Examination 1932,F 27,22:1

Fealy, Maude
Laugh and get Rich 1931,Mr 28,15:3

Fearing, Kenneth (Original Author)
Big Clock, The 1948,Ap 22,34:2

Feber, Frederick (Director)
That Murder in Berlin 1929,Mr 12,26:2

Fecher, Kurt
Big Show, The 1961,My 11,42:4

Fechner, Ellen (Screenwriter)
Film Without a Name 1950,O 20,32:2

Fedck, Sari
Iza Neni 1934,Je 5,28:6
Mami 1938,F 19,19:5
Erik/a/Buzakalasz; Wheat Ripens, The 1939,S 11,15:2
Oeroek Titok, Az; Eternal Secret, The 1940,Mr 9,19:3

Feder, Moishe
I Want to Be a Mother 1937,F 27,9:2
Mirele Efros 1939,O 21,12:2

Feder, Sid (Cinematographer)
ThIs is Russia 1957,D 10,45:1

Feder, Sid (Director)
ThIs is Russia 1957,D 10,45:1

Feder, Sid (Original Author)
Murder, Inc 1960,Je 29,26:6

Feder, Sid (Producer)
ThIs is Russia 1957,D 10,45:1

Feder Sisters
Catskill Honeymoon 1950,Ja 28,10:3

Federman, Simon (Producer)
Jews in Poland 1957,Ap 17,37:1

Federof, V F (Director)
House of Death 1932,Ag 13,18:6

Federspiel, Birgitte
Ordet 1957,D 16,33:6
Stranger Knocks, A 1965,Ap 1,30:1

Federspiel, Ejner
Ordet 1957,D 16,33:6

Fedin, Konstantin (Original Author)
No Ordinary Summer 1958,O 6,36:3

Fedor, Tania
Si l'Empereur Savait Ca 1931,F 23,20:3
Fantomas 1934,Mr 13,27:4
Crossroads 1939,Mr 14,17:5
Open Road, The 1940,O 5,20:2
Queen and the Cardinal, The 1944,Je 1,17:3
Sins of the Borgias 1956,Mr 5,21:1
Take it All; A Tout Prendre 1966,Ap 26,55:1

Fedorova, I
No Greater Love 1944,F 25,23:3
Heroes Are Made 1944,Mr 11,10:2

Fedorova, Z
Three Women 1936,F 12,25:4
Great Citizen, The 1939,Ja 16,11:2
Man With the Gun, The 1939,Ja 30,9:3
Soviet Border 1939,F 20,13:2
Grown-Up Children 1963,Ap 15,36:5

Fedorovsky, F
Amangeldy 1939,Je 16,27:4

Fedosyef, B
Golden Mountains 1932,Ap 14,25:3

Fedotoff, Dimitry
Journey, The 1959,F 20,19:1

Feeney, Francis
Secrets 1924,Mr 25,25:2
Unknown, The 1924,N 18,22:1
K-The Unknown 1924,N 18,22:1

Feeney, John (Composer)
Spell of Ireland, The 1954,My 11,25:5

Fegan, John
Massacre Hill 1950,D 14,51:3
Kangaroo 1952,My 17,22:7

Fehdmer, Helene
Luise, Koenigin von Preussen 1932,O 5,26:6
Die vom Niederrhein; Lower Rhine Folks 1935,My 20,20:6

Feher, Freidrich (Director)
Gehetzie Menschen 1934,Je 2,22:5

Feher, Friedrich (Composer)
Robber Symphony 1937,Ja 27,17:2

Feher, Friedrich (Director)
Maria Stuart 1928,Mr 11,VIII,5:1
Mata Hari: The Red Dancer 1928,N 12,18:2
Robber Symphony 1937,Ja 27,17:2

Feher, Friedrich (Screenwriter)
Robber Symphony 1937,Ja 27,17:2

Feher, Hans
Gehetzie Menschen 1934,Je 2,22:5
Robber Symphony 1937,Ja 27,17:2

Fehmiu, Bekim
Feverish Years, The 1967,S 22,57:2
I Even Met Happy Gypsies 1968,Mr 21,57:1

Fehr, Rudi (Producer)
Desert Song, The 1953,My 21,39:2

Fei-Kwong, Ho (Director)
Maid of Formosa 1949,Ag 8,10:5

Feibleman, Peter S (Screenwriter)
Ensign Pulver 1964,Ag 1,13:2

Feilding, Edward
I Wanted Wings 1941,Mr 27,29:4

Feiler, Hertha
Manner Mussen so Sein; Men Are That Way 1939,My 13,11:6

Feinberg, Marve (Screenwriter)
Ambush Bay 1966,S 15,51:4

Feindt, Cilly
  Ferien vom Ich 1935,Ap 1,17:2
  Ferien vom Ich 1935,Ap 1,17:2
Feinsilber, Samson
  Porteuse de Pain, La 1936,Jl 1,29:5
Feinstein, Barry (Cinematographer)
  You Are What You Eat 1968,S 25,38:1
  Monterey Pop 1968,D 27,44:1
Feinstein, Barry (Director)
  You Are What You Eat 1968,S 25,38:1
Feinstein, Barry (Producer)
  You Are What You Eat 1968,S 25,38:1
Feinzimmer, A (Director)
  Czar wants to Sleep, The 1934,D 10,16:3
  Men of the Sea 1938,Je 20,11:2
  Secret Brigade 1951,Mr 19,23:2
  Gadfly, The 1956,S 17,22:2
Feist, Felix (Director)
  Deluge 1933,O 9,22:3
  All by Myself 1943,Jl 16,20:3
  ThIs is the Life 1944,Ap 28,23:3
  George White's Scandals 1945,O 11,26:2
  Devil Thumbs a Ride, The 1947,Mr 22,10:2
  Threat, The 1949,D 2,35:4
  Guilty of Treason 1950,Ap 11,26:2
  Man Who Cheated Himself, The 1951,F 9,21:2
  Tomorrow Is Another Day 1951,Ag 9,17:5
  Basketball Fix, the 1951,S 14,21:2
  Big Trees, The 1952,F 6,24:2
  ThIs Woman is Dangerous 1952,F 28,23:2
  Donovan's Brain 1954,Ja 21,28:2
  Pirates of Tripoli 1955,F 24,21:2
Feist, Felix (Original Author)
  Devil Thumbs a Ride, The 1947,Mr 22,10:2
Feist, Felix (Screenwriter)
  Donovan's Brain 1954,Ja 21,28:2
  Babes in Bagdad 1954,Ap 5,21:3
Feist, Harry
  Open City; Citta Aperta 1946,F 26,21:2
Fejos, Paul (Director)
  Lonesome 1928,O 2,23:5
  Broadway 1929,My 28,36:2
  Last Performance, The 1929,N 4,28:1
  Fantomas 1934,Mr 13,27:4
Fejos, Paul (Producer)
  Last Moment, The 1928,Mr 12,26:1
Fejos, Paul (Screenwriter)
  Last Moment, The 1928,Mr 12,26:1
Fekete, Paul (Screenwriter)
  Queen and the Cardinal, The 1944,Je 1,17:3
  Francis the First 1947,N 20,38:4
Fekets, Laszoo Bus (Original Author)
  Roadhouse Murder 1932,Ap 29,13:4
Feld, Eliot
  West Side Story 1961,O 19,39:3
Feld, Fritz
  Broadway 1929,My 28,36:2
  I Met Him in Paris 1937,Je 3,29:2
  Lancer Spy 1937,N 4,29:1
  True Confession 1937,D 16,35:2
  Tovarich 1937,D 31,9:2
  Expensive Husbands 1938,Ja 8,19:3
  Hollywood Hotel 1938,Ja 13,17:3
  Bringing Up Baby 1938,Mr 4,17:5
  Romance in the Dark 1938,Mr 21,18:2
  Gold Diggers in Paris 1938,Je 2,19:2
  Go Chase Yourself 1938,Je 15,27:1
  I'll Give a Million 1938,Jl 16,7:2
  Campus Confessions 1938,S 23,35:1
  Affairs of Annabel, The 1938,O 13,29:2
  Artists and Models Abroad 1938,D 22,25:3
  Idiot's Delight 1939,F 3,13:1
  When Tomorrow Comes 1939,Ag 17,16:2
  At the Circus 1939,N 17,17:2
  Everything Happens at Night 1939,D 16,12:6
  Little Old New York 1940,F 3,9:2
  It's a Date 1940,Mr 23,16:2
  I Was an Adventuress 1940,My 20,13:2
  Sandy Is a Lady 1940,Je 28,22:2
  Victory 1940,D 23,23:2
  World Premiere 1941,Ag 21,15:2
  You Belong to Me 1941,N 29,14:2
  Maisie Gets her Man 1942,Jl 16,23:2
  Iceland 1942,O 15,27:1
  Phantom of the Opera, The 1943,O 15,15:2
  Knickerbocker Holiday 1944,Ap 20,22:7
  Great John L, The 1945,Jl 9,14:6
  George White's Scandals 1945,O 11,26:2
  Wife of Monte Cristo, The 1946,Ap 8,31:2
  Catman of Paris, The 1946,Jl 13,12:2
  I've Always Loved You 1946,S 7,11:1
  Her Sister's Secret 1947,Ja 23,31:3
  Carnival in Costa Rica 1947,Mr 29,21:2
  Secret Life of Walter Mitty, The 1947,Ag 15,12:2
  My Girl Tisa 1948,F 21,9:2
  If You Knew Susie 1948,F 23,19:2
  Julia Misbehaves 1948,O 8,30:2
  Mexican Hayride 1949,Ja 12,33:3
  Jackpot, The 1950,N 23,55:2
  Aaron Slick From Punkin Crick 1952,Ap 19,18:6
  O Henry's Full House (The Gift of the Magi); Gift
    of the Magi, The (O Henry's Full House)
    1952,O 17,33:1

Barefoot in the Park 1967,My 26,51:1
Feld, Milton H (Producer)
  Big Town Girl 1937,D 13,23:4
Feldary, Eric
  Hold Back the Dawn 1941,O 2,29:1
  For Whom the Bell Tolls 1943,Jl 15,25:2
  Hostages 1943,O 11,23:2
  Master Race, The 1944,N 2,22:1
  I, Jane Doe 1948,Jl 5,8:4
  16 Fathoms Deep 1948,O 7,35:2
  Sealed Cargo 1951,My 24,47:1
Felder, Robert
  Stormy Weather 1943,Jl 22,15:1
Feldkamp, Fred (Producer)
  Silken Affair, The 1957,O 31,41:1
Feldman, Charles K (Producer)
  Follow the Boys 1944,Ap 26,24:6
  Glass Menagerie, The 1950,S 29,31:5
  Streetcar Named Desire, A 1951,S 30,27:1
  Seven Year Itch, The 1955,Je 4,9:1
  Walk on the Wild Side 1962,F 22,20:1
  Seventh Dawn, The 1964,S 3,24:1
  What's New Pussycat? 1965,Je 23,49:1
  Casino Royale 1967,Ap 29,25:1
Feldman, Gladys
  West of the Water Tower 1923,D 31,9:3
Feldman, Louis F (Producer)
  Jazz Singer, The 1953,Ja 14,27:3
Feldman, Phil (Producer)
  You're a Big Boy Now 1967,Mr 21,35:3
Feldon, Barbara
  Fitzwilly 1967,D 21,45:1
Felette, Nicole
  Father Goose 1964,D 11,55:1
Feli, Maurizio Lodi (Producer)
  Girl With a Suitcase 1961,S 12,36:2
Feliciani, Mario
  Everybody go Home!; Tutti a Casa 1962,N 6,38:1
  Greco, El 1967,My 24,52:2
Felicioni, Fernando (Producer)
  Constantine and the Cross 1963,Mr 14,8:2
Felio, Gordon
  Secret Cinema, The 1968,My 2,57:1
Feliu y Codina (Original Author)
  Heritage 1940,N 5,33:2
Felix, Alfonso San
  Kid Rodelo 1966,F 23,46:1
Felix, Maria
  Enamorada 1949,D 3,8:6
  Hidden River 1950,D 1,31:2
  French-Cancan 1956,Ap 17,26:2
  Heroes and Sinners; (Heros Sont Fatigues, Les)
    1959,My 12,38:2
  Cucaracha, La 1961,N 2,42:1
  Empty Star, The; Estrella Vacia, La
    1962,Mr 28,36:4
Felix, Seymour (Director)
  Girls Demand Excitement 1931,F 7,11:1
  Stepping Sisters 1932,Ja 9,21:1
Felix, Seymour (Miscellaneous)
  Kid Millions 1934,N 12,17:2
  Great Ziegfeld, The 1936,Ap 9,21:2
Feliz, Alice
  Desire 1936,Ap 13,15:1
Felko, Anton (Screenwriter)
  Four Hearts 1946,F 25,21:5
Fell, Norman
  Pork Chop Hill 1959,My 30,9:2
  Inherit the Wind 1960,O 13,41:1
  Killers, The 1964,Jl 18,10:4
  Quick, Before it Melts 1965,Ap 1,30:2
  Fitzwilly 1967,D 21,45:1
  Graduate, The 1967,D 22,44:4
  Sergeant Ryker 1968,Mr 21,56:2
  Young Runaways, The 1968,S 12,54:3
  Bullitt 1968,O 18,41:2
Feller, Bob
  Untitled-Baseball Technique 1941,Ja 17,11:3
  Ninth Inning, The 1942,Ja 8,30:3
Feller, Catherine
  Curse of the Werewolf, The 1961,Je 8,40:2
  Waltz of the Toreadors 1962,Ag 14,34:1
Fellini, Federico
  Ways of Love (The Miracle); Miracle, The (Ways
    of Love) 1950,D 13,50:2
Fellini, Federico (Director)
  White Sheik, The 1956,Ap 26,37:4
  Strada, La 1956,Jl 17,19:2
  Vitelloni 1956,O 24,43:1
  Cabiria 1957,O 29,34:2
  Dolce Vita, La 1961,Ap 20,30:1
  Boccaccio '70 (The Temptation of Dr Antonio);
    Temptation of Dr Antonio, The (Boccaccio '70)
    1962,Je 27,40:1
  Eight and One Half 1963,Je 26,36:1
  Bidone, Il 1964,N 20,42:1
  Variety Lights; Luci del Varieta 1965,My 7,34:1
Fellini, Federico (Original Author)
  Ways of Love (The Temptation of Dr Antonio);
    Miracle, The (Ways
    of Love) 1950,D 13,50:2
  White Sheik, The 1956,Ap 26,37:4
  Vitelloni 1956,O 24,43:1
  Bidone, Il 1964,N 20,42:1

Fellini, Federico (Original Author)— Cont
  Variety Lights; Luci del Varieta 1965,My 7,34:1
  Juliet of the Spirits 1965,N 4,57:1
Fellini, Federico (Producer)
  Variety Lights; Luci del Varieta 1965,My 7,34:1
Fellini, Federico (Screenwriter)
  Open City; Citta Aperta 1946,F 26,21:2
  Paisan 1948,Mr 30,26:2
  Mafia; (In Nome Della Legge) 1950,Mr 2,33:2
  Without Pity; (Senza Pieta) 1950,Mr 16,40:4
  Bullet for Stefano 1950,O 26,38:7
  Flesh will Surrender 1950,O 26,38:7
  Mill on the Po, The 1951,O 23,35:2
  Path of Hope, The (II Cammino Della Speranza)
    1952,Ag 5,15:5
  Flowers of St Francis 1952,O 7,26:2
  Strada, La 1956,Jl 17,19:2
  Vitelloni 1956,O 24,43:1
  Cabiria 1957,O 29,34:2
  Dolce Vita, La 1961,Ap 20,30:1
  Boccaccio '70 (The Temptation of Dr Antonio);
    Temptation of Dr Antonio, The (Boccaccio '70)
    1962,Je 27,40:1
  Eight and One Half 1963,Je 26,36:1
  Bidone, Il 1964,N 20,42:1
  Variety Lights; Luci del Varieta 1965,My 7,34:1
  Juliet of the Spirits 1965,N 4,57:1
Fellini, Riccardo
  Vitelloni 1956,O 24,43:1
  Conjugal Bed, The 1963,S 17,30:1
Fellowes, Rockliffe
  Friendly Husband 1918,Ag 5,7:1
  In Search of a Sinner 1920,Mr 8,9:6
  In Search of a Sinner 1920,Mr 8,9:5
  Yes or No 1920,Jl 5,12:4
  Bits of Life 1921,O 17,18:1
  Stranger's Banquet, The 1923,Ja 1,18:1
  Trifling With Honor 1923,My 30,10:4
  Penrod and Sam 1923,Je 25,16:5
  Spoilers, The 1923,Ag 6,14:2
  Boy of Mine 1923,D 24,12:1 (In Addenda)
  Signal Tower, The 1924,Jl 21,14:4
  Garden of Weeds, The 1924,N 4,24:1
  East of Suez 1925,Ja 26,22:1
  Declassee 1925,Mr 23,14:2
  Golden Princess 1925,S 7,15:3
  Rose of the World 1925,N 10,25:3
  Silence 1926,My 19,29:3
  Syncopating Sue 1926,N 2,35:1
  Third Degree, The 1927,F 15,23:1
  Taxi Dancer, The 1927,Mr 8,18:4
  Understanding Heart, The 1927,My 10,24:5
  Satin Woman, The 1927,Ag 10,21:4
  Crystal Cup, The 1927,O 25,33:3
  Charlatan, The 1929,Ap 15,22:6
  Outside the Law 1930,S 1,16:1
  Vice Squad, The 1931,Je 6,15:5
  Monkey Business 1931,O 8,22:6
  Ladies of the Big House 1932,Ja 1,31:1
  Hotel Continental 1932,Mr 21,19:5
  Huddle 1932,Je 17,24:1
  Lawyer Man 1932,D 27,10:2
  Phantom Broadcast, The 1933,Jl 31,16:2
Fellows, Edith
  His Greatest Gamble 1934,Jl 18,20:2
  Mrs Wiggs of the Cabbage Patch 1934,O 29,14:2
  Black Fury 1935,Ap 11,27:2
  Keeper of the Bees, The 1935,Ag 17,18:5
  She Married her Boss 1935,S 27,25:3
  One Way Ticket 1936,Ja 1,35:2
  And So They Were Married 1936,My 14,29:3
  Pennies From Heaven 1936,D 10,35:2
  City Streets 1938,Jl 25,18:2
  Music in My Heart 1940,Ja 4,19:2
Fellows, John (Producer)
  Hondo 1953,N 27,99:9
Fellows, Robert (Producer)
  Bombardier 1943,Jl 2,15:2
  Fallen Sparrow, The 1943,Ag 20,13:1
  Iron Major, The 1943,N 1,12:5
  Marine Raiders 1944,Jl 1,10:7
  Step Lively 1944,Jl 27,14:1
  Heavenly Days 1944,O 21,15:2
  Tall in the Saddle 1944,D 15,25:3
  Having Wonderful Crime 1945,Ap 13,15:2
  Back to Bataan 1945,S 13,26:3
  Man Alive 1945,N 17,14:5
  Blaze of Noon 1947,Mr 5,31:2
  Wild Harvest 1947,N 13,33:2
  Beyond Glory 1948,Ag 4,18:2
  Sealed Verdict 1948,N 3,36:2
  Connecticut Yankee in King Arthur's Court, A
    1949,Ap 8,31:2
  Streets of Laredo 1949,My 12,28:2
  Red, Hot and Blue 1949,O 20,39:2
  Chicago Deadline 1949,N 3,37:2
  Let's Dance 1950,N 30,42:2
  Appointment With Danger 1951,My 10,38:2
  Big Jim McLain 1952,S 18,35:2
  Plunder of the Sun 1953,Ag 27,22:1
  Hondo 1953,N 27,99:9
  Ring of Fear 1954,Jl 29,18:3
  Screaming Mimi 1958,Je 26,23:3

Felmy, Hansjorg
Aren't We Wonderful? 1959,O 16,27:1
Shadows Grow Longer, The 1962,Je 11,36:4
Torn Curtain 1966,Jl 28,23:1
Felmy, Jorg
Station Six-Sahara 1964,N 12,40:2
Felsenstein, Walter (Director)
Fidelio 1961,My 13,10:1
Felsenstein, Walter (Screenwriter)
Fidelio 1961,My 13,10:1
Felsette, Laurelle
Father Goose 1964,D 11,55:1
Felton, Bostic
Cool World, The 1964,Ap 21,42:1
Felton, Earl (Original Author)
Man Hunt 1936,Ja 30,14:2
Bengal Tiger 1936,Jl 30,22:1
World Premiere 1941,Ag 21,15:2
Criminal Court 1946,N 16,15:3
Angel on the Amazon 1948,D 27,16:4
Trapped 1949,N 26,10:6
Felton, Earl (Screenwriter)
Fish 1936,Ja 25,18:5
Freshman Love 1936,Ja 25,18:5
Bengal Tiger 1936,Jl 30,22:1
Bad Guy 1937,Ag 26,25:2
Prison Nurse 1938,Mr 4,17:5
Calling All Marines 1939,O 26,27:2
Lone Wolf Takes a Chance, The 1941,Ap 7,13:2
World Premiere 1941,Ag 21,15:2
Pittsburgh Kid, The 1941,S 23,27:4
Pardon my Past 1946,Ja 28,15:5
Trapped 1949,N 26,10:6
Las Vegas Story, The 1952,Ja 31,37:6
Narrow Margin, The 1952,My 5,18:7
Happy Time, The 1952,O 31,30:2
20,000 Leagues Under the Sea 1954,D 24,7:2
Rawhide Years, The 1956,Je 16,12:2
Felton, Felix
Adventures of Sadie, The 1955,My 18,35:2
2nd Best Secret Agent in the Whole Wide World,
The 1966,Ap 28,49:1
Felton, Mariene
Three bad Sisters 1956,F 13,24:1
Felton, Verna
She Wrote the Book 1946,Je 20,20:3
Buccaneer's Girl 1950,Mr 27,19:2
Gunfighter, The 1950,Je 24,7:2
Don't Bother to Knock 1952,Jl 19,8:2
Picnic 1956,F 17,13:3
Oklahoman, The 1957,My 15,39:1
Fenady, Andrew J (Producer)
Stakeout on Dope Street 1958,Ap 24,38:1
Ride Beyond Vengance 1966,S 29,60:1
Fenady, Andrew J (Screenwriter)
Stakeout on Dope Street 1958,Ap 24,38:1
Ride Beyond Vengance 1966,S 29,60:1
Fenderson, Reginald
Green Pastures, The 1936,Jl 17,20:1
Fenemore, Stephen
Yellow Balloon, The 1954,O 13,28:2
Feng, Julie Yeh
Shepherd Girl, The 1965,S 2,36:3
Feng, Lin
Shepherd Girl, The 1965,S 2,36:3
Feng, Tien
Last Woman of Shang, The 1964,D 15,56:2
Feng, Yueh (Director)
Last Woman of Shang, The 1964,D 15,56:2
Lady General, The 1965,F 12,19:1
Fenin, L A
Petersburg Nights 1934,S 10,20:4
Alexander Nevsky 1939,Mr 23,27:1
Secret Brigade 1951,Mr 19,23:2
Sadko 1953,Je 1,18:6
Fenisch, Erna (Screenwriter)
Confession of Ina Kahn, The 1958,Ja 1,31:4
Fenn, Jean
Serenade 1956,Mr 24,21:1 (Incorrect in this
edition; use 1956,Mr 23,21:1 elsewhere)
Fennell, Albert (Producer)
Green Scarf, The 1955,Ja 15,10:2
Next to no Time 1960,My 28,13:2
Innocents, The 1961,D 26,15:2
Burn, Witch, Burn 1962,Jl 5,21:2 (In Addenda)
Fennell, Rufus
Dark Sands 1938,Ag 17,23:4
Fennelly, Parker
Lost Boundaries 1949,Jl 1,14:4
Whistle at Eaton Falls, The 1951,O 11,49:2
Trouble With Harry, The 1955,O 18,46:2
It Happened to Jane 1959,Ag 6,18:3
Russians are Coming the Russians are Coming,
The 1966,My 26,55:1
Fennelly, Vincent (Producer)
Seven Angry Men 1955,Ap 2,15:2
At Gunpoint 1956,F 4,24:5
Crime in the Streets 1956,My 24,27:4
Fenneman, George (Narrator)
Tanga Tika 1953,O 6,34:4
World Dances 1954,N 8,24:6

Fenner, Walter
Sap From Syracuse, The 1930,Jl 26,16:4
Juarez 1939,Ap 26,27:1
You Can't Fool Your Wife 1940,My 24,23:4
Lost Angel 1944,Ap 10,14:1
Fennerty, Warren
Murder, Inc 1960,Je 29,26:6
Fenton, Earl (Original Author)
Beautiful Blonde From Bashful Bend, The
1949,My 28,11:2
Fenton, Earl (Screenwriter)
Lone Wolf Keeps a Date, The 1941,Ja 2,24:3
Night Plane From Chungking 1943,My 31,13:2
Fenton, Frank
Navy Comes Through, The 1942,N 12,30:3
Lady of Burlesque 1943,My 14,17:2
Claudia 1943,N 5,23:2
Buffalo Bill 1944,Ap 20,22:6
Secret Command 1944,Je 14,16:2
Big Noise, The 1944,S 23,16:1
Destiny 1945,F 3,16:5
Hold That Blonde 1945,N 8,17:2
If I'm Lucky 1946,S 20,41:3
Hit Parade of 1947 1947,My 5,32:8
Magic Town 1947,O 8,29:2
Relentless 1948,Mr 6,17:3
Hazard 1948,Je 3,19:2
Mexican Hayride 1949,Ja 12,33:3
Lawless, The 1950,Je 23,29:2
Wyoming Mail 1950,O 23,26:5
Rogue River 1951,F 16,21:4
Fenton, Frank (Original Author)
Woman Chases Man 1937,Je 11,26:2
International Settlement 1938,F 12,20:3
Keep Smiling 1938,Ag 10,15:2
While New York Sleeps 1938,D 22,25:3
Golden Fleecing, The 1940,N 7,33:4
Nocturne 1946,N 11,42:2
Fenton, Frank (Screenwriter)
Step Lively, Jeeves 1937,Ap 2,19:6
Angel's Holiday 1937,My 29,20:2
Wild and Woolly 1937,S 6,20:1
Saint in London, The 1939,Jl 19,23:3
Saint Takes Over, The 1940,My 28,29:3
Millionaires in Prison 1940,Jl 16,21:3
Date With the Falcon, A 1941,N 25,33:2
Falcon takes Over, The 1942,My 30,9:2
Sky's the Limit, The 1943,S 3,15:2
Lady Luck 1946,O 31,22:3
Night Song 1948,Ja 29,27:5
Malaya 1950,F 23,33:1
Walk Softly Stranger 1950,O 16,30:5
His Kind of Woman 1951,Ag 30,20:2
Man With a Cloak, The 1951,N 28,37:2
Wild North, The 1952,My 12,21:2
Ride Vaquero 1953,Jl 16,17:2
Escape from Fort Bravo 1954,Ja 23,11:2
River of no Return 1954,My 1,13:2
Garden of Evil 1954,Jl 10,17:1
Untamed 1955,Mr 12,11:6
These Wilder Years 1956,Ag 18,11:2
Wings of Eagles, The 1957,F 1,28:1
Fenton, Leslie
What Price Glory 1926,N 24,26:4
Gateway of the Moon, The 1928,Ja 9,20:1
Showdown, The 1928,Mr 5,21:1
Drag Net, The 1928,Je 4,13:2
First Kiss, The 1928,Ag 20,21:3
Girls Gone Wild 1929,Ap 22,23:1
Dangerous Woman, A 1929,My 20,22:6
Broadway 1929,My 28,36:2
Man I Love, The 1929,My 28,36:2
Woman Trap 1929,Ag 31,13:4
Paris Bound 1929,S 21,17:1
Last Performance, The 1929,N 4,28:1
Dynamite 1929,D 28,11:1
Man Who Came Back, The 1931,Ja 3,21:2
Public Enemy, The 1931,Ap 24,27:1
Kick In 1931,My 25,17:1
Murder at Midnight 1931,O 5,17:3
Guilty Generation, The 1931,N 21,20:4
Hatchet Man, The 1932,F 4,25:2
Famous Ferguson Case, The 1932,Ap 25,18:6
Strange Love of Molly Louvain, The
1932,My 9,19:5
Thunder Below 1932,Je 20,11:2
Air Mail 1932,N 7,20:3
F P 1 1933,S 16,9:3
Night Flight 1933,O 7,18:4
Lady Killer 1934,Ja 1,28:2
I Believed in You 1934,Ap 11,25:3
Marie Galante 1934,N 21,23:4
Star of Midnight 1935,Ap 12,26:5
Casino Murder Case, The 1935,Ap 17,26:5
Stolen Harmony 1935,Ap 20,16:2
Chinatown Squad 1935,My 30,21:1
Men Without Names 1935,Je 29,16:2
Two in the Dark 1936,F 1,9:2
Murder on a Bridle Path 1936,Ap 11,19:2
Sworn Enemy 1936,S 12,20:1
Longest Night, The 1936,O 17,21:2
House of Secrets 1937,F 22,13:1
China Passage 1937,Ap 16,27:2

Fenton, Leslie— Cont
Boys Town 1938,S 9,25:1
Fenton, Leslie (Director)
Tell no Tales 1939,Je 2,27:3
Stronger Than Desire 1939,Je 30,17:3
Man From Dakota, The 1940,F 22,29:2
Golden Fleecing, The 1940,N 7,33:4
Saint's Vacation, The 1941,Je 13,22:2
Tomorrow the World 1944,D 22,12:4
Pardon my Past 1946,Ja 28,15:5
Miracle Can Happen, A 1948,F 4,28:4
Saigon 1948,Ap 1,30:5
Lulu Belle 1948,Je 21,18:3
Whispering Smith 1949,F 15,28:2
Streets of Laredo 1949,My 12,28:2
Redhead and the Cowboy, The 1951,Je 6,37:2
Fenton, Leslie (Producer)
Pardon my Past 1946,Ja 28,15:5
Fenton, Lucile
Citizen Saint 1948,My 28,28:2
Fenton, Mabel
How Molly Made Good 1915,O 20,5:5
Fenton, Mark
Behold my Wife 1920,O 11,19:3
Name the Man 1924,F 4,23:3
Spirit of the U S A, The 1924,My 21,22:3
Thank You 1925,O 6,30:1
Four Horsemen of the Apocalypse, The
1926,S 27,27:3
Fenton, Shane
Dream Maker, The 1964,Ap 23,34:1
Fenton, Verna
Little Egypt 1951,Ag 30,20:3
Fentsch, Erna
Klosterjaeger, Der 1936,Ja 3,13:7
Fenwick, Jean
Mary of Scotland 1936,Jl 31,22:2
Arrest Bulldog Drummond 1939,Ja 12,23:2
Tell no Tales 1939,Je 2,27:3
That Uncertain Feeling 1941,My 2,25:1
Ellery Queen and the Murder Ring
1941,O 21,29:4
Street Corner 1948,D 4,9:4
Fenwick, Peg (Screenwriter)
All That Heaven Allows 1956,F 29,35:1
Fenyes, Szaboles (Composer)
Maria Noever 1937,Ap 9,19:2
Feodoroff, Leo
Music Master, The 1927,Ja 17,12:4 (In Addenda)
Ferar, Rahela
I Even Met Happy Gypsies 1968,Mr 21,57:1
Feraude, Maurice de
Bill or Crainquebille 1923,S 3,9:3
Feraudy, Jacques
Tillers of the Soil 1927,Ap 5,30:7
Heart of a Clown 1928,Ja 17,23:2
Marianne of my Youth; (Marianne de ma
Jeunesse) 1959,Ja 20,43:1
Ferber, Edna (Original Author)
Our Mrs McChesney 1918,Ag 19,7:1
So Big 1925,Ja 5,19:1
Welcome Home 1925,My 18,12:1
Classified 1925,N 2,20:1
Gigolo 1926,O 5,27:1
Mother Knows Best 1928,S 17,27:1
Show Boat 1929,Ap 18,32:3
Hard to Get 1929,S 28,17:3
Royal Family of Broadway, The 1930,D 23,25:1
Cimarron 1931,Ja 27,20:5
Expert, The 1932,F 27,22:1
So Big 1932,Ap 30,19:3
Dinner at Eight 1933,Ag 24,18:1
Glamour 1934,My 12,12:3
Show Boat 1936,My 15,29:4
Come and Get It 1936,N 12,31:1
Stage Door 1937,O 8,27:2
Saratoga Trunk 1945,N 22,39:2
Show Boat 1951,Jl 20,14:1
So Big 1953,O 22,34:2
Giant 1956,O 11,51:1
Ice Palace 1960,Je 30,22:1
Cimarron 1961,F 17,12:2
Ferber, Nat (Original Author)
Circumstantial Evidence 1945,Ap 21,18:3
Fercella, Enzo (Screenwriter)
Hands Over the City 1964,S 18,28:1
Ferdi, Weiss
Schuetzen Koenig, Der 1933,My 3,15:5 (In
Addenda)
Ferdin, Pamelyn
One and Only Genuine Original Family Band,
The 1968,Mr 22,55:1
Ferdinand, Roger (Screenwriter)
Man and his Wife, A 1939,Mr 28,20:1
Ferdl, Weiss
Meisterdetektiv, Der 1934,F 13,23:2
Die Mutter der Kompagnie 1934,Mr 9,22:3
Beiden Seehunde, Die 1935,Mr 9,19:2
Konjunkturritter 1935,Ap 29,12:4
Pantoffelhelden 1935,O 21,22:5
Alles Weg'n Dem Hund 1936,Mr 31,17:3
Muede Theodor, Der 1936,O 24,23:2
Gordian, Der Tyrann 1937,Je 21,15:3
Lachdoktor, Der; Laugh Doctor, The

Ferdl, Weiss— Cont
1938,Mr 12,13:4
Arme Millionar, Der; Poor Millionaire, The
1939,D 30,9:2
Ferenczy, Karoly
Oeroek Titok, Az; Eternal Secret, The
1940,Mr 9,19:3
Feres, Marcel
Easiest Profession, The 1960,Mr 26,15:7
Ferez, Christian
Gervaise 1957,N 12,46:1
Ferguson, Anna
Wee Geordie 1956,O 8,31:1
Ferguson, Casson
Flame of the Desert 1919,O 27,9:3
Madame X 1920,S 27,18:1
Bunty Pulls the Strings 1921,Ja 9,VI,2:1 (In Addenda)
At the End of the World 1921,Ag 15,14:3
Law and the Woman, The 1922,Ja 22,VI,3:1 (In Addenda)
Borderland 1922,Jl 24,10:2
Drums of Fate 1923,Ja 15,18:3
Gentleman of Leisure, A 1923,Jl 16,14:2
Road to Yesterday, The 1925,D 1,22:4
Cobra 1925,D 7,19:1
For Alimony Only 1926,S 21,33:1
King of Kings, The 1927,Ap 20,29:2
Tenth Avenue 1928,O 9,35:1
Ferguson, Elsie
Barbary Sheep 1917,S 10,11:3
Rise of Jennie Cushing, The 1917,N 12,11:3
Song of Songs, The 1918,F 19,11:2
Lie, The 1918,Ap 15,13:3
Danger Mark, The 1918,Jl 8,9:4
Heart of the Wilds 1918,Ag 19,7:1
Under the Greenwood Tree 1918,D 9,11:4
His Parisian Wife 1919,Ja 20,13:2
Marriage Price, The 1919,Mr 17,13:2
Eyes of the Soul 1919,Ap 21,13:4
Avalanche, The 1919,Je 30,16:3
Society Exile, A 1919,Ag 18,9:2
Witness for the Defense, The 1919,S 15,16:3
His House in Order 1920,Mr 8,9:5
His House in Order 1920,Mr 8,9:6
Lady Rose's Daughter 1920,Ag 30,12:3
Footlights 1921,S 9,IV,4:1
Peter Ibbetson; (Forever) 1921,O 17,18:1
Scarlet Pages 1930,D 6,21:3
Ferguson, Frank
Beginning or the End, The 1947,F 21,15:1
They Won't Believe Me 1947,Jl 17,16:2
Variety Girl 1947,O 16,34:4
Miracle of the Bells, The 1948,Mr 17,30:1
Vicious Circle, The 1948,Jl 22,27:2
Abbott and Costello Meet Frankenstein
1948,Jl 29,17:2
Walls of Jericho, The 1948,Ag 5,16:2
Rachel and the Stranger 1948,S 20,21:2
Walk a Crooked Mile 1948,O 13,31:2
That Wonderful Urge 1948,D 22,29:6
Caught 1949,F 18,26:4
Slightly French 1949,My 27,25:3
Follow Me Quietly 1949,Jl 8,14:5
Roseanna McCoy 1949,O 13,33:2
Good Humor Man, The 1950,Jl 14,17:2
Furies, The 1950,Ag 17,23:2
He's a Cockeyed Wonder 1950,O 20,32:4
West Point Story, The 1950,D 23,11:3
Frenchie 1951,F 12,19:2
On Dangerous Ground 1952,F 13,35:2
Rancho Notorious 1952,My 15,39:5
Winning Team, The 1952,Je 21,12:2
Million Dollar Mermaid 1952,D 5,35:2
Beast From 20,000 Fathoms, The 1953,Je 25,23:1
Wicked Woman 1954,Mr 27,13:6
Johnny Guitar 1954,My 28,19:2
Drum Beat 1954,N 18,42:1
Young at Heart 1955,Ja 20,35:1
McConnell Story, The 1955,S 30,23:1
This Could Be the Night 1957,My 15,39:1
Light in the Forest, The 1958,Jl 11,15:2
Andy Hardy Comes Home 1958,D 24,00:0
Sunrise at Campobello 1960,S 29,32:1
Hush...Hush, Sweet Charlotte 1965,Mr 4,36:1
Ferguson, Graeme (Director)
Love Goddesses, The 1965,Mr 4,36:2
Ferguson, Graeme (Producer)
Love Goddesses, The 1965,Mr 4,36:2
Ferguson, Graeme (Screenwriter)
Love Goddesses, The 1965,Mr 4,36:2
Ferguson, Helen
Miss Lulu Bett 1921,D 25,VI,2:1
Hungry Hearts 1922,N 27,18:1
Famous Mrs Fair, The 1923,Ap 23,18:3
Within the Law 1923,Ap 30,11:2
Unknown Purple, The 1924,Mr 24,13:1
Ferguson, Margaret (Original Author)
Sign of the Ram, The 1948,Mr 4,30:2
Ferguson, Myrtle
Topsy and Eva 1927,Ag 8,10:3
Ferguson, Norman
Reluctant Dragon, The 1941,Jl 25,12:2

Ferguson, Norman (Director)
Three Caballeros, The 1945,F 5,20:1
Ferguson, Norman (Producer)
Saludos Amigos 1943,F 13,8:2
Ferguson, Ron (Original Author)
Big Business 1937,Je 1,27:2
Hot Water 1937,N 5,19:4
Ferguson, W B (Original Author)
Garrison's Finish 1923,My 28,18:2
Man With 100 Faces 1938,N 1,27:2
Ferguson, W J
Passers By 1920,Je 21,13:1
To Have and to Hold 1922,N 6,13:1
Fergusson, Harvey (Original Author)
Wolf Song 1929,F 25,16:1
Hot Saturday 1932,N 5,12:5
Fergusson, Harvey (Screenwriter)
It Happened in Hollywood 1937,O 2,18:1
Stand up and Fight 1939,Ja 27,17:2
Feriac, Anouck
Live for Life 1967,D 19,59:1
Ferida, Luisa
Re Burlone, Il 1936,Mr 28,11:3
Tutta la Vita in una Notte; All of Life in one
Night 1940,My 2,29:6
Stella del Mare; Star of the Sea 1940,My 3,17:6
Avventura di Salvator Rosa, Un; Adventure of
Salvator Rosa, An 1940,S 20,27:3
Conte di Brechard, Il; Count of Brechard, The
1940,O 24,31:3
Iron Crown 1949,Je 11,11:2
Ferjac, Anouck
We Are all Murderers 1957,Ja 9,27:2
Ferkauf, Betty
Broken Hearts 1926,Mr 3,26:1
Ferman, Robert (Producer)
Sweet Love, Bitter 1967,Ja 31,50:1
Fermas, Nicos
Barefoot Battalion 1954,My 29,13:4
Girl in Black, A 1957,S 17,39:2
Fernanda, Maria
Amazon Trader, The 1956,N 17,17:6
Fernandel
Paris-Beguin 1932,D 31,10:1
He 1933,D 27,23:6
Ordonnance, L'; Orderly, The 1935,Jl 1,22:3
Porteuse de Pain, La 1936,Jl 1,29:5
Carnet de Bal, Un 1938,Mr 26,12:1
Heartbeat 1939,S 5,21:3
Harvest 1939,O 3,19:4
Well-Digger's Daughter, The 1946,S 30,21:4
Francis the First 1947,N 20,38:4
Fric-Frac 1948,My 29,8:6
Nais 1948,Je 16,37:2
Ignace 1950,S 19,39:4
Hoboes in Paradise 1950,O 9,21:5
Three Sinners 1952,Jl 8,23:2
Topaze 1952,O 28,37:1
Cupboard was Bare, The; (Armoire Volante, L')
1952,N 4,33:1
Little World of Don Camillo, The
1953,Ja 14,27:1
Red Inn, The 1954,Je 8,25:2
French Touch, The 1954,S 2,18:2
Sheep Has Five Legs, The 1955,Ag 10,19:2
Return of Don Camillo, The 1956,Mr 27,41:1
Wild Oat, The 1956,Je 28,33:2
Around the World in 80 Days 1956,O 18,37:1
Pantaloons 1956,D 26,34:1
Three Feet in a Bed 1957,My 18,23:2
Fernandel the Dressmaker 1957,Jl 1,19:2
Paris Holiday 1958,My 10,19:2
Man in the Raincoat, The 1958,Jl 15,21:2
Senechal the Magnificent 1958,O 14,44:1
Forbidden Fruit 1959,F 23,19:1
Law Is the Law, The 1959,Mr 11,41:2
Virtuous Bigamist, The 1959,My 28,34:3
Easiest Profession, The 1960,Mr 26,15:7
Big Chief, The 1960,Ap 27,32:1
Cow and I, The 1961,Je 6,42:2
Devil and the 10 Commandments, The (Episode
5) 1963,O 15,44:1
My Wife's Husband 1965,Ja 27,26:1
Fernandez, Abel
Second Chance 1953,Jl 23,20:2
Target Zero 1955,N 16,43:2
Harder They Fall, The 1956,My 10,26:3
Last Wagon, The 1956,S 22,20:2
Pork Chop Hill 1959,My 30,9:2
Fernandez, Bijou
New Toys 1925,F 17,18:1
Just Suppose 1926,Ja 18,26:2
Fernandez, Carlos
Brave One, The 1957,Mr 22,26:1
Fernandez, E L
Eye for Eye 1918,D 23,9:1
Fernandez, Emilio
Buenaventura, La 1934,S 15,20:3
Cruz Diablo 1935,Ap 6,10:1
Adios, Nicanor 1938,Mr 14,13:2
Amor con Amor se Paga; Love for Love
1940,Mr 16,8:2
Flor Sylvestre 1945,Ja 16,17:2

Fernandez, Emilio— Cont
Cucaracha, La 1961,N 2,42:1
Reward, The 1965,S 16,55:1
Appaloosa, The 1966,S 15,51:1
Return of the Seven 1966,O 20,52:5
Covenant with Death, A 1967,F 16,32:3
Fernandez, Emilio (Director)
Passion Island 1943,My 1,11:2
Maria Candelaria 1944,S 12,23:7
Flor Sylvestre 1945,Ja 16,17:2
Pearl, The 1948,F 18,36:4
Enamorada 1949,D 3,8:6
Torch, The 1950,Ag 21,15:2
Hidden River 1950,D 1,31:2
Rosanna 1956,My 17,37:2
Fernandez, Emilio (Screenwriter)
Adios, Nicanor 1938,Mr 14,13:2
Passion Island 1943,My 1,11:2
Pearl, The 1948,F 18,36:4
Enamorada 1949,D 3,8:6
Torch, The 1950,Ag 21,15:2
Hidden River 1950,D 1,31:2
Rosanna 1956,My 17,37:2
Fernandez, Esther
Alla en el Rancho Grande 1936,N 23,17:3
Baul Macabro, El; Macabre Trunk, The
1937,N 30,26:3
Adelita, La 1938,O 12,35:2
Tierra Brava 1938,O 29,15:6
Mi Candidato; My Candidate 1938,O 31,12:3
Hombres de Mar; Men of the Sea 1938,N 7,23:6
Rancho Grande 1938,D 2,27:2
Ojos Tapatios 1939,F 13,13:3
Luces de Barriada; Neighborhood Lights
1940,S 2,19:2
Alla en el Tropico; Down in the Tropics
1943,My 8,19:3
Two Years Before the Mast 1946,S 25,39:2
Pancho Villa Returns 1950,O 24,34:6
Fernandez, Felix
Mad Queen, The 1950,O 27,24:3
Rocket From Calabuch 1958,O 8,41:1
Fernandez, Fernando
Fugitive, The 1947,D 26,22:2
Enamorada 1949,D 3,8:6
Hidden River 1950,D 1,31:2
Fernandez, Jaime
Adventures of Robinson Crusoe, The
1954,Ag 6,10:5
Massacre 1956,Je 2,13:5
Guns for San Sebastian 1968,Mr 21,57:2
Fernandez, Jesus
Nazarin 1968,Je 21,48:1
Fernandez, Juano
Two Loves 1961,Je 22,23:2
Fernandez, Nani
Don Quixote 1949,My 13,29:3
Fernandez, Peter
City Across the River 1949,Ap 8,31:3
Fernandez, Severo
Noches de Buenos Aires 1935,D 10,31:3
Noches de Buenos Aires; Buenos Aires Nights
1935,D 12,33:4
Fernau, Rudolf
Verraeter 1937,Ja 23,13:1
Confess, Dr Corda 1960,O 24,25:5
Ferney, Ernest
Stolen Life 1939,Je 15,27:2
Ferno, John (Cinematographer)
Spanish Earth, The 1937,Ag 21,7:2
400,000,000, The 1939,Mr 8,19:2
Ferno, John (Director)
400,000,000, The 1939,Mr 8,19:2
Fernside, John
Uncivilized 1937,N 17,27:4
Overlanders, The 1946,D 20,31:2
Bush Christmas 1947,N 27,50:4
Massacre Hill 1950,D 14,51:3
Ferny
Moscow Nights 1938,My 3,19:3
Ferra, Margot
Lied vom Leben, Das 1931,O 19,28:1
Ferracuti, Aldo
Lucia di Lammermoor 1947,N 1,11:3
Ferraday, Lisa
Belle of New York, The 1952,Mr 6,25:6
California Conquest 1952,Je 7,22:6
Merry Widow, The 1952,S 25,38:1
Kentuckian, The 1955,S 2,13:2
Death of a Scoundrel 1956,N 6,30:1
Ferrandis, Gloria
Dark River 1956,F 27,19:4
Ferrandi, Maria Giuseppina
Tomorrow is too Late 1952,Ap 14,22:2
Ferrare, Christina
Impossible Years, The 1968,D 6,54:1
Ferrari, Angelo
Cyrano de Bergerac 1925,Jl 6,12:2
Richthofen: The Red Knight of the Air
1929,S 2,16:1
Acht Tage Glueck 1931,Jl 24,22:1
Ferrari, Mario
Passaporto Rosso 1936,S 2,18:2
Giovanni De Medici, The Leader 1940,Ja 5,15:4

Ferrari, Mario— Cont
Between Two Worlds 1940,F 9,15:2
Terra di Nessuno; Nobody's Land 1940,O 25,25:4
Women Without Names 1951,Ag 7,22:2
Life of Donizetti, The 1952,Ap 26,19:2
Tormento 1953,Ap 4,9:2
Queen of Sheba, The 1953,N 4,29:3
Ten Commandments, The 1958,Ap 7,26:1

Ferrari, Paglo
White Voices; Voci Blanche 1965,Ap 13,32:2

Ferraro, Enrique
Where Words Fail; Donde Mueren las Palabraso 1948,Ag 19,18:4

Ferraro, Luigi
Hell Raiders of the Deep 1954,Jl 3,9:2

Ferrayra, Jose A (Director)
Ayudame a Vivir; Help Me to Live 1938,My 7,18:2

Ferraz, Catherina
Snowbound 1949,F 21,20:2
Flame and the Flesh 1954,My 3,21:2

Ferre, Cliff
About Face 1952,My 24,15:3
She's Back on Broadway 1953,Mr 12,24:2

Ferreira, Bibi
End of the River, The 1948,Je 21,18:2

Ferreira, Roberto
Given Word, The 1964,Mr 25,47:1

Ferrell, Ray
Hell's Five Hours 1957,Jl 24,18:1
Strangers When we Meet 1960,Je 30,22:2

Ferrell, Raymond
Zero Hour 1957,N 14,41:1

Ferrell, Tony
Great Flamario, The 1945,Ja 15,15:5

Ferrer, Aurelia
Where Words Fail; Donde Mueren las Palabraso 1948,Ag 19,18:4

Ferrer, Jose
Joan of Arc 1948,N 12,30:5
Whirlpool 1950,Ja 14,9:2
Crisis 1950,Jl 4,10:2
Cyrano De Bergerac 1950,N 17,31:2
Anything Can Happen 1952,Ap 4,21:1
Moulin Rouge 1953,F 11,33:5
Miss Sadie Thompson 1953,D 24,9:1
Caine Mutiny, The 1954,Je 25,17:1
Deep in my Heart 1954,D 10,35:2
Shrike, The 1955,Jl 8,15:2
Cockleshell Heroes, The 1956,Je 4,25:2
Great Man, The 1957,Ja 2,28:2
I Accuse! 1958,Mr 6,32:1
High Cost of Loving, The 1958,My 17,12:1
Lawrence of Arabia 1962,D 17,5:6
Nine Hours to Rama 1963,Ap 4,58:2
Cyrano and D'Artagnan 1964,S 26,16:1
Stop Train 349 1964,N 12,40:2
Greatest Story Ever Told, The 1965,F 16,40:2
Ship of Fools 1965,Jl 29,18:1
Enter Laughing 1967,Ag 1,24:1

Ferrer, Jose (Director)
Shrike, The 1955,Jl 8,15:2
Cockleshell Heroes, The 1956,Je 4,25:2
Great Man, The 1957,Ja 2,28:2
I Accuse! 1958,Mr 6,32:1
High Cost of Loving, The 1958,My 17,12:1
Return to Peyton Place 1961,My 6,26:1
State Fair 1962,Ap 12,41:4

Ferrer, Jose (Screenwriter)
Great Man, The 1957,Ja 2,28:2

Ferrer, Mel
Lost Boundaries 1949,Jl 1,14:4
Born to be Bad 1950,S 29,31:5
Brave Bulls, The 1951,Ap 19,39:2
Scaramouche 1952,My 9,20:2
Rancho Notorious 1952,My 15,39:5
Lili 1953,Mr 11,36:7
Knights of the Round Table 1954,Ja 8,17:2
Saadia 1954,Mr 20,10:5
War and Peace 1956,Ag 22,26:2
Paris Does Strange Things 1957,Mr 30,13:2
Vintage, The 1957,My 9,36:5
Sun Also Rises, The 1957,Ag 24,12:2
Fraulein 1958,Je 9,27:2
World, The Flesh and the Devil, The 1959,My 21,35:1
Blood and Roses 1961,O 12,41:4
Longest Day, The 1962,O 5,28:1
Devil and the 10 Commandments, The (Episode 4) 1963,O 15,44:1
Fall of the Roman Empire, The 1964,Mr 27,14:2
Sex and the Single Girl 1964,D 26,9:2
Greco, El 1967,My 24,52:2

Ferrer, Mel (Director)
Secret Fury, The 1950,Je 22,34:2
Vendetta 1950,D 26,19:1
Green Mansions 1959,Mr 20,26:1

Ferrer, Mel (Producer)
Greco, El 1967,My 24,52:2
Wait Until Dark 1967,O 27,48:1

Ferrer, Tony
Vengeance of Fu Manchu, The 1968,F 15,47:1

Ferreri, Marco
Casanova 1965,Jl 21,43:1

Ferreri, Marco (Director)
Conjugal Bed, The 1963,S 17,30:1
Ape Woman, The 1964,S 23,55:1
Man With the Balloons, The 1968,Je 25,33:2

Ferreri, Marco (Original Author)
Conjugal Bed, The 1963,S 17,30:1
Man With the Balloons, The 1968,Je 25,33:2

Ferreri, Marco (Screenwriter)
Conjugal Bed, The 1963,S 17,30:1
Mafioso 1964,Jl 1,42:1
Ape Woman, The 1964,S 23,55:1
Man With the Balloons, The 1968,Je 25,33:2

Ferrero, Anna Maria
We Lived Through Buchenwald 1947,Jl 24,27:3
Sky Is Red, The 1952,My 27,30:2
Count of St Elmo, The 1953,Mr 14,13:2
Strange Deception 1953,My 27,28:2
War and Peace 1956,Ag 22,26:2
Life and Music of Giuseppe Verdi, The 1957,My 2,26:2
It Happened in the Park 1957,Ag 13,23:2
Notte Brava, La 1962,Ja 25,25:2
Love and Larceny 1963,F 2,5:6

Ferrero, Danton
Secret Seven, The 1940,Ag 12,11:6

Ferretti, Jacobo (Composer)
Cinderella 1953,My 15,20:2

Ferreyra, Jose A (Director)
Besos Brujos; Bewitching Kisses 1939,O 21,12:3
Ley que Olvidaron, La; Law They Forgot, The 1940,Ja 13,11:3

Ferreyro, Dora
Oro entre Barro; Gold in Clay 1940,Jl 1,23:2

Ferri, Liana (Screenwriter)
Beautiful but Dangerous 1958,F 6,24:1

FERRIS
See Also FARIS

Ferris, Audrey
Silver Slave, The 1928,Ja 3,28:2
Beware of Married Men 1928,Ap 10,33:2
Powder my Back 1928,Ag 7,25:4
Women They Talk About 1928,O 15,16:1
Little Wildcat, The 1929,Ja 21,18:4
Glad Rag Doll, The 1929,Je 3,27:2
Honky Tonk 1929,Je 5,32:3

Ferris, Barbara
Tom Thumb 1958,D 24,00:0
Sparrows Don't Sing 1963,My 7,46:2
Children of the Damned 1964,Ja 30,24:2
Pair of Briefs, A 1964,F 3,22:2
Having a Wild Weekend 1965,Ag 19,35:1
Girl-Getters, The 1966,Ap 13,37:6
Interlude 1968,Jl 3,26:1

Ferris, Mercedes
Dama de las Camelias, La 1944,S 26,16:1

Ferris, Walter (Original Author)
Susannah of the Mounties 1939,Je 24,13:2

Ferris, Walter (Screenwriter)
Under Two Flags 1936,My 1,19:1
Lloyds of London 1936,N 26,39:1
Maid of Salem 1937,Mr 4,27:2
Heidi 1937,N 6,14:2
Yank at Oxford, A 1938,F 25,15:1
Four Men and a Prayer 1938,My 7,18:1
Little Princess, The 1939,Mr 11,21:1
Magnificent Fraud, The 1939,Jl 20,16:2
Swiss Family Robinson 1940,F 9,15:3
Tom Brown's School Days 1940,Je 28,22:2
Gallant Blade 1948,O 13,31:3
At Swords Point 1952,Ap 10,37:1

Ferriz, F Nava
Juarez y Maximiliano 1935,F 16,9:2

Ferriz, Miguel A
Mano in Mano 1933,F 20,11:6
Mano a Mano 1938,S 19,16:3
Beso Mortal, El; Fatal Kiss, The 1939,Ja 21,19:3
Night of the Mayas 1941,Ja 14,16:7
Passion Island 1943,My 1,11:2
Creo en Dios 1943,Jl 17,8:3
Flor Sylvestre 1945,Ja 16,17:2

Ferroni, Giorgio (Director)
Tombolo 1949,D 31,9:4

Ferroni, Giorgio (Screenwriter)
Tombolo 1949,D 31,9:4

Ferrusquilla
Littlest Outlaw, The 1955,D 27,31:1
Massacre 1956,Je 2,13:5

Ferry, Christian (Producer)
Rapture 1965,Ag 24,25:3
Blue Max, The 1966,Je 22,38:1

Ferry, Jean (Original Author)
Impossible on Saturday 1966,F 17,29:1

Ferry, Jean (Screenwriter)
Jenny Lamour 1948,Mr 6,17:2
Manon 1950,D 26,19:1
Miquette 1951,F 5,18:2
Daughters of Destiny (Lysistrata); Lysistrata (Daughters of Destiny) 1954,Jl 6,19:1
Wayward Wife, The 1955,Ap 11,29:3
If all the Guys in the World 1957,Ap 23,34:1
Sinners of Paris 1959,Ap 24,23:1

Ferry, Jean (Screenwriter)— Cont
Babette Goes to War 1960,Je 8,46:1
Madame 1963,Mr 21,8:6
Impossible on Saturday 1966,F 17,29:1

Ferry, Minna
Girls Gone Wild 1929,Ap 22,23:1

Fersen, Alessandro
Theodora, Slave Empress 1955,Ja 12,24:2

Ferte, Rene
Last Will of Dr Mabuse, The 1943,Mr 20,11:1

Fertis, Yannis
Electra 1962,D 18,5:2

Ferval
Francis the First 1947,N 20,38:4

Ferzetti, Gabriele
Three Forbidden Stories 1953,N 16,21:4
Wayward Wife, The 1955,Ap 11,29:3
House of Ricordi 1956,Mr 13,32:1
Sins of Casanova 1957,O 7,23:2
Defend my Love; (Difendo il Mio Amore) 1959,O 8,48:7
Hannibal 1960,Ag 4,17:1
Avventura, L' 1961,Ap 5,30:1
Jessica 1962,Ap 20,20:2
Crime Does Not Pay (The Mask); Mask, The (Crime Does Not Pay) 1962,O 17,35:2
Cross of the Living 1963,F 5,5:5
Red Lips 1964,Mr 19,28:2
Bible, The 1966,S 29,60:1
We Still Kill the Old Way 1968,F 29,28:1
Devil in Love, The 1968,Jl 4,13:4

Fescourt, Henri (Director)
Miserables, Les 1926,Jl 9,17:1
Miserables, Les 1927,Ag 23,29:4

Fescourt, Henri (Producer)
Occident, L' 1928,D 16,IX,8:2

Feshenko, S
Land, The 1955,Ap 11,29:3

Fessier, Michael (Producer)
Her Primitive Man 1944,Ap 1,11:1
Merry Monahans, The 1944,O 13,16:2
San Diego, I Love You 1944,N 10,25:1
That's the Spirit 1945,Je 2,11:2
Frontier Gal 1945,D 15,14:2
Lover Come Back 1946,Je 20,20:3
Slave Girl 1947,Jl 18,21:3

Fessier, Michael (Screenwriter)
Society Doctor 1935,F 4,11:3
Exclusive Story 1936,Ja 18,19:2
Speed 1936,My 16,11:2
Valley of the Giants 1938,S 10,20:2
Wings of the Navy 1939,F 4,11:1
Angels Wash Their Faces 1939,S 4,16:2
Espionage Agent 1939,S 23,22:2
It all Came True 1940,Ap 6,13:2
He Stayed for Breakfast 1940,Ag 31,16:2
You'll Never Get Rich 1941,O 24,27:2
You Were Never Lovelier 1942,D 4,31:1
Fired Wife 1943,O 1,15:2
Her Primitive Man 1944,Ap 1,11:1
Greenwich Village 1944,S 28,26:2
Merry Monahans, The 1944,O 13,16:2
San Diego, I Love You 1944,N 10,25:1
That's the Spirit 1945,Je 2,11:2
Frontier Gal 1945,D 15,14:2
Lover Come Back 1946,Je 20,20:3
Slave Girl 1947,Jl 18,21:3
Red Garters 1954,Mr 27,13:5

Fessler, O (Producer)
We Live Again 1948,S 6,17:2

Festa, Pasquale (Producer)
Holiday Island; (Vacanzie a Izchia) 1959,S 22,46:1

Fetchit, Stepin
In old Kentucky 1927,N 21,20:1
Ghost Talks, The 1929,F 18,28:1
Hearts in Dixie 1929,F 28,30:3
Thru Different Eyes 1929,Ap 15,22:6
Show Boat 1929,Ap 18,32:3
William Fox Movietone Follies of 1929 1929,My 27,22:1
Big Time 1929,S 9,30:2
Salute 1929,O 5,22:5
Cameo Kirby 1930,F 8,12:5
Swing High 1930,Je 27,26:3
Big Fight, The 1930,Je 28,9:2
Prodigal, The 1931,Je 27,20:3
Carolina 1934,F 16,17:2
David Harum 1934,Mr 2,23:2
Stand up and Cheer 1934,Ap 20,17:1
World Moves On, The 1934,Je 30,18:5
Judge Priest 1934,O 12,33:1
Marie Galante 1934,N 21,23:4
Helldorado 1935,Ja 7,13:2
County Chairman, The 1935,Ja 19,8:1
One More Spring 1935,F 22,27:1
Charlie Chan in Egypt 1935,Je 24,12:2
Steamboat Around the Bend 1935,S 20,17:2
36 Hours to Live 1936,Ag 15,6:3
Dimples 1936,O 10,21:2
On the Avenue 1937,F 5,17:3
Love Is News 1937,Mr 6,10:1
Fifty Roads to Town 1937,Je 5,21:1
Zenobia 1939,My 15,15:2

Fetchit, Stepin— Cont
  Miracle in Harlem 1949,O 24,19:4
  Bend of the River 1952,Ap 10,37:1
  Sun Shines Bright, The 1954,Mr 17,25:2
Fetherston, Eddie
  Old Ironsides 1926,D 7,21:2
  True to the Navy 1930,My 24,21:2
  Movie Crazy 1932,S 15,19:3
  Cheating Blondes 1933,My 20,11:4
  Lost City, The 1935,F 21,23:3
  Shadows of the Orient 1937,O 11,26:6
  Shadow, The 1937,D 17,33:3
  Women in Prison 1938,Mr 1,19:3
  Who Killed Gail Preston? 1938,My 6,27:2
  Lone Wolf in Paris, The 1938,My 23,21:2
  Homicide Bureau 1939,F 2,17:2
  Second Chance 1947,S 20,12:4
Fetin, V (Director)
  Colt, The 1961,Je 5,37:4
Fetter, Ted (Composer)
  I Dood It 1943,N 11,29:1
Feuchtwanger, Lion (Original Author)
  Power 1934,O 5,29:3
  Oppenheim Family, The 1939,My 24,29:2
Feuermann, Emanuel
  Adventure in Music 1944,Mr 6,17:3
Feuillade, Louis (Director)
  Vampires, Les 1965,S 14,54:1
Feuillade, Louis (Screenwriter)
  Judex 1966,Ap 26,55:1
Feuillere, Edwige
  Topaze 1935,F 16,9:2
  Lucrezia Borgia 1937,O 13,27:2
  Mayerling to Sarajevo 1940,O 30,27:6
  Compliments of Mr Iflow 1941,F 17,10:7
  Marthe Richard 1944,N 9,23:2
  Idiot, The 1948,F 5,26:2
  Blind Desire 1948,Je 10,28:4
  Honorable Catherine, The 1948,Ag 23,13:3
  Eagle with Two Heads 1948,D 30,24:2
  Wicked Duchess, The 1949,N 5,10:5
  Pit of Loneliness 1954,Ap 9,19:2
  Game of Love, The 1954,D 15,41:1
  Adorable Creatures 1956,Ja 11,36:2
  Fruits of Summer 1956,Jl 18,22:2
  Love Is my Profession 1959,Ap 28,41:1
Feuillere, Pierre
  Dawn Over France 1945,Mr 17,17:2
Feyday, Jean (Miscellaneous)
  Dark Eyes 1938,Ap 19,24:5
Feydean, Georges (Original Author)
  Flea in her Ear, A 1968,N 28,66:1
Feydeau, Georges (Original Author)
  Oh, Amelia 1951,D 3,22:2
  Hotel Paradiso 1966,O 15,34:2
Feydeau, J P (Screenwriter)
  Symphonie Fantastique, La 1947,D 8,35:2
Feydeau, Jacques (Original Author)
  Dame de Chez Maxim, La; Woman at Maxim's,
    The 1933,Je 11,IX,2:5
Feyder, Jacques (Director)
  Faces of Children 1926,Je 30,18:1
  Carmen 1928,My 7,29:1
  Shadows of Fear 1928,N 6,35:1
  Nouveaux Messieurs, Les 1929,Ja 13,VIII,7:4
  Kiss, The 1929,N 16,25:2
  Nouveau Messieurs, Les; New Gentlemen, The
    1929,D 15,X,6:5
  Spectre Vert, Le 1930,Je 8,IX,6:1
  Olympia 1930,D 7,IX,6:4
  Anna Christie 1931,Ja 6,25:1
  Si l'Empereur Savait Ca 1931,F 23,20:3
  Daybreak 1931,Je 1,15:1
  Son of India 1931,Jl 25,11:6
  Pension Mimosas 1936,My 6,27:1
  Kermesse Heroique, La 1936,S 23,29:1
  Knight Without Armor 1937,Jl 9,18:1
  Portrait of a Woman 1946,Ap 22,26:2
Feyder, Jacques (Producer)
  Pension Mimosas 1936,My 6,27:1
  Portrait of a Woman 1946,Ap 22,26:2
  Back Streets of Paris 1948,O 16,9:2
Feyder, Jacques (Screenwriter)
  Missing Husbands 1922,My 13,16:1
  Pension Mimosas 1936,My 6,27:1
  Portrait of a Woman 1946,Ap 22,26:2
Ffrangcon-Davies, Gwen
  Nine Days a Queen 1936,O 3,21:1
  Devil's Own, The 1967,Mr 16,53:2
Fiala, Karel
  Lemonade Joe 1967,N 21,53:1
Fialova, Kveta
  Closely Watched Trains 1967,O 16,59:2
  Lemonade Joe 1967,N 21,53:1
  Murder Czech Style 1968,Ag 20,33:1
Fiastri, Jara (Screenwriter)
  Love and Marriage (Saturday, July 18); Saturday,
    July 18 (Love and Marriage) 1966,Ag 5,20:1
  Love and Marriage (The First Night); First Night,
    The (Love and Marriage) 1966,Ag 5,20:1
  Love and Marriage (The Last Resort); Last Resort,
    The (Love and Marriage) 1966,Ag 5,20:1
  Love and Marriage (One Moment Is Enough); One
    Moment Is Enough (Love and Marriage)

  1966,Ag 5,20:1
Fichelseher, W F (Original Author)
  Dancing Heart, The 1958,Ja 18,10:3
Fichter, Jean (Cinematographer)
  Gri-Gri 1956,S 29,12:2
Fickett, Mary
  Man on Fire 1957,Ag 23,10:1
  Kathy O' 1958,S 25,29:2
FIDLER
  See Also FIEDLER
Fidler, Jimmie
  Garden of the Moon 1938,S 24,13:1
Fieberling, Hal
  Set-Up, The 1949,Mr 30,31:2
  Crooked Way, The 1949,S 5,13:2
  Yes Sir, That's my Baby 1949,N 11,31:2
  Sands of Iwo Jima 1949,D 31,9:2
  Dial 1119 1950,D 4,32:6
FIEDLER
  See Also FIDLER
Fiedler, Erich
  Eine Tuer geht Auf 1933,F 6,11:5
  Dell Etappenhase 1938,Ja 1,11:3
  Kleines Bezirksgericht; Little Country Court
    1939,F 18,12:4
  Kluge Schwiegermutter, Die; Wise Mother-in-Law,
    The 1939,O 9,15:3
Fiedler, Franz
  Kadetten 1933,D 26,19:3
Fiedler, John
  12 Angry Men 1957,Ap 15,24:1
  Stage Struck 1958,Ap 23,40:1
  Raisin in the Sun, A 1961,Mr 30,24:1
  That Touch of Mink 1962,Je 15,16:2
  World of Henry Orient, The 1964,Mr 20,27:2
  Kiss Me, Stupid 1964,D 23,22:2
  Fine Madness, A 1966,Je 30,28:2
  Fitzwily 1967,D 21,45:1
  Odd Couple, The 1968,My 3,42:1
Fiedling, Margaret
  You Can't Buy Luck 1937,My 14,21:2
Field, Alexander
  Red Wagon 1936,Je 22,22:1
  Human Monster, The 1940,Mr 25,11:2
  Next of Kin 1943,My 6,25:2
Field, Alice
  Femme Nue, La 1933,Ag 25,12:3
  Celle Vielle Canaille 1935,Ja 12,12:2
  Cette Vielle Canaille 1935,Ja 12,12:2
Field, Arthur L (Producer)
  Twice Blessed 1945,Jl 7,7:5
  Dangerous Partners 1945,N 2,22:4
Field, Ben
  Silver King, The 1929,S 2,16:1
  Michael and Mary 1932,Mr 5,11:2
  Reserved for Ladies 1932,My 21,9:2
  Night and Day 1933,My 29,22:2
  Loyalties 1934,O 26,25:1
  Clairvoyant, The 1935,Je 8,12:2
Field, Betty
  What a Life 1939,O 12,33:1
  Of Mice and Men 1940,F 17,9:2
  Seventeen 1940,F 29,15:2
  Victory 1940,D 23,23:2
  Shepherd of the Hills, The 1941,Jl 31,13:2
  Blues in the Night 1941,D 12,35:2
  Kings Row 1942,F 3,23:2
  Are Husbands Necessary? 1942,Jl 9,17:2
  Flesh and Fantasy 1943,N 18,29:1
  Great Moment, The 1944,N 13,15:2
  Tomorrow the World 1944,D 22,12:4
  Southerner, The 1945,Ag 27,22:3
  Great Gatsby, The 1949,Jl 14,20:5
  Picnic 1956,F 17,13:3
  Bus Stop 1956,S 1,19:2
  Peyton Place 1957,D 13,35:1
  Hound-Dog Man 1960,Ap 28,29:1
  Butterfield 8 1960,N 17,46:1
  Birdman of Alcatraz 1962,Jl 19,19:2
  7 Women 1966,My 5,59:1
  How to Save a Marriage - And Ruin Your Life
    1968,Ja 19,30:1
  Coogan's Bluff 1968,O 3,56:1
Field, Crystal
  Splendor in the Grass 1961,O 11,53:1
Field, Elvin
  None Shall Escape 1944,Ap 7,23:2
Field, Esther
  Mothers of Today 1939,Mr 2,19:2
Field, George
  Blood and Sand 1922,Ag 7,14:2
  Stephen Steps Out 1923,N 19,19:3
Field, Grace
  Avalanche, The 1919,Je 30,16:3
Field, Gustave (Original Author)
  Flight to Hong Kong 1957,Ja 3,28:2
Field, Harry
  Ebb Tide 1937,N 18,27:2
Field, Harry (Producer)
  Go Go Mania 1965,My 20,52:4
Field, Margaret
  Beyond Glory 1948,Ag 4,18:2
  My Friend Irma 1949,S 29,39:2

Field, Margaret— Cont
  Man From Planet X, The 1951,Ap 9,31:2
  For Men Only 1952,Ja 16,21:2
  Raiders, The 1952,D 13,19:2
  So This Is Love 1953,Ag 12,22:1
  Inside Detroit 1956,Ja 28,10:5
Field, Mary
  Prince and the Pauper, The 1937,My 6,23:1
  Call it a Day 1937,My 7,29:2
  White Banners 1938,Je 23,27:1
  Cowboy From Brooklyn 1938,Jl 14,17:1
  Eternally Yours 1939,O 7,11:2
  Dancing Co-Ed 1939,N 10,27:3
  Convicted Woman 1940,F 26,11:2
  Girls of the Road 1940,Jl 22,20:2
  Howards of Virginia, The 1940,S 27,27:1
  Wild Geese Calling 1941,Ag 30,10:2
  Ball of Fire 1942,Ja 16,25:2
  Miss Annie Rooney 1942,Je 8,11:1
  You Were Never Lovelier 1942,D 4,31:1
  Great Gildersleeve, The 1942,D 18,36:8
  Gorilla Man, The 1943,Ja 15,21:4
  Crystal Ball, The 1943,F 19,22:2
  Hello, Frisco, Hello 1943,Mr 25,25:1
  Lady Takes a Chance, A 1943,S 16,25:2
  Frenchman's Creek 1944,S 21,26:2
  Ministry of Fear 1945,F 8,15:2
  Affairs of Susan, The 1945,Mr 29,18:2
  Unseen, The 1945,My 14,20:5
  Miracle on 34th Street 1947,Je 5,32:1
  Life With Father 1947,Ag 16,6:6
  Corpse came C O D, The 1947,Ag 19,27:2
  Up in Central Park 1948,My 27,29:3
  Mr Peabody and the Mermaid 1948,Ag 14,6:5
  Song Is Born, A 1948,O 20,37:2
  Chicken every Sunday 1949,Ja 19,34:2
  Top o' the Morning 1949,S 1,25:2
  Dear Wife 1950,F 2,31:2
  Cheaper by the Dozen 1950,Ap 1,12:2
  Edge of Doom 1950,Ag 4,13:2
  Passage West 1951,Ag 31,12:2
  Private War of Major Benson, The
    1955,Ag 3,27:2
  To Hell and Back 1955,S 23,21:2
  Seven Ways From Sundown 1960,D 22,18:4
Field, Norman
  Invitation 1952,Ja 30,22:6
Field, Pat
  Quiet Week-End 1948,Ag 20,13:2
Field, Percy
  This Freedom 1923,N 28,15:1
Field, Rachel (Original Author)
  All This and Heaven, Too 1940,Jl 5,10:2
  And Now Tomorrow 1944,N 23,38:2
  Time Out of Mind 1947,Ap 7,20:1
Field, Salisbury (Original Author)
  Twin Beds 1920,N 1,13:2
  Wedding Bells 1921,Ag 15,14:3
  Zander the Great 1925,My 4,16:2
  His Greatest Gamble 1934,Jl 18,20:2
  On Such a Night 1937,S 17,29:2
  Twin Beds 1942,My 1,23:4
Field, Sally
  Way West, The 1967,My 25,54:1
Field, Shirley Anne
  Horrors of the Black Museum 1959,Ap 30,37:2
  Once More With Feeling 1960,F 12,22:2
  Entertainer, The 1960,O 4,49:2
  Saturday Night and Sunday Morning
    1961,Ap 4,44:2
  Man in the Moon 1961,Je 13,29:2
  War Lover, The 1963,Mr 7,8:5
  King of the Sun 1963,D 26,33:4
  These Are the Damned 1965,Jl 8,35:1
  Alfie 1966,Ag 25,42:1
Field, Sydney (Screenwriter)
  Spree 1967,N 30,59:2
Field, Sylvia
  Voice of the City, The 1929,Ap 29,29:2
  Her Primitive Man 1944,Ap 1,11:1
  Junior Miss 1945,Je 18,15:4
  All Mine to Give 1959,Ag 4,32:5
Field, Virginia
  Lady is Willing, The 1934,Ag 11,16:5
  Sing, Baby, Sing 1936,S 12,20:1
  Thank You, Jeeves 1936,O 5,25:1
  Ladies in Love 1936,O 29,31:1
  Lloyds of London 1936,N 26,39:1
  London by Night 1937,Ag 13,13:1
  Think Fast, Mr Moto 1937,Ag 16,15:3
  Ali Baba Goes to Town 1937,O 23,14:1
  Lancer Spy 1937,N 4,29:1
  Charlie Chan at Monte Carlo 1937,D 18,18:1
  Mr Moto's Last Warning 1939,Ja 27,17:3
  Captain Fury 1939,My 26,20:2
  Bridal Suite 1939,My 26,20:2
  Sun Never Sets, The 1939,Je 9,26:2
  Mr Moto Takes a Vacation 1939,Je 19,12:6
  Eternally Yours 1939,O 7,11:2
  Cisco Kid and the Lady, The 1939,D 25,29:2
  Waterloo Bridge 1940,My 17,23:2
  Dance, Girl, Dance 1940,O 11,25:2
  Hudson's Bay 1941,Ja 10,23:2
  Singapore Woman 1941,My 12,13:6
  Atlantic Convoy 1942,Jl 6,18:5

Field, Virginia— Cont

Crystal Ball, The 1943,F 19,22:2
Stage Door Canteen 1943,Je 25,13:2
Ladies' Man 1947,Ja 13,18:5
Perfect Marriage, The 1947,Ja 16,30:3
Imperfect Lady, The 1947,My 22,34:5
Repeat Performance 1947,Jl 2,19:2
Christmas Eve 1947,N 28,30:2
Dream Girl 1948,Je 17,29:2
John Loves Mary 1949,F 5,11:2
Connecticut Yankee in King Arthur's Court, A 1949,Ap 8,31:2
Dial 1119 1950,D 4,32:6
Veils of Bagdad, The 1953,N 27,99:9
Appointment With a Shadow 1959,Ja 8,24:2
Explosive Generation, The 1962,F 15,24:2

Fielder, Ann

Dark Angel, The 1935,S 6,12:2

Fielding, Clarissa

Isle of Lost Ships, The 1929,O 26,15:1

Fielding, Claude

Garden of Allah, The 1927,S 3,13:5

Fielding, Edward

Invisible Man Returns, The 1940,Ja 16,19:2
House Across the Bay, The 1940,Mr 22,23:2
Rebecca 1940,Mr 29,25:2
Down Argentine Way 1940,O 18,25:1
Kitty Foyle 1941,Ja 9,27:2
Scotland Yard 1941,Ap 9,33:3
Parachute Battalion 1941,Ag 29,13:2
Belle Starr 1941,N 1,20:2
In This our Life 1942,My 9,10:2
Ten Gentlemen From West Point 1942,Je 5,23:3
Pacific Rendezvous 1942,Jl 8,27:4
Pride of the Yankees, The 1942,Jl 16,23:1
Major and the Minor, The 1942,S 17,21:3
Star Spangled Rhythm 1942,D 31,20:1
Mr Lucky 1943,Jl 23,21:2
What a Woman 1943,D 3,27:2
Lady in the Dark 1944,F 23,17:1
See Here Private Hargrove 1944,Mr 22,17:2
Dead Man's Eyes 1944,O 7,11:2
My Pal, Wolf 1944,O 9,17:2
Belle of the Yukon 1945,Mr 30,18:4
Guest Wife 1945,O 18,21:2

Fielding, Fenella

Foxhole in Cairo 1961,F 16,25:2
Follow a Star 1961,Ap 26,34:1
No Love for Johnnie 1961,D 13,55:1
Old Dark House, The 1963,O 31,26:3
Doctor in Distress 1964,Jl 8,38:2
Arrivederci, Baby! 1966,D 29,22:1

Fielding, Gerald

Garden of Allah, The 1927,S 3,13:5
Just a Gigolo 1931,Je 13,20:4
Night Club Lady, The 1932,Ag 27,13:4
Chump at Oxford, A 1940,F 20,17:3

Fielding, Henry (Original Author)

Tom Jones 1963,O 8,48:1

Fielding, Lorraine (Original Author)

This Time for Keeps 1947,D 5,33:4

Fielding, Margaret

If Winter Comes 1923,S 4,14:1
Drag 1929,Je 21,17:2
Paris 1929,N 8,31:2
Moon's our Home, The 1936,My 13,29:2
To Mary-With Love 1936,Ag 27,16:1
Nancy Steele is Missing 1937,Mr 8,22:1

Fielding, Marjorie

Quiet Wedding 1941,D 29,27:4
Jeannie 1943,S 13,14:2
Yellow Canary, The 1944,Ap 14,24:7
Adventure for Two 1945,D 14,24:5
Quiet Week-End 1948,Ag 20,13:2
Easy Money (Episode 1) 1949,F 14,15:3
Spring in Park Lane 1949,S 21,38:2
Fame Is the Spur 1949,N 8,34:2
Amazing Mr Beecham, The 1949,D 26,33:4
Conspirator 1950,Ap 28,26:2
Mudlark, The 1950,D 25,25:1
Circle of Danger 1951,Jl 12,21:6
Lavender Hill Mob, The 1951,O 16,35:2
Portrait of Clare 1951,D 26,19:6
Franchise Affair, The 1952,Je 6,19:2
Magic Box, The 1952,S 24,40:2
Story of Mandy, The 1953,F 24,21:3
Project M 7 1953,N 27,22:5
Rob Roy 1954,F 4,21:5
Woman's Angle, The 1954,Ag 27,11:6

Fielding, Romaine

Rose of the Golden West 1927,S 26,27:1
Shepherd of the Hills, The 1928,F 20,14:1

Fielding, Sol Baer (Producer)

Jeopardy 1953,Mr 31,36:2
Bright Road 1953,Ap 29,33:5
Trooper Hook 1957,Jl 13,11:2

Fields, Arabella

Love in Morocco 1933,Mr 20,18:3

Fields, Benny

Big Broadcast of 1937, The 1936,O 22,31:1
Minstrel Man 1944,Jl 17,18:5

Fields, Benny (Miscellaneous)

Somebody Loves Me 1952,S 25,38:1

Fields, Dorothy

Stage Door Canteen 1943,Je 25,13:2

Fields, Dorothy (Composer)

Meet the Baron 1933,O 28,20:3
Dancing Lady 1933,D 1,23:2
I Dream too Much 1935,N 29,24:1
In Person 1935,D 13,31:5
When You're in Love 1937,F 19,15:2
One Night in the Tropics 1940,D 20,33:2
Mexican Hayride 1949,Ja 12,33:3
Mr Imperium 1951,O 15,22:2
Lovely to Look At 1952,My 30,11:2

Fields, Dorothy (Miscellaneous)

Roberta 1935,Mr 8,25:2
Hooray for Love 1935,Jl 13,16:2
Every Night at Eight 1935,Ag 3,16:2
King Steps Out, The 1936,My 29,15:2
Swing Time 1936,Ag 28,21:2
Joy of Living 1938,My 6,27:1

Fields, Dorothy (Original Author)

Joy of Living 1938,My 6,27:1
Let's Face It 1943,Ag 5,18:1
Something for the Boys 1944,N 30,19:1
Up in Central Park 1948,My 27,29:3
Annie Get Your Gun 1950,My 18,37:1

Fields, Dorothy (Screenwriter)

Father takes a Wife 1941,S 5,19:3

Fields, Gracie

It's Love I'm After 1937,N 11,31:2
We're Going to Be Rich 1938,Jl 4,10:2
Smiling Along 1939,F 20,13:2
Shipyard Sally 1940,Ja 18,27:3
Stage Door Canteen 1943,Je 25,13:2
Holy Matrimony 1943,S 16,25:2
Molly and Me 1945,My 26,18:2
Paris Underground 1945,O 20,8:2

Fields, Herbert (Composer)

Mexican Hayride 1949,Ja 12,33:3

Fields, Herbert (Original Author)

Let's Fall in Love 1934,Ja 22,12:3
Down to Their Last Yacht 1934,S 24,14:1
Joy of Living 1938,My 6,27:1
Honolulu 1939,F 23,19:2
Panama Hattie 1942,O 2,31:2
Let's Face It 1943,Ag 5,18:1
Du Barry Was a Lady 1943,Ag 20,13:1
Something for the Boys 1944,N 30,19:1
Up in Central Park 1948,My 27,29:3
Slightly French 1949,My 27,25:3
Annie Get Your Gun 1950,My 18,37:1
Hit the Deck 1955,Mr 4,17:1

Fields, Herbert (Screenwriter)

Hot Heiress, The 1931,Mr 14,23:2
Mississippi 1935,Ap 18,27:2
People Will Talk 1935,Je 17,20:2
Accent on Youth 1935,Ag 12,10:3
Hands Across the Table 1935,N 2,13:2
Love Before Breakfast 1936,Mr 14,10:1
Luckiest Girl in the World, The 1936,D 5,16:3
Fools for Scandal 1938,Mr 25,15:3
Honolulu 1939,F 23,19:2
Father takes a Wife 1941,S 5,19:3

Fields, John (Original Author)

Bride for Sale 1949,N 21,29:4 (In Addenda)

Fields, Joseph (Original Author)

Annie Oakley 1935,D 24,10:5
Walking Dead, The 1936,Mr 2,13:2
Mexican Spitfire 1940,Ja 10,16:4
My Sister Eileen 1942,O 23,15:1
Doughgirls, The 1944,Ag 31,14:1
Junior Miss 1945,Je 18,15:4
Gentlemen Prefer Blondes 1953,Jl 16,17:2
My Sister Eileen 1955,S 23,21:1
Tunnel of Love 1958,N 22,27:4
Happy Anniversary 1959,N 11,41:1

Fields, Joseph (Producer)

Man From Texas 1948,Ag 12,16:5
Tunnel of Love 1958,N 22,27:4

Fields, Joseph (Screenwriter)

$1,000 a Minute 1935,D 21,11:1
Grand Jury 1936,Ag 1,16:3
When Love Is Young 1937,Ap 17,15:1
Reported Missing 1937,S 3,12:2
Fools for Scandal 1938,Mr 25,15:3
Rich Man, Poor Girl 1938,Ag 19,13:3
Girl From Mexico, The 1939,Je 8,31:4
Girl and the Gambler, The 1939,Je 28,17:3
Spellbinder, The 1939,Ag 24,17:3
Mexican Spitfire 1940,Ja 10,16:4
Two Girls on Broadway 1940,Ap 25,28:4
Dulcy 1940,N 28,28:2
Louisiana Purchase 1942,Ja 1,37:1
My Sister Eileen 1942,O 23,15:1
Night in Casablanca, A 1946,Ag 12,17:2
Lost Honeymoon 1947,Je 20,25:6
Man From Texas 1948,Ag 12,16:5
Farmer Takes a Wife, The 1953,Je 13,11:2
Tunnel of Love 1958,N 22,27:4
Happy Anniversary 1959,N 11,41:1
Flower Drum Song 1961,N 10,40:1

Fields, Leonard (Original Author)

Devil's Mate 1933,S 23,11:7

Fields, Lew

Friendly Enemies 1925,My 5,24:2
Story of Vernon and Irene Castle, The 1939,Mr 31,19:2

Fields, Ralph (Producer)

Happy Anniversary 1959,N 11,41:1

Fields, Robert

Incident, The 1967,N 6,65:1

Fields, Shep and his orchestra

Big Broadcast of 1938, The 1938,Mr 10,16:2

Fields, Sidney

Strike Me Pink 1936,Ja 17,15:2
Mexican Hayride 1949,Ja 12,33:3

Fields, Stanley

Street of Chance 1930,F 3,17:1
Mammy 1930,Mr 27,24:5
Ladies Love Brutes 1930,My 16,20:4
Border Legion, The 1930,Je 30,22:6
Manslaughter 1930,Jl 24,26:4
See America Thirst 1930,D 12,35:3
Hook, Line and Sinker 1930,D 25,31:5
Little Casear 1931,Ja 10,19:2
Cimarron 1931,Ja 27,20:5
Cracked Nuts 1931,Ap 6,24:1
City Streets 1931,Ap 18,17:3
Holy Terror, A 1931,Jl 20,20:4
Traveling Husbands 1931,Ag 8,16:3
Riders of the Purple Sage 1931,S 26,25:3
Skyline 1931,O 5,17:3
Girl of the Rio 1932,Ja 9,21:1
Way Back Home 1932,Ja 16,13:1
Two Kinds of Women 1932,Ja 16,13:1
Girl Crazy 1932,Mr 25,23:3
Mouthpiece, The 1932,Ap 21,25:2
Painted Woman, The 1932,S 16,24:4
Hell's Highway 1932,S 26,18:2
Rackety Rax 1932,N 5,12:5
Sherlock Holmes 1932,N 12,20:5
Kid From Spain, The 1932,N 18,23:2
Island of Lost Souls 1933,Ja 13,19:2
Destination Unknown 1933,Ap 8,16:2
Palooka 1934,F 28,23:2
Sing and Like It 1934,Ap 14,18:2
Many Happy Returns 1934,Je 9,18:2
Kid Millions 1934,N 12,17:2
Helldorado 1935,Ja 7,13:2
Daring Young Man, The 1935,Jl 18,15:2
Mutiny on the Bounty 1935,N 9,19:2
It Had to Happen 1936,F 15,18:6
O'Malley of the Mounted 1936,Ap 6,18:1
Show Boat 1936,My 15,29:4
Mine With the Iron Door, The 1936,Jl 11,11:3
Gay Desperado, The 1936,O 9,31:4
Devil is a Sissy, The 1936,O 17,21:2
Midnight Court 1937,Mr 4,27:3
Way out West 1937,My 4,29:1
Three Legionnaires 1937,Jl 10,18:2
Toast of New York, The 1937,Jl 23,16:2
Souls at Sea 1937,Ag 10,23:2
Counsel for Crime 1937,O 9,16:1
Ali Baba Goes to Town 1937,O 23,14:1
Wells Fargo 1937,D 30,15:2
Wide Open Faces 1938,Ap 15,23:2
Algiers 1938,Jl 15,13:2
Painted Desert 1938,S 14,26:5
Straight, Place and Show 1938,O 1,10:2
Flirting With Fate 1938,D 15,35:3
Blackwell's Island 1939,Mr 2,19:1
Kid From Kokomo, The 1939,My 20,11:2
Hell's Kitchen 1939,Jl 3,10:5
Exile Express 1939,Ag 16,21:3
Pack up Your Troubles 1939,O 27,27:2
Fugitive at Large 1939,N 13,15:2
Viva Cisco Kid 1940,Mr 22,23:4
Ski Patrol 1940,My 21,29:4
New Moon 1940,Jl 19,22:2
Great Plane Robbery, The 1940,N 15,25:2
Lady From Cheyenne, The 1941,Ap 18,18:2
Adventures of Marco Polo, The 1965,Ap 8,17:2

Fields, Tommy

Smiling Along 1939,F 20,13:2

Fields, W C

Janice Meredith 1924,Ag 6,13:3
That Royle Girl 1926,Ja 4,33:1
It's the old Army Game 1926,Jl 5,6:4
So's Your Old Man 1926,N 1,28:2
Potters, The 1927,Ja 18,23:1
Running Wild 1927,Je 14,33:2
Two Flaming Youths 1928,Ja 2,28:1
Fools for Luck 1928,Je 12,33:5
Her Majesty, Love 1931,N 26,37:2
Million Dollar Legs 1932,Jl 9,7:5
If I Had a Million 1932,D 3,21:4
International House 1933,My 27,11:5
Tillie and Gus 1933,N 13,21:1
Alice in Wonderland 1933,D 23,19:1
Six of a Kind 1934,Mr 10,18:3
You're Telling Me 1934,Ap 7,19:1
Old-Fashioned Way, The 1934,Jl 14,16:5
Mrs Wiggs of the Cabbage Patch 1934,O 29,14:2
It's a Gift 1935,Ja 5,20:2
David Copperfield 1935,Ja 19,8:1
Mississippi 1935,Ap 18,27:2

Fields, W C— Cont
Man on the Flying Trapeze 1935,Ag 3,16:2
Poppy 1936,Je 18,19:1
Big Broadcast of 1938, The 1938,Mr 10,16:2
You Can't Cheat an Honest Man 1939,F 20,13:2
My Little Chickadee 1940,Mr 16,8:2
Bank Dick, The 1940,D 13,29:2
Never Give a Sucker an Even Break
1941,O 27,21:2
Follow the Boys 1944,Ap 26,24:6
Song of the Open Road 1944,Je 7,13:3
Sensations of 1945 1944,Jl 7,13:2
W C Fields Comedy Festival 1966,F 23,46:1
Fields, W C (Otis Criblecoblis) (Original Author)
Never Give a Sucker an Even Break
1941,O 27,21:2
Fields, W C (Screenwriter)
My Little Chickadee 1940,Mr 16,8:2
Fienburgh, Wilfred (Original Author)
No Love for Johnnie 1961,D 13,55:1
Fier, Jack (Producer)
Mystery Ship 1941,Ag 16,18:3
Sabotage Squad 1942,Ag 5,16:1
What's Buzzin Cousin 1943,Jl 23,21:4
Fiermonte, Enzo
Merchant of Slaves 1949,O 27,35:4
Romeo and Juliet 1954,D 22,28:1
Naked Maja, The 1959,Je 11,36:2
Slave, The 1963,My 30,20:1
Fierro, Iole
Angelo 1951,Mr 26,19:4
Fierro, Paul
Red River 1948,O 1,31:2
Amazon Quest 1949,My 14,9:3
Abbott and Costello in the Foreign Legion
1950,Ag 14,14:4
Wings of the Hawk 1953,Ag 27,22:1
Creature Walks among Us, The 1956,Ap 27,21:6
Fierro, Roberto (Producer)
Beso Mortal, El; Fatal Kiss, The 1939,Ja 21,19:3
Fiesch, Jean-Andre
Alphaville 1965,O 26,49:1
Fife, Maxine
One Body too Many 1944,N 25,21:2
Figdor, Carl (Original Author)
Dragon's Claw, The 1922,Mr 6,9:3
Figman, Max
Old Home Week 1925,My 25,21:3
Figman, Oscar
Manhattan 1924,O 29,18:1
Figueroa, Miguel
Wave, The 1937,Ap 21,18:1
Figurovsky, Nicolia (Screenwriter)
When the Trees Were Tall 1965,F 22,14:1
Figurovsky (Screenwriter)
Miles of Fire 1958,N 10,36:6 (In Addenda)
Fijewska, Barbara
Last Stop, The 1949,Mr 22,31:2
Fijewski, T
Ulica 1933,Ja 27,13:2
Border Street 1950,Ap 26,35:2
Filacuridi, Nicola
Madame Butterfly 1956,Ap 24,26:2
Filauri, Antonio
Road to Happiness 1942,Mr 27,27:4
Wilson 1944,Ag 2,18:1
Mother Wore Tights 1947,Ag 21,33:2
Too Young to Kiss 1951,N 23,32:2
Fildes, Audrey
Kind Hearts and Coronets 1950,Je 15,41:2
Filho, Napoleao Lopes
Given Word, The 1964,Mr 25,47:1
Filidoro, Giovanni
It Started in Naples 1960,S 3,7:6
Filimonov, Anatol (Screenwriter)
Winner, The 1947,D 1,27:2
Filip, Josef
Do You Keep a Lion at Home? 1966,S 18,78:1
Filiposky, Frantisck
Emperor and the Golem, The 1955,Ja 10,27:4
Filippeschi, Mario
Lucia di Lammermoor 1947,N 1,11:3
Rigoletto 1949,N 10,41:4
Filippidou, Vana
Madame X 1960,O 3,34:5
Filippo, Eduardo de
Seven Deadly Sins, The (Avarice and Anger);
Avarice and Anger (The Seven Deadly Sins)
1953,My 12,31:3
Filippo, Eduardo de (Director)
Seven Deadly Sins, The (Avarice and Anger);
Avarice and Anger (The Seven Deadly Sins)
1953,My 12,31:3
Filippov, F (Director)
Chelkash 1964,Ja 27,19:1
Filippov, S
Tiger Girl 1955,S 5,8:2
Filkovskaya, Lena
Scandal? 1929,O 28,20:1
Fillacier, Sylvette
Maternelle, La 1935,O 15,19:1
Filler, Leo
They Were Ten; (Heym Hayu Assara)
1961,Ap 18,44:2

Fillmore, Clyde
Nurse Marjorie 1920,My 24,20:3
Moonlight Follies 1921,S 19,12:1
Shanghai Gesture, The 1941,D 26,21:2
Unholy Partners 1941,D 29,21:4
Remarkable Andrew, The 1942,Mr 6,17:2
Two Yanks in Trinidad 1942,Ap 6,19:4
Mystery of Marie Roget, The 1942,My 5,17:3
Talk of the Town, The 1942,Ag 28,22:3
My Sister Eileen 1942,O 23,15:1
Margin for Error 1943,Ja 25,10:7
When Johnny Comes Marching Home
1943,Mr 5,20:4
Taxi, Mister 1943,Ap 15,20:2
More the Merrier, The 1943,My 14,17:1
Fall In 1943,My 15,13:3
Watch on the Rhine 1943,Ag 28,15:1
Swing Fever 1944,Ja 28,14:1
Laura 1944,O 12,24:1
3 Is a Family 1944,D 20,20:3
Filmer, June
Rockabye 1932,D 5,21:2
One Man's Journey 1933,S 1,15:2
Filmer, Robert
Thunderhead 1945,Mr 16,21:2
Filmer, Vic
Old Curiosity Shop, The 1935,D 23,15:5
Filmer-Sankey, Patrick (Producer)
S O S Pacific 1960,O 13,41:3
Fils, Baron
Venus 1929,O 14,20:2
Il est Charmant 1932,Ap 9,18:1
Meet Miss Mozart 1937,N 27,21:3
Fils, Numes
Ces Dames aux Chapeaux Verts; Ladies in the
Green Hats, The 1945,Ap 5,26:2
Filson, Al
String Beans 1918,D 30,7:3
Widow by Proxy 1919,S 22,8:1
Home Spun Folks 1920,O 4,14:3
Fimberg, Hal (Composer)
Big Store, The 1941,Je 27,14:4
Fimberg, Hal (Original Author)
Boogie Man Will Get You, The 1942,O 12,12:4
Our Man Flint 1966,Ja 26,23:4
Fimberg, Hal (Screenwriter)
Big Store, The 1941,Je 27,14:4
Wave, A Wac and a Marine, A 1944,Ag 14,11:4
In Society 1944,Ag 17,20:2
Naughty Nineties, The 1945,Je 21,16:2
Our Man Flint 1966,Ja 26,23:4
Finaly, Pierre
Paris-Beguin 1932,D 31,10:1
Finance, Ernesto
Padre Mercader; Merchant Father 1939,Jl 15,8:3
Fincato, Serio
Climax, The 1967,S 12,55:1
Finch, Flora
When Knighthood Was in Flower 1922,S 15,17:2
(In Addenda)
Monsieur Beaucaire 1924,Ag 12,12:1 (In
Addenda)
Men and Women 1925,Mr 30,21:3
Brown Derby, The 1926,Je 14,24:1
Oh Baby! 1926,Ag 11,25:2
Captain Salvation 1927,Je 27,25:2
Cat and the Canary, The 1927,S 10,9:4
Rose of the Golden West 1927,S 26,27:1
Quality Street 1927,N 2,24:5
Haunted House, The 1928,D 17,23:1
Finch, Peter
Miniver Story, The 1950,O 27,24:2
Massacre Hill 1950,D 14,51:3
Rats of Tobruk, The 1951,My 24,47:3
Train of Events 1952,My 26,18:4
Story of Robin Hood, The 1952,Je 27,18:3
Gilbert and Sullivan 1953,O 28,36:3
Elephant Walk 1954,Ap 22,37:2
Detective, The 1954,N 2,25:2
Heart of the Matter, The 1954,N 19,20:2
Warriors, The 1955,S 10,11:2
Make Me an Offer 1956,F 29,35:2
Simon and Laura 1956,Jl 3,17:2
Pursuit of the Graf Spee 1957,D 27,33:2
Town Like Alice, A 1958,S 22,27:1
Windom's Way 1958,O 1,45:1
Nun's Story, The 1959,Je 19,30:1
Kidnapped 1960,My 19,44:3
Trials of Oscar Wilde, The 1960,Je 28,26:1
Operation Amsterdam 1960,Jl 7,26:1
Sins of Rachel Cade, The 1961,Ag 6,30:3
No Love for Johnnie 1961,D 13,55:1
I Thank a Fool 1962,S 15,15:1
In the Cool of the Day 1963,My 30,20:1
Girl With Green Eyes 1964,Ag 11,37:2
Pumpkin Eater, The 1964,N 10,58:1
Judith 1966,Ja 21,22:1
Flight of the Phoenix, The 1966,F 1,26:1
10:30 PM Summer 1966,O 20,52:1
Far From the Madding Crowd 1967,O 19,59:1
Legend of Lylah Clare, The 1968,Ag 23,33:1

Finch, Peter (Narrator)
Queen in Australia, The 1954,Je 16,37:3
Finch, Scot
French Mistress, A 1960,D 19,34:2
Kitchen, The 1961,N 2,42:1
Why Bother to Knock 1965,F 4,24:2
Finch, Scot (Screenwriter)
Shalako 1968,N 6,32:1
FINCK
See Also FINK
Finck, Werner
Freundin Eines Grossen Mannes, Die
1934,S 11,24:5
Wenn am Sonntagabend die Dorfmusik Spielt
1935,D 9,25:3
Graue Dame, Die; Gray Lady, The
1938,D 17,10:4
Affairs of Julie, The 1958,D 10,53:1
Finden, Amy Woodford (Composer)
Hers to Hold 1943,Jl 22,15:1
Findlater, John
With Six You Get Egg Roll 1968,O 10,59:6
Findlay, Ruth
Heroes of the Alamo 1938,Ap 2,18:2
Findlay, Thomas
Hellotrope 1920,N 29,20:3
Little Old New York 1923,Ag 2,10:3
Yolanda 1924,F 20,23:1
Let's Get Married 1926,Mr 2,22:1
Findley, Ferguson (Original Author)
Mob, The 1951,O 18,32:2
Findley, Sylvia
Black Tuesday 1955,Ja 1,16:2
FINE
See Also FAIN
Fine, Budd
Battling Butler 1926,Ag 23,9:1
Wreck of the Hesperus, The 1927,N 28,18:5
Be Yourself 1930,Mr 7,20:5
Fine, Harry (Producer)
Pleasure Girls, The 1966,Ap 21,43:1
Penthouse, The 1967,O 4,38:3
Long Day's Dying, The 1968,My 29,20:1
Fine, Larry
Rockin' in The Rockies 1945,Jl 5,7:2
Fine, Morton (Screenwriter)
Pawnbroker, The 1965,Ap 21,51:1
Fine, Sylvia (Composer)
Kid From Brooklyn, The 1946,Ap 19,25:2
Secret Life of Walter Mitty, The 1947,Ag 15,12:2
Knock on Wood 1954,Ap 15,34:2
Court Jester, The 1956,F 2,19:1
Fine, Sylvia (Miscellaneous)
Wonder Man 1945,Je 9,17:2
Fineman, B P (Original Author)
Appointment in Berlin 1943,Jl 17,8:2
Fineman, B P (Producer)
Smashing the Rackets 1938,Ag 9,22:5
Tarnished Angel 1938,N 15,27:2
Beauty for the Asking 1939,F 10,19:1
Tarzan's Secret Treasure 1941,D 25,33:1
Journey for Margaret 1942,D 18,36:7
Pilot No 5 1943,Je 25,13:4
Fineman, Irving (Original Author)
Rome Adventure 1962,Mr 16,25:1
Fineman, Irving (Screenwriter)
Once Upon a Time 1944,Je 30,17:2
Fineschi, Onella
Lost One, The; La Traviata 1948,Mr 30,26:2
FINK
See Also FINCK
Fink, Harry Julian (Screenwriter)
Major Dundee 1965,Ap 8,45:1
Ice Station Zebra 1968,D 21,49:1
Fink, Henry
Kibitzer, The 1929,D 21,17:1
Goldie Gets Along 1933,Je 3,16:4
Finkel, Abem (Original Author)
Deceiver, The 1931,N 23,22:1
Road Gang 1936,F 24,14:1
Finkel, Abem (Screenwriter)
Black Fury 1935,Ap 11,27:2
Special Agent 1935,S 19,28:1
Public Enemy's Wife 1936,Jl 9,17:2
Black Legion 1937,Ja 18,21:1
Marked Woman 1937,Ap 12,15:2
Jezebel 1938,Mr 11,15:2
White Banners 1938,Je 23,27:1
Sergeant York 1941,Jl 3,15:1
Big Shot, The 1942,Jl 18,8:2
Tonight and Every Night 1945,Mr 9,16:2
Time Out of Mind 1947,Ap 7,20:1
Finkenzeller, Heli
Ehestreik 1935,Ag 31,16:3
Hoehere Befehl, Der 1936,Mr 31,17:3
Royal Waltz, The 1936,Ap 10,27:1
Weiberregiment 1936,S 14,25:2
Boccaccio 1937,F 27,9:3
Drama on the Threshing Floor 1937,O 30,22:3
Mustergatte, Der; Model Husband
1938,Mr 19,11:3
Gleisdreieck 1938,Je 11,9:1
Schimmelkrieg von Holledau, Der 1938,Jl 19,15:4

Finkenzeller, Heli — Cont
Konzert in Tirol 1939,Ja 7,6:4
Diskretion-Ehrensache; Discretion with Honor
    1939,Mr 13,12:3
Kleine Nachtmusik, Eine 1940,Mr 2,9:5
Opernball; Opera Ball 1940,O 15,29:2
Finklehoffe, Fred F (Composer)
Mr Ace 1946,S 30,21:3
Finklehoffe, Fred F (Original Author)
Brother Rat 1938,N 5,15:2
Babes on Broadway 1942,Ja 1,37:1
Mr Ace 1946,S 30,21:3
About Face 1952,My 24,15:3
Stooge, The 1953,F 5,19:2
Finklehoffe, Fred F (Producer)
Egg and I, The 1947,Ap 25,29:2
At War With the Army 1951,Ja 25,21:5
Finklehoffe, Fred F (Screenwriter)
Brother Rat and a Baby 1940,Ja 27,9:4
Strike up the Band 1940,S 30,13:2
Babes on Broadway 1942,Ja 1,37:1
For Me and My Gal 1942,O 22,25:1
Best Foot Forward 1943,Je 30,25:2
Girl Crazy 1943,D 3,27:2
Meet Me in St Louis 1944,N 29,20:2
Mr Ace 1946,S 30,21:3
Egg and I, The 1947,Ap 25,29:2
Words and Music 1948,D 10,34:2
At War With the Army 1951,Ja 25,21:5
Stooge, The 1953,F 5,19:2
Finklestein, I
My Father's House 1947,S 26,28:3
Finlavson, James
Thunder Below 1932,Je 20,11:2
Finlay, Frank
Underworld Informers 1965,O 14,53:1
Othello 1966,F 2,24:1
Walk in the Shadow 1966,S 12,52:5
Study in Terror, A 1966,N 3,45:3
Jokers, The 1967,My 16,50:1
Deadly Bees, The 1967,My 20,39:2
Robbery 1967,S 28,58:2
I'll Never Forget What's 'Isname
    1968,Ap 15,51:1
Inspector Clouseau 1968,Jl 25,26:1
Finlay, Pierre
Tender Enemy, The 1938,Mr 31,15:2 (In
    Addenda)
Finlayson, Alex
D-Day, The Sixth of June 1956,My 30,13:1
Journey to the Center of the Earth
    1959,D 17,51:1
Finlayson, James
Small Town Idol, A 1921,Ap 17,VI,2:1 (In
    Addenda)
Ladies' Night in a Turkish Bath 1928,Ap 9,18:2
Lady Be Good 1928,My 28,23:2
Show Girl 1928,N 5,26:1
Two Weeks Off 1929,Je 24,27:1
Hard to Get 1929,S 28,17:3
Wall Street 1929,N 25,22:1
Dawn Patrol, The 1930,Jl 11,22:1
For the Defense 1930,Jl 19,7:5
Pardon Us 1931,Ag 22,7:5
Pack up Your Troubles 1932,O 1,10:4
Devil's Brother, The 1933,Je 10,16:4
Bohemian Girl, The 1936,F 17,21:1
Our Relations 1936,N 11,55:1
Way out West 1937,My 4,29:1
Pick a Star 1937,My 28,17:2
Block-Heads 1938,Ag 30,14:2
Hollywood Cavalcade 1939,O 14,13:2
Flying Deuces, The 1939,N 24,29:2
Great Victor Herbert, The 1939,D 7,35:1
Perils of Pauline, The 1947,Jl 10,17:2
Thunder in the Valley 1947,N 28,30:1
Royal Wedding 1951,Mr 9,30:2
When Comedy Was King 1960,Mr 30,42:1
Laurel and Hardy's Laughing 20's 1965,N 18,55:2
Further Perils of Laurel and Hardy, The
    1968,Ap 1,56:6
Finlayson, Marion
Incredible Journey, The 1963,N 21,43:2
Finley, Irene (Producer)
Chumming With Chipmunks 1921,F 14,12:2
Finley, Murrel
Sin Takes a Holliday 1930,N 28,23:1
Finley, William
Murder a la Mod 1968,My 2,57:1
Finley, William L (Producer)
Chumming With Chipmunks 1921,F 14,12:2
Finn, Catherine
Deadly Bees, The 1967,My 20,39:2
Finn, Elsie (Original Author)
I Dream too Much 1935,N 29,24:1
Finn, James Hilary (Original Author)
Lawyer's Secret, The 1931,My 30,9:2
Finn, Jonathan (Original Author)
Jailbreak 1936,Ag 6,22:1
You Can't Get Away With Murder
    1939,Mr 25,19:2
Angels Wash Their Faces 1939,S 4,16:2
Invisible Stripes 1940,Ja 13,11:2
Lady From Cheyenne, The 1941,Ap 18,18:2

Finn, Mickey
Sergeants 3 1962,F 12,28:2
Finn, Sheila
Hallelujah the Hills 1963,D 17,49:1
Finnerty, Warren
Connection, The 1962,O 4,44:1
Brig, The 1964,S 21,37:4
Andy 1965,Ja 22,21:2
Pawnbroker, The 1965,Ap 21,51:1
Cool Hand Luke 1967,N 2,58:1
Finney, Albert
Entertainer, The 1960,O 4,49:2
Saturday Night and Sunday Morning
    1961,Ap 4,44:2
Tom Jones 1963,O 8,48:1
Victors, The 1963,D 20,21:2
Night Must Fall 1964,Mr 19,28:1
Two for the Road 1967,Ap 28,36:2
Charlie Bubbles 1968,F 12,47:2
Finney, Albert (Director)
Charlie Bubbles 1968,F 12,47:2
Finney, Albert (Producer)
Night Must Fall 1964,Mr 19,28:1
Finney, Benjamin F Jr
Miami 1924,Je 3,22:2
Finney, Charles G (Original Author)
7 Faces of Dr Lao 1964,Jl 23,19:1
Finney, Edward (Producer)
Mystery of the Hooded Horsemen, The
    1937,Ag 13,13:2
Corregidor 1943,My 28,19:2
Finney, Jack (Original Author)
Five Against the House 1955,Je 11,8:7
House of Numbers 1957,S 13,15:2
Good Neighbor Sam 1964,Jl 23,19:1
Assault on a Queen 1966,Jl 28,23:3
Finniel, E
Chalutzim 1934,Ap 2,13:3
Finos, Filopimin (Producer)
Stefania 1968,N 29,56:1
Fins, Bernard (Original Author)
Noose Hangs High, The 1948,My 29,8:6
Finston, Nat W (Composer)
Last of the Pagans 1936,Ja 9,25:2
Finston, Nathaniel (Producer)
Song of my Heart 1948,Mr 5,17:3
Finter, Alec
Hue and Cry 1951,Ja 9,25:2
Fio-Riot, Ted (Composer)
Young and Beautiful 1934,S 18,18:4
Fiore, Maria
Two Cents Worth of Hope 1952,D 16,44:2
Half a Century of Songs 1954,O 30,15:6
Gran Varieta 1955,Ap 11,29:5
Neapolitan Carousel 1961,O 12,41:3
Let's Talk About Women 1964,S 29,52:5
Fiorelli, Aldo
Escape into Dreams 1950,Ap 13,34:5
Anthony of Padua 1952,Mr 29,19:2
Fiorelli, Nada
Tombolo 1949,D 31,9:4
Golden Coach, The 1954,Ja 22,30:2
Fiorentini, Fiorenzo
Tiger and the Pussycat, The 1967,S 21,56:4
Fiorentini, Fiorenzo (Screenwriter)
Anthony of Padua 1952,Mr 29,19:2
Fiori, Agala
Operation Kid Brother 1967,N 23,58:2
Fiorito, Ted and his orchestra
Silver Skates 1943,Mr 19,15:3
Firbank, Ann
Servant, The 1964,Mr 17,30:2
Darling 1965,Ag 4,20:1
Accident 1967,Ap 18,33:1
Firestone, Eddie
With a Song in my Heart 1952,Ap 5,20:2
Good Morning, Miss Dove 1955,N 24,41:1
Revolt of Mamie Stover, The 1956,My 12,12:7
Great Locomotive Chase, The 1956,Je 27,35:1
Bailout at 43,000 1957,Je 8,13:2
Law and Jake Wade, the 1958,Je 7,11:1
Two for the Seesaw 1962,N 22,43:1
Firmans, Lothar
Marriage in the Shadows 1948,S 17,28:3
Firschke, Trixie
Broadway Melody of 1940 1940,Mr 29,25:3
FIRTH
See Also FURTH
Firth, Anne
Spitfire 1943,Je 14,13:2
FISCHER
See Also FISHER
Fischer, Adolf
Kuhle Wampe 1933,Ap 24,11:4
Fischer, Arthur
Baldvins Brollop; Baldwin's Wedding
    1938,D 27,13:2
Skanor-Falsterbo 1939,Ap 17,13:2
Fischer, Charles
Goldstein 1965,My 8,19:7
Fischer, Gloria
Beloved Brat 1938,My 2,13:2

Fischer, H L
Gretel and Liesel; (Kohlhiesel's Daughters)
    1931,Ja 26,21:1
Long Is the Road 1948,N 12,30:5
Fischer, Hugo
Drei von der Kavallerie 1935,Ap 13,11:4
Fischer, Jakob
Long Is the Road 1948,N 12,30:5
Fischer, Jane
Athena 1954,D 22,28:2
Oklahoma! 1955,O 11,49:1
Fischer, Kai
Girls of the Night 1959,Mr 21,13:2
Escape from East Berlin 1962,D 6,55:3
Great British Train Robbery, The 1967,Ap 6,45:2
Fischer, Margarita
Unknown, The 1924,N 18,22:1
Any Woman 1925,My 27,26:2
Uncle Tom's Cabin 1927,N 5,16:2
Fischer, O W
Anton der Letzte; Anthony the Last
    1940,Mr 30,11:2
Lysistrata 1948,Je 19,19:2
Desires 1954,Jl 2,10:2
Portrait of an Unknown Woman 1958,Ap 26,14:6
Dreaming Lips; (Traumende Mund, The)
    1958,N 1,14:3
Arms and the Man 1962,F 24,21:7
Fischer, Robert
Oath, The 1921,Ap 11,9:1
Loves of an Actress 1928,Jl 30,21:2
Wiser Sex, The 1932,Mr 12,19:5
Expensive Husbands 1938,Ja 8,19:3
Zaza 1939,Ja 5,17:1
Zanzibar 1940,Ap 1,15:3
Birthright 1952,F 15,17:2
Fischer, Sigge
Swedish Wedding Night 1965,N 15,48:1
Fischer, Tyra
Sunshine Follows Rain 1949,S 29,39:2
Fischer-Koeppe, Hugo
Der Schrecken der Garnison 1932,Je 1,19:5
Gloria 1932,O 28,22:4
Ja, Treu Ist die Soldatenliebe 1934,Ap 28,11:4
Wie Man Maenner Fesselt 1934,My 21,20:3
Im Heidekrug 1934,D 31,9:7
Traum vom Rhein, Der 1935,D 9,25:2
Wackere Schustermeister, Der 1936,Jl 7,22:4
Grosse Bluff, Der; Big Bluff, The 1937,S 6,20:2
Fischer-White, J
Old Curiosity Shop, The 1935,D 23,15:5
Fiser, Ruzena (Original Author)
Seventh Continent, The 1968,Jl 30,33:2
Fiser, Stanislav
Lady on the Tracks, The 1968,N 26,39:2
Fish, G (Screenwriter)
Ski Battalion 1938,Mr 14,13:1
Fish, Nancy
Funnyman 1967,S 25,56:3
Fishbein, Benjamin
Overture to Glory 1940,F 12,14:2
Vilna Legend, A (American Cast) 1949,S 26,17:1
FISHER
See Also FISCHER
Fisher, A S
Prince of Peace, The 1951,Mr 24,8:3
Fisher, Al
Mister Rock and Roll 1957,O 17,42:2
Fisher, Alfred
Fighting American, The 1924,My 13,24:1
Home Maker, The 1925,Ag 10,8:2
Fisher, Bob (Original Author)
Impossible Years, The 1968,D 6,54:1
Fisher, Bob (Screenwriter)
Snow Queen, The 1960,Ap 14,34:1
Global Affair, A 1964,My 7,31:2
I'll Take Sweden 1965,Ag 12,30:4
Eight on the Lam 1967,Ap 27,52:1
Fisher, Clay (Original Author)
Tall Men, The 1955,O 12,36:2
Yellowstone Kelly 1959,N 12,27:1
Fisher, Diane
Swanee River 1939,D 30,9:2
Blue Bird, The 1940,Ja 20,11:2
Lillian Russell 1940,My 18,11:2
Young People 1940,Ag 24,16:2
Fisher, Doris (Composer)
Thrill of Brazil, The 1946,S 6,18:3
Down to Earth 1947,S 12,18:2
Fisher, Eddie
All About Eve 1950,O 14,13:2
Bundle of Joy 1956,D 20,36:1
Butterfield 8 1960,N 17,46:1
Fisher, Elliot
Love Takes Flight 1937,S 27,24:3
Fisher, Freddie (Composer)
Seven Days Ashore 1944,Ap 26,24:7
Oh, You Beautiful Doll 1949,N 12,8:4
Fisher, Freddie Band
Seven Days Ashore 1944,Ap 26,24:7
Fisher, George
Moonlight Follies 1921,S 19,12:1
Champagne for Caesar 1950,My 12,33:2

Fisher, George— Cont
Hard, Fast and Beautiful 1951,Jl 2,16:6
Fisher, Ham (Original Author)
Palooka 1934,F 28,23:2
Fisher, James B (Original Author)
Within These Walls 1945,Jl 16,8:4
Fisher, Larry
Long Live the King 1923,D 4,24:1
Boy of Flanders, A 1924,Ap 15,24:1
Into her Kingdom 1926,Ag 10,19:2
Fisher, Laurence
Winds of Chance 1925,Ag 17,10:3
Fisher, Leck (Screenwriter)
Red Meadows 1950,Ja 19,35:2
Fisher, Margarita
K-The Unknown 1924,N 18,22:1
Fisher, Mary Gale
One Million BC 1940,Ap 27,9:2
Fisher, Michael (Screenwriter)
Savage Seven, The 1968,Ag 22,47:1
Fisher, Millicent
Alarm Clock Andy 1920,Mr 15,13:2
Fisher, Nelle
Up in Central Park 1948,My 27,29:3
Fisher, Norman (Cinematographer)
Royal Tour of Queen Elizabeth and Philip, The
1954,Je 22,24:2
Fisher, Richard (Original Author)
Showtime 1948,My 20,35:3
Fisher, Shug
Mister Roberts 1955,Jl 15,14:1
Fisher, Steve (Original Author)
Typhoon 1940,My 23,28:4
I Wake up Screaming 1942,Ja 17,13:2
To the Shores of Tripoli 1942,Mr 26,27:2
Destination Tokyo 1944,Ja 1,9:2
That's my Man 1947,Ap 7,20:2
Tokyo Joe 1949,O 27,35:2
Vickie 1953,S 8,26:3
Hell's Half Acre 1954,F 27,11:3
Susan Slept Here 1954,Jl 30,9:1
September Storm 1960,O 29,26:7
Johnny Reno 1966,Mr 10,26:3
Fisher, Steve (Screenwriter)
Berlin Correspondent 1942,S 4,19:2
Johnny Angel 1945,D 28,12:2
Dead Reckoning 1947,Ja 23,31:2
Lady in the Lake 1947,Ja 24,18:3
Song of the Thin Man 1947,Ag 29,14:2
Battle Zone 1952,N 1,17:2
Flat Top 1952,D 6,17:2
City That Never Sleeps 1953,Ag 8,14:2
Man From the Alamo, The 1953,S 12,13:2
Shanghai Story, The 1954,S 25,10:7
Las Vegas Shakedown 1955,Je 18,14:2
Black Spurs 1965,My 29,17:1
Johnny Reno 1966,Mr 10,26:3
Fort Utah 1967,My 25,54:3
Fisher, Terence (Director)
Girl in the Painting, The 1949,Ag 22,13:1
Astonished Heart, The 1950,F 15,23:2
So Long at the Fair 1951,Ja 22,14:2
Marry Me 1952,Mr 14,27:3
Four Sided Triangle 1953,My 16,10:1
Blackout 1954,My 22,8:2
Unholy Four, The 1954,N 20,10:2
Curse of Frankenstein, The 1957,Ag 8,15:5
Horror of Dracula 1958,My 29,24:4
Hounds of the Baskervilles, The 1959,Jl 4,9:4
Mummy, The 1959,D 17,51:4
Brides of Dracula, The 1960,S 6,41:4
Sword of Sherwood Forest 1961,Ja 26,32:3
Curse of the Werewolf, The 1961,Je 8,40:2
House of Fright 1961,Ag 24,25:4
Phantom of the Opera, The 1962,Ag 23,25:2
Devil's Bride, The 1968,D 19,60:1
Fisher, Terence (Screenwriter)
Four Sided Triangle 1953,My 16,10:1
Fiske, Bert
Frisco Sal 1945,F 17,11:2
Fiske, Richard
Homicide Bureau 1939,F 2,17:2
Blondie Meets the Boss 1939,Ap 27,31:1
Behind Prison Gates 1939,Ag 21,9:3
Parents on Trial 1939,S 18,15:5
Men Without Souls 1940,My 13,21:2
Devil Commands, The 1941,F 14,15:3
Lone Wolf Takes a Chance, The 1941,Ap 7,13:2
Officer and the Lady, The 1941,Ag 11,17:4
Valley of the Sun 1942,Mr 19,29:2
Fiske, Robert
Sky Parade, The 1936,Ap 20,17:1
Flight Into Nowhere 1938,My 2,13:3
Adventure in Sahara 1938,D 19,19:2
Racketeers of the Range 1939,Je 8,31:4
East Side Kids 1940,F 19,21:6
Passport to Alcatraz 1940,Je 15,12:2
Before I Hang 1940,O 3,31:3
Fisz, S Benjamin (Producer)
Operation Snafu 1965,My 22,18:1
Heroes of Telemark, The 1966,Mr 10,26:1
Fitch, Clyde (Original Author)
Barbara Frietchie 1915,N 29,11:3
Woman in the Case, The 1916,Ag 7,9:5

Virtuous Vamp, A 1919,N 17,20:1
Beau Brummell 1924,Mr 31,20:1
Climbers, The 1927,My 4,29:2
Wiser Sex, The 1932,Mr 12,19:5
Beau Brummell 1954,O 21,31:5
Fitch, George (Original Author)
Those Were the Days 1940,Jl 15,18:4
Fite, Hugh Major (Screenwriter)
Parachute Battalion 1941,Ag 29,13:2
Fithian, Ted (Original Author)
Captive Wild Woman 1943,Je 7,9:4
Fitinghoff, Laura (Original Author)
Children, The 1949,D 23,17:1
Fitts, Margaret (Original Author)
King and Four Queens, The 1956,D 22,13:7
Fitts, Margaret (Screenwriter)
Sun comes up, The 1949,My 13,29:2
Stars in my Crown 1950,D 22,19:1
Moonfleet 1955,Je 25,9:2
King and Four Queens, The 1956,D 22,13:7
Fitz, Veronika
Spessart Inn, The 1961,F 18,12:3
Fitz-Richards, Arthur (Original Author)
Sun Never Sets, The 1939,Je 9,26:2
Ruby Gentry 1952,D 26,20:2
Fitzgerald, Aubrey
Widecombe Fair 1929,O 28,20:1
Magic Night 1932,N 3,25:3
Fitzgerald, Barry
Juno and the Paycock 1930,Je 30,22:6
Plough and the Stars, The 1937,Ja 29,15:1
Ebb Tide 1937,N 18,27:2
Bringing Up Baby 1938,Mr 4,17:5
Four Men and a Prayer 1938,My 7,18:1
Dawn Patrol 1938,D 24,12:1
Pacific Liner 1939,Ja 18,17:3
Saint Strikes Back, The 1939,Mr 9,18:2
Full Confession 1939,S 28,29:4
Long Voyage Home, The 1940,O 9,30:2 (In
Addenda)
San Francisco Docks 1940,D 26,23:3
Sea Wolf, The 1941,Mr 26,27:3
How Green Was my Valley 1941,O 29,27:2
Tarzan's Secret Treasure 1941,D 25,33:1
Amazing Mrs Holliday, The 1943,F 22,20:2
Two Tickets to London 1943,Jl 3,11:2
Corvette K-225 1943,O 21,30:1
Going my Way 1944,My 3,25:2
I Love a Soldier 1944,N 2,22:2
None but the Lonely Heart 1944,N 18,16:6
None but the Lonely Heart 1944,D 3,II,1:8
Incendiary Blonde 1945,Jl 26,13:2
Duffy's Tavern 1945,S 6,23:3
And Then There Were None 1945,N 1,20:2
Stork Club, The 1945,D 20,18:2
Two Years Before the Mast 1946,S 25,39:2
California 1947,Ja 15,31:2
Easy Come, Easy Go 1947,F 6,29:2
Welcome Stranger 1947,Ag 7,15:2
Naked City, The 1948,Mr 5,17:2
Sainted Sisters, The 1948,My 20,35:2
Miss Tatlock's Millions 1948,N 25,47:2
Top o' the Morning 1949,S 1,25:2
Story of Seabiscuit, The 1949,N 12,8:4
Union Station 1950,O 5,38:3
Quiet Man, The 1952,Ag 22,13:1
Tonight's the Night 1954,D 23,13:4
Catered Affair, The 1956,Je 15,32:4
Rooney 1958,Je 6,29:2
Broth of a Boy 1959,D 28,18:1
Fitzgerald, Cissy
Flowing Gold 1924,Mr 10,18:2
Lilies of the Field 1924,Mr 17,19:1
Babbitt 1924,Jl 15,9:4
Vanity's Price 1924,O 8,16:2
If Marriage Fails 1925,Je 2,16:3
I'll Show You the Town 1925,Je 8,19:1
Crown of Lies 1926,Mr 30,20:6
Her big Night 1926,O 13,21:1
Matinee Ladies 1927,Ap 13,29:4
Women's Wares 1927,N 15,27:1
Two Flaming Youths 1928,Ja 2,28:1
Laugh, Clown, Laugh 1928,My 28,23:2
Ladies of the Night Club 1928,Jl 17,15:3
Transgression 1931,Je 15,23:3
Fitzgerald, Dallas M (Director)
Passionate Youth 1925,Je 30,14:3
Fitzgerald, Edith (Original Author)
Illicit 1931,Ja 19,25:1
Compromised 1931,N 7,16:5
Ex-Lady 1933,My 15,16:2
Fitzgerald, Edith (Screenwriter)
Painted Veil, The 1934,D 7,29:1
Wedding Night, The 1935,Mr 16,19:1
Small Town Girl 1936,Ap 11,19:1
My American Wife 1936,Ag 21,12:3
Within the Law 1939,Ap 6,31:2
Fitzgerald, Ella
Ride 'Em Cowboy 1942,Mr 5,27:3
Pete Kelly's Blues 1955,Ag 19,10:1
St Louis Blues 1958,Ap 12,13:1
Let no Man Write my Epitaph 1960,N 11,36:2

Fitzgerald, F Scott (Original Author)
Beautiful and Damned, The 1922,D 11,22:1
Great Gatsby, The 1926,N 22,28:3
Great Gatsby, The 1949,Jl 14,20:5
Last Time I saw Paris, The 1954,N 19,20:2
Tender is the Night 1962,Ja 20,13:2
Fitzgerald, F Scott (Screenwriter)
Three Comrades 1938,Je 3,17:1
Fitzgerald, Geraldine
Wuthering Heights 1939,Ap 14,28:2
Dark Victory 1939,Ap 21,27:2
Mill On the Floss, The 1939,N 15,19:3
Child Is Born, A 1940,Ja 11,19:2
'Til We Meet Again 1940,Ap 14,14:2
Flight From Destiny 1941,Mr 28,26:7
Shining Victory 1941,My 31,14:1
Gay Sisters, The 1942,Ag 15,14:2
Watch on the Rhine 1943,Ag 28,15:1
Ladies Courageous 1944,Mr 16,17:2
Wilson 1944,Ag 2,18:1
Uncle Harry 1945,Ag 24,14:5
Three Strangers 1946,F 23,20:2
O S S 1946,My 27,15:5
Nobody Lives Forever 1946,N 2,12:2
So Evil my Love 1948,Jl 22,27:2
Obsessed 1952,F 6,24:2
Ten North Frederick 1958,My 23,29:2
Fiercest Heart, The 1961,Ag 3,13:5
Pawnbroker, The 1965,Ap 21,51:1
Rachel Rachel 1968,Ag 27,36:1
Fitzgerald, Johnny
Boy Slaves 1939,F 9,17:3
Fitzgerald, Josephine
Spring in Park Lane 1949,S 21,38:2
You Can't Fool an Irishman 1950,D 7,45:4
Broth of a Boy 1959,D 28,18:1
Fitzgerald, Lillian
Some Like It Hot 1939,My 25,31:2
Fitzgerald, Neil
Informer, The 1935,My 10,25:2
Bride of Frankenstein, The 1935,My 11,21:2
Charlie Chan in Shanghai 1935,O 14,21:1
Mary of Scotland 1936,Jl 31,22:2
Plough and the Stars, The 1937,Ja 29,15:1
Parnell 1937,Je 4,27:2
London by Night 1937,Ag 13,13:1
Arrest Bulldog Drummond 1939,Ja 12,23:2
Sergeant Madden 1939,Mr 24,27:2
Bulldog Drummond's Secret Police
1939,Mr 30,19:3
Mirage 1965,My 27,28:1
Fitzgerald, Walter
This England 1941,N 18,33:2
In Which We Serve 1942,D 24,18:1
Squadron Leader X 1943,Jl 23,21:2
Blanche Fury 1948,N 24,20:2
This Was a Woman 1949,Ja 5,22:2
Mine Own Executioner 1949,Ja 19,34:2
Edward my Son 1949,Je 3,21:2
Fallen Idol, The 1949,N 16,39:2
Winslow Boy, The 1950,Je 7,34:4
Treasure Island 1950,Ag 16,24:2
Project M 7 1953,N 27,22:5
Pickwick Papers, The 1954,Ap 5,21:2
Personal Affair 1954,O 23,13:2
Front Page Story 1955,Ap 19,28:1
Adventures of Sadie, The 1955,My 18,35:2
Lease of Life 1956,F 10,18:1
Something of Value 1957,My 11,24:6
Camp on Blood Island, The 1958,S 18,37:2
Darby O'Gill and the Little People 1959,Jl 1,26:1
Third Man on the Mountain 1959,N 12,27:1
Damn the Defiant 1962,S 20,29:2
Fitzgerald, William
Cockleshell Heroes, The 1956,Je 4,25:2
Fitzgibbon, Patrick
Fixed Bayonets 1951,N 21,20:2
Fitzherbert, Victor
Uncivilized 1937,N 17,27:4
Fitzmaurice, George
Avalanche, The 1919,Je 30,16:3
Fitzmaurice, George (Director)
Society Exile, A 1919,Ag 18,9:2
Witness for the Defense, The 1919,S 15,16:3
On With the Dance 1920,F 16,8:1
Right to Love, The 1920,Ag 23,9:2
Idols of Clay 1920,N 21,VI,2:3
Experience 1921,Ag 8,12:2
Peter Ibbetson; (Forever) 1921,O 17,18:1
Three Live Ghosts 1922,Ja 2,20:1
Man From Home, The 1922,My 1,20:3
To Have and to Hold 1922,N 6,13:1
Kick In 1922,D 18,22:2
Bella Donna 1923,Ap 16,20:2
Cheat, The 1923,Ag 27,14:3
Eternal City, The 1924,Ja 21,20:1
Cytherea 1924,My 26,21:1
Tarnish 1924,O 13,21:1
Thief in Paradise, A 1925,Ja 26,14:1
His Supreme Moment 1925,Ap 13,24:1
Dark Angel, The 1925,O 12,19:3
Son of the Sheik, The 1926,Jl 26,13:2
Night of Love, The 1927,Ja 25,18:4

Fitzmaurice, George (Director) — Cont

Tender Hour, The 1927,Je 7,27:4
Rose of the Golden West 1927,S 26,27:1
Love Mart, The 1927,D 26,16:6
Lilac Time 1928,Ag 4,7:2
Barker, The 1928,D 6,35:1
His Captive Woman 1929,Ap 3,26:4
Tiger Rose 1929,D 25,23:1
Locked Door, The 1930,Ja 20,21:1
Bad One, The 1930,Je 13,28:3
Devil to Pay, The 1930,D 19,30:1
One Heavenly Night 1931,Ja 10,19:2
Strangers May Kiss 1931,Ap 13,17:1
Unholy Garden, The 1931,O 29,27:1
Mata Hari 1932,Ja 1,31:1
As You Desire Me 1932,Je 3,23:4
Petticoat Fever 1936,Mr 21,13:2
Suzy 1936,Jl 25,16:1
Emperor's Candlesticks, The 1937,Jl 9,18:1
Live, Love and Learn 1937,N 19,27:2
Arsene Lupin Returns 1938,Mr 9,21:1
Vacation From Love 1938,N 10,33:2
Adventure in Diamonds 1940,Ap 4,27:2

Fitzmaurice, Michael

House of a Thousand Candles, The
   1936,Ap 2,29:2
Reported Missing 1937,S 3,12:2
Fourteen Hours 1951,Mr 7,43:2

Fitzpatrick, Coleen

Pleasure Girls, The 1966,Ap 21,43:1

Fitzpatrick, Pat

Mozart 1940,O 4,29:2

Fitzpatrick, Ronald

Winning Ticket, The 1935,F 11,14:2

Fitzroy, Emily

Driven 1923,F 12,13:4
Purple Highway, The 1923,Jl 24,14:3 (In
   Addenda)
Strangers of the Night 1923,O 8,20:1
Secrets 1924,Mr 25,25:2
Man Who Came Back, The 1924,S 1,9:1
Red Lily, The 1924,S 29,10:1
His Hour 1924,O 7,26:1
Love's Wilderness 1924,D 22,20:2
Her Night of Romance 1925,Ja 13,16:1
Lady, The 1925,Ja 27,11:2
Learning to Love 1925,F 23,24:1
Denial, The 1925,Mr 10,19:3
Zander the Great 1925,My 4,16:2
Bobbed Hair 1925,N 4,17:4
What Happened to Jones 1926,F 9,22:1
Bat, The 1926,Mr 15,18:3
Bardelys The Magnificent 1926,N 1,28:1 (In
   Addenda)
Cheerful Fraud, The 1926,D 28,17:1
Orchids and Ermine 1927,Ap 19,24:4
Mockery 1927,Ag 22,21:3
Love 1927,N 30,22:4
Gentlemen Prefer Blondes 1928,Ja 16,24:1
Love Me and the World Is Mine 1928,F 6,12:3
Trail of '98, The 1928,Mr 21,30:3
Case of Lena Smith, The 1929,Ja 15,22:4
Show Boat 1929,Ap 18,32:3
Bridge of San Luis Rey, The 1929,My 20,22:6
Song O' my Heart 1930,Mr 12,32:6
Man From Blankley's, The 1930,Mr 29,23:1
She's my Weakness 1930,Je 21,20:5
Flirting Widow, The 1930,Ag 2,16:4
New Moon 1930,D 25,18:6
Unfaithful 1931,Mr 7,17:2
Way Down East 1931,Mr 16,25:1
It's a Wise Child 1931,My 16,13:3
Aren't We All? 1932,Jl 1,19:3
Man With two Faces, The 1934,Jl 12,20:2
Captain Hates the Sea, The 1934,N 29,33:2
Don Quixote 1934,D 24,17:1
Vigil in the Night 1940,Mr 9,19:2

Fitzroy, Katie

Playboy of the Western World, The
   1963,Mr 19,8:2

FITZSIMMONS

See Also FITZSIMONS

Fitzsimmons, Bob

Legendary Champions, The 1968,O 29,54:1

Fitzsimmons, Cortland (Original Author)

70,000 Witnesses 1932,S 3,16:2
Death on the Diamond 1934,S 24,14:1
Longest Night, The 1936,O 17,21:2
Earl Carroll Vanities 1945,Ap 2,15:6

Fitzsimmons, Cortland (Screenwriter)

Death of a Champion 1939,Ag 24,17:3
Devil With Hitler, The 1942,O 19,15:2

Fitzsimmons, Freddie

Safe at Home 1941,N 26,31:2

FITZSIMONS

See Also FITZSIMMONS

FitzSimons, Charles

Quiet Man, The 1952,Ag 22,13:1
What Price Glory 1952,Ag 23,10:2
Titanic 1953,My 28,27:5
Last Hurrah, The 1958,O 24,40:1

Fitzsimons, Charles (Producer)

Deadly Companions, The 1962,Ap 12,41:7

FitzSimons, Foster (Original Author)

Bright Leaf 1950,Je 17,7:2

Fitzsimons, Margot

Captive Heart, The 1947,Ap 28,27:2
I Know Where I'm Going 1947,Ag 20,25:2

Fix, Paul

First Kiss, The 1928,Ag 20,21:3
Lucky Star 1929,Jl 22,17:1
Ladies Love Brutes 1930,My 16,20:4
Three Girls Lost 1931,My 2,23:4
Good Bad Girl, The 1931,My 15,20:6
Dancers in the Dark 1932,Mr 19,11:2
Last Mile, The 1932,Ag 26,20:3
Back Street 1932,Ag 29,9:2
Zoo in Budapest 1933,Ap 28,15:2
Devil's Mate 1933,S 23,11:7
Avenger, The 1933,O 3,28:3
Little Man, What Now? 1934,Je 1,29:1
World Accuses, The 1935,Mr 21,27:2
Men Without Names 1935,Je 29,16:2
Prisoner of Shark Island, The 1936,F 13,25:2
Ex-Mrs Bradford, The 1936,My 28,19:2
Road to Glory, The 1936,Ag 6,22:1
Winterset 1936,D 4,31:1
Plot Thickens, The 1936,D 9,35:2
After the Thin Man 1936,D 25,19:2
Border Cafe 1937,Je 8,30:2
King of Gamblers 1937,Jl 3,18:1
Armored Car 1937,Jl 26,15:2
Souls at Sea 1937,Ag 10,23:2
Paid to Dance 1937,D 6,19:1
Daughter of Shanghai 1937,D 24,21:2
Penitentiary 1938,Mr 7,13:2
When G-Men Step In 1938,Mr 14,13:2
Crime Ring 1938,Jl 22,10:3
Smashing the Rackets 1938,Ag 9,22:5
Crime Takes a Holiday 1938,N 28,11:2
Undercover Doctor 1939,Je 1,31:2
Girl and the Gambler, The 1939,Je 28,17:3
News Is Made at Night 1939,Jl 13,17:2
Mutiny on the Blackhawk 1939,Ag 2,17:2
Behind Prison Gates 1939,Ag 21,9:3
Those High Grey Walls 1939,O 19,27:2
Black Friday 1940,Mr 22,23:3
Outside the Three-Mile Limit 1940,Ap 8,15:2
Crooked Road, The 1940,Je 11,33:4
Ghost Breakers, The 1940,Jl 4,12:2
Black Diamonds 1940,S 10,26:6
Great Plane Robbery, The 1940,N 15,25:2
Jail House Blues 1942,F 6,23:2
Escape From Crime 1942,O 12,12:3
Sherlock Holmes and the Secret Weapon
   1943,Ja 5,15:2
Pittsburgh 1943,F 25,27:2
Hitler-Dead or Alive 1943,Mr 31,23:3
In old Oklahoma 1943,D 6,21:1
Fighting Seabees, The 1944,Mr 20,14:2
Tall in the Saddle 1944,D 15,25:3
Flame of Barbary Coast 1945,My 28,22:2
Back to Bataan 1945,S 13,26:3
Dakota 1945,D 17,17:2
Tycoon 1947,D 26,22:6
Red River 1948,O 1,31:2
Plunders, The 1948,N 1,28:2
Force of Evil 1948,D 27,16:2
Wake of the Red Witch 1949,Ja 10,19:2
Hellfire 1949,My 30,9:4
Fighting Kentuckian, The 1949,S 19,18:3
Surrender 1950,O 9,21:5
California Passage 1950,D 16,10:5
What Price Glory 1952,Ag 23,10:2
Hondo 1953,N 27,99:9
Johnny Guitar 1954,My 28,19:2
High and the Mighty, The 1954,Jl 1,21:2
Blood Alley 1955,O 6,25:3
Santiago 1956,Jl 14,13:2
Bad Seed, The 1956,S 13,39:6
Toward the Unknown 1956,S 28,24:4
Giant 1956,O 11,51:1
Night Passage 1957,Jl 25,28:1
Jet Pilot 1957,O 5,8:6
To Kill a Mockingbird 1963,F 15,10:2
Outrage, The 1964,O 8,48:2
Baby, the Rain Must Fall 1965,Ja 14,44:1
Shenandoah 1965,Jl 29,18:3
Sons of Katie Elder, The 1965,Ag 26,40:3
Nevada Smith 1966,Je 24,28:1 (Incorrect in this
   edition; use 1966,Je 30,28:1 elsewhere)
Ride Beyond Vengance 1966,S 29,60:1
Welcome to Hard Times 1967,My 2,56:1
Dorado, El 1967,Je 29,32:1
Day of the Evil Gun 1968,Ap 25,53:2

Fix, Paul (Screenwriter)

Tall in the Saddle 1944,D 15,25:3
Ring of Fear 1954,Jl 29,18:3

Fjeldstad, Jack

Nine Lives 1959,Ja 6,28:1

Fjellstrom, Emil

Kryss med Albertina, Paa; Cruise in the Albertina,
   A 1940,Mr 25,11:3
Lasse-Maja 1943,Mr 22,15:4
Himlaspelet 1944,O 9,17:3

Fjord, Olaf

Monna Vanna 1923,S 25,8:2
Madonna of the Sleeping Cars, The
   1929,O 14,20:2

Flack, Karen

High Wind in Jamaica, A 1965,Je 17,27:2

Flagg, James Montgomers (Original Author)

Independence B'Gosh 1918,D 2,11:3

Flagg, James Montgomery

Good Sport, The 1918,My 6,11:3
Perfectly Fiendish Flanagan 1918,D 16,13:3
Good Sport, The 1918,My 6,11:3
Spoiled Girl, The 1918,Je 3,9:3
Tell That to the Marines 1918,O 14,15:1
Perfectly Fiendish Flanagan 1918,D 16,13:3
One Every Minute 1919,Ja 13,9:3
Beresford and the Baboons 1919,F 17,11:3

Flagg, James Montgomery (Screenwriter)

Spirit of the Red Cross, The 1918,Ap 21,IV,11:8

Flagstad, Kirsten

Big Broadcast of 1938, The 1938,Mr 10,16:2

Flaherty, Frances (Original Author)

Louisiana Story 1948,S 29,36:2

Flaherty, Howard (Screenwriter)

PT 109 1963,Je 27,23:1

Flaherty, Pat

20th Century 1934,My 4,24:2
My Man Godfrey 1936,S 19,18:1 (Incorrect in
   this edition; use 1936,S 18,18:1 elsewhere)
Pigskin Parade 1936,N 14,23:3
Flying Hostess 1936,D 14,29:4
Woman Wise 1937,Ja 23,13:1
Hold 'Em Navy 1937,N 6,14:2
Navy Blue and Gold 1937,D 24,21:2
She Loved a Fireman 1938,Ja 21,15:3
Stadium Murders, The 1938,Ap 9,11:2
Main Event, The 1938,Je 20,11:3
Always in Trouble 1938,N 3,27:1
Only Angels Have Wings 1939,My 12,25:2
Legion of Lost Flyers 1939,O 30,13:3
Black Diamonds 1940,S 10,26:6
Flight Command 1941,Ja 17,21:2
Meet John Doe 1941,Mr 13,25:2
Sergeant York 1941,Jl 3,15:1
Who Is Hope Schuyler 1942,My 22,27:1
It Happened in Flatbush 1942,Jl 3,12:8
Gentleman Jim 1942,N 26,40:3
Jackie Robinson Story, The 1950,My 17,36:1
Winning Team, The 1952,Je 21,12:2

Flaherty, Robert (Director)

Elephant Boy 1937,Ap 6,20:2
Louisiana Story 1948,S 29,36:2

Flaherty, Robert (Miscellaneous)

St Matthew Passion 1952,Ja 29,17:4

Flaherty, Robert (Original Author)

Tabu 1931,Mr 19,21:3
Louisiana Story 1948,S 29,36:2

Flaherty, Robert (Producer)

Nanook of the North 1922,Je 12,16:2 (Incorrect
   in this edition; use 1922,Je 12,10:2 elsewhere)
Moana 1926,F 8,24:2
Man of Aran 1934,O 19,27:1
Louisiana Story 1948,S 29,36:2

Flaherty, Vincent X (Original Author)

Jim Thorpe - All American 1951,Ag 25,7:2

Flaherty, Vincent X (Screenwriter)

PT 109 1963,Je 27,23:1

Flaiano, Ennio (Miscellaneous)

Rocket From Calabuch 1958,O 8,41:1

Flaiano, Ennio (Original Author)

Vitelloni 1956,O 24,43:1
Bidone, Il 1964,N 20,42:1

Flaiano, Ennio (Screenwriter)

Flight Into France 1949,Jl 22,16:2
Too Bad She's Bad 1955,D 26,23:2
Vitelloni 1956,O 24,43:1
Woman of Rome 1956,N 6,30:1
It Happened in the Park 1957,Ag 13,23:2
Cabiria 1957,O 29,34:2
Dolce Vita, La 1961,Ap 20,30:1
Night; The; Notte, La 1962,F 20,29:4
Boccaccio '70 (The Temapation of Dr Antonio);
   Temptation of Dr Antonio, The (Boccaccio '70)
   1962,Je 27,40:1
Eight and One Half 1963,Je 26,36:1
Bidone, Il 1964,N 20,42:1
Not on Your Life; Verdugo, El 1965,Mr 30,52:1
Variety Lights; Luci del Varieta 1965,My 7,34:1
Juliet of the Spirits 1965,N 4,57:1
10th Victim, The 1965,D 21,46:1
Tonio Kroger 1968,Ja 16,24:1
Oldest Profession, The (Prehistoric Era);
   Prehistoric Era (The Oldest Profession)
   1968,N 8,42:1
Oldest Profession, The (Roman Nights); Roman
   Nights (The Oldest Profession) 1968,N 8,42:1

Flake, Snow

Cabin in the Cotton 1932,S 30,17:3
Lawless Nineties, The 1936,Je 29,11:1

Flame (Dog)

Miraculous Journey 1948,S 20,21:2

Flament, Edouard (Composer)
Maternelle, La 1935,O 15,19:1
Flament, Georges
It Happened in Gibraltar 1943,N 16,27:1
Marked Girls 1949,Je 25,8:7
Young Girls Beware 1959,Ag 22,8:2
Flanagan, Bud
13 Hours by Air 1936,Ap 30,17:2
Girl From Scotland Yard, The 1937,My 31,11:2
Flanagan, Fionnuala
Ulysses 1967,Mr 14,55:1
Flanagan, Ray
Passages From James Joyce's Finnegans Wake
1967,O 10,56:1
Flandrau, Grace H (Original Author)
Being Respectable 1924,Ag 4,16:3
Flannery, Jerrilyn
I Want You 1951,D 24,9:1
Flannery, Walter
By the Light of the Silvery Moon
1953,Mr 27,28:2
Flanz, Marta (Director)
Kochaj Tylko Mnie 1937,Ap 20,29:2
Flassmire, Gus
Woman Doctor 1939,Mr 24,27:3
Flateau, Georges
Katia 1939,D 23,9:2
Flateau, Joel
Sans Famille 1959,S 5,11:4
Fanny 1961,Jl 7,16:1
Victors, The 1963,D 20,21:2
Flaubert, Gustave (Original Author)
Madame Bovary 1937,O 30,22:2
Madame Bovary 1949,Ag 26,15:2
Flavin, James
King Kong 1933,Mr 3,12:1
Baby, Take a Bow 1934,Je 30,18:6
Gift of Gab 1934,S 26,17:6
One Way Ticket 1936,Ja 1,35:2
My Man Godfrey 1936,S 19,18:1 (Incorrect in
this edition; use 1936,S 18,18:1 elsewhere)
League of Frightened Men, The 1937,Jl 2,25:1
Wives Under Suspicion 1938,Jl 1,22:3
Thanks For Everything 1938,D 10,13:2
Duke of West Point, The 1938,D 16,33:2
Ride a Crooked Mile 1938,D 29,15:2
Gracie Allen Murder Case, The 1939,Je 8,31:3
Mickey, the Kid 1939,Jl 6,27:1
Mister Wong in Chinatown 1939,Jl 31,9:2 (In
Addenda)
Calling All Marines 1939,O 26,27:2
Cisco Kid and the Lady, The 1939,D 25,29:2
South of Pago-Pago 1940,Ag 2,12:2
Great Profile, The 1940,O 18,25:1
Devil's Pipeline, The 1940,N 11,22:4
Belle Starr 1941,N 1,20:2
Kathleen 1941,D 19,35:3
Treat 'Em Rough 1942,Ja 19,21:3
Juke Box Jenny 1942,Ap 17,21:3
Fingers at the Window 1942,Ap 23,27:3
Ten Gentlemen From West Point 1942,Je 5,23:3
Iceland 1942,O 15,27:1
Gentleman Jim 1942,N 26,40:3
Life Begins at Eight-Thirty 1942,D 10,35:2
Air Force 1943,F 4,29:1
Corvette K-225 1943,O 21,30:1
Uncertain Glory 1944,Ap 8,9:2
Laura 1944,O 12,24:1
Abroad With two Yanks 1944,O 26,19:7
Conflict 1945,Je 16,10:2
Anchors Aweigh 1945,Jl 20,15:2
Tars and Spars 1946,F 15,29:2
Easy to Wed 1946,Jl 12,14:2
Strange Love of Martha Ivers, The
1946,Jl 25,18:4
Cloak and Dagger 1946,O 5,13:2
Angel on my Shoulder 1946,O 21,27:2
Nobody Lives Forever 1946,N 2,12:2
Fabulous Dorseys, The 1947,My 30,25:3
Desert Fury 1947,S 25,35:4
Nightmare Alley 1947,O 10,31:3
One Touch of Venus 1948,O 29,29:5
Plunders, The 1948,N 1,28:2
Mighty Joe Young 1949,Jl 28,19:3
Blondie Hits the Jackpot 1949,S 9,28:3
Abbott and Costello Meet the Killer Boris Karloff
1949,S 19,18:3
Prison Warden 1949,O 21,31:2
South Sea Sinner 1950,Ja 16,18:4
Oh! Susanna 1951,Mr 30,28:5
Million Dollar Mermaid 1952,D 5,35:2
Mister Roberts 1955,Jl 15,14:1
Francis in the Haunted House 1956,Jl 21,9:2
Wild Is the Wind 1957,D 12,35:1
In Cold Blood 1967,D 15,60:1
Flavin, Martin (Original Author)
Criminal Code, The 1931,Ja 5,21:3
Too Young to Marry 1931,My 4,15:3
Age of Consent, The 1932,S 3,16:2
Love Begins at 20 1936,S 19,20:1
Penitentiary 1938,Mr 7,13:2

Flaws, Jessie
I, A Lover 1968,My 4,46:2
Fleck, F (Director)
Wenn die Soldaten 1932,O 31,18:4
Fleck, J (Director)
Die Csikos Baroness 1932,Mr 28,11:2
Pfarrer von Kirchfeld, Der; Pastor of Kirchfeld,
The 1939,Ap 22,15:3
Fleck, James
Tell-Tale Heart, The 1934,Je 15,26:3
Fleck, L (Director)
Die Csikos Baroness 1932,Mr 28,11:2
Wenn die Soldaten 1932,O 31,18:4
Pfarrer von Kirchfeld, Der; Pastor of Kirchfeld,
The 1939,Ap 22,15:3
Fleck, T L (Director)
Mein Liebster Ist ein Jaegersmann 1936,S 15,37:6
Fleet, Jo Van
Wild River 1960,My 27,22:1
Fleeting, John
Forty Thousand Horsemen 1941,Ag 15,13:2
Fleetwing, John
Pacific Adventure 1947,N 26,18:2
Fleetwood, Betty
This Happy Breed 1947,Ap 14,24:2
Fleigel, Gustaf
City Without Jews, The 1928,Jl 9,25:1
Fleisch, Walter (Original Author)
Countess of Monte Cristo, The 1934,Ap 2,13:2
Fleischer, Dave (Director)
Gulliver's Travels 1939,D 21,29:1
Mr Bug Goes to Town 1942,F 20,21:3
Fleischer, Dave (Original Author)
Mr Bug Goes to Town 1942,F 20,21:3
Fleischer, Max (Director)
Out of the Ink Well 1919,Ap 21,13:4
Fleischer, Max (Producer)
Out of the Inkwell 1919,D 1,9:3
Gulliver's Travels 1939,D 21,29:1
Mr Bug Goes to Town 1942,F 20,21:3
Fleischer, Richard (Director)
Follow Me Quietly 1949,Jl 8,14:5
Trapped 1949,N 26,10:6
Narrow Margin, The 1952,My 5,18:7
Vikings, The 1952,Je 12,35:2
Arena 1953,Jl 23,20:2
20,000 Leagues Under the Sea 1954,D 24,7:2
Violent Saturday 1955,My 12,32:2
Girl in the Red Velvet Swing, The
1955,O 20,41:2
Between Heaven and Hell 1956,O 12,33:2
Compulsion 1959,Ap 2,26:2
These Thousand Hills 1959,My 7,36:1
Crack in the Mirror 1960,My 20,26:1
Big Gamble, The 1961,S 2,19:2
Barabbas 1962,O 11,49:1
Fantastic Voyage 1966,S 8,43:1
Doctor Dolittle 1967,D 20,55:1
Boston Strangler, The 1968,O 17,52:1
Fleischer, Richard O (Producer)
Design for Death 1948,Je 11,27:2
Fleischman, A S (Original Author)
Blood Alley 1955,O 6,25:3
Fleischman, A S (Screenwriter)
Blood Alley 1955,O 6,25:3
Lafayette Escadrille 1958,Ap 19,10:4
Deadly Companions, The 1962,Ap 12,41:7
Fleischman, Harry
Crossroads 1942,Jl 27,18:2
Stand by for Action 1943,Mr 12,12:2
Fleischman, Sid (Original Author)
Adventures of Bullwhip Griffin, The
1967,Mr 9,43:2
FLEISHER
See FLEISCHER
FLEISHMAN
See FLEISCHMAN
Fleming, Alice
Playmates 1941,D 26,21:3
Storm Over Lisbon 1944,S 11,14:1
It's a Pleasure 1945,My 4,23:3
Fleming, Athol
Alias Bulldog Drummond 1935,S 10,26:2
Fleming, Berry (Original Author)
Colonel Effingham's Raid 1946,Ap 5,21:3
Fleming, Bob
Nugget Nell 1919,Jl 28,8:5
Fleming, Claude
Mamba 1930,Mr 11,25:2
Captain of the Guard 1930,Mr 29,23:1
Bride of the Regiment 1930,My 22,32:6
One Night at Susie's 1930,N 24,26:5
Fleming, Eric
Conquest of Space 1955,My 28,7:6
Glass Bottom Boat, The 1966,Je 10,54:1
Fleming, Ian
Sherlock Holmes's Fatal Hour 1931,Jl 13,13:5
Missing Rembrandt, The 1932,Mr 26,17:2
Triumph of Sherlock Holmes, The
1935,My 27,20:6
Crouching Beast, The 1936,Ag 22,6:1
When Thief Meets Thief 1937,Je 15,26:2
Hatter's Castle 1948,Jl 3,8:6

Fleming, Ian— Cont
Murder Will Out 1953,Ap 6,24:2
Trials of Oscar Wilde, The 1960,Je 28,26:1
Return of Mr Moto 1965,D 2,48:1
Fleming, Ian (Original Author)
Dr No 1963,My 30,20:1
From Russia with Love 1964,Ap 9,25:1
Goldfinger 1964,D 22,36:1
Thunderball 1965,D 22,23:1
Casino Royale 1967,Ap 29,25:1
Poppy is Also a Flower, The 1967,D 14,62:4
Chitty Chitty Bang Bang 1968,D 19,64:4
Fleming, Jane
Viscount, The 1967,My 11,50:1
Fleming, John (Original Author)
Larceny 1948,S 4,8:6
Fleming, Rhonda
Spellbound 1945,N 2,22:2
Spiral Staircase, The 1946,F 7,29:3
Abilene Town 1946,Mr 4,16:5
Adventure Island 1947,O 20,29:2
Out of the Past 1947,N 26,18:2
Connecticut Yankee in King Arthur's Court, A
1949,Ap 8,31:2
Great Lover, The 1949,N 24,48:2
Eagle and the Hawk, The 1950,Jl 6,31:2
Cry Danger 1951,F 22,27:3
Redhead and the Cowboy, The 1951,Je 6,37:2
Last Outpost, The 1951,Je 22,16:3
Little Egypt 1951,Ag 30,20:3
Crosswinds 1951,D 7,35:4
Hong Kong 1952,Ap 5,20:3
Golden Hawk, The 1952,O 18,16:4
Pony Express 1953,Je 6,8:6
Inferno 1953,Ag 12,22:2
Those Redheads From Seattle 1953,O 1,34:2
Jivaro 1954,F 13,11:5
Yankee Pasha 1954,Ap 19,19:2
Tennessee's Partner 1955,N 5,22:8
Killer is Loose, The 1956,Mr 3,17:2
Slightly Scarlet 1956,Mr 17,13:2
While the City Sleeps 1956,My 17,37:1
Buster Keaton Story, The 1957,Ap 22,31:6
Gunfight at the O K Corral 1957,My 30,23:2
Gun Glory 1957,Jl 20,8:7
Home Before Dark 1958,N 7,23:1
Alias Jesse James 1959,My 18,31:2
Big Circus, The 1959,Jl 18,6:1
Crowded Sky, The 1961,F 11,27:2
Revolt of the Slaves, The 1961,N 8,41:1
Fleming, Susan
Lover Come Back 1931,Je 5,26:5
Men Are Like That 1931,Ag 17,18:2
Dangerous Affair, A 1931,N 23,22:1
Million Dollar Legs 1932,Jl 9,7:5
My Weakness 1933,S 22,14:1
Call it Luck 1934,Jl 10,24:5
Break of Hearts 1935,My 17,24:3
Star for a Night 1936,S 5,7:2
Gold Diggers of 1937 1936,D 25,19:2
God's Country and the Woman 1937,Ja 11,15:5
Fleming, Suzanne
Ace of Cads, The 1926,O 18,18:1 (In Addenda)
Fleming, Victor (Director)
When Clouds Roll by 1919,D 29,7:2
Mollycoddle, The 1920,Je 14,13:2
Woman's Place 1921,O 23,VI,4:1 (In Addenda)
Lane That had no Turning, The 1922,Ja 9,15:2
Red Hot Romance 1922,Ja 23,11:4
Law of the Lawless, The 1923,Je 19,22:4
To the Last Man 1923,Ag 28,12:1
Call of the Canyon, The 1923,D 17,23:1
Empty Hands 1924,Ag 18,8:2
Devil's Cargo, The 1925,F 3,24:1
Adventure 1925,Ap 15,16:1
Son of his Father, A 1925,S 29,31:3
Lord Jim 1925,N 16,19:4
Blind Goddess 1926,Ap 6,26:4 (In Addenda)
Rough Riders, The 1927,Mr 16,28:2
Way of all Flesh, The 1927,Je 27,25:2
Hula 1927,Ag 29,21:1
Way of all Flesh, The 1928,Ja 29,VIII,6:2
Abie's Irish Rose 1928,Ap 20,26:7
Awakening, The 1928,D 31,9:1
Wolf Song 1929,F 25,16:1
Virginian, The 1929,D 23,18:2
Renegades 1930,N 8,21:3
Wet Parade, The 1932,Ap 22,23:2
Red Dust 1932,N 5,12:5
White Sister, The 1933,Mr 18,9:3
Bombshell 1933,O 21,11:2
Treasure Island 1934,Ag 18,5:5
Reckless 1935,Ap 20,16:1
Farmer Takes a Wife, The 1935,Ag 9,21:2
Captains Courageous 1937,My 12,27:1
Test Pilot 1938,Ap 16,17:1
Wizard of Oz, The 1939,Ag 18,16:2
Gone With the Wind 1939,D 20,31:2
Dr Jekyll and Mr Hyde 1941,Ag 13,13:2
Tortilla Flat 1942,My 22,27:1
Guy Named Joe, A 1943,D 24,17:2
Adventure 1946,F 8,23:2
Joan of Arc 1948,N 12,30:5

Flemyne, Gordon (Director)
Split, The 1968,N 5,55:2
Flemyng, Robert
Head Over Heels in Love 1937,F 13,9:1
Guinea Pig, The 1949,My 2,20:2
Bond Street 1950,Mr 30,40:6
Conspirator 1950,Ap 28,26:2
Blue Lamp, The 1951,Ja 9,25:1
Holly and the Ivy, The 1954,F 5,16:1
Man Who Never Was, The 1956,Ap 4,24:1
Funny Face 1957,Mr 29,16:1
Let's Be Happy 1957,My 25,25:1
Cast a Dark Shadow 1957,N 28,57:1
Windom's Way 1958,O 1,45:1
Touch of Larceny, A 1960,Mr 17,28:1
Chance Meeting 1960,O 27,45:2
Horrible Dr Hitchcock, The 1964,D 3,58:3
Quiller Memorandum, The 1966,D 16,59:1
Spy With a Cold Nose, The 1966,D 20,58:2
Deadly Affair, The 1967,Ja 27,31:1
Flender, Harold (Original Author)
Paris Blues 1961,N 8,41:1
Flers, R de (Original Author)
Nouveaux Messieurs, Les 1929,Ja 13,VIII,7:4
Nouveau Messieurs, Les; New Gentlemen, The
  1929,D 15,X,6:5
Flers, R De (Original Author)
Royal Affair, A; (Roi, Le) 1950,Mr 9,25:2
Flers, Robert de (Composer)
Ciboulette 1934,Ja 7,X,4:2
Fletcher, Bill
Rebellion in Cuba 1961,Jl 1,9:1
Fletcher, Bramwell
So This Is London 1930,My 24,21:2
Raffles 1930,Jl 25,20:4
Millionaire, The 1931,Ap 9,30:5
Svengali 1931,My 1,30:3
Daughter of the Dragon 1931,Ag 22,7:5
Once a Lady 1931,N 9,22:4
Silent Witness, The 1932,F 8,21:1
Bill of Divorcement, A 1932,O 3,15:2
Mummy, The 1933,Ja 7,11:2
Scarlet Pimpernel, The 1935,F 8,27:2
White Cargo 1942,N 27,27:2
Random Harvest 1942,D 18,36:6
Immortal Sergeant 1943,F 4,29:2
Fletcher, Cecil
Song of Songs, The 1918,F 19,11:2
Fletcher, Charlotte
Big Fisherman, The 1959,Ag 6,18:1
Fletcher, Jack
Any Wednesday 1966,O 14,50:1
Tiger Makes Out, The 1967,S 19,53:1
Fletcher, Jerry
Submarine D-1 1937,D 30,15:4
Fletcher, Kent
Lord of the Flies 1963,Ag 20,37:1
Fletcher, Lester
Operation Eichmann 1961,My 4,40:7
Fletcher, Lucille (Original Author)
Blindfold 1966,My 26,55:2
Fletcher, Lucille (Screenwriter)
Sorry, Wrong Number 1948,S 2,18:2
Fletcher, Maria Garcia
Bravados, The 1958,Je 26,23:2
Fletcher, Robin
M 1951,Je 11,20:7
Fletscher, Richard (Director)
Happy Time, The 1952,O 31,30:2
Fleullen, Joel
Burning Cross, The 1948,F 20,19:1
Flexner, Anne Crawford (Original Author)
Mrs Wiggs of the Cabbage Patch 1934,O 29,14:2
Fliangoltz, Dmitri (Composer)
Lucky Bride, The 1948,Ja 26,15:2
Flick, Pat C
Black Legion 1937,Ja 18,21:1
Missing Guest, The 1938,S 7,30:7
Flick, Pat C (Miscellaneous)
Stars Over Broadway 1935,N 14,17:3
Miss Pacific Fleet 1935,D 7,22:2
Wide Open Faces 1938,Ap 15,23:2
Flick, Pat C (Original Author)
Nobody's Baby 1937,My 20,17:3
Flick, Pat C (Screenwriter)
Singing Kid, The 1936,Ap 4,11:1
Stage Struck 1936,S 28,14:4
Nobody's Baby 1937,My 20,17:3
Marry the Girl 1937,Jl 31,6:2
Flickenschildt, Elisabeth
Stefanie 1959,Je 18,36:1
Scampolo 1959,Ag 6,18:4
Faust 1961,Ap 16,31:1
Flicker, Theodore J
Troublemaker, The 1964,Je 23,25:1
Flicker, Theodore J (Director)
Troublemaker, The 1964,Je 23,25:1
President's Analyst, The 1967,D 22,44:4
Flicker, Theodore J (Original Author)
Troublemaker, The 1964,Je 23,25:1
Flicker, Theodore J (Screenwriter)
Troublemaker, The 1964,Je 23,25:1
Spinout 1966,D 15,60:1

President's Analyst, The 1967,D 22,44:4
Flint, Eva K (Original Author)
Reckless Living 1931,D 5,21:2
Flint, Helen
Uncle Sam of Freedom Ridge 1920,S 27,15:2
Ninth Guest, The 1934,Mr 3,8:5
Midnight 1934,Mr 10,18:3
Broadway Bill 1934,N 30,22:2
While the Patient Slept 1935,Mr 2,18:2
Doubting Thomas 1935,Jl 11,24:2
Ah, Wilderness! 1935,D 25,30:2
Fury 1936,Je 6,21:1
Early to Bed 1936,Jl 16,20:2
Give Me your Heart 1936,S 17,18:2
Black Legion 1937,Ja 18,21:1
Step Lively, Jeeves 1937,Ap 2,19:6
Married Before Breakfast 1937,Jl 23,16:2
Blonde Trouble 1937,Ag 7,7:2
Time to Kill 1942,D 25,15:4
Flint, Kelly (Narrator)
Roosevelt Story, The 1947,Ag 22,11:2
Flint, Sam
Mrs Wiggs of the Cabbage Patch 1934,O 29,14:2
Florida Special 1936,My 29,15:2
Lawless Nineties, The 1936,Je 29,11:1
Accusing Finger, The 1936,N 17,35:4
Road to Happiness 1942,Mr 27,27:4
My Pal Trigger 1946,Ag 17,16:3
Four Faces West 1948,Ag 4,18:3
Rock Island Trail 1950,Je 5,19:3
Steel Trap, The 1952,N 13,35:2
Ruby Gentry 1952,D 26,20:2
Soldier in the Rain 1963,N 29,67:6 (Incorrect in
  this edition; use 1963,N 28,67:6 elsewhere)
Flippen, Jay C
Marie Galante 1934,N 21,23:4
Intrigue 1948,Ap 24,11:2
Down to the Sea in Ships 1949,F 23,31:2
They Live by Night 1949,N 4,33:2
Oh, You Beautiful Doll 1949,N 12,8:4
Yellow Cab Man, The 1950,Mr 27,19:2
Buccaneer's Girl 1950,Mr 27,19:2
Love That Brute 1950,My 27,10:6
Winchester 73 1950,Je 8,38:2
Two Flags West 1950,O 13,23:2
Lemon Drop Kid, The 1951,Mr 22,41:2
People Against O'Hara, The 1951,S 6,39:3
Flying Leathernecks 1951,S 20,37:1
Model and the Marriage Broker, The
  1952,Ja 12,10:6
Las Vegas Story, The 1952,Ja 31,37:6
Bend of the River 1952,Ap 10,37:1
Woman of the North Country 1952,Ag 30,6:2
Thunder Bay 1953,My 21,39:2
Devil's Canyon 1953,O 3,14:2
Wild One, The 1953,D 31,9:2
Carnival Story 1954,Ap 17,8:2
Six Bridges to Cross 1955,Ja 22,8:2
Far Country, The 1955,F 14,24:2
Man Without a Star 1955,Mr 25,19:3
Strategic Air Command 1955,Ap 21,33:1
It's Always Fair Weather 1955,S 16,19:1
Oklahoma! 1955,O 11,49:1
Kismet 1955,D 9,32:2
Killing, The 1956,My 21,20:1
King and Four Queens, The 1956,D 22,13:7
Public Pigeon No 1 1957,My 18,23:2
Midnight Story, The 1957,Jl 5,14:2
Night Passage 1957,Jl 25,28:1
Run of the Arrow 1957,Ag 3,8:6
Jet Pilot 1957,O 5,8:6
From Hell to Texas 1958,Je 5,39:2
Wild River 1960,My 27,22:1
Studs Lonigan 1960,D 15,59:1
Cat Ballou 1965,Je 25,36:1
Firecreek 1968,F 22,36:2
Flippen, Ruth Brooks (Original Author)
Three Guys Named Mike 1951,Mr 2,21:2
Because You're Mine 1952,S 26,18:2
Flippen, Ruth Brooks (Screenwriter)
Love Is Better Than Ever 1952,Mr 4,23:2
Gidget Goes Hawaiian 1961,Ag 10,17:4
Sail a Crooked Ship 1962,F 3,12:6
Ticklish Affair, A 1963,Ag 22,19:2
Gidget Goes to Rome 1963,S 12,32:2
Flippov, S
Twelfth Night 1956,Mr 5,21:1
Flo, Janett
As du Turf, Les; Aces of Turf 1935,My 11,21:3
Floden, Torsten (Original Author)
Lasse-Maja 1943,Mr 22,15:4
Flodqvist, Barbro
Sun Over Klara 1944,My 1,20:8
Flom, Suzanne
Train, The 1965,Mr 18,25:1
Flon, Suzanne
Moulin Rouge 1953,F 11,33:5
Miracle of Saint Therese 1959,F 10,38:4 (In
  Addenda)
Mr Arkadin 1962,O 12,26:1
Monkey in Winter 1963,F 1,7:2
Trial, The 1963,F 21,5:1
Chateau en Suede; Castle in Switzerland
  1964,O 14,51:1

Flon, Suzanne— Cont
Zita 1968,Ag 12,40:2
Flood, Dorothy
Resurrection 1931,Ja 24,15:1
Flood, James (Director)
Woman Hater, The 1925,Jl 13,20:2
Wife Who Wasn't Wanted, The 1925,S 9,23:1
Satan in Sables 1925,O 15,27:3
Why Girls Go Back Home 1926,My 18,28:2
Lady in Ermine, The 1927,Ja 3,16:2
Three Hours 1927,Mr 8,18:4
Count of Ten, The 1928,Mr 13,23:3
Marriage by Contract 1928,N 13,37:1
She-Wolf 1931,My 28,30:6
Mouthpiece, The 1932,Ap 21,25:2
Life Begins 1932,Ag 26,20:3
Under-Cover Man 1932,D 5,21:2
All of Me 1934,F 5,19:2
Such Women Are Dangerous 1934,Je 9,18:3
Wings in the Dark 1935,F 2,10:1
Shanghai 1935,Jl 20,16:2
We're Only Human 1936,Ja 18,19:2
Everybody's Old Man 1936,Mr 26,27:2
Midnight Madonna 1937,Jl 17,18:1
Off the Record 1939,F 18,12:2
Big Fix, The 1947,My 3,10:3
Florat, Robert (Producer)
Sins of Paris 1954,Ja 30,9:6
Florath, Albert
Berlin-Alexanderplatz 1933,My 11,14:1
Spiel in Sommerwind; Play in the Summer
  Breezes 1939,Ap 1,17:2
Biberpelz, Der; Beaver Coat, The 1939,S 9,11:3
Hurra! Ich bin Papa; Hurrah! I'm a Papa
  1940,Je 1,12:3
Florelle
Dame de Chez Maxim, La; Woman at Maxim's,
  The 1933,Je 11,IX,2:5
Femme Nue, La 1933,Ag 25,12:3
Opera de Quat' Sous, L' 1933,D 9,18:4
Liliom 1935,Mr 18,14:4
Miserables, Les 1936,O 28,31:2
Amphitryon 1937,Mr 24,29:1
Gervaise 1957,N 12,46:1
Oasis 1960,Jl 7,26:1
Crime of Monsieur Lange, The 1964,Ap 4,15:5
Florence
On Demande un Compagnon 1933,Je 5,18:5
Florence and Alvarez
Student Tour 1934,O 31,17:3
Florencie
Panic 1947,N 27,50:2
Florent, Napoleon
Kisenga, Man of Africa 1952,Mr 7,18:2
Florenz, Nyall
Singer not the Song, The 1962,My 3,25:4
Flores, Beatriz
Roots, The (The Cows); Cows, The (The Roots)
  1957,S 3,23:2
Flores, Felipe
My Outlaw Brother 1951,Ag 23,19:2
Flores, Iris
Ride the Pink Horse 1947,O 9,32:3
Woman in the Night 1948,Ja 10,16:2
Flores, John (Producer)
Suicide Attack 1951,Jl 14,7:2
Flores, Marta
Goyescas 1944,My 29,18:3
Flores Brothers
That Night in Rio 1941,Mr 10,21:2
Mexican Hayride 1949,Ja 12,33:3
Florey, Robert (Director)
Hole in the Wall, The 1929,Ap 15,22:6
Cocoanuts, The 1929,My 25,17:3
Night Club 1929,Ag 12,22:2
Murders in the Rue Morgue 1932,F 11,16:1
Man Called Back, The 1932,Jl 30,16:5
Girl Missing 1933,Ap 1,18:2
Ex-Lady 1933,My 15,16:2
House on 56th Street, The 1933,D 2,9:3
Bedside 1934,Mr 7,23:4
I Sell Anything 1934,D 27,25:2
I am a Thief 1935,Ja 1,24:1
Woman in Red, The 1935,Mr 23,11:3
Florentine Dagger, The 1935,Ap 27,20:6
Don't Bet on Blondes 1935,Jl 20,16:2
Pay-Off, The 1935,N 13,25:3
Preview Murder Mystery, The 1936,Mr 21,13:2
Till We Meet Again 1936,My 9,11:2
Hollywood Boulevard 1936,S 21,26:4
Outcast 1937,Mr 3,27:2
Mountain Music 1937,Je 24,30:3
King of Gamblers 1937,Jl 3,18:1
This Way Please 1937,O 8,27:2
Daughter of Shanghai 1937,D 24,21:2
Dangerous to Know 1938,Mr 11,15:4
King of Alcatraz 1938,O 7,21:2
Disbarred 1939,Ja 19,17:2
Hotel Imperial 1939,My 11,31:3
Magnificent Fraud, The 1939,Jl 20,16:2
Death of a Champion 1939,Ag 24,17:3
Parole Fixer 1940,Ap 18,28:5
Women Without Names 1940,My 9,26:4
Face Behind the Mask, The 1941,F 7,23:2

Florey, Robert (Director) — Cont
Meet Boston Blackie 1941,F 26,17:2
Dangerously They Live 1942,Ap 11,9:2
Desert Song, The 1943,D 18,10:6
Roger Touhy, Gangster 1944,Je 5,14:7
Man From Frisco 1944,Je 16,14:7
God is my Co-Pilot 1945,Mr 24,22:6
Danger Signal 1945,N 22,39:2
Beast With Five Fingers, The 1946,D 26,28:3
Tarzan and the Mermaids 1948,Mr 30,26:4
Rogues' Regiment 1948,D 20,31:2
Outpost in Morocco 1949,Mr 25,28:3
Crooked Way, The 1949,S 5,13:2
Johnny One-Eye 1950,N 17,31:2
Florey, Robert (Original Author)
Rogues' Regiment 1948,D 20,31:2
Florey, Robert (Producer)
Coffin Maker, The 1928,O 9,35:1
Florfeld, M
Chalutzim 1934,Ap 2,13:3
Florian
Mayor's Dilemma, The 1940,Ap 23,19:2
Florian, Barbara
Times Gone By (A Pot-Pourri of Songs);
Pot-Pourri of Songs, A (Times Gone By)
1953,D 30,16:2
Heaven on Earth 1960,O 11,55:3
Flotats, Jose Marie
Zita 1968,Ag 12,40:2
Flothow, Rudolph C (Producer)
Whistler, The 1944,Ap 29,12:2
Shadows in the Night 1944,Jl 29,16:2
Mark of the Whistler, The 1944,N 11,19:2
Key Witness 1947,Jl 30,27:6
Prison Warden 1949,O 21,31:2
Mary Ryan, Detective 1949,N 4,33:3
Bodyhold 1949,D 12,29:4
He's a Cockeyed Wonder 1950,O 20,32:4
Al Jennings of Oklahoma 1951,My 18,34:6
Criminal Lawyer 1951,Ag 24,11:4
Flournoy, Elizabeth
Adam's Rib 1949,D 26,33:2
Flournoy, Richard
Beware, Spooks 1939,N 3,17:4
Affairs of Susan, The 1945,Mr 29,18:2
Flournoy, Richard (Original Author)
Pick a Star 1937,My 28,17:2
Wide Open Faces 1938,Ap 15,23:2
Blondie Meets the Boss 1939,Ap 27,31:1
Beware, Spooks 1939,N 3,17:4
Affair With a Stranger 1953,Jl 11,8:2
Flournoy, Richard (Screenwriter)
Pick a Star 1937,My 28,17:2
Riding on Air 1937,Je 26,20:2 (In Addenda)
Fit for a King 1937,O 15,18:5
Blondie 1938,D 22,25:4
So You Won't Talk 1940,O 17,33:2
Blondie Goes Latin 1941,F 26,17:3
Go West, Young Lady 1941,N 24,11:6
Bedtime Story 1942,Mr 20,25:4
Night to Remember, A 1943,Ja 1,27:2
More the Merrier, The 1943,My 14,17:1
One Last Fling 1949,Jl 1,14:6
Affair With a Stranger 1953,Jl 11,8:2
She Couldn't Say No 1954,F 27,11:3
Flournoy, Richard F (Original Author)
Here Comes the Groom 1934,Je 16,20:2
Flower, Alice
Home Maker, The 1925,Ag 10,8:2
Flower, David
Slow Run 1968,O 11,39:1
Flowers, Bess
Irene 1926,Mr 1,17:1
Ghost Talks, The 1929,F 18,28:1
Bachelor Apartment 1931,My 16,13:3
Paid to Dance 1937,D 6,19:1
Shadow, The 1937,D 17,33:3
Lone Wolf in Paris, The 1938,My 23,21:2
Meet John Doe 1941,Mr 13,25:2
Song of the Thin Man 1947,Ag 29,14:2
Born to be Bad 1950,S 29,31:5
Flowers, Harry
Frogmen, The 1951,Je 30,8:6
Floyd, Henrietta
Lost-a Wife 1925,Je 22,10:2
Fluellen, Joel
Jackie Robinson Story, The 1950,My 17,36:1
Duffy of San Quentin 1954,F 10,38:5
Sitting Bull 1954,N 26,24:4
Friendly Persuasion 1956,N 2,30:1
Decks Ran Red, The 1958,O 11,18:2
Porgy and Bess 1959,Je 25,20:3
Raisin in the Sun, A 1961,Mr 30,24:1
He Rides Tall 1964,F 27,28:1
Fluker, Mack
Win That Girl 1928,O 1,23:1
Flying Zacchinis
Phantom of the Rue Morgue 1954,Mr 20,10:5
Flynn, Charles
Second Chance 1947,S 20,12:4
Milkman, The 1951,Ja 1,13:6
Flynn, Edythe
Broadway 1929,My 28,36:2

Flynn, Elinor
Ladies in Love 1930,Je 14,9:4
She-Wolf 1931,My 28,30:6
Flynn, Emmett (Director)
Shame 1921,Ag 1,8:3 (Incorrect in this edition;
use 1921,Ag 1,6:4 elsewhere)
Monte Cristo 1922,Ag 15,20:3
In the Palace of the King 1923,D 3,14:1
Nellie, the Beautiful Cloak Model
1924,Ap 14,14:1
Man Who Came Back, The 1924,S 1,9:1
Yankee Senor, The 1926,Ja 28,14:4
Hold Your Man 1929,O 14,20:2
Shannons of Broadway, The 1929,D 21,17:1
Flynn, Emmett (Original Author)
Dancers, The 1925,Ja 26,22:1
Flynn, Emmett (Producer)
Connecticut Yankee in King Arthur's Court, A
1921,Mr 15,14:3
Flynn, Emmett (Screenwriter)
Shame 1921,Ag 1,8:3 (Incorrect in this edition;
use 1921,Ag 1,6:4 elsewhere)
Flynn, Errol
Case of the Curious Bride, The 1935,Ap 5,21:3
Don't Bet on Blondes 1935,Jl 20,16:2
Captain Blood 1935,D 27,14:1
Charge of the Light Brigade, The 1936,N 2,24:1
Green Light 1937,F 13,9:1
Prince and the Pauper, The 1937,My 6,23:1
Another Dawn 1937,Je 18,25:3
Perfect Specimen, The 1937,O 28,29:2
Adventures of Robin Hood, The 1938,My 13,17:2
Four's a Crowd 1938,Ag 12,11:1
Sisters, The 1938,O 15,21:3
Dawn Patrol 1938,D 24,12:1
Dodge City 1939,Ap 8,19:1
Private Lives of Elizabeth and Essex, The
1939,D 2,21:2
Sea Hawk, The 1940,Ag 10,16:2
Santa Fe Trail 1940,D 21,21:2
Footsteps in the Dark 1941,Mr 15,13:2
Dive Bomber 1941,Ag 30,10:2
They Died With Their Boots On 1941,N 21,23:3
Desperate Journey 1942,S 26,11:2
Gentleman Jim 1942,N 26,40:3
Edge of Darkness 1943,Ap 10,12:4
Thank Your Lucky Stars 1943,O 2,19:2
Northern Pursuit 1943,N 26,29:2
Uncertain Glory 1944,Ap 8,9:2
Objective Burma 1945,Ja 27,15:2
San Antonio 1945,D 29,19:5
Never Say Goodbye 1946,N 23,12:2
Cry Wolf 1947,Jl 19,10:2
Escape me Never 1947,N 8,11:2
Silver River 1948,My 22,8:3
Adventures of Don Juan 1948,D 25,10:1
That Forsyte Woman 1949,N 11,31:2
Montana 1950,F 4,9:2
Rocky Mountain 1950,N 4,13:2
Kim 1950,D 8,40:4
Adventures of Captain Fabian 1951,D 14,36:2
Mara Maru 1952,Ap 24,38:1
Against all Flags 1952,D 25,34:6
Master of Ballantrae, The 1953,Ag 6,16:2
Warriors, The 1955,S 10,11:2
Istanbul 1957,Ja 24,34:1
Big Boodle, The 1957,Mr 12,38:1
Sun Also Rises, The 1957,Ag 24,12:2
Too Much, Too Soon 1958,My 10,19:2
Roots of Heaven, The 1958,O 16,46:1
Cuban Rebel Girls 1959,D 26,7:3
Flynn, Errol (Original Author)
Cuban Rebel Girls 1959,D 26,7:3
Flynn, Errol (Screenwriter)
Adventures of Captain Fabian 1951,D 14,36:2
Flynn, Gertrude
Barefoot Contessa, The 1954,S 30,37:1
Boy on a Dolphin 1957,Ap 20,21:2
I Want to Live 1958,N 19,45:1
Funny Girl 1968,S 20,42:1
Flynn, Joe
Portland Expose 1957,S 27,16:6
This Happy Feeling 1958,Je 19,28:2
Cry for Happy 1961,Mr 4,16:1
Last Time I Saw Archie, The 1961,My 29,9:6
Lover Come Back 1962,F 9,21:1
McHale's Navy 1964,Jl 11,15:2
Divorce American Style 1967,Jl 20,30:2
Flynn, John (Director)
Sergeant, The 1968,D 26,53:5
Flynn, Maria
Intermezzo, A Love Story 1939,O 6,31:1
Born to Sing 1942,F 19,23:2
Flynn, Maurice B (Lefty)
Drums of Fate 1923,Ja 15,18:3
Snow Bride, The 1923,Jl 22,12:2
Open all Night 1924,S 9,19:1
Flynn, Rita
Girl From Woolworth's, The 1929,D 21,17:1
Be Yourself 1930,Mr 7,20:5
Lord Byron of Broadway 1930,Mr 8,21:1
Sweet Mamma 1930,Jl 12,16:4
Top Speed 1930,Ag 30,7:4

Flynn, Sean
Stop Train 349 1964,N 12,40:2
Flynn, Thomas (Original Author)
Man From Laramie, The 1955,S 1,20:2
Fnetsch, Erna (Miscellaneous)
White Hell of Pitz Palu, The 1953,N 14,14:2
Foa, Arnoldo
Verginita 1953,Ap 18,17:2
Stranger on the Prowl 1953,N 10,38:1
Times Gone By (A Question of Property);
Question of Property, A (Times Gone By)
1953,D 30,16:2
Genoese Dragnet 1954,F 12,20:5
Angela 1955,Je 4,9:2
Sins of the Borgias 1956,Mr 5,21:1
Nights of Lucretia Borgia, The 1960,O 6,51:4
Heaven on Earth 1960,O 11,55:3
Tartars, The 1962,Je 21,26:2
Barabbas 1962,O 11,49:1
Reluctant Saint, The 1962,D 4,47:2
Trial, The 1963,F 21,5:1
Judith 1966,Ja 21,22:1
Sailor From Gibraltar, The 1967,Ap 25,38:2
Focaccia, Piero
Bambole; Dolls, The (Treatise on Eugenics);
Treatise on Eugenics (The Dolls)
1965,Je 29,26:1
Focas, Spiros
Rocco and his Brothers 1961,Je 28,40:2
Psycosissimo 1962,S 8,16:2
Run With the Devil 1963,Jl 16,25:1
Fear, The 1967,O 10,56:3
Stefania 1968,N 29,56:1
Foch, Nina
Return of the Vampire, The 1944,Ja 29,10:1
Shadows in the Night 1944,Jl 29,16:2
Cry of the Werewolf, The 1944,Ag 12,16:5
Song to Remember, A 1945,Ja 26,16:4
My Name is Julia Ross 1945,N 9,16:3
Johnny O'Clock 1947,Mr 27,39:2
Guilt of Janet Ames, The 1947,My 23,31:2
Dark Past, The 1948,D 23,25:2
Undercover Man, The 1949,Ap 21,30:2
Johnny Allegro 1949,My 31,19:2
American in Paris, An 1951,O 5,24:2
Scaramouche 1952,My 9,20:2
Young Man With Ideas 1952,Je 7,22:6
Sombrero 1953,Ap 23,37:2
Executive Suite 1954,My 7,19:1
Four Guns to the Border 1954,N 6,15:3
You're Never too Young 1955,Ag 26,10:2
Illegal 1955,O 29,12:6
Ten Commandments, The 1956,N 9,35:2
Three Brave Men 1957,Mr 16,13:2
Cash McCall 1960,Ja 28,26:1
Spartacus 1960,O 7,28:1
Fodebav, Kieta African Ballet
Neapolitan Carousel 1961,O 12,41:3
Fodor, Ladislas (Original Author)
Beauty and the Boss 1932,Ap 2,13:2
Unguarded Hour, The 1936,Ap 4,11:1
Girls' Dormitory 1936,Ag 29,16:2
Wives Under Suspicion 1938,Jl 1,22:3
Charlie Chan in City in Darkness 1939,D 18,29:2
Seven Sinners 1940,N 18,23:2
Night Before the Divorce, The 1942,Ap 10,21:3
Girl Trouble 1942,O 8,31:2
Cairo 1942,N 6,27:2
Tampico 1944,Je 2,21:2
Imperfect Lady, The 1947,My 22,34:5
Great Sinner, The 1949,Je 30,19:2
South Sea Sinner 1950,Ja 16,18:4
Man From Cairo, The 1953,D 17,52:4
Corrupt Ones, The 1967,F 23,41:3
Fodor, Ladislas (Screenwriter)
Tales of Manhattan 1942,S 25,25:1
Girl Trouble 1942,O 8,31:2
Other Love, The 1947,My 15,32:4
Great Sinner, The 1949,Je 30,19:2
Tom Thumb 1958,D 24,00:0
Fodor, Laszlo (Original Author)
Jewel Robbery 1932,Jl 23,6:6
Kiss Before the Mirror, The 1933,My 15,16:2
Footsteps in the Dark 1941,Mr 15,13:2
North to Alaska 1960,N 11,36:1
Fodosyuk, Nina
Tanya 1942,Mr 5,27:1
Foeldes, Emeric (Screenwriter)
Man's Past, A 1927,O 4,34:2
Fogel, V P
Yellow Ticket, The 1928,D 10,25:1
Fogelson, E E Col
Pepe 1960,D 22,18:1
Fogg, Fay
I'd Climb the Highest Mountain 1951,My 10,38:1
Fogg, Kay
I'd Climb the Highest Mountain 1951,My 10,38:1
Foile, Ian
Pollyanna 1960,My 20,26:1
Fokine, Michel (Miscellaneous)
Royal Ballet, The (The Firebird); Firebird, The
(The Royal Ballet) 1960,O 5,45:2

Foldes, Yolanda (Original Author)
My Own True Love 1949,F 3,27:3
Foldessy, Geza
Szerelmi Almok 1937,Ja 5,19:2
Once a Week 1937,O 2,18:1
Foley, Bill
Broth of a Boy 1959,D 28,18:1
Mark, The 1961,O 3,46:2
Foley, Clare
Janie 1944,Ag 5,16:2
Janie Gets Married 1946,Je 15,24:2
Foley, Joe
Whistle at Eaton Falls, The 1951,O 11,49:2
Folgar, Tino
Cancion del Dia, La 1933,Ag 26,14:3
Folger, Byron
Christmas in July 1940,N 6,35:2
Foltin, Senta
Kleine Nachtmusik, Eine 1940,Mr 2,9:5
Fomchenko, Igor
Violin and Roller 1962,Ag 20,18:2
Fonda, Henry
Farmer Takes a Wife, The 1935,Ag 9,21:2
Way Down East 1935,O 31,16:2
I Dream too Much 1935,N 29,24:1
Trail of the Lonesome Pine, The 1936,F 20,23:5
Moon's our Home, The 1936,My 13,29:2
Spendthrift 1936,Jl 23,24:1
You Only Live Once 1937,F 1,15:2
Wings of the Morning 1937,Mr 12,19:1
Slim 1937,Je 24,30:2
That Certain Woman 1937,S 16,29:1
I Met my Love Again 1938,Ja 15,19:1
Jezebel 1938,Mr 11,15:2
Blockade 1938,Je 17,25:1
Spawn of the North 1938,S 8,27:1
Mad Miss Manton, The 1938,O 21,27:2
Jesse James 1939,Ja 14,13:1
Let Us Live 1939,Mr 30,19:2
Story of Alexander Graham Bell, The 1939,Ap 1,17:2
Young Mr Lincoln 1939,Je 3,11:2
Drums Along the Mohawk 1939,N 4,11:2
Grapes of Wrath, The 1940,Ja 25,17:2
Lillian Russell 1940,My 18,11:2
Return of Frank James, The 1940,Ag 10,16:4
Chad Hanna 1940,D 26,23:1
Lady Eve, The 1941,F 26,17:1
Wild Geese Calling 1941,Ag 30,10:2
You Belong to Me 1941,N 29,14:2
Male Animal, The 1942,Mr 28,11:1
Rings on her Fingers 1942,Ap 24,21:4
Magnificent Dope, The 1942,Jl 3,12:5
Big Street, The 1942,Ag 14,13:1
Tales of Manhattan 1942,S 25,25:1
Immortal Sergeant 1943,F 4,29:2
Ox-Bow Incident, The 1943,My 10,15:2 (In Addenda)
My Darling Clementine 1946,D 4,44:5
Long Night, The 1947,S 17,31:2
Daisy Kenyon 1947,D 25,32:1
Fugitive, The 1947,D 26,22:2
Miracle Can Happen, A 1948,F 4,28:4
Fort Apache 1948,Je 25,26:2
Mister Roberts 1955,Jl 15,14:1
War and Peace 1956,Ag 22,26:2
Wrong Man, The 1956,D 24,8:1
12 Angry Men 1957,Ap 15,24:1
Tin Star, The 1957,O 24,37:2
Stage Struck 1958,Ap 23,40:1
Warlock 1959,My 1,34:1
Man Who Understood, The 1959,O 3,14:7
Advise and Consent 1962,Je 7,31:2
Longest Day, The 1962,O 5,28:1
How the West Was Won 1963,Ap 1,54:1
Spencer's Mountain 1963,My 17,26:6
Best Man, The 1964,Ap 7,29:1
Fail Safe 1964,S 16,36:1
Sex and the Single Girl 1964,D 26,9:2
In Harm's Way 1965,Ap 7,36:1
Rounders, The 1965,Ap 29,40:2
Battle of the Bulge 1965,D 18,36:1
Big Hand for the Little Lady, A 1966,Je 9,54:2
Welcome to Hard Times 1967,My 2,56:1
Firecreek 1968,F 22,36:2
Madigan 1968,Mr 30,22:2
Yours, Mine and Ours 1968,Ap 25,53:1
Boston Strangler, The 1968,O 17,52:1
Fonda, Henry (Narrator)
Pictura 1952,Ap 8,35:3
Fonda, Henry (Original Author)
Miracle Can Happen, A 1948,F 4,28:4
Fonda, Henry (Producer)
12 Angry Men 1957,Ap 15,24:1
Fonda, Jane
Tall Story 1960,Ap 7,46:1
Walk on the Wild Side 1962,F 22,20:1
Chapman Report, The 1962,O 18,49:2
Period of Adjustment 1962,N 1,34:1
In the Cool of the Day 1963,My 30,20:1
Sunday in New York 1964,F 12,30:2
Joy House 1965,F 18,29:1
Circle of Love 1965,Mr 25,42:4

Cat Ballou 1965,Je 25,36:1
Chase, The 1966,F 19,24:1
Any Wednesday 1966,O 14,50:1
Game is Over, The 1967,Ja 10,34:1
Hurry Sundown 1967,Mr 24,22:1
Barefoot in the Park 1967,My 26,51:1
Barbarella 1968,O 12,43:1
Fonda, Peter
Tammy and the Doctor 1963,Je 27,23:2
Victors, The 1963,D 20,21:2
Lilith 1964,S 21,37:2
Young Lovers, The 1965,F 11,45:1
Wild Angels, The 1966,D 22,40:4
Trip, The 1967,Ag 24,43:1
Fondane, Benjamin (Screenwriter)
Mystic Mountain, The 1936,Mr 31,17:2
Fondat, Marcel (Original Author)
Blood and Black Lace 1965,N 11,58:3
Fondat, Marcel (Screenwriter)
Blood and Black Lace 1965,N 11,58:3
Fondato, Marcello (Screenwriter)
Everybody go Home!; Tutti a Casa 1962,N 6,38:1
Bebo's Girl 1964,N 12,40:1
Fondra, Elena
Juliet of the Spirits 1965,N 4,57:1
Fong, Benson
Behind the Rising Sun 1943,O 14,26:2
Purple Heart, The 1944,Mr 9,15:2
Keys of the Kingdom, The 1944,D 30,15:2
China Sky 1945,My 25,22:3
Deception 1946,O 19,15:3
Calcutta 1947,Ap 24,30:2
Woman in the Night 1948,Ja 10,16:2
Peking Express 1951,Jl 19,20:2
His Majesty O'Keefe 1954,F 6,17:2
Conquest of Space 1955,My 28,7:6
Left Hand of God, The 1955,S 22,34:5
Walk Like a Dragon 1960,S 16,24:1
Flower Drum Song 1961,N 10,40:1
Fong, Harold
Steel Helmet, The 1951,Ja 25,21:5
Peking Express 1951,Jl 19,20:2
Pleasure of his Company, The 1961,Je 2,36:1
Diamond Head 1963,F 21,5:2
Fong, Jon
Donovan's Reef 1963,Jl 25,14:1
Fong, Willie
Cocktail Hour 1933,Je 5,18:5
Fons, Angelino (Screenwriter)
Hunt, The 1967,Ap 25,38:1
Fonseca, Lew (Director)
Untitled-Baseball Technique 1941,Ja 17,11:3
Ninth Inning, The 1942,Ja 8,30:3
Fonseca, Lew (Screenwriter)
Untitled-Baseball Technique 1941,Ja 17,11:3
Ninth Inning, The 1942,Ja 8,30:3
Font, Roberto
Molinos de Viento; Windmills 1940,F 26,11:2
Fontaine, Eddie
Girl Can't Help It, The 1957,F 9,12:7
Fontaine, Frank
Nancy Goes to Rio 1950,Ap 7,22:2
Stella 1950,Ag 19,9:2
Call Me Mister 1951,F 1,21:2
Model and the Marriage Broker, The 1952,Ja 12,10:6
Fontaine, Jacqueline
Outlaw Woman 1952,Ap 5,20:3
Country Girl, The 1954,D 16,51:2
Lieutenant Wore Skirts, The 1956,Ja 12,22:1
Fontaine, Joan
Quality Street 1937,Ap 9,19:2
Man Who Found Himself, The 1937,Ap 9,19:3
You Can't Beat Love 1937,Je 25,25:3
Music for Madame 1937,O 23,14:1
Damsel in Distress, A 1937,N 25,37:1
Sky Giant 1938,Jl 20,22:2
Duke of West Point, The 1938,D 16,33:2
Gunga Din 1939,Ja 28,19:2
Man of Conquest 1939,Ap 28,31:2
Women, The 1939,S 22,27:2
Rebecca 1940,Mr 29,25:2
Suspicion 1941,N 21,23:2
This Above All 1942,My 13,14:3
Constant Nymph, The 1943,Jl 24,8:2
Jane Eyre 1944,F 4,12:5
Frenchman's Creek 1944,S 21,26:2
Affairs of Susan, The 1945,Mr 29,18:2
From This Day Forward 1946,Ap 20,16:2
Ivy 1947,Je 26,19:1
Letters From an Unknown Woman 1948,Ap 29,20:6
Emperor Waltz, The 1948,Je 18,19:2
Kiss the Blood off my Hands 1948,O 30,10:2
You Gotta Stay Happy 1948,N 5,29:2
Born to be Bad 1950,S 29,31:5
September Affair 1951,F 2,19:2
Darling, How Could You! 1951,N 9,22:4
Something to Live For 1952,Mr 8,11:2
Ivanhoe 1952,Ag 1,8:2
Decameron Nights 1953,N 17,38:2
Flight to Tangier 1953,N 26,50:4
Bigamist, The 1953,D 26,10:4

Fontaine, Joan—Cont
Casanova's Big Night 1954,Ap 19,19:1
Serenade 1956,Mr 24,21:1 (Incorrect in this edition; use 1956,Mr 23,21:1 elsewhere)
Beyond a Reasonable Doubt 1956,S 14,27:2
Island in the Sun 1957,Je 13,37:1
Until They Sail 1957,O 9,41:2
Certain Smile, A 1958,Ag 1,13:2
Voyage to the Bottom of the Sea 1961,Jl 20,32:2
Tender is the Night 1962,Ja 20,13:2
Devil's Own, The 1967,Mr 16,53:2
Fontaine, John
Battle Zone 1952,N 1,17:2
Fontaine, Lilian
Lost Weekend, The 1945,D 3,17:2
Suddenly It's Spring 1947,F 27,26:2
Locket, The 1947,Mr 20,38:2
Time Out of Mind 1947,Ap 7,20:1
Ivy 1947,Je 26,19:1
Fontaine, Robert (Original Author)
Happy Time, The 1952,O 31,30:2
Fontan, Gabrielle
Ces Dames aux Chapeaux Verts; Ladies in the Green Hats, The 1950,Ap 5,26:2
Francois Villon 1950,Jl 3,9:2
Ways of Love (A Day in the Country); Day in the Country, A (Ways of Love) 1950,D 13,50:2
Deadlier Than the Male 1957,O 9,41:1
Gates of Paris 1958,Ja 15,24:1
Crime and Punishment 1958,S 16,23:2
Premier May 1958,S 17,44:2
Julie the Redhead 1963,O 15,44:1
Fontana, Anna
Richiamo del Cuore, Il; Appeal of the Heart, The 1931,Mr 2,19:1
Fontana, Eugenio (Producer)
Albero di Adamo, L'; Adam's Tree 1938,Ja 20,19:2
Carmela 1949,My 14,9:2
Strange Deception 1953,My 27,28:2
Fontana, Jimmy
Crazy Desire 1964,Jl 3,13:2
Fontane, Theodor (Original Author)
Schritt vom Wege, Der; False Step, The 1939,Ap 29,13:3
Fontanne, Lynn
Second Youth 1924,Ap 22,19:3
Man Who Found Himself, The 1925,Ag 24,17:3
Guardsman, The 1931,S 10,22:4
Stage Door Canteen 1943,Je 25,13:2
Fonteney, Catherine
Poil de Carotte 1933,My 26,24:2
Late Mathias Pascal, The 1937,N 18,27:2
Tender Enemy, The 1938,Mr 31,15:2 (In Addenda)
Shop-Girls of Paris; Au Bonheur de Dames 1947,Je 23,14:4
Symphonie Fantastique, La 1947,D 8,35:2
Under the Paris Sky 1952,My 6,35:1
Miracle of Saint Therese 1959,F 10,38:4 (In Addenda)
Fonteyn, Margot
Little Ballerina, The 1951,F 28,33:2
Royal Ballet, The (Ondine); Ondine (The Royal Ballet) 1960,O 5,45:2
Royal Ballet, The (Swan Lake Act II); Swan Lake Act II (The Royal Ballet) 1960,O 5,45:2
Royal Ballet, The (The Firebird); Firebird, The (The Royal Ballet) 1960,O 5,45:2
Evening With the Royal Ballet, An 1965,D 9,60:1
Romeo and Juliet 1966,O 6,55:1
Fontini, Anagleto (Producer)
Gladiators Seven 1964,My 7,31:2
Foo, Lee Tong
Mister Wong in Chinatown 1939,Jl 31,9:2 (In Addenda)
Foo, Lee Tung
General Died at Dawn, The 1936,S 3,17:2
Across the Pacific 1942,S 5,9:2
Behind the Rising Sun 1943,O 14,26:2
Laura 1944,O 12,24:1
There's a Girl in my Heart 1950,Ja 20,29:2
Foo, Mah
Beachcomber, The 1938,D 26,29:3
Foote, Bradbury (Original Author)
Billy the Kid 1941,Je 20,28:2
High Wall 1947,D 26,22:2
Foote, Bradbury (Screenwriter)
Bride Wore Red, The 1937,O 15,18:4
Of Human Hearts 1938,F 18,23:1
Young Tom Edison 1940,Mr 15,27:2
Edison the Man 1940,Je 7,27:2
Foote, Courtenay
His Parisian Wife 1919,Ja 20,13:2
Passion Flower, The 1921,Ap 4,18:1
Little Old New York 1923,Jl 10,10:3
Ashes of Vengeance 1923,Ag 7,20:2
Tess of the D'Urbervilles 1924,Jl 28,12:2
Madonna of the Streets 1924,O 28,23:4
Foote, Dick
Bride of Vengeance 1949,Ap 7,38:2
Streets of Laredo 1949,My 12,28:2
Blue Grass of Kentucky 1950,Ja 27,29:2

Foote, Horton (Original Author)
Baby, the Rain Must Fall 1965,Ja 14,44:1
Chase, The 1966,F 19,24:1
Foote, Horton (Screenwriter)
Storm Fear 1955,D 17,19:2
To Kill a Mockingbird 1963,F 15,10:2
Baby, the Rain Must Fall 1965,Ja 14,44:1
Hurry Sundown 1967,Mr 24,22:1
Foote, John Tainton (Original Author)
Toby's Bow 1919,D 15,20:1
Foote, John Taintor (Original Author)
Convoy 1927,My 9,26:4
Kentucky 1938,D 24,12:1
Broadway Serenade 1939,Ap 7,25:2
Foote, John Taintor (Producer)
Great Dan Patch, The 1949,N 9,37:2
Foote, John Taintor (Screenwriter)
Kentucky 1938,D 24,12:1
Swanee River 1939,D 30,9:2
Mark of Zorro, The 1940,N 4,23:2
Great Dan Patch, The 1949,N 9,37:2
Story of Seabiscuit, The 1949,N 12,8:4
Foran, Dick
Shipmates Forever 1935,O 17,29:3
Dangerous 1935,D 27,14:1
Petrified Forest, The 1936,F 7,14:2
Song of the Saddle 1936,Mr 21,13:3
Golden Arrow, The 1936,My 4,16:1
Treachery Rides the Range 1936,My 30,7:3
Public Enemy's Wife 1936,Jl 9,17:2
Black Legion 1937,Ja 18,21:1
Perfect Specimen, The 1937,O 28,29:2
She Loved a Fireman 1938,Ja 21,15:3
Love, Honor and Behave 1938,Mr 21,18:2
Over the Wall 1938,Mr 28,19:2
Cowboy From Brooklyn 1938,Jl 14,17:1
Four Daughters 1938,Ag 19,13:3
Boy Meets Girl 1938,Ag 27,7:2
Sisters, The 1938,O 15,21:3
Secrets of a Nurse 1938,D 12,26:2
Heart of the North 1938,D 21,29:2
Daughters Courageous 1939,Je 24,14:2
I Stole a Million 1939,Ag 7,11:2
Four Wives 1939,D 23,9:1
Fighting 69th, The 1940,Ja 27,9:2
My Little Chickadee 1940,Mr 16,8:2
House of the Seven Gables, The 1940,Ap 15,21:3
Rangers of Fortune 1940,S 19,27:2
Mummy's Hand, The 1940,S 20,27:2
Four Mothers 1941,Ja 11,12:7
Horror Island 1941,Mr 31,11:3
In the Navy 1941,Je 12,29:2
Unfinished Business 1941,S 2,20:2
Mob Town 1941,N 20,39:3
Keep 'Em Flying 1941,N 27,29:2
Kid From Kansas, The 1941,D 2,29:4
Ride 'Em Cowboy 1942,Mr 5,27:3
Butch Minds the Baby 1942,My 1,23:3
Private Buckaroo 1942,Je 25,27:4
Mummy's Tomb, The 1942,O 26,19:2
He's my Guy 1943,Mr 12,12:3
Guest Wife 1945,O 18,21:2
Easy Come, Easy Go 1947,F 6,29:2
Fort Apache 1948,Je 25,26:2
El Paso 1949,Mr 24,35:2
Deputy Marshal 1949,N 11,31:3
Al Jennings of Oklahoma 1951,My 18,34:6
Chicago Confidential 1957,Ag 31,19:1
Big Night, The 1960,F 18,37:4
Atomic Submarine, The 1960,Ap 20,45:2
Studs Lonigan 1960,D 15,59:1
Taggart 1964,D 25,24:4
Foran, Nick
Stand up and Cheer 1934,Ap 20,17:1
Gentlemen are Born 1934,N 22,27:2
One More Spring 1935,F 22,27:1
Accent on Youth 1935,Ag 12,10:3
Big Noise, The 1936,Jl 4,18:3
Earthworm Tractors 1936,Jl 25,16:1
Foray, June (Narrator)
Snow Queen, The 1960,Ap 14,34:1
Forbes, Alan
Another Sky 1960,O 25,40:2
Forbes, Archibald (Original Author)
China 1943,Ap 22,31:2
Forbes, Brenda
Perfect Gentleman, The 1935,D 19,33:4
Vigil in the Night 1940,Mr 9,19:2
Mrs Miniver 1942,Je 5,23:1
White Cliffs of Dover, The 1944,My 12,15:2
Forbes, Bryan
All Over the Town 1949,My 26,34:4
World in His Arms, The 1952,O 10,21:2
Sea Devils 1953,Jl 31,11:5
Man With a Million 1954,Je 29,21:2
Inspector Calls, An 1954,N 26,24:4
Satellite in the Sky 1956,S 4,32:7
Baby and the Battleship, The 1957,O 1,37:2
Colditz Story, The 1957,O 25,23:2
Key, The 1958,Jl 2,23:3
League of Gentlemen, The 1961,Ja 25,30:4
Guns of Navarone, The 1961,Je 23,19:1

Forbes, Bryan (Director)
Whistle Down the Wind 1962,Ap 23,34:2
L-Shaped Room, The 1963,My 28,32:1
Seance on a Wet Afternoon 1964,N 6,30:1
King Rat 1965,O 28,48:1
Wrong Box 1966,Jl 20,46:1
Whisperers, The 1967,Ag 1,24:1
Deadfall 1968,S 12,54:1
Forbes, Bryan (Miscellaneous)
Black Knight, The 1954,O 29,27:2
Forbes, Bryan (Producer)
Angry Silence, The 1960,D 13,25:2
Wrong Box 1966,Jl 20,46:1
Forbes, Bryan (Screenwriter)
Cockleshell Heroes, The 1956,Je 4,25:2
Triple Deception 1957,O 7,23:2
Captain's Table, The 1960,S 27,40:1
Angry Silence, The 1960,D 13,25:2
League of Gentlemen, The 1961,Ja 25,30:4
Man in the Moon 1961,Je 13,29:2
Only Two Can Play 1962,Mr 21,33:2
L-Shaped Room, The 1963,My 28,32:1
Of Human Bondage 1964,S 24,46:2
Seance on a Wet Afternoon 1964,N 6,30:1
Station Six-Sahara 1964,N 12,40:2
King Rat 1965,O 28,48:1
Whisperers, The 1967,Ag 1,24:1
Deadfall 1968,S 12,54:1
Forbes, C Scott (Original Author)
Penthouse, The 1967,O 4,38:3
Forbes, Esther (Original Author)
Johnny Tremain 1957,Jl 11,21:1
Forbes, Hazel
Down to Their Last Yacht 1934,S 24,14:1
Forbes, James (Original Author)
Traveling Salesman, The 1916,D 18,9:3
Famous Mrs Fair, The 1923,Ap 23,18:3
Bachelor's Affairs 1932,Je 25,18:2
Forbes, Kathryn (Original Author)
I Remember Mama 1948,Mr 12,29:2
Forbes, Kenneth
At War With the Army 1951,Ja 25,21:5
Forbes, Lou (Composer)
Pot o'Gold 1941,Ap 4,25:2
Forbes, Madeleine
Wilson 1944,Ag 2,18:1
Forbes, Mary
Sunny Side Up 1929,O 4,24:5
Trespasser, The 1929,N 2,14:6
So This Is London 1930,My 24,21:2
East Is West 1930,N 1,23:2
Devil to Pay, The 1930,D 19,30:1
Man Who Came Back, The 1931,Ja 3,21:2
Born to Love 1931,Ap 25,23:4
Chances 1931,Je 12,27:1
Brat, The 1931,Ag 24,13:4
Stepping Sisters 1932,Ja 9,21:1
Silent Witness, The 1932,F 8,21:1
Farewell to Arms, A 1932,D 9,26:5
Cavalcade 1933,Ja 6,23:2
Bombshell 1933,O 21,11:2
You Can't Buy Everything 1934,F 3,9:2
Blind Date 1934,S 1,16:3
Happiness Ahead 1934,O 11,28:2
Miserables, Les 1935,Ap 22,14:2
Laddie 1935,My 6,22:3
Anna Karenina 1935,Ag 31,16:2
Perfect Gentleman, The 1935,D 19,33:4
Captain Blood 1935,D 27,14:1
Women of Glamour 1937,Mr 6,10:1
Another Dawn 1937,Je 18,25:3
Wee Willie Winkie 1937,Jl 24,12:1
Awful Truth, The 1937,N 5,19:3
Everybody Sing 1938,Mr 11,15:3
Always Goodbye 1938,Je 25,7:2
You Can't Take It With You 1938,S 2,21:2
You Can't Cheat an Honest Man 1939,F 20,13:2
Risky Business 1939,Mr 23,27:2
Sun Never Sets, The 1939,Je 9,26:2
Adventures of Sherlock Holmes, The 1939,S 2,20:1
Private Affairs 1940,Jl 5,10:3
South of Suez 1940,D 19,33:2
Nothing but the Truth 1941,O 23,27:1
Two Tickets to London 1943,Jl 3,11:2
Woman in Bondage 1944,Mr 27,17:2
Tender Comrade 1944,Je 2,21:2
Picture of Dorian Gray, The 1945,Mr 2,15:2
Earl Carroll Vanities 1945,Ap 2,15:6
Terror by Night 1946,F 9,9:2
Other Love, The 1947,My 15,32:4
Ivy 1947,Je 26,19:1
Exile, The 1947,D 26,22:4
You Gotta Stay Happy 1948,N 5,29:2
Forbes, Meriel
Mr Cohen Takes a Walk 1936,F 13,25:2
Long Dark Hall, The 1951,My 10,38:3
Murder on Monday 1953,O 7,35:2
Forbes, Murray (Original Author)
Hollow Triumph 1948,O 29,29:5
Forbes, Ralph
Beau Geste 1926,Ag 26,17:3
Mr Wu 1927,My 16,24:2

Forbes, Ralph — Cont
Enemy, The 1927,D 28,26:6
Latest From Paris, The 1928,F 27,16:2
Trail of '98, The 1928,Mr 21,30:3
Actress, The 1928,Jl 9,25:1
Whip, The 1928,S 17,28:2
Masks of the Devil, The 1928,N 26,30:2
Restless Youth 1929,Ja 1,60:1
Green Goddess, The 1930,F 14,20:1
Lilies of the Field 1930,F 22,13:1
Mamba 1930,Mr 11,25:2
Lady of Scandal, The 1930,Je 14,9:4
Inside the Lines 1930,S 29,19:1
Her Wedding Night 1930,S 29,19:1
Beau Ideal 1931,Ja 19,25:1
Bachelor Father, The 1931,F 2,23:1
Thunder Below 1932,Je 20,11:2
Smilin' Through 1932,O 15,13:1
Christopher Strong 1933,Mr 10,19:2
Pleasure Cruise 1933,Ap 3,13:3
Phantom Broadcast, The 1933,Jl 31,16:2
Solitaire Man, The 1933,S 23,11:5
Avenger, The 1933,O 3,28:3
Bombay Mail 1934,Ja 6,18:2
Mystery of Mr X, The 1934,F 26,21:3
Riptide 1934,Mr 31,8:2
20th Century 1934,My 4,24:2
Fountain, The 1934,Ag 31,14:1
Barretts of Wimpole Street, The 1934,S 29,12:2
Outcast Lady 1934,N 3,20:3
Enchanted April 1935,Mr 9,19:1
Age of Indiscretion 1935,My 18,21:2
Goose and the Gander, The 1935,S 12,29:2
Three Musketeers, The 1935,N 1,25:1
Mary of Scotland 1936,Jl 31,22:2
Romeo and Juliet 1936,Ag 21,12:2
Piccadilly Jim 1936,Ag 31,19:1
Daniel Boone 1936,O 24,23:2
Last of Mrs Cheyney, The 1937,F 19,15:1
Thirteenth Chair, The 1937,Je 18,25:3
Make a Wish 1937,S 23,33:1
Women Are Like That 1938,Ap 11,12:2
Kidnapped 1938,My 28,9:2
If I Were King 1938,S 29,31:1
Annabel Takes a Tour 1938,D 29,15:3
Hound of the Baskervilles, The 1939,Mr 25,19:2
Magnificent Fraud, The 1939,Jl 20,16:2
Private Lives of Elizabeth and Essex, The 1939,D 2,21:2
Tower of London 1939,D 12,37:2
Calling Philo Vance 1940,F 9,15:3
Adventure in Diamonds 1940,Ap 4,27:2
Curtain Call 1940,Ap 19,25:2
Frenchman's Creek 1944,S 21,26:2
Forbes, Rosita (Original Author)
Fighting Love 1927,My 23,27:2
White Sheik, The 1929,D 9,32:5
Forbes, Scott
Rocky Mountain 1950,N 4,13:2
Operation Pacific 1951,F 3,10:2
Raton Pass 1951,Ap 20,25:1
Inside the Walls of Folsom Prison 1951,My 28,17:4
Forbes, Sheila
Psychomania 1964,F 15,14:3
Forbes-Robertson, John
Kathleen 1938,Ja 24,17:1
Forboess, Conny
Elusive Corporal, The 1963,F 19,5:1
Forbstein, Leo (Composer)
Call it a Day 1937,My 7,29:2
Force, Jean (Screenwriter)
Border Street 1950,Ap 26,35:2
FORD
See Also FORDE
Ford, Alexander (Director)
Ulica 1933,Ja 27,13:2
Chalutzim 1934,Ap 2,13:3
Children Must Laugh; Mir Kumen an 1938,Mr 26,12:2
Border Street 1950,Ap 26,35:2
Young Chopin 1952,D 25,34:7
Five From Barska Street 1955,Mr 14,29:4
Eighth Day of the Week, The 1959,Mr 24,45:2
Ford, Alexander (Screenwriter)
Border Street 1950,Ap 26,35:2
Young Chopin 1952,D 25,34:7
Five From Barska Street 1955,Mr 14,29:4
Eighth Day of the Week, The 1959,Mr 24,45:2
Ford, Cecil
Men of Ireland 1938,S 30,24:2
Ford, Cecil F (Producer)
633 Squadron 1964,Je 25,25:1
Ford, Constance
Last Hunt, The 1956,Mr 1,37:2
Bailout at 43,000 1957,Je 8,13:2
Summer Place, A 1959,O 23,24:1
Home from the Hill 1960,Mr 4,19:1
Claudelle Inglish 1961,S 21,40:2
Rome Adventure 1962,Mr 16,25:1
House of Women 1962,Ap 12,41:6
All Fall Down 1962,Ap 12,41:3
Cabinet of Caligari, The 1962,My 26,13:5
Caretakers, The 1963,Ag 22,19:2

Ford, Corey (Original Author)
Sophomore, The 1929,Ag 24,11:5
Her Bodyguard 1933,Ag 7,18:2
Start Cheering 1938,Mr 17,17:3
Remember? 1939,D 15,33:4
Cloak and Dagger 1946,O 5,13:2
Ford, Corey (Screenwriter)
Topper Takes a Trip 1938,D 30,11:2
Ford, Damon
Wedding Present 1936,N 19,31:3
Ford, David
Middle of the Night 1959,Je 18,36:1
Ford, Derek (Original Author)
Study in Terror, A 1966,N 3,45:3
Ford, Derek (Screenwriter)
Study in Terror, A 1966,N 3,45:3
Corruption 1968,D 5,59:1
Ford, Donald (Original Author)
Study in Terror, A 1966,N 3,45:3
Ford, Donald (Screenwriter)
Study in Terror, A 1966,N 3,45:3
Corruption 1968,D 5,59:1
Ford, Dorothy
Love Laughs at Andy Hardy 1947,Ja 8,28:2
Miracle Can Happen, A 1948,F 4,28:4
Three Godfathers 1949,Mr 4,25:2
Jack and the Beanstalk 1952,Ap 8,35:3
Seven Year Itch, The 1955,Je 4,9:1
Ford, Francis
Wreck of the Hesperus, The 1927,N 28,18:5
Drake Case, The 1929,S 16,30:1
Pilgrimage 1933,Jl 13,17:5
Charlie Chan's Greatest Case 1933,O 7,18:4
Murder in Trinidad 1934,My 16,22:2
Judge Priest 1934,O 12,33:1
Informer, The 1935,My 10,25:2
Goin' to Town 1935,My 11,21:2
Arizonian, The 1935,Jl 27,16:2
Steamboat Around the Bend 1935,S 20,17:2
Paddy O'Day 1936,F 8,19:2
Prisoner of Shark Island, The 1936,F 13,25:2
Charlie Chan at the Circus 1936,Mr 19,22:4
Gentle Julia 1936,Ap 11,19:1
Sins of Man 1936,Je 19,17:2
Educating Father 1936,Je 20,22:2
Slave Ship 1937,Je 17,19:2
Kentucky Moonshine 1938,My 21,9:2
Texans, The 1938,Jl 28,23:2
Stagecoach 1939,Mr 3,21:1
Young Mr Lincoln 1939,Je 3,11:2
Bad Lands 1939,Ag 9,15:2
Drums Along the Mohawk 1939,N 4,11:2
Geronimo 1940,F 8,18:3
Viva Cisco Kid 1940,Mr 22,23:4
Lucky Cisco Kid 1940,Je 24,19:5
South of Pago-Pago 1940,Ag 2,12:2
Diamond Frontiers 1940,O 4,29:2
Tobacco Road 1941,F 21,16:2
Man Who Wouldn't Die, The 1942,Ap 28,25:5
Loves of Edgar Allan Poe, The 1942,S 21,19:2
Ox-Bow Incident, The 1943,My 10,15:2 (In
 Addenda)
Hangover Square 1945,F 8,15:2
My Darling Clementine 1946,D 4,44:5
High Tide 1947,N 8,11:2
Plunders, The 1948,N 1,28:2
Wagonmaster 1950,Je 19,17:2
Quiet Man, The 1952,Ag 22,13:1
Sun Shines Bright, The 1954,Mr 17,25:2
Ford, Fred (Cinematographer)
Zanzabuku 1956,Ag 16,30:3
Ford, Fred Jr (Cinematographer)
Zanzabuku 1956,Ag 16,30:3
Ford, Fritz
Mister Roberts 1955,Jl 15,14:1
Ford, Garrett (Screenwriter)
Zero Hour, The 1939,Jl 5,20:3
Ford, Glenn
My Son Is Guilty 1940,Ja 15,11:2
Convicted Woman 1940,F 26,11:2
Men Without Souls 1940,My 13,21:2
Lady in Question, The 1940,D 10,33:2
So Ends our Night 1941,F 28,17:2
Texas 1941,O 17,27:3
Go West, Young Lady 1941,N 24,11:6
Adventures of Martin Eden 1942,Mr 16,19:2
Flight Lieutenant 1942,Jl 31,11:1
Desperadoes, The 1943,My 13,17:2
Destroyer 1943,S 2,15:3
Gilda 1946,Mr 15,27:2
Stolen Life, A 1946,My 2,27:4
Gallant Journey 1946,O 10,33:2
Framed 1947,My 26,24:2
Mating of Millie, The 1948,Mr 13,12:2
Loves of Carmen, The 1948,S 3,16:2
Man From Colorado 1949,Ja 21,24:3
Return of October, The 1949,F 23,31:2
Undercover Man, The 1949,Ap 21,30:2
Lust for Gold 1949,Jl 4,9:2
Doctor and the Girl, The 1949,O 31,20:2
White Tower, The 1950,Jl 3,9:2
Flying Missile, The 1950,D 25,25:1
Follow the Sun 1951,Ap 26,34:4

Redhead and the Cowboy, The 1951,Je 6,37:2
Secret of Convict Lake, The 1951,Ag 4,7:2
Green Glove, The 1952,Ap 24,38:1
Young Man With Ideas 1952,Je 7,22:6
Affair in Trinidad 1952,Jl 31,14:2
Plunder of the Sun 1953,Ag 27,22:1
Man From the Alamo, The 1953,S 12,13:2
Big Heat, The 1953,O 15,43:2
Appointment in Honduras 1953,N 19,41:4
Human Desire 1954,Ag 7,7:2
Americano, The 1955,Ja 20,35:1
Violent Men, The 1955,Ja 27,17:2
Blackboard Jungle 1955,Mr 21,21:5
Interrupted Melody 1955,My 6,18:1
Trial 1955,O 14,21:2
Ransom 1956,Ja 25,28:3
Jubal 1956,Ap 25,39:1
Fastest Gun Alive, The 1956,Jl 13,23:3
Teahouse of the August Moon, The
 1956,N 30,19:1
3:10 to Yuma 1957,Ag 29,22:1
Don't Go Near the Water 1957,N 15,37:1
Cowboy 1958,F 20,29:5
Sheepman, The 1958,My 8,36:1
Imitation General 1958,Ag 21,22:2
Torpedo Run 1958,O 25,16:2
It Started With a Kiss 1959,Ag 20,14:2
Gazebo, The 1960,Ja 16,14:4
Cimarron 1961,F 17,12:2
Cry for Happy 1961,Mr 4,16:1
Pocketful of Miracles 1961,D 19,39:1
4 Horsemen of the Apocalypse, The
 1962,Mr 10,10:2
Experiment in Terror 1962,Ap 14,14:1
Courtship of Eddie's Father, The 1963,Mr 7,8:5
 (Incorrect in this edition; use 1963,Mr 28,8:5
 elsewhere)
Love Is a Ball 1963,Ap 25,38:1
Advance to the Rear 1964,Je 11,27:3
Fate Is the Hunter 1964,D 10,61:1
Dear Heart 1965,Mr 8,33:1
Rounders, The 1965,Ap 29,40:2
Money Trap, The 1966,My 5,59:1
Is Paris Burning? 1966,N 11,36:1
Last Challenge, The 1967,D 28,25:1
Day of the Evil Gun 1968,Ap 25,53:2
Ford, Grace
Devil Doll, The 1936,Ag 8,5:2
Between Two Women 1937,Ag 6,21:1
Big City 1937,S 17,29:2
Ford, Harriet (Miscellaneous)
I Married a Doctor 1936,Ap 20,17:1
Ford, Harriet (Original Author)
Dummy, The 1929,Mr 4,20:2
Argyle Case, The 1929,Ag 31,13:4
Case of the Black Parrot, The 1941,Ja 10,23:3
Make Your own Bed 1944,My 27,12:2
Ford, Harrison
Mysterious Mrs M, The 1917,Ja 22,9:1
Cruise of the Make-Believe, The 1918,S 2,7:1
Veiled Adventure, The 1919,Jl 7,18:5
Lottery Man, The 1919,O 6,15:1
Lottery Man, The 1919,N 17,20:1
Hawthorne of the U.S.A. 1919,N 17,20:1
Passion Flower, The 1921,Ap 4,18:1
Wedding Bells 1921,Ag 15,14:3
Love's Redemption 1922,Ja 9,15:2
Foolish Wives 1922,Ja 12,15:2
Old Homestead, The 1922,O 9,10:2
Vanity Fair 1923,My 7,19:3
Little Old New York 1923,Ag 2,10:3
Three Miles Out 1924,Ja 1,20:1
Maytime 1924,Je 2,14:3
Janice Meredith 1924,Ag 6,13:3
Price of a Party, The 1924,N 26,17:3
Proud Flesh 1925,Ap 14,26:1
Zander the Great 1925,My 4,16:2
Marriage Whirl, The 1925,Jl 15,22:3
Lovers in Quarantine 1925,O 13,20:1
That Royle Girl 1926,Ja 4,33:1
Song and Dance Man, The 1926,F 1,16:1
Up in Mabel's Room 1926,Je 29,21:2
Nervous Wreck, The 1926,O 12,30:2
Rubber Tires 1927,Mr 9,29:1
Night Bride, The 1927,Mr 30,22:6
Rejuvenation of Aunt Mary, The 1927,Jl 27,27:4
Girl on the Pullman, The 1927,N 1,21:1 (In
 Addenda)
Let 'Er go, Gallegher 1928,Ja 16,24:1
Rush Hour, The 1928,Ja 31,29:1
Just Married 1928,Ag 13,23:2
Three Week Ends 1928,D 10,25:1
Her Husband's Women 1929,Ag 13,23:2
Ford, Helen
Apartment for Peggy 1948,O 16,9:2
Model and the Marriage Broker, The
 1952,Ja 12,10:6
Ford, Henry (Narrator)
Battle of Midway, The 1942,S 15,19:3
Ford, Hugh (Director)
Danger Mark, The 1918,Jl 8,9:4
Woman Thou Gavest Me, The 1919,Je 9,16:3
Secret Service 1919,Je 23,10:3

Ford, Hugh (Director) — Cont
In Mizzoura 1919,O 13,16:3
His House in Order 1920,Mr 8,9:5
His House in Order 1920,Mr 8,9:6
Ford, James
Outcast 1928,N 26,30:2
Wedding Rings 1930,My 10,25:3
Ford, John
Hangman's House Last of the Pagans
 1928,My 14,25:1
Man of Affairs 1937,F 20,9:2
At the Front 1943,Mr 19,15:5
Tales of Hoffmann 1951,Ap 5,34:2
Ford, John (Cinematographer)
Battle of Midway, The 1942,S 15,19:3
Ford, John (Director)
Silver Wings 1922,My 18,14:4
Village Blacksmith, The 1922,N 3,17:5
Iron Horse, The 1924,Ag 29,6:1
Lightnin 1925,Jl 22,14:4
Four Sons 1928,F 14,27:1
Mother Machree 1928,Mr 6,20:3
Napoleon's Barber 1928,N 26,30:2
Riley, The Cop 1928,D 4,29:1
Strong Boy 1929,Ap 1,22:1
Black Watch, The 1929,My 23,26:3
Salute 1929,O 5,22:5
Men Without Women 1930,F 1,15:1
Born Reckless 1930,Je 7,10:4
Up the River 1930,O 11,21:3
Brat, The 1931,Ag 24,13:4
Arrowsmith 1931,D 8,36:4
Air Mail 1932,N 7,20:3
Flesh 1932,D 10,19:3
Pilgrimage 1933,Jl 13,17:5
Doctor Bull 1933,O 6,21:2
Lost Patrol, The 1934,Ap 2,13:2
World Moves On, The 1934,Je 30,18:5
Judge Priest 1934,O 12,33:1
Whole Town's Talking, The 1935,Mr 1,16:2
Informer, The 1935,My 10,25:2
Steamboat Around the Bend 1935,S 20,17:2
Prisoner of Shark Island, The 1936,F 13,25:2
Mary of Scotland 1936,Jl 31,22:2
Plough and the Stars, The 1937,Ja 29,15:1
Wee Willie Winkie 1937,Jl 24,12:1
Hurricane, The 1937,N 10,31:2
Four Men and a Prayer 1938,My 7,18:1
Submarine Patrol 1938,N 19,9:2
Stagecoach 1939,Mr 3,21:1
Young Mr Lincoln 1939,Je 3,11:2
Drums Along the Mohawk 1939,N 4,11:2
Grapes of Wrath, The 1940,Ja 25,17:2
Long Voyage Home, The 1940,O 9,30:2 (In
 Addenda)
Tobacco Road 1941,F 21,16:2
How Green Was my Valley 1941,O 29,27:2
They Were Expendable 1945,D 21,25:2
My Darling Clementine 1946,D 4,44:5
Fugitive, The 1947,D 26,22:2
Fort Apache 1948,Je 25,26:2
Three Godfathers 1949,Mr 4,25:2
She Wore a Yellow Ribbon 1949,N 18,35:2
When Willie Comes Marching Home
 1950,F 18,9:2
Wagonmaster 1950,Je 19,17:2
Rio Grande 1950,N 20,21:2
This Is Korea 1951,Ag 20,14:2
Quiet Man, The 1952,Ag 22,13:1
What Price Glory 1952,Ag 23,10:2
Mogambo 1953,O 2,18:1
Sun Shines Bright, The 1954,Mr 17,25:2
Long Gray Line, The 1955,F 11,19:2
Mister Roberts 1955,Jl 15,14:1
Searchers, The 1956,My 31,21:4
Wings of Eagles, The 1957,F 1,28:1
Rising of the Moon, The (The Majesty of the
 Law); Majesty of the Law, The (The Rising of
 the Moon) 1957,Jl 10,23:1
Rising of the Moon, The (1921); 1921 (The Rising
 of the Moon) 1957,Jl 10,23:1
Rising of the Moon, The (A Minute's Wait);
 Minute's Wait, A (The Rising of the Moon)
 1957,Jl 10,23:1
Last Hurrah, The 1958,O 24,40:1
Gideon of Scotland Yard 1959,My 20,38:2
Horse Soldiers, The 1959,Je 26,13:1
Sergeant Rutledge 1960,My 26,37:1
Two Rode Together 1961,Jl 27,23:3
Man Who Shot Liberty Valance, The
 1962,My 24,29:2
How the West Was Won 1963,Ap 1,54:1
Donovan's Reef 1963,Jl 25,14:1
Cheyenne Autumn 1964,D 24,8:1
7 Women 1966,My 5,59:1
Ford, John (Miscellaneous)
Young Cassidy 1965,Mr 23,35:1
Ford, John (Original Author)
Men Without Women 1930,F 1,15:1
Last Outlaw, The 1936,Je 15,24:1
Ford, John (Producer)
Long Voyage Home, The 1940,O 9,30:2 (In
 Addenda)
They Were Expendable 1945,D 21,25:2

Ford, John (Producer)— Cont

Fugitive, The 1947,D 26,22:2
Fort Apache 1948,Je 25,26:2
Three Godfathers 1949,Mr 4,25:2
Rio Grande 1950,N 20,21:2
Sun Shines Bright, The 1954,Mr 17,25:2
Last Hurrah, The 1958,O 24,40:1
Gideon of Scotland Yard 1959,My 20,38:2
Donovan's Reef 1963,Jl 25,14:1

Ford, Montgomery
Last Blitzkrieg, The 1959,Ja 31,13:5

Ford, Patrick (Original Author)
Wagonmaster 1950,Je 19,17:2

Ford, Patrick (Producer)
Sergeant Rutledge 1960,My 26,37:1

Ford, Paul
House on Ninety-Second Street, The
1945,S 27,24:7
Lust for Gold 1949,Jl 4,9:2
Perfect Strangers 1950,Mr 11,8:2
Kid From Texas, The 1950,Je 2,26:2
Teahouse of the August Moon, The
1956,N 30,19:1
Matchmaker, The 1958,Ag 13,22:1
Advise and Consent 1962,Je 7,31:2
Music Man, The 1962,Ag 24,14:1
Who's Got the Action? 1962,D 26,5:4
It's a Mad, Mad, Mad, Mad World
1963,N 19,47:1
Never too Late 1965,N 5,28:1
Russians are Coming the Russians are Coming,
The 1966,My 26,55:1
Big Hand for the Little Lady, A 1966,Je 9,54:2
Spy With a Cold Nose, The 1966,D 20,58:2
Comedians, The 1967,N 1,37:1

Ford, Peter
Lieutenant Craig-Missing 1951,My 19,9:4

Ford, Philip (Director)
Last Crooked Mile, The 1946,S 14,10:8

Ford, Ross
Sign of the Ram, The 1948,Mr 4,30:2
Fuller Brush Man, The 1948,My 15,18:2
Gallant Blade 1948,O 13,31:3
Night Unto Night 1949,Je 11,11:2
Barbary Pirate 1949,O 28,29:3
Girl's School 1950,F 3,29:2
Challenge to Lassie 1950,Ap 7,22:3
He's a Cockeyed Wonder 1950,O 20,32:4
Flying Missile, The 1950,D 25,25:1
Force of Arms 1951,Ag 14,20:2

Ford, Ruth
Lady is Willing, The 1942,Ap 24,21:2
Murder in the Big House 1942,My 8,27:3
Lady Gangster 1942,Jl 10,13:2
Escape From Crime 1942,O 12,12:3
Hidden Hand, The 1942,N 26,40:4
Gorilla Man, The 1943,Ja 15,21:4
Truck Busters 1943,Ja 29,23:5
Princess O'Rourke 1943,N 6,16:2
Wilson 1944,Ag 2,18:1
Circumstantial Evidence 1945,Ap 21,18:3
Dragonwyck 1946,Ap 11,35:2
Act One 1963,D 27,17:2

Ford, Vera
Song of the Lark 1937,N 15,15:3

Ford, Wallace
Possessed 1931,N 28,20:4
X Marks the Spot 1931,D 7,16:1
Beast of the City, The 1932,Mr 14,13:3
Wet Parade, The 1932,Ap 22,23:2
Freaks 1932,Jl 9,7:5
Skyscraper Souls 1932,Ag 5,11:2
Central Park 1932,D 7,29:3
Hypnotized 1933,Ja 16,13:3
Employees' Entrance 1933,Ja 21,10:6
Big Cage, The 1933,My 9,20:5
Three-Cornered Moon 1933,Ag 12,14:2
Good-Bye Again 1933,S 2,15:2
My Woman 1933,O 16,20:3
Headline Shooters 1933,O 23,18:3
Lost Patrol, The 1934,Ap 2,13:2
Men in White 1934,Je 9,18:2
Man Who Reclaimed his Head, The
1935,Ja 9,22:1
Whole Town's Talking, The 1935,Mr 1,16:2
Mysterious Mr Wong, The 1935,Mr 7,26:1
Nut Farm, The 1935,Ap 8,23:3
Informer, The 1935,My 10,25:2
She Couldn't Take It 1935,N 7,27:1
Mary Burns, Fugitive 1935,N 16,19:2
Two in the Dark 1936,F 1,9:2
Absolute Quiet 1936,My 2,11:1
Son Comes Home, A 1936,S 5,7:1
You're in the Army Now 1937,Ap 16,27:2
Swing It, Sailor 1937,D 13,23:5
Dark Sands 1938,Ag 17,23:4
Back Door to Heaven 1939,Ap 20,21:2
Isle of Destiny 1940,Ap 8,15:2
Two Girls on Broadway 1940,Ap 25,28:4
Mummy's Hand, The 1940,S 20,27:2
Give Us Wings 1940,N 21,43:3
Man Betrayed, A 1941,Mr 27,29:5
Murder by Invitation 1941,Jl 23,15:4
Blues in the Night 1941,D 12,35:2

All Through the Night 1942,Ja 24,13:2
Mummy's Tomb, The 1942,O 26,19:2
Seven Days' Leave 1942,D 11,33:2
Shadow of a Doubt 1943,Ja 13,18:2
Cross of Lorraine, The 1943,D 3,27:4
Secret Command 1944,Je 14,16:2
Blood on the Sun 1945,Je 29,12:2
Great John L, The 1945,Jl 9,14:6
Spellbound 1945,N 2,22:2
Green Years, The 1946,Ap 5,21:2
Lover Come Back 1946,Je 20,20:3
Crack-Up 1946,S 7,11:1
Rendezvous With Annie 1946,S 23,29:3
Black Angel 1946,S 26,32:4
Dead Reckoning 1947,Ja 23,31:2
Magic Town 1947,O 8,29:2
T-Men 1948,Ja 23,28:3
Man From Texas 1948,Ag 12,16:5
Belle Star's Daughter 1949,Ja 10,19:2
Set-Up, The 1949,Mr 30,31:2
Red Stallion in the Rockies 1949,Ag 26,15:2
Dakota Lil 1950,Mr 3,21:5
Furies, The 1950,Ag 17,23:2
Breaking Point, The 1950,O 7,10:6
Harvey 1950,D 22,19:1
He Ran all the Way 1951,Je 21,24:2
Painting the Clouds With Sunshine 1951,S 1,9:6
Warpath 1951,N 23,32:2
Flesh and Fury 1952,Mr 28,27:4
She Couldn't Say No 1954,F 27,11:3
Three Ring Circus 1954,D 25,7:2
Man From Laramie, The 1955,S 1,20:2
Lucy Gallant 1955,O 21,30:1
Spoilers, The 1955,D 24,10:2
Maverick Queen, the 1956,Je 4,25:2
First Texan, The 1956,Je 23,20:2
Johnny Concho 1956,Ag 16,30:1
Rainmaker, The 1956,D 13,51:1
Twilight for the Gods 1958,Ag 7,21:1
Matchmaker, The 1958,Ag 13,22:1
Last Hurrah, The 1958,O 24,40:1
Warlock 1959,My 1,34:1
Patch of Blue, A 1965,D 16,63:1

Ford, Whitey
Safe at Home 1962,Ap 14,14:1

FORDE
See Also FORD

Forde, Eugene (Director)
Smoky 1934,Ja 1,28:2
Charlie Chan in London 1934,S 13,26:1
Mystery Woman 1935,Ja 9,22:2
Great Hotel Murder, The 1935,F 28,17:4
Your Uncle Dudley 1935,D 12,33:4
Country Beyond, The 1936,Ap 30,17:3
36 Hours to Live 1936,Ag 15,6:3
Step Lively, Jeeves 1937,Ap 2,19:6
Charlie Chan on Broadway 1937,S 20,19:1
Charlie Chan at Monte Carlo 1937,D 18,18:1
One Wild Night 1938,Je 3,17:2
Meet the Girls 1938,S 3,16:6
Inspector Hornleigh 1939,Je 15,27:3
Honeymoon's Over, The 1939,D 15,33:3
Charlie Chan's Murder Cruise 1940,My 3,17:5
Pier 13 1940,Ag 9,19:3
Michael Shayne, Private Detective
1940,D 19,33:2
Sleepers West 1941,Mr 20,25:3
Dressed to Kill 1941,Ag 22,19:3
Man at Large 1941,O 11,21:4
Buy Me That Town 1941,O 23,27:2
Berlin Correspondent 1942,S 4,19:2
Shadows in the Night 1944,Jl 29,16:2
Jewels of Brandenburg 1947,My 24,10:5
Backlash 1947,My 24,10:5
Crimson Key, The 1947,O 18,9:2
Invisible Wall, The 1947,N 1,11:2

Forde, Eugenie
Strictly Confidential 1919,O 6,15:1
Memory Lane 1926,F 2,20:4
That's My Baby 1926,Ap 12,18:4
Captain Salvation 1927,Je 27,25:2

Forde, Hal
Great White Way, The 1924,Ja 4,10:1

Forde, Stanley
Great White Way, The 1924,Ja 4,10:1

Forde, Walter (Director)
Ringer, The 1932,Je 2,25:2
Condemned to Death 1932,Jl 14,24:2
Rome Express 1932,D 18,X,6:5
Ghost Train, The 1933,F 18,13:3
Rome Express 1933,F 27,11:2
Night and Day 1933,My 29,22:2
Orders Is Orders 1934,My 7,20:2
Chu Chin Chow 1934,S 22,12:2
Jack Ahoy 1935,F 9,11:2
Alias Bulldog Drummond 1935,S 10,26:2
Born for Glory 1935,O 21,22:4
King of the Damned 1936,F 1,9:2
Forbidden Music 1938,D 27,13:2
Secret Four, The 1940,Ap 22,13:2
Three Cockeyed Sailors 1942,Ja 26,18:3
Flying Fortress 1942,D 19,22:2
Master of Bankdam 1949,O 17,18:2

Fordred, Dorice
Day Dreams 1930,F 4,28:3
As You Like It 1936,N 6,29:3
Knight Without Armor 1937,Jl 9,18:1
Stolen Life 1939,Je 15,27:2

FOREMAN
See Also FORMAN

Foreman, Carl (Director)
Victors, The 1963,D 20,21:2

Foreman, Carl (Original Author)
Spooks Run Wild 1941,N 1,20:3
Dakota 1945,D 17,17:2

Foreman, Carl (Producer)
Guns of Navarone, The 1961,Je 23,19:1
Victors, The 1963,D 20,21:2

Foreman, Carl (Screenwriter)
Spooks Run Wild 1941,N 1,20:3
Champion 1949,Ap 11,29:2
Home of the Brave 1949,My 13,29:1
Young Man With a Horn 1950,F 10,18:4
Men, The 1950,Jl 21,15:2
Cyrano De Bergerac 1950,N 17,31:2
High Noon 1952,Jl 25,14:2
Key, The 1958,Jl 2,23:3
Guns of Navarone, The 1961,Je 23,19:1
Victors, The 1963,D 20,21:2

Foreman, L L (Original Author)
Savage, The 1953,Ja 2,11:1
Arrow in the Dust 1954,My 1,13:2

Forest, Ann
Man Who Played God, The 1922,O 2,21:2

Forest, Chet (Miscellaneous)
Sweethearts 1938,D 23,16:2

Forest, Frank
Big Broadcast of 1937, The 1936,O 22,31:1
Champagne Waltz 1937,F 4,17:2
I'll Take Romance 1937,D 17,33:2

Forest, Jean-Claude (Original Author)
Barbarella 1968,O 12,43:1

Forest, Jean-Claude (Screenwriter)
Barbarella 1968,O 12,43:1

Forest, Karl
Der Falsche Feldmarschall 1932,Je 30,26:2

Forest, Mark
Goliath and the Dragon 1961,Ja 5,27:2
Son of Samson 1962,S 27,33:4
Goliath and the Sins of Babylon 1964,Mr 5,36:2

Forest, Michael
Deathwatch 1967,Je 28,38:1

Forest, William
In This our Life 1942,My 9,10:2
Race Street 1948,Ag 23,13:3

Forester, C S (Original Author)
Born for Glory 1935,O 21,22:4
Eagle Squadron 1942,Jl 3,12:5
Forever and a Day 1943,Mr 13,9:2
Captain Horatio Hornblower 1951,S 14,21:2
African Queen, The 1952,F 21,24:3
Sailor of the King 1953,S 3,15:2
Commandos Strike at Dawn 1954,Ja 14,25:1
Pride and the Passion, The 1957,Je 29,10:6
Sink the Bismarck! 1960,F 12,22:3

Forgay, Wenonah
Loves of Ricardo, The 1926,Ag 16,10:1

Forge, Huguette
Landru 1963,Ap 10,31:1

Foriani, Remo (Miscellaneous)
Sans Famille 1959,S 5,11:4

Foriani, Remo (Screenwriter)
Sans Famille 1959,S 5,11:4

Forie, Sidney J (Director)
Leather Boys, The 1965,N 9,50:1

Forli, Giuseppe
Monte Cassino 1948,N 25,47:3

Forlong, Michael (Director)
Green Helmet, The 1961,Jl 20,32:2

FORMAN
See Also FOREMAN

Forman, Carol
Falcon's Adventure, The 1946,D 14,19:2
San Quentin 1947,F 10,24:3
Mozart Story, The 1948,N 15,21:5

Forman, Henry James (Original Author)
Pony Express, The 1925,S 14,16:1

Forman, Joey
Andy Hardy Comes Home 1958,D 24,00:0
Wheeler Dealers, The 1963,N 15,25:2
Wicked Dreams of Paula Schultz, The
1968,Ja 4,28:1

Forman, Mary
Resurrection 1931,Ja 24,15:1

Forman, Milos (Director)
Loves of a Blonde 1966,S 13,51:2
Loves of a Blonde 1966,O 27,55:1
Loves of a Blonde 1967,Je 19,41:1
Audition 1968,Jl 4,13:2
Firemen's Ball, The 1968,S 30,60:1

Forman, Milos (Original Author)
Audition 1968,Jl 4,13:2

Forman, Milos (Screenwriter)
Loves of a Blonde 1966,O 27,55:1
Audition 1968,Jl 4,13:2
Firemen's Ball, The 1968,S 30,60:1

Forman, Tom
For Better, For Worse 1919,Ap 28,13:2
Kosher Kitty Kelly 1926,S 28,30:2
Rawhide 1938,Ap 25,19:2
Forman, Tom (Director)
Easy Road, The 1921,F 20,VI,2:2 (In Addenda)
White and Unmarried 1921,My 30,12:5
Cappy Ricks 1921,Ag 22,13:6
Prince There Was 1921,N 14,18:1
Broken Wing, The 1923,O 9,17:4
Fighting American, The 1924,My 13,24:1
Crimson Runner, The 1925,My 27,26:2
Formby, George
Let George Do It 1940,O 14,25:5
It's in the Air 1940,D 10,33:2
Formby, George (Composer)
Let George Do It 1940,O 14,25:5
It's in the Air 1940,D 10,33:2
Formichi, Enrico
Cinderella 1953,My 15,20:2
Aida 1954,N 12,17:1
Forney, Pauline (Original Author)
Jazz Heaven 1929,O 30,29:2
Foronda, Pituka de
Serpiente Roja, La; Red Serpent, The
  1937,S 27,24:3
Ahora Seremos Felices; Now We Shall Be Happy
  1940,Mr 16,8:2
Forquet, Philippe
In the French Style 1963,S 19,23:1
Take Her, She's Mine 1963,N 14,41:1
Forrell, Gene (Composer)
To the Fair 1965,F 13,10:2
Forrest, Alan
Long Live the King 1923,D 4,24:1
Dressmaker from Paris, The 1925,Mr 18,19:2
Old Clothes 1925,N 9,25:1
Rose of the World 1925,N 10,25:3
Partners Again, With Potash and Perlmutter
  1926,F 15,16:4
Forrest, Allan
Man From Lost River, The 1922,Ja 16,18:3
Wandering Daughters 1923,Jl 2,16:2
Captain Blood 1924,S 9,19:1
Pampered Youth 1925,F 10,20:1
Great Divide, The 1925,F 11,19:4
Summer Bachelors 1926,D 20,28:3
Ankles Preferred 1927,Ap 18,21:2
Lovelorn, The 1927,D 19,30:1
Sally of the Scandals 1928,Jl 3,19:3
Forrest, Allen
Siren of Seville, The 1924,N 17,16:1 (In
  Addenda)
Forrest, Ann
Behold my Wife 1920,O 11,19:3
Faith Healer, The 1921,Mr 14,9:2
Marriage Morals 1923,Ag 14,10:3
If Winter Comes 1923,S 4,14:1
Forrest, Arthur
When Knighthood Was in Flower 1922,S 15,17:2
  (In Addenda)
Forrest, Arthur (Screenwriter)
Crowded Paradise 1956,Je 22,15:1
Forrest, Chet (Composer)
Good Old Soak 1937,Ap 20,25:3
Saratoga 1937,Jl 23,16:3
Mannequin 1938,Ja 21,15:2
First 100 Years, The 1938,My 13,17:2
Three Comrades 1938,Je 3,17:1
Let Freedom Ring 1939,Mr 10,19:2
Music in My Heart 1940,Ja 4,19:2
Blondie Goes Latin 1941,F 26,17:3
I Married an Angel 1942,Jl 10,13:2
Forrest, Chet (Miscellaneous)
After the Thin Man 1936,D 25,19:2
Maytime 1937,Mr 19,27:1
Firefly, The 1937,S 2,17:2
Broadway Serenade 1939,Ap 7,25:2
Forrest, George (Composer)
Kismet 1955,D 9,32:2
Forrest, Gladys
Mad Wednesday 1951,Ja 25,21:5
Forrest, Helen
Two Girls and a Sailor 1944,Je 15,16:1
Bathing Beauty 1944,Je 28,20:1
Forrest, Jack (Producer)
Werewolf in a Girls Dormitory 1963,Je 7,37:1
Forrest, John
Great Expectations 1947,My 23,31:1
Guinea Pig, The 1949,My 2,20:2
Adam and Evalyn 1950,My 12,33:4
Tom Brown's School Days 1952,Ja 8,23:5
Glory at Sea 1953,Mr 11,36:7
Coming-Out Party, A 1962,Jl 31,19:2
Forrest, Lottie Pickford
Don Q, Son of Zorro 1925,Je 16,24:1
Forrest, Mabel
Holiday 1930,Jl 3,25:4
Hollywood Boulevard 1936,S 21,26:4
Forrest, Robert
Ransom 1956,Ja 25,28:3

Forrest, Sally
Not Wanted 1949,Jl 25,11:4
Mystery Street 1950,Jl 28,12:5
Vengeance Valley 1951,F 16,21:2
Excuse my Dust 1951,Je 28,21:2
Hard, Fast and Beautiful 1951,Jl 2,16:6
Strange Door, The 1951,D 10,34:6
Son of Sinbad 1955,Jl 28,18:2
While the City Sleeps 1956,My 17,37:1
Forrest, Steve
Clown, The 1953,Ja 29,25:1
Dream Wife 1953,Jl 30,20:1
So Big 1953,O 22,34:2
Take the High Ground 1953,N 20,19:2
Phantom of the Rue Morgue 1954,Mr 20,10:5
Prisoner of War 1954,My 10,20:2
Rogue Cop 1954,S 18,12:2
Bedevilled 1955,Ap 23,23:1
Living Idol, The 1957,My 3,18:1
It Happened to Jane 1959,Ag 6,18:3
Heller in Pink Tights 1960,Mr 17,28:1
Five Branded Women 1960,Je 2,27:2
Flaming Star 1960,D 17,19:1
Second Time Around, The 1961,D 23,16:1
Longest Day, The 1962,O 5,28:1
Yellow Canary, The 1963,My 16,42:1
Forrest, William
Lone Wolf Meets a Lady, The 1940,Je 17,19:2
Secret Seven, The 1940,Ag 12,11:6
Flight From Destiny 1941,Mr 28,26:7
Lone Wolf Takes a Chance, The 1941,Ap 7,13:2
Joe Smith, American 1942,Ap 2,27:4
Spy Ship 1942,Jl 11,8:2
Fighting Seabees, The 1944,Mr 20,14:2
Mr Winkle Goes to War 1944,Ag 3,16:1
Abroad With two Yanks 1944,O 26,19:7
Sign of the Cross 1944,D 21,16:3
Caribbean Mystery, The 1945,Ag 20,22:4
Jolson Story, The 1946,O 11,28:2
Dead Reckoning 1947,Ja 23,31:2
Corpse came C O D, The 1947,Ag 19,27:2
Mother Wore Tights 1947,Ag 21,33:2
Spirit of West Point 1947,O 3,31:2
Younger Brothers, The 1949,My 28,11:2
Girl from Jones Beach, The 1949,Jl 30,9:2
Story of Seabiscuit, The 1949,N 12,8:4
I'll See You in my Dreams 1951,D 7,35:1
Story of Will Rogers, The 1952,Jl 18,10:5
Night Without Sleep 1952,S 27,13:2
Eddie Cantor Story, The 1953,D 26,10:2
Band of Angels 1957,Jl 11,21:1
Good Neighbor Sam 1964,Jl 23,19:1
Forrester, Cay
Blonde Savage 1947,O 4,9:2
D O A 1950,My 1,18:2
Forrester, Elizabeth
Holiday 1930,Jl 3,25:4
Born to Love 1931,Ap 25,23:4
American Tragedy, An 1931,Ag 6,22:5
Forrester, Frederick
These Thirty Years 1934,My 24,28:3
Forrester, Izola (Screenwriter)
White Moth, The 1924,Je 16,18:3
Forrester, Larry (Original Author)
Fathom 1967,D 14,62:1
Forsberg, Carin
I Am With You 1949,Mr 1,30:5
Forsch, Robert
Murderers Among Us 1948,Ag 17,19:6
Forsh, Olga (Screenwriter)
Pugachev 1938,Jl 4,10:2
Forslund, Bengst (Screenwriter)
Here's Your Life 1968,D 20,60:1
Forssell, Lars (Original Author)
Doll, The 1964,Ja 14,27:1
Forst, Emil (Original Author)
Parisian Nights 1925,Je 2,16:3
Forst, Garrett (Screenwriter)
Jalna 1935,S 14,8:4
Forst, Willi
Burning Secret 1933,My 28,IX,2:5 (In Addenda)
Maskerade 1934,O 14,X,4:2 (In Addenda)
Forst, Willi (Director)
Maskerade 1934,O 14,X,4:2 (In Addenda)
Forst, Willi (Screenwriter)
Maskerade 1934,O 14,X,4:2 (In Addenda)
Forst, Willy
Zwei Hertzen in Drei-Viertel Takt
  1930,O 13,31:1
Lustigen Weiber von Wien, Die 1931,Jl 10,22:2
Ein Burschenlied aus Heidelberg 1931,S 14,15:3
Raub der Mona Lisa, Der; Theft of the Mona Lisa,
  The 1931,S 27,VIII,7:1
Sein Liebeslied 1931,N 19,27:5
Das Lied ist Aus 1932,Ja 29,13:2
Raub der Mona Lisa, Der 1932,Mr 30,15:2
Blonder Tram, Ein; Blond Dream, A
  1932,N 13,IX,4:2
Liebling vom Wien, Der 1933,Je 10,16:5
So ein Maedel Vergisst Man nicht 1935,S 28,12:3
Ich Kenn' Dich Nicht und Liebe Dich; I Don't
  Know You, but I Love You 1935,N 18,20:1
Royal Waltz, The 1936,Ap 10,27:1

Forst, Willy— Cont
Operetta 1949,Je 6,15:4
Forst, Willy (Director)
Unfinished Symphony 1935,Ja 14,11:2
Masquerade in Vienna 1937,Ja 26,16:4
Vienna Burgtheater 1937,O 27,47:1
Operetta 1949,Je 6,15:4
Sunderin 1954,D 24,7:2
Cabaret 1957,N 9,31:2 (Incorrect in this edition;
  use 1957,N 7,43:4 elsewhere)
White Horse Inn, The 1957,D 4,50:3
Forst, Willy (Narrator)
Wonderful Times 1951,Ap 24,35:2
Forst, Willy (Original Author)
Vienna Burgtheater 1937,O 27,47:1
Forst, Willy (Producer)
Vienna Burgtheater 1937,O 27,47:1
Operetta 1949,Je 6,15:4
Forst, Willy (Screenwriter)
Operetta 1949,Je 6,15:4
Sunderin 1954,D 24,7:2
Forster, Margaret (Original Author)
Georgy Girl 1966,O 18,48:1
Forster, Margaret (Screenwriter)
Georgy Girl 1966,O 18,48:1
Forster, Robert
Reflections in a Golden Eye 1967,O 12,59:1
Forster, Rudolf
At the Grey House 1927,N 8,33:1
Dreigroschenoper, Die; Beggar's Opera, The
  1931,My 18,21:2
Yorck 1932,N 24,35:2
Morgenrot 1933,My 16,15:2
Traeumende Mund, Der 1934,F 5,19:2
Hohe Schule; College 1939,Ap 8,19:3
White Horse Inn, The 1957,D 4,50:3
Liane, Jungle Goddess 1959,F 23,19:1
Threepenny Opera, The 1960,Jl 11,24:4
Rest Is Silence, The 1960,Ag 2,22:6
Tonio Kroger 1968,Ja 16,24:1
Forster, Rudolph
Graefin von Monte Christo, Die; Countess of
  Monte Christo, The 1932,My 15,VIII,4:2 (In
  Addenda)
Forster, Thilde (Screenwriter)
Woman Commands, A 1932,Ja 28,13:2
Forster, Walter (Screenwriter)
Togger 1937,Mr 14,XI,4:5 (In Addenda)
Forster-Larrinaga, Frau
Kreuzer Emden 1932,S 8,17:2
Forsyne, Ida
Green Pastures, The 1936,Jl 17,20:1
Forsyth, Bruce
Star! 1968,O 23,36:2
Forsyth, Charles
Every Night at Eight 1935,Ag 3,16:2
Forsyth, Frank
Psycopath, The 1966,S 29,60:1
Forsyth, James (Screenwriter)
Francis of Assisi 1961,Jl 29,8:2
Forsyth, Rosemary
Shenandoah 1965,Jl 29,18:3
War Lord, The 1965,N 18,55:2
Texas Across the River 1966,N 24,65:1
Forsyth, Steve
Love and Marriage (One Moment Is Enough); One
  Moment Is Enough (Love and Marriage)
  1966,Ag 5,20:1
Forsythe, John
Destination Tokyo 1944,Ja 1,9:2
Captive City, The 1952,Mr 27,34:2
Glass Web, The 1953,N 12,37:5
Escape from Fort Bravo 1954,Ja 23,11:2
Trouble With Harry, The 1955,O 18,46:2
Ambassador's Daughter, The 1956,Ag 30,19:1
Kitten With a Whip 1964,N 5,50:4
Madame X 1966,Ap 28,49:1
In Cold Blood 1967,D 15,60:1
Forsythe, Mimi
Three Russian Girls 1944,F 5,13:2
Sensations of 1945 1944,Jl 7,13:2
Fort, Garrett (Original Author)
Dangerous Nan McGrew 1930,Je 21,20:5
Panama Flo 1932,Ja 20,17:4
Dracula's Daughter 1936,My 18,14:2
Twelve Crowded Hours 1939,F 24,15:2
Lady for a Night 1942,F 12,27:2
Blood on the Sun 1945,Je 29,12:2
Inside Job 1946,Je 15,24:3
Fort, Garrett (Screenwriter)
Outside the Law 1930,S 1,16:1
Dracula's Daughter 1936,My 18,14:2
Devil Doll, The 1936,Ag 8,5:2
Storm Over Bengal 1938,D 8,34:4
Mark of Zorro, The 1940,N 4,23:2
Ladies in Retirement 1941,N 7,27:1
Among the Living 1941,D 13,25:2
Street Of Chance 1942,N 19,31:3
Man in Half Moon Street, The 1945,Ja 20,16:2
Forte, Rene
6 1/2 x 11 1929,Ag 13,23:2
Forterre (Composer)
Man and his Wife, A 1939,Mr 28,20:1

Fortescue, Kenneth
Barretts of Wimpole Street, The 1957,Ja 18,15:3
How to Murder a Rich Uncle 1957,O 26,19:2
Forti, Fiorella C
Voice in Your Heart, A 1952,F 23,7:5
Fortune, Jan (Screenwriter)
Man of Conquest 1939,Ap 28,31:2
Vanishing Virginian, The 1942,My 28,13:3
Forvay, Jose
Treasure of Sierra Madre 1948,Ja 24,11:2
Forwood, Anthony
Story of Robin Hood, The 1952,Je 27,18:3
Knights of the Round Table 1954,Ja 8,17:2
Forwood, Gareth
Bofors Gun, The 1968,S 23,42:3
Forzane, Jacqueline
Nana 1929,Jl 30,19:4
Forzano, Andrea (Director)
Stranger on the Prowl 1953,N 10,38:1
Forzano, Andrea (Screenwriter)
Stranger on the Prowl 1953,N 10,38:1
Forzano, Giovacchino (Director)
Man of Courage 1934,N 14,23:2
One Hundred Days of Napoleon 1936,S 14,25:1
Padre delle Patria, Il; Father of his Country, The
1938,Ag 30,14:2
Forzano, Giovacchino (Original Author)
Padre delle Patria, Il; Father of his Country, The
1938,Ag 30,14:2
Forzano, Giovacchino (Screenwriter)
Conte di Brechard, Il; Count of Brechard, The
1940,O 24,31:3
Fosca, Pietro
Man of Courage 1934,N 14,23:2
Fosge, Bunty
This Freedom 1923,N 28,15:1
Foshay, Harold
To Mary-With Love 1936,Ag 27,16:1
Foss, Tore
En Glad Gutt 1933,N 24,25:7
Fosse, Bob
Kiss Me Kate 1953,N 6,23:2
My Sister Eileen 1955,S 23,21:1
Fossey, Brigitte
Forbidden Games 1952,D 9,43:2
Happy Road, The 1957,Je 21,20:2
Fossier, Michael (Producer)
That Night With You 1945,N 9,16:2
Fossier, Michael (Screenwriter)
That Night With You 1945,N 9,16:2
Fostel, S
Yiddle With his Fiddle 1937,Ja 2,15:1
Tkies Khaf; (Vow, The) 1938,S 15,29:3
Foster, Art
Gentleman Jim 1942,N 26,40:3
Gorilla Man, The 1943,Ja 15,21:4
Mysterious Doctor, The 1943,My 20,26:4
Action in the North Atlantic 1943,My 22,10:2
Enter Arsene Lupin 1944,D 2,17:6
Confidential Agent 1945,N 3,11:2
Blonde Savage 1947,O 4,9:2
Foster, Barry
Surprise Package 1960,O 15,26:2
King and Country 1964,S 24,46:2
King and Country 1966,Ja 28,20:4
Family Way, The 1967,Je 29,32:1
Inspector Clouseau 1968,Jl 25,26:1
Foster, Dan
Scaramouche 1952,My 9,20:2
Foster, Dianne
Bad for Each Other 1953,D 24,9:3
Drive a Crooked Road 1954,Ap 3,19:3
Three Hours to Kill 1954,S 4,6:4
Violent Men, The 1955,Ja 27,17:2
Monkey on my Back 1957,My 30,23:2
Night Passage 1957,Jl 25,28:1
Deep Six, The 1958,Ja 16,32:1
Last Hurrah, The 1958,O 24,40:1
Gideon of Scotland Yard 1959,My 20,38:2
King of the Roaring Twenties 1961,O 5,43:1
Who's Been Sleeping in My Bed? 1963,D 26,33:2
Foster, Dudley
Term of Trial 1963,Ja 31,5:2
Little Ones, The 1965,S 16,55:2
Foster, Eddie
Midnight Court 1937,Mr 4,27:3
Highway Patrol 1938,Ag 4,15:2
Mutiny in the Big House 1939,D 11,26:2
Mummy's Hand, The 1940,S 20,27:2
Angels Over Broadway 1940,N 18,23:2
Foster, Frances
Take a Giant Step 1961,Mr 6,28:2
Foster, Gloria
Cool World, The 1964,Ap 21,42:1
Nothing but a Man 1964,S 21,37:2
Comedians, The 1967,N 1,37:1
Foster, Harold (Original Author)
Prince Valiant 1954,Ap 7,40:2
Foster, Harry (Miscellaneous)
Spain Fights on 1939,F 13,13:2
Foster, Helen
Hell-Ship Bronson 1928,Je 19,31:1
Mating Call, The 1928,O 8,14:2

Gold Diggers of Broadway, The 1929,Ag 31,13:4
So Long Letty 1930,F 8,12:5
Road to Ruin, The 1934,F 21,23:2
Foster, Isabelle
Scoundrel, The 1935,My 3,23:2
Soak the Rich 1936,F 5,14:2
Foster, Jack (Original Author)
This Is China 1937,O 6,29:4
Foster, Jerry
Frontier Marshal 1934,Ja 31,20:3
Foster, Julia
Loneliness of the Long Distance Runner, The
1962,O 9,44:1
Small World of Sammy Lee, The 1963,Ag 14,28:1
One Way Pendulum 1965,Mr 3,34:3
Girl-Getters, The 1966,Ap 13,37:6
Alfie 1966,Ag 25,42:1
Half a Sixpence 1968,F 21,60:3
Foster, Lewis (Director)
Armored Car 1937,Jl 26,15:2
Lucky Stiff, The 1949,Ja 31,14:2
El Paso 1949,Mr 24,35:2
Manhandled 1949,My 26,34:2
Captain China 1950,Mr 2,33:2
Eagle and the Hawk, The 1950,Jl 6,31:2
Last Outpost, The 1951,Je 22,16:3
Passage West 1951,Ag 31,12:2
Hong Kong 1952,Ap 5,20:3
Those Redheads From Seattle 1953,O 1,34:2
Crashout 1955,Jl 9,9:2
Bold and the Brave, The 1956,My 26,15:2
Dakota Incident 1956,N 10,14:2
Tonka 1959,Mr 26,27:1
Sign of Zorro, The 1961,S 5,37:6
Foster, Lewis (Miscellaneous)
Stolen Harmony 1935,Ap 20,16:2
Foster, Lewis (Original Author)
Let's Talk It Over 1934,Je 16,20:2
Two in a Crowd 1936,O 5,25:1
Sons of the Legion 1938,S 30,24:3
Illegal Traffic 1938,N 17,29:3
Mr Smith Goes to Washington 1939,O 20,27:2
Comin' Round the Mountain 1940,S 26,27:3
I Live on Danger 1942,Ag 22,16:2
It Happened Tomorrow 1944,My 29,18:2
Crashout 1955,Jl 9,9:2
Foster, Lewis (Screenwriter)
Two in a Crowd 1936,O 5,25:1
Magnificent Brute, The 1936,O 24,23:1
Armored Car 1937,Jl 26,15:2
Sons of the Legion 1938,S 30,24:3
Illegal Traffic 1938,N 17,29:3
Some Like It Hot 1939,My 25,31:2
Farmer's Daughter, The 1940,F 16,23:4
Golden Gloves 1940,Ag 21,23:6
Comin' Round the Mountain 1940,S 26,27:3
Adventure in Washington 1941,Ag 1,11:3
Mayor of Forty-Fourth Street, The
1942,Je 11,27:4
I Live on Danger 1942,Ag 22,16:2
More the Merrier, The 1943,My 14,17:1
Hers to Hold 1943,Jl 22,15:1
Can't Help Singing 1944,D 26,22:4
Never Say Goodbye 1946,N 23,12:2
I Wonder Who's Kissing Her Now
1947,Jl 24,27:2
Lucky Stiff, The 1949,Ja 31,14:2
El Paso 1949,Mr 24,35:2
Manhandled 1949,My 26,34:2
Special Agent 1949,Ag 22,13:1
Captain China 1950,Mr 2,33:2
Eagle and the Hawk, The 1950,Jl 6,31:2
Passage West 1951,Ag 31,12:2
Crosswinds 1951,D 7,35:4
Those Redheads From Seattle 1953,O 1,34:2
Tonka 1959,Mr 26,27:1
Foster, Linda
Ambushers, The 1967,D 23,29:1
Foster, Maralee
Yours, Mine and Ours 1968,Ap 25,53:1
Foster, Marion
Emil 1938,Ap 15,23:2
Foster, Maurice (Producer)
Jokers, The 1967,My 16,50:1
Assignment K 1968,Jl 20,18:2
Foster, Maurice (Screenwriter)
Assignment K 1968,Jl 20,18:2
Foster, Maximillian
When Strangers Marry 1933,My 25,24:3
Foster, Maximillian (Original Author)
Silent Partner, The 1923,Ag 20,4:2
Foster, May
Woman of the World, A 1925,D 14,18:2
Crown of Lies 1926,Mr 30,20:6
Docks of New York, The 1928,S 17,28:2
Foster, Norman
Gentlemen of the Press 1929,My 13,27:2
Young Man of Manhattan 1930,Ap 19,15:1
No Limit 1931,Ja 17,23:1
Pays to Advertise, It 1931,F 21,15:2
It Pays to Advertise 1931,F 21,15:2
Up Pops the Devil 1931,My 16,13:3
Men Call it Love 1931,Je 20,20:4

Foster, Norman— Cont
Confessions of a Co-Ed 1931,Je 20,20:4
Reckless Living 1931,D 5,21:2
Under Eighteen 1931,D 26,15:5
Girl of the Rio 1932,Ja 9,21:1
Alias the Doctor 1932,Mr 3,22:3
Play Girl 1932,Mr 19,11:2
Cohens and Kellys in Hollywood, The
1932,Ap 22,23:2
Week-End Marriage 1932,Je 4,9:2
Skyscraper Souls 1932,Ag 5,11:2
Strange Justice 1932,O 20,24:2
Prosperity 1932,N 26,11:4
State Fair 1933,Ja 27,13:2
Pilgrimage 1933,Jl 13,17:5
Professional Sweetheart 1933,Jl 14,15:3
Walls of Gold 1933,O 21,11:3
Orient Express 1934,F 28,23:2
Strictly Dynamite 1934,Jl 4,18:2
Behind the Evidence 1935,Ja 26,13:2
Behind the Green Lights 1935,Ap 22,14:2
Escape from Devil's Island 1935,N 25,22:2
Everybody's Old Man 1936,Mr 26,27:2
High Tension 1936,Jl 11,11:4
Fatal Lady 1936,Jl 11,11:3
Murder Ahoy 1964,S 23,55:3
Merry Wives of Windsor, The 1966,F 28,21:1
Foster, Norman (Director)
Think Fast, Mr Moto 1937,Ag 16,15:3
Thank You, Mr Moto 1938,Ja 3,16:2
Walking Down Broadway 1938,Ap 1,17:3
Mr Moto Takes a Chance 1938,Je 13,15:4
Mysterious Mr Moto of Devil's Island
1938,S 19,16:2
Mr Moto's Last Warning 1939,Ja 27,17:3
Charlie Chan in Reno 1939,My 31,27:2
Mr Moto Takes a Vacation 1939,Je 19,12:6
Charlie Chan at Treasure Island 1939,S 1,15:5
Charlie Chan in Panama 1940,F 23,19:3
Viva Cisco Kid 1940,Mr 22,23:4
Scotland Yard 1941,Ap 9,33:3
Journey Into Fear 1943,Mr 19,15:3
Rachel and the Stranger 1948,S 20,21:2
Kiss the Blood off my Hands 1948,O 30,10:2
Father Is a Bachelor 1950,F 23,33:3
Woman on the Run 1950,N 30,24:2
Navajo 1952,F 21,24:4
Sombrero 1953,Ap 23,37:2
Davy Crockett, King of the Wild Frontier
1955,My 26,36:1
Sign of Zorro, The 1961,S 5,37:6
Foster, Norman (Original Author)
Mr Moto Takes a Chance 1938,Je 13,15:4
Mr Moto Takes a Vacation 1939,Je 19,12:6
Foster, Norman (Producer)
Merry Wives of Windsor, The 1966,F 28,21:1
Foster, Norman (Screenwriter)
Think Fast, Mr Moto 1937,Ag 16,15:3
Thank You, Mr Moto 1938,Ja 3,16:2
Mysterious Mr Moto of Devil's Island
1938,S 19,16:2
Mr Moto's Last Warning 1939,Ja 27,17:3
Woman on the Run 1950,N 30,24:2
Navajo 1952,F 21,24:4
Sombrero 1953,Ap 23,37:2
Sign of Zorro, The 1961,S 5,37:6
Merry Wives of Windsor, The 1966,F 28,21:1
Foster, Phil
Conquest of Space 1955,My 28,7:6
Foster, Phoebe
Tarnished Lady 1931,Ap 30,29:3
Night Angel, The 1931,Je 11,28:4
Our Betters 1933,F 24,13:2
Dinner at Eight 1933,Ag 24,18:1
Anna Karenina 1935,Ag 31,16:2
White Angel, The 1936,Je 25,24:1
Foster, Preston
Follow the Leader 1930,D 6,21:3
Two Seconds 1932,My 19,25:3
Doctor X 1932,Ag 4,17:2
Life Begins 1932,Ag 26,20:3
Last Mile, The 1932,Ag 26,20:3
All American, The 1932,O 22,18:4
I Am a Fugitive From a Chain Gang
1932,N 11,17:2
You Said a Mouthful 1932,N 18,23:2
Ladies They Talk About 1933,F 25,20:4
Elmer the Great 1933,My 26,24:2
Corruption 1933,Je 20,22:7
Man Who Dared, The 1933,S 9,9:3
Devil's Mate 1933,S 23,11:7
Hoopla 1933,D 1,23:3
Heat Lightning 1934,Mr 8,23:2
Wharf Angel 1934,Ap 21,12:1
Band Plays on, The 1934,D 22,21:2
People's Enemy, The 1935,Ap 30,13:7
Informer, The 1935,My 10,25:2
Arizonian, The 1935,Jl 27,16:2
Last Days of Pompeii, The 1935,O 17,29:2
Annie Oakley 1935,D 24,10:5
We're Only Human 1936,Ja 18,19:2
Muss 'Em Up 1936,F 3,21:2
Love Before Breakfast 1936,Mr 14,10:1
We Who Are About to Die 1937,Ja 2,15:1

Foster, Preston— Cont

Plough and the Stars, The 1937,Ja 29,15:1
Sea Devils 1937,Mr 16,26:4
Outcasts of Poker Flat, The 1937,Ap 27,18:3
You Can't Beat Love 1937,Je 25,25:3
Westland Case, The 1937,O 23,14:2
First Lady 1937,D 23,25:1
Double Danger 1938,F 10,17:5
Lady in the Morgue, The 1938,My 9,13:3
Army Girl 1938,Ag 12,11:1
Storm, The 1938,O 31,12:2
Submarine Patrol 1938,N 19,9:2
Up the River 1938,D 3,11:2
Last Warning, The 1938,D 8,34:4
News Is Made at Night 1939,Jl 13,17:2
20,000 Men a Year 1939,O 28,11:2
Missing Evidence 1939,N 17,17:3
Street of Missing Women 1940,Ja 8,11:2
Geronimo 1940,F 8,18:3
North West Mounted Police 1940,N 7,33:2
Moon Over Burma 1940,D 12,37:4
Roundup, The 1941,Mr 13,25:4
Unfinished Business 1941,S 2,20:2
Secret Agent of Japan 1942,Mr 23,19:3
Gentleman After Dark, A 1942,Ap 17,21:2
Night in New Orleans 1942,Jl 2,25:2
Little Tokyo, USA 1942,Ag 7,13:2
Thunder Birds 1942,O 29,19:2
American Empire 1943,Ja 14,25:4
My Friend Flicka 1943,My 27,21:4
Guadalcanal Diary 1943,N 18,29:1
Bermuda Mystery 1944,My 13,17:1
Roger Touhy, Gangster 1944,Je 5,14:7
Thunderhead 1945,Mr 16,21:2
Valley of Decision, The 1945,My 4,23:2
Twice Blessed 1945,Jl 7,7:5
Harvey Girls, The 1946,Ja 25,26:2
Tangier 1946,Je 7,II,16:4
Inside Job 1946,Je 15,24:3
Ramrod 1947,Je 30,25:6
I Shot Jesse James 1949,Ap 2,12:2
Big Cat, The 1949,Jl 29,12:2
Tomahawk 1951,F 19,19:2
Big Night, The 1952,Mr 20,37:5
Kansas City Confidential 1952,N 29,11:2
I, The Jury 1953,Ag 22,8:2
Man From Galveston, The 1964,Ja 23,26:3

Foster, Richard
River, The 1951,S 11,33:2

Foster, Ron
Operation Bottleneck 1961,S 7,40:2
Secret of Deep Harbor 1961,O 26,39:7

Foster, Roy (Miscellaneous)
Enchanted City, The 1922,F 6,9:1

Foster, Royal (Composer)
Bill and Coo 1948,Mr 29,17:4

Foster, Royal (Screenwriter)
Bill and Coo 1948,Mr 29,17:4

Foster, Stephen Collins (Miscellaneous)
Harmony Lane 1935,O 24,19:4

Foster, Susanna
Great Victor Herbert, The 1939,D 7,35:1
There's Magic in Music 1941,Je 5,27:2
Phantom of the Opera, The 1943,O 15,15:2
Top Man 1943,O 29,23:2
This is the Life 1944,Ap 28,23:3
Bowery to Broadway 1944,N 30,19:2
Climax, The 1944,D 14,28:5
Frisco Sal 1945,F 17,11:2
That Night With You 1945,N 9,16:2

Foster-Jones, Glenna
Joanna 1968,N 25,54:1

Fostini, Giovanni
Angela 1955,Je 4,9:2

Fostini, John
Burning Cross, The 1948,F 20,19:1
Three Steps North 1951,Je 29,14:2

Fotiou, Elli
Fear, The 1967,O 10,56:3

Fotopoulos, Mimis
Taxi Driver, The 1958,Mr 3,24:8
Golfo-Girl of the Mountains 1958,My 19,19:5
Hurdy Gurdy, The 1958,S 22,27:1
Counterfeit Coin 1960,My 16,39:1
Madame X 1960,O 3,34:5
Castle in Greece 1960,D 12,38:2
Grouch, The 1961,F 27,23:2
Fortune Teller, The 1961,My 22,37:5

Fotre, Vincent (Screenwriter)
Missle to the Moon 1958,N 17,37:2

Foucaud, Pierre (Screenwriter)
OSS 117-Mission for a Killer 1966,O 13,50:3

Fouche, Andre
Cesar 1948,O 28,36:2

Fouchet, Max-Pol (Narrator)
Masters of the Congo Jungle 1960,My 5,41:2

Fouille, Edwige
Crime Does Not Pay (The Mask); Mask, The
(Crime Does Not Pay) 1962,O 17,35:2

Fouleau, Raymond
Argent, L' 1968,S 23,42:5

Foulger, Byron
Prisoner of Zenda, The 1937,S 3,12:1
Tenth Avenue Kid 1938,S 2,21:3

Tarnished Angel 1938,N 15,27:2
Mutiny on the Blackhawk 1939,Ag 2,17:2
Exile Express 1939,Ag 16,21:3
Man With Nine Lives, The 1940,Ap 29,12:3
Edison the Man 1940,Je 7,27:2
Sky Murder 1940,N 14,28:3
Ellery Queen, Master Detective 1940,D 19,33:1
Arizona 1941,F 7,23:3
Man Made Monster 1941,Mr 19,25:4
Mystery Ship 1941,Ag 16,18:3
Sullivan's Travels 1942,Ja 29,25:2
Quiet Please, Murder 1942,D 22,31:1
Human Comedy, The 1943,Mr 3,19:2
Stand by for Action 1943,Mr 12,12:2
Hangmen Also Die 1943,Ap 16,24:2
Sweet Rosie O'Grady 1943,O 21,30:2
In old Oklahoma 1943,D 6,21:1
Whistler, The 1944,Ap 29,12:2
Enemy of Women 1944,S 12,23:6
Circumstantial Evidence 1945,Ap 21,18:3
Snafu 1945,D 26,15:2
Dick Tracy vs Cueball 1946,N 23,12:2
Till the Clouds Roll By 1946,D 6,27:4
Michigan Kid 1947,F 22,16:3
I Shot Jesse James 1949,Ap 2,12:2
Dancing in the Dark 1949,D 3,8:6
Inspector General, The 1949,D 31,9:2
Champagne for Caesar 1950,My 12,33:2
My Six Convicts 1952,Mr 28,27:3
Magnetic Monster, The 1953,My 14,32:5

Foulk, Robert
San Francisco Story, The 1952,My 10,16:4
Hot Blood 1956,Mr 24,14:2
Backlash 1956,Ap 21,11:2
Great Man, The 1957,Ja 2,28:2
Untamed Youth 1957,My 11,24:6
Hell's Five Hours 1957,Jl 24,18:1
Hell's Five Hours 1958,Jl 24,18:1
State Fair 1962,Ag 12,41:4
Tammy and the Doctor 1963,Je 27,23:2

Foundas, Georges
Stella 1957,Je 11,40:1
Girl in Black, A 1957,S 17,39:2
Wind of Hate; (O Anemos Tou Missous)
1958,N 17,37:2
Never on Sunday 1960,O 19,54:1
Take Me Away, My Love 1962,Jl 30,15:5
Zorba, The Greek 1964,D 18,25:1
Red Lanterns 1965,Ap 1,30:1

Fountaine, William
Hallelujah 1929,Ag 21,33:1

Four Freshmen Quartet
Rich, Young and Pretty 1951,Jl 26,17:3

Four Pennies, The
Go Go Mania 1965,My 20,52:4

Four Step Brothers
When Johnny Comes Marching Home
1943,Mr 5,20:4
Greenwich Village 1944,S 28,26:2
Here Come the Girls 1953,D 26,10:1

Fourcade, Christian
Little Boy Lost 1953,S 22,38:2
Little Boy Lost 1953,S 22,38:2
Paris Incident 1954,Ag 18,20:2
Companions of the Night 1954,N 25,44:2

Fourmost, The
Go Go Mania 1965,My 20,52:4

Fourneau, Jean-Claude
Trial of Joan of Arc, The 1965,F 12,19:1

Fournier, Camille
Mlle Desiree 1948,N 19,35:2

Fournier, Clairette
Generals Without Buttons 1938,Mr 8,23:2

Foursome and Wills, The
Go West, Young Lady 1941,N 24,11:6

Fourton, Reynaud (Original Author)
Symphony for a Massacre 1965,My 28,40:1

Fowldes, Derek
Hotel Paradiso 1966,O 15,34:2

Fowler, Almeda
Party Girl 1930,Ja 2,28:2
Carolina 1934,F 16,17:2
Damaged Lives 1937,Je 14,26:2

Fowler, Brenda
World Moves On, The 1934,Je 30,18:5
Judge Priest 1934,O 12,33:1
Ruggles of Red Gap 1935,Mr 7,26:1
Case Against Mrs Ames, The 1936,My 28,19:2
Second Wife 1936,Ag 29,16:3
Comin' Round the Mountain 1940,S 26,27:3

Fowler, Clement
Hamlet 1964,S 24,46:1

Fowler, Douglas
Miracle of the White Stallions 1963,My 23,31:2

Fowler, Gene (Original Author)
Union Depot 1932,Ja 15,24:4
Way to Love, The 1933,N 11,10:3
Shoot the Works 1934,Jl 7,16:5
Ali Baba Goes to Town 1937,O 23,14:1
Some Like It Hot 1939,My 25,31:2
Earl of Chicago, The 1940,Mr 14,29:3
Beau James 1957,Je 27,21:1

Fowler, Gene (Screenwriter)
Mighty Barnum, The 1934,D 24,17:1
Call of the Wild 1935,Ag 15,15:2
Professional Soldier 1936,Ja 30,14:2
Message to Garcia, A 1936,Ap 10,27:1
Half Angel 1936,My 30,7:3
White Fang 1936,Jl 18,18:2
Nancy Steele is Missing 1937,Mr 8,22:1
Love Under Fire 1937,Ag 28,8:2
Billy the Kid 1941,Je 20,28:2
Big Jack 1949,My 23,27:4

Fowler, Gene Jr (Director)
Oregon Trail, The 1959,D 10,51:6

Fowler, Gene Jr (Screenwriter)
My Outlaw Brother 1951,Ag 23,19:2
Oregon Trail, The 1959,D 10,51:6

Fowler, George (Producer)
Three on a Spree 1961,Ag 31,22:3

Fowler, H (Screenwriter)
Phantom Fiend 1935,Ap 22,14:2

Fowler, H Waller Jr
Panic in the Streets 1950,Ag 5,9:2

Fowler, Harry
48 Hours 1944,Je 26,21:2
Girl in the Canal, The 1947,O 9,32:3
Champagne Charlie 1948,Ag 7,8:2
Don't Take it to Heart 1948,D 25,10:3
Hue and Cry 1951,Ja 9,25:2
High Treason 1952,My 21,23:3
I Believe in You 1953,My 5,34:3
Pickwick Papers, The 1954,Ap 5,21:2
Fuss Over Feathers 1954,D 27,22:6

Fowler, J
Passionate Youth 1925,Je 30,14:3
Ranson's Folly 1926,My 31,10:2
Wolf's Clothing 1927,Mr 28,26:4
Are We Civilized? 1934,Je 14,28:5

Fowler, Jean
Under Western Stars 1938,Je 25,7:3

Fowler, L D Pvt Jr
Sands of Iwo Jima 1949,D 31,9:2

Fowler, Lawrence (Cinematographer)
Deliverance 1919,Ag 19,10:1

Fowler, Phyllis
Fort Ti 1953,My 30,7:1

Fowler, Will
This Man's Navy 1945,Ap 16,18:6

Fowles, John (Original Author)
Collector, The 1965,Je 18,28:1
Magus, The 1968,D 11,57:1

Fowles, John (Screenwriter)
Magus, The 1968,D 11,57:1

Fowley, Douglas
Let's Talk It Over 1934,Je 16,20:2
Student Tour 1934,O 31,17:3
Night Life of the Gods 1935,F 23,14:6
Transient Lady 1935,Mr 11,15:1
Two for Tonight 1935,Ag 31,16:2
Small Town Girl 1936,Ap 11,19:1
Big Brown Eyes 1936,My 2,11:1
Crash Donovan 1936,Ag 10,10:3
36 Hours to Live 1936,Ag 15,6:3
Sing, Baby, Sing 1936,S 12,20:1
Fifteen Maiden Lane 1936,O 17,21:3
Woman Wise 1937,Ja 23,13:1
On the Avenue 1937,F 5,17:3
Time Out for Romance 1937,Mr 13,23:2
Wake up and Live 1937,Ap 24,16:2
This Is my Affair 1937,My 28,17:1
Fifty Roads to Town 1937,Je 5,21:1
She Had to Eat 1937,Jl 24,12:1
One Mile From Heaven 1937,Ag 19,23:1
Wild and Woolly 1937,S 6,20:1
Charlie Chan on Broadway 1937,S 20,19:1
Love and Hisses 1938,Ja 1,11:1
City Girl 1938,F 4,17:3
Mr Moto's Gamble 1938,Ap 8,17:2
Passport Husband 1938,Ag 5,11:2
Alexander's Ragtime Band 1938,Ag 6,7:2
Keep Smiling 1938,Ag 10,15:2
Time Out for Murder 1938,O 7,21:2
Submarine Patrol 1938,N 19,9:2
Dodge City 1939,Ap 8,19:1
Lucky Night 1939,My 5,29:3
It Could Happen to You 1939,Je 9,26:3
Charlie Chan at Treasure Island 1939,S 1,15:5
Street of Missing Women 1940,Ja 8,11:2
Twenty-Mule Team 1940,My 10,26:6
Slightly Honorable 1940,My 17,23:4
Wagons Westward 1940,Jl 8,13:2
Pier 13 1940,Ag 9,19:3
East of the River 1940,O 28,21:2
Cherokee Strip 1940,N 4,23:2
Ellery Queen, Master Detective 1940,D 19,33:1
Great Swindle, The 1941,My 14,25:4
Parson of Panamint, The 1941,Jl 26,18:2
Tanks a Million 1941,O 9,27:2
Mr Wise Guy 1942,Mr 5,27:2
I Live on Danger 1942,Ag 22,16:2
Devil With Hitler, The 1942,O 19,15:2
Man in the Trunk, The 1942,O 23,25:1
Stand by for Action 1943,Mr 12,12:2 -
Jitterbugs 1943,Je 5,12:2

Fowley, Douglas— Cont

Gildersleeve's Bad Day 1943,Je 11,23:1
Kansan, The 1943,O 1,15:3
See Here Private Hargrove 1944,Mr 22,17:2
Rationing 1944,Ap 10,14:2
One Body too Many 1944,N 25,21:2
Backlash 1947,My 24,10:5
Hucksters, The 1947,Jl 18,21:2
Merton of the Movies 1947,N 7,20:3
Roses Are Red 1947,N 15,11:2
If You Knew Susie 1948,F 23,19:2
Mighty Joe Young 1949,Jl 28,19:3
Battleground 1949,N 12,8:4
Edge of Doom 1950,Ag 4,13:2
He's a Cockeyed Wonder 1950,O 20,32:4
Stage to Tucson 1951,My 5,14:2
Criminal Lawyer 1951,Ag 24,11:4
Across the Wide Missouri 1951,N 7,35:4
Just This Once 1952,Mr 18,22:3
Singin' in the Rain 1952,Mr 28,27:2
Cat-Women of the Moon 1954,Mr 20,10:7
Naked Jungle, The 1954,Ap 3,19:2
High and the Mighty, The 1954,Jl 1,21:2
Desire in the Dust 1960,O 12,47:2
Barabbas 1962,O 11,49:1

Fox, Allen
Street Scene 1931,Ag 27,22:5
Love Starved 1932,Ap 15,23:1
Forgotten Commandments 1932,Je 2,25:2
Dr Cyclops 1940,Ap 11,32:3

Fox, Bernard
Honeymoon Hotel 1964,Je 4,28:1

Fox, Edward
Jokers, The 1967,My 16,50:1

Fox, Elsie (Original Author)
Last Train from Madrid, The 1937,Je 19,20:2

Fox, Finis (Screenwriter)
Should a Woman Tell? 1920,Ja 5,15:1

Fox, Frank
Clouds Over Europe 1939,Je 16,27:2

Fox, Frederic Louis (Original Author)
Dakota Incident 1956,N 10,14:2

Fox, Gerald
Fame Is the Spur 1949,N 8,34:2
Hue and Cry 1951,Ja 9,25:2

Fox, James
Servant, The 1964,Mr 17,30:2
Those Magnificent Men in Their Flying Machines
  (Or How I Flew From London to Paris in 25
  Hours and 11 Minutes) 1965,Je 17,27:1
King Rat 1965,O 28,48:1
Chase, The 1966,F 19,24:1
Thoroughly Modern Millie 1967,Mr 23,25:1
Duffy 1968,S 17,50:3

Fox, Janet
They Knew What They Wanted 1940,O 11,25:2

Fox, Jimmie
Washington Story 1952,Jl 2,22:3

Fox, John Jr
One Glorious Day 1922,Ja 30,16:2
When a Man's a Man 1924,F 5,20:1
Lady, The 1925,Ja 27,11:2
Contraband 1925,Mr 24,20:6
Pony Express, The 1925,S 14,16:1

Fox, John Jr (Original Author)
Trail of the Lonesome Pine 1916,F 14,11:2
Heart o' the Hills 1919,D 1,9:3
Trail of the Lonesome Pine, The 1923,Mr 20,24:3
Hill Billy, The 1924,Mr 12,19:4
Trail of the Lonesome Pine, The 1936,F 20,23:5

Fox, Lucy
Lone Wolf, The 1924,My 7,19:4
Miami 1924,Je 3,22:2

Fox, Michael
Magnetic Monster, The 1953,My 14,32:5
Beast From 20,000 Fathoms, The 1953,Je 25,23:1
Gog 1954,Ag 14,8:2
Running Wild 1955,N 12,23:2
Top Secret Affair 1957,Ja 31,21:1
Girl in the Kremlin, The 1957,My 22,29:2
New Interns, The 1964,Ag 20,34:2

Fox, Norman (Original Author)
Rawhide Years, The 1956,Je 16,12:2
Night Passage 1957,Jl 25,28:1

Fox, Paul Hervey (Original Author)
Dangerously Yours 1933,F 23,20:3
Mandalay 1934,F 15,15:6
Last Train from Madrid, The 1937,Je 19,20:2
Safari 1940,Je 20,29:2
Gentleman at Heart, A 1942,F 23,25:2
Stars Are Singing, The 1953,Mr 12,24:2

Fox, Reginald
Livingstone in Africa 1929,Mr 25,32:2

Fox, Sidney
Bad Sister 1931,Mr 30,25:2
Six Cylinder Love 1931,My 16,31:3
Strictly Dishonorable 1931,N 11,27:1
Murders in the Rue Morgue 1932,F 11,16:1
Nice Women 1932,F 20,11:2
Mouthpiece, The 1932,Ap 21,25:2
Once in a Lifetime 1932,O 29,18:4
Afraid to Talk 1932,D 19,19:5
Midnight 1934,Mr 10,18:3
Down to Their Last Yacht 1934,S 24,14:1

Don Quixote 1934,D 24,17:1

Fox, Sidney (Producer)
Upturned Glass, The 1947,N 5,34:4

Fox, Sonny
Christmas That Almost Wasn't 1966,N 24,65:2

Fox, Stephen (Screenwriter)
Victory 1919,D 28,4:4
Treasure Island 1920,Ap 12,13:1

Fox, Wallace (Director)
Yellow Dust 1936,F 24,14:1
Powdersmoke Range 1936,Mr 9,20:2
Bowery Blitzkrieg 1941,O 1,24:5
Spooks Run Wild 1941,N 1,20:3
Pillow of Death 1946,Ja 26,19:3

Fox, William
Miniver Story, The 1950,O 27,24:2
Magnet, The 1951,F 27,22:6

Foxe, Earle
Black Panther's Cub, The 1921,My 30,12:5
Vanity Fair 1923,My 7,19:3
Fashion Row 1924,Ja 28,12:1
Last Man on Earth, The 1924,D 13,12:4
Slaves of Beauty 1927,Je 8,23:3
Ladies Must Dress 1927,D 31,31:1
Four Sons 1928,F 14,27:1
Sailors' Wives 1928,F 28,18:4
Hangman's House 1928,My 14,25:1
News Parade, The 1928,My 29,17:2
River Pirate, The 1928,S 17,27:1
Ghost Talks, The 1929,F 18,28:1
Thru Different Eyes 1929,Ap 15,22:6
Good Intentions 1930,Jl 26,16:4
Dance, Fools, Dance 1931,Mr 21,15:1
Transatlantic 1931,Jl 31,15:2
Spider, The 1931,S 5,7:4
Ladies of the Big House 1932,Ja 1,31:1
Union Depot 1932,Ja 15,24:4
Expert, The 1932,F 27,22:1
Strangers in Love 1932,Mr 5,11:2
So Big 1932,Ap 30,19:3
Midnight Patrol, The 1932,My 7,11:5
They Never Come Back 1932,Je 4,9:2
Passport to Hell, A 1932,Ag 27,13:4
Scarlet Dawn 1932,N 4,25:4
Blondie Johnson 1933,F 27,11:2
Mind Reader, The 1933,Ap 7,22:4
Bedtime Story, A 1933,Ap 20,20:3
Arizona to Broadway 1933,Jl 22,14:3
Little Man, What Now? 1934,Je 1,29:1
Golden Arrow, The 1936,My 4,16:1
Mary of Scotland 1936,Jl 31,22:2
Crack-Up 1937,Ja 4,20:4
We're on the Jury 1937,F 10,18:5
Dangerously Yours 1937,O 18,14:2
Military Academy 1940,Ag 5,10:4

Foxter, Helen
13 Washington Square 1928,Ja 30,18:1

Foxwell, Ivan (Miscellaneous)
Stowaway Girl 1957,N 6,43:3
Touch of Larceny, A 1960,Mr 17,28:1

Foxwell, Ivan (Producer)
No Room at the Inn 1949,D 26,33:4
Guilt is my Shadow 1954,Mr 25,36:4
Intruder, The 1955,Ja 26,22:1
Colditz Story, The 1957,O 25,23:2
Stowaway Girl 1957,N 6,43:3
Touch of Larceny, A 1960,Mr 17,28:1
Tiara Tahiti 1963,N 6,32:1
Quiller Memorandum, The 1966,D 16,59:1

Foxwell, Ivan (Screenwriter)
No Room at the Inn 1949,D 26,33:4
Guilt is my Shadow 1954,Mr 25,36:4
Colditz Story, The 1957,O 25,23:2
Tiara Tahiti 1963,N 6,32:1

Foxx, Jimmy
Untitled-Baseball Technique 1941,Ja 17,11:3

Foy, Bryan (Director)
Home Towners, The 1928,O 24,26:4
Queen of the Night Clubs 1929,Mr 18,30:6
Gorilla, The 1931,F 23,20:3

Foy, Bryan (Original Author)
College 1927,S 12,29:1

Foy, Bryan (Producer)
Little Tokyo, USA 1942,Ag 7,13:2
Berlin Correspondent 1942,S 4,19:2
Loves of Edgar Allan Poe, The 1942,S 21,19:2
Guadalcanal Diary 1943,N 18,29:1
Take It or Leave It 1944,Jl 13,14:2
Doll Face 1946,Mr 28,35:3
If I'm Lucky 1946,S 20,41:3
Trapped 1949,N 26,10:6
Great Jewel Robber, The 1950,Ag 4,13:2
Breakthrough 1950,N 18,10:2
Highway 301 1950,D 9,13:2
I Was a Communist for the F B I 1951,My 3,34:4
Inside the Walls of Folsom Prison
  1951,My 28,17:4
Tanks are Coming, The 1951,D 6,42:4
Lion and the Horse, The 1952,My 19,12:2
Winning Team, The 1952,Je 21,12:2
Miracle of Our Lady Fatima, The
  1952,Ag 21,16:2
House of Wax 1953,Ap 11,15:2

Foy, Bryan (Producer)— Cont
Crime Wave 1954,Ja 13,26:2
Mad Magician, The 1954,My 20,38:2
Women's Prison 1955,F 3,18:5
Blueprint for Robbery 1961,F 2,24:3
House of Women 1962,Ap 12,41:6
PT 109 1963,Je 27,23:1

Foy, Charles
Hot Money 1936,Jl 25,16:2
Polo Joe 1936,N 5,35:1
Fugitive in the Sky 1937,Ja 16,21:1
Midnight Court 1937,Mr 4,27:3
Melody for Two 1937,My 21,19:5
Dance Charlie Dance 1937,Ag 26,25:2
Torchy Blane, The Adventurous Blonde
  1937,D 18,18:1
Daredevil Drivers, The 1938,F 23,27:2
Penrod and his Twin Brother 1938,Ap 18,11:1
King of the Underworld 1939,Ja 7,6:2
Blackwell's Island 1939,Mr 2,19:1
Conspiracy 1939,Ag 23,19:2
Mutiny in the Big House 1939,D 11,26:2
East of the River 1940,O 28,21:2
Wagons Roll at Night, The 1941,My 10,20:4
Woman of the Town, The 1944,Mr 6,17:2

Foy, Eddie Jr
Queen of the Night Clubs 1929,Mr 18,30:6
Leathernecking 1930,S 13,9:3
Myrt and Marge 1934,Ja 17,23:2
Secret Service of the Air 1939,Mr 2,19:2
Women in the Wind 1939,Ap 13,27:2
Frontier Marshal 1939,Jl 29,18:2
Smashing the Money Ring 1939,N 17,17:2
Lillian Russell 1940,My 18,11:2
Murder in the Air 1940,Jl 4,12:2
Fugitive From Justice, A 1940,Jl 8,13:3
Case of the Black Parrot, The 1941,Ja 10,23:3
Rookies on Parade 1941,My 22,25:2
Yankee Doodle Dandy 1942,My 30,9:1
Powder Town 1942,Je 8,11:2
Dixie Dugan 1943,Ap 9,25:5
Dixie 1943,Je 24,26:2
And the Angels Sing 1944,Jl 13,14:2
Wilson 1944,Ag 2,18:1
Farmer Takes a Wife, The 1953,Je 13,11:2
Lucky Me 1954,Ap 10,11:2
Pajama Game, The 1957,Ag 30,12:2
Bells Are Ringing 1960,Je 24,31:2
Gidget Goes Hawaiian 1961,Ag 10,17:4
30 Is a Dangerous Age, Cynthia 1968,Mr 5,34:1

Foy, Eddie 3d
Run Silent, Run Deep 1958,Mr 28,29:1

Foy, Gloria
Dancing Lady 1933,D 1,23:2

Foy, Mary
Icebound 1924,Mr 3,22:3 (In Addenda)
Hoosier Schoolmaster, The 1924,Mr 18,25:2
Dangerous Money 1924,O 14,21:5
Manicure Girl, The 1925,Je 15,10:1
Irish Luck 1925,N 24,28:4
It's the old Army Game 1926,Jl 5,6:4
Ankles Preferred 1927,Ap 18,21:2
Slaves of Beauty 1927,Je 8,23:3
Mad Hour, The 1928,Ap 16,20:5
Man From Wyoming, A 1930,Jl 12,16:4
Dumbbells in Ermine 1930,Jl 28,22:1
Ladies of the Big House 1932,Ja 1,31:1
Strange People 1933,Je 17,16:5
Once to Every Woman 1934,Mr 26,22:3
Love in Bloom 1935,Ap 20,16:2
Little Big Shot 1935,O 7,11:2

Foy Willing and orchestra
Texas Carnival 1951,O 13,9:1

Foyer, Eddie
Big House, The 1930,Je 25,31:2

Fracassi, Clemente (Director)
Sensualita 1954,Ap 29,40:2
Aida 1954,N 12,17:1

Fraction, Edward
Betrayal, The 1948,Je 26,10:5

Fraenkel, Helene (Miscellaneous)
It Happened Tomorrow 1944,My 29,18:2

Fraenkel, Yael
Dream no More 1950,Ja 6,25:2

Fraganza, Trixie
Charmer, The 1925,Ap 6,17:3

Fragrance, Lotus
Revenge of General Ling, The 1938,F 21,15:1

Fraju, Georges (Director)
Thomas the Imposter 1965,S 13,42:1

Frambes, William
Janie 1944,Ag 5,16:2
Circumstantial Evidence 1945,Ap 21,18:3
Junior Miss 1945,Je 18,15:4
Janie Gets Married 1946,Je 15,24:2
Bringing Up Father 1946,N 22,27:3
Shocking Miss Pilgrim, The 1947,F 12,34:2

Frame, Grazina
Alphabet Murders, The 1966,Jl 12,36:2

Franc, Frederic M (Screenwriter)
Samson and Delilah 1949,D 22,29:2

Franca, Herminia
Dark River 1956,F 27,19:4

Francan, Victor
   Madame Curie 1943,D 17,23:1
FRANCE
   See Also FRANTZ, FRANZ
France, Anatole (Original Author)
   Bill or Crainquebille 1923,S 3,9:3
   Red Lily, The 1924,S 29,10:1
   Twilight 1949,D 30,13:2
France, Annie
   Moulin Rouge 1944,N 23,38:2
France, C V
   Skin Game, The 1931,Je 20,20:4
   Scrooge 1935,D 14,11:1
   Broken Blossoms 1937,Ja 14,16:3
   Victoria the Great 1937,O 29,19:1
   Yank at Oxford, A 1938,F 25,15:1
   If I Were King 1938,S 29,31:1
   Ware Case, The 1939,Jl 22,12:2
   Night Train 1940,D 30,21:1
   Missing Ten Days 1941,Ap 21,15:5 (In Addenda)
   48 Hours 1944,Je 26,21:2
France, Claude Mlle
   Madonna of the Sleeping Cars, The
      1929,O 14,20:2
France, Dawson
   It's Great to be Young 1957,D 26,23:3
France, Marie
   Golden Mask, The 1954,Mr 20,10:5
France, Rolla
   A Nous la Liberte 1932,Ja 10,VIII,5:1
   Nous, La Liberte, A 1932,My 18,25:2
Francell, Fernand
   Trois Mousquetaires, Les 1933,My 1,10:2
   Call, The 1938,Mr 29,18:3
Francell, Jacqueline
   Mirages De Paris 1933,D 25,28:3
   Call, The 1938,Mr 29,18:3
   Glory of Faith, The 1938,N 24,37:2
   Symphonie d'Amour 1946,Mr 11,19:2
Francen, Victor
   End of the World, The 1934,Ap 18,23:3
   Sacrifice d'Honneur 1938,D 2,27:2
   Vierge Folle, La 1938,D 30,11:3
   Crime in the Maginot Line 1939,My 8,21:2
   End of a Day, The 1939,S 12,28:4
   That They May Live 1939,N 7,31:2
   Entente Cordiale 1939,D 26,23:2
   Living Corpse, The 1940,S 23,21:4
   Open Road, The 1940,O 5,20:2
   Hold Back the Dawn 1941,O 2,29:1
   King, The 1941,O 23,29:3
   Tuttles of Tahiti, The 1942,Ap 30,14:1
   Ten Gentlemen From West Point 1942,Je 5,23:3
   Great Temptation, The 1942,Jl 10,13:3
   Tales of Manhattan 1942,S 25,25:1
   Mission to Moscow 1943,Ap 30,25:2
   In our Time 1944,F 12,11:2
   Passage to Marseille 1944,F 17,12:5
   Mask of Dimitrios, The 1944,Je 24,16:2
   Conspirators, The 1944,O 21,15:2
   Hollywood Canteen 1944,D 16,19:2
   Confidential Agent 1945,N 3,11:2
   San Antonio 1945,D 29,19:5
   Devotion 1946,Ap 6,10:5
   Night and Day 1946,Jl 26,16:2
   Beast With Five Fingers, The 1946,D 26,28:3
   Beginning or the End, The 1947,F 21,15:1
   To the Victor 1948,Ap 17,11:2
   Forbidden Love 1948,Ag 26,16:4
   Stolen Affections 1951,Mr 12,20:2
   Adventures of Captain Fabian 1951,D 14,36:2
   Hell and High Water 1954,F 2,20:6
   Bedevilled 1955,Ap 23,23:1
   Farewell to Arms, A 1958,Ja 25,14:1
   Fanny 1961,Jl 7,16:1
FRANCES
   See Also FRANCIS
Frances, Noel
   Good Dame 1934,Mr 17,11:4
Frances, Vera
   Waterloo Road 1948,D 25,10:3
Frances, Victor
   Desert Song, The 1943,D 18,10:6
Francesci, Paul
   Arab, The 1924,Jl 14,11:5
Francey, Bill
   Out all Night 1927,S 27,31:1
Francey, Jean
   Frochard et les Deux Orphelines, La
      1934,F 7,16:2
Francey, Micheline
   Devil Is an Empress, The 1939,D 4,18:4
   Charrette Fantome, La 1940,My 28,29:2
   Cage aux Rossignols, La; (Cage of Nightingales,
      A) 1947,Ap 3,31:2
   Midnight in Paris 1947,O 9,32:3
   Corbeau, Le; Raven, The 1948,F 24,21:1
   Francois Villon 1950,Jl 3,9:2
   Strollers, The 1952,Jl 22,22:7
   Holiday for Henrietta 1955,Ja 25,21:1
Franch, Harold (Screenwriter)
   Paris Express, The 1953,Je 6,8:6

Franchetti, Rina
   Passa L'Amore 1933,N 25,10:3
   Eye of the Needle, The 1965,Je 22,25:2
Franchi, Alfredo
   Condemned of Altona, The 1963,O 31,26:1
Franchina, B (Screenwriter)
   Rome, 11 O'Clock 1953,Ap 30,39:2
   Fall of the Roman Empire, The 1964,Mr 27,14:2
Franchina, Sandro
   Greatest Love, The 1954,Ja 12,19:2
Franci, Adolfo (Screenwriter)
   Shoe-Shine 1947,Ag 27,19:2
Franci, Diana
   Schoolgirl Diary 1947,O 18,9:2
Franci, Pier Giuseppi (Screenwriter)
   Lucia di Lammermoor 1947,N 1,11:3
Francia, Maria Grazia
   Angelina 1948,Ap 6,27:2
   Bitter Rice 1950,S 19,39:2
   Under the Olive Tree 1951,O 5,24:4
   Rome, 11 O'Clock 1953,Ap 30,39:2
Francinci, Pietro (Director)
   Hercules Unchained 1960,Jl 14,23:1
Francinci, Pietro (Screenwriter)
   Hercules Unchained 1960,Jl 14,23:1
Francine, Anne
   Juliet of the Spirits 1965,N 4,57:1
Francioli, Armando
   Paolo and Francesca 1953,F 14,8:3
   Rome, 11 O'Clock 1953,Ap 30,39:2
   Wife for a Night 1958,Je 12,35:2
Franciolini, Gianni (Director)
   Hello Elephant 1954,S 10,18:5
   Bed, The (The Divorce); Divorce, The (The Bed)
      1955,Je 8,26:4
   It Happened in the Park 1957,Ag 13,23:2
Franciosa, Campanile (Screenwriter)
   Holiday Island; (Vacanzie a Izchia)
      1959,S 22,46:1
Franciosa, Massimo (Director)
   White Voices; Voci Blanche 1965,Ap 13,32:2
Franciosa, Massimo (Original Author)
   Girl and the General, The 1967,D 7,60:1
Franciosa, Massimo (Screenwriter)
   Poor but Beautiful 1958,Je 11,39:4
   Holiday Island; (Vacanzie a Izchia)
      1959,S 22,46:1
   Rocco and his Brothers 1961,Je 28,40:2
   Viaccia, La 1962,S 21,35:1
   Four Days of Naples, The 1963,Mr 20,5:1
   Leopard, The 1963,Ag 13,25:1
   White Voices; Voci Blanche 1965,Ap 13,32:2
Franciosa, Tony
   This Could Be the Night 1957,My 15,39:1
   Face in the Crowd, A 1957,My 29,33:1
   Hatful of Rain, A 1957,Jl 18,19:2
   Wild Is the Wind 1957,D 12,35:1
   Long, Hot Summer, The 1958,Ap 4,16:1
   Naked Maja, The 1959,Je 11,36:2
   Career 1959,O 9,24:1
   Story of Page One, The 1960,Ja 14,28:1
   Go Naked in the World 1961,Mr 11,15:1
   Period of Adjustment 1962,N 1,34:1
   Rio Conchos 1964,O 29,38:1
   Pleasure Seekers, The 1964,D 26,9:1
   Man Could Get Killed, A 1966,My 12,54:2
   Assault on a Queen 1966,Jl 28,23:3
   Swinger, The 1966,D 15,60:1
   Fathom 1967,D 14,62:1
   Sweet Ride, The 1968,Je 13,57:2
FRANCIS
   See Also FRANCES
Francis, Alec B
   Heartsease 1919,Ag 25,8:5
   Lord and Lady Algy 1919,S 29,16:1
   Flame of the Desert 1919,O 27,9:3
   Paliser Case, The 1920,F 16,8:1
   Godless Men 1921,Ja 31,11:1
   Voice in the Dark, A 1921,Je 6,16:4
   Great Moment, The 1921,Jl 25,8:3
   Children of Jazz 1923,Jl 9,8:4
   Gentleman of Leisure, A 1923,Jl 16,14:2
   Three Wise Fools 1923,Jl 23,13:4
   Eternal Three, The 1923,O 12,7:2 (Incorrect in
      this edition; use 1927,O 1,7:2 elsewhere)
   Drivin' Fool, The 1923,O 29,18:1
   Lucretia Lombard 1923,D 17,23:1
   Beau Brummell 1924,Mr 31,20:1
   Thief in Paradise, A 1925,Ja 26,14:1
   Capital Punishment 1925,F 5,23:3
   Charley's Aunt 1925,F 9,15:3
   Bridge of Sighs, The 1925,Mr 23,14:2
   Waking up the Town 1925,Mr 31,17:4
   Man and Maid 1925,Ap 7,17:3
   Mad Whirl, The 1925,Jl 1,16:1
   Coast of Folly, The 1925,Ag 31,19:3
   Circle, The 1925,S 22,22:3
   Thank You 1925,O 6,30:1
   Rose of the World 1925,N 10,25:3
   Yankee Senor, The 1926,Ja 28,14:4
   Tramp, Tramp, Tramp 1926,My 24,24:3
   Forever After 1926,N 9,31:1
   Music Master, The 1927,Ja 17,12:4 (In Addenda)

   Camille 1927,Ap 22,19:1
   Tender Hour, The 1927,Je 7,27:4
   Shepherd of the Hills, The 1928,F 20,14:1
   Lion and the Mouse, The 1928,Je 16,11:4
   Terror, The 1928,Ag 16,25:3
   Evangeline 1929,Jl 29,23:3
   Evidence 1929,O 5,22:5
   Mississippi Gambler, The 1929,O 28,20:1
   Sacred Flame, The 1929,N 23,18:5
   Bishop Murder Case, The 1930,F 1,15:1
   Case of Sergeant Grischa, The 1930,Mr 8,21:1
   Murder Will Out 1930,Ap 14,24:2
   Outward Bound 1930,S 18,28:3
   Feet First 1930,O 31,20:1
   Arrowsmith 1931,D 8,36:4
   Mata Hari 1932,Ja 1,31:1
   No Greater Love 1932,My 14,11:5
   Last Mile, The 1932,Ag 26,20:3
   Last Man, The 1932,S 17,18:4
   Oliver Twist 1933,Ap 13,15:3
   Looking Forward 1933,My 1,10:2
   Alice in Wonderland 1933,D 23,19:1
   Mystery of Mr X, The 1934,F 26,21:3
   I'll Tell the World 1934,Ap 21,12:2
   Outcast Lady 1934,N 3,20:3
Francis, Anne
   Summer Holiday 1948,Je 12,8:5
   So Young, So Bad 1950,Jl 24,15:2
   Whistle at Eaton Falls, The 1951,O 11,49:2
   Elopement 1951,D 21,21:3
   Lydia Bailey 1952,My 31,12:5
   Dreamboat 1952,Jl 26,9:2
   Lion Is in the Streets, A 1953,S 24,39:2
   Susan Slept Here 1954,Jl 30,9:1
   Rogue Cop 1954,S 18,12:2
   Bad Day at Black Rock 1955,F 2,22:2
   Battle Cry 1955,F 3,18:1
   Blackboard Jungle 1955,Mr 21,21:5
   Scarlet Coat, The 1955,Jl 30,14:2
   Forbidden Planet 1956,My 4,21:2
   Rack, The 1956,N 6,30:1
   Don't Go Near the Water 1957,N 15,37:1
   Girl of the Night 1960,N 12,15:1
   Crowded Sky, The 1961,F 11,27:2
   Satan Bug, The 1965,Ap 15,38:1
   Brainstorm 1965,Je 10,38:1
   Funny Girl 1968,S 20,42:1
Francis, Arlene
   Stage Door Canteen 1943,Je 25,13:2
   All my Sons 1948,Mr 29,17:3
   With These Hands 1950,Je 16,28:4
   One, Two, Three 1961,D 22,17:1
   Thrill of it All, The 1963,Ag 2,15:3
Francis, C
   Uncivilized 1937,N 17,27:4
   Howards of Virginia, The 1940,S 27,27:1
   Black Swan, The 1942,D 24,18:3
Francis, Cedric (Producer)
   Amazon Trader, The 1956,N 17,17:6
   Manhunt in the Jungle 1958,Ap 12,13:1
Francis, Clive
   Inspector Clouseau 1968,Jl 25,26:1
Francis, Connie
   Where the Boys Are 1961,Ja 20,22:1
   Follow the Boys 1963,F 28,8:2
   When the Boys Meet the Girls 1966,Ja 20,29:1
Francis, Derek
   Tomb of Ligeia 1965,My 6,44:1
   Little Ones, The 1965,S 16,55:2
Francis, Eugene
   Pride of the Bowery 1941,Ja 24,15:2
   Flying Wild 1941,Ap 12,19:3
Francis, Eve
   Club De Femmes 1937,O 20,27:2
Francis, Freddie (Director)
   Paranoiac 1963,My 23,31:2
   Evil of Frankenstein, The 1964,Je 18,29:2
   Nightmare 1964,Je 18,29:2
   Hysteria 1965,S 9,36:3
   Psycopath, The 1966,S 29,60:1
   Deadly Bees, The 1967,My 20,39:2
   Torture Garden 1968,Jl 20,18:2
Francis, Kay
   Gentlemen of the Press 1929,My 13,27:2
   Cocoanuts, The 1929,My 25,17:3
   Dangerous Curves 1929,Jl 15,25:1
   Illusion 1929,S 28,17:3
   Marriage Playground, The 1929,D 14,22:4
   Behind the Makeup 1930,Ja 18,21:1
   Street of Chance 1930,F 3,17:1
   Notorious Affair, A 1930,Ap 26,11:1
   For the Defense 1930,Jl 19,7:5
   Raffles 1930,Jl 25,20:4
   Let's Go Native 1930,Ag 30,7:4
   Virtuous Sin 1930,N 2,VIII,5:2 (In Addenda)
   Passion Flower 1930,D 22,16:2
   Scandal Sheet 1931,F 9,25:3
   Ladies' Man 1931,My 1,30:3
   Vice Squad, The 1931,Je 6,15:5
   Transgression 1931,Je 15,23:3
   Guilty Hands 1931,Ag 29,16:3
   Twenty-Four Hours 1931,O 3,20:2
   Girls About Town 1931,N 2,27:1

Francis, Kay — Cont

Strangers in Love 1932,Mr 5,11:2
Man Wanted 1932,Ap 16,11:2
Street of Women 1932,My 30,16:5
Jewel Robbery 1932,Jl 23,6:6
One Way Passage 1932,O 14,23:2
Trouble in Paradise 1932,N 9,28:5
Cynara 1932,D 26,26:2
Keyhold, The 1933,Mr 31,23:3
Storm at Daybreak 1933,Jl 22,14:4
Mary Stevens, M D 1933,Ag 5,9:6
I Loved a Woman 1933,S 22,14:2
House on 56th Street, The 1933,D 2,9:3
Mandalay 1934,F 15,15:6
Wonder Bar 1934,Mr 1,23:2
Dr Monica 1934,Je 21,28:2
British Agent 1934,S 20,20:1
Living on Velvet 1935,Mr 8,25:4
Stranded 1935,Je 20,16:2
Goose and the Gander, The 1935,S 12,29:2
I Found Stella Parish 1935,N 4,24:4
White Angel, The 1936,Je 25,24:1
Give Me your Heart 1936,S 17,18:2
Stolen Holiday 1937,F 1,15:3
Another Dawn 1937,Je 18,25:3
Confession 1937,Ag 19,23:1
First Lady 1937,D 23,25:1
Women Are Like That 1938,Ap 11,12:2
My Bill 1938,Jl 7,22:4
Secrets of an Actress 1938,O 8,10:2
Comet over Broadway 1938,D 16,33:3
King of the Underworld 1939,Ja 7,6:2
Women in the Wind 1939,Ap 13,27:2
In Name Only 1939,Ag 4,11:3
It's a Date 1940,Mr 23,16:2
When the Daltons Rode 1940,Ag 23,13:3
Little Men 1940,D 9,23:2
Play Girl 1941,Ja 30,19:3
Charley's Aunt 1941,Ag 2,18:2
Feminine Touch, The 1941,D 12,35:3
Always in my Heart 1942,Mr 14,19:2
Between Us Girls 1942,S 25,25:3
Four Jills in a Jeep 1944,Ap 6,27:2
Allotment Wives 1945,N 22,39:3
Francis, Kay (Miscellaneous)
Four Jills in a Jeep 1944,Ap 6,27:2
Francis, Kay (Producer)
Allotment Wives 1945,N 22,39:3
Francis, Melvin
Story of Dr Wassell, The 1944,Je 7,13:2
Francis, Noel
Rough Romance 1930,Je 16,25:3
New Movietone Follies of 1930, The
1930,Je 21,20:5
Up the River 1930,O 11,21:3
Bachelor Apartment 1931,My 16,13:3
Smart Money 1931,Je 19,21:1
Smart Woman 1931,O 12,28:2
Blonde Crazy 1931,D 4,28:2
Ladies of the Big House 1932,Ja 1,31:1
Expert, The 1932,F 27,22:1
Mouthpiece, The 1932,Ap 21,25:2
Night Court 1932,My 27,27:5
Man About Town 1932,My 28,18:2
Guilty as Hell 1932,Ag 6,14:5
My Pal the King 1932,O 4,26:4
I Am a Fugitive From a Chain Gang
1932,N 11,17:2
Under-Cover Man 1932,D 5,21:2
Frisco Jenny 1933,Ja 7,11:2
Hold Me Tight 1933,My 22,18:6
Bureau of Missing Persons 1933,S 9,9:2
Only Yesterday 1933,N 10,25:1
Francis, Olin
Kid Brother, The 1927,Ja 24,14:1
Win That Girl 1928,O 1,23:1
Hard Rock Harrigan 1935,Jl 30,16:2
O'Malley of the Mounted 1936,Ap 6,18:1
Francis, Owen (Original Author)
No Other Woman 1933,Ja 30,9:4 (In Addenda)
Magnificent Brute, The 1936,O 24,23:1
Francis, Owen (Screenwriter)
Magnificent Brute, The 1936,O 24,23:1
Criminals of the Air 1937,O 28,29:2
Pack up Your Troubles 1939,O 27,27:2
20,000 Men a Year 1939,O 28,11:2
Shooting High 1940,Ap 12,19:2
Francis, Raymond
Court Martial 1955,Ag 2,17:1
Storm over the Nile 1956,Je 9,14:2
Francis, Robert
Caine Mutiny, The 1954,Je 25,17:1
Long Gray Line, The 1955,F 11,19:2
Francis, Tom
Traveling Husbands 1931,Ag 8,16:3
Ladies of the Jury 1932,Ap 2,13:2
Francis, Wilma
Sudden Death, And 1936,Jl 18,18:2
Lady, Be Careful 1936,O 10,21:1
Hideaway Girl 1937,Ja 13,20:4
Trade Winds 1939,Ja 13,17:2
Guest Wife 1945,O 18,21:2

Francisci, Mario (Producer)
Queen of Sheba, The 1953,N 4,29:3
Francisci, Pietro (Director)
Escape into Dreams 1950,Ap 13,34:5
Anthony of Padua 1952,Mr 29,19:2
Queen of Sheba, The 1953,N 4,29:3
Attila 1958,My 19,19:4
Hercules 1959,Jl 23,32:2
Warrior Empress, The 1961,Ag 10,17:4
Siege of Syracuse, The 1962,Ag 9,17:8
Hercules, Samson and Ulysses 1965,N 4,57:2
Francisci, Pietro (Screenwriter)
Escape into Dreams 1950,Ap 13,34:5
Anthony of Padua 1952,Mr 29,19:2
Queen of Sheba, The 1953,N 4,29:3
Hercules 1959,Jl 23,32:2
Warrior Empress, The 1961,Ag 10,17:4
Siege of Syracuse, The 1962,Ag 9,17:8
Hercules, Samson and Ulysses 1965,N 4,57:2
Francisco, Betty
Poor Men's Wives 1923,Ja 29,11:1
Ashes of Vengeance 1923,Ag 7,20:2
Flaming Youth 1923,N 26,15:6
Darling of New York, The 1924,Ja 18,20:1
Maytime 1924,Je 2,14:3
Fifth Avenue Models 1925,My 4,16:2
Private Affairs 1925,Jl 15,22:3
Seven Keys to Baldpate 1925,N 3,25:4
Man Bait 1927,Ja 19,21:1
Gingham Girl, The 1927,Jl 19,27:2
Gay Retreat, The 1927,O 10,24:1
Broadway 1929,My 28,36:2
Smiling Irish Eyes 1929,Jl 24,23:2
Street of Chance 1930,F 3,17:1
Widow From Chicago, The 1930,D 20,20:6
Charlie Chan Carries On 1931,Mr 21,15:1
Good Sport 1931,D 12,23:3
Mystery Ranch 1932,Je 30,26:2
Franciscus, James
Mugger, The 1959,Je 25,20:7
I Passed for White 1960,Ag 18,19:3
Outsider, The 1962,F 8,25:1
Miracle of the White Stallions 1963,My 23,31:2
Youngblood Hawke 1964,N 6,30:1
FRANCK
See Also FRANK, FRANKE
Franck, Walter
Herr Der Welt, Der 1935,D 16,23:3
For Her Country's Sake 1937,N 27,21:3
Gouverneur, Der 1939,S 11,15:2
Francke, Caroline (Original Author)
Bombshell 1933,O 21,11:2
Francks, Don
Circle, The 1967,Ag 16,36:1
Finian's Rainbow 1968,O 10,59:5
Franco, Dominick (Producer)
Heaven on Earth 1960,O 11,55:3
Franco, Fulvia
Of Wayward Love (The Soldier); Soldier, The (Of
Wayward Love) 1964,Mr 24,29:1
High Infidelity (The Scandal); Scandal, The (High
Infidelity) 1965,Jl 2,17:1
Franco, Herminia
Nobleza Gaucha; Gaucho Chivalry
1938,Ap 2,18:2
Franco, Jess (Director)
Awful Dr Orlof, The 1964,D 3,58:3
Francoeur, Richard
Devil in the Flesh 1949,My 10,29:2
Francois, Jacques
Barkleys of Broadway, The 1949,My 5,34:2
Just a big Simple Girl; Une Grande Fille Toute
Simple 1949,O 28,29:2
Encore (Winter Cruise); Winter Cruise (Encore)
1952,Ap 3,45:1
Edward and Caroline 1952,Ap 30,33:3
Skipper Next to God 1953,Ja 13,24:2
Golden Mask, The 1954,Mr 20,10:5
To Paris With Love 1955,Mr 29,33:4
Grand Maneuver, The 1956,O 2,39:1
Francois, Michel
Extenuating Circumstances; Circostanze
Attenuantes 1946,S 24,41:3
Francoise, Jacqueline
Affaire, L' 1950,N 13,23:2
Francy, Neddy
Palermo 1938,O 22,14:2
Termina Siempre Asi; It Always Ends That Way
1940,S 3,21:3
Franden, David (Screenwriter)
Ferry Cross the Mersey 1965,F 20,16:2
Frandon, David
State Fair 1962,Ap 12,41:4
Frandsen, Andreas John
Young Have no Time, The 1959,N 23,41:2
Frandsen, Robert
Great Moment, The 1944,N 13,15:2
Franey, William
Senor Daredevil 1926,Ag 17,15:3
She's a Shiek 1927,N 21,20:1
No More Women 1934,Mr 15,27:4

Frangadakis, Vassilos
Barefoot Battalion 1954,My 29,13:4
Franju, Georges (Director)
Therese 1963,N 13,35:2
Judex 1966,Ap 26,55:1
Franju, Georges (Screenwriter)
Therese 1963,N 13,35:2
FRANK
See Also FRANCK, FRANKE
Frank, Amy
Broken Journey 1949,My 26,34:3
While the Sun Shines 1950,Jl 1,9:2
Frank, Bruno (Miscellaneous)
Royal Scandal, A 1945,Ap 12,19:2
Frank, Bruno (Original Author)
Sutter's Gold 1936,Mr 27,25:2
Storm in a Teacup 1938,Mr 22,18:4
Frank, Bruno (Screenwriter)
Heart's Desire 1937,Jl 12,20:4
Hunchback of Notre Dame, The 1940,Ja 1,29:2
Frank, Carl
Lady From Shanghai, The 1948,Je 10,28:2
Frank, Charles (Director)
Inheritance, The 1951,F 12,19:2
Intimate Relations 1954,F 22,15:4
Frank, Charles (Screenwriter)
Obsessed 1952,F 6,24:2
Intimate Relations 1954,F 22,15:4
Frank, Christian
Ragged Edge, The 1923,Je 5,24:5
Black Cyclone 1925,My 19,24:2
Ancient Highway, The 1925,N 11,27:3
Chicago After Midnight 1928,Mr 6,20:3
Easy Come, Easy Go 1928,My 8,25:3
Cavalier, The 1928,O 31,28:4
My Pal the King 1932,O 4,26:4
Frank, Consuelo
Tierra, Amor y Dolor 1935,Ag 10,16:5
Clemencia 1935,Ag 20,25:4
Rosa de Francia 1935,O 28,16:3
Sueno de Amor 1936,Ja 11,9:3
Familia Dressel, La 1936,My 4,16:2
Calvario de una Esposa, El 1936,S 26,11:2
Nostradamus 1937,S 6,20:1
Ora, Ponciano; Come on, Ponciano
1937,D 18,18:2
Tierra del Mariachi, La; Country of the Mariachi,
The 1938,D 3,11:2
Indio, El 1939,My 13,11:5
Viejo Amor, Un; Old Love, An 1940,Ja 29,11:6
Caballo a Caballo; Horse for Horse
1940,F 10,19:2
Herencia Macabra; Macabre Legacy, A
1940,My 4,13:2
El Conde de Monte Cristo 1943,N 9,26:2
Frank, Ernst L (Director)
Nagana 1933,F 16,23:2
Frank, Fredric (Original Author)
Submarine Zone; (Escape To Glory)
1941,Ap 7,13:2
Harmon of Michigan 1941,O 2,29:2
Greatest Show on Earth, The 1952,Ja 11,17:2
Frank, Fredric (Screenwriter)
Unconquered 1947,O 11,11:2
Greatest Show on Earth, The 1952,Ja 11,17:2
Ten Commandments, The 1956,N 9,35:2
Cid, El 1961,D 15,49:1
Frank, Gerold (Original Author)
I'll Cry Tomorrow 1956,Ja 13,18:1
Too Much, Too Soon 1958,My 10,19:2
Beloved Infidel 1959,N 18,46:1
Boston Strangler, The 1968,O 17,52:1
Frank, Harriet Jr (Original Author)
Run for Cover 1955,Ap 30,10:6
Frank, Harriet Jr (Screenwriter)
Silver River 1948,My 22,8:3
Whiplash 1948,D 27,16:3
Long, Hot Summer, The 1958,Ap 4,16:1
Sound and the Fury, The 1959,Mr 28,11:1
Home from the Hill 1960,Mr 4,19:1
Hud 1963,My 29,36:1
Hombre 1967,Mr 22,41:1
Frank, Harry
Tiger von Berlin, Der 1930,S 15,29:3
Lumpenball 1931,Ap 27,25:1
Grosse Sehnsucht, Die 1931,O 8,22:6
Der Falsche Feldmarschall 1932,Je 30,26:2
Madame Blaubart 1933,My 11,14:2
Choral von Leuthen, Der 1935,Ja 21,19:4
Razzia 1948,Je 14,19:2
Frank, Horst
Head, The 1963,Je 20,29:1
Frank, Jacob
Mother's Boy 1929,My 8,34:6
Frank, Jerry
Lost City, The 1935,F 21,23:3
Frank, Joanna
America America 1963,D 16,44:1
Savage Seven, The 1968,Ag 22,47:1
Born Wild 1968,D 12,62:6
Frank, L (Producer)
Spain Fights on 1939,F 13,13:2

Frank, Leonhard (Original Author)
Homecoming 1928,N 19,16:7
Sieger, Der; Victor, The 1932,My 15,VIII,4:4 (In Addenda)
Desire Me 1947,S 26,28:3
Frank, Leonhard (Screenwriter)
Murderer Dimitri Karamasoff, The 1931,Mr 1,VIII,6:7 (In Addenda)
Niemandsland; No Man's Land 1932,Ja 24,VIII,5:1
Frank, Louis (Narrator)
Fury Over Spain 1937,Jl 21,19:2
Frank, Melvin (Director)
Reformer and the Redhead, The 1950,Ap 10,15:2
Strictly Dishonorable 1951,Jl 12,21:6
Callaway Went Thataway 1951,D 6,42:1
Above and Beyond 1953,Ja 31,10:6
Knock on Wood 1954,Ap 15,34:2
Court Jester, The 1956,F 2,19:1
That Certain Felling 1956,Je 21,35:2
Li'l Abner 1959,D 12,19:2
Facts of Life, The 1961,F 11,27:1
Strange Bedfellows 1965,Mr 11,38:1
Frank, Melvin (Original Author)
My Favorite Blonde 1942,Ap 2,27:2
Southern Yankee, A 1948,N 25,47:2
Callaway Went Thataway 1951,D 6,42:1
Knock on Wood 1954,Ap 15,34:2
Court Jester, The 1956,F 2,19:1
Li'l Abner 1959,D 12,19:2
Strange Bedfellows 1965,Mr 11,38:1
Not With my Wife, You Don't! 1966,N 3,45:2
Frank, Melvin (Producer)
Mr Blandings Builds his Dream House 1948,Mr 26,26:2
Reformer and the Redhead, The 1950,Ap 10,15:2
Strictly Dishonorable 1951,Jl 12,21:6
Callaway Went Thataway 1951,D 6,42:1
Above and Beyond 1953,Ja 31,10:6
Knock on Wood 1954,Ap 15,34:2
Court Jester, The 1956,F 2,19:1
That Certain Felling 1956,Je 21,35:2
Trap, The 1959,Ja 29,18:4
Road to Hong Kong, The 1962,Je 28,21:1
Strange Bedfellows 1965,Mr 11,38:1
Funny Thing Happened on the Way to the Forum, A 1966,O 17,48:1
Frank, Melvin (Screenwriter)
Happy Go Lucky 1943,Mr 25,25:1
Thank Your Lucky Stars 1943,O 2,19:2
And the Angels Sing 1944,Jl 13,14:2
Duffy's Tavern 1945,S 6,23:3
Road to Utopia 1946,F 28,20:2
Our Hearts Were Growing Up 1946,Ag 12,17:2
Monsieur Beaucaire 1946,S 5,23:1
It Had to be You 1947,D 8,35:2
Mr Blandings Builds his Dream House 1948,Mr 26,26:2
Return of October, The 1949,F 23,31:2
Reformer and the Redhead, The 1950,Ap 10,15:2
Strictly Dishonorable 1951,Jl 12,21:6
Above and Beyond 1953,Ja 31,10:6
White Christmas 1954,O 15,16:3
That Certain Felling 1956,Je 21,35:2
Li'l Abner 1959,D 12,19:2
Facts of Life, The 1961,F 11,27:1
Road to Hong Kong, The 1962,Je 28,21:1
Strange Bedfellows 1965,Mr 11,38:1
Funny Thing Happened on the Way to the Forum, A 1966,O 17,48:1
Frank, Milo O Jr (Original Author)
High Cost of Loving, The 1958,My 17,12:1
Frank, Milo O Jr (Producer)
High Cost of Loving, The 1958,My 17,12:1
Frank, Nino (Screenwriter)
Vie de Boheme, La 1947,N 28,37:4
Frank, Pat (Original Author)
Man's Favorite Sport? 1964,F 20,22:1
Frank, Paul (Original Author)
Beauty and the Boss 1932,Ap 2,13:2
Adorable 1933,My 19,20:2
Josette 1938,Je 11,9:1
Invisible Wall, The 1947,N 1,11:2
Frank, Paul (Screenwriter)
Drei von ver Tankstelle, Die 1931,Je 20,20:4
Frank, Robert (Cinematographer)
Chappaqua 1967,N 6,65:2
Frank, Robert (Miscellaneous)
Pull my Daisy 1960,Ap 10,II,1:8 (In Addenda)
Frank, T C (Director)
Born Losers, The 1967,Ag 19,16:2
Frank, W R (Producer)
Enemy of Women 1944,S 12,23:6
Cry Danger 1951,F 22,27:3
Frank, Will
Last Edition, The 1925,N 11,27:3
Frank, Zoe
Hell on Earth 1934,Ja 29,10:2
Frankau, Gilbert (Original Author)
If I Marry Again 1925,Ja 12,11:2
Christopher Strong 1933,Mr 10,19:2

Frankau, Ronald
Skin Game, The 1931,Je 20,20:4
FRANKE
See Also FRANCK, FRANK
Franke, Ingeborg
Kampf, Der 1936,S 11,29:3
Frankel, Cyril (Director)
Make Me an Offer 1956,F 29,35:2
Man of Africa 1956,O 11,51:1
It's Great to be Young 1957,D 26,23:3
She Didn't Say No 1963,Jl 30,18:1
Why Bother to Knock 1965,F 4,24:2
Operation Snafu 1965,My 22,18:1
Devil's Own, The 1967,Mr 16,53:2
Frankel, Cyril (Original Author)
Man of Africa 1956,O 11,51:1
Frankel, Isadore (Screenwriter)
God, Man and Devil 1950,Ja 23,16:2
Franken, Rose (Original Author)
Another Language 1933,Ag 5,9:5
Claudia 1943,N 5,23:2
Claudia and David 1946,Ag 15,19:2
Secret Heart, The 1946,D 26,28:2
Franken, Rose (Screenwriter)
Alias Mary Dow 1935,Je 29,16:2
Beloved Enemy 1936,D 26,15:2
Claudia and David 1946,Ag 15,19:2
Franken, Steve
Americanization of Emily, The 1964,O 28,51:1
Follow Me, Boys! 1966,D 2,46:1
Frankenheimer, John (Director)
Young Stranger, The 1957,Ap 9,40:1
Young Savages, The 1961,My 25,31:1
All Fall Down 1962,Ap 12,41:3
Birdman of Alcatraz 1962,Jl 19,19:2
Manchurian Candidate, The 1962,O 25,48:3
Seven Days in May 1964,F 20,22:1
Train, The 1965,Mr 18,25:1
Seconds 1966,O 6,56:1
Grand-Prix 1966,D 22,40:1
Fixer, The 1968,D 9,59:1
Frankenheimer, John (Producer)
Manchurian Candidate, The 1962,O 25,48:3
Frankeur, Paul
Enfants du Paradis, Les 1947,F 20,32:2
Mr Orchid; Pere Tranquille, Le 1948,Mr 29,17:3
Devil's Daughter 1949,F 26,11:2
Counter Investigation 1949,D 30,13:2
Jour de Fete 1952,F 20,26:4
Under the Paris Sky 1952,My 6,35:1
We Are all Murderers 1957,Ja 9,27:2
Nana 1957,Ap 13,12:3
Winner's Circle, The 1957,My 6,25:2
Every Second Counts 1957,O 15,39:4
Grisbi 1959,Jl 13,23:1
Speaking of Murder 1959,O 12,14:1
Marie Octobre 1960,Ag 16,25:2
Come Dance With Me!; Voulez-Vous Danser Avec Moi 1960,N 8,32:6
Rue de Paris 1960,D 23,14:3
Night Affair 1961,O 13,27:1
Magnificent Tramp, The 1962,Ap 25,30:1
Viaccia, La 1962,S 21,35:1
Monkey in Winter 1963,F 1,7:2
Frankham, David
Master of the World 1961,S 16,9:1
Tales of Terror 1962,Jl 5,21:2 (In Addenda)
Franklin, Chester M (Director)
You Never Can Tell 1920,O 4,14:3
Private Scandal, A 1921,Je 13,16:1
Case of Becky, The 1921,O 10,16:1
Toll of the Sea, The 1922,N 27,18:1
Where the North Begins 1923,Ag 27,14:3
Song of Love, The 1924,F 25,13:1
Silent Accuser, The 1924,N 25,26:1
Thirteenth Hour, The 1927,N 28,18:5
File No 113 1932,F 20,11:2
Stoker, The 1932,Jl 16,5:5
Iron Master, The 1933,F 4,11:3
Sequoia 1935,F 23,14:6
Tough Guy 1936,Mr 14,10:1
Franklin, Chester M (Original Author)
Thirteenth Hour, The 1927,N 28,18:5
Franklin, Dave (Composer)
That's Right, You're Wrong 1939,N 30,25:3
Pot o'Gold 1941,Ap 4,25:2
Utah 1945,Mr 12,22:7
See my Lawyer 1945,My 4,23:4
Franklin, Dean (Original Author)
Tombstone, The Town too Tough to Die 1942,Jl 27,18:2
Franklin, Dean (Screenwriter)
Fighting 69th, The 1940,Ja 27,9:2
Franklin, Edgar (Original Author)
Don't Ever Marry 1920,Ap 19,13:3
$20 a Week 1924,Je 10,24:4
Poker Faces 1926,S 14,25:4
Working Man, The 1933,Ap 21,20:3
Everybody's Old Man 1936,Mr 26,27:2
Rich Man, Poor Girl 1938,Ag 19,13:3
Franklin, Edgar (Screenwriter)
Where Was I 1925,Ag 19,14:4

Franklin, Gloria
Lady of the Tropics 1939,S 8,28:3
Franklin, Harold B (Producer)
Gambling 1934,D 4,22:3
Franklin, Harry (Screenwriter)
Brave One, The 1957,Mr 22,26:1
Franklin, Hugh
Curse of the Living Corpse, The 1964,Ap 30,30:1
Franklin, Irene
Lazy River 1934,Ap 4,26:2
Change of Heart 1934,My 11,24:2
Down to Their Last Yacht 1934,S 24,14:1
President Vanishes, The 1934,D 8,18:5
Whipsaw 1936,Ja 25,18:4
Timothy's Quest 1936,F 29,11:2
Song and Dance Man 1936,Mr 12,18:2
Fatal Lady 1936,Jl 11,11:3
Wanted: Jane Turner 1936,N 30,24:7
Midnight Madonna 1937,Jl 17,18:1
Married Before Breakfast 1937,Jl 23,16:2
Fixer Dugan 1939,My 6,21:2
Franklin, Irwin (Screenwriter)
Minstrel Man 1944,Jl 17,18:5
Franklin, Judy
Rock-a-Bye Baby 1958,Jl 24,18:1
Franklin, Martha
Don Q, Son of Zorro 1925,Je 16,24:1
Duchess of Buffalo, The 1926,Ag 9,10:3
Serenade 1927,D 19,30:1
Wheels of Chance 1928,Jl 2,11:2
Woman From Moscow, The 1928,N 5,26:1
Franklin, Miriam
Duffy's Tavern 1945,S 6,23:3
Franklin, Muriel
Tramplers, The 1966,D 8,64:1
Franklin, Pamela
Innocents, The 1961,D 26,15:2
Lion, The 1962,D 22,5:2
Third Secret, The 1964,Ap 29,27:1
Tiger Walks, A 1964,Ag 27,28:2
Flipper's New Adventure 1964,Ag 27,28:2
Nanny, The 1965,N 4,57:2
Our Mother's House 1967,O 10,56:1
Franklin, Paul (Original Author)
Power Dive 1941,My 29,15:4
Franklin, Paul (Screenwriter)
Trouble in Morocco 1937,Mr 15,27:1
Roaring Timber 1937,Ag 19,23:1
Outlaws of the Orient 1937,S 25,10:2
Headin' East 1938,Ja 15,19:2
Franklin, Sidney
Fashion Row 1924,Ja 28,12:1
Boy of Flanders, A 1924,Ap 15,24:1
In Hollywood with Potash and Perlmutter 1924,S 30,27:3
Wheels of Chance 1928,Jl 2,11:2
Puttin' on the Ritz 1930,F 15,15:1
Kid From Spain, The 1932,N 18,23:2
Franklin, Sidney (Director)
Forbidden City, The 1918,O 7,11:3
Heart of the Wetona, The 1919,Ja 6,11:3
Heart o' the Hills 1919,D 1,9:3
Two Weeks 1920,Ja 26,16:1
Smilin' Through 1922,Ap 17,22:3
Primitive Lover, The 1922,My 15,20:3
Brass 1923,Mr 12,18:1
Dulcy 1923,S 17,18:2
Tiger Rose 1923,D 3,14:1
Her Night of Romance 1925,Ja 13,16:1
Learning to Love 1925,F 23,24:1
Beverly of Graustark 1926,Ap 19,24:3
Duchess of Buffalo, The 1926,Ag 9,10:3
Quality Street 1927,N 2,24:5
Wild Orchids 1929,Ap 1,22:1
Last of Mrs Cheyney, The 1929,Ag 12,22:2
Devil May Care 1929,D 23,18:2
Lady of Scandal, The 1930,Je 14,9:4
Lady's Morals, A 1930,N 8,21:3
Guardsman, The 1931,S 10,22:4
Private Lives 1931,D 19,16:4
Smilin' Through 1932,O 15,13:1
Reunion in Vienna 1933,Ap 29,14:2
Barretts of Wimpole Street, The 1934,S 29,12:2
Dark Angel, The 1935,S 6,12:2
Good Earth, The 1937,F 3,27:1
Barretts of Wimpole Street, The 1957,Ja 18,15:3
Franklin, Sidney (Producer)
On Borrowed Time 1939,Jl 7,13:2
Waterloo Bridge 1940,My 17,23:2
Mrs Miniver 1942,Je 5,23:1
Random Harvest 1942,D 18,36:6
Madame Curie 1943,D 17,23:1
White Cliffs of Dover, The 1944,My 12,15:2
Yearling, The 1947,Ja 24,18:2
Homecoming 1948,Ap 30,28:4
Command Decision 1949,Ja 20,34:2
Miniver Story, The 1950,O 27,24:2
Story of Three Loves, The (Mademoiselle); Mademoiselle (The Story of Three Loves) 1953,Mr 6,29:2
Story of Three Loves, The (Equilibrium); Equilibrium (The Story of Three Loves) 1953,Mr 6,29:2

Franklin, Sidney (Producer)— Cont

Story of Three Loves, The (The Jealous Lover);
   Jealous Lover, The (The Story of Three Loves)
   1953,Mr 6,29:2
Story of Three Loves, The 1953,Mr 6,29:2
Equilibrium 1953,Mr 6,29:2
Young Bess 1953,My 22,31:1
Torch Song 1953,O 13,34:2
Franklin, Wendell
Fourth Commandment, The 1927,Ap 6,25:1
Four Sons 1928,F 14,27:1
Franklyn, John
Young Cassidy 1965,Mr 23,35:1
Franklyn, William
Flesh is Weak, The 1957,N 9,31:2
Snorkel, The 1958,S 18,37:2
Breakout 1960,My 19,44:3
Cul de Sac 1966,N 8,44:2
Frankovich, M J (Producer)
Fugitive Lady 1951,Ag 25,7:2
Decameron Nights 1953,N 17,38:2
Fire over Africa 1954,N 22,29:5
Footsteps of the Fog 1955,S 15,39:2
Joe Macbeth 1956,Ap 7,13:1
Frankovitch, Mike
Buck Privates 1941,F 14,15:2
Franquelli, Fely
Leopard Man, The 1943,My 20,26:4
Cry Havoc 1943,N 24,16:2
Back to Bataan 1945,S 13,26:3
FRANTZ
See Also FRANCE, FRANZ
Frantz, Dalies
Sweethearts 1938,D 23,16:2
Balalaika 1939,D 15,33:2
I Take This Woman 1940,F 16,23:3
FRANZ
See Also FRANTZ, FRANCE
Franz, Arthur
Red Stallion in the Rockies 1949,Ag 26,15:2
Roseanna McCoy 1949,O 13,33:2
Doctor and the Girl, The 1949,O 31,20:2
Sands of Iwo Jima 1949,D 31,9:2
Red Light 1950,Ja 16,18:4
Three Secrets 1950,O 21,10:6
Abbott and Costello Meet the Invisible Man
   1951,Ap 13,18:6
Strictly Dishonorable 1951,Jl 12,21:6
Submarine Command 1952,Ja 19,13:2
Sniper, The 1952,My 10,16:3
Member of the Wedding, The 1952,D 31,10:2
Eight Iron Men 1953,Ja 2,11:1
Invaders From Mars 1953,My 30,7:1
Bad for Each Other 1953,D 24,9:3
Eddie Cantor Story, The 1953,D 26,10:2
Flight Nurse 1954,Ja 30,9:6
Caine Mutiny, The 1954,Je 25,17:1
New Orleans Uncensored 1955,Ap 30,10:8
Beyond a Reasonable Doubt 1956,S 14,27:2
Wild Party, The 1956,D 22,13:1
Unholy Wife, The 1958,Mr 7,17:1
Young Lions, The 1958,Ap 3,23:1
Atomic Submarine, The 1960,Ap 20,45:2
Carpetbaggers, The 1964,Jl 2,24:4
Alvarez Kelly 1966,N 17,55:2
Franz, Eduard
Iron Curtain, The 1948,My 13,31:2
Hollow Triumph 1948,O 29,29:5
Wake of the Red Witch 1949,Ja 10,19:2
Outpost in Morocco 1949,Mr 25,28:3
Oh, You Beautiful Doll 1949,N 12,8:4
Whirlpool 1950,Ja 14,9:2
Francis 1950,Mr 16,40:2
Emergency Wedding 1950,D 22,19:2
Magnificent Yankee, The 1951,Ja 19,21:2
Molly 1951,Mr 8,37:2
Thing, The 1951,My 3,34:4
Great Caruso, The 1951,My 11,32:2
Desert Fox, The 1951,O 18,32:1
Unknown Man, The 1951,N 17,9:5
Shadow in the Sky 1952,Jl 19,8:2
One Minute to Zero 1952,S 20,13:2
Because You're Mine 1952,S 26,18:2
Everything I Have is Yours 1952,O 30,40:5
Jazz Singer, The 1953,Ja 14,27:3
Dream Wife 1953,Jl 30,20:1
Latin Lovers 1953,Ag 13,17:2
Sins of Jezebel 1954,Ja 9,12:2
Beachhead 1954,Ap 17,8:2
Broken Lance 1954,Jl 30,9:1
Sign of the Pagan 1955,F 14,24:2
White Feather 1955,F 17,23:1
Lady Godiva 1955,D 3,13:3
Indian Fighter, The 1955,D 22,20:1
Three for Jamie Dawn 1956,Jl 7,11:3
Burning Hills, The 1956,Ag 24,15:2
Ten Commandments, The 1956,N 9,35:2
Man Afraid 1957,Ap 5,24:2
Day of the Badman 1958,Ja 30,19:2
Certain Smile, A 1958,Ag 1,13:2
Story of Ruth, The 1960,Je 18,12:3
Francis of Assisi 1961,Jl 29,8:2
Fiercest Heart, The 1961,Ag 3,13:5
Hatari 1962,Jl 12,19:1

President's Analyst, The 1967,D 22,44:4
Franz, Joseph
Easy Come, Easy Go 1928,My 8,25:3
Franz, Joseph J (Director)
Fightin' Mad 1921,N 21,20:1
Franz, Uta
Forever My Love 1962,Mr 28,36:4
Franzero, C M (Original Author)
Cleopatra 1963,Je 13,29:1
Frapie, Leon (Original Author)
Maternelle, La 1935,O 15,19:1
Frasca, Paolo (Producer)
Angelina 1948,Ap 6,27:2
FRASER
See Also FRAZER, FRAZIER
Fraser, Alex
Good Companions, The 1933,O 10,24:1
Mutiny of the Elsinore, The 1939,F 16,17:2
Moss Rose 1947,Jl 3,14:2
Blonde Savage 1947,O 4,9:2
Fraser, Bill
Captain's Paradise, The 1953,S 29,25:5
Barefoot Contessa, The 1954,S 30,37:1
Masquerade 1965,Ap 29,40:2
Fraser, Dan
Lilies of the Field 1963,O 2,51:1
Fraser, Elizabeth
One Foot in Heaven 1941,N 14,28:3
Man Who Came to Dinner, The 1942,Ja 2,25:2
Busses Roar 1942,S 25,25:4
Hidden Hand, The 1942,N 26,40:4
All my Sons 1948,Mr 29,17:3
Roseanna McCoy 1949,O 13,33:2
Dear Wife 1950,F 2,31:2
Callaway Went Thataway 1951,D 6,42:1
Death of a Salesman 1951,D 21,21:3
So Big 1953,O 22,34:2
Commandos Strike at Dawn 1954,Ja 14,25:1
Young at Heart 1955,Ja 20,35:1
Tunnel of Love 1958,N 22,27:4
Ask any Girl 1959,My 22,32:1
I'm All Right Jack 1960,Ap 26,40:2
Two-Way Stretch 1961,Ja 24,20:3
Pure Hell of St Trinian's, The 1961,S 26,31:1
Double Bunk 1961,N 17,41:3
Doctor in Love 1962,Ap 27,27:2
Two for the Seesaw 1962,N 22,43:1
Pair of Briefs, A 1964,F 3,22:2
Americanization of Emily, The 1964,O 28,51:1
Patch of Blue, A 1965,D 16,63:1
Glass Bottom Boat, The 1966,Je 10,54:1
Seconds 1966,O 6,56:1
Tony Rome 1967,N 16,58:1
Graduate, The 1967,D 22,44:4
Fraser, Georg (Original Author)
Josette 1938,Je 11,9:1
Fraser, George (Director)
Voice of the Hurricane 1964,Je 3,36:4
Fraser, Harry (Director)
Spirit of Youth 1938,F 28,19:1
Heroes of the Alamo 1938,Ap 2,18:2
Fraser, Helen
Billy Liar 1963,D 17,49:1
Uncle, The 1966,Jl 19,34:1
Birthday Party, The 1968,D 10,54:1
Fraser, Jeri Lynne
Two Tickets to Paris 1962,N 29,46:5
Fraser, John
Touch and go 1956,Mr 20,13:2
Wind Cannot Read, The 1960,Mr 10,36:1
Trials of Oscar Wilde, The 1960,Je 28,26:1
Tunes of Glory 1960,D 21,38:2
Cid, El 1961,D 15,49:1
Waltz of the Toreadors 1962,Ag 14,34:1
Tamahine 1964,Jl 16,23:1
Operation Crossbow 1965,Ap 2,29:1
Repulsion 1965,O 4,7:6
Study in Terror, A 1966,N 3,45:3
Fraser, Moyra
Madeleine 1950,S 1,17:2
Man Who Loved Redheads, The 1955,Jl 26,29:2
Left, Right and Centre 1961,F 10,19:1
Here We Go Around the Mulberry Bush
   1968,Mr 5,34:5
Fraser, Phyllis
Lucky Devils 1933,F 20,11:5
Little Men 1935,F 18,19:3
Fighting Youth 1935,N 2,13:3
Every Saturday Night 1936,Mr 14,10:2
Harvester, The 1936,Jl 4,18:2
Fraser, Richard
Yank in the R A F, A 1941,S 27,11:3
How Green Was my Valley 1941,O 29,27:2
Joan of Paris 1942,Ja 26,18:2
Busses Roar 1942,S 25,25:4
Desperate Journey 1942,S 26,11:2
Gorilla Man, The 1943,Ja 15,21:4
Truck Busters 1943,Ja 29,23:5
Edge of Darkness 1943,Ap 10,12:4
Holy Matrimony 1943,S 16,25:2
Ladies Courageous 1944,Mr 16,17:2
Picture of Dorian Gray, The 1945,Mr 2,15:2
Bedlam 1946,Ap 20,16:4

Fraser, Richard— Cont

Private Affairs of Bel Ami, The 1947,Je 16,25:4
Blackmail 1947,Ag 5,26:3
Lone Wolf in London, The 1947,N 22,10:3
Rogues' Regiment 1948,D 20,31:2
Fraser, Ronald
Sundowners, The 1960,D 9,39:1
Jungle Fighters 1962,Mr 15,28:2
V I P's, The 1963,S 20,29:1
Model Murder Case, The 1964,N 25,45:1
Code 7...Victim 5 1965,My 20,52:1
Flight of the Phoenix, The 1966,F 1,26:1
Counterfeit Constable, The 1966,N 22,32:2
Whisperers, The 1967,Ag 1,24:1
Fathom 1967,D 14,62:1
Sebastian 1968,Ja 25,33:2
Killing of Sister George, The 1968,D 17,58:4
Fraser, Sally
It's a Dog's Life 1955,D 23,14:3
Fraser, Shelagh
History of Mr Polly, The 1951,O 25,36:3
Raising a Riot 1957,My 8,44:1
Fraser, Stanley
Maze, The 1953,Jl 11,8:2
Frasheri, Naim
Skanderbeg 1954,Jl 5,6:4
Frassineti, Augusto (Screenwriter)
Giant of Marathon, The 1960,My 26,37:3
Thief of Baghdad, The 1961,Ag 17,18:2
Italiano Brava Gente 1966,F 4,20:1
Fratellini, Annie
Zazie 1961,N 21,45:5
Cloportes 1966,Ap 19,36:1
Fratellinis
Die Galavorstellung 1933,D 11,23:4
Frattari, Benito (Cinematographer)
Mondo Cane; Dog's World, A 1963,Ap 4,58:1 (In
   Addenda)
Women of the World 1963,Jl 3,14:1
Frattini, Galo (Screenwriter)
Hercules 1959,Jl 23,32:2
Hercules Unchained 1960,Jl 14,23:1
Frau, Maria
My Seven Little Sins 1956,My 2,27:1
Margaret of Cortona 1957,Ja 21,20:4
Frausto, Antonio R
Prisionero 13, El 1934,Ap 30,11:4
Enemigos 1934,Ag 18,5:6
Tigre de Yautepec, El 1934,O 20,20:3
Compadre Mendoza, El 1934,N 19,13:2
Juarez y Maximiliano 1935,F 16,9:2
Payasada de la Vida; Tricks of Life
   1935,Mr 18,14:5
Heroe de Nacozari, El 1935,S 23,20:4
Rayo, El 1935,O 19,21:3
Tesoro de Pancho Villa, El 1936,Ja 27,20:4
Adelita, La 1938,O 12,35:2
Mexico Lindo 1939,F 4,11:1
Asi es mi Tierra; Such Is my Country
   1939,Mr 18,9:3
Cobarde, El; Coward, The 1939,Mr 27,11:2
Vamonus con Pancho Villa; Let's Go With Pancho
   Villa 1939,Ap 15,15:2
Tia de las Muchachas, La; Girls' Aunt, The
   1939,O 30,13:3
Bestia Negra, La; Black Beast, The 1940,Je 3,11:2
Asi Se Quiere En Jalisco 1943,Ag 7,6:2
Frawley, James
Greenwich Village Story 1963,Jl 12,14:3
Ladybug, Ladybug 1963,D 24,9:1
Troublemaker, The 1964,Je 23,25:1
Frawley, William
Surrender 1931,N 28,20:4
Moonlight and Pretzels 1933,Ag 23,21:2
Hell and Highwater 1933,D 18,24:4
Miss Fane's Baby is Stolen 1934,Ja 20,12:2
Bolero 1934,F 17,20:3
Witching Hour, The 1934,Ap 28,11:3
Crime Doctor, The 1934,My 11,24:3
Shoot the Works 1934,Jl 7,16:5
Lemon Drop Kid, The 1934,O 27,20:2
Here is my Heart 1934,D 22,21:1
Car 99 1935,F 23,14:7
Hold 'Em Yale 1935,Ap 27,20:6
Alibi Ike 1935,Jl 17,22:1
Harmony Lane 1935,O 24,19:4
Strike Me Pink 1936,Ja 17,15:2
Desire 1936,Ap 13,15:1
F-Man 1936,My 4,16:1
Princess Comes Across, The 1936,Je 4,27:2
Three Cheers for Love 1936,Ag 1,16:2
General Died at Dawn, The 1936,S 3,17:2
Rose Bowl 1936,D 2,35:2
High, Wide and Handsome 1937,Jl 22,15:1
Double or Nothing 1937,S 2,17:3
Something to Sing About 1937,S 21,29:4
Blossoms On Broadway 1937,D 3,29:2
Mad About Music 1938,Mr 12,13:2
Professor Beware 1938,Jl 14,17:1
Sons of the Legion 1938,S 30,24:3
Touchdown Army 1938,O 28,27:2
St Louis Blues 1939,F 9,17:2
Ambush 1939,Jl 9,17:2
Persons in Hiding 1939,Mr 2,19:2

Frawley, William— Cont
Huckleberry Finn 1939,Mr 3,21:2
Rose of Washington Square 1939,My 6,21:2
Ex-Champ 1939,My 12,25:3
Grand Jury Secrets 1939,Je 29,19:2
Stop, Look and Love 1939,S 8,28:5
Farmer's Daughter, The 1940,F 16,23:4
Untamed 1940,Jl 25,14:3
Golden Gloves 1940,Ag 21,23:6
Rhythm on the River 1940,Ag 29,23:2
Quarterback, The 1940,O 17,33:3
One Night in the Tropics 1940,D 20,33:2
Six Lessons From Madame La Zonga
  1941,F 19,25:2
Footsteps in the Dark 1941,Mr 15,13:2
Bride Came C O D, The 1941,Jl 26,18:2
Treat 'Em Rough 1942,Ja 19,21:3
Roxie Hart 1942,F 20,21:1
It Happened in Flatbush 1942,Jl 3,12:8
Give Out, Sisters 1942,Ag 28,22:3
Gentleman Jim 1942,N 26,40:3
We've Never Been Licked 1943,Ag 19,23:1
Fighting Seabees, The 1944,Mr 20,14:2
Whistling in Brooklyn 1944,Mr 24,17:3
Lake Placid Serenade 1944,D 25,15:6
Flame of Barbary Coast 1945,My 28,22:2
Lady on a Train 1945,S 15,21:2
Ziegfeld Follies 1946,Mr 23,8:3
Virginian, The 1946,Ap 18,22:2
Rendezvous With Annie 1946,S 23,29:3
Hit Parade of 1947 1947,My 5,32:8
Miracle on 34th Street 1947,Je 5,32:1
I Wonder Who's Kissing Her Now
  1947,Jl 24,27:2
Mother Wore Tights 1947,Ag 21,33:2
Down to Earth 1947,S 12,18:2
My Wild Irish Rose 1947,D 25,32:2
Babe Ruth Story, The 1948,Jl 29,17:2
Good Sam 1948,S 17,28:2
Chicken every Sunday 1949,Ja 19,34:2
Lady Takes a Sailor, The 1949,D 17,15:2
East Side, West Side 1949,D 23,17:2
Kill the Umpire 1950,My 29,10:6
Pretty Baby 1950,S 23,11:2
Lemon Drop Kid, The 1951,Mr 22,41:2
Abbott and Costello Meet the Invisible Man
  1951,Ap 13,18:6
Rhubarb 1951,Ag 31,12:2
Rancho Notorious 1952,My 15,39:5
Safe at Home 1962,Ap 14,14:1
Frayne, Josephine
Mark, The 1961,O 3,46:2
Frazee, Jane
Buck Privates 1941,F 14,15:2
Moonlight in Hawaii 1941,O 10,26:6
Hellzapoppin 1941,D 26,21:4
What's Cookin' 1942,F 26,15:5
Almost Married 1942,Je 5,23:2
Get Help to Love 1942,O 19,15:3
Hi 'Ya Chum 1943,F 26,17:4
When Johnny Comes Marching Home
  1943,Mr 5,20:4
Big Bonanza, The 1945,F 26,14:5
Practically Yours 1945,Mr 29,18:2
Frazee, Steve (Original Author)
Many Rivers to Cross 1955,F 24,21:2
Gold of the Seven Saints 1961,Ap 6,30:3
Frazen, Stanley (Producer)
Man Trap 1961,N 30,40:4
FRAZER
See Also FRASER, FRAZIER
Frazer, Robert
Without Limit 1921,Mr 21,11:3
Love Piker, The 1923,Jl 16,14:2
When a Man's a Man 1924,F 5,20:1
Men 1924,My 5,18:3
Women Who Give 1924,Je 3,22:1
Bread 1924,Jl 21,14:4
Broken Barriers 1924,Ag 4,16:3
Miss Bluebeard 1925,Ja 28,14:1
Charmer, The 1925,Ap 6,17:3
White Desert, The 1925,Jl 8,12:4
Keeper of the Bees, The 1925,O 28,29:2
Desert Gold 1926,Mr 23,24:5
Splendid Road, The 1926,Je 13,31:1
Back to God's Country 1927,O 24,24:3
Out of the Ruins 1928,Ag 20,21:3
Careers 1929,Je 10,23:1
Drake Case, The 1929,S 16,30:1
Frozen Justice 1929,O 26,15:1
Ten Nights in a Barroom 1931,F 28,15:2
Rainbow Trail, The 1932,Ja 30,13:2
White Zombie 1932,Jl 29,18:2
Vampire Bat, The 1933,Ja 23,9:1
Found Alive 1934,F 12,19:2
World Accuses, The 1935,Mr 21,27:2
Frazer, William
Sherlock Holmes's Fatal Hour 1931,Jl 13,13:5
FRAZIER
See Also FRASER, FRAZER
Frazier, Richard
Wizard, The 1927,N 28,18:5

Frazin, Gladys
Let Not Man Put Asunder 1924,Ja 15,16:1
Frebel
Story of a Cheat, The 1938,S 27,25:2
Freberg, Stan
Callaway Went Thataway 1951,D 6,42:1
Tom Thumb 1958,D 24,00:0
Frechiman, Bernard (Screenwriter)
Game is Over, The 1967,Ja 10,34:1
Freda, Riccardo (Director)
Miserables, Les 1952,Mr 25,23:2
Theodora, Slave Empress 1955,Ja 12,24:2
See Naples and Die 1959,Ag 31,16:2
White Warrior, The 1961,F 11,27:2
Freda, Riccardo (Original Author)
Theodora, Slave Empress 1955,Ja 12,24:2
Freda, Riccardo (Screenwriter)
Miserables, Les 1952,Mr 25,23:2
Theodora, Slave Empress 1955,Ja 12,24:2
Frede, Richard (Original Author)
Interns, The 1962,Ag 9,17:5
New Interns, The 1964,Ag 20,34:2
Frederic, Marc (Producer)
Missle to the Moon 1958,N 17,37:2
Frankenstein's Daughter 1958,N 17,37:2
Frederici, Blanche
Gentlemen Prefer Blondes 1928,Ja 16,24:1
Sadie Thompson 1928,F 6,12:3
Wonder of Women 1929,Jl 22,17:1
Jazz Heaven 1929,O 30,29:2
Soldiers and Women 1930,My 12,27:3
Courage 1930,My 23,21:1
Numbered Men 1930,Je 9,23:3
Bad One, The 1930,Je 13,28:3
Last of the Duanes 1930,S 13,9:3
Office Wife, The 1930,S 27,21:3
Billy the Kid 1930,O 18,23:2
Kismet 1930,O 31,20:1
Ten Cents a Dance 1931,Mr 7,17:2
Woman Hungry 1931,Mr 23,24:7
Night Nurse 1931,Jl 17,23:4
Murder by the Clock 1931,Jl 18,16:6
Wicked 1931,S 19,10:2
Honor of the Family 1931,O 17,20:1
Woman Between, The 1931,O 24,20:3
Friends and Lovers 1931,N 7,16:5
Dangerous Affair, A 1931,N 23,22:1
Mata Hari 1932,Ja 1,31:1
Hatchet Man, The 1932,F 4,25:2
Lady With a Past 1932,F 22,23:2
Love Starved 1932,Ap 15,23:1
So Big 1932,Ap 30,19:3
Miss Pinkerton 1932,Jl 9,7:5
Love Me Tonight 1932,Ag 19,20:6
Night Club Lady, The 1932,Ag 27,13:4
Thirteen Women 1932,O 15,13:1
Farewell to Arms, A 1932,D 9,26:5
Secrets 1933,Mr 16,21:2
Alimony Madness 1933,My 5,18:1
Barbarian, The 1933,My 13,16:2
Adorable 1933,My 19,20:2
Hold Your Man 1933,Jl 1,16:6
Aggie Appleby, Maker of Men 1933,O 20,14:2
Way to Love, The 1933,N 11,10:3
All of Me 1934,F 5,19:2
It Happened One Night 1934,F 23,23:2
Frederick, Freddie Burke
Crowd, The 1928,F 20,14:1
Evidence 1929,O 5,22:5
Wall Street 1929,N 25,22:1
Second Wife 1930,F 10,20:4
Ladies Love Brutes 1930,My 16,20:4
Iron Master, The 1933,F 4,11:3
Frederick, Geoffrey
Hell is a City 1961,Ja 19,26:3
Frederick, Harlow (Producer)
Yellowback 1957,Ap 5,24:2
Frederick, John
Corvette K-225 1943,O 21,30:1
Frederick, Pauline
Bella Donna 1915,N 15,11:1
Audrey 1916,Mr 27,9:2
Slave Island, The 1917,Ja 1,10:2
Sleeping Fires 1917,Ap 16,9:2
Resurrection 1918,My 20,9:7
Her Final Reckoning 1918,Je 24,9:1
Fedora 1918,Ag 5,7:1
Out of the Shadow 1919,Ja 13,9:3
One Week of Life 1919,My 19,20:5
Peace of Roaring River, The 1919,Ag 11,9:1
Bonds of Love 1919,N 3,13:3
Paliser Case, The 1920,F 16,8:1
Madame X 1920,S 27,18:1
Tosca, La 1921,N 21,20:1
Let Not Man Put Asunder 1924,Ja 15,16:1
Three Women 1924,O 6,25:1
Married Flirts 1924,N 19,19:3
Smouldering Fires 1925,Mr 31,17:4
Her Honor the Governor 1926,Jl 20,17:3
Devil's Island 1926,Ag 2,21:2
On Trial 1928,N 15,26:5
Evidence 1929,O 5,22:5
Sacred Flame, The 1929,N 23,18:5

Frederick, Pauline— Cont
This Modern Age 1931,S 7,19:3
Wayward 1932,F 15,13:1
Phantom of Crestwood, The 1932,O 17,18:3
My Marriage 1936,F 22,12:2
Ramona 1936,O 7,32:4
Thank You, Mr Moto 1938,Ja 3,16:2
Fredericks, Charles
Tender is the Night 1962,Ja 20,13:2
Cabinet of Caligari, The 1962,My 26,13:5
Fredericks, Dean
Savage Sam 1963,Ag 1,17:3
Fredericks, Lee
Sun Sets at Dawn, The 1951,Ja 15,13:1
Fredersdorf, Herbert B (Director)
Long Is the Road 1948,N 12,30:5
Fredric, Norman
Light in the Forest, The 1958,Jl 11,15:2
FREED
See Also FRIED
Freed, Alan
Don't Knock the Rock 1957,F 23,13:1
Mister Rock and Roll 1957,O 17,42:2
Freed, Arthur (Composer)
Hold Your Man 1933,Jl 1,16:6
Stage Mother 1933,S 30,18:5
Going Hollywood 1933,D 23,19:2
Sadie McKee 1934,My 18,18:3 (Incorrect in this
  edition; use 1934,My 19,18:3 elsewhere)
Hollywood Party 1934,My 26,12:2
Student Tour 1934,O 31,17:3
Broadway Melody of 1936 1935,S 19,28:1
Night at the Opera, A 1935,D 7,22:1
Broadway Melody of 1938 1937,S 3,12:1
Thoroughbreds Don't Cry 1937,N 26,27:4
Babes in Arms 1939,O 20,27:2
Lady Be Good 1941,S 19,27:1
Yolanda and the Thief 1945,N 23,26:2
Ziegfeld Follies 1946,Mr 23,8:3
Pagan Love Song 1950,D 26,19:1
Freed, Arthur (Miscellaneous)
Devil is a Sissy, The 1936,O 17,21:2
After the Thin Man 1936,D 25,19:2
Freed, Arthur (Producer)
Babes in Arms 1939,O 20,27:2
Strike up the Band 1940,S 30,13:2
Lady Be Good 1941,S 19,27:1
Babes on Broadway 1942,Ja 1,37:1
Panama Hattie 1942,O 2,31:2
For Me and My Gal 1942,O 22,25:1
Cabin in the Sky 1943,My 28,19:3
Best Foot Forward 1943,Je 30,25:2
Du Barry Was a Lady 1943,Ag 20,13:1
Girl Crazy 1943,D 3,27:2
Meet Me in St Louis 1944,N 29,20:2
Clock, The 1945,My 4,23:2
Yolanda and the Thief 1945,N 23,26:2
Harvey Girls, The 1946,Ja 25,26:2
Ziegfeld Follies 1946,Mr 23,8:3
Till the Clouds Roll By 1946,D 6,27:4
Good News 1947,D 5,33:2
Pirate, The 1948,My 21,19:2
Summer Holiday 1948,Je 12,8:5
Easter Parade 1948,Jl 1,19:3
Words and Music 1948,D 10,34:2
Take Me Out to the Ball Game 1949,Mr 10,35:2
Barkleys of Broadway, The 1949,My 5,34:2
Any Number Can Play 1949,Jl 1,14:4
On the Town 1949,D 9,37:2
Annie Get Your Gun 1950,My 18,37:1
Crisis 1950,Jl 4,10:2
Pagan Love Song 1950,D 26,19:1
Royal Wedding 1951,Mr 9,30:2
Show Boat 1951,Jl 20,14:1
American in Paris, An 1951,O 5,24:2
Belle of New York, The 1952,Mr 6,25:6
Singin' in the Rain 1952,Mr 28,27:2
Band Wagon, The 1953,Jl 10,10:2
Brigadoon 1954,S 17,18:2
It's Always Fair Weather 1955,S 16,19:1
Kismet 1955,D 9,32:2
Invitation to the Dance (Circus); Circus (Invitation
  to the Dance) 1956,My 23,35:7
Invitation to the Dance (Sinbad the Sailor); Sinbad
  the Sailor (Invitation to the Dance)
  1956,My 23,35:7
Invitation to the Dance (Ring Around the Rosy);
  Ring Around the Rosy (Invitation to the
  Dance) 1956,My 23,35:7
Silk Stockings 1957,Jl 19,11:1
Gigi 1958,My 16,21:1
Bells Are Ringing 1960,Je 24,31:2
Subterraneans, The 1960,Jl 7,26:1
Light in the Piazza 1962,F 8,25:1
Freed, Arthur (Screenwriter)
Those Three French Girls 1930,O 11,21:3
Freed, Bert
Black Hand 1950,Mr 13,15:2
Where the Sidewalk Ends 1950,Jl 8,7:4
711 Ocean Drive 1950,Jl 20,21:2
No Way Out 1950,Ag 17,23:1
Halls of Montezuma, The 1951,Ja 6,9:6
Company She Keeps, The 1951,Ja 29,14:4
Detective Story 1951,N 7,35:2

Freed, Bert — Cont
Red Mountain 1952,Ap 26,19:2
Atomic City, The 1952,My 2,21:1
Take the High Ground 1953,N 20,19:2
Long, Long Trailer, The 1954,F 19,24:3
Men of the Fighting Lady 1954,My 8,15:2
Cobweb, The 1955,Ag 6,13:3
Desperate Hours, The 1955,O 6,25:1
Paths of Glory 1957,D 26,23:2
Goddess, The 1958,Je 25,24:1
Gazebo, The 1960,Ja 16,14:4
Subterraneans, The 1960,Jl 7,26:1
Why Must I Die? 1960,S 15,45:4
Swinger, The 1966,D 15,60:1
Wild in the Streets 1968,My 30,21:1

Freed, Lazar
Salome of the Tenements 1925,F 24,17:3
Overture to Glory 1940,F 12,14:2

Freed, Ralph (Composer)
Swing High, Swing Low 1937,Ap 15,19:1
Babes on Broadway 1942,Ja 1,37:1
Seven Sweethearts 1942,N 13,28:1
Thousands Cheer 1943,S 14,27:1
I Dood It 1943,N 11,29:1
Two Sisters From Boston 1946,Je 7,16:2

Freed, Ralph (Miscellaneous)
College Holiday 1936,D 24,21:2

Freed, Stan (Narrator)
Mr Bug Goes to Town 1942,F 20,21:3

Freedland, George (Miscellaneous)
Russian Story, The 1943,Je 9,17:2

Freedley, Vinton
Stage Door Canteen 1943,Je 25,13:2

FREEDMAN
See Also FRIEDMAN, FRIEDMANN

Freedman, Benedict (Original Author)
Mrs Mike 1950,F 9,36:5

Freedman, Benedict (Screenwriter)
Atomic Kid, The 1954,D 4,14:2
Everything's Ducky 1961,D 21,30:6

Freedman, David (Miscellaneous)
Palmy Days 1931,S 24,21:2
New Faces of 1937 1937,Jl 2,25:1

Freedman, David (Screenwriter)
Palmy Days 1931,S 24,21:2

Freedman, Nancy (Original Author)
Mrs Mike 1950,F 9,36:5

Freedom Singers
Festival 1967,O 24,53:2

Freeland, Thornton (Director)
Three Live Ghosts 1929,S 30,23:1
Be Yourself 1930,Mr 7,20:5
Whoopee 1930,O 1,26:3
Six Cylinder Love 1931,My 16,31:3
Secret Witness, The 1931,D 21,28:4
Week-End Marriage 1932,Je 4,9:2
They Call It Sin 1932,O 21,25:4
Flying Down to Rio 1933,D 22,25:2
Brewster's Millions 1935,Ap 8,23:3
Amateur Gentleman, The 1936,Ap 27,19:2
Accused 1936,D 17,35:1
Gaiety Girls, The 1938,Mr 31,15:1
Dark Sands 1938,Ag 17,23:4
Marry the Boss's Daughter 1941,D 4,33:4
Meet Me at Dawn 1948,My 18,26:2
Dear Mr Prohack 1950,Jl 15,7:2

Freeman, Al Jr
Black Like Me 1964,My 21,42:1
Troublemaker, The 1964,Je 23,25:1
Dutchman 1967,F 28,32:1
Detective, The 1968,My 29,20:3
Finian's Rainbow 1968,O 10,59:5

Freeman, Arny
Phffft 1954,N 11,43:2

Freeman, Dave (Screenwriter)
Those Fantastic Flying Fools 1967,O 19,59:2

Freeman, Denis (Screenwriter)
Gay Lady, The 1951,Ap 16,21:2
Across the Bridge 1957,O 30,24:1

Freeman, Devery (Miscellaneous)
Public Pigeon No 1 1957,My 18,23:2

Freeman, Devery (Original Author)
Kiss in the Dark, A 1949,Mr 26,10:6
Borderline 1950,Mr 6,17:2
Francis in the Navy 1955,Ag 6,13:4
Three bad Sisters 1956,F 13,24:1

Freeman, Devery (Screenwriter)
Thrill of Brazil, The 1946,S 6,18:3
Guilt of Janet Ames, The 1947,My 23,31:2
Fuller Brush Man, The 1948,My 15,18:2
Borderline 1950,Mr 6,17:2
Yellow Cab Man, The 1950,Mr 27,19:2
Watch the Birdie 1950,D 12,46:4
Dear Brat 1951,Jl 5,21:2
Three Sailors and a Girl 1953,N 23,32:2
Francis Joins the Wacs 1954,Jl 31,6:3
Ain't Misbehavin' 1955,Jl 2,13:2
Francis in the Navy 1955,Ag 6,13:4
Dance With Me Henry 1956,D 24,8:2
Girl Most Likely, The 1958,O 9,47:1

Freeman, Eric
Do You Love Me 1946,My 25,12:2

Freeman, Everett (Original Author)
$1,000 a Minute 1935,D 21,11:1
Thank Your Lucky Stars 1943,O 2,19:2
Kiss in the Dark, A 1949,Mr 26,10:6
Too Young to Kiss 1951,N 23,32:2

Freeman, Everett (Producer)
Jim Thorpe - All American 1951,Ag 25,7:2
Sunday in New York 1964,F 12,30:2
Glass Bottom Boat, The 1966,Je 10,54:1
Where Were You When the Lights Went Out?
1968,Ag 9,30:2

Freeman, Everett (Screenwriter)
Married Before Breakfast 1937,Jl 23,16:2
Chaser, The 1938,Ag 2,15:3
Larceny, Inc 1942,Ap 25,9:1
George Washington Slept Here 1942,O 31,11:1
Princess and the Pirate, The 1945,F 10,16:2
It Happened on Fifth Avenue 1947,Je 11,33:2
Secret Life of Walter Mitty, The 1947,Ag 15,12:2
Lulu Belle 1948,Je 21,18:3
Lady Takes a Sailor, The 1949,D 17,15:2
Pretty Baby 1950,S 23,11:2
Jim Thorpe - All American 1951,Ag 25,7:2
Million Dollar Mermaid 1952,D 5,35:2
Destination Gobi 1953,My 30,7:1
My Man Godfrey 1957,O 12,23:1
Marjorie Morningstar 1958,Ap 25,32:2
Where Were You When the Lights Went Out?
1968,Ag 9,30:2

Freeman, Frank
Iron Duke, The 1935,Ja 25,27:2

Freeman, Frank Jr (Producer)
Omar Khayyam 1957,Ag 24,12:4

Freeman, Gillian (Screenwriter)
Leather Boys, The 1965,N 9,50:1

Freeman, Helen
Abraham Lincoln 1930,Ag 26,24:1
Symphony of Six Million 1932,Ap 15,23:1
Song of Songs 1933,Jl 20,22:2
Doctor Bull 1933,O 6,21:2
Right to Romance, The 1933,D 15,28:2
Sadie McKee 1934,My 18,18:3 (Incorrect in this
edition; use 1934,My 19,18:3 elsewhere)
Doubting Thomas 1935,Jl 11,24:2
Ah, Wilderness! 1935,D 25,30:2
Bulldog Drummond Comes Back 1937,S 4,8:3
Safety in Numbers 1938,S 6,17:2
Don Juan Quilligan 1945,Jl 30,16:2
Saratoga Trunk 1945,N 22,39:2
Unknown, The 1946,Jl 20,10:3
So Dark the Night 1946,D 7,16:2
Late George Apley, The 1947,Mr 21,29:2

Freeman, Herbie
Three Legionnaires 1937,Jl 10,18:2

Freeman, Howard
Margin for Error 1943,Ja 25,10:7
Slightly Dangerous 1943,Ap 2,17:2
Air Raid Wardens 1943,Ap 5,15:5
Pilot No 5 1943,Je 25,13:4
Hitler's Madman 1943,Ag 28,15:1
Girl Crazy 1943,D 3,27:2
Whistling in Brooklyn 1944,Mr 24,17:3
Rationing 1944,Ap 10,14:2
Lost Angel 1944,Ap 10,14:1
Secret Command 1944,Je 14,16:2
Once Upon a Time 1944,Je 30,17:2
Meet The People 1944,S 8,16:2
Carolina Blues 1944,D 8,26:6
Song to Remember, A 1945,Ja 26,16:4
Where Do We Go From Here? 1945,Je 7,25:2
Mexicana 1945,N 17,14:6
House of Horrors 1946,F 23,20:3
Abilene Town 1946,Mr 4,16:5
So Goes my Love 1946,My 2,3:7
Blue Dahlia, The 1946,My 9,27:3
Inside Job 1946,Je 15,24:3
Monsieur Beaucaire 1946,S 5,23:1
Cross my Heart 1946,D 19,42:3
California 1947,Ja 15,31:2
Perfect Marriage, The 1947,Ja 16,30:3
Swell Guy 1947,Ja 27,17:2
That Way With Women 1947,F 15,20:4
My Brother Talks to Horses 1947,Je 19,27:4
Long Night, The 1947,S 17,31:2
Magic Town 1947,O 8,29:2
Cass Timberlane 1947,N 7,20:2
If You Knew Susie 1948,F 23,19:2
Letters From an Unknown Woman
1948,Ap 29,20:6
Up in Central Park 1948,My 27,29:3
Time of your Life, The 1948,My 27,29:2
Summer Holiday 1948,Je 12,8:5
Give my Regards to Broadway 1948,Je 23,32:2
Cry of the City 1948,S 30,32:4
Snake Pit, the 1948,N 5,29:2
Take one False Step 1949,Je 23,33:2
Perfect Strangers 1950,Mr 11,8:2
Double Dynamite 1951,D 26,19:4
Scaramouche 1952,My 9,20:2
Million Dollar Mermaid 1952,D 5,35:2
Dear Brigitte 1965,Ja 28,20:1

Freeman, Joan
Come September 1961,S 8,34:1
Three Stooges Go Around the World in a Daze,
The 1963,D 19,40:2
Roustabout 1964,N 11,38:1
Rounders, The 1965,Ap 29,40:2
Fastest Guitar Alive, The 1968,F 15,47:1

Freeman, Joel (Producer)
Heart is a Lonely Hunter, The 1968,Ag 1,24:1

Freeman, Joseph (Miscellaneous)
Cities and Years 1931,Ap 4,23:1

Freeman, Kathleen
Reformer and the Redhead, The 1950,Ap 10,15:2
House by the River 1950,My 2,25:2
Once a Thief 1951,Ja 19,21:3
Love Is Better Than Ever 1952,Mr 4,23:2
Far Country, The 1955,F 14,24:2
Midnight Story, The 1957,Jl 5,14:2
Fly, The 1958,Ag 30,6:6
North to Alaska 1960,N 11,36:1
Ladies Man, The 1961,Jl 13,26:3
Madison Avenue 1962,Mr 29,28:2
Nutty Professor, The 1963,Jl 18,15:2
Disorderly Orderly, The 1964,D 24,8:3
Rounders, The 1965,Ap 29,40:2
3 on a Couch 1966,Jl 7,30:1

Freeman, Kenneth
Miracle in Harlem 1949,O 24,19:4

Freeman, Lea David (Original Author)
Lazy River 1934,Ap 4,26:2

Freeman, Leonard (Original Author)
Steel Town 1952,My 10,16:4

Freeman, Leonard (Producer)
Gold of the Seven Saints 1961,Ap 6,30:3
Claudelle Inglish 1961,S 21,40:2
Hang 'Em High 1968,Ag 8,27:3

Freeman, Leonard (Screenwriter)
Gold of the Seven Saints 1961,Ap 6,30:3
Claudelle Inglish 1961,S 21,40:2
Hang 'Em High 1968,Ag 8,27:3

Freeman, Maurice
Stephen Steps Out 1923,N 19,19:3
Strangers on a Honeymoon 1937,Mr 13,23:2

Freeman, Michael
Eight on the Lam 1967,Ap 27,52:1

Freeman, Mona
Till We Meet Again 1944,Ag 30,15:1
Together Again 1944,N 24,19:2
Junior Miss 1945,Je 18,15:4
Danger Signal 1945,N 22,39:2
Black Beauty 1946,Ag 30,13:2
That Brennan Girl 1946,D 9,34:3
Dear Ruth 1947,Je 11,33:3
Mother Wore Tights 1947,Ag 21,33:2
Isn't It Romantic? 1948,O 7,35:2
Streets of Laredo 1949,My 12,28:2
Heiress, The 1949,O 7,35:2
Dear Wife 1950,F 2,31:2
I Was a Shoplifter 1950,Ap 28,26:3
Copper Canyon 1950,N 16,39:2
Branded 1951,Ja 11,28:5
Dear Brat 1951,Jl 5,21:2
Darling, How Could You! 1951,N 9,22:4
Flesh and Fury 1952,Mr 28,27:4
Jumping Jacks 1952,Jl 24,30:2
Thunderbirds 1953,Mr 12,24:4
Angel Face 1953,Ap 25,11:5
Battle Cry 1955,F 3,18:1
Huk! 1956,D 15,20:4
Dragoon Wells Massacre 1957,My 6,25:2

Freeman, Robert (Director)
Touchables, The 1968,N 21,41:1

Freeman, Robert (Miscellaneous)
Touchables, The 1968,N 21,41:1

Freeman, Russ
Subterraneans, The 1960,Jl 7,26:1

Freeman, William
Mirandy Smiles 1918,D 16,13:3

Frees, Paul
Red Light 1950,Ja 16,18:4
Place in the Sun, A 1951,Ag 29,20:1
Big Sky, The 1952,Ag 20,21:1
Star, The 1953,Ja 29,25:1
War of the Worlds, The 1953,Ag 14,10:2
Riot in Cell Block 11 1954,F 19,24:5
Suddenly 1954,O 8,27:2
Gay Purr--ee 1962,D 6,55:3

Frees, Paul (Narrator)
Snow Queen, The 1960,Ap 14,34:1

Frees, Wolf
Odette 1951,Mr 28,33:2
Day They Robbed the Bank of England, The
1960,S 5,11:2

FREESE
See Also FRIES

Fregis, Lucien
Mr Hulot's Holiday 1954,Je 17,36:2
My Uncle 1958,N 4,30:2

Fregonese, Hugo (Director)
Where Words Fail; Donde Mueren las Palabraso
1948,Ag 19,18:4
One Way Street 1950,My 12,33:3
Saddle Tramp 1950,N 24,31:4

Fregonese, Hugo (Director) — Cont
Apache Drums 1951,My 7,22:2
Mark of the Renegade 1951,S 7,24:2
My Six Convicts 1952,Mr 28,27:3
Untamed Frontier 1952,Ag 23,10:2
Blowing Wild 1953,O 8,37:5
Decameron Nights 1953,N 17,38:2
Man in the Attic 1954,F 6,17:2
Raid, The 1954,Ag 21,10:4
Black Tuesday 1955,Ja 1,16:2
Harry Black and the Tiger 1958,S 19,24:4
Marco Polo 1962,S 20,29:2
Shatterhand 1968,Je 6,54:1

Fregoso, Arturo
Torero! 1957,My 22,29:2

Freiberger, Fred (Original Author)
Garden of Evil 1954,Jl 10,17:1
Massacre 1956,Je 2,13:5

Freiberger, Fred (Screenwriter)
Beast From 20,000 Fathoms, The 1953,Je 25,23:1
Beginning of the End 1957,Jl 4,16:1

Freidkin, Joel
Angel on my Shoulder 1946,O 21,27:2

Freinditch, V
Don Quixote 1961,Ja 21,18:1

Freindlich, Bruno
Fathers and Sons 1960,D 26,27:2

Frell, Dick (Screenwriter)
Crackerjack, The 1925,My 18,12:1

Freman, Everett (Screenwriter)
Glass Bottom Boat, The 1966,Je 10,54:1

Fremault, Anita
4 Devils 1928,O 4,26:3
Wonder of Women 1929,Jl 22,17:1

Fremont, Al
She's a Shiek 1927,N 21,20:1

French, Charles
Stronger Than Death 1920,Ja 12,7:1
Abysmal Brute, The 1923,Ap 18,24:5
Woman of Paris, A 1923,O 2,7:2
Extra Girl, The 1924,Ja 21,20:1
Being Respectable 1924,Ag 4,16:3
Way of a Girl, The 1925,Mr 30,21:3
Free and Equal 1925,Ap 20,22:1
Texas Trail, The 1925,Jl 9,14:2
Flaming Frontier, The 1926,Ap 5,24:1
Rainmaker, The 1926,My 18,28:2
Fast and Furious 1927,Jl 4,20:3
Man, Woman and Sin 1927,D 5,26:2
Last Warning, The 1929,Ja 7,36:2

French, Charles K
Hands Up 1926,Ja 18,26:2

French, Dick
Half Way to Heaven 1929,D 7,19:3
Hold 'Em Navy 1937,N 6,14:2

French, George
Sawdust Paradise, The 1928,Ag 27,23:1

French, Harold (Director)
Avengers, The 1942,N 25,18:2
Jeannie 1943,S 13,14:2
Mr Emmanuel 1945,Ja 8,15:2
Randolph Family 1945,Mr 13,19:4
Quiet Week-End 1948,Ag 20,13:2
Quartet (The Alien Corn); Alien Corn, The
  (Quartet) 1949,Mr 29,30:3
Her Man Gilbey 1949,Je 9,35:2
Blind Goddess, The 1949,Je 23,33:3
My Brother Jonathan 1949,Je 29,34:4
Adam and Evalyn 1950,My 12,33:4
Trio 1950,O 11,42:1
Dancing Years, The 1951,Ja 29,14:4
Encore (The Ant and the Grasshopper); Ant and
  the Grasshopper, The (Encore) 1952,Ap 3,45:1
Encore (Gigolo and Gigolette); Gigolo and
  Gigolette (Encore) 1952,Ap 3,45:1
Encore (Winter Cruise); Winter Cruise (Encore)
  1952,Ap 3,45:1
Hour of 13, The 1952,O 28,37:1
Paris Express, The 1953,Je 6,8:6
Rob Roy 1954,F 4,21:5
Man Who Loved Redheads, The 1955,Jl 26,29:2

French, Harold (Producer)
Blind Goddess, The 1949,Je 23,33:3
Adam and Evalyn 1950,My 12,33:4

French, Hugh
If Winter Comes 1948,Ja 23,28:4
Woman's Vengeance, A 1948,Ja 30,19:2
Mr Peabody and the Mermaid 1948,Ag 14,6:5
Sword in the Desert 1949,Ag 25,20:2
Fancy Pants 1950,Ag 31,21:2
Lucky Nick Cain 1951,Ap 23,21:2

French, Leslie
This England 1941,N 18,33:2
Orders to Kill 1958,N 18,41:2
Singer not the Song, The 1962,My 3,25:4
Leopard, The 1963,Ag 13,25:1
More Than a Miracle 1967,N 2,58:2

French, Mary Meade
In Like Flint 1967,Mr 16,53:2

French, Pauline
Little Johnny Jones 1923,Ag 13,16:1
Last Man on Earth, The 1924,D 13,12:4

French, Susan
Impossible Years, The 1968,D 6,54:1

French, Valerie
Jubal 1956,Ap 25,39:1
Garment Jungle, The 1957,My 16,28:2
Shalako 1968,N 6,32:1

French National Opera Symphony
Ballerina 1938,N 15,27:1

French Resistance, Members of
School for Danger 1947,N 10,21:3

Frend, Charles (Director)
Johnny Frenchman 1946,O 21,27:3
Run for Your Money, A 1950,Ap 10,15:3
Scott of the Antarctic 1951,F 26,20:2
Magnet, The 1951,F 27,22:6
Cruel Sea, The 1953,Ag 11,18:5
Lease of Life 1956,F 10,18:1
Third Key, The 1957,Je 3,30:2
All at Sea 1957,D 23,18:2
Trouble in the Sky 1961,Jl 13,26:3

Frend, Charles (Screenwriter)
Run for Your Money, A 1950,Ap 10,15:3

Freni, Mirella
Boheme, La 1965,O 20,51:2

Frenke, Eugene (Director)
Two Who Dared 1937,Jl 10,18:2

Frenke, Eugene (Producer)
Two Who Dared 1937,Jl 10,18:2
Exile Express 1939,Ag 16,21:3
Let's Live a Little 1948,D 10,34:2
Lady in the Iron Mask 1952,Jl 5,7:2
Heaven Knows Mr Allison 1957,Mr 15,22:1
Barbarian and the Geisha 1958,O 3,25:1
Last Sunset, The 1961,Je 15,51:1

Fresco, Robert M (Original Author)
Private Navy of Sgt O'Farrell, The
  1968,My 9,54:1

Freshman, William
Widecombe Fair 1929,O 28,20:1
F P 1 1933,S 16,9:3

Freshman, William (Director)
Conspiracy in Teheran 1950,Mr 11,8:3

Fresnay, Pierre
Vierge Folle, La 1929,Ja 13,VIII,7:4
Marius 1933,Ap 14,22:5
Dame aux Camelias, La 1935,Mr 21,27:1
Man Who Knew too Much, The 1935,Mr 23,11:2
Razumov 1937,Mr 9,27:2
Grand Illusion 1938,S 13,28:2
Three Waltzes 1939,Ap 25,19:2
S O S Mediterranean 1940,Ja 1,29:2
Charrette Fantome, La 1940,My 28,29:2
Carnival of Sinners 1947,Ap 8,34:2
Murderer Lives at Number 21, The
  1947,Ag 18,12:3
Fanny 1948,F 13,26:2
Corbeau, Le; Raven, The 1948,F 24,21:1
Cesar 1948,O 28,36:2
Street of Shadows 1948,N 20,9:2
Monsieur Vincent 1948,D 21,33:2
Devil's Daughter 1949,F 26,11:2
Strangers in the House 1949,O 13,33:3
Tainted 1950,Ja 21,10:2
Paris Waltz, The 1950,Ag 23,35:2
God Needs Men 1951,Mr 27,35:1
Au Grand Balcon 1951,My 5,14:2
Perfectionist, The 1952,My 2,21:3
Amazing Monsieur Fabre, The 1952,S 9,21:2
Voyage to America 1952,O 20,18:2
Ostrich Has two Eggs, The 1960,S 27,40:1

Fresnay, Pierre (Narrator)
Days of our Years 1951,D 6,42:2

Fresno, Maruchi
Agua en el Suelo, El 1935,F 4,11:4
Vidas Rotas 1935,Ag 3,16:3
Night Heaven Fell, The 1958,O 22,40:4

Fresson, Bernard
Hiroshima, Mon Amour 1960,My 17,43:1
Zita 1968,Ag 12,40:2

Freuchen, Peter (Original Author)
Eskimo 1933,N 15,25:2

Freud, Ralph
Police Call 1933,Ag 22,20:3
My Woman 1933,O 16,20:3

Freud, Sigmund Dr (Original Author)
Secrets of the Soul 1927,Ap 25,20:4

Freund, Charles
Pagan Love Song 1950,D 26,19:1

Freund, Eric
Spitfire 1943,Je 14,13:2
Mr Emmanuel 1945,Ja 8,15:2

Freund, Karl (Director)
Mummy, The 1933,Ja 7,11:2
Madame Spy 1934,F 10,20:1
Countess of Monte Cristo, The 1934,Ap 2,13:2
I Give my Love 1934,Jl 17,24:2
Gift of Gab 1934,S 26,17:6
Mad Love 1935,Ag 5,20:2

Freund, Karl (Miscellaneous)
Uneasy Money 1928,D 11,35:3

Freund, Karl (Producer)
Berlin, A Symphony of a Big City
  1928,My 14,25:1

FREY
See Also FRY, FRYE

Frey, Arno
Best of Enemies 1933,Jl 17,19:5
Hell in the Heavens 1934,D 12,28:2
Mystery Woman 1935,Ja 9,22:2
Jungle Siren 1942,O 10,11:3

Frey, Barbara
Love at Twenty 1963,F 7,5:6

Frey, Derek (Screenwriter)
Sleeping Tiger, The 1954,O 9,8:7

Frey, Eric
Last ten Days, The 1956,Ap 12,26:1
Cardinal, The 1963,D 13,41:1

Frey, Evelyn
Powers Girl, The 1943,Mr 26,14:2 (In Addenda)

Frey, Nathaniel
Kiss Them for Me 1957,N 9,31:2
Damn Yankees 1958,S 27,12:7
What's so bad About Feeling Good?
  1968,My 25,27:1

Frey, Sami
Truth, The 1961,Je 27,23:2
7 Capital Sins (Pride); Pride (7 Capital Sins)
  1963,Ja 17,5:2
Therese 1963,N 13,35:2
Disorder 1964,My 26,44:2
Band of Outsiders 1964,S 19,19:1
Band of Outsiders; Bande a Part 1966,Mr 16,48:3

Freybe, Jutta
Zwischen den Eltern; Between the Parents
  1938,Jl 30,10:3
Jugend von Heute; Youth of Today
  1938,N 5,15:3
Pour le Merite 1939,Ap 8,19:2

Freydeau, Jean Pierre (Screenwriter)
Extenuating Circumstances; Circostances
  Attenuantes 1946,S 24,41:3

Freylich, Semyon (Screenwriter)
Sun Shines for All 1961,Jl 10,25:3

Freytag, Robert
Decision Before Dawn 1951,D 22,12:2
Circus of Love 1958,Ag 16,10:2

Frez, Ilya (Director)
Dimka 1964,Mr 21,13:5

Fric, Mac (Director)
Zinker, Der 1931,O 4,VIII,7:1
Adjutant Seiner Hoheit, Der 1934,O 22,12:3
Doppelbraeutigam, Der; Double Fiance, The
  1935,Mr 23,11:3
Gaesschen zum Paradies, Das 1937,Ag 21,7:3
Inspector General, The 1937,N 25,37:1
World Is Ours, The 1939,Ag 14,11:5

Fric, Martin (Director)
Emperor and the Golem, The 1955,Ja 10,27:4

Fric, Martin (Screenwriter)
Emperor and the Golem, The 1955,Ja 10,27:4

FRICK
See Also FRICKE

Frick, Billy
Is Paris Burning? 1966,N 11,36:1

Frick and Frack
Silver Skates 1943,Mr 19,15:3

FRICKE
See Also FRICK

Fricke, Florian
Signs of Life; Lebenszeichen 1968,S 26,60:1

Frickert, Joseph (Screenwriter)
One Million BC 1940,Ap 27,9:2

Frickhoffer, Gerhard
Merry Wives of Windsor, The 1952,S 22,19:2

Friday
Eyes in the Night 1942,O 16,23:1

Fridell, Ake
I Am With You 1949,Mr 1,30:5
Smiles of a Summer Night 1957,D 24,11:1
Seventh Seal 1958,O 14,44:1
Wild Strawberries 1959,Je 23,37:1
Magician, The 1959,Ag 28,27:1

Friderici, Blanche
Trespasser, The 1929,N 2,14:6

Fridh, Gertrud
Frustration 1949,Ag 27,7:3
Wild Strawberries 1959,Je 23,37:1
Magician, The 1959,Ag 28,27:1
Devil's Eye, The 1961,O 31,27:4
All These Women 1964,O 6,35:1
Hour of the Wolf 1968,Ap 10,50:2

FRIED
See Also FREED

Fried, George (Original Author)
Mary Ryan, Detective 1949,N 4,33:3

Fried, Harry (Original Author)
Dancing Sweeties 1930,Ag 16,8:3
Humanity 1933,Ap 22,16:3

Fried, Harry (Screenwriter)
Fools for Luck 1928,Je 12,33:5

Fried, Olivia
Antenato, L'; Ancestor, The 1938,O 22,14:3

Fried, Ralph (Composer)
Champagne Waltz 1937,F 4,17:2

Fried, Valeri (Screenwriter)
There Was an old Couple 1967,My 22,53:1
Fried, Y
Othello 1960,My 16,39:1
Fried, Y (Director)
Twelfth Night 1956,Mr 5,21:1
Fried, Y (Screenwriter)
Twelfth Night 1956,Mr 5,21:1
Friedhofer, Hugo (Composer)
Valley of the Giants 1938,S 10,20:2
Friedkin, David (Screenwriter)
Pawnbroker, The 1965,Ap 21,51:1
Friedkin, Joel
Great John L, The 1945,Jl 9,14:6
Friedkin, William (Director)
Good Times 1967,Ag 3,26:4
Birthday Party, The 1968,D 10,54:1
Night They Raided Minsky's, The
1968,D 23,43:1
Friedland, Dahlia
Impossible on Saturday 1966,F 17,29:1
Friedlander, Louis (Director)
Raven, The 1935,Jl 5,9:2
Parole 1936,Je 27,21:1
Friedlob, Bert (Producer)
Fireball, The 1950,N 10,35:4
Millionaire for Christy, A 1951,O 5,24:3
Steel Trap, The 1952,N 13,35:2
Star, The 1953,Ja 29,25:1
Untamed 1955,Mr 12,11:6
While the City Sleeps 1956,My 17,37:1
Friedlova, Helena
Merry Wives, The 1940,N 12,28:3
FRIEDMAN
See Also FREEDMAN, FRIEDMANN
Friedman, Alan (Original Author)
She Went to the Races 1946,F 1,29:2
Friedman, Jane
To Love; Att Alska 1964,S 23,45:3 (Incorrect in
this edition; use 1964,S 23,54:1 elsewhere)
Friedman, Monk
Crime Incorporated 1945,Je 23,9:7
Friedman, Seymour (Director)
Prison Warden 1949,O 21,31:2
Chinatown at Midnight 1949,N 18,35:3
Bodyhold 1949,D 12,29:4
Criminal Lawyer 1951,Ag 24,11:4
Lone Shark 1952,My 12,21:2
Khyber Patrol 1954,S 20,19:2
African Manhunt 1957,Ap 20,21:4
Friedman, Shrada
Sallah 1965,O 13,39:1
Judith 1966,Ja 21,22:1
Friedman, Walter
Some Blondes Are Dangerous 1937,N 3,29:3
FRIEDMANN
See Also FREEDMAN, FRIEDMAN
Friedmann, Semmy
Pettersson & Bendel 1934,F 22,25:2
Friedmann-Frederich, Fritz (Director)
Friederike 1933,F 27,11:3
Friedmann-Frederick, Fritz (Director)
Der Herr Finanzdirektor 1932,Je 25,18:2
Friedrichsen, Uwe
Faust 1963,Ap 16,31:1
Friend, Cliff (Composer)
New Movietone Follies of 1930, The
1930,Je 21,20:5
Down to Their Last Yacht 1934,S 24,14:1
George White's 1935 Scandals 1935,Ap 29,12:3
Hit Parade, The 1937,My 31,11:2
Shine on Harvest Moon 1944,Mr 11,10:2
Friend, Helene
Love Parade, The 1929,N 20,32:6
Friend, Philip
Mister V 1942,F 13,24:4
In Which We Serve 1942,D 24,18:1
Enchantment 1948,D 27,16:2
My Own True Love 1949,F 3,27:3
Sword in the Desert 1949,Ag 25,20:2
Buccaneer's Girl 1950,Mr 27,19:2
Spy Hunt 1950,S 8,25:2
Smuggler's Island 1951,My 24,47:2
Thunder on the Hill 1951,O 18,32:3
Desperate Moment 1953,S 1,19:4
Edge of Divorce 1954,Jl 2,10:1
Diamond Wizard, The 1954,Jl 17,7:4
Friendich, B
Twelfth Night 1956,Mr 5,21:1
Friendlich, V
Mussorgsky 1951,Ag 20,14:3
Friendly, Fred W (Producer)
Satchmo the Great 1958,Mr 1,12:1
FRIES
See Also FREESE
Fries, Otto
Hotel Imperial 1927,Ja 3,16:2
Surrender 1927,O 11,27:1
Riley, The Cop 1928,D 4,29:1
Monkey Business 1931,O 8,22:6
Expensive Husbands 1938,Ja 8,19:3

Friese-Greene, Claude (Cinematographer)
Widdicombe Fair 1929,Ja 13,VIII,5:2 (In
Addenda)
Friganza, Trixie
Proud Flesh 1925,Ap 14,26:1
Coming of Amos, The 1925,S 8,29:1
Road to Yesterday, The 1925,D 1,22:4
Gentlemen Prefer Blondes 1928,Ja 16,24:1
Thanks For The Buggy Ride 1928,Ja 23,18:3
Free and Easy 1930,Ap 19,15:1
Myrt and Marge 1934,Ja 17,23:2
If I Had my Way 1940,My 6,13:2
Frigerto, Jone
Maestrina, La; Little School Mistress, The
1938,Ap 29,17:2
Friml, Rudolf (Composer)
Lottery Bride, The 1930,N 29,21:4
Rose Marie 1936,F 1,9:2
Firefly, The 1937,S 2,17:2
Music for Madame 1937,O 23,14:1
Northwest Outpost 1947,Ag 8,10:2
Vagabond King, The 1956,S 13,39:6
Friml, Rudolf (Original Author)
Vagabond King, The 1930,Mr 2,IX,5:1
Vagabond King, The 1956,S 13,39:6
Frings, Ketti (Original Author)
Hold Back the Dawn 1941,O 2,29:1
Company She Keeps, The 1951,Ja 29,14:4
Frings, Ketti (Screenwriter)
Guest in the House 1945,F 16,19:2
Accused, The 1949,Ja 13,26:2
Thelma Jordon 1950,Ja 19,35:2
Dark City 1950,O 19,40:5
Company She Keeps, The 1951,Ja 29,14:4
Because of You 1952,D 4,47:3
Come Back, Little Sheba 1952,D 24,13:2 (In Addenda)
About Mrs Leslie 1954,Je 28,16:2
Shrike, The 1955,Jl 8,15:2
Foxfire 1955,Jl 14,19:1
Frinton, Freddie
Make Mine Mink 1960,D 20,43:4
Fris, Maria
Dancing Heart, The 1958,Ja 18,10:3
Frisch, Larry (Director)
Tel Aviv Taxi 1956,D 31,10:7
Pillar of Fire, The 1963,Ap 8,35:2
Casablan 1964,D 14,50:1
Frisch, Larry (Producer)
Pillar of Fire, The 1963,Ap 8,35:2
Frisch, Larry (Screenwriter)
Tel Aviv Taxi 1956,D 31,10:7
Frisches, Axel
Livet paa Hegnsgaard; Life on the Hegn Farm
1939,N 13,15:2
Frisches, Axel (Original Author)
65, 66 Och Jag (65, 66 And Me)
1937,Ag 30,25:2
Frisco, Albert
Love Light, The 1921,Ja 10,9:1
Frisco, Joe
Gorilla, The 1931,F 23,20:3
Atlantic City 1944,Ag 14,11:4
Shady Lady 1945,O 11,26:2
That's my Man 1947,Ap 7,20:2
Riding High 1950,Ap 11,26:2
Sweet Smell of Success 1957,Je 28,29:2
Frisk, Elizabeth
Dream Waltz, The 1930,D 27,16:3
Frissell, Varick (Cinematographer)
Swilin' Racket, The 1928,Ap 24,29:3
Frissell, Varick (Producer)
Viking, The 1931,Je 17,32:5
Fritchie, Barbara
Last Round-Up, The 1934,My 10,25:2
Murder at the Vanities 1934,My 21,20:2
Murder on the Blackboard 1934,Je 20,24:2
Thunder Mountain 1935,O 2,27:2
Gay Deception, The 1935,O 11,31:1
Frith, Leslie
Dreyfus Case, The 1931,Ag 31,11:5
Murder in the Old Red Barn 1936,Ag 19,18:3
Fritsch, Gunther V (Director)
Curse of the Cat People, The 1944,Mr 4,11:1
Fritsch, Thomas
Adorable Julia 1964,Ap 8,33:1
And so to Bed 1965,Jl 31,11:3
Fritsch, Willi
Schuldig 1928,Mr 11,VIII,7:6 (In Addenda)
Fritsch, Willy
Last Waltz, The 1927,N 14,26:1
Spione; Spies 1928,My 20,VIII,8:5
Guilty 1928,S 18,33:2
Spies 1929,Mr 5,29:1
His Late Excellency 1929,Je 11,27:2
Hungarian Rhapsody 1929,Ag 5,25:2
Docks of Hamburg 1930,Jl 7,22:3
Hocuspocus 1930,Ag 3,VIII,4:1
Melody of The Heart 1930,S 1,16:1
By Rocket to the Moon 1931,F 7,11:1
Liebeswalzer 1931,My 4,15:3
Drei von ver Tankstelle, Die 1931,Je 20,20:4
In Geheimdienst; In the Employ of the Secret
Service 1931,O 25,VIII,6:1

Fritsch, Willy — Cont
Ihre Hoheit Befiehlt 1931,N 7,16:5
Congress Dances, The 1931,N 22,VIII,6:6
Ronny 1932,Ap 14,25:3
Mad Idea, A; Toller Einfall, Ein 1932,Jl 31,IX,3:4
Blonder Tram, Ein; Blond Dream, A
1932,N 13,IX,4:2
Saison in Kairo 1933,D 25,28:2
Frechdachs, Der 1934,Ja 6,18:3
Eines Prinzen Junge Liebe 1934,Mr 24,20:4
Toller Einfall, Ein 1934,My 21,20:3
Waltz Time in Vienna 1934,N 19,13:2
Prinzessin, Turandot 1935,Ja 16,21:2
Boccaccio 1937,F 27,9:3
Glueckskinder 1937,Je 5,21:1
Sieben Ohrfeigen; Seven Slaps 1938,F 12,20:5
Aus den Wolken Kommt das Glueck; Luck Comes
From the Clouds 1938,Ap 16,17:2
Meadchen von Gestern Nacht, Das; Girl of Last
Night, The 1938,Je 18,18:2
Zwischen den Eltern; Between the Parents
1938,Jl 30,10:3
Streitum den Knaben Jo; Strife Over the Boy Jo
1938,D 10,13:2
Volk Will Leben, Ein; People Wants to Live, A
1939,Mr 27,11:2
Fledermaus, Die; Bat, The 1948,Mr 15,26:2
Film Without a Name 1950,O 20,32:2
Vienna Blood 1951,F 22,27:4
Fritz, Bruno
Escape from East Berlin 1962,D 6,55:3
Fritz, Hans
Last Illusion, The 1951,Mr 8,37:2
Fritzell, Jim (Screenwriter)
Good Neighbor Sam 1964,Jl 23,19:1
Ghost and Mr Chicken, The 1966,S 22,57:2
Shakiest Gun in the West, The 1968,Jl 11,30:1
Fritzsche, K J (Producer)
Grapes are Ripe, The 1953,O 15,43:2
Frobe, Gert
Berliner, The 1952,O 28,37:1
He Who Must Die 1958,D 29,21:1
Heroes and Sinners; (Heros Sont Fatigues, Les)
1959,My 12,38:2
Rosemary 1960,Ja 19,40:2
It Happened in Broad Daylight 1960,S 30,33:1
Longest Day, The 1962,O 5,28:1
Goldfinger 1964,D 22,36:1
Banana Peel; Peau de Banane 1965,Ja 19,29:1
Backfire 1965,Ap 27,27:1
High Wind in Jamaica, A 1965,Je 17,27:2
Those Magnificent Men in Their Flying Machines
(Or How I Flew From London to Paris in 25
Hours and 11 Minutes) 1965,Je 17,27:1
Greed in the Sun 1965,Ag 19,35:3
Enough Rope 1966,Jl 15,34:3
Is Paris Burning? 1966,N 11,36:1
Triple Cross 1967,Jl 20,20:2
Upper Hand, The 1967,Jl 29,29:3
Those Fantastic Flying Fools 1967,O 19,59:2
Tonio Kroger 1968,Ja 16,24:1
Chitty Chitty Bang Bang 1968,D 19,64:4
FROEHLICH
See Also FROELICH, FROHLICH
Froehlich, Gustav
Metropolis 1927,Mr 7,16:3
Homecoming 1928,N 19,16:7
Eva and the Grasshopper 1928,N 19,16:7
Temptation 1929,Jl 14,IX,4:5
Meistersinger 1929,D 16,34:2
Asphalt 1930,My 6,33:4
Burning Heart, The 1930,My 12,27:3
Hurrah I'm Alive 1930,Je 16,25:3
Brand in der Oper; Fire in the Opera House
1930,N 23,IX,6:2
Voruntersuchung; Inquest 1931,My 24,VIII,4:1
Immortal Vagabond, The 1931,Ag 3,15:5
Immortal Vagabond, The 1931,Ag 3,15:5
Zwei Menschen 1931,D 23,27:3
Ein Walzer vom Strauss 1932,F 11,16:1
Mein Leopold 1932,Ap 1,17:4
Liebeskommando 1932,Ap 27,13:6
Der Unsterbliche Lump 1932,My 20,22:3
Brand in der Oper 1932,Jl 11,11:4
Gitta Entdeckt Ihr Herz 1932,S 30,17:3
Herzblut 1932,O 3,15:2
Gloria 1932,O 28,22:4
Ich Will Nicht Wissen Wer Du Bist
1933,F 16,23:2
Was Frauen Traeumen; What Women Dream
1933,Jl 2,IX,2:2
Geld Regiert die Welt 1934,My 12,12:4
Fluechtling aus Chicago, Der 1936,Mr 16,21:4
Liebe und Trompetenklang 1936,Ap 13,15:2
Oberwachtmeister Schwenke 1936,My 5,26:7
Liebesleute 1936,O 3,21:2
Barcarole 1936,O 21,35:3
Ein Lied, Ein Kuss, Ein Maeder 1936,D 12,29:4
Night of the Great Love, The 1937,O 1,19:5
Liebe auf Umwegen; Love by Indirection
1937,D 18,18:2
Gleisdreieck 1938,Je 11,9:1
Abduction, The 1938,Je 11,9:2

Froehlich, Gustav — Cont

Kleine und die Grosse Liebe, Die; Minor Love and the Real Thing, The 1938,Jl 23,10:5
Teufelskerl, Ein; Devil of a Fellow, A 1938,O 1,10:3
Secrets of a Soul 1950,S 16,12:6
Sunderin 1954,D 24,7:2

Froehlich, Gustav (Director)
Liebe und Trompetenklang 1936,Ap 13,15:2

Froehlich, Marianne
Brand in der Oper 1932,Jl 11,11:4

FROELICH
See Also FROEHLICH, FROHLICH

Froelich, Carl (Director)
Brand in der Oper; Fire in the Opera House 1930,N 23,IX,6:2
Brand in der Oper 1932,Jl 11,11:4
Gitta Entdeckt Ihr Herz 1932,S 30,17:3
Luise, Koenigin von Preussen 1932,O 5,26:6
Die oder Keine; Her or Nobody 1932,N 13,IX,4:2
Die-oder Keine 1934,O 29,14:3
Choral von Leuthen, Der 1935,Ja 21,19:4
Krach um Iolanthe 1935,My 11,21:3
Fruehlingsmaerchen 1935,My 20,20:5
Reifende Jugend 1936,Ja 4,19:1
Private Life of Louis XIV, The 1936,Ja 9,25:2
Oberwachtmeister Schwenke 1936,My 5,26:7
Traumulus 1936,S 19,20:1
Wenn der Hahn Kraeht 1936,N 14,23:3
If We All Were Angels 1937,O 9,16:2
Magda 1938,S 10,20:2
Es War eine Rauschende Ballnacht; It Was a Gay Ball Night 1939,N 4,11:3

Froelich, Carl (Miscellaneous)
Nacht Gehoert Uns, Die; Night Belongs to Us, The 1930,My 11,IX,4:2 (In Addenda)

Froelich, Carl (Producer)
Krach um Iolanthe 1935,My 11,21:3
Fruehlingsmaerchen 1935,My 20,20:5
Reifende Jugend 1936,Ja 4,19:1
Private Life of Louis XIV, The 1936,Ja 9,25:2
Oberwachtmeister Schwenke 1936,My 5,26:7
Traumulus 1936,S 19,20:1
If We All Were Angels 1937,O 9,16:2

Froelick, Anne (Screenwriter)
Shining Victory 1941,My 31,14:1
Master Race, The 1944,N 2,22:1
Miss Susie Slagle's 1946,F 7,29:2
Easy Come, Easy Go 1947,F 6,29:2
Harriet Craig 1950,N 3,31:2

Froeschel, George (Original Author)
I Aim at the Stars 1960,O 20,42:2

Froeschel, George (Screenwriter)
Waterloo Bridge 1940,My 17,23:2
Mortal Storm, The 1940,Je 21,25:2
We Were Dancing 1942,My 1,23:2
Mrs Miniver 1942,Je 5,23:1
Random Harvest 1942,D 18,36:6
White Cliffs of Dover, The 1944,My 12,15:2
Command Decision 1949,Ja 20,34:2
Miniver Story, The 1950,O 27,24:2
Unknown Man, The 1951,N 17,9:5
Scaramouche 1952,My 9,20:2
Story of Three Loves, The (Equilibrium); Equilibrium (The Story of Three Loves) 1953,Mr 6,29:2
Story of Three Loves, The (Mademoiselle); Mademoiselle (The Story of Three Loves) 1953,Mr 6,29:2
Story of Three Loves, The (The Jealous Lover); Jealous Lover, The (The Story of Three Loves) 1953,Mr 6,29:2
Story of Three Loves, The 1953,Mr 6,29:2
Equilibrium 1953,Mr 6,29:2
Never Let Me Go 1953,Je 11,37:2
Rose Marie 1954,Ap 2,22:2
Betrayed 1954,S 9,36:1
Quentin Durward 1955,N 24,41:1
Gaby 1956,My 10,26:3
Me and the Colonel 1958,Ag 27,33:1

FROHLICH
See Also FROEHLICH, FROELICH

Frohman, Bert
Back Door to Heaven 1939,Ap 20,21:2

Frolke, Jozka
Mizici Svet; Vanishing World 1935,My 30,21:2

Frolov, Andrei (Director)
Winner, The 1947,D 1,27:2

Froman, Jane
Stars Over Broadway 1935,N 14,17:3
Radio City Revels 1938,Mr 21,18:3

Frome, Milton
You're Never too Young 1955,Ag 26,10:2
Birds and the Bees, The 1956,Ap 23,22:1
Pardners 1956,Jl 26,20:2
Delicate Delinquent, The 1957,Jl 4,16:1
Fuzzy Pink Nightgown, The 1957,O 31,41:1
John Goldfarb, Please Come Home 1965,Mr 25,42:4
Family Jewels, The 1965,Ag 12,30:4
Swinger, The 1966,D 15,60:1

Froment, Raymond (Producer)
Anatomy of a Marriage; My Days With Jean Marc; My Nights With Francoise 1964,O 27,42:2
Young World, A 1966,My 17,52:1

Fromiot, Maxime
Poil de Carotte 1933,My 26,24:2

Fromkess, Leon (Producer)
Minstrel Man 1944,Jl 17,18:5
Wife of Monte Cristo, The 1946,Ap 8,31:2

Fromont, Pierre
Diary of a Bad Girl 1958,My 30,13:2

Frondale, Pierre (Original Author)
Fazil 1928,Je 5,21:1
Eau du Nil, L' 1928,D 16,IX,8:2
Homme a l'Hispano, L'; Man in the Hispano-Suiza, The 1933,Je 11,IX,2:5

Frondale, Pierre (Screenwriter)
I Give my Life 1941,S 1,18:4

Fronde, Louis
Shriek of Araby, The 1923,Je 11,16:2

Frondi, Signor
Loves of Ricardo, The 1926,Ag 16,10:1

Front, Phillip
Mill On the Floss, The 1939,N 15,19:3

Froos, Sylvia
Stand up and Cheer 1934,Ap 20,17:1

Frost, Jackie
O K Nero 1953,Je 20,8:6

Frost, Leila
Sentimental Tommy 1921,My 9,16:2

Frost, Philip
Scrooge 1935,D 14,11:1
Wings of the Morning 1937,Mr 12,19:1
Kipps 1942,My 25,11:2

Frost, Terry
Apache Rose 1947,Jl 23,19:3
Man Who Cheated Himself, The 1951,F 9,21:2

Frost, Toni
To Paris With Love 1955,Mr 29,33:4

Fruen, Patricia
Way Down East 1931,Mr 16,25:1

Fruges, Thalie
Marriage Came Tumbling Down, The 1968,N 6,32:3

FRY
See Also FREY, FRYE

Fry, Christopher (Miscellaneous)
Queen is Crowned, A 1953,Je 8,26:2

Fry, Christopher (Screenwriter)
Beggar's Opera, The 1953,Ag 25,18:2
Barabbas 1962,O 11,49:1
Bible, The 1966,S 29,60:1

Fryd, Joseph (Producer)
Hercules, Samson and Ulysses 1965,N 4,57:2

Frydenschildt, Elizabeth
Aren't We Wonderful? 1959,O 16,27:1

FRYE
See Also FREY, FRY

Frye, Cathy
Three Russian Girls 1944,F 5,13:2
Woman in the Night 1948,Ja 10,16:2

Frye, Clayton
Old Home Week 1925,My 25,21:3

Frye, Dwight
Man to Man 1931,Ja 3,21:2
Dracula 1931,F 13,21:3
Maltese Falcon, The 1931,My 29,26:5
Black Camel, The 1931,Jl 4,11:5
Frankenstein 1931,D 5,21:2
Attorney for the Defense 1932,My 28,18:2
Vampire Bat, The 1933,Ja 23,9:1
Circus Queen Murder, The 1933,My 9,20:5
Bride of Frankenstein, The 1935,My 11,21:2
Great Impersonation, The 1935,D 14,11:1
Crime of Dr Crespi, The 1936,Ja 13,14:3
Florida Special 1936,My 29,15:2
Man Who Found Himself, The 1937,Ap 9,19:3
Something to Sing About 1937,S 21,29:4
Shadow, The 1937,D 17,33:3
Invisible Enemy 1938,Ap 30,18:2
Fast Company 1938,Jl 6,21:2
Adventure in Sahara 1938,D 19,19:2
Conspiracy 1939,Ag 23,19:2
Gangs of Chicago 1940,Je 13,29:2
Phantom Raiders 1940,Je 24,19:5
Mystery Ship 1941,Ag 16,18:3
Frankenstein Meets the Wolf Man 1943,Mr 6,8:3

Frye, Ellen
Crazy Quilt, The 1966,O 4,50:1

Frye, John W
Boots Malone 1952,Mr 13,26:2

Frye, Peter (Producer)
Hill 24 Doesn't Answer 1955,N 3,37:1

Frye, Peter (Screenwriter)
Hill 24 Doesn't Answer 1955,N 3,37:1

Frye, William (Producer)
Trouble With Angels, The 1966,Ap 7,45:1
Where Angels Go-Trouble Follows 1968,Ap 11,51:1

Fryer, Robert (Producer)
Boston Strangler, The 1968,O 17,52:1

Fryland, Alphons
Quo Vadis 1925,F 16,24:1

Fryo, Joseph (Producer)
Wild, Wild Planet 1967,Ag 10,45:5

Fu, Ah
Tanga Tika 1953,O 6,34:4

Fu, Chang
Samarang 1933,Je 29,22:2

Fuchs, Claire
Fruehlingsmaerchen 1935,My 20,20:5
Oberwachtmeister Schwenke 1936,My 5,26:7

Fuchs, Daniel (Original Author)
Day the Bookies Wept, The 1939,S 14,18:2
Gangster, The 1947,O 31,29:3
Love Me or Leave Me 1955,My 27,14:1
Jeanne Eagels 1957,Ag 31,19:1

Fuchs, Daniel (Screenwriter)
Big Shot, The 1942,Jl 18,8:2
Hard Way, The 1943,Mr 13,9:2
Between Two Worlds 1944,My 6,11:2
Gangster, The 1947,O 31,29:3
Hollow Triumph 1948,O 29,29:5
Criss Cross 1949,Mr 12,10:2
Panic in the Streets 1950,Ag 5,9:2
Storm Warning 1951,Mr 3,8:2
Taxi 1953,Ja 22,20:3
Human Jungle, The 1954,N 26,24:6
Love Me or Leave Me 1955,My 27,14:1
Jeanne Eagels 1957,Ag 31,19:1

Fuchs, Eugen
Marriage of Figaro 1950,N 3,31:2

Fuchs, Gianni (Producer)
Goliath and the Dragon 1961,Ja 5,27:2

Fuchs, Heinrich
Der Schrecken der Garnison 1932,Je 1,19:5

Fuchs, Leo
I Want to Be a Mother 1937,F 27,9:2
Americaner Shadchen; American Matchmaker 1940,My 7,31:3
Story of Ruth, The 1960,Je 18,12:3

Fuchs, Leo (Producer)
Gambit 1966,D 22,40:2

Fuchs, Vivian Sir (Miscellaneous)
Antarctic Crossing 1959,My 11,30:1

Fuchsberger, Joachim
How to Seduce a Playboy 1968,My 16,53:2

Fuentes, Alma
Young and the Damned, The 1952,Mr 25,23:2

Fuentes, Fernando de (Director)
Zandunga, La 1938,My 14,18:2
Bajo el Cielo de Mexico; Beneath the Sky of Mexico 1938,D 31,7:3
Casa del Ogro, La; House of the Ogre, The 1939,F 13,13:2
Su Gran Aventura; His Great Adventure 1939,Ap 3,11:6

Fuentes, Fernando de (Producer)
Papacito Lindo; Sugar Daddy 1939,N 18,22:6

Fuentes, Franciso de (Director)
Vamonus con Pancho Villa; Let's Go With Pancho Villa 1939,Ap 15,15:2

Fuerbringer, E F
Truxa 1937,Jl 26,15:2

Fuerburg, De Garcia
Scaramouche 1923,O 12,7:2 (Incorrect in this edition; use 1927,O 1,7:2 elsewhere)

Fuerstenberg, Betsy
Women Without Names 1951,Ag 7,22:2

Fuerstenberg, Ilsa
Lustige Witwenball, Der; Merry Widows' Ball, The 1939,My 1,21:2
Captain from Koepenick, The 1958,Jl 26,6:1

Fuerstenberg, Ilse
Hauptmann von Koepenick, Der 1933,Ja 17,22:6
Friesennot 1936,O 26,20:1
Golden Plaque, The 1963,Ag 10,8:6

Fueter, Willy
Snowbound 1949,F 21,20:2
One Night With You 1949,F 21,20:2

Fuetterer, Werner
Faust 1926,D 7,21:2
Uneasy Money 1928,D 11,35:3
Love Commandment, The 1928,D 25,31:3
Survival 1930,Ja 13,21:1
Rheinlandmaedel, Das 1931,S 18,29:1
O Alte Burschenherrlichkeit 1932,Je 18,9:2
Kreuzer Emden 1932,S 8,17:2
Das Nachtigall Maedel 1933,Ja 23,9:2
Ich Glaub' nie Mehr an Eine Frau 1933,O 13,25:4
Tochter des Regiments, Die 1934,Mr 31,8:3
In Wien Hab' Ich Einmal ein Maedel Geliebt 1934,My 26,12:3
Adjutant Seiner Hoheit, Der 1934,O 22,12:3
Einmal Eine Grosse Dame Sein 1934,O 27,20:3
Heimat am Rhein 1934,D 11,29:4
Mustergatte, Der; Model Husband 1938,Mr 19,11:3
Ziel den Wolken; Goal in the Clouds 1939,My 27,13:3

Fugazot
Boliche 1935,My 28,30:2

Fuhr, Charles (Director)
Bomber's Moon 1943,Jl 31,8:2
Fuhrer, Beni
Avalanche 1932,Mr 26,17:2
Fujikawa
Ana-Ta-Han 1954,My 18,38:2
Fujikawa, Jerry
Journey, The 1959,F 20,19:1
Fujiki, Yu
King Kong vs. Godzilla 1963,Je 27,23:4
Samurai (Part II) 1967,O 21,16:1
Fujima Japanese Dancers
World Dances 1954,N 8,24:6
Fujimaki, Jun
Majin 1968,Ag 10,15:5
Fujimoto, Fumiyo
Marines, Lets Go! 1961,Ag 16,37:2
Fujimoto, Masumi (Producer)
Saga of the Vagabonds 1964,O 7,31:1 (Incorrect
in this edition; use 1964,O 7,51:1 elsewhere)
Fujimoto, Sanezumi (Producer)
Happiness of Us Alone 1963,Ap 10,31:5
My Hobo 1963,Jl 24,27:3
Fujimura, Shiho
Zatoichi 1968,Je 28,37:1
Fujino, Hideo
Daughter of Two Fathers, A 1929,Mr 12,26:3
Fujino, Takako
Prodigal Son 1964,Ja 30,24:3 (Incorrect in this
edition; use 1964,Ja 31,16:1 elsewhere)
Fujita, Susumu
Escapde in Japan 1957,D 24,11:1
Men Who Tread on the Tiger's Tail, The
1960,Ja 11,35:7
Hidden Fortress The 1962,Ja 24,24:2
Fujita, Toyo
Dragon Painter, The 1919,O 5,IV,5:3 (In
Addenda)
Garden of Weeds, The 1924,N 4,24:1
Fujiwara, Kamatari
Kimiko 1937,Ap 13,31:3
Magnificent Seven, The 1956,N 20,46:2
Ikiru; To Live 1960,Ja 30,13:5
Yojimbo 1962,O 16,34:1
Different Sons 1964,F 13,25:1
Fujiwara, Reiko
Zatoichi 1968,Je 28,37:1
Fujiyama, Yoko
Different Sons 1964,F 13,25:1
Fujli, Hiroaki (Original Author)
Phantom Horse, the 1956,Jl 25,16:1
Fujlwara, Kamatari
Bad Sleep Well, The 1963,Ja 23,5:2
Fukazawa, Shichiro (Original Author)
Ballad of Narayama 1961,Je 20,27:1
Fukunaga, Akira
Go for Broke 1951,My 25,31:2
Beachhead 1954,Ap 17,8:2
Fulchignoni, Enrico (Miscellaneous)
First Opera Film Festival 1948,My 31,12:7
Fulchignoni, Enrico (Screenwriter)
Difficult Years 1950,Ag 22,31:2
Fulchignoni, Felice
Juliet of the Spirits 1965,N 4,57:1
Fulci, Lucio (Screenwriter)
Day in Court, A 1963,My 11,15:2
Fulda, Ludwig (Original Author)
Two Faced Woman 1942,Ja 1,37:2
Fuliaara, Kamatari
Hidden Fortress The 1962,Ja 24,24:2
Fulimoto, Sanezomi (Producer)
Sword of Doom, The 1967,Ap 15,35:2
Fuller, Barbara
Red Menace, The 1949,Je 27,18:2
Rock Island Trail 1950,Je 5,19:3
Fuller, Clem
Sundowners, The 1950,My 5,17:2
High Lonesome 1950,D 8,40:4
Fuller, Dale
Merry Go Round 1923,Jl 2,16:2
Reno 1924,Ja 8,27:1
Three Weeks 1924,Ap 1,19:3
Babbitt 1924,Jl 15,9:4
His Hour 1924,O 7,26:1
Greed 1924,D 5,28:1
Husbands and Lovers 1924,D 9,23:3
Tomorrow's Love 1925,Ja 7,33:5
Devil's Cargo, The 1925,F 3,24:1
Lady of the Night 1925,Mr 2,14:1
Woman Hater, The 1925,Jl 13,20:2
Only Thing, The 1925,N 23,25:4
Ben Hur 1925,D 31,10:5 (In Addenda)
Midnight Lovers 1926,O 26,23:1
Canadian, The 1926,N 30,27:1
Fazil 1928,Je 5,21:1
Cossacks, The 1928,Je 25,27:1
Wedding March, The 1928,O 15,26:1
Glad Rag Doll, The 1929,Je 3,27:2
Sacred Flame, The 1929,N 23,18:5
Man From Blankley's, The 1930,Mr 29,23:1
Office Wife, The 1930,S 27,21:3
Ben Hur 1931,D 4,28:2
Emma 1932,F 6,14:4

20th Century 1934,My 4,24:2
We Live Again 1934,N 2,27:2
Fuller, Edward (Narrator)
Beyond Endurance 1946,My 20,18:8
Fuller, Frances
One Sunday Afternoon 1933,S 2,14:4
Elmer and Elsie 1934,Ag 4,14:5
Girl in the Red Velvet Swing, The
1955,O 20,41:2
Fuller, James
Green Pastures, The 1936,Jl 17,20:1
Fuller, Jean
Fire in the Straw 1943,Jl 2,15:2
Fuller, Lance
Cattle Queen of Montana 1955,Ja 26,22:1
This Island Earth 1955,Je 11,8:7
Pearl of the South Pacific 1955,S 17,12:2
Slightly Scarlet 1956,Mr 17,13:2
God's Little Acre 1958,Ag 14,23:2
Fuller, Lester (Screenwriter)
Three Steps North 1951,Je 29,14:2
Fuller, Maude
High Wind in Jamaica, A 1965,Je 17,27:2
Fuller, Robert
Return of the Seven 1966,O 20,52:5
Fuller, Rosalinde
Unwritten Law, The 1929,D 24,14:5
Perfect Understanding 1933,F 23,20:2
Escape me Never 1935,My 24,24:2
Fuller, Samuel (Director)
I Shot Jesse James 1949,Ap 2,12:2
Baron of Arizona, The 1950,Je 23,29:2
Steel Helmet, The 1951,Ja 25,21:5
Fixed Bayonets 1951,N 21,20:2
Park Row 1952,D 22,20:2
Pickup on South Street 1953,Je 18,38:2
Hell and High Water 1954,F 2,20:6
House of Bamboo 1955,Jl 2,13:2
China Gate 1957,My 23,40:2
Run of the Arrow 1957,Ag 3,8:6
Verboten 1960,Jl 12,39:1
Underworld, U S A 1961,My 13,10:1
Merrill's Marauders 1962,Je 14,23:4
Shock Corridor 1963,S 12,32:1
Naked Kiss, The 1964,O 29,38:1
Fuller, Samuel (Original Author)
Gangs of New York 1938,My 28,9:2
Adventure in Sahara 1938,D 19,19:2
Confirm or Deny 1941,D 19,35:2
Tanks are Coming, The 1951,D 6,42:4
Scandal Sheet 1952,Ja 17,23:1
Fuller, Samuel (Producer)
Steel Helmet, The 1951,Ja 25,21:5
Park Row 1952,D 22,20:2
China Gate 1957,My 23,40:2
Run of the Arrow 1957,Ag 3,8:6
Verboten 1960,Jl 12,39:1
Underworld, U S A 1961,My 13,10:1
Shock Corridor 1963,S 12,32:1
Naked Kiss, The 1964,O 29,38:1
Fuller, Samuel (Screenwriter)
It Happened in Hollywood 1937,O 2,18:1
Gangs of New York 1938,My 28,9:2
I Shot Jesse James 1949,Ap 2,12:2
Baron of Arizona, The 1950,Je 23,29:2
Steel Helmet, The 1951,Ja 25,21:5
Fixed Bayonets 1951,N 21,20:2
Park Row 1952,D 22,20:2
Pickup on South Street 1953,Je 18,38:2
Command, The 1954,Ja 16,10:5
Hell and High Water 1954,F 2,20:6
China Gate 1957,My 23,40:2
Run of the Arrow 1957,Ag 3,8:6
Verboten 1960,Jl 12,39:1
Underworld, U S A 1961,My 13,10:1
Merrill's Marauders 1962,Je 14,23:4
Shock Corridor 1963,S 12,32:1
Naked Kiss, The 1964,O 29,38:1
Fuller, Starita (Original Author)
Their own Desire 1930,Ja 25,13:2
Fullmer, Gene
Devil's Brigade, The 1968,My 23,56:2
Fullwood, Yemiko
Naked Maja, The 1959,Je 11,36:2
Fulop-Miller, Rene (Original Author)
Great Moment, The 1944,N 13,15:2
Great Sinner, The 1949,Je 30,19:2
Fulstorff, Max
Ich Will Nicht Wissen Wer Du Bist
1933,F 16,23:2
Fulton, Eileen
Girl of the Night 1960,N 12,15:1
Fulton, Ian
Tom Brown's School Days 1940,Je 28,22:2
Fulton, James F
Eternal Three, The 1923,O 12,7:2
Fulton, James F (Original Author)
Love Piker, The 1923,Jl 16,14:2
Fulton, Joan
House of Horrors 1946,F 23,20:3
Runaround, The 1946,Je 7,16:3
Inside Job 1946,Je 15,24:3

Fulton, Joan— Cont
Lover Come Back 1946,Je 20,20:3
White Tie and Tails 1946,N 8,28:2
I'll Be Yours 1947,F 22,16:2
Michigan Kid 1947,F 22,16:3
Buck Privates Come Home 1947,Ap 12,11:3
Vigilantes Return, The 1947,Jl 1,30:2
Fulton, June
Yes Sir, That's my Baby 1949,N 11,31:2
Fulton, Maude
Gingham Girl, The 1927,Jl 19,27:2
Silk Legs 1927,D 26,26:6
Nix on Dames 1929,N 23,18:5
Cohens and Kellys in Trouble, The
1933,Ap 17,16:4
Fulton, Maude (Original Author)
Brat, The 1919,N 3,13:3
Humming Bird, The 1924,Ja 14,2:1
Nix on Dames 1929,N 23,18:5
Other Men's Women 1931,Ap 20,16:3
Brat, The 1931,Ag 24,13:4
Under Eighteen 1931,D 26,15:5
Fulton, Maude (Screenwriter)
Song and Dance Man 1936,Mr 12,18:2
Fulton, Rad
Last Sunset, The 1961,Je 15,51:1
No, My Darling Daughter 1964,Mr 28,13:5
Fulvio (Screenwriter)
Streets of Sorrow 1952,N 18,37:4
Fumaroli, Judge
Casta Oiva 1937,O 5,29:2
Funai, Helen
Our Man Flint 1966,Ja 26,23:4
Funakoshi, Eiji
Golden Demon 1956,Ja 31,34:3
Fires on the Plain 1963,S 25,39:1
Funal, Helen
Funny Thing Happened on the Way to the Forum,
A 1966,O 17,48:1
Funes, Louis de
Seven Deadly Sins, The (Sloth); Sloth (The Seven
Deadly Sins) 1953,My 12,31:3
Game of Love, The 1954,D 15,41:1
Sheep Has Five Legs, The 1955,Ag 10,19:2
Inside a Girls' Dormitory 1956,F 6,27:7
Mama, Papa, the Maid and I 1956,Ag 28,31:1
Four Bags Full 1957,S 5,32:1
Virtuous Scoundrel, The 1957,O 23,37:1
Crazy in the Noodle 1957,D 15,45:4 (Incorrect in
this edition; use 1957,D 17,45:4 elsewhere)
Belle Americaine, La 1961,D 18,42:1
Crime Does Not Pay (The Man on the Avenue);
Man on the Avenue, The (Crime Does Not
Pay) 1962,O 17,35:2
Candide 1962,N 20,39:1
Devil and the 10 Commandments, The (Episode
7) 1963,O 15,44:1
Fantomas 1966,Ap 6,36:2
Sucker, The 1967,O 9,61:1
Funes, Mimi
Liliom 1935,Mr 18,14:4
Fung, Paul
Remember Pearl Harbor 1942,Je 4,22:4
Bombs Over Burma 1942,Ag 10,15:2
China Girl 1943,Ja 21,27:2
Samurai 1945,Ag 25,7:5
Lone Wolf in London, The 1947,N 22,10:3
Fung, Willie
Two-Gun Man, The 1926,Jl 13,19:3
Dangerous Paradise 1930,F 16,III,8:1
Gun Smoke 1931,Ap 24,27:1
Hatchet Man, The 1932,F 4,25:2
Red Dust 1932,N 5,12:5
Narrow Corner, The 1933,Jl 14,15:3
Lost Lady, A 1934,O 4,19:1
Sequoia 1935,F 23,14:6
Ruggles of Red Gap 1935,Mr 7,26:1
Oil for the Lamps of China 1935,Je 6,25:2
Shanghai 1935,Jl 20,16:2
One Way Ticket 1936,Ja 1,35:2
Small Town Girl 1936,Ap 11,19:1
White Hunter 1936,N 26,39:2
Stowaway 1936,D 19,16:1
We Who Are About to Die 1937,Ja 2,15:1
Secret Valley 1937,Ja 25,22:2
Wee Willie Winkie 1937,Jl 24,12:1
Wells Fargo 1937,D 30,15:2
Sinners in Paradise 1938,My 20,17:2
too Hot To Handle 1938,S 30,24:2
Honolulu 1939,F 23,19:2
Gracie Allen Murder Case, The 1939,Je 8,31:3
Six Thousand Enemies 1939,Je 9,26:2
Maisie 1939,Je 23,23:1
Hollywood Cavalcade 1939,O 14,13:2
Barricade 1939,D 9,18:2
Great Profile, The 1940,O 18,25:1
Letter, The 1940,N 23,12:6
Burma Convoy 1941,O 7,26:7
North to the Klondike 1942,Mr 12,24:3
Destination Unknown 1942,O 29,19:3
Black Swan, The 1942,D 24,18:3
Funicello, Annette
Shaggy Dog, The 1959,Mr 20,26:2
Babes in Toyland 1961,D 15,49:1

Funicello, Annette— Cont
Beach Party 1963,S 26,40:2
Misadventures of Merlin Jones, The
1964,Mr 26,40:4
Muscle Beach Party 1964,My 28,40:1
Bikini Beach 1964,S 17,52:6
Fireball 500 1966,N 24,65:4
How to Stuff a Wild Bikini 1967,Ja 12,48:1
Thunder Valley 1967,S 14,55:1
Thunder Alley 1967,S 14,55:1
Head 1968,N 7,51:1
Funk, Peter V K (Original Author)
My Six Loves 1963,Ap 4,58:4
Funkquist, Georg
Crime and Punishment 1948,Mr 1,17:2
Illicit Interlude 1954,O 27,32:6
Devil's Eye, The 1961,O 31,27:4
All These Women 1964,O 6,35:1
Furber, Douglas (Composer)
Good Companions, The 1933,O 10,24:1
Furber, Douglas (Miscellaneous)
Brewster's Millions 1935,Ap 8,23:3
Furber, Douglas (Original Author)
Thirteenth Hour, The 1927,N 28,18:5
Night and Day 1933,My 29,22:2
Furber, Douglas (Screenwriter)
When Knights Were Bold 1942,Mr 31,29:2
Furberg, Curt
Berlin Correspondent 1942,S 4,19:2
Furberg, Hans
Air Mail 1932,N 7,20:3
Furet, Yves
Sins of Paris 1954,Ja 30,9:6
Furft, Joseph
Freud 1962,D 13,37:1
Furguson, Ron (Screenwriter)
Blind Alibi 1938,My 20,17:2
Furia, Giacomo
Too Bad She's Bad 1955,D 26,23:2
Gold of Naples (Pizza on Credit); Pizza on Credit
(Gold of Naples) 1957,F 12,30:1
Variety Lights; Luci del Varieta 1965,My 7,34:1
Furia, John Jr (Original Author)
Singing Nun, The 1966,Mr 18,33:1
Furia, John Jr (Screenwriter)
Singing Nun, The 1966,Mr 18,33:1
Furia, Lina
Too Bad She's Bad 1955,D 26,23:2
Furie, Sidney J (Director)
Three on a Spree 1961,Ag 31,22:3
Ipcress File, The 1965,Ag 3,35:1
Appaloosa, The 1966,S 15,51:1
Naked Runner, The 1967,Jl 20,30:2
Furlong (Tinker)
Song of Love 1947,O 10,31:2
Furlop, Ilona (Miscellaneous)
Marie 1933,Mr 19,IX,4:2 (In Addenda)
Furnasof, N V
Rivals 1933,Ap 5,22:6
Furneaux, Yvonne
Tonight at 8:30 (Ways and Means); Ways and
Means (Tonight at 8:30) 1953,My 26,33:2
Master of Ballantrae, The 1953,Ag 6,16:2
Beggar's Opera, The 1953,Ag 25,18:2
Warriors, The 1955,S 10,11:2
Lisbon 1956,Ag 30,19:2
Mummy, The 1959,D 17,51:4
Dolce Vita, La 1961,Ap 20,30:1
Story of Monte Cristo, The 1962,N 7,48:1
Run With the Devil 1963,Jl 16,25:1
Enough Rope 1966,Jl 15,34:3
Champagne Murders, The 1968,Ap 25,53:1
Furnell, John (Original Author)
Trials of Oscar Wilde, The 1960,Je 28,26:1
Furnell, Peter
Reach for Glory 1963,S 10,46:1
Furness, Betty
Great Jasper, The 1933,F 17,5:3
Lucky Devils 1933,F 20,11:5
Emergency Call 1933,Je 24,16:2
Aggie Appleby, Maker of Men 1933,O 20,14:2
Midshipman Jack 1933,N 20,18:2
Let's Fall in Love 1934,Ja 22,12:3
Beggars in Ermine 1934,Ap 25,25:3
Life of Vergie Winters, The 1934,Je 15,26:1
Band Plays on, The 1934,D 22,21:2
Wicked Woman, A 1935,Ja 1,24:1
Shadow of Doubt 1935,Mr 11,15:1
McFadden's Flats 1935,Mr 13,16:2
Keeper of the Bees, The 1935,Ag 17,18:5
Here Comes Cookie 1935,O 12,12:2
Magnificent Obsession 1935,D 31,11:2
Three Wise Guys, The 1936,My 23,12:2
Swing Time 1936,Ag 28,21:2
President's Mystery, The 1936,O 19,22:1
Good Old Soak 1937,Ap 20,25:3
It Can't Last Forever 1937,Jl 30,22:5
Furness, George
Last Voyage, The 1960,F 20,14:2
Furse, Judith
Goodbye Mr Chips 1939,My 16,27:2
Black Narcissus 1947,Ag 14,29:2
One Night With You 1949,F 21,20:2
While the Sun Shines 1950,Jl 1,9:2

Dear Mr Prohack 1950,Jl 15,7:2
Doctor at Large 1957,Jl 29,15:5
Blue Murder at St Trinian's 1958,My 27,27:1
Scent of Mystery 1960,F 19,23:1
Furse, Roger (Miscellaneous)
Henry V 1946,Je 18,30:2
Furst, Jill
Goodbye Mr Chips 1939,My 16,27:2
Furst, Manfred
Question 7 1961,S 29,30:2
Furst, Sigge
Lesson in Love, A 1960,Mr 15,46:1
Shame 1968,D 24,14:1
Furstenberg, Ira Princess
Matchless 1967,N 11,26:3
FURTH
See Also FIRTH
Furth, George
Best Man, The 1964,Ap 7,29:1
New Interns, The 1964,Ag 20,34:2
Very Special Favor, A 1965,Ag 26,40:3
Cool Ones, The 1967,My 11,50:1
Games 1967,S 18,58:2
What's so bad About Feeling Good?
1968,My 25,27:1
Furth, Jaro
Streets of Sorrow 1927,Jl 6,23:2
Because I Loved You 1930,Ja 25,13:2
Furthman, Charles (Original Author)
Hard Rock Harrigan 1935,Jl 30,16:2
Furthman, Charles (Screenwriter)
City Gone Wild, The 1927,D 6,27:1
Thunderbolt 1929,Je 21,17:2
Furthman, Jules (Miscellaneous)
Peking Express 1951,Jl 19,20:2
Furthman, Jules (Original Author)
You'd Be Surprised 1926,S 27,27:3
Girl in 419 1933,My 20,11:5
Way of all Flesh, The 1940,Je 6,33:2
Outlaw, The 1947,S 12,18:4
Pretty Baby 1950,S 23,11:2
Furthman, Jules (Producer)
Jet Pilot 1957,O 5,8:6
Furthman, Jules (Screenwriter)
City Gone Wild, The 1927,D 6,27:1
Thunderbolt 1929,Je 21,17:2
China Seas 1935,Ag 10,16:4
Mutiny on the Bounty 1935,N 9,19:2
Come and Get It 1936,N 12,31:1
Spawn of the North 1938,S 8,27:1
Only Angels Have Wings 1939,My 12,25:2
Shanghai Gesture, The 1941,D 26,21:2
To Have and Have Not 1944,O 12,24:1
Moss Rose 1947,Jl 3,14:2
Outlaw, The 1947,S 12,18:4
Nightmare Alley 1947,O 10,31:3
Jet Pilot 1957,O 5,8:6
Rio Bravo 1959,Mr 19,40:2
Furuhata, Koji
Love at Twenty 1963,F 7,5:6
Fury, Barney
Winds of Chance 1925,Ag 17,10:3
Fury, Billy
Play it Cool 1963,Jl 18,15:3
Fury, Ed
Mighty Ursus, The 1962,Jl 26,17:1
Furze, Judith
Quiet Week-End 1948,Ag 20,13:2
Fushimi, Kazuko
Golden Demon 1956,Ja 31,34:3
Fusi, Irma
Pierpin, La Figlia Ritrovata 1936,Mr 27,25:3
Fusier-Gir, Jeanne
Couturiere de Luneville, La 1932,O 14,23:2
Crainquebille 1934,D 10,16:3
Claudine 1940,Ap 1,15:2
Fire in the Straw 1943,Jl 2,15:2
Corbeau, Le; Raven, The 1948,F 24,21:1
Miquette 1951,F 5,18:2
Simple Case of Money, A 1952,F 2,11:2
Fruits of Summer 1956,Jl 18,22:2
Witches of Salem 1958,D 9,54:2
Marie Octobre 1960,Ag 16,25:2
Fusier-Gir, Jeannie
Parole Fixer 1940,Ap 18,28:5
Pop Always Pays 1940,Ag 30,16:6
Honorable Catherine, The 1948,Ag 23,13:3
Fuss, Harry
Marika 1953,F 18,27:2
Futcher, Hugh
Rattle of a Simple Man 1964,D 21,42:2
Futrelle, Jacques (Original Author)
My Lady's Garter 1920,Mr 15,13:2
Futter, Walter (Original Author)
Dark Sands 1938,Ag 17,23:4
Futter, Walter (Producer)
India Speaks 1933,My 8,10:1
Amazing Monsieur Fabre, The 1952,S 9,21:2
Fyedotova, I
University of Life 1941,F 26,17:1
Fyffe, Will
Love in Exile 1936,D 10,35:3
Sez O'Reilly to MacNab 1938,F 19,19:4

Fyffe, Will— Cont
To the Victor 1938,Ap 13,21:2
Rulers of the Sea 1939,N 9,27:1
Prime Minister, The 1942,F 4,23:2
Brothers, The 1948,My 5,30:4
Fyodorina, Olga
Girl From Leningrad 1941,D 20,25:2
Fyodorova, Maria (Director)
Gift for Music 1957,Jl 15,15:2
Fyodorova, Maria (Producer)
Gift for Music 1957,Jl 15,15:2
Fyodorova, Victorie
Ballad of Love, A 1966,F 21,51:1
Fyodorova, Zoya
Girl From Leningrad 1941,D 20,25:2
Marriage 1945,F 22,31:3

G

Gaal, Bela (Director)
Filleres Gyoers 1933,Mr 27,13:7
As Uj Rokon; New Relative, The
1935,Mr 12,25:3
Az Uj Rokon 1935,Mr 12,25:3
Csunya Lany, A 1935,O 18,27:4
Budai Cukraszda 1936,Ja 2,21:5
Cimzett Ismeretlen 1936,F 7,14:2
Az uj Foeldesur 1936,S 22,30:5
Meseauto 1936,N 10,31:4
Aranyember 1937,My 7,29:3
Hotel Sunrise 1937,O 30,22:3
Pesti Mese; Tales of Budapest 1938,Ja 3,16:3
Maga Lesz a Ferjem; You Will Be my Husband
1938,O 12,35:3
Majd a Zsuzsi 1938,O 22,14:3
Janos Vitez; John, The Hero 1939,Ap 8,19:2
Gaal, Bella (Director)
Az Ember Neha Teved; Man Sometimes Errs
1938,Mr 28,19:3
Gaal, Erno (Producer)
Torockoi Menyasszony; Torockoi Bride
1938,Mr 5,11:2
Gaal, Franciska
Pesti Szerelem 1934,My 10,25:3
Buccaneer, The 1938,F 17,17:2
Girl Downstairs, The 1939,Ja 26,17:1
Paris Honeymoon 1939,Ja 26,17:1
Gaal, Franziska
Wie Man Maenner Fesselt 1934,My 21,20:3
Gruss und Kuss, Veronika 1936,F 24,14:2
Gaavle, Hilding
Rena Rama Sanningen; Nothing but the Truth
1939,O 7,11:2
Gabai, G (Director)
Forty-Nine Days 1964,Ja 27,19:1
Gabai, Yehuda
They Were Ten; (Heym Hayu Assara)
1961,Ap 18,44:2
Gabel, Martin
Fourteen Hours 1951,Mr 7,43:2
M 1951,Je 11,20:7
Deadline U S A 1952,Mr 15,8:2
Thief, The 1952,O 16,37:1
Tip on a Dead Jockey 1957,S 7,12:7
Marnie 1964,Je 23,19:1
Lord Love a Duck 1966,F 22,14:6
Divorce American Style 1967,Jl 20,30:2
Lady in Cement 1968,N 21,41:1
Gabel, Martin (Director)
Lost Moment, The 1947,N 22,10:2
Gabel, Martin (Narrator)
Pictura 1952,Ap 8,35:3
Gabel, Scilla
Tarzan's Greatest Adventure 1959,Jl 9,22:1
White Warrior, The 1961,F 11,27:2
Queen of the Pirates 1961,Jl 27,23:4
How to Seduce a Playboy 1968,My 16,53:2
Gabin, Jean
Paris-Beguin 1932,D 31,10:1
Adieu les Beaux Jours 1934,Ap 23,20:2
Maria Chapdelaine 1935,S 25,18:2
Lower Depths, The 1937,S 11,20:1
They Were Five 1938,Je 1,19:5
Grand Illusion 1938,S 13,28:2
Bete Humaine, La 1939,F 26,IX,5:6 (In Addenda)
Escape From Yesterday 1939,My 3,27:2
Port of Shadows 1939,O 30,13:2
Human Beast, The 1940,F 20,17:2
Daybreak 1940,Jl 30,16:2
Pepe le Moko 1941,Mr 4,20:2
Moontide 1942,Ap 30,14:1
Impostor, The 1944,Mr 27,17:2
Stormy Waters 1946,Je 17,32:2
Room Upstairs, The 1948,S 4,8:6
Walls of Malapaga, The 1950,Mr 21,34:2
Marie du Port 1951,Jl 24,21:2
Night is my Kingdom, The 1953,S 30,37:1
His Last Twelve Hours 1953,N 13,24:7
Moment of Truth, The 1954,Ap 27,36:2
Plaisir, Le (The House of Madame Tellier); House
of Madame Tellier (Le Plaisir)
1954,My 20,38:1
French-Cancan 1956,Ap 17,26:2

Gabin, Jean— Cont
Four Bags Full 1957,S 5,32:1
Deadlier Than the Male 1957,O 9,41:1
Razzi 1957,N 19,39:4
Case of Dr Laurent, The 1958,Je 26,23:2
Crime and Punishment 1958,S 16,23:2
Inspector Maigret 1958,O 9,47:1
House on the Waterfront, The 1959,F 21,25:2
Love Is my Profession 1959,Ap 28,41:1
Grisbi 1959,Jl 13,23:1
Possessors, The 1959,Jl 21,24:1
Speaking of Murder 1959,O 12,14:1
Rue de Paris 1960,D 23,14:3
Night Affair 1961,O 13,27:1
Money, Money, Money 1962,Jl 18,20:1
Monkey in Winter 1963,F 1,7:2
Any Number Can Win 1963,O 9,47:2
Upper Hand, The 1967,Jl 29,29:3

Gable, Clark
Easiest Way, The 1931,F 28,15:2
Painted Desert, The 1931,Mr 9,19:1
Dance, Fools, Dance 1931,Mr 21,15:1
Finger Points, The 1931,Mr 28,15:3
Secret Six, The 1931,My 2,23:4
Free Soul, A 1931,Je 3,29:2
Laughing Sinners 1931,Jl 4,11:5
Night Nurse 1931,Jl 17,23:4
Sporting Blood 1931,Ag 15,18:3
Susan Lenox; Her Fall and Rise 1931,O 17,20:1
Possessed 1931,N 28,20:4
Hell Divers 1931,D 23,27:3
Pente, La; Dance Fools Dance 1932,Ja 10,VIII,5:1
Polly of the Circus 1932,Mr 19,11:2
Strange Interlude 1932,S 1,24:3
Red Dust 1932,N 5,12:5
No Man of her Own 1932,D 31,10:1
White Sister, The 1933,Mr 18,9:3
Hold Your Man 1933,Jl 1,16:6
Night Flight 1933,O 7,18:4
Dancing Lady 1933,D 1,23:2
It Happened One Night 1934,F 23,23:2
Manhattan Melodrama 1934,My 5,22:2
Men in White 1934,Je 9,18:2
Chained 1934,S 1,16:2
Forsaking all Others 1934,D 21,18:1
After Office Hours 1935,Mr 9,19:1
China Seas 1935,Ag 10,16:4
Call of the Wild 1935,Ag 15,15:2
Mutiny on the Bounty 1935,N 9,19:2
Wife vs Secretary 1936,F 29,11:1
San Francisco 1936,Je 27,21:1
Cain and Mabel 1936,O 19,22:1
Love on the Run 1936,N 28,13:3
Parnell 1937,Je 4,27:2
Saratoga 1937,Jl 23,16:3
Test Pilot 1938,Ap 16,17:1
too Hot To Handle 1938,S 30,24:2
Idiot's Delight 1939,F 3,13:1
Gone With the Wind 1939,D 20,31:2
Strange Cargo 1940,Ap 26,25:2
Boom Town 1940,S 6,25:2
Comrade X 1940,D 26,23:1
They Met in Bombay 1941,Jl 4,17:1
Honky Tonk 1941,O 3,27:3
Somewhere I'll Find You 1942,Ag 28,22:4
Adventure 1946,F 8,23:2
Hucksters, The 1947,Jl 18,21:2
Homecoming 1948,Ap 30,28:4
Command Decision 1949,Ja 20,34:2
Any Number Can Play 1949,Jl 1,14:4
Key to the City 1950,F 2,31:2
To Please a Lady 1950,O 27,24:3
Across the Wide Missouri 1951,N 7,35:4
Lone Star 1952,F 2,11:4
Never Let Me Go 1953,Je 11,37:2
Mogambo 1953,O 2,18:1
Betrayed 1954,S 9,36:1
Soldier of Fortune 1955,My 28,7:4
Tall Men, The 1955,O 12,36:2
King and Four Queens, The 1956,D 22,13:7
Band of Angels 1957,Jl 11,21:1
Teacher's Pet 1958,Mr 20,33:1
Run Silent, Run Deep 1958,Mr 28,29:1
But Not for Me 1959,O 3,14:6
It Started in Naples 1960,S 3,7:6
Misfits, The 1961,F 2,24:2
Gone With the Wind 1967,O 11,41:1
Gable, Clark (Narrator)
Wing Up 1943,My 28,19:1
Gable, Toni
French Without Tears 1940,Ap 29,12:2
Gabor, Eva
Pacific Blackout 1942,Ja 15,25:2
Royal Scandal, A 1945,Ap 12,19:2
Wife of Monte Cristo, The 1946,Ap 8,31:2
Mad Magician, The 1954,My 20,38:2
Last Time I saw Paris, The 1954,N 19,20:2
Artists and Models 1955,D 22,20:1
My Man Godfrey 1957,O 12,23:1
Don't Go Near the Water 1957,N 15,37:1
Gigi 1958,My 16,21:1
Truth About Women, The 1958,Ag 29,18:2
It Started With a Kiss 1959,Ag 20,14:2

New Kind of Love, A 1963,O 31,26:2
Youngblood Hawke 1964,N 6,30:1
Gabor, Miklos
It Happened in Europe 1949,O 4,32:4
Age of Illusions 1967,Mr 30,55:1
Father 1967,S 29,53:1
Gabor, Zsa Zsa
Lovely to Look At 1952,My 30,11:2
We're not Married 1952,Jl 12,16:2
Moulin Rouge 1953,F 11,33:5
Story of Three Loves, The (Mademoiselle);
  Mademoiselle (The Story of Three Loves)
  1953,Mr 6,29:2
Lili 1953,Mr 11,36:7
Three Ring Circus 1954,D 25,7:2
Death of a Scoundrel 1956,N 6,30:1
Girl in the Kremlin, The 1957,My 22,29:2
For the First Time 1959,Ag 15,8:7
Pepe 1960,D 22,18:1
Boys' Night Out 1962,Je 22,15:2
Arrivederci, Baby! 1966,D 29,22:1
Gaboriau, Emile (Original Author)
File No 113 1932,F 20,11:2
Gabourie, Fred
Shack out on 101 1956,Ja 10,26:2
Gabriel
Ways of Love (A Day in the Country); Day in the
  Country, A (Ways of Love) 1950,D 13,50:2
Gabriel, Gilbert (Original Author)
This Woman Is Mine 1941,O 13,21:2
Gabriel, Gilbert (Screenwriter)
Hotel Imperial 1939,My 11,31:3
Magnificent Fraud, The 1939,Jl 20,16:2
Gabriel, John
Hunters, The 1958,Ag 27,33:1
Story of Ruth, The 1960,Je 18,12:3
Stagecoach 1966,Je 16,53:1
Gabriello
Lower Depths, The 1937,S 11,20:1
Simple Case of Money, A 1952,F 2,11:2
Gabrielson, Frank (Screenwriter)
Something for the Boys 1944,N 30,19:1
Don Juan Quilligan 1945,Jl 30,16:2
It Shouldn't Happen to a Dog 1946,S 7,11:2
Gabrilovich, E (Screenwriter)
Last Night, The 1937,Ap 28,18:3
Two Soldiers 1944,Jl 27,14:2
Girl No 217 1945,S 3,17:2
In the Name of Life 1947,O 20,29:2
Vasili's Return 1953,S 28,21:4
Gadfly, The 1956,S 17,22:2
Resurrection 1963,O 7,35:2
Gabrio, Gabriel
Miserables, Les 1926,Jl 9,17:1
Miserables, Les 1927,Ag 23,29:4
Frochard et les Deux Orphelines, La
  1934,F 7,16:2
Razumov 1937,Mr 9,27:2
Lucrezia Borgia 1937,O 13,27:2
Harvest 1939,O 3,19:4
Pepe le Moko 1941,Mr 4,20:2
Devil's Own Envoy, The 1947,Ag 30,8:6
Gaby, Frank
Mr Dynamite 1941,Mr 13,25:2
Gacel, Lili
Casa del Angel, La 1960,Ag 30,25:1
Gadd, Renee
Aren't We All? 1932,Jl 1,19:3
White Face 1933,D 4,22:3
Love Captive, The 1934,Je 8,18:1
Crimson Circle, The 1936,D 28,12:3
They Came to a City 1945,F 19,21:3
Frieda 1947,Ag 15,12:3
Gaddis, Thomas E (Original Author)
Birdman of Alcatraz 1962,Jl 19,19:2
Gade, Sven (Director)
Hamlet 1921,N 9,20:3 (In Addenda)
Gade, Svend (Director)
Fifth Avenue Models 1925,My 4,16:2
Siege 1925,Je 16,24:1
Into her Kingdom 1926,Ag 10,19:2
Blonde Saint, The 1926,N 23,27:1
Gades, Antonio
Tarantos, Los 1964,Je 30,22:1
Pleasure Seekers, The 1964,D 26,9:1
Gadson, Jacqueline
Goldfish, The 1924,My 20,15:2
His Hour 1924,O 7,26:1
Wife of the Centaur, The 1925,Ja 7,33:5
Man and Maid 1925,Ap 7,17:3
Not so Long Ago 1925,Jl 28,24:4
Merry Widow, The 1925,Ag 27,14:1
Regular Fellow, A 1925,O 5,25:2
Thirteenth Hour, The 1927,N 28,18:5
Red Hair 1928,Mr 26,26:2
Scarlet Lady, The 1928,Ag 15,19:4
Gael, Anna
Benjamin 1968,Mr 26,41:2
Therese and Isabelle 1968,My 15,41:4
Gael, Bela (Director)
Erik/a/Buzakalasz; Wheat Ripens, The
  1939,S 11,15:2

Gael, Josseline
Miserables, Les 1936,O 28,31:2
Champs-Elysees 1939,F 28,17:2
Man and his Wife, A 1939,Mr 28,20:1
Miserables, Les 1946,D 26,28:4
Carnival of Sinners 1947,Ap 8,34:2
Gaela, Genevieve
Carabiniers, Les 1968,Ap 26,31:1
Gaffney, Arch (Original Author)
No Marriage Ties 1933,Ag 4,18:2
Gaffney, Edward
Greed 1924,D 5,28:1
Gaffney, Liam
Irish and Proud of It 1938,O 31,12:3
Macushla 1940,Ja 6,9:2
Captain Boycott 1947,D 6,11:2
Curtain Up 1953,F 2,17:3
Gaffney, Marjorie (Miscellaneous)
Head Over Heels in Love 1937,F 13,9:1
Gaffney, Marjorie (Original Author)
First a Girl 1936,Ja 4,19:1
Gaffney, Marjorie (Screenwriter)
First a Girl 1936,Ja 4,19:1
Gaffney, Robert (Producer)
Troublemaker, The 1964,Je 23,25:1
Gafliff, Frank
Ipcress File, The 1965,Ag 3,35:1
Gage, Erford
Seven Miles From Alcatraz 1942,N 19,31:3
Hitler's Children 1943,F 25,27:1
Falcon Strikes Back, The 1943,Ap 2,17:4
Mr Lucky 1943,Jl 23,21:2
Falcon in Danger, The 1943,Jl 23,21:2
Seventh Victim, The 1943,S 18,11:3
Days of Glory 1944,Je 17,10:2
Gage, John (Director)
Velvet Touch, The 1948,Ag 26,16:2
Gage, Leona
Tales of Terror 1962,Jl 5,21:2 (In Addenda)
Gage, Walter (Screenwriter)
Bus Riley's Back in Town 1965,Ap 8,45:2
Gagin, Jean
Magnificent Tramp, The 1962,Ap 25,30:1
Gagnon, J Lee
Thirteenth Letter, The 1951,F 22,27:2
Gagnon, Rene A
Sands of Iwo Jima 1949,D 31,9:2
Gahagan, Helen
She 1935,Jl 26,18:2
Gahndo, Nacho
Hitch-Hiker, The 1953,Ap 30,39:3
Gai, G
Garnet Bracelet, The 1966,My 28,11:6
Gaidar, Arkady (Original Author)
Chuk and Gek 1953,D 21,27:4
School of Courage 1957,S 9,21:2
Gaidarov, V
Victors and the Vanquished, The 1950,My 1,18:2
Gaidarov, Vladimir
Manon Lescaut 1926,N 30,27:1
Michael Strogoff 1926,D 6,28:3
Russia-1908 1929,Ja 7,36:2
Scandal In Paris, A 1929,Je 10,23:1
Rasputin 1929,O 21,30:1
Luise, Koenigin von Preussen 1932,O 5,26:6
First Front, The 1949,N 14,19:2
Gaige, Russell
Forever Female 1954,Ja 13,26:2
Gail, Albert (Screenwriter)
Five Weeks in a Balloon 1962,Ag 27,18:1
Gail, Zoe
No Orchids for Miss Blandish 1951,F 23,33:2
Gaillaudet, John
Wagons Westward 1940,Jl 8,13:2
Gaillard, Roger
Strange Ones, The 1952,Jl 29,17:3
Gaillard, Slim
Go, Man, Go 1954,Mr 10,29:5
Gailmor, William S (Miscellaneous)
Day After Day 1943,N 6,16:3
Gailmor, William S (Narrator)
Great Betrayal, The 1947,Je 6,27:2
Gaines, Ernestine
Aloma of the South Seas 1926,My 17,19:1
Gaines, Harris
Betrayal, The 1948,Je 26,10:5
Gaines, Richard
Howards of Virginia, The 1940,S 27,27:1
Night to Remember, A 1943,Ja 1,27:2
More the Merrier, The 1943,My 14,17:1
Mr Winkle Goes to War 1944,Ag 3,16:1
Double Indemnity 1944,S 7,21:1
Enchanted Cottage, The 1945,Ap 28,19:2
Twice Blessed 1945,Jl 7,7:5
Don Juan Quilligan 1945,Jl 30,16:2
So Goes my Love 1946,My 2,3:7
Do You Love Me 1946,My 25,12:2
Nobody Lives Forever 1946,N 2,12:2
White Tie and Tails 1946,N 8,28:2
Humoresque 1946,D 26,28:1
Brute Force 1947,Jl 17,16:2
Hucksters, The 1947,Jl 18,21:2
Ride the Pink Horse 1947,O 9,32:3

Gaines, Richard — Cont
Unconquered 1947,O 11,11:2
Invisible Wall, The 1947,N 1,11:2
Cass Timberlane 1947,N 7,20:2
That Wonderful Urge 1948,D 22,29:6
Lucky Stiff, The 1949,Ja 31,14:2
Strange Bargain 1949,S 30,28:3
Drum Beat 1954,N 18,42:1
Love Me or Leave Me 1955,My 27,14:1
Ransom 1956,Ja 25,28:3
Francis in the Haunted House 1956,Jl 21,9:2
Five Steps to Danger 1957,Ja 31,21:1
Gaines, Robert (Original Author)
Front Page Story 1955,Ap 19,28:1
Gaines, William
Brown of Harvard 1926,My 3,27:1
Gainey, Michael
Blue Denim 1959,Jl 31,21:1
Gainotti, Enzo
Serpente a Sonagli, Il 1936,Ag 17,9:2
Gainsbourg, Serge
Come Dance With Me!; Voulez-Vous Danser Avec
    Moi 1960,N 8,32:6
Marriage Came Tumbling Down, The
    1968,N 6,32:3
Gaioni, Cristina
Mighty Ursus, The 1962,Jl 26,17:1
Love at Twenty 1963,F 7,5:6
Run With the Devil 1963,Jl 16,25:1
Steppe, The 1963,O 1,33:1
Successo, Il 1965,Ap 29,40:2
Facts of Murder, The 1965,Jl 1,34:1
Lady Killer From Rome, The 1966,Je 9,54:3
Gaisseau, Pierre (Cinematographer)
Gri-Gri 1956,S 29,12:2
Gaisseau, Pierre Dominique (Director)
Flame and the Fire 1966,Mr 29,37:1
Round Trip 1967,Jl 20,30:2
Gaisseau, Pierre-Dominique (Director)
Sky Above, The-Mud Below, The 1962,Je 20,40:1
Gaisseau, Pierre-Dominique (Screenwriter)
Sky Above, The-Mud Below, The 1962,Je 20,40:1
Gaither, David (Director)
Forest Ring, The 1930,Ap 26,11:1
Gaither, Gant (Producer)
My Six Loves 1963,Ap 4,58:4
Gal, Ernest (Producer)
Borcsa Amerikaben; Barbara in America
    1939,F 11,13:2
Janos Vitez; John, The Hero 1939,Ap 8,19:2
Galabru, Michel
War of the Buttons, The 1963,D 19,40:2
My Wife's Husband 1965,Ja 27,26:1
Galan, Alberto
Maria Candelaria 1944,S 12,23:7
Galan, Aurelia
Tarantos, Los 1964,Je 30,22:1
Galang, Fred
Walls of Hell, The 1965,N 18,55:3
Beach Red 1967,Ag 4,18:1
Galanos, Alecos (Original Author)
Red Lanterns 1965,Ap 1,30:1
Galanos, Alecos (Screenwriter)
Red Lanterns 1965,Ap 1,30:1
Galas, Lucien
Grandeur et Decadence 1937,My 31,11:3
Galassi, Angelo
Jessica 1962,Ap 20,20:2
Galdeburov, P
Admiral Nakhimov 1948,N 25,47:4
Galdieri, Michele (Original Author)
Escape into Dreams 1950,Ap 13,34:5
Galdieri, Michele (Screenwriter)
Escape into Dreams 1950,Ap 13,34:5
Galdini, Marcello
Gospel According to St Matthew, The
    1966,F 18,23:1
Galdos, Benito Perez (Original Author)
Nazarin 1968,Je 21,48:1
Gale, Diedre
Little Princess, The 1939,Mr 11,21:1
Mozart 1940,O 4,29:2
Gale, Edra
Eight and One Half 1963,Je 26,36:1
What's New Pussycat? 1965,Je 23,49:1
Gale, Gladys
Smart Woman 1931,O 12,28:2
Gale, Joan
Blind Date 1934,S 1,16:3
Nut Farm, The 1935,Ap 8,23:3
Gale, June
Time Out for Murder 1938,O 7,21:2
While New York Sleeps 1938,D 22,25:3
It Could Happen to You 1939,Je 9,26:3
Hotel for Women 1939,Ag 26,20:2
Charlie Chan at Treasure Island 1939,S 1,15:5
Escape, The 1939,N 3,17:4
Honeymoon's Over, The 1939,D 15,33:3
City of Chance 1940,Ja 22,11:3
Gale, Norah
Give Me a Sailor 1938,Ag 11,31:1
Gale, Richard
Miniver Story, The 1950,O 27,24:2

Gale, Roberta
Bachelor Apartment 1931,My 16,13:3
Are These our Children 1931,N 14,15:3
Girl of the Rio 1932,Ja 9,21:1
Police Call 1933,Ag 22,20:3
Gale, Shirley
Uncle Vanya 1958,Ap 29,26:2
Gale, Sondra
Glory Stompers, The 1968,Mr 28,52:4
Gale, Zona (Original Author)
Miss Lulu Bett 1921,D 25,VI,2:1
Galea, Bud
Enter Madame 1935,Ja 12,12:1
Galea, Genevieve
Carabiniers, Les 1967,S 28,58:3
Galeati, Giuseppe
Last Chance, The 1945,N 28,21:6
Galeen, Henrik (Director)
Alraune 1928,My 20,VIII,8:4
Man Who Cheated Life, The 1929,F 11,26:3
After the Verdict 1930,Ja 18,21:1
Salon Dora Green 1937,Jl 26,15:3
Galentine, Wheaton (Director)
To the Fair 1965,F 13,10:2
Galento, Tony
On the Waterfront 1954,Jl 29,18:1
Best Things in Life are Free, The 1956,S 29,12:2
Wind Across the Everglades 1958,S 12,21:1
Galey, Louis Emile (Producer)
24 Hours in a Woman's Life 1968,S 25,39:1
Galich, A (Screenwriter)
True Friends 1954,N 15,33:2
House on the Front Line, The 1963,S 2,18:1
Galindo, Alejandro (Director)
Rebel Souls 1937,N 13,11:2
Muerto Murio, El; Dead Man Died, The
    1939,Jl 29,18:3
Corazon de Nino; Heart of a Child
    1940,Ja 1,29:4
Mientras Mexico Duerme; While Mexico Sleeps
    1940,F 12,14:3
Galindo, Nacho
South of St Louis 1949,Mr 7,17:2
Borderline 1950,Mr 6,17:2
Surrender 1950,O 9,21:5
Lightning Strikes Twice 1951,Ap 13,18:7
Lone Star 1952,F 2,11:4
Green Fire 1954,D 25,7:1
Wetbacks 1956,My 5,13:2
Galindo, Pedro (Composer)
Silk, Blood and Sun 1943,Ja 30,10:6
Galio, Maria Rosa
Hand in the Trap 1963,Jl 2,16:2
Gall, E
Cain and Artem 1930,Je 7,10:4
Masquerade 1943,My 17,11:2
Gall, Raymond
Club De Femmes 1937,O 20,27:2
Gall, Robert
Sez O'Reilly to MacNab 1938,F 19,19:4
Gallabher, Jack
Sand 1949,Ag 5,23:2
GALLAGHER
See Also GALLAHER
Gallagher, Carole
Falcon out West, The 1944,Mr 18,18:2
Gallagher, Desmond
Doctor Rhythm 1938,My 19,25:2
Gallagher, Donald
Johnny Holiday 1950,My 17,36:1
Gallagher, Edward (Composer)
Ziegfeld Girl 1941,Ap 25,17:2
Gallagher, Helen
Strangers When we Meet 1960,Je 30,22:2
Gallagher, Johnny
Great White Way, The 1924,Ja 4,10:1
Gallagher, Raymond
Argyle Case, The 1929,Ag 31,13:4
Gallagher, Richard (Skeets)
Potters, The 1927,Ja 18,23:1
New York 1927,Ja 31,13:1
For the Love of Mike 1927,Ag 24,27:5
Alex The Great 1928,My 1,33:3
Racket, The 1928,Jl 9,25:1
Stocks and Blondes 1928,O 23,33:1
Close Harmony 1929,Ap 29,29:2
Fast Company 1929,O 5,22:5
Pointed Heels 1929,D 28,11:1
Honey 1930,Mr 29,23:1
Social Lion, The 1930,Je 14,9:4
Love Among the Millionaires 1930,Jl 5,17:4
Let's Go Native 1930,Ag 30,7:4
Her Wedding Night 1930,S 29,19:1
Pays to Advertise, It 1931,F 21,15:2
Up Pops the Devil 1931,My 16,13:3
Road to Reno, The 1931,O 10,20:4
Possessed 1931,N 28,20:4
Trial of Vivienne Ware, The 1932,Ap 30,19:3
Merrily We Go to Hell 1932,Je 11,9:3
Night Club Lady, The 1932,Ag 27,13:4
Bird of Paradise 1932,S 10,18:5
Phantom of Crestwood, The 1932,O 17,18:3
Conquerors, The 1932,N 21,21:1

Gallagher, Richard (Skeets) — Cont
Sport Parade, The 1932,D 17,22:3
Past of Mary Holmes, The 1933,My 1,10:3
Too Much Harmony 1933,S 23,11:5
Alice in Wonderland 1933,D 23,19:1
Riptide 1934,Mr 31,8:2
Perfect Clue, The 1935,Mr 14,18:1
Yours for the Asking 1936,Ag 20,14:2
Man I Marry, The 1936,O 31,24:3
Polo Joe 1936,N 5,35:1
Espionage 1937,Mr 9,27:3
Idiot's Delight 1939,F 3,13:1
Gallagher, Thomas
Babes in Bagdad 1954,Ap 5,21:3
I Like Money 1962,My 19,18:2
Gallagher and Shean
Atlantic City 1944,Ag 14,11:4
GALLAHER
See Also GALLAGHER
Gallaher, Donald
Eye for Eye 1918,D 23,9:1
Thru Different Eyes 1929,Ap 15,22:6
Collegiate 1936,Ja 23,25:2
Magnificent Fraud, The 1939,Jl 20,16:2
Gallaher, Donald (Director)
Nix on Dames 1929,N 23,18:5
Temple Tower 1930,My 10,25:3
Gallaher, Donald (Original Author)
Sh! The Octopus 1937,D 24,21:2
Galland, Jean
Fantomas 1934,Mr 13,27:4
Serment, Le 1934,Mr 14,23:2
Cessez le Feu; Cease Firing 1934,Ag 12,IX,2:1
Scandale, Le 1934,Ag 12,IX,2:1
Second Bureau 1936,F 17,21:2
Barbier de Seville, Le 1936,S 23,29:2
Entente Cordiale 1939,D 26,23:2
Whirlpool; (Remous) 1940,O 8,31:2
Marthe Richard 1944,N 9,23:2
Savage Brigade 1948,D 3,33:4
Edward and Caroline 1952,Ap 30,33:3
Plaisir, Le (The Mask); Mask, The (Le Plaisir)
    1954,My 20,38:1
What Price Murder 1958,N 11,26:1
Marianne of my Youth; (Marianne de ma
    Jeunesse) 1959,Ja 20,43:1
Gallandet, John
Who Killed Gail Preston? 1938,My 6,27:2
Second Woman, The 1951,F 2,19:2
Gallant, Kathleen
Bravados, The 1958,Je 26,23:2
Gallardo, Antonio
Desperate Moment 1953,S 1,19:4
Gallardo, L Lucas J (Screenwriter)
Teacher and the Miracle, The 1961,Ap 24,36:4
Gallardo, Lucy
Exterminating Angel, The 1967,Ag 22,33:1
Gallardo, Lupita
Tigre de Yautepec, El 1934,O 20,20:3
Cruz Diablo 1935,Ap 6,10:1
Cielito Lindo 1936,N 9,22:5
Cancion del Milagro, La; Miracle Song, The
    1940,My 11,15:2
Gallardo, Roberto (Producer)
Herencia Macabra; Macabre Legacy, A
    1940,My 4,13:2
Gallaudet, Frank
Julie 1956,N 22,51:1
Gallaudet, John
Counterfeit 1936,Jl 20,11:1
Final Hour, The 1936,Ag 1,16:3
Shakedown 1936,Ag 17,9:2
Adventure in Manhattan 1936,O 23,27:5
Come Closer, Folks 1936,N 23,17:3
Pennies From Heaven 1936,D 10,35:2
Devil's Playground 1937,F 15,12:5
Racketeers in Exile 1937,Ag 12,15:3
I Promise to Pay 1937,Ap 26,15:2
Double or Nothing 1937,S 2,17:3
Criminals of the Air 1937,O 28,29:2
Devil's Party, The 1938,My 31,8:3
Main Event, The 1938,Je 20,11:3
Federal Man-Hunt 1939,F 2,17:3
Wings of the Navy 1939,F 4,11:1
Twelve Crowded Hours 1939,F 24,15:2
Street of Missing Men 1939,Je 1,31:3
They all Come Out 1939,Ag 3,15:4
One Hour to Live 1939,N 4,11:3
Fugitive From Justice, A 1940,Jl 8,13:3
No Greater Sin 1941,Ag 29,18:2
Flight Lieutenant 1942,Jl 31,11:1
Shady Lady 1945,O 11,26:2
So Goes my Love 1946,My 2,3:7
Beginning or the End, The 1947,F 21,15:1
April Showers 1948,Mr 27,10:2
Task Force 1949,O 1,8:6
Quicksand 1950,Je 16,28:4
Right Cross 1950,N 16,39:2
Angels in the Outfield 1951,O 18,32:1
Confidence Girl 1952,Je 21,12:2
Everything I Have is Yours 1952,O 30,40:5
Kid From Left Field, The 1953,S 26,15:3

Gallaudet, John — Cont
Decks Ran Red, The 1958,O 11,18:2
In Cold Blood 1967,D 15,60:1
Gallaway, Cheryl
Night of the Hunter, The 1955,S 30,23:1
Gallcia, Joseph
Iron Mistress, The 1952,N 20,39:2
Galle, Raymond
Lie of Nina Petrovna, The 1938,Mr 30,19:2
Glory of Faith, The 1938,N 24,37:2
Champs-Elysees 1939,F 28,17:2
Passionnelle 1948,Mr 1,17:2
Gallery, Tom
Eternal Three, The 1923,O 12,7:2 (Incorrect in this edition; use 1927,O 1,7:2 elsewhere)
Limited Mail, The 1925,S 1,18:2
Gallet, Gustave
Francois Villon 1950,Jl 3,9:2
Galletti, Giovanna
Open City; Citta Aperta 1946,F 26,21:2
Bible, The 1966,S 29,60:1
Galley, Georges
Secret Document-Vienna 1954,Mr 29,22:4
Galli, Augusto
Sei tu l'Amore 1930,N 18,28:4
Galli, Dina
Frenesia; Frenzy 1940,Je 6,33:4
My Widow and I 1950,Ag 30,27:5
Galli, Eola
Carnegie Hall 1947,My 3,10:2
Galli, Ida
Leopard, The 1963,Ag 13,25:1
Galli, Leonid
Train Goes East, The 1949,S 5,13:3
Galli, Rosina
Blockade 1938,Je 17,25:1
Fisherman's Wharf 1939,F 24,15:2
Housekeeper's Daughter, The 1939,D 2,21:4
You Can't Fool Your Wife 1940,My 24,23:4
You're not so Tough 1940,Jl 9,25:3
This Thing Called Love 1941,F 14,15:2
They Met in Bombay 1941,Jl 4,17:1
Mad Doctor of Market Street, The 1942,Ja 5,21:5
Where Do We Go From Here? 1945,Je 7,25:2
Gallian, Ketti
Marie Galante 1934,N 21,23:4
Under the Pampas Moon 1935,My 31,11:1
Espionage 1937,Mr 9,27:3
Shall We Dance 1937,My 14,21:1
Gallico, Bob
Secret Door, The 1964,Je 4,28:1
Gallico, Paul (Original Author)
Wedding Present 1936,N 19,31:3
No Time to Marry 1938,F 23,27:2
Joe Smith, American 1942,Ap 2,27:4
Pride of the Yankees, The 1942,Jl 16,23:1
Clock, The 1945,My 4,23:2
Never Take No for an Answer 1952,Ap 29,32:2
Assignment-Paris 1952,O 25,12:6
Lili 1953,Mr 11,36:7
Merry Andrews 1958,Mr 21,17:1
Next to no Time 1960,My 28,13:2
Three Lives of Thomasina, The 1963,D 12,46:1
Gallico, Paul (Screenwriter)
Wedding Present 1936,N 19,31:3
Never Take No for an Answer 1952,Ap 29,32:2
Gallico, Pauline (Original Author)
Clock, The 1945,My 4,23:2
Assignment-Paris 1952,O 25,12:6
Gallico, Pauline (Screenwriter)
Never Take No for an Answer 1952,Ap 29,32:2
Gallina, Mario
Marco Visconti 1947,S 20,12:4
Island of Procida, The 1952,Mr 15,8:2
Gallina, Pina
Contessa di Parma, La 1938,F 24,23:2
Four Steps in the Clouds 1948,N 22,25:2
Gallis, L
Problem Child 1955,Ja 24,20:5
Devotion 1955,Ag 1,15:2
Gift for Music 1957,Jl 15,15:2
Gallo, Jacques
Little Boy Lost 1953,S 22,38:2
Gallo, Julio
Romance del Palmar, El 1939,My 1,21:2
Gallo, Lew
Pork Chop Hill 1959,My 30,9:2
Odds Against Tomorrow 1959,O 16,27:1
PT 109 1963,Je 27,23:1
Soldier in the Rain 1963,N 29,67:6 (Incorrect in this edition; use 1963,N 28,67:6 elsewhere)
Gallo, Maresa
Lupa, La 1954,F 18,36:2
Gallo, Nunzio
Tarantella Napoletana 1954,Ap 19,19:3
Gallone, Carmine (Director)
Pawns of Passion 1929,My 27,22:1
Bride 68 1930,Ap 15,28:5
Soir de Rafle, Un 1931,O 16,27:1
Die Singende Stadt 1932,My 10,25:4
Farewell to Love 1933,N 25,10:2
My Heart Is Calling 1935,Ap 15,16:3
Wenn die Musik Nicht Waer 1937,Ap 3,17:2
Thank You, Madame 1937,Ap 27,18:2

Casta Oiva 1937,O 5,29:2
Stimme des Blutes; Blood Bond 1937;D 28,29:2
Dingehort mein Herz; My Heart Belongs to Thee 1939,Mr 25,19:2
Scipio Africanus 1939,S 23,22:2
Das Erlebnis Geht Weiter; Another Experience 1940,F 3,9:3
Dream of Butterfly, The 1941,F 13,25:2
Manon Lescaut 1941,Ap 14,23:5
Before Him all Rome Trembled 1947,F 22,16:2
Eternal Melodies 1948,F 14,17:3
Lost One, The; La Traviata 1948,Mr 30,26:2
Trovatore, Il 1950,F 9,36:7
Faust and the Devil 1950,My 1,18:2
Her Wonderful Lie 1950,Jl 17,15:2
Two Orphans, The 1950,O 19,40:6
Forza del Destino, La 1952,O 17,33:1
Singing Taxi Driver 1953,My 16,10:1
House of Ricordi 1956,Mr 13,32:1
Madame Butterfly 1956,Ap 24,26:2
Tosca 1958,O 24,40:3
Michael Strogoff 1960,My 21,15:1
Carthage in Flames 1961,Ja 26,32:3
Gallone, Carmine (Producer)
Trovatore, Il 1950,F 9,36:7
Forza del Destino, La 1952,O 17,33:1
Gallone, Carmine (Screenwriter)
Pawns of Passion 1929,My 27,22:1
Before Him all Rome Trembled 1947,F 22,16:2
Eternal Melodies 1948,F 14,17:3
Trovatore, Il 1950,F 9,36:7
Madame Butterfly 1956,Ap 24,26:2
Gallone, Garmine (Director)
Only for Thee; Solo per To 1938,S 12,13:2
Gallone, Riccardo
Hell Raiders of the Deep 1954,Jl 3,9:2
Galloway, Don
Rare Breed, The 1966,Ap 14,42:3
Rough Night in Jericho 1967,N 9,56:4
Galloway, Morgan
Ladies of the Jury 1932,Ap 2,13:2
Lena Rivers 1932,My 21,9:2
Galludet, John
Lonelyhearts 1959,Mr 5,35:3
Galperson, Alexander (Producer)
Mr Perrin and Mr Traill 1949,Ja 17,15:2
Galsworthy, John (Original Author)
Stranger, The 1924,F 5,20:1
Escape 1930,N 1,23:2
Skin Game, The 1931,Je 20,20:4
One More River 1934,Ag 10,21:1
Loyalties 1934,O 26,25:1
21 Days Together 1940,My 23,28:4
Escape 1948,Ag 16,12:2
That Forsyte Woman 1949,N 11,31:2
Galter, Irene
Sins of Casanova 1957,O 7,23:2
Liane, Jungle Goddess 1959,F 23,19:1
Galton, Ray (Original Author)
Call Me Genius 1961,O 17,47:1
Spy With a Cold Nose, The 1966,D 20,58:2
Galton, Ray (Screenwriter)
Call Me Genius 1961,O 17,47:1
Spy With a Cold Nose, The 1966,D 20,58:2
Galvani, Ciro
Scipio Africanus 1939,S 23,22:2
Galvani, Dino
Missing Rembrandt, The 1932,Mr 26,17:2
In a Monastery Garden 1935,Mr 13,16:2
Princess Charming 1935,Je 22,18:5
Sleeping Car to Trieste 1949,Ap 18,18:6
Three Steps North 1951,Je 29,14:2
Always a Bride 1954,My 28,19:2
Galvert, E H
Wizard, The 1927,N 28,18:5
Galvez, Jose
Macario 1961,S 28,48:6
Galzer, Benjamin (Producer)
Love in Bloom 1935,Ap 20,16:2
Gam, Rita
Thief, The 1952,O 16,37:1
Night People 1954,Mr 13,11:2
Saadia 1954,Mr 20,10:5
Sign of the Pagan 1955,F 14,24:2
Hannibal 1960,Ag 4,17:1
King of Kings 1961,O 12,41:2
No Exit 1962,D 6,55:2
Gamal, Samia
Little Miss Devil 1951,D 8,9:2
Valley of the Kings 1954,Jl 22,15:2
Gaman, Tom
Lord of the Flies 1963,Ag 20,37:1
Gamar, Maria E
Riachuelo 1934,D 8,18:5
Gamba, Pierino
Great Dawn, The 1947,Ag 28,28:3
Gambarelli, Maria
Here's to Romance 1935,O 3,29:2
Dottor Antonio, Il 1939,D 7,35:1
Gambarelli, Mlle (Miscellaneous)
High Sign, The 1922,Mr 20,10:3

Gambashidze, S
They Wanted Peace 1940,Ja 8,11:3
Keto and Kote 1954,Ap 5,21:4
Dragonfly, The 1955,Je 27,18:2
Gambier, Claude
Search, The 1948,Mr 24,30:3
Gambino, Charles
Lonely Night, The 1954,Mr 29,22:2
Gambino, Domenico
Tatras Zauber 1933,F 18,13:4
His Young Wife 1949,Mr 12,10:2
Gambino, Domenico (Director)
Lotte nell Ombra; Battles in the Shadow 1939,Mr 21,27:3
Gambino, Gloria
Lonely Night, The 1954,Mr 29,22:2
Gambino, Lillian
Lonely Night, The 1954,Mr 29,22:2
Gamble, Fred
Tornado, The 1924;D 15,14:1
Tumbleweeds 1925,D 21,27:2
Gamble, Jerry
13 Washington Square 1928,Ja 30,18:1
Gamble, Warburton
Silver King, The 1919,Ja 13,9:3
Society Exile, A 1919,Ag 18,9:2
Paliser Case, The 1920,F 16,8:1
Tonight or Never 1931,D 18,29:2
As You Desire Me 1932,Je 3,23:4
Fast Life 1932,D 24,11:4
Tonight Is Ours 1933,Ja 21,10:6
Child of Manhattan 1933,F 13,11:4
Study in Scarlet, A 1933,Je 1,15:3
By Candlelight 1934,Ja 6,18:2
Gamboa, Federico
Suprema Ley; Supreme Law 1938,Ja 15,19:2
Gamboa, Federico (Original Author)
Liaga, La; Torment, The 1937,O 4,17:2
Gambold, Fred
Black Oxen 1924,Ja 7,23:1
Red Mill, The 1927,F 14,15:1
Gamet, Kenneth (Original Author)
Flying Tigers 1942,O 23,25:2
Thunderbirds 1953,Mr 12,24:4
Gamet, Kenneth (Screenwriter)
Smart Blonde 1937,Ja 9,21:1
Midnight Court 1937,Mr 4,27:3
Fly Away Baby 1937,Jl 9,18:2
Missing Witness 1937,D 10,33:3
Broadway Musketeers 1938,O 14,27:1
You Can't Get Away With Murder 1939,Mr 25,19:2
Tear Gas Squad 1940,My 31,15:3
Devil's Island 1940,Jl 12,11:4
South of Pago-Pago 1940,Ag 2,12:2
Flowing Gold 1940,S 2,19:3
Strange Alibi 1941,Ap 28,11:2
Highway West 1941,Ag 8,13:4
Smiling Ghost, The 1941,S 26,26:5
Juke Girl 1942,Je 20,9:2
Flying Tigers 1942,O 23,25:2
Pittsburgh 1943,F 25,27:2
Bomber's Moon 1943,Jl 31,8:2
Tampico 1944,Je 2,21:2
Betrayal From the East 1945,Ap 25,27:2
Wake of the Red Witch 1949,Ja 10,19:2
Canadian Pacific 1949,My 20,32:4
Santa Fe 1951,My 4,31:2
Fighting Coast Guard 1951,My 12,14:6
Stranger Wore a Gun, The 1953,Jl 30,20:3
Hell's Outpost 1955,F 26,13:3
Maverick Queen, the 1956,Je 4,25:2
Gamez, Maria
Molinos de Viento; Windmills 1940,F 26,11:2
Gamilin, Lionel
Seance on a Wet Afternoon 1964,N 6,30:1
Gamis, Celia
Murio el Sargento Laprida; Sergeant Laprida Died 1939,Mr 20,13:2
Gamis, Jose Alcalde
Dos Cadetes, Los 1938,S 26,13:3
Gamore, Charles
Swiss Miss 1938,Je 4,18:2
Gampu, Ken
Dingaka 1965,Jl 1,34:1
Naked Prey, The 1966,Je 15,40:1
Gamse, Albert (Composer)
Thrill of Brazil, The 1946,S 6,18:3
Gamut, David
Last of the Mohicans, The 1921,Ja 3,20:2
Gamy, Yvonne
Letters From my Windmill (The Three Low Masses); Three Low Masses, The (Letters From my Windmill) 1955,D 19,33:1
Gan, Chester
West of Shanghai 1937,O 29,19:2
Shadows Over Shanghai 1938,D 1,29:2
'Til We Meet Again 1940,Ap 14,14:2
Victory 1940,D 23,23:2
Man Made Monster 1941,Mr 19,25:4
Get-Away, The 1941,Jl 17,23:4
Burma Convoy 1941,O 7,26:7
Moontide 1942,Ap 30,14:1

Gan, Chester— Cont
　Across the Pacific　1942,S　5,9:2
　Flying Tigers　1942,O　23,25:2
　China Girl　1943,Ja　21,27:2
Gance, Abel
　End of the World, The　1934,Ap　18,23:3
Gance, Abel (Director)
　I Accuse; (J'Accuse)　1921,O　10,16:1
　Napoleon　1928,Mr　4,IX,6:3
　Napoleon　1929,F　12,23:1
　Serment, Le　1934,Mr　14,23:2
　Lucrezia Borgia　1937,O　13,27:2
　Life and Loves of Beethoven, The
　　1937,N　22,15:1
　That They May Live　1939,N　7,31:2
　Louise　1940,F　3,9:4
　Four Flights to Love　1942,Ap　13,12:2
　Queen and the Cardinal, The　1944,Je　1,17:3
　Cyrano and D'Artagnan　1964,S　26,16:1
Gance, Abel (Original Author)
　J'Accuse　1920,My　23,VI,2:2
　Serment, Le　1934,Mr　14,23:2
　Life and Loves of Beethoven, The
　　1937,N　22,15:1
Gance, Abel (Producer)
　J'Accuse　1920,My　23,VI,2:2
　Life and Loves of Beethoven, The
　　1937,N　22,15:1
　Napoleon　1967,S　25,56:5
　Napoleon　1967,O　2,58:2
Gance, Abel (Screenwriter)
　That They May Live　1939,N　7,31:2
　Cyrano and D'Artagnan　1964,S　26,16:1
Gance, M Abel (Miscellaneous)
　Napoleon　1927,Je　5,VII,5:6　(In Addenda)
Gandera, Felix (Director)
　Mysteres de Paris, Les　1937,Ja　30,21:2
　Crime in the Maginot Line　1939,My　8,21:2
Gandera, Felix (Producer)
　Mysteres de Paris, Les　1937,Ja　30,21:2
　Crime in the Maginot Line　1939,My　8,21:2
Gandera, Felix (Screenwriter)
　Crime in the Maginot Line　1939,My　8,21:2
Gandos, Giorgio
　Seven Hills of Rome　1958,Ja　28,24:2　(Incorrect
　　in this edition; use 1958,Ja　31,24:2 elsewhere)
Gandron, Leroy (Original Author)
　City That Never Sleeps, The　1924,S　29,10:1
Gandusio, Antonio
　I Tre Innamorati　1937,Je　17,19:2
　Signora Fortuna; Lady Luck　1937,N　29,19:3
　Albero di Adamo, L'; Adam's Tree
　　1938,Ja　20,19:2
　Antenato, L'; Ancestor, The　1938,O　22,14:3
　Eravamo Sette Sorelle; We Were Seven Sisters
　　1939,Mr　3,21:3
　Per Vomini Soli; For Men Only　1939,Ap　21,27:4
　Eravamo Sette Vedove; We Were Seven Widows
　　1940,F　16,23:4
　Frenesia; Frenzy　1940,Je　6,33:4
Gandy Dancers
　World Dances　1954,N　8,24:6
Gangelin, Paul (Miscellaneous)
　Cover Girl　1944,Mr　31,26:1
Gangelin, Paul (Original Author)
　Racketeer, The　1930,Ja　6,30:8
　Beloved　1934,Ja　27,9:3
　Scarlet Claw, The　1944,My　19,12:1
　My Pal Trigger　1946,Ag　17,16:3
Gangelin, Paul (Screenwriter)
　Ten Modern Commandments　1927,Jl　11,23:4
　Rolled Stockings　1927,Jl　19,27:2
　Tarzan's Secret Treasure　1941,D　25,33:1
　Nazi Agent　1942,Je　13,11:2
　Murder in Times Square　1943,My　31,13:2
　Big Bonanza, The　1945,F　26,14:5
　Daltons Ride Again, The　1945,D　8,21:2
Gangopadhaya, Rama
　Pather Panchali　1958,S　23,37:2
Ganley, Gail
　Don't Knock the Rock　1957,F　23,13:1
Gann, Ernest K (Original Author)
　Blaze of Noon　1947,Mr　5,31:2
　Island in the Sky　1953,S　10,22:2
　Soldier of Fortune　1955,My　28,7:4
　Twilight for the Gods　1958,Ag　7,21:1
　Fate Is the Hunter　1964,D　10,61:1
Gann, Ernest K (Screenwriter)
　Island in the Sky　1953,S　10,22:2
　High and the Mighty, The　1954,Jl　1,21:2
　Soldier of Fortune　1955,My　28,7:4
　Twilight for the Gods　1958,Ag　7,21:1
Gannaway, Albert C (Director)
　Rebellion in Cuba　1961,Jl　1,9:1
Gannaway, Albert C (Producer)
　Rebellion in Cuba　1961,Jl　1,9:1
Gannon, Kim (Composer)
　Powers Girl, The　1943,Mr　26,14:2　(In Addenda)
　Shine on Harvest Moon　1944,Mr　11,10:2
　Earl Carroll Vanities　1945,Ap　2,15:6
　Melody Time　1948,My　28,28:2
　Innocent Affair, An　1948,S　29,36:2

Gannon, Kim (Miscellaneous)
　Song of the Open Road　1944,Je　7,13:3
Gannon, Robert I Very Rev S J (Narrator)
　Holy Year 1950　1950,Ag　16,24:3
Ganor, Rina
　Cast a Giant Shadow　1966,Mr　31,43:3
Ganpatrao
　Gyandev of India　1943,Ap　10,12:5
Gansard, Clara
　Money, Money, Money　1962,Jl　18,20:1
Gant, Steven
　In Love and War　1958,N　1,14:2
Gantarina, P
　Eagle of the Caucasus, The　1932,S　17,18:4
Gantiler, Vallejo
　Till We Meet Again　1936,My　9,11:2
Gantillon, Simon (Miscellaneous)
　Personal Column　1941,F　3,13:2
Gantillon, Simon (Screenwriter)
　Rumors　1949,Mr　19,10:7
Gantkowski, Romuald (Original Author)
　Hearts Aflame　1937,O　14,22:3
Gantkowski, Romuald (Screenwriter)
　Hearts Aflame　1937,O　14,22:3
Gantvoori, Carl
　When Romance Rides　1922,Ap　10,18:2
Ganzer, Alvin (Director)
　Girls of Pleasure Island, The　1953,My　16,10:1
　Leather Saint, The　1956,Je　16,12:2
　When the Boys Meet the Girls　1966,Ja　20,29:1
　Three Bites of the Apple　1967,My　25,54:2
Ganzer, Alvin (Producer)
　Three Bites of the Apple　1967,My　25,54:2
Ganzer, Alvin (Screenwriter)
　Leather Saint, The　1956,Je　16,12:2
Ganzhern, Jack
　Iron Horse, The　1924,Ag　29,6:1
Garabedian, John
　Cyanamide　1954,Mr　26,17:6
Garard, Christian
　Indiscretions　1939,My　1,21:1
Garasa, Angel
　Romeo and Juliet　1944,Je　17,10:3
Garat, Henry
　Il est Charmant; He is Charming
　　1932,Mr　27,VIII,6:2
　Fille et le Garcon, La; Girl and the Boy, The
　　1932,Mr　27,VIII,6:2
　Il est Charmant　1932,Ap　9,18:1
　Congress Dances　1932,My　12,23:2
　Roi des Resquilleurs, Le　1932,Je　13,19:3
　Adorable　1933,My　19,20:2
　Soir de Reveillon　1935,Ja　19,8:2
　Amphitryon　1937,Mr　24,29:1
　Avocate d'Amour　1938,S　8,27:2
Garavaglia, Leo
　Shoe-Shine　1947,Ag　27,19:2
Garay, Joaquin
　Three Caballeros, The　1945,F　5,20:1
　Latin Lovers　1953,Ag　13,17:2
Garber, Anna
　Action of the Tiger　1957,N　14,41:1
Garber, Jan, and Orchestra
　Jam Session　1944,My　3,25:3
Garber, Matthew
　Three Lives of Thomasina, The　1963,D　12,46:1
　Mary Poppins　1964,S　25,34:1
　Gnome-Mobile, The　1967,Jl　20,30:2
Garbinetti, Guilio
　Romeo and Juliet　1954,D　22,28:1
Garbini, Aristide
　Messalina　1924,Ag　25,16:2
Garbo, Greta
　Ibanez's Torrent　1926,F　22,14:1
　Temptress, The　1926,O　11,18:1
　Flesh and the Devil　1927,Ja　10,20:2
　Streets of Sorrow　1927,Jl　6,23:2
　Love　1927,N　30,22:4
　Divine Woman, The　1928,Ja　16,24:1
　Mysterious Lady, The　1928,Ag　6,15:2
　Legend of Gosta Berling, The　1928,O　29,29:1
　Woman of Affairs, A　1929,Ja　21,18:4
　Wild Orchids　1929,Ap　1,22:1
　Single Standard, The　1929,Jl　29,23:3
　Kiss, The　1929,N　16,25:2
　Anna Christie　1930,Mr　15,22:5
　Romance　1930,Ag　23,7:3
　Anna Christie　1931,Ja　6,25:1
　Inspiration　1931,F　9,25:3
　Susan Lenox; Her Fall and Rise　1931,O　17,20:1
　Mata Hari　1932,Ja　1,31:1
　Grand Hotel　1932,Ap　13,23:2
　As You Desire Me　1932,Je　3,23:4
　Grand Hotel　1933,Je　4,IX,2:1　(In Addenda)
　Queen Christina　1933,D　27,23:3
　Painted Veil, The　1934,D　7,29:1
　Anna Karenina　1935,Ag　31,16:2
　Camille　1937,Ja　23,13:1
　Conquest　1937,N　5,19:1
　Ninotchka　1939,N　10,27:2
　Two Faced Woman　1942,Ja　1,37:2

Garbo, Sven
　Nar Rosorna Sla Ut　1931,F　10,24:4
Garces, Delia
　Gente Bien　1939,O　9,15:2
　Vida de Carlos Gardel, A　1940,Ja　6,9:2
　Alas de mi Patria; My Country's Wingo
　　1940,Je　4,19:4
　This Strange Passion　1955,D　5,34:2
Garces, John
　Robby　1968,Ag　15,46:3
Garchery
　Francois Villon　1950,Jl　3,9:2
Garcia, Allan
　Circus, The　1928,Ja　9,20:1
　City Lights　1931,F　7,11:1
　Deceiver, The　1931,N　23,22:1
　Modern Times　1936,F　6,23:2
　Gay Desperado, The　1936,O　9,31:4
Garcia, Amapola
　Tarantos, Los　1964,Je　30,22:1
Garcia, Antonio (Cinematographer)
　Fury Over Spain　1937,Jl　21,19:2
Garcia, Juan
　Pearl, The　1948,F　18,36:4
　Plunder of the Sun　1953,Ag　27,22:1
　Vera Cruz　1954,D　27,22:4
　Tall Men, The　1955,O　12,36:2
Garcia, Lea
　Black Orpheus　1959,D　22,41:1
Garcia, Mercedes
　Semana de Felicidad, Una; One Week of
　　Happiness　1935,Je　15,20:3
Garcia, Rosita
　Love in Morocco　1933,Mr　20,18:3
　Beachcomber, The　1938,D　26,29:3
　Padre de Mas de Cuatro; Father of More Than
　　Four　1939,Ap　24,13:3
Garcia, Sara
　Malditas Sean las Mujeres　1936,Ag　29,16:3
　Asi es la Mujer　1936,O　21,35:3
　No te Enganes, Corazon; Don't Fool Thyself,
　　Heart　1937,D　14,33:6
　no Basta ser Madre; Motherhood Is Not Enough
　　1938,Ja　31,15:2
　Traidor, El　1938,Ap　9,11:3
　Dos Cadetes, Los　1938,S　26,13:3
　Perjura　1939,Ja　16,11:2
　Su Gran Aventura; His Great Adventure
　　1939,Ap　3,11:6
　Por Mis Pistolas; By My Pistols　1939,Je　10,14:3
　Soy Chato, Pero las Huelo; I Am Snub-nosed but I
　　Can Smell　1939,Jl　22,12:3
　Capitan Aventurero, El; Adventureous Captain,
　　The　1939,O　3,19:5
　Papacito Lindo; Sugar Daddy　1939,N　18,22:6
　En un Burro Tres Baturros; Three Rustics on one
　　Donkey　1940,S　21,13:3
　Mi Madrecita; My Little Mother　1940,S　24,26:6
　Alla en el Tropico; Down in the Tropics
　　1943,My　8,19:3
　Living Idol, The　1957,My　3,18:1
Garcia, Violetta
　Hunt, The　1967,Ap　25,38:1
Garcin, Henri
　Vie de Chateau, La　1967,Mr　21,35:1
Gard, Kathryn
　Undercurrent　1946,N　29,36:2
Gardan, Julius
　Moj Wujaszek Z Ameryki　1933,O　25,25:3
　Tredowata　1936,D　31,21:2
Gardan, Julius (Director)
　Halka　1938,Ja　17,11:3
Garday, Lajos
　Oeroek Titok, Az; Eternal Secret, The
　　1940,Mr　9,19:3
Garde, Betty
　Lady Lies, The　1929,S　7,15:1
　Queen High　1930,Ag　9,16:5
　Damaged Love　1931,Ja　19,25:1
　Girl Habit, The　1931,Jl　4,11:5
　Secrets of a Secretary　1931,Ag　29,16:3
　Call Northside 777　1948,F　19,29:2
　Cry of the City　1948,S　30,32:4
　Caged　1950,My　20,8:6
　Prince Who Was a Thief, The　1951,Jl　4,13:2
　One Desire　1955,S　3,9:1
Gardel, Carlos
　Esperame　1933,Jl　3,14:6
　Melodia de Arrabal　1933,Ag　5,9:5
　Cuesta Abajo　1934,Ag　15,13:5
　Tango en Broadway, El　1934,D　29,11:3
　Tango-Bar　1935,Jl　6,16:3
　Dia que me Quieras, El; Day You Love Me, The
　　1935,Ag　27,23:3
Garden, Faith
　This Freedom　1923,N　28,15:1
Garden, Helen
　Monte Carlo　1930,Ag　28,22:4
Garden, John (Original Author)
　Double Confession　1953,My　1,17:2
Garden, Mary
　Thais　1917,D　31,5:2
　Splendid Sinner, The　1918,Ap　1,9:3

Garden, Viola
Living Corpse, The 1931,Ja 4,27:2
Gardenas, Vicente (Maera)
Brave Bulls, The 1951,Ap 19,39:2
Gardener, Shayle
Blame the Woman 1932,O 25,24:5
Gardenia, Vincent
Mad Dog Coll 1961,My 13,10:1
View From the Bridge, A 1962,Ja 23,36:1
Gardes, Renee
We Are all Murderers 1957,Ja 9,27:2
Gardett, Maurice
Belle Americaine, La 1961,D 18,42:1
Gardin, V
Dom Zhadnosti 1934,Ag 13,9:6
Miracles 1934,O 22,12:3
Pesnya O Stchasti 1935,Ap 8,23:4
Peasants 1935,Ag 29,25:2
Dubrovsky 1936,Mr 30,17:6
Beethoven Concerto 1937,Mr 24,29:1
Young Pushkin 1937,D 16,35:3
Pugachev 1938,Jl 4,10:2
Conquests of Peter The Great, The
1939,Ag 24,17:2
Spring Song 1942,S 12,9:2
Russian Ballerina 1947,S 11,31:2
GARDINER
See Also GARDNER
Gardiner, Becky (Original Author)
Coming-Out Party 1934,Mr 17,11:3
Gardiner, Betty (Screenwriter)
New York 1927,Ja 31,13:1
Gardiner, Douglas
Our Town 1940,Je 14,25:3
Gardiner, Reginald
Just Smith 1934,Ap 23,20:2
Born to Dance 1936,D 5,16:1
Damsel in Distress, A 1937,N 25,37:1 ·
Everybody Sing 1938,Mr 11,15:3
Marie Antoinette 1938,Ag 17,23:2
Sweethearts 1938,D 23,16:2
Girl Downstairs, The 1939,Ja 26,17:1
Flying Deuces, The 1939,N 24,29:2
Night of Nights, The 1939,D 28,17:1
Doctor Takes a Wife, The 1940,Je 15,12:2
Great Dictator, The 1940,O 16,29:1
Dulcy 1940,N 28,28:2
Yank in the R A F, A 1941,S 27,11:3
My Life With Caroline 1941,O 30,27:1
Man Who Came to Dinner, The 1942,Ja 2,25:2
Captains of the Clouds 1942,F 13,24:2
Immortal Sergeant 1943,F 4,29:2
Sweet Rosie O'Grady 1943,O 21,30:2
Claudia 1945,N 5,23:2 ·
Horn Blows at Midnight, The 1945,Ap 21,18:2
Molly and Me 1945,My 26,18:2
Christmas in Connecticut 1945,Jl 28,7:2
Dolly Sisters, The 1945,N 15,24:6
Do You Love Me 1946,My 25,12:2
One More Tomorrow 1946,My 25,12:2
Cluny Brown 1946,Je 3,27:3
I Wonder Who's Kissing Her Now
1947,Jl 24,27:2
Fury at Furnace Creek 1948,Jl 12,11:2
That Lady in Ermine 1948,Ag 25,31:2
That Wonderful Urge 1948,D 22,29:6
Wabash Avenue 1950,Ap 29,8:3
Halls of Montezuma, The 1951,Ja 6,9:6
Elopement 1951,D 21,21:3
Androcles and the Lion 1953,Ja 15,23:2
Black Widow 1954,O 28,46:6
Ain't Misbehavin' 1955,Jl 2,13:2
Birds and the Bees, The 1956,Ap 23,22:1
Story of Mankind, The 1957,N 9,31:2
Rock-a-Bye Baby 1958,Jl 24,18:1
Back Street 1961,O 13,27:1
Mr Hobbs Takes a Vacation 1962,Je 16,11:2
What a Way to Go! 1964,My 15,44:1
Sergeant Deadhead 1965,O 23,17:3
Do Not Disturb 1965,D 25,17:2
GARDNER
See Also GARDINER
Gardner, Arthur
Heart of the North 1938,D 21,29:2
Waterfront 1939,Jl 17,10:2
Gardner, Arthur (Producer)
Vice Squad 1953,Ag 26,23:2
Down Three Dark Streets 1954,S 4,6:4
Clambake 1967,D 14,62:3
Scalphunters, The 1968,Ap 3,40:1
Gardner, Ava
Three Men in White 1944,My 26,23:3
Maisie Goes to Reno 1944,S 29,18:1
She Went to the Races 1946,F 1,29:2
Whistle Stop 1946,Mr 18,24:2
Killers, The 1946,Ag 29,24:2
Hucksters, The 1947,Jl 18,21:2
Singapore 1947,S 17,31:2
One Touch of Venus 1948,O 29,29:5
Bribe, The 1949,F 4,31:2
Great Sinner, The 1949,Je 30,19:2
East Side, West Side 1949,D 23,17:2
My Forbidden Past 1951,Ap 26,34:2

Show Boat 1951,Jl 20,14:1
Pandora and the Flying Dutchman 1951,D 7,35:2
Lone Star 1952,F 2,11:4
Snows of Kilimanjaro, The 1952,S 19,19:2
Ride Vaquero 1953,Jl 16,17:2
Mogambo 1953,O 2,18:1
Knights of the Round Table 1954,Ja 8,17:2
Barefoot Contessa, The 1954,S 30,37:1
Bhowani Junction 1956,My 25,26:1
Little Hut, The 1957,My 4,25:1
Sun Also Rises, The 1957,Ag 24,12:2
Naked Maja, The 1959,Je 11,36:2
On the Beach 1959,D 18,34:1
Angel Wore Red, The 1960,S 29,32:1
55 Days at Peking 1963,My 30,20:1
Seven Days in May 1964,F 20,22:1
Night of the Iguana, The 1964,Jl 1,42:1
Bible, The 1966,S 29,60:1
Gardner, Betty
This Freedom 1923,N 28,15:1
Gardner, Buster
Deadwood Coach, The 1925,Ja 21,19:3
Best Bad Man, The 1925,D 2,23:1
Circus Ace, The 1927,Jl 6,23:2
Gardner, Cyril (Director)
Only Saps Work 1930,D 13,22:2
Royal Family of Broadway, The 1930,D 23,25:1
Reckless Living 1931,D 5,21:2
Doomed Battalion, The 1932,Je 11,9:3
Perfect Understanding 1933,F 23,20:2
Gardner, Diane
Gigot 1962,S 28,26:1
Gardner, Ed
Duffy's Tavern 1945,S 6,23:3
Gardner, Edward F (Producer)
Man With my Face, The 1951,Je 15,27:5
Gardner, Erle Stanley (Original Author)
Case of the Howling Dog, The 1934,O 18,26:5
Case of the Curious Bride, The 1935,Ap 5,21:3
Case of the Lucky Legs, The 1935,N 1,25:1
Special Investigator 1936,Ap 25,21:1
Case of the Velvet Claws, The 1936,Ag 29,16:3
Case of the Black Cat, The 1936,D 26,15:4
Gardner, Helen
Sandra 1924,D 22,20:2
Gardner, Herb (Original Author)
Thousand Clowns, A 1965,D 14,54:2
Gardner, Herb (Screenwriter)
Thousand Clowns, A 1965,D 14,54:2
Gardner, Hunter
Gambling 1934,D 4,22:3
Gardner, Jack
Wild Bill Hickok 1923,N 21,22:1
To the Ladies 1923,N 26,15:6
Bluff 1924,Ap 28,18:2
Three Russian Girls 1944,F 5,13:2
It Happened Tomorrow 1944,My 29,18:2
Gardner, Joan
Catherine the Great 1934,F 15,15:6
Private Life of Don Juan, The 1934,D 10,16:2
Scarlet Pimpernel, The 1935,F 8,27:2
Men of Tomorrow 1935,Ap 16,27:2
Man Who Could Work Miracles, The
1937,F 22,13:1
Forever Yours 1937,Je 7,22:2
Dark Journey 1937,Ag 23,22:1
Challenge, The 1939,O 2,15:2
Gardner, John (Original Author)
Liquidator, The 1966,O 29,34:1
Gardner, Kenny (Narrator)
Mr Bug Goes to Town 1942,F 20,21:3
Gardner, Nancy
Doctors' Wives 1931,Ap 25,23:4
Gardner, Richard
Young Lions, The 1958,Ap 3,23:1
Gardner, Rita
1 ■ 1 1961,N 8,41:1
Gardner, Robert W Rev (Narrator)
our Lady Of Paris 1943,Mr 13,9:4
Gardner, Robert W Rev (Screenwriter)
our Lady Of Paris 1943,Mr 13,9:4
Gardner, Shayle
Three Live Ghosts 1929,S 30,23:1
Disraeli 1929,O 3,27:5
New Adventures of Dr Fu Manchu, The
1930,My 3,23:1
Phantom Fiend 1935,Ap 22,14:2
Garey, Peter
Young Widow 1946,Jl 29,12:8
Garfein, Jack (Director)
Strange One, The 1957,Ap 13,12:3
Something Wild 1961,D 24,30:6
Garfein, Jack (Screenwriter)
Something Wild 1961,D 24,30:6
Garfield, John
Four Daughters 1938,Ag 19,13:3
They Made Me a Criminal 1939,Ja 21,19:2
Blackwell's Island 1939,Mr 2,19:1
Juarez 1939,Ap 26,27:1
Daughters Courageous 1939,Je 24,14:2
Dust Be my Destiny 1939,O 7,11:2
Castle on the Hudson 1940,Mr 4,11:2
Saturday's Children 1940,My 4,13:1

Garfield, John— Cont
Flowing Gold 1940,S 2,19:3
East of the River 1940,O 28,21:2
Sea Wolf, The 1941,Mr 26,27:3
Out of the Fog 1941,Je 21,20:2
Dangerously They Live 1942,Ap 11,9:2
Tortilla Flat 1942,My 22,27:1
Air Force 1943,F 4,29:1
Fallen Sparrow, The 1943,Ag 20,13:1
Thank Your Lucky Stars 1943,O 2,19:2
Destination Tokyo 1944,Ja 1,9:2
Destination Tokyo 1944,Ja 9,II,3:1
Between Two Worlds 1944,My 6,11:2
Hollywood Canteen 1944,D 16,19:2
Pride of the Marines 1945,Ag 25,7:3
Postman Always Rings Twice, The
1946,My 3,15:3
Nobody Lives Forever 1946,N 2,12:2
Humoresque 1946,D 26,28:1
Body and Soul 1947,N 10,21:2
Gentleman's Agreement 1947,N 12,36:2
Force of Evil 1948,D 27,16:2
We Were Strangers 1949,Ap 28,28:2
Under my Skin 1950,Mr 18,9:2
Breaking Point, The 1950,O 7,10:6
He Ran all the Way 1951,Je 21,24:2
Garfield, John (Narrator)
Difficult Years 1950,Ag 22,31:2
Garfield, John Jr
Warning Shot 1967,Je 8,52:2
Swimmer, The 1968,My 16,53:1
Garfield, Warren (Screenwriter)
Stranger in Town, A 1968,Ap 25,53:4
Garfinkle, Louis (Screenwriter)
Minute to Pray, A Second to Die, A
1968,My 23,56:2
Gargan, Edward
Girl in 419 1933,My 20,11:5
20th Century 1934,My 4,24:2
Wild Gold 1934,Jl 24,20:2
Belle of the Nineties 1934,S 22,12:2
Gilded Lily, The 1935,F 9,11:2
Behold My Wife 1935,F 18,19:3
Hands Across the Table 1935,N 2,13:2
Bride Comes Home, The 1935,D 25,30:2
Ceiling Zero 1936,Ja 20,22:2
Dangerous Waters 1936,Ja 22,15:5
Anything Goes 1936,F 6,23:3
Nobody's Fool 1936,Je 4,27:2
My Man Godfrey 1936,S 19,18:1 (Incorrect in
this edition; use 1936,S 18,18:1 elsewhere)
Two in a Crowd 1936,O 5,25:1
Great Guy 1937,Ja 1,19:2
We're on the Jury 1937,F 10,18:5
Wake up and Live 1937,Ap 24,16:2
You Can't Buy Luck 1937,My 14,21:2
Go Getter, The 1937,Je 4,27:2
Danger Patrol 1937,N 19,27:3
Girl With Ideas, A 1938,Ja 1,11:2
Crime School 1938,My 11,17:2
Devil's Party, The 1938,My 31,8:3
Texans, The 1938,Jl 28,23:2
Straight, Place and Show 1938,O 1,10:2
Up the River 1938,D 3,11:2
Thanks for the Memory 1938,D 8,34:3
While New York Sleeps 1938,D 22,25:3
Annabel Takes a Tour 1938,D 29,15:3
Honolulu 1939,F 23,19:2
Saint Strikes Back, The 1939,Mr 9,18:2
Lucky Night 1939,My 5,29:3
Fixer Dugan 1939,My 6,21:2
They all Come Out 1939,Ag 3,15:4
Pack up Your Troubles 1939,O 27,27:2
20,000 Men a Year 1939,O 28,11:2
Brother Rat and a Baby 1940,Ja 27,9:4
Three Cheers for the Irish 1940,Mr 9,19:2
Girl From God's Country 1940,S 9,18:5
Spring Parade 1940,O 4,29:2
San Francisco Docks 1940,D 26,23:3
Lone Wolf Keeps a Date, The 1941,Ja 2,24:3
Meet the Chump 1941,F 27,23:4
Tight Shoes 1941,Je 19,25:2
Date With the Falcon, A 1941,N 25,33:2
Dr Kildare's Victory 1942,F 5,25:2
Falcon takes Over, The 1942,My 30,9:2
They all Kissed the Bride 1942,Jl 31,11:1
A-Haunting We Will Go 1942,Ag 3,18:4
Falcon's Brother, The 1942,O 3,9:5
Over my Dead Body 1942,D 26,15:2
Falcon Strikes Back, The 1943,Ap 2,17:4
Falcon in Danger, The 1943,Jl 23,21:2
My Kingdom for a Cook 1943,O 15,15:3
Falcon out West, The 1944,Mr 18,18:2
Bullfighters, The 1945,My 12,10:3
Wonder Man 1945,Je 9,17:2
Cinderella Jones 1946,Mr 16,9:6
Bedtime for Bonzo 1951,Ap 6,31:4
Gargan, William
Misleading Lady, The 1932,Ap 9,18:1
Rain 1932,O 13,22:3
Sport Parade, The 1932,D 17,22:3
Animal Kingdom, The 1932,D 30,14:2
Lucky Devils 1933,F 20,11:5
Sweepings 1933,Mr 24,22:3

Gargan, William— Cont

Story of Temple Drake, The 1933,My 6,11:2
Emergency Call 1933,Je 24,16:2
Night Flight 1933,O 7,18:4
Aggie Appleby, Maker of Men 1933,O 20,14:2
Headline Shooters 1933,O 23,18:3
Four Frightened People 1934,Ja 27,9:2
Strictly Dynamite 1934,Jl 4,18:2
British Agent 1934,S 20,20:1
Traveling Saleslady 1935,Mr 29,26:2
Black Fury 1935,Ap 11,27:2
Night at the Ritz, A 1935,My 16,20:2
Broadway Gondolier 1935,Jl 18,15:2
Don't Bet on Blondes 1935,Jl 20,16:2
Bright Lights 1935,Ag 15,15:2
Man Hunt 1936,Ja 30,14:2
Milky Way, The 1936,Mr 26,27:2
Sky Parade, The 1936,Ap 20,17:1
Flying Hostess 1936,D 14,29:4
You Only Live Once 1937,F 1,15:2
Breezing Home 1937,Mr 20,23:5
Wings Over Honolulu 1937,My 29,20:1
Fury and the Woman 1937,Je 22,26:2
Reported Missing 1937,S 3,12:2
Some Blondes Are Dangerous 1937,N 3,29:3
You're a Sweetheart 1937,D 25,10:5
Behind the Mike 1938,Ja 28,12:1
Crime of Dr Hallet, The 1938,Mr 24,21:3
Devil's Party, The 1938,My 31,8:3
Crowd Roars, The 1938,Ag 5,11:1
Personal Secretary 1938,O 5,20:2
Within the Law 1939,Ap 6,31:2
Broadway Serenade 1939,Ap 7,25:2
Women in the Wind 1939,Ap 13,27:2
Three Sons 1939,N 24,29:3
Housekeeper's Daughter, The 1939,D 2,21:4
Joe and Ethel Turp Call on the President
  1940,Ja 4,19:2
Double Alibi 1940,Mr 11,11:2
Isle of Destiny 1940,Ap 8,15:2
Star Dust 1940,My 4,13:1
Sporting Blood 1940,Jl 22,20:2
Turnabout 1940,Jl 27,17:6
They Knew What They Wanted 1940,O 11,25:2
Cheers for Miss Bishop 1941,Mr 14,17:2
Flying Cadets 1941,O 14,29:2
Keep 'Em Flying 1941,N 27,29:2
Bombay Clipper 1942,Ja 12,23:3
I Wake up Screaming 1942,Ja 17,13:2
Miss Annie Rooney 1942,Je 8,11:1
Mayor of Forty-Fourth Street, The
  1942,Je 11,27:4
Enemy Agents meet Ellery Queen
  1942,Ag 22,16:2
Destination Unknown 1942,O 29,19:3
Who Done It 1942,D 3,35:2
Swing Fever 1944,Ja 28,14:1
Canterville Ghost, The 1944,Jl 29,16:2
She Gets her Man 1945,F 9,20:5
Midnight Manhunt 1945,Ag 18,12:5
Bells of St Mary's, The 1945,D 7,26:2
Behind Green Lights 1946,F 16,10:2
Night Editor 1946,Mr 30,11:2
Murder in the Music Hall 1946,Ap 15,22:2
Till the End of Time 1946,Jl 24,24:1
Swell Guy 1947,Ja 27,17:2
Miracle in the Rain 1956,Ap 2,18:1
Rawhide Years, The 1956,Je 16,12:2

Gargiullo, Giorgio
Wild Eye, The 1968,Ag 22,47:1

Gargoet, Jean
I Am a Camera 1955,Ag 9,29:1

Garibay, Emilio
Adventures of Robinson Crusoe, The
  1954,Ag 6,10:5

Garin, E
Czar wants to Sleep, The 1934,D 10,16:3
Soviet Border 1939,F 20,13:2
Marriage 1945,F 22,31:3
Inspector General, The 1954,My 3,21:2

Garinel, Enzo
Most Wonderful Moment, The 1959,Je 1,23:6

Gariss, Jack (Screenwriter)
Ten Commandments, The 1956,N 9,35:2

Garity, William E (Miscellaneous)
Fantasia 1940,N 14,28:2

Garkavy, M
Victors and the Vanquished, The 1950,My 1,18:2

Garko, Gianni
Crazy Desire 1964,Jl 3,13:2

Garl, Giulio
Traviata, La 1953,D 28,17:2

Garland, Beverly
Miami Story, The 1954,My 15,13:2
New Orleans Uncensored 1955,Ap 30,10:8
Steel Jungle, The 1956,Mr 10,9:5
Chicago Confidential 1957,Ag 31,19:1
Joker Is Wild, The 1957,S 27,16:6
Twice Told Tales (The House of the Seven
  Gables); House of the Seven Gables, The (Twice
  Told Tales) 1964,My 28,40:1
Pretty Poison 1968,O 25,55:1

Garland, Geoff
Hamlet 1964,S 24,46:1

Garland, Jane
Lady in a Jam 1942,S 11,25:2

Garland, Judy
Pigskin Parade 1936,N 14,23:3
Broadway Melody of 1938 1937,S 3,12:1
Thoroughbreds Don't Cry 1937,N 26,27:4
Everybody Sing 1938,Mr 11,15:3
Love Finds Andy Hardy 1938,Jl 22,10:2
Listen, Darling 1938,N 24,37:2
Wizard of Oz, The 1939,Ag 18,16:2
Babes in Arms 1939,O 20,27:2
Andy Hardy Meets Debutante 1940,Ag 2,12:2
Strike up the Band 1940,S 30,13:2
Little Nellie Kelly 1940,D 25,33:2
Ziegfeld Girl 1941,Ap 25,17:2
Life Begins for Andy Hardy 1941,Ag 22,19:4
Babes on Broadway 1942,Ja 1,37:1
For Me and My Gal 1942,O 22,25:1
Presenting Lily Mars 1943,Ap 30,25:3
Thousands Cheer 1943,S 14,27:1
Girl Crazy 1943,D 3,27:2
Meet Me in St Louis 1944,N 29,20:2
Clock, The 1945,My 4,23:2
Harvey Girls, The 1946,Ja 25,26:2
Ziegfeld Follies 1946,Mr 23,8:3
Till the Clouds Roll By 1946,D 6,27:4
Pirate, The 1948,My 21,19:2
Easter Parade 1948,Jl 1,19:3
Words and Music 1948,D 10,34:2
In the Good Old Summertime 1949,Ag 5,23:2
Summer Stock 1950,S 1,17:2
Star is Born, A 1954,O 12,23:1
Judgment at Nuremberg 1961,D 20,36:1
Gay Purr--ee 1962,D 6,55:3
Child Is Waiting, A 1963,F 14,5:6
I Could go on Singing 1963,My 16,42:1

Garland, Maria
Child of Man 1950,F 1,25:2
Invisible Army, The 1950,Je 26,17:3

Garland, Timothy
Charlie Bubbles 1968,F 12,47:2

Garland Hamlin (Original Author)
Ranger of the big Trees, The 1925,Jl 28,24:4

Garmes, Lee (Director)
Angels Over Broadway 1940,N 18,23:2

Garmes, Lee (Producer)
Beyond Tomorrow 1940,S 27,27:1

Garner, Cindy
Red Ball Express 1952,My 30,11:2

Garner, Don
My Darling Clementine 1946,D 4,44:5
Lady Without Passport, A 1950,Ag 4,13:2

Garner, James
Toward the Unknown 1956,S 28,24:4
Girl He Left Behind, The 1956,O 27,17:1
Soyonara 1957,D 6,39:4
Sayonara 1957,D 6,39:4
Darby's Rangers 1958,F 13,23:2
Up Periscope 1959,Mr 5,35:4
Cash McCall 1960,Ja 28,26:1
Childrens Hour, The 1962,Mr 15,28:2
Boys' Night Out 1962,Je 22,15:2
Thrill of it All, The 1963,Ag 2,15:3
Great Escape, The 1963,Ag 8,19:1
Wheeler Dealers, The 1963,N 15,25:2
Move Over Darling 1963,D 26,33:1
Americanization of Emily, The 1964,O 28,51:1
36 Hours 1965,Ja 29,25:2
Art of Love, The 1965,Jl 1,34:1
Man Could Get Killed, A 1966,My 12,54:2
Duel at Diablo 1966,Je 16,53:1
Mister Buddwing 1966,O 12,36:1
Grand-Prix 1966,D 22,40:1
Hour of the Gun 1967,N 2,58:4
How Sweet It Is 1968,Ag 22,47:1
Pink Jungle, The 1968,O 17,52:1

Garner, Paullyn
Imitation of Life 1934,N 24,19:1

Garner, Peggy Ann
In Name Only 1939,Ag 4,11:3
Pied Piper, The 1942,Ag 13,15:3
Jane Eyre 1944,F 4,12:5
Keys of the Kingdom, The 1944,D 30,15:2
Tree Grows in Brooklyn, A 1945,Mr 1,25:5
Junior Miss 1945,Je 18,15:4
Nob Hill 1945,Jl 4,10:3
Home Sweet Homicide 1946,S 12,5:7
Thunder in the Valley 1947,N 28,30:1
Daisy Kenyon 1947,D 25,32:1
Sign of the Ram, The 1948,Mr 4,30:2
Bomba, the Jungle Boy 1949,Ap 16,11:4
Big Cat, The 1949,Jl 29,12:2
Teresa 1951,Ap 6,31:2
Black Widow 1954,O 28,46:6

Garnett, Cara
Fanny Hill 1965,D 2,48:1

Garnett, Tay
Eternally Yours 1939,O 7,11:2

Garnett, Tay (Director)
Spieler, The 1929,F 25,16:1
Officer O'Brien 1930,F 24,18:1

Garnett, Tay (Director)— Cont

Her Man 1930,O 4,15:2
Bad Company 1931,N 7,16:5
Prestige 1932,F 5,25:2
Okay America 1932,S 10,18:5
One Way Passage 1932,O 14,23:2
Destination Unknown 1933,Ap 8,16:2
S O S Iceberg 1933,S 25,18:4
China Seas 1935,Ag 10,16:4
She Couldn't Take It 1935,N 7,27:1
Professional Soldier 1936,Ja 30,14:2
Love Is News 1937,Mr 6,10:1
Slave Ship 1937,Je 17,19:2
Stand-In 1937,N 19,27:2
Joy of Living 1938,My 6,27:1
Trade Winds 1939,Ja 13,17:2
Eternally Yours 1939,O 7,11:2
Slightly Honorable 1940,My 17,23:4
Seven Sinners 1940,N 18,23:2
Cheers for Miss Bishop 1941,Mr 14,17:2
My Favorite Spy 1942,My 29,13:4
Bataan 1943,Je 4,17:2
Cross of Lorraine, The 1943,D 3,27:4
Mrs Parkington 1944,O 13,16:1
Valley of Decision, The 1945,My 4,23:2
Postman Always Rings Twice, The
  1946,My 3,15:3
Wild Harvest 1947,N 13,33:2
Connecticut Yankee in King Arthur's Court, A
  1949,Ap 8,31:2
Fireball, The 1950,N 10,35:4
Soldiers Three 1951,Mr 30,28:5
Cause for Alarm 1951,Mr 30,28:5
One Minute to Zero 1952,S 20,13:2
Main Street to Broadway 1953,O 14,34:1
Black Knight, The 1954,O 29,27:2
Seven Wonders of the World 1956,Ap 11,29:1
Night Fighters, The 1960,D 15,59:1

Garnett, Tay (Original Author)
Her Man 1930,O 4,15:2
Trade Winds 1939,Ja 13,17:2
Street of Missing Women 1940,Ja 8,11:2

Garnett, Tay (Producer)
Eternally Yours 1939,O 7,11:2
Unexpected Uncle 1941,S 25,29:1
Week End for Three 1941,O 24,27:4

Garnett, Tay (Screenwriter)
Fireball, The 1950,N 10,35:4

Garnier, Christine (Original Author)
Heroes and Sinners; (Heros Sont Fatigues, Les)
  1959,My 12,38:2

Garon, Pauline
You Can't Fool Your Wife 1923,Ap 24,25:3
Wine of Youth 1924,Ag 11,16:1
Passionate Youth 1925,Je 30,14:3
Where Was I 1925,Ag 19,14:4
Compromise 1925,O 27,23:3
Rose of the World 1925,N 10,25:3
Splendid Road, The 1926,Je 13,31:1
Ladies at Ease 1927,O 5,31:1
College Hero, The 1927,N 22,32:2
Gamblers, The 1929,Ag 24,11:5
White Cockatoo, The 1935,Ja 16,21:1
Becky Sharp 1935,Je 14,27:2
Her Husband's Secretary 1937,Mr 20,23:6

Garr, Eddie
Obey the Law 1933,Mr 13,18:3

Garralaga, Martin
Gay Caballero, The 1932,Mr 26,17:2
Message to Garcia, A 1936,Ap 10,27:1
Rose of the Rio Grande 1938,Jl 9,10:3
Di que me Quieres; Say That You Love Me
  1939,Ap 24,13:2
Papa Soltero; Bachelor Father 1939,N 6,20:3
For Whom the Bell Tolls 1943,Jl 15,25:2
Purple Heart, The 1944,Mr 9,15:2
Voice in the Wind 1944,Mr 16,17:2
Perilous Holiday 1946,Je 1,10:4
Outlaw, The 1947,S 12,18:4
Ride the Pink Horse 1947,O 9,32:3
Tycoon 1947,D 26,22:6
Rogues' Regiment 1948,D 20,31:2
Bribe, The 1949,F 4,31:2
Last Bandit, The 1949,Mr 21,19:2
There's a Girl in my Heart 1950,Ja 20,29:2
Outriders, The 1950,Mr 9,25:2
Kid From Texas, The 1950,Je 2,26:2
Branded 1951,Ja 11,28:5
Fighter, The 1952,My 31,12:6
Hitch-Hiker, The 1953,Ap 30,39:3
Secret of the Incas 1954,My 29,13:3
Blackjack Ketchum Desperado 1956,Ap 5,26:2

Garralaga, William
Four Faces West 1948,Ag 4,18:3

Garrani, Ivo
Hercules 1959,Jl 23,32:2
Black Sunday 1961,Mr 9,23:1
Slave, The 1963,My 30,20:1
Cyrano and D'Artagnan 1964,S 26,16:1
Love a la Carte 1965,Ja 12,31:1

Garrasa, Angel
Que Lindo es Michoacan 1944,Ap 22,8:7

Garraway, T V (Producer)
Jesse James' Women 1954,S 29,23:4
Garrel, S
Czar Ivan the Terrible 1928,Mr 12,26:1
Garrett, Andi
I Saw What You Did 1965,Jl 22,24:2
Garrett, Betty
Big City 1948,My 17,23:3
Words and Music 1948,D 10,34:2
Take Me Out to the Ball Game 1949,Mr 10,35:2
Neptune's Daughter 1949,Je 10,32:2
On the Town 1949,D 9,37:2
My Sister Eileen 1955,S 23,21:1
Garrett, George (Screenwriter)
Young Lovers, The 1965,F 11,45:1
Playground, The 1965,O 4,00:0
Garrett, Grant (Original Author)
Bedtime Story 1942,Mr 20,25:4
Barbary Coast Gent 1944,S 29,18:2
Garrett, Grant (Screenwriter)
Home on the Range 1935,F 13,24:4
Rainmakers, The 1935,N 2,13:2
This Way Please 1937,O 8,27:2
Thrill of a Lifetime 1937,D 9,30:2
Model Wife 1941,Ap 24,25:3
He's my Guy 1943,Mr 12,12:3
Rationing 1944,Ap 10,14:2
Barbary Coast Gent 1944,S 29,18:2
Bad Bascomb 1946,My 23,18:4
Mighty McGurk, The 1947,Ap 4,19:4
Garrett, Martyn
Baby and the Battleship, The 1957,O 1,37:2
Garrett, Michael
Walk East on Beacon 1952,My 29,17:2
Garrett, Oliver H P (Miscellaneous)
Hurricane, The 1937,N 10,31:2
Garrett, Oliver H P (Original Author)
Drag Net, The 1928,Je 4,13:2
Vice Squad, The 1931,Je 6,15:5
Her Husband Lies 1937,Mr 18,20:1
Underground 1941,Je 23,13:2
Garrett, Oliver H P (Screenwriter)
Forgotten Faces 1928,Ag 6,15:2
Street of Chance 1930,F 3,17:1
She Couldn't Take It 1935,N 7,27:1
One Way Ticket 1936,Ja 1,35:2
One Third of a Nation 1939,F 11,13:2
Four Feathers 1939,Ag 4,11:1
Man I Married, The 1940,Ag 3,9:2
Flight for Freedom 1943,Ap 16,24:2
Dead Reckoning 1947,Ja 23,31:2
Duel in the Sun 1947,My 8,30:2
Sealed Cargo 1951,My 24,47:1
Garrett, Otis (Director)
Black Doll, The 1938,F 7,10:2
Lady in the Morgue, The 1938,My 9,13:3
Personal Secretary 1938,O 5,20:2
Last Express, The 1938,O 11,24:4
Exile Express 1939,Ag 16,21:3
Witness Vanishes, The 1939,O 23,15:2
Garrett, Otis (Miscellaneous)
O'Shaughnessy's Boy 1935,O 5,18:2
Garrett, Otis (Original Author)
Meet the Chump 1941,F 27,23:4
Garrett, Otis (Screenwriter)
Age of Indiscretion 1935,My 18,21:2
Garrett, Robert (Producer)
Curtain Up 1953,F 2,17:3
Always a Bride 1954,My 28,19:2
Garrick, Ann (Original Author)
Side Streets 1934,Ag 15,13:5
Garrick, Gene
Road Back, The 1937,Je 18,25:2
Green Hell 1940,Ja 30,15:6
Paris Calling 1942,Ja 19,21:2
Garrick, John
Married in Hollywood 1929,S 23,24:3
Sky Hawk, The 1929,D 12,36:4
Song O' my Heart 1930,Mr 12,32:6
Just Imagine 1930,N 22,21:3
Lottery Bride, The 1930,N 29,21:4
Charlie Chan Carries On 1931,Mr 21,15:1
Always Good-Bye 1931,My 23,13:4
Bad Company 1931,N 7,16:5
Bride of the Lake, The 1934,S 11,24:5
Chu Chin Chow 1934,S 22,12:2
Broken Melody, The 1934,O 31,17:3
High Treason 1937,Ja 27,17:3
Two Who Dared 1937,Jl 10,18:2
Great Victor Herbert, The 1939,D 7,35:1
Suicide Legion 1940,My 6,13:3
Garrick, Pauline
Rats of Tobruk, The 1951,My 24,47:3
Garrick, Rian
Flying Fontaines, The 1959,D 24,13:6
Edge of Eternity 1960,F 25,34:2
Garrick, Richard
Boomerang 1947,Mr 6,36:2
Green Grass of Wyoming 1948,Je 10,28:3
Streetcar Named Desire, A 1951,S 30,27:1
Viva Zapata 1952,F 8,19:2
Dreamboat 1952,Jl 26,9:2
O Henry's Full House (The Last Leaf 1952,O 17,33:1

Stars and Stripes Forever 1952,D 23,17:2
Man Called Peter, A 1955,Ap 1,22:1
Hilda Crane 1956,My 3,35:2
High Society 1956,Ag 10,9:2
Garrido, Alberto
Romance del Palmar, El 1939,My 1,21:2
Ultima Melodia, La; Last Melody, The 1939,Ag 5,18:3
Garrison, Greg (Director)
Hey, Lets Twist 1962,F 8,25:1
Two Tickets to Paris 1962,N 29,46:5
Garrison, J (Screenwriter)
Crooked Road, The 1965,F 4,24:2
Garrison, Jan
Beach Red 1967,Ag 4,18:1
Garrison, Michael (Producer)
Crowded Sky, The 1961,F 11,27:2
Garrison, Pat
Harpoon 1948,D 9,48:8
Flying Saucer, The 1950,Ja 5,28:3
Garrison, Robert
Chained 1926,D 15,30:4
Garrison, Sean
Onionhead 1958,O 2,44:1
Up Periscope 1959,Mr 5,35:4
Splendor in the Grass 1961,O 11,53:1
Bridge to the Sun 1961,O 18,50:1
Moment to Moment 1966,Mr 3,28:1
Garrone, Riccardo
Most Wonderful Moment, The 1959,Je 1,23:6
Tailor's Maid, The; (Patri e Figli) 1959,S 2,35:4
Dolce Vita, La 1961,Ap 20,30:1
Warrior Empress, The 1961,Ag 10,17:4
Girl With a Suitcase 1961,S 12,36:2
Swordsman of Siena 1962,D 6,55:3
Fiasco in Milan 1963,Ap 11,29:2
Successo, Il 1965,Ap 29,40:2
Eva 1965,Je 5,21:2
GARRY
See Also GARY
Garry, Joe
Back Door to Heaven 1939,Ap 20,21:2
Garson, Greer
Goodbye Mr Chips 1939,My 16,27:2
Remember? 1939,D 15,33:4
Pride and Prejudice 1940,Ag 9,19:1
Blossoms in the Dust 1941,Je 27,14:4
When Ladies Meet 1941,S 5,19:2
Mrs Miniver 1942,Je 5,23:1
Random Harvest 1942,D 18,36:6
Youngest Profession, The 1943,Je 25,13:3
Madame Curie 1943,D 17,23:1
Madame Curie 1944,Ja 9,II,3:1
Mrs Parkington 1944,O 13,16:1
Valley of Decision, The 1945,My 4,23:2
Adventure 1946,F 8,23:2
Desire Me 1947,S 26,28:3
Julia Misbehaves 1948,O 8,30:2
That Forsyte Woman 1949,N 11,31:2
Miniver Story, The 1950,O 27,24:2
Law and the Lady, The 1951,Ag 16,23:2
Julius Caesar 1953,Je 5,19:1
Scandal at Scourie 1953,Je 16,24:2
Her Twelve Men 1954,Ag 12,23:2
Strange Lady in Town 1955,My 21,11:1
Sunrise at Campobello 1960,S 29,32:1
Pepe 1960,D 22,18:1
Singing Nun, The 1966,Mr 18,33:1
Happiest Millionaire, The 1967,D 1,56:1
Garson, Harry (Director)
Hush 1921,Ap 25,9:2
Garson, Harry (Producer)
Unpardonable Sin, The 1919,My 3,11:3
Garson, Henry (Screenwriter)
Reckless Moment, The 1949,D 30,13:2
Don't Give up the Ship 1959,Jl 9,22:1
Visit to a Small Planet 1960,Ap 14,34:1
G I Blues 1960,N 5,28:1
Garson, Natalie
Dangerously Yours 1937,O 18,14:2
Garstin, Crosbie (Original Author)
China Seas 1935,Ag 10,16:4
Garth, David (Original Author)
Hideaway Girl 1937,Ja 13,20:4
there Goes The Groom 1937,D 25,10:6
Four Men and a Prayer 1938,My 7,18:1
Fury at Furnace Creek 1948,Jl 12,11:2
Garth, Michael
Pork Chop Hill 1959,My 30,9:2
Gartside, Ernest (Producer)
Obsessed 1952,F 6,24:2
Count Five and Die 1958,My 15,25:1
Garve, Andrew (Original Author)
Touch of Larceny, A 1960,Mr 17,28:1
Garver, Kathy
Monkey on my Back 1957,My 30,23:2
Garvey, Ed
East Side, West Side 1927,O 18,33:2
Smiling Faces 1932,Ag 31,12:3
Soak the Rich 1936,F 5,14:2
Garvey, Stanley (Original Author)
Every Night at Eight 1935,Ag 3,16:2

Garvin, Anita
Bertha, The Sewing Machine Girl 1927,Ja 4,21:1
Play Girl, The 1928,Ap 23,20:2
Swiss Miss 1938,Je 4,18:2
Laurel and Hardy's Laughing 20's 1965,N 18,55:2
Garwood, John
Hells Angels on Wheels 1967,Jl 29,29:3
Savage Seven, The 1968,Ag 22,47:1
GARY
See Also GARRY
Gary, Gene
Paris After Dark 1943,O 23,11:1
Gary, Harold
Undercover Girl 1950,N 8,37:2
Gary, Inez
Hidden Hand, The 1942,N 26,40:4
Gary, Micheline
Picnic on the Grass 1960,O 12,47:1
Gary, Romain (Director)
Birds in Peru 1968,N 7,51:2
Gary, Romain (Original Author)
Roots of Heaven, The 1958,O 16,46:1
Man Who Understood, The 1959,O 3,14:7
Lady L 1966,My 19,51:1
Birds in Peru 1968,N 7,51:2
Gary, Romain (Screenwriter)
Roots of Heaven, The 1958,O 16,46:1
Longest Day, The 1962,O 5,28:1
Birds in Peru 1968,N 7,51:2
Gary, Sheila
Illiac Passion, The 1968,Ap 19,40:1
Garyine, Anita
Night Watch, The 1928,O 8,14:2
Garza, Lorenzo
Domingo en la Tarde, Un; On a Sunday Afternoon 1939,Ja 7,6:3
Novillero 1939,Mr 4,18:5
Torero! 1957,My 22,29:2
Garzay, Dario
Where Words Fail; Donde Mueren las Palabraso 1948,Ag 19,18:4
Gasanof, K
Twenty-Six Commissars 1933,Jl 1,16:6
Gasiorowski, Waclaw (Original Author)
Conquest 1937,N 5,19:1
Gasket, Harold
Moulin Rouge 1953,F 11,33:5
Gasnier, L (Director)
Rich Men's Wives 1922,Ag 21,6:2
Poor Men's Wives 1923,Ja 29,11:1
Daughters of the Rich 1923,Je 18,13:5
Maytime 1924,Je 2,14:3
Poisoned Paradise 1924,Ag 11,16:1
Breath of Scandal, The 1924,N 26,17:3
Parasite, The 1925,F 16,24:1
Boomerang, The 1925,Jl 1,16:1
Streets of Shanghai 1928,F 21,19:3
Slightly Scarlet 1930,Mr 1,23:1
Shadow of the Law 1930,Je 7,10:4
Lawyer's Secret, The 1931,My 30,9:2
Silence 1931,Ag 15,18:3
Strange Case of Clara Deane, The 1932,My 6,15:3
Forgotten Commandments 1932,Je 2,25:2
Esperame 1933,Jl 3,14:6
Gambling Ship 1933,Jl 13,17:5
Melodia de Arrabal 1933,Ag 5,9:5
Cuesta Abajo 1934,Ag 15,13:5
Tango en Broadway, El 1934,D 29,11:3
Topaze 1935,F 16,9:2
Gold Racket, The 1937,Ag 2,10:3
Juan Soldado, o Venganza; John the Soldier or Vengeance 1939,Jl 24,9:3
Gasnier, L (Producer)
Kismet 1920,N 15,12:2
Gasnier, Louis (Director)
Virtuous Sin 1930,N 2,VIII,5:2 (In Addenda)
Gaspard-Huit, P (Director)
Maid in Paris 1957,Jl 13,11:1
Girl on the Third Floor, The; (Sophie et le Crime) 1958,O 11,47:1 (Incorrect in this edition; use 1958,O 11,18:4 elsewhere)
Gaspard-Huit, P (Screenwriter)
Girl on the Third Floor, The; (Sophie et le Crime) 1958,O 11,47:1 (Incorrect in this edition; use 1958,O 11,18:4 elsewhere)
Gassman, Vittorio
Wandering Jew, The 1949,Mr 11,33:2
Shamed 1949,O 13,33:3
Bitter Rice 1950,S 19,39:2
Voice in Your Heart, A 1952,F 23,7:5
Streets of Sorrow 1952,N 18,37:4
Anna 1953,F 19,20:5
Sombrero 1953,Ap 23,37:2
Lure of the Sira 1953,D 26,10:7
Rhapsody 1954,Mr 12,17:1
Mambo 1955,Mr 31,23:3
War and Peace 1956,Ag 22,26:2
Beautiful but Dangerous 1958,F 6,24:1
Tempest 1959,Mr 27,19:2
Defend my Love; (Difendo il Mio Amore) 1959,O 8,48:7
Miracle, The 1959,N 13,25:4

Gassman, Vittorio— Cont
Big Deal on Madonna Street, The 1960,N 23,20:1
Great War; (Grande Guerra, La) 1961,Ag 31,22:3
Barabbas 1962,O 11,49:1
Love and Larceny 1963,F 2,5:6
Fiasco in Milan 1963,Ap 11,29:2
Easy Life, The 1963,D 23,18:2
...And Suddenly It's Murder! 1964,Ja 24,21:1
Let's Talk About Women 1964,S 29,52:5
Successo, Il 1965,Ap 29,40:2
Eye of the Needle, The 1965,Je 22,25:2
Woman Times Seven 1967,Je 28,38:1
Tiger and the Pussycat, The 1967,S 21,56:4
Devil in Love, The 1968,Jl 4,13:4

Gast, Michael (Director)
I Spit on Your Grave 1963,Je 29,13:5

Gaston, William
Billy Rose's Diamond Horseshoe 1945,My 3,37:1

Gastoni, Lisa
Dance Little Lady 1955,D 26,23:3
Baby and the Battleship, The 1957,O 1,37:2
Blue Murder at St Trinian's 1958,My 27,27:1
Intent to Kill 1959,Ap 1,43:2
3 Men in a Boat 1959,Jl 29,33:2
Passport to China 1961,Mr 23,28:1
Gidget Goes to Rome 1963,S 12,32:2
Eva 1965,Je 5,21:2
Wild, Wild Planet 1967,Ag 10,45:5

Gatehouse, Richard
Mouse That Roared, The 1959,O 27,40:1

Gates, Eleanor (Original Author)
Poor Little Rich Girl, The 1917,Mr 5,9:3
Cupid, the Cowpuncher 1920,Jl 26,9:5
Poor Little Rich Girl, The 1936,Je 26,16:1

Gates, H L (Original Author)
Joanna 1925,D 15,14:5
Half Way to Heaven 1929,D 7,19:3

Gates, Harvey
Allotment Wives 1945,N 22,39:3

Gates, Harvey (Original Author)
Crimson Runner, The 1925,My 27,26:2
Madame Racketeer 1932,Jl 23,6:6
O'Shaughnessy's Boy 1935,O 5,18:2
Meet Doctor Christian 1939,D 1,27:2
Men Without Souls 1940,My 13,21:2

Gates, Harvey (Screenwriter)
Forward Pass, The 1929,N 29,25:1
Band Plays on, The 1934,D 22,21:2
Voice of Bugle Ann, The 1936,F 27,23:1
Flying Hostess 1936,D 14,29:4
Fugitive at Large 1939,N 13,15:2
Meet Doctor Christian 1939,D 1,27:2
Mr Wise Guy 1942,Mr 5,27:2

Gates, Joseph (Director)
Girl of the Night 1960,N 12,15:1

Gates, Larry
Has Anybody Seen My Gal 1952,Jl 5,7:2
Glory Alley 1952,Jl 30,20:8
Above and Beyond 1953,Ja 31,10:6
Strange One, The 1957,Ap 13,12:3
Jeanne Eagels 1957,Ag 31,19:1
Cat on a Hot Tin Roof 1958,S 19,24:1
Some Came Running 1959,Ja 23,17:1
Remarkable Mr Pennypacker, The 1959,F 21,25:2
One Foot in Hell 1960,O 20,42:2
Great Impostor, The 1961,Mr 30,24:1
Hoodlum Priest, The 1961,Ap 3,28:5
Underworld, U S A 1961,My 13,10:1
Young Savages, The 1961,My 25,31:1
Ada 1961,Ag 26,15:1
Spiral Road, The 1962,Ag 4,11:2
Toys in the Attic 1963,Ag 1,17:2
Sand Pebbles, The 1966,D 21,48:1
In the Heat of the Night 1967,Ag 3,26:1
Hour of the Gun 1967,N 2,58:4

Gates, Nancy
Great Gildersleeve, The 1942,D 18,36:8
Hitler's Children 1943,F 25,27:1
This Land Is Mine 1943,My 28,19:1
Gildersleeve's Bad Day 1943,Je 11,23:1
Night of Adventure, A 1944,Je 3,10:4
Bride by Mistake 1944,S 16,20:2
Master Race, The 1944,N 2,22:1
Spanish Main, The 1945,N 7,20:2
At Swords Point 1952,Ap 10,37:1
Atomic City, The 1952,My 2,21:1
Member of the Wedding, The 1952,D 31,10:2
Hell's Half Acre 1954,F 27,11:3
Suddenly 1954,O 8,27:2
Bottom of the Bottle, The 1956,F 2,19:2
Wetbacks 1956,My 5,13:2
Death of a Scoundrel 1956,N 6,30:1
Some Came Running 1959,Ja 23,17:1

Gates, Tudor (Screenwriter)
Barbarella 1968,O 12,43:1
Danger Diabolik 1968,D 12,62:6

Gateson, Marjorie
Beloved Bachelor, The 1931,O 17,20:1
Husband's Holiday 1931,D 25,29:2
Street of Women 1932,My 30,16:5
Society Girl 1932,Je 10,22:3
Okay America 1932,S 10,18:5
Silver Dollar 1932,D 23,20:1
King's Vacation, The 1933,Ja 20,21:2

Employees' Entrance 1933,Ja 21,10:6
Cocktail Hour 1933,Je 5,18:5
Lilly Turner 1933,Je 15,21:2
Melody Cruise 1933,Je 23,15:2
Bureau of Missing Persons 1933,S 9,9:2
Walls of Gold 1933,O 21,11:3
World Changes, The 1933,O 27,22:3
Blind Adventure 1933,O 31,24:3
Lady Killer 1934,Ja 1,28:2
Let's Fall in Love 1934,Ja 22,12:3
Hi, Nellie! 1934,F 1,15:5
Coming-Out Party 1934,Mr 17,11:3
Operator 13 1934,Je 23,16:5
Side Streets 1934,Ag 15,13:5
Chained 1934,S 1,16:2
Million Dollar Ransom 1934,S 19,15:2
Down to Their Last Yacht 1934,S 24,14:1
Happiness Ahead 1934,O 11,28:2
Big Hearted Herbert 1934,N 14,23:2
Gentlemen are Born 1934,N 22,27:2
Goin' to Town 1935,My 11,21:2
Your Uncle Dudley 1935,D 12,33:4
Wife vs Secretary 1936,F 29,11:1
Milky Way, The 1936,Mr 26,27:2
Big Brown Eyes 1936,My 2,11:1
Private Number 1936,Je 12,19:1
Man I Marry, The 1936,O 31,24:3
We Have our Moments 1937,Ap 30,17:3
Turn off the Moon 1937,My 20,17:2
Vogues of 1938 1937,Ag 20,21:1
First Lady 1937,D 23,25:1
No Time to Marry 1938,F 23,27:2
Making the Headlines 1938,Ap 1,17:2
Gateway 1938,Ag 8,9:2
Stablemates 1938,O 21,27:2
Spring Madness 1938,D 1,29:3
Duke of West Point, The 1938,D 16,33:2
Geronimo 1940,F 8,18:3
'Til We Meet Again 1940,Ap 14,14:2
Back Street 1941,F 12,25:2
Submarine Zone; (Escape To Glory)
  1941,Ap 7,13:2
Moonlight in Hawaii 1941,O 10,26:6
You'll Never Get Rich 1941,O 24,27:2
International Lady 1941,N 11,29:2
Obliging Young Lady 1942,F 13,24:4
Juke Box Jenny 1942,Ap 17,21:3
Rings on her Fingers 1942,Ap 24,21:4
Sky's the Limit, The 1943,S 3,15:2
I Dood It 1943,N 11,29:1
No Time for Love 1943,D 2,30:1
Seven Days Ashore 1944,Ap 26,24:7
One More Tomorrow 1946,My 25,12:2
Caddy, The 1953,S 18,16:6

Gatica, Malu
Target Unknown 1951,Mr 5,24:2

Gatlin, Jerry
Run, Appaloosa, Run! 1966,Jl 14,28:1

Gattegne, Cesar
Pickpocket 1963,My 22,36:2

Gatti, Attilio Comdr (Director)
Bitter Spears 1956,N 10,14:2

Gatti, Attilio Comdr (Producer)
Bitter Spears 1956,N 10,14:2

Gattiker, Albert
Ramparts We Watch, The 1940,S 20,27:1

Gatto, Alfonso
Gospel According to St Matthew, The
  1966,F 18,23:1

Gaubert, Daniele
Flight From Ashiya 1964,Ap 23,34:1
And so to Bed 1965,Jl 31,11:3

Gaubert, Ginette
Kermesse Heroique, La 1936,S 23,29:1

Gaudeau, Yvonne
Resistance; Peleton d'Execution 1946,Jl 5,15:3
Sextette (Part I-The Gun); Gun, The (Sextette)
  1953,Mr 2,19:2
Marriage of Figaro, The 1963,Ap 30,26:1

Gaudsmith Brothers
Pirate, The 1948,My 21,19:2

Gauge, Alexander
Interrupted Journey 1951,My 29,20:2
Murder in the Cathedral 1952,Mr 26,35:2
Penny Princess 1953,Mr 25,37:3
Martin Luther 1953,S 10,22:1
Pickwick Papers, The 1954,Ap 5,21:2
Will any Gentleman? 1955,S 28,70:6
Iron Petticoat, The 1957,F 2,12:2

Gaugler, Hans
It Happened in Broad Daylight 1960,S 30,33:1

Gauglitz, Hans Otto
Jugend von Heute; Youth of Today
  1938,N 5,15:3

Gaulden, Ray (Original Author)
5 Card Stud 1968,Ag 1,24:1

Gauldi, Massimo (Producer)
Stranger Returns, The 1968,S 12,54:3

Gaulle, Charles de
Liberation of Europe, The 1968,S 29,IV,7:1

Gaultier, Henry
Passion Of Joan Of Arc, The 1929,Mr 29,21:1
Passion of Jeanne d'Arc, The 1929,Mr 31,VIII,7:1

Gaumont, C L M (Producer)
Lovers and Thieves 1958,Ag 5,23:2

Gaunt, Valerie
Curse of Frankenstein, The 1957,Ag 8,15:5
Horror of Dracula 1958,My 29,24:4

Gaunt, William
Virtuous Vamp, A 1919,N 17,20:1

Gauthier, Jacqueline
Loves of Casanova 1948,S 18,11:4

Gauthier, Jacques (Producer)
Tempest in the Flesh 1957,Ja 19,12:2
Lover's Net 1957,Jl 23,23:1

Gauthier, Jacques (Screenwriter)
Light Across the Street, The; Lumiere d'en Face,
  La 1957,Jl 30,20:2

Gauthier Ballet
Tarantella Napoletana 1954,Ap 19,19:3

Gautier, Jacqueline
Louise 1940,F 3,9:4
Shop-Girls of Paris; Au Bonheur de Dames
  1947,Je 23,14:4
Scandals of Clochemerle, The 1950,Mr 28,28:2

Gautier, Leonard Bricklayers
Follow the Boys 1944,Ap 26,24:6

Gautier, Richard (Screenwriter)
Maryjane 1968,Mr 14,51:4

Gauvreau, Emile (Miscellaneous)
Heroes All 1931,N 12,30:2

Gauvreau, Emile (Original Author)
Scandal for Sale 1932,Ap 3,26:2

Gavaldon, Roberto (Director)
Adventures of Casanova 1948,Mr 22,18:3
Littlest Outlaw, The 1955,D 27,31:1
Macario 1961,S 28,48:6

Gavaldon, Roberto (Screenwriter)
Macario 1961,S 28,48:6

Gaven, Jean
If all the Guys in the World 1957,Ap 23,34:1
Girl on the Third Floor, The; (Sophie et le Crime)
  1958,O 11,47:1 (Incorrect in this edition; use
  1958,O 11,18:4 elsewhere)
Witches of Salem 1958,D 9,54:2
Young Girls Beware 1959,Ag 22,8:2
Riff Raff Girls 1962,O 20,13:5

Gavin, Grace
Scotch on the Rocks 1954,Je 14,18:2

Gavin, John
Four Girls in Town 1957,Ja 17,34:5
Quantez 1957,S 7,12:7
Time to Love and a Time to Die, A
  1958,Jl 10,22:1
Imitation of Life 1959,Ap 18,18:1
Psycho 1960,Je 17,37:1
Spartacus 1960,O 7,28:1
Midnight Lace 1960,O 14,27:1
Breath of Scandal, A 1960,D 17,19:1
Romanoff and Juliet 1961,Je 9,26:1
Tammy Tell me True 1961,Jl 27,23:2
Back Street 1961,O 13,27:1
Thoroughly Modern Millie 1967,Mr 23,25:1

Gavras, Costa (Director)
Sleeping Car Murder, The 1966,Mr 8,45:1

Gavras, Costa (Screenwriter)
Sleeping Car Murder, The 1966,Mr 8,45:1

Gavrilidis, George
Policeman of the 16th Precinct, The
  1963,Ap 22,23:2

Gavrilovitch, E (Screenwriter)
Mashenka 1942,N 21,10:7

Gavronsky, M (Director)
Beethoven Concerto 1937,Mr 24,29:1

Gawthorne, Peter
Behind That Curtain 1929,Jl 1,31:2
Sunny Side Up 1929,O 4,24:5
Temple Tower 1930,My 10,25:3
Man Who Came Back, The 1931,Ja 3,21:2
Charlie Chan Carries On 1931,Mr 21,15:1
Perfect Understanding 1933,F 23,20:2
Night and Day 1933,My 29,22:2
Blarney Kiss, The 1933,Ag 19,14:4
Phantom Fiend 1935,Ap 22,14:2
Gangway 1937,Ag 21,7:3
Mister V 1942,F 13,24:4

Gaxton, William
It's the old Army Game 1926,Jl 5,6:4
Fifty Million Frenchmen 1931,Mr 26,31:2
Their big Moment 1934,S 6,22:4
Something to Shout About 1943,Ap 8,27:3
Best Foot Forward 1943,Je 30,25:2
Heat's on, The 1943,N 26,29:2

Gay, Betsy
What's Buzzin Cousin 1943,Jl 23,21:4

Gay, Dixie
Two Weeks Off 1929,Je 24,27:1

Gay, F T (Producer)
Hired Killer, The 1967,Mr 2,30:3

Gay, Git
Dreams; Kvinnodrom 1960,Je 1,42:1

Gay, Inez
Father's Son 1941,F 13,25:3

Gay, John (Original Author)
Beggar's Opera, The 1953,Ag 25,18:2
Threepenny Opera, The 1960,Jl 11,24:4

Gay, John (Screenwriter)
Run Silent, Run Deep 1958,Mr 28,29:1
Separate Tables 1958,D 19,2:7
Happy Thieves, The 1962,F 5,19:4
4 Horsemen of the Apocalypse, The
  1962,Mr 10,10:2
Courtship of Eddie's Father, The 1963,Mr 7,8:5
  (Incorrect in this edition; use 1963,Mr 28,8:5
  elsewhere)
Hallelujah Trail, The 1965,Jl 2,17:1
Power, The 1968,Mr 7,52:2
No Way to Treat a Lady 1968,Mr 21,56:1
Gay, Noel (Composer)
Sleepless Nights 1933,Jl 22,14:2
Woman in Command, The 1934,My 29,22:2
You Made Me Love You 1934,My 30,14:3
Gay, Noel (Screenwriter)
There Goes the Bride 1933,Mr 4,11:3
Gay, Ramon
Empty Star, The; Estrella Vacia, La
  1962,Mr 28,36:4
Gaye, Gregory
They Had to See Paris 1929,O 12,11:1
High Society Blues 1930,Ap 19,15:1
What a Widow 1930,O 4,15:2
Renegades 1930,N 8,21:3
Young as You Feel 1931,Ag 8,16:3
Once in a Lifetime 1932,O 29,18:4
Affairs of a Gentleman 1934,Je 23,16:7
Handy Andy 1934,Ag 4,14:5
British Agent 1934,S 20,20:1
Dodsworth 1936,S 24,29:1
Under Your Spell 1936,N 7,15:2
Charlie Chan at the Opera 1936,D 5,16:2
That Girl From Paris 1937,Ja 1,19:1
Lancer Spy 1937,N 4,29:1
First Lady 1937,D 23,25:1
Tovarich 1937,D 31,9:2
Wise Girl 1938,Ja 10,13:3
Love, Honor and Behave 1938,Mr 21,18:2
Straight, Place and Show 1938,O 1,10:2
Thanks For Everything 1938,D 10,13:2
Paris Honeymoon 1939,Ja 26,17:1
Three Musketeers, The 1939,F 18,12:2
Hotel for Women 1939,Ag 26,20:2
Ninotchka 1939,N 10,27:2
Down Argentine Way 1940,O 18,25:1
Flight Lieutenant 1942,Jl 31,11:1
Purple Heart, The 1944,Mr 9,15:2
Conspirators, The 1944,O 21,15:2
Cornered 1945,D 26,15:1
So Dark the Night 1946,D 7,16:2
Bachelor and the Bobby-Soxer, The
  1947,Jl 25,12:5
Blackmail 1947,Ag 5,26:3
Unfinished Dance, The 1947,O 31,29:2
Black Magic 1949,N 9,37:2
Cargo to Capetown 1950,Mr 31,36:3
Peking Express 1951,Jl 19,20:2
World in His Arms, The 1952,O 10,21:2
Bailout at 43,000 1957,Je 8,13:2
Gaye, Howard
Scaramouche 1923,O 12,7:2 (Incorrect in this
  edition; use 1927,O 1,7:2 elsewhere)
Dante's Inferno 1924,S 30,27:3
Prince of Lovers, The 1927,N 29,31:1
Gaye, Lisa
Ten Thousand Bedrooms 1957,Ap 4,37:1
Gayer, Echlin
Her Love Story 1924,O 7,26:1
Gaylor, Anna
Elephant Gun 1959,Je 20,11:2
Inside Out 1964,S 25,32:1
Life Upside Down; Inside Out 1965,Ag 18,41:4
Killing Game, The 1968,Ag 27,36:1
Gaylord, Gerry
Five Gates to Hell 1959,D 10,51:6
Gaynes, Page
Inheritance, The 1964,N 9,42:2
Gaynor, Janet
Seventh Heaven 1927,My 26,22:1
Sunrise 1927,S 24,15:3 (In Addenda)
Two Girls Wanted 1927,N 14,26:1
Sunrise; Song of two Human Beings
  1928,Ja 29,VIII,6:2
Street Angel 1928,Ap 10,33:2
4 Devils 1928,O 4,26:3
Christina 1929,Ap 1,22:1
Lucky Star 1929,Jl 22,17:1
Sunny Side Up 1929,O 4,24:5
Happy Days 1930,F 14,20:1
High Society Blues 1930,Ap 19,15:1
Man Who Came Back, The 1931,Ja 3,21:2
Daddy Long Legs 1931,Je 6,15:5
Merely Mary Ann 1931,S 12,15:4
Delicious 1931,D 26,15:5
First Year, The 1932,Ag 22,20:2
Tess of the Storm Country 1932,N 19,20:2
State Fair 1933,Ja 27,13:2
Adorable 1933,My 19,23:2
Paddy the Next Best Thing 1933,Ag 25,12:2
Carolina 1934,F 16,17:2
Change of Heart 1934,My 11,24:2

Servants' Entrance 1934,S 27,25:2
One More Spring 1935,F 22,27:1
Farmer Takes a Wife, The 1935,Ag 9,21:2
Small Town Girl 1936,Ap 11,19:1
Ladies in Love 1936,O 29,31:1
Star Is Born, A 1937,Ap 23,25:1
Three Loves Has Nancy 1938,S 2,21:2
Young in Heart, The 1938,N 4,27:2
Bernardine 1957,Jl 25,28:1
Gaynor, Mitzi
My Blue Heaven 1950,S 16,12:6
Take Care of my Little Girl 1951,Jl 19,20:2
Golden Girl 1951,N 21,20:3
We're not Married 1952,Jl 12,16:2
Bloodhounds of Broadway 1952,N 15,15:2
Down Among the Sheltering Palms
  1953,Je 13,11:2
Three Young Texans 1954,Ap 17,8:2
There's no Business Like Show Business
  1954,D 17,37:3
Anything Goes 1956,Mr 22,38:1
Birds and the Bees, The 1956,Ap 23,22:1
Joker Is Wild, The 1957,S 27,16:6
Girls, Les 1957,O 4,27:2
South Pacific 1958,Mr 20,33:1
Happy Anniversary 1959,N 11,41:1
Surprise Package 1960,O 15,26:2
For Love or Money 1963,Ag 8,19:1
Gayson, Eunice
Miss Robin Hood 1953,Je 27,7:2
Dance Little Lady 1955,D 26,23:3
Zarak 1956,D 27,22:1
Ship Was Loaded, The 1958,Ja 20,20:1
Dr No 1963,My 30,20:1
From Russia with Love 1964,Ap 9,25:1
Gazaille, Gilbert L Pfc
Cease Fire! 1953,N 25,17:1
Gaze, Gwen
I Cover the War 1937,Ag 2,10:2
Partners of the Plains 1938,F 12,20:4
Gazlades, Michael (Director)
Anna of Rhodes 1950,Mr 23,34:2
Gazon, Gyula
Vasember 1935,D 9,25:3
Pentek Rezi; Friday Rose 1939,D 23,9:2
Gazy, V (Screenwriter)
Sandu Follows the Sun 1965,Ap 19,37:1
Gazzano, Sam (Miscellaneous)
Scorched Earth 1942,S 12,9:2
Gazzara, Ben
Strange One, The 1957,Ap 13,12:3
Anatomy of a Murder 1959,Jl 3,10:1
Young Doctors, The 1961,Ag 24,25:2
Convicts 4 1962,O 4,44:2
Rage to Live, A 1965,O 21,57:1
Gazzo, Michael V (Original Author)
Hatful of Rain, A 1957,Jl 18,19:2
Gazzo, Michael V (Screenwriter)
Hatful of Rain, A 1957,Jl 18,19:2
King Creole 1958,Jl 4,15:2
Gazzolo, Lauro
Documento Fatale, Il 1940,S 26,27:3
Eternal Melodies 1948,F 14,17:3
Merry Chase, The 1948,S 18,11:4
Four Steps in the Clouds 1948,N 22,25:2
Shamed 1949,O 13,33:3
Peddlin' in Society 1950,F 23,33:3
Tomorrow is too Late 1952,Ap 14,22:2
Sky Is Red, The 1952,My 27,30:2
Father's Dilemma 1952,S 23,25:1
Ring Around the Clock 1953,My 19,36:2
Gazzolo, Nando
Hills Run Red, The 1967,N 11,26:3
Gear, Luella
Carefree 1938,S 23,35:1
Perfect Marriage, The 1947,Ja 16,30:3
Jigsaw 1949,My 30,9:4
Phffft 1954,N 11,43:2
Gear, Will
Kid From Texas, The 1950,Je 2,26:2
Gearon, Valerie
Nine Hours to Rama 1963,Ap 4,58:2
Geary, Alex
Rock-a-Bye Baby 1958,Jl 24,18:1
Geary, Bud
Trail of the Lonesome Pine, The 1936,F 20,23:5
Smoky 1946,Je 27,29:1
Geary, Maine
Hill Billy, The 1924,Mr 12,19:4
Soft Living 1928,F 27,16:2
Geary, Pat
Gay Intruders, The 1946,Mr 18,24:2
Geay, Pierre
Siroco 1931,N 26,37:2
Gebauer, Olly
Ein Ausgekochter Junge 1932,My 3,25:5
Marion, Das Gehoert Sich Nicht 1934,D 15,9:4
Kaiserwalzer 1934,D 29,11:2
Madonna, Wo Bist Du? 1936,Mr 21,13:3
Ein Liebesroman im Hause Habsburg
  1936,O 12,23:2
Podoroso Caballero 1936,O 26,20:2
Wir Sind vom K u K Infantrie-Regiment
  1938,N 19,9:2

Gebel, Bruno
Before Him all Rome Trembled 1947,F 22,16:2
Gebert, Gordon
Holiday Affair 1949,N 24,48:2
Flame and the Arrow, The 1950,Jl 8,7:2
House on Telegraph Hill 1951,My 14,29:1
Night Into Morning 1951,Je 11,20:7
Narrow Margin, The 1952,My 5,18:7
Summer Love 1958,Je 26,23:4
Gebler, Ernest (Original Author)
Plymouth Adventure 1952,N 14,20:3
Gebrail, Joseph
Broken Wings, The 1968,Mr 16,34:1
Gebuehr, Otto
Waterloo 1929,Ap 16,32:5
Floetenkonzert von Sanssouci, Das
  1931,O 17,20:1
Barberina, Die Taenzerin Von Sans-Souci
  1932,O 26,15:4
Choral von Leuthen, Der 1935,Ja 21,19:4
Pretty Miss Schragg 1937,S 25,10:2
Nanon 1938,N 26,18:2
Fridericus 1939,F 25,19:2
Leidenschaft; Passion 1940,S 24,26:6
City of Torment 1950,Je 10,11:4
Devil Makes Three, The 1952,Ag 30,6:2
Angelika 1954,S 25,10:7
Gebuhr, Otto
Fredericus Rex 1922,Je 25,III,13:1 (In Addenda)
Gee, Donald
Bofors Gun, The 1968,S 23,42:3
Gee, Z
Uncivilized 1937,N 17,27:4
GEER
See Also GEYER
Geer, Andrew (Original Author)
Wild Blue Yonder, The 1952,Ja 2,20:1
Sea Chase, The 1955,Je 11,8:7
Geer, Lennie
Great Locomotive Chase, The 1956,Je 27,35:1
Geer, Will
Misleading Lady, The 1932,Ap 9,18:1
Deep Waters 1948,Jl 23,12:4
Johnny Allegro 1949,My 31,19:2
Lust for Gold 1949,Jl 4,9:2
Anna Lucasta 1949,Ag 12,13:2
Intruder in the Dust 1949,N 23,19:1
Comanche Territory 1950,Ap 8,9:3
Winchester 73 1950,Je 8,38:2
Broken Arrow 1950,Jl 21,15:2
To Please a Lady 1950,O 27,24:3
Double Crossbones 1951,Ap 27,19:2
Bright Victory 1951,Ag 1,19:2
Tall Target, The 1951,S 28,26:2
Salt of the Earth 1954,Mr 15,20:2
Advise and Consent 1962,Je 7,31:2
Black Like Me 1964,My 21,42:1
Salt of the Earth 1965,N 1,57:1
Seconds 1966,O 6,56:1
In Cold Blood 1967,D 15,60:1
President's Analyst, The 1967,D 22,44:4
Bandolero 1968,Jl 18,26:2
Geeson, Judy
To Sir, With Love 1967,Je 15,56:1
Berserk! 1968,Ja 11,42:2
Here We Go Around the Mulberry Bush
  1968,Mr 5,34:5
Prudence and the Pill 1968,My 24,37:1
Hammerhead 1968,S 12,54:3
Geffroy, Jean-Pierre
Portrait of Innocence 1948,Je 9,35:2
Geftman, C (Director)
Confessions of a Rogue 1948,Mr 30,26:3
Geftman, C (Producer)
Pasha's Wives, The 1942,Ap 6,19:2
Friend Will come Tonight, A; Ami Viendra Ce
  Soir, Un 1948,Jl 12,11:2
Gegauff, Paul
Weekend 1968,S 28,36:1
Gegauff, Paul (Miscellaneous)
Cousins, The (Les Cousins) 1959,N 24,44:1
Gegauff, Paul (Screenwriter)
Leda 1961,Jl 19,33:1
Purple Noon 1961,S 1,12:1
Bonnes Femmes, Les 1966,My 13,32:1
Biches, Les 1968,S 27,34:1
Gegechkori, G
Dragonfly, The 1955,Je 27,18:2
Scrapper, The 1959,D 14,42:2
Gegol, Nikolai (Original Author)
Overcoat, The 1965,Mr 2,31:2
Gehien, Fritz
Young Torless 1968,Jl 23,27:2
Gehret, Jean
Boudu Saved From Drowning; Boudu Sauve Des
  Eaux 1967,F 24,26:2
Gehret, Jean (Producer)
Boudu Saved From Drowning; Boudu Sauve Des
  Eaux 1967,F 24,26:2
Gehrig, Lou
Rawhide 1938,Ap 25,19:2
Ninth Inning, The 1942,Ja 8,30:3

Gehring, Viktor
Monna Vanna 1923,S 25,8:2
Schloss Hubertus 1935,F 9,11:3
Gehrman, Lucy
Brivele der Mamen, A; Little Letter to Mother, A
1939,S 15,26:4
God, Man and Devil 1950,Ja 23,16:2
Geibart, Larry (Original Author)
Thrill of it All, The 1963,Ag 2,15:3
Geiber, Stasia
Echoes of Silence 1967,Ap 7,32:2
Geiger, Franz (Screenwriter)
Lola Montes 1968,S 23,42:6
Geiger, Miriam (Original Author)
Woman Doctor 1939,Mr 24,27:3
Geiger, Rod E (Producer)
Give Us This Day 1949,D 21,41:2
Geimi, Pietro
And There Came a Man 1968,Ap 5,56:4
Geiovani, M G
Lenin in 1918 1939,Je 27,27:2
Geirod, A
Men and Jobs 1933,Ja 3,19:3
Geisel, Helen (Original Author)
Design for Death 1948,Je 11,27:2
Geisel, Theodor S (Original Author)
Design for Death 1948,Je 11,27:2
Geiser, Linda
Pawnbroker, The 1965,Ap 21,51:1
Geist, Irving (Miscellaneous)
Dybbuk, The 1938,Ja 28,17:2
Gelabuzsky, F A (Director)
Station Master, The 1928,Je 18,13:2
Gelba, Eugenjusz
Przysieglas 1932,My 16,19:5
Gelbart, Larry (Original Author)
Funny Thing Happened on the Way to the Forum,
A 1966,O 17,48:1
Gelbart, Larry (Screenwriter)
Notorious Landlady, The 1962,Jl 27,15:2
Not With my Wife, You Don't! 1966,N 3,45:2
Gelbert, Larry (Screenwriter)
Wrong Box 1966,Jl 20,46:1
Geldert, Clarence
Woman of Paris, A 1923,O 2,7:2
Richard the Lion-Hearted 1923,O 22,17:1
Love's Whirlpool 1924,Mr 11,16:2
Fighting American, The 1924,My 13,24:1
North of 36 1924,D 8,13:3
Oh, Doctor! 1925,F 23,24:1
Young April 1926,Ag 31,15:3
Flaming Forest, The 1926,N 22,28:3
Dress Parade 1927,O 31,22:1
Bishop Murder Case, The 1930,F 1,15:1
White Eagle 1932,S 24,18:4
Jungle Bride 1933,My 13,16:3
In Love With Life 1934,My 12,12:3
Man Trailer, The 1934,My 23,22:3
Mississippi 1935,Ap 18,27:2
Geleva, E
Tsar's Bride, The 1966,Mr 12,13:2
Gelin, Daniel
Her First Affair; (Children of Paradise)
1947,F 20,32:3
Friend Will come Tonight, A; Ami Viendra Ce
Soir, Un 1948,Jl 12,11:2
Edward and Caroline 1952,Ap 30,33:3
Ronde, La 1954,Mr 17,27:2
Dirty Hands 1954,My 11,25:5
Plaisir, Le (The Model); Model, The (Le Plaisir)
1954,My 20,38:1
Adorable Creatures 1956,Ja 11,36:2
Man Who Knew too Much, The 1956,My 17,37:1
Snow Was Black, The 1956,O 16,36:5
Woman of Rome 1956,N 6,30:1
Royal Affairs in Versailles 1957,Mr 9,16:1
Maid in Paris 1957,Jl 13,11:1
Lover's Net 1957,Jl 23,23:1
Please Mr Balzac 1957,N 18,37:2
There's Always a Price Tag 1958,My 26,25:2
Port of Desire 1960,N 3,49:2
Carthage in Flames 1961,Ja 26,32:3
Testament of Orpheus 1962,Ap 10,48:1
Julie the Redhead 1963,O 15,44:1
Bonne Soupe, La 1964,Mr 16,37:1
Is Paris Burning? 1966,N 11,36:1
Gell, William (Producer)
Lilli Marlene 1952,Mr 29,19:2
Rattle of a Simple Man 1964,D 21,42:2
Gellenbeck, Benno
Sunderin 1954,D 24,7:2
Geller
Stormy Waters 1946,Je 17,32:2
Geller, Bruce (Screenwriter)
Sail a Crooked Ship 1962,F 3,12:6
Geller, Jack (Original Author)
Connection, The 1962,O 4,44:1
Geller, Jack (Screenwriter)
Connection, The 1962,O 4,44:1
Geller, James J (Producer)
Love From a Stranger 1947,N 28,30:1

Geller, Joyce (Original Author)
Cool Ones, The 1967,My 11,50:1
Geller, Joyce (Screenwriter)
Cool Ones, The 1967,My 11,50:1
Geller, Stephen (Original Author)
Pretty Poison 1968,O 25,55:1
Gellert, Baby
Please Don't Eat the Daisies 1960,Ap 1,37:1
Gellin, Daniel
Season for Love, The 1963,My 9,40:2
Gellow, Janet Ann
Ghost of Frankenstein, The 1942,Ap 4,19:2
Gelovani, I (Screenwriter)
Ballet Tales 1956,O 25,40:5
Gelovani, M
Man With the Gun, The 1939,Ja 30,9:3
New Horizons 1939,My 12,25:3
They Wanted Peace 1940,Ja 8,11:3
Wings of Victory 1941,N 17,15:2
Fortress on the Volga 1942,D 25,15:3
Vow, The 1947,Je 23,14:3
Fall of Berlin 1952,Je 9,19:2
Gelsey, Erwin (Original Author)
Swing Time 1936,Ag 28,21:2
Big Broadcast of 1937, The 1936,O 22,31:1
Campus Confessions 1938,S 23,35:1
Touchdown Army 1938,O 28,27:2
Sing Your Worries Away 1942,My 15,25:2
Cover Girl 1944,Mr 31,26:1
This Time for Keeps 1947,D 5,33:4
Gelsey, Erwin (Screenwriter)
Sweet Adeline 1935,Ja 7,13:2
Muss 'Em Up 1936,F 3,21:2
Double or Nothing 1937,S 2,17:3
Hold 'Em Navy 1937,N 6,14:2
Campus Confessions 1938,S 23,35:1
Touchdown Army 1938,O 28,27:2
Gelzer, Jay (Original Author)
Driven 1923,F 12,13:4
Gemier, Firmin
Magician, The 1926,O 25,15:1
Grandeur et Decadence 1937,My 31,11:3
Gemini, Marco
Eight and One Half 1963,Je 26,36:1
Gemma, Giuliano
My Son, The Hero 1963,S 19,23:1
Goliath and the Sins of Babylon 1964,Mr 5,36:2
Gemma, Irene
It's Forever Springtime 1951,D 29,7:7
Gemmiti, Arturo (Director)
Monte Cassino 1948,N 25,47:3
Gemmiti, Arturo (Producer)
Monte Cassino 1948,N 25,47:3
Gemmiti, Arturo (Screenwriter)
Monte Cassino 1948,N 25,47:3
Gemmo, Biulo
Cieca di Sorrento, La 1936,Ag 3,11:3
Gemmo, Donatella
Passion of St Francis, The 1932,D 17,22:3
Gemorov, Mikhail (Director)
Skanderbeg 1954,Jl 5,6:4
Genait, Marcelle
Crossroads 1939,Mr 14,17:5
Gence, Denise
Pot Bouille 1958,O 28,39:1
Marriage of Figaro, The 1963,Ap 30,26:1
Gencel, Jack
Face to the Wind 1951,Ja 16,34:2
Here Comes the Groom 1951,S 21,19:2
Gendron, Pierre
Bashful Suitor, The 1921,D 12,20:2
Young Painter, The 1922,F 26,VI,3:1 (In
Addenda)
Three Women 1924,O 6,25:1
Lover of Camille, The 1924,N 11,14:1
Gendron, Pierre (Screenwriter)
Minstrel Man 1944,Jl 17,18:5
Generalis, Thanos
Mademoiselle-Age 39 1956,Mr 26,34:2
Policeman of the 16th Precinct, The
1963,Ap 22,23:2
Genest, Emile
Nikki, Wild Dog of the North 1961,S 5,37:6
Big Red 1962,S 3,11:2
Rampage 1963,O 17,39:2
Incredible Journey, The 1963,N 21,43:2
Genet, Jean (Original Author)
Balcony, The 1963,Mr 22,7:1
Deathwatch 1967,Je 28,38:1
Genet, Jean (Screenwriter)
Mademoiselle 1966,Ag 2,23:1
Genette, Adam
Three Steps North 1951,Je 29,14:2
Genevois, Emile
Miserables, Les 1936,O 28,31:2
Miserables, Les 1946,D 26,28:4
Portrait of Innocence 1948,Je 9,35:2
Genia, Claude
Honorable Catherine, The 1948,Ag 23,13:3
Geniat, Gilberte
Act of Love 1954,F 12,20:5
Belle Americaine, La 1961,D 18,42:1

Geniat, Marcelle
Mysteres de Paris, Les 1937,Ja 30,21:2
Grandeur et Decadence 1937,My 31,11:3
They Were Five 1938,Je 1,19:5
Man of the Hour, The 1940,N 21,43:2
Genin, Rene
Lower Depths, The 1937,S 11,20:1
Orage 1938,D 12,26:2
Boys' School 1939,Je 6,26:2
Port of Shadows 1939,O 30,13:2
Charrette Fantome, La 1940,My 28,29:2
It Happened at the Inn; Goupi Mains Rouge
1945,D 22,16:2
Cage aux Rossignols, La; (Cage of Nightingales,
A) 1947,Ap 3,31:2
Francis the First 1947,N 20,38:4
Savage Triangle 1952,S 30,38:2
Ramuntcho 1953,Mr 2,19:2
Moment of Truth, The 1954,Ap 27,36:2
Sheep Has Five Legs, The 1955,Ag 10,19:2
Forbidden Fruit 1959,F 23,19:1
Law Is the Law, The 1959,Mr 11,41:2
Judex 1966,Ap 26,55:1
Genina, Augusto (Director)
Cyrano de Bergerac 1925,Jl 6,12:2
Paris-Beguin 1932,D 31,10:1
Blumen aus Nizza; Flowers From Nice
1939,Ap 1,17:3
Squadrone Bianco, Lo; White Squadrone, The
1939,D 1,27:2
Kiss of Fire, The 1940,N 20,27:4
Devotion 1953,Ja 31,10:6
Three Forbidden Stories 1953,N 16,21:4
Genina, Augusto (Original Author)
Three Forbidden Stories 1953,N 16,21:4
Genina, Augusto (Screenwriter)
Devotion 1953,Ja 31,10:6
Three Forbidden Stories 1953,N 16,21:4
Genius
Juliet of the Spirits 1965,N 4,57:1
Genn, Leo
When Thief Meets Thief 1937,Je 15,26:2
Rat, The 1938,F 28,19:1
Missing Ten Days 1941,Ap 21,15:5 (In Addenda)
Way Ahead, The 1945,Je 4,22:3
Henry V 1946,Je 18,30:2
Green for Danger 1947,Ag 8,10:2
Mourning Becomes Electra 1947,N 20,38:2
Velvet Touch, The 1948,Ag 26,16:2
Snake Pit, the 1948,N 5,29:2
Miniver Story, The 1950,O 27,24:2
No Place for Jennifer 1951,Jl 17,31:2
Wooden Horse, The 1951,Ag 29,20:2
Magic Box, The 1952,S 24,40:2
Plymouth Adventure 1952,N 14,20:3
Girls of Pleasure Island, The 1953,My 16,10:1
Paratrooper 1953,D 31,9:3
Personal Affair 1954,O 23,13:2
Green Scarf, The 1955,Ja 15,10:2
Moby Dick 1956,Jl 5,18:1
Beyond Mombasa 1957,My 31,14:2
I Accuse! 1958,Mr 6,32:1
Lady Chatterley's Lover 1959,Jl 11,11:1
Longest Day, The 1962,O 5,28:1
55 Days at Peking 1963,My 30,20:1
Ten Little Indians 1966,F 10,33:1
Genn, Leo (Narrator)
Tunisian Victory 1944,Mr 24,17:2
Elizabeth is Queen 1953,Je 29,20:4
Genna, Irene
Verginita 1953,Ap 18,17:2
Life and Music of Giuseppe Verdi, The
1957,My 2,26:2
Gennari, Lina
Lacrime e Sorrisi 1936,D 17,35:2
Umberto D 1955,N 8,37:1
Gennaro, Peter (Miscellaneous)
Unsinkable Molly Brown, The 1964,Jl 17,15:1
Genock, Edward (Director)
Cassino to Korea 1950,O 4,38:2
Genoino, Arnaldo (Screenwriter)
Fear No Evil 1949,Mr 31,31:2
Genov, N
Heroes of Shipka 1956,S 3,10:5
Genoves, Andre (Producer)
Biches, Les 1968,S 27,34:1
Gensac, Claudia
Virtuous Scoundrel, The 1957,O 23,37:1
Genschow, Fritz
Morgenrot 1933,My 16,15:2
Ferien vom Ich 1935,Ap 1,17:2
Gleisdreieck 1938,Je 11,9:1
Seefahrt die Ist Lustig, Eine; Merry Sea Trip, A
1938,O 22,14:2
Drei Unteroffiziere; Three Non-Coms
1939,My 20,11:3
Henker Fraven und Soldaten; Hangmen, Women
and Soldiers 1940,Ja 13,11:3
Genske, Margaret
Cliff of Sin, The 1952,N 22,16:5
Gensler, Lewis E (Composer)
Here is my Heart 1934,D 22,21:1

Gensler, Lewis E (Original Author)
Yours for the Asking 1936,Ag 20,14:2
Gensler, Lewis E (Producer)
Yours for the Asking 1936,Ag 20,14:2
Big Broadcast of 1937, The 1936,O 22,31:1
Artists and Models 1937,Ag 5,19:2
College Swing 1938,Ap 28,27:2
Gentile, Robert
Strangers in the City 1962,Jl 17,19:2
Gentilli, Olga V
Serpente a Sonagli, Il 1936,Ag 17,9:2
Al Buio Insieme 1937,Ag 6,21:3
Gentilomo, Giacomo
Carnevale di Venezia, Il; Carnival of Venice, The 1940,O 11,25:2
Gentilomo, Giacomo (Director)
Lieutenant Craig-Missing 1951,My 19,9:4
Young Caruso, The 1953,O 13,34:4
Last of the Vikings 1962,S 27,33:4
Gentilomo, Giacomo (Original Author)
Lieutenant Craig-Missing 1951,My 19,9:4
Gentilomo, Giacomo (Screenwriter)
Lieutenant Craig-Missing 1951,My 19,9:4
Young Caruso, The 1953,O 13,34:4
Gentle, Alice
Song of the Flame 1930,My 7,24:5
Golden Dawn 1930,Jl 26,16:4
Gentle, Lili
Teenage Rebel 1956,N 17,17:6
Will Success Spoil Rock Hunter 1957,S 12,37:5
Sing Boy Sing 1958,F 22,9:4
Mr Hobbs Takes a Vacation 1962,Je 16,11:2
Gentle Maniacs
Hit Parade, The 1937,My 31,11:2
Gentry, Race
Bold and the Brave, The 1956,My 26,15:2
Men in War 1957,Mr 20,32:4
Gentzel, Ludde
Dreams; Kvinnodrom 1960,Je 1,42:1
Geoffrey, Madeleine
Curtain Rises, The 1939,Ap 22,15:2
Personal Column 1941,F 3,13:2
Geoffrey, Wallace
Flying Fool 1931,O 19,28:1
Spy 77 1936,F 10,15:1
Geoffrey, Wallace (Original Author)
Scotland Yard Mystery, The 1936,Mr 16,21:4
Perfect Woman, The 1951,F 17,10:7
George, Christopher
Dorado, El 1967,Je 29,32:1
George, Don
Sit Tight 1931,F 19,20:4
George, Eliot (Original Author)
Leather Boys, The 1965,N 9,50:1
George, Florence
College Swing 1938,Ap 28,27:2
Tell no Tales 1939,Je 2,27:3
George, George S (Screenwriter)
Heat's on, The 1943,N 26,29:2
George, George W (Director)
James Dean Story, The 1957,O 19,16:7
George, George W (Miscellaneous)
Thunder Bay 1953,My 21,39:2
George, George W (Original Author)
Nevadan, The 1950,Ja 13,19:4
Woman on Pier 13, The 1950,Je 16,28:4
George, George W (Producer)
James Dean Story, The 1957,O 19,16:7
Matter of Innocence, A 1968,F 22,36:1
George, George W (Screenwriter)
Nevadan, The 1950,Ja 13,19:4
Peggy 1950,Jl 21,15:4
Mystery Submarine 1951,F 2,19:2
Red Mountain 1952,Ap 26,19:2
City of Bad Men 1953,O 21,37:6
Desert Sands 1955,N 19,22:7
Fort Dobbs 1958,Ap 19,10:4
George, Gladys
Red Hot Dollars 1919,D 29,7:2
Home Spun Folks 1920,O 4,14:3
Straight Is the Way 1934,Ag 29,13:2
Valiant Is the Word for Carrie 1936,O 8,27:2
They Gave Him a Gun 1937,My 14,21:1
Madame X 1937,O 25,23:1
Love Is a Headache 1938,Ja 28,17:3
Marie Antoinette 1938,Ag 17,23:2
I'm From Missouri 1939,Mr 23,27:1
Here I Am a Stranger 1939,S 30,11:2
Roaring Twenties, The 1939,N 11,12:1
Child Is Born, A 1940,Ja 11,19:2
House Across the Bay, The 1940,Mr 22,23:2
Way of all Flesh, The 1940,Je 6,33:2
Lady From Cheyenne, The 1941,Ap 18,18:2
Hit the Road 1941,Jl 3,15:3
Maltese Falcon, The 1941,O 4,18:2
Crystal Ball, The 1943,F 19,22:2
Hard Way, The 1943,Mr 13,9:2
Christmas Holiday 1944,Je 29,16:1
Minstrel Man 1944,Jl 17,18:5
Best Years of our Lives, The 1946,N 22,27:2
Flamingo Road 1949,My 7,10:2
Bright Leaf 1950,Je 17,7:2
Undercover Girl 1950,N 8,37:2

Lullaby of Broadway 1951,Mr 27,35:2
He Ran all the Way 1951,Je 21,24:2
Detective Story 1951,N 7,35:2
George, Grace
Johnny Come Lately 1943,S 24,26:1
George, Heinrich
Metropolis 1927,Mr 7,16:3
Bondage 1928,N 6,35:1
Armored Vault 1928,N 13,37:2 (In Addenda)
Whirl of Life, The 1929,Mr 25,32:2
Wrath of the Seas, The 1929,Ag 19,22:1
Theatre 1929,Ag 25,VIII,5:1
Wasted Love 1929,D 30,16:4
Mann der den Mord Beging, Der; Man Who Committed the Murder, The 1931,F 22,VIII,6:2
Berlin-Alexanderplatz 1931,N 15,VIII,6:1
Andere, Der 1932,Ja 15,24:4
1914: The Last Days Before the War 1932,S 5,9:6
Berlin-Alexanderplatz 1933,My 11,14:1
Unsere Fahne Flattert Uns Voran 1934,Jl 7,16:6
Hermine und die Sieben Aufrechten 1935,S 21,18:2
Maedchen Johanna, Das 1935,O 9,27:2 (In Addenda)
Reifende Jugend 1936,Ja 4,19:1
Stuetzen der Gesellschaft 1936,N 7,15:3
Wenn der Hahn Kraeht 1936,N 14,23:3
Promise Me Nothing 1937,N 13,11:3
Ball im Metropol 1938,Mr 5,11:3
Unternehmen Michael; Private's Job, The 1938,My 14,18:2
Magda 1938,S 10,20:2
Biberpelz, Der; Beaver Coat, The 1939,S 9,11:3
Unsterbliche Herz, Das; Immortal Heart, The 1939,O 21,12:2
Frau Sylvelin 1939,D 9,18:3
Dreyfus Case, The 1940,O 30,29:3
George, Jack
Song of my Heart 1948,Mr 5,17:3
That Lady in Ermine 1948,Ag 25,31:2
Harpoon 1948,D 9,48:8
Amazon Quest 1949,My 14,9:3
George, John
Where the Pavement Ends 1923,Ap 2,22:1
Scaramouche 1923,O 12,7:2 (Incorrect in this edition; use 1927,O 1,7:2 elsewhere)
Road to Mandalay, The 1926,Je 29,21:2
Don Juan 1926,Ag 7,6:1 (In Addenda)
Night of Love, The 1927,Ja 25,18:4
Unknown, The 1927,Je 13,17:1
Big City, The 1928,Mr 26,26:2
Outside the Law 1930,S 1,16:1
Trick for Trick 1933,Je 10,16:4
George, Mary
Native Land 1942,My 12,16:3
George, Maude
Devil's Pass Key, The 1920,Ag 9,6:3
Madame X 1920,S 27,18:1
Monte Cristo 1922,Ag 15,20:3
Merry Go Round 1923,Jl 2,16:2
Six Days 1923,S 24,5:4
Worldly Goods 1924,N 3,20:1
Garden of Eden, The 1928,Mr 19,26:2
After the Storm 1928,My 8,25:3
Wedding March, The 1928,O 15,26:1
Woman From Moscow, The 1928,N 5,26:1
George, Muriel
My Song For You 1935,My 27,20:6
Voice in the Night, The 1941,My 23,25:4
48 Hours 1944,Je 26,21:2
Vacation From Marriage 1946,Mr 15,27:2
Years Between, The 1947,Mr 10,25:2
Last Holiday 1950,N 14,39:4
Dancing Years, The 1951,Ja 29,14:4
George, Ott
Under my Skin 1950,Mr 18,9:2
George, Paul
Passion of Jeanne d'Arc, The 1929,Mr 31,VIII,7:1
George, Peter (Original Author)
Dr Strangelove or: How I Learned to Stop Worrying and Love the Bomb 1964,Ja 31,16:1 (Incorrect in this edition; use 1964,Ja 30,24:1 elsewhere)
George, Peter (Screenwriter)
Dr Strangelove or: How I Learned to Stop Worrying and Love the Bomb 1964,Ja 31,16:1 (Incorrect in this edition; use 1964,Ja 30,24:1 elsewhere)
George, Richard
Invaders, The 1942,Mr 6,17:1
Tower of Terror 1942,Je 29,11:4
Great Expectations 1947,My 23,31:1
Quiet Week-End 1948,Ag 20,13:2
George, Robert
One Third of a Nation 1939,F 11,13:2
George, Sue
Gidget 1959,Ap 23,27:4
Strange Affair, The 1968,Jl 25,26:2
George, Tony
Three bad Sisters 1956,F 13,24:1
Chicago Confidential 1957,Ag 31,19:1

George, Voya
Legion of the Condemned, The 1928,Mr 19,26:2
Georges
Born to Dance 1936,D 5,16:1
Georges, Edith
Folies Bergere 1958,My 28,37:2
Man in the Raincoat, The 1958,Jl 15,21:2
House on the Waterfront, The 1959,F 21,25:2
Georges-Michel, Michel (Original Author)
Modigliani of Montparnasse 1961,Mr 1,27:3
Georgette
Club De Femmes 1937,O 20,27:2
Georgi, Mally
Pechmarie 1935,Ap 22,14:3
Georgi, Wolf
Lumpenball 1931,Ap 27,25:1
Georgia Sea Island Singers
Festival 1967,O 24,53:2
Georgiou, Margarita
Windfall in Athens 1956,O 1,31:1
Georgitis, Phaedon
Red Lanterns 1965,Ap 1,30:1
Georgiyevskaya, A
Inspector General, The 1954,My 3,21:2
Georgladis, Vassilis (Director)
Red Lanterns 1965,Ap 1,30:1
Georgouli, Alice
Policeman of the 16th Precinct, The 1963,Ap 22,23:2
Geprtova, Libuse
Lady on the Tracks, The 1968,N 26,39:2
Gerace, Liliana
Behind Closed Shutters 1952,Je 10,22:7
Fist in his Pocket 1968,My 28,40:1
Geraga, Piotr
Wait for Me 1945,Mr 19,23:3
Geraghty, Carmelita
Black Oxen 1924,Ja 7,23:1
Through the Dark 1924,Ja 8,27:1
Under the Rouge 1925,Jl 22,14:4
Great Gatsby, The 1926,N 22,28:3
Last Trail, The 1927,Ja 26,17:1
Venus of Venice 1927,My 3,25:1
My Best Girl 1927,N 7,26:4
Good-Bye Kiss, The 1928,N 12,18:2
Paris Bound 1929,S 21,17:1
Mississippi Gambler, The 1929,O 28,20:1
This Thing Called Love 1929,D 14,22:4
Millie 1931,F 7,11:1
Fifty Million Frenchmen 1931,Mr 26,31:2
Prestige 1932,F 5,25:2
Escapade 1932,My 28,18:2
Geraghty, Gerald (Original Author)
Her Jungle Love 1938,Ap 14,27:2
Cat Creeps, The 1946,My 18,12:4
Geraghty, Gerald (Screenwriter)
Jungle Princess 1936,D 24,21:3
Wells Fargo 1937,D 30,15:2
Badlands of Dakota 1941,S 9,27:6
South of Tahiti 1941,N 10,21:3
Sin Town 1942,O 17,11:2
Falcon Strikes Back, The 1943,Ap 2,17:4
Frontier Badmen 1943,Ag 14,12:8
Falcon in Mexico, The 1944,Ag 5,16:2
Falcon in Hollywood, The 1944,D 9,21:2
Frisco Sal 1945,F 17,11:2
Shady Lady 1945,O 11,26:2
Apache Rose 1947,Jl 23,19:3
Wyoming 1947,Jl 25,12:5
Plunders, The 1948,N 1,28:2
Red Menace, The 1949,Je 27,18:2
Geraghty, Maurice (Director)
Sword of Monte Cristo, The 1951,Ap 23,21:2
Geraghty, Maurice (Original Author)
Good Morning, Judge 1943,Ap 30,25:4
Sword of Monte Cristo, The 1951,Ap 23,21:2
Love Me Tender 1956,N 16,23:1
Geraghty, Maurice (Producer)
Falcon's Brother, The 1942,O 3,9:5
Falcon Strikes Back, The 1943,Ap 2,17:4
Falcon in Danger, The 1943,Jl 23,21:2
Action in Arabia 1944,F 19,18:7
Falcon out West, The 1944,Mr 18,18:2
Falcon in Mexico, The 1944,Ag 5,16:2
Falcon in Hollywood, The 1944,D 9,21:2
China Sky 1945,My 25,22:3
Falcon in San Francisco, The 1945,Jl 21,7:2
Geraghty, Maurice (Screenwriter)
Good Morning, Judge 1943,Ap 30,25:4
Whiplash 1948,D 27,16:3
Red Canyon 1949,Ap 28,28:2
Calamity Jane and Sam Bass 1949,Jl 18,14:2
Dakota Lil 1950,Mr 3,21:5
Tomahawk 1951,F 19,19:2
Geraghty, Tom (Original Author)
Fireman, Save My Child 1927,O 10,24:1
Mr Robinson Crusoe 1932,S 22,25:4
Geraghty, Tom (Screenwriter)
Mollycoddle, The 1920,Je 14,13:2
Hollywood 1923,Jl 30,11:4
Pied Piper Malone 1924,Ja 28,12:1
Old Home Week 1925,My 25,21:3
Irish Luck 1925,N 24,28:4

Geraghty, Tom (Screenwriter) — Cont
New Klondike, The 1926,Mr 22,16:1
Harold Teen 1928,Ag 14,15:4
Wings of the Morning 1937,Mr 12,19:1
Gerald, Ara
White Angel, The 1936,Je 25,24:1
Gerald, Jim
Nuit est a Nous, La; (Night is Ours, The)
1931,F 21,15:2
Horse Ate the Hat, The 1931,S 1,30:6
Constant Nymph, The 1934,Ap 7,19:1
Robber Symphony 1937,Ja 27,17:2
Bulldog Drummond at Bay 1937,O 25,23:2
French Without Tears 1940,Ap 29,12:2
Last Will of Dr Mabuse, The 1943,Mr 20,11:1
Adventures of Captain Fabian 1951,D 14,36:2
Pardon my French 1952,Mr 31,17:2
Moulin Rouge 1953,F 11,33:5
Moment of Truth, The 1954,Ap 27,36:2
Barefoot Contessa, The 1954,S 30,37:1
Gerald, Minoque
Innocents in Paris 1955,Mr 5,9:6
GERARD
See Also GIRARD
Gerard, Barney (Original Author)
Bringing Up Father 1946,N 22,27:3
Gerard, Barney (Producer)
Bringing Up Father 1946,N 22,27:3
Gerard, Carl
Voice From the Minaret, The 1923,F 5,18:2
Wild Bill Hickok 1923,N 21,22:1
Up in Mabel's Room 1926,Je 29,21:2
Ladies of the Mob 1928,Je 18,13:2
Public Defender, The 1931,Ag 1,16:4
Gerard, Claire
Ballerina 1938,N 15,27:1
Portrait of a Woman 1946,Ap 22,26:2
Voyage Surprise 1948,F 14,17:3
Happy Road, The 1957,Je 21,20:2
Gerard, Douglas
Lighthouse by the Sea, The 1924,D 29,11:4
Madonna of Avenue A 1929,Ag 12,22:2
Manhattan Parade 1931,D 25,29:2
Gerard, Hal
Lady in the Iron Mask 1952,Jl 5,7:2
Gerard, James W (Original Author)
My Four Years in Germany 1918,Mr 11,9:5
Gerard, Marguerite
Mr Hulot's Holiday 1954,Je 17,36:2
Gerard, Merwin (Original Author)
Winning Team, The 1952,Je 21,12:2
Gerard, Merwin (Screenwriter)
Winning Team, The 1952,Je 21,12:2
Gerasch, Alfred
Modern du Barry, A 1928,Mr 19,26:2
Carnival Crime, The 1929,Jl 8,17:3
Spy of Madame de Pompadour, The
1929,S 10,27:1
Gerasimov, S
Alone 1932,My 25,23:6
Gerasimov, S (Director)
Seven Brave Men 1936,Je 15,24:2
City of Youth 1938,S 5,30:4
New Teacher, The 1941,Ap 7,13:3
Masquerade 1943,My 17,11:2
Ural Front, The 1945,Je 7,25:3
Moscow Music Hall 1946,S 9,20:1
Young Guard 1949,D 26,33:6
New China, The 1952,Mr 10,18:4
Country Doctor, The 1953,F 16,16:2
And Quiet Flows the Don 1960,My 25,45:2
Gerasimov, S (Screenwriter)
Seven Brave Men 1936,Je 15,24:2
New Teacher, The 1941,Ap 7,13:3
Ural Front, The 1945,Je 7,25:3
Young Guard 1949,D 26,33:6
And Quiet Flows the Don 1960,My 25,45:2
Geraskina, L (Screenwriter)
Problem Child 1955,Ja 24,20:5
Geray, Steven
Dance Band 1936,Ja 4,19:2
Inspector Hornleigh 1939,Je 15,27:3
Man at Large 1941,O 11,21:4
Gentleman at Heart, A 1942,F 23,25:2
Secret Agent of Japan 1942,Mr 23,19:3
Eyes in the Night 1942,O 16,23:1
Moon and Sixpence, The 1942,O 28,26:4
Night Plane From Chungking 1943,My 31,13:2
Pilot No 5 1943,Je 25,13:4
Appointment in Berlin 1943,Jl 17,8:2
Phantom of the Opera, The 1943,O 15,15:2
Whistling in Brooklyn 1944,Mr 24,17:3
Mask of Dimitrios, The 1944,Je 24,16:2
In Society 1944,Ag 17,20:2
Meet The People 1944,S 8,16:2
Seventh Cross, The 1944,S 29,18:1
Conspirators, The 1944,O 21,15:2
Hotel Berlin 1945,Mr 3,11:2
Tarzan and the Amazons 1945,Ap 30,13:4
Spellbound 1945,N 2,22:2
Mexicana 1945,N 17,14:6
Cornered 1945,D 26,15:1
Gilda 1946,Mr 15,27:2
So Dark the Night 1946,D 7,16:2

Return of Monte Cristo, The 1947,Ja 3,16:4
Mr District Attorney 1947,F 28,27:3
Unfaithful, The 1947,Je 28,10:2
Gunfighters 1947,Jl 25,12:5
Dark Past, The 1948,D 23,25:2
El Paso 1949,Mr 24,35:2
Once More, my Darling 1949,S 26,17:1
Holiday in Havana 1949,O 14,33:5
Under my Skin 1950,Mr 18,9:2
In a Lonely Place 1950,My 18,37:2
Lady Without Passport, A 1950,Ag 4,13:2
Woman on the Run 1950,N 30,24:2
Second Woman, The 1951,F 2,19:2
Target Unknown 1951,Mr 5,24:2
I Can Get It for You Wholesale 1951,Ap 5,34:4
House on Telegraph Hill, The 1951,My 14,29:1
Little Egypt 1951,Ag 30,20:3
Lady Possessed 1952,F 15,17:2
Affair in Trinidad 1952,Jl 31,14:2
Big Sky, The 1952,Ag 20,21:1
Night Without Sleep 1952,S 27,13:2
O Henry's Full House (The Last Leaf
1952,O 17,33:1
Tonight We Sing 1953,F 13,17:2
Call Me Madam 1953,Mr 26,37:1
Knock on Wood 1954,Ap 15,34:2
French Line, The 1954,My 15,13:2
New York Confidential 1955,F 19,18:1
Daddy Long Legs 1955,My 6,17:5
Birds and the Bees, The 1956,Ap 23,22:1
Attack! 1956,S 20,29:4
Certain Smile, A 1958,Ag 1,13:2
Count Your Blessings 1959,Ap 24,23:1
Verboten 1960,Jl 12,39:1
Dime With a Halo 1963,Je 27,23:3
Gerber, Emil
Marie-Louise 1945,N 13,24:2
Last Chance, The 1945,N 28,21:6
Gerbidon, M (Original Author)
French Touch, The 1954,S 2,18:2
Gerdes, Emily
Ella Cinders 1926,Je 7,23:2
Geret, Georges
Diary of a Chambermaid; Journal d'une Femme de
Chambre, Le 1964,S 22,44:1
Cloportes 1966,Ap 19,36:1
Weekend at Dunkirk 1966,My 19,51:2
Poppy is Also a Flower, The 1967,D 14,62:4
Gerhard, Peter
April 1, 2000 1954,F 17,27:2
Story of Vickie, The 1958,Ja 30,19:2
Gerhardt, Elfi
Konzert in Tirol 1939,Ja 7,6:4
Gerhardt, Gherardo (Original Author)
Doctor, Beware 1951,Ap 30,16:3
Gerhardt, Karl
Immortal Vagabond, The 1931,Ag 3,15:5
Der Unsterbliche Lump 1932,My 20,22:3
Geri, Adolfo
Eredita dello Zio, L' 1935,Je 29,16:3
Fiat Voluntas Dei 1936,Jl 6,11:5
Geri, Iska
Montpi 1959,Ap 21,40:1
Gericke, Eugene
I Was a Male War Bride 1949,Ag 27,7:2
Gerin, Pierre (Producer)
Night is my Kingdom, The 1953,S 30,37:1
Would-Be Gentleman, The 1960,Mr 23,31:1
Marriage of Figaro, The 1963,Ap 30,26:1
Gering, Marion (Director)
I Take This Woman 1931,Je 13,20:4
Twenty-Four Hours 1931,O 3,20:2
Ladies of the Big House 1932,Ja 1,31:1
Devil and the Deep 1932,Ag 20,7:4
Madame Butterfly 1932,D 26,26:2
Pick Up 1933,Mr 25,13:4
Jennie Gerhardt 1933,Je 9,20:2
Good Dame 1934,Mr 17,11:4
Thirty Day Princess 1934,My 12,12:3
Rumba 1935,F 25,13:2
Rose of the Rancho 1936,Ja 9,25:2
Lady of Secrets 1936,F 22,12:1
Thunder in the City 1937,Ap 23,25:2
She Married an Artist 1938,F 25,15:2
Gerlatta
Hoboes in Paradise 1950,O 9,21:5
Gerlich, Jackie
East Side of Heaven 1939,My 5,29:3
Germain, Andre
Golden Mistress, The 1954,O 30,15:6
Germain, Lud
Red Inn, The 1954,Je 8,25:2
Germaine, Mary
Laughter in Paradise 1951,N 12,21:2
Where's Charley? 1952,Je 27,18:3
German, Edward (Miscellaneous)
Nell Gwyn 1935,Je 20,16:2
German, J (Screenwriter)
Case of Sergei Rumyantsev, The 1956,N 26,22:7
German, U (Screenwriter)
Seven Brave Men 1936,Je 15,24:2

German, Yuri (Screenwriter)
My Beloved 1959,Je 15,31:4
Germi, Pietro
Flight Into France 1949,Jl 22,16:2
Viaccia, La 1962,S 21,35:1
Facts of Murder, The 1965,Jl 1,34:1
Railroad Man, The; Ferroviere, Il 1965,O 25,46:2
Germi, Pietro (Director)
Lost Youth 1949,O 27,35:4
Mafia; (In Nome Della Legge) 1950,Mr 2,33:2
Path of Hope, The (Il Cammino Della Speranza)
1952,Ag 5,15:5
Mademoiselle Gobette 1955,F 5,13:3
Divorce-Italian Style 1962,S 18,34:1
Seduced and Abandoned 1964,Jl 16,23:1
Facts of Murder, The 1965,Jl 1,34:1
Railroad Man, The; Ferroviere, Il 1965,O 25,46:2
Birds, the Bees and the Italians, The
1967,Ag 8,33:2
Climax, The 1967,S 12,55:1
Germi, Pietro (Original Author)
Seduced and Abandoned 1964,Jl 16,23:1
Birds, the Bees and the Italians, The
1967,Ag 8,33:2
Germi, Pietro (Producer)
Birds, the Bees and the Italians, The
1967,Ag 8,33:2
Climax, The 1967,S 12,55:1
Germi, Pietro (Screenwriter)
Lost Youth 1949,O 27,35:4
Path of Hope, The (Il Cammino Della Speranza)
1952,Ag 5,15:5
Divorce-Italian Style 1962,S 18,34:1
Seduced and Abandoned 1964,Jl 16,23:1
Facts of Murder, The 1965,Jl 1,34:1
Railroad Man, The; Ferroviere, Il 1965,O 25,46:2
Birds, the Bees and the Italians, The
1967,Ag 8,33:2
Climax, The 1967,S 12,55:1
Germon, Nane
Stormy Waters 1946,Je 17,32:2
Beauty and the Beast 1947,D 24,12:2
Red Inn, The 1954,Je 8,25:2
Inside Out 1964,S 25,32:1
Biches, Les 1968,S 27,34:1
Gerner, L
Reiter von Deutsch-Ostafrika, Die 1935,Je 8,12:3
Gerold, Luis
Rebel, The 1933,Jl 25,17:2
Gerome, Raymond
Dangerous Exile 1958,O 11,18:3
Loss of Innocence 1961,N 22,27:1
Geronimi, Clyde (Director)
Make Mine Music 1946,Ap 22,26:2
Melody Time 1948,My 28,28:2
Adventures of Ichabod and Mr Toad, The
1949,O 10,18:2
Cinderella 1950,F 23,33:1
Peter Pan 1953,F 12,23:1
Lady and the Tramp 1955,Je 24,17:1
Sleeping Beauty 1959,F 18,36:1
one Hundred and One Dalmations
1961,F 11,27:1
Geronimi, Clyde (Miscellaneous)
Three Caballeros, The 1945,F 5,20:1
Geronimi, Jerome (Screenwriter)
Diabolique 1955,N 22,41:1
Grand Maneuver, The 1956,O 2,39:1
If all the Guys in the World 1957,Ap 23,34:1
Gerotti, Massimo
Fabiola 1951,My 30,14:2
Gerould, Katherine Fullerton (Original Author)
Yankee Senor, The 1926,Ja 28,14:4
Romance of Rio Grande 1929,N 9,22:5
Romance of the Rio Grande 1940,D 25,33:4
Gerrani, Ivo
Leopard, The 1963,Ag 13,25:1
Gerrard, Charles
Hun Within, The 1918,Ag 26,9:1
New Moon, The 1919,My 12,11:4
Isle of Conquest, The 1919,O 27,9:3
Mary Ellen Comes to Town 1920,Mr 22,12:1
World and his Wife, The 1920,Jl 19,16:3
Passionate Pilgrim, The 1921,Ja 3,20:2
When Knighthood Was in Flower 1922,S 15,17:2
(In Addenda)
Glimpses of the Moon 1923,Ap 3,23:4
Richard the Lion-Hearted 1923,O 22,17:1
Dangerous Maid, The 1923,D 11,26:2
Her Temporary Husband 1924,Ja 1,20:1
Lilies of the Field 1924,Mr 17,19:1
Circe the Enchantress 1924,D 9,23:3
Man on the Box, The 1925,S 28,24:1
California Straight Ahead 1926,Ja 12,27:5
Nervous Wreck, The 1926,O 12,30:2
For Wives Only 1926,D 1,24:5
Cheerful Fraud, The 1926,D 28,17:1
Heart Thief, The 1927,Ap 27,22:5
Framed 1927,Je 20,25:3
Painting the Town 1927,Ag 2,19:2
Home Made 1927,D 13,33:2
Port of Missing Girls, The 1928,Jl 31,13:4
Caught in the Fog 1928,D 4,29:1

Gerrard, Charles — Cont
Lone Wolf's Daughter, The 1929,Mr 4,20:2
Men Without Women 1930,F 1,15:1
Journey's End 1930,Ap 9,25:1
Anybody's Woman 1930,Ag 16,8:3
Dracula 1931,F 13,21:3
Menace, The 1932,Ja 30,13:2

Gerrard, Douglas
Footloose Windows 1926,Je 22,21:2
Wolf's Clothing 1927,Mr 28,26:4
Million Bid, A 1927,My 31,25:2
First Auto, The 1927,Je 28,28:4
Dearie 1927,Jl 4,20:3
Desired Woman, The 1927,Ag 30,21:3
College Widow, The 1927,N 7,26:4
Ladies of the Night Club 1928,Jl 17,15:3
Glad Rag Doll, The 1929,Je 3,27:2
Argyle Case, The 1929,Ag 31,13:4
Hottentot, The 1929,S 7,15:1
Road to Singapore, The 1931,O 1,25:2
Tenderfoot, The 1932,My 23,18:4
One Way Passage 1932,O 14,23:2
King's Vacation, The 1933,Ja 20,21:2
Bulldog Drummond Strikes Back 1934,Ag 16,20:2
Ghost Walks, The 1935,Mr 30,11:2
Under Two Flags 1936,My 1,19:1

Gerrard, Gene
Mister Hobo 1936,F 8,19:2

Gerringer, Robert
Black Like Me 1964,My 21,42:1
Fail Safe 1964,S 16,36:1

Gerrits, Paul
Stolen Harmony 1935,Ap 20,16:2
On the Avenue 1937,F 5,17:3

Gerrogiannis, X (Screenwriter)
Moment of Passion 1960,N 21,34:1

Gerron, Kurt
Manege 1928,Mr 11,VIII,7:6 (In Addenda)
Strange Case of Captain Ramper, The
 1928,Je 4,13:2
Berlin After Dark 1929,My 28,36:2
Survival 1930,Ja 13,21:1
Liebe im Ring 1930,Ag 11,13:1
Blue Angel, The 1930,D 6,21:3
Drei von ver Tankstelle, Die 1931,Je 20,20:4
Dolly Macht Karriere 1931,Jl 18,16:6
Man Braucht Kein Geld; You Don't Need any
 Money 1932,F 28,VIII,6:1
Trapeze 1932,My 3,25:2
Man Braucht Kein Geld 1932,N 16,15:3
Ihre Majestaet die Liebe 1933,F 7,23:4
Marquise von Pompadour, Die 1936,F 3,21:3

Gerron, Kurt (Director)
Meine Frau, Die Hochstaplerin 1932,F 6,14:4
Es Wird Schon Wieder Besser 1934,Ja 24,21:3
Toller Einfall, Ein 1934,My 21,20:3

Gerry, Alex
Whirlpool 1950,Ja 14,9:2
Young Man With a Horn 1950,F 10,18:4
Woman of Distinction, A 1950,Mr 17,28:2
Reformer and the Redhead, The 1950,Ap 10,15:2
Excuse my Dust 1951,Je 28,21:2
Invitation 1952,Ja 30,22:6
Love Is Better Than Ever 1952,Mr 4,23:2
Jazz Singer, The 1953,Ja 14,27:3
Lili 1953,Mr 11,36:7
Kid From Left Field, The 1953,S 26,15:3
Eddie Cantor Story, The 1953,D 26,10:2
Come on, The 1956,Ap 7,13:1
Funny Face 1957,Mr 29,16:1
This Happy Feeling 1958,Je 19,28:2
Pillow Talk 1959,O 7,47:2
Bellboy, The 1960,Jl 21,17:1
Back Street 1961,O 13,27:1
Tammy and the Doctor 1963,Je 27,23:2
Brass Bottle, The 1964,My 21,42:1

Gerry, Toni
Boots Malone 1952,Mr 13,26:2
Lust for Life 1956,S 18,39:1

Gershe, Leonard (Composer)
Star is Born, A 1954,O 12,23:1
Funny Face 1957,Mr 29,16:1

Gershe, Leonard (Original Author)
Funny Face 1957,Mr 29,16:1

Gershe, Leonard (Screenwriter)
Silk Stockings 1957,Jl 19,11:1

Gershenson, Joe (Producer)
Little Giant 1946,My 9,27:5
Runaround, The 1946,Je 7,16:3
She Wrote the Book 1946,Je 20,20:3

Gershwin, George (Composer)
King of Jazz 1930,My 3,23:1
Shall We Dance 1937,My 14,21:1
Damsel in Distress, A 1937,N 25,37:1
Goldwyn Follies, The 1938,F 21,15:1
Lady Be Good 1941,S 19,27:1
Girl Crazy 1943,D 3,27:2
Broadway Rhythm 1944,Ap 14,24:6
Ziegfeld Follies 1946,Mr 23,8:3
Shocking Miss Pilgrim, The 1947,F 12,34:2
Lullaby of Broadway 1951,Mr 27,35:2
Three for the Show 1955,F 25,16:1
Funny Face 1957,Mr 29,16:1
Porgy and Bess 1959,Je 25,20:3

Gershwin, Henry (Miscellaneous)
Ecstasy 1940,D 25,33:2

Gershwin, Ira (Composer)
Shall We Dance 1937,My 14,21:1
Goldwyn Follies, The 1938,F 21,15:1
Lady Be Good 1941,S 19,27:1
Girl Crazy 1943,D 3,27:2
Lady in the Dark 1944,F 23,17:1
Cover Girl 1944,Mr 31,26:1
Broadway Rhythm 1944,Ap 14,24:6
Where Do We Go From Here? 1945,Je 7,25:2
Ziegfeld Follies 1946,Mr 23,8:3
Shocking Miss Pilgrim, The 1947,F 12,34:2
Star is Born, A 1954,O 12,23:1
Three for the Show 1955,F 25,16:1
Funny Face 1957,Mr 29,16:1
Porgy and Bess 1959,Je 25,20:3

Gershwin, Ira (Miscellaneous)
Damsel in Distress, A 1937,N 25,37:1

Gershwin, Jerry (Producer)
Harper 1966,Mr 31,43:1
Bobo, The 1967,S 29,53:1
Sweet November 1968,F 9,55:1

Gerson, Betty Lou
Red Menace, The 1949,Je 27,18:2
Annapolis Story, An 1955,Ap 9,8:2

Gerson, Charles
Pony Express, The 1925,S 14,16:1

Gerss, Sol
Bullet Scars 1942,Ap 24,21:4

Gersten, Berta
Mirele Efros 1939,O 21,12:2
God, Man and Devil 1950,Ja 23,16:2
Benny Goodman Story 1956,F 22,22:1

Gerstle, Frank
Magnetic Monster, The 1953,My 14,32:5
Autumn Leaves 1956,Ag 2,21:2
Between Heaven and Hell 1956,O 12,33:2
Silencers, The 1966,Mr 17,35:1

Gert, Valeska
Nana 1928,Ja 22,VIII,7:7
Nana 1929,Jl 30,19:4
Dreigroschenoper, Die; Beggar's Opera, The
 1931,My 18,21:2
Threepenny Opera, The 1960,Jl 11,24:4
Juliet of the Spirits 1965,N 4,57:1

Gertier, Sam
Youth of Russia, The 1934,N 10,19:3

Gertler, Victor (Director)
Maria Noever 1937,Ap 9,19:2
A Ferfi Mind Oeruelt; All Men Are Crazy
 1937,D 11,22:3
Marika 1938,N 19,9:3
Ele serelt Ember; Changed Man 1939,F 25,19:3
Leanyvari Boszorkany; Witch of Leanyvar
 1939,N 25,13:2

Gervais, Gerard
Paris Incident 1954,Ag 18,20:2

Gervasi, Frank (Screenwriter)
Beautiful but Dangerous 1958,F 6,24:1

Gervay, Marica
Igloi Diakok 1935,My 24,24:3
Szent Peter Esernyoeje 1936,Ja 8,22:2
111-es Szobaban; In Room 111 1938,Ap 2,18:2

Gervon, Sammy
Iron Man 1931,Ap 18,17:3

Geschonneck, Erwin
Naked Among the Wolves 1967,Ap 19,54:7

Gesner, Adrienne
No Time for Flowers 1952,D 26,20:3

Gessner, Robert (Original Author)
Massacre 1934,Ja 18,19:2

Gest, Inna
Ghost Creeps, The 1940,Ag 19,13:3

Gest, Morris (Miscellaneous)
Hearts of the World 1918,Ap 5,13:1

Gest, Morris (Original Author)
Chu Chin Chow 1925,F 11,19:4

Gestettenbaur, Gusti Stark
Silence of the Forest, The; Schweigen im Walde,
 Das 1937,D 6,19:2

Getchell, Summer
Daybreak 1931,Je 1,15:1

Getchell, Sumner
Flying Fleet, The 1929,F 11,26:3
College Love 1929,Ag 5,25:2
Maybe It's Love 1930,O 18,23:2
Crooner 1932,Ag 20,7:4
That's my Boy 1932,N 21,21:1
there Goes The Groom 1937,D 25,10:6
Campus Confessions 1938,S 23,35:1
These Glamour Girls 1939,Ag 31,14:2
Lady in Question, The 1940,D 10,33:2
My Girl Tisa 1948,F 21,9:2
No Sad Songs for Me 1950,Ap 28,26:2

Getler, Israel
Dream no More 1950,Ja 6,25:2

Gets, Gerosha
Red and White 1932,N 29,23:5

Gettman, Lorraine
Navy Blues 1941,S 20,11:2

GETZ
See Also GOETZ

Geunod (Composer)
Ballerina 1938,N 15,27:1

Geurin-Catelain, Raymond
Nana 1929,Jl 30,19:4

Geuvremont, Paul
Luck of Ginger Coffey, The 1964,S 22,44:1

Geva, Tamara
Night Club 1929,Ag 12,22:2
Girl Habit, The 1931,Jl 4,11:5
Their big Moment 1934,S 6,22:4
Manhattan Merry-Go-Round 1937,D 31,9:3
Orchestra Wives 1942,S 24,23:2
Night Plane From Chungking 1943,My 31,13:2
Gay Intruders, The 1949,Je 28,33:4

Geva, Tamara (Miscellaneous)
Specter of the Rose 1946,S 2,12:4

Gevers, Joseph
We Lived Through Buchenwald 1947,Jl 24,27:3

Gevrey, Andre
We Lived Through Buchenwald 1947,Jl 24,27:3

Gewland, Gibson
Red Lily, The 1924,S 29,10:1

GEYER
See Also GEER

Geyer, Siegfried (Original Author)
By Candlelight 1934,Ja 6,18:2

Ghane, Marina
Dorado, El 1967,Je 29,32:1

Ghdjibekov, Uzair (Composer)
Arshin Takes a Wife 1950,Jl 31,13:6

Ghedevanshvili, S (Director)
Keto and Kote 1954,Ap 5,21:4

Ghedini, Francesco (Screenwriter)
Disorder 1964,My 26,44:2

Ghenzi, Sandro (Producer)
It's Forever Springtime 1951,D 29,7:7
Romeo and Juliet 1954,D 22,28:1

Gheorghiu, C Virgil (Original Author)
25th Hour, The 1967,F 17,45:1

Gheraldi, Cesarina
Behind Closed Shutters 1952,Je 10,22:7

Gherard, G (Screenwriter)
Before Him all Rome Trembled 1947,F 22,16:2
Doctor, Beware 1951,Ap 30,16:3

Gherdeman, Ted (Screenwriter)
Big Show, The 1961,My 11,42:4

Ghere, High
Spitfire 1934,Mr 9,22:3

Ghosal, Smaran
Aparajito 1959,Ap 29,30:1

Ghosh, Charu
Aparajito 1959,Ap 29,30:1

Ghostley, Alice
New Faces 1954,F 20,8:7
My Six Loves 1963,Ap 4,58:4
Flim Flam Man, The 1967,Ag 23,40:1
Graduate, The 1967,D 22,44:4
With Six You Get Egg Roll 1968,O 10,59:6

Giacalone, A (Director)
Solo per Danne 1939,My 30,13:3
Legittima Difesa; Self Defense 1940,Ap 6,13:3

Giacalone, Alberto (Producer)
Forever Yours 1937,Je 7,22:2
Streets of Sorrow 1952,N 18,37:4

Giachetti, Fosco
Luci Sommerse 1936,Je 22,22:2
Scipio Africanus 1939,S 23,22:2
Squadrone Bianco, Lo; White Squadrone, The
 1939,D 1,27:2
Napoli che mon Muore; Naples That Never Dies
 1940,Mr 4,11:3
Life of Giuseppe Verdi 1940,Ap 3,19:2
Ultima Nemica, L'; Last Enemy, The
 1940,Ap 18,28:5
Dream of Butterfly, The 1941,F 13,25:2
Life Begins Anew; Vita Ricomincia, La
 1947,Ap 7,20:5
Damned, The; Maudits, Les 1948,Ap 26,27:2
Fear No Evil 1949,Mr 31,31:2
House of Ricordi 1956,Mr 13,32:1
Virtuous Bigamist, The 1959,My 28,34:3
Love and Larceny 1963,F 2,5:6

Giachetti, Gianfranco
Figaro E La Sua Gran Giornata 1933,O 28,20:4
Gesuzza, La Sposa Garibaldina 1936,N 3,33:4
Piccolo Eroe 1937,Jl 1,33:2

Giacobini, Franco
Crazy Desire 1964,Jl 3,13:2
Greco, El 1967,My 24,52:2

Giacos, Luigi (Original Author)
Revenge 1947,N 28,37:4

Giacosa, Giuseppe (Miscellaneous)
Boheme, La 1965,O 20,51:2

Giacosi, L (Original Author)
Island of Procida, The 1952,Mr 15,8:2

Giagni, Giandomenico (Screenwriter)
Woman in the Painting, The 1959,Ja 15,27:1
Italiano Brava Gente 1966,F 4,20:1

Giagnoni, Piero
Land of the Pharaohs 1955,Jl 27,15:2
Boy on a Dolphin 1957,Ap 20,21:2

Giakonis, V
Golfo-Girl of the Mountains 1958,My 19,19:5
Giallelis, Stathis
America America 1963,D 16,44:1
Cast a Giant Shadow 1966,Mr 31,43:3
Eavesdropper, The 1966,S 15,51:1
Blue 1968,My 11,28:1
Giambartolomei, Guido (Producer)
Bigamist, The 1958,My 12,25:1
Tailor's Maid, The; (Patri e Figli) 1959,S 2,35:4
Taboos of the World 1965,My 20,52:4
Gianakopoulos, D (Screenwriter)
Trouble for Father 1958,Ja 6,26:4
Gianetti, Alfredo (Screenwriter)
Facts of Murder, The 1965,Jl 1,34:1
Giannetti, Alfredo (Director)
Engagement Italiano 1966,Je 21,35:1
Giannetti, Alfredo (Screenwriter)
Divorce-Italian Style 1962,S 18,34:1
Railroad Man, The; Ferroviere, Il 1965,O 25,46:2
Engagement Italiano 1966,Je 21,35:1
Climax, The 1967,S 12,55:1
Gianni, Giuliana
Ultima Nemica, L'; Last Enemy, The
1940,Ap 18,28:5
Giannides, John
Taxi Driver, The 1958,Mr 3,24:8
Giannini, Ettore
Greatest Love, The 1954,Ja 12,19:2
Giannini, Ettore (Director)
Neapolitan Carousel 1961,O 12,41:3
Giannini, Ettore (Screenwriter)
Neapolitan Carousel 1961,O 12,41:3
Giannopoulou, E (Director)
Take Me Away, My Love 1962,Jl 30,15:5
Giannuzzi-Savelli, Giacomo (Producer)
Two Orphans, The 1950,O 19,40:6
Gianviti, Roberto (Screenwriter)
Psycosissimo 1962,S 8,16:2
Goliath and the Sins of Babylon 1964,Mr 5,36:2
Giascoss, Giuseppe (Composer)
Tosca 1958,O 24,40:3
Giascoss, Giuseppe (Screenwriter)
Tosca 1958,O 24,40:3
Giason, Fred (Screenwriter)
Savage Sam 1963,Ag 1,17:3
Gibb, Wendy
Rugged O'Riordans, The 1950,Ja 6,25:2
Cinerama-South Seas Adventure 1958,Jl 16,26:1
Gibberson, William
Tattooed Stranger, The 1950,F 10,18:6
Gibbons, Ann
Servants' Entrance 1934,S 27,25:2
Gibbons, Ayliene
Loved One, The 1965,O 12,57:1
Gibbons, Carroll and his Orchestra
Sidewalks of London 1940,F 15,15:1
Gibbons, Cedric (Director)
Tarzan and his Mate 1934,Ap 21,12:1
Gibbons, Eliot (Original Author)
Give Us Wings 1940,N 21,43:3
Gibbons, Eliot (Screenwriter)
Flight at Midnight 1939,S 7,29:2
Honeymoon Deferred 1940,F 16,23:4
Gibbons, Floyd (Narrator)
With Byrd at the South Pole 1930,Je 20,6:3
Gibbons, Javier
As the Earth Turns 1934,Ap 12,27:2
Gibbons, Tom
Shanghai Bound 1927,N 7,26:4
Gibbs, A (Original Author)
Whirlwind of Youth, The 1927,Je 6,27:2
Chances 1931,Je 12,27:1
Men of Tomorrow 1935,Ap 16,27:2
Gibbs, George (Original Author)
Sackcloth and Scarlet 1925,Mr 25,24:2
Great Deception, The 1926,Ag 9,10:3
Voltaire 1933,Ag 23,21:2
Gibbs, Jill
No Room at the Inn 1949,D 26,33:4
Gibbs, Philip Sir (Original Author)
Reckless Lady, The 1926,Ja 25,21:2
Out of the Ruins 1928,Ag 20,21:3
Paradise 1929,N 4,28:1
Captured 1933,Ag 18,18:3
Gibbs, Sheila Shand
High and Dry 1954,Ag 31,25:5
Gibbs, Suzanne
Blanche Fury 1948,N 24,20:2
Miss Robin Hood 1953,Je 27,7:2
Lolita 1962,Je 14,23:2
Gibchman, K
Peter the First 1937,D 25,10:4
Giblin, Charles
Her Wild Oat 1928,F 6,12:3
Woman Trap 1929,Ag 31,13:4
Giblyn, Charles
Insidious Dr Fu Manchu, The 1929,Jl 22,17:1
Party Girl 1930,Ja 2,28:2
Playboy of Paris 1930,N 1,23:2
Only Saps Work 1930,D 13,22:2
Five and Ten 1931,Jl 11,7:6
Prosperity 1932,N 26,11:4

What! No Beer? 1933,F 11,11:3
Giblyn, Charles (Director)
Black Is White 1920,Mr 8,9:6
Price of a Party, The 1924,N 26,17:3
Gibney, Sheridan (Original Author)
World Changes, The 1933,O 27,22:3
Story of Louis Pasteur, The 1936,F 10,15:1
South of Suez 1940,D 19,33:2
Once Upon a Honeymoon 1942,N 13,28:1
Gibney, Sheridan (Screenwriter)
Story of Louis Pasteur, The 1936,F 10,15:1
Green Pastures, The 1936,Jl 17,20:1
Anthony Adverse 1936,Ag 27,16:1
Letter of Introduction 1938,S 1,17:1
Disputed Passage 1939,O 26,27:2
Cheers for Miss Bishop 1941,Mr 14,17:2
Once Upon a Honeymoon 1942,N 13,28:1
Our Hearts Were Young and Gay 1944,O 12,24:2
Locket, The 1947,Mr 20,38:2
Gibran, Kahlil (Original Author)
Broken Wings, The 1968,Mr 16,34:1
Gibshman, K
Conquests of Peter The Great, The
1939,Ag 24,17:2
Gibson, Althea
Horse Soldiers, The 1959,Je 26,13:1
Gibson, Colin
John and Julie 1957,My 7,40:1
Gibson, Diana
Dangerous Waters 1936,Ja 22,15:5
Flying Hostess 1936,D 14,29:4
Man Who Found Himself, The 1937,Ap 9,19:3
Behind the Headlines 1937,Je 1,27:2
Adventure's End 1937,D 20,23:2
Gibson, Hoot
Flaming Frontier, The 1926,Ap 5,24:1
Long, Long Trail, The 1929,N 4,28:1
Powdersmoke Range 1936,Mr 9,20:2
Last Outlaw, The 1936,Je 15,24:1
Horse Soldiers, The 1959,Je 26,13:1
Gibson, James
Arizona Kid, The 1930,My 17,21:2
Social Lion, The 1930,Je 14,9:4
Battle of the Sexes, The 1960,Ap 19,40:4
Gibson, Judith
Holiday Inn 1942,Ag 5,16:1
Bombs Over Burma 1942,Ag 10,15:2
Gibson, Julie
Are You With It? 1948,Ap 15,31:2
Gibson, Kenneth
Ashes of Vengeance 1923,Ag 7,20:2
Idle Rich, The 1929,Je 17,29:1
Gibson, Mimi
I'll See You in my Dreams 1951,D 7,35:1
Bottom of the Bottle, The 1956,F 2,19:2
Three Faces of Eve, The 1957,S 27,16:6
No Down Payment 1957,O 31,41:1
Houseboat 1958,N 14,24:1
Buccaneer, The 1958,D 24,00:0
Gibson, Virginia
Goodbye, my Fancy 1951,My 30,14:2
Painting the Clouds With Sunshine 1951,S 1,9:6
Starlift 1951,D 15,11:2
About Face 1952,My 24,15:3
Stop, You're Killing Me 1952,D 11,45:3
Seven Brides for Seven Brothers 1954,Jl 23,8:3
Athena 1954,D 22,28:2
Funny Face 1957,Mr 29,16:1
Gibson, Vivian
Scandal In Paris, A 1929,Je 10,23:1
Gibson, William (Original Author)
Cobweb, The 1955,Ag 6,13:3
Miracle Worker, The 1962,My 24,29:2
Two for the Seesaw 1962,N 22,43:1
Gibson, William (Screenwriter)
Miracle Worker, The 1962,My 24,29:2
Gibson, Wynne
Nothing but the Truth 1929,Ap 22,23:1
Fall Guy, The 1930,My 27,27:2
Gang Buster, The 1931,Ja 24,15:1
June Moon 1931,Mr 14,23:2
Man of the World 1931,Mr 21,15:1
City Streets 1931,Ap 18,17:3
Kick In 1931,My 25,17:1
Road to Reno, The 1931,O 10,20:4
Ladies of the Big House 1932,Ja 1,31:1
Two Kinds of Women 1932,Ja 16,13:1
Strange Case of Clara Deane, The
1932,My 6,15:3
Lady and Gent 1932,Jl 16,5:5
Night after Night 1932,O 31,18:4
If I Had a Million 1932,D 3,21:4
Devil Is Driving, The 1932,D 16,25:5
Crime of the Century, The 1933,Mr 13,18:2
Emergency Call 1933,Je 24,16:2
Her Bodyguard 1933,Ag 7,18:2
Aggie Appleby, Maker of Men 1933,O 20,14:2
I Give my Love 1934,Jl 17,24:2
Captain Hates the Sea, The 1934,N 29,33:2
Gambling 1934,D 4,22:3
Crouching Beast, The 1936,Ag 22,6:1
Come Closer, Folks 1936,N 23,17:3
Racketeers in Exile 1937,Ap 12,15:3

Gibson, Wynne— Cont
Trapped by G-Men 1937,N 4,29:1
Gangs of New York 1938,My 28,9:2
Flirting With Fate 1938,D 15,35:3
Street of Missing Women 1940,Ja 8,11:2
My Son Is Guilty 1940,Ja 15,11:2
Falcon Strikes Back, The 1943,Ap 2,17:4
Gick, Judith
School for Husbands 1939,F 7,16:2
Gicognini, Alessandro (Composer)
Faust and the Devil 1950,My 1,18:2
Gidding, Nelson (Screenwriter)
Helen Morgan Story, The 1957,O 3,33:2
Onionhead 1958,O 2,44:1
I Want to Live 1958,N 19,45:1
Lisa 1962,My 25,28:1
Nine Hours to Rama 1963,Ap 4,58:2
Haunting, The 1963,S 19,23:1
Lost Command 1966,S 15,51:1
Giddings, Jack
Open all Night 1924,S 9,19:1
Gide, Andre
Life Begins Tomorrow 1952,N 18,37:2
Gide, Andre (Original Author)
Symphonie Pastorale 1948,S 14,34:3
Gide, Andre (Producer)
Symphonie Pastorale 1948,S 14,34:3
Gideon, Melville
Co-Optimists, The 1930,F 5,27:2
Gideon, Ralph (Director)
Place Called Glory, A 1966,Ag 11,27:4
Giehse, Therese
Acht Tage Glueck 1931,Jl 24,22:1
Meisterdetektiv, Der 1934,F 13,23:2
Last Chance, The 1945,N 28,21:6
Madchen in Uniform 1965,Ag 18,41:2
Gielgud, Gwen Bagni (Original Author)
Last Wagon, The 1956,S 22,20:2
Gielgud, Gwen Bagni (Screenwriter)
Last Wagon, The 1956,S 22,20:2
Gielgud, Irwin (Original Author)
Amazon Quest 1949,My 14,9:3
Abandoned Woman 1949,O 27,35:3
I Was a Shoplifter 1950,Ap 28,26:3
Gielgud, Irwin (Screenwriter)
Abandoned Woman 1949,O 27,35:3
I Was a Shoplifter 1950,Ap 28,26:3
Gielgud, John
Secret Agent 1936,Je 13,13:1
Prime Minister, The 1942,F 4,23:2
Julius Caesar 1953,Je 5,19:1
Romeo and Juliet 1954,D 22,28:1
Richard III 1956,Mr 12,1:4
Around the World in 80 Days 1956,O 18,37:1
Barretts of Wimpole Street, The 1957,Ja 18,15:3
Saint Joan 1957,Je 27,21:1
Becket 1964,Mr 12,40:2
Hamlet 1964,S 24,46:1
Loved One, The 1965,O 12,57:1
Falstaff; Chimes at Midnight 1967,Mr 18,19:2
Sebastian 1968,Ja 25,33:2
Charge of the Light Brigade, The 1968,O 7,59:1
Shoes of the Fisherman, The 1968,N 15,40:3
Gielgud, John (Narrator)
To Die in Madrid 1965,S 16,00:0
Gielgud, John (Screenwriter)
Hamlet 1964,S 24,46:1
Gielgud, Val
Good Companions, The 1933,O 10,24:1
Men Are not Gods 1937,Ja 19,28:1
Gierasch, Stefan
Hustler, The 1961,S 27,35:1
Gierasinski
Co Moj Maz Robi W Nocy?; What Is my Husband
Doing Tonight? 1935,N 29,24:2
Giere, Helen
Time to Love 1927,Je 23,23:3
Loves of an Actress 1928,Jl 30,21:2
Giermann, Frederick
Beasts of Berlin 1939,N 20,15:6
British Intelligence 1940,F 12,14:2
Hitler-Dead or Alive 1943,Mr 31,23:3
Strange Death of Adolf Hitler, The 1943,O 9,11:5
Hostages 1943,O 11,23:2
Cross of Lorraine, The 1943,D 3,27:4
Counter-Attack 1945,My 17,15:2
Night in Casablanca, A 1946,Ag 12,17:2
Gifford, Alan
Satellite in the Sky 1956,S 4,32:7
Iron Petticoat, The 1957,F 2,12:2
Across the Bridge 1957,O 30,24:1
Screaming Mimi 1958,Je 26,23:3
Passport to China 1961,Mr 23,28:1
Town Without Pity 1961,O 11,53:1
Gifford, Frances
Reluctant Dragon, The 1941,Jl 25,12:2
West Point Widow 1941,Jl 11,21:5
Louisiana Purchase 1942,Ja 1,37:1
Tombstone, The Town too Tough to Die
1942,Jl 27,18:2
Glass Key, The 1942,O 16,23:1
American Empire 1943,Ja 14,25:4
Tarzan Triumphs 1943,F 5,16:3
Cry Havoc 1943,N 24,16:2

Gifford, Frances— Cont
Marriage Is a Private Affair 1944,O 27,17:7
Thrill of a Romance 1945,My 25,22:2
Our Vines Have Tender Grapes 1945,S 7,21:2
She Went to the Races 1946,F 1,29:2
Arnelo Affair, The 1947,S 13,8:5
Luxury Liner 1948,S 10,19:2
Riding High 1950,Ap 11,26:2

Gifford, Frank
Up Periscope 1959,Mr 5,35:4
Paper Lion 1968,O 24,54:1

Gifford, Harry (Composer)
Let George Do It 1940,O 14,25:5
It's in the Air 1940,D 10,33:2
Mister Big 1943,Je 14,13:4

Gifford, Lillie Bea
Orders to Kill 1958,N 18,41:2

Giffra, Geza (Director)
Zsivany Becsuelet 1935,O 30,16:3

Gift, Denn
Yearling, The 1947,Ja 24,18:2
Fighting Father Dunne 1948,Je 25,26:2

Gigli, Beniamino
Forever Yours 1937,Je 7,22:2
Ave Maria 1937,O 2,18:1
Only for Thee; Solo per To 1938,S 12,13:2
Dingehort mein Herz; My Heart Belongs to Thee
  1939,Mr 25,19:2
Du Bist mein Gluck; Thou Art my Joy
  1940,Ja 6,9:2
Legittima Difesa; Self Defense 1940,Ap 6,13:3
Laugh Pagliacci 1948,Ja 31,14:2
Singing Taxi Driver 1953,My 16,10:1

Gigli, Beniamino (Composer)
Manon Lescaut 1941,Ap 14,23:5

Giglio, Sandro
Strictly Dishonorable 1951,Jl 12,21:6
Saturday's Hero 1951,S 12,37:2
When Worlds Collide 1952,F 7,30:2
Holiday for Sinners 1952,S 20,13:2
Assignment-Paris 1952,O 25,12:6
Second Chance 1953,Jl 23,20:2
War of the Worlds, The 1953,Ag 14,10:2
House of Bamboo 1955,Jl 2,13:2
Rose Tattoo, The 1955,D 13,55:1
Big Boodle, The 1957,Mr 12,38:1
For the First Time 1959,Ag 15,8:7

Gignoux, Regis (Original Author)
Between Us Girls 1942,S 25,25:3

Gil, Antonio
Dos Mujeres y un Don Juan 1934,Je 4,12:4

Gil, Carlos Robles
Roots, The (The Filly); Filly, The (The Roots)
  1957,S 3,23:2

Gil, Enrique
Desheredados, Los 1936,Mr 23,22:6

Gil, Gilbert
Abused Confidence 1938,D 1,29:1
Heart of Paris 1939,Ja 13,17:3
Pepe le Moko 1941,Mr 4,20:2
Midnight in Paris 1947,O 9,32:3
Symphonie Fantastique, La 1947,D 8,35:2
Portrait of Innocence 1948,Je 9,35:2
Foolish Husbands 1948,O 11,27:2

Gil, Margarita
Backfire 1965,Ap 27,27:1

Gil, Rafael (Director)
Don Quixote 1949,My 13,29:3
Nail, The 1949,Jl 1,14:6

Gil, Rafael (Screenwriter)
Don Quixote 1949,My 13,29:3

Gilardoni, Eugenio
Retribution 1922,Je 7,22:3

Gilasenko, L
Rimsky-Korsakov 1954,Mr 1,16:3

Gilberg, Lewis (Director)
Reach for the Sky 1957,My 1,40:1

Gilbert, Anna
Partners Again, With Potash and Perlmutter
  1926,F 15,16:4

Gilbert, Anthony (Original Author)
My Name is Julia Ross 1945,N 9,16:3

Gilbert, Billy
Million Dollar Legs 1932,Jl 9,7:5
Pack up Your Troubles 1932,O 1,10:4
Sutter's Gold 1936,Mr 27,25:2
Kelly the Second 1936,O 3,21:2
Big Game, The 1936,O 24,23:1
Night Waitress 1936,D 18,31:5
On the Avenue 1937,F 5,17:3
We're on the Jury 1937,F 10,18:5
Man Who Found Himself, The 1937,Ap 9,19:3
Outcasts of Poker Flat, The 1937,Ap 27,18:3
Toast of New York, The 1937,Jl 23,16:2
Firefly, The 1937,S 2,17:2
Broadway Melody of 1938 1937,S 3,12:1
100 Men and a Girl 1937,S 18,15:2
Life of the Party, The 1937,O 4,17:1
Music for Madame 1937,O 23,14:1
Fight for Your Lady 1937,N 20,21:2
Rosalie 1937,D 31,9:2
She's Got Everything 1938,Ja 14,21:3
Happy Landing 1938,Ja 22,19:1
Joy of Living 1938,My 6,27:1

Army Girl 1938,Ag 12,11:1
Block-Heads 1938,Ag 30,14:2
My Lucky Star 1938,S 10,20:2
Breaking the Ice 1938,S 23,35:3
Mr Doodle Kicks Off 1938,S 28,29:4
Peck's bad Boy With the Circus 1939,Ja 11,17:4
Girl Downstairs, The 1939,Ja 26,17:1
Star Maker, The 1939,Ag 31,14:2
Under-Pup, The 1939,S 5,21:2
Rio 1939,O 27,27:2
Destry Rides Again 1939,N 30,25:1
His Girl Friday 1940,Ja 12,13:2
Women in War 1940,My 30,21:2
Safari 1940,Je 20,29:2
Sandy Is a Lady 1940,Je 28,22:2
Cross Country Romance 1940,Jl 19,22:3
Great Dictator, The 1940,O 16,29:1
Little Bit of Heaven, A 1940,N 8,24:2
Seven Sinners 1940,N 18,23:2
Tin Pan Alley 1940,N 22,27:3
No, No, Nanette 1940,D 20,33:1
Model Wife 1941,Ap 24,25:3
Reaching for the Sun 1941,My 8,21:1
One Night in Lisbon 1941,Je 12,29:3
Week-End in Havana 1941,N 8,11:2
New Wine 1942,F 2,11:2
Mr Wise Guy 1942,Mr 5,27:2
Song of the Islands 1942,Mr 12,24:4
Valley of the Sun 1942,Mr 19,29:2
Arabian Nights 1942,D 26,15:1
Crazy House 1943,D 16,33:3
Anchors Aweigh 1945,Jl 20,15:2
Kissing Bandit, The 1948,N 19,35:2
Bride of Vengeance 1949,Ap 7,38:2
Down Among the Sheltering Palms
  1953,Je 13,11:2
Five Weeks in a Balloon 1962,Ag 27,18:1
Sound of Laughter, The 1963,D 18,44:2

Gilbert, Bob
Never the Twain Shall Meet 1931,Je 6,15:5

Gilbert, Claire
Wench, The 1949,Mr 14,15:5

Gilbert, Doris (Original Author)
Ladies Courageous 1944,Mr 16,17:2

Gilbert, Doris (Screenwriter)
Ladies Courageous 1944,Mr 16,17:2
Atlantic City 1944,Ag 14,11:4
Storm Over Lisbon 1944,S 11,14:1
Lake Placid Serenade 1944,D 25,15:6
Little Egypt 1951,Ag 30,20:3

Gilbert, Edwin (Original Author)
Blues in the Night 1941,D 12,35:2

Gilbert, Edwin (Screenwriter)
All Through the Night 1942,Ja 24,13:2
Larceny, Inc 1942,Ap 25,9:1

Gilbert, Eugenie
Sinners in Silk 1924,S 8,15:3
So This Is Marriage 1924,D 23,16:2
After the Storm 1928,My 8,25:3

Gilbert, Helen
Andy Hardy Gets Spring Fever 1939,Jl 19,23:2
Secret of Dr Kildare, The 1939,D 8,33:5
Florian 1940,Je 6,33:2
Falcon takes Over, The 1942,My 30,9:2
Beyond the Blue Horizon 1942,Je 25,27:2
Music for Millions 1944,D 22,12:4
Thief of Damascus 1952,My 8,37:2

Gilbert, Henry
Long John Silver 1955,Ap 7,24:1
Return of Mr Moto 1965,D 2,48:1

Gilbert, J Charles
Once in a Blue Moon 1936,D 2,35:1

Gilbert, Jack
Widow by Proxy 1919,S 22,8:1
White Circle, The 1920,Ag 23,9:2
Ladies Must Live 1921,N 21,20:1

Gilbert, Jean (Composer)
Zwei Herzen und ein Schlag 1932,S 9,17:5

Gilbert, Jean (Miscellaneous)
Theaternaechte von Berlin 1932,Ja 11,28:5

Gilbert, Jo
Too Young to Kiss 1951,N 23,32:2
Red Garters 1954,Mr 27,13:5
Big Fisherman, The 1959,Ag 6,18:1
Boheme, La 1926,F 25,26:2

Gilbert, Joanne
Great Man, The 1957,Ja 2,28:2
High Cost of Loving, The 1958,My 17,12:1

Gilbert, Jody
Everything Happens at Night 1939,D 16,12:6
Little Old New York 1940,F 3,9:2
Seventeen 1940,F 29,15:2
Star Dust 1940,My 4,13:1
Flowing Gold 1940,S 2,19:3
Wild Geese Calling 1941,Ag 30,10:2
Ride 'Em Cowboy 1942,My 5,27:3
Hard Way, The 1943,Mr 13,9:2
Deadline for Murder 1946,Je 29,22:7
Albuquerque 1948,Mr 1,17:2
Are You With It? 1948,Ap 15,31:2
My Dear Secretary 1949,F 14,15:4
Hellfire 1949,My 30,9:4
One Last Fling 1949,Jl 1,14:6

Gilbert, Jody— Cont
House by the River 1950,My 2,25:2
Actors and Sin; (Woman of Sin) 1952,My 30,11:3

Gilbert, John
Shame 1921,Ag 1,8:3 (Incorrect in this edition;
  use 1921,Ag 1,6:4 elsewhere)
Monte Cristo 1922,Ag 15,20:3
His Hour 1924,O 7,26:1
He Who Gets Slapped 1924,N 10,20:1
Snob, The 1924,D 15,14:1
Wife of the Centaur, The 1925,Ja 7,33:5
Merry Widow, The 1925,Ag 27,14:1
Big Parade, The 1925,N 20,18:1 (In Addenda)
Bardelys The Magnificent 1926,N 1,28:1 (In
  Addenda)
Flesh and the Devil 1927,Ja 10,20:2
Show, The 1927,Mr 14,16:1
Twelve Miles Out 1927,Jl 26,17:1
Love 1927,N 30,22:4
Man, Woman and Sin 1927,D 5,26:2
Cossacks, The 1928,Je 25,27:1
Four Walls 1928,Ag 20,21:3
Masks of the Devil, The 1928,N 26,30:2
Woman of Affairs, A 1929,Ja 21,18:4
Desert Nights 1929,My 6,30:4
Hollywood Revue, The 1929,Ag 15,20:5
His Glorious Night 1929,O 5,22:5
Redemption 1930,My 3,23:1
Way for a Sailor 1930,D 13,22:2
Gentleman's Fate 1931,Je 27,20:3
Phantom of Paris, The 1931,N 14,15:3
Downstairs 1932,O 8,15:4
Fast Workers 1933,Mr 20,18:2
Queen Christina 1933,D 27,23:3
Captain Hates the Sea, The 1934,N 29,33:2
Show People 1967,O 2,58:2

Gilbert, John (Original Author)
Olympia 1930,D 7,IX,6:4

Gilbert, John (Screenwriter)
Downstairs 1932,O 8,15:4

Gilbert, L Wolfe (Composer)
Roman Scandals 1933,D 25,28:2

Gilbert, Lauren
Close-Up 1948,Ap 5,24:2
Girl of the Night 1960,N 12,15:1
X-15 1962,Ap 5,30:2
Unsinkable Molly Brown, The 1964,Jl 17,15:1

Gilbert, Leatrice Joy
Of Human Hearts 1938,F 18,23:1

Gilbert, Lewis
Hound of the Baskervilles, The 1922,S 11,20:2
Viva Zapata 1952,F 8,19:2

Gilbert, Lewis (Director)
Little Ballerina, The 1951,F 28,33:2
Wall of Death 1952,My 19,12:4
Hundred Hour Hunt 1953,Je 17,32:2
Time, Gentlemen, Please 1953,S 24,39:2
Cast a Dark Shadow 1957,N 28,57:1
Admirable Crichton, The 1957,D 15,45:4
  (Incorrect in this edition; use 1957,D 17,45:4
  elsewhere)
Cry From the Streets, A 1959,F 24,32:2
Sink the Bismarck! 1960,F 12,22:3
Ferry to Hong Kong 1961,Ap 27,27:7
Loss of Innocence 1961,N 22,27:1
Damn the Defiant 1962,S 20,29:2
Seventh Dawn, The 1964,S 3,24:1
Alfie 1966,Ag 25,42:1
You Only Live Twice 1967,Je 14,40:1

Gilbert, Lewis (Miscellaneous)
Admirable Crichton, The 1957,D 15,45:4
  (Incorrect in this edition; use 1957,D 17,45:4
  elsewhere)

Gilbert, Lewis (Producer)
Alfie 1966,Ag 25,42:1

Gilbert, Lewis (Screenwriter)
Little Ballerina, The 1951,F 28,33:2
Marry Me 1952,Mr 14,27:3
Hundred Hour Hunt 1953,Je 17,32:2
Reach for the Sky 1957,My 1,40:1
Ferry to Hong Kong 1961,Ap 27,27:7

Gilbert, Lou
Requiem for a Heavyweight 1962,O 17,35:1
Across the River 1965,Ap 27,27:1
Goldstein 1965,My 8,19:7
Juliet of the Spirits 1965,N 4,57:1

Gilbert, Michael (Original Author)
Breakout 1960,My 19,44:3

Gilbert, Nina
Service de Luxe 1938,O 24,13:2

Gilbert, Olive
Dancing Years, The 1951,Ja 29,14:4
Festival 1967,O 24,53:2

Gilbert, Paul
So This Is Paris 1955,F 12,11:1
Second Greatest Sex, The 1956,F 11,12:2
Sylvia 1965,F 11,45:1
Cat Ballou 1965,Je 25,36:1

Gilbert, Philip
Checkpoint 1957,S 19,25:2
Frozen Dead, The 1967,N 16,58:1

Gilbert, Ray (Composer)
Three Caballeros, The 1945,F 5,20:1
Make Mine Music 1946,Ap 22,26:2

Gilbert, Ray (Composer) — Cont
Melody Time 1948,My 28,28:2
Gilbert, Raye
George Washington Carver 1940,Ap 17,26:4
Gilbert, Robert (Composer)
Schlacht von Bademuende, Die 1931,N 21,20:4
Gilbert, Ronnie
Festival 1967,O 24,53:2
Windflowers 1968,F 23,43:1
Gilbert, Ruth
Alice in Wonderland 1931,D 28,22:1
Gilbert, W S (Composer)
Mikado, The 1967,Mr 15,53:1
Gilbert, Walter
Gambling 1934,D 4,22:3
Gilbert, Wolfe (Composer)
Love, Live and Laugh 1929,N 2,14:6
Gilbert and Sullivan (Original Author)
Mikado, The 1939,Je 2,27:2
Gilberts, O P (Original Author)
drame De Shanghai; Shanghai Drama, The
1945,Ja 11,19:2
Gilbreth, Frank B Jr (Original Author)
Cheaper by the Dozen 1950,Ap 1,12:2
Belles on Their Toes 1952,My 3,17:5
Gilchrist, Connie
Woman's Face, A 1941,My 16,21:2
Barnacle Bill 1941,Jl 25,12:4
Johnny Eager 1942,F 20,21:2
We Were Dancing 1942,My 1,23:2
Sunday Punch 1942,My 11,19:2
Tortilla Flat 1942,My 22,27:1
Grand Central Murder 1942,My 23,8:8
War Against Mrs Hadley, The 1942,N 26,40:2
Presenting Lily Mars 1943,Ap 30,25:3
Swing Shift Maisie 1943,S 10,29:2
Cry Havoc 1943,N 24,16:2
Heavenly Body, The 1944,Mr 24,17:3
Rationing 1944,Ap 10,14:2
Junior Miss 1945,Je 18,15:4
Bad Bascomb 1946,My 23,18:4
Young Widow 1946,Jl 29,12:8
Hucksters, The 1947,Jl 18,21:2
Song of the Thin Man 1947,Ag 29,14:2
Good News 1947,D 5,33:2
Big City 1948,My 17,23:3
Chicken every Sunday 1949,Ja 19,34:2
Letter to Three Wives, A 1949,Ja 21,24:2
Act of Violence 1949,Ja 24,16:2
Little Women 1949,Mr 11,33:2
Story of Molly X, The 1949,D 2,35:4
Buccaneer's Girl 1950,Mr 27,19:2
Ticket to Tomahawk, A 1950,My 20,8:6
Peggy 1950,Jl 21,15:4
Louisa 1950,O 25,45:2
Undercover Girl 1950,N 8,37:2
Tripoli 1950,N 10,35:2
Stars in my Crown 1950,D 22,19:1
Killer That Stalked New York, The
1951,Ja 5,17:2
Here Comes the Groom 1951,S 21,19:2
Thunder on the Hill 1951,O 18,32:3
Flesh and Fury 1952,Mr 28,27:4
Houdini 1953,Jl 3,10:2
It Should Happen to You 1954,Ja 16,10:5
Far Country, The 1955,F 14,24:2
Long John Silver 1955,Ap 7,24:1
Man in the Gray Flannel Suit, The
1956,Ap 13,21:1
Auntie Mame 1958,D 5,39:1
Some Came Running 1959,Ja 23,17:1
Say One for Me 1959,Je 20,11:2
Swingin' Along 1962,Ag 27,18:1
Misadventures of Merlin Jones, The
1964,Mr 26,40:4
Tiger Walks, A 1964,Ag 27,28:2
House is not a Home, A 1964,S 2,33:1
Two on a Guillotine 1965,Ja 14,44:3
Gilden, K B (Original Author)
Hurry Sundown 1967,Mr 24,22:1
Giler, Berne (Original Author)
No Questions Asked 1951,Ag 10,13:2
Affair in Trinidad 1952,Jl 31,14:2
Giler, Berne (Screenwriter)
Turnabout 1940,Jl 27,17:6
C-Man 1949,My 28,11:4
Tarzan the Magnificent 1960,Jl 21,17:1
Giler, Bernie (Screenwriter)
Tarzan's Greatest Adventure 1959,Jl 9,22:1
Giles, Miranda
Mountain Music 1937,Je 24,30:3
Gilette, Ruth
Everybody Does It 1949,O 26,32:2
Gilford, Jack
Mister Buddwing 1966,O 12,36:1
Funny Thing Happened on the Way to the Forum,
A 1966,O 17,48:1
Enter Laughing 1967,Ag 1,24:1
Incident, The 1967,N 6,65:1
Who's Minding the Mint? 1967,D 7,60:3
Gilger, Glenn
Eight on the Lam 1967,Ap 27,52:1

Gilgi, Susy
Warrior Empress, The 1961,Ag 10,17:4
Gilier, Walter
Tonio Kroger 1968,Ja 16,24:1
Gill, Basil
Should a Doctor Tell 1931,Ag 22,7:5
Rembrandt 1936,D 3,31:1
Man of Affairs 1937,F 20,9:2
Knight Without Armor 1937,Jl 9,18:1
Citadel, The 1938,N 4,27:2
Sidewalks of London 1940,F 15,15:1
Gill, Florence
Every Night at Eight 1935,Ag 3,16:2
Reluctant Dragon, The 1941,Jl 25,12:2
Gill, Frank Jr (Screenwriter)
Hit Parade of 1943 1943,Ap 16,24:3
Chatterbox 1943,Jl 2,15:3
Atlantic City 1944,Ag 14,11:4
Brazil 1944,N 20,25:2
Earl Carroll Vanities 1945,Ap 2,15:6
Mexicana 1945,N 17,14:6
Earl Carroll Sketchbook 1946,Ag 30,13:2
McHale's Navy 1964,Jl 11,15:2
Gill, Geoffrey
Peg o'my Heart 1933,My 20,11:4
Gill, Gwen
Come on Marines 1934,Mr 24,20:3
Behold My Wife 1935,F 18,19:3
Irish and Proud of It 1938,O 31,12:3
Gill, Gwenllian
Menace 1934,N 22,27:2
Gill, Inga
Miss Julie 1952,Ap 8,35:2
Seventh Seal 1958,O 14,44:1
Gill, Maud
Farmer's Wife, The 1930,Ja 7,28:3
Gill, Moss Sergeant
Unbeliever, The 1918,F 12,9:2
Gill, Renja
Shadows Grow Longer, The 1962,Je 11,36:4
Gill, Tom
This Man Is News 1939,Jl 20,16:4
Hotel Sahara 1952,Ja 1,21:4
Mister Drake's Duck 1952,Ja 28,15:2
Mr Lord Says No! 1952,F 12,22:5
Gill, Tom (Original Author)
Gay Caballero, The 1932,Mr 26,17:2
Border Cafe 1937,Je 8,30:2
Gillatt, Sidney (Screenwriter)
Lady Vanishes, The 1938,D 26,29:1
Gille, Andre
Stowaway in the Sky 1962,Je 19,28:1
Gille, Jean
Tawny Pipit 1947,S 8,25:5
Gillen, Ernest
Any Woman 1925,My 27,26:2
His Secretary 1925,D 21,27:2
Auction Block, The 1926,F 15,16:4
Giller, Walter
Captain from Koepenick, The 1958,Jl 26,6:1
Roses for the Prosecutor; (Rosen fur den
Staarsanwalt) 1961,O 10,38:2
Hippodrome 1962,Mr 12,36:1
Burning Court, The 1963,Ag 1,17:2
Conjugal Bed, The 1963,S 17,30:1
Fanny Hill 1965,D 2,48:1
Gillespie, Arnold (Miscellaneous)
Wizard of Oz, The 1939,Ag 18,16:2
Gillespie, William
Blues in the Night 1941,D 12,35:2
Gillette, Betty
Crooner 1932,Ag 20,7:4
Big City Blues 1932,S 10,18:5
Scarlet Dawn 1932,N 4,25:4
Gillette, Roland
Blame the Woman 1932,O 25,24:5
Gillette, Ruth
Frontier Marshal 1934,Ja 31,20:3
Wild Gold 1934,Jl 24,20:2
Life Begins at 40 1935,Ap 5,21:3
Off to the Races 1937,F 6,15:2
In Old Chicago 1938,Ja 7,15:2
Rebecca of Sunnybrook Farm 1938,Mr 26,12:1
Josette 1938,Je 11,9:1
Chaser, The 1938,Ag 2,15:3
Return of the Cisco Kid, The 1939,Ap 29,13:2
In a Lonely Place 1950,My 18,37:2
Gillette, William (Original Author)
Secret Service 1919,Je 23,10:3
Sherlock Holmes 1922,My 8,14:3
Secret Service 1931,D 14,16:3
Adventures of Sherlock Holmes, The
1939,S 2,20:1
Gilliat, Leslie (Producer)
Ring of Treason 1964,My 28,40:3 (Incorrect in
this edition; use 1964,My 29,15:1 elsewhere)
Gilliat, Sidney (Director)
Notorious Gentleman 1946,N 14,39:3
Green for Danger 1947,Ag 8,10:2
Dulcimer Street 1948,N 8,24:2
Waterloo Road 1948,D 25,10:3
State Secret 1950,O 5,38:2
Gilbert and Sullivan 1953,O 28,36:3

Gilliat, Sidney (Director) — Cont
Constant Husband, The 1957,Jl 26,10:3
Left, Right and Centre 1961,F 10,19:1
Only Two Can Play 1962,Mr 21,33:2
Gilliat, Sidney (Miscellaneous)
My Heart Is Calling 1935,Ap 15,16:3
Jamaica Inn 1939,O 12,33:1
Gilliat, Sidney (Original Author)
Friday the 13th 1934,My 15,18:1
Jack Ahoy 1935,F 9,11:2
Adventures, The 1947,Ap 4,19:2
Green Man, The 1957,My 23,40:1
Gilliat, Sidney (Producer)
Notorious Gentleman 1946,N 14,39:3
Adventures, The 1947,Ap 4,19:2
Green for Danger 1947,Ag 8,10:2
Captain Boycott 1947,D 6,11:2
Dulcimer Street 1948,N 8,24:2
Happiest Days of Your Life, The 1950,S 18,19:2
Gilbert and Sullivan 1953,O 28,36:3
Folly to be Wise 1953,D 28,17:2
Wee Geordie 1956,O 8,31:1
Green Man, The 1957,My 23,40:1
Constant Husband, The 1957,Jl 26,10:3
Blue Murder at St Trinian's 1958,My 27,27:1
Left, Right and Centre 1961,F 10,19:1
Pure Hell of St Trinian's, The 1961,S 26,31:1
Gilliat, Sidney (Screenwriter)
Jack Ahoy 1935,F 9,11:2
Alias Bulldog Drummond 1935,S 10,26:2
King of the Damned 1936,F 1,9:2
Seven Sinners 1936,Ag 22,6:1
Man Who Lived Again, The 1936,D 16,35:4
Strangers on a Honeymoon 1937,Mr 13,23:2
Jamaica Inn 1939,O 12,33:1
Night Train 1940,D 30,21:1
Girl in the News, The 1941,My 5,13:2
Kipps 1942,My 25,11:2
Young Mr Pitt, The 1943,Mr 11,17:1
Notorious Gentleman 1946,N 14,39:3
Green for Danger 1947,Ag 8,10:2
Dulcimer Street 1948,N 8,24:2
Waterloo Road 1948,D 25,10:3
State Secret 1950,O 5,38:2
Gilbert and Sullivan 1953,O 28,36:3
Belles of St Trinian's, The 1954,D 23,13:4
Wee Geordie 1956,O 8,31:1
Green Man, The 1957,My 23,40:1
Constant Husband, The 1957,Jl 26,10:3
Blue Murder at St Trinian's 1958,My 27,27:1
Left, Right and Centre 1961,F 10,19:1
Pure Hell of St Trinian's, The 1961,S 26,31:1
Gillibert, Jean
Trial of Joan of Arc, The 1965,F 12,19:1
Gillie, Jean
This'll Make You Whistle 1938,N 1,27:2
Decoy 1946,N 2,12:2
Macomber Affair, The 1947,Ap 21,21:2
Gilliespie, Harold Commodore
Cinerama-South Seas Adventure 1958,Jl 16,26:1
Gilligan, Edmund (Original Author)
Sealed Cargo 1951,My 24,47:1
Gilliland, Helen
Storm, The 1938,O 31,12:2
Gilling, John (Director)
Murder Will Out 1953,Ap 6,24:2
White Fire 1954,S 18,12:4
Man Inside, The 1959,F 5,24:7
Shadow of the Cat, The 1961,Je 8,40:2
It Takes a Thief 1963,Ag 15,24:7
Where the Bullets Fly 1967,S 7,50:4
Gilling, John (Screenwriter)
Murder Will Out 1953,Ap 6,24:2
White Fire 1954,S 18,12:4
Killers of Kilimanjaro 1960,Ap 7,46:1
It Takes a Thief 1963,Ag 15,24:7
Gillingwater, Claude
Little Lord Fauntleroy 1921,S 16,17:3
Dust Flower, The 1922,Jl 3,8:6
Fools First 1922,Jl 31,12:3
Remembrance 1922,O 2,21:2
Stranger's Banquet, The 1923,Ja 1,18:1
Three Wise Fools 1923,Jl 23,13:4
Dulcy 1923,S 17,18:2
Tiger Rose 1923,D 3,14:1
Daddies 1924,F 11,18:3
Madonna of the Streets 1924,O 28,23:4
Thief in Paradise, A 1925,Ja 26,14:1
Cheaper to Marry 1925,F 2,14:1
Winds of Chance 1925,Ag 17,10:3
Seven Sinners 1925,D 8,28:5
We Moderns 1925,D 8,28:5
That's My Baby 1926,Ap 12,18:4
Into her Kingdom 1926,Ag 10,19:2
Fast and Furious 1927,Jl 4,20:3
Naughty but Nice 1927,Jl 5,19:2
Barbed Wire 1927,Ag 8,10:3
Gorilla, The 1927,N 21,20:1
Kentucky Courage 1928,My 14,25:1
Oh, Kay! 1928,Ag 27,23:1
Women They Talk About 1928,O 15,16:1
Glad Rag Doll, The 1929,Je 3,27:2
Smiling Irish Eyes 1929,Jl 24,23:2
So Long Letty 1930,F 8,12:5

Gillingwater, Claude— Cont

Great Divide, The 1930,F 17,17:6
Dumbbells in Ermine 1930,Jl 28,22:1
Flirting Widow, The 1930,Ag 2,16:4
Kiss Me Again 1931,Ja 8,21:4
Illicit 1931,Ja 19,25:1
Conquering Horde, The 1931,Mr 30,25:2
Gold Dust Gertie 1931,My 30,9:2
Daddy Long Legs 1931,Je 6,15:5
Compromised 1931,N 7,16:5
Tess of the Storm Country 1932,N 19,20:2
Ann Carver's Profession 1933,Je 9,20:2
Avenger, The 1933,O 3,28:3
Before Midnight 1934,Ja 10,24:3
You Can't Buy Everything 1934,F 3,9:2
Show-Off, The 1934,Mr 17,11:3
Unknown Blonde 1934,Ap 24,27:2
In Love With Life 1934,My 12,12:3
Captain Hates the Sea, The 1934,N 29,33:2
Broadway Bill 1934,N 30,22:2
Woman in Red, The 1935,Mr 23,11:3
Mississippi 1935,Ap 18,27:2
Tale of Two Cities, A 1935,D 26,21:2
Prisoner of Shark Island, The 1936,F 13,25:2
Florida Special 1936,My 29,15:2
Poor Little Rich Girl, The 1936,Je 26,16:1
Counterfeit 1936,Jl 20,11:1
Ticket to Paradise 1936,Ag 8,5:3
Wives Never Know 1936,O 31,24:2
Top of the Town 1937,Mr 27,19:2
Conquest 1937,N 5,19:1
Yank at Oxford, A 1938,F 25,15:1
Little Miss Broadway 1938,Jl 23,10:4
There Goes my Heart 1938,O 14,27:1
Just Around the Corner 1938,D 3,11:2
Cafe Society 1939,F 23,19:2

Gillis, Ann

Off to the Races 1937,F 6,15:2
Adventures of Tom Sawyer, The 1938,F 18,23:1
Peck's bad Boy With the Circus 1939,Ja 11,17:4
Under-Pup, The 1939,S 5,21:2
Edison the Man 1940,Je 7,27:2
All This and Heaven, Too 1940,Jl 5,10:2
My Love Came Back 1940,Jl 13,16:5
Little Men 1940,D 9,23:2
Mr Dynamite 1941,Mr 13,25:2
Nice Girl 1941,Mr 27,29:6
Janie 1944,Ag 5,16:2
Wave, A Wac and a Marine, A 1944,Ag 14,11:4
In Society 1944,Ag 17,20:2
Cheaters, The 1945,Jl 21,7:2
Janie Gets Married 1946,Je 15,24:2
Time of Their Lives, The 1946,N 28,40:2

Gillmore, Margalo

Wayward 1932,F 15,13:1
Perfect Strangers 1950,Mr 11,8:2
Cause for Alarm 1951,Mr 30,28:5
Law and the Lady, The 1951,Ag 16,23:2
Behave Yourself 1951,N 8,35:2
Elopement 1951,D 21,21:3
Skirts Ahoy! 1952,My 29,17:2
Scandal at Scourie 1953,Je 16,24:2
Woman's World 1954,S 29,23:4
Gaby 1956,My 10,26:3
High Society 1956,Ag 10,9:2

Gillstrom, Arvid E (Director)

Legionnaires in Paris 1927,D 26,26:6

Gilly, Renee

Barber of Seville 1949,Jl 21,21:2

Gilman, Lucy

Gangster's Boy 1938,N 7,23:6

Gilman, Mildred (Original Author)

Sob Sister 1931,O 3,20:2

Gilman, Peter (Original Author)

Diamond Head 1963,F 21,5:2

Gilman, Sam

Full of Life 1957,F 13,38:1
Young Lions, The 1958,Ap 3,23:1
One Eyed Jacks 1961,Mr 31,21:1

Gilmore, Arthur

It Should Happen to You 1954,Ja 16,10:5

Gilmore, Barney

South Sea Love 1928,F 7,30:3

Gilmore, Denis

Three Lives of Thomasina, The 1963,D 12,46:1

Gilmore, Dorothy

Chocolate Soldier, The 1941,N 1,20:2

Gilmore, Douglas

Sally, Irene and Mary 1925,D 7,19:1
Dance Madness 1926,Ja 25,21:2
Paris 1926,Je 1,29:3
Taxi Dancer, The 1927,Mr 8,18:4
Kiss in a Taxi, A 1927,Mr 15,29:2
Rough House Rosie 1927,My 23,27:2
One Woman Idea, The 1929,Je 10,23:1
Pleasure Crazed 1929,Jl 15,25:1
Married in Hollywood 1929,S 23,24:3
Cameo Kirby 1930,F 8,12:5
Hell's Angels 1930,Ag 16,8:3
Unfaithful 1931,Mr 7,17:2
Naughty Flirt, The 1931,Ap 13,17:1
Girl Habit, The 1931,Jl 4,11:5

Gilmore, Helen

Sensation Seekers 1927,Mr 16,28:2

Gilmore, J H

Democracy, The Vision Restored 1920,Ag 25,6:4

Gilmore, Lowell

Days of Glory 1944,Je 17,10:2
Picture of Dorian Gray, The 1945,Mr 2,15:2
Johnny Angel 1945,D 28,12:2
Step by Step 1946,Ag 24,6:7
Calcutta 1947,Ap 24,30:2
Arnelo Affair, The 1947,S 13,8:5
Dream Girl 1948,Je 17,29:2
Black Arrow, The 1948,O 4,14:2
Walk a Crooked Mile 1948,O 13,31:2
Sword in the Desert 1949,Ag 25,20:2
Fortunes of Captain Blood 1950,Je 10,11:3
Tripoli 1950,N 10,35:2
King Solomon's Mines 1950,N 10,35:1
Lone Star 1952,F 2,11:4
Plymouth Adventure 1952,N 14,20:3
Androcles and the Lion 1953,Ja 15,23:2
Saskatchewan 1954,Mr 11,26:2

Gilmore, Stuart (Director)

Virginian, The 1946,Ap 18,22:2
Half Breed, The 1952,Jl 5,7:2

Gilmore, Virginia

Winter Carnival 1939,Jl 28,14:2
Tall, Dark and Handsome 1941,Ja 24,15:2
Western Union 1941,F 7,23:2
Swamp Water 1941,N 17,15:2
Pride of the Yankees, The 1942,Jl 16,23:1
Berlin Correspondent 1942,S 4,19:2
Loves of Edgar Allan Poe, The 1942,S 21,19:2
Orchestra Wives 1942,S 24,23:2
Chetniks 1943,Mr 19,15:3
Wonder Man 1945,Je 9,17:2
Close-Up 1948,Ap 5,24:2
Walk East on Beacon 1952,My 29,17:2

Gilpatric, Guy (Original Author)

Action in the North Atlantic 1943,My 22,10:2

Gilpin, J

Southerner, The 1945,Ag 27,22:3
They Were Sisters 1946,Jl 24,24:2
Years Between, The 1947,Mr 10,25:2

Gilroy, Bert (Producer)

Gun Law 1938,Je 24,15:1
Painted Desert 1938,S 14,26:5
Renegade Ranger, The 1939,F 17,17:3
Racketeers of the Range 1939,Je 8,31:4
Pop Always Pays 1940,Ag 30,16:6
Mexican Spitfire's Elephant 1942,S 18,25:2
Army Surgeon 1942,N 5,35:2
Ladies' Day 1943,Mr 26,14:3

Gilroy, Frank D (Original Author)

Fastest Gun Alive, The 1956,Jl 13,23:3
Subject Was Roses, The 1968,O 14,53:2

Gilroy, Frank D (Screenwriter)

Fastest Gun Alive, The 1956,Jl 13,23:3
Gallant Hours, The 1960,Je 23,19:4
Subject Was Roses, The 1968,O 14,53:2

Gilson, Tom

Rally Round the Flag Boys! 1958,D 24,2:7

Gilyazova, Fatima

Children of the New Day 1930,Je 30,22:6

Gimenez, John

Way Out 1967,O 26,54:3

Gimenez, John (Original Author)

Way Out 1967,O 26,54:3

Gimpel, Jakob

Gaslight 1944,My 5,17:2

Ging, Jack

Desire in the Dust 1960,O 12,47:2
Sniper's Ridge 1961,Ag 24,25:3

Gingold, Hermione

Pickwick Papers, The 1954,Ap 5,21:2
Around the World in 80 Days 1956,O 18,37:1
Gigi 1958,My 16,21:1
Bell, Book and Candle 1958,D 27,2:7
Naked Edge 1961,Jl 1,9:1
Music Man, The 1962,Ag 24,14:1
Gay Purr--ee 1962,D 6,55:3
I'd Rather Be Rich 1964,S 3,24:2
Harvey Middleman, Fireman 1965,Jl 13,39:1
Promise her Anything 1966,F 23,46:1
Munster, Go Home 1966,Je 16,53:4
Those Fantastic Flying Fools 1967,O 19,59:2

Ginju

Flute and the Arrow, The 1960,O 11,55:1

Ginna, Robert Emmett (Producer)

Young Cassidy 1965,Mr 23,35:1

Ginna, Robert Emmett (Screenwriter)

Last Challenge, The 1967,D 28,25:1

GINSBERG

See Also GINSBURG

Ginsberg, Allen

Chappaqua 1967,N 6,65:2

Ginsberg, Allen (Narrator)

Guns of the Trees 1964,F 29,12:2

Ginsberg, Henry (Producer)

Giant 1956,O 11,51:1

GINSBURG

See Also GINSBERG

Ginsburg, Alexei (Director)

Fortress on the Volga 1942,D 25,15:3

Ginter, Lee (Miscellaneous)

Wednesday's Child 1934,D 15,9:3

Ginty, E B (Original Author)

Man From Texas 1948,Ag 12,16:5

Ginzburg, Alexander (Screenwriter)

Cinderella 1961,D 19,39:1

Giocchino

Dream of Butterfly, The 1941,F 13,25:2

Giol, Vivi

Frenesia; Frenzy 1940,Je 6,33:4
Tragic Hunt 1948,O 22,30:2
Earth Cries Out, The; Grido Della Terra, Il 1949,Ag 31,26:2
Women Without Names 1951,Ag 7,22:2
Mistress of the Mountains 1954,My 27,34:5

Giono, Jean (Original Author)

Heartbeat 1939,S 5,21:3
Harvest 1939,O 3,19:4
Baker's Wife, The 1940,F 27,17:2
Ways of Love (Jofroi); Jofroi (Ways of Love) 1950,D 13,50:2

Giorda, Marcello

Albero di Adamo, L'; Adam's Tree 1938,Ja 20,19:2
Scipio Africanus 1939,S 23,22:2
Rigoletto 1949,N 10,41:4

Giordano, Mariangela

Eye of the Needle, The 1965,Je 22,25:2

Giordano, Salvatore

Webb Singing Pictures 1917,Ja 15,7:1

Giorgi, Elsa de

Eredita dello Zio, L 1935,Je 29,16:3
Delitto di Mastrovanni, Il 1935,Jl 30,16:2
But It's Nothing Serious 1939,O 10,27:2
Grande Luce, La; Great Light, The 1940,Mr 15,27:4

Giorgi, Paola

Passa L'Amore 1933,N 25,10:3

Giorgielli, Gabriella

Arturo Island 1962,D 22,5:2
Organizer, The 1964,My 7,31:2

Giouli, Smaroula

Taxi Driver, The 1958,Mr 3,24:8
House on Stournara Street, The 1960,O 17,33:4
Castle in Greece 1960,D 12,38:2

Giovampietro, Renzo

Duel Without Honor 1953,F 28,8:8
Greco, El 1967,My 24,52:2

Giovanna, Marco Della

Climax, The 1967,S 12,55:1

Giovanni, Jose

Symphony for a Massacre 1965,My 28,40:1

Giovanni, Jose (Original Author)

Night Watch, The; Trou, Le 1964,My 27,46:1

Giovanni, Jose (Screenwriter)

Riff Raff Girls 1962,O 20,13:5
Night Watch, The; Trou, Le 1964,My 27,46:1
Symphony for a Massacre 1965,My 28,40:1

Gipson, Fred (Original Author)

Return of the Texan 1952,F 14,23:1
Old Yeller 1957,D 26,23:4
Hound-Dog Man 1960,Ap 28,29:1

Gipson, Fred (Screenwriter)

Old Yeller 1957,D 26,23:4
Hound-Dog Man 1960,Ap 28,29:1

Gir

Honorable Catherine, The 1948,Ag 23,13:3

Gir, Jeanne Fusler

Crazy for Love 1960,N 26,13:2

Giraci, May

Miss Lulu Bett 1921,D 25,VI,2:1
Lorna Doone 1922,D 4,20:2
Secrets 1924,Mr 25,25:2

Giradon, Michele

Anatomy of a Marriage; My Days With Jean Marc; My Nights With Francoise 1964,O 27,42:2

Giraldi, Duccia

Miserables, Les 1952,Mr 25,23:2

Giraldi, Franco (Director)

Minute to Pray, A Second to Die, A 1968,My 23,56:2

GIRARD

See Also GERARD

Girard, Aime-Simon

Francis the First 1947,N 20,38:4

Girard, Bernard (Director)

Dead Heat on a Merry-Go-Round 1966,O 13,50:1

Girard, Bernard (Original Author)

This Woman is Dangerous 1952,F 28,23:2

Girard, Bernard (Screenwriter)

Breakthrough 1950,N 18,10:2
Dead Heat on a Merry-Go-Round 1966,O 13,50:1

Girard, Joseph

In Hollywood with Potash and Perlmutter 1924,S 30,27:3
Fireman, Save My Child 1927,O 10,24:1
Partners in Crime 1928,Ap 30,18:3
Terror, The 1928,Ag 16,25:3

Girard, Joseph— Cont

Fleet's In, The 1928,O 1,23:1
Redskin 1929,Ja 28,21:1
Leatherneck, The 1929,Ap 22,23:1
One Woman Idea, The 1929,Je 10,23:1
Girl from Havana, The 1929,S 2,16:1
Troopers Three 1930,F 17,17:6
Just Imagine 1930,N 22,21:3
Gang Buster, The 1931,Ja 24,15:1
Sky Spider, The 1931,Ag 31,11:5
Strictly Dishonorable 1931,N 11,27:1
Radio Patrol 1932,Jl 14,24:2
Crusader, The 1932,O 8,15:4
Racetrack 1933,Mr 6,16:6
Mystery of the Hooded Horsemen, The
  1937,Ag 13,13:2

Girard, William (Producer)

Circumstantial Evidence 1945,Ap 21,18:3
Bullfighters, The 1945,My 12,10:3
Caribbean Mystery, The 1945,Ag 20,22:4
It Shouldn't Happen to a Dog 1946,S 7,11:2

Girardi, Mirna

Grido, Il 1962,O 23,42:1

Girardi, Toni

Die vom Rummelplatz 1932,Ja 2,14:2

Girardon, Michele

Hatari 1962,Jl 12,19:1
7 Capital Sins (Pride); Pride (7 Capital Sins)
  1963,Ja 17,5:2
Adventures of Scaramouche, The 1964,N 23,34:1
  (Incorrect in this edition; use 1964,N 21,34:1
  elsewhere)
Magnificent Cuckold 1965,Ap 20,42:1
Tender Scoundrel 1967,N 16,58:2

Girardot, Annie

Inspector Maigret 1958,O 9,47:1
Speaking of Murder 1959,O 12,14:1
Love and the Frenchwoman; (Francaise et
  l'Amour, La) 1961,F 28,38:2
Rocco and his Brothers 1961,Je 28,40:2
Crime Does Not Pay (The Fenayrou Case);
  Fenayrou Case, The (Crime Does Not Pay)
  1962,O 17,35:2
Lovers on a Tightrope 1962,O 25,48:3
Bonne Soupe, La 1964,Mr 16,37:1
Organizer, The 1964,My 7,31:2
Ape Woman, The 1964,S 23,55:1
Vice and Virtue 1965,Mr 18,25:1
Male Companion 1966,F 15,33:2
Engagement Italiano 1966,Je 21,35:1
Live for Life 1967,D 19,59:1

Girardot, Etienne

Kennel Murder Case, The 1933,O 30,14:2
Advice to the Lovelorn 1933,D 14,28:2
Fashions of 1934 1934,Ja 20,12:2
Mandalay 1934,F 15,15:6
20th Century 1934,My 4,24:2
Little Man, What Now? 1934,Je 1,29:1
Return of the Terror 1934,Jl 11,20:2
Dragon Murder Case, The 1934,Ag 23,13:3
Firebird, The 1934,N 15,25:2
Clive of India 1935,Ja 18,29:1
Grand Old Girl 1935,F 26,16:4
Whole Town's Talking, The 1935,Mr 1,16:2
Hooray for Love 1935,Jl 13,16:2
Curly Top 1935,Ag 2,22:3
Metropolitan 1935,O 18,27:4
Old Kentucky, In 1935,N 29,24:1
Music Goes 'Round, The 1936,F 22,12:1
Garden Murder Case, The 1936,Mr 2,13:2
Half Angel 1936,My 30,7:3
Hearts Divided 1936,Je 13,13:1
Devil is a Sissy, The 1936,O 17,21:2
Longest Night, The 1936,O 17,21:2
Go West, Young Man 1936,N 19,31:3
College Holiday 1936,D 24,21:2
Wake up and Live 1937,Ap 24,16:2
Road Back, The 1937,Je 18,25:2
Great Garrick, The 1937,O 25,23:1
Breakfast for Two 1937,N 20,21:2
Danger-Love at Work 1937,D 11,22:2
Professor Beware 1938,Jl 14,17:1
Port of Seven Seas 1938,Jl 15,13:2
There Goes my Heart 1938,O 14,27:1
Fast and Loose 1939,Mr 9,18:1
Story of Vernon and Irene Castle, The
  1939,Mr 31,19:2
Exile Express 1939,Ag 16,21:3
Hawaiian Nights 1939,S 29,19:4
Little Accident 1939,N 24,29:3
Hunchback of Notre Dame, The 1940,Ja 1,29:2
Isle of Destiny 1940,Ap 8,15:2

Giraud, Claude

Circle of Love 1965,Mr 25,42:4

Giraud, Octavio

Message to Garcia, A 1936,Ap 10,27:1

Giraud, Wesley

No Greater Glory 1934,My 5,22:2

Giraudoux, Jean (Miscellaneous)

Angels of the Streets 1950,Ja 17,24:2

Giraudoux, Jean (Producer)

Wicked Duchess, The 1949,N 5,10:5

Giraudoux, Jean (Screenwriter)

Angels of the Streets 1950,Ja 17,24:2

Girelli, Arturito

Vidas Rotas 1935,Ag 3,16:3

Girelli, Margherita

Divorce-Italian Style 1962,S 18,34:1

Giret, Francoise

Seventh Juror, The 1964,Ja 28,25:1

Girodoux (Original Author)

Amphitryon 38 1935,O 13,IX,4:6 (In Addenda)

Giron, Adolfo

Sobre Las Olas 1934,Mr 17,11:4
Obre las Olas 1934,Mr 17,11:4
Oro y Plata 1934,Ag 29,13:2
Maria Elena 1936,F 18,27:1

Girosi, Marcello (Producer)

Bread, Love and Dreams 1954,S 21,24:1
Scandal in Sorrento 1957,Je 13,37:1
Monte Carlo Story, The 1958,F 13,23:2
Black Orchid, The 1959,F 13,33:2
That Kind of Woman 1959,S 12,12:2
Heller in Pink Tights 1960,Mr 17,28:1
Breath of Scandal, A 1960,D 17,19:1

Girosi, Marcello (Screenwriter)

Frisky 1955,O 25,37:3
Scandal in Sorrento 1957,Je 13,37:1

Girotti, Mario

Wonders of Aladdin, The 1961,D 23,16:1
Story of Joseph and his Brethern, The
  1962,D 1,17:1
Leopard, The 1963,Ag 13,25:1

Girotti, Massimo

Tragic Hunt 1948,O 22,30:2
Woman Trouble 1949,My 26,34:2
Iron Crown 1949,Je 11,11:2
Shamed 1949,O 13,33:3
Lost Youth 1949,O 27,35:4
Woman 1950,F 9,36:6
Mafia; (In Nome Della Legge) 1950,Mr 2,33:2
Escape into Dreams 1950,Ap 13,34:5
Difficult Years 1950,Ag 22,31:2
Behind Closed Shutters 1952,Je 10,22:7
Duel Without Honor 1953,F 28,8:8
Rome, 11 O'Clock 1953,Ap 30,39:2
Ten Commandments, The 1958,Ap 7,26:1
Cossacks, The 1960,S 6,41:4
Head of a Tyrant 1962,Je 7,31:2
Duel of the Titans 1963,Ag 8,19:1
Marco the Magnificent 1966,D 15,60:1
Senso 1968,Jl 9,31:1

Giroud, Francoise (Miscellaneous)

Antoine and Antoinette 1948,Ap 16,29:2

Giroud, Francoise (Screenwriter)

Antoine and Antoinette 1948,Ap 16,29:2
Julietta 1957,Je 18,38:2

Gish, Dorothy

Jordan Is a Hard Road 1915,N 15,11:1
Little Meena's Romance 1916,Ap 3,11:4
Hearts of the World 1918,Ap 5,13:1
Hun Within, The 1918,Ag 26,9:1
Battling Jane 1918,S 30,7:1
Hope Chest, The 1919,Ja 6,11:3
Boots 1919,Mr 10,9:3
Peppy Polly 1919,Ap 7,11:5
Nugget Nell 1919,Jl 28,8:5
Hearts of the World 1919,Ag 12,7:6
Nobody Home 1919,Ag 25,8:5
Turning the Tables 1919,N 3,13:3
Mary Ellen Comes to Town 1920,Mr 22,12:1
Remodeling her Husband 1920,Je 7,20:3 (In
  Addenda)
Little Miss Rebellion 1920,S 20,13:1
Country Flapper, The 1922,Jl 31,12:3
Bright Shawl, The 1923,Ap 23,18:3
Romola 1924,D 2,13:2
Night Life of New York 1925,Jl 14,14:1
Beautiful City, The 1925,N 23,25:4
Clothes Make the Pirate 1925,N 30,17:1
Nell Gwyn 1926,Jl 19,13:1
London 1926,O 25,15:1
Madame Pompadour 1927,Ag 2,19:2
Wanted Men 1937,Jl 8,15:2
Our Hearts Were Young and Gay 1944,O 12,24:2
Centennial Summer 1946,Jl 18,20:2
Whistle at Eaton Falls, The 1951,O 11,49:2
Cardinal, The 1963,D 13,41:1

Gish, Lillian

Hearts of the World 1918,Ap 5,13:1
Great Love, The 1918,Ag 12,7:1
Greatest Thing in Life, The 1918,D 23,9:1
Romance of Happy Valley, A 1919,Ja 27,11:4
Broken Blossoms 1919,My 14,15:5
I'll Get Him yet 1919,My 19,20:5
True Heart Susie 1919,Je 2,20:4
Hearts of the World 1919,Ag 12,7:6
Greatest Question, The 1919,D 29,7:2
Birth of a Nation, The 1921,My 2,12:1
Birth of a Nation, The 1922,D 5,24:3
White Sister, The 1923,S 6,10:2
Romola 1924,D 2,13:2
Boheme, La 1926,F 25,26:2
Scarlet Letter, The 1926,Ag 10,19:2
Annie Laurie 1927,My 12,24:3

Gish, Lillian— Cont

Enemy, The 1927,D 28,26:6
White Sister, The 1928,My 21,25:1
Wind, The 1928,N 5,26:1
One Romantic Night 1930,My 31,19:4
Birth of a Nation, The 1930,D 22,16:2
Way Down East 1931,Mr 16,25:1
His Double Life 1933,D 16,12:3
Top Man 1943,O 29,23:2
Miss Susie Slagle's 1946,F 7,29:2
Duel in the Sun 1947,My 8,30:2
Portrait of Jennie 1949,Mr 30,31:2
Commandos Strike at Dawn 1954,Ja 14,25:1
Cobweb, The 1955,Ag 6,13:3
Night of the Hunter, The 1955,S 30,23:1
Orders to Kill 1958,Ag 18,41:2
Unforgiven, The 1960,Ap 7,46:1
Follow Me, Boys! 1966,D 2,46:1
Warning Shot 1967,Je 8,52:2
Comedians, The 1967,N 1,37:1

Gish, Lillian (Director)

Remodeling her Husband 1920,Je 7,20:3 (In
  Addenda)

Giskes, H J (Original Author)

House of Intrigue, The 1960,Mr 10,36:3

Gist, Robert

Jigsaw 1949,My 30,9:4
Scene of the Crime 1949,Jl 29,12:2
Dangerous Profession, A 1949,D 12,29:4
I Was a Shoplifter 1950,Ap 28,26:3
Jackpot, The 1950,N 23,55:2
Strangers on a Train 1951,Jl 4,13:2
One Minute to Zero 1952,S 20,13:2
Band Wagon, The 1953,Jl 10,10:2
D-Day, The Sixth of June 1956,My 30,13:1
Naked and the Dead, The 1958,Ag 7,21:1
Al Capone 1959,Mr 26,27:1
Operation Petticoat 1959,D 6,38:1
Blueprint for Robbery 1961,F 2,24:3

Gist, Robert (Director)

American Dream, An 1966,S 1,28:2

Gittelson, June

White Parade, The 1934,N 10,19:1
Mark of the Vampire 1935,My 3,23:4
Convicted Woman 1940,F 26,11:2

Gittens, Wyndham (Screenwriter)

Mars Attacks the World 1938,N 8,26:3

Gittler, Lewis F (Screenwriter)

Earth Cries Out, The; Grido Della Terra, Il
  1949,Ag 31,26:2

Gitzer, G W (Cinematographer)

True Heart Susie 1919,Je 2,20:4

Giudice, F Del (Miscellaneous)

Fame Is the Spur 1949,N 8,34:2

Giudies, Sonia Lo

Journey to Love 1953,O 9,32:8

Giuffre, Aldo

Best of Enemies, The 1962,Ag 7,35:2
Yesterday, Today and Tomorrow (Part 1-Adelina
  Naples); Adelina Naples (Yesterday, Today and
  Tomorrow) 1964,Mr 18,46:1
Hercules, Samson and Ulysses 1965,N 4,57:2

Giuffre, Carlo

Seven Hills of Rome 1958,Ja 28,24:2 (Incorrect
  in this edition; use 1958,Ja 31,24:2 elsewhere)
Madame 1963,Mr 21,8:6
Railroad Man, The; Ferroviere, Il 1965,O 25,46:2

Giuffre, Jimmy Trio

Jazz on a Summer's Day 1960,Mr 29,46:2

Giuliani, Massimo

Hippodrome 1962,Mr 12,36:1

Giulianni, Luigi

Boccaccio '70 (The Raffle); Raffle, The (Boccaccio
  '70) 1962,Je 27,40:1
Arturo Island 1962,D 22,5:2

Giussani, Angela (Original Author)

Danger Diabolik 1968,D 12,62:6

Giussani, Luciana (Original Author)

Danger Diabolik 1968,D 12,62:6

Giussani, Mario

Conjugal Bed, The 1963,S 17,30:1

Giustini, Carlo

Naked Maja, The 1959,Je 11,36:2
Story of Joseph and his Brethern, The
  1962,D 1,17:1

Givanpietro, Enzo

House of Ricordi 1956,Mr 13,32:1

Givney, Kathryn

Lover Come Back 1931,Je 5,26:5
Isn't It Romantic? 1948,O 7,35:2
My Friend Irma 1949,S 29,39:2
Operation Pacific 1951,F 3,10:2
Lightning Strikes Twice 1951,Ap 13,18:7
Double Crossbones 1951,Ap 27,19:2
Place in the Sun, A 1951,Ag 29,20:1
Little Egypt 1951,Ag 30,20:3
Too Young to Kiss 1951,N 23,32:2
Three Coins in the Fountain 1954,My 21,18:2
Daddy Long Legs 1955,My 6,17:5
Guys and Dolls 1955,N 4,23:2
Congo Crossing 1956,Jl 14,13:2
Wayward Bus, The 1957,Je 6,35:2
Certain Smile, A 1958,Ag 1,13:2
Man in the Net, The 1959,Je 11,36:2

Givney, Kathryn— Cont
4 Horsemen of the Apocalypse, The 1962,Mr 10,10:2

Givot, George
Chief, The 1933,D 2,9:4
Hollywood Party 1934,My 26,12:2
Riffraff 1936,Ja 13,14:2
Paddy O'Day 1936,F 8,19:2
Step Lively, Jeeves 1937,Ap 2,19:6
Wake up and Live 1937,Ap 24,16:2
Hit Parade, The 1937,My 31,11:2
Thin Ice 1937,S 4,8:2
Conquest 1937,N 5,19:1
Beg, Borrow or Steal 1937,D 10,33:2
45 Fathers 1937,D 11,22:2
Hollywood Cavalcade 1939,O 14,13:2
Young as You Feel 1940,Mr 8,25:3
Road to Morocco 1942,N 12,30:1
Du Barry Was a Lady 1943,Ag 20,13:1
Behind the Rising Sun 1943,O 14,26:2
Government Girl 1944,Ja 7,13:2
Riff-Raff 1947,Je 30,25:7
April in Paris 1952,D 25,34:5
Three Sailors and a Girl 1953,N 23,32:2
Miracle in the Rain 1956,Ap 2,18:1
China Gate 1957,My 23,40:2

Givray, Claude de (Director)
army Game, The; Tire Au Flanc 1963,Ap 24,40:1
Givray, Claude de (Miscellaneous)
army Game, The; Tire Au Flanc 1963,Ap 24,40:1
Givray, Claude de (Screenwriter)
army Game, The; Tire Au Flanc 1963,Ap 24,40:1

Gizzi, Loris
Giovanni De Medici, The Leader 1940,Ja 5,15:4
Great Dawn, The 1947,Ag 28,28:3
Difficult Years 1950,Ag 22,31:2
Theodora, Slave Empress 1955,Ja 12,24:2

Gladkov, Alexander (Screenwriter)
Ballad of a Hussar, The 1963,Jl 15,25:5
Glado, Albert
Devil's Daughter 1949,F 26,11:2
Gladstone, Richard (Producer)
Set-Up, The 1949,Mr 30,31:2
Gladtstone, J (Miscellaneous)
Overture to Glory 1940,F 12,14:2

Glaessner, Erika
Die Lustigen Musikanten 1933,My 27,11:6
Madame Wuenscht Keine Kinder 1933,Je 2,22:4
Hochtourist, Der 1934,Ja 13,16:4
Schoen Ist Es Verliebt zu Sein 1936,Ap 7,31:2
Ganzer Kerl, Ein 1936,Ap 25,21:2
Muede Theodor, Der 1936,O 24,23:2
Ist Mein Mann Nicht Fabelhaft 1936,D 8,31:3
Besuch am Abend 1937,Jl 3,18:2
Hummel-Hummel 1939,Mr 11,21:2

Glahn, Heinz
Rosenmontag 1931,Mr 28,15:3
Glaisyer, David
Strange Affair, The 1968,Jl 25,26:2
Gland, Warner
Charlie Chan in Paris 1935,Ja 22,23:2
Glanville, Brian (Narrator)
Goal 1967,Ja 19,26:1
Glas, Ned
Papa's Delicate Condition 1963,Mr 7,8:5

GLASER
See Also GLASSER, GLAZER
Glaser, Lulu
How Molly Made Good 1915,O 20,5:5
Glaser, Miles (Producer)
Oratorio for Prague 1968,S 30,60:1
Glaser, Vaughan
What a Life 1939,O 12,33:1
Rulers of the Sea 1939,N 9,27:1
Those Were the Days 1940,Jl 15,18:4
Adventure in Washington 1941,Ag 1,11:3
Henry Aldrich for President 1941,O 18,22:2
Saboteur 1942,My 8,27:2
Arsenic and old Lace 1944,S 2,17:2
Glaser, Vaughn
My Favorite Spy 1942,My 29,13:4
Glasgow, Ellen (Original Author)
In This our Life 1942,My 9,10:2
Glasgow, Pat
Alice in Wonderland 1931,D 28,22:1
Glasgow Orpheus Choir (Miscellaneous)
Edge of the World, The 1938,S 12,13:2
Glashen, Terressta
George Washington Carver 1940,Ap 17,26:4
Glasmire, Gus
Fugitive From Justice, A 1940,Jl 8,13:3
Glasmon, Kubec (Original Author)
Public Enemy, The 1931,Ap 24,27:1
Smart Money 1931,Je 19,21:1
Blonde Crazy 1931,D 4,28:2
False Faces 1932,N 25,19:2
Bolero 1934,F 17,20:3
Show Them no Mercy 1935,D 9,25:2
Parole 1936,Je 27,21:1
Man in Blue, The 1937,Ag 30,25:2
Glasmon, Kubec (Screenwriter)
Three on a Match 1932,O 29,18:4
Glass Key, The 1935,Je 15,20:2
Men Without Names 1935,Je 29,16:2

Show Them no Mercy 1935,D 9,25:2
Parole 1936,Je 27,21:1
Glaspell, Susan (Original Author)
Right to Love, The 1931,Ja 2,25:1
Glass, Everett
Petty Girl, The 1950,Ag 18,17:2
Two Flags West 1950,O 13,23:2
Inferno 1953,Ag 12,22:2
Demetrius and the Gladiators 1954,Je 19,9:1
Friendly Persuasion 1956,N 2,30:1
Elmer Gantry 1960,Jl 8,16:1
Marriage-Go-Round 1961,Ja 7,12:2
Glass, Gaston
Open Your Eyes 1919,Je 30,16:3
Humoresque 1920,My 31,14:2
World and his Wife, The 1920,Jl 19,16:3
Monte Cristo 1922,Ag 15,20:3
Gimme 1923,Ja 15,18:3
Daughters of the Rich 1923,Je 18,13:5
I Am the Man 1925,Mr 6,23:1
Parisian Nights 1925,Je 2,16:3
Subway Sadie 1926,S 13,18:1
Gorilla, The 1927,N 21,20:1
Red Mark, The 1928,O 30,27:3
Geraldine 1929,Mr 4,20:2
She Got What She Wanted 1930,D 29,18:1
Sutter's Gold 1936,Mr 27,25:2
Mary of Scotland 1936,Jl 31,22:2
Glass, Gaston (Original Author)
Legong 1935,O 2,27:1
Glass, George (Producer)
Naked Edge 1961,Jl 1,9:1
Paris Blues 1961,N 8,41:1
Julie the Redhead 1963,O 15,44:1
Glass, Max (Producer)
Unbekannte Gast, Der; Unknown Guest, The 1935,Je 1,18:3
Rasputin 1939,O 17,31:4
Entente Cordiale 1939,D 26,23:2
Glass, Montague (Miscellaneous)
Hungry Hearts 1922,N 27,18:1
Glass, Montague (Original Author)
Potash and Perlmutter 1923,S 24,5:4
In Hollywood with Potash and Perlmutter 1924,S 30,27:3
Partners Again, With Potash and Perlmutter 1926,F 15,16:4
Glass, Ned
Give Me a Sailor 1938,Ag 11,31:1
He's a Cockeyed Wonder 1950,O 20,32:4
Storm Warning 1951,Mr 3,8:2
Stop, You're Killing Me 1952,D 11,45:3
West Side Story 1961,O 19,39:3
Experiment in Terror 1962,Ap 14,14:1
Kid Galahad 1963,Mr 7,8:5
Charade 1963,D 6,40:1
Never a Dull Moment 1968,Ag 15,46:2
Glass, Paul
Guests are Coming; Jada Goscie Jada 1967,Ja 13,15:1
Glassburn, Robert Major (Original Author)
Dress Parade 1927,O 31,22:1
GLASSER
See Also GLASER, GLAZER
Glasser, Bernard (Producer)
Crack in the World 1965,My 13,32:2
Glasshoff, Alexander (Director)
Jailbreakers, The 1961,Ja 5,27:2
Glasshoff, Alexander (Producer)
Jailbreakers, The 1961,Ja 5,27:2
Glasshoff, Alexander (Screenwriter)
Jailbreakers, The 1961,Ja 5,27:2
Glassmire, Gus
Our Leading Citizen 1939,Ag 24,17:1
Wilson 1944,Ag 2,18:1
Glaubrecht, Frank
Bridge, The; (Bruecke, Die) 1961,My 2,42:1
Glaum, Louise
Honor Thy Name 1916,Jl 17,9:4
Sahara 1919,Je 30,16:3
GLAZER
See Also GLASER, GLASSER
Glazer, Benjamin (Director)
Strange Cargo 1929,F 18,28:1
Song of my Heart 1948,Mr 5,17:3
Glazer, Benjamin (Miscellaneous)
Thy Name Is Woman 1924,Mr 4,17:1
Glazer, Benjamin (Original Author)
No Man of her Own 1932,D 31,10:1
Way to Love, The 1933,N 11,10:3
We're not Dressing 1934,Ap 26,27:2
Arise my Love 1940,O 17,33:2
Glazer, Benjamin (Producer)
Enter Madame 1935,Ja 12,12:1
Paris in Spring 1935,Jl 13,16:2
Big Broadcast of 1936, The 1935,S 16,15:2
Anything Goes 1936,F 6,23:3
Rhythm on the Range 1936,Jl 30,22:1
Internes Can't Take Money 1937,My 6,23:2
Mountain Music 1937,Je 24,30:3
Exclusive 1937,Jl 22,15:1
Double or Nothing 1937,S 2,17:3
Paris Calling 1942,Ja 19,21:2

Glazer, Benjamin (Screenwriter)
Sinners in Silk 1924,S 8,15:3
Memory Lane 1926,F 2,20:4
Street of Sin, The 1928,My 28,23:2
Strange Cargo 1929,F 18,28:1
Mata Hari 1932,Ja 1,31:1
Paris Calling 1942,Ja 19,21:2
Tortilla Flat 1942,My 22,27:1
Song of my Heart 1948,Mr 5,17:3
Carousel 1956,F 17,13:1
Glazer, Ernest (Original Author)
Lady in Ermine, The 1927,Ja 3,16:2
Glazer, Jay (Original Author)
Compromise 1925,O 27,23:3
Glazier, Sidney (Producer)
Eleanor Roosevelt Story, The 1965,N 9,50:1
Producers, The 1968,Mr 19,38:1
Glazov, Alexei
Country Doctor, The 1953,F 16,16:2
GLEASON
See Also GLEESON
Gleason, Adda
Ramona 1916,Ap 6,11:1
How Baxter Buttered In 1925,Je 23,24:3
Man Bait 1927,Ja 19,21:1
College Coquette, The 1929,Ag 26,17:1
Spider Woman Strikes Back, The 1946,Mr 23,8:3
Gleason, Jackie
Navy Blues 1941,S 20,11:2
Larceny, Inc 1942,Ap 25,9:1
Orchestra Wives 1942,S 24,23:2
Springtime in the Rockies 1942,N 12,30:2
Desert Hawk, The 1950,Ag 26,9:2
Hustler, The 1961,S 27,35:1
Gigot 1962,S 28,26:1
Requiem for a Heavyweight 1962,O 17,35:1
Papa's Delicate Condition 1963,Mr 7,8:5
Soldier in the Rain 1963,N 29,67:6 (Incorrect in this edition; use 1963,N 28,67:6 elsewhere)
Gleason, Jackie (Original Author)
Gigot 1962,S 28,26:1
Gleason, Jackie C
All Through the Night 1942,Ja 24,13:2
Lady Gangster 1942,Jl 10,13:2
Escape From Crime 1942,O 12,12:3
Gleason, James
Count of Ten, The 1928,Mr 13,23:3
Shannons of Broadway, The 1929,D 21,17:1
Puttin' on the Ritz 1930,F 15,15:1
Dumbbells in Ermine 1930,Jl 28,22:1
Matrimonial Bed, The 1930,Ag 25,14:2
Her Man 1930,O 4,15:2
Big Money 1930,N 22,21:3
Beyond Victory 1931,Ap 6,24:1
It's a Wise Child 1931,My 16,13:3
Free Soul, A 1931,Je 3,29:2
Sweepstakes 1931,Je 25,23:5
Big Gamble, The 1931,S 21,20:2
Suicide Fleet 1931,N 23,22:1
Lady and Gent 1932,Jl 16,5:5
Blondie of the Follies 1932,S 2,19:2
All American, The 1932,O 22,18:4
Devil Is Driving, The 1932,D 16,25:5
Billion Dollar Scandal, The 1933,Ja 9,23:1
Clear all Wires 1933,Mr 4,11:2
Hoopla 1933,D 1,23:3
Search for Beauty 1934,F 10,20:2
Orders Is Orders 1934,My 7,20:2
Murder on the Blackboard 1934,Je 20,24:2
Helldorado 1935,Ja 7,13:2
Murder on a Honeymoon 1935,Mr 4,12:2
West Point of the Air 1935,Ap 6,10:1
We're Only Human 1936,Ja 18,19:2
Murder on a Bridle Path 1936,Ap 11,19:2
Ex-Mrs Bradford, The 1936,My 28,19:2
Yours for the Asking 1936,Ag 20,14:2
Don't Turn 'em Loose 1936,S 25,20:2
Big Game, The 1936,O 24,23:1
Plot Thickens, The 1936,D 9,35:2
Forty Naughty Girls 1937,S 18,15:3
Manhattan Merry-Go-Round 1937,D 31,9:3
Dawn Over Ireland 1938,F 19,19:2
Army Girl 1938,Ag 12,11:1
On Your Toes 1939,O 21,12:2
Meet John Doe 1941,Mr 13,25:2
Affectionally Yours 1941,My 24,18:2
Here Comes Mr Jordan 1941,Ag 8,13:2
Tanks a Million 1941,O 9,27:2
Nine Loves Are not Enough 1941,O 30,27:2
Date With the Falcon, A 1941,N 25,33:2
Safe at Home 1941,N 26,31:2
Babes on Broadway 1942,Ja 1,37:1
My Gal Sal 1942,My 1,23:1
Falcon takes Over, The 1942,My 30,9:2
Footlight Serenade 1942,S 10,30:3
Tales of Manhattan 1942,S 25,25:1
Manila Calling 1942,S 28,13:1
Crash Dive 1943,Ap 29,25:2
Guy Named Joe, A 1943,D 24,17:2
Once Upon a Time 1944,Je 30,17:2
Arsenic and old Lace 1944,S 2,17:2
Keys of the Kingdom, The 1944,D 30,15:2
Tree Grows in Brooklyn, A 1945,Mr 1,25:5

Gleason, James— Cont

This Man's Navy 1945,Ap 16,18:6
Clock, The 1945,My 4,23:2
Captain Eddie 1945,Ag 9,24:2
Well Groomed Bride, The 1946,My 11,22:5
Hoodlum Saint, The 1946,Je 27,29:1
Home Sweet Homicide 1946,S 12,5:7
Lady Luck 1946,O 31,22:3
Homestretch, The 1947,Ap 24,30:2
Down to Earth 1947,S 12,18:2
Bishop's Wife, The 1947,D 10,44:2
Tycoon 1947,D 26,22:6
When my Baby Smiles at Me 1948,N 24,20:2
Return of October, The 1949,F 23,31:2
Bad Boy 1949,Mr 23,35:2
Life of Riley, The 1949,Ap 18,18:4
Take one False Step 1949,Je 23,33:2
Key to the City 1950,F 2,31:2
Yellow Cab Man, The 1950,Mr 27,19:2
Riding High 1950,Ap 11,26:2
Jackpot, The 1950,N 23,55:2
Come Fill the Cup 1951,N 22,47:2
I'll See You in my Dreams 1951,D 7,35:1
We're not Married 1952,Jl 12,16:2
Story of Will Rogers, The 1952,Jl 18,10:5
What Price Glory 1952,Ag 23,10:2
Forever Female 1954,Ja 13,26:2
Suddenly 1954,O 8,27:2
Night of the Hunter, The 1955,S 30,23:1
Spring Reunion 1957,My 6,25:2
Last Hurrah, The 1958,O 24,40:1

Gleason, James (Original Author)

Is Zat So? 1927,My 17,27:2
Two Fisted 1935,O 5,18:3
Goodbye Broadway 1938,My 14,18:1

Gleason, Lucille

Shannons of Broadway, The 1929,D 21,17:1
Girls About Town 1931,N 2,27:1
Girl of the Rio 1932,Ja 9,21:1
Nice Women 1932,F 20,11:2
Don't Bet on Love 1933,Jl 31,16:2
Solitaire Man, The 1933,S 23,11:5
Love, Honor and Oh, Baby! 1933,O 28,20:3
Beloved 1934,Ja 27,9:3
I Like It That Way 1934,Ap 18,23:3
Klondike Annie 1936,Mr 12,18:2
Ex-Mrs Bradford, The 1936,My 28,19:2
Rhythm on the Range 1936,Jl 30,22:1
First Lady 1937,D 23,25:1
Beloved Brat 1938,My 2,13:2
Nurse From Brooklyn 1938,My 13,17:3
Lucky Partners 1940,S 6,25:2
Stage Door Canteen 1943,Je 25,13:2
Clock, The 1945,My 4,23:2

Gleason, Pat

23 1/2 Hours Leave 1937,My 17,23:2
Criminal Court 1946,N 16,15:3

Gleason, Russell

Strange Cargo 1929,F 18,28:1
Shady Lady, The 1929,Mr 25,32:2
Sophomore, The 1929,Ag 24,11:5
Seven Faces 1929,N 16,25:2
Officer O'Brien 1930,F 24,18:1
All Quiet On the Western Front 1930,Ap 30,29:1
Laugh and get Rich 1931,Mr 28,15:3
Beyond Victory 1931,Ap 6,24:1
Homicide Squad 1931,O 19,28:1
Nice Women 1932,F 20,11:2
Strange Case of Clara Deane, The
  1932,My 6,15:3
Private Jones 1933,Mr 25,13:3
Off to the Races 1937,F 6,15:2
Big Business 1937,Je 1,27:2
Hot Water 1937,N 5,19:4
Trip to Paris, A 1938,Je 10,18:2
Safety in Numbers 1938,S 6,17:2
News Is Made at Night 1939,Jl 13,17:2
Here I Am a Stranger 1939,S 30,11:2
Young as You Feel 1940,Mr 8,25:3
Unexpected Uncle 1941,S 25,29:1
Fingers at the Window 1942,Ap 23,27:3
Salute to the Marines 1943,Ag 30,11:3
Adventures of Mark Twain, The 1944,My 4,25:5

Gleaves, Abraham

Green Pastures, The 1936,Jl 17,20:1

Glebov, G

Secret Brigade 1951,Mr 19,23:2

Glebov, Pyotr

And Quiet Flows the Don 1960,My 25,45:2
Yolanta 1964,D 23,22:3

Glebova, Tatiana

Spring Song 1942,S 12,9:2

Gleckler, Robert

Mother's Boy 1929,My 8,34:6
Sea God, The 1930,S 6,9:2
Finger Points, The 1931,Mr 28,15:3
Take a Chance 1933,N 27,20:3
Now I'll Tell 1934,My 26,12:2
Personality Kid, The 1934,Ag 1,14:2
Defense Rests, The 1934,Ag 16,20:3
Million Dollar Ransom 1934,S 19,15:2
Great Hotel Murder, The 1935,F 28,17:4
Perfect Clue, The 1935,Mr 14,18:1
It Happened in New York 1935,Ap 6,10:1

Mr Dynamite 1935,My 25,12:1
Glass Key, The 1935,Je 15,20:2
Daring Young Man, The 1935,Jl 18,15:2
Dante's Inferno 1935,Ag 1,15:1
Farmer Takes a Wife, The 1935,Ag 9,21:2
Whipsaw 1936,Ja 25,18:4
Absolute Quiet 1936,My 2,11:1
Forgotten Faces 1936,Jl 4,18:2
I'd Give my Life 1936,Ag 17,9:1
Yours for the Asking 1936,Ag 20,14:2
Sworn Enemy 1936,S 12,20:1
Love Begins at 20 1936,S 19,20:1
Girl on the Front Page, The 1936,N 7,15:2
Great Guy 1937,Ja 1,19:2
Pick a Star 1937,My 28,17:2
Hot Water 1937,N 5,19:4
Bulldog Drummond's Revenge 1937,D 17,33:2
Rascals 1938,My 27,12:2
Gangs of New York 1938,My 28,9:2
Gun Law 1938,Je 24,15:1
Little Miss Broadway 1938,Jl 23,10:4
Alexander's Ragtime Band 1938,Ag 6,7:2
They Made Me a Criminal 1939,Ja 21,19:2
Stand up and Fight 1939,Ja 27,17:2

Glee Club

Bitter Sweet 1940,N 22,27:1

Gleeder, Mikhail (Cinematographer)

August 14; One Day in the USSR
  1948,Ag 16,12:2

GLEESON

See Also GLEASON

Gleize, Maurice (Director)

Madonna of the Sleeping Cars, The
  1929,O 14,20:2

Glen, John (Original Author)

Kathleen 1938,Ja 24,17:1

Glendenning, Raymond

Galloping Major, The 1951,D 17,27:2

Glendinning, Ernest

When Knighthood Was in Flower 1922,S 15,17:2
  (In Addenda)

Glendinning, Ethel

Song of the Road 1940,My 6,13:2

Glendon, Frank

Tale of Two Worlds, A 1921,Mr 14,9:2
Lights of Old Broadway 1925,N 2,20:1
Upstage 1926,N 15,19:1

Glendon, J Frank

What Do Men Want? 1921,N 14,18:1
Strange People 1933,Je 17,16:5

Glenn, Grosvenor

Julius Caesar 1952,N 25,33:5

Glenn, Jerry

Babes in Toyland 1961,D 15,49:1

Glenn, Montgomery

Horrible Dr Hitchcock, The 1964,D 3,58:3

Glenn, Raymond

Ladies at Ease 1927,O 5,31:1

Glenn, Roy

Lydia Bailey 1952,My 31,12:5
Carmen Jones 1954,O 29,27:2
Sound and the Fury, The 1959,Mr 28,11:1
Raisin in the Sun, A 1961,Mr 30,24:1
Dead Heat on a Merry-Go-Round
  1966,O 13,50:1
Guess Who's Coming to Dinner 1967,D 12,56:1

Glennon, Bert (Director)

Air Legion, The 1928,N 13,37:1
Gang War 1928,N 19,16:7
Syncopation 1929,Ap 8,32:1

Glennon, Gordon (Miscellaneous)

Wicked Lady, The 1946,D 23,19:5

Glenville, Peter

Madonna of the Seven Moons 1946,My 23,18:4
Good Time Girl 1950,S 25,18:5
Hotel Paradiso 1966,O 15,34:2

Glenville, Peter (Director)

Prisoner, The 1955,D 12,37:1
Me and the Colonel 1958,Ag 27,33:1
Summer and Smoke 1961,N 17,41:1
Term of Trial 1963,Ja 31,5:2
Becket 1964,Mr 12,40:2
Hotel Paradiso 1966,O 15,34:2
Comedians, The 1967,N 1,37:1

Glenville, Peter (Producer)

Hotel Paradiso 1966,O 15,34:2
Comedians, The 1967,N 1,37:1

Glenville, Peter (Screenwriter)

Term of Trial 1963,Ja 31,5:2
Hotel Paradiso 1966,O 15,34:2

Glersberg, Max (Original Author)

All the King's Horses 1935,Mr 9,19:1

Glesnes, Lawrence (Producer)

Will It Happen Again 1948,My 17,23:4

Gliese, Rochus (Director)

Lost Shadow, The 1928,Mr 20,20:3

Glinski, Wieczyslaw

Kanal 1961,My 10,52:1

Gloag, Julian (Original Author)

Our Mother's House 1967,O 10,56:1

Glockner-Kramer, Pepi

Verliebte Herzen; Hearts in Love 1939,Je 10,14:2

Glori, Enrico

Pearls of the Crown, The 1938,Ap 12,26:2
Man of the Sea 1948,Ja 24,11:2
Spirit and the Flesh, The 1948,N 1,28:2
Lost in the Dark 1949,My 14,9:2
Stranger on the Prowl 1953,N 10,38:1

Glori, Gianni

Angelina 1948,Ap 6,27:2
I Cadetti di Guascogna 1952,O 6,22:2
Side Street Story 1954,Je 24,30:4

Glori, Vittorio Musy (Director)

Sign of the Gladiator 1959,D 3,46:1

Glori, Vittorio Musy (Producer)

Fuga, La 1966,Mr 22,33:1

Gloria, Angelo

Amore e Morte; (Love and Death) 1932,O 4,26:4

Gloria, Leda

Terra Madre 1931,O 31,22:2
Figaro E La Sua Gran Giornata 1933,O 28,20:4
Milizia Territoriale 1936,Ap 6,18:2
Cappello a Tre Punte, Il 1936,S 28,14:5
Armata Azzurra, La; Blue Fleet, The
  1937,D 13,23:4
Avventura di Giacomo Casanova 1938,D 2,27:3
Aria del Continente, L'; Continental Atmosphere
  1939,N 17,17:3
Grande Luce, La; Great Light, The
  1940,Mr 15,27:4
Mill on the Po, The 1951,O 23,35:2
Ring Around the Clock 1953,My 19,36:2
Three Girls From Rome 1953,O 14,34:2
Side Street Story 1954,Je 24,30:4
Return of Don Camillo, The 1956,Mr 27,41:1
Wild Oat, The 1956,Je 28,33:2
It Happened in the Park 1957,Ag 13,23:2
Guendalina 1958,Je 30,23:2
Law Is the Law, The 1959,Mr 11,41:2
Virtuous Bigamist, The 1959,My 28,34:3

Glory, Marie

Tu Seras Duchesse 1932,My 7,11:5
Mon Coeur Balance 1933,F 3,21:4
Paquebot Tenacity 1934,Ag 12,IX,2:1
Charlemagne 1935,Ag 24,18:3
With a Smile 1939,F 6,8:4
Napoli che mon Muore; Naples That Never Dies
  1940,Mr 4,11:3
Moglie in Pericolo, Una; Wife in Danger, A
  1940,Je 7,27:3
Adorable Creatures 1956,Ja 11,36:2
And God Created Woman 1957,O 22,41:1

Glory, Mary

Argent, L' 1929,Mr 3,VII,7:2 (Incorrect in this
  edition; use 1929,Mr 3,VIII,8:5 in film)
Argent, L' 1968,S 23,42:5

Glossop, Marcia

Mikado, The 1967,Mr 15,53:1

Glosz, Rosemary

One Night of Love 1934,S 7,25:3

Glover, Edmund

Courageous Dr Christian, The 1940,Mr 29,25:3
Ghost Ship, The 1943,D 25,19:4
Night of Adventure, A 1944,Je 3,10:4
Marine Raiders 1944,Jl 1,10:7
Two O'Clock Courage 1945,Ap 14,13:3

Glover, Guy (Producer)

Stratford Adventure, The 1954,Ag 3,14:2

Glover, Julian

Tom Jones 1963,O 8,48:1
Girl With Green Eyes 1964,Ag 11,37:2
Alphabet Murders, The 1966,Jl 12,36:2
Time Lost and Time Remembered
  1966,Ag 30,35:2
Five Million Years to Earth 1968,My 30,21:4
Magus, The 1968,D 11,57:1

Glucksman, Ernest D (Producer)

Errand Boy, The 1962,F 8,25:1
Nutty Professor, The 1963,Jl 18,15:2
Patsy, The 1964,Ag 13,24:2

Glyn, Elinor

It 1927,F 13,VII,7:2 (In Addenda)

Glyn, Elinor (Original Author)

Career of Catherine Bush, The 1919,Ag 4,8:3
Beyond the Rocks 1922,My 8,14:3
Three Weeks 1924,Ap 1,19:3
His Hour 1924,O 7,26:1
Man and Maid 1925,Ap 7,17:3
Only Thing, The 1925,N 23,25:4
Soul Mates 1926,Ja 4,16:1
Ritzy 1927,Je 20,25:3
Mad Hour, The 1928,Ap 16,20:5
Such Men Are Dangerous 1930,Mr 8,21:1
Knowing Men 1930,Mr 9,IX,6:1

Glyn, Elinor (Screenwriter)

Great Moment, The 1921,Jl 25,8:3
Six Days 1923,S 24,5:4
Red Hair 1928,Mr 26,26:2

Glyn, Patricia

Inheritance, The 1951,F 12,19:2

Glyn-Jones, John

Court Martial 1955,Ag 2,17:1
Man in the Moon 1961,Je 13,29:2
Waltz of the Toreadors 1962,Ag 14,34:1

Glynne, Angela
Happiest Days of Your Life, The 1950,S 18,19:2
Glynne, Mary
Bonnie Brier Bush, The 1921,N 28,16:1
Good Companions, The 1933,O 10,24:1
Scrooge 1935,D 14,11:1
Emil 1938,Ap 15,23:2
Glynne, Maureen
Gay Intruders, The 1946,Mr 18,24:2
Guinea Pig, The 1949,My 2,20:2
Glynos, George
Lily of the Harbor 1958,Ap 16,38:3
Golfo-Girl of the Mountains 1958,My 19,19:5
Gmilevsky, Gregory
Christmas Slippers 1945,D 24,19:2
Gnass, Fritz
M 1933,Ap 3,13:3
Gobbi, A (Screenwriter)
Aida 1954,N 12,17:1
Gobbi, Jean-Francois
Echoes of Silence 1967,Ap 7,32:2
Gobbi, Tito
Giovanni De Medici, The Leader 1940,Ja 5,15:4
Barber of Seville, The 1947,My 6,35:2
Lost One, The; La Traviata 1948,Mr 30,26:2
This Wine of Love 1948,Ap 19,27:2
First Opera Film Festival 1948,My 31,12:7
Rigoletto 1949,N 10,41:4
Love of a Clown (Pagliacci) 1950,Ap 17,18:5
Glass Mountain, The 1950,My 18,37:3
Forza del Destino, La 1952,O 17,33:1
House of Ricordi 1956,Mr 13,32:1
Gobbs, Anthony (Original Author)
For Love or Money 1934,Jl 26,14:2
Gobel, Art
Lost Squadron, The 1932,Mr 11,15:4
Gobel, George
Birds and the Bees, The 1956,Ap 23,22:1
I Married a Woman 1958,N 5,42:5
Gobert, Boy
Rest Is Silence, The 1960,Ag 2,22:6
Fledermaus, Die 1964,F 8,15:2
Gobet, Jean
King, The 1941,O 23,29:3
Gobin, Gabriel
Riptide 1951,Ap 7,9:2
Up From the Beach 1965,Je 10,38:1
Gobin, Jean
Cheat, The 1950,O 2,19:3
Godard, Jean-Luc
Breathless 1961,F 8,26:1
Two or Three Things I Know About Her
1968,S 26,60:1
Godard, Jean-Luc (Director)
Breathless 1961,F 8,26:1
7 Capital Sins (Laziness); Laziness (7 Capital
Sins) 1963,Ja 17,5:2
My Life to Live 1963,S 24,43:2
Woman Is a Woman, A 1964,S 19,19:1
Band of Outsiders 1964,S 19,19:1
Contempt 1964,D 19,25:2
Married Woman, The; Femme Mariee, La
1965,Ag 17,39:1
Alphaville 1965,S 8,51:1
Six in Paris 1965,S 16,54:2
Alphaville 1965,O 26,49:1
Band of Outsiders; Bande a Part 1966,Mr 16,48:3
Masculine Feminine 1966,S 19,57:1
Pierre le Fou; Peter the Crazy 1966,S 22,57:2
Petit Soldat, Le 1967,Ap 21,48:1
Made in U S A 1967,S 28,58:2
Carabiniers, Les 1967,S 28,58:3
Chinoise, La 1968,Ap 4,58:2
Carabiniers, Les 1968,Ap 26,31:1
Far From Vietnam 1968,Je 7,32:1
Two or Three Things I Know About Her
1968,S 26,60:1
Weekend 1968,S 28,36:1
Oldest Profession, The (Anticipation); Anticipation
(The Oldest Profession) 1968,N 8,42:1
Godard, Jean-Luc (Narrator)
Far from Vietnam 1967,O 2,58:1
Godard, Jean-Luc (Screenwriter)
Breathless 1961,F 8,26:1
7 Capital Sins (Laziness); Laziness (7 Capital
Sins) 1963,Ja 17,5:2
My Life to Live 1963,S 24,43:2
Woman Is a Woman, A 1964,S 19,19:1
Band of Outsiders 1964,S 19,19:1
Contempt 1964,D 19,25:2
Married Woman, The; Femme Mariee, La
1965,Ag 17,39:1
Alphaville 1965,O 26,49:1
Band of Outsiders; Bande a Part 1966,Mr 16,48:3
Masculine Feminine 1966,S 19,57:1
Petit Soldat, Le 1967,Ap 21,48:1
Carabiniers, Les 1967,S 28,58:3
Made in U S A 1967,S 28,58:2
Chinoise, La 1968,Ap 4,58:2
Carabiniers, Les 1968,Ap 26,31:1
Two or Three Things I Know About Her
1968,S 26,60:1
Weekend 1968,S 28,36:1

Oldest Profession, The (Anticipation); Anticipation
(The Oldest Profession) 1968,N 8,42:1
Godau, Irma
Susanne Macht Ordnung 1931,O 12,28:2
Godbout, Claude
Cat in the Sack 1967,My 12,53:1
Goddard, Alf
Jaws of Hell 1931,Ja 5,21:3
King Solomon's Mines 1937,Jl 3,18:1
Troopship 1938,Ap 26,18:2
Sidewalks of London 1940,F 15,15:1
Lady in Distress 1942,F 16,21:2
Way Ahead, The 1945,Je 4,22:3
Goddard, Charles W (Original Author)
Ghost Breaker, The 1922,S 11,20:2
Broken Wing, The 1923,O 9,17:4
Broken Wing, The 1932,Mr 26,17:2
Ghost Breakers, The 1940,Jl 4,12:2
Scared Stiff 1953,Jl 3,10:2
Perils of Pauline, The 1967,Ag 3,26:3
Goddard, Doris
Wee Geordie 1956,O 8,31:1
Goddard, John
Sniper's Ridge 1961,Ag 24,25:3
Goddard, Mark
Rage to Live, A 1965,O 21,57:1
Love-Ins, The 1967,Ag 19,16:1
Goddard, Paulette
Modern Times 1936,F 6,23:2
Young in Heart, The 1938,N 4,27:2
Dramatic School 1938,D 9,31:2
Women, The 1939,S 22,27:2
Cat and the Canary, The 1939,N 23,38:5
Ghost Breakers, The 1940,Jl 4,12:2
Great Dictator, The 1940,O 16,29:1
North West Mounted Police 1940,N 7,33:2
Second Chorus 1941,Ja 16,25:2
Pot o'Gold 1941,Ap 4,25:2
Hold Back the Dawn 1941,O 2,29:1
Nothing but the Truth 1941,O 23,27:1
Lady Has Plans, The 1942,Mr 5,27:1
Reap the Wild Wind 1942,Mr 27,27:2
Forest Rangers, The 1942,O 22,25:2
Star Spangled Rhythm 1942,D 31,20:1
Crystal Ball, The 1943,F 19,22:2
So Proudly We Hail 1943,S 10,29:1
Standing Room Only 1944,F 23,17:2
I Love a Soldier 1944,N 2,22:2
Duffy's Tavern 1945,S 6,23:3
Kitty 1946,Ap 1,23:1
Diary of a Chambermaid, The 1946,Je 23,28:2
Suddenly It's Spring 1947,F 27,26:2
Unconquered 1947,O 11,11:2
Ideal Husband, An 1948,Ja 15,28:2
Miracle Can Happen, A 1948,F 4,28:4
Hazard 1948,Je 3,19:2
Bride of Vengeance 1949,Ap 7,38:2
Anna Lucasta 1949,Ag 12,13:2
Torch, The 1950,Ag 21,15:2
Vice Squad 1953,Ag 26,23:2
Sins of Jezebel 1954,Ja 9,12:2
Babes in Bagdad 1954,Ap 5,21:3
Unholy Four, The 1954,N 20,10:2
Time of Indifference 1965,O 13,50:1
Time of Indifference 1966,O 13,50:1
Goddard, Victor Sir Air Marshal (Original Author)
Night my Number Came up, The 1955,D 20,39:5
Goddard, Willoughby
In the Wake of a Stranger 1961,Je 22,23:3
Godde, Ruth (Original Author)
Tonight We Sing 1953,F 13,17:2
Godden, Bill
Born Free 1966,Je 23,29:1
Godden, Rudi
Truxa 1937,Jl 26,15:2
Musketier Meier III 1938,D 31,7:2
Godden, Rumer (Original Author)
Black Narcissus 1947,Ag 14,29:2
Enchantment 1948,D 27,16:2
River, The 1951,S 11,33:2
Loss of Innocence 1961,N 22,27:1
Battle of the Villa Fiorita, The 1965,My 27,28:1
Godden, Rumer (Screenwriter)
River, The 1951,S 11,33:2
Gode, Annelle
Madame 1963,Mr 21,8:6
Godeau, Yvonne
Monsieur Vincent 1948,D 21,33:2
Godet, Danielle
Singing Taxi Driver 1953,My 16,10:1
Godey, John (Original Author)
Never a Dull Moment 1968,Ag 15,46:2
Godfrey, Arthur
Glass Bottom Boat, The 1966,Je 10,54:1
Where Angels Go-Trouble Follows
1968,Ap 11,51:1
Godfrey, Derek
Guns of Darkness 1962,Ag 18,10:1
Vengance of She, The 1968,My 30,21:4
Godfrey, George
Old Ironsides 1926,D 7,21:2

Godfrey, Peter
Blockade 1938,Je 17,25:1
Raffles 1940,Ja 13,11:2
Earl of Chicago, The 1940,Mr 14,29:3
Edison the Man 1940,Je 7,27:2
Dr Jekyll and Mr Hyde 1941,Ag 13,13:2
Two Mrs Carrolls, The 1947,Ap 7,20:1
Godfrey, Peter (Director)
Lone Wolf Spy Hunt, The 1939,Mr 6,11:3
Unexpected Uncle 1941,S 25,29:1
Make Your own Bed 1944,My 27,12:2
Hotel Berlin 1945,Mr 3,11:2
Christmas in Connecticut 1945,Jl 28,7:2
One More Tomorrow 1946,My 25,12:2
Two Mrs Carrolls, The 1947,Ap 7,20:1
Cry Wolf 1947,Jl 19,10:2
That Hagen Girl 1947,O 25,13:2
Escape me Never 1947,N 8,11:2
Woman in White, The 1948,My 8,12:2
Decision of Christopher Blake, The
1948,D 11,12:2
One Last Fling 1949,Jl 1,14:6
Girl from Jones Beach, The 1949,Jl 30,9:2
Barricade 1950,Mr 25,8:6
Great Jewel Robber, The 1950,Ag 4,13:2
He's a Cockeyed Wonder 1950,O 20,32:4
Godfrey, Peter (Original Author)
Forever and a Day 1943,Mr 13,9:2
Godfrey, Philip
Jeannie 1943,S 13,14:2
Godfrey, Renee
Bedside Manner 1945,Je 23,9:6
Terror by Night 1946,F 9,9:2
Inherit the Wind 1960,O 13,41:1
Godfrey, Sam
Washington Merry-Go-Round 1932,O 24,18:5
Frisco Jenny 1933,Ja 7,11:2
Blondie Johnson 1933,F 27,11:2
Parole Girl 1933,Ap 10,8:2
I Loved a Woman 1933,S 22,14:2
After Tonight 1933,N 3,23:2
Private Worlds 1935,Mr 28,25:2
Godfurt, Frederick (Screenwriter)
Why Bother to Knock 1965,F 4,24:2
Godik, W
Border Street 1950,Ap 26,35:2
Godinet, Henreetta
Return to Paradise 1953,S 11,24:2
Godowsky, Dagmar
Red Lights 1923,S 10,15:4
Common Law, The 1923,O 29,18:1
Virtuous Liars 1924,Mr 31,20:1
Story Without a Name, The 1924,O 6,25:1
Sainted Devil, A 1924,N 24,15:3
Price of a Party, The 1924,N 26,17:3
Godoy, Frank
Safari 1940,Je 20,29:2
Godridge, Constance
First a Girl 1936,Ja 4,19:1
Godsell, Vanda
Hell is a City 1961,Ja 19,26:3
This Sporting Life 1963,Jl 17,19:2
Shot in the Dark, A 1964,Je 24,28:1
Godwin, Frank (Producer)
Small World of Sammy Lee, The 1963,Ag 14,28:1
Why Bother to Knock 1965,F 4,24:2
Goehr, Walter (Composer)
Great Expectations 1947,My 23,31:1
Goelet, Robert Jr (Producer)
Rapture 1950,D 14,51:3
Goell, Kermit (Composer)
Bachelor's Daughters, The 1946,O 7,23:2
Torch Song 1953,O 13,34:2
Tom Thumb 1958,D 24,00:0
Goerling, Anne
Sein Liebeslied 1931,N 19,27:5
Week-End Im Paradies 1932,O 24,18:5
Goerling, Nathan (Composer)
Lasse-Maja 1943,Mr 22,15:4
Goethals, Stanley
Outside the Law 1926,My 12,31:1
Goethe (Original Author)
Faust and the Devil 1950,My 1,18:2
Faust 1963,Ap 16,31:1
Goettinger, Lisiott
Girl With Green Eyes 1964,Ag 11,37:2
GOETZ
See Also GETZ
Goetz, Augustus (Original Author)
Heiress, The 1949,O 7,35:2
Goetz, Augustus (Screenwriter)
Heiress, The 1949,O 7,35:2
Carrie 1952,Jl 17,20:2
Rhapsody 1954,Mr 12,17:1
Stage Struck 1958,Ap 23,40:1
Goetz, Carl
Pandora's Box 1929,D 2,28:2
Die Frau von der Man Spricht 1933,Ap 22,16:4
Goetz, E Ray (Composer)
For Me and My Gal 1942,O 22,25:1
Goetz, Hans
Versuchen Sie Meine Schwester 1931,Je 20,20:4
Liebe im Dreiviertel Takt; Love in Waltz Time
1938,S 24,13:1

Goetz, Hayes (Producer)
Hour of 13, The 1952,O 28,37:1
Arrow in the Dust 1954,My 1,13:2
Human Jungle, The 1954,N 26,24:6
Three for Jamie Dawn 1956,Jl 7,11:3

Goetz, John (Director)
Uncle Vanya 1958,Ap 29,26:2

Goetz, Kurt (Original Author)
Hocuspocus 1930,Ag 3,VIII,4:1
People Will Talk 1951,Ag 30,20:1

Goetz, Ruth (Original Author)
Heiress, The 1949,O 7,35:2

Goetz, Ruth (Screenwriter)
Heiress, The 1949,O 7,35:2
Carrie 1952,Jl 17,20:2
Rhapsody 1954,Mr 12,17:1
Stage Struck 1958,Ap 23,40:1

Goetz, Walter (Screenwriter)
Assignment-Paris 1952,O 25,12:6

Goetz, William (Producer)
Jane Eyre 1944,F 4,12:5
Autumn Leaves 1956,Ag 2,21:2
Soyonara 1957,D 6,39:4
Sayonara 1957,D 6,39:4
Me and the Colonel 1958,Ag 27,33:1
They Came to Cordura 1959,O 22,47:2
Mountain Road, The 1960,Je 30,22:3
Song Without End 1960,Ag 12,10:2
Cry for Happy 1961,Mr 4,16:1
Assault on a Queen 1966,Jl 28,23:3

Goetzke, Bernhard
Peter the Great 1923,Je 25,16:5
Between Worlds 1924,Jl 7,10:4
Slums of Berlin 1927,Ja 26,17:1
Schuldig 1928,Mr 11,VIII,7:6 (In Addenda)
Vanina 1928,Mr 20,20:3
Children of no Importance 1928,Ap 3,33:2
Guilty 1928,S 18,33:2
Kriemhild's Revenge 1928,O 16,29:1
Wrath of the Seas, The 1929,Ag 19,22:1
Cities and Years 1931,Ap 4,23:1
Alraune 1934,My 5,22:4

Goetzman, Gary
Yours, Mine and Ours 1968,Ap 25,53:1

Gofe, Richard
Rembrandt 1936,D 3,31:1
Forever Yours 1937,Je 7,22:2

GOFF
See Also GOUGH

Goff, Ivan (Original Author)
Glory at Sea 1953,Mr 11,36:7
Portrait in Black 1960,Jl 28,19:1

Goff, Ivan (Screenwriter)
My Love Came Back 1940,Jl 13,16:5
White Heat 1949,S 3,7:2
Backfire 1950,Ja 27,29:2
Goodbye, my Fancy 1951,My 30,14:2
Captain Horatio Hornblower 1951,S 14,21:2
Come Fill the Cup 1951,N 22,47:2
O Henry's Full House (The Cop and the Anthem);
  Cop and the Anthem, The (O Henry's Full
  House) 1952,O 17,33:1
O Henry's Full House (The Gift of the Magi); Gift
  of the Magi, The (O Henry's Full House)
  1952,O 17,33:1
O Henry's Full House (The Last Leaf)
  1952,O 17,33:1
O Henry's Full House (The Clarion Call); Clarion
  Call, The (O Henry's Full House)
  1952,O 17,33:1
White Witch Doctor 1953,Jl 2,19:3
King of the Khyber Rifles 1953,D 23,21:1
Green Fire 1954,D 25,7:1
Serenade 1956,Mr 24,21:1 (Incorrect in this
  edition; use 1956,Mr 23,21:1 elsewhere)
Band of Angels 1957,Jl 11,21:1
Man of a Thousand Faces 1957,Ag 14,21:1
Shake Hands With the Devil 1959,Je 25,20:7
Portrait in Black 1960,Jl 28,19:1
Midnight Lace 1960,O 14,27:1

Goff, Lloyd
Body and Soul 1947,N 10,21:2

Goff, Peter
Hurry Sundown 1967,Mr 24,22:1

Gofman, P
Men of the Sea 1938,Je 20,11:2

Gog, Gregor
Kampf, Der 1936,S 11,29:3

Gogal (Miscellaneous)
Bespoke Overcoat, The 1956,O 8,31:1

Gogol, Nikolai (Original Author)
Taras Bulba 1927,D 28,26:6
Christmas Slippers 1945,D 24,19:2
Stars of the Ukraine 1953,Jl 13,22:4
May Night 1953,Jl 13,22:4
Overcoat, The 1953,O 13,34:1
Inspector General, The 1954,My 3,21:2
Black Sunday 1961,Mr 9,23:1
Taras Bulba 1962,D 26,5:2
Night Before Christmas, A 1963,D 16,44:4
Sofi 1968,Mr 28,52:3

Gogolieva, E N
Gobsek 1937,Jl 16,22:1

Gola, Jose
Poor Perez 1937,N 1,24:6
Palermo 1938,O 22,14:2
Fuera de la Ley; Outside the Law
  1940,My 13,21:2

Golan, Gila
Our Man Flint 1966,Ja 26,23:4
3 on a Couch 1966,Jl 7,30:1

Golan, Menaheim (Director)
Trunk to Cairo 1966,D 29,22:1

Golan, Menaheim (Producer)
Sallah 1965,O 13,39:1
Trunk to Cairo 1966,D 29,22:1

Golbert, Boy
Montpi 1959,Ap 21,40:1

Gold, Jack (Director)
Bofors Gun, The 1968,S 23,42:3

Gold, Kaethe
Aus den Wolken Kommt das Glueck; Luck Comes
  From the Clouds 1938,Ap 16,17:2

Gold, Kathe
Sins of Rose Bernd, The 1959,Ja 24,13:4 (In
  Addenda)

Gold, Lee (Screenwriter)
Tamango 1959,S 17,48:4

Gold, Michael (Miscellaneous)
Jew at War, A 1931,Jl 25,11:6

Gold, Zachary (Screenwriter)
Top Man 1943,O 29,23:2
Humoresque 1946,D 26,28:1
South of St Louis 1949,Mr 7,17:2

Goldbaum, P (Producer)
Arms and the Man 1962,F 24,21:7

Goldbeck, Willis (Director)
Rationing 1944,Ap 10,14:2
Three Men in White 1944,My 26,23:3
Between Two Women 1945,Mr 29,18:3
She Went to the Races 1946,F 1,29:2
Love Laughs at Andy Hardy 1947,Ja 8,28:2
Dark Delusion 1947,Je 26,19:2
Johnny Holiday 1950,My 17,36:1
Ten Tall Men 1951,O 27,10:5

Goldbeck, Willis (Original Author)
Dr Kildare's Strange Case 1940,Ap 12,19:2
Dr Kildare's Crisis 1940,D 19,33:1
Ten Tall Men 1951,O 27,10:5

Goldbeck, Willis (Producer)
I Died a Thousand Times 1955,N 10,45:2
Lone Ranger, The 1956,F 11,12:1
Sergeant Rutledge 1960,My 26,37:1
Man Who Shot Liberty Valance, The
  1962,My 24,29:2

Goldbeck, Willis (Screenwriter)
Wednesday's Child 1934,D 15,9:3
Young Doctor Kildare 1938,O 28,27:1
Calling Dr Kildare 1939,My 12,25:4
Secret of Dr Kildare, The 1939,D 8,33:5
Dr Kildare's Strange Case 1940,Ap 12,19:2
Dr Kildare Goes Home 1940,S 19,27:4
Dr Kildare's Crisis 1940,D 19,33:1
People vs Dr Kildare, The 1941,My 8,21:1
Dr Kildare's Wedding Day 1941,S 18,31:1
Dr Kildare's Victory 1942,F 5,25:2
Calling Dr Gillespie 1942,Jl 9,17:4
Johnny Holiday 1950,My 17,36:1
Sergeant Rutledge 1960,My 26,37:1
Man Who Shot Liberty Valance, The
  1962,My 24,29:2

Goldberg, Dina
Catskill Honeymoon 1950,Ja 28,10:3

Goldberg, Heinz (Screenwriter)
1914: The Last Days Before the War 1932,S 5,9:6
Dreyfus Case, The 1940,O 30,29:3

Goldberg, Jack (Miscellaneous)
Unknown Soldier Speaks, The 1934,My 26,12:3

Goldberg, Jack (Producer)
We've Come a Long, Long Way 1944,Je 26,21:3
Miracle in Harlem 1949,O 24,19:4

Goldberg, Jakub (Screenwriter)
Knife in the Water 1963,O 29,31:2

Goldberg, Maurice (Director)
Feeling of Inferiority, The 1948,D 27,16:4

Goldberg, Mel (Screenwriter)
Lively Set, The 1964,O 15,54:1
Hang 'Em High 1968,Ag 8,27:3

Goldberg, R
Chalutzim 1934,Ap 2,13:3

Goldberg, Sam
Fallen Sparrow, The 1943,Ag 20,13:1

Goldberg, William (Miscellaneous)
Victims of Persecution 1933,Je 17,16:6

Goldblatt, Harold
Rising of the Moon, The (A Minute's WaitE
  1957,Jl 10,23:1
Rooney 1958,Je 6,29:2
A Night to Remember 1958,D 17,2:7
Francis of Assisi 1961,Jl 29,8:2
Lisa 1962,My 25,28:1
Reluctant Saint, The 1962,D 4,47:2
Nine Hours to Rama 1963,Ap 4,58:2
Mind Benders, The 1963,My 2,40:2

Goldblatt, Harold— Cont
Running Man, The 1963,O 3,31:1
Young Cassidy 1965,Mr 23,35:1

Goldblatt, M (Director)
Gypsies 1936,Jl 30,22:2

GOLDEN
See Also GOLDIN

Golden, Alfred (Original Author)
One Mile From Heaven 1937,Ag 19,23:1

Golden, Eddie
Broth of a Boy 1959,D 28,18:1
Poacher's Daughter, The 1960,F 16,31:2
Home Is the Hero 1961,Ja 26,32:1
Ulysses 1967,Mr 14,55:1

Golden, Edward A (Producer)
Hitler's Children 1943,F 25,27:1
Master Race, The 1944,N 2,22:1

Golden, Eleanor (Original Author)
Spring Madness 1938,D 1,29:3

Golden, Eve (Original Author)
Moon Over her Shoulder 1941,N 5,31:2

Golden, Geoffrey
Ulysses 1967,Mr 14,55:1

Golden, Harvey
Canterbury Tale, A 1949,Ja 24,16:2

Golden, John (Original Author)
Three Wise Fools 1923,Jl 23,13:4
After Tomorrow 1932,Mr 7,13:5
Her First Mate 1933,S 2,14:5

Golden, Marta
Revenge 1928,D 10,25:1

Golden, Max (Producer)
Every Saturday Night 1936,Mr 14,10:2
Little Tough Guys in Society 1938,N 21,14:4

Golden, Max H (Producer)
Hawaiian Nights 1939,S 29,19:4

Golden, Michael
Hungry Hill 1947,O 11,11:2
Escape 1948,Ag 16,12:2
Blue Lamp, The 1951,Ja 9,25:1
Pool of London 1951,N 28,37:2
Murder She Said 1962,Ja 8,27:2

Golden, Olive
Trader Horn 1931,F 4,21:3

Golden, Ray (Composer)
Kentucky Moonshine 1938,My 21,9:2
Big Store, The 1941,Je 27,14:4

Golden, Ray (Miscellaneous)
Life Begins In College 1937,O 9,16:1
Kentucky Moonshine 1938,My 21,9:2
Three Musketeers, The 1939,F 18,12:2
Hit Parade of 1941 1940,D 5,33:2

Golden, Ray (Screenwriter)
Argentine Nights 1940,O 11,25:3
Big Store, The 1941,Je 27,14:4
Nothing but Trouble 1945,Mr 10,14:1

Golden, Robert (Producer)
Breakfast in Hollywood 1946,Jl 15,21:1
Guilty of Treason 1950,Ap 11,26:2

Golden Gate Quartet
Star Spangled Rhythm 1942,D 31,20:1
Hit Parade of 1943 1943,Ap 16,24:3
Hollywood Canteen 1944,D 16,19:2
Song Is Born, A 1948,O 20,37:2

Goldenberg, Samuel
Shir Hashirim 1935,O 11,31:1

Golder, Lew (Producer)
Spirit of Youth 1938,F 28,19:1

Goldfaden, Wolf
Broken Hearts 1926,Mr 3,26:1
Youth of Russia, The 1934,N 10,19:3

Goldie, Wyndham
Sixty Glorious Years 1938,N 18,25:2
Night Train 1940,D 30,21:1
Girl in the News, The 1941,My 5,13:2
Cosmic Monster, The 1959,Ja 1,38:1

Goldie, Wyndham
Under the Red Robe 1937,Je 1,27:2

GOLDIN
See Also GOLDEN

Goldin, Pat
Bringing Up Father 1946,N 22,27:3
Glory Alley 1952,Jl 30,20:8

Goldina, Marian
Flaming Star 1960,D 17,19:1

Goldina, Miriam
Ladies of the Big House 1932,Ja 1,31:1

Golding, Louis (Original Author)
Mr Emmanuel 1945,Ja 8,15:2

Golding, Louis (Screenwriter)
Proud Valley 1941,My 17,19:2
Voice in the Night, The 1941,My 23,25:4
Mr Emmanuel 1945,Ja 8,15:2

Golding, Richard
Tales of Hoffmann 1951,Ap 5,34:2

Golding, Samuel R (Original Author)
Buccaneer's Girl 1950,Mr 27,19:2

Golding, William (Original Author)
Lord of the Flies 1963,Ag 20,37:1

Goldman, Harold (Screenwriter)
Petticoat Fever 1936,Mr 21,13:2
Emperor's Candlesticks, The 1937,Jl 9,18:1
Girl Downstairs, The 1939,Ja 26,17:1
Haunted Honeymoon 1940,O 31,28:2

Goldman, Harold (Screenwriter) — Cont
 Little Bit of Heaven, A 1940,N 8,24:2
 My Kingdom for a Cook 1943,O 15,15:3
Goldman, James (Screenwriter)
 Lion in Winter, The 1968,O 31,54:1
Goldman, Lawrence L (Screenwriter)
 Kronos 1957,My 11,24:6
Goldman, Peter (Cinematographer)
 Echoes of Silence 1967,Ap 7,32:2
Goldman, Peter (Director)
 Echoes of Silence 1967,Ap 7,32:2
Goldman, Peter (Producer)
 Echoes of Silence 1967,Ap 7,32:2
Goldman, Peter (Screenwriter)
 Echoes of Silence 1967,Ap 7,32:2
Goldman, William (Original Author)
 Soldier in the Rain 1963,N 29,67:6 (Incorrect in
  this edition; use 1963,N 28,67:6 elsewhere)
 No Way to Treat a Lady 1968,Mr 21,56:1
Goldman, William (Screenwriter)
 Harper 1966,Mr 31,43:1
Goldner, Charles
 One Night With You 1949,F 21,20:2
 Black Magic 1949,N 9,37:2
 Give Us This Day 1949,D 21,41:2
 Laughing Lady, The 1950,Ja 23,16:3
 Bond Street 1950,Mr 30,40:6
 Rocking Horse Winner, The 1950,Je 9,29:2
 Dear Mr Prohack 1950,Jl 15,7:2
 No Orchids for Miss Blandish 1951,F 23,33:2
 Lucky Nick Cain 1951,Ap 23,21:2
 Encore (Gigolo and Gigolette); Gigolo and
  Gigolette (Encore) 1952,Ap 3,45:1
 Master of Ballantrae, The 1953,Ag 6,16:2
 Captain's Paradise, The 1953,S 29,25:5
 Golden Mask, The 1954,Mr 20,10:5
 Flame and the Flesh 1954,My 3,21:2
 Always a Bride 1954,My 28,19:2
 Racers, The 1955,F 5,13:2
 End of the Affair, The 1955,Ap 29,28:2
Goldoni, Lelia
 Shadows 1961,Mr 22,37:1
 Hysteria 1965,S 9,36:3
Goldsborough, Arnold
 Seventh Veil, The 1945,D 26,15:1
Goldsmith, Charles
 Journey to the Beginning of Time 1967,F 11,20:1
Goldsmith, Clifford (Original Author)
 What a Life 1939,O 12,33:1
 Life With Henry 1941,F 6,25:2
 Father Was a Fullback 1949,O 13,33:3
Goldsmith, Clifford (Screenwriter)
 Life With Henry 1941,F 6,25:2
Goldsmith, I (Original Author)
 Screen, The 1951,Ap 23,21:2
Goldsmith, I (Producer)
 Stars Look Down, The 1941,Jl 24,15:2
 Bedelia 1947,F 8,10:2
 Hatter's Castle 1948,Jl 3,8:6
 Three Husbands 1951,Mr 9,30:2
 Screen, The 1951,Ap 23,21:2
Goldsmith, I (Screenwriter)
 Bedelia 1947,F 8,10:2
Goldsmith, Ken (Miscellaneous)
 Little Men 1935,F 18,19:3
Goldsmith, Ken (Original Author)
 Top Man 1943,O 29,23:2
Goldsmith, Ken (Producer)
 Little Tough Guy 1938,Ag 18,23:3
 Invisible Man Returns, The 1940,Ja 16,19:2
 Honeymoon Deferred 1940,F 16,23:4
Goldsmith, Ken (Screenwriter)
 Slightly Tempted 1940,N 1,33:1
Goldsmith, L S (Original Author)
 Manhandled 1949,My 26,34:2
Goldsmith, Martin (Original Author)
 Hell's Island 1955,My 7,10:2
Goldsmith, Martin (Screenwriter)
 Shakedown 1950,S 4,11:2
 Mission Over Korea 1953,S 19,7:2
Goldsmith, Myron (Original Author)
 I Was an American Spy 1951,Jl 4,13:2
Goldsmith, Oliver (Original Author)
 Vicar of Wakefield, The 1917,F 26,10:2
Goldsmith, William (Screenwriter)
 Masquerade 1965,Ap 29,40:2
Goldstein, Bob (Producer)
 Black Tuesday 1955,Ja 1,16:2
 Dance With Me Henry 1956,D 24,8:2
 Crime of Passion 1957,Ja 10,25:1
Goldstein, Charlotte
 Power of Life 1938,Ap 29,17:2
Goldstein, Howard
 Newly Rich 1931,Jl 3,22:1
Goldstein, Jennie
 Two Sisters 1938,D 1,29:3
Goldstein, Leonard (Producer)
 Black Bart 1948,Mr 4,30:4
 River Lady 1948,My 21,19:5
 Larceny 1948,S 4,8:6
 Red Canyon 1949,Ap 28,28:2
 Calamity Jane and Sam Bass 1949,Jl 18,14:2
 Ma and Pa Kettle 1949,Ag 12,13:2
 Arctic Manhunt 1949,Ag 19,12:5

 Yes Sir, That's my Baby 1949,N 11,31:2
 Comanche Territory 1950,Ap 8,9:3
 I Was a Shoplifter 1950,Ap 28,26:3
 One Way Street 1950,My 12,33:3
 Desert Hawk, The 1950,Ag 26,9:2
 Sleeping City, The 1950,S 21,20:2
 Saddle Tramp 1950,N 24,31:4
 Tomahawk 1951,F 19,19:2
 Up Front 1951,Mr 26,19:2
 Double Crossbones 1951,Ap 27,19:2
 Ma and Pa Kettle Back on the Farm
  1951,My 11,32:3
 Hollywood Story 1951,Je 7,40:6
 Prince Who Was a Thief, The 1951,Jl 4,13:2
 Francis Goes to the Races 1951,Jl 25,19:2
 Flame of Araby 1951,D 20,41:7
 Meet Danny Wilson 1952,Mr 27,34:4
 Flesh and Fury 1952,Mr 28,27:4
 Battle at Apache Pass, The 1952,My 10,16:4
 Steel Town 1952,My 10,16:4
 Scarlet Angel 1952,Je 21,12:2
 Just Across the Street 1952,Je 28,12:4
 Ma and Pa Kettle at the Fair 1952,Jl 12,16:2
 Duel at Silver Creek 1952,Ag 2,7:6
 Son of Ali Baba 1952,Ag 16,7:4
 Untamed Frontier 1952,Ag 23,10:2
 Francis Goes to West Point 1952,Ag 23,10:2
 It Grows on Trees 1952,N 29,11:2
 Redhead From Wyoming, The 1953,Ja 9,17:4
 Mister Scoutmaster 1953,Ag 29,10:1
 Vickie 1953,S 8,26:3
 Kid From Left Field, The 1953,S 26,15:3
 City of Bad Men 1953,O 21,37:6
 Siege at Red River, The 1954,Ap 3,19:2
 Three Young Texans 1954,Ap 17,8:2
 Gambler From Natchez, The 1954,Ag 14,8:2
 Raid, The 1954,Ag 21,10:4
 White Feather 1955,F 17,23:1
 Chief Crazy Horse 1955,Ap 28,25:1
 Life in the Balance, A 1955,Jl 14,19:1
Goldstein, Marek (Director)
 Long Is the Road 1948,N 12,30:5
Goldstein, Michael
 Green Fields 1937,O 12,31:4
 Singing Blacksmith, The 1938,N 3,27:1
Goldstein, Ruby
 Joe Louis Story, The 1953,N 4,29:4
Goldston, Robert (Producer)
 Uncle, The 1966,Jl 19,34:1
 Georgy Girl 1966,O 18,48:1
 Bofors Gun, The 1968,S 23,42:3
Goldstone, Harry (Miscellaneous)
 Just a big Simple Girl; Une Grande Fille Toute
  Simple 1949,O 28,29:2
Goldstone, James (Director)
 Jigsaw 1968,Je 6,54:2
Goldstone, Nat G (Producer)
 Casbah 1948,My 3,27:4
Goldstone, Phil (Director)
 Sin of Nora Moran, The 1933,D 13,29:3
Goldstone, Phil (Producer)
 Age of Indiscretion 1935,My 18,21:2
 O'Shaughnessy's Boy 1935,O 5,18:2
 Last of the Pagans 1936,Ja 9,25:2
 Marriage Forbidden 1938,Jl 16,7:2
Goldstone, Richard (Director)
 Cinerama-South Seas Adventure 1958,Jl 16,26:1
 No Man is an Island 1962,O 11,49:2
Goldstone, Richard (Original Author)
 Harmon of Michigan 1941,O 2,29:2
Goldstone, Richard (Producer)
 Outriders, The 1950,Mr 9,25:2
 Yellow Cab Man, The 1950,Mr 27,19:2
 Dial 1119 1950,D 4,32:6
 Inside Straight 1951,Mr 16,34:2
 Tall Target, The 1951,S 28,26:2
 Devil Makes Three, The 1952,Ag 30,6:2
 Cinerama-South Seas Adventure 1958,Jl 16,26:1
 No Man is an Island 1962,O 11,49:2
 Sergeant, The 1968,D 26,53:5
Goldstone, Richard (Screenwriter)
 No Man is an Island 1962,O 11,49:2
Goldsworthy, John
 Hangover Square 1945,F 8,15:2
 Emperor Waltz, The 1948,Je 18,19:2
 Everybody Does It 1949,O 26,32:2
Goldvani, M (Director)
 Power of Evil, The 1929,Ag 12,22:2
Goldwater, Patricia
 Captive City, The 1952,Mr 27,34:2
Goldwyn, Samuel (Producer)
 Street Scene 1931,Ag 27,22:5
 Greeks Had a Word for Them, The 1932,F 4,25:2
 Kid From Spain, The 1932,N 18,23:2
 Dodsworth 1936,S 24,29:1
 Stella Dallas 1937,Ag 6,21:1
 Goldwyn Follies, The 1938,F 21,15:1
 They Shall Have Music 1939,Jl 26,17:2
 Real Glory, The 1939,S 15,26:2
 Raffles 1940,Ja 13,11:2
 Westerner, The 1940,O 25,25:2
 Little Foxes, The 1941,Ag 22,19:2
 Ball of Fire 1942,Ja 16,25:2

Goldwyn, Samuel (Producer) — Cont
 Pride of the Yankees, The 1942,Jl 16,23:1
 North Star, The 1943,N 5,23:1
 Up in Arms 1944,Mr 3,19:2
 Princess and the Pirate, The 1945,F 10,16:2
 Wonder Man 1945,Je 9,17:2
 Kid From Brooklyn, The 1946,Ap 19,25:2
 Best Years of our Lives, The 1946,N 22,27:2
 Secret Life of Walter Mitty, The 1947,Ag 15,12:2
 Bishop's Wife, The 1947,D 10,44:2
 Song Is Born, A 1948,O 20,37:2
 Enchantment 1948,D 27,16:2
 Our Very Own 1950,Jl 28,12:5
 Edge of Doom 1950,Ag 4,13:2
 I Want You 1951,D 24,9:1
 Hans Christian Andersen 1952,N 26,20:2
 Guys and Dolls 1955,N 5,26:1
 Porgy and Bess 1959,Je 25,20:3
 Adventures of Marco Polo, The 1965,Ap 8,17:2
Goldwyn, Samuel Jr (Director)
 Young Lovers, The 1965,F 11,45:1
Goldwyn, Samuel Jr (Producer)
 Man With the Gun 1955,D 23,14:2
 Proud Rebel, The 1958,Jl 2,23:4
 Adventures of Huckleberry Finn, The
  1960,Ag 4,17:1
 Young Lovers, The 1965,F 11,45:1
Goldwyn Girls
 Secret Life of Walter Mitty, The 1947,Ag 15,12:2
 Guys and Dolls 1955,N 5,26:1
Goler, Harry
 We're not Married 1952,Jl 12,16:2
Golisano, Francesco
 Under the Sun of Rome 1949,O 6,40:4
 Miracle in Milan 1951,D 18,42:2
Golizin, Natalie
 Napoleon's Barber 1928,N 26,30:2
Golki, Elena
 Ivan 1933,F 27,11:3
Golling, Alexander
 Tiger von Eschnapur, Der 1938,Ap 30,18:2
 Indian Tomb, The; Tiger von Eschnapur, Der
  1938,My 14,18:2
Gollino, Federico
 Passaporto Rosso 1936,S 2,18:2
Gollomb, Joseph (Composer)
 Murder at the Vanities 1934,My 21,20:2
Gollong, Christian
 Kluge Schwiegermutter, Die; Wise Mother-in-Law,
  The 1939,O 9,15:3
 Heimatland; Homeland 1939,O 28,11:2
Gollova, Natasa
 Emperor and the Golem, The 1955,Ja 10,27:4
Golm, Lisa
 Underground 1941,Je 23,13:2
 Journey for Margaret 1942,D 18,36:7
 Anna Lucasta 1949,Ag 12,13:2
 Doctor and the Girl, The 1949,O 31,20:2
 East Side, West Side 1949,D 23,17:2
 Hoodlum, The 1951,Jl 6,14:6
 Invitation 1952,Ja 30,22:6
 Monkey on my Back 1957,My 30,23:2
Golm, Liza
 Come Back, Little Sheba 1952,D 24,13:2
Golonka, Arlene
 Harvey Middleman, Fireman 1965,Jl 13,39:1
 Penelope 1966,N 11,36:6
 Welcome to Hard Times 1967,My 2,56:1
 Busy Body, The 1967,Je 8,52:2
 Hang 'Em High 1968,Ag 8,27:3
Golos, Len (Original Author)
 Man Made Monster 1941,Mr 19,25:4
Golovanov, N (Screenwriter)
 Boris Godunov 1956,Ja 23,21:4
Golovin, Ivon
 Rasputin, The Holy Sinner 1929,Ja 15,22:4
Golovin, V
 Victors and the Vanquished, The 1950,My 1,18:2
Golovko, Kira Ivanova
 War and Peace 1968,Ap 29,50:5
Golow, Natan
 End of St Petersberg, The 1928,My 31,21:2 (In
  Addenda)
Golsova, Anna
 My Beloved 1959,Je 15,31:4
Golubinski, Daniel
 Zygmunt Kolosowski 1947,N 13,13:3
Golubkina, Larissa
 Ballad of a Hussar, The 1963,Jl 15,25:5
Gombaszogi, Ella
 Iza Neni 1934,Je 5,28:6
 My Wife, The Miss 1934,S 13,26:2
 Mindent a Noert! 1934,O 17,26:3
 Huszarszerelem 1935,Ap 23,24:5
 Elnoek Kisasszony 1935,O 12,12:3
 Csunya Lany, A 1935,O 18,27:4
 Szent Peter Esernyoeje 1936,Ja 8,22:2
 Legy Jo Mindhalalig 1936,O 26,20:2
 Meseauto 1936,N 10,31:4
 Fizessen Nagysag 1937,Je 4,27:3
 Az en Lanyom nem olyan; My Daughter Is
  Different 1938,Ap 30,18:2
 Pokhalo 1938,My 7,18:2

Gombault, Anita
Heart of a Nation, The 1943,Ap 8,27:2
Gombell, Minna
Bad Girl 1931,Ag 15,18:3
Sob Sister 1931,O 3,20:2
Good Sport 1931,D 12,23:3
Stepping Sisters 1932,Ja 9,21:1
Rainbow Trail, The 1932,Ja 30,13:2
Careless Lady 1932,Ap 18,19:2
Bachelor's Affairs 1932,Je 25,18:2
First Year, The 1932,Ag 22,20:2
Pleasure Cruise 1933,Ap 3,13:3
Hello Sister! 1933,My 6,11:2
What Price Innocence? 1933,Je 26,16:3
Big Brain, The 1933,Ag 5,9:5
Wild Boys of the Road 1933,S 22,14:1
Way to Love, The 1933,N 11,10:3
Hoopla 1933,D 1,23:3
Cross Country Cruise 1934,Ja 20,12:3
No More Women 1934,Mr 15,27:4
Thin Man, The 1934,Je 30,18:5
Strictly Dynamite 1934,Jl 4,18:2
Hell Cat, The 1934,Jl 7,16:5
Merry Widow, The 1934,O 12,33:1
Lemon Drop Kid, The 1934,O 27,20:2
Babbitt 1934,D 17,24:2
White Cockatoo, The 1935,Ja 16,21:1
Miss Pacific Fleet 1935,D 7,22:2
Champagne Charlie 1936,My 7,21:2
Banjo on My Knee 1936,D 12,15:1
Make Way for Tomorrow 1937,My 10,23:1
Slave Ship 1937,Je 17,19:2
Wife, Doctor and Nurse 1937,O 11,26:5
Block-Heads 1938,Ag 30,14:2
Great Waltz, The 1938,N 25,19:1
Comet over Broadway 1938,D 16,33:3
Going Places 1939,Ja 7,6:1
Second Fiddle 1939,Jl 1,11:2
Stop, Look and Love 1939,S 8,28:5
Hunchback of Notre Dame, The 1940,Ja 1,29:2
Boom Town 1940,S 6,25:2
High Sierra 1941,Ja 25,11:2
Mexican Spitfire Sees a Ghost 1942,Jl 31,11:2
Chip off the Old Block 1944,Mr 17,14:2
Destiny 1945,F 3,16:5
Man Alive 1945,N 17,14:5
Perilous Holiday 1946,Je 1,10:4
Best Years of our Lives, The 1946,N 22,27:2
Wyoming 1947,Jl 25,12:5
Snake Pit, the 1948,N 5,29:2
Last Bandit, The 1949,Mr 21,19:2
Pagan Love Song 1950,D 26,19:1
Here Comes the Groom 1951,S 21,19:2
I'll See You in my Dreams 1951,D 7,35:1
Gomberg, Sy (Original Author)
When Willie Comes Marching Home
1950,F 18,9:2
Summer Stock 1950,S 1,17:2
Because You're Mine 1952,S 26,18:2
Gomberg, Sy (Producer)
Kathy O' 1958,S 25,29:2
Gomberg, Sy (Screenwriter)
Summer Stock 1950,S 1,17:2
Toast of New Orleans, The 1950,S 30,13:3
Bloodhounds of Broadway 1952,N 15,15:2
Joe Butterfly 1957,My 30,23:2
Kathy O' 1958,S 25,29:2
Gombo
Son of Mongolia 1936,N 21,21:4
Gomes, Dias (Original Author)
Given Word, The 1964,Mr 25,47:1
Gomez, Antonio
Bullfighter and the Lady, The 1951,Ap 27,19:2
Gomez, Augie
Old Los Angeles 1948,Jl 12,11:2
Gomez, Guillermo Hernandez (Director)
Adelita, La 1938,O 12,35:2
Gomez, Inez
Temptress, The 1926,O 11,18:1
Under a Texas Moon 1930,Ap 4,22:1
Gomez, Leonor
Mexican Bus ride 1954,Jl 21,18:3
Gomez, Marie
Professionals, The 1966,N 3,45:1
Gomez, Ramon
Dancer of Barcelona, The 1929,N 25,22:1
Gomez, Thomas
Sherlock Holmes and the Voice Of Terror
1942,S 19,9:2
Who Done It 1942,D 3,35:2
Arabian Nights 1942,D 26,15:1
Pittsburgh 1943,F 25,27:2
White Savage 1943,Ap 26,15:2
Frontier Badmen 1943,Ag 14,12:8
Corvette K-225 1943,O 21,30:1
Crazy House 1943,D 16,33:3
Phantom Lady 1944,F 18,15:2
In Society 1944,Ag 17,20:2
Dead Man's Eyes 1944,O 7,11:2
Bowery to Broadway 1944,N 30,19:2
Climax, The 1944,D 14,28:5
Can't Help Singing 1944,D 26,22:4
Frisco Sal 1945,F 17,11:2

Patrick the Great 1945,Ap 13,15:2
Daltons Ride Again, The 1945,D 8,21:2
Night in Paradise 1946,Je 6,16:3
Swell Guy 1947,Ja 27,17:2
Johnny O'Clock 1947,Mr 27,39:2
Singapore 1947,S 17,31:2
Ride the Pink Horse 1947,O 9,32:3
Captain from Castile 1947,D 26,22:4
Casbah 1948,My 3,27:4
Key Largo 1948,Jl 17,6:6
Force of Evil 1948,D 27,16:2
Sorrowful Jones 1949,Je 6,15:2
Come to the Stable 1949,Jl 28,19:1
That Midnight Kiss 1949,S 23,28:2
Woman on Pier 13, The 1950,Je 16,28:4
Eagle and the Hawk, The 1950,Jl 6,31:2
Furies, The 1950,Ag 17,23:2
Kim 1950,D 8,40:4
Anne of the Indies 1951,O 25,36:3
Macao 1952,My 1,34:2
Sellout, The 1952,My 31,12:7
Merry Widow, The 1952,S 25,38:1
Pony Soldier 1952,D 20,15:2
Sombrero 1953,Ap 23,37:2
Gambler From Natchez, The 1954,Ag 14,8:2
Adventures of Haji Baba, The 1954,O 9,8:7
Magnificent Matador, The 1955,My 25,38:1
Las Vegas Shakedown 1955,Je 18,14:2
Conqueror, The 1956,Mr 31,13:3
Trapeze 1956,Je 5,39:2
John Paul Jones 1959,Je 17,39:1
But Not for Me 1959,O 3,14:6
Summer and Smoke 1961,N 17,41:1
Gomez, Vincente
Blood and Sand 1941,My 23,25:3
Kissing Bandit, The 1948,N 19,35:2
Snows of Kilimanjaro, The 1952,S 19,19:2
Gomi, Kosuke (Original Author)
Secret Scrolls-Part I 1968,My 9,54:3
Secret Scrolls-Part II; Ninjitsu 1968,My 23,56:3
Gomi, Ryutaro
Majin 1968,Ag 10,15:5
Gomikawa, Jumpei (Original Author)
Human Condition, The 1959,D 16,56:1
Gomolyak, V
Sunny Youth 1935,Ag 19,18:2
Gomori, Vilma
Te Csak Pipalj Ladanyi; Keep On Smoking,
Ladanyi 1938,My 18,9:3
Gonatos, John
16 Fathoms Deep 1948,O 7,35:2
Gonda, Greta
Rossini 1948,Ja 31,14:2
Gonder, Bill
Woman Proof 1923,O 30,16:1
Gondo, Gene
Tokyo Joe 1949,O 27,35:2
Gondrell, Adolf
Mit dir Durch Dick und Duenn 1934,N 24,19:2
Grobe Adele, Die 1937,My 15,23:5
Gonichev, Tolya
Village Teacher 1948,Jl 5,8:4
Gonn, Leo
Quo Vadis 1951,N 9,22:2
Gonneau, George (Narrator)
To Die in Madrid 1965,S 16,00:0
Gonta, Maria
Road to Life 1932,Ja 28,24:2
Gonzales, Carl
Little Ones, The 1965,S 16,55:2
Gonzales, Cesareo (Producer)
Flamenco 1954,My 24,24:2
Uninhibited, The 1968,Je 13,57:2
Gonzales, Cesareo (Screenwriter)
Uninhibited, The 1968,Je 13,57:2
Gonzales, Dr
Roots, The (Our Lady); Our Lady (The Roots)
1957,S 3,23:2
Gonzales, Enrique
Manhunt in the Jungle 1958,Ap 12,13:1
Gonzales, Francisco (Original Author)
Roots, The (The Filly); Filly, The (The Roots)
1957,S 3,23:2
Roots, The (The One-Eyed Boy); One-Eyed Boy,
The (The Roots) 1957,S 3,23:2
Roots, The (The Cows); Cows, The (The Roots)
1957,S 3,23:2
Roots, The (Our Lady); Our Lady (The Roots)
1957,S 3,23:2
Gonzales, Gilberto
Pearl, The 1948,F 18,36:4
Littlest Outlaw, The 1955,D 27,31:1
Gonzales, Jose Gonzales
Wetbacks 1956,My 5,13:2
Kronos 1957,My 11,24:6
Gonzales, Lolita
Cuna Vacia, La; Empty Cradle, The
1938,Mr 21,18:3
Rapsodia Mexicana 1938,N 26,18:2
Estrellita; Starlet 1939,Ap 12,27:3
Ultima Melodia, La; Last Melody, The
1939,Ag 5,18:3

Gonzales, Mark
Argentine Love 1924,D 23,16:2
Great Deception, The 1926,Ag 9,10:3
Gonzales, Ricardo
Littlest Outlaw, The 1955,D 27,31:1
Gonzales-Gonzales, Pedro
Wings of the Hawk 1953,Ag 27,22:1
High and the Mighty, The 1954,Jl 1,21:2
Strange Lady in Town 1955,My 21,11:1
I Died a Thousand Times 1955,N 10,45:2
Bottom of the Bottle, The 1956,F 2,19:2
Sheepman, The 1958,My 8,36:1
Rio Bravo 1959,Mr 19,40:2
Gonzales, Augustin
That Man in Istanbul 1966,My 19,51:2
Gonzalez, David
Wave, The 1937,Ap 21,18:1
Ay Jalisco no te Rajes 1943,Ap 24,17:3
Gonzalez, Felix
Sitting Bull 1954,N 26,24:4
Gonzalez, Gilberto
Amor con Amor se Paga; Love for Love
1940,Mr 16,8:2
Gonzalez, Julian S (Director)
Rayo, El 1935,O 19,21:3
Gonzalez, Servando (Director)
Yanco 1964,Je 18,29:2
Gonzalez, Servando (Screenwriter)
Yanco 1964,Je 18,29:2
Gonzalez, Teodulo
Roots, The (The Filly); Filly, The (The Roots)
1957,S 3,23:2
Gonzelez, Carmen
Mexican Bus ride 1954,Jl 21,18:3
Gonzelez, Miguel (Producer)
Yanco 1964,Je 18,29:2
Good, Jack
Father Goose 1964,D 11,55:1
Good, John
Avalanche 1946,Jl 8,25:2
Letters From an Unknown Woman
1948,Ap 29,20:6
Good, Peter B
Brother Rat and a Baby 1940,Ja 27,9:4
Goodale, Elois
Broadway Gold 1923,Jl 31,12:4
Goodall, Grace
Handy Andy 1934,Ag 4,14:5
Make Way for a Lady 1936,D 12,15:1
City Streets 1938,Jl 25,18:2
Goodchild, George (Original Author)
Condemned to Death 1932,Jl 14,24:2
Goode, Frederic (Director)
Go Go Mania 1965,My 20,52:4
Goode, Reginald (Original Author)
Syncopating Sue 1926,N 2,35:1
Goodhart, Al (Composer)
Gangway 1937,Ag 21,7:3
Goodhart, Geoffrey
Always a Bride 1954,My 28,19:2
Goodhart, Sigler (Composer)
First a Girl 1936,Ja 4,19:1
This'll Make You Whistle 1938,N 1,27:2
Goodhue, Willis Maxwell (Original Author)
Sin of Nora Moran, The 1933,D 13,29:3
Goodier, Robert
Oedipus Rex 1957,Ja 8,26:1
Goodin, Peggy (Original Author)
Mickey 1948,Jl 19,11:2
Take Care of my Little Girl 1951,Jl 19,20:2
Goodis, David (Original Author)
Dark Passage 1947,S 6,11:2
Shoot the Piano Player 1962,Jl 24,19:1
Goodis, David (Screenwriter)
Unfaithful, The 1947,Je 28,10:2
Goodkin, J
Fragment of an Empire, A 1930,Ja 27,18:4
China Express, The 1930,Mr 10,24:1
Goodliffe, Michael
Cry, the Beloved Country 1952,Ja 24,23:2
Sea Devils 1953,Jl 31,11:5
Rob Roy 1954,F 4,21:5
Front Page Story 1955,Ap 19,28:1
End of the Affair, The 1955,Ap 29,28:2
Quentin Durward 1955,N 24,41:1
Pursuit of the Graf Spee 1957,D 27,33:2
One That Got Away, The 1958,Ag 23,40:2
Camp on Blood Island, The 1958,S 18,37:2
Conspiracy of Hearts 1960,Ap 8,24:1
39 Steps, The 1960,O 11,55:2
No Love for Johnnie 1961,D 13,55:1
Day the Earth Caught Fire, The 1962,Mr 16,25:1
Man in the Middle 1964,Mr 5,36:1
Seventh Dawn, The 1964,S 3,24:1
Von Ryan's Express 1965,Je 24,28:1
Jokers, The 1967,My 16,50:1
Goodloe, A Carter (Original Author)
I Live my Life 1935,O 12,12:2
Goodly, David (Original Author)
Nightfall 1957,Ja 24,34:1
Goodman, Al (Composer)
She Shall Have Music 1942,O 31,11:2

Goodman, Benny
Powers Girl, The 1943,Mr 26,14:2 (In Addenda)
Sweet and Low Down 1944,O 19,19:2
Song Is Born, A 1948,O 20,37:2
Goodman, Benny and his orchestra
Big Broadcast of 1937, The 1936,O 22,31:1
Goodman, Benny and his Orchestra
Powers Girl, The 1943,Mr 26,14:2 (In Addenda)
Stage Door Canteen 1943,Je 25,13:2
Gang's All Here, The 1943,D 23,26:4
Goodman, Benny and his Swing Band
Hollywood Hotel 1938,Ja 13,17:3
Goodman, D Carson (Miscellaneous)
Escape, The 1914,Je 2,11:5
Goodman, D Carson (Original Author)
Wonder Man, The 1920,My 30,6:4
Battle of The Sexes, The 1928,O 15,16:1
Goodman, Dody
Bedtime Story 1964,Je 11,27:1
Goodman, Edward (Director)
Women Love Once 1931,Je 27,20:3
Goodman, George J W (Original Author)
Wheeler Dealers, The 1963,N 15,25:2
Goodman, George J W (Screenwriter)
Wheeler Dealers, The 1963,N 15,25:2
Goodman, Hal (Original Author)
Invitation to a Gunfighter 1964,O 28,51:3
Goodman, Jack (Original Author)
Meet the Missus 1937,Jl 2,25:2
Goodman, Jules Eckert (Original Author)
Man Who Played God, The 1922,O 2,21:2
Man Who Came Back, The 1924,S 1,9:1
Partners Again, With Potash and Perlmutter 1926,F 15,16:4
Man Who Played God, The 1932,F 11,16:1
Goodman, Lee
Imitation of Life 1959,Ap 18,18:1
Goodman, Lee (Producer)
With These Hands 1950,Je 16,28:4
Goodner, Carol
Ringer, The 1932,Je 2,25:2
There Goes the Bride 1933,Mr 4,11:3
Just Smith 1934,Ap 23,20:2
Mimi 1936,Ja 10,16:3
Student's Romance, The 1936,O 12,23:2
Goodrich, Arthur (Original Author)
Yes or No 1920,Jl 5,12:4
So This Is London 1930,My 24,21:2
Goodrich, C W
Show-Off, The 1926,Ag 23,9:1
Goodrich, Frances (Original Author)
Up Pops the Devil 1931,My 16,13:3
Thanks for the Memory 1938,D 8,34:3
Easter Parade 1948,Jl 1,19:3
Diary of Anne Frank, The 1959,Mr 19,40:1
Goodrich, Frances (Screenwriter)
Naughty Marietta 1935,Mr 23,11:2
Ah, Wilderness! 1935,D 25,30:2
Rose Marie 1936,F 1,9:2
After the Thin Man 1936,D 25,19:2
Firefly, The 1937,S 2,17:2
Society Lawyer 1939,Mr 31,19:2
Another Thin Man 1939,N 24,29:1
Lady in the Dark 1944,F 23,17:1
Hitler Gang, The 1944,My 8,15:2
Virginian, The 1946,Ap 18,22:2
It's a Wonderful Life 1946,D 23,19:2
Pirate, The 1948,My 21,19:2
Summer Holiday 1948,Je 12,8:5
Easter Parade 1948,Jl 1,19:3
In the Good Old Summertime 1949,Ag 5,23:2
Father of the Bride 1950,My 19,31:2
Father's Little Dividend 1951,Ap 13,18:5
Too Young to Kiss 1951,N 23,32:2
Long, Long Trailer, The 1954,F 19,24:3
Seven Brides for Seven Brothers 1954,Jl 23,8:3
Gaby 1956,My 10,26:3
Certain Smile, A 1958,Ag 1,13:2
Diary of Anne Frank, The 1959,Mr 19,40:1
Five Finger Exercise 1962,Ap 20,20:2
Goodrich, John (Original Author)
Crack-Up 1937,Ja 4,20:4
Goodrich, John Fish (Screenwriter)
Rough Riders, The 1927,Mr 16,28:2
Goodrich, Louis
Sherlock Holmes's Fatal Hour 1931,Jl 13,13:5
Goodrich, Marcus (Screenwriter)
Night Waitress 1936,D 18,31:5
Goodrich, William (Director)
Red Mill, The 1927,F 14,15:1
Special Delivery 1927,Ap 26,33:3
Goodrow, Garry
Connection, The 1962,O 4,44:1
Goodschild, George (Original Author)
Public Defender, The 1931,Ag 1,16:4
Goodsell, Major
Sweetheart of Sigma Chi, The 1933,N 9,27:1
Goodstein, Gerald
Cyanamide 1954,Mr 26,17:6
Goodwin, Aline
Desert Gold 1926,Mr 23,24:5

Goodwin, Bill
Wake Island 1942,S 2,19:2
So Proudly We Hail 1943,S 10,29:1
No Time for Love 1943,D 2,30:1
Riding High 1943,D 23,26:4
Bathing Beauty 1944,Je 28,20:1
Incendiary Blonde 1945,Jl 26,13:2
River Gang 1945,O 6,9:7
Spellbound 1945,N 2,22:2
Stork Club, The 1945,D 20,18:2
House of Horrors 1946,F 23,20:3
To Each his Own 1946,My 24,15:2
Earl Carroll Sketchbook 1946,Ag 30,13:2
Jolson Story, The 1946,O 11,28:2
Hit Parade of 1947 1947,My 5,32:8
Heaven Only Knows 1947,N 14,29:3
Mickey 1948,Jl 19,11:2
Life of Riley, The 1949,Ap 18,18:4
It's a Great Feeling 1949,Ag 13,6:6
Jolson Sings Again 1949,Ag 18,16:6
Tea for Two 1950,S 2,11:2
Lucky Me 1954,Ap 10,11:2
Atomic Kid, The 1954,D 4,14:2
Opposite Sex, The 1956,N 16,23:2
Bundle of Joy 1956,D 20,36:1
Big Beat, The 1958,Je 26,23:4
Goodwin, Frank (Producer)
Woman in a Dressing Gown 1957,S 13,15:2
Goodwin, Fred
Way of a Man With a Maid, The 1919,Ja 20,13:2
Goodwin, Harold
Heart o' the Hills 1919,D 1,9:3
Suds 1920,Je 28,13:2
Madonna of the Streets 1924,O 28,23:4
Riders of the Purple Sage 1925,Ap 15,16:1
Talker, The 1925,My 12,26:2
Midshipman, The 1925,O 13,20:1
Flaming Frontier, The 1926,Ap 5,24:1
College 1927,S 12,29:1
Cameraman, The 1928,S 17,27:1
Flight 1929,S 14,17:1
Widow From Chicago, The 1930,D 20,20:6
Dirigible 1931,Ap 6,24:1
Lawyer's Secret, The 1931,My 30,9:2
Sky Bride 1932,Ap 23,11:5
Hat Check Girl 1932,O 8,15:4
Fight to the Finish, A 1937,Je 26,20:2 (In Addenda)
It Happened in Hollywood 1937,O 2,18:1
Jesse James 1939,Ja 14,13:1
Viva Cisco Kid 1940,Mr 22,23:4
Charlie Chan At the Wax Museum 1940,S 28,9:3
Tanks a Million 1941,O 9,27:2
Ride the Pink Horse 1947,O 9,32:3
Tokyo Joe 1949,O 27,35:2
Great Rupert, The 1950,Ap 14,27:2
Magnet, The 1951,F 27,22:6
Man in the White Suit, The 1952,Ap 1,35:2
Ship That Died of Shame, The 1956,Ag 21,33:2
Prince and the Showgirl 1957,Je 14,22:2
All at Sea 1957,D 23,18:2
Law and Disorder 1958,Ag 6,20:1
Goodwin, Jimmy
Attack! 1956,S 20,29:4
Second to Hell 1959,Jl 18,6:3
Goodwin, John (Original Author)
Avenger, The 1933,O 3,28:3
Goodwin, Laurel
Papa's Delicate Condition 1963,Mr 7,8:5
Goodwin, Leslie (Director)
Radio Stars on Parade 1945,S 22,14:2
Goodwin, Robert
Watusi 1959,Jl 2,15:2
Goodwin, Ruby
View From Pompey's Head, The 1955,N 5,22:5
Goodwin, Thomas
Into the Net 1924,Ag 23,10:2
Goodwins, Leslie (Director)
Crime Ring 1938,Jl 22,10:3
Fugitives for a Night 1938,S 21,30:4
Mr Doodle Kicks Off 1938,S 28,29:4
Tarnished Angel 1938,N 15,27:2
Girl From Mexico, The 1939,Je 8,31:4
Day the Bookies Wept, The 1939,S 14,18:2
Mexican Spitfire 1940,Ja 10,16:4
Sued for Libel 1940,Ja 19,15:3
Millionaire Playboy 1940,Mr 16,8:2
Pop Always Pays 1940,Ag 30,16:6
Men Against the Sky 1940,S 12,31:2
Mexican Spitfire out West 1940,O 30,29:3
Let's Make Music 1941,Ja 23,19:2
Parachute Battalion 1941,Ag 29,13:2
Mexican Spitfire at Sea 1942,Je 26,16:5
Mexican Spitfire Sees a Ghost 1942,Jl 31,11:2
Mexican Spitfire's Elephant 1942,S 18,25:2
Silver Skates 1943,Mr 19,15:3
Ladies' Day 1943,Mr 26,14:3
Gals, Inc 1943,Ag 13,13:4
Murder in the Blue Room 1944,O 28,12:2
Mummy's Curse, The 1945,Mr 31,16:1
Lone Wolf in London, The 1947,N 22,10:3

Goodwins, Leslie (Original Author)
Mexican Spitfire's Elephant 1942,S 18,25:2
Goodwins, Leslie (Screenwriter)
Rainmakers, The 1935,N 2,13:2
Goolden, Richard
School for Husbands 1939,F 7,16:2
Goorney, Howard
Bedazzled 1967,D 11,65:2
Goossens, Ray (Director)
Pinnocchio in Outer Space 1965,D 23,21:4
Gopal, Ram
Outpost in Malaya 1952,N 27,49:2
Purple Plain, The 1955,Ap 11,29:1
Gora, Catherine
Tempest in the Flesh 1957,Ja 19,12:2
Gora, Claudio
Shamed 1949,O 13,33:3
Island of Procida, The 1952,Mr 15,8:2
Tempest 1959,Mr 27,19:2
Slave, The 1963,My 30,20:1
Run With the Devil 1963,Jl 16,25:1
Poupee, La 1963,Ag 28,39:1
Gidget Goes to Rome 1963,S 12,32:2
Easy Life, The 1963,D 23,18:2
Love a la Carte 1965,Ja 12,31:1
Facts of Murder, The 1965,Jl 1,34:1
Tramplers, The 1966,D 8,64:1
Gora, Claudio (Director)
Sky Is Red, The 1952,My 27,30:2
Gora, Claudio (Screenwriter)
Sky Is Red, The 1952,My 27,30:2
Gorashvill, M
Magdana's Donkey 1958,Ja 27,21:7
Gorassini, Annie
Eight and One Half 1963,Je 26,36:1
Successo, Il 1965,Ap 29,40:2
Little Nuns, The 1966,Ap 28,49:1
Gorbachev, I
Inspector General, The 1954,My 3,21:2
Gorbatov, Boris (Original Author)
Taras Family, The 1946,D 9,34:4
Gorbatov, Boris (Screenwriter)
Taras Family, The 1946,D 9,34:4
Miners of the Don 1951,N 12,21:2
Gorbe, Janos
Goose Boy, The 1951,O 13,9:2
Gorbin, Gloria
Torn Curtain 1966,Jl 28,23:1
Gorbunov, G
Red Tanks 1942,Je 6,9:2
Gorcey, Bernard
Abie's Irish Rose 1928,Ap 20,26:7
Great Dictator, The 1940,O 16,29:1
Out of the Fog 1941,Je 21,20:2
No Minor Vices 1949,F 26,11:2
Pickup 1951,Ag 31,12:2
Gorcey, David
Little Tough Guy 1938,Ag 18,23:3
Juvenile Court 1938,S 12,13:2
Little Tough Guys in Society 1938,N 21,14:4
Newsboys' Home 1939,Ja 23,8:2
Sergeant Madden 1939,Mr 24,27:2
Ghost Creeps, The 1940,Ag 19,13:3
Pride of the Bowery 1941,Ja 24,15:2
Flying Wild 1941,Ap 12,19:3
Bowery Blitzkrieg 1941,O 1,24:5
Spooks Run Wild 1941,N 1,20:3
Mr Wise Guy 1942,Mr 5,27:2
Gorcey, Leo
Dead End 1937,Ag 25,25:1
Mannequin 1938,Ja 21,15:2
Crime School 1938,My 11,17:2
Angels With Dirty Faces 1938,N 26,18:1
They Made Me a Criminal 1939,Ja 21,19:2
Hell's Kitchen 1939,Jl 3,10:5
Angels Wash Their Faces 1939,S 4,16:2
Dress Parade 1939,O 28,11:2
Invisible Stripes 1940,Ja 13,11:2
Ghost Creeps, The 1940,Ag 19,13:3
Gallant Sons 1940,D 12,37:2
Pride of the Bowery 1941,Ja 24,15:2
Road to Zanzibar 1941,Ap 10,29:2
Flying Wild 1941,Ap 12,19:3
Out of the Fog 1941,Je 21,20:2
Bowery Blitzkrieg 1941,O 1,24:5
Spooks Run Wild 1941,N 1,20:3
Born to Sing 1942,F 19,23:2
Mr Wise Guy 1942,Mr 5,27:2
Sunday Punch 1942,My 11,19:2
Maisie Gets her Man 1942,Jl 16,23:2
Destroyer 1943,S 2,15:3
Midnight Manhunt 1945,Ag 18,12:5
Gorczunska
Co Moj Maz Robi W Nocy?; What Is my Husband Doing Tonight? 1935,N 29,24:2
Gorde, Eugene (Director)
International Settlement 1938,F 12,20:3
Gordeaux, Paul (Screenwriter)
Crime Does Not Pay (The Fenayrou Case); Fenayrou Case, The (Crime Does Not Pay) 1962,O 17,35:2
Crime Does Not Pay (The Man on the Avenue); Man on the Avenue, The (Crime Does Not Pay) 1962,O 17,35:2

Gordeaux, Paul (Screenwriter) — Cont
Crime Does Not Pay (The Mask); Mask, The
(Crime Does Not Pay) 1962,O 17,35:2
Crime Does Not Pay (The Hugues Case); Hugues
Case, The (Crime Does Not Pay)
1962,O 17,35:2
Gordeichuk, Ludmilla
House With an Attic 1964,D 21,42:5
Gordin, Jacob (Original Author)
Without a Home 1939,Ap 1,17:3
Mirele Efros 1939,O 21,12:2
God, Man and Devil 1950,Ja 23,16:2
Gordin (Director)
Czar and Poet 1928,Ja 15,VIII,5:2 (In Addenda)
Gordine, Sacha (Producer)
Jericho 1946,D 16,31:2
Idiot, The 1948,F 5,26:2
Premier May 1958,S 17,44:2
Black Orpheus 1959,D 22,41:1
Gordon
Go Go Mania 1965,My 20,52:4
Gordon, Alex
Paris Incident 1954,Ag 18,20:2
Gordon, Alex (Producer)
Atomic Submarine, The 1960,Ap 20,45:2
Gordon, Arthur (Original Author)
One Man's Way 1964,Mr 12,40:3
Gordon, Barry
Girl Can't Help It, The 1957,F 9,12:7
Pressure Point 1962,O 11,49:3
Thousand Clowns, A 1965,D 14,54:2
Gordon, Bernard (Screenwriter)
Flesh and Fury 1952,Mr 28,27:4
Crime Wave 1954,Ja 13,26:2
55 Days at Peking 1963,My 30,20:1
Cry of Battle 1963,O 12,27:2
Thin Red Line, The 1964,O 29,38:1
Custer of the West 1968,Jl 4,13:2
Gordon, Bert
New Faces of 1937 1937,Jl 2,25:1
Sing for Your Supper 1941,D 1,15:5
Gordon, Bert I (Director)
Beginning of the End 1957,Jl 4,16:1
Amazing Colossal Man, The 1957,O 26,19:2
Boy and the Pirates, The 1960,N 24,48:3
Picture Mommy Dead 1966,N 3,45:4
Gordon, Bert I (Producer)
Beginning of the End 1957,Jl 4,16:1
Amazing Colossal Man, The 1957,O 26,19:2
Boy and the Pirates, The 1960,N 24,48:3
Picture Mommy Dead 1966,N 3,45:4
Gordon, Bert I (Screenwriter)
Amazing Colossal Man, The 1957,O 26,19:2
Gordon, Bobby
Main Street 1923,Je 12,22:2
Cohens and the Kellys, The 1926,F 23,26:5
Jazz Singer, The 1927,O 7,24:4
Big Business Girl 1931,Je 12,27:1
Counsellor-At-Law 1933,D 8,31:2
Student Tour 1934,O 31,17:3
Gordon, Bruce
Smooth as Satin 1925,Je 23,24:3
Vanishing American, The 1925,O 16,18:2
Born to the West 1926,Je 30,18:1 (In Addenda)
Pals in Paradise 1926,N 24,26:4
Partners in Crime 1928,Ap 30,18:3
Elephant Boy 1937,Ap 6,20:2
Love Happy 1950,Ap 8,9:4
Buccaneer, The 1958,D 24,00:0
Slow Run 1968,O 11,39:1
Gordon, C Henry
Renegades 1930,N 8,21:3
Once a Sinner 1931,Ja 17,23:1
Charlie Chan Carries On 1931,Mr 21,15:1
Black Camel, The 1931,Jl 4,11:5
Woman of Experience, A 1931,Jl 9,26:5
Hush Money 1931,Jl 11,7:6
Young as You Feel 1931,Ag 8,16:3
Mata Hari 1932,Ja 1,31:1
Gay Caballero, The 1932,Mr 26,17:2
Strange Love of Molly Louvain, The
1932,My 9,19:5
Scarface, The Shame of the Nation
1932,My 20,22:3
Doomed Battalion, The 1932,Je 11,9:3
Miss Pinkerton 1932,Jl 9,7:5
Washington Masquerade, The 1932,Jl 22,18:2
Jewel Robbery 1932,Jl 23,6:6
Roar of the Dragon 1932,Jl 25,11:2
Hell's Highway 1932,S 26,18:2
Thirteen Women 1932,O 15,13:1
Scarlet Dawn 1932,N 4,25:4
Kongo 1932,N 17,22:5
Rasputin and the Empress 1932,D 24,11:4
Secret of Madame Blanche, The 1933,F 4,11:3
Whistling in the Dark 1933,F 5,IX,5:1
Clear all Wires 1933,Mr 4,11:2
Gabriel Over the White House 1933,Ap 1,18:2
Made on Broadway 1933,Jl 8,14:5
Storm at Daybreak 1933,Jl 22,14:2
Devil's in Love, The 1933,Jl 28,18:2
Turn Back the Clock 1933,Ag 26,14:2
Penthouse 1933,S 9,9:2
Stage Mother 1933,S 30,18:5

Night Flight 1933,O 7,18:4
Broadway Thru a Keyhole 1933,N 2,18:3
Chief, The 1933,D 2,9:4
Advice to the Lovelorn 1933,D 14,28:2
Fugitive Lovers 1934,Ja 13,16:3
Women in his Life, The 1934,Ja 27,9:3
This Side of Heaven 1934,F 10,21:2
Lazy River 1934,Ap 4,26:2
Men in White 1934,Je 9,18:2
Stamboul Quest 1934,Jl 14,16:6
Hide-Out 1934,Ag 25,16:5
Straight Is the Way 1934,Ag 29,13:2
Death on the Diamond 1934,S 24,14:1
Great Hotel Murder, The 1935,F 28,17:4
Crusades, The 1935,Ag 22,21:3
Big Broadcast of 1936, The 1935,S 16,15:2
Professional Soldier 1936,Ja 30,14:2
Under Two Flags 1936,My 1,19:1
Hollywood Boulevard 1936,S 21,26:4
Big Game, The 1936,O 24,23:1
Charge of the Light Brigade, The 1936,N 2,24:1
Trouble in Morocco 1937,Mr 15,27:1
Charlie Chan at the Olympics 1937,My 24,23:1
Sophie Lang Goes West 1937,S 30,19:2
Trapped by G-Men 1937,N 4,29:1
Conquest 1937,N 5,19:1
Stand-In 1937,N 19,27:2
Tarzan's Revenge 1938,Ja 10,13:3
Black Doll, The 1938,F 7,10:2
Invisible Enemy 1938,Ap 30,18:2
Sharpshooters 1938,D 5,19:2
Adventure in Sahara 1938,D 19,19:2
Man of Conquest 1939,Ap 28,31:2
Return of the Cisco Kid, The 1939,Ap 29,13:2
Charlie Chan in City in Darkness 1939,D 18,29:2
Passport to Alcatraz 1940,Je 15,12:2
Charlie Chan At the Wax Museum 1940,S 28,9:3
Kit Carson 1940,N 15,25:3
Gordon, Charles
Black Book, The 1949,O 17,18:2
Gordon, Christine
I Walked With a Zombie 1943,Ap 22,31:5
Gordon, Claire
Konga 1961,S 16,9:1
Gordon, Clark
Cold Wind in August, A 1961,Jl 27,23:2
Gordon, Colin
Edward my Son 1949,Je 3,21:2
Circle of Danger 1951,Jl 12,21:6
Man in the White Suit, The 1952,Ap 1,35:2
Hour of 13, The 1952,O 28,37:1
Folly to be Wise 1953,D 28,17:2
Heart of the Matter, The 1954,N 19,20:2
Green Man, The 1957,My 23,40:1
Escapade 1957,Ag 6,30:2
Safecracker, The 1958,Mr 6,32:1
One That Got Away, The 1958,Ap 23,40:2
Doctor's Dilemma, A 1958,D 18,2:7
Mouse That Roared, The 1959,O 27,40:1
Virgin Island 1960,Mr 24,39:5
Day They Robbed the Bank of England, The
1960,S 5,11:2
Please Turn Over 1961,Ap 29,12:2
Three on a Spree 1961,Ag 31,22:3
Burn, Witch, Burn 1962,Jl 5,21:2 (In Addenda)
Coming-Out Party, A 1962,Jl 31,19:2
Heavens Above! 1963,My 21,28:2
Pink Panther, The 1964,Ap 24,25:1
Psycopath, The 1966,S 29,60:1
Gordon, Dan (Original Author)
Mr Bug Goes to Town 1942,F 20,21:3
Gordon, Dan (Screenwriter)
Gulliver's Travels 1939,D 21,29:1
Mr Bug Goes to Town 1942,F 20,21:3
Gordon, Don
Silver Fleet, The 1945,Mr 24,22:6
Girls in the Night 1953,Ja 16,19:3
Cry Tough 1959,S 17,48:4
Bullitt 1968,O 18,41:2
Gordon, Donald
Force of Arms 1951,Ag 14,20:2
Gordon, Dorothy
Tonight at 8:30 (Fumed Oak); Fumed Oak
(Tonight at 8:30) 1953,My 26,33:2
Hobson's Choice 1954,Je 15,37:1
Haunted Strangler, The 1958,Jl 4,15:3
Gordon, Douglas
Adventure in Diamonds 1940,Ap 4,27:2
Gordon, Eddie
Lady of Burlesque 1943,My 14,17:2
Gordon, Eva
Chechahcos, The 1924,My 19,14:2
Lost Lady, A 1925,Ja 19,14:1
Gordon, Gale
Here We Go Again 1942,O 12,12:3
Woman of Distinction, A 1950,Mr 17,28:2
Rally Round the Flag Boys! 1958,D 24,2:7
Don't Give up the Ship 1959,Jl 9,22:1
Visit to a Small Planet 1960,Ap 14,34:1
All in a Nights Work 1961,Mr 23,28:1
All Hands on Deck 1961,Ap 1,10:2
Sergeant Deadhead 1965,O 23,17:3
Speedway 1968,Je 14,43:1

Gordon, Gavin
His First Command 1929,D 23,18:2
Romance 1930,Ag 23,7:3
Silver Horde, The 1930,O 25,20:6
Great Meadow, The 1931,Mr 14,23:2
Shipmates 1931,My 23,13:4
Secret Service 1931,D 14,16:3
American Madness 1932,Ag 6,14:5
Two Against the World 1932,Ag 19,20:6
Phantom of Crestwood, The 1932,O 17,18:3
Man Against Woman 1932,D 17,22:3
Bitter Tea of General Yen, The 1933,Ja 12,20:6
Hard to Handle 1933,F 2,21:5
Mystery of the Wax Museum, The
1933,F 18,13:3
Female 1933,N 4,18:3
Scralet Empress, The 1934,S 15,20:2
Happiness Ahead 1934,O 11,28:2
Wake up and Dream 1934,O 11,28:3
Bordertown 1935,Ja 24,22:5
Grand Old Girl 1935,F 26,16:4
Red Hot Tires 1935,Mr 1,16:3
Bride of Frankenstein, The 1935,My 11,21:2
Page Miss Glory 1935,Ag 29,25:2
As You Like It 1936,N 6,29:3
Toast of New York, The 1937,Jl 23,16:2
Murder by Invitation 1941,Jl 23,15:4
Gangs Incorporated 1941,Ag 4,16:6
Centennial Summer 1946,Jl 18,20:2
Knock on Wood 1954,Ap 15,34:2
Vagabond King, The 1956,S 13,39:6
Chicago Confidential 1957,Ag 31,19:1
Matchmaker, The 1958,Ag 13,22:1
Bat, The 1959,D 17,51:4
Gordon, Gay
Room for One More 1952,Ja 16,21:2
Gordon, Gene
Brig, The 1964,S 21,37:4
Gordon, Gloria
My Friend Irma 1949,S 29,39:2
Beneath the 12-Mile Reef 1953,D 17,52:2
Man Called Peter, A 1955,Ap 1,22:1
Gordon, Gordon (Original Author)
Experiment in Terror 1962,Ap 14,14:1
That Darn Cat 1965,D 3,44:1
Gordon, Gordon (Screenwriter)
Down Three Dark Streets 1954,S 4,6:4
Experiment in Terror 1962,Ap 14,14:1
That Darn Cat 1965,D 3,44:1
Gordon, Grace
Butterflies in the Rain 1926,D 25,10:5
Million Bid, A 1927,My 31,25:2
Gordon, Grant
Subject Was Roses, The 1968,O 14,53:2
Gordon, Hal
Dance Band 1936,Ja 4,19:2
We're Going to Be Rich 1938,Jl 4,10:2
Let George Do It 1940,O 14,25:5
It's in the Air 1940,D 10,33:2
Gordon, Harold
Viva Zapata 1952,F 8,19:2
Iron Mistress, The 1952,N 20,39:2
Jazz Singer, The 1953,Ja 14,27:3
East of Eden 1955,Mr 10,33:1
Yellowback 1957,Ap 5,24:2
Gordon, Harris
Dawn of a Tomorrow, The 1924,Mr 26,19:2
Our Daily Bread 1934,O 3,25:2
Gordon, Harry (Composer)
You Can't Have Everything 1937,Ag 4,15:2
Gordon, Hilda (Screenwriter)
Truth About Murder, The 1946,Jl 27,12:6
Gordon, Huntley
Famous Mrs Fair, The 1923,Ap 23,18:3
Bluebeard's 8th Wife 1923,Ag 7,20:2
Pleasure Mad 1924,Ja 7,23:1
Shadows of Paris 1924,F 18,13:1
True as Steel 1924,Je 17,22:4
Enemy Sex, The 1924,Jl 1,21:4
Married Flirts 1924,N 19,19:3
My Wife and I 1925,My 20,26:2
Never the Twain Shall Meet 1925,Jl 29,24:4
Love Hour, The 1925,S 2,21:3
Wife Who Wasn't Wanted, The 1925,S 9,23:1
Golden Cocoon, The 1925,D 15,14:5
Other Women's Husbands 1926,Ap 27,23:2
Silken Shackles 1926,My 25,25:1
Don't Tell the Wife 1927,F 22,23:2
Sensation Seekers 1927,Mr 16,28:2
Certain Young Man, A 1928,Je 11,27:1
Our Dancing Daughters 1928,O 8,14:2
Sinners in Love 1928,N 19,16:7
Outcast 1928,N 26,30:2
Scandal 1929,Ap 22,23:1
Melody Lane 1929,Jl 16,23:5
Marriage Playground, The 1929,D 14,22:4
New Movietone Follies of 1930, The
1930,Je 21,20:5
Anybody's Woman 1930,Ag 16,8:3
Night World 1932,My 28,18:2
Red-Haired Alibi 1932,O 24,18:5
Sailor Be Good 1933,F 27,11:2
Racetrack 1933,Mr 6,16:6

Gordon, Huntley — Cont

Corruption 1933,Je 20,22:7
Dancing Man 1934,Jl 16,11:3
Their big Moment 1934,S 6,22:4
It Happened in New York 1935,Ap 6,10:1
Yours for the Asking 1936,Ag 20,14:2
Daniel Boone 1936,O 24,23:2
Idol of the Crowd 1937,D 4,21:1
Mister Wong in Chinatown 1939,Jl 31,9:2 (In Addenda)

Gordon, Huntly

Other Men's Wives 1926,My 2,VIII,5:3 (In Addenda)

Gordon, Jack

Crime Incorporated 1945,Je 23,9:7

Gordon, James

Wanderer of the Wasteland, The 1924,Jl 8,14:2
Iron Horse, The 1924,Ag 29,6:1
Man Who Came Back, The 1924,S 1,9:1
Tumbleweeds 1925,D 21,27:2
Social Highwayman, The 1926,Je 15,23:3
Publicity Madness 1927,D 12,30:6
Escape, The 1928,My 7,29:1
Bachelor Father, The 1931,F 2,23:1
Front Page, The 1931,Mr 20,29:1

Gordon, James B (Original Author)

Don't Knock the Rock 1957,F 23,13:1

Gordon, James B (Screenwriter)

Inside Detroit 1956,Ja 28,10:5
Twist Around the Clock 1962,Ja 27,13:4
Don't Knock the Twist 1962,Ap 14,14:2
Hold On! 1966,Je 23,29:4

Gordon, Joan

Queen of Sheba 1921,Ap 11,9:1

Gordon, John

Circle, The 1959,Ap 16,29:2

Gordon, John (Screenwriter)

Siege of Leningrad 1943,F 11,22:4

Gordon, John J (Director)

This Is Your Army 1954,D 15,41:1

Gordon, Julia Swayne

Hellotrope 1920,N 29,20:3
You Can't Fool Your Wife 1923,Ap 24,25:3
Scaramouche 1923,O 12,7:2 (Incorrect in this edition; use 1927,O 1,7:2 elsewhere)
Lights of Old Broadway 1925,N 2,20:1
Bride of the Storm 1926,Ap 5,24:1
Diplomacy 1926,S 13,18:1
Children of Divorce 1927,Ap 26,33:3
Wings 1927,Ag 13,10:4
13 Washington Square 1928,Ja 30,18:1
Smart Set, The 1928,Mr 5,21:1
Viking, The 1928,N 29,32:4
Three Week Ends 1928,D 10,25:1
Scandal 1929,Ap 22,23:1
Gold Diggers of Broadway, The 1929,Ag 31,13:4
Is Everybody Happy? 1929,N 2,14:6
Dumbbells in Ermine 1930,Jl 28,22:1
Secrets of the French Police 1932,D 12,18:4
Hello, Everybody 1933,Ja 30,9:4

Gordon, Kilbourn (Original Author)

West of Zanzibar 1928,D 31,9:1
Kongo 1932,N 17,22:5

Gordon, Leo

Hondo 1953,N 27,99:9
All the Brothers Were Valiant 1953,D 29,19:2
Riot in Cell Block 11 1954,F 19,24:5
Seven Angry Men 1955,Ap 2,15:2
Soldier of Fortune 1955,My 28,7:4
Tennessee's Partner 1955,N 5,22:8
Man With the Gun 1955,D 23,14:2
Steel Jungle, The 1956,Mr 10,9:5
Conqueror, The 1956,Mr 31,13:3
Great Day in the Morning 1956,My 19,12:6
Baby Face Nelson 1957,D 12,35:1
Black Patch 1958,Ap 24,38:1
Intruder, The 1962,My 15,48:1
Tarzan Goes to India 1962,S 6,37:2
King of the Sun 1963,D 26,33:4
Haunted Palace, The 1964,Ja 30,24:1
Beau Geste 1966,S 8,43:1
Tobruk 1967,F 9,33:2
Devil's Angels 1967,O 5,46:1

Gordon, Leo (Screenwriter)

Black Patch 1958,Ap 24,38:1
Tobruk 1967,F 9,33:2

Gordon, Leon

Sandra 1924,D 22,20:2

Gordon, Leon (Original Author)

Garden of Weeds, The 1924,N 4,24:1
White Cargo 1930,F 24,18:1
Transatlantic Merry-Go-Round 1934,N 1,25:2
Stolen Harmony 1935,Ap 20,16:2
I Love You Again 1940,Ag 16,11:2
White Cargo 1942,N 27,27:2

Gordon, Leon (Producer)

Mrs Parkington 1944,O 13,16:1
Green Years, The 1946,Ap 5,21:2
That Forsyte Woman 1949,N 11,31:2
Kim 1950,D 8,40:4

Gordon, Leon (Screenwriter)

Stolen Harmony 1935,Ap 20,16:2
Age of Indiscretion 1935,My 18,21:2
Unguarded Hour, The 1936,Ap 4,11:1

His Brother's Wife 1936,Ag 15,6:2
Last of Mrs Cheyney, The 1937,F 19,15:1
Society Lawyer 1939,Mr 31,19:2
Balalaika 1939,D 15,33:2
Broadway Melody of 1940 1940,Mr 29,25:3
They Met in Bombay 1941,Jl 4,17:1
White Cargo 1942,N 27,27:2
Kim 1950,D 8,40:4
Hour of 13, The 1952,O 28,37:1

Gordon, Mack

Sitting Pretty 1933,D 2,9:3
Collegiate 1936,Ja 23,25:2
You're my Everything 1949,Jl 23,7:2

Gordon, Mack (Composer)

Smiling Faces 1932,Ag 31,12:3
Broadway Thru a Keyhole 1933,N 2,18:3
White Woman 1933,N 18,18:5
Sitting Pretty 1933,D 2,9:3
We're not Dressing 1934,Ap 26,27:2
Shoot the Works 1934,Jl 7,16:5
Old-Fashioned Way, The 1934,Jl 14,16:5
She Loves Me Not 1934,S 8,18:5
Now and Forever 1934,O 13,10:1
Gay Divorcee, The 1934,N 16,27:1
College Rhythm 1934,N 24,19:1
Stolen Harmony 1935,Ap 20,16:2
Love in Bloom 1935,Ap 20,16:2
Big Broadcast of 1936, The 1935,S 16,15:2
Head Over Heels in Love 1937,F 13,9:1
Wake up and Live 1937,Ap 24,16:2
This Is my Affair 1937,My 28,17:1
Thin Ice 1937,S 4,8:2
Ali Baba Goes to Town 1937,O 23,14:1
Love and Hisses 1938,Ja 1,11:1
In Old Chicago 1938,Ja 7,15:2
Sally, Irene and Mary 1938,F 26,9:2
Rebecca of Sunnybrook Farm 1938,Mr 26,12:1
Josette 1938,Je 11,9:1
Love Finds Andy Hardy 1938,Jl 22,10:2
My Lucky Star 1938,S 10,20:2
Hold That Co-ed 1938,S 24,13:1
Thanks For Everything 1938,D 10,13:2
Rose of Washington Square 1939,My 6,21:2
Lillian Russell 1940,My 18,11:2
Young People 1940,Ag 24,16:2
Down Argentine Way 1940,O 18,25:1
Tin Pan Alley 1940,N 22,27:3
That Night in Rio 1941,Mr 10,21:2
Great American Broadcast, The 1941,My 2,25:2
Dance Hall 1941,Jl 19,16:2
Sun Valley Serenade 1941,S 6,20:1
Week-End in Havana 1941,N 8,11:2
Song of the Islands 1942,Mr 12,24:4
Orchestra Wives 1942,S 24,23:2
Iceland 1942,O 15,27:1
Springtime in the Rockies 1942,N 12,30:2
Sweet Rosie O'Grady 1943,O 21,30:2
Pin Up Girl 1944,My 11,25:6
Billy Rose's Diamond Horseshoe 1945,My 3,37:1
Dolly Sisters, The 1945,N 15,24:6
Three Little Girls in Blue 1946,S 26,32:3
Mother Wore Tights 1947,Ag 21,33:2
Call Me Mister 1951,F 1,21:2

Gordon, Mack (Miscellaneous)

Paris in Spring 1935,Jl 13,16:2
Two for Tonight 1935,Ag 31,16:2
Collegiate 1936,Ja 23,25:2
Poor Little Rich Girl, The 1936,Je 26,16:1
Stowaway 1936,D 19,16:1

Gordon, Mack (Producer)

Three Little Girls in Blue 1946,S 26,32:3

Gordon, Marjorie

After You, Comrade 1967,Ap 11,54:1

Gordon, Mary

Home Maker, The 1925,Ag 10,8:2
Clancy's Kosher Wedding 1927,S 7,35:2
Black Camel, The 1931,Jl 4,11:5
Little Minister, The 1934,D 28,25:1
Vanessa: Her Love Story 1935,Ap 13,11:3
Bride of Frankenstein, The 1935,My 11,21:2
Irish in US, The 1935,Ag 1,15:1
Laughing Irish Eyes 1936,Ag 4,11:2
Forgotten Faces 1936,Jl 4,18:2
Mary of Scotland 1936,Jl 31,22:2
Great Guy 1937,Ja 1,19:2
Plough and the Stars, The 1937,Ja 29,15:1
Great O'Malley, The 1937,Mr 6,10:1
Double Wedding 1937,O 22,27:2
Lady Behave 1938,Ja 28,17:3
Kidnapped 1938,My 28,9:2
City Streets 1938,Jl 25,18:2
Hound of the Baskervilles, The 1939,Mr 25,19:2
Captain Fury 1939,My 26,20:2
Adventures of Sherlock Holmes, The 1939,S 2,20:1
Parents on Trial 1939,S 18,15:5
Rulers of the Sea 1939,N 9,27:1
Joe and Ethel Turp Call on the President 1940,Ja 4,19:2
Tear Gas Squad 1940,My 31,15:3
When the Daltons Rode 1940,Ag 23,13:3
No, No, Nanette 1940,D 20,33:1
Flight From Destiny 1941,Mr 28,26:7

Gordon, Mary — Cont

Pot o'Gold 1941,Ap 4,25:2
Appointment for Love 1941,N 7,27:1
Bombay Clipper 1942,Ja 12,23:3
Powder Town 1942,Je 8,11:2
Sherlock Holmes and the Voice Of Terror 1942,S 19,9:2
Mummy's Tomb, The 1942,O 26,19:2
Sherlock Holmes and the Secret Weapon 1943,Ja 5,15:2
Sarong Girl 1943,Je 18,16:6
Two Tickets to London 1943,Jl 3,11:2
Sherlock Holmes Faces Death 1943,O 8,15:3
Spider Woman 1944,Ja 17,14:5
Hour Before the Dawn, The 1944,My 11,25:6
See my Lawyer 1945,My 4,23:4
Woman in Green, The 1945,Je 16,10:3
Strange Confession 1945,N 8,17:3
Sentimental Journey 1946,Mr 7,33:2
Little Giant 1946,My 9,27:5
Hoodlum Saint, The 1946,Je 27,29:1
Invisible Wall, The 1947,N 1,11:2

Gordon, Maude Turner

Homeward Bound 1923,Jl 31,12:4
Little French Girl, The 1925,Je 1,10:3
Cheating Cheaters 1927,D 6,27:1
Home Made 1927,D 13,33:2
Sporting Goods 1928,F 13,16:2
Just Married 1928,Ag 13,23:2
Glad Rag Doll, The 1929,Je 3,27:2
Illusion 1929,S 28,17:3
Marriage Playground, The 1929,D 14,22:4
Sally 1929,D 24,14:4
Florodora Girl, The 1930,My 31,19:4
Ladies' Man 1931,My 1,30:3
Shopworn 1932,Ap 4,13:6
Back Street 1932,Ag 29,9:2
She Loves Me Not 1934,S 8,18:5
Living on Velvet 1935,Mr 8,25:4

Gordon, Max (Producer)

Abe Lincoln in Illinois 1940,F 23,19:2
My Sister Eileen 1942,O 23,15:1

Gordon, Michael (Director)

Crime Doctor 1943,Jl 5,11:4
Web, The 1947,Je 5,32:1
Another Part of the Forest 1948,My 19,30:2
Live Today for Tomorrow 1948,D 6,29:2
Lady Gambles, The 1949,My 21,9:2
Woman in Hiding 1950,F 23,33:2
Cyrano De Bergerac 1950,N 17,31:2
I Can Get It for You Wholesale 1951,Ap 5,34:4
Secret of Convict Lake, The 1951,Ag 4,7:2
Wherever She Goes 1953,Ja 28,24:4
Pillow Talk 1959,O 7,47:2
Portrait in Black 1960,Jl 28,19:1
Boys' Night Out 1962,Je 22,15:2
For Love or Money 1963,Ag 8,19:1
Move Over Darling 1963,D 26,33:1
Very Special Favor, A 1965,Ag 26,40:3
Texas Across the River 1966,N 24,65:1
Impossible Years, The 1968,D 6,54:1

Gordon, Michael (Original Author)

Wherever She Goes 1953,Ja 28,24:4

Gordon, Michael (Producer)

Wherever She Goes 1953,Ja 28,24:4

Gordon, Michael (Screenwriter)

All Over the Town 1949,My 26,34:4

Gordon, Mildred (Original Author)

Experiment in Terror 1962,Ap 14,14:1
That Darn Cat 1965,D 3,44:1

Gordon, Mildred (Screenwriter)

Down Three Dark Streets 1954,S 4,6:4
Experiment in Terror 1962,Ap 14,14:1
That Darn Cat 1965,D 3,44:1

Gordon, Noele

Facts of Love, The 1949,O 31,20:2

Gordon, Nora

Fallen Idol, The 1949,N 16,39:2

Gordon, Phyllis

Another Thin Man 1939,N 24,29:1

Gordon, R Wells

Howards of Virginia, The 1940,S 27,27:1

Gordon, Richard

13 Rue Madeleine 1947,Ja 16,30:2

Gordon, Richard (Original Author)

Doctor in the House 1955,F 19,18:3
Doctor at Sea 1956,Mr 1,37:3
Doctor at Large 1957,Jl 29,15:5
Captain's Table, The 1960,S 27,40:1
Doctor in Love 1962,Ap 27,27:2

Gordon, Richard (Screenwriter)

Doctor in the House 1955,F 19,18:3
Doctor at Sea 1956,Mr 1,37:3

Gordon, Robert (Director)

Joe Louis Story, The 1953,N 4,29:4
Black Zoo 1963,My 16,42:1

Gordon, Roy

Cocoanut Grove 1938,Je 16,21:2
Campus Confessions 1938,S 23,35:1
Great Man Votes, The 1939,Ja 20,15:2
Boy Slaves 1939,F 9,17:3
Spellbinder, The 1939,Ag 24,17:3
Real Glory, The 1939,S 15,26:2
Sued for Libel 1940,Ja 19,15:3

Gordon, Roy — Cont
Lone Wolf Strikes, The 1940,F 5,13:2
Boom Town 1940,S 6,25:2
Night of January 16th, The 1941,D 19,35:1
Powder Town 1942,Je 8,11:2
What's Buzzin Cousin 1943,Jl 23,21:4
Take It or Leave It 1944,Jl 13,14:2
Caribbean Mystery, The 1945,Ag 20,22:4
Titanic 1953,My 28,27:5
Sangaree 1953,Je 5,19:1
So This Is Love 1953,Ag 12,22:1
Crooked Web, The 1955,D 10,19:1
Slightly Scarlet 1956,Mr 17,13:2
Gordon, Roy Turner
Palm Beach Girl, The 1926,Je 22,21:2
Gordon, Ruth
Abe Lincoln in Illinois 1940,F 23,19:2
Dr Ehrlich's Magic Bullet 1940,F 24,9:2
Two Faced Woman 1942,Ja 1,37:2
Edge of Darkness 1943,Ap 10,12:4
Action in the North Atlantic 1943,My 22,10:2
Inside Daisy Clover 1966,F 18,23:1
Lord Love a Duck 1966,F 22,14:6
Rosemary's Baby 1968,Je 13,57:1
Gordon, Ruth (Original Author)
Over 21 1945,Ag 17,20:2
Actress, The 1953,O 13,34:1
Gordon, Ruth (Screenwriter)
Double Life, A 1948,F 20,19:1
Adam's Rib 1949,D 26,33:2
Marrying Kind, The 1952,Mr 14,27:1
Pat and Mike 1952,Je 19,32:6
Actress, The 1953,O 13,34:1
Rosie 1968,F 8,36:1
Gordon, Sidney
Behind Closed Shutters 1952,Je 10,22:7
Gordon, Susan
Five Pennies, The 1959,Je 19,30:1
Boy and the Pirates, The 1960,N 24,48:3
Picture Mommy Dead 1966,N 3,45:4
Gordon, Vera
Humoresque 1920,My 31,14:2
North Wind's Malice, The 1920,O 18,13:1
Potash and Perlmutter 1923,S 24,5:4
In Hollywood with Potash and Perlmutter 1924,S 30,27:3
Cohens and the Kellys, The 1926,F 23,26:5
Sweet Daddies 1926,Je 23,28:1
Kosher Kitty Kelly 1926,S 28,30:2
Private Izzy Murphy 1926,N 10,25:1
Cohens and the Kellys In Paris, The 1928,F 6,12:3
Four Walls 1928,Ag 20,21:3
Cohens and the Kellys In Atlantic City, The 1929,Mr 18,30:6
Cohens and Kellys in Africa, The 1930,D 20,20:6
Fifty Million Frenchmen 1931,Mr 26,31:2
Big Street, The 1942,Ag 14,13:1
Abie's Irish Rose 1946,D 23,19:4
Gordon, William (Original Author)
Back to Bataan 1945,S 13,26:3
Gordon, William D (Screenwriter)
Sergeant Ryker 1968,Mr 21,56:2
Gordon, Zita
Az uj Foeldesur 1936,S 22,30:5
Gordy, John
Paper Lion 1968,O 24,54:1
Gore, Claudio
Made in Italy 1967,My 1,44:2
Gore, Laura
His Young Wife 1949,Mr 12,10:2
Voice of Love, The 1950,Ja 7,11:2
Peddlin' in Society 1950,F 23,33:3
Gore, Lesley
Ski Party 1965,O 23,17:3
Gore, Rosa
Madonna of the Streets 1924,O 28,23:4
Seven Days 1925,Ag 31,19:3
Lovey Mary 1926,Je 21,17:2
Gore-Browne, R (Original Author)
Cynara 1932,D 26,26:2
Key, The 1934,My 30,14:3
Gorecka, Antonina
Last Stop, The 1949,Mr 22,31:2
Gorecka, Tatjana
Last Stop, The 1949,Mr 22,31:2
Gorelov, V
School of Courage 1957,S 9,21:2
Goreva, Olga
Dark Is The Night 1946,Mr 18,24:3
Gorgemo, Guiseppe (Original Author)
Outcry 1949,Mr 14,15:5
Gorham, Charles
In the Palace of the King 1923,D 3,14:1
Gori, Claudio
White Voices; Voci Blanche 1965,Ap 13,32:2
Gori, Gorella
Roman Holiday 1953,Ag 28,13:1
Gori, Mario Cecchi (Producer)
Love and Larceny 1963,F 2,5:6
Easy Life, The 1963,D 23,18:2
Let's Talk About Women 1964,S 29,52:5
Successo, Il 1965,Ap 29,40:2
Tiger and the Pussycat, The 1967,S 21,56:4

Devil in Love, The 1968,Jl 4,13:4
Goricheva, M M
Prisoners 1937,F 20,9:2
Gorikker, Vladimir (Director)
Yolanta 1964,D 23,22:3
Tsar's Bride, The 1966,Mr 12,13:2
Gorikker, Vladimir (Producer)
Tsar's Bride, The 1966,Mr 12,13:2
Gorikker, Vladimir (Screenwriter)
Tsar's Bride, The 1966,Mr 12,13:2
Gorin, Charles Igor
Broadway Melody of 1938 1937,S 3,12:1
Gorin, Gabriel
Mademoiselle 1966,Ag 2,23:1
Gorin, Helmuth
Ace of Aces 1933,N 11,10:4
Gorin, Igor
Merry Wives of Windsor, The 1966,F 28,21:1
Goring, Marius
Rembrandt 1936,D 3,31:1
Dead Men Tell no Tales 1939,Jl 24,9:2
U-Boat 29 1939,O 6,31:3
Pastor Hall 1940,S 21,13:2
Frightened Lady 1941,N 10,21:3
Stairway to Heaven 1946,D 26,28:1
Red Shoes, The 1948,O 23,9:2
Mr Perrin and Mr Traill 1949,Ja 17,15:2
Take my Life 1949,Ja 19,34:2
Odette 1951,Mr 28,33:2
Circle of Danger 1951,Jl 12,21:6
Pandora and the Flying Dutchman 1951,D 7,35:2
Paris Express, The 1953,Je 6,8:6
So Little Time 1953,Jl 28,23:2
Barefoot Contessa, The 1954,S 30,37:1
Quentin Durward 1955,N 24,41:1
Night Ambush 1958,Ap 25,32:4
Truth About Women, The 1958,Ag 29,18:2
Angry Hills, The 1959,Jl 16,31:3
Exodus 1960,D 16,44:1
Lisa 1962,My 25,28:1
Crooked Road, The 1965,F 4,24:2
Up From the Beach 1965,Je 10,38:1
25th Hour, The 1967,F 17,45:1
Girl on a Motorcycle, The 1968,N 28,66:5
Goringoryanof, B
Czar wants to Sleep, The 1934,D 10,16:3
Gorini, Arianna
Blood and Black Lace 1965,N 11,58:3
Goritcheva, A D
Laughter Through Tears 1933,N 13,21:2
Goriunov, A
Paris Commune 1937,Je 2,20:4
Gorky, Maxim
Soviets on Parade 1933,Mr 6,16:7
Gorky, Maxim (Original Author)
Cain and Artem 1930,Je 7,10:4
Lower Depths, The 1937,S 11,20:1
Childhood of Maxim Gorky 1938,S 28,29:3
On his Own 1939,S 13,31:3
University of Life 1941,F 26,17:1
Lower Depths, The 1947,D 1,27:2
Mistress, The 1954,My 31,9:2
1905 1956,Jl 9,27:2
Malva 1957,D 23,18:2
Gordeyev Family, The 1961,O 16,33:6
Lower Depths, The 1962,F 10,12:5
Chelkash 1964,Ja 27,19:1
Gorley, Edward
Nell Gwyn 1926,Jl 19,13:1
Gorlin, Helga
John Ericsson Victor of Hampton Roads 1938,My 18,17:2
Gorlin-Hilton, Helga
Karl Fredrik Reigns 1938,F 2,15:2
Gorling, Lars (Director)
Guilt 1967,N 21,53:1
Gorling, Lars (Original Author)
491 1967,D 21,45:1
Gorling, Lars (Screenwriter)
Guilt 1967,N 21,53:1
491 1967,D 21,45:1
Gorlitzhi, Illy (Narrator)
Six Days to Eternity 1968,O 31,54:3
Gorlov, N
Ballad of Cossack Gloota, The 1938,F 28,19:1
On his Own 1939,S 13,31:3
Last Hill, The 1945,Je 26,13:2
Gorman, Annette
Five Finger Exercise 1962,Ap 20,20:2
Gorman, Bill
Finders Keepers 1928,Mr 5,21:3
Gorman, Charles
Gay Retreat, The 1927,O 10,24:1
Gorman, Eric
Saints and Sinners 1949,S 12,17:2
Quiet Man, The 1952,Ag 22,13:1
Rising of the Moon, The (The Majesty of the Law); Majesty of the Law, The (The Rising of the Moon) 1957,Jl 10,23:1
Gorman, Herbert (Original Author)
Suzy 1936,Jl 25,16:1

Gorman, Roger (Director)
Masque of the Red Death, The 1964,S 17,52:6
Gorman, Roger (Producer)
Masque of the Red Death, The 1964,S 17,52:6
Gorman, Shay
Eyes of Annie Jones, The 1964,My 14,39:1
Gorn, Lester (Screenwriter)
Beginning of the End 1957,Jl 4,16:1
Gorney, Jay (Composer)
Moonlight and Pretzels 1933,Ag 23,21:2
Take a Chance 1933,N 27,20:3
Jimmy and Sally 1933,D 16,12:3
Stand up and Cheer 1934,Ap 20,17:1
Romance in the Rain 1934,S 8,18:5
Heat's on, The 1943,N 26,29:2
Gorney, Jay (Miscellaneous)
Romance in the Dark 1938,Mr 21,18:2
Gorney, Jay (Original Author)
Romance in the Rain 1934,S 8,18:5
Gorney, Jay (Screenwriter)
College Holiday 1936,D 24,21:2
Gorog, L (Original Author)
Affairs of Susan, The 1945,Mr 29,18:2
Gorog, L (Screenwriter)
Tales of Manhattan 1942,S 25,25:1
Affairs of Susan, The 1945,Mr 29,18:2
Murder in the Music Hall 1946,Ap 15,22:2
Of Love and Desire 1963,S 12,32:1
Gorse, Saul
Love Begins at 20 1936,S 19,20:1
Gorsen, Norah
Wee Geordie 1956,O 8,31:1
Gorshin, Frank
Portland Expose 1957,S 27,16:6
Bells Are Ringing 1960,Je 24,31:2
Studs Lonigan 1960,D 15,59:1
Where the Boys Are 1961,Ja 20,22:1
Great Impostor, The 1961,Mr 30,24:1
Ring of Fire 1961,Ag 17,18:2
Sail a Crooked Ship 1962,F 3,12:6
George Raft Story, The 1962,Mr 22,40:1
That Darn Cat 1965,D 3,44:1
Batman 1966,Ag 25,42:4
Gorska, Lala
Jego Wielka Milosc 1936,Mr 24,27:5
Gorski, Peter (Director)
Faust 1963,Ap 16,31:1
Gorsline, Anthony
One-Way Ticket to Hell 1955,D 8,45:1
Gorss, Sol
Flowing Gold 1940,S 2,19:3
Gorst, Eldon
Mill On the Floss, The 1939,N 15,19:3
Exile, The 1947,D 26,22:4
Gorstle, Frank
Slightly Scarlet 1956,Mr 17,13:2
Gort, Alberto (Screenwriter)
St Francis of Assisi 1947,Ap 5,12:5
Gorvin, Joana Maria
Original Sin, The 1950,Ag 21,15:2
Goryunof, A
Petersburg Nights 1934,S 10,20:4
Anna 1936,Jl 17,20:2
Revolutionists 1936,D 26,15:3
Boule de Suif 1958,My 5,24:1
Goryunof, Anatoli
Tovaristchi 1935,My 25,12:2
Gosch, Martin A (Original Author)
Abbott and Costello in Hollywood 1945,N 23,26:2
Gosch, Martin A (Producer)
Abbott and Costello in Hollywood 1945,N 23,26:2
Gosden, Freeman F
Check and Double Check 1930,N 1,23:1 (In Addenda)
Gosfield, Maurice
Teenage Millionaire 1962,Ja 12,29:2
Gosho, Heinosuke (Director)
Daughter of Two Fathers, A 1929,Mr 12,26:3
Goskind, S (Director)
Al Khet; I Have Sinned 1937,S 9,19:2
Goslar, Jurgen
Aren't We Wonderful? 1959,O 16,27:1
Gosnell, Evelyn
Under the Red Robe 1923,N 13,25:3
Goss, Helen
Wicked Lady, The 1946,D 23,19:5
Place of One's Own, A 1949,F 8,30:2
Pink String and Sealing Wax 1950,O 4,38:2
Outpost in Malaya 1952,N 27,49:2
Goss, James
Subway Express 1931,My 2,23:4
Goss, Walter
Fine Manners 1926,Ag 30,10:3
Fireman, Save My Child 1927,O 10,24:1
Gossage, John W (Producer)
Angels One Five 1954,Ap 30,28:2
Gosset, Georges
Face to the Wind 1951,Ja 16,34:2
Gosset, Gerald
Pardon my French 1952,Mr 31,17:2

Gosset, Pierre (Original Author)
Cinerama Holiday 1955,F 9,31:1
Gosset, Renee (Original Author)
Cinerama Holiday 1955,F 9,31:1
Gosset, Viviane
Babette Goes to War 1960,Je 8,46:1
Gossett, Charles
Greenwich Village Story 1963,Jl 12,14:3
Gossett, Louis
Raisin in the Sun, A 1961,Mr 30,24:1
Goszkowski, Henry Cpl
Cease Fire! 1953,N 25,17:1
Got, Archie
Thunder Birds 1942,O 29,19:2
Got, Roland
Across the Pacific 1942,S 5,9:2
Gotell, Walter
Desperate Moment 1953,S 1,19:4
Road to Hong Kong, The 1962,Je 28,21:1
From Russia with Love 1964,Ap 9,25:1
Lord Jim 1965,F 26,18:1
These Are the Damned 1965,Jl 8,35:1
Gotfurt, Frederick (Screenwriter)
Temptation Harbor 1949,My 11,34:7
Goth, Sandor
Borcsa Amerikaben; Barbara in America
1939,F 11,13:2
Gothard, Michael
Up the Junction 1968,Mr 14,51:1
Gothie, Robert
Palm Springs Weekend 1963,N 6,32:1
Goto, James T
Gallant Hours, The 1960,Je 23,19:4
Goto, Shikeaki
Angry Island 1960,F 28,31:1
Gotovzev, V
1812 1944,S 11,14:1
Gott, Barbara
Mystery at the Villa Rose 1930,Je 2,25:4
Beloved Vagabond, The 1937,F 8,12:5
Gottafavi, Vittorio (Screenwriter)
Legions of the Nile 1961,Mr 4,16:1
Gottel, Oscar
Greed 1924,D 5,28:1
Gottel, Otto
Greed 1924,D 5,28:1
Gotthardt, Eva
Seven Journeys 1951,Mr 12,20:2
Gottler, Archie
William Fox Movietone Follies of 1929
1929,My 27,22:1
Gottler, Archie (Composer)
Wine, Women and Song 1934,Mr 21,24:3
Tin Pan Alley 1940,N 22,27:3
Silver Skates 1943,Mr 19,15:3
Gottler, Archie (Miscellaneous)
William Fox Movietone Follies of 1929
1929,My 27,22:1
I Like It That Way 1934,Ap 18,23:3
Gottlieb, Alex (Miscellaneous)
I Stand Accused 1939,Ja 5,17:1
Gottlieb, Alex (Original Author)
Convicted Woman 1940,F 26,11:2
Meet the Wildcat 1940,O 23,27:2
Horror Island 1941,Mr 31,11:3
Mystery Ship 1941,Ag 16,18:3
I Live on Danger 1942,Ag 22,16:2
Susan Slept Here 1954,Jl 30,9:1
Three Hours to Kill 1954,S 4,6:4
Gottlieb, Alex (Producer)
It Ain't Hay 1943,Mr 11,17:3
Hit the Ice 1943,S 23,27:2
Janie 1944,Ag 5,16:2
Hollywood Canteen 1944,D 16,19:2
Escape in the Desert 1945,My 12,10:2
Janie Gets Married 1946,Je 15,24:2
Two Guys From Milwaukee 1946,Jl 27,12:5
Time; The Place And The Girl, The
1946,D 27,14:3
Stallion Road 1947,Ap 5,12:5
That Hagen Girl 1947,O 25,13:2
Always Together 1947,D 11,46:1
Wallflower 1948,Je 12,8:5
Romance on the High Seas 1948,Je 26,10:5
Girl from Jones Beach, The 1949,Jl 30,9:2
It's a Great Feeling 1949,Ag 13,6:6
Jack and the Beanstalk 1952,Ap 8,35:3
Macao 1952,My 1,34:2
Fighter, The 1952,My 31,12:6
Blue Gardenia, The 1953,Ap 28,31:1
Gottlieb, Alex (Screenwriter)
Invisible Enemy 1938,Ap 30,18:2
Arson Racket Squad 1938,Je 18,18:2
Gambling Ship 1939,Ja 21,19:2
Fugitive From Justice, A 1940,Jl 8,13:3
Meet the Wildcat 1940,O 23,27:2
Dark Streets of Cairo 1940,D 2,19:3
Meet the Chump 1941,F 27,23:4
Susan Slept Here 1954,Jl 30,9:1
Frankie and Johnny 1966,Jl 21,20:2
Gottlieb, M L
Stars of the Russian Ballet (The Flames of Paris);
Flames of Paris, The (Stars of the Russian
Ballet) 1954,S 6,9:2

Gottlieb, Theodore
So Dark the Night 1946,D 7,16:2
Gottowt
Three Way Works, The 1926,Mr 19,25:1
Gottschalk, Ferdinand
Zaza 1923,S 17,18:2
Tonight or Never 1931,D 18,29:2
Grand Hotel 1932,Ap 13,23:2
Sign of the Cross, The 1932,D 1,25:1
Grand Slam 1933,F 22,25:2
Girl Missing 1933,Ap 1,18:2
Parole Girl 1933,Ap 10,8:2
Warrior's Husband, The 1933,My 12,20:4
Ex-Lady 1933,My 15,16:2
Gold Diggers of 1933 1933,Je 8,22:3
She Had to Say Yes 1933,Jl 29,14:2
Midnight Club 1933,Jl 29,14:2
Berkeley Square 1933,S 14,26:2
Female 1933,N 4,18:3
Bombay Mail 1934,Ja 6,18:2
Long Lost Father 1934,F 19,18:2
Gambling Lady 1934,Ap 5,25:2
Witching Hour, The 1934,Ap 28,11:3
Upper World 1934,My 25,25:4
Notorious Sophie Lang, The 1934,Jl 21,14:2
Madame Du Barry 1934,O 25,26:2
I Sell Anything 1934,D 27,25:2
I am a Thief 1935,Ja 1,24:1
Man Who Reclaimed his Head, The
1935,Ja 9,22:1
Clive of India 1935,Ja 18,29:1
Sing Sing Nights 1935,Ja 26,13:2
Night Life of the Gods 1935,F 23,14:6
Folies Bergere 1935,F 25,13:2
Miserables, Les 1935,Ap 22,14:2
Break of Hearts 1935,My 17,24:3
Vagabond Lady 1935,Je 15,20:2
Gay Deception, The 1935,O 11,31:1
Melody Lingers on, The 1935,N 7,27:1
Man Who Broke the Bank at Monte Carlo, The
1935,N 15,20:2
Bunker Bean 1936,Je 27,21:2
Man I Marry, The 1936,O 31,24:3
That Girl From Paris 1937,Ja 1,19:1
Crime Nobody Saw, The 1937,Ap 5,17:2
Cafe Metropole 1937,Ap 29,17:1
Ali Baba Goes to Town 1937,O 23,14:1
I'll Take Romance 1937,D 17,33:2
Romance in the Dark 1938,Mr 21,18:2
Josette 1938,Je 11,9:1
Adventures of Marco Polo, The 1965,Ap 8,17:2
Gottschalk, Joachim
Aufruhr in Damaskus; Tumult in Damascus
1939,My 6,21:2
Gottschalk, Louis F (Composer)
Broken Blossoms 1919,My 14,15:5
Gottschlich, Hugo
Good Soldier Schweik, The 1963,Ag 21,38:1
Gotz, Carl
That Murder in Berlin 1929,Mr 12,26:2
Gotz, Frantisek (Original Author)
Thunder in the Hills 1947,My 24,10:5
Goudal, Jetta
Bright Shawl, The 1923,Ap 23,18:3
Green Goddess, The 1923,Ag 15,21:1
Open all Night 1924,S 9,19:1
Salome of the Tenements 1925,F 24,17:3
Coming of Amos, The 1925,S 8,29:1
Road to Yesterday, The 1925,D 1,22:4
Three Faces West 1926,F 16,22:4
White Gold 1927,Ap 11,18:3
Fighting Love 1927,My 23,27:2
Forbidden Woman, The 1927,O 31,22:1
Cardboard Lover, The 1928,S 3,14:2
Lady of the Pavements 1929,Mr 11,22:2
Spectre Vert, Le 1930,Je 8,IX,6:1
Business and Pleasure 1932,F 13,23:4
Goude, Ingrid
Never Steal Anything Small 1959,F 12,23:1
Goudge, Elizabeth (Original Author)
Green Dolphin Street 1947,O 16,34:2
Gouget
Maternite 1937,Je 8,30:2
GOUGH
See Also GOFF
Gough, John
Smooth as Satin 1925,Je 23,24:3
Judgment of the Hills 1927,Ag 2,19:2
Street of Sin, The 1928,My 28,23:2
Circus Kid, The 1928,D 17,23:1
Two for Tonight 1935,Ag 31,16:2
Gough, Lloyd
Black Bart 1948,Mr 4,30:4
All my Sons 1948,Mr 29,17:3
River Lady 1948,My 21,19:5
Babe Ruth Story, The 1948,Jl 29,17:2
Southern Yankee, A 1948,N 25,47:2
That Wonderful Urge 1948,D 22,29:6
Tulsa 1949,My 27,25:2
Roseanna McCoy 1949,O 13,33:2
Always Leave Them Laughing 1949,N 24,48:2
Tension 1950,Ja 12,32:4
Outside the Wall 1950,Mr 15,34:8

Gough, Lloyd — Cont
Sunset Boulevard 1950,Ag 11,15:2
Storm Warning 1951,Mr 3,8:2
Valentino 1951,Ap 20,25:1
Screen, The 1951,Ap 23,21:2
Rancho Notorious 1952,My 15,39:5
Tony Rome 1967,N 16,58:1
Madigan 1968,Mr 30,22:2
Gough, Michael
Anna Karenina 1948,Ap 28,32:2
Blanche Fury 1948,N 24,20:2
Saraband 1949,Je 13,16:3
Small Back Room, The 1952,F 2,11:3
Man in the White Suit, The 1952,Ap 1,35:2
No Resting Place 1952,My 5,18:5
Sword and the Rose, The 1953,Ag 20,18:3
Rob Roy 1954,F 4,21:5
Richard III 1956,Mr 12,1:4
Horror of Dracula 1958,My 29,24:4
Horse's Mouth, The 1958,N 12,41:1
Horrors of the Black Museum 1959,Ap 30,37:2
Konga 1961,S 16,9:1
I Like Money 1962,My 19,18:2
Phantom of the Opera, The 1962,Ag 23,25:2
No Place Like Homicide 1962,S 13,32:1
Black Zoo 1963,My 16,42:1
Berserk! 1968,Ja 11,42:2
Gough, Wilfred Captain
His Hour 1924,O 7,26:1
Goula, Jose R
Honeymoon 1947,My 19,27:2
Goulard, Didier (Screenwriter)
Backfire 1965,Ap 27,27:1
Gould, Billy
Great White Way, The 1924,Ja 4,10:1
Gould, Bruce (Original Author)
Reunion 1936,N 27,27:1
Gould, Chester (Original Author)
Dick Tracy 1946,Ja 12,10:7
Dick Tracy vs Cueball 1946,N 23,12:2
Dick Tracy's Dilemma 1947,Jl 14,14:5
Dick Tracy and Gruesome 1947,S 27,11:2
Gould, Dan
Rebellion in Cuba 1961,Jl 1,9:1
Gould, Dave (Miscellaneous)
Folies Bergere 1935,F 25,13:2
Broadway Melody of 1936 1935,S 19,28:1
Broadway Melody of 1938 1937,S 3,12:1
Gould, Dave (Original Author)
Gals, Inc 1943,Ag 13,13:4
Gould, Dorothy
Ladies in Love 1930,Je 14,9:4
Gould, Elliott
Night They Raided Minsky's, The
1968,D 23,43:1
Gould, Gertrude
Autumn Crocus 1934,O 25,26:2
Gould, Greta
Min and Bill 1930,N 24,26:5
Gould, Harold
Yellow Canary, The 1963,My 16,42:1
Harper 1966,Mr 31,43:1
Gould, Laurence M
Explorers of the World 1931,D 18,29:3
Gould, Merle S
Body Is a Shell, The 1957,S 9,21:2
Gould, Merle S (Director)
Body Is a Shell, The 1957,S 9,21:2
Gould, Merle S (Producer)
Body Is a Shell, The 1957,S 9,21:2
Gould, Morton (Composer)
Delightfully Dangerous 1945,Je 9,17:3
Cinerama Holiday 1955,F 9,31:1
Gould, Morton and Orchestra
Delightfully Dangerous 1945,Je 9,17:3
Gould, Richard
Yank in Korea, A 1951,Ap 2,29:2
Gould, Rita
Girls' Dormitory 1936,Ag 29,16:2
Vicious Circle, The 1948,Jl 22,27:2
Gould, Sandra
June Bride 1948,O 30,10:2
Honeymoon Hotel 1964,Je 4,28:1
Gould, Sid
Teenage Millionaire 1962,Ja 12,29:2
Gould, William
Flirting With Love 1924,S 1,9:1
Hard Rock Harrigan 1935,Jl 30,16:2
Renfrew of the Royal Mounted 1937,N 3,29:4
Mr Wong, Detective 1938,N 21,14:4
Dress Parade 1939,O 28,11:2
Three Cheers for the Irish 1940,Mr 9,19:2
Tear Gas Squad 1940,My 31,15:3
Murder in the Air 1940,Jl 4,12:2
Pot o'Gold 1941,Ap 4,25:2
No Greater Sin 1941,Ag 29,18:2
Tanks a Million 1941,O 9,27:2
Murder in the Big House 1942,My 8,27:3
Yellow Sky 1949,F 2,36:1
Man Who Cheated Himself, The 1951,F 9,21:2
Gould-Porter, A
Kind Lady 1951,Ag 8,21:2
Virgin Queen, The 1955,Ag 6,13:2
Lady Godiva 1955,D 3,13:3

Gould-Porter, A— Cont
 Top Secret Affair 1957,Ja 31,21:1
Goulding, Alf
 Lady, The 1925,Ja 27,11:2
 Learning to Love 1925,F 23,24:1
Goulding, Alf (Director)
 Excuse Me 1925,Ja 27,11:2
 Chump at Oxford, A 1940,F 20,17:3
Goulding, Edmund (Director)
 Sun Up 1925,Ag 18,14:3
 Sally, Irene and Mary 1925,D 7,19:1
 Love 1927,N 30,22:4
 Trespasser, The 1929,N 2,14:6
 Devil's Holiday, The 1930,My 10,25:3
 Reaching for the Moon 1930,D 30,24:2
 Night Angel, The 1931,Je 11,28:4
 Grand Hotel 1932,Ap 13,23:2
 Blondie of the Follies 1932,S 2,19:2
 Riptide 1934,Mr 31,8:2
 Flame Within, The 1935,Je 1,18:2
 That Certain Woman 1937,S 16,29:1
 White Banners 1938,Je 23,27:1
 Dawn Patrol 1938,D 24,12:1
 Dark Victory 1939,Ap 21,27:2
 Old Maid, The 1939,Ag 12,16:2
 We Are not Alone 1939,D 1,27:1
 'Til We Meet Again 1940,Ap 14,14:2
 Great Lie, The 1941,Ap 12,19:2
 Forever and a Day 1943,Mr 13,9:2
 Constant Nymph, The 1943,Jl 24,8:2
 Claudia 1943,N 5,23:2
 Of Human Bondage 1946,Jl 6,11:2
 Razor's Edge, The 1946,N 20,42:2
 Nightmare Alley 1947,O 10,31:3
 Everybody Does It 1949,O 26,32:2
 Mister 880 1950,S 30,13:2
 We're not Married 1952,Jl 12,16:2
 Down Among the Sheltering Palms
  1953,Je 13,11:2
 Teenage Rebel 1956,N 17,17:6
 Mardi Gras 1958,N 19,45:2
Goulding, Edmund (Original Author)
 Dancing Mothers 1926,F 18,21:1
 Paris 1926,Je 1,29:3
 No Man of her Own 1932,D 31,10:1
 Riptide 1934,Mr 31,8:2
 That Certain Woman 1937,S 16,29:1
 Two Girls on Broadway 1940,Ap 25,28:4
Goulding, Edmund (Producer)
 Flame Within, The 1935,Je 1,18:2
 Forever and a Day 1943,Mr 13,9:2
Goulding, Edmund (Screenwriter)
 Bright Shawl, The 1923,Ap 23,18:3
 Dante's Inferno 1924,S 30,27:3
 Beautiful City, The 1925,N 23,25:4
 Broadway Melody, The 1929,F 9,15:3
 Trespasser, The 1929,N 2,14:6
 Grand Parade, Tne 1930,F 1,15:1
 Devil's Holiday, The 1930,My 10,25:3
 Reaching for the Moon 1930,D 30,24:2
 Night Angel, The 1931,Je 11,28:4
 Flesh 1932,D 10,19:3
 Flame Within, The 1935,Je 1,18:2
 That Certain Woman 1937,S 16,29:1
Goulds, William
 Bad Men of Missouri 1941,Ag 16,18:2
Goulet, Robert
 Gay Purr--ee 1962,D 6,55:3
 Honeymoon Hotel 1964,Je 4,28:1
 I'd Rather Be Rich 1964,S 3,24:2
Goulet, Teddy Burns
 Big Red 1962,S 3,11:2
Goulette, Arthur
 Nine Days a Queen 1936,O 3,21:1
 Caravan 1949,Ap 21,30:4
Goulian, Madame (Producer)
 Paris Incident 1954,Ag 18,20:2
Goulin, Alfred
 Deadlier Than the Male 1957,O 9,41:1
Goullett, Arthur
 King Solomon's Mines 1937,Jl 3,18:1
 Non-Stop New York 1937,N 29,19:2
Goulven, Jerome
 Rumors 1949,Mr 19,10:7
Goulven, Jerome (Producer)
 Thank Heaven for Small Favors 1965,Ja 14,44:2
Goupil, Pierre (Cinematographer)
 World Without Sun 1964,D 23,22:1
Goupillieres, Roger (Director)
 Dr Knock 1937,My 1,16:4
Gourfain, Harry A (Original Author)
 Buy Me That Town 1941,O 23,27:2
Gourgaud, Baron (Miscellaneous)
 Truth About Africa, The 1933,Ap 17,16:3
Gourvitch, Rolla
 Devil's Island 1940,Jl 12,11:4
Gouse-Renal, Christine (Producer)
 Very Private Affair, A 1962,S 29,15:1
 This Special Friendship 1967,N 8,56:1
Gout, Albert (Director)
 Adam and Eve 1958,O 18,17:5
Gout, Albert (Producer)
 Adam and Eve 1958,O 18,17:5

Gout, Alberto (Director)
 St Francis of Assisi 1947,Ap 5,12:5
Gouth, Michael
 Night Ambush 1958,Ap 25,32:4
Gouthier, Louis
 Poil de Carotte 1933,My 26,24:2
Gouzenko, Igor (Original Author)
 Iron Curtain, The 1948,My 13,31:2
Govar, Yvan (Director)
 Cross of the Living 1963,F 5,5:5
Govar, Yvan (Screenwriter)
 Cross of the Living 1963,F 5,5:5
Gover, Michael
 Strange Affair, The 1968,Jl 25,26:2
Gover, Mildred
 Little Miss Marker 1934,My 19,18:3
 Mrs Wiggs of the Cabbage Patch 1934,O 29,14:2
 High School Girl 1935,Mr 16,19:1
 Daytime Wife 1939,N 24,29:1
 Ladies Must Live 1940,S 6,25:3
Govind
 Gyandev of India 1943,Ap 10,12:5
Govolny, M (Composer)
 Two Soldiers 1944,Jl 27,14:2
Govoni, Marcella
 Rigoletto 1949,N 10,41:4
Govorkova, Tamara
 Taxi to Heaven 1944,My 25,16:3
 Winner, The 1947,D 1,27:2
Govrin, Gloria
 Midsummer Night's Dream, A 1967,Ap 18,32:1
Gow, Frances
 Return to Paradise 1953,S 11,24:2
Gow, James (Original Author)
 Tomorrow the World 1944,D 22,12:4
Gow, James (Screenwriter)
 I Dream too Much 1935,N 29,24:1
 Murder on a Bridle Path 1936,Ap 11,19:2
 Bunker Bean 1936,Je 27,21:2
 Moonlight in Hamaii 1941,O 10,26:6
Gower, Ruth
 Family Way, The 1967,Je 29,32:1
Gowing, Gene
 Heads Up 1930,O 13,31:1
Gowland, Gibson
 Blind Husbands 1919,D 8,20:4
 Fighting Shepherdess, The 1920,Mr 29,18:1
 Love and Glory 1924,Ag 5,10:2
 Greed 1924,D 5,28:1
 Phantom of the Opera, The 1925,S 7,15:3
 First Auto, The 1927,Je 28,28:4
 Topsy and Eva 1927,Ag 8,10:3
 Rose-Marie 1928,F 13,16:2
 Mysterious Island, The 1929,D 21,17:1
 Hell Harbor 1930,Mr 28,22:6
 Doomed Battalion, The 1932,Je 11,9:3
 S O S Iceberg 1933,S 25,18:4
 Private Life of Don Juan, The 1934,D 10,16:2
 Revenge of General Ling, The 1938,F 21,15:1
Goya, Chantel
 Masculine Feminine 1966,S 19,57:1
Goya, Francisco (Original Author)
 Naked Maja, The 1959,Je 11,36:2
Goya, Mona
 Flame of Love, The 1930,N 3,19:3
 Coiffeur Pour Dames 1932,O 31,18:4
 Porteuse de Pain, La 1936,Jl 1,29:5
 Juggernaut 1937,Jl 15,16:1
 Francis the First 1947,N 20,38:4
 Babette Goes to War 1960,Je 8,46:1
Goza, Boros
 Csokolj Meg Edes 1932,N 25,19:2
Gozier, Bernie
 Green Dolphin Street 1947,O 16,34:2
 Viva Zapata 1952,F 8,19:2
 Creature from the Black Lagoon 1954,My 1,13:4
Gozon, Gyula
 Key Balvany, A 1933,Ap 18,13:6
 Kek Balvany, A; Blue Idol, The 1933,Ap 18,13:6
 Csunya Lany, A 1935,O 18,27:4
 Zsivany Becsuelet 1935,O 30,16:3
 Edes Mostoha 1935,N 21,27:2
 Budai Cukraszda 1936,Ja 2,21:5
 Kiralyne Huszarja, A 1936,Ja 17,15:3
 Nem Elhetek Muzsikaszo Nelkuel 1936,F 21,21:2
 Segitseg Oeroekoeltem; Help, I'm an Heiress
  1937,O 28,29:2
 Az Ember Neha Teved; Man Sometimes Errs
  1938,Mr 28,19:3
Gozon, Julius
 My Wife, The Miss 1934,S 13,26:2
 Noszty Flu Este Toth Marival 1938,My 16,14:4
Gozzi, Chantal
 Gervaise 1957,N 12,46:1
 Witches of Salem 1958,D 9,54:2
Gozzi, Patricia
 Sundays and Cybele 1962,N 13,43:3
 Rapture 1965,Ag 24,25:3
Graavey, Fernand
 Bitter Sweet 1933,Ag 24,18:2
Grabe, Christine
 Jugend von Heute; Youth of Today
  1938,N 5,15:3

Grable, Betty
 Hold 'Em Jail! 1932,Ag 20,7:4
 Child of Manhattan 1933,F 13,11:4
 What Price Innocence? 1933,Je 26,16:3
 Student Tour 1934,O 31,17:3
 Collegiate 1936,Ja 23,25:2
 Follow the Fleet 1936,F 21,21:2
 Don't Turn 'em Loose 1936,S 25,20:2
 Pigskin Parade 1936,N 14,23:3
 This Way Please 1937,O 8,27:2
 Thrill of a Lifetime 1937,D 9,30:2
 College Swing 1938,Ap 28,27:2
 Give Me a Sailor 1938,Ag 11,31:1
 Campus Confessions 1938,S 23,35:1
 Man About Town 1939,Je 29,19:1
 Day the Bookies Wept, The 1939,S 14,18:2
 Down Argentine Way 1940,O 18,25:1
 Tin Pan Alley 1940,N 22,27:3
 Moon Over Miami 1941,Jl 5,14:2
 Yank in the R A F, A 1941,S 27,11:3
 I Wake up Screaming 1942,Ja 17,13:2
 Song of the Islands 1942,Mr 12,24:4
 Footlight Serenade 1942,S 10,30:3
 Springtime in the Rockies 1942,N 12,30:2
 Coney Island 1943,Je 17,17:2
 Sweet Rosie O'Grady 1943,O 21,30:2
 Four Jills in a Jeep 1944,Ap 6,27:2
 Pin Up Girl 1944,My 11,25:6
 Billy Rose's Diamond Horseshoe 1945,My 3,37:1
 Dolly Sisters, The 1945,N 15,24:6
 Shocking Miss Pilgrim, The 1947,F 12,34:2
 Mother Wore Tights 1947,Ag 21,33:2
 That Lady in Ermine 1948,Ag 25,31:2
 When my Baby Smiles at Me 1948,N 24,20:2
 Beautiful Blonde From Bashful Bend, The
  1949,My 28,11:2
 Wabash Avenue 1950,Ap 29,8:3
 My Blue Heaven 1950,S 16,12:6
 Call Me Mister 1951,F 1,21:2
 Meet Me After the Show 1951,Ag 16,23:2
 Farmer Takes a Wife, The 1953,Je 13,11:2
 How to Marry a Millionaire 1953,N 11,37:1
 Three for the Show 1955,F 25,16:1
 How to be Very, Very Popular 1955,Jl 23,10:1
Grabley, Ursula
 Und das Ist die Hauptsache; That's All That
  Matters 1931,My 24,VIII,4:1
 Der Storch Streikt 1932,My 2,13:2
 Schwartze Husar, Der 1932,D 23,20:1
 Einmal Moecht' Ich Keine Sorgen Haben
  1933,My 25,24:4
 Ja, Treu Ist die Soldatenliebe 1934,Ap 28,11:4
 Im Heidekrug 1934,D 31,9:7
 Schuechterne Felix, Der 1935,S 7,19:5
 Zu Strassburg auf der Schanz; At the Strassburg
  1936,F 15,18:7
 Frauen vom Tannhof, Die 1936,F 18,27:1
 Annette in Paradise 1936,Mr 7,11:4
 Heisses Blut 1936,S 26,11:2
 Ist Mein Mann Nicht Fabelhaft 1936,D 8,31:3
 1A in Oberbayern; 1A in Upper Bavaria
  1939,N 18,22:6
 Arme Millionar, Der; Poor Millionaire, The
  1939,D 30,9:2
 Hurra! Ich bin Papa; Hurrah! I'm a Papa
  1940,Je 1,12:3
Grabowski, Norman
 Misadventures of Merlin Jones, The
  1964,Mr 26,40:4
 Monkey's Uncle, The 1965,Ag 19,35:4
Grabowski, W
 Cabman No 13 1937,N 1,24:6
Graccio, Ugo
 Kif Tebbi 1929,My 20,22:6
Grace, Dick
 Lost Squadron, The 1932,Mr 11,15:4
Grace, Dick (Original Author)
 Lost Squadron, The 1932,Mr 11,15:4
Grace, Henry
 Longest Day, The 1962,O 5,28:1
Grace, Meyer
 Alice in Wonderland 1933,D 23,19:1
Grace, Princess of Monaco
 Poppy is Also a Flower, The 1967,D 14,62:4
Grace, Richard V (Original Author)
 Devil's Squadron 1936,My 11,16:2
Grachev, V
 Problem Child 1955,Ja 24,20:5
Gracie, Sally
 Patterns 1956,Mr 28,26:1
 Stage Struck 1958,Ap 23,40:1
 Fugitive Kind, The 1960,Ap 15,13:1
Grade, Kjell (Director)
 Hugo and Josephine 1968,S 30,60:1
Gradin, Vladimir
 Pozor 1933,Mr 11,18:4
Gradopolof, K
 Peter Vinogradof 1935,Je 28,24:1
Gradov, P (Screenwriter)
 Sailor From the Comet, The 1959,Ag 3,21:2
Gradus, Ben (Producer)
 Crowded Paradise 1956,Je 22,15:1

Grady, H G
Ramparts We Watch, The 1940,S 20,27:1
Grady, William Jr (Producer)
Summer Love 1958,Je 26,23:4
Graef, G
Guerrilla Brigade 1942,Ap 14,17:2
Graeme, Bruce (Original Author)
Missing Ten Days 1941,Ap 21,15:5 (In Addenda)
Graetz, Paul
Monna Vanna 1923,S 25,8:2
Fight for Matterhorn, The 1929,Jl 29,23:3
Wien Du Stadt der Lieder; (Vienna City of Song) 1931,Mr 20,29:1
Power 1934,O 5,29:3
Alias Bulldog Drummond 1935,S 10,26:2
Mimi 1936,Ja 10,16:3
Mr Cohen Takes a Walk 1936,F 13,25:2
Red Wagon 1936,Je 22,22:1
Hot Money 1936,Jl 25,16:2
Bengal Tiger 1936,Jl 30,22:1
April Romance 1937,Ja 27,17:4
Heart's Desire 1937,Jl 12,20:4
Graetz, Paul (Producer)
Heart of a Nation, The 1943,Ap 8,27:2
Devil in the Flesh 1949,My 10,29:2
God Needs Men 1951,Mr 27,35:1
Lovers, Happy Lovers 1954,O 1,19:2
Doctors, The 1956,Ag 7,19:2
Women Are Weak 1959,Je 9,44:2
From a Roman Balcony 1961,O 16,33:5
View From the Bridge, A 1962,Ja 23,36:1
Is Paris Burning? 1966,N 11,36:1
Graf, Otto
Third Sex, The 1959,Mr 26,27:1
Graf, Robert
Jonas 1959,Ap 30,37:1
Aren't We Wonderful? 1959,O 16,27:1
Great Escape, The 1963,Ag 8,19:1
Young Cassidy 1965,Mr 23,35:1
Graf, Suse
Stuetzen der Gesellschaft 1936,N 7,15:3
Hilde Petersen, Postlagernd 1937,Je 26,20:3 (In Addenda)
Wenn Du eine Schwiegermutter hast; When You Have a Mother-in-Law 1938,Ja 29,12:1
Kater Lampe 1938,Ap 23,19:3
Mit versiegelter Order; Under Sealed Orders 1938,Jl 30,10:2
Graf, William N (Producer)
Man for all Seasons, A 1966,D 13,60:1
Graff, Fred
Cry of the Werewolf, The 1944,Ag 12,16:5
Union Station 1950,O 5,38:3
Graff, Wilton
Strange Confession 1945,N 8,17:3
Pillow of Death 1946,Ja 26,19:3
Avalanche 1946,Jl 8,25:2
Unknown, The 1946,Jl 20,10:3
Web, The 1947,Je 5,32:1
Key Witness 1947,Jl 30,27:6
Corpse came C O D, The 1947,Ag 19,27:2
Gentleman's Agreement 1947,N 12,36:2
Double Life, A 1948,F 20,19:1
Another Part of the Forest 1948,My 19,30:2
Gallant Blade 1948,O 13,31:3
Mozart Story, The 1948,N 15,21:5
Dark Past, The 1948,D 23,25:2
Caught 1949,F 18,26:4
Once More, my Darling 1949,S 26,17:1
Black Book, The 1949,O 17,18:2
And Baby Makes Three 1949,D 23,17:3
Fortunes of Captain Blood 1950,Je 10,11:3
West Point Story, The 1950,D 23,11:3
Springfield Rifle 1952,O 23,40:2
Operation Secret 1952,N 6,37:2
Million Dollar Mermaid 1952,D 5,35:2
Lili 1953,Mr 11,36:7
Scandal at Scourie 1953,Je 16,24:2
Miss Sadie Thompson 1953,D 24,9:1
King Richard and the Crusaders 1954,Ag 23,20:5
Benny Goodman Story 1956,F 22,22:1
Lust for Life 1956,S 18,39:1
Compulsion 1959,Ap 2,26:2
Grafton, Edith (Original Author)
System, The 1953,My 23,19:3
Grafton, Gloria
Cry Havoc 1943,N 24,16:2
Up Goes Maisie 1946,Ja 25,26:7
Grafton, Louise
Irish Luck 1925,N 24,28:4
Grafton, Samuel (Original Author)
System, The 1953,My 23,19:3
Gragaglia, Arturo
Heart and Soul 1950,Je 15,41:3
Gragnani, Emilio (Composer)
Bertoldo, Bertoldino, Cacasenno 1937,D 22,32:3
Gragnon, Francois
Fire Within, The 1964,F 18,27:1
Graham, Betty Jane
Night Nurse 1931,Jl 17,23:4
Penrod and Sam 1931,S 26,25:3
Young America 1932,My 7,11:5
No Greater Love 1932,My 14,11:5

Humanity 1933,Ap 22,16:3
Band Plays on, The 1934,D 22,21:2
Wicked Woman, A 1935,Ja 1,24:1
Winning Ticket, The 1935,F 11,14:2
Graham, Bob
People Are Funny 1946,Ja 28,15:6
Graham, Captain (Miscellaneous)
Girl From Maxim's, The 1936,S 16,29:1
Graham, Carroll (Original Author)
Bordertown 1935,Ja 24,22:5
Graham, Charles
Making of O'Malley 1925,Je 22,10:2
Untamed Lady, The 1926,Mr 16,22:5
Graham, Denys
Dunkirk 1958,S 11,42:2
Graham, Emily
Forest Ring, The 1930,Ap 26,11:1
Graham, Frank
Three Caballeros, The 1945,F 5,20:1
Graham, Fred
Fighting Kentuckian, The 1949,S 19,18:3
Woman on Pier 13, The 1950,Je 16,28:4
Angels in the Outfield 1951,O 18,32:1
San Francisco Story, The 1952,My 10,16:4
20,000 Leagues Under the Sea 1954,D 24,7:2
Last Hunt, The 1956,Mr 1,37:2
Woman Obsessed 1959,My 28,34:1
Graham, Frederick
Pleasure Crazed 1929,Jl 15,25:1
Nix on Dames 1929,N 23,18:5
Graham, Garrett (Screenwriter)
Gambling 1934,D 4,22:3
Graham, Gerritt
Greetings 1968,D 16,61:2
Graham, Harry Captain (Screenwriter)
Girl From Maxim's, The 1936,S 16,29:1
Graham, Jo (Director)
Always in my Heart 1942,Mr 14,19:2
You Can't Escape Forever 1942,O 17,11:1
Graham, John
Lost World, The 1960,Jl 14,23:1
Graham, Laura
Midsummer Night's Dream, A 1961,D 19,39:1
Graham, Lewis (Screenwriter)
Crime of Dr Crespi, The 1936,Ja 13,14:3
Graham, Martha
Arabian Duet 1922,My 15,20:3
Spanish Dance 1922,Jl 3,8:6
Graham, Mary Jane
Scandal for Sale 1932,Ap 3,26:2
Graham, Morland
I Stand Condemned 1936,Jl 2,27:2
Jamaica Inn 1939,O 12,33:1
Night Train 1940,D 30,21:1
Voice in the Night, The 1941,My 23,25:4
This England 1941,N 18,33:2
Ships With Wings 1942,My 25,11:2
Tower of Terror 1942,Je 29,11:4
Gay Intruders, The 1946,Mr 18,24:2
Henry V 1946,Je 18,30:2
Upturned Glass, The 1947,N 5,34:4
Brothers, The 1948,My 5,30:4
Showtime 1948,My 20,35:3
Tight Little Island 1949,D 26,33:2
Bonnie Prince Charlie 1952,Ja 7,14:3
Graham, Peter (Director)
Headless Ghost, The 1959,Ap 30,37:2
Graham, Richard
Bomber's Moon 1943,Jl 31,8:2
In old Oklahoma 1943,D 6,21:1
Graham, Robert
Last Parade, The 1931,Mr 2,19:1
Graham, Ronny
New Faces 1954,F 20,8:7
Graham, Ronny (Screenwriter)
New Faces 1954,F 20,8:7
Graham, Sheilah (Original Author)
Beloved Infidel 1959,N 18,46:1
Graham, William (Director)
Waterhole #3 1967,O 11,41:4
Graham, Winston (Screenwriter)
Take my Life 1949,Ja 19,34:2
Night Without Stars 1953,Jl 14,19:4
Grahame, Gloria
It's a Wonderful Life 1946,D 23,19:2
It Happened in Brooklyn 1947,Mr 14,28:5
Crossfire 1947,Jl 23,19:2
Song of the Thin Man 1947,Ag 29,14:2
Merton of the Movies 1947,N 7,20:3
Roughshod 1949,Je 17,27:2
In a Lonely Place 1950,My 18,37:2
Greatest Show on Earth, The 1952,Ja 11,17:2
Macao 1952,My 1,34:2
Sudden Fear 1952,Ag 8,9:2
Bad and the Beautiful, The 1953,Ja 16,19:1
Man on a Tightrope 1953,Je 5,19:1
Big Heat, The 1953,O 15,43:2
Human Desire 1954,Ag 7,7:2
Naked Alibi 1954,O 2,21:2
Not as a Stranger 1955,Je 29,24:1
Cobweb, The 1955,Ag 6,13:3
Oklahoma! 1955,O 11,49:1
Man Who Never Was, The 1956,Ap 4,24:1

Grahame, Gloria — Cont
Odds Against Tomorrow 1959,O 16,27:1
Ride Beyond Vengance 1966,S 29,60:1
Grahame, Kenneth (Original Author)
Adventures of Ichabod and Mr Toad, The 1949,O 10,18:2
Grahame, Margot
Love Habit, The 1931,F 2,23:1
Sorrell and Son 1934,My 29,22:1
Broken Melody, The 1934,O 31,17:3
Informer, The 1935,My 10,25:2
Arizonian, The 1935,Jl 27,16:2
Three Musketeers, The 1935,N 1,25:1
Two in the Dark 1936,F 1,9:2
Counterfeit 1936,Jl 20,11:1
Trouble Ahead 1936,S 21,26:5
Make Way for a Lady 1936,D 12,15:1
Night Waitress 1936,D 18,31:5
Criminal Lawyer 1937,Ja 27,17:3
Soldier and the Lady, The 1937,Ap 10,11:1
Fight for Your Lady 1937,N 20,21:2
Buccaneer, The 1938,F 17,17:2
Crime Over London 1938,Jl 28,23:2
Broken Journey 1949,My 26,34:3
Black Magic 1949,N 9,37:2
Lucky Nick Cain 1951,Ap 23,21:2
Crimson Pirate, The 1952,Ag 28,21:2
Assassin, The 1953,Ap 18,17:2
Beggar's Opera, The 1953,Ag 25,18:2
Grahame, Shirley
Royal Ballet, The (Swan Lake Act II); Swan Lake Act II (The Royal Ballet) 1960,O 5,45:2
GRAINGER
See Also GRANGER
Grainger, Edmund (Director)
One Minute to Zero 1952,S 20,13:2
Grainger, Edmund (Producer)
Sutter's Gold 1936,Mr 27,25:2
Oh, Doctor 1937,Je 19,20:3
Jury's Secret, The 1938,F 4,17:2
Devil's Party, The 1938,My 31,8:3
Wives Under Suspicion 1938,Jl 1,22:3
Flying Tigers 1942,O 23,25:2
Fabulous Texan, The 1947,D 26,22:5
Sands of Iwo Jima 1949,D 31,9:2
Flying Leathernecks 1951,S 20,37:1
Racket, The 1951,D 13,44:2
Blackbeard the Pirate 1952,D 26,20:3
Split Second 1953,My 13,34:2
French Line, The 1954,My 15,13:2
Treasure of Pancho Villa, The 1955,N 25,38:2
Bundle of Joy 1956,D 20,36:1
Sheepman, The 1958,My 8,36:1
Torpedo Run 1958,O 25,16:2
Green Mansions 1959,Mr 20,26:1
Never so Few 1960,Ja 22,15:2
Home from the Hill 1960,Mr 4,19:1
Cimarron 1961,F 17,12:2
Grainger, Jimmy Jr
Joy Girl, The 1927,S 6,34:3
Grainger, Meta
Luck of the Irish, The 1937,Ja 16,21:1
Grainger, Ron (Composer)
Finest Hours, The 1964,N 11,38:1
Gralla, Dina
Madame Wants no Children 1927,Je 21,23:3
K und K Balletmaedel, Das; Royal Ballet Girl, The 1928,Ja 15,VIII,7:6 (In Addenda)
Love Commandment, The 1928,D 25,31:3
Why Cry at Parting 1930,F 4,28:3
Acht Tage Glueck 1931,Jl 24,22:1
Keine Feier Ohne Meyer 1932,O 29,18:4
Schwebende Jungfrau, Die 1937,Ag 7,7:2
Gramatica, Emma
Vecchia Signora, La 1932,D 10,19:3
Delitto di Mastrovanni, Il 1935,Jl 30,16:2
Destino, Il 1938,F 8,17:3
Miracle in Milan 1951,D 18,42:2
Gran, Albert
Tarnish 1924,O 13,21:1
Her Night of Romance 1925,Ja 13,16:1
Graustark 1925,S 8,29:1
Beverly of Graustark 1926,Ap 19,24:3
Seventh Heaven 1927,My 26,22:1
Hula 1927,Ag 29,21:1
Soft Cushions 1927,S 12,29:1
Breakfast at Sunrise 1927,N 14,26:1
Four Sons 1928,F 14,27:1
We Americans 1928,Mr 29,25:3
Blue Danube, The 1928,Ap 30,18:3
Whip, The 1928,S 17,28:2
Mother Knows Best 1928,S 17,27:1
Dry Martini 1928,N 5,26:5 (In Addenda)
Geraldine 1929,Mr 4,20:2
Glad Rag Doll, The 1929,Je 3,27:2
Gold Diggers of Broadway, The 1929,Ag 31,13:4
Our Modern Maidens 1929,S 7,15:1
Show of Shows 1929,N 21,24:5
Tanned Legs 1929,D 2,28:2
Kibitzer, The 1929,D 21,17:1
Man From Blankley's, The 1930,Mr 29,23:1
Little Accident 1930,Ag 4,13:4
Kiss Me Again 1931,Ja 8,21:4
Brat, The 1931,Ag 24,13:4

Gran, Albert— Cont
Fast Life 1932,D 24,11:4
Employees' Entrance 1933,Ja 21,10:6
Gran, Vera
Without a Home 1939,Ap 1,17:3
Grana, Jesus
Don Juan Tenorio 1937,D 28,29:3
Granach, Alexander
Warning Shadows 1927,Ag 10,21:4
Nosferatu the Vampire 1929,Je 4,29:3
Danton 1931,S 7,19:3
Raub der Mona Lisa, Der 1932,Mr 30,15:2
1914: The Last Days Before the War 1932,S 5,9:6
Kameradschaft 1932,N 9,28:5
Gypsies 1936,Jl 30,22:2
Kämpf, Der 1936,S 11,29:3
Ninotchka 1939,N 10,27:2
So Ends our Night 1941,F 28,17:2
Man Betrayed, A 1941,Mr 27,29:5
Joan of Paris 1942,Ja 26,18:2
Hangmen Also Die 1943,Ap 16,24:2
For Whom the Bell Tolls 1943,Jl 15,25:2
Three Russian Girls 1944,F 5,13:2
Voice in the Wind 1944,Mr 16,17:2
Hitler Gang, The 1944,My 8,15:2
Seventh Cross, The 1944,S 29,18:1
Granada, Manuel
Tia Tula, A 1965,Je 3,24:1
Granada, Maria
Gunfighters of Casa Grande 1965,S 2,36:1
Granada, Rosita
Quando el Amor Rie 1933,O 17,26:3
Granado, Manuel
Bandolero, The 1924,O 27,27:1
Granados, Enrique (Composer)
Goyescas 1944,My 29,18:3
Granass, Gardy
If all the Guys in the World 1957,Ap 23,34:1
Granat, Frank (Producer)
Matter of Innocence, A 1968,F 22,36:1
Granatz, Graziella
White Voices; Voci Blanche 1965,Ap 13,32:2
Granberg, A (Screenwriter)
Garnet Bracelet, The 1966,My 28,11:6
Granberg, Olle
Vaaran Pojke 1936,O 10,21:3
Granby, Joseph
Great Flamario, The 1945,Ja 15,15:5
Amazon Quest 1949,My 14,9:3
Written on the Wind 1957,Ja 12,12:6
Grandee, George
Stranded in Paris 1926,D 13,27:1
Dance, Girl, Dance 1933,O 25,23:3
Grandel, Janine
Sunrise at Campobello 1960,S 29,32:1
Grandi, Eugenia
Tragic Hunt 1948,O 22,30:2
Grandin, Ethel
Tailor Made Man, A 1922,O 16,20:2
Grandjacquet, Francesco
Open City; Citta Aperta 1946,F 26,21:2
Grandstedt, Greta
Excess Baggage 1928,S 24,25:1
Manhattan Parade 1931,D 25,29:2
Johnny Holiday 1950,My 17,36:1
Grandval, Berthe
Tales of Paris (The Tale of Sophie); Tale of Sophie,
The (Tales of Paris) 1962,Ag 27,18:1
Grandval, Charles
Boudu Saved From Drowning; Boudu Sauve Des
Eaux 1967,F 24,26:2
Granelli, Mireille
Fascist, The 1965,Je 18,28:3
Graneman, Eddie (Screenwriter)
Lost City, The 1935,F 21,23:3
Graner, Gertrude
Glass Menagerie, The 1950,S 29,31:5
Witness to Murder 1954,Ap 16,16:4
Granet, Bert (Original Author)
Annabel Takes a Tour 1938,D 29,15:3
Millionaire Playboy 1940,Mr 16,8:2
Time Out for Rhythm 1941,Jl 10,16:3
Show Business 1944,My 11,25:7
Do You Love Me 1946,My 25,12:2
Granet, Bert (Producer)
Bride by Mistake 1944,S 16,20:2
Locket, The 1947,Mr 20,38:2
Berlin Express 1948,My 21,19:3
Marrying Kind, The 1952,Mr 14,27:1
Granet, Bert (Screenwriter)
Legion of Terror 1936,N 2,24:2
Meet the Missus 1937,Jl 2,25:2
Big Shot, The 1937,Ag 13,13:1
Law of the Underworld 1938,Ap 28,27:2
Go Chase Yourself 1938,Je 15,27:1
Mr Doodle Kicks Off 1938,S 28,29:4
Affairs of Annabel, The 1938,O 13,29:2
Annabel Takes a Tour 1938,D 29,15:3
Fixer Dugan 1939,My 6,21:2
Career 1939,Jl 28,14:2
Day the Bookies Wept, The 1939,S 14,18:2
Cross Country Romance 1940,Jl 19,22:3
Girl, a Guy and a Gob, A 1941,Ap 24,25:3
Obliging Young Lady 1942,F 13,24:4

Grange, Red
One Minute to Play 1926,S 6,16:2
GRANGER
See Also GRAINGER
Granger, Dorothy
Love, Honor and Oh, Baby! 1933,O 28,20:3
I'll Tell the World 1934,Ap 21,12:2
Dramatic School 1938,D 9,31:2
When the Daltons Rode 1940,Ag 23,13:3
Lady From Cheyenne, The 1941,Ap 18,18:2
North to the Klondike 1942,Mr 12,24:3
One Body too Many 1944,N 25,21:2
Southerner, The 1945,Ag 27,22:3
Granger, Farley
North Star, The 1943,N 5,23:1
Purple Heart, The 1944,Mr 9,15:2
Rope 1948,Ag 27,12:4
Enchantment 1948,D 27,16:2
Roseanna McCoy 1949,O 13,33:2
They Live by Night 1949,N 4,33:2
Side Street 1950,Mr 24,29:2
Our Very Own 1950,Jl 28,12:5
Edge of Doom 1950,Ag 4,13:2
Strangers on a Train 1951,Jl 4,13:2
Behave Yourself 1951,N 8,35:2
I Want You 1951,D 24,9:1
O Henry's Full House (The Gift of the Magi); Gift
of the Magi, The (O Henry's Full House)
1952,O 17,33:1
Hans Christian Andersen 1952,N 26,20:2
Story of Three Loves, The (Mademoiselle);
Mademoiselle (The Story of Three Loves)
1953,Mr 6,29:2
Small Town Girl 1953,My 7,37:2
Naked Street, The 1955,O 1,11:2
Girl in the Red Velvet Swing, The
1955,O 20,41:2
Senso 1968,Jl 9,31:1
Granger, John
Advise and Consent 1962,Je 7,31:2
Granger, Michael
Hiawatha 1952,D 26,20:4
Salome 1953,Mr 25,37:1
White Witch Doctor 1953,Jl 2,19:3
Big Heat, The 1953,O 15,43:2
Granger, Stewart
Fanny by Gaslight 1944,Jl 16,II,3:4
Man in Grey, The 1945,N 30,18:6
Madonna of the Seven Moons 1946,My 23,18:4
Caesar and Cleopatra 1946,S 6,18:2
Lady Surrenders, A 1947,Je 20,25:6
Magic Bow, The 1947,Jl 7,13:2
Captain Boycott 1947,D 6,11:2
Man of Evil 1948,Mr 26,26:2
Blanche Fury 1948,N 24,20:2
Waterloo Road 1948,D 25,10:3
Caravan 1949,Ap 21,30:4
Saraband 1949,Je 13,16:3
Adam and Evalyn 1950,My 12,33:4
King Solomon's Mines 1950,N 10,35:1
Soldiers Three 1951,Mr 30,28:5
Light Touch, The 1952,Ja 17,23:1
Scaramouche 1952,My 9,20:2
Wild North, The 1952,My 12,21:2
Prisoner of Zenda, The 1952,N 5,36:2
Salome 1953,Mr 25,37:1
Young Bess 1953,My 22,31:1
All the Brothers Were Valiant 1953,D 29,19:2
Beau Brummell 1954,O 21,31:5
Green Fire 1954,D 25,7:1
Moonfleet 1955,Je 25,9:2
Footsteps of the Fog 1955,S 15,39:2
Last Hunt, The 1956,Mr 1,37:2
Bhowani Junction 1956,My 25,26:1
Little Hut, The 1957,My 4,25:1
Gun Glory 1957,Jl 20,8:7
Harry Black and the Tiger 1958,S 19,24:4
North to Alaska 1960,N 11,36:1
Swordsman of Siena 1962,D 6,55:3
Sodom and Gomorrah 1963,Ja 24,5:3
Secret Invasion, The 1964,S 17,52:5
Secret Invasion, The 1964,S 17,52:5
Crooked Road, The 1965,F 4,24:2
Granger, William
6-Day Bike Rider 1934,N 3,20:3
Grangier, Gilles (Director)
Speaking of Murder 1959,O 12,14:1
Night Affair 1961,O 13,27:1
Magnificent Tramp, The 1962,Ap 25,30:1
My Wife's Husband 1965,Ja 27,26:1
Grangier, Gilles (Screenwriter)
Speaking of Murder 1959,O 12,14:1
Night Affair 1961,O 13,27:1
Money, Money, Money 1962,Jl 18,20:1
Granhagen, Lena
Puss and Kram 1967,S 25,56:1
Hugs and Kisses 1968,Ag 19,44:1
Granier, Saint
Criez-Le sur les Toits; Shout it From the
Housetops 1935,Je 22,18:5
Granier-Deferre, Pierre (Director)
Cloportes 1966,Ap 19,36:1
Paris in the Month of August 1968,Ag 26,46:4

Granier-Deferre, Pierre (Screenwriter)
Paris in the Month of August 1968,Ag 26,46:4
Granischdaetten (Composer)
Paris-Mediterranee 1932,Mr 27,VIII,6:2
Granowski, W
Dodek na Froncie 1936,Mr 30,17:6
Granowsky, Alexis (Director)
Close Harmony 1929,Ap 29,29:2
Lied vom Leben, Das 1931,O 19,28:1
Moscow Nights 1938,My 3,19:3
Granowsky, Alexis (Producer)
I Stand Condemned 1936,Jl 2,27:2
Granowsky (Director)
Koffer des Herrn O F, Die; Trunks of Mr O F,
The 1932,Ja 17,VIII,6:1
Granstedt, Greta
Sunny Skies 1930,My 17,21:2
What a Man 1930,Jl 21,20:3
Street Scene 1931,Ag 27,22:5
Deceiver, The 1931,N 23,22:1
Secret Witness, The 1931,D 21,28:4
After Tomorrow 1932,Mr 7,13:5
Night World 1932,My 28,15:2
They Never Come Back 1932,Je 4,9:2
Night Club Lady, The 1932,Ag 27,13:4
Crime Without Passion 1934,S 1,16:2
Last Express, The 1938,O 11,24:4
Beasts of Berlin 1939,N 20,15:6
Our Vines Have Tender Grapes 1945,S 7,21:2
Crooked Way, The 1949,S 5,13:2
Juggler, The 1953,My 6,39:2
Eddie Cantor Story, The 1953,D 26,10:2
Grant, A Cameron
Beloved Infidel 1959,N 18,46:1
Grant, Alexande
Royal Ballet, The (Ondine); Ondine (The Royal
Ballet) 1960,O 5,45:2
Grant, Alfred
Well, The 1951,S 27,37:2
Grant, Beverly
Illiac Passion, The 1968,Ap 19,40:1
Grant, Campbell (Miscellaneous)
Pinocchio 1940,F 8,18:3
Adventures of Ichabod and Mr Toad, The
1949,O 10,18:2
Grant, Cary
This is the Night 1932,Ap 16,11:2
Sinners in the Sun 1932,My 14,11:5
Merrily We Go to Hell 1932,Je 11,9:3
Devil and the Deep 1932,Ag 20,7:4
Blonde Venus 1932,S 24,18:4
Hot Saturday 1932,N 5,12:5
Madame Butterfly 1932,D 26,26:2
She Done Him Wrong 1933,F 10,12:3
Woman Accused, The 1933,Mr 13,18:2
Eagle and the Hawk, The 1933,My 13,16:2
Gambling Ship 1933,Jl 13,17:5
I'm no Angel 1933,O 14,18:2
Alice in Wonderland 1933,D 23,19:1
Thirty Day Princess 1934,My 12,12:3
Born to be Bad 1934,My 31,22:6
Kiss and Make-Up 1934,Je 29,17:1
Ladies Should Listen 1934,Jl 28,16:6
Enter Madame 1935,Ja 12,12:1
Wings in the Dark 1935,F 2,10:1
Last Outpost, The 1935,O 5,18:2
Sylvia Scarlett 1936,Ja 10,16:2
Big Brown Eyes 1936,My 2,11:1
Suzy 1936,Jl 25,16:1
Wedding Present 1936,N 19,31:3
When You're in Love 1937,F 19,15:2
Toast of New York, The 1937,Jl 23,16:2
Topper 1937,Ag 20,21:2
Awful Truth, The 1937,N 5,19:3
Bringing Up Baby 1938,Mr 4,17:5
Holiday 1938,Je 24,15:1
Gunga Din 1939,Ja 28,19:2
Only Angels Have Wings 1939,My 12,25:2
In Name Only 1939,Ag 4,11:3
His Girl Friday 1940,Ja 12,13:2
My Favorite Wife 1940,My 31,15:2
Howards of Virginia, The 1940,S 27,27:1
Philadelphia Story, The 1940,D 27,22:2
Penny Serenade 1941,My 23,25:2
Suspicion 1941,N 21,23:2
Talk of the Town, The 1942,Ag 28,22:3
Once Upon a Honeymoon 1942,N 13,28:1
Mr Lucky 1943,Jl 23,21:2
Destination Tokyo 1944,Ja 1,9:2
Destination Tokyo 1944,Ja 9,II,3:1
Once Upon a Time 1944,My 30,17:2
Arsenic and old Lace 1944,S 2,17:2
None but the Lonely Heart 1944,N 18,16:6
None but the Lonely Heart 1944,D 3,II,1:8
Night and Day 1946,Jl 26,16:2
Notorious 1946,Ag 16,19:2
Bachelor and the Bobby-Soxer, The
1947,Jl 25,12:5
Bishop's Wife, The 1947,D 10,44:2
Mr Blandings Builds his Dream House
1948,Mr 26,26:2
Every Girl Should be Married 1948,D 24,14:2
I Was a Male War Bride 1949,Ag 27,7:2

Grant, Cary — Cont

Crisis 1950,Jl 4,10:2
People Will Talk 1951,Ag 30,20:1
Room for One More 1952,Ja 16,21:2
Monkey Business 1952,S 6,12:6
Dream Wife 1953,Jl 30,20:1
To Catch a Thief 1955,Ag 5,14:2
Pride and the Passion, The 1957,Je 29,10:6
Affair to Remember, An 1957,Jl 20,8:5
Kiss Them for Me 1957,N 9,31:2
Indiscreet 1958,Je 27,18:2
Houseboat 1958,N 14,24:1
North by Northwest 1959,Ag 7,28:1
Operation Petticoat 1959,D 6,38:1
Grass is Greener, The 1960,D 24,8:2
That Touch of Mink 1962,Je 15,16:2
Charade 1963,D 6,40:1
Father Goose 1964,D 11,55:1
Walk, Don't Run 1966,Ag 25,42:3

Grant, Cy

Safari 1956,Je 21,35:2
Sea Wife 1957,D 5,45:2

Grant, Frances

Doubting Thomas 1935,Jl 11,24:2
Thunder Mountain 1935,O 2,27:2

Grant, Frances Miller

Dancers of Paris, The 1926,Mr 29,24:3

Grant, Gogi

Big Beat, The 1958,Je 26,23:4

Grant, Harry Allen

Danger Street 1928,S 25,29:4 (In Addenda)

Grant, Harvey

Take Me to Town 1953,Je 20,8:6

Grant, Helena

Quality Street 1937,Ap 9,19:2

Grant, James Edward (Director)

Angel and the Badman 1947,Mr 3,28:4
Ring of Fear 1954,Jl 29,18:3

Grant, James Edward (Original Author)

Whipsaw 1936,Ja 25,18:4
Muss 'Em Up 1936,F 3,21:2
Big Brown Eyes 1936,My 2,11:1
Ex-Mrs Bradford, The 1936,My 28,19:2
Grand Jury 1936,Ag 1,16:3
Great Guy 1937,Ja 1,19:2
She Had to Eat 1937,Jl 24,12:1
She's no Lady 1937,Ag 12,14:3
Danger-Love at Work 1937,D 11,22:2
We're Going to Be Rich 1938,Jl 4,10:2
Music in My Heart 1940,Ja 4,19:2
Boom Town 1940,S 6,25:2
They Dare not Love 1941,My 16,21:4
Johnny Eager 1942,F 20,21:2
Lady is Willing, The 1942,Ap 24,21:2
Angel and the Badman 1947,Mr 3,28:4
Plunders, The 1948,N 1,28:2
Johnny Allegro 1949,My 31,19:2
Father Is a Bachelor 1950,F 23,33:3
Surrender 1950,O 9,21:5
Two of a Kind 1951,Je 30,8:6
Sheepman, The 1958,My 8,36:1
Proud Rebel, The 1958,Jl 2,23:4

Grant, James Edward (Producer)

Great John L, The 1945,Jl 9,14:6

Grant, James Edward (Screenwriter)

Danger-Love at Work 1937,D 11,22:2
Josette 1938,Je 11,9:1
There's That Woman Again 1939,Ja 6,25:4
Miracles for Sale 1939,Ag 10,15:2
Music in My Heart 1940,Ja 4,19:2
Johnny Eager 1942,F 20,21:2
Lady is Willing, The 1942,Ap 24,21:2
Belle of the Yukon 1945,Mr 30,18:4
Great John L, The 1945,Jl 9,14:6
Sands of Iwo Jima 1949,D 31,9:2
Father Is a Bachelor 1950,F 23,33:3
Rock Island Trail 1950,Je 5,19:3
Surrender 1950,O 9,21:5
California Passage 1950,D 16,10:5
Bullfighter and the Lady, The 1951,Ap 27,19:2
Flying Leathernecks 1951,S 20,37:1
Big Jim McLain 1952,S 18,35:2
Hondo 1953,N 27,99:9
Ring of Fear 1954,Jl 29,18:3
Last Wagon, The 1956,S 22,20:2
Three Violent People 1957,F 11,34:2
Sheepman, The 1958,My 8,36:1
Alamo, The 1960,O 27,45:1
Comancheros, The 1961,N 2,42:1
Donovan's Reef 1963,Jl 25,14:1
McLintock 1963,N 14,41:3
Circus World 1964,Je 26,34:2

Grant, Joe (Miscellaneous)

Pinocchio 1940,F 8,18:3
Reluctant Dragon, The 1941,Jl 25,12:2
Make Mine Music 1946,Ap 22,26:2

Grant, Joe (Original Author)

Saludos Amigos 1943,F 13,8:2

Grant, Joe (Screenwriter)

Dumbo 1941,O 24,27:2

Grant, John (Miscellaneous)

Rio Rita 1942,My 8,27:3
Time of Their Lives, The 1946,N 28,40:2
Double Crossbones 1951,Ap 27,19:2

Grant, John (Producer)

Bowery to Broadway 1944,N 30,19:2
Here Come the Co-Eds 1945,F 19,21:1

Grant, John (Screenwriter)

In the Navy 1941,Je 12,29:2
Hold That Ghost 1941,Ag 8,13:3
Keep 'Em Flying 1941,N 27,29:2
Ride 'Em Cowboy 1942,Mr 5,27:3
Pardon my Sarong 1942,Ag 27,15:1
Who Done It 1942,D 3,35:2
It Ain't Hay 1943,Mr 11,17:3
Hit the Ice 1943,S 23,27:2
In Society 1944,Ag 17,20:2
Lost in a Harem 1944,N 9,23:2
Here Come the Co-Eds 1945,F 19,21:1
Naughty Nineties, The 1945,Je 21,16:2
Buck Privates Come Home 1947,Ap 12,11:3
Wistful Widow of Wagon Gap, The
  1947,N 21,36:2
Noose Hangs High, The 1948,My 29,8:6
Abbott and Costello Meet Frankenstein
  1948,Jl 29,17:2
Mexican Hayride 1949,Ja 12,33:3
Abbott and Costello Meet the Killer Boris Karloff
  1949,S 19,18:3
Abbott and Costello in the Foreign Legion
  1950,Ag 14,14:4
Abbott and Costello Meet the Invisible Man
  1951,Ap 13,18:6
Ma and Pa Kettle at the Fair 1952,Jl 12,16:2

Grant, Kathryn

Phenix City Story, The 1955,S 3,9:1
Storm Center 1956,O 22,25:4
Wild Party, The 1956,D 22,13:1
Mister Cory 1957,F 23,13:1
Operation Mad Ball 1957,N 21,38:1
Seventh Voyage of Sinbad 1958,D 24,00:0
Anatomy of a Murder 1959,Jl 3,10:1
Big Circus, The 1959,Jl 18,6:1

Grant, Kirby

Blondie Goes Latin 1941,F 26,17:3
Hello, Frisco, Hello 1943,Mr 25,25:1
Ghost Catchers 1944,My 31,22:3
In Society 1944,Ag 17,20:2
Spider Woman Strikes Back, The 1946,Mr 23,8:3
She Wrote the Book 1946,Je 20,20:3
Comin' Round the Mountain 1951,Jl 27,15:2

Grant, Lawrence

Happiness 1924,Mr 11,16:2
His Hour 1924,O 7,26:1
Grand Duchess and the Waiter, The
  1926,F 9,22:1
Duchess of Buffalo, The 1926,Ag 9,10:3
Service for Ladies 1927,Ag 15,22:5
Gentleman of Paris, A 1927,O 3,20:1
Serenade 1927,D 19,30:1
Red Hair 1928,Mr 26,26:2
Doomsday 1928,Ap 2,25:1
Something Always Happens 1928,My 21,25:1
At Yale 1928,Jl 30,21:2
Woman From Moscow, The 1928,N 5,26:1
Case of Lena Smith, The 1929,Ja 15,22:4
Canary Murder Case, The 1929,Mr 11,22:2
Bulldog Drummond 1929,My 3,23:2
Is Everybody Happy? 1929,N 2,14:6
Cat Creeps, The 1930,N 8,21:3
Boudoir Diplomat, The 1930,D 8,26:1
Daughter of the Dragon 1931,Ag 22,7:5
Squaw Man, The 1931,S 19,10:2
Unholy Garden, The 1931,O 29,27:1
Shanghai Express 1932,F 18,25:3
Man About Town 1932,My 28,18:2
Jewel Robbery 1932,Jl 23,6:6
Speak Easily 1932,Ag 19,20:6
Faithless 1932,N 19,20:2
Mask of Fu Manchu, The 1932,D 3,21:4
Clear all Wires 1933,Mr 4,11:2
Looking Forward 1933,My 1,10:2
By Candlelight 1934,Ja 6,18:2
Nana 1934,F 2,20:3
I'll Tell the World 1934,Ap 21,12:2
Count of Monte Cristo, The 1934,S 27,25:2
Man Who Reclaimed his Head, The
  1935,Ja 9,22:1
Vanessa: Her Love Story 1935,Ap 13,11:3
Devil is a Woman, The 1935,My 4,17:2
Werewolf of London, The 1935,My 10,25:2
Dark Angel, The 1935,S 6,12:2
Three Kids and a Queen 1935,N 9,19:2
Tale of Two Cities, A 1935,D 26,21:2
House of a Thousand Candles, The
  1936,Ap 2,29:2
Mary of Scotland 1936,Jl 31,22:2
Under the Red Robe 1937,Je 1,27:2
Prisoner of Zenda, The 1937,S 3,12:1
Bluebeard's Eighth Wife 1938,Mr 24,21:2
Service de Luxe 1938,O 24,13:2
Young in Heart, The 1938,N 4,27:2
Women in War 1940,My 30,21:2
Dr Jekyll and Mr Hyde 1941,Ag 13,13:2
Confidential Agent 1945,N 3,11:2

Grant, Lee

Detective Story 1951,N 7,35:2
Storm Fear 1955,D 17,19:2
Middle of the Night 1959,Je 18,36:1
Balcony, The 1963,Mr 22,7:1
Affair of the Skin, An 1963,N 21,43:2
Terror in the City 1966,N 9,43:4
Divorce American Style 1967,Jl 20,30:2
In the Heat of the Night 1967,Ag 3,26:1
Valley of the Dolls 1967,D 16,51:1

Grant, Louis

Native Land 1942,My 12,16:3

Grant, Marian (Original Author)

Hunted Men 1938,My 21,9:2

Grant, Marshall (Producer)

Treat 'Em Rough 1942,Ja 19,21:3

Grant, Maxwell (Original Author)

Shadow Strikes, The 1937,S 13,17:1

Grant, Morton (Original Author)

Younger Brothers, The 1949,My 28,11:2
Holiday in Havana 1949,O 14,33:5

Grant, Morton (Screenwriter)

Love Is on the Air 1937,N 12,27:3
She Loved a Fireman 1938,Ja 21,15:3
Moonlight in Hawaii 1941,O 10,26:6
Falcon out West, The 1944,Mr 18,18:2
Song of the South 1946,N 28,40:2
Gallant Blade 1948,O 13,31:3
Big Cat, The 1949,Jl 29,12:2

Grant, Neil (Original Author)

Man of Affairs 1937,F 20,9:2

Grant, Richard

Forbidden Planet 1956,My 4,21:2

Grant, Robert (Original Author)

Mystery Sea Raider 1940,Ag 26,11:4

Grant, Shelby

Pleasure Seekers, The 1964,D 26,9:1
Our Man Flint 1966,Ja 26,23:4

Grant, Stephen

Angel and the Badman 1947,Mr 3,28:4

Granval

End of a Day, The 1939,S 12,28:4

Granval, Charles

They Were Five 1938,Je 1,19:5
Midnight in Paris 1947,O 9,32:3
Honorable Catherine, The 1948,Ag 23,13:3

Granval, J P

Picnic on the Grass 1960,O 12,47:1

Granval, Lillie

Pearls of the Crown, The 1938,Ap 12,26:2

Granville, Bonita

Westward Passage 1932,Je 4,9:2
Cradle Song 1933,N 20,18:2
Ah, Wilderness! 1935,D 25,30:2
These Three 1936,Mr 19,22:4
Plough and the Stars, The 1937,Ja 29,15:1
Maid of Salem 1937,Mr 4,27:2
Quality Street 1937,Ap 9,19:2
Call it a Day 1937,My 7,29:2
It's Love I'm After 1937,N 11,31:2
Merrily We Live 1938,Mr 18,23:3
Beloved Brat 1938,My 2,13:2
White Banners 1938,Je 23,27:1
My Bill 1938,Jl 7,22:4
Hard To Get 1938,N 14,15:2
Angels Wash Their Faces 1939,S 4,16:2
Forty Little Mothers 1940,Ap 19,25:2
Mortal Storm, The 1940,Je 21,25:2
Those Were the Days 1940,Jl 15,18:4
Escape 1940,N 1,33:1
Third Finger, Left Hand 1940,D 12,37:2
Gallant Sons 1940,D 12,37:2
People vs Dr Kildare, The 1941,My 8,21:1
H M Pulham, Esq 1941,D 19,35:1
Syncopation 1942,My 29,13:3
Glass Key, The 1942,O 16,23:1
Now, Voyager 1942,O 23,25:3
Seven Miles From Alcatraz 1942,N 19,31:3
Hitler's Children 1943,F 25,27:1
Andy Hardy's Blonde Trouble 1944,My 5,17:3
Song of the Open Road 1944,Je 7,13:3
Youth Runs Wild 1944,S 2,17:2
Suspense 1946,Jl 5,15:3
Breakfast in Hollywood 1946,Jl 15,21:1
Truth About Murder, The 1946,Jl 27,12:6
Love Laughs at Andy Hardy 1947,Ja 8,28:2
Guilty, The 1947,My 19,27:2
Guilty of Treason 1950,Ap 11,26:2
Lone Ranger, The 1956,F 11,12:1

Granville, Charlotte

Just a Gigolo 1931,Je 13,20:4
Twenty-Four Hours 1931,O 3,20:2
Now and Forever 1934,O 13,10:1
Behold My Wife 1935,F 18,19:3
Werewolf of London, The 1935,My 10,25:2
Rose of the Rancho 1936,Ja 9,25:2

Grapewin, Charley

Only Saps Work 1930,D 13,22:2
Hell's House 1932,F 12,24:5
Disorderly Conduct 1932,Ap 11,19:2
Woman From Room 13, The 1932,My 21,9:2
Night of June 13th, The 1932,S 17,18:4
Hello, Everybody 1933,Ja 30,9:4

Grapewin, Charley — Cont
Kiss Before the Mirror, The 1933,My 15,16:2
Pilgrimage 1933,Jl 13,17:5
Heroes for Sale 1933,Jl 22,14:3
Don't Bet on Love 1933,Jl 31,16:2
Torch Singer 1933,O 7,18:5
Hell and Highwater 1933,D 18,24:4
Quitter, The 1934,Mr 14,23:3
She Made her Bed 1934,Ap 27,25:1
Caravan 1934,S 28,27:1
Judge Priest 1934,O 12,33:1
President Vanishes, The 1934,D 8,18:5
Anne of Green Gables 1934,D 22,21:1
Shanghai 1935,Jl 20,16:2
Alice Adams 1935,Ag 16,11:3
King Solomon of Broadway 1935,O 19,12:2
Rendezvous 1935,O 26,12:2
Ah, Wilderness! 1935,D 25,30:2
Petrified Forest, The 1936,F 7,14:2
Voice of Bugle Ann, The 1936,F 27,23:1
Small Town Girl 1936,Ap 11,19:1
Libeled Lady 1936,O 31,24:2
Without Orders 1936,N 4,41:3
Sinner Take All 1937,F 3,27:1
Good Earth, The 1937,F 3,27:1
Family Affair, A 1937,Ap 20,29:2
Captains Courageous 1937,My 12,27:1
Between Two Women 1937,Ag 6,21:1
Bad Guy 1937,Ag 26,25:2
Broadway Melody of 1938 1937,S 3,12:1
Big City 1937,S 17,29:2
Bad Man of Brimstone, The 1938,F 4,17:2
Of Human Hearts 1938,F 18,23:1
Three Comrades 1938,Je 3,17:1
Three Loves Has Nancy 1938,S 2,21:2
Listen, Darling 1938,N 24,37:2
Artists and Models Abroad 1938,D 22,25:3
Stand up and Fight 1939,Ja 27,17:2
Wizard of Oz, The 1939,Ag 18,16:2
Dust Be my Destiny 1939,O 7,11:2
Sabotage 1939,N 16,29:5
Grapes of Wrath, The 1940,Ja 25,17:2
Johnny Apollo 1940,Ap 13,21:2
Earthbound 1940,Je 7,27:4
Rhythm on the River 1940,Ag 29,23:2
Ellery Queen, Master Detective 1940,D 19,33:1
Texas Rangers Ride Again 1941,Ja 9,27:4
Tobacco Road 1941,F 21,16:2
Ellery Queen's Penthouse Mystery
   1941,Mr 7,17:2
Ellery Queen and the Perfect Crime
   1941,Ag 11,17:3
Ellery Queen and the Murder Ring
   1941,O 21,29:4
They Died With Their Boots On 1941,N 21,23:3
Enemy Agents meet Ellery Queen
   1942,Ag 22,16:2
Crash Dive 1943,Ap 29,25:2
Follow the Boys 1944,Ap 26,24:6
Atlantic City 1944,Ag 14,11:4
Impatient Years, The 1944,S 20,20:1
Gunfighters 1947,Jl 25,12:5
Sand 1949,Ag 5,23:2

Gras, Enrico (Miscellaneous)
Pictura 1952,Ap 8,35:3
Gras, Jean
Day and the Hour, The 1964,F 20,22:2
Mademoiselle 1966,Ag 2,23:1
Gras, Marcel (Director)
Heritage 1940,N 5,33:2
Gras, Marcel (Producer)
Heritage 1940,N 5,33:2
Gras, Marcel (Screenwriter)
Heritage 1940,N 5,33:2
Grashin, Mauri (Original Author)
Hide-Out 1934,Ag 25,16:5
I'll Wait for You 1941,Je 2,13:6
Grasiosi, Giorgio (Screenwriter)
Queen of Sheba, The 1953,N 4,29:3
Grassby, Bertram
Borderland 1922,Jl 24,10:2
Tiger's Claw, The 1923,Mr 19,22:2
Pioneer Trails 1923,N 12,15:3
Man From Brodney's, The 1923,D 18,16:3
Fools in the Dark 1924,Ag 18,8:2
Captain Blood 1924,S 9,19:1
His Hour 1924,O 7,26:1
Midnight Express, The 1924,N 19,19:3
When a Man Loves 1927,F 4,16:6
Beloved Rogue, The 1927,Mr 14,16:1
Grasse, Joseph De
So Big 1925,Ja 5,19:1
Grasse, Joseph de (Director)
Girl I Loved, The 1923,My 14,18:2
Grasse, Sam De
Sally, Irene and Mary 1925,D 7,19:1
Black Pirate, The 1926,Mr 9,21:4
Eagle of the Sea, The 1926,N 17,21:6
Grasset, Pierre
Rififi 1956,Je 6,37:1
Grasso, Angelo
Path of Hope, The (Il Cammino Della Speranza)
   1952,Ag 5,15:5

Grasso, Giovanni
Delitto di Mastrovanni, Il 1935,Jl 30,16:2
Sotto la Croce del Sud; Under the Southern Cross
   1939,Ap 10,13:4
Great Dawn, The 1947,Ag 28,28:3
Ruy Blas 1948,O 4,14:2
Margaret of Cortona 1957,Ja 21,20:4
Gratton, Stephen
Snow Bride, The 1923,Je 12,22:2
Grau, Harold
Stage Struck 1958,Ap 23,40:1
Graue, Siegfried
Artists Under the Big Top Perplexed
   1968,S 27,34:1
Grauer, Ben (Miscellaneous)
Kon-Tiki 1951,Ap 4,35:2
Grauer, Ben (Narrator)
Norway Replies! 1944,F 26,10:3
Grauer, Bunny
Town That Forgot God, The 1922,N 1,16:3
Grault, Jean (Screenwriter)
Jules and Jim 1962,Ap 24,32:1
Paris Belongs to Us 1962,N 6,38:1
Grauman, Ben (Original Author)
American Empire 1943,Ja 14,25:4
Grauman, Sid
Mad About Music 1938,Mr 12,13:2
Dancing in the Dark 1949,D 3,8:6
Grauman, Walter (Director)
Lady in a Cage 1964,Je 11,27:1
633 Squadron 1964,Je 25,25:1
Rage to Live, A 1965,O 21,57:1
Graumann, Karl
Waterloo 1929,Ap 16,32:5
Spy of Madame de Pompadour, The
   1929,S 10,27:1
Grauthoff, Christine
Night of the Great Love, The 1937,O 1,19:5
Grave, Neville
Mikado, The 1967,Mr 15,53:1
Grave, Serge
Sans Famille 1935,Je 4,26:5
Generals Without Buttons 1938,Mr 8,23:2
Story of a Cheat, The 1938,S 27,25:2
Flight Into Darkness (L'Equipage)
   1938,O 17,12:1
Boys' School 1939,Je 6,26:2
Queen and the Cardinal, The 1944,Je 1,17:3
Red Angel, The 1950,N 4,13:2
Gravelotte (horse)
Veilchen vom Potsdamer Platz, La; Violet of
   Potsdam Square, The 1939,Ap 8,19:3
Gravers, Steve
Operation Eichmann 1961,My 4,40:7
Graves, Diana
Lady Possessed 1952,F 15,17:2
Graves, Ernest
Walk East on Beacon 1952,My 29,17:2
1 ■ 1 1961,N 8,41:1
Graves, Frank (Screenwriter)
Rebellion in Cuba 1961,Jl 1,9:1
Graves, George
Robber Symphony 1937,Ja 27,17:2
Tenth Man, The 1937,N 15,15:2
Graves, Peter
Waltz Time 1946,F 11,25:2
Showtime 1948,My 20,35:3
Spring in Park Lane 1949,S 21,38:2
Laughing Lady, The 1950,Ja 23,16:3
Mrs Fitzherbert 1950,My 11,37:2
Rogue River 1951,F 16,21:4
Encore (The Ant and the Grasshopper); Ant and
   the Grasshopper, The (Encore) 1952,Ap 3,45:1
Maytime in Mayfair 1952,Ap 23,23:5
Red Planet Mars 1952,Je 16,15:2
Stalag 17 1953,Jl 2,19:2
Beneath the 12-Mile Reef 1953,D 17,52:2
Raid, The 1954,Ag 21,10:4
Black Tuesday 1955,Ja 1,16:2
Long Gray Line, The 1955,F 11,19:2
Night of the Hunter, The 1955,S 30,23:1
Naked Street, The 1955,O 1,11:2
Court-Martial of Billy Mitchell, The
   1955,D 23,14:2
Beginning of the End 1957,Jl 4,16:1
Admirable Crichton, The 1957,D 15,45:4
   (Incorrect in this edition; use 1957,D 17,45:4
   elsewhere)
Stranger in my Arms 1959,Mr 4,34:2
Rage to Live, A 1965,O 21,57:1
Texas Across the River 1966,N 24,65:1
Jokers, The 1967,My 16,50:1
Ballad of Josie, The 1968,Mr 14,51:2
Sergeant Ryker 1968,Mr 21,56:2
Graves, Ralph
Sporting Life 1918,S 16,9:3
Nobody Home 1919,Ag 25,8:5
Scarlet Days 1919,N 10,18:2
Mary Ellen Comes to Town 1920,Mr 22,12:1
Little Miss Rebellion 1920,S 20,13:1
Kindred of the Dust 1922,Ag 28,14:1
Prodigal Daughters 1923,Ap 17,26:3
Extra Girl, The 1924,Ja 21,20:1

Graves, Ralph — Cont
Yolanda 1924,F 20,23:1
Daughters of Today 1924,Mr 4,17:1
Alias the Deacon 1927,Je 21,29:2
Submarine 1928,Ag 31,23:3
Flying Fleet, The 1929,F 11,26:3
Glad Rag Doll, The 1929,Je 3,27:2
Flight 1929,S 14,17:1
Song of Love, The 1929,N 14,24:3
Ladies of Leisure 1930,My 24,21:2
Hell's Island 1930,Jl 19,7:5
Dirigible 1931,Ap 6,24:1
Salvation Nell 1931,Jl 6,24:4
Dangerous Affair, A 1931,N 23,22:1
When a Feller Needs a Friend 1932,My 14,11:5
Huddle 1932,Je 17,24:1
War Correspondent 1932,Ag 13,18:6
Street of Missing Men 1939,Je 1,31:3
Eternally Yours 1939,O 7,11:2
Graves, Ralph (Original Author)
Flight 1929,S 14,17:1
Born to be Bad 1934,My 31,22:6
Outlaws of the Orient 1937,S 25,10:2
Graves, Robert
Sherlock Holmes 1932,N 12,20:5
Sisters Under the Skin 1934,Je 8,18:1
King and the Chorus Girl, The 1937,Mr 29,14:4
Graves, Stephanie
I, A Man 1967,Ag 25,28:1
Graves, Taylor
Miss Lulu Bett 1921,D 25,VI,2:1
Men of Steel 1926,Jl 12,24:4
Graves, Ralph
Amazon Quest 1949,My 14,9:3
Gravet, Fernand
King and the Chorus Girl, The 1937,Mr 29,14:4
Fools for Scandal 1938,Mr 25,15:3
Lie of Nina Petrovna, The 1938,Mr 30,19:2
Great Waltz, The 1938,N 25,19:1
Compliments of Mr Iflow 1941,F 17,10:7
Four Flights to Love 1942,Ap 13,12:2
Symphonie d'Amour 1946,Mr 11,19:2
Foolish Husbands 1948,O 11,27:2
Ronde, La 1954,Mr 17,27:2
Graveure, Louis
Ich Sehne Mich Nach Dir 1936,S 9,32:4
Ein Walzer fuer Dich 1936,S 29,35:2
Gibt nur eine Liebe, Es 1937,Ja 23,23:2
Gravey, Fernand
Tu Seras Duchesse 1932,My 7,11:5
Coiffeur Pour Dames 1932,O 31,18:4
Royal Affairs in Versailles 1957,Mr 9,16:1
Mitsou 1958,Ap 15,42:5
How to Steal a Million 1966,Jl 15,34:1
Gravina, Carla
Five Branded Women 1960,Je 2,27:2
Big Deal on Madonna Street, The 1960,N 23,20:1
Everybody go Home!; Tutti a Casa 1962,N 6,38:1
Violent Four, The 1968,Ag 15,46:2
Gravina, Cesare
Scratch my Back 1920,Je 5,19:3
Madame X 1920,S 27,18:1
Daddy 1923,Ap 16,20:2
Circus Days 1923,Ag 6,14:2
Humming Bird, The 1924,Ja 14,2:1
Greed 1924,D 5,28:1
Contraband 1925,Mr 24,20:6
Charmer, The 1925,Ap 6,17:3
Woman's Faith, A 1925,Jl 27,17:3
Phantom of the Opera, The 1925,S 7,15:3
Flower of the Night 1925,O 19,26:1
Midnight Sun, The 1926,Ap 24,20:4
Blonde Saint, The 1926,N 23,27:1
Road to Romance, The 1927,O 10,24:1
Cheating Cheaters 1927,D 6,27:1
Divine Woman, The 1928,Ja 16,24:1
Trail of '98, The 1928,Mr 21,30:3
Man Who Laughs, The 1928,Ap 28,12:3
How to Handle Women 1928,Je 18,13:2
Wedding March, The 1928,O 15,26:1
GRAY
See Also GREY
Gray, Alexander
Show of Shows 1929,N 21,24:5
Sally 1929,D 24,14:4
No, No, Nanette 1930,Ja 4,21:1
Song of the Flame 1930,My 7,24:5
Viennese Nights 1930,N 27,32:5
Gray, Arlene
Strange Bargain 1949,S 30,28:3
Gray, Arnold
Mummy, The 1933,Ja 7,11:2
Phantom Broadcast, The 1933,Jl 31,16:2
Private Worlds 1935,Mr 28,25:2
Nut Farm, The 1935,Ap 8,23:3
Gray, Baby
Beiden Seehunde, Die 1935,Mr 9,19:2
Gray, Barbara (Screenwriter)
Istanbul 1957,Ja 24,34:1
Gray, Bernice
Song of the Flame 1930,My 7,24:5
Gray, Billy
Specter of the Rose 1946,S 2,12:4
Fighting Father Dunne 1948,Je 25,26:2

Gray, Billy — Cont

Singing Guns 1950,Je 5,19:3
On Moonlight Bay 1951,Jl 27,15:2
Guy Who Came Back, The 1951,Ag 17,13:2
Jim Thorpe - All American 1951,Ag 25,7:2
Day the Earth Stood Still, The 1951,S 19,37:1
By the Light of the Silvery Moon
  1953,Mr 27,28:2
All I Desire 1953,Ag 29,10:1
Girl Next Door, The 1953,S 5,7:4
Seven Little Foys, The 1955,Je 30,18:2
Some Like It Hot 1959,Mr 30,23:1
Explosive Generation, The 1962,F 15,24:2
Two for the Seesaw 1962,N 22,43:1

Gray, Campbell

Odette 1951,Mr 28,33:2

Gray, Carole

Rattle of a Simple Man 1964,D 21,42:2

Gray, Charles

Man in the Moon 1961,Je 13,29:2
Night of the Generals, The 1967,F 3,38:1
You Only Live Twice 1967,Je 14,40:1
Secret War of Harry Frigg, The 1968,Mr 5,34:5
Devil's Bride, The 1968,D 19,60:1

Gray, Charles (Original Author)

River Gang 1945,O 6,9:7

Gray, Coleen

Kiss of Death 1947,Ag 28,28:2
Nightmare Alley 1947,O 10,31:3
Fury at Furnace Creek 1948,Jl 12,11:2
Red River 1948,O 1,31:2
Sand 1949,Ag 5,23:2
Father Is a Bachelor 1950,F 23,33:3
Riding High 1950,Ap 11,26:2
Sleeping City, The 1950,S 21,20:2
Lucky Nick Cain 1951,Ap 23,21:2
Apache Drums 1951,My 7,22:2
Models, Inc 1952,My 26,18:4
Kansas City Confidential 1952,N 29,11:2
Sabre Jet 1953,N 3,34:1
Arrow in the Dust 1954,My 1,13:2
Las Vegas Shakedown 1955,Je 18,14:2
Tennessee's Partner 1955,N 5,22:8
Killing, The 1956,My 21,20:1
Death of a Scoundrel 1956,N 6,30:1
Hell's Five Hours 1957,Jl 24,18:1
Hell's Five Hours 1958,Jl 24,18:1
P J 1968,Mr 7,52:3

Gray, David (Original Author)

Best People 1925,O 21,21:3
Fast and Loose 1930,D 1,21:1

Gray, Dolores

Mr Skeffington 1944,My 26,23:2
It's Always Fair Weather 1955,S 16,19:1
Kismet 1955,D 9,32:2
Opposite Sex, The 1956,N 16,23:2
Designing Woman 1957,My 17,20:2

Gray, Donald

Four Feathers 1939,Ag 4,11:1

Gray, Dorian

My Heart Sings 1954,Mr 5,15:5
Cabiria 1957,O 29,34:2
Grido, Il 1962,O 23,42:1
Love and Larceny 1963,F 2,5:6
...And Suddenly It's Murder! 1964,Ja 24,21:1

Gray, Dorothy

As the Earth Turns 1934,Ap 12,27:2
Black Fury 1935,Ap 11,27:2
Princess O'Hara 1935,Ap 13,11:3
Three Russian Girls 1944,F 5,13:2

Gray, Dulcie

Madonna of the Seven Moons 1946,My 23,18:4
They Were Sisters 1946,Jl 24,24:2
Wanted for Murder 1946,D 12,38:4
Years Between, The 1947,Mr 10,25:2
Mine Own Executioner 1949,Ja 19,34:2
Place of One's Own, A 1949,F 8,30:2
Man About the House, A 1949,Mr 9,33:2
My Brother Jonathan 1949,Je 29,34:4
Glass Mountain, The 1950,My 18,37:3
Franchise Affair, The 1952,Je 6,19:2
Angels One Five 1954,Ap 30,28:2
Man Could Get Killed, A 1966,My 12,54:2

Gray, Eddie

First a Girl 1936,Ja 4,19:1
Smiling Along 1939,F 20,13:2

Gray, Eden

Lovers in Quarantine 1925,O 13,20:1

Gray, Elspet

Blind Goddess, The 1949,Je 23,33:3

Gray, Eve

Moulin Rouge 1929,Ap 30,33:2
Night Birds 1931,Ja 3,21:2
Scrooge 1935,D 14,11:1
Last Journey, The 1936,Je 8,22:4

Gray, Gary

Address Unknown 1944,Ap 17,20:1
Rachel and the Stranger 1948,S 20,21:2
Girl from Jones Beach, The 1949,Jl 30,9:2
Great Lover, The 1949,N 24,48:2
Next Voice You Hear, The 1950,Je 30,18:2
Two Weeks With Love 1950,N 24,31:2

Gray, Gilda

Aloma of the South Seas 1926,My 17,19:1
Cabaret 1927,My 2,26:4
Devil Dancer, The 1927,D 19,30:1
Piccadilly 1929,Jl 15,25:1
Rose Marie 1936,F 1,9:2

Gray, Gilda (Miscellaneous)

Aloma of the South Seas 1926,My 17,19:1

Gray, Glen and his Casa Loma Orchestra

Time Out for Rhythm 1941,Jl 10,16:3
Gals, Inc 1943,Ag 13,13:4
Jam Session 1944,My 3,25:3

Gray, Harry

Hallelujah 1929,Ag 21,33:1

Gray, Hugh (Miscellaneous)

Kiss the Blood off my Hands 1948,O 30,10:2

Gray, Hugh (Original Author)

River Gang 1945,O 6,9:7

Gray, Hugh (Screenwriter)

Forever Yours 1937,Je 7,22:2
Drums 1938,S 30,24:4
Ulysses 1955,Ag 18,17:2
Helen of Troy 1956,Ja 27,21:4

Gray, Iris

Fascinating Youth 1926,My 10,19:1
Popular Sin, The 1926,D 20,28:3
Love's Greatest Mistake 1927,F 21,14:2

Gray, Janine

Pumpkin Eater, The 1964,N 10,58:1
Quick, Before it Melts 1965,Ap 1,30:2

Gray, John

Abandon Ship 1957,Ap 18,35:1

Gray, Lawrence

Dressmaker from Paris, The 1925,Mr 18,19:2
Are Parents People 1925,Je 9,16:3
Coast of Folly, The 1925,Ag 31,19:3
Stage Struck 1925,N 16,19:4
American Venus, The 1926,Ja 26,25:2
Untamed Lady, The 1926,Mr 16,22:5
Palm Beach Girl, The 1926,Je 22,21:2
Kid Boots 1926,O 11,18:2
Everybody's Acting 1926,N 8,19:2
Love 'Em and Leave 'Em 1926,D 8,24:3
Ankles Preferred 1927,Ap 18,21:2
Convoy 1927,My 9,26:4
Telephone Girl, The 1927,My 16,24:2
Callahans and the Murphys, The 1927,Jl 12,29:3
After Midnight 1927,Ag 16,31:2
Pajamas 1927,N 7,26:4
Ladies Must Dress 1927,D 31,31:1
Love Hungry 1928,Ap 16,20:5
Patsy, The 1928,Ap 23,20:2
Oh, Kay! 1928,Ag 27,23:1
Marriage by Contract 1928,N 13,37:1
Marianne 1929,O 19,22:6
It's a Great Life 1930,Ja 18,21:1
Florodora Girl, The 1930,My 31,19:4
Sunny 1930,D 27,16:3
Going Wild 1931,Ja 26,21:1
Man of the World 1931,Mr 21,15:1
She-Wolf 1931,My 28,30:6
Here Comes the Groom 1934,Je 16,20:2

Gray, Lilian

Life of Beethoven, The 1929,Mr 12,26:3

Gray, Lorna

Adventure in Sahara 1938,D 19,19:2
Convicted Woman 1940,F 26,11:2
So Proudly We Hail 1943,S 10,29:1

Gray, Mack

Car 99 1935,F 23,14:7
Broadway 1942,Je 5,23:2
Johnny Angel 1945,D 28,12:2
Nocturne 1946,N 11,42:2
Race Street 1948,Ag 23,13:3

Gray, Madeline

Nothing but the Truth 1929,Ap 22,23:1

Gray, Nadia

Silver King, The 1919,Ja 13,9:3
Valley of the Eagles 1952,Ap 11,19:2
Spider and the Fly, The 1952,Jl 29,17:3
Night Without Stars 1953,Jl 14,19:4
Mr Potts Goes to Moscow 1953,S 3,15:2
House of Ricordi 1956,Mr 13,32:1
Sins of Casanova 1957,O 7,23:2
Folies Bergere 1958,My 28,37:2
Wife for a Night 1958,Je 12,35:2
Parisienne, La 1958,Jl 31,27:1
Senechal the Magnificent 1958,O 14,44:1
Holiday Island; (Vacanzie a Izchia)
  1959,S 22,46:1
Captain's Table, The 1960,S 27,40:1
Dolce Vita, La 1961,Ap 20,30:1
Neapolitan Carousel 1961,O 12,41:3
I Like Money 1962,My 19,18:2
Candide 1962,N 20,39:1
Maniac 1963,O 31,26:3
Crooked Road, The 1965,F 4,24:2
Two for the Road 1967,Ap 28,36:2
Naked Runner, The 1967,Jl 20,30:2
Oldest Profession, The (Paris Today); Paris Today
  (The Oldest Profession) 1968,N 8,42:1

Gray, Nan

Firebird, The 1934,N 15,25:2

Gray, Peter

House of Bamboo 1955,Jl 2,13:2

Gray, Roger

Hit the Deck 1930,Ja 15,28:6
George White's Scandals 1934,Mr 16,24:2
Come on Marines 1934,Mr 24,20:3
Barbary Coast 1935,O 14,21:1
Fury 1936,Je 6,21:1
Westerner, The 1940,O 25,25:2

Gray, Sally

Saint in London, The 1939,Jl 19,23:3
Saint's Vacation, The 1941,Je 13,22:2
Lady in Distress 1942,F 16,21:2
Suicide Squadron 1942,My 14,23:2
Green for Danger 1947,Ag 8,10:2
Silent Dust 1949,D 30,13:2
Hidden Room, The 1950,Ja 9,19:2

Gray, Sidney de

Amateur Gentleman, The 1926,Ag 17,15:3

Gray, Thomas J (Screenwriter)

Hot Water 1924,O 27,27:1

Gray, Vernon

To Paris With Love 1955,Mr 29,33:4
Barretts of Wimpole Street, The 1957,Ja 18,15:3

Grayam, Dan

Look in any Window 1962,Mr 22,40:1

Grayson, Charles (Original Author)

Newsboys' Home 1939,Ja 23,8:2
Wild Blue Yonder, The 1952,Ja 2,20:1

Grayson, Charles (Screenwriter)

Crash Donovan 1936,Ag 10,10:3
Breezing Home 1937,Mr 20,23:5
Top of the Town 1937,Mr 27,19:2
You're a Sweetheart 1937,D 25,10:5
Personal Secretary 1938,O 5,20:2
Risky Business 1939,Mr 23,27:2
Unexpected Father 1939,Ag 11,12:2
Hawaiian Nights 1939,S 29,19:4
Double Alibi 1940,Mr 11,11:2
Ma! He's Making Eyes at Me 1940,Ap 26,25:2
Sandy Is a Lady 1940,Je 28,22:2
Private Affairs 1940,Jl 5,10:3
She Couldn't Say No 1941,Ja 17,21:3
Underground 1941,Je 23,13:2
Bad Men of Missouri 1941,Ag 16,18:2
Law of the Tropics 1941,O 10,26:5
Wild Bill Hickok Rides 1942,F 7,13:5
Noose Hangs High, The 1948,My 29,8:6
Outpost in Morocco 1949,Mr 25,28:3
Woman on Pier 13, The 1950,Je 16,28:4
Battle Hymn 1957,F 16,14:1
Barbarian and the Geisha 1958,O 3,25:1

Grayson, Eunice

Out of the Clouds 1957,Ag 1,20:4

Grayson, Jessie

Little Foxes, The 1941,Ag 22,19:2
Syncopation 1942,My 29,13:3
Youngest Profession, The 1943,Je 25,13:3
Claudia 1943,N 5,23:2
Cass Timberlane 1947,N 7,20:2
Our Very Own 1950,Jl 28,12:5

Grayson, Kathryn

Andy Hardy's Private Secretary 1941,Mr 7,17:2
Rio Rita 1942,My 8,27:3
Vanishing Virginian, The 1942,My 28,13:3
Seven Sweethearts 1942,N 13,28:1
Thousands Cheer 1943,S 14,27:1
Anchors Aweigh 1945,Jl 20,15:2
Ziegfeld Follies 1946,Mr 23,8:3
Two Sisters From Boston 1946,Je 7,16:2
Till the Clouds Roll By 1946,D 6,27:4
It Happened in Brooklyn 1947,Mr 14,28:5
Kissing Bandit, The 1948,N 19,35:2
That Midnight Kiss 1949,S 23,28:2
Toast of New Orleans, The 1950,S 30,13:3
Grounds for Marriage 1951,Ja 12,24:6
Show Boat 1951,Jl 20,14:1
Lovely to Look At 1952,My 30,11:2
Desert Song, The 1953,My 21,39:2
So This Is Love 1953,Ag 12,22:1
Kiss Me Kate 1953,N 6,23:2
Vagabond King, The 1956,S 13,39:6

Grayson, Madelon

Girls of the Road 1940,Jl 22,20:2

Grayson, Richard

Eight Iron Men 1953,Ja 2,11:1

Grayson, Victoria

Another Sky 1960,O 25,40:2

Grazer, Wanda

Dramatic Life of Abraham Lincoln, The
  1924,Ja 22,17:3

Graziano, Rocky

Mister Rock and Roll 1957,O 17,42:2
Teenage Millionaire 1962,Ja 12,29:2
Tony Rome 1967,N 16,58:1

Graziosi, Giorgio (Screenwriter)

Anthony of Padua 1952,Mr 29,19:2

Graziosi, Paolo

China Is Near 1968,Ja 9,37:1

Greanin, Leon
Toast to Love 1951,N 7,35:5
Greason, John
Desert Patrol 1962,Ja 18,23:5
Great Mendoza
Three Little Words 1950,Ag 10,21:2
Greatorex, Wilfred (Screenwriter)
High Commissioner, The 1968,D 12,62:5
Greaves, William
Lost Boundaries 1949,Jl 1,14:4
Miracle in Harlem 1949,O 24,19:4
Greaza, Walter
Boomerang 1947,Mr 6,36:2
Street with no Name, The 1948,Jl 15,26:6
Larceny 1948,S 4,8:6
It Happened to Jane 1959,Ag 6,18:3
Grebel, Stevan
Lovers of Teruel, The 1962,D 15,5:1
Grebeshkova, N
Devotion 1955,Ag 1,15:2
Mumu 1961,Je 5,37:4
Grebner, G (Screenwriter)
General Suvorov 1941,S 20,11:2
Adventure in Odessa 1954,Je 21,19:6
Grechani, A
Mother and Sons 1938,S 15,29:2
In the Rear of the Enemy 1942,O 10,11:2
Greci, Jose
Goliath and the Sins of Babylon 1964,Mr 5,36:2
Greco
Orpheus 1950,N 30,42:2
Greco, Cosetta
Three Girls From Rome 1953,O 14,34:2
Wild Love; (Gli Inamorati) 1961,Ap 6,30:2
Greco, Francesco
Island Sinner, The 1960,S 5,11:2
Greco, Jose
Sombrero 1953,Ap 23,37:2
Around the World in 80 Days 1956,O 18,37:1
Holiday for Lovers 1959,Jl 25,10:2
Ship of Fools 1965,Jl 29,18:1
Greco, Juliette
Green Glove, The 1952,Ap 24,38:1
Paris Does Strange Things 1957,Mr 30,13:2
Sun Also Rises, The 1957,Ag 24,12:2
Bonjour Tristesse 1958,Ja 16,32:1
Naked Earth 1958,Ag 29,18:1
Roots of Heaven, The 1958,O 16,46:1
Crack in the Mirror 1960,My 20,26:1
Big Gamble, The 1961,S 2,19:2
Greco, Perlita
Cancion del Regreso, La; Home-Coming Song
1940,Je 22,18:4
Grede, Kjell (Screenwriter)
Hugo and Josephine 1968,S 30,60:1
Gredy, Jean-Pierre (Screenwriter)
Beauties of the Night 1954,Mr 23,23:5
Greear, Geraine
Gaucho, The 1927,N 22,32:2
Greek Folk Dances and Songs Society (Panegyris)
Boy on a Dolphin 1957,Ap 20,21:2
Green, Abel
Copacabana 1947,Jl 12,7:2
Green, Adolph (Original Author)
On the Town 1949,D 9,37:2
Singin' in the Rain 1952,Mr 28,27:2
Bells Are Ringing 1960,Je 24,31:2
Green, Adolph (Screenwriter)
Good News 1947,D 5,33:2
Barkleys of Broadway, The 1949,My 5,34:2
On the Town 1949,D 9,37:2
Singin' in the Rain 1952,Mr 28,27:2
Band Wagon, The 1953,Jl 10,10:2
Auntie Mame 1958,D 5,39:1
Bells Are Ringing 1960,Je 24,31:2
What a Way to Go! 1964,My 15,44:1
Green, Alan (Original Author)
Love on the Run 1936,N 28,13:3
Green, Alan (Screenwriter)
Long Wait, The 1954,Jl 3,9:2
Green, Alfred (Director)
Just Out of College 1921,F 7,8:2
Through the Back Door 1921,My 6,20:2
(Incorrect in this edition; use 1921,My 16,20:2
elsewhere)
Little Lord Fauntleroy 1921,S 16,17:3
Our Leading Citizen 1922,Je 12,16:2 (Incorrect in
this edition; use 1922,Je 12,10:2 elsewhere)
Ghost Breaker, The 1922,S 11,20:2
Back Home and Broke 1922,D 25,21:1
Ne'er Do-Well, The 1923,My 1,24:3
Woman Proof 1923,O 30,16:1
Pied Piper Malone 1924,Ja 28,12:1
In Hollywood with Potash and Perlmutter
1924,S 30,27:3
Inez From Hollywood 1924,D 16,28:1
Sally 1925,Mr 16,16:1
Talker, The 1925,My 12,26:2
Man Who Found Himself, The 1925,Ag 24,17:3
Irene 1926,Mr 1,17:1
Ella Cinders 1926,Je 7,23:2
It Must Be Love 1926,O 4,20:2
Ladies at Play 1926,N 16,25:3

Is Zat So? 1927,My 17,27:2
Two Girls Wanted 1927,N 14,26:1
Come to My House 1928,Ja 16,24:1
Honor Bound 1928,Ap 30,18:3
Disraeli 1929,O 3,27:5
Green Goddess, The 1930,F 14,20:1
Man From Blankley's, The 1930,Mr 29,23:1
Sweet Kitty Bellairs 1930,S 6,9:2
Smart Money 1931,Je 19,21:1
Road to Singapore, The 1931,O 1,25:2
Union Depot 1932,Ja 15,24:4
It's Tough to be Famous 1932,Ap 9,18:1
Rich are Always With Us, The 1932,My 16,19:5
Dark Horse, The 1932,Je 9,27:3
Silver Dollar 1932,D 23,20:1
Parachute Jumper 1933,Ja 26,12:2
Baby Face 1933,Je 24,16:2
Narrow Corner, The 1933,Jl 14,15:3
I Loved a Woman 1933,S 22,14:2
Dark Hazard 1934,F 23,23:3
As the Earth Turns 1934,Ap 12,27:2
Housewife 1934,Ag 10,21:2
Side Streets 1934,Ag 15,13:5
Lost Lady, A 1934,O 4,19:1
Gentlemen are Born 1934,N 22,27:2
Sweet Music 1935,F 21,23:2
Girl From 10th Avenue, The 1935,My 27,20:6
Goose and the Gander, The 1935,S 12,29:2
Here's to Romance 1935,O 3,29:2
Dangerous 1935,D 27,14:1
Colleen 1936,Mr 9,20:2
Golden Arrow, The 1936,My 4,16:1
They Met in a Taxi 1936,S 7,20:5
Two in a Crowd 1936,O 5,25:1
More Than a Secretary 1936,D 11,35:2
League of Frightened Men, The 1937,Jl 2,25:1
Mr Dodd Takes the Air 1937,Ag 12,14:2
Thoroughbreds Don't Cry 1937,N 26,27:4
Duke of West Point, The 1938,D 16,33:2
Ride a Crooked Mile 1938,D 29,15:2
King of the Turf 1939,My 8,21:2
Gracie Allen Murder Case, The 1939,Je 8,31:3
20,000 Men a Year 1939,O 28,11:2
Shooting High 1940,Ap 12,19:2
South of Pago-Pago 1940,Ag 2,12:2
Flowing Gold 1940,S 2,19:3
East of the River 1940,O 28,21:2
Adventure in Washington 1941,Ag 1,11:3
Badlands of Dakota 1941,S 9,27:6
Mayor of Forty-Fourth Street, The
1942,Je 11,27:4
Appointment in Berlin 1943,Jl 17,8:2
Mr Winkle Goes to War 1944,Ag 3,16:1
Thousand and one Nights, A 1945,Jl 12,8:2
Tars and Spars 1946,F 15,29:2
Jolson Story, The 1946,O 11,28:2
Fabulous Dorseys, The 1947,My 30,25:3
Copacabana 1947,Jl 12,7:2
Four Faces West 1948,Ag 4,18:3
Jackie Robinson Story, The 1950,My 17,36:1
Sierra 1950,S 15,31:2
Invasion USA 1953,Ap 30,39:4
Eddie Cantor Story, The 1953,D 26,10:2
Top Banana 1954,F 20,8:6
Green, Amy
Inspector Calls, An 1954,N 26,24:4
Green, Anne (Screenwriter)
Her Sister's Secret 1947,Ja 23,31:3
Green, Billy
Frisco Sal 1945,F 17,11:2
Tangier 1946,Je 7,II,16:4
Life of Riley, The 1949,Ap 18,18:4
Green, Bud (Composer)
Baby, Take a Bow 1934,Je 30,18:6
Green, Charles
Bluebeard's 8th Wife 1923,Ag 7,20:2
Three Weeks 1924,Ap 1,19:3
Empty Hands 1924,Ag 18,8:2
Green, Danny
Crime Over London 1938,Jl 28,23:2
Smugglers, The 1948,Mr 29,17:1
No Orchids for Miss Blandish 1951,F 23,33:2
Ladykillers 1956,F 21,37:2
Kid for two Farthings, A 1956,Ap 18,25:1
Abandon Ship 1957,Ap 18,35:1
In the Wake of a Stranger 1961,Je 22,23:3
Old Dark House, The 1963,O 31,26:3
Green, Dee Dee
Enemies of the Law 1931,Jl 13,13:5
Cold Wind in August, A 1961,Jl 27,23:2
Green, Denis
Witness Vanishes, The 1939,O 23,15:2
Dr Jekyll and Mr Hyde 1941,Ag 13,13:2
Yank in the R A F, A 1941,S 27,11:3
Frenchman's Creek 1944,S 21,26:2
Lone Wolf in London, The 1947,N 22,10:3
Mighty Joe Young 1949,Jl 28,19:3
Green, Dorothy
Big Heat, The 1953,O 15,43:2
Helen Morgan Story, The 1957,O 3,33:2
Palm Springs Weekend 1963,N 6,32:1

Green, Duke
Call of the Wild 1935,Ag 15,15:2
Green, Eddie
Duffy's Tavern 1945,S 6,23:3
Green, F L (Original Author)
Odd Man Out 1947,Ap 24,30:2
Green, F L (Screenwriter)
Odd Man Out 1947,Ap 24,30:2
Green, George
Native Son 1951,Je 18,19:2
Green, George (Original Author)
Tom Brown of Culver 1932,Jl 30,16:5
Green, George Grafton (Producer)
Palaces of a Queen 1967,Je 27,32:1
Green, Gerald (Original Author)
His Majesty O'Keefe 1954,F 6,17:2
Last Angry Man, The 1959,O 23,24:1
Green, Gerald (Screenwriter)
Last Angry Man, The 1959,O 23,24:1
Green, Gertrude
Devil's Squadron 1936,My 11,16:2
Green, Gilbert
By Love Possessed 1961,Jl 20,32:2
Experiment in Terror 1962,Ap 14,14:1
Dark Intruder 1965,Jl 22,24:2
Green, Guy (Director)
Tears for Simon 1957,Ap 18,35:2
Triple Deception 1957,O 7,23:2
Snorkel, The 1958,S 18,37:2
S O S Pacific 1960,O 13,41:3
Angry Silence, The 1960,D 13,25:2
Mark, The 1961,O 3,46:2
Desert Patrol 1962,Ja 18,23:5
Light in the Piazza 1962,F 8,25:1
Diamond Head 1963,F 21,5:2
Patch of Blue, A 1965,D 16,63:1
Matter of Innocence, A 1968,F 22,36:1
Magus, The 1968,D 11,57:1
Green, Guy (Screenwriter)
Patch of Blue, A 1965,D 16,63:1
Green, Harry
Close Harmony 1929,Ap 29,29:2
Man I Love, The 1929,My 28,36:2
Why Bring That Up? 1929,O 5,22:5
Kibitzer, The 1929,D 21,17:1
Be Yourself 1930,Mr 7,20:5
Honey 1930,Mr 29,23:1
Paramount on Parade 1930,Ap 21,20:4
Light of Western Stars, The 1930,Ap 26,11:1
True to the Navy 1930,My 24,21:2
Spoilers, The 1930,S 20,15:4
Sea Legs 1930,N 11,29:1
No Limit 1931,Ja 17,23:1
This Day and Age 1933,S 1,15:4
Too Much Harmony 1933,S 23,11:5
Mr Skitch 1933,D 23,19:1
Coming-Out Party 1934,Mr 17,11:3
Bottoms Up 1934,Mr 23,29:2
Born to be Bad 1934,My 31,22:6
Wild Gold 1934,Jl 24,20:2
She Learned About Sailors 1934,Jl 30,9:4
Cisco Kid and the Lady, The 1939,D 25,29:2
Star Dust 1940,My 4,13:1
Joe Macbeth 1956,Ap 7,13:1
Alligator Named Daisy, An 1957,O 7,23:2
Next to no Time 1960,My 28,13:2
Green, Howard (Miscellaneous)
Song of Love, The 1929,N 14,24:3
New Faces of 1937 1937,Jl 2,25:1
Green, Howard (Original Author)
Dangerous Affair, A 1931,N 23,22:1
Maker of Men 1931,D 19,16:4
Cohens and Kellys in Hollywood, The
1932,Ap 22,23:2
Making the Headlines 1938,Ap 1,17:2
Invisible Wall, The 1947,N 1,11:2
Green, Howard (Producer)
Meet the Girls 1938,S 3,16:6
Time Out for Murder 1938,O 7,21:2
Green, Howard (Screenwriter)
Broadway Scandals 1929,O 29,35:1
Song of Love, The 1929,N 14,24:3
Rumba 1935,F 25,13:2
Star of Midnight 1935,Ap 12,26:5
Men Without Names 1935,Je 29,16:2
If You Could Only Cook 1935,D 26,21:4
Devil's Squadron 1936,My 11,16:2
Meet Nero Wolfe 1936,Jl 16,20:1
They Met in a Taxi 1936,S 7,20:5
This Way Please 1937,O 8,27:2
Making the Headlines 1938,Ap 1,17:2
Mad Doctor, The 1941,F 27,23:4
Harmon of Michigan 1941,O 2,29:2
Reveille With Beverly 1943,Ap 24,17:2
Having Wonderful Crime 1945,Ap 13,15:2
George White's Scandals 1945,O 11,26:2
San Quentin 1947,F 10,24:3
Green, Hugh
Tom Brown's School Days 1940,Je 28,22:2
If Winter Comes 1948,Ja 23,28:4
Hills of Home 1948,N 26,32:2

Green, Jane
Marriage Is a Private Affair 1944,O 27,17:7
Bad Bascomb 1946,My 23,18:4
Courage of Lassie 1946,Jl 25,18:5
Cockeyed Miracle, The 1946,O 25,28:1
Good News 1947,D 5,33:2
Green, Janet (Original Author)
Clouded Yellow, The 1951,N 13,33:2
Tears for Simon 1957,Ap 18,35:2
Cast a Dark Shadow 1957,N 28,57:1
Midnight Lace 1960,O 14,27:1
Green, Janet (Screenwriter)
Clouded Yellow, The 1951,N 13,33:2
Third Key, The 1957,Je 3,30:2
Sapphire 1959,N 3,27:1
Victim 1962,F 6,27:2
7 Women 1966,My 5,59:1
Walk in the Shadow 1966,S 12,52:5
Green, Johnny (Composer)
Start Cheering 1938,Mr 17,17:3
Stage Door Canteen 1943,Je 25,13:2
Fiesta 1947,Je 27,17:3
Something in the Wind 1947,Ag 29,14:3
Toast of New Orleans, The 1950,S 30,13:3
Green, Johnny and his orchestra
Start Cheering 1938,Mr 17,17:3
Green, Joseph
Baron of Arizona, The 1950,Je 23,29:2
Green, Joseph (Director)
Yiddle With his Fiddle 1937,Ja 2,15:1
Purimspieler, Der 1937,D 6,19:2
Mamele; Little Mothers 1938,D 26,29:1
Brivele der Mamen, A; Little Letter to Mother, A 1939,S 15,26:4
Green, Judd
Chu Chin Chow 1925,F 11,19:4
Nell Gwyn 1926,Jl 19,13:1
Woman Tempted, The 1928,Ap 24,29:3
Green, Laurence (Original Author)
Fugitive, The 1940,Jl 23,22:2
Green, Marika
Pickpocket 1963,My 22,36:2
Green, Martyn
Mikado, The 1939,Je 2,27:2
Gilbert and Sullivan 1953,O 28,36:3
Lovely Way to Die, A 1968,Jl 13,18:1
Green, Millicent
They Knew What They Wanted 1940,O 11,25:2
Green, Mitzi
Honey 1930,Mr 29,23:1
Paramount on Parade 1930,Ap 21,20:4
Love Among the Millionaires 1930,Jl 5,17:4
Sante Fe Trail, The 1930,O 18,23:2
Tom Sawyer 1930,D 20,20:6
Finn and Hattie 1931,Ja 31,15:1
Skippy 1931,Ap 4,23:1
Dude Ranch 1931,Ap 25,23:4
Newly Rich 1931,Jl 3,22:1
Huckleberry Finn 1931,Ag 8,16:3
Girl Crazy 1932,Mr 25,23:3
Transatlantic Merry-Go-Round 1934,N 1,25:2
Bloodhounds of Broadway 1952,N 15,15:2
Green, Morris Lee (Screenwriter)
This Rebel Breed 1960,My 5,41:2
Green, Nigel
Reach for the Sky 1957,My 1,40:1
Sword of Sherwood Forest 1961,Ja 26,32:3
Mysterious Island 1961,D 21,30:6
Zulu 1964,Jl 8,38:1
Masque of the Red Death, The 1964,S 17,52:6
Ipcress File, The 1965,Ag 3,35:1
Face of Fu Manchu, The 1965,N 11,58:3
Khartoum 1966,Jl 14,28:1
Let's Kill Uncle 1966,N 19,26:1
Tobruk 1967,F 9,33:2
Deadlier Than the Male 1967,F 22,21:1
Africa-Texas Style! 1967,Jl 13,30:2
Pink Jungle, The 1968,O 17,52:1
Green, Paul (Original Author)
Carolina 1934,F 16,17:2
Green, Paul (Screenwriter)
State Fair 1945,Ag 31,14:3
State Fair 1962,Ap 12,41:4
Green, Reita
Stranger in my Arms 1959,Mr 4,34:2
Green, Ronald
Diane 1956,Ja 13,18:1
Green, Walon (Director)
Spree 1967,N 30,59:2
Green, Walton (Original Author)
Corsair 1931,N 19,27:5
Private Affairs 1940,Jl 5,10:3
Green, William H (Cinematographer)
Legong 1935,O 2,27:1
Greenbaum, Everett (Screenwriter)
Good Neighbor Sam 1964,Jl 23,19:1
Ghost and Mr Chicken, The 1966,S 22,57:2
Shakiest Gun in the West, The 1968,Jl 11,30:1
Greenbaum, Marty
Hallelujah the Hills 1963,D 17,49:1
Greenberg, Esther
Sallah 1965,O 13,39:1

Greenberg, Hank
Untitled-Baseball Technique 1941,Ja 17,11:3
Greenberg, Henry (Screenwriter)
Al Capone 1959,Mr 26,27:1
Caretakers, The 1963,Ag 22,19:2
Greenbill, Dorothy (Original Author)
For Love or Money 1934,Jl 26,14:2
Greene, Angela
Time, The Place And The Girl, The 1946,D 27,14:3
Stallion Road 1947,Ap 5,12:5
Love and Learn 1947,My 3,10:3
At War With the Army 1951,Ja 25,21:5
Greene, Barbara
Moonlight Sonata 1937,Je 6,XI,4:4 (In Addenda)
Moonlight Sonata 1938,My 10,17:2
Greene, Billy
Shrike, The 1955,Jl 8,15:2
Slaughter on Tenth Avenue 1957,N 6,43:1
Never Steal Anything Small 1959,F 12,23:1
Lolita 1962,Je 14,23:2
Greene, Clarence (Original Author)
Pillow Talk 1959,O 7,47:2
Greene, Clarence (Producer)
Well, The 1951,S 27,37:2
Thief, The 1952,O 16,37:1
Wicked Woman 1954,Mr 27,13:6
New York Confidential 1955,F 19,18:1
Unidentified Flying Objects 1956,Je 13,46:2
Fastest Gun Alive, The 1956,Jl 13,23:3
Thunder in the Sun 1959,Ap 9,37:2
House is not a Home, A 1964,S 2,33:1
Oscar, The 1966,Mr 5,16:1
Caper of the Golden Bulls, The 1967,Je 22,46:1
Greene, Clarence (Screenwriter)
D O A 1950,My 1,18:2
Well, The 1951,S 27,37:2
Thief, The 1952,O 16,37:1
Wicked Woman 1954,Mr 27,13:6
New York Confidential 1955,F 19,18:1
House is not a Home, A 1964,S 2,33:1
Oscar, The 1966,Mr 5,16:1
Greene, David
Golden Madonna, The 1949,S 5,13:4
Wooden Horse, The 1951,Ag 29,20:2
Greene, David (Director)
Sebastian 1968,Ja 25,33:2
Shuttered Room, The 1968,F 15,47:1
Strange Affair, The 1968,Jl 25,26:2
Greene, David Allen (Cinematographer)
Come Back Baby 1968,Je 14,43:1
Greene, David Allen (Director)
Come Back Baby 1968,Je 14,43:1
Greene, David Allen (Miscellaneous)
Come Back Baby 1968,Je 14,43:1
Greene, David Allen (Producer)
Come Back Baby 1968,Je 14,43:1
Greene, David Allen (Screenwriter)
Come Back Baby 1968,Je 14,43:1
Greene, Eve (Miscellaneous)
Artists and Models 1937,Ag 5,19:2
Greene, Eve (Original Author)
Moonlight in Hamaii 1941,O 10,26:6
Greene, Eve (Screenwriter)
Great Impersonation, The 1935,D 14,11:1
Yours for the Asking 1936,Ag 20,14:2
Her Husband Lies 1937,Mr 18,20:1
When Love Is Young 1937,Ap 17,15:1
Stolen Heaven 1938,My 12,27:2
Little Accident 1939,N 24,29:3
Night of January 16th, The 1941,D 19,35:1
Sweater Girl 1942,Jl 13,18:3
Born to Kill 1947,My 1,34:2
Greene, Felix (Cinematographer)
China 1965,My 26,41:1
North Vietnam 1967,D 11,65:3
Greene, Felix (Narrator)
North Vietnam 1967,D 11,65:3
Greene, Felix (Producer)
China 1965,My 26,41:1
North Vietnam-A Personal Report 1968,Ja 23,79:1
Greene, Felix (Screenwriter)
China 1965,My 26,41:1
North Vietnam 1967,D 11,65:3
Greene, Frances Nimmo (Original Author)
One Clear Call 1922,Je 19,10:3
Greene, Graham (Miscellaneous)
Stranger's Hand, The 1955,F 16,24:5
Greene, Graham (Original Author)
Orient Express 1934,F 28,23:2
This Gun for Hire 1942,My 14,23:2
48 Hours 1944,Je 26,21:2
Ministry of Fear 1945,F 8,15:2
Confidential Agent 1945,N 3,11:2
Green Cockatoo, The 1947,Jl 19,10:2
Fugitive, The 1947,D 26,22:2
Smugglers, The 1948,Mr 29,17:1
Fallen Idol, The 1949,N 16,39:2
Third Man, The 1950,F 3,29:2
Young Scarface 1951,N 8,35:2
Heart of the Matter, The 1954,N 19,20:2
End of the Affair, The 1955,Ap 29,28:2

Greene, Graham (Original Author) — Cont
Across the Bridge 1957,O 30,24:1
Quiet American, The 1958,F 6,24:1
Our Man in Havana 1960,Ja 28,26:1
Comedians, The 1967,N 1,37:1
Greene, Graham (Screenwriter)
Fallen Idol, The 1949,N 16,39:2
Third Man, The 1950,F 3,29:2
Young Scarface 1951,N 8,35:2
Saint Joan 1957,Je 27,21:1
Our Man in Havana 1960,Ja 28,26:1
Comedians, The 1967,N 1,37:1
Greene, Harold (Original Author)
Great Plane Robbery, The 1940,N 15,25:2
Kansas City Confidential 1952,N 29,11:2
Hide and Seek 1964,Mr 12,40:3
Greene, Harold (Screenwriter)
Criminal Lawyer 1951,Ag 24,11:4
Texas Across the River 1966,N 24,65:1
Greene, Harrison
Vampire Bat, The 1933,Ja 23,9:1
International House 1933,My 27,11:5
Midnight Court 1937,Mr 4,27:3
Career 1939,Jl 28,14:2
You Can't Fool Your Wife 1940,My 24,23:4
Greene, Howard
Kitchen, The 1961,N 2,42:1
Greene, Ira (Producer)
George Washington Carver 1940,Ap 17,26:4
Greene, Jaclynne
Girls in the Night 1953,Ja 16,19:3
Greene, Joe (Composer)
See my Lawyer 1945,My 4,23:4
Greene, John L (Original Author)
Private Navy of Sgt O'Farrell, The 1968,My 9,54:1
Greene, Leon
Funny Thing Happened on the Way to the Forum, A 1966,O 17,48:1
Devil's Bride, The 1968,D 19,60:1
Greene, Lorne
Silver Chalice, The 1954,D 27,22:5
Tight Spot 1955,Mr 19,11:7
Autumn Leaves 1956,Ag 2,21:2
Peyton Place 1957,D 13,35:1
Gift of Love, The 1958,F 12,32:2
Buccaneer, The 1958,D 24,00:0
Trap, The 1959,Ja 29,18:4
Greene, Max (Director)
Man From Morocco, The 1946,N 25,38:2
Greene, Mort (Composer)
Hold That Ghost 1941,Ag 8,13:3
Call out the Marines 1942,Ja 26,18:3
Sing Your Worries Away 1942,My 15,25:2
Seven Days Ashore 1944,Ap 26,24:7
Greene, Otis
White Witch Doctor 1953,Jl 2,19:3
Sunrise at Campobello 1960,S 29,32:1
Greene, Patricia
Kitchen, The 1961,N 2,42:1
Greene, Richard
Four Men and a Prayer 1938,My 7,18:1
My Lucky Star 1938,S 10,20:2
Submarine Patrol 1938,N 19,9:2
Kentucky 1938,D 24,12:1
Little Princess, The 1939,Mr 11,21:1
Hound of the Baskervilles, The 1939,Mr 25,19:2
Stanley and Livingstone 1939,Ag 5,18:2
Here I Am a Stranger 1939,S 30,11:2
Little Old New York 1940,F 3,9:2
I Was an Adventuress 1940,My 20,13:2
Flying Fortress 1942,D 19,22:2
Yellow Canary, The 1944,Ap 14,24:7
Forever Amber 1947,O 23,31:2
Showtime 1948,My 20,35:3
Don't Take it to Heart 1948,D 25,10:3
Fighting O'Flynn, The 1949,F 28,16:2
Fan, The 1949,Ap 2,12:2
If This Be Sin 1950,Jl 1,9:2
Desert Hawk, The 1950,Ag 26,9:2
Operation X 1950,D 11,31:2
Lorna Doone 1951,S 21,19:4
Black Castle, The 1952,D 26,20:4
Sword of Sherwood Forest 1961,Ja 26,32:3
Greene, Sarah P McLean (Original Author)
Women Who Give 1924,Je 3,22:1
Greene, Shecky
Tony Rome 1967,N 16,58:1
Greene, Stanley
For Love of Ivy 1968,Jl 18,26:1
Greene, Ward (Original Author)
They Won't Forget 1937,Jl 15,16:1
Lady and the Tramp 1955,Je 24,17:1
Greenlaw, Verina
Father Goose 1964,D 11,55:1
Greenleaf, Raymond
Deep Waters 1948,Jl 23,12:4
For the Love of Mary 1948,S 23,37:2
Kiss in the Dark, A 1949,Mr 26,10:6
Slattery's Hurricane 1949,Ag 13,6:6
Pinky 1949,S 30,28:2
All the King's Men 1949,N 9,37:2
East Side, West Side 1949,D 23,17:2
No Sad Songs for Me 1950,Ap 28,26:2

Greenleaf, Raymond — Cont

Ticket to Tomahawk, A 1950,My 20,8:6
Harriet Craig 1950,N 3,31:2
Storm Warning 1951,Mr 3,8:2
Al Jennings of Oklahoma. 1951,My 18,34:6
Millionaire for Christy, A 1951,O 5,24:3
Washington Story 1952,Jl 2,22:3
She's Working her Way Through College 1952,Jl 10,27:2
Paula 1952,Jl 16,21:2
South Sea Woman 1953,Je 4,33:6
Powder River 1953,Jl 4,7:2
Never Say Goodbye 1956,Ap 14,20:1
Monkey on my Back 1957,My 30,23:2
Story of Page One, The 1960,Ja 14,28:1
From the Terrace 1960,Jl 16,10:1
Wild in the Country 1961,Je 10,12:2
Birdman of Alcatraz 1962,Jl 19,19:2

Greenman, Alvin

Miracle on 34th Street 1947,Je 5,32:1
Mr Belvedere Goes to College 1949,Ap 16,11:2
Down Among the Sheltering Palms 1953,Je 13,11:2
Beast From 20,000 Fathoms, The 1953,Je 25,23:1

Greenspan, Peter

French Mistress, A 1960,D 19,34:2

Greenstreet, Sydney

Maltese Falcon, The 1941,O 4,18:2
They Died With Their Boots On 1941,N 21,23:3
Across the Pacific 1942,S 5,9:2
Casablanca 1942,N 27,27:1
Background to Danger 1943,Jl 3,11:2
Passage to Marseille 1944,F 17,12:5
Between Two Worlds 1944,My 6,11:2
Mask of Dimitrios, The 1944,Je 24,16:2
Conspirators, The 1944,O 21,15:2
Hollywood Canteen 1944,D 16,19:2
Pillow to Post 1945,My 26,18:2
Conflict 1945,Je 16,10:2
Christmas in Connecticut 1945,Jl 28,7:2
Three Strangers 1946,F 23,20:2
Devotion 1946,Ap 6,10:5
Verdict, The 1946,D 13,29:4
That Way With Women 1947,F 15,20:4
Hucksters, The 1947,Jl 18,21:2
Woman in White, The 1948,My 8,12:2
Velvet Touch, The 1948,Ag 26,16:2
Ruthless 1948,S 4,8:7
Flamingo Road 1949,My 7,10:2
Malaya 1950,F 23,33:1

Greenwald, Harold Dr (Original Author)

Girl of the Night 1960,N 12,15:1

Greenwald, Hazel (Screenwriter)

Tomorrow's a Wonderful Day 1949,Ap 11,29:4

Greenway, Ann

Half Marriage 1929,Ag 19,22:1

Greenway, Tom

Outcasts of Poker Flat 1952,My 16,19:3
Winning Team, The 1952,Je 21,12:2
Miami Story, The 1954,My 15,13:2
Nice Little Bank That Should Be Robbed, A 1958,D 11,17:4
Story of Page One, The 1960,Ja 14,28:1
Second Time Around, The 1961,D 23,16:1

Greenwood, Charlotte

Baby Mine 1928,Ja 9,20:1
So Long Letty 1930,F 8,12:5
Parlor, Bedroom and Bath 1931,Ap 4,23:1
Man in Possession, The 1931,Jl 18,16:6
Palmy Days 1931,S 24,21:2
Flying High 1931,D 12,23:3
Cheaters at Play 1932,F 27,22:1
Orders Is Orders 1934,My 7,20:2
Star Dust 1940,My 4,13:1
Young People 1940,Ag 24,16:2
Down Argentine Way 1940,O 18,25:1
Tall, Dark and Handsome 1941,Ja 24,15:2
Moon Over Miami 1941,Jl 5,14:2
Springtime in the Rockies 1942,N 12,30:2
Dixie Dugan 1943,Ap 9,25:5
Gang's All Here, The 1943,D 23,26:4
Up in Mabel's Room 1944,Ap 22,8:6
Home in Indiana 1944,Je 22,23:1
Wake up and Dream 1947,Ja 24,18:4
Great Dan Patch, The 1949,N 9,37:2
Oh, You Beautiful Doll 1949,N 12,8:4
Peggy 1950,Jl 21,15:4
Dangerous When Wet 1953,Je 19,18:1
Oklahoma! 1955,O 11,49:1
Opposite Sex, The 1956,N 16,23:2

Greenwood, E

Jamaica Inn 1939,O 12,33:1

Greenwood, E (Director)

Co-Optimists, The 1930,F 5,27:2

Greenwood, E (Original Author)

East Meets West 1936,O 31,24:2

Greenwood, E (Screenwriter)

Man Who Knew too Much, The 1935,Mr 23,11:2
East Meets West 1936,O 31,24:2
Girl Was Young, The 1938,F 11,27:2

Greenwood, Edwin (Director)

To What Red Hell 1929,O 6,IX,9:4 (In Addenda)

Greenwood, Edwin (Producer)

To What Red Hell 1929,O 6,IX,9:4 (In Addenda)

Greenwood, Joan

Frenzy 1946,Jl 20,10:3
Smugglers, The 1948,Mr 29,17:1
October Man, The 1948,Ap 16,29:2
Bad Sister 1948,Je 11,27:3
Saraband 1949,Je 13,16:3
Tight Little Island 1949,D 26,33:2
Kind Hearts and Coronets 1950,Je 15,41:2
Girl in a Million, A 1950,Jl 24,15:2
Mr Peek-A-Boo 1951,S 19,37:1
Bad Lord Byron, The 1952,Mr 20,37:5
Man in the White Suit, The 1952,Ap 1,35:2
Young Wives' Tale 1952,N 4,33:1
Importance of Being Earnest, The 1952,D 23,17:2
Lovers, Happy Lovers 1954,O 1,19:2
Detective, The 1954,N 2,25:2
Moonfleet 1955,Je 25,9:2
Stage Struck 1958,Ap 23,40:1
Mysterious Island 1961,D 21,30:6
Tom Jones 1963,O 8,48:1
Moonspinners, The 1964,N 4,47:1

Greenwood, John (Composer)

Man of Aran 1934,O 19,27:1
Drums 1938,S 30,24:4

Greenwood, Rosamund

Men Are not Gods 1937,Ja 19,28:1
Prince and the Showgirl 1957,Je 14,22:2

Greenwood, Walter (Original Author)

Love on the Dole 1945,O 13,11:2

Greenwood, Walter (Screenwriter)

Love on the Dole 1945,O 13,11:2
Massacre Hill 1950,D 14,51:3
Chance of a Lifetime 1951,Mr 15,37:2

Greenwood, Winifred

Life of the Party, The 1920,N 22,13:3
To the Last Man 1923,Ag 28,12:1

Greer, Bette Jane

Two O'Clock Courage 1945,Ap 14,13:3
George White's Scandals 1945,O 11,26:2

Greer, Dabbs

House of Wax 1953,Ap 11,15:2
Trouble Along the Way 1953,My 7,37:2
Affair With a Stranger 1953,Jl 11,8:2
Riot in Cell Block 11 1954,F 19,24:5
Private Hell 36 1954,S 4,6:4
I Want to Live 1958,N 19,45:1

Greer, Ethel

Road to Zanzibar 1941,Ap 10,29:2

Greer, Jane

Dick Tracy 1946,Ja 12,10:7
Falcon's Alibi, The 1946,Ap 13,23:2
Sinbad the Sailor 1947,Ja 23,31:2
They Won't Believe Me 1947,Jl 17,16:2
Out of the Past 1947,N 26,18:2
Big Steal, The 1949,Jl 11,13:2
Company She Keeps, The 1951,Ja 29,14:4
U S S Teakettle 1951,F 24,11:2
You for Me 1952,S 25,38:3
Prisoner of Zenda, The 1952,N 5,36:2
Clown, The 1953,Ja 29,25:1
Down Among the Sheltering Palms 1953,Je 13,11:2
Run for the Sun 1956,Ag 25,7:2
Man of a Thousand Faces 1957,Ag 14,21:1
Where Love Has Gone 1964,N 3,26:1
Billie 1965,S 16,55:3

Greer, Jimmy and his Orchestra

Transatlantic Merry-Go-Round 1934,N 1,25:2

Greet, Clare

Manxman, The 1929,D 17,28:7
Should a Doctor Tell 1931,Ag 22,7:5
Sign of the Four, The 1932,Ag 20,7:4
White Face 1933,D 4,22:3
Murder in the Old Red Barn 1936,Ag 19,18:3
Emil 1938,Ap 15,23:2
Jamaica Inn 1939,O 12,33:1
Sidewalks of London 1940,F 15,15:1

Greet, Jose

Ben Hur 1959,N 19,50:2

Gregery, Jackson (Original Author)

Man to Man 1922,Mr 28,17:4

Gregg, Arnold

Skyrocket, The 1926,Ja 26,25:2

Gregg, Christina

Young Racers, The 1963,O 10,49:3

Gregg, Everley

Private Life of Henry VIII, The 1933,O 13,25:2
Scoundrel, The 1935,My 3,23:2
Ghost Goes West, The 1936,Ja 11,9:2
Pygmalion 1938,D 8,34:2
Spies of the Air 1940,Jl 4,12:3
Adventure for Two 1945,D 14,24:5
Brief Encounter 1946,Ag 26,21:2
Great Expectations 1947,My 23,31:1
Room at the Top 1959,Mr 31,26:1

Gregg, Frances

Mary Burns, Fugitive 1935,N 16,19:2

Gregg, Hubert

In Which We Serve 1942,D 24,18:1
Once Upon a Dream 1949,Jl 15,17:2
Facts of Love, The 1949,O 31,20:2

Gregg, Hubert — Cont

Story of Robin Hood, The 1952,Je 27,18:3
High and Dry 1954,Ag 31,25:5
Svengali 1955,S 26,18:2
Doctor at Sea 1956,Mr 1,37:3
Simon and Laura 1956,Jl 3,17:2

Gregg, Hubert (Screenwriter)

3 Men in a Boat 1959,Jl 29,33:2

Gregg, Olive

Psycopath, The 1966,S 29,60:1

Gregg, Virginia

Body and Soul 1947,N 10,21:2
Casbah 1948,My 3,27:4
Gay Intruders, The 1949,Je 28,33:4
Dragnet 1954,Ag 21,10:2
Love Is a Many-Splendored Thing 1955,Ag 19,10:1
I'll Cry Tomorrow 1956,Ja 13,18:1
Crime in the Streets 1956,My 24,27:4
Fastest Gun Alive, The 1956,Jl 13,23:3
D I, The 1957,Je 6,35:2
Portland Expose 1957,S 27,16:6
Hanging Tree, The 1959,F 12,23:1
Operation Petticoat 1959,D 6,38:1
Man Trap 1961,N 30,40:4
House of Women 1962,Ap 12,41:6
Spencer's Mountain 1963,My 17,26:6
Two on a Guillotine 1965,Ja 14,44:3

Gregor, Arthur (Director)

Women's Wares 1927,N 15,27:1
What Price Decency? 1933,Mr 2,20:6

Gregor, Arthur (Original Author)

What Price Decency? 1933,Mr 2,20:6

Gregor, Manfred (Original Author)

Bridge, The; (Bruecke, Die) 1961,My 2,42:1
Town Without Pity 1961,O 11,53:1

Gregor, Martin

Transport From Paradise 1967,F 8,22:1

Gregor, Nora

Olympia 1930,D 7,IX,6:4
Und das Ist die Hauptsache; That's All That Matters 1931,My 24,VIII,4:1
But the Flesh Is Weak 1932,Ap 16,11:2
Was Frauen Traeumen; What Women Dream 1933,Jl 2,IX,2:2
Rules of the Game, The 1950,Ap 10,15:3
Rules of the Game, The 1961,Ja 19,26:1

Gregoretti, Ugo (Director)

New Angels, The; I Nuovi Angeli 1965,My 4,49:1

Gregoretti, Ugo (Screenwriter)

New Angels, The; I Nuovi Angeli 1965,My 4,49:1

Gregory, Charles

Battle for Music 1945,O 15,13:2

Gregory, Dick

Sweet Love, Bitter 1967,Ja 31,50:1

Gregory, Dora

Skin Game, The 1931,Je 20,20:4
In Which We Serve 1942,D 24,18:1

Gregory, Edna

In the Palace of the King 1923,D 3,14:1
Desert Flower, The 1925,Je 1,10:3

Gregory, Frank

Casanova 1965,Jl 21,43:1
After You, Comrade 1967,Ap 11,54:1

Gregory, Iain

Sword of Lancelot 1963,O 10,49:2

Gregory, Ian

Girl-Getters, The 1966,Ap 13,37:6

Gregory, Jackson (Original Author)

Everlasting Whisper, The 1925,O 12,19:3

Gregory, James

Frogmen, The 1951,Je 30,8:6
Nightfall 1957,Ja 24,34:1
Big Caper, The 1957,Mr 29,16:1
Young Stranger, The 1957,Ap 9,40:1
Gun Glory 1957,Jl 20,8:7
Onionhead 1958,O 2,44:1
Al Capone 1959,Mr 26,27:1
Hey Boy! Hey Girl! 1959,Je 6,18:3
X-15 1962,Ap 5,30:2
Two Weeks in Another Town 1962,Ag 18,10:1
Manchurian Candidate, The 1962,O 25,48:3
PT 109 1963,Je 27,23:1
Twilight of Honor 1963,N 14,41:2
Captain Newman, MD 1964,F 21,36:1
Distant Trumpet, A 1964,My 28,40:1
Quick, Before it Melts 1965,Ap 1,30:2
Sons of Katie Elder, The 1965,Ag 26,40:3
Rage to Live, A 1965,O 21,57:1
Silencers, The 1966,Mr 17,35:1
Murderers' Row 1966,D 22,40:3
Clambake 1967,Je 4,62:3
Ambushers, The 1967,D 23,29:1
Secret War of Harry Frigg, The 1968,Mr 5,34:5

Gregory, Lady (Miscellaneous)

Rising of the Moon, The (1921); 1921 (The Rising of the Moon) 1957,Jl 10,23:1
Rising of the Moon, The (A Minute's Wait); Minute's Wait, A (The Rising of the Moon) 1957,Jl 10,23:1

Gregory, Lady (Original Author)
Rising of the Moon, The (The Majesty of the Law); Majesty of the Law, The (The Rising of the Moon) 1957,Jl 10,23:1
Gregory, Martin
Shop on Main Street, The 1966,Ja 25,47:1
Gregory, Paul
Whoopee 1930,O 1,26:3
Sit Tight 1931,F 19,20:4
Children of Dreams 1931,Jl 20,20:4
Wine, Women and Song 1934,Mr 21,24:3
Gregory, Paul (Producer)
Night of the Hunter, The 1955,S 30,23:1
Naked and the Dead, The 1958,Ag 7,21:1
Gregory, Stephen
Hail the Conquering Hero 1944,Ag 10,14:2
Gregory, Thea
Satellite in the Sky 1956,S 4,32:7
Gregory, Will
Sensation Seekers 1927,Mr 16,28:2
Gregos, Zoltan
Falu Rossza, A; Village Rogue, The 1938,Ap 18,11:2
Gregson, Florence
Good Companions, The 1933,O 10,24:1
Gregson, John
Tight Little Island 1949,D 26,33:2
Treasure Island 1950,Ag 16,24:2
Lavender Hill Mob, The 1951,O 16,35:2
Submarine Command 1952,Ja 19,13:2
Brave Don't Cry, The 1952,N 6,37:2
Assassin, The 1953,Ap 18,17:2
Titfield Thunderbolt, The 1953,O 6,34:2
Holly and the Ivy, The 1954,F 5,16:1
Genevieve 1954,F 16,30:2
Angels One Five 1954,Ap 30,28:2
Weak and the Wicked, The 1954,Ag 21,10:3
Fuss Over Feathers 1954,D 27,22:6
Three Cases of Murder (You Killed Elizabeth); You Killed Elizabeth (Three Cases of Murder) 1955,Mr 16,39:4
Cash on Delivery 1956,S 1,19:3
Above Us the Waves 1957,Ap 18,35:2
Value for Money 1957,Ag 1,20:4
Pursuit of the Graf Spee 1957,D 27,33:2
Rooney 1958,Je 6,29:2
Captain's Table, The 1960,S 27,40:1
S O S Pacific 1960,O 13,41:3
Hand in Hand 1961,F 7,41:3
Longest Day, The 1962,O 5,28:1
Night of the Generals, The 1967,F 3,38:1
Gregson, Richard (Original Author)
Angry Silence, The 1960,D 13,25:2
Gregson, Warwick
Enchantment 1948,D 27,16:2
Greguss, Zoltan
Az en Lanyom nem olyan; My Daughter Is Different 1938,Ap 30,18:2
Fekete Gyemantok; Black Diamonds 1939,Ap 24,13:2
Gyimesi Vadvirag; Wildflower of Gyimes 1939,O 21,12:3
Tiszavirag; Flower of the Tisza 1939,D 30,9:3
Zigeunerweisen; Gypsy Ways 1940,My 11,15:3
Grehan, Joseph
Adventures of Mark Twain, The 1944,My 4,25:5
Man Alive 1945,N 17,14:5
GREIFF
See Also GRIEF
Greiff, Heins
Kampf, Der 1936,S 11,29:3
Greig, Richard
Animal Crackers 1930,Ag 29,20:3
Greig, Robert
Tonight or Never 1931,D 18,29:2
Stepping Sisters 1932,Ja 9,21:1
Beauty and the Boss 1932,Ap 2,13:2
Man Wanted 1932,Ap 16,11:2
Cohens and Kellys in Hollywood, The 1932,Ap 22,23:2
Tenderfoot, The 1932,My 23,18:4
Merrily We Go to Hell 1932,Je 11,9:3
Jewel Robbery 1932,Jl 23,6:6
Horse Feathers 1932,Ag 11,12:2
Love Me Tonight 1932,Ag 19,20:6
Trouble in Paradise 1932,N 9,28:5
They Just Had to Get Married 1933,F 13,11:4
Dangerously Yours 1933,F 23,20:3
Men Must Fight 1933,Mr 11,18:3
Pleasure Cruise 1933,Ap 3,13:3
Mind Reader, The 1933,Ap 7,22:4
Peg o'my Heart 1933,My 20,11:4
It's Great to be Alive 1933,Jl 8,14:6
Easy to Love 1934,Ja 15,12:2
Cockeyed Cavaliers 1934,Jl 25,22:2
One More River 1934,Ag 10,21:1
Clive of India 1935,Ja 18,29:1
Folies Bergere 1935,F 25,13:2
Gay Deception, The 1935,O 11,31:1
I Live for Love 1935,O 19,21:2
Rose Marie 1936,F 1,9:2
Unguarded Hour, The 1936,Ap 4,11:1
Small Town Girl 1936,Ap 11,19:1

Trouble for Two 1936,My 30,7:2
Devil Doll, The 1936,Ag 8,5:2
Theodora Goes Wild 1936,N 13,27:4
Lloyds of London 1936,N 26,39:1
Stowaway 1936,D 19,16:1
Easy Living 1937,Jl 8,20:1
Lady Behave 1938,Ja 28,17:3
Algiers 1938,Jl 15,13:2
It Could Happen to You 1939,Je 9,26:3
Way Down South 1939,Ag 18,16:4
Drums Along the Mohawk 1939,N 4,11:2
No Time for Comedy 1940,S 7,9:2
Hudson's Bay 1941,Ja 10,23:2
Lady Eve, The 1941,F 26,17:1
Moon Over Miami 1941,Jl 5,14:2
Sullivan's Travels 1942,Ja 29,25:2
Moon and Sixpence, The 1942,O 28,26:4
I Married a Witch 1942,N 20,27:2
Palm Beach Story, The 1942,D 11,33:1
Summer Storm 1944,O 23,14:3
Great Moment, The 1944,N 13,15:2
Picture of Dorian Gray, The 1945,Mr 2,15:2
Earl Carroll Vanities 1945,Ap 2,15:6
Cheaters, The 1945,Jl 21,7:2
Adventures of Marco Polo, The 1965,Ap 8,17:2
Greiner, Fritz
Manon Lescaut 1926,N 30,27:1
Hungarian Rhapsody 1929,Ag 5,25:2
Greinerer, Fritz
Kreuzer Emden 1932,S 8,17:2
Greiter, Lewis (Screenwriter)
Cash on Demand 1962,My 17,31:1
Greley, Jack
Canadians, The 1961,Je 1,31:1
Grellier, Michele
Pot Bouille 1958,O 28,39:1
Would-Be Gentleman, The 1960,Mr 23,31:1
Marriage of Figaro, The 1963,Ap 30,26:1
Grello, Jacques
Pot Bouille 1958,O 28,39:1
Gremillon, Jean (Director)
Woman Who Dared, The 1949,Mr 19,10:7
Gremin, Alexander
Fortress on the Volga 1942,D 25,15:3
Grenade, Sylvie
End of the World, The 1934,Ap 18,23:3
Grendel, Frederic (Miscellaneous)
Three Fables of Love (Two Pigeons); Two Pigeons (Three Fables of Love) 1963,Ag 21,38:1
Three Fables of Love (The Fox and the Crow); Fox and the Crow, The (Three Fables of Love) 1963,Ag 21,38:1
Three Fables of Love (The Tortoise and the Hare); Tortoise and the Hare, The (Three Fables of Love) 1963,Ag 21,38:1
Three Fables of Love (The Fox and the Crow); Fox and the Crow, The (Three Fables of Love) 1963,Ag 21,38:1
Grendel, Frederic (Original Author)
Ceremony, The 1964,My 14,39:1
Grendel, Frederic (Screenwriter)
Ostrich Has two Eggs, The 1960,S 27,40:1
Grene, Karl (Director)
Spy of Madame de Pompadour, The 1929,S 10,27:1
Grenfell, Joyce
Stage Fright 1950,F 24,27:2
Run for Your Money, A 1950,Ap 10,15:3
While the Sun Shines 1950,Jl 1,9:2
Happiest Days of Your Life, The 1950,S 18,19:2
Laughter in Paradise 1951,N 12,21:2
Galloping Major, The 1951,D 17,27:2
Genevieve 1954,F 16,30:2
Pickwick Papers, The 1954,Ap 5,21:2
Man With a Million 1954,Je 29,21:2
Belles of St Trinian's, The 1954,D 23,13:4
Blue Murder at St Trinian's 1958,My 27,27:1
Happy is the Bride 1959,Je 30,27:2
Pure Hell of St Trinian's, The 1961,S 26,31:1
Old Dark House, The 1963,O 31,26:3
Americanization of Emily, The 1964,O 28,51:1
Yellow Rolls-Royce, The 1965,My 14,42:2
Grenfell, Wilfred Sir (Miscellaneous)
Viking, The 1931,Je 17,32:5
Grenier, Jean-Pierre
Skipper Next to God 1953,Ja 13,24:2
Justice Is Done 1953,Mr 3,23:2
Grenier, Philippe
And God Created Woman 1957,O 22,41:1
Gresac, Fred de (Original Author)
Boheme, La 1926,F 25,26:2
Gresham, William Lindsay (Original Author)
Nightmare Alley 1947,O 10,31:3
Greshler, Abner J (Director)
Yesterday and Today 1954,Mr 13,11:3
Greshler, Abner J (Producer)
At War With the Army 1951,Ja 25,21:5
Yesterday and Today 1954,Mr 13,11:3
Gresley, Marjorie
Tony Draws a Horse 1951,My 15,38:6
Gretchany, A
Ballad of Cossack Gloota, The 1938,F 28,19:1

Grethe, Hildegard
Robert Koch 1939,N 25,13:2
Gretillat, Jacques
Nero 1922,My 26,17:2
Porteuse de Pain, La 1936,Jl 1,29:5
Heart of Paris 1939,Ja 13,17:3
Devil Is an Empress, The 1939,D 4,18:4
Entente Cordiale 1939,D 26,23:2
Gretler, Heinrich
William Tell 1925,My 20,26:2
Marie-Louise 1945,N 13,24:2
Devil Makes Three, The 1952,Ag 30,6:2
White Hell of Pitz Palu, The 1953,N 14,14:2
Heidi 1953,D 21,27:2
Heidi and Peter 1955,D 13,55:2
It Happened in Broad Daylight 1960,S 30,33:1
Money, Money, Money 1962,Jl 18,20:1
Grevellius, Nils (Composer)
Karl Fredrik Reigns 1938,F 2,15:2
Grevenberg, Auguste Prasch
Unsterbliche Herz, Das; Immortal Heart, The 1939,O 21,12:2
Grevenhorst, Klaus Detlef
Man Escaped, A 1957,Ag 27,33:2
Grevenius, Herbert (Screenwriter)
Illicit Interlude 1954,O 27,32:6
Greville, Edmond
Sous les Toits de Paris; (Under the Roofs of Paris) 1930,D 16,34:4
Greville, Edmond T (Director)
Whirlpool; (Remous) 1940,O 8,31:2
Passionnelle 1948,Mr 1,17:2
House on the Waterfront, The 1959,F 21,25:2
Temptation 1962,N 10,16:2
Greville, Edmond T (Miscellaneous)
Passionnelle 1948,Mr 1,17:2
Greville, Edmond T (Screenwriter)
Passionnelle 1948,Mr 1,17:2
Temptation 1962,N 10,16:2
Greville, Wanda
Bal, Le 1932,S 28,22:5
Grew, William A (Original Author)
Nice Women 1932,F 20,11:2
GREY
See Also GRAY
Grey, Anne
Faithful Heart 1933,Ag 15,20:2
Blarney Kiss, The 1933,Ag 19,14:4
Just Smith 1934,Ap 23,20:2
Break of Hearts 1935,My 17,24:3
Grey, Clifford
Carnival 1921,Je 27,16:3
Grey, Clifford (Composer)
Woman in Command, The 1934,My 29,22:2
You Made Me Love You 1934,My 30,14:3
Hit the Deck 1955,Mr 4,17:1
Grey, Clifford (Original Author)
Rome Express 1933,F 27,11:2
Sleeping Car to Trieste 1949,Ap 18,18:6
Grey, Clifford (Screenwriter)
Brewster's Millions 1935,Ap 8,23:3
Mimi 1936,Ja 10,16:3
Grey, Denise
Honorable Catherine, The 1948,Ag 23,13:3
Devil in the Flesh 1949,My 10,29:2
Inside a Girls' Dormitory 1956,F 6,27:7
Julietta 1957,Je 18,38:2
Dog, a Mouse and a Sputnik, A; Pied, a Cheval et un Sputnik, A 1960,N 1,46:2
Love and the Frenchwoman; (Francaise et l'Amour, La) 1961,F 28,38:2
Bonne Soupe, La 1964,Mr 16,37:1
Grey, Ethel
Too Much Business 1922,My 1,20:3
Grey, Frances
Day the Earth Stood Still, The 1951,S 19,37:1
Grey, George
Champs-Elysees 1939,F 28,17:2
Nine Bachelors 1942,F 9,19:2
Well-Digger's Daughter, The 1946,S 30,21:4
Grey, Gloria
Spirit of the U S A, The 1924,My 21,22:3
Little Robinson Crusoe 1924,S 3,17:1
Dante's Inferno 1924,S 30,27:3
Lucky Star 1929,Jl 22,17:1
Married in Hollywood 1929,S 23,24:3
Grey, Harry (Original Author)
Portrait of a Mobster 1961,Ap 20,30:4
Grey, Harry (Producer)
Tenth Avenue Kid 1938,S 2,21:3
Grey, Jack
Hell Bound 1931,My 9,15:4
Grey, Jane
Little Gray Lady, The 1914,Jl 14,9:5
Grey, Jeanne
Follow the Fleet 1936,F 21,21:2
Grey, Joel
About Face 1952,My 24,15:3
Come September 1961,S 8,34:1
Grey, John (Original Author)
Hawaiian Nights 1939,S 29,19:4

Grey, John (Screenwriter)
Hot Water 1924,O 27,27:1
Freshman, The 1925,S 21,12:4
Feet First 1930,O 31,20:1
Movie Crazy 1932,S 15,19:3
Farmer in the Dell, The 1936,Mr 7,11:4
Mysterious Crossing 1937,F 2,20:5
Forty Naughty Girls 1937,S 18,15:3
I'm From the City 1938,Ag 19,13:4
Rockin' in The Rockies 1945,Jl 5,7:2

Grey, Lynda
Shadows Over Shanghai 1938,D 1,29:2
Holiday Inn 1942,Ag 5,16:1
Happy Go Lucky 1943,Mr 25,25:1

Grey, Mina
Choosing a Wife 1919,Ag 11,9:1

Grey, Nan
Babbitt 1934,D 17,24:2
Sutter's Gold 1936,Mr 27,25:2
Dracula's Daughter 1936,My 18,14:2
Crash Donovan 1936,Ag 10,10:3
Three Smart Girls 1937,Ja 25,22:2
Let Them Live 1937,Je 8,30:3
Man in Blue, The 1937,Ag 30,25:2
Some Blondes Are Dangerous 1937,N 3,29:3
Jury's Secret, The 1938,F 4,17:2
Black Doll, The 1938,F 7,10:2
Storm, The 1938,O 31,12:2
Girls' School 1938,N 3,27:1
Three Smart Girls Grow Up 1939,Mr 18,9:2
Ex-Champ 1939,My 12,25:3
Under-Pup, The 1939,S 5,21:2
Tower of London 1939,D 12,37:2
Invisible Man Returns, The 1940,Ja 16,19:2
House of the Seven Gables, The 1940,Ap 15,21:3
Sandy Is a Lady 1940,Je 28,22:2
You're not so Tough 1940,Jl 9,25:3
Little Bit of Heaven, A 1940,N 8,24:2

Grey, Ray
Shriek of Araby, The 1923,Je 11,16:2

Grey, Richard
Sanders of the River 1935,Je 27,16:1

Grey, Schuyler E (Original Author)
Search for Beauty 1934,F 10,20:2

Grey, Shirley
Public Defender, The 1931,Ag 1,16:4
Secret Service 1931,D 14,16:3
Back Street 1932,Ag 29,9:2
Uptown New York 1932,D 10,19:3
From Hell to Heaven 1933,Mr 18,9:3
Private Jones 1933,Mr 25,13:3
Out all Night 1933,Ap 8,16:2
Girl in 419 1933,My 20,11:5
Little Giant, The 1933,My 27,11:5
Life of Jimmy Dolan, The 1933,Je 14,22:3
Don't Bet on Love 1933,Jl 31,16:2
Too Much Harmony 1933,S 23,11:5
Bombay Mail 1934,Ja 6,18:2
I Like It That Way 1934,Ap 18,23:3
Sisters Under the Skin 1934,Jl 8,18:1
His Greatest Gamble 1934,Jl 18,20:2
Defense Rests, The 1934,Ag 16,20:3
Transatlantic Merry-Go-Round 1934,N 1,25:2
Wednesday's Child 1934,D 15,9:3
People's Enemy, The 1935,Ap 30,13:7
Stranded 1935,Je 20,16:2

Grey, Virginia
Uncle Tom's Cabin 1927,N 5,16:2
Michigan Kid, The 1928,Jl 2,11:2
Heart to Heart 1928,S 10,29:2
Old Hutch 1936,D 7,27:4
Secret Valley 1937,Ja 25,22:2
Bad Guy 1937,Ag 26,25:2
Rosalie 1937,D 31,9:2
Test Pilot 1938,Ap 16,17:1
Rich Man, Poor Girl 1938,Ag 19,13:3
Youth Takes a Fling 1938,O 17,12:1
Dramatic School 1938,D 9,31:2
Idiot's Delight 1939,F 3,13:1
Broadway Serenade 1939,Ap 7,25:2
Hardys Ride High, The 1939,Ap 14,28:2
Women, The 1939,S 22,27:2
Thunder Afloat 1939,O 13,27:2
Another Thin Man 1939,N 24,29:1
Three Cheers for the Irish 1940,Mr 9,19:2
Golden Fleecing, The 1940,N 7,33:4
Hullabaloo 1940,D 19,33:1
Washington Melodrama 1941,My 26,15:3
Big Store, The 1941,Je 27,14:4
Whistling in the Dark 1941,Ag 28,23:2
Mr and Mrs North 1942,Ja 22,13:2
Grand Central Murder 1942,My 23,8:8
Tarzan's New York Adventure 1942,Ag 7,13:2
Tish 1942,S 18,25:2
Stage Door Canteen 1943,Je 25,13:2
Sweet Rosie O'Grady 1943,O 21,30:2
Flame of Barbary Coast 1945,My 28,22:2
Men in her Diary 1945,S 24,16:5
House of Horrors 1946,F 23,20:3
Swamp Fire 1946,Ag 26,21:4
Wyoming 1947,Jl 25,12:5
Unconquered 1947,O 11,11:2
Miraculous Journey 1948,S 20,21:2

Jungle Jim 1949,Ja 1,9:2
Unknown Island 1949,Ja 8,11:4
Mexican Hayride 1949,Ja 12,33:3
Threat, The 1949,D 2,35:4
Highway 301 1950,D 9,13:2
Bullfighter and the Lady, The 1951,Ap 27,19:2
Eternal Sea, The 1955,Je 10,16:2
Rose Tattoo, The 1955,D 13,55:1
All That Heaven Allows 1956,F 29,35:1
Crime of Passion 1957,Ja 10,25:1
Jeanne Eagels 1957,Ag 31,19:1
Portrait in Black 1960,Jl 28,19:1
Tammy Tell me True 1961,Jl 27,23:2
Back Street 1961,O 13,27:1
Bachelor in Paradise 1961,N 17,41:2
Black Zoo 1963,My 16,42:1
Naked Kiss, The 1964,O 29,38:1
Love Has Many Faces 1965,F 25,24:1
Madame X 1966,Ap 28,49:1

Grey, Zane (Original Author)
Border Legion, The 1918,Jl 29,9:3
Last of the Duanes, The 1919,S 15,16:3
Riders of the Dawn 1920,My 3,18:1
When Romance Rides 1922,Ap 10,18:2
To the Last Man 1923,Ag 28,12:1
Call of the Canyon, The 1923,D 17,23:1
Heritage of the Desert, The 1924,Ja 24,15:1
Wanderer of the Wasteland, The 1924,Jl 8,14:2
Code of the West 1925,Ap 13,24:1
Riders of the Purple Sage 1925,Ap 15,16:1
Rainbow Trail, The 1925,Je 3,26:4
Wild Horse Mesa 1925,Ag 10,8:2
Vanishing American, The 1925,O 16,18:2
Born to the West 1926,Je 30,18:1 (In Addenda)
Last Trail, The 1927,Ja 26,17:1
Water Hole, The 1928,S 3,14:2
Light of Western Stars, The 1930,Ap 26,11:1
Border Legion, The 1930,Je 30,22:6
Last of the Duanes 1930,S 13,9:3
Fighting Caravans 1931,Ja 26,21:1
Riders of the Purple Sage 1931,S 26,25:3
Rainbow Trail, The 1932,Ja 30,13:2
Heritage of the Desert 1933,Mr 11,18:3
Woman Accused, The 1933,Mr 13,18:2
Last Round-Up, The 1934,My 10,25:2
Dude Ranger, The 1934,O 2,18:5
Wagon Wheels 1934,O 4,19:1
West of the Pecos 1934,D 29,11:2
Home on the Range 1935,F 13,24:4
Thunder Mountain 1935,O 2,27:2
King of the Royal Mounted 1936,N 29,35:2
Thunder Trail 1938,F 5,19:3
Western Union 1941,F 7,23:2
Wanderer of the Wasteland 1945,S 29,12:2
Gunfighters 1947,Jl 25,12:5
Red Canyon 1949,Ap 28,28:2
Maverick Queen, the 1956,Je 4,25:2

Grey, Zane (Screenwriter)
Light of the Western Stars, The 1925,Je 24,14:3

Greyff, Edna
Sein bester Freund; His Best Friend 1938,Jl 2,10:4

Greyn, Clinton
Robbery 1967,S 28,58:2

Grgic, Zlatk (Producer)
Little and Big 1968,Ja 20,21:3

Griault, Jean (Screenwriter)
Carabiniers, Les 1968,Ap 26,31:1

Gribble, Donna Jo
Dolly Sisters, The 1945,N 15,24:6
Somebody up There Likes Me 1956,Jl 6,16:1

Gribble, Harry Wagstaff (Director)
Madame Racketeer 1932,Jl 23,6:6

Gribble, Harry Wagstaff (Original Author)
Trick for Trick 1933,Je 10,16:4

Gribble, Harry Wagstaff (Screenwriter)
Stella Dallas 1937,Ag 6,21:1

Gribbon, Eddie
Crossroads of New York, The 1922,My 22,18:4
East of Broadway 1924,N 12,13:1
Code of the West 1925,Ap 13,24:1
Seven Days 1925,Ag 31,19:3
Limited Mail, The 1925,S 1,18:2
Bat, The 1926,Mr 15,18:3
Flaming Frontier, The 1926,Ap 5,24:1
Tell It to the Marines 1926,D 24,18:2
Man Bait 1927,Ja 19,21:1
Convoy 1927,My 9,26:4
Callahans and the Murphys, The 1927,Jl 12,29:3
Cheating Cheaters 1927,D 6,27:1
Night Life 1927,D 20,33:2
Buck Privates 1928,Ja 30,18:1
Streets of Shanghai 1928,F 21,19:3
Stop That Man 1928,Ap 17,27:2
United States Smith 1928,Jl 24,13:3
Gang War 1928,N 19,16:7
Two Weeks Off 1929,Je 24,27:1
Twin Beds 1929,Jl 15,25:1
Dames Ahoy 1930,Mr 29,23:1
Born Reckless 1930,Je 7,10:4
Good Intentions 1930,Jl 26,16:4
Mr Lemon of Orange 1931,Mr 28,15:3
Three Rogues 1931,Ap 4,23:1

Gribbon, Eddie — Cont
Love on a Bet 1936,Mr 5,25:2
You Can't Buy Luck 1937,My 14,21:2
Big Shot, The 1937,Ag 13,13:1
Great Dictator, The 1940,O 16,29:1

Gribbon, Harry
Knockout Reilly 1927,Ap 18,21:2
Rose-Marie 1928,F 13,16:2
Cameraman, The 1928,S 17,27:1
Show People 1928,N 12,18:2
Shakedown, The 1929,Ap 8,32:1
On With the Show 1929,My 29,28:6
Mysterious Island, The 1929,D 21,17:1
So Long Letty 1930,F 8,12:5
Lottery Bride, The 1930,N 29,21:4
Gorilla, The 1931,F 23,20:3
You Said a Mouthful 1932,N 18,23:2
Ladies They Talk About 1933,F 25,20:4
Baby Face 1933,Je 24,16:2

Gribic, Bratislav
Legends of Anika 1956,Ap 19,35:1

Gribkov, V
Last Night, The 1937,Ap 28,18:3
Taxi to Heaven 1944,My 25,16:3
Winner, The 1947,D 1,27:2

Gribov, A
Red Army Days 1935,O 21,22:4
Concentration Camp 1939,Mr 20,13:2
Marriage 1945,F 22,31:3
Military Secret 1945,Ag 2,16:2
Inspector General, The 1954,My 3,21:2
True Friends 1954,N 15,33:2
Safety Match, The 1955,Mr 28,24:5
Sound of Life, The 1962,F 12,28:2
Grown-Up Children 1963,Ap 15,36:5

Gridoux, Lucas
Mystic Mountain, The 1936,Mr 31,17:2
Life and Loves of Beethoven, The 1937,N 22,15:1
Citadel of Silence, The 1939,D 25,29:1
Pepe le Moko 1941,Mr 4,20:2
Panic 1947,N 27,50:2

Gridov, T
Horsemen, The 1951,Ja 29,14:5

Grieben, Marisa
Inheritance, The; Herencia, La 1964,S 16,36:3

Grieco, Sergio (Director)
Nights of Lucretia Borgia, The 1960,O 6,51:4

GRIEF
See Also GREIFF

Grief, Gregory
Girl No 217 1945,S 3,17:2

Grief (dog)
Sein bester Freund; His Best Friend 1938,Jl 2,10:4

Grieg-Halvorsen, Sten
Ungkarlspappan 1936,Ja 4,19:1

Grierson, John (Producer)
Drifting 1930,Je 30,22:6
Song of Ceylon 1937,Ag 16,15:1
Now the Peace; World in Action 1945,Jl 1,II,3:1
World in Action 1945,Jl 1,II,3:1
War Clouds in the Pacific; World in Action 1945,Jl 11,3:1
Brave Don't Cry, The 1952,N 6,37:2
Time, Gentlemen, Please 1953,S 24,39:2
Scotch on the Rocks 1954,Je 14,18:2
Man of Africa 1956,O 11,51:1

Gries, Tom (Producer)
Donovan's Brain 1954,Ja 21,28:2
Hunters of the Deep 1954,D 17,37:4

Gries, Tom (Screenwriter)
Hunters of the Deep 1954,D 17,37:4

Grieve, Andrew
Bitter Sweet 1940,N 22,27:1

Grieve, Helen
Overlanders, The 1946,D 20,31:2
Bush Christmas 1947,N 27,50:4

Griffe, Maurice (Miscellaneous)
Antoine and Antoinette 1948,Ap 16,29:2

Griffe, Maurice (Screenwriter)
Paris Frills 1946,N 25,38:3
Antoine and Antoinette 1948,Ap 16,29:2
Razzi 1957,N 19,39:4
Grisbi 1959,Jl 13,23:1

GRIFFEN
See Also GRIFFIN

Griffi, Peppino Patroni (Screenwriter)
More Than a Miracle 1967,N 2,58:2

Griffies, Ethel
Waterloo Bridge 1931,S 5,7:4
Road to Singapore, The 1931,O 1,25:2
Once a Lady 1931,N 9,22:4
Manhattan Parade 1931,D 25,29:2
Impatient Maiden, The 1932,Mr 4,17:3
Westward Passage 1932,Je 4,9:2
Love Me Tonight 1932,Ag 19,20:6
Tonight Is Ours 1933,Ja 21,10:6
Lady's Profession, A 1933,Mr 25,13:3
Alice in Wonderland 1933,D 23,19:1
Bulldog Drummond Strikes Back 1934,Ag 16,20:2
We Live Again 1934,N 2,27:2
Mystery of Edwin Drood, The 1935,Mr 21,27:1
Vanessa: Her Love Story 1935,Ap 13,11:3

Griffies, Ethel — Cont

Hold 'Em Yale 1935,Ap 27,20:6
Werewolf of London, The 1935,My 10,25:2
Anna Karenina 1935,Ag 31,16:2
Return of Peter Grimm, The 1935,O 4,25:2
Kathleen 1938,Ja 24,17:1
Man With 100 Faces 1938,N 1,27:2
I'm From Missouri 1939,Mr 23,27:1
We Are not Alone 1939,D 1,27:1
Vigil in the Night 1940,Mr 9,19:2
Irene 1940,My 24,23:3
Anne of Windy Poplars 1940,Ag 23,13:3
Stranger on the Third Floor 1940,S 2,19:2
Dead Men Tell 1941,Ap 17,29:3
Yank in the R A F, A 1941,S 27,11:3
Great Guns 1941,O 3,27:2
How Green Was my Valley 1941,O 29,27:2
Between Us Girls 1942,S 25,25:3
Time to Kill 1942,D 25,15:4
Holy Matrimony 1943,S 16,25:2
Jane Eyre 1944,F 4,12:5
Music for Millions 1944,D 22,12:4
Horn Blows at Midnight, The 1945,Ap 21,18:2
Thrill of a Romance 1945,My 25,22:2
Molly and Me 1945,My 26,18:2
Uncle Harry 1945,Ag 24,14:5
Saratoga Trunk 1945,N 22,39:2
Devotion 1946,Ap 6,10:5
Homestretch, The 1947,Ap 24,30:2
Birds, The 1963,Jl 1,5:5 (Incorrect in this
    edition; use 1963,Ap 1,54:1 elsewhere)
Billy Liar 1963,D 17,49:1

GRIFFIN
See Also GRIFFEN

Griffin, Carlton
Girl Shy 1924,Ap 21,21:4

Griffin, David (Cinematographer)
Pledge to Bataan 1943,Jl 2,15:2

Griffin, David (Director)
Pledge to Bataan 1943,Jl 2,15:2
Orders From Tokyo 1945,Ag 3,3:8

Griffin, Eleanore (Original Author)
Time Out for Romance 1937,Mr 13,23:2
When Love Is Young 1937,Ap 17,15:1
Thoroughbreds Don't Cry 1937,N 26,27:4
Boys Town 1938,S 9,25:1
St Louis Blues 1939,F 9,17:2
Street of Missing Men 1939,Je 1,31:3
I Wanted Wings 1941,Mr 27,29:4
Nob Hill 1945,Jl 4,10:3

Griffin, Eleanore (Screenwriter)
In old Oklahoma 1943,D 6,21:1
Man Called Peter, A 1955,Ap 1,22:1
Good Morning, Miss Dove 1955,N 24,41:1
Imitation of Life 1959,Ap 18,18:1
Third Man on the Mountain 1959,N 12,27:1
Back Street 1961,O 13,27:1
One Man's Way 1964,Mr 12,40:3

Griffin, Harold
Luck of the Irish, The 1937,Ja 16,21:1

Griffin, John Howard (Original Author)
Black Like Me 1964,My 21,42:1

Griffin, Josephine
Purple Plain, The 1955,Ap 11,29:1
Man Who Never Was, The 1956,Ap 4,24:1
Spanish Gardner, The 1957,S 9,21:2

Griffin, Merv
So This Is Love 1953,Ag 12,22:1
Phantom of the Rue Morgue 1954,Mr 20,10:5

Griffin, Robert
Barricade 1950,Mr 25,8:6
Broken Arrow 1950,Jl 21,15:2
Inside Detroit 1956,Ja 28,10:5
Crime of Passion 1957,Ja 10,25:1
Fury at Showdown 1957,Ap 20,21:3

Griffin, Russell
Marriage Morals 1923,Ag 14,10:3
Man Who Found Himself, The 1925,Ag 24,17:3

Griffin, Stephanie
Last Wagon, The 1956,S 22,20:2

Griffin, Tom
Edge, The 1968,Mr 28,52:1

Griffin, Z Wayne (Producer)
Family Honeymoon 1949,F 25,28:2
Key to the City 1950,F 2,31:2
Lone Star 1952,F 2,11:4

Griffith, Andy
Face in the Crowd, A 1957,My 29,33:1
No Time for Sergeants 1958,My 30,13:2
Onionhead 1958,O 2,44:1
Second Time Around, The 1961,D 23,16:1

Griffith, Charles (Screenwriter)
Atlas 1961,Ag 10,17:4
Wild Angels, The 1966,D 22,40:4
Devil's Angels 1967,O 5,46:1

Griffith, Corinne
Yellow Girl, The 1922,Mr 13,18:2
Six Days 1923,S 24,5:4
Common Law, The 1923,O 29,18:1
Black Oxen 1924,Ja 7,23:1
Lilies of the Field 1924,Mr 17,19:1
Single Wives 1924,Jl 29,9:2
Love's Wilderness 1924,D 22,20:2

Declassee 1925,Mr 23,14:2
Marriage Whirl, The 1925,Jl 15,22:3
Classified 1925,N 2,20:1
Infatuation 1926,Ja 4,16:1
Mlle Modiste 1926,Ap 26,25:1
Into her Kingdom 1926,Ag 10,19:2
Syncopating Sue 1926,N 2,35:1
Lady in Ermine, The 1927,Ja 3,16:2
Three Hours 1927,Mr 8,18:4
Garden of Eden, The 1928,Mr 19,26:2
Outcast 1928,N 26,30:2
Divine Lady, The 1929,Mr 23,22:4
Saturday's Children 1929,Ap 29,29:2
Lilies of the Field 1930,F 22,13:1
Back Pay 1930,My 31,19:4
Lily Christine 1932,My 29,VIII,4:4 (In Addenda)

Griffith, Corinne (Original Author)
Papa's Delicate Condition 1963,Mr 7,8:5

Griffith, D W (Composer)
Broken Blossoms 1919,My 14,15:5

Griffith, D W (Director)
Escape, The 1914,Je 2,11:5
Birth of a Nation, The 1915,Mr 4,9:4
Sable Lorcha, The 1915,O 18,9:1
Greatest Thing in Life, The 1918,D 23,9:1
Idol Dancer, The 1920,Mr 22,12:1
Love Flower, The 1920,Ag 23,9:2
Orphans of the Storm 1922,Ja 29,VI,2:1 (In
    Addenda)
One Exciting Night 1922,O 24,17:3
Birth of a Nation, The 1922,D 5,24:3
White Rose, The 1923,My 23,18:3
America 1924,F 22,20:1
Isn't Life Wonderful? 1924,D 1,17:3
That Royle Girl 1926,Ja 4,33:1
Sorrows of Satan, The 1926,O 13,21:1
Drums of Love 1928,Ja 25,20:4
Battle of The Sexes, The 1928,O 15,16:1
Lady of the Pavements 1929,Mr 11,22:2
Abraham Lincoln 1930,Ag 26,24:1
Struggle, The 1931,D 11,35:1

Griffith, D W (Producer)
Don Quixote 1915,D 20,11:1
Intolerance 1916,S 6,7:4
Great Love, The 1918,Ag 12,7:1
Romance of Happy Valley, A 1919,Ja 27,11:4
Girl Who Stayed Home, The 1919,Mr 24,11:3
Broken Blossoms 1919,My 14,15:5
True Heart Susie 1919,Je 2,20:4
Fall of Babylon, The 1919,Jl 22,10:2
Hearts of the World 1919,Ag 12,7:6
Mother and the Law, The 1919,Ag 19,10:1
Scarlet Days 1919,N 10,18:2
Greatest Question, The 1919,D 29,7:2
Birth of a Nation, The 1921,My 2,12:1
One Exciting Night 1922,O 24,17:3
Birth of a Nation, The 1930,D 22,16:2
Way Down East 1931,Mr 16,25:1
Intolerance 1936,Mr 5,25:2

Griffith, David
Man Upstairs, The 1959,Ag 11,23:2

Griffith, E H (Director)
Go-Getter 1923,Ap 9,14:3 (In Addenda)

Griffith, Edward H (Director)
Scrambled Wives 1921,My 23,16:3
Unseeing Eyes 1923,O 22,17:1
Bad Company 1925,Mr 16,16:1
Afraid to Love 1927,Ap 12,25:3
Alias the Lone Wolf 1927,S 20,32:2
Shady Lady, The 1929,Mr 25,32:2
Paris Bound 1929,S 21,17:1
Rebound 1931,Ag 29,16:3
Lady With a Past 1932,F 22,23:2
Animal Kingdom, The 1932,D 30,14:2
Another Language 1933,Ag 5,9:5
Biography of a Bachelor Girl 1935,Mr 2,18:2
No More Ladies 1935,Je 22,18:5
Next Time We Love 1936,Ja 31,16:2
Ladies in Love 1936,O 29,31:1
Cafe Metropole 1937,Ap 29,17:1
I'll Take Romance 1937,D 17,33:2
Cafe Society 1939,F 23,19:2
Honeymoon in Bali 1939,S 21,21:1
Safari 1940,Je 20,29:2
Virginia 1941,Ja 29,21:2
One Night in Lisbon 1941,Je 12,29:3
Bahama Passage 1942,F 19,23:2
Sky's the Limit, The 1943,S 3,15:2
Perilous Holiday 1946,Je 1,10:4

Griffith, Edward H (Original Author)
Virginia 1941,Ja 29,21:2

Griffith, Edward H (Producer)
Virginia 1941,Ja 29,21:2
One Night in Lisbon 1941,Je 12,29:3
Bahama Passage 1942,F 19,23:2

Griffith, Eleanor
Alibi 1929,Ap 9,29:1

Griffith, Gordon
Huckleberry Finn 1920,F 23,11:2
Village Blacksmith, The 1922,N 3,17:5
Little Annie Rooney 1925,O 19,26:1

Griffith, Harry
Found Alive 1934,F 12,19:2

Griffith, Hugh
Dulcimer Street 1948,N 8,24:2
Dolwyn 1949,Ag 30,18:4
Run for Your Money, A 1950,Ap 10,15:3
Kind Hearts and Coronets 1950,Je 15,41:2
Laughter in Paradise 1951,N 12,21:2
Galloping Major, The 1951,D 17,27:2
Wild Heart, The 1952,My 29,17:2
Beggar's Opera, The 1953,Ag 25,18:2
Titfield Thunderbolt, The 1953,O 6,34:2
Sleeping Tiger, The 1954,O 9,8:7
Lucky Jim 1958,S 1,8:6
Ben Hur 1959,N 19,50:2
Story of Page One, The 1960,Ja 14,28:1
Day They Robbed the Bank of England, The
    1960,S 5,11:2
Exodus 1960,D 16,44:1
Counterfeit Traitor, The 1962,Ap 18,28:1
Lisa 1962,My 25,28:1
Mutiny on the Bounty 1962,N 9,31:2
Term of Trial 1963,Ja 31,5:2
Tom Jones 1963,O 8,48:1
Hide and Seek 1964,Mr 12,40:3
How to Steal a Million 1966,Jl 15,34:1
Oh Dad, Poor Dad, Mamma's Hung You in the
    Closet and I'm Feeling so Sad 1967,F 16,32:1
Sailor From Gibraltar, The 1967,Ap 25,38:2
Poppy is Also a Flower, The 1967,D 14,62:4
Fixer, The 1968,D 9,59:1
Oliver! 1968,D 11,57:1

Griffith, J J (Screenwriter)
Shalako 1968,N 6,32:1

Griffith, James
Bright Leaf 1950,Je 17,7:2
*Breaking Point, The 1950,O 7,10:6
Apache Drums 1951,My 7,22:2
Rhubarb 1951,Ag 31,12:2
Eight Iron Men 1953,Ja 2,11:1
Black Dakotas, The 1954,O 2,21:2
Anything Goes 1956,Mr 22,38:1
Tribute to a Bad Man 1956,Mr 31,13:3
First Texan, The 1956,Je 23,20:2
Big Fisherman, The 1959,Ag 6,18:1
Amazing Transparent Man, The 1961,Mr 30,24:2

Griffith, Katherine
Woman Thou Gavest Me, The 1919,Je 9,16:3

Griffith, Kay
Wife, Husband and Friend 1939,F 25,19:2

Griffith, Kenneth
Love on the Dole 1945,O 13,11:2
Bond Street 1950,Mr 30,40:6
High Treason 1952,My 21,23:3
Prisoner, The 1955,D 12,37:1
Private's Progress 1956,Jl 24,19:2
1984 1956,O 1,31:1
Your Past Is Showing 1958,Jl 1,36:2
Lucky Jim 1958,S 1,8:6
Two-Headed Spy, The 1959,Mr 3,38:4
Man Upstairs, The 1959,Ag 11,23:2
Tiger Bay 1959,D 15,50:1
I'm All Right Jack 1960,Ap 26,40:2
Circus of Horrors 1960,S 1,31:1
Risk, The 1961,S 25,41:2
Only Two Can Play 1962,Mr 21,33:2
Payroll 1963,My 11,15:2
Rotten to the Core 1965,Jl 20,39:2
Whisperers, The 1967,Ag 1,24:1
Bobo, The 1967,S 29,53:1

Griffith, Nona
Unseen, The 1945,My 14,20:5
Perfect Marriage, The 1947,Ja 16,30:3

Griffith, O W (Producer)
Hearts of the World 1918,Ap 5,13:1

Griffith, R
Nellie, the Beautiful Cloak Model
    1924,Ap 14,14:1

Griffith, Raymond
Fools First 1922,Jl 31,12:3
Eternal Three, The 1923,O 12,7:2 (Incorrect in
    this edition; use 1927,O 1,7:2 elsewhere)
Day of Faith, The 1923,N 27,11:2
Dawn of a Tomorrow, The 1924,Mr 26,19:2
Changing Husbands 1924,Je 23,22:4
Poisoned Paradise 1924,Ag 11,16:1
Lily of the Dust 1924,Ag 25,16:2
Open all Night 1924,S 9,19:1
Miss Bluebeard 1925,Ja 28,14:1
Forty Winks 1925,F 3,24:1
Paths to Paradise 1925,Je 30,14:3
Paths to Paradise 1925,Jl 5,VII,2:1
Regular Fellow, A 1925,O 5,25:2
Fine Clothes 1925,O 20,28:1
Hands Up 1926,Ja 18,26:2
Wet Paint 1926,My 17,19:1
You'd Be Surprised 1926,S 27,27:3
Time to Love 1927,Je 23,23:3
Wedding Bills 1927,Je 29,29:3
All Quiet on The Western Front 1930,Ap 30,29:1

Griffith, Raymond (Producer)
Fifty Roads to Town 1937,Je 5,21:1
Thin Ice 1937,S 4,8:2

Griffith, Raymond (Producer) — Cont
Wife, Doctor and Nurse 1937,O 11,26:5
Heidi 1937,N 6,14:2
Second Honeymoon 1937,N 13,11:2
Baroness and the Butler, The 1938,F 19,19:2
Rebecca of Sunnybrook Farm 1938,Mr 26,12:1
Three Blind Mice 1938,Je 18,18:2
Always Goodbye 1938,Je 25,7:2
Three Musketeers, The 1939,F 18,12:2
Griffith, Robert
Night Club, The 1925,My 5,24:2
Girl in the Canal, The 1947,O 9,32:3
Griffith, Wallace
Stand up and Fight 1939,Ja 27,17:2
Griffith, William
Time Out for Romance 1937,Mr 13,23:2
Griffiths, Fred
Ladykillers 1956,F 21,37:2
I'm All Right Jack 1960,Ap 26,40:2
Griffiths, Howard (Screenwriter)
2nd Best Secret Agent in the Whole Wide World,
The 1966,Ap 28,49:1
Griffiths, Jane
Man With a Million 1954,Je 29,21:2
Green Scarf, The 1955,Ja 15,10:2
Grigg, Ricky
Surfari 1967,Jl 19,26:2
Grigg, Thelma
Bush Christmas 1947,N 27,50:4
Griggs, John
Annapolis Salute 1937,O 2,18:1
Grignon, Marcel (Cinematographer)
Fixer, The 1968,D 9,59:1
Grigoriev, Anton
Khovanschina 1960,S 19,41:2
Grigoriev, Feodor
Life in Bloom 1949,My 9,20:4
Grigoriev, Y
Bolshoi Ballet 67 1966,S 30,54:1
Grigoryev, R (Director)
Day in Moscow, A 1957,D 23,18:2
Grigoryev, R (Screenwriter)
Day in Moscow, A 1957,D 23,18:2
Grigoryeva, G
Dubrovsky 1936,Mr 30,17:6
Grika, Herb
Last Blitzkrieg, The 1959,Ja 31,13:5
Grilikhes, Michel (Screenwriter)
Duel at Diablo 1966,Je 16,53:1
Grill, Willi
Ronny 1932,Ap 14,25:3
Grimaldi, Alberto (Producer)
For a Few Dollars More 1967,Jl 4,23:1
Good, The Bad and the Ugly, The
1968,Ja 25,33:1
Big Gundown, The 1968,Ag 23,33:1
Grimaldi, Giovanni (Screenwriter)
Slave, The 1963,My 30,20:1
Grimblat, Pierre (Director)
How Not to Rob a Department Store
1965,D 29,23:1
Grimblat, Pierre (Screenwriter)
How Not to Rob a Department Store
1965,D 29,23:1
Grimes, Henry
Jazz on a Summer's Day 1960,Mr 29,46:2
Grimes, Karolyn
Pardon my Past 1946,Ja 28,15:5
It's a Wonderful Life 1946,D 23,19:2
Bishop's Wife, The 1947,D 10,44:2
Albuquerque 1948,Mr 1,17:2
Rio Grande 1950,N 20,21:2
Grimes, Rosemary
Island of Lost Souls 1933,Ja 13,19:2
Grimes, Tammy
Three Bites of the Apple 1967,My 25,54:2
Grimm, Brothers (Original Author)
Snow White 1916,D 25,7:1
Tom Thumb 1958,D 24,00:0
Snow White and the Three Stooges 1961,Jl 1,9:1
Grimm, Oliver
Reaching for the Stars 1958,My 24,18:2
Reach for Glory 1963,S 10,46:1
Grimm (Original Author)
Snow White and the Seven Dwarfs
1938,Ja 14,21:1 (In Addenda)
Grimwood, Herbert
Romola 1924,D 2,13:2
Amateur Gentleman, The 1926,Ag 17,15:3
Grin, Guillermina
Don Quixote 1949,My 13,29:3
Grinde, Nick (Director)
Bishop Murder Case, The 1930,F 1,15:1
Good News 1930,S 6,9:2
Remote Control 1930,D 8,26:1
This Modern Age 1931,S 7,19:3
Shopworn 1932,Ap 4,13:6
Vanity Street 1932,O 15,13:1
Public Enemy's Wife 1936,Jl 9,17:2
Jailbreak 1936,Ag 6,22:1
Fugitive in the Sky 1937,Ja 16,21:1
White Bondage 1937,Ag 6,21:3
Love Is on the Air 1937,N 12,27:3
Federal Man-Hunt 1939,F 2,17:3

King of Chinatown 1939,Mr 16,27:2
Woman Is the Judge, A 1939,S 28,29:5
Convicted Woman 1940,F 26,11:2
Man With Nine Lives, The 1940,Ap 29,12:3
Men Without Souls 1940,My 13,21:2
Girls of the Road 1940,Jl 22,20:2
Before I Hang 1940,O 3,31:3
Hitler-Dead or Alive 1943,Mr 31,23:3
Grinde, Nick (Screenwriter)
Babes in Toyland 1934,D 13,28:2
We've Never Been Licked 1943,Ag 19,23:1
Grindel, Gerhard (Screenwriter)
City of Torment 1950,Je 10,11:4
Gringer, Judy
Venum 1968,Ja 11,42:1
Grinstead, Durward (Screenwriter)
Maid of Salem 1937,Mr 4,27:2
Gripe, Maria (Original Author)
Hugo and Josephine 1968,S 30,60:1
Gripe, Maria (Screenwriter)
Hugo and Josephine 1968,S 30,60:1
Gripp, Harry
Honor Bound 1928,Ap 30,18:3
Grisham, Walter
Captain's Paradise, The 1953,S 29,25:5
Grishko, M
Cossack Beyond the Danube, A 1954,F 8,18:5
Grishkov, Sergei
Conflict 1955,D 26,23:4
Grissell, Wallace (Director)
Wanderer of the Wasteland 1945,S 29,12:2
Griswold, Grace
One Exciting Night 1922,O 24,17:3
Griswold, Herbert Spencer
Hogan's Alley 1925,N 24,28:4
Gritcher, G (Director)
Laughter Through Tears 1933,N 13,21:2
Gritsch, Willy
Waltz Dream, The 1926,Jl 26,13:2
Gritsenko, L
True Friends 1954,N 15,33:2
1905 1956,Jl 9,27:2
Gritsenko, N
Lucky Bride, The 1948,Ja 26,15:2
Dream of a Cossack 1952,F 18,15:2
Big Family, A 1955,Je 6,24:1
Sisters 1959,My 25,33:2
Gritsenko, Olympiada
Christmas Slippers 1945,D 24,19:2
Grizzard, George
From the Terrace 1960,Jl 16,10:1
Advise and Consent 1962,Je 7,31:2
Warning Shot 1967,Je 8,52:2
Grodski, Nikolas
Zygmunt Kolosowski 1947,N 13,13:3
Grodsky, M
Golden Taiga 1935,Ag 2,22:3
Groenberg, Ake
Naked Night, The 1956,Ap 10,27:5
Lesson in Love, A 1960,Mr 15,46:1
Groeneveld
Man to Men 1949,F 21,20:2
Grofe, Ferde (Composer)
King of Jazz 1930,My 3,23:1
Thousands Cheer 1943,S 14,27:1
Grofe, Ferde Jr (Screenwriter)
Steel Claw, The 1961,S 21,40:2
Samar 1962,Ap 12,41:6
Walls of Hell, The 1965,N 18,55:3
Grogan, Reb
Stark Love 1927,F 28,22:3
Groh, Herbert Ernst
Lied vom Glueck, Das; Song of Happiness, The
1935,N 30,12:7
Schoen Ist Es Verliebt zu Sein 1936,Ap 7,31:2
Groll, Herbert
Keepers of the Night 1953,Je 9,24:2
Gromof, A I
Rivals 1933,Ap 5,22:6
Gromoff, Gregoire
Edward and Caroline 1952,Ap 30,33:3
Anastasia 1956,D 14,35:6
Gromyko, Margarita
In the Name of Life 1947,O 20,29:2
Gronau
Ich Kenn' Dich Nicht und Liebe Dich; I Don't
Know You, but I Love You 1935,N 18,20:1
Gronau, Ernst
His Late Excellency 1929,Je 11,27:2
Gronda, Greta
Eravamo Sette Vedove; We Were Seven Widows
1940,F 16,23:4
Gronstedt, Olle
Doll, The 1964,Ja 14,27:1
Groom, Pelham (Original Author)
Angels One Five 1954,Ap 30,28:2
Groom, Sam
Act One 1963,D 27,17:2
Gropper, Milton Herbert (Original Author)
We Americans 1928,Mr 29,25:3
Thru Different Eyes 1929,Ap 15,22:6
Ladies of Leisure 1930,My 24,21:2
Women of Glamour 1937,Mr 6,10:1

Gropper, Milton Herbert (Screenwriter)
New Toys 1925,F 17,18:1
Grosbard, Ulu (Director)
Subject Was Roses, The 1968,O 14,53:2
Grose, Lionel
Blanche Fury 1948,N 24,20:2
Snowbound 1949,F 21,20:2
Groser, John Father
Murder in the Cathedral 1952,Mr 26,35:2
Groser, Michael
Murder in the Cathedral 1952,Mr 26,35:2
Grosmith, Lawrence
No Time for Comedy 1940,S 7,9:2
Gross, Cordelia Baird (Original Author)
This Could Be the Night 1957,My 15,39:1
Gross, Edward (Producer)
Mrs Mike 1950,F 9,36:5
Gross, Erwin
Fidelio 1961,My 13,10:1
Gross, Helen
Dodek na Froncie 1936,Mr 30,17:6
Gross, Irmgard
Brand in der Oper 1932,Jl 11,11:4
Gross, Jack (Producer)
Big Steal, The 1949,Jl 11,13:2
Woman on Pier 13, The 1950,Je 16,28:4
Little Egypt 1951,Ag 30,20:3
Mark of the Renegade 1951,S 7,24:2
Gross, Jerry (Director)
Teenage Mother 1968,S 19,62:4
Gross, Jerry (Producer)
Teenage Mother 1968,S 19,62:4
Gross, Jerry (Screenwriter)
Teenage Mother 1968,S 19,62:4
Gross, Joseph
Judith 1966,Ja 21,22:1
Gross, Laurence (Original Author)
Whistling in the Dark 1933,F 5,IX,5:1
Whistling in the Dark 1941,Ag 28,23:2
Gross, Milt (Screenwriter)
Sis Hopkins 1941,My 1,27:5
Rookies on Parade 1941,My 22,25:2
Gross, Robert (Producer)
Will It Happen Again 1948,My 17,23:4
Gross, Stephen
Beggars in Ermine 1934,Ap 25,25:3
Gross, Stephen (Screenwriter)
Thank You, Jeeves 1936,O 5,25:1
Gross, Walter
Razzia 1948,Je 14,19:2
Gross, Walter (Composer)
Torch Song 1953,O 13,34:2
Gross, William J
Prunelia 1918,Je 3,9:3
Grossac, Gil
Five Day Lover, The 1961,D 14,55:4
Grosse, Arthur
Rebel, The 1933,Jl 25,17:2
Grossett, John
Miss Sadie Thompson 1953,D 24,9:1
Grossi, Thomas (Original Author)
Marco Visconti 1947,S 20,12:4
Grossinger, Fred
Wind Across the Everglades 1958,S 12,21:1
Grossland, Marjorie
Day the Earth Stood Still, The 1951,S 19,37:1
Grossley, Syd
Suspense 1930,N 8,21:3
Grosslicht, Trude
Fall des Oberst Redl, Der 1932,Ag 18,23:3
Grosslichtova, T
Inspector General, The 1937,N 25,37:1
Grossman, Albert
Don't Look Back 1967,S 7,50:2
Grossman, Albert (Producer)
Don't Look Back 1967,S 7,50:2
Grossman, Bernie (Composer)
Young and Beautiful 1934,S 18,18:4
Wake up and Dream 1934,O 11,28:3
Grossman, Budd (Original Author)
Bachelor Flat 1962,Ja 13,14:1
Grossman, Budd (Screenwriter)
Bachelor Flat 1962,Ja 13,14:1
Grossman, F Maury (Original Author)
Swing That Cheer 1938,N 11,31:2
Grossman, Helen
Tevya 1939,D 22,15:3
Grossman, Irving
Catskill Honeymoon 1950,Ja 28,10:3
Grossman, Ladislav (Screenwriter)
Shop on Main Street, The 1966,Ja 25,47:1
Grossmith, George
Women Everywhere 1930,Je 23,15:1
Those Three French Girls 1930,O 11,21:3
Reserved for Ladies 1932,My 21,9:2
Homme a l'Hispano, L'; Man in the Hispano-Suiza,
The 1933,Je 11,IX,2:5
Princess Charming 1935,Je 22,18:5
Girl From Maxim's, The 1936,S 16,29:1
Amoureux, Les 1940,D 9,23:3
Grossmith, George (Original Author)
Women Everywhere 1930,Je 23,15:1

Grossmith, Lawrence
Private Life of Don Juan, The 1934,D 10,16:2
Men Are not Gods 1937,Ja 19,28:1
I'm From Missouri 1939,Mr 23,27:1
Captain Fury 1939,My 26,20:2
Larceny Street 1941,Ja 6,11:2
Gaslight 1944,My 5,17:2

Grossowna, Helen
Krolowa Przedmiescia; Queen of the Market
Place 1937,D 29,17:2
Pietro Wyzej; Apartment Above 1938,Ja 10,13:4
Dyplomatyczna Zona 1938,O 24,13:2
Neighbors; Shekhonim 1938,D 9,31:3

Grothe, Franz
Ihr Groesster Erfolg; Her Greatest Success
1939,F 12,20:4

Grothe, Fritz (Miscellaneous)
Rendez-Vous 1932,Ap 30,19:3

Grottesi, Rosalba
Shoot Loud, Louder... I Don't Understand
1967,S 21,56:4

Grotti, Aldo
Red Desert 1965,F 9,43:1

Grouix, Gilles (Director)
Cat in the Sack 1967,My 12,53:1

Grouix, Gilles (Original Author)
Cat in the Sack 1967,My 12,53:1

Grove, Gerald
Man and Maid 1925,Ap 7,17:3

Grove, Sybil
His Private Life 1928,N 12,18:2
Let Us Be Gay 1930,Jl 12,16:4
Strauss's Great Waltz 1935,Ap 8,23:3
Men Are not Gods 1937,Ja 19,28:1

Grover, Mildred
Who Killed Gail Preston? 1938,My 6,27:2

Groves, Clemence
Constant Nymph, The 1943,Jl 24,8:2

Groves, Fred
Suspense 1930,N 8,21:3
Beachcomber, The 1938,D 26,29:3
21 Days Together 1940,My 23,28:4
My Brothers Keeper 1949,F 14,15:3

Groves, Scotty
Give Me a Sailor 1938,Ag 11,31:1

Gruault, Jean (Screenwriter)
Carabiniers, Les 1967,S 28,58:3
Religieuse, La 1968,S 23,42:3

Grubb, Davis (Original Author)
Night of the Hunter, The 1955,S 30,23:1

Gruber, Frank (Original Author)
Death of a Champion 1939,Ag 24,17:3
Kansan, The 1943,O 1,15:3
Fighting Man of the Plains 1949,N 17,35:6
Dakota Lil 1950,Mr 3,21:5
Great Missouri Raid, The 1951,Ap 9,31:2
Texas Rangers, The 1951,Jl 14,7:2
Warpath 1951,N 23,32:2
Denver and Rio Grande, The 1952,My 17,22:7
Pony Express 1953,Je 6,8:6
Backlash 1956,Ap 21,11:2
Big Land, The 1957,Mr 2,18:2

Gruber, Frank (Screenwriter)
Mask of Dimitrios, The 1944,Je 24,16:2
Terror by Night 1946,F 9,9:2
Dressed to Kill 1946,My 25,12:4
Fighting Man of the Plains 1949,N 17,35:6
Cariboo Trail, The 1950,S 1,17:2
Great Missouri Raid, The 1951,Ap 9,31:2
Warpath 1951,N 23,32:2
Denver and Rio Grande, The 1952,My 17,22:7
Hurricane Smith 1952,O 4,15:2

Gruber, Georg Dr (Composer)
Orphan Boy of Vienna, An 1937,S 9,19:2

Gruber, Herbert (Producer)
Fledermaus, Die 1964,F 8,15:2

Gruber, Mercle
Shir Hashirim 1935,O 11,31:1

Grubnik, P
Land, The 1955,Ap 11,29:3

Grudberg, I
Tkies Khaf; (Vow, The) 1938,S 15,29:3

Gruen, James (Miscellaneous)
Everybody Sing 1938,Mr 11,15:3

Gruen, James (Original Author)
Leathernecks Have Landed, The 1936,Mr 23,22:5

Gruen, James (Screenwriter)
Marines are Coming, The 1935,F 23,14:7

Gruen, John
8 X 8 1957,Mr 16,13:2

Gruen, Margaret (Original Author)
Road House 1948,N 8,24:2

Gruenbaum, Fritz
Meine Frau, Die Hochstaplerin 1932,F 6,14:4
Es Wird Schon Wieder Besser; Things Will Soon
Get Better 1932,F 28,VIII,6:1
Brave Suender, Der 1933,Mr 29,13:2
Einmal Moecht' Ich Keine Sorgen Haben
1933,My 25,24:4
Es Wird Schon Wieder Besser 1934,Ja 24,21:3
Ein Lied, Ein Kuss, Ein Maeder 1936,D 12,29:4

Gruenberg, Louis (Composer)
Fight for Life, The 1940,Mr 7,19:2

Gruenberger, Manne
Pettersson & Bendel 1934,F 22,25:2

Gruendgens, Gustaf
Maedchen Johanna, Das 1935,O 9,27:2 (In
Addenda)

Gruendgens, Gustav
Hocuspocus 1930,Ag 3,VIII,4:1
Brand in der Oper; Fire in the Opera House
1930,N 23,IX,6:2
Danton 1931,S 7,19:3
Raub der Mona Lisa, Der 1932,Mr 30,15:2
Brand in der Oper 1932,Jl 11,11:4
Luise, Koenigin von Preussen 1932,O 5,26:6
Yorck 1932,N 24,35:2
Teilnehmer Antwortet Nicht 1932,N 30,23:6
M 1933,Ap 3,13:3
Voce del Sangue, La 1933,Ap 17,16:4
Ich Glaub' nie Mehr an Eine Frau
1933,O 13,25:4
Schwarzer Jaeger Johanna 1935,Ap 1,17:2
Liebelei 1936,F 28,18:2
Erbe in Pretoria, Das 1936,Ap 18,19:3
Frau Ohne Bedeutung, Ein 1938,Ap 16,17:2
Liebe im Gleitflug; Love in Stunt Flying
1938,Je 18,18:3
Faust 1963,Ap 16,31:1

Gruendgens, Gustav (Director)
Eine Stadt Steht Kopf 1934,Ja 29,10:2
Finanzen des Grossherzogs, Die; Grand Duke's
Finances, The 1935,Ap 6,10:3
Liebe im Gleitflug; Love in Stunt Flying
1938,Je 18,18:3
Schritt vom Wege, Der; False Step, The
1939,Ap 29,13:3

Gruendgens, Gustav (Miscellaneous)
Faust 1963,Ap 16,31:1

Gruener, Allan
Underworld, U S A 1961,My 13,10:1

Grueter, Alexander (Producer)
Bimbo the Great 1961,Je 29,26:1
World in my Pocket, The 1962,My 10,30:2

Gruman, Francis (Cinematographer)
Festival 1967,O 24,53:2

Grummer, Elisabeth
Don Giovanni 1956,D 27,22:1

Grun, Bernard (Composer)
Balalaika 1939,D 15,33:2

Grundgens, Gustav
Graefin von Monte Christo, Die; Countess of
Monte Christo, The 1932,My 15,VIII,4:2 (In
Addenda)

Grune, Karl (Director)
Street, The 1927,S 6,34:3
Am Rande der Welt; On the Edge of the World
1928,Ja 15,VIII,7:4 (In Addenda)
Jealousy 1928,D 4,29:1
Waterloo 1929,Ap 16,32:5
At the Edge of the World 1929,Je 18,29:4
Abdul the Damned 1936,My 11,16:2
Clown Must Laugh, A 1938,O 12,35:2

Grunewald, Berdine
Cry, the Beloved Country 1952,Ja 24,23:2

Gruning, Ilka
Drunter und Drueber 1932,D 19,19:5
Underground 1941,Je 23,13:2
Kings Row 1942,F 3,23:2
Dangerously They Live 1942,Ap 11,9:2
Friendly Enemies 1942,Je 22,19:1
Desperate Journey 1942,S 26,11:2
Iceland 1942,O 15,27:1
Casablanca 1942,N 27,27:1
This Is the Army 1943,Jl 29,11:6
Repeat Performance 1947,Jl 2,19:2
Captain China 1950,Mr 2,33:2

Grunnbaum, Herbert
Threepenny Opera, The 1960,Jl 11,24:4

Grusczynski, Stanislaw
Noc Listopadowa 1933,My 1,10:3

Gruskin, Jerry (Original Author)
Lady Takes a Sailor, The 1949,D 17,15:2

Gruskin, Jerry (Screenwriter)
Tarzan and the Huntress 1947,Ap 7,20:4

Gruter, Alexander (Producer)
For the First Time 1959,Ag 15,8:7

Gruzdev, I (Screenwriter)
Childhood of Maxim Gorky 1938,S 28,29:3
On his Own 1939,S 13,31:3
University of Life 1941,F 26,17:1

Gryaznof, E (Director)
Born Anew 1933,Jl 1,14:3

Gstettenbaur, Gustl Starck
By Rocket to the Moon 1931,F 7,11:1

Guadalajara Trio
Masquerade in Mexico 1945,N 29,27:2

Gualdieri, Michele (Screenwriter)
Gran Varieta 1955,Ap 11,29:5

Guard, Kit
Legionnaires in Paris 1927,D 26,26:6
Beau Broadway 1928,Jl 30,21:2
Unholy Garden, The 1931,O 29,27:1
Last Man, The 1932,S 17,18:4

Guard, Kit — Cont
Corruption 1933,Je 20,22:7
Shadows of the Orient 1937,O 11,26:6
Johnny O'Clock 1947,Mr 27,39:2

Guard, Philip
Angel Who Pawned her Harp, The
1956,F 29,35:2

Guardino, Harry
Houseboat 1958,N 14,24:1
Pork Chop Hill 1959,My 30,9:2
Five Pennies, The 1959,Je 19,30:1
Five Branded Women 1960,Je 2,27:2
King of Kings 1961,O 12,41:2
Hell is for Heroes 1962,Jl 12,19:3
Pigeon That Took Rome, The 1962,Ag 23,25:1
Rhino! 1964,Ag 27,28:2
Adventures of Bullwhip Griffin, The
1967,Mr 9,43:2
Treasure of San Gennaro 1968,F 27,36:1
Madigan 1968,Mr 30,22:2
Jigsaw 1968,Je 6,54:2
Hell With Heroes, The 1968,S 3,54:2

Guardiola, Jose
Spanish Affair 1958,F 6,24:1

Guarducci, Corrado
Cousins, The (Les Cousins) 1959,N 24,44:1

Guareschi, Giovanni (Original Author)
Little World of Don Camillo, The
1953,Ja 14,27:1
Mistress of the Mountains 1954,My 27,34:5
Return of Don Camillo, The 1956,Mr 27,41:1

Guarini, Alfredo (Original Author)
Walls of Malapaga, The 1950,Mr 21,34:2

Guarnieri, Gianna
Streets of Sorrow 1952,N 18,37:4

Guarracino, Umberto
Maciste in Hell 1931,Je 29,20:3

Guazoni, Enrico (Director)
Re Burlone, Il 1936,Mr 28,11:3

Guazzoni, Enrico (Director)
Messalina 1924,Ag 25,16:2
Ho Perduto mio Marito; I Have Lost My
Husband 1939,O 20,27:4
Dottor Antonio, Il 1939,D 7,35:1
Re di Danari; Money King 1939,D 22,15:2

Guazzoni, Enrico (Screenwriter)
Messalina 1924,Ag 25,16:2

Gubanova, Irina
War and Peace 1968,Ap 29,50:5

Gubin, S
Scandal? 1929,O 28,20:1

Gude, John
Garden of Eden 1957,D 18,45:3

Gudegast, Hans
Dayton's Devils 1968,O 3,56:4

Guderman, Linda
Macabre 1958,Jl 24,18:1

Gudkin, G
Pozor 1933,Mr 11,18:4

Gudrun, Ann
Trouble in the Glen 1955,Ap 11,29:2

Guedel, John (Original Author)
People Are Funny 1946,Ja 28,15:6

Gueden, Nicole
Bride Is Much too Beautiful, The 1958,Ja 21,35:1
Inside Out 1964,S 25,32:1

Guedes, Alvarez
Big Boodle, The 1957,Mr 12,38:1

Guedon, Nicole
Life Upside Down; Inside Out 1965,Ag 18,41:4

Guedry, C T
Louisiana Story 1948,S 29,36:2

Gueera, Tonino (Screenwriter)
Wild Eye, The 1968,Ag 22,47:1

Guelis, Jean
Minne 1951,Ap 17,35:2

Guelstorff, Max
Meistersinger 1929,D 16,34:2
Hurrah I'm Alive 1930,Je 16,25:3
Grosse Tenor, Der 1931,My 29,26:5
Raub der Mona Lisa, Der 1932,Mr 30,15:2
Ich Geh' aus und Du Bleibst da 1932,N 21,21:1
Hauptmann von Koepenick, Der 1933,Ja 17,22:6
Liebe Muss Verstanden Sein 1934,Mr 21,24:3
Sonne Geht auf, Die 1935,F 18,19:4
Ich Sing Mich in Dein Herz Hinein
1935,Je 3,22:3
Frischer Wind aus Kanada 1935,S 21,18:2
So ein Maedel Vergisst Man nicht 1935,S 28,12:3
Ich Kenn' Dich Nicht und Liebe Dich; I Don't
Know You, but I Love You 1935,N 18,20:1
Schloss im Sueden, Das 1936,F 24,14:2
Annette in Paradise 1936,Mr 7,11:4
Heisses Blut 1936,S 26,11:2
Raub der Sabinerinnen, Der 1937,Ja 16,21:1
Falscher Fuffziger, Ein 1937,F 13,9:1
Kirschen in Nachbars Garten 1937,My 15,23:6
Schabernack 1937,Ag 14,16:5
Susanne im Bade; Susanna in the Bath
1937,S 11,20:1
Zerbrochene Krug, Der; Broken Jugi, The
1938,Ja 15,19:2
Herzensclieb; Heart Thief 1938,Jl 2,10:4
Schritt vom Wege, Der; False Step, The
1939,Ap 29,13:3

Guelstorff, Max— Cont
  Kleine Nachtmusik, Eine 1940,Mr 2,9:5
  Congo Express 1940,My 11,15:3
Guenette, Robert (Screenwriter)
  Defector, The 1966,N 17,55:1
GUENTHER
  See Also GUNTHER
Guenther, Carl
  Aufforderung zum Tanz; Invitation to the Dance
    1935,N 23,23:3
  Vienna Burgtheater 1937,O 27,47:1
  Maria Ilona 1940,Ap 20,14:3
Guerin, Bruce
  Drifting 1923,Ag 20,4:2
  Country Kid, The 1923,O 30,16:1
  Revelation 1924,Je 24,18:2
  Salvation Hunters, The 1925,F 2,14:1
  Parasite, The 1925,F 16,24:1
Guerin, Francois
  Virtuous Scoundrel, The 1957,O 23,37:1
  Mitsou 1958,Ap 15,42:5
  Diary of a Bad Girl 1958,My 30,13:2
  Sinners of Paris 1959,Ap 24,23:1
Guerini, Camille
  Gigot 1962,S 28,26:1
  Two Are Guilty 1964,F 29,12:1
Guerlais, Pierre (Director)
  Pecheurs d'Islande 1935,S 21,18:2
Guerlais, Pierre (Producer)
  Pecheurs d'Islande 1935,S 21,18:2
Guerner, Enrique (Cinematographer)
  Flamenco 1954,My 24,24:2
Guerney, Claude (Screenwriter)
  Green for Danger 1947,Ag 8,10:2
Guernsey, Otis L (Original Author)
  13 Frightened Girls 1963,S 12,32:2
Guerra, Mario (Screenwriter)
  Sword and the Cross, The 1960,Jl 7,26:1
Guerra, Tonino (Original Author)
  Casanova 1965,Jl 21,43:1
Guerra, Tonino (Screenwriter)
  Night, The; Notte, La 1962,F 20,29:4
  Eclipse 1962,D 21,5:1
  Empty Canvas, The 1964,My 16,21:1 (Incorrect
    in this edition; use 1964,My 16,12:1 elsewhere)
  Marriage Italian Style 1964,D 21,42:1
  Red Desert 1965,F 9,43:1
  10th Victim, The 1965,D 21,46:1
  Blow-Up 1966,D 19,52:2
  More Than a Miracle 1967,N 2,58:2
  Queens, The (Queen Armenia); Queen Armenia
    (The Queens) 1968,Mr 11,49:1
Guerrero, Carmen
  Mano in Mano 1933,F 20,11:6
  Cascarrabias 1933,O 30,14:2
  Sombra de Pancho Villa, La 1934,Ja 8,20:3
  Obre las Olas 1934,Mr 17,11:4
  Sobre Las Olas 1934,Mr 17,11:4
  Oro y Plata 1934,Ag 29,13:2
  El Escandalo 1934,S 22,12:3
  Compadre Mendoza, El 1934,N 19,13:2
  Maria Elena 1936,F 18,27:1
  Calandria, La 1936,O 12,23:3
  Mujeres Sin Alma 1936,D 12,29:4
  Mano a Mano 1938,S 19,16:3
Guerrini, Mino (Director)
  Love and Marriage (The First Night); First Night,
    The (Love and Marriage) 1966,Ag 5,20:1
  Love and Marriage (Saturday, July 18); Saturday,
    July 18 (Love and Marriage) 1966,Ag 5,20:1
  Love and Marriage (The Last Resort); Last Resort,
    The (Love and Marriage) 1966,Ag 5,20:1
  Love and Marriage (One Moment Is Enough); One
    Moment Is Enough (Love and Marriage)
    1966,Ag 5,20:1
Guerrini, Mino (Original Author)
  New Angels, The; I Nuovi Angeli
    1965,My 4,49:1
Guerrini, Mino (Screenwriter)
  New Angels, The; I Nuovi Angeli
    1965,My 4,49:1
  Love and Marriage (The Last Resort); Last Resort,
    The (Love and Marriage) 1966,Ag 5,20:1
  Love and Marriage (Saturday, July 18); Saturday,
    July 18 (Love and Marriage) 1966,Ag 5,20:1
  Love and Marriage (The First Night); First Night,
    The (Love and Marriage) 1966,Ag 5,20:1
  Love and Marriage (One Moment Is Enough); One
    Moment Is Enough (Love and Marriage)
    1966,Ag 5,20:1
Guers, Paul
  Marie Octobre 1960,Ag 16,25:2
  Tales of Paris (The Tale of Francoise); Tale of
    Francoise, The (Tales of Paris) 1962,Ag 27,18:1
  Crime Does Not Pay (The Fenayrou Case);
    Fenayrou Case, The (Crime Does Not Pay)
    1962,O 17,35:2
  I Spit on Your Grave 1963,Je 29,13:5
  Bay of the Angels; Baie des Anges, La
    1964,N 24,44:1
  Magnificent Cuckold 1965,Ap 20,42:1
  Fuga, La 1966,Mr 22,33:1

Guertzman, Paul
  His Private Life 1928,N 12,18:2
Guerzoni, Fausto
  Bertoldo, Bertoldino, Cacasenno 1937,D 22,32:3
  Great Dawn, The 1947,Ag 28,28:3
Guest, Paul
  Girl With the Golden Eyes, The 1962,Ag 21,36:2
Guest, Val (Director)
  Mister Drake's Duck 1952,Ja 28,15:2
  Penny Princess 1953,Mr 25,37:3
  Runaway Bus, The 1954,O 25,30:7
  Dance Little Lady 1955,D 26,23:3
  Ship Was Loaded, The 1958,Ja 20,20:1
  Camp on Blood Island, The 1958,S 18,37:2
  Up the Creek 1958,N 11,26:2
  Yesterday's Enemy 1960,Mr 4,19:1
  Expresso Bongo 1960,Ap 13,44:1
  Hell is a City 1961,Ja 19,26:3
  Stop Me Before I Kill 1961,Je 22,23:4
  Day the Earth Caught Fire, The 1962,Mr 16,25:1
  Where the Spies Are 1966,Ja 27,29:1
  Casino Royale 1967,Ap 29,25:1
  Assignment K 1968,Jl 20,18:2
Guest, Val (Original Author)
  Penny Princess 1953,Mr 25,37:3
  Runaway Bus, The 1954,O 25,30:7
  Up the Creek 1958,N 11,26:2
Guest, Val (Producer)
  Penny Princess 1953,Mr 25,37:3
  Runaway Bus, The 1954,O 25,30:7
  Expresso Bongo 1960,Ap 13,44:1
  Stop Me Before I Kill 1961,Je 22,23:4
  Day the Earth Caught Fire, The 1962,Mr 16,25:1
  Where the Spies Are 1966,Ja 27,29:1
Guest, Val (Screenwriter)
  Happy Go Lovely 1951,Jl 26,17:2
  Another Man's Poison 1952,Ja 7,14:3
  Mister Drake's Duck 1952,Ja 28,15:2
  Dance Little Lady 1955,D 26,23:3
  Ship Was Loaded, The 1958,Ja 20,20:1
  Camp on Blood Island, The 1958,S 18,37:2
  Up the Creek 1958,N 11,26:2
  Hell is a City 1961,Ja 19,26:3
  Stop Me Before I Kill 1961,Je 22,23:4
  Day the Earth Caught Fire, The 1962,Mr 16,25:1
  Where the Spies Are 1966,Ja 27,29:1
  Assignment K 1968,Jl 20,18:2
Guetary, Georges
  Loves of Casanova 1948,S 18,11:4
  American in Paris, An 1951,O 5,24:2
Guevara, Fernanda Ladron de
  Hombre que se Reia del Amor, El 1935,Jl 18,15:3
Guevara, Maria Ladron de
  Odio 1935,Je 24,12:3
Guevremont, Paul
  Thirteenth Letter, The 1951,F 22,27:2
  Quebec 1951,Mr 16,34:2
Guezel, Yvon (Miscellaneous)
  Male Hunt; Chasse a l'Homme, La
    1965,Ap 20,42:1
Guezel, Yvon (Producer)
  Maid in Paris 1957,Jl 13,11:1
  Time Out for Love 1963,Ap 23,31:2
  Burning Court, The 1963,Ag 1,17:2
Gug, Madeleine (Miscellaneous)
  Farrebique 1948,F 24,21:2
Guggenheim, Charles (Director)
  Great St Louis Bank Robbery, The 1960,F 4,34:1
Guggenheim, Charles (Producer)
  Great St Louis Bank Robbery, The 1960,F 4,34:1
Guglielmi, Marco
  Always Victorious 1960,Ap 7,46:1
  Savage Innocents, The 1961,My 25,31:1
  Stranger Returns, The 1968,S 12,54:3
Guglielmi, Riccardo
  Eight and One Half 1963,Je 26,36:1
Guglielmi, Vandina
  Grande Luce, La; Great Light, The
    1940,Mr 15,27:4
Gugoika, John
  Our Mother's House 1967,O 10,56:1
Gugushe, Tsepo
  Cry, the Beloved Country 1952,Ja 24,23:2
Guha, Bhupesh
  Bwana Devil 1953,F 19,20:5
Guhl, George
  Sing Me a Love Song 1936,D 26,15:2
  Fly Away Baby 1937,Jl 9,18:2
  Night Club Scandal 1937,N 12,27:2
  Torchy Blane, The Adventurous Blonde
    1937,D 18,18:1
  Torchy Gets her Man 1938,N 18,25:3
  What a Life 1939,O 12,33:1
  Buck Benny Rides Again 1940,Ap 25,28:4
  Murder by Invitation 1941,Jl 23,15:4
Guhne, Erich
  Germany Year Zero 1949,S 20,35:2
Guibert, Andre
  Diary of a Country Priest 1954,Ap 6,35:2
Guibert, J P (Producer)
  There's Always a Price Tag 1958,My 26,25:2
  Inspector Maigret 1958,O 9,47:1

Guibourg, Edmundo (Director)
  Bodas de Sangre; Bloody Wedding
    1939,N 13,15:3
Guichard, Charles (Director)
  Kreutzer Sonata, The 1938,D 20,30:2
Guida, Ernesto (Screenwriter)
  Constantine and the Cross 1963,Mr 14,8:2
Guida, Wandisa
  Revolt of the Slaves, The 1961,N 8,41:1
Guide, Paul
  Miserables, Les 1926,Jl 9,17:1
  Miserables, Les 1927,Ag 23,29:4
  Loves of Casanova, The 1929,Ap 30,33:2
Guidi, Paolo
  Accattone! 1968,Ap 5,56:1
Guido, Beatriz (Original Author)
  Casa del Angel, La 1960,Ag 30,25:1
  Hand in the Trap 1963,Jl 2,16:2
Guido, Beatriz (Screenwriter)
  Casa del Angel, La 1960,Ag 30,25:1
  Summerskin 1962,My 29,22:2
  Hand in the Trap 1963,Jl 2,16:2
  Terrace, The 1964,N 25,45:1
  Eavesdropper, The 1966,S 15,51:1
Guilbert, J C
  Mouchette 1968,S 21,26:1
Guilbert, Pierre
  World Without Sun 1964,D 23,22:1
Guilbert, Yvette
  Faust 1926,D 7,21:2
  Argent, L' 1929,Mr 3,VII,7:2 (Incorrect in this
    edition; use 1929,Mr 3,VIII,8:5 in film)
  Frochard et les Deux Orphelines, La
    1934,F 7,16:2
  Pecheurs d'Islande 1935,S 21,18:2
  Argent, L' 1968,S 23,42:5
Guild, Nancy
  Somewhere in the Night 1946,Je 13,24:2
  Brasher Doubloon, The 1947,My 22,34:5
  Give my Regards to Broadway 1948,Je 23,32:2
  Black Magic 1949,N 9,37:2
  Abbott and Costello Meet the Invisible Man
    1951,Ap 13,18:6
  Little Egypt 1951,Ag 30,20:3
Guilfoyle, James
  Speakeasy 1929,Mr 11,22:2
  Criminal Code, The 1931,Ja 5,21:3
  Alimony 1949,Jl 22,16:3
Guilfoyle, Paul
  Special Agent 1935,S 19,28:1
  Crime of Dr Crespi, The 1936,Ja 13,14:3
  Two-Fisted Gentleman 1936,Ag 24,11:2
  Wanted: Jane Turner 1936,N 30,24:7
  Winterset 1936,D 4,31:1
  Soldier and the Lady, The 1937,Ap 10,11:1
  Woman I Love, The 1937,Ap 16,27:2
  You Can't Buy Luck 1937,My 14,21:2
  Behind the Headlines 1937,Je 1,27:2
  You Can't Beat Love 1937,Je 25,25:3
  Super-Sleuth 1937,Jl 17,18:1
  Flight From Glory 1937,S 11,20:1
  Hideaway 1937,S 25,10:2
  Danger Patrol 1937,N 19,27:3
  Fight for Your Lady 1937,N 20,21:2
  Crashing Hollywood 1938,Ja 8,19:2
  Double Danger 1938,F 10,17:5
  Law of the Underworld 1938,Ap 28,27:2
  Blind Alibi 1938,My 20,17:2
  Saint in New York, The 1938,My 26,31:2
  Sky Giant 1938,Jl 20,22:2
  I'm From the City 1938,Ag 19,13:4
  Fugitives for a Night 1938,S 21,30:4
  Mad Miss Manton, The 1938,O 21,27:2
  Tarnished Angel 1938,N 15,27:2
  Law West of Tombstone, The 1938,N 25,19:1
  Pacific Liner 1939,Ja 18,17:3
  Society Lawyer 1939,Mr 31,19:2
  News Is Made at Night 1939,Jl 13,17:2
  Unexpected Father 1939,Ag 11,12:2
  Our Leading Citizen 1939,Ag 24,17:1
  One Hour to Live 1939,N 4,11:3
  Sabotage 1939,N 16,29:5
  Thou Shalt Not Kill 1940,Ja 8,11:2
  Remember the Night 1940,Ja 18,27:2
  Grapes of Wrath, The 1940,Ja 25,17:2
  Saint Takes Over, The 1940,My 28,29:3
  Millionaires in Prison 1940,Jl 16,21:3
  One Crowded Night 1940,Ag 27,17:2
  East of the River 1940,O 28,21:2
  Saint in Palm Springs, The 1941,Ja 31,15:5
  Who Is Hope Schuyler 1942,My 22,27:1
  Time to Kill 1942,D 25,15:4
  White Savage 1943,Ap 26,15:2
  North Star, The 1943,N 5,23:1
  Three Russian Girls 1944,F 5,13:2
  It Happened Tomorrow 1944,My 29,18:2
  Seventh Cross, The 1944,S 29,18:1
  Master Race, The 1944,N 2,22:1
  Mark of the Whistler, The 1944,N 11,19:2
  Why Girls Leave Home 1945,Ag 4,7:3
  Virginian, The 1946,Ap 18,22:2
  Second Chance 1947,S 20,12:4
  Roses Are Red 1947,N 15,11:2

Guilfoyle, Paul— Cont
  Mighty Joe Young 1949,Jl 28,19:3
  White Heat 1949,S 3,7:2
  There's a Girl in my Heart 1950,Ja 20,29:2
  Davy Crockett, Indian Scout 1950,Mr 17,28:3
  Woman on Pier 13, The 1950,Je 16,28:4
  Torch Song 1953,O 13,34:2
  Apache 1954,Jl 10,7:2
  Chief Crazy Horse 1955,Ap 28,25:1
  Boy and the Pirates, The 1960,N 24,48:3
Guillemaud, M (Original Author)
  Million, Le 1931,My 21,33:2
Guillermin, John (Director)
  Miss Robin Hood 1953,Je 27,7:2
  Tarzan's Greatest Adventure 1959,Jl 9,22:1
  Day They Robbed the Bank of England, The
    1960,S 5,11:2
  Waltz of the Toreadors 1962,Ag 14,34:1
  Tarzan Goes to India 1962,S 6,37:2
  Never Let Go 1963,Je 15,10:2
  Guns at Batasi 1964,N 17,47:1
  Rapture 1965,Ag 24,25:3
  Blue Max, The 1966,Je 22,38:1
  P J 1968,Mr 7,52:3
Guillermin, John (Original Author)
  Never Let Go 1963,Je 15,10:2
Guillermin, John (Screenwriter)
  Tarzan's Greatest Adventure 1959,Jl 9,22:1
  Tarzan Goes to India 1962,S 6,37:2
Guillot, Olga
  Heroina 1965,N 11,58:2
Guinan, Texas
  Queen of the Night Clubs 1929,Mr 18,30:6
  Broadway Thru a Keyhole 1933,N 2,18:3
Guinee, Jean (Screenwriter)
  Atalante, L' 1947,Je 23,14:5
Guingand, Pierre de
  Equipage, L' 1928,My 20,VIII,5:7
  Last Flight, The 1929,Je 17,29:1
  Chance, La 1932,My 28,18:2
  Bal, Le 1932,S 28,22:5
  Call, The 1938,Mr 29,18:3
Guinn, Earl
  Mad Empress, The 1940,F 15,15:1
Guinness, Alec
  Great Expectations 1947,My 23,31:1
  Run for Your Money, A 1950,Ap 10,15:3
  Kind Hearts and Coronets 1950,Je 15,41:2
  Last Holiday 1950,N 14,39:4
  Mudlark, The 1950,D 25,25:1
  Oliver Twist 1951,Jl 31,17:2
  Lavender Hill Mob, The 1951,O 16,35:2
  Man in the White Suit, The 1952,Ap 1,35:2
  Promoter, The 1952,O 29,36:2
  Captain's Paradise, The 1953,S 29,25:5
  Malta Story 1954,Jl 17,7:2
  Detective, The 1954,N 2,25:2
  To Paris With Love 1955,Mr 29,33:4
  Prisoner, The 1955,D 12,37:1
  Ladykillers 1956,F 21,37:2
  Swan, The 1956,Ap 27,21:5
  Bridge on the River Kwai 1957,D 19,39:1
  All at Sea 1957,D 23,18:2
  Horse's Mouth, The 1958,N 12,41:1
  Scapegoat, The 1959,Ag 7,28:1
  Our Man in Havana 1960,Ja 28,26:1
  Tunes of Glory 1960,D 21,38:2
  Majority of One, A 1962,Ja 12,29:2
  Damn the Defiant 1962,S 20,29:2
  Lawrence of Arabia 1962,D 17,5:6
  Fall of the Roman Empire, The 1964,Mr 27,14:2
  Situation Hopeless-But not Serious
    1965,O 14,53:1
  Doctor Zhivago 1965,D 23,21:1
  Hotel Paradiso 1966,O 15,34:2
  Quiller Memorandum, The 1966,D 16,59:1
  Comedians, The 1967,N 1,37:1
Guinness, Alec (Screenwriter)
  Horse's Mouth, The 1958,N 12,41:1
Guiol, Fred (Composer)
  Kentucky Kernels 1935,Ja 5,20:2
Guiol, Fred (Director)
  Rainmakers, The 1935,N 2,13:2
  Silly Billies 1936,Ap 6,18:1
  Tanks a Million 1941,O 9,27:2
  Here Comes Trouble 1948,Ap 15,31:4
Guiol, Fred (Original Author)
  Kentucky Kernels 1935,Ja 5,20:2
  Rainmakers, The 1935,N 2,13:2
  Silly Billies 1936,Ap 6,18:1
  Abroad With two Yanks 1944,O 26,19:7
Guiol, Fred (Producer)
  Taxi, Mister 1943,Ap 15,20:2
  Fall In 1943,My 15,13:3
  Prairie Chickens 1943,Jl 9,21:6
  Here Comes Trouble 1948,Ap 15,31:4
Guiol, Fred (Screenwriter)
  Kentucky Kernels 1935,Ja 5,20:2
  Gunga Din 1939,Ja 28,19:2
  Vigil in the Night 1940,Mr 9,19:2
  Giant 1956,O 11,51:1
Guiomar, Julien
  King of Hearts 1967,Je 20,34:1
  Thief of Paris, The 1967,Ag 24,43:2

Guise, Janine
  Slipper Episode, The 1938,My 19,25:2
Guise, Tom
  Twenty-three and a Half Hours' Leave
    1919,O 27,9:3
  Alarm Clock Andy 1920,Mr 15,13:2
  Don't Ever Marry 1920,Ap 19,13:3
  Black Oxen 1924,Ja 7,23:1
  Free and Equal 1925,Ap 20,22:1
  Claw, The 1927,My 11,28:3
  Wedding Bills 1927,Je 29,29:3
Guisol, Henri
  Vierge Folle, La 1938,D 30,11:3
  Bizarre, Bizarre 1939,Mr 21,27:2
  Three Waltzes 1939,Ap 25,19:2
  Crime in the Maginot Line 1939,My 8,21:2
  Portrait of a Woman 1946,Ap 22,26:2
  Affaire, L' 1950,N 13,23:2
  Lady Paname 1951,Mr 20,35:4
  Dream Ballerina 1951,Ap 16,21:2
  Theodora, Slave Empress 1955,Ja 12,24:2
  Fruits of Summer 1956,Jl 18,22:2
  Crime of Monsieur Lange, The 1964,Ap 4,15:5
Guissart, Rene (Director)
  Tu Seras Duchesse 1932,My 7,11:5
  Chance, La 1932,My 28,18:2
  Coiffeur Pour Dames 1932,O 31,18:4
  Mon Coeur Balance 1933,F 3,21:4
Guistini, Carlo
  Savage Innocents, The 1961,My 25,31:1
Guiton, Jean (Original Author)
  Forty Little Mothers 1938,D 23,16:3
Guitry, Genevieve
  Nine Bachelors 1942,F 9,19:2
  Mlle Desiree 1948,N 19,35:2
Guitry, Sacha
  Pasteur 1936,Ja 30,14:3
  Pearls of the Crown, The 1938,Ap 12,26:2
  Story of a Cheat, The 1938,S 27,25:2
  Champs-Elysees 1939,F 28,17:2
  Indiscretions 1939,My 1,21:1
  Nine Bachelors 1942,F 9,19:2
  Private Life of an Actor; En Scene 1948,S 7,21:3
  Mlle Desiree 1948,N 19,35:2
  Royal Affairs in Versailles 1957,Mr 9,16:1
Guitry, Sacha (Director)
  Pasteur 1936,Ja 30,14:3
  Pearls of the Crown, The 1938,Ap 12,26:2
  Story of a Cheat, The 1938,S 27,25:2
  Champs-Elysees 1939,F 28,17:2
  Indiscretions 1939,My 1,21:1
  Nine Bachelors 1942,F 9,19:2
  Private Life of an Actor; En Scene 1948,S 7,21:3
  Mlle Desiree 1948,N 19,35:2
  Royal Affairs in Versailles 1957,Mr 9,16:1
  Virtuous Scoundrel, The 1957,O 23,37:1
  Lovers and Thieves 1958,Ag 5,23:2
Guitry, Sacha (Original Author)
  Lover of Camille, The 1924,N 11,14:1
  Sleeping Partners 1930,D 13,22:2
  Lucky Partners 1940,S 6,25:2
  Royal Affairs in Versailles 1957,Mr 9,16:1
  Lovers and Thieves 1958,Ag 5,23:2
Guitry, Sacha (Producer)
  Private Life of an Actor; En Scene 1948,S 7,21:3
  Mlle Desiree 1948,N 19,35:2
  Royal Affairs in Versailles 1957,Mr 9,16:1
  Virtuous Scoundrel, The 1957,O 23,37:1
Guitry, Sacha (Screenwriter)
  Pearls of the Crown, The 1938,Ap 12,26:2
  Story of a Cheat, The 1938,S 27,25:2
  Champs-Elysees 1939,F 28,17:2
  Indiscretions 1939,My 1,21:1
  Nine Bachelors 1942,F 9,19:2
  Private Life of an Actor; En Scene 1948,S 7,21:3
  Mlle Desiree 1948,N 19,35:2
  Virtuous Scoundrel, The 1957,O 23,37:1
Guitton, Jean (Original Author)
  Forty Little Mothers 1940,Ap 19,25:2
Guitton, Jean (Screenwriter)
  Rothchild 1938,O 12,35:2
Guitty, Madeleine
  Madame Sans Gene 1925,Ap 18,19:1
  Celle Vielle Canaille 1935,Ja 12,12:2
  Cette Vielle Canaille 1935,Ja 12,12:2
  Avec l'Assurance 1935,My 4,17:3
  Sans Famille 1935,Je 4,26:5
  Porteuse de Pain, La 1936,Jl 1,29:5
Guizar, Susana
  Juntos pero no Revueltos; United but not Mixed
    1939,O 23,15:3
  Reina del Rio, La; Queen of the River, The
    1940,F 24,9:3
Guizar, Tito
  Alla en el Rancho Grande 1936,N 23,17:3
  Big Broadcast of 1938, The 1938,Mr 10,16:2
  Tropic Holiday 1938,Je 30,21:2
  Rancho Grande 1938,D 2,27:2
  St Louis Blues 1939,F 9,17:2
  Papa Soltero; Bachelor Father 1939,N 6,20:3
  Blondie Goes Latin 1941,F 26,17:3
  Alla en el Tropico; Down in the Tropics
    1943,My 8,19:3

Guizar, Tito— Cont
  Que Lindo es Michoacan 1944,Ap 22,8:7
  Brazil 1944,N 20,25:2
  Mexicana 1945,N 17,14:6
  Thrill of Brazil, The 1946,S 6,18:3
Gulager, Clu
  Killers, The 1964,Jl 18,10:4
Gulaya, Inna
  When the Trees Were Tall 1965,F 22,14:1
Guldbrandsen, Peer (Producer)
  I, A Lover 1968,My 4,46:2
Guldbrandsen, Peer (Screenwriter)
  I, A Woman 1966,O 12,36:3
  I, A Lover 1968,My 4,46:2
Gulick, Bill (Original Author)
  Bend of the River 1952,Ap 10,37:1
  Hallelujah Trail, The 1965,Jl 2,17:1
Gulino, Giuseppe
  Gesuzza, La Sposa Garibaldina 1936,N 3,33:4
Gullan, Campbell
  Pleasure Crazed 1929,Jl 15,25:1
  Power 1934,O 5,29:3
  Iron Duke, The 1935,Ja 25,27:2
  Song of the Road 1940,My 6,13:2
Gulliver, Dorothy
  Shield of Honor 1927,D 13,33:2
  Good Morning, Judge 1928,Je 26,29:1
  College Love 1929,Ag 5,25:2
  Night Parade 1929,N 11,20:2
  Troopers Three 1930,F 17,17:6
  Cheating Blondes 1933,My 20,11:4
  Faces 1968,S 23,42:4
Gullmain, Ofelia
  Nazarin 1968,Je 21,48:1
Gulowski, Gene (Producer)
  Cul de Sac 1966,N 8,44:2
Gumley, Leonard
  Sands of Iwo Jima 1949,D 31,9:2
Gump, Irving
  Bullfighters, The 1945,My 12,10:3
Gunan, Eileen
  Men of Ireland 1938,S 30,24:2
Gundelach, Gustel
  Code 7...Victim 5 1965,My 20,52:1
Gunia, V
  Eagle of the Caucasus, The 1932,S 17,18:4
Gunji, Jiromasa (Original Author)
  Samurai Assassin 1965,Mr 19,27:5
Gunn, Earl
  We Are From Kronstadt 1936,My 2,11:1
  Missing Witness 1937,D 10,33:3
  Island Of Doomed Men 1940,Je 10,21:2
  Devil's Island 1940,Jl 12,11:4
  Swamp Woman 1941,D 27,15:2
  Great Commandment, The 1942,O 17,11:1
Gunn, Franzi
  Folly of Vanity 1925,Ja 28,14:1
Gunn, Gilbert (Director)
  Cosmic Monster, The 1959,Ja 1,38:1
Gunn, Gilbert (Screenwriter)
  Landfall 1953,My 11,25:2
Gunn, Herbert
  Always in my Heart 1942,Mr 14,19:2
Gunn, James (Original Author)
  Born to Kill 1947,My 1,34:2
Gunn, James (Screenwriter)
  Lady of Burlesque 1943,My 14,17:2
  Unfaithful, The 1947,Je 28,10:2
  Harriet Craig 1950,N 3,31:2
  Flying Missile, The 1950,D 25,25:1
  Two of a Kind 1951,Je 30,8:6
  Affair in Trinidad 1952,Jl 31,14:2
  All I Desire 1953,Ag 29,10:1
  Young Philadelphians, The 1959,My 22,32;1
Gunn, Judy
  Last Journey, The 1936,Je 8,22:4
Gunn, William
  Sound and the Fury, The 1959,Mr 28,11:1
Gunner, Robert
  Planet of the Apes 1968,F 9,55:2
Gunning, Wid (Producer)
  What Do Men Want? 1921,N 14,18:1
GUNTHER
  See Also GUENTHER
Gunther, Isa
  Heidi 1953,D 21,27:2
  Heidi and Peter 1955,D 13,55:2
Gunther, John (Miscellaneous)
  Thunder Birds 1942,O 29,19:2
Gunther, John (Screenwriter)
  Lost Continent 1957,Mr 12,38:1
Gunther, Karl
  Lied der Wuste, Das; Desert Song 1940,F 3,9:3
Gunther, Paul
  Luise, Koenigin von Preussen 1932,O 5,26:6
Gunty, Morty
  What's so bad About Feeling Good?
    1968,My 25,27:1
Gunzberg, Milton (Screenwriter)
  Devil Commands, The 1941,F 14,15:3
Gupta, Anubha
  Kanchenjungha 1966,Jl 26,27:2

Gupta, Pinaki Sen
Aparajito 1959,Ap 29,30:1
Gupta, Ramani Sen
Aparajito 1959,Ap 29,30:1
Gupta, S
Gyandev of India 1943,Ap 10,12:5
Gupta, Santi
Aparajito 1959,Ap 29,30:1
Gupta, Sarada
Throw of the Dice 1930,Ja 6,30:5
Gupta, Uma Das
Pather Panchali 1958,S 23,37:2
Gur, Alizia
Night Train to Paris 1964,D 3,58:2
Kill a Dragon 1967,D 7,60:2
Gur, Sergei
Horsemen, The 1951,Ja 29,14:5
Gurchenko, Lyudmila
Carnival in Moscow 1957,N 4,40:1
Girl With the Guitar, The 1960,F 1,22:4
Marriage of Baezaminov, The 1966,Je 11,20:2
Guretskaya, T
Pozor 1933,Mr 11,18:4
Miracles 1934,O 22,12:3
Professor Mamlock 1938,N 8,26:2
Guretskaya, Tatiana
Tovaristchi 1935,My 25,12:2
Gurevitch, I
Mass Struggle 1934,S 17,20:3
Gurie, Sigrid
Algiers 1938,Jl 15,13:2
Forgotten Woman, The 1939,Ag 4,11:2
Rio 1939,O 27,27:2
Three Faces West 1940,Ag 19,13:2
Dark Streets of Cairo 1940,D 2,19:3
Voice in the Wind 1944,Mr 16,17:2
Enemy of Women 1944,S 12,23:6
Sword of the Avenger 1948,Ag 26,16:4
Sofia 1948,S 4,8:7
Adventures of Marco Polo, The 1965,Ap 8,17:2
Gurienko, Misha
We Are From Kronstadt 1936,My 2,11:1
Gurin, I (Screenwriter)
Private Ivan 1957,Ap 3,28:2
Gurnaby, Davy
Co-Optimists, The 1930,F 5,27:2
Gurney, Rachel
Tom Brown's School Days 1952,Ja 8,23:5
Port Afrique 1956,N 3,27:5
Touch of Larceny, A 1960,Mr 17,28:1
Funeral in Berlin 1966,D 23,17:1
Gurnyak, K
Her Way of Love 1929,Ag 19,22:1
Deserter 1934,O 13,10:1
Gurov, S (Director)
U S S R Today 1953,Ap 20,21:2
Daring Circus Youth 1953,D 21,27:4
Spring Voices 1956,O 25,40:5
Gurov, S (Screenwriter)
Daring Circus Youth 1953,D 21,27:4
Gurso, S
Young Guard 1949,D 26,33:6
Gurtler, George D
Strange Case of Captain Ramper, The
1928,Je 4,13:2
Guschtchinsky, V
Defense of Volotchayevsk, The 1938,Ag 11,13:3
Gusev, P A
Stars of the Russian Ballet (The Fountain of
Bakhchisarai); Fountain of Bakhchisarai (Stars of
the Russian Ballet) 1954,S 6,9:2
Gusev, V
Girl With the Guitar, The 1960,F 1,22:4
Apartment in Moscow 1962,My 28,25:5
Resurrection 1963,O 7,35:2
Gusev, Victor (Screenwriter)
Six PM 1946,Ja 28,15:5
Gusian-Jade, A
Arshin Takes a Wife 1950,Jl 31,13:6
Gusman, Chinto
Apache Drums 1951,My 7,22:2
Guss, Jack (Screenwriter)
Lady in Cement 1968,N 21,41:1
Gussev, Victor (Screenwriter)
They Met in Moscow 1944,Je 7,13:2
Gustafson, Besse (Screenwriter)
Obession 1968,Ag 29,46:3
Gustafsson, Nils
Himlaspelet 1944,O 9,17:3
Gustavson, Gunoild
To Bed...Or not to Bed 1963,D 23,18:2
Gustavsson, Gosta
One Summer of Happiness 1955,Mr 22,35:2
Gutemberg, Linda
Naked Childhood 1968,S 28,36:1
Guter, Johannes (Director)
Der Falsche Ehemann 1932,O 17,18:3
Guterson, Mischa (Composer)
Siren of Seville, The 1924,N 17,16:1 (In
Addenda)
Guterson, Mischa (Miscellaneous)
Lover of Camille, The 1924,N 11,14:1

Guthier, M (Producer)
Light Across the Street, The; Lumiere d'en Face,
La 1957,Jl 30,20:2
Guthrie, A B Jr (Original Author)
Big Sky, The 1952,Ag 20,21:1
These Thousand Hills 1959,My 7,36:1
Way West, The 1967,My 25,54:1
Guthrie, A B Jr (Screenwriter)
Shane 1953,Ap 24,30:3
Kentuckian, The 1955,S 2,13:2
Guthrie, Lester D (Director)
Amazing Transparent Man, The 1961,Mr 30,24:2
Guthrie, Tyrone
Beachcomber, The 1938,D 26,29:3
Sidewalks of London 1940,F 15,15:1
Guthrie, Tyrone (Director)
Oedipus Rex 1957,Ja 8,26:1
Gutierrez (Original Author)
Trovatore, Il 1950,F 9,36:7
GUTMAN
See Also GUTTMAN
Gutman, D
New Babylon, The 1929,D 2,28:2
Cities and Years 1931,Ap 4,23:1
Return of Nathan Becker, The 1933,Ap 15,16:3
Gutman, D (Director)
Captain Grant's Children 1939,Ja 12,23:3
Untitled-Capt Grant's Children 1939,Ja 12,23:3
Gutman, Walter
Unstrap Me 1968,N 21,41:2
Gutman, Walter (Original Author)
Unstrap Me 1968,N 21,41:2
Gutowski, Gene (Producer)
Fearless Vampire Killers, The, or Pardon Me but
Your Teeth are in my Neck 1967,N 14,52:1
Gutschwager, Helo
Counterfeit Traitor, The 1962,Ap 18,28:1
Guttenberg, Bertha
Cantor's Son, The 1937,D 27,11:1
Gutter, Johanne (Director)
Fraeulein Liselott 1935,My 27,20:7
Fraulein Liselott 1935,My 27,20:7
GUTTMAN
See Also GUTMAN
Guttman, Henry
They Got Me Covered 1943,Mr 5,20:2
Night Has a Thousand Eyes 1948,O 14,38:3
Guttmann, Arthur (Composer)
Der Schrecken der Garnison 1932,Je 1,19:5
Guttmann, Arthur (Miscellaneous)
Ein Walzer vom Strauss 1932,F 11,16:1
Ein Prinz Verliebt Sich 1932,Ap 29,13:4
Guy, Edmonde
Kreutzer Sonata, The 1938,D 20,30:2
Devil Is an Empress, The 1939,D 4,18:4
Guy, Eula
Over the Hill 1931,N 21,20:4
Rich are Always With Us, The 1932,My 16,19:5
Rebecca of Sunnybrook Farm 1932,Jl 30,16:5
Expensive Husbands 1938,Ja 8,19:3
Moon Over her Shoulder 1941,N 5,31:2
Spider Woman Strikes Back, The 1946,Mr 23,8:3
Paula 1952,Jl 16,21:2
Guyau, Victor
Oh, Amelia 1951,D 3,22:2
Guyse, Sheila
Miracle in Harlem 1949,O 24,19:4
Guzeyev, A
Inspector General, The 1954,My 3,21:2
Guzmab, Robert E
Desert Song, The 1929,My 2,20:6
Guzman, Enrique
Juarez y Maximiliano 1935,F 16,9:2
Gvale, Ragnar
Four Sons 1940,Je 8,18:4
Gwaltney, Francis (Original Author)
Between Heaven and Hell 1956,O 12,33:2
Gwenn, Edmund
Real Thing at Last, The 1916,Mr 9,11:2
How He Lied to her Husband 1931,Ja 17,23:1
Skin Game, The 1931,Je 20,20:4
Money for Nothing 1932,F 21,VIII,5:2 (In
Addenda)
Condemned to Death 1932,Jl 14,24:2
Be Mine Tonight 1933,Ap 14,22:5
Good Companions, The 1933,O 10,24:1
I Was a Spy 1934,Ja 15,12:2
Friday the 13th 1934,My 15,18:1
Channel Crossing 1934,My 24,28:3
For Love or Money 1934,Jl 26,14:2
Strauss's Great Waltz 1935,Ap 8,23:3
Java Head 1935,Jl 31,21:4
Sylvia Scarlett 1936,Ja 10,16:2
Walking Dead, The 1936,Mr 2,13:2
Anthony Adverse 1936,Ag 27,16:1
Mad Holiday 1936,N 26,39:2
Parnell 1937,Je 4,27:2
Yank at Oxford, A 1938,F 25,15:1
South Riding 1938,Ag 2,15:2
Earl of Chicago, The 1940,Mr 14,29:3
Doctor Takes a Wife, The 1940,Je 15,12:2
Pride and Prejudice 1940,Ag 9,19:1
Foreign Correspondent 1940,Ag 28,15:2

Gwenn, Edmund— Cont
Cheers for Miss Bishop 1941,Mr 14,17:2
Scotland Yard 1941,Ap 9,33:3
Devil and Miss Jones, The 1941,My 16,21:2
One Night in Lisbon 1941,Je 12,29:3
Charley's Aunt 1941,Ag 2,18:2
Laburnum Grove 1941,D 2,29:2
Yank at Eton, A 1942,O 16,23:1
Meanest Man in the World, The 1943,F 25,27:3
Lassie Come Home 1943,O 8,15:4
Between Two Worlds 1944,My 6,11:2
Keys of the Kingdom, The 1944,D 30,15:2
Bewitched 1945,Ag 17,20:3
Dangerous Partners 1945,N 2,22:4
She Went to the Races 1946,F 1,29:2
Of Human Bondage 1946,Jl 6,11:2
Undercurrent 1946,N 29,36:2
Miracle on 34th Street 1947,Je 5,32:1
Life With Father 1947,Ag 16,6:6
Green Dolphin Street 1947,O 16,34:2
Thunder in the Valley 1947,N 28,30:1
Apartment for Peggy 1948,O 16,9:2
Hills of Home 1948,N 26,32:2
Woman of Distinction, A 1950,Mr 17,28:2
Challenge to Lassie 1950,Ap 7,22:3
Pretty Baby 1950,S 23,11:2
Mister 880 1950,S 30,13:2
Louisa 1950,O 25,45:2
For Heaven's Sake 1950,D 16,10:5
Peking Express 1951,Jl 19,20:2
Miserables, Les 1952,Ag 15,11:2
Something for the Birds 1952,N 15,15:2
Mister Scoutmaster 1953,Ag 29,10:1
Bigamist, The 1953,D 26,10:4
Student Prince, The 1954,Je 16,18:2
Them 1954,Je 17,36:2
Trouble With Harry, The 1955,O 18,46:2
It's a Dog's Life 1955,D 23,14:3
Rocket From Calabuch 1958,O 8,41:1
Gwiazdowski, Tadeusz
Kanal 1961,My 10,52:1
Gwillim, Jack
Pursuit of the Graf Spee 1957,D 27,33:2
One That Got Away, The 1958,Ap 23,40:2
Sink the Bismarck! 1960,F 12,22:3
Flame Over India 1960,Ap 30,14:1
Midsummer Night's Dream, A 1961,D 19,39:1
In Search of the Castaways 1962,D 22,5:2
Gwyn, Nell (Miscellaneous)
Nell Gwyn 1935,Je 20,16:2
Gwynn, Michael
Dunkirk 1958,S 11,42:2
Camp on Blood Island, The 1958,S 18,37:2
Doctor's Dilemma, A 1958,D 18,2:7
Question 7 1961,S 29,30:2
Barabbas 1962,O 11,49:1
Cleopatra 1963,Je 13,29:1
Gwynne, Anne
Unexpected Father 1939,Ag 11,12:2
Honeymoon Deferred 1940,F 16,23:4
Black Friday 1940,Mr 22,23:3
Sandy Is a Lady 1940,Je 28,22:2
Spring Parade 1940,O 4,29:2
Give Us Wings 1940,N 21,43:3
Nice Girl 1941,Mr 27,29:6
Black Cat, The 1941,Ap 26,20:3
Washington Melodrama 1941,My 26,15:3
Tight Shoes 1941,Je 19,25:2
Mob Town 1941,N 20,39:3
Jail House Blues 1942,F 6,23:2
Ride 'Em Cowboy 1942,Mr 5,27:3
Strange Case of Dr Rx 1942,Mr 28,11:2
Broadway 1942,Je 5,23:2
Men of Texas 1942,Jl 13,18:3 (In Addenda)
Sin Town 1942,O 17,11:2
Frontier Badmen 1943,Ag 14,12:8
We've Never Been Licked 1943,Ag 19,23:1
Top Man 1943,O 29,23:2
Ladies Courageous 1944,Mr 16,17:2
Weird Woman 1944,Ap 1,11:1
Murder in the Blue Room 1944,O 28,12:2
House of Frankenstein 1944,D 16,19:3
Dick Tracy and Gruesome 1947,S 27,11:2
Gwynne, Fred
On the Waterfront 1954,Jl 29,18:1
Munster, Go Home 1966,Je 16,53:4
Gwynne, Michael
Village of the Damned 1960,D 8,43:3
Gyarfas, Laszlo
Paul Street Boys, The 1929,Jl 15,25:1
Gyergyai, Istvan
Csokolj Meg Edes 1932,N 25,19:2
Majd a Zsuzsi 1938,O 22,14:3
Busuini Nem Jo; Don't Worry 1938,O 29,15:5
Gyldtenungae, Annita
Kalle paa Spaangen 1940,Ja 27,9:3
Gyllenspetz, Ann-Marie
Brink of Life; (Nara Livet) 1959,N 9,36:2
Gyni, Ketty
Barefoot Battalion 1954,My 29,13:4
Gynt, Greta
Road Back, The 1937,Je 18,25:2
Human Monster, The 1940,Mr 25,11:2
At Dawn We Die 1943,My 8,19:2

Gynt, Greta— Cont
Mr Emmanuel 1945,Ja 8,15:2
Mr Perrin and Mr Traill 1949,Ja 17,15:2
Take my Life 1949,Ja 19,34:2
Easy Money (Episode 3) 1949,F 14,15:3
Soldiers Three 1951,Mr 30,28:5
Lucky Nick Cain 1951,Ap 23,21:2
Gyoergy, Istvan
Igloi Diakok 1935,My 24,24:3
Gyoergy, Istvan (Director)
Nagymama 1935,D 30,15:1
Kiralyne Huszarja, A 1936,Ja 17,15:3
Zivatar a Pusztan 1937,Ap 24,16:2
Oeroek Titok, Az; Eternal Secret, The
1940,Mr 9,19:3
Gyoergy, Istvan (Producer)
Zivatar a Pusztan 1937,Ap 24,16:2
Gyoergy, Istvan (Screenwriter)
Zivatar a Pusztan 1937,Ap 24,16:2
Gypsies
Love in the Afternoon 1957,Ag 24,12:1
Gyula, Csortos
Hyppolit, A Lakaj 1933,Ja 4,22:6
Gyula, Gozon
Csokolj Meg Edes 1932,N 25,19:2
Gyula, Kabos
Hyppolit, A Lakaj 1933,Ja 4,22:6

H

Haack, Kaethe
Skandal Um Eva 1931,Ap 21,35:2
Emil und die Detektive 1931,D 21,28:4
Hauptmann von Koepenick, Der 1933,Ja 17,22:6
Liebe Muss Verstanden Sein 1934,Mr 21,24:3
Tannenberg 1934,Ap 3,26:6
Alraune 1934,My 5,22:4
Konjunkturritter 1935,Ap 29,12:4
Pantoffelhelden 1935,O 21,22:5
Vier Musketiere, Die; Four Musketeers, The
1935,N 9,19:3
Falscher Fuffziger, Ein 1937,F 13,9:1
Urlaub auf Ehrenwort; Furlough on Word of
Honor 1938,Mr 28,19:2
Krach und Glueckum Kuennemann; Row and Joy
About Kuennemann 1938,S 17,20:3
Fridericus 1939,F 25,19:2
Schritt vom Wege, Der; False Step, The
1939,Ap 29,13:3
Familie Schimek 1939,S 2,20:2
Gluck auf den Lande; Rural Happiness
1940,F 10,19:3
Tag Nach der Scheidung, Der; Day After the
Divorce, The 1940,Mr 2,9:5
Keepers of the Night 1953,Je 9,24:2
Haade, William
Kid Galahad 1937,My 27,21:3
Missing Witness 1937,D 10,33:3
Invisible Menace, The 1938,F 14,20:6
Stadium Murders, The 1938,Ap 9,11:2
Texans, The 1938,Jl 28,23:2
If I Were King 1938,S 29,31:1
Shadows Over Shanghai 1938,D 1,29:2
Union Pacific 1939,My 11,31:2
Full Confession 1939,S 28,29:4
Kid Nightingale 1939,D 8,33:6
Reno 1939,D 21,29:2
Invisible Stripes 1940,Ja 13,11:2
Geronimo 1940,F 8,18:3
Man From Dakota, The 1940,F 22,29:2
One Crowded Night 1940,Ag 27,17:2
Cherokee Strip 1940,N 4,23:2
Roundup, The 1941,Mr 13,25:4
Penalty, The 1941,Ap 10,29:3
Dance Hall 1941,Jl 19,16:2
Rise and Shine 1941,D 6,14:3
You're in the Army Now 1941,D 26,21:4
Juke Girl 1942,Je 20,9:2
Jackass Mail 1942,Jl 2,25:2
Just off Broadway 1942,Ag 29,18:4
Star Spangled Rhythm 1942,D 31,20:1
Pittsburgh 1943,F 25,27:2
Dancing Masters, The 1943,D 2,30:2
Down to Earth 1947,S 12,18:2
Lulu Belle 1948,Je 21,18:3
Scene of the Crime 1949,Jl 29,12:2
Rawhide 1951,Mr 26,19:2
Oh! Susanna 1951,Mr 30,28:5
Yank in Korea, A 1951,Ap 2,29:2
Haagen, Margarete
Seven Journeys 1951,Mr 12,20:2
Reaching for the Stars 1958,My 24,18:2
Haakin, Byron (Director)
I Walk Alone 1948,Ja 22,36:3
Haal, Renee
Unexpected Uncle 1941,S 25,29:1
Haaland, Ingjald
En Saga 1938,Ja 8,19:2
Haardt, Georges-Marie (Miscellaneous)
Croisiere Jaune, La; Yellow Journey, The
1934,My 6,IX,4:5 (In Addenda)

Haaria, Saulo
Milkmaid, The 1959,My 2,14:5
Haarleman, Nita
Soederkaakar 1936,D 19,16:2
HAAS
See Also HASS
Haas, Charles (Director)
Summer Love 1958,Je 26,23:4
Beat Generation, The 1959,O 22,47:4
Platinum High School 1960,My 26,37:3
Haas, Charles (Producer)
Moonrise 1949,Mr 7,17:2
Haas, Charles (Screenwriter)
Moonrise 1949,Mr 7,17:2
Haas, Dolly
Dolly Macht Karriere; Dolly's Way to Stardom
1930,N 23,IX,6:2
Dolly Macht Karriere 1931,Jl 18,16:6
Liebeskommando 1932,Ap 27,13:6
Brave Suender, Der 1933,Mr 29,13:2
Ein Maedel der Strasse 1933,Ap 6,22:5
Es Wird Schon Wieder Besser 1934,Ja 24,21:3
Page vom Dalmasse-Hotel, Der 1935,Mr 25,12:3
So ein Maedel Vergisst Man nicht 1935,S 28,12:3
Die Privatsekretaerin Heiratet 1936,D 5,16:4
Broken Blossoms 1937,Ja 14,16:3
Spy of Napoleon 1939,Ag 19,18:4
I Confess 1953,Mr 23,28:2
Haas, Hugo
Skeleton on Horseback 1940,F 5,13:3
Days of Glory 1944,Je 17,10:2
Summer Storm 1944,O 23,14:3
Princess and the Pirate, The 1945,F 10,16:2
Bell for Adano, A 1945,Jl 6,8:3
Dakota 1945,D 17,17:2
What Next Corporal Hargrove? 1945,D 26,15:2
Holiday in Mexico 1946,Ag 16,19:3
Two Smart People 1947,F 15,20:4
Fiesta 1947,Je 27,17:3
Northwest Outpost 1947,Ag 8,10:2
Foxes of Harrow, The 1947,S 25,35:4
Merton of the Movies 1947,N 7,20:3
My Girl Tisa 1948,F 21,9:2
Casbah 1948,My 3,27:4
For the Love of Mary 1948,S 23,37:2
Fighting Kentuckian, The 1949,S 19,18:3
King Solomon's Mines 1950,N 10,35:1
Vendetta 1950,D 26,19:1
Pickup 1951,Ag 31,12:2
Bait 1954,F 24,21:3
Lizzie 1957,Ap 5,24:2
Haas, Hugo (Director)
Skeleton on Horseback 1940,F 5,13:3
Pickup 1951,Ag 31,12:2
Bait 1954,F 24,21:3
Lizzie 1957,Ap 5,24:2
Night of the Quarter Moon 1959,Mr 5,35:5
Haas, Hugo (Producer)
Pickup 1951,Ag 31,12:2
Bait 1954,F 24,21:3
Haas, Hugo (Screenwriter)
Pickup 1951,Ag 31,12:2
Haas, Waltraut
Beggar Student, The 1958,Ja 25,14:3
Haase, John (Original Author)
Petulia 1968,Je 11,54:4
Habay, Andre
Quo Vadis 1925,F 16,24:1
Habe, Hans (Original Author)
Cross of Lorraine, The 1943,D 3,27:4
Haber, Sandy (Screenwriter)
Mask, The 1961,O 28,12:4
Habib, Eli (Producer)
Hatikvah; (Hope, The) 1959,O 27,40:4
Habib, Nuri (Director)
Hatikvah; (Hope, The) 1959,O 27,40:4
Habib, Nuri (Screenwriter)
Hatikvah; (Hope, The) 1959,O 27,40:4
Habib, Ralph (Director)
Companions of the Night 1954,N 25,44:2
Bed, The (Riviera Express); Riviera Express (The
Bed) 1955,Je 8,26:4
Doctors, The 1956,Ag 7,19:2
Tempest in the Flesh 1957,Ja 19,12:2
Hachey, Joe
Amateur Daddy 1932,Ap 23,11:5
Hachler, Horst
Last Bridge, The 1957,Ag 21,22:2
HACK
See Also HOCH
Hack, Kaethe
Toerichte Jungfrau, Die 1935,S 9,24:3
Hermine und die Sieben Aufrechten
1935,S 21,18:2
Hack, Stan
Safe at Home 1941,N 26,31:2
Hackady, Hal (Screenwriter)
Hey, Lets Twist 1962,F 8,25:1
Two Tickets to Paris 1962,N 29,46:5
Hackathorne, George
Heart of Humanity, The 1918,D 22,17:3
To Please one Woman 1920,D 20,11:2

Hackathorne, George— Cont
Last of the Mohicans, The 1921,Ja 3,20:2
What Do Men Want? 1921,N 14,18:1
Village Blacksmith, The 1922,N 3,17:5
Human Wreckage 1923,Je 28,10:2
When a Man's a Man 1924,F 5,20:1
Lady, The 1925,Ja 27,11:2
Capital Punishment 1925,F 5,23:3
Night Life of New York 1925,Jl 14,14:1
Squall, The 1929,My 10,32:5
Captain of the Guard 1930,Mr 29,23:1
Hackel, A W (Producer)
Murder by Invitation 1941,Jl 23,15:4
Hackenschmied, Alexander (Cinematographer)
Lights Out In Europe 1940,Ap 15,21:2
Forgotten Village, The 1941,N 19,26:3
Hackenschmied, Alexander (Miscellaneous)
Crisis 1939,Mr 13,12:2
Hacker, David
It Ain't Hay 1943,Mr 11,17:3
Hackett, Albert
Whoopee 1930,O 1,26:3
Hackett, Albert (Miscellaneous)
Summer Holiday 1948,Je 12,8:5
Hackett, Albert (Original Author)
Up Pops the Devil 1931,My 16,13:3
Thanks for the Memory 1938,D 8,34:3
Easter Parade 1948,Jl 1,19:3
Diary of Anne Frank, The 1959,Mr 19,40:1
Hackett, Albert (Screenwriter)
Naughty Marietta 1935,Mr 23,11:2
Ah, Wilderness! 1935,D 25,30:2
Rose Marie 1936,F 1,9:2
After the Thin Man 1936,D 25,19:2
Firefly, The 1937,S 2,17:2
Society Lawyer 1939,Mr 31,19:2
Another Thin Man 1939,N 24,29:1
Lady in the Dark 1944,F 23,17:1
Hitler Gang, The 1944,My 8,15:2
Virginian, The 1946,Ap 18,22:2
It's a Wonderful Life 1946,D 23,19:2
Pirate, The 1948,My 21,19:2
Easter Parade 1948,Jl 1,19:3
In the Good Old Summertime 1949,Ag 5,23:2
Father of the Bride 1950,My 19,31:2
Father's Little Dividend 1951,Ap 13,18:5
Too Young to Kiss 1951,N 23,32:2
Long, Long Trailer, The 1954,F 19,24:3
Seven Brides for Seven Brothers 1954,Jl 23,8:3
Gaby 1956,My 10,26:3
Certain Smile, A 1958,Ag 1,13:2
Diary of Anne Frank, The 1959,Mr 19,40:1
Five Finger Exercise 1962,Ap 20,20:2
Hackett, Buddy
Walking my Baby Back Home 1954,Ja 16,10:5
God's Little Acre 1958,Ag 14,23:2
All Hands on Deck 1961,Ap 1,10:2
Everything's Ducky 1961,D 21,30:6
Wonderful World of the Brothers Grimm, The
(The Singing Bone); Singing Bone, The (The
Wonderful World of the Brothers Grimm)
1962,Ag 8,35:1
Music Man, The 1962,Ag 24,14:1
It's a Mad, Mad, Mad, Mad World
1963,N 19,47:1
Hackett, Hal
Love Laughs at Andy Hardy 1947,Ja 8,28:2
Summer Holiday 1948,Je 12,8:5
Hackett, Joan
Group, The 1966,Mr 17,35:1
Will Penny 1968,Ap 11,51:2
Hackett, Karl
Down Under the Sea 1936,Ag 10,10:2
Frontier Town 1938,Mr 12,13:3
Chip of the Flying U 1940,Ja 22,11:3
Hackett, Lillian
In Hollywood with Potash and Perlmutter
1924,S 30,27:3
Ladies at Ease 1927,O 5,31:1
Hackett, Raymond
Cruise of the Make-Believe, The 1918,S 2,7:1
Trial of Mary Dugan, The 1929,Mr 29,21:1
Madame X 1929,Ap 25,32:3
Footlights and Fools 1929,N 9,22:5
Not so Dumb 1930,F 8,12:5
Numbered Men 1930,Je 9,23:3
Let Us Be Gay 1930,Jl 12,16:4
Our Blushing Brides 1930,Ag 2,16:4
On Your Back 1930,S 15,29:3
Sea Wolf, The 1930,O 6,21:1
Cat Creeps, The 1930,N 8,21:3
Seed 1931,My 15,20:6
Hackett, Walter (Original Author)
Strangers of the Night 1923,O 8,20:1
Sweethearts and Wives 1930,Je 28,9:2
Their big Moment 1934,S 6,22:4
Espionage 1937,Mr 9,27:3
Love Under Fire 1937,Ag 28,8:2
Hackett, Walter (Screenwriter)
Pays to Advertise, It 1931,F 21,15:2
It Pays to Advertise 1931,F 21,15:2
Hackman, Gene
Lilith 1964,S 21,37:2
Hawaii 1966,O 11,54:1

Hackman, Gene— Cont
First to Fight 1967,Mr 30,55:1
Bonnie and Clyde 1967,Ag 14,36:1
Split, The 1968,N 5,55:2

Hackney, Alan (Original Author)
Private's Progress 1956,Jl 24,19:2

Hackney, Alan (Screenwriter)
I'm All Right Jack 1960,Ap 26,40:2
Sword of Sherwood Forest 1961,Ja 26,32:3
Operation Snatch 1962,S 25,31:4

Hadank, Guenther
August der Starke 1937,Ja 30,21:3

Hadar, Moshe (Screenwriter)
Clouds Over Israel 1966,My 10,48:6

Hadden, George (Director)
Charlie Chan's Courage 1934,Ag 25,16:6

Haddick, Victor (Original Author)
Luck of the Irish, The 1937,Ja 16,21:1

HADDON
See Also HAYDEN, HEIDEN

Haddon, Harriette
Give Me a Sailor 1938,Ag 11,31:1

Haddon, Peter
Beloved Vagabond, The 1937,F 8,12:5
Secret of Stamboul, The 1941,My 31,14:1

Hadely, Reed
Stadium Murders, The 1938,Ap 9,11:2

Haden, Charles
Synanon 1965,My 6,44:1

Haden, Sara
Spitfire 1934,Mr 9,22:3
Finishing School 1934,Ap 30,11:4
Life of Vergie Winters, The 1934,Je 15,26:1
Affairs of a Gentleman 1934,Je 23,16:7
Hat, Coat and Glove 1934,Jl 27,21:2
Fountain, The 1934,Ag 31,14:1
White Parade, The 1934,N 10,19:1
Music in the Air 1934,D 14,29:3
Anne of Green Gables 1934,D 22,21:1
Black Fury 1935,Ap 11,27:2
Mad Love 1935,Ag 5,20:2
O'Shaughnessy's Boy 1935,O 5,18:2
Way Down East 1935,O 31,16:2
Magnificent Obsession 1935,D 31,11:2
Captain January 1936,Ap 25,21:1
Half Angel 1936,My 30,7:3
Little Miss Nobody 1936,Je 6,21:1
Poor Little Rich Girl, The 1936,Je 26,16:1
Crime of Dr Forbes, The 1936,Jl 6,11:4
Reunion 1936,N 27,27:1
Under Cover of Night 1937,Ja 20,18:4
Last of Mrs Cheyney, The 1937,F 19,15:1
Family Affair, A 1937,Ap 20,29:2
Barrier, The 1937,N 27,21:2
First Lady 1937,D 23,25:1
You're Only Young Once 1938,Ja 3,16:2
Out West With the Hardys 1938,D 9,31:2
Four Girls in White 1939,F 23,19:3
Hardys Ride High, The 1939,Ap 14,28:2
Tell no Tales 1939,Je 2,27:3
Andy Hardy Gets Spring Fever 1939,Jl 19,23:2
Secret of Dr Kildare, The 1939,D 8,33:5
Remember? 1939,D 15,33:4
Judge Hardy and Son 1940,Ja 18,27:3 (In Addenda)
Shop Around the Corner, The 1940,Ja 26,13:2
Andy Hardy Meets Debutante 1940,Ag 2,12:2
Boom Town 1940,S 6,25:2
Trial of Mary Dugan, The 1941,Mr 6,25:4
Andy Hardy's Private Secretary 1941,Mr 7,17:2
Washington Melodrama 1941,My 26,15:3
Love Crazy 1941,Je 6,25:5
Barnacle Bill 1941,Jl 25,12:4
Life Begins for Andy Hardy 1941,Ag 22,19:4
H M Pulham, Esq 1941,D 19,35:1
Woman of the Year 1942,F 6,23:2
Courtship of Andy Hardy, The 1942,Ap 10,21:2
Andy Hardy's Double Life 1943,Ja 12,23:3
Youngest Profession, The 1943,Je 25,13:3
Best Foot Forward 1943,Je 30,25:2
Above Suspicion 1943,Ag 6,10:3
Thousands Cheer 1943,S 14,27:1
Lost Angel 1944,Ap 10,14:1
Andy Hardy's Blonde Trouble 1944,My 5,17:3
Our Vines Have Tender Grapes 1945,S 7,21:2
She Wouldn't Say Yes 1946,Ja 12,10:7
She Wolf of London 1946,Ap 6,10:6
So Goes my Love 1946,My 2,3:7
Bad Bascomb 1946,My 23,18:4
Our Hearts Were Growing Up 1946,Ag 12,17:2
Mr Ace 1946,S 30,21:3
Love Laughs at Andy Hardy 1947,Ja 8,28:2
Bishop's Wife, The 1947,D 10,44:2
Rachel and the Stranger 1948,S 20,21:2
Roughshod 1949,Je 17,27:2
Big Cat, The 1949,Jl 29,12:2
Great Rupert, The 1950,Ap 14,27:2
Life of her Own, A 1950,O 12,43:2
Lion Is in the Streets, A 1953,S 24,39:2
Andy Hardy Comes Home 1958,D 24,00:0

Hadfield, Abby
Mikado, The 1967,Mr 15,53:1

Hadge, Michael
Mister Buddwing 1966,O 12,36:1

Hadie, Russell
Costello Case, The 1930,N 4,36:1

Hadjirchristos, Costos
Policeman of the 16th Precinct, The 1963,Ap 22,23:2

Hadley, Bert
Yankee Consul, The 1924,F 11,18:3

Hadley, Fred
Price of a Party, The 1924,N 26,17:3

Hadley, Reed
Female Fugitive 1938,Ap 11,12:3
Calling Dr Kildare 1939,My 12,25:4
I Take This Woman 1940,F 16,23:3
Ski Patrol 1940,My 21,29:4
Bank Dick, The 1940,D 13,29:2
I'll Wait for You 1941,Je 2,13:6
Whistling in the Dark 1941,Ag 28,23:2
Jail House Blues 1942,F 6,23:2
Juke Box Jenny 1942,Ap 17,21:3
Guadalcanal Diary 1943,N 18,29:1
Roger Touhy, Gangster 1944,Je 5,14:7
Wing and a Prayer 1944,Ag 31,14:1
Rainbow Island 1944,O 26,19:6
Circumstantial Evidence 1945,Ap 21,18:3
Caribbean Mystery, The 1945,Ag 20,22:4
Shock 1946,Mr 9,10:2
Doll Face 1946,Mr 28,35:3
Dark Corner, The 1946,My 9,27:3
It Shouldn't Happen to a Dog 1946,S 7,11:2
If I'm Lucky 1946,S 20,41:3
Fabulous Texan, The 1947,D 26,22:5
Man From Texas 1948,Ag 12,16:5
Southern Yankee, A 1948,N 25,47:2
I Shot Jesse James 1949,Ap 2,12:2
Baron of Arizona, The 1950,Je 23,29:2
Dallas 1951,Ja 13,10:4
Little Big Horn 1951,Jl 27,15:2
Half Breed, The 1952,Jl 5,7:2
Highway Dragnet 1954,F 20,8:7
Big House U S A 1955,Mr 12,11:6

Haechler, Horst (Director)
As the Sea Rages 1961,My 18,41:1

Haedrich, Marcel (Original Author)
Crack in the Mirror 1960,My 20,26:1

Haedrich, Rolf (Director)
Stop Train 349 1964,N 12,40:2

Haefeli, Charles
Miserables, Les 1935,Ap 22,14:2

Haefelin, Trude
Ich Kenn' Dich Nicht und Liebe Dich; I Don't Know You, but I Love You 1935,N 18,20:1
Arme Millionar, Der; Poor Millionaire, The 1939,D 30,9:2

Haenckels, Paul
Trial of Donald Westhof, The 1928,F 18,11:2

Haenel, Gunther
Miracle of the White Stallions 1963,My 23,31:2

Haenning, Gitte
Hagbard and Signe 1968,My 17,56:1

Haerlin, Friedl
Gross Reinemachen; General Housecleaning 1938,Je 23,27:2

Haesaerts, Paul (Director)
Rubens 1949,Ap 30,9:2

Haesaerts, Paul (Producer)
Rubens 1949,Ap 30,9:2

Haeussler, Richard
Drama on the Threshing Floor 1937,O 30,22:3
Schimmelkrieg von Holledau, Der 1938,Jl 19,15:4
Secrets of a Soul 1950,S 16,12:6

Hafiz, Achmed
Signs of Life; Lebenszeichent 1968,S 26,60:1

Hafner, Ingrid
Bluebeard's Ten Honeymoons 1960,N 8,32:6

HAGAN
See Also HAGEN

Hagan, Edna
Struggle, The 1931,D 11,35:1

Hagan, James (Original Author)
One Sunday Afternoon 1933,S 2,14:4
Strawberry Blonde 1941,F 22,11:2
One Sunday Afternoon 1948,D 27,16:3

Hagberg, Guniog
Unmarried Mothers 1956,F 23,32:5

Hage, Douglas
Night is my Future 1963,Ja 9,5:6

Hagedorn, Hermann (Original Author)
Rough Riders, The 1927,Mr 16,28:2

Hageman, Richard
Hi Diddle Diddle 1943,S 24,26:2
New Orleans 1947,Je 20,25:6
Toast of New Orleans, The 1950,S 30,13:3
Grounds for Marriage 1951,Ja 12,24:6
Great Caruso, The 1951,My 11,32:2
Rhapsody 1954,Mr 12,17:1

HAGEN
See Also HAGAN

Hagen, George
Way to Love, The 1933,N 11,10:3

Hagen, Holger
Man on a String 1960,My 21,15:1

Hagen, Jack
Johnny Holiday 1950,My 17,36:1

Hagen, Jean
Adam's Rib 1949,D 26,33:2
Ambush 1950,Ja 19,35:2
Side Street 1950,Mr 24,29:2
Asphalt Jungle, The 1950,Je 9,29:3
Life of her Own, A 1950,O 12,43:2
Night Into Morning 1951,Je 11,20:7
No Questions Asked 1951,Ag 10,13:2
Singin' in the Rain 1952,Mr 28,27:2
Carbine Williams 1952,My 8,37:2
Shadow in the Sky 1952,Jl 19,8:2
Arena 1953,Jl 23,20:2
Latin Lovers 1953,Ag 13,17:2
Big Knife, The 1955,N 9,41:2
Spring Reunion 1957,My 6,25:2
Shaggy Dog, The 1959,Mr 20,26:2
Sunrise at Campobello 1960,S 29,32:1
Dead Ringer 1964,F 20,22:3

Hagen, Julius (Producer)
Wandering Jew, The 1935,Ja 14,11:3
Triumph of Sherlock Holmes, The 1935,My 27,20:6
Morals of Marcus, The 1936,Ja 13,14:2
Last Journey, The 1936,Je 8,22:4
Broken Blossoms 1937,Ja 14,16:3
Juggernaut 1937,Jl 15,16:1
She Shall Have Music 1942,O 31,11:2

Hagen, Kevin
Man From Galveston, The 1964,Ja 23,26:3
Last Challenge, The 1967,D 28,25:1

Hagen, Paul
Crazy Paradise 1965,Ag 11,41:2
I, A Lover 1968,My 4,46:2

Hagen, Peter (Director)
Friesennot 1936,O 26,20:1

Hagen, Ross
Speedway 1968,Je 14,43:1
Mini-Skirt Mob, The 1968,O 24,55:5

Hager, Clyde
Strike Me Pink 1936,Ja 17,15:2

Hager, James (Producer)
Stranger in Town, A 1968,Ap 25,53:4

Hagerman, Helge
Pettersson & Bendel 1934,F 22,25:2
Raggen, Det Aer Jag Det 1936,My 22,19:1
Sun Over Sweden 1938,Ap 9,11:2
Children, The 1949,D 23,17:1
Lesson in Love, A 1960,Mr 15,46:1

Hagerman, Jan
Miss Julie 1952,Ap 8,35:2

Hagerthy, Ron
I Was a Communist for the F B I 1951,My 3,34:4
Force of Arms 1951,Ag 14,20:2
Starlift 1951,D 15,11:2
Charge at Feather River, The 1953,Jl 16,17:2
City That Never Sleeps 1953,Ag 8,14:2
Make Haste to Live 1954,Mr 26,16:2
Eighteen and Anxious 1957,D 14,16:6
Saintly Sinners 1962,Mr 29,28:2

Haggard, H Rider (Original Author)
Moon of Israel 1927,Je 29,29:3
She 1935,Jl 26,18:2
King Solomon's Mines 1937,Jl 3,18:1
King Solomon's Mines 1950,N 10,35:1
Watusi 1959,Jl 2,15:2
She 1965,S 2,36:1
Vengance of She, The 1968,My 30,21:4

Haggard, Stephen
Jamaica Inn 1939,O 12,33:1
Mozart 1940,O 4,29:2
Young Mr Pitt, The 1943,Mr 11,17:1

Haggart, Bob (Composer)
Let's Make Music 1941,Ja 23,19:2

Haggerty, Billie
Ex-Flame 1931,Ja 24,15:1

Haggerty, Diane
Good Times 1967,Ag 3,26:4

Haggerty, Don
Canadian Pacific 1949,My 20,32:4
Sundowners, The 1950,My 5,17:2
Kid From Texas, The 1950,Je 2,26:2
Quebec 1951,Mr 16,34:2
Gambling House 1951,Mr 19,23:2
Cause for Alarm 1951,Mr 30,28:5
Go for Broke 1951,My 25,31:2
Angels in the Outfield 1951,O 18,32:1
Callaway Went Thataway 1951,D 6,42:1
Loophole 1954,Mr 13,11:3
Cry Vengence 1955,F 19,18:3
Private War of Major Benson, The 1955,Ag 3,27:2

Haggiag, Brahim
Battle of Algiers, The 1967,S 21,56:1

Haggiag, Robert (Producer)
Thief of Venice, The 1952,N 28,22:7
Birds, the Bees and the Italians, The 1967,Ag 8,33:2
Candy 1968,D 18,54:2

Haggiani, Serge
 25th Hour, The 1967,F 17,45:1
Hagman, Britt
 Intermezzo 1937,D 25,10:6
Hagman, Calle
 For Her Sake 1930,N 11,29:1
Hagman, Harriet
 Thirteen Women 1932,O 15,13:1
Hagman, Larry
 Ensign Pulver 1964,Ag 1,13:2
 Fail Safe 1964,S 16,36:1
 In Harm's Way 1965,Ap 7,36:1
 Cavern, The 1965,D 25,17:2
 Group, The 1966,Mr 17,35:1
Hagman, Victor
 Soederkaakar 1936,D 19,16:2
Hagney, Frank
 Roaring Rails 1924,O 15,27:3
 Hogan's Alley 1925,N 24,28:4
 Two-Gun Man, The 1926,Jl 13,19:3
 Ice Flood, The 1926,O 19,26:2
 Last Trail, The 1927,Ja 26,17:1
 All Abroad 1927,Ap 19,24:4
 On Your Toes 1928,Ja 9,20:1
 Burning Daylight 1928,Ap 23,20:2
 Captain Lash 1929,F 4,20:1
 Fighting Caravans 1931,Ja 26,21:1
 Sit Tight 1931,F 19,20:4
 Squaw Man, The 1931,S 19,10:2
 House Divided, A 1932,Ja 9,21:1
 You Said a Mouthful 1932,N 18,23:2
 Conflict 1937,Ja 18,21:2
 Hollywood Cowboy 1937,Jl 24,12:1
 Glass Key, The 1942,O 16,23:1
 It's a Wonderful Life 1946,D 23,19:2
 San Francisco Story, The 1952,My 10,16:4
Haguet, Andre (Director)
 Secret Document-Vienna 1954,Mr 29,22:4
Haguet, Andre (Producer)
 Miracle of Saint Therese 1959,F 10,38:4 (In
 Addenda)
Haguet, Andre (Screenwriter)
 Miracle of Saint Therese 1959,F 10,38:4 (In
 Addenda)
Hahn, Jess
 Happy Road, The 1957,Je 21,20:2
 Cartouche 1964,Jl 22,39:1
 Topkapi 1964,S 18,25:1
 What's New Pussycat? 1965,Je 23,49:1
 Up to his Ears 1966,My 18,37:1
 Great Spy Chase, The 1966,O 6,56:4
Hahn, Otto
 Two Girls on Broadway 1940,Ap 25,28:4
Hahn, Paul
 Angry Red Planet, The 1960,My 5,41:2
Haid, Grit
 Die Mutter der Kompagnie 1934,Mr 9,22:3
 Drei Kaiserjaeger 1935,Mr 16,19:1
 Fuerst Sepp'l 1937,Jl 17,18:1
Haid, Liana
 Bei der Blonden Kathrein 1934,D 3,15:2
Haid, Liane
 Last Waltz, The 1927,N 14,26:1
 Explosion 1927,D 13,33:2
 Two Brothers, The 1928,Ag 21,27:4
 Lucrecia Borgia 1928,D 25,31:3
 Spy of Madame de Pompadour, The
  1929,S 10,27:1
 Immortal Vagabond, The 1931,Ag 3,15:5
 Opernredoute; Opera ball 1931,O 4,VIII,7:1
 Opern-Ball, Der; Opera Ball 1931,N 6,28:3
 Kaiserliebchen 1931,N 12,30:2
 Das Lied ist Aus 1932,Ja 29,13:2
 Der Unsterbliche Lump 1932,My 20,22:3
 Zirkus Leben 1932,D 28,14:7
 Ich Will Nicht Wissen Wer Du Bist
  1933,F 16,23:2
 Madame Wuenscht Keine Kinder 1933,Je 2,22:4
 Stern von Valencia, Der 1934,Ap 21,12:2
 Roman Einer Nacht 1934,Je 22,24:2
 Frau wie Du, Eine 1934,D 24,17:3
 Keine Angst vor Liebe 1936,Ja 21,27:6
 Schloss im Sueden, Das 1936,F 24,14:2
 Madonna, Wo Bist Du? 1936,Mr 21,13:3
 Tanzmusik 1936,My 26,27:2
 Fahrt in Die Jugend, Die 1936,Ag 31,19:2
 Besuch am Abend 1937,Jl 3,18:2
 Herzensclieb; Heart Thief 1938,Jl 2,10:4
 Mozart 1940,O 4,29:2
Haidarhodzic, Izef
 Kaya 1968,S 25,39:1
Haiflit, Harvey (Screenwriter)
 Secret Land, The 1948,D 2,39:2
Haig, Douglas
 Sins of the Fathers 1929,Ja 28,21:1
 Betrayal 1929,My 6,30:4
 Caught Short 1930,Je 21,20:5
 Cisco Kid, The 1931,O 24,20:3
 Attorney for the Defense 1932,My 28,18:2
Haigh, Kenneth
 Saint Joan 1957,Je 27,21:1
 Cleopatra 1963,Je 13,29:1
 Hard Day's Night, A 1964,Ag 12,41:1

Weekend at Dunkirk 1966,My 19,51:2
 Deadly Affair, The 1967,Ja 27,31:1
 Lovely Way to Die, A 1968,Jl 13,18:1
Haight, George (Miscellaneous)
 Goldwyn Follies, The 1938,F 21,15:1
Haight, George (Original Author)
 Good-Bye Again 1933,S 2,15:2
 Gold Diggers of 1937 1936,D 25,19:2
 Honeymoon for Three 1941,F 8,19:2
Haight, George (Producer)
 Beloved Enemy 1936,D 26,15:2
 Story of Vernon and Irene Castle, The
  1939,Mr 31,19:2
 In Name Only 1939,Ag 4,11:3
 Lucky Partners 1940,S 6,25:2
 Whistling in the Dark 1941,Ag 28,23:2
 Kathleen 1941,D 19,35:3
 Whistling in Dixie 1942,D 31,20:4
 Swing Shift Maisie 1943,S 10,29:2
 See Here Private Hargrove 1944,Mr 22,17:2
 Whistling in Brooklyn 1944,Mr 24,17:3
 Maisie Goes to Reno 1944,S 29,18:1
 Lost in a Harem 1944,N 9,23:2
 Keep Your Powder Dry 1945,Mr 12,22:6
 What Next Corporal Hargrove? 1945,D 26,15:2
 Up Goes Maisie 1946,Ja 25,26:7
 Lady in the Lake 1947,Ja 24,18:3
Haik, Jacques (Miscellaneous)
 Legion of Honor, The 1928,Jl 20,8:4
Haik, Jacques (Producer)
 Great Test, The 1928,Ap 27,8:2
 Soul of France, The 1929,O 12,11:1
 Mystere de la Villa Rose, Le 1932,Ja 11,28:5
 Ronde des Heures, La 1932,Ja 25,20:3
Hail
 Good Morning and Goodbye! 1968,F 20,53:1
Hailer, Daniel (Producer)
 War Gods of the Deep 1965,Je 3,24:3
Hailey, Arthur (Original Author)
 Zero Hour 1957,N 14,41:1
 Hotel 1967,Ja 20,27:1
Hailey, Arthur (Screenwriter)
 Zero Hour 1957,N 14,41:1
Haim, Harry
 Bondage 1928,N 6,35:1
Haimson, Abrasha (Producer)
 Mozart Story, The 1948,N 15,21:5
HAINES
 See Also HAYNES
Haines, Alan
 Madonna of the Seven Moons 1946,My 23,18:4
Haines, Connie
 Wave, A Wac and a Marine, A 1944,Ag 14,11:4
 Duchess of Idaho 1950,Jl 21,15:3
Haines, David
 Woman Trap 1936,Mr 7,11:4
Haines, Donald
 Skippy 1931,Ap 4,23:1
 When a Feller Needs a Friend 1932,My 14,11:5
 No Greater Glory 1934,My 5,22:2
 Little Man, What Now? 1934,Je 1,29:1
 Tale of Two Cities, A 1935,D 26,21:2
 Invisible Ray, The 1936,Ja 11,9:3
 Little Miss Nobody 1936,Je 6,21:1
 Kidnapped 1938,My 28,9:2
 Sergeant Madden 1939,Mr 24,27:2
 Seventeen 1940,F 29,15:2
 Prison Camp 1940,Ag 3,9:3
 Ghost Creeps, The 1940,Ag 19,13:3
 Pride of the Bowery 1941,Ja 24,15:2
 Flying Wild 1941,Ap 12,19:3
 Bowery Blitzkrieg 1941,O 1,24:5
 Spooks Run Wild 1941,N 1,20:3
Haines, Fred (Screenwriter)
 Ulysses 1967,Mr 14,55:1
Haines, Larry
 Odd Couple, The 1968,My 3,42:1
Haines, Rhea
 Scarlet Days 1919,N 10,18:2
 Mary Ellen Comes to Town 1920,Mr 22,12:1
Haines, Robert
 Lone Wolf, The 1924,My 7,19:4
 Noose, The 1928,My 19,26:4
 How to Handle Women 1928,Je 18,13:2
 Guilty 1930,Ap 7,21:1
 These Thirty Years 1934,My 24,28:3
 Gigolette 1935,My 13,18:6
Haines, Sol
 Song of Scheherazade 1947,F 27,26:2
Haines, William
 Three Weeks 1924,Ap 1,19:3
 True as Steel 1924,Je 17,22:4
 Wine of Youth 1924,Ag 11,16:1
 Midnight Express, The 1924,N 19,19:3
 Circe the Enchantress 1924,D 9,23:3
 Wife of the Centaur 1925,Ja 7,33:5
 Denial, The 1925,Mr 10,19:3
 Slave of Fashion, A 1925,Jl 21,26:2
 Tower of Lies, The 1925,S 28,24:1
 Little Annie Rooney 1925,O 19,26:1
 Sally, Irene and Mary 1925,D 7,19:1
 Mike 1926,Ja 11,33:1
 Memory Lane 1926,F 2,20:4

Haines, William— Cont
 Lovey Mary 1926,Je 21,17:2
 Tell It to the Marines 1926,D 24,18:2
 Little Journey, A 1927,Ja 4,21:1
 Slide, Kelly, Slide 1927,Mr 23,19:2
 Spring Fever 1927,O 18,33:2
 West Point 1928,Ja 2,28:1
 Smart Set, The 1928,Mr 5,21:1
 Telling the World 1928,Jl 16,25:3
 Excess Baggage 1928,S 24,25:1
 Show People 1928,N 12,18:2
 Alias Jimmy Valentine 1928,N 16,28:6
 Duke Steps Out, The 1929,Ap 15,22:6
 Man's Man, A 1929,Je 3,27:2
 Hollywood Revue, The 1929,Ag 15,20:5
 Speedway 1929,S 21,17:1
 Navy Blues 1930,Ja 11,21:3
 Girl Said No, The 1930,Ap 5,23:3
 Free and Easy 1930,Ap 19,15:1
 Way out West 1930,Ag 18,24:1
 Remote Control 1930,D 8,26:1
 Tailor-Made Man, A 1931,Ap 25,23:4
 Just a Gigolo 1931,Je 13,20:4
 New Adventures of Get-Rich-Quick Wallingford
  1931,O 10,20:4
 Fast Life 1932,D 24,11:4
 Young and Beautiful 1934,S 18,18:4
 Marines are Coming, The 1935,F 23,14:7
 Show People 1967,O 2,58:2
Haines, William Wister (Original Author)
 Slim 1937,Je 24,30:2
 Command Decision 1949,Ja 20,34:2
 Eternal Sea, The 1955,Je 10,16:2
Haines, William Wister (Screenwriter)
 Alibi Ike 1935,Jl 17,22:1
 Man of Iron 1935,D 7,22:2
 Black Legion 1937,Ja 18,21:1
 Mr Dodd Takes the Air 1937,Ag 12,14:2
 Texans, The 1938,Jl 28,23:2
 Beyond Glory 1948,Ag 4,18:2
 Racket, The 1951,D 13,44:2
 One Minute to Zero 1952,S 20,13:2
 Wings of Eagles, The 1957,F 1,28:1
 Torpedo Run 1958,O 25,16:2
Hainey, Betty Jean
 Little Miss Nobody 1936,Je 6,21:1
 Dimples 1936,O 10,21:2
Hainia, Marcelle
 It Happened at the Inn; Goupi Mains Rouge
  1945,D 22,16:2
 Boudu Saved From Drowning; Boudu Sauve Des
  Eaux 1967,F 24,26:2
Hainisch, Leopold
 Last ten Days, The 1956,Ap 12,26:1
Hainisch, Leopold (Director)
 Kleine Nachtmusik, Eine 1940,Mr 2,9:5
Hairston, Jester
 Alamo, The 1960,O 27,45:1
Hairston, Margaret
 Porgy and Bess 1959,Je 25,20:3
Hairston, William
 Take the High Ground 1953,N 20,19:2
Haislip, Harvey (Original Author)
 Thunder Afloat 1939,O 13,27:2
 Flight Command 1941,Ja 17,21:2
 Stand by for Action 1943,Mr 12,12:2
 Flying Missile, The 1950,D 25,25:1
Haislip, Harvey (Screenwriter)
 Thunder Afloat 1939,O 13,27:2
 Flight Command 1941,Ja 17,21:2
Haisman, Irene
 Time, The Place and the Girl, The 1929,Jl 8,17:3
Haitto, Heimo
 There's Magic in Music 1941,Je 5,27:2
Hajdu, Emery (Composer)
 Rad Bizom a Felesegem; I Entrust my Wife to
  You 1939,My 6,21:3
Hajdukova, Zlata
 Janosik 1936,D 25,19:3
Hajman, L
 Honor 1929,S 10,27:1
Hajmay, Tibor von
 Liebeskommando 1932,Ap 27,13:6
Hajos, Joe (Composer)
 Lie of Nina Petrovna, The 1938,Mr 30,19:2
Hakim, Andre (Producer)
 Mr Belvedere Rings the Bell 1951,Ag 2,18:1
 O Henry's Full House (The Last Leaf
  1952,O 17,33:1
 O Henry's Full House (The Gift of the Magi); Gift
  of the Magi, The (O Henry's Full House)
  1952,O 17,33:1
 O Henry's Full House (The Cop and the Anthem);
  Cop and the Anthem, The (O Henry's Full
  House) 1952,O 17,33:1
 O Henry's Full House (The Clarion Call); Clarion
  Call, The (O Henry's Full House)
  1952,O 17,33:1
 Naughty Martine 1953,Ap 13,32:4
 Powder River 1953,Jl 4,7:2
 Man Who Never Was, The 1956,Ap 4,24:1
 Sea Wife 1957,D 5,45:2
 Bonne Soupe, La 1964,Mr 16,37:1
 Friend of the Family 1965,N 18,55:3

Hakim, Rafael (Producer)
Marthe Richard 1944,N 9,23:2
Hakim, Raymond (Producer)
Heartbeat 1946,My 11,22:4
Long Night, The 1947,S 17,31:2
Without Honor 1950,Jl 3,9:2
Hunchback of Notre Dame, The 1957,D 12,35:1
Pot Bouille 1958,O 28,39:1
Leda 1961,Jl 19,33:1
Purple Noon 1961,S 1,12:1
Eclipse 1962,D 21,5:1
Circle of Love 1965,Mr 25,42:4
Bonnes Femmes, Les 1966,My 13,32:1
Weekend at Dunkirk 1966,My 19,51:2
Belle de Jour 1968,Ap 11,51:1
Hakim, Robert (Producer)
Marthe Richard 1944,N 9,23:2
Southerner, The 1945,Ag 27,22:3
Heartbeat 1946,My 11,22:4
Long Night, The 1947,S 17,31:2
Without Honor 1950,Jl 3,9:2
Hunchback of Notre Dame, The 1957,D 12,35:1
Pot Bouille 1958,O 28,39:1
Leda 1961,Jl 19,33:1
Purple Noon 1961,S 1,12:1
Eclipse 1962,D 21,5:1
Circle of Love 1965,Mr 25,42:4
Bonnes Femmes, Les 1966,My 13,32:1
Weekend at Dunkirk 1966,My 19,51:2
Belle de Jour 1968,Ap 11,51:1
Hakin, Raphael (Producer)
Her Husband's Affairs 1947,N 14,29:2
Halain, Jean (Miscellaneous)
Simple Case of Money, A 1952,F 2,11:2
Simple Case of Money, A 1952,F 2,11:2
Halain, Jean (Screenwriter)
Story of Monte Cristo, The 1962,N 7,48:1
Fantomas 1966,Ap 6,36:2
OSS 117-Mission for a Killer 1966,O 13,50:3
Halama, Loda
Kocha, Lubi, Szanuje 1934,N 3,20:4
Manewry Milosne 1936,N 11,55:1
Halas, John (Director)
Animal Farm 1954,D 30,14:1
Halas, John (Producer)
Animal Farm 1954,D 30,14:1
Here Comes the Mad Martian 1965,Je 4,39:1
Halas, John (Screenwriter)
Animal Farm 1954,D 30,14:1
Halasz, Judit
Age of Illusions 1967,Mr 30,55:1
Halasz, Nicholas (Original Author)
I Accuse! 1958,Mr 6,32:1
Hald, Grit
Zigeunerblut 1935,Ap 8,23:5
Hald, Ragnhild
En Glad Gutt 1933,N 24,25:7
Halda, Katsuhiko
Tokyo File 212 1951,Je 1,20:7
Escapde in Japan 1957,D 24,11:1
Haldmuller, C M
Spy 77 1936,F 10,15:1
Hale, Alan
Four Horsemen of the Apocalypse 1921,Mr 7,8:1
One Glorious Day 1922,Ja 30,16:2
Main Street 1923,Je 12,22:2
Eleventh Hour, The 1923,Ag 28,12:1
Long Live the King 1923,D 4,24:1
Black Oxen 1924,Ja 7,23:1
Code of the Wilderness, The 1924,Jl 1,21:4
Dick Turpin 1925,Ja 26,14:1
Crimson Runner, The 1925,My 27,26:2
Four Horsemen of the Apocalypse, The
  1926,S 27,27:3
Vanity 1927,Je 15,31:4
Wreck of the Hesperus, The 1927,N 28,18:5
Leopard Lady, The 1928,F 27,16:2
Skyscraper 1928,Ap 9,18:2
Oh, Kay! 1928,Ag 27,23:1
Cop, The 1928,N 6,35:1
Power 1928,N 27,34:1
Sal of Singapore 1929,Ja 29,27:1
Spieler, The 1929,F 25,16:1
Leatherneck, The 1929,Ap 22,23:1
Sailor's Holiday 1929,O 21,30:1
She Got What She Wanted 1930,D 29,18:1
Night Angel, The 1931,Je 11,28:4
Rebound 1931,Ag 29,16:3
Susan Lenox; Her Fall and Rise 1931,O 17,20:1
Sin of Madelon Claudet, The 1931,O 31,22:2
Union Depot 1932,Ja 15,24:4
So Big 1932,Ap 30,19:3
Rebecca of Sunnybrook Farm 1932,Jl 30,16:5
Match King, The 1932,D 8,25:3
What Price Decency? 1933,Mr 2,20:6
Destination Unknown 1933,Ap 8,16:2
Miss Fane's Baby is Stolen 1934,Ja 20,12:4
It Happened One Night 1934,F 23,23:2
Lost Patrol, The 1934,Ap 2,13:2
Little Man, What Now? 1934,Je 1,29:1
Fog over Frisco 1934,Je 7,26:2
Of Human Bondage 1934,Je 29,17:1
There's Always Tomorrow 1934,N 10,19:2

Imitation of Life 1934,N 24,19:1
Broadway Bill 1934,N 30,22:2
Babbitt 1934,D 17,24:2
Little Minister, The 1934,D 28,25:1
Good Fairy, The 1935,F 1,18:1
Grand Old Girl 1935,F 26,16:4
Crusades, The 1935,Ag 22,21:3
Last Days of Pompeii, The 1935,O 17,29:2
Two in the Dark 1936,F 1,9:2
Message to Garcia, A 1936,Ap 10,27:1
Country Beyond, The 1936,Ap 30,17:3
Parole 1936,Je 27,21:1
Our Relations 1936,N 11,55:1
God's Country and the Woman 1937,Ja 11,15:5
Prince and the Pauper, The 1937,My 6,23:1
When Thief Meets Thief 1937,Je 15,26:2
High, Wide and Handsome 1937,Jl 22,15:1
Stella Dallas 1937,Ag 6,21:1
Thin Ice 1937,S 4,8:2
Music for Madame 1937,O 23,14:1
Four Men and a Prayer 1938,My 7,18:1
Adventures of Robin Hood, The 1938,My 13,17:2
Algiers 1938,Jl 15,13:2
Valley of the Giants 1938,S 10,20:2
Sisters, The 1938,O 15,21:3
Listen, Darling 1938,N 24,37:2
Pacific Liner 1939,Ja 18,17:3
Dodge City 1939,Ap 8,19:1
Man in the Iron Mask, The 1939,Jl 14,11:1
Dust Be my Destiny 1939,O 7,11:2
On Your Toes 1939,O 21,12:2
Private Lives of Elizabeth and Essex, The
  1939,D 2,21:2
Fighting 69th, The 1940,Ja 27,9:2
Green Hell 1940,Ja 30,15:6
Three Cheers for the Irish 1940,Mr 9,19:2
They Drive by Night 1940,Jl 27,17:5
Sea Hawk, The 1940,Ag 10,16:2
Tugboat Annie Sails Again 1940,N 9,20:2
Santa Fe Trail 1940,D 21,21:2
Strawberry Blonde 1941,F 22,11:2
Footsteps in the Dark 1941,Mr 15,13:2
Manpower 1941,Jl 5,14:2
Smiling Ghost, The 1941,S 26,26:5
Captains of the Clouds 1942,F 13,24:2
Juke Girl 1942,Je 20,9:2
Desperate Journey 1942,S 26,11:2
Gentleman Jim 1942,N 26,40:3
Action in the North Atlantic 1943,My 22,10:2
This Is the Army 1943,Jl 29,11:6
Thank Your Lucky Stars 1943,O 2,19:2
Destination Tokyo 1944,Ja 1,9:2
Destination Tokyo 1944,Ja 9,II,3:1
Adventures of Mark Twain, The 1944,My 4,25:5
Make Your own Bed 1944,My 27,12:2
Janie 1944,Ag 5,16:2
Hollywood Canteen 1944,D 16,19:2
Roughly Speaking 1945,F 1,18:4
Hotel Berlin 1945,Mr 3,11:2
God is my Co-Pilot 1945,Mr 24,22:6
Escape in the Desert 1945,My 12,10:2
Perilous Holiday 1946,Je 1,10:4
Night and Day 1946,Jl 26,16:2
Time, The Place And The Girl, The
  1946,D 27,14:3
Man I Love, The 1947,Ja 25,12:2
That Way With Women 1947,F 15,20:4
Pursued 1947,Mr 8,10:2
Cheyenne 1947,Je 7,9:2
My Wild Irish Rose 1947,D 25,32:2
My Girl Tisa 1948,F 21,9:2
Adventures of Don Juan 1948,D 25,10:1
Whiplash 1948,D 27,16:3
South of St Louis 1949,Mr 7,17:2
Younger Brothers, The 1949,My 28,11:2
House Across the Street 1949,S 2,14:4
Always Leave Them Laughing 1949,N 24,48:2
Inspector General, The 1949,D 31,9:2
Stars in my Crown 1950,D 22,19:1
Young at Heart 1955,Ja 20,35:1
Killer is Loose, The 1956,Mr 3,17:2
Battle Hymn 1957,F 16,14:1
True Story of Jesse James, The 1957,Mr 23,17:2
Up Periscope 1959,Mr 5,35:4
All Mine to Give 1959,Ag 4,32:5
Swingin' Maiden, The 1964,Ja 1,16:2
Adventures of Marco Polo, The 1965,Ap 8,17:2
Hale, Alan (Director)
Risky Business 1926,S 8,19:3
Rubber Tires 1927,Mr 9,29:1
Hale, Alan Jr
To the Shores of Tripoli 1942,Mr 26,27:2
Eagle Squadron 1942,Jl 3,12:5
It Happened on Fifth Avenue 1947,Je 11,33:2
Spirit of West Point 1947,O 3,31:2
One Sunday Afternoon 1948,D 27,16:3
It Happens Every Spring 1949,Je 11,11:2
Kill the Umpire 1950,My 29,10:6
Four Days' Leave 1950,Je 9,29:4
Gunfighter, The 1950,Je 24,7:2
Underworld Story, The 1950,Jl 27,29:4
West Point Story, The 1950,D 23,11:3
Short Grass 1951,Ja 13,10:4

Hale, Alan Jr— Cont
Big Trees, The 1952,F 6,24:2
At Swords Point 1952,Ap 10,37:1
Wait Till the Sun Shines, Nellie 1952,Je 28,12:2
Lady in the Iron Mask 1952,Jl 5,7:2
Springfield Rifle 1952,O 23,40:2
Rogue Cop 1954,S 18,12:2
Indian Fighter, The 1955,D 22,20:1
Hale, Allan
Robin Hood 1922,O 31,15:4 (In Addenda)
Hale, Barbara
Higher and Higher 1944,Ja 22,8:4
Falcon out West, The 1944,Mr 18,18:2
Heavenly Days 1944,O 21,15:2
Falcon in Hollywood, The 1944,D 9,21:2
West of the Pecos 1945,Ag 11,14:6
First Yank into Tokyo 1945,O 25,18:2
Lady Luck 1946,O 31,22:3
Boy With Green Hair, The 1949,Ja 13,26:2
Window, The 1949,Ag 8,10:5
Jolson Sings Again 1949,Ag 18,16:6
And Baby Makes Three 1949,D 23,17:3
Jackpot, The 1950,N 23,55:2
Emergency Wedding 1950,D 22,19:2
Lorna Doone 1951,S 21,19:4
Lone Hand 1953,Je 27,7:2
Lion Is in the Streets, A 1953,S 24,39:2
Unchained 1955,Ja 28,15:2
Far Horizons, The 1955,My 21,11:1
Oklahoman, The 1957,My 15,39:1
Hale, Binnie
Love From a Stranger 1937,Ap 19,27:2
Hale, Chanin
Synanon 1965,My 6,44:1
Hale, Creighton
Idol Dancer, The 1920,Mr 22,12:1
Orphans of the Storm 1922,Ja 29,VI,2:1 (In
  Addenda)
Trilby 1923,Jl 30,11:4
Name the Man 1924,F 4,23:3
Marriage Circle, The 1924,F 4,23:3
Wine of Youth 1924,Ag 11,16:1
This Woman 1924,O 21,21:3
Bridge of Sighs, The 1925,Mr 23,14:2
Seven Days 1925,Ag 31,19:3
Circle, The 1925,S 22,22:3
Exchange of Wives 1925,O 5,25:2
Time, the Comedian 1925,D 14,18:2
Beverly of Graustark 1926,Ap 19,24:3
Oh Baby! 1926,Ag 11,25:2
Annie Laurie 1927,My 12,24:3
Cat and the Canary, The 1927,S 10,9:4
Rose-Marie 1928,F 13,16:2
Holiday 1930,Jl 3,25:4
Way Down East 1931,Mr 16,25:1
Prestige 1932,F 5,25:2
Masquerader, The 1933,S 4,9:5
Hollywood Boulevard 1936,S 21,26:4
Return Of Doctor X, The 1939,N 23,38:5
Calling Philo Vance 1940,F 9,15:3
Bullet Scars 1942,Ap 24,21:4
Gorilla Man, The 1943,Ja 15,21:4
Mysterious Doctor, The 1943,My 20,26:4
Two Mrs Carrolls, The 1947,Ag 7,20:1
Perils of Pauline, The 1947,Jl 10,17:2
Hale, Diana
My Friend Flicka 1943,My 27,21:4
Thunderhead 1945,Mr 16,21:2
Hale, Dorothy
Catherine the Great 1934,F 15,15:6
Hale, Edward Everett (Original Author)
Man Without a Country, The 1925,F 12,16:1
Hale, Elvi
Happy is the Bride 1959,Je 30,27:2
Hale, Frank J (Producer)
Dr Coppelius 1968,D 26,56:1
Hale, Georgia
Salvation Hunters, The 1925,F 2,14:1
Gold Rush, The 1925,Ag 17,10:3
Rainmaker, The 1926,My 18,28:2
Great Gatsby, The 1926,N 22,28:3
Last Moment, The 1928,Mr 12,26:1
Gold Rush, The 1942,Ap 20,17:1
Hale, Grace
Front Page Woman 1935,Jl 12,15:1
Harvester, The 1936,Jl 4,18:2
Hale, Jean
Psychomania 1964,F 15,14:3
In Like Flint 1967,Mr 16,53:2
St Valentine's Day Massacre, The 1967,Jl 27,29:2
Hale, John
Singing Kid, The 1936,Ap 4,11:1
Inside Daisy Clover 1966,F 18,23:1
Hale, Jonathan
Alice Adams 1935,Ag 16,11:3
Charlie Chan's Secret 1936,Ja 18,19:4
Voice of Bugle Ann, The 1936,F 27,23:1
Case Against Mrs Ames, The 1936,My 28,19:2
Fury 1936,Je 6,21:1
Educating Father 1936,Je 20,22:2
Charlie Chan at the Race Track 1936,Ag 15,6:2
36 Hours to Live 1936,Ag 15,6:3
Devil is a Sissy, The 1936,O 17,21:2
You Only Live Once 1937,F 1,15:2

Hale, Jonathan— Cont

John Meade's Woman 1937,F 18,19:1
Man of the People 1937,F 23,25:4
Racketeers in Exile 1937,Ap 12,15:3
Charlie Chan at the Olympics 1937,My 24,23:1
This Is my Affair 1937,My 28,17:1
League of Frightened Men, The 1937,Jl 2,25:1
Midnight Madonna 1937,Jl 17,18:1
Saratoga 1937,Jl 23,16:3
Madame X 1937,O 25,23:1
Arsene Lupin Returns 1938,Mr 9,21:1
Over the Wall 1938,Mr 28,19:2
Judge Hardy's Children 1938,Ap 8,17:2
Her Jungle Love 1938,Ap 14,27:2
Yellow Jack 1938,My 20,17:2
Saint in New York, The 1938,My 26,31:2
Gangs of New York 1938,My 28,9:2
Wives Under Suspicion 1938,Jl 1,22:3
Boys Town 1938,S 9,25:1
Fugitives for a Night 1938,S 21,30:4
Breaking the Ice 1938,S 23,35:3
Tarnished Angel 1938,N 15,27:2
Duke of West Point, The 1938,D 16,33:2
Blondie 1938,D 22,25:4
There's That Woman Again 1939,Ja 6,25:4
Stand up and Fight 1939,Ja 27,17:2
Wings of the Navy 1939,F 4,11:1
Tail Spin 1939,F 11,13:2
Saint Strikes Back, The 1939,Mr 9,18:2
Story of Alexander Graham Bell, The 1939,Ap 1,17:2
Blondie Meets the Boss 1939,Ap 27,31:1
In Name Only 1939,Ag 4,11:3
Thunder Afloat 1939,O 13,27:2
Barricade 1939,D 9,18:2
Big Guy, The 1940,Ja 1,29:2
Amazing Mr Williams, The 1940,Ja 19,15:2
Saint's Double Trouble, The 1940,F 13,27:2
Johnny Apollo 1940,Ap 13,21:2
Saint Takes Over, The 1940,My 28,29:3
Private Affairs 1940,Jl 5,10:3
We Who are Young 1940,S 13,27:2
Dulcy 1940,N 28,28:2
Saint in Palm Springs, The 1941,Ja 31,15:5
Blondie Goes Latin 1941,F 26,17:3
Flight From Destiny 1941,Mr 28,26:7
Great Swindle, The 1941,My 14,25:4
Ringside Maisie 1941,Ag 1,11:2
Pittsburgh Kid, The 1941,S 23,27:4
Joe Smith, American 1942,Ap 2,27:4
Bugle Sounds, The 1942,Ap 3,25:2
Miss Annie Rooney 1942,Je 8,11:1
Calling Dr Gillespie 1942,Jl 9,17:4
Flight Lieutenant 1942,Jl 31,11:1
Amazing Mrs Holliday, The 1943,F 22,20:2
Hangmen Also Die 1943,Ap 16,24:2
Sweet Rosie O'Grady 1943,O 21,30:2
Jack London 1944,Mr 3,19:3
This is the Life 1944,Ap 28,23:3
Dead Man's Eyes 1944,O 7,11:2
And Now Tomorrow 1944,N 23,38:2
Man Alive 1945,N 17,14:5
Allotment Wives 1945,N 22,39:3
Dakota 1945,D 17,17:2
Cat Creeps, The 1946,My 18,12:4
Easy to Wed 1946,Jl 12,14:2
Angel on my Shoulder 1946,O 21,27:2
Walls Came Tumbling Down, The 1946,N 9,13:5
Beginning or the End, The 1947,F 21,15:1
Vigilantes Return, The 1947,Jl 1,30:2
Her Husband's Affairs 1947,N 14,29:2
Silver River 1948,My 22,8:3
Stampede 1949,S 16,36:2
Short Grass 1951,Ja 13,10:4
Three Husbands 1951,Mr 9,30:2
Strangers on a Train 1951,Jl 4,13:2
Scandal Sheet 1952,Ja 17,23:1
Duffy of San Quentin 1954,F 10,38:5

Hale, Louise Closser

Hole in the Wall, The 1929,Ap 15,22:6
Paris 1929,N 8,31:2
Dangerous Nan McGrew 1930,Je 21,20:5
Big Boy 1930,S 13,9:3
Princess and the Plumber, The 1930,D 23,25:1
Born to Love 1931,Ap 25,23:4
Daddy Long Legs 1931,Je 6,15:5
Rebound 1931,Ag 29,16:3
Devotion 1931,O 3,20:2
Platinum Blonde 1931,O 31,22:2
Man Who Played God, The 1932,F 11,16:1
Shanghai Express 1932,F 18,25:3
Sky Bride 1932,Ap 23,11:5
Letty Lynton 1932,Ap 30,19:3
New Morals for Old 1932,Je 24,15:3
Rebecca of Sunnybrook Farm 1932,Jl 30,16:5
Movie Crazy 1932,S 15,19:3
Faithless 1932,N 19,20:2
Son-Daughter, The 1933,Ja 2,29:2
No More Orchids 1933,Ja 2,29:2
White Sister, The 1933,Mr 18,9:3
Today We Live 1933,Ap 15,16:2
Barbarian, The 1933,My 13,16:2
Storm at Daybreak 1933,Jl 22,14:2
Another Language 1933,Ag 5,9:5

Dinner at Eight 1933,Ag 24,18:1

Hale, Martin (Original Author)

Caprice 1967,Je 8,52:2

Hale, Monte

Big Bonanza, The 1945,F 26,14:5
Giant 1956,O 11,51:1

Hale, Patty

Always in my Heart 1942,Mr 14,19:2
I Was Framed 1942,Je 12,16:6

Hale, Richard

None Shall Escape 1944,Ap 7,23:2
Knickerbocker Holiday 1944,Ap 20,22:7
Counter-Attack 1945,My 17,15:2
Thousand and one Nights, A 1945,Jl 12,8:2
Abilene Town 1946,Mr 4,16:5
Badman's Territory 1946,My 31,27:2
Other Love, The 1947,My 15,32:4
Beautiful Blonde From Bashful Bend, The 1949,My 28,11:2
All the King's Men 1949,N 9,37:2
Kim 1950,D 8,40:4
Soldiers Three 1951,Mr 30,28:5
Man With a Cloak, The 1951,N 28,37:2
Scaramouche 1952,My 9,20:2
Miracle of Our Lady Fatima, The 1952,Ag 21,16:2
Springfield Rifle 1952,O 23,40:2
Julius Caesar 1953,Je 5,19:1
Diamond Queen, The 1954,Ja 27,24:2
Red Garters 1954,Mr 27,13:5
Friendly Persuasion 1956,N 2,30:1
Sergeants 3 1962,F 12,28:2

Hale, Robert

Strauss's Great Waltz 1935,Ap 8,23:3
It's Love Again 1936,My 23,12:1
Storm in a Teacup 1938,Mr 22,18:4
Hangover Square 1945,F 8,15:2

Hale, Sonnie

Be Mine Tonight 1933,Ap 14,22:5
Friday the 13th 1934,My 15,18:1
Are You a Mason? 1934,O 30,23:5
Evergreen 1935,Ja 11,29:1
My Heart Is Calling 1935,Ap 15,16:3
My Song For You 1935,My 27,20:6
First a Girl 1936,Ja 4,19:1
It's Love Again 1936,My 23,12:1

Hale, Sonnie (Director)

Head Over Heels in Love 1937,F 13,9:1
Gangway 1937,Ag 21,7:3
Sailing Along 1938,Ap 16,17:1

Hale, Sonnie (Screenwriter)

Gangway 1937,Ag 21,7:3
Sailing Along 1938,Ap 16,17:1

Halevy, Julian (Original Author)

Young Lovers, The 1965,F 11,45:1

Halevy, Julian (Screenwriter)

Psyche 39 1964,Ap 30,30:1
Circus World 1964,Je 26,34:2
Custer of the West 1968,Jl 4,13:2

Haley, Aileen

Happy Go Lucky 1943,Mr 25,25:1

Haley, Jack

Follow Thru 1930,S 13,9:3
Sitting Pretty 1933,D 2,9:3
Here Comes the Groom 1934,Je 16,20:2
Girl Friend, The 1935,S 28,12:2
Coronado 1935,D 19,33:4
F-Man 1936,My 4,16:1
Poor Little Rich Girl, The 1936,Je 26,16:1
Pigskin Parade 1936,N 14,23:3
Wake up and Live 1937,Ap 24,16:2
Pick a Star 1937,My 28,17:2
She Had to Eat 1937,Jl 24,12:1
Danger-Love at Work 1937,D 11,22:2
Rebecca of Sunnybrook Farm 1938,Mr 26,12:1
Alexander's Ragtime Band 1938,Ag 6,7:2
Hold That Co-ed 1938,S 24,13:1
Thanks For Everything 1938,D 10,13:2
Wizard of Oz, The 1939,Ag 18,16:2
Moon Over Miami 1941,Jl 5,14:2
Navy Blues 1941,S 20,11:2
Beyond the Blue Horizon 1942,Je 25,27:2
Higher and Higher 1944,Ja 22,8:4
One Body too Many 1944,N 25,21:2
George White's Scandals 1945,O 11,26:2
People Are Funny 1946,Ja 28,15:6

Halff, Robert (Screenwriter)

Swing Shift Maisie 1943,S 10,29:2

Halfpenny, Tony

Young Woodley 1930,S 27,21:3

Haliatt, May

Human Monster, The 1940,Mr 25,11:2

Haliday, Bryant (Miscellaneous)

Bullfight 1956,Jl 4,15:2

Haliroua, Maria

Mizici Svet; Vanishing World 1935,My 30,21:2

Halkova, Elen

Merry Wives, The 1940,N 12,28:3

Hall, Adam (Original Author)

Quiller Memorandum, The 1966,D 16,59:1

Hall, Adelaide

Thief of Bagdad, The 1940,D 6,28:2

Hall, Adrian

Chitty Chitty Bang Bang 1968,D 19,64:4

Hall, Al K

Come and Get It 1936,N 12,31:1
Woman Chases Man 1937,Je 11,26:2

Hall, Alexander (Director)

Sinners in the Sun 1932,My 14,11:5
Madame Racketeer 1932,Jl 23,6:6
Girl in 419 1933,My 20,11:5
Midnight Club 1933,Jl 29,14:2
Torch Singer 1933,O 7,18:5
Miss Fane's Baby is Stolen 1934,Ja 20,12:2
Little Miss Marker 1934,My 19,18:3
Pursuit of Happiness, The 1934,O 26,25:1
Limehouse Blues 1934,D 12,28:2
Goin' to Town 1935,My 11,21:2
Annapolis Farewell 1935,Ag 24,18:2
Give Us This Night 1936,Ap 6,18:1
Yours for the Asking 1936,Ag 20,14:2
Exclusive 1937,Jl 22,15:1
There's Always a Woman 1938,Ap 29,17:2
I Am the Law 1938,Ag 26,14:2
There's That Woman Again 1939,Ja 6,25:4
Lady's From Kentucky, The 1939,Ap 27,31:1
Good Girls Go to Paris 1939,Je 23,23:1
Amazing Mr Williams, The 1940,Ja 19,15:2
Doctor Takes a Wife, The 1940,Je 15,12:2
He Stayed for Breakfast 1940,Ag 31,16:2
This Thing Called Love 1941,F 14,15:2
Here Comes Mr Jordan 1941,Ag 8,13:2
Bedtime Story 1942,Mr 20,25:4
They all Kissed the Bride 1942,Jl 31,11:1
My Sister Eileen 1942,O 23,15:1
Heavenly Body, The 1944,Mr 24,17:3
Once Upon a Time 1944,Je 30,17:2
She Wouldn't Say Yes 1946,Ja 12,10:7
Down to Earth 1947,S 12,18:2
Great Lover, The 1949,N 24,48:2
Love That Brute 1950,My 27,10:6
Louisa 1950,O 25,45:2
Up Front 1951,Mr 26,19:2
Because You're Mine 1952,S 26,18:2
Let's Do It Again 1953,O 14,34:3
Forever, Darling 1956,F 10,18:1

Hall, Anthony

Atlantis the Lost Continent 1961,My 27,12:1

Hall, Ben

Skyrocket, The 1926,Ja 26,25:2
Hot News 1928,Jl 23,11:2
Harold Teen 1928,Ag 14,15:4
Hot Stuff 1929,My 13,27:2
Nix on Dames 1929,N 23,18:5
South Sea Rose 1929,D 7,19:3
Girl From Woolworth's, The 1929,D 21,17:1
Man From Wyoming, A 1930,Jl 12,16:4
Newly Rich 1931,Jl 3,22:1
Strictly Personal 1933,Mr 20,18:2
Sequoia 1935,F 23,14:6
You Only Live Once 1937,F 1,15:2
Algiers 1938,Jl 15,13:2
Service de Luxe 1938,O 24,13:2
My Darling Clementine 1946,D 4,44:5

Hall, Bert Lieutenant

Romance of the Air, A 1918,N 11,13:3

Hall, Berta

One Summer of Happiness 1955,Mr 22,35:2

Hall, Cameron

Adventure's End 1937,D 20,23:2
Madeleine 1950,S 1,17:2
Reach for Glory 1963,S 10,46:1

Hall, Charles

Crooks Can't Win 1928,My 29,17:2
Why Bring That Up? 1929,O 5,22:5
Chump at Oxford, A 1940,F 20,17:3
You Can't Fool Your Wife 1940,My 24,23:4
Top Sergeant Mulligan 1941,N 12,31:3

Hall, Charles D (Miscellaneous)

Modern Times 1936,F 6,23:2

Hall, Charlie

Further Perils of Laurel and Hardy, The 1968,Ap 1,56:6

Hall, Deanna Jean

West Point Widow 1941,S 11,21:5

Hall, Devon

Dutchman 1967,F 28,32:1

Hall, Donald

Unguarded Women 1924,Je 24,18:2
Her Love Story 1924,O 7,26:1

Hall, Dorothy

Nothing but the Truth 1929,Ap 22,23:1
Laughing Lady, The 1930,Ja 4,21:1

Hall, Ella

In the Name of the Law 1922,Jl 10,9:5
Third Alarm, The 1923,Ja 10,28:5
Bitter Tea of General Yen, The 1933,Ja 12,20:6

Hall, Evelyn

My Best Girl 1927,N 7,26:4
Our Dancing Daughters 1928,O 8,14:2
Divine Lady, The 1929,Mr 22:4
She Goes to War 1929,Je 10,23:1
Married in Hollywood 1929,S 23,24:3
New Adventures of Dr Fu Manchu, The 1930,My 3,23:1

Hall, Evelyn — Cont

Hell's Angels 1930,Ag 16,8:3
Five Star Final 1931,S 11,24:2
Lovers Courageous 1932,F 20,11:2

Hall, G

As You Like It 1936,N 6,29:3

Hall, Genee

I Met my Love Again 1938,Ja 15,19:1
Santa Fe Stampede 1939,Ap 26,27:3

Hall, Geraldine

More Than a Secretary 1936,D 11,35:2
Ace in the Hole 1951,Je 30,8:6
Captive City, The 1952,Mr 27,34:2

Hall, Grayson

Satan in High Heels 1962,Mr 24,15:6
Night of the Iguana, The 1964,Jl 1,42:1
That Darn Cat 1965,D 3,44:1

Hall, H S (Original Author)

Steel Preferred 1925,D 22,13:1

Hall, Hal (Miscellaneous)

African Holiday 1937,Je 4,27:3

Hall, Harvey

I'll Never Forget What's 'Isname
1968,Ap 15,51:1

Hall, Henry

Story of Temple Drake, The 1933,My 6,11:2
Dude Ranger, The 1934,O 2,18:5
Our Daily Bread 1934,O 3,25:2
Jailbreak 1936,Ag 6,22:1
Chip of the Flying U 1940,Ja 22,11:3
Ape, The 1940,N 28,28:3
Beginning or the End, The 1947,F 21,15:1

Hall, Holly

Follow the Leader 1930,D 6,21:3

Hall, Holworthy (Original Author)

Valiant, The 1929,My 13,27:2
Man Who Wouldn't Talk, The 1940,Ja 12,13:3

Hall, Huntz

Dead End 1937,Ag 25,25:1
Crime School 1938,My 11,17:2
Little Tough Guy 1938,Ag 18,23:3
Angels With Dirty Faces 1938,N 26,18:1
They Made Me a Criminal 1939,Ja 21,19:2
Hell's Kitchen 1939,Jl 3,10:5
Angels Wash Their Faces 1939,S 4,16:2
Dress Parade 1939,O 28,11:2
Return Of Doctor X, The 1939,N 23,38:5
You're not so Tough 1940,Jl 9,25:3
Give Us Wings 1940,N 21,43:3
Hit the Road 1941,Jl 3,15:3
Bowery Blitzkrieg 1941,O 1,24:5
Spooks Run Wild 1941,N 1,20:3
Mob Town 1941,N 20,39:3
Mr Wise Guy 1942,Mr 5,27:2
Private Buckaroo 1942,Je 25,27:4
Bring on the Girls 1945,Mr 1,25:5
Wonder Man 1945,Je 9,17:2
Walk in the Sun, A 1946,Ja 12,10:6
Gentle Giant 1968,Ap 20,26:1

Hall, James

Campus Flirt, The 1926,S 22,31:1
Stranded in Paris 1926,D 13,27:1
Hotel Imperial 1927,Ja 3,16:2
Love's Greatest Mistake 1927,F 21,14:2
Senorita 1927,My 9,26:4
Ritzy 1927,Je 20,25:3
Rolled Stockings 1927,Jl 19,27:2
Swim, Girl, Swim 1927,S 5,13:2
Four Sons 1928,F 14,27:1
Fifty-Fifty Girl, The 1928,My 14,25:1
Just Married 1928,Ag 13,23:2
Fleet's In, The 1928,O 1,23:1
Case of Lena Smith, The 1929,Ja 15,22:4
Canary Murder Case, The 1929,Mr 11,22:2
This Is Heaven 1929,My 27,22:1
Smiling Irish Eyes 1929,Jl 24,23:2
Saturday Night Kid, The 1929,N 16,25:2
Dangerous Nan McGrew 1930,Je 21,20:5
Hell's Angels 1930,Ag 16,8:3
Let's Go Native 1930,Ag 30,7:4
Maybe It's Love 1930,O 18,23:2
Millie 1931,F 7,11:1
Divorce Among Friends 1931,Ap 2,30:4
Good Bad Girl, The 1931,My 15,20:6
She-Wolf 1931,My 28,30:6
Sporting Chance 1931,N 28,20:4

Hall, James Norman (Original Author)

Mutiny on the Bounty 1935,N 9,19:2
Hurricane, The 1937,N 10,31:2
Tuttles of Tahiti, The 1942,Ap 30,14:1
Passage to Marseille 1944,F 17,12:5
High Barbaree 1947,Je 6,27:2
Botany Bay 1953,O 30,27:2
Mutiny on the Bounty 1962,N 9,31:2

Hall, Jane (Original Author)

These Glamour Girls 1939,Ag 31,14:2
It's a Date 1940,Mr 23,16:2
Patrick the Great 1945,Ap 13,15:2
Nancy Goes to Rio 1950,Ap 7,22:2

Hall, Jane (Screenwriter)

These Glamour Girls 1939,Ag 31,14:2

Hall, Jon

Hurricane, The 1937,N 10,31:2
Sailor's Lady 1940,Je 29,12:2

South of Pago-Pago 1940,Ag 2,12:2
Kit Carson 1940,N 15,25:3
Aloma of the South Seas 1941,Ag 28,23:4
Tuttles of Tahiti, The 1942,Ap 30,14:1
Eagle Squadron 1942,Jl 3,12:5
Invisible Agent 1942,Ag 6,23:2
Arabian Nights 1942,D 26,15:1
White Savage 1943,Ap 26,15:2
Lady in the Dark 1944,F 23,17:1
Ali Baba and the Forty Thieves 1944,Mr 16,17:3
Cobra Woman 1944,My 18,17:2
Invisible Man's Revenge, The 1944,Je 10,12:2
Gypsy Wildcat 1944,O 5,18:6
San Diego, I Love You 1944,N 10,25:1
Sudan 1945,Ap 19,22:8
Men in her Diary 1945,S 24,16:5
Michigan Kid 1947,F 22,16:3
Vigilantes Return, The 1947,Jl 1,30:2
Last of the Redmen 1947,Ag 30,8:6
Zamba 1949,N 7,33:2
Deputy Marshal 1949,N 11,31:3

Hall, Josephine

Love Parade, The 1929,N 20,32:6

Hall, Juanita

Miracle in Harlem 1949,O 24,19:4
South Pacific 1958,Mr 20,33:1
Flower Drum Song 1961,N 10,40:1

Hall, Juanita Choir

Miracle in Harlem 1949,O 24,19:4

Hall, Ken G (Director)

Wild Innocence 1938,N 11,31:2
Pacific Adventure 1947,N 26,18:2

Hall, Ken G (Original Author)

Pacific Adventure 1947,N 26,18:2

Hall, Ken G (Producer)

Wild Innocence 1938,N 11,31:2

Hall, Lillian

Quo Vadis 1925,F 16,24:1

Hall, Manley P (Original Author)

When Were You Born? 1938,Je 9,27:2

Hall, Marian

Hidden Hand, The 1942,N 26,40:4
Gorilla Man, The 1943,Ja 15,21:4

Hall, Mel

Sensations of 1945 1944,Jl 7,13:2

Hall, Michael

Best Years of our Lives, The 1946,N 22,27:2

Hall, Newton

Penrod and Sam 1923,Je 25,16:5

Hall, Norman S (Original Author)

Brimstone 1949,O 7,35:3

Hall, Norman S (Screenwriter)

Mars Attacks the World 1938,N 8,26:3
Montana Belle 1952,N 8,9:2

Hall, O W

Hoosier Schoolmaster, The 1924,Mr 18,25:2

Hall, Oakley (Original Author)

Warlock 1959,My 1,34:1

Hall, Porter

Thin Man, The 1934,Je 30,18:5
Case of the Lucky Legs, The 1935,N 1,25:1
Petrified Forest, The 1936,F 7,14:2
Story of Louis Pasteur, The 1936,F 10,15:1
Snowed Under 1936,Mr 30,17:5
Princess Comes Across, The 1936,Je 4,27:2
Sudden Death, And 1936,Jl 18,18:2
Satan Met a Lady 1936,Jl 23,24:2
General Died at Dawn, The 1936,S 3,17:2
Plainsman, The 1937,Ja 14,16:2
Make Way for Tomorrow 1937,My 10,23:1
King of Gamblers 1937,Jl 3,18:1
Souls at Sea 1937,Ag 10,23:2
This Way Please 1937,O 8,27:2
True Confession 1937,D 16,35:2
Wells Fargo 1937,D 30,15:2
Scandal Street 1938,F 5,19:2 (In Addenda)
Dangerous to Know 1938,Mr 11,15:4
Bulldog Drummond's Peril 1938,Mr 18,23:2
Stolen Heaven 1938,My 12,27:2
Prison Farm 1938,Jl 15,13:3
King of Alcatraz 1938,O 7,21:2
Men With Wings 1938,O 27,27:2
Arkansas Traveler, The 1938,N 17,29:2
Grand Jury Secrets 1939,Je 29,19:2
They Shall Have Music 1939,Jl 26,17:2
Mr Smith Goes to Washington 1939,O 20,27:2
His Girl Friday 1940,Ja 12,13:2
Dark Command 1940,My 11,15:2
Trail of the Vigilantes 1940,D 7,13:2
Arizona 1941,F 7,23:3
Parson of Panamint, The 1941,Jl 26,18:2
Mr and Mrs North 1942,Ja 22,13:2
Sullivan's Travels 1942,Ja 29,25:2
Remarkable Andrew, The 1942,Mr 6,17:2
Butch Minds the Baby 1942,My 1,23:3
Desperadoes, The 1943,My 13,17:2
Miracle of Morgan's Creek, The 1944,Ja 20,15:2
Standing Room Only 1944,F 23,17:2
Woman of the Town, The 1944,Mr 6,17:2
Going my Way 1944,My 3,25:2
Double Indemnity 1944,S 7,21:1
Mark of the Whistler, The 1944,N 11,19:2
Great Moment, The 1944,N 13,t5:2

Hall, Porter — Cont

Bring on the Girls 1945,Mr 1,25:5
Murder, He Says 1945,Je 25,20:3
Blood on the Sun 1945,Je 29,12:2
Kiss and Tell 1945,O 26,16:2
Miracle on 34th Street 1947,Je 5,32:1
Singapore 1947,S 17,31:2
Unconquered 1947,O 11,11:2
You Gotta Stay Happy 1948,N 5,29:2
That Wonderful Urge 1948,D 22,29:6
Chicken every Sunday 1949,Ja 19,34:2
Beautiful Blonde From Bashful Bend, The
1949,My 28,11:2
Intruder in the Dust 1949,N 23,19:1
Ace in the Hole 1951,Je 30,8:6
Carbine Williams 1952,My 8,37:2
Half Breed, The 1952,Jl 5,7:2
Pony Express 1953,Je 6,8:6
Vice Squad 1953,Ag 26,23:2

Hall, Richard

Shadow of the Thin Man 1941,N 21,23:2
Born to Sing 1942,F 19,23:2
Rationing 1944,Ap 10,14:2

Hall, Robert

Barabbas 1962,O 11,49:1
Custer of the West 1968,Jl 4,13:2

Hall, Robert (Producer)

Franchise Affair, The 1952,Je 6,19:2

Hall, Robert (Screenwriter)

Franchise Affair, The 1952,Je 6,19:2

Hall, Ruth

Monkey Business 1931,O 8,22:6
Her Majesty, Love 1931,N 26,37:2
Local Boy Makes Good 1931,N 27,29:3
Union Depot 1932,Ja 15,24:4
Heart of New York, The 1932,Mr 2,15:3
Miss Pinkerton 1932,Jl 9,7:5
Blessed Event 1932,S 3,16:2
Kid From Spain, The 1932,N 18,23:2
Laughing at Life 1933,Jl 15,14:2
Beloved 1934,Ja 27,9:3
Farmer Takes a Wife, The 1953,Je 13,11:2

Hall, Sheridan (Director)

Steadfast Heart, The 1923,D 25,26:1

Hall, Sherry

Dancing Masters, The 1943,D 2,30:2
Prowler, The 1951,Jl 2,16:6

Hall, Sibyl

8 X 8 1957,Mr 16,13:2

Hall, Stuart

Cavalcade 1933,Ja 6,23:2
Dawn Patrol 1938,D 24,12:1

Hall, Thurston

Cleopatra 1917,O 15,11:2
We Can't Have Everything 1918,Jl 15,9:3
Iron Trail, The 1921,O 31,19:3
Love Me Forever 1935,Je 28,24:1
Hooray for Love 1935,Jl 13,16:2
Girl Friend, The 1935,S 28,12:2
Metropolitan 1935,O 18,27:4
Feather in her Hat, A 1935,O 25,24:5
Crime and Punishment 1935,N 22,18:2
Case of the Missing Man, The 1935,N 23,23:2
One Way Ticket 1936,Ja 1,35:2
Lone Wolf Returns, The 1936,F 4,25:5
Don't Gamble With Love 1936,Mr 2,13:3
Pride of the Marines 1936,Ap 27,19:2
Three Wise Guys, The 1936,My 23,12:2
King Steps Out, The 1936,My 29,15:2
Trapped by Television 1936,Je 15,24:3
Shakedown 1936,Ag 17,9:2
Two-Fisted Gentleman 1936,Ag 24,11:2
Man Who Lived Twice, The 1936,O 12,23:2
Killer at Large 1936,O 26,20:1
Theodora Goes Wild 1936,N 13,27:4
Lady From Nowhere 1936,D 21,19:2
Don't Tell the Wife 1937,F 19,15:2
Women of Glamour 1937,Mr 6,10:1
Parole Racket 1937,Mr 8,22:1
We Have our Moments 1937,Ap 30,17:3
Oh, Doctor 1937,Je 19,20:3
It Can't Last Forever 1937,Jl 30,22:5
Counsel for Crime 1937,O 9,16:1
Murder in Greenwich Village 1937,O 30,22:2
No Time to Marry 1938,F 23,27:2
Women Are Like That 1938,Ap 11,12:2
There's Always a Woman 1938,Ap 29,17:2
Main Event, The 1938,Je 20,11:3
Fast Company 1938,Jl 6,21:2
Professor Beware 1938,Jl 14,17:1
Amazing Dr Clitterhouse, The 1938,Jl 21,14:2
Campus Confessions 1938,S 23,35:1
Affairs of Annabel, The 1938,O 13,29:2
Hard To Get 1938,N 14,15:2
Going Places 1939,Ja 7,6:1
You Can't Cheat an Honest Man 1939,F 20,13:2
Each Dawn I Die 1939,Jl 22,12:2
Mutiny on the Blackhawk 1939,Ag 2,17:2
Star Maker, The 1939,Ag 31,14:2
Day the Bookies Wept, The 1939,S 14,18:2
Hawaiian Nights 1939,S 29,19:4
Dancing Co-Ed 1939,N 10,27:3
Sued for Libel 1940,Ja 19,15:3
Blue Bird, The 1940,Ja 20,11:2

Hall, Thurston— Cont

Our Neighbors-The Carters 1940,F 15,15:2
Alias the Deacon 1940,My 14,27:5
Lone Wolf Meets a Lady, The 1940,Je 17,19:2
Millionaires in Prison 1940,Jl 16,21:3
Great McGinty, The 1940,Ag 15,23:1
City for Conquest 1940,S 28,9:2
Golden Fleecing, The 1940,N 7,33:4
Lone Wolf Keeps a Date, The 1941,Ja 2,24:3
Flight From Destiny 1941,Mr 28,26:7
Lone Wolf Takes a Chance, The 1941,Ap 7,13:2
Great Lie, The 1941,Ap 12,19:2
Washington Melodrama 1941,My 26,15:3
She Knew All the Answers 1941,Je 20,28:4
Pacific Blackout 1942,Ja 15,25:2
Design for Scandal 1942,F 6,23:3
Night Before the Divorce, The 1942,Ap 10,21:3
Great Man's Lady, The 1942,Ap 30,14:3
Counter-Espionage 1942,S 28,13:2
Great Gildersleeve, The 1942,D 18,36:8
Hard Way, The 1943,Mr 13,9:2
This Land Is Mine 1943,My 28,19:1
He Hired the Boss 1943,Je 4,17:4
I Dood It 1943,N 11,29:1
Cover Girl 1944,Mr 31,26:1
Wilson 1944,Ag 2,18:1
In Society 1944,Ag 17,20:2
Great Moment, The 1944,N 13,15:2
Something for the Boys 1944,N 30,19:1
Bring on the Girls 1945,Mr 1,25:5
Brewster's Millions 1945,Ap 27,23:2
Don Juan Quilligan 1945,Jl 30,16:2
West of the Pecos 1945,Ag 11,14:6
Lady on a Train 1945,S 15,21:2
Colonel Effingham's Raid 1946,Ap 5,21:3
One More Tomorrow 1946,My 25,12:2
Two Sisters From Boston 1946,Je 7,16:2
Without Reservations 1946,Je 8,17:2
She Wrote the Book 1946,Je 20,20:3
Farmer's Daughter, The 1947,Mr 26,31:2
Secret Life of Walter Mitty, The 1947,Ag 15,12:2
Black Gold 1947,S 5,16:4
Unfinished Dance, The 1947,O 31,29:2
Mourning Becomes Electra 1947,N 20,38:2
It Had to be You 1947,D 8,35:2
Up in Central Park 1948,My 27,29:3
Miraculous Journey 1948,S 20,21:2
Girl's School 1950,F 3,29:2
Bright Leaf 1950,Je 17,7:2
Belle le Grand 1951,My 18,34:6

Hall, Tommy

Seven Brides for Seven Brothers 1954,Jl 23,8:3

Hall, Virginia

Eight Girls in a Boat 1934,Ja 13,16:3

Hall, Willard Lee

Scaramouche 1923,O 12,7:2 (Incorrect in this edition; use 1927,O 1,7:2 elsewhere)

Hall, William

Magnificent Brute, The 1936,O 24,23:1
Flying Hostess 1936,D 14,29:4
Oh, Doctor 1937,Je 19,20:3
Spy Ring, The 1938,Ja 15,19:1
Officer and the Lady, The 1941,Ag 11,17:4
Harmon of Michigan 1941,O 2,29:2
Time of Their Lives, The 1946,N 28,40:2
Bachelor and the Bobby-Soxer, The 1947,Jl 25,12:5

Hall, Willis (Original Author)

Jungle Fighters 1962,Mr 15,28:2
Billy Liar 1963,D 17,49:1

Hall, Willis (Screenwriter)

Whistle Down the Wind 1962,Ap 23,34:2
Valiant, The 1962,Je 14,23:4
Kind of Loving, A 1962,O 2,46:1
Billy Liar 1963,D 17,49:1
Man in the Middle 1964,Mr 5,36:1
Matter of Innocence, A 1968,F 22,36:1

Hall, Winifred

Almost a Honeymoon 1931,Ja 10,19:2

Hall, Winter

Turn in the Road, The 1919,Mr 30,IV,6:1
Money Corporal, The 1919,Ap 21,13:4
Why Smith Left Home 1919,O 13,16:3
Forbidden Woman, The 1920,F 23,11:2
Behold my Wife 1920,O 11,19:3
Ashes of Vengeance 1923,Ag 7,20:2
Day of Faith 1923,N 27,11:2
Name the Man 1924,F 4,23:3
Secrets 1924,Mr 25,25:2
Only Woman, The 1924,N 3,20:1
Husbands and Lovers 1924,D 9,23:3
Boomerang, The 1925,Jl 1,16:1
Graustark 1925,S 8,29:1
Compromise 1925,O 27,23:3
Ben Hur 1925,D 31,10:5 (In Addenda)
Kitty 1929,Je 11,27:2
Wrecker, The 1929,Ag 13,23:2
Woman to Woman 1929,N 12,34:4
Lost Zeppelin, The 1930,F 3,17:1
Passion Flower 1930,D 22,16:2
Road to Paradise, The 1931,Ja 20,21:3
Girls Demand Excitement 1931,F 7,11:1
Confessions of a Co-Ed 1931,Je 20,20:4
Ben Hur 1931,D 4,28:2

Tomorrow and Tomorrow 1932,Ja 30,13:2
Pursuit of Happiness, The 1934,O 26,25:1

Hall, Zooey

Born Wild 1968,D 12,62:6

Hall-Davis, Lilian

White Sheik, The 1929,D 9,32:5
Farmer's Wife, The 1930,Ja 7,28:3
Volga, Volga 1933,D 15,28:3

Hall Johnson Choir, The

Dimples 1936,O 10,21:2
Follow Your Heart 1936,O 22,31:1
Banjo on My Knee 1936,D 12,15:1
Rainbow on the River 1936,D 18,31:4
Way Down South 1939,Ag 18,16:4
Tales of Manhattan 1942,S 25,25:1

Hall-King, Magdalen (Original Author)

Wicked Lady, The 1946,D 23,19:5

Halland, Herman E Comdr (Miscellaneous)

This Man's Navy 1945,Ap 16,18:6

Hallaran, Susan

Marrying Kind, The 1952,Mr 14,27:1

Hallard, C

Two Worlds 1930,N 22,21:3
Almost a Honeymoon 1931,Ja 10,19:2
W Plan, The 1931,Mr 23,24:7
Battle of Gallipoli, The 1931,D 7,16:1
King of the Damned 1936,F 1,9:2
I Stand Condemned 1936,Jl 2,27:2

Hallatt, Henry

Gangway 1937,Ag 21,7:3
Victoria the Great 1937,O 29,19:1
Sixty Glorious Years 1938,N 18,25:2

Hallatt, May

Black Narcissus 1947,Ag 14,29:2
Girl in the Canal, The 1947,O 9,32:3
Spider and the Fly, The 1952,Jl 29,17:3
Separate Tables 1958,D 19,2:7

Hallback, Ivar

Sunshine Follows Rain 1949,S 29,39:2

Hallberg, Nils

One Summer of Happiness 1955,Mr 22,35:2
Time of Desire 1959,N 21,26:5

Hallberg, Ruth

Hertha's Erwachen 1933,Mr 14,18:3 (Incorrect in this edition; use 1933,Mr 14,19:2 elsewhere)

Haller, Barbara

It Happened in Broad Daylight 1960,S 30,33:1

Haller, Daniel (Director)

Devil's Angels 1967,O 5,46:1

Haller, Else

Comrades of 1918 1931,F 20,18:5

Haller, Ernest (Cinematographer)

Gone With the Wind 1939,D 20,31:2

Haller, Magda

Monjes, Des 1935,Ja 21,19:3
Noches de Gloria; Glorious Nights 1938,Ap 23,19:3
Beso Mortal, El; Fatal Kiss, The 1939,Ja 21,19:3
Infidelidad 1939,My 8,21:3
A lo Macho; In Rough Style 1939,Je 3,11:3
Perfidia; Perfidy 1940,F 17,9:3
Odio; Hate 1940,Ap 6,13:2

Haller, Ray

Courtship of Myles Standish, The 1923,D 31,9:3
Red Dice 1926,Ap 16,20:3

Haller, Richard

Corrupt Ones, The 1967,F 23,41:3

Hallett, Henry

Ringer, The 1932,Je 2,25:2

Hallett, Mary

Horse's Mouth, The 1958,N 12,41:1

Halley, Ina

Our Daily Bread 1950,O 9,21:6
Merry Wives of Windsor, The 1952,S 22,19:2

Halliburton, Richard (Narrator)

India Speaks 1933,My 8,10:1

HALLIDAY

See Also HOLIDAY, HOLLIDAY

Halliday, Brett (Original Author)

Michael Shayne, Private Detective 1940,D 19,33:2
Sleepers West 1941,Mr 20,25:3
Dressed to Kill 1941,Ag 22,19:3
Man Who Wouldn't Die, The 1942,Ap 28,25:5
Just off Broadway 1942,Ag 29,18:4
Time to Kill 1942,D 25,15:4

Halliday, Clive L

Mary Poppins 1964,S 25,34:1

Halliday, Frank

Deceiver, The 1931,N 23,22:1

Halliday, Jackson

Struggle, The 1931,D 11,35:1

Halliday, John

Woman Gives, The 1920,Ap 12,13:1
Recaptured Love 1930,Ag 9,16:5
Scarlet Pages 1930,D 6,21:3
Once a Sinner 1931,Ja 17,23:1
Millie 1931,F 7,11:1
Father's Son 1931,F 21,15:2
Fifty Million Frenchmen 1931,Mr 26,31:2

Halliday, John— Cont

Transatlantic 1931,Jl 31,15:2
Smart Woman 1931,O 12,28:2
Consolation Marriage 1931,O 30,26:4
Ruling Voice, The 1931,N 5,29:3
Men of Chance 1931,D 28,22:1
Impatient Maiden, The 1932,Mr 4,17:3
Week Ends Only 1932,Je 18,9:2
Man Called Back, The 1932,Jl 30,16:5
Age of Consent, The 1932,S 3,16:2
Bird of Paradise 1932,S 10,18:5
Perfect Understanding 1933,F 23,20:2
Woman Accused, The 1933,Mr 13,18:2
Bed of Roses 1933,Je 30,20:3
House on 56th Street, The 1933,D 2,9:3
Witching Hour, The 1934,Ap 28,11:3
Finishing School 1934,Ap 30,11:4
Return of the Terror 1934,Jl 11,20:2
Housewife 1934,Ag 10,21:2
Desirable 1934,S 15,20:5
Happiness Ahead 1934,O 11,28:2
Mystery Woman 1935,Ja 9,22:2
Dark Angel, The 1935,S 6,12:2
Melody Lingers on, The 1935,N 7,27:1
Peter Ibbetson 1935,N 8,18:2
Desire 1936,Ap 13,15:1
Fatal Lady 1936,Jl 11,11:3
Three Cheers for Love 1936,Ag 1,16:2
Hollywood Boulevard 1936,S 21,26:4
Arsene Lupin Returns 1938,Mr 9,21:1
Blockade 1938,Je 17,25:1
That Certain Age 1938,N 5,15:2
Hotel for Women 1939,Ag 26,20:2
Intermezzo, A Love Story 1939,O 6,31:1
Philadelphia Story, The 1940,D 27,22:2
Submarine Zone; (Escape To Glory) 1941,Ap 7,13:2
Lydia 1941,S 19,27:1

Halliday, Peter

Dunkirk 1958,S 11,42:2

Halligan, William

Follow the Leader 1930,D 6,21:3
Public Defender, The 1931,Ag 1,16:4
Lady and Gent 1932,Jl 16,5:5
Crooner 1932,Ag 20,7:4
Blessed Event 1932,S 3,16:2
You Can't Fool Your Wife 1940,My 24,23:4
Hired Wife 1940,S 14,11:2
Gangs Incorporated 1941,Ag 4,16:6
Moontide 1942,Ap 30,14:1
Life Begins at Eight-Thirty 1942,D 10,35:2
He's my Guy 1943,Mr 12,12:3
Dick Tracy 1946,Ja 12,10:7
Spider, The 1946,Je 21,20:3
If I'm Lucky 1946,S 20,41:3
Till the Clouds Roll By 1946,D 6,27:4
Shocking Miss Pilgrim, The 1947,F 12,34:2

Hallis, Hal (Producer)

Thelma Jordon 1950,Ja 19,35:2

Hallor, Edith

Inside of the Cup, The 1921,Ja 16,VI,2:1 (In Addenda)

Hallor, Ray

Dangerous Maid, The 1923,D 11,26:2
Inez From Hollywood 1924,D 16,28:1
Learning to Love 1925,F 23,24:1
Sally 1925,Mr 16,16:1
Man Crazy 1927,D 19,30:1
Haunted Ship, The 1928,Ja 23,18:3
Fast Life 1929,Ag 17,5:3
Truth About Youth, The 1930,D 13,22:2

Halloran, John

Blood on the Sun 1945,Je 29,12:2
Badman's Territory 1946,My 31,27:2
Angel and the Badman 1947,Mr 3,28:4
Kiss Tomorrow Goodbye 1950,Ag 5,9:2

Halls, Ethel May

Thou Shalt Not Kill 1940,Ja 8,11:2

Hallward, Joy

Born to be Bad 1950,S 29,31:5
Witness to Murder 1954,Ap 16,16:4

Hallyday, Johnny

Tales of Paris (The Tale of Sophie); Tale of Sophie, The (Tales of Paris) 1962,Ag 27,18:1

Halm, Alfred (Screenwriter)

Youth Astray 1928,My 29,17:2

Halm, Harry

It's Easy to Become a Father 1929,Je 24,27:1
Why Cry at Parting 1930,F 4,28:3
Rosenmontag 1931,Mr 28,15:3
Wahre Jakob, Der 1931,Ag 7,20:2
Blonde Nachtigall, Die 1931,Ag 22,7:5
Kyritz-Pyritz 1932,Ag 9,20:5
Eine Liebesnacht 1933,My 15,16:2
Toller Einfall, Ein 1934,My 21,20:3
Zu Befehl, Herr Unteroffizier 1934,Je 16,20:3

Halm, Harry (Screenwriter)

White Horse Inn, The 1957,D 4,50:3

Halmay, Tibor

Der Falsche Ehemann 1932,O 17,18:3
Teilnehmer Antwortet Nicht 1932,N 30,23:6
Und Es Leuchtet die Puszta 1934,Ja 30,17:2
Mindent a Noert! 1934,O 17,26:3
Jo as a Haznal; Father Knows Best 1935,F 5,22:4

Halmay, Tibor— Cont

3:1 a Szerelem Javara; 3 to 1 for Love 1939,Mr 25,19:3

Halme, Kurt (Producer)

Wozzeck 1962,Mr 3,13:1

Halmey-Clifford, Molly

Magnet, The 1951,F 27,22:6

Halop, Billy

Dead End 1937,Ag 25,25:1

Crime School 1938,My 11,17:2

Little Tough Guy 1938,Ag 18,23:3

Angels With Dirty Faces 1938,N 26,18:1

They Made Me a Criminal 1939,Ja 21,19:2

You Can't Get Away With Murder 1939,Mr 25,19:2

Hell's Kitchen 1939,Jl 3,10:5

Angels Wash Their Faces 1939,S 4,16:2

Dust Be my Destiny 1939,O 7,11:2

Dress Parade 1939,O 28,11:2

Call a Messenger 1939,N 11,12:1

Tom Brown's School Days 1940,Je 28,22:2

You're not so Tough 1940,Jl 9,25:3

Give Us Wings 1940,N 21,43:3

Hit the Road 1941,Jl 3,15:3

Mob Town 1941,N 20,39:3

Blues in the Night 1941,D 12,35:2

Mister Buddwing 1966,O 12,36:1

Halperin, Edward (Producer)

Revolt of the Zombies 1936,Je 5,17:2

Halperin, Victor (Director)

School for Wives 1925,Ap 1,21:3

Dance Magic 1927,Jl 13,21:2

Party Girl 1930,Ja 2,28:2

Ex-Flame 1931,Ja 24,15:1

White Zombie 1932,Jl 29,18:2

Supernatural 1933,Ap 22,16:3

Revolt of the Zombies 1936,Je 5,17:2

Halperin, Victor (Screenwriter)

Revolt of the Zombies 1936,Je 5,17:2

Halpern, Diana

Dybbuk, The 1938,Ja 28,17:2

Tkies Khaf; (Vow, The) 1938,S 15,29:3

Halpin, Luke

Flipper 1963,S 19,23:1

Flipper's New Adventure 1964,Ag 27,28:2

Halsey, Brett

To Hell and Back 1955,S 23,21:2

Three bad Sisters 1956,F 13,24:1

Best of Everything 1959,O 9,24:2

Atomic Submarine, The 1960,Ap 20,45:2

Desire in the Dust 1960,O 12,47:2

Return to Peyton Place 1961,My 6,26:1

Twice Told Tales (Rappaccini's Daughter); Rappaccini's Daughter (Twice Told Tales) 1964,Mr 28,40:1

Halsey, Forrest (Original Author)

Whip Woman, The 1928,F 13,16:2

Alias Mary Dow 1935,Je 29,16:2

Halsey, Forrest (Screenwriter)

Ruling Passion, The 1922,Ja 23,11:4

Ragged Edge, The 1923,Je 5,24:5

Halsey, Genitha

Angel Who Pawned her Harp, The 1956,F 29,35:2

Halsey, Mary

Falcon's Brother, The 1942,O 3,9:5

Cat People 1942,D 7,22:2

Halstan, Margaret

Middle Watch, The 1930,D 20,20:6

Quiet Wedding 1941,D 29,27:4

Holly and the Ivy, The 1954,F 5,16:1

Touch and go 1956,Mr 20,13:2

Halsted, Henry (Producer)

Up the Creek 1958,N 11,26:2

Halston, Howard

It's a Great Life 1920,Ag 30,12:3

Halt, James

Silk Legs 1927,D 26,26:6

Halton, Charles

Come and Get It 1936,N 12,31:1

More Than a Secretary 1936,D 11,35:2

Gold Diggers of 1937 1936,D 25,19:2

Sing Me a Love Song 1936,D 26,15:2

Black Legion 1937,Ja 18,21:1

Stolen Holiday 1937,F 1,15:3

Ready, Willing and Able 1937,Mr 15,27:1

Penrod and Sam 1937,Mr 29,14:3

Pick a Star 1937,My 28,17:2

Woman Chases Man 1937,Je 11,26:2

Talent Scout 1937,Ag 20,21:3

Blossoms On Broadway 1937,D 3,29:2

Penrod and his Twin Brother 1938,Ap 18,11:1

Stolen Heaven 1938,My 12,27:2

I'll Give a Million 1938,Jl 16,7:2

I Am the Law 1938,Ag 26,14:2

Room Service 1938,S 22,27:1

Man to Remember, A 1938,N 7,23:2

Jesse James 1939,Ja 14,13:1

Federal Man-Hunt 1939,F 2,17:3

They Made Her a Spy 1939,Mr 29,21:4

Dodge City 1939,Ap 8,19:1

Young Mr Lincoln 1939,Je 3,11:2

They Asked for It 1939,Je 30,17:4

News Is Made at Night 1939,Jl 13,17:2

Indianapolis Speedway 1939,Jl 15,8:2

Charlie Chan at Treasure Island 1939,S 1,15:5

Reno 1939,D 21,29:2

Dr Ehrlich's Magic Bullet 1940,F 24,9:2

Dr Cyclops 1940,Ap 11,32:3

Twenty-Mule Team 1940,My 10,26:6

Gangs of Chicago 1940,Je 13,29:2

Doctor Takes a Wife, The 1940,Je 15,12:2

They Drive by Night 1940,Jl 27,17:5

Young People 1940,Ag 24,16:2

Stranger on the Third Floor 1940,S 2,19:2

Westerner, The 1940,O 25,25:2

Tugboat Annie Sails Again 1940,N 9,20:2

Behind the News 1941,Ja 16,25:3

Tobacco Road 1941,F 21,16:2

Mr and Mrs Smith 1941,F 21,16:3

Meet the Chump 1941,F 27,23:4

Mr District Attorney 1941,Ap 17,29:3

Million Dollar Baby 1941,Je 7,20:2

Dance Hall 1941,Jl 19,16:2

I Was a Prisoner on Devil's Island 1941,Jl 28,16:4

Smiling Ghost, The 1941,S 26,26:5

H M Pulham, Esq 1941,D 19,35:1

Look Who's Laughing 1941,D 25,33:2

Unholy Partners 1941,D 29,21:4

Body Disappears, The 1942,Ja 31,13:2

Captains of the Clouds 1942,F 13,24:2

To Be or not to Be 1942,Mr 7,13:2

Juke Box Jenny 1942,Ap 17,21:3

Whispering Ghosts 1942,My 18,19:4

Spoilers, The 1942,My 22,27:2

In old California 1942,Je 18,25:3

Across the Pacific 1942,S 5,9:2

You Can't Escape Forever 1942,O 17,11:1

Jitterbugs 1943,Je 5,12:2

My Kingdom for a Cook 1943,O 15,15:3

Rationing 1944,Ap 10,14:2

Address Unknown 1944,Ap 17,20:1

Shadows in the Night 1944,Jl 29,16:2

Wilson 1944,Ag 2,18:1

Tree Grows in Brooklyn, A 1945,Mr 1,25:5

Fighting Guardsman, The 1945,O 6,9:6

Because of Him 1946,Ja 25,26:6

She Went to the Races 1946,F 1,29:2

Three Little Girls in Blue 1946,S 26,32:3

Three Godfathers 1949,Mr 4,25:2

Traveling Saleswoman 1950,Ja 6,25:3

When Willie Comes Marching Home 1950,F 18,9:2

Stella 1950,Ag 19,9:2

Carrie 1952,Jl 17,20:2

Friendly Persuasion 1956,N 2,30:1

Halton, Jo

Yellow Canary, The 1963,My 16,42:1

Hama, Mie

King Kong vs. Godzilla 1963,Je 27,23:4

What's Up, Tiger Lily? 1966,N 18,33:1

You Only Live Twice 1967,Je 14,40:1

King Kong Escapes 1968,Jl 11,30:1

Hamada, Harry

Go for Broke 1951,My 25,31:2

Frogmen, The 1951,Je 30,8:6

Hamaguchi, Yoshihiro

Fires on the Plain 1963,S 25,39:1

Hamamura, Jon

Odd Obsession 1961,D 27,16:1

Temptress and the Monk, The 1963,My 28,32:1

Hambledon, Phyllis (Original Author)

No Place for Jennifer 1951,Jl 17,31:2

Hambleton, Harry

Long John Silver 1955,Ap 7,24:1

Hambling, Arthur

Secret Four, The 1940,Ap 22,13:2

Wings and the Woman 1942,O 8,31:1

Henry V 1946,Je 18,30:2

Odd Man Out 1947,Ap 24,30:2

Lavender Hill Mob, The 1951,O 16,35:2

Hamby, William H (Screenwriter)

Percy 1925,Mr 25,24:2

Hameiri, Y (Director)

Six Days to Eternity 1968,O 31,54:3

Hamel, Peter

Film Without a Name 1950,O 20,32:2

HAMER

See Also HAMMER

Hamer, Fannie Lou

Festival 1967,O 24,53:2

Hamer, Gerald

Swing Time 1936,Ag 28,21:2

Bulldog Drummond's Bride 1939,Jl 13,17:2

Sherlock Holmes Faces Death 1943,O 8,15:3

Scarlet Claw, The 1944,My 19,12:1

Enter Arsene Lupin 1944,D 2,17:6

Sign of the Ram, The 1948,Mr 4,30:2

Hamer, Gladys

This Freedom 1923,N 28,15:1

Magician, The 1926,O 25,15:1

Hamer, Robert (Director)

Dead of Night 1946,Je 29,22:6

It Always Rains on Sunday 1949,F 14,15:5

Kind Hearts and Coronets 1950,Je 15,41:2

Pink String and Sealing Wax 1950,O 4,38:2

Hamer, Robert (Director)— Cont

Spider and the Fly, The 1952,Jl 29,17:3

Long Memory, The 1953,Jl 27,15:2

Detective, The 1954,N 2,25:2

To Paris With Love 1955,Mr 29,33:4

His Excellency 1956,F 2,19:3

Scapegoat, The 1959,Ag 7,28:1

School for Scoundrels 1960,Jl 12,39:1

Hamer, Robert (Screenwriter)

Always Rains on Sunday, It 1949,F 14,15:5

Kind Hearts and Coronets 1950,Je 15,41:2

Long Memory, The 1953,Jl 27,15:2

Detective, The 1954,N 2,25:2

His Excellency 1956,F 2,19:3

Scapegoat, The 1959,Ag 7,28:1

They all Died Laughing 1964,Mr 16,37:2

Hamer, Rusty

Dance With Me Henry 1956,D 24,8:2

Hamilton, Aileen (Original Author)

Slightly Dangerous 1943,Ap 2,17:2

Christmas in Connecticut 1945,Jl 28,7:2

Hamilton, Bernie

Jackie Robinson Story, The 1950,My 17,36:1

Let no Man Write my Epitaph 1960,N 11,36:2

Young One, The 1961,Ja 19,26:1

Devil at 4 O'Clock, The 1961,O 19,39:3

One Potato, Two Potato 1964,Jl 30,16:1

Synanon 1965,My 6,44:1

Swimmer, The 1968,My 16,53:1

Hamilton, Betty

Victims of Persecution 1933,Je 17,16:6

Hamilton, Bruce

Whirlpool 1950,Ja 14,9:2

Hamilton, Charles

Strange Cargo 1929,F 18,28:1

Big Broadcast of 1936, The 1935,S 16,15:2

Hamilton, Chico Quintet

Sweet Smell of Success 1957,Je 28,29:2

Jazz on a Summer's Day 1960,Mr 29,46:2

Hamilton, Clayton (Original Author)

Thirty Days 1922,D 11,22:1

Girl Habit, The 1931,Jl 4,11:5

Hamilton, Cosmo (Original Author)

One Week of Life 1919,My 19,20:5

Midsummer Madness 1920,D 6,19:1

Rustle of Silk, The 1923,My 8,22:4

Exchange of Wives 1925,O 5,25:2

Paradise 1926,O 4,20:2

Perfect Gentleman, The 1935,D 19,33:4

Exile, The 1947,D 26,22:4

Hamilton, Donald (Original Author)

Violent Men, The 1955,Ja 27,17:2

Five Steps to Danger 1957,Ja 31,21:1

Big Country, The 1958,O 2,44:1

Silencers, The 1966,Mr 17,35:1

Murderers' Row 1966,D 22,40:3

Ambushers, The 1967,D 23,29:1

Hamilton, Frank

Subterraneans, The 1960,Jl 7,26:1

Hamilton, George

Well, The 1951,S 27,37:2

Crime and Punishment, U S A 1959,Je 17,39:3

Home from the Hill 1960,Mr 4,19:1

All the Fine Young Cannibals 1960,S 23,33:1

Where the Boys Are 1961,Ja 20,22:1

By Love Possessed 1961,Jl 20,32:2

Thunder of Drums, A 1961,S 27,35:1

Angel Baby 1961,O 5,43:1

Light in the Piazza 1962,F 8,25:1

Two Weeks in Another Town 1962,Ag 18,10:1

Victors, The 1963,D 20,21:2

Act One 1963,D 27,17:2

Your Cheatin' Heart 1965,My 20,52:2

Viva Maria 1965,D 20,48:2

Doctor, You've Got to be Kidding 1967,My 11,50:1

Jack of Diamonds 1967,N 11,26:3

Power, The 1968,Mr 7,52:2

Hamilton, Gilbert P (Director)

Open Your Eyes 1919,Je 30,16:3

Hamilton, Gladys

This Freedom 1923,N 28,15:1

Hamilton, Grace (Composer)

Wake up and Dream 1934,O 11,28:3

Hamilton, Guy (Director)

Inspector Calls, An 1954,N 26,24:4

Intruder, The 1955,Ja 26,22:1

Colditz Story, The 1957,O 25,23:2

Stowaway Girl 1957,N 6,43:3

Devil's Disciple, The 1959,Ag 21,12:1

Touch of Larceny, A 1960,Mr 17,28:1

Best of Enemies, The 1962,Ag 7,35:2

Man in the Middle 1964,Mr 5,36:1

Goldfinger 1964,D 22,36:1

Funeral in Berlin 1966,D 23,17:1

Hamilton, Guy (Miscellaneous)

Stowaway Girl 1957,N 6,43:3

Touch of Larceny, A 1960,Mr 17,28:1

Hamilton, Guy (Screenwriter)

Colditz Story, The 1957,O 25,23:2

Hamilton, Hale

His Children's Children 1923,N 5,15:1

Manicure Girl, The 1925,Je 15,10:1

Tin Gods 1926,S 20,21:3

413

Hamilton, Hale— Cont

Great Gatsby, The 1926,N 22,28:3
Summer Bachelors 1926,D 20,28:3
Telephone Girl, The 1927,My 16,24:2
Good Intentions 1930,Jl 26,16:4
Common Clay 1930,Ag 2,16:4
Paid 1931,Ja 3,21:2
Beau Ideal 1931,Ja 19,25:1
Dance, Fools, Dance 1931,Mr 21,15:1
Strangers May Kiss 1931,Ap 13,17:1
Tailor-Made Man, A 1931,Ap 25,23:4
Never the Twain Shall Meet 1931,Je 6,15:5
Great Lover, The 1931,Ag 24,13:4
Murder at Midnight 1931,O 5,17:3
New Adventures of Get-Rich-Quick Wallingford
  1931,O 10,20:4
Susan Lenox; Her Fall and Rise 1931,O 17,20:1
Champ, The 1931,N 10,29:4
Cuban Love Song, The 1931,D 5,21:2
Life Begins 1932,Ag 26,20:3
Successful Calamity, A 1932,S 23,22:2
Three on a Match 1932,O 29,18:4
I Am a Fugitive From a Chain Gang
  1932,N 11,17:2
Call Her Savage 1932,N 25,19:2
Billion Dollar Scandal, The 1933,Ja 9,23:1
Employees' Entrance 1933,Ja 21,10:6
Parole Girl 1933,Ap 10,8:2
Strange People 1933,Je 17,16:5
One Man's Journey 1933,S 1,15:2
Sitting Pretty 1933,D 2,9:3
Quitter, The 1934,Mr 14,23:3
Dr Monica 1934,Je 21,28:2
Girl From Missouri, The 1934,Ag 4,14:6
Big Hearted Herbert 1934,N 14,23:2
Marines are Coming, The 1935,F 23,14:7
Grand Old Girl 1935,F 26,16:4
After Office Hours 1935,Mr 9,19:1
Woman in Red, The 1935,Mr 23,11:3
Hold 'Em Yale 1935,Ap 27,20:6
Let 'Em Have It 1935,My 30,21:1
Three Kids and a Queen 1935,N 9,19:2
Adventures of Marco Polo, The 1965,Ap 8,17:2

Hamilton, Hale (Original Author)

Purple Highway, The 1923,Jl 24,14:3 (In
  Addenda)

Hamilton, Harry (Original Author)

Banjo on My Knee 1936,D 12,15:1
Main Street Lawyer 1939,N 9,27:2

Hamilton, J Frank

Men of Texas 1942,Jl 13,18:3 (In Addenda)
Amazing Mrs Holliday, The 1943,F 22,20:2

Hamilton, James (Original Author)

Man Who Fights Alone, The 1924,Jl 28,12:2
Ankles Preferred 1927,Ap 18,21:2

Hamilton, Jane

Paid to Dance 1937,D 6,19:1
That Hagen Girl 1947,O 25,13:2

Hamilton, John

White Cargo 1930,F 24,18:1
Mystery at the Villa Rose 1930,Je 2,25:4
Heads Up 1930,O 13,31:1
Legion of Terror 1936,N 2,24:2
Bad Guy 1937,Ag 26,25:2
Criminals of the Air 1937,O 28,29:2
Over the Wall 1938,Mr 28,19:2
Mr Moto's Gamble 1938,Ap 8,17:2
Doctor Rhythm 1938,My 19,25:2
Mr Wong, Detective 1938,N 21,14:4
I Stand Accused 1939,Ja 5,17:1
Allegheny Uprising 1939,N 10,27:3
Roaring Twenties, The 1939,N 11,12:1
Saint's Double Trouble, The 1940,F 13,27:2
Johnny Apollo 1940,Ap 13,21:2
Tear Gas Squad 1940,My 31,15:3
Gold Rush Maisie 1940,S 2,19:2
Tugboat Annie Sails Again 1940,N 9,20:2
Great Plane Robbery, The 1940,N 15,25:2
Maltese Falcon, The 1941,O 4,18:2
Always in my Heart 1942,Mr 14,19:2
In This our Life 1942,My 9,10:2
Big Shot, The 1942,Jl 18,8:2
Enemy Agents meet Ellery Queen
  1942,Ag 22,16:2
Across the Pacific 1942,S 5,9:2
Escape From Crime 1942,O 12,12:3
Over my Dead Body 1942,D 26,15:2
Swingtime Johnny 1943,D 17,23:3
Action in Arabia 1944,F 19,18:7
Great Flamario, The 1945,Ja 15,15:5
Circumstantial Evidence 1945,Ap 21,18:3
Step by Step 1946,Ag 24,6:7
Beginning or the End, The 1947,F 21,15:1
Song of my Heart 1948,Mr 5,17:3
Undercover Man, The 1949,Ap 21,30:2
Canadian Pacific 1949,My 20,32:4
Bodyhold 1949,D 12,29:4
Davy Crockett, Indian Scout 1950,Mr 17,28:3
Her Wonderful Lie 1950,Jl 17,15:2
Guy Who Came Back, The 1951,Ag 17,13:2
On the Waterfront 1954,Jl 29,18:1
Sitting Bull 1954,N 26,24:4

Hamilton, Joseph H

Hoodlum Priest, The 1961,Ap 3,28:5

Hamilton, Kim

Odds Against Tomorrow 1959,O 16,27:1

Hamilton, Kipp

Good Morning, Miss Dove 1955,N 24,41:1
Bigger Than Life 1956,Ag 3,11:2
Never so Few 1960,Ja 22,15:2
Unforgiven, The 1960,Ap 7,46:1

Hamilton, Lillian

Outrage 1950,O 16,30:5

Hamilton, Lloyd

His Darker Self 1924,Mr 26,19:2
Show of Shows 1929,N 21,24:5

Hamilton, Mahlon

Her Kingdom of Dreams 1919,S 22,8:1
Earthbound 1920,Ag 11,9:4
Ladies Must Live 1921,N 21,20:1
Lane That had no Turning, The 1922,Ja 9,15:2
Peg o'my Heart 1923,Ja 22,10:1
Christian, The 1923,F 12,13:4
Heart Raider, The 1923,Je 6,24:5
Little Old New York 1923,Ag 2,10:3
His Children's Children 1923,N 5,15:1
Recoil, The 1924,Je 30,16:1
Honky Tonk 1929,Je 5,32:3
Single Standard, The 1929,Jl 29,23:3
Sporting Chance 1931,N 28,20:4
Strangers of the Evening 1932,Je 4,9:2
High School Girl 1935,Mr 16,19:1
Mississippi 1935,Ap 18,27:2

Hamilton, Marc

Great Locomotive Chase, The 1956,Je 27,35:1

Hamilton, Margaret

Another Language 1933,Ag 5,9:5
Hat, Coat and Glove 1934,Jl 27,21:2
There's Always Tomorrow 1934,N 10,19:2
Broadway Bill 1934,N 30,22:2
Farmer Takes a Wife, The 1935,Ag 9,21:2
Way Down East 1935,O 31,16:2
Chatterbox 1936,F 15,18:6
These Three 1936,Mr 19,22:4
Witness Chair, The 1936,Ap 18,19:2
You Only Live Once 1937,F 1,15:2
When's Your Birthday? 1937,Mr 19,27:2
Good Old Soak 1937,Ap 20,25:3
Mountain Justice 1937,My 13,31:2
Nothing Sacred 1937,N 26,27:2
I'll Take Romance 1937,D 17,33:2
Adventures of Tom Sawyer, The 1938,F 18,23:1
Slight Case of Murder, A 1938,F 28,19:1
Mother Carey's Chickens 1938,Ag 5,11:1
Four's a Crowd 1938,Ag 12,11:1
Breaking the Ice 1938,S 23,35:3
Stablemates 1938,O 21,27:2
Wizard of Oz, The 1939,Ag 18,16:2
Angels Wash Their Faces 1939,S 4,16:2
Babes in Arms 1939,O 20,27:2
Main Street Lawyer 1939,N 9,27:2
My Little Chickadee 1940,Mr 16,8:2
Play Girl 1941,Ja 30,19:3
Twin Beds 1942,My 1,23:4
Johnny Come Lately 1943,S 24,26:1
Guest in the House 1945,F 16,19:2
George White's Scandals 1945,O 11,26:2
Janie Gets Married 1946,Je 15;24:2
Dishonored Lady 1947,My 24,10:5
State of the Union 1948,Ap 23,28:1
Red Pony, The 1949,Mr 9,33:2
Sun comes up, The 1949,My 13,29:2
Beautiful Blonde From Bashful Bend, The
  1949,My 28,11:2
Riding High 1950,Ap 11,26:2
Wabash Avenue 1950,Ap 29,8:3
Mad Wednesday 1951,Ja 25,21:5
People Will Talk 1951,Ag 30,20:1
13 Ghosts 1960,Ag 6,9:2
Rosie 1968,F 8,36:1

Hamilton, Mark

Rainbow Trail, The 1925,Je 3,26:4
Light of the Western Stars, The 1925,Je 24,14:3
Sparrows 1926,S 20,21:3

Hamilton, Murray

Bright Victory 1951,Ag 1,19:2
Whistle at Eaton Falls, The 1951,O 11,49:2
Toward the Unknown 1956,S 28,24:4
Girl He Left Behind, The 1956,O 27,17:1
Spirit of St Louis, The 1957,F 22,25:1
Darby's Rangers 1958,F 13,23:2
Too Much, Too Soon 1958,My 10,19:2
No Time for Sergeants 1958,My 30,13:2
Houseboat 1958,N 14,24:1
Anatomy of a Murder 1959,Jl 3,10:1
F B I Story, The 1959,S 25,23:1
Tall Story 1960,Ap 7,46:1
Hustler, The 1961,S 27,35:1
13 Frightened Girls 1963,S 12,32:2
American Dream, An 1966,S 1,28:2
Seconds 1966,O 6,56:1
Graduate, The 1967,D 22,44:4
No Way to Treat a Lady 1968,Mr 21,56:1
Sergeant Ryker 1968,Mr 21,56:2
Boston Strangler, The 1968,O 17,52:1

Hamilton, Nancy (Miscellaneous)

Unconquered, The; (Helen Keller in Her Story)
  1954,Je 16,37:1

Hamilton, Nancy (Original Author)

Fools for Scandal 1938,Mr 25,15:3

Hamilton, Nancy (Screenwriter)

Du Barry Was a Lady 1943,Ag 20,13:1

Hamilton, Neil

White Rose, The 1923,My 23,18:3
America 1924,F 22,20:1
Side Show of Life, The 1924,Jl 22,9:1
Isn't Life Wonderful? 1924,D 1,17:3
Men and Women 1925,Mr 30,21:3
Little French Girl, The 1925,Je 1,10:3
Street of Forgotten Men, The 1925,Jl 21,26:2
Golden Princess 1925,S 7,15:3
New Brooms 1925,N 4,17:4
Splendid Crime, The 1925,D 17,27:1
Desert Gold 1926,Mr 23,24:5
Beau Geste 1926,Ag 26,17:3
Diplomacy 1926,S 13,18:1
Great Gatsby, The 1926,N 22,28:3
Music Master, The 1927,Ja 17,12:4 (In Addenda)
Ten Modern Commandments 1927,Jl 11,23:4
Joy Girl, The 1927,S 6,34:3
Spotlight, The 1927,N 28,18:5
Shield of Honor 1927,D 13,33:2
Showdown, The 1928,Mr 5,21:1
Mother Machree 1928,Mr 6,20:3
Something Always Happens 1928,My 21,25:1
Don't Marry 1928,My 21,25:1
Grip of the Yukon, The 1928,Jl 10,17:3
Hot News 1928,Jl 23,11:2
Patriot, The 1928,Ag 18,7:2 (In Addenda)
Take Me Home 1928,O 23,33:1
Three Week Ends 1928,D 10,25:1
What a Night! 1928,D 24,11:1
Why Be Good? 1929,My 6,30:4
Dangerous Woman, A 1929,My 20,22:6
Studio Murder Mystery, The 1929,Je 10,23:1
Insidious Dr Fu Manchu, The 1929,Jl 22,17:1
Mysterious Dr Fu Manchu, The
  1929,Jl 28,VIII,3:7 (In Addenda)
Kibitzer, The 1929,D 21,17:1
New Adventures of Dr Fu Manchu, The
  1930,My 3,23:1
Anybody's War 1930,Jl 11,22:1
Dawn Patrol, The 1930,Jl 11,22:1
Cat Creeps, The 1930,N 8,21:3
Widow From Chicago, The 1930,D 20,20:6
Ex-Flame 1931,Ja 24,15:1
Strangers May Kiss 1931,Ap 13,17:1
Laughing Sinners 1931,Jl 4,11:5
Great Lover, The 1931,Ag 24,13:4
This Modern Age 1931,S 7,19:3
Sin of Madelon Claudet, The 1931,O 31,22:2
Tarzan, The Ape Man 1932,Mr 28,11:2
Wet Parade, The 1932,Ap 22,23:2
Woman in Room 13, The 1932,My 21,9:2
What Price Hollywood 1932,Jl 16,5:5
Two Against the World 1932,Ag 19,20:6
Payment Deferred 1932,N 8,26:3
Animal Kingdom, The 1932,D 30,14:2
World Gone Mad, The 1933,Ap 15,16:3
Silk Express, The 1933,Je 28,24:2
One Sunday Afternoon 1933,S 2,14:4
Tarzan and his Mate 1934,Ap 21,12:1
Here Comes the Groom 1934,Je 16,20:2
Blind Date 1934,S 1,16:3
Daring Young Man, The 1935,Jl 18,15:2
Keeper of the Bees, The 1935,Ag 17,18:5
Portia on Trial 1937,D 3,29:2
Lady Behave 1938,Ja 28,17:3
Stadium Murders, The 1938,Ap 9,11:2
Army Girl 1938,Ag 12,11:1
Saint Strikes Back, The 1939,Mr 9,18:2
Father takes a Wife 1941,S 5,19:3
Look Who's Laughing 1941,D 25,33:2
All by Myself 1943,Jl 16,20:3
Brewster's Millions 1945,Ap 27,23:2
Good Neighbor Sam 1964,Jl 23,19:1
Family Jewels, The 1965,Ag 12,30:4
Batman 1966,Ag 25,42:4

Hamilton, Patrick (Original Author)

Gaslight 1944,My 5,17:2
Hangover Square 1945,F 8,15:2
Rope 1948,Ag 27,12:4
Angel Street 1952,N 11,25:2

Hamilton, Phyllis

Flight Angels 1940,My 27,23:2

Hamilton, Richard

Ladybug, Ladybug 1963,D 24,9:1
Greetings 1968,D 16,61:2

Hamilton, Rita

Our Very Own 1950,Jl 28,12:5

Hamilton, Robert

Big Game, The 1936,O 24,23:1

Hamilton, Roy (Screenwriter)

Cat-Women of the Moon 1954,Mr 20,10:7

Hamilton, William (Director)

Freckles 1935,O 26,12:2
Seven Keys to Baldpate 1935,D 14,11:2
Murder on a Bridle Path 1936,Ap 11,19:2

Hamilton, William (Director)— Cont
Bunker Bean 1936,Je 27,21:2
Call out the Marines 1942,Ja 26,18:3
Hamilton, William (Screenwriter)
Call out the Marines 1942,Ja 26,18:3
Hamlin, Mary (Original Author)
Alexander Hamilton 1931,S 17,21:4
Hamlon, Bert
Decision of Christopher Blake, The
1948,D 11,12:2
HAMMER
See Also HAMER
Hammer, Al
Walk in the Sun, A 1946,Ja 12,10:6
Hammer, Alvin
Hollow Triumph 1948,O 29,29:5
Ma and Pa Kettle 1949,Ag 12,13:2
Hammer, Mike
Catskill Honeymoon 1950,Ja 28,10:3
Hammerstein, Elaine
One Week of Love 1923,Ja 8,22:1
Rupert of Hentzau 1923,Jl 9,8:4
Broadway Gold 1923,Jl 31,12:4
Midnight Express, The 1924,N 19,19:3
Parisian Nights 1925,Je 2,16:3
After Business Hour 1925,Je 17,16:2
Hammerstein, Oscar 2d
Main Street to Broadway 1953,O 14,34:1
Hammerstein, Oscar 2d (Composer)
New Moon 1930,D 25,18:6
Sweet Adeline 1935,Ja 7,13:2
Reckless 1935,Ap 20,16:1
Give Us This Night 1936,Ap 6,18:1
One Night in the Tropics 1940,D 20,33:2
Lady Be Good 1941,S 19,27:1
Broadway Rhythm 1944,Ap 14,24:6
State Fair 1945,Ag 31,14:3
Oklahoma! 1955,O 11,49:1
King and I, The 1956,Je 29,15:6
South Pacific 1958,Mr 20,33:1
Sound of Music, The 1965,Mr 3,34:1
Hammerstein, Oscar 2d (Miscellaneous)
Music in the Air 1934,D 14,29:3
Night is Young, The 1935,Ja 14,11:2
Rose Marie 1936,F 1,9:2
Show Boat 1936,My 15,29:4
High, Wide and Handsome 1937,Jl 22,15:1
I'll Take Romance 1937,D 17,33:2
Great Waltz, The 1938,N 25,19:1
Sunny 1941,Je 13,22:2
Hammerstein, Oscar 2d (Original Author)
Song of the West 1930,F 28,20:7
Viennese Nights 1930,N 27,32:5
New Moon 1930,D 25,18:6
Music in the Air 1934,D 14,29:3
Sweet Adeline 1935,Ja 7,13:2
Show Boat 1936,My 15,29:4
High, Wide and Handsome 1937,Jl 22,15:1
New Moon 1940,Jl 19,22:2
Desert Song, The 1943,D 18,10:6
Show Boat 1951,Jl 20,14:1
Desert Song, The 1953,My 21,39:2
Rose Marie 1954,Ap 2,22:2
Carmen Jones 1954,O 29,27:2
Carousel 1956,F 17,13:1
Hammerstein, Oscar 2d (Screenwriter)
New Toys 1925,F 17,18:1
Children of Dreams 1931,Jl 20,20:4
Show Boat 1936,My 15,29:4
Swing High, Swing Low 1937,Ap 15,19:1
High, Wide and Handsome 1937,Jl 22,15:1
Story of Vernon and Irene Castle, The
1939,Mr 31,19:2
State Fair 1945,Ag 31,14:3
State Fair 1962,Ap 12,41:4
Hammett, Dashiell (Original Author)
City Streets 1931,Ap 18,17:3
Maltese Falcon, The 1931,My 29,26:5
Thin Man, The 1934,Je 30,18:5
Mr Dynamite 1935,My 25,12:1
Glass Key, The 1935,Je 15,20:2
Satan Met a Lady 1936,Jl 23,24:2
After the Thin Man 1936,D 25,19:2
Another Thin Man 1939,N 24,29:1
Maltese Falcon, The 1941,O 4,18:2
Shadow of the Thin Man 1941,N 21,23:2
Glass Key, The 1942,O 16,23:1
Thin Man Goes Home, The 1945,Ja 26,16:5
Song of the Thin Man 1947,Ag 29,14:2
Hammett, Dashiell (Screenwriter)
Watch on the Rhine 1943,Ag 28,15:1
Hammid, Alexander (Director)
Hymn of the Nations 1946,Ap 22,26:2
Of Men and Music 1951,F 15,27:2
To the Fair 1965,F 13,10:2
HAMMOND
See Also HEYMAN, HEYMANN
Hammond, Brian
Tiger Bay 1959,D 15,50:1
Hammond, Charles
Manon Lescaut 1914,Je 14,15:1
Irish Luck 1925,N 24,28:4

Hammond, Earl
Satan in High Heels 1962,Mr 24,15:6
Hammond, Edward (Original Author)
Ghost Talks, The 1929,F 18,28:1
Hammond, Frank
Our Daily Bread 1934,O 3,25:2
Hammond, Hally
Pistol for Ringo, A 1966,N 3,45:4
Hammond, Harriet
Bits of Life 1921,O 17,18:1
Man and Maid 1925,Ap 7,17:3
Midshipman, The 1925,O 13,20:1
Hammond, John (Miscellaneous)
Sandra 1924,D 22,20:2
Hammond, Kay
Trespasser, The 1929,N 2,14:6
Her Private Affair 1930,Ja 11,21:3
Abraham Lincoln 1930,Ag 26,24:1
Racetrack 1933,Mr 6,16:6
Double Harness 1933,Jl 21,20:2
Eight Girls in a Boat 1934,Ja 13,16:3
Jeannie 1943,S 13,14:2
Blithe Spirit 1945,O 4,27:2
Five Golden Hours 1961,O 19,39:3
Hammond, Len (Original Author)
too Hot To Handle 1938,S 30,24:2
Hammond, Len (Producer)
Confirm or Deny 1941,D 19,35:2
Hammond, Nicholas
Lord of the Flies 1963,Ag 20,37:1
Sound of Music, The 1965,Mr 3,34:1
Hammond, Peter
Holiday Camp 1948,Ja 24,11:2
Operation Disaster 1951,Ja 15,13:1
Reluctant Widow, The 1951,S 8,8:6
Hammond, Virginia
Anybody's Woman 1930,Ag 16,8:3
Newly Rich 1931,Jl 3,22:1
No One Man 1932,Ja 23,18:4
Rich are Always With Us, The 1932,My 16,19:5
Crash, The 1932,S 9,17:5
Cabin in the Cotton 1932,S 30,17:3
Chandu the Magician 1932,O 1,10:4
Rockabye 1932,D 5,21:2
Eagle and the Hawk, The 1933,My 13,16:2
Chance at Heaven 1933,D 26,19:3
Come on Marines 1934,Mr 24,20:3
Dr Monica 1934,Je 21,28:2
Desirable 1934,S 15,20:5
Rumba 1935,F 25,13:2
Romeo and Juliet 1936,Ag 21,12:2
Hamner, Earl Jr (Original Author)
Spencer's Mountain 1963,My 17,26:6
Hamner, Earl Jr (Screenwriter)
Palm Springs Weekend 1963,N 6,32:1
Hamon, Lucienne (Original Author)
Zita 1968,Ag 12,40:2
Hamon, Lucienne (Screenwriter)
Zita 1968,Ag 12,40:2
Hamory, Imre
Borcsa Amerikaben; Barbara in America
1939,F 11,13:2
Leanyvari Boszorkany; Witch of Leanyvar
1939,N 25,13:2
Hampden, Walter
Hunchback of Notre Dame, The 1940,Ja 1,29:2
All This and Heaven, Too 1940,Jl 5,10:2
North West Mounted Police 1940,N 7,33:2
They Died With Their Boots On 1941,N 21,23:3
Reap the Wild Wind 1942,Mr 27,27:2
Adventures of Mark Twain, The 1944,My 4,25:5
All About Eve 1950,O 14,13:2
First Legion, The 1951,Ap 28,9:2
Five Fingers 1952,F 23,7:5
Sombrero 1953,Ap 23,37:2
Treasure of the Golden Condor 1953,My 23,19:2
Sabrina 1954,S 23,43:2
Silver Chalice, The 1954,D 27,22:5
Prodigal, The 1955,My 14,10:7
Strange Lady in Town 1955,My 21,11:1
Vagabond King, The 1956,S 13,39:6
Hamper, Genevieve
Under the Red Robe 1923,N 13,25:3
Hampshire, Melanie
Blow-Up 1966,D 19,52:2
Hampshire, Susan
Woman in the Hall, The 1949,Ja 24,16:2
Three Lives of Thomasina, The 1963,D 12,46:1
Night Must Fall 1964,Mr 19,28:1
Fighting Prince of Donegal, The 1966,N 10,64:1
Paris in the Month of August 1968,Ag 26,46:4
Hampton, Benjamin B (Producer)
Westerners, The 1919,Ag 4,8:3
When Romance Rides 1922,Ap 10,18:2
Hampton, Bruce
Sailor's Lady 1940,Je 29,12:2
Hampton, Grace
Bat Whispers, The 1931,Ja 16,27:1
Gigolette 1935,My 13,18:6
Piccadilly Jim 1936,Ag 31,19:1
Shanghai Gesture, The 1941,D 26,21:2
Exile, The 1947,D 26,22:4
Sitting Pretty 1948,Mr 11,35:2

Hampton, Grace— Cont
Love That Brute 1950,My 27,10:6
Hampton, Hope
Star Dust 1922,F 6,9:1
Lawful Larceny 1923,Jl 24,14:3 (In Addenda)
Price of a Party, The 1924,N 26,17:3
Road to Reno, The 1938,O 3,11:2
Hampton, Lionel
Song Is Born, A 1948,O 20,37:2
Benny Goodman Story 1956,F 22,22:1
Hampton, Lionel and his Band
Mister Rock and Roll 1957,O 17,42:2
Hampton, Louise
Goodbye Mr Chips 1939,My 16,27:2
Hell's Cargo 1940,S 16,15:2
Haunted Honeymoon 1940,O 31,28:2
Bedelia 1947,F 8,10:2
Story of Robin Hood, The 1952,Je 27,18:3
Horse's Mouth, The 1954,Ja 20,33:4
Hampton, Myra
Trial of Mary Dugan, The 1929,Mr 29,21:1
Once a Sinner 1931,Ja 17,23:1
Hampton, Orville H (Screenwriter)
Outlaw Woman 1952,Ap 5,20:3
New Orleans Uncensored 1955,Ap 30,10:8
Atomic Submarine, The 1960,Ap 20,45:2
Young Jesse James 1960,Ag 25,25:1
Operation Bottleneck 1961,S 7,40:2
Jack the Giant Killer 1962,Jl 26,17:1
One Potato, Two Potato 1964,Jl 30,16:1
Young Runaways, The 1968,S 12,54:3
Hampton, Robert (Director)
Horrible Dr Hitchcock, The 1964,D 3,58:3
Hampton, Ruth
Johnny Dark 1954,Je 26,7:2
Hamrin, Folke
Vi paa Solglantan; We at Solglantan
1940,O 9,30:3
Hamsen, Max
Wien Du Stadt der Lieder; (Vienna City of Song)
1931,Mr 20,29:1
Hamshire, Keith
In Search of the Castaways 1962,D 22,5:2
Hamsun, Knut (Original Author)
Hunger 1966,S 14,53:2
Hunger 1968,Ag 13,45:2
Hamza, A (Producer)
We Live Again 1948,S 6,17:2
Han, Chin
Lady General, The 1965,F 12,19:1
Han, Otto
Cadet Girl 1941,D 11,39:1
Tokyo Joe 1949,O 27,35:2
Han-hsiang, Li (Director)
Love Eterne, The; Liang Shan Po and Chu
Ying-lai 1965,Ja 16,14:1
Empress Wu 1965,Mr 16,42:2
Han-hsiang, Li (Screenwriter)
Love Eterne, The; Liang Shan Po and Chu
Ying-lai 1965,Ja 16,14:1
Hana, Hajime
Alone on the Pacific 1964,S 24,46:2
Hana, Sonya
Outpost in Malaya 1952,N 27,49:2
Hanabusa, Eiko
House of Bamboo 1955,Jl 2,13:2
Hanabusa, Yuriko
Kimiko 1937,Ap 13,31:3
Hanalis, Blanche (Miscellaneous)
Weddings and Babies 1960,O 6,51:3
Hanalis, Blanche (Screenwriter)
Trouble With Angels, The 1966,Ap 7,45:1
Where Angels Go-Trouble Follows
1968,Ap 11,51:1
Hanbury, Victor (Director)
No Funny Business 1934,Mr 9,22:4
Crouching Beast, The 1936,Ag 22,6:1
Sleeping Tiger, The 1954,O 9,8:7
Hanbury, Victor (Producer)
It Happened to One Man 1941,F 24,11:6
Squadron Leader X 1943,Jl 23,21:2
Sleeping Tiger, The 1954,O 9,8:7
Hancock, Barbara
Finian's Rainbow 1968,O 10,59:5
Hancock, Sheila
Night Must Fall 1964,Mr 19,28:1
Moonspinners, The 1964,N 4,47:1
Carry on Cleo 1965,O 23,17:2
Anniversary, The 1968,Mr 21,57:2
Hancock, Tony
Call Me Genius 1961,O 17,47:1
Those Magnificent Men in Their Flying Machines
(Or How I Flew From London to Paris in 25
Hours and 11 Minutes) 1965,Je 17,27:1
Wrong Box 1966,Jl 20,46:1
Hancock, Tony (Original Author)
Call Me Genius 1961,O 17,47:1
Hancza, Wladyslaw
Guests are Coming; Jada Goscie Jada
1967,Ja 13,15:1
Hand, David (Director)
Snow White and the Seven Dwarfs
1938,Ja 14,21:1 (In Addenda)
Bambi 1942,Ag 14,13:1

Hand, David (Miscellaneous)
Victory Through Air Power 1943,Jl 19,13:1
Handel, Aben (Screenwriter)
They Won't Forget 1937,Jl 15,16:1
Handel, Wolfram
Naked Among the Wolves 1967,Ap 19,54:7
Handel (Composer)
Great Mr Handel, The 1943,S 10,29:3
Handl, Irene
Girl in the News, The 1941,My 5,13:2
Temptation Harbor 1949,My 11,34:7
Silent Dust 1949,D 30,13:2
Perfect Woman, The 1951,F 17,10:7
Belles of St Trinian's, The 1954,D 23,13:4
Kid for two Farthings, A 1956,Ap 18,25:1
Brothers in Law 1957,Ag 20,22:1
Key, The 1958,Jl 2,23:3
Happy is the Bride 1959,Je 30,27:2
I'm All Right Jack 1960,Ap 26,40:2
Man in a Cocked Hat 1960,Je 15,50:2
School for Scoundrels 1960,Jl 12,39:1
French Mistress, A 1960,D 19,34:2
Make Mine Mink 1960,D 20,43:4
Two-Way Stretch 1961,Ja 24,20:3
Pure Hell of St Trinian's, The 1961,S 26,31:1
Call Me Genius 1961,O 17,47:1
Week-End With Lulu, A 1962,My 24,29:2
Heavens Above! 1963,My 21,28:2
Morgan! 1966,Ap 5,42:2
Wrong Box 1966,Jl 20,46:1
Smashing Time 1967,D 21,44:1
Handleman, Stanley
Harvey Middleman, Fireman 1965,Jl 13,39:1
HANDLEY
See Also HANLEY
Handley, Jack (Original Author)
Appointment in Tokyo 1945,D 8,21:3
Handley, Thomas
On the Waterfront 1954,Jl 29,18:1
Handman, Lou (Composer)
Hit Parade, The 1937,My 31,11:2
Handschiezl, Max (Cinematographer)
Heritage of the Red Man, The 1920,O 4,14:3
Handy, W C
Satchmo the Great 1958,Mr 1,12:1
Handysides, Clarence
Turn of the Wheel 1918,S 2,7:1
Handzlik, Jan
Auntie Mame 1958,D 5,39:1
Hanebelle, Andre (Director)
Fantomas 1966,Ap 6,36:2
Hanemann, H W (Screenwriter)
Silver Streak, The 1935,Ja 16,21:1
Riffraff 1936,Ja 13,14:2
House of a Thousand Candles, The
1936,Ap 2,29:2
Cadet Girl 1941,D 11,39:1
Tahiti Honey 1943,My 13,17:2
Haney, Carol
Kiss Me Kate 1953,N 6,23:2
Pajama Game, The 1957,Ag 30,12:2
Hanfstaengl, Ernst (Composer)
Horst Wessel; Hans Westmar 1934,F 4,IX,4:4
Hanft, Jules
Dramatic Life of Abraham Lincoln, The
1924,Ja 22,17:3
Hani, Susumu (Director)
She and He 1964,S 26,16:1
Hani, Susumu (Original Author)
She and He 1964,S 26,16:1
Hanighen, Bernie (Composer)
Second Chorus 1941,Ja 16,25:2
Hanin, Israel
Faithful City 1952,Ap 8,35:2
Hanin, Roger
He Who Must Die 1958,D 29,21:1
Cat, The 1959,Ap 13,35:1
Tamango 1959,S 17,48:4
Rocco and his Brothers 1961,Je 28,40:2
Night Affair 1961,O 13,27:1
Riff Raff Girls 1962,O 20,13:5
Hankinson, Hank
Kid Galahad 1937,My 27,21:3
HANLEY
See Also HANDLEY
Hanley, Clifford (Original Author)
Why Bother to Knock 1965,F 4,24:2
Hanley, Gerald (Screenwriter)
Blue Max, The 1966,Je 22,38:1
Hanley, James (Composer)
New Movietone Follies of 1930, The
1930,Je 21,20:5
Rose of Washington Square 1939,My 6,21:2
Lullaby of Broadway 1951,Mr 27,35:2
Hanley, James (Screenwriter)
Rainbow Man, The 1929,Ap 17,30:6
Hanley, Jimmy
Little Friend 1934,O 20,20:2
Born for Glory 1935,O 21,22:4
Transatlantic Tunnel 1935,O 28,16:2
Red Wagon 1936,Je 22,22:1
Housemaster 1939,Ap 10,13:2
Way Ahead, The 1945,Je 4,22:3

Henry V 1946,Je 18,30:2
Murder in Reverse 1947,Ja 11,23:5
Captive Heart, The 1947,Ap 28,27:2
Holiday Camp 1948,Ja 24,11:2
It Always Rains on Sunday 1949,F 14,15:5
Master of Bankdam 1949,O 17,18:2
Facts of Love, The 1949,O 31,20:2
It's Hard to be Good 1950,D 25,25:3
Blue Lamp, The 1951,Ja 9,25:1
Galloping Major, The 1951,D 17,27:2
Angel Street 1952,N 11,25:2
Deep Blue Sea, The 1955,O 13,35:2
Satellite in the Sky 1956,S 4,32:7
Hanline, Maurice (Composer)
One Rainy Afternoon 1936,My 14,29:2
Hanline, Maurice (Original Author)
It's Love I'm After 1937,N 11,31:2
Hanline, Maurice (Screenwriter)
Four Wives 1939,D 23,9:1
Hanlon, Bert
Surrender 1931,N 28,20:4
Trial of Vivienne Ware, The 1932,Ap 30,19:3
Society Girl 1932,Je 10,22:3
Me and my Gal 1932,D 12,18:4
Wings in the Dark 1935,F 2,10:1
Slight Case of Murder, A 1938,F 28,19:1
Amazing Dr Clitterhouse, The 1938,Jl 21,14:2
Boy Meets Girl 1938,Ag 27,7:2
Hanlon, Bert (Miscellaneous)
Every Night at Eight 1935,Ag 3,16:2
Hanlon, Bert (Screenwriter)
Big Brown Eyes 1936,My 2,11:1
Spendthrift 1936,Jl 23,24:1
Hanlon, Brooke (Original Author)
It Must Be Love 1926,O 4,20:2
Hanlon, Jack
Shakedown, The 1929,Ap 8,32:1
Parade of the West 1930,Mr 3,18:4
Hanlon, Tom
Gift of Gab 1934,S 26,17:6
Father Was a Fullback 1949,O 13,33:3
I'll Get by 1950,N 2,39:3
Guy Who Came Back, The 1951,Ag 17,13:2
HANNA
See Also HANNAH
Hanna, Emil
Tripoli 1950,N 10,35:2
Hanna, Franklin
Democracy, The Vision Restored 1920,Ag 25,6:4
Hanna, Mark
Southwest Passage 1954,S 11,11:2
Pirates of Tripoli 1955,F 24,21:2
Hanna, Mark (Screenwriter)
Amazing Colossal Man, The 1957,O 26,19:2
Rebellion in Cuba 1961,Jl 1,9:1
Hanna, William (Director)
Hey There, It's Yogi Bear 1964,Jl 30,16:1
Man Called Flintstone, The 1967,N 25,42:1
Hanna, William (Producer)
Hey There, It's Yogi Bear 1964,Jl 30,16:1
Man Called Flintstone, The 1967,N 25,42:1
HANNAH
See Also HANNA
Hannah, Dorothy (Screenwriter)
Brasher Doubloon, The 1947,My 22,34:5
Hannah, Link (Original Author)
All by Myself 1943,Jl 16,20:3
Hannassey, Buck
Big Country, The 1958,O 2,44:1
Hannassey, Rufus
Big Country, The 1958,O 2,44:1
Hanneford, Poodles
Circus Kid, The 1928,D 17,23:1
Our Little Girl 1935,Je 7,24:4
Springfield Rifle 1952,O 23,40:2
Hannemann, Karl
August der Starke 1937,Ja 30,21:3
Marriage in the Shadows 1948,S 17,28:3
Hannen, Nicholas
Man they Couldn't Arrest, The 1933,Mr 14,19:3
F P 1 1933,S 16,9:3
Loves of a Dictator 1935,Je 1,18:2
Prime Minister, The 1942,F 4,23:2
Henry V 1946,Je 18,30:2
Winslow Boy, The 1950,Je 7,34:4
Quo Vadis 1951,N 9,22:2
Quentin Durward 1955,N 24,41:1
Richard III 1956,Mr 12,1:4
Dunkirk 1958,S 11,42:2
Hanney, James
Native Land 1942,My 12,16:3
Hannon, Chick
Mystery of the Hooded Horsemen, The
1937,Ag 13,13:2
Hannum, Alberta (Original Author)
Roseanna McCoy 1949,O 13,33:2
Hanold, Marilyn
Solid Gold Cadillac, The 1956,O 25,40:3
Hanray, Lawrence
There Goes the Bride 1933,Mr 4,11:3
Faithful Heart 1933,Ag 15,20:2
Private Life of Henry VIII, The 1933,O 13,25:2
Chu Chin Chow 1934,S 22,12:2

Hanray, Lawrence — Cont
Loyalties 1934,O 26,25:1
Scarlet Pimpernel, The 1935,F 8,27:2
Brewster's Millions 1935,Ap 8,23:3
Mimi 1936,Ja 10,16:3
As You Like It 1936,N 6,29:3
Rembrandt 1936,D 3,31:1
Man Who Could Work Miracles, The
1937,F 22,13:1
Knight Without Armor 1937,Jl 9,18:1
Moonlight Sonata 1938,My 10,17:2
21 Days Together 1940,My 23,28:4
Mozart 1940,O 4,29:2
On Approval 1945,Ja 29,17:1
Nicholas Nickleby 1947,D 1,27:2
Hatter's Castle 1948,Jl 3,8:6
Mine Own Executioner 1949,Ja 19,34:2
Hansard, Paul
One That Got Away, The 1958,Ap 23,40:2
Hansberry, Lorraine (Original Author)
Raisin in the Sun, A 1961,Mr 30,24:1
Hansberry, Lorraine (Screenwriter)
Raisin in the Sun, A 1961,Mr 30,24:1
HANSEN
See Also HANSON
Hansen, Alfred (Cinematographer)
Loves of Pharaoh 1922,F 22,13:3 (In Addenda)
Hansen, Ann Elizabeth
Ordet 1957,D 16,33:6
Hansen, Cecil Dan (Screenwriter)
Second Time Around, The 1961,D 23,16:1
Hansen, Eleanor
Crime of Dr Hallet, The 1938,Mr 24,21:3
Mad Miss Manton, The 1938,O 21,27:2
Hansen, Else Marie
Nar Rosorna Sla Ut 1931,F 10,24:4
Hansen, Helen
Against the Wind 1949,Je 27,18:3
Hansen, Janis
Oh Dad, Poor Dad, Mamma's Hung You in the
Closet and I'm Feeling so Sad 1967,F 16,32:1
Hansen, Juanita
Midnight Romance, A 1919,Mr 10,9:3
Hansen, Karen
Telephone Girl, The 1927,My 16,24:2
Hansen, Max
His Late Excellency 1929,Je 11,27:2
Jumping Jack, The; Hampelmann, Der
1931,My 24,VIII,4:1
Hampelmann, Der 1931,S 8,38:7
Kabinett des Dr. Larifari, Das 1931,S 11,24:2
Wer Nimmt die Liebe Ernst; Who Takes Love
Seriously 1931,D 27,VIII,7:1
Einmal Moecht' Ich Keine Sorgen Haben
1933,My 25,24:4
Die-oder Keine 1934,O 29,14:3
Glueckliche Reise 1936,Ja 20,22:3
Wer Nimmt die Liebe Ernst? 1936,F 10,15:2
Die Privatsekretaerin Heiratet 1936,D 5,16:4
Csardas, Ihre Tollste Nacht 1937,Je 21,15:3
Hansen, Myrna
So This Is Paris 1955,F 12,11:1
Man Without a Star 1955,Mr 25,19:3
Purple Mask, The 1955,Je 16,35:7
Party Girl 1958,O 29,30:1
Hansen, Nina
Vicious Circle, The 1948,Jl 22,27:2
Stage Struck 1958,Ap 23,40:1
Hansen, Peter
Five Steps to Danger 1957,Ja 31,21:1
Hansen, Richard (Original Author)
Victory at Sea 1954,Jl 14,33:2
Hansen, Rolf (Director)
White Hell of Pitz Palu, The 1953,N 14,14:2
Desires 1954,Jl 2,10:2
Angelika 1954,S 25,10:7
Hansen, Sverre
Nine Lives 1959,Ja 6,28:1
Hansen, William
Pinky 1949,S 30,28:2
Member of the Wedding, The 1952,D 31,10:2
Fail Safe 1964,S 16,36:1
Hanser, Richard (Narrator)
Savage Splendor 1949,N 4,37:2
Hanses, Friedel
Im Heidekrug 1934,D 31,9:7
Hansi
Man on a Tightrope 1953,Je 5,19:1
Hanslip, Ann
Gilbert and Sullivan 1953,O 28,36:3
Knights of the Round Table 1954,Ja 8,17:2
Three Cases of Murder (In the Picture); In the
Picture (Three Cases of Murder)
1955,Mr 16,39:4
HANSON
See Also HANSEN
Hanson, Arthur
They Came to Cordura 1959,O 22,47:2
Hanson, Elnar
Into her Kingdom 1926,Ag 10,19:2
Her big Night 1926,O 13,21:1
Lady in Ermine, The 1927,Ja 3,16:2
Fashions For Women 1927,Mr 28,26:4
Children of Divorce 1927,Ap 26,33:3

Hanson, Elnar — Cont
Streets of Sorrow 1927,Jl 6,23:2
Barbed Wire 1927,Ag 8,10:3
Woman on Trial, The 1927,S 26,27:1
Hanson, Kristina
Dinosaurusi 1960,S 9,36:4
Hanson, Lars
Scarlet Letter, The 1926,Ag 10,19:2
Flesh and the Devil 1927,Ja 10,20:2
Captain Salvation 1927,Je 27,25:2
Divine Woman, The 1928,Ja 16,24:1
Legend of Gosta Berling, The 1928,O 29,29:1
Wind, The 1928,N 5,26:1
Homecoming 1928,N 19,16:7
Paa Solsidan 1936,Ag 26,16:3
491 1967,D 21,45:1
Hanson, Paul
Lost Patrol, The 1934,Ap 2,13:2
Hanson, Peter
Branded 1951,Ja 11,28:5
Molly 1951,Mr 8,37:2
Last Outpost, The 1951,Je 22,16:3
Passage West 1951,Ag 31,12:2
Darling, How Could You! 1951,N 9,22:4
When Worlds Collide 1952,F 7,30:2
Savage, The 1953,Ja 2,11:1
Drum Beat 1954,N 18,42:1
Bullet for Joey, A 1955,Ap 16,12:1
Hell on Frisco Bay 1956,Ja 7,21:1
Proud and Profane, The 1956,Je 14,41:2
Harlow 1965,Jl 22,24:1
Hansson, Lena
Swedish Wedding Night 1965,N 15,48:1
Hansson, Maud
Seventh Seal 1958,O 14,44:1
Wild Strawberries 1959,Je 23,37:1
Hansson, Siv
Children, The 1949,D 23,17:1
Hara, Izumi
Happiness of Us Alone 1963,Ap 10,31:5
Hara, Setsuko
Country Doctor, The 1963,Ag 14,28:1
Harakas, James
Beneath the 12-Mile Reef 1953,D 17,52:2
Haran, Ronnie
Come September 1961,S 8,34:1
Harareet, Haya
Hill 24 Doesn't Answer 1955,N 3,37:1
Ben Hur 1959,N 19,50:2
Interns, The 1962,Ag 9,17:5
Harareet, Haya (Screenwriter)
Our Mother's House 1967,O 10,56:1
Harari, Clement
Demoniaque 1958,Mr 4,34:5
Me and the Colonel 1958,Ag 27,33:1
Monkeys Go Home 1967,Mr 30,55:1
Harari, Robert (Original Author)
Hitting a new High 1937,D 27,11:1
Sun Valley Serenade 1941,S 6,20:1
Three Steps North 1951,Je 29,14:2
Millionaire for Christy, A 1951,O 5,24:3
Harari, Robert (Screenwriter)
Music for Madame 1937,O 23,14:1
Daytime Wife 1939,N 24,29:1
Everything Happens at Night 1939,D 16,12:6
Ice-Capades 1941,S 25,29:1
Foreign Affair, A 1948,Jl 1,19:3
Harbach, Otto (Composer)
Lovely to Look At 1952,My 30,11:2
Harbach, Otto (Miscellaneous)
Roberta 1935,Mr 8,25:2
Rose Marie 1936,F 1,9:2
No, No, Nanette 1940,D 20,33:1
Sunny 1941,Je 13,22:2
Harbach, Otto (Original Author)
Going Up 1923,O 10,16:2
Cat and the Fiddle, The 1934,F 17,20:2
Roberta 1935,Mr 8,25:2
Firefly, The 1937,S 2,17:2
No, No, Nanette 1940,D 20,33:1
Desert Song, The 1943,D 18,10:6
Up in Mabel's Room 1944,Ap 22,8:6
Tea for Two 1950,S 2,11:2
Desert Song, The 1953,My 21,39:2
Rose Marie 1954,Ap 2,22:2
Harbacher, Karl
Gretel and Liesel; (Kohlhiesel's Daughters)
1931,Ja 26,21:1
Lumpenball 1931,Ap 27,25:1
Der Schrecken der Garnison 1932,Je 1,19:5
Harbaugh, Carl
Silent Command, The 1923,S 5,15:3
College 1927,S 12,29:1
Devil's Brother, The 1933,Je 10,16:4
Harbaugh, Carl (Director)
Other Man's Wife, The 1919,Je 9,16:3
North Wind's Malice, The 1920,O 18,13:1
Harbaugh, Carl (Original Author)
College 1927,S 12,29:1
Harbaugh, Carl (Screenwriter)
Mademoiselle Midnight 1924,My 27,14:1
Steamboat Bill, Jr 1928,My 15,17:3
Three Legionnaires 1937,Jl 10,18:2

Harben, Hubert
Battle of Gallipoli, The 1931,D 7,16:1
Fires of Fate 1933,Ap 3,13:4
Scrooge 1935,D 14,11:1
Victoria the Great 1937,O 29,19:1
Suicide Legion 1940,My 6,13:3
Mozart 1940,O 4,29:2
Harben, Joan
Encore (Winter Cruise); Winter Cruise (Encore)
1952,Ap 3,45:1
Harber, Harry Paul (Screenwriter)
Terror is a Man 1960,Jl 14,23:1
Harbin, Suzette
Foxes of Harrow, The 1947,S 25,35:4
Harbord, Carl
Battle of Gallipoli, The 1931,D 7,16:1
Heart's Desire 1937,Jl 12,20:4
Sahara 1943,N 12,25:2
Dressed to Kill 1946,My 25,12:4
Macomber Affair, The 1947,Ap 21,21:2
Christmas Eve 1947,N 28,30:2
Woman's Vengeance, A 1948,Ja 30,19:2
Harbou, Thea von (Screenwriter)
Spione; Spies 1928,My 20,VIII,8:5
Woman of No Importance 1936,D 13,XI,6:6 (In
Addenda)
Harburg, E Y (Composer)
Moonlight and Pretzels 1933,Ag 23,21:2
Take a Chance 1933,N 27,20:3
Babes in Arms 1939,O 20,27:2
At the Circus 1939,N 17,17:2
Babes on Broadway 1942,Ja 1,37:1
Rio Rita 1942,My 8,27:3
Ship Ahoy 1942,Je 26,16:5
Panama Hattie 1942,O 2,31:2
Cairo 1942,N 6,27:2
Presenting Lily Mars 1943,Ap 30,25:3
Cabin in the Sky 1943,My 28,19:3
Thousands Cheer 1943,S 14,27:1
Song of Russia 1944,F 11,17:2
Can't Help Singing 1944,D 26,22:4
Harburg, E Y (Miscellaneous)
Singing Kid, The 1936,Ap 4,11:1
Stage Struck 1936,S 28,14:4
Gold Diggers of 1937 1936,D 25,19:2
Wizard of Oz, The 1939,Ag 18,16:2
Harburg, E Y (Original Author)
Broadway Gondolier 1935,Jl 18,15:2
Finian's Rainbow 1968,O 10,59:5
Harburg, E Y (Producer)
Meet The People 1944,S 8,16:2
Harburg, E Y (Screenwriter)
Finian's Rainbow 1968,O 10,59:5
Harburgh, Bert
Silken Shackles 1926,My 25,25:1
Harcourt, Cyril (Original Author)
Silk Stockings 1927,N 29,31:1
They Just Had to Get Married 1933,F 13,11:4
Harcourt, James
Old Curiosity Shop, The 1935,D 23,15:5
Seven Sinners 1936,Ag 22,6:1
Men Are not Gods 1937,Ja 19,28:1
I Met a Murderer 1939,O 2,15:2
Night Train 1940,D 30,21:1
This England 1941,N 18,33:2
Laburnum Grove 1941,D 2,29:2
Courageous Mr Penn 1943,D 23,26:5
Adventures, The 1947,Ap 4,19:2
Captive Heart, The 1947,Ap 28,27:2
Meet Me at Dawn 1948,My 18,26:2
End of the River, The 1948,Je 21,18:2
Hidden Room, The 1950,Ja 9,19:2
HARDEN
See Also HARDIN
Harden, Jacques
Gervaise 1957,N 12,46:1
Lola 1962,O 15,32:2
Hardenburg, William von
Slave of Desire 1923,D 11,26:2
Harder, Emil (Director)
William Tell 1925,My 20,26:2
Harder, Emil Jr
William Tell 1925,My 20,26:2
Hardeyn, Jeanne
Shameless Old Lady, The 1966,S 27,52:1
HARDIE
See Also HARDY
Hardie, Russell
Broadway to Hollywood 1933,S 2,14:4
Stage Mother 1933,S 30,18:5
Christopher Bean 1933,N 25,10:2
As the Earth Turns 1934,My 12,27:2
Men in White 1934,Je 9,18:2
Operator 13 1934,Je 23,16:5
Hell in the Heavens 1934,D 12,28:2
Band Plays on, The 1934,D 22,21:2
Sequoia 1935,F 23,14:6
West Point of the Air 1935,Ap 6,10:1
Old Kentucky, In 1935,N 29,24:1
Harvester, The 1936,Jl 4,18:2
Meet Nero Wolfe 1936,Jl 16,20:1
Down Under the Sea 1936,Ag 10,10:2
Killer at Large 1936,O 26,20:1

Hardie, Russell — Cont
Camille 1937,Ja 23,13:1
Frogmen, The 1951,Je 30,8:6
Whistle at Eaton Falls, The 1951,O 11,49:2
Cop Hater 1958,O 2,44:3
HARDIN
See Also HARDEN
Hardin, Danny
Enemies of the Law 1931,Jl 13,13:5
Hardin, Sasha
China Gate 1957,My 23,40:2
Hardin, Ty
Merrill's Marauders 1962,Je 14,23:4
Chapman Report, The 1962,O 18,49:2
PT 109 1963,Je 27,23:1
Wall of Noise 1963,S 5,27:1
Palm Springs Weekend 1963,N 6,32:1
Battle of the Bulge 1965,D 18,36:1
Berserk! 1968,Ja 11,42:2
Custer of the West 1968,Jl 4,13:2
Harding, Alan
I've Lived Before 1956,Ag 4,13:1
Harding, Ann
Paris Bound 1929,S 21,17:1
Condemned 1929,N 4,28:1
Her Private Affair 1930,Ja 11,21:3
Holiday 1930,Jl 3,25:4
Girl of the Golden West, The 1930,O 27,17:1
East Lynne 1931,F 21,15:2
Devotion 1931,O 3,20:2
Prestige 1932,F 5,25:2
Westward Passage 1932,Je 4,9:2
Conquerors, The 1932,N 21,21:1
Animal Kingdom, The 1932,D 30,14:2
When Ladies Meet 1933,Je 24,16:2
Double Harness 1933,Jl 21,20:2
Right to Romance, The 1933,D 15,28:2
Gallant Lady 1934,Ja 22,12:3
Life of Vergie Winters, The 1934,Je 15,26:1
Fountain, The 1934,Ag 31,14:1
Biography of a Bachelor Girl 1935,Mr 2,18:2
Enchanted April 1935,Mr 9,19:1
Flame Within, The 1935,Je 1,18:2
Peter Ibbetson 1935,N 8,18:2
Lady Consents, The 1936,F 6,23:4
Witness Chair, The 1936,Ap 18,19:2
Love From a Stranger 1937,Ap 19,27:2
Eyes in the Night 1942,O 16,23:1
Mission to Moscow 1943,Ap 30,25:2
North Star, The 1943,N 5,23:1
Janie 1944,Ag 5,16:2
Those Endearing Young Charms 1945,Je 20,26:5
Janie Gets Married 1946,Je 15,24:2
It Happened on Fifth Avenue 1947,Je 11,33:2
Christmas Eve 1947,N 28,30:2
Two Weeks With Love 1950,N 24,31:2
Magnificent Yankee, The 1951,Ja 19,21:2
Unknown Man, The 1951,N 17,9:5
Man in the Gray Flannel Suit, The
1956,Ap 13,21:1
Harding, Ben
Busher, The 1919,My 26,19:4
Harding, Bertita (Original Author)
Juarez 1939,Ap 26,27:1
Harding, Gilbert
Alligator Named Daisy, An 1957,O 7,23:2
Expresso Bongo 1960,Ap 13,44:1
Harding, Jackie Lou
Weird Woman 1944,Ap 1,11:1
Harding, John
Love Me or Leave Me 1955,My 27,14:1
Crime and Punishment, U S A 1959,Je 17,39:3
Please Don't Eat the Daisies 1960,Ap 1,37:1
This Property is Condemned 1966,Ag 4,24:1
Hawaii 1966,O 11,54:1
Impossible Years, The 1968,D 6,54:1
Harding, John Briard (Original Author)
My Wife's Best Friend 1952,O 11,17:2
Harding, John Briard (Screenwriter)
Kissing Bandit, The 1948,N 19,35:2
Harding, June
Trouble With Angels, The 1966,Ap 7,45:1
Harding, Kay
Scarlet Claw, The 1944,My 19,12:1
Mummy's Curse, The 1945,Mr 31,16:1
Harding, Lyn
When Knighthood Was in Flower 1922,S 15,17:2
(In Addenda)
Yolanda 1924,F 20,23:1
Sleeping Partners 1930,D 13,22:2
Speckled Band, The 1931,N 7,16:5
Constant Nymph, The 1934,Ap 7,19:1
Man Who Changed his Name, The
1934,O 17,26:2
Escape me Never 1935,My 24,24:2
Man Who Lived Again, The 1936,D 16,35:4
Fire Over England 1937,Mr 5,16:2
Knight Without Armor 1937,Jl 9,18:1
Pearls of the Crown, The 1938,Ap 12,26:2
Mutiny of the Elsinore, The 1939,F 16,17:2
Goodbye Mr Chips 1939,My 16,27:2
Spy of Napoleon 1939,Ag 19,18:4
Prime Minister, The 1942,F 4,23:2

Harding, Lynn
Triumph of Sherlock Holmes, The
1935,My 27,20:6
Hardman, Karl
Night of the Living Dead 1968,D 5,59:2
Hardman, Karl (Producer)
Night of the Living Dead 1968,D 5,59:2
Hardman, R (Screenwriter)
Big Night, The 1960,F 18,37:4
Rare Breed, The 1966,Ap 14,42:3
Hardmuth, Paul
Wonder Boy 1951,D 26,19:5
Hardt, Eloise
Games 1967,S 18,58:2
Hardt, Harry
Hungarian Nights 1930,Je 10,32:2
Verklungene Traume 1930,D 9,31:3
Koenigin der Unterwelt 1932,D 9,26:5
Verlorene Tal, Das 1936,My 30,7:3
Hardt, Karin
Die Blonde Christl 1934,F 23,23:3
Ein Gewisser Herr Gran 1934,F 24,18:5
Abel Mit Der Mundharmonika 1934,S 1,16:3
Zwischen Himmel und Erde; Between Heaven and
Earth 1935,Ja 21,19:3
Liebe und die Erste Eisenbahn, Die; Love and the
First Railroad 1935,F 18,19:4
Toerichte Jungfrau, Die 1935,S 9,24:3
Schoen Ist Es Verliebt zu Sein 1936,Ap 7,31:2
Abenteurer von Paris, Der 1937,My 29,20:3
Starker als die Liebe; Stronger Than Love
1939,My 6,21:3
Verliebte Herzen; Hearts in Love 1939,Je 10,14:2
Town Without Pity 1961,O 11,53:1
Hardt, Karl
Hermine und die Sieben Aufrechten
1935,S 21,18:2
Hardt, Ludwig
Arizona 1941,F 7,23:3
Hardtmuth, Paul
Desperate Moment 1953,S 1,19:4
Hardwick, Paul
Prince and the Showgirl 1957,Je 14,22:2
Hardwicke, Cedric Sir
Dreyfus Case, The 1931,Ag 31,11:5
Rome Express 1932,D 18,X,6:5
Rome Express 1933,F 27,11:2
Ghoul, The 1934,Ja 27,9:2
Orders Is Orders 1934,My 7,20:2
Lady is Willing, The 1934,Ag 11,16:5
Power 1934,O 5,29:3
Bella Donna 1935,F 26,16:4
Miserables, Les 1935,Ap 22,14:2
Becky Sharp 1935,Je 14,27:2
Nell Gwyn 1935,Je 20,16:2
Peg of Old Drury 1936,Ap 13,15:1
Things to Come 1936,Ap 18,19:2
Tudor Rose 1936,My 24,IX,3:8 (In Addenda)
Nine Days a Queen 1936,O 3,21:1
Green Light 1937,F 13,9:1
King Solomon's Mines 1937,Jl 3,18:1
On Borrowed Time 1939,Jl 7,13:2
Stanley and Livingstone 1939,Ag 5,18:2
Hunchback of Notre Dame, The 1940,Ja 1,29:2
Invisible Man Returns, The 1940,Ja 16,19:2
Tom Brown's School Days 1940,Je 28,22:2
Howards of Virginia, The 1940,S 27,27:1
Victory 1940,D 23,23:2
Suspicion 1941,N 21,23:2
Laburnum Grove 1941,D 2,29:2
Valley of the Sun 1942,Mr 19,29:2
Ghost of Frankenstein, The 1942,Ap 4,19:2
Invisible Agent 1942,Ag 6,23:2
Forever and a Day 1943,Mr 13,9:2
Moon Is Down, The 1943,Mr 27,8:6
Cross of Lorraine, The 1943,D 3,27:4
Lodger, The 1944,Ja 20,15:3
Wilson 1944,Ag 2,18:1
Wing and a Prayer 1944,Ag 31,14:1
Keys of the Kingdom, The 1944,D 30,15:2
Sentimental Journey 1946,Mr 7,33:2
Imperfect Lady, The 1947,My 22,34:5
Ivy 1947,Je 26,19:1
Lured 1947,Ag 29,14:4
Beware of Pity 1947,N 1,11:2
Nicholas Nickleby 1947,D 1,27:2
Tycoon 1947,D 26,22:6
Woman's Vengeance, A 1948,Ja 30,19:2
Song of my Heart 1948,Mr 5,17:3
I Remember Mama 1948,Mr 12,29:2
Rope 1948,Ag 27,12:4
Connecticut Yankee in King Arthur's Court, A
1949,Ap 8,31:2
Winslow Boy, The 1950,Je 7,34:4
White Tower, The 1950,Jl 3,9:2
Mr Imperium 1951,O 15,22:2
Desert Fox, The 1951,O 18,32:1
Green Glove, The 1952,Ap 24,38:1
Salome 1953,Mr 25,37:1
War of the Worlds, The 1953,Ag 14,10:2
Botany Bay 1953,O 30,27:2
Commandos Strike at Dawn 1954,Ja 14,25:1
Diane 1956,Ja 13,18:1

Helen of Troy 1956,Ja 27,21:4
Richard III 1956,Mr 12,1:4
Gaby 1956,My 10,26:3
Vagabond King, The 1956,S 13,39:6
Power and The Prize, the 1956,S 27,42:1
Around the World in 80 Days 1956,O 18,37:1
Ten Commandments, The 1956,N 9,35:2
Story of Mankind, The 1957,N 9,31:2
Baby Face Nelson 1957,D 12,35:1
Five Weeks in a Balloon 1962,Ag 27,18:1
Pumpkin Eater, The 1964,N 10,58:1
Hardwicke, Cedric Sir (Director)
Forever and a Day 1943,Mr 13,9:2
Hardwicke, Cedric Sir (Producer)
Forever and a Day 1943,Mr 13,9:2
Hardwicke, Edward
Othello 1966,F 2,24:1
Flea in her Ear, A 1968,N 28,66:1
HARDY
See Also HARDIE
Hardy, Arthur
Atlantic 1930,O 6,21:1
Dreyfus Case, The 1931,Ag 31,11:5
Hardy, Elizabeth
Amazing Monsieur Fabre, The 1952,S 9,21:2
Hardy, Francoise
Chateau en Suede; Castle in Switzerland
1964,O 14,51:1
Grand-Prix 1966,D 22,40:1
Hardy, Frank
Louisiana Story 1948,S 29,36:2
Hardy, Glenn
Day the Earth Stood Still, The 1951,S 19,37:1
Hardy, J L (Original Author)
Key, The 1934,My 30,14:3
Hardy, John
Botany Bay 1953,O 30,27:2
Hardy, Laurence
Love Is a Ball 1963,Ap 25,38:1
Woman of Straw 1964,O 1,30:6
Hardy, Lindsay (Original Author)
Love Is a Ball 1963,Ap 25,38:1
Hardy, Lindsay (Screenwriter)
World for Ransom 1954,Je 5,11:2
Hardy, Oliver
Wizard of Oz, The 1925,Ap 14,26:1
Rogue Song, The 1930,Ja 29,26:4
Pardon Us 1931,Ag 22,7:5
Pack up Your Troubles 1932,O 1,10:4
Devil's Brother, The 1933,Je 10,16:4
Sons of the Desert 1934,Ja 12,29:3
Hollywood Party 1934,My 26,12:2
Babes in Toyland 1934,D 13,28:2
Bohemian Girl, The 1936,F 17,21:1
Our Relations 1936,N 11,55:1
Way out West 1937,My 4,29:1
Pick a Star 1937,My 28,17:2
Swiss Miss 1938,Je 4,18:2
Block-Heads 1938,Ag 30,14:2
Zenobia 1939,My 15,15:2
Flying Deuces, The 1939,N 24,29:2
Chump at Oxford, A 1940,F 20,17:3
Great Guns 1941,O 3,27:2
Air Raid Wardens 1943,Ap 5,15:5
Jitterbugs 1943,Je 5,12:2
Nothing but Trouble 1945,Mr 10,14:1
Bullfighters, The 1945,My 12,10:3
Fighting Kentuckian, The 1949,S 19,18:3
Riding High 1950,Ap 11,26:2
Utopia 1954,D 15,41:1
When Comedy Was King 1960,Mr 30,42:1
Days of Thrills and Laughter 1961,Mr 22,37:1
30 Years of Fun 1963,D 26,33:4
Laurel and Hardy's Laughing 20's 1965,N 18,55:2
Further Perils of Laurel and Hardy, The
1968,Ap 1,56:6
Hardy, Patricia
Girls in the Night 1953,Ja 16,19:3
Don't Knock the Rock 1957,F 23,13:1
Hardy, Paul
Pamela, Pamela You Are.... 1968,D 21,49:4
Hardy, Rene (Screenwriter)
Triple Cross 1967,Jl 20,20:2
Hardy, Robert
Torpedo Run 1958,O 25,16:2
Berserk! 1968,Ja 11,42:2
Hardy, Sam
Woman's Experience, A 1918,N 11,13:3
Get-Rich-Quick Wallingford 1921,D 5,20:1
Mighty Lak' a Rose 1923,Mr 20,24:3
Little Old New York 1923,Ag 2,10:3
Half-Way Girl, The 1925,Jl 29,24:4
Bluebeard's Seven Wives 1925,D 28,19:2
Great Deception, The 1926,Ag 9,10:3
Prince of Tempters, The 1926,O 18,18:1
Perfect Sap, The 1927,Ja 11,18:2
Orchids and Ermine 1927,Ap 19,24:4
Broadway Nights 1927,Je 28,29:4
Life of Riley, The 1927,S 5,13:2
Life of Riley, The 1927,S 11,VIII,5:1
Texas Steer, A 1928,Ja 2,28:1
Big Noise, The 1928,My 7,29:1
Butter and Egg Man, The 1928,Ag 28,27:4

Hardy, Sam — Cont
Night Bird, The 1928,O 2,23:5
Outcast 1928,N 26,30:2
Give and Take 1928,D 27,27:1
Rainbow Man, The 1929,Ap 17,30:6
On With the Show 1929,My 29,28:6
Man's Man, A 1929,Je 3,27:2
Fast Company 1929,O 5,22:5
Big News 1929,O 7,22:1
Burning Up 1930,F 8,12:5
Song of the West 1930,F 28,20:7
Florodora Girl, The 1930,My 31,19:4
Reno 1930,N 4,36:1
June Moon 1931,Mr 14,23:2
Millionaire, The 1931,Ap 9,30:5
Annabelle's Affairs 1931,Je 29,20:3
Magnificent Lie, The 1931,Jl 25,11:6
Miracle Woman, The 1931,Ag 17,18:2
Peach O'Reno 1931,D 24,20:8
Dark Horse, The 1932,Je 9,27:3
Make Me a Star 1932,Jl 1,19:3
Phantom of Crestwood, The 1932,O 17,18:3
Face in the Sky 1933,F 20,11:5
King Kong 1933,Mr 3,12:1
Goldie Gets Along 1933,Je 3,16:4
Big Brain, The 1933,Ag 5,9:5
One Sunday Afternoon 1933,S 2,14:4
Ann Vickers 1933,S 29,24:1
Little Miss Marker 1934,My 19,18:3
Along Came Sally 1934,Je 16,20:3
I Give my Love 1934,Jl 17,24:2
Transatlantic Merry-Go-Round 1934,N 1,25:2
Gay Bride, The 1934,D 19,27:2
Break of Hearts 1935,My 17,24:3
Hooray for Love 1935,Jl 13,16:2
Powdersmoke Range 1936,Mr 9,20:2
Hardy, Sam (Original Author)
Man on the Flying Trapeze 1935,Ag 3,16:2
Hardy, Sam (Screenwriter)
Man on the Flying Trapeze 1935,Ag 3,16:2
Hardy, Stuart (Original Author)
Sierra 1950,S 15,31:2
Hardy, Thomas (Original Author)
Tess of the D'Urbervilles 1924,Jl 28,12:2
Far From the Madding Crowd 1967,O 19,59:1
HARE
See Also HEER
Hare, Doris
Another Time Another Place 1958,My 3,10:4
Hare, Harry
Geisha Boy, The 1958,D 24,00:0
Hare, Lumsden
Avalanche, The 1919,Je 30,16:3
On the Banks of the Wabash 1923,O 23,21:3
Second Youth 1924,Ap 22,19:3
Girls Gone Wild 1929,Ap 22,23:1
Black Watch, The 1929,My 23,26:3
Salute 1929,O 5,22:5
Sky Hawk, The 1929,D 12,36:4
So This Is London 1930,My 24,21:2
Scotland Yard 1930,O 20,28:2
Charlie Chan Carries On 1931,Mr 21,15:1
Svengali 1931,My 1,30:3
Always Good-Bye 1931,My 23,13:4
Road to Singapore, The 1931,O 1,25:2
Arrowsmith 1931,D 8,36:4
Silent Witness, The 1932,F 8,21:1
International House 1933,My 27,11:5
His Double Life 1933,D 16,12:3
Man of Two Worlds 1934,Ja 12,29:2
House of Rothschild, The 1934,Mr 15,27:2
Black Moon 1934,Je 28,26:2
World Moves On, The 1934,Je 30,18:5
Outcast Lady 1934,N 3,20:3
Little Minister, The 1934,D 28,25:1
Lives of a Bengal Lancer, The 1935,Ja 12,12:2
Clive of India 1935,Ja 18,29:1
Folies Bergere 1935,F 25,13:2
Cardinal Richelieu 1935,Ap 19,24:2
Lady Tubbs 1935,Jl 22,20:2
She 1935,Jl 26,18:2
Crusades, The 1935,Ag 22,21:3
Freckles 1935,O 26,12:2
Three Musketeers, The 1935,N 1,25:1
Great Impersonation, The 1935,D 14,11:1
Professional Soldier 1936,Ja 30,14:2
Under Two Flags 1936,My 1,19:1
Princess Comes Across, The 1936,Je 4,27:2
Charge of the Light Brigade, The 1936,N 2,24:1
Lloyds of London 1936,N 26,39:1
Last of Mrs Cheyney, The 1937,F 19,15:1
Life of Emile Zola, The 1937,Ag 12,14:2
Gunga Din 1939,Ja 28,19:2
Captain Fury 1939,My 26,20:2
Northwest Passage 1940,Mr 8,25:1
Rebecca 1940,Mr 29,25:2
Dispatch From Reuters, A 1940,D 12,37:2
Hudson's Bay 1941,Ja 10,23:2
Dr Jekyll and Mr Hyde 1941,Ag 13,13:2
Gorilla Man, The 1943,Ja 15,21:4
Mission to Moscow 1943,Ap 30,25:2
Lodger, The 1944,Ja 20,15:3
Canterville Ghost, The 1944,Jl 29,16:2
Three Strangers 1946,F 23,20:2

Hare, Lumsden— Cont

Swordsman, The 1947,O 17,18:4
Exile, The 1947,D 26,22:4
Mr Peabody and the Mermaid 1948,Ag 14,6:5
Hills of Home 1948,N 26,32:2
Fighting O'Flynn, The 1949,F 28,16:2
Challenge to Lassie 1950,Ap 7,22:3
Fortunes of Captain Blood 1950,Je 10,11:3
David and Bathsheba 1951,Ag 15,23:2
My Cousin Rachel 1952,D 26,20:2
Young Bess 1953,My 22,31:1
Count Your Blessings 1959,Ap 24,23:1

Hare, Marilyn
Lady for a Night 1942,F 12,27:2

Hare, Robertson
Friday the 13th 1934,My 15,18:1
It's a Boy 1934,Je 8,18:2
Are You a Mason? 1934,O 30,23:5
Adventures of Sadie, The 1955,My 18,35:2
Hotel Paradiso 1966,O 15,34:2

Hare, Walter B (Original Author)
Aaron Slick From Punkin Crick 1952,Ap 19,18:6

Harell, Marte
Wiener Geschichten; Vienna Tales 1940,S 28,9:3
Opernball; Opera Ball 1940,O 15,29:2
Fledermaus, Die; Bat, The 1948,Mr 15,26:2

Harens, Dean
Christmas Holiday 1944,Je 29,16:1
Suspect, The 1945,F 1,18:5

Harford, Alec
Secret Sharer, The 1953,Ja 14,27:2
Botany Bay 1953,O 30,27:2
Lady Godiva 1955,D 3,13:3

Harford, Betty
Inside Daisy Clover 1966,F 18,23:1

Hargitay, Mickey
Will Success Spoil Rock Hunter 1957,S 12,37:5
Slaughter on Tenth Avenue 1957,N 6,43:1

Hargrave, Ron
Dance With Me Henry 1956,D 24,8:2

Hargreaves, Gerald Sir (Original Author)
Atlantis the Lost Continent 1961,My 27,12:1

Hargreaves, L Z (Original Author)
Battle Beneath the Earth 1968,S 12,54:3

Hargreaves, L Z (Screenwriter)
Battle Beneath the Earth 1968,S 12,54:3

Hargreaves, Robert (Composer)
Charming Deceiver, The 1933,D 9,18:3

Hargrove, Dean (Screenwriter)
One Spy too Many 1966,D 8,64:1

Hargrove, Marion (Original Author)
See Here Private Hargrove 1944,Mr 22,17:2
Girl He Left Behind, The 1956,O 27,17:1

Hargrove, Marion (Screenwriter)
Joe Butterfly 1957,My 30,23:2
Cash McCall 1960,Ja 28,26:1
Boys' Night Out 1962,Je 22,15:2
Music Man, The 1962,Ag 24,14:1
40 Pounds of Trouble 1963,Ja 24,5:2

Hari, Wilfred
Melody in Spring 1934,Mr 31,8:2
Affairs of a Gentleman 1934,Je 23,16:7

Harian, Kenneth
Drusilla With a Million 1925,My 25,21:3
Man, Woman and Wife 1928,N 5,26:5 (In Addenda)

Harian, Richard (Director)
Odio 1935,Je 24,12:3

Harien, Macey
Woman and the Puppet 1920,Ap 5,20:1

Harifal, Zaharira
Sallah 1965,O 13,39:1

Haring, Franke (Composer)
Stingaree 1934,My 18,27:1

Haritai, Zahariar (Narrator)
Six Days to Eternity 1968,O 31,54:3

Harker, Gordon
Ring, The 1927,D 25,VIII,7:7 (In Addenda)
Wrecker, The 1929,Ag 13,23:2
Farmer's Wife, The 1930,Ja 7,28:3
Escape 1930,N 1,23:2
W Plan, The 1931,Mr 23,24:7
Ringer, The 1932,Je 2,25:2
Condemned to Death 1932,Jl 14,24:2
Rome Express 1932,D 18,X,6:5
Rome Express 1933,F 27,11:2
Man they Couldn't Arrest, The 1933,Mr 14,19:3
White Face 1933,D 4,22:3
Criminal at Large 1933,D 20,27:2
Friday the 13th 1934,My 15,18:1
Amateur Gentleman, The 1936,Ap 27,19:2
Inspector Hornleigh 1939,Je 15,27:3
Facts of Love, The 1949,O 31,20:2

Harker, Jane
Love and Learn 1947,My 3,10:3
Unfaithful, The 1947,Je 28,10:2

Harkin, Dennis
Brief Encounter 1946,Ag 26,21:2
Holiday Camp 1948,Ja 24,11:2
Mr Know-All 1950,O 11,42:1

Harkins, John
Tiger Makes Out, The 1967,S 19,53:1

Harlam, Macey
Flame of the Desert 1919,O 27,9:3
Toby's Bow 1919,D 15,20:1
Right to Love, The 1920,Ag 23,9:2
When Knighthood Was in Flower 1922,S 15,17:2 (In Addenda)
Bella Donna 1923,Ap 16,20:2

Harlam, Otis
Welcome Stranger 1924,O 14,21:5

Harlan, Cris
Shepherd of the Hills, The 1928,F 20,14:1

Harlan, Kenneth
Mamma's Affair 1921,Ja 24,16:2
Nobody 1921,Jl 25,8:3
Toll of the Sea, The 1922,N 27,18:1
Beautiful and Damned, The 1922,D 11,22:1
Broken Wing, The 1923,O 9,17:4
Poisoned Paradise 1924,Ag 11,16:1
Crowded Hour, The 1925,Ap 27,15:2
Marriage Whirl, The 1925,Jl 15,22:3
Ranger of the big Trees, The 1925,Jl 28,24:4
Bobbed Hair 1925,N 4,17:4
Ice Flood, The 1926,O 19,26:2
Twinkletoes 1926,D 27,20:3
Easy Pickings 1927,Mr 25,25:3
Cheating Cheaters 1927,D 6,27:1
Streets of Shanghai 1928,F 21,19:3
United States Smith 1928,Jl 24,13:3
Women Men Marry 1931,Jl 13,13:5
Man Hunt 1936,Ja 30,14:2
Song of the Saddle 1936,Mr 21,13:3
San Francisco 1936,Je 27,21:1
Public Enemy's Wife 1936,Jl 9,17:2
China Clipper 1936,Ag 12,14:3
Case of the Velvet Claws, The 1936,Ag 29,16:3
They Met in a Taxi 1936,S 7,20:5
Flying Hostess 1936,D 14,29:4
Penrod and Sam 1937,Mr 29,14:3
Shadow Strikes, The 1937,S 13,17:1
Renfrew of the Royal Mounted 1937,N 3,29:4
Accidents Will Happen 1938,Ap 25,19:2
Under Western Stars 1938,Je 25,7:3
Duke of West Point, The 1938,D 16,33:2
On Trial 1939,Ap 5,31:2
Murder in the Air 1940,Jl 4,12:2
Little Bit of Heaven, A 1940,N 8,24:2
Pride of the Bowery 1941,Ja 24,15:2
Hitler-Dead or Alive 1943,Mr 31,23:3

Harlan, Marion
Wings of Youth 1925,Ap 20,18:1 (Incorrect in this edition; use 1925,Ap 28,18:1 elsewhere)
Thank You 1925,O 6,30:1
Tony Runs Wild 1926,Ap 28,28:3

Harlan, Martin (Director)
Papa Soltero; Bachelor Father 1939,N 6,20:3

Harlan, Otis
Barefoot Boy, The 1923,N 11,6:1
Pioneer Trails 1923,N 12,15:3
Dramatic Life of Abraham Lincoln, The 1924,Ja 22,17:3
Mademoiselle Midnight 1924,My 27,14:1
Code of the Wilderness, The 1924,Jl 1,21:4
Captain Blood 1924,S 9,19:1
Clean Heart, The 1924,S 15,28:1
Dixie Handicap, The 1924,D 30,15:3
Redeeming Sin, The 1925,Ja 20,18:2
Oh, Doctor! 1925,F 23,24:1
How Baxter Buttered In 1925,Je 23,24:3
Lightnin 1925,Jl 22,14:4
Where Was I 1925,Ag 19,14:4
Limited Mail, The 1925,S 1,18:2
What Happened to Jones 1926,F 9,22:1
Cheerful Fraud, The 1926,D 28,17:1
Don't Tell the Wife 1927,F 22,23:2
Student Prince, The 1927,S 22,33:2
Silk Stockings 1927,N 29,31:1
Good Morning, Judge 1928,Je 26,29:1
Grip of the Yukon, The 1928,Jl 10,17:3
Clear the Decks 1929,Ap 1,22:1
Show Boat 1929,Ap 18,32:3
Broadway 1929,My 28,36:2
Mississippi Gambler, The 1929,O 28,20:1
Parade of the West 1930,Mr 3,18:4
Captain of the Guard 1930,Mr 29,23:1
Dames Ahoy 1930,Mr 29,23:1
Man to Man 1931,Ja 3,21:2
Millie 1931,F 7,11:1
Big Shot, The 1932,Ja 2,14:2
That's my Boy 1932,N 21,21:1
Let's Talk It Over 1934,Je 16,20:2
Diamond Jim 1935,Ag 24,18:2
Midsummer Night's Dream, A 1935,O 10,31:1
Texans, The 1938,Jl 28,23:2

Harlan, Otis (Original Author)
Code of the Wilderness, The 1924,Jl 1,21:4

Harlan, Richard
Classmates 1924,D 30,15:3

Harlan, Veit
Meistersinger 1929,D 16,34:2
Hungarian Nights 1930,Je 10,32:2

Harlan, Veit (Director)
Muede Theodor, Der 1936,O 24,23:2
Kreutzer Sonata 1937,Mr 14,XI,4:6 (In Addenda)

Harlan, Veit (Director)— Cont

Maria, Die Magd 1937,My 22,19:2
Ruler, The 1937,O 16,22:3
Trouble Back Stairs; Krach im Hinterhaus 1937,D 4,21:1
Kater Lampe 1938,Ap 23,19:3
Kreutzer Sonata, The 1938,My 28,9:3
Alles Fuer Veronika 1939,F 4,11:2
Verwehte Spuren; Covered Tracks 1939,O 14,13:3
Unsterbliche Herz, Das; Immortal Heart, The 1939,O 21,12:2
Reise Nach Tilsit, Die; Trip to Tilsit, The 1940,F 10,19:2
Third Sex, The 1959,Mr 26,27:1

Harlan, Veit (Producer)
Jugend; Youth 1939,D 9,18:2

Harlem Globetrotters
Go, Man, Go 1954,Mr 10,29:5

Harlin, Friedl
Tanzhusar, Der 1933,Ap 10,8:4

Harline, Leigh (Composer)
Snow White and the Seven Dwarfs 1938,Ja 14,21:1 (In Addenda)
Pinocchio 1940,F 8,18:3
Music in Manhattan 1944,O 7,11:2
George White's Scandals 1945,O 11,26:2

Harline, Leigh (Miscellaneous)
Mr Bug Goes to Town 1942,F 20,21:3

Harling, Jack
Gift of Gab 1934,S 26,17:6

Harlow, Jean
Hell's Angels 1930,Ag 16,8:3
Iron Man 1931,Ap 18,17:3
Public Enemy, The 1931,Ap 24,27:1
Secret Six, The 1931,My 2,23:4
Goldie 1931,Je 29,20:3
Platinum Blonde 1931,O 31,22:2
Three Wise Girls 1932,F 6,14:4
Beast of the City, The 1932,Mr 14,13:3
Red Headed Woman 1932,Jl 1,19:3
Red Dust 1932,N 5,12:5
Hold Your Man 1933,Jl 1,16:6
Dinner at Eight 1933,Ag 24,18:1
Bombshell 1933,O 21,11:2
Girl From Missouri, The 1934,Ag 4,14:6
Reckless 1935,Ap 20,16:1
China Seas 1935,Ag 10,16:4
Riffraff 1936,Ja 13,14:2
Wife vs Secretary 1936,F 29,11:1
Suzy 1936,Jl 25,16:1
Libeled Lady 1936,O 31,24:2
Personal Property 1937,Ap 11,27:2
Saratoga 1937,Jl 23,16:3
Further Perils of Laurel and Hardy, The 1968,Ap 1,56:6
Queen, The 1968,Je 18,37:1

Harlow, John (Director)
Agitator, The 1949,Ag 19,12:5
Appointment With Crime 1951,F 19,19:3

Harlow, John (Screenwriter)
Appointment With Crime 1951,F 19,19:3

Harmer, Elsie
Bowery, The 1933,O 5,24:2

Harmer, Lillian
She-Wolf 1931,My 28,30:6
Huckleberry Finn 1931,Ag 8,16:3
Smart Woman 1931,O 12,28:2
New Morals for Old 1932,Je 24,15:3
Guilty as Hell 1932,Ag 6,14:5
No Man of her Own 1932,D 31,10:1
Shriek in the Night, A 1933,Jl 24,11:2
Alice in Wonderland 1933,D 23,19:1
Lady by Choice 1934,N 17,12:1
Romance in Manhattan 1935,Ja 18,29:2
Public Hero No 1 1935,Je 8,12:2
Three Kids and a Queen 1935,N 9,19:2
Don't Get Personal 1936,F 22,12:1
Dancing Feet 1936,Mr 28,11:2
Fugitive in the Sky 1937,Ja 16,21:1

Harmon, David (Original Author)
Johnny Concho 1956,Ag 16,30:1
Big Beat, The 1958,Je 26,23:4

Harmon, David (Screenwriter)
Johnny Concho 1956,Ag 16,30:1
Wonderful World of the Brothers Grimm, The 1962,Ag 8,35:1
Wonderful World of the Brothers Grimm, The (The Singing Bone); Singing Bone, The (The Wonderful World of the Brothers Grimm) 1962,Ag 8,35:1
Wonderful World of the Brothers Grimm, The (The Cobbler and the Elves); Cobbler and the Elves, The (The Wonderful World of the Brothers Grimm) 1962,Ag 8,35:1
Wonderful World of the Brothers Grimm, The (The Dancing Princess); Dancing Princess, The (The Wonderful World of the Brothers Grimm) 1962,Ag 8,35:1
Dark Purpose 1964,F 6,36:4

Harmon, Francis S (Miscellaneous)
Land of Liberty 1939,Je 16,27:3
Land of Liberty 1941,Ja 30,19:2

Harmon, Henry
Out of the Fog 1919,F 10,11:3
Stronger Than Death 1920,Ja 12,7:1
Old Lady 31 1920,My 24,20:3
Harmon, John
Gambling Ship 1939,Ja 21,19:2
Gangs of Chicago 1940,Je 13,29:2
Fugitive From Justice, A 1940,Jl 8,13:3
Devil's Island 1940,Jl 12,11:4
Hit the Road 1941,Jl 3,15:3
Pittsburgh Kid, The 1941,S 23,27:4
Dangerously They Live 1942,Ap 11,9:2
I Was Framed 1942,Je 12,16:6
Truck Busters 1943,Ja 29,23:5
Lady Gambles, The 1949,My 21,9:2
Crooked Way, The 1949,S 5,13:2
Man in the Dark 1953,Ap 9,31:5
Jack Slade 1953,O 29,42:6
Harmon, Julian (Screenwriter)
Unknown, The 1946,Jl 20,10:3
Harmon, Marie
Ladies Courageous 1944,Mr 16,17:2
Not Wanted 1949,Jl 25,11:4
Harmon, Pat
Eternal Struggle, The 1923,O 16,21:3
Midnight Express, The 1924,N 19,19:3
Barriers Burned Away 1925,Mr 12,17:2
Freshman, The 1925,S 21,12:4
Barrier, The 1926,Mr 22,16:1
Haunted Ship, The 1928,Ja 23,18:3
Waterfront 1928,O 22,29:1
Sal of Singapore 1929,Ja 29,27:1
Gang Buster, The 1931,Ja 24,15:1
Teen Age 1944,Je 19,17:1
Freshman, The 1953,Ap 28,31:6
Harmon, Sidney (Original Author)
Hand in Hand 1961,F 7,41:3
Harmon, Sidney (Producer)
Big Combo, The 1955,Mr 26,13:2
Wild Party, The 1956,D 22,13:1
Men in War 1957,Mr 20,32:4
God's Little Acre 1958,Ag 14,23:2
Anna Lucasta 1959,Ja 15,27:1
Thin Red Line, The 1964,O 29,38:1
Harmon, Sidney (Screenwriter)
Mutiny 1952,Mr 20,37:5
Harmon, Stanley (Original Author)
Mara Maru 1952,Ap 24,38:1
Harmon, Steve
One and Only Genuine Original Family Band,
The 1968,Mr 22,55:1
Harmon, Tom
Harmon of Michigan 1941,O 2,29:2
Spirit of West Point 1947,O 3,31:2
That's My Boy 1951,Ag 2,18:1
Off Limits 1953,Mr 30,25:5
Harnack, Falk (Director)
Tempestous Love 1958,N 22,27:4
Harnett, Sunny
Funny Face 1957,Mr 29,16:1
Harney, Lilian
Hocuspocus 1930,Ag 3,VIII,4:1
Harold
Pan-Americana 1945,Mr 23,13:2
Harolde, Ralf
Officer O'Brien 1930,F 24,18:1
Framed 1930,Mr 29,23:1
Dixiana 1930,S 5,21:1
Hook, Line and Sinker 1930,D 25,31:5
Smart Money 1931,Je 19,21:1
Night Nurse 1931,Jl 17,23:4
Alexander Hamilton 1931,S 17,21:4
Tip Off, The 1931,O 26,22:1
Safe in Hell 1931,D 19,16:4
Secret Witness, The 1931,D 21,28:4
Expert, The 1932,F 27,22:1
Winner Take All 1932,Je 18,9:2
Hollywood Speaks 1932,Ag 12,18:2
Billion Dollar Scandal, The 1933,Ja 9,23:1
Picture Snatcher 1933,My 19,20:3
Cheating Blondes 1933,My 20,11:4
Night Flight 1933,O 7,18:4
Deluge 1933,O 9,22:3
I'm no Angel 1933,O 14,18:2
Jimmy the Gent 1934,Mr 26,22:3
Witching Hour, The 1934,Ap 28,11:3
He Was her Man 1934,My 17,28:2
Baby, Take a Bow 1934,Je 30,18:6
She Loves Me Not 1934,S 8,18:5
Perfect Clue, The 1935,Mr 14,18:1
Stolen Harmony 1935,Ap 20,16:2
Million Dollar Baby 1935,My 6,22:3
Great God Gold 1935,My 6,22:3
Silk Hat Kid 1935,Ag 7,22:5
Tale of Two Cities, A 1935,D 26,21:2
If You Could Only Cook 1935,D 26,21:4
Song and Dance Man 1936,Mr 12,18:2
Fifteen Maiden Lane 1936,O 17,21:3
Our Relations 1936,N 11,55:1
Accusing Finger, The 1936,N 17,35:4
Her Husband Lies 1937,Mr 18,20:1
One Mile From Heaven 1937,Ag 19,23:1
Conquest 1937,N 5,19:1

Sea Wolf, The 1941,Mr 26,27:3
Horror Island 1941,Mr 31,11:3
No Greater Sin 1941,Ag 29,18:2
Broadway 1942,Je 5,23:2
Sin Town 1942,O 17,11:2
Murder, my Sweet 1945,Mr 9,16:2
Jewels of Brandenburg 1947,My 24,10:5
Harp, Kenneth
Fear and Desire 1953,Ap 1,35:2
Harper, Betty
Jigsaw 1949,My 30,9:4
Harper, Bruce
Guilt of Janet Ames, The 1947,My 23,31:2
Harper, Gerald
Admirable Crichton, The 1957,D 15,45:4
(Incorrect in this edition; use 1957,D 17,45:4
elsewhere)
Tunes of Glory 1960,D 21,38:2
Harper, Kenneth (Producer)
Blonde Sinner 1957,Ja 24,34:1
Action of the Tiger 1957,N 14,41:1
Prudence and the Pill 1968,My 24,37:1
Harper, Rand
Rear Window 1954,Ag 5,18:2
Harper's Bizarre
You Are What You Eat 1968,S 25,38:1
Harprecht, Bruno
Streitum den Knaben Jo; Strife Over the Boy Jo
1938,D 10,13:2
Harradine, Archie
Mr Perrin and Mr Traill 1949,Ja 17,15:2
Harrat, Robert
Road to Rio 1948,F 19,29:3
Harriet, Judy
Say One for Me 1959,Je 20,11:2
Harrigan, Nedda
Laughing Lady, The 1930,Ja 4,21:1
I'll Fix It 1934,N 12,17:3
Charlie Chan at the Opera 1936,D 5,16:2
Case of the Black Cat, The 1936,D 26,15:4
Fugitive in the Sky 1937,Ja 16,21:1
Thank You, Mr Moto 1938,Ja 3,16:2
Trip to Paris, A 1938,Je 10,18:2
Men Are Such Fools 1938,Je 17,25:1
On Trial 1939,Ap 5,31:2
Castle on the Hudson 1940,Mr 4,11:2
Devil's Island 1940,Jl 12,11:4
Harrigan, Robert
Cardinal Richelieu 1935,Ap 19,24:2
Harrigan, William
Cabaret 1927,My 2,26:4
Nix on Dames 1929,N 23,18:5
Born Reckless 1930,Je 7,10:4
On the Level 1930,Jl 5,17:4
Pick Up 1933,Mr 25,13:4
Girl in 419 1933,My 20,11:5
Disgraced 1933,Jl 15,14:2
Invisible Man, The 1933,N 18,18:4
G Men 1935,My 2,17:1
Stranded 1935,Je 20,16:2
Silk Hat Kid 1935,Ag 7,22:5
Melody Lingers on, The 1935,N 7,27:1
Whipsaw 1936,Ja 25,18:4
Over the Goal 1937,O 16,22:2
Federal Bullets 1937,D 27,11:1
Hawaii Calls 1938,Ap 29,17:2
Back Door to Heaven 1939,Ap 20,21:2
Farmer's Daughter, The 1947,Mr 26,31:2
Desert Fury 1947,S 25,35:4
Citizen Saint 1948,My 28,28:2
Flying Leathernecks 1951,S 20,37:1
Steel Town 1952,My 10,16:4
Harring, Aggie
Island in the Sky 1938,My 14,18:1
Harrington, Curtis (Director)
Night Tide 1963,Je 7,37:1
Games 1967,S 18,58:2
Harrington, Curtis (Original Author)
Mardi Gras 1958,N 19,45:2
Games 1967,S 18,58:2
Harrington, Curtis (Screenwriter)
Night Tide 1963,Je 7,37:1
Harrington, James
Red Menace, The 1949,Je 27,18:2
Harrington, Joe
Freshman, The 1925,S 21,12:4
Freshman, The 1953,Ap 28,31:6
Harrington, John
Street of Forgotten Men, The 1925,Jl 21,26:2
Man Who Found Himself, The 1925,Ag 24,17:3
Tin Gods 1926,S 20,21:3
Rubber Heels 1927,Je 28,29:4
Local Boy Makes Good 1931,N 27,29:3
Swing Time 1936,Ag 28,21:2
Big Game, The 1936,O 24,23:1
Counterfeit Lady 1937,Ja 11,15:6
Step Lively, Jeeves 1937,Ap 2,19:6
Dangerously Yours 1937,O 18,14:2
Harrington, Joseph (Original Author)
Dr Kildare's Victory 1942,F 5,25:2
Harrington, Joy
My Name is Julia Ross 1945,N 9,16:3
Madness of the Heart 1950,O 12,43:2

Harrington, Kate
Rachel Rachel 1968,Ag 27,36:1
Harrington, Mary Lou
My Favorite Wife 1940,My 31,15:2
It Comes up Love 1943,Ja 22,25:3
Harrington, Mildred (Original Author)
Turn off the Moon 1937,My 20,17:2
Harrington, Pat Jr
Stage Struck 1958,Ap 23,40:1
Wheeler Dealers, The 1963,N 15,25:2
Move Over Darling 1963,D 26,33:1
Easy Come, Easy Go 1967,Je 15,56:1
President's Analyst, The 1967,D 22,44:4
Harris, Al
Tevya 1939,D 22,15:3
Harris, Albert
State Fair 1962,Ap 12,41:4
Harris, Averill
Secrets of a Secretary 1931,Ag 29,16:3
His Woman 1931,D 5,21:2
Harris, Barbara
Thousand Clowns, A 1965,D 14,54:2
Oh Dad, Poor Dad, Mamma's Hung You in the
Closet and I'm Feeling so Sad 1967,F 16,32:1
Harris, Brad
Monkey on my Back 1957,My 30,23:2
Harris, Buddy
Lying Wives 1925,Je 17,16:2
Harris, Charles K
After the Ball 1929,O 8,24:5
Harris, Charles K (Original Author)
Bridge of Sighs, The 1925,Mr 23,14:2
Chicago After Midnight 1928,Mr 6,20:3
Harris, Christopher
Lord of the Flies 1963,Ag 20,37:1
Harris, Corra (Original Author)
I'd Climb the Highest Mountain 1951,My 10,38:1
Harris, Crampton (Original Author)
Professor Beware 1938,Jl 14,17:1
Harris, Dare
I'll Be Seeing You 1945,Ap 6,20:6
Harris, Dorothy
White Witch Doctor 1953,Jl 2,19:3
Harris, Edna M
Green Pastures, The 1936,Jl 17,20:1
Spirit of Youth 1938,F 28,19:1
Harris, Eleanor (Original Author)
Every Girl Should be Married 1948,D 24,14:2
Harris, Eleanor (Screenwriter)
Kidnapped 1938,My 28,9:2
Harris, Elmer
Garrison's Finish 1923,My 28,18:2
Harris, Elmer (Original Author)
Sham 1921,My 6,20:2
Forbidden Woman, The 1927,O 31,22:1
Father and Son 1929,Je 4,29:3
Let 'Em Have It 1935,My 30,21:1
Johnny Belinda 1948,O 2,11:2
Harris, Elmer (Screenwriter)
Lottery Man, The 1919,O 6,15:1
Three Wise Guys, The 1936,My 23,12:2
Harris, Frank (Original Author)
Cowboy 1958,F 20,29:5
Harris, George
Lights of Old Broadway 1925,N 2,20:1
Harris, Gordon
Touch of Larceny, A 1960,Mr 17,28:1
Murder at the Gallop 1963,Je 25,23:2
Harris, Howard (Miscellaneous)
Higher and Higher 1944,Ja 22,8:4
Harris, Howard (Screenwriter)
Copacabana 1947,Jl 12,7:2
Noose Hangs High, The 1948,My 29,8:6
Harris, Ivy
Fascinating Youth 1926,My 10,19:1
Potters, The 1927,Ja 18,23:1
Gentleman of Paris, A 1927,O 3,20:1
Three Sinners 1928,Ap 23,20:2
Just Married 1928,Ag 13,23:2
Harris, Jack H (Producer)
Dinosaurusi 1960,S 9,36:4
Oldest Profession, The (Mademoiselle Mimi);
Mademoiselle Mimi (The Oldest Profession)
1968,N 8,42:1
Oldest Profession, The (Anticipation); Anticipation
(The Oldest Profession) 1968,N 8,42:1
Oldest Profession, The (Paris Today); Paris Today
(The Oldest Profession) 1968,N 8,42:1
Oldest Profession, The (Gay Nineties, The); Gay
Nineties, The (The Oldest Profession)
1968,N 8,42:1
Oldest Profession, The (Roman Nights); Roman
Nights (The Oldest Profession) 1968,N 8,42:1
Oldest Profession, The (Prehistoric Era);
Prehistoric Era (The Oldest Profession)
1968,N 8,42:1
Harris, James B (Director)
Bedford Incident, The 1965,N 3,43:1
Harris, James B (Producer)
Killing, The 1956,My 21,20:1
Paths of Glory 1957,D 26,23:2
Lolita 1962,Je 14,23:2
Bedford Incident, The 1965,N 3,43:1

Harris, Jane
River, The 1951,S 11,33:2
Harris, Jed (Original Author)
Light Touch, The 1952,Ja 17,23:1
Night People 1954,Mr 13,11:2
Harris, Jed (Producer)
Operation Mad Ball 1957,N 21,38:1
Harris, Jed (Screenwriter)
Operation Mad Ball 1957,N 21,38:1
Harris, Jennifer
River, The 1951,S 11,33:2
Harris, Jeel Chandler (Original Author)
Song of the South 1946,N 28,40:2
Harris, Jonathan
Botany Bay 1953,O 30,27:2
Big Fisherman, The 1959,Ag 6,18:1
Harris, Judy
Wild River 1960,My 27,22:1
Harris, Julie
Member of the Wedding, The 1952,D 31,10:2
East of Eden 1955,Mr 10,33:1
I Am a Camera 1955,Ag 9,29:1
Truth About Women, The 1958,Ag 29,18:2
Poacher's Daughter, The 1960,F 16,31:2
Requiem for a Heavyweight 1962,O 17,35:1
Haunting, The 1963,S 19,23:1
Harper 1966,Mr 31,43:1
You're a Big Boy Now 1967,Mr 21,35:3
Reflections in a Golden Eye 1967,O 12,59:1
Split, The 1968,N 5,55:2
Harris, Julius
Nothing but a Man 1964,S 21,37:2
Harris, Katherine
Bitter Sweet 1940,N 22,27:1
Harris, Kathlyn (Screenwriter)
Broadway Gold 1923,Jl 31,12:4
Harris, Kay
Parachute Nurse 1942,Jl 27,18:2
Sabotage Squad 1942,Ag 5,16:1
Harris, Leland
All About Eve 1950,O 14,13:2
Harris, Lionel
Tales of Hoffmann 1951,Ap 5,34:2
Ivanhoe 1952,Ag 1,8:2
Brandy for the Parson 1952,Ag 18,13:4
Harris, Marcia
Prunelia 1918,Je 3,9:3
Anne of Green Gables 1919,D 22,18:3
Fighting Blade, The 1923,O 15,15:4
On the Banks of the Wabash 1923,O 23,21:3
Isn't Life Wonderful? 1924,D 1,17:3
King on Main Street, The 1925,O 26,25:2
Reckless Lady, The 1926,Ja 25,21:2
Sorrows of Satan, The 1926,O 13,21:1
So's Your Old Man 1926,N 1,28:2
Love 'Em and Leave 'Em 1926,D 8,24:3
Music Master, The 1927,Ja 17,12:4 (In Addenda)
Take Me Home 1928,O 23,33:1
Saturday's Children 1929,Ap 29,29:2
Greene Murder Case, The 1929,Ag 10,11:3
Big Trail, The 1930,O 25,20:3
Young as You Feel 1931,Ag 8,16:3
Three Wise Girls 1932,F 6,14:4
Harris, Maria
Sinners in Heaven 1924,S 10,21:3
Harris, Marilyn
Frankenstein 1931,D 5,21:2
Wicked Woman, A 1935,Ja 1,24:1
Harris, Marion
Devil May Care 1929,D 23,18:2
Harris, Marion Jr
Galloping Major, The 1951,D 17,27:2
Harris, Mildred
For Husbands Only 1918,S 2,7:1
Prince There Was 1921,N 14,18:1
Fool's Paradise 1921,D 10,11:4
Flaming Love 1925,Ja 19,14:1
Dressmaker from Paris, The 1925,Mr 18,19:2
Private Affairs 1925,Jl 15,22:3
Heart of a Follies Girl, The 1928,Mr 12,26:1
Melody of Love 1928,O 22,29:1
No, No, Nanette 1930,Ja 4,21:1
Harris, Mitchell
Sea Wolf, The 1930,O 6,21:1
Connecticut Yankee, A 1931,Ap 13,17:1
Peach O'Reno 1931,D 24,20:8
Scandal for Sale 1932,Ap 3,26:2
Hypnotized 1933,Ja 16,13:3
Victims of Persecution 1933,Je 17,16:6
Connecticut Yankee at the Court of King Arthur, A 1936,My 4,16:1
Harris, Owen (Screenwriter)
Secret of Deep Harbor 1961,O 26,39:7
Incident in an Alley 1962,My 17,31:1
Harris, Pamela (Original Author)
Tin Pan Alley 1940,N 22,27:3
I'll Get by 1950,N 2,39:3
Harris, Phil
Melody Cruise 1933,Je 23,15:2
Man About Town 1939,Je 29,19:1
Buck Benny Rides Again 1940,Ap 25,28:4
Wabash Avenue 1950,Ap 29,8:3
Here Comes the Groom 1951,S 21,19:2

Starlift 1951,D 15,11:2
Wild Blue Yonder, The 1952,Ja 2,20:1
Glenn Miller Story, the 1954,F 11,33:2
High and the Mighty, The 1954,Jl 1,21:2
Anything Goes 1956,Mr 22,38:1
Wheeler Dealers, The 1963,N 15,25:2
Patsy, The 1964,Ag 13,24:2
Cool Ones, The 1967,My 11,50:1
Harris, Ray (Original Author)
Story of Alexander Graham Bell, The 1939,Ap 1,17:2
Harris, Ray (Screenwriter)
Youth for Sale 1924,S 3,17:1
Say It Again 1926,Je 7,23:2
Rubber Heels 1927,Je 28,29:4
Man Power 1927,Jl 26,17:1
Sporting Goods 1928,F 13,16:2
Enchanted April 1935,Mr 9,19:1
Laddie 1935,My 6,22:3
Hooray for Love 1935,Jl 13,16:2
Man on the Flying Trapeze 1935,Ag 3,16:2
Dancing Pirate 1936,Je 18,19:1
Harris, Richard
Wreck of the Mary Deare, The 1959,N 7,27:1
Night Fighters, The 1960,D 15,59:1
Guns of Navarone, The 1961,Je 23,19:1
Jungle Fighters 1962,Mr 15,28:2
Mutiny on the Bounty 1962,N 9,31:2
This Sporting Life 1963,Jl 17,19:2
Red Desert 1965,F 9,43:1
Major Dundee 1965,Ap 8,45:1
Heroes of Telemark, The 1966,Mr 10,26:1
Bible, The 1966,S 29,60:1
Hawaii 1966,O 11,54:1
Caprice 1967,Je 8,52:2
Camelot 1967,O 26,54:1
Harris, Robert
How He Lied to her Husband 1931,Ja 17,23:1
For Them that Trespass 1950,S 27,37:2
Laughing Anne 1954,My 8,15:2
Big Caper, The 1957,Mr 29,16:1
Abandon Ship 1957,Ap 18,35:1
No Down Payment 1957,O 31,41:1
Fuzzy Pink Nightgown, The 1957,O 31,41:1
Peyton Place 1957,D 13,35:1
Oscar Wilde 1960,Je 21,28:2
Convicts 4 1962,O 4,44:2
America America 1963,D 16,44:1
Model Murder Case, The 1964,N 25,45:1
Mirage 1965,My 27,28:1
Valley of the Dolls 1967,D 16,51:1
Harris, Robert (Original Author)
Werewolf of London, The 1935,My 10,25:2
Harris, Robin (Original Author)
One Mile From Heaven 1937,Ag 19,23:1
Harris, Robin (Screenwriter)
City Girl 1938,F 4,17:3
Harris, Ronald
Rebecca of Sunnybrook Farm 1932,Jl 30,16:5
Jane Eyre 1944,F 4,12:5
Harris, Rosemary
Beau Brummell 1954,O 21,31:5
Flea in her Ear, A 1968,N 28,66:1
Harris, Roy
Flying Cadets 1941,O 14,29:2
Bombay Clipper 1942,Ja 12,23:3
North to the Klondike 1942,Mr 12,24:3
Harris, Sam Major
I Cover the War 1937,Ag 2,10:2
Harris, Sibyl
Bunker Bean 1936,Je 27,21:2
Mountain Justice 1937,My 13,31:2
They Won't Forget 1937,Jl 15,16:1
Crime School 1938,My 11,17:2
Federal Man-Hunt 1939,F 2,17:3
Untamed 1940,Jl 25,14:3
Harris, Slim
Safari 1956,Je 21,35:2
Harris, Stacy
Appointment With Danger 1951,My 10,38:2
Great Sioux Uprising, The 1953,Jl 18,6:2
Dragnet 1954,Ag 21,10:2
New Orleans Uncensored 1955,Ap 30,10:8
Harris, Steve
Ice Palace 1960,Je 30,22:1
Yellow Canary, The 1963,My 16,42:1
Harris, Theresa
Baby Face 1933,Je 24,16:2
Hold Your Man 1933,Jl 1,16:6
Jezebel 1938,Mr 11,15:2
Toy Wife, The 1938,Je 24,15:1
Tell no Tales 1939,Je 2,27:3
Buck Benny Rides Again 1940,Ap 25,28:4
Love Thy Neighbor 1940,D 18,32:5
Flame of New Orleans, The 1941,Ap 26,20:2
Blossoms in the Dust 1941,Je 27,14:4
Our Wife 1941,S 18,31:1
Cat People 1942,D 7,22:2
I Walked With a Zombie 1943,Ap 22,31:5
What's Buzzin Cousin 1943,Jl 23,21:4
Miracle on 34th Street 1947,Je 5,32:1
Thelma Jordon 1950,Ja 19,35:2
Grounds for Marriage 1951,Ja 12,24:6

Harris, Vernon
Troopship 1938,Ap 26,18:2
Harris, Vernon (Screenwriter)
Hundred Hour Hunt 1953,Je 17,32:2
Admirable Crichton, The 1957,D 15,45:4 (Incorrect in this edition; use 1957,D 17,45:4 elsewhere)
Cry From the Streets, A 1959,F 24,32:2
3 Men in a Boat 1959,Jl 29,33:2
Ferry to Hong Kong 1961,Ap 27,27:7
Almost Angels 1962,N 1,34:2
Oliver! 1968,D 11,57:1
Harris, Winifred
Love Doctor, The 1929,N 9,22:5
Fast and Loose 1930,D 1,21:1
Night Must Fall 1937,Ap 30,17:2
Life of the Party, The 1937,O 4,17:1
Kid From Kokomo, The 1939,My 20,11:2
Kid Nightingale 1939,D 8,33:6
British Intelligence 1940,F 12,14:2
Claudia 1943,N 5,23:2
Four Jills in a Jeep 1944,Ap 6,27:2
That Hagen Girl 1947,O 25,13:2
Harris and Shore
Letter, The 1940,N 23,12:6
Harrison, Charles
We're Going to Be Rich 1938,Jl 4,10:2
Harrison, David
Darling 1965,Ag 4,20:1
Harrison, Dennis
Guilty Bystander 1950,Ap 21,18:2
Harrison, Edward (Producer)
Kanchenjungha 1966,Jl 26,27:2
Harrison, George
Hard Day's Night, A 1964,Ag 12,41:1
Help! 1965,Ag 24,25:1
Harrison, Howard (Producer)
Strange Affair, The 1968,Jl 25,26:2
Harrison, Irma
One Exciting Night 1922,O 24,17:3
Alibi 1929,Ap 9,29:1
Harrison, James
Charley's Aunt 1925,F 9,15:3
Stop Flirting 1925,Je 18,16:3
Lawless Nineties, The 1936,Je 29,11:1
Vengeance Valley 1951,F 16,21:2
Harrison, Joan (Producer)
Uncle Harry 1945,Ag 24,14:5
Nocturne 1946,N 11,42:2
They Won't Believe Me 1947,Jl 17,16:2
Ride the Pink Horse 1947,O 9,32:3
Once More, my Darling 1949,S 26,17:1
Eye Witness 1950,Ag 28,13:2
Circle of Danger 1951,Jl 12,21:6
Harrison, Joan (Screenwriter)
Jamaica Inn 1939,O 12,33:1
Rebecca 1940,Mr 29,25:2
Foreign Correspondent 1940,Ag 28,15:2
Suspicion 1941,N 21,23:2
Saboteur 1942,My 8,27:2
Dark Waters 1944,N 22,25:2
Harrison, June
Bringing Up Father 1946,N 22,27:3
Citizen Saint 1948,My 28,28:2
Harrison, Kathleen
Ghoul, The 1934,Ja 27,9:2
Broken Blossoms 1937,Ja 14,16:3
Night Must Fall 1937,Ap 30,17:2
Outsider, The 1940,Mr 18,13:2
Girl in the News, The 1941,My 5,13:2
Girl Must Live, A 1942,Mr 24,25:2
In Which We Serve 1942,D 24,18:1
Wanted for Murder 1946,D 12,38:4
Holiday Camp 1948,Ja 24,11:2
Temptation Harbor 1949,My 11,34:7
Bond Street 1950,Mr 30,40:6
Winslow Boy, The 1950,Je 7,34:4
Verger, The 1950,O 11,42:1
Here Come the Huggetts 1950,D 25,25:3
Oliver Twist 1951,Jl 31,17:2
Christmas Carol, A 1951,N 29,41:2
Mr Lord Says No! 1952,F 12,22:5
Double Confession 1953,My 1,17:2
Landfall 1953,My 11,25:2
Turn the Key Softly 1954,F 4,21:6
Pickwick Papers, The 1954,Ap 5,21:2
Gay Adventure, The 1954,S 16,35:7
Cast a Dark Shadow 1957,N 28,57:1
Cry From the Streets, A 1959,F 24,32:2
Operation Snafu 1965,My 22,18:1
Harrison, Linda
Planet of the Apes 1968,F 9,55:2
Harrison, Lottie
Lost in a Harem 1944,N 9,23:2
Harrison, Marguerite (Producer)
Grass 1925,Mr 31,17:4
Harrison, Michael
Stage Door Canteen 1943,Je 25,13:2
Janie 1944,Ag 5,16:2
Harrison, Noel
Best of Enemies, The 1962,Ag 7,35:2

Harrison, Rex
Men Are not Gods 1937,Ja 19,28:1
Storm in a Teacup 1938,Mr 22,18:4
Citadel, The 1938,N 4,27:2
School for Husbands 1939,F 7,16:2
Sidewalks of London 1940,F 15,15:1
Night Train 1940,D 30,21:1
Missing Ten Days 1941,Ap 21,15:5 (In Addenda)
Major Barbara 1941,My 15,27:1
Continental Express 1942,Ap 7,26:3
Blithe Spirit 1945,O 4,27:2
Yank in London, A 1946,Ap 20,16:3
Anna and the King of Siam 1946,Je 21,20:2
Notorious Gentleman 1946,N 14,39:3
Ghost and Mrs Muir, The 1947,Je 27,17:2
Foxes of Harrow, The 1947,S 25,35:4
Escape 1948,Ag 16,12:2
Unfaithfully Yours 1948,N 6,9:2
Long Dark Hall, The 1951,My 10,38:3
Four Poster, The 1952,O 16,37:1
Main Street to Broadway 1953,O 14,34:1
King Richard and the Crusaders 1954,Ag 23,20:5
Constant Husband, The 1957,Jl 26,10:3
Reluctant Debutante, The 1958,Ag 15,17:1
Midnight Lace 1960,O 14,27:1
Happy Thieves, The 1962,F 5,19:4
Cleopatra 1963,Je 13,29:1
My Fair Lady 1964,O 22,41:1
Yellow Rolls-Royce, The 1965,My 14,42:2
Agony and the Ecstacy, The 1965,O 9,5:6
Honey Pot, The 1967,My 23,52:1
Doctor Dolittle 1967,D 20,55:1
Flea in her Ear, A 1968,N 28,66:1
Harrison, Richard
Constant Husband, The 1955,N 7,55:1
Kronos 1957,My 11,24:6
Master of the World 1961,S 16,9:1
Gladiators Seven 1964,My 7,31:2
Harrison, Stephen S
Blue Grass of Kentucky 1950,Ja 27,29:2
Harrison, Susan
Sweet Smell of Success 1957,Je 28,29:2
Harrison, Tom (Miscellaneous)
Mr Perrin and Mr Traill 1949,Ja 17,15:2
Harrison, Walter
Juliet of the Spirits 1965,N 4,57:1
Harrity, Rory
Where the Boys Are 1961,Ja 20,22:1
Harrold, Scott
This'll Make You Whistle 1938,N 1,27:2
Harron, Donald
Best of Everything 1959,O 9,24:2
Harron, John
Penrod 1922,F 20,7:1
Dulcy 1923,S 17,18:2
Learning to Love 1925,F 23,24:1
My Wife and I · 1925,My 20,26:2
Woman Hater, The 1925,Jl 13,20:2
Wife Who Wasn't Wanted, The 1925,S 9,23:1
Below the Line 1925,S 21,12:4
Satan in Sables 1925,O 15,27:3
Bride of the Storm 1926,Ap 5,24:1
Night Cry, The 1926,Ap 7,26:6
Hell-Bent for Heaven 1926,My 4,31:1
Little Irish Girl, The 1926,My 11,24:3
Closed Gates 1927,Je 1,25:2
Silk Stockings 1927,N 29,31:1
Night Life 1927,D 20,33:2
Finders Keepers 1928,Mr 5,21:3
Street Girl 1929,Jl 31,17:3
Czar of Broadway, The 1930,Je 30,22:6
Big Boy 1930,S 13,9:3
Laugh and get Rich 1931,Mr 28,15:3
White Zombie 1932,Jl 29,18:2
Missing Witness 1937,O 10,33:3
Invisible Menace, The 1938,F 14,20:6
Torchy Gets her Man 1938,N 18,25:3
Indianapolis Speedway 1939,Jl 15,8:2
Harron, Robert
Marriage of Molly-O, The 1916,Jl 24,7:4
Hearts of the World 1918,Ap 5,13:1
Great Love, The 1918,Ag 12,7:1
Greatest Thing in Life, The 1918,D 23,9:1
Romance of Happy Valley, A 1919,Ja 27,11:4
Girl Who Stayed Home, The 1919,Mr 24,11:3
True Heart Susie 1919,Je 2,20:4
Hearts of the World 1919,Ag 12,7:6
Mother and the Law, The 1919,Ag 19,10:1
Greatest Question, The 1919,D 29,7:2
Birth of a Nation, The 1921,My 2,12:1
Birth of a Nation, The 1922,D 5,24:3
Harryhausen, Ray (Composer)
Seventh Voyage of Sinbad 1958,D 24,00:0
Harryhausen, Ray (Miscellaneous)
Animal World, The 1956,My 31,21:6
Harsanyi, Rezso
Iza Neni 1934,Je 5,28:6
Oeroek Titok, Az; Eternal Secret, The
1940,Mr 9,19:3
HART
See Also HARTE

Hart, Adriana
Seven Hills of Rome 1958,Ja 28,24:2 (Incorrect
in this edition; use 1958,Ja 31,24:2 elsewhere)
Hart, Al
Doubling for Romeo 1921,O 24,13:1
Man Without a Country, The 1925,F 12,16:1
Pony Express, The 1925,S 14,16:1
Honor Bound 1928,Ap 30,18:3
American Tragedy, An 1931,Ag 6,22:5
Hart, Bertha
Power of Life 1938,Ap 29,17:2
Hart, Bob
Joanna 1925,D 15,14:5
Hart, Charles
Juvenile Court 1938,S 12,13:2
Green Grass of Wyoming 1948,Je 10,28:3
Hart, David
Long Is the Road 1948,N 12,30:5
Hart, Diane
Forbidden Street, The 1949,My 14,9:2
Happy Go Lovely 1951,Jl 26,17:2
Pickwick Papers, The 1954,Ap 5,21:2
Hart, Dolores
Loving You 1957,Jl 18,19:2
Wild Is the Wind 1957,D 12,35:1
King Creole 1958,Jl 4,15:2
Lonelyhearts 1959,Mr 5,35:3
Where the Boys Are 1961,Ja 20,22:1
Francis of Assisi 1961,Jl 29,8:2
Sail a Crooked Ship 1962,F 3,12:6
Lisa 1962,My 25,28:1
Come Fly With Me 1963,My 2,40:2
Hart, Dorothy
Gunfighters 1947,Jl 25,12:5
Naked City, The 1948,Mr 5,17:2
Larceny 1948,S 4,8:6
Take one False Step 1949,Je 23,33:2
Calamity Jane and Sam Bass 1949,Jl 18,14:2
Story of Molly X, The 1949,D 2,35:4
Undertow 1949,D 16,37:2
Outside the Wall 1950,Mr 15,34:8
Raton Pass 1951,Ap 20,25:1
I Was a Communist for the F B I 1951,My 3,34:4
Inside the Walls of Folsom Prison
1951,My 28,17:4
Lone Shark 1952,My 12,21:2
Hart, Eddie
Hell's Highway 1932,S 26,18:2
I'll Wait for You 1941,Je 2,13:6
Mayor of Forty-Fourth Street, The
1942,Je 11,27:4
Hart, Eloise
Powers Girl, The 1943,Mr 26,14:2 (In Addenda)
Hart, Ferdinand
1914: The Last Days Before the War 1932,S 5,9:6
Golem, The 1937,Mr 22,27:2
Dreyfus Case, The 1940,O 30,29:3
Hart, Frances Noyes (Screenwriter)
Bellamy Trial, The 1929,Ja 24,30:5
Hart, Gordon
Dracula's Daughter 1936,My 18,14:2
Charge of the Light Brigade, The 1936,N 2,24:1
Fugitive in the Sky 1937,Ja 16,21:1
Midnight Court 1937,Mr 4,27:3
Her Husband's Secretary 1937,Mr 20,23:6
Melody for Two 1937,My 21,19:5
Fly Away Baby 1937,Jl 9,18:2
Back in Circulation 1937,O 4,17:1
West of Shanghai 1937,O 29,19:2
Lady in the Morgue, The 1938,My 9,13:3
On Trial 1939,Ap 5,31:2
Hart, Harvey (Director)
Bus Riley's Back in Town 1965,Ap 8,45:2
Dark Intruder 1965,Jl 22,24:2
Sweet Ride, The 1968,Je 13,57:2
Hart, Henry
D O A 1950,My 1,18:2
Hart, John
Prison Farm 1938,Jl 15,13:3
King of Alcatraz 1938,O 7,21:2
Disbarred 1939,Ja 19,17:2
Champagne for Caesar 1950,My 12,33:2
Man Who Loved Redheads, The 1955,Jl 26,29:2
Crooked Web, The 1955,D 10,19:1
Hart, June
Dance Band 1936,Ja 4,19:2
Hart, Lorenz (Composer)
Dancing Lady 1933,D 1,23:2
Manhattan Melodrama 1934,My 5,22:2
Hollywood Party 1934,My 26,12:2
Evergreen 1935,Ja 11,29:1
Mississippi 1935,Ap 18,27:2
Fools for Scandal 1938,Mr 25,15:3
Babes in Arms 1939,O 20,27:2
I Married an Angel 1942,Jl 10,13:2
Stage Door Canteen 1943,Je 25,13:2
Higher and Higher 1944,Ja 22,8:4
Pal Joey 1957,O 28,30:1
Jumbo 1962,D 7,49:1
Hart, Lorenz (Miscellaneous)
Hot Heiress, The 1931,Mr 14,23:2
Dancing Pirate 1936,Je 18,19:1
Too Many Girls 1940,N 21,43:1

Hart, Lorenz (Original Author)
Babes in Arms 1939,O 20,27:2
On Your Toes 1939,O 21,12:2
Boys From Syracuse, The 1940,Ag 1,25:2
I Married an Angel 1942,Jl 10,13:2
Hart, Ludwig
Rage in Heaven 1941,Mr 21,19:2
Hart, Mabel
Over the Wall 1938,Mr 28,19:2
Hart, Maria
Lusty Men, The 1952,O 25,12:6
Hart, Mary
Love Is on the Air 1937,N 12,27:3
Everything's on Ice 1939,O 6,31:1
Hart, Moss (Original Author)
Once in a Lifetime 1932,O 29,18:4
Broadway Melody of 1936 1935,S 19,28:1
You Can't Take It With You 1938,S 2,21:2
Man Who Came to Dinner, The 1942,Ja 2,25:2
George Washington Slept Here 1942,O 31,11:1
Lady in the Dark 1944,F 23,17:1
Decision of Christopher Blake, The
1948,D 11,12:2
Act One 1963,D 27,17:2
Hart, Moss (Screenwriter)
Winged Victory 1944,D 21,16:2
Gentleman's Agreement 1947,N 12,36:2
Hans Christian Andersen 1952,N 26,20:2
Star is Born, A 1954,O 12,23:1
Prince of Players 1955,Ja 12,24:2
Hart, Neal
Renegade Ranger, The 1939,F 17,17:3
Hart, Pamela
Young Girls of Rochefort, The 1968,Ap 12,50:1
Hart, Richard
Desire Me 1947,S 26,28:3
Green Dolphin Street 1947,O 16,34:2
B F's Daughter 1948,Mr 25,35:2
Black Book, The 1949,O 17,18:2
Hart, Sunshine
Syncopating Sue 1926,N 2,35:1
My Best Girl 1927,N 7,26:4
Hart, Susan
Ride the Wild Surf 1964,D 24,8:4
War Gods of the Deep 1965,Je 3,24:3
Dr Goldfoot and the Bikini Machine
1966,F 17,29:3
Hart, Teddy
Million Dollar Legs 1932,Jl 9,7:5
Diplomaniacs 1933,Ap 29,14:2
Three Men on a Horse 1936,N 26,39:1
After the Thin Man 1936,D 25,19:2
Ready, Willing and Able 1937,Mr 15,27:1
That Man's Here Again 1937,My 6,23:3
Marry the Girl 1937,Jl 31,6:2
Talent Scout 1937,Ag 20,21:3
Footloose Heiress 1937,O 9,16:2
You're the One 1941,F 20,23:2
My Favorite Spy 1942,My 29,13:4
Lady Luck 1946,O 31,22:3
Ma and Pa Kettle Back on the Farm
1951,My 11,32:3
Fat Man, The 1951,My 25,31:2
Girl in Every Port, A 1952,F 14,23:1
Mickey One 1965,S 9,36:1
Hart, Vivian
Girl Said No, The 1937,O 18,14:1
Hart, Walter (Director)
Molly 1951,Ag 8,37:2
Hart, Walter (Original Author)
Primrose Path 1940,Mr 23,16:2
Hart, Wilfred
Enter Madame 1935,Ja 12,12:1
Hart, William S
Disciple, The 1915,O 18,9:1
Apostle of Vengeance, The 1916,Je 12,9:3 (In
Addenda)
Captive God, The 1916,Jl 3,7:4
Patriot, The 1916,Ag 14,7:6
Return of Draw Egan, The 1916,O 2,9:4
Truthful Tolliver 1916,D 18,9:3
Blue Blazes Rawden 1918,F 19,9:2
Selfish Yates 1918,My 13,11:3
Shark Monroe 1918,Jl 1,9:3
Riddle Gawne 1918,Ag 12,7:1
Border Wireless, The 1918,S 30,7:1
Branding Broadway 1918,D 16,13:3
Poppy Girl's Husband, The 1919,Mr 24,11:3
Money Corporal, The 1919,Ap 21,13:4
Toll Gate, The 1920,Ap 19,13:3
Sand 1920,Je 21,13:1
Cradle of Courage, The 1920,S 20,13:1
O'Malley of the Mounted 1921,F 7,8:2
White Oak 1921,O 31,19:3
Hollywood 1923,Jl 30,11:4
Wild Bill Hickok 1923,N 21,22:1
Singer Jim McKee 1924,Mr 24,13:1
Tumbleweeds 1925,D 21,27:2
Hart, William S (Director)
Money Corporal, The 1919,Ap 21,13:4
Hart, William S (Original Author)
Money Corporal, The 1919,Ap 21,13:4
O'Malley of the Mounted 1936,Ap 6,18:1

Hart, William S (Producer)
Singer Jim McKee 1924,Mr 24,13:1
Hart, William S (Screenwriter)
White Oak 1921,O 31,19:3
HARTE
See Also HART
Harte, Bret (Original Author)
Half Breed, The 1916,Jl 10,9:5
M'liss 1918,My 6,11:3
Golden Princess 1925,S 7,15:3
M'liss 1936,Ag 8,5:2
Outcasts of Poker Flat, The 1937,Ap 27,18:3
Outcasts of Poker Flat 1952,My 16,19:3
Tennessee's Partner 1955,N 5,22:8
Hartegg, Vera
Soldaten-Kameraden 1936,O 5,25:1
Hartfield, Jack (Original Author)
Forever and a Day 1943,Mr 13,9:2
Hartford, David
Rough Romance 1930,Je 16,25:3
Hartford, David M (Director)
Nomads of the North 1920,S 27,18:1
Golden Snare, The 1921,Jl 11,9:3
Hartford, Dee
Girl in Every Port, A 1952,F 14,23:1
Hartford, Huntington (Producer)
Bride Comes to Yellow Sky, The 1953,Ja 14,27:2
Secret Sharer, The 1953,Ja 14,27:2
Face to Face 1953,Ja 14,27:2
Hartford-Davis, Robert (Director)
Corruption 1968,D 5,59:1
Hartieben, Jerry
Buccaneer, The 1958,D 24,00:0
Hartigan, Pat
Where the North Begins 1923,Ag 27,14:3
Darling of New York, The 1924,Ja 18,20:1
Dramatic Life of Abraham Lincoln, The
1924,Ja 22,17:3
Find Your Man 1924,S 23,26:1
Welcome Stranger 1924,O 14,21:5
Code of the West 1925,Ap 13,24:1
Below the Line 1925,S 21,12:4
Bobbed Hair 1925,N 4,17:4
Clash of the Wolves, The 1925,N 18,27:4
Oh! What a Nurse! 1926,F 22,14:1
Ranson's Folly 1926,My 31,10:2
Tenderloin 1928,Mr 15,28:3
State Street Sadie 1928,S 3,14:2
Midnight Taxi, The 1928,O 29,29:1
Handle with Care 1932,D 24,11:4
Hartl, Karl (Director)
Ein Burschenlied aus Heidelberg 1931,S 14,15:3
Graefin von Monte Christo, Die; Countess of
Monte Christo, The 1932,My 15,VIII,4:2 (In
Addenda)
F P 1 1933,S 16,9:3
Gold 1934,O 22,12:3
Zigeunerbaron 1935,S 14,8:5
Ritt in die Freiheit 1937,My 8,23:3
Zwei lustige Abenteurer; Two Merry Adventures
1938,Ja 1,11:2
Mozart Story, The 1948,N 15,21:5
Eroica; (The Beethoven Story) 1951,O 29,19:2
Wonder Boy 1951,D 26,19:5
Life and Loves of Mozart, The 1958,Ja 7,28:2
Hartl, Karl (Original Author)
Wonder Boy 1951,D 26,19:5
Hartl, Karl (Producer)
Angel With the Trumpet 1951,D 21,21:5
Wonder Boy 1951,D 26,19:5
Hartl, Karl (Screenwriter)
Eroica; (The Beethoven Story) 1951,O 29,19:2
Angel With the Trumpet 1951,D 21,21:5
Life and Loves of Mozart, The 1958,Ja 7,28:2
Hartleben, Dale
Her Twelve Men 1954,Ag 12,23:2
Hartleben, Jerry
3:10 to Yuma 1957,Ag 29,22:1
Hartleben, Otto Erich (Original Author)
Rosenmontag 1931,Mr 28,15:3
Hartley, Charles
Prunelia 1918,Je 3,9:3
Hartley, Irving
Man and Maid 1925,Ap 7,17:3
Fascinating Youth 1926,My 10,19:1
Hartley, John
Grand Jury Secrets 1939,Je 29,19:2
$1,000 a Touchdown 1939,O 5,27:2
Hartley, Mariette
Ride the High Country 1962,Je 21,26:2
Drums of Africa 1963,Jl 4,9:1
Marnie 1964,Je 23,19:1
Hartley, Neil (Producer)
Sailor From Gibraltar, The 1967,Ap 25,38:2
Charge of the Light Brigade, The 1968,O 7,59:1
Hartley, Pete
Great White Way, The 1924,Ja 4,10:1
Hartley, Ted
Walk, Don't Run 1966,Ag 25,42:3
Barefoot in the Park 1967,My 26,51:1
Hartley-Milburn, Julie
This Freedom 1923,N 28,15:1

Hartling, Lore
Stefanie 1959,Je 18,36:1
HARTMAN
See Also HARTMANN
Hartman, David
Ballad of Josie, The 1968,Mr 14,51:2
Nobody's Perfect 1968,Ap 4,58:3
Hartman, Don (Composer)
Romance in the Rain 1934,S 8,18:5
Waikiki Wedding 1937,Mr 25,29:1
Hartman, Don (Director)
It Had to be You 1947,D 8,35:2
Every Girl Should be Married 1948,D 24,14:2
Holiday Affair 1949,N 24,48:2
Mr Imperium 1951,O 15,22:2
It's a big Country 1952,Ja 9,25:2
Hartman, Don (Original Author)
Romance in Manhattan 1935,Ja 18,29:2
Here Comes Cookie 1935,O 12,12:2
Coronado 1935,D 19,33:4
Waikiki Wedding 1937,Mr 25,29:1
Tropic Holiday 1938,Je 30,21:2
Life With Henry 1941,F 6,25:2
Road to Zanzibar 1941,Ap 10,29:2
It Had to be You 1947,D 8,35:2
Hartman, Don (Producer)
Down to Earth 1947,S 12,18:2
It Had to be You 1947,D 8,35:2
Every Girl Should be Married 1948,D 24,14:2
Holiday Affair 1949,N 24,48:2
Desire Under the Elms 1958,Mr 13,24:2
Matchmaker, The 1958,Ag 13,22:1
Hartman, Don (Screenwriter)
Gay Deception, The 1935,O 11,31:1
Here Comes Cookie 1935,O 12,12:2
Coronado 1935,D 19,33:4
Princess Comes Across, The 1936,Je 4,27:2
Champagne Waltz 1937,F 4,17:2
Waikiki Wedding 1937,Mr 25,29:1
Tropic Holiday 1938,Je 30,21:2
Paris Honeymoon 1939,Ja 26,17:1
Never Say Die 1939,Mr 9,18:1
Star Maker, The 1939,Ag 31,14:2
Road to Singapore 1940,Mr 14,29:2
Those Were the Days 1940,Jl 15,18:4
Life With Henry 1941,F 6,25:2
Road to Zanzibar 1941,Ap 10,29:2
Nothing but the Truth 1941,O 23,27:1
My Favorite Blonde 1942,Ap 2,27:2
Road to Morocco 1942,N 12,30:1
True to Life 1943,O 14,26:1
Up in Arms 1944,Mr 3,19:2
Princess and the Pirate, The 1945,F 10,16:2
Wonder Man 1945,Je 9,17:2
Kid From Brooklyn, The 1946,Ap 19,25:2
Down to Earth 1947,S 12,18:2
Every Girl Should be Married 1948,D 24,14:2
Mr Imperium 1951,O 15,22:2
Hartman, Eddie
Ship Ahoy 1942,Je 26,16:5
Hartman, Edward (Original Author)
Big Noise, The 1936,Jl 4,18:3
Hartman, Elizabeth
Patch of Blue, A 1965,D 16,63:1
Group, The 1966,Mr 17,35:1
You're a Big Boy Now 1967,Mr 21,35:3
Fixer, The 1968,D 9,59:1
Hartman, Ena
Our Man Flint 1966,Ja 26,23:4
Hartman, Grace
Sunny 1941,Je 13,22:2
Higher and Higher 1944,Ja 22,8:4
Hartman, Gretchen
Time, The Place and the Girl, The 1929,Jl 8,17:3
College Coquette, The 1929,Ag 26,17:1
Hartman, Margot
Psychomania 1964,F 15,14:3
Curse of the Living Corpse, The 1964,Ap 30,30:1
Hartman, Paul
Tatjana 1927,My 18,29:3
At the Grey House 1927,N 8,33:1
Vanina 1928,Mr 20,20:3
Schwarzer Jaeger Johanna 1935,Ap 1,17:2
Alles um Eine Frau 1935,D 21,11:1
Erbe in Pretoria, Das 1936,Ag 18,19:3
Salon Dora Green 1937,Jl 26,15:3
Schloss im Flandern, Das 1937,Ag 7,7:3
Stronger Than the Rule 1937,S 25,10:2
Freiheit und Liebe, Um; For Freedom and Love
1938,F 5,19:3
Dreikland; Triad 1938,Jl 23,10:5
Mit versiegelter Order; Under Sealed Orders
1938,Jl 30,10:2
Pour le Merite 1939,Ap 8,19:2
Schritt vom Wege, Der; False Step, The
1939,Ap 29,13:3
Sunny 1941,Je 13,22:2
Higher and Higher 1944,Ja 22,8:4
Man on a Tightrope 1953,Je 5,19:1
Inherit the Wind 1960,O 13,41:1
Longest Day, The 1962,O 5,28:1
How to Succeed in Business Without Really
Trying 1967,Mr 10,30:1

Hartman, Paul— Cont
Luv 1967,Jl 27,29:1
HARTMANN
See Also HARTMAN
Hartman, Edmund L (Original Author)
Don't Get Personal 1936,F 22,12:1
Beauty for the Asking 1939,F 10,19:1
Keep 'Em Flying 1941,N 27,29:2
Ride 'Em Cowboy 1942,Mr 5,27:3
Ghost Catchers 1944,My 31,22:3
Here Come the Co-Eds 1945,F 19,21:1
Here Come the Girls 1953,D 26,10:1
Hartmann, Edmund L (Producer)
Ghost Catchers 1944,My 31,22:3
In Society 1944,Ag 17,20:2
See my Lawyer 1945,My 4,23:4
Naughty Nineties, The 1945,Je 21,16:2
Hartmann, Edmund L (Screenwriter)
Without Orders 1936,N 4,41:3
Man Who Found Himself, The 1937,Ap 9,19:3
China Passage 1937,Ap 16,27:2
Behind the Headlines 1937,Je 1,27:2
Hideaway 1937,S 25,10:2
Law of the Underworld 1938,Ap 28,27:2
Last Express, The 1938,O 11,24:4
Last Warning, The 1938,D 8,34:4
Big Town Czar 1939,My 4,27:3
Enemy Agent 1940,Ap 22,13:3
Ma! He's Making Eyes at Me 1940,Ap 26,25:2
South to Karanga 1940,Ag 9,19:1
Diamond Frontiers 1940,O 4,29:2
San Francisco Docks 1940,D 26,23:3
Time Out for Rhythm 1941,Jl 10,16:3
Feminine Touch, The 1941,D 12,35:3
Sherlock Holmes and the Secret Weapon
1943,Ja 5,15:2
Hi 'Ya Chum 1943,F 26,17:4
Ali Baba and the Forty Thieves 1944,Mr 16,17:3
Scarlet Claw, The 1944,My 19,12:1
In Society 1944,Ag 17,20:2
Sudan 1945,Ap 19,22:8
See my Lawyer 1945,My 4,23:4
Naughty Nineties, The 1945,Je 21,16:2
Dangerous Partners 1945,N 2,22:4
Variety Girl 1947,O 16,34:4
Paleface, The 1948,D 16,41:2
Sorrowful Jones 1949,Je 6,15:2
Fancy Pants 1950,Ag 31,21:2
Lemon Drop Kid, The 1951,Mr 22,41:2
My Favorite Spy 1951,D 26,19:3
Caddy, The 1953,S 18,16:6
Here Come the Girls 1953,D 26,10:1
Casanova's Big Night 1954,Ap 19,19:1
Shakiest Gun in the West, The 1968,Jl 11,30:1
Hartmann, Otto
Fall des Oberst Redl, Der 1932,Ag 18,23:3
Orphan Boy of Vienna, An 1937,S 9,19:2
Hartmann, Paul
Togger 1937,Mr 14,XI,4:5 (In Addenda)
Hartmann, Rudolf (Miscellaneous)
Rosenkavalier, Der 1962,O 10,57:1
Hartmann, Sadakichi
Thief of Bagdad, The 1924,Mr 19,19:1
Hartmans, The
45 Fathers 1937,D 11,22:2
Hartnell, William
Way Ahead, The 1945,Je 4,22:3
Murder in Reverse 1947,Ja 11,23:5
Odd Man Out 1947,Ap 24,30:2
Escape 1948,Ag 16,12:2
Temptation Harbor 1949,My 11,34:7
Agitator, The 1949,Ag 19,12:5
Lost People, The 1950,O 2,19:4
Appointment With Crime 1951,F 19,19:3
Young Scarface 1951,N 8,35:2
Double Confession 1953,My 1,17:2
Holly and the Ivy, The 1954,F 5,16:1
Pickwick Papers, The 1954,Ap 5,21:2
Will any Gentleman? 1955,S 28,70:6
Private's Progress 1956,Jl 24,19:2
Battle Hell 1957,Ag 22,23:1
Mouse That Roared, The 1959,O 27,40:1
Carry on Sergeant 1959,O 28,40:5
Heavens Above! 1963,My 21,28:2
This Sporting Life 1963,Jl 17,19:2
Hartwig, Knut
Marriage in the Shadows 1948,S 17,28:3
Harty, Patricia
Harvey Middleman, Fireman 1965,Jl 13,39:1
Hartzband, Moe (Cinematographer)
Lovely Way to Die, A 1968,Jl 13,18:1
Harukawa, Masumi
Insect Woman, The; Nippon Konchuki
1964,Jl 1,42:1
Unholy Desire 1964,N 18,54:1
Utamaro, Painter of Women 1964,D 2,57:1
Haruko, Togo
I Live in Fear; Ikimono no Kiroku
1967,Ja 26,25:1
Harven, Jaroslav (Composer)
Crisis 1939,Mr 13,12:2
Harvel, John (Director)
Captivation 1931,S 28,17:4

Harvey, Anthony
Caesar and Cleopatra 1946,S 6,18:2
Harvey, Anthony (Director)
Dutchman 1967,F 28,32:1
Lion in Winter, The 1968,O 31,54:1
Harvey, Anthony (Original Author)
Lion in Winter, The 1968,O 31,54:1
Harvey, Clarence
Zaza 1939,Ja 5,17:1
Harvey, Clem
Thunder of Drums, A 1961,S 27,35:1
State Fair 1962,Ap 12,41:4
Harvey, Don C
Women's Prison 1955,F 3,18:5
Picnic 1956,F 17,13:3
Blackjack Ketchum Desperado 1956,Ap 5,26:2
Harvey, Forrester
White Sheik, The 1929,D 9,32:5
Tailor-Made Man, A 1931,Ap 25,23:4
Man in Possession, The 1931,Jl 18,16:6
Guilty Hands 1931,Ag 29,16:3
Devotion 1931,O 3,20:2
Sky Devils 1932,Mr 4,17:3
Tarzan, The Ape Man 1932,Mr 28,11:2
But the Flesh Is Weak 1932,Ap 16,11:2
Wet Parade, The 1932,Ap 22,23:2
Mystery Ranch 1932,Je 30,26:2
Smilin' Through 1932,O 15,13:1
Red Dust 1932,N 5,12:5
Kongo 1932,N 17,22:5
Destination Unknown 1933,Ap 8,16:2
Eagle and the Hawk, The 1933,My 13,16:2
Invisible Man, The 1933,N 18,18:4
Man of Two Worlds 1934,Ja 12,29:2
Mystery of Mr X, The 1934,F 26,21:3
Tarzan and his Mate 1934,Ap 21,12:1
Menace 1934,N 22,27:2
Painted Veil, The 1934,D 7,29:1
Limehouse Blues 1934,D 12,28:2
Best Man Wins 1935,Ja 2,22:4
Mystery of Edwin Drood, The 1935,Mr 21,27:1
Vagabond Lady 1935,Je 15,20:2
Jalna 1935,S 14,8:4
Perfect Gentleman, The 1935,D 19,33:4
Captain Blood 1935,D 27,14:1
Petticoat Fever 1936,Mr 21,13:2
White Hunter 1936,N 26,39:2
Lloyds of London 1936,N 26,39:1
Personal Property 1937,Ap 11,27:2
Prince and the Pauper, The 1937,My 6,23:1
Thoroughbreds Don't Cry 1937,N 26,27:4
Kidnapped 1938,My 28,9:2
Bulldog Drummond in Africa 1938,Ag 25,15:1
Mysterious Mr Moto of Devil's Island
  1938,S 19,16:2
Bulldog Drummond's Secret Police
  1939,Mr 30,19:3
Lady's From Kentucky, The 1939,Ap 27,31:1
Witness Vanishes, The 1939,O 23,15:2
Invisible Man Returns, The 1940,Ja 16,19:2
Chump at Oxford, A 1940,F 20,17:3
Rebecca 1940,Mr 29,25:2
Tom Brown's School Days 1940,Je 28,22:2
Little Nellie Kelly 1940,D 25,33:2
Free and Easy 1941,Ap 3,29:4
Dr Jekyll and Mr Hyde 1941,Ag 13,13:2
Wolf Man, The 1941,D 22,24:5
Mysterious Doctor, The 1943,My 20,26:4
Harvey, Frank
Love Storm 1931,O 19,28:1
Harvey, Frank (Miscellaneous)
Burma Victory 1949,Ap 2,12:2
Harvey, Frank (Original Author)
Love Storm 1931,O 19,28:1
High Treason 1952,My 21,23:3
Heavens Above! 1963,My 21,28:2
No, My Darling Daughter 1964,Mr 28,13:5
Harvey, Frank (Screenwriter)
My Brothers Keeper 1949,F 14,15:3
Girl in the Painting, The 1949,Ag 22,13:1
Seven Days to Noon 1950,D 19,41:3
High Treason 1952,My 21,23:3
Long Memory, The 1953,Jl 27,15:2
Crest of the Wave 1954,N 11,43:2
Private's Progress 1956,Jl 24,19:2
Brothers in Law 1957,Ag 20,22:1
I'm All Right Jack 1960,Ap 26,40:2
39 Steps, The 1960,O 11,55:2
Upstairs and Downstairs 1960,D 2,53:4
World in my Pocket, The 1962,My 10,30:2
Heavens Above! 1963,My 21,28:2
No, My Darling Daughter 1964,Mr 28,13:5
Harvey, George Y
Wife Savers 1928,Ja 17,23:2
Harvey, Georgette
Back Door to Heaven 1939,Ap 20,21:2
Harvey, Harry
Pride of the Yankees, The 1942,Jl 16,23:1
Step by Step 1946,Ag 24,6:7
Trail Street 1947,Ap 10,35:2
They Won't Believe Me 1947,Jl 17,16:2
Arctic Manhunt 1949,Ag 19,12:5
They Live by Night 1949,N 4,33:2

Ace in the Hole 1951,Je 30,8:6
Outcasts of Poker Flat 1952,My 16,19:3
Highway Dragnet 1954,F 20,8:7
Harvey, Harry Jr
Forbidden Planet 1956,My 4,21:2
Harvey, Jack (Screenwriter)
Let's Live a Little 1948,D 10,34:2
Unknown Island 1949,Ja 8,11:4
City Beneath the Sea 1953,Mr 12,24:3
Harvey, Jean
Dream Maker, The 1964,Ap 23,34:1
Harvey, Joan
Pretty Boy Floyd 1960,N 3,49:2
Harvey, John
Four Jills in a Jeep 1944,Ap 6,27:2
Pin Up Girl 1944,My 11,25:6
Spider, The 1946,Je 21,20:3
Chance of a Lifetime 1951,Mr 15,37:2
Man With my Face, The 1951,Je 15,27:5
High Treason 1952,My 21,23:3
Psycopath, The 1966,S 29,60:1
Harvey, John Joseph (Director)
Night of the Pub, The 1920,Ja 26,16:1
Harvey, Laurence
Black Rose, The 1950,S 2,11:2
Man on the Run 1952,F 27,22:5
Wall of Death 1952,My 19,12:4
Cairo Road 1952,N 1,17:2
I Believe in You 1953,My 5,34:3
King Richard and the Crusaders 1954,Ag 23,20:5
Romeo and Juliet 1954,D 22,28:1
Innocents in Paris 1955,Mr 5,9:6
I Am a Camera 1955,Ag 9,29:1
Storm over the Nile 1956,Je 9,14:2
Truth About Women, The 1958,Ag 29,18:2
Room at the Top 1959,Mr 31,26:1
3 Men in a Boat 1959,Jl 29,33:2
Expresso Bongo 1960,Ap 13,44:1
Alamo, The 1960,O 27,45:1
Butterfield 8 1960,N 17,46:1
Two Loves 1961,Je 22,23:2
Summer and Smoke 1961,N 17,41:1
Walk on the Wild Side 1962,F 22,20:1
Jungle Fighters 1962,Mr 15,28:2
Wonderful World of the Brothers Grimm, The
  (The Cobbler and the Elves); Cobbler and the
  Elves, The (The Wonderful World of the
  Brothers Grimm) 1962,Ag 8,35:1
Wonderful World of the Brothers Grimm, The
  1962,Ag 8,35:1
Manchurian Candidate, The 1962,O 25,48:3
Girl Named Tamiku, A 1963,Mr 15,8:2
Running Man, The 1963,O 3,31:1
Ceremony, The 1964,My 14,39:1
Of Human Bondage 1964,S 24,46:2
Outrage, The 1964,O 8,48:2
Darling 1965,Ag 4,20:1
Life at the Top 1965,D 15,53:1
Spy With a Cold Nose, The 1966,D 20,58:2
Dandy in Aspic, A 1968,Ap 3,40:1
Harvey, Laurence (Director)
Ceremony, The 1964,My 14,39:1
Harvey, Laurence (Producer)
Ceremony, The 1964,My 14,39:1
Harvey, Lew
Broadway After Dark 1924,My 20,15:2
Find Your Man 1924,S 23,26:1
Lady of the Night 1925,Mr 2,14:1
Wolf's Clothing 1927,Mr 28,26:4
Argyle Case, The 1929,Ag 31,13:4
Hold Everything 1930,Ap 23,24:1
Big Boy 1930,S 13,9:3
Oklahoma Kid, The 1939,Mr 11,21:1
Honky Tonk 1941,O 3,27:3
Harvey, Lilian
Love Commandment, The 1928,D 25,31:3
It's Easy to Become a Father 1929,Je 24,27:1
Murder for Sale 1930,Ag 3,4:1
Liebeswalzer 1931,My 4,15:3
Drei von ver Tankstelle, Die 1931,Je 20,20:4
Nie Wieder Liebe; No More Love
  1931,O 4,VIII,7:1
Congress Dances, The 1931,N 22,VIII,6:6
Nie Wieder Liebe 1932,Ja 16,13:1
Fille et le Garcon, La; Girl and the Boy, The
  1932,Mr 27,VIII,6:2
Congress Dances, The; Congre's s'Amuse, Le
  1932,Mr 27,VIII,6:2
Congress Dances 1932,My 12,23:2
Zwei Herzen und ein Schlag 1932,S 9,17:5
Blonder Tram, Ein; Blond Dream, A
  1932,N 13,IX,4:2
Ich und die Kaiserin 1933,My 28,IX,2:5 (In
  Addenda)
My Weakness 1933,S 22,14:1
My Lips Betray 1933,N 4,18:3
Quick, Koenig der Clowns 1933,D 9,18:3
I Am Suzanne 1934,Ja 19,24:3
Heart Song 1934,Je 6,24:6
Let's Live Tonight 1935,Mr 18,14:4
Glueckskinder 1937,Je 5,21:1
Untitled-Dance 1937,D 25,10:4
Sieben Ohrfeigen; Seven Slaps 1938,F 12,20:5

Harvey, Lilian— Cont
Invitation to the Waltz 1938,Jl 2,10:3
Schubert's Serenade 1940,S 3,21:2
Harvey, Michael
Drums 1938,S 30,24:4
Tycoon 1947,D 26,22:6
Berlin Express 1948,My 21,19:3
Return of the Badmen 1948,Ag 5,16:2
Harvey, Morris
Office Girl 1932,Je 27,20:7
Scrooge 1935,D 14,11:1
21 Days Together 1940,My 23,28:4
Great Mr Handel, The 1943,S 10,29:3
Harvey, Paul
Wiser Sex, The 1932,Mr 12,19:5
Advice to the Lovelorn 1933,D 14,28:2
House of Rothschild, The 1934,Mr 15,27:2
Looking for Trouble 1934,Ap 12,27:2
Handy Andy 1934,Ag 4,14:5
She Was a Lady 1934,Ag 22,21:2
Charlie Chan's Courage 1934,Ag 25,16:6
Affairs of Cellini, The 1934,S 6,22:3
Kid Millions 1934,N 12,17:2
Broadway Bill 1934,N 30,22:2
President Vanishes, The 1934,D 8,18:5
Wicked Woman, A 1935,Ja 1,24:1
Whole Town's Talking, The 1935,Mr 1,16:2
I'll Love You Always 1935,Mr 30,11:2
Four Hours to Kill 1935,Ap 11,27:3
Goin' to Town 1935,My 11,21:2
Alibi Ike 1935,Jl 17,22:1
Broadway Melody of 1936 1935,S 19,28:1
Thanks a Million 1935,N 14,17:1
Rose of the Rancho 1936,Ja 9,25:2
Petrified Forest, The 1936,F 7,14:2
Walking Dead, The 1936,Mr 2,13:2
Witness Chair, The 1936,Ap 18,19:2
Private Number 1936,Je 12,19:1
Return of Sophie Lang, The 1936,Jl 24,13:1
Three Men on a Horse 1936,N 26,39:1
Plainsman, The 1937,Ja 14,16:2
Black Legion 1937,Ja 18,21:1
Soldier and the Lady, The 1937,Ap 10,11:1
23 1/2 Hours Leave 1937,My 17,23:2
Devil is Driving, The 1937,Jl 16,22:1
Big City 1937,S 17,29:2
On Again-Off Again 1937,S 18,15:3
Slight Case of Murder, A 1938,F 28,19:1
Mr Moto in Danger Island 1938,Mr 20,13:3
Rebecca of Sunnybrook Farm 1938,Mr 26,12:1
Algiers 1938,Jl 15,13:2
I'll Give a Million 1938,Jl 16,7:2
If I Were King 1938,S 29,31:1
Charlie Chan in Honolulu 1938,D 31,7:3
There's That Woman Again 1939,Ja 6,25:4
Never Say Die 1939,Mr 9,18:1
Gorilla, The 1939,My 28,6:2
News Is Made at Night 1939,Jl 13,17:2
They Shall Have Music 1939,Jl 26,17:2
Forgotten Woman, The 1939,Ag 4,11:2
Stanley and Livingstone 1939,Ag 5,18:2
Meet Doctor Christian 1939,D 1,27:2
Brother Rat and a Baby 1940,Ja 27,9:4
Typhoon 1940,My 23,28:4
Maryland 1940,Jl 13,16:5
Behind the News 1941,Ja 16,25:3
High Sierra 1941,Ja 25,11:2
Arizona 1941,F 7,23:3
Great Guns 1941,O 3,27:2
Law of the Tropics 1941,O 10,26:5
You Belong to Me 1941,N 29,14:2
You're in the Army Now 1941,D 26,21:4
Man Who Wouldn't Die, The 1942,Ap 28,25:5
You Can't Escape Forever 1942,O 17,11:1
Four Jills in a Jeep 1944,Ap 6,27:2
Chicago Kid, The 1945,F 12,24:3
Pillow to Post 1945,My 26,18:2
Spellbound 1945,N 2,22:2
Up Goes Maisie 1946,Ja 25,26:7
Easy to Wed 1946,Jl 12,14:2
Beginning or the End, The 1947,F 21,15:1
Late George Apley, The 1947,Mr 21,29:2
High Barbaree 1947,Je 6,27:2
Wyoming 1947,Jl 25,12:5
Call Northside 777 1948,F 19,29:2
Give my Regards to Broadway 1948,Je 23,32:2
John Loves Mary 1949,F 5,11:2
Down to the Sea in Ships 1949,F 23,31:2
Family Honeymoon 1949,F 25,28:2
Mr Belvedere Goes to College 1949,Ap 16,11:2
Take one False Step 1949,Je 23,33:2
Fountainhead, The 1949,Jl 9,8:5
Girl from Jones Beach, The 1949,Jl 30,9:2
Side Street 1950,Mr 24,29:2
Yellow Cab Man, The 1950,Mr 27,19:2
Riding High 1950,Ap 11,26:2
Father of the Bride 1950,My 19,31:2
Lawless, The 1950,Je 23,29:2
Skipper Surprised his Wife, The 1950,Je 30,18:2
Three Little Words 1950,Ag 10,21:2
Stella 1950,Ag 19,9:2
Flying Missile, The 1950,D 25,25:1
Milkman, The 1951,Ja 1,13:6
Up Front 1951,Mr 26,19:2

Harvey, Paul— Cont
Father's Little Dividend 1951,Ap 13,18:5
Excuse my Dust 1951,Je 28,21:2
Dreamboat 1952,Jl 26,9:2
April in Paris 1952,D 25,34:5
Calamity Jane 1953,N 5,40:2
Three for the Show 1955,F 25,16:1
Harvey, Phil
Why Must I Die? 1960,S 15,45:4
Harvey, Tom
Luck of Ginger Coffey, The 1964,S 22,44:1
Harvey, William Fryer (Original Author)
Beast With Five Fingers, The 1946,D 26,28:3
Harwin, Dixon R (Producer)
Corregidor 1943,My 28,19:2
Harwood, H M (Original Author)
Man in Possession, The 1931,Jl 18,16:6
Cynara 1932,D 26,26:2
Iron Duke, The 1935,Ja 25,27:2
Personal Property 1937,Ap 11,27:2
Harwood, Johanna (Screenwriter)
Dr No 1963,My 30,20:1
Call Me Bwana 1963,Jl 4,9:1
Harwood, John
Persecution and Assassination of Jean-Paul Marat
as Performed by the Inmates of the Asylum of
Charenton Under the Direction of the Marquis
De Sade, The 1967,F 23,41:1
Harwood, Ronald (Screenwriter)
High Wind in Jamaica, A 1965,Je 17,27:2
Arrivederci, Baby! 1966,D 29,22:1
Haryton, George
Moon of Israel 1927,Je 29,29:3
Has, Woiciech J (Director)
Partings 1962,N 28,44:1
Has, Woiciech J (Screenwriter)
Partings 1962,N 28,44:1
Hasbrouck, Olive
Two-Gun Man, The 1926,Jl 13,19:3
Clear the Decks 1929,Ap 1,22:1
Hascal, Lon
His Woman 1931,D 5,21:2
Hasebe, Keiji (Miscellaneous)
Odd Obsession 1961,D 27,16:1
Hasebe, Keiji (Screenwriter)
Insect Woman, The; Nippon Konchuki
1964,Jl 1,42:1
Enjo 1964,S 23,54:1
Hasegawa, Kazuo
Gate of Hell 1954,D 14,45:2
Utamaro, Painter of Women 1964,D 2,57:1
Hasegawa, Kimyuki (Screenwriter)
Phantom Horse, the 1956,Jl 25,16:1
Hasegawa, Uhei
Scoundrel, The 1935,My 3,23:2
Hasek, Jaroslav (Original Author)
Good Soldier Schweik, The 1963,Ag 21,38:1
Hasek, Vlastimal
Devil's Trap, The 1964,Ag 14,16:1
Hasek, Vlastimil
Death of Tarzan, The 1968,Jl 4,13:2
Hasenclever, Walter (Miscellaneous)
Rendez-Vous 1932,Ap 30,19:3
Hashim, Edmund
Outsider, The 1962,F 8,25:1
Hashimoto, Shinobu (Screenwriter)
Rasho-Mon 1951,D 27,18:3
Magnificent Seven, The 1956,N 20,46:2
Ikiru; To Live 1960,Ja 30,13:5
Throne of Blood 1961,N 23,50:2
Hidden Fortress The 1962,Ja 24,24:2
Lower Depths, The 1962,F 10,12:5
Bad Sleep Well, The 1963,Ja 23,5:2
Harakiri 1964,Ag 5,24:2
Samurai Assassin 1965,Mr 19,27:5
I Live in Fear; Ikimono no Kiroku
1967,Ja 26,25:1
Sword of Doom, The 1967,Ap 15,35:2
Rebellion 1968,O 26,27:4
Haskeil, Virginia
Happy is the Bride 1959,Je 30,27:2
Haskel, Leonhard
Explosion 1927,D 13,33:2
Haskell, Jean
True as Steel 1924,Je 17,22:4
Haskell, Peter
Passages From James Joyce's Finnegans Wake
1967,O 10,56:1
Haskin, Byron (Cinematographer)
Midsummer Night's Dream, A 1935,O 10,31:1
Haskin, Byron (Director)
Matinee Ladies 1927,Ap 13,29:4
Man-Eater of Kumaon 1948,Jl 2,24:2
Too Late for Tears 1949,Ag 15,12:3
Treasure Island 1950,Ag 16,24:2
Warpath 1951,N 23,32:2
Denver and Rio Grande, The 1952,My 17,22:7
War of the Worlds, The 1953,Ag 14,10:2
His Majesty O'Keefe 1954,F 6,17:2
Naked Jungle, The 1954,Ap 3,19:2
Long John Silver 1955,Ap 7,24:1
Conquest of Space 1955,My 28,7:6
First Texan, The 1956,Je 23,20:2
From the Earth to the Moon 1958,N 27,52:2

Jet Over the Atlantic 1960,Ja 7,24:6
September Storm 1960,O 29,26:7
Armored Command 1961,O 7,14:3
Captain Sindbad 1963,Jl 4,9:1
Robinson Crusoe on Mars 1964,Ag 27,28:2
Power, The 1968,Mr 7,52:2
Haslett, Jessie
Seventh Heaven 1927,My 26,22:1
HASS
See Also HAAS
Hass, Hans Dr (Director)
Under the Red Sea 1952,N 19,37:3
Hass, Hans Dr (Producer)
Under the Red Sea 1952,N 19,37:3
Hassall, Imogen
Long Duel, The 1967,N 2,58:3
Hassan, Ibrahim Bin
Spiral Road, The 1962,Ag 4,11:2
Hasse, Charles (Director)
Shrine of Victory 1943,Ag 20,13:2
Hasse, Clemens
Muede Theodor, Der 1936,O 24,23:2
Glueckspilze 1936,O 26,21:1
Hasse, Laura (Screenwriter)
Captain Lash 1929,F 4,20:1
Hasse, O E
Ganzer Kerl, Ein 1936,Ap 25,21:2
Big Lift, The 1950,Ap 27,37:2
Decision Before Dawn 1951,D 22,12:2
Berliner, The 1952,O 28,37:1
I Confess 1953,Mr 23,28:2
Betrayed 1954,S 9,36:1
Last Waltz, The 1958,Ap 12,13:1
Deadly Decision 1958,Ap 29,26:2
No Sun in Venice 1958,Je 10,40:2
Glass Tower, The; (Glaserne Turm, Der)
1959,Ag 27,24:4
Elusive Corporal, The 1963,F 19,5:1
Vice and Virtue 1965,Mr 18,25:1
Hassein, Robert
No Sun in Venice 1958,Je 10,40:2
Madame 1963,Mr 21,8:6
Hassell, George
Boheme, La 1926,F 25,26:2
Night Life of the Gods 1935,F 23,14:6
Flame Within, The 1935,Je 1,18:2
Becky Sharp 1935,Je 14,27:2
Captain Blood 1935,D 27,14:1
Petticoat Fever 1936,Mr 21,13:2
King Steps Out, The 1936,My 29,15:2
Girls' Dormitory 1936,Ag 29,16:2
White Hunter 1936,N 26,39:2
Woman Wise 1937,Ja 23,13:1
Hasselquist, Jenny
Aftermath 1927,D 6,27:1
Guilty 1928,S 18,33:2
Dream Waltz, The 1930,D 27,16:3
Hassen, Jamie
Behind That Curtain 1929,Jl 1,31:2
Hasso, Signe
Vi Tvaa; We Two 1939,D 2,21:3
Assignment in Brittany 1943,Ap 22,31:2
Heaven Can Wait 1943,Ag 12,15:1
Story of Dr Wassell, The 1944,Je 7,13:2
Seventh Cross, The 1944,S 29,18:1
House on Ninety-Second Street, The
1945,S 27,24:7
Dangerous Partners 1945,N 2,22:4
Johnny Angel 1945,D 28,12:2
Scandal In Paris, A 1946,S 16,9:7
Where There's Life 1947,D 25,32:1
To the Ends of the Earth 1948,F 13,26:2
Double Life, A 1948,F 20,19:1
Outside the Wall 1950,Mr 15,34:8
Crisis 1950,Jl 4,10:2
Hasson, Jamiel
Action in Arabia 1944,F 19,18:7
Hasson, Thomas
In Like Flint 1967,Mr 16,53:2
Hastings, Bob
McHale's Navy 1964,Jl 11,15:2
Hastings, Charlotte (Original Author)
Thunder on the Hill 1951,O 18,32:3
Hastings, Harry
Fury and the Woman 1937,Je 22,26:2
Hastings, Hugh (Original Author)
Crest of the Wave 1954,N 11,43:2
Hastings, Hugh (Screenwriter)
Glory at Sea 1953,Mr 11,36:7
Hastings, Marie
Ulysses 1967,Mr 14,55:1
Hastings, Patrick (Original Author)
Notorious Lady, The 1927,Ap 11,18:3
Blind Goddess, The 1949,Je 23,33:3
Hastings, Phyllis (Original Author)
Rapture 1965,Ag 24,25:3
Hasty, John Eugene (Original Author)
There's a Girl in my Heart 1950,Ja 20,29:2
Hasty, John Eugene (Screenwriter)
There's a Girl in my Heart 1950,Ja 20,29:2
Haswell, Ara
Second Hand Wife 1933,Ja 14,8:4

Hatch, Eric (Miscellaneous)
My Man Godfrey 1957,O 12,23:1
Hatch, Eric (Original Author)
Spendthrift 1936,Jl 23,24:1
My Man Godfrey 1936,S 19,18:1 (Incorrect in
this edition; use 1936,S 18,18:1 elsewhere)
Road Show 1941,F 19,25:2
Unexpected Uncle 1941,S 25,29:1
My Man Godfrey 1957,O 12,23:1
Horse in the Gray Flannel Suit, The
1968,D 21,49:3
Hatch, Eric (Screenwriter)
My Man Godfrey 1936,S 19,18:1 (Incorrect in
this edition; use 1936,S 18,18:1 elsewhere)
Topper 1937,Ag 20,21:2
Hatch, Helen
Boomerang 1947,Mr 6,36:2
Hatch, Ike
Dark Sands 1938,Ag 17,23:4
Hatch, Kurt
Mummy's Curse, The 1945,Mr 31,16:1
Hatch, Riley
Little Miss Rebellion 1920,S 20,13:1
Little Old New York 1923,Ag 2,10:3
If Winter Comes 1923,S 4,14:1
Zaza 1923,S 17,18:2
West of the Water Tower 1923,D 31,9:3
America 1924,F 22,20:1
Hatcher, Mary
Our Hearts Were Growing Up 1946,Ag 12,17:2
Variety Girl 1947,O 16,34:4
Isn't It Romantic? 1948,O 7,35:2
Holiday in Havana 1949,O 14,33:5
Hatfield, Hurd
Dragon Seed 1944,Jl 21,16:4
Picture of Dorian Gray, The 1945,Mr 2,15:2
Diary of a Chambermaid, The 1946,Je 23,28:2
Beginning or the End, The 1947,F 21,15:1
Unsuspected, The 1947,O 4,9:2
Joan of Arc 1948,N 12,30:5
Chinatown at Midnight 1949,N 18,35:3
Tarzan and the Slave Girl 1950,Je 24,7:3
Left Handed Gun, The 1958,My 8,36:2
King of Kings 1961,O 12,41:2
Cid, El 1961,D 15,49:1
Mickey One 1965,S 9,36:1
Boston Strangler, The 1968,O 17,52:1
Hathaway, Henry (Director)
Heritage of the Desert 1933,Mr 11,18:3
Come on Marines 1934,Mr 24,20:3
Witching Hour, The 1934,Ap 28,11:3
Last Round-Up, The 1934,My 10,25:2
Now and Forever 1934,O 13,10:1
Lives of a Bengal Lancer, The 1935,Ja 12,12:2
Peter Ibbetson 1935,N 8,18:2
Trail of the Lonesome Pine, The 1936,F 20,23:5
Go West, Young Man 1936,N 19,31:3
Souls at Sea 1937,Ag 10,23:2
Spawn of the North 1938,S 8,27:1
Real Glory, The 1939,S 15,26:2
Johnny Apollo 1940,Ap 13,21:2
Brigham Young - Frontiersman 1940,S 21,13:2
Shepherd of the Hills 1941,Jl 31,13:2
Sundown 1941,D 26,21:3
Ten Gentlemen From West Point 1942,Je 5,23:3
China Girl 1943,Ja 21,27:2
Home in Indiana 1944,Je 22,23:1
Wing and a Prayer 1944,Ag 31,14:1
Nob Hill 1945,Jl 4,10:3
House on Ninety-Second Street, The
1945,S 27,24:7
Dark Corner, The 1946,My 9,27:3
13 Rue Madeleine 1947,Ja 16,30:2
Kiss of Death 1947,Ag 28,28:2
Call Northside 777 1948,F 19,29:2
Down to the Sea in Ships 1949,F 23,31:2
Black Rose, The 1950,S 2,11:2
U S S Teakettle 1951,F 24,11:2
Fourteen Hours 1951,Mr 7,43:2
Rawhide 1951,Mr 26,19:2
Desert Fox, The 1951,O 18,32:1
Desert Fox, The 1951,O 28,II,1:8
Diplomatic Courier 1952,Je 14,12:2
O Henry's Full House (The Gift of the Magi); Gift
of the Magi, The (O Henry's Full House)
1952,O 17,33:1
O Henry's Full House (The Last Leaf
1952,O 17,33:1
O Henry's Full House (The Clarion Call); Clarion
Call, The (O Henry's Full House)
1952,O 17,33:1
O Henry's Full House (The Cop and the Anthem);
Cop and the Anthem, The (O Henry's Full
House) 1952,O 17,33:1
Niagara 1953,Ja 22,20:3
White Witch Doctor 1953,Jl 2,19:3
Prince Valiant 1954,Ap 7,40:2
Garden of Evil 1954,Jl 10,17:1
Racers, The 1955,F 5,13:2
Bottom of the Bottle, The 1956,F 2,19:2
23 Paces to Baker Street 1956,My 19,12:6
Legend of the Lost 1957,D 23,18:2
From Hell to Texas 1958,Je 5,39:2

Hathaway, Henry (Director) — Cont
Woman Obsessed 1959,My 28,34:1
Seven Thieves 1960,Mr 12,14:5
North to Alaska 1960,N 11,36:1
How the West Was Won 1963,Ap 1,54:1
Circus World 1964,Je 26,34:2
Sons of Katie Elder, The 1965,Ag 26,40:3
Nevada Smith 1966,Je 24,28:1 (Incorrect in this edition; use 1966,Je 30,28:1 elsewhere)
5 Card Stud 1968,Ag 1,24:1
Hathaway, Henry (Miscellaneous)
Of Human Bondage 1964,S 24,46:2
Hathaway, Henry (Producer)
Souls at Sea 1937,Ag 10,23:2
Legend of the Lost 1957,D 23,18:2
North to Alaska 1960,N 11,36:1
Nevada Smith 1966,Je 24,28:1 (Incorrect in this edition; use 1966,Je 30,28:1 elsewhere)
Hathaway, Rod
Bigger Than Barnum's 1926,Jl 13,19:3
Hatheyer, Heidemarie
Zigeunerweisen; Gypsy Ways 1940,My 11,15:3
Desires 1954,Jl 2,10:2
Angelika 1954,S 25,10:7
Hatswell, D R O
Peg o'my Heart 1923,Ja 22,10:1
Hattan, Raymond
Triumph 1924,Ap 21,21:4
Top of the World, The 1925,F 17,18:1
Hattie, Hilo
Song of the Islands 1942,Mr 12,24:4
Miss Tatlock's Millions 1948,N 25,47:2
Hatton, Bradford
Smiling Faces 1932,Ag 31,12:3
Top Banana 1954,F 20,8:6
Hatton, Charles
Lorna Doone 1922,D 4,20:2
Hatton, Fanny (Miscellaneous)
Fall of Eve, The 1929,Je 18,29:4
Hatton, Fanny (Original Author)
Upstairs and Down 1919,Je 16,11:2
Waning Sex, The 1926,S 21,33:1
Synthetic Sin 1929,Ja 7,36:2
Great Lover, The 1931,Ag 24,13:4
Hatton, Fanny (Screenwriter)
Manicure Girl, The 1925,Je 15,10:1
Money Talks 1926,My 11,24:3
Hatton, Frances
Day of Faith, The 1923,N 27,11:2
Confessions of a Queen 1925,Mr 24,20:6
Hatton, Frank (Original Author)
Great Lover, The 1931,Ag 24,13:4
Hatton, Frederic (Miscellaneous)
Waning Sex, The 1926,S 21,33:1
Fall of Eve, The 1929,Je 18,29:4
Hatton, Frederic (Original Author)
Upstairs and Down 1919,Je 16,11:2
Hatton, Frederic (Screenwriter)
Manicure Girl, The 1925,Je 15,10:1
Money Talks 1926,My 11,24:3
Hatton, Frederick (Original Author)
Synthetic Sin 1929,Ja 7,36:2
Hatton, Raymond
Oliver Twist 1916,D 11,7:3
We Can't Have Everything 1918,Jl 15,9:3
Source, The 1918,S 9,9:1
You're Fired 1919,Je 16,11:2
Love Burglar, The 1919,Jl 28,8:5
Male and Female 1919,N 24,13:1
Everywoman 1919,D 15,20:1
Dancin' Fool, The 1920,My 3,18:1
Jes' Call Me Jim 1920,My 24,20:3
Bunty Pulls the Strings 1921,Ja 9,VI,2:1 (In Addenda)
Concert, The 1921,F 21,16:1
Affairs of Anatol, The 1921,S 12,16:1
Doubling for Romeo 1921,O 24,13:1
To Have and to Hold 1922,N 6,13:1
Ebb Tide 1922,N 20,21:3
Hottentot, The 1923,F 19,10:1
Man of Action, A 1923,Je 4,13:3
Hunchback of Notre Dame, The 1923,S 3,9:3
Barefoot Boy, The 1923,N 11,6:1
Big Brother 1923,D 24,12:1 (In Addenda)
Fighting American, The 1924,My 13,24:1
True as Steel 1924,Je 17,22:4
Tomorrow's Love 1925,Ja 7,33:5
Devil's Cargo, The 1925,F 3,24:1
Contraband 1925,Mr 24,20:6
Adventure 1925,Ap 15,16:1
In the Name of Love 1925,Ag 27,14:1
Son of his Father, A 1925,S 29,31:3
Lord Jim 1925,N 16,19:4
Behind the Front 1926,F 10,16:2
Silence 1926,My 19,29:3
Born to the West 1926,Je 30,18:1 (In Addenda)
We're in the Navy Now 1926,N 8,19:2
Fashions For Women 1927,Mr 28,26:4
Fireman, Save My Child 1927,O 10,24:1
We're in the Air Now 1927,D 31,31:1
Wife Savers 1928,Ja 17,23:2
Partners in Crime 1928,Ap 30,18:3
Big Killing, The 1928,Jl 2,11:2
Hell's Heroes 1929,D 28,11:1

Mighty, The 1929,D 30,16:4
Midnight Mystery 1930,Je 2,25:4
Road to Paradise 1930,S 30,23:1
Silver Horde, The 1930,O 25,20:6
Road to Paradise, The 1931,Ja 20,21:3
Woman Hungry 1931,Mr 23,24:7
Honeymoon Lane 1931,Ag 1,16:4
Squaw Man, The 1931,S 19,10:2
Law and Order 1932,F 29,21:3
Polly of the Circus 1932,Mr 19,11:2
Stranger in Town 1932,Jl 8,22:5
Vanity Street 1932,O 15,13:1
Uptown New York 1932,D 10,19:3
Terror Trail 1933,F 11,11:3
State Trooper 1933,Mr 27,13:6
Big Cage, The 1933,My 9,20:5
Penthouse 1933,S 9,9:2
Alice in Wonderland 1933,D 23,19:1
Lady Killer 1934,Ja 1,28:2
Lazy River 1934,Ap 4,26:2
Defense Rests, The 1934,Ag 16,20:3
Straight Is the Way 1934,Ag 29,13:2
Wagon Wheels 1934,O 4,19:1
Times Square Lady 1935,Mr 15,25:3
G Men 1935,My 2,17:1
Daring Young Man, The 1935,Jl 18,15:2
Steamboat Around the Bend 1935,S 20,17:2
Exclusive Story 1936,Ja 18,19:2
Timothy's Quest 1936,F 29,11:2
Laughing Irish Eyes 1936,Ap 4,11:2
Mad Holiday 1936,N 26,39:2
Marked Woman 1937,Ap 12,15:2
Fly Away Baby 1937,Jl 9,18:2
Roaring Timber 1937,Ag 19,23:1
Over the Goal 1937,O 16,22:2
Love Is on the Air 1937,N 12,27:3
Missing Witness 1937,D 10,33:3
Torchy Blane, The Adventurous Blonde 1937,D 18,18:1
Over the Wall 1938,Mr 28,19:2
Love Finds Andy Hardy 1938,Jl 22,10:2
Texans, The 1938,Jl 28,23:2
Touchdown Army 1938,O 28,27:2
Paris Honeymoon 1939,Ja 26,17:1
Ambush 1939,F 9,17:2
I'm From Missouri 1939,Mr 23,27:1
Undercover Doctor 1939,Je 1,31:2
Six Thousand Enemies 1939,Je 9,26:2
Career 1939,Jl 28,14:2
Kit Carson 1940,N 15,25:3
Tall in the Saddle 1944,D 15,25:3
Black Gold 1947,S 5,16:4
Golden Hawk, The 1952,O 18,16:4
Hatton, Rondo
In Old Chicago 1938,Ja 7,15:2
Ox-Bow Incident, The 1943,My 10,15:2 (In Addenda)
Pearl of Death 1944,Ag 26,15:2
Jungle Captive 1945,Jl 7,7:5
House of Horrors 1946,F 23,20:3
Spider Woman Strikes Back, The 1946,Mr 23,8:3
Hatvany, Lili (Original Author)
My Kingdom for a Cook 1943,O 15,15:3
Hatziagyrf, Helen
You Came too Late 1962,N 12,35:8
Hatzihristos, Kostas
Castle in Greece 1960,D 12,38:2
Lisa, Tosca of Athens 1961,Je 20,27:1
Hauber, William
Midnight Taxi, The 1928,O 29,29:1
Haudepin, Didier
Moderato Cantabile 1964,Ja 7,24:1
This Special Friendship 1967,N 8,56:1
Haudepin, Sabine
Jules and Jim 1962,Ap 24,32:1
Hauer, Jerry
Go, Man, Go 1954,Mr 10,29:5
Hauff, Angelika
Marriage of Figaro 1950,N 3,31:2
Haufler, Max
Town Without Pity 1961,O 11,53:1
Saboteur, The: Code Name-Mori Turi 1965,Ag 26,40:2
Haulani, Mylee
Elephant Walk 1954,Ap 22,37:2
Haupt, Dietrich
Wonder of Women 1929,Jl 22,17:1
Haupt, Ullrich
Tempest 1928,My 18,27:3
Captain Swagger 1928,D 24,17:7
Iron Mask, The 1929,F 22,18:6
Madame X 1929,Ap 25,32:3
Wonder of Women 1929,Jl 22,17:1
Greene Murder Case, The 1929,Ag 10,11:3
Frozen Justice 1929,O 26,15:1
Rogue Song, The 1930,Ja 29,26:4
Bad One, The 1930,Je 13,28:3
Du Barry, Woman of Passion 1930,N 3,19:3
Morocco 1930,N 17,29:1
Man Who Came Back, The 1931,Ja 3,21:2
Unholy Garden, The 1931,O 29,27:1

Hauptmann, Gerhardt (Original Author)
Weavers, The 1929,O 7,22:1
Ruler, The 1937,O 16,22:3
Biberpelz, Der; Beaver Coat, The 1939,S 9,11:3
Sins of Rose Bernd, The 1959,Ja 24,13:4 (In Addenda)
Hause, Newton
Which Shall It Be? 1924,Ap 7,15:3
Hauser, Armando (Composer)
Wife, Husband and Friend 1939,F 25,19:2
Hauser, Dwight (Screenwriter)
Legend of Lobo, The 1962,N 10,16:2
Hauser, Gilgi
Divided Heart, The 1955,Ag 4,16:1
Hauser, Kurt (Screenwriter)
Trial, The 1952,Mr 15,8:2
Hauser, Lionel (Original Author)
Girl From Mexico, The 1939,Je 8,31:4
Hauser, Philo
Girl in the Painting, The 1949,Ag 22,13:1
Give Us This Day 1949,D 21,41:2
House of the Seven Hawks, The 1959,D 17,51:2
Under ten Flags 1960,S 16,24:1
HAUSMAN
See Also HOUSMAN
Hausman, Ernst
Four Sons 1940,Je 8,18:4
Hausmeister, Ruth
Girls Behind Bars 1950,My 10,41:2
Hausner, Jerry
Outrage 1950,O 16,30:5
Just This Once 1952,Mr 18,22:3
Off Limits 1953,Mr 30,25:5
Private Hell 36 1954,S 4,6:4
Paths of Glory 1957,D 26,23:2
Who's Minding the Store? 1963,N 29,67:6 (Incorrect in this edition; use 1963,N 28,67:6 elsewhere)
Haussermann, Ernst H
Cimzett Ismeretler 1936,F 7,14:2
Haussermann, Reinbold
Moon of Israel 1927,Je 29,29:3
Haussler, Richard
Girls Behind Bars 1950,My 10,41:2
Wozzeck 1962,Mr 3,13:1
Hautzik, Selma (Composer)
Let's Sing Again 1936,My 9,11:2
Havard, Rene
Crime and Punishment 1958,S 16,23:2
Babette Goes to War 1960,Je 8,46:1
Cow and I, The 1961,Je 6,42:2
Gigot 1962,S 28,26:1
Havelkova, Libuse
Closely Watched Trains 1967,O 16,59:2
Havelock-Allan, Anthony (Director)
This Happy Breed 1947,Ap 14,24:2
Evening With the Royal Ballet, An 1965,D 9,60:1
Havelock-Allan, Anthony (Producer)
Continental Express 1942,Ap 7,26:3
Blanche Fury 1948,N 24,20:2
Take my Life 1949,Ja 19,34:2
Interrupted Journey 1951,My 29,20:2
Never Take No for an Answer 1952,Ap 29,32:2
Tonight at 8:30 (Fumed Oak); Fumed Oak (Tonight at 8:30) 1953,My 26,33:2
Tonight at 8:30 (Ways and Means); Ways and Means (Tonight at 8:30) 1953,My 26,33:2
Orders to Kill 1958,N 18,41:2
Quare Fellow 1963,F 20,6:1
Othello 1966,F 2,24:1
Mikado, The 1967,Mr 15,53:1
Up the Junction 1968,Mr 14,51:1
Romeo and Juliet 1968,O 9,41:1
Havelock-Allan, Anthony (Screenwriter)
Blithe Spirit 1945,O 4,27:2
Havemann, Alexander D
Untamed 1955,Mr 12,11:6
Haven, Adrian
City of Secrets 1963,Jl 27,10:2
Haven, Ruth
Song of the Road 1940,My 6,13:2
Haver, June
Home in Indiana 1944,Je 22,23:1
Irish Eyes Are Smiling 1944,N 8,27:1
Where Do We Go From Here? 1945,Je 7,25:2
Dolly Sisters, The 1945,N 15,24:6
Three Little Girls in Blue 1946,S 26,32:3
Wake up and Dream 1947,Ja 24,18:4
I Wonder Who's Kissing Her Now 1947,Jl 24,27:2
Scudda-Hoo! Scudda-Hay! 1948,Ap 15,31:1
Look for the Silver Lining 1949,Je 24,29:2
Oh, You Beautiful Doll 1949,N 12,8:4
Daughter of Rosie O'Grady, The 1950,Mr 31,36:2
I'll Get by 1950,N 2,39:3
Girl Next Door, The 1953,S 5,7:4
Haver, Phylis
Wise Wife 1927,N 1,21:1 (In Addenda)
Haver, Phyllis
Small Town Idol, A 1921,Ap 17,VI,2:1 (In Addenda)

Haver, Phyllis — Cont

Christian, The 1923,F 12,13:4
Temple of Venus, The 1923,N 1,24:3
Fighting Coward, The 1924,Mr 17,19:1
Lilies of the Field 1924,Mr 17,19:1
Singer Jim McKee 1924,Mr 24,13:1
Perfect Flapper, The 1924,Je 23,22:4
Single Wives 1924,Jl 29,9:2
Midnight Express, The 1924,N 19,19:3
Breath of Scandal, The 1924,N 26,17:3
Snob, The 1924,D 15,14:1
So Big 1925,Ja 5,19:1
I Want my Man 1925,Ap 6,17:3
After Business Hour 1925,Je 17,16:2
Golden Princess 1925,S 7,15:3
New Brooms 1925,N 4,17:4
Cave Man, The 1926,Mr 1,17:1
Other Women's Husbands 1926,Ap 27,23:2
Up in Mabel's Room 1926,Je 29,21:2
Don Juan 1926,Ag 7,6:1 (In Addenda)
Nervous Wreck, The 1926,O 12,30:2
What Price Glory 1926,N 24,26:4
Nobody's Widow 1927,Ja 13,29:1
Way of all Flesh, The 1927,Je 27,25:2
Rejuvenation of Aunt Mary, The 1927,Jl 27,27:4
Fighting Eagle, The 1927,Ag 15,22:5
Chicago 1927,D 24,9:1
Way of all Flesh, The 1928,Ja 29,VIII,6:2
Tenth Avenue 1928,O 9,35:1
Battle of The Sexes, The 1928,O 15,16:1
Sal of Singapore 1929,Ja 29,27:1
Shady Lady, The 1929,Mr 25,32:2
Thunder 1929,Jl 8,17:3
30 Years of Fun 1963,D 26,33:4

Havez, Jean (Screenwriter)
Sherlock Jr 1924,My 26,21:1
Navigator, The 1924,O 13,21:1

Havien, J Alex
They Were Expendable 1945,D 21,25:2

Havier, J Alex
Bataan 1943,Je 4,17:2
Back to Bataan 1945,S 13,26:3

Haviland-Taylor, Katharine (Original Author)
One Man's Journey 1933,S 1,15:2
Man to Remember, A 1938,N 7,23:2

Havoc, June
Sing Your Worries Away 1942,My 15,25:2
Powder Town 1942,Je 8,11:2
My Sister Eileen 1942,O 23,15:1
Hello, Frisco, Hello 1943,Mr 25,25:1
Hi Diddle Diddle 1943,S 24,26:2
No Time for Love 1943,D 2,30:1
Brewster's Millions 1945,Ap 27,23:2
Gentleman's Agreement 1947,N 12,36:2
Intrigue 1948,Ap 24,11:2
Iron Curtain, The 1948,My 13,31:2
When my Baby Smiles at Me 1948,N 24,20:2
Red, Hot and Blue 1949,O 20,39:2
Chicago Deadline 1949,N 3,37:2
Story of Molly X, The 1949,D 2,35:4
Mother Didn't Tell Me 1950,Mr 4,11:2
Once a Thief 1951,Ja 19,21:3
Follow the Sun 1951,Ap 26,34:4
Lady Possessed 1952,F 15,17:2
Three for Jamie Dawn 1956,Jl 7,11:3

Havrilla, Alois (Narrator)
ThIs is America 1933,Jl 20,22:2
This Is China 1937,O 6,29:4
Norway Replies! 1944,F 26,10:3

Hawdon, Robin
Day the Earth Caught Fire, The 1962,Mr 16,25:1

HAWES
See Also HOWES

Hawes, Mary
Soul Mates 1926,Ja 4,16:1

Hawes, Stanley (Director)
Monkey Into Man 1941,My 31,14:1

Hawes, Stanley (Producer)
Queen in Australia, The 1954,Je 16,37:3

Hawes, William
Slattery's Hurricane 1949,Ag 13,6:6

Hawk, Jeremy
Lucky Jim 1958,S 1,8:6

Hawkes, J Kerby (Original Author)
Guilty Generation, The 1931,N 21,20:4

Hawkes, Mary
Scarlet Letter, The 1926,Ag 10,19:2

Hawkesworth, John (Producer)
Tiger Bay 1959,D 15,50:1

Hawkesworth, John (Screenwriter)
Tiger Bay 1959,D 15,50:1

Hawkins, Dolores
Adventures of Huckleberry Fin, The 1960,Ag 4,17:1

Hawkins, Geoffrey
Town Like Alice, A 1958,S 22,27:1

Hawkins, J N A (Miscellaneous)
Fantasia 1940,N 14,28:2

Hawkins, Jack
Good Companions, The 1933,O 10,24:1
Autumn Crocus 1934,O 25,26:2
Phantom Fiend 1935,Ap 22,14:2
Peg of Old Drury 1936,Ap 13,15:1
Next of Kin 1943,My 6,25:2

Fallen Idol, The 1949,N 16,39:2
Black Rose, The 1950,S 2,11:2
State Secret 1950,O 5,38:2
No Highway in the Sky 1951,S 22,8:6
Bonnie Prince Charlie 1952,Ja 7,14:3
Small Back Room, The 1952,F 2,11:3
Outpost in Malaya 1952,N 27,49:2
Story of Mandy, The 1953,F 24,21:3
Cruel Sea, The 1953,Ag 11,18:5
Murder on Monday 1953,O 7,35:2
Fighting Pimpernel, The 1954,Ap 19,19:1
Angels One Five 1954,Ap 30,28:2
Malta Story 1954,Jl 17,7:2
Intruder, The 1955,Ja 26,22:1
Front Page Story 1955,Ap 19,28:1
Land of Fury 1955,My 3,37:4
Land of the Pharaohs 1955,Jl 27,15:2
Prisoner, The 1955,D 12,37:1
Touch and go 1956,Mr 20,13:2
Third Key, The 1957,Je 3,30:2
Bridge on the River Kwai 1957,D 19,39:1
Two-Headed Spy, The 1959,Mr 3,38:4
Gideon of Scotland Yard 1959,My 20,38:2
Ben Hur 1959,N 19,50:2
League of Gentlemen, The 1961,Ja 25,30:4
Two Loves 1961,Je 22,23:2
Five Finger Exercise 1962,Ap 20,20:2
Lawrence of Arabia 1962,D 17,5:6
Lafayette 1963,Ap 11,29:1
Rampage 1963,O 17,39:2
Third Secret, The 1964,Ap 29,27:1
Zulu 1964,Jl 8,38:1
Guns at Batasi 1964,N 17,47:1
Lord Jim 1965,F 26,18:1
Masquerade 1965,Ap 29,40:2
Judith 1966,Ja 21,22:1
Poppy is Also a Flower, The 1967,D 14,62:4
Shalako 1968,N 6,32:1

Hawkins, Jimmy
It's a Wonderful Life 1946,D 23,19:2
Caught 1949,F 18,26:4
Red Menace, The 1949,Je 27,18:2
Love That Brute 1950,My 27,10:6
Mister Scoutmaster 1953,Ag 29,10:1
Private Hell 36 1954,S 4,6:4

Hawkins, John (Original Author)
Secret Command 1944,Je 14,16:2
Crime Wave 1954,Ja 13,26:2
Killer is Loose, The 1956,Mr 3,17:2

Hawkins, Ward (Original Author)
Secret Command 1944,Je 14,16:2
Crime Wave 1954,Ja 13,26:2
Killer is Loose, The 1956,Mr 3,17:2

Hawks, Howard (Director)
Cradle Snatchers 1927,My 31,25:2
Paid to Love 1927,Jl 25,25:3
Girl in Every Port, A 1928,F 20,14:1
Fazil 1928,Je 5,21:1
Air Circus, The 1928,S 3,14:2
Criminal Code, The 1931,Ja 5,21:3
Crowd Roars, The 1932,Mr 23,25:4
Crowd Roars, The 1932,Ap 3,VIII,4:4
Scarface, The Shame of the Nation 1932,My 20,22:3
Tiger Shark 1932,S 23,22:2
Today We Live 1933,Ap 15,16:2
20th Century 1934,My 4,24:2
Barbary Coast 1935,O 14,21:1
Ceiling Zero 1936,Ja 20,22:2
Road to Glory, The 1936,Ag 6,22:1
Come and Get It 1936,N 12,31:1
Bringing Up Baby 1938,Mr 4,17:5
Only Angels Have Wings 1939,My 12,25:2
His Girl Friday 1940,Ja 12,13:2
Sergeant York 1941,Jl 3,15:1
Ball of Fire 1942,Ja 16,25:2
Air Force 1943,F 4,29:1
To Have and Have Not 1944,O 12,24:1
Big Sleep, The 1946,Ag 24,6:6
Red River 1948,O 1,31:2
Song Is Born, A 1948,O 20,37:2
I Was a Male War Bride 1949,Ag 27,7:2
Big Sky, The 1952,Ag 20,21:1
Monkey Business 1952,S 6,12:6
Gentlemen Prefer Blondes 1953,Jl 16,17:2
Land of the Pharaohs 1955,Jl 27,15:2
Rio Bravo 1959,Mr 19,40:2
Hatari 1962,Jl 12,19:1
Man's Favorite Sport? 1964,F 20,22:1
Red Line 7000 1965,D 9,60:4
Dorado, El 1967,Je 29,32:1

Hawks, Howard (Original Author)
Only Angels Have Wings 1939,My 12,25:2
Indianapolis Speedway 1939,Jl 15,8:2
Red Line 7000 1965,D 9,60:4

Hawks, Howard (Producer)
Bringing Up Baby 1938,Mr 4,17:5
Only Angels Have Wings 1939,My 12,25:2
His Girl Friday 1940,Ja 12,13:2
Corvette K-225 1943,O 21,30:1
To Have and Have Not 1944,O 12,24:1
Big Sleep, The 1946,Ag 24,6:6
Red River 1948,O 1,31:2

Hawks, Howard (Producer) — Cont

Thing, The 1951,My 3,34:4
Big Sky, The 1952,Ag 20,21:1
Land of the Pharaohs 1955,Jl 27,15:2
Rio Bravo 1959,Mr 19,40:2
Hatari 1962,Jl 12,19:1
Man's Favorite Sport? 1964,F 20,22:1
Red Line 7000 1965,D 9,60:4
Dorado, El 1967,Je 29,32:1

Hawks, Howard (Screenwriter)
Dressmaker from Paris, The 1925,Mr 18,19:2
Crowd Roars, The 1932,Mr 23,25:4

Hawks, Kenneth (Director)
Big Time 1929,S 9,30:2
Such Men Are Dangerous 1930,Mr 8,21:1

Hawks, William (Producer)
Tall Men, The 1955,O 12,36:2
Law and Jake Wade, the 1958,Je 7,11:1
Imitation General 1958,Ag 21,22:2

Hawks, William B (Producer)
Last Wagon, The 1956,S 22,20:2

Hawley, Cameron (Original Author)
Executive Suite 1954,My 7,19:1
Cash McCall 1960,Ja 28,26:1

Hawley, Helen
Laughing Lady, The 1930,Ja 4,21:1

Hawley, Lowell S (Screenwriter)
Swiss Family Robinson 1960,D 24,8:4
Sign of Zorro, The 1961,S 5,37:6
Babes in Toyland 1961,D 15,49:1
In Search of the Castaways 1962,D 22,5:2
Tiger Walks, A 1964,Ag 27,28:2
Adventures of Bullwhip Griffin, The 1967,Mr 9,43:2
One and Only Genuine Original Family Band, The 1968,Mr 22,55:1

Hawley, Neil
Stop the World-I Want to Get Off 1966,My 12,54:2

Hawley, Robert
Caressed 1965,S 16,54:2

Hawley, Wanda
We Can't Have Everything 1918,Jl 15,9:3
Way of a Man With a Maid, The 1919,Ja 20,13:2
For Better, For Worse 1919,Ap 28,13:2
Greased Lightning 1919,Ap 28,13:2
You're Fired 1919,Je 16,11:2
Secret Service 1919,Je 23,10:3
Lottery Man, The 1919,O 6,15:1
Everywoman 1919,D 15,20:1
Double Speed 1920,F 2,10:1
Affairs of Anatol, The 1921,S 12,16:1
Young Rajah, The 1922,N 6,13:1
Thirty Days 1922,D 11,22:1
Masters of Men 1923,My 15,22:1
Man From Brodney's, The 1923,D 18,16:3
Bread 1924,Jl 21,14:4
Barriers Burned Away 1925,Mr 12,17:2
Smouldering Fires 1925,Mr 31,17:4
Stop Flirting 1925,Je 18,16:3
Graustark 1925,S 8,29:1

Haworth, Gail
Goddess, The 1958,Je 25,24:1

Haworth, Jill
Exodus 1960,D 16,44:1
Your Shadow Is Mine 1963,My 15,32:1
Cardinal, The 1963,D 13,41:1
In Harm's Way 1965,Ap 7,36:1
It 1967,N 16,58:1

Haworth, Joe
Salome, Where She Danced 1945,My 3,27:1
I Was a Male War Bride 1949,Ag 27,7:2
Father Was a Fullback 1949,O 13,33:3
Gun Belt 1953,Ag 1,8:2

Haworth, Vinton
Without Orders 1936,N 4,41:3
Night Waitress 1936,D 18,31:5
That Girl From Paris 1937,Ja 1,19:1
We're on the Jury 1937,F 10,18:5
China Passage 1937,Ap 16,27:2
You Can't Buy Luck 1937,My 14,21:2
Riding on Air 1937,Je 26,20:2 (In Addenda)
Hitting a new High 1937,D 27,11:1

Hawthorne, David
Prince of Lovers, The 1927,N 29,31:1
Escape 1930,N 1,23:2
Laburnum Grove 1941,D 2,29:2

Hawthorne, Nathaniel (Original Author)
Scarlet Letter, The 1926,Ag 10,19:2
House of the Seven Gables, The 1940,Ap 15,21:3

Hawtrey, Charles
Canterbury Tale, A 1949,Ja 24,16:2
Galloping Major, The 1951,D 17,27:2
Brandy for the Parson 1952,Ag 18,13:4
Carry on Sergeant 1959,O 28,40:5
Carry on Nurse 1960,S 10,11:1
Carry on Cleo 1965,O 23,17:2

Hawtrey, Nicholas
Barretts of Wimpole Street, The 1957,Ja 18,15:3

Hay, Alexandra
Guess Who's Coming to Dinner 1967,D 12,56:1

Hay, Charles
Return of Sherlock Holmes, The 1929,O 19,22:6

Hay, Ian (Miscellaneous)
Thirty-Nine Steps, The 1935,S 14,8:4
Secret Agent 1936,Je 13,13:1
Woman Alone, The 1937,F 27,9:2
Troopship 1938,Ap 26,18:2
Hay, Ian (Original Author)
Middle Watch, The 1930,D 20,20:6
Orders Is Orders 1934,My 7,20:2
Widow From Monte Carlo, The 1936,Ja 23,25:2
Housemaster 1939,Ap 10,13:2
Ship Was Loaded, The 1958,Ja 20,20:1
Hay, Jacob (Original Author)
Sheriff of Fractured Jaw, The 1959,Mr 14,27:4
Hay, Mary
New Toys 1925,F 17,18:1
Way Down East 1931,Mr 16,25:1
Hayabusa, Hideto
Tokyo File 212 1951,Je 1,20:7
Hayakawa, Sessue
Alien Souls 1916,My 15,7:1
Dragon Painter, The 1919,O 5,IV,5:3 (In Addenda)
Bonds of Honor 1919,O 5,IV,5:3 (In Addenda)
First Born, The 1921,Ja 31,11:1
Where Lights Are Low 1921,Ag 1,8:3 (Incorrect in this edition; use 1921,Ag 1,6:4 elsewhere)
Daughter of the Dragon 1931,Ag 22,7:5
Tokyo Joe 1949,O 27,35:2
Three Came Home 1950,F 21,22:5
House of Bamboo 1955,Jl 2,13:2
Bridge on the River Kwai 1957,D 19,39:1
Geisha Boy, The 1958,D 24,00:0
Green Mansions 1959,Mr 20,26:1
Hell to Eternity 1960,O 13,41:1
Swiss Family Robinson 1960,D 24,8:4
Hayakawa, Yuki
Golden Demon 1956,Ja 31,34:3
Hayama, Ryoji
Temptress and the Monk, The 1963,My 28,32:1
Hayashi, Chizu
Showdown for Zatoichi 1968,O 5,40:1
Hayashi, Yoichi
Kwaidan (Hoichi, The Earless); Hoichi, The Earless (Kwaidan) 1965,N 23,51:1
Hayashida, Shigeo (Cinematographer)
Tokyo Olympiad 1966,N 17,55:1
Haycox, Ernest (Original Author)
Stagecoach 1939,Mr 3,21:1
Union Pacific 1939,My 11,31:2
Abilene Town 1946,Mr 4,16:5
Canyon Passage 1946,Ag 8,18:2
Montana 1950,F 4,9:2
Bugles in the Afternoon 1952,Mr 5,32:2
Stagecoach 1966,Je 16,53:1
Haycox, Ernest (Screenwriter)
Heaven Only Knows 1947,N 14,29:3
HAYDEN
See Also HADDON, HEIDEN
Hayden, Don
Margie 1946,O 17,28:3
Hayden, Harry
I Married a Doctor 1936,Ap 20,17:1
Public Enemy's Wife 1936,Jl 9,17:2
Killer at Large 1936,O 26,20:1
Man I Marry, The 1936,O 31,24:3
God's Country and the Woman 1937,Ja 11,15:5
Black Legion 1937,Ja 18,21:1
John Meade's Woman 1937,F 18,19:1
Melody for Two 1937,My 21,19:5
Ever Since Eve 1937,Je 25,25:2
Love Is on the Air 1937,N 12,27:3
Double Danger 1938,F 10,17:5
I'll Give a Million 1938,Jl 16,7:2
Kentucky 1938,D 24,12:1
Hidden Power 1939,Jl 26,17:3
Frontier Marshal 1939,Jl 29,18:2
Flight at Midnight 1939,S 7,29:2
Rains Came, The 1939,S 9,11:2
Barricade 1939,D 9,18:2
Cisco Kid and the Lady, The 1939,D 25,29:2
Swanee River 1939,D 30,9:2
He Married his Wife 1940,Ja 20,11:2
Sleepers West 1941,Mr 20,25:3
Man Betrayed, A 1941,Mr 27,29:5
Parson of Panamint, The 1941,Jl 26,18:2
Night of January 16th, The 1941,D 19,35:1
Remember the Day 1941,D 26,21:2
Whispering Ghosts 1942,My 18,19:4
Tales of Manhattan 1942,S 25,25:1
Springtime in the Rockies 1942,N 12,30:2
Palm Beach Story, The 1942,D 11,33:1
Meanest Man in the World, The 1943,F 25,27:3
Hello, Frisco, Hello 1943,Mr 25,25:1
Weird Woman 1944,Ap 1,11:1
Up in Mabel's Room 1944,Ap 22,8:6
Hail the Conquering Hero 1944,Ag 10,14:2
Great Moment, The 1944,N 13,15:2
Two Sisters From Boston 1946,Je 7,16:2
Killers, The 1946,Ag 29,24:2
If I'm Lucky 1946,S 20,41:3
Till the Clouds Roll By 1946,D 6,27:4
My Brother Talks to Horses 1947,Je 19,27:4
Key Witness 1947,Jl 30,27:6

Unfinished Dance, The 1947,O 31,29:2
Merton of the Movies 1947,N 7,20:3
Good Sam 1948,S 17,28:2
Beautiful Blonde From Bashful Bend, The 1949,My 28,11:2
Judge Steps Out, The 1949,Je 3,21:4
Intruder in the Dust 1949,N 23,19:1
Traveling Saleswoman 1950,Ja 6,25:3
Union Station 1950,O 5,38:3
Carrie 1952,Jl 17,20:2
Hayden, Jeffrey (Director)
Vintage, The 1957,My 9,36:5
Hayden, Julie
Song of the Eagle 1933,Ap 29,14:3
Dawn to Dawn 1933,D 27,23:5
Hayden, Melissa
Limelight 1952,O 24,27:2
Hayden, Nora
Angry Red Planet, The 1960,My 5,41:2
Hayden, Russell
Hopalong Rides Again 1938,Ja 22,19:1
Partners of the Plains 1938,F 12,20:4
Heart of Arizona 1938,Ap 16,17:1
Albuquerque 1948,Mr 1,17:2
Hayden, Sterling
Virginia 1941,Ja 29,21:2
Blaze of Noon 1947,Mr 5,31:2
El Paso 1949,Mr 24,35:2
Manhandled 1949,My 26,34:2
Asphalt Jungle, The 1950,Je 9,29:3
Journey Into Light 1951,O 5,24:4
Denver and Rio Grande, The 1952,My 17,22:7
Golden Hawk, The 1952,O 18,16:4
Flat Top 1952,D 6,17:2
Star, The 1953,Ja 29,25:1
Take Me to Town 1953,Je 20,8:6
So Big 1953,O 22,34:2
Crime Wave 1954,Ja 13,26:2
Prince Valiant 1954,Ap 7,40:2
Arrow in the Dust 1954,My 1,13:2
Johnny Guitar 1954,My 28,19:2
Naked Alibi 1954,O 2,21:2
Suddenly 1954,O 8,27:2
Timberjack 1955,Mr 10,33:3
Eternal Sea, The 1955,Je 10,16:2
Come on, The 1956,My 7,13:1
Killing, The 1956,My 21,20:1
Crime of Passion 1957,Ja 10,25:1
Five Steps to Danger 1957,Ja 31,21:1
Zero Hour 1957,N 14,41:1
Dr Strangelove or: How I Learned to Stop Worrying and Love the Bomb 1964,Ja 31,16:1 (Incorrect in this edition; use 1964,Ja 30,24:1 elsewhere)
Hayden, Stirling
Bahama Passage 1942,F 19,23:2
Hayden-Coffin, Adeline
This Freedom 1923,N 28,15:1
Woman Tempted, The 1928,Ap 24,29:3
Haydn, Richard
Charley's Aunt 1941,Ag 2,18:2
Ball of Fire 1942,Ja 16,25:2
Are Husbands Necessary? 1942,Jl 9,17:2
Thunder Birds 1942,O 29,19:2
No Time for Love 1943,D 2,30:1
And Then There Were None 1945,N 1,20:2
Adventure 1946,F 8,23:2
Green Years, The 1946,Ap 5,21:2
Cluny Brown 1946,Je 3,27:3
Beginning or the End, The 1947,F 21,15:1
Late George Apley, The 1947,Mr 21,29:2
Singapore 1947,S 17,31:2
Foxes of Harrow, The 1947,S 25,35:4
Forever Amber 1947,O 23,31:2
Sitting Pretty 1948,Mr 11,35:2
Emperor Waltz, The 1948,Je 18,19:2
Miss Tatlock's Millions 1948,N 25,47:2
Mr Music 1950,D 21,34:3
Merry Widow, The 1952,S 25,38:1
Never Let Me Go 1953,Je 11,37:2
Money From Home 1954,F 27,11:3
Her Twelve Men 1954,Ag 12,23:2
Jupiter's Darling 1955,F 18,18:4
Toy Tiger 1956,Je 30,11:2
Twilight for the Gods 1958,Ag 7,21:1
Please Don't Eat the Daisies 1960,Ap 1,37:1
Lost World, The 1960,Jl 14,23:1
Five Weeks in a Balloon 1962,Ag 27,18:1
Mutiny on the Bounty 1962,N 9,31:2
Sound of Music, The 1965,Mr 3,34:1
Clarence, the Cross-Eyed Lion 1965,Ag 5,15:3
Adventures of Bullwhip Griffin, The 1967,Mr 9,43:2
Haydn, Richard (Director)
Miss Tatlock's Millions 1948,N 25,47:2
Dear Wife 1950,F 2,31:2
Mr Music 1950,D 21,34:3
Haydon, Julie
Thirteen Women 1932,O 15,13:1
Conquerors, The 1932,N 21,21:1
Lucky Devils 1933,F 20,11:5
Their big Moment 1934,S 6,22:4
Age of Innocence, The 1934,O 19,27:1

Haydon, Julie— Cont
Scoundrel, The 1935,My 3,23:2
Son Comes Home, A 1936,S 5,7:1
Longest Night, The 1936,O 17,21:2
Family Affair, A 1937,Ap 20,29:2
Citizen Saint 1948,My 28,28:2
Haye, Helen
Atlantic 1930,O 6,21:1
Skin Game, The 1931,Je 20,20:4
Congress Dances 1932,My 12,23:2
Monte Carlo Madness 1932,Je 4,9:2
Its a Boy 1933,Jl 23,IX,2:2 (In Addenda)
It's a Boy 1934,Je 8,18:2
Loves of a Dictator 1935,Je 1,18:2
Thirty-Nine Steps, The 1935,S 14,8:4
Wings of the Morning 1937,Mr 12,19:1
U-Boat 29 1939,O 6,31:3
Sidewalks of London 1940,F 15,15:1
Frightened Lady 1941,N 10,21:3
Kipps 1942,My 25,11:2
Randolph Family 1945,Mr 13,19:4
Man of Evil 1948,Mr 26,26:2
Anna Karenina 1948,Ap 28,32:2
Mine Own Executioner 1949,Ja 19,34:2
Place of One's Own, A 1949,F 8,30:2
Conspirator 1950,Ap 28,26:2
Mrs Fitzherbert 1950,My 11,37:2
Hobson's Choice 1954,Je 15,37:1
Front Page Story 1955,Ap 19,28:1
Richard III 1956,Mr 12,1:4
Haye, Ina de la
Give Us This Day 1949,D 21,41:2
Night Without Stars 1953,Jl 14,19:4
Rob Roy 1954,F 4,21:5
Dance Little Lady 1955,D 26,23:3
Anastasia 1956,D 14,35:6
Spanish Gardner, The 1957,S 9,21:2
Hayers, Sidney (Director)
Circus of Horrors 1960,S 1,31:1
Burn, Witch, Burn 1962,Jl 5,21:2 (In Addenda)
Payroll 1963,My 11,15:2
HAYES
See Also HAYS
Hayes, Alfred (Original Author)
Teresa 1951,Ap 6,31:2
Act of Love 1954,F 12,20:5
Hayes, Alfred (Screenwriter)
Paisan 1948,Mr 30,26:2
Clash by Night 1952,Je 19,32:6
Human Desire 1954,Ag 7,7:2
Left Hand of God, The 1955,S 22,34:5
Island in the Sun 1957,Je 13,37:1
Hatful of Rain, A 1957,Jl 18,19:2
These Thousand Hills 1959,My 7,36:1
Mountain Road, The 1960,Je 30,22:3
Joy in the Morning 1965,Je 10,38:1
Double Man, The 1968,My 2,57:1
Hayes, Allison
So This Is Paris 1955,F 12,11:1
Sign of the Pagan 1955,F 14,24:2
Chicago Syndicate 1955,Je 21,37:1
Steel Jungle, The 1956,Mr 10,9:5
Hayes, Anthony
Ride the Wild Surf 1964,D 24,8:4
Hayes, Bernadene
Absolute Quiet 1936,My 2,11:1
Parole 1936,Je 27,21:1
Accusing Finger, The 1936,N 17,35:4
Great Guy 1937,Ja 1,19:2
Emperor's Candlesticks, The 1937,Jl 9,18:1
Prison Nurse 1938,Mr 4,17:5
You and Me 1938,Je 2,19:1
Idiot's Delight 1939,F 3,13:1
King of Chinatown 1939,Mr 16,27:2
Lucky Night 1939,My 5,29:3
Some Like It Hot 1939,My 25,31:2
Day the Bookies Wept, The 1939,S 14,18:2
Sing for Your Supper 1941,D 1,15:5
Mr Winkle Goes to War 1944,Ag 3,16:1
Dick Tracy's Dilemma 1947,Jl 14,14:5
Living in a Big Way 1947,O 10,31:4
Crimson Key, The 1947,O 18,9:2
Woman in the Night 1948,Ja 10,16:2
Caught 1949,F 18,26:4
Hayes, Bettina
Hotel Sahara 1952,Ja 1,21:4
Hayes, Bill
Stop, You're Killing Me 1952,D 11,45:3
Li'l Abner 1959,D 12,19:2
Cardinal, The 1963,D 13,41:1
Hayes, Cardinal
Pope Speaks, The 1933,Ap 17,13:3 (In Addenda)
Hayes, Charles
Safari 1956,Je 21,35:2
Africa-Texas Style! 1967,Jl 13,30:2
Hayes, Danny
New Klondike, The 1926,Mr 22,16:1
Hayes, Elton
Story of Robin Hood, The 1952,Je 27,18:3
Isabel 1968,Jl 24,47:1
Hayes, Flora
Hurricane, The 1937,N 10,31:2

Hayes, Frank
Greed 1924,D 5,28:1
Hayes, George (Gabby)
Rainbow Man, The 1929,Ap 17,30:6
Smiling Irish Eyes 1929,Jl 24,23:2
Beggars in Ermine 1934,Ap 25,25:3
Lost City, The 1935,F 21,23:3
Thunder Mountain 1935,O 2,27:2
$1,000 a Minute 1935,D 21,11:1
Mister Hobo 1936,F 8,19:2
Three on the Trail 1936,My 5,26:5
Lawless Nineties, The 1936,Je 29,11:1
Plainsman, The 1937,Ja 14,16:2
Mountain Music 1937,Je 24,30:3
Hopalong Rides Again 1938,Ja 22,19:1
Gold Is Where You Find It 1938,F 14,20:6
Emil 1938,Ap 15,23:2
Heart of Arizona 1938,Ap 16,17:1
Forbidden Music 1938,D 27,13:2
Let Freedom Ring 1939,Mr 10,19:2
Man of Conquest 1939,Ap 28,31:2
Dark Command 1940,My 11,15:2
Wagons Westward 1940,Jl 8,13:2
Melody Ranch 1940,D 26,23:3
Voice in the Night, The 1941,My 23,25:4
Frightened Lady 1941,N 10,21:3
In old Oklahoma 1943,D 6,21:1
Tall in the Saddle 1944,D 15,25:3
Big Bonanza, The 1945,F 26,14:5
Utah 1945,Mr 12,22:7
Badman's Territory 1946,My 31,27:2
My Pal Trigger 1946,Ag 17,16:3
Trail Street 1947,Ap 10,35:2
Great Expectations 1947,My 23,31:1
Wyoming 1947,Jl 25,12:5
Albuquerque 1948,Mr 1,17:2
Return of the Badmen 1948,Ag 5,16:2
El Paso 1949,Mr 24,35:2
Cariboo Trail, The 1950,S 1,17:2
Hayes, Grace
King of Jazz 1930,My 3,23:1
Myrt and Marge 1934,Ja 17,23:2
Babes in Arms 1939,O 20,27:2
Always Leave Them Laughing 1949,N 24,48:2
Hayes, Helen
Sin of Madelon Claudet, The 1931,O 31,22:2
Arrowsmith 1931,D 8,36:4
Farewell to Arms, A 1932,D 9,26:5
Son-Daughter, The 1933,Ja 2,29:2
White Sister, The 1933,Mr 18,9:3
Another Language 1933,Ag 5,9:5
Night Flight 1933,O 7,18:4
What Every Woman Knows 1934,O 27,20:2
Vanessa: Her Love Story 1935,Ap 13,11:3
Stage Door Canteen 1943,Je 25,13:2
My Son John 1952,Ap 9,27:1
Main Street to Broadway 1953,O 14,34:1
Anastasia 1956,D 14,35:6
Hayes, Ira H
Sands of Iwo Jima 1949,D 31,9:2
Hayes, Jack (Original Author)
Mr Lemon of Orange 1931,Mr 28,15:3
Hayes, Jimmy
Tea and Sympathy 1956,S 28,24:4
Hayes, John Anthony
Strait Jacket 1964,Ja 23,26:1
Hayes, John Maxwell
Song of Bernadette, The 1944,Ja 27,15:2
Hayes, John Michael (Original Author)
Thunder Bay 1953,My 21,39:2
Hayes, John Michael (Screenwriter)
Red Ball Express 1952,My 30,11:2
Thunder Bay 1953,My 21,39:2
Torch Song 1953,O 13,34:2
Rear Window 1954,Ag 5,18:2
To Catch a Thief 1955,Ag 5,14:2
Trouble With Harry, The 1955,O 18,46:2
It's a Dog's Life 1955,D 23,14:3
Man Who Knew too Much, The 1956,My 17,37:1
Peyton Place 1957,D 13,35:1
Matchmaker, The 1958,Ag 13,22:1
But Not for Me 1959,O 3,14:6
Childrens Hour, The 1962,Mr 15,28:2
Chalk Garden, The 1964,My 22,42:2
Carpetbaggers, The 1964,Jl 2,24:4
Where Love Has Gone 1964,N 3,26:1
Harlow 1965,Jl 22,24:1
Judith 1966,Ja 21,22:1
Nevada Smith 1966,Je 24,28:1 (Incorrect in this edition; use 1966,Je 30,28:1 elsewhere)
Hayes, Joseph (Original Author)
Desperate Hours, The 1955,O 6,25:1
Bon Voyage! 1962,My 18,34:2
Third Day, The 1965,Ag 5,15:3
Hayes, Joseph (Screenwriter)
Desperate Hours, The 1955,O 6,25:1
Young Doctors, The 1961,Ag 24,25:2
Hayes, Linda
Girl From Mexico, The 1939,Je 8,31:4
Conspiracy 1939,Ag 23,19:2
Spellbinder, The 1939,Ag 24,17:3
Mexican Spitfire 1940,Ja 10,16:4
Sued for Libel 1940,Ja 19,15:3

Millionaires in Prison 1940,Jl 16,21:3
I'm Still Alive 1940,O 11,25:4
Mexican Spitfire out West 1940,O 30,29:3
Saint in Palm Springs, The 1941,Ja 31,15:5
Ellery Queen and the Perfect Crime 1941,Ag 11,17:3
Hayes, Margaret
Night of January 16th, The 1941,D 19,35:1
Sullivan's Travels 1942,Ja 29,25:2
Lady Has Plans, The 1942,Mr 5,27:1
Glass Key, The 1942,O 16,23:1
They Got Me Covered 1943,Mr 5,20:2
Blackboard Jungle 1955,Mr 21,21:5
Violent Saturday 1955,My 12,32:2
Bottom of the Bottle, The 1956,F 2,19:2
Omar Khayyam 1957,Ag 24,12:4
Fraulein 1958,Je 9,27:2
Beat Generation, The 1959,O 22,47:4
House of Women 1962,Ap 12,41:6
13 West Street 1962,Je 7,31:2
Hayes, Marrijane (Original Author)
Bon Voyage! 1962,My 18,34:2
Hayes, Marvin
Carmen Jones 1954,O 29,27:2
Hayes, Maxwell
Climax, The 1944,D 14,28:5
Hayes, Melvyn
Man Who Loved Redheads, The 1955,Jl 26,29:2
Curse of Frankenstein, The 1957,Ag 8,15:5
Hayes, Nelson (Original Author)
Bahama Passage 1942,F 19,23:2
Hayes, Patricia
48 Hours 1944,Je 26,21:2
Nicholas Nickleby 1947,D 1,27:2
Battle of the Sexes, The 1960,Ap 19,40:4
Hayes, Peter Lind
These Glamour Girls 1939,Ag 31,14:2
Seventeen 1940,F 29,15:2
Playmates 1941,D 26,21:3
Seven Days' Leave 1942,D 11,33:2
Winged Victory 1944,D 21,16:2
Senator Was Indiscreet, The 1947,D 27,9:2
5,000 Fingers of Dr T, The 1953,Je 20,8:6
Hayes, Raphael (Screenwriter)
One Potato, Two Potato 1964,Jl 30,16:1
Hayes, Ron
Around the World Under the Sea 1966,Jl 21,20:2
Hayes, Russell (Screenwriter)
Hey Boy! Hey Girl! 1959,Ag 6,18:3
Hayes, Sam
Rebecca of Sunnybrook Farm 1938,Mr 26,12:1
Hitch-Hiker, The 1953,Ap 30,39:3
Hayes, William Edward (Original Author)
Black Doll, The 1938,F 7,10:2
Haygood, Paula
Birthright 1952,F 15,17:2
Hayle, Grace
Tovarich 1937,D 31,9:2
Our Neighbors-The Carters 1940,F 15,15:2
Great Dictator, The 1940,O 16,29:1
Let's Face It 1943,Ag 5,18:1
Don't Bother to Knock 1952,Jl 19,8:2
Haymes, Bob
Two Senoritas From Chicago 1943,Ag 6,10:4
Mr Winkle Goes to War 1944,Ag 3,16:1
Haymes, Dick
Four Jills in a Jeep 1944,Ap 6,27:2
Irish Eyes Are Smiling 1944,N 8,27:1
Billy Rose's Diamond Horseshoe 1945,My 3,37:1
State Fair 1945,Ag 31,14:3
Do You Love Me 1946,My 25,12:2
Shocking Miss Pilgrim, The 1947,F 12,34:2
Carnival in Costa Rica 1947,Mr 29,21:2
Up in Central Park 1948,My 27,29:3
One Touch of Venus 1948,O 29,29:5
HAYNES
See Also HAINES
Haynes, Arthur
Strange Bedfellows 1965,Mr 11,38:1
Haynes, Daniel
Hallelujah 1929,Ag 21,33:1
Last Mile, The 1932,Ag 26,20:3
Escape from Devil's Island 1935,N 25,22:2
So Red the Rose 1935,N 28,39:1
Haynes, Dick
Fuzzy Pink Nightgown, The 1957,O 31,41:1
Haynes, Hilda
Gone are the Days! 1963,S 24,43:2
Haynes, Manning (Director)
Should a Doctor Tell 1931,Ag 22,7:5
Haynes, Roberta
Fighter, The 1952,My 31,12:6
Return to Paradise 1953,S 11,24:2
Haynes, Stanley (Producer)
Madeleine 1950,S 1,17:2
Haynes, Stanley (Screenwriter)
One Woman's Story 1949,My 18,33:2
Madeleine 1950,S 1,17:2
Oliver Twist 1951,Jl 31,17:2
HAYS
See Also HAYES

Hays, Guerney
Chechahcos, The 1924,My 19,14:2
Hays, Kathryn
Ladybug, Ladybug 1963,D 24,9:1
Ride Beyond Vengance 1966,S 29,60:1
Counterpoint 1968,Mr 14,51:2
Hays, Will H Jr (Screenwriter)
You're my Everything 1949,Jl 23,7:2
Hayse, Emil
Moon of Israel 1927,Je 29,29:3
Haystead, Mercy
Admirable Crichton, The 1957,D 15,45:4 (Incorrect in this edition; use 1957,D 17,45:4 elsewhere)
Hayter, James
Nicholas Nickleby 1947,D 1,27:2
End of the River, The 1948,Je 21,18:2
All Over the Town 1949,My 26,34:4
Blue Lagoon, The 1949,O 3,13:2
Fallen Idol, The 1949,N 16,39:2
No Room at the Inn 1949,D 26,33:4
Silent Dust 1949,D 30,13:2
Eye Witness 1950,Ag 28,13:2
For Them that Trespass 1950,S 27,37:2
Verger, The 1950,O 11,42:1
Operation Disaster 1951,Ja 15,13:1
Her Panelled Door 1951,Ag 28,18:2
Tom Brown's School Days 1952,Ja 8,23:5
Story of Robin Hood, The 1952,Je 27,18:3
Crimson Pirate, The 1952,Ag 28,21:2
Four Sided Triangle 1953,My 16,10:1
Pickwick Papers, The 1954,Ap 5,21:2
Always a Bride 1954,My 28,19:2
Beau Brummell 1954,O 21,31:5
Land of the Pharaohs 1955,Jl 27,15:2
Will any Gentleman? 1955,S 28,70:6
Touch and go 1956,Mr 20,13:2
Port Afrique 1956,N 3,27:5
Abandon Ship 1957,Ap 18,35:1
Captain's Table, The 1960,S 27,40:1
39 Steps, The 1960,O 11,55:2
Haythorne, Joan
Svengali 1955,S 26,18:2
3 Men in a Boat 1959,Jl 29,33:2
Coming-Out Party, A 1962,Jl 31,19:2
Haythorne, Reed N (Cinematographer)
Human Adventure, The 1935,O 30,16:3
Hayton, Lennie (Composer)
Born to Sing 1942,F 19,23:2
Hayuting, Harvey (Producer)
Tarzan's Greatest Adventure 1959,Jl 9,22:1
Hayward, Brooke
Mad Dog Coll 1961,My 13,10:1
Hayward, Helen
Chaser, The 1928,Ap 10,33:2
Hayward, Jim
Vengeance Valley 1951,F 16,21:2
Excuse my Dust 1951,Je 28,21:2
Rhubarb 1951,Ag 31,12:2
Let's Make It Legal 1951,N 7,35:3
Pony Soldier 1952,D 20,15:2
Arena 1953,Jl 23,20:2
No Down Payment 1957,O 31,41:1
Hayward, Leland (Miscellaneous)
Mister Roberts 1955,Jl 15,14:1
Hayward, Leland (Original Author)
Whip Woman, The 1928,F 13,16:2
Hayward, Leland (Producer)
Mister Roberts 1955,Jl 15,14:1
Spirit of St Louis, The 1957,F 22,25:1
Old Man and the Sea, The 1958,O 8,41:1
Hayward, Lillie (Original Author)
Man Hunter, The 1930,Ap 5,23:3
Frisco Jenny 1933,Ja 7,11:2
Housewife 1934,Ag 10,21:2
Sons of the Legion 1938,S 30,24:3
Hayward, Lillie (Screenwriter)
White Cockatoo, The 1935,Ja 16,21:1
Front Page Woman 1935,Jl 12,15:1
Walking Dead, The 1936,Mr 2,13:2
Her Husband's Secretary 1937,Mr 20,23:6
Penrod and Sam 1937,Mr 29,14:3
That Man's Here Again 1937,My 6,23:3
Ever Since Eve 1937,Je 25,25:2
Blonde Trouble 1937,Ag 7,7:2
Night Club Scandal 1937,N 12,27:2
Expensive Husbands 1938,Ja 8,19:3
Her Jungle Love 1938,Ap 14,27:2
Sons of the Legion 1938,S 30,24:3
Disbarred 1939,Ja 19,17:2
King of Chinatown 1939,Mr 16,27:2
Biscuit Eater, The 1940,My 23,28:5
Aloma of the South Seas 1941,Ag 28,23:4
Margin for Error 1943,Ja 25,10:7
My Friend Flicka 1943,My 27,21:4
My Pal, Wolf 1944,O 9,17:2
Smoky 1946,Je 27,29:1
Black Beauty 1946,Ag 30,13:2
Blood on the Moon 1948,N 12,30:5
Northwest Stampede 1948,D 10,34:3
Follow Me Quietly 1949,Jl 8,14:5
Strange Bargain 1949,S 30,28:3
Cattle Drive 1951,Ag 9,17:5

Hayward, Lillie (Screenwriter) — Cont

Raiders, The 1952,D 13,19:2
Tarzan and the Lost Safari 1957,Ap 13,12:3
Proud Rebel, The 1958,Jl 2,23:4
Shaggy Dog, The 1959,Mr 20,26:2
Tonka 1959,Mr 26,27:1
Toby Tyler 1960,Ap 20,45:2
Boy and the Pirates, The 1960,N 24,48:3
Lad: A Dog 1963,My 2,40:2

Hayward, Louis

Sorrell and Son 1934,My 29,22:1
Flame Within, The 1935,Je 1,18:2
Feather in her Hat, A 1935,O 25,24:5
Absolute Quiet 1936,My 2,11:1
Trouble for Two 1936,My 30,7:2
Anthony Adverse 1936,Ag 27,16:1
Luckiest Girl in the World, The 1936,D 5,16:3
Woman I Love, The 1937,Ap 16,27:2
Condemned Woman 1938,Ap 22,15:5
Saint in New York, The 1938,My 26,31:2
Rage of Paris 1938,Jl 2,10:2
Duke of West Point, The 1938,D 16,33:2
Man in the Iron Mask, The 1939,Jl 14,11:1
My Son, My Son! 1940,My 10,26:6
Dance, Girl, Dance 1940,O 11,25:2
Son of Monte Cristo, The 1940,D 5,33:1
Ladies in Retirement 1941,N 7,27:1
And Then There Were None 1945,N 1,20:2
Young Widow 1946,Jl 29,12:8
Return of Monte Cristo, The 1947,Ja 3,16:4
Strange Woman, The 1947,F 24,16:4
Repeat Performance 1947,Jl 2,19:2
Ruthless 1948,S 4,8:7
Black Arrow, The 1948,O 4,14:2
Walk a Crooked Mile 1948,O 13,31:2
Pirates of Capri, The 1949,D 26,33:5
House by the River 1950,My 2,25:2
Fortunes of Captain Blood 1950,Je 10,11:3
Lady in the Iron Mask 1952,Jl 5,7:2
Duffy of San Quentin 1954,F 10,38:5
Chuka 1967,N 2,58:3

Hayward, Richard

Luck of the Irish, The 1937,Ja 16,21:1
Irish and Proud of It 1938,O 31,12:3

Hayward, Susan

Girls on Probation 1938,O 21,27:3
Beau Geste 1939,Ag 3,15:2
Our Leading Citizen 1939,Ag 24,17:1
$1,000 a Touchdown 1939,O 5,27:2
Adam Had Four Sons 1941,Mr 28,26:6
Sis Hopkins 1941,My 1,27:5
Among the Living 1941,D 13,25:2
Reap the Wild Wind 1942,Mr 27,27:2
Forest Rangers, The 1942,O 22,25:2
I Married a Witch 1942,N 20,27:2
Star Spangled Rhythm 1942,D 31,20:1
Hit Parade of 1943 1943,Ap 16,24:3
Jack London 1944,Mr 3,19:3
Fighting Seabees, The 1944,Mr 20,14:2
Hairy Ape, The 1944,Jl 3,8:3
And Now Tomorrow 1944,N 23,38:2
Deadline at Dawn 1946,Ap 4,33:2
Canyon Passage 1946,Ag 8,18:2
Smash-Up, The Story of a Woman 1947,Ap 11,31:2
They Won't Believe Me 1947,Jl 17,16:2
Lost Moment, The 1947,N 22,10:2
Tap Roots 1948,Ag 26,16:3
Saxon Charm, The 1948,S 30,32:3
Tulsa 1949,My 27,25:2
House of Strangers 1949,Jl 2,8:2
My Foolish Heart 1950,Ja 20,29:2
Rawhide 1951,Mr 26,19:2
I Can Get It for You Wholesale 1951,Ap 5,34:4
I'd Climb the Highest Mountain 1951,My 10,38:1
David and Bathsheba 1951,Ag 15,23:2
With a Song in my Heart 1952,Ap 5,20:2
Snows of Kilimanjaro, The 1952,S 19,19:2
Lusty Men, The 1952,O 25,12:6
President's Lady, The 1953,My 22,31:1
White Witch Doctor 1953,Jl 2,19:3
Demetrius and the Gladiators 1954,Je 19,9:1
Garden of Evil 1954,Jl 10,17:1
Untamed 1955,Mr 12,11:6
Soldier of Fortune 1955,My 28,7:4
I'll Cry Tomorrow 1956,Ja 13,18:1
Conqueror, The 1956,Mr 31,13:3
Top Secret Affair 1957,Ja 31,21:1
I Want to Live 1958,N 19,45:1
Thunder in the Sun 1959,Ap 9,37:2
Woman Obsessed 1959,My 28,34:1
Marriage-Go-Round 1961,Ja 7,12:2
Ada 1961,Ag 26,15:1
Back Street 1961,O 13,27:1
! Thank a Fool 1962,S 15,15:1
Stolen Hours 1963,O 17,39:1
Where Love Has Gone 1964,N 3,26:1
Honey Pot, The 1967,My 23,52:1
Valley of the Dolls 1967,D 16,51:1

HAYWOOD

See Also HEYWOOD

Haywood, George

Santa Fe Trail 1940,D 21,21:2

Hayworth, Rita

Criminals of the Air 1937,O 28,29:2
Paid to Dance 1937,D 6,19:1
Shadow, The 1937,D 17,33:3
Who Killed Gail Preston? 1938,My 6,27:2
Convicted 1938,Ag 22,9:3
Juvenile Court 1938,S 12,13:2
Homicide Bureau 1939,F 2,17:2
Renegade Ranger, The 1939,F 17,17:3
Lone Wolf Spy Hunt, The 1939,Mr 6,11:3
Only Angels Have Wings 1939,My 12,25:2
Music in My Heart 1940,Ja 4,19:2
Susan and God 1940,Jl 12,11:2
Angels Over Broadway 1940,N 18,23:2
Lady in Question, The 1940,D 10,33:2
Strawberry Blonde 1941,F 22,11:2
Blood and Sand 1941,My 23,25:3
Affectionaly Yours 1941,My 24,18:2
You'll Never Get Rich 1941,O 24,27:2
My Gal Sal 1942,My 1,23:1
Tales of Manhattan 1942,S 25,25:1
You Were Never Lovelier 1942,D 4,31:1
Cover Girl 1944,Mr 31,26:1
Tonight and Every Night 1945,Mr 9,16:2
Gilda 1946,Mr 15,27:2
Down to Earth 1947,S 12,18:2
Lady From Shanghai, The 1948,Je 10,28:2
Loves of Carmen, The 1948,S 3,16:2
Affair in Trinidad 1952,Jl 31,14:2
Salome 1953,Mr 25,37:1
Miss Sadie Thompson 1953,D 24,9:1
Fire Down Below 1957,Ag 9,11:2
Pal Joey 1957,O 28,30:1
Separate Tables 1958,D 19,2:7
They Came to Cordura 1959,O 22,47:2
Story of Page One, The 1960,Ja 14,28:1
Happy Thieves, The 1962,F 5,19:4
Circus World 1964,Je 26,34:2
Money Trap, The 1966,My 5,59:1
Poppy is Also a Flower, The 1967,D 14,62:4

Hayworth, Rita (Cansino)

Under the Pampas Moon 1935,My 31,11:1
Charlie Chan in Egypt 1935,Je 24,12:2
Dante's Inferno 1935,Ag 1,15:1
Paddy O'Day 1936,F 8,19:2
Human Cargo 1936,My 16,11:2
Meet Nero Wolfe 1936,Jl 16,20:1

Hayworth, Vinton

Girl He Left Behind, The 1956,O 27,17:1
Great Man, The 1957,Ja 2,28:2

Hazama, Michio

Beach Red 1967,Ag 4,18:1

HAZARD

See Also HAZZARD

Hazard, Jayne

Cadet Girl 1941,D 11,39:1
Powers Girl, The 1943,Mr 26,14:2 (In Addenda)
Black Market Babies 1946,Ap 1,23:1

Hazard, John W (Original Author)

U S S Teakettle 1951,F 24,11:2

Hazard, Lawrence (Miscellaneous)

Maybe It's Love 1935,F 11,14:2

Hazard, Lawrence (Original Author)

From Hell to Heaven 1933,Mr 18,9:3
Man's Castle 1933,D 30,9:2
I'll Love You Always 1935,Mr 30,11:2
Destination Unknown 1942,O 29,19:3
Forever and a Day 1943,Mr 13,9:2

Hazard, Lawrence (Screenwriter)

Hooray for Love 1935,Jl 13,16:2
Feather in her Hat, A 1935,O 25,24:5
Thoroughbreds Don't Cry 1937,N 26,27:4
Mannequin 1938,Ja 21,15:2
Strange Cargo 1940,Ap 26,25:2
Sporting Blood 1940,Jl 22,20:2
Spoilers, The 1942,My 22,27:2
Jackass Mail 1942,Jl 2,25:2
Gentle Annie 1945,My 5,11:5
Dakota 1945,D 17,17:2
She Went to the Races 1946,F 1,29:2
Wyoming 1947,Jl 25,12:5
Fabulous Texan, The 1947,D 26,22:5

Haze, Jonathon

Stakeout on Dope Street 1958,Ap 24,38:1

Hazel

Guide, The 1965,F 10,44:2

Hazell, Hy

Meet Me at Dawn 1948,My 18,26:2
Franchise Affair, The 1952,Je 6,19:2
Yellow Balloon, The 1954,O 13,28:2

Hazeltine, Horace (Original Author)

Sable Lorcha, The 1915,O 18,9:1

Hazelton, Phillip (Producer)

Cold Wind in August, A 1961,Jl 27,23:2
Psyche 39 1964,Ap 30,30:1
Shuttered Room, The 1968,F 15,47:1

Hazlet, Bill

Go West, Young Lady 1941,N 24,11:6

Hazlewood, Jean (Screenwriter)

Secret Ways, The 1961,My 25,31:1

HAZZARD

See Also HAZARD

Hazzard, John E (Original Author)

Turn to the Right 1922,Ja 24,11:1

Head, Bob

Treasure Island 1950,Ag 16,24:2

Head, Edith

Oscar, The 1966,Mr 5,16:1

Head, Jack Big

Jim Thorpe - All American 1951,Ag 25,7:2

Head, Murray

Family Way, The 1967,Je 29,32:1

Head, Ruby

Up the Junction 1968,Mr 14,51:1

Headrick, Richard

Rich Men's Wives 1922,Ag 21,6:2

Heal, Joan

Pickwick Papers, The 1954,Ap 5,21:2
Make Mine Mink 1960,D 20,43:4

Heald, Heinz (Screenwriter)

Great Flamario, The 1945,Ja 15,15:5

HEALEY

See Also HEALY

Healey, Myron

Man From Colorado 1949,Ja 21,24:3
Slightly French 1949,My 27,25:3
Short Grass 1951,Ja 13,10:4
Monsoon 1953,S 26,15:2
Cattle Queen of Montana 1955,Ja 26,22:1
African Manhunt 1957,Ap 20,21:4

Healey, Ted

Mad Holiday 1936,N 26,39:2

HEALY

See Also HEALEY

Healy, Betty

Our Relations 1936,N 11,55:1

Healy, Dan

Laughing Lady, The 1930,Ja 4,21:1
Glorifying the American Girl 1930,Ja 11,21:3

Healy, Eunice

Follow Your Heart 1936,O 22,31:1

Healy, Harold

Enemies of the Law 1931,Jl 13,13:5
Sign of the Cross, The 1932,D 1,25:1
Parachute Jumper 1933,Ja 26,12:2
Ladies They Talk About 1933,F 25,20:4
Gambling 1934,D 4,22:3

Healy, Mary

Second Fiddle 1939,Jl 1,11:2
Hotel for Women 1939,Ag 26,20:2
20,000 Men a Year 1939,O 28,11:2
He Married his Wife 1940,Ja 20,11:2
Star Dust 1940,My 4,13:1
5,000 Fingers of Dr T, The 1953,Je 20,8:6

Healy, Michael (Producer)

You Can't Fool an Irishman 1950,D 7,45:4

Healy, Myron

Mask of the Himalayas 1953,Ag 12,22:3

Healy, Ted

Stage Mother 1933,S 30,18:5
Bombshell 1933,O 21,11:2
Meet the Baron 1933,O 28,20:3
Dancing Lady 1933,D 1,23:2
Fugitive Lovers 1934,Ja 13,16:3
Myrt and Marge 1934,Ja 17,23:2
Lazy River 1934,Ap 4,26:2
Hollywood Party 1934,My 26,12:2
Operator 13 1934,Je 23,16:5
Paris Interlude 1934,Jl 28,16:5
Death on the Diamond 1934,S 24,14:1
Band Plays on, The 1934,D 22,21:2
Winning Ticket, The 1935,F 11,14:2
Casino Murder Case, The 1935,Ap 17,26:5
Reckless 1935,Ap 20,16:1
Murder in the Fleet 1935,Je 3,22:2
Mad Love 1935,Ag 5,20:2
It's in the Air 1935,N 8,18:2
Speed 1936,My 16,11:2
San Francisco 1936,Je 27,21:1
Sing, Baby, Sing 1936,S 12,20:1
Longest Night, The 1936,O 17,21:2
Man of the People 1937,F 23,25:4
Good Old Soak 1937,Ap 20,25:3
Varsity Show 1937,S 2,17:2
Hollywood Hotel 1938,Ja 13,17:3
Love Is a Headache 1938,Ja 28,17:3

Heaps, Alan

Lord of the Flies 1963,Ag 20,37:1

Heaps, Jonathan

Lord of the Flies 1963,Ag 20,37:1

HEARD

See Also HURD

Heard, H F (Original Author)

Deadly Bees, The 1967,My 20,39:2

Hearn, Edward

When a Man's a Man 1924,F 5,20:1
Daughters of Today 1924,Mr 4,17:1
Man Without a Country, The 1925,F 12,16:1
Harvester, The 1927,N 7,33:1
Ned McCobb's Daughter 1929,F 18,28:1
Donovan Affair, The 1929,Ap 29,29:2
Drake Case, The 1929,S 16,30:1
Hide Out 1930,Ap 12,23:1
Rainbow Trail, The 1932,Ja 30,13:2
Young and Beautiful 1934,S 18,18:4

Hearn, Lafcadio (Original Author)
Kwaidan (In the Cup of Tea); In the Cup of Tea (Kwaidan) 1965,N 23,51:1
Kwaidan (Black Hair); Black Hair (Kwaidan) 1965,N 23,51:1
Kwaidan (Hoichi, The Earless); Hoichi, The Earless (Kwaidan) 1965,N 23,51:1
Hearn, Lew
See America Thirst 1930,D 12,35:3
International Crime 1938,My 16,14:4
Specter of the Rose 1946,S 2,12:4
Inspector General, The 1949,D 31,9:2
Go, Man, Go 1954,Mr 10,29:5
Hearn, Mary
Conquering Power, The 1921,Jl 10,VI,2:1 (In Addenda)
Hearn, Sam
Florida Special 1936,My 29,15:2
Inspector General, The 1949,D 31,9:2
Hearne, James A
Shore Acres 1920,My 17,19:3
Hearne, Richard
Dance Band 1936,Ja 4,19:2
Captain Horatio Hornblower 1951,S 14,21:2
Miss Robin Hood 1953,Je 27,7:2
HEARST
See HURST
Heasley, John
5,000 Fingers of Dr T, The 1953,Je 20,8:6
Heater, Claude
Ben Hur 1959,N 19,50:2
Heath, Ariel
Leopard Man, The 1943,My 20,26:4
Heath, Dody
Brigadoon 1954,S 17,18:2
Diary of Anne Frank, The 1959,Mr 19,40:1
Ask any Girl 1959,My 22,32:1
Seconds 1966,O 6,56:1
Heath, George (Screenwriter)
Rats of Tobruk, The 1951,My 24,47:3
Heath, Gordon
Heroes and Sinners; (Heros Sont Fatigues, Les) 1959,My 12,38:2
Sapphire 1959,N 3,27:1
Heath, Hy (Composer)
That's Right, You're Wrong 1939,N 30,25:3
Pot o'Gold 1941,Ap 4,25:2
Heath, Len (Original Author)
Up the Creek 1958,N 11,26:2
Heath, Len (Screenwriter)
Up the Creek 1958,N 11,26:2
Two-Way Stretch 1961,Ja 24,20:3
Wrong Arm of the Law, The 1963,Ap 3,39:1
Heath, Mark
Call Me Bwana 1963,Jl 4,9:1
Heath, Percy (Original Author)
Slightly Scarlet 1930,Mr 1,23:1
Safety in Numbers 1930,My 31,19:4
Gang Buster, The 1931,Ja 24,15:1
Heath, Percy (Screenwriter)
Impossible Mrs Bellew, The 1922,O 23,10:1
Rolled Stockings 1927,Jl 19,27:2
Tell It to Sweeney 1927,O 17,20:2
Two Flaming Youths 1928,Ja 2,28:1
Close Harmony 1929,Ap 29,29:2
Let's Go Native 1930,Ag 30,7:4
Heath, William L (Original Author)
Violent Saturday 1955,My 12,32:2
Heathcote, Thomas
Sword and the Rose, The 1953,Ag 20,18:3
Heather, Jean
Going my Way 1944,My 3,25:2
Double Indemnity 1944,S 7,21:1
Our Hearts Were Young and Gay 1944,O 12,24:2
Murder, He Says 1945,Je 25,20:3
Well Groomed Bride, The 1946,My 11,22:5
Red Stallion in the Rockies 1949,Ag 26,15:2
Heatherley, Clifford
Love Habit, The 1931,F 2,23:1
Magic Night 1932,N 3,25:3
After the Ball 1933,Mr 20,18:3
Fires of Fate 1933,Ap 3,13:4
Bitter Sweet 1933,Ag 24,18:2
Catherine the Great 1934,F 15,15:6
Private Life of Don Juan, The 1934,D 10,16:2
Heatherton, Joey
Twilight of Honor 1963,N 14,41:2
Where Love Has Gone 1964,N 3,26:1
My Blood Runs Cold 1965,Mr 25,42:4
Heaton, Tom
Bandolero 1968,Jl 18,26:2
Heatter, Gabriel
Champagne for Caesar 1950,My 12,33:2
Hebay, Jean
Avocate d'Amour 1938,S 8,27:2
Hebert, Paul
Mouchette 1968,S 21,26:1
Hebey, Jean
Queen's Necklace, The 1947,My 17,8:5
Ma Pomme 1951,O 15,22:2
Strollers, The 1952,Jl 22,22:7
To Catch a Thief 1955,Ag 5,14:2

HECHT
See Also HECK
Hecht, Ben (Director)
Crime Without Passion 1934,S 1,16:2
Scoundrel, The 1935,My 3,23:2
Soak the Rich 1936,F 5,14:2
Once in a Blue Moon 1936,D 2,35:1
Angels Over Broadway 1940,N 18,23:2
Specter of the Rose 1946,S 2,12:4
Actors and Sin; (Actor's Blood) 1952,My 30,11:3
Actors and Sin; (Woman of Sin) 1952,My 30,11:3
Hecht, Ben (Original Author)
Underworld 1927,Ag 22,21:3
Great Gabbo, The 1929,S 13,33:1
Unholy Night, The 1929,O 12,11:1
Roadhouse Nights 1930,F 22,13:1
Roadhouse Nights 1930,Mr 2,IX,5:1
Front Page, The 1931,Mr 20,29:1
Unholy Garden, The 1931,O 29,27:1
Hallelujah, I'm a Bum 1933,F 9,15:2
Turn Back the Clock 1933,Ag 26,14:2
20th Century 1934,My 4,24:2
Upper World 1934,My 25,25:4
Shoot the Works 1934,Jl 7,16:5
Florentine Dagger, The 1935,Ap 27,20:6
Once in a Blue Moon 1936,D 2,35:1
Goldwyn Follies, The 1938,F 21,15:1
Gunga Din 1939,Ja 28,19:2
Let Freedom Ring 1939,Mr 10,19:2
It's a Wonderful World 1939,My 19,27:2
Some Like It Hot 1939,My 25,31:2
His Girl Friday 1940,Ja 12,13:2
Specter of the Rose 1946,S 2,12:4
Perfect Strangers 1950,Mr 11,8:2
Miracle in the Rain 1956,Ap 2,18:1
Jumbo 1962,D 7,49:1
Hecht, Ben (Producer)
Crime Without Passion 1934,S 1,16:2
Scoundrel, The 1935,My 3,23:2
Soak the Rich 1936,F 5,14:2
Once in a Blue Moon 1936,D 2,35:1
Angels Over Broadway 1940,N 18,23:2
China Girl 1943,Ja 21,27:2
Specter of the Rose 1946,S 2,12:4
Actors and Sin; (Woman of Sin) 1952,My 30,11:3
Actors and Sin; (Actor's Blood) 1952,My 30,11:3
Hecht, Ben (Screenwriter)
Crime Without Passion 1934,S 1,16:2
Scoundrel, The 1935,My 3,23:2
Barbary Coast 1935,O 14,21:1
Soak the Rich 1936,F 5,14:2
Nothing Sacred 1937,N 26,27:2
Goldwyn Follies, The 1938,F 21,15:1
Let Freedom Ring 1939,Mr 10,19:2
Wuthering Heights 1939,Ap 14,28:2
It's a Wonderful World 1939,My 19,27:2
Lady of the Tropics 1939,S 8,28:3
Angels Over Broadway 1940,N 18,23:2
Comrade X 1940,D 26,23:1
Lydia 1941,S 19,27:1
Ten Gentlemen From West Point 1942,Je 5,23:3
Tales of Manhattan 1942,S 25,25:1
Black Swan, The 1942,D 24,18:3
China Girl 1943,Ja 21,27:2
Spellbound 1945,N 2,22:2
Notorious 1946,Ag 16,19:2
Kiss of Death 1947,Ag 28,28:2
Ride the Pink Horse 1947,O 9,32:3
Her Husband's Affairs 1947,N 14,29:2
Miracle of the Bells, The 1948,Mr 17,30:1
Whirlpool 1950,Ja 14,9:2
Where the Sidewalk Ends 1950,Jl 8,7:4
Actors and Sin; (Woman of Sin) 1952,My 30,11:3
Actors and Sin; (Actor's Blood) 1952,My 30,11:3
Monkey Business 1952,S 6,12:6
Ulysses 1955,Ag 18,17:2
Indian Fighter, The 1955,D 22,20:1
Miracle in the Rain 1956,Ap 2,18:1
Legend of the Lost 1957,D 23,18:2
Farewell to Arms, A 1958,Ja 25,14:1
Circus World 1964,Je 26,34:2
Hecht, Harold (Producer)
Flame and the Arrow, The 1950,Jl 8,7:2
Ten Tall Men 1951,O 27,10:5
Crimson Pirate, The 1952,Ag 28,21:2
His Majesty O'Keefe 1954,F 6,17:2
Apache 1954,Jl 10,7:2
Marty 1955,Ap 12,25:3
Kentuckian, The 1955,S 2,13:2
Bachelor Party, The 1957,Ap 10,37:2
Run Silent, Run Deep 1958,Mr 28,29:1
Separate Tables 1958,D 19,2:7
Devil's Disciple, The 1959,Ag 21,12:1
Taras Bulba 1962,D 26,5:2
Wild and Wonderful 1964,Je 11,27:4
Cat Ballou 1965,Je 25,36:1
Way West, The 1967,My 25,54:1
Hecht, Jenny
Actors and Sin; (Woman of Sin) 1952,My 30,11:3
Hecht, Ted
Time to Kill 1942,D 25,15:4
So Proudly We Hail 1943,S 10,29:1
Tarzan and the Huntress 1947,Ap 7,20:4

Hecht, Ted— Cont
Gangster, The 1947,O 31,29:3
Man-Eater of Kumaon 1948,Jl 2,24:2
Bad Men of Tombstone 1949,Mr 5,10:2
Song of India 1949,Je 10,32:3
Blue Grass of Kentucky 1950,Ja 27,29:2
HECK
See Also HECHT
Heck, Stanton
Bad Man, The 1923,O 9,17:4
Courtship of Myles Standish, The 1923,D 31,9:3
Woman on the Jury, The 1924,My 19,14:2
Silent Sanderson 1925,Je 11,14:3
Mystic, The 1925,Ag 31,19:3
Old Clothes 1925,N 9,25:1
Her Honor the Governor 1926,Jl 20,17:3
Yankee Clipper, The 1927,My 3,25:1
Heckart, Eileen
Miracle in the Rain 1956,Ap 2,18:1
Somebody up There Likes Me 1956,Jl 6,16:1
Bus Stop 1956,S 1,19:2
Bad Seed, The 1956,S 13,39:6
Hot Spell 1958,S 18,37:2
Heller in Pink Tights 1960,Mr 17,28:1
My Six Loves 1963,Ap 4,58:4
Up the Down Staircase 1967,Ag 18,36:2
No Way to Treat a Lady 1968,Mr 21,56:1
Heckelmann, Charles (Original Author)
Deputy Marshal 1949,N 11,31:3
Heckers, Jean (Screenwriter)
Backfire 1965,Ap 27,27:1
Heckstall-Smith, V (Original Author)
Unwritten Law, The 1929,D 24,14:5
Hector, Louis
Northwest Passage 1940,Mr 8,25:1
Hedeby, Kerstin
Dreams; Kvinnodrom 1960,Je 1,42:1
Hedengran, Solveig
Skaergaards-Flirt 1936,Ap 8,26:3
Raggen, Det Aer Jag Det 1936,My 22,19:1
Familjen Som Var En Karusel 1937,My 22,19:3
Children, The 1949,D 23,17:1
Hedge, Ray
Myrt and Marge 1934,Ja 17,23:2
Hedges, Lionel
Battle of Gallipoli, The 1931,D 7,16:1
Hedin, June
I Remember Mama 1948,Mr 12,29:2
Thirteenth Letter, The 1951,F 22,27:2
Member of the Wedding, The 1952,D 31,10:2
Hedison, Al
Enemy Below, The 1957,D 26,23:2
Fly, The 1958,Ag 30,6:6
Hedison, David
Lost World, The 1960,Jl 14,23:1
Marines, Lets Go! 1961,Ag 16,37:2
Greatest Story Ever Told, The 1965,F 16,40:2
Hedley, Jack
Make Mine Mink 1960,D 20,43:4
Left, Right and Centre 1961,F 10,19:1
In the French Style 1963,S 19,23:1
Of Human Bondage 1964,S 24,46:2
How I Won the War 1967,N 9,56:1
Anniversary, The 1968,Mr 21,57:2
Hedlund, Guy
Last of the Redmen 1947,Ag 30,8:6
Hedquist, Ivan
Youth 1927,N 30,22:4
Vaermlaenningarna 1932,N 18,23:2
Hedren, Tippi
Birds, The 1963,Ap 1,5:5 (Incorrect in this edition; use 1963,Ap 1,54:1 elsewhere)
Marnie 1964,Je 23,19:1
Countess from Hong Kong, A 1967,Mr 17,35:1
Hedstrom, Tina
My Sister, My Love 1967,F 20,45:2
Guilt 1967,N 21,53:1
Hedwall, Frithiof
Sun Over Klara 1944,My 1,20:8
Hee, T (Miscellaneous)
Reluctant Dragon, The 1941,Jl 25,12:2
Hee, T (Screenwriter)
Victory Through Air Power 1943,Jl 19,13:1
HEER
See Also HARE
Heer, Jacob Christopher (Original Author)
Eternal Love 1929,My 13,27:2
Heerer, Astrid
Thomas Crown Affair, The 1968,Je 27,48:2
Heerman, Victor (Director)
Rupert of Hentzau 1923,Jl 9,8:4
Dangerous Maid, The 1923,D 11,26:2
Confidence Man, The 1924,Ap 15,24:1
Old Home Week 1925,My 25,21:3
For Wives Only 1926,D 1,24:5
Rubber Heels 1927,Je 28,29:4
Ladies Must Dress 1927,D 31,31:1
Love Hungry 1928,Ap 16,20:5
Animal Crackers 1930,Ag 29,20:3
Sea Legs 1930,N 11,29:1
Heerman, Victor (Screenwriter)
Little Minister, The 1934,D 28,25:1
Break of Hearts 1935,My 17,24:3
Magnificent Obsession 1935,D 31,11:2

Heerman, Victor (Screenwriter)— Cont
Golden Boy 1939,S 8,28:2
Little Women 1949,Mr 11,33:2
Magnificent Obsession 1954,Ag 5,18:4
Heermance, Richard (Producer)
Maze, The 1953,Jl 11,8:2
Heesters, Johannes
Bettelstudent, Der 1936,D 28,12:3
Wenn Frauen Schweigen; When Women Keep
  Silent 1937,S 11,20:2
Gasparone 1938,Mr 12,13:4
Nanon 1938,N 26,18:2
Das Erlebnis Geht Weiter; Another Experience
  1940,F 3,9:3
Fledermaus, Die; Bat, The 1948,Mr 15,26:2
White Horse Inn, The 1957,D 4,50:3
Heesters, Nicole
Cabaret 1957,N 9,31:2 (Incorrect in this edition;
  use 1957,N 7,43:4 elsewhere)
Heffley, Warren
Crime and Punishment, U S A 1959,Je 17,39:3
Heffley, Wayne
Outsider, The 1962,F 8,25:1
Heffron, Richard (Screenwriter)
Great St Louis Bank Robbery, The 1960,F 4,34:1
Heffron, Thomas (Director)
City of Masks, The 1920,Jl 12,12:4
Sham 1921,My 6,20:2
Heflin, Van
Woman Rebels, A 1936,O 30,27:2
Outcasts of Poker Flat, The 1937,Ap 27,18:3
Flight From Glory 1937,S 11,20:1
Annapolis Salute 1937,O 2,18:1
Saturday's Heroes 1937,O 16,22:2
Santa Fe Trail 1940,D 21,21:2
Feminine Touch, The 1941,D 12,35:3
H M Pulham, Esq 1941,D 19,35:1
Johnny Eager 1942,F 20,21:2
Kid Glove Killer 1942,Ap 17,21:4
Grand Central Murder 1942,My 23,8:8
Seven Sweethearts 1942,N 13,28:1
Tennessee Johnson 1943,Ja 13,18:2
Presenting Lily Mars 1943,Ap 30,25:3
Strange Love of Martha Ivers, The
  1946,Jl 25,18:4
Till the Clouds Roll By 1946,D 6,27:4
Possessed 1947,My 30,25:2
Green Dolphin Street 1947,O 16,34:2
B F's Daughter 1948,Mr 25,35:2
Tap Roots 1948,Ag 26,16:3
Three Musketeers, The 1948,O 21,33:2
Act of Violence 1949,Ja 24,16:2
Madame Bovary 1949,Ag 26,15:2
East Side, West Side 1949,D 23,17:2
Tomahawk 1951,F 19,19:2
Prowler, The 1951,Jl 2,16:6
My Son John 1952,Ap 9,27:1
Shane 1953,Ap 24,30:3
Wings of the Hawk 1953,Ag 27,22:1
Golden Mask, The 1954,Mr 20,10:5
Tanganyika 1954,Je 19,9:2
Raid, The 1954,Ag 21,10:4
Woman's World 1954,S 29,23:4
Black Widow 1954,O 28,46:6
Battle Cry 1955,F 3,18:1
Patterns 1956,Mr 28,26:1
3:10 to Yuma 1957,Ag 29,22:1
Tempest 1959,Mr 27,19:2
They Came to Cordura 1959,O 22,47:2
Five Branded Women 1960,Je 2,27:2
Under ten Flags 1960,S 16,24:1
Cry of Battle 1963,O 12,27:2
Wastrel, The 1963,N 5,24:1
Greatest Story Ever Told, The 1965,F 16,40:2
Once a Thief 1965,S 9,36:1
Stagecoach 1966,Je 16,53:1
Heflin, Van (Narrator)
Secret Land, The 1948,D 2,39:2
Hegarth, Alexander
Jack of Diamonds 1967,N 11,26:3
Hegeman, Alice
Laughing Lady, The 1930,Ja 4,21:1
Heger, Karl
Livet paa Hegnsgaard; Life on the Hegn Farm
  1939,N 13,15:2
Hegetschweiler, Emil
Heidi and Peter 1955,D 13,55:2
Heggen, Thomas (Original Author)
Mister Roberts 1955,Jl 15,14:1
Heggie, O P
Actress, The 1928,Jl 9,25:1
Letter, The 1929,Mr 8,30:1
Wheel of Life, The 1929,Je 24,27:1
Insidious Dr Fu Manchu, The 1929,Jl 22,17:1
Mysterious Dr Fu Manchu, The
  1929,Jl 28,VIII,3:7 (In Addenda)
Mighty, The 1929,D 30,16:4
Vagabond King, The 1930,F 20,22:4
Vagabond King, The 1930,Mr 2,IX,5:1
New Adventures of Dr Fu Manchu, The
  1930,My 3,23:1
One Romantic Night 1930,My 31,19:4
Playboy of Paris 1930,N 1,23:2
Sunny 1930,D 27,16:3

East Lynne 1931,F 21,15:2
Too Young to Marry 1931,My 4,15:3
Devotion 1931,O 3,20:2
Woman Between, The 1931,O 24,20:3
Smilin' Through 1932,O 15,13:1
King's Vacation, The 1933,Ja 20,21:2
Zoo in Budapest 1933,Ap 28,15:2
Midnight 1934,Mr 10,18:3
Count of Monte Cristo, The 1934,S 27,25:2
Peck's bad Boy 1934,O 6,20:1
Anne of Green Gables 1934,D 22,21:1
Bride of Frankenstein, The 1935,My 11,21:2
Ginger 1935,Jl 19,13:2
Prisoner of Shark Island, The 1936,F 13,25:2
Hegira, Anne
On the Waterfront 1954,Jl 29,18:1
Hehn, Albert
Drei Unteroffiziere; Three Non-Coms
  1939,My 20,11:3
Heiberc, Christina
Legittima Difesa; Self Defense 1940,Ap 6,13:3
Heid, Trevor
How to Murder a Rich Uncle 1957,O 26,19:2
Heideman, Leonard (Miscellaneous)
Walk East on Beacon 1952,My 29,17:2
Heidemann, Paul
Jumping Jack, The; Hampelmann, Der
  1931,My 24,VIII,4:1
Hampelmann, Der 1931,S 8,38:7
Ihre Hoheit Befiehlt 1931,N 7,16:5
Kyritz-Pyritz 1932,Ag 9,20:5
Schoen Ist die Manoeverzeit 1932,Ag 19,20:6
Pension Schoeller 1932,S 20,26:3
Wenn die Soldaten 1932,O 31,18:4
Die Mutter der Kompagnie 1934,Mr 9,22:3
Ja, Treu Ist die Soldatenliebe 1934,Ap 28,11:4
Wie Man Maenner Fesselt 1934,My 21,20:3
Abel Mit Der Mundharmonika 1934,S 1,16:3
Liebe in Uniform 1934,O 9,17:2
Drei von der Kavallerie 1935,Ap 13,11:4
Schuechterne Felix, Der 1935,S 7,19:5
Tolle Bomberg, Der 1935,O 26,12:2
Vetter aus Dingsda, Der 1936,F 1,9:3
Die Ganze Welt Dreht Sich um Liebe
  1936,N 27,27:2
Ist Mein Mann Nicht Fabelhaft 1936,D 8,31:3
Junge Graf, Der 1936,D 14,15:2
Freuhling im Wien 1937,F 6,15:2
Hilde Petersen, Postlagernd 1937,Je 26,20:3 (In
  Addenda)
Unwiderst Ehliche, Der; Irresistable Man, The
  1937,D 20,23:3
Lachdoktor, Der; Laugh Doctor, The
  1938,Mr 12,13:4
Peter, Paul und Nanette 1940,My 25,20:1
HEIDEN
See Also HADDON, HAYDEN
Heiden, Eddie Dale
Little Men 1935,F 18,19:3
Heidt, Horace
Pot o'Gold 1941,Ap 4,25:2
Heidt, Horace, Orchestra
Pot o'Gold 1941,Ap 4,25:2
Heifetz, Jascha
They Shall Have Music 1939,Jl 26,17:2
Carnegie Hall 1947,My 3,10:2
Of Men and Music 1951,F 15,27:2
Heifetz, Joseph (Director)
Baltic Deputy 1937,S 4,8:2
Heifetz, L (Original Author)
International House 1933,My 27,11:5
I Have Lived 1933,S 6,24:4
Shadows of the Orient 1937,O 11,26:6
Heifetz, Vladimir (Composer)
Green Fields 1937,O 12,31:4
Last Chapter, The 1966,F 22,14:5
Heifitz, Josef (Director)
Red Army Days 1935,O 21,22:4
Last Hill, The 1945,Je 26,13:2
In the Name of Life 1947,O 20,29:2
Big Family, A 1955,Je 6,24:1
My Beloved 1959,Je 15,31:4
Lady With the Dog, The 1962,N 7,48:1
Heifitz, Josef (Producer)
Lady With the Dog, The 1962,N 7,48:1
Heifitz, Josef (Screenwriter)
Baltic Deputy 1937,S 4,8:2
Last Hill, The 1945,Je 26,13:2
In the Name of Life 1947,O 20,29:2
Lady With the Dog, The 1962,N 7,48:1
Heigh, Helene
Her Sister's Secret 1947,Ja 23,31:3
Heilbron, Adelaide (Original Author)
French Dressing 1927,D 13,33:2
It's all Yours 1938,Ja 7,15:3
Heilbron, Adelaide (Screenwriter)
Girl of the Golden West, The 1923,My 21,12:2
New Lives for Old 1925,F 25,16:7
Dressmaker from Paris, The 1925,Mr 18,19:2
Mantrap 1926,Jl 12,24:4
Cheers for Miss Bishop 1941,Mr 14,17:2
Friendly Enemies 1942,Je 22,19:1

Heillinger, Heinrich
Heideschulmeister uwe Karsten 1934,Ap 14,18:3
Drei Kaiserjaeger 1935,Mr 16,19:1
Heilman, Claude (Producer)
Earth Is Mine, The 1959,Je 27,13:1
Heim, Emery H (Composer)
Ecstasy 1940,D 25,33:2
HEIMANN
See Also HYMAN
Heimann, Peter (Miscellaneous)
Dolly Macht Karriere 1931,Jl 18,16:6
Heims, Jo (Screenwriter)
Double Trouble 1967,My 25,54:2
Heindorf, Ray (Composer)
Rhapsody in Blue 1945,Je 28,22:2
Love and Learn 1947,My 3,10:3
HEINE
See Also HINE
Heine, Albert
Tochter des Regiments, Die 1934,Mr 31,8:3
Heinlein, Robert (Original Author)
Destination Moon 1950,Je 28,32:2
Heinlein, Robert (Screenwriter)
Destination Moon 1950,Je 28,32:2
Heinrich, Andre (Producer)
Le Joli Mai 1966,Je 10,54:2
Heinrich, George
Waterloo 1929,Ap 16,32:5
Constant Nymph, The 1929,Je 10,23:1
Heinrich, Mimi
Journey to the Seventh Planet 1962,My 25,28:3
Heinrich, Susanne
Eric Soya's 17 1967,Ja 25,37:1
Heintel, Kurt
Embezzled Heaven 1959,Ap 24,23:1
Heinz, Gerard
Caravan 1949,Ap 21,30:4
Broken Journey 1949,My 26,34:3
Girl in the Painting, The 1949,Ag 22,13:1
Fallen Idol, The 1949,N 16,39:2
If This Be Sin 1950,Jl 1,9:2
Lost People, The 1950,O 2,19:4
Clouded Yellow, The 1951,N 13,33:2
Desperate Moment 1953,S 1,19:4
Prisoner, The 1955,D 12,37:1
His Excellency 1956,F 2,19:3
Mark of the Hawk, The 1958,Mr 6,32:1
House of the Seven Hawks, The 1959,D 17,51:2
I Aim at the Stars 1960,O 20,42:2
Heinze, Peter
Bible, The 1966,S 29,60:1
Heisler, Stuart (Director)
Biscuit Eater, The 1940,My 23,28:5
Monster and the Girl, The 1941,Mr 20,25:3
Among the Living 1941,D 13,25:2
Remarkable Andrew, The 1942,Mr 6,17:2
Glass Key, The 1942,O 16,23:1
Along Came Jones 1945,Jl 19,8:7
Blue Skies 1946,O 17,28:2
Smash-Up, The Story of a Woman
  1947,Ap 11,31:2
Tulsa 1949,My 27,25:2
Tokyo Joe 1949,O 27,35:2
Chain Lightning 1950,F 20,21:2
Dallas 1951,Ja 13,10:4
Storm Warning 1951,Mr 3,8:2
Journey Into Light 1951,O 5,24:4
Star, The 1953,Ja 29,25:1
Beachhead 1954,Ap 17,8:2
This is my Love 1954,D 25,7:3
I Died a Thousand Times 1955,N 10,45:2
Lone Ranger, The 1956,F 11,12:1
Burning Hills, The 1956,Ag 24,15:2
Heiss, Carol
Snow White and the Three Stooges 1961,Jl 1,9:1
Helbert, Jack
Stephen Steps Out 1923,N 19,19:3
Helbig, Heinz (Director)
Seine Tochter Ist der Peter; His Daughter is Peter
  1938,Mr 28,19:3
Helbling, Jeanne
Avec l'Assurance 1935,My 4,17:3
Helene 1938,Ja 22,19:1
Three Waltzes 1939,Ap 25,19:2
Fire in the Straw 1943,Jl 2,15:2
Held, Anna
Madame la Presidente 1916,F 7,9:3
Held, Karl
That Darn Cat 1965,D 3,44:1
Held, Martin
Deadly Decision 1958,Ap 29,26:2
Captain from Koepenick, The 1958,Jl 26,6:1
Roses for the Prosecutor; (Rosen fur den
  Staarsanwalt) 1961,O 10,38:2
And so to Bed 1965,Jl 31,11:3
Oldest Profession, The (Gay Nineties, The); Gay
  Nineties, The (The Oldest Profession)
  1968,N 8,42:1
Held, Tania
Long Dark Hall, The 1951,My 10,38:3
Heldabrand, John
On the Waterfront 1954,Jl 29,18:1
Wrong Man, The 1956,D 24,8:1

Helfon, Samy
Trans-Europ-Express 1968,My 13,52:1
Helfon, Samy (Producer)
Trans-Europ-Express 1968,My 13,52:1
Helgar, Eric
Du Bist mein Gluck; Thou Art my Joy 1940,Ja 6,9:2
Helia, Jenny
Amours de Toni, Les 1936,N 5,35:1
Marseillaise 1939,N 6,20:2
Human Beast, The 1940,F 20,17:2
Toni 1968,S 19,62:2
Helier, Ivy St
Henry V 1946,Je 18,30:2
Hell, Arthur
Blonde Nachtigall, Die 1931,Ag 22,7:5
Hell, Erik
Frustration 1949,Ag 27,7:3
One Summer of Happiness 1955,Mr 22,35:2
Sorciere, La 1956,D 28,17:2
Dear John 1966,Mr 9,46:1
Hellard, Simone
Coiffeur Pour Dames 1932,O 31,18:4
Mistigri 1933,Ja 13,19:3
Topaze 1935,F 16,9:2
Criez-Le sur les Toits; Shout it From the Housetops 1935,Je 22,18:5
Hellberg, Ruth
Kleine Suenderin, Die; Little Sinner, The 1938,D 3,11:3
Drei Unteroffiziere; Three Non-Coms 1939,My 20,11:3
Hellen, Marjorie
Virgin Queen, The 1955,Ag 6,13:2
Heller, Cindy
Singing in the Dark 1956,Mr 8,32:5
Heller, E
Asphalt 1930,My 6,33:4
Thirteen Men and a Girl 1931,Ag 17,18:2
Adventures in Bokhara 1944,Ag 21,9:4
Heller, Gloria
Wine of Youth 1924,Ag 11,16:1
So This Is Marriage 1924,D 23,16:2
Heller, Joseph (Screenwriter)
Sex and the Single Girl 1964,D 26,9:2
Heller, Lukas (Miscellaneous)
Sapphire 1959,N 3,27:1
Heller, Lukas (Screenwriter)
What Ever Happened to Baby Jane? 1962,N 7,48:1
Hush...Hush, Sweet Charlotte 1965,Mr 4,36:1
Agent 8 3/4 1965,O 14,53:1
Flight of the Phoenix, The 1966,F 1,26:1
Dirty Dozen, The 1967,Je 16,36:1
Killing of Sister George, The 1968,D 17,58:4
Heller, Paul M (Producer)
David and Lisa 1962,D 27,5:5
Eavesdropper, The 1966,S 15,51:1
Come Spy with Me 1967,F 22,21:1
Heller, Ray
It Must Be Love 1926,O 4,20:2
Helliman, Earl
Giant 1956,O 11,51:1
Hellinger, Mark (Original Author)
Night Court 1932,My 27,27:5
Broadway Bill 1934,N 30,22:2
Roaring Twenties, The 1939,N 11,12:1
Riding High 1950,Ap 11,26:2
Hellinger, Mark (Producer)
Rise and Shine 1941,D 6,14:3
Moontide 1942,Ap 30,14:1
Thank Your Lucky Stars 1943,O 2,19:2
Between Two Worlds 1944,My 6,11:2
Doughgirls, The 1944,Ag 31,14:1
Horn Blows at Midnight, The 1945,Ap 21,18:2
Killers, The 1946,Ag 29,24:2
Two Mrs Carrolls, The 1947,Ap 7,20:1
Brute Force 1947,Jl 17,16:2
Naked City, The 1948,Mr 5,17:2
Hellinger, Mark (Screenwriter)
Comet over Broadway 1938,D 16,33:3
Hellman, George S (Original Author)
Night in Paradise 1946,Je 6,16:3
Hellman, Jerome (Producer)
World of Henry Orient, The 1964,Mr 20,27:2
Fine Madness, A 1966,Je 30,28:2
Hellman, Lillian (Miscellaneous)
Watch on the Rhine 1943,Ag 28,15:1
Hellman, Lillian (Original Author)
These Three 1936,Mr 19,22:4
Spanish Earth, The 1937,Ag 21,7:2
Little Foxes, The 1941,Ag 22,19:2
Watch on the Rhine 1943,Ag 28,15:1
North Star, The 1943,N 5,23:1
Another Part of the Forest 1948,My 19,30:2
Childrens Hour, The 1962,Mr 15,28:2
Toys in the Attic 1963,Ag 1,17:2
Hellman, Lillian (Screenwriter)
Dark Angel, The 1935,S 6,12:2
These Three 1936,Mr 19,22:4
Dead End 1937,Ag 25,25:1
Little Foxes, The 1941,Ag 22,19:2
North Star, The 1943,N 5,23:1

Searching Wind, The 1946,Je 27,29:1
Chase, The 1966,F 19,24:1
Hellman, Marcel (Producer)
Amateur Gentleman, The 1936,Ap 27,19:2
Accused 1936,D 17,35:1
When Thief Meets Thief 1937,Je 15,26:2
Crime Over London 1938,Jl 28,23:2
Jeannie 1943,S 13,14:2
Wanted for Murder 1946,D 12,38:4
Meet Me at Dawn 1948,My 18,26:2
This Was a Woman 1949,Ja 5,22:2
Happy Go Lovely 1951,Jl 26,17:2
Duel in the Jungle 1954,Ag 9,13:2
Let's Be Happy 1957,My 25,25:1
Flame Over India 1960,Ap 30,14:1
Amorous Adventures of Moll Flanders, The 1965,My 27,28:1
Hellman, Sam (Miscellaneous)
Daring Young Man, The 1935,Jl 18,15:2
Stanley and Livingstone 1939,Ag 5,18:2
Hellman, Sam (Original Author)
My Darling Clementine 1946,D 4,44:5
Powder River 1953,Jl 4,7:2
Hellman, Sam (Screenwriter)
County Chairman, The 1935,Ja 19,8:1
Old Kentucky, In 1935,N 29,24:1
Captain January 1936,Ap 25,21:1
Poor Little Rich Girl, The 1936,Je 26,16:1
Reunion 1936,N 27,27:1
Slave Ship 1937,Je 17,19:2
Baroness and the Butler, The 1938,F 19,19:2
We're Going to Be Rich 1938,Jl 4,10:2
Three Musketeers, The 1939,F 18,12:2
Frontier Marshal 1939,Jl 29,18:2
Here I Am a Stranger 1939,S 30,11:2
He Married his Wife 1940,Ja 20,11:2
Return of Frank James, The 1940,Ag 10,16:4
Shine on Harvest Moon 1944,Mr 11,10:2
Doughgirls, The 1944,Ag 31,14:1
Horn Blows at Midnight, The 1945,Ap 21,18:2
Runaround, The 1946,Je 7,16:3
Pirates of Monterey 1947,D 17,41:4
Hellmer, Karl
Liebe, Tod und Teufel 1935,My 25,12:2
Leichte Kavallerie 1936,F 8,19:2
Schloss Vogeloed 1936,My 9,11:2
Marriage in the Shadows 1948,S 17,28:3
Hellor, Ray
Last Edition, The 1925,N 11,27:3
Hellstrom, Eric
Sorciere, La 1956,D 28,17:2
Hellstrom, Gunnar
Return to Peyton Place 1961,My 6,26:1
Hellwell, David (Producer)
3:10 to Yuma 1957,Ag 29,22:1
Hellwig, Judith
Rosenkavalier, Der 1962,O 10,57:1
Helly, Jane
Lady Paname 1951,Mr 20,35:4
Helm, Anne
Desire in the Dust 1960,O 12,47:2
Couch, The 1962,F 22,20:3
Interns, The 1962,Ag 9,17:5
Follow That Dream 1962,Ag 9,17:7
Swingin' Maiden, The 1964,Ja 1,16:2
Honeymoon Hotel 1964,Je 4,28:1
Helm, Brigitte
Metropolis 1927,Mr 7,16:3
Love of Jeanne Ney, The 1928,Ja 15,VIII,7:5
Am Rande der Welt; On the Edge of the World 1928,Ja 15,VIII,7:4 (In Addenda)
Alraune 1928,My 20,VIII,8:4
Loves of Jeanne Ney, The 1928,Jl 10,17:3
Argent, L' 1929,Mr 3,VII,7:2 (Incorrect in this edition; use 1929,Mr 3,VIII,8:5 in film)
At the Edge of the World 1929,Je 18,29:4
Wonderful Life, The 1929,Jl 14,IX,4:5
Wonderful Lies of Nova Petrova, The 1930,Je 30,27:2
In Geheimdienst; In the Employ of the Secret Service 1931,O 25,VIII,6:1
Die Singende Stadt 1932,My 10,25:4
Graefin von Monte Christo, Die; Countess of Monte Christo, The 1932,My 15,VIII,4:2 (In Addenda)
Atlantide, L' 1932,Ag 7,IX,2:1
Gloria 1932,O 28,22:4
Inge und die Millionen 1934,Ap 13,25:1
Adieux les Beaux Jours 1934,Ap 23,20:2
Alraune 1934,My 5,22:4
Gold 1934,O 22,12:3
Blue Danube 1934,N 8,27:1
Fuerst Woronzeff 1934,N 17,12:2
Idealer Gatte, Ein 1937,Ja 11,15:7
Gilgi Eine Von Uns 1937,Jl 10,18:2
Argent, L' 1968,S 23,42:5
Helm, Fay
Racket Busters 1938,Ag 11,13:1
I Am the Law 1938,Ag 26,14:2
Peck's bad Boy With the Circus 1939,Ja 11,17:4
Dark Victory 1939,Ap 21,27:2
Our Leading Citizen 1939,Ag 24,17:1

Helm, Fay— Cont
Light That Failed, The 1939,D 25,19:1
Child Is Born, A 1940,Ja 11,19:2
Abe Lincoln in Illinois 1940,F 23,19:2
Dr Kildare's Strange Case 1940,Ap 12,19:2
Women Without Names 1940,My 9,26:4
Untamed 1940,Jl 25,14:3
Million Dollar Baby 1941,Je 7,20:2
Wolf Man, The 1941,D 22,24:5
Wings for the Eagle 1942,Ag 1,14:2
Give Out, Sisters 1942,Ag 28,22:3
You Can't Escape Forever 1942,O 17,11:1
Night Monster 1942,N 30,18:5
Crystal Ball, The 1943,F 19,22:2
Captive Wild Woman 1943,Je 7,9:4
Calling Dr Death 1944,F 12,11:3
Phantom Lady 1944,F 18,15:2
Lady in the Dark 1944,F 23,17:1
Son of Lassie 1945,Je 11,12:1
Falcon in San Francisco, The 1945,Jl 21,7:2
Sister Kenny 1946,S 30,21:2
That Brennan Girl 1946,D 9,34:3
Locket, The 1947,Mr 20,38:2
Helman, John (Producer)
Secret Ceremony 1968,O 24,55:1
Helmer, E
Gaesschen zum Paradies, Das 1937,Ag 21,7:3
Helmers, Peter
Tampico 1944,Je 2,21:2
Days of Glory 1944,Je 17,10:2
Helmi, Katerina
Red Lanterns 1965,Ap 1,30:1
Helmore, Tom
White Cargo 1930,F 24,18:1
Three Daring Daughters 1948,F 13,26:3
Malaya 1950,F 23,33:1
Shadow on the Wall 1950,My 19,31:3
Trouble Along the Way 1953,My 7,37:2
Let's Do It Again 1953,O 14,34:3
Lucy Gallant 1955,O 21,30:1
Tender Trap, The 1955,N 11,29:6
This Could Be the Night 1957,My 15,39:1
Designing Woman 1957,My 17,20:2
Vertigo 1958,My 29,24:2
Count Your Blessings 1959,Ap 24,23:1
Man in the Net, The 1959,Je 11,36:2
Time Machine, The 1960,Ag 18,19:1
Flipper's New Adventure 1964,Ag 27,28:2
Helmore, William (Composer)
Loose Ends 1930,O 18,23:2
Helmuth, Frits
Young Have no Time, The 1959,N 23,41:2
Helmuth, Osvald
En Fuldendt Gentleman 1937,O 14,22:3
Helpmann, Robert
One of our Aircraft Is Missing 1942,N 2,17:2
Henry V 1946,Je 18,30:2
Red Shoes, The 1948,O 23,9:2
Caravan 1949,Ap 21,30:4
Tales of Hoffmann 1951,Ap 5,34:2
Iron Petticoat, The 1957,F 2,12:2
55 Days at Peking 1963,My 30,20:1
Quiller Memorandum, The 1966,D 16,59:1
Chitty Chitty Bang Bang 1968,D 19,64:4
Helpmann, Robert (Miscellaneous)
Red Shoes, The 1948,O 23,9:2
Helseth, Henry Edward (Original Author)
Cry of the City 1948,S 30,32:4
Outside the Wall 1950,Mr 15,34:8
Helsig, Helmut
Our Daily Bread 1950,O 9,21:6
Helton, Charles
Saint in New York, The 1938,My 26,31:2
Helton, Percy
Silver Wings 1922,My 18,14:4
Hazard 1948,Je 3,19:2
Larceny 1948,S 4,8:6
Chicken every Sunday 1949,Ja 19,34:2
Criss Cross 1949,Mr 12,10:2
Set-Up, The 1949,Mr 30,31:2
Crooked Way, The 1949,S 5,13:2
My Friend Irma 1949,S 29,39:2
Copper Canyon 1950,N 16,39:2
Cyrano De Bergerac 1950,N 17,31:2
Sun Sets at Dawn, The 1951,Ja 15,13:1
Girl in Every Port, A 1952,F 14,23:1
Call Me Madam 1953,Mr 26,37:1
How to Marry a Millionaire 1953,N 11,37:1
Wicked Woman 1954,Mr 27,13:6
20,000 Leagues Under the Sea 1954,D 24,7:2
Helu, Antonio (Director)
Obligation to Assassinate, The 1937,O 19,29:6
Alma Jarocha 1938,Ap 30,18:2
India Bonita, La; Pretty Indian Girl, The 1939,Ap 15,15:2
Hotel de los Chiflados, El 1939,Ag 28,17:2
Helu, Antonio (Screenwriter)
Obligation to Assassinate, The 1937,O 19,29:6
Helvick, James (Original Author)
Beat the Devil 1954,Mr 13,11:2
Helwig, Warner (Original Author)
As the Sea Rages 1961,My 18,41:1

Helzmeister, Judith
Lysistrata 1948,Je 19,19:2
Hem, Narie
Dragon Sky 1964,Ag 25,28:2
Hemery, Annie
Rumors 1949,Mr 19,10:7
Heming, Violet
Turn of the Wheel 1918,S 2,7:1
Everywoman 1919,D 15,20:1
Man Who Played God, The 1932,F 11,16:1
Hemingway, Ernest (Original Author)
Farewell to Arms, A 1932,D 9,26:5
For Whom the Bell Tolls 1943,Jl 15,25:2
To Have and Have Not 1944,O 12,24:1
Killers, The 1946,Ag 29,24:2
Macomber Affair, The 1947,Ap 21,21:2
Under my Skin 1950,Mr 18,9:2
Breaking Point, The 1950,O 7,10:6
Snows of Kilimanjaro, The 1952,S 19,19:2
Sun Also Rises, The 1957,Ag 24,12:2
Farewell to Arms, A 1958,Ja 25,14:1
Old Man and the Sea, The 1958,O 8,41:1
Hemingway's Adventures of a Young Man
1962,Jl 26,17:1
Killers, The 1964,Jl 18,10:4
Hemingway, Ernest (Screenwriter)
Spanish Earth, The 1937,Ag 21,7:2
Hemmings, David
Girl-Getters, The 1966,Ap 13,37:6
Blow-Up 1966,D 19,52:2
Camelot 1967,O 26,54:1
Eye of the Devil 1967,D 7,60:1
Long Day's Dying, The 1968,My 29,20:1
Charge of the Light Brigade, The 1968,O 7,59:1
Barbarella 1968,O 12,43:1
Only When I Larf 1968,O 24,55:3
Hemon, Louis (Original Author)
Maria Chapdelaine 1935,S 25,18:2
Hemphill, Ray
This Property is Condemned 1966,Ag 4,24:1
Hempstead, David (Original Author)
Finishing School 1934,Ap 30,11:4
Hell and High Water 1954,F 2,20:6
Hempstead, David (Producer)
Kitty Foyle 1941,Ja 9,27:2
Joan of Paris 1942,Ja 26,18:2
Flight for Freedom 1943,Ap 16,24:2
Mr Lucky 1943,Jl 23,21:2
Sky's the Limit, The 1943,S 3,15:2
Tender Comrade 1944,Je 2,21:2
None but the Lonely Heart 1944,N 18,16:6
King and Four Queens, The 1956,D 22,13:7
Hemsley, Estelle
Edge of the City 1957,Ja 30,33:2
Green Mansions 1959,Mr 20,26:1
Take a Giant Step 1961,Mr 6,28:2
America America 1963,D 16,44:1
Baby, the Rain Must Fall 1965,Ja 14,44:1
Henabery, Joseph
Birth of a Nation, The 1930,D 22,16:2
Henabery, Joseph (Director)
Life of the Party, The 1920,N 22,13:3
North of the Rio Grande 1922,My 15,20:3
While Satan Sleeps 1922,Je 26,16:2
Man Unconquerable, The 1922,Jl 17,16:3
Tiger's Claw, The 1923,Mr 19,22:2
Gentleman of Leisure, A 1923,Jl 16,14:2
Stephen Steps Out 1923,N 19,19:3
Stranger, The 1924,F 5,20:1
Guilty One, The 1924,Je 17,22:4
Sainted Devil, A 1924,N 24,15:3
Tongues of Flame 1924,D 16,28:1
Cobra 1925,D 7,19:1
See You in Jail 1927,Ap 4,30:5
Lonesome Ladies 1927,Ag 2,19:2
Sailors' Wives 1928,F 28,18:4
Hell-Ship Bronson 1928,Je 19,31:1
Red Hot Speed 1929,F 5,26:3
Clear the Decks 1929,Ap 1,22:1
Hench, John (Miscellaneous)
Fun and Fancy Free 1947,S 29,17:2 (In
Addenda)
Henckels, Paul
Shadows of Fear 1928,N 6,35:1
Hungarian Nights 1930,Je 10,32:2
Mother Love 1931,F 16,17:1
Skandal Um Eva 1931,Ap 21,35:2
Wahre Jakob, Der 1931,Ag 7,20:2
Lindenwirtin vom Rhein, Die 1931,S 25,28:7
Ungetreue Eckehart, Der 1932,Ja 23,18:4
Man Braucht Kein Geld 1932,N 16,15:3
Die-oder Keine 1934,O 29,14:3
Finanzen des Grossherzogs, Die; Grand Duke's
Finances, The 1935,Ap 6,10:3
Hermine und die Sieben Aufrechten
1935,S 21,18:2
Pantoffelhelden 1935,O 21,22:5
Tolle Bomberg, Der 1935,O 26,12:2
Glueckliche Reise 1936,Ja 20,22:3
Zwichen Zwei Herzen; Between Two Hearts
1936,Ja 28,15:3
Erbe in Pretoria, Das 1936,Ap 18,19:3
Alte Kameraden 1936,Ap 27,19:3

Wackere Schustermeister, Der 1936,Jl 7,22:4
Alle Tage Ist Kein Sonntag 1936,Jl 11,11:4
Einmaleins der Liebe, Das 1937,Ja 2,15:2
Idealer Gatte, Ein 1937,Ja 11,15:7
Schabernack 1937,Ag 14,16:5
Seefahrt die Ist Lustig, Eine; Merry Sea Trip, A
1938,O 22,14:2
Zweimal zwei im Himmelbett; Twice Two in a
Four-Post Bed 1939,F 5,19:3
Hummel-Hummel 1939,Mr 11,21:2
Lustige Witwenball, Der; Merry Widows' Ball,
The 1939,My 1,21:2
Florentiner Hut, Der; Leghorn Hat, The
1939,Je 3,11:3
Glaserne Kugel, Die; Glass Ball, The
1939,Je 17,12:3
Unsterbliche Herz, Das; Immortal Heart, The
1939,O 21,12:2
Peter, Paul und Nanette 1940,My 25,20:1
Palace Scandal 1949,Je 6,15:5
Dancing Heart, The 1958,Ja 18,10:3
Confessions of Felix Krull, The 1958,Mr 5,38:1
Reaching for the Stars 1958,My 24,18:2
Hendel, Nehama
Pillar of Fire, The 1963,Ap 8,35:2
Hendergran, Solveg
En Saga 1938,Ja 8,19:2
Henderson, Betty
39 Steps, The 1960,O 11,55:2
Henderson, Brenda
My Son, My Son! 1940,My 10,26:6
Henderson, Charles (Composer)
Utah 1945,Mr 12,22:7
Do You Love Me 1946,My 25,12:2
Henderson, Charles (Miscellaneous)
New Faces of 1937 1937,Jl 2,25:1
Henderson, Del
Getting Gertie's Garter 1927,F 9,17:3
Crowd, The 1928,F 20,14:1
Patsy, The 1928,Ap 23,20:2
Show People 1928,N 12,18:2
Riley, The Cop 1928,D 4,29:1
Hit the Deck 1930,Ja 15,28:6
Newly Rich 1931,Jl 3,22:1
From Hell to Heaven 1933,Mr 18,9:3
I Have Lived 1933,S 6,24:4
Bottoms Up 1934,Mr 23,29:2
You're Telling Me 1934,Ap 7,19:1
Old-Fashioned Way, The 1934,Jl 14,16:5
Notorious Sophie Lang, The 1934,Jl 21,14:2
It's a Gift 1935,Ja 5,20:2
Ruggles of Red Gap 1935,Mr 7,26:1
Make Way for Tomorrow 1937,My 10,23:1
Goodbye Broadway 1938,My 14,18:1
Frontier Marshal 1939,Jl 29,18:2
You Can't Fool Your Wife 1940,My 24,23:4
Laurel and Hardy's Laughing 20's 1965,N 18,55:2
Henderson, Dick
Man From Blankley's, The 1930,Mr 29,23:1
Cavalcade 1933,Ja 6,23:2
Henderson, Donald (Producer)
Born Losers, The 1967,Ag 19,16:2
Henderson, Douglas
Eight Iron Men 1953,Ja 2,11:1
From Here to Eternity 1953,Ag 6,16:2
Sniper's Ridge 1961,Ag 24,25:3
Manchurian Candidate, The 1962,O 25,48:3
Americanization of Emily, The 1964,O 28,51:1
Henderson, Ivo
Bulldog Drummond Comes Back 1937,S 4,8:3
Henderson, Jack
Strange Victory 1948,S 27,27:2
Henderson, Jane
Belles of St Trinian's, The 1954,D 23,13:4
Green Scarf, The 1955,Ja 15,10:2
Henderson, Jessie (Original Author)
Perfect Flapper, The 1924,Je 23,22:4
Henderson, John M
Luck of the Irish, The 1937,Ja 16,21:1
Henderson, Joseph
Three Miles Out 1924,Ja 1,20:1
Henderson, Kay
Little Ballerina, The 1951,F 28,33:2
Henderson, Lorna
Belles of St Trinian's, The 1954,D 23,13:4
Henderson, Lucius
Man Must Live, A 1925,Ja 29,12:2
New Commandment, The 1925,N 10,25:3
Great Deception, The 1926,Ag 9,10:3
Henderson, Marcia
Thunder Bay 1953,My 21,39:2
All I Desire 1953,Ag 29,10:1
Glass Web, The 1953,N 12,37:5
Naked Alibi 1954,O 2,21:2
Henderson, Ray (Composer)
Hold Everything 1930,Ap 23,24:1
George White's Scandals 1934,Mr 16,24:2
George White's Scandals 1945,O 11,26:2
Henderson, Ray (Miscellaneous)
Curly Top 1935,Ag 2,22:3
Henderson, Robert
Penny Princess 1953,Mr 25,37:3
Never Let Me Go 1953,Je 11,37:2

Henderson (Composer)
Sunny Side Up 1929,O 4,24:5
Just Imagine 1930,N 22,21:3
Henderson (Miscellaneous)
Just Imagine 1930,N 22,21:3
Henderson (Original Author)
Sunny Side Up 1929,O 4,24:5
Follow Thru 1930,S 13,9:3
Indscreet 1931,My 7,21:4
Hendrian, Dutch
Vanity Street 1932,O 15,13:1
That's my Boy 1932,N 21,21:1
Air Hostess 1933,Ja 23,9:2
Bulldog Drummond's Secret Police
1939,Mr 30,19:3
Little Old New York 1940,F 3,9:2
Hendrichs, Josef
Eternal Waltz, The; (Ewiger Walzer)
1959,Jl 9,22:1
Hendrick, Richard
Should a Woman Tell? 1920,Ja 5,15:1
HENDRICKS
See Also HENDRIX
Hendricks, Arch
Flying Cadets 1941,O 14,29:2
Hendricks, Ben
Temperamental Wife, A 1919,S 15,16:3
Headless Horseman, The 1922,D 25,21:1
Tides of Passion 1925,Ap 20,22:1
Welcome Home 1925,My 18,12:1
What Happened to Jones 1926,F 9,22:1
Skinner's Dress Suit 1926,My 3,27:1
Rolling Home 1926,Je 8,22:1
One Minute to Play 1926,S 6,16:2
Take It From Me 1926,N 2,35:1
Barbed Wire 1927,Ag 8,10:3
Out all Night 1927,S 27,31:1
Waterfront 1928,O 22,29:1
Synthetic Sin 1929,Ja 7,36:2
Wild Party, The 1929,Ap 2,28:4
Twin Beds 1929,Jl 15,25:1
Men Without Women 1930,F 1,15:1
Ladies Love Brutes 1930,My 16,20:4
Girl of the Golden West, The 1930,O 27,17:1
Sunny 1930,D 27,16:3
Road to Paradise, The 1931,Ja 20,21:3
Public Enemy, The 1931,Ap 24,27:1
Woman From Monte Carlo, The 1931,D 31,17:6
Fireman, Save My Child 1932,F 18,25:3
Rain 1932,O 13,22:3
Kid From Spain, The 1932,N 18,23:2
Fast Life 1932,D 24,11:4
Big Shakedown, The 1934,F 12,19:2
We're not Dressing 1934,Ap 26,27:2
Blind Date 1934,S 1,16:3
O'Shaughnessy's Boy 1935,O 5,18:2
Slim 1937,Je 24,30:2
Roaring Timber 1937,Ag 19,23:1
Hendricks, Ben (Original Author)
City That Never Sleeps, The 1924,S 29,10:1
Hendricks, Louis
Conquest of Canaan, The 1921,Jl 11,9:3
Hendricks, Seble
Imitation of Life 1934,N 24,19:1
Hendrie, Ernest (Original Author)
Choosing a Wife 1919,Ag 11,9:1
Hendriks, Jan
Arms and the Man 1962,F 24,21:7
HENDRIX
See Also HENDRICKS
Hendrix, Wanda
Confidential Agent 1945,N 3,11:2
Nora Prentiss 1947,F 22,16:2
Welcome Stranger 1947,Ag 7,15:2
Ride the Pink Horse 1947,O 9,32:3
Miss Tatlock's Millions 1948,N 25,47:2
My Own True Love 1949,F 3,27:3
Prince of Foxes 1949,D 24,11:2
Captain Carey U S A 1950,Mr 30,40:5
Sierra 1950,S 15,31:2
Admiral Was a Lady, The 1950,O 13,23:3
Saddle Tramp 1950,N 24,31:4
My Outlaw Brother 1951,Ag 23,19:2
Highway Dragnet 1954,F 20,8:7
Golden Mask, The 1954,Mr 20,10:5
Black Dakotas, The 1954,O 2,21:2
Johnny Cool 1963,O 3,31:1
Hendry, Ian
Children of the Damned 1964,Ja 30,24:2
Model Murder Case, The 1964,N 25,45:1
Hill, The 1965,O 4,00:0
Repulsion 1965,O 4,7:6
Hendry, Len
Hail the Conquering Hero 1944,Ag 10,14:2
Heneghan, Patricia
Whistle Down the Wind 1962,Ap 23,34:2
Henie, Sonja
One in a Million 1937,Ja 1,19:3
Thin Ice 1937,S 4,8:2
Happy Landing 1938,Ja 22,19:1
My Lucky Star 1938,S 10,20:2
Second Fiddle 1939,Jl 1,11:2
Everything Happens at Night 1939,D 16,12:6

Henie, Sonja— Cont
Sun Valley Serenade 1941,S 6,20:1
Iceland 1942,O 15,27:1
Wintertime 1943,S 30,27:2
It's a Pleasure 1945,My 4,23:3
Henigson, Henry (Producer)
Port of Seven Seas 1938,Jl 15,13:2
Henkels, Dieterle
Holzapfel Weiss Alles 1933,Ja 7,11:3
Henkels, Paul
Maulkorb, Der 1938,Ap 9,11:3
Wozzeck 1962,Mr 3,13:1
Henkina, C (Narrator)
Great is my Country 1959,Jl 1,26:1
Henle, Ray
Untitled-News, Life of Herbert Hoover
1955,N 7,55:1
Henlere, Herschel
Woman in Command, The 1934,My 29,22:2
Henley, David (Producer)
Crooked Road, The 1965,F 4,24:2
Henley, Drewe
Nothing but the Best 1964,Jl 14,28:1
25th Hour, The 1967,F 17,45:1
Henley, Dusty
Take Me to Town 1953,Je 20,8:6
Henley, Hobart (Director)
Sin That Was His, The 1920,D 6,19:1
Star Dust 1922,F 6,9:1
Abysmal Brute, The 1923,Ap 18,24:5
Sinners in Silk 1924,S 8,15:3
So This Is Marriage 1924,D 23,16:2
Denial, The 1925,Mr 10,19:3
Slave of Fashion, A 1925,Jl 21,26:2
Exchange of Wives 1925,O 5,25:2
His Secretary 1925,D 21,27:2
Auction Block, The 1926,F 15,16:4
Tillie the Toiler 1927,Je 7,27:4
His Tiger Lady 1928,My 28,23:2
Certain Young Man, A 1928,Je 11,27:1
Lady Lies, The 1929,S 7,15:1
Roadhouse Nights 1930,F 22,13:1
Roadhouse Nights 1930,Mr 2,IX,5:1
Big Pond, The 1930,My 19,21:1
Mothers Cry 1930,D 6,21:3
Free Love 1930,D 15,29:1
Bad Sister 1931,Mr 30,25:2
Expensive Women 1931,N 14,15:3
Night World 1932,My 28,18:2
Unknown Blonde 1934,Ap 24,27:2
Henley, Hobart (Miscellaneous)
Flirt, The 1922,D 31,VII,2:2 (In Addenda)
Henley, Jack (Original Author)
Blondie Hits the Jackpot 1949,S 9,28:3
Girl's School 1950,F 3,29:2
Henley, Jack (Screenwriter)
Mr Wise Guy 1942,Mr 5,27:2
Night to Remember, A 1943,Ja 1,27:2
Reveille With Beverly 1943,Ap 24,17:2
My Kingdom for a Cook 1943,O 15,15:3
Thousand and one Nights, A 1945,Jl 12,8:2
Blondie Hits the Jackpot 1949,S 9,28:3
He's a Cockeyed Wonder 1950,O 20,32:4
Ma and Pa Kettle Back on the Farm
1951,My 11,32:3
Henley, James F (Composer)
Listen, Darling 1938,N 24,37:2
Hennequin, Maurice (Original Author)
Mademoiselle Gobette 1955,F 5,13:3
Hennery
Light Across the Street, The; Lumiere d'en Face,
La 1957,Jl 30,20:2
Hennessey, Johnny
Great White Way, The 1924,Ja 4,10:1
Hennessy, April
Love and Marriage (The Last Resort); Last Resort,
The (Love and Marriage) 1966,Ag 5,20:1
Hennessy, Michael
Home is the Hero 1961,Ja 26,32:1
Hennessy, Monique
Doulos-The Finger Man 1964,Mr 3,31:1
Hennessy, Robert
No Resting Place 1952,My 5,18:5 —
Hennesy, Hugh (Miscellaneous)
Fun and Fancy Free 1947,S 29,17:2 (In
Addenda)
Henney, Nella Braddy (Miscellaneous)
Unconquered, The; (Helen Keller in Her Story)
1954,Je 16,37:1
Henning, Carlos
Run for the Sun 1956,Ag 25,7:2
Henning, Eva
Devil's Wanton, The 1962,Jl 5,21:2
Henning, Pat
Man on a Tightrope 1953,Je 5,19:1
On the Waterfront 1954,Jl 29,18:1
Wind Across the Everglades 1958,S 12,21:1
Henning, Paul (Screenwriter)
Lover Come Back 1962,F 9,21:1
Bedtime Story 1964,Je 11,27:1
Henning, Tim
That Certain Woman 1937,S 16,29:1
Perfect Specimen, The 1937,O 28,29:2

Henning, Uno
Love of Jeanne Ney, The 1928,Ja 15,VIII,7:5
Loves of Jeanne Ney, The 1928,Jl 10,17:3
Three Loves 1929,S 9,30:2
Escaped From Dartmoor 1930,Ap 12,23:1
Nar Rosorna Sla Ut 1931,F 10,24:4
Natt, En 1935,Ja 29,24:1
Henning-Jensen, Bjarne (Director)
Child of Man 1950,F 1,25:2
Henning-Jensen, Bjarne (Screenwriter)
Child of Man 1950,F 1,25:2
Hennings, Fred
Bei der Blonden Kathrein 1934,D 3,15:2
Hennion, Robert (Director)
Sextette (Part 6-Ski Champ); Ski Champ
(Sextette) 1953,Mr 2,19:2
Sextette (Part 5-Seducer's Fate); Seducer's Fate
(Sextette) 1953,Mr 2,19:2
Sextette (Part 2-Female Affair); Female Affair
(Sextette) 1953,Mr 2,19:2
Sextette (Part 4-Snow Queen); Snow Queen
(Sextette) 1953,Mr 2,19:2
Sextette (Part 3-The Key to Sin); Key to Sin, The
(Sextette) 1953,Mr 2,19:2
Sextette (Part I-The Gun); Gun, The (Sextette)
1953,Mr 2,19:2
Hennion, Robert (Producer)
Sextette (Part 5-Seducer's Fate); Seducer's Fate
(Sextette) 1953,Mr 2,19:2
Sextette (Part 6-Ski Champ); Ski Champ
(Sextette) 1953,Mr 2,19:2
Sextette (Part 4-Snow Queen); Snow Queen
(Sextette) 1953,Mr 2,19:2
Sextette (Part I-The Gun); Gun, The (Sextette)
1953,Mr 2,19:2
Sextette (Part 3-The Key to Sin); Key to Sin, The
(Sextette) 1953,Mr 2,19:2
Sextette (Part 2-Female Affair); Female Affair
(Sextette) 1953,Mr 2,19:2
Henreid, Monika
Blues for Lovers 1966,S 8,43:1
Henreid, Paul
Goodbye Mr Chips 1939,My 16,27:2
Night Train 1940,D 30,21:1
Now, Voyager 1942,O 23,25:3
Casablanca 1942,N 27,27:1
In our Time 1944,F 12,11:2
Between Two Worlds 1944,My 6,11:2
Conspirators, The 1944,O 21,15:2
Hollywood Canteen 1944,D 16,19:2
Spanish Main, The 1945,N 7,20:2
Devotion 1946,Ap 6,10:5
Of Human Bondage 1946,Jl 6,11:2
Deception 1946,O 19,15:3
Song of Love 1947,O 10,31:2
Hollow Triumph 1948,O 29,29:5
Rope of Sand 1949,Ag 4,19:2
So Young, So Bad 1950,Jl 24,15:2
Last of the Buccaneers 1950,D 15,43:2
For Men Only 1952,Ja 16,21:2
Pardon my French 1952,Mr 31,17:2
Deep in my Heart 1954,D 10,35:2
Meet Me in Las Vegas 1956,Mr 14,39:2
Woman's Devotion, A 1957,Mr 22,26:1
Ten Thousand Bedrooms 1957,Ap 4,37:1
Holiday for Lovers 1959,Jl 25,10:2
Never so Few 1960,Ja 22,15:2
4 Horsemen of the Apocalypse, The
1962,Mr 10,10:2
Operation Crossbow 1965,Ap 2,29:1
Henreid, Paul (Director)
For Men Only 1952,Ja 16,21:2
Woman's Devotion, A 1957,Mr 22,26:1
Dead Ringer 1964,F 20,22:3
Blues for Lovers 1966,S 8,43:1
Henreid, Paul (Original Author)
Blues for Lovers 1966,S 8,43:1
Henreid, Paul (Producer)
Hollow Triumph 1948,O 29,29:5
For Men Only 1952,Ja 16,21:2
Henrey, Bobby
Fallen Idol, The 1949,N 16,39:2
Wonder Boy 1951,D 26,19:5
Henrich, Linda
State Fair 1962,Ap 12,41:4
Henried, Paul
Joan of Paris 1942,Ja 26,18:2
Thief of Damascus 1952,My 8,37:2
Pirates of Tripoli 1955,F 24,21:2
Cabaret 1957,N 9,31:2 (Incorrect in this edition;
use 1957,N 7,43:4 elsewhere)
Henrikson, Anders
John Ericsson Victor of Hampton Roads
1938,My 18,17:2
Frun Tillhanda; Servant Girls 1938,D 30,9:2
Hennes Lilla Majestat; Her Little Majesty
1940,Ap 20,14:2
Himlaspelet 1944,O 9,17:3
Blood and Fire 1950,Je 24,7:4
Miss Julie 1952,Ap 8,35:2
Of Love and Lust (On Payment); On Payment (Of
Love and Lust) 1959,My 26,31:2
Devil's Wanton, The 1962,Jl 5,21:2

Henrikson, Anders (Director)
65, 66 Och Jag (65, 66 And Me)
1937,Ag 30,25:2
Blood and Fire 1950,Je 24,7:4
Of Love and Lust (Doll's House, A); Doll's House,
A (Of Love and Lust) 1959,My 26,31:2
Of Love and Lust (On Payment); On Payment (Of
Love and Lust) 1959,My 26,31:2
Henrikson, Matthias
Obession 1968,Ag 29,46:3
Henriques, Basil
Children on Trial 1947,N 10,21:3
Henriques, Vilhelm
Girls are Willing, The 1959,My 11,30:1
Henry, Bill
Gentleman After Dark, A 1942,Ap 17,21:2
Sweater Girl 1942,Jl 13,18:3
Sarong Girl 1943,Je 18,16:6
Calaboose 1943,Jl 30,19:2
Johnny Come Lately 1943,S 24,26:1
Woman in Bondage 1944,Mr 27,17:2
Lady and the Monster, The 1944,Ap 8,9:2
Adventures of Mark Twain, The 1944,My 4,25:5
Sergeant Rutledge 1960,My 26,37:1
Henry, Bruce (Screenwriter)
Two Before Zero 1962,N 1,34:1
Henry, Buck
Troublemaker, The 1964,Je 23,25:1
Graduate, The 1967,D 22,44:4
Henry, Buck (Original Author)
Troublemaker, The 1964,Je 23,25:1
Henry, Buck (Screenwriter)
Troublemaker, The 1964,Je 23,25:1
Graduate, The 1967,D 22,44:4
Candy 1968,D 18,54:2
Henry, Buzz
Last of the Redmen 1947,Ag 30,8:6
Rocky Mountain 1950,N 4,13:2
Indian Fighter, The 1955,D 22,20:1
Cowboy 1958,F 20,29:5
Sheepman, The 1958,My 8,36:1
In Like Flint 1967,Mr 16,53:2
Henry, Buzzy
Blue Grass of Kentucky 1950,Ja 27,29:2
Henry, Charlotte
Courage 1930,My 23,21:1
Huckleberry Finn 1931,Ag 8,16:3
Arrowsmith 1931,D 8,36:4
Forbidden 1932,Ja 11,28:5
Lena Rivers 1932,My 21,9:2
Rebecca of Sunnybrook Farm 1932,Jl 30,16:5
Alice in Wonderland 1933,D 23,19:1
Human Side, The 1934,S 15,20:3
Last Gentleman, The 1934,O 18,26:5
Babes in Toyland 1934,D 13,28:2
Laddie 1935,My 6,22:3
Three Kids and a Queen 1935,N 9,19:2
Charlie Chan at the Opera 1936,D 5,16:2
Bowery Blitzkrieg 1941,O 1,24:5
Henry, Ella
Flower Thief, The 1962,Jl 14,11:5
Henry, Gale
Merton of the Movies 1924,S 8,15:3
Open all Night 1924,S 9,19:1
New Lives for Old 1925,F 25,16:7
Declassee 1925,Mr 23,14:2
Love Doctor, The 1929,N 9,22:5
Henry, Gloria
Johnny Allegro 1949,My 31,19:2
Kill the Umpire 1950,My 29,10:6
Al Jennings of Oklahoma 1951,My 18,34:6
Rancho Notorious 1952,My 15,39:5
Henry, Gustav
Our Mother's House 1967,O 10,56:1
Henry, Hank
Pal Joey 1957,O 28,30:1
Pepe 1960,D 22,18:1
Sergeants 3 1962,F 12,28:2
Henry, Harriet (Original Author)
Bought 1931,Ag 15,18:3
Lady With a Past 1932,F 22,23:2
Henry, Jack (Screenwriter)
Play it Cool 1963,Jl 18,15:3
Henry, Jay
We're not Dressing 1934,Ap 26,27:2
Henry, Joan (Original Author)
Weak and the Wicked, The 1954,Ag 21,10:3
Blonde Sinner 1957,Ja 24,34:1
Henry, Joan (Screenwriter)
Blonde Sinner 1957,Ja 24,34:1
Henry, Louise
Paris Interlude 1934,Jl 28,16:5
Hide-Out 1934,Ag 25,16:5
Society Doctor 1935,F 4,11:3
Casino Murder Case, The 1935,Ap 17,26:5
Reckless 1935,Ap 20,16:1
King Solomon of Broadway 1935,O 19,12:2
Remember Last Night? 1935,N 21,27:2
Old Kentucky, In 1935,N 29,24:1
Exclusive Story 1936,Ja 18,19:2
Hit Parade, The 1937,My 31,11:2
Charlie Chan on Broadway 1937,S 20,19:1
45 Fathers 1937,D 11,22:2

Henry, Louise— Cont

there Goes The Groom 1937,D 25,10:6
Charlie Chan in Reno 1939,My 31,27:2
Henry, Louise (Screenwriter)
Remember Last Night? 1935,N 21,27:2
Henry, Marguerite (Original Author)
Misty 1961,Jl 18,33:2
Henry, Mike
Tarzan and the Valley of Gold 1967,Mr 30,55:1
Henry, Noell (Original Author)
So Little Time 1953,Jl 28,23:2
Henry, O (Original Author)
Green Door, The 1917,My 7,10:4
You're Fired 1919,Je 16,11:2
In old Arizona 1929,Ja 21,18:4
Texan, The 1930,My 17,21:2
Cisco Kid, The 1931,O 24,20:3
Doctor Rhythm 1938,My 19,25:2
Return of the Cisco Kid, The 1939,Ap 29,13:2
Lucky Cisco Kid 1940,Je 24,19:5
Gay Caballero, The 1940,O 25,25:3
Romance of the Rio Grande 1940,D 25,33:4
Ride on Vaquero 1941,Ap 19,20:2
O Henry's Full House (The Last Leaf 1952,O 17,33:1
O Henry's Full House (The Gift of the Magi); Gift of the Magi, The (O Henry's Full House) 1952,O 17,33:1
O Henry's Full House (The Cop and the Anthem); Cop and the Anthem, The (O Henry's Full House) 1952,O 17,33:1
O Henry's Full House (The Clarion Call); Clarion Call, The (O Henry's Full House) 1952,O 17,33:1
Big Chief, The 1960,Ap 27,32:1
Henry, Pat
Lady in Cement 1968,N 21,41:1
Henry, Tom Browne
Johnny Allegro 1949,My 31,19:2
House of Strangers 1949,Jl 2,8:2
Winning Team, The 1952,Je 21,12:2
Operation Secret 1952,N 6,37:2
Stars and Stripes Forever 1952,D 23,17:2
Sitting Bull 1954,N 26,24:4
Earth vs the Flying Saucers 1956,Ag 2,21:2
Power and The Prize, the 1956,S 27,42:1
Beginning of the End 1957,Jl 4,16:1
Henry, Will (Original Author)
Pillars of the Sky 1956,O 13,15:2
Henry, William
Thin Man, The 1934,Je 30,18:5
Wicked Woman, A 1935,Ja 1,24:1
Society Doctor 1935,F 4,11:3
China Seas 1935,Ag 10,16:4
Exclusive Story 1936,Ja 18,19:2
Tarzan Escapes 1936,N 20,27:2
Double or Nothing 1937,S 2,17:3
Madame X 1937,O 25,23:1
Four Men and a Prayer 1938,My 7,18:1
Yellow Jack 1938,My 20,17:2
Campus Confessions 1938,S 23,35:1
Man to Remember, A 1938,N 7,23:2
Ambush 1939,F 9,17:2
Persons in Hiding 1939,Mr 2,19:2
I'm From Missouri 1939,Mr 23,27:1
Geronimo 1940,F 8,18:3
Parole Fixer 1940,Ap 18,28:5
Way of all Flesh, The 1940,Je 6,33:2
Queen of the Mob 1940,Jl 1,23:2
Cherokee Strip 1940,N 4,23:2
Blossoms in the Dust 1941,Je 27,14:4
Dance Hall 1941,Jl 19,16:2
Woman in the Night 1948,Ja 10,16:2
Secret of the Incas 1954,My 29,13:3
New Orleans Uncensored 1955,Ap 30,10:8
Mister Roberts 1955,Jl 15,14:1
Henshaw, Marjorie
Here Come the Waves 1944,D 28,25:2
Hensley, John
Good Morning, Miss Dove 1955,N 24,41:1
Henson, Basil
Dr Crippen 1964,F 15,14:1
Darling 1965,Ag 4,20:1
Frozen Dead, The 1967,N 16,58:1
Henson, Elizabeth
Alice in Wonderland 1951,Jl 27,15:2
Henson, Gladys
Captive Heart, The 1947,Ap 28,27:2
Frieda 1947,Ag 15,12:3
Dulcimer Street 1948,N 8,24:2
Happiest Days of Your Life, The 1950,S 18,19:2
Blue Lamp, The 1951,Ja 9,25:1
Magnet, The 1951,F 27,22:6
Happy Go Lovely 1951,Jl 26,17:2
Cage of Gold 1952,Ja 19,13:3
Case of Gold 1952,Ja 19,13:3
Prince and the Showgirl 1957,Je 14,22:2
Doctor at Large 1957,Jl 29,15:5
Leather Boys, The 1965,N 9,50:1
Henson, Leslie
Its a Boy 1933,Jl 23,IX,2:1 (In Addenda)
It's a Boy 1934,Je 8,18:2
Girl From Maxim's, The 1936,S 16,29:1

Henson, Nicky
Conqueror Worm, The 1968,Ag 15,46:2
Henze, Hans Werner (Composer)
Royal Ballet, The (Ondine); Ondine (The Royal Ballet) 1960,O 5,45:2
Hepburn, Audrey
Laughter in Paradise 1951,N 12,21:2
Young Wives' Tale 1952,N 4,33:1
Roman Holiday 1953,Ag 28,13:1
Monte Carlo Baby 1954,My 29,13:4
Sabrina 1954,S 23,43:2
War and Peace 1956,Ag 22,26:2
Funny Face 1957,Mr 29,16:1
Love in the Afternoon 1957,Ag 24,12:1
Green Mansions 1959,Mr 20,26:1
Nun's Story, The 1959,Je 19,30:1
Unforgiven, The 1960,Ap 7,46:1
Breakfast at Tiffany's 1961,O 6,28:1
Childrens Hour, The 1962,Mr 15,28:2
Charade 1963,D 6,40:1
Paris When it Sizzles 1964,Ap 9,25:3
My Fair Lady 1964,O 22,41:1
How to Steal a Million 1966,Jl 15,34:1
Two for the Road 1967,Ap 28,36:2
Wait Until Dark 1967,O 27,48:1
Hepburn, Barton
Dynamite 1929,D 28,11:1
Hi Diddle Diddle 1943,S 24,26:2
Bridge of San Luis Rey, The 1944,Mr 4,11:1
Hepburn, Katharine
Bill of Divorcement, A 1932,O 3,15:2
Christopher Strong 1933,Mr 10,19:2
Morning Glory 1933,Ag 18,18:2
Little Women 1933,N 17,22:3
Spitfire 1934,Mr 9,22:3
Little Minister, The 1934,D 28,25:1
Break of Hearts 1935,My 17,24:3
Alice Adams 1935,Ag 16,11:3
Sylvia Scarlett 1936,Ja 10,16:2
Mary of Scotland 1936,Jl 31,22:2
Woman Rebels, A 1936,O 30,27:2
Quality Street 1937,Ap 9,19:2
Stage Door 1937,O 8,27:2
Bringing Up Baby 1938,Mr 4,17:5
Holiday 1938,Je 24,15:1
Philadelphia Story, The 1940,D 27,22:2
Woman of the Year 1942,F 6,23:2
Keeper of the Flame 1943,Mr 19,15:2
Stage Door Canteen 1943,Je 25,13:2
Dragon Seed 1944,Jl 21,16:4
Without Love 1945,Mr 23,13:1
Undercurrent 1946,N 29,36:2
Sea of Grass, The 1947,F 28,27:2
Song of Love 1947,O 10,31:2
State of the Union 1948,Ap 23,28:1
Adam's Rib 1949,D 26,33:2
African Queen, The 1952,F 21,24:3
Pat and Mike 1952,Je 19,32:6
Summertime 1955,Je 22,25:1
Rainmaker, The 1956,D 13,51:1
Iron Petticoat, The 1957,F 2,12:2
Desk Set 1957,My 16,28:2
Suddenly, Last Summer 1959,D 23,22:1
Long Day's Journey Into Night 1962,O 10,57:2
Guess Who's Coming to Dinner 1967,D 12,56:1
Lion in Winter, The 1968,O 31,54:1
Hepburn, Philip
Bright Road 1953,Ap 29,33:5
Heppell, Michael
Convicted 1938,Ag 22,9:3
Hepper, William (Miscellaneous)
Tsar to Lenin 1966,My 27,33:3
Hepworth, Henry
Housemaster 1939,Ap 10,13:2
Herald, Douglas
Q Ships 1928,S 17,27:1
Herald, Heinz (Original Author)
Life of Emile Zola, The 1937,Ag 12,14:2
Vicious Circle, The 1948,Jl 22,27:2
Herald, Heinz (Screenwriter)
Life of Emile Zola, The 1937,Ag 12,14:2
Dr Ehrlich's Magic Bullet 1940,F 24,9:2
Vicious Circle, The 1948,Jl 22,27:2
Herbe, Herbert
Last ten Days, The 1956,Ap 12,26:1
Herben, Swei
Landstreicher, Die; Hoboes, The 1938,N 26,18:1
Herbert, A J
Fool, The 1925,Ap 13,24:1
Herbert, A P (Original Author)
House by the River 1950,My 2,25:2
Herbert, Alan
Pacific Adventure 1947,N 26,18:2
Herbert, Bryan
Human Monster, The 1940,Mr 25,11:2
Lady Surrenders, A 1947,Je 20,25:6
Blanche Fury 1948,N 24,20:2
Herbert, Charles
No Down Payment 1957,O 31,41:1
Fly, The 1958,Ag 30,6:6
Houseboat 1958,N 14,24:1
Please Don't Eat the Daisies 1960,Ap 1,37:1
13 Ghosts 1960,Ag 6,9:2

Herbert, Charles— Cont

Boy and the Pirates, The 1960,N 24,48:3
Herbert, Charles W (Cinematographer)
Land of Promise, The 1935,N 21,27:2
Herbert, David
Knowing Men 1930,Mr 9,IX,6:1
Herbert, Diana
Margie 1946,O 17,28:3
Herbert, Don (Producer)
Queen, The 1968,Je 18,37:1
Herbert, F Hugh (Director)
He Knew Women 1930,Ap 23,24:1
Scudda-Hoo! Scudda-Hay! 1948,Ap 15,31:1
Girls of Pleasure Island, The 1953,My 16,10:1
Herbert, F Hugh (Original Author)
Hotel Continental 1932,Mr 21,19:5
Women in his Life, The 1934,Ja 27,9:3
People Will Talk 1935,Je 17,20:2
If You Could Only Cook 1935,D 26,21:4
That Certain Age 1938,N 5,15:2
Kiss and Tell 1945,O 26,16:2
This Happy Feeling 1958,Je 19,28:2
Herbert, F Hugh (Producer)
Little Hut, The 1957,My 4,25:1
Herbert, F Hugh (Screenwriter)
Adam and Evil 1927,Ag 10,21:4
Secret Bride, The 1935,F 2,10:1
Traveling Saleslady 1935,Mr 29,26:2
Widow From Monte Carlo, The 1936,Ja 23,25:2
Colleen 1936,Mr 9,20:2
Snowed Under 1936,Mr 30,17:5
Case of the Black Cat, The 1936,D 26,15:4
As Good as Married 1937,My 22,19:2
Dark Command 1940,My 11,15:2
Women in War 1940,My 30,21:2
Three Faces West 1940,Ag 19,13:2
Hit Parade of 1941 1940,D 5,33:2
Melody Ranch 1940,D 26,23:3
West Point Widow 1941,S 11,21:5
Together Again 1944,N 24,19:2
Men in her Diary 1945,S 24,16:5
Kiss and Tell 1945,O 26,16:2
Home Sweet Homicide 1946,S 12,5:7
Margie 1946,O 17,28:3
Sitting Pretty 1948,Mr 11,35:2
Scudda-Hoo! Scudda-Hay! 1948,Ap 15,31:1
Our Very Own 1950,Jl 28,12:5
Let's Make It Legal 1951,N 7,35:3
Girls of Pleasure Island, The 1953,My 16,10:1
Moon Is Blue, The 1953,Jl 9,18:3
Little Hut, The 1957,My 4,25:1
Herbert, Hans
Phantom of the Opera, The 1943,O 15,15:2
Herbert, Henry
Day of Faith, The 1923,N 27,11:2
Captain Blood 1924,S 9,19:1
So Big 1925,Ja 5,19:1
Enchanted Hill, The 1925,D 29,19:2 (In Addenda)
Their own Desire 1930,Ja 25,13:2
Herbert, Holmes
White Heather, The 1919,My 5,11:1
Black Is White 1920,Mr 8,9:6
His House in Order 1920,Mr 8,9:5
His House in Order 1920,Mr 8,9:6
My Lady's Garter 1920,Mr 15,13:2
Right to Love, The 1920,Ag 23,9:2
Lady Rose's Daughter 1920,Ag 30,12:3
Heedless Moths 1921,Je 4,14:2
Enchanted Cottage, The 1924,Ap 14,14:1
Sinners in Heaven 1924,S 10,21:3
Love's Wilderness 1924,D 22,20:2
Daddy's Gone A-Hunting 1925,F 24,17:3
Wildfire 1925,Je 10,18:2
Woman of the World, A 1925,D 14,18:2
Fire Brigade, The 1926,D 21,20:2
When a Man Loves 1927,F 4,16:6
Lovers 1927,Ap 19,24:4
Mr Wu 1927,My 16,24:2
Heart of a Salome, The 1927,Je 6,27:2
Slaves of Beauty 1927,Je 8,23:3
Gay Retreat, The 1927,O 10,24:1
East Side, West Side 1927,O 18,33:2
Silver Slave, The 1928,Ja 3,28:2
Gentlemen Prefer Blondes 1928,Ja 16,24:1
Terror, The 1928,Ag 16,25:3
On Trial 1928,N 15,26:5
Charlatan, The 1929,Ap 15,22:6
Madame X 1929,Ap 25,32:3
Careers 1929,Je 10,23:1
Say It With Songs 1929,Ag 7,29:2
Careless Age, The 1929,S 21,17:1
Kiss, The 1929,N 16,25:2
Untamed 1929,N 30,23:1
Ship From Shanghai, The 1930,Ap 26,11:1
Hot Heiress, The 1931,Mr 14,23:2
Single Sin, The 1931,Mr 17,34:3
Chances 1931,Je 12,27:1
Daughter of the Dragon 1931,Ag 22,7:5
Dr Jekyll and Mr Hyde 1932,Ja 2,14:2
Miss Pinkerton 1932,Jl 9,7:5
Central Park 1932,D 7,29:3
Mystery of the Wax Museum, The 1933,F 18,13:3

Herbert, Holmes— Cont

Invisible Man, The 1933,N 18,18:4
House of Rothschild, The 1934,Mr 15,27:2
Count of Monte Cristo, The 1934,S 27,25:2
Pursuit of Happiness, The 1934,O 26,25:1
Sons of Steel 1935,Ap 15,16:3
Mark of the Vampire 1935,My 3,23:4
Accent on Youth 1935,Ag 12,10:3
Captain Blood 1935,D 27,14:1
Country Beyond, The 1936,Ap 30,17:3
Fifteen Maiden Lane 1936,O 17,21:3
Lloyds of London 1936,N 26,39:1
House of Secrets 1937,F 22,13:1
Slave Ship 1937,Je 17,19:2
Thirteenth Chair, The 1937,Je 18,25:3
Love Under Fire 1937,Ag 28,8:2
Lancer Spy 1937,N 4,29:1
Black Doll, The 1938,F 7,10:2
Say It in French 1938,D 1,29:1
Little Princess, The 1939,Mr 11,21:1
Juarez 1939,Ap 26,27:1
Stanley and Livingstone 1939,Ag 5,18:2
Adventures of Sherlock Holmes, The
  1939,S 2,20:1
We Are not Alone 1939,D 1,27:1
Everything Happens at Night 1939,D 16,12:6
British Intelligence 1940,F 12,14:2
Man Hunt 1941,Je 14,20:2
International Squadron 1941,N 14,28:4
Ghost of Frankenstein, The 1942,Ap 4,19:2
Invisible Agent 1942,Ag 6,23:2
Sherlock Holmes and the Secret Weapon
  1943,Ja 5,15:2
Two Tickets to London 1943,Jl 3,11:2
Corvette K-225 1943,O 21,30:1
Calling Dr Death 1944,F 12,11:3
Our Hearts Were Young and Gay 1944,O 12,24:2
Enter Arsene Lupin 1944,D 2,17:6
House of Fear, The 1945,Mr 19,23:3
Mummy's Curse, The 1945,Mr 31,16:1
Confidential Agent 1945,N 3,11:2
Verdict, The 1946,D 13,29:4
Singapore 1947,S 17,31:2
Swordsman, The 1947,O 17,18:4
This Time for Keeps 1947,D 5,33:4
Jungle Jim 1949,Ja 1,9:2
Barbary Pirate 1949,O 28,29:3
David and Bathsheba 1951,Ag 15,23:2
Anne of the Indies 1951,O 25,36:3

Herbert, Holmes E

Stage Romance, A 1922,Mr 26,VI,2:1 (In
  Addenda)

Herbert, Hugh

Caught in the Fog 1928,D 4,29:1
Danger Lights 1930,D 15,29:1
Hook, Line and Sinker 1930,D 25,31:5
Laugh and get Rich 1931,Mr 28,15:3
Traveling Husbands 1931,Ag 8,16:3
Friends and Lovers 1931,N 7,16:5
Lost Squadron, The 1932,Mr 11,15:4
Million Dollar Legs 1932,Jl 9,7:5
Faithless 1932,N 19,20:2
Strictly Personal 1933,Mr 20,18:2
Diplomaniacs 1933,Ap 29,14:2
She Had to Say Yes 1933,Jl 29,14:2
Good-Bye Again 1933,S 2,15:2
Bureau of Missing Persons 1933,S 9,9:2
Footlight Parade 1933,O 6,21:3
College Coach 1933,N 11,10:4
From Headquarters 1933,N 17,22:4
Convention City 1933,D 25,28:2
Easy to Love 1934,Ja 15,12:2
Fashions of 1934 1934,Ja 20,12:2
Wonder Bar 1934,Mr 1,23:2
Fog over Frisco 1934,Je 7,26:2
Dames 1934,Ag 16,20:2
Kansas City Princess 1934,N 5,23:1
Sweet Adeline 1935,Ja 7,13:2
Gold Diggers of 1935 1935,Mr 15,25:2
Traveling Saleslady 1935,Mr 29,26:2
We're In the Money 1935,Ag 22,21:4
Midsummer Night's Dream, A 1935,O 10,31:1
To Beat the Band 1935,N 23,23:2
Miss Pacific Fleet 1935,D 7,22:2
Colleen 1936,Mr 9,20:2
One Rainy Afternoon 1936,My 14,29:2
We Went to College 1936,Jl 27,20:2
Love Begins at 20 1936,S 19,20:1
Sing Me a Love Song 1936,D 26,15:2
Top of the Town 1937,Mr 27,19:2
That Man's Here Again 1937,My 6,23:3
Singing Marine, The 1937,Jl 1,33:2
Marry the Girl 1937,Jl 31,6:2
Perfect Specimen, The 1937,O 28,29:2
Sh! The Octopus 1937,D 24,21:2
Hollywood Hotel 1938,Ja 13,17:3
Gold Diggers in Paris 1938,Je 2,19:2
Men Are Such Fools 1938,Je 17,25:1
Four's a Crowd 1938,Ag 12,11:1
Great Waltz, The 1938,N 25,19:1
Lady's From Kentucky, The 1939,Ap 27,31:1
Family Next Door, The 1939,Ap 28,31:2
Eternally Yours 1939,O 7,11:2
Little Accident 1939,N 24,29:3

Conga Nights, La 1940,Je 5,33:5
Private Affairs 1940,Jl 5,10:3
Slightly Tempted 1940,N 1,33:1
Little Bit of Heaven, A 1940,N 8,24:2
Hit Parade of 1941 1940,D 5,33:2
Meet the Chump 1941,F 27,23:4
Black Cat, The 1941,Ap 26,20:3
Badlands of Dakota 1941,S 9,27:6
Hellzapoppin 1941,D 26,21:4
Stage Door Canteen 1943,Je 25,13:2
Kismet 1944,Ag 23,16:1
Music for Millions 1944,D 22,12:4
Miracle Can Happen, A 1948,F 4,28:4
Song Is Born, A 1948,O 20,37:2
Beautiful Blonde From Bashful Bend, The
  1949,My 28,11:2

Herbert, Joe

Seven Keys to Baldpate 1929,D 26,21:1

Herbert, Percy

Cockleshell Heroes, The 1956,Je 4,25:2
Bridge on the River Kwai 1957,D 19,39:1
All at Sea 1957,D 23,18:2
Tunes of Glory 1960,D 21,38:2
Mysterious Island 1961,D 21,30:6
Mutiny on the Bounty 1962,N 9,31:2
Call Me Bwana 1963,Jl 4,9:1
Becket 1964,Mr 12,40:2
Guns at Batasi 1964,N 17,47:1
Tobruk 1967,F 9,33:2

Herbert, Pitt

Hud 1963,My 29,36:1

Herbert, Sydney

If Winter Comes 1923,S 4,14:1
Under the Red Robe 1923,N 13,25:3
Her Love Story 1924,O 7,26:1

Herbert, T H (Original Author)

Citadel of Silence, The 1939,D 25,29:1

Herbert, Tom

Belle of the Nineties 1934,S 22,12:2

Herbert, Victor (Composer)

Fall of a Nation, The 1916,Je 7,11:1
Yolanda 1924,F 20,23:1
Mlle Modiste 1926,Ap 26,25:1
Naughty Marietta 1935,Mr 23,11:2
Sweethearts 1938,D 23,16:2
Babes in Toyland 1961,D 15,49:1

Herbert, Victor (Original Author)

Red Mill, The 1927,F 14,15:1
Kiss Me Again 1931,Ja 8,21:4
Babes in Toyland 1934,D 13,28:2

Herbert-Bond, John

Tower of London 1939,D 12,37:2

Herbier, Marcel L' (Director)

Scandale, Le 1934,Ag 12,IX,2:1
Citadel of Silence, The 1939,D 25,29:1

Herbier, Marcel L' (Original Author)

New Enchantment, The 1926,Mr 15,18:3

Herbst, I (Director)

Six Days to Eternity 1968,O 31,54:3

Herbst, Jo

Rosemary 1960,Ja 19,40:2

Herczeg, Arpad Dr (Original Author)

Rapture 1950,D 14,51:3

Herczeg, Geza (Miscellaneous)

Capture of Budapest 1945,Ag 31,14:4

Herczeg, Geza (Original Author)

Wonder Bar 1934,Mr 1,23:2
Life of Emile Zola, The 1937,Ag 12,14:2
Vicious Circle, The 1948,Jl 22,27:2
Rapture 1950,D 14,51:3

Herczeg, Geza (Screenwriter)

Life of Emile Zola, The 1937,Ag 12,14:2
Florian 1940,Je 6,33:2
Shanghai Gesture, The 1941,D 26,21:2
Rapture 1950,D 14,51:3
Women Without Names 1951,Ag 7,22:2

Herde, Rene

We Lived Through Buchenwald 1947,Jl 24,27:3

Herder, Andrzei

Barrier 1967,S 27,39:3

Herdman, John

Lady, The 1925,Ja 27,11:2

Herdman, Virginia

Mystery Ranch 1932,Je 30,26:2

Heredia, Father (Original Author)

Virgin of Guadalupe, The 1943,My 15,13:3

Herendeen, Frederick (Original Author)

All the King's Horses 1935,Mr 9,19:1

Hergesheimer, Joseph (Original Author)

Tol'able David 1922,Ja 2,20:1
Bright Shawl, The 1923,Ap 23,18:3
Wild Oranges 1924,Mr 3,22:3
Cytherea 1924,My 26,21:1
Flower of the Night 1925,O 19,26:1
Tol'able David 1930,N 17,29:1
Woman I Stole, The 1933,Je 28,24:3
Java Head 1935,Jl 31,21:4

Heriat, Philippe

Miracle of the Wolves, The 1925,F 24,17:3
Sea-Fever 1929,O 28,20:1
Miracle des Loups, Le 1930,Jl 28,22:1
Rothchild 1938,O 12,35:2

Heriat, Philippi (Original Author)

Rosie 1968,F 8,36:1

Heribel, Renee

Madame Sans Gene 1925,Ap 18,19:1
Appassionata 1929,Jl 8,17:3
Three Masques, The 1929,N 24,X,8:4
Trois Masques, The 1929,N 24,X,8:4 (In
  Addenda)

HERING

See HERRING

Herking, Ursula

Rote Orchideen; Red Orchids 1939,Ap 15,15:2
Heimatland; Homeland 1939,O 28,11:2

Herlen, Jacques

Tiger and the Pussycat, The 1967,S 21,56:4

Herlie, Eileen

Hungry Hill 1947,O 11,11:2
Hamlet 1948,S 30,32:2
Angel With the Trumpet 1951,D 21,21:5
Gilbert and Sullivan 1953,O 28,36:3
Freud 1962,D 13,37:1
She Didn't Say No 1963,Jl 30,18:1
Hamlet 1964,S 24,46:1
Sea Gull, The 1968,D 24,14:1

Herlihy, James Leo

In the French Style 1963,S 19,23:1

Herlihy, James Leo (Original Author)

Blue Denim 1959,Jl 31,21:1
All Fall Down 1962,Ap 12,41:3

Herm, Charles F (Producer)

Untitled-Science, Natural History 1920,Je 21,13:1

HERMAN

See Also HERMANN, HERRMAN,
  HERRMANN

Herman

Vier Musketiere, Die; Four Musketeers, The
  1935,N 9,19:3

Herman, Al

Bad Company 1931,N 7,16:5
Hollywood Cowboy 1937,Jl 24,12:1
Talent Scout 1937,Ag 20,21:3
Paid to Dance 1937,D 6,19:1
Torchy Blane, The Adventurous Blonde
  1937,D 18,18:1
Headin' East 1938,Ja 15,19:2
Conspiracy 1939,Ag 23,19:2
Swanee River 1939,D 30,9:2

Herman, Al (Director)

Sporting Chance 1931,N 28,20:4
Renfrew of the Royal Mounted 1937,N 3,29:4

Herman, Billy

Safe at Home 1941,N 26,31:2

Herman, Freddie

World in my Corner 1956,F 18,12:5

Herman, Gil

When Willie Comes Marching Home
  1950,F 18,9:2

Herman, Henry (Producer)

Torch Song 1953,O 13,34:2

Herman, Tommy

Harder They Fall, The 1956,My 10,26:3

Herman, Woody

What's Cookin' 1942,F 26,15:5
New Orleans 1947,Je 20,25:6

Herman, Woody and his Orchestra

Wintertime 1943,S 30,27:2
Sensations of 1945 1944,Jl 7,13:2
Earl Carroll Vanities 1945,Ap 2,15:6
Hit Parade of 1947 1947,My 5,32:8

Herman (Pigeon)

Gazebo, The 1960,Ja 16,14:4

Herman (Rabbit)

Eternally Yours 1939,O 7,11:2

HERRMANN

See Also HERMAN, HERRMAN,
  HERRMANN

Hermann, Dr

Tatras Zauber 1933,F 18,13:4

Hermann, Nori Elisabeth

Bridge to the Sun 1961,O 18,50:1

Hermann, Peter

Journey to the Beginning of Time 1967,F 11,20:1

Hermanos, Rodriguez (Producer)

Vivire Otra Vez; I Shall Live Again
  1940,O 23,27:2

Herman's Hermits

Go Go Mania 1965,My 20,52:4
Hold On! 1966,Je 23,29:4

Hermantier, Raymond

Under the Paris Sky 1952,My 6,35:1

Hermine's Midgets

Court Jester, The 1956,F 2,19:1

Hermitage, Roy

Nicholas Nickleby 1947,D 1,27:2

Hermosillo, Carmen

Madres del Mundo 1936,Ag 17,9:3
Tras la Reja 1937,Ja 11,15:7
Domingo en la Tarde, Un; On a Sunday
  Afternoon 1939,Ja 7,6:3
Nobleza Ranchero; Rural Chivalry
  1939,F 20,13:3

Hern, Pepe
Borderline 1950,Mr 6,17:2
Make Haste to Live 1954,Mr 26,16:2
Hernadi, Gyula (Screenwriter)
Red and the White, The 1968,S 21,26:1
Hernandez, Anna
Leave It to Susan 1919,My 26,19:4
Extra Girl, The 1924,Ja 21,20:1
Name the Man 1924,F 4,23:3
Hernandez, Antonia
Roots, The (The One-Eyed Boy); One-Eyed Boy,
The (The Roots) 1957,S 3,23:2
Hernandez, George
Mary Regan 1919,My 5,11:1
Village Sleuth 1920,S 13,12:1
Hernandez, Joe
That's my Man 1947,Ap 7,20:2
Hernandez, Juano
Intruder in the Dust 1949,N 23,19:1
Young Man With a Horn 1950,F 10,18:4
Breaking Point, The 1950,O 7,10:6
Stars in my Crown 1950,D 22,19:1
Trial 1955,O 14,21:2
Ransom 1956,Ja 25,28:3
Something of Value 1957,My 11,24:6
Roots, The (Our Lady); Our Lady (The Roots)
1957,S 3,23:2
Mark of the Hawk, The 1958,Mr 6,32:1
St Louis Blues 1958,Ap 12,13:1
Sergeant Rutledge 1960,My 26,37:1
Sins of Rachel Cade, The 1961,Ap 6,30:3
Hemingway's Adventures of a Young Man
1962,Jl 26,17:1
Pawnbroker, The 1965,Ap 21,51:1
Hernandez, Rafael (Composer)
Perfidia; Perfidy 1940,F 17,9:3
Hernandez, Regelio
Big Boodle, The 1957,Mr 12,38:1
Hernandez, Silvio
Wave, The 1937,Ap 21,18:1
Hernandez, Tom
Third Voice, The 1960,Mr 7,24:5
Herne, Julie (Original Author)
Heart Raider, The 1923,Je 6,24:5
Snow Bride, The 1923,Je 12,22:2
Hero, Teresa
Holiday in Mexico 1946,Ag 16,19:3
Hero, Tonia
Holiday in Mexico 1946,Ag 16,19:3
Heron, Joyce
Agitator, The 1949,Ag 19,12:5
Herrand, Marcel
Enfants du Paradis, Les 1947,F 20,32:2
Star Without Light; Etoile Sans Lumiere
1947,Ag 4,14:2
Devil's Own Envoy, The 1947,Ag 30,8:6
Room Upstairs, The 1948,S 4,8:6
Ruy Blas 1948,O 4,14:2
Fanfan the Tulip 1953,My 5,34:2
Respectful Prostitute, The 1957,Jl 11,21:1
Herrera, Daniel
Night of the Mayas 1941,Ja 14,16:7
Herrera, Enrique
Noche del Pecado, La 1933,D 26,19:4
Juarez y Maximiliano 1935,F 16,9:2
Paloma, La 1938,F 26,9:4
Huapango 1938,Je 11,9:1
Cada Loco con su Tema; Every Madman to his
Specialty 1939,Ap 29,13:3
Tia de las Muchachas, La; Girls' Aunt, The
1939,O 30,13:3
Caballo a Caballo; Horse for Horse
1940,F 10,19:2
Herrera, Jacoba
Night of the Mayas 1941,Ja 14,16:7
Herrera, Luis Bayon (Director)
Je Hatore 1940,Ag 27,17:2
Jettatore 1940,Ag 27,17:2
Herrera, Mario
Roots, The (The One-Eyed Boy); One-Eyed Boy,
The (The Roots) 1957,S 3,23:2
Herrera R (Director)
Oro entre Barro; Gold in Clay 1940,Jl 1,23:2
Herrero, Goyita
Esperame 1933,Jl 3,14:6
Herrestrup, Hugo
Eric Soya's 17 1967,Ja 25,37:1
Herrick, F Herrick (Director)
Norway Replies! 1944,F 26,10:3
Herrick, F Herrick (Screenwriter)
Norway Replies! 1944,F 26,10:3
Herrick, Jack
Dick Turpin 1925,Ja 26,14:1
Way of a Girl, The 1925,Mr 30,21:3
Is Zat So? 1927,My 17,27:2
Beau Broadway 1928,Jl 30,21:2
Arizona Kid, The 1930,My 17,21:2
Tip Off, The 1931,O 26,22:1
Herrick, Joseph
White Fang 1936,Jl 18,18:2
Herrick, Robert
No Time for Love 1943,D 2,30:1

Herrick, Robert (Original Author)
Dangerous Money 1924,O 14,21:5
Herrick, Samuel R
Tall Texan, The 1953,Ap 13,32:4
Herriman, E H
How to Handle Women 1928,Je 18,13:2
Herring, Aggie
Hairpins 1920,Ag 2,12:2
Isle of Lost Ships, The 1923,My 14,18:2
Pioneer Trails 1923,N 12,15:3
Pampered Youth 1925,F 10,20:1
Any Woman 1925,My 27,26:2
Sally, Irene and Mary 1925,D 7,19:1
Kosher Kitty Kelly 1926,S 28,30:2
Gorilla, The 1927,N 21,20:1
Lady Be Good 1928,My 28,23:2
Smiling Irish Eyes 1929,Jl 24,23:2
In the Next Room 1930,Ap 7,21:1
Clancy in Wall Street 1930,My 3,23:1
Billy the Kid 1930,O 18,23:2
Millie 1931,F 7,11:1
She Done Him Wrong 1933,F 10,12:3
Quitter, The 1934,Mr 14,23:3
Daniel Boone 1936,O 24,23:2
Man in Blue, The 1937,Ag 30,25:2
Herring, Jess
Beloved Brute, The 1924,N 10,20:1
Herriot, Edouard (Original Author)
Madame Recamier 1928,Je 17,6:3
Madame Recamier 1928,Jl 15,VIII,3:3
Herriot, Mary
Three Russian Girls 1944,F 5,13:2
HERRMAN
See Also HERMAN, HERMANN,
HERRMANN
Herrman, Leo (Producer)
Land of Promise, The 1935,N 21,27:2
HERRMANN
See Also HERMAN, HERMANN, HERRMAN
Herrmann, Bernard (Composer)
Citizen Kane 1941,My 2,25:1
Herrmann, John L (Cinematographer)
Little America 1935,O 15,19:2
Herrmann, Lucille Fletcher (Original Author)
Once Upon a Time 1944,Je 30,17:2
Herrod, Julie
Wait Until Dark 1967,O 27,48:1
Herschensohn, Bruce (Composer)
John F Kennedy: Years of Lightning, Day of
Drums 1966,Ap 11,41:1
Herschensohn, Bruce (Director)
John F Kennedy: Years of Lightning, Day of
Drums 1966,Ap 11,41:1
Herschensohn, Bruce (Screenwriter)
John F Kennedy: Years of Lightning, Day of
Drums 1966,Ap 11,41:1
Hersent, Philippe
King, The 1941,O 23,29:3
Goliath and the Dragon 1961,Ja 5,27:2
Mighty Crusaders, The 1961,S 23,17:1
Hersey, John (Original Author)
Bell for Adano, A 1945,Jl 6,8:3
War Lover, The 1963,Mr 7,8:5
Hershey, Barbara
With Six You Get Egg Roll 1968,O 10,59:6
Hershey, Burnet (Original Author)
Dealers in Death 1934,D 15,9:3
Hershfield, Harry
Great White Way, The 1924,Ja 4,10:1
Hersholt, Jean
Tess of the Storm Country 1922,N 13,12:1
Red Lights 1923,S 10,15:4
Woman on the Jury, The 1924,My 19,14:2
Goldfish, The 1924,My 20,15:2
Sinners in Silk 1924,S 8,15:3
Greed 1924,D 5,28:1
So Big 1925,Ja 5,19:1
Her Night of Romance 1925,Ja 13,16:1
Fifth Avenue Models 1925,My 4,16:2
If Marriage Fails 1925,Je 2,16:3
Dangerous Innocence 1925,Je 8,19:1
Don Q, Son of Zorro 1925,Je 16,24:1
Woman's Faith, A 1925,Jl 27,17:3
Stella Dallas 1925,N 17,30:2
Greater Glory, The 1926,My 4,31:1
Four Horsemen of the Apocalypse, The
1926,S 27,27:3
It Must Be Love 1926,O 4,20:2
Alias the Deacon 1927,Je 21,29:2
Student Prince, The 1927,S 22,33:2
13 Washington Square 1928,Ja 30,18:1
Secret Hour, The 1928,Mr 12,26:1
Abie's Irish Rose 1928,Ap 20,26:7
Battle of The Sexes, The 1928,O 15,16:1
Give and Take 1928,D 27,27:1
Girl on the Barge, The 1929,F 26,31:1
Younger Generation, The 1929,Mr 11,22:2
Case of Sergeant Grischa, The 1930,Mr 8,21:1
Mamba 1930,Mr 11,25:2
Hell Harbor 1930,Mr 28,22:6
Cat Creeps, The 1930,N 8,21:3

Hersholt, Jean— Cont
Viennese Nights 1930,N 27,32:5
Soldiers Plaything, A 1931,My 2,23:4
Daybreak 1931,Je 1,15:1
Transatlantic 1931,Jl 31,15:2
Susan Lenox; Her Fall and Rise 1931,O 17,20:1
Sin of Madelon Claudet, The 1931,O 31,22:2
Phantom of Paris, The 1931,N 14,15:3
Private Lives 1931,D 19,16:4
Emma 1932,F 6,14:4
Beast of the City, The 1932,Mr 14,13:3
Grand Hotel 1932,Ap 13,23:2
Night Court 1932,My 27,27:5
New Morals for Old 1932,Je 24,15:3
Unashamed 1932,Jl 15,13:4
Skyscraper Souls 1932,Ag 5,11:2
Mask of Fu Manchu, The 1932,D 3,21:4
Flesh 1932,D 10,19:3
Crime of the Century, The 1933,Mr 13,18:2
Song of the Eagle 1933,Ap 29,14:3
Dinner at Eight 1933,Ag 24,18:1
Christopher Bean 1933,N 25,10:2
Cat and the Fiddle, The 1934,F 17,20:2
Men in White 1934,Je 9,18:2
Fountain, The 1934,Ag 31,14:1
Painted Veil, The 1934,D 7,29:1
Mark of the Vampire 1935,My 3,23:4
Break of Hearts 1935,My 17,24:3
Murder in the Fleet 1935,Je 3,22:2
Country Doctor, The 1936,Mr 13,32:2 (Incorrect
in this edition; use 1936,Mr 13,27:2 elsewhere)
Tough Guy 1936,Mr 14,10:1
Sins of Man 1936,Je 19,17:2
His Brother's Wife 1936,Ag 15,6:2
Reunion 1936,N 27,27:1
One in a Million 1937,Ja 1,19:3
Seventh Heaven 1937,Mr 26,25:1
Heidi 1937,N 6,14:2
Happy Landing 1938,Ja 22,19:1
Mr Moto in Danger Island 1938,Mr 20,13:3
I'll Give a Million 1938,Jl 16,7:2
Alexander's Ragtime Band 1938,Ag 6,7:2
Five of a Kind 1938,O 31,12:2
Meet Doctor Christian 1939,D 1,27:2
Courageous Dr Christian, The 1940,Mr 29,25:3
Stage Door Canteen 1943,Je 25,13:2
Dancing in the Dark 1949,D 3,8:6
Run for Cover 1955,Ap 30,10:6
Hershorn, Robert (Producer)
Take it All; A Tout Prendre 1966,Ap 26,55:1
Hersko, Janos (Director)
Dialogue 1967,O 14,13:2
Hersko, Janos (Screenwriter)
Dialogue 1967,O 14,13:2
Hertejandy, John (Producer)
C'mon Let's Live a Little 1967,My 4,34:1
Hertel, Ingeborg
Waldwinter 1936,N 14,23:3
Herter, Francis
Prince and the Pauper, The 1922,Ag 14,12:4
Herter, Gerard
White Warrior, The 1961,F 11,27:2
Any Gun Can Play 1968,S 14,34:2
Herterich, Franz
Vienna Burgtheater 1937,O 27,47:1
Hertz, B Russell (Original Author)
Grand Slam 1933,F 22,25:2
Hertz, David (Miscellaneous)
Beloved Enemy 1936,D 26,15:2
Hertz, David (Original Author)
Love Crazy 1941,Je 6,25:5
Pilot No 5 1943,Je 25,13:4
Hertz, David (Screenwriter)
I Met my Love Again 1938,Ja 15,19:1
Three Loves Has Nancy 1938,S 2,21:2
Stronger Than Desire 1939,Je 30,17:3
Blackmail 1939,S 15,26:3
Love Crazy 1941,Je 6,25:5
Journey for Margaret 1942,D 18,36:7
Pilot No 5 1943,Je 25,13:4
Marriage Is a Private Affair 1944,O 27,17:7
Daisy Kenyon 1947,D 25,32:1
Hertz, Lone
Crazy Paradise 1965,Ag 11,41:2
Hertz, Ralph
Alice in Wonderland 1931,D 28,22:1
Hertzogs, The Five
Crazy House 1943,D 16,33:3
Herubel, Michael
Trial of Joan of Arc, The 1965,F 12,19:1
Hervey, Grizelda
Informer, The 1935,My 10,25:2
Girl in the Street 1938,My 26,31:2
Kiss the Blood off my Hands 1948,O 30,10:2
Gideon of Scotland Yard 1959,My 20,38:2
Hervey, Harry (Miscellaneous)
Green Hell 1940,Ja 30,15:6
Hervey, Harry (Original Author)
Devil Dancer, The 1927,D 19,30:1
Prestige 1932,F 5,25:2
Shanghai Express 1932,F 18,25:3
Devil and the Deep 1932,Ag 20,7:4
Passport to Hell, A 1932,Ag 27,13:4
Devil's in Love, The 1933,Jl 28,18:2

Hervey, Harry (Original Author)— Cont

Son Comes Home, A 1936,S 5,7:1
Road to Singapore 1940,Mr 14,29:2
Night Plane From Chungking 1943,My 31,13:2
Peking Express 1951,Jl 19,20:2

Hervey, Irene

Stranger's Return, The 1933,Jl 28,18:2
Women in his Life, The 1934,Ja 27,9:3
Let's Try Again 1934,Je 22,24:1
Count of Monte Cristo, The 1934,S 27,25:2
Dude Ranger, The 1934,O 2,18:5
Winning Ticket, The 1935,F 11,14:2
Hard Rock Harrigan 1935,Jl 30,16:2
Charlie Chan in Shanghai 1935,O 14,21:1
His Night Out 1935,N 16,19:2
Three Godfathers, The 1936,Mr 9,20:2
Absolute Quiet 1936,My 2,11:1
League of Frightened Men, The 1937,Jl 2,25:1
Girl Said No, The 1937,O 18,14:1
Say It in French 1938,D 1,29:1
East Side of Heaven 1939,My 5,29:3
Missing Evidence 1939,N 17,17:3
Destry Rides Again 1939,N 30,25:1
Three Cheers for the Irish 1940,Mr 9,19:2
Crooked Road, The 1940,Je 11,33:4
Boys From Syracuse, The 1940,Ag 1,25:2
San Francisco Docks 1940,D 26,23:3
Mr Dynamite 1941,Mr 13,25:2
Bombay Clipper 1942,Ja 12,23:3
Frisco Lil 1942,F 12,27:2
Destination Unknown 1942,O 29,19:3
Night Monster 1942,N 30,18:5
He's my Guy 1943,Mr 12,12:3
Mickey 1948,Jl 19,11:2
Mr Peabody and the Mermaid 1948,Ag 14,6:5
Lucky Stiff, The 1949,Ja 31,14:2
Manhandled 1949,My 26,34:2
Chicago Deadline 1949,N 3,37:2
Cry in the Night, A 1956,S 1,19:4
Teenage Rebel 1956,N 17,17:6

Hervil, Rene (Director)

Douceur D'Aimer, La 1931,D 14,16:3

Herwich, Mme

Legion of Honor, The 1928,Jl 20,8:4

Herzig, Sig (Miscellaneous)

Artists and Models 1937,Ag 5,19:2

Herzig, Sig (Original Author)

Moonlight and Pretzels 1933,Ag 23,21:2
Romance in the Rain 1934,S 8,18:5
Broadway Gondolier 1935,Jl 18,15:2
Varsity Show 1937,S 2,17:2
Forever and a Day 1943,Mr 13,9:2
Where Do We Go From Here? 1945,Je 7,25:2
Because of Him 1946,Ja 25,26:6

Herzig, Sig (Screenwriter)

Broadway Gondolier 1935,Jl 18,15:2
Millions in the Air 1935,D 12,33:4
Sing Me a Love Song 1936,D 26,15:2
Ready, Willing and Able 1937,Mr 15,27:1
Marry the Girl 1937,Jl 31,6:2
Four's a Crowd 1938,Ag 12,11:1
Going Places 1939,Ja 7,6:1
They Made Me a Criminal 1939,Ja 21,19:2
Indianapolis Speedway 1939,Jl 15,8:2
On Your Toes 1939,O 21,12:2
I Wanted Wings 1941,Mr 27,29:4
Sunny 1941,Je 13,22:2
My Favorite Spy 1942,My 29,13:4
I Dood It 1943,N 11,29:1
Meet the People 1944,S 8,16:2
Brewster's Millions 1945,Ap 27,23:2

Herzinger, Carl (Miscellaneous)

Around the World 1943,N 25,39:2

Herzinger, Charles

Bat, The 1926,Mr 15,18:3

Herzog, Fred

Scarlet Letter, The 1926,Ag 10,19:2

Herzog, Maurice (Miscellaneous)

Annapurna 1953,D 14,45:4

Herzog, Maurice (Narrator)

Annapurna 1953,D 14,45:4

Herzog, Werner (Director)

Signs of Life; Lebenszeichen 1968,S 26,60:1

Herzog, Werner (Producer)

Signs of Life; Lebenszeichen 1968,S 26,60:1

Herzog, Werner (Screenwriter)

Signs of Life; Lebenszeichen 1968,S 26,60:1

Herzog (Original Author)

Dreyfus Case, The 1931,Ag 31,11:5

Heslop, Charles

Man With 100 Faces 1938,N 1,27:2
Flying Fortress 1942,D 19,22:2
Follow a Star 1961,Ap 26,34:1
Pair of Briefs, A 1964,F 3,22:2

Hesperia, Alda Mme

Little Corporal, The 1927,O 25,33:3

Hess, John D (Producer)

Matter of Morals, A 1961,Je 1,31:1

Hess, John D (Screenwriter)

Matter of Morals, A 1961,Je 1,31:1

Hess, Karl Heinz

Great British Train Robbery, The 1967,Ap 6,45:2

Hesse, Julia

Dramatic Life of Abraham Lincoln, The
1924,Ja 22,17:3

Hesse, Otto (Screenwriter)

Voruntersuchung; Inquest 1931,My 24,VIII,4:1

Hessens, Robert (Miscellaneous)

Pictura 1952,Ap 8,35:3

Hessler, Gordon (Director)

Woman Who Wouldn't Die, The 1965,Je 10,38:1

Hessling, Catherine

Nana 1928,Ja 22,VIII,7:7
Nana 1929,Jl 30,19:4
Sea-Fever 1929,O 28,20:1

Hessmann, Gabriele

Girls Behind Bars 1950,My 10,41:2

Hesterberg, Trude

Manon Lescaut 1926,N 30,27:1
Madame Wants no Children 1927,Je 21,23:3
Forbidden Love 1929,Ja 14,20:1
Strauss, The Waltz King 1929,Jl 22,17:1
Stuerme der Leidenschaft 1932,Mr 16,17:3
In Wien Hab' Ich Einmal ein Maedel Geliebt
1934,My 26,12:3
Page vom Dalmasse-Hotel, Der 1935,Mr 25,12:3
Grosse Chance, Die 1935,My 6,22:4
Alles Weg'n Dem Hund 1936,Mr 31,17:3
Ist Mein Mann Nicht Fabelhaft 1936,D 8,31:3
Unwiderst Ehliche, Der; Irresistable Man, The
1937,D 20,23:3

Heston, Charlton

Dark City 1950,O 19,40:5
Greatest Show on Earth, The 1952,Ja 11,17:2
Julius Caesar 1952,N 25,33:5
Ruby Gentry 1952,D 26,20:2
Savage, The 1953,Ja 2,11:1
President's Lady, The 1953,My 22,31:1
Pony Express 1953,Je 6,8:6
Arrowhead 1953,S 16,38:6
Bad for Each Other 1953,D 24,9:3
Naked Jungle, The 1954,Ap 3,19:2
Secret of the Incas 1954,My 29,13:3
Far Horizons, The 1955,My 21,11:1
Private War of Major Benson, The
1955,Ag 3,27:2
Lucy Gallant 1955,O 21,30:1
Ten Commandments, The 1956,N 9,35:2
Three Violent People 1957,F 11,34:2
Touch of Evil 1958,My 22,25:2
Buccaneer, The 1958,D 24,00:0
Wreck of the Mary Deare, The 1959,N 7,27:1
Ben Hur 1959,N 19,50:2
Cid, El 1961,D 15,49:1
Pigeon That Took Rome, The 1962,Ag 23,25:1
Diamond Head 1963,F 21,5:2
55 Days at Peking 1963,My 30,20:1
Greatest Story Ever Told, The 1965,F 16,40:2
Major Dundee 1965,Ap 8,45:1
Agony and the Ecstasy, The 1965,O 9,5:6
War Lord, The 1965,N 18,55:2
Khartoum 1966,Jl 14,28:1
Planet of the Apes 1968,F 9,55:2
Counterpoint 1968,Mr 14,51:2
Will Penny 1968,Ap 11,51:2

Heth, Edward Harris (Original Author)

Any Number Can Play 1949,Jl 1,14:4

Heuberger, Edmund (Director)

Verlorene Tal, Das 1936,My 30,7:3

Heugly, Archie

Macbeth 1950,D 28,22:6

Heuse, Andre (Original Author)

Diary of a Chambermaid, The 1946,Je 23,28:2

Heuser, Herman

My Father's House 1947,S 26,28:3

Heuser, Loni

Liebe in Uniform 1934,O 9,17:2

Heuze, Andre

Legion of Honor, The 1928,Jl 20,8:4

Hevdt, Louis Jean

Gung Ho! 1944,Ja 26,23:2

Hewer, John

Law and Disorder 1958,Ag 6,20:1

Hewitt, Alan

Private's Affair, A 1959,Ag 15,8:7
Bachelor in Paradise 1961,N 17,41:2
That Touch of Mink 1962,Je 15,16:2
Misadventures of Merlin Jones, The
1964,Mr 26,40:4
How to Murder Your Wife 1965,Ja 27,26:1
Monkey's Uncle, The 1965,Ag 19,35:4

Hewitt, Christopher

Pool of London 1951,N 28,37:2
Producers, The 1968,Mr 19,38:1

Hewitt, Henry

Rembrandt 1936,D 3,31:1
Avengers, The 1942,N 25,18:2
Young Mr Pitt, The 1943,Mr 11,17:1
Happy Go Lovely 1951,Jl 26,17:2
Where's Charley? 1952,Je 27,18:3
Hundred Hour Hunt 1953,Je 17,32:2
Your Past Is Showing 1958,Jl 1,36:2

Hewitt, Lew (Screenwriter)

Golden Mistress, The 1954,O 30,15:6

Hewitt, Russell

Anne of Green Gables 1919,D 22,18:3

Hewitt, Virginia

My Dear Secretary 1949,F 14,15:4
Flying Saucer, The 1950,Ja 5,28:3

Hewitt-Jones, Brian

Quare Fellow 1963,F 20,6:1

Hewland, Philip

Sherlock Holmes's Fatal Hour 1931,Jl 13,13:5
Missing Rembrandt, The 1932,Mr 26,17:2

Hewlett, Ben

Not Quite Decent 1929,My 6,30:4
On the Level 1930,Jl 5,17:4
Woman Is the Judge, A 1939,S 28,29:5

Heyburn, Weldon

Silent Witness, The 1932,F 8,21:1
Gay Caballero, The 1932,Mr 26,17:2
Careless Lady 1932,Ap 18,19:2
Chandu the Magician 1932,O 1,10:4
Call Her Savage 1932,N 25,19:2
West of Singapore 1933,Ap 1,18:3
Speed 1936,My 16,11:2
Sea Racketeers 1937,O 4,17:2
Atlantic Flight 1937,N 1,24:5
Thirteenth Man, The 1938,Ja 1,11:2
Crime School 1938,My 11,17:2
Fugitive at Large 1939,N 13,15:2
Flight From Destiny 1941,Mr 28,26:7

Heydel, Rolf

Lied der Wuste, Das; Desert Song 1940,F 3,9:3

Heydt, Louis Jean

Make Way for Tomorrow 1937,My 10,23:1
Test Pilot 1938,Ap 16,17:1
I Am the Law 1938,Ag 26,14:2
Let Freedom Ring 1939,Mr 10,19:2
They Made Her a Spy 1939,Mr 29,21:4
Each Dawn I Die 1939,Jl 22,12:2
Charlie Chan at Treasure Island 1939,S 1,15:5
Reno 1939,D 21,29:2
Joe and Ethel Turp Call on the President
1940,Ja 4,19:2
Child Is Born, A 1940,Ja 11,19:2
Abe Lincoln in Illinois 1940,F 23,19:2
Dr Ehrlich's Magic Bullet 1940,F 24,9:2
Man Who Talked too Much, The 1940,Je 29,12:2
Pier 13 1940,Ag 9,19:3
Great McGinty, The 1940,Ag 15,23:1
Let's Make Music 1941,Ja 23,19:2
Sleepers West 1941,Mr 20,25:3
Power Dive 1941,My 29,15:4
Dive Bomber 1941,Ag 30,10:2
Pacific Blackout 1942,Ja 15,25:2
Captains of the Clouds 1942,F 13,24:2
Ten Gentlemen From West Point 1942,Je 5,23:3
Manila Calling 1942,S 28,13:1
Stage Door Canteen 1943,Je 25,13:2
Her Primitive Man 1944,Ap 1,11:1
Great Moment, The 1944,N 13,15:2
Thirty Seconds Over Tokyo 1944,N 16,19:1
Betrayal From the East 1945,Ap 25,27:2
Zombies on Broadway 1945,Ap 27,23:2
They Were Expendable 1945,D 21,25:2
Bad Men of Tombstone 1949,Mr 5,10:2
Come to the Stable 1949,Jl 28,19:1
Kid From Cleveland, The 1949,S 5,13:2
Paid in Full 1950,F 16,28:2
Furies, The 1950,Ag 17,23:2
Rawhide 1951,Mr 26,19:2
Great Missouri Raid, The 1951,Ap 9,31:2
Raton Pass 1951,Ap 20,25:1
Models, Inc 1952,My 26,18:4
Commandos Strike at Dawn 1954,Ja 14,25:1
Wings of Eagles, The 1957,F 1,28:1

Heyerdahl, Thor (Cinematographer)

Kon-Tiki 1951,Ap 4,35:2

Heyerdahl, Thor (Narrator)

Kon-Tiki 1951,Ap 4,35:2

Heyes, Douglas (Director)

Kitten With a Whip 1964,N 5,50:4
Beau Geste 1966,S 8,43:1

Heyes, Douglas (Screenwriter)

Drums of Tahiti 1954,Ap 24,14:5
Kitten With a Whip 1964,N 5,50:4
Beau Geste 1966,S 8,43:1
Ice Station Zebra 1968,D 21,49:1

Heyes, Herbert

Destination Unknown 1942,O 29,19:3
Teen Age 1944,Je 19,17:1
T-Men 1948,Ja 23,28:3
Kiss Tomorrow Goodbye 1950,Ag 5,9:2
Union Station 1950,O 5,38:3
Tripoli 1950,N 10,35:2
Three Guys Named Mike 1951,Mr 2,21:2
Bedtime for Bonzo 1951,Ap 6,31:4
Only the Valiant 1951,Ap 14,9:6
Place in the Sun, A 1951,Ag 29,20:1
Something to Live For 1952,Mr 8,11:2
Carbine Williams 1952,My 8,37:2
Park Row 1952,D 22,20:2
Ruby Gentry 1952,D 26,20:2
Far Horizons, The 1955,My 21,11:1
Seven Little Foys, The 1955,Je 30,18:2
Love Is a Many-Splendored Thing
1955,Ag 19,10:1

Heyes, Herbert— Cont
Sincerely Yours 1955,N 3,37:1
Court-Martial of Billy Mitchell, The
1955,D 23,14:2
Heyl, Kaiser
Kreuzer Emden 1932,S 8,17:2
Heym, Stefan (Original Author)
Hostages 1943,O 11,23:2
HEYMAN
See Also HAMMOND, HEYMANN
Heyman, Claude
Shoot the Piano Player 1962,Jl 24,19:1
Heyman, Edward (Composer)
Anything Goes 1936,F 6,23:3
Delightfully Dangerous 1945,Je 9,17:3
On an Island With You 1948,Jl 30,13:2
Heyman, Edward (Miscellaneous)
Curly Top 1935,Ag 2,22:3
That Girl From Paris 1937,Ja 1,19:1
Northwest Outpost 1947,Ag 8,10:2
Heyman, John (Producer)
Privilege 1967,Jl 25,30:2
Boom! 1968,My 27,56:1
HEYMANN
See Also HAMMOND, HEYMAN
Heymann, Claude (Screenwriter)
Jericho 1946,D 16,31:2
Premier May 1958,S 17,44:2
Heymann, Werner R (Composer)
Ihre Hoheit Befiehlt 1931,N 7,16:5
Liebe Ist Liebe 1932,Je 2,25:2
Monte Carlo Madness 1932,Je 4,9:2
Bal, Le 1932,S 28,22:5
Blonder Tram, Ein; Blond Dream, A
1932,N 13,IX,4:2
Adorable 1933,My 19,20:2
Caravan 1934,S 28,27:1
King and the Chorus Girl, The 1937,Mr 29,14:4
Shop Around the Corner, The 1940,Ja 26,13:2
Knickerbocker Holiday 1944,Ap 20,22:7
Heymann, Werner R (Miscellaneous)
Liebeswalzer 1931,My 4,15:3
Drei von ver Tankstelle, Die 1931,Je 20,20:4
Heyne, Kurd E (Original Author)
Original Sin, The 1950,Ag 21,15:2
Heyward, Dorothy (Original Author)
Porgy and Bess 1959,Je 25,20:3
Heyward, DuBose (Composer)
Porgy and Bess 1959,Je 25,20:3
Porgy and Bess 1959,Je 25,20:3
Heyward, DuBose (Original Author)
Porgy and Bess 1959,Je 25,20:3
Heyward, Louis M (Producer)
Conqueror Worm, The 1968,Ag 15,46:2
Heyward, Louis M (Screenwriter)
War Gods of the Deep 1965,Je 3,24:3
Sergeant Deadhead 1965,O 23,17:3
HEYWOOD
See Also HAYWOOD
Heywood, Anne
Doctor at Large 1957,Jl 29,15:5
Checkpoint 1957,S 19,25:2
Dangerous Exile 1958,O 11,18:3
Upstairs and Downstairs 1960,D 2,53:4
Night Fighters, The 1960,D 15,59:1
Carthage in Flames 1961,Ja 26,32:3
90 Degrees in the Shade 1966,N 16,52:1
Fox, The 1968,F 8,36:1
Heywood, Herbert
Escape from Devil's Island 1935,N 25,22:2
Three Blind Mice 1938,Je 18,18:2
Little Old New York 1940,F 3,9:2
No Time for Comedy 1940,S 7,9:2
Strawberry Blonde 1941,F 22,11:2
Blues in the Night 1941,D 12,35:2
Swingtime Johnny 1943,D 17,23:3
Smoky 1946,Je 27,29:1
Green Grass of Wyoming 1948,Je 10,28:3
Heywood, Pat
Romeo and Juliet 1968,O 9,41:1
Heyworth, John
Forbidden Music 1938,D 27,13:2
Heyworth, Mimi
Three Came Home 1950,F 21,22:5
Hiatt, Phillipa
Half-Way House 1945,Ag 13,22:4
Hiatt, Ruth
His First Flame 1927,My 2,26:4
Missing Link, The 1927,My 7,15:2
Hibbert, Christopher (Miscellaneous)
Palaces of a Queen 1967,Je 27,32:1
Hibbert, Geoffrey
Love on the Dole 1945,O 13,11:2
Hundred Hour Hunt 1953,Je 17,32:2
Hibbs, Jesse (Director)
Rails Into Laramie 1954,My 13,34:2
To Hell and Back 1955,S 23,21:2
Spoilers, The 1955,D 24,10:2
World in my Corner 1956,F 18,12:5
Walk the Proud Land 1956,S 8,20:6 (In
Addenda)
Joe Butterfly 1957,My 30,23:2

Hibler, Winston (Miscellaneous)
Cinderella 1950,F 23,33:1
Hibler, Winston (Narrator)
Water Birds 1952,Je 27,18:3
Living Desert, The 1953,N 10,38:1
Vanishing Prairie, The 1954,Ag 17,17:3
African Lion, The 1955,S 15,39:2
Secrets of Life 1956,N 21,20:1
Perri 1957,O 2,27:5
White Wilderness 1958,Ag 13,22:1
Hibler, Winston (Producer)
Perri 1957,O 2,27:5
Hound that Thought he was a Racoon, The
1960,Ag 18,19:2
Nikki, Wild Dog of the North 1961,S 5,37:6
Big Red 1962,S 3,11:2
Ugly Dachshund, The 1966,Ap 7,45:1
Follow Me, Boys! 1966,D 2,46:1
Horse in the Gray Flannel Suit, The
1968,D 21,49:3
Hibler, Winston (Screenwriter)
Living Desert, The 1953,N 10,38:1
Vanishing Prairie, The 1954,Ag 17,17:3
African Lion, The 1955,S 15,39:2
Perri 1957,O 2,27:5
Nikki, Wild Dog of the North 1961,S 5,37:6
Hichens, Robert (Original Author)
Bella Donna 1915,N 15,11:1
Voice From the Minaret, The 1923,F 5,18:2
Bella Donna 1923,Ap 16,20:2
Garden of Allah, The 1927,S 3,13:5
Garden of Allah, The 1927,S 11,VIII,5:1
After the Verdict 1930,Ja 18,21:1
Bella Donna 1935,F 26,16:4
Garden of Allah, The 1936,N 20,27:2
Temptation 1946,D 25,33:6
Hickey, Donna Lee
Farmer Takes a Wife, The 1953,Je 13,11:2
Hickey, William
Hatful of Rain, A 1957,Jl 18,19:2
Hickman, Alfred
Here Comes the Bride 1919,F 3,13:2
Enchanted Cottage, The 1924,Ap 14,14:1
Rescue, The 1929,Ja 14,20:1
Woman of Experience, A 1931,Jl 9,26:5
Phantom of Paris, The 1931,N 14,15:3
Hickman, Bill
To Please a Lady 1950,O 27,24:3
Hickman, Cordell
Biscuit Eater, The 1940,My 23,28:5
Tarzan's Secret Treasure 1941,D 25,33:1
Tales of Manhattan 1942,S 25,25:1
Big Bonanza, The 1945,F 26,14:5
Hickman, Darryl
Grapes of Wrath, The 1940,Ja 25,17:2
Untamed 1940,Jl 25,14:3
Young People 1940,Ag 24,16:2
Men of Boys Town 1941,Ap 11,24:6
Mob Town 1941,N 20,39:3
Joe Smith, American 1942,Ap 2,27:4
Jackass Mail 1942,Jl 2,25:2
Human Comedy, The 1943,Mr 3,19:2
Keeper of the Flame 1943,Mr 19,15:2
Assignment in Brittany 1943,Ap 22,31:2
Song of Russia 1944,F 11,17:2
Captain Eddie 1945,Ag 9,24:2
Kiss and Tell 1945,O 26,16:2
Leave Her to Heaven 1945,D 26,15:1
Strange Love of Martha Ivers, The
1946,Jl 25,18:4
Boy's Ranch 1946,Ag 9,12:2
Two Years Before the Mast 1946,S 25,39:2
Sainted Sisters, The 1948,My 20,35:2
Fighting Father Dunne 1948,Je 25,26:2
Alias Nick Beal 1949,Mr 10,35:2
Set-Up, The 1949,Mr 30,31:2
Any Number Can Play 1949,Jl 1,14:4
Lightning Strikes Twice 1951,Ap 13,18:7
Criminal Lawyer 1951,Ag 24,11:4
Submarine Command 1952,Ja 19,13:2
Destination Gobi 1953,My 30,7:1
Prisoner of War 1954,My 10,20:2
Southwest Passage 1954,S 11,11:2
Tea and Sympathy 1956,S 28,24:4
Hickman, Dwayne
Secret Heart, The 1946,D 26,28:2
Boy With Green Hair, The 1949,Ja 13,26:2
Rally Round the Flag Boys! 1958,D 24,2:7
Cat Ballou 1965,Je 25,36:1
Ski Party 1965,O 23,17:3
How to Stuff a Wild Bikini 1967,Ja 12,48:1
Doctor, You've Got to be Kidding
1967,My 11,50:1
Hickman, Howard
Alias Jimmy Valentine 1928,N 16,28:6
His First Command 1929,D 23,18:2
Brothers 1930,N 15,15:3
Sisters Under the Skin 1934,Je 8,18:1
Here Comes the Navy 1934,Jl 21,14:2
Rendezvous 1935,O 26,12:2
Fury 1936,Je 6,21:1
Fifteen Maiden Lane 1936,O 17,21:3
We Who Are About to Die 1937,Ja 2,15:1

Hickman, Howard— Cont
Crack-Up 1937,Ja 4,20:4
Crime Nobody Saw, The 1937,Ap 5,17:2
Charlie Chan at the Olympics 1937,My 24,23:1
One Mile From Heaven 1937,Ag 19,23:1
100 Men and a Girl 1937,S 18,15:2
Start Cheering 1938,Mr 17,17:3
Flight Into Nowhere 1938,My 2,13:3
Rascals 1938,My 27,12:2
Juvenile Court 1938,S 12,13:2
Come on Leathernecks 1938,S 15,29:3
I Stand Accused 1939,Ja 5,17:1
Good Girls Go to Paris 1939,Je 23,23:1
Espionage Agent 1939,S 23,22:2
Return Of Doctor X, The 1939,N 23,38:5
Gone With the Wind 1939,D 20,31:2
It all Came True 1940,Ap 6,13:2
Slightly Honorable 1940,My 17,23:4
Gangs of Chicago 1940,Je 13,29:2
Girls of the Road 1940,Jl 22,20:2
Secret Seven, The 1940,Ag 12,11:6
Strike up the Band 1940,S 30,13:2
Cheers for Miss Bishop 1941,Mr 14,17:2
Washington Melodrama 1941,My 26,15:3
Nine Loves Are not Enough 1941,O 30,27:2
Belle Starr 1941,N 1,20:2
Tarzan's New York Adventure 1942,Ag 7,13:2
Hickman, Joan
Secret of my Success, The 1965,N 4,57:2
Hickox, Harry
Music Man, The 1962,Ag 24,14:1
Hotel 1967,Ja 20,27:1
Hicks, Barbara
Touch of Larceny, A 1960,Mr 17,28:1
Hand in Hand 1961,F 7,41:3
Hicks, Don
Twelve O'Clock High 1950,Ja 28,10:2
Halls of Montezuma, The 1951,Ja 6,9:6
Hicks, Johnny
Free, White and 21 1963,Je 20,29:3
Hicks, Leonard
Guns of the Trees 1964,F 29,12:2
Santa Claus Conquers the Martians
1964,D 17,50:2
Hicks, Maxine Elliott
Babbitt 1924,Jl 15,9:4
Enticement 1925,Mr 21,16:3
Hicks, Russell
Happiness Ahead 1934,O 11,28:2
Case of the Howling Dog, The 1934,O 18,26:5
Firebird, The 1934,N 15,25:2
Gentlemen are Born 1934,N 22,27:2
Babbitt 1934,D 17,24:2
Murder in the Clouds 1934,D 26,18:1
Devil Dogs of the Air 1935,F 7,23:2
Sweet Music 1935,F 21,23:2
While the Patient Slept 1935,Mr 2,18:2
Living on Velvet 1935,Mr 8,25:4
Woman in Red, The 1935,Mr 23,11:3
Cardinal Richelieu 1935,Ap 19,24:2
Lady Tubbs 1935,Jl 22,20:2
Charlie Chan in Shanghai 1935,O 14,21:1
$1,000 a Minute 1935,D 21,11:1
Follow the Fleet 1936,F 21,21:2
Woman Trap 1936,Mr 7,11:4
Special Investigator 1936,Ap 25,21:1
Bunker Bean 1936,Je 27,21:2
Grand Jury 1936,Ag 1,16:3
Ticket to Paradise 1936,Ag 8,5:3
Fifteen Maiden Lane 1936,O 17,21:3
Secret Valley 1937,Ja 25,22:2
Girl Overboard 1937,Mr 1,15:1
23 1/2 Hours Leave 1937,My 17,23:2
Pick a Star 1937,My 28,17:2
Toast of New York, The 1937,Jl 23,16:2
Big Shot, The 1937,Ag 13,13:1
On Again-Off Again 1937,S 18,15:3
Fit for a King 1937,O 15,18:5
Westland Case, The 1937,O 23,14:2
Criminals of the Air 1937,O 28,29:2
Big Broadcast of 1938, The 1938,Mr 10,16:2
Kidnapped 1938,My 28,9:2
Gateway 1938,Ag 8,9:2
Fugitives for a Night 1938,S 21,30:4
Hold That Co-ed 1938,S 24,13:1
Kentucky 1938,D 24,12:1
Three Musketeers, The 1939,F 18,12:2
I Was a Convict 1939,Mr 23,27:2
Story of Alexander Graham Bell, The
1939,Ap 1,17:2
East Side of Heaven 1939,My 5,29:3
Stanley and Livingstone 1939,Ag 5,18:2
Real Glory, The 1939,S 15,26:2
Hollywood Cavalcade 1939,O 14,13:2
Honeymoon's Over, The 1939,D 15,33:3
Swanee River 1939,D 30,9:2
Big Guy, The 1939,Ja 1,29:2
Blue Bird, The 1940,Ja 20,11:2
Johnny Apollo 1940,Ap 13,21:2
Enemy Agent 1940,Ap 22,13:3
Earthbound 1940,Je 7,27:4
Mortal Storm, The 1940,Je 21,25:2
Sporting Blood 1940,Jl 22,20:2
Return of Frank James, The 1940,Ag 10,16:4

Hicks, Russell — Cont

East of the River 1940,O 28,21:2
Bank Dick, The 1940,D 13,29:2
Love Thy Neighbor 1940,D 18,32:5
No, No, Nanette 1940,D 20,33:1
Night at Earl Carroll's, A 1941,Ja 23,19:1
Western Union 1941,F 7,23:2
Ellery Queen's Penthouse Mystery
  1941,Mr 7,17:2
Man Made Monster 1941,Mr 19,25:4
Man Betrayed, A 1941,Mr 27,29:5
Great Lie, The 1941,Ap 12,19:2
Big Store, The 1941,Je 27,14:4
Parson of Panamint, The 1941,Jl 26,18:2
Hold That Ghost 1941,Ag 8,13:3
Little Foxes, The 1941,Ag 22,19:2
Great Guns 1941,O 3,27:2
To the Shores of Tripoli 1942,Mr 26,27:2
Joe Smith, American 1942,Ap 2,27:4
We Were Dancing 1942,My 1,23:2
Pacific Rendezvous 1942,Jl 8,27:4
Tarzan's New York Adventure 1942,Ag 7,13:2
Tennessee Johnson 1943,Ja 13,18:2
Hitler-Dead or Alive 1943,Mr 31,23:3
Air Raid Wardens 1943,Ap 5,15:5
Woman of the Town, The 1944,Mr 6,17:2
Janie 1944,Ag 5,16:2
She Gets her Man 1945,F 9,20:5
Flame of Barbary Coast 1945,My 28,22:2
Game of Death, A 1945,N 24,22:4
Scarlet Street 1946,F 15,29:2
Bandit of Sherwood Forest, The 1946,Mr 23,8:4
Bachelor's Daughters, The 1946,O 7,23:2
Plainsman and the Lady, The 1946,N 4,33:1
Sea of Grass, The 1947,F 28,27:2
Race Street 1948,Ag 23,13:3
Black Arrow, The 1948,O 4,14:2
Plunders, The 1948,N 1,28:2
My Dear Secretary 1949,F 14,15:4
Barbary Pirate 1949,O 28,29:3
Flying Saucer, The 1950,Ja 5,28:3
Blue Grass of Kentucky 1950,Ja 27,29:2
Big Hangover, The 1950,My 26,20:3

Hicks, Seymour

Sleeping Partners 1930,D 13,22:2
Love Habit, The 1931,F 2,23:1
Money for Nothing 1932,F 21,VIII,5:2 (In
  Addenda)
Scrooge 1935,D 14,11:1
Sleeping Partners 1937,Mr 23,IX,6:1
Pastor Hall 1940,S 21,13:2
Haunted Honeymoon 1940,O 31,28:2
Young Man's Fancy, A 1943,D 4,11:2
Fame Is the Spur 1949,N 8,34:2
Silent Dust 1949,D 30,13:2

Hicks, Seymour (Director)

Sleeping Partners 1930,D 13,22:2

Hicks, Seymour (Screenwriter)

Sleeping Partners 1930,D 13,22:2
Love Habit, The 1931,F 2,23:1
Money for Nothing 1932,F 21,VIII,5:2 (In
  Addenda)

Hicks, Walter (Miscellaneous)

Baboona 1935,Ja 23,21:2

Hickson, Joan

Love From a Stranger 1937,Ap 19,27:2
Don't Take it to Heart 1948,D 25,10:3
This Was a Woman 1949,Ja 5,22:2
Guinea Pig, The 1949,My 2,20:2
Seven Days to Noon 1950,D 19,41:3
High Treason 1952,My 21,23:3
Promoter, The 1952,O 29,36:2
Curtain Up 1953,F 2,17:3
Dance Little Lady 1955,D 26,23:3
Man Who Never Was, The 1956,Ap 4,24:1
Law and Disorder 1958,Ag 6,20:1
39 Steps, The 1960,O 11,55:2
Upstairs and Downstairs 1960,D 2,53:4
Murder She Said 1962,Ja 8,27:2

Hidaka, Ayako

Escapde in Japan 1957,D 24,11:1

Hidari, Bokuzen

Magnificent Seven, The 1956,N 20,46:2
Lower Depths, The 1962,F 10,12:5

Hidari, Sachiko

This Madding Crowd 1964,Je 17,48:1
Insect Woman, The; Nippon Konchuki
  1964,Jl 1,42:1
She and He 1964,S 26,16:1

Hidey, Jean

Savage Eye, The 1960,Je 7,27:1

Hielsen, Helen (Original Author)

Blackout 1954,My 22,8:2

Hiers, Walter

Leave It to Susan 1919,My 26,19:4
Why Smith Left Home 1919,O 13,16:3
Sham 1921,My 6,20:2
Bought and Paid For 1922,Mr 13,18:2
Is Matrimony a Failure 1922,Ap 17,22:3
Ghost Breaker, The 1922,S 11,20:2
Mr Billings Spends his Dime 1923,Mr 5,15:3
Sixty Cents an Hour 1923,My 15,22:1
Hollywood 1923,Jl 30,11:4
Flaming Barriers 1924,Ja 29,16:1

Christine of the Hungry Heart 1924,D 8,13:3
Excuse Me 1925,Ja 27,11:2
Hold That Lion 1926,S 6,16:2
Beware of Widows 1927,My 24,23:4
Night Life 1927,D 20,33:2
Dancers in the Dark 1932,Mr 19,11:2
70,000 Witnesses 1932,S 3,16:2

Hiestand, John

I Wanted Wings 1941,Mr 27,29:4

Higashi, Emiko

Insect Woman, The; Nippon Konchuki
  1964,Jl 1,42:1

Higashiyama, Chieko

Idiot, The 1963,My 1,35:1

Higby, Wilbur

Nugget Nell 1919,Jl 28,8:5
Richard the Lion-Hearted 1923,O 22,17:1
Confessions of a Queen 1925,Mr 24,20:6
Lights of Old Broadway 1925,N 2,20:1
Hat, Coat and Glove 1934,Jl 27,21:2

Higgin, Howard (Director)

In the Name of Love 1925,Ag 27,14:1
New Commandment, The 1925,N 10,25:3
Reckless Lady, The 1926,Ja 25,21:2
Wilderness Woman, The 1926,My 10,19:1
Great Deception, The 1926,Ag 9,10:3
Perfect Sap, The 1927,Ja 11,18:2
Skyscraper 1928,Ap 9,18:2
Power 1928,N 27,34:1
Sal of Singapore 1929,Ja 29,27:1
Leatherneck, The 1929,Ap 22,23:1
Racketeer, The 1930,Ja 6,30:8
Painted Desert, The 1931,Mr 9,19:1
Hell's House 1932,F 12,24:5
Final Edition, The 1932,F 22,23:2
Last Man, The 1932,S 17,18:4

Higgin, Howard (Original Author)

Her Man 1930,O 4,15:2
Invisible Ray, The 1936,Ja 11,9:3
Gold Racket, The 1937,Ag 2,10:3
Street of Missing Women 1940,Ja 8,11:2

Higgin, Howard (Screenwriter)

Fashion Row 1924,Ja 28,12:1
Trouble With Wives, The 1925,Ag 5,12:4
Painted Desert, The 1931,Mr 9,19:1
Hell's House 1932,F 12,24:5
Revolt of the Zombies 1936,Je 5,17:2

Higgins, David

Confidence Man, The 1924,Ap 15,24:1

Higgins, George

Golden Coach, The 1954,Ja 22,30:2
Paris Does Strange Things 1957,Mr 30,13:2

Higgins, Joe

Flipper's New Adventure 1964,Ag 27,28:2

Higgins, John C (Original Author)

They all Come Out 1939,Ag 3,15:4
Kid Glove Killer 1942,Ap 17,21:4
Adventures of Tartu, The 1943,S 24,26:1
Main Street After Dark 1945,Ja 13,15:4
Border Incident 1949,N 21,29:2

Higgins, John C (Screenwriter)

Murder Man, The 1935,Jl 27,16:2
They all Come Out 1939,Ag 3,15:4
Penalty, The 1941,Ap 10,29:3
Kid Glove Killer 1942,Ap 17,21:4
Main Street After Dark 1945,Ja 13,15:4
T-Men 1948,Ja 23,28:3
Raw Deal 1948,Jl 9,11:4
He Walked by Night 1949,F 7,15:2
Border Incident 1949,N 21,29:2
Pony Soldier 1952,D 20,15:2
Diamond Wizard, The 1954,Jl 17,7:4
Shield for Murder 1954,Ag 28,8:3
Big House U S A 1955,Mr 12,11:6
Seven Cities of Gold 1955,O 8,13:2
Untamed Youth 1957,My 11,24:6
Robinson Crusoe on Mars 1964,Ag 27,28:2

Higgins, Kenneth (Original Author)

He's my Guy 1943,Mr 12,12:3

Higgins, Michael

Terror in the City 1966,N 9,43:4

Higgins, Rose

Northern Pursuit 1943,N 26,29:2

**High Altitude Observatory of Harvard Univ
/(Cinematographer)**

Action on the Sun 1949,D 29,1:6

Highes, Gareth

Sentimental Tommy 1921,My 9,16:2

Highsmith, Patricia (Original Author)

Strangers on a Train 1951,Jl 4,13:2
Purple Noon 1961,S 1,12:1
Enough Rope 1966,Jl 15,34:3

Hightower, Harold

Four Feathers, The 1929,Je 13,35:4

Hightower, Rosella

Neapolitan Carousel 1961,O 12,41:3

Higley, Philip (Original Author)

Remember the Day 1941,D 26,21:2

Hignett, H R

Caravan 1949,Ap 21,30:4
Spring in Park Lane 1949,S 21,38:2

Hiken, Gerald

Uncle Vanya 1958,Ap 29,26:2
Goddess, The 1958,Je 25,24:1

Hilary, Jennifer

Becket 1964,Mr 12,40:2
Heroes of Telemark, The 1966,Mr 10,26:1
Idol, The 1966,Ag 11,27:1

Hilbeck, Fernando

Kid Rodelo 1966,F 23,46:1

Hilber, Winston (Screenwriter)

Adventures of Ichabod and Mr Toad, The
  1949,O 10,18:2

Hilburn, Betty

Sinners in Heaven 1924,S 10,21:3

Hildebrand, Hilde

Kleine Seitensprung, Der 1932,Ja 1,31:1
Wenn die Liebe Mode Macht 1933,O 30,14:3
Das Schicksal der Renate Langen 1933,N 4,18:4
Liebe Muss Verstanden Sein 1934,Mr 21,24:3
Viktor und Viktoria 1935,Ja 28,10:5
Gretl Zieht das Grosse Los 1935,F 11,14:2
Drei von der Kavallerie 1935,Ap 13,11:4
Unbekannte Gast, Der; Unknown Guest, The
  1935,Je 1,18:3
Klein Dorrit 1935,O 19,21:2
Polenblut; Polish Blood 1935,N 16,19:3
Private Life of Louis XIV, The 1936,Ja 9,25:2
Gruss und Kuss, Veronika 1936,F 24,14:2
Falscher Fuffziger, Ein 1937,F 13,9:1
Maria, Die Magd 1937,My 22,19:2
Selige Exzellenz, Die 1937,Je 15,26:2
Meadehen von Gestern Nacht, Das; Girl of Last
  Night, The 1938,Je 18,18:2
Only for Thee; Solo per To 1938,S 12,13:2
Alles Fuer Veronika 1939,F 4,11:2
Tag Nach der Scheidung, Der; Day After the
  Divorce, The 1940,Mr 2,9:5
Peter, Paul und Nanette 1940,My 25,20:1

Hildebrand, Rodney

Mother Machree 1928,Mr 6,20:3

Hildebrand, Weyler

Soederkaakar 1936,D 19,16:2
Surf, The 1949,D 17,15:2

Hildebrand, Weyler (Director)

Soederkaakar 1936,D 19,16:2
Rena Rama Sanningen; Nothing but the Truth
  1939,O 7,11:2

Hill, Al

Me, Gangster 1928,O 22,29:1
Half Way to Heaven 1929,D 7,19:3
Racketeer, The 1930,Ja 6,30:8
Last Mile, The 1932,Ag 26,20:3
Night after Night 1932,O 31,18:4
Death Kiss, The 1933,F 5,IX,5:3
Private Jones 1933,Mr 25,13:3
Air Hawks 1935,Je 4,26:5
Pay-Off, The 1935,N 13,25:3
Three on the Trail 1936,My 5,26:5
Border Patrolman 1936,Je 29,11:2
Crash Donovan 1936,Ag 10,10:3
Hollywood Cowboy 1937,Jl 24,12:1
Big Shot, The 1937,Ag 13,13:1
Partners of the Plains 1938,F 12,20:4
Lady in the Morgue, The 1938,My 9,13:3
Gambling Ship 1939,Ja 21,19:2
Bank Dick, The 1940,D 13,29:2
Perilous Holiday 1946,Je 1,10:4
Sealed Cargo 1951,My 24,47:1

Hill, Arthur

Deep Blue Sea, The 1955,O 13,35:2
Young Doctors, The 1961,Ag 24,25:2
Ugly American, The 1963,Ap 12,30:2
In the Cool of the Day 1963,My 30,20:1
Moment to Moment 1966,Mr 3,28:1
Harper 1966,Mr 31,43:1
Petulia 1968,Je 11,54:4

Hill, Benny

Those Magnificent Men in Their Flying Machines
  (Or How I Flew From London to Paris in 25
  Hours and 11 Minutes) 1965,Je 17,27:1
Chitty Chitty Bang Bang 1968,D 19,64:4

Hill, Craig

Cheaper by the Dozen 1950,Ap 1,12:2
All About Eve 1950,O 14,13:2
Detective Story 1951,N 7,35:2
Fixed Bayonets 1951,N 21,20:2
Outcasts of Poker Flat 1952,My 16,19:3
What Price Glory 1952,Ag 23,10:2
Siege at Red River, The 1954,Ap 3,19:2
Black Shield of Falworth, The 1954,O 7,16:2
Tammy and the Bachelor 1957,Je 15,10:7
Follow Me, Boys! 1966,D 2,46:1
Swinger, The 1966,D 15,60:1

Hill, Doris

Rough House Rosie 1927,My 23,27:2
Tell It to Sweeney 1927,O 17,20:2
Take Me Home 1928,O 23,33:1
Studio Murder Mystery, The 1929,Je 10,23:1
His Glorious Night 1929,O 5,22:5

Hill, Edwin C (Miscellaneous)

Hitler's Reign of Terror 1934,My 1,26:6

Hill, Elizabeth (Original Author)
Streets of Laredo 1949,My 12,28:2
Hill, Elizabeth (Screenwriter)
Citadel, The 1938,N 4,27:2
H M Pulham, Esq 1941,D 19,35:1
Hill, Ethel (Miscellaneous)
When You're in Love 1937,F 19,15:2
Hill, Ethel (Original Author)
Virtue 1932,O 25,24:5
Side Streets 1934,Ag 15,13:5
More Than a Secretary 1936,D 11,35:2
Maisie Gets her Man 1942,Jl 16,23:2
Hill, Ethel (Screenwriter)
I'll Fix It 1934,N 12,17:3
Best Man Wins 1935,Ja 2,22:4
It Happened in Hollywood 1937,O 2,18:1
Just Around the Corner 1938,D 3,11:2
Little Princess, The 1939,Mr 11,21:1
Maryland 1940,Jl 13,16:5
Dance Hall 1941,Jl 19,16:2
In old Oklahoma 1943,D 6,21:1
Man From Frisco 1944,Je 16,14:7
Twice Blessed 1945,Jl 7,7:5
Two Smart People 1947,F 15,20:4
Hill, Frank
Arizona 1941,F 7,23:3
Hill, George (Director)
Through the Dark 1924,Ja 8,27:1
Hill Billy, The 1924,Mr 12,19:4
Midnight Express, The 1924,N 19,19:3
Zander the Great 1925,My 4,16:2
Limited Mail, The 1925,S 1,18:2
Barrier, The 1926,Mr 22,16:1
Tell It to the Marines 1926,D 24,18:2
Callahans and the Murphys, The 1927,Jl 12,29:3
Cossacks, The 1928,Je 25,27:1
Flying Fleet, The 1929,F 11,26:3
Big House, The 1930,Je 25,31:2
Min and Bill 1930,N 24,26:5
Secret Six, The 1931,My 2,23:4
Hell Divers 1931,D 23,27:3
Clear all Wires 1933,Mr 4,11:2
Hill, George (Original Author)
Secret of Stamboul, The 1941,My 31,14:1
Hill, George (Screenwriter)
Midnight Express, The 1924,N 19,19:3
Hill, George Roy (Director)
Period of Adjustment 1962,N 1,34:1
Toys in the Attic 1963,Ag 1,17:2
World of Henry Orient, The 1964,Mr 20,27:2
Hawaii 1966,O 11,54:1
Thoroughly Modern Millie 1967,Mr 23,25:1
Hill, Gladys (Screenwriter)
Marika 1953,F 18,27:2
Reflections in a Golden Eye 1967,O 12,59:1
Hill, Grundy
Pacific Adventure 1947,N 26,18:2
Hill, Gus (Original Author)
McFadden's Flats 1935,Mr 13,16:2
Hill, Howard
Last Wildermess, The 1935,My 15,26:2
Adventures of Robin Hood, The 1938,My 13,17:2
Hill, James (Director)
Trapeze 1956,Je 5,39:2
Kitchen, The 1961,N 2,42:1
Trial and Error 1962,N 17,17:2
Born Free 1966,Je 23,29:1
Study in Terror, A 1966,N 3,45:3
Corrupt Ones, The 1967,F 23,41:3
Hill, James (Producer)
Vera Cruz 1954,D 27,22:4
Sweet Smell of Success 1957,Je 28,29:2
Unforgiven, The 1960,Ap 7,46:1
Hill, James (Screenwriter)
Hoodlum Saint, The 1946,Je 27,29:1
His Majesty O'Keefe 1954,F 6,17:2
Hill, Jerome
Hallelujah the Hills 1963,D 17,49:1
Hill, Jerome (Director)
Grandma Moses 1950,O 24,34:6
Albert Schweitzer 1957,Ja 21,20:2
Sand Castle, The 1961,Ag 16,37:2
Open the Door and See all the People
1964,Ap 2,28:1
Hill, Jerome (Miscellaneous)
Albert Schweitzer 1957,Ja 21,20:2
Hill, Jerome (Producer)
Albert Schweitzer 1957,Ja 21,20:2
Sand Castle, The 1961,Ag 16,37:2
Open the Door and See all the People
1964,Ap 2,28:1
Hill, Jerome (Screenwriter)
Sand Castle, The 1961,Ag 16,37:2
Open the Door and See all the People
1964,Ap 2,28:1
Hill, Kathryn
Wanderer, The 1925,Ag 20,22:1
Yankee Senor, The 1926,Ja 28,14:4
Hill, Marianna
Red Line 7000 1965,D 9,60:4
Hill, Mary
Models, Inc 1952,My 26,18:4
Beast From 20,000 Fathoms, The 1953,Je 25,23:1

Hill, Maude
Puritan Passions 1923,O 15,15:4
Hill, Maurice J (Screenwriter)
Track of Thunder 1968,F 1,28:4
Hill, Morgan
23 1/2 Hours Leave 1937,My 17,23:2
Hill, Peter Murray
Outsider, The 1940,Mr 18,13:2
Madonna of the Seven Moons 1946,My 23,18:4
They Were Sisters 1946,Jl 24,24:2
Hill, Phyllis
Singing in the Dark 1956,Mr 8,32:5
Hill, Ramsey
Down to Their Last Yacht 1934,S 24,14:1
Crusades, The 1935,Ag 22,21:3
Bwana Devil 1953,F 19,20:5
Hill, Riley
Short Grass 1951,Ja 13,10:4
Hill, Robert
Nobody Waved Goodbye 1964,S 17,52:1
Hill, Robert (Director)
Tarzan, The Fearless 1933,Ag 12,14:3
Mars Attacks the World 1938,N 8,26:3
East Side Kids 1940,F 19,21:6
Hill, Robert (Original Author)
Female on the Beach 1955,Ag 20,20:2
Hill, Robert (Screenwriter)
Female on the Beach 1955,Ag 20,20:2
Raw Edge 1956,Jl 28,10:7
Woman's Devotion, A 1957,Mr 22,26:1
Girl in the Kremlin, The 1957,My 22,29:2
Female Animal, The 1958,Ja 23,24:3
Fanny Hill 1965,D 2,48:1
Hill, Shirley
Moon Over her Shoulder 1941,N 5,31:2
Hill, Sinclair (Director)
Unwritten Law, The 1929,D 24,14:5
First Mrs Fraser, The 1932,My 29,VIII,4:5 (In
Addenda)
Hill, Steven
Lady Without Passport, A 1950,Ag 4,13:2
Storm Fear 1955,D 17,19:2
Goddess, The 1958,Je 25,24:1
Child Is Waiting, A 1963,F 14,5:6
Slender Thread, The 1965,D 24,24:2
Hill, Thelma
Fair Co-ed, The 1927,O 24,24:3
Play Girl, The 1928,Ap 23,20:2
Crooks Can't Win 1928,My 29,17:2
Miracle Woman, The 1931,Ag 17,18:2
Hill, Trevor
Village, The 1953,S 23,37:2
Hill, Weldon (Original Author)
Onionhead 1958,O 2,44:1
Hillaire, Marcel
Sabrina 1954,S 23,43:2
Seven Thieves 1960,Mr 12,14:5
Honeymoon Machine, The 1961,Ag 24,25:2
4 Horsemen of the Apocalypse, The
1962,Mr 10,10:2
Wheeler Dealers, The 1963,N 15,25:2
Very Special Favor, A 1965,Ag 26,40:3
Made in Paris 1966,F 17,29:1
Hillberg, Linnea
Med Folket Foer Fosterlandet 1939,F 21,14:2
Hille, Ellen
Gordian, Der Tyrann 1937,Je 21,15:3
Hille, Heinz (Director)
Frechdachs, Der 1934,Ja 6,18:3
Und Es Leuchtet die Puszta 1934,Ja 30,17:2
Szerelmi Almok 1937,Ja 5,19:2
Hille, Heinz (Screenwriter)
Szerelmi Almok 1937,Ja 5,19:2
Hiller, Arthur (Director)
Careless Years, The 1957,N 28,57:3
Miracle of the White Stallions 1963,My 23,31:2
Wheeler Dealers, The 1963,N 15,25:2
Americanization of Emily, The 1964,O 28,51:1
Penelope 1966,N 11,36:6
Tobruk 1967,F 9,33:2
Tiger Makes Out, The 1967,S 19,53:1
Hiller, Kurt
Last Laugh, The 1925,Ja 28,14:1
Hiller, Lejaren a' (Director)
Beggar Maid, The 1921,S 26,18:1
Beggar Maid, The 1921,O 2,VII,3:1
Bashful Suitor, The 1921,D 12,20:2
Young Painter, The 1922,F 26,VI,3:1 (In
Addenda)
Hiller, Wendy
Pygmalion 1938,D 8,34:2
Major Barbara 1941,My 15,27:1
I Know Where I'm Going 1947,Ag 20,25:2
Outcast of the Islands 1952,My 16,19:2
Sailor of the King 1953,S 3,15:2
Something of Value 1957,My 11,24:6
How to Murder a Rich Uncle 1957,O 26,19:2
Separate Tables 1958,D 19,2:7
Sons and Lovers 1960,Ag 3,35:1
Toys in the Attic 1963,Ag 1,17:2
Man for all Seasons, A 1966,D 13,60:1

Hilliard, Bob (Composer)
She's Back on Broadway 1953,Mr 12,24:2
Hilliard, Ernest
Little Child Shall Lead Them, A 1922,S 2,10:4
Recoil, The 1924,Je 30,16:1
Smile, Brother, Smile 1927,Ag 29,21:1
Matinee Idol, The 1928,Ap 24,29:3
Sinners in Love 1928,N 19,16:7
Wall Street 1929,N 25,22:1
Dynamite 1929,D 28,11:1
Soul of a Monster, The 1944,S 9,12:4
Hilliard, Harriet
Follow the Fleet 1936,F 21,21:2
New Faces of 1937 1937,Jl 2,25:1
Life of the Party, The 1937,O 4,17:1
Cocoanut Grove 1938,Je 16,21:2
Letter, The 1940,N 23,12:6
Confessions of Boston Blackie 1941,D 8,31:2
Canal Zone 1942,Mr 30,21:2
Juke Box Jenny 1942,Ap 17,21:3
Falcon Strikes Back, The 1943,Ap 2,17:4
Gals, Inc 1943,Ag 13,13:4
Swingtime Johnny 1943,D 17,23:3
Hilliard, Harry
Romeo and Juliet 1916,O 23,10:3
Hilliard, Jacqueline Dalya
Mystery Submarine 1951,F 2,19:2
Hilliard, Patricia
Private Life of Don Juan, The 1934,D 10,16:2
Ghost Goes West, The 1936,Ja 11,9:2
Things to Come 1936,Ap 18,19:2
Troopship 1938,Ap 26,18:2
Hilliard, Richard (Director)
Playground, The 1965,O 4,00:0
Hilliard, Richard (Producer)
Playground, The 1965,O 4,00:0
Hilliard, Richard L (Director)
Psychomania 1964,F 15,14:3
Hilliard, Richard L (Screenwriter)
Horror of Party Beach, The 1964,Ap 30,30:1
Hillias, Peg
Streetcar Named Desire, A 1951,S 30,27:1
Hillie, Verna
From Hell to Heaven 1933,Mr 18,9:3
Duck Soup 1933,N 23,24:2
Search for Beauty 1934,F 10,20:2
Princess O'Hara 1935,Ap 13,11:3
Mr Dynamite 1935,My 25,12:1
Hillier, Fiorette
House of Fear, The 1945,Mr 19,23:3
Hillies, Peg
Peyton Place 1957,D 13,35:1
Hilliker, Katherine (Miscellaneous)
Cameraing Through Africa (part two)
1919,Ap 28,13:2
Some Speed to Surago 1920,Mr 8,9:5
Some Speed to Surago 1920,Mr 8,9:6
Passion 1921,Ja 30,VI,2:1 (In Addenda)
Cabinet of Dr Caligari, The 1921,Ap 4,18:1
Singed 1927,Jl 12,29:3
Hilliker, Katherine (Screenwriter)
Theodora 1921,O 15,16:2
Hilling, Jacques
Gervaise 1957,N 12,46:1
Inspector Maigret 1958,O 9,47:1
Babette Goes to War 1960,Je 8,46:1
Hillman, Gordon Malherbe (Original Author)
Great Man Votes, The 1939,Ja 20,15:2
Here I Am a Stranger 1939,S 30,11:2
Hillon, George
Any Gun Can Play 1968,S 14,34:2
Hills, Beverly
Breakfast at Tiffany's 1961,O 6,28:1
Hills, Gillian
Tales of Paris (The Tale of Sophie); Tale of Sophie,
The (Tales of Paris) 1962,Ag 27,18:1
Inadmissible Evidence 1968,Je 24,44:1
Hills, H F
White Corridors 1952,Jl 16,21:1
Hills, Padua Players
Three Caballeros, The 1945,F 5,20:1
Hillworth (Producer)
Happy Thieves, The 1962,F 5,19:4
Hillyer, Lambert (Director)
Toll Gate, The 1920,Ap 19,13:3
Cradle of Courage, The 1920,S 20,13:1
O'Malley of the Mounted 1921,F 7,8:2
White Oak 1921,O 31,19:3
Skin Deep 1922,O 23,10:1
Scars of Jealousy 1923,My 7,19:3
Spoilers, The 1923,Ag 6,14:2
Those Who Dance 1924,Je 30,16:1
I Want my Man 1925,Ap 6,17:3
Making of O'Malley 1925,Je 22,10:2
Knockout, The 1925,O 27,23:3
Unguarded Hour, The 1926,Ja 5,25:2 (In
Addenda)
Beau Bandit 1930,Je 14,9:4
White Eagle 1932,S 24,18:4
Master of Men 1933,N 29,23:4
Before Midnight 1934,Ja 10,24:3
Once to Every Woman 1934,Mr 26,22:3
Man Trailer, The 1934,My 23,22:3

Hillyer, Lambert (Director)— Cont

Defense Rests, The 1934,Ag 16,20:3
Behind the Evidence 1935,Ja 26,13:2
Invisible Ray, The 1936,Ja 11,9:3
Dangerous Waters 1936,Ja 22,15:5
Dracula's Daughter 1936,My 18,14:2
Women in Prison 1938,Mr 1,19:3

Hillyer, Lambert (Original Author)

State Trooper 1933,Mr 27,13:6
Man Trailer, The 1934,My 23,22:3
Highway Patrol 1938,Ag 4,15:2
Officer and the Lady, The 1941,Ag 11,17:4

Hillyer, Lambert (Screenwriter)

Cradle of Courage, The 1920,S 20,13:1
Hide Out 1930,Ap 12,23:1
Parents on Trial 1939,S 18,15:5
Officer and the Lady, The 1941,Ag 11,17:4

Hilm, Harry (Miscellaneous)

Vienna Burgtheater 1937,O 27,47:1

Hilmar, Gustav

Thunder in the Hills 1947,My 24,10:5

Hilpert, Heinz

Golden Plaque, The 1963,Ag 10,8:6

Hilpert, Heinz (Director)

Drei Tage Liebe; Three Days of Love 1931,Mr 15,IX,6:1
Liebe, Tod und Teufel 1935,My 25,12:2

Hilpert, Heinz (Screenwriter)

Drei Tage Liebe; Three Days of Love 1931,Mr 15,IX,6:1

Hilton, Arthur (Director)

Cat-Women of the Moon 1954,Mr 20,10:7

Hilton, Daisy

Freaks 1932,Jl 9,7:5

Hilton, Edward

David and Goliath 1961,O 7,14:3

Hilton, James (Miscellaneous)

Foreign Correspondent 1940,Ag 28,15:2

Hilton, James (Narrator)

Lights Out In Europe 1940,Ap 15,21:2
Madame Curie 1943,D 17,23:1

Hilton, James (Original Author)

Lost Horizon 1937,Mr 4,27:1
Knight Without Armor 1937,Jl 9,18:1
Goodbye Mr Chips 1939,My 16,27:2
We Are not Alone 1939,D 1,27:1
Rage in Heaven 1941,Mr 21,19:2
Random Harvest 1942,D 18,36:6
Forever and a Day 1943,Mr 13,9:2
Story of Dr Wassell, The 1944,Je 7,13:2
So Well Remembered 1947,N 5,34:3

Hilton, James (Screenwriter)

Camille 1937,Ja 23,13:1
We Are not Alone 1939,D 1,27:1
Tuttles of Tahiti, The 1942,Ap 30,14:1
Mrs Miniver 1942,Je 5,23:1

Hilton, Paul

Strange Holiday 1945,O 20,8:2

Hilton, Tony (Screenwriter)

No Place Like Homicide 1962,S 13,32:1

Hilton, Violet

Freaks 1932,Jl 9,7:5

Himbold, Karin

Tale of Five Women, A 1953,Ja 16,19:2

Himes, Madelyn

Love and Kisses 1965,D 23,21:4

Hincks, Reginald

What Price Vengeance 1937,My 26,30:3
Fury and the Woman 1937,Je 22,26:2

Hindemith, Harry

Somewhere in Berlin 1949,Ag 16,19:3
Our Daily Bread 1950,O 9,21:6

Hindrich, Heinz

Roman Holiday 1953,Ag 28,13:1

Hinds, Anthony (Producer)

Curse of Frankenstein, The 1957,Ag 8,15:5
Horror of Dracula 1958,My 29,24:4
Camp on Blood Island, The 1958,S 18,37:2
Hounds of the Baskervilles, The 1959,Jl 4,9:4
Brides of Dracula, The 1960,S 6,41:4
Phantom of the Opera, The 1962,Ag 23,25:2
Paranoiac 1963,My 23,31:2
Kiss of the Vampire 1963,O 10,49:2
Evil of Frankenstein, The 1964,Je 18,29:2
Die! Die! My Darling 1965,My 20,52:1
These Are the Damned 1965,Jl 8,35:1

Hinds, Samuel S

Shore Leave 1925,S 14,16:1
Crime of the Century, The 1933,Mr 13,18:2
Gabriel Over the White House 1933,Ap 1,18:2
Nuisance, The 1933,My 29,22:2
Bed of Roses 1933,Je 30,20:3
One Man's Journey 1933,S 1,15:2
Berkeley Square 1933,S 14,26:2
Deluge 1933,O 9,22:3
Little Women 1933,N 17,22:3
Son of a Sailor 1933,N 30,38:4
Women in his Life, The 1934,Ja 27,9:3
Ninth Guest, The 1934,Mr 3,8:5
No Greater Glory 1934,My 5,22:2
Sisters Under the Skin 1934,Je 8,18:1
Men in White 1934,Je 9,18:2
Hat, Coat and Glove 1934,Jl 27,21:2
Lost Lady, A 1934,O 4,19:1

Have a Heart 1934,O 20,20:2
West of the Pecos 1934,D 29,11:2
Behind the Evidence 1935,Ja 26,13:2
Sequoia 1935,F 23,14:6
Rumba 1935,F 25,13:2
Living on Velvet 1935,Mr 8,25:4
Shadow of Doubt 1935,Mr 11,15:1
Private Worlds 1935,Mr 28,25:2
Raven, The 1935,Jl 5,9:2
She 1935,Jl 26,18:2
Accent on Youth 1935,Ag 12,10:3
Annapolis Farewell 1935,Ag 24,18:2
Big Broadcast of 1936, The 1935,S 16,15:2
Dr Socrates 1935,O 3,29:2
Two Fisted 1935,O 5,18:3
Rendezvous 1935,O 26,12:2
Millions in the Air 1935,D 12,33:4
In Person 1935,D 13,31:5
Woman Trap 1936,Mr 7,11:4
Border Flight 1936,Je 22,22:1
Fatal Lady 1936,Jl 11,11:3
Rhythm on the Range 1936,Jl 30,22:1
His Brother's Wife 1936,Ag 15,6:2
Sworn Enemy 1936,S 12,20:1
Black Legion 1937,Ja 18,21:1
Top of the Town 1937,Mr 27,19:2
Night Key 1937,Ap 19,27:2
Wings Over Honolulu 1937,My 29,20:1
Road Back, The 1937,Je 18,25:2
Double or Nothing 1937,S 2,17:3
Stage Door 1937,O 8,27:2
Navy Blue and Gold 1937,D 24,21:2
Girl With Ideas, A 1938,Ja 1,11:2
Jury's Secret, The 1938,F 4,17:2
Double Danger 1938,F 10,17:5
Test Pilot 1938,Ap 16,17:1
Devil's Party, The 1938,My 31,8:3
Wives Under Suspicion 1938,Jl 1,22:3
Rage of Paris 1938,Jl 2,10:2
You Can't Take It With You 1938,S 2,21:2
Road to Reno, The 1938,O 3,11:2
Personal Secretary 1938,O 5,20:2
Young Doctor Kildare 1938,O 28,27:1
Storm, The 1938,O 31,12:2
Swing That Cheer 1938,N 11,31:2
Secrets of a Nurse 1938,D 12,26:2
Newsboys' Home 1939,Ja 23,8:2
Within the Law 1939,Ap 6,31:2
Ex-Champ 1939,My 12,25:3
Calling Dr Kildare 1939,My 12,25:4
Career 1939,Jl 28,14:2
Under-Pup, The 1939,S 5,21:2
Tropic Fury 1939,S 8,28:4
Hawaiian Nights 1939,S 29,19:4
Rio 1939,O 27,27:2
One Hour to Live 1939,N 4,11:3
First Love 1939,N 9,27:3
Destry Rides Again 1939,N 30,25:1
Secret of Dr Kildare, The 1939,D 8,33:5
Charlie McCarthy, Detective 1939,D 25,29:2
It's a Date 1940,Mr 23,16:2
Zanzibar 1940,Ap 1,15:3
Dr Kildare's Strange Case 1940,Ap 12,19:2
Ski Patrol 1940,My 21,29:4
Boys From Syracuse, The 1940,Ag 1,25:2
Dr Kildare Goes Home 1940,S 19,27:4
Spring Parade 1940,O 4,29:2
Seven Sinners 1940,N 18,23:2
Back Street 1941,F 12,25:2
Buck Privates 1941,F 14,15:2
Man Made Monster 1941,Mr 19,25:4
Lady From Cheyenne, The 1941,Ap 18,18:2
Tight Shoes 1941,Je 19,25:2
Blossoms in the Dust 1941,Je 27,14:4
Shepherd of the Hills, The 1941,Jl 31,13:2
Adventure in Washington 1941,Ag 1,11:3
Unfinished Business 1941,S 2,20:2
Badlands of Dakota 1941,S 9,27:6
Dr Kildare's Wedding Day 1941,S 18,31:1
Jail House Blues 1942,F 6,23:2
Frisco Lil 1942,F 12,27:2
Ride 'Em Cowboy 1942,Mr 5,27:3
Strange Case of Dr Rx 1942,Mr 28,11:2
Kid Glove Killer 1942,Ap 17,21:4
Spoilers, The 1942,My 22,27:2
Grand Central Murder 1942,My 23,8:8
Pardon my Sarong 1942,Ag 27,15:1
Lady in a Jam 1942,S 11,25:2
Pittsburgh 1943,F 25,27:2
It Ain't Hay 1943,Mr 11,17:3
He's my Guy 1943,Mr 12,12:3
Good Morning, Judge 1943,Ap 30,25:4
Mister Big 1943,Je 14,13:4
Hers to Hold 1943,Jl 22,15:1
Fired Wife 1943,O 1,15:2
Top Man 1943,O 29,23:2
Son of Dracula 1943,N 6,16:4
Ladies Courageous 1944,Mr 16,17:2
Cobra Woman 1944,My 18,17:2
Jungle Woman 1944,Jl 15,19:6
Frisco Sal 1945,F 17,11:2
Escape in the Desert 1945,My 12,10:2
Uncle Harry 1945,Ag 24,14:5

Hinds, Samuel S— Cont

Lady on a Train 1945,S 15,21:2
Men in her Diary 1945,S 24,16:5
Week-End at the Waldorf 1945,O 5,27:2
Scarlet Street 1946,F 15,29:2
Runaround, The 1946,Je 7,16:3
Inside Job 1946,Je 15,24:3
White Tie and Tails 1946,N 8,28:2
It's a Wonderful Life 1946,D 23,19:2
Time Out of Mind 1947,Ap 7,20:1
Egg and I, The 1947,Ap 25,29:2
Boy With Green Hair, The 1949,Ja 13,26:2
Bribe, The 1949,F 4,31:2
Return of October, The 1949,F 23,31:2

HINE

See Also HEINE

Hine, Al (Original Author)

Lord Love a Duck 1966,F 22,14:6

Hine, Lee (Original Author)

Fifth Avenue Models 1925,My 4,16:2

Hines, Charles (Director)

Speed Spook, The 1924,O 21,21:3
Crackerjack, The 1925,My 18,12:1
Brown Derby, The 1926,Je 14,24:1
Home Made 1927,D 13,33:2

Hines, Harry

Mr Belvedere Rings the Bell 1951,Ag 2,18:1
Boots Malone 1952,Mr 13,26:2

Hines, Johnny

Little Johnny Jones 1923,Ag 13,16:1
Speed Spook, The 1924,O 21,21:3
Crackerjack, The 1925,My 18,12:1
Brown Derby, The 1926,Je 14,24:1
All Abroad 1927,Ap 19,24:4
Home Made 1927,D 13,33:2
Run Around, The 1931,Ag 10,18:3
Whistling in the Dark 1933,F 5,IX,5:1
Girl in 419 1933,My 20,11:5
Her Bodyguard 1933,Ag 7,18:2
Society Doctor 1935,F 4,11:3
too Hot To Handle 1938,S 30,24:2

Hines, Leonard (Original Author)

Ghoul, The 1934,Ja 27,9:2

Hines, Ronald

Dunkirk 1958,S 11,42:2
Seance on a Wet Afternoon 1964,N 6,30:1

Hines, Wilmer

They Won't Forget 1937,Jl 15,16:1

Hingle, Pat

Strange One, The 1957,Ap 13,12:3
No Down Payment 1957,O 31,41:1
Splendor in the Grass 1961,O 11,53:1
Ugly American, The 1963,Ap 12,30:2
All the Way Home 1963,O 30,46:1
Invitation to a Gunfighter 1964,O 28,51:3
Nevada Smith 1966,Je 24,28:1 (Incorrect in this edition; use 1966,Je 30,28:1 elsewhere)
Jigsaw 1968,Je 6,54:2
Sol Madrid 1968,Je 14,43:1
Hang 'Em High 1968,Ag 8,27:3

Hingst, Elfriede

Marriage of Figaro 1950,N 3,31:2

Hinkle, Ed

Dementia 1955,D 23,14:4

Hinrich, Hans (Director)

Dreikland; Triad 1938,Jl 23,10:5
Zwischen den Eltern; Between the Parents 1938,Jl 30,10:3

Hinrich, John

Miserables, Les 1952,Mr 25,23:2

Hintermann, Carlo

Breath of Scandal, A 1960,D 17,19:1
Girl With a Suitcase 1961,S 12,36:2

Hintington, Lawrence (Screenwriter)

Vulture, The 1967,My 20,39:2

Hinton, Ed

Lion and the Horse, The 1952,My 19,12:2
River of no Return 1954,My 1,13:2
Julie 1956,N 22,51:1

Hinton, James (Original Author)

God's Gift to Women 1931,Ap 18,17:3

Hinton, Jane (Miscellaneous)

I'll Be Yours 1947,F 22,16:2

Hinton, Mary

Hatter's Castle 1948,Jl 3,8:6
Broken Journey 1949,My 26,34:3
Gay Lady, The 1951,Ap 16,21:2
White Corridors 1952,Jl 16,21:1
Angel Street 1952,N 11,25:2
Village, The 1953,S 23,37:2

Hinton Ed

Harpoon 1948,D 9,48:8

Hinz, Michael

Bridge, The; (Bruecke, Die) 1961,My 2,42:1

Hinz, Werner

Alte und der Junge Koenig, Der 1935,D 10,31:2
Weisse Sklaven 1937,Jl 31,6:2
Freiheit und Liebe, Um; For Freedom and Love 1938,F 5,19:3
Jugend; Youth 1939,D 9,18:2
Longest Day, The 1962,O 5,28:1
Tonio Kroger 1968,Ja 16,24:1

Hinze, Ingetraude
Germany Year Zero 1949,S 20,35:2
Hiort, Barbo of Ornas
Brink of Life; (Nara Livet) 1959,N 9,36:2
Hirano, Robert
Geisha Boy, The 1958,D 24,00:0
Hirata, Akihiko
Godzilla, King of the Monsters 1956,Ap 28,11:1
Mysterians, The 1959,Jl 2,15:2
Ghidrah, The Three-Headed Monster 1965,D 16,63:3
Samurai (Part II) 1967,O 21,16:1
Hirata, Daizaburo
Insect Woman, The; Nippon Konchuki 1964,Jl 1,42:1
Hirata, Noshiomi (Miscellaneous)
Kimiko 1937,Ap 13,31:3
Hird, Thora
48 Hours 1944,Je 26,21:2
Corridor of Mirrors 1949,Mr 23,35:3
Weaker Sex, The 1949,Jl 11,13:2
Conspirator 1950,Ap 28,26:2
Madness of the Heart 1950,O 12,43:2
Magnet, The 1951,F 27,22:6
Maytime in Mayfair 1952,Ap 23,23:5
Hundred Hour Hunt 1953,Je 17,32:2
Long Memory, The 1953,Jl 27,15:2
Turn the Key Softly 1954,F 4,21:6
Edge of Divorce 1954,Jl 2,10:1
Personal Affair 1954,O 23,13:2
Simon and Laura 1956,Jl 3,17:2
Panic in the Parlor 1957,D 18,45:1
Entertainer, The 1960,O 4,49:2
Kind of Loving, A 1962,O 2,46:1
Term of Trial 1963,Ja 31,5:2
Rattle of a Simple Man 1964,D 21,42:2
Hire, Gail
Red Line 7000 1965,D 9,60:4
Hirliman, George A (Producer)
Daniel Boone 1936,O 24,23:2
Navy Spy 1937,Mr 22,27:3
Hollywood Cowboy 1937,Jl 24,12:1
Hirsch, Charles (Producer)
Greetings 1968,D 16,61:2
Hirsch, Charles (Screenwriter)
Greetings 1968,D 16,61:2
Hirsch, Elroy
Unchained 1955,Ja 28,15:2
Zero Hour 1957,N 14,41:1
Hirsch, Emi Florence
Bridge to the Sun 1961,O 18,50:1
Hirsch, Klaus
Wonder Boy 1951,D 26,19:5
Hirsch, Kurt (Narrator)
Russia on Parade 1946,S 9,20:1
Hirsch, Louis A (Original Author)
Going Up 1923,O 10,16:2
Hirsch, Robert
Please Mr Balzac 1957,N 18,37:2
Hunchback of Notre Dame, The 1957,D 12,35:1
Impossible on Saturday 1966,F 17,29:1
Hirsch, Walter (Composer)
Hit Parade, The 1937,My 31,11:2
Hirsch, Walter (Miscellaneous)
Ecstasy 1940,D 25,33:2
Hirschmeier, Alfred (Screenwriter)
Naked Among the Wolves 1967,Ap 19,54:7
Hirshbein, Peretz (Screenwriter)
Green Fields 1937,O 12,31:4
Hitler's Madman 1943,Ag 28,15:1
Hirshberg, Albert S (Original Author)
Fear Strikes Out 1957,Mr 21,37:2
Hirson, Stan (Miscellaneous)
Journey to Jerusalem, A 1968,N 18,59:1
HIRST
See HURST
Hirt, Al
Rome Adventure 1962,Mr 16,25:1
Hirt, Eleanore
What's New Pussycat? 1965,Je 23,49:1
Killing Game, The 1968,Ag 27,36:1
Hisaita, Eijiro
Bad Sleep Well, The 1963,Ja 23,5:2
Hisaita, Eijiro (Screenwriter)
Idiot, The 1963,My 1,35:1
High and Low 1963,N 27,30:1
Hisamatsu, Seiji (Director)
Angry Island 1960,F 28,31:1
Hiscott, Leslie (Director)
Mystery at the Villa Rose 1930,Je 2,25:4
Sherlock Holmes's Fatal Hour 1931,Jl 13,13:5
Missing Rembrandt, The 1932,Mr 26,17:2
She Shall Have Music 1942,O 31,11:2
Hiscott, Leslie S (Director)
Triumph of Sherlock Holmes, The 1935,My 27,20:6
Hisle, Betsy Ann
Nellie, the Beautiful Cloak Model 1924,Ap 14,14:1
Sorrell and Son 1927,N 14,26:1
Jennie Gerhardt 1933,Je 9,20:2

Hislop, Geraldine
Suicide Legion 1940,My 6,13:3
Hislop, Joseph
Loves of Robert Burns, The 1930,Mr 23,IX,6:1
Hispano, Don Cornelio (Miscellaneous)
Life of Simon Bolivar, The 1943,Je 18,16:5
Hitchcock, Alfred (Director)
Case of Jonathan Drew, The 1928,Je 11,27:1
Blackmail 1929,Jl 14,IX,4:5
Blackmail 1929,O 7,22:1
Manxman, The 1929,D 17,28:7
Farmer's Wife, The 1930,Ja 7,28:3
Elstree Calling 1930,Mr 9,IX,6:1
Skin Game, The 1931,Je 20,20:4
Man Who Knew too Much, The 1935,Mr 23,11:2
Strauss's Great Waltz 1935,Ap 8,23:3
Thirty-Nine Steps, The 1935,S 14,8:4
Secret Agent 1936,Je 13,13:1
Woman Alone, The 1937,F 27,9:2
Girl Was Young, The 1938,F 11,27:2
Lady Vanishes, The 1938,D 26,29:1
Jamaica Inn 1939,O 12,33:1
Rebecca 1940,Mr 29,25:2
Foreign Correspondent 1940,Ag 28,15:2
Mr and Mrs Smith 1941,F 21,16:3
Suspicion 1941,N 21,23:2
Saboteur 1942,My 8,27:2
Shadow of a Doubt 1943,Ja 13,18:2
Lifeboat 1944,Ja 13,17:1
Spellbound 1945,N 2,22:2
Notorious 1946,Ag 16,19:2
Paradine Case, The 1948,Ja 9,26:2
Rope 1948,Ag 27,12:4
Under Capricorn 1949,S 9,28:3
Stage Fright 1950,F 24,27:2
Strangers on a Train 1951,Jl 4,13:2
I Confess 1953,Mr 23,28:2
Dial M for Murder 1954,My 29,13:2
Rear Window 1954,Ag 5,18:2
To Catch a Thief 1955,Ag 5,14:2
Trouble With Harry, The 1955,O 18,46:2
Man Who Knew too Much, The 1956,My 17,37:1
Wrong Man, The 1956,D 24,8:1
Vertigo 1958,My 29,24:2
North by Northwest 1959,Ag 7,28:1
Psycho 1960,Je 17,37:1
Birds, The 1963,Ap 1,5:5 (Incorrect in this edition; use 1963,Ap 1,54:1 elsewhere)
Marnie 1964,Je 23,19:1
Torn Curtain 1966,Jl 28,23:1
Hitchcock, Alfred (Producer)
Ring, The 1927,D 25,VIII,7:7 (In Addenda)
Notorious 1946,Ag 16,19:2
Strangers on a Train 1951,Jl 4,13:2
To Catch a Thief 1955,Ag 5,14:2
Trouble With Harry, The 1955,O 18,46:2
Vertigo 1958,My 29,24:2
North by Northwest 1959,Ag 7,28:1
Psycho 1960,Je 17,37:1
Birds, The 1963,Ap 1,5:5 (Incorrect in this edition; use 1963,Ap 1,54:1 elsewhere)
Marnie 1964,Je 23,19:1
Torn Curtain 1966,Jl 28,23:1
Hitchcock, Edward
Never Take No for an Answer 1952,Ap 29,32:2
Hitchcock, Keith
Raffles 1940,Ja 13,11:2
Blue Bird, The 1940,Ja 20,11:2
Man Hunt 1941,Je 14,20:2
Black Swan, The 1942,D 24,18:3
Hitchcock, Pat
Stage Fright 1950,F 24,27:2
Strangers on a Train 1951,Jl 4,13:2
Psycho 1960,Je 17,37:1
Hitchcock, Raymond
Everybody's Acting 1926,N 8,19:2
Monkey Talks, The 1927,Ap 5,30:7
Hitchens, Robert (Original Author)
Barbary Sheep 1917,S 10,11:3
Hitchins, B (Original Author)
Band of Outsiders 1964,S 19,19:1
Hitchins, D (Original Author)
Band of Outsiders 1964,S 19,19:1
Band of Outsiders; Bande a Part 1966,Mr 16,48:3
Hite, Les and His Orchestra
Fools for Scandal 1938,Mr 25,15:3
Hitler, Adolf
Liberation of Europe, The 1968,S 29,IV,7:1
Hittleman, Carl K (Producer)
I Shot Jesse James 1949,Ap 2,12:2
Baron of Arizona, The 1950,Je 23,29:2
Little Big Horn 1951,Jl 27,15:2
Hitu
Tabu 1931,Mr 19,21:3
Hively, Jack (Director)
They Made Her a Spy 1939,Mr 29,21:4
Spellbinder, The 1939,Ag 24,17:3
Three Sons 1939,N 24,29:3
Saint's Double Trouble, The 1940,F 13,27:2
Saint Takes Over, The 1940,My 28,29:3
Anne of Windy Poplars 1940,Ag 23,13:3
Saint in Palm Springs, The 1941,Ja 31,15:5
Father takes a Wife 1941,S 5,19:3

Hively, Jack (Director) — Cont
Street Of Chance 1942,N 19,31:3
Appointment in Tokyo 1945,D 8,21:3
Are You With It? 1948,Ap 15,31:2
Hivley, Wells (Miscellaneous)
Drums of Love 1928,Ja 25,20:4
Hixon, Butler
Strangers on a Honeymoon 1937,Mr 13,23:2
Hjelm, Keve
Night Games 1966,D 20,58:1
Hlasko, Marek (Original Author)
Eighth Day of the Week, The 1959,Mr 24,45:2
Hlasko, Marek (Screenwriter)
Eighth Day of the Week, The 1959,Mr 24,45:2
Hlinomaz, Josef
Happy End 1968,Je 11,54:4
Hlubi, Makubalo
King Solomon's Mines 1937,Jl 3,18:1
Ho, Andy
Outpost in Malaya 1952,N 27,49:2
World of Suzie Wong, The 1960,N 11,36:1
Satan Never Sleeps 1962,F 22,20:1
Ho, Chew
Percy 1925,Mr 25,24:2
Ho, F K
Fight to the Last 1938,D 22,25:3
Ho, Peter Chen
Sons of Good Earth 1967,S 16,37:5
Ho, T S
Fight to the Last 1938,D 22,25:3
Ho-Chang, King
Piccadilly 1929,Jl 15,25:1
HOAG
See Also HOGG, HOGUE
Hoag, Doane R (Original Author)
Count the Hours 1953,Je 24,30:4
Hoag, Doane R (Screenwriter)
Count the Hours 1953,Je 24,30:4
Hoag, Mitzi
Tammy and the Doctor 1963,Je 27,23:2
Hoare, John (Original Author)
Red Planet Mars 1952,Je 16,15:2
Hobart, Alice Tisdale (Original Author)
Oil for the Lamps of China 1935,Je 6,25:2
Law of the Tropics 1941,O 10,26:5
Earth Is Mine, The 1959,Je 27,13:1
Hobart, George V (Original Author)
Experience 1921,Ag 8,12:2
Wildfire 1925,Je 10,18:2
Hobart, Rose
Liliom 1930,O 4,15:2
Lady Surrenders, A 1930,O 4,15:2
Chances 1931,Je 12,27:1
East of Borneo 1931,S 26,25:3
Compromised 1931,N 7,16:5
Dr Jekyll and Mr Hyde 1932,Ja 2,14:2
Scandal for Sale 1932,Ap 3,26:2
Tower of London 1939,D 12,37:2
Susan and God 1940,Jl 12,11:2
Night at Earl Carroll's, A 1941,Ja 23,19:1
Ziegfeld Girl 1941,Ap 25,17:2
Singapore Woman 1941,My 12,13:6
Lady Be Good 1941,S 19,27:1
Nothing but the Truth 1941,O 23,27:1
No Hands on the Clock 1941,D 22,24:6
Mr and Mrs North 1942,Ja 22,13:2
Gentleman at Heart, A 1942,F 23,25:2
Who Is Hope Schuyler 1942,My 22,27:1
Salute to the Marines 1943,Ag 30,11:3
Mad Ghoul, The 1943,D 11,11:2
Song of the Open Road 1944,Je 7,13:3
Soul of a Monster, The 1944,S 9,12:4
Brighton Strangler, The 1945,My 19,15:2
Conflict 1945,Je 16,10:2
Cat Creeps, The 1946,My 18,12:4
Canyon Passage 1946,Ag 8,18:2
Claudia and David 1946,Ag 15,19:2
Farmer's Daughter, The 1947,Mr 26,31:2
Trouble With Women, The 1947,Jl 14,14:4
Mickey 1948,Jl 19,11:2
Hobbes, Halliwell
Jealousy 1929,S 14,17:1
Lucky in Love 1929,D 14,22:4
Grumpy 1930,Ag 2,16:4
Scotland Yard 1930,O 20,28:2
Charley's Aunt 1930,D 26,18:4
Bachelor Father, The 1931,F 2,23:1
Right of Way, The 1931,Mr 24,31:2
Five and Ten 1931,Jl 11,7:6
Woman Between, The 1931,O 24,20:3
Sin of Madelon Claudet, The 1931,O 31,22:2
Platinum Blonde 1931,O 31,22:2
Dr Jekyll and Mr Hyde 1932,Ja 2,14:2
Forbidden 1932,Ja 11,28:5
Menace, The 1932,Ja 30,13:2
Lovers Courageous 1932,Ap 20,11:2
Devil's Lottery 1932,Ap 2,13:2
Man About Town 1932,My 28,18:2
Week Ends Only 1932,Je 18,9:2
Six Hours to Live 1932,O 22,18:4
Payment Deferred 1932,N 8,26:3
Looking Forward 1933,My 1,10:2
Study in Scarlet, A 1933,Je 1,15:3
Masquerader, The 1933,S 4,9:5

Hobbes, Halliwell— Cont

Should Ladies Behave? 1933,D 18,24:3
I Am Suzanne 1934,Ja 19,24:3
Mandalay 1934,F 15,15:6
Riptide 1934,Mr 31,8:2
Double Door 1934,My 5,22:3
Key, The 1934,My 30,14:3
Bulldog Drummond Strikes Back 1934,Ag 16,20:2
British Agent 1934,S 20,20:1
Madame Du Barry 1934,O 25,26:2
Menace 1934,N 22,27:2
Folies Bergere 1935,F 25,13:2
Cardinal Richelieu 1935,Ap 19,24:2
Jalna 1935,S 14,8:4
Charlie Chan in Shanghai 1935,O 14,21:1
Millions in the Air 1935,D 12,33:4
Story of Louis Pasteur, The 1936,F 10,15:1
Dracula's Daughter 1936,My 18,14:2
Hearts Divided 1936,Je 13,13:1
White Angel, The 1936,Je 25,24:1
Spendthrift 1936,Jl 23,24:1
Give Me your Heart 1936,S 17,18:2
Maid of Salem 1937,Mr 4,27:2
Prince and the Pauper, The 1937,My 6,23:1
Varsity Show 1937,S 2,17:2
Fit for a King 1937,O 15,18:5
Jury's Secret, The 1938,F 4,17:2
Bulldog Drummond's Peril 1938,Mr 18,23:2
Kidnapped 1938,My 28,9:2
You Can't Take It With You 1938,S 2,21:2
Service de Luxe 1938,O 24,13:2
Storm Over Bengal 1938,D 8,34:4
Pacific Liner 1939,Ja 18,17:3
Hardys Ride High, The 1939,Ap 14,28:2
Tell no Tales 1939,Je 2,27:3
Naughty but Nice 1939,Je 23,23:2
Remember? 1939,D 15,33:4
Light That Failed, The 1939,D 25,19:1
Earl of Chicago, The 1940,Mr 14,29:3
Third Finger, Left Hand 1940,D 12,37:2
That Hamilton Woman 1941,Ap 4,25:1
Here Comes Mr Jordan 1941,Ag 8,13:2
Son of Fury 1942,Ja 30,23:2
To Be or not to Be 1942,Mr 7,13:2
War Against Mrs Hadley, The 1942,N 26,40:2
Journey for Margaret 1942,D 18,36:7
Sherlock Holmes Faces Death 1943,O 8,15:3
Gaslight 1944,My 5,17:2
Mr Skeffington 1944,My 26,23:2
Invisible Man's Revenge, The 1944,Je 10,12:2
Casanova Brown 1944,S 15,16:1
Canyon Passage 1946,Ag 8,18:2
If Winter Comes 1948,Ja 23,28:4
Black Arrow, The 1948,O 4,14:2
You Gotta Stay Happy 1948,N 5,29:2
Miracle in the Rain 1956,Ap 2,18:1

Hobbes, Peter
Barretts of Wimpole Street, The 1934,S 29,12:2
Kiss the Blood off my Hands 1948,O 30,10:2

Hobbie, Duke
For Singles Only 1968,Je 6,54:1

Hobbs, Carleton (Narrator)
King's Story, A 1967,My 25,57:2

Hobbs, Jack
It's in the Air 1940,D 10,33:2

Hobbs, Peter
Top Hat 1935,Ag 30,12:2
Good Neighbor Sam 1964,Jl 23,19:1

Hobhouse, Adam (Original Author)
Remember Last Night? 1935,N 21,27:2

Hobl, Pavel (Director)
Do You Keep a Lion at Home? 1966,S 18,78:1

Hobson, Laura Z (Original Author)
Gentleman's Agreement 1947,N 12,36:2

Hobson, Laura Z (Screenwriter)
Her Twelve Men 1954,Ag 12,23:2

Hobson, Valerie
Mystery of Edwin Drood, The 1935,Mr 21,27:1
Werewolf of London, The 1935,My 10,25:2
Bride of Frankenstein, The 1935,My 11,21:2
Chinatown Squad 1935,My 30,21:1
Great Impersonation, The 1935,D 14,11:1
When Thief Meets Thief 1937,Je 15,26:2
Drums 1938,S 30,24:4
Clouds Over Europe 1939,Je 16,27:2
This Man Is News 1939,Jl 20,16:4
U-Boat 29 1939,O 6,31:3
Blackout 1940,D 2,19:2
Secret of Stamboul, The 1941,My 31,14:1
Continental Express 1942,Ap 7,26:3
Adventures of Tartu, The 1943,S 24,26:1
Years Between, The 1947,Mr 10,25:2
Great Expectations 1947,My 23,31:1
Blanche Fury 1948,N 24,20:2
Rocking Horse Winner, The 1950,Je 9,29:2
Kind Hearts and Coronets 1950,Je 15,41:2
Train of Events 1952,My 26,18:4
Promoter, The 1952,O 29,36:2
Murder Will Out 1953,Ap 6,24:2
Tonight at 8:30 (Ways and Means); Ways and
    Means (Tonight at 8:30) 1953,My 26,33:2
Passionate Sentry, The 1953,N 12,37:5
Edge of Divorce 1954,Jl 2,10:1
Lovers, Happy Lovers 1954,O 1,19:2

HOCH
See Also HACK

Hoch, Emil
Stage Struck 1925,N 16,19:4

Hochbaum, Werner (Director)
Leichte Kavallerie 1936,F 8,19:2
Eternal Mask, The 1937,Ja 13,20:3
Wir Sind vom K u K Infanterie-Regiment
    1938,N 19,9:2
Drei Unteroffiziere; Three Non-Coms
    1939,My 20,11:3
Schatten der Vergangeheit; Shadows of the Past
    1940,Ap 20,14:2

Hocking, Joseph (Original Author)
Prodigal Daughters 1923,Ap 17,26:3

Hockner, David
London Scene, The (Tonite Let's All Make Love
    in London); Tonite Let's All Make Love in
    London (The London Scene) 1967,S 27,39:1

Hoctor, Harriet
Great Ziegfeld, The 1936,Ap 9,21:2
Shall We Dance 1937,My 14,21:1

Hoctor, Harriet (Composer)
Great Ziegfeld, The 1936,Ap 9,21:2

Hodeir, Andre (Composer)
World Without Sun 1964,D 23,22:1

Hodes, Robert (Director)
Now Cinema! (The Game); Game, The (Now
    Cinema!) 1968,Ap 9,56:1

Hodes, Roberta O (Screenwriter)
Lad: A Dog 1963,My 2,40:2

Hodges, Douglas (Original Author)
Invisible Ray, The 1936,Ja 11,9:3

Hodges, Eddie
Hole in the Head, A 1959,Jl 16,31:2
Adventures of Huckleberry Fin, The
    1960,Ag 4,17:1
Advise and Consent 1962,Je 7,31:2
Summer Magic 1963,Ag 22,19:2
C'mon Let's Live a Little 1967,My 4,34:1
Happiest Millionaire, The 1967,D 1,56:1

Hodges, Horace
Escape 1930,N 1,23:2
Girl in the Street 1938,My 26,31:2
Jamaica Inn 1939,O 12,33:1

Hodges, Horace (Original Author)
Grumpy 1923,Mr 26,16:2

Hodges, Jimmie (Composer)
Sioux City Sue 1947,Jl 23,19:3

Hodges, Joy
Follow the Fleet 1936,F 21,21:2
Merry-Go-Round of 1938 1937,N 26,27:2
Personal Secretary 1938,O 5,20:2
Service de Luxe 1938,O 24,13:2
Family Next Door, The 1939,Ap 28,31:2
They Asked for It 1939,Je 30,17:4
Unexpected Father 1939,Ag 11,12:2
Little Accident 1939,N 24,29:3

Hodges, Ralph
Yank in Korea, A 1951,Ap 2,29:2
Millionaire for Christy, A 1951,O 5,24:3

Hodgins, Earl
I Cover the War 1937,Ag 2,10:2
Headin' East 1938,Ja 15,19:2
Partners of the Plains 1938,F 12,20:4
Heroes of the Alamo 1938,Ap 2,18:2
Bachelor's Daughters, The 1946,O 7,23:2
Old Los Angeles 1948,Jl 12,11:2
Slightly French 1949,My 27,25:3
Thunder Over the Plains 1953,D 10,64:4

Hodgins, Eric (Original Author)
Mr Blandings Builds his Dream House
    1948,Mr 26,26:2

Hodgson, Frances Mrs (Original Author)
Dawn of a Tomorrow, The 1924,Mr 26,19:2

Hodgson, Leyland
Case of Sergeant Grischa, The 1930,Mr 8,21:1
Ladies of the Jury 1932,Ap 2,13:2
Under-Cover Man 1932,D 5,21:2
Eagle and the Hawk, The 1933,My 13,16:2
Trouble for Two 1936,My 30,7:2
Beloved Enemy 1936,D 26,15:2
Torchy Blane, The Adventurous Blonde
    1937,D 18,18:1
Mr Moto's Last Warning 1939,Ja 27,17:3
Susannah of the Mounties 1939,Je 24,13:2
Eternally Yours 1939,O 7,11:2
Witness Vanishes, The 1939,O 23,15:2
He Married his Wife 1940,Ja 20,11:2
Case of the Black Parrot, The 1941,Ja 10,23:3
Scotland Yard 1941,Ap 9,33:3
International Lady 1941,N 11,29:2
Secret Agent of Japan 1942,Mr 23,19:3
Ghost of Frankenstein, The 1942,Ap 4,19:2
Just off Broadway 1942,Ag 29,18:4
Sherlock Holmes and the Voice Of Terror
    1942,S 19,9:2
Enter Arsene Lupin 1944,D 2,17:6
Hangover Square 1945,F 8,15:2
Terror by Night 1946,F 9,9:2
Bedlam 1946,Ap 20,16:4
Black Beauty 1946,Ag 30,13:2
Thunder in the Valley 1947,N 28,30:1

Hodgson, Leyland— Cont

Woman's Vengeance, A 1948,Ja 30,19:2
Kiss the Blood off my Hands 1948,O 30,10:2

Hodgson, Phoebe
Pandora and the Flying Dutchman 1951,D 7,35:2

Hodgson, Red (Miscellaneous)
Music Goes 'Round, The 1936,F 22,12:1

Hodiak, John
I Dood It 1943,N 11,29:1
Lifeboat 1944,Ja 13,17:1
Song of Russia 1944,F 11,17:2
Maisie Goes to Reno 1944,S 29,18:1
Marriage Is a Private Affair 1944,O 27,17:7
Sunday Dinner for a Soldier 1945,Ja 25,16:2
Bell for Adano, A 1945,Jl 6,8:3
Harvey Girls, The 1946,Ja 25,26:2
Somewhere in the Night 1946,Je 13,24:2
Two Smart People 1947,F 15,20:4
Arnelo Affair, The 1947,S 13,8:5
Desert Fury 1947,S 25,35:4
Love From a Stranger 1947,N 28,30:1
Homecoming 1948,Ap 30,28:4
Command Decision 1949,Ja 20,34:2
Bribe, The 1949,F 4,31:2
Battleground 1949,N 12,8:4
Ambush 1950,Ja 19,35:2
Malaya 1950,F 23,33:1
Lady Without Passport, A 1950,Ag 4,13:2
Miniver Story, The 1950,O 27,24:2
Night Into Morning 1951,Je 11,20:7
People Against O'Hara, The 1951,S 6,39:3
Across the Wide Missouri 1951,N 7,35:4
Sellout, The 1952,My 31,12:7
Battle Zone 1952,N 1,17:2
Mission Over Korea 1953,S 19,7:2
Trial 1955,O 14,21:2
On the Threshold of Space 1956,Mr 30,10:5

Hodson, J L (Original Author)
Tunisian Victory 1944,Mr 24,17:2
Something Money Can't Buy 1953,O 1,34:3
King and Country 1964,S 24,46:2
King and Country 1966,Ja 28,20:4

Hodson, J L (Screenwriter)
Under the Red Robe 1937,Je 1,27:2
Something Money Can't Buy 1953,O 1,34:3

Hoe, William Soo
China Gate 1957,My 23,40:2

Hoeberg, Albert
Day of Wrath 1948,Ap 26,27:2

Hoebiger, Paul
Blaufuchs; Blue Fox 1939,Mr 4,18:5
Mozart Story, The 1948,N 15,21:5

Hoecker, Oscar
Johannisnact 1935,F 25,13:4
Threepenny Opera, The 1960,Jl 11,24:4

Hoefelin, Trude
Gordian, Der Tyrann 1937,Je 21,15:3

Hoeffich, Lucie
1914: The Last Days Before the War 1932,S 5,9:6

Hoefler, Paul L (Cinematographer)
Africa Speaks 1930,S 20,15:4

Hoefler, Paul L Dr (Producer)
Leopard Men of Africa, The 1940,Jl 29,10:6

Hoeflich, Lucie
Raub der Sabinerinnen, Der 1937,Ja 16,21:1
Freiheit und Liebe, Um; For Freedom and Love
    1938,F 5,19:3
Peer Gynt 1939,N 11,12:2

Hoeglund, Peter
En Saga 1938,Ja 8,19:2

Hoehn, Carola
Ferien vom Ich 1935,Ap 1,17:2
Royal Waltz, The 1936,Ap 10,27:1
Koenigin der Liebe 1936,My 4,16:2
Schloss Vogeloed 1936,My 9,11:2
Alle Tage Ist Kein Sonntag 1936,Jl 11,11:4
Bettelstudent, Der 1936,D 28,12:3
Zweimal zwei im Himmelbett; Twice Two in a
    Four-Post Bed 1939,F 5,19:3
Kamera den auf See; Comrades at Sea
    1939,Ap 22,15:3
Hurra! Ich bin Papa; Hurrah! I'm a Papa
    1940,Je 1,12:3

Hoel, Carloa
Alte und der Junge Koenig, Der 1935,D 10,31:2

Hoellering, George (Director)
Murder in the Cathedral 1952,Mr 26,35:2

Hoellering, George (Producer)
Murder in the Cathedral 1952,Mr 26,35:2

Hoellering, George M (Producer)
Kuhle Wampe 1933,Ap 24,11:4

Hoelzlin, Friedrich
Fall des Oberst Redl, Der 1932,Ag 18,23:3

Hoengen, Elisabeth
St Matthew Passion 1952,Ja 29,17:4

Hoerberger, Paul
Reserve Hat Ruh 1932,Ap 11,19:2

Hoerbiger, Attila
Zwischen Himmel und Erde; Between Heaven and
    Earth 1935,Ja 21,19:3
Punks Kommt aus Amerika 1937,Je 12,8:2
Stimme des Blutes; Blood Bond 1937,D 28,29:2

Hoerbiger, Otto
Prinzessin Sissy 1939,Ja 14,13:2
Hoerbiger, Paul
Why Cry at Parting 1930,F 4,28:3
Zwei Hertzen in Drei-Viertel Takt
1930,O 13,31:1
Lustigen Weiber von Wien, Die 1931,Jl 10,22:2
Zinker, Der 1931,O 4,VIII,7:1
Ihre Hoheit Befiehlt 1931,N 7,16:5
Ungetreue Eckehart, Der 1932,Ja 23,18:4
Sein Scheidungsgrund 1932,F 20,11:2
Kyritz-Pyritz 1932,Ag 9,20:5
Friederike 1933,F 27,11:3
Walzerparadies 1933,Mr 4,11:3
Ein Maedel der Strasse 1933,Ap 6,22:5
Drei Tage Mittelarrest 1933,My 18,17:4
Liebling von Wien, Der 1933,Je 10,16:5
Hellseher, Der 1933,S 11,20:4
Ich Glaub' nie Mehr an Eine Frau
1933,O 13,25:4
Wiener Blut 1933,N 13,21:2
Zwel Gute Kameraden 1933,D 4,22:3
Quick, Koenig der Clowns 1933,D 9,18:3
Luegen auf Reisen 1934,Ja 1,28:2
Eines Prinzen Junge Liebe 1934,Mr 24,20:4
Trenck 1934,Ap 7,19:2
Pesti Szerelem 1934,My 10,25:3
Wie Man Maenner Fesselt 1934,My 21,20:3
Es War Einmal ein Walzer 1934,O 15,20:5
Waltz Time in Vienna 1934,N 19,13:2
Spiel mit dem Feuer 1934,N 26,12:2
Annemarie, Die Braut der Kompanie
1934,D 8,18:6
Kaiserwalzer 1934,D 29,11:2
Drei von der Kavallerie 1935,Ap 13,11:4
Rosen aus dem Sueden; Roses from the South
1935,Ap 23,24:5
Csardasfuerstin 1935,Ap 25,18:3
Frischer Wind aus Kanada 1935,S 21,18:2
So, ein Maedel Vergisst Man nicht 1935,S 28,12:3
Gruss und Kuss, Veronika 1936,F 24,14:2
Liebelei 1936,F 28,18:2
Royal Waltz, The 1936,Ap 10,27:1
Koenigin der Liebe 1936,My 4,16:2
Ein Liebesroman im Hause Habsburg
1936,O 12,23:2
Einmaleins der Liebe, Das 1937,Ja 2,15:2
Drei Maeoerl um Schubert 1937,Je 5,21:2
Besuch am Abend 1937,Jl 3,18:2
Fraeulein Frau 1937,Jl 3,18:2
Endstation 1937,Jl 17,18:1
Schabernack 1937,Ag 14,16:5
Grosse Bluff, Der; Big Bluff, The 1937,S 6,20:2
Fiakerlied, Das; (Cabbie's Song, The)
1937,S 6,20:2
Dr Engel, Child Specialist 1937,S 20,19:2
Seine Tochter Ist der Peter; His Daughter is Peter
1938,Mr 28,19:3
Magda 1938,S 10,20:2
Landstreicher, Die; Hoboes, The 1938,N 26,18:1
O Schwarzwald, O Heimat; Oh Black Forest, Oh
Home 1939,Ap 24,13:2
Manner Mussen so Sein; Men Are That Way
1939,My 13,11:6
Unsterblicher Walzer; Immortal Waltz
1939,N 18,22:6
Maria Ilona 1940,Ap 20,14:3
Laugh Pagliacci 1948,Ja 31,14:2
Operetta 1949,Je 6,15:4
Third Man, The 1950,F 3,29:2
Dancing Heart, The 1958,Ja 18,10:3
Gypsy Baron, The 1959,N 14,13:1
City of Secrets 1963,Jl 27,10:2
Hoeree, Arthur (Composer)
Mystic Mountain, The 1936,Mr 31,17:2
Hoerl, Arthur (Original Author)
Cross Examination 1932,F 27,22:1
Midnight Patrol, The 1932,My 7,11:5
They Never Come Back 1932,Je 4,9:2
There's a Girl in my Heart 1950,Ja 20,29:2
She Shoulda Said No 1957,Ja 31,21:1
African Manhunt 1957,Ap 20,21:4
For Singles Only 1968,Je 6,54:1
Hoerl, Arthur (Screenwriter)
Spirit of Youth 1938,F 28,19:1
Cipher Bureau 1938,D 14,32:6
Isle of Destiny 1940,Ap 8,15:2
Sarong Girl 1943,Je 18,16:6
There's a Girl in my Heart 1950,Ja 20,29:2
African Manhunt 1957,Ap 20,21:4
Young Dillinger 1965,My 13,32:3
Hoerle, Micheline
Girls Behind Bars 1950,My 10,41:2
Hoessrich, Hanna
Comrades of 1918 1931,F 20,18:5
Hoey, Dennis
Battle of Gallipoli, The 1931,D 7,16:1
Love in Morocco 1933,Mr 20,18:3
Good Companions, The 1933,O 10,24:1
Bride of the Lake, The 1934,S 11,24:5
Chu Chin Chow 1934,S 22,12:2
Wandering Jew, The 1935,Ja 14,11:3
Brewster's Millions 1935,Ap 8,23:3

Murder in the Old Red Barn 1936,Ag 19,18:3
Uncivilized 1937,N 17,27:4
This Above All 1942,My 13,14:3
Cairo 1942,N 6,27:2
Sherlock Holmes and the Secret Weapon
1943,Ja 5,15:2
Frankenstein Meets the Wolf Man 1943,Mr 6,8:3
They Came to Blow up America
1943,My 15,13:2
Bomber's Moon 1943,Jl 31,8:2
Sherlock Holmes Faces Death 1943,O 8,15:3
Spider Woman 1944,Ja 17,14:5
Uncertain Glory 1944,Ap 8,9:2
Pearl of Death 1944,Ag 26,15:2
House of Fear, The 1945,Mr 19,23:3
Thousand and one Nights, A 1945,Jl 12,8:2
Terror by Night 1946,F 9,9:2
Tarzan and the Leopard Woman 1946,F 11,25:2
Kitty 1946,Ap 1,23:1
She Wolf of London 1946,Ap 6,10:6
Anna and the King of Siam 1946,Je 21,20:2
Strange Woman, The 1947,F 24,16:4
Second Chance 1947,S 20,12:4
Foxes of Harrow, The 1947,S 25,35:4
Crimson Key, The 1947,O 18,9:2
Christmas Eve 1947,N 28,30:2
Golden Earrings 1947,D 4,41:3
Where There's Life 1947,D 25,32:1
If Winter Comes 1948,Ja 23,28:4
Ruthless 1948,S 4,8:7
Joan of Arc 1948,N 12,30:5
Wake of the Red Witch 1949,Ja 10,19:2
Kid From Texas, The 1950,Je 2,26:2
David and Bathsheba 1951,Ag 15,23:2
Hoey, Iris
Tenth Man, The 1937,N 15,15:2
Hoey, John
Home Is the Hero 1961,Ja 26,32:1
Hoey, Michael A (Producer)
Palm Springs Weekend 1963,N 6,32:1
Hof, Uti
Francis of Assisi 1961,Jl 29,8:2
Hofelich, Harry L Pfc
Cease Fire! 1953,N 25,17:1
Hofer, Johanna
Above Suspicion 1943,Ag 6,10:3
Hitler's Madman 1943,Ag 28,15:1
Last Illusion, The 1951,Mr 8,37:2
Farewell to Arms, A 1958,Ja 25,14:1
Hofer, Sigi
Wien Du Stadt der Lieder; (Vienna City of Song)
1931,Mr 20,29:1
Hoff, Carl, Orchestra
Hit Parade, The 1937,My 31,11:2
Hoffe, Monckton (Original Author)
Panthea 1917,Ja 8,9:2
Faithful Heart 1933,Ag 15,20:2
Lady Eve, The 1941,F 26,17:1
Daybreak 1949,Jl 4,9:2
Birds and the Bees, The 1956,Ap 23,22:1
Hoffe, Monckton (Screenwriter)
Flame of Love, The 1930,Mr 23,IX,6:1
Last of Mrs Cheyney, The 1937,F 19,15:1
Emperor's Candlesticks, The 1937,Jl 9,18:1
Girl in the Street 1938,My 26,31:2
Clown Must Laugh, A 1938,O 12,35:2
Haunted Honeymoon 1940,O 31,28:2
Julia Misbehaves 1948,O 8,30:2
Hoffe, Monkton (Original Author)
Street Angel 1928,Ap 10,33:2
Hoffenberg, Mason (Original Author)
Candy 1968,D 18,54:2
Hoffenstein, Samuel (Miscellaneous)
Gay Divorcee, The 1934,N 16,27:1
That Night in Rio 1941,Mr 10,21:2
Hoffenstein, Samuel (Screenwriter)
Enchanted April 1935,Mr 9,19:1
Paris in Spring 1935,Jl 13,16:2
Voice of Bugle Ann, The 1936,F 27,23:1
Desire 1936,Ap 13,15:1
Conquest 1937,N 5,19:1
Great Waltz, The 1938,N 25,19:1
Bridal Suite 1939,My 26,20:2
Lydia 1941,S 19,27:1
Loves of Edgar Allan Poe, The 1942,S 21,19:2
Tales of Manhattan 1942,S 25,25:1
Phantom of the Opera, The 1943,O 15,15:2
Flesh and Fantasy 1943,N 18,29:1
His Butler's Sister 1943,D 30,13:2
Laura 1944,O 12,24:1
Sentimental Journey 1946,Mr 7,33:2
Cluny Brown 1946,Je 3,27:3
Carnival in Costa Rica 1947,Mr 29,21:2
Give my Regards to Broadway 1948,Je 23,32:2
Hoffert, Paul (Composer)
Winter Kept Us Warm 1968,F 9,55:3
Hoffman, Aaron (Original Author)
Welcome Stranger 1924,O 14,21:5
Friendly Enemies 1925,My 5,24:2
Cohens and the Kellys, The 1926,F 23,26:5
Friendly Enemies 1942,Je 22,19:1

Hoffman, Al (Composer)
First a Girl 1936,Ja 4,19:1
Gangway 1937,Ag 21,7:3
This'll Make You Whistle 1938,N 1,27:2
Listen, Darling 1938,N 24,37:2
She Shall Have Music 1942,O 31,11:2
Cinderella 1950,F 23,33:1
Hoffman, Bern
Nocturne 1946,N 11,42:2
Man Who Understood, The 1959,O 3,14:7
Li'l Abner 1959,D 12,19:2
Hoffman, Bernd (Screenwriter)
Woman of No Importance 1936,D 13,XI,6:6 (In
Addenda)
Hoffman, Carl von (Cinematographer)
Jungle Gods 1927,D 11,IX,6:2 (In Addenda)
Hoffman, Charles (Miscellaneous)
Voice of the Turtle, The 1947,D 26,22:4
Hoffman, Charles (Original Author)
Affairs of Annabel, The 1938,O 13,29:2
Annabel Takes a Tour 1938,D 29,15:3
It Could Happen to You 1939,Je 9,26:3
Somewhere I'll Find You 1942,Ag 28,22:4
Her Kind of Man 1946,My 4,10:6
Hoffman, Charles (Producer)
Voice of the Turtle, The 1947,D 26,22:4
Hoffman, Charles (Screenwriter)
Janie 1944,Ag 5,16:2
Pillow to Post 1945,My 26,18:2
Cinderella Jones 1946,Mr 16,9:6
One More Tomorrow 1946,My 25,12:2
Night and Day 1946,Jl 26,16:2
Two Guys From Milwaukee 1946,Jl 27,12:5
That Hagen Girl 1947,O 25,13:2
Woman of Distinction, A 1950,Mr 17,28:2
West Point Story, The 1950,D 23,11:3
Blue Gardenia, The 1953,Ap 28,31:1
So This Is Paris 1955,F 12,11:1
Spoilers, The 1955,D 24,10:2
Second Greatest Sex, The 1956,F 11,12:2
Never Say Goodbye 1956,Ap 14,20:1
Hoffman, David
Mask of Dimitrios, The 1944,Je 24,16:2
Beast With Five Fingers, The 1946,D 26,28:3
Desire Me 1947,S 26,28:3
Backfire 1950,Ja 27,29:2
Hoffman, Dustin
Graduate, The 1967,D 22,44:4
Hoffman, Ferdie
All the Way Home 1963,O 30,46:1
Hoffman, George
Song of the Eagle 1933,Ap 29,14:3
Hoffman, Gerard
My Life to Live 1963,S 24,43:2
Hoffman, Gertrude
Before Dawn 1933,O 17,26:2
Hell and Highwater 1933,D 18,24:4
Son Comes Home, A 1936,S 5,7:1
Untamed 1940,Jl 25,14:3
Foreign Correspondent 1940,Ag 28,15:2
Ape, The 1940,N 28,28:3
Thelma Jordon 1950,Ja 19,35:2
Hoffman, Gunther
Bridge, The; (Bruecke, Die) 1961,My 2,42:1
Hoffman, Herman (Director)
It's a Dog's Life 1955,D 23,14:3
Hoffman, Herman (Screenwriter)
Attack on the Iron Coast 1968,Je 6,54:2
Hoffman, Howard
Macabre 1958,Jl 24,18:1
Hoffman, Irmgard
Lachdoktor, Der; Laugh Doctor, The
1938,Mr 12,13:4
Hoffman, Jane
Ladybug, Ladybug 1963,D 24,9:1
Hoffman, Jerry (Producer)
Speed to Burn 1938,S 9,25:1
Hoffman, John (Director)
Strange Confession 1945,N 8,17:3
Hoffman, Joseph (Miscellaneous)
Charlie Chan's Secret 1936,Ja 18,19:4
Arson Racket Squad 1938,Je 18,18:2
Gung Ho! 1944,Ja 26,23:2
Gypsy Wildcat 1944,O 5,18:6
Air Cadet 1951,My 11,32:3
Hoffman, Joseph (Original Author)
Headin' East 1938,Ja 15,19:2
Hollywood Round-Up 1938,Mr 5,11:2
Swing Fever 1944,Ja 28,14:1
Sex and the Single Girl 1964,D 26,9:2
Hoffman, Joseph (Screenwriter)
Your Uncle Dudley 1935,D 12,33:4
Jailbreak 1936,Ag 6,22:1
Thank You, Jeeves 1936,O 5,25:1
Under Suspicion 1937,D 20,23:2 (In Addenda)
Hollywood Round-Up 1938,Mr 5,11:2
Marriage Forbidden 1938,Jl 16,7:2
Safety in Numbers 1938,S 6,17:2
Shadows Over Shanghai 1938,D 1,29:2
Young as You Feel 1940,Mr 8,25:3
Officer and the Lady, The 1941,Ag 11,17:4
My Kingdom for a Cook 1943,O 15.15:3
Carolina Blues 1944,D 8,26:6

Hoffman, Joseph (Screenwriter) — Cont

China Sky 1945,My 25,22:3
Innocent Affair, An 1948,S 29,36:2
And Baby Makes Three 1949,D 23,17:3
Buccaneer's Girl 1950,Mr 27,19:2
At Swords Point 1952,Ap 10,37:1
No Room for the Groom 1952,Je 14,12:2
Has Anybody Seen My Gal 1952,Jl 5,7:2
Duel at Silver Creek 1952,Ag 2,7:6
Against all Flags 1952,D 25,34:6
Lone Hand 1953,Je 27,7:2
Yankee Pasha 1954,Ap 19,19:2
Rails Into Laramie 1954,My 13,34:2
Chicago Syndicate 1955,Je 21,37:1

Hoffman, Kurt (Director)

Paradies der Junggesellen; Bachelors' Paradise 1940,Ap 13,21:3
Hurra! Ich bin Papa; Hurrah! I'm a Papa 1940,Je 1,12:3
Secrets of a Soul 1950,S 16,12:6
Confessions of Felix Krull, The 1958,Mr 5,38:1
Flying Classroom, The 1958,Je 28,13:7
Aren't We Wonderful? 1959,O 16,27:1
Spessart Inn, The 1961,F 18,12:3

Hoffman, Leonard (Miscellaneous)

Call Northside 777 1948,F 19,29:2

Hoffman, Leonard (Screenwriter)

Honeymoon's Over, The 1939,D 15,33:3

Hoffman, Max

Sailor Be Good 1933,F 27,11:2
Counterfeit Lady 1937,Ja 11,15:6
Swing It, Sailor 1937,D 13,23:5
Accidents Will Happen 1938,Ap 25,19:2
Sky Giant 1938,Jl 20,22:2
Wings of the Navy 1939,F 4,11:1
Kid Nightingale 1939,D 8,33:6

Hoffman, Otto

String Beans 1918,D 30,7:3
Sheriff's Son, The 1919,Mr 31,11:3
Busher, The 1919,My 26,19:4
City of Comrades, The 1919,Jl 14,12:2
Egg Crate Wallop, The 1919,S 29,16:1
Homer Comes Home 1920,Je 28,13:2
It's a Great Life 1920,Ag 30,12:3
Sin Flood, The 1922,O 30,11:1
Human Wreckage 1923,Je 28,10:2
Strangers of the Night 1923,O 8,20:1
Lucretia Lombard 1923,D 17,23:1
Daddies 1924,F 11,18:3
Broadway After Dark 1924,My 20,15:2
This Woman 1924,O 21,21:3
Dixie Handicap, The 1924,D 30,15:3
Price She Paid, The 1925,Ja 13,16:1
Confessions of a Queen 1925,Mr 24,20:6
Circle, The 1925,S 22,22:3
Satan in Sables 1925,O 15,27:3
Beware of Widows 1927,My 24,23:4
Fourflusher, The 1928,Ja 16,24:1
Terror, The 1928,Ag 16,25:3
Noah's Ark 1929,Mr 13,28:6
Desert Song, The 1929,My 2,20:6
Madonna of Avenue A 1929,Ag 12,22:2
Is Everybody Happy? 1929,N 2,14:6
Abraham Lincoln 1930,Ag 26,24:1
Kismet 1930,O 31,20:1
Criminal Code, The 1931,Ja 5,21:3
Cimarron 1931,Ja 27,20:5
Side Show 1931,S 19,10:2
Two Seconds 1932,My 19,25:3
Downstairs 1932,O 8,15:4
Iron Master, The 1933,F 4,11:3
Death Takes a Holiday 1934,F 24,18:4
Murder at the Vanities 1934,My 21,20:2
Kid Millions 1934,N 12,17:2
Behold My Wife 1935,F 18,19:3
Barbary Coast 1935,O 14,21:1
Hideaway 1937,S 25,10:2
Our Leading Citizen 1939,Ag 24,17:1
Lucky Cisco Kid 1940,Je 24,19:5
Stranger on the Third Floor 1940,S 2,19:2
This is the Life 1944,Ap 28,23:3

Hoffman, Paul

Untitled-Dance 1937,D 25,10:4
Meine Freundin Barbara; My Firend Barbara 1938,Je 4,18:3
Gleisdreieck 1938,Je 11,9:1
Mystery Submarine 1951,F 2,19:2
Last Illusion, The 1951,Mr 8,37:2
Portrait of an Unknown Woman 1958,Ap 26,14:6

Hoffman, Renaud (Director)

Which Shall It Be? 1924,Ap 7,15:3
Private Affairs 1925,Jl 15,22:3
Unknown Soldier, The 1926,My 31,10:2
Blaze O' Glory 1929,D 31,15:1

Hoffman, Renaud (Original Author)

Wanted by the Police 1938,S 26,13:2
Our Neighbors-The Carters 1940,F 15,15:2

Hoffman, Renaud (Screenwriter)

Which Shall It Be? 1924,Ap 7,15:3

Hoffman, Robert

Grand Slam 1968,F 21,60:4
Assignment K 1968,Jl 20,18:2
24 Hours in a Woman's Life 1968,S 25,39:1

Hoffman, Stan

Singing in the Dark 1956,Mr 8,32:5

Hoffmann, Benno

Tomorrow Is my Turn 1962,F 2,24:2

Hoffmann, Guy

Take it All; A Tout Prendre 1966,Ap 26,55:1

Hoffmann, Karl (Cinematographer)

In Geheimdienst; In the Employ of the Secret Service 1931,O 25,VIII,6:1
Yorck 1932,Ja 31,6:1

Hoffmann, Karl (Director)

Einmaleins der Liebe, Das 1937,Ja 2,15:2

Hofler, Franz (Director)

Drei Kaiserjaeger 1935,Mr 16,19:1

Hoflich, Lucie

Sky Without Stars 1959,My 30,9:2

Hofmann, Ernest

U-Boat 9 1929,Ja 22,23:1

Hogan, Brenda

Guinea Pig, The 1949,My 2,20:2

Hogan, Dick

Annapolis Salute 1937,O 2,18:1
Saturday's Heroes 1937,O 16,22:2
Submarine Patrol 1938,N 19,9:2
Five came Back 1939,Jl 5,20:2
Three Sons 1939,N 24,29:3
One Crowded Night 1940,Ag 27,17:2
Pot o'Gold 1941,Ap 4,25:2
Army Surgeon 1942,N 5,35:2
Action in the North Atlantic 1943,My 22,10:2
So Proudly We Hail 1943,S 10,29:1
Blaze of Noon 1947,Mr 5,31:2
Beyond Glory 1948,Ag 4,18:2
Rope 1948,Ag 27,12:4

Hogan, Earl

Haunted Ship, The 1928,Ja 23,18:3

Hogan, Eddie

Invitation to Happiness 1939,Je 8,31:2

Hogan, James (Director)

Steel Preferred 1925,D 22,13:1
Accusing Finger, The 1936,N 17,35:4
Last Train from Madrid, The 1937,Je 19,20:2
Ebb Tide 1937,N 18,27:2
Scandal Street 1938,F 5,19:2 (In Addenda)
Bulldog Drummond's Peril 1938,Mr 18,23:2
Texans, The 1938,Jl 28,23:2
Sons of the Legion 1938,S 30,24:3
Arrest Bulldog Drummond 1939,Ja 12,23:2
Bulldog Drummond's Secret Police 1939,Mr 30,19:3
Grand Jury Secrets 1939,Je 29,19:2
Bulldog Drummond's Bride 1939,Jl 13,17:2
$1,000 a Touchdown 1939,O 5,27:2
Farmer's Daughter, The 1940,F 16,23:4
Queen of the Mob 1940,Jl 1,23:2
Texas Rangers Ride Again 1941,Ja 9,27:4
Ellery Queen's Penthouse Mystery 1941,Mr 7,17:2
Power Dive 1941,My 29,15:4
Ellery Queen and the Perfect Crime 1941,Ag 11,17:3
Ellery Queen and the Murder Ring 1941,O 21,29:4
Enemy Agents meet Ellery Queen 1942,Ag 22,16:2
Strange Death of Adolf Hitler, The 1943,O 9,11:5
Mad Ghoul, The 1943,D 11,11:2

Hogan, James (Original Author)

Gypsy Wildcat 1944,O 5,18:6

Hogan, James (Screenwriter)

Gypsy Wildcat 1944,O 5,18:6

Hogan, Michael

Last Journey, The 1936,Je 8,22:4

Hogan, Michael (Miscellaneous)

Born for Glory 1935,O 21,22:4
Dr Syn 1937,N 15,15:1

Hogan, Michael (Original Author)

Forever and a Day 1943,Mr 13,9:2
Bride of Vengeance 1949,Ap 7,38:2

Hogan, Michael (Screenwriter)

Passing of the Third Floor Back, The 1936,Ap 29,19:2
Nurse Edith Cavell 1939,S 22,27:4
Rebecca 1940,Mr 29,25:2
Lady From Louisiana 1941,My 15,27:2
Prime Minister, The 1942,F 4,23:2
Arabian Nights 1942,D 26,15:1
Appointment in Berlin 1943,Jl 17,8:2
Hour Before the Dawn, The 1944,My 11,25:6
Tall in the Saddle 1944,D 15,25:3
Woman on the Beach, The 1947,Je 9,26:6
Bride of Vengeance 1949,Ap 7,38:2
Blue Lagoon, The 1949,O 3,13:2
Fortunes of Captain Blood 1950,Je 10,11:3

Hogan, Pat

Lure of the Wilderness 1952,O 4,15:2
Davy Crockett, King of the Wild Frontier 1955,My 26,36:1
Last Frontier, The 1955,D 8,45:1

Hogan, Paul

Sand 1949,Ag 5,23:2

Hogan, Robert

Greenwich Village Story 1963,Jl 12,14:3

Hogan, Society Kid

Lemon Drop Kid, The 1951,Mr 22,41:2

Hogarth, Michael

Men Are not Gods 1937,Ja 19,28:1
S O S Mediterranean 1940,Ja 1,29:2

Hogarth, William (Miscellaneous)

Bedlam 1946,Ap 20,16:4

Hoger, Hannelore

Artists Under the Big Top Perplexed 1968,S 27,34:1

Hoger, Karel

Krakatit 1951,Ap 30,16:2

HOGG

See Also HOAG, HOGUE

Hogg, Ian

Persecution and Assassination of Jean-Paul Marat as Performed by the Inmates of the Asylum of Charenton Under the Direction of the Marquis De Sade, The 1967,F 23,41:1

Hoglund, Gunnar (Director)

Obession 1968,Ag 29,46:3

Hoglund, Gunnar (Screenwriter)

Obession 1968,Ag 29,46:3

HOGUE

See Also HOAG, HOGG

Hogue, Eades

Baby Doll 1956,D 19,40:2

Hogue, Roland

His Double Life 1933,D 16,12:3

Hohart, George V (Original Author)

Sonny 1922,My 29,14:1

Hohenzollern

Hiding in Holland 1919,Je 30,16:3

Hohl, Arthur

Cheat, The 1931,D 12,23:3
Sign of the Cross, The 1932,D 1,25:1
Island of Lost Souls 1933,Ja 13,19:2
Infernal Machine 1933,Ap 8,16:3
Life of Jimmy Dolan, The 1933,Je 14,22:3
Baby Face 1933,Je 24,16:2
Silk Express, The 1933,Je 28,24:2
Private Detective 62 1933,Jl 7,20:2
Captured 1933,Ag 18,18:3
Wild Boys of the Road 1933,S 22,14:1
Brief Moment 1933,S 30,18:5
Footlight Parade 1933,O 6,21:3
World Changes, The 1933,O 27,22:3
Kennell Murder Case, The 1933,O 30,14:2
College Coach 1933,N 11,10:4
Man's Castle 1933,D 30,9:2
Massacre 1934,Ja 18,19:2
Jimmy the Gent 1934,Mr 26,22:3
As the Earth Turns 1934,Ap 12,27:2
Modern Hero, A 1934,Ap 20,17:1
Bulldog Drummond Strikes Back 1934,Ag 16,20:2
Defense Rests, The 1934,Ag 16,20:3
Cleopatra 1934,Ag 17,12:1
Lady by Choice 1934,N 17,12:1
Romance in Manhattan 1935,Ja 18,29:2
Whole Town's Talking, The 1935,Mr 1,16:2
I'll Love You Always 1935,Mr 30,11:2
Case of the Missing Man, The 1935,N 23,23:2
We're Only Human 1936,Ja 18,19:2
Show Boat 1936,My 15,29:4
Forgotten Faces 1936,Jl 4,18:2
Devil Doll, The 1936,Ag 8,5:2
Lloyds of London 1936,N 26,39:1
Slave Ship 1937,Je 17,19:2
Road Back, The 1937,Je 18,25:2
Mountain Music 1937,Je 24,30:3
Trapped by G-Men 1937,N 4,29:1
Hot Water 1937,N 5,19:4
Bad Man of Brimstone, The 1938,F 4,17:2
Penitentiary 1938,Mr 7,13:2
Kidnapped 1938,My 28,9:2
Stablemates 1938,O 21,27:2
Crime Takes a Holiday 1938,N 28,11:2
Boy Slaves 1939,F 9,17:3
You Can't Cheat an Honest Man 1939,F 20,13:2
They Shall Have Music 1939,Jl 26,17:2
Adventures of Sherlock Holmes, The 1939,S 2,20:1
Blackmail 1939,S 15,26:3
Fugitive at Large 1939,N 13,15:2
Hunchback of Notre Dame, The 1940,Ja 1,29:2
Twenty-Mule Team 1940,My 10,26:6
Men of Boys Town 1941,Ap 11,24:6
Ride on Vaquero 1941,Ap 19,20:2
Son of Fury 1942,Ja 30,23:2
Moontide 1942,Ap 30,14:1
Whispering Ghosts 1942,My 18,19:4
Spider Woman 1944,Ja 17,14:5
Woman of the Town, The 1944,Mr 6,17:2
Scarlet Claw, The 1944,My 19,12:1
Salome, Where She Danced 1945,My 3,27:1
Yearling, The 1947,Ja 24,18:2
It Happened on Fifth Avenue 1947,Je 11,33:2
Vigilantes Return, The 1947,Jl 1,30:2

Hoile, Edward V (Original Author)

Caretaker's Daughter, The 1953,Ag 20,18:5

Hoiree, Arthur
Lover's Return, A; Revenant, Le 1948,Ja 26,15:2
Hojgaard, Else
Young Have no Time, The 1959,N 23,41:2
Hojo, Hideji (Original Author)
Samurai 1956,Ja 10,26:1
Hokanson, Mary Alan
Them 1954,Je 17,36:2
Private War of Major Benson, The
1955,Ag 3,27:2
Guys and Dolls 1955,N 5,26:1
Ransom 1956,Ja 25,28:3
Lonelyhearts 1959,Mr 5,35:3
Holbert, Robinson (Original Author)
Ladies' Man 1947,Ja 13,18:5
Holbrook, Hal
Group, The 1966,Mr 17,35:1
Wild in the Streets 1968,My 30,21:1
Holbrook, Walter
Charge of the Light Brigade, The 1936,N 2,24:1
Holcolmb, Helen
Wild, Wild Susan 1925,Ag 5,12:4
Holcomb, Thomas Major
Unbeliever, The 1918,F 12,9:2
Holcombe, Harry
Unsinkable Molly Brown, The 1964,Jl 17,15:1
Kisses for my President 1964,Ag 22,13:1
Fortune Cookie, The 1966,O 20,52:1
Holcombe, Jean
How to be Very, Very Popular 1955,Jl 23,10:1
Hold, Marianne
Marianne of my Youth; (Marianne de ma
Jeunesse) 1959,Ja 20,43:1
Holdaway, Jim (Original Author)
Modesty Blaise 1966,Ag 11,27:1
Holden, Alan (Miscellaneous)
Symmetry 1967,Ja 21,35:1
Holden, Eddie
Battle of Broadway 1938,Ap 25,19:2
Holden, Fay
Wives Never Know 1936,O 31,24:2
Polo Joe 1936,N 5,35:1
Exclusive 1937,Jl 22,15:1
Double or Nothing 1937,S 2,17:3
You're Only Young Once 1938,Ja 3,16:2
Love Is a Headache 1938,Ja 28,17:3
Judge Hardy's Children 1938,Ap 8,17:2
Hold That Kiss 1938,Je 11,9:1
Love Finds Andy Hardy 1938,Jl 22,10:2
Out West With the Hardys 1938,D 9,31:2
Sweethearts 1938,D 23,16:2
Sergeant Madden 1939,Mr 24,27:2
Hardys Ride High, The 1939,Ap 14,28:2
Andy Hardy Gets Spring Fever 1939,Jl 19,23:2
Judge Hardy and Son 1940,Ja 18,27:3 (In
Addenda)
Andy Hardy Meets Debutante 1940,Ag 2,12:2
Bitter Sweet 1940,N 22,27:1
Andy Hardy's Private Secretary 1941,Mr 7,17:2
Ziegfeld Girl 1941,Ap 25,17:2
Washington Melodrama 1941,My 26,15:3
I'll Wait for You 1941,Je 2,13:6
Blossoms in the Dust 1941,Je 27,14:4
Life Begins for Andy Hardy 1941,Ag 22,19:4
H M Pulham, Esq 1941,D 19,35:1
Courtship of Andy Hardy, The 1942,Ap 10,21:2
Andy Hardy's Double Life 1943,Ja 12,23:3
Andy Hardy's Blonde Trouble 1944,My 5,17:3
Canyon Passage 1946,Ag 8,18:2
Love Laughs at Andy Hardy 1947,Ja 8,28:2
Whispering Smith 1949,F 15,28:2
Samson and Delilah 1949,D 22,29:2
Big Hangover, The 1950,My 26,20:3
Andy Hardy Comes Home 1958,D 24,00:0
Holden, Gloria
Wife vs Secretary 1936,F 29,11:1
Dracula's Daughter 1936,My 18,14:2
Life of Emile Zola, The 1937,Ag 12,14:2
Test Pilot 1938,Ap 16,17:1
Hawaii Calls 1938,Ap 29,17:2
Girls' School 1938,N 3,27:1
Dodge City 1939,Ap 8,19:1
Miracles for Sale 1939,Ag 10,15:2
Child Is Born, A 1940,Ja 11,19:2
This Thing Called Love 1941,F 14,15:2
Corsican Brothers, The 1942,Ja 16,25:4
Gentleman After Dark, A 1942,Ap 17,21:2
Miss Annie Rooney 1942,Je 8,11:1
Behind the Rising Sun 1943,O 14,26:2
Strange Holiday 1945,O 20,8:2
Hucksters, The 1947,Jl 18,21:2
Killer McCoy 1948,F 12,31:2
Dream Wife 1953,Jl 30,20:1
Eddy Duchin Story, The 1956,Je 22,15:1
This Happy Feeling 1958,Je 19,28:2
Holden, Harry
Yankee Clipper, The 1927,My 3,25:1
Gay Defender, The 1927,D 26,26:6
Holden, James
Fighter Squadron 1948,N 20,9:2
House Across the Street 1949,S 2,14:4
Task Force 1949,O 1,8:6
Sands of Iwo Jima 1949,D 31,9:2

Flight Nurse 1954,Ja 30,9:6
Holden, Jennifer
Jailhouse Rock 1957,N 14,41:1
Holden, Joyce
Milkman, The 1951,Ja 1,13:6
Target Unknown 1951,Mr 5,24:2
Iron Man 1951,Ag 20,14:2
Girls in the Night 1953,Ja 16,19:3
Holden, June
Hatter's Castle 1948,Jl 3,8:6
Holden, Lansing G (Director)
She 1935,Jl 26,18:2
Holden, Maxine
Lolita 1962,Je 14,23:2
Holden, Michael (Producer)
Ferry Cross the Mersey 1965,F 20,16:2
Holden, Peter
Great Man Votes, The 1939,Ja 20,15:2
Holden, William
Three Week Ends 1928,D 10,25:1
Weary River 1929,Ja 25,20:6
His Captive Woman 1929,Ap 3,26:4
Fast Life 1929,Ag 17,5:3
Trespasser, The 1929,N 2,14:6
Dynamite 1929,D 28,11:1
Not so Dumb 1930,F 8,12:5
Framed 1930,Mr 29,23:1
Numbered Men 1930,Je 9,23:3
Holiday 1930,Jl 3,25:4
Three Faces East 1930,S 6,9:2
What a Widow 1930,O 4,15:2
Man Who Came Back, The 1931,Ja 3,21:2
Charlie Chan Carries On 1931,Mr 21,15:1
Dance, Fools, Dance 1931,Mr 21,15:1
Six Cylinder Love 1931,My 16,31:3
Golden Boy 1939,S 8,28:2
Invisible Stripes 1940,Ja 13,11:2
Our Town 1940,Je 14,25:3
Those Were the Days 1940,Jl 15,18:4
Arizona 1941,F 7,23:3
I Wanted Wings 1941,Mr 27,29:4
Texas 1941,O 17,27:3
Remarkable Andrew, The 1942,Mr 6,17:2
Fleet's In, The 1942,Mr 12,24:2
Blaze of Noon 1947,Mr 5,31:2
Dear Ruth 1947,Je 11,33:3
Rachel and the Stranger 1948,S 20,21:2
Apartment for Peggy 1948,O 16,9:2
Dark Past, The 1948,D 23,25:2
Man From Colorado 1949,Ja 21,24:3
Streets of Laredo 1949,My 12,28:2
Dear Wife 1950,F 2,31:2
Father Is a Bachelor 1950,F 23,33:3
Sunset Boulevard 1950,Ag 11,15:2
Union Station 1950,O 5,38:3
Born Yesterday 1950,D 27,30:2
Force of Arms 1951,Ag 14,20:2
Submarine Command 1952,Ja 19,13:2
Boots Malone 1952,Mr 13,26:2
Turning Point, The 1952,N 15,15:2
Stalag 17 1953,Jl 2,19:2
Moon Is Blue, The 1953,Jl 9,18:3
Forever Female 1954,Ja 13,26:2
Escape from Fort Bravo 1954,Ja 23,11:2
Executive Suite 1954,My 7,19:1
Sabrina 1954,S 23,43:2
Country Girl, The 1954,D 16,51:2
Bridges at Toko-Ri, The 1955,Ja 21,20:2
Love Is a Many-Splendored Thing
1955,Ag 19,10:1
Picnic 1956,F 17,13:3
Proud and Profane, The 1956,Je 14,41:2
Toward the Unknown 1956,S 28,24:4
Bridge on the River Kwai 1957,D 19,39:1
Key, The 1958,Jl 2,23:3
Horse Soldiers, The 1959,Je 26,13:1
World of Suzie Wong, The 1960,N 11,36:1
Satan Never Sleeps 1962,F 22,20:1
Counterfeit Traitor, The 1962,Ap 18,28:1
Lion, The 1962,D 22,5:2
Paris When it Sizzles 1964,Ap 9,25:3
Seventh Dawn, The 1964,S 3,24:1
Alvarez Kelly 1966,N 17,55:2
Casino Royale 1967,Ap 29,25:1
Holder, Erich (Director)
Frischer Wind aus Kanada 1935,S 21,18:2
Holder, Geoffrey
Doctor Dolittle 1967,D 20,55:1
Holder, Roy
Whistle Down the Wind 1962,Ap 23,34:2
Murder Ahoy 1964,S 23,55:3
Othello 1966,F 2,24:1
Taming of the Shrew, The 1967,Mr 9,43:1
Holderness, Fay
Last Man on Earth, The 1924,D 13,12:4
Dick Turpin 1925,Ja 26,14:1
Lonesome 1928,O 2,23:5
Holding, Elisabeth Sanxay (Original Author)
Bride Comes Home, The 1935,D 25,30:2
Reckless Moment, The 1949,D 30,13:2
Holding, Thomas
Peace of Roaring River, The 1919,Ag 11,9:1
Without Benefit of Clergy 1921,Je 20,17:2

Holding, Thomas — Cont
Stranger's Banquet, The 1923,Ja 1,18:1
Ruggles of Red Gap 1923,S 10,15:4
Courtship of Myles Standish, The 1923,D 31,9:3
White Monkey, The 1925,Je 9,16:3
Holdren, Judd
Lady in the Iron Mask 1952,Jl 5,7:2
Holdridge, Desmond (Original Author)
End of the River, The 1948,Je 21,18:2
Hole, Jonathan
Riot in Cell Block 11 1954,F 19,24:5
Opposite Sex, The 1956,N 16,23:2
Holgate, Diane
Whistle Down the Wind 1962,Ap 23,34:2
Holiday, Billie
New Orleans 1947,Je 20,25:6
Holiday, Bryant (Narrator)
Bullfight 1956,Jl 4,15:2
Holiday, Hope
Apartment, The 1960,Je 16,37:2
Irma la Douce 1963,Je 6,39:1
Rounders, The 1965,Ap 29,40:2
Holl, Fritz (Director)
Nanu, Sie Kennen Korff noch Nicht?; So, You
Don't Know Korff Yet? 1939,My 22,15:3
Holl, Milo
Fabulous World of Jules Verne, The
1961,Je 29,26:1
Hollaender, Freiderich (Director)
Heart Song 1934,Je 6,24:6
Hollaender, Freidrich (Miscellaneous)
Stuerme der Leidenschaft 1932,Mr 16,17:3
Holland, Anthony
Goldstein 1965,My 8,19:7
Last Mohican, The 1966,S 13,51:2
Bye Bye Braverman 1968,F 22,36:1
Holland, Betty Lou
Goddess, The 1958,Je 25,24:1
Man in the Net, The 1959,Je 11,36:2
Holland, Catherine
Dog of Flanders, A 1960,Ap 1,37:1
Holland, Cecil
Name the Man 1924,F 4,23:3
Holland, Charles
Youth Will Be Served 1940,N 15,25:2
Hullabaloo 1940,D 19,33:1
Holland, Clifford
Summer Bachelors 1926,D 20,28:3
Rich but Honest 1927,My 18,29:3
Secret Studio, The 1927,Je 15,31:4
Holland, E C (Original Author)
Virtuous Liars 1924,Mr 31,20:1
Holland, Edna
Bachelor Mother 1939,Je 30,17:2
Between Two Women 1945,Mr 29,18:3
Kiss and Tell 1945,O 26,16:2
Intrigue 1948,Ap 24,11:2
Criss Cross 1949,Mr 12,10:2
Once More, my Darling 1949,S 26,17:1
Holland, Erik
Torn Curtain 1966,Jl 28,23:1
Holland, Gene
Song of the South 1946,N 28,40:2
Holland, George (Original Author)
Don't Tell the Wife 1937,F 19,15:2
Holland, Gilbert (Screenwriter)
Escapade 1957,Ag 6,30:2
Holland, Gladys
Lydia Bailey 1952,My 31,12:5
Holland, James G (Original Author)
Jes' Call Me Jim 1920,My 24,20:3
Holland, John
She Goes to War 1929,Je 10,23:1
College Coquette, The 1929,Ag 26,17:1
Hell Harbor 1930,Mr 28,22:6
Guilty 1930,Ap 7,21:1
Eyes of the World 1930,Ag 15,20:5
Ladies' Man 1931,My 1,30:3
Morals for Women 1931,N 16,23:1
Dance Band 1936,Ja 4,19:2
Voice of the Turtle, The 1947,D 26,22:4
State Department-File 649 1949,F 21,20:2
Rock Island Trail 1950,Je 5,19:3
Open the Door and See all the People
1964,Ap 2,28:1
My Fair Lady 1964,O 22,41:1
Naked Brigade, The 1965,Je 17,27:2
Holland, Marty (Original Author)
Fallen Angel 1946,F 7,29:4
Thelma Jordon 1950,Ja 19,35:2
Holland, William
Violated 1953,D 12,23:8
Holland, William (Producer)
Violated 1953,D 12,23:8
Hollander, Felix (Original Author)
Trial of Donald Westhof, The 1928,F 18,11:2
Hollander, Frederick (Composer)
I Am Suzanne 1934,Ja 19,24:3
Millions in the Air 1935,D 12,33:4
Anything Goes 1936,Je 23:3
Desire 1936,Ap 13,15:1
Champagne Waltz 1937,F 4,17:2
Thrill of a Lifetime 1937,D 9,30:2
Man About Town 1939,Je 29,19:1

Hollander, Frederick (Composer)— Cont
That Lady in Ermine 1948,Ag 25,31:2
Hollander, Frederick (Miscellaneous)
Artists and Models 1937,Ag 5,19:2
Hollander, Friedrich (Director)
Ich und die Kaiserin 1933,My 28,IX,2:5 (In Addenda)
Hollander, Hannah
I Want to Be a Mother 1937,F 27,9:2
Hollander, Jack
Miracle Worker, The 1962,My 24,29:2
Hollering, Franz (Screenwriter)
Scampolo 1959,Ag 6,18:4
Madchen in Uniform 1965,Ag 18,41:2
Holles, Anthony
Missing Rembrandt, The 1932,Mr 26,17:2
Brewster's Millions 1935,Ap 8,23:3
Things to Come 1936,Ap 18,19:2
Seven Sinners 1936,Ag 22,6:1
Tenth Man, The 1937,N 15,15:2
Gaiety Girls, The 1938,Mr 31,15:1
This'll Make You Whistle 1938,N 1,27:2
Larceny Street 1941,Ja 6,11:2
Battle for Music 1945,O 15,13:2
Magic Bow, The 1947,Jl 7,13:2
Rocking Horse Winner, The 1950,Je 9,29:2
Holles, Antony
Missing Ten Days 1941,Ap 21,15:5 (In Addenda)
Holles, Robert (Original Author)
Guns at Batasi 1964,N 17,47:1
Holles, Robert (Screenwriter)
Guns at Batasi 1964,N 17,47:1
Holley, Ruth
Sherlock Jr 1924,My 26,21:1
HOLLIDAY
See Also HALLIDAY, HOLIDAY
Holliday, Jason
Portrait of Jason 1967,S 30,26:1
Holliday, Judy
Winged Victory 1944,D 21,16:2
Adam's Rib 1949,D 26,33:2
Born Yesterday 1950,D 27,30:2
Marrying Kind, The 1952,Mr 14,27:1
It Should Happen to You 1954,Ja 16,10:5
Phffft 1954,N 11,43:2
Solid Gold Cadillac, The 1956,O 25,40:3
Full of Life 1957,F 13,38:1
Bells Are Ringing 1960,Je 24,31:2
Holliday, Martha
George White's Scandals 1945,O 11,26:2
Holliman, Earl
Destination Gobi 1953,My 30,7:1
Broken Lance 1954,Jl 30,9:1
Bridges at Toko-Ri, The 1955,Ja 21,20:2
Big Combo, The 1955,Mr 26,13:2
I Died a Thousand Times 1955,N 10,45:2
Forbidden Planet 1956,My 4,21:2
Burning Hills, The 1956,Ag 24,15:2
Rainmaker, The 1956,D 13,51:1
Gunfight at the O K Corral 1957,My 30,23:2
Trooper Hook 1957,Jl 13,11:2
Don't Go Near the Water 1957,N 15,37:1
Hot Spell 1958,S 18,37:2
Trap, The 1959,Ja 29,18:4
Last Train from Gun Hill 1959,Jl 30,31:2
Visit to a Small Planet 1960,Ap 14,34:1
Armored Command 1961,O 7,14:3
Summer and Smoke 1961,N 17,41:1
Sons of Katie Elder, The 1965,Ag 26,40:3
Covenant with Death, A 1967,F 16,32:3
Power, The 1968,Mr 7,52:2
Anzio 1968,Jl 25,26:1
Hollingsworth, Alfred
Leave It to Susan 1919,My 26,19:4
Hollingsworth, Harry
Sing Me a Love Song 1936,D 26,15:2
My Favorite Blonde 1942,Ap 2,27:2
Hollister, Alice
Voice in the Dark, A 1921,Je 6,16:4
Married Flirts 1924,N 19,19:3
Dancers, The 1925,Ja 26,22:1
Hollister, Len D (Original Author)
Gold Dust Gertie 1931,My 30,9:2
Hollman, Werner
Karamazof 1931,S 21,20:2
Holloway, Carol
Saphead, The 1921,F 14,12:2
Rainbow Trail, The 1925,Je 3,26:4
Chicken a la King 1928,Je 11,27:1
Holloway, Jean (Original Author)
Words and Music 1948,D 10,34:2
Holloway, Jean (Screenwriter)
Till the Clouds Roll By 1946,D 6,27:4
Summer Holiday 1948,Je 12,8:5
Madame X 1966,Ap 28,49:1
Holloway, Stanley
Co-Optimists, The 1930,F 5,27:2
Bride of the Lake, The 1934,S 11,24:5
Way Ahead, The 1945,Je 4,22:3
Johnny in the Clouds 1945,N 16,16:2
Brief Encounter 1946,Ag 26,21:2
Wanted for Murder 1946,D 12,38:4
This Happy Breed 1947,Ap 14,24:2
Nicholas Nickleby 1947,D 1,27:2
Meet Me at Dawn 1948,My 18,26:2
Champagne Charlie 1948,Ag 7,8:2
Hamlet 1948,S 30,32:2
Snowbound 1949,F 21,20:2
One Night With You 1949,F 21,20:2
Passport to Pimlico 1949,O 27,35:2
Another Shore 1951,F 12,19:3
Perfect Woman, The 1951,F 17,10:7
Lavender Hill Mob, The 1951,O 16,35:2
Mr Lord Says No! 1952,F 12,22:5
Magic Box, The 1952,S 24,40:2
Tonight at 8:30 (Fumed Oak); Fumed Oak (Tonight at 8:30) 1953,My 26,33:2
Beggar's Opera, The 1953,Ag 25,18:2
Titfield Thunderbolt, The 1953,O 6,34:2
Midnight Episode 1955,My 19,25:5
Alligator Named Daisy, An 1957,O 7,23:2
No Love for Johnnie 1961,D 13,55:1
My Fair Lady 1964,O 22,41:1
In Harm's Way 1965,Ap 7,36:1
Operation Snafu 1965,My 22,18:1
Ten Little Indians 1966,F 10,33:1
Holloway, Sterling
Casey at the Bat 1927,Ap 4,30:5
Blondie Johnson 1933,F 27,11:2
Fast Workers 1933,Mr 20,18:2
Hell Below 1933,Ap 26,13:2
Elmer the Great 1933,My 26,24:2
Gold Diggers of 1933 1933,Je 8,22:3
Wild Boys of the Road 1933,S 22,14:1
Dancing Lady 1933,D 1,23:2
Advice to the Lovelorn 1933,D 14,28:2
Alice in Wonderland 1933,D 23,19:1
Strictly Dynamite 1934,Jl 4,18:2
Down to Their Last Yacht 1934,S 24,14:1
Gift of Gab 1934,S 26,17:6
Merry Widow, The 1934,O 12,33:1
Wicked Woman, A 1935,Ja 1,24:1
Life Begins at 40 1935,Ap 5,21:3
Doubting Thomas 1935,Jl 11,24:2
$1,000 a Minute 1935,D 21,11:1
Girl From Maxim's, The 1936,S 16,29:1
Maid of Salem 1937,Mr 4,27:2
Woman I Love, The 1937,Ap 16,27:2
When Love Is Young 1937,Ap 17,15:1
Varsity Show 1937,S 2,17:2
Of Human Hearts 1938,F 18,23:1
Doctor Rhythm 1938,My 19,25:2
Professor Beware 1938,Jl 14,17:1
Spring Madness 1938,D 1,29:3
Nick Carter, Master Detective 1939,D 14,35:2
Remember the Night 1940,Ja 18,27:2
Blue Bird, The 1940,Ja 20,11:2
Hit Parade of 1941 1940,D 5,33:2
Little Men 1940,D 9,23:2
Meet John Doe 1941,Mr 13,25:2
Cheers for Miss Bishop 1941,Mr 14,17:2
Top Sergeant Mulligan 1941,N 12,31:3
New Wine 1942,F 2,11:2
Iceland 1942,O 15,27:1
Star Spangled Rhythm 1942,D 31,20:1
Three Caballeros, The 1945,F 5,20:1
Walk in the Sun, A 1946,Ja 12,10:6
Sioux City Sue 1947,Jl 23,19:3
Beautiful Blonde From Bashful Bend, The 1949,My 28,11:2
Her Wonderful Lie 1950,Jl 17,15:2
Adventures of Huckleberry Fin, The 1960,Ag 4,17:1
It's a Mad, Mad, Mad, Mad World 1963,N 19,47:1
Holloway, W
Elephant Boy 1937,Ap 6,20:2
Mill On the Floss, The 1939,N 15,19:3
Hollstrom, Gunnar (Director)
Name of the Game Is Kill, The 1968,Je 6,54:1
Hellubar, Allen (Director)
Right to Happiness, The 1919,S 1,5:6
Hollubar, Allen (Original Author)
Right to Happiness, The 1919,S 1,5:6
Man-Woman-Marriage 1921,Mr 28,11:4
Holly, Ellen
Take a Giant Step 1961,Mr 6,28:2
Holly, Martin
Shop on Main Street, The 1966,Ja 25,47:1
Holly, Ruth
Friendly Enemies 1942,Je 22,19:1
Hollyman, Burnes
Lord of the Flies 1963,Ag 20,37:1
Hollywood, Jimmy
Every Night at Eight 1935,Ag 3,16:2
Hollywood Blondes, The
It Ain't Hay 1943,Mr 11,17:3
Hollywood Canteen Kids
Song of the Open Road 1944,Je 7,13:3
Holm, Astrid
Stroke of Midnight, The 1922,Je 5,16:2
Holm, Celeste
Three Little Girls in Blue 1946,S 26,32:3
Carnival in Costa Rica 1947,Mr 29,21:2
Gentleman's Agreement 1947,N 12,36:2
Snake Pit, the 1948,N 5,29:2
Road House 1948,N 8,24:2
Holm, Celeste— Cont
Chicken every Sunday 1949,Ja 19,34:2
Come to the Stable 1949,Jl 28,19:1
Everybody Does It 1949,O 26,32:2
Champagne for Caesar 1950,My 12,33:2
All About Eve 1950,O 14,13:2
Tender Trap, The 1955,N 11,29:6
High Society 1956,Ag 10,9:2
Bachelor Flat 1962,Ja 13,14:1
Doctor, You've Got to be Kidding 1967,My 11,50:1
Holm, Charles
Bimbo the Great 1961,Je 29,26:1
Holm, Claus
Marriage in the Shadows 1948,S 17,28:3
Merry Wives of Windsor, The 1952,S 22,19:2
Devil Strikes at Night, The 1959,Ja 30,31:3
Girls of the Night 1959,Mr 21,13:2
Journey to the Lost City 1960,D 8,43:3
Holm, Darry
Wrath of the Seas, The 1929,Ag 19,22:1
Holm, Eleanor
Tarzan's Revenge 1938,Ja 10,13:3
Holm, Erik (Screenwriter)
Face of War, The 1963,N 1,30:2
Holm, Gustav (Original Author)
Ich Will Nicht Wissen Wer Du Bist 1933,F 16,23:2
King Steps Out, The 1936,My 29,15:2
Her Wonderful Lie 1950,Jl 17,15:2
Holm, Ian
Bofors Gun, The 1968,S 23,42:3
Fixer, The 1968,D 9,59:1
Holm, Jan
My Bill 1938,Jl 7,22:4
Broadway Musketeers 1938,O 14,27:1
Holm, John Cecil
It Happened to Jane 1959,Ag 6,18:3
Holm, John Cecil (Original Author)
Three Men on a Horse 1936,N 26,39:1
Best Foot Forward 1943,Je 30,25:2
Holm, Kat
Child of Man 1950,F 1,25:2
Holm, Klaus
Razzia 1948,Je 14,19:2
Holm, Richard
Fidelio 1961,My 13,10:1
Holm, Rut
Tjocka Slaekten; Near Relatives 1935,My 20,20:5
Larsson I Andra Giftet 1935,O 19,21:3
Skaergaards-Flirt 1936,Ap 8,26:3
Familjen Som Var En Karusel 1937,My 22,19:3
Sun Over Sweden 1938,Ap 9,11:2
Frun Tillhanda; Servant Girls 1938,D 30,9:2
Skanor-Falsterbo 1939,Ap 17,13:2
Skicka Hem Nr 7; Send Home No 7 1939,My 9,29:2
Vi paa Solglantan; We at Solglantan 1940,O 9,30:3
Flickorna Fran Gamla Stan 1934,D 27,25:4
Soederkaakar 1936,D 19,16:2
Holm, S (Original Author)
I, A Woman 1966,O 12,36:3
I, A Lover 1968,My 4,46:2
Holm, Sonia
Miranda 1949,Ap 25,20:2
Broken Journey 1949,My 26,34:3
Bad Lord Byron, The 1952,Mr 20,37:5
Holm, Valso
Girls are Willing, The 1959,My 11,30:1
Holman, Bryce
Small Hours, The 1962,Ag 14,34:1
Holman, Harry
Sporting Blood 1931,Ag 15,18:3
Her Majesty, Love 1931,N 26,37:2
So Big 1932,Ap 30,19:3
Week-End Marriage 1932,Je 4,9:2
Dark Horse, The 1932,Je 9,27:3
Doctor X 1932,Ag 4,17:2
Conquerors, The 1932,N 21,21:1
Central Park 1932,D 7,29:3
Silver Dollar 1932,D 23,20:1
Woman Accused, The 1933,Mr 13,18:2
Oliver Twist 1933,Ap 13,15:3
Circus Queen Murder, The 1933,My 9,20:5
Devil's Mate 1933,S 23,11:7
My Woman 1933,O 16,20:3
Traveling Saleslady 1935,Mr 29,26:2
Here Comes Cookie 1935,O 12,12:2
Gentle Julia 1936,Ap 11,19:1
Slightly Tempted 1940,N 1,33:1
Meet John Doe 1941,Mr 13,25:2
Bride Came C O D, The 1941,Jl 26,18:2
Mexican Spitfire at Sea 1942,Je 26,16:5
Seven Days' Leave 1942,D 11,33:2
Badman's Territory 1946,My 31,27:2
Magic Town 1947,O 8,29:2
Holman, Libby (Narrator)
Russian Story, The 1943,Je 9,17:2
Holman, Robert
Thirteenth Man, The 1938,Ja 1,11:2
Holman, Vincent
Lady Surrenders, A 1947,Je 20,25:6
Breaking Through the Sound Barrier 1952,N 7,19:1

Holmes, Ben
Expert, The 1932,F 27,22:1
Holmes, Ben (Director)
Farmer in the Dell, The 1936,Mr 7,11:4
Plot Thickens, The 1936,D 9,35:2
We're on the Jury 1937,F 10,18:5
There Goes my Girl 1937,Je 12,8:2
Saint in New York, The 1938,My 26,31:2
I'm From the City 1938,Ag 19,13:4
Holmes, Ben (Original Author)
Melody Cruise 1933,Je 23,15:2
Cockeyed Cavaliers 1934,Jl 25,22:2
I'm From the City 1938,Ag 19,13:4
Holmes, Ben (Screenwriter)
Saint's Double Trouble, The 1940,F 13,27:2
Holmes, Brown (Miscellaneous)
While the Patient Slept 1935,Mr 2,18:2
Case of the Curious Bride, The 1935,Ap 5,21:3
Florentine Dagger, The 1935,Ap 27,20:6
Holmes, Brown (Original Author)
Hollywood Cavalcade 1939,O 14,13:2
Holmes, Brown (Screenwriter)
I Sell Anything 1934,D 27,25:2
Case of the Lucky Legs, The 1935,N 1,25:1
Snowed Under 1936,Mr 30,17:5
Satan Met a Lady 1936,Jl 23,24:2
Flying Hostess 1936,D 14,29:4
Top of the Town 1937,Mr 27,19:2 ·
Oh, Doctor 1937,Je 19,20:3
Crime of Dr Hallet, The 1938,Mr 24,21:3
Three Blind Mice 1938,Je 18,18:2
Castle on the Hudson 1940,Mr 4,11:2
Moon Over Miami 1941,Jl 5,14:2
Three Little Girls in Blue 1946,S 26,32:3
Holmes, Burton (Producer)
Mirrors of Nature 1920,Ja 19,16:3
Holmes, Dennis
Woman Obsessed 1959,My 28,34:1
Return of Mr Moto 1965,D 2,48:1
Holmes, Douglas
Strangers When we Meet 1960,Je 30,22:2
Holmes, Elsie
Rhubarb 1951,Ag 31,12:2
Marrying Kind, The 1952,Mr 14,27:1
Holmes, George
It Happened in Flatbush 1942,Jl 3,12:8
Man in the Trunk, The 1942,O 23,25:1
Crash Dive 1943,Ap 29,25:2
Falcon in San Francisco, The 1945,Jl 21,7:2
Holmes, Herbert
Up the Ladder 1925,My 12,26:2
Holmes, Ione
Convoy 1927,My 9,26:4
Mad Hour, The 1928,Ap 16,20:5
Hit of the Show 1928,Jl 9,25:1
Jazz Age, The 1929,Ja 7,36:2
Holmes, J B (Director)
Coastal Command 1944,Ap 19,26:1
Holmes, Leon
Poker Faces 1926,S 14,25:4
Frisco Sally Levy 1927,Ap 13,29:4
Holmes, Marian
Miracle in the Rain 1956,Ap 2,18:1
Holmes, Mary J (Original Author)
Lena Rivers 1932,My 21,9:2
Holmes, Maynard
Dancing Lady 1933,D 1,23:2
Madame Du Barry 1934,O 25,26:2
Leathernecks Have Landed, The 1936,Mr 23,22:5
Satan Met a Lady 1936,Jl 23,24:2
Go West, Young Man 1936,N 19,31:3
Top Sergeant Mulligan 1941,N 12,31:3
Remember Pearl Harbor 1942,Je 4,22:4
Star Spangled Rhythm 1942,D 31,20:1
Holmes, Milton
Wreck of the Hesperus, The 1927,N 28,18:5
Holmes, Milton (Original Author)
Salty O'Rourke 1945,Ap 26,26:2
Johnny O'Clock 1947,Mr 27,39:2
Holmes, Milton (Producer)
Boots Malone 1952,Mr 13,26:2
Matter of Who, A 1962,Jl 25,29:2
Holmes, Milton (Screenwriter)
Mr Lucky 1943,Jl 23,21:2
Salty O'Rourke 1945,Ap 26,26:2
Boots Malone 1952,Mr 13,26:2
Naked Earth 1958,Ag 29,18:1
Matter of Who, A 1962,Jl 25,29:2
Holmes, Phillips
Varsity 1928,O 29,29:1
Wild Party, The 1929,Ap 2,28:4
Return of Sherlock Holmes, The 1929,O 19,22:6
Pointed Heels 1929,D 28,11:1
Only the Brave 1930,Mr 8,21:1
Devil's Holiday, The 1930,My 10,25:3
Grumpy 1930,Ag 2,16:4
Her Man 1930,O 4,15:2
Man to Man 1931,Ja 3,21:2
Criminal Code, The 1931,Ja 5,21:3
Stolen Heaven 1931,F 14,11:4
Confessions of a Co-Ed 1931,Je 20,20:4
American Tragedy, An 1931,Ag 6,22:5
Two Kinds of Women 1932,Ja 16,13:1

Holmes, Robert
Jaws of Hell 1931,Ja 5,21:3
Holmes, Stuart
Other Man's Wife, The 1919,Je 9,16:3
Prisoner of Zenda, The 1922,Ag 1,14:3
Under Two Flags 1922,S 25,10:2
Daughters of the Rich 1923,Je 18,13:5
Unknown Purple, The 1924,Mr 24,13:1
Three Weeks 1924,Ap 1,19:3
Between Friends 1924,My 12,14:4
Tess of the D'Urbervilles 1924,Jl 28,12:2
Vanity's Price 1924,O 8,16:2
Beloved Brute, The 1924,N 10,20:1
Siren of Seville, The 1924,N 17,16:1 (In Addenda)
Salvation Hunters, The 1925,F 2,14:1
Friendly Enemies 1925,My 5,24:2
Steele of the Royal Mounted 1925,Je 18,16:3
Good and Naughty 1926,Je 14,24:1
Four Horsemen of the Apocalypse, The 1926,S 27,27:3
Everybody's Acting 1926,N 8,19:2
When a Man Loves 1927,F 4,16:6
Beware of Married Men 1928,Ap 10,33:2
Burning Daylight 1928,Ap 23,20:2
Man Who Laughs, The 1928,Ap 28,12:3
Hawk's Nest, The 1928,Je 25,27:1
Cavalier, The 1928,O 31,28:4
My Pal the King 1932,O 4,26:4
Are We Civilized? 1934,Je 14,28:5
Belle of the Nineties 1934,S 22,12:2
Murder by an Aristocrat 1936,Je 13,13:2
Case of the Velvet Claws, The 1936,Ag 29,16:3
Her Husband's Secretary 1937,Mr 20,23:6
British Intelligence 1940,F 12,14:2
Devil's Island 1940,Jl 12,11:4
Holmes, Taylor
$20 a Week 1924,Je 10,24:4
Crimson Runner, The 1925,My 27,26:2
Dancers, The 1930,N 15,15:3
Crime of Dr Forbes, The 1936,Jl 6,11:4
Make Way for a Lady 1936,D 12,15:1
Boomerang 1947,Mr 6,36:2
Kiss of Death 1947,Ag 28,28:2
Nightmare Alley 1947,O 10,31:3
Plunders, The 1948,N 1,28:2
Joan of Arc 1948,N 12,30:5
That Wonderful Urge 1948,D 22,29:6
Act of Violence 1949,Ja 24,16:2
Mr Belvedere Goes to College 1949,Ap 16,11:2
Once More, my Darling 1949,S 26,17:1
Woman in Hiding 1950,F 23,33:2
Father of the Bride 1950,My 19,31:2
Quicksand 1950,Je 16,28:4
Bright Leaf 1950,Je 17,7:2
Copper Canyon 1950,N 16,39:2
First Legion, The 1951,Ap 28,9:2
Rhubarb 1951,Ag 31,12:2
Two Tickets to Broadway 1951,N 22,47:2
Hoodlum Empire 1952,Mr 6,25:6
Woman of the North Country 1952,Ag 30,6:2
Beware my Lovely 1952,S 13,10:5
Gentlemen Prefer Blondes 1953,Jl 16,17:2
Outcast, The 1954,Jl 3,9:2
Hell's Outpost 1955,F 26,13:3
Maverick Queen, the 1956,Je 4,25:2
Holmes, Tracy
Ghost Train, The 1933,F 18,13:3
Holmes, W
Terror Trail 1933,F 11,11:3
Lost Boundaries 1949,Jl 1,14:4
Elmer Gantry 1960,Jl 8,16:1
Holmquist, Elsa
Baldvins Brollop; Baldwin's Wedding 1938,D 27,13:2
Holmquist, Sigrid
Gentleman of Leisure, A 1923,Jl 16,14:2
Light That Failed, The 1923,N 27,11:2
Youth for Sale 1924,S 3,17:1
School for Wives 1925,Ap 1,21:3
Crackerjack, The 1925,My 18,12:1

Holmsen, Egil (Director)
Time of Desire 1959,N 21,26:5
Holmsen, Egil (Screenwriter)
Time of Desire 1959,N 21,26:5
Holmsten, Karl-Arne
Frun Tillhanda; Servant Girls 1938,D 30,9:2
Du Gamla, Du Fria; Thou old, Tho Free 1939,Mr 21,27:2
Kustens Glada Kavaljerer; Coast's Happy Cavaliers, The 1939,My 23,27:2
Secrets of Woman 1961,Jl 12,36:1
Holodenko, I (Producer)
We Live Again 1948,S 6,17:2
Holoubek, Gustaw
Partings 1962,N 28,44:1
Salto 1966,O 4,50:1
Holsboer, Max Dr
S O S Iceberg 1933,S 25,18:4
Holsey, Reva
Sonne Geht auf, Die 1935,F 18,19:4
Holst, Maria
Operetta 1949,Je 6,15:4
Vienna Blood 1951,F 22,27:4
Holst-Jensen, J
Nine Lives 1959,Ja 6,28:1
Holt, Andrew (Screenwriter)
Avalanche 1946,Jl 8,25:2
Holt, Charlene
If a Man Answers 1962,N 22,43:1
Man's Favorite Sport? 1964,F 20,22:1
Red Line 7000 1965,D 9,60:4
Dorado, El 1967,Je 29,32:1
Holt, David
Cat's Paw, The 1934,Ag 17,12:2
You Belong to Me 1934,S 13,26:1
Age of Indiscretion 1935,My 18,21:2
Men Without Names 1935,Je 29,16:2
Last Days of Pompeii, The 1935,O 17,29:2
Adventures of Tom Sawyer, The 1938,F 18,23:1
Military Academy 1940,Ag 5,10:4
Pride of the Yankees, The 1942,Jl 16,23:1
Human Comedy, The 1943,Mr 3,19:2
Top Man 1943,O 29,23:2
Cheaters, The 1945,Jl 21,7:2
Courage of Lassie 1946,Jl 25,18:5
Holt, Denis (Producer)
Stolen Hours 1963,O 17,39:1
Holt, Evelyn
Das Ekel 1932,Ja 30,13:2
Namensheirat 1933,Ja 9,23:1
Aschermittwoch; Ash Wednesday 1935,Mr 11,15:2
Holt, Felix (Original Author)
Kentuckian, The 1955,S 2,13:2
Holt, George
Bigger Than Barnum's 1926,Jl 13,19:3
Holt, Gloria
Lovey Mary 1926,Je 21,17:2
Holt, Hans
Liebe im Dreiviertel Takt; Love in Waltz Time 1938,S 24,13:1
Konzert in Tirol 1939,Ja 7,6:4
Diskretion-Ehrensache; Discretion with Honor 1939,Mr 13,12:3
Fasching in Wien 1939,Mr 18,9:2
Unsterblicher Walzer; Immortal Waltz 1939,N 18,22:6
Ekel, Das; Grouch, The 1939,D 4,18:4
Mutterliebe; Mother Love 1940,Mr 16,8:3
Mozart Story, The 1948,N 15,21:5
Singing Angels 1952,Ja 16,21:2
Embezzled Heaven 1959,Ap 24,23:1
Trapp Family, The 1961,Ag 31,22:4
Almost Angels 1962,N 1,34:2
Holt, Jack
Cheating Cheaters 1919,Ja 27,11:4
Midnight Romance, A 1919,Mr 10,9:3
Woman Thou Gavest Me, The 1919,Je 9,16:3
Sporting Chance, A 1919,Jl 14,12:2
Life Line, The 1919,S 29,16:1
Victory 1919,D 28,4:4
Best of Luck, The 1920,Jl 5,12:4
Midsummer Madness 1920,D 6,19:1
Lost Romance, The 1921,My 9,16:2
Bought and Paid For 1922,Mr 13,18:2
North of the Rio Grande 1922,My 15,20:3
While Satan Sleeps 1922,Je 26,16:2
Man Unconquerable, The 1922,Jl 17,16:3
On the High Seas 1922,O 8,VI,3:1 (In Addenda)
Tiger's Claw, The 1923,Mr 19,22:2
Gentleman of Leisure, A 1923,Jl 16,14:2
Cheat, The 1923,Ag 27,14:3
Don't Call it Love 1923,D 25,26:1
Lone Wolf, The 1924,My 7,19:4
Wanderer of the Wasteland, The 1924,Jl 8,14:2
Empty Hands 1924,Ag 18,8:2
North of 36 1924,D 8,13:3
Eve's Secret 1925,Je 11,14:3
Light of the Western Stars, The 1925,Je 24,14:3
Wild Horse Mesa 1925,Ag 10,8:2
Ancient Highway, The 1925,N 11,27:3
Enchanted Hill, The 1925,D 29,19:2 (In Addenda)

Holt, Jack— Cont

Sea Horses 1926,F 23,26:5
Blind Goddess 1926,Ap 6,26:4 (In Addenda)
Born to the West 1926,Je 30,18:1 (In Addenda)
Smart Set, The 1928,Mr 5,21:1
Submarine 1928,Ag 31,23:3
Water Hole, The 1928,S 3,14:2
Donovan Affair, The 1929,Ap 29,29:2
Father and Son 1929,Je 4,29:3
Flight 1929,S 14,17:1
Border Legion, The 1930,Je 30,22:6
Hell's Island 1930,Jl 19,7:5
Squealer, The 1930,S 8,17:1
Last Parade, The 1931,Mr 2,19:1
Dirigible 1931,Ap 6,24:1
Subway Express 1931,My 2,23:4
White Shoulders 1931,Je 5,26:5
Fifty Fathoms Deep 1931,S 19,10:2
Dangerous Affair, A 1931,N 23,22:1
Maker of Men 1931,D 19,16:4
Behind the Mask 1932,My 2,13:2
War Correspondent 1932,Ag 13,18:6
This Sporting Age 1932,O I,10:4
Man Against Woman 1932,D 17,22:3
When Strangers Marry 1933,My 25,24:3
Woman I Stole, The 1933,Je 28,24:3
Wrecker, The 1933,Ag 7,18:3
Master of Men 1933,N 29,23:4
Whirlpool 1934,My 5,22:3
Black Moon 1934,Je 28,26:2
Defense Rests, The 1934,Ag 16,20:3
I'll Fix It 1934,N 12,17:3
Best Man Wins 1935,Ja 2,22:4
Littlest Rebel, The 1935,D 20,30:1
Dangerous Waters 1936,Ja 22,15:5
San Francisco 1936,Je 27,21:1
Crash Donovan 1936,Ag 10,10:3
Trouble in Morocco 1937,Mr 15,27:1
Roaring Timber 1937,Ag 19,23:1
Outlaws of the Orient 1937,S 25,10:2
Trapped by G-Men 1937,N 4,29:1
Under Suspicion 1937,D 20,23:2 (In Addenda)
Making the Headlines 1938,Ap 1,17:2
Flight Into Nowhere 1938,My 2,13:3
Reformatory 1938,Je 27,13:6
Crime Takes a Holiday 1938,N 28,11:2
Hidden Power 1939,Jl 26,17:3
Fugitive at Large 1939,N 13,15:2
Outside the Three-Mile Limit 1940,Ap 8,15:2
Passport to Alcatraz 1940,Je 15,12:2
Prison Camp 1940,Ag 3,9:3
Great Plane Robbery, The 1940,N 15,25:2
Great Swindle, The 1941,My 14,25:4
Thunder Birds 1942,O 29,19:2
Cat People 1942,D 7,22:2
They Were Expendable 1945,D 21,25:2
My Pal Trigger 1946,Ag 17,16:3
Chase, The 1946,N 18,31:2
Last Bandit, The 1949,Mr 21,19:2
Task Force 1949,O 1,8:6
Brimstone 1949,O 7,35:3
Return of the Frontiersman 1950,Je 10,11:3
Across the Wide Missouri 1951,N 7,35:4

Holt, Jany

Golem, The 1937,Mr 22,27:2
Lower Depths, The 1937,S 11,20:1
Life and Loves of Beethoven, The
   1937,N 22,15:1
Alibi, L' 1939,Ap 10,13:3
Rasputin 1939,O 17,31:4
Sirocco 1946,Ag 12,17:3
Not Guilty 1948,Ap 23,28:2
Rumors 1949,Mr 19,10:7
Counter Investigation 1949,D 30,13:2
Angels of the Streets 1950,Ja 17,24:2
Green Glove, The 1952,Ap 24,38:1
Gervaise 1957,N 12,46:1

Holt, Jennifer

Private Buckaroo 1942,Je 25,27:4
Cowboy in Manhattan 1943,My 28,19:2

Holt, Kealoha

Honolulu 1939,F 23,19:2

Holt, Nat (Producer)

Badman's Territory 1946,My 31,27:2
Trail Street 1947,Ap 10,35:2
Riff-Raff 1947,Je 30,25:7
Return of the Badmen 1948,Ag 5,16:2
Race Street 1948,Ag 23,13:3
Canadian Pacific 1949,My 20,32:4
Fighting Man of the Plains 1949,N 17,35:6
Cariboo Trail, The 1950,S 1,17:2
Great Missouri Raid, The 1951,Ap 9,31:2
Warpath 1951,N 23,32:2
Denver and Rio Grande, The 1952,My 17,22:7
Hurricane Smith 1952,O 4,15:2
Pony Express 1953,Je 6,8:6
Arrowhead 1953,S 16,38:6
Flight to Tangier 1953,N 26,50:4

Holt, Olinpio

Voice in Your Heart, A 1952,F 23,7:5

Holt, Patrick

Frieda 1947,Ag 15,12:3
October Man, The 1948,Ap 16,29:2
Girl in the Painting, The 1949,Ag 22,13:1

Master of Bankdam 1949,O 17,18:2
Marry Me 1952,Mr 14,27:3
Ivanhoe 1952,Ag 1,8:2
Guilt is my Shadow 1954,Mr 25,36:4
Unholy Four, The 1954,N 20,10:2
Warriors, The 1955,S 10,11:2
Guns at Batasi 1964,N 17,47:1
Genghis Khan 1965,Je 24,28:2
Hammerhead 1968,S 12,54:3

Holt, Paul (Screenwriter)

Bad Lord Byron, The 1952,Mr 20,37:5

Holt, Robert I (Screenwriter)

Rampage 1963,O 17,39:2

Holt, Seth (Director)

Scream of Fear 1961,Ag 23,29:1
Station Six-Sahara 1964,N 12,40:2
Nanny, The 1965,N 4,57:2
Danger Route 1968,Je 6,54:2

Holt, Tim

Stella Dallas 1937,Ag 6,21:1
I Met my Love Again 1938,Ja 15,19:1
Gold Is Where You Find It 1938,F 14,20:6
Sons of the Legion 1938,S 30,24:3
Law West of Tombstone, The 1938,N 25,19:1
Renegade Ranger, The 1939,F 17,17:3
Stagecoach 1939,Mr 3,21:1
Spirit of Culver 1939,Mr 9,18:1
Girl and the Gambler, The 1939,Je 28,17:3
Fifth Avenue Girl 1939,Ag 25,12:2
Swiss Family Robinson 1940,F 9,15:3
Back Street 1941,F 12,25:2
Magnificent Ambersons, The 1942,Ag 14,13:3
Hitler's Children 1943,F 25,27:1
My Darling Clementine 1946,D 4,44:5
Treasure of Sierra Madre 1948,Ja 24,11:2
His Kind of Woman 1951,Ag 30,20:2

Holt, Ula

New Adventures of Tarzan, The 1935,O 15,19:3

Holtby, Winifred (Original Author)

South Riding 1938,Ag 2,15:2

Holton, Charles

Road Back, The 1937,Je 18,25:2
Midnight Manhunt 1945,Ag 18,12:5

Holton, Robert

Young Widow 1946,Jl 29,12:8
Monkey on my Back 1957,My 30,23:2

Holtz, Bernd

Artists Under the Big Top Perplexed
   1968,S 27,34:1

Holtz, Lou

Follow the Leader 1930,D 6,21:3

Holtz, Tenen

Upstage 1926,N 15,19:1
Frisco Sally Levy 1927,Ap 13,29:4
Latest From Paris, The 1928,F 27,16:2
Bringing Up Father 1928,Mr 19,26:2
Trail of '98, The 1928,Mr 21,30:3
Cardboard Lover, The 1928,S 3,14:2
Duke Steps Out, The 1929,Ap 15,22:6
Three Live Ghosts 1929,S 30,23:1
Kibitzer, The 1929,D 21,17:1
Gentleman's Fate 1931,Je 27,20:3
Whistling in the Dark 1933,F 5,IX,5:1
British Agent 1934,S 20,20:1
International Crime 1938,My 16,14:4
Cipher Bureau 1938,D 14,32:6

Holtz, Tubea

Show People 1928,N 12,18:2

Holtzman, Iris

Unstrap Me 1968,N 21,41:2

Holtzmann, Thomas

Funeral in Berlin 1966,D 23,17:1

Holubar, Allen (Director)

Heart of Humanity, The 1918,D 22,17:3
Paid in Advance 1919,D 1,9:3
Slander the Woman 1923,My 28,18:2

Holzmann, Olly

Hotel Sacher 1939,Je 10,14:2
Wiener Geschichten; Vienna Tales 1940,S 28,9:3

Holzmeister, Judith

Eroica; (The Beethoven Story) 1951,O 29,19:2
April 1, 2000 1954,F 17,27:2

Holzschuh, Lizzi

Himmel auf Erden, Der 1935,D 26,21:4
Vetter aus Dingsda, Der 1936,F 1,9:3
Mein Liebster Ist ein Jaegersmann 1936,S 15,37:6
Rendezvous in Wien 1938,F 19,19:4
Unsterbliche Melodien; Immortal Melodies
   1938,Ap 23,19:3
Liebe im Dreiviertel Takt; Love in Waltz Time
   1938,S 24,13:1
Teufelskerl, Ein; Devil of a Fellow, A
   1938,O 1,10:3

Homans, Robert

Fast and Furious 1927,Jl 4,20:3
Smiling Irish Eyes 1929,Jl 24,23:2
Son of the Gods 1930,Ja 31,24:1
Black Camel, The 1931,Jl 4,11:5
Silence 1931,Ag 15,18:3
Young America 1932,My 7,11:5
Madame Racketeer 1932,Jl 23,6:6
She Done Him Wrong 1933,F 10,12:3
President's Mystery, The 1936,O 19,22:1

Homans, Robert— Cont

Plough and the Stars, The 1937,Ja 29,15:1
Penrod and Sam 1937,Mr 29,14:3
Dance Charlie Dance 1937,Ag 26,25:2
Kid Comes Back, The 1938,F 7,10:2
Gold Is Where You Find It 1938,F 14,20:6
Over the Wall 1938,Mr 28,19:2
Stadium Murders, The 1938,Ap 9,11:2
Amazing Dr Clitterhouse, The 1938,Jl 21,14:2
Hell's Kitchen 1939,Jl 3,10:5
Grapes of Wrath, The 1940,Ja 25,17:2
West of Carson City 1940,My 7,31:3
Beyond Tomorrow 1940,S 27,27:1
East of the River 1940,O 28,21:2
Out of the Fog 1941,Je 21,20:2
Lady in a Jam 1942,S 11,25:2
Night Monster 1942,N 30,18:5
Frontier Badmen 1943,Ag 14,12:8
Jack London 1944,Mr 3,19:3
Whistler, The 1944,Ap 29,12:2
Pin Up Girl 1944,My 11,25:6
It Happened Tomorrow 1944,My 29,18:2
Merry Monahans, The 1944,O 13,16:2
River Gang 1945,O 6,9:7
Earl Carroll Sketchbook 1946,Ag 30,13:2

Home, William Douglas (Miscellaneous)

Eye Witness 1950,Ag 28,13:2

Home, William Douglas (Original Author)

Reluctant Debutante, The 1958,Ag 15,17:1

Home, William Douglas (Screenwriter)

Amazing Mr Beecham, The 1949,D 26,33:4
Reluctant Debutante, The 1958,Ag 15,17:1

Homeier, Skip

Tomorrow the World 1944,D 22,12:4
Boy's Ranch 1946,Ag 9,12:2
Mickey 1948,Jl 19,11:2
Big Cat, The 1949,Jl 29,12:2
Gunfighter, The 1950,Je 24,7:2
Halls of Montezuma, The 1951,Ja 6,9:6
Sealed Cargo 1951,My 24,47:1
Fixed Bayonets 1951,N 21,20:2
Sailor Beware 1952,F 1,17:1
Has Anybody Seen My Gal 1952,Jl 5,7:2
Beachhead 1954,Ap 17,8:2
Dawn at Socorro 1954,Ag 28,8:2
Black Widow 1954,O 28,46:6
Cry Vengence 1955,F 19,18:3
At Gunpoint 1956,F 4,24:5
Burning Hills, The 1956,Ag 24,15:2
Between Heaven and Hell 1956,O 12,33:2
Dakota Incident 1956,N 10,14:2
Ghost and Mr Chicken, The 1966,S 22,57:2

Homer, Peter Sr

Outsider, The 1962,F 8,25:1

Homer (Original Author)

Ulysses 1955,Ag 18,17:2
Helen of Troy 1956,Ja 27,21:4

Homes, Geoffrey (Original Author)

No Hands on the Clock 1941,D 22,24:6
Tall Target, The 1951,S 28,26:2

Homes, Geoffrey (Screenwriter)

Swamp Fire 1946,Ag 26,21:4
Out of the Past 1947,N 26,18:2
Roughshod 1949,Je 17,27:2
Big Steal, The 1949,Jl 11,13:2
Lawless, The 1950,Je 23,29:2
Eagle and the Hawk, The 1950,Jl 6,31:2
Last Outpost, The 1951,Je 22,16:3
This Woman is Dangerous 1952,F 28,23:2
Bugles in the Afternoon 1952,Mr 5,32:2
Powder River 1953,Jl 4,7:2
Those Redheads From Seattle 1953,O 1,34:2
Alaska Seas 1954,Mr 6,13:5
Southwest Passage 1954,S 11,11:2
Annapolis Story, An 1955,Ap 9,8:2
Bullet for Joey, A 1955,Ap 16,12:1

Homma, Fumiko

Rasho-Mon 1951,D 27,18:3

Homola, Miroslav

Thunder in the Hills 1947,My 24,10:5
Krakatit 1951,Ap 30,16:2

Homolka, Oscar

Aftermath 1927,D 6,27:1
Trial of Donald Westhof, The 1928,F 18,11:2
Women Without Men 1928,N 12,18:2
Uneasy Money 1928,D 11,35:3
Prince of Rogues, The 1929,Jl 30,19:4
Hocuspocus 1930,Ag 3,VIII,4:1
In Geheimdienst; In the Employ of the Secret
   Service 1931,O 25,VIII,6:1
1914: The Last Days Before the War 1932,S 5,9:6
Rhodes 1936,F 29,11:1
Woman Alone, The 1937,F 27,9:2
Ebb Tide 1937,N 18,27:2
Dreyfus Case, The 1940,O 30,29:3
Seven Sinners 1940,N 18,23:2
Comrade X 1940,D 26,23:1
Invisible Woman, The 1941,Ja 9,27:2
Rage in Heaven 1941,Mr 21,19:2
Ball of Fire 1942,Ja 16,25:2
Mission to Moscow 1943,Ap 30,25:2
Hostages 1943,O 11,23:2
I Remember Mama 1948,Mr 12,29:2
Anna Lucasta 1949,Ag 12,13:2

Homolka, Oscar— Cont
White Tower, The 1950,Jl 3,9:2
Mr Potts Goes to Moscow 1953,S 3,15:2
Prisoner of War 1954,My 10,20:2
Seven Year Itch, The 1955,Je 4,9:1
War and Peace 1956,Ag 22,26:2
Farewell to Arms, A 1958,Ja 25,14:1
Key, The 1958,Jl 2,23:3
Tempest 1959,Mr 27,19:2
Mr Sardonicus 1961,O 19,39:3
Boys' Night Out 1962,Je 22,15:2
Wonderful World of the Brothers Grimm, The 1962,Ag 8,35:1
Long Ships, The 1964,Je 25,25:1
Joy in the Morning 1965,Je 10,38:1
Funeral in Berlin 1966,D 23,17:1
Happening, The 1967,My 18,56:3
Billion Dollar Brain 1967,D 23,29:1

Homolka, Oskar
Zwischen Nacht und Morgen 1931,O 25,VIII,6:1

Honda, Inoshiro (Director)
Godzilla, King of the Monsters 1956,Ap 28,11:1
Mysterians, The 1959,Jl 2,15:2
Battle in Outer Space 1960,Jl 9,10:5
Mothra 1962,Jl 12,19:4
King Kong vs. Godzilla 1963,Je 27,23:4
Gozdilla vs the Thing 1964,N 26,52:2
Ghidrah, The Three-Headed Monster 1965,D 16,63:3
King Kong Escapes 1968,Jl 11,30:1

Honda, Inoshiro (Screenwriter)
Godzilla, King of the Monsters 1956,Ap 28,11:1

Hondo, Med
Zita 1968,Ag 12,40:2

Honegger, Arthur
Lover's Return, A; Revenant, Le 1948,Ja 26,15:2

Honegger, Arthur (Composer)
Mystic Mountain, The 1936,Mr 31,17:2
Mayerling 1937,S 14,27:1
Pygmalion 1938,D 8,34:2
Harvest 1939,O 3,19:4
Citadel of Silence, The 1939,D 25,29:1
Lover's Return, A; Revenant, Le 1948,Ja 26,15:2

Honegger, Arthur (Miscellaneous)
Miserables, Les 1936,O 28,31:2

Honeth, Fiffi
Children, The 1949,D 23,17:1

Honeycombs, The
Go Go Mania 1965,My 20,52:4

Hong, James
Love Is a Many-Splendored Thing 1955,Ag 19,10:1
China Gate 1957,My 23,40:2
One Spy too Many 1966,D 8,64:1
Sand Pebbles, The 1966,D 21,48:1

Hongo, Kohiro
Buddha 1965,Je 17,27:4
Great Wall, The 1965,D 16,63:2

Honl, Arthur
Narrow Corner, The 1933,Jl 14,15:3

Honneger, Arthur (Composer)
Miserables, Les 1946,D 26,28:4

Honnett, Mickie
It's the old Army Game 1926,Jl 5,6:4

Hononet, Robert
Sextette (Part 5-Seducer's Fate); Seducer's Fate (Sextette) 1953,Mr 2,19:2

Honorat, Roger
Trial of Joan of Arc, The 1965,F 12,19:1

Hoo, Hayward Soo
Bombs Over Burma 1942,Ag 10,15:2

Hoo, Hugh
Betrayal From the East 1945,Ap 25,27:2

Hood, Ann (Screenwriter)
Singing in the Dark 1956,Mr 8,32:5

Hood, Daria
Bohemian Girl, The 1936,F 17,21:1
Born to Sing 1942,F 19,23:2

Hood, Gordon
Dingaka 1965,Jl 1,34:1

Hood, Miki
Girl in the Street 1938,My 26,31:2
This'll Make You Whistle 1938,N 1,27:2
Inspector Hornleigh 1939,Je 15,27:3

Hood, Noel
Curse of Frankenstein, The 1957,Ag 8,15:5
How to Murder a Rich Uncle 1957,O 26,19:2

Hooker, Brian (Miscellaneous)
Rose of the Rancho 1936,Ja 9,25:2
Cyrano De Bergerac 1950,N 17,31:2

Hooker, Brian (Original Author)
Coronado 1935,D 19,33:4
Vagabond King, The 1956,S 13,39:6

Hooks, David
Dark Odyssey 1961,Je 26,22:2

Hooks, Robert
Sweet Love, Bitter 1967,Ja 31,50:1
Hurry Sundown 1967,Mr 24,22:1

Hoolahahn, Bill
Diamond Jim 1935,Ag 24,18:2

Hooper, Ewan
How I Won the War 1967,N 9,56:1

Hoopts, Fritz
Krach um Iolanthe 1935,My 11,21:3
Wenn der Hahn Kraeht 1936,N 14,23:3

Hoose, Fred
East Side Kids 1940,F 19,21:6

Hooser, William S
Spirit of the U S A, The 1924,My 21,22:3

Hoosier Hotshots
Rockin' in The Rockies 1945,Jl 5,7:2

Hoover, Clara
Illiac Passion, The 1968,Ap 19,40:1

Hoover, Herbert
Untitled-News, Life of Herbert Hoover 1955,N 7,55:1

Hoover, J Edgar (Miscellaneous)
Next of Kin 1943,My 6,25:2

Hoover, J Edgar (Original Author)
Persons in Hiding 1939,Mr 2,19:2
Undercover Doctor 1939,Je 1,31:2
Parole Fixer 1940,Ap 18,28:5
Queen of the Mob 1940,Jl 1,23:2
Walk East on Beacon 1952,My 29,17:2

Hoover, Joseph
Hell is for Heroes 1962,Jl 12,19:3

Hope, Ann
Along Came Sally 1934,Je 16,20:3

Hope, Anthony (Original Author)
Prisoner of Zenda, The 1922,Ag 1,14:3
Rupert of Hentzau 1923,Jl 9,8:4
Prisoner of Zenda, The 1937,S 3,12:1
Prisoner of Zenda, The 1952,N 5,36:2

Hope, Avis
Eight on the Lam 1967,Ap 27,52:1

Hope, Bob
Big Broadcast of 1938, The 1938,Mr 10,16:2
College Swing 1938,Ap 28,27:2
Give Me a Sailor 1938,Ag 11,31:1
Thanks for the Memory 1938,D 8,34:3
Never Say Die 1939,Mr 9,18:1
Some Like It Hot 1939,My 25,31:2
Cat and the Canary, The 1939,N 23,38:5
Road to Singapore 1940,Mr 14,29:2
Ghost Breakers, The 1940,Jl 4,12:2
Road to Zanzibar 1941,Ap 10,29:2
Caught in the Draft 1941,Je 26,27:3
Nothing but the Truth 1941,O 23,27:1
Louisiana Purchase 1942,Ja 1,37:1
My Favorite Blonde 1942,Ap 2,27:2
Road to Morocco 1942,N 12,30:1
Star Spangled Rhythm 1942,D 31,20:1
They Got Me Covered 1943,Mr 5,20:2
Let's Face It 1943,Ag 5,18:1
Princess and the Pirate, The 1945,F 10,16:2
Road to Utopia 1946,F 28,20:2
Monsieur Beaucaire 1946,S 5,23:1
My Favorite Brunette 1947,Mr 20,38:2
Where There's Life 1947,D 25,32:1
Road to Rio 1948,F 19,29:3
Paleface, The 1948,D 16,41:2
Sorrowful Jones 1949,Je 6,15:2
Great Lover, The 1949,N 24,48:2
Fancy Pants 1950,Ag 31,21:2
Lemon Drop Kid, The 1951,Mr 22,41:2
My Favorite Spy 1951,D 26,19:3
Son of Paleface 1952,O 2,32:3
Road to Bali 1953,Ja 30,25:1
Off Limits 1953,Mr 30,25:5
Here Come the Girls 1953,D 26,10:1
Casanova's Big Night 1954,Ap 19,19:1
Seven Little Foys, The 1955,Je 30,18:2
That Certain Felling 1956,Je 21,35:2
Iron Petticoat, The 1957,F 2,12:2
Beau James 1957,Je 27,21:1
Paris Holiday 1958,My 10,19:2
Alias Jesse James 1959,My 18,31:2
Facts of Life, The 1961,F 11,27:1
Bachelor in Paradise 1961,N 17,41:2
Road to Hong Kong, The 1962,Je 28,21:1
Critic's Choice 1963,My 2,40:2
Call Me Bwana 1963,Jl 4,9:1
Sound of Laughter, The 1963,D 18,44:2
Global Affair, A 1964,My 7,31:2
I'll Take Sweden 1965,Ag 12,30:4
Boy, Did I Get a Wrong Number! 1966,Je 9,54:2
Eight on the Lam 1967,Ap 27,52:1
Eight on the Lam 1967,Ap 27,52:1
Private Navy of Sgt O'Farrell, The 1968,My 9,54:1

Hope, Bob (Original Author)
Paris Holiday 1958,My 10,19:2

Hope, Bob (Producer)
Paris Holiday 1958,My 10,19:2
Alias Jesse James 1959,My 18,31:2

Hope, Diana
Man From Blankley's, The 1930,Mr 29,23:1

Hope, Dorothy (Original Author)
No Funny Business 1934,Mr 9,22:4
At Dawn We Die 1943,My 8,19:2
Candlelight in Algeria 1944,Jl 31,10:2
Golden Madonna, The 1949,S 5,13:4

Hope, Edward (Original Author)
She Loves Me Not 1934,S 8,18:5
Marry the Girl 1937,Jl 31,6:2

Hope, Edward (Original Author)— Cont
Down Among the Sheltering Palms 1953,Je 13,11:2
How to be Very, Very Popular 1955,Jl 23,10:1

Hope, Edward (Screenwriter)
Long Gray Line, The 1955,F 11,19:2
Three for the Show 1955,F 25,16:1

Hope, Gloria
Great Love, The 1918,Ag 12,7:1
Tess of the Storm Country 1922,N 13,12:1
Free and Equal 1925,Ap 20,22:1
Twice Blessed 1945,Jl 7,7:5

Hope, Jack (Producer)
Alias Jesse James 1959,My 18,31:2

Hope, Laurence (Composer)
Hers to Hold 1943,Jl 22,15:1

Hope, Maidie
This'll Make You Whistle 1938,N 1,27:2

Hope, Vida
Johnny in the Clouds 1945,N 16,16:2
Nicholas Nickleby 1947,D 1,27:2
While the Sun Shines 1950,Jl 1,9:2
For Them that Trespass 1950,S 27,37:2
Interrupted Journey 1951,My 29,20:2
Woman in Question, The 1952,F 19,24:2
Man in the White Suit, The 1952,Ap 1,35:2
Hundred Hour Hunt 1953,Je 17,32:2
Long Memory, The 1953,Jl 27,15:2
Lease of Life 1956,F 10,18:1

Hopf, Heinz
Loving Couples 1966,S 20,38:1

Hopfer, Konstantin
World Dances 1954,N 8,24:6

Hopkins, Anthony
Lion in Winter, The 1968,O 31,54:1

Hopkins, Arthur (Director)
His Double Life 1933,D 16,12:3

Hopkins, Arthur (Original Author)
Swing High, Swing Low 1937,Ap 15,19:1
When my Baby Smiles at Me 1948,N 24,20:2

Hopkins, Betty (Original Author)
Flight Lieutenant 1942,Jl 31,11:1

Hopkins, Bob
Lucky Stiff, The 1949,Ja 31,14:2
Kid From Left Field, The 1953,S 26,15:3
Autumn Leaves 1956,Ag 2,21:2

Hopkins, George (Screenwriter)
Top of New York, The 1922,Je 19,10:3
Woman With Four Faces, The 1923,Je 18,13:5

Hopkins, Joan
Temptation Harbor 1949,My 11,34:7
Weaker Sex, The 1949,Jl 11,13:2
Man on the Run 1952,F 27,22:5
Double Confession 1953,My 1,17:2

Hopkins, John (Screenwriter)
Thunderball 1965,D 22,23:1

Hopkins, Maurice
This Freedom 1923,N 28,15:1

Hopkins, Miriam
Fast and Loose 1930,D 1,21:1
Smiling Lieutenant, The 1931,My 23,13:4
Twenty-Four Hours 1931,O 3,20:2
Dr Jekyll and Mr Hyde 1932,Ja 2,14:2
Two Kinds of Women 1932,Ja 16,13:1
Dancers in the Dark 1932,Mr 19,11:2
World and the Flesh, The 1932,My 7,11:5
Trouble in Paradise 1932,N 9,28:5
Story of Temple Drake, The 1933,My 6,11:2
Stranger's Return, The 1933,Jl 28,18:2
Design for Living 1933,N 23,24:2
All of Me 1934,F 5,19:2
She Loves Me Not 1934,S 8,18:5
Richest Girl in the World, The 1934,S 21,29:2
Becky Sharp 1935,Je 14,27:2
Barbary Coast 1935,O 14,21:1
Splendor 1935,N 23,23:2
These Three 1936,Mr 19,22:4
Men Are not Gods 1937,Ja 19,28:1
Woman I Love, The 1937,Ap 16,27:2
Woman Chases Man 1937,Je 11,26:2
Wise Girl 1938,Ja 10,13:3
Old Maid, The 1939,Ag 12,16:2
Lady With red Hair 1940,D 6,28:2
Gentleman After Dark, A 1942,Ap 17,21:2
Old Acquaintance 1943,N 3,20:2
Heiress, The 1949,O 7,35:2
Mating Season, The 1951,Ap 12,41:2
Outcasts of Poker Flat 1952,My 16,19:3
Carrie 1952,Jl 17,20:2
Childrens Hour, The 1962,Mr 15,28:2
Fanny Hill 1965,D 2,48:1
Chase, The 1966,F 19,24:1

Hopkins, Robert (Miscellaneous)
Florodora Girl, The 1930,My 31,19:4

Hopkins, Robert (Original Author)
What! No Beer? 1933,F 11,11:3
Chief, The 1933,D 2,9:4
San Francisco 1936,Je 27,21:1
Saratoga 1937,Jl 23,16:3

Hopkins, Robert (Screenwriter)
Saratoga 1937,Jl 23,16:3

Hopkins, Steven G (Producer)
Matter of Morals, A 1961,Je 1,31:1

Hopp, Johnny
Safe at Home 1941,N 26,31:2
Hoppe, Marianne
Heideschulmeister uwe Karsten 1934,Ap 14,18:3
Schimmelreiter, Der; Rider of the White Horse, The 1935,F 25,13:3
Schwarzer Jaeger Johanna 1935,Ap 1,17:2
Judas von Tirol, Der 1935,Ap 27,20:7
Krach um Iolanthe 1935,My 11,21:3
Oberwachtmeister Schwenke 1936,My 5,26:7
Wenn der Hahn Kraeht 1936,N 14,23:3
Ruler, The 1937,O 16,22:3
Liebe auf Umwegen; Love by Indirection 1937,D 18,18:2
Frau Ohne Bedeutung, Ein 1938,Ap 16,17:2
Werf zum Graven Hecht, Die; Gray Pikes Wharf, The 1938,Ap 18,11:2
Liebe im Gleitflug; Love in Stunt Flying 1938,Je 18,18:3
Schritt vom Wege, Der; False Step, The 1939,Ap 29,13:3
Congo Express 1940,My 11,15:3
Secrets of a Soul 1950,S 16,12:6
Ten Little Indians 1966,F 10,33:1
Hopper, Bill
Sitting Bull 1954,N 26,24:4
Hopper, De Wolf
Don Quixote 1915,D 20,11:1
Sunshine Dad 1916,Ap 17,9:3
Puppets 1916,S 11,11:4
Old Maid, The 1939,Ag 12,16:2
Return Of Doctor X, The 1939,N 23,38:5
Fighting 69th, The 1940,Ja 27,9:2
Flight Angels 1940,My 27,23:2
Tear Gas Squad 1940,My 31,15:3
Ladies Must Live 1940,S 6,25:3
Flight From Destiny 1941,Mr 28,26:7
Bullets for O'Hara 1941,Jl 28,16:4
They Died With Their Boots On 1941,N 21,23:3
Lady Gangster 1942,Jl 10,13:2
Hopper, De Wolf Jr
Sunshine Dad 1916,Ap 17,9:3
Hopper, De Wolf Mrs
Virtuous Wives 1918,D 30,7:3
Hopper, Dennis
Rebel without a Cause 1955,O 27,28:3
Giant 1956,O 11,51:1
Gunfight at the O K Corral 1957,My 30,23:2
Story of Mankind, The 1957,N 9,31:2
From Hell to Texas 1958,Je 5,39:2
Key Witness 1960,N 12,15:1
Night Tide 1963,Je 7,37:1
Sons of Katie Elder, The 1965,Ag 26,40:3
Trip, The 1967,Ag 24,43:1
Cool Hand Luke 1967,N 2,58:1
Glory Stompers, The 1968,Mr 28,52:4
Hopper, E Mason (Director)
Edgar and the Teacher's Pet 1920,Mr 28,V,9:1
Edgar's Hamlet 1920,Ap 19,13:3
Dangerous Curve Ahead 1921,O 3,16:2
Glorious Fool, The 1922,Mr 20,10:3
Brothers Under the Skin 1922,N 13,12:1
Hungry Hearts 1922,N 27,18:1
Daddy 1923,Ap 16,20:2
Love Piker, The 1923,Jl 16,14:2
Crowded Hour, The 1925,Ap 27,15:2
Up in Mabel's Room 1926,Je 29,21:2
Getting Gertie's Garter 1927,F 9,17:3
Night Bride, The 1927,Mr 30,22:6
Wise Wife 1927,N 1,21:1 (In Addenda)
Rush Hour, The 1928,Ja 31,29:1
Carnation Kid, The 1929,F 25,16:1
Their own Desire 1930,Ja 25,13:2
Her mad Night 1932,N 15,24:5
Hopper, Frank
Rough Riders, The 1927,Mr 16,28:2
Hopper, Hal (Screenwriter)
Shalako 1968,N 6,32:1
Hopper, Hedda
Man Who Lost Himself, The 1920,My 31,14:2
Heedless Moths 1921,Je 4,14:2
Sherlock Holmes 1922,My 8,14:3
Reno 1924,Ja 8,27:1
Happiness 1924,Mr 11,16:2
Why Men Leave Home 1924,My 12,14:4
Miami 1924,Je 3,22:2
Sinners in Silk 1924,S 8,15:3
Snob, The 1924,D 15,14:1
Declassee 1925,Mr 23,14:2
Zander the Great 1925,My 4,16:2
Dangerous Innocence 1925,Je 8,19:1
Teaser, The 1925,Je 15,10:1
Dance Madness 1926,Ja 25,21:2
Cave Man, The 1926,Mr 1,17:1
Skinner's Dress Suit 1926,My 3,27:1
Don Juan 1926,Ag 7,6:1 (In Addenda)
Matinee Ladies 1927,Ap 13,29:4
Orchids and Ermine 1927,Ap 19,24:4
Children of Divorce 1927,Ap 26,33:3
Venus of Venice 1927,My 3,25:1
Adam and Evil 1927,Ag 10,21:4
Wings 1927,Ag 13,10:4

One Woman to Another 1927,S 19,30:3
Drop Kick, The 1927,S 20,32:2
Whip Woman, The 1928,F 13,16:2
Love and Learn 1928,F 20,14:1
Port of Missing Girls, The 1928,Jl 31,13:4
Harold Teen 1928,Ag 14,15:4
Girls Gone Wild 1929,Ap 22,23:1
Last of Mrs Cheyney, The 1929,Ag 12,22:2
His Glorious Night 1929,O 5,22:5
Such Men Are Dangerous 1930,Mr 8,21:1
Murder Will Out 1930,Ap 14,24:2
High Society Blues 1930,Ap 19,15:1
Holiday 1930,Jl 3,25:4
Let Us Be Gay 1930,Jl 12,16:4
War Nurse 1930,O 24,31:1
Tailor-Made Man, A 1931,Ap 25,23:4
Shipmates 1931,My 23,13:4
Men Call it Love 1931,Je 20,20:4
Prodigal, The 1931,Je 27,20:3
Common Law, The 1931,Jl 20,20:4
Rebound 1931,Ag 29,16:3
Good Sport 1931,D 12,23:3
Flying High 1931,D 12,23:3
Man Who Played God, The 1932,F 11,16:1
Night World 1932,My 28,18:2
As You Desire Me 1932,Je 3,23:4
Skyscraper Souls 1932,Ag 5,11:2
Speak Easily 1932,Ag 19,20:6
Downstairs 1932,O 8,15:4
Men Must Fight 1933,Mr 11,18:3
Barbarian, The 1933,My 13,16:2
Pilgrimage 1933,Jl 13,17:5
Beauty for Sale 1933,S 16,9:3
Bombay Mail 1934,Ja 6,18:2
Little Man, What Now? 1934,Je 1,29:1
Lady Tubbs 1935,Jl 22,20:2
Alice Adams 1935,Ag 16,11:3
Dracula's Daughter 1936,My 18,14:2
Bunker Bean 1936,Je 27,21:2
You Can't Buy Luck 1937,My 14,21:2
Artists and Models 1937,Ag 5,19:2
Topper 1937,Ag 20,21:2
Vogues of 1938 1937,Ag 20,21:1
Tarzan's Revenge 1938,Ja 10,13:3
Dangerous to Know 1938,Mr 11,15:4
Thanks for the Memory 1938,D 8,34:3
Midnight 1939,Ap 6,31:1
Women, The 1939,S 22,27:2
What a Life 1939,O 12,33:1
Queen of the Mob 1940,Jl 1,23:2
Cross Country Romance 1940,Jl 19,22:3
Life With Henry 1941,F 6,25:2
Reap the Wild Wind 1942,Mr 27,27:2
Breakfast in Hollywood 1946,Jl 15,21:1
Sunset Boulevard 1950,Ag 11,15:2
Pepe 1960,D 22,18:1
Oscar, The 1966,Mr 5,16:1
Hopper, Jerry (Director)
Atomic City, The 1952,My 2,21:1
Hurricane Smith 1952,O 4,15:2
Pony Express 1953,Je 6,8:6
Alaska Seas 1954,Mr 6,13:5
Secret of the Incas 1954,My 29,13:3
Naked Alibi 1954,O 2,21:2
Private War of Major Benson, The 1955,Ag 3,27:2
One Desire 1955,S 3,9:1
Square Jungle, The 1955,D 31,17:2
Never Say Goodbye 1956,Ap 14,20:1
Toy Tiger 1956,Je 30,11:2
Blueprint for Robbery 1961,F 2,24:3
Hopper, Victoria
Constant Nymph, The 1934,Ap 7,19:1
Mill On the Floss, The 1939,N 15,19:3
Mozart 1940,O 4,29:2
Laburnum Grove 1941,D 2,29:2
Hopper, William
Footloose Heiress 1937,O 9,16:2
Over the Goal 1937,O 16,22:2
Love Is on the Air 1937,N 12,27:3
Torchy Blane, The Adventurous Blonde 1937,D 18,18:1
Mystery House 1938,Je 29,15:5
Track of the Cat 1954,D 2,38:2
One Desire 1955,S 3,9:1
Rebel without a Cause 1955,O 27,28:3
First Texan, The 1956,Je 23,20:2
Bad Seed, The 1956,S 13,39:6
Hopson, Violet
Widecombe Fair 1929,O 28,20:1
Hopton, Russell
Call of the Flesh 1930,S 13,9:3
Min and Bill 1930,N 24,26:5
College Lovers 1930,N 28,23:1
Remote Control 1930,D 8,26:1
Dance, Fools, Dance 1931,Mr 21,15:1
Miracle Woman, The 1931,Ag 17,18:2
Street Scene 1931,Ag 27,21:2
Reckless Living 1931,D 5,21:2
Arrowsmith 1931,D 8,36:4
Man Who Played God, The 1932,F 11,16:1
Law and Order 1932,F 29,21:3
Famous Ferguson Case, The 1932,Ap 25,18:6

Hopton, Russell — Cont
Night World 1932,My 28,18:2
Radio Patrol 1932,Jl 14,24:2
Tom Brown of Culver 1932,Jl 30,16:5
Once in a Lifetime 1932,O 29,18:4
Air Mail 1932,N 7,20:3
Destination Unknown 1933,Ap 8,16:2
Elmer the Great 1933,My 26,24:2
Little Giant, The 1933,My 27,11:5
Secret of the Blue Room, The 1933,S 13,22:1
I'm no Angel 1933,O 14,18:2
Lady Killer 1934,Ja 1,28:2
Good Dame 1934,Mr 17,11:4
He Was her Man 1934,My 17,28:2
Born to be Bad 1934,My 31,22:6
Men in White 1934,Je 9,18:2
Half a Sinner 1934,Je 23,16:5
Desirable 1934,S 15,20:5
I Sell Anything 1934,D 27,25:2
Wings in the Dark 1935,F 2,10:1
Times Square Lady 1935,Mr 15,25:3
World Accuses, The 1935,Mr 21,27:2
Star of Midnight 1935,Ap 12,26:5
G Men 1935,My 2,17:1
Rose of the Rancho 1936,Ja 9,25:2
Last Outlaw, The 1936,Je 15,24:1
We Who Are About to Die 1937,Ja 2,15:1
Angel's Holiday 1937,My 29,20:2
High, Wide and Handsome 1937,Jl 22,15:1
One Mile From Heaven 1937,Ag 19,23:1
Idol of the Crowd 1937,D 4,21:1
Crime Takes a Holiday 1938,N 28,11:2
Made for Each Other 1939,F 17,17:2
Saint Strikes Back, The 1939,Mr 9,18:2
Mutiny in the Big House 1939,D 11,26:2
Night of Adventure, A 1944,Je 3,10:4
Zombies on Broadway 1945,Ap 27,23:2
Hopwood, Avery (Original Author)
Why Men Leave Home 1924,My 12,14:4
Seven Days 1925,Ag 31,19:3
Best People 1925,O 21,21:3
Bat, The 1926,Mr 15,18:3
Good and Naughty 1926,Je 14,24:1
Nobody's Widow 1927,Ja 13,29:1
Getting Gertie's Garter 1927,F 9,17:3
Gold Diggers of Broadway, The 1929,Ag 31,13:4
Her Wedding Night 1930,S 29,19:1
Fast and Loose 1930,D 1,21:1
Gold Diggers of 1933 1933,Je 8,22:3
Solo per Danne 1939,My 30,13:3
Our Little Wife 1940,Ja 27,9:2
Getting Gertie's Garter 1946,F 4,21:2
Painting the Clouds With Sunshine 1951,S 1,9:6
Bat, The 1959,D 17,51:4
Hopwood, Avery (Screenwriter)
Ladies' Night in a Turkish Bath 1928,Ap 9,18:2
Horace, Johnny
Stormy Weather 1943,Jl 22,15:1
Horalek, Adolf
Song of the Lark 1937,N 15,15:3
Horan, Edward (Original Author)
All the King's Horses 1935,Mr 9,19:1
Horbiger, Attila
Die Grosse Liebe 1932,F 22,23:2
Affairs of Maupassant, The 1938,F 12,20:2
Julika, Die 1939,D 23,9:1
Spiegel des Lebens, Der; Life's Mirror 1940,F 17,9:3
Zigeunerweisen; Gypsy Ways 1940,My 11,15:3
Horbiger, Paul
Verliebte Herzen; Hearts in Love 1939,Je 10,14:2
Mutterliebe; Mother Love 1940,Mr 16,8:3
Walzerlange; Waltz Melodies 1940,Ap 27,9:3
Wiener Geschichten; Vienna Tales 1940,S 28,9:3
Opernball; Opera Ball 1940,O 15,29:2
Story of Vickie, The 1958,Ja 30,19:2
Hordern, Michael
Verger, The 1950,O 11,42:1
Christmas Carol, A 1951,N 29,41:2
Tom Brown's School Days 1952,Ja 8,23:5
Story of Robin Hood, The 1952,Je 27,18:3
Hour of 13, The 1952,O 28,37:1
Promoter, The 1952,O 29,36:2
Both Sides of the Law 1954,Ja 12,19:2
Personal Affair 1954,O 23,13:2
Heart of the Matter, The 1954,N 19,20:2
Beachcomber, The 1955,Ja 17,27:5
Warriors, The 1955,S 10,11:2
Night my Number Came up, The 1955,D 20,39:5
Alexander the Great 1956,Mr 29,23:1
Man Who Never Was, The 1956,Ap 4,24:1
Storm over the Nile 1956,Je 9,14:2
Constant Husband, The 1957,Jl 26,10:3
Spanish Gardner, The 1957,S 21,22:2
Baby and the Battleship, The 1957,O 1,37:2
Windom's Way 1958,O 1,45:1
Sink the Bismarck! 1960,F 12,22:3
Man in the Moon 1961,Je 13,29:2
Cid, El 1961,D 15,49:1
Malaga 1962,F 22,20:3
Cleopatra 1963,Je 13,29:1
V I P's, The 1963,S 20,29:1
Genghis Khan 1965,Je 24,28:2
Spy Who Came in From the Cold, The 1965,D 24,24:1

Hordern, Michael— Cont
Khartoum 1966,Jl 14,28:1
Funny Thing Happened on the Way to the Forum,
A 1966,O 17,48:1
Taming of the Shrew, The 1967,Mr 9,43:1
Jokers, The 1967,My 16,50:1
How I Won the War 1967,N 9,56:1
I'll Never Forget What's 'Isname
1968,Ap 15,51:1
Horens, Dean
Crack-Up 1946,S 7,11:1
Horeschowski, Melanie
Cabaret 1957,N 9,31:2 (Incorrect in this edition;
use 1957,N 7,43:4 elsewhere)
Horgan, P
Thomas Crown Affair, The 1968,Je 27,48:2
Horgan, P (Original Author)
Distant Trumpet, A 1964,My 28,40:1
Horikawa, Hiromichi (Director)
Prodigal Son 1964,Ja 30,24:3 (Incorrect in this
edition; use 1964,Ja 31,16:1 elsewhere)
Naked General, The 1964,D 16,51:2
Blue Beast, The 1965,Ja 30,18:2
Horikoshi, Setsuko
Kimiko 1937,Ap 13,31:3
Horimoto, Masanori
Island, The; Hadaka No Shima 1962,S 11,27:2
Horle, Ken-ichi (Original Author)
Alone on the Pacific 1964,S 24,46:2
Horman, Arthur T (Original Author)
Double Danger 1938,F 10,17:5
When G-Men Step In 1938,Mr 14,13:2
In the Navy 1941,Je 12,29:2
Navy Blues 1941,S 20,11:2
Obliging Young Lady 1942,F 13,24:4
Runaround, The 1946,Je 7,16:3
Undertow 1949,D 16,37:2
Horman, Arthur T (Screenwriter)
You Can't Buy Luck 1937,My 14,21:2
Big Shot, The 1937,Ag 13,13:1
Shadow, The 1937,D 17,33:3
Double Danger 1938,F 10,17:5
Lone Wolf in Paris, The 1938,My 23,21:2
They Asked for It 1939,Je 30,17:4
Missing Evidence 1939,N 17,17:3
You're not so Tough 1940,Jl 9,25:3
Argentine Nights 1940,O 11,25:3
Slightly Tempted 1940,N 1,33:1
Give Us Wings 1940,N 21,43:3
Buck Privates 1941,F 14,15:2
In the Navy 1941,Je 12,29:2
Navy Blues 1941,S 20,11:2
Captains of the Clouds 1942,F 13,24:2
Desperate Journey 1942,S 26,11:2
Bowery to Broadway 1944,N 30,19:2
Suspect, The 1945,F 1,18:5
Here Come the Co-Eds 1945,F 19,21:1
Conflict 1945,Je 16,10:2
Runaround, The 1946,Je 7,16:3
Noose Hangs High, The 1948,My 29,8:6
Undertow 1949,D 16,37:2
Horn, Aloysius (Original Author)
Trader Horn 1931,F 4,21:3
Horn, Camilla
Faust 1926,D 7,21:2
Tempest 1928,My 18,27:3
Eva and the Grasshopper 1928,N 19,16:7
Eternal Love 1929,My 13,27:2
Royal Box, The 1929,D 15,X,8:6
Grosse Sehnsucht, Die 1931,O 8,22:6
Ich Geh' aus und Du Bleibst da 1932,N 21,21:1
Frechdachs, Der 1934,Ja 6,18:3
Geld Regiert die Welt 1934,My 12,12:4
Grosse Chance, Die 1935,My 6,22:4
Ich Sehne Mich Nach Dir 1936,S 9,32:4
Ein Walzer fuer Dich 1936,S 29,35:2
Weisse Sklaven 1937,Jl 31,6:2
Mother Love 1938,My 7,18:2
Rote Orchideen; Red Orchids 1939,Ap 15,15:2
Horn, Dimitri
Windfall in Athens 1956,O 1,31:1
Girl in Black, A 1957,S 17,39:2
Counterfeit Coin 1960,My 16,39:1
We Have Only one Life 1963,Je 24,21:4
Horn, Marilynn
Carmen Jones 1954,O 29,27:2
Horn, Mildred (Screenwriter)
Prince of Peace, The 1951,Mr 24,8:3
Mom and Dad 1957,Ja 31,21:1
Horna, Mario
No Exit 1962,D 6,55:2
Hornbeck, William (Screenwriter)
Men Are not Gods 1937,Ja 19,28:1
Hornblow, Arthur (Original Author)
Isle of Conquest, The 1919,O 27,9:3
Hornblow, Arthur (Producer)
Swing High, Swing Low 1937,Ap 15,19:1
Tropic Holiday 1938,Je 30,21:2
Hornblow, Arthur Jr (Producer)
Limehouse Blues 1934,D 12,28:2
Wings in the Dark 1935,F 2,10:1
Ruggles of Red Gap 1935,Mr 7,26:1
Mississippi 1935,Ap 18,27:2

Princess Comes Across, The 1936,Je 4,27:2
Waikiki Wedding 1937,Mr 25,29:1
Easy Living 1937,Jl 8,20:1
High, Wide and Handsome 1937,Jl 22,15:1
Artists and Models Abroad 1938,D 22,25:3
Midnight 1939,Ap 6,31:1
Man About Town 1939,Je 29,19:1
Cat and the Canary, The 1939,N 23,38:5
Ghost Breakers, The 1940,Jl 4,12:2
Arise my Love 1940,O 17,33:2
I Wanted Wings 1941,Mr 27,29:4
Hold Back the Dawn 1941,O 2,29:1
Nothing but the Truth 1941,O 23,27:1
Major and the Minor, The 1942,S 17,21:3
Heavenly Body, The 1944,Mr 24,17:3
Gaslight 1944,My 5,17:2
Week-End at the Waldorf 1945,O 5,27:2
Hucksters, The 1947,Jl 18,21:2
Desire Me 1947,S 26,28:3
Cass Timberlane 1947,N 7,20:2
Conspirator 1950,Ap 28,26:2
Million Dollar Mermaid 1952,D 5,35:2
Oklahoma! 1955,O 11,49:1
Witness for the Prosecution 1958,F 7,16:1
War Lover, The 1963,Mr 7,8:5
Horne, Andrew
Lord of the Flies 1963,Ag 20,37:1
Horne, David
It's Love Again 1936,My 23,12:1
Seven Sinners 1936,Ag 22,6:1
21 Days Together 1940,My 23,28:4
Wings and the Woman 1942,O 8,31:1
Avengers, The 1942,N 25,18:2
Spitfire 1943,Je 14,13:2
Yellow Canary, The 1944,Ap 14,24:7
They Were Sisters 1946,Jl 24,24:2
Notorious Gentleman 1946,N 14,39:3
Man From Morocco, The 1946,N 25,38:2
Wicked Lady, The 1946,D 23,19:5
Smugglers, The 1948,Mr 29,17:1
Showtime 1948,My 20,35:3
Saraband 1949,Je 13,16:3
Once Upon a Dream 1949,Jl 15,17:2
Madeleine 1950,S 1,17:2
Martin Luther 1953,S 10,22:1
Beau Brummell 1954,O 21,31:5
Three Cases of Murder (Lord Mountdrago); Lord
Mountdrago (Three Cases of Murder)
1955,Mr 16,39:4
Lust for Life 1956,S 18,39:1
Prince and the Showgirl 1957,Je 14,22:2
Safecracker, The 1958,Mr 6,32:1
Sheriff of Fractured Jaw, The 1959,Mr 14,27:4
Devil's Disciple, The 1959,Ag 21,12:1
Goodbye Again 1961,Je 30,32:2
Horne, Geoffrey
Strange One, The 1957,Ap 13,12:3
Bridge on the River Kwai 1957,D 19,39:1
Bonjour Tristesse 1958,Ja 16,32:1
Tempest 1959,Mr 27,19:2
Story of Joseph and his Brethern, The
1962,D 1,17:1
Horne, James (Director)
Hottentot, The 1923,F 19,10:1
Man of Action, A 1923,Je 4,13:3
Yankee Consul, The 1924,F 11,18:3
Kosher Kitty Kelly 1926,S 28,30:2
College 1927,S 12,29:1
Bohemian Girl, The 1936,F 17,21:1
Way out West 1937,My 4,29:1
Horne, Jimmy
Other Love, The 1947,My 15,32:4
Horne, John
Roman Holiday 1953,Ag 28,13:1
Barefoot Contessa, The 1954,S 30,37:1
Horne, Lena
Panama Hattie 1942,O 2,31:2
Cabin in the Sky 1943,My 28,19:3
Stormy Weather 1943,Jl 22,15:1
Thousands Cheer 1943,S 14,27:1
I Dood It 1943,N 11,29:1
Swing Fever 1944,Ja 28,14:1
Broadway Rhythm 1944,Ap 14,24:6
Two Girls and a Sailor 1944,Je 15,16:1
Ziegfeld Follies 1946,Mr 23,8:3
Till the Clouds Roll By 1946,D 6,27:4
Words and Music 1948,D 10,34:2
Duchess of Idaho 1950,Jl 21,15:3
Meet Me in Las Vegas 1956,Mr 14,39:2
Horne, Victoria
Scarlet Claw, The 1944,My 19,12:1
Unseen, The 1945,My 14,20:5
That's the Spirit 1945,Je 2,11:2
Pillow of Death 1946,Ja 26,19:3
In old Sacramento 1946,Ap 29,24:4
To Each his Own 1946,My 24,15:2
She Wrote the Book 1946,Je 20,20:3
Blue Skies 1946,O 17,28:2
Suddenly It's Spring 1947,F 27,26:2
Ghost and Mrs Muir, The 1947,Je 27,17:2
Crimson Key, The 1947,O 18,9:2
Daisy Kenyon 1947,D 25,32:1
Life of Riley, The 1949,Ap 18,18:4

Horne, Victoria— Cont
Mary Ryan, Detective 1949,N 4,33:3
Harvey 1950,D 22,19:1
Affair With a Stranger 1953,Jl 11,8:2
Horner, Harry (Director)
Red Planet Mars 1952,Je 16,15:2
Beware my Lovely 1952,S 13,10:5
Vickie 1953,S 8,26:3
New Faces 1954,F 20,8:7
Life in the Balance, A 1955,Jl 14,19:1
Wild Party, The 1956,D 22,13:1
Horner, Jackie
Smilin' Through 1941,D 5,29:2
Panama Hattie 1942,O 2,31:2
Horner, Penelope
Angry Silence, The 1960,D 13,25:2
Half a Sixpence 1968,F 21,60:3
Horney, Brigitte
Heideschulmeister uwe Karsten 1934,Ap 14,18:3
Mann Will Nach Deutschland, Ein
1934,N 13,22:4
Liebe, Tod und Teufel 1935,My 25,12:2
Katzensteg 1938,Ja 22,19:2
Verklungene Melodie; Dead Melody
1938,Je 25,7:2
Winter Stuerme; Winter Storms 1938,O 1,10:2
Aufruhr in Damaskus; Tumult in Damascus
1939,My 6,21:2
Ziel den Wolken; Goal in the Clouds
1939,My 27,13:3
Gouverneur, Der 1939,S 11,15:2
Befreite Hande; Freed Hans 1940,My 25,20:1
Glass Tower, The; (Glaserne Turm, Der)
1959,Ag 27,24:4
Miracle of the White Stallions 1963,My 23,31:2
Horniman, Roy (Original Author)
Gentleman of Paris, A 1927,O 3,20:1
Bedtime Story, A 1933,Ap 20,20:3
Hornung, E W (Original Author)
Raffles 1930,Jl 25,20:4
Stingaree 1934,My 18,27:1
Raffles 1940,Ja 13,11:2
Hornung, Paul
Devil's Brigade, The 1968,My 23,56:2
HOROWITZ
See HURWITZ
Horrocks, Cyril
As You Like It 1936,N 6,29:3
Horse, Yellow
Romance in the Rain 1934,S 8,18:5
Horsfall, Bernard
Man in the Moon 1961,Je 13,29:2
Guns at Batasi 1964,N 17,47:1
Horsley, David
No More Ladies 1935,Je 22,18:5
Horsley, John
Encore (Winter Cruise); Winter Cruise (Encore)
1952,Ap 3,45:1
Sailor of the King 1953,S 3,15:2
Night People 1954,Mr 13,11:2
Runaway Bus, The 1954,O 25,30:7
Sink the Bismarck! 1960,F 12,22:3
Operation Amsterdam 1960,Jl 7,26:1
Horton, Clara
Girl From Outside, The 1919,N 10,18:2
Everywoman 1919,D 15,20:1
It's a Great Life 1920,Ag 30,12:3
Nineteen and Phyllis 1920,D 27,11:3
Prisoners of Love 1921,Ja 17,9:1
Fortune Hunter, The 1928,Ja 10,28:4
Horton, Edward Everett
Too Much Business 1922,My 1,20:3
Ruggles of Red Gap 1923,S 10,15:4
To the Ladies 1923,N 26,15:6
Man Who Fights Alone, The 1924,Jl 28,12:2
Beggar on Horseback 1925,Je 6,9:2
Marry Me 1925,Jl 13,20:2
Boheme, La 1926,F 25,26:2
Poker Faces 1926,S 14,25:4
Taxi, Taxi 1927,F 15,23:1
Terror, The 1928,Ag 16,25:3
Miss Information 1928,N 18,IX,7:6
Sonny Boy 1929,Mr 9,24:3
Hottentot, The 1929,S 7,15:1
Aviator, The 1930,Ja 11,21:3
Wide Open 1930,Mr 22,22:6
Holiday 1930,Jl 3,25:4
Once a Gentleman 1930,O 4,15:2
Reaching for the Moon 1930,D 30,24:2
Kiss Me Again 1931,Ja 8,21:4
Lonely Wives 1931,Mr 16,25:1
Front Page, The 1931,Mr 20,29:1
Six Cylinder Love 1931,My 16,31:3
Smart Woman 1931,O 12,28:2
Age for Love, The 1931,N 13,27:2
But the Flesh Is Weak 1932,Ap 16,11:2
Roar of the Dragon 1932,Jl 25,11:2
Trouble in Paradise 1932,N 9,28:5
Bedtime Story, A 1933,Ap 20,20:3
Its a Boy 1933,Jl 23,IX,2:2 (In Addenda)
Way to Love, The 1933,N 11,10:3
Way to Love, The 1933,N 20,18:2
Design for Living 1933,N 23,24:2
Alice in Wonderland 1933,D 23,19:1

Horton, Edward Everett— Cont
Easy to Love 1934,Ja 15,12:2
Sing and Like It 1934,Ap 14,18:2
Success at any Price 1934,My 4,24:2
Woman in Command, The 1934,My 29,22:2
It's a Boy 1934,Je 8,18:2
Kiss and Make-Up 1934,Je 29,17:1
Ladies Should Listen 1934,Jl 28,16:6
Merry Widow, The 1934,O 12,33:1
Gay Divorcee, The 1934,N 16,27:1
Night is Young, The 1935,Ja 14,11:2
Biography of a Bachelor Girl 1935,Mr 2,18:2
All the King's Horses 1935,Mr 9,19:1
Devil is a Woman, The 1935,My 4,17:2
In Caliente 1935,Je 27,16:1
Top Hat 1935,Ag 30,12:2
Little Big Shot 1935,O 7,11:2
His Night Out 1935,N 16,19:2
Your Uncle Dudley 1935,D 12,33:4
Singing Kid, The 1936,Ap 4,11:1
Nobody's Fool 1936,Je 4,27:2
Hearts Divided 1936,Je 13,13:1
Lost Horizon 1937,Mr 4,27:1
King and the Chorus Girl, The 1937,Mr 29,14:4
Shall We Dance 1937,My 14,21:1
Oh, Doctor 1937,Je 19,20:3
Great Garrick, The 1937,O 25,23:1
Perfect Specimen, The 1937,O 28,29:2
Angel 1937,N 4,29:1
Danger-Love at Work 1937,D 11,22:2
Hitting a new High 1937,D 27,11:1
Bluebeard's Eighth Wife 1938,Mr 24,21:2
College Swing 1938,Ap 28,27:2
Holiday 1938,Je 24,15:1
Little Tough Guys in Society 1938,N 21,14:4
Paris Honeymoon 1939,Ja 26,17:1
That's Right, You're Wrong 1939,N 30,25:3
You're the One 1941,F 20,23:2
Ziegfeld Girl 1941,Ap 25,17:2
Sunny 1941,Je 13,22:2
Here Comes Mr Jordan 1941,Ag 8,13:2
Week End for Three 1941,O 24,27:4
Body Disappears, The 1942,Ja 31,13:2
Magnificent Dope, The 1942,Jl 3,12:5
I Married an Angel 1942,Jl 10,13:2
Springtime in the Rockies 1942,N 12,30:2
Thank Your Lucky Stars 1943,O 2,19:2
Gang's All Here, The 1943,D 23,26:4
Her Primitive Man 1944,Ap 1,11:1
Arsenic and old Lace 1944,S 2,17:2
Summer Storm 1944,O 23,14:3
San Diego, I Love You 1944,N 10,25:1
Brazil 1944,N 20,25:2
Lady on a Train 1945,S 15,21:2
Cinderella Jones 1946,Mr 16,9:6
Earl Carroll Sketchbook 1946,Ag 30,13:2
Down to Earth 1947,S 12,18:2
Her Husband's Affairs 1947,N 14,29:2
Story of Mankind, The 1957,N 9,31:2
Pocketful of Miracles 1961,D 19,39:1
It's a Mad, Mad, Mad, Mad World
  1963,N 19,47:1
Sex and the Single Girl 1964,D 26,9:2
Perils of Pauline, The 1967,Ag 3,26:3
Horton, Harold H (Cinematographer)
Bali, the Unknown; (Ape Man Island)
  1921,F 28,16:2
Horton, Helen
Village, The 1953,S 23,37:2
Horton, Louisa
All my Sons 1948,Mr 29,17:3
Walk East on Beacon 1952,My 29,17:2
Horton, Robert
Blarney Kiss, The 1933,Ag 19,14:4
When Knights Were Bold 1942,Mr 31,29:2
Tanks are Coming, The 1951,D 6,42:4
Return of the Texan 1952,F 14,23:1
Pony Soldier 1952,D 20,15:2
Bright Road 1953,Ap 29,33:5
Arena 1953,Jl 23,20:2
Men of the Fighting Lady 1954,My 8,15:2
Prisoner of War 1954,My 10,20:2
Horton, Russell
Teen Age 1944,Je 19,17:1
Horton, Walter
Fighting Blade, The 1923,O 15,15:4
Horvath, Charles
Strange Door, The 1951,D 10,34:6
His Majesty O'Keefe 1954,F 6,17:2
Vera Cruz 1954,D 27,22:4
Francis in the Haunted House 1956,Jl 21,9:2
Pillars of the Sky 1956,O 13,15:2
Horvath, Laci
It Happened in Europe 1949,O 4,32:4
Horvath, Teri
Goose Boy, The 1951,O 13,9:2
Horwin, Jerry (Miscellaneous)
Gold Diggers in Paris 1938,Je 2,19:2
Horwin, Jerry (Original Author)
Sport Parade, The 1932,D 17,22:3
Rose of Washington Square 1939,My 6,21:2
Sun Never Sets, The 1939,Je 9,26:2
Stormy Weather 1943,Jl 22,15:1

Horwin, Jerry (Screenwriter)
Two Against the World 1932,Ag 19,20:6
Horwitz, Howie (Producer)
Appointment With a Shadow 1959,Ja 8,24:2
Horwitz, Kurt
Was Frauen Traeumen; What Women Dream
  1933,Jl 2,IX,2:2
Fuerst Sepp'l 1937,Jl 17,18:1
Hosford, Maud
Mrs Wiggs of the Cabbage Patch 1919,F 17,11:3
Hoshelle, Marjorie
Make Your own Bed 1944,My 27,12:2
Mask of Dimitrios, The 1944,Je 24,16:2
Black Market Babies 1946,Ap 1,23:1
One More Tomorrow 1946,My 25,12:2
Cloak and Dagger 1946,O 5,13:2
Riding High 1950,Ap 11,26:2
Dangerous Crossing 1953,S 30,37:2
Hoshi, Hikaru
Fires on the Plain 1963,S 25,39:1
Hoshi, Yuriko
Gozdilla vs the Thing 1964,N 26,52:2
Ghidrah, The Three-Headed Monster
  1965,D 16,63:3
Rabble, The 1968,Mr 29,31:1
Whirlwind 1968,Jl 27,15:1
Hoskins, Basil
Millionairess, The 1961,F 10,19:1
Hosokawa, Chikako
Kimiko 1937,Ap 13,31:3
Hosokawa, Shoji (Miscellaneous)
New Japanese Cinema, The (Won't You Have
  Some Milk); Won't You Have Some Milk (The
  New Japanese Cinema) 1968,My 3,42:1
Hosoya, Tatsuo (Producer)
Harakiri 1964,Ag 5,24:2
Hossein, Robert
Rififi 1956,Je 6,37:1
Crime and Punishment 1958,S 16,23:2
Young Girls Beware 1959,Ag 22,8:2
Nude in a White Car 1960,O 27,47:2
Riff Raff Girls 1962,O 20,13:5
Paris Pick-Up 1963,Ag 29,36:2
Love on a Pillow 1963,D 17,49:1
Vice and Virtue 1965,Mr 18,25:1
Enough Rope 1966,Jl 15,34:3
Marco the Magnificent 1966,D 15,60:1
Hossein, Robert (Director)
Nude in a White Car 1960,O 27,47:2
Hossein, Robert (Screenwriter)
Nude in a White Car 1960,O 27,47:2
Host, Per (Director)
Last of the Nomads 1958,S 29,32:6
Host, Per (Producer)
Last of the Nomads 1958,S 29,32:6
Hoster, Anita
Situation Hopeless-But not Serious
  1965,O 14,53:1
Hostetler, Paul
Panic in the Streets 1950,Ag 5,9:2
Hotchner, A E (Screenwriter)
Hemingway's Adventures of a Young Man
  1962,Jl 26,17:1
Hotivari, L (Screenwriter)
Dragonfly, The 1955,Je 27,18:2
Hotton, Lucille
Any Woman 1925,My 27,26:2
Houcke, Gilbert
Artists Under the Big Top Perplexed
  1968,S 27,34:1
Houdini, Harry
Days of Thrills and Laughter 1961,Mr 22,37:1
Hough, Donald (Original Author)
Prairie Chickens 1943,Jl 9,21:6
Calaboose 1943,Jl 30,19:2
Hough, E Morton (Screenwriter)
Women's Wares 1927,N 15,27:1
Hough, Emerson (Original Author)
Man Next Door, The 1923,My 29,10:3
North of 36 1924,D 8,13:3
Conquering Horde, The 1931,Mr 30,25:2
Texans, The 1938,Jl 28,23:2
Hough, Paul
In Cold Blood 1967,D 15,60:1
Hough, R L (Director)
Silent Witness, The 1932,F 8,21:1
Hough, Stanley L (Original Author)
Bandolero 1968,Jl 18,26:2
Houghton, Katharine
Guess Who's Coming to Dinner 1967,D 12,56:1
Houidini, Harry
Grim Game, The 1919,Ag 26,11:3
Man From Beyond, The 1922,Ap 4,15:3
Houidini, Harry (Screenwriter)
Man From Beyond, The 1922,Ap 4,15:3
Houk, Ralph
Safe at Home 1962,Ap 14,14:1
Hould, Ra
Beloved Enemy 1936,D 26,15:2
Doctor's Diary, A 1937,F 17,16:4
Boots and Saddles 1937,N 8,19:2

Houlihan, James
Hide and Seek 1964,Mr 12,40:3
House, Allan (Screenwriter)
Meanest Man in the World, The 1943,F 25,27:3
House, Billy
God's Gift to Women 1931,Ap 18,17:3
Smart Money 1931,Je 19,21:1
Merry-Go-Round of 1938 1937,N 26,27:2
Bedlam 1946,Ap 20,16:4
Stranger, The 1946,Jl 11,18:2
Trail Street 1947,Ap 10,35:2
Egg and I, The 1947,Ap 25,29:2
Where Danger Lives 1951,Ja 1,13:6
Santa Fe 1951,My 4,31:2
People Will Talk 1951,Ag 30,20:1
House, Eric
Oedipus Rex 1957,Ja 8,26:1
House, Jimmie
White Eagle 1932,S 24,18:4
House, Newton
Spirit of the U S A, The 1924,My 21,22:3
House, Son
Festival 1967,O 24,53:2
House, William
Reckless Hour, The 1931,Ag 1,16:4
Expensive Women 1931,N 14,15:3
Household, Geoffrey (Original Author)
Man Hunt 1941,Je 14,20:2
Brandy for the Parson 1952,Ag 18,13:4
Household, Geoffrey (Screenwriter)
Brandy for the Parson 1952,Ag 18,13:4
Houseman, John
Seven Days in May 1964,F 20,22:1
Houseman, John (Producer)
Miss Susie Slagle's 1946,F 7,29:2
Blue Dahlia, The 1946,My 9,27:3
Letters From an Unknown Woman
  1948,Ap 29,20:6
They Live by Night 1949,N 4,33:2
Company She Keeps, The 1951,Ja 29,14:4
On Dangerous Ground 1952,F 13,35:2
Holiday for Sinners 1952,S 20,13:2
Bad and the Beautiful, The 1953,Ja 16,19:1
Julius Caesar 1953,Je 5,19:1
Executive Suite 1954,My 7,19:1
Her Twelve Men 1954,Ag 12,23:2
Moonfleet 1955,Je 25,9:2
Cobweb, The 1955,Ag 6,13:3
Lust for Life 1956,S 18,39:1
All Fall Down 1962,Ap 12,41:3
Two Weeks in Another Town 1962,Ag 18,10:1
In the Cool of the Day 1963,My 30,20:1
This Property is Condemned 1966,Ag 4,24:1
Houseman, John (Screenwriter)
Jane Eyre 1944,F 4,12:5
Houser, Lionel (Original Author)
Condemned Woman 1938,Ap 22,15:5
Sky Giant 1938,Jl 20,22:2
They Made Her a Spy 1939,Mr 29,21:4
Houser, Lionel (Producer)
Cargo to Capetown 1950,Mr 31,36:3
Houser, Lionel (Screenwriter)
Grand Exit 1935,N 4,24:5
Lone Wolf Returns, The 1936,F 4,25:5
Devil's Squadron 1936,My 11,16:2
I Promise to Pay 1937,Ap 26,15:2
Border Cafe 1937,Je 8,30:2
Love Takes Flight 1937,S 27,24:3
Condemned Woman 1938,Ap 22,15:5
Blind Alibi 1938,My 20,17:2
Sky Giant 1938,Jl 20,22:2
Smashing the Rackets 1938,Ag 9,22:5
Tell no Tales 1939,Je 2,27:3
Girl From Mexico, The 1939,Je 8,31:4
Forgotten Woman, The 1939,Ag 4,11:2
First Love 1939,N 9,27:3
Sabotage 1939,N 16,29:5
Dark Command 1940,My 11,15:2
Third Finger, Left Hand 1940,D 12,37:2
Design for Scandal 1942,F 6,23:3
Yank at Eton, A 1942,O 16,23:1
Three Hearts for Julia 1943,My 21,22:4
Christmas in Connecticut 1945,Jl 28,7:2
Courage of Lassie 1946,Jl 25,18:5
Adventure in Baltimore 1949,Ap 29,27:2
Cargo to Capetown 1950,Mr 31,36:3
Secret Fury, The 1950,Je 22,34:2
Houser, Mervin (Original Author)
Rhythm on the Range 1936,Jl 30,22:1
Pardners 1956,Jl 26,20:2
Houser, Mervin (Screenwriter)
Love Takes Flight 1937,S 27,24:3
HOUSMAN
See Also HAUSMAN
Housman, Arthur
Under the Red Robe 1923,N 13,25:3
Nellie, the Beautiful Cloak Model
  1924,Ap 14,14:1
Manhandled 1924,Jl 29,9:2
Man Must Live, A 1925,Ja 29,12:2
Coast of Folly, The 1925,Ag 31,19:3
Bat, The 1926,Mr 15,18:3
Bertha, The Sewing Machine Girl 1927,Ja 4,21:1

Housman, Arthur— Cont
Rough House Rosie 1927,My 23,27:2
Sunrise 1927,S 24,15:3 (In Addenda)
Spotlight, The 1927,N 28,18:5
Publicity Madness 1927,D 12,30:6
Partners in Crime 1928,Ap 30,18:3
Fools for Luck 1928,Je 12,33:5
Singing Fool, The 1928,S 20,33:2
Sins of the Fathers 1929,Ja 28,21:1
Queen of the Night Clubs 1929,Mr 18,30:6
Broadway 1929,My 28,36:2
Side Street 1929,S 9,30:2
Fast Company 1929,O 5,22:5
Song of Love, The 1929,N 14,24:3
Officer O'Brien 1930,F 24,18:1
Squealer, The 1930,S 8,17:1
Girl of the Golden West, The 1930,O 27,17:1
Five and Ten 1931,Jl 11,7:6
No More Orchids 1933,Ja 2,29:2
She Done Him Wrong 1933,F 10,12:3
Way to Love, The 1933,N 11,10:3
Mrs Wiggs of the Cabbage Patch 1934,O 29,14:2
Here is my Heart 1934,D 22,21:1
Our Relations 1936,N 11,55:1
Step Lively, Jeeves 1937,Ap 2,19:6
Houston, Branch (Original Author)
Safe in Hell 1931,D 19,16:4
Houston, Charles
Man Upstairs, The 1959,Ag 11,23:2
Houston, Donald
Blue Lagoon, The 1949,O 3,13:2
Run for Your Money, A 1950,Ap 10,15:3
Paratrooper 1953,D 31,9:3
Doctor in the House 1955,F 19,18:3
Battle Hell 1957,Ag 22,23:1
Room at the Top 1959,Mr 31,26:1
Man Upstairs, The 1959,Ag 11,23:2
Breakout 1960,My 19,44:3
Question of Adultery, A 1961,Jl 6,18:2
Mark, The 1961,O 3,46:2
300 Spartans, The 1962,S 20,29:2
Maniac 1963,O 31,26:3
633 Squadron 1964,Je 25,25:1
Doctor in Distress 1964,Jl 8,38:2
Study in Terror, A 1966,N 3,45:3
Houston, George
Melody Lingers on, The 1935,N 7,27:1
Let's Sing Again 1936,My 9,11:2
Conquest 1937,N 5,19:1
Blockade 1938,Je 17,25:1
Great Waltz, The 1938,N 25,19:1
Howards of Virginia, The 1940,S 27,27:1
Houston, Glyn
Verger, The 1950,O 11,42:1
Turn the Key Softly 1954,F 4,21:6
Houston, John (Director)
We Were Strangers 1949,Ap 28,28:2
Houston, Josephine
On With the Show 1929,My 29,28:6
Houston, Julian (Miscellaneous)
Strangers on a Honeymoon 1937,Mr 13,23:2
Houston, Norman
Make a Million 1935,N 9,19:3
Houston, Norman (Original Author)
Man Bait 1927,Ja 19,21:1
Broadway Nights 1927,Je 28,29:4
High Tension 1936,Jl 11,11:4
Battle of Broadway 1938,Ap 25,19:2
Woman of the Town, The 1944,Mr 6,17:2
Houston, Norman (Screenwriter)
Great God Gold 1935,My 6,22:3
Hopalong Rides Again 1938,Ja 22,19:1
Heart of Arizona 1938,Ap 16,17:1
Cherokee Strip 1940,N 4,23:2
West of the Pecos 1945,Ag 11,14:6
Wanderer of the Wasteland 1945,S 29,12:2
Game of Death, A 1945,N 24,22:4
Trail Street 1947,Ap 10,35:2
Houston, Renee
Girl Must Live, A 1942,Mr 24,25:2
Belles of St Trinian's, The 1954,D 23,13:4
Time Without Pity 1957,N 23,11:2
Town Like Alice, A 1958,S 22,27:1
Horse's Mouth, The 1958,N 12,41:1
Three on a Spree 1961,Ag 31,22:3
Cul de Sac 1966,N 8,44:2
Houston, Warren
Dark Odyssey 1961,Je 26,22:2
Hoven, Adrian
White Hell of Pitz Palu, The 1953,N 14,14:2
Story of Vickie, The 1958,Ja 30,19:2
Deadly Decision 1958,Ap 29,26:2
I Aim at the Stars 1960,O 20,42:2
Foxhole in Cairo 1961,F 16,25:2
Hovey, Ann
Wild Boys of the Road 1933,S 22,14:1
Annapolis Salute 1937,O 2,18:1
Danger Patrol 1937,N 19,27:3
Hovey, Tamara (Original Author)
Bagdad 1949,D 24,11:4
Hovey, Tamara (Screenwriter)
That Midnight Kiss 1949,S 23,28:2
Tamango 1959,S 17,48:4

Hovey, Tim
Private War of Major Benson, The
 1955,Ag 3,27:2
Queen Bee 1955,N 23,18:2
Toy Tiger 1956,Je 30,11:2
Man Afraid 1957,Ap 5,24:2
Hovick, Louise
You Can't Have Everything 1937,Ag 4,15:2
Ali Baba Goes to Town 1937,O 23,14:1
Sally, Irene and Mary 1938,F 26,9:2
Battle of Broadway 1938,Ap 25,19:2
My Lucky Star 1938,S 10,20:2
Hovick, Louise (Original Author)
Doll Face 1946,Mr 28,35:3
Howal, Clark
Hitch-Hiker, The 1953,Ap 30,39:3
Howard, Al
Spirit of Notre Dame, The 1931,O 16,27:1
Howard, Ann
Royal Ballet, The (Swan Lake Act II); Swan Lake
 Act II (The Royal Ballet) 1960,O 5,45:2
Howard, Anne
Princess O'Hara 1935,Ap 13,11:3
Little Men 1940,D 9,23:2
Howard, Arthur
Lady is Willing, The 1934,Ag 11,16:5
Dulcimer Street 1948,N 8,24:2
One Woman's Story 1949,My 18,33:2
Happiest Days of Your Life, The 1950,S 18,19:2
Intruder, The 1955,Ja 26,22:1
Joy House 1965,F 18,29:1
Howard, Arthur (Narrator)
Flute and the Arrow, The 1960,O 11,55:1
Howard, Billy
No Room at the Inn 1949,D 26,33:4
Howard, Boothe
Hot Pepper 1933,Ja 23,9:2
Avenger, The 1933,O 3,28:3
My Woman 1933,O 16,20:3
Midnight Alibi 1934,Jl 4,18:3
Every Night at Eight 1935,Ag 3,16:2
Mary Burns, Fugitive 1935,N 16,19:2
Show Them no Mercy 1935,D 9,25:2
Robin Hood of El Dorado, The 1936,Mr 14,10:1
Charlie Chan at the Circus 1936,Mr 19,22:4
Howard, Bruce (Screenwriter)
King Kong vs. Godzilla 1963,Je 27,23:4
Howard, Cal (Screenwriter)
Gulliver's Travels 1939,D 21,29:1
Mr Bug Goes to Town 1942,F 20,21:3
Howard, Charles
Night Angel, The 1931,Je 11,28:4
Howard, Christopher
Ladybug, Ladybug 1963,D 24,9:1
Howard, Clint
Gentle Giant 1968,Ap 20,26:1
Howard, Constance
Hold That Lion 1926,S 6,16:2
White Black Sheep, The 1926,D 21,20:2
Night Bride, The 1927,Mr 30,22:6
Smart Set, The 1928,Mr 5,21:1
Mother Machree 1928,Mr 6,20:3
Howard, Cy (Original Author)
My Friend Irma 1949,S 29,39:2
My Friend Irma Goes West 1950,Ag 3,20:2
That's My Boy 1951,Ag 2,18:1
Howard, Cy (Screenwriter)
My Friend Irma 1949,S 29,39:2
My Friend Irma Goes West 1950,Ag 3,20:2
That's My Boy 1951,Ag 2,18:1
Marriage on the Rocks 1965,S 16,00:0
Howard, David (Director)
Rainbow Trail, The 1932,Ja 30,13:2
Mystery Ranch 1932,Je 30,26:2
Quando el Amor Rie 1933,O 17,26:3
Lost Jungle, The 1934,Je 8,18:1
Crimson Romance 1934,O 13,10:1
Marines are Coming, The 1935,F 23,14:7
Hard Rock Harrigan 1935,Jl 30,16:2
Thunder Mountain 1935,O 2,27:2
Whispering Smith Speaks 1936,F 17,21:1
O'Malley of the Mounted 1936,Ap 6,18:1
Border Patrolman 1936,Je 29,11:2
Mine With the Iron Door, The 1936,Jl 11,11:3
Daniel Boone 1936,O 24,23:2
Conflict 1937,Ja 18,21:2
Stadium Murders, The 1938,Ap 9,11:2
Gun Law 1938,Je 24,15:1
Painted Desert 1938,S 14,26:5
Renegade Ranger, The 1939,F 17,17:3
Howard, Duke
Murderers' Row 1966,D 22,40:3
Howard, Elden (Screenwriter)
Telltale Heart, The 1963,My 16,42:1
Howard, Esther
Vice Squad, The 1931,Je 6,15:5
Ladies of the Big House 1932,Ja 1,31:1
Cohens and Kellys in Hollywood, The
 1932,Ag 22,23:2
Merrily We Go to Hell 1932,Je 11,9:3
Winner Take All 1932,Je 18,9:2
Rackety Rax 1932,N 5,12:5
Second Hand Wife 1933,Ja 14,8:4

Howard, Esther— Cont
Iron Master, The 1933,F 4,11:3
Below the Sea 1933,Je 3,16:4
Klondike Annie 1936,Mr 12,18:2
M'liss 1936,Ag 8,5:2
Scandal Street 1938,F 5,19:2 (In Addenda)
Great McGinty, The 1940,Ag 15,23:1
Sullivan's Travels 1942,Ja 29,25:2
Palm Beach Story, The 1942,D 11,33:1
Miracle of Morgan's Creek, The 1944,Ja 20,15:2
Hail the Conquering Hero 1944,Ag 10,14:2
Big Noise, The 1944,S 23,16:1
Great Flamario, The 1945,Ja 15,15:5
Murder, my Sweet 1945,Mr 9,16:2
Falcon's Alibi, The 1946,Ap 13,23:2
Dick Tracy vs Cueball 1946,N 23,12:2
Born to Kill 1947,My 1,34:2
Beautiful Blonde From Bashful Bend, The
 1949,My 28,11:2
Hellfire 1949,My 30,9:4
Howard, Eugene
Vitaphone 1926,O 8,23:2
Howard, Frances
Swan, The 1925,Mr 2,14:1
Too Many Kisses 1925,Mr 3,20:1
Shock Punch, The 1925,My 11,14:3
Howard, Frankie
Runaway Bus, The 1954,O 25,30:7
Ladykillers 1956,F 21,37:2
Alligator Named Daisy, An 1957,O 7,23:2
Howard, Fred
Numbered Men 1930,Je 9,23:3
Front Page, The 1931,Mr 20,29:1
Two Seconds 1932,My 19,25:3
Rain 1932,O 13,22:3
Richest Girl in the World, The 1934,S 21,29:2
Howard, George Bronson (Original Author)
Come Through 1917,Je 18,7:2
Howard, George Bronson (Screenwriter)
Spy, The 1917,Ag 28,7:6
Howard, George W
I Want my Man 1925,Ap 6,17:3
Howard, Gertrude
Easy Pickings 1927,Mr 25,25:3
On Your Toes 1928,Ja 9,20:1
Synthetic Sin 1929,Ja 7,36:2
Hearts in Dixie 1929,F 28,30:3
His Captive Woman 1929,Ap 3,26:4
Show Boat 1929,Ap 18,32:3
Father's Son 1931,F 21,15:2
Prodigal, The 1931,Je 27,20:3
Strangers in Love 1932,Mr 5,11:2
Wet Parade, The 1932,Ap 22,23:2
I'm no Angel 1933,O 14,18:2
Peck's bad Boy 1934,O 6,20:1
Howard, Hartley (Original Author)
Assignment K 1968,Jl 20,18:2
Howard, Helen
Brass Buttons 1919,Ap 7,11:5
Captain Blood 1924,S 9,19:1
Howard, Henry
Brig, The 1964,S 21,37:4
Howard, Jack
Loves of Ricardo, The 1926,Ag 16,10:1
Blue Grass of Kentucky 1950,Ja 27,29:2
Howard, Jane
Gun for a Coward 1957,Ja 31,21:1
Howard, Jean
Broadway to Hollywood 1933,S 2,14:4
Prizefighter and the Lady, The 1933,N 11,11:3
Break of Hearts 1935,My 17,24:3
We're on the Jury 1937,F 10,18:5
Claudia 1943,N 5,23:2
Bermuda Mystery 1944,My 13,17:1
Howard, Jeff
Up the Down Staircase 1967,Ag 18,36:2
Howard, Jennifer
Return to Peyton Place 1961,My 6,26:1
All Fall Down 1962,Ap 12,41:3
Chapman Report, The 1962,O 18,49:2
Howard, Jerry
Rockin' in The Rockies 1945,Jl 5,7:2
Howard, Joan
Swing Your Lady 1938,Ja 27,17:2
Woman Doctor 1939,Mr 24,27:3
Howard, John
Annapolis Farewell 1935,Ag 24,18:2
Millions in the Air 1935,D 12,33:4
Soak the Rich 1936,F 5,14:2
13 Hours by Air 1936,Ap 30,17:2
Border Flight 1936,Je 22,22:1
Valiant Is the Word for Carrie 1936,O 8,27:2
Lost Horizon 1937,Mr 4,27:1
Let Them Live 1937,Je 8,30:3
Mountain Music 1937,Je 24,30:3
Bulldog Drummond Comes Back 1937,S 4,8:3
Hold 'Em Navy 1937,N 6,14:2
Bulldog Drummond's Revenge 1937,D 17,33:2
Hitting a new High 1937,D 27,11:1
Penitentiary 1938,Mr 7,13:2
Bulldog Drummond's Peril 1938,Mr 18,23:2
Prison Farm 1938,Jl 15,13:3
Bulldog Drummond in Africa 1938,Ag 25,15:1
Touchdown Army 1938,O 28,27:2

Howard, John— Cont
Arrest Bulldog Drummond 1939,Ja 12,23:2
Bulldog Drummond's Secret Police
1939,Mr 30,19:3
Grand Jury Secrets 1939,Je 29,19:2
Bulldog Drummond's Bride 1939,Jl 13,17:2
What a Life 1939,O 12,33:1
Disputed Passage 1939,O 26,27:2
Green Hell 1940,Ja 30,15:6
Man From Dakota, The 1940,F 22,29:2
Philadelphia Story, The 1940,D 27,22:2
Invisible Woman, The 1941,Ja 9,27:2
Texas Rangers Ride Again 1941,Ja 9,27:4
Mad Doctor, The 1941,F 27,23:4
Tight Shoes 1941,Je 19,25:2
Father takes a Wife 1941,S 5,19:3
Overlanders, The 1946,D 20,31:2
Love From a Stranger 1947,N 28,30:1
They Are not Angels 1948,My 22,8:3
I, Jane Doe 1948,Jl 5,8:4
Fighting Kentuckian, The 1949,S 19,18:3
Models, Inc 1952,My 26,18:4
Make Haste to Live 1954,Mr 26,16:2
High and the Mighty, The 1954,Jl 1,21:2
Howard, Joyce
Voice in the Night, The 1941,My 23,25:4
Love on the Dole 1945,O 13,11:2
Mrs Fitzherbert 1950,My 11,37:2
Appointment With Crime 1951,F 19,19:3
Howard, Kathleen
Death Takes a Holiday 1934,F 24,18:4
You're Telling Me 1934,Ap 7,19:1
One More River 1934,Ag 10,21:1
It's a Gift 1935,Ja 5,20:2
Stolen Holiday 1937,F 1,15:3
First Love 1939,N 9,27:3
Young People 1940,Ag 24,16:2
Mystery Sea Raider 1940,Ag 26,11:4
Girl, a Guy and a Gob, A 1941,Ap 24,25:3
Blossoms in the Dust 1941,Je 27,14:4
Ball of Fire 1942,Ja 16,25:2
You Were Never Lovelier 1942,D 4,31:1
Crash Dive 1943,Ap 29,25:2
My Kingdom for a Cook 1943,O 15,15:3
Laura 1944,O 12,24:1
Shady Lady 1945,O 11,26:2
Snafu 1945,D 26,15:2
Centennial Summer 1946,Jl 18,20:2
Late George Apley, The 1947,Mr 21,29:2
Cynthia 1947,S 19,27:2
Bride Goes Wild, The 1948,Je 4,27:2
Cry of the City 1948,S 30,32:4
Petty Girl, The 1950,Ag 18,17:2
Born to be Bad 1950,S 29,31:5
Howard, Langley
Talk of the Devil 1937,My 15,23:5
Howard, Leigh (Original Author)
Chance Meeting 1960,O 27,45:2
Howard, Leslie
Outward Bound 1930,S 18,28:3
Free Soul, A 1931,Je 3,29:2
Never the Twain Shall Meet 1931,Je 6,15:5
Five and Ten 1931,Jl 11,7:6
Devotion 1931,O 3,20:2
Reserved for Ladies 1932,My 21,9:2
Smilin' Through 1932,O 15,13:1
Animal Kingdom, The 1932,D 30,14:2
Secrets 1933,Mr 16,21:2
Captured 1933,Ag 18,18:3
Berkeley Square 1933,S 14,26:2
Of Human Bondage 1934,Je 29,17:1
Lady is Willing, The 1934,Ag 11,16:5
British Agent 1934,S 20,20:1
Scarlet Pimpernel, The 1935,F 8,27:2
Petrified Forest, The 1936,F 7,14:2
Romeo and Juliet 1936,Ag 21,12:2
It's Love I'm After 1937,N 11,31:2
Stand-In 1937,N 19,27:2
Pygmalion 1938,D 8,34:2
Intermezzo, A Love Story 1939,O 6,31:1
Gone With the Wind 1939,D 20,31:2
Mister V 1942,F 13,24:4
Invaders, The 1942,Mr 6,17:1
Spitfire 1943,Je 14,13:2
Of Human Bondage 1965,S 15,41:1
Howard, Leslie (Director)
Pygmalion 1938,D 8,34:2
Mister V 1942,F 13,24:4
Spitfire 1943,Je 14,13:2
Howard, Leslie (Producer)
Mister V 1942,F 13,24:4
Spitfire 1943,Je 14,13:2
Howard, Lewis
First Love 1939,N 9,27:3
It's a Date 1940,Mr 23,16:2
San Francisco Docks 1940,D 26,23:3
Meet the Chump 1941,F 27,23:4
Horror Island 1941,Mr 31,11:3
Hellzapoppin 1941,D 26,21:4
Seven Sweethearts 1942,N 13,28:1
Up Goes Maisie 1946,Ja 25,26:7
I've Always Loved You 1946,S 7,11:1
Song of my Heart 1948,Mr 5,17:3
In a Lonely Place 1950,My 18,37:2

Howard, Lisa
Man Who Cheated Himself, The 1951,F 9,21:2
Donovan's Brain 1954,Ja 21,28:2
Howard, Mary
My Weakness 1933,S 22,14:1
Fast Company 1938,Jl 6,21:2
Love Finds Andy Hardy 1938,Jl 22,10:2
Four Girls in White 1939,F 23,19:3
Nurse Edith Cavell 1939,S 22,27:4
Abe Lincoln in Illinois 1940,F 23,19:2
Billy the Kid 1941,Je 20,28:2
Swamp Water 1941,N 17,15:2
Who Is Hope Schuyler 1942,My 22,27:1
Loves of Edgar Allan Poe, The 1942,S 21,19:2
Howard, Mary (Original Author)
Spirit of West Point 1947,O 3,31:2
Howard, Meredith
Kentucky 1938,D 24,12:1
Howard, Michael
Adventures, The 1947,Ap 4,19:2
It Always Rains on Sunday 1949,F 14,15:5
Front Page Story 1955,Ap 19,28:1
Howard, Moe
Rockin' in The Rockies 1945,Jl 5,7:2
Howard, Noel (Director)
Marco the Magnificent 1966,D 15,60:1
Howard, Norah
Condemned to Death 1932,Jl 14,24:2
Saint in London, The 1939,Jl 19,23:3
Two Loves 1961,Je 22,23:2
Howard, Olin
Beresford and the Baboons 1919,F 17,11:3
Case of the Velvet Claws, The 1936,Ag 29,16:3
Comin' Round the Mountain 1940,S 26,27:3
Howard, Peter (Original Author)
Voice of the Hurricane 1964,Je 3,36:4
Howard, Ray
Sally, Irene and Mary 1925,D 7,19:1
Howard, Richard
Vanishing American, The 1925,O 16,18:2
Desert Gold 1926,Mr 23,24:5
Howard, Ronald
My Brother Jonathan 1949,Je 29,34:4
Queen of Spades, The 1949,Jl 1,14:4
Bond Street 1950,Mr 30,40:6
While the Sun Shines 1950,Jl 1,9:2
Browning Version, The 1951,O 30,33:2
Portrait of Clare 1951,D 26,19:6
Double Confession 1953,My 1,17:2
Both Sides of the Law 1954,Ja 12,19:2
Gideon of Scotland Yard 1959,My 20,38:2
Babette Goes to War 1960,Je 8,46:1
Naked Edge 1961,Jl 1,9:1
Come September 1961,S 8,34:1
Murder She Said 1962,Ja 8,27:2
Weekend at Dunkirk 1966,My 19,51:2
Africa-Texas Style! 1967,Jl 13,30:2
Howard, Ronny
Music Man, The 1962,Ag 24,14:1
Courtship of Eddie's Father, The 1963,Mr 7,8:5
(Incorrect in this edition; use 1963,Mr 28,8:5
elsewhere)
Howard, Sandy (Producer)
Jack of Diamonds 1967,N 11,26:3
Howard, Sandy (Screenwriter)
Jack of Diamonds 1967,N 11,26:3
Howard, Shemp
Headin' East 1938,Ja 15,19:2
Hollywood Round-Up 1938,Mr 5,11:2
Millionaires in Prison 1940,Jl 16,21:3
Give Us Wings 1940,N 21,43:3
Bank Dick, The 1940,D 13,29:2
Buck Privates 1941,F 14,15:2
Six Lessons From Madame La Zonga
1941,F 19,25:2
Meet the Chump 1941,F 27,23:4
Mr Dynamite 1941,Mr 13,25:2
In the Navy 1941,Je 12,29:2
Tight Shoes 1941,Je 19,25:2
Hit the Road 1941,Jl 3,15:3
Hold That Ghost 1941,Ag 8,13:3
Hellzapoppin 1941,D 26,21:4
Strange Case of Dr Rx 1942,Mr 28,11:2
Butch Minds the Baby 1942,My 1,23:3
Private Buckaroo 1942,Je 25,27:4
Arabian Nights 1942,D 26,15:1
Pittsburgh 1943,F 25,27:2
It Ain't Hay 1943,Mr 11,17:3
Crazy House 1943,D 16,33:3
Africa Screams 1949,My 5,34:2
Howard, Sidney (Miscellaneous)
He Stayed for Breakfast 1940,Ag 31,16:2
Howard, Sidney (Original Author)
We're all Gamblers 1927,O 12,30:6
Secret Hour, The 1928,Mr 12,26:1
Ned McCobb's Daughter 1929,F 18,28:1
Lady to Love, A 1930,Mr 1,23:1
Free Love 1930,D 15,29:1
Silver Cord, The 1933,My 5,18:1
Christopher Bean 1933,N 25,10:2
Yellow Jack 1938,My 20,17:2
They Knew What They Wanted 1940,O 11,25:2

Howard, Sidney (Screenwriter)
Raffles 1930,Jl 25,20:4
One Heavenly Night 1931,Ja 10,19:2
Dodsworth 1936,S 24,29:1
Gone With the Wind 1939,D 20,31:2
Raffles 1940,Ja 13,11:2
Howard, Sydney
French Leave 1931,D 7,16:1
Transatlantic Merry-Go-Round 1934,N 1,25:2
Shipyard Sally 1940,Ja 18,27:3
Howard, Ted
Moby Dick 1956,Jl 5,18:1
Howard, Tom
Rain or Shine 1930,Ag 8,11:1
Howard, Trevor
Johnny in the Clouds 1945,N 16,16:2
Brief Encounter 1946,Ag 26,21:2
Adventures, The 1947,Ap 4,19:2
Green for Danger 1947,Ag 8,10:2
So Well Remembered 1947,N 5,34:3
One Woman's Story 1949,My 18,33:2
Third Man, The 1950,F 3,29:2
Golden Salamander 1951,Mr 24,8:3
Odette 1951,Mr 28,33:2
Clouded Yellow, The 1951,N 13,33:2
Outcast of the Islands 1952,My 16,19:2
Glory at Sea 1953,Mr 11,36:7
Heart of the Matter, The 1954,N 19,20:2
Stranger's Hand, The 1955,F 16,24:5
Cockleshell Heroes, The 1956,Je 4,25:2
Run for the Sun 1956,Ag 25,7:2
Around the World in 80 Days 1956,O 18,37:1
Lover's Net 1957,Jl 23,23:1
Stowaway Girl 1957,N 6,43:3
Key, The 1958,Jl 2,23:3
Sons and Lovers 1960,Ag 3,35:1
Malaga 1962,F 22,20:3
Mutiny on the Bounty 1962,N 9,31:2
Lion, The 1962,D 22,5:2
Man in the Middle 1964,Mr 5,36:1
Father Goose 1964,D 11,55:1
Operation Crossbow 1965,Ap 2,29:1
Von Ryan's Express 1965,Je 24,28:1
Saboteur, The: Code Name-Mori Turi
1965,Ag 26,40:2
Liquidator, The 1966,O 29,34:1
Triple Cross 1967,Jl 20,20:2
Long Duel, The 1967,N 2,58:3
Poppy is Also a Flower, The 1967,D 14,62:4
Matter of Innocence, A 1968,F 22,36:1
Charge of the Light Brigade, The 1968,O 7,59:1
Howard, Vanessa
Here We Go Around the Mulberry Bush
1968,Mr 5,34:5
Howard, Veronica
Taste of Honey, A 1962,My 1,33:3
Howard, Violet
Dreyfus Case, The 1931,Ag 31,11:5
Howard, William K (Director)
East of Broadway 1924,N 12,13:1
Code of the West 1925,Ap 13,24:1
Light of the Western Stars, The 1925,Je 24,14:3
Red Dice 1926,Ap 16,20:3
Gigolo 1926,O 5,27:1
White Gold 1927,Ap 11,18:3
Main Event, The 1927,O 31,22:1
Ship Comes in, A 1928,S 4,21:2
River Pirate, The 1928,S 17,27:1
Christina 1929,Ap 1,22:1
Valiant, The 1929,My 13,27:2
Love, Live and Laugh 1929,N 2,14:6
Scotland Yard 1930,O 20,28:2
Don't Bet on Women 1931,Mr 7,17:2
Transatlantic 1931,Jl 31,15:2
Trial of Vivienne Ware, The 1932,Ap 30,19:3
First Year, The 1932,Ag 22,20:2
Sherlock Holmes 1932,N 12,20:5
Power and the Glory, The 1933,Ag 17,13:2
This Side of Heaven 1934,F 10,21:2
Cat and the Fiddle, The 1934,F 17,20:2
Evelyn Prentice 1934,N 10,19:1
Vanessa: Her Love Story 1935,Ap 13,11:3
Rendezvous 1935,O 26,12:2
Mary Burns, Fugitive 1935,N 16,19:2
Princess Comes Across, The 1936,Je 4,27:2
Murder on Diamond Row 1937,N 12,27:2
Back Door to Heaven 1939,Ap 20,21:2
Money and the Woman 1940,A 29:2
Bullets for O'Hara 1941,Jl 28,16:4
Johnny Come Lately 1943,S 24,26:1
Howard, William K (Original Author)
Back Door to Heaven 1939,Ap 20,21:2
Howard, William K (Producer)
Back Door to Heaven 1939,Ap 20,21:2
Green Cockatoo, The 1947,Jl 19,10:2
Howard, Willie
Vitaphone 1926,O 8,23:2
Millions in the Air 1935,D 12,33:4
Rose of the Rancho 1936,Ja 9,25:2
Broadway Melody of 1938 1937,S 3,12:1
Howarth, David (Original Author)
Nine Lives 1959,Ja 6,28:1

Howarth, Jack
Hobson's Choice 1954,Je 15,37:1
Howat, Clark
Glass Web, The 1953,N 12,37:5
Howatt, Nina (Screenwriter)
Mysterious Mr Wong, The 1935,Mr 7,26:1
Howatt, William
Greatest Love of All, The 1924,N 11,14:1
Howe, Dorothy
Big Broadcast of 1938, The 1938,Mr 10,16:2
Her Jungle Love 1938,Ap 14,27:2
Cocoanut Grove 1938,Je 16,21:2
King of Alcatraz 1938,O 7,21:2
Howe, George (Original Author)
Decision Before Dawn 1951,D 22,12:2
Howe, James Wong (Cinematographer)
Outrage, The 1964,O 8,48:2
Howe, James Wong (Director)
Go, Man, Go 1954,Mr 10,29:5
Howe, Lyman (Producer)
Runaway Train, The 1921,My 6,20:2
Howe, Sonny
Tomorrow Is Forever 1946,F 22,21:2
Howe, Wally
Why Worry? 1923,S 3,9:3
$20 a Week 1924,Je 10,24:4
Tundra 1936,D 3,31:2
Howell, Alice
Wandering Daughters 1923,Jl 2,16:2
Howell, Clift (Narrator)
Scorched Earth 1942,S 12,9:2
Howell, Dorothy (Miscellaneous)
Song of Love, The 1929,N 14,24:3
Howell, Dorothy (Original Author)
Fifty Fathoms Deep 1931,S 19,10:2
Howell, Dorothy (Screenwriter)
Song of Love, The 1929,N 14,24:3
I'll Fix It 1934,N 12,17:3
Howell, E Gilburt
Uncivilized 1937,N 17,27:4
Howell, Hazel
Beware of Blondes 1928,Ag 21,27:4
Girls About Town 1931,N 2,27:1
Howell, Kenneth
Eagle and the Hawk, The 1933,My 13,16:2
I Give my Love 1934,Jl 17,24:2
Every Saturday Night 1936,Mr 14,10:2
Educating Father 1936,Je 20,22:2
Off to the Races 1937,F 6,15:2
Big Business 1937,Je 1,27:2
Hot Water 1937,N 5,19:4
Trip to Paris, A 1938,Je 10,18:2
Safety in Numbers 1938,S 6,17:2
Girls' School 1938,N 3,27:1
Young as You Feel 1940,Mr 8,25:3
Pride of the Bowery 1941,Ja 24,15:2
Henry Aldrich for President 1941,O 18,22:2
Hurry, Charlie, Hurry 1941,N 12,31:3
Sweater Girl 1942,Jl 13,18:3
Howell, Lottice
In Gay Madrid 1930,Je 7,10:4
Howell, Maude (Miscellaneous)
Mister Hobo 1936,F 8,19:2
Howell, Maude (Screenwriter)
Cardinal Richelieu 1935,Ap 19,24:2
East Meets West 1936,O 31,24:2
Howell, Paul (Director)
Borderland 1922,Jl 24,10:2
Howell, Virginia
They Just Had to Get Married 1933,F 13,11:4
Our Betters 1933,F 24,13:2
Spitfire 1934,Mr 9,22:3
Double Door 1934,My 5,22:3
Alice Adams 1935,Ag 16,11:3
Goodbye Broadway 1938,My 14,18:1
Girls' School 1938,N 3,27:1
St Louis Blues 1939,F 9,17:2
Howell, Yvonne
Fashions For Women 1927,Mr 28,26:4
Take Me Home 1928,O 23,33:1
Howells, Jack (Screenwriter)
Front Page Story 1955,Ap 19,28:1
Howells, Ursula
I Believe in You 1953,My 5,34:3
Horse's Mouth, The 1954,Ja 20,33:4
Third Key, The 1957,Je 3,30:2
HOWES
See Also HAWES
Howes, Bobby
Happy Go Lovely 1951,Jl 26,17:2
Howes, Reed
Bobbed Hair 1925,N 4,17:4
Rough House Rosie 1927,My 23,27:2
Ladies' Night in a Turkish Bath 1928,Ap 9,18:2
Hell-Ship Bronson 1928,Je 19,31:1
Sawdust Paradise, The 1928,Ag 27,23:1
Singing Fool, The 1928,S 20,33:2
Hell Divers 1931,D 23,27:3
Stage to Tucson 1951,My 5,14:2
Hangman's Knot 1952,D 11,45:3
Stranger Wore a Gun, The 1953,Jl 30,20:3

Howes, Sally Ann
Half-Way House 1945,Ag 13,22:4
Dead of Night 1946,Je 29,22:6
Nicholas Nickleby 1947,D 1,27:2
Anna Karenina 1948,Ap 28,32:2
Pink String and Sealing Wax 1950,O 4,38:2
History of Mr Polly, The 1951,O 25,36:3
Admirable Crichton, The 1957,D 15,45:4
(Incorrect in this edition; use 1957,D 17,45:4
elsewhere)
Chitty Chitty Bang Bang 1968,D 19,64:4
Howicki, Jan
Barrier 1967,S 27,39:3
Howland, Chris
Fanny Hill 1965,D 2,48:1
Howland, Gibson
Ladies Must Live 1921,N 21,20:1
Howland, Jobyna
Way of a Woman, The 1919,Jl 28,8:5
Second Youth 1924,Ap 22,19:3
Honey 1930,Mr 29,23:1
Cuckoos, The 1930,Ap 26,11:1
Dixiana 1930,S 5,21:1
Virtuous Sin 1930,N 2,VIII,5:2 (In Addenda)
Lady's Morals, A 1930,N 8,21:3
Hook, Line and Sinker 1930,D 25,31:5
Stepping Sisters 1932,Ja 9,21:1
Big City Blues 1932,S 10,18:5
Once in a Lifetime 1932,O 29,18:4
Rockabye 1932,D 5,21:2
Silver Dollar 1932,D 23,20:1
Topaze 1933,F 10,12:2
Cohens and Kellys in Trouble, The
1933,Ap 17,16:4
Story of Temple Drake, The 1933,My 6,11:2
Howland, Kathleen
Man on the Flying Trapeze 1935,Ag 3,16:2
Howland, Lucille
Dementia 1955,D 23,14:4
Howland, Olin
Independence B'Gosh 1918,D 2,11:3
Great White Way, The 1924,Ja 4,10:1
Janice Meredith 1924,Ag 6,13:3
Zander the Great 1925,My 4,16:2
Over the Hill 1931,N 21,20:4
Cheaters at Play 1932,F 27,22:1
Blondie Johnson 1933,F 27,11:2
Wagon Wheels 1934,O 4,19:1
Behold My Wife 1935,F 18,19:3
Folies Bergere 1935,F 25,13:2
Case of the Curious Bride, The 1935,Ap 5,21:3
Case of the Lucky Legs, The 1935,N 1,25:1
Road Gang 1936,F 24,14:1
I Married a Doctor 1936,Ap 20,17:1
Big Noise, The 1936,Jl 4,18:3
Satan Met a Lady 1936,Jl 23,24:2
Earthworm Tractors 1936,Jl 25,16:1
Gold Diggers of 1937 1936,D 25,19:2
Mountain Music 1937,Je 24,30:3
Nothing Sacred 1937,N 26,27:2
Swing Your Lady 1938,Ja 27,17:2
Girl of the Golden West, The 1938,Mr 25,15:2
Mad Miss Manton, The 1938,O 21,27:2
Brother Rat 1938,N 5,15:2
Sweethearts 1938,D 23,16:2
Made for Each Other 1939,F 17,17:2
Zenobia 1939,My 15,15:2
One Hour to Live 1939,N 4,11:3
Return Of Doctor X, The 1939,N 23,38:5
Young People 1940,Ag 24,16:2
Chad Hanna 1940,D 26,23:1
Great Lie, The 1941,Ap 12,19:2
Buy Me That Town 1941,O 23,27:2
Belle Starr 1941,N 1,20:2
One Foot in Heaven 1941,N 14,28:3
Man Who Wouldn't Die, The 1942,Ap 28,25:5
Almost Married 1942,Je 5,23:2
When Johnny Comes Marching Home
1943,Mr 5,20:4
Man From Frisco 1944,Je 16,14:7
Can't Help Singing 1944,D 26,22:4
Dakota 1945,D 17,17:2
Fallen Angel 1946,F 7,29:4
Home Sweet Homicide 1946,S 12,5:7
Angel and the Badman 1947,Mr 3,28:4
Apache Rose 1947,Jl 23,19:3
Wistful Widow of Wagon Gap, The
1947,N 21,36:2
Little Women 1949,Mr 11,33:2
Massacre River 1949,Jl 15,17:2
Ticket to Tomahawk, A 1950,My 20,8:6
Rock Island Trail 1950,Je 5,19:3
Stage to Tucson 1951,My 5,14:2
Them 1954,Je 17,36:2
Blob, The 1958,N 7,23:1
Howland, Tom
Good Morning and Goodbye! 1968,F 20,53:1
Howlett, Noel
Men Are not Gods 1937,Ja 19,28:1
Yank at Oxford, A 1938,F 25,15:1
This Was a Woman 1949,Ja 5,22:2
Corridor of Mirrors 1949,Mr 23,35:3
Saraband 1949,Je 13,16:3

Howlett, Noel— Cont
Once Upon a Dream 1949,Jl 15,17:2
Eye Witness 1950,Ag 28,13:2
Detective, The 1954,N 2,25:2
Lust for Life 1956,S 18,39:1
Scapegoat, The 1959,Ag 7,28:1
Battle of the Sexes, The 1960,Ap 19,40:4
Howson, Albert S (Original Author)
Matinee Ladies 1927,Ap 13,29:4
Hoy, Danny
Tess of the Storm Country 1922,N 13,12:1
Dramatic Life of Abraham Lincoln, The
1924,Ja 22,17:3
Hoy, John
Last Chance, The 1945,N 28,21:6
Hoy, Renate
Certain Smile, A 1958,Ag 1,13:2
Hoy, Robert
Gun for a Coward 1957,Ja 31,21:1
Slender Thread, The 1965,D 24,24:2
Hoyko, Ferenc
Sarga Csiko 1937,Ja 29,15:2
Hoyos, Rodolfo
Raton Pass 1951,Ap 20,25:1
Fighter, The 1952,My 31,12:6
Second Chance 1953,Jl 23,20:2
Americano, The 1955,Ja 20,35:1
Timetable 1956,Mr 17,13:2
First Texan, The 1956,Je 23,20:2
Brave One, The 1957,Mr 22,26:1
Villa 1958,D 24,00:0
Hoyt, Arthur
Nurse Marjorie 1920,My 24,20:3
Love Piker, The 1923,Jl 16,14:2
To the Ladies 1923,N 26,15:6
When a Man's a Man 1924,F 5,20:1
Bluff 1924,Ap 28,18:2
Sundown 1924,D 1,17:3
Lost World, The 1925,F 9,15:3
Sporting Venus, The 1925,My 11,14:3
Any Woman 1925,My 27,26:2
Coming of Amos, The 1925,S 8,29:1
Crown of Lies 1926,Mr 30,20:6
Midnight Sun, The 1926,Ap 24,20:4
Footloose Windows 1926,Je 22,21:2
Affair of the Follies, An 1927,F 28,22:3
Love Thrill, The 1927,My 10,24:5
Tillie the Toiler 1927,Je 7,27:4
Ten Modern Commandments 1927,Jl 11,23:4
Rejuvenation of Aunt Mary, The 1927,Jl 27,27:4
Shanghai Bound 1927,N 7,26:4
Texas Steer, A 1928,Ja 2,28:1
Just Married 1928,Ag 13,23:2
Home James 1928,S 11,31:3
My Man 1928,D 22,14:3
Wheel of Life, The 1929,Je 24,27:1
Her Private Affair 1930,Ja 11,21:3
Seven Days' Leave 1930,Ja 25,13:2
Dumbbells in Ermine 1930,Jl 28,22:1
Life of the Party, The 1930,N 10,16:2
Criminal Code, The 1931,Ja 5,21:3
Going Wild 1931,Ja 26,21:1
Inspiration 1931,F 9,25:3
Flood, The 1931,Ap 27,25:1
Gold Dust Gertie 1931,My 30,9:2
Peach O'Reno 1931,D 24,20:8
Impatient Maiden, The 1932,Mr 4,17:3
Make Me a Star 1932,Jl 1,19:3
Madame Racketeer 1932,Jl 23,6:6
American Madness 1932,Ag 6,14:5
Devil and the Deep 1932,Ag 20,7:4
Crusader, The 1932,O 8,15:4
Vanity Street 1932,O 15,13:1
Washington Merry-Go-Round 1932,O 24,18:5
Red-Haired Alibi 1932,O 24,18:5
Call Her Savage 1932,N 25,19:2
20,000 Years in Sing Sing 1933,Ja 10,26:2
Dangerously Yours 1933,F 23,20:3
Daring Daughters 1933,Mr 25,13:4
Pleasure Cruise 1933,Ap 3,13:3
Goldie Gets Along 1933,Je 3,16:4
Shriek in the Night, A 1933,Jl 24,11:2
Shanghai Madness 1933,S 23,11:6
Only Yesterday 1933,N 10,25:1
It Happened One Night 1934,F 23,23:2
Let's Try Again 1934,Je 22,24:1
Notorious Sophie Lang, The 1934,Jl 21,14:2
Wake up and Dream 1934,O 11,28:3
Kansas City Princess 1934,N 5,23:1
Murder on a Honeymoon 1935,Mr 4,12:2
Night at the Ritz, A 1935,My 16,20:2
Chinatown Squad 1935,My 30,21:1
Raven, The 1935,Jl 5,9:2
$1,000 a Minute 1935,D 21,11:1
Magnificent Obsession 1935,D 31,11:2
Mr Deeds Goes to Town 1936,Ap 17,17:2
Poor Little Rich Girl, The 1936,Je 26,16:1
M'liss 1936,Ag 8,5:2
Star Is Born, A 1937,Ap 23,25:1
Ever Since Eve 1937,Je 25,25:2
She's no Lady 1937,Ag 12,14:3
Love Takes Flight 1937,S 27,24:3
It's all Yours 1938,Ja 7,15:3
Devil's Party, The 1938,My 31,8:3

Hoyt, Arthur— Cont
Cowboy and the Lady, The 1938,N 25,19:3
East Side of Heaven 1939,My 5,29:3
Hail the Conquering Hero 1944,Ag 10,14:2
Mad Wednesday 1951,Ja 25,21:5
Hoyt, Charles (Original Author)
Midnight Bell, A 1921,Ag 8,12:2
Texas Steer, A 1928,Ja 2,28:1
Hoyt, Harry (Director)
Woman on the Jury, The 1924,My 19,14:2
Sundown 1924,D 1,17:3
Jungle Bride 1933,My 13,16:3
Hoyt, Harry (Original Author)
Hero for a Night, A 1927,D 26,26:6
Hoyt, Harry (Screenwriter)
Painting the Town 1927,Ag 2,19:2
Hoyt, John
O S S 1946,My 27,15:5
My Favorite Brunette 1947,Mr 20,38:2
Unfaithful, The 1947,Je 28,10:2
Brute Force 1947,Jl 17,16:2
To the Ends of the Earth 1948,F 13,26:2
Winter Meeting 1948,Ap 8,31:2
Sealed Verdict 1948,N 3,36:2
Decision of Christopher Blake, The
1948,D 11,12:2
Bribe, The 1949,F 4,31:2
Lady Gambles, The 1949,My 21,9:2
Everybody Does It 1949,O 26,32:2
Great Dan Patch, The 1949,N 9,37:2
Trapped 1949,N 26,10:6
Outside the Wall 1950,Mr 15,34:8
Lawless, The 1950,Je 23,29:2
Company She Keeps, The 1951,Ja 29,14:4
Inside Straight 1951,Mr 16,34:2
Quebec 1951,Mr 16,34:2
Desert Fox, The 1951,O 18,32:1
When Worlds Collide 1952,F 7,30:2
Lone Shark 1952,My 12,21:2
Androcles and the Lion 1953,Ja 15,23:2
Julius Caesar 1953,Je 5,19:1
Sins of Jezebel 1954,Ja 9,12:2
Casanova's Big Night 1954,Ap 19,19:1
Student Prince, The 1954,Je 16,18:2
Desiree 1954,N 18,42:1
Blackboard Jungle 1955,Mr 21,21:5
Big Combo, The 1955,Mr 26,13:2
Purple Mask, The 1955,Je 16,35:7
Moonfleet 1955,Je 25,9:2
Trial 1955,O 14,21:2
Girl in the Red Velvet Swing, The
1955,O 20,41:2
Forever, Darling 1956,F 10,18:1
Conqueror, The 1956,Mr 31,13:3
Come on, The 1956,Ap 7,13:1
Wetbacks 1956,My 5,13:2
Death of a Scoundrel 1956,N 6,30:1
Never so Few 1960,Ja 22,15:2
Spartacus 1960,O 7,28:1
Cleopatra 1963,Je 13,29:1
X - The Man With X-Ray Eyes 1963,O 24,37:1
Two on a Guillotine 1965,Ja 14,44:3
Young Dillinger 1965,My 13,32:3
Duel at Diablo 1966,Je 16,53:1
Hoyt, Julia
Man Who Found Himself, The 1925,Ag 24,17:3
Hoyt, Vance Joseph (Original Author)
Sequoia 1935,F 23,14:6
Hrabal, Bohumil (Original Author)
Closely Watched Trains 1967,O 16,59:2
Boring Afternoon, A 1968,Jl 4,13:2
Hrabal, Bohumil (Screenwriter)
Closely Watched Trains 1967,O 16,59:2
Boring Afternoon, A 1968,Jl 4,13:2
Hrach, Dora
Wien Du Stadt der Lieder; (Vienna City of Song)
1931,Mr 20,29:1
Hruba, Vera
Ice-Capades 1941,S 25,29:1
Hruby, Margarete
Traeumende Mund, Der 1934,F 5,19:2
Hrusinsky, Rudolf
90 Degrees in the Shade 1966,N 16,52:1
Death of Tarzan, The 1968,Jl 4,13:2
Murder Czech Style 1968,Ag 20,33:1
Capricious Summer 1968,S 18,50:2
Capricious Summer 1968,S 25,38:2
Hrust, Brandon
Seventh Heaven 1927,My 26,22:1
Hsalo, Suzanne
Genghis Khan 1965,Je 24,28:2
Hsia, Julia
Sons of Good Earth 1967,S 16,37:5
Hsieh, Warren
China Gate 1957,My 23,40:2
South Pacific 1958,Mr 20,33:1
Hsu, Mary
Sable Cicada 1939,Ja 14,13:1
Hsueh, Nancy
Targets 1968,Ag 14,34:1
Hua, Li Li
China Doll 1958,D 4,52:1

Huba, Mikulas
Seventh Continent, The 1968,Jl 30,33:2
Hubay, Jenoe
Hello Budapest 1935,N 14,17:4
Hubbard, Elbert (Original Author)
Message to Garcia, A 1936,Ap 10,27:1
Hubbard, John
Housekeeper's Daughter, The 1939,D 2,21:4
One Million BC 1940,Ap 27,9:2
Turnabout 1940,Jl 27,17:6
Road Show 1941,F 19,25:2
She Knew All the Answers 1941,Je 20,28:4
Our Wife 1941,S 18,31:1
You'll Never Get Rich 1941,O 24,27:2
Canal Zone 1942,Mr 30,21:2
Mummy's Tomb, The 1942,O 26,19:2
Chatterbox 1943,Jl 2,15:3
What's Buzzin Cousin 1943,Jl 23,21:4
Up in Mabel's Room 1944,Ap 22,8:6
Mexican Hayride 1949,Ja 12,33:3
Bullfighter and the Lady, The 1951,Ap 27,19:2
Big Jim McLain 1952,S 18,35:2
Buccaneer, The 1958,D 24,00:0
Hubbard, Lucien (Director)
Rose-Marie 1928,F 13,16:2
Mysterious Island, The 1929,D 21,17:1
Hubbard, Lucien (Original Author)
Star Witness, The 1931,Ag 4,19:5
Hubbard, Lucien (Producer)
Society Doctor 1935,F 4,11:3
Shadow of Doubt 1935,Mr 11,15:1
Times Square Lady 1935,Mr 15,25:3
Casino Murder Case, The 1935,Ap 17,26:5
Murder in the Fleet 1935,Je 3,22:2
Public Hero No 1 1935,Je 8,12:2
Exclusive Story 1936,Ja 18,19:2
Garden Murder Case, The 1936,Mr 2,13:2
Moonlight Murder 1936,Mr 28,11:2
Speed 1936,My 16,11:2
Sworn Enemy 1936,S 12,20:1
Longest Night, The 1936,O 17,21:2
Under Cover of Night 1937,Ja 20,18:4
Sinner Take All 1937,F 3,27:1
Man of the People 1937,F 23,25:4
Family Affair, A 1937,Ap 20,29:2
Ebb Tide 1937,N 18,27:2
Texans, The 1938,Jl 28,23:2
Six Thousand Enemies 1939,Je 9,26:2
Nick Carter, Master Detective 1939,D 14,35:2
Hubbard, Lucien (Screenwriter)
Wild Honey 1922,F 28,17:4
Gung Ho! 1944,Ja 26,23:2
Hubbard, Tom
Highway Dragnet 1954,F 20,8:7
Port of Hell 1954,D 18,12:2
Hubbard, Tom (Screenwriter)
Port of Hell 1954,D 18,12:2
Legion of the Doomed 1959,Mr 12,27:5
Hubbare, John
Hold 'Em Navy 1937,N 6,14:2
Hubbell, Carl
Safe at Home 1941,N 26,31:2
Hubbell, Edwin
Lady, The 1925,Ja 27,11:2
Huber, Gottlieb
Next Time We Love 1936,Ja 31,16:2
Huber, Gusti
Tanzmusik 1936,My 26,27:2
Freuhling im Wien 1937,F 6,15:2
Fiakerlied, Das; (Cabbie's Song, The)
1937,S 6,20:2
Meadchen von Gestern Nacht, Das; Girl of Last
Night, The 1938,Je 18,18:2
Zwischen den Eltern; Between the Parents
1938,Jl 30,10:3
Diary of Anne Frank, The 1959,Mr 19,40:1
Huber, Harold
Central Park 1932,D 7,29:3
Match King, The 1932,D 8,25:3
Frisco Jenny 1933,Ja 7,11:2
20,000 Years in Sing Sing 1933,Ja 10,26:2
Parachute Jumper 1933,Ja 26,12:2
Ladies They Talk About 1933,F 25,20:4
Girl Missing 1933,Ap 1,18:2
Central Airport 1933,My 4,20:5
Life of Jimmy Dolan, The 1933,Je 14,22:3
Silk Express, The 1933,Je 28,24:2
Mayor of Hell, The 1933,Jl 1,16:5
Bowery, The 1933,O 5,24:2
No More Women 1934,Mr 15,27:4
He Was her Man 1934,My 17,28:2
Thin Man, The 1934,Je 30,18:5
Defense Rests, The 1934,Ag 16,20:3
Hide-Out 1934,Ag 25,16:5
Naughty Marietta 1935,Mr 23,11:2
G Men 1935,My 2,17:1
We're Only Human 1936,Ja 18,19:2
Muss 'Em Up 1936,F 3,21:2
Klondike Annie 1936,Mr 12,18:2
San Francisco 1936,Je 27,21:1
Kelly the Second 1936,O 3,21:2
Gay Desperado, The 1936,O 9,31:4
Devil is a Sissy, The 1936,O 17,21:2

Huber, Harold— Cont
Good Earth, The 1937,F 3,27:1
Trouble in Morocco 1937,Mr 15,27:1
Angel's Holiday 1937,My 29,20:2
You Can't Beat Love 1937,Je 25,25:3
Love Under Fire 1937,Ag 28,8:2
Charlie Chan on Broadway 1937,S 20,19:1
Outlaws of the Orient 1937,S 25,10:2
Charlie Chan at Monte Carlo 1937,D 18,18:1
International Settlement 1938,F 12,20:3
Slight Case of Murder, A 1938,F 28,19:1
Mr Moto's Gamble 1938,Ap 8,17:2
Gangs of New York 1938,My 28,9:2
Trip to Paris, A 1938,Je 10,18:2
Passport Husband 1938,Ag 5,11:2
Little Tough Guys in Society 1938,N 21,14:4
While New York Sleeps 1938,D 22,25:3
Going Places 1939,Ja 7,6:1
You Can't Get Away With Murder
1939,Mr 25,19:2
King of the Turf 1939,My 8,21:2
Six Thousand Enemies 1939,Je 9,26:2
Main Street Lawyer 1939,N 9,27:2
Charlie Chan in City in Darkness 1939,D 18,29:2
Charlie McCarthy, Detective 1939,D 25,29:2
Dance, Girl, Dance 1940,O 11,25:2
Kit Carson 1940,N 15,25:3
Man Betrayed, A 1941,Mr 27,29:5
Gentleman After Dark, A 1942,Ap 17,21:2
Little Tokyo, USA 1942,Ag 7,13:2
Manila Calling 1942,S 28,13:1
Crime Doctor 1943,Jl 5,11:4
My Friend Irma Goes West 1950,Ag 3,20:2
Let's Dance 1950,N 30,42:2
Adventures of Marco Polo, The 1965,Ap 8,17:2
Hubert, Ali (Miscellaneous)
Loves of Pharaoh 1922,F 22,13:3 (In Addenda)
Hubert, Roger
Forbidden Games 1952,D 9,43:2
Light Across the Street, The; Lumiere d'en Face,
La 1957,Jl 30,20:2
Hubler, Richard G (Screenwriter)
Man-Eater of Kumaon 1948,Jl 2,24:2
Hubley, Faith (Miscellaneous)
Of Stars and Men 1964,Ap 29,47:1
Hubley, Faith (Producer)
Of Stars and Men 1964,Ap 29,47:1
Hubley, John (Director)
Four Poster, The 1952,O 16,37:1
Of Stars and Men 1964,Ap 29,47:1
Hubley, John (Miscellaneous)
Of Stars and Men 1964,Ap 29,47:1
Hubley, John (Producer)
Of Stars and Men 1964,Ap 29,47:1
Hubner, Herbert
Hotel Sacher 1939,Je 10,14:2
Third Sex, The 1959,Mr 26,27:1
Hubschmid, Paul
Maria Ilona 1940,Ap 20,14:3
Affairs of Julie, The 1958,D 10,53:1
Scampolo 1959,Ag 6,18:4
And so to Bed 1965,Jl 31,11:3
Mozambique 1966,F 10,33:1
Funeral in Berlin 1966,D 23,17:1
That Woman 1968,Jl 19,30:3
Hudd, Walter
I Stand Condemned 1936,Jl 2,27:2
Rembrandt 1936,D 3,31:1
Elephant Boy 1937,Ap 6,20:2
Housemaster 1939,Ap 10,13:2
Black Limelight 1939,Je 26,12:2
Outsider, The 1940,Mr 18,13:2
Major Barbara 1941,My 15,27:1
Yank in London, A 1946,Ap 20,16:3
Lady Surrenders, A 1947,Je 20,25:6
I Know Where I'm Going 1947,Ag 20,25:2
Escape 1948,Ag 16,12:2
Importance of Being Earnest, The 1952,D 23,17:2
Landfall 1953,My 11,25:2
Cast a Dark Shadow 1957,N 28,57:1
Two-Headed Spy, The 1959,Mr 3,38:4
Man Upstairs, The 1959,Ag 11,23:2
Sink the Bismarck! 1960,F 12,22:3
Huddleston, David
Black Like Me 1964,My 21,42:1
Huddleston, Floyd (Composer)
Duchess of Idaho 1950,Jl 21,15:3
Hudepin, Didier
Uninhibited, The 1968,Je 13,57:2
Hudis, Norman (Screenwriter)
Carry on Sergeant 1959,O 28,40:5
Carry on Nurse 1960,S 10,11:1
Please Turn Over 1961,Ap 29,12:2
Hudman, Wes
Blackjack Ketchum Desperado 1956,Ap 5,26:2
Hudson, Beverly
Born to Sing 1942,F 19,23:2
True to Life 1943,O 14,26:1
Sweet and Low Down 1944,O 19,19:2
Hudson, Bill
Steel Trap, The 1952,N 13,35:2
Hudson, E (Screenwriter)
For Sale 1924,Jl 14,11:5
Single Wives 1924,Jl 29,9:2

Hudson, E (Screenwriter) — Cont
Sundown 1924,D 1,17:3
Hudson, Eddy
Junior Miss 1945,Je 18,15:4
Hudson, Ethel
Ramparts We Watch, The 1940,S 20,27:1
Hudson, Eva
End of the River, The 1948,Je 21,18:2
Hudson, Hal (Original Author)
Meet the Chump 1941,F 27,23:4
Hudson, John
Hue and Cry 1951,Ja 9,25:2
Bright Victory 1951,Ag 1,19:2
Battle at Apache Pass, The 1952,My 10,16:4
Return to Paradise 1953,S 11,24:2
Racers, The 1955,F 5,13:2
Gunfight at the O K Corral 1957,My 30,23:2
Hudson, Larry
Solid Gold Cadillac, The 1956,O 25,40:3
Hudson, Rochelle
Fanny Foley Herself 1931,O 26,22:1
Are These our Children 1931,N 14,15:3
Hell's Highway 1932,S 26,18:2
She Done Him Wrong 1933,F 10,12:3
Wild Boys of the Road 1933,S 22,14:1
Doctor Bull 1933,O 6,21:2
Walls of Gold 1933,O 21,11:3
Mr Skitch 1933,D 23,19:1
Such Women Are Dangerous 1934,Je 9,18:3
Judge Priest 1934,O 12,33:1
Imitation of Life 1934,N 24,19:1
Mighty Barnum, The 1934,D 24,17:1
Life Begins at 40 1935,Ap 5,21:3
Miserables, Les 1935,Ap 22,14:2
Curly Top 1935,Ag 2,22:3
Way Down East 1935,O 31,16:2
Show Them no Mercy 1935,D 9,25:2
Music Goes 'Round, The 1936,F 22,12:1
Everybody's Old Man 1936,Mr 26,27:2
Country Beyond, The 1936,Ap 30,17:3
Poppy 1936,Je 18,19:1
Reunion 1936,N 27,27:1
Woman Wise 1937,Ja 23,13:1
That I May Live 1937,My 10,23:2
She Had to Eat 1937,Jl 24,12:1
Born Reckless 1937,Jl 30,22:6
Rascals 1938,My 27,12:2
Mr Moto Takes a Chance 1938,Je 13,15:4
Storm Over Bengal 1938,D 8,34:4
Missing Daughters 1939,Je 12,14:5
Woman Is the Judge, A 1939,S 28,29:5
Convicted Woman 1940,F 26,11:2
Men Without Souls 1940,My 13,21:2
Island Of Doomed Men 1940,Je 10,21:2
Girls Under 21 1940,N 11,22:4
Meet Boston Blackie 1941,F 26,17:2
Officer and the Lady, The 1941,Ag 11,17:4
Rebel without a Cause 1955,O 27,28:3
Strait Jacket 1964,Ja 23,26:1
Night Walker, The 1965,Ja 21,22:1
Hudson, Rock
Winchester 73 1950,Je 8,38:2
Peggy 1950,Jl 21,15:4
Desert Hawk, The 1950,Ag 26,9:2
Tomahawk 1951,F 19,19:2
Air Cadet 1951,My 11,32:3
Fat Man, The 1951,My 25,31:2
Iron Man 1951,Ag 20,14:2
Bend of the River 1952,Ap 10,37:1
Scarlet Angel 1952,Je 21,12:2
Has Anybody Seen My Gal 1952,Jl 5,7:2
Horizons West 1952,N 22,16:5
Sea Devils 1953,Jl 31,11:5
Magnificent Obsession 1954,Ag 5,18:4
Bengal Brigade 1954,N 13,13:2
One Desire 1955,S 3,9:1
All That Heaven Allows 1956,F 29,35:1
Never Say Goodbye 1956,Ap 14,20:1
Giant 1956,O 11,51:1
Written on the Wind 1957,Ja 12,12:6
Battle Hymn 1957,F 16,14:1
Something of Value 1957,My 11,24:6
Tarnished Angels, The 1958,Ja 7,31:1
Farewell to Arms, A 1958,Ja 25,14:1
Twilight for the Gods 1958,Ag 7,21:1
Earth Is Mine, The 1959,Je 27,13:1
Pillow Talk 1959,O 7,47:2
Last Sunset, The 1961,Je 15,51:1
Come September 1961,S 8,34:1
Lover Come Back 1962,F 9,21:1
Spiral Road, The 1962,Ag 4,11:2
Gathering of Eagles, A 1963,Jl 11,21:2
Man's Favorite Sport? 1964,F 20,22:1
Send Me no Flowers 1964,N 13,30:1
Strange Bedfellows 1965,Mr 11,38:1
Very Special Favor, A 1965,Ag 26,40:3
Blindfold 1966,My 26,55:2
Seconds 1966,O 6,56:1
Tobruk 1967,F 9,33:2
Ice Station Zebra 1968,D 21,49:1
Hudson, Rock (Narrator)
Marilyn 1963,Jl 18,15:1

Hudson, Vanda
Circus of Horrors 1960,S 1,31:1
Hudson, W H (Original Author)
Green Mansions 1959,Mr 20,26:1
Hudson, William
Objective Burma 1945,Ja 27,15:2
Hard, Fast and Beautiful 1951,Jl 2,16:6
Mister Roberts 1955,Jl 15,14:1
Amazing Colossal Man, The 1957,O 26,19:2
Huebler-Kahla, J A (Director)
Tanzmusik 1936,My 26,27:2
Freuhling im Wien 1937,F 6,15:2
Veilchen vom Potsdamer Platz, La; Violet of
Potsdam Square, The 1939,Ap 8,19:3
Geheimnisvolle Mister X, Der; Mysterious Mr X,
The 1939,Jl 1,11:2
Huebner, Bruno
Flying Classroom, The 1958,Je 28,13:7
Huebner, Herbert
Die Blumenfrau von Lindenau 1932,Jl 8,22:5
Karneval und Liebe 1936,Ap 4,11:2
Traumulus 1936,S 19,20:1
Gruene Hoelle, Die; Green Hell, The
1939,Ja 21,19:2
Rote Orchideen; Red Orchids 1939,Ap 15,15:2
Affair Blum, The 1949,O 18,35:2
Spessart Inn, The 1961,F 18,12:3
Huelsenback, Richard
8 X 8 1957,Mr 16,13:2
Huemer, Dick (Miscellaneous)
Reluctant Dragon, The 1941,Jl 25,12:2
Huemer, Dick (Original Author)
Saludos Amigos 1943,F 13,8:2
Huemer, Dick (Screenwriter)
Dumbo 1941,O 24,27:2
Huet, Henri-Jacques
Breathless 1961,F 8,26:1
Petit Soldat, Le 1967,Ap 21,48:1
Huff, Jack
Sackcloth and Scarlet 1925,Mr 25,24:2
Zander the Great 1925,My 4,16:2
Limited Mail, The 1925,S 1,18:2
Huff, Louise
Reward of Patience, The 1916,S 11,11:4
Disraeli 1921,Ag 22,13:6
Huffaker, Clair (Original Author)
Flaming Star 1960,D 17,19:1
Seven Ways From Sundown 1960,D 22,18:4
Rio Conchos 1964,O 29,38:1
War Wagon, The 1967,Ag 3,26:3
Huffaker, Clair (Screenwriter)
Flaming Star 1960,D 17,19:1
Seven Ways From Sundown 1960,D 22,18:4
Comancheros, The 1961,N 2,42:1
Rio Conchos 1964,O 29,38:1
Tarzan and the Valley of Gold 1967,Mr 30,55:1
War Wagon, The 1967,Ag 3,26:3
Huggins, Roy (Director)
Hangman's Knot 1952,D 11,45:3
Huggins, Roy (Miscellaneous)
Woman in Hiding 1950,F 23,33:2
Huggins, Roy (Original Author)
Fuller Brush Man, The 1948,My 15,18:2
Too Late for Tears 1949,Ag 15,12:3
Good Humor Man, The 1950,Jl 14,17:2
Huggins, Roy (Producer)
Fever in the Blood 1961,Ap 20,30:4
Huggins, Roy (Screenwriter)
Lady Gambles, The 1949,My 21,9:2
Too Late for Tears 1949,Ag 15,12:3
Sealed Cargo 1951,My 24,47:1
Hangman's Knot 1952,D 11,45:3
Pushover 1954,Jl 31,6:3
Three Hours to Kill 1954,S 4,6:4
Fever in the Blood 1961,Ap 20,30:4
Hugh, R John (Director)
Yellowback 1957,Ap 5,24:2
Hugh, R John (Original Author)
Yellowback 1957,Ap 5,24:2
Hugh, R John (Producer)
Johnny Tiger 1966,Je 16,53:4
Hugh, R John (Screenwriter)
Johnny Tiger 1966,Je 16,53:4
Hugham, Oxley (Director)
Queen's Royal Tour, A 1954,Mr 3,22:2
Hughes, Adelaide (Original Author)
Gimme 1923,Ja 15,18:3
Hughes, Andrew
Last Voyage, The 1960,F 20,14:2
Hughes, Anthony
In Old Chicago 1938,Ja 7,15:2
Call of the Yukon 1938,My 6,27:1
Wives Under Suspicion 1938,Jl 1,22:3
Diamond Frontiers 1940,O 4,29:2
Hughes, Arthur
Hue and Cry 1951,Ja 9,25:2
Hughes, Barnard
Hamlet 1964,S 24,46:1
Hughes, C Anthony
Heads Up 1930,O 13,31:1
Hughes, Carol
Golden Arrow, The 1936,My 4,16:1
Earthworm Tractors 1936,Jl 25,16:1

Hughes, Carol — Cont
Case of the Velvet Claws, The 1936,Ag 29,16:3
Stage Struck 1936,S 28,14:4
Polo Joe 1936,N 5,35:1
Three Men on a Horse 1936,N 26,39:1
Ready, Willing and Able 1937,Mr 15,27:1
Ever Since Eve 1937,Je 25,25:2
Marry the Girl 1937,Jl 31,6:2
Westland Case, The 1937,O 23,14:2
Renfrew of the Royal Mounted 1937,N 3,29:4
Under Western Stars 1938,Je 25,7:3
Day the Bookies Wept, The 1939,S 14,18:2
Married and in Love 1940,F 2,13:2
Flight Angels 1940,My 27,23:2
Scattergood Baines 1941,Ap 4,25:2
I'll Wait for You 1941,Je 2,13:6
Top Sergeant Mulligan 1941,N 12,31:3
What's Buzzin Cousin 1943,Jl 23,21:4
Pillow to Post 1945,My 26,18:2
Bachelor and the Bobby-Soxer, The
1947,Jl 25,12:5
Scaramouche 1952,My 9,20:2
Hughes, Charles A
Touchdown Army 1938,O 28,27:2
Hughes, Charles Anthony
Women in the Wind 1939,Ap 13,27:2
Hughes, David
Grapes of Wrath, The 1940,Ja 25,17:2
Long Voyage Home, The 1940,O 9,30:2 (In
Addenda)
Hughes, David (Screenwriter)
Loving Couples 1966,S 20,38:1
Night Games 1966,D 20,58:1
Hughes, Dorothy
Sorrows of Satan, The 1926,O 13,21:1
Hughes, Dorothy B (Original Author)
Fallen Sparrow, The 1943,Ag 20,13:1
Ride the Pink Horse 1947,O 9,32:3
In a Lonely Place 1950,My 18,37:2
Hughes, Gareth
Mrs Wiggs of the Cabbage Patch 1919,F 17,11:3
Eyes of Youth 1919,D 1,9:3
Forget Me Not 1922,Jl 24,10:2
Kick In 1922,D 18,22:2
Enemies of Women 1923,Ap 1,5:4
Penrod and Sam 1923,Je 25,16:5
Spanish Dancer, The 1923,O 8,20:1
Shadows of Paris 1924,F 18,13:1
Whirlwind of Youth, The 1927,Je 6,27:2
Hughes, Gwenyth
Corn is Green, The 1945,Mr 30,18:2
Hughes, Hatcher (Original Author)
Hell-Bent for Heaven 1926,My 4,31:1
Hughes, Hazel
Ireland's Border Line 1939,O 13,27:3
Hughes, Howard (Director)
Hell's Angels 1930,Ag 16,8:3
Outlaw, The 1947,S 12,18:4
Hughes, Howard (Producer)
Front Page, The 1931,Mr 20,29:1
Cock of the Air 1932,Ja 25,20:3
Sky Devils 1932,Mr 4,17:3
Outlaw, The 1947,S 12,18:4
Vendetta 1950,D 26,19:1
Affair With a Stranger 1953,Jl 11,8:2
Hughes, J Anthony
Whipsaw 1936,Ja 25,18:4
Country Doctor, The 1936,Mr 13,32:2 (Incorrect
in this edition; use 1936,Mr 13,27:2 elsewhere)
Educating Father 1936,Je 20,22:2
Tail Spin 1939,F 11,13:2
Cisco Kid and the Lady, The 1939,D 25,29:2
Beyond Tomorrow 1940,S 27,27:1
Hughes, Jackie
Gentle Julia 1936,Ap 11,19:1
Hughes, John B
Rhapsody in Blue 1945,Je 28,22:2
Hughes, Kathleen
Mother is a Freshman 1949,Mr 12,10:2
Mr Belvedere Goes to College 1949,Ap 16,11:2
Mister 880 1950,S 30,13:2
Take Care of my Little Girl 1951,Jl 19,20:2
For Men Only 1952,Ja 16,21:2
It Came From Outer Space 1953,Je 18,38:2
Glass Web, The 1953,N 12,37:5
Dawn at Socorro 1954,Ag 28,8:2
Three bad Sisters 1956,F 13,24:1
Hughes, Kay
Robin Hood of El Dorado, The 1936,Mr 14,10:1
Every Saturday Night 1936,Mr 14,10:2
Singing Kid, The 1936,Ap 4,11:1
Hughes, Ken (Director)
Joe Macbeth 1956,Ap 7,13:1
Trials of Oscar Wilde, The 1960,Je 28,26:1
Small World of Sammy Lee, The 1963,Ag 14,28:1
Of Human Bondage 1964,S 24,46:2
Arrivederci, Baby! 1966,D 29,22:1
Casino Royale 1967,Ap 29,25:1
Chitty Chitty Bang Bang 1968,D 19,64:4
Hughes, Ken (Original Author)
Small World of Sammy Lee, The 1963,Ag 14,28:1
Hughes, Ken (Producer)
Arrivederci, Baby! 1966,D 29,22:1

Hughes, Ken (Screenwriter)
Trials of Oscar Wilde, The 1960,Je 28,26:1
Small World of Sammy Lee, The 1963,Ag 14,28:1
Arrivederci, Baby! 1966,D 29,22:1
Chitty Chitty Bang Bang 1968,D 19,64:4
Hughes, Langston (Original Author)
Way Down South 1939,Ag 18,16:4
Hughes, Langston (Screenwriter)
Way Down South 1939,Ag 18,16:4
Hughes, Leonora
Rejected Woman, The 1924,My 5,18:3
Hughes, Llewellyn (Original Author)
Sky Hawk, The 1929,D 12,36:4
Heartbreak 1931,O 17,20:1
Hughes, Lloyd
Turn in the Road, The 1919,Mr 30,IV,6:1
Below the Surface 1920,Je 7,20:3 (In Addenda)
Home Spun Folks 1920,O 4,14:3
Hail the Woman 1922,Ja 16,18:3
Tess of the Storm Country 1922,N 13,12:1
Scars of Jealousy 1923,My 7,19:3
Heritage of the Desert, The 1924,Ja 24,15:1
Sea Hawk, The 1924,Je 3,22:1
Welcome Stranger 1924,O 14,21:5
Dixie Handicap, The 1924,D 30,15:3
If I Marry Again 1925,Ja 12,11:2
Lost World, The 1925,F 9,15:3
Sally 1925,Mr 16,16:1
Declassee 1925,Mr 23,14:2
Desert Flower, The 1925,Je 1,10:3
Half-Way Girl, The 1925,Jl 29,24:4
Irene 1926,Mr 1,17:1
Ella Cinders 1926,Je 7,23:2
Forever After 1926,N 9,31:1
Ladies at Play 1926,N 16,25:3
Loose Ankles 1926,N 21,VIII,7:3 (In Addenda)
Valencia 1926,D 27,20:3
Affair of the Follies, An 1927,F 28,22:3
Stolen Bride, The 1927,Ag 10,21:4
American Beauty 1927,O 11,27:1
Sailors' Wives 1928,F 28,18:4
Heart to Heart 1928,S 10,29:2
Where East Is East 1929,My 27,22:1
Mysterious Island, The 1929,D 21,17:1
Love Comes Along 1930,F 1,15:1
Runaway Bride 1930,My 17,21:2
Moby Dick 1930,Ag 15,20:5
Big Boy 1930,S 13,9:3
Extravagance 1930,D 9,31:3
Hell Bound 1931,My 9,15:4
Deceiver, The 1931,N 23,22:1
Miracle Man, The 1932,Ap 21,25:2
Harmony Lane 1935,O 24,19:4
Romance of the Redwoods 1939,Ap 24,13:2
Hughes, Mary Beth
These Glamour Girls 1939,Ag 31,14:2
Women, The 1939,S 22,27:2
Fast And Furious 1939,O 12,33:3
Dancing Co-Ed 1939,N 10,27:3
Free, Blonde and 21 1940,Ap 5,25:2
Star Dust 1940,My 4,13:1
Four Sons 1940,Je 8,18:4
Lucky Cisco Kid 1940,Je 24,19:5
Great Profile, The 1940,O 18,25:1
Sleepers West 1941,Mr 20,25:3
Ride on Vaquero 1941,Ap 19,20:2
Dressed to Kill 1941,Ag 22,19:3
Design for Scandal 1942,F 6,23:3
Night Before the Divorce, The 1942,Ap 10,21:3
Orchestra Wives 1942,S 24,23:2
Over my Dead Body 1942,D 26,15:2
Good Morning, Judge 1943,Ap 30,25:4
Ox-Bow Incident, The 1943,My 10,15:2 (In Addenda)
Great Flamario, The 1945,Ja 15,15:5
Rockin' in The Rockies 1945,Jl 5,7:2
El Paso 1949,Mr 24,35:2
Young Man With a Horn 1950,F 10,18:4
Highway Dragnet 1954,F 20,8:7
Loophole 1954,Mr 13,11:3
Las Vegas Shakedown 1955,Je 18,14:2
Hughes, Richard (Miscellaneous)
It Had to Happen 1936,F 15,18:6
Hughes, Richard (Original Author)
High Wind in Jamaica, A 1965,Je 17,27:2
Hughes, Richard (Screenwriter)
Run for Your Money, A 1950,Ap 10,15:3
Hughes, Robin
Flame and the Arrow, The 1950,Jl 8,7:2
Cyrano De Bergerac 1950,N 17,31:2
Dial M for Murder 1954,My 29,13:2
Manhunt in the Jungle 1958,Ap 12,13:1
Thing That Couldn't Die, The 1958,Je 28,13:7
Auntie Mame 1958,D 5,39:1
Hughes, Roddy
Old Curiosity Shop, The 1935,D 23,15:5
Quiet Wedding 1941,D 29,27:4
So Well Remembered 1947,N 5,34:3
Hatter's Castle 1948,Jl 3,8:6
Hidden Room, The 1950,Ja 9,19:2
Christmas Carol, A 1951,N 29,41:2
Man in the White Suit, The 1952,Ap 1,35:2

Hughes, Rupert (Director)
Wall Flower, The 1922,Je 26,16:2
Remembrance 1922,O 2,21:2
Gimme 1923,Ja 15,18:3
Souls for Sale 1923,Ap 9,14:3
Reno 1924,Ja 8,27:1
True as Steel 1924,Je 17,22:4
Hughes, Rupert (Miscellaneous)
Concert, The 1921,F 21,16:1
Hughes, Rupert (Original Author)
Gloria's Romance 1916,My 23,9:2
We Can't Have Everything 1918,Jl 15,9:3
Unpardonable Sin, The 1919,My 3,11:3
Scratch my Back 1920,Je 5,19:3
Old Nest, The 1921,Je 29,10:3
Dangerous Curve Ahead 1921,O 3,16:2
Gimme 1923,Ja 15,18:3
Reno 1924,Ja 8,27:1
Excuse Me 1925,Ja 27,11:2
Money Talks 1926,My 11,24:3
Patent Leather Kid, The 1927,Ag 16,31:2
Girl on the Barge, The 1929,F 26,31:1
She Goes to War 1929,Je 10,23:1
Ladies' Man 1931,My 1,30:3
No One Man 1932,Ja 23,18:4
Woman Accused, The 1933,Mr 13,18:2
Tillie and Gus 1933,N 13,21:1
Miss Fane's Baby is Stolen 1934,Ja 20,12:2
President's Mystery, The 1936,O 19,22:1
Hughes, Rupert (Screenwriter)
Wall Flower, The 1922,Je 26,16:2
Remembrance 1922,O 2,21:2
Souls for Sale 1923,Ap 9,14:3
True as Steel 1924,Je 17,22:4
Hughes, Rupert Mrs (Original Author)
Gloria's Romance 1916,My 23,9:2
Hughes, Rush
Ashes of Vengeance 1923,Ag 7,20:2
Reno 1924,Ja 8,27:1
Love and Hisses 1938,Ja 1,11:1
Hughes, Russell (Screenwriter)
House Across the Street 1949,S 2,14:4
This Side of the Law 1950,Jl 7,15:2
Sugarfoot 1951,F 12,19:4
Thunder Over the Plains 1953,D 10,64:4
Command, The 1954,Ja 16,10:5
Them 1954,Je 17,36:2
Last Frontier, The 1955,D 8,45:1
Jubal 1956,Ap 25,39:1
Hughes, Stanley
Storm, The 1938,O 31,12:2
Swing That Cheer 1938,N 11,31:2
Secrets of a Nurse 1938,D 12,26:2
Hughes, Thomas (Original Author)
Tom Brown's School Days 1940,Je 28,22:2
Tom Brown's School Days 1952,Ja 8,23:5
Hughes, Tony
Armored Car 1937,Jl 26,15:2
Just Around the Corner 1938,D 3,11:2
Hughes, William
Amazing Colossal Man, The 1957,O 26,19:2
Hughes, Yvonne
Zaza 1923,S 17,18:2
Society Scandal, A 1924,Mr 10,18:2
Hugill, John
Mikado, The 1967,Mr 15,53:1
Hugo, Jean Victor (Miscellaneous)
Passion Of Joan Of Arc, The 1929,Mr 29,21:1
Passion of Jeanne d'Arc, The 1929,Mr 31,VIII,7:1
Hugo, Laurence
Three Hours to Kill 1954,S 4,6:4
Hugo, Mauritz
Wanted by the Police 1938,S 26,13:2
Iron Curtain, The 1948,My 13,31:2
Ticket to Tomahawk, A 1950,My 20,8:6
No Questions Asked 1951,Ag 10,13:2
Hugo, Victor (Original Author)
Miserables, Les 1917,D 5,13:2
Miserables, Les 1926,Jl 9,17:1
Miserables, Les 1927,Ag 23,29:4
Man Who Laughs, The 1928,Ap 28,12:3
Miserables, Les 1934,Mr 25,X,4:2
Miserables, Les 1935,Ap 22,14:2
Miserables, Les 1936,O 28,31:2
Hunchback of Notre Dame, The 1940,Ja 1,29:2
Miserables, Los 1944,O 24,17:2
Miserables, Les 1946,D 26,28:4
King's Jester, The 1947,Je 26,19:3
Ruy Blas 1948,O 4,14:2
Miserables, Les 1952,Mr 25,23:2
Miserables, Les 1952,Ag 15,11:2
Hunchback of Notre Dame, The 1957,D 12,35:1
Hugon, Andre (Director)
Marche Nuptiale, La 1929,Mr 3,VIII,7:2
Heroes of the Marne; (Famille Lefrancois, Le) 1939,Ap 24,13:2
Dawn Over France 1945,Mr 17,17:2
Hugon, Andre (Producer)
Heroes of the Marne; (Famille Lefrancois, Le) 1939,Ap 24,13:2
Moulin Rouge 1944,N 23,38:2

Hugon, Andre (Screenwriter)
Three Masques, The 1929,N 24,X,8:4
Trois Masques, The 1929,N 24,X,8:4 (In Addenda)
Heroes of the Marne; (Famille Lefrancois, Le) 1939,Ap 24,13:2
Huguenin, Jean-Rene (Screenwriter)
Your Shadow Is Mine 1963,My 15,32:1
Hugueny, Sharon
Parrish 1961,My 5,22:1
Caretakers, The 1963,Ag 22,19:2
Young Lovers, The 1965,F 11,45:1
Hugues, Jean
Orage 1938,D 12,26:2
Huie, Donald
Dulcy 1940,N 28,28:2
Huillet, Daniele (Screenwriter)
Chronicle of Anna Magdalena Bach 1968,S 20,37:7
Hulbert, Claude
Alias Bulldog Drummond 1935,S 10,26:2
Hulbert, Claude (Composer)
Jack Ahoy 1935,F 9,11:2
Hulbert, Jack
Office Girl 1932,Je 27,20:7
Ghost Train, The 1933,F 18,13:3
Night and Day 1933,My 29,22:2
Jack Ahoy 1935,F 9,11:2
Alias Bulldog Drummond 1935,S 10,26:2
Gaiety Girls, The 1938,Mr 31,15:1
Queen of Crime 1941,F 19,25:2
Man in the Dinghy 1951,N 1,34:2
Hulbert, Jack (Director)
Elstree Calling 1930,Mr 9,IX,6:1
Hulbert, Jack (Miscellaneous)
Jack Ahoy 1935,F 9,11:2
Queen of Crime 1941,F 19,25:2
Hulbert, Jack (Original Author)
Night and Day 1933,My 29,22:2
Woman in Command, The 1934,My 29,22:2
Alias Bulldog Drummond 1935,S 10,26:2
Hulburd, Merritt (Producer)
Come and Get It 1936,N 12,31:1
Hurricane, The 1937,N 10,31:2
Hule, William Bradford (Original Author)
Revolt of Mamie Stover, The 1956,My 12,12:7
Wild River 1960,My 27,22:1
Outsider, The 1962,F 8,25:1
Americanization of Emily, The 1964,O 28,51:1
Hulett, Otto
One Third of a Nation 1939,F 11,13:2
Saturday's Hero 1951,S 12,37:2
Mob, The 1951,O 18,32:2
Carbine Williams 1952,My 8,37:2
Paula 1952,Jl 16,21:2
Francis Goes to West Point 1952,Ag 23,10:2
You for Me 1952,S 25,38:3
City That Never Sleeps 1953,Ag 8,14:2
Phenix City Story, The 1955,S 3,9:1
Hulette, Gladys
Secrets of Paris 1923,Ja 8,22:1
Iron Horse, The 1924,Ag 29,6:1
Private Affairs 1925,Jl 15,22:3
Mystic, The 1925,Ag 31,19:3
Go Straight 1925,O 6,30:1
Skyrocket, The 1926,Ja 26,25:2
Hull, Alexander (Original Author)
Homer Comes Home 1920,Je 28,13:2
Hull, Arthur
Prince There Was 1921,N 14,18:1
Hull, Arthur S
Within the Law 1923,Ap 30,11:2
Man of Action, A 1923,Je 4,13:3
Going Up 1923,O 10,16:2
Yankee Consul, The 1924,F 11,18:3
Woman on the Jury, The 1924,My 19,14:2
Bought 1931,Ag 15,18:3
Sisters Under the Skin 1934,Je 8,18:1
Hull, Edith M (Original Author)
Sheik, The 1921,N 7,20:1
Old Loves and New 1926,Ap 20,24:7
Hull, Henry
One Exciting Night 1922,O 24,17:3
Hoosier Schoolmaster, The 1924,Mr 18,25:2
Midnight 1934,Mr 10,18:3
Transient Lady 1935,Mr 11,15:1
Werewolf of London, The 1935,My 10,25:2
Paradise for Three 1938,F 16,17:1
Yellow Jack 1938,My 20,17:2
Three Comrades 1938,Je 3,17:1
Boys Town 1938,S 9,25:1
Great Waltz, The 1938,N 25,19:1
Jesse James 1939,Ja 14,13:1
Spirit of Culver 1939,Mr 9,18:1
Return of the Cisco Kid, The 1939,Ap 29,13:2
Stanley and Livingstone 1939,Ag 5,18:2
Miracles for Sale 1939,Ag 10,15:2
Babes in Arms 1939,O 20,27:2
Nick Carter, Master Detective 1939,D 14,35:2
Judge Hardy and Son 1940,Ja 18,27:3 (In Addenda)
My Son, My Son! 1940,My 10,26:6
Return of Frank James, The 1940,Ag 10,16:4

Hull, Henry — Cont

High Sierra 1941,Ja 25,11:2
Lifeboat 1944,Ja 13,17:1
Woman of the Town, The 1944,Mr 6,17:2
Objective Burma 1945,Ja 27,15:2
High Barbaree 1947,Je 6,27:2
Deep Valley 1947,Ag 23,7:2
Mourning Becomes Electra 1947,N 20,38:2
Scudda-Hoo! Scudda-Hay! 1948,Ap 15,31:1
Walls of Jericho, The 1948,Ag 5,16:2
Fighter Squadron 1948,N 20,9:2
El Paso 1949,Mr 24,35:2
Portrait of Jennie 1949,Mr 30,31:2
Colorado Territory 1949,Je 25,8:6
Fountainhead, The 1949,Jl 9,8:5
Great Gatsby, The 1949,Jl 14,20:5
Great Dan Patch, The 1949,N 9,37:2
Hollywood Story 1951,Je 7,40:6
Inferno 1953,Ag 12,22:2
Thunder Over the Plains 1953,D 10,64:4
Man With the Gun 1955,D 23,14:2
Proud Rebel, The 1958,Jl 2,23:4
Buccaneer, The 1958,D 24,00:0
Sheriff of Fractured Jaw, The 1959,Mr 14,27:4
Oregon Trail, The 1959,D 10,51:6
Master of the World 1961,S 16,9:1
Chase, The 1966,F 19,24:1

Hull, Josephine

After Tomorrow 1932,Mr 7,13:5
Careless Lady 1932,Ap 18,19:2
Arsenic and old Lace 1944,S 2,17:2
Harvey 1950,D 22,19:1

Hull, Mary

Swamp Woman 1941,D 27,15:2

Hull, Warren

Miss Pacific Fleet 1935,D 7,22:2
Fish 1936,Ja 25,18:5
Freshman Love 1936,Ja 25,18:5
Walking Dead, The 1936,Mr 2,13:2
Law in her Hands, The 1936,Je 6,21:2
Big Noise, The 1936,Jl 4,18:3
Bengal Tiger 1936,Jl 30,22:1
Love Begins at 20 1936,S 19,20:1
Fugitive in the Sky 1937,Ja 16,21:1
Her Husband's Secretary 1937,Mr 20,23:6
Night Key 1937,Ap 19,27:2
Hawaii Calls 1938,Ap 29,17:2
Lone Wolf Meets a Lady, The 1940,Je 17,19:2
Wagons Westward 1940,Jl 8,13:2
Bowery Blitzkrieg 1941,O 1,24:5

Hull, Wayne

Wagons Westward 1940,Jl 8,13:2

Hullei, Stephen (Original Author)

Variety 1926,Je 28,15:5

Hullinger, Edwin Ware (Screenwriter)

Private Life of Mussolini, The 1938,Je 24,15:2

Hulme, Kathryn (Original Author)

Nun's Story, The 1959,Je 19,30:1

Hulper, Ilse

Christina 1951,Ja 15,13:1

Hulswit, Mart

Come Spy with Me 1967,F 22,21:1

Hultberg, Paul

Edge, The 1968,Mr 28,52:1

Hultman, Rune Sgt

Winged Victory 1944,D 21,16:2

Hulton, Richard

Friday the 13th 1934,My 15,18:1

Hulzen, Joop von

Before Him all Rome Trembled 1947,F 22,16:2

Hulzen, Van

Open City; Citta Aperta 1946,F 26,21:2

Humbart, George

Night Club Lady, The 1932,Ag 27,13:4

Humberstone, Bruce (Director)

Strangers of the Evening 1932,Je 4,9:2
If I Had a Million 1932,D 3,21:4
King of the Jungle 1933,F 25,20:3
Dragon Murder Case, The 1934,Ag 23,13:3
Silk Hat Kid 1935,Ag 7,22:5
Charlie Chan at the Race Track 1936,Ag 15,6:2
Charlie Chan at the Opera 1936,D 5,16:2
Charlie Chan at the Olympics 1937,My 24,23:1
Rascals 1938,My 27,12:2
Time Out for Murder 1938,O 7,21:2
While New York Sleeps 1938,D 22,25:3
Charlie Chan in Honolulu 1938,D 31,7:3
Pack up Your Troubles 1939,O 27,27:2
Lucky Cisco Kid 1940,Je 24,19:5
Quarterback, The 1940,O 17,33:3
Tall, Dark and Handsome 1941,Ja 24,15:2
Sun Valley Serenade 1941,S 6,20:1
I Wake up Screaming 1942,Ja 17,13:2
To the Shores of Tripoli 1942,Mr 26,27:2
Iceland 1942,O 15,27:1
Hello, Frisco, Hello 1943,Mr 25,25:1
Pin Up Girl 1944,My 11,25:6
Wonder Man 1945,Je 9,17:2
Within These Walls 1945,Jl 16,8:4
Three Little Girls in Blue 1946,S 26,32:3
Homestretch, The 1947,Ap 24,30:2
Fury at Furnace Creek 1948,Jl 12,11:2
South Sea Sinner 1950,Ja 16,18:4
Happy Go Lovely 1951,Jl 26,17:2

She's Working her Way Through College 1952,Jl 10,27:2
Desert Song, The 1953,My 21,39:2
Purple Mask, The 1955,Je 16,35:7
Tarzan and the Lost Safari 1957,Ap 13,12:3
Tarzan's Fight for Life 1958,Ag 16,10:2
Madison Avenue 1962,Mr 29,28:2

Humberstone, Bruce (Producer)

Madison Avenue 1962,Mr 29,28:2

Humbert, George

Greatest Love of All, The 1924,N 11,14:1
Street Scene 1931,Ag 27,22:5
Ladies of the Jury 1932,Ap 2,13:2
Farewell to Arms, A 1932,D 9,26:5
I Cover the Waterfront 1933,My 18,17:3
Whom the Gods Destroy 1934,Jl 13,14:2
Redhead 1934,N 16,27:1
In Caliente 1935,Je 27,16:1
Hard Rock Harrigan 1935,Jl 30,16:2
Winterset 1936,D 4,31:1
Banjo on My Knee 1936,D 12,15:1
You Can't Have Everything 1937,Ag 4,15:2
Dead End 1937,Ag 25,25:1
Love Under Fire 1937,Ag 28,8:2
Heidi 1937,N 6,14:2
Girl With Ideas, A 1938,Ja 1,11:2
Expensive Husbands 1938,Ja 8,19:3
No Time to Marry 1938,F 23,27:2
Island in the Sky 1938,My 14,18:1
Professor Beware 1938,Jl 14,17:1
City Streets 1938,Jl 25,18:2
Fisherman's Wharf 1939,F 24,15:2
Daughters Courageous 1939,Je 24,14:2
Song of the Street 1939,S 5,21:2
Full Confession 1939,S 28,29:4
Music in My Heart 1940,Ja 4,19:2
Ghost Creeps, The 1940,Ag 19,13:3
Hired Wife 1940,S 14,11:2
Moon Over Miami 1941,Jl 5,14:2
Truck Busters 1943,Ja 29,23:5
Rose Tattoo, The 1955,D 13,55:1

Hume, Benita

Wrecker, The 1929,Ag 13,23:2
High Treason 1929,Ag 25,VIII,4:7 (In Addenda)
Jaws of Hell 1931,Ja 5,21:3
Flying Fool 1931,O 19,28:1
Reserved for Ladies 1932,My 21,9:2
Blame the Woman 1932,O 25,24:5
Clear all Wires 1933,Mr 4,11:2
Looking Forward 1933,My 1,10:2
Gambling Ship 1933,Jl 13,17:5
Only Yesterday 1933,N 10,25:1
Worst Woman in Paris, The 1933,N 25,10:3
Power 1934,O 5,29:3
Private Life of Don Juan, The 1934,D 10,16:2
Gay Deception, The 1935,O 11,31:1
Garden Murder Case, The 1936,Mr 2,13:2
Moonlight Murder 1936,Mr 28,11:2
Suzy 1936,Jl 25,16:1
Tarzan Escapes 1936,N 20,27:2
Rainbow on the River 1936,D 18,31:4
Last of Mrs Cheyney, The 1937,F 19,15:1
Peck's bad Boy With the Circus 1939,Ja 11,17:4

Hume, Cyril (Original Author)

Wife of the Centaur, The 1925,Ja 7,33:5
Bugle Sounds, The 1942,Ap 3,25:2

Hume, Cyril (Screenwriter)

Limehouse Blues 1934,D 12,28:2
Yellow Dust 1936,F 24,14:1
Tarzan Escapes 1936,N 20,27:2
Jungle Princess 1936,D 24,21:3
They Gave Him a Gun 1937,My 14,21:1
Live, Love and Learn 1937,N 19,27:2
Bad Man of Brimstone, The 1938,F 4,17:2
Tarzan Finds a Son 1939,Je 15,27:2
Twenty-Mule Team 1940,My 10,26:6
Bugle Sounds, The 1942,Ap 3,25:2
High Barbaree 1947,Je 6,27:2
Bride of Vengeance 1949,Ap 7,38:2
Great Gatsby, The 1949,Jl 14,20:5
Tokyo Joe 1949,O 27,35:2
Lady Without Passport, A 1950,Ag 4,13:2
Branded 1951,Ja 11,28:5
Ransom 1956,Ja 25,28:3
Forbidden Planet 1956,My 4,21:2
Bigger Than Life 1956,Ag 3,11:2

Hume, David (Original Author)

Patient Vanishes, The 1947,My 23,31:2

Hume, Doris (Original Author)

Susan Slade 1961,N 11,14:6

Hume, Douglas

This Rebel Breed 1960,My 5,41:2

Hume, Margaret

Triumph of the Scarlet Pimpernel, The 1929,Jl 8,17:3

Hume, Marjorie

Prince of Lovers, The 1927,N 29,31:1
Curse of Frankenstein, The 1957,Ag 8,15:5

Humes, Fred

Circus Rookies 1928,My 14,25:1

Hummel, Wilson

First Born, The 1921,Ja 31,11:1
Dangerous Maid, The 1923,D 11,26:2

Hummel, Wilson — Cont

Ladies Must Dress 1927,D 31,31:1
Woman Trap 1929,Ag 31,13:4

Hummert, Frank (Original Author)

Manhattan Merry-Go-Round 1937,D 31,9:3

Humphrey, Cavada

Thoroughly Modern Millie 1967,Mr 23,25:1

Humphrey, John

Three Cases of Murder (Lord Mountdrago); Lord Mountdrago (Three Cases of Murder) 1955,Mr 16,39:4

Humphrey, Orral

Huckleberry Finn 1920,F 23,11:2

Humphrey, William

Scaramouche 1923,O 12,7:2 (Incorrect in this edition; use 1927,O 1,7:2 elsewhere)
Dramatic Life of Abraham Lincoln, The 1924,Ja 22,17:3
Beau Brummell 1924,Mr 31,20:1
Drusilla With a Million 1925,My 25,21:3
Dangerous Innocence 1925,Je 8,19:1
Unholy Three, The 1925,Ag 4,14:3
Silent Lover, The 1926,N 15,19:1
Actress, The 1928,Jl 9,25:1
Devil May Care 1929,D 23,18:2
Murder at Midnight 1931,O 5,17:3
Manhattan Parade 1931,D 25,29:2
Vampire Bat, The 1933,Ja 23,9:1
Cheating Blondes 1933,My 20,11:4
Are We Civilized? 1934,Je 14,28:5

Humphrey, William (Original Author)

Home from the Hill 1960,Mr 4,19:1

Humphreys, Cecil

Irish Luck 1925,N 24,28:4
Unfinished Symphony 1935,Ja 14,11:2
Accused 1936,D 17,35:1
Wuthering Heights 1939,Ap 14,28:2
Razor's Edge, The 1946,N 20,42:2
Desire Me 1947,S 26,28:3
Woman's Vengeance, A 1948,Ja 30,19:2

Humphreys, Dick

If You Knew Susie 1948,F 23,19:2

Humphreys, Griffith

Condemned to Death 1932,Jl 14,24:2
Loyalties 1934,O 26,25:1
Wanted Men 1936,Jl 8,15:2

Humphries, Barry

Bedazzled 1967,D 11,65:2

Humphries, Joe

Great White Way, The 1924,Ja 4,10:1

Hundar, Robert

Marco Polo 1962,S 20,29:2

Hunebelle, Andre (Director)

Simple Case of Money, A 1952,F 2,11:2
OSS 117-Mission for a Killer 1966,O 13,50:3

Hunebelle, Andre (Producer)

Simple Case of Money, A 1952,F 2,11:2

Hunebelle, Andre (Screenwriter)

OSS 117-Mission for a Killer 1966,O 13,50:3

Hung, Pat Tind

Last Woman of Shang, The 1964,D 15,56:2

Hunger, Anna (Original Author)

Secret of Convict Lake, The 1951,Ag 4,7:2
Pearl of the South Pacific 1955,S 17,12:2

Hunnicutt, Arthur

Fall In 1943,My 15,13:3
Johnny Come Lately 1943,S 24,26:1
Abroad With two Yanks 1944,O 26,19:7
Lust for Gold 1949,Jl 4,9:2
Pinky 1949,S 30,28:2
Great Dan Patch, The 1949,N 9,37:2
Border Incident 1949,N 21,29:2
Ticket to Tomahawk, A 1950,My 20,8:6
Broken Arrow 1950,Jl 21,15:2
Two Flags West 1950,O 13,23:2
Stars in my Crown 1950,D 22,19:1
Sugarfoot 1951,F 12,19:4
Red Badge of Courage, The 1951,O 19,22:2
Distant Drums 1951,D 26,19:3
Big Sky, The 1952,Ag 20,21:1
Lusty Men, The 1952,O 25,12:6
Split Second 1953,My 13,34:2
Devil's Canyon 1953,O 3,14:2
She Couldn't Say No 1954,F 27,11:3
French Line, The 1954,My 15,13:2
Cardinal, The 1963,D 13,41:1
Tiger Walks, A 1964,Ag 27,28:2
Cat Ballou 1965,Je 25,36:1
Adventures of Bullwhip Griffin, The 1967,Mr 9,43:2
Dorado, El 1967,Je 29,32:1

Hunnicutt, Gayle

P J 1968,Mr 7,52:3

Hunt, Albert (Screenwriter)

Tell Me Lies 1968,F 13,46:3

Hunt, Eleanor

Whoopee 1930,O 1,26:3
Goldie 1931,Je 29,20:3
Navy Spy 1937,Mr 22,27:3
Gold Racket, The 1937,Ag 2,10:3

Hunt, Frances

You're a Sweetheart 1937,D 25,10:5

Hunt, Harry
Crazy Quilt, The 1966,O 4,50:1
Hunt, Heidy
Tobruk 1967,F 9,33:2
Hunt, Helen
Sawdust Paradise, The 1928,Ag 27,23:1
Wagon Wheels 1934,O 4,19:1
Hunt, Irene
Forget Me Not 1922,Jl 24,10:2
Eternal Three, The 1923,O 12,7:2 (Incorrect in
this edition; use 1927,O 1,7:2 elsewhere)
Hunt, Jay
Hunchback of Notre Dame, The 1923,S 3,9:3
Lightnin 1925,Jl 22,14:4
My Own Pal 1926,Mr 15,18:3
One Minute to Play 1926,S 6,16:2
Captain Salvation 1927,Je 27,25:2
Harvester, The 1927,N 7,33:1
Sky Spider, The 1931Ag 31,11:5
Hunt, Jimmy
Mating of Millie, The 1948,Mr 13,12:2
Sainted Sisters, The 1948,My 20,35:2
Pitfall 1948,Ag 25,31:2
Sorry, Wrong Number 1948,S 2,18:2
Family Honeymoon 1949,F 25,28:2
Top o' the Morning 1949,S 1,25:2
Cheaper by the Dozen 1950,Ap 1,12:2
Shadow on the Wall 1950,My 19,31:3
Capture, The 1950,My 20,8:6
Rock Island Trail 1950,Je 5,19:3
Louisa 1950,O 25,45:2
Invaders From Mars 1953,My 30,7:1
Lone Hand 1953,Je 27,7:2
Hunt, Leslie
Uncle Sam of Freedom Ridge 1920,S 27,15:2
Old Home Week 1925,My 25,21:3
Hunt, Marsha
Gentle Julia 1936,Ap 11,19:1
Hollywood Boulevard 1936,S 21,26:4
Accusing Finger, The 1936,N 17,35:4
College Holiday 1936,D 24,21:2
Annapolis Salute 1937,O 2,18:1
Thunder Trail 1938,F 5,19:3
Come on Leathernecks 1938,S 15,29:3
Hardys Ride High, The 1939,Ap 14,28:2
Winter Carnival 1939,Jl 28,14:2
These Glamour Girls 1939,Ag 31,14:2
Joe and Ethel Turp Call on the President
1940,Ja 4,19:2
Irene 1940,My 24,23:3
Pride and Prejudice 1940,Ag 9,19:1
Ellery Queen, Master Detective 1940,D 19,33:1
Flight Command 1941,Ja 17,21:2
Trial of Mary Dugan, The 1941,Mr 6,25:4
Cheers for Miss Bishop 1941,Mr 14,17:2
Penalty, The 1941,Ap 10,29:3
I'll Wait for You 1941,Je 2,13:6
Blossoms in the Dust 1941,Je 27,14:4
Unholy Partners 1941,D 29,21:4
Joe Smith, American 1942,Ap 2,27:4
Kid Glove Killer 1942,Ap 17,21:4
Panama Hattie 1942,O 2,31:2
Seven Sweethearts 1942,N 13,28:1
Human Comedy, The 1943,Mr 3,19:2
Pilot No 5 1943,Je 25,13:4
Thousands Cheer 1943,S 14,27:1
Cry Havoc 1943,N 24,16:2
None Shall Escape 1944,Ap 7,23:2
Lost Angel 1944,Ap 10,14:1
Bride by Mistake 1944,S 16,20:2
Music for Millions 1944,D 22,12:4
Valley of Decision, The 1945,My 4,23:2
Letter for Evie, A 1946,Je 28,17:4
Smash-Up, The Story of a Woman
1947,Ap 11,31:2
Carnegie Hall 1947,My 3,10:2
Raw Deal 1948,Jl 9,11:4
Take one False Step 1949,Je 23,33:2
Mary Ryan, Detective 1949,N 4,33:3
Actors and Sin; (Actor's Blood) 1952,My 30,11:3
Happy Time, The 1952,O 31,30:2
Bombers B-52 1957,N 23,11:2
Blue Denim 1959,Jl 31,21:1
Hunt, Martita
Reserved for Ladies 1932,My 21,9:2
I Was a Spy 1934,Ja 15,12:2
Friday the 13th 1934,My 15,18:1
First a Girl 1936,Ja 4,19:1
Nine Days a Queen 1936,O 3,21:1
Troopship 1938,Ap 26,18:2
Prison Without Bars 1939,Ap 10,13:2
Mill On the Floss, The 1939,N 15,19:3
When Knights Were Bold 1942,Mr 31,29:2
Wings and the Woman 1942,O 8,31:1
Young Man's Fancy, A 1943,D 4,11:2
Man in Grey, The 1945,N 30,18:6
Wicked Lady, The 1946,D 23,19:5
Great Expectations 1947,My 23,31:1
Anna Karenina 1948,Ap 28,32:2
So Evil my Love 1948,Jl 22,27:2
Fan, The 1949,Ap 2,12:2
Little Ballerina, The 1951,F 28,33:2
Story of Robin Hood, The 1952,Je 27,18:3

Melba 1953,Je 25,23:1
It Started in Paradise 1953,Jl 25,8:2
Folly to be Wise 1953,D 28,17:2
Anastasia 1956,D 14,35:6
Admirable Crichton, The 1957,D 15,45:4
(Incorrect in this edition; use 1957,D 17,45:4
elsewhere)
Bonjour Tristesse 1958,Ja 16,32:1
Me and the Colonel 1958,Ag 27,33:1
Dangerous Exile 1958,O 11,18:3
3 Men in a Boat 1959,Jl 29,33:2
Song Without End 1960,Ag 12,10:2
Brides of Dracula, The 1960,S 6,41:4
I Like Money 1962,My 19,18:2
Wonderful World of the Brothers Grimm, The
1962,Ag 8,35:1
Becket 1964,Mr 12,40:2
Unsinkable Molly Brown, The 1964,Jl 17,15:1
Bunny Lake is Missing 1965,O 4,00:0
Hunt, Robert B (Original Author)
Boogie Man Will Get You, The 1942,O 12,12:4
Hunt, Ronald Leigh
Khartoum 1966,Jl 14,28:1
Hunter, Alastair
Tight Little Island 1949,D 26,33:2
Martin Luther 1953,S 10,22:1
Hunter, Ann
Hi Diddle Diddle 1943,S 24,26:2
Hunter, Barbara
Trouble With Angels, The 1966,Ap 7,45:1
Where Angels Go-Trouble Follows
1968,Ap 11,51:1
Hunter, Evan (Original Author)
Blackboard Jungle 1955,Mr 21,21:5
Strangers When we Meet 1960,Je 30,22:2
Young Savages, The 1961,My 25,31:1
Mister Buddwing 1966,O 12,36:1
Hunter, Evan (Screenwriter)
Strangers When we Meet 1960,Je 30,22:2
Birds, The 1963,Ap 1,5:5 (Incorrect in this
edition; use 1963,Ap 1,54:1 elsewhere)
Hunter, Glenn
Case of Becky, The 1921,O 10,16:1
Cradle Buster, The 1922,My 22,18:4
Country Flapper, The 1922,Jl 31,12:3
Puritan Passions 1923,O 15,15:4
West of the Water Tower 1923,D 31,9:3
Merton of the Movies 1924,S 8,15:3
Hunter, Hall (Original Author)
Bengal Brigade 1954,N 13,13:2
Hunter, Henry
Nobody's Fool 1936,Je 4,27:2
Parole 1936,Je 27,21:1
Road Back, The 1937,Je 18,25:2
Girl With Ideas, A 1938,Ja 1,11:2
Calling Dr Kildare 1939,My 12,25:4
Good Girls Go to Paris 1939,Je 23,23:1
Thunder Afloat 1939,O 13,27:2
Hunter, Ian
Ring, The 1927,D 25,VIII,7:7 (In Addenda)
Syncopation 1929,Ap 8,32:1
Escape 1930,N 1,23:2
Love Storm 1931,O 19,28:1
Sign of the Four, The 1932,Ag 20,7:4
Orders Is Orders 1934,My 7,20:2
Girl From 10th Avenue, The 1935,My 27,20:6
Jalna 1935,S 14,8:4
Midsummer Night's Dream, A 1935,O 10,31:1
I Found Stella Parish 1935,N 4,24:4
Morals of Marcus, The 1936,Ja 13,14:2
White Angel, The 1936,Je 25,24:1
To Mary-With Love 1936,Je 27,16:1
Devil is a Sissy, The 1936,O 17,21:2
Stolen Holiday 1937,F 1,15:3
Call it a Day 1937,My 7,29:2
Another Dawn 1937,Je 18,25:3
Confession 1937,Ag 19,23:1
That Certain Woman 1937,S 16,29:1
52d Street 1937,N 15,15:1
Adventures of Robin Hood, The 1938,My 13,17:2
Always Goodbye 1938,Je 25,7:2
Secrets of an Actress 1938,O 8,10:2
Sisters, The 1938,O 15,21:3
Comet over Broadway 1938,D 16,33:3
Yes, My Darling Daughter 1939,F 27,11:2
Little Princess, The 1939,Mr 11,21:1
Broadway Serenade 1939,Ap 7,25:2
Tarzan Finds a Son 1939,Je 15,27:2
Maisie 1939,Je 23,23:1
Tower of London 1939,D 12,37:2
Broadway Melody of 1940 1940,Mr 29,25:3
Strange Cargo 1940,Ap 26,25:2
Long Voyage Home, The 1940,O 9,30:2 (In
Addenda)
Bitter Sweet 1940,N 22,27:1
Dulcy 1940,N 28,28:2
Gallant Sons 1940,D 12,37:2
Come Live With Me 1941,F 28,17:3
Andy Hardy's Private Secretary 1941,Mr 7,17:2
Ziegfeld Girl 1941,Ap 25,17:2
Billy the Kid 1941,Je 20,28:2
Dr Jekyll and Mr Hyde 1941,Ag 13,13:2
Smilin' Through 1941,D 5,29:2

Hunter, Ian— Cont
Yank at Eton, A 1942,O 16,23:1
It Comes up Love 1943,Ja 22,25:3
Forever and a Day 1943,Mr 13,9:2
Bedelia 1947,F 8,10:2
Bad Sister 1948,Je 11,27:3
Edward my Son 1949,Je 3,21:2
It Started in Paradise 1953,Jl 25,8:2
Eight O'Clock Walk 1955,Ap 30,10:6
Pursuit of the Graf Spee 1957,D 27,33:2
Mad Little Island 1958,D 31,12:1
Flame Over India 1960,Ap 30,14:1
Guns of Darkness 1962,Ag 18,10:1
Door in the Wall 1965,Ja 22,21:2
Hunter, Ian McLellan (Original Author)
Slightly Dangerous 1943,Ap 2,17:2
Woman of Distinction, A 1950,Mr 17,28:2
Roman Holiday 1953,Ag 28,13:1
Hunter, Ian McLellan (Screenwriter)
Fisherman's Wharf 1939,F 24,15:2
Meet Doctor Christian 1939,D 1,27:2
Courageous Dr Christian, The 1940,Mr 29,25:3
Second Chorus 1941,Ja 16,25:2
Mr District Attorney 1947,F 28,27:3
Eye Witness 1950,Ag 28,13:2
Roman Holiday 1953,Ag 28,13:1
Hunter, J (Original Author)
Killers of Kilimanjaro 1960,Ap 7,46:1
Blue Max, The 1966,Je 22,38:1
Hunter, Jack (Screenwriter)
Glass Mountain, The 1950,My 18,37:3
Hunter, James
King and Country 1966,Ja 28,20:4
Hunter, Jeffrey
Call Me Mister 1951,F 1,21:2
Fourteen Hours 1951,Mr 7,43:2
Frogmen, The 1951,Je 30,8:6
Take Care of my Little Girl 1951,Jl 19,20:2
Smoke Jumpers 1952,Mr 22,9:6
Belles on Their Toes 1952,My 3,17:5
Dreamboat 1952,Jl 26,9:2
Lure of the Wilderness 1952,O 4,15:2
Sailor of the King 1953,S 3,15:2
Three Young Texans 1954,Ap 17,8:2
Princess of the Nile 1954,Je 12,13:2
White Feather 1955,F 17,23:1
Seven Angry Men 1955,Ap 2,15:2
Seven Cities of Gold 1955,O 8,13:2
Searchers, The 1956,My 31,21:4
Great Locomotive Chase, The 1956,Je 27,35:1
Proud Ones, The 1956,Ag 11,10:2
Gun for a Coward 1957,Ja 31,21:1
True Story of Jesse James, The 1957,Mr 23,17:2
Way to*the Gold, The 1957,My 11,24:6
No Down Payment 1957,O 31,41:1
Count Five and Die 1958,My 15,25:1
Last Hurrah, The 1958,O 24,40:1
In Love and War 1958,N 1,14:2
Sergeant Rutledge 1960,My 26,37:1
Hell to Eternity 1960,O 13,41:1
Key Witness 1960,N 12,15:1
King of Kings 1961,O 12,41:2
Man Trap 1961,N 30,40:4
Longest Day, The 1962,O 5,28:1
No Man is an Island 1962,O 11,49:2
Man From Galveston, The 1964,Ja 23,26:3
Brainstorm 1965,Je 10,38:1
Private Navy of Sgt O'Farrell, The
1968,My 9,54:1
Custer of the West 1968,Jl 4,13:2
Hunter, Jerry
Date with Judy, A 1948,Ag 7,8:2
Great Lover, The 1949,N 24,48:2
Hunter, John
Odette 1951,Mr 28,33:2
Hunter, John (Screenwriter)
Intruder, The 1955,Ja 26,22:1
Court Martial 1955,Ag 2,17:1
Hunter, Kenneth
League of Frightened Men, The 1937,Jl 2,25:1
Lancer Spy 1937,N 4,29:1
Adventures of Robin Hood, The 1938,My 13,17:2
Little Princess, The 1939,Mr 11,21:1
Moon and Sixpence, The 1942,O 28,26:4
Hunter, Kim
Seventh Victim, The 1943,S 18,11:3
Tender Comrade 1944,Je 2,21:2
You Came Along 1945,Jl 5,7:2
Stairway to Heaven 1946,D 26,28:1
Canterbury Tale, A 1949,Ja 24,16:2
Streetcar Named Desire, A 1951,S 30,27:1
Deadline U S A 1952,Mr 15,8:2
Anything Can Happen 1952,Ap 4,21:1
Storm Center 1956,O 22,25:4
Young Stranger, The 1957,Ap 9,40:1
Lilith 1964,S 21,37:2
Planet of the Apes 1968,F 9,55:2
Swimmer, The 1968,My 16,53:1
Hunter, Nita
White Tie and Tails 1946,N 8,28:2
Men, The 1950,Jl 21,15:2
Hunter, Raymond
Way Back Home 1932,Ja 16,13:1

Hunter, Robert
Big Sky, The 1952,Ag 20,21:1
Hunter, Ross (Producer)
Take Me to Town 1953,Je 20,8:6
All I Desire 1953,Ag 29,10:1
Magnificent Obsession 1954,Ag 5,18:4
Naked Alibi 1954,O 2,21:2
One Desire 1955,S 3,9:1
Spoilers, The 1955,D 24,10:2
There's Always Tomorrow 1956,Ja 21,18:2
All That Heaven Allows 1956,F 29,35:1
Battle Hymn 1957,F 16,14:1
Tammy and the Bachelor 1957,Je 15,10:7
My Man Godfrey 1957,O 12,23:1
This Happy Feeling 1958,Je 19,28:2
Stranger in my Arms 1959,Mr 4,34:2
Imitation of Life 1959,Ap 18,18:1
Pillow Talk 1959,O 7,47:2
Portrait in Black 1960,Jl 28,19:1
Midnight Lace 1960,O 14,27:1
Tammy Tell me True 1961,Jl 27,23:2
Back Street 1961,O 13,27:1
Flower Drum Song 1961,N 10,40:1
If a Man Answers 1962,N 22,43:1
Tammy and the Doctor 1963,Je 27,23:2
Thrill of it All, The 1963,Ag 2,15:3
Chalk Garden, The 1964,My 22,42:2
I'd Rather Be Rich 1964,S 3,24:2
Art of Love, The 1965,Jl 1,34:1
Madame X 1966,Ap 28,49:1
Pad, The (And How to Use It) 1966,Ag 18,27:2
Thoroughly Modern Millie 1967,Mr 23,25:1
Hunter, Russell
Lilli Marlene 1952,Mr 29,19:2
Hunter, T Hayes (Director)
Border Legion, The 1918,Jl 29,9:3
Earthbound 1920,Ag 11,9:4
Recoil, The 1924,Je 30,16:1
Wildfire 1925,Je 10,18:2
Silver King, The 1929,S 2,16:1
Man they Couldn't Arrest, The 1933,Mr 14,19:3
White Face 1933,D 4,22:3
Criminal at Large 1933,D 20,27:2
Ghoul, The 1934,Ja 27,9:2
Hunter, Tab
Lawless, The 1950,Je 23,29:2
Gun Belt 1953,Ag 1,8:2
Track of the Cat 1954,D 2,38:2
Battle Cry 1955,F 3,18:1
Sea Chase, The 1955,Je 11,8:7
Burning Hills, The 1956,Ag 24,15:2
Girl He Left Behind, The 1956,O 27,17:1
Lafayette Escadrille 1958,Ap 19,10:4
Damn Yankees 1958,S 27,12:7
That Kind of Woman 1959,S 12,12:2
They Came to Cordura 1959,O 22,47:2
Pleasure of his Company, The 1961,Je 2,36:1
Ride the Wild Surf 1964,D 24,8:4
War Gods of the Deep 1965,Je 3,24:3
Loved One, The 1965,O 12,57:1
Hunter, Thomas
Hills Run Red, The 1967,N 11,26:3
Anzio 1968,Jl 25,26:1
Hunter, Virginia
Mating of Millie, The 1948,Mr 13,12:2
Huntington, Lawrence (Director)
Tower of Terror 1942,Je 29,11:4
Wanted for Murder 1946,D 12,38:4
Patient Vanishes, The 1947,My 23,31:2
Upturned Glass, The 1947,N 5,34:4
Mr Perrin and Mr Traill 1949,Ja 17,15:2
Man on the Run 1952,F 27,22:5
Franchise Affair, The 1952,Je 6,19:2
Vulture, The 1967,My 20,39:2
Huntington, Lawrence (Producer)
Trunk, The 1962,N 1,34:3
Vulture, The 1967,My 20,39:2
Huntington, Lawrence (Screenwriter)
Patient Vanishes, The 1947,My 23,31:2
Man on the Run 1952,F 27,22:5
Franchise Affair, The 1952,Je 6,19:2
Vulture, The 1967,My 20,39:2
Huntington, Louise
Three Rogues 1931,Ap 4,23:1
Viking, The 1931,Je 17,32:5
Huntington, Sheila
Upturned Glass, The 1947,N 5,34:4
Huntley, Chet
Arctic Manhunt 1949,Ag 19,12:5
Huntley, Chet (Narrator)
Mau Mau 1955,Jl 14,19:1
Huntley, Fred
Heart of the Wetona, The 1919,Ja 6,11:3
Heart o' the Hills 1919,D 1,9:3
Everywoman 1919,D 15,20:1
Prince There Was 1921,N 14,18:1
Borderland 1922,Jl 24,10:2
Law of the Lawless, The 1923,Je 19,22:4
Where the North Begins 1923,Ag 27,14:3
To the Last Man 1923,Ag 28,12:1
Call of the Canyon, The 1923,D 17,23:1

Huntley, G P
Merely Mary Ann 1931,S 12,15:4
As Husbands Go 1934,Ja 26,20:3
Death Takes a Holiday 1934,F 24,18:4
Now I'll Tell 1934,My 26,12:2
Little Man, What Now? 1934,Je 1,29:1
Servants' Entrance 1934,S 27,25:2
Imitation of Life 1934,N 24,19:1
Becky Sharp 1935,Je 14,27:2
Two Fisted 1935,O 5,18:3
Golden Arrow, The 1936,My 4,16:1
Sons o'Guns 1936,My 14,29:2
Charlie Chan at the Race Track 1936,Ag 15,6:2
Charge of the Light Brigade, The 1936,N 2,24:1
Another Dawn 1937,Je 18,25:3
Say It in French 1938,D 1,29:1
Artists and Models Abroad 1938,D 22,25:3
I'm From Missouri 1939,Mr 23,27:1
Mr Moto Takes a Vacation 1939,Je 19,12:6
Tower of London 1939,D 12,37:2
Private Affairs 1940,Jl 5,10:3
Cross Country Romance 1940,Jl 19,22:3
Play Girl 1941,Ja 30,19:3
Shining Victory 1941,My 31,14:1
They Died With Their Boots On 1941,N 21,23:3
Great Man's Lady, The 1942,Ap 30,14:3
Journey for Margaret 1942,D 18,36:7
Huntley, Hugh
Steadfast Heart, The 1923,D 25,26:1
Second Youth 1924,Ap 22,19:3
Social Celebrity, A 1926,Ap 19,24:3
Second Wife 1930,F 10,20:4
Eyes of the World 1930,Ag 15,20:5
Bat Whispers, The 1931,Ja 16,27:1
Double Harness 1933,Jl 21,20:2
Whom the Gods Destroy 1934,Jl 13,14:2
Lloyds of London 1936,N 26,39:1
Huntley, Raymond
Rembrandt 1936,D 3,31:1
Knight Without Armor 1937,Jl 9,18:1
Dinner at the Ritz 1937,D 4,21:1
Night Train 1940,D 30,21:1
Voice in the Night, The 1941,My 23,25:4
Mister V 1942,F 13,24:4
They Came to a City 1945,F 19,21:3
Way Ahead, The 1945,Je 4,22:3
Adventures, The 1947,Ap 4,19:2
So Evil my Love 1948,Jl 22,27:2
Mr Perrin and Mr Traill 1949,Ja 17,15:2
Broken Journey 1949,My 26,34:3
Passport to Pimlico 1949,O 27,35:2
Sanitorium 1950,O 11,42:1
It's Hard to be Good 1950,D 25,25:3
Long Dark Hall, The 1951,My 10,38:3
I'll Never Forget You 1951,D 8,9:2
Secret Flight 1952,Jl 3,16:2
Mr Denning Drives North 1953,S 2,20:1
Scotch on the Rocks 1954,Je 14,18:2
Hobson's Choice 1954,Je 15,37:1
Teckman Mystery, The 1955,Ag 22,18:2
Prisoner, The 1955,D 12,37:1
Doctor at Sea 1956,Mr 1,37:3
Wee Geordie 1956,O 8,31:1
Green Man, The 1957,My 23,40:1
Constant Husband, The 1957,Jl 26,10:3
Brothers in Law 1957,Ag 20,22:1
Room at the Top 1959,Mr 31,26:1
Our Man in Havana 1960,Ja 28,26:1
I'm All Right Jack 1960,Ap 26,40:2
Man in a Cocked Hat 1960,Je 15,50:2
French Mistress, A 1960,D 19,34:2
Make Mine Mink 1960,D 20,43:4
Risk, The 1961,S 25,41:2
Pure Hell of St Trinian's, The 1961,S 26,31:1
Only Two Can Play 1962,Mr 21,33:2
Waltz of the Toreadors 1962,Ag 14,34:1
Rotten to the Core 1965,Jl 20,39:2
Huntley, Tim
Sword of the Avenger 1948,Ag 26,16:4
Gallant Blade 1948,O 13,31:3
Adventures of Don Juan 1948,D 25,10:1
Come to the Stable 1949,Jl 28,19:1
Huntoon, Helen
Loves of Ricardo, The 1926,Ag 16,10:1
Hunyady, Sandor (Original Author)
Storm at Daybreak 1933,Jl 22,14:2
Girl Downstairs, The 1939,Ja 26,17:1
Eb Ura Fako 1940,Mr 23,16:4
Huper, Harold
Mysterious Mr Moto of Devil's Island 1938,S 19,16:2
Hupfeld, Herman (Composer)
Moonlight and Pretzels 1933,Ag 23,21:2
Take a Chance 1933,N 27,20:3
Huppertz, Toni (Director)
Soldaten-Kameraden 1936,O 5,25:1
HURD
See Also HEARD
Hurd, Earl (Screenwriter)
Fresh Fish 1922,Ag 14,12:4
Snow White and the Seven Dwarfs 1938,Ja 14,21:1 (In Addenda)

Hurd, Hugh
Shadows 1961,Mr 22,37:1
Hurdalek, Georg (Screenwriter)
Devil's General, The 1957,Ap 16,38:2
Roses for the Prosecutor; (Rosen fur den Staarsanwalt) 1961,O 10,38:2
Town Without Pity 1961,O 11,53:1
Hurka, Hans
Monna Vanna 1923,S 25,8:2
Hurlbut, Gladys
Mating Season, The 1951,Ap 12,41:2
Captive City, The 1952,Mr 27,34:2
Shadow in the Sky 1952,Jl 19,8:2
Something for the Birds 1952,N 15,15:2
President's Lady, The 1953,My 22,31:1
Long, Long Trailer, The 1954,F 19,24:3
Man Called Peter, A 1955,Ap 1,22:1
Rains of Ranchipur, The 1955,D 16,38:2
Hurlbut, Gladys (Original Author)
Higher and Higher 1944,Ja 22,8:4
Hurlbut, Gladys (Screenwriter)
Love on the Run 1936,N 28,13:3
Hurlbut, William (Miscellaneous)
Make a Wish 1937,S 23,33:1
Hurlbut, William (Original Author)
Lilies of the Field 1924,Mr 17,19:1
Lilies of the Field 1930,F 22,13:1
Good Sport 1931,D 12,23:3
Hurlbut, William (Screenwriter)
There's Always Tomorrow 1934,N 10,19:2
Imitation of Life 1934,N 24,19:1
Bride of Frankenstein, The 1935,My 11,21:2
Daring Young Man, The 1935,Jl 18,15:2
Orchids to You 1935,Ag 10,16:4
Way Down East 1935,O 31,16:2
Rainbow on the River 1936,D 18,31:4
Adam Had Four Sons 1941,Mr 28,26:6
Hurley, Harold (Producer)
Home on the Range 1935,F 13,24:4
Millions in the Air 1935,D 12,33:4
Timothy's Quest 1936,F 29,11:2
Woman Trap 1936,Mr 7,11:4
Preview Murder Mystery, The 1936,Mr 21,13:2
Sky Parade, The 1936,Ap 20,17:1
Bulldog Drummond in Africa 1938,Ag 25,15:1
Hurley, Julia
Argentine Love 1924,D 23,16:2
Little French Girl, The 1925,Je 1,10:3
Hurlic, Philip
Helldorado 1935,Ja 7,13:2
Hearts Divided 1936,Je 13,13:1
Penrod and Sam 1937,Mr 29,14:3
Adventures of Tom Sawyer, The 1938,F 18,23:1
Penrod and his Twin Brother 1938,Ap 18,11:1
Zenobia 1939,My 15,15:2
Father's Son 1941,F 13,25:3
Hurlock, Madeline
When Comedy Was King 1960,Mr 30,42:1
Hurn, Philip D (Original Author)
Wings in the Dark 1935,F 2,10:1
Hurok, Sol (Original Author)
Tonight We Sing 1953,F 13,17:2
Hurst, Brandon
Thief of Bagdad, The 1924,Mr 19,19:1
Cytherea 1924,My 26,21:1
He Who Gets Slapped 1924,N 10,20:1
Lover of Camille, The 1924,N 11,14:1
Lady, The 1925,Ja 27,11:2
Enchanted Hill, The 1925,D 29,19:2 (In Addenda)
Grand Duchess and the Waiter, The 1926,F 9,22:1
Rainmaker, The 1926,My 18,28:2
Amateur Gentleman, The 1926,Ag 17,15:3
Annie Laurie 1927,My 12,24:3
High School Hero 1927,O 24,24:3
Love 1927,N 30,22:4
Man Who Laughs, The 1928,Ap 28,12:3
News Parade, The 1928,My 29,17:2
Interference 1928,N 17,23:1
Greene Murder Case, The 1929,Ag 10,11:3
High Society Blues 1930,Ap 19,15:1
Eyes of the World 1930,Ag 15,20:5
Right of Way, The 1931,Mr 24,31:2
Connecticut Yankee, A 1931,Ap 13,17:1
Young as You Feel 1931,Ag 8,16:3
Murder at Midnight 1931,O 5,17:3
Murders in the Rue Morgue 1932,F 11,16:1
Midnight Lady 1932,Jl 1,19:3
White Zombie 1932,Jl 29,18:2
Down to Earth 1932,S 2,19:2
Sherlock Holmes 1932,N 12,20:5
Bombay Mail 1934,Ja 6,18:2
Lost Patrol, The 1934,Ap 2,13:2
Bright Eyes 1934,D 21,31:1
While the Patient Slept 1935,Mr 2,18:2
Great Impersonation, The 1935,D 14,11:1
Connecticut Yankee at the Court of King Arthur, A 1936,My 4,16:1
Moon's our Home, The 1936,My 13,29:2
Mary of Scotland 1936,Jl 31,22:2

Hurst, Brandon— Cont

Plough and the Stars, The 1937,Ja 29,15:1
Wee Willie Winkie 1937,Jl 24,12:1
Suez 1938,O 15,21:2
Stanley and Livingstone 1939,Ag 5,18:2
Blue Bird, The 1940,Ja 20,11:2
Rhythm on the River 1940,Ag 29,23:2
Remarkable Andrew, The 1942,Mr 6,17:2
Road to Happiness 1942,Mr 27,27:4
Man in Half Moon Street, The 1945,Ja 20,16:2
Princess and the Pirate, The 1945,F 10,16:2

Hurst, Brian Desmond (Director)

Tell-Tale Heart, The 1934,Je 15,26:3
Norah O'Neale 1934,O 25,26:3
Ourselves Alone 1937,Jl 31,6:2
Tenth Man, The 1937,N 15,15:2
Prison Without Bars 1939,Ap 10,13:2
Lion Has Wings, The 1940,Ja 22,11:2
Fugitive, The 1940,Jl 23,22:2
Suicide Squadron 1942,My 14,23:2
Hungry Hill 1947,O 11,11:2
Gay Lady, The 1951,Ap 16,21:2
Christmas Carol, A 1951,N 29,41:2
Simba 1955,O 22,24:2
Dangerous Exile 1958,O 11,18:3
Playboy of the Western World, The
  1963,Mr 19,8:2

Hurst, Brian Desmond (Producer)

Christmas Carol, A 1951,N 29,41:2

Hurst, Brian Desmond (Screenwriter)

Fugitive, The 1940,Jl 23,22:2
Playboy of the Western World, The
  1963,Mr 19,8:2

Hurst, David

Tony Draws a Horse 1951,My 15,38:6
So Little Time 1953,Jl 28,23:2
Always a Bride 1954,My 28,19:2

Hurst, Fannie (Miscellaneous)

Skeleton on Horseback 1940,F 5,13:3

Hurst, Fannie (Original Author)

Humoresque 1920,My 31,14:2
Star Dust 1922,F 6,9:1
Back Pay 1922,F 13,10:1
Nth Commandment, The 1923,Ap 10,24:3
Mannequinn 1926,Ja 12,27:5
Untamed Lady, The 1926,Mr 16,22:5
Younger Generation, The 1929,Mr 11,22:2
Lummox 1930,Mr 24,25:1
Back Pay 1930,My 31,19:4
Five and Ten 1931,Jl 11,7:6
Back Street 1932,Ag 29,9:2
Hello, Everybody 1933,Ja 30,9:4
Imitation of Life 1934,N 24,19:1
Four Daughters 1938,Ag 19,13:3
Four Wives 1939,D 23,9:1
Back Street 1941,F 12,25:2
Humoresque 1946,D 26,28:1
Young at Heart 1955,Ja 20,35:1
Imitation of Life 1959,Ap 18,18:1
Back Street 1961,O 13,27:1

Hurst, Fannie (Screenwriter)

Symphony of Six Million 1932,Ap 15,23:1

Hurst, Hawthorne (Original Author)

Goldie Gets Along 1933,Je 3,16:4

Hurst, Paul

Red Raiders, The 1927,S 28,28:3
Valley of the Giants, The 1927,D 5,26:2
Sailor's Holiday 1929,O 21,30:1
Racketeer, The 1930,Ja 6,30:8
Officer O'Brien 1930,F 24,18:1
Runaway Bride 1930,My 17,21:2
Shadow of the Law 1930,Je 7,10:4
Single Sin, The 1931,Mr 17,34:3
Secret Six, The 1931,My 2,23:4
Kick In 1931,My 25,17:1
Sweepstakes 1931,Je 25,23:5
Public Defender, The 1931,Ag 1,16:4
Bad Company 1931,N 7,16:5
Secret Witness, The 1931,D 21,28:4
Panama Flo 1932,Ja 20,17:4
Hold 'Em Jail! 1932,Ag 20,7:4
My Pal the King 1932,O 4,26:4
Island of Lost Souls 1933,Ja 13,19:2
Hold Your Man 1933,Jl 1,16:6
Sphinx, The 1933,Jl 6,26:5
Tugboat Annie 1933,Ag 12,14:2
Saturday's Millions 1933,O 14,18:3
Day of Reckoning 1933,N 4,18:2
Midnight Alibi 1934,Jl 4,18:3
Sequoia 1935,F 23,14:6
Shadow of Doubt 1935,Mr 11,15:1
Star of Midnight 1935,Ap 12,26:5
Mississippi 1935,Ap 18,27:2
Public Hero No 1 1935,Je 8,12:2
Gay Deception, The 1935,O 11,31:1
Riffraff 1936,Ja 13,14:2
Robin Hood of El Dorado, The 1936,Mr 14,10:1
I'd Give my Life 1936,Ag 17,9:1
To Mary-With Love 1936,Ag 27,16:1
Gay Desperado, The 1936,O 9,31:4
We Who Are About to Die 1937,Ja 2,15:1
Trouble in Morocco 1937,Mr 15,27:1
Wake up and Live 1937,Ap 24,16:2
This Is my Affair 1937,My 28,17:1

Angel's Holiday 1937,My 29,20:2
Fifty Roads to Town 1937,Je 5,21:1
Slave Ship 1937,Je 17,19:2
You Can't Beat Love 1937,Je 25,25:3
Super-Sleuth 1937,Jl 17,18:1
She's no Lady 1937,Ag 12,14:3
Wife, Doctor and Nurse 1937,O 11,26:5
Second Honeymoon 1937,N 13,11:2
In Old Chicago 1938,Ja 7,15:2
No Time to Marry 1938,F 23,27:2
Rebecca of Sunnybrook Farm 1938,Mr 26,12:1
Island in the Sky 1938,My 14,18:1
Josette 1938,Je 11,9:1
Prison Break 1938,Jl 13,17:4
Alexander's Ragtime Band 1938,Ag 6,7:2
My Lucky Star 1938,S 10,20:2
Hold That Co-ed 1938,S 24,13:1
Last Express, The 1938,O 11,24:4
Thanks For Everything 1938,D 10,13:2
Secrets of a Nurse 1938,D 12,26:2
Topper Takes a Trip 1938,D 30,11:2
Kid From Kokomo, The 1939,My 20,11:2
It Could Happen to You 1939,Je 9,26:3
Each Dawn I Die 1939,Jl 22,12:2
Bad Lands 1939,Ag 9,15:2
On Your Toes 1939,O 21,12:2
Gone With the Wind 1939,D 20,31:2
Star Dust 1940,My 4,13:1
Torrid Zone 1940,My 18,11:3
Edison the Man 1940,Je 7,27:2
They Drive by Night 1940,Jl 27,17:5
South to Karanga 1940,Ag 9,19:1
Westerner, The 1940,O 25,25:2
Tugboat Annie Sails Again 1940,N 9,20:2
Tall, Dark and Handsome 1941,Ja 24,15:2
Virginia 1941,Ja 29,21:2
Caught in the Draft 1941,Je 26,27:3
Parson of Panamint, The 1941,Jl 26,18:2
This Woman Is Mine 1941,O 13,21:2
Ellery Queen and the Murder Ring
  1941,O 21,29:4
Hi 'Ya Chum 1943,F 26,17:4
Ox-Bow Incident, The 1943,My 10,15:2 (In
  Addenda)
Coney Island 1943,Je 17,17:2
Calaboose 1943,Jl 30,19:2
Jack London 1944,Mr 3,19:3
Barbary Coast Gent 1944,S 29,18:2
Something for the Boys 1944,N 30,19:1
Midnight Manhunt 1945,Ag 18,12:5
Dolly Sisters, The 1945,N 15,24:6
Dakota 1945,D 17,17:2
In old Sacramento 1946,Ap 29,24:4
Plainsman and the Lady, The 1946,N 4,33:1
Angel and the Badman 1947,Mr 3,28:4
Yellow Sky 1949,F 2,36:1

Hurst, Veronica

Laughter in Paradise 1951,N 12,21:2
Maze, The 1953,Jl 11,8:2
Angels One Five 1954,Ap 30,28:2
Yellow Balloon, The 1954,O 13,23:2
Will any Gentleman? 1955,S 28,70:6
Boy Cried Murder, The 1966,Ap 14,42:3
2nd Best Secret Agent in the Whole Wide World,
  The 1966,Ap 28,49:1

Hurst, Vida (Original Author)

Blind Date 1934,S 1,16:3

Hurt, John

Man for all Seasons, A 1966,D 13,60:1

Hurt, Mississippi John

Festival 1967,O 24,53:2

Hurtado, Luis

Spirit and the Flesh, The 1948,N 1,28:2

Hurtado, Maria

Where Words Fail; Donde Mueren las Palabraso
  1948,Ag 19,18:4

Hurtado, Pepe

Silk, Blood and Sun 1943,Ja 30,10:6

Hurter, Albert (Miscellaneous)

Pinocchio 1940,F 8,18:3

Hurton, Clarence

Navigator, The 1924,O 13,21:1

Hurwicz, Angelika

Our Daily Bread 1950,O 9,21:6

Hurwitz, L

Chalutzim 1934,Ap 2,13:3

Hurwitz, Leo (Director)

Native Land 1942,My 12,16:3
Strange Victory 1948,S 27,27:2

Hurwitz, Leo (Miscellaneous)

Wave, The 1937,Ap 21,18:1

Hurwitz, Leo (Screenwriter)

Strange Victory 1948,S 27,27:2

Husberg, Rolf (Director)

Children, The 1949,D 23,17:1

Husberg, Rolf (Screenwriter)

Children, The 1949,D 23,17:1

Hush, Lisabeth

X-15 1962,Ap 5,30:2
Thoroughly Modern Millie 1967,Mr 23,25:1

Husing, Ted

To Please a Lady 1950,O 27,24:3

Husing, Ted (Narrator)

Olympic Games of 1948, The 1948,S 25,11:2

Husmann, Ron

Love Has Many Faces 1965,F 25,24:1

Huson, Paul

Richard III 1956,Mr 12,1:4

Hussaini, Zafir

Island of Allah 1956,Je 27,35:1

Hussan, Sanny Bin

Windom's Way 1958,O 1,45:1

Hussein, Anwar

Guide, The 1965,F 10,44:2

Hussein, M

Angelo 1951,Mr 26,19:4

Hussels, Jupp

Herbst-Monoever; Fall Manoeuvres
  1939,Mr 18,9:3

Hussenot, Olivier

Amazing Monsieur Fabre, The 1952,S 9,21:2
Voyage to America 1952,O 20,18:2
Fanfan the Tulip 1953,My 5,34:2
Paris Incident 1954,Ag 18,20:2
Grand Maneuver, The 1956,O 2,39:1
Inspector Maigret 1958,O 9,47:1
Roots of Heaven, The 1958,O 16,46:1
Pot Bouille 1958,O 28,39:1

Hussey, John

Persecution and Assassination of Jean-Paul Marat
  as Performed by the Inmates of the Asylum of
  Charenton Under the Direction of the Marquis
  De Sade, The 1967,F 23,41:1

Hussey, Olivia

Battle of the Villa Fiorita, The 1965,My 27,28:1
Romeo and Juliet 1968,O 9,41:1

Hussey, Ruth

Madame X 1937,O 25,23:1
Man-Proof 1938,Ja 14,21:1
Judge Hardy's Children 1938,Ap 8,17:2
Hold That Kiss 1938,Je 11,9:1
Rich Man, Poor Girl 1938,Ag 19,13:3
Time Out for Murder 1938,O 7,21:2
Spring Madness 1938,D 1,29:3
Honolulu 1939,F 23,19:2
Within the Law 1939,Ap 6,31:2
Maisie 1939,Je 23,23:1
Blackmail 1939,S 15,26:3
Women, The 1939,S 22,27:2
Fast And Furious 1939,O 12,33:3
Another Thin Man 1939,N 24,29:1
Northwest Passage 1940,Mr 8,25:1
Susan and God 1940,Jl 12,11:2
Philadelphia Story, The 1940,D 27,22:2
Flight Command 1941,Ja 17,21:2
Free and Easy 1941,Ap 3,29:4
Our Wife 1941,S 18,31:1
Married Bachelor 1941,O 16,25:3
H M Pulham, Esq 1941,D 19,35:1
Pierre of the Plains 1942,Jl 30,17:3
Tennessee Johnson 1943,Ja 13,18:2
Uninvited, The 1944,F 21,19:3
Tender Comrade 1944,Je 2,21:2
Marine Raiders 1944,Jl 1,10:7
Bedside Manner 1945,Je 23,9:6
I, Jane Doe 1948,Jl 5,8:4
Great Gatsby, The 1949,Jl 14,20:5
Louisa 1950,O 25,45:2
Mr Music 1950,D 21,34:3
That's My Boy 1951,Ag 2,18:1
Woman of the North Country 1952,Ag 30,6:2
Stars and Stripes Forever 1952,D 23,17:2
Lady Wants Mink, The 1953,Ap 6,24:2
Facts of Life, The 1961,F 11,27:1

Huston, John

Cardinal, The 1963,D 13,41:1
Bible, The 1966,S 29,60:1
Casino Royale 1967,Ap 29,25:1
Candy 1968,D 18,54:2

Huston, John (Cinematographer)

Report From the Aleutians 1943,Jl 31,8:2

Huston, John (Director)

Maltese Falcon, The 1941,O 4,18:2
In This our Life 1942,My 9,10:2
Across the Pacific 1942,S 5,9:2
San Pietro 1945,Ja 12,8:2
Treasure of Sierra Madre 1948,Ja 24,11:2
Key Largo 1948,Jl 17,6:6
Asphalt Jungle, The 1950,Je 9,29:3
Red Badge of Courage, The 1951,O 19,22:2
African Queen, The 1952,F 21,24:3
Moulin Rouge 1953,F 11,33:5
Beat the Devil 1954,Mr 13,11:2
Moby Dick 1956,Jl 5,18:1
Heaven Knows Mr Allison 1957,Mr 15,22:1
Barbarian and the Geisha 1958,O 3,25:1
Roots of Heaven, The 1958,O 16,46:1
Unforgiven, The 1960,Ap 7,46:1
Misfits, The 1962,F 2,24:2
Freud 1962,D 13,37:1
List of Adrian Messenger, The 1963,My 30,20:1
Night of the Iguana, The 1964,Jl 1,42:1
Bible, The 1966,S 29,60:1

Huston, John (Director)— Cont

Casino Royale 1967,Ap 29,25:1
Reflections in a Golden Eye 1967,O 12,59:1
Huston, John (Original Author)
Three Strangers 1946,F 23,20:2
Huston, John (Producer)
Asphalt Jungle, The 1950,Je 9,29:3
Moby Dick 1956,Jl 5,18:1
Huston, John (Screenwriter)
Jezebel 1938,Mr 11,15:2
Amazing Dr Clitterhouse, The 1938,Jl 21,14:2
Juarez 1939,Ap 26,27:1
Dr Ehrlich's Magic Bullet 1940,F 24,9:2
High Sierra 1941,Ja 25,11:2
Sergeant York 1941,Jl 3,15:1
Maltese Falcon, The 1941,O 4,18:2
Three Strangers 1946,F 23,20:2
Treasure of Sierra Madre 1948,Ja 24,11:2
Key Largo 1948,Jl 17,6:6
We Were Strangers 1949,Ap 28,28:2
Asphalt Jungle, The 1950,Je 9,29:3
Red Badge of Courage, The 1951,O 19,22:2
African Queen, The 1952,F 21,24:3
Moulin Rouge 1953,F 11,33:5
Beat the Devil 1954,Mr 13,11:2
Moby Dick 1956,Jl 5,18:1
Heaven Knows Mr Allison 1957,Mr 15,22:1
Night of the Iguana, The 1964,Jl 1,42:1
Huston, Patricia
Experiment in Terror 1962,Ap 14,14:1
Synanon 1965,My 6,44:1
Huston, Paul (Original Author)
Devil's Pipeline, The 1940,N 11,22:4
Mutiny in the Arctic 1941,My 3,20:5
Huston, Paul (Screenwriter)
Ski Patrol 1940,My 21,29:4
Devil's Pipeline, The 1940,N 11,22:4
Drums of the Congo 1942,Jl 20,16:4
Huston, Philip
Big Game, The 1936,O 24,23:1
We're on the Jury 1937,F 10,18:5
Man Who Found Himself, The 1937,Ap 9,19:3
Behind the Headlines 1937,Je 1,27:2
Close-Up 1948,Ap 5,24:2
Huston, Tony
List of Adrian Messenger, The 1963,My 30,20:1
Huston, Virginia
Nocturne 1946,N 11,42:2
Out of the Past 1947,N 26,18:2
Flamingo Road 1949,My 7,10:2
Racket, The 1951,D 13,44:2
Sudden Fear 1952,Ag 8,9:2
Knock on Wood 1954,Ap 15,34:2
Huston, Walter
Gentlemen of the Press 1929,My 13,27:2
Lady Lies, The 1929,S 7,15:1
Virginian, The 1929,D 23,18:2
Abraham Lincoln 1930,Ag 26,24:1
Bad Man, The 1930,S 27,21:3
Virtuous Sin 1930,N 2,VIII,5:2 (In Addenda)
Criminal Code, The 1931,Ja 5,21:3
Star Witness, The 1931,Ag 4,19:5
Ruling Voice, The 1931,N 5,29:3
Woman From Monte Carlo, The 1931,D 31,17:6
House Divided, A 1932,Ja 9,21:1
Law and Order 1932,F 29,21:3
Beast of the City, The 1932,Mr 14,13:3
Wet Parade, The 1932,Ap 22,23:2
Night Court 1932,My 27,27:5
American Madness 1932,Ag 6,14:5
Rain 1932,O 13,22:3
Kongo 1932,N 17,22:5
Gabriel Over the White House 1933,Ap 1,18:2
Hell Below 1933,Ap 26,13:2
Storm at Daybreak 1933,Jl 22,14:2
Ann Vickers 1933,S 29,24:1
Prizefighter and the Lady, The 1933,N 11,11:3
Transatlantic Tunnel 1935,O 28,16:2
Rhodes 1936,F 29,11:1
Dodsworth 1936,S 24,29:1
Of Human Hearts 1938,F 18,23:1
Light That Failed, The 1939,D 25,19:1
All That Money Can Buy 1941,O 17,27:2
Swamp Water 1941,N 17,15:2
Shanghai Gesture, The 1941,D 26,21:2
Always in my Heart 1942,Mr 14,19:2
Yankee Doodle Dandy 1942,My 30,9:1
Edge of Darkness 1943,Ap 10,12:4
Mission to Moscow 1943,Ap 30,25:2
North Star, The 1943,N 5,23:1
Dragon Seed 1944,Jl 21,16:4
And Then There Were None 1945,N 1,20:2
Dragonwyck 1946,Ap 11,35:2
Duel in the Sun 1947,My 8,30:2
Outlaw, The 1947,S 12,18:4
Treasure of Sierra Madre 1948,Ja 24,11:2
Summer Holiday 1948,Je 12,8:5
Great Sinner, The 1949,Je 30,19:2
Furies, The 1950,Ag 17,23:2
Huston, Walter (Narrator)
Our Russian Front 1942,F 12,27:2
Prelude to War 1943,My 14,16:1

Huszar-Puffy, Karl
Between Worlds 1924,Jl 7,10:4
Bride 68 1930,Ap 15,28:5
Blue Angel, The 1930,D 6,21:3
Ein Ausgekochter Junge 1932,My 3,25:5
I Kiss Your Hand, Madame 1932,Ag 29,9:2
Pesti Szerelem 1934,My 10,25:3
Iza Neni 1934,Je 5,28:6
Hutchens, Robert (Original Author)
Paradine Case, The 1948,Ja 9,26:2
Hutcherson, Le Vern
Carmen Jones 1954,O 29,27:2
Hutcheson, David
Fast and Loose 1930,D 1,21:1
This'll Make You Whistle 1938,N 1,27:2
Convoy 1941,Ja 17,21:2
Next of Kin 1943,My 6,25:2
Life and Death of Colonel Blimp, The
  1945,Mr 30,18:2
Madness of the Heart 1950,O 12,43:2
Operation X 1950,D 11,31:2
Encore (Gigolo and Gigolette); Gigolo and
  Gigolette (Encore) 1952,Ap 3,45:1
Something Money Can't Buy 1953,O 1,34:3
Law and Disorder 1958,Ag 6,20:1
Evil of Frankenstein, The 1964,Je 18,29:2
Hutchings, Linda
Best of Everything 1959,O 9,24:2
Marines, Lets Go! 1961,Ag 16,37:2
Hutchins, Peter
Bedazzled 1967,D 11,65:2
Hutchins, Will
No Time for Sergeants 1958,My 30,13:2
Merrill's Marauders 1962,Je 14,23:4
Spinout 1966,D 15,60:1
Clambake 1967,D 14,62:3
Hutchinson, A S M (Original Author)
Clean Heart, The 1924,S 15,28:1
If Winter Comes 1948,Ja 23,28:4
Hutchinson, David
Sleeping Car to Trieste 1949,Ap 18,18:6
Hutchinson, Harry
Adventures, The 1947,Ap 4,19:2
Hutchinson, Jerry (Screenwriter)
Two in Revolt 1936,Ap 25,21:1
Hutchinson, Josephine
Happiness Ahead 1934,O 11,28:2
Right to Live, The 1935,F 16,9:1
Oil for the Lamps of China 1935,Je 6,25:2
Melody Lingers on, The 1935,N 7,27:1
Story of Louis Pasteur, The 1936,F 10,15:1
I Married a Doctor 1936,Ap 20,17:1
Mountain Justice 1937,My 13,31:2
Crime of Dr Hallet, The 1938,Mr 24,21:3
Son of Frankenstein 1939,Ja 30,9:2
My Son, My Son! 1940,My 10,26:6
Tom Brown's School Days 1940,Je 28,22:2
Somewhere in the Night 1946,Je 13,24:2
Cass Timberlane 1947,N 7,20:2
Adventure in Baltimore 1949,Ap 29,27:2
Love Is Better Than Ever 1952,Mr 4,23:2
Ruby Gentry 1952,D 26,20:2
Miracle in the Rain 1956,Ap 2,18:1
Gun for a Coward 1957,Ja 31,21:1
Sing Boy Sing 1958,F 22,9:4
North by Northwest 1959,Ag 7,28:1
Adventures of Huckleberry Fin, The
  1960,Ag 4,17:1
Walk Like a Dragon 1960,S 16,24:1
Baby, the Rain Must Fall 1965,Ja 14,44:1
Nevada Smith 1966,Je 24,28:1 (Incorrect in this
  edition; use 1966,Je 30,28:1 elsewhere)
Hutchison, Charles (Director)
Women Men Marry 1931,Jl 13,13:5
Found Alive 1934,F 12,19:2
Hutchison, Muriel
One Third of a Nation 1939,F 11,13:2
Women, The 1939,S 22,27:2
Another Thin Man 1939,N 24,29:1
Huth, Harold
Triumph of the Scarlet Pimpernel, The
  1929,Jl 8,17:3
Silver King, The 1929,S 2,16:1
Jaws of Hell 1931,Ja 5,21:3
Outsider, The 1931,Je 7,VIII,6:1
First Mrs Fraser, The 1932,My 29,VIII,4:5 (In
  Addenda)
Aren't We All? 1932,Jl 1,19:3
Rome Express 1932,D 18,X,6:5
Rome Express 1933,F 27,11:2
Ghoul, The 1934,Ja 27,9:2
Huth, Harold (Director)
Hell's Cargo 1940,S 16,15:2
Huth, Harold (Producer)
They Were Sisters 1946,Jl 24,24:2
Lady Surrenders, A 1947,Je 20,25:6
Bad Sister 1948,Je 11,27:3
Caravan 1949,Ap 21,30:4
Trials of Oscar Wilde, The 1960,Je 28,26:1
Hellions, The 1962,Mr 15,28:2
Huth, Harold (Screenwriter)
Hellions, The 1962,Mr 15,28:2

Huth, Jochen (Original Author)
Vienna Burgtheater 1937,O 27,47:1
Hutshing, Edward Everett (Screenwriter)
Andy Hardy Comes Home 1958,D 24,00:0
Hutt, William
Oedipus Rex 1957,Ja 8,26:1
Hutt, William (Narrator)
To Die in Madrid 1965,S 16,00:0
Hutton, Betty
Fleet's In, The 1942,Mr 12,24:2
Star Spangled Rhythm 1942,D 31,20:1
Happy Go Lucky 1943,Mr 25,25:1
Let's Face It 1943,Ag 5,18:1
Miracle of Morgan's Creek, The 1944,Ja 20,15:2
And the Angels Sing 1944,Jl 13,14:2
Here Come the Waves 1944,D 28,25:2
Incendiary Blonde 1945,Jl 26,13:2
Duffy's Tavern 1945,S 6,23:3
Stork Club, The 1945,D 20,18:2
Cross my Heart 1946,D 19,42:3
Perils of Pauline, The 1947,Jl 10,17:2
Dream Girl 1948,Je 17,29:2
Red, Hot and Blue 1949,O 20,39:2
Annie Get Your Gun 1950,My 18,37:1
Let's Dance 1950,N 30,42:2
Greatest Show on Earth, The 1952,Ja 11,17:2
Somebody Loves Me 1952,S 25,38:1
Spring Reunion 1957,My 6,25:2
Hutton, Brian
Fear Strikes Out 1957,Mr 21,37:2
Gunfight at the O K Corral 1957,My 30,23:2
Last Train from Gun Hill 1959,Jl 30,31:2
Big Fisherman, The 1959,Ag 6,18:1
Hutton, Brian G (Director)
Pad, The (And How to Use It) 1966,Ag 18,27:2
Sol Madrid 1968,Je 14,43:1
Hutton, Jim
Subterraneans, The 1960,Jl 7,26:1
Where the Boys Are 1961,Ja 20,22:1
Honeymoon Machine, The 1961,Ag 24,25:2
Bachelor in Paradise 1961,N 17,41:2
Horizontal Lieutenant, The 1962,My 12,15:3
Period of Adjustment 1962,N 1,34:1
Major Dundee 1965,Ag 8,45:1
Hallelujah Trail, The 1965,Jl 2,17:1
Never too Late 1965,N 5,28:1
Walk, Don't Run 1966,Ag 25,42:3
Who's Minding the Mint? 1967,D 7,60:3
Green Berets, The 1968,Je 20,49:1
Hutton, Lauren
Paper Lion 1968,O 24,54:1
Hutton, Lucille
Ladies Must Live 1921,N 21,20:1
Wine of Youth 1924,Ag 11,16:1
Dick Turpin 1925,Ja 26,14:1
Hutton, Marion
In Society 1944,Ag 17,20:2
Love Happy 1950,Ap 8,9:4
Hutton, Michael Clayton (Original Author)
Mr Lord Says No! 1952,F 12,22:5
Hutton, Raymond
Three Wise Fools 1923,Jl 23,13:4
Hutton, Robert
Destination Tokyo 1944,Ja 1,9:2
Janie 1944,Ag 5,16:2
Hollywood Canteen 1944,D 16,19:2
Roughly Speaking 1945,F 1,18:4
Too Young to Know 1945,D 8,21:2
Janie Gets Married 1946,Je 15,24:2
Time Out of Mind 1947,Ap 7,20:1
Love and Learn 1947,My 3,10:3
Always Together 1947,D 11,46:1
Wallflower 1948,Je 12,8:5
Younger Brothers, The 1949,My 28,11:2
And Baby Makes Three 1949,D 23,17:3
Man on the Eiffel Tower, The 1950,Ja 30,12:2
Beauty on Parade 1950,Ag 18,17:2
Steel Helmet, The 1951,Ja 25,21:5
New Mexico 1951,Jl 14,7:2
Racket, The 1951,D 13,44:2
Casanova's Big Night 1954,Ap 19,19:1
Cinderfella 1960,D 17,19:2
Jailbreakers, The 1961,Ja 5,27:2
Secret Door, The 1964,Je 4,28:1
Vulture, The 1967,My 20,39:2
Huxley, Aldous (Original Author)
Woman's Vengeance, A 1948,Ja 30,19:2
Prelude to Fame 1950,N 10,35:3
Huxley, Aldous (Screenwriter)
Pride and Prejudice 1940,Ag 9,19:1
Jane Eyre 1944,F 4,12:5
Woman's Vengeance, A 1948,Ja 30,19:2
Huxley, Julian (Miscellaneous)
Monkey Into Man 1941,My 31,14:1
Huxley, Rick
Having a Wild Weekend 1965,Ag 19,35:1
Huxley, Sophie
Saratoga Trunk 1945,N 22,39:2
Huxtable, Judy
Psycopath, The 1966,S 29,60:1
Touchables, The 1968,N 21,41:1

Hwang, Lier
World of Suzie Wong, The 1960,N 11;36:1
Hyams, John
Broadway Scandals 1929,O 29,35:1
Cameo Kirby 1930,F 8,12:5
Mighty Barnum, The 1934,D 24,17:1
Sudden Death, And 1936,Jl 18,18:2
Pick a Star 1937,My 28,17:2
Housekeeper's Daughter, The 1939,D 2,21:4
Hyams, Leila
Sandra 1924,D 22,20:2
Summer Bachelors 1926,D 20,28:3
Brute, The 1927,Ap 21,25:1
Wizard, The 1927,N 28,18:5
Honor Bound 1928,Ap 30,18:3
Alias Jimmy Valentine 1928,N 16,28:6
Spite Marriage 1929,Mr 25,32:2
Idle Rich, The 1929,Je 17,29:1
Wonder of Women 1929,Jl 22,17:1
Bishop Murder Case, The 1930,F 1,15:1
Girl Said No, The 1930,Ap 5,23:3
Big House, The 1930,Je 25,31:2
Sweethearts and Wives 1930,Je 28,9:2
Sins of the Children 1930,Jl 26,16:4
Flirting Widow, The 1930,Ag 2,16:4
Way out West 1930,Ag 18,24:1
Way for a Sailor 1930,D 13,22:2
Shepper - Newfounder, The 1930,D 25,31:5
Men Call it Love 1931,Je 20,20:4
Gentleman's Fate 1931,Je 27,20:3
New Adventures of Get-Rich-Quick Wallingford
  1931,O 10,20:4
Phantom of Paris, The 1931,N 14,15:3
Surrender 1931,N 28,20:4
Red Headed Woman 1932,Jl 1,19:3
Freaks 1932,Jl 9,7:5
Big Broadcast, The 1932,O 15,13:1
Island of Lost Souls 1933,Ja 13,19:2
Sing Sinner Sing 1933,Ag 15,20:2
Saturday's Millions 1933,O 14,18:3
Affairs of a Gentleman 1934,Je 23,16:7
Ruggles of Red Gap 1935,Mr 7,26:1
People Will Talk 1935,Je 17,20:2
$1,000 a Minute 1935,D 21,11:1
Yellow Dust 1936,F 24,14:1
Hyams, Nicholas (Original Author)
Good Times 1967,Ag 3,26:4
Hyans, Eddie Jr
Jungle Woman 1944,Jl 15,19:6
Hyatt, Bobby
Miracle on 34th Street 1947,Je 5,32:1
Mr Peabody and the Mermaid 1948,Ag 14,6:5
Dark Past, The 1948,D 23,25:2
No Minor Vices 1949,F 26,11:2
He Ran all the Way 1951,Je 21,24:2
Tomorrow Is Another Day 1951,Ag 9,17:5
Basketball Fix, the 1951,S 14,21:2
It's a big Country 1952,Ja 9,25:2
Carbine Williams 1952,My 8,37:2
Miserables, Les 1952,Ag 15,11:2
Careless Years, The 1957,N 28,57:3
Hyatt, Daniel (Screenwriter)
Gorgo 1961,Mr 30,24:2
Hyde, Dora
Prelude to Fame 1950,N 10,35:3
Hyde, Mary Ann
Flesh and Fantasy 1943,N 18,29:1
Hyde, Montgomery (Original Author)
Trials of Oscar Wilde, The 1960,Je 28,26:1
Hyde-White, Wilfrid
One Woman's Story 1949,My 18,33:2
Man on the Eiffel Tower, The 1950,Ja 30,12:2
Third Man, The 1950,F 3,29:2
Conspirator 1950,Ap 28,26:2
Mr Know-All 1950,O 11,42:1
Last Holiday 1950,N 14,39:4
Golden Salamander 1951,Mr 24,8:3
Mister Drake's Duck 1952,Ja 28,15:2
Outcast of the Islands 1952,My 16,19:2
Truth About Women, The 1958,Ag 29,18:2
Circle, The 1959,Ap 16,29:2
John Goldfarb, Please Come Home
  1965,Mr 25,42:4
Operation Snafu 1965,My 22,18:1
Ten Little Indians 1966,F 10,33:1
Chamber of Horrors 1966,O 20,52:5
Liquidator, The 1966,O 29,34:1
P J 1968,Mr 7,52:3
Hydes, David
Red Danube, The 1949,D 9,37:3
Hyer, Georgette (Original Author)
Reluctant Widow, The 1951,S 8,8:6
Hyer, Martha
Judge Steps Out, The 1949,Je 3,21:4
Roughshod 1949,Je 17,27:2
Lawless, The 1950,Je 23,29:2
So Big 1953,O 22,34:2
Riders to the Stars 1954,Mr 20,10:7
Lucky Me 1954,Ap 10,11:2
Scarlet Spear, The 1954,Ap 10,11:4
Down Three Dark Streets 1954,S 4,6:4
Sabrina 1954,S 23,43:2
Cry Vengence 1955,F 19,18:3

Francis in the Navy 1955,Ag 6,13:4
Kiss of Fire 1955,S 24,11:2
Battle Hymn 1957,F 16,14:1
Mister Cory 1957,F 23,13:1
Delicate Delinquent, The 1957,Jl 4,16:1
My Man Godfrey 1957,O 12,23:1
Paris Holiday 1958,My 10,19:2
Houseboat 1958,N 14,24:1
Some Came Running 1959,Ja 23,17:1
Big Fisherman, The 1959,Ag 6,18:1
Best of Everything 1959,O 9,24:2
Ice Palace 1960,Je 30,22:1
Desire in the Dust 1960,O 12,47:2
Right Approach, The 1961,My 18,41:1
Last Time I Saw Archie, The 1961,My 29,9:6
Girl Named Tamiku, A 1963,Mr 15,8:2
Man From the Diners' Club, The
  1963,Ap 18,39:1
Hot Horse 1963,Jl 25,14:2
Wives and Lovers 1963,Ag 29,36:1
Carpetbaggers, The 1964,Jl 2,24:4
Bikini Beach 1964,S 17,52:6
First Men in the Moon 1964,N 26,52:2
Sons of Katie Elder, The 1965,Ag 26,40:3
Chase, The 1966,F 19,24:1
Night of the Grizzly, The 1966,Je 23,29:1
Picture Mommy Dead 1966,N 3,45:4
Happening, The 1967,My 18,56:3
House of 1,000 Dolls 1968,Mr 14,51:4
Hyers, Frank
At War With the Army 1951,Ja 25,21:5
Hyke, Ray
Red River 1948,O 1,31:2
Captain China 1950,Mr 2,33:2
Frogmen, The 1951,Je 30,8:6
Beast From 20,000 Fathoms, The 1953,Je 25,23:1
Hyland, Diana
One Man's Way 1964,Mr 12,40:3
Chase, The 1966,F 19,24:1
Jigsaw 1968,Je 6,54:2
Hyland, Dick (Original Author)
Her Primitive Man 1944,Ap 1,11:1
Wave, A Wac and a Marine, A 1944,Ag 14,11:4
Night Song 1948,Ja 29,27:5
Hyland, Dick (Screenwriter)
Lake Placid Serenade 1944,D 25,15:6
Love, Honor and Goodbye 1945,S 8,12:2
New Orleans 1947,Je 20,25:6
Night Song 1948,Ja 29,27:5
Threat, The 1949,D 2,35:4
Hyland, Frances (Miscellaneous)
Hit Parade of 1943 1943,Ap 16,24:3
Hyland, Frances (Original Author)
Morals for Women 1931,N 16,23:1
Crime of Dr Forbes, The 1936,Jl 6,11:4
Step Lively, Jeeves 1937,Ap 2,19:6
Cheaters, The 1945,Jl 21,7:2
Hyland, Frances (Screenwriter)
Lost Zeppelin, The 1930,F 3,17:1
Helldorado 1935,Ja 7,13:2
My Marriage 1936,F 22,12:2
Crime of Dr Forbes, The 1936,Jl 6,11:4
Under Your Spell 1936,N 7,15:2
45 Fathers 1937,D 11,22:2
City Girl 1938,F 4,17:3
Island in the Sky 1938,My 14,18:1
Keep Smiling 1938,Ag 10,15:2
While New York Sleeps 1938,D 22,25:3
Charlie Chan in Reno 1939,My 31,27:2
Cisco Kid and the Lady, The 1939,D 25,29:2
Free, Blonde and 21 1940,Ap 5,25:2
In old California 1942,Je 18,25:3
Cheaters, The 1945,Jl 21,7:2
Murder in the Music Hall 1946,Ap 15,22:2
In old Sacramento 1946,Ap 29,24:4
Hyland, Jim
Crime and Punishment, U S A 1959,Je 17,39:3
Hyland, Ricky
Emil 1938,Ap 15,23:2
Hylten-Cavallius, Rangar (Producer)
Youth 1927,N 30,22:4
Hylton, Jack
She Shall Have Music 1942,O 31,11:2
Battle for Music 1945,O 15,13:2
Hylton, Jane
Upturned Glass, The 1947,N 5,34:4
Dear Murderer 1948,My 8,12:2
My Brothers Keeper 1949,F 14,15:3
Daybreak 1949,Jl 4,9:2
Passport to Pimlico 1949,O 27,35:2
Here Come the Huggetts 1950,D 25,25:3
It Started in Paradise 1953,Jl 25,8:2
Frightened Bride, The 1953,Ag 20,18:5
Weak and the Wicked, The 1954,Ag 21,10:3
Circus of Horrors 1960,S 1,31:1
Hylton, Richard
Lost Boundaries 1949,Jl 1,14:4
Halls of Montezuma, The 1951,Ja 6,9:6
Fixed Bayonets 1951,N 21,20:2
Pride of St Louis, The 1952,My 3,17:5
HYMAN
See Also HEIMANN

Hyman, Bernard H (Producer)
Forsaking all Others 1934,D 21,18:1
After Office Hours 1935,Mr 9,19:1
Escapade 1935,Jl 6,16:2
I Live my Life 1935,O 12,12:2
San Francisco 1936,Je 27,21:1
Saratoga 1937,Jl 23,16:3
Conquest 1937,N 5,19:1
Great Waltz, The 1938,N 25,19:1
Hyman, Bynunsky
Son of the Sheik, The 1926,Jl 26,13:2
Hyman, Kenneth (Producer)
Gigot 1962,S 28,26:1
Hill, The 1965,O 4,00:0
Dirty Dozen, The 1967,Je 16,36:1
Hyman, Louis
Broken Hearts 1926,Mr 3,26:1
Hyman, Mac (Original Author)
No Time for Sergeants 1958,My 30,13:2
Hymer, John B (Miscellaneous)
Law of the Underworld 1938,Ap 28,27:2
Hymer, John B (Original Author)
Alias the Deacon 1927,Je 21,29:2
Fast Life 1929,Ag 17,5:3
Love, Live and Laugh 1929,N 2,14:6
East Is West 1930,N 1,23:2
Pay-Off, The 1930,N 10,16:2
Scarlet Pages 1930,D 6,21:3
Half a Sinner 1934,Je 23,16:5
Alias the Deacon 1940,My 14,27:5
Hymer, John B (Screenwriter)
Alamo of the South Seas 1926,My 17,19:1
Aloma of the South Seas 1926,My 17,19:1
Hymer, Warren
Speakeasy 1929,Mr 11,22:2
William Fox Movietone Follies of 1929
  1929,My 27,22:1
Girl from Havana, The 1929,S 2,16:1
Men Without Women 1930,F 1,15:1
Born Reckless 1930,Je 7,10:4
Sinners' Holiday 1930,O 11,21:3
Up the River 1930,O 11,21:3
Seas Beneath 1931,Ja 31,15:1
Charlie Chan Carries On 1931,Mr 21,15:1
Goldie 1931,Je 29,20:3
Spider, The 1931,S 5,7:4
Unholy Garden, The 1931,O 29,27:1
Love Is a Racket 1932,Je 11,9:3
Hold 'Em Jail! 1932,Ag 20,7:4
Madison Square Garden 1932,O 12,26:5
One Way Passage 1932,O 14,23:2
Night Mayor, The 1932,N 25,19:2
Billion Dollar Scandal, The 1933,Ja 9,23:1
20,000 Years in Sing Sing 1933,Ja 10,26:2
Lady's Profession, A 1933,Mr 25,13:3
I Love That Man 1933,Jl 10,11:7
Midnight Mary 1933,Jl 15,14:2
Her First Mate 1933,S 2,14:5
My Woman 1933,O 16,20:3
King for a Night 1933,D 11,23:4
George White's Scandals 1934,Mr 16,24:2
Little Miss Marker 1934,My 19,18:3
Cat's Paw, The 1934,Ag 17,12:2
She Loves Me Not 1934,S 8,18:5
Young and Beautiful 1934,S 18,18:4
Belle of the Nineties 1934,S 22,12:2
Kid Millions 1934,N 12,17:2
Case of the Curious Bride, The 1935,Ap 5,21:3
Hold 'Em Yale 1935,Ap 27,20:6
Daring Young Man, The 1935,Jl 18,15:2
Silk Hat Kid 1935,Ag 7,22:5
Show Them no Mercy 1935,D 9,25:2
Everybody's Old Man 1936,Mr 26,27:2
Laughing Irish Eyes 1936,Ap 4,11:2
Mr Deeds Goes to Town 1936,Ap 17,17:2
Nobody's Fool 1936,Je 4,27:2
San Francisco 1936,Je 27,21:1
Rhythm on the Range 1936,Jl 30,22:1
36 Hours to Live 1936,Ag 15,6:3
You Only Live Once 1937,F 1,15:2
Wake up and Live 1937,Ap 24,16:2
We Have our Moments 1937,Ap 30,17:3
Married Before Breakfast 1937,Jl 23,16:2
Bad Guy 1937,Ag 26,25:2
Sea Racketeers 1937,O 4,17:2
Ali Baba Goes to Town 1937,O 23,14:1
Lady Behave 1938,Ja 28,17:3
Mr Moto in Danger Island 1938,Mr 20,13:3
Bluebeard's Eighth Wife 1938,Mr 24,21:2
Joy of Living 1938,My 6,27:1
You and Me 1938,Je 2,19:1
Arson Racket Squad 1938,Je 18,18:2
Gateway 1938,Ag 8,9:2
Submarine Patrol 1938,N 19,9:2
Thanks For Everything 1938,D 10,13:2
Calling All Marines 1939,O 26,27:2
Destry Rides Again 1939,N 30,25:1
Charlie McCarthy, Detective 1939,D 25,29:2
Buy Me That Town 1941,Ap 23,27:2
Birth of the Blues 1941,D 11,39:1
Jail House Blues 1942,F 6,23:2
Mr Wise Guy 1942,Mr 5,27:2
Dr Broadway 1942,Je 25,27:3

Hymer, Warren — Cont
 Hitler-Dead or Alive 1943,Mr 31,23:3
 3 Is a Family 1944,D 20,20:3
Hynd, Alan (Original Author)
 Betrayal From the East 1945,Ap 25,27:2
Hynd, Ronald
 Romeo and Juliet 1966,O 6,55:1
Hynes, Neal
 Incident, The 1967,N 6,65:1
Hyson, Dorothy
 Ghoul, The 1934,Ja 27,9:2
 Woman in Command, The 1934,My 29,22:2
Hyspa, Vincent
 Nous, La Liberte, A 1932,My 18,25:2
 They Were Five 1938,Je 1,19:5
Hytten, Olaf
 Salvation Hunters, The 1925,F 2,14:1
 Chu Chin Chow 1925,F 11,19:4
 Kitty 1929,Je 11,27:2
 Grumpy 1930,Ag 2,16:4
 Daughter of the Dragon 1931,Ag 22,7:5
 Berkeley Square 1933,S 14,26:2
 Becky Sharp 1935,Je 14,27:2
 Dark Angel, The 1935,S 6,12:2
 White Hunter 1936,N 26,39:2
 Good Earth, The 1937,F 3,27:1
 I Cover the War 1937,Ag 2,10:2
 First Lady 1937,D 23,25:1
 Lone Wolf in Paris, The 1938,My 23,21:2
 Andy Hardy Gets Spring Fever 1939,Jl 19,23:2
 Our Leading Citizen 1939,Ag 24,17:1
 Rulers of the Sea 1939,N 9,27:1
 Allegheny Uprising 1939,N 10,27:3
 Our Neighbors-The Carters 1940,F 15,15:2
 That Hamilton Woman 1941,Ap 4,25:1
 Washington Melodrama 1941,My 26,15:3
 Bedtime Story 1942,Mr 20,25:4
 Ghost of Frankenstein, The 1942,Ap 4,19:2
 Sherlock Holmes and the Voice Of Terror
  1942,S 19,9:2
 Great Commandment, The 1942,O 17,11:1
 Destination Unknown 1942,O 29,19:3
 Black Swan, The 1942,D 24,18:3
 Sherlock Holmes Faces Death 1943,O 8,15:3
 Lodger, The 1944,Ja 20,15:3
 Brighton Strangler, The 1945,My 19,15:2
 My Name is Julia Ross 1945,N 9,16:3
 Black Beauty 1946,Ag 30,13:2
 That Way With Women 1947,F 15,20:4
Hyun, Peter Lee
 White Heat 1934,Je 16,20:2

I

Iatrites, Stavros
 Moussitsa 1960,O 31,25:2
Ibanez, Bonaventure
 Romola 1924,D 2,13:2
Ibanez, Maria Fernanda
 Madrina del Diablo, La; Devil's Godmother, The
  1938,F 21,15:2
 Dos Cadetes, Los 1938,S 26,13:3
Ibanez, Ramon
 White Sister, The 1923,S 6,10:2
 White Sister, The 1928,My 21,25:1
Ibanez, Roger
 Zita 1968,Ag 12,40:2
Ibarra, Pedro
 Mexican Bus ride 1954,Jl 21,18:3
Ibbs, Ronald
 Blue Murder at St Trinian's 1958,My 27,27:1
Ibert, Jacques (Composer)
 Don Quichotte 1933,Ap 23,X,4:1
 Maternite 1937,Je 8,30:2
 Invitation to the Dance (Ring Around the Rosy);
  Ring Around the Rosy (Invitation to the
  Dance) 1956,My 23,35:7
 Invitation to the Dance (Sinbad the Sailor); Sinbad
  the Sailor (Invitation to the Dance)
  1956,My 23,35:7
 Invitation to the Dance (Circus); Circus (Invitation
  to the Dance) 1956,My 23,35:7
Ibert, Jacques (Original Author)
 Don Quixote 1934,D 24,17:1
Ibrahim, Moulay
 Itto 1936,Ja 29,15:5
Ibsen, Henrik (Original Author)
 Peer Gynt 1915,S 20,9:1
 Man There Was, A 1920,Ap 26,18:1
 Doll's House, A 1922,F 13,10:1
 Peer Gynt 1939,N 11,12:2
Icardo, Rafael
 Forgive Me, Son 1937,O 23,14:2
 Corazon de Nino; Heart of a Child
  1940,Ja 1,29:4
 Silk, Blood and Sun 1943,Ja 30,10:6
 Marvels of the Bull Ring 1943,Jl 3,11:3
 Maria Candelaria 1944,S 12,23:7
Ichac, Marcel (Cinematographer)
 Annapurna 1953,D 14,45:4
Ichac, Marcel (Miscellaneous)
 Annapurna 1953,D 14,45:4

Ichikawa, Chusha
 Chushingura 1963,O 4,26:1
Ichikawa, Danko
 Ballad of Narayama 1961,Je 20,27:1
Ichikawa, Kilchi (Producer)
 Woman in the Dunes; Suno no Onna
  1964,S 17,52:1
Ichikawa, Kodaya
 Imposter, The 1955,Mr 23,27:1
 Barbarian and the Geisha 1958,O 3,25:1
Ichikawa, Kon (Director)
 Odd Obsession 1961,D 27,16:1
 Fires on the Plain 1963,S 25,39:1
 Enjo 1964,S 23,54:1
 Alone on the Pacific 1964,S 24,46:2
 Tokyo Olympiad 1966,N 17,55:1
 Burmese Harp, The 1967,Ap 29,25:1
Ichikawa, Kon (Narrator)
 Tokyo Olympiad 1966,N 17,55:1
Ichikawa, Kon (Screenwriter)
 Odd Obsession 1961,D 27,16:1
Ichikawa, Raizo
 Taira Clan, The; Shin Heike Monagatari
  1964,S 21,37:4
 Enjo 1964,S 23,54:1
 Buddha 1965,Je 17,27:4
 Great Wall, The 1965,D 16,63:2
Ichikawa, Somegoro
 Bandits on the Wind 1964,Ja 15,27:3
 Young Swordsman 1964,O 30,29:1
 Rabble, The 1968,Mr 29,31:1
 Whirlwind 1968,Jl 27,15:1
Ichikawa, Utaemon
 Imposter, The 1955,Mr 23,27:1
Ichioaka, Mia
 West of Shanghai 1937,O 29,19:2
Icube, Madame (Screenwriter)
 Street of Shadows 1948,N 20,9:2
Iczenko, D
 Border Street 1950,Ap 26,35:2
Idam, Fatma
 Stampede 1930,Ap 28,24:5
Ide, Leonard (Original Author)
 Secret Bride, The 1935,F 2,10:1
Ide, Masato (Screenwriter)
 Bandits on the Wind 1964,Ja 15,27:3
 Rabble, The 1968,Mr 29,31:1
 Red Beard 1968,D 20,60:4
Ide, Toshirc (Screenwriter)
 School for Sea 1967,D 2,48:5
Idell, Albert E (Original Author)
 Centennial Summer 1946,Jl 18,20:2
Idriss, Ramez (Composer)
 If You Knew Susie 1948,F 23,19:2
Ienard, Kay (Screenwriter)
 Wings of the Hawk 1953,Ag 27,22:1
Ieschenko, Nikolai (Producer)
 Arshin Takes a Wife 1950,Jl 31,13:6
Iflikhar
 Guide, The 1965,F 10,44:2
Igin-Khorlo
 Son of Mongolia 1936,N 21,21:4
Iglesias, Emilia
 Morena Clara 1938,Je 18,18:3
Iglesias, Eugene
 Brave Bulls, The 1951,Ap 19,39:2
 Mask of the Avenger 1951,Je 27,25:2
 California Conquest 1952,Je 7,22:6
 Duel at Silver Creek 1952,Ag 2,7:6
 Hiawatha 1952,D 26,20:4
 Underwater! 1955,F 10,27:2
 Cowboy 1958,F 20,29:5
 Safe at Home 1962,Ap 14,14:1
Ignatyev, A
 Vasili's Return 1953,S 28,21:4
Ignon, Gui
 Nurse Edith Cavell 1939,S 22,27:4
Igoa, Luis F de (Original Author)
 Age of Infidelity 1958,Ag 19,23:2
Igual, Francisco
 Pandora and the Flying Dutchman 1951,D 7,35:2
Ihnat, Steve
 Hour of the Gun 1967,N 2,58:4
 Madigan 1968,Mr 30,22:2
 Countdown 1968,My 2,57:3
Iida, Choko
 Mistress, The 1959,F 3,36:2
 Girl in the Mist 1959,D 23,22:1
 Drunken Angel 1959,D 31,12:1
 Rikisha Man, The 1960,My 4,57:1
Ikawa, Kuniko
 Imposter, The 1955,Mr 23,27:1
Ike, Baby
 World in my Corner 1956,F 18,12:5
Ikebe, Ryo
 Battle in Outer Space 1960,Jl 9,10:5
Ikeda, Tadashi
 Wind Cannot Read, The 1960,Mr 10,36:1
Ikeuchi, Junko
 This Madding Crowd 1964,Je 17,48:1
 Young Swordsman 1964,O 30,29:1
 Illusion of Blood 1968,N 28,66:5

Ikonen, Ansa
 Jumalen Tuomio; Judgement of God, The
  1939,O 27,27:2
Ikonikoff, Alexander
 Man Who Played God, The 1932,F 11,16:1
Ilchenko, Danilo
 And Quiet Flows the Don 1960,My 25,45:2
Iles, Francis (Original Author)
 Suspicion 1941,N 21,23:2
Ilg, J Kaspar
 Mystic Mountain, The 1936,Mr 31,17:2
Ilich-Djukich, Vera
 Magic Sword, The 1952,N 19,37:2
Ilinsky, B
 Three Thieves 1933,O 30,14:3
Ilinsky, Igor
 Volga-Volga 1941,My 17,19:2
Ilisa, Amelia de
 Bohemios 1935,S 16,15:3
 Muertos Hablan, Los; Dead Speak, The
  1935,N 25,22:2
Iliuschenko, Yelena
 Ballet of Romeo and Juliet, The 1956,Ap 3,31:2
Illery, Pola
 Sous les Toits de Paris; (Under the Roofs of
  Paris) 1930,D 16,34:4
 Quatorez Juillet 1933,O 20,14:2
Illiard, Elisa
 Aufforderung zum Tanz; Invitation to the Dance
  1935,N 23,23:3
Illica, Luigi (Composer)
 Tosca 1958,O 24,40:3
Illica, Luigi (Miscellaneous)
 Boheme, La 1965,O 20,51:2
Illica, Luigi (Screenwriter)
 Tosca 1958,O 24,40:3
Illing, Peter
 Against the Wind 1949,Je 27,18:3
 State Secret 1950,O 5,38:2
 Operation X 1950,D 11,31:2
 Massacre Hill 1950,D 14,51:3
 Lucky Nick Cain 1951,Ap 23,21:2
 Outcast of the Islands 1952,My 16,19:2
 Never Let Me Go 1953,Je 11,37:2
 Flame and the Flesh 1954,My 3,21:2
 West of Zanzibar 1955,Ja 18,31:2
 Innocents in Paris 1955,Mr 5,9:6
 Chance Meeting 1955,Ap 20,38:1
 Svengali 1955,S 26,18:2
 Bhowani Junction 1956,My 25,26:1
 Fire Down Below 1957,Ag 9,11:2
 Pursuit of the Graf Spee 1957,D 27,33:2
 I Accuse! 1958,Mr 6,32:1
 Angry Hills, The 1959,Jl 16,31:3
 Campbell's Kingdom 1960,Ja 11,35:5
 Secret Door, The 1964,Je 4,28:1
 Man Could Get Killed, A 1966,My 12,54:2
Illington, Margaret
 Sacrifice 1917,My 14,9:3
Illopoulos, Dinos
 Grouch, The 1961,F 27,23:2
Ilo, Yunosoke
 Samurai Assassin 1965,Mr 19,27:5
Ilyinsky, Igor
 Carnival in Moscow 1957,N 4,40:1
 Ballad of a Hussar, The 1963,Jl 15,25:5
Imadashvilli, A
 Caucasian Love 1929,D 3,28:4
Imal, Tadashi (Director)
 Bushido 1964,S 13,39:1
Imamura, Shohei (Director)
 Insect Woman, The; Nippon Konchuki
  1964,Jl 1,42:1
 Unholy Desire 1964,N 18,54:1
Imamura, Shohei (Screenwriter)
 Insect Woman, The; Nippon Konchuki
  1964,Jl 1,42:1
 Unholy Desire 1964,N 18,54:1
Imani, Besa
 Skanderbeg 1954,Jl 5,6:4
Imbert, Christiane (Screenwriter)
 Sorciere, La 1956,D 28,17:2
Imboden, David
 King of Kings, The 1927,Ap 20,29:2
Imbry, Aimes
 Volga Boatman, The 1938,Ap 15,23:3
Imhof, Roger
 Paddy the Next Best Thing 1933,Ag 25,12:2
 Charlie Chan's Greatest Case 1933,O 7,18:4
 Hoopla 1933,D 1,23:3
 David Harum 1934,Mr 2,23:2
 Ever Since Eve 1934,Mr 28,27:5
 Grand Canary 1934,Jl 20,11:1
 Wild Gold 1934,Jl 24,20:2
 Handy Andy 1934,Ag 4,14:5
 Judge Priest 1934,O 12,33:1
 Music in the Air 1934,D 14,29:3
 Under Pressure 1935,F 4,11:3
 One More Spring 1935,F 22,27:1
 Life Begins at 40 1935,Ap 5,21:3
 Farmer Takes a Wife, The 1935,Ag 9,21:2

Imhof, Roger— Cont

Steamboat Around the Bend 1935,S 20,17:2
Riffraff 1936,Ja 13,14:2
San Francisco 1936,Je 27,21:1
Son Comes Home, A 1936,S 5,7:1
In His Steps 1936,O 29,31:1
there Goes The Groom 1937,D 25,10:6
Every Day's a Holiday 1938,Ja 27,17:2
Drums Along the Mohawk 1939,N 4,11:2
Everything Happens at Night 1939,D 16,12:6
Grapes of Wrath, The 1940,Ja 25,17:2
Little Old New York 1940,F 3,9:2
Abe Lincoln in Illinois 1940,F 23,19:2
I Was an Adventuress 1940,My 20,13:2
Way of all Flesh, The 1940,Je 6,33:2
Man Hunt 1941,Je 14,20:2
Mystery Ship 1941,Ag 16,18:3
This Gun for Hire 1942,My 14,23:2
It Happened in Flatbush 1942,Jl 3,12:8

Imhoff, Fritz

Thank You, Madame 1937,Ap 27,18:2
Kleines Bezirksgericht; Little Country Court
1939,F 18,12:4
You Are the World for Me 1964,D 26,9:4

Imholz, Joseph

William Tell 1925,My 20,26:2

Imlay, Agnes

High Treason 1937,Ja 27,17:3

Impekoven, Toni (Original Author)

Palace Scandal 1949,Je 6,15:5

Imperio, Rosario

On the Riviera 1951,My 24,47:1

Impet, Ernie

Fury and the Woman 1937,Je 22,26:2

Imre, Raday

Csokolj Meg Edes 1932,N 25,19:2

Imrie, Richard (Screenwriter)

Operation Crossbow 1965,Ap 2,29:1

Inaba, Yoshio

Magnificent Seven, The 1956,N 20,46:2
Harakiri 1964,Ag 5,24:2

Inagaki, Hiroshi (Director)

Samurai 1956,Ja 10,26:1
Rikisha Man, The 1960,My 4,57:1
Chushingura 1963,O 4,26:1
Bandits on the Wind 1964,Ja 15,27:3
Young Swordsman 1964,O 30,29:1
Samurai (Part II) 1967,O 21,16:1
Rabble, The 1968,Mr 29,31:1
Secret Scrolls-Part I 1968,My 9,54:3
Secret Scrolls-Part II; Ninjitsu 1968,My 23,56:3
Whirlwind 1968,Jl 27,15:1
Kojiro 1968,Ag 30,23:1

Inagaki, Hiroshi (Original Author)

Young Swordsman 1964,O 30,29:1

Inagaki, Hiroshi (Screenwriter)

Samurai 1956,Ja 10,26:1
Rikisha Man, The 1960,My 4,57:1
Samurai (Part II) 1967,O 21,16:1
Rabble, The 1968,Mr 29,31:1
Secret Scrolls-Part I 1968,My 9,54:3
Secret Scrolls-Part II; Ninjitsu 1968,My 23,56:3
Whirlwind 1968,Jl 27,15:1
Kojiro 1968,Ag 30,23:1

Inagaki, Horishi (Director)

Country Doctor, The 1963,Ag 14,28:1

Inanovsky, Alexander (Director)

Spring Song 1942,S 12,9:2

Ince, John

Alias French Gertie 1930,Ap 14,24:2
Moby Dick 1930,Ag 15,20:5
Old Kentucky, In 1935,N 29,24:1
Don't Turn 'em Loose 1936,S 25,20:2

Ince, John (Director)

Should a Woman Tell? 1920,Ja 5,15:1
Old Lady 31 1920,My 24,20:3
If Marriage Fails 1925,Je 2,16:3

Ince, Ralph

Land of Opportunity, The 1920,F 9,10:3
Bigger Than Barnum's 1926,Jl 13,19:3
Shanghaied 1927,S 13,36:2
Chicago After Midnight 1928,Mr 6,20:3
Wall Street 1929,N 25,22:1
Numbered Men 1930,Je 9,23:3
Big Fight, The 1930,Je 28,9:2
Little Casear 1931,Ja 10,19:2
Hell Bound 1931,My 9,15:4
Gentleman's Fate 1931,Je 27,20:3
Star Witness, The 1931,Ag 4,19:5
Big Gamble, The 1931,S 21,20:2
Men of Chance 1931,D 28,22:1
Girl of the Rio 1932,Ja 9,21:1
Hatchet Man, The 1932,F 4,25:2
Law and Order 1932,F 29,21:3
Lost Squadron, The 1932,Mr 11,15:4
Mouthpiece, The 1932,Ap 21,25:2
State's Attorney 1932,My 6,15:3
Tenderfoot, The 1932,My 23,18:4
Guilty as Hell 1932,Ag 6,14:5
Big Pay-Off, The 1933,Ja 17,22:7
Havana Widows 1933,N 23,24:3

Ince, Ralph (Director)

Man's Home, A 1921,D 19,13:1
Success 1923,Jl 10,22:5

Homeward Bound 1923,Jl 31,12:4
Moral Sinner, The 1924,Ap 7,15:3
Playing With Souls 1925,Ap 20,18:1 (Incorrect in
this edition; use 1925,Ap 28,18:1 elsewhere)
Smooth as Satin 1925,Je 23,24:3
Bigger Than Barnum's 1926,Jl 13,19:3
Shanghaied 1927,S 13,36:2
South Sea Love 1928,F 7,30:3
Coney Island 1928,F 14,27:1 (In Addenda)
Chicago After Midnight 1928,Mr 6,20:3
Lucky Devils 1933,F 20,11:5

Ince, Thomas H (Director)

Disciple, The 1915,O 18,9:1
Civilization 1916,Je 3,11:2

Ince, Thomas H (Miscellaneous)

Scars of Jealousy 1923,My 7,19:3
Those Who Dance 1924,Je 30,16:1

Ince, Thomas H (Producer)

Fuss and Feathers 1918,D 9,11:4
String Beans 1918,D 30,7:3
False Faces, The 1919,F 17,11:3
Busher, The 1919,My 26,19:4
Hay Foot, Straw Foot 1919,Je 23,10:3
Stepping Out 1919,S 22,8:1
Egg Crate Wallop, The 1919,S 29,16:1
Twenty-three and a Half Hours' Leave
1919,O 27,9:3
Behind the Door 1920,Ja 5,15:1
Black Is White 1920,Mr 8,9:6
Let's Be Fashionable 1920,Je 14,13:2
Homer Comes Home 1920,Je 28,13:2
Hairpins 1920,Ag 2,12:2
Home Spun Folks 1920,O 4,14:3
Lying Lips 1921,Mr 7,8:1
Three Musketeers, The 1921,O 2,VII,3:1
Hail the Woman 1922,Ja 16,18:3
Skin Deep 1922,O 23,10:1
Hottentot, The 1923,F 19,10:1
Free and Equal 1925,Ap 20,22:1

Inclan, Lupe

Asi Se Quiere En Jalisco 1943,Ag 7,6:2

Inclan, Manuel

Maria Candelaria 1944,S 12,23:7

Inclan, Miguel

Creo en Dios 1943,Jl 17,8:3
Fugitive, The 1947,D 26,22:2
Fort Apache 1948,Je 25,26:2
Young and the Damned, The 1952,Mr 25,23:2

Incontrera, Annabella

Devil in Love, The 1968,Jl 4,13:4

Incrocci, Agenore (Original Author)

I Cadetti di Guascogna 1952,O 6,22:2

Incrocci, Agenore (Screenwriter)

I Cadetti di Guascogna 1952,O 6,22:2
Casanova 1965,Jl 21,43:1
Tiger and the Pussycat, The 1967,S 21,56:4

Incrocci, Zoe

Eredita dello Zio, L' 1935,Je 29,16:3

Inda, Estela

Cancion del Milagro, La; Miracle Song, The
1940,My 11,15:2
Night of the Mayas 1941,Ja 14,16:7
Young and the Damned, The 1952,Mr 25,23:2

Indiana Boys School, Staff and Boys

Johnny Holiday 1950,My 17,36:1

Indovina, Franco (Director)

Oldest Profession, The (Prehistoric Era);
Prehistoric Era (The Oldest Profession)
1968,N 8,42:1

Indrisano, John

Winning Ticket, The 1935,F 11,14:2
Ringside Maisie 1941,Ag 1,11:2
Lulu Belle 1948,Je 21,18:3
Yellow Cab Man, The 1950,Mr 27,19:2
Callaway Went Thataway 1951,D 6,42:1

Indwig, William (Screenwriter)

Love Finds Andy Hardy 1938,Jl 22,10:2

Inerney, Frances Mac

Waterloo Bridge 1940,My 17,23:2

Inescort, Frieda

Dark Angel, The 1935,S 6,12:2
If You Could Only Cook 1935,D 26,21:4
Garden Murder Case, The 1936,Mr 2,13:2
King Steps Out, The 1936,My 29,15:2
Mary of Scotland 1936,Jl 31,22:2
Give Me your Heart 1936,S 17,18:2
Hollywood Boulevard 1936,S 21,26:4
Great O'Malley, The 1937,Mr 6,10:1
Call it a Day 1937,My 7,29:2
Another Dawn 1937,Je 18,25:3
Portia on Trial 1937,D 3,29:2
Beauty for the Asking 1939,F 10,19:1
Woman Doctor 1939,Mr 24,27:3
Tarzan Finds a Son 1939,Je 15,27:2
Zero Hour, The 1939,Jl 5,20:3
Woman Is the Judge, A 1939,S 28,29:5
Convicted Woman 1940,F 26,11:2
Pride and Prejudice 1940,Ag 9,19:1
Letter, The 1940,N 23,12:6
Father's Son 1941,F 13,25:3
Trial of Mary Dugan, The 1941,Mr 6,25:4
Sunny 1941,Je 13,22:2
You'll Never Get Rich 1941,O 24,27:2

Inescort, Frieda— Cont

Remember the Day 1941,D 26,21:2
Courtship of Andy Hardy, The 1942,Ap 10,21:2
Sweater Girl 1942,Jl 13,18:3
Street Of Chance 1942,N 19,31:3
It Comes up Love 1943,Ja 22,25:3
Amazing Mrs Holliday, The 1943,F 22,20:2
Return of the Vampire, The 1944,Ja 29,10:1
Heavenly Days 1944,O 21,15:2
Judge Steps Out, The 1949,Je 3,21:4
Underworld Story, The 1950,Jl 27,29:4
Place in the Sun, A 1951,Ag 29,20:1
Never Wave at a Wac 1953,Ap 24,30:2
Casanova's Big Night 1954,Ap 19,19:1
Foxfire 1955,Jl 14,19:1
Flame of the Islands 1956,F 25,12:4
Eddy Duchin Story, The 1956,Je 22,15:1

Iness, Sim

Lady Godiva 1955,D 3,13:3

Infante, Eddie

American Guerrilla in the Philippines
1950,N 8,37:2

Infascelli, Carlo (Screenwriter)

Half a Century of Songs 1954,O 30,15:6

Infascelli, Roberto (Producer)

Stranger Returns, The 1968,S 12,54:3

Infuhr, Teddy

Amazing Mrs Holliday, The 1943,F 22,20:2
Spider Woman 1944,Ja 17,14:5
That Night With You 1945,N 9,16:2
Boy With Green Hair, The 1949,Ja 13,26:2
Traveling Saleswoman 1950,Ja 6,25:3
David and Bathsheba 1951,Ag 15,23:2

Inge, William

Splendor in the Grass 1961,O 11,53:1

Inge, William (Original Author)

Come Back, Little Sheba 1952,D 24,13:2 (In Addenda)
Picnic 1956,F 17,13:3
Bus Stop 1956,S 1,19:2
Stripper, The 1963,Je 20,29:1

Inge, William (Screenwriter)

Splendor in the Grass 1961,O 11,53:1
All Fall Down 1962,Ap 12,41:3

Ingels, Marty

Horizontal Lieutenant, The 1962,My 12,15:3
Wild and Wonderful 1964,Je 11,27:4
Busy Body, The 1967,Je 8,52:2
For Singles Only 1968,Je 6,54:1

Inger, Manfred

Magic Face, The 1951,O 1,19:2
No Time for Flowers 1952,D 26,20:3
Arms and the Man 1962,F 24,21:7

Ingersoll, William

Partners of the Night 1920,Mr 1,16:2
Cheat, The 1931,D 12,23:3
Mary Burns, Fugitive 1935,N 16,19:2
Whipsaw 1936,Ja 25,18:4

Inglesakis, Jean

Merlusse 1938,Mr 17,17:2

Ingleton, E Magnus (Screenwriter)

On the High Seas 1922,O 8,VI,3:1 (In Addenda)

Ingleton, George

Clean Heart, The 1924,S 15,28:1
Beloved Brute, The 1924,N 10,20:1

Inglis, Brand

White Corridors 1952,Jl 16,21:1

Inglis, Elizabeth

Thunder in the City 1937,Ap 23,25:2

Inglis, Hamilton G (Producer)

No Place for Jennifer 1951,Jl 17,31:2
Will any Gentleman? 1955,S 28,70:6

Ingraham, Lloyd

Scaramouche 1923,O 12,7:2 (Incorrect in this
edition; use 1927,O 1,7:2 elsewhere)
Rainbow Man, The 1929,Ap 17,30:6
Night Parade 1929,N 11,20:2
Untamed 1929,N 30,23:1
Montana Moon 1930,Ap 14,24:2
Last of the Duanes 1930,S 13,9:3
Spoilers, The 1930,S 20,15:4
Lady Who Dared, The 1931,Je 6,15:5
Crusader, The 1932,O 8,15:4
Sixteen Fathoms Deep 1934,Ja 19,24:3
In Love With Life 1934,My 12,12:3
Dude Ranger, The 1934,O 2,18:5
Reformatory 1938,Je 27,13:6
Painted Desert 1938,S 14,26:5
Twenty-Mule Team 1940,My 10,26:6
Merry Monahans, The 1944,O 13,16:2

Ingraham, Lloyd (Director)

Mary's Ankle 1920,Mr 1,16:2
Let's Be Fashionable 1920,Je 14,13:2
Going Up 1923,O 10,16:2
Jesse James 1927,O 17,20:2

Ingraham, Roy (Composer)

Silver Skates 1943,Mr 19,15:3

Ingram, Amo

Wild Party, The 1929,Ap 2,28:4

Ingram, Clifford

Hearts in Dixie 1929,F 28,30:3

Ingram, Jack

Short Grass 1951,Ja 13,10:4

Ingram, Rex
Love in Morocco 1933,Mr 20,18:3
Green Pastures, The 1936,Jl 17,20:1
Huckleberry Finn 1939,Mr 3,21:2
Thief of Bagdad, The 1940,D 6,28:2
Talk of the Town, The 1942,Ag 28,22:3
Cabin in the Sky 1943,My 28,19:3
Fired Wife 1943,O 1,15:2
Sahara 1943,N 12,25:2
Dark Waters 1944,N 22,25:2
Thousand and one Nights, A 1945,Jl 12,8:2
Moonrise 1949,Mr 7,17:2
Congo Crossing 1956,Jl 14,13:2
God's Little Acre 1958,Ag 14,23:2
Watusi 1959,Jl 2,15:2
Elmer Gantry 1960,Jl 8,16:1
Desire in the Dust 1960,O 12,47:2
Hurry Sundown 1967,Mr 24,22:1
Ingram, Rex (Director)
Four Horsemen of the Apocalypse 1921,Mr 7,8:1
Conquering Power, The 1921,Jl 10,VI,2:1 (In Addenda)
Turn to the Right 1922,Ja 24,11:1
Prisoner of Zenda, The 1922,Ag 1,14:3
Trifling Women 1922,O 4,23:4
Where the Pavement Ends 1923,Ap 2,22:1
Scaramouche 1923,O 12,7:2 (Incorrect in this edition; use 1927,O 1,7:2 elsewhere)
Arab, The 1924,Jl 14,11:5
Mare Nostrum 1926,F 16,22:4
Garden of Allah, The 1927,S 3,13:5
Garden of Allah, The 1927,S 11,VIII,5:1
Love in Morocco 1933,Mr 20,18:3
Ingram, Rex (Miscellaneous)
Four Horsemen of the Apocalypse, The 1926,S 27,27:3
Magician, The 1926,O 25,15:1
Ingram, Rex (Original Author)
Love in Morocco 1933,Mr 20,18:3
Ingram, Rex (Screenwriter)
Trifling Women 1922,O 4,23:4
Ingrams, Michael (Director)
Palaces of a Queen 1967,Je 27,32:1
Ingro, Dina
Games Men Play, The 1968,Mr 15,30:1
Ingster, Boris (Director)
Stranger on the Third Floor 1940,S 2,19:2
Judge Steps Out, The 1949,Je 3,21:4
Southside 1-1000 1950,N 3,31:2
Ingster, Boris (Miscellaneous)
Last Days of Pompeii, The 1935,O 17,29:2
Amazing Mrs Holliday, The 1943,F 22,20:2
Ingster, Boris (Original Author)
Happy Landing 1938,Ja 22,19:1
Cloak and Dagger 1946,O 5,13:2
California 1947,Ja 15,31:2
Something for the Birds 1952,N 15,15:2
Ingster, Boris (Screenwriter)
Dancing Pirate 1936,Je 18,19:1
Thin Ice 1937,S 4,8:2
I'll Give a Million 1938,Jl 16,7:2
Paris Underground 1945,O 20,8:2
Judge Steps Out, The 1949,Je 3,21:4
Southside 1-1000 1950,N 3,31:2
Something for the Birds 1952,N 15,15:2
Iniutina, G
Men of the Sea 1938,Je 20,11:2
Ink Spots, The Four
Great American Broadcast, The 1941,My 2,25:2
Pardon my Sarong 1942,Ag 27,15:1
Inkijinoff, V
Tempete sur l'Asie; Storm Over Asia 1929,N 17,IX,5:6
Storm Over Asia 1930,S 8,17:1
Battle, The 1934,N 23,23:2
Friesennot 1936,O 26,20:1
Revenge of General Ling, The 1938,F 21,15:1
Volga Boatman, The 1938,Ap 15,23:3
drame De Shanghai; Shanghai Drama, The 1945,Ja 11,19:2
Corinna Darling 1958,Je 14,14:3
Michael Strogoff 1960,My 21,15:1
Journey to the Lost City 1960,D 8,43:3
Up to his Ears 1966,My 18,37:1
Innemann, S (Director)
Song of the Lark 1937,N 15,15:3
Sextanerin, Die; Erste Liebe; First Love 1938,S 12,13:3
Innes, George
Billy Liar 1963,D 17,49:1
Innes, Hammond (Miscellaneous)
Snowbound 1949,F 21,20:2
Innes, Hammond (Original Author)
Wreck of the Mary Deare, The 1959,N 7,27:1
Campbell's Kingdom 1960,Ja 11,35:5
Inness, Jean
Mrs Mike 1950,F 9,36:5
Gunfighter, The 1950,Je 24,7:2
Edge of Doom 1950,Ag 4,13:2
I'd Climb the Highest Mountain 1951,My 10,38:1
Innocenti, Camillo (Producer)
Retribution 1922,Je 7,22:3

Inocencio, Benny
Real Glory, The 1939,S 15,26:2
Inouye, Masso
Daughter of Two Fathers, A 1929,Mr 12,26:3
Interlenghi, Franco
Shoe-Shine 1947,Ag 27,19:2
Teresa 1951,Ap 6,31:2
Little World of Don Camillo, The 1953,Ja 14,27:1
Barefoot Contessa, The 1954,S 30,37:1
Wayward Wife, The 1955,Ap 11,29:3
Ulysses 1955,Ag 18,17:2
Vitelloni 1956,O 24,43:1
Farewell to Arms, A 1958,Ja 25,14:1
Love Is my Profession 1959,Ap 28,41:1
Wild Love; (Gli Inamorati) 1961,Ap 6,30:2
Notte Brava, La 1962,Ja 25,25:2
International Film Foundation (Miscellaneous)
Cry of the World, The 1932,My 5,23:5
International Velvet
**** 1967,D 17,94:5
Intrator, Jerald (Director)
Satan in High Heels 1962,Mr 24,15:6
Inuzuka, Minoru (Screenwriter)
Zatoichi 1968,Je 28,37:1
Invader, Tiverton
Biscuit Eater, The 1940,My 23,28:5
Ioannidou, Theano
Electra 1962,D 18,5:2
Ioganson, Edward (Director)
Son of the Land, A 1931,My 23,13:4
Iordanogiou, B (Producer)
House on Stournara Street, The 1960,O 17,33:4
Iplician, Anaid
Tonio Kroger 1968,Ja 16,24:1
Ipsen, Bodil (Director)
Red Meadows 1950,Ja 19,35:2
Ir-Kan
Son of Mongolia 1936,N 21,21:4
Iracheta (Producer)
Adelita, La 1938,O 12,35:2
Irazoqul, Enrique
Gospel According to St Matthew, The 1966,F 18,23:1
Ireland, Anthony
When Thief Meets Thief 1937,Je 15,26:2
Juggernaut 1937,Jl 15,16:1
Prime Minister, The 1942,F 4,23:2
Ireland, Jean
Pink String and Sealing Wax 1950,O 4,38:2
Ireland, Jill
3 Men in a Boat 1959,Jl 29,33:2
Ireland, John
Walk in the Sun, A 1946,Ja 12,10:6
Behind Green Lights 1946,F 16,10:2
It Shouldn't Happen to a Dog 1946,S 7,11:2
My Darling Clementine 1946,D 4,44:5
Wake up and Dream 1947,Ja 24,18:4
Gangster, The 1947,O 31,29:3
Open Secret 1948,F 2,15:2
Raw Deal 1948,Jl 9,11:4
Red River 1948,O 1,31:2
Joan of Arc 1948,N 12,30:5
Southern Yankee, A 1948,N 25,47:2
I Shot Jesse James 1949,Ap 2,12:2
Roughshod 1949,Je 17,27:2
Anna Lucasta 1949,Ag 12,13:2
All the King's Men 1949,N 9,37:2
Cargo to Capetown 1950,Mr 31,36:3
Vengeance Valley 1951,F 16,21:2
Screen, The 1951,Ap 23,21:2
Little Big Horn 1951,Jl 27,15:2
Basketball Fix, the 1951,S 14,21:2
Red Mountain 1952,Ap 26,19:2
Hurricane Smith 1952,O 4,15:2
Southwest Passage 1954,S 11,11:2
Queen Bee 1955,N 23,18:2
Gunfight at the O K Corral 1957,My 30,23:2
Party Girl 1958,O 29,30:1
Spartacus 1960,O 7,28:1
Wild in the Country 1961,Je 10,12:2
55 Days at Peking 1963,My 30,20:1
Fall of the Roman Empire, The 1964,Mr 27,14:2
Ceremony, The 1964,My 14,39:1
I Saw What You Did 1965,Ji 22,24:2
Fort Utah 1967,My 25,54:3
Ireland, John Jr
C'mon Let's Live a Little 1967,My 4,34:1
Irene, Lilyan
Sweet Rosie O'Grady 1943,O 21,30:2
What a Woman 1943,D 3,27:2
Iriarte, Miquel A
No Exit 1962,D 6,55:2
Iribe, Paul (Director)
Changing Husbands 1924,Je 23,22:4
Forty Winks 1925,F 3,24:1
Night Club, The 1925,My 5,24:2
Iris, Esperanza
Mater Nostra 1936,S 9,32:4
Noches de Gloria; Glorious Nights 1938,Ap 23,19:3

Irish, Kitty
That's my Man 1947,Ap 7,20:2
Irish, Tom
Father of the Bride 1950,My 19,31:2
Father's Little Dividend 1951,Ap 13,18:5
Sabre Jet 1953,N 3,34:1
Hondo 1953,N 27,99:9
Irish, William (Original Author)
Phantom Lady 1944,F 18,15:2
Deadline at Dawn 1946,Ap 4,33:2
Fear in the Night 1947,Ap 19,11:3
No Man of her Own 1950,My 4,32:3
Irish, William (Woolrich, Cornell) (Original Author)
Bride Wore Black, The 1968,Je 26,42:1
Irish Rovers
World Dances 1954,N 8,24:6
Irmanov, Vyacheslav
Murder Czech Style 1968,Ag 20,33:1
Iron, Simonyi
Csokolj Meg Edes 1932,N 25,19:2
Irusta, Augustin
Boliche 1935,My 28,30:2
Puerta Cerrada; Closed Door 1940,F 5,13:3
Matrero, El; Outlaw, The 1940,Mr 18,13:2
IRVIN
See ERVIN, IRVINE
IRVINE
See Also ERVIN
Irvine, Blanaid (Screenwriter)
Broth of a Boy 1959,D 28,18:1
Poacher's Daughter, The 1960,F 16,31:2
Irving, Charles
Face in the Crowd, A 1957,My 29,33:1
Irving, Ellis
As You Like It 1936,N 6,29:3
Sea Hawk, The 1940,Ag 10,16:2
Irving, George
Wanderer of the Wasteland, The 1924,Jl 8,14:2
For Sale 1924,Jl 14,11:5
Man Who Fights Alone, The 1924,Jl 28,12:2
Madonna of the Streets 1924,O 28,23:4
North of 36 1924,D 8,13:3
Goose Hangs High, The 1925,Mr 10,19:3
Air Mail, The 1925,Mr 17,18:1
Wild Horse Mesa 1925,Ag 10,8:2
Golden Princess 1925,S 7,15:3
Desert Gold 1926,Mr 23,24:5
Risky Business 1926,S 8,19:3
Eagle of the Sea, The 1926,N 17,21:6
Wings 1927,Ag 13,10:4
Shanghai Bound 1927,N 7,26:4
Two Flaming Youths 1928,Ja 2,28:1
Feel my Pulse 1928,F 27,16:2
Partners in Crime 1928,Ap 30,18:3
Port of Missing Girls, The 1928,Jl 31,13:4
Craig's Wife 1928,D 4,29:1
Coquette 1929,Ap 6,14:4 (In Addenda)
Thunderbolt 1929,Je 21,17:2
Dance of Life, The 1929,Ag 16,18:6
Paris Bound 1929,S 21,17:1
Last Performance 1929,N 4,28:1
Puttin' on the Ritz 1930,F 15,15:1
Young Eagles 1930,Mr 22,22:6
Divorcee, The 1930,My 10,25:3
Shadow of the Law 1930,Je 7,10:4
Spoilers, The 1930,S 20,15:4
Maybe It's Love 1930,O 18,23:2
Only Saps Work 1930,D 13,22:2
Free Love 1930,D 15,29:1
Resurrection 1931,Ja 24,15:1
Girls Demand Excitement 1931,F 7,11:1
Naughty Flirt, The 1931,Ap 13,17:1
Shipmates 1931,My 23,13:4
Confessions of a Co-Ed 1931,Je 20,20:4
Five and Ten 1931,Jl 11,7:6
Touchdown 1931,N 16,23:1
Lady With a Past 1932,F 22,23:2
Merrily We Go to Hell 1932,Je 11,9:3
Island of Lost Souls 1933,Ja 13,19:2
Humanity 1933,Ap 22,16:3
Worst Woman in Paris, The 1933,N 25,10:3
Son of a Sailor 1933,N 30,38:4
George White's Scandals 1934,Mr 16,24:2
World Moves On, The 1934,Je 30,18:5
Here Comes the Navy 1934,Jl 21,14:2
Bright Eyes 1934,D 21,31:1
Age of Indiscretion 1935,My 18,21:2
Under the Pampas Moon 1935,My 31,11:1
Dangerous 1935,D 27,14:1
It Had to Happen 1936,F 15,18:6
Captain January 1936,Ap 25,21:1
Private Number 1936,Je 12,19:1
Hearts Divided 1936,Je 13,13:1
Charlie Chan at the Race Track 1936,Ag 15,6:2
Don't Tell the Wife 1937,F 19,15:2
Man Who Found Himself, The 1937,Ap 9,19:3
China Passage 1937,Ap 16,27:2
You Can't Buy Luck 1937,My 14,21:2
Border Cafe 1937,Je 8,30:2
Damaged Lives 1937,Je 14,26:2
Toast of New York, The 1937,Jl 23,16:2
Big Shot, The 1937,Ag 13,13:1

Irving, George— Cont

Life of the Party, The 1937,O 4,17:1
Saturday's Heroes 1937,O 16,22:2
there Goes The Groom 1937,D 25,10:6
Crashing Hollywood 1938,Ja 8,19:2
She's Got Everything 1938,Ja 14,21:3
Bringing Up Baby 1938,Mr 4,17:5
Condemned Woman 1938,Ap 22,15:5
Blind Alibi 1938,My 20,17:2
Go Chase Yourself 1938,Je 15,27:1
Crime Ring 1938,Jl 22,10:3
Mother Carey's Chickens 1938,Ag 5,11:1
Smashing the Rackets 1938,Ag 9,22:5
Mr Doodle Kicks Off 1938,S 28,29:4
Law West of Tombstone, The 1938,N 25,19:1
Hardys Ride High, The 1939,Ap 14,28:2
Streets of New York 1939,My 1,21:1
Dust Be my Destiny 1939,O 7,11:2
New Moon 1940,Jl 19,22:2
Spy Ship 1942,Jl 11,8:2
Son of Dracula 1943,N 6,16:4
Magic Town 1947,O 8,29:2

Irving, George (Director)
Silver King, The 1919,Ja 13,9:3

Irving, Harry R (Original Author)
Black Fury 1935,Ap 11,27:2

Irving, Hollis
Facts of Life, The 1961,F 11,27:1

Irving, Laurence (Producer)
Inheritance, The 1951,F 12,19:2

Irving, Laurence (Screenwriter)
Inheritance, The 1951,F 12,19:2

Irving, Margaret
Animal Crackers 1930,Ag 29,20:3
Thanks a Million 1935,N 14,17:1
Wife vs Secretary 1936,F 29,11:1
I Married a Doctor 1936,Ap 20,17:1
San Francisco 1936,Je 27,21:1
Follow Your Heart 1936,O 22,31:1
Three Men on a Horse 1936,N 26,39:1
Charlie Chan at the Opera 1936,D 5,16:2
Outcasts of Poker Flat, The 1937,Ap 27,18:3
Wife, Doctor and Nurse 1937,O 11,26:5
Under Suspicion 1937,D 20,23:2 (In Addenda)
Sh! The Octopus 1937,D 24,21:2
Baroness and the Butler, The 1938,F 19,19:2
Love, Honor and Behave 1938,Mr 21,18:2
Mr Moto's Last Warning 1939,Ja 27,17:3
In Society 1944,Ag 17,20:2

Irving, Mary Jane
Brand, The 1919,Mr 17,13:2
Borderland 1922,Jl 24,10:2
Light That Failed, The 1923,N 27,11:2
Stranger, The 1924,F 5,20:1
Golden Bed, The 1925,Ja 20,18:2
Splendid Road, The 1926,Je 13,31:1
Lovey Mary 1926,Je 21,17:2
Flaming Forest, The 1926,N 22,28:3
Tom Sawyer 1930,D 20,20:6
Arsene Lupin 1932,F 27,22:1

Irving, Paul
Count of Monte Cristo, The 1934,S 27,25:2
Great Ziegfeld, The 1936,Ap 9,21:2
Gold Diggers of 1937 1936,D 25,19:2
On the Avenue 1937,F 5,17:3
Battle of Broadway 1938,Ap 25,19:2
Balalaika 1939,D 15,33:2

Irving, Richard
Violence 1947,My 10,8:5
Canon City 1948,Jl 8,19:2
Borderline 1950,Mr 6,17:2
On Dangerous Ground 1952,F 13,35:2

Irving, Roy
Odd Man Out 1947,Ap 24,30:2

Irving, Stanley (Director)
Forever Yours 1937,Je 7,22:2

Irving, Washington (Original Author)
Headless Horseman, The 1922,D 25,21:1
Adventures of Ichabod and Mr Toad, The
  1949,O 10,18:2

Irving, William
Pampered Youth 1925,F 10,20:1
Coney Island 1928,F 14,27:1 (In Addenda)
Hearts in Exile 1929,N 29,25:1
All Quiet on The Western Front 1930,Ap 30,29:1
Her Majesty, Love 1931,N 26,37:2
Manhattan Parade 1931,D 25,29:2
Diplomaniacs 1933,Ap 29,14:2
Orient Express 1934,F 28,23:2
Melody in Spring 1934,Mr 31,8:2
Air Hawks 1935,Je 4,26:5
Shadow, The 1937,D 17,33:3
Convicted 1938,Ag 22,9:3

Irwin, Boyd
Ashes of Vengeance 1923,Ag 7,20:2
Captain Blood 1924,S 9,19:1
Man From Yesterday, The 1932,Je 25,18:2
Pursuit of Happiness, The 1934,O 26,25:1
Cardinal Richelieu 1935,Ap 19,24:2
Devil's Squadron 1936,My 11,16:2
Meet Nero Wolfe 1936,Jl 16,20:1
Killer at Large 1936,O 26,20:1
Prisoner of Zenda, The 1937,S 3,12:1
Man in the Iron Mask, The 1939,Jl 14,11:1

Great Swindle, The 1941,My 14,25:4

Irwin, Caroline
Tornado, The 1924,D 15,14:1

Irwin, Charles
King of Jazz 1930,My 3,23:1
Looking Forward 1933,My 1,10:2
Blind Adventure 1933,O 31,24:3
Mystery of Mr X, The 1934,F 26,21:3
Gilded Lily, The 1935,F 9,11:2
Whipsaw 1936,Ja 25,18:4
White Angel, The 1936,Je 25,24:1
League of Frightened Men, The 1937,Jl 2,25:1
Lord Jeff 1938,Jl 1,22:2
Susannah of the Mounties 1939,Je 24,13:2
Light That Failed, The 1939,D 25,19:1
Man I Married, The 1940,Ag 3,9:2
International Squadron 1941,N 14,28:4
Desperate Journey 1942,S 26,11:2
Black Swan, The 1942,D 24,18:3
Gorilla Man, The 1943,Ja 15,21:4
Hangover Square 1945,F 8,15:2
Foxes of Harrow, The 1947,S 25,35:4
Thunder in the Valley 1947,N 28,30:1
My Wild Irish Rose 1947,D 25,32:2
Bomba, the Jungle Boy 1949,Ap 16,11:4
Montana 1950,F 4,9:2
Challenge to Lassie 1950,Ap 7,22:3

Irwin, Charles W (Screenwriter)
He Rides Tall 1964,F 27,28:1

Irwin, Coulter
Night Editor 1946,Mr 30,11:2

Irwin, John
Barker, The 1928,D 6,35:1
We're not Dressing 1934,Ap 26,27:2

Irwin, Margaret (Original Author)
Young Bess 1953,My 22,31:1

Irwin, Ralph (Composer)
One Rainy Afternoon 1936,My 14,29:2

Irwin, Theodore D (Original Author)
Unknown Blonde 1934,Ap 24,27:2

Irwin, Wallace (Original Author)
Woman in Red, The 1935,Mr 23,11:3

Irwin, Wallace (Screenwriter)
Golden Bed, The 1925,Ja 20,18:2

Irwin, Will (Miscellaneous)
Love and Hisses 1938,Ja 1,11:1

Irwin, Will (Original Author)
Al Jennings of Oklahoma 1951,My 18,34:6

Isabelita
Pan-Americana 1945,Mr 23,13:2

Isakov, Valeri
She-Wolf, The 1963,S 2,18:1

Isakovic, Antonije (Original Author)
Three 1967,Je 30,30:1

Isakovic, Antonije (Screenwriter)
Three 1967,Je 30,30:1

Isaksson, Ulla (Screenwriter)
Brink of Life; (Nara Livet) 1959,N 9,36:2
Virgin Spring, The; Jungfrukallan 1960,N 15,46:1

Isasi, Anthony (Director)
That Man in Istanbul 1966,My 19,51:2

Isasi, Anthony (Producer)
That Man in Istanbul 1966,My 19,51:2

Isasmendi, Antonio Isasi (Director)
Adventures of Scaramouche, The 1964,N 23,34:1
  (Incorrect in this edition; use 1964,N 21,34:1
  elsewhere)

Isasmendi, Antonio Isasi (Screenwriter)
Adventures of Scaramouche, The 1964,N 23,34:1
  (Incorrect in this edition; use 1964,N 21,34:1
  elsewhere)

Isayev, K (Screenwriter)
Secret Agent 1949,F 10,37:3
Sadko 1953,Je 1,18:6
May Night 1953,Jl 13,22:4
Stars of the Ukraine 1953,Jl 13,22:4
True Friends 1954,N 15,33:2

Isayev, Vladimir
Life in Bloom 1949,My 9,20:4

Isbert, Jose
Man Who Wagged his Tail, The 1961,S 19,39:1
Not on Your Life; Verdugo, El 1965,Mr 30,52:1

Isbert, Lolita
Rocket From Calabuch 1958,O 8,41:1

Isbert, Maruja
Not on Your Life; Verdugo, El 1965,Mr 30,52:1

Isedal, Tor
Virgin Spring, The; Jungfrukallan 1960,N 15,46:1
Doll, The 1964,Ja 14,27:1
Swedish Wedding Night 1965,N 15,48:1

Isham, Frederic S (Original Author)
Three Live Ghosts 1922,Ja 2,20:1
Three Live Ghosts 1929,S 30,23:1
Nothing but the Truth 1941,O 23,27:1

Isham, Gyles
Iron Duke, The 1935,Ja 25,27:2
Anna Karenina 1935,Ag 31,16:2

Ishenko, F
Shors 1939,N 21,19:4
Last Hill, The 1945,Je 26,13:2

Isher, Guy
Clear all Wires 1933,Mr 4,11:2

Isherwood, Christopher (Original Author)
Forever and a Day 1943,Mr 13,9:2
Adventure in Baltimore 1949,Ap 29,27:2

Isherwood, Christopher (Screenwriter)
Rage in Heaven 1941,Mr 21,19:2
Great Sinner, The 1949,Je 30,19:2
Diane 1956,Ja 13,18:1
Loved One, The 1965,O 12,57:1
Sailor From Gibraltar, The 1967,Ap 25,38:2

Ishiguro, Tatsuya
Gate of Hell 1954,D 14,45:2
Yang Kwei Fei 1956,S 11,41:2

Ishihama, Akira
Harakiri 1964,Ag 5,24:2

Ishihara, Shintaro
Love at Twenty 1963,F 7,5:6

Ishihara, Yujiro
Alone on the Pacific 1964,S 24,46:2
Those Magnificent Men in Their Flying Machines
  (Or How I Flew From London to Paris in 25
  Hours and 11 Minutes) 1965,Je 17,27:1

Ishikaza, Yojiro (Original Author)
Girl in the Mist 1959,D 23,22:1

Ishiyama, Kenjiro
Kojiro 1968,Ag 30,23:1

Ismatov, P
Vow, The 1947,Je 23,14:3

Israel, Charles (Original Author)
Mark, The 1961,O 3,46:2

Israel, Steven Ben
Brig, The 1964,S 21,37:4

Isrdel Philharmonic
Journey to Jerusalem, A 1968,N 18,59:1

Israeli Folk Dancers
World Dances 1954,N 8,24:6

Israell, Shimon
Clouds Over Israel 1966,My 10,48:6

Israels, Josef (Miscellaneous)
Bashful Suitor, The 1921,D 12,20:2

Isralow, Dvora
World Dances 1954,N 8,24:6

Issacs, Jorge (Original Author)
Maria 1939,Ap 10,13:4

Istvan, Szekely (Director)
Hyppolit, A Lakaj 1933,Ja 4,22:6

Isunza, Agustin
Hidden River 1950,D 1,31:2

Itami, Ichizo
Lord Jim 1965,F 26,18:1

Itami, Mansaku (Screenwriter)
Rikisha Man, The 1960,My 4,57:1

Itch, Jerry
Walleyed Nippon 1963,S 3,36:1

Ito, Corley Z (Producer)
Breath of the Gods, The 1920,Jl 26,9:5

Ito, Daisuke (Screenwriter)
Showdown for Zatoichi 1968,O 5,40:1

Ito, Emi
Ghidrah, The Three-Headed Monster
  1965,D 16,63:3

Ito, Hisaya
Ghidrah, The Three-Headed Monster
  1965,D 16,63:3

Ito, Sachio (Original Author)
She Was Like a Wild Chrysanthemum
  1960,Ja 22,15:2

Ito, Takashi
Girl in the Mist 1959,D 23,22:1

Ito, Yumi
Ghidrah, The Three-Headed Monster
  1965,D 16,63:3

Ito, Yunosuke
Ikiru; To Live 1960,Ja 30,13:5
Ballad of Narayama 1961,Je 20,27:1

Itoga, Haruo
Unholy Desire 1964,N 18,54:1

Itoh, Kaoru
Kimiko 1937,Ap 13,31:3

Itoh, Noboru (Composer)
Kimiko 1937,Ap 13,31:3

Itoh, Sister
Mothra 1962,Jl 12,19:4

Itoh, Tomoko
Kimiko 1937,Ap 13,31:3

Itoya, Hisao (Producer)
Onibaba 1965,F 10,44:3

Itter, Kaethe
Grobe Adele, Die 1937,My 15,23:5

Iturbe, Gloria
Una Vida Por Otra 1933,F 11,11:3
Vida por Otra, Una 1933,F 11,11:3

Iturbe, Amparo
Holiday in Mexico 1946,Ag 16,19:3
That Midnight Kiss 1949,S 23,28:2

Iturbi, John
Adventure in Music 1944,Mr 6,17:3

Iturbi, Jose
Thousands Cheer 1943,S 14,27:1
Two Girls and a Sailor 1944,Je 15,16:1
Music for Millions 1944,D 22,12:4
Anchors Aweigh 1945,Jl 20,15:2
Holiday in Mexico 1946,Ag 16,19:3
Three Daring Daughters 1948,F 13,26:3

Iturbi, Jose— Cont
  That Midnight Kiss 1949,S 23,28:2
Iturbide, Rebecca
  Of Love and Desire 1963,S 12,32:1
Itzenplitz, Eberhard
  Streitum den Knaben Jo; Strife Over the Boy Jo
    1938,D 10,13:2
Ivakin, N
  We Are From Kronstadt 1936,My 2,11:1
  In the Far East 1937,O 20,27:3
Ivan, Perry
  Sun Sets at Dawn, The 1951,Ja 15,13:1
Ivan, Rosalind
  Suspect, The 1945,F 1,18:5
  Corn is Green, The 1945,Mr 30,18:2
  Pursuit to Algiers 1945,O 27,12:2
  Pillow of Death 1946,Ja 26,19:3
  Scarlet Street 1946,F 15,29:2
  Three Strangers 1946,F 23,20:2
  That Brennan Girl 1946,D 9,34:3
  Verdict, The 1946,D 13,29:4
  Ivy 1947,Je 26,19:1
  Johnny Belinda 1948,O 2,11:2
  Elephant Walk 1954,Ap 22,37:2
Ivanitski, Boris
  Son of the Land, A 1931,My 23,13:4
Ivano, Paul (Miscellaneous)
  Dawn to Dawn 1933,D 27,23:5
Ivanoff, V (Director)
  End of the World, The 1934,Ap 18,23:3
Ivanov, A (Director)
  Transport of Fire 1931,Mr 24,31:2
  Soviet Border 1939,F 20,13:2
  Road Home, The 1947,My 2,28:3
Ivanov, B (Director)
  Lad From our Town 1943,O 7,26:2
  Wait for Me 1945,Mr 19,23:3
  Song and Dance Over the Vistula 1956,Je 25,19:7
Ivanov, B (Screenwriter)
  Song and Dance Over the Vistula 1956,Je 25,19:7
Ivanov, D
  They Wanted Peace 1940,Ja 8,11:3
Ivanov, Lev (Miscellaneous)
  Royal Ballet, The (Swan Lake Act II); Swan Lake
    Act II (The Royal Ballet) 1960,O 5,45:2
Ivanov, S (Cinematographer)
  Concert of Stars 1953,Mr 2,19:4
Ivanov, V (Screenwriter)
  Amangeldy 1939,Je 16,27:4
Ivanov, Vladimir
  Young Guard 1949,D 26,33:6
Ivanov-Barkov, E (Director)
  Under Sunny Skies 1950,D 26,19:3
Ivanova, Katya
  Great Glinka, The 1947,D 22,30:2
Ivanova, L
  Idiot, The 1960,Jl 22,11:2
Ivanova, M
  Young Guard 1949,D 26,33:6
Ivanova, Nina
  Once There Was a Girl 1945,D 24,19:2
Ivanovsky, A (Director)
  Dom Zhadnosti 1934,Ag 13,9:6
  Dubrovsky 1936,Mr 30,17:6
  Russian Ballerina 1947,S 11,31:2
  Concert of Stars 1953,Mr 2,19:4
  Tiger Girl 1955,S 5,8:2
Ivanovsky, A (Screenwriter)
  Russian Ballerina 1947,S 11,31:2
  Eugene Onegin 1959,S 14,33:1
Ivans, Perry
  Girl Without a Room 1933,D 7,26:3
Ivasheva, V
  Young Pushkin 1937,D 16,35:3
  Alexander Nevsky 1939,Mr 23,27:1
Ivasheva, Valentina
  Nightingale 1936,N 4,41:2
Ivasheva, Vera
  Rainbow, The 1944,O 23,14:3
Ivashov, Vladimir
  Ballad of a Soldier 1960,D 27,22:1
Ivens, Joris (Cinematographer)
  400,000,000, The 1939,Mr 8,19:2
Ivens, Joris (Director)
  400,000,000, The 1939,Mr 8,19:2
  Peace Will Win 1952,Ja 21,11:2
  Far from Vietnam 1968,Je 7,32:1
  17th Parallel: Vietnam in War 1968,S 27,36:1
Ivens, Joris (Miscellaneous)
  Our Russian Front 1942,F 12,27:2
  17th Parallel: Vietnam in War 1968,S 27,36:1
Ivens, Joris (Narrator)
  Far from Vietnam 1967,O 2,58:1
Ivens, Joris (Producer)
  Spanish Earth, The 1937,Ag 21,7:2
Ivensen, Edith
  Redhead and the Cowboy, The 1951,Je 6,37:2
Iveria, Miki
  Adventures of Tartu, The 1943,S 24,26:1
  Orders to Kill 1958,N 18,41:2
Ivernel, Daniel
  Under the Paris Sky 1952,My 6,35:1
  Daughters of Destiny (Jeanne); Jeanne (Daughters
    of Destiny) 1954,Jl 6,19:1

  Holiday for Henrietta 1955,Ja 25,21:1
  Ulysses 1955,Ag 18,17:2
  Snow Was Black, The 1956,O 16,36:5
  Marie Octobre 1960,Ag 16,25:2
  Sundays and Cybele 1962,N 13,43:3
  Diary of a Chambermaid; Journal d'une Femme de
    Chambre, Le 1964,S 22,44:1
  Paris in the Month of August 1968,Ag 26,46:4
Ivers, Julia Crawford (Screenwriter)
  Nurse Marjorie 1920,My 24,20:3
  Jenny, Be Good 1920,Je 28,13:2
  Green Temptation, The 1922,Mr 20,10:3
Ivers, Robert
  Delicate Delinquent, The 1957,Jl 4,16:1
  G I Blues 1960,N 5,28:1
Ives, Burl
  Smoky 1946,Je 27,29:1
  Green Grass of Wyoming 1948,Je 10,28:3
  So Dear to my Heart 1949,Ja 31,14:2
  Sierra 1950,S 15,31:2
  East of Eden 1955,Mr 10,33:1
  Power and The Prize, the 1956,S 27,42:1
  Desire Under the Elms 1958,Mr 13,24:2
  Wind Across the Everglades 1958,S 12,21:1
  Cat on a Hot Tin Roof 1958,S 19,24:1
  Our Man in Havana 1960,Ja 28,26:1
  Let no Man Write my Epitaph 1960,N 11,36:2
  Spiral Road, The 1962,Ag 4,11:2
  Summer Magic 1963,Ag 22,19:2
  Brass Bottle, The 1964,My 21,42:1
  Ensign Pulver 1964,Ag 1,13:2
  Those Fantastic Flying Fools 1967,O 19,59:2
Ives, Burl (Narrator)
  Mediterannean Holiday 1964,D 16,51:1
Ives, Norman
  Loves of Ricardo, The 1926,Ag 16,10:1
Ivins, Perry
  Reckless Living 1931,D 5,21:2
  Charlie Chan in London 1934,S 13,26:1
  Charlie Chan in Paris 1935,Ja 22,23:2
  Miserables, Les 1935,Ap 22,14:2
  Hooray for Love 1935,Jl 13,16:2
  Streets of Laredo 1949,My 12,28:2
  Redhead and the Cowboy, The 1951,Je 6,37:2
Ivo, Tommy
  Earl Carroll Vanities 1945,Ap 2,15:6
  Carnival in Costa Rica 1947,Mr 29,21:2
  I Remember Mama 1948,Mr 12,29:2
  Plymouth Adventure 1952,N 14,20:3
Ivory, James (Director)
  Householder, The 1963,O 22,43:2
  Shakespeare Wallah 1965,S 13,42:1
  Shakespeare Wallah 1966,Mr 23,40:2
Ivory, James (Original Author)
  Shakespeare Wallah 1966,Mr 23,40:2
Ivory, James (Screenwriter)
  Shakespeare Wallah 1966,Mr 23,40:2
Iwai, Hanshiro
  Men Who Tread on the Tiger's Tail, The
    1960,Ja 11,35:7
Iwasaki, Kaneko
  Showdown for Zatoichi 1968,O 5,40:1
Iwashita, Akira
  Harakiri 1964,Ag 5,24:2
Iwashita, Shunsaku (Original Author)
  Rikisha Man, The 1960,My 4,57:1
Iwaskiewicz, Jaroslav (Original Author)
  Joan of the Angels? 1962,My 8,43:6
Iwatare, Yukokiko
  Phantom Horse, the 1956,Jl 25,16:1
Izard, Forrest (Miscellaneous)
  Champs-Elysees 1939,F 28,17:2
  Fabiola 1951,My 30,14:2
Izewska, Teresa
  Kanal 1961,My 10,52:1
Izmatlova, Elena
  Secret Agent 1949,F 10,37:3
Izumi, Kyoka (Original Author)
  Temptress and the Monk, The 1963,My 28,32:1
Izunza, Agustin
  Juntos pero no Revueltos; United but not Mixed
    1939,O 23,15:3
Izvitskaya, Isolda
  Forty-First, The 1957,Je 15,10:7
  Fathers and Sons 1960,D 26,27:2

J

Jabotinsky, Vladimir (Miscellaneous)
  Samson and Delilah 1949,D 22,29:2
Jabour, Gabriel
  Poupee, La 1963,Ag 28,39:1
Jachino, Silvana
  Corsaro Nero, Il; Black Corsair, The
    1939,My 8,21:3
  Aria del Continente, L'; Continental Atmosphere
    1939,N 17,17:3
  Eravamo Sette Vedove; We Were Seven Widows
    1940,F 16,23:4
  Cuore Napoletano; Neapolitan Heart
    1940,O 8,31:2
  Juliet of the Spirits 1965,N 4,57:1

Jack, Roland
  Tulsa 1949,My 27,25:2
Jack, Stephen
  Treasure Island 1950,Ag 16,24:2
  Room at the Top 1959,Mr 31,26:1
Jackie (Lion)
  Mad Wednesday 1951,Ja 25,21:5
Jackler, Jackie
  Cuban Rebel Girls 1959,D 26,7:3
Jackley, Jolyon
  Breaking Through the Sound Barrier
    1952,N 7,19:1
Jackman, Fred (Cinematographer)
  Midsummer Night's Dream, A 1935,O 10,31:1
Jackman, Frederick Wood (Director)
  Black Cyclone 1925,My 19,24:2
Jacks, Robert L (Producer)
  Lure of the Wilderness 1952,O 4,15:2
  Desert Rats, The 1953,My 9,13:2
  Man on a Tightrope 1953,Je 5,19:1
  Man in the Attic 1954,F 6,17:2
  Prince Valiant 1954,Ap 7,40:2
  Princess of the Nile 1954,Je 12,13:2
  Gorilla at Large 1954,Je 12,13:2
  White Feather 1955,F 17,23:1
  Killer is Loose, The 1956,Mr 3,17:2
  Proud Ones, The 1956,Ag 11,10:2
  Bandolero 1968,Jl 18,26:2
Jackson, Alfred (Original Author)
  Run Around, The 1931,Ag 10,18:3
Jackson, Anne
  So Young, So Bad 1950,Jl 24,15:2
  Journey, The 1959,F 20,19:1
  Tall Story 1960,Ap 7,46:1
  Tiger Makes Out, The 1967,S 19,53:1
  How to Save a Marriage - And Ruin Your Life
    1968,Ja 19,30:1
  Secret Life of an American Wife, The
    1968,Je 26,42:2
Jackson, Avonne
  Little Colonel, The 1935,Mr 22,26:2
Jackson, Barry
  Bofors Gun, The 1968,S 23,42:3
Jackson, Bee
  Lying Wives 1925,Je 17,16:2
Jackson, Brad
  It Came From Outer Space 1953,Je 18,38:2
  April Love 1957,N 28,57:2
Jackson, Charles R (Original Author)
  Lost Weekend, The 1945,D 3,17:2
Jackson, Charles Tenney (Original Author)
  Eagle of the Sea, The 1926,N 17,21:6
  Show, The 1927,Mr 14,16:1
Jackson, Charlotte
  Prince There Was 1921,N 14,18:1
Jackson, Colette
  Seven Days in May 1964,F 20,22:1
Jackson, Curtis Loys Jr
  Great Lover, The 1949,N 24,48:2
Jackson, Dan
  Beautiful Blonde From Bashful Bend, The
    1949,My 28,11:2
  Beyond Mombasa 1957,My 31,14:2
  Roots of Heaven, The 1958,O 16,46:1
  Mysterious Island 1961,D 21,30:6
Jackson, Earl
  Porgy and Bess 1959,Je 25,20:3
Jackson, Eddie
  Roadhouse Nights 1930,F 22,13:1
Jackson, Eugene
  Little Annie Rooney 1925,O 19,26:1
  Hearts in Dixie 1929,F 28,30:3
  Dixiana 1930,S 5,21:1
  Sporting Blood 1931,Ag 15,18:3
  Sporting Chance 1931,N 28,20:4
  Lady's From Kentucky, The 1939,Ap 27,31:1
Jackson, Eugene Jr
  Shenandoah 1965,Jl 29,18:3
Jackson, Felix (Original Author)
  Rage of Paris 1938,Jl 2,10:2
  Bachelor Mother 1939,Je 30,17:2
  Bundle of Joy 1956,D 20,36:1
Jackson, Felix (Producer)
  Hers to Hold 1943,Jl 22,15:1
  His Butler's Sister 1943,D 30,13:2
  Christmas Holiday 1944,Je 29,16:1
  Can't Help Singing 1944,D 26,22:4
  Lady on a Train 1945,S 15,21:2
  Because of Him 1946,Ja 25,26:6
  I'll Be Yours 1947,F 22,16:2
Jackson, Felix (Screenwriter)
  Mad About Music 1938,Mr 12,13:2
  Rage of Paris 1938,Jl 2,10:2
  Girl Downstairs, The 1939,Ja 26,17:1
  Three Smart Girls Grow Up 1939,Mr 18,9:2
  Destry Rides Again 1939,N 30,25:1
  Spring Parade 1940,O 4,29:2
  Back Street 1941,F 12,25:2
  Appointment for Love 1941,N 7,27:1
  Broadway 1942,Je 5,23:2
Jackson, Freda
  Henry V 1946,Je 18,30:2
  Great Expectations 1947,My 23,31:1

Jackson, Freda — Cont

Beware of Pity 1947,N 1,11:2
Canterbury Tale, A 1949,Ja 24,16:2
No Room at the Inn 1949,D 26,33:4
Bhowani Junction 1956,My 25,26:1
Flesh is Weak, The 1957,N 9,31:2
Tale of Two Cities, A 1958,Ag 5,23:1
Brides of Dracula, The 1960,S 6,41:4
Shadow of the Cat, The 1961,Je 8,40:2
Tom Jones 1963,O 8,48:1

Jackson, Frederick (Original Author)

My Sin 1931,S 11,24:2
School for Husbands 1939,F 7,16:2
Sensations of 1945 1944,Jl 7,13:2

Jackson, Frederick (Screenwriter)

Great Gambini, The 1937,Jl 12,20:4
Wells Fargo 1937,D 30,15:2
Stolen Heaven 1938,My 12,27:2
Say It in French 1938,D 1,29:1
School for Husbands 1939,F 7,16:2
There's Magic in Music 1941,Je 5,27:2
Stormy Weather 1943,Jl 22,15:1
Hi Diddle Diddle 1943,S 24,26:2
Bedside Manner 1945,Je 23,9:6

Jackson, G J Montgomery

Pacific Adventure 1947,N 26,18:2

Jackson, Gary Lee

Mrs Mike 1950,F 9,36:5

Jackson, Gene

Penrod and Sam 1923,Je 25,16:5

Jackson, George Captain

Unfaithful 1931,Mr 7,17:2

Jackson, Glenda

Persecution and Assassination of Jean-Paul Marat
  as Performed by the Inmates of the Asylum of
  Charenton Under the Direction of the Marquis
  De Sade, The 1967,F 23,41:1
Negatives 1968,O 15,40:1

Jackson, Gordon

Somewhere in France 1943,Jl 12,11:2
Captive Heart, The 1947,Ap 28,27:2
Against the Wind 1949,Je 27,18:3
Tight Little Island 1949,D 26,33:2
Pink String and Sealing Wax 1950,O 4,38:2
Massacre Hill 1950,D 14,51:3
Happy Go Lovely 1951,Jl 26,17:2
Abandon Ship 1957,Ap 18,35:1
Panic in the Parlor 1957,D 18,45:1
Mad Little Island 1958,D 31,12:1
Bridal Path, The 1959,D 21,34:2
Yesterday's Enemy 1960,Mr 4,19:1
Chance Meeting 1960,O 27,45:2
Tunes of Glory 1960,D 21,38:2
Trouble in the Sky 1961,Jl 13,26:3
Greyfriars' Bobby 1961,O 12,41:4
Mutiny on the Bounty 1962,N 9,31:2
Great Escape, The 1963,Ag 8,19:1
Ipcress File, The 1965,Ag 3,35:1
Cast a Giant Shadow 1966,Mr 31,43:3
Fighting Prince of Donegal, The 1966,N 10,64:1
Danger Route 1968,Je 6,54:2

Jackson, Helen Hunt (Original Author)

Ramona 1916,Ap 6,11:1
Ramona 1928,My 15,17:3
Ramona 1936,O 7,32:4

Jackson, Horace (Miscellaneous)

Biography of a Bachelor Girl 1935,Mr 2,18:2

Jackson, Horace (Original Author)

Bedtime Story 1942,Mr 20,25:4

Jackson, Horace (Screenwriter)

No More Ladies 1935,Je 22,18:5
Suzy 1936,Jl 25,16:1
Women Are Like That 1938,Ap 11,12:2
Men Are Such Fools 1938,Je 17,25:1
Model Wife 1941,Ap 24,25:3

Jackson, Howard (Composer)

Great Gabbo, The 1929,S 13,33:1
Beloved 1934,Ja 27,9:3

Jackson, Jackie

Red Pony, The 1949,Mr 9,33:2
Great Lover, The 1949,N 24,48:2

Jackson, Jay

Days of Thrills and Laughter 1961,Mr 22,37:1

Jackson, Jay (Narrator)

30 Years of Fun 1963,D 26,33:4
Further Perils of Laurel and Hardy, The
  1968,Ap 1,56:6

Jackson, Joseph (Original Author)

Is Everybody Happy? 1929,N 2,14:6
Be Yourself 1930,Mr 7,20:5

Jackson, Joy

Bright Road 1953,Ap 29,33:5

Jackson, Leigh (Director)

Okinawa 1952,Ap 24,38:3

Jackson, Louis H (Producer)

Waltz Time 1946,F 11,25:2
Frenzy 1946,Jl 20,10:3
Murder in Reverse 1947,Ja 11,23:5
Agitator, The 1949,Ag 19,12:5
Laughing Lady, The 1950,Ja 23,16:3
Mrs Fitzherbert 1950,My 11,37:2
Appointment With Crime 1951,F 19,19:3
Lisbon Story, The 1951,S 6,39:4
Devil's Plot 1953,Je 19,18:1

Jackson, Mahalia

St Louis Blues 1958,Ap 12,13:1
Imitation of Life 1959,Ap 18,18:1
Jazz on a Summer's Day 1960,Mr 29,46:2
Best Man, The 1964,Ap 7,29:1

Jackson, Marion (Original Author)

Senor Daredevil 1926,Ag 17,15:3
Red Raiders, The 1927,S 28,28:3
Carnival Boat 1932,Mr 21,19:5

Jackson, Mary

Targets 1968,Ag 14,34:1

Jackson, Pat (Director)

Raider, The; Western Approaches 1946,S 28,13:2
Shadow on the Wall 1950,My 19,31:3
Encore (The Ant and the Grasshopper); Ant and
  the Grasshopper, The (Encore) 1952,Ap 3,45:1
Encore (Winter Cruise); Winter Cruise (Encore)
  1952,Ap 3,45:1
Encore (Gigolo and Gigolette); Gigolo and
  Gigolette (Encore) 1952,Ap 3,45:1
White Corridors 1952,Jl 16,21:1
Something Money Can't Buy 1953,O 1,34:3
Virgin Island 1960,Mr 24,39:5
No Place Like Homicide 1962,S 13,32:1

Jackson, Pat (Original Author)

Raider, The; Western Approaches 1946,S 28,13:2
Something Money Can't Buy 1953,O 1,34:3

Jackson, Pat (Screenwriter)

White Corridors 1952,Jl 16,21:1
Something Money Can't Buy 1953,O 1,34:3
Virgin Island 1960,Mr 24,39:5

Jackson, Peaches

Greatest Thing in Life, The 1918,D 23,9:1
Circus Days 1923,Ag 6,14:2
Eternal Three, The 1923,O 12,7:2 (Incorrect in
  this edition; use 1927,O 1,7:2 elsewhere)
Pied Piper Malone 1924,Ja 28,12:1
Oytherea 1924,My 26,21:1
Poisoned Paradise 1924,Ag 11,16:1

Jackson, Ray

Frieda 1947,Ag 15,12:3
Final Test, The 1954,Ja 26,21:5
Crest of the Wave 1954,N 11,43:2
Dunkirk 1958,S 11,42:2

Jackson, Samadu

Something of Value 1957,My 11,24:6

Jackson, Sammy

Fastest Guitar Alive, The 1968,F 15,47:1

Jackson, Selmer

Thru Different Eyes 1929,Ap 15,22:6
Why Bring That Up? 1929,O 5,22:5
Lovin' the Ladies 1930,Mr 22,22:6
Dirigible 1931,Ap 6,24:1
Subway Express 1931,My 2,23:4
Secret Call, The 1931,Jl 13,13:5
Leftover Ladies 1931,N 9,22:4
You Said a Mouthful 1932,N 18,23:2
Sisters Under the Skin 1934,Je 8,18:1
Traveling Saleslady 1935,Mr 29,26:2
Black Fury 1935,Ap 11,27:2
Public Hero No 1 1935,Je 8,12:2
Front Page Woman 1935,Jl 12,15:1
Grand Exit 1935,N 4,24:5
Parole 1936,Je 27,21:1
Public Enemy's Wife 1936,Jl 9,17:2
Magnificent Brute, The 1936,O 24,23:1
Family Affair, A 1937,Ap 20,29:2
Man in Blue, The 1937,Ag 30,25:2
West of Shanghai 1937,O 29,19:2
Hot Water 1937,N 5,19:4
Federal Bullets 1937,D 27,11:1
Manhattan Merry-Go-Round 1937,D 31,9:3
Thirteenth Man, The 1938,Ja 1,11:2
You're Only Young Once 1938,Ja 3,16:2
Prison Nurse 1938,Mr 4,17:5
Arson Racket Squad 1938,Je 18,18:2
Missing Guest, The 1938,S 7,30:7
Personal Secretary 1938,O 5,20:2
Secrets of an Actress 1938,O 8,10:2
Gangster's Boy 1938,N 7,23:6
Gambling Ship 1939,Ja 21,19:2
Stand up and Fight 1939,Ja 27,17:2
Off the Record 1939,F 18,12:2
Calling All Marines 1939,O 26,27:2
Dress Parade 1939,O 28,11:2
Grapes of Wrath, The 1940,Ja 25,17:2
Johnny Apollo 1940,Ap 13,21:2
Sailor's Lady 1940,Je 29,12:2
Wagons Westward 1940,Jl 8,13:2
Millionaires in Prison 1940,Jl 16,21:3
Men Against the Sky 1940,S 12,31:2
Hired Wife 1940,S 14,11:2
Lady With red Hair 1940,D 6,28:2
Play Girl 1941,Ja 30,19:3
Tight Shoes 1941,Je 19,25:2
Parachute Battalion 1941,Ag 29,13:2
International Squadron 1941,N 14,28:4
They Died With Their Boots On 1941,N 21,23:3
Secret Agent of Japan 1942,Mr 23,19:3
Road to Happiness 1942,Mr 27,27:4
Ten Gentlemen From West Point 1942,Je 5,23:3
Margin for Error 1943,Ja 25,10:7
Circumstantial Evidence 1945,Ap 21,18:3

Jackson, Selmer — Cont

Allotment Wives 1945,N 22,39:3
Dakota 1945,D 17,17:2
Black Market Babies 1946,Ap 1,23:1
Pretender, The 1947,Ag 12,26:2
Magic Town 1947,O 8,29:2
Fuller Brush Man, The 1948,My 15,18:2
Pitfall 1948,Ag 25,31:2
That's My Boy 1951,Ag 2,18:1
Elopement 1951,D 21,21:3
Deadline U S A 1952,Mr 15,8:2
Autumn Leaves 1956,Ag 2,21:2

Jackson, Sherry

Breaking Point, The 1950,O 7,10:6
Lion and the Horse, The 1952,My 19,12:2
Miracle of Our Lady Fatima, The
  1952,Ag 21,16:2
Trouble Along the Way 1953,My 7,37:2
Adventures of Huckleberry Fin, The
  1960,Ag 4,17:1
Gunn 1967,Je 29,32:1
Mini-Skirt Mob, The 1968,O 24,55:5

Jackson, Shirley (Original Author)

Lizzie 1957,Ap 5,24:2
Haunting, The 1963,S 19,23:1

Jackson, Stanley (Narrator)

Moontrap, The; Pour la Suite du Monde
  1964,N 11,38:1

Jackson, Theron

Zamba 1949,N 7,33:2

Jackson, Thomas

Broadway 1929,My 28,36:2
Double Cross Roads 1930,Ap 29,31:1
Fall Guy, The 1930,My 27,27:2
For the Defense 1930,Jl 19,7:5
Good News 1930,S 6,9:2
Little Casear 1931,Ja 10,19:2
Lawless Woman, The 1931,Je 8,21:1
Sweepstakes 1931,Je 25,23:5
Twenty-Four Hours 1931,O 3,20:2
Women Go on Forever 1931,O 19,28:1
Reckless Living 1931,D 5,21:2
Escapade 1932,My 28,18:2
Unashamed 1932,Jl 15,13:4
Doctor X 1932,Ag 4,17:2
Big City Blues 1932,S 10,18:5
Strange Justice 1932,O 20,24:2
Afraid to Talk 1932,D 19,19:5
Parachute Jumper 1933,Ja 26,12:2
Mystery of the Wax Museum, The
  1933,F 18,13:3
From Hell to Heaven 1933,Mr 18,9:3
Strictly Personal 1933,Mr 20,18:2
Avenger, The 1933,O 3,28:3
Myrt and Marge 1934,Ja 17,23:2
George White's Scandals 1934,Mr 16,24:2
Melody in Spring 1934,Mr 31,8:2
Manhattan Melodrama 1934,My 5,22:2
Personality Kid, The 1934,Ag 1,14:2
Carnival 1935,F 16,9:1
Gold Diggers of 1935 1935,Mr 15,25:2
Case of the Curious Bride, The 1935,Ap 5,21:3
Irish in US, The 1935,Ag 1,15:1
It Had to Happen 1936,F 15,18:6
Preview Murder Mystery, The 1936,Mr 21,13:2
Little Miss Nobody 1936,Je 6,21:1
Son Comes Home, A 1936,S 5,7:1
Magnificent Brute, The 1936,O 24,23:1
Fugitive in the Sky 1937,Ja 16,21:1
She's no Lady 1937,Ag 12,14:3
Lady in the Morgue, The 1938,My 9,13:3
International Crime 1938,My 16,14:4
Torchy Gets her Man 1938,N 18,25:3
Crime Takes a Holiday 1938,N 28,11:2
I Stand Accused 1939,Ja 5,17:1
Free, Blonde and 21 1940,Ap 5,25:2
Fugitive From Justice, A 1940,Jl 8,13:3
Millionaires in Prison 1940,Jl 16,21:3
Girl From God's Country 1940,S 9,18:5
Law of the Tropics 1941,O 10,26:5
Woman in the Window, The 1945,Ja 26,16:4
Circumstantial Evidence 1945,Ap 21,18:3
Why Girls Leave Home 1945,Ag 4,7:3
Shady Lady 1945,O 11,26:2
Guilty, The 1947,My 19,27:2
Guilt of Janet Ames, The 1947,My 23,31:2
Here Comes Trouble 1948,Ap 15,31:4
Phone Call From a Stranger 1952,F 2,11:2

Jackson, Tony (Composer)

Broadway Rhythm 1944,Ap 14,24:6

Jackson, Warren

Hollywood Round-Up 1938,Mr 5,11:2
Oh, You Beautiful Doll 1949,N 12,8:4

Jackson, Wilfred (Director)

Saludos Amigos 1943,F 13,8:2
Melody Time 1948,My 28,28:2
Cinderella 1950,F 23,33:1
Peter Pan 1953,F 12,23:1
Lady and the Tramp 1955,Je 24,17:1

Jackson and Lynam

Ice-Capades 1941,S 25,29:1

Jacobeni, Marie

Strange Case of District Attorney M, The
  1930,Mr 17,20:3

JACOBI
See Also JACOBY
Jacobi, Derek
Othello 1966,F 2,24:1
Jacobi, Lieselotte
Zapfenstreich am Rhein 1933,F 2,21:6
Jacobi, Lou
Kid for two Farthings, A 1956,Ap 18,25:1
Diary of Anne Frank, The 1959,Mr 19,40:1
Song Without End 1960,Ag 12,10:2
Irma la Douce 1963,Je 6,39:1
Last of the Secret Agents, The? 1966,Je 23,29:1
Penelope 1966,N 11,36:6
Jacobini, Diomira
Last Night, The 1930,Ja 27,18:4
Jacobini, Marta
Living Corpse, The 1931,Ja 4,27:2
Eternal Melodies 1948,F 14,17:3
Jacobs, Alexander (Screenwriter)
Point Blank 1967,S 19,53:1
Jacobs, Angela
Counsellor-At-Law 1933,D 8,31:2
Jacobs, Arthur P (Producer)
What a Way to Go! 1964,My 15,44:1
Doctor Dolittle 1967,D 20,55:1
Planet of the Apes 1968,F 9,55:2
Jacobs, Harrison (Miscellaneous)
Barrier, The 1937,N 27,21:2
Jacobs, Harrison (Original Author)
Little Big Shot 1935,O 7,11:2
Jacobs, Harrison (Screenwriter)
Partners of the Plains 1938,F 12,20:4
Wagons Westward 1940,Jl 8,13:2
Jacobs, Jack (Original Author)
Man on Fire 1957,Ag 23,10:1
Jacobs, Lewis (Producer)
Sweet Love, Bitter 1967,Ja 31,50:1
Jacobs, Lewis (Screenwriter)
Sweet Love, Bitter 1967,Ja 31,50:1
Jacobs, Robert
South Pacific 1958,Mr 20,33:1
Jacobs, Seaman (Screenwriter)
It Happened at the World's Fair 1963,My 30,20:1
Jacobs, W W (Original Author)
Our Relations 1936,N 11,55:1
Jacobs, Werner (Director)
Beggar Student, The 1958,Ja 25,14:3
Guitars of Love 1958,Jl 12,18:1
Heidi 1968,S 23,42:4
Jacobs, William (Original Author)
Song of the Saddle 1936,Mr 21,13:3
Treachery Rides the Range 1936,My 30,7:3
Hot Money 1936,Jl 25,16:2
Over the Goal 1937,O 16,22:2
Jacobs, William (Producer)
Shine on Harvest Moon 1944,Mr 11,10:2
Conflict 1945,Je 16,10:2
Too Young to Know 1945,D 8,21:2
Verdict, The 1946,D 13,29:4
Beast With Five Fingers, The 1946,D 26,28:3
My Wild Irish Rose 1947,D 25,32:2
April Showers 1948,Mr 27,10:2
Whiplash 1948,D 27,16:3
Look for the Silver Lining 1949,Je 24,29:2
Story of Seabiscuit, The 1949,N 12,8:4
Montana 1950,F 4,9:2
Daughter of Rosie O'Grady, The
 1950,Mr 31,36:2
Rocky Mountain 1950,N 4,13:2
Lullaby of Broadway 1951,Mr 27,35:2
On Moonlight Bay 1951,Jl 27,15:2
Painting the Clouds With Sunshine 1951,S 1,9:6
About Face 1952,My 24,15:3
She's Working her Way Through College
 1952,Jl 10,27:2
April in Paris 1952,D 25,34:5
By the Light of the Silvery Moon
 1953,Mr 27,28:2
Calamity Jane 1953,N 5,40:2
Jacobs, William (Screenwriter)
Song of the Saddle 1936,Mr 21,13:3
Treachery Rides the Range 1936,My 30,7:3
Big Noise, The 1936,Jl 4,18:3
Hot Money 1936,Jl 25,16:2
Talent Scout 1937,Ag 20,21:3
Dance Charlie Dance 1937,Ag 26,25:2
Over the Goal 1937,O 16,22:2
Penrod and his Twin Brother 1938,Ap 18,11:1
Jacobsen, Johan (Director)
Invisible Army, The 1950,Je 26,17:3
Stranger Knocks, A 1965,Ap 1,30:1
Jacobsen, Johan (Producer)
Stranger Knocks, A 1965,Ap 1,30:1
Jacobson, Arthur (Director)
Home on the Range 1935,F 13,24:4
Jacobson, H J
Shanghaied 1927,S 13,36:2
Jacobson, Henrietta
Catskill Honeymoon 1950,Ja 28,10:3
Jacobson, Henrik
Hotel Sahara 1952,Ja 1,21:4

Jacobson, Hy (Composer)
Catskill Honeymoon 1950,Ja 28,10:3
Jacobson, Hymie
Purimspieler, Der 1937,D 6,19:2
Jacobson, Joel (Miscellaneous)
Catskill Honeymoon 1950,Ja 28,10:3
Jacobson, Paul (Producer)
Santa Claus Conquers the Martians
 1964,D 17,50:2
Jacobsson, Nils
Tjocka Slaekten; Near Relatives 1935,My 20,20:5
Jacobsson, Ulla
One Summer of Happiness 1955,Mr 22,35:2
Smiles of a Summer Night 1957,D 24,11:1
Crime and Punishment 1958,S 16,23:2
Love Is a Ball 1963,Ap 25,38:1
Zulu 1964,Jl 8,38:1
Heroes of Telemark, The 1966,Mr 10,26:1
JACOBY
See Also JACOBI
Jacoby, Annalee Whitmore (Screenwriter)
Tish 1942,S 18,25:2
Jacoby, Carl (Original Author)
Riddle Woman, The 1920,N 8,20:2
Jacoby, Georg (Director)
Vendetta 1921,D 19,13:1
Quo Vadis 1925,F 16,24:1
Mother Love 1931,F 16,17:1
Lindenwirtin vom Rhein, Die 1931,S 25,28:7
Hurra! Ein Junge! 1932,Je 21,19:6
Die Blumenfrau von Lindenau 1932,Jl 8,22:5
Pension Schoeller 1932,S 20,26:3
Kadetten 1933,D 26,19:3
Ja, Treu Ist die Soldatenliebe 1934,Ap 28,11:4
Melodie der Liebe 1934,S 17,20:3
Liebe in Uniform 1934,O 9,17:2
Csardasfuerstin 1935,Ap 25,18:3
Ehestreik 1935,Ag 31,16:3
Geschichten aus dem Wienerwald; Tales From the
 Vienna Woods 1935,N 2,13:3
Madonna, Wo Bist Du? 1936,Mr 21,13:3
Heisses Blut 1936,S 26,11:2
Ist Mein Mann Nicht Fabelhaft 1936,D 8,31:3
Bettelstudent, Der 1936,D 28,12:3
Letzte Walzer, Der 1937,Ap 17,15:1
Besuch am Abend 1937,Jl 3,18:2
Zwei im Sonnenschein 1937,Jl 31,6:2
Grosse Bluff, Der; Big Bluff, The 1937,S 6,20:2
Drama on the Threshing Floor 1937,O 30,22:3
Gasparone 1938,Mr 12,13:4
Husaren Heraus 1938,Mr 19,11:3
Teufelskerl, Ein; Devil of a Fellow, A
 1938,O 1,10:3
Nacht im Mai, Eine; Night in May, A
 1938,N 12,10:3
Herbst-Monoever; Fall Manoeuvres
 1939,Mr 18,9:3
Marika 1953,F 18,27:2
Jacoby, Georg (Original Author)
Tradition 1921,Jl 1,8:1
Vendetta 1921,D 19,13:1
Jacoby, Hans (Original Author)
Taxi 1953,Ja 22,20:3
Jacoby, Hans (Screenwriter)
Tarzan and the Amazons 1945,Ap 30,13:4
Champagne for Caesar 1950,My 12,33:2
Tarzan and the Slave Girl 1950,Je 24,7:3
Sirocco 1951,Je 14,31:2
Carnival Story 1954,Ap 17,8:2
Portrait of an Unknown Woman 1958,Ap 26,14:6
Circus of Love 1958,Ag 16,10:2
It Happened in Broad Daylight 1960,S 30,33:1
Good Soldier Schweik, The 1963,Ag 21,38:1
Judge and the Sinner, The 1964,Je 6,14:2
Jacoby, Irving (Director)
Lonely Night, The 1954,Mr 29,22:2
Jacoby, Irving (Original Author)
Lonely Night, The 1954,Mr 29,22:2
Jacoby, John (Screenwriter)
Between Us Girls 1942,S 25,25:3
Amazing Mrs Holliday, The 1943,F 22,20:2
Happy Go Lucky 1943,Mr 25,25:1
Phantom of the Opera, The 1943,O 15,15:2
She Wouldn't Say Yes 1946,Ja 12,10:7
Tars and Spars 1946,F 15,29:2
Jacoby, Madame
Notorious Sophie Lang, The 1934,Jl 21,14:2
Jacoby, Michel (Original Author)
Charge of the Light Brigade, The 1936,N 2,24:1
Here Comes Carter 1936,N 14,23:3
Doomed to Die 1940,Jl 30,16:3
They Came to Blow up America
 1943,My 15,13:2
Jacoby, Michel (Screenwriter)
Charge of the Light Brigade, The 1936,N 2,24:1
Love, Honor and Behave 1938,Mr 21,18:2
Betrayal 1939,S 16,20:2
No Greater Sin 1941,Ag 29,18:2
Frisco Lil 1942,F 12,27:2
Mystery of Marie Roget, The 1942,My 5,17:3
Are These our Parents? 1944,Ag 23,16:2

Jaconson, Nils
Roeda Dagen 1932,My 21,9:2
Jacopetti, Gualtiero (Director)
Women of the World 1963,Jl 3,14:1
Mondo Pazzo 1965,Ap 1,30:3
Africa Addio 1967,Mr 13,47:3
Jacopetti, Gualtiero (Original Author)
Africa Addio 1967,Mr 13,47:3
Jacopetti, Gualtiero (Producer)
Mondo Cane; Dog's World, A 1963,Ap 4,58:1 (In
 Addenda)
Jacopetti, Gualtiero (Screenwriter)
Mondo Cane; Dog's World, A 1963,Ap 4,58:1 (In
 Addenda)
Women of the World 1963,Jl 3,14:1
Mondo Pazzo 1965,Ap 1,30:3
Africa Addio 1967,Mr 13,47:3
Jacovides, Leles
Anna of Rhodes 1950,Mr 23,34:2
Jacovoni, Alessandro (Cinematographer)
Wild, Wild World 1965,N 22,48:2
Jacovoni, Alessandro (Miscellaneous)
Wild, Wild World 1965,N 22,48:2
Jacovoni, Alessandro (Producer)
Wild Love; (Gli Inamorati) 1961,Ap 6,30:2
Duel of the Titans 1963,Ag 8,19:1
Jacqot, Tony
Youth in Revolt 1939,My 16,27:3
Jacques, Andre (Director)
Noah's Ark 1950,Ag 21,15:1
Jacques, Franz (Original Author)
Beware of Married Men 1928,Ap 10,33:2
Jacques, Fred (Original Author)
Hole in the Wall, The 1929,Ap 15,22:6
Jacques, Hattie
Chance of a Lifetime 1951,Mr 15,37:2
Gay Lady, The 1951,Ap 16,21:2
Adventures of Sadie, The 1955,My 18,35:2
Carry on Sergeant 1959,O 28,40:5
School for Scoundrels 1960,Jl 12,39:1
Carry on Nurse 1960,S 10,11:1
Make Mine Mink 1960,D 20,43:4
Follow a Star 1961,Ap 26,34:1
Bobo, The 1967,S 29,53:1
Jacques, Le Petit
Merlusse 1938,Mr 17,17:2
Jacques, Ted
Flaming Star 1960,D 17,19:1
Jacquet, Dany
Burning Court, The 1963,Ag 1,17:2
Jacquet, Gaston
Living Image, The 1928,Je 4,13:2
David Golder 1932,O 20,24:2
Charlemagne 1935,Ag 24,18:3
Golem, The 1937,Mr 22,27:2
Jacquier, Marc
Trial of Joan of Arc, The 1965,F 12,19:1
Jacquin, Abel
Ultimatum 1940,F 5,13:2
It Happened in Gibraltar 1943,N 16,27:1
Dame de Pique, La 1944,O 19,19:2
Resistance; Peleton d'Execution 1946,Jl 5,15:3
Man to Men 1949,F 21,20:2
Counter Investigation 1949,D 30,13:2
Au Grand Balcon 1951,My 5,14:2
Jacquin, Maurice (Producer)
Lafayette 1963,Ap 11,29:1
Upper Hand, The 1967,Jl 29,29:3
Jacquot, Tony
End of a Day, The 1939,S 12,28:4
Jadjiarghiri, Helen
Lily of the Harbor 1958,Ap 16,38:3
Jaeckel, Antonie
Der Falsche Feldmarschall 1932,Je 30,26:2
Letzte Rose 1936,O 10,21:3
Jaeckel, Richard
Guadalcanal Diary 1943,N 18,29:1
Wing and a Prayer 1944,Ag 31,14:1
City Across the River 1949,Ap 8,31:3
Battleground 1949,N 12,8:4
Sands of Iwo Jima 1949,D 31,9:2
Gunfighter, The 1950,Je 24,7:2
Wyoming Mail 1950,O 23,26:5
Fighting Coast Guard 1951,My 12,14:6
Hoodlum Empire 1952,Mr 6,25:6
My Son John 1952,Ap 9,27:1
Come Back, Little Sheba 1952,D 24,13:2 (In Addenda)
Shanghai Story, The 1954,S 25,10:7
Violent Men, The 1955,Ja 27,17:2
Attack! 1956,S 20,29:4
3:10 to Yuma 1957,Ag 29,22:1
Cowboy 1958,F 20,29:5
Naked and the Dead, The 1958,Ag 7,21:1
Platinum High School 1960,My 26,37:3
Gallant Hours, The 1960,Je 23,19:4
Flaming Star 1960,D 17,19:1
Town Without Pity 1961,O 11,53:1
Dirty Dozen, The 1967,Je 16,36:1
Devil's Brigade, The 1968,My 23,56:2
Jaeger, Claude (Producer)
Devil and the 10 Commandments, The (Episode
 7) 1963,O 15,44:1
Devil and the 10 Commandments, The (Episode
 6) 1963,O 15,44:1

Jaeger Claude (Producer)— Cont
Devil and the 10 Commandments, The (Episode 5) 1963,O 15,44:1
Devil and the 10 Commandments, The (Episode 3) 1963,O 15,44:1
Devil and the 10 Commandments, The (Episode 4) 1963,O 15,44:1
Devil and the 10 Commandments, The (Episode 1) 1963,O 15,44:1
Devil and the 10 Commandments, The (Episode 2) 1963,O 15,44:1

Jaekel, Antoine
Why Cry at Parting 1930,F 4,28:3

Jaerrell, Stig
Larsson I Andra Giftet 1935,O 19,21:3
Raggen, Det Aer Jag Det 1936,My 22,19:1

Jaffe, Carl
Saint in London, The 1939,Jl 19,23:3
Continental Express 1942,Ap 7,26:3
Life and Death of Colonel Blimp, The 1945,Mr 30,18:2
State Secret 1950,O 5,38:2
Dancing Years, The 1951,Ja 29,14:4
Lilli Marlene 1952,Mr 29,19:2
Ivanhoe 1952,Ag 1,8:2
Desperate Moment 1953,S 1,19:4
Mad Little Island 1958,D 31,12:1
Roman Spring of Mrs Stone, The 1961,D 29,11:1

Jaffe, Rona (Original Author)
Best of Everything 1959,O 9,24:2

Jaffe, Sam
Scralet Empress, The 1934,S 15,20:2
We Live Again 1934,N 2,27:2
Lost Horizon 1937,Mr 4,27:1
Gunga Din 1939,Ja 28,19:2
Stage Door Canteen 1943,Je 25,13:2
13 Rue Madeleine 1947,Ja 16,30:2
Gentleman's Agreement 1947,N 12,36:2
Accused, The 1949,Ja 13,26:2
Rope of Sand 1949,Ag 4,19:2
Asphalt Jungle, The 1950,Je 9,29:3
Under the Gun 1951,F 23,33:2
I Can Get It for You Wholesale 1951,Ap 5,34:4
Day the Earth Stood Still, The 1951,S 19,37:1
Barbarian and the Geisha 1958,O 3,25:1
Ben Hur 1959,N 19,50:2
Guns for San Sebastian 1968,Mr 21,57:2

Jaffe, Sam (Producer)
Sullivans, The 1944,F 10,19:2
Damon and Pythias 1962,S 6,37:2

Jaffrey, Madhur
Shakespeare Wallah 1965,S 13,42:1
Shakespeare Wallah 1966,Mr 23,40:2

Jaffrey, William
Woman Chases Man 1937,Je 11,26:2

Jagadish
Kanchenjungha 1966,Jl 26,27:2

Jagaeus, Christina
Children, The 1949,D 23,17:1

Jagaeus, Paula
Children, The 1949,D 23,17:1

Jagger, Dean
You Belong to Me 1934,S 13,26:1
Wings in the Dark 1935,F 2,10:1
Home on the Range 1935,F 13,24:4
Behold My Wife 1935,F 18,19:3
Car 99 1935,F 23,14:7
People Will Talk 1935,Je 17,20:2
Men Without Names 1935,Je 29,16:2
13 Hours by Air 1936,Ap 30,17:2
Revolt of the Zombies 1936,Je 5,17:2
Pepper 1936,Ag 24,11:2
Star for a Night 1936,S 5,7:2
Under Cover of Night 1937,Ja 20,18:4
Dangerous Number 1937,Mr 12,19:2
Brigham Young - Frontiersman 1940,S 21,13:2
Western Union 1941,F 7,23:2
Men In her Life, The 1941,D 12,35:1
Valley of the Sun 1942,Mr 19,29:2
North Star, The 1943,N 5,23:1
Yank in London, A 1946,Ap 20,16:3
Sister Kenny 1946,S 30,21:2
Pursued 1947,Mr 8,10:2
C-Man 1949,My 28,11:4
Twelve O'Clock High 1950,Ja 28,10:2
Sierra 1950,S 15,31:2
Dark City 1950,O 19,40:5
Rawhide 1951,Mr 26,19:2
Warpath 1951,N 23,32:2
My Son John 1952,Ap 9,27:1
Denver and Rio Grande, The 1952,My 17,22:7
It Grows on Trees 1952,N 29,11:2
Robe, The 1953,S 17,32:6
Executive Suite 1954,My 7,19:1
White Christmas 1954,O 15,16:3
Bad Day at Black Rock 1955,F 2,22:2
Eternal Sea, The 1955,Je 10,16:2
It's a Dog's Life 1955,D 23,14:3
On the Threshold of Space 1956,Mr 30,10:5
Great Man, The 1957,Ja 2,28:2
Three Brave Men 1957,Mr 16,13:2
Bernardine 1957,Jl 25,28:1
Proud Rebel, The 1958,Jl 2,23:4
King Creole 1958,Jl 4,15:2

Nun's Story, The 1959,Je 19,30:1
Cash McCall 1960,Ja 28,26:1
Elmer Gantry 1960,Jl 8,16:1
Parrish 1961,My 5,22:1
Honeymoon Machine, The 1961,Ag 24,25:2
Jumbo 1962,D 7,49:1
First to Fight 1967,Mr 30,55:1
Firecreek 1968,F 22,36:2
Day of the Evil Gun 1968,Ap 25,53:2

Jaglom, Henry
Psych-Out 1968,Mr 28,52:1

Jago, June
Please Turn Over 1961,Ap 29,12:2

Jago, Syme
Incredible Journey, The 1963,N 21,43:2

Jahn, Otto Heinz (Screenwriter)
Girls Behind Bars 1950,My 10,41:2

Jahnberg, Hakan
Silence, The 1964,F 4,28:1

Jahnen, Margarete
Question 7 1961,S 29,30:2

Jahr, Adolf
Pettersson & Bendel 1934,F 22,25:2
Adolf Armstrong 1937,O 1,19:5
Kryss med Albertina, Paa; Cruise in the Albertina, A 1940,Mr 25,11:3

Jahrblum, Charles (Miscellaneous)
Harvest 1939,O 3,19:4

Jai
Tarzan Goes to India 1962,S 6,37:2

Jaimison, William
Chaser, The 1928,Ap 10,33:2

Jairaj
Nine Hours to Rama 1963,Ap 4,58:2

Jairal
Maya 1966,Je 23,29:4

Jakisch, Mara
Hummel-Hummel 1939,Mr 11,21:2

Jakov, O
We Are From Kronstadt 1936,My 2,11:1
Seven Brave Men 1936,Je 15,24:2
Concentration Camp 1939,Mr 20,13:2

Jakubowska, Wanda (Director)
Last Stop, The 1949,Mr 22,31:2

Jakubowska, Wanda (Producer)
Last Stop, The 1949,Mr 22,31:2

Jakubowska, Wanda (Screenwriter)
Last Stop, The 1949,Mr 22,31:2

Jalabert, Mme
Legion of Honor, The 1928,Jl 20,8:4

Jalna
Born to Dance 1936,D 5,16:1

Jaloma, Adela
Prisionero 13, El 1934,Ap 30,11:4
Cuna Vacia, La; Empty Cradle, The 1938,Mr 21,18:3

Jalovec, Vasa
Ecstasy of Young Love 1936,Mr 10,27:3

Jambrina, Francisco
Padre Mercader; Merchant Father 1939,Jl 15,8:3
Life of Simon Bolivar, The 1943,Je 18,16:5
Young and the Damned, The 1952,Mr 25,23:2

Jamerson, Peter
Between Us Girls 1942,S 25,25:3

James, Alfred P
Everything's Rosie 1931,My 22,28:5
Heaven on Earth 1931,D 19,16:4
Six of a Kind 1934,Mr 10,18:3
Cockeyed Cavaliers 1934,Jl 25,22:2
Elmer and Elsie 1934,Ag 4,14:5

James, Anthony
Dolwyn 1949,Ag 30,18:4
In the Heat of the Night 1967,Ag 3,26:1

James, Barbara
Patient Vanishes, The 1947,My 23,31:2

James, Claire
Navy Blues 1941,S 20,11:2

James, Clifton
Strange One, The 1957,Ap 13,12:3
Something Wild 1961,D 24,30:6
Experiment in Terror 1962,Ap 14,14:1
David and Lisa 1962,D 27,5:5
Black Like Me 1964,My 21,42:1
Happening, The 1967,My 18,56:3
Caper of the Golden Bulls, The 1967,Je 22,46:1
Cool Hand Luke 1967,N 2,58:1
Will Penny 1968,Ap 11,51:2

James, Dan (Screenwriter)
Three Russian Girls 1944,F 5,13:2

James, David
Charley's Aunt 1925,F 9,15:3
Stop Flirting 1925,Je 18,16:3
Lady is Willing, The 1942,Ap 24,21:2
Frenchman's Creek 1944,S 21,26:2

James, Edward (Screenwriter)
Private Buckaroo 1942,Je 25,27:4
Over my Dead Body 1942,D 26,15:2

James, Elizabeth
Born Losers, The 1967,Ag 19,16:2

James, Forrest
Stark Love 1927,F 28,22:3

James, Francis
Laburnum Grove 1941,D 2,29:2

James, Gardner
Silent Sanderson 1925,Je 11,14:3
Happy Warrior, The 1925,Jl 7,24:2
Hell-Bent for Heaven 1926,My 4,31:1
Amateur Gentleman, The 1926,Ag 17,15:3
Flaming Forest, The 1926,N 22,28:3
Ladies at Ease 1927,O 5,31:1
Kentucky Courage 1928,My 14,25:1
Big Killing, The 1928,Jl 2,11:2
Mating Call, The 1928,O 8,14:2
Flying Fleet, The 1929,F 11,26:3
Studio Murder Mystery, The 1929,Je 10,23:1
Dawn Patrol, The 1930,Jl 11,22:1
Captain Blood 1935,D 27,14:1
Crash Donovan 1936,Ag 10,10:3

James, Gertie Des Wentworth (Original Author)
Cheating Blondes 1933,My 20,11:4

James, Gladden
Heart of the Wetona, The 1919,Ja 6,11:3
Yes or No 1920,Jl 5,12:4
Foot Falls 1921,S 9,18:3
His Captive Woman 1929,Ap 3,26:4

James, Gordon
Weary River 1929,Ja 25,20:6
Clown Must Laugh, A 1938,O 12,35:2

James, Harry
Do You Love Me 1946,My 25,12:2
If I'm Lucky 1946,S 20,41:3
Carnegie Hall 1947,My 3,10:2
Miracle Can Happen, A 1948,F 4,28:4
I'll Get by 1950,N 2,39:3
Benny Goodman Story 1956,F 22,22:1
Opposite Sex, The 1956,N 16,23:2

James, Harry (Composer)
New Faces of 1937 1937,Jl 2,25:1
Do You Love Me 1946,My 25,12:2

James, Harry (Original Author)
Waltz Time 1946,F 11,25:2

James, Harry (Screenwriter)
Waltz Time 1946,F 11,25:2

James, Harry and his Music Makers
Private Buckaroo 1942,Je 25,27:4
Springtime in the Rockies 1942,N 12,30:2
Best Foot Forward 1943,Je 30,25:2
Two Girls and a Sailor 1944,Je 15,16:1
Bathing Beauty 1944,Je 28,20:1
If I'm Lucky 1946,S 20,41:3

James, Henry (Original Author)
Spitfire 1943,Je 14,13:2
Lost Moment, The 1947,N 22,10:2
Heiress, The 1949,O 7,35:2
Innocents, The 1961,D 26,15:2

James, Horace
Guns at Batasi 1964,N 17,47:1

James, Inez (Composer)
Mister Big 1943,Je 14,13:4
Patrick the Great 1945,Ap 13,15:2
Are You With It? 1948,Ap 15,31:2

James, Jason (Screenwriter)
Fury at Showdown 1957,Ap 20,21:3

James, Jeri Lou
Glass Web, The 1953,N 12,37:5

James, Jesse E (Miscellaneous)
Jesse James 1927,O 17,20:2

James, Jo Frances (Screenwriter)
Jesse James 1939,Ja 14,13:1

James, John
Flying Tigers 1942,O 23,25:2
Gung Ho! 1944,Ja 26,23:2
Sign of the Cross 1944,D 21,16:3
Bedside Manner 1945,Je 23,9:6

James, Keith
Dutchman 1967,F 28,32:1

James, Kyle
Donovan's Brain 1954,Ja 21,28:2

James, Leon
Cabin in the Sky 1943,My 28,19:3

James, Lisa
Two Tickets to Paris 1962,N 29,46:5

James, Olga
Carmen Jones 1954,O 29,27:2

James, Polly (Screenwriter)
Mrs Parkington 1944,O 13,16:1
Raiders, The 1952,D 13,19:2
Redhead From Wyoming, The 1953,Ja 9,17:4

James, Rian (Director)
Best of Enemies 1933,Jl 17,19:5

James, Rian (Original Author)
Love Is a Racket 1932,Je 11,9:3
Crooner 1932,Ag 20,7:4
Hat Check Girl 1932,O 8,15:4
Parachute Jumper 1933,Ja 26,12:2
White Parade, The 1934,N 10,19:1
Down Argentine Way 1940,O 18,25:1
Dead Ringer 1964,F 20,22:3

James, Rian (Screenwriter)
White Parade, The 1934,N 10,19:1
It Happened in New York 1935,Ap 6,10:1
To Beat the Band 1935,N 23,23:2
We're Only Human 1936,Ja 18,19:2
Witness Chair, The 1936,Ap 18,19:2

James, Rian (Screenwriter) — Cont
Internes Can't Take Money 1937,My 6,23:2
Exclusive 1937,Jl 22,15:1
Submarine Patrol 1938,N 19,9:2
Gorilla, The 1939,My 28,6:2
Housekeeper's Daughter, The 1939,D 2,21:4
Broadway Limited 1941,Je 16,11:6
Parachute Nurse 1942,Jl 27,18:2
Whispering City 1948,My 10,25:5

James, Robert
Bridal Path, The 1959,D 21,34:2

James, Sidney
Give Us This Day 1949,D 21,41:2
Last Holiday 1950,N 14,39:4
Lavender Hill Mob, The 1951,O 16,35:2
You Can't Beat the Irish 1952,My 1,34:4
Assassin, The 1953,Ap 18,17:2
I Believe in You 1953,My 5,34:3
Hundred Hour Hunt 1953,Je 17,32:2
Miss Robin Hood 1953,Je 27,7:2
Titfield Thunderbolt, The 1953,O 6,34:2
Detective, The 1954,N 2,25:2
Crest of the Wave 1954,N 11,43:2
Will any Gentleman? 1955,S 28,70:6
Joe Macbeth 1956,Ap 7,13:1
Kid for two Farthings, A 1956,Ap 18,25:1
Trapeze 1956,Je 5,39:2
Iron Petticoat, The 1957,F 2,12:2
John and Julie 1957,My 7,40:1
Smallest Show on Earth, The 1957,N 23,11:2
Another Time Another Place 1958,My 3,10:4
Sheriff of Fractured Jaw, The 1959,My 14,27:4
Too Many Crooks 1959,Ap 25,14:2
Campbell's Kingdom 1960,Ja 11,35:5
39 Steps, The 1960,O 11,55:2
Upstairs and Downstairs 1960,D 2,53:4
Green Helmet, The 1961,Jl 20,32:2
Pure Hell of St Trinian's, The 1961,S 26,31:1
Double Bunk 1961,N 17,41:3
No Place Like Homicide 1962,S 13,32:1
Carry on Cleo 1965,O 23,17:2

James, Susan Saint
Where Angels Go-Trouble Follows
 1968,Ap 11,51:1
What's so bad About Feeling Good?
 1968,My 25,27:1
Jigsaw 1968,Je 6,54:2

James, Walter
Monster, The 1925,F 16,24:1
Everlasting Whisper, The 1925,O 12,19:3
Little Annie Rooney 1925,O 19,26:1
Battling Butler 1926,Ag 23,9:1
Kid Brother, The 1927,Ja 24,14:1
Blood Ship, The 1927,Jl 19,27:2
Irresistible Lover, The 1927,O 19,24:4
Me, Gangster 1928,O 22,29:1
Shadow of the Law 1930,Je 7,10:4
Street Scene 1931,Ag 27,22:5

James, Will (Original Author)
Smoky 1934,Ja 1,28:2
Smoky 1946,Je 27,29:1
Sand 1949,Ag 5,23:2

JAMESON
See Also JAMISON, JAMIESON

Jameson, Conrad
Playground, The 1965,O 4,00:0

Jameson, House
Naked City, The 1948,Mr 5,17:2
Mirage 1965,My 27,28:1
Swimmer, The 1968,My 16,53:1

Jameson, Joyce
Tip on a Dead Jockey 1957,S 7,12:7
Apartment, The 1960,Je 16,37:2
Balcony, The 1963,Mr 22,7:1
Comedy of Terrors, The 1964,Ja 23,26:2
Good Neighbor Sam 1964,Jl 23,19:1
Boy, Did I Get a Wrong Number! 1966,Je 9,54:2

Jameson, Pauline
I Could go on Singing 1963,My 16,42:1
Crooks Anonymous 1963,O 31,26:3

JAMIESON
See Also JAMISON, JAMESON

Jamieson, Harold
Treasure Island 1950,Ag 16,24:1
Lisbon 1956,Ag 30,19:2

Jamieson, Hazel (Screenwriter)
Dangerous Waters 1936,Ja 22,15:5

Jamieson, Peter
Crystal Ball, The 1943,F 19,22:2

Jamin, Georges
Bouquets From Nicholas 1939,Mr 2,19:1

JAMISON
See Also JAMESON, JAMIESON

Jamison, Bud
Dante's Inferno 1924,S 30,27:3
His First Flame 1927,My 2,26:4
Texas Steer, A 1928,Ja 2,28:1
Buck Privates 1928,Ja 30,18:1
Grand Parade, The 1930,F 1,15:1

Jamison, C V Mrs (Original Author)
Rainbow on the River 1936,D 18,31:4

Jamois, Marguerite
Secret of Mayerling, The 1951,My 8,39:2

Jamot, Armand (Screenwriter)
Tomorrow Is my Turn 1962,F 2,24:2

Jan, Paulette
Antoine and Antoinette 1948,Ap 16,29:2

Jana, La
Shadows of Fear 1928,N 6,35:1
Schlemihl, Der 1934,N 5,23:1
Truxa 1937,Jl 26,15:2

Janatsch, Helmut
No Time for Flowers 1952,D 26,20:3

Janaver, Richard
1 ∎ 1 1961,N 8,41:1

Janclaire, Camille
Three Stripes in the Sun 1955,N 24,41:2

Jancso, Miklos (Director)
Red and the White, The 1968,S 21,26:1

Jancso, Miklos (Screenwriter)
Red and the White, The 1968,S 21,26:1

Janczar, Tadeusz
Five From Barska Street 1955,Mr 14,29:4
Kanal 1961,My 10,52:1
Partings 1962,N 28,44:1

Jandeline
Girls of the Night 1959,Mr 21,13:2

Jandl, Ivan
Search, The 1948,Mr 24,30:3

Jane, Baby
Imitation of Life 1934,N 24,19:1
Man Who Reclaimed his Head, The
 1935,Ja 9,22:1
Alias Mary Dow 1935,Je 29,16:2

Jane, Margot
Yours, Mine and Ours 1968,Ap 25,53:1

Jane, Topsy
Loneliness of the Long Distance Runner, The
 1962,O 9,44:1

Janecka, Janina
Moj Wujaszek Z Ameryki 1933,O 25,25:3

Janeway, Elizabeth (Original Author)
Daisy Kenyon 1947,D 25,32:1

Janey, William
Crooner 1932,Ag 20,7:4

Jani, Bice
Passion of St Francis, The 1932,D 17,22:3

Janis, Conrad
Snafu 1945,D 26,15:2
Margie 1946,O 17,28:3
Brasher Doubloon, The 1947,My 22,34:5
That Hagen Girl 1947,O 25,13:2
Beyond Glory 1948,Ag 4,18:2

Janis, Dorothy
Pagan, The 1929,My 14,29:1
Lummox 1930,Mr 24,25:1

Janis, Elsie
Regular Girl, A 1919,N 11,13:3
Vitaphone 1926,O 8,23:2
Women in War 1940,My 30,21:2

Janis, Elsie (Miscellaneous)
Paramount on Parade 1930,Ap 21,20:4

Janis, Elsie (Original Author)
Oh, Kay! 1928,Ag 27,23:1
Close Harmony 1929,Ap 29,29:2

Jankowsky, Waclaw
Treasure, The 1951,Mr 29,24:4

Jankuhn, Walter
Because I Loved You 1930,Ja 25,13:2
Marquise von Pompadour, Die 1936,F 3,21:3

Janney, Leon
Courage 1930,My 23,21:1
Doorway to Hell, The 1930,N 1,23:2
Father's Son 1931,F 21,15:2
Penrod and Sam 1931,S 26,25:3
Fame Street 1932,Ap 2,13:2
Last Mile, The 1959,F 19,27:1
Charly 1968,S 24,55:1

Janney, Russell (Original Author)
Miracle of the Bells, The 1948,Mr 17,30:1

Janney, Sam (Original Author)
Ladies at Play 1926,N 16,25:3

Janney, William
Coquette 1929,Ap 6,14:4 (In Addenda)
Salute 1929,O 5,22:5
Girl Said No, The 1930,Ap 5,23:3
Those Who Dance 1930,Jl 7,22:3
Dawn Patrol, The 1930,Jl 11,22:1
Pay-Off, The 1930,N 10,16:2
Girls Demand Excitement 1931,F 7,11:1
Right of Way, The 1931,Mr 24,31:2
Man Who Played God, The 1932,F 11,16:1
Mouthpiece, The 1932,Ap 21,25:2
Two Seconds 1932,My 19,25:3
Successful Calamity, A 1932,S 23,22:2
Under-Cover Man 1932,D 5,21:2
Iron Master, The 1933,F 4,11:3
Crime of the Century, The 1933,Mr 13,18:2
Secret of the Blue Room, The 1933,S 13,22:1
World Changes, The 1933,O 27,22:3
Should Ladies Behave? 1933,D 18,24:3
As the Earth Turns 1934,Ap 12,27:2
Modern Hero, A 1934,Ap 20,17:1
Great Hotel Murder, The 1935,F 28,17:4
Sutter's Gold 1936,Mr 27,25:2

Janni, Joseph (Miscellaneous)
Romeo and Juliet 1954,D 22,28:1

Janni, Joseph (Producer)
Glass Mountain, The 1950,My 18,37:3
White Corridors 1952,Jl 16,21:1
Something Money Can't Buy 1953,O 1,34:3
Town Like Alice, A 1958,S 22,27:1
Captain's Table, The 1960,S 27,40:1
Kind of Loving, A 1962,O 2,46:1
Billy Liar 1963,D 17,49:1
Darling 1965,Ag 4,20:1
Far From the Madding Crowd 1967,O 19,59:1
Poor Cow 1968,F 1,28:2

Janni, Joseph (Screenwriter)
Glass Mountain, The 1950,My 18,37:3

Jannig, Hans
Rebel, The 1933,Jl 25,17:2

Jannings, Emil
All for a Woman 1921,D 5,20:1
Vendetta 1921,D 19,13:1
Loves of Pharaoh 1922,F 22,13:3 (In Addenda)
Othello 1923,F 26,15:1
Peter the Great 1923,Je 25,16:5
Passion 1923,Je 26,14:2
Last Laugh, The 1925,Ja 28,14:1
Quo Vadis 1925,F 16,24:1
Three Way Works, The 1926,Mr 19,25:1
Variety 1926,Je 28,15:5
Faust 1926,D 7,21:2
Way of all Flesh, The 1927,Je 27,25:2
Way of all Flesh, The 1927,Jl 3,VII,3:1
Tartuffe 1927,Jl 25,25:3
Husbands or Lovers 1927,N 22,32:2
Last Command, The 1928,Ja 23,18:3
Way of all Flesh, The 1928,Ja 29,VIII,6:2
Street of Sin, The 1928,My 28,23:2
Street of Sin, The 1928,Je 3,VIII,5:1
Power 1928,Jl 16,25:3
Fortune's Fool 1928,Ag 13,23:2
Patriot, The 1928,Ag 18,7:2 (In Addenda)
Sins of the Fathers 1929,Ja 28,21:1
Betrayal 1929,My 6,30:4
Darling of the Gods; Liebling der Gotter
 1930,N 30,IX,6:5
Blue Angel, The 1930,D 6,21:3
Grosse Tenor, Der 1931,My 29,26:5
Stuerme der Leidenschaft; Storms of Passion
 1932,F 14,VIII,6:1
Stuerme der Leidenschaft 1932,Mr 16,17:3
Alte und der Junge Koenig, Der 1935,D 10,31:2
Traumulus 1936,S 19,20:1
Zerbrochene Krug, Der; Broken Jugi, The
 1938,Ja 15,19:2
Robert Koch 1939,N 25,13:2

Jannings, Orin (Original Author)
She's Back on Broadway 1953,Mr 12,24:2

Jannings, Orin (Screenwriter)
Force of Arms 1951,Ag 14,20:2
Time to Love and a Time to Die, A
 1958,Jl 10,22:1
Gene Krupa Story, The 1959,D 26,7:1

Jannssen, Walter
Alles Fuer Veronika 1939,F 4,11:2

Janos, Vaszary (Original Author)
I Married an Angel 1942,Jl 10,13:2

Janov, Eleen
Horse in the Gray Flannel Suit, The
 1968,D 21,49:3

Janowitz, Hans (Original Author)
Cabinet of Dr Caligari, The 1921,Mr 20,VI,2:1

Janowska, Alina
Treasure, The 1951,Mr 29,24:4

Jans, Alice
Picture Snatcher 1933,My 19,20:3

Jans, Harry
Murder on a Bridle Path 1936,Ap 11,19:2
Special Investigator 1936,Ap 25,21:1
Two in Revolt 1936,Ap 25,21:1
Last Outlaw, The 1936,Je 15,24:1
Grand Jury 1936,Ag 1,16:3
Charlie Chan at the Race Track 1936,Ag 15,6:2
Don't Turn 'em Loose 1936,S 25,20:2
That Girl From Paris 1937,Ja 1,19:1
Don't Tell the Wife 1937,F 19,15:2

Jansen, Dirk
Counterfeit Traitor, The 1962,Ap 18,28:1

Jansen, Pierre (Composer)
Bonnes Femmes, Les 1966,My 13,32:1

Jansen, Viktor (Director)
Hilde Petersen, Postlagernd 1937,Je 26,20:3 (In
 Addenda)

Jansky, Ladislav
Diamonds of the Night 1968,Mr 15,30:1

Janson, Christopher (Original Author)
Witch Woman, The 1929,Ap 8,32:1

Janson, Victor
At the Edge of the World 1929,Je 18,29:4
1914: The Last Days Before the War 1932,S 5,9:6
Walzerkoenig, Der 1932,D 5,21:2
Nanu, Sie Kennen Korff noch Nicht?; So, You
 Don't Know Korff Yet? 1939,My 22,15:3
Marriage of Figaro 1950,N 3,31:2

Janson, Victor (Director)
Love Commandment, The 1928,D 25,31:3
Hungarian Nights 1930,Je 10,32:2
Holzapfel Weiss Alles 1933,Ja 7,11:3
Die Frau von der Man Spricht 1933,Ap 22,16:4
Bettelstudent, Der 1933,O 14,18:3
Luegen auf Ruegen 1934,Ja 1,28:2
Blaue Vom Himmel, Das 1934,S 8,18:6
Es War Einmal ein Walzer 1934,O 15,20:5
Page vom Dalmasse-Hotel, Der 1935,Mr 25,12:3
Grosse Chance, Die 1935,My 6,22:4
Stimme der Liebe, Die 1936,My 16,11:2
Eine Frau die Weiss Was sie Will 1936,Jl 18,18:3
Rendezvous in Wien 1938,F 19,19:4
Sie und die Drei; She and the Three
1938,D 10,13:3
Ueber Alles die Treue 1939,F 13,13:3
Blonde Carmen, Die 1939,O 7,11:3
Janssen, David
Chief Crazy Horse 1955,Ap 28,25:1
To Hell and Back 1955,S 23,21:2
Square Jungle, The 1955,D 31,17:2
Never Say Goodbye 1956,Ap 14,20:1
Toy Tiger 1956,Je 30,11:2
Francis in the Haunted House 1956,Jl 21,9:2
Girl He Left Behind, The 1956,O 27,17:1
Hell to Eternity 1960,O 13,41:1
Ring of Fire 1961,Ag 17,18:2
King of the Roaring Twenties 1961,O 5,43:1
Man Trap 1961,N 30,40:4
Belle Sommers 1962,My 31,23:2
My Six Loves 1963,Ap 4,58:4
Warning Shot 1967,Je 8,52:2
Green Berets, The 1968,Je 20,49:1
Shoes of the Fisherman, The 1968,N 15,40:3
Janssen, Eilene
Green Years, The 1946,Ap 5,21:2
Miracle Can Happen, A 1948,F 4,28:4
About Mrs Leslie 1954,Je 28,16:2
Janssen, Elsa
Great Lover, The 1931,Ag 24,13:4
Journal of a Crime 1934,Ap 28,11:3
Pride of the Yankees, The 1942,Jl 16,23:1
They Came to Blow up America
1943,My 15,13:2
Claudia 1943,N 5,23:2
His Butler's Sister 1943,D 30,13:2
3 Is a Family 1944,D 20,20:3
Claudia and David 1946,Ag 15,19:2
Song of Love 1947,O 10,31:2
Commandos Strike at Dawn 1954,Ja 14,25:1
Janssen, Julia
Himmel auf Erden, Der 1935,D 26,21:4
Orphan Boy of Vienna, An 1937,S 9,19:2
Janssen, Walter
Peter the Great 1923,Je 25,16:5
Between Worlds 1924,Jl 7,10:4
Zwei Hertzen in Drei-Viertel Takt
1930,O 13,31:1
Floetenkonzert von Sanssouci, Das
1931,O 17,20:1
Kaiserliebchen 1931,N 12,30:2
Theaternaechte von Berlin 1932,Ja 11,28:5
Die Singende Stadt 1932,My 10,25:4
Yorck 1932,N 24,35:2
Lachende Erben 1933,N 18,18:6
Choral von Leuthen, Der 1935,Ja 21,19:4
Schwarzwaldmaedel 1935,O 12,12:3
Herr Der Welt, Der 1935,D 16,23:3
Masquerade in Vienna 1937,Ja 26,16:4
Rote Orchideen; Red Orchids 1939,Ap 15,15:2
Mozart Story, The 1948,N 15,21:5
Janssen, Walter (Director)
Rosen aus dem Sueden; Roses from the South
1935,Ag 23,24:5
Schoen Ist Es Verliebt zu Sein 1936,Ap 7,31:2
Alle Tage Ist Kein Sonntag 1936,Jl 11,11:4
Leidenschaft; Passion 1940,S 24,26:6
Janssen, Werner
Abduction, The 1938,Je 11,9:2
Janssen, Werner (Composer)
Lights Out In Europe 1940,Ap 15,21:2
Slightly Honorable 1940,My 17,23:4
Jantzen, Kitty
Es geht um mein Leben; My Life Is at Stake
1938,Ap 11,12:3
Tiger von Eschnapur, Der 1938,Ap 30,18:2
Indian Tomb, The; Tiger von Eschnapur, Der
1938,My 14,18:2
January, Lois
By Candlelight 1934,Ja 6,18:2
One Rainy Afternoon 1936,My 14,29:2
Japaridze, Revas (Screenwriter)
Stepchildren 1962,Jl 2,22:2
Japrisot, Sebastian (Original Author)
Sleeping Car Murder, The 1966,Mr 8,45:1
Jaque, Christian (Director)
Pearls of the Crown, The 1938,Ap 12,26:2
Boys' School 1939,Je 6,26:2
Carmen 1946,N 27,20:2
Angel and Sinner 1947,F 24,16:5
Bellman, The 1947,Ap 7,20:5
Lover's Return, A; Revenant, Le 1948,Ja 26,15:2

Who Killed Santa Claus? 1948,Ap 21,33:2
Daughters of Destiny (Lysistrata); Lysistrata
(Daughters of Destiny) 1954,Jl 6,19:1
Adorable Creatures 1956,Ja 11,36:2
Nana 1957,Ap 13,12:3
If all the Guys in the World 1957,Ap 23,34:1
Jaque, Christian (Miscellaneous)
Lover's Return, A; Revenant, Le 1948,Ja 26,15:2
Jaque, Christian (Producer)
Carmen 1946,N 27,20:2
Jaque, Christian (Screenwriter)
Angel and Sinner 1947,F 24,16:5
Adorable Creatures 1956,Ja 11,36:2
Nana 1957,Ap 13,12:3
If all the Guys in the World 1957,Ap 23,34:1
Jaquet, Frank
War Is a Racket 1934,D 10,16:2
Crime School 1938,My 11,17:2
When Were You Born? 1938,Je 9,27:2
Stanley and Livingstone 1939,Ag 5,18:2
Dust Be my Destiny 1939,O 7,11:2
Eternally Yours 1939,O 7,11:2
No Greater Sin 1941,Ag 29,18:2
None Shall Escape 1944,Ap 7,23:2
Ace in the Hole 1951,Je 30,8:6
Jaquet, William
Barbary Pirate 1949,O 28,29:3
Jara, Maurice
Lawless, The 1950,Je 23,29:2
Second Chance 1953,Jl 23,20:2
Take the High Ground 1953,N 20,19:2
They Came to Cordura 1959,O 22,47:2
Jaracz, Stefan
Noc Listopadowa 1933,My 1,10:3
Jego Wielka Milosc 1936,Mr 24,27:5
Jaraczowna, Hanna
Dziewczeta z Nowolipek; Girls of Nowolipek
1938,N 25,19:2
Jaray, Hans
Loves of Jeanne Ney, The 1928,Jl 10,17:3
Unfinished Symphony 1935,Ja 14,11:2
Affairs of Maupassant, The 1938,F 12,20:2
Letzte Liebe; Last; Last Love 1938,Jl 19,15:4
Pfarrer von Kirchfeld, Der; Pastor of Kirchfeld,
The 1939,Ap 22,15:3
Jardin, Pascal (Screenwriter)
Joy House 1965,F 18,29:1
Jardine, Betty
Girl in the News, The 1941,My 5,13:2
Canterbury Tale, A 1949,Ja 24,16:2
Jarlo, Gerard (Screenwriter)
Moderato Cantabile 1964,Ja 7,24:1
Jarman, Claude Jr
Yearling, The 1947,Ja 24,18:2
High Barbaree 1947,Je 6,27:2
Sun comes up, The 1949,My 13,29:2
Roughshod 1949,Je 17,27:2
Intruder in the Dust 1949,N 23,19:1
Outriders, The 1950,Mr 9,25:2
Rio Grande 1950,N 20,21:2
Inside Straight 1951,Mr 16,34:2
Hangman's Knot 1952,D 11,45:3
Fair Wind to Java 1953,Ag 28,13:3
Great Locomotive Chase, The 1956,Je 27,35:1
Jarmyn, Jil
Tarzan's Fight for Life 1958,Ag 16,10:2
Jarninska, Amelja
Noc Listopadowa 1933,My 1,10:3
Jaron, Janusz
First Start, The 1953,F 2,17:3
Jaroslav (Screenwriter)
Krakatit 1951,Ap 30,16:2
Jaroslawzeff, W
Flames on the Volga 1929,Ap 2,28:4
Jaroslow, Ruth
Harvey Middleman, Fireman 1965,Jl 13,39:1
Jarre, Maurice (Composer)
Dragon Sky 1964,Ag 25,28:2
To Die in Madrid 1965,S 16,00:0
Fixer, The 1968,D 9,59:1
Jarrel, Stig
Vi Tvaa; We Two 1939,D 2,21:3
Torment 1947,Ap 22,34:2
Interlude 1949,Ja 3,19:2
Incorrigible 1949,Jl 2,8:2
Affairs of a Model 1952,Ag 7,12:8
Devil's Eye, The 1961,O 31,27:4
Jarrett, Arthur
Ace of Aces 1933,N 11,10:4
Dancing Lady 1933,D 1,23:2
Let's Fall in Love 1934,Ja 22,12:3
Riptide 1934,Mr 31,8:2
Tattooed Stranger, The 1950,F 10,18:6
Jarrett, Arthur (Original Author)
Moonlight and Pretzels 1933,Ag 23,21:2
Jarrett, Dan (Original Author)
Her First Mate 1933,S 2,14:5
Let's Sing Again 1936,My 9,11:2
Rawhide 1938,Ap 25,19:2
Flirting With Fate 1938,D 15,35:3
Tomahawk 1951,F 19,19:2

Jarrett, Dan (Screenwriter)
Hard Rock Harrigan 1935,Jl 30,16:2
Thunder Mountain 1935,O 2,27:2
Calling of Dan Matthews, The 1936,Ja 25,18:4
O'Malley of the Mounted 1936,Ap 6,18:1
Let's Sing Again 1936,My 9,11:2
Border Patrolman 1936,Je 29,11:2
Mine With the Iron Door, The 1936,Jl 11,11:3
Daniel Boone 1936,O 24,23:2
Secret Valley 1937,Ja 25,22:2
Hollywood Cowboy 1937,Jl 24,12:1
Rawhide 1938,Ap 25,19:2
Jarrett, David
Angry Silence, The 1960,D 13,25:2
Jarrett, W O
Birthright 1952,F 15,17:2
Jarrett, W O Mrs
Birthright 1952,F 15,17:2
Jarrico, Paul (Original Author)
Tom, Dick and Harry 1941,Jl 18,22:2
Thousands Cheer 1943,S 14,27:1
Little Giant 1946,My 9,27:5
Not Wanted 1949,Jl 25,11:4
Jarrico, Paul (Producer)
Salt of the Earth 1954,Mr 15,20:2
Salt of the Earth 1965,N 1,57:1
Jarrico, Paul (Screenwriter)
No Time to Marry 1938,F 23,27:2
Beauty for the Asking 1939,F 10,19:1
Face Behind the Mask, The 1941,F 7,23:2
Tom, Dick and Harry 1941,Jl 18,22:2
Thousands Cheer 1943,S 14,27:1
Song of Russia 1944,F 11,17:2
Search, The 1948,Mr 24,30:3
Not Wanted 1949,Jl 25,11:4
White Tower, The 1950,Jl 3,9:2
Jarrige, Bernard la
Simple Case of Money, A 1952,F 2,11:2
Beauties of the Night 1954,Mr 23,23:5
Three Feet in a Bed 1957,My 18,23:2
Four Bags Full 1957,S 5,32:1
Bernadette of Lourdes 1962,Ja 30,20:2
Mistress for the Summer, A 1964,Mr 28,13:5
Creatures, Les 1966,S 16,31:2
Jarry, Ashton
Uncivilized 1937,N 17,27:4
Jarvis, Francesca
Lilies of the Field 1963,O 2,51:1
Jarvis, Greg
Slender Thread, The 1965,D 24,24:2
Jarvis, Nina (Screenwriter)
It Happened to One Man 1941,F 24,11:6
Jarvis, Sydney
Casey at the Bat 1927,Ap 4,30:5
Circus Rookies 1928,My 14,25:1
Unholy Night, The 1929,O 12,11:1
Movie Crazy 1932,S 15,19:3
Count of Monte Cristo, The 1934,S 27,25:2
Jasiukiewicz, Stanislaw
Joan of the Angels? 1962,My 8,43:6
Jasmyn, Joan (Composer)
Myrt and Marge 1934,Ja 17,23:2
Freshman Love 1936,Ja 25,18:5
Times Square Playboy 1936,My 2,11:2
Jasmyn, Joan (Miscellaneous)
Fish 1936,Ja 25,18:5
Jasny, Vojtech (Director)
When the Cat Comes; Cat, The 1967,Je 19,41:1
Jason
Top of the Town 1937,Mr 27,19:2
Jason, Jay (Original Author)
Caprice 1967,Je 8,52:2
Jason, Jay (Screenwriter)
Caprice 1967,Je 8,52:2
Jason, Leigh (Director)
High Gear 1933,Ap 15,16:2
Love on a Bet 1936,Mr 5,25:2
Bride Walks Out, The 1936,Jl 10,15:1
That Girl From Paris 1937,Ja 1,19:1
New Faces of 1937 1937,Jl 2,25:1
Wise Girl 1938,Ja 10,13:3
Mad Miss Manton, The 1938,O 21,27:2
Flying Irishman, The 1939,Ap 12,27:2
Career 1939,Jl 28,14:2
Model Wife 1941,Ap 24,25:3
Lady for a Night 1942,F 12,27:2
Carolina Blues 1944,D 8,26:6
Lost Honeymoon 1947,Je 20,25:6
Man From Texas 1948,Ag 12,16:5
Jason, Leigh (Original Author)
High Gear 1933,Ap 15,16:2
Model Wife 1941,Ap 24,25:3
Jason, Leigh (Producer)
Model Wife 1941,Ap 24,25:3
Jason, Rick
Sombrero 1953,Ap 23,37:2
Saracen Blade, The 1954,My 15,13:4
ThIs is my Love 1954,D 25,7:3
Lieutenant Wore Skirts, The 1956,Ja 12,22:1
Wayward Bus, The 1957,Je 6,35:2
Jason, Sybil
Little Big Shot 1935,O 7,11:2
I Found Stella Parish 1935,N 4,24:4

Jason, Sybil— Cont
Singing Kid, The 1936,Ap 4,11:1
Great O'Malley, The 1937,Mr 6,10:1
Comet over Broadway 1938,D 16,33:3
Little Princess, The 1939,Mr 11,21:1
Woman Doctor 1939,Mr 24,27:3
Blue Bird, The 1940,Ja 20,11:2

Jason, Will (Composer)
Girl Without a Room 1933,D 7,26:3
Cockeyed Cavaliers 1934,Jl 25,22:2
Down to Their Last Yacht 1934,S 24,14:1

Jason, Will (Director)
Soul of a Monster, The 1944,S 9,12:4
Thief of Damascus 1952,My 8,37:2

Jaubert, Maurice (Composer)
End of a Day, The 1939,S 12,28:4
Pasha's Wives, The 1942,Ap 6,19:2

Jaubert, Soeurs
Claudine 1940,Ap 1,15:2

Jaubert (Composer)
Carnet de Bal, Un 1938,Mr 26,12:1

Jaun, Elizabeth
William Tell 1925,My 20,26:2

Javal, Bertrand (Producer)
Time Out for Love 1963,Ap 23,31:2
Cloportes 1966,Ap 19,36:1

Javor, Pal
Kek Balvany, A; Blue Idol, The 1933,Ap 18,13:6

Javor, Paul
Key Balvany, A 1933,Ap 18,13:6
Iza Neni 1934,Je 5,28:6
My Wife, The Miss 1934,S 13,26:2
Rakoczi Indulo 1934,N 21,23:4
Huszarszerelem 1935,Ap 23,24:5
Koeszoenoem Hogy Elgazolt 1935,My 7,28:2
Igloi Diakok 1935,My 24,24:3
Elnoek Kisasszony 1935,O 12,12:3
Csunya Lany, A 1935,O 18,27:4
Nem Elhetek Muzsikaszo Nelkuel 1936,F 21,21:2
Az uj Foeldesur 1936,S 22,30:5
Salary, 200 a Month 1937,Ja 15,17:3
Naszut Felaron 1937,F 13,9:2
Fizessen Nagysag 1937,Je 4,27:3
Viki 1937,N 29,19:3
A Ferfi Mind Oeruelt; All Men Are Crazy 1937,D 11,22:3
Pusztai Szel; Beauty of the Pusta 1938,Ja 10,13:4
Torockoi Menyasszony; Torockoi Bride 1938,Mr 5,11:2
111-es Szobaban; In Room 111 1938,Ap 2,18:2
Mother Love 1938,My 7,18:2
Noszty Flu Este Toth Marival 1938,My 16,14:4
Maga Lesz a Ferjem; You Will Be my Husband 1938,O 12,35:3
Marika 1938,N 19,9:3
Ket Fogoly; Two Prisoners 1938,D 31,7:3
Fekete Gyemantok; Black Diamonds 1939,Ap 24,13:2
Toprini Nasz; Wedding in Toprin 1939,N 6,20:2
Uz Bence 1940,Ja 15,11:2
Carmela 1949,My 14,9:2
Great Caruso, The 1951,My 11,32:2

Jaworsky, J von (Cinematographer)
Verraeter; Traitors 1936,N 22,XI,4:2 (In Addenda)

Jay, Ernest
Iron Duke, The 1935,Ja 25,27:2
Broken Blossoms 1937,Ja 14,16:3
Blanche Fury 1948,N 24,20:2
Edward my Son 1949,Je 3,21:2
Secret Flight 1952,Jl 3,16:2
I Believe in You 1953,My 5,34:3
Sword and the Rose, The 1953,Ag 20,18:3
Mr Potts Goes to Moscow 1953,S 3,15:2
Doctor at Large 1957,Jl 29,15:5

Jay, Griffin (Original Author)
Mummy's Hand, The 1940,S 20,27:2
Kid From Kansas, The 1941,D 2,29:4
Mummy's Ghost, The 1944,Jl 1,10:7

Jay, Griffin (Screenwriter)
Air Hawks 1935,Je 4,26:5
Mummy's Hand, The 1940,S 20,27:2
Kid From Kansas, The 1941,D 2,29:4
Mummy's Tomb, The 1942,O 26,19:2
Captive Wild Woman 1943,Je 7,9:4
Return of the Vampire, The 1944,Ja 29,10:1
Mummy's Ghost, The 1944,Jl 1,10:7
Cry of the Werewolf, The 1944,Ag 12,16:5

Jay, Jean
Silver King, The 1929,S 2,16:1

Jay, Jean (Original Author)
Palais de Danse 1928,Ag 19,VII,3:7

Jayashri
Shakuntala 1947,D 26,22:3

Jayne, Jennifer
Crawling Eye, The 1959,Ja 1,38:1
Hysteria 1965,S 9,36:3

Jaynes, Betty
Sweethearts 1938,D 23,16:2
Babes in Arms 1939,O 20,27:2
Swing Shift Maisie 1943,S 10,29:2
Meet The People 1944,S 8,16:2

Jaynes, Clare (Original Author)
My Reputation 1946,Ja 26,19:2

Jeakins, Dorothy
Hawaii 1966,O 11,54:1

Jean
Tabu 1931,Mr 19,21:3

Jean, Gloria
Under-Pup, The 1939,S 5,21:2
If I Had my Way 1940,My 6,13:2
Little Bit of Heaven, A 1940,N 8,24:2
Never Give a Sucker an Even Break 1941,O 27,21:2
What's Cookin' 1942,F 26,15:5
Get Help to Love 1942,O 19,15:3
It Comes up Love 1943,Ja 22,25:3
When Johnny Comes Marching Home 1943,Mr 5,20:4
Mister Big 1943,Je 14,13:4
Ghost Catchers 1944,My 31,22:3
Destiny 1945,F 3,16:5
River Gang 1945,O 6,9:7
Copacabana 1947,Jl 12,7:2
There's a Girl in my Heart 1950,Ja 20,29:2

Jean, Guy Saint
Inside Out 1964,S 25,32:1
Killing Game, The 1968,Ag 27,36:1

Jean, Ursula
Friday the 13th 1934,My 15,18:1

Jean-Max
Second Bureau 1936,F 17,21:2
I Give my Life 1941,S 1,18:4

Jeane, Edward
Stolen Heaven 1931,F 14,11:4

Jeanine, Jean (Screenwriter)
Thirst of Men, The 1952,O 28,37:1

Jeanmaire
Anything Goes 1956,Mr 22,38:1
Folies Bergere 1958,My 28,37:2
Black Tights 1962,F 21,54:2

Jeanmaire, Renee
Hans Christian Andersen 1952,N 26,20:2

Jeans, Desmond
Blame the Woman 1932,O 25,24:5
Blue Danube 1934,N 8,27:1
Girl From Maxim's, The 1936,S 16,29:1

Jeans, Isabel
Loves of a Dictator 1935,Je 1,18:2
Crouching Beast, The 1936,Ag 22,6:1
Tovarich 1937,D 31,9:2
Fools for Scandal 1938,Mr 25,15:3
Garden of the Moon 1938,S 24,13:1
Secrets of an Actress 1938,O 8,10:2
Youth Takes a Fling 1938,O 17,12:1
Hard To Get 1938,N 14,15:2
Good Girls Go to Paris 1939,Je 23,23:1
Man About Town 1939,Je 29,19:1
Suspicion 1941,N 21,23:2
Gigi 1958,My 16,21:1
Breath of Scandal, A 1960,D 17,19:1
Heavens Above! 1963,My 21,28:2

Jeans, Marjorie (Screenwriter)
River of Unrest 1937,N 27,21:2

Jeans, Ursula
Love Habit, The 1931,F 2,23:1
Flying Fool 1931,O 19,28:1
Cavalcade 1933,Ja 6,23:2
Dark Journey 1937,Ag 23,22:1
Storm in a Teacup 1938,Mr 22,18:4
Mr Emmanuel 1945,Ja 8,15:2
Life and Death of Colonel Blimp, The 1945,Mr 30,18:2
Showtime 1948,My 20,35:3
Woman in the Hall, The 1949,Ja 24,16:2
Weaker Sex, The 1949,Jl 11,13:2
Night my Number Came up, The 1955,D 20,39:5
Flame Over India 1960,Ap 30,14:1
Green Helmet, The 1961,Jl 20,32:2
Battle of the Villa Fiorita, The 1965,My 27,28:1

Jeanson, Francis
Chinoise, La 1968,Ap 4,58:2

Jeanson, Henri (Director)
Lady Paname 1951,Mr 20,35:4

Jeanson, Henri (Miscellaneous)
Carnet de Bal, Un 1938,Mr 26,12:1
Lie of Nina Petrovna, The 1938,Mr 30,19:2
Curtain Rises, The 1939,Ap 22,15:2
Lover's Return, A; Revenant, Le 1948,Ja 26,15:2
Damned, The; Maudits, Les 1948,Ap 26,27:2
Loves of Colette 1949,D 3,8:6
Sinners, The 1950,N 11,11:2
Three Sinners 1952,Jl 8,23:2
Savage Triangle 1952,S 30,38:2
Moment of Truth, The 1954,Ap 27,36:2
Maxime 1962,O 25,48:3

Jeanson, Henri (Original Author)
Cow and I, The 1961,Je 6,42:2
Paris When it Sizzles 1964,Ap 9,25:3

Jeanson, Henri (Screenwriter)
Curtain Rises, The 1939,Ap 22,15:2
Compliments of Mr Iflow 1941,F 17,10:7
Pepe le Moko 1941,Mr 4,20:2
Mad Emperor, The 1941,Mr 10,21:3
Angel and Sinner 1947,F 24,16:5

Jeanson, Henri (Screenwriter)— Cont
Lover's Return, A; Revenant, Le 1948,Ja 26,15:2
Confessions of a Rogue 1948,Mr 30,26:3
Loves of Colette 1949,D 3,8:6
Monelle 1950,F 3,29:2
Souvenir 1950,O 3,34:4
Lady Paname 1951,Mr 20,35:4
Savage Triangle 1952,S 30,38:2
Fanfan the Tulip 1953,My 5,34:2
His Last Twelve Hours 1953,N 13,24:7
Moment of Truth, The 1954,Ap 27,36:2
Daughters of Destiny (Lysistrata); Lysistrata (Daughters of Destiny) 1954,Jl 6,19:1
Holiday for Henrietta 1955,Ja 25,21:1
Nana 1957,Ap 13,12:3
Pot Bouille 1958,O 28,39:1
Modigliani of Montparnasse 1961,Mr 1,27:3
Cow and I, The 1961,Je 6,42:2
Madame 1963,Mr 21,8:6
Devil and the 10 Commandments, The (Episode 1) 1963,O 15,44:1
Devil and the 10 Commandments, The (Episode 2) 1963,O 15,44:1
Devil and the 10 Commandments, The (Episode 3) 1963,O 15,44:1
Devil and the 10 Commandments, The (Episode 4) 1963,O 15,44:1
Devil and the 10 Commandments, The (Episode 5) 1963,O 15,44:1
Devil and the 10 Commandments, The (Episode 6) 1963,O 15,44:1
Devil and the 10 Commandments, The (Episode 7) 1963,O 15,44:1
Don't Tempt the Devil 1964,Ap 28,43:1

Jeayes, Allan
Hound of the Baskervilles, The 1922,S 11,20:2
Hate Ship, The 1930,N 15,15:3
Woman in Chains 1932,N 21,21:1
Ghost Train, The 1933,F 18,13:3
Catherine the Great 1934,F 15,15:6
Sanders of the River 1935,Je 27,16:1
Things to Come 1936,Ap 18,19:2
Seven Sinners 1936,Ag 22,6:1
Rembrandt 1936,D 3,31:1
Man of Affairs 1937,F 20,9:2
Elephant Boy 1937,Ap 6,20:2
Forever Yours 1937,Je 7,22:2
Murder on Diamond Row 1937,N 12,27:2
Return of the Scarlet Pimpernel, The 1938,Ap 11,12:2
Four Feathers 1939,Ag 4,11:1
Thief of Bagdad, The 1940,D 6,28:2
Convoy 1941,Ja 17,21:2
Proud Valley 1941,My 17,19:2
Stars Look Down, The 1941,Jl 24,15:2
Mister V 1942,F 13,24:4
At Dawn We Die 1943,My 8,19:2
Green Cockatoo, The 1947,Jl 19,10:2
Ideal Husband, An 1948,Ja 15,28:2
Smugglers, The 1948,Mr 29,17:1
Blanche Fury 1948,N 24,20:2
Saraband 1949,Je 13,16:3
Hidden Room, The 1950,Ja 9,19:2

Jeeves, Mahatma Kane (Screenwriter)
Bank Dick, The 1940,D 13,29:2

Jefferies, Douglas
Channel Crossing 1934,My 24,28:3
Frieda 1947,Ag 15,12:3

Jefferies, James J
Beau Broadway 1928,Jl 30,21:2

Jefferson, L V (Original Author)
Redeeming Sin, The 1929,F 16,14:6

Jefferson, Thomas
Sis 1919,Mr 3,11:2
Sis Hopkins 1919,Mr 3,11:2
Paid to Love 1927,Jl 25,25:3
Fortune Hunter, The 1928,Ja 10,28:4
Soft Living 1928,F 27,16:2
On With the Show 1929,My 29,28:6
Double Cross Roads 1930,Ap 29,31:1
Lightnin' 1930,N 29,21:4
Ten Nights in a Barroom 1931,F 28,15:2
Forbidden 1932,Ja 11,28:5

Jefferson-Cohn, Marcelle
Collier de la Reine, Le; Queen's Necklace, The 1929,D 8,X,7:1

Jefford, Barbara
Midsummer Night's Dream, A 1961,D 19,39:1
Ulysses 1967,Mr 14,55:1
Shoes of the Fisherman, The 1968,N 15,40:3

Jeffrey, Peter
Becket 1964,Mr 12,40:2

Jeffrey, R E
Skin Game, The 1931,Je 20,20:4

Jeffrey, William
Eyes of the World 1930,Ag 15,20:5
My Woman 1933,O 16,20:3
Before Midnight 1934,Ja 10,24:3

Jeffreys, Anne
I Married an Angel 1942,Jl 10,13:2
Chatterbox 1943,Jl 2,15:3
Step Lively 1944,Jl 27,14:1
Dillinger 1945,Ap 26,26:2
Zombies on Broadway 1945,Ap 27,23:2

Jeffreys, Anne— Cont
Dick Tracy 1946,Ja 12,10:7
Step by Step 1946,Ag 24,6:7
Dick Tracy vs Cueball 1946,N 23,12:2
Trail Street 1947,Ap 10,35:2
Riff-Raff 1947,Je 30,25:7
Return of the Badmen 1948,Ag 5,16:2
Boys' Night Out 1962,Je 22,15:2
Jeffreys, Ellis
Perfect Alibi, The 1931,Ap 20,16:3
Jeffries, Fran
Buccaneer, The 1958,D 24,00:0
Pink Panther, The 1964,Ap 24,25:1
Sex and the Single Girl 1964,D 26,9:2
Harum Scarum 1965,D 16,63:3
Jeffries, James J
Legendary Champions, The 1968,O 29,54:1
Jeffries, Lang
Revolt of the Slaves, The 1961,N 8,41:1
Don't Knock the Twist 1962,Ap 14,14:2
Jeffries, Lionel
Bhowani Junction 1956,My 25,26:1
Lust for Life 1956,S 18,39:1
Doctor at Large 1957,Jl 29,15:5
Blue Murder at St Trinian's 1958,My 27,27:1
Law and Disorder 1958,Ag 6,20:1
Up the Creek 1958,N 11,26:2
Orders to Kill 1958,N 18,41:2
Circle, The 1959,Ap 16,29:2
Nun's Story, The 1959,Je 19,30:1
Trials of Oscar Wilde, The 1960,Je 28,26:1
Tarzan the Magnificent 1960,Jl 21,17:1
Two-Way Stretch 1961,Ja 24,20:3
Please Turn Over 1961,Ap 29,12:2
Fanny 1961,Jl 7,16:1
Hellions, The 1962,Mr 15,28:2
Notorious Landlady, The 1962,Jl 27,15:2
Operation Snatch 1962,S 25,31:4
Kill or Cure 1962,N 13,43:4
Wrong Arm of the Law, The 1963,Ap 3,39:1
Call Me Bwana 1963,Jl 4,9:1
Long Ships, The 1964,Je 25,25:1
Murder Ahoy 1964,S 23,55:3
First Men in the Moon 1964,N 26,52:2
Truth About Spring, The 1965,Je 17,27:2
Secret of my Success, The 1965,N 4,57:2
Spy With a Cold Nose, The 1966,D 20,58:2
Arrivederci, Baby! 1966,D 29,22:1
Oh Dad, Poor Dad, Mamma's Hung You in the
  Closet and I'm Feeling so Sad 1967,F 16,32:1
Those Fantastic Flying Fools 1967,O 19,59:2
Camelot 1967,O 26,54:1
Chitty Chitty Bang Bang 1968,D 19,64:4
Jeffries, Oliver (Original Author)
Reckless 1935,Ap 20,16:1
Jehanne, Edith
Love of Jeanne Ney, The 1928,Ja 15,VIII,7:5
Loves of Jeanne Ney, The 1928,Jl 10,17:3
Chess Player, The 1930,My 19,21:1
Jehara, Misa
Saga of the Vagabonds 1964,O 7,31:1 (Incorrect
  in this edition; use 1964,O 7,51:1 elsewhere)
Jeimo, Yannina
Vanka 1943,Mr 25,25:3
Jelic, Milan
Feverish Years, The 1967,S 22,57:2
Jelinek, Karel
Bohemian Rapture 1948,F 16,16:2
Jell, Colette
Kaiserliebchen 1931,N 12,30:2
Jellicoe, Admiral
Q Ships 1928,S 17,27:1
Jellicoe, Ann (Original Author)
Knack...and how to get it, The 1965,Je 30,42:1
Jelm, Carlotta
One Foot in Heaven 1941,N 14,28:3
Jemima, Aunt
Stand up and Cheer 1934,Ap 20,17:1
Jemma, Jean-Louis
Would-Be Gentleman, The 1960,Mr 23,31:1
Jen, C
Fight to the Last 1938,D 22,25:3
Jenbach, Ida (Original Author)
Opern-Ball, Der; Opera Ball 1931,N 6,28:3
Jencks, Clinton
Salt of the Earth 1954,Mr 15,20:2
Salt of the Earth 1965,N 1,57:1
Jencks, Virginia
Salt of the Earth 1954,Mr 15,20:2
Jenkins, Allen
Girl Habit, The 1931,Jl 4,11:5
Blessed Event 1932,S 3,16:2
Rackety Rax 1932,N 5,12:5
I Am a Fugitive From a Chain Gang
  1932,N 11,17:2
Lawyer Man 1932,D 27,10:2
Employees' Entrance 1933,Ja 21,10:6
Hard to Handle 1933,F 2,21:5
Blondie Johnson 1933,F 27,11:2
42d Street 1933,Mr 10,19:3
Keyhold, The 1933,Mr 31,23:3
Mind Reader, The 1933,Ap 7,22:4
Silk Express, The 1933,Je 28,24:2
Mayor of Hell, The 1933,Jl 1,16:5

Tomorrow at Seven 1933,Jl 3,14:6
Professional Sweetheart 1933,Jl 14,15:3
Bureau of Missing Persons 1933,S 9,9:2
Havana Widows 1933,N 23,24:3
I've Got Your Number 1934,F 3,9:3
Big Shakedown, The 1934,F 12,19:2
Bedside 1934,Mr 7,23:4
Jimmy the Gent 1934,Mr 26,22:3
20 Million Sweethearts 1934,Ap 27,25:1
Whirlpool 1934,My 5,22:3
Happiness Ahead 1934,O 11,28:2
Case of the Howling Dog, The 1934,O 18,26:5
St Louis Kid, The 1934,N 1,25:2
Sweet Music 1935,F 21,23:2
While the Patient Slept 1935,Mr 2,18:2
Case of the Curious Bride, The 1935,Ap 5,21:3
Night at the Ritz, A 1935,My 16,20:2
Irish in US, The 1935,Ag 1,15:1
Page Miss Glory 1935,Ag 29,25:2
I Live for Love 1935,O 19,21:2
Case of the Lucky Legs, The 1935,N 1,25:1
Miss Pacific Fleet 1935,D 7,22:2
Broadway Hostess 1935,D 16,23:3
Singing Kid, The 1936,Ap 4,11:1
Sins of Man 1936Je 19,17:2
Cain and Mabel 1936,O 19,22:1
Three Men on a Horse 1936,N 26,39:1
Sing Me a Love Song 1936,D 26,15:2
Ready, Willing and Able 1937,Mr 15,27:1
Marked Woman 1937,Ap 12,15:2
Ever Since Eve 1937,Je 25,25:2
Singing Marine, The 1937,Jl 1,33:2
Marry the Girl 1937,Jl 31,6:2
Dead End 1937,Ag 25,25:1
Dance Charlie Dance 1937,Ag 26,25:2
Perfect Specimen, The 1937,O 28,29:2
Sh! The Octopus 1937,D 24,21:2
Swing Your Lady 1938,Ja 27,17:2
Slight Case of Murder, A 1938,F 28,19:1
Fools for Scandal 1938,Mr 25,15:3
Gold Diggers in Paris 1938,Je 2,19:2
Amazing Dr Clitterhouse, The 1938,Jl 21,14:2
Racket Busters 1938,Ag 11,13:1
Hard To Get 1938,N 14,15:2
Heart of the North 1938,D 21,29:2
Going Places 1939,Ja 7,6:1
Naughty but Nice 1939,Je 23,23:2
Five came Back 1939,Jl 5,20:2
Destry Rides Again 1939,N 30,25:1
Brother Orchid 1940,Je 8,18:2
Meet the Wildcat 1940,O 23,27:2
Tin Pan Alley 1940,N 22,27:3
Footsteps in the Dark 1941,Mr 15,13:2
Time Out for Rhythm 1941,Jl 10,16:3
Dive Bomber 1941,Ag 30,10:2
Go West, Young Lady 1941,N 24,11:6
Date With the Falcon, A 1941,N 25,33:2
Ball of Fire 1942,Ja 16,25:2
Tortilla Flat 1942,My 22,27:1
Falcon takes Over, The 1942,My 30,9:2
Maisie Gets her Man 1942,Jl 16,23:2
They all Kissed the Bride 1942,Jl 31,11:1
Eyes in the Night 1942,O 16,23:1
Stage Door Canteen 1943,Je 25,13:2
Wonder Man 1945,Je 9,17:2
Lady on a Train 1945,S 15,21:2
Easy Come, Easy Go 1947,F 6,29:2
Wild Harvest 1947,N 13,33:2
Senator Was Indiscreet, The 1947,D 27,9:2
Bodyhold 1949,D 12,29:4
Behave Yourself 1951,N 8,35:2
Pillow Talk 1959,O 7,47:2
Doctor, You've Got to be Kidding
  1967,My 11,50:1
Jenkins, Jackie (Butch)
Human Comedy, The 1943,Mr 3,19:2
National Velvet 1944,D 15,25:2
Our Vines Have Tender Grapes 1945,S 7,21:2
Boy's Ranch 1946,Ag 9,12:2
My Brother Talks to Horses 1947,Je 19,27:4
Big City 1948,My 17,23:3
Bride Goes Wild, The 1948,Je 4,27:2
Summer Holiday 1948,Je 12,8:5
Jenkins, James
Bridges at Toko-Ri, The 1955,Ja 21,20:2
Jenkins, Megs
Continental Express 1942,Ap 7,26:3
Green for Danger 1947,Ag 8,10:2
Girl in the Canal, The 1947,O 9,32:3
Brothers, The 1948,My 5,30:4
Saraband 1949,Je 13,16:3
Facts of Love, The 1949,O 31,20:2
No Place for Jennifer 1951,Jl 17,31:2
History of Mr Polly, The 1951,O 25,36:3
Ivanhoe 1952,Ag 1,8:2
Cruel Sea, The 1953,Ag 11,18:5
Personal Affair 1954,O 23,13:2
Trouble in Store 1956,Ja 14,13:2
John and Julie 1957,My 7,40:1
Indiscreet 1958,Je 27,18:2
Tiger Bay 1959,D 15,50:1
Conspiracy of Hearts 1960,Ap 8,24:1
Green Helmet, The 1961,Jl 20,32:2

Jenkins, Megs— Cont
Innocents, The 1961,D 26,15:2
Murder Most Foul 1965,My 24,36:2
Walk in the Shadow 1966,S 12,52:5
Jenkins, Warren
It's Love Again 1936,My 23,12:1
Gangway 1937,Ag 21,7:3
Jenkins, Will (Original Author)
Torchy Blane in Chinatown 1939,F 3,13:2
Jenks, Frank
Farmer in the Dell, The 1936,Mr 7,11:4
Witness Chair, The 1936,Ap 18,19:2
Last Outlaw, The 1936,Je 15,24:1
That Girl From Paris 1937,Ja 1,19:1
We Who Are About to Die 1937,Ja 2,15:1
When's Your Birthday? 1937,Mr 19,27:2
Angel's Holiday 1937,My 29,20:2
There Goes my Girl 1937,Je 12,8:2
100 Men and a Girl 1937,S 18,15:2
Saturday's Heroes 1937,O 16,22:2
Westland Case, The 1937,O 23,14:2
You're a Sweetheart 1937,D 25,10:5
Love Is a Headache 1938,Ja 28,17:3
Lady in the Morgue, The 1938,My 9,13:3
Goodbye Broadway 1938,My 14,18:1
Devil's Party, The 1938,My 31,8:3
Youth Takes a Fling 1938,O 17,12:1
Storm, The 1938,O 31,12:2
Last Warning, The 1938,D 8,34:4
Big Town Czar 1939,My 4,27:3
S O S Tidal Wave 1939,Je 22,19:3
Under-Pup, The 1939,S 5,21:2
First Love 1939,N 9,27:3
His Girl Friday 1940,Ja 12,13:2
Three Cheers for the Irish 1940,Mr 9,19:2
Little Bit of Heaven, A 1940,N 8,24:2
Tall, Dark and Handsome 1941,Ja 24,15:2
Back Street 1941,F 12,25:2
Flame of New Orleans, The 1941,Ap 26,20:2
Two Yanks in Trinidad 1942,Ap 6,19:4
Syncopation 1942,My 29,13:3
Maisie Gets her Man 1942,Jl 16,23:2
Navy Comes Through, The 1942,N 12,30:3
Seven Miles From Alcatraz 1942,N 19,31:3
Corregidor 1943,My 28,19:2
Gildersleeve's Bad Day 1943,Je 11,23:1
Thousands Cheer 1943,S 14,27:1
His Butler's Sister 1943,D 30,13:2
Ladies Courageous 1944,Mr 16,17:2
This is the Life 1944,Ap 28,23:3
Roger Touhy, Gangster 1944,Je 5,14:7
Two Girls and a Sailor 1944,Je 15,16:1
Take It or Leave It 1944,Jl 13,14:2
Impatient Years, The 1944,S 20,20:1
Falcon in Hollywood, The 1944,D 9,21:2
Zombies on Broadway 1945,Ap 27,23:2
Bedside Manner 1945,Je 23,9:6
Christmas in Connecticut 1945,Jl 28,7:2
White Tie and Tails 1946,N 8,28:2
That Brennan Girl 1946,D 9,34:3
Blonde Savage 1947,O 4,9:2
Petty Girl, The 1950,Ag 18,17:2
To Please a Lady 1950,O 27,24:3
Woman on the Run 1950,N 30,24:2
Jenks, Si
Sixteen Fathoms Deep 1934,Ja 19,24:3
Captain January 1936,Ap 25,21:1
Special Investigator 1936,Ap 25,21:1
President's Mystery, The 1936,O 19,22:1
Follow Your Heart 1936,O 22,31:1
Pigskin Parade 1936,N 14,23:3
Outcasts of Poker Flat, The 1937,Ap 27,18:3
Topper 1937,Ag 20,21:2
Rawhide 1938,Ap 25,19:2
Kentucky Moonshine 1938,My 21,9:2
Frontier Marshal 1939,Jl 29,18:2
Drums Along the Mohawk 1939,N 4,11:2
Girl From God's Country 1940,S 9,18:5
Jennings, Al
Sea Hawk, The 1924,Je 3,22:1
Jennings, Al (Original Author)
Al Jennings of Oklahoma 1951,My 18,34:6
Jennings, Dean (Original Author)
Duffy of San Quentin 1954,F 10,38:5
Jennings, DeWitt
Within the Law 1923,Ap 30,11:2
Circus Days 1923,Ag 6,14:2
Name the Man 1924,F 4,23:3
Enemy Sex, The 1924,Jl 1,21:4
Merton of the Movies 1924,S 8,15:3
Mystic, The 1925,Ag 31,19:3
Go Straight 1925,O 6,30:1
Splendid Road, The 1926,Je 13,31:1
Ice Flood, The 1926,O 19,26:2
Fire Brigade, The 1926,D 21,20:2
Great Mail Robbery, The 1927,Jl 20,29:3
Two Arabian Knights 1927,O 24,24:3
Home Made 1927,D 13,33:2
Night Flyer, The 1928,Mr 13,23:3
Red Hot Speed 1929,F 5,26:3
Trial of Mary Dugan, The 1929,Mr 29,21:1
Alibi 1929,Ap 9,29:1
Thru Different Eyes 1929,Ap 15,22:6
Valiant, The 1929,My 13,27:2

Jennings, DeWitt— Cont

William Fox Movietone Follies of 1929
  1929,My 27,22:1
Seven Keys to Baldpate 1929,D 26,21:1
Night Ride 1930,Ja 20,21:1
In the Next Room 1930,Ap 7,21:1
Big House, The 1930,Je 25,31:2
Those Who Dance 1930,Jl 7,22:3
Outside the Law 1930,S 1,16:1
Min and Bill 1930,N 24,26:5
Scarlet Pages 1930,D 6,21:3
Criminal Code, The 1931,Ja 5,21:3
Bat Whispers, The 1931,Ja 16,27:1
Secret Six, The 1931,My 2,23:4
Salvation Nell 1931,Jl 6,24:4
Caught Plastered 1931,S 12,15:4
Squaw Man, The 1931,S 19,10:2
Deceiver, The 1931,N 23,22:1
Dangerous Affair, A 1931,N 23,22:1
Arrowsmith 1931,D 8,36:4
Dancers in the Dark 1932,Mr 19,11:2
Tess of the Storm Country 1932,N 19,20:2
Central Park 1932,D 7,29:3
Match King, The 1932,D 8,25:3
Silver Dollar 1932,D 23,20:1
Mystery of the Wax Museum, The
  1933,F 18,13:3
Ladies They Talk About 1933,F 25,20:4
Strictly Personal 1933,Mr 20,18:2
Lady's Profession, A 1933,Mr 25,13:3
Massacre 1934,Ja 18,19:2
Little Man, What Now? 1934,Je 1,29:1
Death on the Diamond 1934,S 24,14:1
President Vanishes, The 1934,D 8,18:5
Wicked Woman, A 1935,Ja 1,24:1
Murder on a Honeymoon 1935,Mr 4,12:2
Mutiny on the Bounty 1935,N 9,19:2
Sins of Man 1936,Je 19,17:2
Crime of Dr Forbes, The 1936,Jl 6,11:4
Kelly the Second 1936,O 3,21:2
Accusing Finger, The 1936,N 17,35:4
We Who Are About to Die 1937,Ja 2,15:1
That I May Live 1937,My 10,23:2
Slave Ship 1937,Je 17,19:2

Jennings, Gladys
Should a Doctor Tell 1931,Ag 22,7:5
Jennings, Gordon (Miscellaneous)
Crusades, The 1935,Ag 22,21:3
Jennings, Hilde
Women Without Men 1928,N 12,18:2
Jennings, Humphrey (Producer)
Silent Village, The 1943,O 2,19:2
Jennings, Jane
Case of Becky, The 1921,O 10,16:1
Man Must Live, A 1925,Ja 29,12:2
Little French Girl, The 1925,Je 1,10:3
Song and Dance Man, The 1926,F 1,16:1
Jennings, Maxine
Muss 'Em Up 1936,F 3,21:2
Witness Chair, The 1936,Ap 18,19:2
Last Outlaw, The 1936,Je 15,24:1
Bunker Bean 1936,Je 27,21:2
Walking on Air 1936,S 12,20:2
Don't Turn 'em Loose 1936,S 25,20:2
Make Way for a Lady 1936,D 12,15:1
We're on the Jury 1937,F 10,18:5
You Can't Buy Luck 1937,My 14,21:2
There Goes my Girl 1937,Je 12,8:2
Big Shot, The 1937,Ag 13,13:1
On Again-Off Again 1937,S 18,15:3
Mr Wong, Detective 1938,N 21,14:4
Jennings, S E
Bat Whispers, The 1931,Ja 16,27:1
Jennings, Talbot (Miscellaneous)
Pearl of the South Pacific 1955,S 17,12:2
Jennings, Talbot (Original Author)
Across the Wide Missouri 1951,N 7,35:4
Naked Maja, The 1959,Je 11,36:2
Sons of Katie Elder, The 1965,Ag 26,40:3
Jennings, Talbot (Screenwriter)
Mutiny on the Bounty 1935,N 9,19:2
Romeo and Juliet 1936,Ag 21,12:2
Good Earth, The 1937,F 3,27:1
Rulers of the Sea 1939,N 9,27:1
Northwest Passage 1940,Mr 8,25:1
Edison the Man 1940,Je 7,27:2
So Ends our Night 1941,F 28,17:2
Frenchman's Creek 1944,S 21,26:2
Anna and the King of Siam 1946,Je 21,20:2
Black Rose, The 1950,S 2,11:2
Across the Wide Missouri 1951,N 7,35:4
Landfall 1953,My 11,25:2
Knights of the Round Table 1954,Ja 8,17:2
Untamed 1955,Mr 12,11:6
Escape to Burma 1955,My 21,11:2
Jenns, Elizabeth
Star Is Born, A 1937,Ap 23,25:1
Jeno, Sandor (Composer)
Csokolj Meg Edes 1932,N 25,19:2
Jens, Arnette
Balcony, The 1963,Mr 22,7:1
Jens, Salome
Angel Baby 1961,O 5,43:1
Seconds 1966,O 6,56:1

Jensen, Ake
Kaera Slaekten 1934,My 14,20:4
Sangen Till Henne; Song to Her, The
  1935,F 22,27:3
Jensen, Cleo
Elvira Madigan 1967,S 30,26:1
Jensen, Eugen
Loves of Jeanne Ney, The 1928,Jl 10,17:3
Tausend Fuer Eine Nacht 1934,F 12,19:2
Jensen, Eulalie
Passion Flower, The 1921,Ap 4,18:1
Hunchback of Notre Dame, The 1923,S 3,9:3
Slave of Desire 1923,D 11,26:2
Being Respectable 1924,Ag 4,16:3
Wine of Youth 1924,Ag 11,16:1
Charley's Aunt 1925,F 9,15:3
Ranger of the big Trees, The 1925,Jl 28,24:4
Circle, The 1925,S 22,22:3
Flower of the Night 1925,O 19,26:1
Forever After 1926,N 9,31:1
Kiss in a Taxi, A 1927,Mr 15,29:2
Heart Thief, The 1927,Ap 27,22:5
Uncle Tom's Cabin 1927,N 5,16:2
Mother Machree 1928,Mr 6,20:3
Kentucky Courage 1928,My 14,25:1
Strong Boy 1929,Ap 1,22:1
She Goes to War 1929,Je 10,23:1
Up Pops the Devil 1931,My 16,13:3
Never the Twain Shall Meet 1931,Je 6,15:5
Confessions of a Co-Ed 1931,Je 20,20:4
Union Depot 1932,Ja 15,24:4
So Big 1932,Ap 30,19:3
Miss Pinkerton 1932,Jl 9,7:5
Hat Check Girl 1932,O 8,15:4
Jensen, Eulallo
Yankee Consul, The 1924,F 11,18:3
Jensen, Frederik
David Copperfield 1923,N 6,23:3
Jensen, Jesper
Weekend 1964,Ap 27,24:1
Jensen, Karen
Ballad of Josie, The 1968,Mr 14,51:2
Jenson, Roy
Harper 1966,Mr 31,43:1
Waterhole #3 1967,O 11,41:4
Ambushers, The 1967,D 23,29:1
Jigsaw 1968,Je 6,54:2
Jenssens, Wiers (Original Author)
Day of Wrath 1948,Ap 26,27:2
Jeppsen, Jorn
Young Have no Time, The 1959,N 23,41:2
Jepsen, Klaus
Funeral in Berlin 1966,D 23,17:1
Jepson, Helen
Goldwyn Follies, The 1938,F 21,15:1
Jepson, Selwyn (Original Author)
Sailing Along 1938,Ap 16,17:1
Stage Fright 1950,F 24,27:2
Jeremy, Kenneth Augustus
Ivory Hunter 1952,Ag 19,19:1
Jergens, Adele
Thousand and one Nights, A 1945,Jl 12,8:2
She Wouldn't Say Yes 1946,Ja 12,10:7
Corpse came C O D, The 1947,Ag 19,27:2
Down to Earth 1947,S 12,18:2
Fuller Brush Man, The 1948,My 15,18:2
Dark Past, The 1948,D 23,25:2
Slightly French 1949,My 27,25:3
Traveling Saleswoman 1950,Ja 6,25:3
Side Street 1950,Mr 24,29:2
Edge of Doom 1950,Ag 4,13:2
Sugarfoot 1951,F 12,19:4
Abbott and Costello Meet the Invisible Man
  1951,Ap 13,18:6
Try and Get Me 1951,My 7,22:2
Aaron Slick From Punkin Crick 1952,Ap 19,18:6
Somebody Loves Me 1952,S 25,38:1
Miami Story, The 1954,My 15,13:2
Strange Lady in Town 1955,My 21,11:1
Cobweb, The 1955,Ag 6,13:3
Jergens, Diane
Bob Mathias Story, The 1954,O 16,14:6
Teenage Rebel 1956,N 17,17:6
Three Brave Men 1957,Mr 16,13:2
Desk Set 1957,My 16,28:2
High School Confidential 1958,My 31,6:6
F B I Story, The 1959,S 25,23:1
Teenage Millionaire 1962,Ja 12,29:2
Jerger, Alfred
Unsterbliche Melodien; Immortal Melodies
  1938,Ap 23,19:3
Jerome, Edwin
House on Ninety-Second Street, The
  1945,S 27,24:7
Tattered Dress, The 1957,Mr 15,22:3
Three Faces of Eve, The 1957,S 27,16:6
Man Who Understood, The 1959,O 3,14:7
Jerome, Helen (Miscellaneous)
Conquest 1937,N 5,19:1
Jerome, Helen (Original Author)
Pride and Prejudice 1940,Ag 9,19:1

Jerome, Jerome K (Original Author)
Strictly Confidential 1919,O 6,15:1
Passing of the Third Floor Back, The
  1936,Ap 29,19:2
3 Men in a Boat 1959,Jl 29,33:2
Jerome, Jerry
I'll Wait for You 1941,Je 2,13:6
Jerome, M K (Composer)
Myrt and Marge 1934,Ja 17,23:2
Miss Pacific Fleet 1935,D 7,22:2
Freshman Love 1936,Ja 25,18:5
Song of the Saddle 1936,Mr 21,13:3
Times Square Playboy 1936,My 2,11:2
Melody for Two 1937,My 21,19:5
Kid Galahad 1937,My 27,21:3
Dance Charlie Dance 1937,Ag 26,25:2
She Loved a Fireman 1938,Ja 21,15:3
Slight Case of Murder, A 1938,F 28,19:1
Over the Wall 1938,Mr 28,19:2
Shine on Harvest Moon 1944,Mr 11,10:2
Love and Learn 1947,My 3,10:3
Jerome, M K (Miscellaneous)
Fish 1936,Ja 25,18:5
Treachery Rides the Range 1936,My 30,7:3
Talent Scout 1937,Ag 20,21:3
Swing Your Lady 1938,Ja 27,17:2
Jerome, Mark (Original Author)
Invitation to Happiness 1939,Je 8,31:2
Jerre, Sam (Producer)
Born Free 1966,Je 23,29:1
Jerrems, Jeanne
Dark Odyssey 1961,Je 26,22:2
Jerrold, Jean (Director)
Monte Carlo Baby 1954,My 29,13:4
Jerrold, Jean (Screenwriter)
Monte Carlo Baby 1954,My 29,13:4
Jerrold, Mary
W Plan, The 1931,Mr 23,24:7
Perfect Understanding 1933,F 23,20:2
Friday the 13th 1934,My 15,18:1
Magic Bow, The 1947,Jl 7,13:2
Mr Perrin and Mr Traill 1949,Ja 17,15:2
Bond Street 1950,Mr 30,40:6
Marry Me 1952,Mr 14,27:3
Tonight at 8:30 (Ways and Means); Ways and
  Means (Tonight at 8:30) 1953,My 26,33:2
Jersey, William C (Miscellaneous)
Time for Burning, A 1967,F 24,26:2
Jeske, George (Screenwriter)
Day the Bookies Wept, The 1939,S 14,18:2
Jesse, F Tennyson (Original Author)
Lovers in Quarantine 1925,O 13,20:1
Half Angel 1936,My 30,7:3
Jessel, George
Other Man's Wife, The 1919,Je 9,16:3
Vitaphone 1926,O 8,23:2
Private Izzy Murphy 1926,N 10,25:1
Lucky Boy 1929,F 25,16:1
Love, Live and Laugh 1929,N 2,14:6
Stage Door Canteen 1943,Je 25,13:2
Four Jills in a Jeep 1944,Ap 6,27:2
Busy Body, The 1967,Je 8,52:2
Jessel, George (Composer)
Life of the Party, The 1937,O 4,17:1
Golden Girl 1951,N 21,20:3
Jessel, George (Narrator)
Yesterday and Today 1954,Mr 13,11:3
Jessel, George (Original Author)
You're my Everything 1949,Jl 23,7:2
Jessel, George (Producer)
Do You Love Me 1946,My 25,12:2
I Wonder Who's Kissing Her Now
  1947,Jl 24,27:2
Nightmare Alley 1947,O 10,31:3
When my Baby Smiles at Me 1948,N 24,20:2
Oh, You Beautiful Doll 1949,N 12,8:4
Dancing in the Dark 1949,D 3,8:6
Meet Me After the Show 1951,Ag 16,23:2
Anne of the Indies 1951,O 25,36:3
Golden Girl 1951,N 21,20:3
Wait Till the Sun Shines, Nellie 1952,Je 28,12:2
Bloodhounds of Broadway 1952,N 15,15:2
Tonight We Sing 1953,F 13,17:2
Jessel, George (Screenwriter)
Yesterday and Today 1954,Mr 13,11:3
Jessel, Patricia
Flesh is Weak, The 1957,N 9,31:2
Man Upstairs, The 1959,Ag 11,23:2
Horror Hotel 1963,Je 20,29:1
They all Died Laughing 1964,Mr 16,37:2
Funny Thing Happened on the Way to the Forum,
  A 1966,O 17,48:1
Jessell, George
Valley of the Dolls 1967,D 16,51:1
Jessell, George (Producer)
Dolly Sisters, The 1945,N 15,24:6
Jessop, Clytie
Innocents, The 1961,D 26,15:2
Jessua, Alain (Director)
Inside Out 1964,S 25,32:1
Life Upside Down; Inside Out 1965,Ag 18,41:4
Killing Game, The 1968,Ag 27,36:1

Jessua, Alain (Original Author)
Life Upside Down; Inside Out 1965,Ag 18,41:4
Jessua, Alain (Producer)
Inside Out 1964,S 25,32:1
Life Upside Down; Inside Out 1965,Ag 18,41:4
Jessua, Alain (Screenwriter)
Inside Out 1964,S 25,32:1
Killing Game, The 1968,Ag 27,36:1
Jessup, Richard (Original Author)
Young Don't Cry, The 1957,Jl 27,10:7
Cincinnati Kid, The 1965,O 28,48:1
Chuka 1967,N 2,58:3
Jessup, Richard (Screenwriter)
Young Don't Cry, The 1957,Jl 27,10:7
Chuka 1967,N 2,58:3
Jessye, Eva
Black Like Me 1964,My 21,42:1
Jestpovici, Jean (Miscellaneous)
Passionnelle 1948,Mr 1,17:2
Jetley, Trilak
River, The 1951,S 11,33:2
Jetsam
Chu Chin Chow 1934,S 22,12:2
Jevne, Jack (Miscellaneous)
Our Relations 1936,N 11,55:1
Jevne, Jack (Original Author)
Way out West 1937,My 4,29:1
Wyoming 1940,O 3,31:4
Barnacle Bill 1941,Jl 25,12:4
Jevne, Jack (Screenwriter)
Kelly the Second 1936,O 3,21:2
Topper 1937,Ag 20,21:2
Merrily We Live 1938,Mr 18,23:3
There Goes my Heart 1938,O 14,27:1
Topper Takes a Trip 1938,D 30,11:2
Captain Fury 1939,My 26,20:2
Wyoming 1940,O 3,31:4
Barnacle Bill 1941,Jl 25,12:4
Air Raid Wardens 1943,Ap 5,15:5
Wintertime 1943,S 30,27:2
Wonder Man 1945,Je 9,17:2
Autumn Leaves 1956,Ag 2,21:2
Jewell, Austin
Greed 1924,D 5,28:1
Wild Geese 1927,D 5,26:2
Jewell, Betty
Rejected Woman, The 1924,My 5,18:3
Partners Again, With Potash and Perlmutter
1926,F 15,16:4
Jewell, Estelle
Shadow of a Doubt 1943,Ja 13,18:2
Jewell, Hollis
Grapes of Wrath, The 1940,Ja 25,17:2
Jewell, Isabel
Blessed Event 1932,S 3,16:2
Bondage 1933,Ap 24,11:3
Beauty for Sale 1933,S 16,9:3
Bombshell 1933,O 21,11:2
Day of Reckoning 1933,N 4,18:2
Design for Living 1933,N 23,24:2
Counsellor-at-Law 1933,D 8,31:2
Advice to the Lovelorn 1933,D 14,28:2
Women in his Life, The 1934,Ja 27,9:3
Manhattan Melodrama 1934,My 5,22:2
Here Comes the Groom 1934,Je 16,20:2
Evelyn Prentice 1934,N 10,19:1
Shadow of Doubt 1935,Mr 11,15:1
Times Square Lady 1935,Mr 15,25:3
Casino Murder Case, The 1935,Ap 17,26:5
Tale of Two Cities, A 1935,D 26,21:2
Ceiling Zero 1936,Ja 20,22:2
Leathernecks Have Landed, The 1936,Mr 23,22:5
Dancing Feet 1936,Mr 28,11:2
Small Town Girl 1936,Ap 11,19:1
Big Brown Eyes 1936,My 2,11:1
36 Hours to Live 1936,Ag 15,6:3
Valiant Is the Word for Carrie 1936,O 8,27:2
Man Who Lived Twice, The 1936,O 12,23:2
Go West, Young Man 1936,N 19,31:3
Lost Horizon 1937,Mr 4,27:1
Marked Woman 1937,Ap 12,15:2
Swing It, Sailor 1937,D 13,23:5
Crowd Roars, The 1938,Ag 5,11:1
Missing Daughters 1939,Je 12,14:5
They Asked for It 1939,Je 30,17:4
Gone With the Wind 1939,D 20,31:2
Northwest Passage 1940,Mr 8,25:1
Irene 1940,My 24,23:3
Little Men 1940,D 9,23:2
High Sierra 1941,Ja 25,11:2
Leopard Man, The 1943,My 20,26:4
Seventh Victim, The 1943,S 18,11:3
Merry Monahans, The 1944,O 13,16:2
Badman's Territory 1946,My 31,27:2
Born to Kill 1947,My 1,34:2
Belle Star's Daughter 1949,Ja 10,19:2
Man in the Attic 1954,F 6,17:2
Drum Beat 1954,N 18,42:1
Bernardine 1957,Jl 25,28:1
Jewell, Stuart V (Cinematographer)
Living Desert, The 1953,N 10,38:1

Jewison, Norman (Director)
40 Pounds of Trouble 1963,Ja 24,5:2
Thrill of it All, The 1963,Ag 2,15:3
Send Me no Flowers 1964,N 13,30:1
Art of Love, The 1965,Jl 1,34:1
Cincinnati Kid, The 1965,O 28,48:1
Russians are Coming the Russians are Coming,
The 1966,My 26,55:1
In the Heat of the Night 1967,Ag 3,26:1
Thomas Crown Affair, The 1968,Je 27,48:2
Jewison, Norman (Producer)
Russians are Coming the Russians are Coming,
The 1966,My 26,55:1
Thomas Crown Affair, The 1968,Je 27,48:2
Jewkes, Delos
Stars and Stripes Forever 1952,D 23,17:2
Jeydt, Louis Jean
Big Sleep, The 1946,Ag 24,6:6
Jezkova, Marie
Firemen's Ball, The 1968,S 30,60:1
Jezkova, Milada
Loves of a Blonde 1966,S 13,51:2
Loves of a Blonde 1966,O 27,55:1
Jhabvala, R Prawer (Original Author)
Householder, The 1963,O 22,43:2
Shakespeare Wallah 1966,Mr 23,40:2
Jhabvala, R Prawer (Screenwriter)
Householder, The 1963,O 22,43:2
Shakespeare Wallah 1966,Mr 23,40:2
Jianacopolou, Chris (Screenwriter)
Mademoiselle-Age 39 1956,Mr 26,34:2
Jiggs (chimpanzee)
Her Jungle Love 1938,Ap 14,27:2
Jiling, Lene
Nur am Rhein 1931,S 25,28:7
Jilliann, Ann
Babes in Toyland 1961,D 15,49:1
Gypsy 1962,N 2,24:1
Jillson, Williard
Abroad With two Yanks 1944,O 26,19:7
Jim, Marion
King and I, The 1956,Je 29,15:6
Jim the Crow
Enchanted Forest, The 1945,D 17,17:2
Jimenez, Carlos Sanchez
Tia Tula, A 1965,Je 3,24:1
Jimenez, Sharyn
Way Out 1967,O 26,54:3
Jiminez, J L
Pecados de Amor 1934,Ap 24,27:2
Virgin of Guadalupe, The 1943,My 15,13:3
St Francis of Assisi 1947,Ap 5,12:5
Macario 1961,S 28,48:6
Jiminez, Maria Rosa
Loyola, The Soldier Saint 1952,Ap 25,19:2
Jiminez, Soledad
In old Arizona 1929,Ja 21,18:4
Cock Eyed World, The 1929,Ag 5,25:2
Romance of Rio Grande 1929,N 9,22:5
Arizona Kid, The 1930,My 17,21:2
Texan, The 1930,My 17,21:2
Broken Wing, The 1932,Mr 26,17:2
Bordertown 1935,Ja 24,22:5
Under the Pampas Moon 1935,My 31,11:1
Robin Hood of El Dorado, The 1936,Mr 14,10:1
Man of the People 1937,F 23,25:4
Kid Galahad 1937,My 27,21:3
Black Bart 1948,Mr 4,30:4
Red Light 1950,Ja 16,18:4
Jimmy (Crow)
Miraculous Journey 1948,S 20,21:2
Jimmy Dorsey and his band
Hollywood Canteen 1944,D 16,19:2
Jimmy Dorsey and his orchestra
I Dood It 1943,N 11,29:1
Jinadas, E R
Four Frightened People 1934,Ja 27,9:2
Jivin' Jacks and Jills, The
What's Cookin' 1942,F 26,15:5
Private Buckaroo 1942,Je 25,27:4
Give Out, Sisters 1942,Ag 28,22:3
Get Help to Love 1942,O 19,15:3
Mister Big 1943,Je 14,13:4
Joachimson, Felix (Screenwriter)
Affairs of Maupassant, The 1938,F 12,20:2
Joannon, Leo (Director)
S O S Mediterranean 1940,Ja 1,29:2
Children of Chaos 1950,Ap 20,37:2
Utopia 1954,D 15,41:1
Joannon, Leo (Original Author)
Hell's Cargo 1940,S 16,15:2
Utopia 1954,D 15,41:1
Joannon, Leo (Screenwriter)
S O S Mediterranean 1940,Ja 1,29:2
Joano, Clotilde
Your Shadow Is Mine 1963,My 15,32:1
Bonnes Femmes, Les 1966,My 13,32:1
Job, Thomas (Miscellaneous)
Siren of Atlantis 1949,Ag 22,13:1
Job, Thomas (Original Author)
Uncle Harry 1945,Ag 24,14:5

Job, Thomas (Screenwriter)
Escape in the Desert 1945,My 12,10:2
Two Mrs Carrolls, The 1947,Ap 7,20:1
Job, William
Privilege 1967,Jl 25,30:2
Jobert, Marlene
Masculine Feminine 1966,S 19,57:1
Thief of Paris, The 1967,Ag 24,43:2
Jobs, Lisskulla
Crime and Punishment 1948,Mr 1,17:2
Jobson, Edward
City of Masks, The 1920,Jl 12,12:4
Jobst, Jola
Our Little Wife 1940,Ja 27,9:2
Joby, Hans
Hell's Angels 1930,Ag 16,8:3
Suicide Fleet 1931,N 23,22:1
I Met Him in Paris 1937,Je 3,29:2
Thunder Afloat 1939,O 13,27:2
Beasts of Berlin 1939,N 20,15:6
Jocelyn, Andre
Leda 1961,Jl 19,33:1
Jochim, Anthony
Dangerous Crossing 1953,S 30,37:2
Joeken, Carl
Schubert's Fruehlingstraum 1932,Je 22,19:4
Joel, Dennis
Toby Tyler 1960,Ap 20,45:2
Joffe, Alex
Shoot the Piano Player 1962,Jl 24,19:1
Joffe, Alex (Director)
Every Second Counts 1957,O 15,39:4
Riff Raff Girls 1962,O 20,13:5
Impossible on Saturday 1966,F 17,29:1
Joffe, Alex (Original Author)
Devil's Daughter 1949,F 26,11:2
Impossible on Saturday 1966,F 17,29:1
Joffe, Alex (Screenwriter)
Devil's Daughter 1949,F 26,11:2
Simple Case of Money, A 1952,F 2,11:2
Taxi 1953,Ja 22,20:3
Monte Carlo Baby 1954,My 29,13:4
Paris Incident 1954,Ag 18,20:2
Every Second Counts 1957,O 15,39:4
Riff Raff Girls 1962,O 20,13:5
Impossible on Saturday 1966,F 17,29:1
Joffre
Orage 1938,D 12,26:2
End of a Day, The 1939,S 12,28:4
Johann, Albert
Murderers Among Us 1948,Ag 17,19:6
Johann, Zita
Struggle, The 1931,D 11,35:1
Tiger Shark 1932,S 23,22:2
Mummy, The 1933,Ja 7,11:2
Luxury Liner 1933,F 3,21:3
Man Who Dared, The 1933,S 9,9:3
Sin of Nora Moran, The 1933,D 13,29:3
Grand Canary 1934,Jl 20,11:1
Johanne
Take it All; A Tout Prendre 1966,Ap 26,55:1
Johannsen, Ernst (Original Author)
Western Front 1918, The 1930,Je 22,VIII,4:2
Comrades of 1918 1931,F 20,18:5
Johansen, Aud
Lilli Marlene 1952,Mr 29,19:2
Johanson, Erik
Soederkaakar 1936,D 19,16:2
Johansson, Aake
Med Folket Foer Fosterlandet 1939,F 21,14:2
Johansson, Ingemar
All the Young Men 1960,Ag 27,8:6
Johansson, Ivar (Director)
Haelsingar 1934,S 25,25:2
Sangen Till Henne; Song to Her, The
1935,F 22,27:3
Froeken Blir Piga 1937,Je 12,8:3
Surf, The 1949,D 17,15:2
Johar, I S
Harry Black and the Tiger 1958,S 19,24:4
Flame Over India 1960,Ap 30,14:1
Lawrence of Arabia 1962,D 17,5:6
Maya 1966,Je 23,29:4
John, Alice
These Thirty Years 1934,My 24,28:3
John, Bertram
Take It From Me 1926,N 2,35:1
John, Carl
Wenn der Hahn Kraeht 1936,N 14,23:3
John, Errol
Sins of Rachel Cade, The 1961,Ap 6,30:3
PT 109 1963,Je 27,23:1
Man in the Middle 1964,Mr 5,36:1
Guns at Batasi 1964,N 17,47:1
Assault on a Queen 1966,Jl 28,23:3
John, Georg
Last Laugh, The 1925,Ja 28,14:1
M 1933,Ap 3,13:3
Tod Ueber Schanghai 1933,D 16,12:4
John, H W (Original Author)
I Aim at the Stars 1960,O 20,42:2

John, Karl
Weisse Sklaven 1937,Jl 31,6:2
Lachdoktor, Der; Laugh Doctor, The 1938,Mr 12,13:4
Seven Journeys 1951,Mr 12,20:2
Man Between, The 1953,N 19,41:2
No Way Back 1955,My 19,25:5
Devil's General, The 1957,Ap 16,38:2
John, Peter
Town Like Alice, A 1958,S 22,27:1
John, Rosamund
Spitfire 1943,Je 14,13:2
Johnny in the Clouds 1945,N 16,16:2
Green for Danger 1947,Ag 8,10:2
Tawny Pipit 1947,S 8,25:5
Upturned Glass, The 1947,N 5,34:4
Fame Is the Spur 1949,N 8,34:2
No Place for Jennifer 1957,Jl 17,31:2
Both Sides of the Law 1954,Ja 12,19:2
John, Rupert
Moulin Rouge 1953,F 11,33:5
Johns, Bertram
Conrad in Quest of his Youth 1920,N 8,20:2
Stephen Steps Out 1923,N 19,19:3
Declassee 1925,Mr 23,14:2
Claw, The 1927,My 11,28:3
Johns, Glynis
Big Game, The 1936,O 24,23:1
South Riding 1938,Ag 2,15:2
Prison Without Bars 1939,Ap 10,13:2
Fugitive, The 1940,Jl 23,22:2
Adventures of Tartu, The 1943,S 24,26:1
Half-Way House 1945,Ag 13,22:4
Vacation From Marriage 1946,Mr 15,27:2
Frieda 1947,Ag 15,12:3
Ideal Husband, An 1948,Ja 15,28:2
Miranda 1949,Ap 25,20:2
Dear Mr Prohack 1950,Jl 15,7:2
State Secret 1950,O 5,38:2
No Highway in the Sky 1951,S 22,8:6
Encore (Gigolo and Gigolette); Gigolo and Gigolette (Encore) 1952,Ap 3,45:1
Island Rescue 1952,Jl 1,19:4
Promoter, The 1952,O 29,36:2
Sword and the Rose, The 1953,Ag 20,18:3
Rob Roy 1954,F 4,21:5
Weak and the Wicked, The 1954,Ag 21,10:3
Personal Affair 1954,O 23,13:2
Beachcomber, The 1955,Ja 17,27:5
Land of Fury 1955,My 3,37:4
Court Jester, The 1956,F 2,19:1
Around the World in 80 Days 1956,O 18,37:1
Another Time Another Place 1958,My 3,10:4
Shake Hands With the Devil 1959,Je 25,20:7
All Mine to Give 1959,Ag 4,32:5
Sundowners, The 1960,D 9,39:1
Cabinet of Caligari, The 1962,My 26,13:5
Chapman Report, The 1962,O 18,49:2
Papa's Delicate Condition 1963,Mr 7,8:5
Mary Poppins 1964,S 25,34:1
Dear Brigitte 1965,Ja 28,20:1
Don't Just Stand There 1968,S 3,54:2
Johns, Harriette
Ideal Husband, An 1948,Ja 15,28:2
Edward my Son 1949,Je 3,21:2
Two-Headed Spy, The 1959,Mr 3,38:4
Johns, Jane
Idol of the Crowd 1937,D 4,21:1
Johns, Larry
Beginning or the End, The 1947,F 21,15:1
Dakota Lil 1950,Mr 3,21:5
Johns, Margo
Konga 1961,S 16,9:1
Johns, Mervyn
Jamaica Inn 1939,O 12,33:1
Convoy 1941,Ja 17,21:2
Girl in the News, The 1941,My 5,13:2
Next of Kin 1943,My 6,25:2
48 Hours 1944,Je 26,21:2
Half-Way House 1945,Ag 13,22:4
Dead of Night 1946,Je 29,22:6
Captive Heart, The 1947,Ap 28,27:2
Captain Boycott 1947,D 6,11:2
Easy Money (Episode 2) 1949,F 14,15:3
Quartet (The Kite); Kite, The (Quartet) 1949,Mr 29,30:3
Edward my Son 1949,Je 3,21:2
Pink String and Sealing Wax 1950,O 4,38:2
Tony Draws a Horse 1951,My 15,38:6
Christmas Carol, A 1951,N 29,41:2
Magic Box, The 1952,S 24,40:2
Devil's Plot 1953,Je 19,18:1
Master of Ballantrae, The 1953,Ag 6,16:2
Frightened Bride, The 1953,Ag 20,18:5
Horse's Mouth, The 1954,Ja 20,33:4
Romeo and Juliet 1954,D 22,28:1
Moby Dick 1956,Jl 5,18:1
1984 1956,O 1,31:1
Circle, The 1959,Ap 16,29:2
Devil's Disciple, The 1959,Ag 21,12:1
Once More With Feeling 1960,F 12,22:2
Sundowners, The 1960,D 9,39:1
Francis of Assisi 1961,Jl 29,8:2

Call Me Genius 1961,O 17,47:1
No Love for Johnnie 1961,D 13,55:1
Day of the Triffids 1963,My 11,15:2
Never Let Go 1963,Je 15,10:2
Old Dark House, The 1963,O 31,26:3
Victors, The 1963,D 20,21:2
They all Died Laughing 1964,Mr 16,37:2
Heroes of Telemark, The 1966,Mr 10,26:1
Johns, Shirley
Cynthia 1947,S 19,27:2
Summer Holiday 1948,Je 12,8:5
Johns, Stratford
Those Fantastic Flying Fools 1967,O 19,59:2
JOHNSON
See Also JOHNSTON, JOHNSTONE
Johnson, Arch
Somebody up There Likes Me 1956,Jl 6,16:1
Gun Glory 1957,Jl 20,8:7
G I Blues 1960,N 5,28:1
Johnson, Arte
Subterraneans, The 1960,Jl 7,26:1
Third Day, The 1965,Ag 5,15:3
Johnson, Bari
Call Me Bwana 1963,Jl 4,9:1
Johnson, Ben
Three Godfathers 1949,Mr 4,25:2
Mighty Joe Young 1949,Jl 28,19:3
She Wore a Yellow Ribbon 1949,N 18,35:2
Wagonmaster 1950,Je 19,17:2
Rio Grande 1950,N 20,21:2
Shane 1953,Ap 24,30:3
Simba 1955,O 22,24:2
One Eyed Jacks 1961,Mr 31,21:1
Major Dundee 1965,Ap 8,45:1
Will Penny 1968,Ap 11,51:2
Johnson, Bill
Keep Your Powder Dry 1945,Mr 12,22:6
It's a Pleasure 1945,My 4,23:3
Johnson, Byron (Original Author)
Air Mail, The 1925,Mr 17,18:1
Johnson, Candy
Beach Party 1963,S 26,40:2
Johnson, Carmencita
Wonder of Women 1929,Jl 22,17:1
Mrs Wiggs of the Cabbage Patch 1934,O 29,14:2
These Three 1936,Mr 19,22:4
Beloved Brat 1938,My 2,13:2
Keep Smiling 1938,Ag 10,15:2
Johnson, Casey
Five came Back 1939,Jl 5,20:2
One Crowded Night 1940,Ag 27,17:2
Boom Town 1940,S 6,25:2
Little Men 1940,D 9,23:2
One Foot in Heaven 1941,N 14,28:3
Johnson, Celia
In Which We Serve 1942,D 24,18:1
Randolph Family 1945,Mr 13,19:4
Brief Encounter 1946,Ag 26,21:2
This Happy Breed 1947,Ap 14,24:2
Astonished Heart, The 1950,F 15,23:2
I Believe in You 1953,My 5,34:3
Captain's Paradise, The 1953,S 29,25:5
Holly and the Ivy, The 1954,F 5,16:1
Kid for two Farthings, A 1956,Ap 18,25:1
Johnson, Chic
Fifty Million Frenchmen 1931,Mr 26,31:2
Gold Dust Gertie 1931,My 30,9:2
Hellzapoppin 1941,D 26,21:4
Crazy House 1943,D 16,33:3
See my Lawyer 1945,My 4,23:4
Johnson, Chic (Miscellaneous)
Hellzapoppin 1941,D 26,21:4
Johnson, Chubby
Rocky Mountain 1950,N 4,13:2
Bend of the River 1952,Ap 10,37:1
Calamity Jane 1953,N 5,40:2
Cattle Queen of Montana 1955,Ja 26,22:1
Far Country, The 1955,F 14,24:2
Tennessee's Partner 1955,N 5,22:8
Tribute to a Bad Man 1956,Mr 31,13:3
Rawhide Years, The 1956,Je 16,12:2
First Texan, The 1956,Je 23,20:2
Fastest Gun Alive, The 1956,Jl 13,23:3
True Story of Jesse James, The 1957,Mr 23,17:2
River's Edge, The 1957,Ap 12,20:2
Johnson, Claude
Papa's Delicate Condition 1963,Mr 7,8:5
Johnson, Dick Winslow
Love, Live and Laugh 1929,N 2,14:6
Johnson, Dolores
Strong Boy 1929,Ap 1,22:1
Thru Different Eyes 1929,Ap 15,22:6
Johnson, Don
Good Morning and Goodbye! 1968,F 20,53:1
Johnson, Dorothy (Original Author)
Hanging Tree, The 1959,F 12,23:1
Man Who Shot Liberty Valance, The 1962,My 24,29:2
Johnson, Dots
Paisan 1948,Mr 30,26:2
No Way Out 1950,Ag 17,23:1
Joe Louis Story, The 1953,N 4,29:4

Johnson, Earl
Biscuit Eater, The 1940,My 23,28:5
Johnson, Earl (Original Author)
Two in Revolt 1936,Ap 25,21:1
Johnson, Ed
Egg Crate Wallop, The 1919,S 29,16:1
Johnson, Eddie
Star Spangled Rhythm 1942,D 31,20:1
Johnson, Edward
West of Zanzibar 1955,Ja 18,31:2
Johnson, Emilie (Original Author)
In the Name of the Law 1922,Jl 10,9:5
Third Alarm, The 1923,Ja 10,28:5
Johnson, Emilie (Screenwriter)
Last Edition, The 1925,N 11,27:3
Fourth Commandment, The 1927,Ap 6,25:1
Shield of Honor 1927,D 13,33:2
Johnson, Emory
Woman Next Door, The 1919,My 19,20:5
In the Name of the Law 1922,Jl 10,9:5
Johnson, Emory (Director)
In the Name of the Law 1922,Jl 10,9:5
Third Alarm, The 1923,Ja 10,28:5
Spirit of the U S A, The 1924,My 21,22:3
Last Edition, The 1925,N 11,27:3
Fourth Commandment, The 1927,Ap 6,25:1
Shield of Honor 1927,D 13,33:2
Lone Eagle, The 1927,D 20,33:2
Phantom Express, The 1932,S 20,26:3
Johnson, Emory (Screenwriter)
Phantom Express, The 1932,S 20,26:3
Johnson, Ernest W
Street of Sin, The 1928,My 28,23:2
Johnson, Eyvind (Original Author)
Here's Your Life 1968,D 20,60:1
Johnson, Fred
Native Land 1942,My 12,16:3
Adam and Evelyn 1950,My 12,33:4
Martin Luther 1953,S 10,22:1
Naked Heart, The 1955,Mr 9,22:4
Brides of Dracula, The 1960,S 6,41:4
Scream of Fear 1961,Ag 23,29:1
Johnson, George
Intruder, The 1962,My 15,48:1
Johnson, George Clayton (Original Author)
Ocean's Eleven 1960,Ag 11,19:1
Johnson, Gladys (Original Author)
Home James 1928,S 11,31:3
Johnson, Hal (choir)
Lady for a Night 1942,F 12,27:2
Johnson, Hall (Miscellaneous)
Green Pastures, The 1936,Jl 17,20:1
Johnson, Hall Choir
Hearts Divided 1936,Je 13,13:1
Green Pastures, The 1936,Jl 17,20:1
Swanee River 1939,D 30,9:2
Johnson, Helen
Divorcee, The 1930,My 10,25:3
Soldiers and Women 1930,My 12,27:3
Sin Takes a Holliday 1930,N 28,23:1
Pays to Advertise, It 1931,F 21,15:2
It Pays to Advertise 1931,F 21,15:2
Vice Squad, The 1931,Je 6,15:5
Women Love Once 1931,Je 27,20:3
Johnson, Henry (Miscellaneous)
Under the Pampas Moon 1935,My 31,11:1
Old Kentucky, In 1935,N 29,24:1
Johnson, Henry (Original Author)
Arizona to Broadway 1933,Jl 22,14:3
Johnson, Henry (Screenwriter)
Devil With Women, A 1930,O 20,28:2
365 Nights in Hollywood 1934,N 7,32:1
Fighting Youth 1935,N 2,13:3
F-Man 1936,My 4,16:1
Johnson, Howard
Voice in the Wind 1944,Mr 16,17:2
Johnson, J (Composer)
Klondike Annie 1936,Mr 12,18:2
Hit Parade of 1943 1943,Ap 16,24:3
Johnson, J Lewis
Miss Susie Slagle's 1946,F 7,29:2
Unknown, The 1946,Jl 20,10:3
Johnson, Jack
Legendary Champions, The 1968,O 29,54:1
Johnson, James
Ring of Fire 1961,Ag 17,18:2
Johnson, Janet
Proud Valley 1941,My 17,19:2
Johnson, Jean
Last Man on Earth, The 1924,D 13,12:4
Born to the West 1926,Je 30,18:1 (In Addenda)
Johnson, Jessie
Betrayal, The 1948,Je 26,10:5
Johnson, John L
Radio Patrol 1932,Jl 14,24:2
Tarzan's Revenge 1938,Ja 10,13:3
Johnson, Julian (Miscellaneous)
With Byrd at the South Pole 1930,Je 20,6:3
Johnson, Julian (Original Author)
Lucky Cisco Kid 1940,Je 24,19:5
Johnson, June
Double Danger 1938,F 10,17:5

Johnson, Katie
  Voice in the Night, The 1941,My 23,25:4
  Hellzapoppin 1941,D 26,21:4
  Jeannie 1943,S 13,14:2
  Years Between, The 1947,Mr 10,25:2
  Meet Me at Dawn 1948,My 18,26:2
  I Believe in You 1953,My 5,34:3
  Ladykillers 1956,F 21,37:2
  How to Murder a Rich Uncle 1957,O 26,19:2
  Studs Lonigan 1960,D 15,59:1
Johnson, Kay
  Dynamite 1929,D 28,11:1
  Ship From Shanghai, The 1930,Ap 26,11:1
  This mad World 1930,Jl 21,20:3
  Spoilers, The 1930,S 20,15:4
  Madam Satan 1930,O 6,21:1
  Billy the Kid 1930,O 18,23:2
  Passion Flower 1930,D 22,16:2
  Single Sin, The 1931,Mr 17,34:3
  American Madness 1932,Ag 6,14:5
  Thirteen Women 1932,O 15,13:1
  Eight Girls in a Boat 1934,Ja 13,16:3
  This Man is Mine 1934,Ap 13,25:1
  Of Human Bondage 1934,Je 29,17:1
  Their big Moment 1934,S 6,22:4
  Jalna 1935,S 14,8:4
  White Banners 1938,Je 23,27:1
  Real Glory, The 1939,S 15,26:2
  Son of Fury 1942,Ja 30,23:2
  Mr Lucky 1943,Jl 23,21:2
Johnson, Lamont
  Retreat Hell! 1952,F 20,26:2
Johnson, Lamont (Director)
  Covenant with Death, A 1967,F 16,32:3
Johnson, Laraine
  Scandal Street 1938,F 5,19:2 (In Addenda)
  Painted Desert 1938,S 14,26:5
Johnson, Larry H (Screenwriter)
  Lord Love a Duck 1966,F 22,14:6
Johnson, Laurence E (Original Author)
  It's a Wise Child 1931,My 16,13:3
Johnson, Lawrence
  Silver King, The 1919,Ja 13,9:3
Johnson, Les
  Girl He Left Behind, The 1956,O 27,17:1
Johnson, Lydia
  Due Madri, Le; Two Mothers, The
    1940,My 17,23:3
  French-Cancan 1956,Ap 17,26:2
Johnson, Mae E
  Stormy Weather 1943,Jl 22,15:1
Johnson, Malcolm (Original Author)
  On the Waterfront 1954,Jl 29,18:1
Johnson, Margaret
  Burn, Witch, Burn 1962,Jl 5,21:2 (In Addenda)
Johnson, Martin (Cinematographer)
  Baboona 1935,Ja 23,21:2
Johnson, Martin (Miscellaneous)
  Head Hunters of the South Seas 1923,Ja 9,27:2
    (In Addenda)
  Wonders of the Congo 1931,D 5,21:2
Johnson, Martin (Producer)
  Among the Cannibal Isles of the South Pacific
    1918,Jl 22,9:1
  Jungle Adventures 1921,S 12,16:1
  Trailing African Wild Animals 1923,My 21,12:2
  Congorilla 1932,Jl 22,18:2
  Baboona 1935,Ja 23,21:2
  Borneo 1937,S 4,8:3
Johnson, Martin Mrs (Miscellaneous)
  Wonders of the Congo 1931,D 5,21:2
Johnson, Martin Mrs (Producer)
  Trailing African Wild Animals 1923,My 21,12:2
  Congorilla 1932,Jl 22,18:2
  Baboona 1935,Ja 23,21:2
  Borneo 1937,S 4,8:3
Johnson, Mary
  Three Who Were Doomed, The 1928,Ja 10,28:4
  Manege 1928,Mr 11,VIII,7:6 (In Addenda)
  Youth Astray 1928,My 29,17:2
  Strange Case of Captain Ramper, The
    1928,Je 4,13:2
Johnson, Melodie
  Coogan's Bluff 1968,O 3,56:1
Johnson, Mike
  Smiling Along 1939,F 20,13:2
Johnson, Moffat
  Midnight 1934,Mr 10,18:3
Johnson, Muriel
  As You Like It 1936,N 6,29:3
Johnson, Noble
  Ten Commandments, The 1923,D 22,8:1
  Thief of Bagdad, The 1924,Mr 19,19:1
  Little Robinson Crusoe 1924,S 3,17:1
  Navigator, The 1924,O 13,21:1
  Midnight Express, The 1924,N 19,19:3
  Adventure 1925,Ap 15,16:1
  Hands Up 1926,Ja 18,26:2
  Flaming Frontier, The 1926,Ap 5,24:1
  When a Man Loves 1927,F 4,16:6
  Vanity 1927,Js 15,31:4
  Topsy and Eva 1927,Ag 8,10:3
  Soft Cushions 1927,S 12,29:1

Gateway of the Moon, The 1928,Ja 9,20:1
Redskin 1929,Ja 28,21:1
Sal of Singapore 1929,Ja 29,27:1
Noah's Ark 1929,Mr 13,28:6
Four Feathers, The 1929,Je 13,35:4
Insidious Dr Fu Manchu, The 1929,Jl 22,17:1
Moby Dick 1930,Ag 15,20:5
East of Borneo 1931,S 26,25:3
Safe in Hell 1931,D 19,16:4
Murders in the Rue Morgue 1932,F 11,16:1
Mystery Ranch 1932,Je 30,26:2
Most Dangerous Game, The 1932,N 21,21:1
Mummy, The 1933,Ja 7,11:2
Nagana 1933,F 16,23:2
King Kong 1933,Mr 3,12:1
Murder in Trinidad 1934,My 16,22:2
Lives of a Bengal Lancer, The 1935,Ja 12,12:2
She 1935,Jl 26,18:2
Escape from Devil's Island 1935,N 25,22:2
Conquest 1937,N 5,19:1
Tropic Fury 1939,S 8,28:4
Ghost Breakers, The 1940,Jl 4,12:2
Aloma of the South Seas 1941,Ag 28,23:4
Hurry, Charlie, Hurry 1941,N 12,31:3
Mad Doctor of Market Street, The 1942,Ja 5,21:5
Jungle Book 1942,Ap 6,19:1
Ten Gentlemen From West Point 1942,Je 5,23:3
Game of Death, A 1945,N 24,22:4
She Wore a Yellow Ribbon 1949,N 18,35:2
Johnson, Nora (Original Author)
  World of Henry Orient, The 1964,Mr 20,27:2
Johnson, Nora (Screenwriter)
  World of Henry Orient, The 1964,Mr 20,27:2
Johnson, Norris
  Lorna Doone 1922,D 4,20:2
Johnson, Nunnally (Director)
  Night People 1954,Mr 13,11:2
  Black Widow 1954,O 28,46:6
  How to be Very, Very Popular 1955,Jl 23,10:1
  Man in the Gray Flannel Suit, The
    1956,Ap 13,21:1
  Oh Men! Oh Women! 1957,F 22,25:2
  Three Faces of Eve, The 1957,S 27,16:6
  Man Who Understood, The 1959,O 3,14:7
  Angel Wore Red, The 1960,S 29,32:1
Johnson, Nunnally (Original Author)
  Moulin Rouge 1934,F 8,14:4
Johnson, Nunnally (Producer)
  Dimples 1936,O 10,21:2
  Nancy Steele is Missing 1937,Mr 8,22:1
  Cafe Metropole 1937,Ap 29,17:1
  Slave Ship 1937,Je 17,17:1
  Love Under Fire 1937,Ag 28,8:2
  Roxie Hart 1942,F 20,21:1
  Pied Piper, The 1942,Ag 13,15:3
  Life Begins at Eight-Thirty 1942,D 10,35:2
  Moon Is Down, The 1943,Mr 27,8:6
  Holy Matrimony 1943,S 16,25:2
  Casanova Brown 1944,S 15,16:1
  Woman in the Window, The 1945,Ja 26,16:4
  Dark Mirror, The 1946,O 19,15:2
  Senator Was Indiscreet, The 1947,D 27,9:2
  Mr Peabody and the Mermaid 1948,Ag 14,6:5
  Everybody Does It 1949,O 26,32:2
  Three Came Home 1950,F 21,22:5
  Gunfighter, The 1950,Je 24,7:2
  Mudlark, The 1950,D 25,25:1
  Desert Fox, The 1951,O 18,32:1
  Desert Fox, The 1951,O 28,II,1:8
  Phone Call From a Stranger 1952,F 2,11:2
  We're not Married 1952,Jl 12,16:2
  My Cousin Rachel 1952,D 26,20:2
  How to Marry a Millionaire 1953,N 11,37:1
  Night People 1954,Mr 13,11:2
  Black Widow 1954,O 28,46:6
  How to be Very, Very Popular 1955,Jl 23,10:1
  Oh Men! Oh Women! 1957,F 22,25:2
  Three Faces of Eve, The 1957,S 27,16:6
  Man Who Understood, The 1959,O 3,14:7
Johnson, Nunnally (Screenwriter)
  Rough House Rosie 1927,My 23,27:2
  Kid Millions 1934,N 12,17:2
  Thanks a Million 1935,N 14,17:1
  Man Who Broke the Bank at Monte Carlo, The
    1935,N 15,20:2
  Prisoner of Shark Island, The 1936,F 13,25:2
  Banjo on My Knee 1936,D 12,15:1
  Jesse James 1939,Ja 14,13:1
  Wife, Husband and Friend 1939,F 25,19:2
  Rose of Washington Square 1939,My 6,21:2
  Grapes of Wrath, The 1940,Ja 25,17:2
  Chad Hanna 1940,D 26,23:1
  Tobacco Road 1941,F 21,16:2
  Roxie Hart 1942,F 20,21:1
  Pied Piper, The 1942,Ag 13,15:3
  Life Begins at Eight-Thirty 1942,D 10,35:2
  Moon Is Down, The 1943,Mr 27,8:6
  Holy Matrimony 1943,S 16,25:2
  Casanova Brown 1944,S 15,16:1
  Keys of the Kingdom, The 1944,D 30,15:2
  Woman in the Window, The 1945,Ja 26,16:4
  Along Came Jones 1945,Jl 19,8:7
  Dark Mirror, The 1946,O 19,15:2

  Mr Peabody and the Mermaid 1948,Ag 14,6:5
  Everybody Does It 1949,O 26,32:2
  Three Came Home 1950,F 21,22:5
  Mudlark, The 1950,D 25,25:1
  Long Dark Hall, The 1951,My 10,38:3
  Desert Fox, The 1951,O 18,32:1
  Phone Call From a Stranger 1952,F 2,11:2
  We're not Married 1952,Jl 12,16:2
  My Cousin Rachel 1952,D 26,20:2
  How to Marry a Millionaire 1953,N 11,37:1
  Night People 1954,Mr 13,11:2
  Black Widow 1954,O 28,46:6
  How to be Very, Very Popular 1955,Jl 23,10:1
  Man in the Gray Flannel Suit, The
    1956,Ap 13,21:1
  True Story of Jesse James, The 1957,Mr 23,17:2
  Three Faces of Eve, The 1957,S 27,16:6
  Man Who Understood, The 1959,O 3,14:7
  Angel Wore Red, The 1960,S 29,32:1
  Flaming Star 1960,D 17,19:1
  Mr Hobbs Takes a Vacation 1962,Je 16,11:2
  Take Her, She's Mine 1963,N 14,41:1
  World of Henry Orient, The 1964,Mr 20,27:2
  Dirty Dozen, The 1967,Je 16,36:1
Johnson, Osa (Producer)
  I Married Adventure 1940,S 24,26:5
Johnson, Oscar
  Ice Follies of 1939 1939,Mr 17,25:2
Johnson, Owen (Original Author)
  Virtuous Wives 1918,D 30,7:3
  Woman Gives, The 1920,Ap 12,13:1
  Enemy Sex, The 1924,Jl 1,21:4
  Children of Divorce 1927,Ap 26,33:3
Johnson, Page
  Passages From James Joyce's Finnegans Wake
    1967,O 10,56:1
Johnson, Pauline
  Wrecker, The 1929,Ag 13,23:2
Johnson, Payne
  Blue Bird, The 1940,Ja 20,11:2
Johnson, Rafer
  Wild in the Country 1961,Je 10,12:2
  Fiercest Heart, The 1961,Ag 3,13:5
Johnson, Ray
  Born to Dance 1936,D 5,16:1
Johnson, Richard
  Never so Few 1960,Ja 22,15:2
  Haunting, The 1963,S 19,23:1
  Pumpkin Eater, The 1964,N 10,58:1
  Operation Crossbow 1965,Ap 2,29:1
  Amorous Adventures of Moll Flanders, The
    1965,My 27,28:1
  Khartoum 1966,Jl 14,28:1
  Deadlier Than the Male 1967,F 22,21:1
  Danger Route 1968,Je 6,54:2
  Oedipus the King 1968,S 19,62:2
Johnson, Rita
  London by Night 1937,Ag 13,13:1
  Man-Proof 1938,Ja 14,21:1
  Smashing the Rackets 1938,Ag 9,22:5
  Rich Man, Poor Girl 1938,Ag 19,13:3
  Letter of Introduction 1938,S 1,17:1
  Girl Downstairs, The 1939,Ja 26,17:1
  Honolulu 1939,F 23,19:2
  Within the Law 1939,Ap 6,31:2
  Broadway Serenade 1939,Ap 7,25:2
  Six Thousand Enemies 1939,Je 9,26:2
  Stronger Than Desire 1939,Jl 30,17:3
  They all Come Out 1939,Ag 3,15:4
  Nick Carter, Master Detective 1939,D 14,35:2
  Congo Maisie 1940,F 8,18:4
  Forty Little Mothers 1940,Ap 19,25:2
  Edison the Man 1940,Je 7,27:2
  Golden Fleecing, The 1940,N 7,33:4
  Here Comes Mr Jordan 1941,Ag 8,13:2
  Appointment for Love 1941,N 7,27:1
  Major and the Minor, The 1942,S 17,21:3
  My Friend Flicka 1943,My 27,21:4
  Thunderhead 1945,Mr 16,21:2
  Affairs of Susan, The 1945,Mr 29,18:2
  Naughty Nineties, The 1945,Je 21,16:2
  Pardon my Past 1946,Ja 28,15:5
  Perfect Marriage, The 1947,Ja 16,30:3
  Michigan Kid 1947,F 22,16:3
  They Won't Believe Me 1947,Jl 17,16:2
  Sleep, My Love 1948,F 19,29:4
  Big Clock, The 1948,Ap 22,34:2
  Innocent Affair, An 1948,S 29,36:2
  Family Honeymoon 1949,F 25,28:2
  Second Face, The 1951,Mr 2,21:3
Johnson, Robert Lee (Original Author)
  Gentlemen are Born 1934,N 22,27:2
  Hit the Road 1941,Jl 3,15:3
Johnson, Robert Lee (Screenwriter)
  Gentlemen are Born 1934,N 22,27:2
  Harvester, The 1936,Jl 4,18:2
  Down Under the Sea 1936,Ag 10,10:2
  Tarzan's Revenge 1938,Ja 10,13:3
  Girl From God's Country 1940,S 9,18:5
  Hit the Road 1941,Jl 3,15:3
  Canal Zone 1942,Mr 30,21:2
  Atlantic Convoy 1942,Jl 6,18:5
  Enchanted Forest, The 1945,D 17,17:2

Johnson, Russell
For Men Only 1952,Ja 16,21:2
It Came From Outer Space 1953,Je 18,38:2
This Island Earth 1955,Je 11,8:7
Johnson, Seesal A
Riders of the Purple Sage 1925,Ap 15,16:1
Johnson, Slim
Petrified Forest, The 1936,F 7,14:2
Johnson, Stan
Song of my Heart 1948,Mr 5,17:3
What Price Glory 1952,Ag 23,10:2
Johnson, Tefft
New Klondike, The 1926,Mr 22,16:1
Johnson, Thomas (Miscellaneous)
Mr Bug Goes to Town 1942,F 20,21:3
Johnson, Tor
Man on the Flying Trapeze 1935,Ag 3,16:2
Abbott and Costello in the Foreign Legion
1950,Ag 14,14:4
Lemon Drop Kid, The 1951,Mr 22,41:2
San Francisco Story, The 1952,My 10,16:4
Johnson, Ulf
Hour of the Wolf 1968,Ap 10,50:2
Johnson, Van
Murder in the Big House 1942,My 8,27:3
War Against Mrs Hadley, The 1942,N 26,40:2
Human Comedy, The 1943,Mr 3,19:2
Pilot No 5 1943,Je 25,13:4
Madame Curie 1943,D 17,23:1
Guy Named Joe, A 1943,D 24,17:2
White Cliffs of Dover, The 1944,My 12,15:2
Three Men in White 1944,My 26,23:3
Two Girls and a Sailor 1944,Je 15,16:1
Thirty Seconds Over Tokyo 1944,N 16,19:1
Between Two Women 1945,Mr 29,18:3
Thrill of a Romance 1945,My 25,22:2
Week-End at the Waldorf 1945,O 5,27:2
Easy to Wed 1946,Jl 12,14:2
No Leave, No Love 1946,O 18,29:2
Till the Clouds Roll By 1946,D 6,27:4
High Barbaree 1947,Je 6,27:2
Romance of Rosy Ridge, The 1947,S 12,18:3
State of the Union 1948,Ap 23,28:1
Bride Goes Wild, The 1948,Je 4,27:2
Command Decision 1949,Ja 20,34:2
Mother is a Freshman 1949,Mr 12,10:2
Scene of the Crime 1949,Jl 29,12:2
In the Good Old Summertime 1949,Ag 5,23:2
Battleground 1949,N 12,8:4
Big Hangover, The 1950,My 26,20:3
Duchess of Idaho 1950,Jl 21,15:3
Grounds for Marriage 1951,Ja 12,24:6
Three Guys Named Mike 1951,Mr 2,21:2
Go for Broke 1951,My 25,31:2
Too Young to Kiss 1951,N 23,32:2
It's a big Country 1952,Ja 9,25:2
Invitation 1952,Ja 30,22:6
When in Rome 1952,My 12,21:2
Washington Story 1952,Jl 2,22:3
Plymouth Adventure 1952,N 14,20:3
Easy to Love 1953,N 27,99:9
Siege at Red River, The 1954,Ap 3,19:2
Men of the Fighting Lady 1954,My 8,15:2
Caine Mutiny, The 1954,Je 25,17:1
Brigadoon 1954,S 17,18:2
Last Time I saw Paris, The 1954,N 19,20:2
End of the Affair, The 1955,Ap 29,28:2
Bottom of the Bottle, The 1956,F 2,19:2
Miracle in the Rain 1956,Ap 2,18:1
23 Paces to Baker Street 1956,My 19,12:6
Slander 1957,Ja 17,34:4
Action of the Tiger 1957,N 14,41:1
Last Blitzkrieg, The 1959,Ja 31,13:5
Enemy General, The 1960,O 20,42:2
Wives and Lovers 1963,Ag 29,36:1
Divorce American Style 1967,Jl 20,30:2
Where Angels Go-Trouble Follows
1968,Ap 11,51:1
Yours, Mine and Ours 1968,Ap 25,53:1
Johnson, Walter
Charlie Chan in London 1934,S 13,26:1
White Parade, The 1934,N 10,19:1
Bright Eyes 1934,D 21,31:1
Fighting Youth 1935,N 2,13:3
Fish 1936,Ja 25,18:5
Freshman Love 1936,Ja 25,18:5
Love on a Bet 1936,Mr 5,25:2
Johnson Brothers
Sensations of 1945 1944,Jl 7,13:2
Johnsson, Bo (Producer)
Hugs and Kisses 1968,Ag 19,44:1
JOHNSTON
See Also JOHNSON, JOHNSTONE
Johnston, Agnes Christine (Original Author)
Village Sleuth 1920,S 13,12:1
Old Fashioned Boy, An 1920,N 1,13:2
Poor Men's Wives 1923,Ja 29,11:1
Nobody's Fool 1936,Je 4,27:2
Johnston, Agnes Christine (Screenwriter)
Twenty-three and a Half Hours' Leave
1919,O 27,9:3
Homer Comes Home 1920,Je 28,13:2
Rich Men's Wives 1922,Ag 21,6:2

Movie Crazy 1932,S 15,19:3
When a Man's a Man 1935,F 22,27:2
Out West With the Hardys 1938,D 9,31:2
Hardys Ride High, The 1939,Ap 14,28:2
Seventeen 1940,F 29,15:2
Life Begins for Andy Hardy 1941,Ag 22,19:4
Courtship of Andy Hardy, The 1942,Ap 10,21:2
Andy Hardy's Double Life 1943,Ja 12,23:3
Andy Hardy's Blonde Trouble 1944,My 5,17:3
Janie 1944,Ag 5,16:2
Janie Gets Married 1946,Je 15,24:2
Black Beauty 1946,Ag 30,13:2
Time, The Place And The Girl, The
1946,D 27,14:3
Black Gold 1947,S 5,16:4
Mickey 1948,Jl 19,11:2
Johnston, Andrew
Sea Hawk, The 1924,Je 3,22:1
Johnston, Anges Christine (Original Author)
Alarm Clock Andy 1920,Mr 15,13:2
Johnston, Anges Christine (Screenwriter)
Show People 1928,N 12,18:2
Johnston, Annie Fellows (Original Author)
Little Colonel, The 1935,Mr 22,26:2
Johnston, Arthur (Composer)
College Humor 1933,Je 23,15:4
Too Much Harmony 1933,S 23,11:5
Murder at the Vanities 1934,My 21,20:2
Many Happy Returns 1934,Je 9,18:2
Belle of the Nineties 1934,S 22,12:2
Gilded Lily, The 1935,F 9,11:2
Thanks a Million 1935,N 14,17:1
Millions in the Air 1935,D 12,33:4
Double or Nothing 1937,S 2,17:3
Sailing Along 1938,Ap 16,17:1
Johnston, Arthur (Miscellaneous)
Pennies From Heaven 1936,D 10,35:2
Johnston, Calvin (Original Author)
Without Limit 1921,Mr 21,11:3
Johnston, Clint (Screenwriter)
Naked Prey, The 1966,Je 15,40:1
Beach Red 1967,Ag 4,18:1
Johnston, Cullen
Power and the Glory, The 1933,Ag 17,13:2
Johnston, Dennis (Screenwriter)
River of Unrest 1937,N 27,21:2
Johnston, Gladys
Hunchback of Notre Dame, The 1923,S 3,9:3
Chechahcos, The 1924,My 19,14:2
Johnston, Isabel (Screenwriter)
Peaceful Valley 1920,O 11,19:3
Johnston, J L
Winds of Chance 1925,Ag 17,10:3
Johnston, J W
Unseeing Eyes 1923,O 22,17:1
New Klondike, The 1926,Mr 22,16:1
Sawdust Paradise, The 1928,Ag 27,23:1
Take Me Home 1928,O 23,33:1
Johnston, Johnnie
Sweater Girl 1942,Jl 13,18:3
Priorities on Parade 1942,Jl 23,19:2
Star Spangled Rhythm 1942,D 31,20:1
This Time for Keeps 1947,D 5,33:4
Man From Texas 1948,Ag 12,16:5
Unchained 1955,Ja 28,15:2
Johnston, Julanne
Thief of Bagdad, The 1924,Mr 19,19:1
Aloma of the South Seas 1926,My 17,19:1
Twinkletoes 1926,D 27,20:3
Venus of Venice 1927,My 3,25:1
Good Time Charley 1927,N 21,20:1
Her Wild Oat 1928,F 6,12:3
Whip Woman, The 1928,F 13,16:2
Oh, Kay! 1928,Ag 27,23:1
Smiling Irish Eyes 1929,Jl 24,23:2
City of Temptation 1929,S 2,16:1
Strictly Modern 1930,My 3,23:1
Johnston, Lorimer
Scaramouche 1923,O 12,7:2 (Incorrect in this
edition; use 1927,O 1,7:2 elsewhere)
Dante's Inferno 1924,S 30,27:3
Top of the World, The 1925,F 17,18:1
Enticement 1925,Mr 21,16:3
Ex-Flame 1931,Ja 24,15:1
Johnston, Margaret
Notorious Gentleman 1946,N 14,39:3
Man About the House, A 1949,Mr 9,33:2
Portrait of Clare 1951,D 26,19:6
Magic Box, The 1952,S 24,40:2
Lovers, Happy Lovers 1954,O 1,19:2
Touch and go 1956,Mr 20,13:2
Model Murder Case, The 1964,N 25,45:1
Life at the Top 1965,D 15,53:1
Psycopath, The 1966,S 29,60:1
Sebastian 1968,Ja 25,33:2
Johnston, Mary (Original Author)
To Have and to Hold 1916,Mr 6,11:1
Audrey 1916,Mr 27,9:2
To Have and to Hold 1922,N 6,13:1
Johnston, Oliver
Indiscreet 1958,Je 27,18:2
Touch of Larceny, A 1960,Mr 17,28:1
Francis of Assisi 1961,Jl 29,8:2

Johnston, Oliver— Cont
Dr Crippen 1964,F 15,14:1
Tomb of Ligeia 1965,My 6,44:1
Countess from Hong Kong, A 1967,Mr 17,35:1
Johnston, Renita
If I Were King 1920,Ag 10,10:3
Johnston, William (Original Author)
When a Feller Needs a Friend 1932,My 14,11:5
Alias Mary Dow 1935,Je 29,16:2
JOHNSTONE
See Also JOHNSON, JOHNSTON
Johnstone, Archie (Screenwriter)
Festival in Moscow 1958,F 17,19:1
Johnstone, Belle
No More Orchids 1933,Ja 2,29:2
Johnstone, Justine
Never the Twain Shall Meet 1925,Jl 29,24:4
Johnstone, Will B (Miscellaneous)
Reported Missing 1922,Ap 24,18:3
Johnstone, Will B (Original Author)
Take It From Me 1926,N 2,35:1
Johnstone, Will B (Screenwriter)
Monkey Business 1931,O 8,22:6
Johnstone, William
Enchantment 1948,D 27,16:2
Titanic 1953,My 28,27:5
Joiner, Pat
Men, The 1950,Jl 21,15:2
Enforcer, The 1951,Ja 26,19:2
Joint, Alf
Goldfinger 1964,D 22,36:1
Jokai, Maurice (Original Author)
Fekete Gyemantok; Black Diamonds
1939,Ap 24,13:2
Joken, Carl
Kabinett des Dr. Larifari, Das 1931,S 11,24:2
Jolivet, Rene (Original Author)
Affaire, L' 1950,N 13,23:2
Jolivet, Rita
Lest We Forget 1918,Ja 28,13:2
Theodora 1921,O 15,16:2
Jolley, I Stanford
Baron of Arizona, The 1950,Je 23,29:2
Curtain Call at Cactus Creek 1950,S 22,35:4
Long, Hot Summer, The 1958,Ap 4,16:1
Jolley, Norman (Screenwriter)
I've Lived Before 1956,Ag 4,13:1
Appointment With a Shadow 1959,Ja 8,24:2
Joloff, Friedrich
Desperate Moment 1953,S 1,19:4
Third Sex, The 1959,Mr 26,27:1
Man on a String 1960,My 21,15:1
Jolson, Al
Vitaphone 1926,O 8,23:2
Jazz Singer, The 1927,O 7,24:4
Singing Fool, The 1928,S 20,33:2
Say It With Songs 1929,Ag 7,29:2
Mammy 1930,Mr 27,24:5
Big Boy 1930,S 13,9:3
Hallelujah, I'm a Bum 1933,F 9,15:2
Wonder Bar 1934,Mr 1,23:2
Go Into Your Dance 1935,My 4,17:2
Singing Kid, The 1936,Ap 4,11:1
Rose of Washington Square 1939,My 6,21:2
Swanee River 1939,D 30,9:2
Rhapsody in Blue 1945,Je 28,22:2
Jolson, Al (Composer)
Hold That Ghost 1941,Ag 8,13:3
Joly, Max (Miscellaneous)
Passionnelle 1948,Mr 1,17:2
Joly, Max (Screenwriter)
Heritage 1940,N 5,33:2
Passionnelle 1948,Mr 1,17:2
Joly, Monique
Take it All; A Tout Prendre 1966,Ap 26,55:1
Joly, Paul (Producer)
Seventh Juror, The 1964,Ja 28,25:1
Jonak, Julius
Last ten Days, The 1956,Ap 12,26:1
Jonasson, Frank
Fighting Coward, The 1924,Mr 17,19:1
Merton of the Movies 1924,S 8,15:3
Top of the World, The 1925,F 17,18:1
Cock O' the Walk 1930,Ap 12,23:1
Jonay, Roberta
Ladies' Man 1947,Ja 13,18:5
Suddenly It's Spring 1947,F 27,26:2
Emperor Waltz, The 1948,Je 18,19:2
Jones, Al Q
Men in War 1957,Mr 20,32:4
Jones, Allan
Reckless 1935,Ap 20,16:1
Night at the Opera, A 1935,D 7,22:1
Rose Marie 1936,F 1,9:2
Show Boat 1936,My 15,29:4
Day at the Races, A 1937,Je 18,25:2
Firefly, The 1937,S 2,17:2
Everybody Sing 1938,Mr 11,15:3
Honeymoon in Bali 1939,S 21,21:1
Great Victor Herbert, The 1939,D 7,35:1
Boys From Syracuse, The 1940,Ag 1,25:2
One Night in the Tropics 1940,D 20,33:2
There's Magic in Music 1941,Je 5,27:2
True to the Army 1942,Je 15,15:4

Jones, Allan— Cont
When Johnny Comes Marching Home
1943,Mr 5,20:4
Jones, Arthur V (Miscellaneous)
Kelly the Second 1936,O 3,21:2
Jones, Arthur V (Original Author)
Pick a Star 1937,My 28,17:2
Frisco Lil 1942,F 12,27:2
Jones, Arthur V (Screenwriter)
Pick a Star 1937,My 28,17:2
Juke Box Jenny 1942,Ap 17,21:3
Jones, Barry
Squadron Leader X 1943,Jl 23,21:2
Frieda 1947,Ag 15,12:3
Madeleine 1950,S 1,17:2
Seven Days to Noon 1950,D 19,41:3
Clouded Yellow, The 1951,N 13,33:2
Island Rescue 1952,Jl 1,19:4
White Corridors 1952,Jl 16,21:1
Plymouth Adventure 1952,N 14,20:3
Return to Paradise 1953,S 11,24:2
Prince Valiant 1954,Ap 7,40:2
Demetrius and the Gladiators 1954,Je 19,9:1
Brigadoon 1954,S 17,18:2
Glass Slipper, The 1955,Mr 25,19:2
Alexander the Great 1956,Mr 29,23:1
War and Peace 1956,Ag 22,26:2
Saint Joan 1957,Je 27,21:1
Safecracker, The 1958,Mr 6,32:1
39 Steps, The 1960,O 11,55:2
Heroes of Telemark, The 1966,Mr 10,26:1
Study in Terror, A 1966,N 3,45:3
Jones, Beulah Hall
Cameo Kirby 1930,F 8,12:5
Drums Along the Mohawk 1939,N 4,11:2
Jones, Billy (Screenwriter)
Falcon out West, The 1944,Mr 18,18:2
Jones, Buck
White Eagle 1932,S 24,18:4
Man Trailer, The 1934,My 23,22:3
Stone of Silver Creek 1935,Ap 8,23:3
Headin' East 1938,Ja 15,19:2
Hollywood Round-Up 1938,Mr 5,11:2
Wagons Westward 1940,Jl 8,13:2
Jones, Burne (Miscellaneous)
Beggar Maid, The 1921,S 26,18:1
Jones, Carolyn
Off Limits 1953,Mr 30,25:5
House of Wax 1953,Ap 11,15:2
Big Heat, The 1953,O 15,43:2
Saracen Blade, The 1954,My 15,13:4
Shield for Murder 1954,Ag 28,8:3
Desiree 1954,N 18,42:1
Seven Year Itch, The 1955,Je 4,9:1
Tender Trap, The 1955,N 11,29:6
Man Who Knew too Much, The 1956,My 17,37:1
Opposite Sex, The 1956,N 16,23:2
Bachelor Party, The 1957,Ap 10,37:2
Baby Face Nelson 1957,D 12,35:1
Marjorie Morningstar 1958,Ap 25,32:2
King Creole 1958,Jl 4,15:2
Man in the Net, The 1959,Je 11,36:2
Hole in the Head, A 1959,Jl 16,31:2
Last Train from Gun Hill 1959,Jl 30,31:2
Career 1959,O 9,24:1
Ice Palace 1960,Je 30,22:1
Sail a Crooked Ship 1962,F 3,12:6
How the West Was Won 1963,Ap 1,54:1
Ticklish Affair, A 1963,Ag 22,19:2
Jones, Charles
Fast Mail, The 1922,Jl 10,9:5
Eleventh Hour, The 1923,Ag 28,12:1
Child of Manhattan 1933,F 13,11:4
Jones, Charles Reed (Original Author)
Enemies of the Law 1931,Jl 13,13:5
Jones, Christopher
Wild in the Streets 1968,My 30,21:1
Jones, Chuck (Screenwriter)
Gay Purr--ee 1962,D 6,55:3
Jones, Clifford
Power and the Glory, The 1933,Ag 17,13:2
Man Who Dared, The 1933,S 9,9:3
Tillie and Gus 1933,N 13,21:1
Catherine the Great 1934,F 15,15:6
Coming-Out Party 1934,Mr 17,11:3
Transient Lady 1935,Mr 11,15:1
Princess O'Hara 1935,Ap 13,11:3
Don't Gamble With Love 1936,Mr 2,13:3
Parole 1936,Je 27,21:1
Girl on the Front Page, The 1936,N 7,15:2
Jones, Constance (Original Author)
Mr Peabody and the Mermaid 1948,Ag 14,6:5
Luck of the Irish, The 1948,S 16,34:1
Jones, Cyril (Miscellaneous)
Tsar to Lenin 1966,My 27,33:3
Jones, Darby
Tarzan Escapes 1936,N 20,27:2
Virginia 1941,Ja 29,21:2
White Cargo 1942,N 27,27:2
I Walked With a Zombie 1943,Ap 22,31:5
Zombies on Broadway 1945,Ap 27,23:2
Zamba 1949,N 7,33:2

Jones, David
Betrayal, The 1948,Je 26,10:5
Shadows 1961,Mr 22,37:1
Head 1968,N 7,51:1
Jones, Dean
Tea and Sympathy 1956,S 28,24:4
Ten Thousand Bedrooms 1957,Ap 4,37:1
Imitation General 1958,Ag 21,22:2
Torpedo Run 1958,O 25,16:2
Night of the Quarter Moon 1959,Mr 5,35:5
Never so Few 1960,Ja 22,15:2
Under the Yum Yum Tree 1963,N 21,43:2
New Interns, The 1964,Ag 20,34:2
Two on a Guillotine 1965,Ja 14,44:3
That Darn Cat 1965,D 3,44:1
Ugly Dachshund, The 1966,Ap 7,45:1
Any Wednesday 1966,O 14,50:1
Monkeys Go Home 1967,Mr 30,55:1
Blackbeard's Ghost 1968,Ap 11,51:3
Horse in the Gray Flannel Suit, The
1968,D 21,49:3
Jones, Dickie
Little Men 1935,F 18,19:3
Daniel Boone 1936,O 24,23:2
Black Legion 1937,Ja 18,21:1
Stella Dallas 1937,Ag 6,21:1
Renfrew of the Royal Mounted 1937,N 3,29:4
Love Is on the Air 1937,N 12,27:3
Kid Comes Back, The 1938,F 7,10:2
Hollywood Round-Up 1938,Mr 5,11:2
Devil's Party, The 1938,My 31,8:3
Man to Remember, A 1938,N 7,23:2
Woman Doctor 1939,Mr 24,27:3
Sergeant Madden 1939,Mr 24,27:2
Destry Rides Again 1939,N 30,25:1
Brigham Young - Frontiersman 1940,S 21,13:2
Howards of Virginia, The 1940,S 27,27:1
Adventure in Washington 1941,Ag 1,11:3
Vanishing Virginian, The 1942,My 28,13:3
Heaven Can Wait 1943,Ag 12,15:1
Adventures of Mark Twain, The 1944,My 4,25:5
Rocky Mountain 1950,N 4,13:2
Fort Worth 1951,Jl 13,12:7
Jones, Dorothy (Screenwriter)
Gay Purr--ee 1962,D 6,55:3
Jones, Duane
Night of the Living Dead 1968,D 5,59:2
Jones, Edna Mae
George White's Scandals 1934,Mr 16,24:2
Cadet Girl 1941,D 11,39:1
Ten Gentlemen From West Point 1942,Je 5,23:3
Jones, Elizabeth
Drums Along the Mohawk 1939,N 4,11:2
Jones, Emrys
One of our Aircraft Is Missing 1942,N 2,17:2
Beware of Pity 1947,N 1,11:2
Nicholas Nickleby 1947,D 1,27:2
Holiday Camp 1948,Ja 24,11:2
This Was a Woman 1949,Ja 5,22:2
Small Back Room, The 1952,F 2,11:3
Three Cases of Murder (You Killed Elizabeth);
You Killed Elizabeth (Three Cases of Murder)
1955,Mr 16,39:4
Trials of Oscar Wilde, The 1960,Je 28,26:1
Jones, Eugene S (Cinematographer)
Face of War, A 1968,My 11,28:1
Jones, Eugene S (Director)
Face of War, A 1968,My 11,28:1
Jones, Eugene S (Producer)
Face of War, A 1968,My 11,28:1
Jones, Evan (Screenwriter)
King and Country 1964,S 24,46:2
Eva 1965,Je 5,21:2
These Are the Damned 1965,Jl 8,35:1
King and Country 1966,Ja 28,20:4
Modesty Blaise 1966,Ag 11,27:1
Funeral in Berlin 1966,D 23,17:1
Jones, F Richard (Director)
Molly O 1921,N 21,20:1
Crossroads of New York, The 1922,My 22,18:4
Country Flapper, The 1922,Jl 31,12:3
Suzanna 1923,Mr 26,16:2
Shriek of Araby, The 1923,Je 11,16:2
Gaucho, The 1927,N 22,32:2
Water Hole, The 1928,S 3,14:2
Bulldog Drummond 1929,My 3,23:2
Jones, Fred C
Fool, The 1925,Ap 13,24:1
Jones, Freddie
Persecution and Assassination of Jean-Paul Marat
as Performed by the Inmates of the Asylum of
Charenton Under the Direction of the Marquis
De Sade, The 1967,F 23,41:1
Jones, Gilbert Hackforth (Screenwriter)
Baby and the Battleship, The 1957,O 1,37:2
Jones, Glyn (Screenwriter)
King's Story, A 1967,My 25,57:2
Jones, Glynis
Invaders, The 1942,Mr 6,17:1
Jones, Gordon
Let 'Em Have It 1935,My 30,21:1
Red Salute 1935,S 30,13:1
Strike Me Pink 1936,Ja 17,15:2

Jones, Gordon— Cont
Devil's Squadron 1936,My 11,16:2
Walking on Air 1936,S 12,20:2
Don't Turn 'em Loose 1936,S 25,20:2
Night Waitress 1936,D 18,31:5
We Who Are About to Die 1937,Ja 2,15:1
China Passage 1937,Ap 16,27:2
There Goes my Girl 1937,Je 12,8:2
Big Shot, The 1937,Ag 13,13:1
Fight for Your Lady 1937,N 20,21:2
Rich Man, Poor Girl 1938,Ag 19,13:3
Out West With the Hardys 1938,D 9,31:2
I Stand Accused 1939,Ja 5,17:1
Big Town Czar 1939,My 4,27:3
Disputed Passage 1939,O 26,27:2
Doctor Takes a Wife, The 1940,Je 15,12:2
You Belong to Me 1941,N 29,14:2
Feminine Touch, The 1941,D 12,35:3
Among the Living 1941,D 13,25:2
True to the Army 1942,Je 15,15:4
They all Kissed the Bride 1942,Jl 31,11:1
Flying Tigers 1942,O 23,25:2
My Sister Eileen 1942,O 23,15:1
Secret Life of Walter Mitty, The 1947,Ag 15,12:2
Wistful Widow of Wagon Gap, The
1947,N 21,36:2
Foreign Affair, A 1948,Jl 1,19:3
Easy Living 1949,O 13,33:3
Tokyo Joe 1949,O 27,35:2
Bodyhold 1949,D 12,29:4
Dear Wife 1950,F 2,31:2
Winning Team, The 1952,Je 21,12:2
Spring Reunion 1957,My 6,25:2
Perfect Furlough, The 1959,Ja 22,27:4
Jones, Griffith
Escape me Never 1935,My 24,24:2
First a Girl 1936,Ja 4,19:1
Revenge of General Ling, The 1938,F 21,15:1
Yank at Oxford, A 1938,F 25,15:1
Mill On the Floss, The 1939,N 15,19:3
Secret Four, The 1940,Ap 22,13:2
Avengers, The 1942,N 25,18:2
Young Man's Fancy, A 1943,D 4,11:2
Henry V 1946,Je 18,30:2
Notorious Gentleman 1946,N 14,39:3
Wicked Lady, The 1946,D 23,19:5
Miranda 1949,Ap 25,20:2
Once Upon a Dream 1949,Jl 15,17:2
Good Time Girl 1950,S 25,18:5
Jones, Grover (Director)
Dangerous Paradise 1930,Mr 2,IX,5:1
Hell and Highwater 1933,D 18,24:4
Jones, Grover (Miscellaneous)
Annapolis Farewell 1935,Ag 24,18:2
Jones, Grover (Narrator)
One Million BC 1940,Ap 27,9:2
Jones, Grover (Original Author)
What a Night! 1928,D 24,11:1
Gun Smoke 1931,Ap 24,27:1
Sky Bride 1932,Ap 23,11:5
Lady and Gent 1932,Jl 16,5:5
Little Bit of Heaven, A 1940,N 8,24:2
Girl, a Guy and a Gob, A 1941,Ap 24,25:3
Jones, Grover (Producer)
Souls at Sea 1937,Ag 10,23:2
Captain Caution 1940,O 21,21:3
Jones, Grover (Screenwriter)
Wedding Bills 1927,Je 29,29:3
Gay Defender, The 1927,D 26,26:6
Partners in Crime 1928,Ap 30,18:3
Take Me Home 1928,O 23,33:1
Derelict 1930,N 22,21:3
Limehouse Blues 1934,D 12,28:2
Lives of a Bengal Lancer, The 1935,Ja 12,12:2
Behold My Wife 1935,F 18,19:3
One Way Ticket 1936,Ja 1,35:2
Trail of the Lonesome Pine, The 1936,F 20,23:5
Milky Way, The 1936,Mr 26,27:2
Souls at Sea 1937,Ag 10,23:2
52d Street 1937,N 15,15:1
Lucky Night 1939,My 5,29:3
Captain Fury 1939,My 26,20:2
Under-Pup, The 1939,S 5,21:2
Abe Lincoln in Illinois 1940,F 23,19:2
Dark Command 1940,My 11,15:2
Captain Caution 1940,O 21,21:3
Shepherd of the Hills, The 1941,Jl 31,13:2
Kid From Brooklyn, The 1946,Ap 19,25:2
Jones, Guy (Original Author)
Mr Peabody and the Mermaid 1948,Ag 14,6:5
Luck of the Irish, The 1948,S 16,34:1
Jones, Hannah
Piccadilly 1929,Jl 15,25:1
Blackmail 1929,O 7,22:1
Jones, Harmon (Director)
As Young as You Feel 1951,Ag 3,10:6
Pride of St Louis, The 1952,My 3,17:5
Bloodhounds of Broadway 1952,N 15,15:2
Kid From Left Field, The 1953,S 26,15:3
City of Bad Men 1953,O 21,37:6
Gorilla at Large 1954,Je 12,13:2
Princess of the Nile 1954,Je 12,13:2
Target Zero 1955,N 16,43:2

Jones, Harry
Soft Cushions 1927,S 12,29:1
Jones, Hazel
Strictly Personal 1933,Mr 20,18:2
Jones, Henry
Lady Says No, The 1952,Ja 7,14:3
Bad Seed, The 1956,S 13,39:6
Girl He Left Behind, The 1956,O 27,17:1
Girl Can't Help It, The 1957,F 9,12:7
3:10 to Yuma 1957,Ag 29,22:1
Will Success Spoil Rock Hunter 1957,S 12,37:5
Cash McCall 1960,Ja 28,26:1
Bramble Bush, The 1960,F 25,34:2
Angel Baby 1961,O 5,43:1
Never too Late 1965,N 5,28:1
Champagne Murders, The 1968,Ap 25,53:1
Jones, Henry Arthur (Original Author)
Lie, The 1918,Ap 15,13:3
Silver King, The 1919,Ja 13,9:3
Society Exile, A 1919,Ag 18,9:2
Beyond 1921,S 5,12:4
Silver King, The 1929,S 2,16:1
Jones, Herbert A Commander (Original Author)
Suicide Fleet 1931,N 23,22:1
Jones, Ike
Prisoner of War 1954,My 10,20:2
Jones, Ike (Producer)
Man Called Adam, A 1966,Ag 4,24:2
Jones, Isaac
Joe Louis Story, The 1953,N 4,29:4
About Mrs Leslie 1954,Je 28,16:2
Anna Lucasta 1959,Ja 15,27:1
Jones, Jack (Screenwriter)
Proud Valley 1941,My 17,19:2
Jones, James (Original Author)
From Here to Eternity 1953,Ag 6,16:2
Some Came Running 1959,Ja 23,17:1
Thin Red Line, The 1964,O 29,38:1
Jones, James (Screenwriter)
Longest Day, The 1962,O 5,28:1
Jones, James Earl
Dr Strangelove or: How I Learned to Stop
Worrying and Love the Bomb 1964,Ja 31,16:1
(Incorrect in this edition; use 1964,Ja 30,24:1
elsewhere)
Comedians, The 1967,N 1,37:1
Jones, Jane
Slave Ship 1937,Je 17,19:2
Port of Missing Girls, The 1938,Ap 4,12:5
East Side of Heaven 1939,My 5,29:3
Night Song 1948,Ja 29,27:5
Jones, Jennifer
Song of Bernadette, The 1944,Ja 27,15:2
Since You Went Away 1944,Jl 21,16:2
Love Letters 1945,Ag 27,22:3
Cluny Brown 1946,Je 3,27:3
Duel in the Sun 1947,My 8,30:2
Portrait of Jennie 1949,Mr 30,31:2
We Were Strangers 1949,Ap 28,28:2
Madame Bovary 1949,Ag 26,15:2
Wild Heart, The 1952,My 29,17:2
Carrie 1952,Jl 17,20:2
Ruby Gentry 1952,D 26,20:2
Beat the Devil 1954,Mr 13,11:2
Indiscretion of an American Wife 1954,Je 26,7:2
Love Is a Many-Splendored Thing
1955,Ag 19,10:1
Good Morning, Miss Dove 1955,N 24,41:1
Man in the Gray Flannel Suit, The
1956,Ap 13,21:1
Barretts of Wimpole Street, The 1957,Ja 18,15:3
Farewell to Arms, A 1958,Ja 25,14:1
Tender is the Night 1962,Ja 20,13:2
Idol, The 1966,Ag 11,27:1
Jones, Jenny
Front Page Story 1955,Ap 19,28:1
Devil's Disciple, The 1959,Ag 21,12:1
Jones, John Glyn
Convoy 1941,Ja 17,21:2
Jones, John Paul
Parole Girl 1933,Ap 10,8:2
Jones, John R
Island of Allah 1956,Je 27,35:1
Jones, Johnny
Edgar and the Teacher's Pet 1920,Mr 28,V,9:1
Edgar's Little Saw 1920,D 27,11:3
Old Nest, The 1921,Je 29,10:3
Jones, Juan
Summerskin 1962,My 29,22:2
Jones, L Q
Annapolis Story, An 1955,Ap 9,8:2
Target Zero 1955,N 16,43:2
Santiago 1956,Jl 14,13:2
Toward the Unknown 1956,S 28,24:4
Operation Mad Ball 1957,N 21,38:1
Young Lions, The 1958,Ap 3,23:1
Naked and the Dead, The 1958,Ag 7,21:1
Torpedo Run 1958,O 25,16:2
Flaming Star 1960,D 17,19:1
Ride the High Country 1962,Je 21,26:2
Major Dundee 1965,Ap 8,45:1

Jones, LeRoi (Screenwriter)
Dutchman 1967,F 28,32:1
Jones, Macon
Whom the Gods Destroy 1934,Jl 13,14:2
Jones, Marc Edmund (Original Author)
Skin Deep 1922,O 23,10:1
Jones, Marcia Mae
Night Nurse 1931,Jl 17,23:4
Champ, The 1931,N 10,29:4
These Three 1936,Mr 19,22:4
Mountain Justice 1937,My 13,31:2
Life of Emile Zola, The 1937,Ag 12,14:2
Heidi 1937,N 6,14:2
Lady Behave 1938,Ja 28,17:3
Adventures of Tom Sawyer, The 1938,F 18,23:1
Mad About Music 1938,Mr 12,13:2
Little Princess, The 1939,Mr 11,21:1
First Love 1939,N 9,27:3
Meet Doctor Christian 1939,D 1,27:2
Dr Kildare's Strange Case 1940,Ap 12,19:2
Anne of Windy Poplars 1940,Ag 23,13:3
Nice Girl 1941,Mr 27,29:6
Youngest Profession, The 1943,Je 25,13:3
Top Man 1943,O 29,23:2
Snafu 1945,D 26,15:2
Street Corner 1948,D 4,9:4
Daughter of Rosie O'Grady, The
1950,Mr 31,36:2
Jones, Mark
Persecution and Assassination of Jean-Paul Marat
as Performed by the Inmates of the Asylum of
Charenton Under the Direction of the Marquis
De Sade, The 1967,F 23,41:1
Jones, Marry
Magic Box, The 1952,S 24,40:2
Jones, Maurice
Mr Perrin and Mr Traill 1949,Ja 17,15:2
Oliver Twist 1951,Jl 31,17:2
Jones, Morgan
Forbidden Planet 1956,My 4,21:2
Jones, Olive
Goose and the Gander, The 1935,S 12,29:2
Jones, Park
Deliverance 1919,Ag 19,10:1
Old Nest, The 1921,Je 29,10:3
Jones, Parry
Waltz Time 1933,S 29,24:2
Jones, Pat
Slow Run 1968,O 11,39:1
Jones, Paul
Privilege 1967,Jl 25,30:2
Jones, Paul (Producer)
Never Say Die 1939,Mr 9,18:1
I'm From Missouri 1939,Mr 23,27:1
Untamed 1940,Jl 25,14:3
Great McGinty, The 1940,Ag 15,23:1
Lady Eve, The 1941,F 26,17:1
Road to Zanzibar 1941,Ap 10,29:2
Kiss the Boys Goodbye 1941,Ag 14,21:2
Sullivan's Travels 1942,Ja 29,25:2
Medal for Benny, A 1945,My 24,15:2
Hold That Blonde 1945,N 8,17:2
Road to Utopia 1946,F 28,20:2
Virginian, The 1946,Ap 18,22:2
Monsieur Beaucaire 1946,S 5,23:1
Dear Ruth 1947,Je 11,33:3
Where There's Life 1947,D 25,32:1
Southern Yankee, A 1948,N 25,47:2
My Favorite Spy 1951,D 26,19:3
Girls of Pleasure Island, The 1953,My 16,10:1
Caddy, The 1953,S 18,16:6
Here Come the Girls 1953,D 26,10:1
Casanova's Big Night 1954,Ap 19,19:1
Living It Up 1954,Jl 24,6:6
You're Never too Young 1955,Ag 26,10:2
Birds and the Bees, The 1956,Ap 23,22:1
Pardners 1956,Jl 26,20:2
It's Only Money 1962,N 22,43:1
Who's Minding the Store? 1963,N 29,67:6
(Incorrect in this edition; use 1963,N 28,67:6
elsewhere)
Jones, Paul M (Original Author)
You're Telling Me 1934,Ap 7,19:1
Jones, Paul Whitsun
Tunes of Glory 1960,D 21,38:2
Jones, Peggy Ann
Mikado, The 1967,Mr 15,53:1
Jones, Peter
Blue Lagoon, The 1949,O 3,13:2
Chance of a Lifetime 1951,Mr 15,37:2
Browning Version, The 1951,O 30,33:2
Miss Robin Hood 1953,Je 27,7:2
Private's Progress 1956,Jl 24,19:2
School for Scoundrels 1960,Jl 12,39:1
Romanoff and Juliet 1961,Je 9,26:1
Never Let Go 1963,Je 15,10:2
Jones, Peter (Screenwriter)
Always a Bride 1954,My 28,19:2
Jones, Raymond F (Original Author)
This Island Earth 1955,Je 11,8:7
Jones, Robert Earl
Wild River 1960,My 27,22:1
One Potato, Two Potato 1964,Jl 30,16:1

Jones, Robert Earl— Cont
Terror in the City 1966,N 9,43:4
Jones, Robert Edmond (Miscellaneous)
Becky Sharp 1935,Je 14,27:2
Dancing Pirate 1936,Je 18,19:1
Jones, Shirley
Oklahoma! 1955,O 11,49:1
Carousel 1956,F 17,13:1
April Love 1957,N 28,57:2
Never Steal Anything Small 1959,F 12,23:1
Elmer Gantry 1960,Jl 8,16:1
Pepe 1960,D 22,18:1
Two Rode Together 1961,Jl 27,23:3
Music Man, The 1962,Ag 24,14:1
Courtship of Eddie's Father, The 1963,Mr 7,8:5
(Incorrect in this edition; use 1963,Mr 28,8:5
elsewhere)
Ticklish Affair, A 1963,Ag 22,19:2
Dark Purpose 1964,F 6,36:4
Bedtime Story 1964,Je 11,27:1
Fluffy 1965,O 21,57:2
Secret of my Success, The 1965,N 4,57:2
Jones, Spike and His City Slickers
Thank Your Lucky Stars 1943,O 2,19:2
Meet The People 1944,S 8,16:2
Breakfast in Hollywood 1946,Jl 15,21:1
Ladies' Man 1947,Ja 13,18:5
Jones, Stan
Rio Grande 1950,N 20,21:2
Great Locomotive Chase, The 1956,Je 27,35:1
Horse Soldiers, The 1959,Je 26,13:1
Jones, Stan (Composer)
Wagonmaster 1950,Je 19,17:2
Jones, Tiny
Greed 1924,D 5,28:1
Man From Blankley's, The 1930,Mr 29,23:1
Jones, W W
America 1924,F 22,20:1
Jones, Winston (Director)
Unidentified Flying Objects 1956,Je 13,46:2
Jonson, Ben (Original Author)
Volpone 1947,D 27,9:3
Jonson, Julian
Sara Laer Sig Folkvett 1938,F 16,17:1
Joost, Eddie
Safe at Home 1941,N 26,31:2
Joplin, Gareth
King of Burlesque 1936,Ja 16,25:2
Joppolo, Benjamin (Original Author)
Carabiniers, Les 1967,S 28,58:3
Carabiniers, Les 1968,Ap 26,31:1
Jorda, Lou
Safe at Home 1941,N 26,31:2
Jordan, Anne (Original Author)
Luckiest Girl in the World, The 1936,D 5,16:3
Jordan, Bobby
Dead End 1937,Ag 25,25:1
Slight Case of Murder, A 1938,F 28,19:1
Crime School 1938,My 11,17:2
Reformatory 1938,Je 27,13:6
My Bill 1938,Jl 7,22:4
Angels With Dirty Faces 1938,N 26,18:1
They Made Me a Criminal 1939,Ja 21,19:2
Off the Record 1939,F 18,12:2
Hell's Kitchen 1939,Jl 3,10:5
Angels Wash Their Faces 1939,S 4,16:2
Dust Be my Destiny 1939,O 7,11:2
Dress Parade 1939,O 28,11:2
Young Tom Edison 1940,Mr 15,27:2
You're not so Tough 1940,Jl 9,25:3
Military Academy 1940,Ag 5,10:4
Ghost Creeps, The 1940,Ag 19,13:3
Give Us Wings 1940,N 21,43:3
Pride of the Bowery 1941,Ja 24,15:2
Flying Wild 1941,Ap 12,19:3
Bowery Blitzkrieg 1941,O 1,24:5
Spooks Run Wild 1941,N 1,20:3
Mr Wise Guy 1942,Mr 5,27:2
Jordan, Charles
Penrod and his Twin Brother 1938,Ap 18,11:1
Native Land 1942,My 12,16:3
711 Ocean Drive 1950,Jl 20,21:2
Edge of the City 1957,Ja 30,33:2
Terror in the City 1966,N 9,43:4
Jordan, Dorothy
Taming of the Shrew, The 1929,N 30,23:1
Devil May Care 1929,D 23,18:2
In Gay Madrid 1930,Je 7,10:4
Call of the Flesh 1930,S 13,9:3
Love in the Rough 1930,S 27,21:3
Min and Bill 1930,N 24,26:5
Tailor-Made Man, A 1931,Ap 25,23:4
Young Sinners 1931,My 9,15:4
Shipmates 1931,My 23,13:4
Beloved Bachelor, The 1931,O 17,20:1
Hell Divers 1931,D 23,27:3
Lost Squadron, The 1932,Mr 11,15:4
Wet Parade, The 1932,Ap 22,23:2
Roadhouse Murder 1932,Ap 29,13:4
Down to Earth 1932,S 2,19:2
70,000 Witnesses 1932,S 3,16:2
Cabin in the Cotton 1932,S 30,17:3
That's my Boy 1932,N 21,21:1
Strictly Personal 1933,Mr 20,18:2

Jordan, Dorothy— Cont
Bondage 1933,Ap 24,11:3
One Man's Journey 1933,S 1,15:2
Sun Shines Bright, The 1954,Mr 17,25:2
Jordan, Egon v
Richthofen: The Red Knight of the Air
1929,S 2,16:1
Jordan, Elizabeth (Original Author)
Make Way for a Lady 1936,D 12,15:1
Jordan, Henry (Original Author)
Johnny Stool Pigeon 1949,S 23,28:3
Jordan, Jack
Best Foot Forward 1943,Je 30,25:2
Jordan, Jim
This Way Please 1937,O 8,27:2
Look Who's Laughing 1941,D 25,33:2
Here We Go Again 1942,O 12,12:3
Heavenly Days 1944,O 21,15:2
Jordan, Joanne
Farmer Takes a Wife, The 1953,Je 13,11:2
Bottom of the Bottle, The 1956,F 2,19:2
Faces 1968,S 23,42:4
Jordan, Kate (Original Author)
Poor Little Peppina 1916,F 21,9:2
Time, the Comedian 1925,D 14,18:2
Transgression 1931,Je 15,23:3
Jordan, Louis and Orchestra
Follow the Boys 1944,Ap 26,24:6
Jordan, Marian
This Way Please 1937,O 8,27:2
Look Who's Laughing 1941,D 25,33:2
Here We Go Again 1942,O 12,12:3
Heavenly Days 1944,O 21,15:2
Jordan, Miriam
Six Hours to Live 1932,O 22,18:4
Sherlock Holmes 1932,N 12,20:5
Dangerously Yours 1933,F 23,20:3
I Loved You Wednesday 1933,Je 16,20:2
Let's Fall in Love 1934,Ja 22,12:3
Jordan, Patrick
Man Upstairs, The 1959,Ag 11,23:2
Jordan, Pierre
Heart of a Nation, The 1943,Ap 8,27:2
Jordan, Sid
Deadwood Coach, The 1925,Ja 21,19:3
Dude Ranger, The 1934,O 2,18:5
Hollywood Cowboy 1937,Jl 24,12:1
Jordon, Kerry
Zulu 1964,Jl 8,38:1
Jordon, Romaine
William Tell 1925,My 20,26:2
Jorge, Paul
Miserables, Les 1926,Jl 9,17:1
Miserables, Les 1927,Ag 23,29:4
Passion Of Joan Of Arc, The 1929,Mr 29,21:1
Jory, Nicholas (Screenwriter)
New Wine 1942,F 2,11:2
Jory, Victor
Second Hand Wife 1933,Ja 14,8:4
Big Pay-Off, The 1933,Ja 17,22:7
State Fair 1933,Ja 27,13:2
Broadway Bad 1933,Mr 6,16:6
Sailor's Luck 1933,Mr 17,21:2
Infernal Machine 1933,Ap 8,16:3
Trick for Trick 1933,Je 10,16:4
I Loved You Wednesday 1933,Je 16,20:2
Devil's in Love, The 1933,Jl 28,18:2
My Woman 1933,O 16,20:3
Smoky 1934,Ja 1,28:2
I Believed in You 1934,Ap 11,25:3
Murder in Trinidad 1934,My 16,22:2
He Was her Man 1934,My 17,28:2
Madame Du Barry 1934,O 25,26:2
Midsummer Night's Dream, A 1935,O 10,31:1
Escape from Devil's Island 1935,N 25,22:2
King Steps Out, The 1936,My 29,15:2
Meet Nero Wolfe 1936,Jl 16,20:1
Bulldog Drummond at Bay 1937,O 25,23:2
First Lady 1937,D 23,25:1
Adventures of Tom Sawyer, The 1938,F 18,23:1
Wings of the Navy 1939,F 4,11:1
Blackwell's Island 1939,Mr 2,19:1
Dodge City 1939,Ap 8,19:1
Women in the Wind 1939,Ap 13,27:2
Man of Conquest 1939,Ap 28,31:2
Susannah of the Mounties 1939,Je 24,13:2
Each Dawn I Die 1939,Jl 22,12:2
I Stole a Million 1939,Ag 7,11:2
Gone With the Wind 1939,D 20,31:2
Lone Wolf Meets a Lady, The 1940,Je 17,19:2
River's End 1940,Ag 26,11:4
Cherokee Strip 1940,N 4,23:2
Give Us Wings 1940,N 21,43:3
Lady With red Hair 1940,D 6,28:2
Bad Men of Missouri 1941,Ag 16,18:2
Tombstone, The Town too Tough to Die
1942,Jl 27,18:2
Kansan, The 1943,O 1,15:3
Loves of Carmen, The 1948,S 3,16:2
Gallant Blade 1948,O 13,31:3
South of St Louis 1949,Mr 7,17:2
Canadian Pacific 1949,My 20,32:4
Fighting Man of the Plains 1949,N 17,35:6
Capture, The 1950,My 20,8:6

Cariboo Trail, The 1950,S 1,17:2
Son of Ali Baba 1952,Ag 16,7:4
Man From the Alamo, The 1953,S 12,13:2
Cat-Women of the Moon 1954,Mr 20,10:7
Valley of the Kings 1954,Jl 22,15:2
Blackjack Ketchum Desperado 1956,Ap 5,26:2
Death of a Scoundrel 1956,N 6,30:1
Fugitive Kind, The 1960,Ap 15,13:1
Miracle Worker, The 1962,My 24,29:2
Cheyenne Autumn 1964,D 24,8:1
Jigsaw 1968,Je 6,54:2
Josane, Lola
Pawns of Passion 1929,My 27,22:1
Jose, Edward (Director)
Private Peat 1918,O 14,15:1
Woman of Impulse, A 1918,O 21,15:1
My Cousin 1918,N 25,11:3
Fires of Faith 1919,My 6,16:2
Isle of Conquest, The 1919,O 27,9:3
Fighting Shepherdess, The 1920,Mr 29,18:1
Riddle Woman, The 1920,N 8,20:2
Prodigal Judge, The 1922,F 5,VI,3:1 (In
Addenda)
Daughter of Israel, A 1928,My 21,25:1
Jose, Jaspe
Queen of the Pirates 1961,Jl 27,23:4
Josef, Ben
Faithful City 1952,Ap 8,35:2
Joselillo, Novillero
Torero! 1957,My 22,29:2
Joseph, A (Original Author)
Be Mine Tonight 1933,Ap 14,22:5
Hitler's Madman 1943,Ag 28,15:1
Joseph, Edmund (Original Author)
Bowery to Broadway 1944,N 30,19:2
Joseph, Edmund (Screenwriter)
Yankee Doodle Dandy 1942,My 30,9:1
Who Done It 1942,D 3,35:2
Make Your own Bed 1944,My 27,12:2
Bowery to Broadway 1944,N 30,19:2
Naughty Nineties, The 1945,Je 21,16:2
Joseph, Michael (Miscellaneous)
Brewster's Millions 1935,Ap 8,23:3
Joseph, Peter (Director)
Richthofen: The Red Knight of the Air
1929,S 2,16:1
Joseph, Robert (Producer)
Third Secret, The 1964,Ap 29,27:1
Joseph, Robert (Screenwriter)
Hitch-Hiker, The 1953,Ap 30,39:3
Third Secret, The 1964,Ap 29,27:1
Josephson, Erland
Magician, The 1959,Ag 28,27:1
Brink of Life; (Nara Livet) 1959,N 9,36:2
Hour of the Wolf 1968,Ap 10,50:2
Josephson, Erland (Screenwriter)
All These Women 1964,O 6,35:1
Josephson, Julien (Screenwriter)
Home Spun Folks 1920,O 4,14:3
Man Unconquerable, The 1922,Jl 17,16:3
Brass 1923,Mr 12,18:1
Main Street 1923,Je 12,22:2
Ship Comes in, A 1928,S 4,21:2
Wee Willie Winkie 1937,Jl 24,12:1
Heidi 1937,N 6,14:2
Suez 1938,O 15,21:2
Stanley and Livingstone 1939,Ag 5,18:2
Rains Came, The 1939,S 9,11:2
Great Gildersleeve, The 1942,D 18,36:8
Happy Land 1943,D 9,33:3
Josephson, Matthew (Original Author)
Toast of New York, The 1937,Jl 23,16:2
Josephson, Sam
Power of Life 1938,Ap 29,17:2
Josephson, Saul
Power of Life 1938,Ap 29,17:2
Josephy, Alvin (Original Author)
Captive City, The 1952,Mr 27,34:2
Operation Secret 1952,N 6,37:2
Something for the Birds 1952,N 15,15:2
Josephy, Alvin (Screenwriter)
Captive City, The 1952,Mr 27,34:2
Josipovich, Dagmar
Romeo and Juliet 1954,D 22,28:1
Josipovici, Jean (Director)
Flesh and Desire 1958,N 27,52:4
Josipovici, Jean (Screenwriter)
Flesh and Desire 1958,N 27,52:4
Joslin, Howard
Quebec 1951,Mr 16,34:2
Detective Story 1951,N 7,35:2
Joslyn, Allyn
They Won't Forget 1937,Jl 15,16:1
Expensive Husbands 1938,Ja 8,19:3
Hollywood Hotel 1938,Ja 13,17:3
Sweethearts 1938,D 23,16:2
Shining Hour, The 1939,Ja 20,15:2
Cafe Society 1939,F 23,19:2
Only Angels Have Wings 1939,My 12,25:2
Fast and Furious 1939,O 12,33:3
If I Had my Way 1940,My 6,13:2
Great McGinty, The 1940,Ag 15,23:1
No Time for Comedy 1940,S 7,9:2

Joslyn, Allyn— Cont
Spring Parade 1940,O 4,29:2
This Thing Called Love 1941,F 14,15:2
I Wake up Screaming 1942,Ja 17,13:2
Bedtime Story 1942,Mr 20,25:4
Wife Takes a Flyer, The 1942,Je 19,19:1
My Sister Eileen 1942,O 23,15:1
Immortal Sergeant 1943,F 4,29:2
Heaven Can Wait 1943,Ag 12,15:1
Impostor, The 1944,Mr 27,17:2
Bride by Mistake 1944,S 16,20:2
Sweet and Low Down 1944,O 19,19:2
Horn Blows at Midnight, The 1945,Ap 21,18:2
Junior Miss 1945,Je 18,15:4
Colonel Effingham's Raid 1946,Ap 5,21:3
Thrill of Brazil, The 1946,S 6,18:3
It Shouldn't Happen to a Dog 1946,S 7,11:2
Shocking Miss Pilgrim, The 1947,F 12,34:2
If You Knew Susie 1948,F 23,19:2
Moonrise 1949,Mr 7,17:2
Lady Takes a Sailor, The 1949,D 17,15:2
Harriet Craig 1950,N 3,31:2
As Young as You Feel 1951,Ag 3,10:6
Jazz Singer, The 1953,Ja 14,27:3
I Love Melvin 1953,Ap 10,18:4
Titanic 1953,My 28,27:5
Island in the Sky 1953,S 10,22:2
Fastest Gun Alive, The 1956,Jl 13,23:3
Public Pigeon No 1 1957,My 18,23:2
Joslyn, Don
Hoodlum Priest, The 1961,Ap 3,28:5
Jostyn, Jay
Kiss of Death 1947,Ag 28,28:2
Josyane
Morgane, the Enchantress 1929,Je 21,17:2
As du Turf, Les; Acres of Turf 1935,My 11,21:3
Marie-Louise 1945,N 13,24:2
Josz, Marcel
We Lived Through Buchenwald 1947,Jl 24,27:3
Jou-Jerville, Jacques
Enigmatique Monsieur Parkes, L' 1930,S 2,19:3
Jouanneau, Jacques
Crazy in the Noodle 1957,D 15,45:4 (Incorrect in
this edition; use 1957,D 17,45:4 elsewhere)
Elusive Corporal, The 1963,F 19,5:1
Judex 1966,Ap 26,55:1
Joube, Romuald
J'Accuse 1920,My 23,VI,2:2
I Accuse; (J'Accuse) 1921,O 10,16:1
Miracle of the Wolves, The 1925,F 24,17:3
Miracle des Loups, Le 1930,Jl 28,22:1
Passion of St Francis, The 1932,D 17,22:3
Jourdan, Andre
Shameless Old Lady, The 1966,S 27,52:1
Jourdan, Catherine
Girl on a Motorcycle, The 1968,N 28,66:5
Jourdan, Louis
Her First Affair; (Children of Paradise)
1947,F 20,32:3
Vie de Boheme, La 1947,N 28,37:4
Paradine Case, The 1948,Ja 9,26:2
Letters From an Unknown Woman
1948,Ap 29,20:6
No Minor Vices 1949,F 26,11:2
Madame Bovary 1949,Ag 26,15:2
Twilight 1949,D 30,13:2
Bird of Paradise 1951,Mr 15,37:2
Anne of the Indies 1951,O 25,36:3
Happy Time, The 1952,O 31,30:2
Decameron Nights 1953,N 17,38:2
Three Coins in the Fountain 1954,My 21,18:2
Swan, The 1956,Ap 27,21:5
Julie 1956,N 22,51:1
Bride Is Much too Beautiful, The 1958,Ja 21,35:1
Gigi 1958,My 16,21:1
Dangerous Exile 1958,O 11,18:3
Best of Everything 1959,O 9,24:2
Can-Can 1960,Mr 10,36:1
Story of Monte Cristo, The 1962,N 7,48:1
V I P's, The 1963,S 20,29:1
Disorder 1964,My 26,44:2
Made in Paris 1966,F 17,29:1
Flea in her Ear, A 1968,N 28,66:1
Jourdan, Pierre
Midnight in Paris 1947,O 9,32:3
Rouge et Noir 1958,Ap 9,42:1
Jourdan, Raymond
Picnic on the Grass 1960,O 12,47:1
Rise of Louis XIV, The 1967,S 26,54:2
Jourfier, Lucienne
Barber of Seville 1949,Jl 21,21:2
Journet, Marcel
Foxes of Harrow, The 1947,S 25,35:4
To the Ends of the Earth 1948,F 13,26:2
Letters From an Unknown Woman
1948,Ap 29,20:6
Sealed Verdict 1948,N 3,36:2
Desperate Decision 1954,N 9,31:5
Jouvenet, Pierre
Stolen Life 1939,Je 15,27:2
Jouvet, Louis
Topaze 1935,F 16,9:2
Kermesse Heroique, La 1936,S 23,29:1
Dr Knock 1937,My 1,16:4

Jouvet, Louis— Cont
Lower Depths, The 1937,S 11,20:1
Carnet de Bal, Un 1938,Mr 26,12:1
Bizarre, Bizarre 1939,Mr 21,27:2
Alibi, L' 1939,Ap 10,13:3
Curtain Rises, The 1939,Ap 22,15:2
End of a Day, The 1939,S 12,28:4
Marseillaise 1939,N 6,20:2
Charrette Fantome, La 1940,My 28,29:2
Schubert's Serenade 1940,S 3,21:2
Hotel du Nord 1940,D 30,21:2
Compliments of Mr Iflow 1941,F 17,10:7
Heart of a Nation, The 1943,Ap 8,27:2
drame De Shanghai; Shanghai Drama, The
 1945,Ja 11,19:2
Barge-Keeper's Daughter, The 1945,S 6,23:3
Sirocco 1946,Ag 12,17:3
Volpone 1947,D 27,9:3
Lover's Return, A; Revenant, Le 1948,Ja 26,15:2
Jenny Lamour 1948,Mr 6,17:2
Confessions of a Rogue 1948,Mr 30,26:3
Street of Shadows 1948,N 20,9:2
Monelle 1950,F 3,29:2
Between Eleven and Midnight 1950,F 23,33:3
Miquette 1951,F 5,18:2
Lady Paname 1951,Mr 20,35:4
Ramuntcho 1953,Mr 2,19:2
Dr Knock 1955,O 10,31:2
Jouvet, Louis (Director)
Dr Knock 1937,My 1,16:4
Jouvet, Louis (Miscellaneous)
Dr Knock 1955,O 10,31:2
Joux, Francois
Antoine and Antoinette 1948,Ap 16,29:2
Not Guilty 1948,Ap 23,28:2
Royal Affair, A; (Roi, Le) 1950,Mr 9,25:2
We Are all Murderers 1957,Ja 9,27:2
Julietta 1957,Je 18,38:2
Jovanovic, Gordana
I Even Met Happy Gypsies 1968,Mr 21,57:1
Jowitt, Anthony
Little French Girl, The 1925,Je 1,10:3
Coast of Folly, The 1925,Ag 31,19:3
Splendid Crime, The 1925,D 17,27:1
Call Her Savage 1932,N 25,19:2
Joy, Beatrice
Manslaughter 1922,S 18,14:2
Joy, Dennis
If Winter Comes 1948,Ja 23,28:4
Joy, Gloria
Old Fashioned Boy, An 1920,N 1,13:2
Joy, Leatrice
Bunty Pulls the Strings 1921,Ja 9,VI,2:1 (In
 Addenda)
Tale of Two Worlds, A 1921,Mr 14,9:2
Marriage Cheat, The 1921,Je 2,14:3
Ladies Must Live 1921,N 21,20:1
You Can't Fool Your Wife 1923,Ap 24,25:3
Hollywood 1923,Jl 30,11:4
Silent Partner, The 1923,Ag 20,4:2
Triumph 1924,Ap 21,21:4
Changing Husbands 1924,Je 23,22:4
Dressmaker from Paris, The 1925,Mr 18,19:2
Hell's Highroad 1925,Ag 26,14:2
For Alimony Only 1926,S 21,33:1
Nobody's Widow 1927,Ja 13,29:1
Vanity 1927,Je 15,31:4
Angel of Broadway 1927,N 1,21:1 (In Addenda)
Blue Danube, The 1928,Ap 30,18:3
Man Made Women 1928,S 18,33:2
Bellamy Trial, The 1929,Ja 24,30:5
Strong Boy 1929,Ap 1,22:1
Most Immoral Lady, A 1929,O 21,30:1
First Love 1939,N 9,27:3
Red Stallion in the Rockies 1949,Ag 26,15:2
Show People 1967,O 2,58:2
Joy, Nicholas
Dishonored Lady 1947,My 24,10:5
Gentleman's Agreement 1947,N 12,36:2
Daisy Kenyon 1947,D 25,32:1
Iron Curtain, The 1948,My 13,31:2
Fuller Brush Man, The 1948,My 15,18:2
Larceny 1948,S 4,8:6
Bride of Vengeance 1949,Ap 7,38:2
Sun comes up, The 1949,My 13,29:2
Great Gatsby, The 1949,Jl 14,20:5
Abbott and Costello Meet the Killer Boris Karloff
 1949,S 19,18:3
And Baby Makes Three 1949,D 23,17:3
Native Son 1951,Je 18,19:2
Here Comes the Groom 1951,S 21,19:2
Man With a Cloak, The 1951,N 28,37:2
Affair With a Stranger 1953,Jl 11,8:2
Desk Set 1957,My 16,28:2
Joyce, Alice
Courage of Silence, The 1917,Ja 29,11:2
Within the Law 1917,Ap 30,11:3
Lion and the Mouse, The 1919,F 17,11:3
Green Goddess, The 1923,Ag 15,21:1
Daddy's Gone A-Hunting 1925,F 24,17:3
Little French Girl, The 1925,Je 1,10:3
Home Maker, The 1925,Ag 10,8:2
Stella Dallas 1925,N 17,30:2
Mannequinn 1926,Ja 12,27:5

Dancing Mothers 1926,F 18,21:1
Beau Geste 1926,Ag 26,17:3
Ace of Cads, The 1926,O 18,18:1 (In Addenda)
So's Your Old Man 1926,N 1,28:2
Sorrell and Son 1927,N 14,26:1
13 Washington Square 1928,Ja 30,18:1
Noose, The 1928,Mr 19,26:4
Squall, The 1929,My 10,32:5
Green Goddess, The 1930,F 14,20:1
Song O' my Heart 1930,Mr 12,32:6
He Knew Women 1930,Ap 23,24:1
Joyce, Brenda
Rains Came, The 1939,S 9,11:2
Here I Am a Stranger 1939,S 30,11:2
Little Old New York 1940,F 3,9:2
Maryland 1940,Jl 13,16:5
Public Deb No 1 1940,S 18,19:2
Private Nurse 1941,Ag 29,13:3
Marry the Boss's Daughter 1941,D 4,33:4
Whispering Ghosts 1942,My 18,19:4
Little Tokyo, USA 1942,Ag 7,13:2
Tarzan and the Amazons 1945,Ap 30,13:4
Strange Confession 1945,N 8,17:3
Enchanted Forest, The 1945,D 17,17:2
Pillow of Death 1946,Ja 26,19:3
Tarzan and the Leopard Woman 1946,F 11,25:2
Spider Woman Strikes Back, The 1946,Mr 23,8:3
Little Giant 1946,My 9,27:5
Tarzan and the Huntress 1947,Ap 7,20:4
Tarzan and the Mermaids 1948,Mr 30,26:4
Tarzan's Magic Fountain 1949,F 7,15:2
Joyce, Debbie
Private's Affair, A 1959,Ag 15,8:7
Joyce, Dorothy
Blue Bird, The 1940,Ja 20,11:2
Joyce, Eileen
Battle for Music 1945,O 15,13:2
Girl in a Million, A 1950,Jl 24,15:2
Joyce, Jack
New Lives for Old 1925,F 25,16:7
Joyce, James
Too Late Blues 1962,Mr 1,27:4
Joyce, James (Original Author)
Ulysses 1967,Mr 14,55:1
Passages From James Joyce's Finnegans Wake
 1967,O 10,56:1
Joyce, Kathleen
Ringer, The 1932,Je 2,25:2
Joyce, Natalie
Circus Ace, The 1927,Jl 6,23:2
Girl in Every Port, A 1928,F 20,14:1
Dance Hall 1929,D 16,34:2
Cock O' the Walk 1930,Ap 12,23:1
Joyce, Peggy Hopkins
Skyrocket, The 1926,Ja 26,25:2
International House 1933,My 27,11:5
Joyce, Teddy
Crooner 1932,Ag 20,7:4
Joyce, Willian Ogden
This Could Be the Night 1957,My 15,39:1
Joyce, Yootha
Die! Die! My Darling 1965,My 20,52:1
Having a Wild Weekend 1965,Ag 19,35:1
Man for all Seasons, A 1966,D 13,60:1
Joyeux, Odette
Luc Aux Dames 1936,Ja 15,14:4
Curtain Rises, The 1939,Ap 22,15:2
Youth in Revolt 1939,My 16,27:3
Passionnelle 1948,Mr 1,17:2
Love Story 1949,Je 27,18:4
Sylvie and the Phantom 1950,O 16,30:5
Ronde, La 1954,Mr 17,27:2
Bride Is Much too Beautiful, The 1958,Ja 21,35:1
Joyeux, Odette (Screenwriter)
Bride Is Much too Beautiful, The 1958,Ja 21,35:1
Joyner, Joyzelle
Sign of the Cross, The 1932,D 1,25:1
I Believed in You 1934,Ap 11,25:3
Juan, Olga San
Blue Skies 1946,O 17,28:2
Third Voice, The 1960,Mr 7,24:5
Juan, San
Thirst of Men, The 1952,O 28,37:1
Judd, Edward
Man Upstairs, The 1959,Ag 11,23:2
Day the Earth Caught Fire, The 1962,Mr 16,25:1
It Takes a Thief 1963,Ag 15,24:7
Stolen Hours 1963,O 17,39:1
Long Ships, The 1964,Je 25,25:1
First Men in the Moon 1964,N 26,52:2
Strange Bedfellows 1965,Mr 11,38:1
Vengance of She, The 1968,My 30,21:4
Judd, Forrest (Producer)
Monsoon 1953,S 26,15:2
Judd, Forrest (Screenwriter)
16 Fathoms Deep 1948,O 7,35:2
Monsoon 1953,S 26,15:2
Judeis, Charles
High Pressure 1932,F 1,22:3
Judell, Ben (Producer)
Hitler-Dead or Alive 1943,Mr 31,23:3

Judels, Charles
Little Old New York 1923,Ag 2,10:3
Under the Red Robe 1923,N 13,25:3
Hot for Paris 1930,Ja 4,21:1
Let's Go Places 1930,Mr 1,23:1
Doorway to Hell, The 1930,N 1,23:2
Life of the Party, The 1930,N 10,16:2
Fifty Million Frenchmen 1931,Mr 26,31:2
Captain Thunder 1931,My 11,15:4
Gold Dust Gertie 1931,My 30,9:2
Women of all Nations 1931,My 30,9:2
One Hour with You 1932,Mr 24,17:5
Night is Young, The 1935,Ja 14,11:2
Enchanted April 1935,Mr 9,19:1
Florentine Dagger, The 1935,Ap 27,20:6
Great Ziegfeld, The 1936,Ap 9,21:2
San Francisco 1936,Je 27,21:1
Suzy 1936,Jl 25,16:1
Love on the Run 1936,N 28,13:3
Plainsman, The 1937,Ja 14,16:2
When's Your Birthday? 1937,Mr 19,27:2
Maytime 1937,Mr 19,27:1
Swing High, Swing Low 1937,Ap 15,19:1
It Can't Last Forever 1937,Jl 30,22:5
Life of the Party, The 1937,O 4,17:1
Ebb Tide 1937,N 18,27:2
Live, Love and Learn 1937,N 19,27:2
Fight for Your Lady 1937,N 20,21:2
Love and Hisses 1938,Ja 1,11:1
You're Only Young Once 1938,Ja 3,16:2
Stolen Heaven 1938,My 12,27:2
Swiss Miss 1938,Je 4,18:2
Flirting With Fate 1938,D 15,35:3
Viva Cisco Kid 1940,Mr 22,23:4
It all Came True 1940,Ap 6,13:2
Gold Rush Maisie 1940,S 2,23:2
Public Deb No 1 1940,S 18,19:2
Down Argentine Way 1940,O 18,25:1
Law of the Tropics 1941,O 10,26:5
This Woman Is Mine 1941,O 13,21:2
Chocolate Soldier, The 1941,N 1,20:2
Kathleen 1941,D 19,35:3
Hard Way, The 1943,Mr 13,9:2
Bell for Adano, A 1945,Jl 6,8:3
Whistle Stop 1946,Mr 18,24:2
In old Sacramento 1946,Ap 29,24:4
Tangier 1946,Je 7,II,16:4
Mighty McGurk, The 1947,Ap 4,19:4
Judge, Arline
Bachelor Apartment 1931,My 16,13:3
American Tragedy, An 1931,Ag 6,22:5
Are These our Children 1931,N 14,15:3
Girl Crazy 1932,Mr 25,23:3
Love Starved 1932,Ap 15,23:1
Is my Face red 1932,Je 11,9:3
Roar of the Dragon 1932,Jl 25,11:2
Age of Consent, The 1932,S 3,16:2
Flying Devils 1933,Ag 26,14:3
Looking for Trouble 1934,Ap 12,27:2
Shoot the Works 1934,Jl 7,16:5
Mysterious Mr Wong, The 1935,Mr 7,26:1
George White's 1935 Scandals 1935,Ap 29,12:3
Million Dollar Baby 1935,My 6,22:3
King of Burlesque 1936,Ja 16,25:2
It Had to Happen 1936,F 15,18:6
Star for a Night 1936,S 5,7:2
Valiant Is the Word for Carrie 1936,O 8,27:2
Pigskin Parade 1936,N 14,23:3
One in a Million 1937,Ja 1,19:3
Lady is Willing, The 1942,Ap 24,21:2
From This Day Forward 1946,Ap 20,16:2
Mad Wednesday 1951,Ja 25,21:5
Judge, James P (Original Author)
Baby, Take a Bow 1934,Je 30,18:6
Judge, Joel (Director)
Golden Mistress, The 1954,O 30,15:6
Judge, Joel (Screenwriter)
Golden Mistress, The 1954,O 30,15:6
Judge, Naomi
Terror Trail 1933,F 11,11:3
Judis, Gary
Incident in an Alley 1962,My 17,31:1
Judson, Lester
Sand Castle, The 1961,Ag 16,37:2
Open the Door and See all the People
 1964,Ap 2,28:1
Judy, Anne and Zeke
Artists and Models 1937,Ag 5,19:2
Juel, Inger
Each Heart Has Its Own Story 1953,Mr 28,15:2
Juergensen, Helke
Schloss im Sueden, Das 1936,F 24,14:2
Jug, Little Brown
Red Pony, The 1949,Mr 9,33:2
Jugert, Rudolph (Director)
Film Without a Name 1950,O 20,32:2
Jugert, Rudolph (Screenwriter)
Film Without a Name 1950,O 20,32:2
Jugo, Jenny
Casanova 1927,Je 23,23:3
Looping the Loop 1929,F 11,26:3
Loves of Casanova, The 1929,Ap 30,33:2
Royal Scandal, A 1929,S 23,24:3

Jugo, Jenny— Cont
Docks of Hamburg 1930,Jl 7,22:3
Wer Nimmt die Liebe Ernst; Who Takes Love
 Seriously 1931,D 27,VIII,7:1
Fuenf von der Jazzband; Five of the Jazzband
 1932,My 15,VIII,4:4 (In Addenda)
Heute Nacht-Eventuell 1933,Je 24,16:3
Lied fur Dich, Ein; Song for You, A
 1933,Jl 2,IX,2:2
Eine Stadt Steht Kopf 1934,Ja 29,10:2
Pechmarie 1935,Ap 22,14:3
Wer Nimmt die Liebe Ernst? 1936,F 10,15:2
Gibt nur eine Liebe, Es 1937,Ja 23,23:2
Fraeulein Frau 1937,Jl 3,18:2
Nacht mit dem Kaiser, Die 1937,Ag 14,16:5
Kleine und die Grosse Liebe, Die; Minor Love and
 the Real Thing, The 1938,Jl 23,10:5
Ein Hoffnungsloser Fall 1939,S 18,15:5

Juhasz, Josef
Harom Sarkany 1936,D 22,32:3
Te Csak Pipalj Ladanyi; Keep On Smoking,
 Ladanyi 1938,My 18,9:3
Marika 1938,N 19,9:3
Kolcsonkert Kastely; Borrowed Castle, The
 1938,D 17,10:4
Pentek Rezi; Friday Rose 1939,D 23,9:2
Tiszavirag; Flower of the Tisza 1939,D 30,9:3

Juhnke, Harald
Guitars of Love 1958,Jl 12,18:1

Jui-feng, Ke (Screenwriter)
Lady General, The 1965,F 12,19:1

Juillard, Argus Speare
Guns of the Trees 1964,F 29,12:2

Jukes, Bernard
Sap From Syracuse, The 1930,Jl 26,16:4

Jules
Tabu 1931,Mr 19,21:3

JULIAN
See Also JULIEN

Julian, Joe
That Night 1957,O 15,39:3

Julian, Joseph (Narrator)
Secrets of the Reef 1956,Jl 24,19:2

Julian, Marcel (Screenwriter)
Sucker, The 1967,O 9,61:1

Julian, Ray
Guilty Bystander 1950,Ap 21,18:2
Guerrilla Girl 1953,Jl 7,23:7

Julian, Rupert
Kaiser, The Beast of Berlin, The 1918,Mr 10,18:8

Julian, Rupert (Director)
Merry Go Round 1923,Jl 2,16:2
Love and Glory 1924,Ag 5,10:2
Hell's Highroad 1925,Ag 26,14:2
Phantom of the Opera, The 1925,S 7,15:3
Three Faces West 1926,F 16,22:4
Silence 1926,My 19,29:3
Yankee Clipper, The 1927,My 3,25:1
Leopard Lady, The 1928,F 27,16:2
Love Comes Along 1930,F 1,15:1
Phantom of the Opera 1930,F 10,20:4
Cat Creeps, The 1930,N 8,21:3

Julie, Jarl
Smiles of a Summer Night 1957,D 24,11:1

Julie, Lady
Love Master, The 1924,My 19,14:2

JULIEN
See Also JULIAN

Julien, Arthur (Original Author)
Happy Road, The 1957,Je 21,20:2

Julien, Arthur (Screenwriter)
Happy Road, The 1957,Je 21,20:2

Julien, Max
Psych-Out 1968,Mr 28,52:1
Savage Seven, The 1968,Ag 22,47:1
Up Tight 1968,D 19,62:1

Jullen, A M
Children of Chaos 1950,Ap 20,37:2

Jullien, Henri
As du Turf, Les; Acres of Turf 1935,My 11,21:3

Juma
West of Zanzibar 1955,Ja 18,31:2
Safari 1956,Je 21,35:2

Junco, Tito
Virgin of Guadalupe, The 1943,My 15,13:3
Life of Simon Bolivar, The 1943,Je 18,16:5
Romeo and Juliet 1944,Je 17,10:3

June, Mildred
Crossroads of New York, The 1922,My 22,18:4

Jung, Allen
China Girl 1943,Ja 21,27:2
Night Plane From Chungking 1943,My 31,13:2

Jung, Rudolph
William Tell 1925,My 20,26:2

Jung, Shia
Charlie Chan at the Circus 1936,Mr 19,22:4

Junge, Alfred (Miscellaneous)
Stairway to Heaven 1946,D 26,28:1

Jungke, Max (Original Author)
Eleven Who Were Loyal 1929,My 20,22:6

Jungmeyer, Jack (Original Author)
Shady Lady, The 1929,Mr 25,32:2
When the Daltons Rode 1940,Ag 23,13:3

Jungmeyer, Jack (Screenwriter)
Street Corner 1948,D 4,9:4

Jungmeyer, Jack Jr (Producer)
Highway Dragnet 1954,F 20,8:7

Jungo, Jenny
Madchenjahre einer Konigin; Girlhood of a
 Queen 1936,Ap 26,IX,4:4 (In Addenda)

Junkermann, Hans
Anna Christie 1931,Ja 6,25:1
Liebeswalzer 1931,My 4,15:3
Ein Walzer vom Strauss 1932,F 11,16:1
Ein Prinz Verliebt Sich 1932,Ap 29,13:4
Der Storch Streikt 1932,My 2,13:2
Barberina, Die Taenzerin Von Sans-Souci
 1932,O 26,15:4
Man Braucht Kein Geld 1932,N 16,15:3
Zapfenstreich am Rhein 1933,F 2,21:6
Traum von Schoenbrunn 1933,Je 1,15:4
In Wien Hab' Ich Einmal ein Maedel Geliebt
 1934,My 26,12:3
Liebe in Uniform 1934,O 9,17:2
Hochzeit am Wolfgangsee 1934,N 17,12:2
Heimat am Rhein 1934,D 11,29:4
Aschermittwoch; Ash Wednesday
 1935,Mr 11,15:2
Page vom Dalmasse-Hotel, Der 1935,Mr 25,12:3
Rosen aus dem Sueden; Roses from the South
 1935,Ap 23,24:5
Pantoffelhelden 1935,O 21,22:5
Ist Mein Mann Nicht Fabelhaft 1936,D 8,31:3
Junge Graf, Der 1936,D 14,15:2
Ueber Alles die Treue 1939,F 13,13:3
Hummel-Hummel 1939,Mr 11,21:2
Lustige Witwenball, Der; Merry Widows' Ball,
 The 1939,My 1,21:2
Ekel, Das; Grouch, The 1939,D 4,18:4
Peter, Paul und Nanette 1940,My 25,20:1
Leidenschaft; Passion 1940,S 24,26:6

Junkin, Harry (Original Author)
Slander 1957,Ja 17,34:4

Junkin, John
Hard Day's Night, A 1964,Ag 12,41:1
Kaleidoscope 1966,S 23,45:1

Junosza-Stepowski, K
Znachor; Miracle Man, The 1938,F 21,15:2
Rena 1939,Ja 27,17:3
Za Winy niepopelnione; For Crimes Not Theirs
 1939,F 20,13:3
Dzien Upragniony; Anticipated Day, The
 1939,Mr 13,12:3

Jura, Walter
Hirsekorn Greift Ein 1932,Je 10,22:3

Juracek, Pavel (Director)
Joseph Kilian 1966,Jl 19,34:1

Juracek, Pavel (Original Author)
Daisies 1967,O 26,54:2

Juracek, Pavel (Screenwriter)
Joseph Kilian 1966,Jl 19,34:1

Jurado, Arthur
Men, The 1950,Jl 21,15:2

Jurado, Elena
What Price Glory 1926,N 24,26:4
Girl in Every Port, A 1928,F 20,14:1

Jurado, Katy
Bullfighter and the Lady, The 1951,Ap 27,19:2
High Noon 1952,Jl 25,14:2
Arrowhead 1953,S 16,38:6
Broken Lance 1954,Jl 30,9:1
Racers, The 1955,F 5,13:2
Trial 1955,O 14,21:2
Sword of Granada 1956,My 19,12:6
Trapeze 1956,Je 5,39:2
Dragoon Wells Massacre 1957,My 6,25:2
Badlanders, The 1958,S 4,33:1
One Eyed Jacks 1961,Mr 31,21:1
Barabbas 1962,O 11,49:1
Covenant with Death, A 1967,F 16,32:3

Juran, Nathan (Director)
Black Castle, The 1952,D 26,20:4
Highway Dragnet 1954,F 20,8:7
Crooked Web, The 1955,D 10,19:1
Flight of the Lost Balloon 1962,My 24,29:2
First Men in the Moon 1964,N 26,52:2

Juran, Nathan (Screenwriter)
Flight of the Lost Balloon 1962,My 24,29:2

Jurgens, Curt
Royal Waltz, The 1936,Ap 10,27:1
Mozart Story, The 1948,N 15,21:5
Operetta 1949,Je 6,15:4
April 1, 2000 1954,F 17,27:2
Devil's General, The 1957,Ap 16,38:2
And God Created Woman 1957,O 22,41:1
Enemy Below, The 1957,D 26,23:2
Confession of Ina Kahn, The 1958,Ja 1,31:4
Last Waltz, The 1958,Ap 12,13:1
This Happy Feeling 1958,Je 19,28:2
Circus of Love 1958,Ag 16,10:2
Me and the Colonel 1958,Ag 27,33:1
Inn of the Sixth Happiness, The 1958,D 14,2:7
Heroes and Sinners; (Heros Sont Fatigues, Les)
 1959,My 12,38:2
Blue Angel, The 1959,S 5,11:4
Tamango 1959,S 17,48:4

Jurgens, Curt— Cont
House of Intrigue, The 1960,Mr 10,36:3
Michael Strogoff 1960,My 21,15:1
I Aim at the Stars 1960,O 20,42:2
Eye for an Eye, An 1961,F 10,19:1
Ferry to Hong Kong 1961,Ap 27,27:7
Longest Day, The 1962,O 5,28:1
Magnificent Sinner 1963,Ap 25,38:1
Miracle of the White Stallions 1963,My 23,31:2
Of Love and Desire 1963,S 12,32:1
Hide and Seek 1964,Mr 12,40:3
Psyche 39 1964,Ap 30,30:1
Disorder 1964,My 26,44:2
Chateau en Suede; Castle in Switzerland
 1964,O 14,51:1
Lord Jim 1965,F 26,18:1
Artists Under the Big Top Perplexed
 1968,S 27,34:1

Jurgensen, Edwin
Graue Dame, Die; Gray Lady, The
 1938,D 17,10:4

Jurinac, Sena
Rosenkavalier, Der 1962,O 10,57:1

Jurmann, Walter (Composer)
Hirsekorn Greift Ein 1932,Je 10,22:3
Perfect Gentleman, The 1935,D 19,33:4
Seven Sweethearts 1942,N 13,28:1
Presenting Lily Mars 1943,Ap 30,25:3
Thousands Cheer 1943,S 14,27:1

Jurmann, Walter (Miscellaneous)
Escapade 1935,Jl 6,16:2
Day at the Races, A 1937,Je 18,25:2

Juross, Albert
Carabiniers, Les 1967,S 28,58:3
Carabiniers, Les 1968,Ap 26,31:1

Jurow, Martin (Producer)
Hanging Tree, The 1959,F 12,23:1
Fugitive Kind, The 1960,Ap 15,13:1
Love in a Goldfish Bowl 1961,Jl 13,26:3
Breakfast at Tiffany's 1961,O 6,28:1
Soldier in the Rain 1963,N 29,67:6 (Incorrect in
 this edition; use 1963,N 28,67:6 elsewhere)
Pink Panther, The 1964,Ap 24,25:1
Great Race, The 1965,S 16,00:0

Jurow, Nathan (Director)
Jack the Giant Killer 1962,Jl 26,17:1

Jurow, Nathan (Screenwriter)
Jack the Giant Killer 1962,Jl 26,17:1

Just, Monigue
Psycosissimo 1962,S 8,16:2

Justian, Kazimierz
Dziesieciu z Pawiaka 1932,Ap 21,25:2

Justice, Barry
King and Country 1964,S 24,46:2
King and Country 1966,Ja 28,20:4

Justice, James Robertson
Against the Wind 1949,Je 27,18:3
Christopher Columbus 1949,O 13,33:2
Tight Little Island 1949,D 26,33:2
Black Rose, The 1950,S 2,11:2
Prelude to Fame 1950,N 10,35:3
Operation X 1950,D 11,31:2
Scott of the Antarctic 1951,F 26,20:2
David and Bathsheba 1951,Ag 15,23:2
Captain Horatio Hornblower 1951,S 14,21:2
Anne of the Indies 1951,O 25,36:3
Pool of London 1951,N 28,37:2
Lady Says No, The 1952,Ja 7,14:3
Story of Robin Hood, The 1952,Je 27,18:3
Miserables, Les 1952,Ag 15,11:2
Murder Will Out 1953,Ap 6,24:2
Miss Robin Hood 1953,Je 27,7:2
Sword and the Rose, The 1953,Ag 20,18:3
Rob Roy 1954,F 4,21:5
Doctor in the House 1955,F 19,18:3
Land of the Pharaohs 1955,Jl 27,15:2
Doctor at Sea 1956,Mr 1,37:3
Storm over the Nile 1956,Je 9,14:2
Moby Dick 1956,Jl 5,18:1
Iron Petticoat, The 1957,F 2,12:2
Above Us the Waves 1957,Ap 18,35:2
Living Idol, The 1957,My 3,18:1
Doctor at Large 1957,Jl 29,15:5
Out of the Clouds 1957,Ag 1,20:4
Checkpoint 1957,S 19,25:2
Alligator Named Daisy, An 1957,O 7,23:2
Orders to Kill 1958,N 18,41:2
Campbell's Kingdom 1960,Ja 11,35:5
Upstairs and Downstairs 1960,D 2,53:4
French Mistress, A 1960,D 19,34:2
Foxhole in Cairo 1961,F 16,25:2
Guns of Navarone, The 1961,Je 23,19:1
Murder She Said 1962,Ja 8,27:2
Doctor in Love 1962,Ap 27,27:2
Coming-Out Party, A 1962,Jl 31,19:2
Guns of Darkness 1962,Ag 18,10:1
Crooks Anonymous 1963,O 31,26:3
Love on a Pillow 1963,D 17,49:1
Pair of Briefs, A 1964,F 3,22:2
Dr Crippen 1964,F 15,14:1
Doctor in Distress 1964,Jl 8,38:2
Up From the Beach 1965,Je 10,38:1
Chitty Chitty Bang Bang 1968,D 19,64:4

Justice, Katherine
  Way West, The 1967,My 25,54:1
  5 Card Stud 1968,Ag 1,24:1
Justin, Charles
  Wild, Wild Planet 1967,Ag 10,45:5
Justin, George (Producer)
  Middle of the Night 1959,Je 18,36:1
  Something Wild 1961,D 24,30:6
  Tiger Makes Out, The 1967,S 19,53:1
Justin, John
  Thief of Bagdad, The 1940,D 6,28:2
  Angel With the Trumpet 1951,D 21,21:5
  Breaking Through the Sound Barrier
    1952,N 7,19:1
  Melba 1953,Je 25,23:1
  Village, The 1953,S 23,37:2
  King of the Khyber Rifles 1953,D 23,21:1
  Crest of the Wave 1954,N 11,43:2
  Untamed 1955,Mr 12,11:6
  Man Who Loved Redheads, The 1955,Jl 26,29:2
  Teckman Mystery, The 1955,Ag 22,18:2
  Safari 1956,Je 21,35:2
  Island in the Sun 1957,Je 13,37:1
Justini, Carlo
  Novel Affair, A 1957,Ag 28,22:1
  Intent to Kill 1959,Ap 1,43:2
Jutra, Claude
  Take it All; A Tout Prendre 1966,Ap 26,55:1
Jutra, Claude (Director)
  Take it All; A Tout Prendre 1966,Ap 26,55:1
Jutra, Claude (Miscellaneous)
  Take it All; A Tout Prendre 1966,Ap 26,55:1
Jutra, Claude (Producer)
  Take it All; A Tout Prendre 1966,Ap 26,55:1
Jutzi, Phil (Director)
  Berlin-Alexanderplatz 1931,N 15,VIII,6:1
  Berlin-Alexanderplatz 1933,My 11,14:1
Juul, Einar
  Red Meadows 1950,Ja 19,35:2
Juul, Ole (Original Author)
  Red Meadows 1950,Ja 19,35:2
  Crazy Paradise 1965,Ag 11,41:2
Juvelier, Jeanne
  Johnny Holiday 1950,My 17,36:1
Juvenet, Pierre
  Barbier de Seville, Le 1936,S 23,29:2
  Call, The 1938,Mr 29,18:3
  Dawn Over France 1945,Mr 17,17:2
  Devil's Daughter 1949,F 26,11:2
  Gigi 1950,Ja 31,20:2
  Sextette (Part 2-Female Affair); Female Affair
    (Sextette) 1953,Mr 2,19:2

K

K Yurushkina, N (Cinematographer)
  Life in the Arctic 1953,S 7,15:2
Kaapa, Hanna
  Weird Woman 1944,Ap 1,11:1
Kaaren, Suzanne
  Bottoms Up 1934,Mr 23,29:2
  When's Your Birthday? 1937,Mr 19,27:2
Kabaneles, Jakovos (Screenwriter)
  Horse and Carriage 1958,Je 30,23:3
Kabayashi, Katsuhiko
  Buddha 1965,Je 17,27:4
Kaberidze, O
  Italiano Brava Gente 1966,F 4,20:1
Kabes, Gyula
  Huszarszerelem 1935,Ap 23,24:5
Kabibble, Ish
  That's Right, You're Wrong 1939,N 30,25:3
  You'll Find Out 1940,N 15,25:2
  Playmates 1941,D 26,21:3
  Around the World 1943,N 25,39:2
Kabos, Gyula
  Piri Mindont Tud 1933,Ja 26,12:3
  Mindent a Noert! 1934,O 17,26:3
  As Uj Rokon; New Relative, The
    1935,Mr 12,25:3
  Az Uj Rokon 1935,Mr 12,25:3
  Koeszoenoem Hogy Elgazolt 1935,My 7,28:2
  Lila Akac 1935,My 15,26:3
  Elnoek Kisasszony 1935,O 12,12:3
  Csunya Lany, A 1935,O 18,27:4
  Zsivany Becsuelet 1935,O 30,16:3
  Hello Budapest 1935,N 14,17:4
  Vasember 1935,D 9,25:3
  Budai Cukraszda 1936,Ja 2,21:5
  Cimzett Ismeretlen 1936,F 7,14:2
  Okos Mama, Az 1936,Ap 13,15:2
  Fizessen Nagysag 1937,Je 4,27:3
  Affair of Honor, An 1937,S 20,19:1
  Hotel Sunrise 1937,O 30,22:3
  Torockoi Menyasszony; Torockoi Bride
    1938,Mr 5,11:2
  Doentoe Pillanat, A; Crucial Moment, The
    1938,S 17,20:3
  Maga Lesz a Ferjem; You Will Be my Husband
    1938,O 12,35:3
  Harapos Ferj; Biting Husbank 1939,Ja 28,19:2
  Pillanatnyi Pezzavar; Temporarily Broke
    1939,My 20,11:3

Kabos, Julius
  Meseauto 1936,N 10,31:4
  Naszut Felaron 1937,F 13,9:2
  Szensacio 1937,Mr 1,15:2
  Once a Week 1937,O 2,18:1
  Viki 1937,N 29,19:3
  Szerelemboel Noesueltem; I Married for Love
    1938,F 7,10:3
  Urilany Szobat Keres; Lady Seeks Room
    1938,Mr 19,11:2
  Az en Lanyom nem olyan; My Daughter Is
    Different 1938,Ap 30,18:2
  Kolcsonkert Kastely; Borrowed Castle, The
    1938,D 17,10:4
  Fehervari Huszarok; Hussars of Fehervari
    1939,S 16,20:3
Kachalov, Vassili Ivanovich
  Lower Depths, The 1947,D 1,27:2
Kacyzna, S A (Screenwriter)
  Dybbuk, The 1938,Ja 28,17:2
Kadar, Jan (Director)
  Shop on Main Street, The 1966,Ja 25,47:1
Kadechnikov, P
  Road to Life 1956,Je 11,26:6
Kadelburg, Gustav (Original Author)
  Is Matrimony a Failure 1922,Ap 17,22:3
Kadin, Paul (Producer)
  Born Free 1966,Je 23,29:1
Kadish, Ben (Original Author)
  Indian Fighter, The 1955,D 22,20:1
Kadison, Ellis (Original Author)
  Don't Give up the Ship 1959,Jl 9,22:1
Kadison, Ellis (Screenwriter)
  Gnome-Mobile, The 1967,Jl 20,30:2
Kadison, Louis
  Vilna Legend, A (American Cast) 1949,S 26,17:1
Kadler-Ben-Salem
  Return of Nathan Becker, The 1933,Ap 15,16:3
Kadochnikov, P
  Spring Song 1942,S 12,9:2
  Fortress on the Volga 1942,D 25,15:3
  Ivan the Terrible, Part I 1947,Mr 10,25:2
  Secret Agent 1949,F 10,37:3
  Far for Moscow 1951,Jl 2,16:6
  Boys From Leningrad, The 1955,My 2,16:5
  Big Family, A 1955,Je 6,24:1
  Tiger Girl 1955,S 5,8:2
  Ivan the Terrible, Part II 1959,N 25,22:4
Kaeired, Katharine
  Enlighten Thy Daughter 1917,Ja 29,11:2
  Mamma's Affair 1921,Ja 24,16:2
Kaestner, Erich (Original Author)
  Emil und die Detektive 1931,D 21,28:4
Kafa, Elizabeth (Original Author)
  Patch of Blue, A 1965,D 16,63:1
Kafka, Franz (Original Author)
  Trial, The 1963,F 21,5:1
Kafka, John (Original Author)
  Crossroads 1939,Mr 14,17:5
  They Met in Bombay 1941,Jl 4,17:1
  Crossroads 1942,Jl 27,18:2
  Destination Unknown 1942,O 29,19:3
Kafka, John (Screenwriter)
  Man on a String 1960,My 21,15:1
Kaganovitch, L
  Soviets on Parade 1933,Mr 6,16:7
Kagansky, Michel (Producer)
  Dame de Pique, La 1944,O 19,19:2
Kagawa, Kenjiro
  High and Low 1963,N 27,30:1
Kagawa, Kyoko
  Lower Depths, The 1962,F 10,12:5
  Mothra 1962,Jl 12,19:4
  Bad Sleep Well, The 1963,Ja 23,5:2
  Prodigal Son 1964,Ja 30,24:3 (Incorrect in this
    edition; use 1964,Ja 31,16:1 elsewhere)
  Secret Scrolls-Part II; Ninjitsu 1968,My 23,56:3
  Red Beard 1968,D 20,60:4
Kagawa, Ryosuke
  Ugetsu 1954,S 8,40:3
Kage, Ivar
  John Ericsson Victor of Hampton Roads
    1938,My 18,17:2
Kagno, Marcia
  Hole in the Wall, The 1929,Ap 15,22:6
Kahal, Irving (Composer)
  Footlight Parade 1933,O 6,21:3
  Strictly Dynamite 1934,Jl 4,18:2
  Dames 1934,Ag 16,20:2
  Happiness Ahead 1934,O 11,28:2
  Gentlemen are Born 1934,N 22,27:2
  Sweet Music 1935,F 21,23:2
  Goin' to Town 1935,My 11,21:2
  See my Lawyer 1945,My 4,23:4
Kahanamoku, Duke
  Adventure 1925,Ap 15,16:1
  Lord Jim 1925,N 16,19:4
  Rescue, The 1929,Ja 14,20:1
  Wake of the Red Witch 1949,Ja 10,19:2
  Mister Roberts 1955,Jl 15,14:1

Kahane, B B (Producer)
  There's That Woman Again 1939,Ja 6,25:4
  Lady in Question, The 1940,D 10,33:2
Kahanovitsch, Amnon
  They Were Ten; (Heym Hayu Assara)
    1961,Ap 18,44:2
KAHN
  See Also CAHN
Kahn, Art and his Orchestra
  Angel of Broadway 1927,N 1,21:1 (In Addenda)
Kahn, E J Jr (Original Author)
  Three Stripes in the Sun 1955,N 24,41:2
Kahn, Florence
  Secret Agent 1936,Je 13,13:1
Kahn, Gordon (Original Author)
  X Marks the Spot 1931,D 7,16:1
  Gigolette 1935,My 13,18:6
  Tenth Avenue Kid 1938,S 2,21:3
  Ex-Champ 1939,My 12,25:3
  World Premiere 1941,Ag 21,15:2
Kahn, Gordon (Screenwriter)
  People's Enemy, The 1935,Ap 30,13:7
  Gigolette 1935,My 13,18:6
  Tenth Avenue Kid 1938,S 2,21:3
  I Stand Accused 1939,Ja 5,17:1
  Newsboys' Home 1939,Ja 23,8:2
  S O S Tidal Wave 1939,Je 22,19:3
  Mickey, the Kid 1939,Jl 6,27:1
  Buy Me That Town 1941,O 23,27:2
  Yank on the Burma Road, A 1942,Ja 29,25:3
  Her Kind of Man 1946,My 4,10:6
  Ruthless 1948,S 4,8:7
  Whiplash 1948,D 27,16:3
Kahn, Gus (Composer)
  Bottoms Up 1934,Mr 23,29:2
  Stingaree 1934,My 18,27:1
  Hollywood Party 1934,My 26,12:2
  Operator 13 1934,Je 23,16:5
  Caravan 1934,S 28,27:1
  Kid Millions 1934,N 12,17:2
  Thanks a Million 1935,N 14,17:1
  Let's Sing Again 1936,My 9,11:2
  Bride Wore Red, The 1937,O 15,18:4
  Music for Madame 1937,O 23,14:1
  Everybody Sing 1938,Mr 11,15:3
  Honolulu 1939,F 23,19:2
  Lillian Russell 1940,My 18,11:2
  Spring Parade 1940,O 4,29:2
  Go West 1941,F 21,16:2
  Ziegfeld Girl 1941,Ap 25,17:2
  Chocolate Soldier, The 1941,N 1,20:2
  Broadway Rhythm 1944,Ap 14,24:6
Kahn, Gus (Miscellaneous)
  Storm at Daybreak 1933,Jl 22,14:2
  Flying Down to Rio 1933,D 22,25:2
  One Night of Love 1934,S 7,25:3
  Kid Millions 1934,N 12,17:2
  Naughty Marietta 1935,Mr 23,11:2
  Love Me Forever 1935,Je 28,24:1
  Escapade 1935,Jl 6,16:2
  Rose Marie 1936,F 1,9:2
  Captains Courageous 1937,My 12,27:1
  Day at the Races, A 1937,Je 18,25:2
  Firefly, The 1937,S 2,17:2
  Girl of the Golden West, The 1938,Mr 25,15:2
  Broadway Serenade 1939,Ap 7,25:2
Kahn, Ivan (Original Author)
  Star Dust 1940,My 4,13:1
Kahn, Lily
  Tale of Five Women, A 1953,Ja 16,19:2
Kahn, Richard (Director)
  Hombre Peligroso, Un; Dangerous Man, A
    1935,O 14,21:2
Kahn, Ronald (Producer)
  Prudence and the Pill 1968,My 24,37:1
Kahn, Sajid
  Maya 1966,Je 23,29:4
Kai, Francis
  Hurricane, The 1937,N 10,31:2
Kaieda, Jogi
  Imposter, The 1955,Mr 23,27:1
KAIN
  See KANE, CANE, CAIN, CAINE
Kains, Maurice
  Tell It to the Marines 1926,D 24,18:2
Kaiser, George (Original Author)
  Brand in der Oper 1932,Jl 11,11:4
Kaiser, Helen
  Rio Rita 1929,O 7,22:1
  Dance Hall 1929,D 16,34:2
Kaiser, Roland
  Affairs of Julie, The 1958,D 10,53:1
  Roses for the Prosecutor; (Rosen fur den
    Staarsanwalt) 1961,O 10,38:2
Kaiser-Heyl, W
  Anna und Elisabeth 1936,Je 13,13:1
Kaiser-Tietz, Erich
  Hungarian Rhapsody 1929,Ag 5,25:2
Kaiss-Arrowa, Eugenie
  Das Nachtigall Maedel 1933,Ja 23,9:2
Kaitz, Armand
  Fast and Furious 1927,Jl 4,20:3

Kaja, Katrina
　End of St Petersberg, The　1928,My 31,21:2 (In
　　Addenda)
Kakavas, Kostas
　Moment of Passion　1960,N 21,34:1
　Lisa, Tosca of Athens　1961,Je 20,27:1
Kalais, Manus
　Antigone　1962,S 19,30:1
Kalamandir, Rajkamal (Producer)
　Shakuntala　1947,D 26,22:3
Kalanian, Vassily (Director)
　Cinerama's Russian Adventure　1966,Ap 14,42:1
Kalantarly, M
　Arshin Takes a Wife　1950,Jl 31,13:6
Kalapu
　Return to Paradise　1953,S 11,24:2
Kalatozov, Mikhail (Director)
　Wings of Victory　1941,N 17,15:2
　Moscow Music Hall　1946,S 9,20:1
　True Friends　1954,N 15,33:2
　Cranes are Flying, The　1960,Mr 22,31:2
　Letter That Was Never Sent, The　1962,N 19,39:2
Kalatozov, Mikhail (Producer)
　Cranes are Flying, The　1960,Mr 22,31:2
Kalatusiva, Marina
　Song Over Moscow　1964,N 23,52:1
Kaler, James Otis (Original Author)
　Toby Tyler　1960,Ap 20,45:2
Kaley, Charles
　Lord Byron of Broadway　1930,Mr 8,21:1
Kalfon, Jean-Pierre
　To be a Crook　1967,F 7,33:2
　Weekend　1968,S 28,36:1
　Birds in Peru　1968,N 7,51:2
Kalich, Bertha
　Scandal　1916,Ap 10,11:3
　Ambition　1916,Je 26,11:3
Kalidasa (Original Author)
　Shakuntala　1947,D 26,22:3
Kalik, Mikhail (Director)
　Lullaby, The　1961,My 15,35:2
　Sandu Follows the Sun　1965,Ap 19,37:1
Kalik, Mikhail (Screenwriter)
　Sandu Follows the Sun　1965,Ap 19,37:1
Kalili, Manuella
　Ebb Tide　1937,N 18,27:2
Kalina, Vladimir (Producer)
　Capricious Summer　1968,S 18,50:2
Kalinin, Mikhail
　Soviets on Parade　1933,Mr 6,16:7
Kalinin, Sergei
　Symphony of Life　1948,D 28,19:7
Kalinina, Marina
　Conflict　1955,D 26,23:4
Kalinoski, Marc
　Adolescents, The (Marie-France and Veronica);
　　Marie-France and Veronica (The Adolescents)
　　1967,Ap 14,33:1
Kaliuzhnaya, L A
　Mother and Sons　1938,S 15,29:2
Kaliz, Armand
　Temperamental Wife, A　1919,S 15,16:3
　Temptress, The　1926,O 11,18:1
　Stolen Bride, The　1927,Ag 10,21:4
　Love Mart, The　1927,D 26,16:6
　That's my Daddy　1928,F 13,16:2
　Noah's Ark　1929,Mr 13,28:6
　Twin Beds　1929,Jl 15,25:1
　Gold Diggers of Broadway, The　1929,Ag 31,13:4
　Marriage Playground, The　1929,D 14,22:4
　Aviator, The　1930,Ja 11,21:3
　Enigmatique Monsieur Parkes, L'　1930,S 2,19:3
　Honeymoon Lane　1931,Ag 1,16:4
　Three Wise Girls　1932,F 6,14:4
　George White's Scandals　1934,Mr 16,24:2
　Caravan　1934,S 28,27:1
　Here's to Romance　1935,O 3,29:2
　King and the Chorus Girl, The　1937,Mr 29,14:4
　Gold Diggers in Paris　1938,Je 2,19:2
　Trip to Paris, A　1938,Je 10,18:2
　Josette　1938,Je 11,9:1
　Vacation From Love　1938,N 10,33:2
　Topper Takes a Trip　1938,D 30,11:2
　Off the Record　1939,F 18,12:2
　Midnight　1939,Ap 6,31:1
Kalkhurst, Eric
　Unfaithful　1931,Mr 7,17:2
Kallay, Sandor
　Madame Butterfly　1932,D 26,26:2
Kallen, Kitty
　Second Greatest Sex, The　1956,F 11,12:2
Kallergis, Lykourgos
　Casablan　1964,D 14,50:1
Kallerud, Arne
　One Summer of Happiness　1955,Mr 22,35:2
Kallina, Anna
　Affairs of Maupassant, The　1938,F 12,20:2
Kallman, Dick
　Doctor, You've Got to be Kidding
　　1967,My 11,50:1
Kalman, Emmerich (Composer)
　Ronny　1932,Ja 31,6:1

Kalman, Emmerich (Miscellaneous)
　Ronny　1932,Ap 14,25:3
Kalmar, Bert (Composer)
　Horse Feathers　1932,Ag 11,12:2
　Kid From Spain, The　1932,N 18,23:2
　Hips, Hips, Hooray　1934,F 24,18:3
　Happiness Ahead　1934,O 11,28:2
　Kentucky Kernels　1935,Ja 5,20:2
　Thanks a Million　1935,N 14,17:1
　Man Who Broke the Bank at Monte Carlo, The
　　1935,N 15,20:2
　Everybody Sing　1938,Mr 11,15:3
Kalmar, Bert (Miscellaneous)
　Bright Lights　1935,Ag 15,15:2
Kalmar, Bert (Original Author)
　Animal Crackers　1930,Ag 29,20:3
　Top Speed　1930,Ag 30,7:4
　Broad Minded　1931,Jl 6,24:4
　Duck Soup　1933,N 23,24:2
　Hips, Hips, Hooray　1934,F 24,18:3
　Circus Clown, The　1934,Je 30,18:6
　Kentucky Kernels　1935,Ja 5,20:2
　Ship Ahoy　1942,Je 26,16:5
　Look for the Silver Lining　1949,Je 24,29:2
　Three Little Words　1950,Ag 10,21:2
Kalmar, Bert (Screenwriter)
　Horse Feathers　1932,Ag 11,12:2
　Kid From Spain, The　1932,N 18,23:2
　Kentucky Kernels　1935,Ja 5,20:2
　Bright Lights　1935,Ag 15,15:2
　Walking on Air　1936,S 12,20:2
　Life of the Party, The　1937,O 4,17:1
Kalmar, Laszlo (Director)
　Sut a Nap (Sun Shines, The); Sun Shines, The
　　1940,Ap 6,13:3
Kalmen, Rozsahegyl
　Csokolj Meg Edes　1932,N 25,19:2
Kalmus, Natalie (Miscellaneous)
　Trail of the Lonesome Pine, The　1936,F 20,23:5
　Gone With the Wind　1939,D 20,31:2
Kalogerikou, Christine
　Horse and Carriage　1958,Je 30,23:3
Kalogeroupoulos, Xenia
　Lisa, Tosca of Athens　1961,Je 20,27:1
　Midwife, The　1961,S 25,41:2
Kalouta, Anna
　Otan o Syzygos Taxeideyei; When the Husband
　　Travels　1939,N 13,15:3
Kalouta, Marika
　Dr Epameinondas　1938,Ap 5,19:6
　Otan o Syzygos Taxeideyei; When the Husband
　　Travels　1939,N 13,15:3
Kalser, Erwin
　Rasputin: The Holy Devil　1930,Ag 25,14:2
　Thirteen Men and a Girl　1931,Ag 17,18:2
　Hertha's Erwachen　1933,Mr 14,18:3 (Incorrect in
　　this edition; use 1933,Mr 14,19:2 elsewhere)
　Submarine Zone; (Escape To Glory)
　　1941,Ap 7,13:2
　Underground　1941,Je 23,13:2
　Dressed to Kill　1941,Ag 22,19:3
　Berlin Correspondent　1942,S 4,19:2
　Watch on the Rhine　1943,Ag 28,15:1
　Address Unknown　1944,Ap 17,20:1
　Hotel Berlin　1945,Mr 3,11:2
　Girl in White, The　1952,My 31,12:5
　Stalag 17　1953,Jl 2,19:2
Kalske, Kullervo
　Jaakarin Morsian; Soldiers' Bride　1939,D 18,29:3
Kaluzhski, E
　1812　1944,S 11,14:1
Kaly Dancers
　Crazy House　1943,D 16,33:3
Kamai, Kolimau
　White Heat　1934,Je 16,20:2
Kamarof, A (Director)
　Road North, The　1932,N 26,11:4
Kamb, Karl (Miscellaneous)
　Lulu Belle　1948,Je 21,18:3
Kamb, Karl (Screenwriter)
　Main Street After Dark　1945,Ja 13,15:4
　Pardon my Past　1946,Ja 28,15:5
　Carnegie Hall　1947,My 3,10:2
　Pitfall　1948,Ag 25,31:2
　Whispering Smith　1949,F 15,28:2
　Kid From Texas, The　1950,Je 2,26:2
　Starlift　1951,D 15,11:2
　Captive City, The　1952,Mr 27,34:2
Kamft, Rudolf
　Last Chance, The　1945,N 28,21:6
Kamikubo, Takeshi
　Three Stripes in the Sun　1955,N 24,41:2
Kamin, Fay (Screenwriter)
　Right Approach, The　1961,My 18,41:1
Kamin, Michael (Screenwriter)
　Right Approach, The　1961,My 18,41:1
Kaminska, Ida
　Without a Home　1939,Ap 1,17:3
　Vilna Legend, A (Russian-Jewish Cast)
　　1949,S 26,17:1
　Shop on High Street, The　1965,S 10,40:1
　Shop on Main Street, The　1966,Ja 25,47:1

Kamiyama, Sojim
　East of Suez　1925,Ja 26,22:1
　Bat, The　1926,Mr 15,18:3
Kamo, Kyoko
　Tokyo Joe　1949,O 27,35:2
Kamp, Irene (Screenwriter)
　Paris Blues　1961,N 8,41:1
　Lion, The　1962,D 22,5:2
Kamp, Louis (Screenwriter)
　Lion, The　1962,D 22,5:2
Kampers, Fritz
　Berlin After Dark　1929,My 28,36:2
　His Late Excellency　1929,Je 11,27:2
　Gretel and Liesel; (Kohlhiesel's Daughters)
　　1931,Ja 26,21:1
　Comrades of 1918　1931,F 20,18:5
　Lumpenball　1931,Ap 27,25:1
　Drei von ver Tankstelle, Die　1931,Je 20,20:4
　Reserve Hat Ruh　1932,Ap 11,19:2
　Stolz der 3 Kompagnie, Der　1932,Jl 21,15:2
　Pension Schoeller　1932,S 20,26:3
　Gloria　1932,O 28,22:4
　Kameradschaft　1932,N 9,28:5
　Korvettenkapitaen, Der　1933,Mr 20,18:3
　Die Lustigen Musikanten　1933,My 27,11:6
　Frau Lehmann's Toechter　1933,O 27,22:3
　Zwei Gute Kameraden　1933,D 4,22:3
　Meisterdetektiv, Der　1934,F 13,23:2
　Strich Durch die Rechnung　1934,Mr 3,8:6
　Blaue Vom Himmel, Das　1934,S 8,18:6
　Liebe in Uniform　1934,O 9,17:2
　Frau wie Du, Eine　1934,D 24,17:3
　Kaiserwalzer　1934,D 29,11:2
　Sonne Geht auf, Die　1935,F 18,19:4
　Liebe und die Erste Eisenbahn, Die; Love and the
　　First Railroad　1935,F 18,19:4
　Drei Kaiserjaeger　1935,Mr 16,19:1
　Drei von der Kavallerie　1935,Ap 13,11:4
　Judas von Tirol, Der　1935,Ap 27,20:7
　Die vom Niederrhein; Lower Rhine Folks
　　1935,My 20,20:6
　Zigeunerbaron　1935,S 14,8:5
　Gruen ist die Heide　1935,O 14,21:2
　Vier Musketiere, Die; Four Musketeers, The
　　1935,N 9,19:3
　Leichte Kavallerie　1936,F 8,19:2
　Fahrt ins Gruene, Die　1936,My 23,12:2
　Ein Lied Geht um die Welt　1936,S 25,20:3
　Letzte Rose　1936,O 10,21:3
　Paloma, La　1936,O 21,35:3
　Bettelstudent, Der　1936,D 28,12:3
　Drei Blaue Jungs-Ein Blondes Maedel
　　1936,D 29,16:3
　Weisse Sklaven　1937,Jl 31,6:2
　Drama on the Threshing Floor　1937,O 30,22:3
　Urlaub auf Ehrenwort; Furlough on Word of
　　Honor　1938,Mr 28,19:2
　Konzert in Tirol　1939,Ja 7,6:4
　Veilchen vom Potsdamer Platz, La; Violet of
　　Potsdam Square, The　1939,Ap 8,19:3
　Pour le Merite　1939,Ap 8,19:2
　Ekel, Das; Grouch, The　1939,D 4,18:4
　Drei um Christine, Die; Three After Christine,
　　The　1940,My 4,13:2
　Joseph Schmidt Story, The　1951,Mr 5,24:2
Kampers, Fritz (Director)
　Konjunkturritter　1935,Ap 29,12:4
　Ich Sing Mich in Dein Herz Hinein
　　1935,Je 3,22:3
Kan, L
　Frontier　1935,D 28,10:5
Kanavan, Richard
　Shoot the Piano Player　1962,Jl 24,19:1
Kanayeva, A
　Dream of a Cossack　1952,F 18,15:2
Kandaurashvill, Asmat
　Stepchildren　1962,Jl 2,22:2
Kandel, Aben (Miscellaneous)
　Big City　1948,My 17,23:3
Kandel, Aben (Original Author)
　Sing and Like It　1934,Ap 14,18:2
　Come Closer, Folks　1936,N 23,17:3
　More Than a Secretary　1936,D 11,35:2
　City for Conquest　1940,S 28,9:2
　What's Buzzin Cousin　1943,Jl 23,21:4
　Berserk!　1968,Ja 11,42:2
Kandel, Aben (Screenwriter)
　Thunder in the City　1937,Ap 23,25:2
　Rio　1939,O 27,27:2
　Iron Major, The　1943,N 1,12:5
　Three Russian Girls　1944,F 5,13:2
　Fighter, The　1952,My 31,12:6
　Singing in the Dark　1956,Mr 8,32:5
　Timetable　1956,Mr 17,13:2
　Horrors of the Black Museum　1959,Ap 30,37:2
　Konga　1961,S 16,9:1
　Berserk!　1968,Ja 11,42:2
Kandel, Stephen (Screenwriter)
　Singing in the Dark　1956,Mr 8,32:5
　Chamber of Horrors　1966,O 20,52:5
KANE
　See Also CANE, CAIN, CAINE

Kane, Byron
Gog 1954,Ag 14,8:2
Kane, Diana
Miss Bluebeard 1925,Ja 28,14:1
Lovers in Quarantine 1925,O 13,20:1
New Commandment, The 1925,N 10,25:3
Bluebeard's Seven Wives 1925,D 28,19:2
Brown Derby, The 1926,Je 14,24:1
Perfect Sap, The 1927,Ja 11,18:2
Kane, Eddie
Broadway Melody, The 1929,F 9,15:3
Street Girl 1929,Jl 31,17:3
Illusion 1929,S 28,17:3
Why Bring That Up? 1929,O 5,22:5
Kibitzer, The 1929,D 21,17:1
Puttin' on the Ritz 1930,F 15,15:1
Framed 1930,Mr 29,23:1
Midnight Patrol, The 1932,My 7,11:5
Love Is a Racket 1932,Je 11,9:3
Once in a Lifetime 1932,O 29,18:4
Mummy, The 1933,Ja 7,11:2
Million Dollar Baby 1935,My 6,22:3
Hooray for Love 1935,Jl 13,16:2
Melody for Two 1937,My 21,19:5
Manhattan Merry-Go-Round 1937,D 31,9:3
Hollywood Round-Up 1938,Mr 5,11:2
Swiss Miss 1938,Je 4,18:2
Give Me a Sailor 1938,Ag 11,31:1
Gladiator, The 1938,Ag 29,10:2
Some Like It Hot 1939,My 25,31:2
Missing Daughters 1939,Je 12,14:5
Music in My Heart 1940,Ja 4,19:2
Jam Session 1944,My 3,25:3
Minstrel Man 1944,Jl 17,18:5
Kane, Gail
Paying the Price 1916,Jl 10,9:5
White Sister, The 1923,S 6,10:2
Convoy 1927,My 9,26:4
White Sister, The 1928,My 21,25:1
Kane, Helen
Nothing but the Truth 1929,Ap 22,23:1
Sweetie 1929,O 26,15:1
Pointed Heels 1929,D 28,11:1
Paramount on Parade 1930,Ap 21,20:4
Dangerous Nan McGrew 1930,Je 21,20:5
Heads Up 1930,O 13,31:1
Kane, Henry (Screenwriter)
Cop Hater 1958,O 2,44:3
Mugger, The 1959,Je 25,20:7
Kane, Jack
Virtuous Vamp, A 1919,N 17,20:1
Wild, Wild Susan 1925,Ag 5,12:4
Kane, Joel (Original Author)
Tin Star, The 1957,O 24,37:2
Kane, Johnny
Man With my Face, The 1951,Je 15,27:5
Kane, Joseph (Director)
Lawless Nineties, The 1936,Je 29,11:1
Boots and Saddles 1937,N 8,19:2
Arson Racket Squad 1938,Je 18,18:2
Under Western Stars 1938,Je 25,7:3
Flame of Barbary Coast 1945,My 28,22:2
Cheaters, The 1945,Jl 21,7:2
Dakota 1945,D 17,17:2
In old Sacramento 1946,Ap 29,24:4
Plainsman and the Lady, The 1946,N 4,33:1
Wyoming 1947,Jl 25,12:5
Old Los Angeles 1948,Jl 12,11:2
Plunders, The 1948,N 1,28:2
Last Bandit, The 1949,Mr 21,19:2
Brimstone 1949,O 7,35:3
Rock Island Trail 1950,Je 5,19:3
California Passage 1950,D 16,10:5
Oh! Susanna 1951,Mr 30,28:5
Fighting Coast Guard 1951,My 12,14:6
Hoodlum Empire 1952,Mr 6,25:6
Woman of the North Country 1952,Ag 30,6:2
Jubilee Trail 1954,My 1,13:3
Hell's Outpost 1955,F 26,13:3
Timberjack 1955,Mr 10,33:3
Maverick Queen, the 1956,Je 4,25:2
Track of Thunder 1968,F 1,28:4
Kane, Joseph (Producer)
In old Sacramento 1946,Ap 29,24:4
Wyoming 1947,Jl 25,12:5
Woman of the North Country 1952,Ag 30,6:2
Kane, Kathryn
Spirit of Culver 1939,Mr 9,18:1
Kane, Lida
Follow the Leader 1930,D 6,21:3
Kane, Louise
Wyoming 1947,Jl 25,12:5
Oh! Susanna 1951,Mr 30,28:5
Kane, Marjorie
Great Gabbo, The 1929,S 13,33:1
Be Yourself 1930,Mr 7,20:5
Sunny Skies 1930,My 17,21:2
Border Romance 1930,My 26,25:3
Merrily We Live 1938,Mr 18,23:3
Kane, Michael
Bedford Incident, The 1965,N 3,43:1

Kane, Mrs (Original Author)
Kisses for my President 1964,Ag 22,13:1
Kane, Robert G (Screenwriter)
Kisses for my President 1964,Ag 22,13:1
Kane, Robert T (Director)
Shipyard Sally 1940,Ja 18,27:3
Kane, Robert T (Producer)
Under Pressure 1935,F 4,11:3
Daring Young Man, The 1935,Jl 18,15:2
Orchids to You 1935,Ag 10,16:4
Wings of the Morning 1937,Mr 12,19:1
Under the Red Robe 1937,Je 1,27:2
Dinner at the Ritz 1937,D 4,21:1
Smiling Along 1939,F 20,13:2
Canon City 1948,Jl 8,19:2
He Walked by Night 1949,F 7,15:2
Kane, Sandra
Mutiny on the Blackhawk 1939,Ag 2,17:2
Kane, Violet
Golden Cocoon, The 1925,D 15,14:5
Kane, Whitford
Hide-Out 1934,Ag 25,16:5
Adventures of Mark Twain, The 1944,My 4,25:5
Ghost and Mrs Muir, The 1947,Je 27,17:2
Walls of Jericho, The 1948,Ag 5,16:2
Judge Steps Out, The 1949,Je 3,21:4
Kaneem, Antonia
Torch, The 1950,Ag 21,15:2
Kaneko, Nobuo
Ikiru; To Live 1960,Ja 30,13:5
Kanin, Fay (Original Author)
Goodbye, my Fancy 1951,My 30,14:2
Kanin, Fay (Screenwriter)
Sunday Punch 1942,My 11,19:2
Rhapsody 1954,Mr 12,17:1
Opposite Sex, The 1956,N 16,23:2
Teacher's Pet 1958,Mr 20,33:1
Kanin, Garson (Director)
Man to Remember, A 1938,N 7,23:2
Next Time I Marry 1938,D 2,27:2
Great Man Votes, The 1939,Ja 20,15:2
Bachelor Mother 1939,Je 30,17:2
My Favorite Wife 1940,My 31,15:2
They Knew What They Wanted 1940,O 11,25:2
Tom, Dick and Harry 1941,Jl 18,22:2
True Glory, The 1945,S 7,1:2
Kanin, Garson (Original Author)
Born Yesterday 1950,D 27,30:2
Rat Race, The 1960,My 26,37:3
High Time 1960,S 17,15:1
Right Approach, The 1961,My 18,41:1
Kanin, Garson (Screenwriter)
From This Day Forward 1946,Ap 20,16:2
Double Life, A 1948,F 20,19:1
Adam's Rib 1949,D 26,33:2
Marrying Kind, The 1952,Mr 14,27:1
Pat and Mike 1952,Je 19,32:6
It Should Happen to You 1954,Ja 16,10:5
Rat Race, The 1960,My 26,37:3
Kanin, Michael (Producer)
Double Life, A 1948,F 20,19:1
Kanin, Michael (Screenwriter)
They Made Her a Spy 1939,Mr 29,21:4
Anne of Windy Poplars 1940,Ag 23,13:3
Woman of the Year 1942,F 6,23:2
Sunday Punch 1942,My 11,19:2
Cross of Lorraine, The 1943,D 3,27:4
Centennial Summer 1946,Jl 18,20:2
Honeymoon 1947,My 19,27:2
Rhapsody 1954,Mr 12,17:1
Opposite Sex, The 1956,N 16,23:2
Teacher's Pet 1958,Mr 20,33:1
Swordsman of Siena 1962,D 6,55:3
Outrage, The 1964,O 8,48:2
Kanizsay, Jozsef (Director)
Pillanatnyi Pezzavar; Temporarily Broke 1939,My 20,11:3
Kankinson, Michael (Original Author)
Broken Melody, The 1934,O 31,17:3
Kann, Lilly
Frenzy 1946,Jl 20,10:3
Woman in the Hall, The 1949,Ja 24,16:2
Mrs Fitzherbert 1950,My 11,37:2
Clouded Yellow, The 1951,N 13,33:2
Edge of Divorce 1954,Jl 2,10:1
Betrayed 1954,S 9,36:1
Eight O'Clock Walk 1955,Ap 30,10:6
Kanner, Alexis
Reach for Glory 1963,S 10,46:1
Kano, Junko
Odd Obsession 1961,D 27,16:1
Kans, Joseph (Director)
Fair Wind to Java 1953,Ag 28,13:3
Kanski, T
Dziesieciu z Pawiaka 1932,Ap 21,25:2
Kantarian, Aram (Producer)
Night Tide 1963,Je 7,37:1
KANTER
See Also KANTOR, CANTOR
Kanter, Hal (Director)
Loving You 1957,Jl 18,19:2
I Married a Woman 1958,N 5,42:5
Hot Horse 1963,Jl 25,14:2

Kanter, Hal (Miscellaneous)
My Favorite Spy 1951,D 26,19:3
Kanter, Hal (Original Author)
Off Limits 1953,Mr 30,25:5
Kanter, Hal (Producer)
Hot Horse 1963,Jl 25,14:2
Kanter, Hal (Screenwriter)
Two Tickets to Broadway 1951,N 22,47:2
Road to Bali 1953,Ja 30,25:1
Off Limits 1953,Mr 30,25:5
Here Come the Girls 1953,D 26,10:1
Money From Home 1954,F 27,11:3
Casanova's Big Night 1954,Ap 19,19:1
About Mrs Leslie 1954,Je 28,16:2
Rose Tattoo, The 1955,D 13,55:1
Artists and Models 1955,D 22,20:1
Loving You 1957,Jl 18,19:2
Mardi Gras 1958,N 19,45:2
Bachelor in Paradise 1961,N 17,41:2
Pocketful of Miracles 1961,D 19,39:1
Blue Hawaii 1962,F 22,20:2
Hot Horse 1963,Jl 25,14:2
Move Over Darling 1963,D 26,33:1
Dear Brigitte 1965,Ja 28,20:1
Kanter, Marianne
Pawnbroker, The 1965,Ap 21,51:1
Kanter, Robert
Thin Red Line, The 1964,O 29,38:1
KANTOR
See Also CANTOR, KANTER
Kantor, Lenard (Original Author)
Tight Spot 1955,Mr 19,11:7
Kantor, MacKinlay
Wind Across the Everglades 1958,S 12,21:1
Kantor, MacKinlay (Original Author)
Voice of Bugle Ann, The 1936,F 27,23:1
Mountain Music 1937,Je 24,30:3
Man From Dakota, The 1940,F 22,29:2
Happy Land 1943,D 9,33:3
Gentle Annie 1945,My 5,11:5
Best Years of our Lives, The 1946,N 22,27:2
Romance of Rosy Ridge, The 1947,S 12,18:3
Follow Me, Boys! 1966,D 2,46:1
Kantor, MacKinley (Original Author)
Gun Crazy 1950,Ag 25,17:5
Kantor, MacKinley (Screenwriter)
Gun Crazy 1950,Ag 25,17:5
Kanturek, Otto (Director)
Student's Romance, The 1936,O 12,23:2
Kanyou, Curtis (Screenwriter)
Love and Hisses 1938,Ja 1,11:1
Kanze, Hideo
Lost Sex 1968,Jl 23,27:2
Kapelyan, Edvard
Flying Carpet, The 1960,F 28,31:1
Kaper, Branislau (Composer)
Night at the Opera, A 1935,D 7,22:1
Kaper, Bronislau (Composer)
Perfect Gentleman, The 1935,D 19,33:4
Everybody Sing 1938,Mr 11,15:3
Lillian Russell 1940,My 18,11:2
Go West 1941,F 21,16:2
Chocolate Soldier, The 1941,N 1,20:2
Kaper, Bronislaw (Miscellaneous)
Escapade 1935,Jl 6,16:2
Day at the Races, A 1937,Je 18,25:2
Kaplan, Boris D (Producer)
Let no Man Write my Epitaph 1960,N 11,36:2
Kaplan, Jacques
Round Trip 1967,Jl 20,30:2
Kaplan, Marvin
Reformer and the Redhead, The 1950,Ap 10,15:2
I Can Get It for You Wholesale 1951,Ap 5,34:4
Criminal Lawyer 1951,Ag 24,11:4
Angels in the Outfield 1951,O 18,32:1
Behave Yourself 1951,N 8,35:2
Wake Me When It's Over 1960,Ap 9,17:2
New Kind of Love, A 1963,O 31,26:2
It's a Mad, Mad, Mad, Mad World 1963,N 19,47:1
Great Race, The 1965,S 16,00:0
Kaplan, Nelly (Screenwriter)
Cyrano and D'Artagnan 1964,S 26,16:1
Kaplan, Richard (Director)
Eleanor Roosevelt Story, The 1965,N 9,50:1
Kaplan, Sol (Composer)
Tales of Manhattan 1942,S 25,25:1
Guns of August, The 1964,D 25,24:2
Kapler, A (Original Author)
Behind the Show Window 1957,Ap 17,37:1
Kapler, A (Screenwriter)
Lenin in October 1938,Ap 2,18:1
Lenin in 1918 1939,Je 27,27:2
Day After Day 1943,N 6,16:3
No Ordinary Summer 1958,O 6,36:3
Kaplunovsky, V (Director)
Mexican, The 1957,Ap 3,28:2
Captain's Daughter, The 1959,N 23,41:3
Kaplunovsky, V (Producer)
Mexican, The 1957,Ap 3,28:2
Captain's Daughter, The 1959,N 23,41:3

Kapoor, A K
   Vagabond, The 1956,Ap 16,30:4
Kapoor, H R
   Vagabond, The 1956,Ap 16,30:4
Kapoor, Jennifer
   Shakespeare Wallah 1966,Mr 23,40:2
Kapoor, Pincho
   Householder, The 1963,O 22,43:2
   Shakespeare Wallah 1966,Mr 23,40:2
Kapoor, Raj
   Vagabond, The 1956,Ap 16,30:4
   Boot Polish 1958,Ag 18,15:2
Kapoor, Raj (Director)
   Vagabond, The 1956,Ap 16,30:4
Kapoor, Raj (Original Author)
   Boot Polish 1958,Ag 18,15:2
Kapoor, Raj (Producer)
   Boot Polish 1958,Ag 18,15:2
Kapoor, S P
   Look Back in Anger 1959,S 16,45:1
Kapoor, Shashi
   Householder, The 1963,O 22,43:2
   Shakespeare Wallah 1965,S 13,42:1
   Shakespeare Wallah 1966,Mr 23,40:2
   Matter of Innocence, A 1968,F 22,36:1
Kapp, David (Composer)
   Patrick the Great 1945,Ap 13,15:2
Kapralof, I
   Polish Terror, The 1933,Mr 13,18:3
Kapsakis, D (Director)
   You Came too Late 1962,N 12,35:8
Kapsaskis, Sokratis (Director)
   Lisa, Tosca of Athens 1961,Je 20,27:1
Kapur, Prithviraj
   Journey Beyond Three Seas 1960,Ap 11,42:6
Kapustin, Lev
   Country Doctor, The 1953,F 16,16:2
Kapustina, Maria
   Girl From Leningrad 1941,D 20,25:2
Kar, Nidal Ash
   Broken Wings, The 1968,Mr 16,34:1
Kara, S (Screenwriter)
   Big Family, A 1955,Je 6,24:1
Kara-Dmitrief, M
   Horizon, The Wandering Jew 1933,My 12,20:4
Karajan, Herbert von (Miscellaneous)
   St Matthew Passion 1952,Ja 29,17:4
   Rosenkavalier, Der 1962,O 10,57:1
   Boheme, La 1965,O 20,51:2
   Boheme, La 1965,O 20,51:2
Karam, Elena
   America America 1963,D 16,44:1
   Ladybug, Ladybug 1963,D 24,9:1
Karamitev, A
   Heroes of Shipka 1956,S 3,10:5
Karas, Anton (Composer)
   Third Man, The 1950,F 3,29:2
Karashvilli, Kokhta
   Caucasian Love 1929,D 3,28:4
Karath, Frances
   M 1951,Je 11,20:7
   Because of You 1952,D 4,47:3
Karath, Kym
   Thrill of it All, The 1963,Ag 2,15:3
   Sound of Music, The 1965,Mr 3,34:1
Karatzopoulos, I (Producer)
   Moussitsa 1960,O 31,25:2
Karavayeva, Valentina
   Mashenka 1942,N 21,10:7
Karbanova, Ivana
   Daisies 1967,O 26,54:2
Kardas, Laszio (Director)
   120 Kilometers an Hour 1937,N 23,27:4
Kardish, Larry (Director)
   Slow Run 1968,O 11,39:1
Kardish, Larry (Producer)
   Slow Run 1968,O 11,39:1
Kardish, Larry (Screenwriter)
   Slow Run 1968,O 11,39:1
Kardo, Alexander (Director)
   Prince and the Pauper, The 1922,Ag 14,12:4
Kardos, Leslie (Director)
   Sportszerelem; Love of Sport 1938,F 14,20:8
   Dark Streets of Cairo 1940,D 2,19:3
   Small Town Girl 1953,My 7,37:2
Kardos, Leslie (Original Author)
   Dance With Me Henry 1956,D 24,8:2
Kardos, Leslie (Screenwriter)
   No Leave, No Love 1946,O 18,29:2
Karef, A M
   Greater Promise, A 1936,O 8,27:3
Karelov, E (Director)
   Last Game, The 1964,O 25,41:5 (Incorrect in this
      edition; use 1964,O 26,41:5 elsewhere)
Karels, Harvey
   Merry Widow, The 1925,Ag 27,14:1
Karelskikh, K D
   Oppenheim Family, The 1939,My 24,29:2
Karen, Bedrich
   Skeleton on Horseback 1940,F 5,13:3
   Merry Wives, The 1940,N 12,28:3

Karenne, Diana
   Casanova 1927,Je 23,23:3
   Marie Antoinette 1929,F 25,16:1
   Loves of Casanova 1929,Ap 30,33:2
   Rasputin: The Holy Devil 1930,Ag 25,14:2
   Collier de la Reine, Le (Queen's Necklace, The)
      1931,F 9,25:3
Karevsky, B (Director)
   Private Ivan 1957,Ap 3,28:2
Karewicz, Emil
   Eighth Day of the Week, The 1959,Mr 24,45:2
   Kanal 1961,My 10,52:1
Karezi, Jenny
   Trouble for Father 1958,Ja 6,26:4
   Hurdy Gurdy, The 1958,S 22,27:1
   Moment of Passion 1960,N 21,34:1
   Red Lanterns 1965,Ap 1,30:1
Karger, Maxwell (Producer)
   Should a Woman Tell? 1920,Ja 5,15:1
Kariakina, E
   Pugachev 1938,Jl 4,10:2
Karin, Ella
   Ugly Ones, The 1968,D 12,62:5
Karin, Zuzanna
   Przysieglas 1932,My 16,19:5
Karina, Anna
   Three Fables of Love (The Fox and the Crow);
      Fox and the Crow, The (Three Fables of Love)
      1963,Ag 21,38:1
   My Life to Live 1963,S 24,43:2
   Woman Is a Woman, A 1964,S 19,19:1
   Band of Outsiders 1964,S 19,19:1
   Sweet and Sour 1964,D 28,34:2
   Circle of Love 1965,Mr 25,42:4
   Alphaville 1965,S 8,51:1
   Alphaville 1965,O 26,49:1
   Band of Outsiders; Bande a Part 1966,Mr 16,48:3
   Pierre le Fou; Peter the Crazy 1966,S 22,57:2
   Petit Soldat, Le 1967,Ap 21,48:1
   Made in U S A 1967,S 28,58:2
   Stranger, The 1967,D 19,59:1
   Religieuse, La 1968,S 23,42:3
   Oldest Profession, The (Anticipation); Anticipation
      (The Oldest Profession) 1968,N 8,42:1
   Magus, The 1968,D 11,57:1
Karina, Sandra
   Port of Missing Girls, The 1938,Ap 4,12:5
KARL
   See Also CARL, CARLE
Karl, Roger
   Living Image, The 1928,Je 4,13:2
   Fantomas 1934,Mr 13,27:4
   Prince Jean, Le 1936,D 12,15:2
   Razumov 1937,Mr 9,27:2
   Golem, The 1937,Mr 22,27:2
   Lucrezia Borgia 1937,O 13,27:2
   Betrayal 1939,S 16,20:2
   Angel and Sinner 1947,F 24,16:5
   Rumors 1949,Mr 19,10:7
Karl, Rudolf
   Landstreicher, Die; Hoboes, The 1938,N 26,18:1
   Verliebte Herzen; Hearts in Love 1939,Je 10,14:2
Karlan, Richard
   Union Station 1950,O 5,38:3
   Racket, The 1951,D 13,44:2
   Wait Till the Sun Shines, Nellie 1952,Je 28,12:2
   O Henry's Full House (The Cop and the Anthem);
      Cop and the Anthem, The (O Henry's Full
      House) 1952,O 17,33:1
   Blowing Wild 1953,O 8,37:5
Karlash, Nicholas
   Cossacks in Exile 1939,Ja 28,19:2
Karlash-Verbitsky, Boris
   False Uniforms 1932,N 19,20:2
Karlin, Miriam
   Hand in Hand 1961,F 7,41:3
   Millionairess, The 1961,F 10,19:1
   Heavens Above! 1963,My 21,28:2
   Small World of Sammy Lee, The 1963,Ag 14,28:1
   Ladies Who Do 1963,N 26,52:2
Karloff, Boris
   Parisian Nights 1925,Je 2,16:3
   Her Honor the Governor 1926,Jl 20,17:3
   Soft Cushions 1927,S 12,29:1
   Two Arabian Knights 1927,O 24,24:3
   Love Mart, The 1927,D 26,16:6
   Behind That Curtain 1929,Jl 1,31:2
   Unholy Night, The 1929,O 12,11:1
   Criminal Code, The 1931,Ja 5,21:3
   Cracked Nuts 1931,Ap 6,24:1
   Donovan's Kid 1931,My 22,28:5
   Smart Money 1931,Je 19,21:1
   Public Defender, The 1931,Ag 1,16:4
   Five Star Final 1931,S 11,24:2
   I Like Your Nerve 1931,S 12,15:4
   Mad Genius, The 1931,O 24,20:3
   Yellow Ticket, The 1931,O 31,22:2
   Guilty Generation, The 1931,N 21,20:4
   Frankenstein 1931,D 5,21:2
   Tonight or Never 1931,D 18,29:2
   Business and Pleasure 1932,F 13,23:4
   Alias the Doctor 1932,Mr 3,22:3
   Miracle Man, The 1932,Ap 21,25:2

Karloff, Boris — Cont
   Behind the Mask 1932,My 2,13:2
   Scarface, The Shame of the Nation
      1932,My 20,22:3
   Night World 1932,My 28,18:2
   Old Dark House, The 1932,O 28,22:4
   Mask of Fu Manchu, The 1932,D 3,21:4
   Mummy, The 1933,Ja 7,11:2
   Ghoul, The 1934,Ja 27,9:2
   House of Rothschild, The 1934,Mr 15,27:2
   Lost Patrol, The 1934,Ap 2,13:2
   Black Cat, The 1934,My 19,18:4
   Bride of Frankenstein, The 1935,My 11,21:2
   Raven, The 1935,Jl 5,9:2
   Invisible Ray, The 1936,Ja 11,9:3
   Walking Dead, The 1936,Mr 2,13:2
   Charlie Chan at the Opera 1936,D 5,16:2
   Man Who Lived Again, The 1936,D 16,35:4
   Night Key 1937,Ap 19,27:2
   Juggernaut 1937,Jl 15,16:1
   West of Shanghai 1937,O 29,19:2
   Invisible Menace, The 1938,F 14,20:6
   Mr Wong, Detective 1938,N 21,14:4
   Son of Frankenstein 1939,Ja 30,9:2
   Mister Wong in Chinatown 1939,Jl 31,9:2 (In
      Addenda)
   Man They Could Not Hang, The 1939,S 21,21:1
   Tower of London 1939,D 12,37:2
   Fatal Hour, The 1940,Ja 13,11:2
   British Intelligence 1940,F 12,14:2
   Black Friday 1940,Mr 22,23:3
   Man With Nine Lives, The 1940,Ap 29,12:3
   Devil's Island 1940,Jl 12,11:4
   Doomed to Die 1940,Jl 30,16:3
   Before I Hang 1940,O 3,31:3
   You'll Find Out 1940,N 15,25:2
   Ape, The 1940,N 28,28:3
   Devil Commands, The 1941,F 14,15:3
   Boogie Man Will Get You, The 1942,O 12,12:4
   Climax, The 1944,D 14,28:5
   House of Frankenstein 1944,D 16,19:3
   Body Snatcher, The 1945,My 26,18:3
   Isle of the Dead 1945,S 8,12:2
   Bedlam 1946,Ap 20,16:4
   Secret Life of Walter Mitty, The 1947,Ag 15,12:2
   Lured 1947,Ag 29,14:4
   Dick Tracy and Gruesome 1947,S 27,11:2
   Unconquered 1947,O 11,11:2
   Tap Roots 1948,Ag 26,16:3
   Abbott and Costello Meet the Killer Boris Karloff
      1949,S 19,18:3
   Strange Door, The 1951,D 10,34:6
   Black Castle, The 1952,D 26,20:4
   Haunted Strangler, The 1958,Jl 4,15:3
   Days of Thrills and Laughter 1961,Mr 22,37:1
   Raven, The 1963,Ja 26,5:8
   Corridors of Blood 1963,Je 6,39:1
   Comedy of Terrors, The 1964,Ja 23,26:2
   Venetian Affair, The 1967,Ja 19,41:2
   Targets 1968,Ag 14,34:1
Karloff, Boris (Narrator)
   Emperor's Nightingale, The 1951,My 14,29:1
Karlowa, Elma
   Cabaret 1957,N 9,31:2 (Incorrect in this edition;
      use 1957,N 7,43:4 elsewhere)
   Beggar Student, The 1958,Ja 25,14:3
   Guitars of Love 1958,Jl 12,18:1
Karlsen, John
   Francis of Assisi 1961,Jl 29,8:2
   Cleopatra 1963,Je 13,29:1
   Christmas That Almost Wasn't 1966,N 24,65:2
Karlson, Phil (Director)
   Black Gold 1947,S 5,16:4
   Big Cat, The 1949,Jl 29,12:2
   Iroquois Trail, The 1950,O 27,24:4
   Mask of the Avenger 1951,Je 27,25:2
   Texas Rangers, The 1951,Jl 14,7:2
   Lorna Doone 1951,S 21,19:4
   Scandal Sheet 1952,Ja 17,23:1
   Brigand, The 1952,Jl 26,9:2
   Kansas City Confidential 1952,N 29,11:2
   99 River Street 1953,O 3,14:2
   Tight Spot 1955,Mr 19,11:7
   Hell's Island 1955,My 7,10:2
   Five Against the House 1955,Je 11,8:7
   Phenix City Story, The 1955,S 3,9:1
   Hell to Eternity 1960,O 13,41:1
   Key Witness 1960,N 12,15:1
   Secret Ways, The 1961,My 25,31:1
   Young Doctors, The 1961,Ag 24,25:2
   Kid Galahad 1963,Mr 7,8:5
   Rampage 1963,O 17,39:2
   Silencers, The 1966,Mr 17,35:1
Karlstadt, Lisl
   Mit dir Durch Dick und Duenn 1934,N 24,19:2
   Kirschen in Nachbars Garten 1937,My 15,23:6
Karlstein, Phil (Director)
   Wave, A Wac and a Marine, A 1944,Ag 14,11:4
Karlukovsky, P
   Heroes of Shipka 1956,S 3,10:5
Karlweis, Oscar
   Zwei Hertzen in Drei-Viertel Takt
      1930,O 13,31:1

Karlweis, Oscar— Cont
Foresterchristl, Die 1931,Ap 27,25:1
Drei von ver Tankstelle, Die 1931,Je 20,20:4
Dolly Macht Karriere 1931,Jl 18,16:6
Sein Liebeslied 1931,N 19,27:5
Tanzhusar, Der 1933,Ap 10,8:4
Five Fingers 1952,F 23,7:5
Anything Can Happen 1952,Ap 4,21:1
Tonight We Sing 1953,F 13,17:2
Juggler, The 1953,My 6,39:2
Meet Me in Las Vegas 1956,Mr 14,39:2

Karlyev, A
Under Sunny Skies 1950,D 26,19:3

Karman, Roman (Director)
Visit to India 1956,Ap 16,30:4

Karmazinski, N (Director)
If War Comes Tomorrow 1938,Jl 14,17:2

Karmel, Alex (Original Author)
Something Wild 1961,D 24,30:6

Karmel, Alex (Screenwriter)
Something Wild 1961,D 24,30:6

Karmen, R (Cinematographer)
Caspian Story 1954,Ag 2,12:3

Karmen, R (Director)
Albania 1946,Jl 15,21:1
Caspian Story 1954,Ag 2,12:3
Great is my Country 1959,Jl 1,26:1
One Day With Russians 1961,Mr 13,36:6
Cinerama's Russian Adventure 1966,Ap 14,42:1

Karmen, R (Narrator)
Great is my Country 1959,Jl 1,26:1

Karmen, R (Producer)
Nuremberg Trials, The 1947,My 26,24:2
Great is my Country 1959,Jl 1,26:1

Karmen, R (Screenwriter)
One Day in Soviet Russia 1941,O 27,21:2

Karn, Roger
Moscow Nights 1938,My 3,19:3

Karnelly, Lelia
Cock Eyed World, The 1929,Ag 5,25:2
Married in Hollywood 1929,S 23,24:3

Karnes, Robert
Daisy Kenyon 1947,D 25,32:1
Captain from Castile 1947,D 26,22:4
Scudda-Hoo! Scudda-Hay! 1948,Ap 15,31:1
Road House 1948,N 8,24:2
Three Husbands 1951,Mr 9,30:2
From Here to Eternity 1953,Ag 6,16:2
Riders to the Stars 1954,Mr 20,10:7

Karnilova, Maria
Unsinkable Molly Brown, The 1964,Jl 17,15:1

Karns, Roscoe
Life of the Party, The 1920,N 22,13:3
Bluff 1924,Ap 28,18:2
Midnight Express, The 1924,N 19,19:3
Ritzy 1927,Je 20,25:3
Ten Modern Commandments 1927,Jl 11,23:4
Beau Sabreur 1928,Ja 23,18:3
Something Always Happens 1928,My 21,25:1
Warming Up 1928,Jl 16,25:3
Beggars of Life 1928,S 24,25:1
Win That Girl 1928,O 1,23:1
This Thing Called Love 1929,D 14,22:4
New York Nights 1930,F 1,15:1
Troopers Three 1930,F 17,17:6
Safety in Numbers 1930,My 31,19:4
Little Accident 1930,Ag 4,13:4
Costello Case, The 1930,N 4,36:1
Gorilla, The 1931,F 23,20:3
Dirigible 1931,Ap 6,24:1
Laughing Sinners 1931,Jl 4,11:5
Leftover Ladies 1931,N 9,22:4
Roadhouse Murder 1932,Ap 29,13:4
Night after Night 1932,O 31,18:4
If I Had a Million 1932,D 3,21:4
Under-Cover Man 1932,D 5,21:2
Lawyer Man 1932,D 27,10:2
Lady's Profession, A 1933,Mr 25,13:3
Today We Live 1933,Ap 15,16:2
Gambling Ship 1933,Jl 13,17:5
One Sunday Afternoon 1933,S 2,14:4
Alice in Wonderland 1933,D 23,19:1
Women in his Life, The 1934,Ja 27,9:3
Search for Beauty 1934,F 10,20:2
It Happened One Night 1934,F 23,23:2
Come on Marines 1934,Mr 24,20:3
20th Century 1934,My 4,24:2
Shoot the Works 1934,Jl 7,16:5
Elmer and Elsie 1934,Ag 4,14:5
I Sell Anything 1934,D 27,25:2
Wings in the Dark 1935,F 2,10:1
Red Hot Tires 1935,Mr 1,16:3
Four Hours to Kill 1935,Ap 11,27:3
Front Page Woman 1935,Jl 12,15:1
Alibi Ike 1935,Jl 17,22:1
Two Fisted 1935,O 5,18:3
Woman Trap 1936,Mr 7,11:4
Border Flight 1936,Je 22,22:1
Three Cheers for Love 1936,Ag 1,16:2
Cain and Mabel 1936,O 19,22:1
On Such a Night 1937,S 17,29:2
Scandal Street 1938,F 5,19:2 (In Addenda)
Dangerous to Know 1938,Mr 11,15:4
Tip-Off Girls 1938,Mr 25,15:3

You and Me 1938,Je 2,19:1
Thanks for the Memory 1938,D 8,34:3
King of Chinatown 1939,Mr 16,27:2
Everything's on Ice 1939,O 6,31:1
Dancing Co-Ed 1939,N 10,27:3
That's Right, You're Wrong 1939,N 30,25:3
His Girl Friday 1940,Ja 12,13:2
Double Alibi 1940,Mr 11,11:2
Saturday's Children 1940,My 4,13:1
They Drive by Night 1940,Jl 27,17:5
Ladies Must Live 1940,S 6,25:3
Footsteps in the Dark 1941,Mr 15,13:2
Woman of the Year 1942,F 6,23:2
Road to Happiness 1942,Mr 27,27:4
You Can't Escape Forever 1942,O 17,11:1
Stage Door Canteen 1943,Je 25,13:2
Old Acquaintance 1943,N 3,20:2
Minstrel Man 1944,Jl 17,18:5
Avalanche 1946,Jl 8,25:2
That's my Man 1947,Ap 7,20:2
Onionhead 1958,O 2,44:1
Man's Favorite Sport? 1964,F 20,22:1

Karns, Todd
Andy Hardy's Private Secretary 1941,Mr 7,17:2
Courtship of Andy Hardy, The 1942,Ap 10,21:2
It's a Wonderful Life 1946,D 23,19:2
Good Sam 1948,S 17,28:2
My Son John 1952,Ap 9,27:1
Battle Zone 1952,N 1,17:2
Mission Over Korea 1953,S 19,7:2

Karns, Virginia
Babes in Toyland 1934,D 13,28:2

Karousos, T
Antigone 1962,S 19,30:1
You Came too Late 1962,N 12,35:8

Karoussos, Giorgos
Phaedra 1962,O 19,24:1

Karp, David (Screenwriter)
Sol Madrid 1968,Je 14,43:1

Karp, Theodore B (Screenwriter)
Feeling of Inferiority, The 1948,D 27,16:4

Karpova, Z A
Mother and Sons 1938,S 15,29:2

KARR
See Also CARR

Karr, David (Producer)
Money Trap, The 1966,My 5,59:1
Welcome to Hard Times 1967,My 2,56:1

Karr, Mabel
Colossus of Rhodes, The 1961,D 14,55:6

Karras, Alex
Paper Lion 1968,O 24,54:1

Karras, Athan
Dark Odyssey 1961,Je 26,22:2

Karsenil, Annette
To be a Crook 1967,F 7,33:2

Karsner, David (Original Author)
Silver Dollar 1932,D 23,20:1

Kartalian, Buck
Mister Roberts 1955,Jl 15,14:1

Kartashova, L
Ski Battalion 1938,Mr 14,13:1
Blue Cliff, The 1943,Mr 25,25:3
Taras Family, The 1946,D 9,34:4

Kasahara, Kenji
Rikisha Man, The 1960,My 4,57:1

Kasatkina, Lena
Tiger Girl 1955,S 5,8:2

Kasatkina, Natalia
Bolshoi Ballet 67 1966,S 30,54:1

Kascoh, Pongracz (Composer)
Janos Vitez; John, The Hero 1939,Ap 8,19:2

Kasday, David
Miami Story, The 1954,My 15,13:2
I'll Cry Tomorrow 1956,Ja 13,18:1
Benny Goodman Story 1956,F 22,22:1
Invitation to the Dance (Sinbad the Sailor); Sinbad
the Sailor (Invitation to the Dance)
1956,My 23,35:7

Kasher, Charles (Producer)
Funeral in Berlin 1966,D 23,17:1

Kasheverova, Nadezhda (Director)
Christmas Slippers 1945,D 24,19:2

Kasheverova, Nadezhda (Screenwriter)
Christmas Slippers 1945,D 24,19:2

Kashey, Abe (King Kong)
That Nazty Nuisance 1943,My 29,10:3
Crime Doctor's Courage, The 1945,Mr 3,11:3

Kashfi, Anna
Mountain, The 1956,N 15,44:6
Battle Hymn 1957,F 16,14:1
Cowboy 1958,F 20,29:5
Night of the Quarter Moon 1959,Mr 5,35:5

Kashinskya, Dora
Youth of Russia, The 1934,N 10,19:3

Kashkarova, Z
Nightingale 1936,N 4,41:2

Kashner, Bruno
Love Commandment, The 1928,D 25,31:3

Kashner, Dave
Sundowners, The 1950,My 5,17:2
High Lonesome 1950,D 8,40:4

Kashnjtskaya, Elena
Return of Nathan Becker, The 1933,Ap 15,16:3

Kashpur
Last Game, The 1964,O 25,41:5 (Incorrect in this
edition; use 1964,O 26,41:5 elsewhere)

Kashyap, J S
Guide, The 1965,F 10,44:2

Kasimov, K
Heroes of Shipka 1956,S 3,10:5

Kasket, Harold
Beau Brummell 1954,O 21,31:5
Stowaway Girl 1957,N 6,43:3
Boy Who Stole a Million, The 1960,D 22,18:3
Return of Mr Moto 1965,D 2,48:1
Arabesque 1966,My 6,54:1

Kasnar, Kurt
Glory Alley 1952,Jl 30,20:8
Ambushers, The 1967,D 23,29:1

Kassagi
Pickpocket 1963,My 22,36:2

Kassen, Mohamed Ben
Battle of Algiers, The 1967,S 21,56:1

Kassewitz, Helene
William Tell 1925,My 20,26:2

Kasslo, Hugo
Sunshine Follows Rain 1949,S 29,39:2

Kassowitz, Peter
My Life to Live 1963,S 24,43:2

Kast, Pierre (Director)
Season for Love, The 1963,My 9,40:2

Kast, Pierre (Screenwriter)
Season for Love, The 1963,My 9,40:2

Kastner, Bruno
Luther 1929,Je 24,27:1
Carnival Crime, The 1929,Jl 8,17:3

Kastner, Elliott (Producer)
Bus Riley's Back in Town 1965,Ap 8,45:2
Harper 1966,Mr 31,43:1
Kaleidoscope 1966,S 23,45:1
Bobo, The 1967,S 29,53:1
Sweet November 1968,F 9,55:1

Kastner, Eric (Original Author)
Paradise for Three 1938,F 16,17:1
Emil 1938,Ap 15,23:2
Parent Trap, The 1961,Je 22,23:1

Kastner, Peter
Nobody Waved Goodbye 1964,S 17,52:1
You're a Big Boy Now 1967,Mr 21,35:3

Kasu, Sanpei (Miscellaneous)
New Japanese Cinema, The (Trap); Trap (The
New Japanese Cinema) 1968,My 3,42:1

Kasyanova, L
Don Quixote 1961,Ja 21,18:1

Kasznar, Kurt
Light Touch, The 1952,Ja 17,23:1
Anything Can Happen 1952,Ap 4,21:1
Lovely to Look At 1952,My 30,11:2
Happy Time, The 1952,O 31,30:2
Lili 1953,Mr 11,36:7
Sombrero 1953,Ap 23,37:2
Ride Vaquero 1953,Jl 16,17:2
Kiss Me Kate 1953,N 6,23:2
All the Brothers Were Valiant 1953,D 29,19:2
Valley of the Kings 1954,Jl 22,15:2
Last Time I saw Paris, The 1954,N 19,20:2
My Sister Eileen 1955,S 23,21:1
Flame of the Islands 1956,F 25,12:4
Anything Goes 1956,Mr 22,38:1
Legend of the Lost 1957,D 23,18:2
Farewell to Arms, A 1958,Ja 25,14:1
Journey, The 1959,F 20,19:1
For the First Time 1959,Ag 15,8:7
Arms and the Man 1962,F 24,21:7
55 Days at Peking 1963,My 30,20:1
Casino Royale 1967,Ap 29,25:1
Perils of Pauline, The 1967,Ag 3,26:3

Katanyan, Vassili (Miscellaneous)
Plisetskaya Dances 1965,Ap 19,37:1

Katayev, Valentin (Original Author)
Lonely White Sail 1938,My 7,18:1
Son of the Regiment 1948,Ap 29,27:3

Katayev, Valentin (Screenwriter)
Lonely White Sail 1938,My 7,18:1
Son of the Regiment 1948,Ap 29,27:3

Katch, Kurt
Tkies Khaf; (Vow, The) 1938,S 15,29:3
Man at Large 1941,O 11,21:4
Secret Agent of Japan 1942,Mr 23,19:3
Berlin Correspondent 1942,S 4,19:2
Counter-Espionage 1942,S 28,13:2
Quiet Please, Murder 1942,D 22,31:1
Mission to Moscow 1943,Ap 30,25:2
Background to Danger 1943,Jl 3,11:2
Watch on the Rhine 1943,Ag 28,15:1
Purple Heart, The 1944,Mr 9,15:2
Make Your own Bed 1944,My 27,12:2
Mask of Dimitrios, The 1944,Je 24,16:2
Seventh Cross, The 1944,S 29,18:1
Conspirators, The 1944,O 21,15:2
Salome, Where She Danced 1945,My 3,27:1
Angel on my Shoulder 1946,O 21,27:2
Song of Love 1947,O 10,31:2
Secret of the Incas 1954,My 29,13:3

Katch, Kurt — Cont
Adventures of Haji Baba, The 1954,O 9,8:7
Girl in the Kremlin, The 1957,My 22,29:2
Katcha, Vahe (Original Author)
Eye for an Eye, An 1961,F 10,19:1
Hook, The 1963,F 16,5:6
Katcha, Vahe (Screenwriter)
Eye for an Eye, An 1961,F 10,19:1
Galia 1966,D 20,50:4
Katchalof, V I
Lash of the Czar, The 1929,F 12,23:1
Path to Life, The 1931,Jl 9,VIII,4:3
Katcher, Aram
Spy Hunt 1950,S 8,25:2
Flight to Hong Kong 1957,Ja 3,28:2
Girl in the Kremlin, The 1957,My 22,29:2
Do Not Disturb 1965,D 25,17:2
Katcher, Leo (Original Author)
Between Midnight and Dawn 1950,O 2,19:2
Naked Street, The 1955,O 1,11:2
Eddy Duchin Story, The 1956,Je 22,15:1
Party Girl 1958,O 29,30:1
King of the Roaring Twenties 1961,O 5,43:1
Island of Love 1963,Je 13,30:4
Katcher, Leo (Screenwriter)
M 1951,Je 11,20:7
Naked Street, The 1955,O 1,11:2
Katcher, Robert
Jack London 1944,Mr 3,19:3
Kath, Katherine
Moulin Rouge 1953,F 11,33:5
Inside a Girls' Dormitory 1956,F 6,27:7
Gigot 1962,S 28,26:1
Circus World 1964,Je 26,34:2
Katharyna
Circus World 1964,Je 26,34:2
Katkov, Notrman (Original Author)
It Happened to Jane 1959,Ag 6,18:3
Katkov, Notrman (Screenwriter)
It Happened to Jane 1959,Ag 6,18:3
Kato, Daisuke
Rasho-Mon 1951,D 27,18:3
Magnificent Seven, The 1956,N 20,46:2
Yojimbo 1962,O 16,34:1
When a Woman Ascends the Stairs
 1963,Je 26,36:4
Naked General, The 1964,D 16,51:2
Samurai (Part II) 1967,O 21,16:1
Kato, Takeshi
Bad Sleep Well, The 1963,Ja 23,5:2
None but the Brave 1965,F 25,24:1
Rebellion 1967,S 25,56:4
Rebellion 1968,O 26,27:4
Katoh, Yoshi
Hiroshima 1955,My 17,32:1
Katona, Victor (Screenwriter)
Once Upon a Dream 1949,Jl 15,17:2
Katrakis, Manos
Electra 1962,D 18,5:2
Red Lanterns 1965,Ap 1,30:1
Katri, Vera
Bed of Grass 1957,D 28,9:2
Katscher, Robert (Original Author)
Wonder Bar 1934,Mr 1,23:2
Katscher, Rudolf (Director)
Teilnehmer Antwortet Nicht 1932,N 30,23:6
Katscher, Rudolph (Screenwriter)
Tiger von Berlin, Der 1930,S 15,29:3
Katsiotes, Nico (Screenwriter)
Barefoot Battalion 1954,My 29,13:4
Katsu, Shintaro
Buddha 1965,Je 17,27:4
Great Wall, The 1965,D 16,63:2
Zatoichi 1968,Je 28,37:1
Showdown for Zatoichi 1968,O 5,40:1
Katsumoto, K
Bridge on the River Kwai 1957,D 19,39:1
Katt, Geraldine
Irene 1936,D 13,XI,6:6 (In Addenda)
Maedchen Irene, Das 1937,My 22,19:3
Katterjohn, Monte M (Original Author)
Social Celebrity, A 1926,Ap 19,24:3
Katterjohn, Monte M (Screenwriter)
Moran of the Lady Letty 1922,F 6,9:1
Green Temptation, The 1922,Mr 20,10:3
Impossible Mrs Bellew, The 1922,O 23,10:1
Prodigal Daughters 1923,Ap 17,26:3
Katz, Joel
Cyanamide 1954,Mr 26,17:6
Katz, Lee (Original Author)
Blackwell's Island 1939,Mr 2,19:1
Kid Nightingale 1939,D 8,33:6
Katz, Lee (Screenwriter)
Heart of the North 1938,D 21,29:2
Women in the Wind 1939,Ap 13,27:2
Waterfront 1939,Jl 17,10:2
Return Of Doctor X, The 1939,N 23,38:5
British Intelligence 1940,F 12,14:2
Katz, Pitzy
Dough Boys 1930,S 30,23:1
Katz, Ruth
Cyanamide 1954,Mr 26,17:6

Katz, Z
Dybbuk, The 1938,Ja 28,17:2
Katzman, Sam (Producer)
East Side Kids 1940,F 19,21:6
Ghost Creeps, The 1940,Ag 19,13:3
Pride of the Bowery 1941,Ja 24,15:2
Flying Wild 1941,Ap 12,19:3
Invisible Ghost, The 1941,My 8,21:2
Spooks Run Wild 1941,N 1,20:3
Mr Wise Guy 1942,Mr 5,27:2
Last of the Redmen 1947,Ag 30,8:6
Jungle Jim 1949,Ja 1,9:2
Barbary Pirate 1949,O 28,29:3
Chinatown at Midnight 1949,N 18,35:3
Mark of the Gorilla 1950,F 17,27:2
Last of the Buccaneers 1950,D 15,43:2
Yank in Korea, A 1951,Ap 2,29:2
Thief of Damascus 1952,My 8,37:2
California Conquest 1952,Je 7,22:6
Golden Hawk, The 1952,O 18,16:4
Fort Ti 1953,My 30,7:1
Drums of Tahiti 1954,Ap 24,14:5
Saracen Blade, The 1954,My 15,13:4
Miami Story, The 1954,My 15,13:2
Pirates of Tripoli 1955,F 24,21:2
New Orleans Uncensored 1955,Ap 30,10:8
Blackjack Ketchum Desperado 1956,Ap 5,26:2
Don't Knock the Rock 1957,F 23,13:1
Last Blitzkrieg, The 1959,Ja 31,13:5
Flying Fontaines, The 1959,D 24,13:6
Enemy General, The 1960,O 20,42:2
Wizard of Baghdad, The 1961,Mr 4,16:1
Twist Around the Clock 1962,Ja 27,13:4
Don't Knock the Twist 1962,Ap 14,14:2
Kissin' Cousins 1964,Ap 2,28:3
Get Yourself a College Girl 1965,Ap 29,40:2
Your Cheatin' Heart 1965,My 20,52:2
Harum Scarum 1965,D 16,63:3
When the Boys Meet the Girls 1966,Ja 20,29:1
Hold On! 1966,Je 23,29:4
Hot Rods to Hell 1967,Ag 10,45:5
Love-Ins, The 1967,Ag 19,16:1
Fastest Guitar Alive, The 1968,F 15,47:1
For Singles Only 1968,Je 6,54:1
Young Runaways, The 1968,S 12,54:3
Kaufman, Allan (Miscellaneous)
Cyanamide 1954,Mr 26,17:6
Kaufman, Bel (Original Author)
Up the Down Staircase 1967,Ag 18,36:2
Kaufman, Boris (Cinematographer)
Now Cinema! (Film); Film (Now Cinema!)
 1968,Ap 9,56:1
Kaufman, Charles (Original Author)
Cinerama-South Seas Adventure 1958,Jl 16,26:1
Freud 1962,D 13,37:1
Kaufman, Charles (Screenwriter)
Saturday's Heroes 1937,O 16,22:2
Breakfast for Two 1937,N 20,21:2
Saint in New York, The 1938,My 26,31:2
Exposed 1938,N 21,14:5
Model Wife 1941,Ap 24,25:3
Paris Calling 1942,Ja 19,21:2
Cynthia 1947,S 19,27:2
Return to Paradise 1953,S 11,24:2
Racers, The 1955,F 5,13:2
Story of Esther Costello, The 1957,N 6,43:1
Bridge to the Sun 1961,O 18,50:1
Freud 1962,D 13,37:1
Kaufman, Edward (Miscellaneous)
Gay Divorcee, The 1934,N 16,27:1
Kaufman, Edward (Original Author)
Cockeyed Cavaliers 1934,Jl 25,22:2
Kaufman, Edward (Producer)
Lady Consents, The 1936,F 6,23:4
Ex-Mrs Bradford, The 1936,My 28,19:2
Life of the Party, The 1937,O 4,17:1
Breakfast for Two 1937,N 20,21:2
Wise Girl 1938,Ja 10,13:3
Radio City Revels 1938,Mr 21,18:3
They all Kissed the Bride 1942,Jl 31,11:1
Song of Scheherazade 1947,F 27,26:2
Kaufman, Edward (Screenwriter)
Romance in Manhattan 1935,Ja 18,29:2
McFadden's Flats 1935,Mr 13,16:2
Star of Midnight 1935,Ap 12,26:5
Affectionally Yours 1941,My 24,18:2
Kaufman, George S (Director)
Senator Was Indiscreet, The 1947,D 27,9:2
Kaufman, George S (Original Author)
Dulcy 1923,S 17,18:2
To the Ladies 1923,N 26,15:6
Merton of the Movies 1924,S 8,15:3
Welcome Home 1925,My 18,12:1
Beggar on Horseback 1925,Je 6,9:2
Butter and Egg Man, The 1928,Ag 28,27:4
Not so Dumb 1930,F 8,12:5
Animal Crackers 1930,Ag 29,20:3
Royal Family of Broadway, The 1930,D 23,25:1
June Moon 1931,Mr 14,23:2

Kaufman, George S (Original Author) — Cont
Tenderfoot, The 1932,My 23,18:4
Make Me a Star 1932,Jl 1,19:3
Once in a Lifetime 1932,O 29,18:4
Dinner at Eight 1933,Ag 24,18:1
Roman Scandals 1933,Ag 25,28:2
Elmer and Elsie 1934,Ag 4,14:5
Blonde Trouble 1937,Ag 7,7:2
Dance Charlie Dance 1937,Ag 26,25:2
Stage Door 1937,O 8,27:2
First Lady 1937,D 23,25:1
You Can't Take It With You 1938,S 2,21:2
Angel From Texas, An 1940,My 10,26:7
Dulcy 1940,N 28,28:2
Man Who Came to Dinner, The 1942,Ja 2,25:2
George Washington Slept Here 1942,O 31,11:1
Late George Apley, The 1947,Mr 21,29:2
Merton of the Movies 1947,N 7,20:3
Three Sailors and a Girl 1953,N 23,32:2
Solid Gold Cadillac, The 1956,O 25,40:3
Kaufman, George S (Screenwriter)
Night at the Opera, A 1935,D 7,22:1
Kaufman, Joseph (Producer)
Lucky Nick Cain 1951,Ap 23,21:2
Pandora and the Flying Dutchman 1951,D 7,35:2
Sudden Fear 1952,Ag 8,9:2
Long John Silver 1955,Ap 7,24:1
Another Time Another Place 1958,My 3,10:4
Black Tights 1962,F 21,54:2
Kaufman, Leonard B (Producer)
Clarence, the Cross-Eyed Lion 1965,Ag 5,15:3
Kaufman, Millard (Director)
Convicts 4 1962,O 4,44:2
Kaufman, Millard (Original Author)
Take the High Ground 1953,N 20,19:2
Kaufman, Millard (Screenwriter)
Gun Crazy 1950,Ag 25,17:5
Take the High Ground 1953,N 20,19:2
Bad Day at Black Rock 1955,F 2,22:2
Raintree County 1957,D 21,22:1
Never so Few 1960,Ja 22,15:2
Convicts 4 1962,O 4,44:2
War Lord, The 1965,N 18,55:2
Kaufman, Philip (Director)
Goldstein 1965,My 8,19:7
Kaufman, Philip (Screenwriter)
Goldstein 1965,My 8,19:7
Kaufman, Robert
Flower Thief, The 1962,Jl 14,11:5
Kaufman, Robert (Original Author)
Divorce American Style 1967,Jl 20,30:2
Kaufman, Robert (Screenwriter)
Ski Party 1965,O 23,17:3
Dr Goldfoot and the Bikini Machine
 1966,F 17,29:3
Cool Ones, The 1967,My 11,50:1
Kaufman, S Jay (Original Author)
Dance Madness 1926,Ja 25,21:2
Kaufman, S Jay (Screenwriter)
Highlowbrow 1929,Ja 28,21:1
Kaufman, Sidney (Miscellaneous)
Behind the Great Wall 1959,D 10,51:6
Kaufman, Sidney (Original Author)
Sorcerers' Village 1958,Jl 3,22:6
Kaufman, Sidney (Producer)
Sorcerers' Village 1958,Jl 3,22:6
Kaufman, Sidney (Screenwriter)
Behind the Great Wall 1959,D 10,51:6
Kaufman, Will
Confessions of a Nazi Spy 1939,Ap 29,13:2
Nurse Edith Cavell 1939,S 22,27:4
Beasts of Berlin 1939,N 20,15:6
British Intelligence 1940,F 12,14:2
Man I Married, The 1940,Ag 3,9:2
Mystery Sea Raider 1940,Ag 26,11:4
Kaufman, Wolfe (Original Author)
Sued for Libel 1940,Ja 19,15:3
Lone Wolf Meets a Lady, The 1940,Je 17,19:2
**Kaufman-Alexander Woollcott, George S (Original
                                      /Author)**
Man With two Faces, The 1934,Jl 12,20:2
Kaufmann, Christine
Embezzled Heaven 1959,Ap 24,23:1
Last Days of Pompeii, The 1960,Ag 11,19:1
Town Without Pity 1961,O 11,53:1
Swordsman of Siena 1962,D 6,55:3
Escape from East Berlin 1962,D 6,55:3
Taras Bulba 1962,D 26,5:2
Constantine and the Cross 1963,Mr 14,8:2
Red Lips 1964,Mr 19,28:2
Wild and Wonderful 1964,Je 11,27:4
Madchen in Uniform 1965,Ag 18,41:2
Kaufmann, Maurice
Shot in the Dark, A 1964,Je 24,28:1
Die! Die! My Darling 1965,My 20,52:1
Kaufmann (Cinematographer)
Moscow Today 1929,My 13,27:2
Kaus, Gina (Miscellaneous)
Whispering City 1948,My 10,25:5
Kaus, Gina (Original Author)
Luxury Liner 1933,F 3,21:3
Prison Without Bars 1939,Ap 10,13:2
Affair Lafont, The; Conflict 1939,O 9,15:2
Charlie Chan in City in Darkness 1939,D 18,29:2

Kaus, Gina (Original Author) — Cont

Night Before the Divorce, The 1942,Ap 10,21:3
Wife Takes a Flyer, The 1942,Je 19,19:1
They all Kissed the Bride 1942,Jl 31,11:1
Her Sister's Secret 1947,Ja 23,31:3
We're not Married 1952,Jl 12,16:2

Kaus, Gina (Screenwriter)

Affair Lafont, The; Conflit 1939,O 9,15:2
Wife Takes a Flyer, The 1942,Je 19,19:1
Julia Misbehaves 1948,O 8,30:2
Red Danube, The 1949,D 9,37:3
Three Secrets 1950,O 21,10:6
Robe, The 1953,S 17,32:6
Tempestous Love 1958,N 22,27:4

Kautner, Helmut

Original Sin, The 1950,Ag 21,15:2

Kautner, Helmut (Director)

Original Sin, The 1950,Ag 21,15:2
Seven Journeys 1951,Mr 12,20:2
Devil's General, The 1957,Ap 16,38:2
Last Bridge, The 1957,Ag 21,22:2
Portrait of an Unknown Woman 1958,Ap 26,14:6
Captain from Koepenick, The 1958,Jl 26,6:1
Affairs of Julie, The 1958,D 10,53:1
Stranger in my Arms 1959,Mr 4,34:2
Montpi 1959,Ap 21,40:1
Sky Without Stars 1959,My 30,9:2
Rest Is Silence, The 1960,Ag 2,22:6

Kautner, Helmut (Original Author)

Seven Journeys 1951,Mr 12,20:2

Kautner, Helmut (Producer)

Rest Is Silence, The 1960,Ag 2,22:6

Kautner, Helmut (Screenwriter)

Original Sin, The 1950,Ag 21,15:2
Film Without a Name 1950,O 20,32:2
Devil's General, The 1957,Ap 16,38:2
Last Bridge, The 1957,Ag 21,22:2
Reaching for the Stars 1958,My 24,18:2
Captain from Koepenick, The 1958,Jl 26,6:1
Affairs of Julie, The 1958,D 10,53:1
Montpi 1959,Ap 21,40:1
Sky Without Stars 1959,My 30,9:2
Rest Is Silence, The 1960,Ag 2,22:6

Kavadia, Tasso

Windfall in Athens 1956,O 1,31:1
Stefania 1968,N 29,56:1

Kavaleridze, E (Director)

Mass Struggle 1934,S 17,20:3
Natalka-Poltavka 1936,D 25,19:4

KAVANAGH

See Also CAVANAGH, CAVANAUGH, KAVANAUGH

Kavanagh, H T (Original Author)

Darby O'Gill and the Little People 1959,Jl 1,26:1

KAVANAUGH

See Also CAVANAGH, CAVANAUGH, KAVANAGH

Kavanaugh, Katharine (Miscellaneous)

Off to the Races 1937,F 6,15:2
Hot Water 1937,N 5,19:4
Trip to Paris, A 1938,Je 10,18:2

Kavanaugh, Katharine (Original Author)

Every Saturday Night 1936,Mr 14,10:2

Kavanaugh, Katharine (Screenwriter)

Educating Father 1936,Je 20,22:2

Kavil, Karin

All These Women 1964,O 6,35:1

Kawaguchi, Hiroshi

Buddha 1965,Je 17,27:4
Great Wall, The 1965,D 16,63:2

Kawaguchi, Matsutaro (Screenwriter)

Ugetsu 1954,S 8,40:3
Yang Kwei Fei 1956,S 11,41:2

Kawalerowicz, Jerzy (Director)

Joan of the Angels? 1962,My 8,43:6

Kawalerowicz, Jerzy (Screenwriter)

Joan of the Angels? 1962,My 8,43:6

Kawasaki, Keizo

Buddha 1965,Je 17,27:4

Kawashima, Yuzo (Director)

This Madding Crowd 1964,Je 17,48:1

Kawazu, Seizaburo

Yojimbo 1962,O 16,34:1
Insect Woman, The; Nippon Konchuki 1964,Jl 1,42:1
Saga of the Vagabonds 1964,O 7,31:1 (Incorrect in this edition; use 1964,O 7,51:1 elsewhere)
Utamaro, Painter of Women 1964,D 2,57:1

Kawinska, Stanislawa

Kazdemu Wolno Kochac 1933,My 24,24:3

Kay, Andrew

Cry, the Beloved Country 1952,Ja 24,23:2

Kay, Arthur

William Fox Movietone Follies of 1929 1929,My 27,22:1
Girl Said No, The 1937,O 18,14:1

Kay, Beatrice

Billy Rose's Diamond Horseshoe 1945,My 3,37:1
Underworld, U S A 1961,My 13,10:1

Kay, Bernard

Shuttered Room, The 1968,F 15,47:1
Interlude 1968,Jl 3,26:1

Kay, Geraldine

Crime of Dr Crespi, The 1936,Ja 13,14:3

Kay, Gilbert L (Director)

Three bad Sisters 1956,F 13,24:1
Secret Door, The 1964,Je 4,28:1

Kay, Gordon (Producer)

Man Afraid 1957,Ap 5,24:2
Quantez 1957,S 7,12:7
Day of the Badman 1958,Ja 30,19:2
Twilight for the Gods 1958,Ag 7,21:1
Voice in the Mirror 1958,Ag 14,23:2
Seven Ways From Sundown 1960,D 22,18:4
6 Black Horses 1962,Ap 25,30:1
He Rides Tall 1964,F 27,28:1
Fluffy 1965,O 21,57:2
Young Warriors, The 1968,F 8,36:1

Kay, Joyce

As the Earth Turns 1934,Ap 12,27:2
Prisoner of Shark Island, The 1936,F 13,25:2

Kay, Karol

Second Hand Wife 1933,Ja 14,8:4

Kay, Kathryn

Artists and Models 1937,Ag 5,19:2

Kay, Mary Ellen

Tarzan and the Slave Girl 1950,Je 24,7:3
Vice Squad 1953,Ag 26,23:2
Long Wait, The 1954,Jl 3,9:2
Francis in the Haunted House 1956,Jl 21,9:2

Kay, Richard (Producer)

Golden Mistress, The 1954,O 30,15:6
She Shoulda Said No 1957,Ja 31,21:1

Kay, Roger (Director)

Cabinet of Caligari, The 1962,My 26,13:5

Kay, Roger (Screenwriter)

Cabinet of Caligari, The 1962,My 26,13:5

Kay, Sylvia

Rapture 1965,Ag 24,25:3

Kay, Wanda

Our Neighbors-The Carters 1940,F 15,15:2

Kayama, Shigeru (Miscellaneous)

Mysterians, The 1959,Jl 2,15:2

Kayama, Yuzo

Happiness of Us Alone 1963,Ap 10,31:5
Sanjuro 1963,My 8,34:2
Chushingura 1963,O 4,26:1
Different Sons 1964,F 13,25:1
Honolulu-Tokyo-Hong Kong 1964,S 2,33:3
Sword of Doom, The 1967,Ap 15,35:2
Red Beard 1968,D 20,60:4

Kaye, Benjamin (Original Author)

She Couldn't Say No 1930,F 16,III,8:1
She Couldn't Say No 1941,Ja 17,21:3

Kaye, Buddy (Composer)

Fun and Fancy Free 1947,S 29,17:2 (In Addenda)

Kaye, Celia

Island of the Blue Dolphins 1964,Jl 4,8:2

Kaye, Claudelle

Manhattan Melodrama 1934,My 5,22:2
Flame Within, The 1935,Je 1,18:2

Kaye, Danny

Up in Arms 1944,Mr 3,19:2
Wonder Man 1945,Je 9,17:2
Kid From Brooklyn, The 1946,Ap 19,25:2
Secret Life of Walter Mitty, The 1947,Ag 15,12:2
Song Is Born, A 1948,O 20,37:2
Inspector General, The 1949,D 31,9:2
On the Riviera 1951,My 24,47:1
Hans Christian Andersen 1952,N 26,20:2
Hans Christian Andersen 1953,S 7,14:6
Knock on Wood 1954,Ap 15,34:2
White Christmas 1954,O 15,16:3
Court Jester, The 1956,F 2,19:1
Merry Andrews 1958,Mr 21,17:1
Me and the Colonel 1958,Ag 27,33:1
Five Pennies, The 1959,Je 19,30:1
On the Double 1961,My 20,12:1
Man From the Diners' Club, The 1963,Ap 18,39:1
Sound of Laughter, The 1963,D 18,44:2

Kaye, Davy

Wrong Arm of the Law, The 1963,Ap 3,39:1
Biggest Bundle of Them All, The 1968,Ja 18,46:1

Kaye, Elaine

Patterns 1956,Mr 28,26:1

Kaye, Leo

Song of my Heart 1948,Mr 5,17:3

Kaye, Maira

Taste of Honey, A 1962,My 1,33:3

Kaye, Paul

Easy to Love 1934,Ja 15,12:2
Romance in the Rain 1934,S 8,18:5
Night Life of the Gods 1935,F 23,14:6

Kaye, Stubby

Taxi 1953,Ja 22,20:3
Guys and Dolls 1955,N 5,26:1
Li'l Abner 1959,D 12,19:2
40 Pounds of Trouble 1963,Ja 24,5:2
Cat Ballou 1965,Je 25,36:1
Way West, The 1967,My 25,54:1

Kaye, Suzie

West Side Story 1961,O 19,39:3
Wild Wild Winter 1966,Ja 6,20:2

Kaye, Suzie — Cont

C'mon Let's Live a Little 1967,My 4,34:1

Kayne, Jan

I Can Get It for You Wholesale 1951,Ap 5,34:4

Kayrouz, Toulic (Producer)

Broken Wings, The 1968,Mr 16,34:1

Kayser, Charles Willy

Waterloo 1929,Ap 16,32:5

Kayssler, Christian

D III 88, Die neue deutsche Luftwaffe greift an; D III 88, The New German Air Force Attacks 1940,F 17,9:3

Kayssler, Friedrich

Modern du Barry, A 1928,Mr 19,26:2
Burning Heart, The 1930,My 12,27:3
Floetenkonzert von Sanssouci, Das 1931,O 17,20:1
Avalanche 1932,Mr 26,17:2
Luise, Koenigin von Preussen 1932,O 5,26:6
Yorck 1932,N 24,35:2
Hauptmann von Koepenick, Der 1933,Ja 17,22:6
Alte und der Junge Koenig, Der 1935,D 10,31:2
Friesennot 1936,O 26,20:1
Zerbrochene Krug, Der; Broken Jug, The 1938,Ja 15,19:2
Zwischen den Eltern; Between the Parents 1938,Jl 30,10:3
Winter Stuerme; Winter Storms 1938,O 1,10:2
Verwehte Spuren; Covered Tracks 1939,O 14,13:3

Kayukov, S

Youth of Maxim, The 1935,Ap 20,16:1
Friends 1939,Ja 2,28:3
University of Life 1941,F 26,17:1
Dream of a Cossack 1952,F 18,15:2
Sadko 1953,Je 1,18:6

Kazab, Ruth

Strangers in the City 1962,Jl 17,19:2

Kazan, Elia

City for Conquest 1940,S 28,9:2
Blues in the Night 1941,D 12,35:2

Kazan, Elia (Director)

Tree Grows in Brooklyn, A 1945,Mr 1,25:5
Sea of Grass, The 1947,F 28,27:2
Boomerang 1947,Mr 6,36:2
Gentleman's Agreement 1947,N 12,36:2
Pinky 1949,S 30,28:2
Panic in the Streets 1950,Ag 5,9:2
Streetcar Named Desire, A 1951,S 30,27:1
Viva Zapata 1952,F 8,19:2
Man on a Tightrope 1953,Je 5,19:1
On the Waterfront 1954,Jl 29,18:1
East of Eden 1955,Mr 10,33:1
Baby Doll 1956,D 19,40:2
Face in the Crowd, A 1957,My 29,33:1
Wild River 1960,My 27,22:1
Splendor in the Grass 1961,O 11,53:1
America America 1963,D 16,44:1

Kazan, Elia (Original Author)

America America 1963,D 16,44:1

Kazan, Elia (Producer)

Face in the Crowd, A 1957,My 29,33:1
Wild River 1960,My 27,22:1
Splendor in the Grass 1961,O 11,53:1
America America 1963,D 16,44:1

Kazan, Elia (Screenwriter)

America America 1963,D 16,44:1

Kazan, Joe

Boomerang 1947,Mr 6,36:2

Kazan, Lainie

Dayton's Devils 1968,O 3,56:4
Lady in Cement 1968,N 21,41:1

Kazanovich, Vladimir

Russian Ballerina 1947,S 11,31:2

Kazansky, G (Director)

Flying Carpet, The 1960,F 28,31:1

Kazantzakis, Nikos (Original Author)

He Who Must Die 1958,D 29,21:1
Zorba, The Greek 1964,D 18,25:1

Kazbek, A (Original Author)

Caucasian Love 1929,D 3,28:4

Kazenov, P

Duel, The 1964,S 7,11:2

Kazis, Nikos

Antigone 1962,S 19,30:1

Kaznovich, Y (Screenwriter)

Lust for Gold 1958,Jl 24,18:1

Keable, Robert (Original Author)

Recompense 1925,Ap 20,22:1

Keach, Stacy Jr

Heart is a Lonely Hunter, The 1968,Ag 1,24:1

Kean, Betty

Gals, Inc 1943,Ag 13,13:4
Murder in the Blue Room 1944,O 28,12:2

Kean, Marie

Rooney 1958,Je 6,29:2
Broth of a Boy 1959,D 28,18:1
Poacher's Daughter, The 1960,F 16,31:2
Home Is the Hero 1961,Ja 26,32:1
Girl With Green Eyes 1964,Ag 11,37:2
Time Lost and Time Remembered 1966,Ag 30,35:2
Cul de Sac 1966,N 8,44:2

Kean, Richard
  Beautiful Blonde From Bashful Bend, The
    1949,My 28,11:2
  Court Jester, The 1956,F 2,19:1
Keane, Charles
  Untamed Fury 1947,Ap 26,10:6
  Yellow Canary, The 1963,My 16,42:1
Keane, Desmond
  Another Shore 1951,F 12,19:3
Keane, Doris
  Romance 1920,My 17,19:3
Keane, Edward
  His Woman 1931,D 5,21:2
  Ann Carver's Profession 1933,Je 9,20:2
  I Am Suzanne 1934,Ja 19,24:3
  Count of Monte Cristo, The 1934,S 27,25:2
  Behind the Evidence 1935,Ja 26,13:2
  Hard Rock Harrigan 1935,Jl 30,16:2
  Man of Iron 1935,D 7,22:2
  Night at the Opera, A 1935,D 7,22:1
  Whispering Smith Speaks 1936,F 17,21:1
  Singing Kid, The 1936,Ap 4,11:1
  Parole 1936,Je 27,21:1
  I Promise to Pay 1937,Ap 26,15:2
  Alcatraz Island 1937,O 14,22:2
  Torchy Gets her Man 1938,N 18,25:3
  Shadows Over Shanghai 1938,D 1,29:2
  Roaring Twenties, The 1939,N 11,12:1
  Fugitive From Justice, A 1940,Jl 8,13:3
  Devil's Island 1940,Jl 12,11:4
  Who Is Hope Schuyler 1942,My 22,27:1
  Invisible Wall, The 1947,N 1,11:2
  Roses Are Red 1947,N 15,11:2
  It Happens Every Spring 1949,Je 11,11:2
  Baron of Arizona, The 1950,Je 23,29:2
Keane, J R Rev
  Eternal Gift, The 1942,Ja 12,23:3
Keane, James
  I Am the Man 1925,Mr 6,23:1
Keane, Raymond
  Midnight Sun, The 1926,Ap 24,20:4
  Lone Eagle, The 1927,D 20,33:2
  How to Handle Women 1928,Je 18,13:2
  Marriage by Contract 1928,N 13,37:1
Keane, Robert Emmett
  Laugh and get Rich 1931,Mr 28,15:3
  Captain Thunder 1931,My 11,15:4
  Men Call it Love 1931,Je 20,20:4
  Big Noise, The 1936,Jl 4,18:3
  Hot Money 1936,Jl 25,16:2
  Grand Jury 1936,Ag 1,16:3
  Jailbreak 1936,Ag 6,22:1
  Man of the People 1937,F 23,25:4
  Under Suspicion 1937,D 20,23:2 (In Addenda)
  Chaser, The 1938,Ag 2,15:3
  Boys Town 1938,S 9,25:1
  Last Express, The 1938,O 11,24:4
  Confessions of a Nazi Spy 1939,Ap 29,13:2
  Spellbinder, The 1939,Ag 24,17:3
  Fifth Avenue Girl 1939,Ag 25,12:2
  Hawaiian Nights 1939,S 29,19:4
  Pack up Your Troubles 1939,O 27,27:2
  One Hour to Live 1939,N 4,11:3
  Double Alibi 1940,Mr 11,11:2
  Saint Takes Over, The 1940,My 28,29:3
  Lone Wolf Meets a Lady, The 1940,Je 17,19:2
  Slightly Tempted 1940,N 1,33:1
  Tin Pan Alley 1940,N 22,27:3
  Men of Boys Town 1941,Ap 11,24:6
  Devil and Miss Jones, The 1941,My 16,21:2
  Wild Geese Calling 1941,Ag 30,10:2
  Man Who Wouldn't Die, The 1942,Ap 28,25:5
  Remember Pearl Harbor 1942,Je 4,22:4
  A-Haunting We Will Go 1942,Ag 3,18:4
  Sabotage Squad 1942,Ag 5,16:1
  He Hired the Boss 1943,Je 4,17:4
  Jitterbugs 1943,Je 5,12:2
  Crazy House 1943,D 16,33:3
  Whistler, The 1944,Ap 29,12:2
  Impatient Years, The 1944,S 20,20:1
  Why Girls Leave Home 1945,Ag 4,7:3
  Beginning or the End, The 1947,F 21,15:1
  Fear in the Night 1947,Ap 19,11:3
  When my Baby Smiles at Me 1948,N 24,20:2
  Jolson Sings Again 1949,Ag 18,16:6
  Everybody Does It 1949,O 26,32:2
  Atomic Kid, The 1954,D 4,14:2
Kearins, Tommy
  High and Dry 1954,Ag 31,25:5
Kearn, Joseph
  Daddy Long Legs 1955,My 6,17:5
KEARNEY
  See Also CARNEY
Kearney, Carolyn
  Thing That Couldn't Die, The 1958,Je 28,13:7
Kearney, Gene (Screenwriter)
  Games 1967,S 18,58:2
Kearney, John
  East Side, West Side 1927,O 18,33:2
  Honor Among Lovers 1931,F 28,15:2
Kearney, Michael
  All the Way Home 1963,O 30,46:1

Kearney, Patrick (Original Author)
  Place in the Sun, A 1951,Ag 29,20:1
Kearney, Patrick (Screenwriter)
  Man's Man, A 1929,Je 3,27:2
Kearns, Allen
  Tanned Legs 1929,D 2,28:2
  Lovin' the Ladies 1930,Mr 22,22:6
Kearns, Bill
  Purple Noon 1961,S 1,12:1
  Five Miles to Midnight 1963,Mr 21,8:6
  Day and the Hour, The 1964,F 20,22:2
Kearns, Joseph
  Hard, Fast and Beautiful 1951,Jl 2,16:6
  Gift of Love, The 1958,F 12,32:2
  Anatomy of a Murder 1959,Jl 3,10:1
Keath, Donna (Narrator)
  Zoya 1945,Ap 16,18:6
Keating, Elizabeth
  Mad Parade, The 1931,S 19,10:2
Keating, Fred
  Captain Hates the Sea, The 1934,N 29,33:2
  Shanghai 1935,Jl 20,16:2
  I Live my Life 1935,O 12,12:2
  To Beat the Band 1935,N 23,23:2
  13 Hours by Air 1936,Ap 30,17:2
  When's Your Birthday? 1937,Mr 19,27:2
  Melody for Two 1937,My 21,19:5
  Doctor Rhythm 1938,My 19,25:2
  Eternally Yours 1939,O 7,11:2
  Tin Pan Alley 1940,N 22,27:3
Keating, Helen
  Mad Parade, The 1931,S 19,10:2
Keating, Henry (Screenwriter)
  Home Is the Hero 1961,Ja 26,32:1
Keating, Larry
  Whirlpool 1950,Ja 14,9:2
  I Was a Shoplifter 1950,Ap 28,26:3
  Stella 1950,Ag 19,9:2
  Mister 880 1950,S 30,13:2
  Three Secrets 1950,O 21,10:6
  Right Cross 1950,N 16,39:2
  Mating Season, The 1951,Ap 12,41:2
  Follow the Sun 1951,Ap 26,34:4
  Bright Victory 1951,Ag 1,19:2
  Come Fill the Cup 1951,N 22,47:2
  Too Young to Kiss 1951,N 23,32:2
  Light Touch, The 1952,Ja 17,23:1
  When Worlds Collide 1952,F 7,30:2
  About Face 1952,My 24,15:3
  Carson City 1952,Je 14,12:2
  Monkey Business 1952,S 6,12:6
  Something for the Birds 1952,N 15,15:2
  Above and Beyond 1953,Ja 31,10:6
  She's Back on Broadway 1953,Mr 12,24:2
  Inferno 1953,Ag 12,22:2
  Lion Is in the Streets, A 1953,S 24,39:2
  Daddy Long Legs 1955,My 6,17:5
  Eddy Duchin Story, The 1956,Je 22,15:1
  Best Things in Life are Free, The 1956,S 29,12:2
  Buster Keaton Story, The 1957,Ap 22,31:6
  Wayward Bus, The 1957,Je 6,35:2
  Stopover Tokyo 1957,D 27,23:4
  Who Was That Lady? 1960,Ap 16,10:1
  Boys' Night Out 1962,Je 22,15:2
  Incredible Mr Limpet, The 1964,Mr 26,40:4
Keating, William J (Original Author)
  Slaughter on Tenth Avenue 1957,N 6,43:1
Keaton, Buster
  One Week 1920,O 25,18:1
  Saphead, The 1921,F 14,12:2
  Scarecrow, The 1921,F 21,16:1
  Neighbors 1921,Ap 11,9:1
  Hard Luck 1921,Je 20,17:2
  High Sign, The 1922,Mr 20,10:3
  Paleface, The 1922,My 8,14:3
  Our Hospitality 1923,D 10,20:1
  Sherlock Jr 1924,My 26,21:1
  Navigator, The 1924,O 13,21:1
  Seven Chances 1925,Mr 17,18:1
  Go West 1925,O 26,25:2
  Battling Butler 1926,Ag 23,9:1
  General, The 1927,F 8,21:1
  College 1927,S 12,29:1
  Steamboat Bill, Jr 1928,My 15,17:3
  Cameraman, The 1928,S 17,27:1
  Spite Marriage 1929,Mr 25,32:2
  Hollywood Revue, The 1929,Ag 15,20:5
  Free and Easy 1930,Ap 19,15:1
  Dough Boys 1930,S 30,23:1
  Parlor, Bedroom and Bath 1932,F 14,VIII,6:1
  Passionate Plumber, The 1932,Mr 12,19:5
  Speak Easily 1932,Ag 19,20:6
  What! No Beer? 1933,F 11,11:3
  Hollywood Cavalcade 1939,O 14,13:2
  Forever and a Day 1943,Mr 13,9:2
  San Diego, I Love You 1944,N 10,25:1
  That's the Spirit 1945,Je 2,11:2
  You're my Everything 1949,Jl 23,7:2
  In the Good Old Summertime 1949,Ag 5,23:2
  Sunset Boulevard 1950,Ag 11,15:2
  Limelight 1952,O 24,27:2
  Around the World in 80 Days 1956,O 18,37:1
  When Comedy Was King 1960,Mr 30,42:1

Keaton, Buster— Cont
  Adventures of Huckleberry Fin, The
    1960,Ag 4,17:1
  It's a Mad, Mad, Mad, Mad World
    1963,N 19,47:1
  Sound of Laughter, The 1963,D 18,44:2
  30 Years of Fun 1963,D 26,33:4
  Seven Chances 1965,S 15,41:1
  Sergeant Deadhead 1965,O 23,17:3
  Funny Thing Happened on the Way to the Forum,
    A 1966,O 17,48:1
  How to Stuff a Wild Bikini 1967,Ja 12,48:1
Keaton, Buster (Director)
  Sherlock Jr 1924,My 26,21:1
  Navigator, The 1924,O 13,21:1
  Seven Chances 1925,Mr 17,18:1
  Go West 1925,O 26,25:2
  Battling Butler 1926,Ag 23,9:1
  General, The 1927,F 8,21:1
Keaton, Buster (Screenwriter)
  Go West 1925,O 26,25:2
  General, The 1927,F 8,21:1
Keaton, Buston
  My Wife's Relations 1922,O 23,10:1
  Parlor, Bedroom and Bath 1931,Ap 4,23:1
Keatos, Joseph
  Sherlock Jr 1924,My 26,21:1
Keats, Viola
  Mister Hobo 1936,F 8,19:2
  Two Who Dared 1937,Jl 10,18:2
Keays, Vernon (Director)
  Rockin' in The Rockies 1945,Jl 5,7:2
Keckley, Jane
  Hill Billy, The 1924,Mr 12,19:4
  Deadwood Coach, The 1925,Ja 21,19:3
  Lady in Ermine, The 1927,Ja 3,16:2
  Angel of Broadway 1927,N 1,21:1 (In Addenda)
  Craig's Wife 1928,D 4,29:1
  Strange People 1933,Je 17,16:5
  Quitter, The 1934,Mr 14,23:3
  World Accuses, The 1935,Mr 21,27:2
  Shot in the Dark, A 1935,My 22,23:2
Kedem, Moshe
  They Were Ten; (Heym Hayu Assara)
    1961,Ap 18,44:2
Kedrof, M
  Sibirsky Patrul 1932,My 14,11:5
Kedrova, Lila
  No Way Back 1955,My 19,25:5
  Razzi 1957,N 19,39:4
  Lovemaker, The 1958,Mr 11,33:4
  Female, The 1960,Ap 28,29:1
  Modigliani of Montparnasse 1961,Mr 1,27:3
  Zorba, The Greek 1964,D 18,25:1
  High Wind in Jamaica, A 1965,Je 17,27:2
  Penelope 1966,N 11,36:6
Keedwell, Norval
  Little Old New York 1923,Ag 2,10:3
Keefe, Cornelius
  Society Scandal, A 1924,Mr 10,18:2
  Unguarded Hour, The 1926,Ja 5,25:2 (In
    Addenda)
  Three's a Crowd 1927,O 3,20:1
  Come to My House 1928,Ja 16,24:1
  Cohens and the Kellys In Atlantic City, The
    1929,Mr 18,30:6
  Those Who Dance 1930,Jl 7,22:3
  Ex-Flame 1931,Ja 24,15:1
  Lady With a Past 1932,F 22,23:2
  Disorderly Conduct 1932,Ap 11,19:2
  Silver Lining, The 1932,My 30,16:5
  Tomorrow at Seven 1933,Jl 3,14:6
  Charlie Chan's Greatest Case 1933,O 7,18:4
  Stagecoach 1939,Mr 3,21:1
  Fifth Avenue Girl 1939,Ag 25,12:2
Keefer, Don
  Death of a Salesman 1951,D 21,21:3
  Girl in White, The 1952,My 31,12:5
  Riot in Cell Block 11 1954,F 19,24:5
  Private War of Major Benson, The
    1955,Ag 3,27:2
  Torpedo Run 1958,O 25,16:2
Keegan, Arthur
  From Here to Eternity 1953,Ag 6,16:2
  On the Waterfront 1954,Jl 29,18:1
Keegan, Barry
  Satellite in the Sky 1956,S 4,32:7
  Hand in Hand 1961,F 7,41:3
Keel, Howard
  Annie Get Your Gun 1950,My 18,37:1
  Pagan Love Song 1950,D 26,19:1
  Three Guys Named Mike 1951,Mr 2,21:2
  Show Boat 1951,Jl 20,14:1
  Texas Carnival 1951,O 13,9:1
  Callaway Went Thataway 1951,D 6,42:1
  Lovely to Look At 1952,My 30,11:2
  Ride Vaquero 1953,Jl 16,17:2
  Calamity Jane 1953,N 5,40:2
  Kiss Me Kate 1953,N 6,23:2
  Rose Marie 1954,Ap 2,22:2
  Seven Brides for Seven Brothers 1954,Jl 23,8:3
  Deep in my Heart 1954,D 10,35:2
  Jupiter's Darling 1955,F 18,18:4
  Kismet 1955,D 9,32:2

Keel, Howard — Cont

Big Fisherman, The 1959,Ag 6,18:1
Armored Command 1961,O 7,14:3
Day of the Triffids 1963,My 11,15:2
War Wagon, The 1967,Ag 3,26:3

Keeler, Harry Stephen (Original Author)

Sing Sing Nights 1935,Ja 26,13:2
Mysterious Mr Wong, The 1935,Mr 7,26:1

Keeler, Ruby

42d Street 1933,Mr 10,19:3
Gold Diggers of 1933 1933,Je 8,22:3
Footlight Parade 1933,O 6,21:3
Dames 1934,Ag 16,20:2
Flirtation Walk 1934,N 29,33:1
Go Into Your Dance 1935,My 4,17:2
Shipmates Forever 1935,O 17,29:3
Colleen 1936,Mr 9,20:2
Ready, Willing and Able 1937,Mr 15,27:1
Mother Carey's Chickens 1938,Ag 5,11:1

Keen, Diana

Here We Go Around the Mulberry Bush
  1968,Mr 5,34:5

Keen, Geoffrey

Fallen Idol, The 1949,N 16,39:2
Treasure Island 1950,Ag 16,24:2
It's Hard to be Good 1950,D 25,25:3
Chance of a Lifetime 1951,Mr 15,37:2
Clouded Yellow, The 1951,N 13,33:2
Cry, the Beloved Country 1952,Ja 24,23:2
High Treason 1952,My 21,23:3
Stranger in Between, The 1952,Ag 20,21:3
Long Memory, The 1953,Jl 27,15:2
Rob Roy 1954,F 4,21:5
Turn the Key Softly 1954,F 4,21:6
Genevieve 1954,F 16,30:2
High and Dry 1954,Ag 31,25:5
Doctor in the House 1955,F 19,18:3
Court Martial 1955,Ag 2,17:1
Divided Heart, The 1955,Ag 4,16:1
His Excellency 1956,F 2,19:3
Doctor at Sea 1956,Mr 1,37:3
Man Who Never Was, The 1956,Ap 4,24:1
Storm over the Nile 1956,Je 9,14:2
Blonde Sinner 1957,Ja 24,34:1
Third Key, The 1957,Je 3,30:2
Spanish Gardner, The 1957,S 9,21:2
Triple Deception 1957,O 7,23:2
Panic in the Parlor 1957,D 18,45:1
Horrors of the Black Museum 1959,Ap 30,37:2
Scapegoat, The 1959,Ag 7,28:1
Sink the Bismarck! 1960,F 12,22:3
Angry Silence, The 1960,D 13,25:2
No Love for Johnnie 1961,D 13,55:1
Matter of Who, A 1962,Jl 25,29:2
Spiral Road, The 1962,Ag 4,11:2
Doctor Zhivago 1965,D 23,21:1
Born Free 1966,Je 23,29:1
Berserk! 1968,Ja 11,42:2

Keen, Malcolm

Manxman, The 1929,D 17,28:7
Wanted Men 1936,Jl 8,15:2
Sixty Glorious Years 1938,N 18,25:2
Great Mr Handel, The 1943,S 10,29:3
Mating Season, The 1951,Ap 12,41:2
Operation Amsterdam 1960,Jl 7,26:1
Francis of Assisi 1961,Jl 29,8:2
Walk in the Shadow 1966,S 12,52:5

Keen, Noah

Caper of the Golden Bulls, The 1967,Je 22,46:1

Keen, Norman (Original Author)

Police Call 1933,Ag 22,20:3

Keen, Pat

Kind of Loving, A 1962,O 2,46:1

Keenan, Frank

Honor Thy Name 1916,Jl 17,9:4
Thoroughbred, The 1916,Ag 21,9:7
More Trouble 1918,My 27,11:3
Bells, The 1918,S 16,9:3
Scars of Jealousy 1923,My 7,19:3
Women Who Give 1924,Je 3,22:1
Dixie Handicap, The 1924,D 30,15:3

Keenan, William J (Screenwriter)

King Kong Escapes 1968,Jl 11,30:1

Keene, Day (Original Author)

Joy House 1965,F 18,29:1

Keene, Hamilton

Lost Patrol, The 1929,D 16,34:2
Middle Watch, The 1930,D 20,20:6
Mutiny of the Elsinore, The 1939,F 16,17:2
Sword and the Rose, The 1953,Ag 20,18:3

Keene, Mike

Satan in High Heels 1962,Mr 24,15:6
Psychomania 1964,F 15,14:3

Keene, Ralph (Screenwriter)

Double Confession 1953,My 1,17:2

Keene, Richard

Why Leave Home 1929,S 16,30:1
Happy Days 1930,F 14,20:1
Her Golden Calf 1930,My 5,27:3
Wild Company 1930,Jl 19,7:5

Keene, Tom

Our Daily Bread 1934,O 3,25:2
Timothy's Quest 1936,F 29,11:2

Keener, Hazel

Empty Hands 1924,Ag 18,8:2
Freshman, The 1925,S 21,12:4
Murder by Invitation 1941,Jl 23,15:4
Freshman, The 1953,Ap 28,31:6

Keesee, Oscar

Terror is a Man 1960,Jl 14,23:1
Badjao 1962,S 21,35:1

Kehlet, Jette

Child of Man 1950,F 1,25:2

Keighley, William

Resurrection 1931,Ja 24,15:1

Keighley, William (Director)

Ladies They Talk About 1933,F 25,20:4
Easy to Love 1934,Ja 15,12:2
Journal of a Crime 1934,Ap 28,11:3
Dr Monica 1934,Je 21,28:2
Kansas City Princess 1934,N 5,23:1
Big Hearted Herbert 1934,N 14,23:2
Babbitt 1934,D 17,24:2
Right to Live, The 1935,F 16,9:1
G Men 1935,My 2,17:1
Special Agent 1935,S 19,28:1
Stars Over Broadway 1935,N 14,17:3
Singing Kid, The 1936,Ap 4,11:1
Bullets or Ballots 1936,My 27,27:1
Green Pastures, The 1936,Jl 17,20:1
God's Country and the Woman 1937,Ja 11,15:5
Prince and the Pauper, The 1937,My 6,23:1
Varsity Show 1937,S 2,17:2
Adventures of Robin Hood, The 1938,My 13,17:2
Valley of the Giants 1938,S 10,20:2
Secrets of an Actress 1938,O 8,10:2
Brother Rat 1938,N 5,15:2
Yes, My Darling Daughter 1939,F 27,11:2
Each Dawn I Die 1939,Jl 22,12:2
Fighting 69th, The 1940,Ja 27,9:2
Torrid Zone 1940,My 18,11:3
No Time for Comedy 1940,S 7,9:2
Four Mothers 1941,Ja 11,12:7
Bride Came C O D, The 1941,Jl 26,18:2
Man Who Came to Dinner, The 1942,Ja 2,25:2
George Washington Slept Here 1942,O 31,11:1
Honeymoon 1947,My 19,27:2
Street with no Name, The 1948,Jl 15,26:6
Rocky Mountain 1950,N 4,13:2
Master of Ballantrae, The 1953,Ag 6,16:2

Keightley, Isabel

Forest Ring, The 1930,Ap 26,11:1

Keil, Ursula (Original Author)

Vintage, The 1957,My 9,36:5

Keiling, Robert Lee

Success 1923,Jl 10,22:5

Keim, Betty Lou

These Wilder Years 1956,Ag 18,11:2
Teenage Rebel 1956,N 17,17:6
Wayward Bus, The 1957,Je 6,35:2
Some Came Running 1959,Ja 23,17:1

Keindorff, Eberhard (Screenwriter)

Arms and the Man 1962,F 24,21:7

Keir, Andrew

Brave Don't Cry, The 1952,N 6,37:2
Scotch on the Rocks 1954,Je 14,18:2
High and Dry 1954,Ag 31,25:5
Day They Robbed the Bank of England, The
  1960,S 5,11:2
Cleopatra 1963,Je 13,29:1
Lord Jim 1965,F 26,18:1
Fighting Prince of Donegal, The 1966,N 10,64:1
Long Duel, The 1967,N 2,58:3
Five Million Years to Earth 1968,My 30,21:4
Attack on the Iron Coast 1968,Je 6,54:2

Keir, David

Ghost Goes West, The 1936,Ja 11,9:2
This Man Is News 1939,Jl 20,16:4
At Dawn We Die 1943,My 8,19:2

Keish, Gerald (Miscellaneous)

Scent of Mystery 1960,F 19,23:1

Keith, Agnes Newton (Original Author)

Three Came Home 1950,F 21,22:5

Keith, Brian

Arrowhead 1953,S 16,38:6
Jivaro 1954,F 13,11:5
Alaska Seas 1954,Mr 6,13:5
Violent Men, The 1955,Ja 27,17:2
Tight Spot 1955,Mr 19,11:7
Five Against the House 1955,Je 11,8:7
Storm Center 1956,O 22,25:4
Nightfall 1957,Ja 24,34:1
Dino 1957,Je 22,9:2
Run of the Arrow 1957,Ag 3,8:6
Chicago Confidential 1957,Ag 31,19:1
Fort Dobbs 1958,Ap 19,10:4
Villa 1958,D 24,00:0
Appointment With a Shadow 1959,Ja 8,24:2
Young Philadelphians, The 1959,My 22,32:1
Parent Trap, The 1961,Je 22,23:1
Moon Pilot 1962,Ap 6,30:2
Deadly Companions, The 1962,Ap 12,41:7
Savage Sam 1963,Ag 1,17:3
Tiger Walks, A 1964,Ag 27,28:2
Pleasure Seekers, The 1964,D 26,9:1
Those Calloways 1965,Ap 15,38:2

Keith, Brian — Cont

Hallelujah Trail, The 1965,Jl 2,17:1
Rare Breed, The 1966,Ap 14,42:3
Russians are Coming the Russians are Coming,
  The 1966,My 26,55:1
Nevada Smith 1966,Je 24,28:1 (Incorrect in this
  edition; use 1966,Je 30,28:1 elsewhere)
Way...Way Out 1966,O 27,55:1
Reflections in a Golden Eye 1967,O 12,59:1
With Six You Get Egg Roll 1968,O 10,59:6

Keith, Byron

Stranger, The 1946,Jl 11,18:2
Dallas 1951,Ja 13,10:4

Keith, Carlos (Screenwriter)

Body Snatcher, The 1945,My 26,18:3
Bedlam 1946,Ap 20,16:4

Keith, Donald

Baree, Son of Kazan 1925,My 19,24:2
Boomerang, The 1925,Jl 1,16:1
Dancing Mothers 1926,F 18,21:1
Plastic Age, The 1926,Jl 19,13:1
Special Delivery 1927,Ap 26,33:3
Whirlwind of Youth, The 1927,Je 6,27:2
Way of all Flesh, The 1927,Je 27,25:2
Wild Geese 1927,D 5,26:2
Lone Wolf's Daughter, The 1929,Mr 4,20:2
Branded Men 1931,D 12,23:3
Midnight Lady, The 1932,Jl 1,19:3

Keith, Eugene

Uncle Sam of Freedom Ridge 1920,S 27,15:2

Keith, Ian

Manhandled 1924,Jl 29,9:2
Her Love Story 1924,O 7,26:1
Christine of the Hungry Heart 1924,D 8,13:3
Love's Wilderness 1924,D 22,20:2
Enticement 1925,Mr 21,16:3
Talker, The 1925,My 12,26:2
Tower of Lies, The 1925,S 28,24:1
Greater Glory, The 1926,My 4,31:1
Prince of Tempters, The 1926,O 18,18:1
Convoy 1927,My 9,26:4
Man's Past, A 1927,O 4,34:2
Two Arabian Knights 1927,O 24,24:3
Divine Lady, The 1929,Mr 23,22:4
Great Divide, The 1930,F 17,17:6
Abraham Lincoln 1930,Ag 26,24:1
Boudoir Diplomat, The 1930,D 8,26:1
Tailor-Made Man, A 1931,Ap 25,23:4
Susan Lenox; Her Fall and Rise 1931,O 17,20:1
Phantom of Paris, The 1931,N 14,15:3
Deceiver, The 1931,N 23,22:1
Sign of the Cross, The 1932,D 1,25:1
Queen Christina 1933,D 27,23:3
Cleopatra 1934,Ag 17,12:1
Crusades, The 1935,Ag 22,21:3
Three Musketeers, The 1935,N 1,25:1
Don't Gamble With Love 1936,Mr 2,13:3
Preview Murder Mystery, The 1936,Mr 21,13:2
Mary of Scotland 1936,Jl 31,22:2
Buccaneer, The 1938,F 17,17:2
Comet over Broadway 1938,D 16,33:3
All This and Heaven, Too 1940,Jl 5,10:2
Sea Hawk, The 1940,Ag 10,16:2
Remember Pearl Harbor 1942,Je 4,22:4
Five Graves to Cairo 1943,My 27,21:2
Corregidor 1943,My 28,19:2
That Nazty Nuisance 1943,My 29,10:3
Spanish Main, The 1945,N 7,20:2
Captain Kidd 1945,N 23,26:3
Dick Tracy vs Cueball 1946,N 23,12:2
Strange Woman, The 1947,F 24,16:4
Dick Tracy's Dilemma 1947,Jl 14,14:5
Nightmare Alley 1947,O 10,31:3
Three Musketeers, The 1948,O 21,33:2
Black Shield of Falworth, The 1954,O 7,16:2
Prince of Players 1955,Ja 12,24:2
New York Confidential 1955,F 19,18:1

Keith, Isabelle

Desert Flower, The 1925,Je 1,10:3
Very Confidential 1927,N 29,31:1

Keith, Jane

Sea Wolf, The 1930,O 6,21:1
Secret Call, The 1931,Jl 13,13:5

Keith, Michael

King Kong vs. Godzilla 1963,Je 27,23:4

Keith, Robert

Bad Company 1931,N 7,16:5
Boomerang 1947,Mr 6,36:2
Kiss of Death 1947,Ag 28,28:2
My Foolish Heart 1950,Ja 20,29:2
Reformer and the Redhead, The 1950,Ap 10,15:2
Edge of Doom 1950,Ag 4,13:2
Woman on the Run 1950,N 30,24:2
Branded 1951,Ja 11,28:5
Fourteen Hours 1951,Mr 7,43:2
Here Comes the Groom 1951,S 21,19:2
I Want You 1951,D 24,9:1
Just Across the Street 1952,Je 28,12:4
Somebody Loves Me 1952,S 25,38:1
Small Town Girl 1953,My 7,37:2
Battle Circus 1953,My 28,27:5
Devil's Canyon 1953,O 3,14:2
Wild One, The 1953,D 31,9:2
Drum Beat 1954,N 18,42:1

Keith, Robert— Cont
Young at Heart 1955,Ja 20,35:1
Underwater! 1955,F 10,27:2
Love Me or Leave Me 1955,My 27,14:1
Guys and Dolls 1955,N 5,26:1
Ransom 1956,Ja 25,28:3
Between Heaven and Hell 1956,O 12,33:2
Written on the Wind 1957,Ja 12,12:6
Men in War 1957,Mr 20,32:4
My Man Godfrey 1957,O 12,23:1
Tempest 1959,Mr 27,19:2
They Came to Cordura 1959,O 22,47:2
Cimarron 1961,F 17,12:2

Keith, Rosalind
Under Suspicion 1937,D 20,23:2 (In Addenda)

Keith, Rosalind
Glass Key, The 1935,Je 15,20:2
Annapolis Farewell 1935,Ag 24,18:2
Poppy 1936,Je 18,19:1
King of the Royal Mounted 1936,S 29,35:2
Theodora Goes Wild 1936,N 13,27:4
Parole Racket 1937,Mr 8,22:1
Fight to the Finish, A 1937,Je 26,20:2 (In Addenda)
Criminals of the Air 1937,O 28,29:2
Arson Racket Squad 1938,Je 18,18:2

Keith, Sydney
Orders Is Orders 1934,My 7,20:2
Battle of the Sexes, The 1960,Ap 19,40:4

Keith-Johnston, Colin
Lucky in Love 1929,D 14,22:4
Berkeley Square 1933,S 14,26:2
Exile, The 1947,D 26,22:4
Kiss the Blood off my Hands 1948,O 30,10:2
Joan of Arc 1948,N 12,30:5
Enchantment 1948,D 27,16:2
Fancy Pants 1950,Ag 31,21:2
Left Handed Gun, The 1958,My 8,36:2

Keithly, Jane
Florodora Girl, The 1930,My 31,19:4

Kelber, Michel (Cinematographer)
Story of a Three Day Pass, The 1968,Jl 9,31:1

Kelberer, A
Othello 1960,My 16,39:1

Kelenyi, Edward Dr (Composer)
Adventures of Chico, The 1938,F 26,9:2

Keleti, Martin (Director)
Viki 1937,N 29,19:3
Torockoi Menyasszony; Torockoi Bride 1938,Mr 5,11:2
Te Csak Pipalj Ladanyi; Keep On Smoking, Ladanyi 1938,My 18,9:3
Harapos Ferj; Biting Husbank 1939,Ja 28,19:2
Borcsa Amerikaben; Barbara in America 1939,F 11,13:2
Fehervari Huszarok; Hussars of Fehervari 1939,S 16,20:3

Kelin, Adelaide
Troublemaker, The 1964,Je 23,25:1

Keliz, Armand
Algiers 1938,Jl 15,13:2

Kelk, Jackie
Born to be Bad 1934,My 31,22:6
Pajama Game, The 1957,Ag 30,12:2

Kell, Harry (Director)
Quantez 1957,S 7,12:7

Kelland, Clarence Budington (Original Author)
Source, The 1918,S 9,9:1
Backbone 1923,Ap 30,11:2
Steadfast Heart, The 1923,D 25,26:1
Woman's Faith, A 1925,Jl 27,17:3
Dance Magic 1927,Jl 13,21:2
Speak Easily 1932,Ag 19,20:6
Thirty Day Princess 1934,My 12,12:3
Cat's Paw, The 1934,Ag 17,12:2
Strike Me Pink 1936,Ja 17,15:2
Mr Deeds Goes to Town 1936,Ap 17,17:2
Florida Special 1936,My 29,15:2
Mr Dodd Takes the Air 1937,Ag 12,14:2
Stand-In 1937,N 19,27:2
Arizona 1941,F 7,23:3
Scattergood Baines 1941,Ap 4,25:2
Valley of the Sun 1942,Mr 19,29:2
Sugarfoot 1951,F 12,19:4

Kellard, Ralph
Restless Sex, The 1920,S 13,12:1
Master Mind, The 1920,S 13,12:1
Virtuous Liars 1924,Mr 31,20:1
Women Everywhere 1930,Je 23,15:1

Kellard, Robert
Battle of Broadway 1938,Ap 25,19:2
Island in the Sky 1938,My 14,18:1
Time Out for Murder 1938,O 7,21:2
Always in Trouble 1938,N 3,27:1
While New York Sleeps 1938,D 22,25:3
Stop, Look and Love 1939,S 8,28:5
Canon City 1948,Jl 8,19:2

Kellaway, Alec
Pacific Adventure 1947,N 26,18:2

Kellaway, Cecil
Double Danger 1938,F 10,17:5
Wuthering Heights 1939,Ap 14,28:2
Intermezzo, A Love Story 1939,O 6,31:1
We Are not Alone 1939,D 1,27:1

Mexican Spitfire 1940,Ja 10,16:4
Invisible Man Returns, The 1940,Ja 16,19:2
House of the Seven Gables, The 1940,Ap 15,21:3
Brother Orchid 1940,Je 8,18:2
Phantom Raiders 1940,Je 24,19:5
Mummy's Hand, The 1940,S 20,27:2
Diamond Frontiers 1940,O 4,29:2
Mexican Spitfire out West 1940,O 30,29:3
Letter, The 1940,N 23,12:6
Lady With red Hair 1940,D 6,28:2
South of Suez 1940,D 19,33:2
West Point Widow 1941,S 11,21:5
Burma Convoy 1941,O 7,26:7
Appointment for Love 1941,N 7,27:1
New York Town 1941,N 13,35:2
Night of January 16th, The 1941,D 19,35:1
Bahama Passage 1942,F 19,23:2
Lady Has Plans, The 1942,Mr 5,27:1
Take a Letter Darling 1942,My 28,13:2
Are Husbands Necessary? 1942,Jl 9,17:2
I Married a Witch 1942,N 20,27:2
Crystal Ball, The 1943,F 19,22:2
It Ain't Hay 1943,Mr 11,17:3
Frenchman's Creek 1944,S 21,26:2
Mrs Parkington 1944,O 13,16:1
And Now Tomorrow 1944,N 23,38:2
Practically Yours 1945,Mr 29,18:2
Love Letters 1945,Ag 27,22:3
Kitty 1946,Ap 1,23:1
Postman Always Rings Twice, The 1946,My 3,15:3
Easy to Wed 1946,Jl 12,14:2
Monsieur Beaucaire 1946,S 5,23:1
Cockeyed Miracle, The 1946,O 25,28:1
Unconquered 1947,O 11,11:2
Always Together 1947,D 11,46:1
Luck of the Irish, The 1948,S 16,34:1
Joan of Arc 1948,N 12,30:5
Decision of Christopher Blake, The 1948,D 11,12:2
Down to the Sea in Ships 1949,F 23,31:2
Portrait of Jennie 1949,Mr 30,31:2
Reformer and the Redhead, The 1950,Ap 10,15:2
Kim 1950,D 8,40:4
Harvey 1950,D 22,19:1
Half Angel 1951,Je 16,9:2
Francis Goes to the Races 1951,Jl 25,19:2
Just Across the Street 1952,Je 28,12:4
My Wife's Best Friend 1952,O 11,17:2
Thunder in the East 1953,F 4,32:2
Young Bess 1953,My 22,31:1
Beast From 20,000 Fathoms, The 1953,Je 25,23:1
Interrupted Melody 1955,My 6,18:1
Prodigal, The 1955,My 14,10:7
Female on the Beach 1955,Ag 20,20:2
Toy Tiger 1956,Je 30,11:2
Proud Rebel, The 1958,Jl 2,23:4
Shaggy Dog, The 1959,Mr 20,26:2
Tammy Tell me True 1961,Jl 27,23:2
Francis of Assisi 1961,Jl 29,8:2
Zotz! 1962,O 4,44:3
Cardinal, The 1963,D 13,41:1
Hush...Hush, Sweet Charlotte 1965,Mr 4,36:1
Spinout 1966,D 15,60:1
Guess Who's Coming to Dinner 1967,D 12,56:1
Fitzwilly 1967,D 21,45:1

Kellener, John V
Passages From James Joyce's Finnegans Wake 1967,O 10,56:1

Keller
Letters From my Windmill (The Three Low Masses); Three Low Masses, The (Letters From my Windmill) 1955,D 19,33:1

Keller, Christa
Sins of Rose Bernd, The 1959,Ja 24,13:4 (In Addenda)

Keller, Edgar (Screenwriter)
Yellow Girl, The 1922,Mr 13,18:2

Keller, Frank
Temple of Venus, The 1923,N 1,24:3

Keller, Harry (Director)
Man Afraid 1957,Ap 5,24:2
Female Animal, The 1958,Ja 23,24:3
Day of the Badman 1958,Ja 30,19:2
Voice in the Mirror 1958,Ag 14,23:2
Seven Ways From Sundown 1960,D 22,18:4
Tammy Tell me True 1961,Jl 27,23:2
6 Black Horses 1962,Ap 25,30:1
Tammy and the Doctor 1963,Je 27,23:2
Brass Bottle, The 1964,My 21,42:1

Keller, Harry (Producer)
Kitten With a Whip 1964,N 5,50:4
Send Me no Flowers 1964,N 13,30:1
Mirage 1965,My 27,28:1
That Funny Feeling 1965,O 21,57:2
Texas Across the River 1966,N 24,65:1

Keller, Helen
Deliverance 1919,Ag 19,10:1

Keller, Ivan (Screenwriter)
Stone Flower 1946,D 30,15:2

Keller, Kate Adams
Deliverance 1919,Ag 19,10:1

Keller, Leon
West Point 1928,Ja 2,28:1

Keller, Martin
Divided Heart, The 1955,Ag 4,16:1

Keller, Phillips Brooks
Deliverance 1919,Ag 19,10:1

Keller, Sam
Jesse James' Women 1954,S 29,23:4

Kellerman, Jucci
Woman 1950,F 9,36:6

Kellerman, Sally
Third Day, The 1965,Ag 5,15:3
Boston Strangler, The 1968,O 17,52:1

Kellermann, Annette
Daughter of the Gods, A 1916,O 18,9:1
Honor System, The 1917,F 13,9:4
Queen of the Sea 1918,S 2,7:1
Art of Diving, The 1920,O 25,18:1

Kellermann, Bernhard (Original Author)
Two Brothers, The 1928,Ag 21,27:4
Transatlantic Tunnel 1935,O 28,16:2

Kelley, Albert (Director)
Jungle Bride 1933,My 13,16:3
Street Corner 1948,D 4,9:4

Kelley, Albert (Original Author)
Street Corner 1948,D 4,9:4

Kelley, Alice
Francis Goes to West Point 1952,Ag 23,10:2
Against all Flags 1952,D 25,34:6

Kelley, Barry
Boomerang 1947,Mr 6,36:2
Force of Evil 1948,D 27,16:2
Knock on any Door 1949,F 23,31:2
Mr Belvedere Goes to College 1949,Ap 16,11:2
Undercover Man, The 1949,Ap 21,30:2
Ma and Pa Kettle 1949,Ag 12,13:2
Too Late for Tears 1949,Ag 15,12:3
Johnny Stool Pigeon 1949,S 23,28:3
Thelma Jordon 1950,Ja 19,35:2
Black Hand 1950,Mr 13,15:2
Wabash Avenue 1950,Ap 29,8:3
Capture, The 1950,My 20,8:6
Love That Brute 1950,My 27,10:6
Singing Guns 1950,Je 5,19:3
Asphalt Jungle, The 1950,Je 9,29:3
711 Ocean Drive 1950,Jl 20,21:2
Southside 1-1000 1950,N 3,31:2
Right Cross 1950,N 16,39:2
Killer That Stalked New York, The 1951,Ja 5,17:2
Great Missouri Raid, The 1951,Ap 9,31:2
Francis Goes to the Races 1951,Jl 25,19:2
Flying Leathernecks 1951,S 20,37:1
Well, The 1951,S 27,37:2
Carrie 1952,Jl 17,20:2
Woman of the North Country 1952,Ag 30,6:2
South Sea Woman 1953,Je 4,33:6
Long Wait, The 1954,Jl 3,9:2
Shanghai Story, The 1954,S 25,10:7
Women's Prison 1955,F 3,18:5
New York Confidential 1955,F 19,18:1
Wings of Eagles, The 1957,F 1,28:1
Monkey on my Back 1957,My 30,23:2
Buccaneer, The 1958,D 24,00:0
Ice Palace 1960,Je 30,22:1
Elmer Gantry 1960,Jl 8,16:1
Secret of Deep Harbor 1961,O 26,39:7
Manchurian Candidate, The 1962,O 25,48:3

Kelley, Bob
Fuzzy Pink Nightgown, The 1957,O 31,41:1

Kelley, De Forest
Fear in the Night 1947,Ap 19,11:3
Variety Girl 1947,O 16,34:4
Canon City 1948,Jl 8,19:2
House of Bamboo 1955,Jl 2,13:2
Gunfight at the O K Corral 1957,My 30,23:2
Raintree County 1957,D 21,22:1
Law and Jake Wade, the 1958,Je 7,11:1
Warlock 1959,My 1,34:1
Where Love Has Gone 1964,N 3,26:1

Kelley, John T (Screenwriter)
Rage to Live, A 1965,O 21,57:1

Kelley, Martin J
Passages From James Joyce's Finnegans Wake 1967,O 10,56:1

Kelley, Virginia
If Winter Comes 1948,Ja 23,28:4
Come to the Stable 1949,Jl 28,19:1
Three Came Home 1950,F 21,22:5
Fancy Pants 1950,Ag 31,21:2

Kelley, Walter
Come Back, Little Sheba 1952,D 24,13:2
Marty 1955,Ap 12,25:3
Men in War 1957,Mr 20,32:4

Kellin, Mike
At War With the Army 1951,Ja 25,21:5
Hurricane Smith 1952,O 4,15:2
Lonelyhearts 1959,Mr 5,35:3
Wackiest Ship in the Army, The 1961,F 9,36:1
Great Impostor, The 1961,Mr 30,24:1
Hell is for Heroes 1962,Jl 12,19:3
Incident, The 1967,N 6,65:1
Banning 1967,D 14,62:2

Kellin, Mike— Cont

Boston Strangler, The 1968,O 17,52:1

Kellino, Pamela

I Met a Murderer 1939,O 2,15:2
They Were Sisters 1946,Jl 24,24:2
Upturned Glass, The 1947,N 5,34:4
Pandora and the Flying Dutchman 1951,D 7,35:2
Lady Possessed 1952,F 15,17:2

Kellino, Pamela (Original Author)

I Met a Murderer 1939,O 2,15:2
Lady Possessed 1952,F 15,17:2

Kellino, Pamela (Screenwriter)

Upturned Glass, The 1947,N 5,34:4
Lady Possessed 1952,F 15,17:2

Kellino, Roy (Director)

I Met a Murderer 1939,O 2,15:2
Lady Possessed 1952,F 15,17:2
Guilt is my Shadow 1954,Mr 25,36:4
Silken Affair, The 1957,O 31,41:1

Kellino, Roy (Screenwriter)

I Met a Murderer 1939,O 2,15:2
Guilt is my Shadow 1954,Mr 25,36:4

Kelljan, Robert

Psych-Out 1968,Mr 28,52:1

Kellock, Harold (Original Author)

Houdini 1953,Jl 3,10:2

Kellogg, Bill

Shadow Strikes, The 1937,S 13,17:1

Kellogg, Bruce

Barbary Coast Gent 1944,S 29,18:2
They Were Expendable 1945,D 21,25:2

Kellogg, Cecil

Rawhide 1938,Ap 25,19:2
Chip of the Flying U 1940,Ja 22,11:3
Geronimo 1940,F 8,18:3

Kellogg, Gayle

Crime Wave 1954,Ja 13,26:2

Kellogg, John

Young Tom Edison 1940,Mr 15,27:2
Mr District Attorney 1947,F 28,27:3
Johnny O'Clock 1947,Mr 27,39:2
Gangster, The 1947,O 31,29:3
Bad Men of Tombstone 1949,Mr 5,10:2
House of Strangers 1949,Jl 2,8:2
Twelve O'Clock High 1950,Ja 28,10:2
Port of New York 1950,F 3,29:2
Kansas Raiders 1951,Ja 26,19:2
Enforcer, The 1951,Ja 26,19:2
Tomorrow Is Another Day 1951,Ag 9,17:5
Come Fill the Cup 1951,N 22,47:2
Greatest Show on Earth, The 1952,Ja 11,17:2
Rancho Notorious 1952,My 15,39:5
Those Redheads From Seattle 1953,O 1,34:2
Gorilla at Large 1954,Je 12,13:2
Edge of the City 1957,Ja 30,33:2
African Manhunt 1957,Ap 20,21:4
Go Naked in the World 1961,Mr 11,15:1
Convicts 4 1962,O 4,44:2

Kellogg, Ray (Director)

Green Berets, The 1968,Je 20,49:1

Kellogg, Virginia (Original Author)

Road to Reno, The 1931,O 10,20:4
Mary Stevens, M D 1933,Ag 5,9:6
Stolen Holiday 1937,F 1,15:3
T-Men 1948,Ja 23,28:3
White Heat 1949,S 3,7:2

Kellogg, Virginia (Screenwriter)

Caged 1950,My 20,8:6

KELLY

See Also KELLEY

Kelly, Al

Singing in the Dark 1956,Mr 8,32:5

Kelly, Anthony Paul (Original Author)

Three Faces West 1926,F 16,22:4
Three Faces East 1930,S 6,9:2
British Intelligence 1940,F 12,14:2

Kelly, Anthony Paul (Screenwriter)

Love's Redemption 1922,Ja 9,15:2
Star Dust 1922,F 6,9:1

Kelly, Barbara

Castle in the Air 1953,Ja 5,19:2
Tale of Five Women, A 1953,Ja 16,19:2

Kelly, Brian

Flipper's New Adventure 1964,Ag 27,28:2
Around the World Under the Sea 1966,Jl 21,20:2

Kelly, Burt (Producer)

People's Enemy, The 1935,Ap 30,13:7
Spirit of Culver 1939,Mr 9,18:1
Ex-Champ 1939,My 12,25:3
I Stole a Million 1939,Ag 7,11:2
Two Bright Boys 1939,S 22,27:3
Swordsman, The 1947,O 17,18:4

Kelly, Carol

Toward the Unknown 1956,S 28,24:4

Kelly, Claire

Badlanders, The 1958,S 4,33:1
Party Girl 1958,O 29,30:1
Ask any Girl 1959,My 22,32:1
Georgy Girl 1966,O 18,48:1
Guide for the Married Man, A 1967,My 27,16:1
Whisperers, The 1967,Ag 1,24:1

Kelly, Craig

Furies, The 1950,Ag 17,23:2

Kelly, Dermot

Broth of a Boy 1959,D 28,18:1
Quare Fellow 1963,F 20,6:1

Kelly, Diarmuid

Treasure Island 1950,Ag 16,24:2

Kelly, Don

Bombers B-52 1957,N 23,11:2

Kelly, Edward

Within These Walls 1945,Jl 16,8:4

Kelly, Emmett

Fat Man, The 1951,My 25,31:2
Greatest Show on Earth, The 1952,Ja 11,17:2
Wind Across the Everglades 1958,S 12,21:1

Kelly, Fred

Deep in my Heart 1954,D 10,35:2

Kelly, Gene

For Me and My Gal 1942,O 22,25:1
Pilot No 5 1943,Je 25,13:4
Du Barry Was a Lady 1943,Ag 20,13:1
Thousands Cheer 1943,S 14,27:1
Cross of Lorraine, The 1943,D 3,27:4
Cover Girl 1944,Mr 31,26:1
Christmas Holiday 1944,Je 29,16:1
Anchors Aweigh 1945,Jl 20,15:2
Ziegfeld Follies 1946,Mr 23,8:3
Living in a Big Way 1947,O 10,31:4
Pirate, The 1948,My 21,19:2
Three Musketeers, The 1948,O 21,33:2
Words and Music 1948,D 10,34:2
Take Me Out to the Ball Game 1949,Mr 10,35:2
On the Town 1949,D 9,37:2
Black Hand 1950,Mr 13,15:2
Summer Stock 1950,S 1,17:2
American in Paris, An 1951,O 5,24:2
It's a big Country 1952,Ja 9,25:2
Singin' in the Rain 1952,Mr 28,27:2
Devil Makes Three, The 1952,Ag 30,6:2
Brigadoon 1954,S 17,18:2
Crest of the Wave 1954,N 11,43:2
Deep in my Heart 1954,D 10,35:2
It's Always Fair Weather 1955,S 16,19:1
Invitation to the Dance (Sinbad the Sailor); Sinbad the Sailor (Invitation to the Dance) 1956,My 23,35:7
Invitation to the Dance (Ring Around the Rosy); Ring Around the Rosy (Invitation to the Dance) 1956,My 23,35:7
Invitation to the Dance (Circus); Circus (Invitation to the Dance) 1956,My 23,35:7
Happy Road, The 1957,Je 21,20:2
Girls, Les 1957,O 4,27:2
Marjorie Morningstar 1958,Ap 25,32:2
Let's Make Love 1960,S 9,36:1
Inherit the Wind 1960,O 13,41:1
What a Way to Go! 1964,My 15,44:1
Young Girls of Rochefort, The 1968,Ap 12,50:1

Kelly, Gene (Director)

On the Town 1949,D 9,37:2
Singin' in the Rain 1952,Mr 28,27:2
It's Always Fair Weather 1955,S 16,19:1
Invitation to the Dance (Sinbad the Sailor); Sinbad the Sailor (Invitation to the Dance) 1956,My 23,35:7
Invitation to the Dance (Circus); Circus (Invitation to the Dance) 1956,My 23,35:7
Invitation to the Dance (Ring Around the Rosy); Ring Around the Rosy (Invitation to the Dance) 1956,My 23,35:7
Happy Road, The 1957,Je 21,20:2
Tunnel of Love 1958,N 22,27:4
Gigot 1962,S 28,26:1
Guide for the Married Man, A 1967,My 27,16:1

Kelly, Gene (Miscellaneous)

Anchors Aweigh 1945,Jl 20,15:2
Pirate, The 1948,My 21,19:2
Invitation to the Dance (Circus); Circus (Invitation to the Dance) 1956,My 23,35:7
Invitation to the Dance (Sinbad the Sailor); Sinbad the Sailor (Invitation to the Dance) 1956,My 23,35:7
Invitation to the Dance (Ring Around the Rosy); Ring Around the Rosy (Invitation to the Dance) 1956,My 23,35:7

Kelly, Gene (Original Author)

Take Me Out to the Ball Game 1949,Mr 10,35:2

Kelly, Gene (Producer)

Happy Road, The 1957,Je 21,20:2

Kelly, George (Original Author)

Craig's Wife 1928,D 4,29:1
Show-Off, The 1934,Mr 17,11:3
Doubting Thomas 1935,Jl 11,24:2
Craig's Wife 1936,O 2,29:3
Harriet Craig 1950,N 3,31:2

Kelly, George (Screenwriter)

Old Hutch 1936,D 7,27:4
Show-Off, The 1947,Mr 20,38:2

Kelly, Grace

Fourteen Hours 1951,Mr 7,43:2
High Noon 1952,Jl 25,14:2
Mogambo 1953,O 2,18:1
Dial M for Murder 1954,My 29,13:2
Rear Window 1954,Ag 5,18:2
Country Girl, The 1954,D 16,51:2

Kelly, Grace— Cont

Green Fire 1954,D 25,7:1
Bridges at Toko-Ri, The 1955,Ja 21,20:2
To Catch a Thief 1955,Ag 5,14:2
Swan, The 1956,Ap 27,21:5
High Society 1956,Ag 10,9:2

Kelly, Gregory

Manhattan 1924,O 29,18:1
Show-Off, The 1926,Ag 23,9:1

Kelly, Jack

Where Danger Lives 1951,Ja 1,13:6
Red Ball Express 1952,My 30,11:2
No Room for the Groom 1952,Je 14,12:2
Redhead From Wyoming, The 1953,Ja 9,17:4
Drive a Crooked Road 1954,Ap 3,19:3
Black Tuesday 1955,Ja 1,16:2
Night Holds Terror, The 1955,S 15,39:2
To Hell and Back 1955,S 23,21:2
Forbidden Planet 1956,My 4,21:2
Julie 1956,N 22,51:1
Fever in the Blood 1961,Ap 20,30:4
FBI Code 98 1964,Ap 9,25:6
Love and Kisses 1965,D 23,21:4

Kelly, James (Screenwriter)

Three on a Spree 1961,Ag 31,22:3
Man in the Dark 1965,Ja 21,22:1

Kelly, James A

12 Angry Men 1957,Ap 15,24:1

Kelly, Jeanne

Crime of Dr Crespi, The 1936,Ja 13,14:3
Devil's Pipeline, The 1940,N 11,22:4
Meet the Chump 1941,F 27,23:4

Kelly, John

Dressed to Kill 1928,Mr 12,26:1
Subway Express 1931,My 2,23:4
Devil Is Driving, The 1932,D 16,25:5
Bowery, The 1933,O 5,24:2
Little Miss Marker 1934,My 19,18:3
Many Happy Returns 1934,Je 9,18:2
Kid Millions 1934,N 12,17:2
Public Hero No 1 1935,Je 8,12:2
Dr Socrates 1935,O 3,29:2
Poor Little Rich Girl, The 1936,Je 26,16:1
Polo Joe 1936,N 5,35:1
Fugitive in the Sky 1937,Ja 16,21:1
You Can't Buy Luck 1937,My 14,21:2
23 1/2 Hours Leave 1937,My 17,23:2
Angel's Holiday 1937,My 29,20:2
Armored Car 1937,Jl 26,15:2
Big Shot, The 1937,Ag 13,13:1
Portia on Trial 1937,D 3,29:2
Bringing Up Baby 1938,Mr 4,17:5
Female Fugitive 1938,Ap 11,12:3
Exposed 1938,N 21,14:5
Sergeant Madden 1939,Mr 24,27:2
Meet Doctor Christian 1939,D 1,27:2
Black Friday 1940,Mr 22,23:3
Pittsburgh Kid, The 1941,S 23,27:4
Jail House Blues 1942,F 6,23:2
Moontide 1942,Ap 30,14:1
No Time for Love 1943,D 2,30:1
Jack London 1943,Mr 3,19:3

Kelly, Judith (Original Author)

Marriage Is a Private Affair 1944,O 27,17:7

Kelly, Judy

At Dawn We Die 1943,My 8,19:2
Dead of Night 1946,Je 29,22:6

Kelly, Karolee

Come on, The 1956,Ap 7,13:1

Kelly, Kitty

Kiss in the Dark, A 1925,Ap 7,17:3
Nuit est a Nous, La; (Night is Ours, The) 1931,F 21,15:2
Behind Office Doors 1931,Mr 21,15:1
Bachelor Apartment 1931,My 16,13:3
White Shoulders 1931,Je 5,26:5
Girl Crazy 1932,Mr 25,23:3
Ladies of the Jury 1932,Ap 2,13:2
Girl in 419 1933,My 20,11:5
Too Much Harmony 1933,S 23,11:5
All of Me 1934,F 5,19:2
Lemon Drop Kid, The 1934,O 27,20:2
Farmer Takes a Wife, The 1935,Ag 9,21:2
Heart's Desire 1937,Jl 12,20:4
Blossoms On Broadway 1937,D 3,29:2
Men With Wings 1938,O 27,27:2
Mutiny of the Elsinore, The 1939,F 16,17:2
Geronimo 1940,F 8,18:3
Women Without Names 1940,My 9,26:4
Mad Doctor, The 1941,F 27,23:4
Lady is Willing, The 1942,Ap 24,21:2
So Proudly We Hail 1943,S 10,29:1

Kelly, Lew

Heaven on Earth 1931,D 19,16:4
Scandal for Sale 1932,Ap 3,26:2
Miracle Man, The 1932,Ap 21,25:2
Laughter in Hell 1933,Ja 2,29:2
State Trooper 1933,Mr 27,13:6
Strange People 1933,Je 17,16:5
Six of a Kind 1934,Mr 10,18:3
Man on the Flying Trapeze 1935,Ag 3,16:2
Diamond Jim 1935,Ag 24,18:2
Man I Marry, The 1936,O 31,24:3
Some Blondes Are Dangerous 1937,N 3,29:3

Kelly, Lew— Cont
Painted Desert 1938,S 14,26:5
Taxi, Mister 1943,Ap 15,20:2
Kelly, Mark (Original Author)
Pigskin Parade 1936,N 14,23:3
Man From Down Under, The 1943,S 27,23:2
Kelly, Mark (Screenwriter)
One in a Million 1937,Ja 1,19:3
Little Men 1940,D 9,23:2
Kelly, Mary
Love Thy Neighbor 1940,D 18,32:5
Model Wife 1941,Ap 24,25:3
Kelly, Matthew Rev (Narrator)
Cloistered 1936,My 20,25:1
Kelly, Maurice
Till the Clouds Roll By 1946,D 6,27:4
Kelly, Nancy
Girl on the Barge, The 1929,F 26,31:1
Submarine Patrol 1938,N 19,9:2
Jesse James 1939,Ja 14,13:1
Tail Spin 1939,F 11,13:2
Frontier Marshal 1939,Jl 29,18:2
Stanley and Livingstone 1939,Ag 5,18:2
He Married his Wife 1940,Ja 20,11:2
Sailor's Lady 1940,Je 29,12:2
Private Affairs 1940,Jl 5,10:3
One Night in the Tropics 1940,D 20,33:2
Scotland Yard 1941,Ap 9,33:3
Parachute Battalion 1941,Ag 29,13:2
To the Shores of Tripoli 1942,Mr 26,27:2
Friendly Enemies 1942,Je 22,19:1
Tarzan's Desert Mystery 1943,D 27,23:3
Woman in Bondage 1944,Mr 27,17:2
Show Business 1944,My 11,25:7
Betrayal From the East 1945,Ap 25,27:2
Murder in the Music Hall 1946,Ap 15,22:2
Crowded Paradise 1956,Je 22,15:1
Bad Seed, The 1956,S 13,39:6
Kelly, P J
Beloved Enemy 1936,D 26,15:2
Adventure's End 1937,D 20,23:2
Missing Guest, The 1938,S 7,30:7
Secret Seven, The 1940,Ag 12,11:6
Kelly, Patsy
Going Hollywood 1933,D 23,19:2
Countess of Monte Cristo, The 1934,Ap 2,13:2
Girl From Missouri, The 1934,Ag 4,14:6
Go Into Your Dance 1935,My 4,17:2
Every Night at Eight 1935,Ag 3,16:2
Page Miss Glory 1935,Ag 29,25:2
Thanks a Million 1935,N 14,17:1
Private Number 1936,Je 12,19:1
Sing, Baby, Sing 1936,S 12,20:1
Kelly the Second 1936,O 3,21:2
Pigskin Parade 1936,N 14,23:3
Wake up and Live 1937,Ap 24,16:2
Nobody's Baby 1937,My 20,17:3
Pick a Star 1937,My 28,17:2
Ever Since Eve 1937,Je 25,25:2
Merrily We Live 1938,Mr 18,23:3
There Goes my Heart 1938,O 14,27:1
Cowboy and the Lady, The 1938,N 25,19:3
Gorilla, The 1939,My 28,6:2
Hit Parade of 1941 1940,D 5,33:2
Road Show 1941,F 19,25:2
Topper Returns 1941,Mr 28,26:6
Broadway Limited 1941,Je 16,11:6
Playmates 1941,D 26,21:3
Sing Your Worries Away 1942,My 15,25:2
In old California 1942,Je 18,25:3
Ladies' Day 1943,Mr 26,14:3
Please Don't Eat the Daisies 1960,Ap 1,37:1
Crowded Sky, The 1961,F 11,27:2
Naked Kiss, The 1964,O 29,38:1
C'mon Let's Live a Little 1967,My 4,34:1
Kelly, Paul
Uncle Sam of Freedom Ridge 1920,S 27,15:2
New Klondike, The 1926,Mr 22,16:1
Slide, Kelly, Slide 1927,Mr 23,19:2
Special Delivery 1927,Ap 26,33:3
Broadway Thru a Keyhole 1933,N 2,18:3
Love Captive, The 1934,Je 8,18:1
Side Streets 1934,Ag 15,13:5
Blind Date 1934,S 1,16:3
Death on the Diamond 1934,S 24,14:1
President Vanishes, The 1934,D 8,18:5
When a Man's a Man 1935,F 22,27:2
Star of Midnight 1935,Ap 12,26:5
Public Hero No 1 1935,Je 8,12:2
Silk Hat Kid 1935,Ag 7,22:5
My Marriage 1936,F 22,12:2
Song and Dance Man 1936,Mr 12,18:2
Country Beyond, The 1936,Ap 30,17:3
Accusing Finger, The 1936,N 17,35:4
Murder With Pictures 1936,N 21,21:4
Parole Racket 1937,Mr 8,22:1
It Happened Out West 1937,Je 7,22:3
Frame-Up 1937,Ag 9,23:2 (In Addenda)
Fit for a King 1937,O 15,18:5
Navy Blue and Gold 1937,D 24,21:2
Torchy Blane in Panama 1938,Ap 18,11:1
Nurse From Brooklyn 1938,My 13,17:3
Island in the Sky 1938,My 14,18:1
Devil's Party, The 1938,My 31,8:3

Missing Guest, The 1938,S 7,30:7
Juvenile Court 1938,S 12,13:2
Adventure in Sahara 1938,D 19,19:2
Within the Law 1939,Ap 6,31:2
Flying Irishman, The 1939,Ap 12,27:2
Six Thousand Enemies 1939,Je 9,26:2
Roaring Twenties, The 1939,N 11,12:1
Invisible Stripes 1940,Ja 13,11:2
Queen of the Mob 1940,Jl 1,23:2
Howards of Virginia, The 1940,S 27,27:1
Wyoming 1940,O 3,31:4
Girls Under 21 1940,N 11,22:4
Flight Command 1941,Ja 17,21:2
Ziegfeld Girl 1941,Ap 25,17:2
I'll Wait for You 1941,Je 2,13:6
Mystery Ship 1941,Ag 16,18:3
Parachute Battalion 1941,Ag 29,13:2
Mr and Mrs North 1942,Ja 22,13:2
Call out the Marines 1942,Ja 26,18:3
Tarzan's New York Adventure 1942,Ag 7,13:2
Flying Tigers 1942,O 23,25:2
Story of Dr Wassell, The 1944,Je 7,13:2
Dead Man's Eyes 1944,O 7,11:2
Allotment Wives 1945,N 22,39:3
San Antonio 1945,D 29,19:5
Cat Creeps, The 1946,My 18,12:4
Deadline for Murder 1946,Je 29,22:7
Fear in the Night 1947,Ap 19,11:3
Crossfire 1947,Jl 23,19:2
Adventure Island 1947,O 20,29:2
Thelma Jordon 1950,Ja 19,35:2
Side Street 1950,Mr 24,29:2
Guilty of Treason 1950,Ap 11,26:2
Secret Fury, The 1950,Je 22,34:2
Frenchie 1951,F 12,19:2
Springfield Rifle 1952,O 23,40:2
Split Second 1953,My 13,34:2
Duffy of San Quentin 1954,F 10,38:5
Johnny Dark 1954,Je 26,7:2
High and the Mighty, The 1954,Jl 1,21:2
Square Jungle, The 1955,D 31,17:2
Storm Center 1956,O 22,25:4
Bailout at 43,000 1957,Je 8,13:2
Kelly, Peggy
School for Wives 1925,Ap 1,21:3
Joy Girl, The 1927,S 6,34:3
Kelly, Seamus
Moby Dick 1956,Jl 5,18:1
Kelly, Sean
Man Inside, The 1959,F 5,24:7
Green Helmet, The 1961,Jl 20,32:2
633 Squadron 1964,Je 25,25:1
Kelly, Skeets (Cinematographer)
Edge of the World, The 1938,S 12,13:2
Kelly, Thomas F (Original Author)
China Doll 1958,D 4,52:1
Kelly, Tommy
Adventures of Tom Sawyer, The 1938,F 18,23:1
Peck's bad Boy With the Circus 1939,Ja 11,17:4
They Shall Have Music 1939,Jl 26,17:2
Irene 1940,My 24,23:3
Military Academy 1940,Ag 5,10:4
Gallant Sons 1940,D 12,37:2
Nice Girl 1941,Mr 27,29:6
Kelly, Walter C
Seas Beneath 1931,Ja 31,15:1
McFadden's Flats 1935,Mr 13,16:2
Laughing Irish Eyes 1936,Ap 4,11:2
Kelly, William J
Lily of the Dust 1924,Ag 25,16:2
Proud Flesh 1925,Ap 14,26:1
Parisian Nights 1925,Je 2,16:3
Woman Accused, The 1933,Mr 13,18:2
Below the Sea 1933,Je 3,16:4
Six of a Kind 1934,Mr 10,18:3
Kelman, Ricky
Critic's Choice 1963,My 2,40:2
Kelsall, Moultie
Man Who Never Was, The 1956,Ap 4,24:1
Kelsall, Moultrie
Last Holiday 1950,N 14,39:4
Captain Horatio Hornblower 1951,S 14,21:2
High and Dry 1954,Ag 31,25:5
Warriors, The 1955,S 10,11:2
Barretts of Wimpole Street, The 1957,Ja 18,15:3
Abandon Ship 1957,Ap 18,35:1
Your Past Is Showing 1958,Jl 1,36:2
Inn of the Sixth Happiness, The 1958,D 14,2:7
Battle of the Sexes, The 1960,Ap 19,40:4
Light in the Piazza 1962,F 8,25:1
Birthday Party, The 1968,D 10,54:1
Kelsey, Frank
That I May Live 1937,My 10,23:2
Knight Without Armor 1937,Jl 9,18:1
Kelsey, Fred
Yankee Consul, The 1924,F 11,18:3
Madonna of the Streets 1924,O 28,23:4
Excuse Me 1925,Ja 27,11:2
Smooth as Satin 1925,Je 23,24:3
Paths to Paradise 1925,Je 30,14:3
Seven Keys to Baldpate 1925,N 3,25:4
Seven Sinners 1925,D 8,28:5
That's My Baby 1926,Ap 12,18:4

Kelsey, Fred— Cont
Social Highwayman, The 1926,Je 15,23:3
Third Degree, The 1927,F 15,23:1
Soft Cushions 1927,S 12,29:1
Gorilla, The 1927,N 21,20:1
Thirteenth Juror, The 1927,N 22,20:1
Thirteenth Hour, The 1927,N 28,18:5
Tenderloin 1928,Mr 15,28:3
On Trial 1928,N 15,26:5
Last Warning, The 1929,Ja 7,36:2
Naughty Baby 1929,F 5,26:3
Donovan Affair, The 1929,Ap 29,29:2
Fall of Eve, The 1929,Je 18,29:4
Smiling Irish Eyes 1929,Jl 24,23:2
Only Saps Work 1930,D 13,22:2
She Got What She Wanted 1930,D 29,18:1
Road to Paradise, The 1931,Ja 20,21:3
Going Wild 1931,Ja 26,21:1
Subway Express 1931,My 2,23:4
Donovan's Kid 1931,My 22,28:5
Guilty as Hell 1932,Ag 6,14:5
Red-Haired Alibi 1932,O 24,18:5
Shadows of Sing Sing 1934,F 21,23:2
Crime Doctor, The 1934,My 11,24:3
Young and Beautiful 1934,S 18,18:4
Carnival 1935,F 16,9:1
Diamond Jim 1935,Ag 24,18:2
Super-Sleuth 1937,Jl 17,18:1
Lone Wolf Strikes, The 1940,F 5,13:2
Lone Wolf Meets a Lady, The 1940,Je 17,19:2
Little Bit of Heaven, A 1940,N 8,24:2
Lone Wolf Keeps a Date, The 1941,Ja 2,24:3
Lone Wolf Takes a Chance, The 1941,Ap 7,13:2
Invisible Ghost, The 1941,My 8,21:2
Counter-Espionage 1942,S 28,13:2
Gentleman Jim 1942,N 26,40:3
Hans Christian Andersen 1952,N 26,20:2
Kelso, Bobby
Jack-Knife Man, The 1920,Ag 2,12:2
Kelso, Edmund (Original Author)
Mystery of the Hooded Horsemen, The
1937,Ag 13,13:2
Kelso, Edmund (Screenwriter)
Mystery of the Hooded Horsemen, The
1937,Ag 13,13:2
Top Sergeant Mulligan 1941,N 12,31:3
Private Buckaroo 1942,Je 25,27:4
Kelso, Jim
Our Leading Citizen 1939,Ag 24,17:1
Kelso, Mayme
Mirandy Smiles 1918,D 16,13:3
Cheating Cheaters 1919,Ja 27,11:4
Men, Women and Money 1919,Je 16,11:2
Why Smith Left Home 1919,O 13,16:3
Conrad in Quest of his Youth 1920,N 8,20:2
Nellie, the Beautiful Cloak Model
1924,Ap 14,14:1
Seven Keys to Baldpate 1925,N 3,25:4
Vanity 1927,Je 15,31:4
Drop Kick, The 1927,S 20,32:2
Kelt, John
Tell-Tale Heart, The 1934,Je 15,26:3
Kelton, Dorrit
Rose Tattoo, The 1955,D 13,55:1
Kelton, Pert
Sally 1929,D 24,14:4
Bed of Roses 1933,Je 30,20:3
Bowery, The 1933,O 5,24:2
Sing and Like It 1934,Ap 14,18:2
Hooray for Love 1935,Jl 13,16:2
Mary Burns, Fugitive 1935,N 16,19:2
Annie Oakley 1935,D 24,10:5
Kelly the Second 1936,O 3,21:2
Cain and Mabel 1936,O 19,22:1
Women of Glamour 1937,Mr 6,10:1
Hit Parade, The 1937,My 31,11:2
Music Man, The 1962,Ag 24,14:1
Love and Kisses 1965,D 23,21:4
Kelvin, Thelda
Fascinating Youth 1926,My 10,19:1
Kemaina, Mousa
Walleyed Nippon 1963,S 3,36:1
Kemble (Director)
America Preparing 1916,Jl 11,7:4
Kemble-Cooper, Lillian
Woman Rebels, A 1936,O 30,27:2
Kemble-Cooper, Violet
Our Betters 1933,F 24,13:2
David Copperfield 1935,Ja 19,8:1
Vanessa: Her Love Story 1935,Ap 13,11:3
Kemeny, John (Producer)
Circle, The 1967,Ag 16,36:1
Kemm, Jean (Director)
Amour Maitre des Choses, L' 1931,Mr 30,25:2
Barbier de Seville, Le 1936,S 23,29:2
Juif Polonais, Le 1937,S 17,29:3
Kemmer, Edward
Too Much, Too Soon 1958,My 10,19:2
Kemp, Hugh (Miscellaneous)
Whispering City 1948,My 10,25:5
Kemp, Jack (Director)
Miracle in Harlem 1949,O 24,19:4

Kemp, Jeremy
Operation Crossbow 1965,Ap 2,29:1
Blue Max, The 1966,Je 22,38:1
Assignment K 1968,Jl 20,18:2
Strange Affair, The 1968,Jl 25,26:2
Kemp, Matty
Magnificent Flirt, The 1928,Je 25,27:1
Good-Bye Kiss, The 1928,N 12,18:2
Common Clay 1930,Ag 2,16:4
Down to Earth 1932,S 2,19:2
Phantom of Crestwood, The 1932,O 17,18:3
Tess of the Storm Country 1932,N 19,20:2
Wine, Women and Song 1934,Mr 21,24:3
Campus Confessions 1938,S 23,35:1
Kemp, Matty (Original Author)
French Line, The 1954,My 15,13:2
Kemp, Paul
Lumpenball 1931,Ap 27,25:1
Dolly Macht Karriere 1931,Jl 18,16:6
Blonde Nachtigall, Die 1931,Ag 22,7:5
Grosse Sehnsucht, Die 1931,O 8,22:6
Gitta Entdeckt Ihr Herz 1932,S 30,17:3
Sehnsucht 202; Longing 202 1932,N 13,IX,4:2
M 1933,Ap 3,13:3
Lied fur Dich, Ein; Song for You, A
  1933,Jl 2,IX,2:2
Verkaufte Braut, Die 1934,Ap 27,25:2
Roman Einer Nacht 1934,Je 22,24:2
Mit dir Durch Dick und Duenn 1934,N 24,19:2
Prinzessin, Turandot 1935,Ja 16,21:2
Csardasfuerstin 1935,Ap 25,18:3
Lied vom Glueck, Das; Song of Happiness, The
  1935,N 30,12:7
Schloss im Sueden, Das 1936,F 24,14:2
Fluechtling aus Chicago, Der 1936,Mr 16,21:4
Schuechterne Casanova, Der 1936,Ag 22,6:2
Heisses Blut 1936,S 26,11:2
Mutige Seefahrer, Der 1936,N 21,21:5
Boccaccio 1937,F 27,9:3
Glueckskinder 1937,Je 5,21:1
Schwebende Jungfrau, Die 1937,Ag 7,7:2
Charm of la Boheme, The 1938,Mr 19,11:2
Aus den Wolken Kommt das Glueck; Luck Comes
  From the Clouds 1938,Ap 16,17:2
Dingehort mein Herz; My Heart Belongs to Thee
  1939,Mr 25,19:2
Blumen aus Nizza; Flowers From Nice
  1939,Ap 1,17:3
Solo per Danne 1939,My 30,13:3
Our Little Wife 1940,Ja 27,9:2
Das Erlebnis Geht Weiter; Another Experience
  1940,F 3,9:3
Lysistrata 1948,Je 19,19:2
Threepenny Opera, The 1960,Jl 11,24:4
Kemp-Welch, Joan
Girl in the Street 1938,My 26,31:2
School for Husbands 1939,F 7,16:2
Haunted Honeymoon 1940,O 31,28:2
Wings and the Woman 1942,O 8,31:1
Jeannie 1943,S 13,14:2
Kemper, Charles
Southerner, The 1945,Ag 27,22:3
Scarlet Street 1946,F 15,29:2
Sister Kenny 1946,S 30,21:2
Gallant Journey 1946,O 10,33:2
Shocking Miss Pilgrim, The 1947,F 12,34:2
Gunfighters 1947,Jl 25,12:5
That Hagen Girl 1947,O 25,13:2
Fighting Father Dunne 1948,Je 25,26:2
Fury at Furnace Creek 1948,Jl 12,11:2
Belle Star's Daughter 1949,Ja 10,19:2
Yellow Sky 1949,F 2,36:1
Adventure in Baltimore 1949,Ap 29,27:2
Intruder in the Dust 1949,N 23,19:1
Nevadan, The 1950,Ja 13,19:4
Ticket to Tomahawk, A 1950,My 20,8:6
Wagonmaster 1950,Je 19,17:2
California Passage 1950,D 16,10:5
Mr Music 1950,D 21,34:3
Stars in my Crown 1950,D 22,19:1
Where Danger Lives 1951,Ja 1,13:6
On Dangerous Ground 1952,F 13,35:2
Kempinsky, Gerard
Beware of Pity 1947,N 1,11:2
Kempler, Kurt (Original Author)
Shriek in the Night, A 1933,Jl 24,11:2
Kempner, Brenda
Persecution and Assassination of Jean-Paul Marat
  as Performed by the Inmates of the Asylum of
  Charenton Under the Direction of the Marquis
  De Sade, The 1967,F 23,41:1
Kempson, Rachel
Jeannie 1943,S 13,14:2
Captive Heart, The 1947,Ap 28,27:2
Woman's Vengeance, A 1948,Ja 30,19:2
Tom Jones 1963,O 8,48:1
Third Secret, The 1964,Ap 29,27:1
Georgy Girl 1966,O 18,48:1
Jokers, The 1967,My 16,50:1
Kenas, Joseph (Screenwriter)
Farewell to Yesterday 1950,D 1,31:2
This Is Your Army 1954,D 15,41:1

Kenda, Jadwiga
Dyplomatyczna Zona 1938,O 24,13:2
Kendall, Betty
Child of Manhattan 1933,F 13,11:4
Kendall, Cy
Dancing Pirate 1936,Je 18,19:1
Hot Money 1936,Jl 25,16:2
Sworn Enemy 1936,S 12,20:1
They Won't Forget 1937,Jl 15,16:1
White Bondage 1937,Ag 6,21:3
Shadow Strikes, The 1937,S 13,17:1
Invisible Menace, The 1938,F 14,20:6
Rawhide 1938,Ap 25,19:2
Hawaii Calls 1938,Ap 29,17:2
Crime School 1938,My 11,17:2
Valley of the Giants 1938,S 10,20:2
Pacific Liner 1939,Ja 18,17:3
Stand up and Fight 1939,Ja 27,17:2
Twelve Crowded Hours 1939,F 24,15:2
Angels Wash Their Faces 1939,S 4,16:2
Calling All Marines 1939,O 26,27:2
Fugitive at Large 1939,N 13,15:2
'Til We Meet Again 1940,Ap 14,14:2
Men Without Souls 1940,My 13,21:2
Saint Takes Over, The 1940,My 28,29:3
Andy Hardy Meets Debutante 1940,Ag 2,12:2
Youth Will Be Served 1940,N 15,25:2
Billy the Kid 1941,Je 20,28:2
Mystery Ship 1941,Ag 16,18:3
Johnny Eager 1942,F 20,21:2
Tarzan's New York Adventure 1942,Ag 7,13:2
Whistler, The 1944,Ap 29,12:2
Wave, A Wac and a Marine, A 1944,Ag 14,11:4
Laura 1944,O 12,24:1
She Gets her Man 1945,F 9,20:5
Kendall, Felicity
Shakespeare Wallah 1965,S 13,42:1
Shakespeare Wallah 1966,Mr 23,40:2
Kendall, Geoffrey
Shakespeare Wallah 1966,Mr 23,40:2
Kendall, Henry
Flying Fool 1931,O 19,28:1
French Leave 1931,D 7,16:1
Innocents of Chicago, The 1932,My 1,VIII,5:4
Man Who Won, The 1933,F 27,11:2
School for Husbands 1939,F 7,16:2
Facts of Love, The 1949,O 31,20:2
Murder Will Out 1953,Ap 6,24:2
Alligator Named Daisy, An 1957,O 7,23:2
Kendall, Kay
Curtain Up 1953,F 2,17:3
Genevieve 1954,F 16,30:2
Doctor in the House 1955,F 19,18:3
Quentin Durward 1955,N 24,41:1
Simon and Laura 1956,Jl 3,17:2
Constant Husband, The 1957,Jl 26,10:3
Girls, Les 1957,O 4,27:2
Reluctant Debutante, The 1958,Ag 15,17:1
Once More With Feeling 1960,F 12,22:2
Kendall, Robert
Song of Scheherazade 1947,F 27,26:2
Kendall, Suzy
To Sir, With Love 1967,Je 15,56:1
Penthouse, The 1967,O 4,38:3
30 Is a Dangerous Age, Cynthia 1968,Mr 5,34:1
Up the Junction 1968,Mr 14,51:1
Kendall, Victor
Chump at Oxford, A 1940,F 20,17:3
Kendall, William
Magic Night 1932,N 3,25:3
This'll Make You Whistle 1938,N 1,27:2
One-Way Ticket to Hell 1955,D 8,45:1
Dance Little Lady 1955,D 26,23:3
Touch of Larceny, A 1960,Mr 17,28:1
Jokers, The 1967,My 16,50:1
Kendig, Betty
In Love With Life 1934,My 12,12:3
Kendis, J D (Producer)
Crusade Against Rackets 1937,Jl 26,15:3
Teen Age 1944,Je 19,17:1
Kendrick, Baynard (Original Author)
Last Express, The 1938,O 11,24:4
Eyes in the Night 1942,O 16,23:1
Hidden Eye, The 1945,Ag 31,14:3
Bright Victory 1951,Ag 1,19:2
Kendrick, Richard
Man on a String 1960,My 21,15:1
Kendricks, Ben Jr
Hook, Line and Sinker 1930,D 25,31:5
Kenedi, Alexander (Original Author)
Marry the Boss's Daughter 1941,D 4,33:4
Kenkhoff, Fita
Krach um Iolanthe 1935,My 11,21:3
Kenna, Marie
Unidentified Flying Objects 1956,Je 13,46:2
Kennaway, James (Original Author)
Tunes of Glory 1960,D 21,38:2
Kennaway, James (Screenwriter)
Tunes of Glory 1960,D 21,38:2
Mind Benders, The 1963,My 2,40:2
Shoes of the Fisherman, The 1968,N 15,40:3

Kenneally, Philip
Man on a Tightrope 1953,Je 5,19:1
Kennedy, A C (Screenwriter)
Painted Woman, The 1932,S 16,24:4
Kennedy, Adam
Men in War 1957,Mr 20,32:4
Bailout at 43,000 1957,Je 8,13:2
Until They Sail 1957,O 9,41:2
Kennedy, Arthur
City for Conquest 1940,S 28,9:2
High Sierra 1941,Ja 25,11:2
Strange Alibi 1941,Ap 28,11:2
Highway West 1941,Ag 8,13:4
Bad Men of Missouri 1941,Ag 16,18:2
They Died With Their Boots On 1941,N 21,23:3
Desperate Journey 1942,S 26,11:2
Air Force 1943,F 4,29:1
Devotion 1946,Ap 6,10:5
Boomerang 1947,Mr 6,36:2
Cheyenne 1947,Je 7,9:2
Champion 1949,Ap 11,29:2
Window, The 1949,Ag 8,10:5
Too Late for Tears 1949,Ag 15,12:3
Chicago Deadline 1949,N 3,37:2
Glass Menagerie, The 1950,S 29,31:5
Bright Victory 1951,Ag 1,19:2
Bend of the River 1952,Ap 10,37:1
Red Mountain 1952,Ap 26,19:2
Rancho Notorious 1952,My 15,39:5
Girl in White, The 1952,My 31,12:5
Lusty Men, The 1952,O 25,12:6
Crashout 1955,Jl 9,9:2
Man From Laramie, The 1955,S 1,20:2
Desperate Hours, The 1955,O 6,25:1
Trial 1955,O 14,21:2
Rawhide Years, The 1956,Je 16,12:2
Peyton Place 1957,D 13,35:1
Twilight for the Gods 1958,Ag 7,21:1
Some Came Running 1959,Ja 23,17:1
Summer Place, A 1959,O 23,24:1
Elmer Gantry 1960,Jl 8,16:1
Home Is the Hero 1961,Ja 26,32:1
Claudelle Inglish 1961,S 21,40:2
Murder She Said 1962,Ja 8,27:2
Hemingway's Adventures of a Young Man
  1962,Jl 26,17:1
Barabbas 1962,O 11,49:1
Lawrence of Arabia 1962,D 17,5:6
Cheyenne Autumn 1964,D 24,8:1
Joy in the Morning 1965,Je 10,38:1
Italiano Brava Gente 1966,F 4,20:1
Nevada Smith 1966,Je 24,28:1 (Incorrect in this
  edition; use 1966,Je 30,28:1 elsewhere)
Fantastic Voyage 1966,S 8,43:1
Day of the Evil Gun 1968,Ap 25,53:2
Minute to Pray, A Second to Die, A
  1968,My 23,56:2
Anzio 1968,Jl 25,26:1
Kennedy, Bill
Destination Tokyo 1944,Ja 1,9:2
Mr Skeffington 1944,My 26,23:2
Make Your own Bed 1944,My 27,12:2
Escape in the Desert 1945,My 12,10:2
Bachelor's Daughters, The 1946,O 7,23:2
That Brennan Girl 1946,D 9,34:3
Red Planet Mars 1952,Je 16,15:2
Unchained 1955,Ja 28,15:2
Kennedy, Burt (Director)
Canadians, The 1961,Je 1,31:1
Mail Order Bride 1964,Je 11,27:3
Rounders, The 1965,Ap 29,40:2
Money Trap, The 1966,My 5,59:1
Return of the Seven 1966,O 20,52:5
Welcome to Hard Times 1967,My 2,56:1
War Wagon, The 1967,Ag 3,26:3
Kennedy, Burt (Screenwriter)
Fort Dobbs 1958,Ap 19,10:4
Yellowstone Kelly 1959,N 12,27:1
Canadians, The 1961,Je 1,31:1
6 Black Horses 1962,Ap 25,30:1
Mail Order Bride 1964,Je 11,27:3
Rounders, The 1965,Ap 29,40:2
Welcome to Hard Times 1967,My 2,56:1
Kennedy, Charles
Little Old New York 1923,Ag 2,10:3
Crime Without Passion 1934,S 1,16:2
Kennedy, Dorothy
Cry Vengence 1955,F 19,18:3
Kennedy, Douglas
Roundup, The 1941,Mr 13,25:4
Possessed 1947,My 30,25:2
Unfaithful, The 1947,Je 28,10:2
Dark Passage 1947,S 6,11:2
That Hagen Girl 1947,O 25,13:2
Always Together 1947,D 11,46:1
To the Victor 1948,Ap 17,11:2
Decision of Christopher Blake, The
  1948,D 11,12:2
Adventures of Don Juan 1948,D 25,10:1
Whiplash 1948,D 27,16:3
South of St Louis 1949,Mr 7,17:2
Look for the Silver Lining 1949,Je 24,29:2
One Last Fling 1949,Jl 1,14:6

Kennedy, Douglas — Cont

Fighting Man of the Plains 1949,N 17,35:6
East Side, West Side 1949,D 23,17:2
Montana 1950,F 4,9:2
Cariboo Trail, The 1950,S 1,17:2
Oh! Susanna 1951,Mr 30,28:5
I Was an American Spy 1951,Jl 4,13:2
Texas Rangers, The 1951,Jl 14,7:2
Callaway Went Thataway 1951,D 6,42:1
For Men Only 1952,Ja 16,21:2
Torpedo Valley 1952,D 20,15:3
Gun Belt 1953,Ag 1,8:2
Sitting Bull 1954,N 26,24:4
Cry Vengence 1955,F 19,18:3
Eternal Sea, The 1955,Je 10,16:2
Last Wagon, The 1956,S 22,20:2
Chicago Confidential 1957,Ag 31,19:1
Amazing Transparent Man, The 1961,Mr 30,24:2

Kennedy, Edgar

Golden Princess 1925,S 7,15:3
Proud Heart 1925,N 3,25:4
Oh! What a Nurse! 1926,F 22,14:1
Wedding Bills 1927,Je 29,29:3
Chinese Parrot, The 1928,Ja 2,28:1
They Had to See Paris 1929,O 12,11:1
Bad Company 1931,N 7,16:5
Carnival Boat 1932,Mr 21,19:5
Hold 'Em Jail! 1932,Ag 20,7:4
Professional Sweetheart 1933,Jl 14,15:3
Tillie and Gus 1933,N 13,21:1
All of Me 1934,F 5,19:2
Heat Lightning 1934,Mr 8,23:2
20th Century 1934,My 4,24:2
Murder on the Blackboard 1934,Je 20,24:2
We're Rich Again 1934,S 1,16:3
Kid Millions 1934,N 12,17:2
Silver Streak, The 1935,Ja 16,21:1
Marines are Coming, The 1935,F 23,14:7
Living on Velvet 1935,Mr 8,25:4
Little Big Shot 1935,O 7,11:2
$1,000 a Minute 1935,D 21,11:1
Bride Comes Home, The 1935,D 25,30:2
Robin Hood of El Dorado, The 1936,Mr 14,10:1
Small Town Girl 1936,Ap 11,19:1
San Francisco 1936,Je 27,21:1
Fatal Lady 1936,Jl 11,11:3
Yours for the Asking 1936,Ag 20,14:2
Mad Holiday 1936,N 26,39:2
Three Men on a Horse 1936,N 26,39:1
When's Your Birthday? 1937,Mr 19,27:2
Star Is Born, A 1937,Ap 23,25:1
Super-Sleuth 1937,Jl 17,18:1
Double Wedding 1937,O 22,27:2
True Confession 1937,D 16,35:2
Hollywood Hotel 1938,Ja 13,17:3
Scandal Street 1938,F 5,19:2 (In Addenda)
Black Doll, The 1938,F 7,10:2
Peck's bad Boy With the Circus 1939,Ja 11,17:4
It's a Wonderful World 1939,My 19,27:2
Everything's on Ice 1939,O 6,31:1
Little Accident 1939,N 24,29:3
Charlie McCarthy, Detective 1939,D 25,29:2
Sandy Is a Lady 1940,Je 28,22:2
Quarterback, The 1940,O 17,33:3
Bride Wore Crutches, The 1941,My 26,15:3
In old California 1942,Je 18,25:3
Falcon Strikes Back, The 1943,Ap 2,17:4
Air Raid Wardens 1943,Ap 5,15:5
Hitler's Madman 1943,Ag 28,15:1
Crazy House 1943,D 16,33:3
It Happened Tomorrow 1944,My 29,18:2
Anchors Aweigh 1945,Jl 20,15:2
Heaven Only Knows 1947,N 14,29:3
Unfaithfully Yours 1948,N 6,9:2
My Dream Is Yours 1949,Ap 16,11:3
Mad Wednesday 1951,Ja 25,21:5
When Comedy Was King 1960,Mr 30,42:1
Sound of Laughter, The 1963,D 18,44:2
Laurel and Hardy's Laughing 20's 1965,N 18,55:2
Further Perils of Laurel and Hardy, The 1968,Ap 1,56:6

Kennedy, Edward

Trouble With Wives, The 1925,Ag 5,12:4
Panic in the Streets 1950,Ag 5,9:2

Kennedy, Fred

Rio Grande 1950,N 20,21:2

Kennedy, George

Charade 1963,D 6,40:1
Strait Jacket 1964,Ja 23,26:1
Island of the Blue Dolphins 1964,Jl 4,8:2
McHale's Navy 1964,Jl 11,15:2
Hush...Hush, Sweet Charlotte 1965,Mr 4,36:1
In Harm's Way 1965,Ap 7,36:1
Mirage 1965,My 27,28:1
Flight of the Phoenix, The 1966,F 1,26:1
Hurry Sundown 1967,Mr 24,22:1
Dirty Dozen, The 1967,Je 16,36:1
Cool Hand Luke 1967,N 2,58:1
Ballad of Josie, The 1968,Mr 14,51:2
Bandolero 1968,Jl 18,26:2
Boston Strangler, The 1968,O 17,52:1
Pink Jungle, The 1968,O 17,52:1

Kennedy, Harold J

Captive City, The 1952,Mr 27,34:2
Riot in Cell Block 11 1954,F 19,24:5

Kennedy, Hazel

Snob, The 1924,D 15,14:1

Kennedy, Jack

Not Quite Decent 1929,My 6,30:4
Skyline 1931,O 5,17:3
Woman From Monte Carlo, The 1931,D 31,17:6
Last Mile, The 1932,Ag 26,20:3
Painted Woman, The 1932,S 16,24:4
Sixteen Fathoms Deep 1934,Ja 19,24:3
Kid Millions 1934,N 12,17:2
Parole 1936,Je 27,21:1
Ape, The 1940,N 28,28:3

Kennedy, Jay Richard (Original Author)

To the Ends of the Earth 1948,F 13,26:2

Kennedy, Jay Richard (Screenwriter)

To the Ends of the Earth 1948,F 13,26:2
I'll Cry Tomorrow 1956,Ja 13,18:1

Kennedy, Joyce

Man From Chicago, The 1931,Ja 16,27:1
Seven Sinners 1936,Ag 22,6:1

Kennedy, King

Seven Days' Leave 1942,D 11,33:2

Kennedy, Lyn Crost (Original Author)

Raiders, The 1952,D 13,19:2

Kennedy, Madge

Baby Mine 1917,S 24,11:2
Danger Game, The 1918,Ap 22,9:1
Fair Pretender, The 1918,My 27,11:3
Service Star, The 1918,Jl 8,9:4
Friendly Husband 1918,Ag 5,7:1
Kingdom of Youth, The 1918,O 7,11:3
Perfect Lady, A 1918,D 2,11:3
Day Dreams 1919,Ja 13,9:3
Leave It to Susan 1919,My 26,19:4
Through the Wrong Door 1919,Jl 21,12:3
Strictly Confidential 1919,O 6,15:1
Blooming Angel, The 1920,F 9,10:3
Purple Highway, The 1923,Jl 24,14:3 (In Addenda)
Three Miles Out 1924,Ja 1,20:1
Bad Company 1925,Mr 16,16:1
Lying Wives 1925,Jl 17,16:2
Oh Baby! 1926,Ag 11,25:2
Marrying Kind, The 1952,Mr 14,27:1
Rains of Ranchipur, The 1955,D 16,38:2
Three bad Sisters 1956,F 13,24:1
Catered Affair, The 1956,Je 15,32:4
Lust for Life 1956,S 18,39:1
Nice Little Bank That Should Be Robbed, A 1958,D 11,17:4
Let's Make Love 1960,S 9,36:1

Kennedy, Margaret (Miscellaneous)

Prison Without Bars 1939,Ap 10,13:2
Take my Life 1949,Ja 19,34:2

Kennedy, Margaret (Original Author)

Constant Nymph, The 1929,Je 10,23:1
Escape me Never 1935,My 24,24:2
Mozart 1940,O 4,29:2
Constant Nymph, The 1943,Jl 24,8:2
Escape me Never 1947,N 8,11:2
If This Be Sin 1950,Jl 1,9:2

Kennedy, Margaret (Screenwriter)

Constant Nymph, The 1934,Ap 7,19:1
Old Curiosity Shop, The 1935,D 23,15:5
Stolen Life 1939,Je 15,27:2
Man in Grey, The 1945,N 30,18:6

Kennedy, Mary

Little Old New York 1923,Ag 2,10:3
Yolanda 1924,F 20,23:1

Kennedy, Merna

Circus, The 1928,Ja 9,20:1
Broadway 1929,My 28,36:2
Skinner Steps Out 1929,D 7,19:3
King of Jazz 1930,My 3,23:1
Lady With a Past 1932,F 22,23:2
All American, The 1932,D 22,18:4
Red-Haired Alibi 1932,O 24,18:5
Laughter in Hell 1933,Ja 2,29:2
Emergency Call 1933,Je 24,16:2
Arizona to Broadway 1933,Jl 22,14:3
Don't Bet on Love 1933,Jl 31,16:2
Police Call 1933,Ag 22,20:3
Wonder Bar 1934,Mr 1,23:2
I Like It That Way 1934,Ap 18,23:3

Kennedy, Neal

Bitter Sweet 1940,N 22,27:1

Kennedy, Phyllis

Stage Door 1937,O 8,27:2
Joy of Living 1938,My 6,27:1
Vivacious Lady 1938,Je 3,17:3
Mother Carey's Chickens 1938,Ag 5,11:1
Artists and Models Abroad 1938,D 22,25:3
Rhythm on the River 1940,Ag 29,23:2
Time to Kill 1942,D 25,15:4
Coney Island 1943,Je 17,17:2
Living in a Big Way 1947,O 10,31:4

Kennedy, Rigs

Dayton's Devils 1968,O 3,56:4

Kennedy, S K (Original Author)

Duel in the Jungle 1954,Ag 9,13:2

Kennedy, Tom

Madonna of the Streets 1924,O 28,23:4
As Man Desires 1925,F 10,20:1
Best Bad Man, The 1925,D 2,23:1
Yankee Senor, The 1926,Ja 28,14:4
Behind the Front 1926,F 10,16:2
Born to the West 1926,Je 30,18:1 (In Addenda)
Mantrap 1926,Jl 12,24:4
We're in the Navy Now 1926,N 8,19:2
Alias the Deacon 1927,Je 21,29:2
Fireman, Save My Child 1927,O 10,24:1
Wife Savers 1928,Ja 17,23:2
At Yale 1928,Jl 30,21:2
Cop, The 1928,N 6,35:1
Cohens and the Kellys In Atlantic City, The 1929,Mr 18,30:6
Big House, The 1930,Je 25,31:2
See America Thirst 1930,D 12,35:3
Gang Buster, The 1931,Ja 24,15:1
Pays to Advertise, It 1931,F 21,15:2
It Pays to Advertise 1931,F 21,15:2
Monkey Business 1931,O 8,22:6
Pack up Your Troubles 1932,O 1,10:4
Devil Is Driving, The 1932,D 16,25:5
She Done Him Wrong 1933,F 10,12:3
Blondie Johnson 1933,F 27,11:2
Hollywood Party 1934,My 26,12:2
Down to Their Last Yacht 1934,S 24,14:1
Smart Blonde 1937,Ja 9,21:1
Behind the Headlines 1937,Je 1,27:2
Fly Away Baby 1937,Jl 9,18:2
Married Before Breakfast 1937,Jl 23,16:2
She Had to Eat 1937,Jl 24,12:1
Armored Car 1937,Jl 26,15:2
Big Shot, The 1937,Ag 13,13:1
Forty Naughty Girls 1937,S 18,15:3
Torchy Blane, The Adventurous Blonde 1937,D 18,18:1
Crashing Hollywood 1938,Ja 8,19:2
Wise Girl 1938,Ja 10,13:3
Making the Headlines 1938,Ap 1,17:2
Torchy Blane in Panama 1938,Ap 18,11:1
Go Chase Yourself 1938,Je 15,27:1
Crime Ring 1938,Jl 22,10:3
Torchy Gets her Man 1938,N 18,25:3
Torchy Blane in Chinatown 1939,F 3,13:2
Society Lawyer 1939,Mr 31,19:2
Day the Bookies Wept, The 1939,S 14,18:2
Remember the Night 1940,Ja 18,27:2
Curtain Call 1940,Ap 19,25:2
Angel From Texas, An 1940,My 10,26:7
Sporting Blood 1940,Jl 22,20:2
Pop Always Pays 1940,Ag 30,16:6
Flowing Gold 1940,S 2,19:3
Mexican Spitfire out West 1940,O 30,29:3
Great Swindle, The 1941,My 14,25:4
Officer and the Lady, The 1941,Ag 11,17:4
Ladies' Day 1943,Mr 26,14:3
Hit Parade of 1943 1943,Ap 16,24:3
Stage Door Canteen 1943,Je 25,13:2
Princess and the Pirate, The 1945,F 10,16:2
Bringing Up Father 1946,N 22,27:3
Pretender, The 1947,Ag 12,26:2
Burning Cross, The 1948,F 20,19:1
Invasion USA 1953,Ap 30,39:4
Further Perils of Laurel and Hardy, The 1968,Ap 1,56:6

Kenneth, Keith

Limehouse Blues 1934,D 12,28:2
Clive of India 1935,Ja 18,29:1
Cardinal Richelieu 1935,Ap 19,24:2
Daniel Boone 1936,O 24,23:2
I Cover the War 1937,Ag 2,10:2
Paris Honeymoon 1939,Ja 26,17:1
Little Princess, The 1939,Mr 11,21:1

Kennett, George (Screenwriter)

Boy, Did I Get a Wrong Number! 1966,Je 9,54:2

Kenney, James

Captain Horatio Hornblower 1951,S 14,21:2
Outcast of the Islands 1952,My 16,19:2
Doctor at Sea 1956,Mr 1,37:3

Kennington, Jill

Blow-Up 1966,D 19,52:2

Kenny, Charles (Composer)

Catskill Honeymoon 1950,Ja 28,10:3

Kenny, Clyde

Enter Arsene Lupin 1944,D 2,17:6

Kenny, Colin

Toby's Bow 1919,D 15,20:1
Black Beauty 1921,F 21,16:1
Grumpy 1930,Ag 2,16:4
Alice in Wonderland 1933,D 23,19:1
Limehouse Blues 1934,D 12,28:2
Captain Blood 1935,D 27,14:1
Charge of the Light Brigade, The 1936,N 2,24:1
Adventures of Robin Hood, The 1938,My 13,17:2
Booloo 1938,Jl 30,10:2
We Are not Alone 1939,D 1,27:1
Two Tickets to London 1943,Jl 3,11:2

Kenny, Elizabeth (Original Author)
Sister Kenny 1946,S 30,21:2
Kenny, Jack
Atlantic City 1944,Ag 14,11:4
Kenny, Joan
You Can't Beat the Irish 1952,My 1,34:4
Kenny, Nick (Composer)
Catskill Honeymoon 1950,Ja 28,10:3
Kent, Allegra
Midsummer Night's Dream, A 1967,Ap 18,32:1
Kent, April
Incredible Shrinking Man, The 1957,F 23,13:1
Tammy and the Bachelor 1957,Je 15,10:7
Kent, Arnold
Hula 1927,Ag 29,21:1
Woman on Trial, The 1927,S 26,27:1
Beau Sabreur 1928,Ja 23,18:3
Showdown, The 1928,Mr 5,21:1
Easy Come, Easy Go 1928,My 8,25:3
Woman Disputed, The 1928,N 10,20:8
Kent, Barbara
Flesh and the Devil 1927,Ja 10,20:2
Drop Kick, The 1927,S 20,32:2
Lone Eagle, The 1927,D 20,33:2
That's my Daddy 1928,F 13,16:2
Stop That Man 1928,Ap 17,27:2
Lonesome 1928,O 2,23:5
Shakedown, The 1929,Ap 8,32:1
Welcome Danger 1929,O 21,30:1
Night Ride 1930,Ja 20,21:1
Dumbbells in Ermine 1930,Jl 28,22:1
Feet First 1930,O 31,20:1
Indiscreet 1931,My 7,21:4
Emma 1932,F 6,14:4
Big Pay-Off, The 1933,Ja 17,22:7
Oliver Twist 1933,Ap 13,15:3
Kent, Carl
Falcon in San Francisco, The 1945,Jl 21,7:2
Try and Get Me 1951,My 7,22:2
Kent, Christopher
Madame Bovary 1949,Ag 26,15:2
Kent, Crauford
Thais 1917,D 31,5:2
Song of Songs, The 1918,F 19,11:2
Good Gracious, Annabelle 1919,Mr 31,11:3
Abysmal Brute, The 1923,Ap 18,24:5
Daddies 1924,F 11,18:3
Flowing Gold 1924,Mr 10,18:2
Lilies of the Field 1924,Mr 17,19:1
Guilty One, The 1924,Je 17,22:4
Man and Maid 1925,Ap 7,17:3
Midshipman, The 1925,O 13,20:1
Seven Keys to Baldpate 1925,N 3,25:4
See You in Jail 1927,Ap 4,30:5
Mother 1927,My 4,29:2
Missing Link, The 1927,My 7,15:2
His Dog 1927,Ag 16,31:2
Foreign Legion, The 1928,Je 25,27:1
Seven Keys to Baldpate 1929,D 26,21:1
Second Story Murder, The 1930,My 3,23:1
Unholy Three, The 1930,Jl 5,17:4
Three Faces East 1930,S 6,9:2
Devil to Pay, The 1930,D 19,30:1
Body and Soul 1931,Mr 14,23:2
Women Men Marry 1931,Jl 13,13:5
Transatlantic 1931,Jl 31,15:2
Menace, The 1932,Ja 30,13:2
File No 113 1932,F 20,11:2
Purchase Price, The 1932,Jl 16,5:5
Western Limited 1932,D 12,18:4
Humanity 1933,Ap 22,16:3
Eagle and the Hawk, The 1933,My 13,16:2
Little Miss Marker 1934,My 19,18:3
Lost Jungle, The 1934,Je 8,18:1
Vanessa: Her Love Story 1935,Ap 13,11:3
Magnificent Obsession 1935,D 31,11:2
O'Malley of the Mounted 1936,Ap 6,18:1
Daniel Boone 1936,O 24,23:2
Love, Honor and Behave 1938,Mr 21,18:2
Service de Luxe 1938,O 24,13:2
We Are not Alone 1939,D 1,27:1
Foreign Correspondent 1940,Ag 28,15:2
International Squadron 1941,N 14,28:4
Constant Nymph, The 1943,Jl 24,8:2
Kent, David
Two Rode Together 1961,Jl 27,23:3
Kent, Dorothea
More Than a Secretary 1936,D 11,35:2
Flying Hostess 1936,D 14,29:4
As Good as Married 1937,My 22,19:2
Some Blondes Are Dangerous 1937,N 3,29:3
Girl With Ideas, A 1938,Ja 1,11:2
Goodbye Broadway 1938,My 14,18:1
Having Wonderful Time 1938,Jl 8,11:2
Last Express, The 1938,O 11,24:4
Youth Takes a Fling 1938,O 17,12:1
Risky Business 1939,Mr 23,27:2
Flight Angels 1940,My 27,23:2
Cross Country Romance 1940,Jl 19,22:3
They Drive by Night 1940,Jl 27,17:5
No, No, Nanette 1940,D 20,33:1
It Started With Eve 1941,O 3,27:1
Stage Door Canteen 1943,Je 25,13:2

Pin Up Girl 1944,My 11,25:6
It Happened on Fifth Avenue 1947,Je 11,33:2
Kent, Ellie
Pal Joey 1957,O 28,30:1
Kent, George (Original Author)
Cockleshell Heroes, The 1956,Je 4,25:2
Kent, Jean
Madonna of the Seven Moons 1946,My 23,18:4
Notorious Gentleman 1946,N 14,39:3
Wicked Lady, The 1946,D 23,19:5
Magic Bow, The 1947,Jl 7,13:2
Man of Evil 1948,Mr 26,26:2
Smugglers, The 1948,Mr 29,17:1
Champagne Charlie 1948,Ag 7,8:2
Sleeping Car to Trieste 1949,Ap 18,18:6
Caravan 1949,Ap 21,30:4
Bond Street 1950,Mr 30,40:6
Good Time Girl 1950,S 25,18:5
Gay Lady, The 1951,Ap 16,21:2
Reluctant Widow, The 1951,S 8,8:6
Browning Version, The 1951,O 30,33:2
Woman in Question, The 1952,F 19,24:2
Prince and the Showgirl 1957,Je 14,22:2
Bonjour Tristesse 1958,Ja 16,32:1
Haunted Strangler, The 1958,Jl 4,15:3
Bluebeard's Ten Honeymoons 1960,N 8,32:6
Please Turn Over 1961,Ap 29,12:2
Kent, Julia
Ramparts We Watch, The 1940,S 20,27:1
Kent, Kenneth
Night Train 1940,D 30,21:1
Suicide Squadron 1942,My 14,23:2
Kent, Larry
Whirlwind of Youth, The 1927,Je 6,27:2
Women's Wares 1927,N 15,27:1
Lovelorn, The 1927,D 19,30:1
Her Wild Oat 1928,F 6,12:3
Heart of a Follies Girl, The 1928,Mr 12,26:1
Mad Hour, The 1928,Ap 16,20:5
Hangman's House 1928,My 14,25:1
Haunted House, The 1928,Jl 17,23:1
Seas Beneath 1931,Ja 31,15:1
Kent, Laurence L (Director)
Caressed 1965,S 16,54:2
Kent, Laurence L (Producer)
Caressed 1965,S 16,54:2
Kent, Lenny
What a Way to Go! 1964,My 15,44:1
Kent, Lois
Four Hours to Kill 1935,Ap 11,27:3
Scandal Street 1938,F 5,19:2 (In Addenda)
Kent, Marjorie
Blondie Hits the Jackpot 1949,S 9,28:3
Kent, Marshall
Last Voyage, The 1960,F 20,14:2
Ring of Fire 1961,Ag 17,18:2
Kent, Mary
Canadian Pacific 1949,My 20,32:4
Kent, Robert
Country Beyond, The 1936,Ap 30,17:3
Crime of Dr Forbes, The 1936,Jl 6,11:4
King of the Royal Mounted 1936,S 29,35:2
Dimples 1936,O 10,21:2
Reunion 1936,N 27,27:1
Nancy Steele is Missing 1937,Mr 8,22:1
Step Lively, Jeeves 1937,Ap 2,19:6
That I May Live 1937,My 10,23:2
Angel's Holiday 1937,My 29,20:2
Born Reckless 1937,Jl 30,22:6
Charlie Chan at Monte Carlo 1937,D 18,18:1
Mr Moto Takes a Chance 1938,Je 13,15:4
Gladiator, The 1938,Ag 30,17:2
Wanted by the Police 1938,S 26,13:2
East Side of Heaven 1939,My 5,29:3
Andy Hardy Gets Spring Fever 1939,Jl 19,23:2
Calling All Marines 1939,O 26,27:2
Secret of Dr Kildare, The 1939,D 8,33:5
Joe Palooka, Champ 1946,Ap 6,10:6
For Heaven's Sake 1950,D 16,10:5
Country Girl, The 1954,D 16,51:2
Kent, Robert E (Miscellaneous)
Zombies on Broadway 1945,Ap 27,23:2
Falcon's Adventure, The 1946,D 14,19:2
Reckless Moment, The 1949,D 30,13:2
Kent, Robert E (Original Author)
King of the Lumberjacks 1940,Ap 15,21:3
Bad Men of Missouri 1941,Ag 16,18:2
Falcon in San Francisco, The 1945,Jl 21,7:2
Fort Ti 1953,My 30,7:1
Drums of Tahiti 1954,Ap 24,14:5
Don't Knock the Rock 1957,F 23,13:1
Kent, Robert E (Producer)
Chicago Confidential 1957,Ag 31,19:1
Operation Bottleneck 1961,S 7,40:2
Secret of Deep Harbor 1961,O 26,39:7
Incident in an Alley 1962,My 17,31:1
Diary of a Madman 1963,Je 6,39:1
Twice Told Tales (Dr Heidegger's Experiment); Dr
Heidegger's Experiment (Twice Told Tales)
1964,Mr 28,40:1
Twice Told Tales (Rappaccini's Daughter);
Rappaccini's Daughter (Twice Told Tales)
1964,Mr 28,40:1

Kent, Robert E (Producer) — Cont
Twice Told Tales (The House of the Seven
Gables); House of the Seven Gables, The (Twice
Told Tales) 1964,My 28,40:1
Kent, Robert E (Screenwriter)
Paid to Dance 1937,D 6,19:1
Who Killed Gail Preston? 1938,My 6,27:2
Highway Patrol 1938,Ag 4,15:2
Juvenile Court 1938,S 12,13:2
Charlie Chan in Reno 1939,My 31,27:2
Ladies Must Live 1940,S 6,25:3
Always a Bride 1940,N 21,43:3
Case of the Black Parrot, The 1941,Ja 10,23:3
Bullet Scars 1942,Ap 24,21:4
Spy Ship 1942,Jl 11,8:2
Truck Busters 1943,Ja 29,23:5
Two O'Clock Courage 1945,Ap 14,13:3
Falcon in San Francisco, The 1945,Jl 21,7:2
Radio Stars on Parade 1945,S 22,14:2
Dick Tracy vs Cueball 1946,N 23,12:2
Red Stallion 1947,N 27,50:3
Where the Sidewalk Ends 1950,Jl 8,7:4
Last of the Buccaneers 1950,D 15,43:2
Thief of Damascus 1952,My 8,37:2
California Conquest 1952,Je 7,22:6
Golden Hawk, The 1952,O 18,16:4
Fort Ti 1953,My 30,7:1
Drums of Tahiti 1954,Ap 24,14:5
Miami Story, The 1954,My 15,13:2
Inside Detroit 1956,Ja 28,10:5
Diary of a Madman 1963,Je 6,39:1
Twice Told Tales (Rappaccini's Daughter);
Rappaccini's Daughter (Twice Told Tales)
1964,Mr 28,40:1
Twice Told Tales (Dr Heidegger's Experiment); Dr
Heidegger's Experiment (Twice Told Tales)
1964,Mr 28,40:1
Twice Told Tales (The House of the Seven
Gables); House of the Seven Gables, The (Twice
Told Tales) 1964,My 28,40:1
Get Yourself a College Girl 1965,Ap 29,40:2
When the Boys Meet the Girls 1966,Ja 20,29:1
Hot Rods to Hell 1967,Ag 10,45:5
Fastest Guitar Alive, The 1968,F 15,47:1
Kent, Robert, E (Producer)
Saintly Sinners 1962,Mr 29,28:2
Kent, Simon (Original Author)
Ferry to Hong Kong 1961,Ap 27,27:7
Kent, Stapleton
Shakedown 1950,S 4,11:2
Invitation 1952,Ja 30,22:6
Donovan's Brain 1954,Ja 21,28:2
Guys and Dolls 1955,N 5,26:1
Kent, Tony
Fixed Bayonets 1951,N 21,20:2
Kent, Walter (Composer)
Song of the Open Road 1944,Je 7,13:3
Earl Carroll Vanities 1945,Ap 2,15:6
Melody Time 1948,My 28,28:2
Innocent Affair, An 1948,S 29,36:2
Kent, Walter (Miscellaneous)
Manhattan Merry-Go-Round 1937,D 31,9:3
Kent, William
When Knighthood Was in Flower 1922,S 15,17:2
(In Addenda)
King of Jazz 1930,My 3,23:1
Saturday's Millions 1933,O 14,18:3
Kent, Willis (Miscellaneous)
Sucker Money 1933,Ap 7,22:5
Kent, Willis (Original Author)
Sucker Money 1933,Ap 7,22:5
Kenter, Heinz (Original Author)
Frischer Wind aus Kanada 1935,S 21,18:2
Kentfield, Calvin
Crazy Quilt, The 1966,O 4,50:1
Kentish, Elizabeth
It's Great to be Young 1957,D 26,23:3
Kenton, Earl (Director)
Small Town Idol, A 1921,Ap 17,VI,2:1 (In
Addenda)
Kenton, Erle (Director)
Other Men's Wives 1926,My 2,VIII,5:3 (In
Addenda)
Kenton, Erle C (Director)
Red Hot Tires 1925,O 20,28:1
Other Women's Husbands 1926,Ap 27,23:2
Palm Beach Girl, The 1926,Je 22,21:2
Rejuvenation of Aunt Mary, The 1927,Jl 27,27:4
Father and Son 1929,Je 4,29:3
Song of Love, The 1929,N 14,24:3
Last Parade, The 1931,Mr 2,19:1
Lover Come Back 1931,Je 5,26:5
Leftover Ladies 1931,N 9,22:4
X Marks the Spot 1931,D 7,16:1
Stranger in Town 1932,Jl 8,22:5
Guilty as Hell 1932,Ag 6,14:5
Island of Lost Souls 1933,Ja 13,19:2
From Hell to Heaven 1933,Mr 18,9:3
Disgraced 1933,Jl 15,14:2
Search for Beauty 1934,F 10,20:2
You're Telling Me 1934,Ap 7,19:1
Best Man Wins 1935,Ja 2,22:4
Grand Exit 1935,N 4,24:5
Devil's Squadron 1936,My 11,16:2

Kenton, Erle C (Director)— Cont
Counterfeit 1936,Jl 20,11:1
Devil's Playground 1937,F 15,12:5
Racketeers in Exile 1937,Ap 12,15:3
Little Tough Guys in Society 1938,N 21,14:4
Everything's on Ice 1939,O 6,31:1
Naval Academy 1941,Je 5,27:3
Flying Cadets 1941,O 14,29:2
Frisco Lil 1942,F 12,27:2
North to the Klondike 1942,Mr 12,24:3
Ghost of Frankenstein, The 1942,Ap 4,19:2
Pardon my Sarong 1942,Ag 27,15:1
Who Done It 1942,D 3,35:2
It Ain't Hay 1943,Mr 11,17:3
House of Frankenstein 1944,D 16,19:3
She Gets her Man 1945,F 9,20:5
House of Dracula 1945,D 22,16:3
Cat Creeps, The 1946,My 18,12:4

Kenton, James B
Search for Beauty 1934,F 10,20:2
You're Telling Me 1934,Ap 7,19:1
Wagon Wheels 1934,O 4,19:1

Kentucky Jubilee Singers
Lost in the Arctic 1928,Jl 26,25:3

Kenward, Allan (Original Author)
Cry Havoc 1943,N 24,16:2
Two Smart People 1947,F 15,20:4

Kenworthy, N Paul Jr (Cinematographer)
Living Desert, The 1953,N 10,38:1

Kenworthy, N Paul Jr (Director)
Perri 1957,O 2,27:5

Kenyon, Charles (Original Author)
Under Eighteen 1931,D 26,15:5
Goose and the Gander, The 1935,S 12,29:2

Kenyon, Charles (Screenwriter)
Iron Horse, The 1924,Ag 29,6:1
Dick Turpin 1925,Ja 26,14:1
Firebird, The 1934,N 15,25:2
Girl From 10th Avenue, The 1935,My 27,20:6
Goose and the Gander, The 1935,S 12,29:2
Midsummer Night's Dream, A 1935,O 10,31:1
Petrified Forest, The 1936,F 7,14:2
Golden Arrow, The 1936,My 4,16:1
Crack-Up 1937,Ja 4,20:4
Road Back, The 1937,Je 18,25:2
100 Men and a Girl 1937,S 18,15:2
Lady With red Hair 1940,D 6,28:2
Highway West 1941,Ag 8,13:4
It Comes up Love 1943,Ja 22,25:3
Man in Half Moon Street, The 1945,Ja 20,16:2

Kenyon, Curtis (Miscellaneous)
Princess and the Pirate, The 1945,F 10,16:2

Kenyon, Curtis (Original Author)
Lloyds of London 1936,N 26,39:1
Wake up and Live 1937,Ap 24,16:2
Bathing Beauty 1944,Je 28,20:1
Two Flags West 1950,O 13,23:2

Kenyon, Curtis (Screenwriter)
Thanks For Everything 1938,D 10,13:2
She Knew All the Answers 1941,Je 20,28:4
Twin Beds 1942,My 1,23:4
Seven Days' Leave 1942,D 11,33:2
Fabulous Dorseys, The 1947,My 30,25:3
Tulsa 1949,My 27,25:2

Kenyon, Doris
Conquest of Canaan, The 1921,Jl 11,9:3
Get-Rich-Quick Wallingford 1921,D 5,20:1
Ruling Passion, The 1922,Ja 23,11:4
Monsieur Beaucaire 1924,Ag 12,12:1 (In Addenda)
If I Marry Again 1925,Ja 12,11:2
Thief in Paradise, A 1925,Ja 26,14:1
I Want my Man 1925,Ap 6,17:3
Half-Way Girl, The 1925,Jl 29,24:4
Unguarded Hour, The 1926,Ja 5,25:2 (In Addenda)
Men of Steel 1926,Jl 12,24:4
Ladies at Play 1926,N 16,25:3
Loose Ankles 1926,N 21,VIII,7:3 (In Addenda)
Blonde Saint, The 1926,N 23,27:1
Valley of the Giants, The 1927,D 5,26:2
Burning Daylight 1928,Ap 23,20:2
Hawk's Nest, The 1928,Je 25,27:1
Home Towners, The 1928,O 24,26:4
Interference 1928,N 17,23:1
Beau Bandit 1930,Je 14,9:4
Bargain, The 1931,S 5,7:4
Alexander Hamilton 1931,S 17,21:4
Road to Singapore, The 1931,O 1,25:2
Ruling Voice, The 1931,N 5,29:3
Young America 1932,My 7,11:5
Man Called Back, The 1932,Jl 30,16:5
No Marriage Ties 1933,Ag 4,18:2
Voltaire 1933,Ag 23,21:2
Counsellor-At-Law 1933,D 8,31:2
Whom the Gods Destroy 1934,Jl 13,14:2
Human Side, The 1934,S 15,20:3
Girls' School 1938,N 3,27:1
Man in the Iron Mask, The 1939,Jl 14,11:1

Kenyon, Ethel
Good Sport 1931,D 12,23:3

Kenyon, Gwen
Hold 'Em Navy 1937,N 6,14:2
Sarong Girl 1943,Je 18,16:6

Kenyon, Joan
Stolen Heaven 1931,F 14,11:4

Kenyon, Nancye
This Freedom 1923,N 28,15:1

Keon, Michael (Original Author)
Seventh Dawn, The 1964,S 3,24:1

Keown, Eric (Original Author)
Ghost Goes West, The 1936,Ja 11,9:2

Keppler, Wolfgang
Mutter und Kind 1934,N 30,22:3

Kept, Robert E (Screenwriter)
I Was Framed 1942,Je 12,16:6

Ker, Evelyn
Playtime; Receation, La 1963,Ja 16,5:2

Keran, Jack
Run, Appaloosa, Run! 1966,Jl 14,28:1

Keraudy, Jean
Night Watch, The; Trou, Le 1964,My 27,46:1

Kerbash, Michele
Battle of Algiers, The 1967,S 21,56:1

Kerbler, Eva
Cabaret 1957,N 9,31:2 (Incorrect in this edition; use 1957,N 7,43:4 elsewhere)
Ballerina 1958,My 10,19:2

Kergy, Albert
Rasputin: The Holy Devil 1930,Ag 25,14:2

Kerien, Jean-Pierre
September Storm 1960,O 29,26:7
Muriel 1963,O 31,26:1

Kerima
Outcast of the Islands 1952,My 16,19:2
Lupa, La 1954,F 18,36:2
Land of the Pharaohs 1955,Jl 27,15:2
Quiet American, The 1958,F 6,24:1
Jessica 1962,Ap 20,20:2

Kerjean, Germaine
It Happened at the Inn; Goupi Mains Rouge 1945,D 22,16:2
Nais 1948,Je 16,37:2
Cupboard was Bare, The; (Armoire Volante, L') 1952,N 4,33:1
Deadlier Than the Male 1957,O 9,41:1
Devil and the 10 Commandments, The (Episode 5) 1963,O 15,44:1

Kerly
Indiscretions 1939,My 1,21:1

Kern, James V (Composer)
That's Right, You're Wrong 1939,N 30,25:3

Kern, James V (Director)
Doughgirls, The 1944,Ag 31,14:1
Never Say Goodbye 1946,N 23,12:2
Stallion Road 1947,Ap 5,12:5
April Showers 1948,Mr 27,10:2
Second Woman, The 1951,F 2,19:2
Two Tickets to Broadway 1951,N 22,47:2

Kern, James V (Original Author)
You'll Find Out 1940,N 15,25:2
Playmates 1941,D 26,21:3
Her Kind of Man 1946,My 4,10:6

Kern, James V (Screenwriter)
That's Right, You're Wrong 1939,N 30,25:3
If I Had my Way 1940,My 6,13:2
You'll Find Out 1940,N 15,25:2
Look Who's Laughing 1941,D 25,33:2
Playmates 1941,D 26,21:3
Thank Your Lucky Stars 1943,O 2,19:2
Shine on Harvest Moon 1944,Mr 11,10:2
Doughgirls, The 1944,Ag 31,14:1
Horn Blows at Midnight, The 1945,Ap 21,18:2
Never Say Goodbye 1946,N 23,12:2

Kern, Jerome (Composer)
Music in the Air 1934,D 14,29:3
Sweet Adeline 1935,Ja 7,13:2
Roberta 1935,Mr 8,25:2
Reckless 1935,Ap 20,16:1
I Dream too Much 1935,N 29,24:1
When You're in Love 1937,F 19,15:2
Joy of Living 1938,My 6,27:1
One Night in the Tropics 1940,D 20,33:2
Sunny 1941,Je 13,22:2
Lady Be Good 1941,S 19,27:1
You Were Never Lovelier 1942,D 4,31:1
Song of Russia 1944,F 11,17:2
Cover Girl 1944,Mr 31,26:1
Broadway Rhythm 1944,Ap 14,24:6
Can't Help Singing 1944,D 26,22:4
Centennial Summer 1946,Jl 18,20:2
Till the Clouds Roll By 1946,D 6,27:4
Lovely to Look At 1952,My 30,11:2

Kern, Jerome (Miscellaneous)
Gloria's Romance 1916,My 23,9:2
Show Boat 1936,My 15,29:4
Swing Time 1936,Ag 28,21:2
High, Wide and Handsome 1937,Jl 22,15:1

Kern, Jerome (Original Author)
Music in the Air 1934,D 14,29:3
Sweet Adeline 1935,Ja 7,13:2
Show Boat 1951,Jl 20,14:1

Kernan, David
Zulu 1964,Jl 8,38:1

Kernan, Reginald
Arturo Island 1962,D 22,5:2
Naked Autumn 1963,N 15,25:3

Kernan, Reginald— Cont
Greed in the Sun 1965,Ag 19,35:3

Kernay, M
Roi des Resquilleurs, Le 1932,Je 13,19:3

Kernell, Harry
Hooray for Love 1935,Jl 13,16:2

Kernell, William (Composer)
It's Great to be Alive 1933,Jl 8,14:6
My Lips Betray 1933,N 4,18:3
Murder on Diamond Row 1937,N 12,27:2

Kernell, William (Miscellaneous)
Gaiety Girls, The 1938,Mr 31,15:1

Kerner, A
Sunny Youth 1935,Ag 19,18:2

Kerness, Donna
Unstrap Me 1968,N 21,41:2

Kernke, Karin
Head, The 1963,Je 20,29:1

Kerns, Hubie
Jim Thorpe - All American 1951,Ag 25,7:2

Kerny, Denise
Vierge Folle, La 1938,D 30,11:3

Kerouac, Jack (Original Author)
Subterraneans, The 1960,Jl 7,26:1

Kerovac, Jack (Narrator)
Pull my Daisy 1960,Ap 10,II,1:8 (In Addenda)

Kerr, Arthur
What Price Vengeance 1937,My 26,30:3
Fury and the Woman 1937,Je 22,26:2

Kerr, Bill
Night my Number Came up, The 1955,D 20,39:5
Wrong Arm of the Law, The 1963,Ap 3,39:1
Pair of Briefs, A 1964,F 3,22:2

Kerr, Bob
They Had to See Paris 1929,O 12,11:1

Kerr, David
Battle for Music 1945,O 15,13:2

Kerr, Deborah
Major Barbara 1941,My 15,27:1
Avengers, The 1942,N 25,18:2
Courageous Mr Penn 1943,D 23,26:5
Life and Death of Colonel Blimp, The 1945,Mr 30,18:2
Love on the Dole 1945,O 13,11:2
Vacation From Marriage 1946,Mr 15,27:2
Adventures, The 1947,Ap 4,19:2
Hucksters, The 1947,Jl 18,21:2
Black Narcissus 1947,Ag 14,29:2
If Winter Comes 1948,Ja 23,28:4
Hatter's Castle 1948,Jl 3,8:6
Edward my Son 1949,Je 3,21:2
Please Believe Me 1950,Je 12,19:4
King Solomon's Mines 1950,N 10,35:1
Quo Vadis 1951,N 9,22:2
Prisoner of Zenda, The 1952,N 5,36:2
Thunder in the East 1953,F 4,32:2
Young Bess 1953,My 22,31:1
Julius Caesar 1953,Je 5,19:1
Dream Wife 1953,Jl 30,20:1
From Here to Eternity 1953,Ag 6,16:2
End of the Affair, The 1955,Ap 29,28:2
Proud and Profane, The 1956,Je 14,41:2
King and I, The 1956,Je 29,15:6
Tea and Sympathy 1956,S 28,24:4
Heaven Knows Mr Allison 1957,Mr 15,22:1
Affair to Remember, An 1957,Jl 20,8:5
Bonjour Tristesse 1958,Ja 16,32:1
Separate Tables 1958,D 19,2:7
Journey, The 1959,F 20,19:1
Count Your Blessings 1959,Ap 24,23:1
Beloved Infidel 1959,N 18,46:1
Sundowners, The 1960,D 9,39:1
Grass is Greener, The 1960,D 24,8:2
Naked Edge 1961,Jl 1,9:1
Innocents, The 1961,D 26,15:2
Chalk Garden, The 1964,My 22,42:2
Night of the Iguana, The 1964,Jl 1,42:1
Marriage on the Rocks 1965,S 16,00:0
Casino Royale 1967,Ap 29,25:1
Eye of the Devil 1967,D 7,60:1
Prudence and the Pill 1968,My 24,37:1

Kerr, Donald
From Hell to Heaven 1933,Mr 18,9:3
Lady in the Morgue, The 1938,My 9,13:3
Four Daughters 1938,Ag 19,13:3
Mars Attacks the World 1938,N 8,26:3
Birth of the Blues 1941,D 11,39:1
Happy Go Lucky 1943,Mr 25,25:1
Oh, You Beautiful Doll 1949,N 12,8:4
Carrie 1952,Jl 17,20:2

Kerr, Ede
Isabel 1968,Jl 24,47:1

Kerr, Frederick
Lady of Scandal, The 1930,Je 14,9:4
Raffles 1930,Jl 25,20:4
Devil to Pay, The 1930,D 19,30:1
Born to Love 1931,Ap 25,23:4
Always Good-Bye 1931,My 23,13:4
Waterloo Bridge 1931,S 5,7:4
Honor of the Family 1931,O 17,20:1
Friends and Lovers 1931,N 7,16:5
Frankenstein 1931,D 5,21:2
Lovers Courageous 1932,F 20,11:2
Beauty and the Boss 1932,Ap 2,13:2

Kerr, Frederick — Cont
But the Flesh Is Weak 1932,Ap 16,11:2
Kerr, Geoffrey
Man From Home, The 1922,My 1,20:3
Just Suppose 1926,Ja 18,26:2
Women Love Once 1931,Je 27,20:3
Run Around, The 1931,Ag 10,18:3
Once a Lady 1931,N 9,22:4
Kerr, Geoffrey (Screenwriter)
Tenth Man, The 1937,N 15,15:2
Break the News 1941,Ja 2,24:2
Jassy 1948,F 20,19:2
Kerr, Jane
Miserables, Les 1935,Ap 22,14:2
Kerr, Jean (Original Author)
That Certain Felling 1956,Je 21,35:2
Please Don't Eat the Daisies 1960,Ap 1,37:1
Mary, Mary 1963,O 25,38:2
Kerr, John
Cobweb, The 1955,Ag 6,13:3
Gaby 1956,My 10,26:3
Tea and Sympathy 1956,S 28,24:4
Vintage, The 1957,My 9,36:5
South Pacific 1958,Mr 20,33:1
Girl of the Night 1960,N 12,15:1
Crowded Sky, The 1961,F 11,27:2
Pit and the Pendulum, The 1961,Ag 24,25:3
Seven Women From Hell 1962,F 1,22:2
Kerr, Laura (Miscellaneous)
My Dream Is Yours 1949,Ap 16,11:3
Kerr, Laura (Original Author)
Battle Circus 1953,My 28,27:5
Kerr, Laura (Screenwriter)
Brazil 1944,N 20,25:2
Farmer's Daughter, The 1947,Mr 26,31:2
Grounds for Marriage 1951,Ja 12,24:6
Kerr, Sophie (Original Author)
Beauty's Worth 1922,Mr 27,12:1
Worldly Goods 1924,N 3,20:1
Woman Accused, The 1933,Mr 13,18:2
Big Hearted Herbert 1934,N 14,23:2
People Will Talk 1935,Je 17,20:2
Kerr, Sophie (Screenwriter)
Big Hearted Herbert 1934,N 14,23:2
Kerridge, Mary
Anna Karenina 1948,Ap 28,32:2
Richard III 1956,Mr 12,1:4
Kerrien, J P
Trapeze 1956,Je 5,39:2
Kerrigan, J M
Little Old New York 1923,Ag 2,10:3
Lucky in Love 1929,D 14,22:4
Song O' my Heart 1930,Mr 12,32:6
New Movietone Follies of 1930, The
1930,Je 21,20:5
Lightnin' 1930,N 29,21:4
Don't Bet on Women 1931,Mr 7,17:2
Black Camel, The 1931,Jl 4,11:5
Merely Mary Ann 1931,S 12,15:4
Rainbow Trail, The 1932,Ja 30,13:2
Careless Lady 1932,Ap 18,19:2
Rockabye 1932,D 5,21:2
Air Hostess 1933,Ja 23,9:2
Study in Scarlet, A 1933,Je 1,15:3
Paddy the Next Best Thing 1933,Ag 25,12:2
Lost Patrol, The 1934,Ap 2,13:2
Modern Hero, A 1934,Ap 20,17:1
Key, The 1934,My 30,14:3
Fountain, The 1934,Ag 31,14:1
Happiness Ahead 1934,O 11,28:2
Informer, The 1935,My 10,25:2
Werewolf of London, The 1935,My 10,25:2
Barbary Coast 1935,O 14,21:1
Feather in her Hat, A 1935,O 25,24:5
Timothy's Quest 1936,F 29,11:2
Colleen 1936,Mr 9,20:2
Laughing Irish Eyes 1936,Ap 4,11:2
Special Investigator 1936,Ap 25,21:1
Spendthrift 1936,Jl 23,24:1
General Died at Dawn, The 1936,S 3,17:2
Lloyds of London 1936,N 26,39:1
Plough and the Stars, The 1937,Ja 29,15:1
London by Night 1937,Ag 13,13:1
Barrier, The 1937,N 27,21:2
Vacation From Love 1938,N 10,33:2
Ride a Crooked Mile 1938,D 29,15:2
Great Man Votes, The 1939,Ja 20,15:2
Flying Irishman, The 1939,Ap 12,27:2
Union Pacific 1939,My 11,31:2
Six Thousand Enemies 1939,Je 9,26:2
Zero Hour, The 1939,Jl 5,20:3
Two Bright Boys 1939,S 22,27:3
Witness Vanishes, The 1939,O 23,15:2
Sabotage 1939,N 16,29:5
Gone With the Wind 1939,D 20,31:2
Congo Maisie 1940,F 8,18:4
Three Cheers for the Irish 1940,Mr 9,19:2
Young Tom Edison 1940,Mr 15,27:2
Untamed 1940,Jl 25,14:3
Sea Hawk, The 1940,Ag 10,16:2
One Crowded Night 1940,Ag 27,17:2
No Time for Comedy 1940,S 7,9:2
Long Voyage Home, The 1940,O 9,30:2 (In
Addenda)

Adventure in Washington 1941,Ag 1,11:3
Appointment for Love 1941,N 7,27:1
Wolf Man, The 1941,D 22,24:5
Captains of the Clouds 1942,F 13,24:2
Vanishing Virginian, The 1942,My 28,13:3
Action in the North Atlantic 1943,My 22,10:2
Mr Lucky 1943,Jl 23,21:2
Fighting Seabees, The 1944,Mr 20,14:2
Wilson 1944,Ag 2,18:1
Big Bonanza, The 1945,F 26,14:5
Tarzan and the Amazons 1945,Ap 30,13:4
Great John L, The 1945,Jl 9,14:6
Spanish Main, The 1945,N 7,20:2
She Went to the Races 1945,F 1,29:2
Black Beauty 1946,Ag 30,13:2
Abie's Irish Rose 1946,D 23,19:4
Luck of the Irish, The 1948,S 16,34:1
Fighting O'Flynn, The 1949,F 28,16:2
Mrs Mike 1950,F 9,36:5
Sealed Cargo 1951,My 24,47:1
Park Row 1952,S 22,20:2
My Cousin Rachel 1952,D 26,20:2
20,000 Leagues Under the Sea 1954,D 24,7:2
It's a Dog's Life 1955,D 23,14:3
Fastest Gun Alive, The 1956,Jl 13,23:3
Kerrigan, J Warren
Girl of the Golden West, The 1923,My 21,12:2
Man From Brodney's, The 1923,D 18,16:3
Captain Blood 1924,S 9,19:1
Kerrigan, Kathleen
Music Master, The 1927,Ja 17,12:4 (In Addenda)
Wicked 1931,S 19,10:2
Kerris, George
Meet Me in Las Vegas 1956,Mr 14,39:2
Kerry, Anita
Case of the Lucky Legs, The 1935,N 1,25:1
Miss Pacific Fleet 1935,D 7,22:2
Murder of Dr Harrigan, The 1936,Ja 21,27:5
Fish 1936,Ja 25,18:5
Freshman Love 1936,Ja 25,18:5
Kerry, Margaret
If You Knew Susie 1948,F 23,19:2
Kerry, Norman
Soldiers of Fortune 1919,N 24,13:1
Get-Rich-Quick Wallingford 1921,D 5,20:1
Three Live Ghosts 1922,Ja 2,20:1
Man From Home, The 1922,My 1,20:3
Brothers Under the Skin 1922,N 13,12:1
Merry Go Round 1923,Jl 2,16:2
Hunchback of Notre Dame, The 1923,S 3,9:3
Acquittal, The 1923,D 12,24:5
Between Friends 1924,My 12,14:4
Oytherea 1924,My 26,21:1
True as Steel 1924,Je 17,22:4
Tarnish 1924,O 13,21:1
Fifth Avenue Models 1925,My 4,16:2
Price of Pleasure, The 1925,My 26,24:2
Phantom of the Opera, The 1925,S 7,15:3
Barrier, The 1926,Mr 22,16:1
Mlle Modiste 1926,Ap 26,25:1
Claw, The 1927,My 11,28:3
Annie Laurie 1927,My 12,24:3
Unknown, The 1927,Je 13,17:1
Irresistible Lover, The 1927,O 19,24:4
Body and Soul 1927,N 8,33:1
Love Me and the World Is Mine 1928,F 6,12:3
Affairs of Hannerl 1928,F 12,VIII,7:2 (In
Addenda)
Foreign Legion, The 1928,Je 25,27:1
Woman From Moscow, The 1928,N 5,26:1
Man, Woman and Wife 1928,N 5,26:5 (In
Addenda)
Phantom of the Opera 1930,F 10,20:4
Ex-Flame 1931,Ja 24,15:1
Bachelor Apartment 1931,My 16,13:3
Tanks a Million 1941,O 9,27:2
Kersh, Gerald (Original Author)
Night and the City 1950,Je 10,11:2
Kershaw, Willette
Sporting Life 1918,S 16,9:3
Vortex, The 1928,Ag 27,23:1
Kershner, Irvin (Director)
Stakeout on Dope Street 1958,Ap 24,38:1
Hoodlum Priest, The 1961,Ap 3,28:5
Luck of Ginger Coffey, The 1964,S 22,44:1
Fine Madness, A 1966,Je 30,28:2
Flim Flam Man, The 1967,Ag 23,40:1
Kershner, Irvin (Screenwriter)
Stakeout on Dope Street 1958,Ap 24,38:1
Kerst, Alexander
Corinna Darling 1958,Je 14,14:3
Kersten, A V
Quick, Koenig der Clowns 1933,D 9,18:3
Kert, Larry
Synanon 1965,My 6,44:1
Kertesz, Gabor
Pesti Szerelem 1934,My 10,25:3
Kertesz, Michael (Director)
Queen of Sin and the Spectacle of Sodom and
Gomorrah 1923,Mr 27,24:3 (In Addenda)
Kerviel, Ketty
Red Angel, The 1950,N 4,13:2

Kerwan, Pat (Screenwriter)
Randolph Family 1945,Mr 13,19:4
Kesel, Lee (Miscellaneous)
Flowers of St Francis 1952,O 7,26:2
Kesler, Henry (Director)
Three Russian Girls 1944,F 5,13:2
Kesler, Henry S (Director)
Five Steps to Danger 1957,Ja 31,21:1
Kesler, Henry S (Producer)
Five Steps to Danger 1957,Ja 31,21:1
Kesler, Henry S (Screenwriter)
Five Steps to Danger 1957,Ja 31,21:1
Kessel, Georges (Original Author)
Joan of Paris 1942,Ja 26,18:2
Paris After Dark 1943,O 23,11:1
Kessel, Georges (Screenwriter)
Oasis 1960,Jl 7,26:1
Kessel, Joseph (Original Author)
Woman I Love, The 1937,Ap 16,27:2
Volga Boatman, The 1938,Ap 15,23:3
Sirocco 1951,Je 14,31:2
Lover's Net 1957,Jl 23,23:1
Belle de Jour 1968,Ap 11,51:1
Kessel, Joseph (Screenwriter)
Mayerling 1937,S 14,27:1
Flight Into Darkness (L'Equipage)
1938,O 17,12:1
They Are not Angels 1948,My 22,8:3
Oasis 1960,Jl 7,26:1
Night of the Generals, The 1967,F 3,38:1
Kessel, M (Original Author)
Equipage, L' 1928,My 20,VIII,5:7
Flight Into Darkness (L'Equipage)
1938,O 17,12:1
Kessel (Director)
Cessez le Feu; Cease Firing 1934,Ag 12,IX,2:1
Kessele, J (Original Author)
Last Flight, The 1929,Je 17,29:1
Kesselring, Joseph (Original Author)
Aggie Appleby, Maker of Men 1933,O 20,14:2
Arsenic and old Lace 1944,S 2,17:2
Kessler, Alice
Beggar Student, The 1958,Ja 25,14:3
Kessler, Bruce (Director)
Angels From Hell 1968,O 24,55:5
Kessler, Edith
To Please one Woman 1920,D 20,11:2
What Do Men Want? 1921,N 14,18:1
Kessler, Ellen
Beggar Student, The 1958,Ja 25,14:3
Kessler, Joseph (Screenwriter)
Au Grand Balcon 1951,My 5,14:2
Kesster, Magnus
En Enda Natt 1942,D 7,22:2
Kester, Karen
Baron of Arizona, The 1950,Je 23,29:2
Kester, Max (Composer)
Princess Charming 1935,Je 22,18:5
Kester, Vaughan (Original Author)
Prodigal Judge, The 1922,F 5,VI,3:1 (In
Addenda)
Kestin, Erich
Blonde Nachtigall, Die 1931,Ag 22,7:5
Schoen Ist Es Verliebt zu Sein 1936,Ap 7,31:2
Ketchum, Cliff
Pork Chop Hill 1959,My 30,9:2
Kettner, Martin
Susanne Macht Ordnung 1931,O 12,28:2
Ketzlin, Hans-Joachim
That Woman 1968,Jl 19,30:3
Keuning, Mark
Three Came Home 1950,F 21,22:5
Dark City 1950,O 19,40:5
Kewksbury, Peter (Director)
Doctor, You've Got to be Kidding
1967,My 11,50:1
Key, Alice
Actors and Sin; (Actor's Blood) 1952,My 30,11:3
Key, Kathleen
Reno 1924,Ja 8,27:1
Sea Hawk, The 1924,Je 3,22:1
Revelation 1924,Je 24,18:2
Midshipman, The 1925,O 13,20:1
Ben Hur 1925,D 31,10:5 (In Addenda)
Flaming Frontier, The 1926,Ap 5,24:1
Money Talks 1926,My 11,24:3
Ben Hur 1931,D 4,28:2
Keyes, Daniel (Original Author)
Charly 1968,S 24,55:1
Keyes, Evelyn
Sons of the Legion 1938,S 30,24:3
Union Pacific 1939,My 11,31:2
Gone With the Wind 1939,D 20,31:2
Slightly Honorable 1940,My 17,23:4
Before I Hang 1940,O 3,31:3
Lady in Question, The 1940,D 10,33:2
Face Behind the Mask, The 1941,F 7,23:2
Here Comes Mr Jordan 1941,Ag 8,13:2
Ladies in Retirement 1941,N 7,27:1
Adventures of Martin Eden 1942,Mr 16,19:2
Flight Lieutenant 1942,Jl 31,11:1
Desperadoes, The 1943,My 13,17:2
Thousand and one Nights, A 1945,Jl 12,8:2

Keyes, Evelyn— Cont
Renegades 1946,Jl 11,18:2
Thrill of Brazil, The 1946,S 6,18:3
Jolson Story, The 1946,O 11,28:2
Johnny O'Clock 1947,Mr 27,39:2
Mating of Millie, The 1948,Mr 13,12:2
Enchantment 1948,D 27,16:2
Mrs Mike 1950,F 9,36:5
Killer That Stalked New York, The
  1951,Ja 5,17:2
Smuggler's Island 1951,My 24,47:2
Prowler, The 1951,Jl 2,16:6
Iron Man 1951,Ag 20,14:2
99 River Street 1953,O 3,14:2
Hell's Half Acre 1954,F 27,11:3
Seven Year Itch, The 1955,Je 4,9:1
Around the World in 80 Days 1956,O 18,37:1

Keyes, John
Rackety Rax 1932,N 5,12:5

Keyhoe, Donald E Maj (Original Author)
Earth vs the Flying Saucers 1956,Ag 2,21:2

Keymas, George
Bait 1954,F 24,21:3
Drums of Tahiti 1954,Ap 24,14:5
Maverick Queen, the 1956,Je 4,25:2

Keys, Anthony Nelson (Producer)
Devil's Own, The 1967,Mr 16,53:2
Five Million Years to Earth 1968,My 30,21:4
Devil's Bride, The 1968,D 19,60:1

Keys, Nelson
Madame Pompadour 1927,Ag 2,19:2
Triumph of the Scarlet Pimpernel, The
  1929,Jl 8,17:3
Last Journey, The 1936,Je 8,22:4

Keys, Robert
Big Jim McLain 1952,S 18,35:2
Wetbacks 1956,My 5,13:2

Keystone, Kops
When Comedy Was King 1960,Mr 30,42:1
Days of Thrills and Laughter 1961,Mr 22,37:1

Keystone,Teddy
When Comedy Was King 1960,Mr 30,42:1

Kezas, George
Woman of the Year 1942,F 6,23:2

Khaidarof, B
City of Youth 1938,S 5,30:4

Khalyutina, Sofia
Ural Front, The 1945,Je 7,25:3

Khamara, Gregory
Crown of Thorns 1934,Mr 28,27:6

Khan, Feroz
Tarzan Goes to India 1962,S 6,37:2

Khan, Pasha
Flight From Glory 1937,S 11,20:1

Khan, Rashid
Guide, The 1965,F 10,44:2

Khan, Salamat
Music Room, The 1963,O 16,50:6

Khanov, A
General Suvorov 1941,S 20,11:2

Kharitonov, L
Private Ivan 1957,Ap 3,28:2
School of Courage 1957,S 9,21:2

Kharitonova, Sophia
Cranes are Flying, The 1960,Mr 22,31:2

Khatchaturian, Aram (Composer)
Pepo 1935,O 10,31:6
First Front, The 1949,N 14,19:2
Othello 1960,My 16,39:1

Khazrevin, Z (Screenwriter)
Son of Mongolia 1936,N 21,21:4

Kheronsky, Chrisauf (Screenwriter)
Mumu 1961,Je 5,37:4

Khikawa, Danshiro
Sword for Hire 1957,S 5,32:1

Khitayeva, L
Night Before Christmas, A 1963,D 16,44:4

Khitrov, Stanislav
Peace to Him Who Enters 1963,N 25,23:5

Khityayeva, Lyudmila
And Quiet Flows the Don 1960,My 25,45:2

Khmelof, N P
House of Death 1932,Ag 13,18:6
Revolutionists 1936,D 26,15:3

Khodursky, A
Gadfly, The 1956,S 17,22:2
Miles of Fire 1958,N 10,36:6 (In Addenda)

Khokhlov, A
Lenin in 1918 1939,Je 27,27:2
Admiral Nakhimov 1948,N 25,47:4

Khokhlov, N
Poet and Tsar 1938,Ag 25,15:1

Khokhryakov, V
Rimsky-Korsakov 1954,Mr 1,16:3

Kholena, Elena
Bolshoi Ballet 67 1966,S 30,54:1

Kholodkov, A
Heroes of Shipka 1956,S 3,10:5

Kholodov, M I
Last Night, The 1937,Ap 28,18:3

Khoniyakov, V
Swan Lake 1960,Ja 26,25:2

Khorava, Anton
Last Hill, The 1945,Je 26,13:2

Khorosh, S
Childred of the Revolution 1936,Ap 6,18:2

Khosa, Lucas
Magic Garden, The 1952,F 6,24:2

Khote, Durga
Householder, The 1963,O 22,43:2

Khoury, Antoine (Producer)
Broken Wings, The 1968,Mr 16,34:1

Khrabrovitsky, D (Screenwriter)
Clear Skies 1963,N 27,30:1
Nine Days of one Year 1964,D 29,19:1

Khrava, Akaki
Skanderbeg 1954,Jl 5,6:4

Khrenikov, Tikhon (Composer)
Six PM 1946,Ja 28,15:5

Khryaschikov, N
Attack From the Sea 1954,Ap 19,19:4

Khudiakov, Genia
Flying Carpet, The 1960,F 28,31:1

Khvilya, A
Shors 1939,N 21,19:4
Heroes Are Made 1944,Mr 11,10:2
Secret Brigade 1951,Mr 19,23:2
Taras Shevchenko 1952,Jl 23,12:6
May Night 1953,Jl 13,22:4
Stars of the Ukraine 1953,Jl 13,22:4
Train Goes to Kiev, The 1961,Ap 10,26:1
Night Before Christmas, A 1963,D 16,44:4

Kiames, Elene
Patterns 1956,Mr 28,26:1

Kibardina, V
Youth of Maxim, The 1935,Ap 20,16:1
Return of Maxim, The 1937,N 2,33:1
New Horizons 1939,My 12,25:3

Kibbee, Guy
Man of the World 1931,Mr 21,15:1
City Streets 1931,Ap 18,17:3
Laughing Sinners 1931,Jl 4,11:5
Side Show 1931,S 19,10:2
New Adventures of Get-Rich-Quick Wallingford
  1931,O 10,20:4
Blonde Crazy 1931,D 4,28:2
Flying High 1931,D 12,23:3
Taxi 1932,Ja 8,27:3
Union Depot 1932,Ja 15,24:4
High Pressure 1932,F 1,22:3
Fireman, Save My Child 1932,F 18,25:3
Play Girl 1932,Mr 19,11:2
Crowd Roars, The 1932,Mr 23,25:4
Mouthpiece, The 1932,Ap 21,25:2
So Big 1932,Ap 30,19:3
Strange Love of Molly Louvain, The
  1932,My 9,19:5
Two Seconds 1932,My 19,25:3
Dark Horse, The 1932,Je 9,27:3
Winner Take All 1932,Je 18,9:2
Crooner 1932,Ag 20,7:4
Big City Blues 1932,S 10,18:5
Rain 1932,O 13,22:3
Scarlet Dawn 1932,N 4,25:4
Conquerors, The 1932,N 21,21:1
Central Park 1932,D 7,29:3
42d Street 1933,Mr 10,19:3
Girl Missing 1933,Ap 1,18:2
Gold Diggers of 1933 1933,Je 8,22:3
Life of Jimmy Dolan, The 1933,Je 14,22:3
Lilly Turner 1933,Je 15,21:2
Silk Express, The 1933,Je 28,24:2
Lady for a Day 1933,S 8,22:2
Footlight Parade 1933,O 6,21:3
World Changes, The 1933,O 27,22:3
Havana Widows 1933,N 23,24:3
Convention City 1933,D 25,28:2
Easy to Love 1934,Ja 15,12:2
Wonder Bar 1934,Mr 1,23:2
Dames 1934,Ag 16,20:2
Big Hearted Herbert 1934,N 14,23:2
Babbitt 1934,D 17,24:2
While the Patient Slept 1935,Mr 2,18:2
Don't Bet on Blondes 1935,Jl 20,16:2
I Live for Love 1935,O 19,21:2
Captain Blood 1935,D 27,14:1
Little Lord Fauntleroy 1936,Ap 3,27:1
I Married a Doctor 1936,Ap 20,17:1
Captain January 1936,Ap 25,21:1
Big Noise, The 1936,Jl 4,18:3
Earthworm Tractors 1936,Jl 25,16:1
M'liss 1936,Ag 8,5:2
Three Men on a Horse 1936,N 26,39:1
Don't Tell the Wife 1937,F 19,15:2
Mountain Justice 1937,My 13,31:2
Riding on Air 1937,Je 26,20:2 (In Addenda)
Big Shot, The 1937,Ag 13,13:1
Bad Man of Brimstone, The 1938,F 4,17:2
Of Human Hearts 1938,F 18,23:1
Joy of Living 1938,My 6,27:1
Three Comrades 1938,Je 3,17:1
Rich Man, Poor Girl 1938,Ag 19,13:3
Three Loves Has Nancy 1938,S 2,21:2
Let Freedom Ring 1939,Mr 10,19:2
It's a Wonderful World 1939,My 19,27:2

Kibbee, Guy— Cont
Mr Smith Goes to Washington 1939,O 20,27:2
Babes in Arms 1939,O 20,27:2
Our Town 1940,Je 14,25:3
Chad Hanna 1940,D 26,23:1
Scattergood Baines 1941,Ap 4,25:2
It Started With Eve 1941,O 3,27:1
Design for Scandal 1942,F 6,23:3
Sunday Punch 1942,My 11,19:2
Miss Annie Rooney 1942,Je 8,11:1
Tish 1942,S 18,25:2
Whistling in Dixie 1942,D 31,20:4
Girl Crazy 1943,D 3,27:2
Horn Blows at Midnight, The 1945,Ap 21,18:2
Romance of Rosy Ridge, The 1947,S 12,18:3
Red Stallion 1947,N 27,50:3
Fort Apache 1948,Je 25,26:2
Three Godfathers 1949,Mr 4,25:2

Kibbee, Milton
Law in her Hands, The 1936,Je 6,21:2
Murder by an Aristocrat 1936,Je 13,13:2
Love Begins at 20 1936,S 19,20:1
Polo Joe 1936,N 5,35:1
White Bondage 1937,Ag 6,21:3
Strike up the Band 1940,S 30,13:2
Mad Doctor of Market Street, The 1942,Ja 5,21:5
In old California 1942,Je 18,25:3
Jungle Siren 1942,O 10,11:3
Strange Holiday 1945,O 20,8:2
Body and Soul 1947,N 10,21:2
State Department-File 649 1949,F 21,20:2

Kibbee, Roland (Screenwriter)
Night in Casablanca, A 1946,Ag 12,17:2
Angel on my Shoulder 1946,O 21,27:2
Painting the Clouds With Sunshine 1951,S 1,9:6
Ten Tall Men 1951,O 27,10:5
Pardon my French 1952,Mr 31,17:2
Crimson Pirate, The 1952,Ag 28,21:2
Desert Song, The 1953,My 21,39:2
Three Sailors and a Girl 1953,N 23,32:2
Vera Cruz 1954,D 27,22:4
Top Secret Affair 1957,Ja 31,21:1
Devil's Disciple, The 1959,Ag 21,12:1
Amorous Adventures of Moll Flanders, The
  1965,My 27,28:1
Appaloosa, The 1966,S 15,51:1

Kibkalo, Yevgeni
Khovanschina 1960,S 19,41:2

Kibler, Beiva
Medium, The 1951,S 6,39:2

Kid, Mary
Rasputin 1929,O 21,30:1
Wasted Love 1929,D 30,16:4
Rubacuori 1932,Mr 5,11:2

Kidd, John
Horse's Mouth, The 1958,N 12,41:1

Kidd, Jonathan
Macabre 1958,Jl 24,18:1

Kidd, Michael
It's Always Fair Weather 1955,S 16,19:1

Kidd, Michael (Composer)
Band Wagon, The 1953,Jl 10,10:2

Kidd, Michael (Director)
Merry Andrews 1958,Mr 21,17:1

Kidder, Edward E (Original Author)
Peaceful Valley 1920,O 11,19:3

Kiefe, Jenny
Ungetreue Eckehart, Der 1932,Ja 23,18:4

Kieling, Wolfgang
Kreutzer Sonata, The 1938,My 28,9:3
Torn Curtain 1966,Jl 28,23:1
Vengeance of Fu Manchu, The 1968,F 15,47:1

Kientzy, Raymond
World Without Sun 1964,D 23,22:1

Kiepura, Jan
Die Singende Stadt 1932,My 10,25:4
Be Mine Tonight 1933,Ap 14,22:5
Lied fur Dich, Ein; Song for You, A
  1933,Jl 2,IX,2:2
Farewell to Love 1933,N 25,10:2
My Heart Is Calling 1935,Ap 15,16:3
My Song For You 1935,My 27,20:6
Give Us This Night 1936,Ap 6,18:1
Thank You, Madame 1937,Ap 27,18:2
Charm of la Boheme, The 1938,Mr 19,11:2
Her Wonderful Lie 1950,Jl 17,15:2

Kiepura, Ladis
Halka 1938,Ja 17,11:3

Kiesler, Frederic
8 X 8 1957,Mr 16,13:2

Kiesler, Hedy
Man Braucht Kein Geld 1932,N 16,15:3

Kieve, Jane (Screenwriter)
Island of the Blue Dolphins 1964,Jl 4,8:2

Kiffe, Karl
Johnny Doughboy 1943,My 6,25:3

Kihle, MimmiHefte, Kristian
Boer Boerson Jr 1939,N 4,11:3

Kihlgren, Sigvard
Great Adventure, The 1955,My 24,34:6

Kikaleishvill, Zurab
Ballet of Othello, The 1964,My 4,35:1

Kiki
Golden Mistress, The 1954,O 30,15:6
Naked Night, The 1956,Ap 10,27:5
Kikuchi, Kan (Original Author)
Gate of Hell 1954,D 14,45:2
Kikume, Al
Hurricane, The 1937,N 10,31:2
Typhoon 1940,My 23,28:4
Mad Doctor of Market Street, The 1942,Ja 5,21:5
Green Dolphin Street 1947,O 16,34:2
Kikumu, Stephen
Africa-Texas Style! 1967,Jl 13,30:2
Kikushima, Ryuzo (Miscellaneous)
Throne of Blood 1961,N 23,50:2
Kikushima, Ryuzo (Producer)
Sanjuro 1963,My 8,34:2
Kikushima, Ryuzo (Screenwriter)
Hidden Fortress The 1962,Ja 24,24:2
Yojimbo 1962,O 16,34:1
Bad Sleep Well, The 1963,Ja 23,5:2
Sanjuro 1963,My 8,34:2
When a Woman Ascends the Stairs
  1963,Je 26,36:4
Country Doctor, The 1963,Ag 14,28:1
High and Low 1963,N 27,30:1
Stray Dog 1964,Mr 4,32:7
Red Beard 1968,D 20,60:4
Kilabayashi, Tanie
Insect Woman, The; Nippon Konchuki
  1964,Jl 1,42:1
Kilbourne, Fannie (Original Author)
Major and the Minor, The 1942,S 17,21:3
You're Never too Young 1955,Ag 26,10:2
Kilbrick, Leonard
Kid Millions 1934,N 12,17:2
Fisherman's Wharf 1939,F 24,15:2
It's a Wonderful World 1939,My 19,27:2
Kilbride, Percy
White Woman 1933,N 18,18:5
George Washington Slept Here 1942,O 31,11:1
Keeper of the Flame 1943,Mr 19,15:2
Crazy House 1943,D 16,33:3
Woman of the Town, The 1944,Mr 6,17:2
Knickerbocker Holiday 1944,Ap 20,22:7
Adventures of Mark Twain, The 1944,My 4,25:5
Guest in the House 1945,F 16,19:2
State Fair 1945,Ag 31,14:3
She Wouldn't Say Yes 1946,Ja 12,10:7
Fallen Angel 1946,F 7,29:4
Well Groomed Bride, The 1946,My 11,22:5
Egg and I, The 1947,Ap 25,29:2
Riff-Raff 1947,Je 30,25:7
Welcome Stranger 1947,Ag 7,15:2
You Were Meant for Me 1948,Ja 29,27:5
Black Bart 1948,Mr 4,30:4
You Gotta Stay Happy 1948,N 5,29:2
Sun comes up, The 1949,My 13,29:2
Ma and Pa Kettle 1949,Ag 12,13:2
Riding High 1950,Ap 11,26:2
Ma and Pa Kettle Back on the Farm
  1951,My 11,32:3
Ma and Pa Kettle at the Fair 1952,Jl 12,16:2
Kilbride, Richard
Playground, The 1965,O 4,00:0
Kilburn, Doris Hume (Original Author)
Dark Purpose 1964,F 6,36:4
Kilburn, Martin
Wild Blue Yonder, The 1952,Ja 2,20:1
Kilburn, Terry
Lord Jeff 1938,Jl 1,22:2
Sweethearts 1938,D 23,16:2
Christmas Carol, A 1938,D 23,16:2
Goodbye Mr Chips 1939,My 16,27:2
Andy Hardy Gets Spring Fever 1939,Jl 19,23:2
They Shall Have Music 1939,Jl 26,17:2
Adventures of Sherlock Holmes, The
  1939,S 2,20:1
Swiss Family Robinson 1940,F 9,15:3
Yank at Eton, A 1942,O 16,23:1
National Velvet 1944,D 15,25:2
Black Beauty 1946,Ag 30,13:2
Song of Scheherazade 1947,F 27,26:2
Only the Valiant 1951,Ap 14,9:6
Fiend Without a Face 1958,Jl 4,15:3
Kilenyi, Edward (Composer)
Midnight Sun, The 1926,Ap 24,20:4
Michael Strogoff 1926,D 6,28:3
African Holiday 1937,Je 4,27:3
Kilenyi, Edward (Miscellaneous)
His Darker Self 1924,Mr 26,19:2
Try and Get It 1924,Ap 2,16:1
Kiley, Jed
Hell's Highway 1932,S 26,18:2
Kiley, Richard
Mob, The 1951,O 18,32:2
Sniper, The 1952,My 10,16:3
Eight Iron Men 1953,Ja 2,11:1
Pickup on South Street 1953,Je 18,38:2
Blackboard Jungle 1955,Mr 21,21:5
Phenix City Story, The 1955,S 3,9:1
Spanish Affair 1958,F 6,24:1

Kilgallen, Dorothy
Sinner Take All 1937,F 3,27:1
Kilgallen, Dorothy (Miscellaneous)
Fly Away Baby 1937,Jl 9,18:2
Kilgas, Nancy
Seven Brides for Seven Brothers 1954,Jl 23,8:3
Athena 1954,D 22,28:2
Kilgour, Joseph
Battle Cry for Peace, The 1915,Ag 7,8:3
Within the Law 1923,Ap 30,11:2
Woman With Four Faces, The 1923,Je 18,13:5
Ponjola 1923,N 19,19:3
Janice Meredith 1924,Ag 6,13:3
Capital Punishment 1925,F 5,23:3
Top of the World, The 1925,F 17,18:1
Percy 1925,Mr 25,24:2
One Year to Live 1925,Jl 6,12:2
King on Main Street, The 1925,O 26,25:2
Let's Get Married 1926,Mr 2,22:1
Kilian, Victor
Wiser Sex, The 1932,Mr 12,19:5
Air Hawks 1935,Je 4,26:5
Girl Friend, The 1935,S 28,12:2
Bad Boy 1935,O 28,16:3
Riffraff 1936,Ja 13,14:2
Music Goes 'Round, The 1936,F 22,12:1
Road to Glory, The 1936,Ag 6,22:1
Shakedown 1936,Ag 17,9:2
Ramona 1936,O 7,32:4
Adventure in Manhattan 1936,O 23,27:5
Banjo on My Knee 1936,D 12,15:1
Lady From Nowhere 1936,D 21,19:2
Seventh Heaven 1937,Mr 26,25:1
League of Frightened Men, The 1937,Jl 2,25:1
It Happened in Hollywood 1937,O 2,18:1
Tovarich 1937,D 31,9:2
It's all Yours 1938,Ja 7,15:3
Adventures of Tom Sawyer, The 1938,F 18,23:1
Gold Diggers in Paris 1938,Je 2,19:2
Prison Break 1938,Jl 13,17:4
Boys Town 1938,S 9,25:1
Paris Honeymoon 1939,Ja 26,17:1
St Louis Blues 1939,F 9,17:2
Huckleberry Finn 1939,Mr 3,21:2
Return of the Cisco Kid, The 1939,Ap 29,13:2
Only Angels Have Wings 1939,My 12,25:2
Dust Be my Destiny 1939,O 7,11:2
Little Old New York 1940,F 3,9:2
Young Tom Edison 1940,Mr 15,27:2
Dr Cyclops 1940,Ap 11,32:3
'Til We Meet Again 1940,Ap 14,14:2
Torrid Zone 1940,My 18,11:3
Return of Frank James, The 1940,Ag 10,16:4
Gold Rush Maisie 1940,S 2,19:2
They Knew What They Wanted 1940,O 11,25:2
Tugboat Annie Sails Again 1940,N 9,20:2
Western Union 1941,F 7,23:2
Blood and Sand 1941,My 23,25:3
I Was a Prisoner on Devil's Island
  1941,Jl 28,16:4
Date With the Falcon, A 1941,N 25,33:2
Reap the Wild Wind 1942,Mr 27,27:2
This Gun for Hire 1942,My 14,23:2
Atlantic Convoy 1942,Jl 6,18:5
Ox-Bow Incident, The 1943,My 10,15:2 (In
  Addenda)
Bomber's Moon 1943,Jl 31,8:2
Hitler's Madman 1943,Ag 28,15:1
Johnny Come Lately 1943,S 24,26:1
Uncertain Glory 1944,Ap 8,9:2
Barbary Coast Gent 1944,S 29,18:2
Belle of the Yukon 1945,Mr 30,18:4
Fighting Guardsman, The 1945,O 6,9:6
Spellbound 1945,N 2,22:2
Spanish Main, The 1945,N 7,20:2
Little Giant 1946,My 9,27:5
Smoky 1946,Je 27,29:1
Gentleman's Agreement 1947,N 12,36:2
Northwest Stampede 1948,D 10,34:3
Yellow Sky 1949,F 2,36:1
I Shot Jesse James 1949,Ap 2,12:2
Flame and the Arrow, The 1950,Jl 8,7:2
Tall Target, The 1951,S 28,26:2
Kiligin, S
General Suvorov 1941,S 20,11:2
Kill, Jorgen
Eric Soya's 17 1967,Ja 25,37:1
Killanin, Michael (Producer)
Rising of the Moon, The (The Majesty of the
  Law); Majesty of the Law, The (The Rising of
  the Moon) 1957,Jl 10,23:1
Rising of the Moon, The (1921); 1921 (The Rising
  of the Moon) 1957,Jl 10,23:1
Rising of the Moon, The (A Minute's Wait);
  Minute's Wait, A (The Rising of the Moon)
  1957,Jl 10,23:1
Killens, John O (Screenwriter)
Odds Against Tomorrow 1959,O 16,27:1
Killer (stallion)
Black Cyclone 1925,My 19,24:2
Killmon, Frank
Take a Giant Step 1961,Mr 6,28:2

Killy, Edward (Director)
Freckles 1935,O 26,12:2
Seven Keys to Baldpate 1935,D 14,11:2
Murder on a Bridle Path 1936,Ap 11,19:2
Bunker Bean 1936,Je 27,21:2
Second Wife 1936,Ag 29,16:3
China Passage 1937,Ap 16,27:2
Big Shot, The 1937,Ag 13,13:1
Saturday's Heroes 1937,O 16,22:2
West of the Pecos 1945,Ag 11,14:6
Wanderer of the Wasteland 1945,S 29,12:2
Killy, Edward (Producer)
Wanted: Jane Turner 1936,N 30,24:7
Kilmonis, Ruta
Seven Brides for Seven Brothers 1954,Jl 23,8:3
Kilpack, Bennett
Way Back Home 1932,Ja 16,13:1
Kilpatrick, Tom (Screenwriter)
Trapped by G-Men 1937,N 4,29:1
Dr Cyclops 1940,Ap 11,32:3
Man Betrayed, A 1941,Mr 27,29:5
Kilzmiller, John
Dr No 1963,My 30,20:1
Kim, I
Frontier 1935,D 28,10:5
Kim, Joseph
Samurai 1945,Ag 25,7:5
Kim, Joy
High and the Mighty, The 1954,Jl 1,21:2
Blood Alley 1955,O 6,25:3
Kim, Suzanna
Good Earth, The 1937,F 3,27:1
Kimball, Edward
Masquerader, The 1922,Ag 14,12:4
Cheat, The 1923,Ag 27,14:3
I'll Show You the Town 1925,Je 8,19:1
Kimball, Ward
Reluctant Dragon, The 1941,Jl 25,12:2
Kimball, Ward (Screenwriter)
Babes in Toyland 1961,D 15,49:1
Kimber, Peggy
Lost Boundaries 1949,Jl 1,14:4
Kimberly, Sharron
Party, The 1968,Ap 5,56:2
Kimble, Lawrence (Original Author)
Bugle Sounds, The 1942,Ap 3,25:2
Kimble, Lawrence (Screenwriter)
Submarine D-1 1937,D 30,15:4
Love, Honor and Behave 1938,Mr 21,18:2
Beloved Brat 1938,My 2,13:2
Off the Record 1939,F 18,12:2
It all Came True 1940,Ap 6,13:2
Pierre of the Plains 1942,Jl 30,17:3
Johnny Doughboy 1943,My 6,25:3
Tahiti Honey 1943,My 13,17:2
Seven Days Ashore 1944,Ap 26,24:7
Music in Manhattan 1944,O 7,11:2
Pan-Americana 1945,Mr 23,13:2
Zombies on Broadway 1945,Ap 27,23:2
Truth About Murder, The 1946,Jl 27,12:6
Criminal Court 1946,N 16,15:3
San Quentin 1947,F 10,24:3
Flame, The 1948,F 20,19:2
I, Jane Doe 1948,Jl 5,8:4
Angel on the Amazon 1948,D 27,16:4
One Way Street 1950,My 12,33:3
Two of a Kind 1951,Je 30,8:6
Kimbrough, Clint
Hot Spell 1958,S 18,37:2
Kimbrough, Emily (Original Author)
Our Hearts Were Young and Gay 1944,O 12,24:2
Kimmell, Leslie
House by the River 1950,My 2,25:2
Kimmich, Max (Original Author)
Madame Spy 1934,F 10,20:1
Kimmins, Anthony (Director)
It's in the Air 1940,D 10,33:2
Mine Own Executioner 1949,Ja 19,34:2
Bonnie Prince Charlie 1952,Ja 7,14:3
Mr Denning Drives North 1953,S 2,20:1
Captain's Paradise, The 1953,S 29,25:5
Passionate Sentry, The 1953,N 12,37:5
Kimmins, Anthony (Producer)
Mine Own Executioner 1949,Ja 19,34:2
Mr Denning Drives North 1953,S 2,20:1
Captain's Paradise, The 1953,S 29,25:5
Passionate Sentry, The 1953,N 12,37:5
Kimmins, Anthony (Screenwriter)
Talk of the Devil 1937,My 15,23:5
It's in the Air 1940,D 10,33:2
Laburnum Grove 1941,D 2,29:2
Kimura, Isao
Magnificent Seven, The 1956,N 20,46:2
Kimura, Keigo (Director)
Utamaro, Painter of Women 1964,D 2,57:1
Kimura, Keigo (Screenwriter)
Utamaro, Painter of Women 1964,D 2,57:1
Kimura, Mitsuko
Three Stripes in the Sun 1955,N 24,41:2
Kimura, Takeshi (Original Author)
Young Swordsman 1964,O 30,29:1

Kimura, Takeshi (Screenwriter)
Mysterians, The 1959,Jl 2,15:2
Secret Scrolls-Part I 1968,My 9,54:3
Secret Scrolls-Part II; Ninjitsu 1968,My 23,56:3
Kimursi
King Solomon's Mines 1950,N 10,35:1
Kin, Joseph
Man of Iron 1935,D 7,22:2
Kinashita, Ryo (Director)
School for Sea 1967,D 2,48:5
Kinberg, Jud (Producer)
Reach for Glory 1963,S 10,46:1
Happening, The 1967,My 18,56:3
Magus, The 1968,D 11,57:1
Kinberg, Jud (Screenwriter)
Reach for Glory 1963,S 10,46:1
Kinburg, Jud (Producer)
Collector, The 1965,Je 18,28:1
Kincaid, Aron
Ski Party 1965,O 23,17:3
Kinch, Myra
Lives of a Bengal Lancer, The 1935,Ja 12,12:2
Kinchalovsky, A (Screenwriter)
Violin and Roller 1962,Ag 20,18:2
Kindahl, Julian
Wild Strawberries 1959,Je 23,37:1
Kindenberg, Etta
Endstation 1937,Jl 17,18:1
Kinderman, Helmo
Question 7 1961,S 29,30:2
Secret Invasion, The 1964,S 17,52:5
Secret Invasion, The 1964,S 17,52:6
King, Alan
Hit the Deck 1955,Mr 4,17:1
Miracle in the Rain 1956,Ap 2,18:1
Girl He Left Behind, The 1956,O 27,17:1
Helen Morgan Story, The 1957,O 3,33:2
Operation Snafu 1965,My 22,18:1
Bye Bye Braverman 1968,F 22,36:1
King, Allan (Director)
Warrendale 1968,S 17,50:1
King, Allan (Producer)
Warrendale 1968,S 17,50:1
King, Allyn
Fighting Blade, The 1923,O 15,15:4
King, Andrea
Very Thought of You, The 1944,N 18,16:7
Hollywood Canteen 1944,D 16,19:2
Roughly Speaking 1945,F 1,18:4
Hotel Berlin 1945,Mr 3,11:2
God is my Co-Pilot 1945,Mr 24,22:6
Beast With Five Fingers, The 1946,D 26,28:3
Man I Love, The 1947,Ja 25,12:2
Ride the Pink Horse 1947,O 9,32:3
My Wild Irish Rose 1947,D 25,32:2
Mr Peabody and the Mermaid 1948,Ag 14,6:5
Buccaneer's Girl 1950,Mr 27,19:2
I Was a Shoplifter 1950,Ap 28,26:3
Southside 1-1000 1950,N 3,31:2
Dial 1119 1950,D 4,32:6
Lemon Drop Kid, The 1951,Mr 22,41:2
Mark of the Renegade 1951,S 7,24:2
Red Planet Mars 1952,Je 16,15:2
World in His Arms, The 1952,O 10,21:2
Band of Angels 1957,Jl 11,21:1
Darby's Rangers 1958,F 13,23:2
King, Basil (Original Author)
Spreading Dawn, The 1917,O 22,13:2
Earthbound 1920,Ag 11,9:4
Dust Flower, The 1922,Jl 3,8:6
Let Not Man Put Asunder 1924,Ja 15,16:1
Tides of Passion 1925,Ap 20,22:1
Earthbound 1940,Je 7,27:4
King, Basil (Producer)
Earthbound 1920,Ag 11,9:4
King, Billy
Hopalong Rides Again 1938,Ja 22,19:1
Heart of Arizona 1938,Ap 16,17:1
King, Bradley (Miscellaneous)
Drag 1929,Je 21,17:2
King, Bradley (Original Author)
Satan in Sables 1925,O 15,27:3
Let's Live Tonight 1935,Mr 18,14:4
Maid of Salem 1937,Mr 4,27:2
That's my Man 1947,Ap 7,20:2
King, Bradley (Screenwriter)
Lying Lips 1921,Mr 7,8:1
Man of Action, A 1923,Je 4,13:3
Mystery of Edwin Drood, The 1935,Mr 21,27:1
Under the Pampas Moon 1935,My 31,11:1
King, Brett
Battleground 1949,N 12,8:4
Payment on Demand 1951,F 16,21:2
Yank in Korea, A 1951,Ap 2,29:2
Racket, The 1951,D 13,44:2
King, Burton (Director)
Man From Beyond, The 1922,Ap 4,15:3
King, Cammie
Gone With the Wind 1939,D 20,31:2
King, Carlotta
Desert Song, The 1929,My 2,20:6

King, Charles
Broadway Melody, The 1929,F 9,15:3
Climbing the Golden Stairs 1929,Ap 25,32:3
Hollywood Revue, The 1929,Ag 15,20:5
Broadway Melody 1929,D 1,X,8:6
Chasing Rainbows 1930,F 22,13:1
Remote Control 1930,D 8,26:1
Branded Men 1931,D 12,23:3
O'Malley of the Mounted 1936,Ap 6,18:1
Lawless Nineties, The 1936,Je 29,11:1
Mystery of the Hooded Horsemen, The 1937,Ag 13,13:2
Frontier Town 1938,Mr 12,13:3
King, Charmion
Nobody Waved Goodbye 1964,S 17,52:1
King, Claude
Judy of Rogues Harbor 1920,Mr 1,16:2
Bella Donna 1923,Ap 16,20:2
Six Days 1923,S 24,5:4
Making of O'Malley 1925,Je 22,10:2
Knockout, The 1925,O 27,23:3
Irish Luck 1925,N 24,28:4
Unguarded Hour, The 1926,Ja 5,25:2 (In Addenda)
Paradise 1926,O 4,20:2
Silent Lover, The 1926,N 15,19:1
Mr Wu 1927,My 16,24:2
London After Midnight 1927,D 31,31:1
Sporting Goods 1928,F 13,16:2
Love and Learn 1928,F 20,14:1
Red Hair 1928,Mr 26,26:2
Night of Mystery, A 1928,Ap 16,20:5
Warming Up 1928,Jl 16,25:3
Oh, Kay! 1928,Ag 27,23:1
Outcast 1928,N 26,30:2
Strange Cargo 1929,F 18,28:1
Madame X 1929,Ap 25,32:3
Behind That Curtain 1929,Jl 1,31:2
Insidious Dr Fu Manchu, The 1929,Jl 22,17:1
Son of the Gods 1930,Ja 31,24:1
Second Story Murder, The 1930,My 3,23:1
In Gay Madrid 1930,Je 7,10:4
Love Among the Millionaires 1930,Jl 5,17:4
Rango 1931,F 19,20:4
Born to Love 1931,Ap 25,23:4
Women Love Once 1931,Je 27,20:3
Transatlantic 1931,Jl 31,15:2
Reckless Hour, The 1931,Ag 1,16:4
Devotion 1931,O 3,20:2
Heartbreak 1931,O 17,20:1
Once a Lady 1931,N 9,22:4
Arrowsmith 1931,D 8,36:4
Shanghai Express 1932,F 18,25:3
Behind the Mask 1932,My 2,13:2
Sherlock Holmes 1932,N 12,20:5
Charlie Chan's Greatest Case 1933,O 7,18:4
White Woman 1933,N 18,18:5
White Woman 1933,D 3,IX,9:4 (In Addenda)
Long Lost Father 1934,F 19,18:2
Murder in Trinidad 1934,My 16,22:2
World Moves On, The 1934,Je 30,18:5
Gilded Lily, The 1935,F 9,11:2
Last Outpost, The 1935,O 5,18:2
Great Impersonation, The 1935,D 14,11:1
$1,000 a Minute 1935,D 21,11:1
Three on the Trail 1936,My 5,26:5
Beloved Enemy 1936,D 26,15:2
Love Under Fire 1937,Ag 28,8:2
Lancer Spy 1937,N 4,29:1
Four Men and a Prayer 1938,My 7,18:1
Booloo 1938,Jl 30,10:2
Within the Law 1939,Ap 6,31:2
New Moon 1940,Jl 19,22:2
King, Colman (Tiger)
Man of Aran 1934,O 19,27:1
King, David
Strange Bedfellows 1965,Mr 11,38:1
King, Dennis
Vagabond King, The 1930,F 20,22:4
Vagabond King, The 1930,Mr 2,IX,5:1
Devil's Brother, The 1933,Je 10,16:4
Between Two Worlds 1944,My 6,11:2
Miracle, The 1959,N 13,25:4
King, Dennis Jr
Let's Make Love 1960,S 9,36:1
King, Diana
Man in Grey, The 1945,N 30,18:6
Die! Die! My Darling 1965,My 20,52:1
King, Edith
Blaze of Noon 1947,Mr 5,31:2
Calcutta 1947,Ap 24,30:2
Gallant Blade 1948,O 13,31:3
Belle Star's Daughter 1949,Ja 10,19:2
King, Eleanore
Private Worlds 1935,Mr 28,25:2
King, Emmett
Trifling With Honor 1923,My 30,10:4
Day of Faith, The 1923,N 27,11:2
Acquittal, The 1923,D 12,24:5
Fighting American, The 1924,My 13,24:1
Captain January 1924,Jl 7,10:4
Devil's Cargo, The 1925,F 3,24:1
Pampered Youth 1925,F 10,20:1

King, Emmett — Cont
Man Without a Country, The 1925,F 12,16:1
Reno 1930,N 4,36:1
Westward Passage 1932,Je 4,9:2
Prisoner of Zenda, The 1937,S 3,12:1
King, Fay
Great White Way, The 1924,Ja 4,10:1
King, Frank (Original Author)
Ghoul, The 1934,Ja 27,9:2
No Place Like Homicide 1962,S 13,32:1
King, Frank (Producer)
Gangster, The 1947,O 31,29:3
Gun Crazy 1950,Ag 25,17:5
Mutiny 1952,Mr 20,37:5
Carnival Story 1954,Ap 17,8:2
Brave One, The 1957,Mr 22,26:1
Captain Sindbad 1963,Jl 4,9:1
Maya 1966,Je 23,29:4
King, George (Director)
Chinese Den 1941,Mr 26,27:3
Frightened Lady 1941,N 10,21:3
At Dawn We Die 1943,My 8,19:2
Candlelight in Algeria 1944,Jl 31,10:2
Showtime 1948,My 20,35:3
King, George (Producer)
Showtime 1948,My 20,35:3
Eight O'Clock Walk 1955,Ap 30,10:6
King, George S (Original Author)
Slave Ship 1937,Je 17,19:2
King, Gerald
Time, The Place and the Girl, The 1929,Jl 8,17:3
King, Henry (Director)
One Hour Before Dawn 1920,Jl 12,12:4
Tol'able David 1922,Ja 2,20:1
Seventh Day, The 1922,Mr 13,18:2
Sonny 1922,My 29,14:1
Bond Boy, The 1922,O 9,10:2
White Sister, The 1923,S 6,10:2
Romola 1924,D 2,13:2
Sackcloth and Scarlet 1925,Mr 25,24:2
Any Woman 1925,My 27,26:2
Stella Dallas 1925,N 17,30:2
Partners Again, With Potash and Perlmutter 1926,F 15,16:4
Winning of Barbara Worth, The 1926,N 29,16:3
Magic Flame, The 1927,S 19,30:3
White Sister, The 1928,My 21,25:1
Woman Disputed, The 1928,N 10,20:8
She Goes to War 1929,Je 10,23:1
Hell Harbor 1930,Mr 28,22:6
Eyes of the World 1930,Ag 15,20:5
Lightnin' 1930,N 29,21:4
Merely Mary Ann 1931,S 12,15:4
Over the Hill 1931,N 21,20:4
Woman in Room 13, The 1932,My 21,9:2
State Fair 1933,Ja 27,13:2
I Loved You Wednesday 1933,Je 16,20:2
Carolina 1934,F 16,17:2
Marie Galante 1934,N 21,23:4
One More Spring 1935,F 22,27:1
Way Down East 1935,O 31,16:2
Country Doctor, The 1936,Mr 13,32:2 (Incorrect in this edition; use 1936,Mr 13,27:2 elsewhere)
Ramona 1936,O 7,32:4
Lloyds of London 1936,N 26,39:1
Seventh Heaven 1937,Mr 26,25:1
In Old Chicago 1938,Ja 7,15:2
Alexander's Ragtime Band 1938,Ag 6,7:2
Jesse James 1939,Ja 14,13:1
Stanley and Livingstone 1939,Ag 5,18:2
Little Old New York 1940,F 3,9:2
Maryland 1940,Jl 13,16:5
Chad Hanna 1940,D 26,23:1 -
Yank in the R A F, A 1941,S 27,11:3
Remember the Day 1941,D 26,21:2
Black Swan, The 1942,D 24,18:3
Song of Bernadette, The 1944,Ja 27,15:2
Wilson 1944,Ag 2,18:1
Bell for Adano, A 1945,Jl 6,8:3
Margie 1946,O 17,28:3
Captain from Castile 1947,D 26,22:4
Deep Waters 1948,Jl 23,12:4
Prince of Foxes 1949,D 24,11:2
Twelve O'Clock High 1950,Ja 28,10:2
Gunfighter, The 1950,Je 24,7:2
I'd Climb the Highest Mountain 1951,My 10,38:1
David and Bathsheba 1951,Ag 15,23:2
Wait Till the Sun Shines, Nellie 1952,Je 28,12:2
Snows of Kilimanjaro, The 1952,S 19,19:2
O Henry's Full House (The Cop and the Anthem); Cop and the Anthem, The (O Henry's Full House) 1952,O 17,33:1
O Henry's Full House (The Gift of the Magi); Gift of the Magi, The (O Henry's Full House) 1952,O 17,33:1
O Henry's Full House (The Last Leaf 1952,O 17,33:1
O Henry's Full House (The Clarion Call); Clarion Call, The (O Henry's Full House) 1952,O 17,33:1
King of the Khyber Rifles 1953,D 23,21:1
Untamed 1955,Mr 12,11:6
Love Is a Many-Splendored Thing 1955,Ag 19,10:1

King, Henry (Director) — Cont
Carousel 1956,F 17,13:1
Sun Also Rises, The 1957,Ag 24,12:2
Bravados, The 1958,Je 26,23:2
Earth Is Mine, The 1959,Je 27,13:1
Beloved Infidel 1959,N 18,46:1
Tender is the Night 1962,Ja 20,13:2

King, Henry (Screenwriter)
Sonny 1922,My 29,14:1

King, Herman (Producer)
Captain Sindbad 1963,Jl 4,9:1

King, Hugh (Original Author)
Storm, The 1938,O 31,12:2
Flight at Midnight 1939,S 7,29:2
Threat, The 1949,D 2,35:4
Dial 1119 1950,D 4,32:6
Underwater! 1955,F 10,27:2

King, Hugh (Producer)
Threat, The 1949,D 2,35:4

King, Hugh (Screenwriter)
Threat, The 1949,D 2,35:4

King, Hyman (Producer)
Bad Men of Tombstone 1949,Mr 5,10:2

King, Jack (Composer)
Reckless 1935,Ap 20,16:1

King, Joe (Narrator)
This Is Your Army 1954,D 15,41:1

King, John
Crash Donovan 1936,Ag 10,10:3
Three Smart Girls 1937,Ja 25,22:2
Road Back, The 1937,Je 18,25:2
Merry-Go-Round of 1938 1937,N 26,27:2
Crime of Dr Hallet, The 1938,Mr 24,21:3
Breaking the Ice 1938,S 23,35:3
Sharpshooters 1938,D 5,19:2
Charlie Chan in Honolulu 1938,D 31,7:3
Three Musketeers, The 1939,F 18,12:2
Hardys Ride High, The 1939,Ap 14,28:2
Mr Moto Takes a Vacation 1939,Je 19,12:6

King, Joseph
Salvation Neil 1921,Je 27,16:3
Twenty-One 1924,F 18,13:1
Unguarded Women 1924,Je 24,18:2
Tin Gods 1926,S 20,21:3
Laughing Lady, The 1930,Ja 4,21:1
Roadhouse Nights 1930,F 22,13:1
Front Page Woman 1935,Jl 12,15:1
Alibi Ike 1935,Jl 17,22:1
Special Agent 1935,S 19,28:1
Shipmates Forever 1935,O 17,29:3
Frisco Kid 1935,N 25,22:1
Broadway Hostess 1935,D 16,23:3
Road Gang 1936,F 24,14:1
Walking Dead, The 1936,Mr 2,13:2
Singing Kid, The 1936,Ap 4,11:1
Sons o'Guns 1936,My 14,29:2
Bullets or Ballots 1936,My 27,27:1
Public Enemy's Wife 1936,Jl 9,17:2
Jailbreak 1936,Ag 6,22:1
China Clipper 1936,Ag 12,14:3
Case of the Velvet Claws, The 1936,Ag 29,16:3
Polo Joe 1936,N 5,35:1
God's Country and the Woman 1937,Ja 11,15:5
That Man's Here Again 1937,My 6,23:3
Slim 1937,Je 24,30:2
Fly Away Baby 1937,Jl 9,18:2
Armored Car 1937,Jl 26,15:2
San Quentin 1937,Ag 4,15:2
White Bondage 1937,Ag 6,21:3
Hot Water 1937,N 5,19:4
City Streets 1938,Jl 25,18:2
Alexander's Ragtime Band 1938,Ag 6,7:2
Heart of the North 1938,D 21,29:2
Off the Record 1939,F 18,12:2
You Can't Get Away With Murder 1939,Mr 25,19:2
Smashing the Money Ring 1939,N 17,17:2
Three Cheers for the Irish 1940,Mr 9,19:2
Black Friday 1940,Mr 22,23:3
It's a Date 1940,Mr 23,16:2
Charlie Chan At the Wax Museum 1940,S 28,9:3
Always a Bride 1940,N 21,43:3
Blondie Goes Latin 1941,F 26,17:3
Strange Alibi 1941,Ap 28,11:2
Bullets for O'Hara 1941,Jl 28,16:4
Big Shot, The 1942,Jl 18,8:2
Glass Key, The 1942,O 16,23:1

King, Judy
Best Bad Man, The 1925,D 2,23:1
Gay Retreat, The 1927,O 10,24:1
Our Neighbors-The Carters 1940,F 15,15:2

King, Kenneth
Illiac Passion, The 1968,Ap 19,40:1

King, Kip
Tea and Sympathy 1956,S 28,24:4

King, L H
Sin Flood, The 1922,O 30,11:1

King, Leslie
Bond Boy, The 1922,O 9,10:2
If Winter Comes 1923,S 4,14:1
Alice in Wonderland 1931,D 28,22:1

King, Louis (Director)
Deceiver, The 1931,N 23,22:1
Fame Street 1932,Ap 2,13:2

Ciudad de Carton, La 1934,F 28,23:3
Murder in Trinidad 1934,My 16,22:2
Julieta Compra un Hijo; Julieta Buys a Baby 1935,Mr 25,12:3
Charlie Chan in Egypt 1935,Je 24,12:2
Angelita 1935,S 11,19:5
Road Gang 1936,F 24,14:1
Song of the Saddle 1936,Mr 21,13:3
Special Investigator 1936,Ap 25,21:1
Bengal Tiger 1936,Jl 30,22:1
That Man's Here Again 1937,My 6,23:3
Melody for Two 1937,My 21,19:5
Bulldog Drummond Comes Back 1937,S 4,8:3
Bulldog Drummond's Revenge 1937,D 17,33:2
Tip-Off Girls 1938,Mr 25,15:3
Hunted Men 1938,My 21,9:2
Prison Farm 1938,Jl 15,13:3
Bulldog Drummond in Africa 1938,Ag 25,15:1
Illegal Traffic 1938,N 17,29:3
Persons in Hiding 1939,Mr 2,19:2
Undercover Doctor 1939,Je 1,31:2
Seventeen 1940,F 29,15:2
Typhoon 1940,My 23,28:4
Way of all Flesh, The 1940,Je 6,33:2
Moon Over Burma 1940,D 12,37:4
Chetniks 1943,Mr 19,15:3
Thunderhead 1945,Mr 16,21:2
Smoky 1946,Je 27,29:1
Thunder in the Valley 1947,N 28,30:1
Green Grass of Wyoming 1948,Je 10,28:3
Sand 1949,Ag 5,23:2
Mrs Mike 1950,F 9,36:5
Frenchie 1951,F 12,19:2
Lion and the Horse, The 1952,My 19,12:2
Powder River 1953,Jl 4,7:2
Sabre Jet 1953,N 3,34:1
Dangerous Mission 1954,Mr 6,13:5
Massacre 1956,Je 2,13:5

King, Lulu B
Act One 1963,D 27,17:2

King, Marie
Cafe in Cairo, A 1925,Mr 18,19:2

King, Maurice (Producer)
Gangster, The 1947,O 31,29:3
Gun Crazy 1950,Ag 25,17:5
Mutiny 1952,Mr 20,37:5
Carnival Story 1954,Ap 17,8:2
Brave One, The 1957,Mr 22,26:1
Maya 1966,Je 23,29:4

King, Michael
Lonely are the Brave 1962,Je 28,21:2

King, Miss (Screenwriter)
Maid of Salem 1937,Mr 4,27:2

King, Nicholas
Long, Hot Summer, The 1958,Ap 4,16:1

King, Owen
China Clipper 1936,Ag 12,14:3
Submarine D-1 1937,D 30,15:4
Murder in the Air 1940,Jl 4,12:2

King, Patty
Long Night, The 1947,S 17,31:2
Red Pony, The 1949,Mr 9,33:2

King, Paul (Original Author)
Operation Petticoat 1959,D 6,38:1

King, Peggy
Zero Hour 1957,N 14,41:1

King, Philip (Original Author)
Curtain Up 1953,F 2,17:3
Panic in the Parlor 1957,D 18,45:1

King, Philip (Screenwriter)
Panic in the Parlor 1957,D 18,45:1

King, Rose
Singing Marine, The 1937,Jl 1,33:2

King, Rufus (Miscellaneous)
Notorious Gentleman, A 1935,F 16,9:1

King, Rufus (Original Author)
Silent Command, The 1923,S 5,15:3
Murder by the Clock 1931,Jl 18,16:6
Murder at the Vanities 1934,My 21,20:2
Hidden Hand, The 1942,N 26,40:4
White Tie and Tails 1946,N 8,28:2
Secret Beyond the Door 1948,Ja 16,25:4

King, Ruth
He Who Gets Slapped 1924,N 10,20:1
Dixie Handicap, The 1924,D 30,15:3
Cafe in Cairo, A 1925,Mr 18,19:2

King, Sherwood (Original Author)
Lady From Shanghai, The 1948,Je 10,28:2

King, Sidney
Sherlock Holmes's Fatal Hour 1931,Jl 13,13:5
Quiet Wedding 1941,D 29,27:4
Flying Fortress 1942,D 19,22:2
Glass Mountain, The 1950,My 18,37:3

King, Simon
Poor Cow 1968,F 1,28:2

King, Sonny
Sergeants 3 1962,F 12,28:2

King, Stevie
Poor Cow 1968,F 1,28:2

King, Vaughn
Native Land 1942,My 12,16:3

King, Walter Woolf
Golden Dawn 1930,Jl 26,16:4
Girl Without a Room 1933,D 7,26:3
One More Spring 1935,F 22,27:1
Ginger 1935,Jl 19,13:2
Night at the Opera, A 1935,D 7,22:1
Call it a Day 1937,My 7,29:2
Swiss Miss 1938,Je 4,18:2
Big Town Czar 1939,My 4,27:3
Balalaika 1939,D 15,33:2
Go West 1941,F 21,16:2
Taxi 1953,Ja 22,20:3
Tonight We Sing 1953,F 13,17:2
Helen Morgan Story, The 1957,O 3,33:2
Householder, The 1963,O 22,43:2

King, Wright
Streetcar Named Desire, A 1951,S 30,27:1

King (Dog)
Proud Rebel, The 1958,Jl 2,23:4

King Brothers (Producer)
Southside 1-1000 1950,N 3,31:2

King-chuan, Hu (Director)
Sons of Good Earth 1967,S 16,37:5

King-chuan, Hu (Screenwriter)
Sons of Good Earth 1967,S 16,37:5

King Cole Trio, The
Pistol Packin' Mama 1943,D 20,27:4
Breakfast in Hollywood 1946,Jl 15,21:1

King-Hall, Stephen (Original Author)
Middle Watch, The 1930,D 20,20:6
Ship Was Loaded, The 1958,Ja 20,20:1

King Sisters
Sing Your Worries Away 1942,My 15,25:2

Kingdon, Edith
Once a Lady 1931,N 9,22:4
Crash, The 1932,S 9,17:5
It's a Gift 1935,Ja 5,20:2

Kingman, Lawrence (Original Author)
His Majesty O'Keefe 1954,F 6,17:2

King's Men
Call out the Marines 1942,Ja 26,18:3
Heavenly Days 1944,O 21,15:2

Kingsford, Guy
That Hamilton Woman 1941,Ap 4,25:1
Get-Away, The 1941,Jl 17,23:4
Sahara 1943,N 12,25:2
Second Chance 1947,S 20,12:4
Lone Wolf in London, The 1947,N 22,10:3
Inside Detroit 1956,Ja 28,10:5

Kingsford, Walter
Pursuit of Happiness, The 1934,O 26,25:1
President Vanishes, The 1934,D 8,18:5
White Cockatoo, The 1935,Ja 16,21:1
Mystery of Edwin Drood, The 1935,Mr 21,27:1
Naughty Marietta 1935,Mr 23,11:2
Shanghai 1935,Jl 20,16:2
I Found Stella Parish 1935,N 4,24:4
Melody Lingers on, The 1935,N 7,27:1
Invisible Ray, The 1936,Ja 11,9:3
Professional Soldier 1936,Ja 30,14:2
Story of Louis Pasteur, The 1936,F 10,15:1
Music Goes 'Round, The 1936,F 22,12:1
Little Lord Fauntleroy 1936,Ap 3,27:1
Trouble for Two 1936,My 30,7:2
Hearts Divided 1936,Je 13,13:1
Meet Nero Wolfe 1936,Jl 16,20:1
Mad Holiday 1936,N 26,39:2
Stolen Holiday 1937,F 1,15:3
Maytime 1937,Mr 19,27:1
Captains Courageous 1937,My 12,27:1
League of Frightened Men, The 1937,Jl 2,25:1
Devil is Driving, The 1937,Jl 16,22:1
Life of Emile Zola, The 1937,Ag 12,14:2
Double or Nothing 1937,S 2,17:3
I'll Take Romance 1937,D 17,33:2
Paradise for Three 1938,F 16,17:1
Yank at Oxford, A 1938,F 25,15:1
There's Always a Woman 1938,Ap 29,17:2
Lone Wolf in Paris, The 1938,My 23,21:2
Toy Wife, The 1938,Je 24,15:1
Lord Jeff 1938,Jl 1,22:2
Algiers 1938,Jl 15,13:2
Carefree 1938,S 23,35:1
If I Were King 1938,S 29,31:1
Young Doctor Kildare 1938,O 28,27:1
Young in Heart, The 1938,N 4,27:2
Say It in French 1938,D 1,29:1
Juarez 1939,Ap 26,27:1
Calling Dr Kildare 1939,My 12,25:4
Man in the Iron Mask, The 1939,Jl 14,11:1
Miracles for Sale 1939,Ag 10,15:2
Witness Vanishes, The 1939,O 23,15:2
Dancing Co-Ed 1939,N 10,27:3
Secret of Dr Kildare, The 1939,D 8,33:5
Adventure in Diamonds 1940,Ap 4,27:2
Dr Kildare's Strange Case 1940,Ap 12,19:2
Star Dust 1940,My 4,13:1
Lucky Partners 1940,S 6,25:2
Dr Kildare Goes Home 1940,S 19,27:4
Dispatch From Reuters, A 1940,D 12,37:2
Dr Kildare's Crisis 1940,D 19,33:1
Kitty Foyle 1941,Ja 9,27:2

Kingsford, Walter— Cont
Lone Wolf Takes a Chance, The 1941,Ap 7,13:2
People vs Dr Kildare, The 1941,My 8,21:1
Devil and Miss Jones, The 1941,My 16,21:2
Ellery Queen and the Perfect Crime
1941,Ag 11,17:3
Dr Kildare's Wedding Day 1941,S 18,31:1
Unholy Partners 1941,D 29,21:4
Corsican Brothers, The 1942,Ja 16,25:4
Dr Kildare's Victory 1942,F 5,25:2
My Favorite Blonde 1942,Ap 2,27:2
Fingers at the Window 1942,Ap 23,27:3
Calling Dr Gillespie 1942,Jl 9,17:4
Loves of Edgar Allan Poe, The 1942,S 21,19:2
Flight for Freedom 1943,Ap 16,24:2
Mr Lucky 1943,Jl 23,21:2
Bomber's Moon 1943,Jl 31,8:2
Hi Diddle Diddle 1943,S 24,26:2
Hitler Gang, The 1944,My 8,15:2
Mr Skeffington 1944,My 26,23:2
Three Men in White 1944,My 26,23:3
Between Two Women 1945,Mr 29,18:3
Velvet Touch, The 1948,Ag 26,16:2
Black Arrow, The 1948,O 4,14:2
Slattery's Hurricane 1949,Ag 13,6:6
My Forbidden Past 1951,Ap 26,34:2
Desert Fox, The 1951,O 18,32:1
Merry Andrews 1958,Mr 21,17:1
Kingsley, Charles (Original Author)
And Women Must Weep 1922,F 20,7:1
Kingsley, Dorothy (Original Author)
Texas Carnival 1951,O 13,9:1
Kingsley, Dorothy (Screenwriter)
Broadway Rhythm 1944,Ap 14,24:6
Bathing Beauty 1944,Je 28,20:1
Easy to Wed 1946,Jl 12,14:2
On an Island With You 1948,Jl 30,13:2
Date with Judy, A 1948,Ag 7,8:2
Neptune's Daughter 1949,Je 10,32:2
Skipper Surprised his Wife, The 1950,Je 30,18:2
Two Weeks With Love 1950,N 24,31:2
Texas Carnival 1951,O 13,9:1
Angels in the Outfield 1951,O 18,32:1
It's a big Country 1952,Ja 9,25:2
When in Rome 1952,My 12,21:2
Small Town Girl 1953,My 7,37:2
Dangerous When Wet 1953,Je 19,18:1
Kiss Me Kate 1953,N 6,23:2
Seven Brides for Seven Brothers 1954,Jl 23,8:3
Jupiter's Darling 1955,F 18,18:4
Pal Joey 1957,O 28,30:1
Don't Go Near the Water 1957,N 15,37:1
Green Mansions 1959,Mr 20,26:1
Can-Can 1960,Mr 10,36:1
Pepe 1960,D 22,18:1
Valley of the Dolls 1967,D 16,51:1
Kingsley, Edward L (Screenwriter)
Torment 1947,Ap 22,34:2
Kingsley, Frank
Fighting American, The 1924,My 13,24:1
Kingsley, Sidney (Original Author)
Men in White 1934,Je 9,18:2
Homecoming 1948,Ap 30,28:4
Detective Story 1951,N 7,35:2
Kingsley International (Miscellaneous)
Viridiana 1962,Mr 20,43:4
Kingston, Jerome (Original Author)
Caught in the Fog 1928,D 4,29:1
Kingston, Lawrence
Knight Without Armor 1937,Jl 9,18:1
Kingston, Natalie
Wet Paint 1926,My 17,19:1
Kid Boots 1926,O 11,18:2
Silent Lover, The 1926,N 15,19:1
Night of Love, The 1927,Ja 25,18:4
His First Flame 1927,My 2,26:4
Lost at the Front 1927,Je 14,33:2
Framed 1927,Je 20,25:3
Harvester, The 1927,N 7,33:1
Girl in Every Port, A 1928,F 20,14:1
Street Angel 1928,Ap 10,33:2
Port of Missing Girls, The 1928,Jl 31,13:4
River of Romance, The 1929,Jl 29,23:3
Her Wedding Night 1930,S 29,19:1
Kingston, Winifred
David Garrick 1916,My 1,9:1
Kinkead, Cleves (Original Author)
Private Number 1936,Je 12,19:1
Kinnear, Roy
Sparrows Don't Sing 1963,My 7,46:2
Heavens Above! 1963,My 21,28:2
Small World of Sammy Lee, The 1963,Ag 14,28:1
Tiara Tahiti 1963,N 6,32:1
Help! 1965,Ag 24,25:1
Hill, The 1965,O 4,00:0
Deadly Affair, The 1967,Ja 27,31:1
How I Won the War 1967,N 9,56:1
Kinnell, Murray
Princess and the Plumber, The 1930,D 23,25:1
Public Enemy, The 1931,Ap 24,27:1
Secret Six, The 1931,My 2,23:4
Black Camel, The 1931,Jl 4,11:5
Honor of the Family 1931,O 17,20:1
Guilty Generation, The 1931,N 21,20:4

Deceiver, The 1931,N 23,22:1
Reckless Living 1931,D 5,21:2
Under Eighteen 1931,D 26,15:5
Menace, The 1932,Ja 30,13:2
Man Who Played God, The 1932,F 11,16:1
Grand Hotel 1932,Ap 13,23:2
Mouthpiece, The 1932,Ap 21,25:2
Purchase Price, The 1932,Jl 16,5:5
Painted Woman, The 1932,S 16,24:4
Successful Calamity, A 1932,S 23,22:2
Match King, The 1932,D 8,25:3
Secrets of the French Police 1932,D 12,18:4
Zoo in Budapest 1933,Ap 28,15:2
Voltaire 1933,Ag 23,21:2
I Loved a Woman 1933,S 22,14:2
Ann Vickers 1933,S 29,24:1
Avenger, The 1933,O 3,28:3
I Am Suzanne 1934,Ja 19,24:3
House of Rothschild, The 1934,Mr 15,27:2
Murder in Trinidad 1934,My 16,22:2
Affairs of a Gentleman 1934,Je 23,16:7
Hat, Coat and Glove 1934,Jl 27,21:2
Charlie Chan's Courage 1934,Ag 25,16:6
Charlie Chan in London 1934,S 13,26:1
Anne of Green Gables 1934,D 22,21:1
Silver Streak, The 1935,Ja 16,21:1
Charlie Chan in Paris 1935,Ja 22,23:2
Cardinal Richelieu 1935,Ap 19,24:2
Last Days of Pompeii, The 1935,O 17,29:2
Three Musketeers, The 1935,N 1,25:1
Fighting Youth 1935,N 2,13:3
Great Impersonation, The 1935,D 14,11:1
Witness Chair, The 1936,Ap 18,19:2
One Rainy Afternoon 1936,My 14,29:2
Mary of Scotland 1936,Jl 31,22:2
Fifteen Maiden Lane 1936,O 17,21:3
Big Game, The 1936,O 24,23:1
Lloyds of London 1936,N 26,39:1
Make Way for a Lady 1936,D 12,15:1
Prince and the Pauper, The 1937,My 6,23:1
Damaged Lives 1937,Je 14,26:2
Think Fast, Mr Moto 1937,Ag 16,15:3
Kinney, Clyde
I'm From the City 1938,Ag 19,13:4
Kinney, Harold
Body and Soul 1931,Mr 14,23:2
Kinney, Jack (Director)
Saludos Amigos 1943,F 13,8:2
Make Mine Music 1946,Ap 22,26:2
Melody Time 1948,My 28,28:2
Adventures of Ichabod and Mr Toad, The
1949,O 10,18:2
1001 Arabian Nights 1959,D 24,13:6
Kinney, Jack (Miscellaneous)
Three Caballeros, The 1945,F 5,20:1
Kinnoch, Ronald (Producer)
Village of the Damned 1960,D 8,43:3
Invasion Quartet 1961,D 11,41:2
Inadmissible Evidence 1968,Je 24,44:1
Kino, Goro
First Born, The 1921,Ja 31,11:1
Kino, Lloyd
Horizontal Lieutenant, The 1962,My 12,15:3
Kino, Robert
Cry for Happy 1961,Mr 4,16:1
Kinogasa, Teinosuke (Director)
Slums of Tokyo 1930,Jl 7,22:3
Kinoshita, Keisuke (Director)
Carmen Comes Home 1959,D 23,22:1
She Was Like a Wild Chrysanthemum
1960,Ja 22,15:2
Ballad of Narayama 1961,Je 20,27:1
Kinoshita, Keisuke (Original Author)
Carmen Comes Home 1959,D 23,22:1
Kinoshita, Keisuke (Screenwriter)
Carmen Comes Home 1959,D 23,22:1
She Was Like a Wild Chrysanthemum
1960,Ja 22,15:2
Ballad of Narayama 1961,Je 20,27:1
Kinsella, Walter
Tattooed Stranger, The 1950,F 10,18:6
Kinskey, Leonid
Duck Soup 1933,N 23,24:2
Girl Without a Room 1933,D 7,26:3
We Live Again 1934,N 2,27:2
Miserables, Les 1935,Ap 22,14:2
Rhythm on the Range 1936,Jl 30,22:1
Road to Glory, The 1936,Ag 6,22:1
General Died at Dawn, The 1936,S 3,17:2
We're on the Jury 1937,F 10,18:5
Espionage 1937,Mr 9,27:3
Cafe Metropole 1937,Ap 29,17:1
Make a Wish 1937,S 23,33:1
Trip to Paris, A 1938,Je 10,18:2
Three Blind Mice 1938,Je 18,18:2
Algiers 1938,Jl 15,13:2
Great Waltz, The 1938,N 25,19:1
Story of Vernon and Irene Castle, The
1939,Mr 31,19:2
Exile Express 1939,Ag 16,21:3
Spellbinder, The 1939,Ag 24,17:3
On Your Toes 1939,O 21,12:2

Kinskey, Leonid— Cont
Daytime Wife 1939,N 24,29:1
Everything Happens at Night 1939,D 16,12:6
He Stayed for Breakfast 1940,Ag 31,16:2
Down Argentine Way 1940,O 18,25:1
So Ends our Night 1941,F 28,17:2
That Night in Rio 1941,Mr 10,21:2
Broadway Limited 1941,Je 16,11:6
Week-End in Havana 1941,N 8,11:2
Ball of Fire 1942,Ja 16,25:2
Lady for a Night 1942,F 12,27:2
I Married an Angel 1942,Jl 10,13:2
Talk of the Town, The 1942,Ag 28,22:3
Casablanca 1942,N 27,27:1
Presenting Lily Mars 1943,Ap 30,25:3
Fighting Seabees, The 1944,Mr 20,14:2
Monsieur Beaucaire 1946,S 5,23:1
Man With the Golden Arm, The 1955,D 16,38:2
Kinski, Klaus
Counterfeit Traitor, The 1962,Ap 18,28:1
Doctor Zhivago 1965,D 23,21:1
Pleasure Girls 1966,Ap 21,43:1
That Man in Istanbul 1966,My 19,51:2
Bang, Bang, You're Dead 1967,Ja 19,41:2
For a Few Dollars More 1967,Jl 4,23:1
Grand Slam 1968,F 21,60:4
Kinsolving, Lee
All the Young Men 1960,Ag 27,8:6
Khovanschina 1960,S 23,33:1
Explosive Generation, The 1962,F 15,24:2
Kinugasa, Teinosuke (Director)
Gate of Hell 1954,D 14,45:2
Kinugasa, Teinosuke (Screenwriter)
Gate of Hell 1954,D 14,45:2
Kinz, Franziska
Tannenberg 1934,Ap 3,26:6
Fluechtlinge 1934,O 15,20:5
Macht der Berge, Die; Power of the Mountains,
The 1938,O 22,14:2
Cow and I, The 1961,Je 6,42:2
Kiousis, Nikos (Screenwriter)
Horse and Carriage 1958,Je 30,23:3
Kipling, Edward
Spanish Dancer, The 1923,O 8,20:1
Shadows of Paris 1924,F 18,13:1
Kipling, Richard
Calling Philo Vance 1940,F 9,15:3
Kipling, Rudyard (Original Author)
Without Benefit of Clergy 1921,Je 20,17:2
Elephant Boy 1937,Ap 6,20:2
Captains Courageous 1937,My 12,27:1
Wee Willie Winkie 1937,Jl 24,12:1
Light That Failed, The 1939,D 25,19:1
Jungle Book 1942,Ap 6,19:1
Kim 1950,D 8,40:4
Soldiers Three 1951,Mr 30,28:5
Jungle Book, The 1967,D 23,29:1
Kipnis, Leonid (Producer)
Pictura 1952,Ap 8,35:3
Leonardo Da Vinci 1952,N 21,21:5
Kippen, Manart
Jungle Siren 1942,O 10,11:3
Mission to Moscow 1943,Ap 30,25:2
Song of Bernadette, The 1944,Ja 27,15:2
Three Russian Girls 1944,F 5,13:2
Flame of Barbary Coast 1945,My 28,22:2
Mildred Pierce 1945,S 29,12:2
Kiraly, Rozsa
Key Balvany, A 1933,Ap 18,13:6
Kek Balvany, A; Blue Idol, The 1933,Ap 18,13:6
Kirby, David
In the Palace of the King 1923,D 3,14:1
Nellie, the Beautiful Cloak Model
1924,Ap 14,14:1
Spirit of the U S A, The 1924,My 21,22:3
Man Who Came Back, The 1924,S 1,9:1
Last Edition, The 1925,N 11,27:3
Shield of Honor 1927,D 13,33:2
Kirby, George
Cynara 1932,D 26,26:2
White Angel, The 1936,Je 25,24:1
Thunder in the Valley 1947,N 28,30:1
Oh Dad, Poor Dad, Mamma's Hung You in the
Closet and I'm Feeling so Sad 1967,F 16,32:1
Kirby, Jay
Rockin' in The Rockies 1945,Jl 5,7:2
Kirby, John
Annapolis Story, An 1955,Ap 9,8:2
Kirby, Joyce
It's a Boy 1934,Je 8,18:2
Are You a Mason? 1934,O 30,23:5
Kirby, Max
There Goes the Bride 1933,Mr 4,11:3
Great Mr Handel, The 1943,S 10,29:3
Maytime in Mayfair 1952,Ap 23,23:5
Kirby, Michael
Summer Holiday 1948,Je 12,8:5
Kirby, William (Producer)
Two-Headed Spy, The 1959,Mr 3,38:4
Oscar Wilde 1960,Je 21,28:2
Kirchhoff, Fritz (Director)
Wenn Frauen Schweigen; When Women Keep
Silent 1937,S 11,20:2
Meine Freundin Barbara; My Firend Barbara
1938,Je 4,18:3

Kirchhoffer, Hugo
Rhapsody in Blue 1945,Je 28,22:2
Kirchner, Jean
Three Godfathers, The 1936,Mr 9,20:2
Kirgo, George
Best Man, The 1964,Ap 7,29:1
Kirgo, George (Screenwriter)
Red Line 7000 1965,D 9,60:4
Spinout 1966,D 15,60:1
Don't Make Waves 1967,Je 21,36:2
Kirienko, Zinaida
And Quiet Flows the Don 1960,My 25,45:2
Kirienko, Zoya
Poem of the Sea 1959,D 21,34:4
Fate of Man 1961,Jl 11,28:1
Kirillov, P
We Are From Kronstadt 1936,My 2,11:1
Ski Battalion 1938,Mr 14,13:1
Men of the Sea 1938,Je 20,11:2
Professor Mamlock 1938,N 8,26:2
Great Citizen, The 1939,Ja 16,11:2
Kirk, Joe
Margin for Error 1943,Ja 25,10:7
Pistol Packin' Mama 1943,D 20,27:4
Here Come the Co-Eds 1945,F 19,21:1
Naughty Nineties, The 1945,Je 21,16:2
My Dear Secretary 1949,F 14,15:4
Kirk, Laurence (Original Author)
Stand by for Action 1943,Mr 12,12:2
Kirk, Phyllis
Our Very Own 1950,Jl 28,12:5
Life of her Own, A 1950,O 12,43:2
Two Weeks With Love 1950,N 24,31:2
Mrs O'Malley and Mr Malone 1951,F 23,33:2
Three Guys Named Mike 1951,Mr 2,21:2
About Face 1952,My 24,15:3
Iron Mistress, The 1952,N 20,39:2
House of Wax 1953,Ap 11,15:2
Thunder Over the Plains 1953,D 10,64:4
Crime Wave 1954,Ja 13,26:2
Johnny Concho 1956,Ag 16,30:1
Back From Eternity 1956,S 8,20:6
Sad Sack, The 1957,N 28,57:1
Kirk, R G (Screenwriter)
Men of Steel 1926,Jl 12,24:4
Kirk, Tommy
Old Yeller 1957,D 26,23:4
Shaggy Dog, The 1959,Mr 20,26:2
Swiss Family Robinson 1960,D 24,8:4
Absent-Minded Professor, The 1961,Mr 16,44:2
Babes in Toyland 1961,D 15,49:1
Moon Pilot 1962,Ap 6,30:2
Bon Voyage! 1962,My 18,34:2
Son of Flubber 1963,F 9,5:2
Savage Sam 1963,Ag 1,17:3
Misadventures of Merlin Jones, The 1964,Mr 26,40:4
Monkey's Uncle, The 1965,Ag 19,35:4
Track of Thunder 1968,F 1,28:4
Kirk, Tommy (Narrator)
Snow Queen, The 1960,Ap 14,34:1
Kirkbride, Ronald (Original Author)
Girl Named Tamiku, A 1963,Mr 15,8:2
Kirke, Donald
Follow the Leader 1930,D 6,21:3
Blondie Johnson 1933,F 27,11:2
Ghost Walks, The 1935,Mr 30,11:2
Border Flight 1936,Je 22,22:1
In His Steps 1936,O 29,31:1
Emperor's Candlesticks, The 1937,Jl 9,18:1
Big Shot, The 1937,Ag 13,13:1
Shadow, The 1937,D 17,33:3
Hawaii Calls 1938,Ap 29,17:2
Kirkham, Kathleen
White Moth, The 1924,Je 16,18:3
Sackcloth and Scarlet 1925,Mr 25,24:2
Regular Fellow, A 1925,O 5,25:2
Kirkland, Alexander
Tarnished Lady 1931,Ap 30,29:3
Surrender 1931,N 28,20:4
Charlie Chan's Chance 1932,Ja 23,18:4
Devil's Lottery 1932,Ap 2,13:2
Passport to Hell, A 1932,Ag 27,13:4
Strange Interlude 1932,S 1,24:3
Humanity 1933,Ap 22,16:3
Bondage 1933,Ap 24,11:3
Face in the Crowd, A 1957,My 29,33:1
Kirkland, David (Director)
Temperamental Wife, A 1919,S 15,16:3
Virtuous Vamp, A 1919,N 17,20:1
Gingham Girl, The 1927,Jl 19,27:2
Pecados de Amor 1934,Ap 24,27:2
Impostor, El 1937,Ap 10,11:2
Kirkland, David (Producer)
Impostor, El 1937,Ap 10,11:2
Kirkland, Hardee
Peace of Roaring River, The 1919,Ag 11,9:1
Woman Proof 1923,O 30,16:1
Kirkland, Jack (Original Author)
Zoo in Budapest 1933,Ap 28,15:2
Now and Forever 1934,O 13,10:1
Gilded Lily, The 1935,F 9,11:2
Tobacco Road 1941,F 21,16:2

Amazing Monsieur Fabre, The 1952,S 9,21:2
Kirkland, Jack (Screenwriter)
Wings in the Dark 1935,F 2,10:1
Sutter's Gold 1936,Mr 27,25:2
Adventure in Manhattan 1936,O 23,27:5
Amazing Monsieur Fabre, The 1952,S 9,21:2
Golden Coach, The 1954,Ja 22,30:2
Kirkland, Muriel
Fast Workers 1933,Mr 20,18:2
Cocktail Hour 1933,Je 5,18:5
Hold Your Man 1933,Jl 1,16:6
Secret of the Blue Room, The 1933,S 13,22:1
Nana 1934,F 2,20:3
Little Man, What Now? 1934,Je 1,29:1
White Parade, The 1934,N 10,19:1
Kirkpatrick, Jess
D O A 1950,My 1,18:2
Well, The 1951,S 27,37:2
Captive City, The 1952,Mr 27,34:2
Long, Hot Summer, The 1958,Ap 4,16:1
Ten North Frederick 1958,My 23,29:2
Kirks, Jeremy (Original Author)
Madison Avenue 1962,Mr 29,28:2
Kirkwood, Gene
Hot Rods to Hell 1967,Ag 10,45:5
Kirkwood, Jack
Fancy Pants 1950,Ag 31,21:2
Never a Dull Moment 1950,N 22,20:2
Kirkwood, James
Man-Woman-Marriage 1921,Mr 28,11:4
Bob Hampton of Placer 1921,My 2,12:1
Man From Home, The 1922,My 1,20:3
Under Two Flags 1922,S 25,10:2
Sin Flood, The 1922,O 30,11:1
Ebb Tide 1922,N 20,21:3
Human Wreckage 1923,Je 28,10:2
Ponjola 1923,N 19,19:3
Love's Whirlpool 1924,Mr 11,16:2
Broken Barriers 1924,Ag 4,16:3
Circe the Enchantress 1924,D 9,23:3
Top of the World, The 1925,F 17,18:1
That Royle Girl 1926,Ja 4,33:1
Reckless Lady, The 1926,Ja 25,21:2
Butterflies in the Rain 1926,D 25,10:5
Some One to Love 1928,D 4,29:1
Time, The Place and the Girl, The 1929,Jl 8,17:3
Hearts in Exile 1929,N 29,25:1
Devil's Holiday, The 1930,My 10,25:3
Spoilers, The 1930,S 20,15:4
Young Sinners 1931,My 9,15:4
Holy Terror, A 1931,Jl 20,20:4
Over the Hill 1931,N 21,20:4
Charlie Chan's Chance 1932,Ja 23,18:4
Rainbow Trail, The 1932,Ja 30,13:2
She Wanted a Millionaire 1932,F 20,11:2
Cheaters at Play 1932,F 27,22:1
Lena Rivers 1932,My 21,9:2
My Pal the King 1932,O 4,26:4
No Hands on the Clock 1941,D 22,24:6
Stage to Tucson 1951,My 5,14:2
Kirkwood, Joe Jr
Joe Palooka, Champ 1946,Ap 6,10:6
Marriage-Go-Round 1961,Ja 7,12:2
Kirkwood, Pat
No Leave, No Love 1946,O 18,29:2
Kirkwood-Hackett, F Madame
Last Holiday 1950,N 14,39:4
Kirman, Patrick (Screenwriter)
Once Upon a Dream 1949,Jl 15,17:2
Kirsanoff, Dimitri (Director)
Mystic Mountain, The 1936,Mr 31,17:2
Kirsanova, T
Problem Child 1955,Ja 24,20:5
Kirscher, Ludwig
Arme Millionar, Der; Poor Millionaire, The 1939,D 30,9:2
Kirschner, Herti
Soldaten-Kameraden 1936,O 5,25:1
Florentiner Hut, Der; Leghorn Hat, The 1939,Je 3,11:3
Kirst, Hans Helmut (Original Author)
Night of the Generals, The 1967,F 3,38:1
Kirsten, Dorothy
Mr Music 1950,D 21,34:3
Great Caruso, The 1951,My 11,32:2
Kirwan, Kitty
Edge of the World, The 1938,S 12,13:2
Macushla 1940,Ja 6,9:2
Odd Man Out 1947,Ap 24,30:2
Kirwan, Patrick (Original Author)
Hotel Sahara 1952,Ja 1,21:4
Kirwan, Patrick (Screenwriter)
Bulldog Drummond at Bay 1937,O 25,23:2
Drums 1938,S 30,24:4
Challenge, The 1939,O 2,15:2
Human Monster, The 1940,Mr 25,11:2
Fugitive, The 1940,Jl 23,22:2
Convoy 1941,Ja 17,21:2
Ships With Wings 1942,My 25,11:2
Avengers, The 1942,N 25,18:2
Amazing Mr Beecham, The 1949,D 26,33:4
Hotel Sahara 1952,Ja 1,21:4
Tale of Five Women, A 1953,Ja 16,19:2

Kirwan, Patrick (Screenwriter)— Cont
Desperate Moment 1953,S 1,19:4
Rooney 1958,Je 6,29:2
Broth of a Boy 1959,D 28,18:1
Poacher's Daughter, The 1960,F 16,31:2
Hellions, The 1962,Mr 15,28:2
Kiryutin, P
Dream of a Cossack 1952,F 18,15:2
Kis, Imre
Paul Street Boys, The 1929,Jl 15,25:1
Kisco, Charley (Composer)
Swing High, Swing Low 1937,Ap 15,19:1
Kiselev, V
Great Citizen, The 1939,Ja 16,11:2
Kiser, Terry
Rachel Rachel 1968,Ag 27,36:1
Kish, Joseph (Director)
World Youth Festival 1950,Jl 10,18:4
Kishen, Epariam (Director)
Sallah 1965,O 13,39:1
Kishen, Epariam (Original Author)
Sallah 1965,O 13,39:1
Kishi, Keiko
Imposter, The 1955,Mr 23,27:1
Kishi, Teruko
Insect Woman, The; Nippon Konchuki 1964,Jl 1,42:1
Kishida, Kyoko
Bushido 1964,S 13,39:1
Woman in the Dunes; Suno no Onna 1964,S 17,52:1
School for Sea 1967,D 2,48:5
Kisimatus, Andreas
Shepherd's Daughter, The 1956,My 14,23:3
Kislinger, Ivana
Naked Maja, The 1959,Je 11,36:2
Kiss, Ferenc
Rakoczi Indulo 1934,N 21,23:4
Sarga Csiko 1937,Ja 29,15:2
Pusztai Szel; Beauty of the Pusta 1938,Ja 10,13:4
Ele serelt Ember; Changed Man 1939,F 25,19:3
Piros Bugyellaris; Red Purse 1939,Mr 11,21:2
Janos Vitez; John, The Hero 1939,Ap 8,19:2
Toprini Nasz; Wedding in Toprin 1939,N 6,20:2
Kiss, Manyi
Noszty Flu Este Toth Marival 1938,My 16,14:4
Goose Boy, The 1951,O 13,9:2
Merry Go-Round 1958,Ap 3,23:3
Kisselev, V
Professor Mamlock 1938,N 8,26:2
Kistemaecker, Henry (Original Author)
Eye for Eye 1918,D 23,9:1
Kistemaeckers, Henry (Original Author)
Occident, L' 1928,D 16,IX,8:2
Nuit est a Nous, La; (Night is Ours, The) 1931,F 21,15:2
Kitabayashi, Tanie
Odd Obsession 1961,D 27,16:1
Burmese Harp, The 1967,Ap 29,25:1
Kitahara, Yoshiro
Phantom Horse, the 1956,Jl 25,16:1
Kitamura, Kazuo
Insect Woman, The; Nippon Konchuki 1964,Jl 1,42:1
Kitau, Johanna
Ivory Hunter 1952,Ag 19,19:1
Kitcheva, G
Under Sunny Skies 1950,D 26,19:3
Kitchin, Jack (Producer)
Mine Own Executioner 1949,Ja 19,34:2
Kitchin, Laurence
Housemaster 1939,Ap 10,13:2
Mister V 1942,F 13,24:4
Kitchin, Laurence (Screenwriter)
Bad Lord Byron, The 1952,Mr 20,37:5
Kithnou, Mlle
Mare Nostrum 1926,F 16,22:4
Kitt, Eartha
New Faces 1954,F 20,8:7
Mark of the Hawk, The 1958,Mr 6,32:1
St Louis Blues 1958,Ap 12,13:1
Anna Lucasta 1959,Ja 15,27:1
Synanon 1965,My 6,44:1
Kitwin, Patrick (Screenwriter)
Johnny Nobody 1965,N 24,35:1
Kitzmiller, John
To Live in Peace 1947,N 25,37:2
Without Pity; (Senza Pieta) 1950,Mr 16,40:4
Lieutenant Craig-Missing 1951,My 19,9:4
Naked Earth 1958,Ag 29,18:1
Island Sinner, The 1960,S 5,11:2
Variety Lights; Luci del Varieta 1965,My 7,34:1
Kiwe, Tile
One, Two, Three 1961,D 22,17:1
Kiyama, Hiroshi
Beach Red 1967,Ag 4,18:1
Kiyokawa, Nijiko
Teahouse of the August Moon, The 1956,N 30,19:1
Kiyokawa, Seji
Men Who Tread on the Tiger's Tail, The 1960,Ja 11,35:7

Kiyokawa, Tamae
Utamaro, Painter of Women 1964,D 2,57:1
Kjaco, Bodil
Invisible Army, The 1950,Je 26,17:3
Kjelgaard, Jim (Original Author)
Big Red 1962,S 3,11:2
Kjellertz, Goesta
Vaermlaenningarna 1932,N 18,23:2
Kjellestroem, Gun
Med Folket Foer Fosterlandet 1939,F 21,14:2
Kjellin, Alf
Torment 1947,Ap 22,34:2
Sunshine Follows Rain 1949,S 29,39:2
My Six Convicts 1952,Mr 28,27:3
Affairs of a Model 1952,Ag 7,12:8
Iron Mistress, The 1952,N 20,39:2
Juggler, The 1953,My 6,39:2
Illicit Interlude 1954,O 27,32:6
Ship of Fools 1965,Jl 29,18:1
Assault on a Queen 1966,Jl 28,23:3
Kjellstroem, Elvor
Loerdagskvaellar 1936,F 13,25:3
Klameth, Thomas
Heidi 1953,D 21,27:2
Heidi and Peter 1955,D 13,55:2
Klaren, Georg (Director)
Wozzeck 1962,Mr 3,13:1
Klaren, Georg (Screenwriter)
Wozzeck 1962,Mr 3,13:1
Klass, Philip
Illiac Passion, The 1968,Ap 19,40:1
Klatchkin, R
Chalutzim 1934,Ap 2,13:3
My Father's House 1947,S 26,28:3
Tel Aviv Taxi 1956,D 31,10:7
Klatzkin, David (Composer)
King Solomon of Broadway 1935,O 19,12:2
Klauber, Gertan
Kitchen, The 1961,N 2,42:1
Klauber, Marcel (Original Author)
Red Ball Express 1952,My 30,11:2
Carnival Story 1954,Ap 17,8:2
Circus of Love 1958,Ag 16,10:2
Klaus, Henry
Four Horsemen of the Apocalypse, The
1926,S 27,27:3
Klavun, Walter
Mob, The 1951,O 18,32:2
It Should Happen to You 1954,Ja 16,10:5
Klaw (Director)
Life and Works of Richard Wagner, The
1913,N 21,9:4
Kleberer, Alexander
Stone Flower 1946,D 30,15:2
Klee, Lawrence M (Narrator)
Roosevelt Story, The 1947,Ag 22,11:2
Klee, Walter (Miscellaneous)
Roosevelt Story, The 1947,Ag 22,11:2
Savage Brigade 1948,D 3,33:4
Kleeb, Helen
Seven Days in May 1964,F 20,22:1
KLEIN
See Also KLINE, CLYNE, CLINE
Klein, Adelaide
Naked City, The 1948,Mr 5,17:2
C-Man 1949,My 28,11:4
Enforcer, The 1951,Ja 26,19:2
Klein, Al
Oh, You Beautiful Doll 1949,N 12,8:4
Klein, Alexander (Original Author)
Counterfeit Traitor, The 1962,Ap 18,28:1
Klein, Allen (Producer)
Stranger in Town, A 1968,Ap 25,53:4
Klein, Charles (Director)
Zigeunerblut 1935,Ap 8,23:5
Wenn am Sonntagabend die Dorfmusik Spielt
1935,D 9,25:3
Klein, Charles (Original Author)
Lion and the Mouse, The 1919,F 17,11:3
Heartsease 1919,Ag 25,8:5
Potash and Perlmutter 1923,S 24,5:4
Music Master, The 1927,Ja 17,12:4 (In Addenda)
Third Degree, The 1927,F 15,23:1
Lion and the Mouse, The 1928,Je 16,11:4
Gamblers, The 1929,Ag 24,11:5
Klein, Ernst (Original Author)
At the End of the World 1921,Ag 15,14:3
Carnival Crime, The 1929,Jl 8,17:3
Klein, Hal (Producer)
Ambush Bay 1966,S 15,51:4
Kill a Dragon 1967,D 7,60:2
Klein, Irwin
Big Game, The 1936,O 24,23:1
Klein, Julius
City of Temptation 1929,S 2,16:1
Klein, Julius (Screenwriter)
Wanted: Jane Turner 1936,N 30,24:7
Klein, Luce
Yo Yo 1967,Mr 1,50:1
Klein, Nita
Muriel 1963,O 31,26:1

Klein, Philip (Original Author)
Night Cry, The 1926,Ap 7,26:6
Hush Money 1931,Jl 11,7:6
Me and my Gal 1932,D 12,18:4
Stand up and Cheer 1934,Ap 20,17:1
Pier 13 1940,Ag 9,19:3
Klein, Philip (Screenwriter)
Dante's Inferno 1935,Ag 1,15:1
Klein, Robert
Dante's Inferno 1924,S 30,27:3
Klein, Wally (Original Author)
Hard To Get 1938,N 14,15:2
Oklahoma Kid, The 1939,Mr 11,21:1
Klein, Wally (Screenwriter)
Indianapolis Speedway 1939,Jl 15,8:2
They Died With Their Boots On 1941,N 21,23:3
Klein, William (Director)
Far From Vietnam 1968,Je 7,32:1
Klein, William (Narrator)
Far from Vietnam 1967,O 2,58:1
Klein-Rogge, Rudolph
Between Worlds 1924,Jl 7,10:4
Peter the Pirate 1927,Ja 7,14:4
Metropolis 1927,Mr 7,16:3
Dr Nabuse 1927,Ag 10,21:4
Spione; Spies 1928,My 20,VIII,8:5
Kriemhild's Revenge 1928,O 16,29:1
Forbidden Love 1929,Ja 14,20:1
Spies 1929,Mr 5,29:1
Loves of Casanova, The 1929,Ap 30,33:2
Zwischen Himmel und Erde; Between Heaven and
Earth 1935,Ja 21,19:3
Frauen vom Tannhof, Die 1936,F 18,27:1
Grenzfeuer 1936,D 19,16:1
Truxa 1937,Jl 26,15:2
Last Will of Dr Mabuse, The 1943,Mr 20,11:1
Kleinau, Willy A
Captain from Koepenick, The 1958,Jl 26,6:1
Tempestous Love 1958,N 22,27:4
Kleinbach, Henry
Babes in Toyland 1934,D 13,28:2
Preview Murder Mystery, The 1936,Mr 21,13:2
Big Brown Eyes 1936,My 2,11:1
Kleine, George (Miscellaneous)
Julius Caesar 1922,F 12,VI,3:1 (In Addenda)
Kleine-Cinca (Producer)
Quo Vadis? 1913,Ap 22,11:4
Kleiner, Arthur (Composer)
Napoleon 1967,S 25,56:5
Kleiner, Harry (Original Author)
King of the Khyber Rifles 1953,D 23,21:1
House of Bamboo 1955,Jl 2,13:2
Kleiner, Harry (Producer)
Garment Jungle, The 1957,My 16,28:2
Cry Tough 1959,S 17,48:4
Rabbit Trap, The 1959,O 15,48:1
Kleiner, Harry (Screenwriter)
Fallen Angel 1946,F 7,29:4
Street with no Name, The 1948,Jl 15,26:6
Smoke Jumpers 1952,Mr 22,9:6
Kangaroo 1952,My 17,22:7
Salome 1953,Mr 25,37:1
Miss Sadie Thompson 1953,D 24,9:1
Carmen Jones 1954,O 29,27:2
Violent Men, The 1955,Ja 27,17:2
Garment Jungle, The 1957,My 16,28:2
Cry Tough 1959,S 17,48:4
Ice Palace 1960,Je 30,22:1
Fever in the Blood 1961,Ap 20,30:4
Fantastic Voyage 1966,S 8,43:1
Bullitt 1968,O 18,41:2
Kleinerman, Isaac (Miscellaneous)
Victory at Sea 1954,Jl 14,33:2
Kleinert, Robert
William Tell 1925,My 20,26:2
Kleinschmidt, F E (Producer)
Primitive Love 1927,My 30,9:4 (In Addenda)
Kleinsinger, George (Composer)
Inheritance, The 1964,N 9,42:2
Kleist, Heinrich von (Original Author)
Zerbrochene Krug, Der; Broken Jugi, The
1938,Ja 15,19:2
Klement, Otto (Original Author)
Fantastic Voyage 1966,S 8,43:1
Klemperer, Werner
Death of a Scoundrel 1956,N 6,30:1
Flight to Hong Kong 1957,Ja 3,28:2
Istanbul 1957,Ja 24,34:1
Five Steps to Danger 1957,Ja 31,21:1
Kiss Them for Me 1957,N 9,31:2
Goddess, The 1958,Je 25,24:1
Operation Eichmann 1961,My 4,40:7
Judgment at Nuremberg 1961,D 20,36:1
Escape from East Berlin 1962,D 6,55:3
Youngblood Hawke 1964,N 6,30:1
Dark Intruder 1965,Jl 22,24:2
Ship of Fools 1965,Jl 29,18:1
Wicked Dreams of Paula Schultz, The
1968,Ja 4,28:1
Klempner, John (Original Author)
Give my Regards to Broadway 1948,Je 23,32:2
Letter to Three Wives, A 1949,Ja 21,24:2

Klempner, John (Screenwriter)
Three for Jamie Dawn 1956,Jl 7,11:3
Klenova, Eva
Thunder in the Hills 1947,My 24,10:5
Kleppel, Gerald (Producer)
Sweet Love, Bitter 1967,Ja 31,50:1
Klering, G
Rainbow, The 1944,O 23,14:3
Zygmunt Kolosowski 1947,N 13,13:3
Klering, Hans
Patrioty 1933,S 25,18:5
Klettenhauer, Elisabeth
Tonio Kroger 1968,Ja 16,24:1
Kletter, Max
Shir Hashirim 1935,O 11,31:1
Kleus, Elena
Gioconda, La 1958,O 13,33:4
Klicks, Rudolf
Tannenberg 1934,Ap 3,26:6
Reiter von Deutsch-Ostafrika, Die 1935,Je 8,12:3
Wackere Schustermeister, Der 1936,Jl 7,22:4
Klimist, Susan
Backlash 1947,My 24,10:5
Klimof, M
Man From the Restaurant, The 1930,Ja 6,30:5
Three Thieves 1933,O 30,14:3
Broken Shoes 1934,Mr 31,8:3
Marionettes 1934,My 8,28:6
Without Dowry 1946,Ap 15,22:2
Klimov, Ilya (Director)
Welcome Kostya! 1965,N 22,48:2
Klinder, Lotte
Tradition 1921,Jl 1,8:1
KLINE
See Also CLYNE, CLINE, KLEIN
Kline, Ed (Director)
Sweet Mamma 1930,Jl 12,16:4
So This Is Africa! 1933,Ap 24,11:3
Kline, Herbert (Director)
Crisis 1939,Mr 13,12:2
Lights Out In Europe 1940,Ap 15,21:2
Forgotten Village, The 1941,N 19,26:3
My Father's House 1947,S 26,28:3
Kid From Cleveland, The 1949,S 5,13:2
Fighter, The 1952,My 31,12:6
Kline, Herbert (Original Author)
Youth Runs Wild 1944,S 2,17:2
Illegal Entry 1949,Je 11,11:2
Kid From Cleveland, The 1949,S 5,13:2
Kline, Herbert (Producer)
Crisis 1939,Mr 13,12:2
Forgotten Village, The 1941,N 19,26:3
My Father's House 1947,S 26,28:3
Kline, Herbert (Screenwriter)
Fighter, The 1952,My 31,12:6
Kline, Marvin
Forest Ring, The 1930,Ap 26,11:1
Counsellor-At-Law 1933,D 8,31:2
Klinge, Ray
Junior Miss 1945,Je 18,15:4
Klingenberg, H
Frau Lehmann's Toechter 1933,O 27,22:3
S A Mann Brand 1934,My 28,16:2
Zwischen Himmel und Erde; Between Heaven and
Earth 1935,Ja 21,19:3
Klinger, Paul
Pretty Miss Schragg 1937,S 25,10:2
Zweimal zwei im Himmelbett; Twice Two in a
Four-Post Bed 1939,F 5,19:3
Marriage in the Shadows 1948,S 17,28:3
Flying Classroom, The 1958,Je 28,13:7
Klinger, Werner
Journey's End 1930,Ap 9,25:1
Tanz Geht Weiter, Der 1931,Ja 6,25:1
Klinger, Werner (Director)
Standschuetze Bruggler 1937,Mr 13,23:3
Razzia 1948,Je 14,19:2
Klippel, Fritz
Fremd im Sudetenland; Strange to the Sudeten
Country 1938,N 5,15:3
Klipstein, Ernst
Johannis fever; St Johns' Fire 1940,Ap 6,13:2
Klipstein, Ernst von (Original Author)
Gouverneur, Der 1939,S 11,15:2
Kliucharev, Vassili
Days and Nights 1946,Ap 29,24:4
Kloepfer, Eugen
Street, The 1927,S 6,34:3
Explosion 1927,D 13,33:2
Luther 1929,Je 24,27:1
1914: The Last Days Before the War 1932,S 5,9:6
Gehetzie Menschen 1934,Je 2,22:5
Fluechtlinge 1934,O 15,20:5
Private Life of Louis XIV, The 1936,Ja 9,25:2
Jugend; Youth 1939,D 9,18:2
Living Dead, The 1940,D 17,33:2
Klorer, John (Original Author)
On Such a Night 1937,S 17,29:2
Seven Miles from Alcatraz 1942,N 19,31:3
Hers to Hold 1943,Jl 22,15:1
Can't Help Singing 1944,D 26,22:4
Good Sam 1948,S 17,28:2
Tension 1950,Ja 12,32:4

Klorer, John (Original Author) — Cont
Pretty Baby 1950,S 23,11:2
Starlift 1951,D 15,11:2

Klorer, John (Screenwriter)
Guest Wife 1945,O 18,21:2
This Love of Ours 1945,N 1,20:2
Starlift 1951,D 15,11:2
Utopia 1954,D 15,41:1
Never Say Goodbye 1956,Ap 14,20:1

Klos, Elmar (Director)
Shop on High Street, The 1965,S 10,40:1
Shop on Main Street, The 1965,S 13,42:1
Shop on Main Street, The 1966,Ja 25,47:1

Klose, Margarete
Marriage of Figaro 1950,N 3,31:2

Klosowski, Roman
Eve Wants to Sleep 1961,Je 6,42:2
Eroica (Second Episode) 1966,F 2,24:1

Klove, Jan (Screenwriter)
...And Now Miguel 1966,S 8,43:1

Kluesner, Karl
Andalusische Naechte; Nights in Andalusia
1938,S 24,13:2

Kluge, Alexander
Yesterday Girl 1967,S 22,57:2

Kluge, Alexander (Director)
Yesterday Girl 1967,S 22,57:2
Artists Under the Big Top Perplexed
1968,S 27,34:1

Kluge, Alexander (Original Author)
Yesterday Girl 1967,S 22,57:2

Kluge, Alexander (Screenwriter)
Yesterday Girl 1967,S 22,57:2
Artists Under the Big Top Perplexed
1968,S 27,34:1

Kluge, George
Citizen Saint 1948,My 28,28:2

Klugman, Jack
Timetable 1956,Mr 17,13:2
12 Angry Men 1957,Ap 15,24:1
Cry Terror 1958,My 15,25:1
Days of Wine and Roses 1963,Ja 18,7:2
I Could go on Singing 1963,My 16,42:1
Yellow Canary, The 1963,My 16,42:1
Act One 1963,D 27,17:2
Detective, The 1968,My 29,20:3
Split, The 1968,N 5,55:2

Klukvin, I
Czar Ivan the Terrible 1928,Mr 12,26:1
Flames on the Volga 1929,Ap 2,28:4
Twenty-Six Commissars 1933,Jl 1,16:6

Klune, Raymond A (Producer)
Hell and High Water 1954,F 2,20:6

Klusak, Jan
Report on the Party and the Guests, A
1968,S 20,37:5
Report on the Party and the Guests, A
1968,S 28,37:1

Klushentsev, P (Director)
Road to the Stars 1958,Je 5,39:2

Klyaro, Ksenia
Transport of Fire 1931,Mr 24,31:2

Kmit, Inna
Lust for Gold 1958,Jl 24,18:1
New Number Comes to Moscow, A
1959,Jl 6,23:1

Kmit, Leonid
Tchapayef 1935,Ja 15,22:1
Pesnya O Stchasti 1935,Ap 8,23:4
Men of the Sea 1938,Je 20,11:2
Guerrilla Brigade 1942,Ap 14,17:2
Blue Cliff, The 1943,Mr 25,25:3

Knaggs, Skelton
Ghost Ship, The 1943,D 25,19:4
House of Dracula 1945,D 22,16:3
Terror by Night 1946,F 9,9:2
Scandal In Paris, A 1946,S 16,9:7
Dick Tracy vs Cueball 1946,N 23,12:2
Dick Tracy and Gruesome 1947,S 27,11:2

Knapp, David
Parrish 1961,My 5,22:1

Knapp, Evalyn
Sinners' Holiday 1930,O 11,21:3
Mothers Cry 1930,D 6,21:3
River's End 1931,Mr 7,17:2
Millionaire, The 1931,Ap 9,30:5
Smart Money 1931,Je 19,21:1
Bargain, The 1931,S 5,7:4
Side Show 1931,S 19,10:2
High Pressure 1932,F 1,22:3
Fireman, Save My Child 1932,F 18,25:3
Strange Love of Molly Louvain, The
1932,My 9,19:5
Madame Racketeer 1932,Jl 23,6:6
Big City Blues 1932,S 10,18:5
Successful Calamity, A 1932,S·23,22:2
This Sporting Age 1932,O 1,10:4
Night Mayor, The 1932,N 25,19:2
Air Hostess 1933,Ja 23,9:2
State Trooper 1933,Mr 27,13:6
Corruption 1933,Je 20,22:7
Dance, Girl, Dance 1933,O 25,23:3
Laughing Irish Eyes 1936,Ap 4,11:2
Rawhide 1938,Ap 25,19:2

Wanted by the Police 1938,S 26,13:2
Lone Wolf Takes a Chance, The 1941,Ap 7,13:2

Knapp, Harry
Manhunt in the Jungle 1958,Ap 12,13:1

Knapp, Josef
Rosenkavalier, Der 1962,O 10,57:1

Knapp, Otto
William Tell 1925,My 20,26:2

Knapp, Robert
Jubal 1956,Ap 25,39:1

Knapp, Terrence
Othello 1966,F 2,24:1

Knapp, Wilfrid
Girl He Left Behind, The 1956,O 27,17:1

Knasnovetsky, V
Diary of a Nazi 1943,Mr 25,25:3

Kneale, Nigel (Original Author)
Five Million Years to Earth 1968,My 30,21:4

Kneale, Nigel (Screenwriter)
Look Back in Anger 1959,S 16,45:1
Entertainer, The 1960,O 4,49:2
Damn the Defiant 1962,S 20,29:2
First Men in the Moon 1964,N 26,52:2
Devil's Own, The 1967,Mr 16,53:2
Five Million Years to Earth 1968,My 30,21:4

Knebel, Fletcher (Original Author)
Seven Days in May 1964,F 20,22:1

Kneebone, Tom
Luck of Ginger Coffey, The 1964,S 22,44:1

Kneeland, Ted (Director)
Dr Coppelius 1968,D 26,56:1

Kneeland, Ted (Screenwriter)
Dr Coppelius 1968,D 26,56:1

Knef, Hildegard
Murderers Among Us 1948,Ag 17,19:6
Lost Continent, The 1968,Je 20,50:2

Knetschke, Charles
Somewhere in Berlin 1949,Ag 16,19:3

Knettles, Robert
Hell and Highwater 1933,D 18,24:4

Kneubuhl, John (Screenwriter)
Two on a Guillotine 1965,Ja 14,44:3

Kniazev, L
Admiral Nakhimov 1948,N 25,47:4

Knibbs, Henry K (Original Author)
Tony Runs Wild 1926,Ap 28,28:3

Kniepert, Erni (Miscellaneous)
Rosenkavalier, Der 1962,O 10,57:1

Knight, Bill
Bigger Than Barnum's 1926,Jl 13,19:3

Knight, Buzzy
These Thousand Hills 1959,My 7,36:1

Knight, Castleton (Director)
Olympic Games of 1948, The 1948,S 25,11:2

Knight, Castleton (Producer)
Plaything, The 1929,O 6,IX,9:4 (In Addenda)
Olympic Games of 1948, The 1948,S 25,11:2
Queen is Crowned, A 1953,Je 8,26:2
Queen's Royal Tour, A 1954,Mr 3,22:2
Royal Symphony, The 1954,Mr 3,22:2

Knight, Christopher
Studs Lonigan 1960,D 15,59:1
If a Man Answers 1962,N 22,43:1

Knight, David
Chance Meeting 1955,Ap 20,38:1
Tears for Simon 1957,Ap 18,35:2
Out of the Clouds 1957,Jl 1,20:4
Across the Bridge 1957,O 30,24:1
Nightmare 1964,Je 18,29:2

Knight, Don
Kill a Dragon 1967,D 7,60:2

Knight, Edmond
Strauss's Great Waltz 1935,Ap 8,23:3
Wild Heart, The 1952,My 29,17:2
Sink the Bismarck! 1960,F 12,22:3

Knight, Eric (Original Author)
This Above All 1942,My 13,14:3
Lassie Come Home 1943,O 8,15:4
Son of Lassie 1945,Je 11,12:1

Knight, Esmond
Ringer, The 1932,Je 2,25:2
Clown Must Laugh, A 1938,O 12,35:2
Blackout 1940,D 2,19:2
This England 1941,N 18,33:2
Silver Fleet, The 1945,Mr 24,22:6
Half-Way House 1945,Ag 13,22:4
Henry V 1946,Je 18,30:2
Black Narcissus 1947,Ag 14,29:2
Holiday Camp 1948,Ja 24,11:2
End of the River, The 1948,Je 21,18:2
Hamlet 1948,S 30,32:2
Red Shoes, The 1948,O 23,9:2
Canterbury Tale, A 1949,Ja 24,16:2
Inheritance, The 1951,F 12,19:2
River, The 1951,S 11,33:2
Richard III 1956,Mr 12,1:4
Prince and the Showgirl 1957,Je 14,22:2

Knight, Felix
Babes in Toyland 1934,D 13,28:2

Knight, Fuzzy
Hell's Highway 1932,S 26,18:2
She Done Him Wrong 1933,F 10,12:3
Her Bodyguard 1933,Ag 7,18:2

Knight, Fuzzy — Cont
Moulin Rouge 1934,F 8,14:4
Last Round-Up, The 1934,My 10,25:2
Operator 13 1934,Je 23,16:5
Music in the Air 1934,D 14,29:3
Home on the Range 1935,F 13,24:4
Behold My Wife 1935,F 18,19:3
Trail of the Lonesome Pine, The 1936,F 20,23:5
Sudden Death, And 1936,Jl 18,18:2
Mountain Justice 1937,My 13,31:2
Mountain Music 1937,Je 24,30:3
Gold Racket, The 1937,Ag 2,10:3
County Fair 1937,D 27,11:1
Singing Outlaw 1937,D 27,11:1
Spawn of the North 1938,S 8,27:1
Cowboy and the Lady, The 1938,N 25,19:3
Union Pacific 1939,My 11,31:2
Chip of the Flying U 1940,Ja 22,11:3
My Little Chickadee 1940,Mr 16,8:2
Johnny Apollo 1940,Ap 13,21:2
West of Carson City 1940,My 7,31:3
Brigham Young - Frontiersman 1940,S 21,13:2
Horror Island 1941,Mr 31,11:3
Shepherd of the Hills, The 1941,Jl 31,13:2
Badlands of Dakota 1941,S 9,27:6
New York Town 1941,N 13,35:2
Butch Minds the Baby 1942,My 1,23:3
Juke Girl 1942,Je 20,9:2
He's my Guy 1943,Mr 12,12:3
Corvette K-225 1943,O 21,30:1
Frisco Sal 1945,F 17,11:2
Frontier Gal 1945,D 15,14:2
Egg and I, The 1947,Ap 25,29:2

Knight, Harlan
Country Flapper, The 1922,Jl 31,12:3
Janice Meredith 1924,Ag 6,13:3
Knockout, The 1925,O 27,23:3
Dance Magic 1927,Jl 13,21:2
Tol'able David 1930,N 17,29:1
Heaven on Earth 1931,D 19,16:4
Story of Temple Drake, The 1933,My 6,11:2

Knight, James
Girl in a Million, A 1950,Jl 24,15:2

Knight, June
Take a Chance 1933,N 27,20:3
Cross Country Cruise 1934,Ja 20,12:3
Wake up and Dream 1934,O 11,28:3
Broadway Melody of 1936 1935,S 19,28:1
Vacation From Love 1938,N 10,33:2
House Across the Bay, The 1940,Mr 22,23:2
Break the News 1941,Ja 2,24:2

Knight, Patricia
Roses Are Red 1947,N 15,11:2
Fabulous Texan, The 1947,D 26,22:5
Second Face, The 1951,Mr 2,21:3
Magic Face, The 1951,O 1,19:2

Knight, Rosalind
Tom Jones 1963,O 8,48:1

Knight, Sandra
Frankenstein's Daughter 1958,N 17,37:2

Knight, Shirley
Ice Palace 1960,Je 30,22:1
Khovanschina 1960,S 23,33:1
Couch, The 1962,F 22,20:3
Sweet Bird of Youth 1962,Mr 29,28:2
House of Women 1962,Ap 12,41:6
Flight From Ashiya 1964,Ap 23,34:1
Group, The 1966,Mr 17,35:1
Dutchman 1967,F 28,32:1
Petulia 1968,Je 11,54:4

Knight, Vick (Miscellaneous)
It Happened on Fifth Avenue 1947,Je 11,33:2

Knight, Vivienne (Screenwriter)
Law and Disorder 1958,Ag 6,20:1
Model Murder Case, The 1964,N 25,45:1

Knight, W R Capt (Narrator)
Filming of the Golden Eagle, The 1929,Ap 2,28:4

Knight, W R Capt (Producer)
Sea Hawks 1930,F 10,20:4

Knipper-Tschech, O
Prisoners of the Sea 1929,Ap 16,32:5

Knoblock, Edward (Miscellaneous)
Evensong 1934,N 17,12:1

Knoblock, Edward (Original Author)
Lost Romance, The 1921,My 9,16:2
Speakeasy 1929,Mr 11,22:2
Love Comes Along 1930,F 1,15:1
Kismet 1930,O 31,20:1
Sin of Madelon Claudet, The 1931,O 31,22:2
Evensong 1934,N 17,12:1
Kismet 1944,Ag 23,16:1
Kismet 1955,D 9,32:2

Knoblock, Edward (Screenwriter)
Rosita 1923,S 4,14:1
Red Wagon 1936,Je 22,22:1
Moonlight Sonata 1938,My 10,17:2

Knoch, Lucille
Sabre Jet 1953,N 3,34:1
Executive Suite 1954,My 7,19:1

Knoles, Harley (Director)
Little Women 1918,N 11,13:3
Carnival 1921,Je 27,16:3
Bohemian Girl, The 1923,F 5,18:2
Oh Baby! 1926,Ag 11,25:2

Knoles, Harley (Director)— Cont
White Sheik, The 1929,D 9,32:5
Knoles, Harley (Screenwriter)
Oh Baby! 1926,Ag 11,25:2
Knopf, Christopher (Screenwriter)
King's Thief, The 1955,Ag 13,7:2
Knopf, Edwin (Composer)
Reckless 1935,Ap 20,16:1
Knopf, Edwin (Director)
Slightly Scarlet 1930,Mr 1,23:1
Light of Western Stars, The 1930,Ap 26,11:1
Sante Fe Trail, The 1930,O 18,23:2
Only Saps Work 1930,D 13,22:2
Nice Women 1932,F 20,11:2
Rebel, The 1933,Jl 25,17:2
Law and the Lady, The 1951,Ag 16,23:2
Knopf, Edwin (Original Author)
Rebel, The 1933,Jl 25,17:2
Wedding Night, The 1935,Mr 16,19:1
Mr Imperium 1951,O 15,22:2
Knopf, Edwin (Producer)
Trial of Mary Dugan, The 1941,Mr 6,25:4
I'll Wait for You 1941,Je 2,13:6
Vanishing Virginian, The 1942,My 28,13:3
Crossroads 1942,Jl 27,18:2
Cry Havoc 1943,N 24,16:2
Cross of Lorraine, The 1943,D 3,27:4
Valley of Decision, The 1945,My 4,23:2
Sailor Takes a Wife, The 1946,Mr 1,17:2
Secret Heart, The 1946,D 26,28:2
Cynthia 1947,S 19,27:2
B F's Daughter 1948,Mr 25,35:2
Edward my Son 1949,Je 3,21:2
Malaya 1950,F 23,33:1
Night Into Morning 1951,Je 11,20:7
Law and the Lady, The 1951,Ag 16,23:2
Mr Imperium 1951,O 15,22:2
Lili 1953,Mr 11,36:7
Glass Slipper, The 1955,Mr 25,19:2
King's Thief, The 1955,Ag 13,7:2
Diane 1956,Ja 13,18:1
Gaby 1956,My 10,26:3
Vintage, The 1957,My 9,36:5
Tip on a Dead Jockey 1957,S 7,12:7
Knopf, Edwin (Screenwriter)
Piccadilly Jim 1936,Ag 31,19:1
Mr Imperium 1951,O 15,22:2
Knopf, Peter
Auto und Kein Geld, Ein; Auto and no Money,
An 1936,Ag 8,5:3
Knorre, Fedor (Screenwriter)
Dark Is The Night 1946,Mr 18,24:3
Road Home, The 1947,My 2,28:3
Knosovsky, D
Zemlya Zhazhdet 1932,My 6,15:3
Knoteck, Hansi
Fuerst Woronzeff 1934,N 17,12:2
Schloss Hubertus 1935,F 9,11:3
Zigeunerbaron 1935,S 14,8:5
Heilige und Ihr Narr, Die; Saint and Her Fool,
The 1935,N 29,24:2
Waldwinter 1936,N 14,23:3
Wenn Frauen Schweigen; When Women Keep
Silent 1937,S 11,20:2
Pretty Miss Schragg 1937,S 25,10:2
Silence of the Forest, The; Schweigen im Walde,
Das 1937,D 6,19:2
Zwei lustige Abenteurer; Two Merry Adventures
1938,Ja 1,11:2
Gewitter im Mai; Storms in May 1938,Mr 5,11:3
Prinzessin Sissy 1939,Ja 14,13:2
Edelweisskoenig, Der 1939,F 4,11:2
Heimatland; Homeland 1939,O 28,11:2
Waldrausch; Forest Fever 1940,Ja 20,11:3
Knott, Adelbert
Percy 1925,Mr 25,24:2
Knott, Clara
Old Lady 31 1920,My 24,20:3
Knott, Else
Morgenrot 1933,My 16,15:2
Knott, Frederick (Original Author)
Wait Until Dark 1967,O 27,48:1
Knott, Frederick (Screenwriter)
Dial M for Murder 1954,My 29,13:2
Knott, George Marion
Rolling Home 1926,Je 8,22:1
Knott, John Major
Four Feathers 1939,Ag 4,11:1
Knott, Lydia
Peaceful Valley 1920,O 11,19:3
Turn to the Right 1922,Ja 24,11:1
Garrison's Finish 1923,My 28,18:2
Woman of Paris, A 1923,O 2,7:2
Perfect Flapper, The 1924,Je 23,22:4
Those Who Dance 1924,Je 30,16:1
Free and Equal 1925,Ap 20,22:1
Rose of the World 1925,N 10,25:3
Guilty 1930,Ap 7,21:1
Knotts, Don
No Time for Sergeants 1958,My 30,13:2
Wake Me When It's Over 1960,Ap 9,17:2
Last Time I Saw Archie, The 1961,My 29,9:6
It's a Mad, Mad, Mad, Mad World
1963,N 19,47:1

Move Over Darling 1963,D 26,33:1
Incredible Mr Limpet, The 1964,Mr 26,40:4
Ghost and Mr Chicken, The 1966,S 22,57:2
Shakiest Gun in the West, The 1968,Jl 11,30:1
Knowland, Alice
Coming Through 1925,F 18,17:3
Knowlden, Marilyn
Women Love Once 1931,Je 27,20:3
Cisco Kid, The 1931,O 24,20:3
Husband's Holiday 1931,D 25,29:2
As the Earth Turns 1934,Ap 12,27:2
Imitation of Life 1934,N 24,19:1
David Copperfield 1935,Ja 19,8:1
Miserables, Les 1935,Ap 22,14:2
Show Boat 1936,My 15,29:4
Anthony Adverse 1936,Ag 27,16:1
Rainbow on the River 1936,D 18,31:4
Four's a Crowd 1938,Ag 12,11:1
Men With Wings 1938,O 27,27:2
Angels With Dirty Faces 1938,N 26,18:1
Just Around the Corner 1938,D 3,11:2
Hidden Power 1939,Jl 26,17:3
Knowles, Bernard (Director)
Magic Bow, The 1947,Jl 7,13:2
Jassy 1948,F 20,19:2
Smugglers, The 1948,Mr 29,17:1
Bad Sister 1948,Je 11,27:3
Place of One's Own, A 1949,F 8,30:2
Easy Money (Episode 4) 1949,F 14,15:3
Easy Money (Episode 2) 1949,F 14,15:3
Easy Money (Episode 3) 1949,F 14,15:3
Easy Money (Episode 1) 1949,F 14,15:3
Lost People, The 1950,O 2,19:4
Perfect Woman, The 1951,F 17,10:7
Reluctant Widow, The 1951,S 8,8:6
Knowles, Bernard (Screenwriter)
Perfect Woman, The 1951,F 17,10:7
Knowles, Patric
Norah O'Neale 1934,O 25,26:3
Mister Hobo 1936,F 8,19:2
Abdul the Damned 1936,My 11,16:2
Give Me your Heart 1936,S 17,18:2
Student's Romance, The 1936,O 12,23:2
Charge of the Light Brigade, The 1936,N 2,24:1
It's Love I'm After 1937,N 11,31:2
Expensive Husbands 1938,Ja 8,19:3
Patient in Room 18, The 1938,Ap 22,15:6
Adventures of Robin Hood, The 1938,My 13,17:2
Four's a Crowd 1938,Ag 12,11:1
Sisters, The 1938,O 15,21:3
Storm Over Bengal 1938,D 8,34:4
Heart of the North 1938,D 21,29:2
Torchy Blane in Chinatown 1939,F 3,13:2
Beauty for the Asking 1939,F 10,19:1
Five came Back 1939,Jl 5,20:2
Spellbinder, The 1939,Ag 24,17:3
Another Thin Man 1939,N 24,29:1
Honeymoon's Over, The 1939,D 15,33:3
Married and in Love 1940,F 2,13:2
Women in War 1940,My 30,21:2
Bill of Divorcement, A 1940,Jl 12,11:2
Anne of Windy Poplars 1940,Ag 23,13:3
How Green Was my Valley 1941,O 29,27:2
Wolf Man, The 1941,D 22,24:5
Strange Case of Dr Rx 1942,Mr 28,11:2
Mystery of Marie Roget, The 1942,My 5,17:3
Lady in a Jam 1942,S 11,25:2
Sin Town 1942,O 17,11:2
Who Done It 1942,D 3,35:2
Frankenstein Meets the Wolf Man 1943,Mr 6,8:3
All by Myself 1943,Jl 16,20:3
Hit the Ice 1943,S 23,27:2
Crazy House 1943,D 16,33:3
Chip off the Old Block 1944,Mr 17,14:2
This is the Life 1944,Ap 28,23:3
Masquerade in Mexico 1945,N 29,27:2
Kitty 1946,Ap 1,23:1
O S S 1946,My 27,15:5
Bride Wore Boots, The 1946,Je 6,16:3
Of Human Bondage 1946,Jl 6,11:2
Monsieur Beaucaire 1946,S 5,23:1
Ivy 1947,Je 26,19:1
Dream Girl 1948,Je 17,29:2
Isn't It Romantic? 1948,O 7,35:2
Big Steal, The 1949,Jl 11,13:2
Three Came Home 1950,F 21,22:5
Quebec 1951,Mr 16,34:2
Mutiny 1952,Mr 20,37:5
World for Ransom 1954,Je 5,11:2
Khyber Patrol 1954,S 20,19:2
Band of Angels 1957,Jl 11,21:1
From the Earth to the Moon 1958,N 27,52:2
Auntie Mame 1958,D 5,39:1
Knox, Alexander
Sea Wolf, The 1941,Mr 26,27:3
This Above All 1942,My 13,14:3
None Shall Escape 1944,Ap 7,23:2
Wilson 1944,Ag 2,18:1
Over 21 1945,Ag 17,20:2
Sister Kenny 1946,S 30,21:2
Sign of the Ram, The 1948,Mr 4,30:2
Judge Steps Out, The 1949,Je 3,21:4
Tokyo Joe 1949,O 27,35:2

Knox, Alexander— Cont
I'd Climb the Highest Mountain 1951,My 10,38:1
Two of a Kind 1951,Je 30,8:6
Saturday's Hero 1951,S 12,37:2
Vikings, The 1952,Je 12,35:2
Paula 1952,Jl 16,21:2
Greatest Love, The 1954,Ja 12,19:2
Commandos Strike at Dawn 1954,Ja 14,25:1
Sleeping Tiger, The 1954,O 9,8:7
Divided Heart, The 1955,Ap 4,16:1
Night my Number Came up, The 1955,D 20,39:5
Reach for the Sky 1957,My 1,40:1
Chase a Crooked Shadow 1958,Mr 25,28:4
Two-Headed Spy, The 1959,Mr 3,38:4
Intent to Kill 1959,Ap 1,43:2
Crack in the Mirror 1960,My 20,26:1
Oscar Wilde 1960,Je 21,28:2
Operation Amsterdam 1960,Jl 7,26:1
Longest Day, The 1962,O 5,28:1
In the Cool of the Day 1963,My 30,20:1
Man in the Middle 1964,Mr 5,36:1
Woman of Straw 1964,O 1,30:6
Crack in the World 1965,My 13,32:2
Mister Moses 1965,My 13,32:1
These Are the Damned 1965,Jl 8,35:1
Khartoum 1966,Jl 14,28:1
Modesty Blaise 1966,Ag 11,27:1
Psycopath, The 1966,S 29,60:1
Accident 1967,Ap 18,33:1
How I Won the War 1967,N 9,56:1
Villa Rides 1968,Jl 18,26:3
Shalako 1968,N 6,32:1
Knox, Alexander (Screenwriter)
Sister Kenny 1946,S 30,21:2
Judge Steps Out, The 1949,Je 3,21:4
Knox, David
Hue and Cry 1951,Ja 9,25:2
Knox, Doris
Servant, The 1964,Mr 17,30:2
Knox, Elyse
Free, Blonde and 21 1940,Ap 5,25:2
Lillian Russell 1940,My 18,11:2
Girl in 313 1940,Je 14,25:3
Youth Will Be Served 1940,N 15,25:2
Tanks a Million 1941,O 9,27:2
Mummy's Tomb, The 1942,O 26,19:2
Mister Big 1943,Je 14,13:4
Hit the Ice 1943,S 23,27:2
Wave, A Wac and a Marine, A 1944,Ag 14,11:4
Joe Palooka, Champ 1946,Ap 6,10:6
Black Gold 1947,S 5,16:4
There's a Girl in my Heart 1950,Ja 20,29:2
Knox, Mickey
I Walk Alone 1948,Ja 22,36:3
Killer McCoy 1948,F 12,31:2
Accused, The 1949,Ja 13,26:2
Knock on any Door 1949,F 23,31:2
City Across the River 1949,Ag 8,31:3
Any Number Can Play 1949,Jl 1,14:4
White Heat 1949,S 3,7:2
Outside the Wall 1950,Mr 15,34:8
Up Front 1951,Mr 26,19:2
Saturday's Hero 1951,S 12,37:2
Singing in the Dark 1956,Mr 8,32:5
Garden of Eden 1957,D 18,45:3
View From the Bridge, A 1962,Ja 23,36:1
10th Victim, The 1965,D 21,46:1
Wild 90 1968,Ja 8,33:1
Beyond the Law 1968,S 30,60:4
Beyond the Law 1968,O 24,55:1
Knox, Patricia
Lady for a Night 1942,F 12,27:2
Knox, W D C
Prince of Lovers, The 1927,N 29,31:1
Knudsen, Elsebet
Weekend 1964,Ap 27,24:1
Knudsen, Kolbjorn
Winter Light 1963,My 14,32:1
Knudsen, Peggy
Stolen Life, A 1946,My 2,27:4
Big Sleep, The 1946,Ag 24,6:6
Never Say Goodbye 1946,N 23,12:2
Humoresque 1946,D 26,28:1
Stallion Road 1947,Ap 5,12:5
Unfaithful, The 1947,Je 28,10:2
Roses Are Red 1947,N 15,11:2
Copper Canyon 1950,N 16,39:2
Unchained 1955,Ja 28,15:2
Good Morning, Miss Dove 1955,N 24,41:1
Bottom of the Bottle, The 1956,F 2,19:2
Hilda Crane 1956,My 3,35:2
Istanbul 1957,Ja 24,34:1
Knudsen, Poul (Screenwriter)
Day of Wrath 1948,Ap 26,27:2
Knuth, Gustav
Lied der Wuste, Das; Desert Song 1940,F 3,9:3
Grapes are Ripe, The 1953,O 15,43:2
Beggar Student, The 1958,Ja 25,14:3
Reaching for the Stars 1958,My 24,18:2
Sky Without Stars 1959,My 30,9:2
Dreimaederlhaus, Das; (House of Three Girls,
The) 1961,N 18,15:1
Hippodrome 1962,Mr 12,36:1
Forever My Love 1962,Mr 28,36:4

Knuth, Gustav— Cont
Heidi 1968,S 23,42:4
Knyazev, L
Clear Skies 1963,N 27,30:1
Ko-Hai
Samarang 1933,Je 29,22:2
Koannidou, T
Loves of a Greek in Paris 1960,Ag 15,19:7
Kobachevitch
Toni 1968,S 19,62:2
Kobart, Ruth
How to Succeed in Business Without Really
Trying 1967,Mr 10,30:1
Kobayashi, Keiju
Happiness of Us Alone 1963,Ap 10,31:5
My Hobo 1963,Jl 24,27:3
Naked General, The 1964,D 16,51:2
Could I but Live 1965,Ja 20,34:2
Samurai Assassin 1965,Mr 19,27:5
Kobayashi, Masaki (Director)
Human Condition, The 1959,D 16,56:1
Harakiri 1964,Ag 5,24:2
Kwaidan (In the Cup of Tea); In the Cup of Tea
(Kwaidan) 1965,N 23,51:1
Kwaidan (Hoichi, The Earless); Hoichi, The
Earless (Kwaidan) 1965,N 23,51:1
Kwaidan (Black Hair); Black Hair (Kwaidan)
1965,N 23,51:1
Rebellion 1967,S 25,56:4
Rebellion 1968,O 26,27:4
Kobayashi, Masaki (Miscellaneous)
Human Condition, The 1959,D 16,56:1
Kobayashi, Masaki (Screenwriter)
Human Condition, The 1959,D 16,56:1
Kobayashi, Tadashi
Temptress and the Monk, The 1963,My 28,32:1
Kobayashi, Toshiko
Carmen Comes Home 1959,D 23,22:1
Kobayashi, Tsuruko
Cry for Happy 1961,Mr 4,16:1
Majority of One, A 1962,Ja 12,29:2
Kober, Arthur (Miscellaneous)
Little Foxes, The 1941,Ag 22,19:2
My Own True Love 1949,F 3,27:3
Kober, Arthur (Original Author)
Hollywood Party 1934,My 26,12:2
Ginger 1935,Jl 19,13:2
Big Broadcast of 1937, The 1936,O 22,31:1
Having Wonderful Time 1938,Jl 8,11:2
Wintertime 1943,S 30,27:2
Kober, Arthur (Screenwriter)
Great Hotel Murder, The 1935,F 28,17:4
Ginger 1935,Jl 19,13:2
Early to Bed 1936,Jl 16,20:2
Having Wonderful Time 1938,Jl 8,11:2
Don Juan Quilligan 1945,Jl 30,16:2
Koberidze, Otar
Stepchildren 1962,Jl 2,22:2
Tsar's Bride, The 1966,Mr 12,13:2
Kobi, Michi
Cry for Happy 1961,Mr 4,16:1
Kobiela, Bogumil
Ashes and Diamonds 1961,My 30,8:1
Kobkolv, E
Tsar's Bride, The 1966,Mr 12,13:2
Kobler, John (Original Author)
Forgotten Woman, The 1939,Ag 4,11:2
Koblock, Edward (Screenwriter)
Three Musketeers, The 1921,Ag 29,14:4
Kobori, Makoto
Ikiru; To Live 1960,Ja 30,13:5
Koch, Carlo (Director)
Story of Tosca, The 1947,D 19,34:2
Koch, Élaine
Big Pond, The 1930,My 19,21:1
Koch, Howard (Director)
Shield for Murder 1954,Ag 28,8:3
Big House U S A 1955,Mr 12,11:6
Untamed Youth 1957,My 11,24:6
Andy Hardy Comes Home 1958,D 24,00:0
Last Mile, The 1959,F 19,27:1
Koch, Howard (Producer)
Beachhead 1954,Ap 17,8:2
Desert Sands 1955,N 19,22:7
Three bad Sisters 1956,F 13,24:1
Sergeants 3 1962,F 12,28:2
President's Analyst, The 1967,D 22,44:4
Odd Couple, The 1968,My 3,42:1
Koch, Howard (Screenwriter)
Sea Hawk, The 1940,Ag 10,16:2
Letter, The 1940,N 23,12:6
Shining Victory 1941,My 31,14:1
Sergeant York 1941,Jl 3,15:1
In This our Life 1942,My 9,10:2
Casablanca 1942,N 27,27:1
Mission to Moscow 1943,Ap 30,25:2
In our Time 1944,F 12,11:2
Rhapsody in Blue 1945,Je 28,22:2
Three Strangers 1946,F 23,20:2
Letters From an Unknown Woman
1948,Ap 29,20:6
Rules of the Game, The 1950,Ap 10,15:3
No Sad Songs for Me 1950,Ap 28,26:2
Thirteenth Letter, The 1951,F 22,27:2

Loss of Innocence 1961,N 22,27:1
War Lover, The 1963,Mr 7,8:5
633 Squadron 1964,Je 25,25:1
Fox, The 1968,F 8,36:1
Koch, Lotte
City of Torment 1950,Je 10,11:4
Koch, Marianne
Night People 1954,Mr 13,11:2
Place Called Glory, A 1966,Ag 11,27:4
Trunk to Cairo 1966,D 29,22:1
Fistful of Dollars, A 1967,F 2,29:1
Koch, Vladimir (Screenwriter)
Ninth Circle, The 1961,S 15,30:3
Kochanska, Maria
Spelnione Marzenia; Fulfilled Dreams
1939,D 14,35:3
Kochetkov, Afanasi
Mumu 1961,Je 5,37:4
Kochetov, V (Screenwriter)
Big Family, A 1955,Je 6,24:1
Kochi, Momoko
Godzilla, King of the Monsters 1956,Ap 28,11:1
Mysterians, The 1959,Jl 2,15:2
Kochitz, Nina
Loves of Casanova, The 1929,Ap 30,33:2
Kochnev, Mikala (Screenwriter)
Sword and the Dragon, The 1960,N 17,46:3
Kochurov, Y (Composer)
Professor Mamlock 1938,N 8,26:2
Kock, Freddy
Red Meadows 1950,Ja 19,35:2
Kocsina, Sylva
Jessica 1962,Ap 20,20:2
Koczewska, Wanda
Guests are Coming; Jada Goscie Jada
1967,Ja 13,15:1
Koczian, Johanna von
For the First Time 1959,Ag 15,8:7
Kodar, Jan (Director)
Shop on Main Street, The 1965,S 13,42:1
Kodet, Jiri
Sweet Light in a Dark Room 1966,Je 30,28:1
Kodo, Kunihori
Magnificent Seven, The 1956,N 20,46:2
Kodor, Jan (Director)
Shop on High Street, The 1965,S 10,40:1
Koechlin, Margot
Aufforderung zum Tanz; Invitation to the Dance
1935,N 23,23:3
Koeck, Edvard
Schimmelkrieg von Holledau, Der 1938,Jl 19,15:4
Waldrausch; Forest Fever 1940,Ja 20,11:3
Koecklin, Charles (Composer)
Return to Life 1938,Ag 4,15:1
KOEHLER
See Also KOLLER, KOHLER
Koehler, Ted (Composer)
Let's Fall in Love 1934,Ja 22,12:3
King of Burlesque 1936,Ja 16,25:2
King and the Chorus Girl, The 1937,Mr 29,14:4
23 1/2 Hours Leave 1937,My 17,23:2
Start Cheering 1938,Mr 17,17:3
Love Affair 1939,Mr 17,25:2
Slightly French 1949,My 27,25:3
Koehler, Ted (Miscellaneous)
Curly Top 1935,Ag 2,22:3
Dimples 1936,O 10,21:2
Artists and Models 1937,Ag 5,19:2
Koehler, Ted (Screenwriter)
Stormy Weather 1943,Jl 22,15:1
Koeller, Ted (Composer)
Rainbow Island 1944,O 26,19:6
Koellner, H F (Screenwriter)
Hippodrome 1962,Mr 12,36:1
Koempel-Pilot, M
S A Mann Brand 1934,My 28,16:2
Grobe Adele, Die 1937,My 15,23:5
Koenan, Frank
Lorna Doone 1922,D 4,20:2
Koene, Rogers
Silent Command, The 1923,S 5,15:3
Koenecke, Heinz
D-Zug 13 Hat Verspaetung 1931,Ag 10,18:3
Das Ekel 1932,Ja 30,13:2
Koenekamp, H F (Cinematographer)
Midsummer Night's Dream, A 1935,O 10,31:1
Koenig, Charles
Magic Face, The 1951,O 1,19:2
Koenig, Hans H (Director)
Rape on the Moor 1957,N 21,38:1
Koenig, Hans H (Producer)
Rape on the Moor 1957,N 21,38:1
Koenig, Hans H (Screenwriter)
Rape on the Moor 1957,N 21,38:1
Koenig, Mabelle
Fighting Kentuckian, The 1949,S 19,18:3
Koenig, Mark
Pride of the Yankees, The 1942,Jl 16,23:1
Babe Ruth Story, The 1948,Jl 29,17:2
Koenigsohn, V
Miles of Fire 1958,N 10,36:6 (In Addenda)

Koeppen, Wolfgang (Screenwriter)
Glass Tower, The; (Glaserne Turm, Der)
1959,Ag 27,24:4
Koerber, Hilde
Maria, Die Magd 1937,My 22,19:2
Kreutzer Sonata, The 1938,My 28,9:3
Third Sex, The 1959,Mr 26,27:1
Koermendy, Janos
Melody of The Heart 1930,S 1,16:1
Koerner, Hermine
Secrets of a Soul 1950,S 16,12:6
Koerner, Karl
Tannenberg 1934,Ap 3,26:6
Koerner, Samson
Knock-Out 1936,F 29,11:2
Koerner, Spider John
Festival 1967,O 24,53:2
Koerpel, Jacques
War Is a Racket 1934,D 10,16:2
Koerpel, Jacques (Director)
War Is a Racket 1934,D 10,16:2
Koerpel, Jacques (Miscellaneous)
Man of Courage 1934,N 14,23:2
Koerpel, Jacques (Producer)
War Is a Racket 1934,D 10,16:2
KOGAN
See Also COGAN
Kogan, Natan
Khamishia-Five Tales From Israel
1954,My 7,19:3
Kogan, Solomon (Director)
Cinerama's Russian Adventure 1966,Ap 14,42:1
Kogio, Tonichi (Miscellaneous)
Tokyo File 212 1951,Je 1,20:7
Kogure, Michiyo
Street of Shame 1959,Je 5,17:2
Drunken Angel 1959,D 31,12:1
Taira Clan, The; Shin Heike Monogatari
1964,S 21,37:4
Koh (Screenwriter)
Don Juan 1956,Mr 6,26:2
KOHLER
See Also KOLLER, KOEHLER
Kohler, Dennis
That Night 1957,O 15,39:3
Portrait in Black 1960,Jl 28,19:1
Kohler, Don
Street with no Name, The 1948,Jl 15,26:6
You Gotta Stay Happy 1948,N 5,29:2
Kohler, Fred
Soldiers of Fortune 1919,N 24,13:1
Iron Horse, The 1924,Ag 29,6:1
Dick Turpin 1925,Ja 26,14:1
Riders of the Purple Sage 1925,Ap 15,16:1
Winds of Chance 1925,Ag 17,10:3
Ice Flood, The 1926,O 19,26:2
Way of all Flesh, The 1927,Je 27,25:2
Blood Ship, The 1927,Jl 19,27:2
Underworld 1927,Ag 22,21:3
Loves of Carmen 1927,S 27,31:1
City Gone Wild, The 1927,D 6,27:1
Gay Defender, The 1927,D 26,26:6
Showdown, The 1928,Mr 5,21:1
Drag Net, The 1928,Je 4,13:2
Forgotten Faces 1928,Ag 6,15:2
Case of Lena Smith, The 1929,Ja 15,22:4
Sal of Singapore 1929,Ja 29,27:1
Spieler, The 1929,F 25,16:1
Dummy, The 1929,Mr 4,20:2
Leatherneck, The 1929,Ap 22,23:1
Thunderbolt 1929,Je 21,17:2
Broadway Babies 1929,Je 30,VIII,3:2 (In
Addenda)
River of Romance, The 1929,Jl 29,23:3
Say It With Songs 1929,Ag 7,29:2
Hell's Heroes 1929,D 28,11:1
Roadhouse Nights 1930,F 22,13:1
Roadhouse Nights 1930,Mr 2,IX,5:1
Under a Texas Moon 1930,Ap 22:1
Light of Western Stars, The 1930,Ap 26,11:1
Lash, The 1931,Ja 1,31:3
Fighting Caravans 1931,Ja 26,21:1
Woman Hungry 1931,Mr 23,24:7
Right of Way, The 1931,Mr 24,31:2
Other Men's Women 1931,Ap 20,16:3
Soldiers Plaything, A 1931,My 2,23:4
Corsair 1931,N 19,27:5
X Marks the Spot 1931,D 7,16:1
Carnival Boat 1932,Mr 21,19:5
Deluge 1933,O 9,22:3
Last Round-Up, The 1934,My 10,25:2
Little Man, What Now? 1934,Je 1,29:1
West of the Pecos 1934,D 29,11:2
Times Square Lady 1935,Mr 15,25:3
Mississippi 1935,Ap 18,27:2
Goin' to Town 1935,My 11,21:2
Hard Rock Harrigan 1935,Jl 30,16:2
Frisco Kid 1935,N 25,22:1
Accusing Finger, The 1936,N 17,35:4
Plainsman, The 1937,Ja 14,16:2
Daughter of Shanghai 1937,D 24,21:2
Buccaneer, The 1938,F 17,17:2
Gangs of New York 1938,My 28,9:2

Kohler, Fred— Cont
Blockade 1938,Je 17,25:1
Painted Desert 1938,S 14,26:5
Why Girls Leave Home 1945,Ag 4,7:3

Kohler, Fred Jr
Corruption 1933,Je 20,22:7
Grand Old Girl 1935,F 26,16:4
Prisoner of Shark Island, The 1936,F 13,25:2
Sins of Man 1936Je 19,17:2
Pigskin Parade 1936,N 14,23:3
Holy Terror, The 1937,Ja 30,21:2
Roaring Timber 1937,Ag 19,23:1
Prison Nurse 1938,Mr 4,17:5
Young Mr Lincoln 1939,Je 3,11:2
Up in Mabel's Room 1944,Ap 22,8:6
Big Bonanza, The 1945,F 26,14:5
Baron of Arizona, The 1950,Je 23,29:2

Kohler, Walter
Affair in Trinidad 1952,Jl 31,14:2

Kohlman, Lee
Strange Case of Clara Deane, The
  1932,My 6,15:3

Kohlmar, Alphonse
Scarlet Dawn 1932,N 4,25:4

Kohlmar, Fred (Producer)
Coast Guard 1939,Ag 28,17:2
Lone Wolf Strikes, The 1940,F 5,13:2
And Now Tomorrow 1944,N 23,38:2
Bring on the Girls 1945,Mr 1,25:5
Dark Corner, The 1946,My 9,27:3
Well Groomed Bride, The 1946,My 11,22:5
Late George Apley, The 1947,Mr 21,29:2
Ghost and Mrs Muir, The 1947,Je 27,17:2
Kiss of Death 1947,Ag 28,28:2
You Were Meant for Me 1948,Ja 29,27:5
Fury at Furnace Creek 1948,Jl 12,11:2
Luck of the Irish, The 1948,S 16,34:1
That Wonderful Urge 1948,D 22,29:6
Father Was a Fullback 1949,O 13,33:3
When Willie Comes Marching Home
  1950,F 18,9:2
Love That Brute 1950,My 27,10:6
Call Me Mister 1951,F 1,21:2
U S S Teakettle 1951,F 24,11:2
Elopement 1951,D 21,21:3
Miserables, Les 1952,Ag 15,11:2
Down Among the Sheltering Palms
  1953,Je 13,11:2
It Should Happen to You 1954,Ja 16,10:5
Phffft 1954,N 11,43:2
My Sister Eileen 1955,S 23,21:1
Three Stripes in the Sun 1955,N 24,41:2
Picnic 1956,F 17,13:3
Solid Gold Cadillac, The 1956,O 25,40:3
Full of Life 1957,F 13,38:1
Pal Joey 1957,O 28,30:1
Last Angry Man, The 1959,O 23,24:1
Wackiest Ship in the Army, The 1961,F 9,36:1
Devil at 4 O'Clock, The 1961,O 19,39:3
Notorious Landlady, The 1962,Jl 27,15:2
Bye Bye Birdie 1963,Ap 5,27:3
How to Steal a Million 1966,Jl 15,34:1
Flea in her Ear, A 1968,N 28,66:1

Kohlmar, Lee
Potash and Perlmutter 1923,S 24,5:4
Kibitzer, The 1929,D 21,17:1
Tenderfoot, The 1932,My 23,18:4
Jewel Robbery 1932,Jl 23,6:6
Scarlet Dawn 1932,N 4,25:4
Silver Dollar 1932,D 23,20:1
She Done Him Wrong 1933,F 10,12:3
Son of Kong 1933,D 30,9:2
20th Century 1934,My 4,24:2
One More Spring 1935,F 22,27:1
Four Hours to Kill 1935,Ap 11,27:3
Love in Bloom 1935,Ap 20,16:2
Break of Hearts 1935,My 17,24:3
Here Comes Cookie 1935,O 12,12:2
Son Comes Home, A 1936,S 5,7:1

KOHN
See Also COEN, COHAN, COHEN

Kohn, Ben G (Original Author)
Best Man Wins 1935,Ja 2,22:4
Lady From Nowhere 1936,D 21,19:2

Kohn, Ben G (Screenwriter)
Adventure's End 1937,D 20,23:2
American Empire 1943,Ja 14,25:4

Kohn, Gabriel
Weddings and Babies 1960,O 6,51:3

Kohn, John (Producer)
Reach for Glory 1963,S 10,46:1
Collector, The 1965,Je 18,28:1
Fathom 1967,D 14,62:1
Magus, The 1968,D 11,57:1

Kohn, John (Screenwriter)
Reach for Glory 1963,S 10,46:1
Collector, The 1965,Je 18,28:1

Kohn, Rose Simon (Original Author)
Pillow to Post 1945,My 26,18:2

Kohner, Frederick (Miscellaneous)
Gidget Goes to Rome 1963,S 12,32:2

Kohner, Frederick (Original Author)
Crise est Finie, La 1935,Mr 14,18:1
Mad About Music 1938,Mr 12,13:2

It's a Date 1940,Mr 23,16:2
Johnny Doughboy 1943,My 6,25:3
Tahiti Honey 1943,My 13,17:2
Lake Placid Serenade 1944,D 25,15:6
Pan-Americana 1945,Mr 23,13:2
Bride for Sale 1949,N 21,29:4 (In Addenda)
Nancy Goes to Rio 1950,Ap 7,22:2
Hollywood Story 1951,Je 7,40:6
Never Wave at a Wac 1953,Ap 24,30:2
Toy Tiger 1956,Je 30,11:2
Gidget 1959,Ap 23,27:4

Kohner, Frederick (Screenwriter)
Sins of Man 1936Je 19,17:2
Men In her Life, The 1941,D 12,35:1
Tahiti Honey 1943,My 13,17:2
Lady and the Monster, The 1944,Ap 8,9:2
Three Daring Daughters 1948,F 13,26:3
Hollywood Story 1951,Je 7,40:6

Kohner, P (Screenwriter)
Utopia 1954,D 15,41:1

Kohner, Paul (Producer)
Next Time We Love 1936,Ja 31,16:2

Kohner, Susan
To Hell and Back 1955,S 23,21:2
Last Wagon, The 1956,S 22,20:2
Dino 1957,Je 22,9:2
Trooper Hook 1957,Jl 13,11:2
Imitation of Life 1959,Ap 18,18:1
Big Fisherman, The 1959,Ag 6,18:1
Gene Krupa Story, The 1959,D 26,7:1
All the Fine Young Cannibals 1960,S 23,33:1
By Love Possessed 1961,Jl 20,32:2
Freud 1962,D 13,37:1

Kohout, Eduard
Bohemian Rapture 1948,F 16,16:2
Distant Journey 1950,Ag 28,13:3

Koiki, Asao
Insect Woman, The; Nippon Konchuki
  1964,Jl 1,42:1

Koizumi, Hiroshi
Mothra 1962,Jl 12,19:4
Gozdilla vs the Thing 1964,N 26,52:2
Ghidrah, The Three-Headed Monster
  1965,D 16,63:3

Kojadinovic, Ugljesa
Kaya 1968,S 25,39:1

Kokler, Henry
Collegiate 1936,Ja 23,25:2

Kokovkin, B
Rimsky-Korsakov 1954,Mr 1,16:3
Big Family, A 1955,Je 6,24:1

Kokriakov, Victor
In the Name of Life 1947,O 20,29:2
Life in Bloom 1949,My 9,20:4

Kolar, Erik (Original Author)
Distant Journey 1950,Ag 28,13:3

Kolar, Erik (Screenwriter)
Distant Journey 1950,Ag 28,13:3

Kolb, Clarence
Toast of New York, The 1937,Jl 23,16:2
Portia on Trial 1937,D 3,29:2
Wells Fargo 1937,D 30,15:2
Gold Is Where You Find it 1938,F 14,20:6
Merrily We Live 1938,Mr 18,23:3
Give Me a Sailor 1938,Ag 11,31:1
Carefree 1938,S 23,35:1
Law West of Tombstone, The 1938,N 25,19:1
Honolulu 1939,F 23,19:2
I Was a Convict 1939,Mr 23,27:2
Society Lawyer 1939,Mr 31,19:2
It Could Happen to You 1939,Je 9,26:3
Good Girls Go to Paris 1939,Je 23,23:1
Our Leading Citizen 1939,Ag 24,17:1
Beware, Spooks 1939,N 3,17:4
His Girl Friday 1940,Ja 12,13:2
Amazing Mr Williams, The 1940,Ja 19,15:2
Man Who Talked too Much, The 1940,Je 29,12:2
No Time for Comedy 1940,S 7,9:2
Tugboat Annie Sails Again 1940,N 9,20:2
Michael Shayne, Private Detective
  1940,D 19,33:2
Caught in the Draft 1941,Je 26,27:3
Nothing but the Truth 1941,O 23,27:1
Night of January 16th, The 1941,N 19,35:1
You're in the Army Now 1941,D 26,21:4
Hellzapoppin 1941,D 26,21:4
Bedtime Story 1942,Mr 20,25:1
True to the Army 1942,Je 15,15:4
Falcon in Danger, The 1943,Jl 23,21:2
True to Life 1943,O 14,26:1
Standing Room Only 1944,F 23,17:2
Irish Eyes Are Smiling 1944,N 8,27:1
Something for the Boys 1944,N 30,19:1
3 Is a Family 1944,D 20,20:3
Kid From Brooklyn, The 1946,Ap 19,25:2
White Tie and Tails 1946,N 8,28:2
Lost Honeymoon 1947,Je 20,25:6
Christmas Eve 1947,N 28,30:2
Adam's Rib 1949,D 26,33:2
Man of a Thousand Faces 1957,Ag 14,21:1

Kolb, Jean
Call, The 1938,Mr 29,18:3
Whirlpool; (Remous) 1940,O 8,31:2

Kolb, John
Knockout, The 1925,O 27,23:3
Men of Steel 1926,Jl 12,24:4
Twinkletoes 1926,D 27,20:3
See You in Jail 1927,Ap 4,30:5
Lost at the Front 1927,Je 14,33:2

Kolb, Josef
Firemen's Ball, The 1968,S 30,60:1

Kolb, Therese
Appassionata 1929,Jl 8,17:3

Kolb, Wallace
If Winter Comes 1923,S 4,14:1

Kolcheff, William T (Director)
Tiara Tahiti 1963,N 6,32:1

Kolchin, V
Safety Match, The 1955,Mr 28,24:5

Kolesnikov, N
First Front, The 1949,N 14,19:2
Victors and the Vanquished, The 1950,My 1,18:2

Kolessov, L
Poet and Tsar 1938,Ag 25,15:1

Kolijamov, L (Director)
Ladies 1955,Je 27,18:2

Kolijamov, L (Screenwriter)
Ladies 1955,Je 27,18:2

Kolin, Nikolai
Edmund Kean, Prince Among Lovers
  1927,Je 1,25:2
Hurrah I'm Alive 1930,Je 16,25:3
Secrets of the Orient 1932,Ja 4,27:3
Keepers of the Night 1953,Je 9,24:2
Portrait of an Unknown Woman 1958,Ap 26,14:6

Kolitz, Zvi (Original Author)
Hill 24 Doesn't Answer 1955,N 3,37:1

Kolitz, Zvi (Producer)
Hill 24 Doesn't Answer 1955,N 3,37:1

Kolitz, Zvi (Screenwriter)
Hill 24 Doesn't Answer 1955,N 3,37:1

Kolk, Scott
Hold Your Man 1929,O 14,20:2
Marianne 1929,O 19,22:6
All Quiet on the Western Front 1930,Ap 30,29:1
For the Defense 1930,Jl 19,7:5
My Sin 1931,S 11,24:2

Kolker, Henry
How Molly Made Good 1915,O 20,5:5
Gloria's Romance 1916,My 23,9:2
Any Woman 1925,My 27,26:2
Sally, Irene and Mary 1925,D 7,19:1
Wet Paint 1926,My 17,19:1
Kiss in a Taxi, A 1927,Mr 15,29:2
Rough House Rosie 1927,My 23,27:2
Soft Living 1928,F 27,16:2
Don't Marry 1928,My 21,25:1
Coquette 1929,Ap 6,14:4 (In Addenda)
Valiant, The 1929,My 13,27:2
Pleasure Crazed 1929,Jl 15,25:1
Love, Live and Laugh 1929,N 2,14:6
Bad One, The 1930,Je 13,28:3
Good Intentions 1930,Jl 26,16:4
East Is West 1930,N 1,23:2
Du Barry, Woman of Passion 1930,N 3,19:3
Don't Bet on Women 1931,Mr 7,17:2
Indiscreet 1931,My 7,21:4
I Like Your Nerve 1931,S 12,15:4
Jewel Robbery 1932,Jl 23,6:6
Devil and the Deep 1932,Ag 20,7:4
First Year, The 1932,Ag 22,20:2
Crash, The 1932,S 9,17:5
Faithless 1932,N 19,20:2
Keyhold, The 1933,Mr 31,23:3
Bedtime Story, A 1933,Ap 20,20:3
Baby Face 1933,Je 24,16:2
Narrow Corner, The 1933,Jl 14,15:3
Power and the Glory, The 1933,Ag 17,13:2
Bureau of Missing Persons 1933,S 9,9:2
I Loved a Woman 1933,S 22,14:2
Meet the Baron 1933,O 28,20:3
Love, Honor and Oh, Baby! 1933,O 28,20:3
Wonder Bar 1934,Mr 1,23:2
Journal of a Crime 1934,Ap 28,11:3
Success at any Price 1934,My 4,24:2
Sisters Under the Skin 1934,Je 8,18:1
Hell Cat, The 1934,Jl 7,16:5
Whom the Gods Destroy 1934,Jl 13,14:2
Girl From Missouri, The 1934,Ag 4,14:6
Blind Date 1934,S 1,16:3
She Loves Me Not 1934,S 8,18:5
Million Dollar Ransom 1934,S 19,15:2
Lost Lady, A 1934,O 4,19:1
Now and Forever 1934,O 13,10:1
Lady by Choice 1934,N 17,12:1
Imitation of Life 1934,N 24,19:1
Band Plays on, The 1934,D 22,21:2
Charlie Chan in Paris 1935,Ja 22,23:2
Sing Sing Nights 1935,Ja 26,13:2
Society Doctor 1935,F 4,11:3
Red Hot Tires 1935,Mr 1,16:3
Times Square Lady 1935,Mr 15,25:3
Ghost Walks, The 1935,Mr 30,11:2
Case of the Curious Bride, The 1935,Ap 5,21:3
Florentine Dagger, The 1935,Ap 27,20:6
Mad Love 1935,Ag 5,20:2

Kolker, Henry— Cont

Diamond Jim 1935,Ag 24,18:2
Red Salute 1935,S 30,13:1
Shipmates Forever 1935,O 17,29:3
Last Days of Pompeii, The 1935,O 17,29:2
My Marriage 1936,F 22,12:2
Bullets or Ballots 1936,My 27,27:1
Romeo and Juliet 1936,Ag 21,12:2
Man Who Lived Twice, The 1936,O 12,23:2
In His Steps 1936,O 29,31:1
Theodora Goes Wild 1936,N 13,27:4
Great Guy 1937,Ja 1,19:2
Under Cover of Night 1937,Ja 20,18:4
Green Light 1937,F 13,9:1
Maid of Salem 1937,Mr 4,27:2
Let Them Live 1937,Je 8,30:3
Devil is Driving, The 1937,Jl 16,22:1
Conquest 1937,N 5,19:1
Thoroughbreds Don't Cry 1937,N 26,27:4
Invisible Menace, The 1938,F 14,20:6
Holiday 1938,Je 24,15:1
Safety in Numbers 1938,S 6,17:2
too Hot To Handle 1938,S 30,24:2
Cowboy and the Lady, The 1938,N 25,19:3
Let Us Live 1939,Mr 30,19:2
Union Pacific 1939,My 11,31:2
Hidden Power 1939,Jl 26,17:3
Real Glory, The 1939,S 15,26:2
Parents on Trial 1939,S 18,15:5
Here I Am a Stranger 1939,S 30,11:2
Main Street Lawyer 1939,N 9,27:2
Money and the Woman 1940,O 4,29:2
Las Vegas Nights 1941,Mr 20,25:2
Great Swindle, The 1941,My 14,25:4
Woman's Face, A 1941,My 16,21:2
Parson of Panamint, The 1941,Jl 26,18:2
Sing for Your Supper 1941,D 1,15:5
Sarong Girl 1943,Je 18,16:6
Adventures of Marco Polo, The 1965,Ap 8,17:2
Kolker, Henry (Director)
Disraeli 1921,Ag 22,13:6
Snow Bride, The 1923,Je 12,22:2
Purple Highway, The 1923,Jl 24,14:3 (In
Addenda)
Kolle, Walter (Miscellaneous)
Theaternaechte von Berlin 1932,Ja 11,28:5
KOLLER
See Also KOEHLER, KOHLER
Koller, Hilde
Unschuld vom Lande, Die 1935,My 13,18:6
Kollmar, Erich
Blast of Silence 1961,D 30,12:1
Kollmar, Richard
Close-Up 1948,Ap 5,24:2
Kollo, Willi (Miscellaneous)
Blonde Nachtigall, Die 1931,Ag 22,7:5
Kolm, Walter (Director)
Csardas, Ihre Tollste Nacht 1937,Je 21,15:3
Kolm-Veltee, Walter (Director)
Eroica; (The Beethoven Story) 1951,O 29,19:2
Kolofldin, N
1905 1956,Jl 9,27:2
Kologyrou, Spyros
Stefania 1968,N 29,56:1
Kolpakchi, Marina
Cinderella 1961,D 19,39:1
Kolpakor, V
Hamlet 1964,S 15,32:1
Kolpe, Max (Screenwriter)
Heartbeat 1946,My 11,22:4
Koltashnikof, V
Jimmie Higgins 1933,F 22,25:3
Koltsava, M
Springtime on the Volga 1961,D 25,27:4
Koltunov, G (Screenwriter)
Forty-First, The 1957,Je 15,10:7
Koltunov, V (Screenwriter)
Maximka 1953,O 12,30:4
Kolyov, Pavel
New Number Comes to Moscow, A
1959,Jl 6,23:1
Kolzumi, Hiroshi
Girl in the Mist 1959,D 23,22:1
Koma, Tetsu
Tokyo Joe 1949,O 27,35:2
Komack, Jimmie
Damn Yankees 1958,S 27,12:7
Hole in the Head, A 1959,Jl 16,31:2
Komai, Tetsu
Moran of the Marines 1928,O 15,16:1
Woman From Moscow, The 1928,N 5,26:1
Chinatown Nights 1929,Ap 1,22:1
East Is West 1930,N 1,23:2
Daughter of the Dragon 1931,Ag 22,7:5
She Wanted a Millionaire 1932,F 20,11:2
War Correspondent 1932,Ag 13,18:6
Island of Lost Souls 1933,Ja 13,19:2
Study in Scarlet, A 1933,Je 1,15:3
Four Frightened People 1934,Ja 27,9:2
Now and Forever 1934,O 13,10:1
Oil for the Lamps of China 1935,Je 6,25:2
Klondike Annie 1936,Mr 12,18:2
Princess Comes Across, The 1936,Je 4,27:2
China Passage 1937,Ap 16,27:2

That Man's Here Again 1937,My 6,23:3
West of Shanghai 1937,O 29,19:2
Real Glory, The 1939,S 15,26:2
Letter, The 1940,N 23,12:6
Komar, Dora
Operetta 1949,Je 6,15:4
Komar, Juliska
Okos Mama, Az 1936,Ap 13,15:2
Sarga Csiko 1937,Ja 29,15:2
Rad Bizom a Felesegem; I Entrust my Wife to
You 1939,My 6,21:3
Komissarjevsky, J (Director)
Enchanted Mirror, The 1959,Jl 22,22:1
Komissarjevsky, J (Screenwriter)
Enchanted Mirror, The 1959,Jl 22,22:1
Komissarov, N
Heroes of the Sea 1941,Ap 28,11:2
Blue Cliff, The 1943,Mr 25,25:3
Victors and the Vanquished, The 1950,My 1,18:2
Chuk and Gek 1953,D 21,27:4
Komissarov, P
Dream of a Cossack 1952,F 18,15:2
Komissarzhevsky, F (Screenwriter)
World Dances, The 1958,Je 5,39:2
Komissarzhevsky, V (Screenwriter)
Circus Stars 1960,Jl 28,19:3
Komroff, Manuel (Miscellaneous)
Scralet Empress, The 1934,S 15,20:2
Komroff, Manuel (Original Author)
Magic Bow, The 1947,Jl 7,13:2
Komuves, Sandor
Gul Baba 1940,O 26,18:8
Kon, H (Composer)
Dybbuk, The 1938,Ja 28,17:2
Konarski, C
Christmas Carol, A 1951,N 29,41:2
Kondo
Ana-Ta-Han 1954,My 18,38:2
Kondor, Ibola
Sportszerelem; Love of Sport 1938,F 14,20:8
Kondrakova, T
Gobsek 1937,Jl 16,22:1
Spring Song 1942,S 12,9:2
Kondrat, Josef
Krolowa Przedmiescia; Queen of the Market
Place 1937,D 29,17:2
Kondrat, Tadeusz
Adventure in Warsaw 1955,O 24,22:2
Kondratiev, N
Poet and Tsar 1938,Ag 25,15:1
Kondratyeva, I
Secret Brigade 1951,Mr 19,23:2
Konev, Ivan S
If Your Home Is Dear to You 1967,O 24,27:1
Kong Na
Tabu 1931,Mr 19,21:3
Konig, Wilhelm
Drei Unteroffiziere; Three Non-Coms
1939,My 20,11:3
Konigfest, J (Producer)
Lie of Nina Petrovna, The 1938,Mr 30,19:2
Konitsiotis, K (Producer)
House on Stournara Street, The 1960,O 17,33:4
Koniukhova, T
Flames on the Volga 1958,Ja 27,21:7
Kononenko, I
Heroes of Shipka 1956,S 3,10:5
Konovalov, Nikolai
Tanya 1942,Mr 5,27:1
Spring Song 1942,S 12,9:2
Marriage 1945,F 22,31:3
Ural Front, The 1945,Je 7,25:3
Spring 1948,Mr 15,26:2
Konrad, Dorothy
Sweet Bird of Youth 1962,Mr 29,28:2
Konradi, Inge
Lysistrata 1948,Je 19,19:2
Singing Angels 1952,Ja 16,21:2
Konsovsky, A
Last Night, The 1937,Ap 28,18:3
Concentration Camp 1939,Mr 20,13:2
Oppenheim Family, The 1939,My 24,29:2
Fathers and Sons 1960,D 26,27:2
Konsovsky, D
Deserter 1934,O 13,10:1
Konsta, Nina
Razzia 1948,Je 14,19:2
Konstam, Phyllis
Murder 1930,O 25,20:6
Skin Game, The 1931,Je 20,20:4
Voice of the Hurricane 1964,Je 3,36:4
Konstantin, Leopoldine
Saison in Kairo 1933,D 25,28:2
Prinzessin, Turandot 1935,Ja 16,21:2
Liebe Dumme Mama; Stupid Mama
1935,Mr 2,18:3
Frischer Wind aus Kanada 1935,S 21,18:2
Alte und der Junge Koenig, Der 1935,D 10,31:2
Notorious 1946,Ag 16,19:2
Konstantinov, Peter
My Beloved 1959,Je 15,31:4

Kontou, Maro
Antigone 1962,S 19,30:1
Konukhova, T
May Night 1953,Jl 13,22:4
Stars of the Ukraine 1953,Jl 13,22:4
Boys From Leningrad, The 1955,My 2,16:5
No Ordinary Summer 1958,O 6,36:3
Sun Shines for All 1961,Jl 10,25:3
Marriage of Baezaminov, The 1966,Je 11,20:2
Red and the White, The 1968,S 21,26:1
Konwicki, Tadeusz (Director)
Salto 1966,O 4,50:1
Konwicki, Tadeusz (Screenwriter)
Joan of the Angels? 1962,My 8,43:6
Salto 1966,O 4,50:1
Konyev, V
Clear Skies 1963,N 27,30:1
Koo, I E
Sable Cicada 1939,Ja 14,13:1
Koo, Violet
Sable Cicada 1939,Ja 14,13:1
Koomar, Asit
Objective Burma 1945,Ja 27,15:2
Koong-woon, Nam
Last Woman of Shang, The 1964,D 15,56:2
Kopalin, I (Director)
Soviet Frontiers on the Danube 1941,Je 30,13:3
Czechoslovakia 1946,Jl 15,21:1
August 14; One Day in the USSR
1948,Ag 16,12:2
Inside the U S S R 1961,N 6,46:5
Kopeck, Miles
Lemonade Joe 1967,N 21,53:1
Kopeczi, Boocz
Naszut Felaron 1937,F 13,9:2
Te Csak Pipalj Ladanyi; Keep On Smoking,
Ladanyi 1938,My 18,9:3
Kopell, Bernie
Loved One, The 1965,O 12,57:1
Kopit, Arthur L (Original Author)
Oh Dad, Poor Dad, Mamma's Hung You in the
Closet and I'm Feeling so Sad 1967,F 16,32:1
Kopp, Rudolph (Miscellaneous)
Crusades, The 1935,Ag 22,21:3
Koppenhoefer, Maria
Schlussakkord 1936,S 10,29:4
Raub der Sabinerinnen, Der 1937,Ja 16,21:1
Winter Stuerme; Winter Storms 1938,O 1,10:2
Kopta, Joseph (Original Author)
Pickup 1951,Ag 31,12:2
Korber, Hilde
Leidenschaft; Passion 1940,S 24,26:6
Desires 1954,Jl 2,10:2
Korchagina-Alexandrovskaya, E
Dom Zhadnosti 1934,Ag 13,9:6
Peasants 1935,Ag 29,25:2
Mother and Sons 1938,S 15,29:2
Korda, Alexander (Director)
Madame Wants no Children 1927,Je 21,23:3
Stolen Bride, The 1927,Ag 10,21:4
Private Life of Helen of Troy, The
1927,D 10,14:7
Modern du Barry, A 1928,Mr 19,26:2
Night Watch, The 1928,O 8,14:2
Squall, The 1929,My 10,32:5
Lilies of the Field 1930,F 22,13:1
Women Everywhere 1930,Je 23,15:1
Princess and the Plumber, The 1930,D 23,25:1
Reserved for Ladies 1932,My 21,9:2
Marius 1933,Ap 14,22:5
Dame de Chez Maxim, La; Woman at Maxim's,
The 1933,Je 11,IX,2:5
Private Life of Henry VIII, The 1933,O 13,25:2
Girl From Maxim's, The 1936,S 16,29:1
Rembrandt 1936,D 3,31:1
That Hamilton Woman 1941,Ap 4,25:1
Vacation From Marriage 1946,Mr 15,27:2
Ideal Husband, An 1948,Ja 15,28:2
Korda, Alexander (Producer)
Private Life of Don Juan, The 1934,D 10,16:2
Scarlet Pimpernel, The 1935,F 8,27:2
Sanders of the River 1935,Je 27,16:1
Ghost Goes West, The 1936,Ja 11,9:2
Things to Come 1936,Ap 18,19:2
Girl From Maxim's, The 1936,S 16,29:1
Man Who Could Work Miracles, The
1937,F 22,13:1
Knight Without Armor 1937,Jl 9,18:1
Murder on Diamond Row 1937,N 12,27:2
Storm in a Teacup 1938,Mr 22,18:4
Divorce of Lady X, The 1938,Ap 1,17:2
Drums 1938,S 30,24:4
Four Feathers 1939,Ag 4,11:1
Lion Has Wings, The 1939,N 19,X,4:1 (In
Addenda)
Lion Has Wings, The 1940,Ja 22,11:2
Thief of Bagdad, The 1940,D 6,28:2
That Hamilton Woman 1941,Ap 4,25:1
Lydia 1941,S 19,27:1
Jungle Book 1942,Ap 6,19:1
Vacation From Marriage 1946,Mr 15,27:2
Ideal Husband, An 1948,Ja 15,28:2
Anna Karenina 1948,Ap 28,32:2

Korda, Alexander (Producer) — Cont
Constant Husband, The 1955,N 7,55:1
Korda, Vincent (Director)
Challenge, The 1939,O 2,15:2
Korda, Zoltan (Director)
Sanders of the River 1935,Je 27,16:1
Elephant Boy 1937,Ap 6,20:2
Drums 1938,S 30,24:4
Four Feathers 1939,Ag 4,11:1
Jungle Book 1942,Ap 6,19:1
Sahara 1943,N 12,25:2
Counter-Attack 1945,My 17,15:2
Macomber Affair, The 1947,Ap 21,21:2
Woman's Vengeance, A 1948,Ja 30,19:2
Cry, the Beloved Country 1952,Ja 24,23:2
Storm over the Nile 1956,Je 9,14:2
Korda, Zoltan (Original Author)
Women Everywhere 1930,Je 23,15:1
Korda, Zoltan (Producer)
Woman's Vengeance, A 1948,Ja 30,19:2
Cry, the Beloved Country 1952,Ja 24,23:2
Storm over the Nile 1956,Je 9,14:2
Korda, Zoltan (Screenwriter)
Sahara 1943,N 12,25:2
Korda, Zolton (Director)
For Love or Money 1934,Jl 26,14:2
Kordium, A (Director)
Black Sea Mutiny, The 1931,Je 22,17:4
Koren, Sergei
Ballet of Romeo and Juliet, The 1956,Ap 3,31:2
Korene, Vera
Second Bureau 1936,F 17,21:2
Volga Boatman, The 1938,Ap 15,23:3
Crime in the Maginot Line 1939,My 8,21:2
Savage Brigade 1948,D 3,33:4
Korff, Arnold
Dough Boys 1930,S 30,23:1
Jazz King, The 1930,N 23,IX,6:2
Olympia 1930,D 7,IX,6:4
Royal Family of Broadway, The 1930,D 23,25:1
American Tragedy, An 1931,Ag 6,22:5
Unholy Garden, The 1931,O 29,27:1
Ambassador Bill 1931,N 14,15:3
Scarlet Dawn 1932,N 4,25:4
Evenings for Sale 1932,N 12,20:5
Secrets of the French Police 1932,D 12,18:4
Black Moon 1934,Je 28,26:2
Wings in the Dark 1935,F 2,10:1
All the King's Horses 1935,Mr 9,19:1
Shanghai 1935,Jl 20,16:2
Korjus, Miliza
Great Waltz, The 1938,N 25,19:1
Korloff, Olga
End of St Petersburg, The 1928,My 31,21:2 (In Addenda)
Korman, Harvey
Lord Love a Duck 1966,F 22,14:6
Don't Just Stand There 1968,S 3,54:2
Korn, Nikolai
Once There Was a Girl 1945,D 24,19:2
Kornapan, Adolph (Composer)
Fool, The 1925,Ap 13,24:1
Kornelia, Irma
You Never Know Women 1926,Jl 27,15:5
Campus Flirt 1926,S 22,31:1
Korner, Max (Screenwriter)
Pepote 1958,D 2,46:1
Kornfeld, Barry
Inheritance, The 1964,N 9,42:2
Kornfeld, Gail
Amateur Daddy 1932,Ap 23,11:5
Korngold, E W (Miscellaneous)
Strauss's Great Waltz 1935,Ap 8,23:3
Korngold, Erich Wolfgang (Composer)
Midsummer Night's Dream, A 1935,O 10,31:1
Give Us This Night 1936,Ap 6,18:1
Prince and the Pauper, The 1937,My 6,23:1
Another Dawn 1937,Je 18,25:3
Adventures of Robin Hood, The 1938,My 13,17:2
Juarez 1939,Ap 26,27:1
Private Lives of Elizabeth and Essex, The 1939,D 2,21:2
Kornman, Mary
Are These our Children 1931,N 14,15:3
College Humor 1933,Je 23,15:4
Quitter, The 1934,Mr 14,23:3
Calling of Dan Matthews, The 1936,Ja 25,18:4
King of the Newsboys 1938,Ap 2,18:2
Kornstein, Malka
Counsellor-At-Law 1933,D 8,31:2
Kornukov, V
Inspector General, The 1954,My 3,21:2
Korobova, K
Lenin in October 1938,Ap 2,18:1
Lenin in 1918 1939,Je 27,27:2
Korolenko, Vladimir (Original Author)
Sound of Life, The 1962,F 12,28:2
Koroleva, Guli
Childred of the Revolution 1936,Ap 6,18:2
Korolevitch, Vladimir (Director)
Killing to Live 1931,D 14,16:3
Korolkevich, Alexei
Spring Song 1942,S 12,9:2

Korolkevich, V
Tiger Girl 1955,S 5,8:2
Koromoitsef, Paul (Director)
Sunny Youth 1935,Ag 19,18:2
Korotkin, Viktor
Song Over Moscow 1964,N 23,52:1
Korov, Ivan
Specter of the Rose 1946,S 2,12:4
Korsak, Lidia
Adventure in Warsaw 1955,O 24,22:2
Korsakof, A
Nightingale 1936,N 4,41:2
Korsakpayev, K
Conquests of Peter The Great, The 1939,Ag 24,17:2
Korseck, Ilse
Stolz der 3 Kompagnie, Der 1932,Jl 21,15:2
Korsh, Vladimir (Director)
Krasnaya Derevnya 1935,My 2,17:1
Korsh-Sablin, V (Director)
Greater Promise, A 1936,O 8,27:3
Korshunov, Viktor
No Ordinary Summer 1958,O 6,36:3
Korska, Marja
Ulica 1933,Ja 27,13:2
Korte, Hans
Yesterday Girl 1967,S 22,57:2
Kortesz, D (Director)
Richthofhen: The Red Knight of the Air 1929,S 2,16:1
Kortman, Robert
Conquering Horde, The 1931,Mr 30,25:2
Twenty-Four Hours 1931,O 3,20:2
White Eagle 1932,S 24,18:4
Island of Lost Souls 1933,Ja 13,19:2
Terror Trail 1933,F 11,11:3
Sixteen Fathoms Deep 1934,Ja 19,24:3
Renegade Ranger, The 1939,F 17,17:3
Wild Harvest 1947,N 13,33:2
Copper Canyon 1950,N 16,39:2
Kortner, Fritz
Backstairs 1926,Je 4,26:2
Beethoven 1927,Mr 22,30:4
Warning Shadows 1927,Ag 10,21:4
Maria Stuart 1928,Mr 11,VIII,5:1
Primanerliebe 1928,Mr 13,23:3
Dame Care 1928,My 20,VIII,8:3
Hands of Orlac, The 1928,Je 5,21:1
Mata Hari: The Red Dancer 1928,N 12,18:2
Life of Beethoven, The 1929,Mr 12,26:3
Scandal In Paris, A 1929,Je 10,23:1
Three Loves 1929,S 9,30:2
Spy of Madame de Pompadour, The 1929,S 10,27:1
Pandora's Box 1929,D 2,28:2
Last Night, The 1930,Ja 27,18:4
Caught in Berlin's Underworld 1930,F 10,20:4
Murderer Dimitri Karamasoff, The 1931,Mr 1,VIII,6:7 (In Addenda)
Danton 1931,S 7,19:3
Karamazof 1931,S 21,20:2
Andere, Der 1932,Ja 15,24:4
Chu Chin Chow 1934,S 22,12:2
Evensong 1934,N 17,12:1
Abdul the Damned 1936,My 11,16:2
Crouching Beast, The 1936,Ag 22,6:1
Dreyfus Case, The 1940,O 30,29:3
Strange Death of Adolf Hitler, The 1943,O 9,11:5
Hitler Gang, The 1944,My 8,15:2
Wife of Monte Cristo, The 1946,Ap 8,31:2
Somewhere in the Night 1946,Je 13,24:2
Razor's Edge, The 1946,N 20,42:2
Brasher Doubloon, The 1947,My 22,34:5
Berlin Express 1948,My 21,19:3
Vicious Circle, The 1948,Jl 22,27:2
Last Illusion, The 1951,Mr 8,37:2
Kortner, Fritz (Director)
Brave Suender, Der; Upright Sinner, The 1931,N 22,VIII,6:6
Brave Suender, Der 1933,Mr 29,13:2
So ein Maedel Vergisst Man nicht 1935,S 28,12:3
City of Secrets 1963,Jl 27,10:2
Kortner, Fritz (Original Author)
Strange Death of Adolf Hitler, The 1943,O 9,11:5
Kortner, Fritz (Screenwriter)
Strange Death of Adolf Hitler, The 1943,O 9,11:5
Last Illusion, The 1951,Mr 8,37:2
City of Secrets 1963,Jl 27,10:2
Korton, Robert
Courtship of Myles Standish, The 1923,D 31,9:3
Kortwich, Werner (Director)
Friesennot 1936,O 26,20:1
Korty, Doug
Crazy Quilt, The 1966,O 4,50:1
Korty, John (Director)
Crazy Quilt, The 1966,O 4,50:1
Funnyman 1967,S 25,56:3
Korty, John (Producer)
Crazy Quilt, The 1966,O 4,50:1
Korty, John (Screenwriter)
Crazy Quilt, The 1966,O 4,50:1
Funnyman 1967,S 25,56:3

Korvin, Charles
Enter Arsene Lupin 1944,D 2,17:6
This Love of Ours 1945,N 1,20:2
Temptation 1946,D 25,33:6
Berlin Express 1948,My 21,19:3
Killer That Stalked New York, The 1951,Ja 5,17:2
Lydia Bailey 1952,My 31,12:5
Sangaree 1953,Je 5,19:1
Ship of Fools 1965,Jl 29,18:1
Korvin-Krukovsky, J V
Golden Mountains 1932,Ap 14,25:3
Kosary, Emmy
Okos Mama, Az 1936,Ap 13,15:2
Varju a Toronyoran; Crow on the Tower 1939,N 18,22:6
Koscina, Sylva
Guendalina 1958,Je 30,23:2
Hercules 1959,Jl 23,32:2
Michael Strogoff 1960,My 21,15:1
Hercules Unchained 1960,Jl 14,23:1
Mighty Crusaders, The 1961,S 23,17:1
Siege of Syracuse, The 1962,Ag 9,17:8
Swordsman of Siena 1962,D 6,55:3
Three Fables of Love (The Tortoise and the Hare); Tortoise and the Hare, The (Three Fables of Love) 1963,Ag 21,38:1
Cyrano and D'Artagnan 1964,S 26,16:1
Let's Talk About Women 1964,S 29,52:5
Agent 8 3/4 1965,O 14,53:1
Railroad Man, The; Ferroviere, Il 1965,O 25,46:2
Juliet of the Spirits 1965,N 4,57:1
Judex 1966,Ap 26,55:1
Little Nuns, The 1966,Ap 28,49:1
That Man in Istanbul 1966,My 19,51:2
Love and Marriage (Saturday, July 18); Saturday, July 18 (Love and Marriage) 1966,Ag 5,20:1
Deadlier Than the Male 1967,F 22,21:1
Made in Italy 1967,My 1,44:2
Three Bites of the Apple 1967,My 25,54:2
Secret War of Harry Frigg, The 1968,Mr 5,34:5
Lovely Way to Die, A 1968,Jl 13,18:1
Koselka, Fritz (Original Author)
Forbidden Music 1938,D 27,13:2
Koshetz, Alexander (Composer)
Marusia 1938,D 12,26:2
Koshetz, Marina
Holiday in Mexico 1946,Ag 16,19:3
No Leave, No Love 1946,O 18,29:2
Luxury Liner 1948,S 10,19:2
On the Riviera 1951,My 24,47:1
Koshetz, Nina
Algiers 1938,Jl 15,13:2
Our Hearts Were Young and Gay 1944,O 12,24:2
Chase, The 1946,N 18,31:2
Hot Blood 1956,Mr 24,14:2
Kosheverova, N (Director)
Tiger Girl 1955,S 5,8:2
Koshevsky, K
Jimmie Higgins 1933,F 22,25:3
Koshiwa, Hideko
Escapde in Japan 1957,D 24,11:1
Koshkina, Nadya
In the Far East 1937,O 20,27:3
Kosikh, Vitya
Welcome Kostya! 1965,N 22,48:2
Kosleck, Martin
Nurse Edith Cavell 1939,S 22,27:4
Nick Carter, Master Detective 1939,D 14,35:2
Calling Philo Vance 1940,F 9,15:3
Foreign Correspondent 1940,Ag 28,15:2
Mad Doctor, The 1941,F 27,23:4
Underground 1941,Je 23,13:2
International Lady 1941,N 11,29:2
All Through the Night 1942,Ja 24,13:2
Nazi Agent 1942,Je 13,11:2
Berlin Correspondent 1942,S 4,19:2
Manila Calling 1942,S 28,13:1
Chetniks 1943,Mr 19,15:3
Bomber's Moon 1943,Jl 31,8:2
North Star, The 1943,N 5,23:1
Hitler Gang, The 1944,My 8,15:2
Mummy's Curse, The 1945,Mr 31,16:1
Frozen Ghost, The 1945,Jl 28,7:3
Strange Holiday 1945,O 20,8:2
Pursuit to Algiers 1945,O 27,12:2
House of Horrors 1946,F 23,20:3
She Wolf of London 1946,Ap 6,10:6
Wife of Monte Cristo, The 1946,Ap 8,31:2
Spider, The 1946,Je 21,20:3
Something Wild 1961,D 24,30:6
Agent for H.A.R.M 1966,Ja 6,20:2
Kosloff, Maurice (Producer)
Hoodlum, The 1951,Jl 6,14:6
Kosloff, Theodore
Woman God Forgot, The 1917,O 29,11:2
Why Change Your Wife 1920,Ap 26,18:1
City of Masks, The 1920,Jl 12,12:4
Forbidden Fruit 1921,Ja 24,16:2
Affairs of Anatol, The 1921,S 12,16:1
Fool's Paradise 1921,D 10,11:4
Lane That had no Turning, The 1922,Ja 9,15:2
Green Temptation, The 1922,Mr 20,10:3

Kosloff, Theodore — Cont
Dictator, The 1922,Jl 3,8:6
To Have and to Hold 1922,N 6,13:1
Law of the Lawless, The 1923,Je 19,22:4
Children of Jazz 1923,Jl 9,8:4
Don't Call it Love 1923,D 25,26:1
Triumph 1924,Ap 21,21:4
Feet of Clay 1924,S 22,16:1
Golden Bed, The 1925,Ja 20,18:2
New Lives for Old 1925,F 25,16:7
Beggar on Horseback 1925,Je 6,9:2
Volga Boatman, The 1926,Ap 14,21:1
King of Kings, The 1927,Ap 20,29:2

Kosma, Jerome (Composer)
Grand Illusion 1938,S 13,28:2

Kosma, Joseph (Composer)
Enfants du Paradis, Les 1947,F 20,32:2

Kosopoulos, Thanos
Shepherd's Daughter, The 1956,My 14,23:3

Kossak, Franz Jan
Soldaten-Kameraden 1936,O 5,25:1

Kosslyn, Jack
Amazing Colossal Man, The 1957,O 26,19:2

Kossoff, David
Chance Meeting 1955,Ap 20,38:1
Svengali 1955,S 26,18:2
Kid for two Farthings, A 1956,Ap 18,25:1
1984 1956,O 1,31:1
Bespoke Overcoat, The 1956,O 8,31:1
Iron Petticoat, The 1957,F 2,12:2
Triple Deception 1957,O 7,23:2
Count Five and Die 1958,My 15,25:1
Indiscreet 1958,Je 27,18:2
Journey, The 1959,F 20,19:1
Mouse That Roared, The 1959,O 27,40:1
House of the Seven Hawks, The 1959,D 17,51:2
Conspiracy of Hearts 1960,Ap 8,24:1
House of Fright 1961,Ag 24,25:4
Freud 1962,D 13,37:1
Mouse on the Moon, The 1963,Je 18,32:1
Ring of Treason 1964,My 28,40:3 (Incorrect in
this edition; use 1964,My 29,15:1 elsewhere)

Kostandaras, Stavros
Madame X 1960,O 3,34:5

Kostant, Anna
Street Scene 1931,Ag 27,22:5

Kostecki, Jozef
Eroica (Second Episode) 1966,F 2,24:1

Kostelanetz, Andre
Artists and Models 1937,Ag 5,19:2

Kostenka, Andrzei (Screenwriter)
Depart, Le 1967,S 23,20:3

KOSTER
See Also COSTER

Koster, Henry (Director)
Three Smart Girls 1937,Ja 25,22:2
100 Men and a Girl 1937,S 18,15:2
Affairs of Maupassant, The 1938,F 12,20:2
Rage of Paris 1938,Jl 2,10:2
Three Smart Girls Grow Up 1939,Mr 18,9:2
First Love 1939,N 9,27:3
Spring Parade 1940,O 4,29:2
It Started With Eve 1941,O 3,27:1
Between Us Girls 1942,S 25,25:3
Music for Millions 1944,D 22,12:4
Two Sisters From Boston 1946,Je 7,16:2
Unfinished Dance, The 1947,O 31,29:2
Bishop's Wife, The 1947,D 10,44:2
Luck of the Irish, The 1948,S 16,34:1
Come to the Stable 1949,Jl 28,19:1
Inspector General, The 1949,D 31,9:2
Wabash Avenue 1950,Ap 29,8:3
My Blue Heaven 1950,S 16,12:6
Harvey 1950,D 22,19:1
Mr Belvedere Rings the Bell 1951,Ag 2,18:1
No Highway in the Sky 1951,S 22,8:6
Elopement 1951,D 21,21:3
O Henry's Full House (The Gift of the Magi); Gift
of the Magi, The (O Henry's Full House)
1952,O 17,33:1
O Henry's Full House (The Clarion Call); Clarion
Call, The (O Henry's Full House)
1952,O 17,33:1
O Henry's Full House (The Last Leaf
1952,O 17,33:1
O Henry's Full House (The Cop and the Anthem);
Cop and the Anthem, The (O Henry's Full
House) 1952,O 17,33:1
Stars and Stripes Forever 1952,D 23,17:2
My Cousin Rachel 1952,D 26,20:2
Robe, The 1953,S 17,32:6
Desiree 1954,N 18,42:1
Man Called Peter, A 1955,Ap 1,22:1
Virgin Queen, The 1955,Ag 6,13:2
Good Morning, Miss Dove 1955,N 24,41:1
D-Day, The Sixth of June 1956,My 30,13:1
Power and The Prize, the 1956,S 27,42:1
My Man Godfrey 1957,O 12,23:1
Fraulein 1958,Je 9,27:2
Naked Maja, The 1959,Je 11,36:2
Flower Drum Song 1961,N 10,40:1
Mr Hobbs Takes a Vacation 1962,Je 16,11:2
Take Her, She's Mine 1963,N 14,41:1
Dear Brigitte 1965,Ja 28,20:1

Singing Nun, The 1966,Mr 18,33:1

Koster, Henry (Producer)
Between Us Girls 1942,S 25,25:3
Take Her, She's Mine 1963,N 14,41:1
Dear Brigitte 1965,Ja 28,20:1

Koster, Nicholas
My Cousin Rachel 1952,D 26,20:2
Desiree 1954,N 18,42:1

Kosterlitz, Henry (Screenwriter)
Moscow Nights 1938,My 3,19:3

Kosterlitz, Hermann (Director)
Storch Hat Uns Getraut, Der 1933,D 1,23:2
Die Privatsekretaerin Heiratet 1936,D 5,16:4

Kosterlitz, Hermann (Screenwriter)
Wer Nimmt die Liebe Ernst; Who Takes Love
Seriously 1931,D 27,VIII,7:1
Fuenf von der Jazzband; Five of the Jazzband
1932,My 15,VIII,4:4 (In Addenda)

Kostic, Aleksandor Dr
Affair of the Heart, An 1967,S 23,20:3

Kostritchkin, A
Cities and Years 1931,Ap 4,23:1
Conquerors of the Night 1933,Jl 31,16:3
Enemies of Progress 1934,Ja 11,19:2

Kosugi, Yoshio
Madame Butterfly 1956,Ap 24,26:2

Kotarz, Henry (Original Author)
Great British Train Robbery, The 1967,Ap 6,45:2

Kotarz, Henry (Screenwriter)
Great British Train Robbery, The 1967,Ap 6,45:2

Kotcheff, Ted (Director)
Life at the Top 1965,D 15,53:1

Kotsiubinsky, Michalo (Original Author)
Shadows of our Forgotten Ancestors
1966,S 20,39:1
Shadows of Forgotten Ancestors 1967,Mr 17,35:3

Kotsonaros, George
Tender Hour, The 1927,Je 7,27:4
Wizard, The 1927,N 28,18:5
Private Life of Helen of Troy, The
1927,D 10,14:7
Fifty-Fifty Girl, The 1928,My 14,25:1
Street of Sin, The 1928,My 28,23:2
Beggars of Life 1928,S 24,25:1
Shakedown, The 1929,Ap 8,32:1
Dangerous Paradise 1930,F 16,III,8:1
Honeymoon Lane 1931,Ag 1,16:4

Kotthaus, Eva
Sky Without Stars 1959,My 30,9:2

Kotto, Yaphet
Thomas Crown Affair, The 1968,Je 27,48:2

Koubitzky, Alexandre
Napoleon 1929,F 12,23:1

Kougoucheff, Prince
Michael Strogoff 1926,D 6,28:3

Kouka, Princess
Dark Sands 1938,Ag 17,23:4

Koulak, Pierre
Birds in Peru 1968,N 7,51:2

Kouprine, Alexander (Original Author)
Sorciere, La 1956,D 28,17:2

Kouprine, Kissa
Club De Femmes 1937,O 20,27:2

Kourkoulos, Nikos
Casablan 1964,D 14,50:1

Kournakoff, Sergei (Narrator)
1812 1944,S 11,14:1

Kourtis, Costas
Red Lanterns 1965,Ap 1,30:1

Kovack, Nancy
Strangers When we Meet 1960,Je 30,22:2
Diary of a Madman 1963,Je 6,39:1
Jason and the Argonauts 1963,Ag 8,19:1
Sylvia 1965,F 11,45:1
Silencers, The 1966,Mr 17,35:1
Frankie and Johnny 1966,Jl 21,20:2
Tarzan and the Valley of Gold 1967,Mr 30,55:1
Enter Laughing 1967,Ag 1,24:1

Kovacs, Bela
Park Row 1952,D 22,20:2

Kovacs, Ernie
Operation Mad Ball 1957,N 21,38:1
Bell, Book and Candle 1958,D 27,2:7
It Happened to Jane 1959,Ag 6,18:3
Our Man in Havana 1960,Ja 28,26:1
Wake Me When It's Over 1960,Ap 9,17:2
Strangers When we Meet 1960,Je 30,22:2
North to Alaska 1960,N 11,36:1
Pepe 1960,D 22,18:1
Five Golden Hours 1961,O 19,39:3
Sail a Crooked Ship 1962,F 3,12:6

Kovaichuk, Lyova
Flying Carpet, The 1960,F 28,31:1

Koval-Samborsky, I
Men on Wings 1935,Je 11,24:5
Concentration Camp 1939,Mr 20,13:2

Kovalesky, D (Composer)
Petersburg Nights 1934,S 10,20:4

Kovaleva, M
Fall of Berlin 1952,Je 9,19:2

Kovanka, Natalie
Michael Strogoff 1926,D 6,28:3
Tales of 1,001 Nights 1927,Ja 24,14:1

Kovarof, S
Patrioty 1933,S 25,18:5

Kovarsky, N (Screenwriter)
1905 1956,Jl 9,27:2
Malva 1957,D 23,18:2
Captain's Daughter, The 1959,N 23,41:3

Kovatchevitch
Amours de Toni, Les 1936,N 5,35:1

Kove, Kenneth
Blame the Woman 1932,O 25,24:5

Kovenberg, J K
Laughter Through Tears 1933,N 13,21:2

Kovrigin, V
Sibirsky Patrul 1932,My 14,11:5
Men and Jobs 1933,Ja 3,19:3
Twenty-Six Commissars 1933,Jl 1,16:6
Deserter 1934,O 13,10:1
Admiral Nakhimov 1948,N 25,47:4

Kovrov, G
Red and White 1932,N 29,23:5
Ural Front, The 1945,Je 7,25:3
Poem of the Sea 1959,D 21,34:4

Kowa, Viktor de
Mein Leben fuer Maria Isabell; My Life for Maria
Isabell 1935,N 5,33:5
Divine Jetta, The 1937,O 2,18:2
Promise Me Nothing 1937,N 13,11:3

Kowakami, Yaguko
Street of Shame 1959,Je 5,17:2

Kowal, Mitchell
Violated 1953,D 12,23:8
Guests are Coming; Jada Goscie Jada
1967,Ja 13,15:1

Kowalski, Wladyslaw
Love at Twenty 1963,F 7,5:6

Koyama, Genki
Beach Red 1967,Ag 4,18:1

Koyama, Shigeru
Rebellion 1968,O 26,27:4

Koyama, Sugisako
Ugetsu 1954,S 8,40:3

Koyo, Ozaki (Original Author)
Golden Demon 1956,Ja 31,34:3

Kozak, Andrzej
Five From Barska Street 1955,Mr 14,29:4

Kozakov, Mikhail
Red and the White, The 1968,S 21,26:1

Kozhamkulov, Serke
Amangeldy 1939,Je 16,27:4

Kozinsky, Maurice (Producer)
Gangs Incorporated 1941,Ag 4,16:6

Kozintsev, Gregory (Director)
New Babylon, The 1929,D 2,28:2
Alone 1932,My 25,23:6
Youth of Maxim, The 1935,Ap 20,16:1
Return of Maxim, The 1937,N 2,33:1
New Horizons 1939,My 12,25:3
Don Quixote 1961,Ja 21,18:1
Hamlet 1964,S 15,32:1
Hamlet 1966,Mr 16,48:1

Kozintsev, Gregory (Screenwriter)
Youth of Maxim, The 1935,Ap 20,16:1
Return of Maxim, The 1937,N 2,33:1
New Horizons 1939,My 12,25:3
Hamlet 1964,S 15,32:1
Hamlet 1966,Mr 16,48:1

Kozintsev Gregory (Producer)
Don Quixote 1961,Ja 21,18:1

Kozlenko, William (Original Author)
Holiday in Mexico 1946,Ag 16,19:3
Raw Edge 1956,Jl 28,10:7
Dance With Me Henry 1956,D 24,8:2

Kozlovsky, I
Boris Godunov 1956,Ja 23,21:4

Kozlovsky, M
Pozor 1933,Mr 11,18:4

Kozminski, S P
Lenin in 1918 1939,Je 27,27:2

Kozniewski, Kazimierz (Screenwriter)
Five From Barska Street 1955,Mr 14,29:4

Kozomara, Liubisa (Screenwriter)
Feverish Years, The 1967,S 22,57:2

Kraa, Tom
Eternal Mask, The 1937,Ja 13,20:3

Kraemer, F W (Director)
Dreyfus Case, The 1931,Ag 31,11:5

Kraerulff-Schmidt, Palle (Director)
Weekend 1964,Ap 27,24:1

Krafft, John W (Screenwriter)
Million Dollar Baby 1935,My 6,22:3
Missing Girls 1936,O 5,25:1
House of Secrets 1937,F 22,13:1
Thirteenth Man, The 1938,Ja 1,11:2

KRAFT
See Also CRAFT

Kraft, Beatrice
Rains of Ranchipur, The 1955,D 16,38:2

Kraft, H S (Original Author)
Champagne Waltz 1937,F 4,17:2

Kraft, H S (Screenwriter)
Stormy Weather 1943,Jl 22,15:1

Kraftschenko, Valerie
Flames on the Volga 1929,Ap 2,28:4
Krah, Marc
Riff-Raff 1947,Je 30,25:7
Intrigue 1948,Ap 24,11:2
Criss Cross 1949,Mr 12,10:2
Black Hand 1950,Mr 13,15:2
Krahl, Hilde
April 1, 2000 1954,F 17,27:2
Eternal Waltz, The; (Ewiger Walzer)
1959,Jl 9,22:1
Krahn, Maria
Maedchenraeuber 1936,Ag 15,6:3
Stuetzen der Gesellschaft 1936,N 7,15:3
August der Starke 1937,Ja 30,21:3
Krach und Glueckum Kuennemann; Row and Joy
About Kuennemann 1938,S 17,20:3
Hummel-Hummel 1939,Mr 11,21:2
Krahn, Martha
Mutige Seefahrer, Der 1936,N 21,21:5
Kraike, Michel (Original Author)
Twice Blessed 1945,Jl 7,7:5
Kraike, Michel (Producer)
Fighting Guardsman, The 1945,O 6,9:6
Renegades 1946,Jl 11,18:2
Criss Cross 1949,Mr 12,10:2
Lady Gambles, The 1949,My 21,9:2
Judge Steps Out, The 1949,Je 3,21:4
South Sea Sinner 1950,Ja 16,18:4
Woman in Hiding 1950,F 23,33:2
Sierra 1950,S 15,31:2
Frenchie 1951,F 12,19:2
Bedtime for Bonzo 1951,Ap 6,31:4
Thunder on the Hill 1951,O 18,32:3
Kraly, Hans (Original Author)
Kiss Me Again 1925,Ag 3,10:1
Broadway Gondolier 1935,Jl 18,15:2
100 Men and a Girl 1937,S 18,15:2
Broadway Serenade 1939,Ap 7,25:2
It Started With Eve 1941,O 3,27:1
Kraly, Hans (Screenwriter)
Three Women 1924,O 6,25:1
Her Night of Romance 1925,Ja 13,16:1
Fortune's Fool 1928,Ag 13,23:2
100 Men and a Girl 1937,S 18,15:2
West Point Widow 1941,S 11,21:5
Mad Ghoul, The 1943,D 11,11:2
Kraly, John (Original Author)
Red Peacock, The 1922,Ap 3,18:2
Kramer, Allen
Stakeout on Dope Street 1958,Ap 24,38:1
Kramer, Billy J
Go Go Mania 1965,My 20,52:4
Kramer, Cecile (Screenwriter)
Silver Queen 1943,Ja 11,18:4
Buffalo Bill 1944,Ap 20,22:6
Ramrod 1947,Je 30,25:6
Kramer, Glen
Pillars of the Sky 1956,O 13,15:2
Kramer, Hope
I Was a Communist for the F B I 1951,My 3,34:4
Kramer, Ida
Abie's Irish Rose 1928,Ap 20,26:7
Kramer, John
Windflowers 1968,F 23,43:1
Kramer, Karl
Sunderin 1954,D 24,7:2
Kramer, Leopold
Hungarian Rhapsody 1929,Ag 5,25:2
Ecstasy 1940,D 25,33:2
Kramer, Marie
Lysistrata 1948,Je 19,19:2
Kramer, Robert (Director)
Edge, The 1968,Mr 28,52:1
Kramer, Robert (Producer)
Edge, The 1968,Mr 28,52:1
Kramer, Robert (Screenwriter)
Edge, The 1968,Mr 28,52:1
Kramer, Searle (Screenwriter)
Mr Universe 1951,Mr 23,16:2
Kramer, Stanley (Director)
Not as a Stranger 1955,Je 29,24:1
Pride and the Passion, The 1957,Je 29,10:6
Defiant Ones, The 1958,S 25,29:1
On the Beach 1959,D 18,34:1
Inherit the Wind 1960,O 13,41:1
Judgment at Nuremberg 1961,D 20,36:1
It's a Mad, Mad, Mad, Mad World
1963,N 19,47:1
Ship of Fools 1965,Jl 29,18:1
Guess Who's Coming to Dinner 1967,D 12,56:1
Kramer, Stanley (Producer)
Champion 1949,Ap 11,29:2
Home of the Brave 1949,My 13,29:1
Men, The 1950,Jl 21,15:2
Cyrano De Bergerac 1950,N 17,31:2
Sniper, The 1952,My 10,16:3
High Noon 1952,Jl 25,14:2
Eight Iron Men 1953,Ja 2,11:1
Caine Mutiny, The 1954,Je 25,17:1
Not as a Stranger 1955,Je 29,24:1
Pride and the Passion, The 1957,Je 29,10:6
Defiant Ones, The 1958,S 25,29:1

On the Beach 1959,D 18,34:1
Inherit the Wind 1960,O 13,41:1
Judgment at Nuremberg 1961,D 20,36:1
Pressure Point 1962,O 11,49:3
Child Is Waiting, A 1963,F 14,5:6
It's a Mad, Mad, Mad, Mad World
1963,N 19,47:1
Ship of Fools 1965,Jl 29,18:1
Guess Who's Coming to Dinner 1967,D 12,56:1
Kramer, Walter
Son of a Sailor 1933,N 30,38:4
Kramer, Wright
Professor Beware 1938,Jl 14,17:1
Gladiator, The 1938,Ag 29,10:2
Anne of Windy Poplars 1940,Ag 23,13:3
Dark Streets of Cairo 1940,D 2,19:3
Kramera, Edythe
Under a Texas Moon 1930,Ap 4,22:1
Kramm, Joseph (Original Author)
Shrike, The 1955,Jl 8,15:2
Kramow, A
Prisoners of the Sea 1929,Ap 16,32:5
Kranicz, Mieczyslaw (Director)
Sluby Ulanskie; Love in the Army 1935,F 22,27:3
Kransnovitsky, V
Heroes Are Made 1944,Mr 11,10:2
Krantz, Lasse
Frustration 1949,Ag 27,7:3
Kranz, Jack
Kid Galahad 1937,My 27,21:3
Krashenikov, G
Forty-Nine Days 1964,Ja 27,19:1
Kraska, George (Miscellaneous)
Masquerade in Vienna 1937,Ja 26,16:4
Krasket, Harold
Mouse That Roared, The 1959,O 27,40:1
Krasna, Maria
Confess, Dr Corda 1960,O 24,25:5
Krasna, Norman (Director)
Princess O'Rourke 1943,N 6,16:2
Big Hangover, The 1950,My 26,20:3
Ambassador's Daughter, The 1956,Ag 30,19:1
Krasna, Norman (Miscellaneous)
Dear Wife 1950,F 2,31:2
Krasna, Norman (Original Author)
So This Is Africa! 1933,Ap 24,11:3
Meet the Baron 1933,O 28,20:3
Richest Girl in the World, The 1934,S 21,29:2
Romance in Manhattan 1935,Ja 18,29:2
Four Hours to Kill 1935,Ap 11,27:3
Fury 1936,Je 6,21:1
As Good as Married 1937,My 22,19:2
Big City 1937,S 17,29:2
First 100 Years, The 1938,My 13,17:2
You and Me 1938,Je 2,19:1
Mr and Mrs Smith 1941,F 21,16:3
Princess O'Rourke 1943,N 6,16:2
Dear Ruth 1947,Je 11,33:3
John Loves Mary 1949,F 5,11:2
Indiscreet 1958,Je 27,18:2
Who Was That Lady? 1960,Ap 16,10:1
Sunday in New York 1964,F 12,30:2
Krasna, Norman (Producer)
Big City 1937,S 17,29:2
First 100 Years, The 1938,My 13,17:2
Three Loves Has Nancy 1938,S 2,21:2
Big Hangover, The 1950,My 26,20:3
Blue Veil, The 1951,O 27,10:5
Behave Yourself 1951,N 8,35:2
Ambassador's Daughter, The 1956,Ag 30,19:1
Who Was That Lady? 1960,Ap 16,10:1
Krasna, Norman (Screenwriter)
Hollywood Speaks 1932,Ag 12,18:2
Four Hours to Kill 1935,Ap 11,27:3
Hands Across the Table 1935,N 2,13:2
Wife vs Secretary 1936,F 29,11:1
King and the Chorus Girl, The 1937,Mr 29,14:4
Bachelor Mother 1939,Je 30,17:2
It's a Date 1940,Mr 23,16:2
Mr and Mrs Smith 1941,F 21,16:3
Flame of New Orleans, The 1941,Ap 26,20:2
Devil and Miss Jones, The 1941,My 16,21:2
It Started With Eve 1941,O 3,27:1
Practically Yours 1945,Mr 29,18:2
Big Hangover, The 1950,My 26,20:3
White Christmas 1954,O 15,16:3
Ambassador's Daughter, The 1956,Ag 30,19:1
Bundle of Joy 1956,D 20,36:1
Indiscreet 1958,Je 27,18:2
Who Was That Lady? 1960,Ap 16,10:1
Let's Make Love 1960,S 9,36:1
My Geisha 1962,Je 14,23:2
Sunday in New York 1964,F 12,30:2
I'd Rather Be Rich 1964,S 3,24:2
Krasne, Philip N (Producer)
Sarong Girl 1943,Je 18,16:6
Boy Cried Murder, The 1966,Ap 14,42:3
Krasner, David (Original Author)
I Loved a Woman 1933,S 22,14:2
Krassina, Olga
Queen of Spades 1961,S 4,10:1

Krassnitzer, Hans
Eroica; (The Beethoven Story) 1951,O 29,19:2
Kraus, Peter
Flying Classroom, The 1958,Je 28,13:7
Krause, Dieter
Man Between, The 1953,N 19,41:2
Krause, Gertrude
Motel, The Operator 1940,Ja 16,19:3
Krause, Willy
Last ten Days, The 1956,Ap 12,26:1
Krauss, Henry
Pathetic Symphony 1928,D 16,IX,8:2
Miserables, Les 1936,O 28,31:2
Krauss, Werner
Cabinet of Dr Caligari, The 1921,Mr 20,VI,2:1
Cabinet of Dr Caligari, The 1921,Ap 4,18:1
All for a Woman 1921,D 5,20:1
Shattered 1921,D 11,VI,3:1 (In Addenda)
Othello 1923,F 26,15:1
Three Way Works, The 1926,Mr 19,25:1
Shattered 1926,Ap 30,17:2
Secrets of the Soul 1927,Ap 25,20:4
Streets of Sorrow 1927,Jl 6,23:2
Tartuffe 1927,Jl 21,25:3
Nana 1928,Ja 22,VIII,7:7
Midsummer Night's Dream 1928,Ja 31,29:1
Decameron Nights 1928,My 29,17:2
Jealousy 1928,D 4,29:1
Man Who Cheated Life, The 1929,F 11,26:3
Looping the Loop 1929,F 11,26:3
Jolly Peasant, The 1929,Jl 1,31:2
Nana 1929,Jl 30,19:4
Royal Scandal, A 1929,S 23,24:3
Yorck 1932,Ja 31,6:1
Mensch Ohne Namen 1932,N 7,20:3
Yorck 1932,N 24,35:2
Crown of Thorns 1934,Mr 28,27:6
Vienna Burgtheater 1937,O 27,47:1
Robert Koch 1939,N 25,13:2
Kraussneck, Arthur
At the Grey House 1927,N 8,33:1
Luther 1929,Je 24,27:1
Krausz, Michael (Composer)
Lindenwirtin vom Rhein, Die 1931,S 25,28:7
Kravchenko, Galina
Island of Doom 1933,Jl 17,9:5
Kravelshvili, V
Keto and Kote 1954,Ap 5,21:4
Krawford, Kathryn
Hide Out 1930,Ap 12,23:1
Krawicz, M (Director)
Kazdemu Wolno Kochac 1933,My 24,24:3
Milosc Wszystko Zwycieza 1936,Ja 28,15:3
Jego Wielka Milosc 1936,Mr 24,27:5
Niedorajda; Good for Nothing 1937,D 27,11:2
Dyplomatyczna Zona 1938,O 24,13:2
Krech, Warren
Town That Forgot God, The 1922,N 1,16:3
Kreczmar, Jan
Passenger 1964,S 21,37:3
Kreig, Frank
No Minor Vices 1949,F 26,11:2
Kreisler, Fritz (Miscellaneous)
King Steps Out, The 1936,My 29,15:2
Kreisova, Jirinka
Bohemian Rapture 1948,F 16,16:2
Kreitsek, Howard (Producer)
Mister Rock and Roll 1957,O 17,42:2
Krejca, Otomar
Distant Journey 1950,Ag 28,13:3
Krellberg, Sherman S (Producer)
Lost City, The 1935,F 21,23:3
Kremer, Theodore (Original Author)
Bertha, The Sewing Machine Girl 1927,Ja 4,21:1
Krepkogorskaya, Maria
Bountiful Summer 1951,D 24,9:1
Kreps, V (Screenwriter)
Frigid Sea, The 1955,N 21,23:4
Kres, Hans
Rosenkavalier, Der 1962,O 10,57:1
Kresadlova, Vera
Intimate Lighting 1966,S 19,57:1
Kresel, Lee
Black Magic 1949,N 9,37:2
Kress, Harold F (Director)
No Questions Asked 1951,Ag 10,13:2
Kressyn, Miriam
Purimspieler, Der 1937,D 6,19:2
Kreuder, Peter (Composer)
Vienna Burgtheater 1937,O 27,47:1
Kreuger, Kurt
Moon Is Down, The 1943,Mr 27,8:6
Strange Death of Adolf Hitler, The 1943,O 9,11:5
Sahara 1943,N 12,25:2
None Shall Escape 1944,Ap 7,23:2
Hotel Berlin 1945,Mr 3,11:2
Escape in the Desert 1945,My 12,10:2
Paris Underground 1945,O 20,8:2
Sentimental Journey 1946,Mr 7,33:2
Dark Corner, The 1946,My 9,27:3
Spider, The 1946,Je 21,20:3
Unfaithfully Yours 1948,N 6,9:2
Spy Hunt 1950,S 8,25:2

Kreuger, Kurt — Cont
Enemy Below, The 1957,D 26,23:2
Legion of the Doomed 1959,Mr 12,27:5
Kreutzer, Guido (Screenwriter)
Hungarian Nights 1930,Je 10,32:2
Krevalid, A
Hamlet 1966,Mr 16,48:1
Krevata, Marika
Trouble for Father 1958,Ja 6,26:4
Policeman of the 16th Precinct, The
1963,Ap 22,23:2
Kreysler, Dorit
Freut Euch des Lebens 1934,N 3,20:3
Jungfrau Gegen Moench; Maiden vs Monk
1935,Mr 16,19:2
Frischer Wind aus Kanada 1935,S 21,18:2
Herr Kobin Geht auf Abenteuer; Mr Kobin Seeks
Adventure 1935,N 26,28:2
Nacht an der Donau, Eine; Night on the Danube,
A 1938,N 19,9:3
Fledermaus, Die; Bat, The 1948,Mr 15,26:2
Vienna Blood 1951,F 22,27:4
Cabaret 1957,N 9,31:2 (Incorrect in this edition;
use 1957,N 7,43:4 elsewhere)
KRIEGER
See Also KRUEGER
Krieger, E (Narrator)
Lenin 1950,Mr 13,15:2
Krieger, E (Screenwriter)
Lenin 1950,Mr 13,15:2
American Farmers Visit Russia 1955,N 3,37:1
Kries, Tom (Director)
Will Penny 1968,Ap 11,51:2
Kries, Tom (Screenwriter)
Will Penny 1968,Ap 11,51:2
Krietsek, Howard B (Producer)
Teenage Millionaire 1962,Ja 12,29:2
Krilov, S
Thirteen, The 1937,Je 19,20:2
City of Youth 1938,S 5,30:4
Soviet Border 1939,F 20,13:2
Red Tanks 1942,Je 6,9:2
Two Soldiers 1944,Jl 27,14:2
My Name Is Ivan (Ivan's Childhood)
1963,Je 28,25:4
Krimer, Harry
Napoleon 1929,F 12,23:1
Heart of a Nation, The 1943,Ap 8,27:2
Krimnus, Nicki
Sandu Follows the Sun 1965,Ap 19,37:1
Krimov, Peter
Lady With the Dog, The 1962,N 7,48:1
Krims, Milton (Original Author)
Dude Ranch 1931,Ap 25,23:4
Young and Beautiful 1934,S 18,18:4
Harmony Lane 1935,O 24,19:4
Speed 1936,My 16,11:2
Krims, Milton (Screenwriter)
West of the Pecos 1934,D 29,11:2
Grand Old Girl 1935,F 26,16:4
Green Light 1937,F 13,9:1
Great O'Malley, The 1937,Mr 6,10:1
Secrets of an Actress 1938,O 8,10:2
Sisters, The 1938,O 15,21:3
Confessions of a Nazi Spy 1939,Ap 29,13:2
We Are not Alone 1939,D 1,27:1
Lady With red Hair 1940,D 6,28:2
Dispatch From Reuters, A 1940,D 12,37:2
Iron Curtain, The 1948,My 13,31:2
Prince of Foxes 1949,D 24,11:2
One Minute to Zero 1952,S 20,13:2
Tennessee's Partner 1955,N 5,22:8
Krinsky, Leonid
Can't Help Singing 1944,D 26,22:4
Krisman, Nino (Producer)
Very Handy Man, A 1966,D 15,60:1
Violent Four, The 1968,Ag 15,46:2
Kristen, Marta
Savage Sam 1963,Ag 1,17:3
Kristi, L (Director)
Enchanted Mirror, The 1959,Jl 22,22:1
Kristi, L (Screenwriter)
Enchanted Mirror, The 1959,Jl 22,22:1
Kristiansen, Cay
Ordet 1957,D 16,33:6
Kristien, Stanley
Young Savages, The 1961,My 25,31:1
Kristy, L (Director)
Circus Stars 1960,Jl 28,19:3
Cinerama's Russian Adventure 1966,Ap 14,42:1
Kristy, L (Screenwriter)
Circus Stars 1960,Jl 28,19:3
Kritayakorn, Renu
King of the White Elephant, The 1941,Ap 5,12:7
Krituchkov, N
Leningrad Symphony 1958,Je 23,19:6
Kritzmiller, John
Tombolo 1949,D 31,9:4
Kriuchkov, Nikolai
Patrioty 1933,S 25,18:5
Thirteen, The 1937,Je 19,20:2
Ski Battalion 1938,Mr 14,13:1
City of Youth 1938,S 5,30:4
Soviet Border 1939,F 20,13:2

In the Rear of the Enemy 1942,O 10,11:2
Lad From our Town 1943,O 7,26:2
They Met in Moscow 1944,Je 7,13:2
Last Hill, The 1945,Je 26,13:2
Bountiful Summer 1951,D 24,9:1
Maximka 1953,O 12,30:4
Frigid Sea, The 1955,N 21,23:4
Immortal Garrison, The 1957,Mr 4,30:2
Forty-First, The 1957,Je 15,10:7
Sailor From the Comet, The 1959,Ag 3,21:2
Ballad of a Soldier 1960,D 27,22:1
Kriuger, V
Eagle of the Caucasus, The 1932,S 17,18:4
Men of the Sea 1938,Je 20,11:2
Kriukov, Nikolai (Composer)
Men on Wings 1935,Je 11,24:5
We Are From Kronstadt 1936,My 2,11:1
Paris Commune 1937,Je 2,20:4
Lenin in 1918 1939,Je 27,27:2
Krivchenya, A
Boris Godunov 1956,Ja 23,21:4
Khovanschina 1960,S 19,41:2
Krizman, Serge
Song of my Heart 1948,Mr 5,17:3
Krochnke, Erich (Screenwriter)
Bimbo the Great 1961,Je 29,26:1
Kroeger, Berry
Iron Curtain, The 1948,My 13,31:2
Cry of the City 1948,S 30,32:4
Dark Past, The 1948,D 23,25:2
Act of Violence 1949,Ja 24,16:2
Down to the Sea in Ships 1949,F 23,31:2
Chicago Deadline 1949,N 3,37:2
Black Magic 1949,N 9,37:2
Fighting Man of the Plains 1949,N 17,35:6
Guilty of Treason 1950,Ap 11,26:2
Gun Crazy 1950,Ag 25,17:5
Sword of Monte Cristo, The 1951,Ap 23,21:2
Blood Alley 1955,O 6,25:3
Yellowback 1957,Ap 5,24:2
Seven Thieves 1960,Mr 12,14:5
Atlantis the Lost Continent 1961,My 27,12:1
Kroff, Arnold
Yellow Ticket, The 1931,O 31,22:2
Kroger, Barry (Miscellaneous)
Pledge to Bataan 1943,Jl 2,15:2
Krohner, Maurice
Overture to Glory 1940,F 12,14:2
Krohner, Sara
Mirele Efros 1939,O 21,12:2
Molly 1951,Mr 8,37:2
Kroiter, Roman (Producer)
Nobody Waved Goodbye 1964,S 17,52:1
Kroll, Harry Harrison (Original Author)
Cabin in the Cotton 1932,S 30,17:3
Kroll, Nathan (Miscellaneous)
Guns of August, The 1964,D 25,24:2
Kroll, Nathan (Producer)
Guns of August, The 1964,D 25,24:2
Kronberg, L
Big Family, A 1955,Je 6,24:1
Kronefeld, Kurt
Damned, The; Maudits, Les 1948,Ap 26,27:2
Kronegger
S O S Mediterranean 1940,Ja 1,29:2
Kroner, Josef
Shop on High Street, The 1965,S 10,40:1
Shop on Main Street, The 1966,Ja 25,47:1
Kroner, Maurice
Motel, The Operator 1940,Ja 16,19:3
Kronhausen, Eberhard Dr (Director)
Now Cinema! (Psychomontage); Psychomontage
(Now Cinema!) 1968,Ap 9,56:1
Kronhausen, Eberhard Dr (Producer)
Now Cinema! (Psychomontage); Psychomontage
(Now Cinema!) 1968,Ap 9,56:1
Kronhausen, Phyllis Dr (Director)
Now Cinema! (Psychomontage); Psychomontage
(Now Cinema!) 1968,Ap 9,56:1
Kronhausen, Phyllis Dr (Producer)
Now Cinema! (Psychomontage); Psychomontage
(Now Cinema!) 1968,Ap 9,56:1
Kronos
David and Goliath 1961,O 7,14:3
Krook, Margareta
Swedish Wedding Night 1965,N 15,48:1
Persona 1967,Mr 7,46:2
Krozos, Stavros
Barefoot Battalion 1954,My 29,13:4
Krska, Vaclav (Director)
Bohemian Rapture 1948,F 16,16:2
Girl With Three Camels, The 1968,Ag 13,45:2
Krska, Vaclav (Screenwriter)
Bohemian Rapture 1948,F 16,16:2
Girl With Three Camels, The 1968,Ag 13,45:2
KRUEGER
See Also KRIEGER
Krueger, Answald (Screenwriter)
Tempestous Love 1958,N 22,27:4
Krueger, Carl (Original Author)
Sabre Jet 1953,N 3,34:1

Krueger, Carl (Producer)
Sabre Jet 1953,N 3,34:1
Krueger, Elsa
Grenzfeuer 1936,D 19,16:1
Krueger, Hilde
Seefahrt die Ist Lustig, Eine; Merry Sea Trip, A
1938,O 22,14:2
Sie und die Drei; She and the Three
1938,D 10,13:3
Peter, Paul und Nanette 1940,My 25,20:1
Krueger, Lorraine
New Faces of 1937 1937,Jl 2,25:1
I'm From the City 1938,Ag 19,13:4
Exposed 1938,N 21,14:5
Idiot's Delight 1939,F 3,13:1
He's my Guy 1943,Mr 12,12:3
Krueger, Vladimir
Island of Doom 1933,Jl 17,9:5
Krueger, Wilhelm
Krach um Iolanthe 1935,My 11,21:3
Alle Tage Ist Kein Sonntag 1936,Jl 11,11:4
Wenn der Hahn Kraeht 1936,N 14,23:3
Kruger, Alma
These Three 1936,Mr 19,22:4
Craig's Wife 1936,O 2,29:3
Breezing Home 1937,Mr 20,23:5
Vogues of 1938 1937,Ag 20,21:1
Man in Blue, The 1937,Ag 30,25:2
100 Men and a Girl 1937,S 18,15:2
Toy Wife, The 1938,Je 24,15:1
Mother Carey's Chickens 1938,Ag 5,11:3
Four's a Crowd 1938,Ag 12,11:1
Tarnished Angel 1938,N 15,27:2
Great Waltz, The 1938,N 25,19:1
Made for Each Other 1939,F 17,17:2
Calling Dr Kildare 1939,My 12,25:4
Secret of Dr Kildare, The 1939,D 8,33:5
Balalaika 1939,D 15,33:2
His Girl Friday 1940,Ja 12,13:2
Dr Kildare's Strange Case 1940,Ap 12,19:2
Anne of Windy Poplars 1940,Ag 23,13:3
Dr Kildare Goes Home 1940,S 19,27:4
You'll Find Out 1940,N 15,25:2
Dr Kildare's Crisis 1940,D 19,33:1
Trial of Mary Dugan, The 1941,Mr 6,25:4
People vs Dr Kildare, The 1941,My 8,21:1
Dr Kildare's Wedding Day 1941,S 18,31:1
Dr Kildare's Victory 1942,F 5,25:2
Saboteur 1942,My 8,27:2
Calling Dr Gillespie 1942,Jl 9,17:4
Three Men in White 1944,My 26,23:3
Our Hearts Were Young and Gay 1944,O 12,24:2
Between Two Women 1945,Mr 29,18:3
Do You Love Me 1946,My 25,12:2
Scandal In Paris, A 1946,S 16,9:7
Dark Delusion 1947,Je 26,19:2
Forever Amber 1947,O 23,31:2
Kruger, Bum
Eighth Day of the Week, The 1959,Mr 24,45:2
Montpi 1959,Ap 21,40:1
Kruger, Hardy
One That Got Away, The 1958,Ap 23,40:2
Liane, Jungle Goddess 1959,F 23,19:1
Rest Is Silence, The 1960,Ag 2,22:6
Confess, Dr Corda 1960,O 24,25:5
Chance Meeting 1960,O 27,45:2
Hatari 1962,Jl 12,19:1
Sundays and Cybele 1962,N 13,43:3
Taxi for Tobruk 1965,Mr 30,52:1
Flight of the Phoenix, The 1966,F 1,26:1
Defector, The 1966,N 17,55:1
Uninhibited, The 1968,Je 13,57:2
Kruger, Otto
Under the Red Robe 1923,N 13,25:3
Turn Back the Clock 1933,Ag 26,14:2
Beauty for Sale 1933,S 16,9:3
Ever in my Heart 1933,O 13,25:3
Prizefighter and the Lady, The 1933,N 11,11:3
Gallant Lady 1934,Ja 22,12:3
Women in his Life, The 1934,Ja 27,9:3
Crime Doctor, The 1934,My 11,24:3
Men in White 1934,Je 9,18:2
Paris Interlude 1934,Jl 28,16:5
Treasure Island 1934,Ag 18,5:5
Chained 1934,S 1,16:2
Vanessa: Her Love Story 1935,Ap 13,11:3
Lady of Secrets 1936,F 22,12:1
Dracula's Daughter 1936,My 18,14:2
They Won't Forget 1937,Jl 15,16:1
Counsel for Crime 1937,O 9,16:1
Barrier, The 1937,N 27,21:2
I Am the Law 1938,Ag 26,14:2
Exposed 1938,N 21,14:5
Thanks for the Memory 1938,D 8,34:3
Disbarred 1939,Ja 19,17:2
Housemaster 1939,Ap 10,13:2
Zero Hour, The 1939,Jl 5,20:3
Woman Is the Judge, A 1939,S 28,29:5
Another Thin Man 1939,N 24,29:1
Dr Ehrlich's Magic Bullet 1940,F 24,9:2
Seventeen 1940,F 29,15:2
Man I Married, The 1940,Ag 3,9:2
Dispatch From Reuters, A 1940,D 12,37:2

Kruger, Otto— Cont
Men In her Life, The 1941,D 12,35:1
Saboteur 1942,My 8,27:2
Friendly Enemies 1942,Je 22,19:1
Hitler's Children 1943,F 25,27:1
Corregidor 1943,My 28,19:2
Night Plane From Chungking 1943,My 31,13:2
Stage Door Canteen 1943,Je 25,13:2
Tarzan's Desert Mystery 1943,D 27,23:3
Cover Girl 1944,Mr 31,26:1
Knickerbocker Holiday 1944,Ap 20,22:7
Storm Over Lisbon 1944,S 11,14:1
Chicago Kid, The 1945,F 12,24:3
Murder, my Sweet 1945,Mr 9,16:2
Earl Carroll Vanities 1945,Ap 2,15:6
Wonder Man 1945,Je 9,17:2
Jungle Captive 1945,Jl 7,7:5
Great John L, The 1945,Jl 9,14:6
Allotment Wives 1945,N 22,39:3
Love and Learn 1947,My 3,10:3
Duel in the Sun 1947,My 8,30:2
Lulu Belle 1948,Je 21,18:3
711 Ocean Drive 1950,Jl 20,21:2
Payment on Demand 1951,F 16,21:2
Valentino 1951,Ap 20,25:1
High Noon 1952,Jl 25,14:2
Magnificent Obsession 1954,Ag 5,18:4
Black Widow 1954,O 28,46:6
Young Philadelphians, The 1959,My 22,32:1
Wonderful World of the Brothers Grimm, The
  (The Singing Bone); Singing Bone, The (The
  Wonderful World of the Brothers Grimm)
  1962,Ag 8,35:1
Kruger, P W
Veilchen vom Potsdamer Platz, La; Violet of
  Potsdam Square, The 1939,Ap 8,19:3
Kruger, Paul
First Auto, The 1927,Je 28,28:4
Fortune Hunter, The 1928,Ja 10,28:4
Midnight Taxi, The 1928,O 29,29:1
Idle Rich, The 1929,Je 17,29:1
Hello, Everybody 1933,Ja 30,9:4
Pursuit of Happiness, The 1934,O 26,25:1
Kruger, Stubby
Mister Roberts 1955,Jl 15,14:1
Krugher, Lea
Blood and Black Lace 1965,N 11,58:3
Krugman, Lou
To the Ends of the Earth 1948,F 13,26:2
I Want to Live 1958,N 19,45:1
Kruk, E
Border Street 1950,Ap 26,35:2
Krukowski, K
Moj Wujaszek Z Ameryki 1933,O 25,25:3
Co Moj Maz Robi W Nocy?; What Is my Husband
  Doing Tonight? 1935,N 29,24:2
Krumbachova, Ester (Original Author)
Daisies 1967,O 26,54:2
Krumbachova, Ester (Screenwriter)
Daisies 1967,O 26,54:2
Report on the Party and the Guests, A
  1968,S 20,37:5
Report on the Party and the Guests, A
  1968,S 28,37:1
Krumgold, Joseph (Director)
Dream no More 1950,Ja 6,25:2
Krumgold, Joseph (Original Author)
Adventure in Manhattan 1936,O 23,27:5
Lady Behave 1938,Ja 28,17:3
Magic Town 1947,O 8,29:2
...And Now Miguel 1966,S 8,43:1
Krumgold, Joseph (Producer)
Dream no More 1950,Ja 6,25:2
Krumgold, Joseph (Screenwriter)
Lone Wolf Returns, The 1936,F 4,25:5
Lady From Nowhere 1936,D 21,19:2
Lady Behave 1938,Ja 28,17:3
Main Street Lawyer 1939,N 9,27:2
Crooked Road, The 1940,Je 11,33:4
Phantom Submarine, The 1941,F 12,25:3
Seven Miles From Alcatraz 1942,N 19,31:3
Dream no More 1950,Ja 6,25:2
Krup, Mara
For a Few Dollars More 1967,Jl 4,23:1
Krupa, Gene
Glenn Miller Story, the 1954,F 11,33:2
Benny Goodman Story 1956,F 22,22:1
Krupa, Gene, and Orchestra
Ball of Fire 1942,Ja 16,25:2
George White's Scandals 1945,O 11,26:2
Kruschen, Jack
Confidence Girl 1952,Je 21,12:2
Blueprint for Murder, A 1953,Jl 25,8:2
War of the Worlds, The 1953,Ag 14,10:2
Money From Home 1954,F 27,11:3
Julie 1956,N 22,51:1
Cry Terror 1958,My 15,25:1
Fraulein 1958,Je 9,27:2
Decks Ran Red, The 1958,O 11,18:2
Last Voyage, The 1960,F 20,14:2
Angry Red Planet, The 1960,My 5,41:2
Apartment, The 1960,Je 16,37:2
Studs Lonigan 1960,D 15,59:1
Lover Come Back 1962,F 9,21:1

Cape Fear 1962,Ap 19,35:2
Convicts 4 1962,O 4,44:2
McLintock 1963,N 14,41:3
Unsinkable Molly Brown, The 1964,Jl 17,15:1
Dear Brigitte 1965,Ja 28,20:1
Harlow 1965,My 15,18:1
Happening, The 1967,My 18,56:3
Caprice 1967,Je 8,52:2
KRUSE
See Also CREWS, CRUZ
Kruse, Hans
Return to Paradise 1953,S 11,24:2
Krustalev, Mikhail
Moscow Music Hall 1946,S 9,20:1
Kruta, Ferdinand
Closely Watched Trains 1967,O 16,59:2
Krynska, Elzbieta
Za Winy niepopelnione; For Crimes Not Theirs
  1939,F 20,13:3
Krzyzewska, Eva
Ashes and Diamonds 1961,My 30,8:1
Ktorof, A
Three Thieves 1933,O 30,14:3
Marionettes 1934,My 8,28:6
Ktorov, A
Without Dowry 1946,Ap 15,22:2
Ktorov, Anatoly
War and Peace 1968,Ap 29,50:5
Kuang-chao, Chiang
Lady General, The 1965,F 12,19:1
Shepherd Girl, The 1965,S 2,36:3
Kuanshbayev, Kalibek
Amangeldy 1939,Je 16,27:4
Kuba, Reiko
Soyonara 1957,D 6,39:4
Sayonara 1957,D 6,39:4
Kubasek, Vaclav (Director)
Thunder in the Hills 1947,My 24,10:5
Kubatsky, A
Frigid Sea, The 1955,N 21,23:4
Kubik, Gail (Composer)
World at War, The 1942,S 4,19:1
Kubler, Ursula
Very Private Affair, A 1962,S 29,15:1
Love on a Pillow 1963,D 17,49:1
Fire Within, The 1964,F 18,27:1
Kubo, Akira
Throne of Blood 1961,N 23,50:2
Kubrick, Stanley (Cinematographer)
Fear and Desire 1953,Ap 1,35:2
Kubrick, Stanley (Director)
Fear and Desire 1953,Ap 1,35:2
Killing, The 1956,My 21,20:1
Paths of Glory 1957,D 26,23:2
Spartacus 1960,O 7,28:1
Lolita 1962,Je 14,23:2
Dr Strangelove or: How I Learned to Stop
  Worrying and Love the Bomb 1964,Ja 31,16:1
  (Incorrect in this edition; use 1964,Ja 30,24:1
  elsewhere)
2001 A Space Odyssey 1968,Ap 4,58:1
Kubrick, Stanley (Miscellaneous)
Fear and Desire 1953,Ap 1,35:2
Kubrick, Stanley (Producer)
Fear and Desire 1953,Ap 1,35:2
Dr Strangelove or: How I Learned to Stop
  Worrying and Love the Bomb 1964,Ja 31,16:1
  (Incorrect in this edition; use 1964,Ja 30,24:1
  elsewhere)
2001 A Space Odyssey 1968,Ap 4,58:1
Kubrick, Stanley (Screenwriter)
Killing, The 1956,My 21,20:1
Paths of Glory 1957,D 26,23:2
Dr Strangelove or: How I Learned to Stop
  Worrying and Love the Bomb 1964,Ja 31,16:1
  (Incorrect in this edition; use 1964,Ja 30,24:1
  elsewhere)
2001 A Space Odyssey 1968,Ap 4,58:1
Kuby, Erich (Screenwriter)
Rosemary 1960,Ja 19,40:2
Kuchar, Erich
Mutterliebe; Mother Love 1940,Mr 16,8:3
Kuchar, George (Director)
Unstrap Me 1968,N 21,41:2
Kuchar, George (Screenwriter)
Unstrap Me 1968,N 21,41:2
Kuchenko, I
Cossack Beyond the Danube, A 1954,F 8,18:5
Kuckelmann, Gertrud
Life and Loves of Mozart, The 1958,Ja 7,28:2
Kude, Jay M (Screenwriter)
Flesh Merchant, The 1956,My 19,12:6
Kudriatsev, I
Concentration Camp 1939,Mr 20,13:2
On his Own 1939,S 13,31:3
Kudryautsef, M
Petersburg Nights 1934,S 10,20:4
Kueckelmann, Gertrud
Dancing Heart, The 1958,Ja 18,10:3
Golden Plaque, The 1963,Ag 10,8:6
Kuenecke, Eduard (Miscellaneous)
Rendez-Vous 1932,Ap 30,19:3

Kuenstler, Frank
Guns of the Trees 1964,F 29,12:2
Kueppers, Topsy
Guitars of Love 1958,Jl 12,18:1
Kufer, Hans (Director)
Luther 1928,Mr 25,IX,5:1
Kufer, Hans (Screenwriter)
Luther 1928,Mr 25,IX,5:1
Kuga, Yoshiko
Idiot, The 1963,My 1,35:1
Taira Clan, The; Shin Heike Monagatari
  1964,S 21,37:4
Ohayo; (Good Morning) 1966,F 2,24:1
Secret Scrolls-Part I 1968,My 9,54:3
Secret Scrolls-Part II; Ninjitsu 1968,My 23,56:3
Kugelmass, J Alvin (Original Author)
Two-Headed Spy, The 1959,Mr 3,38:4
Kuget, Bettina
Greetings 1968,D 16,61:2
Kuh, Anton (Screenwriter)
Maria Stuart 1928,Mr 11,VIII,5:1
Kuhel, Joe
Ninth Inning, The 1942,Ja 8,30:3
Kuhlmann, Carl
Volk Will Leben, Ein; People Wants to Live, A
  1939,Mr 27,11:2
KUHN
See Also COON
Kuhn, Mickey
Juarez 1939,Ap 26,27:1
S O S Tidal Wave 1939,Je 22,19:3
Gone With the Wind 1939,D 20,31:2
I Want a Divorce 1940,O 3,31:2
Dick Tracy 1946,Ja 12,10:7
Strange Love of Martha Ivers, The
  1946,Jl 25,18:4
Magic Town 1947,O 8,29:2
Red River 1948,O 1,31:2
Broken Arrow 1950,Jl 21,15:2
Last Frontier, The 1955,D 8,45:1
Kuhnau, Erik
Weekend 1964,Ap 27,24:1
Kuhne, Wolfgang
Wozzeck 1962,Mr 3,13:1
Kulakof, V
Thirteen, The 1937,Je 19,20:2
City of Youth 1938,S 5,30:4
Kulakov, A
Red Tanks 1942,Je 6,9:2
Kulakov, Victor
We Will Come Back 1943,O 15,15:2
Kulb, Karl Georg (Screenwriter)
Long Is the Road 1948,N 12,30:5
Kuleshof, Lev (Director)
Horizon, The Wandering Jew 1933,My 12,20:4
Kulganek, W
Flames on the Volga 1929,Ap 2,28:4
Kulijanov, Lev (Director)
House I Live in, The 1959,Ap 20,34:2
Home for Tanya, A 1961,Ag 14,28:5
When the Trees Were Tall 1965,F 22,14:1
Kulik, Buzz (Director)
Explosive Generation, The 1962,F 15,24:2
Yellow Canary, The 1963,My 16,42:1
Warning Shot 1967,Je 8,52:2
Sergeant Ryker 1968,Mr 21,56:2
Villa Rides 1968,Jl 18,26:3
Kulik, Ivan (Screenwriter)
Nazar Stodolya 1937,Ag 7,7:2
Kulik, V
Train Goes to Kiev, The 1961,Ap 10,26:1
Kulikov, G
Clear Skies 1963,N 27,30:1
Kulkerni, Shanker
Gyandev of India 1943,Ap 10,12:5
Kulky, Henry
Tarzan's Magic Fountain 1949,F 7,15:2
Bodyhold 1949,D 12,29:4
South Sea Sinner - 1950,Ja 16,18:4
Wabash Avenue 1950,Ap 29,8:3
Guy Who Came Back, The 1951,Ag 17,13:2
Fixed Bayonets 1951,N 21,20:2
World in His Arms, The 1952,O 10,21:2
5,000 Fingers of Dr T, The 1953,Je 20,8:6
Charge at Feather River, The 1953,Jl 16,17:2
Glory Brigade, The 1953,Ag 15,8:4
Up Periscope 1959,Mr 5,35:4
Kull, Edward (Director)
New Adventures of Tarzan, The 1935,O 15,19:3
Kulle, Jarl
Secrets of Woman 1961,Jl 12,36:1
Devil's Eye, The 1961,O 31,27:4
All These Women 1964,O 6,35:1
Swedish Wedding Night 1965,N 15,48:1
Dear John 1966,Mr 9,46:1
My Sister, My Love 1967,F 20,45:2
Kuller, Sid (Composer)
Kentucky Moonshine 1938,My 21,9:2
Big Store, The 1941,Je 27,14:4
Kuller, Sid (Miscellaneous)
Life Begins In College 1937,O 9,16:1
Kentucky Moonshine 1938,My 21,9:2
Three Musketeers, The 1939,F 18,12:2

Kuller, Sid (Miscellaneous) — Cont
Hit Parade of 1941 1940,D 5,33:2
Kuller, Sid (Producer)
Stop! Look! and Laugh! 1961,F 9,36:1
Kuller, Sid (Screenwriter)
Argentine Nights 1940,O 11,25:3
Big Store, The 1941,Je 27,14:4
Stop! Look! and Laugh! 1961,F 9,36:1
Kullmann, Charles
Sonne Geht auf, Die 1935,F 18,19:4
Paloma, La 1936,O 21,35:3
Goldwyn Follies, The 1938,F 21,15:1
Song of Scheherazade 1947,F 27,26:2
Kullock, Bernardo
Terrace, The 1964,N 25,45:1
Kulp, Nancy
Model and the Marriage Broker, The
  1952,Ja 12,10:6
Shane 1953,Ap 24,30:3
Sabrina 1954,S 23,43:2
You're Never too Young 1955,Ag 26,10:2
Forever, Darling 1956,F 10,18:1
Three Faces of Eve, The 1957,S 27,16:6
Parent Trap, The 1961,Je 22,23:1
Who's Minding the Store? 1963,N 29,67:6
  (Incorrect in this edition; use 1963,N 28,67:6
  elsewhere)
Strange Bedfellows 1965,Mr 11,38:1
Night of the Grizzly, The 1966,Je 23,29:1
Kuluva, Will
Abandoned Woman 1949,O 27,35:3
Shrike, The 1955,Jl 8,15:2
Crime in the Streets 1956,My 24,27:4
Odds Against Tomorrow 1959,O 16,27:1
Go Naked in the World 1961,Mr 11,15:1
Spiral Road, The 1962,Ag 4,11:2
Kulyef, Andrei
Thirteen, The 1937,Je 19,20:2
Kuma, Profulla
Light of Asia, The 1928,My 12,8:4
Kumagai, Frank
Tokyo Joe 1949,O 27,35:2
Halls of Montezuma, The 1951,Ja 6,9:6
Pickup on South Street 1953,Je 18,38:2
Kumankov, E (Miscellaneous)
Sadko 1953,Je 1,18:6
Kumar, Raaj
Handful of Grain, A 1959,Jl 4,9:4
Kumar, Rajendra
Handful of Grain, A 1959,Jl 4,9:4
Kumar, Rattan
Boot Polish 1958,Ag 18,15:2
Kumari, Roshan
Music Room, The 1963,O 16,50:6
Kumbera, Antonin
Diamonds of the Night 1968,Mr 15,30:1
Kummer, Clare (Original Author)
Annabelle's Affairs 1931,Je 29,20:3
Successful Calamity, A 1932,S 23,22:2
Kummer, Clare (Screenwriter)
Lost-a Wife 1925,Je 22,10:2
Kummer, Frederic Arnold (Original Author)
Love's Greatest Mistake 1927,F 21,14:2
Kun, Li
Lady General, The 1965,F 12,19:1
Kun, Magda
Filleres Gyoers 1933,Mr 27,13:7
Und Es Leuchtet die Puszta 1934,Ja 30,17:2
Dance Band 1936,Ja 4,19:2
Majd a Zsuzsi 1938,O 22,14:3
Busuini Nem Jo; Don't Worry 1938,O 29,15:5
Kuney, Eva Lee
Penny Serenade 1941,My 23,25:2
Kunkel, George
Leave It to Susan 1919,My 26,19:4
Kunogh, Narla
Jedda the Uncivilized 1957,F 28,18:7
KUNZ
See Also KUNZE
Kunz, Erich
Life and Loves of Mozart, The 1958,Ja 7,28:2
Rosenkavalier, Der 1962,O 10,57:1
Kunz, Werner (Producer)
Isle of Levant 1959,Jl 11,11:1
KUNZE
See Also KUNZ
Kunze, Norbert (Screenwriter)
Last Bridge, The 1957,Ag 21,22:2
Kupfer, Margarete
Bockbierfest 1931,Mr 31,25:3
Die vom Rummelplatz 1932,Ja 2,14:2
Ungetreue Eckehart, Der 1932,Ja 23,18:4
Strich Durch die Rechnung 1934,Mr 3,8:6
Wie Man Maenner Fesselt 1934,My 21,20:3
Blaue Vom Himmel, Das 1934,S 8,18:6
Gretl Zieht das Grosse Los 1935,F 11,14:2
Zu Strassburg auf der Schanz; At the Strassburg
  1936,F 15,18:7
Fahrt ins Gruene, Die 1936,My 23,12:2
Kupper, Margarete
Slums of Berlin 1927,Ja 26,17:1
Storch Hat Uns Getraut, Der 1933,D 1,23:2
Bei der Blonden Kathrein 1934,D 3,15:2
Polenblut; Polish Blood 1935,N 16,19:3

Blinde Passagier; Stowaways 1937,Mr 6,10:1
Kupperman, Joel
Chip off the Old Block 1944,Mr 17,14:2
Kuprin, Alexander (Original Author)
Garnet Bracelet, The 1966,My 28,11:6
Kuralev, Lev
When the Trees Were Tall 1965,F 22,14:1
Kuravlyov, Mazarov
Last Game, The 1964,O 25,41:5 (Incorrect in this
  edition; use 1964,O 26,41:5 elsewhere)
Kurc, A
Dybbuk, The 1938,Ja 28,17:2
Kurdymova, L
Sound of Life, The 1962,F 12,28:2
Kurdyumova, Z D
Clown George 1932,Ag 24,21:4
Kurer, Vilma
Walk East on Beacon 1952,My 29,17:2
Kuri, Yoji (Director)
Two Grilled Fish 1968,Jl 19,30:1
Kurikhin, F N
Moscow Laughs 1935,Mr 25,12:2
Country Bride 1938,Je 4,18:2
Kurilov, S
Maximka 1953,O 12,30:4
Big Family, A 1955,Je 6,24:1
1905 1956,Jl 9,27:2
Leningrad Symphony 1958,Je 23,19:6
Kurnakowicz, J
Kosciuszki 1938,D 27,13:2
Young Chopin 1952,D 25,34:7
Kurnitz, Harry (Miscellaneous)
Heavenly Body, The 1944,Mr 24,17:3
Kurnitz, Harry (Original Author)
Shadow of the Thin Man 1941,N 21,23:2
Thin Man Goes Home, The 1945,Ja 26,16:5
Web, The 1947,Je 5,32:1
Land of the Pharaohs 1955,Jl 27,15:2
Happy Road, The 1957,Je 21,20:2
Once More With Feeling 1960,F 12,22:2
Hatari 1962,Jl 12,19:1
Shot in the Dark, A 1964,Je 24,28:1
Kurnitz, Harry (Producer)
Kiss in the Dark, A 1949,Mr 26,10:6
Pretty Baby 1950,S 23,11:2
Kurnitz, Harry (Screenwriter)
Fast and Loose 1939,Mr 9,18:1
Fast And Furious 1939,O 12,33:3
I Love You Again 1940,Ag 16,11:2
Shadow of the Thin Man 1941,N 21,23:2
Pacific Rendezvous 1942,Jl 8,27:4
They Got Me Covered 1943,Mr 5,20:2
See Here Private Hargrove 1944,Mr 22,17:2
What Next Corporal Hargrove? 1945,D 26,15:2
Something in the Wind 1947,Ag 29,14:3
One Touch of Venus 1948,O 29,29:5
Adventures of Don Juan 1948,D 25,10:1
Kiss in the Dark, A 1949,Mr 26,10:6
My Dream Is Yours 1949,Ap 16,11:3
Inspector General, The 1949,D 31,9:2
Pretty Baby 1950,S 23,11:2
Of Men and Music 1951,F 15,27:2
Tonight We Sing 1953,F 13,17:2
Man Between, The 1953,N 19,41:2
Happy Road, The 1957,Je 21,20:2
Witness for the Prosecution 1958,F 7,16:1
Once More With Feeling 1960,F 12,22:2
Surprise Package 1960,O 15,26:2
Goodbye, Charlie 1964,N 19,49:1
How to Steal a Million 1966,Jl 15,34:1
Kurochkin, N
Safety Match, The 1955,Mr 28,24:5
Kurokawa, Yataro
Gate of Hell 1954,D 14,45:2
Kuromilas, D (Original Author)
Shepherd's Daughter, The 1956,My 14,23:3
Kurosawa, Akira (Director)
Rasho-Mon 1951,D 27,18:3
Magnificent Seven, The 1956,N 20,46:2
Drunken Angel 1959,D 31,12:1
Men Who Tread on the Tiger's Tail, The
  1960,Ja 11,35:7
Ikiru; To Live 1960,Ja 30,13:5
Throne of Blood 1961,N 23,50:2
Hidden Fortress The 1962,Ja 24,24:2
Lower Depths, The 1962,F 10,12:5
Yojimbo 1962,O 16,34:1
Bad Sleep Well, The 1963,Ja 23,5:2
Idiot, The 1963,My 1,35:1
Sanjuro 1963,My 8,34:2
High and Low 1963,N 27,30:1
Stray Dog 1964,Mr 4,32:7
I Live in Fear; Ikimono no Kiroku
  1967,Ja 26,25:1
Red Beard 1968,D 20,60:4
Kurosawa, Akira (Producer)
Throne of Blood 1961,N 23,50:2
Yojimbo 1962,O 16,34:1
Kurosawa, Akira (Screenwriter)
Rasho-Mon 1951,D 27,18:3
Magnificent Seven, The 1956,N 20,46:2
Drunken Angel 1959,D 31,12:1
Men Who Tread on the Tiger's Tail, The
  1960,Ja 11,35:7

Kurosawa, Akira (Screenwriter) — Cont
Throne of Blood 1961,N 23,50:2
Hidden Fortress The 1962,Ja 24,24:2
Lower Depths, The 1962,F 10,12:5
Yojimbo 1962,O 16,34:1
Bad Sleep Well, The 1963,Ja 23,5:2
Idiot, The 1963,My 1,35:1
Sanjuro 1963,My 8,34:2
High and Low 1963,N 27,30:1
Stray Dog 1964,Mr 4,32:7
I Live in Fear; Ikimono no Kiroku
  1967,Ja 26,25:1
Red Beard 1968,D 20,60:4
Kurowska, Bozena
Lotna 1966,My 27,33:1
Kurt, Meisel
Wozzeck 1962,Mr 3,13:1
Kurth, Hans
Pfarrer von Kirchfeld, Der; Pastor of Kirchfeld,
  The 1939,Ap 22,15:3
Kurti, Joszef
Sut a Nap (Sun Shines, The); Sun Shines, The
  1940,Ap 6,13:3
Kurtnitz, Harry (Screenwriter)
Melba 1953,Je 25,23:1
Kurtz, Wilbur G (Miscellaneous)
Gone With the Wind 1939,D 20,31:2
Kurtzel, Sol M (Producer)
Battle of Broadway 1938,Ap 25,19:2
Kurz, Emille
Last Laugh, The 1925,Ja 28,14:1
Manon Lescaut 1926,N 30,27:1
Trial of Donald Westhof, The 1928,F 18,11:2
Kusabue, Mitsuko
Happiness of Us Alone 1963,Ap 10,31:5
Kusell, Daniel (Original Author)
Gingham Girl, The 1927,Jl 19,27:2
Kusell, Harold (Miscellaneous)
New Faces of 1937 1937,Jl 2,25:1
Kusell, Harold (Screenwriter)
there Goes The Groom 1937,D 25,10:6
Kusmin, Veronica
Dr Coppelius 1968,D 26,56:1
Kussell, Maurice (Miscellaneous)
Great Gabbo, The 1929,S 13,33:1
Kusserow, Ingeborg von
Meadehen von Gestern Nacht, Das; Girl of Last
  Night, The 1938,Je 18,18:2
Kusunoki, Ikuko
Unholy Desire 1964,N 18,54:1
Kutai, Ari
Clear all Wires 1933,Mr 4,11:2
Kutchinsky, M
Clown George 1932,Ag 24,21:4
Polish Terror, The 1933,Mr 13,18:3
Kuter, Kay
Guys and Dolls 1955,N 5,26:1
Steel Jungle, The 1956,Mr 10,9:5
Kutner, Nanette (Screenwriter)
Big City 1948,My 17,23:3
Kutter, Anton (Director)
Wiesse Majestat, Die; White Majesty
  1939,My 27,13:3
Kutusow, N
Prisoners of the Sea 1929,Ap 16,32:5
Kuwa, George
Toby's Bow 1919,D 15,20:1
Eternal Struggle, The 1923,O 16,21:3
Broken Barriers 1924,Ag 4,16:3
Oh, Doctor! 1925,F 23,24:1
Wife Who Wasn't Wanted, The 1925,S 9,23:1
Son of his Father, A 1925,S 29,31:3
Enchanted Hill, The 1925,D 29,19:2 (In
  Addenda)
Money Talks 1926,My 11,24:3
Night Bride, The 1927,Mr 30,22:6
Chinese Parrot, The 1928,Ja 2,28:1
Showdown, The 1928,Mr 5,21:1
Secret Hour, The 1928,Mr 12,26:1
After the Storm 1928,My 8,25:3
Kuwayama, Shoichi
Insect Woman, The; Nippon Konchuki
  1964,Jl 1,42:1
Kuyen, Kurt
Ali Baba and the Forty Thieves 1944,Mr 16,17:3
Kuzimina, N
Clear Skies 1963,N 27,30:1
Kuzmicheva, L
Bride with a Dowry 1954,Ag 23,20:5
Kuzmina
Alone 1931,S 13,IX,5:7 (In Addenda)
Kuzmina, Elena
New Babylon, The 1929,D 2,28:2
Alone 1932,My 25,23:6
Horizon, The Wandering Jew 1933,My 12,20:4
Patrioty 1933,S 25,18:5
Thirteen, The 1937,Je 19,20:2
Guerrilla Brigade 1942,Ap 14,17:2
Girl No 217 1945,S 3,17:2
Attack From the Sea 1954,Ap 19,19:4
Kuzmitch, V
Life is Beautiful 1933,F 13,11:5

Kuznetsoff, Alexander
Zoya 1945,Ap 16,18:6
Kuznetsov, Issal (Screenwriter)
Lullaby, The 1961,My 15,35:2
Kuznetsov, Mikhail
Mashenka 1942,N 21,10:7
We Will Come Back 1943,O 15,15:2
Ivan the Terrible, Part I 1947,Mr 10,25:2
In the Name of Life 1947,O 20,29:2
Bountiful Summer 1951,D 24,9:1
Taras Shevchenko 1952,Jl 28,12:6
Adventure in Odessa 1954,Je 21,19:6
Frigid Sea, The 1955,N 21,23:4
Ivan the Terrible, Part II 1959,N 25,22:4
Kuznetsov, P
Peter the First 1937,D 25,10:4
Kuznetsova, E
Mistress, The 1954,My 31,9:2
Kuznetsova, M
Safety Match, The 1955,Mr 28,24:5
Gift for Music 1957,Jl 15,15:2
Kuznetsova, Vera
Boys From Leningrad, The 1955,My 2,16:5
Big Family, A 1955,Je 6,24:1
Home for Tanya, A 1961,Ag 14,28:5
There Was an old Couple 1967,My 22,53:1
Kuznetzof, S
Man From the Restaurant, The 1930,Ja 6,30:5
Krasnaya Derevnya 1935,My 2,17:1
Kuznetzoff, Adia
Madame X 1937,O 25,23:1
Everybody Sing 1938,Mr 11,15:3
Swiss Miss 1938,Je 4,18:2
Pacific Liner 1939,Ja 18,17:3
Bulldog Drummond's Bride 1939,Jl 13,17:2
Tropic Fury 1939,S 8,28:4
Devil's Island 1940,Jl 12,11:4
Second Chorus 1941,Ja 16,25:2
Arabian Nights 1942,D 26,15:1
For Whom the Bell Tolls 1943,Jl 15,25:2
Rainbow Island 1944,O 26,19:6
Lost in a Harem 1944,N 9,23:2
Princess and the Pirate, The 1945,F 10,16:2
Kuznetzov, A
Return of Maxim, The 1937,N 2,33:1
New Horizons 1939,My 12,25:3
Behind the Show Window 1957,Ap 17,37:1
Kuznetzov, G N (Screenwriter)
Cossacks of the Kuban 1950,O 30,22:4
Kuznetzov, Gleb
Transport of Fire 1931,Mr 24,31:2
Rivals 1933,Ap 5,22:6
Kuznetzov, I
Seven Brave Men 1936,Je 15,24:2
Thirteen, The 1937,Je 19,20:2
City of Youth 1938,S 5,30:4
Red Tanks 1942,Je 6,9:2
Two Soldiers 1944,Jl 27,14:2
Moscow Skies 1945,Ja 22,22:5
Dark Is The Night 1946,Mr 18,24:3
Kvrgic, Pero
Steppe, The 1963,O 1,33:1
Kwah-wu, Shang
Song of China 1936,N 10,31:3
Kwan, Nancy
World of Suzie Wong, The 1960,N 11,36:1
Flower Drum Song 1961,N 10,40:1
Main Attraction, The 1963,Je 27,23:3
Honeymoon Hotel 1964,Je 4,28:1
Tamahine 1964,Jl 16,23:1
Fate Is the Hunter 1964,D 10,61:1
Lt Robin Crusoe, USN 1966,Jl 14,28:1
Arrivederci, Baby! 1966,D 29,22:1
Corrupt Ones, The 1967,F 23,41:3
Nobody's Perfect 1968,Ap 4,58:3
Kwarian, Kola
Killing, The 1956,My 21,20:1
Kwen, Li
Love Eterne, The; Liang Shan Po and Chu
Ying-lai 1965,Ja 16,14:1
Kweskin, Jim and the Jug Band
Festival 1967,O 24,53:2
Kwiatkowska, Halina
Ashes and Diamonds 1961,My 30,8:1
Kwolk, Burt
Satan Never Sleeps 1962,F 22,20:1
Kwong-chao, Chiang
Love Eterne, The; Liang Shan Po and Chu
Ying-lai 1965,Ja 16,14:1
Kwong-chao, Ching
Last Woman of Shang, The 1964,D 15,56:2
Kwouk, Bert
Passport to China 1961,Mr 23,28:1
Kyatuk
Igloo 1932,Jl 21,15:2
Kydd, Sam
Treasure Island 1950,Ag 16,24:2
Pool of London 1951,N 28,37:2
Murder Will Out 1953,Ap 6,24:2
Trent's Last Case 1953,N 27,99:9
Law and Disorder 1958,Ag 6,20:1
Up the Creek 1958,N 11,26:2
I'm All Right Jack 1960,Ap 26,40:2

Kyle, Ray
She's Back on Broadway 1953,Mr 12,24:2
Kyne, Peter B (Miscellaneous)
Jim, The Conquerer 1926,D 28,17:1
Kyne, Peter B (Original Author)
Ten-Dollar Raise, The 1921,Je 13,16:1
Cappy Ricks 1921,Ag 22,13:6
While Satan Sleeps 1922,Je 26,16:2
Kindred of the Dust 1922,Ag 28,14:1
Brothers Under the Skin 1922,N 13,12:1
Pride of Palomar, The 1922,N 20,21:3
Go-Getter 1923,Ap 9,14:3 (In Addenda)
Homeward Bound 1923,Jl 31,12:4
Never the Twain Shall Meet 1925,Jl 29,24:4
Enchanted Hill, The 1925,D 29,19:2 (In
Addenda)
Pals in Paradise 1926,N 24,26:4
Understanding Heart, The 1927,My 10,24:5
Valley of the Giants, The 1927,D 5,26:2
Hell's Heroes 1929,D 28,11:1
Never the Twain Shall Meet 1931,Je 6,15:5
Stoker, The 1932,Jl 16,5:5
Big Pay-Off, The 1933,Ja 17,22:7
Three Godfathers, The 1936,Mr 9,20:2
Without Orders 1936,N 4,41:3
Go Getter, The 1937,Je 4,27:2
Valley of the Giants 1938,S 10,20:2
Parson of Panamint, The 1941,Jl 26,18:2
He Hired the Boss 1943,Je 4,17:4
Three Godfathers 1949,Mr 4,25:2
Belle le Grand 1951,My 18,34:6
Kyo, Machika
Odd Obsession 1961,D 27,16:1
Kyo, Machiko
Rasho-Mon 1951,D 27,18:3
Ugetsu 1954,S 8,40:3
Gate of Hell 1954,D 14,45:2
Yang Kwei Fei 1956,S 11,41:2
Teahouse of the August Moon, The
1956,N 30,19:1
Street of Shame 1959,Je 5,17:2
Buddha 1965,Je 17,27:4
Kyokai, Kindai Eiga (Producer)
Lost Sex 1968,Jl 23,27:2
Kyoon, Shin Yung
Last Woman of Shang, The 1964,D 15,56:2
Kyria, Tsyvan
Road to Life 1932,Ja 28,24:2
Kyriakaki, Ero
Red Lanterns 1965,Ap 1,30:1
Kyriakopolos, C (Director)
Loves of a Greek in Paris 1960,Ag 15,19:7
Kyriakopolos, C (Producer)
Loves of a Greek in Paris 1960,Ag 15,19:7
Kyriakos, Petros
Castle in Greece 1960,D 12,38:2
Kyriakou, Anna
Zorba, The Greek 1964,D 18,25:1
Kyriakys, William (Director)
Dark Odyssey 1961,Je 26,22:2
Kyriakys, William (Producer)
Dark Odyssey 1961,Je 26,22:2
Kyriakys, William (Screenwriter)
Dark Odyssey 1961,Je 26,22:2
Kyser, Hans (Director)
Luther 1929,Je 24,27:1
Kyser, Kay
That's Right, You're Wrong 1939,N 30,25:3
You'll Find Out 1940,N 15,25:2
Playmates 1941,D 26,21:3
My Favorite Spy 1942,My 29,13:4
Around the World 1943,N 25,39:2
Swing Fever 1944,Ja 28,14:1
Carolina Blues 1944,D 8,26:6
Kyser, Kay, Band
Playmates 1941,D 26,21:3
My Favorite Spy 1942,My 29,13:4
Stage Door Canteen 1943,Je 25,13:2
Thousands Cheer 1943,S 14,27:1
Around the World 1943,N 25,39:2
Swing Fever 1944,Ja 28,14:1
Carolina Blues 1944,D 8,26:6
Kyveli, Mme
Madame X 1960,O 3,34:5

L

La Barba, Fidel (Original Author)
Susannah of the Mounties 1939,Je 24,13:2
Footlight Serenade 1942,S 10,30:3
La Bern, Arthur (Original Author)
It Always Rains on Sunday 1949,F 14,15:5
La Blanche, Ethel (Screenwriter)
Headin' East 1938,Ja 15,19:2
Flirting With Fate 1938,D 15,35:3
Exile Express 1939,Ag 16,21:3
La Capria, Raffaele (Screenwriter)
More Than a Miracle 1967,N 2,58:2
La Cava, Gregory (Director)
Womanhandled 1926,Ja 5,25:2
Say It Again 1926,Je 7,23:2
Paradise for Two 1927,Ja 25,18:4

La Cava, Gregory (Director) — Cont
Running Wild 1927,Je 14,33:2
Tell It to Sweeney 1927,O 17,20:2
Gay Defender, The 1927,D 26,26:6
Feel my Pulse 1928,F 27,16:2
Saturday's Children 1929,Ap 29,29:2
Big News 1929,O 7,22:1
His First Command 1929,D 23,18:2
Laugh and get Rich 1931,Mr 28,15:3
Smart Woman 1931,O 12,28:2
Symphony of Six Million 1932,Ap 15,23:1
Age of Consent, The 1932,S 3,16:2
Half-Naked Truth, The 1932,D 31,10:1
Gabriel Over the White House 1933,Ap 1,18:2
Bed of Roses 1933,Je 30,20:3
Gallant Lady 1934,Ja 22,12:3
Affairs of Cellini, The 1934,S 6,22:3
What Every Woman Knows 1934,O 27,20:2
Private Worlds 1935,Mr 28,25:2
She Married her Boss 1935,S 27,25:3
My Man Godfrey 1936,S 19,18:1 (Incorrect in
this edition; use 1936,S 18,18:1 elsewhere)
Stage Door 1937,O 8,27:2
Fifth Avenue Girl 1939,Ag 25,12:2
Primrose Path 1940,Mr 23,16:2
Unfinished Business 1941,S 2,20:2
Lady in a Jam 1942,S 11,25:2
Living in a Big Way 1947,O 10,31:4
La Cava, Gregory (Miscellaneous)
So's Your Old Man 1926,N 1,28:2
La Cava, Gregory (Original Author)
Living in a Big Way 1947,O 10,31:4
La Cava, Gregory (Producer)
Fifth Avenue Girl 1939,Ag 25,12:2
Primrose Path 1940,Mr 23,16:2
Unfinished Business 1941,S 2,20:2
Lady in a Jam 1942,S 11,25:2
La Cava, Gregory (Screenwriter)
Running Wild 1927,Je 14,33:2
Living in a Big Way 1947,O 10,31:4
La Cave, Gregory (Screenwriter)
Primrose Path 1940,Mr 23,16:2
La Cheduzzi
Life and Miracles of Blesses Mother Cabrini, The
1946,Jl 8,25:2
La Cressoniere, Georges
Juif Polonais, Le 1937,S 17,29:3
La Fonde, Virginia
Gateway of the Moon, The 1928,Ja 9,20:1
La Franconi, Terry
Cantante de Napoles, El; Singer of Naples, The
1935,F 25,13:4
La Frenais, Ian (Screenwriter)
Jokers, The 1967,My 16,50:1
Touchables, The 1968,N 21,41:1
La Galla, Lina
Seduced and Abandoned 1964,Jl 16,23:1
La Garde, Henri
Marriage Clause, The 1926,S 28,30:2
La Garde, Jocelyne
Hawaii 1966,O 11,54:1
La Guere, George
Way of a Woman, The 1919,Jl 28,8:5
Mamma's Affair 1921,Ja 24,16:2
Men Without Women 1930,F 1,15:1
La Marr, Barbara
Trifling Women 1922,O 4,23:4
Quincy Adams Sawyer 1922,D 18,22:2
Poor Men's Wives 1923,Ja 29,11:1
Souls for Sale 1923,Ap 9,14:3
Brass Bottle, The 1923,Jl 23,13:4
Strangers of the Night 1923,O 8,20:1
Eternal Struggle, The 1923,O 16,21:3
Eternal City, The 1924,Ja 21,20:1
Thy Name Is Woman 1924,Mr 4,17:1
Shooting of Dan McGrew, The 1924,Je 9,14:3
White Moth, The 1924,Je 16,18:3
Sandra 1924,D 22,20:2
Heart of a Siren, The 1925,Ap 8,24:3
White Monkey, The 1925,Je 9,16:3
Girl From Montmarte, The 1926,F 25,26:2
La Marr, Moses
Porgy and Bess 1959,Je 25,20:3
La Mond, John M (Cinematographer)
Flying with the Marines 1918,Je 24,9:1
La Motte, Jean
Folly of Vanity 1925,Ja 28,14:1
La Planche, Louise
Holiday Inn 1942,Ag 5,16:1
Happy Go Lucky 1943,Mr 25,25:1
La Plante, Laura
Old Swimmin' Hole, The 1921,F 28,16:2
Sporting Youth 1924,Ap 2,16:1
Fast Worker, The 1924,N 12,13:1
Smouldering Fires 1925,Mr 31,17:4
Dangerous Innocence 1925,Je 8,19:1
Teaser, The 1925,Je 15,10:1
Midnight Sun, The 1926,Ap 24,20:4
Skinner's Dress Suit 1926,My 3,27:1
Poker Faces 1926,S 14,25:4
Her big Night 1926,O 13,21:1
Butterflies in the Rain 1926,D 25,10:5
Love Thrill, The 1927,My 10,24:5
Beware of Widows 1927,My 24,23:4

La Plante, Laura— Cont
Cat and the Canary, The 1927,S 10,9:4
Silk Stockings 1927,N 29,31:1
Thanks For The Buggy Ride 1928,Ja 23,18:3
Finders Keepers 1928,Mr 5,21:3
Home James 1928,S 11,31:3
Last Warning, The 1929,Ja 7,36:2
Show Boat 1929,Ap 18,32:3
Scandal 1929,Ap 22,23:1
Hold Your Man 1929,O 14,20:2
Captain of the Guard 1930,Mr 29,23:1
King of Jazz 1930,My 3,23:1
Lonely Wives 1931,Mr 16,25:1
God's Gift to Women 1931,Ap 18,17:3
Men Are Like That 1931,Ag 17,18:2
Spring Reunion 1957,My 6,25:2
La Plante, Violet
Clean Heart, The 1924,S 15,28:1
La Porta, Arturo
Lost One, The; Travihta, La 1948,Mr 30,26:2
House of Ricordi 1956,Mr 13,32:1
La Porta, Eliza
Trial of Donald Westhof, The 1928,F 18,11:2
La Raina, Antonio
Scandal in Sorrento 1957,Je 13,37:1
La Reno, Dick
Sea Horses 1926,F 23,26:5
La Roche, Edward
Soul Fire 1925,My 6,26:3
La Roche, Mary
Catskill Honeymoon 1950,Ja 28,10:3
Operation Mad Ball 1957,N 21,38:1
Run Silent, Run Deep 1958,Mr 28,29:1
Gidget 1959,Ap 23,27:4
Bye Bye Birdie 1963,Ap 5,27:3
Swinger, The 1966,D 15,60:1
La Roche, Pete (Screenwriter)
Wetbacks 1956,My 5,13:2
La Rochelle, Drieu (Original Author)
Fire Within, The 1964,F 18,27:1
La Rocque, Rod
Stolen Kiss 1920,Ap 5,20:1
Society Scandal, A 1924,Mr 10,18:2
Triumph 1924,Ap 21,21:4
Feet of Clay 1924,S 22,16:1
Forbidden Paradise 1924,N 17,16:1
Golden Bed, The 1925,Ja 20,18:2
Coming of Amos, The 1925,S 8,29:1
Red Dice 1926,Ap 16,20:3
Gigolo 1926,O 5,27:1
Resurrection 1927,My 17,27:2
Fighting Eagle, The 1927,Ag 15,22:5
Stand and Deliver 1928,Ap 2,25:1
At Yale 1928,Jl 30,21:2
Captain Swagger 1928,D 24,17:7
One Woman Idea, The 1929,Je 10,23:1
Man and the Moment, The 1929,Ag 5,25:2
Our Modern Maidens 1929,S 7,15:1
Forbidden Paradise 1929,O 8,24:5
Locked Door, The 1930,Ja 20,21:1
One Romantic Night 1930,My 31,19:4
Beau Bandit 1930,Je 14,9:4
Let Us Be Gay 1930,Jl 12,16:4
S O S Iceberg 1933,S 25,18:4
Mystery Woman 1935,Ja 9,22:2
Preview Murder Mystery, The 1936,Mr 21,13:2
Till We Meet Again 1936,My 9,11:2
Shadow Strikes, The 1937,S 13,17:1
Taming the Wild 1938,Mr 28,19:2
International Crime 1938,My 16,14:4
Hunchback of Notre Dame, The 1940,Ja 1,29:2
Beyond Tomorrow 1940,S 27,27:1
Dark Streets of Cairo 1940,D 2,19:3
Meet John Doe 1941,Mr 13,25:2
La Rubia, Marga
For Sale 1924,Jl 14,11:5
Flirting With Love 1924,S 1,9:1
La Rue, Fontaine
Faith Healer, The 1921,Mr 14,9:2
Lost Romance, The 1921,My 9,16:2
Daughters of Today 1924,Mr 4,17:1
La Rue, Fontine
Boots 1919,Mr 10,9:3
La Rue, Frank H
Strange People 1933,Je 17,16:5
La Salle, Bobbie
Union Pacific 1939,My 11,31:2
La Salle, Martin
Pickpocket 1963,My 22,36:2
La Shelle, Kirk (Original Author)
Virginian, The 1946,Ap 18,22:2
La Starza, Roland
Convicts 4 1962,O 4,44:2
La Torre, Charles
Louisiana Purchase 1942,Ja 1,37:1
My Sister Eileen 1942,O 23,15:1
Casablanca 1942,N 27,27:1
Life Begins at Eight-Thirty 1942,D 10,35:2
Passage to Marseille 1944,F 17,12:5
Jam Session 1944,My 3,25:3
Hairy Ape, The 1944,Jl 3,8:3
Enter Arsene Lupin 1944,D 2,17:6
Walls Came Tumbling Down, The 1946,N 9,13:5
Double Life, A 1948,F 20,19:1

711 Ocean Drive 1950,Jl 20,21:2
La Toska, Phil
Way Down East 1935,O 31,16:2
La Varre, Myrtland
Knockout Reilly 1927,Ap 18,21:2
La Verne, Jane
That's my Daddy 1928,F 13,16:2
Show Boat 1929,Ap 18,32:3
Melody Lane 1929,Jl 16,23:5
La Verne, Lucille
White Rose, The 1923,My 23,18:3
Zaza 1923,S 17,18:2
America 1924,F 22,20:1
Sun Up 1925,Ag 18,14:3
Last Moment, The 1928,Mr 12,26:1
Abraham Lincoln 1930,Ag 26,24:1
Sinners' Holiday 1930,O 11,21:3
Great Meadow, The 1931,Mr 14,23:2
American Tragedy, An 1931,Ag 6,22:5
Twenty-Four Hours 1931,O 3,20:2
Unholy Garden, The 1931,O 29,27:1
She Wanted a Millionaire 1932,F 20,11:2
Alias the Doctor 1932,Mr 3,22:3
Pilgrimage 1933,Jl 13,17:5
Beloved 1934,Ja 27,9:3
Kentucky Kernels 1935,Ja 5,20:2
Tale of Two Cities, A 1935,D 26,21:2
La Violette, Juliette
White Sister, The 1923,S 6,10:2
Rejected Woman, The 1924,My 5,18:3
White Sister, The 1928,My 21,25:1
La Violette, Wesley
Body Is a Shell, The 1957,S 9,21:2
Laage, Barbara
B F's Daughter 1948,Mr 25,35:2
Act of Love 1954,F 12,20:5
Happy Road, The 1957,Je 21,20:2
Respectful Prostitute, The 1957,Jl 11,21:1
Every Second Counts 1957,O 15,39:4
Paris Blues 1961,N 8,41:1
Therese and Isabelle 1968,My 15,41:4
Labadie, Jean-Loup (Screenwriter)
Tales of Paris (The Tale of Ella); Tale of Ella, The
  (Tales of Paris) 1962,Ag 27,18:1
Labanya
Kanchenjungha 1966,Jl 26,27:2
Labarr, Marta
Break the News 1941,Ja 2,24:2
It Happened to One Man 1941,F 24,11:6
Conspiracy in Teheran 1950,Mr 11,8:3
Labarthe, Andre
Life Begins Tomorrow 1952,N 18,37:2
My Life to Live 1963,S 24,43:2
Labche (Screenwriter)
Horse Ate the Hat, The 1931,S 1,30:6
Labeiskaya, Alta
Gordeyev Family, The 1961,O 16,33:6
Labella, Vincenzo (Screenwriter)
And There Came a Man 1968,Ap 5,56:4
Labissoniere, Erin
Heart of a Salome, The 1927,Je 6,27:2
Laborde, Jean (Original Author)
Don't Tempt the Devil 1964,Ap 28,43:1
Labourdette, Elina
drame De Shanghai; Shanghai Drama, The
  1945,Ja 11,19:2
Edward and Caroline 1952,Ap 30,33:3
Amazing Monsieur Fabre, The 1952,S 9,21:2
To Paris With Love 1955,Mr 29,33:4
Truth About Women, The 1958,Ag 29,18:2
Tales of Paris (The Tale of Sophie); Tale of Sophie,
  The (Tales of Paris) 1962,Ag 27,18:1
Lola 1962,O 15,32:2
Two Are Guilty 1964,F 29,12:1
Dames du Bois de Boulogne, Les; Ladies of the
  Park 1964,Ap 4,15:5
Laboursier, Raymond (Director)
Nais 1948,Je 16,37:2
Labow, John
Winter Kept Us Warm 1968,F 9,55:3
Labry, Pierre
Kermesse Heroique, La 1936,S 23,29:1
Story of a Cheat, The 1938,S 27,25:2
Boys' School 1939,Je 6,26:2
S O S Mediterranean 1940,Ja 1,29:2
Mayor's Dilemma, The 1940,Ap 23,19:2
It Happened at the Inn; Goupi Mains Rouge
  1945,D 22,16:2
Postmaster's Daughter, The 1946,Ag 19,17:6
Bellman, The 1947,Ap 7,20:5
Devil's Own Envoy, The 1947,Ag 30,8:6
Lacasa, Rosita
Patricio miro a una Estrella; Patricio Looked at a
  Star 1938,N 12,10:3
Lacassin, Francis (Screenwriter)
Judex 1966,Ap 26,55:1
Lacca, Yolanda
Chase, The 1946,N 18,31:2
Lace, Ann
Secret Heart, The 1946,D 26,28:2
LaCentra, Peg
Humoresque 1946,D 26,28:1

Laceteen, Frank
Into the Net 1924,Ag 23,10:2
Lacey, Catherine
Lady Vanishes, The 1938,D 26,29:1
October Man, The 1948,Ap 16,29:2
Bad Sister 1948,Je 11,27:3
Tight Little Island 1949,D 26,33:2
Pink String and Sealing Wax 1950,O 4,38:2
Mad Little Island 1958,D 31,12:1
Crack in the Mirror 1960,My 20,26:1
Another Sky 1960,O 25,40:2
Servant, The 1964,Mr 17,30:2
Lacey, Frank (Original Author)
Music Man, The 1962,Ag 24,14:1
Lacey, Margaret
Family Way, The 1967,Je 29,32:1
Lacey, Ronald
Of Human Bondage 1964,S 24,46:2
Having a Wild Weekend 1965,Ag 19,35:1
How I Won the War 1967,N 9,56:1
Lachenal, Louis (Miscellaneous)
Annapurna 1953,Jl 14,45:4
Lachman, Harry (Director)
Compulsory Husband, The 1930,Mr 23,IX,6:1
Outsider, The 1931,Je 7,VIII,6:1
Aren't We All? 1932,Jl 1,19:3
Couturiere de Luneville, La 1932,O 14,23:2
Mistigri 1933,Ja 13,19:3
Face in the Sky 1933,F 20,11:5
Paddy the Next Best Thing 1933,Ag 25,12:2
I Like It That Way 1934,Ap 18,23:3
Baby, Take a Bow 1934,Je 30,18:6
Nada Mas Que Una Mujer 1934,N 26,12:2
Dante's Inferno 1935,Ag 1,15:1
Charlie Chan at the Circus 1936,Mr 19,22:4
Man Who Lived Twice, The 1936,O 12,23:2
Our Relations 1936,N 11,55:1
Devil is Driving, The 1937,Jl 16,22:1
It Happened in Hollywood 1937,O 2,18:1
No Time to Marry 1938,F 23,27:2
Dead Men Tell 1941,Ap 17,29:3
Loves of Edgar Allan Poe, The 1942,S 21,19:2
Lachman, Marc (Original Author)
Hooray for Love 1935,Jl 13,16:2
Lachman, Mort (Screenwriter)
Yours, Mine and Ours 1968,Ap 25,53:1
Lack, Simon
Proud Valley 1941,My 17,19:2
Lackaye, Wilton
Lone Wolf, The 1924,My 7,19:4
Lackey, William (Producer)
Girl of the Limberlost, A 1934,N 9,24:6
Ape, The 1940,N 28,28:3
Lackland, Ben
Boomerang 1947,Mr 6,36:2
Lackteen, Frank
Pony Express, The 1925,S 14,16:1
Desert Gold 1926,Mr 23,24:5
Nagana 1933,F 16,23:2
Escape from Devil's Island 1935,N 25,22:2
I Cover the War 1937,Ag 2,10:2
Girl and the Gambler, The 1939,Je 28,17:3
Moon Over Burma 1940,D 12,37:4
Sea Wolf, The 1941,Mr 26,27:3
South of Tahiti 1941,N 10,21:3
Bombs Over Burma 1942,Ag 10,15:2
Chetniks 1943,Mr 19,15:3
Frontier Badmen 1943,Ag 14,12:8
Frontier Gal 1945,D 15,14:2
Amazon Quest 1949,My 14,9:3
King of the Khyber Rifles 1953,D 23,21:1
Laclos, Choderlos de (Original Author)
Liaisons Dangereuses, Les 1961,D 19,39:1
Lacombe, Georges (Director)
Musiciens du Ciel 1945,Mr 1,26:6
Midnight in Paris 1947,O 9,32:3
Room Upstairs, The 1948,S 4,8:6
Seven Deadly Sins, The (The Eighth Sin); Eighth
  Sin, The (The Seven Deadly Sins)
  1953,My 12,31:3
Night is my Kingdom, The 1953,S 30,37:1
Light Across the Street, The; Lumiere d'en Face,
  La 1957,Jl 30,20:2
Lacombe, Georges (Screenwriter)
32 Rue de Montmartre 1944,S 28,26:3
Lacombrade, Francis
This Special Friendship 1967,N 8,56:1
LaCossitt, Henry (Original Author)
Night Ride 1930,Ja 20,21:1
Homicide Squad 1931,O 19,28:1
Lacoste, M
Legion of Honor, The 1928,Jl 20,8:4
Lacourt, Rene
Mr Hulot's Holiday 1954,Je 17,36:2
Lacuna, Don Vincentre (Miscellaneous)
Life of Simon Bolivar, The 1943,Je 18,16:5
Lacy, Phillipe de
Don Juan 1926,Ag 7,6:1 (In Addenda)
Ladd, Alan
Rulers of the Sea 1939,N 9,27:1
Beasts of Berlin 1939,N 20,15:6
Black Cat, The 1941,Ap 26,20:3
Reluctant Dragon, The 1941,Jl 25,12:2

Gangs Incorporated 1941,Ag 4,16:6
Joan of Paris 1942,Ja 26,18:2
This Gun for Hire 1942,My 14,23:2
Glass Key, The 1942,O 16,23:1
Star Spangled Rhythm 1942,D 31,20:1
Lucky Jordan 1943,Ja 25,10:8
China 1943,Ap 22,31:2
And Now Tomorrow 1944,N 23,38:2
Salty O'Rourke 1945,Ap 26,26:2
Duffy's Tavern 1945,S 6,23:3
Blue Dahlia, The 1946,My 9,27:3
O S S 1946,My 27,15:5
Two Years Before the Mast 1946,S 25,39:2
Calcutta 1947,Ap 24,30:2
Wild Harvest 1947,N 13,33:2
Saigon 1948,Ap 1,30:5
Beyond Glory 1948,Ag 4,18:2
Whispering Smith 1949,F 15,28:2
Great Gatsby, The 1949,Jl 14,20:5
Chicago Deadline 1949,N 3,37:2
Captain Carey U S A 1950,Mr 30,40:5
Branded 1951,Ja 11,28:5
Appointment With Danger 1951,My 10,38:2
Red Mountain 1952,Ap 26,19:2
Iron Mistress, The 1952,N 20,39:2
Thunder in the East 1953,F 4,32:2
Shane 1953,Ap 24,30:3
Desert Legion 1953,My 9,13:2
Botany Bay 1953,O 30,27:2
Paratrooper 1953,D 31,9:3
Saskatchewan 1954,Mr 11,26:2
Hell Below Zero 1954,Jl 17,7:3
Black Knight, The 1954,O 29,27:2
Drum Beat 1954,N 18,42:1
McConnell Story, The 1955,S 30,23:1
Hell on Frisco Bay 1956,Ja 7,21:1
Santiago 1956,Jl 14,13:2
Big Land, The 1957,Mr 2,18:2
Boy on a Dolphin 1957,Ap 20,21:2
Deep Six, The 1958,Ja 16,32:1
Proud Rebel, The 1958,Jl 2,23:4
Badlanders, The 1958,S 4,33:1
Man in the Net, The 1959,Je 11,36:2
All the Young Men 1960,Ag 27,8:6
One Foot in Hell 1960,O 20,42:2
13 West Street 1962,Je 7,31:2
Carpetbaggers, The 1964,Jl 2,24:4

Ladd, David
Big Land, The 1957,Mr 2,18:2
Proud Rebel, The 1958,Jl 2,23:4
Dog of Flanders, A 1960,Ap 1,37:1
Misty 1961,Jl 18,33:2
Ladd, Diane
Wild Angels, The 1966,D 22,40:4
Ladd, Fred (Cinematographer)
Journey to the Beginning of Time 1967,F 11,20:1
Ladd, Fred (Producer)
Pinnocchio in Outer Space 1965,D 23,21:4
Ladd, Hank
Las Vegas Nights 1941,Mr 20,25:2
Ladd, Tom
Men In her Life, The 1941,D 12,35:1
Laddie (Dog)
Son of Lassie 1945,Je 11,12:1
Ladengast, Walter
Toerichte Jungfrau, Die 1935,S 9,24:3
Taiga 1959,Mr 17,42:4
Laderer, Charles (Screenwriter)
His Girl Friday 1940,Ja 12,13:2
Laderman, Ezra (Composer)
Eleanor Roosevelt Story, The 1965,N 9,50:1
Laderman, Fred (Screenwriter)
Pinnocchio in Outer Space 1965,D 23,21:4
Ladesma, Amanda
Senderos de Fe; Paths of Faith 1940,Mr 2,9:5
Ladikou, Alexandra
Red Lanterns 1965,Ap 1,30:1
Ladmiral, Nicole
Diary of a Country Priest 1954,Ap 6,35:2
Lado, Jose
Man's Hope; (Sierra de Teruel) 1947,Ja 21,29:2
Ladoux, Fernand
Trial, The 1963,F 21,5:1
Ladowicz, B (Director)
Jews in Poland 1957,Ap 17,37:1
LaDuke, Jeanne
Green Promise, The 1949,Je 24,29:2
Lady (mare)
Black Cyclone 1925,My 19,24:2
Ladynina, Marina
Grain 1936,Ja 16,25:2
Country Bride 1938,Je 4,18:2
We Will Come Back 1943,O 15,15:2
They Met in Moscow 1944,Je 7,13:2
Six PM 1946,Ja 28,15:5
Symphony of Life 1948,D 28,19:7
Cossacks of the Kuban 1950,O 30,22:4
Devotion 1955,Ag 1,15:2
Laeck, Carsta
Vier Musketiere, Die; Four Musketeers, The
  1935,N 9,19:3

Laemmle, Carl (Producer)
Crashing Through to Berlin 1918,Ag 12,7:3 (In
  Addenda)
Laemmle, Carl Jr (Producer)
Imitation of Life 1934,N 24,19:1
Good Fairy, The 1935,F 1,18:1
Show Boat 1936,My 15,29:4
Laemmle, Edward (Cinematographer)
Shipwrecked Among Cannibals 1920,Jl 5,12:4
Laemmle, Edward (Director)
Thirteenth Juror, The 1927,N 22,20:1
Cheating Cheaters 1927,D 6,27:1
Drake Case, The 1929,S 16,30:1
Notorious Gentleman, A 1935,F 16,9:1
Laeutner, Alfred
Schubert's Fruehlingstraum 1932,Je 22,19:4
Lafaye, George
I Love, You Love 1962,N 10,16:2
Lafayette, Andree
Trilby 1923,Jl 30,11:4
Survival 1930,Ja 13,21:1
Trois Mousquetaires, Les 1933,My 1,10:2
Lafayette, Jeanne
Hans Christian Andersen 1952,N 26,20:2
Lafayette, Ruby
Toby's Bow 1919,D 15,20:1
Day of Faith, The 1923,N 27,11:2
Tomorrow's Love 1925,Ja 7,33:5
Coming of Amos, The 1925,S 8,29:1
Butterflies in the Rain 1926,D 25,10:5
Marriage by Contract 1928,N 13,37:1
Laffan, Patricia
Quo Vadis 1951,N 9,22:2
23 Paces to Baker Street 1956,My 19,12:6
Laffon, Yolande
Life and Loves of Beethoven, The
  1937,N 22,15:1
Angels of the Streets 1950,Ja 17,24:2
Minne 1951,Ap 17,35:2
Lafforgue, Rene-Louis
Lovers of Teruel, The 1962,D 15,5:1
Julie the Redhead 1963,O 15,44:1
Lafitte, Paul (Original Author)
Mister Hobo 1936,F 8,19:2
Rothchild 1938,O 12,35:2
LaFleur, Joy
Whispering City 1948,My 10,25:5
Lafont, Bernadette
Beau Serge, Le 1959,Ag 3,21:1
Leda 1961,Jl 19,33:1
Male Hunt; Chasse a l'Homme, La
  1965,Ap 20,42:1
Bonnes Femmes, Les 1966,My 13,32:1
Thief of Paris, The 1967,Ag 24,43:2
Laforet, Marie
Purple Noon 1961,S 1,12:1
Girl With the Golden Eyes, The 1962,Ag 21,36:2
Male Hunt; Chasse a l'Homme, La
  1965,Ap 20,42:1
How Not to Rob a Department Store
  1965,D 29,23:1
Jack of Diamonds 1967,N 11,26:3
Lafuife, Rene (Miscellaneous)
Sky Above, The-Mud Below, The 1962,Je 20,40:1
Lagache, Daniel
Life Begins Tomorrow 1952,N 18,37:2
Lagano, Jimmy
Black Hand 1950,Mr 13,15:2
Lagar, Pedro Lopez
Bodas de Sangre; Bloody Wedding
  1939,N 13,15:3
Lageard, Theo (Producer)
Midnight Episode 1955,My 19,25:5
Lagerlof, Selma (Original Author)
Girl From the Marsh Croft, The
  1919,Mr 30,IV,6:1
Sir Arne's Treasure 1921,D 25,VI,2:1
Stroke of Midnight, The 1922,Je 5,16:2
Tower of Lies, The 1925,S 28,24:1
Three Who Were Doomed 1928,Ja 10,28:4
Legend of Gosta Berling, The 1928,Ag 29,29:1
Charlotte Loewenskoeld 1932,F 22,23:2
Charrette Fantome, La 1940,My 28,29:2
Wonderful Adventures of Nils, The
  1962,S 14,37:1
Barabbas 1962,O 11,49:1
Lagerwall, Sture
Roeda Dagen 1932,My 21,9:2
Vi Tvaa; We Two 1939,D 2,21:3
Kvinnorna Kring Larsson; Women Around
  Larsson, The 1940,My 18,11:3
Lasse-Maja 1943,Mr 22,15:4
Devil's Eye, The 1961,O 31,27:4
Lagin, L (Original Author)
Flying Carpet, The 1960,F 28,31:1
Lagin, L (Screenwriter)
Flying Carpet, The 1960,F 28,31:1
Lagnell, Ulla
Sorciere, La 1956,D 28,17:2
Lagrange, Louise
Side Show of Life, The 1924,Jl 22,9:1
Sainted Devil, A 1924,N 24,15:3
Marche Nuptiale, La 1929,Mr 3,VIII,7:2

Lagrange, Valerie
Love and the Frenchwoman; (Francaise et
  l'Amour, La) 1961,F 28,38:2
Morgan the Pirate 1961,Jl 20,32:2
Green Mare, The; Jument Verte, La
  1961,O 24,41:2
Male Companion 1966,F 15,33:2
Up to his Ears 1966,My 18,37:1
Man and a Woman, A; Homme et une Femme,
  Un 1966,Jl 13,35:1
Weekend 1968,S 28,36:1
Lagrence, Maurice
Devil in the Flesh 1949,My 10,29:2
Lagutin, I
Lenin in October 1938,Ap 2,18:1
Alexander Nevsky 1939,Mr 23,27:1
Lahiri, Tuisi
Music Room, The 1963,O 16,50:6
Lahner, Lori
Summer Storm 1944,O 23,14:3
Lahr, Bert
Flying High 1931,D 12,23:3
Merry-Go-Round of 1938 1937,N 26,27:2
Love and Hisses 1938,Ja 1,11:1
Josette 1938,Je 11,9:1
Just Around the Corner 1938,D 3,11:2
Zaza 1939,Ja 5,17:1
Wizard of Oz, The 1939,Ag 18,16:2
Sing Your Worries Away 1942,My 15,25:2
Ship Ahoy 1942,Je 26,16:5•
Meet The People 1944,S 8,16:2
Always Leave Them Laughing 1949,N 24,48:2
Mr Universe 1951,Mr 23,16:2
Rose Marie 1954,Ap 2,22:2
Second Greatest Sex, The 1956,F 11,12:2
Sound of Laughter, The 1963,D 18,44:2
Night They Raided Minsky's, The
  1968,D 23,43:1
Lahsen, Itto Bent
Daughter of the Sands 1952,F 18,15:2
Laidlaw, Betty (Screenwriter)
Girl Said No, The 1937,O 18,14:1
Personal Secretary 1938,O 5,20:2
Laidlaw, Ethan
Wolf's Clothing 1927,Mr 28,26:4
Silly Billies 1936,Ap 6,18:1
Special Investigator 1936,Ap 25,21:1
Two in Revolt 1936,Ap 25,21:1
I'm From the City 1938,Ag 19,13:4
Great Missouri Raid, The 1951,Ap 9,31:2
Powder River 1953,Jl 4,7:2
Laidlaw, Roy
Hunchback of Notre Dame, The 1923,S 3,9:3
Snob, The 1924,D 15,14:1
Splendid Road, The 1926,Je 13,31:1
Laidlaw, William R (Screenwriter)
Command Decision 1949,Ja 20,34:2
Laidley, Alice
That Royle Girl 1926,Ja 4,33:1
LAINE
See Also LANE
Laine, Cleo
Roman Spring of Mrs Stone, The 1961,D 29,11:1
Laine, Frankie
Meet Me in Las Vegas 1956,Mr 14,39:2
Laine, Liliane
When Love Calls 1948,O 9,12:6
Fear No Evil 1949,Mr 31,31:2
LAING
See Also LANGE
Laing, Harold
Dance Little Lady 1955,D 26,23:3
Laing, Hugh
Brigadoon 1954,S 17,18:2
Laing, John
Conspiracy 1939,Ag 23,19:2
Laing, Tony
This Freedom 1923,N 28,15:1
Laird, Connie
Guest in the House 1945,F 16,19:2
Laird, Effie
House by the River 1950,My 2,25:2
Laird, Jack (Producer)
Dark Intruder 1965,Jl 22,24:2
Laird, Jenny
Wanted for Murder 1946,D 12,38:4
Black Narcissus 1947,Ag 14,29:2
Girl in the Canal, The 1947,O 9,32:3
Eye Witness 1950,Ag 28,13:2
Village of the Damned 1960,D 8,43:3
Laird, John
Conspiracy 1939,Ag 23,19:2
Laire, Judson
Ugly American, The 1963,Ap 12,30:2
Shock Treatment 1964,Jl 23,19:1
Laison, Jack (Producer)
Chuka 1967,N 2,58:3
Laison Brothers
Crazy House 1943,D 16,33:3
Lait, Jack (Original Author)
Love Burglar, The 1919,Jl 28,8:5
Ten Modern Commandments 1927,Jl 11,23:4
Bad Company 1931,N 7,16:5

Lait, Jack (Original Author)— Cont
  Girl Without a Room 1933,D 7,26:3
  New York Confidential 1955,F 19,18:1
Lait, Jack Jr (Original Author)
  Kentucky Moonshine 1938,My 21,9:2
Laja, Maria
  Paloma, La 1936,O 21,35:3
Lake, Alice
  Come Through 1917,Je 18,7:2
  Should a Woman Tell? 1920,Ja 5,15:1
  Shore Acres 1920,My 17,19:3
  Red Lights 1923,S 10,15:4
  Unknown Purple, The 1924,Mr 24,13:1
  Angel of Broadway 1927,N 1,21:1 (In Addenda)
  Haunted Ship, The 1928,Ja 23,18:3
  Twin Beds 1929,Jl 15,25:1
  Frozen Justice 1929,O 26,15:1
  Wicked 1931,S 19,10:2
Lake, Arthur
  Skinner's Dress Suit 1926,My 3,27:1
  Cradle Snatchers 1927,My 31,25:2
  Irresistible Lover, The 1927,O 19,24:4
  Count of Ten, The 1928,Mr 13,23:3
  Stop That Man 1928,Ap 17,27:2
  Harold Teen 1928,Ag 14,15:4
  Air Circus, The 1928,S 3,14:2
  On With the Show 1929,My 29,28:6
  Tanned Legs 1929,D 2,28:2
  Dance Hall 1929,D 16,34:2
  She's my Weakness 1930,Je 21,20:5
  Indiscreet 1931,My 7,21:4
  Midshipman Jack 1933,N 20,18:2
  Silver Streak, The 1935,Ja 16,21:1
  Orchids to You 1935,Ag 10,16:4
  23 1/2 Hours Leave 1937,My 17,23:2
  Topper 1937,Ag 20,21:2
  Annapolis Salute 1937,O 2,18:1
  Double Danger 1938,F 10,17:5
  There Goes my Heart 1938,O 14,27:1
  Blondie 1938,D 22,25:4
  Blondie Meets the Boss 1939,Ap 27,31:1
  Blondie Goes Latin 1941,F 26,17:3
  3 Is a Family 1944,D 20,20:3
  16 Fathoms Deep 1948,O 7,35:2
  Blondie Hits the Jackpot 1949,S 9,28:3
Lake, Florence
  Thru Different Eyes 1929,Ap 15,22:6
  Rogue Song, The 1930,Ja 29,26:4
  Romance 1930,Ag 23,7:3
  Ladies of the Jury 1932,Ap 2,13:2
  Night World 1932,My 28,18:2
  Sweetheart of Sigma Chi, The 1933,N 9,27:1
  Midshipman Jack 1933,N 20,18:2
  Two Fisted 1935,O 5,18:3
  To Mary-With Love 1936,Ag 27,16:1
  Quality Street 1937,Ap 9,19:2
  I Met my Love Again 1938,Ja 15,19:1
  Condemned Woman 1938,Ap 22,15:5
  Stagecoach 1939,Mr 3,21:1
  Crash Dive 1943,Ap 29,25:2
  San Diego, I Love You 1944,N 10,25:1
Lake, Gladys B
  People vs Dr Kildare, The 1941,My 8,21:1
Lake, Stuart N (Original Author)
  Frontier Marshal 1934,Ja 31,20:3
  Wells Fargo 1937,D 30,15:2
  Frontier Marshal 1939,Jl 29,18:2
  Westerner, The 1940,O 25,25:2
  My Darling Clementine 1946,D 4,44:5
  Winchester 73 1950,Je 8,38:2
Lake, Veronica
  I Wanted Wings 1941,Mr 27,29:4
  Hold Back the Dawn 1941,O 2,29:1
  Sullivan's Travels 1942,Ja 29,25:2
  This Gun for Hire 1942,My 14,23:2
  Glass Key, The 1942,O 16,23:1
  I Married a Witch 1942,N 20,27:2
  Star Spangled Rhythm 1942,D 31,20:1
  So Proudly We Hail 1943,S 10,29:1
  Hour Before the Dawn, The 1944,My 11,25:6
  Bring on the Girls 1945,Mr 1,25:5
  Out of This World 1945,Je 7,25:2
  Duffy's Tavern 1945,S 6,23:3
  Hold That Blonde 1945,N 8,17:2
  Miss Susie Slagle's 1946,F 7,29:2
  Blue Dahlia, The 1946,My 9,27:3
  Ramrod 1947,Je 30,25:6
  Saigon 1948,Ap 1,30:5
  Sainted Sisters, The 1948,My 20,35:2
  Isn't It Romantic? 1948,O 7,35:2
  Slattery's Hurricane 1949,Ag 13,6:6
Lake, Wesley
  4 Devils 1928,O 4,26:3
Lakhtionova, A
  Sunny Youth 1935,Ag 19,18:2
Lakso, Edward J (Screenwriter)
  Gentle Giant 1968,Ap 20,26:1
La'lli
  Return to Paradise 1953,S 11,24:2
Lally, Howard
  Doctor Bull 1933,O 6,21:2
  Mad Game, The 1933,N 13,21:1

Lally, William J
  Red Menace, The 1949,Je 27,18:2
Lalogh, Klari
  Kiralyne Huszarja, A 1936,Ja 17,15:3
Lalor, Frank
  Red Hot Romance 1922,Ja 23,11:4
Lamac, Karl (Director)
  Versuchen Sie Meine Schwester 1931,Je 20,20:4
  Zinker, Der 1931,O 4,VIII,7:1
  Eine Freundin so Goldig wie Du 1931,O 24,20:3
  Die vom Rummelplatz 1932,Ja 2,14:2
  Der Falsche Feldmarschall 1932,Je 30,26:2
  Eine Nacht im Paradies 1933,F 20,11:6
  Tochter des Regiments, Die 1934,Mr 31,8:3
  Klein Dorrit 1935,O 19,21:2
  Polenblut; Polish Blood 1935,N 16,19:3
  Frasquita 1936,Ja 18,19:4
  Knock-Out 1936,F 29,11:2
  Karneval und Liebe 1936,Ap 4,11:2
  Schuechterne Casanova, Der 1936,Ag 22,6:2
  Junge Graf, Der 1936,D 14,15:2
  Postillon of Lonjumeau, The 1937,N 20,21:3
  Gross Reinemachen; General Housecleaning
    1938,Je 23,27:2
  Walzerlange; Waltz Melodies 1940,Ap 27,9:3
Lamande, Jean-Louis
  Shameless Old Lady, The 1966,S 27,52:1
Lamar, Adriana
  Sagrario 1934,Ja 22,12:3
  Tiburon 1934,Ap 18,23:3
  Chucho el Roto 1935,Mr 30,11:3
  Vuelo de la Muerte, El 1935,Ap 16,27:3
  Llorona, La 1935,Jl 20,16:2
  No Mataras; Thou Shalt not Kill 1935,N 11,20:2
  Crimen de Media Noche, El 1936,F 22,12:3
  Malditas Sean las Mujeres 1936,Ag 29,16:3
  Irma la Mala 1936,O 6,28:7
  Mujeres de Hoy 1936,D 7,27:4
  Esos Hombres 1937,Ag 21,7:3
  Cuatro Milpas, Las; Four Corn Patches, The
    1937,S 13,17:2
  Mexico Lindo 1939,F 4,11:1
  Muerto Murio, El; Dead Man Died, The
    1939,Jl 29,18:3
  Olvidados de Dios, Los; Those Forgotten by God
    1940,Ja 15,11:2
  Mexico Lindo 1940,F 10,19:2
  Vivire Otra Vez; I Shall Live Again
    1940,O 23,27:2
Lamar, Mary
  Teacher and the Miracle, The 1961,Ap 24,36:4
Lamarque, Libertad
  Ayudame a Vivir; Help Me to Live
    1938,My 7,18:2
  Madreselva; Honeysuckle 1939,Ag 19,18:4
  Besos Brujos; Bewitching Kisses 1939,O 21,12:3
  Ley que Olvidaron, La; Law They Forgot, The
    1940,Ja 13,11:3
  Puerta Cerrada; Closed Door 1940,F 5,13:3
  Alma del Bandoneon, El; Soul of the Accordion,
    The 1940,Ap 27,9:3
Lamarr, Danielle
  Crazy in the Noodle 1957,D 15,45:4 (Incorrect in
    this edition; use 1957,D 17,45:4 elsewhere)
Lamarr, Hedy
  Algiers 1938,Jl 15,13:2
  Lady of the Tropics 1939,S 8,28:3
  I Take This Woman 1940,F 16,23:3
  Boom Town 1940,S 6,25:2
  Ecstasy 1940,D 25,33:2
  Comrade X 1940,D 26,23:1
  Come Live With Me 1941,F 28,17:3
  Ziegfeld Girl 1941,Ap 25,17:2
  H M Pulham, Esq 1941,D 19,35:1
  Tortilla Flat 1942,My 22,27:1
  Crossroads 1942,Jl 27,18:2
  White Cargo 1942,N 27,27:2
  Heavenly Body, The 1944,Mr 24,17:3
  Conspirators, The 1944,O 21,15:2
  Experiment Perilous 1944,D 30,15:2
  Her Highness and the Bellboy 1945,S 28,16:2
  Strange Woman, The 1947,F 24,16:4
  Dishonored Lady 1947,My 24,10:5
  Let's Live a Little 1948,D 10,34:2
  Samson and Delilah 1949,D 22,29:2
  Lady Without Passport, A 1950,Ag 4,13:2
  Copper Canyon 1950,N 16,39:2
  My Favorite Spy 1951,D 26,19:3
  Story of Mankind, The 1957,N 9,31:2
  Female Animal, The 1958,Ja 23,24:3
Lamas, Carmen
  Amor Manda, El; Love Commands
    1940,My 18,11:3
Lamas, Fernando
  Rich, Young and Pretty 1951,Jl 26,17:3
  Law and the Lady, The 1951,Ag 16,23:2
  Merry Widow, The 1952,S 25,38:1
  Sangaree 1953,Je 5,19:1
  Dangerous When Wet 1953,Je 19,18:1
  Diamond Queen, The 1954,Ja 27,24:2
  Jivaro 1954,F 13,11:5
  Rose Marie 1954,Ap 2,22:2
  Lost World, The 1960,Jl 14,23:1

Lamas, Fernando— Cont
  Kill a Dragon 1967,D 7,60:2
Lamas, Fernando (Screenwriter)
  Place Called Glory, A 1966,Ag 11,27:4
Lamb, Celia
  Man in Grey, The 1945,N 30,18:6
Lamb, Charles
  Galloping Major, The 1951,D 17,27:2
  Curtain Up 1953,F 2,17:3
  Life at the Top 1965,D 15,53:1
Lamb, Gene
  Explorers of the World 1931,D 18,29:3
Lamb, Gil
  Fleet's In, The 1942,Mr 12,24:2
  Star Spangled Rhythm 1942,D 31,20:1
  Riding High 1943,D 23,26:4
  Rainbow Island 1944,O 26,19:6
  Practically Yours 1945,Mr 29,18:2
  Hit Parade of 1947 1947,My 5,32:8
  Her Wonderful Lie 1950,Jl 17,15:2
Lamb, Harold (Miscellaneous)
  Crusades, The 1935,Ag 22,21:3
  Samson and Delilah 1949,D 22,29:2
Lamb, Harold (Screenwriter)
  Crusades, The 1935,Ag 22,21:3
  Plainsman, The 1937,Ja 14,16:2
  Buccaneer, The 1938,F 17,17:2
  Buccaneer, The 1958,D 24,00:0
Lamb, Jane
  Green Scarf, The 1955,Ja 15,10:2
Lamberger, G
  Dybbuk, The 1938,Ja 28,17:2
Lambert, Constant
  Battle for Music 1945,O 15,13:2
Lambert, Diana
  Circle, The 1959,Ap 16,29:2
Lambert, Eddie
  Women Go on Forever 1931,O 19,28:1
  High Gear 1933,Ap 15,16:2
Lambert, Gavin (Director)
  Another Sky 1960,O 25,40:2
Lambert, Gavin (Original Author)
  Inside Daisy Clover 1966,F 18,23:1
Lambert, Gavin (Screenwriter)
  Sons and Lovers 1960,Ag 3,35:1
  Another Sky 1960,O 25,40:2
  Roman Spring of Mrs Stone, The 1961,D 29,11:1
  Inside Daisy Clover 1966,F 18,23:1
Lambert, Irene
  Sally of the Scandals 1928,Jl 3,19:3
Lambert, Jack
  Ghost Goes West, The 1936,Ja 11,9:2
Lambert, Jack
  Cross of Lorraine, The 1943,D 3,27:4
  Harvey Girls, The 1946,Ja 25,26:2
  Abilene Town 1946,Mr 4,16:5
  Killers, The 1946,Ag 29,24:2
  Captive Heart, The 1947,Ap 28,27:2
  Dick Tracy's Dilemma 1947,Jl 14,14:5
  Unsuspected, The 1947,O 4,9:2
  River Lady 1948,My 21,19:5
  Belle Star's Daughter 1949,Ja 10,19:2
  Big Jack 1949,My 23,27:4
  Brimstone 1949,O 7,35:3
  Dakota Lil 1950,Mr 3,21:5
  Massacre Hill 1950,D 14,51:3
  Stars in my Crown 1950,D 22,19:1
  Hue and Cry 1951,Ja 9,25:2
  Enforcer, The 1951,Ja 26,19:2
  Bend of the River 1952,Ap 10,37:1
  Montana Belle 1952,N 8,9:2
  Scared Stiff 1953,Jl 3,10:2
  Vera Cruz 1954,D 27,22:4
  Three Cases of Murder (You Killed Elizabeth);
    You Killed Elizabeth (Three Cases of Murder)
    1955,Mr 16,39:4
  Run for Cover 1955,Ap 30,10:6
  Storm over the Nile 1956,Je 9,14:2
  Little Hut, The 1957,My 4,25:1
  Chicago Confidential 1957,Ag 31,19:1
  Bridal Path, The 1959,D 21,34:2
  Francis of Assisi 1961,Jl 29,8:2
Lambert, Janet
  Up in Mabel's Room 1944,Ap 22,8:6
  Abroad With two Yanks 1944,O 26,19:7
Lambert, Knut
  Larsson I Andra Giftet 1935,O 19,21:3
Lambert, Madeleine
  Bride Is Much too Beautiful, The 1958,Ja 21,35:1
Lambert, Martine
  Love and the Frenchwoman; (Francaise et
    l'Amour, La) 1961,F 28,38:2
Lambert, Michael
  Gay Intruders, The 1946,Mr 18,24:2
Lambert, Paul
  Spartacus 1960,O 7,28:1
  Big Mouth, The 1967,Jl 13,30:2
Lambert, Reita (Original Author)
  Careless Lady 1932,Ap 18,19:2
Lamberti, Prof
  Tonight and Every Night 1945,Mr 9,16:2
Lambertson, Donna
  3 Is a Family 1944,D 20,20:3

Lambertson, Elissa
3 Is a Family 1944,D 20,20:3
Lambetti, Ellie
Youth of Athens 1949,O 31,20:a
Windfall in Athens 1956,O 1,31:1
Girl in Black, A 1957,S 17,39:2
Counterfeit Coin 1960,My 16,39:1
Wastrel, The 1963,N 5,24:1
Lambie, Jack
Atlantic Flight 1937,N 1,24:5
Lamble, Lloyd
Curtain Up 1953,F 2,17:3
Gilbert and Sullivan 1953,O 28,36:3
1954,S 18,12:4
White Fire 1954,S 18,12:4
Belles of St Trinian's, The 1954,D 23,13:4
Blue Murder at St Trinian's 1958,My 27,27:1
Trials of Oscar Wilde, The 1960,Je 28,26:1
Pure Hell of St Trinian's, The 1961,S 26,31:1
Lambrinos, Vassili
Island of Love 1963,Je 13,30:4
Unsinkable Molly Brown, The 1964,Jl 17,15:1
Lamfield, Sidney (Director)
Broadway Bad 1933,Mr 6,16:6
Lamon, Molly
Fury and the Woman 1937,Je 22,26:2
Lamont, B Wayne
Cross Examination 1932,F 27,22:1
Midnight Lady, The 1932,Jl 1,19:3
Lamont, Charles (Director)
World Accuses, The 1935,Mr 21,27:2
Sons of Steel 1935,Ap 15,16:3
Gigolette 1935,My 13,18:6
Shot in the Dark, A 1935,My 22,23:2
International Crime 1938,My 16,14:4
Shadows Over Shanghai 1938,D 1,29:2
Cipher Bureau 1938,D 14,32:6
Verbena Tragica; Tragic Festival, The
1939,Mr 13,12:3
Unexpected Father 1939,Ag 11,12:2
Little Accident 1939,N 24,29:3
Sandy Is a Lady 1940,Je 28,22:2
Give Us Wings 1940,N 21,43:3
Moonlight in Hawaii 1941,O 10,26:6
Almost Married 1942,Je 5,23:2
Get Help to Love 1942,O 19,15:3
It Comes up Love 1943,Ja 22,25:3
When Johnny Comes Marching Home
1943,Mr 5,20:4
Mister Big 1943,Je 14,13:4
Hit the Ice 1943,S 23,27:2
Fired Wife 1943,O 1,15:2
Top Man 1943,O 29,23:2
Chip off the Old Block 1944,Mr 17,14:2
Her Primitive Man 1944,Ap 1,11:1
Merry Monahans, The 1944,O 13,16:2
Bowery to Broadway 1944,N 30,19:2
Salome, Where She Danced 1945,My 3,27:1
That's the Spirit 1945,Je 2,11:2
Frontier Gal 1945,D 15,14:2
Runaround, The 1946,Je 7,16:3
She Wrote the Book 1946,Je 20,20:3
Slave Girl 1947,Jl 18,21:3
Ma and Pa Kettle 1949,Ag 12,13:2
Bagdad 1949,D 24,11:4
I Was a Shoplifter 1950,Ap 28,26:3
Abbott and Costello in the Foreign Legion
1950,Ag 14,14:4
Curtain Call at Cactus Creek 1950,S 22,35:4
Abbott and Costello Meet the Invisible Man
1951,Ap 13,18:6
Comin' Round the Mountain 1951,Jl 27,15:2
Flame of Araby 1951,D 20,41:7
Francis in the Haunted House 1956,Jl 21,9:2
Lamont, Charles (Producer)
Little Accident 1939,N 24,29:3
Lamont, Duncan
Man in the White Suit, The 1952,Ap 1,35:2
Golden Coach, The 1954,Ja 22,30:2
Intruder, The 1955,Ja 26,22:1
Teckman Mystery, The 1955,Ag 22,18:2
Quentin Durward 1955,N 24,41:1
Tale of Two Cities, A 1958,Ag 5,23:1
Touch of Larceny, A 1960,Mr 17,28:1
39 Steps, The 1960,O 11,55:2
Mutiny on the Bounty 1962,N 9,31:2
Murder at the Gallop 1963,Je 25,23:2
Murder Game, The 1966,Mr 31,43:2
Arabesque 1966,My 6,54:1
Devil's Own, The 1967,Mr 16,53:2
Lamont, George
Thru Different Eyes 1929,Ap 15,22:6
Lamont, Jack O (Producer)
Kid Rodelo 1966,F 23,46:1
Lamont, Marten
Music in My Heart 1940,Ja 4,19:2
Pride and Prejudice 1940,Ag 9,19:1
How Green Was my Valley 1941,O 29,27:2
Son of Fury 1942,Ja 30,23:2
Powder Town 1942,Je 8,11:2
Mayor of Forty-Fourth Street, The
1942,Je 11,27:4
Mexican Spitfire at Sea 1942,Je 26,16:5

Mexican Spitfire Sees a Ghost 1942,Jl 31,11:2
Mexican Spitfire's Elephant 1942,S 18,25:2
Navy Comes Through, The 1942,N 12,30:3
Of Human Bondage 1946,Jl 6,11:2
My Dear Secretary 1949,F 14,15:4
Sword in the Desert 1949,Ag 25,20:2
Lamont, Molly
Norah O'Neale 1934,O 25,26:3
Jalna 1935,S 14,8:4
Muss 'Em Up 1936,F 3,21:2
Mary of Scotland 1936,Jl 31,22:2
Jungle Princess 1936,D 24,21:3
Doctor's Diary, A 1937,F 17,16:4
Awful Truth, The 1937,N 5,19:3
Moon and Sixpence, The 1942,O 28,26:4
Mr Skeffington 1944,My 26,23:2
Minstrel Man 1944,Jl 17,18:5
Suspect, The 1945,F 1,18:5
So Goes my Love 1946,My 2,3:7
Dark Corner, The 1946,My 9,27:3
Ivy 1947,Je 26,19:1
Christmas Eve 1947,N 28,30:2
South Sea Sinner 1950,Ja 16,18:4
First Legion, The 1951,Ap 28,9:2
Lamont, Sonny
To Beat the Band 1935,N 23,23:2
Story of Vernon and Irene Castle, The
1939,Mr 31,19:2
Lamont, Syl
Captain Newman, MD 1964,F 21,36:1
Mirage 1965,My 27,28:1
Lost Command 1966,S 15,51:1
Lamore, Isabelle
Last Moment, The 1928,Mr 12,26:1
Lamorisse, Albert (Cinematographer)
White Mane 1953,D 21,27:2
Wonderful Adventures of Nils, The
1962,S 14,37:1
Lamorisse, Albert (Director)
White Mane 1953,D 21,27:2
Red Balloon, The 1957,Mr 12,38:1
Stowaway in the Sky 1962,Je 19,28:1
Lamorisse, Albert (Original Author)
White Mane 1953,D 21,27:2
Red Balloon, The 1957,Mr 12,38:1
Lamorisse, Albert (Producer)
Red Balloon, The 1957,Mr 12,38:1
Lamorisse, Albert (Screenwriter)
Stowaway in the Sky 1962,Je 19,28:1
Lamorisse, Pascal
Red Balloon, The 1957,Mr 12,38:1
Stowaway in the Sky 1962,Je 19,28:1
Lamorisse, Sabine
Red Balloon, The 1957,Mr 12,38:1
LaMotta, Jake
Rebellion in Cuba 1961,Jl 1,9:1
Hustler, The 1961,S 27,35:1
Lamour, Dorothy
Jungle Princess 1936,D 24,21:3
Swing High, Swing Low 1937,Ap 15,19:1
Last Train from Madrid, The 1937,Je 19,20:2
High, Wide and Handsome 1937,Jl 22,15:1
Hurricane, The 1937,N 10,31:2
Thrill of a Lifetime 1937,D 9,30:2
Big Broadcast of 1938, The 1938,Mr 10,16:2
Her Jungle Love 1938,Ap 14,27:2
Tropic Holiday 1938,Je 30,21:2
Spawn of the North 1938,S 8,27:1
St Louis Blues 1939,F 9,17:2
Man About Town 1939,Je 29,19:1
Disputed Passage 1939,O 26,27:2
Road to Singapore 1940,Mr 14,29:2
Johnny Apollo 1940,Ap 13,21:2
Typhoon 1940,My 23,28:4
Moon Over Burma 1940,D 12,37:4
Chad Hanna 1940,D 26,23:1
Road to Zanzibar 1941,Ap 10,29:2
Caught in the Draft 1941,Je 26,27:3
Aloma of the South Seas 1941,Ag 28,23:4
Fleet's In, The 1942,Mr 12,24:2
Beyond the Blue Horizon 1942,Je 25,27:2
Road to Morocco 1942,N 12,30:1
Star Spangled Rhythm 1942,D 31,20:1
They Got Me Covered 1943,Mr 5,20:2
Dixie 1943,Je 24,26:2
Riding High 1943,D 23,26:4
And the Angels Sing 1944,Jl 13,14:2
Rainbow Island 1944,O 26,19:6
Medal for Benny, A 1945,My 24,15:2
Duffy's Tavern 1945,S 6,23:3
Masquerade in Mexico 1945,N 29,27:2
Road to Utopia 1946,F 28,20:2
My Favorite Brunette 1947,Mr 20,38:2
Wild Harvest 1947,N 13,33:2
Miracle Can Happen, A 1948,F 4,28:4
Road to Rio 1948,F 19,29:3
Lulu Belle 1948,Je 21,18:3
Lucky Stiff, The 1949,Ja 31,14:2
Manhandled 1949,My 26,34:2
Slightly French 1949,My 27,25:3
Here Comes the Groom 1951,S 21,19:2
Greatest Show on Earth, The 1952,Ja 11,17:2
Road to Bali 1953,Ja 30,25:1

Lamour, Dorothy— Cont
Road to Hong Kong, The 1962,Je 28,21:1
Donovan's Reef 1963,Jl 25,14:1
L'Amour, Louis (Original Author)
Hondo 1953,N 27,99:9
Blackjack Ketchum Desperado 1956,Ap 5,26:2
Burning Hills, The 1956,Ag 24,15:2
Taggart 1964,D 25,24:4
Kid Rodelo 1966,F 23,46:1
Shalako 1968,N 6,32:1
Lamoureux, Robert
Mama, Papa, the Maid and I 1956,Ag 28,31:1
Love and the Frenchwoman; (Francaise et
l'Amour, La) 1961,F 28,38:2
Lampell, Millard
Inheritance, The 1964,N 9,42:2
Lampell, Millard (Composer)
Walk in the Sun, A 1946,Ja 12,10:6
Inheritance, The 1964,N 9,42:2
Lampell, Millard (Original Author)
Saturday's Hero 1951,S 12,37:2
Lampell, Millard (Screenwriter)
Saturday's Hero 1951,S 12,37:2
Chance Meeting 1960,O 27,45:2
Inheritance, The 1964,N 9,42:2
Idol, The 1966,Ag 11,27:1
Lampert, Zohra
Pay or Die 1960,My 27,22:2
Splendor in the Grass 1961,O 11,53:1
Hey, Lets Twist 1962,F 8,25:1
Bye Bye Braverman 1968,F 22,36:1
Lampin, Georges (Director)
Idiot, The 1948,F 5,26:2
Honorable Catherine, The 1948,Ag 23,13:3
Crime and Punishment 1958,S 16,23:2
Lampin, Georges (Producer)
Vautrin, the Thief 1949,N 11,31:2
Lampin, Georges (Screenwriter)
Slipper Episode, The 1938,My 19,25:2
Lampkin, Charles
Five 1951,Ap 26,34:2
Toys in the Attic 1963,Ag 1,17:2
Lamport, Diane (Composer)
Snow Queen, The 1960,Ap 14,34:1
Lamprecht, Gerhard (Director)
Slums of Berlin 1927,Ja 26,17:1
Children of no Importance 1928,Ap 3,33:2
Emil und die Detektive 1931,D 21,28:4
Schwartze Husar, Der 1932,D 23,20:1
Hertha's Erwachen 1933,Mr 14,18:3 (Incorrect in
this edition; use 1933,Mr 14,19:2 elsewhere)
Ein Gewisser Herr Gran 1934,F 24,18:5
Einmal Eine Grosse Dame Sein 1934,O 27,20:3
Prinzessin, Turandot 1935,Ja 16,21:2
Einer zu viel an Bord 1936,Ja 25,18:5
Hoehere Befehl, Der 1936,Mr 31,17:3
Barcarole 1936,O 21,35:3
Seltsamer Gast, Ein 1937,Jl 10,18:2
Madame Bovary 1937,O 30,22:2
Somewhere in Berlin 1949,Ag 16,19:3
Lamprecht, Gerhard (Original Author)
Somewhere in Berlin 1949,Ag 16,19:3
Lamprecht, Gerhardt (Director)
Zwischen Nacht und Morgen 1931,O 25,VIII,6:1
Lampson, Jacquetta
Echoes of Silence 1967,Ap 7,32:2
Lamson, David (Original Author)
We Who Are About to Die 1937,Ja 2,15:1
LaMure, Pierre (Original Author)
Moulin Rouge 1953,F 11,33:5
Lamy, Charles
Cousine Bette, La 1928,Ag 12,VII,3:4
Paris-Beguin 1932,D 31,10:1
Lan, Wang
Lady General, The 1965,F 12,19:1
Lanak
Igloo 1932,Jl 21,15:2
Lancaster, Betty
Forest Ring, The 1930,Ap 26,11:1
Lancaster, Burt
Killers, The 1946,Ag 29,24:2
Brute Force 1947,Jl 17,16:2
Desert Fury 1947,S 25,35:4
I Walk Alone 1948,Ja 22,36:3
All my Sons 1948,Mr 29,17:3
Sorry, Wrong Number 1948,S 2,18:2
Kiss the Blood off my Hands 1948,O 30,10:2
Criss Cross 1949,Mr 12,10:2
Rope of Sand 1949,Ag 4,19:2
Flame and the Arrow, The 1950,Jl 8,7:2
Mister 880 1950,S 30,13:2
Vengeance Valley 1951,F 16,21:2
Jim Thorpe - All American 1951,Ag 25,7:2
Ten Tall Men 1951,O 27,10:5
Crimson Pirate, The 1952,Ag 28,21:2
Come Back, Little Sheba 1952,D 24,13:2 (In Addenda)
South Sea Woman 1953,Je 4,33:6
From Here to Eternity 1953,Ag 6,16:2
His Majesty O'Keefe 1954,F 6,17:2
Apache 1954,Jl 10,7:2
Vera Cruz 1954,D 27,22:4
Kentuckian, The 1955,S 2,13:2
Rose Tattoo, The 1955,D 13,55:1
Trapeze 1956,Je 5,39:2

Lancaster, Burt— Cont

Rainmaker, The 1956,D 13,51:1
Gunfight at the O K Corral 1957,My 30,23:2
Sweet Smell of Success 1957,Je 28,29:2
Run Silent, Run Deep 1958,Mr 28,29:1
Separate Tables 1958,D 19,2:7
Devil's Disciple, The 1959,Ag 21,12:1
Unforgiven, The 1960,Ap 7,46:1
Elmer Gantry 1960,Jl 8,16:1
Young Savages, The 1961,My 25,31:1
Judgment at Nuremberg 1961,D 20,36:1
Birdman of Alcatraz 1962,Jl 19,19:2
Child Is Waiting, A 1963,F 14,5:6
List of Adrian Messenger, The 1963,My 30,20:1
Leopard, The 1963,Ag 13,25:1
Seven Days in May 1964,F 20,22:1
Train, The 1965,Mr 18,25:1
Hallelujah Trail, The 1965,Jl 2,17:1
Professionals, The 1966,N 3,45:1
Scalphunters, The 1968,Ap 3,40:1
Swimmer, The 1968,My 16,53:1

Lancaster, Burt (Director)
Kentuckian, The 1955,S 2,13:2

Lancaster, C D (Original Author)
Little Irish Girl, The 1926,My 11,24:3

Lancaster, Catherine
Cosmic Monster, The 1959,Ja 1,38:1

Lancaster, G B (Original Author)
Eternal Struggle, The 1923,O 16,21:3

Lancaster, Lucie
Vagabond King, The 1956,S 13,39:6

Lancaster, Stuart
Good Morning and Goodbye! 1968,F 20,53:1

Lance, Lila
Clive of India 1935,Ja 18,29:1

Lancell, Ariane
Gervaise 1957,N 12,46:1

Lancell, Arlane
Babette Goes to War 1960,Je 8,46:1

Lancelot, Sir
I Walked With a Zombie 1943,Ap 22,31:5
Curse of the Cat People, The 1944,Mr 4,11:1
To Have and Have Not 1944,O 12,24:1
Brute Force 1947,Jl 17,16:2
Buccaneer, The 1958,D 24,00:0

Lanchester, Elsa
Day Dreams 1930,F 4,28:3
Love Habit, The 1931,F 2,23:1
Private Life of Henry VIII, The 1933,O 13,25:2
David Copperfield 1935,Ja 19,8:1
Naughty Marietta 1935,Mr 23,11:2
Bride of Frankenstein, The 1935,My 11,21:2
Ghost Goes West, The 1936,Ja 11,9:2
Rembrandt 1936,D 3,31:1
Beachcomber, The 1938,D 26,29:3
Ladies in Retirement 1941,N 7,27:1
Son of Fury 1942,Ja 30,23:2
Tales of Manhattan 1942,S 25,25:1
Forever and a Day 1943,Mr 13,9:2
Lassie Come Home 1943,O 8,15:4
Spiral Staircase, The 1946,F 7,29:3
Razor's Edge, The 1946,N 20,42:2
Northwest Outpost 1947,Ag 8,10:2
Bishop's Wife, The 1947,D 10,44:2
Big Clock, The 1948,Ap 22,34:2
Come to the Stable 1949,Jl 28,19:1
Inspector General, The 1949,D 31,9:2
Buccaneer's Girl 1950,Mr 27,19:2
Mystery Street 1950,Jl 28,12:5
Petty Girl, The 1950,Ag 18,17:2
Frenchie 1951,F 12,19:2
Dreamboat 1952,Jl 26,9:2
Miserables, Les 1952,Ag 15,11:2
Androcles and the Lion 1953,Ja 15,23:2
Girls of Pleasure Island, The 1953,My 16,10:1
Hell's Half Acre 1954,F 27,11:3
Glass Slipper, The 1955,Mr 25,19:2
Witness for the Prosecution 1958,F 7,16:1
Bell, Book and Candle 1958,D 27,2:7
Honeymoon Hotel 1964,Je 4,28:1
Mary Poppins 1964,S 25,34:1
That Darn Cat 1965,D 3,44:1
Easy Come, Easy Go 1967,Je 15,56:1
Blackbeard's Ghost 1968,Ap 11,51:3

Lancret, Bernard
Kermesse Heroique, La 1936,S 23,29:1
Heroes of the Marne; (Famille Lefrancois, Le)
  1939,Ap 24,13:2
Devil Is an Empress, The 1939,D 4,18:4
Citadel of Silence, The 1939,D 25,29:1
Entente Cordiale 1939,D 26,23:2
Ultimatum 1940,F 5,13:2
Schubert's Serenade 1940,S 3,21:2
Foolish Husbands 1948,O 11,27:2
Julietta 1957,Je 18,38:2
Mam'zelle Pigalle 1958,Ap 19,10:4

Lancy, Lucy
Devil's Daughter 1949,F 26,11:2

Land, Gail
Fear Strikes Out 1957,Mr 21,37:2

Land, Robert (Director)
Primanerliebe 1928,Mr 13,23:3
Dame Care 1928,My 20,VIII,8:3
I Kiss Your Hand, Madame 1932,Ag 29,9:2

Week-End Im Paradies 1932,O 24,18:5
Drei Kaiserjaeger 1935,Mr 16,19:1

Landa, Rodolfo
Maria 1939,Ap 10,13:4
Night of the Mayas 1941,Ja 14,16:7

Landau, David
Street Scene 1931,Ag 27,22:5
Arrowsmith 1931,D 8,36:4
Taxi 1932,Ja 8,27:3
This Reckless Age 1932,Ja 9,21:1
Union Depot 1932,Ja 15,24:4
Polly of the Circus 1932,Mr 19,11:2
It's Tough to be Famous 1932,Ap 9,18:1
Amateur Daddy 1932,Ap 23,11:5
Roadhouse Murder 1932,Ap 29,13:4
Purchase Price, The 1932,Jl 16,5:5
Horse Feathers 1932,Ag 11,12:2
70,000 Witnesses 1932,S 3,16:2
Air Mail 1932,N 7,20:3
I Am a Fugitive From a Chain Gang
  1932,N 11,17:2
False Faces 1932,N 25,19:2
Under-Cover Man 1932,D 5,21:2
Lawyer Man 1932,D 27,10:2
She Done Him Wrong 1933,F 10,12:3
They Just Had to Get Married 1933,F 13,11:4
Heritage of the Desert 1933,Mr 11,18:3
Crime of the Century 1933,Mr 13,18:2
Gabriel Over the White House 1933,Ap 1,18:2
Nuisance, The 1933,My 29,22:2
No Marriage Ties 1933,Ag 4,18:2
One Man's Journey 1933,S 1,15:2
Bedside 1934,Mr 7,23:4
As the Earth Turns 1934,Ap 12,27:2
Wharf Angel 1934,Ap 21,12:1
Man With two Faces, The 1934,Jl 12,20:2
Death on the Diamond 1934,S 24,14:1
Judge Priest 1934,O 12,33:1

Landau, David Mrs
Way Down East 1931,Mr 16,25:1

Landau, Ely (Producer)
Long Day's Journey Into Night 1962,O 10,57:2

Landau, Leslie (Producer)
Portrait of Clare 1951,D 26,19:6

Landau, Leslie (Screenwriter)
Portrait of Clare 1951,D 26,19:6

Landau, Leslie L (Screenwriter)
My Brother Jonathan 1949,Je 29,34:4

Landau, Lucy
Thrill of it All, The 1963,Ag 2,15:3

Landau, Martin
Pork Chop Hill 1959,My 30,9:2
North by Northwest 1959,Ag 7,28:1
Gazebo, The 1960,Ja 16,14:4
Cleopatra 1963,Je 13,29:1
Greatest Story Ever Told, The 1965,F 16,40:2
Hallelujah Trail, The 1965,Jl 2,17:1
Nevada Smith 1966,Je 24,28:1 (Incorrect in this
  edition; use 1966,Je 30,28:1 elsewhere)

Landau, Richard (Original Author)
Christmas Eve 1947,N 28,30:2

Landau, Richard (Screenwriter)
Back to Bataan 1945,S 13,26:3
Crooked Way, The 1949,S 5,13:2
Johnny One-Eye 1950,N 17,31:2
Sins of Jezebel 1953,Ja 9,12:2
Blackout 1954,My 22,8:2
She Shoulda Said No 1957,Ja 31,21:1
Up Periscope 1959,Mr 5,35:4

Landau, S
Yiddle With his Fiddle 1937,Ja 2,15:1
Dybbuk, The 1938,Ja 28,17:2
Tkies Khaf; (Vow, The) 1938,S 15,29:3

Landauer, Walter (Miscellaneous)
Die Grosse Liebe 1932,F 22,23:2

Lander, David
Invasion Quartet 1961,D 11,41:2

Landers, Harry
C-Man 1949,My 28,11:4
Guilty Bystander 1950,Ap 21,18:2
Undercover Girl 1950,N 8,37:2
Drive a Crooked Road 1954,Ap 3,19:3
Indian Fighter, The 1955,D 22,20:1
Gallant Hours, The 1960,Je 23,19:4

Landers, Lew (Director)
Without Orders 1936,N 4,41:3
Night Waitress 1936,D 18,31:5
Man Who Found Himself, The 1937,Ap 9,19:3
You Can't Buy Luck 1937,My 14,21:2
Border Cafe 1937,Je 8,30:2
Flight From Glory 1937,S 11,20:1
Danger Patrol 1937,N 19,27:3
Crashing Hollywood 1938,Ja 8,19:2
Double Danger 1938,F 10,17:5
Condemned Woman 1938,Ap 22,15:5
Law of the Underworld 1938,Ap 28,27:2
Blind Alibi 1938,My 20,17:2
Sky Giant 1938,Jl 20,22:2
Smashing the Rackets 1938,Ag 9,22:5
Annabel Takes a Tour 1938,D 29,15:3
Pacific Liner 1939,Ja 18,17:3
Twelve Crowded Hours 1939,F 24,15:2
Fixer Dugan 1939,My 6,21:2

Landers, Lew (Director)— Cont

Girl and the Gambler, The 1939,Je 28,17:3
Bad Lands 1939,Ag 9,15:2
Conspiracy 1939,Ag 23,19:2
Honeymoon Deferred 1940,F 16,23:4
Enemy Agent 1940,Ap 22,13:3
Ski Patrol 1940,My 21,29:4
Conga Nights, La 1940,Je 5,33:5
Wagons Westward 1940,Jl 8,13:2
Slightly Tempted 1940,N 1,33:1
I Was a Prisoner on Devil's Island
  1941,Jl 28,16:4
Mystery Ship 1941,Ag 16,18:3
Canal Zone 1942,Mr 30,21:2
Submarine Raider 1942,Je 22,19:2
Atlantic Convoy 1942,Jl 6,18:5
Sabotage Squad 1942,Ag 5,16:1
Boogie Man Will Get You, The 1942,O 12,12:4
Murder in Times Square 1943,My 31,13:2
Return of the Vampire, The 1944,Ja 29,10:1
Crime Incorporated 1945,Je 23,9:7
Enchanted Forest, The 1945,D 17,17:2
Barbary Pirate 1949,O 28,29:3
Girl's School 1950,F 3,29:2
Davy Crockett, Indian Scout 1950,Mr 17,28:3
Beauty on Parade 1950,Ag 18,17:2
Last of the Buccaneers 1950,D 15,43:2
Yank in Korea, A 1951,Ap 2,29:2
California Conquest 1952,Je 7,22:6
Torpedo Valley 1952,D 20,15:3
Man in the Dark 1953,Ap 9,31:5

Landers, Muriel
Pony Soldier 1952,D 20,15:2
Doctor Dolittle 1967,D 20,55:1

Landfield, David
Bellboy, The 1960,Jl 21,17:1

Landfield, Sydney (Director)
Half Angel 1936,My 30,7:3

Landgard, Janet
Swimmer, The 1968,My 16,53:1

Landgre, Inga
Seventh Seal 1958,O 14,44:1
Dreams; Kvinnodrom 1960,Je 1,42:1
Loving Couples 1966,S 20,38:1

Landgut, Inge
Mother Love 1931,F 16,17:1
Emil und die Detektive 1931,D 21,28:4
M 1933,Ap 3,13:3
Our Daily Bread 1950,O 9,21:6

Landi, Aldo
Dead Woman's Kiss, A 1951,O 6,16:4
Mademoiselle Gobette 1955,F 5,13:3

Landi, Elissa
Underground 1929,F 26,31:1
Betrayal, The 1929,Ap 29,29:2
Knowing Men 1930,Mr 9,IX,6:1
Children of Chance 1931,Ja 24,15:1
Body and Soul 1931,Mr 14,23:2
Always Good-Bye 1931,My 23,13:4
Parisian, The 1931,Ag 22,7:5
Wicked 1931,S 19,10:2
Yellow Ticket, The 1931,O 31,22:2
Devil's Lottery 1932,Ap 2,13:2
Woman in Room 13, The 1932,My 21,9:2
Passport to Hell, A 1932,Ag 27,13:4
Sign of the Cross, The 1932,D 1,25:1
Warrior's Husband, The 1933,My 12,20:4
I Loved You Wednesday 1933,Je 16,20:2
Masquerader, The 1933,S 4,9:5
By Candlelight 1934,Ja 6,18:2
Man of Two Worlds 1934,Ja 12,29:2
Sisters Under the Skin 1934,Je 8,18:1
Great Flirtation, The 1934,Je 22,16:5
Count of Monte Cristo, The 1934,S 27,25:2
Enter Madame 1935,Ja 12,12:1
Amateur Gentleman, The 1936,Ap 27,19:2
Mad Holiday 1936,N 26,39:2
After the Thin Man 1936,D 25,19:2
Thirteenth Chair, The 1937,Je 18,25:3
Corregidor 1943,My 28,19:2

Landi, Maria
Hounds of the Baskervilles, The 1959,Jl 4,9:4

Landi, Marla
Across the Bridge 1957,O 30,24:1
Murder Game, The 1966,Mr 31,43:2

Landicutt, Philip
Unbeliever, The 1918,F 12,9:2

Landin, Hope
Great John L, The 1945,Jl 9,14:6
I Remember Mama 1948,Mr 12,29:2
Walls of Jericho, The 1948,Ag 5,16:2
Sun comes up, The 1949,My 13,29:2
Sugarfoot 1951,F 12,19:4
Scaramouche 1952,My 9,20:2
She Couldn't Say No 1954,F 27,11:3

Landis, Adrian (Screenwriter)
Everything's on Ice 1939,O 6,31:1

Landis, Carole
Four's a Crowd 1938,Ag 12,11:1
One Million BC 1940,Ap 27,9:2
Turnabout 1940,Jl 27,17:6
Mystery Sea Raider 1940,Ag 26,11:4
Road Show 1941,F 19,25:2
Topper Returns 1941,Mr 28,26:6

Landis, Carole— Cont

Moon Over Miami 1941,Jl 5,14:2
Dance Hall 1941,Jl 19,16:2
Cadet Girl 1941,D 11,39:1
I Wake up Screaming 1942,Ja 17,13:2
Gentleman at Heart, A 1942,F 23,25:2
My Gal Sal 1942,My 1,23:1
It Happened in Flatbush 1942,Jl 3,12:8
Orchestra Wives 1942,S 24,23:2
Manila Calling 1942,S 28,13:1
Powers Girl, The 1943,Mr 26,14:2 (In Addenda)
Wintertime 1943,S 30,27:2
Four Jills in a Jeep 1944,Ap 6,27:2
Secret Command 1944,Je 14,16:2
Having Wonderful Crime 1945,Ap 13,15:2
Behind Green Lights 1946,F 16,10:2
It Shouldn't Happen to a Dog 1946,S 7,11:2
Scandal In Paris, A 1946,S 16,9:7

Landis, Carole (Miscellaneous)

Four Jills in a Jeep 1944,Ap 6,27:2

Landis, Cullen

Girl From Outside, The 1919,N 10,18:2
It's a Great Life 1920,Ag 30,12:3
Bunty Pulls the Strings 1921,Ja 9,VI,2:1 (In Addenda)
Snowblind 1921,My 23,16:3
Remembrance 1922,O 2,21:2
Famous Mrs Fair, The 1923,Ap 23,18:3
Masters of Men 1923,My 15,22:1
Soul of the Beast, The 1923,My 22,14:4
Pioneer Trails 1923,N 12,15:3
Fighting Coward, The 1924,Mr 17,19:1
Pampered Youth 1925,F 10,20:1
Sweet Rosie O'Grady 1926,D 9,33:1
We're all Gamblers 1927,O 12,30:6
Lights of New York 1928,Jl 9,25:1

Landis, Jeanette

Persecution and Assassination of Jean-Paul Marat as Performed by the Inmates of the Asylum of Charenton Under the Direction of the Marquis De Sade, The 1967,F 23,41:1

Landis, Jessie Royce

Derelict 1930,N 22,21:3
Mr Belvedere Goes to College 1949,Ap 16,11:2
It Happens Every Spring 1949,Je 11,11:2
My Foolish Heart 1950,Ja 20,29:2
Mother Didn't Tell Me 1950,Mr 4,11:2
Tonight at 8:30 (Ways and Means); Ways and Means (Tonight at 8:30) 1953,My 26,33:2
To Catch a Thief 1955,Ag 5,14:2
Swan, The 1956,Ap 27,21:5
Girl He Left Behind, The 1956,O 27,17:1
My Man Godfrey 1957,O 12,23:1
I Married a Woman 1958,N 5,42:5
North by Northwest 1959,Ag 7,28:1
Private's Affair, A 1959,Ag 15,8:7
Goodbye Again 1961,Je 30,32:2
Bon Voyage! 1962,My 18,34:2
Boys' Night Out 1962,Je 22,15:2
Critic's Choice 1963,My 2,40:2
Gidget Goes to Rome 1963,S 12,32:2

Landis, Margaret

My Man 1924,F 11,18:3
Latest From Paris, The 1928,F 27,16:2

Landis, Monty

Mouse That Roared, The 1959,O 27,40:1
School for Scoundrels 1960,Jl 12,39:1
Targets 1968,Ag 14,34:1

Landis, Winifred

Dante's Inferno 1924,S 30,27:3

Landon, Avice

Guilt is my Shadow 1954,Mr 25,36:4
Wind Cannot Read, The 1960,Mr 10,36:1
Five Golden Hours 1961,O 19,39:3
Nothing but the Best 1964,Jl 14,28:1
Leather Boys, The 1965,N 9,50:1

Landon, Christopher (Screenwriter)

Desert Attack 1961,Mr 23,28:1

Landon, Daniel Michael (Producer)

Wall of Noise 1963,S 5,27:1

Landon, Dinsdale

Operation Snatch 1962,S 25,31:4

Landon, Harold

Gung Ho! 1944,Ja 26,23:2

Landon, Joseph (Original Author)

Hoodlum Priest, The 1961,Ap 3,28:5

Landon, Joseph (Producer)

Finian's Rainbow 1968,O 10,59:5

Landon, Joseph (Screenwriter)

Rise and Fall of Legs' Diamond, The 1960,F 4,34:1
Hoodlum Priest, The 1961,Ap 3,28:5
Explosive Generation, The 1962,F 15,24:2
Wall of Noise 1963,S 5,27:1
Johnny Cool 1963,O 3,31:1
Rio Conchos 1964,O 29,38:1
Stagecoach 1966,Je 16,53:1

Landon, Margaret (Original Author)

Anna and the King of Siam 1946,Je 21,20:2
King and I, The 1956,Je 29,15:6

Landon, Michael

God's Little Acre 1958,Ag 14,23:2

Landry, Gerard

Human Beast, The 1940,F 20,17:2
Mad Emperor, The 1941,Mr 10,21:3
Ces Dames aux Chapeaux Verts; Ladies in the Green Hats, The 1945,Ap 5,26:2
Night Without Stars 1953,Jl 14,19:4
Lovers of Toledo, The 1954,Ap 10,11:3
Trapeze 1956,Je 5,39:2

Landry, Margaret

Leopard Man, The 1943,My 20,26:4

Landshoff, Ruth

Nosferatu the Vampire 1929,Je 4,29:3

Landstrom, Elvor

Himlaspelet 1944,O 9,17:3

Landweer, Ronnie

Last Blitzkrieg, The 1959,Ja 31,13:5

Landy, Hanna

Operation Eichmann 1961,My 4,40:7
Harlow 1965,Jl 22,24:1
In Like Flint 1967,Mr 16,53:2

LANE

See Also LAINE

Lane, Abbe

Americano, The 1955,Ja 20,35:1
Chicago Syndicate 1955,Je 21,37:1

Lane, Allan

Not Quite Decent 1929,My 6,30:4
Love in the Rough 1930,S 27,21:3
Night Nurse 1931,Jl 17,23:4
Honor of the Family 1931,O 17,20:1
Expensive Women 1931,N 14,15:3
Winner Take All 1932,Je 18,9:2
Miss Pinkerton 1932,Jl 9,7:5
Stowaway 1936,D 19,16:1
Charlie Chan at the Olympics 1937,My 24,23:1
Big Business 1937,Je 1,27:2
Fifty Roads to Town 1937,Je 5,21:1
Sing and Be Happy 1937,Je 19,20:2
Crime Ring 1938,Jl 22,10:3
Fugitives for a Night 1938,S 21,30:4
Law West of Tombstone, The 1938,N 25,19:1
Pacific Liner 1939,Ja 18,17:3
Twelve Crowded Hours 1939,F 24,15:2
They Made Her a Spy 1939,Mr 29,21:4
Conspiracy 1939,Ag 23,19:2
Spellbinder, The 1939,Ag 24,17:3
Dancing Masters, The 1943,D 2,30:2

Lane, Brenda

New Klondike, The 1926,Mr 22,16:1

Lane, Burton (Composer)

Dancing Lady 1933,D 1,23:2
Bottoms Up 1934,Mr 23,29:2
Strictly Dynamite 1934,Jl 4,18:2
Kid Millions 1934,N 12,17:2
Folies Bergere 1935,F 25,13:2
Champagne Waltz 1937,F 4,17:2
Swing High, Swing Low 1937,Ap 15,19:1
Double or Nothing 1937,S 2,17:3
College Swing 1938,Ap 28,27:2
Las Vegas Nights 1941,Mr 20,25:2
Babes on Broadway 1942,Ja 1,37:1
Ship Ahoy 1942,Je 26,16:5
Panama Hattie 1942,O 2,31:2
Seven Sweethearts 1942,N 13,28:1
Presenting Lily Mars 1943,Ap 30,25:3
Thousands Cheer 1943,S 14,27:1
Rainbow Island 1944,O 26,19:6

Lane, Burton (Miscellaneous)

College Holiday 1936,D 24,21:2
Artists and Models 1937,Ag 5,19:2

Lane, Charles

Without Limit 1921,Mr 21,11:3
White Sister, The 1923,S 6,10:2
Second Youth 1924,Ap 22,19:3
Romola 1924,D 2,13:2
I Want my Man 1925,Ap 6,17:3
Dark Angel, The 1925,O 12,19:3
Padlocked 1926,Ag 2,21:2
Winning of Barbara Worth, The 1926,N 29,16:3
Music Master, The 1927,Ja 17,12:4 (In Addenda)
Whirlwind of Youth, The 1927,Je 6,27:2
Barbed Wire 1927,Ag 8,10:3
Service for Ladies 1927,Ag 15,22:5
Sadie Thompson 1928,F 6,12:3
White Sister, The 1928,My 21,25:1
Canary Murder Case, The 1929,Mr 11,22:2
Saturday's Children 1929,Ap 29,29:2
Two for Tonight 1935,Ag 31,16:2
Milky Way, The 1936,Mr 26,27:2
Crime of Dr Forbes, The 1936,Jl 6,11:4
36 Hours to Live 1936,Ag 15,6:3
We're on the Jury 1937,F 10,18:5
Ali Baba Goes to Town 1937,O 23,14:1
Trapped by G-Men 1937,N 4,29:1
In Old Chicago 1938,Ja 7,15:2
City Girl 1938,F 4,17:3
Cocoanut Grove 1938,Je 16,21:2
You Can't Take It With You 1938,S 2,21:2
Always in Trouble 1938,N 3,27:1
Thanks For Everything 1938,D 10,13:2
Kentucky 1938,D 24,12:1
Boy Slaves 1939,F 9,17:3
Lucky Night 1939,My 5,29:3

Lane, Charles— Cont

News Is Made at Night 1939,Jl 13,17:2
They all Come Out 1939,Ag 3,15:4
Mr Smith Goes to Washington 1939,O 20,27:2
Johnny Apollo 1940,Ap 13,21:2
You Can't Fool Your Wife 1940,My 24,23:4
Crooked Road, The 1940,Je 11,33:4
Rhythm on the River 1940,Ag 29,23:2
We Who Are Young 1940,S 13,27:2
Great Profile, The 1940,O 18,25:1
Ellery Queen, Master Detective 1940,D 19,33:1
Invisible Woman, The 1941,Ja 9,27:2
Ellery Queen's Penthouse Mystery 1941,Mr 7,17:2
Ellery Queen and the Perfect Crime 1941,Ag 11,17:3
Ball of Fire 1942,Ja 16,25:2
I Wake up Screaming 1942,Ja 17,13:2
Obliging Young Lady 1942,F 13,24:4
Ride 'Em Cowboy 1942,Mr 5,27:3
Lady is Willing, The 1942,Ap 24,21:2
Great Man's Lady, The 1942,Ap 30,14:3
Friendly Enemies 1942,Je 22,19:1
Tarzan's New York Adventure 1942,Ag 7,13:2
Arsenic and old Lace 1944,S 2,17:2
Roses Are Red 1947,N 15,11:2
State of the Union 1948,Ap 23,28:1
Intrigue 1948,Ap 24,11:2
Apartment for Peggy 1948,O 16,9:2
You're my Everything 1949,Jl 23,7:2
Borderline 1950,Mr 6,17:2
Riding High 1950,Ap 11,26:2
For Heaven's Sake 1950,D 16,10:5
I Can Get It for You Wholesale 1951,Ap 5,34:4
Juggler, The 1953,My 6,39:2
Birds and the Bees, The 1956,Ap 23,22:1
Teacher's Pet 1958,Mr 20,33:1
Mating Game, The 1959,Ap 30,37:1
Music Man, The 1962,Ag 24,14:1
Papa's Delicate Condition 1963,Mr 7,8:5
Good Neighbor Sam 1964,Jl 23,19:1
John Goldfarb, Please Come Home 1965,Mr 25,42:4
Billie 1965,S 16,55:3
Ugly Dachshund, The 1966,Ap 7,45:1
What's so bad About Feeling Good? 1968,My 25,27:1

Lane, Eric

Lolita 1962,Je 14,23:2

Lane, Harry

Operation X 1950,D 11,31:2
Fire over Africa 1954,N 22,29:5

Lane, Jackie

Angry Hills, The 1959,Jl 16,31:3
Goodbye Again 1961,Je 30,32:2
Operation Snatch 1962,S 25,31:4

Lane, Jocelyn

Tickle Me 1965,Je 24,28:3
How to Seduce a Playboy 1968,My 16,53:2

Lane, Katheryn

His Children's Children 1923,N 5,15:1

Lane, Lenita

Murder by the Clock 1931,Jl 18,16:6
We're Rich Again 1934,S 1,16:3
Gay Deception, The 1935,O 11,31:1
Dead Men Tell 1941,Ap 17,29:3
Mad Magician, The 1954,My 20,38:2
Bat, The 1959,D 17,51:4

Lane, Leone

Case of Lena Smith, The 1929,Ja 15,22:4

Lane, Lola

Speakeasy 1929,Mr 11,22:2
William Fox Movietone Follies of 1929 1929,My 27,22:1
Girl from Havana, The 1929,S 2,16:1
Let's Go Places 1930,Mr 1,23:1
Big Fight, The 1930,Je 28,9:2
Good News 1930,S 6,9:2
Costello Case, The 1930,N 4,36:1
Hell Bound 1931,My 9,15:4
Murder on a Honeymoon 1935,Mr 4,12:2
Burn 'Em Up Barnes 1935,Mr 30,11:2
Alias Mary Dow 1935,Je 29,16:2
His Night Out 1935,N 16,19:2
Marked Woman 1937,Ap 12,15:2
Hollywood Hotel 1938,Ja 13,17:3
Torchy Blane in Panama 1938,Ap 18,11:1
When Were You Born? 1938,Je 9,27:2
Four Daughters 1938,Ag 19,13:3
Daughters Courageous 1939,Je 24,14:2
Four Wives 1939,D 23,9:1
Convicted Woman 1940,F 26,11:2
Zanzibar 1940,Ap 1,15:3
Gangs of Chicago 1940,Je 13,29:2
Girls of the Road 1940,Jl 22,20:2
Four Mothers 1941,Ja 11,12:7
Mystery Ship 1941,Ag 16,18:3
Why Girls Leave Home 1945,Ag 4,7:3
Deadline at Dawn 1946,Ap 4,33:2

Lane, Lupino

Reporter, The 1922,O 2,21:2
Isn't Life Wonderful? 1924,D 1,17:3
Love Parade, The 1929,N 20,32:6
Show of Shows 1929,N 21,24:5

Lane, Lupino— Cont

Bride of the Regiment 1930,My 22,32:6
Golden Dawn 1930,Jl 26,16:4
Yellow Mask, The 1930,D 8,26:1

Lane, Manda

Fifth Avenue Girl 1939,Ag 25,12:2

Lane, Mara

Innocents in Paris 1955,Mr 5,9:6
Angela 1955,Je 4,9:2
Sins of Casanova 1957,O 7,23:2
Montpi 1959,Ap 21,40:1

Lane, Mark (Original Author)

Rush to Judgement 1967,Je 3,18:1

Lane, Mark (Producer)

Rush to Judgement 1967,Je 3,18:1

Lane, Maryon

Dance Little Lady 1955,D 26,23:3

Lane, Mike

Harder They Fall, The 1956,My 10,26:3

Lane, Nellie

Circus Days 1923,Ag 6,14:2

Lane, Nora

Jesse James 1927,O 17,20:2
Night of Mystery, A 1928,Ap 16,20:5
Marquis Preferred 1929,Ja 21,18:4
Cohens and the Kellys In Atlantic City, The
  1929,Mr 18,30:6
Sally 1929,D 24,14:4
Man Hunter, The 1930,Ap 5,23:3
Rain or Shine 1930,Ag 8,11:1
Young Sinners 1931,My 9,15:4
Cisco Kid, The 1931,O 24,20:3
Dance Team 1932,Ja 16,13:1
After Tomorrow 1932,Mr 7,13:5
Disorderly Conduct 1932,Ap 11,19:2
Careless Lady 1932,Ap 18,19:2
This Sporting Age 1932,O 1,10:4
Jimmy the Gent 1934,Mr 26,22:3
Hopalong Rides Again 1938,Ja 22,19:1
City of Chance 1940,Ja 22,11:3

Lane, Priscilla

Varsity Show 1937,S 2,17:2
Love, Honor and Behave 1938,Mr 21,18:2
Men Are Such Fools 1938,Je 17,25:1
Cowboy From Brooklyn 1938,Jl 14,17:1
Four Daughters 1938,Ag 19,13:3
Brother Rat 1938,N 5,15:2
Yes, My Darling Daughter 1939,F 27,11:2
Daughters Courageous 1939,Je 24,14:2
Dust Be my Destiny 1939,O 7,11:2
Roaring Twenties, The 1939,N 11,12:1
Four Wives 1939,D 23,9:1
Brother Rat and a Baby 1940,Ja 27,9:4
Three Cheers for the Irish 1940,Mr 9,19:2
Four Mothers 1941,Ja 11,12:7
Million Dollar Baby 1941,Je 7,20:2
Blues in the Night 1941,D 12,35:2
Saboteur 1942,My 8,27:2
Silver Queen 1943,Ja 11,18:4
Meanest Man in the World, The 1943,F 25,27:3
Arsenic and old Lace 1944,S 2,17:2

Lane, Richard

Outcasts of Poker Flat, The 1937,Ap 27,18:3
You Can't Buy Luck 1937,My 14,21:2
New Faces of 1937 1937,Jl 2,25:1
Super-Sleuth 1937,Jl 17,18:1
Flight From Glory 1937,S 11,20:1
Life of the Party, The 1937,O 4,17:1
Saturday's Heroes 1937,O 16,22:2
Danger Patrol 1937,N 19,27:3
Crashing Hollywood 1938,Ja 8,19:2
Wise Girl 1938,Ja 10,13:3
Mr Moto in Danger Island 1938,Mr 20,13:3
Radio City Revels 1938,Mr 21,18:3
Blind Alibi 1938,My 20,17:2
Go Chase Yourself 1938,Je 15,27:1
I'm From the City 1938,Ag 19,13:4
Mr Doodle Kicks Off 1938,S 28,29:4
Exposed 1938,N 21,14:5
Charlie Chan in Honolulu 1938,D 31,7:3
Union Pacific 1939,My 11,31:2
It Could Happen to You 1939,Je 9,26:3
Stronger Than Desire 1939,Je 30,17:3
News Is Made at Night 1939,Jl 13,17:2
Mutiny on the Blackhawk 1939,Ag 2,17:2
Unexpected Father 1939,Ag 11,12:2
Day the Bookies Wept, The 1939,S 14,18:2
Escape, The 1939,N 3,17:4
Main Street Lawyer 1939,N 9,27:2
Sued for Libel 1940,Ja 19,15:3
City of Chance 1940,Ja 22,11:3
Free, Blonde and 21 1940,Ap 5,25:2
Two Girls on Broadway 1940,Ap 25,28:4
Biscuit Eater, The 1940,My 23,28:5
Brother Orchid 1940,Je 8,18:2
Sandy Is a Lady 1940,Je 28,22:2
Boom Town 1940,S 6,25:2
Hired Wife 1940,S 14,11:2
Youth Will Be Served 1940,N 15,25:2
Meet Boston Blackie 1941,F 26,17:2
Meet the Chump 1941,F 27,23:4
I Wanted Wings 1941,Mr 27,29:4
Penalty, The 1941,Ap 10,29:3
Girl, a Guy and a Gob, A 1941,Ap 24,25:3

Bride Wore Crutches, The 1941,My 26,15:3
Sunny 1941,Je 13,22:2
Tight Shoes 1941,Je 19,25:2
Time Out for Rhythm 1941,Jl 10,16:3
Navy Blues 1941,S 20,11:2
Man at Large 1941,O 11,21:4
Confessions of Boston Blackie 1941,D 8,31:2
Ride 'Em Cowboy 1942,Mr 5,27:3
Butch Minds the Baby 1942,My 1,23:3
Dr Broadway 1942,Je 25,27:3
Drums of the Congo 1942,Jl 20,16:4
A-Haunting We Will Go 1942,Ag 3,18:4
Time to Kill 1942,D 25,15:4
Arabian Nights 1942,D 26,15:1
Air Force 1943,F 4,29:1
It Ain't Hay 1943,Mr 11,17:3
Fired Wife 1943,O 1,15:2
Corvette K-225 1943,O 21,30:1
Crazy House 1943,D 16,33:3
Gung Ho! 1944,Ja 26,23:2
Bermuda Mystery 1944,My 13,17:1
Secret Command 1944,Je 14,16:2
Mr Winkle Goes to War 1944,Ag 3,16:1
Wave, A Wac and a Marine, A 1944,Ag 14,11:4
One Mysterious Night 1944,O 21,15:3
Brazil 1944,N 20,25:2
Bowery to Broadway 1944,N 30,19:2
Here Come the Co-Eds 1945,F 19,21:1
Two O'Clock Courage 1945,Ap 14,13:3
Bullfighters, The 1945,My 12,10:3
Wonder Man 1945,Je 9,17:2
Song of Scheherazade 1947,F 27,26:2
Hit Parade of 1947 1947,My 5,32:8
Sioux City Sue 1947,Jl 23,19:3
Take Me Out to the Ball Game 1949,Mr 10,35:2
There's a Girl in my Heart 1950,Ja 20,29:2
Jackie Robinson Story, The 1950,My 17,36:1
Admiral Was a Lady, The 1950,O 13,23:3
I Can Get It for You Wholesale 1951,Ap 5,34:4

Lane, Rosemary

Varsity Show 1937,S 2,17:2
Hollywood Hotel 1938,Ja 13,17:3
Gold Diggers in Paris 1938,Je 2,19:2
Four Daughters 1938,Ag 19,13:3
Blackwell's Island 1939,Mr 2,19:1
Oklahoma Kid, The 1939,Mr 11,21:1
Daughters Courageous 1939,Je 24,14:2
Return Of Doctor X, The 1939,N 23,38:5
Four Wives 1939,D 23,9:1
Angel From Texas, An 1940,My 10,26:7
Boys From Syracuse, The 1940,Ag 1,25:2
Ladies Must Live 1940,S 6,25:3
Always a Bride 1940,N 21,43:3
Four Mothers 1941,Ja 11,12:7
Time Out for Rhythm 1941,Jl 10,16:3
Chatterbox 1943,Jl 2,15:3
All by Myself 1943,Jl 16,20:3

Lane, Rusty

House on Ninety-Second Street, The
  1945,S 27,24:7
Harder They Fall, The 1956,My 10,26:3
Bigger Than Life 1956,Ag 3,11:2
Beyond a Reasonable Doubt 1956,S 14,27:2
Johnny Tremain 1957,Jl 11,21:1

Lane, Sarah

I Saw What You Did 1965,Jl 22,24:2

Lane, Tom

Miraculous Journey 1948,S 20,21:2

Lane, Tracy

Lawless Nineties, The 1936,Je 29,11:1

Lane, Vicky

Jungle Captive 1945,Jl 7,7:5

Lanfield, Sidney (Director)

Three Girls Lost 1931,My 2,23:4
Hush Money 1931,Jl 11,7:6
Dance Team 1932,Ja 16,13:1
Society Girl 1932,Je 10,22:3
Hat Check Girl 1932,O 8,15:4
Moulin Rouge 1934,F 8,14:4
Last Gentleman, The 1934,O 18,26:5
Hold 'Em Yale 1935,Ap 27,20:6
Red Salute 1935,S 30,13:1
King of Burlesque 1936,Ja 16,25:2
Sing, Baby, Sing 1936,S 12,20:1
One in a Million 1937,Ja 1,19:3
Wake up and Live 1937,Ap 24,16:2
Thin Ice 1937,S 4,8:2
Love and Hisses 1938,Ja 1,11:1
Always Goodbye 1938,Je 25,7:2
Hound of the Baskervilles, The 1939,Mr 25,19:2
Second Fiddle 1939,Jl 1,11:2
Swanee River 1939,D 30,9:2
You'll Never Get Rich 1941,O 24,27:2
Lady Has Plans, The 1942,Mr 5,27:1
My Favorite Blonde 1942,Ap 27,27:2
Meanest Man in the World, The 1943,F 25,27:3
Let's Face It 1943,Ag 5,18:1
Standing Room Only 1944,F 23,17:2
Well Groomed Bride, The 1946,My 11,22:5
Trouble With Women, The 1947,Jl 14,14:4
Where There's Life 1947,D 25,32:1
Sorrowful Jones 1949,Je 6,15:2
Lemon Drop Kid, The 1951,Mr 22,41:2

Lanfield, Sidney (Director)— Cont

Skirts Ahoy! 1952,My 29,17:2

Lanfield, Sidney (Original Author)

Happy Days 1930,F 14,20:1

Lanfranchi, Mario (Director)

Traviata, La 1968,F 28,43:2

Lang, Andre (Screenwriter)

Miserables, Les 1936,O 28,31:2

Lang, Anthony

Saraband 1949,Je 13,16:3
Tony Draws a Horse 1951,My 15,38:6

Lang, Barbara

House of Numbers 1957,S 13,15:2
Party Girl 1958,O 29,30:1

Lang, Charles

One Crowded Night 1940,Ag 27,17:2
Six Lessons From Madame La Zonga
  1941,F 19,25:2
Hit the Road 1941,Jl 3,15:3
Never Give a Sucker an Even Break
  1941,O 27,21:2
Keep 'Em Flying 1941,N 27,29:2
Bombay Clipper 1942,Ja 12,23:3
Secret Enemies 1943,Ja 1,27:3
Truck Busters 1943,Ja 29,23:5
Tampico 1944,Je 2,21:2
Roger Touhy, Gangster 1944,Je 5,14:7
Wing and a Prayer 1944,Ag 31,14:1

Lang, Charles (Screenwriter)

Magnificent Matador, The 1955,My 25,38:1
Desire in the Dust 1960,O 12,47:2

Lang, Christa

Champagne Murders, The 1968,Ap 25,53:1

Lang, David (Original Author)

People Are Funny 1946,Ja 28,15:6

Lang, David (Screenwriter)

Yank on the Burma Road, A 1942,Ja 29,25:3
Midnight Manhunt 1945,Ag 18,12:5
People Are Funny 1946,Ja 28,15:6

Lang, Doreen

Wrong Man, The 1956,D 24,8:1
Cabinet of Caligari, The 1962,My 26,13:5

Lang, Fritz

Contempt 1964,D 19,25:2

Lang, Fritz (Director)

Between Worlds 1924,Jl 7,10:4
Siegfried 1925,Ag 24,17:3
Beyond the Wall 1927,F 3,18:5
Metropolis 1927,Mr 7,16:3
Dr Nabuse 1927,Ag 10,21:4
Spione; Spies 1928,My 20,VIII,8:5
Kriemhild's Revenge 1928,O 16,29:1
Spies 1929,Mr 5,29:1
By Rocket to the Moon 1931,F 7,11:1
M 1931,Jl 19,VIII,2:6
M 1933,Ap 3,13:3
Liliom 1935,Mr 18,14:4
Fury 1936,Je 6,21:1
You Only Live Once 1937,F 1,15:2
You and Me 1938,Je 2,19:1
Return of Frank James, The 1940,Ag 10,16:4
Western Union 1941,F 7,23:2
Man Hunt 1941,Je 14,20:2
Last Will of Dr Mabuse, The 1943,Mr 20,11:1
Hangmen Also Die 1943,Ap 16,24:2
Woman in the Window, The 1945,Ja 26,16:4
Ministry of Fear 1945,F 8,15:2
Scarlet Street 1946,F 15,29:2
Cloak and Dagger 1946,O 5,13:2
Secret Beyond the Door 1948,Ja 16,25:4
House by the River 1950,My 2,25:2
American Guerrilla in the Philippines
  1950,N 8,37:2
Rancho Notorious 1952,My 15,39:5
Clash by Night 1952,Je 19,32:6
Blue Gardenia, The 1953,Ap 28,31:1
Big Heat, The 1953,O 15,43:2
Human Desire 1954,Ag 7,7:2
Moonfleet 1955,Je 25,9:2
While the City Sleeps 1956,My 17,37:1
Beyond a Reasonable Doubt 1956,S 14,27:2
Journey to the Lost City 1960,D 8,43:3

Lang, Fritz (Original Author)

Hangmen Also Die 1943,Ap 16,24:2

Lang, Fritz (Producer)

By Rockert to the Moon 1931,F 7,11:1
Testament du Dr Mabuse, Le; Dr Mabuse's Will
  1933,Je 11,IX,2:5
You and Me 1938,Je 2,19:1
Hangmen Also Die 1943,Ap 16,24:2
Secret Beyond the Door 1948,Ja 16,25:4
Journey to the Lost City 1960,D 8,43:3

Lang, Fritz (Screenwriter)

Between Worlds 1924,Jl 7,10:4
Fury 1936,Je 6,21:1
Hangmen Also Die 1943,Ap 16,24:2

Lang, Harold

Spider and the Fly, The 1952,Jl 29,17:3
Cairo Road 1952,N 1,17:2
Long Memory, The 1953,Jl 27,15:2
Blackout 1954,My 22,8:2

Lang, Howard

Cradle Song 1933,N 20,18:2
Mystery Woman 1935,Ja 9,22:2

Lang, Howard— Cont
Navy Spy 1937,Mr 22,27:3
Prisoner of Zenda, The 1937,S 3,12:1
Nothing but the Best 1964,Jl 14,28:1
Lang, John Stevenson
Mad Little Island 1958,D 31,12:1
Lang, Julia
Under Capricorn 1949,S 9,28:3
Lang, June
Music in the Air 1934,D 14,29:3
Country Doctor, The 1936,Mr 13,32:2 (Incorrect in this edition; use 1936,Mr 13,27:2 elsewhere)
Every Saturday Night 1936,Mr 14,10:2
Captain January 1936,Ap 25,21:1
Road to Glory, The 1936,Ag 6,22:1
White Hunter 1936,N 26,39:2
Nancy Steele is Missing 1937,Mr 8,22:1
Wee Willie Winkie 1937,Jl 24,12:1
Ali Baba Goes to Town 1937,O 23,14:1
International Settlement 1938,F 12,20:3
One Wild Night 1938,Je 3,17:2
Meet the Girls 1938,S 3,16:6
Zenobia 1939,My 15,15:2
Captain Fury 1939,My 26,20:2
Convicted Woman 1940,F 26,11:2
Isle of Destiny 1940,Ap 8,15:2
Footlight Serenade 1942,S 10,30:3
Stage Door Canteen 1943,Je 25,13:2
Flesh and Fantasy 1943,N 18,29:1
Lang, Lotte
Embezzled Heaven 1959,Ap 24,23:1
Lang, Matheson
Carnival 1921,Je 27,16:3
Triumph of the Scarlet Pimpernel, The 1929,Jl 8,17:3
Carnival 1931,N 22,VIII,6:1
Channel Crossing 1934,My 24,28:3
Little Friend 1934,O 20,20:2
Lang, Matheson (Original Author)
Chinese Den 1941,Mr 26,27:3
Lang, Melvin
Doomed to Die 1940,Jl 30,16:3
Lang, Otto (Director)
Search for Paradise 1957,S 25,25:2
Lang, Otto (Narrator)
Search for Paradise 1957,S 25,25:2
Lang, Otto (Producer)
Call Northside 777 1948,F 19,29:2
Five Fingers 1952,F 23,7:5
White Witch Doctor 1953,Jl 2,19:3
Lang, Otto (Screenwriter)
Search for Paradise 1957,S 25,25:2
Lang, Peter
Dangerous Money 1924,O 14,21:5
Lang, Robert
Othello 1966,F 2,24:1
Lang, Rosemary
Saraband 1949,Je 13,16:3
Lang, Walter (Director)
Satin Woman, The 1927,Ag 10,21:4
College Hero, The 1927,N 22,32:2
Brothers 1930,N 15,15:3
Hell Bound 1931,My 9,15:4
Women Go on Forever 1931,O 19,28:1
No More Orchids 1933,Ja 2,29:2
Warrior's Husband, The 1933,My 12,20:4
Meet the Baron 1933,O 28,20:3
Whom the Gods Destroy 1934,Jl 13,14:2
Mighty Barnum, The 1934,D 24,17:1
Carnival 1935,F 16,9:1
Hooray for Love 1935,Jl 13,16:2
Love Before Breakfast 1936,Mr 14,10:1
Wife, Doctor and Nurse 1937,O 11,26:5
Second Honeymoon 1937,N 13,11:2
Baroness and the Butler, The 1938,F 19,19:2
I'll Give a Million 1938,Jl 16,7:2
Little Princess, The 1939,Mr 11,21:1
Blue Bird, The 1940,Ja 20,11:2
Star Dust 1940,My 4,13:1
Great Profile, The 1940,O 18,25:1
Tin Pan Alley 1940,N 22,27:3
Moon Over Miami 1941,Jl 5,14:2
Week-End in Havana 1941,N 8,11:2
Song of the Islands 1942,Mr 12,24:4
Magnificent Dope, The 1942,Jl 3,12:5
Coney Island 1943,Je 17,17:2
Greenwich Village 1944,S 28,26:2
State Fair 1945,Ag 31,14:3
Sentimental Journey 1946,Mr 7,33:2
Claudia and David 1946,Ag 15,19:2
Mother Wore Tights 1947,Ag 21,33:2
Sitting Pretty 1948,Mr 11,35:2
When my Baby Smiles at Me 1948,N 24,20:2
You're my Everything 1949,Jl 23,7:2
Cheaper by the Dozen 1950,Ap 1,12:2
Jackpot, The 1950,N 23,55:2
On the Riviera 1951,My 24,47:1
With a Song in my Heart 1952,Ap 5,20:2
Call Me Madam 1953,Mr 26,37:1
There's no Business Like Show Business 1954,D 17,37:3
King and I, The 1956,Je 29,15:6
Desk Set 1957,My 16,28:2
But Not for Me 1959,O 3,14:6

Can-Can 1960,Mr 10,36:1
Marriage-Go-Round 1961,Ja 7,12:2
Snow White and the Three Stooges 1961,Jl 1,9:1
Lang, Walter (Screenwriter)
Satin Woman, The 1927,Ag 10,21:4
Langan, Glenn
Return Of Doctor X, The 1939,N 23,38:5
Riding High 1943,D 23,26:4
Four Jills in a Jeep 1944,Ap 6,27:2
Wing and a Prayer 1944,Ag 31,14:1
Something for the Boys 1944,N 30,19:1
Hangover Square 1945,F 8,15:2
Bell for Adano, A 1945,Jl 6,8:3
Sentimental Journey 1946,Mr 7,33:2
Dragonwyck 1946,Ap 11,35:2
Margie 1946,O 17,28:3
Homestretch, The 1947,Ap 24,30:2
Forever Amber 1947,O 23,31:2
Fury at Furnace Creek 1948,Jl 12,11:2
Snake Pit, the 1948,N 5,29:2
Iroquois Trail, The 1950,O 27,24:4
Rapture 1950,D 14,51:3
Hangman's Knot 1952,D 11,45:3
Amazing Colossal Man, The 1957,O 26,19:2
Langan, William
Swing High 1930,Je 27,26:3
Langaner, Clara
Personal Maid 1931,S 5,7:4
Langberg, Ebbe
I, A Lover 1968,My 4,46:2
Langden, John
Atlantic 1930,Ja 26,VIII,6:2
Langdon, Harry
Picking Peaches 1924,Ja 21,20:1
Tramp, Tramp, Tramp 1926,My 24,24:3
Strong Man, The 1926,S 7,44:2
Long Pants 1927,Mr 29,23:2
His First Flame 1927,My 2,26:4
Three's a Crowd 1927,O 3,20:1
Chaser, The 1928,Ap 10,33:2
See America Thirst 1930,D 12,35:3
Soldiers Plaything, A 1931,My 2,23:4
Hallelujah, I'm a Bum 1933,F 9,15:2
My Weakness 1933,S 22,14:1
There Goes my Heart 1938,O 14,27:1
Zenobia 1939,My 15,15:2
Days of Thrills and Laughter 1961,Mr 22,37:1
Sound of Laughter, The 1963,D 18,44:2
30 Years of Fun 1963,D 26,33:4
Langdon, Harry (Director)
Chaser, The 1928,Ap 10,33:2
Langdon, Harry (Original Author)
Block-Heads 1938,Ag 30,14:2
Flying Deuces, The 1939,N 24,29:2
Chump at Oxford, A 1940,F 20,17:3
Langdon, Harry (Screenwriter)
Block-Heads 1938,Ag 30,14:2
Flying Deuces, The 1939,N 24,29:2
Chump at Oxford, A 1940,F 20,17:3
Saps at Sea 1940,Ap 29,12:2
Road Show 1941,F 19,25:2
Langdon, Lillian
Going Up 1923,O 10,16:2
Circe the Enchantress 1924,D 9,23:3
Enticement 1925,Mr 21,16:3
After Business Hour 1925,Je 17,16:2
Cobra 1925,D 7,19:1
Joanna 1925,D 15,14:5
Blonde Saint, The 1926,N 23,27:1
Langdon, Rose
Road to Mandalay, The 1926,Je 29,21:2
Langdon, Sue Anne
Great Impostor, The 1961,Mr 30,24:1
New Interns, The 1964,Ag 20,34:2
Roustabout 1964,N 11,38:1
Rounders, The 1965,Ap 29,40:2
When the Boys Meet the Girls 1966,Ja 20,29:1
Hold On! 1966,Je 23,29:4
Frankie and Johnny 1966,Jl 21,20:2
Guide for the Married Man, A 1967,My 27,16:1
Langdon, Terence
Return of Mr Moto 1965,D 2,48:1
LANGE
See Also LAING
Lange
Last Game, The 1964,O 25,41:5 (Incorrect in this edition; use 1964,O 26,41:5 elsewhere)
Lange, Arthur (Miscellaneous)
Hollywood Revue, The 1929,Ag 15,20:5
Lange, Bernadette
Dr Knock 1955,O 10,31:2
Premier May 1958,S 17,44:2
Lange, Claudie
Bible, The 1966,S 29,60:1
Made in Italy 1967,My 1,44:2
Lange, Hope
Bus Stop 1956,S 1,19:2
True Story of Jesse James, The 1957,Mr 23,17:2
Peyton Place 1957,D 13,35:1
Young Lions, The 1958,Ap 3,23:1
In Love and War 1958,N 1,14:2
Best of Everything 1959,O 9,24:2
Wild in the Country 1961,Je 10,12:2

Lange, Hope— Cont
Pocketful of Miracles 1961,D 19,39:1
Love Is a Ball 1963,Ap 25,38:1
Jigsaw 1968,Je 6,54:2
Lange, Johnny (Composer)
Pick a Star 1937,My 28,17:2
That's Right, You're Wrong 1939,N 30,25:3
Melody Time 1948,My 28,28:2
Langelaan, George (Original Author)
Fly, The 1958,Ag 30,6:6
Langen, Vera von
Verklungene Melodie; Dead Melody 1938,Je 25,7:2
Gruene Hoelle, Die; Green Hell, The 1939,Ja 21,19:2
Fuenf Millionem suchen einen Erben; Five Millions Seek an Heir 1939,O 23,15:3
Langford, Frances
Every Night at Eight 1935,Ag 3,16:2
Broadway Melody of 1936 1935,S 19,28:1
Collegiate 1936,Ja 23,25:2
Born to Dance 1936,D 5,16:1
Hit Parade, The 1937,My 31,11:2
Hollywood Hotel 1938,Ja 13,17:3
Too Many Girls 1940,N 21,43:1
Hit Parade of 1941 1940,D 5,33:2
Yankee Doodle Dandy 1942,My 30,9:1
Cowboy in Manhattan 1943,My 28,19:2
This Is the Army 1943,Jl 29,11:6
Radio Stars on Parade 1945,S 22,14:2
People Are Funny 1946,Ja 28,15:6
Deputy Marshal 1949,N 11,31:3
Glenn Miller Story, the 1954,F 11,33:2
Langham, James R (Original Author)
Night in New Orleans 1942,Jl 2,25:2
Langlenn, Paula
William Fox Movietone Follies of 1929 1929,My 27,22:1
Langler, Max
Night of the Mayas 1941,Ja 14,16:7
Ay Jalisco no te Rajes 1943,Ap 24,17:3
Langley, Adria Locke (Original Author)
Lion Is in the Streets, A 1953,S 24,39:2
Langley, Herbert
Chu Chin Chow 1925,F 11,19:4
Langley, Lee (Screenwriter)
Interlude 1968,Jl 3,26:1
Langley, Noel (Director)
Pickwick Papers, The 1954,Ap 5,21:2
Adventures of Sadie, The 1955,My 18,35:2
Svengali 1955,S 26,18:2
Langley, Noel (Original Author)
Edward my Son 1949,Je 3,21:2
Adam and Evalyn 1950,My 12,33:4
Langley, Noel (Screenwriter)
Maytime 1937,Mr 19,27:1
Wizard of Oz, The 1939,Ag 18,16:2
Florian 1940,Je 6,33:2
Unexpected Uncle 1941,S 25,29:1
Vicious Circle, The 1948,Jl 22,27:2
Trio 1950,O 11,42:1
Christmas Carol, A 1951,N 29,41:2
Tom Brown's School Days 1952,Ja 8,23:5
Ivanhoe 1952,Ag 1,8:2
Prisoner of Zenda, The 1952,N 5,36:2
Knights of the Round Table 1954,Ja 8,17:2
Pickwick Papers, The 1954,Ap 5,21:2
Adventures of Sadie, The 1955,My 18,35:2
Svengali 1955,S 26,18:2
Vagabond King, The 1956,S 13,39:6
Snow White and the Three Stooges 1961,Jl 1,9:1
Langner, Lawrence (Original Author)
Pursuit of Happiness, The 1934,O 26,25:1
Langner, Philip (Producer)
Child Is Waiting, A 1963,F 14,5:6
Pawnbroker, The 1965,Ap 21,51:1
Langre, Inga
Sunshine Follows Rain 1949,S 29,39:2
Langsner, Clara
Counsellor-At-Law 1933,D 8,31:2
Langston, Jean
Belles of St Trinian's, The 1954,D 23,13:4
Langton, David
Abandon Ship 1957,Ap 18,35:1
Langton, Paul
Thirty Seconds Over Tokyo 1944,N 16,19:1
Gentle Annie 1945,My 5,11:5
Hidden Eye, The 1945,Ag 31,14:3
They Were Expendable 1945,D 21,25:2
Till the Clouds Roll By 1946,D 6,27:4
My Brother Talks to Horses 1947,Je 19,27:4
Romance of Rosy Ridge, The 1947,S 12,18:3
Jack Slade 1953,O 29,42:6
Return From the Sea 1954,Jl 10,7:3
To Hell and Back 1955,S 23,21:2
Big Knife, The 1955,N 9,41:2
Incredible Shrinking Man, The 1957,F 23,13:1
Chicago Confidential 1957,Ag 31,19:1
Langtry, Kenneth (Screenwriter)
I Was a Teenage Frankenstein 1958,Ja 30,19:4
Headless Ghost, The 1959,Ap 30,37:2
Lanham, Edwin (Original Author)
It Shouldn't Happen to a Dog 1946,S 7,11:2
Senator Was Indiscreet, The 1947,D 27,9:2

Lani, Lei Prince
Waikiki Wedding 1937,Mr 25,29:1
Bird of Paradise 1951,Mr 15,37:2
Lani, Pua
Hawaii Calls 1938,Ap 29,17:2
Fisherman's Wharf 1939,F 24,15:2
Lania, Leo (Screenwriter)
Ultimatum 1940,F 5,13:2
drame De Shanghai; Shanghai Drama, The
1945,Ja 11,19:2
Lanier, Jean
Modigliani of Montparnasse 1961,Mr 1,27:3
Last Year at Marienbad 1962,Mr 8,26:1
Lanier, Joseph (Composer)
Waltz Time in Vienna 1934,N 19,13:2
Lanner, Susi
Mein Liebster Ist ein Jaegersmann 1936,S 15,37:6
Herbst-Monoever; Fall Manoeuvres
1939,Mr 18,9:3
Lannes, Georges
Collier de la Reine, Le (Queen's Necklace, The)
1931,F 9,25:3
Resistance; Peleton d'Execution 1946,Jl 5,15:3
Moulin Rouge 1953,F 11,33:5
Night is my Kingdom, The 1953,S 30,37:1
Sins of the Borgias 1956,Mr 5,21:1
Lanning, Frank
Huckleberry Finn 1920,F 23,11:2
Bad Man, The 1923,O 9,17:4
Kid Brother, The 1927,Ja 24,14:1
Unknown, The 1927,Je 13,17:1
Stand and Deliver 1928,Ap 2,25:1
Rough Romance 1930,Je 16,25:3
Lanoe, Henri (Screenwriter)
Male Companion 1966,F 15,33:2
Lanoe, Jiguel
Forbidden Woman, The 1920,F 23,11:2
Lanoux, Victor
Shameless Old Lady, The 1966,S 27,52:1
Lanovoi, V
Problem Child 1955,Ja 24,20:5
Lanoy, Andre
Stranded in Paris 1926,D 13,27:1
Blonde or Brunette 1927,Ja 11,18:2
Lanphier, Fay
American Venus, The 1926,Ja 26,25:2
Lanphier, James
Perfect Furlough, The 1959,Ja 22,27:4
Flight of the Lost Balloon 1962,My 24,29:2
Pink Panther, The 1964,Ap 24,25:1
Lanphier, Mary-Madeleine (Miscellaneous)
Weddings and Babies 1960,O 6,51:3
Lansberg, Olle (Original Author)
Dear John 1966,Mr 9,46:1
Lansburgh, Janet (Screenwriter)
Run, Appaloosa, Run! 1966,Jl 14,28:1
Lansburgh, Larry (Director)
Run, Appaloosa, Run! 1966,Jl 14,28:1
Lansburgh, Larry (Original Author)
Littlest Outlaw, The 1955,D 27,31:1
Lansburgh, Larry (Producer)
Littlest Outlaw, The 1955,D 27,31:1
Run, Appaloosa, Run! 1966,Jl 14,28:1
Lansburgh, Larry (Screenwriter)
Jungle Headhunters 1951,D 6,42:5
Lansbury, Angela
Gaslight 1944,My 5,17:2
National Velvet 1944,D 15,25:2
Picture of Dorian Gray, The 1945,Mr 2,15:2
Harvey Girls, The 1946,Ja 25,26:2
Hoodlum Saint, The 1946,Je 27,29:1
Till the Clouds Roll By 1946,D 6,27:4
Private Affairs of Bel Ami, The 1947,Je 16,25:4
If Winter Comes 1948,Ja 23,28:4
State of the Union 1948,Ap 23,28:1
Three Musketeers, The 1948,O 21,33:2
Red Danube, The 1949,D 9,37:3
Samson and Delilah 1949,D 22,29:2
Kind Lady 1951,Ag 8,21:2
Mutiny 1952,Mr 20,37:5
Purple Mask, The 1955,Je 16,35:7
Court Jester, The 1956,F 2,19:1
Long, Hot Summer, The 1958,Ap 4,16:1
Reluctant Debutante, The 1958,Ag 15,17:1
Khovanshina 1960,S 23,33:1
Breath of Scandal, A 1960,D 17,19:1
Blue Hawaii 1962,F 22,20:2
All Fall Down 1962,Ap 12,41:3
Manchurian Candidate, The 1962,O 25,48:3
In the Cool of the Day 1963,My 30,20:1
World of Henry Orient, The 1964,Mr 20,27:2
Greatest Story Ever Told, The 1965,F 16,40:2
Dear Heart 1965,Mr 8,33:1
Amorous Adventures of Moll Flanders, The
1965,My 27,28:1
Harlow 1965,Jl 22,24:1
Mister Buddwing 1966,O 12,36:1
Lansbury, Edgar (Producer)
Subject Was Roses, The 1968,O 14,53:2
Lansfield, Sidney (Director)
Follow the Sun 1951,Ap 26,34:4

Lansford, William Douglas (Original Author)
Villa Rides 1968,Jl 18,26:3
Lansing, Joi
Brave One, The 1957,Mr 22,26:1
Hole in the Head, A 1959,Jl 16,31:2
Who Was That Lady? 1960,Ap 16,10:1
Marriage on the Rocks 1965,S 16,00:0
Lansing, Robert
Gathering of Eagles, A 1963,Jl 11,21:2
Lanta, Leo (Screenwriter)
Threepenny Opera, The 1960,Jl 11,24:4
Lante, Diana
Marcia Nuziale, La 1936,F 27,23:2
Re Burlone, Il 1936,Mr 28,11:3
Lanteau, William
Li'l Abner 1959,D 12,19:2
Facts of Life, The 1961,Jl 11,27:1
Hotel 1967,Ja 20,27:1
Lantszch, Walter
Fuerst Sepp'l 1937,Jl 17,18:1
Lantz, Jim
In Cold Blood 1967,D 15,60:1
Lantz, Louis (Original Author)
Meet The People 1944,S 8,16:2
River of no Return 1954,My 1,13:2
Lantz, Louis (Screenwriter)
Crime Doctor 1943,Jl 5,11:4
Violence 1947,My 10,8:5
Rogue River 1951,F 16,21:4
Lure of the Wilderness 1952,O 4,15:2
Lanvin, Lisette
Orage 1938,D 12,26:2
Champs-Elysees 1939,F 28,17:2
Savage Brigade 1948,D 3,33:4
Lanza, Anthony (Director)
Glory Stompers, The 1968,Mr 28,52:4
Lanza, Mario
That Midnight Kiss 1949,S 23,28:2
Toast of New Orleans, The 1950,S 30,13:3
Great Caruso, The 1951,My 11,32:2
Because You're Mine 1952,S 26,18:2
Serenade 1956,Mr 24,21:1 (Incorrect in this
edition; use 1956,Mr 23,21:1 elsewhere)
Seven Hills of Rome 1958,Ja 28,24:2 (Incorrect
in this edition; use 1958,Ja 31,24:2 elsewhere)
For the First Time 1959,Ag 15,8:7
Lanza, Mila
Life and Miracles of Blesses Mother Cabrini, The
1946,Jl 8,25:2
Lanzi, Dina
Parlami d'Amore Mariu 1934,O 20,20:3
Lanzi, Fulvia
Squadrone Bianco, Lo; White Squadrone, The
1939,D 1,27:2
Lanzi, G (Screenwriter)
What Price Innocence? 1953,My 2,13:3
Lapaire, Leo (Original Author)
Eternal Mask, The 1937,Ja 13,20:3
Lapaire, Leo (Screenwriter)
Eternal Mask, The 1937,Ja 13,20:3
Lapara, Leo
Lover's Return, A; Revenant, Le 1948,Ja 26,15:2
Confessions of a Rogue 1948,Mr 30,26:3
Monelle 1950,F 3,29:2
Between Eleven and Midnight 1950,F 23,33:3
Lapauri, Alexander
Ballet of Romeo and Juliet, The 1956,Ap 3,31:2
Lapeyre, Numa
Daddy Long Legs 1955,My 6,17:5
Lapicki, Andrzei
Salto 1966,O 4,50:1
Lapierre, Dominique (Original Author)
Is Paris Burning? 1966,N 11,36:1
Lapin, B (Screenwriter)
Son of Mongolia 1936,N 21,21:4
LaPlanche, Rosemary
Prairie Chickens 1943,Jl 9,21:6
Lapoknysh, Vasil (Director)
Cossack Beyond the Danube, A 1954,F 8,18:5
Lileia 1960,My 30,8:2
Lapoknysh, Vasil (Producer)
Lileia 1960,My 30,8:2
Lapoknysh, Vasil (Screenwriter)
Lileia 1960,My 30,8:2
Lappan, Patrick
Girl With Green Eyes 1964,Ag 11,37:2
Lapsley, Jimmie
Confidence Man, The 1924,Ap 15,24:1
Lara, Angel
Roots, The (Our Lady); Our Lady (The Roots)
1957,S 3,23:2
Lara, Antonio
Wave, The 1937,Ap 21,18:1
Lara, Augustin
Novillero 1939,Mr 4,18:5
Lara, Augustin (Composer)
Adios, Nicanor 1938,Mr 14,13:2
Tropic Holiday 1938,Je 30,21:2
Three Caballeros, The 1945,F 5,20:1
Lara, Claude Autant (Director)
Devil in the Flesh 1949,My 10,29:2

Larabee, Louise
Act One 1963,D 27,17:2
Larch, John
Phenix City Story, The 1955,S 3,9:1
Killer is Loose, The 1956,Mr 3,17:2
Written on the Wind 1957,Ja 12,12:6
Gun for a Coward 1957,Ja 31,21:1
Quantez 1957,S 7,12:7
Careless Years, The 1957,N 28,57:3
Man With a Shadow 1958,Ja 23,24:3
From Hell to Texas 1958,Je 5,39:2
Hell to Eternity 1960,O 13,41:1
Miracle of the White Stallions 1963,My 23,31:2
Lardner, John (Original Author)
Finger Man 1955,Jl 16,12:4
Lardner, Ring (Original Author)
New Klondike, The 1926,Mr 22,16:1
Fast Company 1929,O 5,22:5
June Moon 1931,Mr 14,23:2
Elmer the Great 1933,My 26,24:2
Alibi Ike 1935,Jl 17,22:1
Blonde Trouble 1937,Ag 7,7:2
Champion 1949,Ap 11,29:2
Lardner, Ring Jr (Miscellaneous)
Four Days' Leave 1950,Je 9,29:4
Lardner, Ring Jr (Screenwriter)
Meet Doctor Christian 1939,D 1,27:2
Courageous Dr Christian, The 1940,Mr 29,25:3
Woman of the Year 1942,F 6,23:2
Cross of Lorraine, The 1943,D 3,27:4
Tomorrow the World 1944,D 22,12:4
Cloak and Dagger 1946,O 5,13:2
Forever Amber 1947,O 23,31:2
Forbidden Street, The 1949,My 14,9:2
Cincinnati Kid, The 1965,O 28,48:1
Largay, Raymond
Soldiers and Women 1930,My 12,27:3
She Wrote the Book 1946,Je 20,20:3
Shocking Miss Pilgrim, The 1947,F 12,34:2
Are You With It? 1948,Ap 15,31:2
Four Faces West 1948,Ag 4,18:3
Force of Evil 1948,D 27,16:2
Petty Girl, The 1950,Ag 18,17:2
Johnny One-Eye 1950,N 17,31:2
Second Woman, The 1951,F 2,19:2
April in Paris 1952,D 25,34:5
LaRiana
Juke Box Jenny 1942,Ap 17,21:3
Larikov
Peter the First 1937,D 25,10:4
Larin, Nikolai (Director)
Rasputin 1929,O 21,30:1
Larinoff, Alexander
Once There Was a Girl 1945,D 24,19:2
Larionova, Alla
Fathers and Sons 1960,D 26,27:2
Larionova, Anna
Sadko 1953,Je 1,18:6
Anna Cross, The 1954,O 25,30:7
Twelfth Night 1956,Mr 5,21:1
Larive, Leon
Passion Of Joan Of Arc, The 1929,Mr 29,21:1
Passion of Jeanne d'Arc, The 1929,Mr 31,VIII,7:1
Lower Depths, The 1937,S 11,20:1
Claudine 1940,Ap 1,15:2
Zero de Conduite 1947,Je 23,14:5
Francois Villon 1950,Jl 3,9:2
Larke, Wynne
Backlash 1947,My 24,10:5
Larkin, John
Smart Money 1931,Je 19,21:1
Prodigal, The 1931,Je 27,20:3
Sporting Blood 1931,Ag 15,18:3
Wet Parade, The 1932,Ap 22,23:2
Stranger in Town 1932,Jl 8,22:5
Great Jasper, The 1933,F 17,5:3
Notorious Gentleman, A 1935,F 16,9:1
Mississippi 1935,Ap 18,27:2
Hearts Divided 1936,Je 13,13:1
Seven Days in May 1964,F 20,22:1
Satan Bug, The 1965,Ap 15,38:1
Those Calloways 1965,Ap 15,38:2
Larkin, John (Director)
Quiet Please, Murder 1942,D 22,31:1
Circumstantial Evidence 1945,Ap 21,18:3
Larkin, John (Narrator)
Farewell to Yesterday 1950,D 1,31:2
Larkin, John (Original Author)
Rose of Washington Square 1939,My 6,21:2
Lone Wolf Meets a Lady 1940,Je 17,19:2
Bermuda Mystery 1944,My 13,17:1
Cloak and Dagger 1946,O 5,13:2
Two Weeks With Love 1950,N 24,31:2
Larkin, John (Screenwriter)
News Is Made at Night 1939,Jl 13,17:2
Charlie Chan at Treasure Island 1939,S 1,15:5
Charlie Chan in Panama 1940,F 23,19:3
Lone Wolf Meets a Lady, The 1940,Je 17,19:2
Charlie Chan At the Wax Museum 1940,S 28,9:3
Gay Caballero, The 1940,O 25,25:3
Dead Men Tell 1941,Ap 17,29:3
Man at Large 1941,O 11,21:4
Secret Agent of Japan 1942,Mr 23,19:3

Larkin, John (Screenwriter) — Cont
Manila Calling 1942,S 28,13:1
Man in the Trunk, The 1942,O 23,25:1
Quiet Please, Murder 1942,D 22,31:1
Dolly Sisters, The 1945,N 15,24:6
Carnival in Costa Rica 1947,Mr 29,21:2
Two Weeks With Love 1950,N 24,31:2
Larkin, John Francis (Original Author)
Frisco Jenny 1933,Ja 7,11:2
She Had to Say Yes 1933,Jl 29,14:2
Larkin, John Jr (Original Author)
Society Girl 1932,Je 10,22:3
LaRoche, Pierre (Miscellaneous)
Portrait of a Woman 1946,Ap 22,26:2
Laroche, Pierre (Screenwriter)
Devil's Own Envoy, The 1947,Ag 30,8:6
Gigi 1950,Ja 31,20:2
Red Angel, The 1950,N 4,13:2
LaRoche, Pierre (Screenwriter)
Minne 1951,Ap 17,35:2
Mitsou 1958,Ap 15,42:5
Larof, M
Polish Terror, The 1933,Mr 13,18:3
Larosa, Viola
Regina di Sparta, La 1931,F 23,20:3
Laroy, Guessippi
Regina di Sparta, La 1931,F 23,20:3
LaRoy, Rita
Dynamite 1929,D 28,11:1
Lovin' the Ladies 1930,Mr 22,22:6
Midnight Mystery 1930,Je 2,25:4
Sin Takes a Holliday 1930,N 28,23:1
Holy Terror, A 1931,Jl 20,20:4
Traveling Husbands 1931,Ag 8,16:3
Gay Diplomat, The 1931,O 10,20:4
Yellow Ticket, The 1931,O 31,22:2
Leftover Ladies 1931,N 9,22:4
Secret Witness, The 1931,D 21,28:4
Amateur Daddy 1932,Ap 23,11:5
So Big 1932,Ap 30,19:3
Sinners in the Sun 1932,My 14,11:5
Bachelor's Affairs 1932,Je 25,18:2
Hollywood Speaks 1932,Ag 12,18:2
Blonde Venus 1932,S 24,18:4
Hot Saturday 1932,N 5,12:5
From Hell to Heaven 1933,Mr 18,9:3
Whirlpool 1934,My 5,22:3
Hollywood Boulevard 1936,S 21,26:4
Lady From Nowhere 1936,D 21,19:2
Flight From Glory 1937,S 11,20:1
Condemned Woman 1938,Ap 22,15:5
Fixer Dugan 1939,My 6,21:2
Larquey, Pierre
Topaze 1935,F 16,9:2
Second Bureau 1936,F 17,21:2
Dr Knock 1937,My 1,16:4
Man and his Wife, A 1939,Mr 28,20:1
Mademoiselle ma Mere 1939,S 19,29:2
Citadel of Silence, The 1939,D 25,29:1
Mayor's Dilemma, The 1940,Ap 23,19:2
Two Women 1940,N 2,19:3
Moulin Rouge 1944,N 23,38:2
Ces Dames aux Chapeaux Verts; Ladies in the
 Green Hats, The 1945,Ap 5,26:2
Jericho 1946,D 16,31:2
Murderer Lives at Number 21, The
 1947,Ag 18,12:3
Blue Veil, The 1947,O 2,32:6
Corbeau, Le; Raven, The 1948,F 24,21:1
Jenny Lamour 1948,Mr 6,17:2
Portrait of Innocence 1948,Je 9,35:2
Sylvie and the Phantom 1950,O 16,30:5
Face to the Wind 1951,Ja 16,34:2
Simple Case of Money, A 1952,F 2,11:2
Topaze 1952,O 28,37:1
Diabolique 1955,N 22,41:1
Witches of Salem 1958,D 9,54:2
Larrabeiti, Carmen
Ley Del Haren, La 1933,Je 17,16:7
Toda una Vida 1933,O 23,18:3
Larranaga, Carlos
Pride and the Passion, The 1957,Je 29,10:6
Larrimore, Francine
John Meade's Woman 1937,F 18,19:1
Larry
Three Stooges Go Around the World in a Daze,
 The 1963,D 19,40:2
Larsen, Elsebeth
Crazy Paradise 1965,Ag 11,41:2
Larsen, Gerd
Romeo and Juliet 1966,O 6,55:1
Larsen, Keith
Flat Top 1952,D 6,17:2
Hiawatha 1952,D 26,20:4
Arrow in the Dust 1954,My 1,13:2
Chief Crazy Horse 1955,Ap 28,25:1
Desert Sands 1955,N 19,22:7
Larsen, Ole
Girls are Willing, The 1959,My 11,30:1
Larsen, Samuel T (Screenwriter)
Prodigal, The 1955,My 14,10:7
Larson, Bobby
Courageous Dr Christian, The 1940,Mr 29,25:3
Design for Scandal 1942,F 6,23:3

Larson, Christine
Well, The 1951,S 27,37:2
Larson, Jack
Fighter Squadron 1948,N 20,9:2
Battle Zone 1952,N 1,17:2
Larssen, Tryggve
En Saga 1938,Ja 8,19:2
Larsson, Barbo
Time of Desire 1959,N 21,26:5
Larteguy, Jean (Original Author)
Lost Command 1966,S 15,51:1
Lartigue, Martin
War of the Buttons, The 1963,D 19,40:2
Larue, Claude
Sleeping Car to Trieste 1949,Ap 18,18:6
Noah's Ark 1950,Ag 21,15:1
Sins of Paris 1954,Ja 30,9:6
LaRue, Frank
Once in a Lifetime 1932,O 29,18:4
It Happened Out West 1937,Je 7,22:3
Prison Camp 1940,Ag 3,9:3
LaRue, Grace
She Done Him Wrong 1933,F 10,12:3
If I Had my Way 1940,My 6,13:2
LaRue, Jack
Mouthpiece, The 1932,Ap 21,25:2
Radio Patrol 1932,Jl 14,24:2
Virtue 1932,O 25,24:5
Farewell to Arms, A 1932,D 9,26:5
Man Against Woman 1932,D 17,22:3
Lawyer Man 1932,D 27,10:2
Christopher Strong 1933,Mr 10,19:2
Woman Accused, The 1933,Mr 13,18:2
Story of Temple Drake, The 1933,My 6,11:2
Girl in 419 1933,My 20,11:5
Gambling Ship 1933,Jl 13,17:5
Headline Shooters 1933,O 23,18:3
Kennell Murder Case, The 1933,O 30,14:2
Miss Fane's Baby is Stolen 1934,Ja 20,12:2
Good Dame 1934,Mr 17,11:4
Straight Is the Way 1934,Ag 29,13:2
Times Square Lady 1935,Mr 15,25:3
Under the Pampas Moon 1935,My 31,11:1
Daring Young Man, The 1935,Jl 18,15:2
Special Agent 1935,S 19,28:1
Little Big Shot 1935,O 7,11:2
His Night Out 1935,N 16,19:2
Remember Last Night? 1935,N 21,27:2
Strike Me Pink 1936,Ja 17,15:2
Dancing Pirate 1936,Je 18,19:1
Her Husband Lies 1937,Mr 18,20:1
That I May Live 1937,My 10,23:2
Captains Courageous 1937,My 12,27:1
Trapped by G-Men 1937,N 4,29:1
Arson Racket Squad 1938,Je 18,18:2
Valley of the Giants 1938,S 10,20:2
Big Town Czar 1939,My 4,27:3
Enemy Agent 1940,Ap 22,13:3
Prison Camp 1940,Ag 3,9:3
Sea Hawk, The 1940,Ag 10,16:2
East of the River 1940,O 28,21:2
Footsteps in the Dark 1941,Mr 15,13:2
Ringside Maisie 1941,Ag 1,11:2
Gangs Incorporated 1941,Ag 4,16:6
Swamp Woman 1941,D 27,15:2
American Empire 1943,Ja 14,25:4
Desert Song, The 1943,D 18,10:6
Pistol Packin' Mama 1943,D 20,27:4
Spanish Main, The 1945,N 7,20:2
Dakota 1945,D 17,17:2
Road to Utopia 1946,F 28,20:2
Murder in the Music Hall 1946,Ap 15,22:2
In old Sacramento 1946,Ap 29,24:4
My Favorite Brunette 1947,Mr 20,38:2
For Heaven's Sake 1950,D 16,10:5
No Orchids for Miss Blandish 1951,F 23,33:2
Lary, P (Screenwriter)
Girl on the Third Floor, The; (Sophie et le Crime)
 1958,O 11,47:1 (Incorrect in this edition; use
 1958,O 11,18:4 elsewhere)
Lasaffre, Roland
Young Girls Beware 1959,Ag 22,8:2
Cheaters, The; (Tricheurs, Les) 1961,Je 5,37:4
Lascoe, Henry
Man With my Face, The 1951,Je 15,27:5
Lasdun, Gary
Gunn 1967,Je 29,32:1
Laserson, Miriam
My Father's House 1947,S 26,28:3
Lash, Harry
Headin' East 1938,Ja 15,19:2
Lashey, Donald
Price of a Party, The 1924,N 26,17:3
Laskari, Zoe
Stefania 1968,N 29,56:1
Lasker, Boris (Composer)
Twins 1947,Jl 28,12:2
Laski, Marghanita (Original Author)
Little Boy Lost 1953,S 22,38:2
Laski, Marghanita (Screenwriter)
It Started in Paradise 1953,Jl 25,8:2

Laskin, Boris (Screenwriter)
Spring Voices 1956,O 25,40:5
Carnival in Moscow 1957,N 4,40:1
Girl With the Guitar, The 1960,F 1,22:4
Lasko, Henry
Tattooed Stranger, The 1950,F 10,18:6
Lasko, Leo (Original Author)
Vendetta 1921,D 19,13:1
Laskos, A (Screenwriter)
Moment of Passion 1960,N 21,34:1
Laskos, G (Director)
Golfo-Girl of the Mountains 1958,My 19,19:5
Laskos, G (Screenwriter)
Golfo-Girl of the Mountains 1958,My 19,19:5
Laskos, Orestes
Moment of Passion 1960,N 21,34:1
Laskos, Orestes (Director)
Madame X 1960,O 3,34:5
Laskos, Orestes (Screenwriter)
Madame X 1960,O 3,34:5
Laskowska, Irena
Salto 1966,O 4,50:1
Lasky, Jesse Jr (Miscellaneous)
Women Without Names 1951,Ag 7,22:2
Lasky, Jesse Jr (Narrator)
Land of Liberty 1939,Je 16,27:3
Land of Liberty 1941,Ja 30,19:2
Lasky, Jesse Jr (Original Author)
Appointment in Tokyo 1945,D 8,21:3
Salome 1953,Mr 25,37:1
Lasky, Jesse Jr (Screenwriter)
White Parade, The 1934,N 10,19:1
Union Pacific 1939,My 11,31:2
North West Mounted Police 1940,N 7,33:2
Reap the Wild Wind 1942,Mr 27,27:2
Attack! The Battle of New Britain 1944,Je 21,1:6
Unconquered 1947,O 11,11:2
Samson and Delilah 1949,D 22,29:2
Mask of the Avenger 1951,Je 27,25:2
Never Trust a Gambler 1951,Jl 20,14:2
Lorna Doone 1951,S 21,19:4
Brigand, The 1952,Jl 26,9:2
Thief of Venice, The 1952,N 28,22:7
Mission Over Korea 1953,S 19,7:2
Hell and High Water 1954,F 2,20:6
Pearl of the South Pacific 1955,S 17,12:2
Hot Blood 1956,Mr 24,14:2
Ten Commandments, The 1956,N 9,35:2
Buccaneer, The 1958,D 24,00:0
John Paul Jones 1959,Je 17,39:1
Wizard of Baghdad, The 1961,Mr 4,16:1
Seven Women From Hell 1962,F 1,22:2
Lasky, Jesse L (Producer)
Helldorado 1935,Ja 7,13:2
Here's to Romance 1935,O 3,29:2
Gay Deception, The 1935,O 11,31:1
Music for Madame 1937,O 23,14:1
Hitting a new High 1937,D 27,11:1
Sergeant York 1941,Jl 3,15:1
Adventures of Mark Twain, The 1944,My 4,25:5
Rhapsody in Blue 1945,Je 28,22:2
Without Reservations 1946,Je 8,17:2
Miracle of the Bells, The 1948,Mr 17,30:1
Lasky, Leo (Director)
Das Nachtigall Maedel 1933,Ja 23,9:2
Lasry, Perre (Producer)
Drifter, The 1967,My 25,54:1
Lass, Barbara
Eve Wants to Sleep 1961,Je 6,42:2
Love at Twenty 1963,F 7,5:6
Werewolf in a Girls Dormitory 1963,Je 6,39:1
Lassen, Casten
Inga 1968,N 21,41:2
Lassie (Dog)
Son of Lassie 1945,Je 11,12:1
Hills of Home 1948,N 26,32:2
Sun comes up, The 1949,My 13,29:2
Challenge to Lassie 1950,Ap 7,22:3
Lassner, Margot
Against the Wind 1949,Je 27,18:3
Lastricato, Giorgio (Screenwriter)
Fear No Evil 1949,Mr 31,31:2
Laszlo, Andres (Original Author)
Pepote 1958,D 2,46:1
Laszlo, Miklos (Original Author)
Big City 1948,My 17,23:3
In the Good Old Summertime 1949,Ag 5,23:2
Laszlo, Nikolaus (Original Author)
Shop Around the Corner, The 1940,Ja 26,13:2
Laszlo, T M
Szerelmi Almok 1937,Ja 5,19:2
Latabar, Kalman
Fizessen Nagysag 1937,Je 4,27:3
Sportszerelem; Love of Sport 1938,F 14,20:8
Latell, Lyle
Wife Takes a Flyer, The 1942,Je 19,19:1
One Mysterious Night 1944,O 21,15:3
Hold That Blonde 1945,N 8,17:2
Dick Tracy 1946,Ja 12,10:7
Dick Tracy vs Cueball 1946,N 23,12:2
Dick Tracy's Dilemma 1947,Jl 14,14:5

Latell, Lyle— Cont
  Dick Tracy and Gruesome 1947,S 27,11:2
Laterza, Giovanni (Director)
  Bullet for Stefano 1950,O 26,38:7
Latham, Louise
  Marnie 1964,Je 23,19:1
  Firecreek 1968,F 22,36:2
Latham, Maxton
  Windflowers 1968,F 23,43:1
Latham, Stuart
  Tawny Pipit 1947,S 8,25:5
  One Night With You 1949,F 21,20:2
  Man in the White Suit, The 1952,Ap 1,35:2
Lathrops
  Manhattan Merry-Go-Round 1937,D 31,9:3
Latimer, Billy
  Spieler, The 1929,F 25,16:1
Latimer, Carl Rocky
  Joe Louis Story, The 1953,N 4,29:4
Latimer, Hugh
  Corridor of Mirrors 1949,Mr 23,35:3
  Cosmic Monster, The 1959,Ja 1,38:1
Latimer, Hurb
  Sniper, The 1952,My 10,16:3
Latimer, Jonathan (Original Author)
  Westland Case, The 1937,O 23,14:2
  Lady in the Morgue, The 1938,My 9,13:3
  Last Warning, The 1938,D 8,34:4
  Phantom Raiders 1940,Je 24,19:5
  Submarine Command 1952,Ja 19,13:2
Latimer, Jonathan (Screenwriter)
  Lone Wolf Spy Hunt, The 1939,Mr 6,11:3
  Topper Returns 1941,Mr 28,26:6
  Night in New Orleans 1942,Jl 2,25:2
  Glass Key, The 1942,O 16,23:1
  Nocturne 1946,N 11,42:2
  They Won't Believe Me 1947,Jl 17,16:2
  Big Clock, The 1948,Ap 22,34:2
  Beyond Glory 1948,Ag 4,18:2
  Night Has a Thousand Eyes 1948,O 14,38:3
  Sealed Verdict 1948,N 3,36:2
  Alias Nick Beal 1949,Mr 10,35:2
  Copper Canyon 1950,N 16,39:2
  Redhead and the Cowboy, The 1951,Je 6,37:2
  Submarine Command 1952,Ja 19,13:2
  Plunder of the Sun 1953,Ag 27,22:1
  Botany Bay 1953,O 30,27:2
  Back From Eternity 1956,S 8,20:6
  Unholy Wife, The 1958,Mr 7,17:1
Latimer, Louise
  There's Always Tomorrow 1934,N 10,19:2
  Murder on a Bridle Path 1936,Ap 11,19:2
  Two in Revolt 1936,Ap 25,21:1
  Bunker Bean 1936,Je 27,21:2
  Grand Jury 1936,Ag 1,16:3
  Don't Turn 'em Loose 1936,S 25,20:2
  Plot Thickens, The 1936,D 9,35:2
  We're on the Jury 1937,F 10,18:5
Latimore, Frank
  Dolly Sisters, The 1945,N 15,24:6
  Shock 1946,Mr 9,10:2
  Three Little Girls in Blue 1946,S 26,32:3
  Razor's Edge, The 1946,N 20,42:2
  13 Rue Madeleine 1947,Ja 16,30:2
  Black Magic 1949,N 9,37:2
  Three Forbidden Stories 1953,N 16,21:4
  Purple Noon 1961,S 1,12:1
  Sergeant, The 1968,D 26,53:5
Latonina, N
  Dom Zhadnosti 1934,Ag 13,9:6
  Peter the First 1937,D 25,10:4
  Pugachev 1938,Jl 4,10:2
Lator, Jill
  Chappaqua 1967,N 6,65:2
Latorre, Don
  Boy of the Streets 1938,Ja 24,17:1
  Juvenile Court 1938,S 12,13:2
Latorre, Jose
  Goyescas 1944,My 29,18:3
Latouche, John
  8 X 8 1957,Mr 16,13:2
Latouche, John (Composer)
  Born to Sing 1942,F 19,23:2
  Cabin in the Sky 1943,My 28,19:3
  I Dood It 1943,N 11,29:1
Latour, Maria
  Viscount, The 1967,My 11,50:1
Latridis, Stavros
  Girl From Corfu, The 1957,My 20,28:2
Latrouitre, Jacques
  Shop-Girls of Paris; Au Bonheur de Dames
    1947,Je 23,14:4
Latson, Candy
  Synanon 1965,My 6,44:1
Latta, Eddie (Composer)
  Let George Do It 1940,O 14,25:5
Lattanzi, Liliana
  Path of Hope, The (Il Cammino Della Speranza)
    1952,Ag 5,15:5
Lattanzi, Tina
  Rubacuori 1932,Mr 5,11:2
  Passaporto Rosso 1936,S 2,18:2
  Amore e Dolore 1937,My 13,31:4
  Avventura di Giacomo Casanova 1938,D 2,27:3

Anna 1953,F 19,20:5
Count of St Elmo, The 1953,Mr 14,13:2
Genoese Dragnet 1954,F 12,20:5
Lattes, Marcel
  Melodia de Arrabal 1933,Ag 5,9:5
Lattes, Marcel (Composer)
  Lucrezia Borgia 1937,O 13,27:2
  Helene 1938,Ja 22,19:1
Lattuada, Alberto (Director)
  Bandit, The 1949,Je 7,26:3
  Without Pity; (Senza Pieta) 1950,Mr 16,40:4
  Flesh will Surrender 1950,O 26,38:7
  Mill on the Po, The 1951,O 23,35:2
  Anna 1953,F 19,20:5
  Overcoat, The 1953,O 13,34:1
  Lupa, La 1954,F 18,36:2
  Guendalina 1958,Je 30,23:2
  Tempest 1959,Mr 27,19:2
  Steppe, The 1963,O 1,33:1
  Mafioso 1964,Jl 1,42:1
  Variety Lights; Luci del Varieta 1965,My 7,34:1
  Mandragola 1966,Je 7,50:2
  Matchless 1967,N 11,26:3
Lattuada, Alberto (Original Author)
  Mandragola 1966,Je 7,50:2
Lattuada, Alberto (Producer)
  Variety Lights; Luci del Varieta 1965,My 7,34:1
Lattuada, Alberto (Screenwriter)
  Flesh will Surrender 1950,O 26,38:7
  Overcoat, The 1953,O 13,34:1
  Lupa, La 1954,F 18,36:2
  Guendalina 1958,Je 30,23:2
  Tempest 1959,Mr 27,19:2
  Steppe, The 1963,O 1,33:1
  Variety Lights; Luci del Varieta 1965,My 7,34:1
  Matchless 1967,N 11,26:3
Lau, Wesley
  I Want to Live 1958,N 19,45:1
  Venetian Affair, The 1967,Ja 19,41:2
Laucknor, Rolf (Original Author)
  Alte und der Junge Koenig, Der 1935,D 10,31:2
Laudenbach, Roland (Screenwriter)
  Voyage to America 1952,O 20,18:2
  Moment of Truth, The 1954,Ap 27,36:2
  End of Desire 1962,Jl 10,29:2
  Lovers on a Tightrope 1962,O 25,48:3
Laudenbach, Rolland (Screenwriter)
  Bed, The (The Pompadour Bed); Pompadour Bed,
    The (The Bed) 1955,Je 8,26:4
Lauder, Harry
  Song of the Road 1940,My 6,13:2
Lauder, Harry (Miscellaneous)
  Song of the Road 1940,My 6,13:2
Lauder, Harry Sir
  Auld Lang Syne 1929,O 6,IX,9:4 (In Addenda)
Lauenstein, Tilly
  Christina 1951,Ja 15,13:1
  Adorable Julia 1964,Ap 8,33:1
Laugeois, Joselle
  Rise of Louis XIV, The 1967,S 26,54:2
Laughlan, Agnes
  U-Boat 29 1939,O 6,31:3
  Once Upon a Dream 1949,Jl 15,17:2
Laughlin, Michael S (Producer)
  Whisperers, The 1967,Ag 1,24:1
  Joanna 1968,N 25,54:1
Laughlin, Tom
  Tea and Sympathy 1956,S 28,24:4
  South Pacific 1958,Mr 20,33:1
  Gidget 1959,Ap 23,27:4
  Tall Story 1960,Ap 7,46:1
  Born Losers, The 1967,Ag 19,16:2
Laughton, Charles
  Piccadilly 1929,Jl 15,25:1
  Day Dreams 1930,F 4,28:3
  Devil and the Deep 1932,Ag 20,7:4
  Old Dark House, The 1932,O 28,22:4
  Payment Deferred 1932,N 8,26:3
  Sign of the Cross, The 1932,D 1,25:1
  If I Had a Million 1932,D 3,21:4
  Island of Lost Souls 1933,Ja 13,19:2
  Private Life of Henry VIII, The 1933,O 13,25:2
  White Woman 1933,N 18,18:5
  White Woman 1933,D 3,IX,9:4 (In Addenda)
  Barretts of Wimpole Street, The 1934,S 29,12:2
  Ruggles of Red Gap 1935,Mr 7,26:1
  Miserables, Les 1935,Ap 22,14:2
  Mutiny on the Bounty 1935,N 9,19:2
  Wanted Men 1936,Jl 8,15:2
  Rembrandt 1936,D 3,31:1
  Beachcomber, The 1938,D 26,29:3
  Jamaica Inn 1939,O 12,33:1
  Hunchback of Notre Dame, The 1940,Ja 1,29:2
  Sidewalks of London 1940,F 15,15:1
  They Knew What They Wanted 1940,O 11,25:2
  It Started With Eve 1941,O 3,27:1
  Tuttles of Tahiti, The 1942,Ap 30,14:1
  Tales of Manhattan 1942,S 25,25:1
  Stand by for Action 1943,Mr 12,12:2
  Forever and a Day 1943,Mr 13,9:2
  This Land Is Mine 1943,My 28,19:1
  Man From Down Under, The 1943,S 27,23:2
  Canterville Ghost, The 1944,Jl 29,16:2

Laughton, Charles— Cont
  Suspect, The 1945,F 1,18:5
  Captain Kidd 1945,N 23,26:3
  Because of Him 1946,Ja 25,26:6
  Paradine Case, The 1948,Ja 9,26:2
  Arch of Triumph 1948,Ap 21,33:2
  Big Clock, The 1948,Ap 22,34:2
  Bribe, The 1949,F 4,31:2
  Man on the Eiffel Tower, The 1950,Ja 30,12:2
  Blue Veil, The 1951,O 27,10:5
  Strange Door, The 1951,D 10,34:6
  O Henry's Full House (The Cop and the Anthem);
    Cop and the Anthem, The (O Henry's Full
    House) 1952,O 17,33:1
  Salome 1953,Mr 25,37:1
  Young Bess 1953,My 22,31:1
  Hobson's Choice 1954,Je 15,37:1
  Witness for the Prosecution 1958,F 7,16:1
  Under ten Flags 1960,S 16,24:1
  Spartacus 1960,O 7,28:1
  Advise and Consent 1962,Je 7,31:2
Laughton, Charles (Director)
  Night of the Hunter, The 1955,S 30,23:1
Laughton, Eddie
  Highway Patrol 1938,Ag 4,15:2
  Convicted 1938,Ag 22,9:3
  Men Without Souls 1940,My 13,21:2
  Girls of the Road 1940,Jl 22,20:2
  Lone Wolf Keeps a Date, The 1941,Ja 2,24:3
  I Was a Prisoner on Devil's Island
    1941,Jl 28,16:4
  Mystery Ship 1941,Ag 16,18:3
  Canal Zone 1942,Mr 30,21:2
  Atlantic Convoy 1942,Jl 6,18:5
  Sabotage Squad 1942,Ag 5,16:1
  Boogie Man Will Get You, The 1942,O 12,12:4
  Shocking Miss Pilgrim, The 1947,F 12,34:2
Laugier, Roger
  Cage aux Rossignols, La; (Cage of Nightingales,
    A) 1947,Ap 3,31:2
  Tainted 1950,Ja 21,10:2
Laugler, Jean
  Man in the Raincoat, The 1958,Jl 15,21:2
Launay, Jean
  Young Torless 1967,S 25,56:2
Launder, Frank (Director)
  Adventures, The 1947,Ap 4,19:2
  Green for Danger 1947,Ag 8,10:2
  Captain Boycott 1947,D 6,11:2
  Happiest Days of Your Life, The 1950,S 18,19:2
  Folly to be Wise 1953,D 28,17:2
  Belles of St Trinian's, The 1954,D 23,13:4
  Wee Geordie 1956,O 8,31:1
  Blue Murder at St Trinian's 1958,My 27,27:1
  Bridal Path, The 1959,D 21,34:2
  Pure Hell of St Trinian's, The 1961,S 26,31:1
Launder, Frank (Original Author)
  Adventures, The 1947,Ap 4,19:2
  Blue Lagoon, The 1949,O 3,13:2
  Green Man, The 1957,My 23,40:1
Launder, Frank (Producer)
  Notorious Gentleman 1946,N 14,39:3
  Adventures, The 1947,Ap 4,19:2
  Green for Danger 1947,Ag 8,10:2
  Captain Boycott 1947,D 6,11:2
  Dulcimer Street 1948,N 8,24:2
  Happiest Days of Your Life, The 1950,S 18,19:2
  Gilbert and Sullivan 1953,O 28,36:3
  Folly to be Wise 1953,D 28,17:2
  Wee Geordie 1956,O 8,31:1
  Green Man, The 1957,My 23,40:1
  Constant Husband, The 1957,Jl 26,10:3
  Blue Murder at St Trinian's 1958,My 27,27:1
  Left, Right and Centre 1961,F 10,19:1
  Pure Hell of St Trinian's, The 1961,S 26,31:1
Launder, Frank (Screenwriter)
  Seven Sinners 1936,Ag 22,6:1
  Lady Vanishes, The 1938,D 26,29:1
  Night Train 1940,D 30,21:1
  Girl Must Live, A 1942,Mr 24,25:2
  Young Mr Pitt, The 1943,Mr 11,17:1
  Notorious Gentleman 1946,N 14,39:3
  Captain Boycott 1947,D 6,11:2
  Blue Lagoon, The 1949,O 3,13:2
  Happiest Days of Your Life, The 1950,S 18,19:2
  Folly to be Wise 1953,D 28,17:2
  Belles of St Trinian's, The 1954,D 23,13:4
  Wee Geordie 1956,O 8,31:1
  Green Man, The 1957,My 23,40:1
  Blue Murder at St Trinian's 1958,My 27,27:1
  Bridal Path, The 1959,D 21,34:2
  Pure Hell of St Trinian's, The 1961,S 26,31:1
  Ring of Treason 1964,My 28,40:3 (Incorrect in
    this edition; use 1964,My 29,15:1 elsewhere)
Launders, Perc
  Falcon out West, The 1944,Mr 18,18:2
  Stork Club, The 1945,D 20,18:2
  Abandoned Woman 1949,O 27,35:3
Laure, Judson
  John Paul Jones 1959,Je 17,39:1
Laure, Marie
  Fantomas 1934,Mr 13,27:4

Laure, Odette
Mitsou 1958,Ap 15,42:5
Laurel, Allen
Horror of Party Beach, The 1964,Ap 30,30:1
Laurel, Stan
Rogue Song, The 1930,Ja 29,26:4
Pardon Us 1931,Ag 22,7:5
Pack up Your Troubles 1932,O 1,10:4
Devil's Brother, The 1933,Je 10,16:4
Sons of the Desert 1934,Ja 12,29:3
Hollywood Party 1934,My 26,12:2
Babes in Toyland 1934,D 13,28:2
Bohemian Girl, The 1936,F 17,21:1
Our Relations 1936,N 11,55:1
Way out West 1937,My 4,29:1
Pick a Star 1937,My 28,17:2
Swiss Miss 1938,Je 4,18:2
Block-Heads 1938,Ag 30,14:2
Flying Deuces, The 1939,N 24,29:2
Chump at Oxford, A 1940,F 20,17:3
Great Guns 1941,O 3,27:2
Air Raid Wardens 1943,Ap 5,15:5
Jitterbugs 1943,Je 5,12:2
Nothing but Trouble 1945,Mr 10,14:1
Bullfighters, The 1945,My 12,10:3
Utopia 1954,D 15,41:1
When Comedy Was King 1960,Mr 30,42:1
Days of Thrills and Laughter 1961,Mr 22,37:1
30 Years of Fun 1963,D 26,33:4
Laurel and Hardy's Laughing 20's 1965,N 18,55:2
Further Perils of Laurel and Hardy, The
  1968,Ap 1,56:6
Laurel and Hardy
A-Haunting We Will Go 1942,Ag 3,18:4
Dancing Masters, The 1943,D 2,30:2
Big Noise, The 1944,S 23,16:1
Laurell, Kay
Brand, The 1919,Mr 17,13:2
Lauren, Rod
Black Zoo 1963,My 16,42:1
Lauren, S K (Original Author)
Men Must Fight 1933,Mr 11,18:3
Sisters Under the Skin 1934,Je 8,18:1
Married and in Love 1940,F 2,13:2
My Blue Heaven 1950,S 16,12:6
Lauren, S K (Screenwriter)
Crime and Punishment 1935,N 22,18:2
Damsel in Distress, A 1937,N 25,37:1
there Goes The Groom 1937,D 25,10:6
Mother Carey's Chickens 1938,Ag 5,11:1
Married and in Love 1940,F 2,13:2
Our Neighbors-The Carters 1940,F 15,15:2
When Ladies Meet 1941,S 5,19:2
Mr and Mrs North 1942,Ja 22,13:2
Flight for Freedom 1943,Ap 16,24:2
Ruthless 1948,S 4,8:7
LAURENCE
See Also LAWRENCE
Laurence, Douglas (Producer)
Quick, Before it Melts 1965,Ap 1,30:2
Mister Buddwing 1966,O 12,36:1
Doctor, You've Got to be Kidding
  1967,My 11,50:1
Speedway 1968,Je 14,43:1
Laurence, Edwin
Orders Is Orders 1934,My 7,20:2
Seven Sinners 1936,Ag 22,6:1
Laurence, Margaret
Reunion in France 1943,Mr 5,20:3
Laurence, Margaret (Original Author)
Rachel Rachel 1968,Ag 27,36:1
Laurence, Michael
Piccadilly Incident 1948,Ag 5,16:2
For Them that Trespass 1950,S 27,37:2
Othello 1955,S 13,27:1
Laurens, Anne
Stormy Waters 1946,Je 17,32:2
Laurent, Agnes
French Mistress, A 1960,D 19,34:2
Sins of Youth 1960,D 24,8:2
Laurent, Andre
Champs-Elysees 1939,F 28,17:2
Laurent, Cecil Saint (Miscellaneous)
Over There, 1914-1918 1965,Mr 11,38:2
Laurent, Eric
Larsson I Andra Giftet 1935,O 19,21:3
Skaergaards-Flirt 1936,Ap 8,26:3
Laurent, J Marie
Shadows of Fear 1928,N 6,35:1
Mystic Mountain, The 1936,Mr 31,17:2
Laurent, Jacqueline
Judge Hardy's Children 1938,Ap 8,17:2
Daybreak 1940,Jl 30,16:2
Laurent, Jacques (Original Author)
Strollers, The 1952,Jl 22,22:7
Laurent, Jacques (Screenwriter)
Strollers, The 1952,Jl 22,22:7
Laurent, Pierre (Director)
Skipper Next to God 1953,Ja 13,24:2
Laurent, Tony
Vautrin, the Thief 1949,N 11,31:2
Battle of the Rails; (Bataille Du Rail)
  1949,D 27,27:2

Laurents, Arthur (Original Author)
Home of the Brave 1949,My 13,29:1
Summertime 1955,Je 22,25:1
Gypsy 1962,N 2,24:1
Laurents, Arthur (Screenwriter)
Rope 1948,Ag 27,12:4
Caught 1949,F 18,26:4
Anna Lucasta 1949,Ag 12,13:2
Anastasia 1956,D 14,35:6
Bonjour Tristesse 1958,Ja 16,32:1
Laurenz, John
Apache Rose 1947,Jl 23,19:3
Tarzan and the Mermaids 1948,Mr 30,26:4
Lauri, John
Dark Sands 1938,Ag 17,23:4
Lauri-Volpi, Giacomo
Canzione del Sole, La 1936,My 6,27:2
LAURIE
See Also LOURIE, LOWREY, LOWRY
Laurie, Joe Jr (Original Author)
Union Depot 1932,Ja 15,24:4
April Showers 1948,Mr 27,10:2
Laurie, John
Juno and the Paycock 1930,Je 30,22:6
Thirty-Nine Steps, The 1935,S 14,8:4
Nine Days a Queen 1936,O 3,21:1
East Meets West 1936,O 31,24:2
As You Like It 1936,N 6,29:3
Troopship 1938,Ap 26,18:2
Edge of the World, The 1938,S 12,13:2
Ware Case, The 1939,Jl 22,12:2
Four Feathers 1939,Ag 4,11:1
Convoy 1941,Ja 17,21:2
Suicide Squadron 1942,My 14,23:2
Life and Death of Colonel Blimp, The
  1945,Mr 30,18:2
Way Ahead, The 1945,Je 4,22:3
Gay Intruders, The 1946,Mr 18,24:2
Henry V 1946,Je 18,30:2
I Know Where I'm Going 1947,Ag 20,25:2
Jassy 1948,F 20,19:2
Man of Evil 1948,Mr 26,26:2
Brothers, The 1948,My 5,30:4
Showtime 1948,My 20,35:3
Hamlet 1948,S 30,32:2
Mine Own Executioner 1949,Ja 19,34:2
Agitator, The 1949,Ag 19,12:9
Treasure Island 1950,Ag 16,24:2
Madeleine 1950,S 1,17:2
Sanitorium 1950,O 11,42:1
Inheritance, The 1951,F 12,19:2
Happy Go Lovely 1951,Jl 26,17:2
Laughter in Paradise 1951,N 12,21:2
Pandora and the Flying Dutchman 1951,D 7,35:2
Bonnie Prince Charlie 1952,Ja 7,14:3
Encore (Winter Cruise); Winter Cruise (Encore)
  1952,Ap 3,45:1
Secret Flight 1952,Jl 3,16:2
Hobson's Choice 1954,Je 15,37:1
Richard III 1956,Mr 12,1:4
Campbell's Kingdom 1960,Ja 11,35:5
Kidnapped 1960,My 19,44:3
Murder Reported 1960,Jl 12,39:1
Laurie, Piper
Louisa 1950,O 25,45:2
Milkman, The 1951,Ja 1,13:6
Prince Who Was a Thief, The 1951,Jl 4,13:2
Francis Goes to the Races 1951,Jl 25,19:2
No Room for the Groom 1952,Je 14,12:2
Has Anybody Seen My Gal 1952,Jl 5,7:2
Son of Ali Baba 1952,Ag 16,7:4
Mississippi Gambler, The 1953,Ja 30,25:1
Dangerous Mission 1954,Mr 6,13:5
Johnny Dark 1954,Je 26,7:2
Dawn at Socorro 1954,Ag 28,8:2
Ain't Misbehavin' 1955,Jl 2,13:2
Until They Sail 1957,O 9,41:2
Hustler, The 1961,S 27,35:1
Laurier, Jay
Waltz Time 1933,S 29,24:2
Lauritzen, Jonreed (Original Author)
Kiss of Fire 1955,S 24,61:2
Lauritzen, Lau
Red Meadows 1950,Ja 19,35:2
Laurner, S John
Marnie 1964,Je 23,19:1
Laury, Agnes
Racers, The 1955,F 5,13:2
Lauter, Harry
Zamba 1949,N 7,33:2
Great Dan Patch, The 1949,N 9,37:2
Blue Grass of Kentucky 1950,Ja 27,29:2
Yankee Pasha 1954,Ap 19,19:2
Crooked Web, The 1955,D 10,19:1
Tarzan's Fight for Life 1958,Ag 16,10:2
Ambush Bay 1966,S 15,51:4
Lautia, Irja
Niskavvoren Naiset; Women of Niskavuori
  1938,N 21,14:5
Lautner, Georges (Director)
Seventh Juror, The 1964,Ja 28,25:1
Great Spy Chase, The 1966,O 6,56:4
Galia 1966,D 20,50:4

Lautner, Georges (Producer)
Great Spy Chase, The 1966,O 6,56:4
Lavagetto, Cookie
Safe at Home 1941,N 26,31:2
Lavalette, Bernard
Belle Americaine, La 1961,D 18,42:1
Tales of Paris (The Tale of Antonio); Tale of
  Antonio, The (Tales of Paris) 1962,Ag 27,18:1
LaVelle, Miriam
Gang's All Here, The 1943,D 23,26:4
Seven Days Ashore 1944,Ap 26,24:7
Meet The People 1944,S 8,16:2
Lavello, Kay
People Will Talk 1951,Ag 30,20:1
Laven, Arnold (Director)
Vice Squad 1953,Ag 26,23:2
Down Three Dark Streets 1954,S 4,6:4
Rack, The 1956,N 6,30:1
Slaughter on Tenth Avenue 1957,N 6,43:1
Anna Lucasta 1959,Ja 15,27:1
Rough Night in Jericho 1967,N 9,56:4
Laven, Arnold (Producer)
Clambake 1967,D 14,62:3
Scalphunters, The 1968,Ap 3,40:1
Laverick, Beryl
Constant Nymph, The 1934,Ap 7,19:1
Unfinished Symphony 1935,Ja 14,11:2
Laverick, June
Follow a Star 1961,Ap 26,34:1
Laverty, Jean
Fleet's In, The 1928,O 1,23:1
Good-Bye Kiss, The 1928,N 12,18:2
Captain Lash 1929,F 4,20:1
Laverty, Johnny
New Faces 1954,F 20,8:7
Lavery, Emmet (Original Author)
Forever and a Day 1943,Mr 13,9:2
Magnificent Yankee, The 1951,Ja 19,21:2
First Legion, The 1951,Ap 28,9:2
Lavery, Emmet (Screenwriter)
Army Surgeon 1942,N 5,35:2
Hitler's Children 1943,F 25,27:1
Behind the Rising Sun 1943,O 14,26:2
Night in Paradise 1946,Je 6,16:3
Guilty of Treason 1950,Ap 11,26:2
Magnificent Yankee, The 1951,Ja 19,21:2
First Legion, The 1951,Ap 28,9:2
Bright Road 1953,Ap 29,33:5
Lavi, Arich
Hill 24 Doesn't Answer 1955,N 3,37:1
Lavi, Daliah
Two Weeks in Another Town 1962,Ag 18,10:1
Candide 1962,N 20,39:1
Cyrano and D'Artagnan 1964,S 26,16:1
Lord Jim 1965,F 26,18:1
And so to Bed 1965,Jl 31,11:3
Ten Little Indians 1966,F 10,33:1
Ten Little Indians 1966,F 10,33:1
Silencers, The 1966,Mr 17,35:1
Spy With a Cold Nose, The 1966,D 30,58:2
Casino Royale 1967,Ap 29,25:1
Those Fantastic Flying Fools 1967,O 19,59:2
Shatterhand 1968,Je 6,54:1
High Commissioner, The 1968,D 12,62:5
Lavialle, Charles
Voyage Surprise 1948,F 14,17:3
Twilight 1949,D 30,13:2
Seventh Juror, The 1964,Ja 28,25:1
Lavikof, A
Beethoven Concerto 1937,Mr 24,29:1
LAVINE
See Also LEVENE, LEVIEN, LEVIN, LEVINE
Lavine, Morris (Original Author)
Day of Reckoning 1933,N 4,18:2
Lavorel, Henri (Director)
Voyage to America 1952,O 20,18:2
Lavorel, Henri (Producer)
Voyage to America 1952,O 20,18:2
Lavorel, Henri (Screenwriter)
Voyage to America 1952,O 20,18:2
Lavrenev, B (Original Author)
Demon of the Steppes 1930,Ja 18,21:1
Break-Up, The 1930,N 29,21:4
Lavrenjuk, Alexander
Bolshoi Ballet 67 1966,S 30,54:1
Lavrof, Yuri
Nightingale 1936,N 4,41:2
Defense of Volotchayevsk, The 1938,Ag 11,13:3
Soviet Border 1939,F 20,13:2
Lavrova, Tamara
Nine Days of one Year 1964,D 29,19:1
Lavrovsky, Leonid (Director)
Ballet of Romeo and Juliet, The 1956,Ap 3,31:2
Bolshoi Ballet 67 1966,S 30,54:1
Lavrovsky, Leonid (Miscellaneous)
Ballet of Romeo and Juliet, The 1956,Ap 3,31:2
Bolshoi Ballet 67 1966,S 30,54:1
Lavrovsky, Leonid (Screenwriter)
Ballet of Romeo and Juliet, The 1956,Ap 3,31:2
Bolshoi Ballet 67 1966,S 30,54:1
Lavsa, Anna
Cabaret 1927,My 2,26:4

Lavut, Martin
Mask, The 1961,O 28,12:4
Law, Burton
Under Two Flags 1922,S 25,10:2
Law, Harold (Original Author)
Nobody's Baby 1937,My 20,17:3
Law, Harold (Screenwriter)
Nobody's Baby 1937,My 20,17:3
Law, John
Spirit of Notre Dame, The 1931,O 16,27:1
Law, John (Screenwriter)
Casino Royale 1967,Ap 29,25:1
Law, John Phillip
High Infidelity (The Scandal); Scandal, The (High Infidelity) 1965,Jl 2,17:1
Russians are Coming the Russians are Coming, The 1966,My 26,55:1
Hurry Sundown 1967,Mr 24,22:1
Barbarella 1968,O 12,43:1
Danger Diabolik 1968,D 12,62:6
Sergeant, The 1968,D 26,53:5
Law, Roberta
Jungle Princess 1936,D 24,21:3
Law, Walter
Perfect Lady, A 1918,D 2,11:3
If I Were King 1920,Ag 10,10:3
Clothes Make the Pirate 1925,N 30,17:1
Whoopee 1930,O 1,26:3
Law, William
After the Thin Man 1936,D 25,19:2
Good Earth, The 1937,F 3,27:1
Lawes, Joan Marie
Up the River 1930,O 11,21:3
Lawes, Lewis E Warden (Original Author)
20,000 Years in Sing Sing 1933,Ja 10,26:2
Over the Wall 1938,Mr 28,19:2
You Can't Get Away With Murder 1939,Mr 25,19:2
Invisible Stripes 1940,Ja 13,11:2
Castle on the Hudson 1940,Mr 4,11:2
Lawford, Betty
Gentlemen of the Press 1929,My 13,27:2
Return of Sherlock Holmes, The 1929,O 19,22:6
Lucky in Love 1929,D 14,22:4
Secrets of a Secretary 1931,Ag 29,16:3
Berkeley Square 1933,S 14,26:2
Gallant Lady 1934,Ja 22,12:3
Human Side, The 1934,S 15,20:3
Love Before Breakfast 1936,Mr 14,10:1
Criminal Lawyer 1937,Ja 27,17:3
Stolen Holiday 1937,F 1,15:3
Stage Door Canteen 1943,Je 25,13:2
Devil Thumbs a Ride, The 1947,Mr 22,10:2
Lawford, Ernest
Irish Luck 1925,N 24,28:4
Personal Maid 1931,S 5,7:4
Lawford, Lady May
Hong Kong 1952,Ap 5,20:3
Lawford, Peter
Lord Jeff 1938,Jl 1,22:2
Yank at Eton, A 1942,O 16,23:1
White Cliffs of Dover, The 1944,My 12,15:2
Picture of Dorian Gray, The 1945,Mr 2,15:2
Son of Lassie 1945,Je 11,12:1
Cluny Brown 1946,Je 3,27:3
Two Sisters From Boston 1946,Je 7,16:2
It Happened in Brooklyn 1947,Mr 14,28:5
My Brother Talks to Horses 1947,Je 19,27:4
Good News 1947,D 5,33:2
Easter Parade 1948,Jl 1,19:3
On an Island With You 1948,Jl 30,13:2
Julia Misbehaves 1948,O 8,30:2
Little Women 1949,Mr 11,33:2
Red Danube, The 1949,D 9,37:3
Please Believe Me 1950,Je 12,19:4
Royal Wedding 1951,Mr 9,30:2
Just This Once 1952,Mr 18,22:3
Kangaroo 1952,My 17,22:7
You for Me 1952,S 25,38:3
Hour of 13, The 1952,O 28,37:1
It Should Happen to You 1954,Ja 16,10:5
Never so Few 1960,Ja 22,15:2
Ocean's Eleven 1960,Ag 11,19:1
Exodus 1960,D 16,44:1
Pepe 1960,D 22,18:1
Sergeants 3 1962,F 12,28:2
Advise and Consent 1962,Je 7,31:2
Longest Day, The 1962,O 5,28:1
Dead Ringer 1964,F 20,22:3
Sylvia 1965,F 11,45:1
Harlow 1965,Jl 22,24:1
Oscar, The 1966,Mr 5,16:1
Man Called Adam, A 1966,Ag 4,24:2
Salt and Pepper 1968,S 19,62:3
Lawford, Peter (Producer)
Johnny Cool 1963,O 3,31:1
Lawler, Anderson
River of Romance, The 1929,Jl 29,23:3
Only Saps Work 1930,D 13,22:2
Girls About Town 1931,N 2,27:1
Hollywood Speaks 1932,Ag 12,18:2
Beloved 1934,Ja 27,9:3
Let's Talk It Over 1934,Je 16,20:2

Fly Away Baby 1937,Jl 9,18:2
Alcatraz Island 1937,O 14,22:2
Torchy Blane, The Adventurous Blonde 1937,D 18,18:1
Invisible Menace, The 1938,F 14,20:6
Accidents Will Happen 1938,Ap 25,19:2
Mystery House 1938,Je 29,15:5
Lawler, Anderson (Producer)
Somewhere in the Night 1946,Je 13,24:2
Lawler, Mary
Shooting Straight 1930,Jl 28,22:1
Good News 1930,S 6,9:2
Lawler, Treva
Miss Pinkerton 1932,Jl 9,7:5
Lawlers, Ray (Original Author)
Season of Passion 1962,F 5,19:4
Lawless, Kavin
Quiet Man, The 1952,Ag 22,13:1
Lawlor, Thomas
Mikado, The 1967,Mr 15,53:1
Lawnhurst, V (Composer)
Pot o'Gold 1941,Ap 4,25:2
Lawo, Anderson
American Madness 1932,Ag 6,14:5
LAWRANCE
See LAWRENCE, LAURENCE
LAWRENCE
See Also LAURENCE
Lawrence, A J (Composer)
Mister Big 1943,Je 14,13:4
Lawrence, Andre
Pleasure Seekers, The 1964,D 26,9:1
Lawrence, Anthony (Screenwriter)
Roustabout 1964,N 11,38:1
Paradise, Hawaiian Style 1966,Je 16,15:3
Easy Come, Easy Go 1967,Je 15,56:1
Lawrence, Arthur
Against the Wind 1949,Je 27,18:3
Lilli Marlene 1952,Mr 29,19:2
Lawrence, Barbara
Margie 1946,O 17,28:3
Captain from Castile 1947,D 26,22:4
You Were Meant for Me 1948,Ja 29,27:5
Give my Regards to Broadway 1948,Je 23,32:2
Street with no Name, The 1948,Jl 15,26:6
Unfaithfully Yours 1948,N 6,9:2
Letter to Three Wives, A 1949,Ja 21,24:2
Mother is a Freshman 1949,Mr 12,10:2
Thieves' Highway 1949,S 24,8:6
Peggy 1950,Jl 21,15:4
Two Tickets to Broadway 1951,N 22,47:2
Star, The 1953,Ja 29,25:1
Arena 1953,Jl 23,20:2
Her Twelve Men 1954,Ag 12,23:2
Oklahoma! 1955,O 11,49:1
Man With the Gun 1955,D 23,14:2
Kronos 1957,My 11,24:6
Man With a Shadow 1958,Ja 23,24:3
Lawrence, Bert (Original Author)
Alias Jesse James 1959,My 18,31:2
Lawrence, Bert (Screenwriter)
Time Out for Rhythm 1941,Jl 10,16:3
Lawrence, Brian
She Shall Have Music 1942,O 31,11:2
Lawrence, Carol
New Faces 1954,F 20,8:7
View From the Bridge, A 1962,Ja 23,36:1
Lawrence, Christy
No Resting Place 1952,My 5,18:5
Lawrence, D H (Original Author)
Lady Chatterley's Lover 1959,Jl 11,11:1
Sons and Lovers 1960,Ag 3,35:1
Fox, The 1968,F 8,36:1
Lawrence, Delphi
Too Many Crooks 1959,Ap 25,14:2
Last Challenge, The 1967,D 28,25:1
Lawrence, Dorothy
Climax, The 1944,D 14,28:5
Lawrence, Edward
Knockout, The 1925,O 27,23:3
Lawrence, Fanya Foss (Original Author)
Why Girls Leave Home 1945,Ag 4,7:3
Lawrence, Fanya Foss (Screenwriter)
Why Girls Leave Home 1945,Ag 4,7:3
Lawrence, Fred
Talent Scout 1937,Ag 20,21:3
Lawrence, Gerald
Iron Duke, The 1935,Ja 25,27:2
As You Like It 1936,N 6,29:3
Lawrence, Gertrude
Aren't We All? 1932,Jl 1,19:3
No Funny Business 1934,Mr 9,22:4
Mimi 1936,Ja 10,16:3
Rembrandt 1936,D 3,31:1
Men Are not Gods 1937,Ja 19,28:1
Glass Menagerie, The 1950,S 29,31:5
Lawrence, Gertrude (Composer)
Stage Door Canteen 1943,Je 25,13:2
Lawrence, H L (Original Author)
These Are the Damned 1965,Jl 8,35:1
Lawrence, Jack (Composer)
Under Western Stars 1938,Je 25,7:3
Bachelor's Daughters, The 1946,O 7,23:2

Lawrence, Jack (Composer) — Cont
Torch Song 1953,O 13,34:2
Lawrence, Jack (Miscellaneous)
Manhattan Merry-Go-Round 1937,D 31,9:3
Lawrence, James (Miscellaneous)
Auntie Mame 1958,D 5,39:1
Lawrence, Jay
Stalag 17 1953,Jl 2,19:2
Lawrence, Jerome (Original Author)
Inherit the Wind 1960,O 13,41:1
Lawrence, Jody
Mask of the Avenger 1951,Je 27,25:2
Ten Tall Men 1951,O 27,10:5
Brigand, The 1952,Jl 26,9:2
Leather Saint, The 1956,Je 16,12:2
Hot Spell 1958,S 18,37:2
Purple Gang, The 1960,Ja 23,15:5
Lawrence, John
Ivory Hunter 1952,Ag 19,19:1
Goddess, The 1958,Je 25,24:1
Seconds 1966,O 6,56:1
Lawrence, John (Producer)
Glory Stompers, The 1968,Mr 28,52:4
Lawrence, John (Screenwriter)
Glory Stompers, The 1968,Mr 28,52:4
Lawrence, John S (Director)
Scarlet Trail, The 1918,D 22,17:3
Lawrence, John S (Original Author)
Scarlet Trail, The 1918,D 22,17:3
Lawrence, Jordan
Love on the Dole 1945,O 13,11:2
Lawrence, Josephine (Original Author)
Make Way for Tomorrow 1937,My 10,23:1
Lawrence, Lillian
Christine of the Hungry Heart 1924,D 8,13:3
Graustark 1925,S 8,29:1
Lawrence, Mady
Week End for Three 1941,O 24,27:4
Lawrence, Marc
Dr Socrates 1935,O 3,29:2
Little Big Shot 1935,O 7,11:2
Road Gang 1936,F 24,14:1
Trapped by Television 1936,Je 15,24:3
Counterfeit 1936,Jl 20,11:1
Final Hour, The 1936,Ag 1,16:3
Night Waitress 1936,D 18,31:5
Racketeers in Exile 1937,Ap 12,15:3
I Promise to Pay 1937,Ap 26,15:2
What Price Vengeance 1937,My 26,30:3
Charlie Chan on Broadway 1937,S 20,19:1
Counsel for Crime 1937,O 9,16:1
Criminals of the Air 1937,O 28,29:2
Murder in Greenwich Village 1937,O 30,22:2
Shadow, The 1937,D 17,33:3
Penitentiary 1938,Mr 7,13:2
Who Killed Gail Preston? 1938,My 6,27:2
Convicted 1938,Ag 22,9:3
I Am the Law 1938,Ag 26,14:2
Adventure in Sahara 1938,D 19,19:2
While New York Sleeps 1938,D 22,25:3
Charlie Chan in Honolulu 1938,D 31,7:3
Homicide Bureau 1939,F 2,17:2
Sergeant Madden 1939,Mr 24,27:2
Ex-Champ 1939,My 12,25:3
Blind Alley 1939,My 23,27:2
S O S Tidal Wave 1939,Je 22,19:3
Dust Be my Destiny 1939,O 7,11:2
Beware, Spooks 1939,N 3,17:4
Housekeeper's Daughter, The 1939,D 2,21:4
Invisible Stripes 1940,Ja 13,11:2
Johnny Apollo 1940,Ap 13,21:2
Brigham Young - Frontiersman 1940,S 21,13:2
Charlie Chan At the Wax Museum 1940,S 28,9:3
Great Profile, The 1940,O 18,25:1
Golden Fleecing, The 1940,N 7,33:4
Tall, Dark and Handsome 1941,Ja 24,15:2
Monster and the Girl, The 1941,Mr 20,25:3
Blossoms in the Dust 1941,Je 27,14:4
Shepherd of the Hills, The 1941,Jl 31,13:2
Lady Scarface 1941,Ag 4,16:6
Hold That Ghost 1941,Ag 8,13:3
This Gun for Hire 1942,My 14,23:2
Nazi Agent 1942,Je 13,11:2
Eyes of the Underworld 1942,O 5,15:2
Ox-Bow Incident, The 1943,My 10,15:2 (In Addenda)
Calaboose 1943,Jl 30,19:2
Hit the Ice 1943,S 23,27:2
Tampico 1944,Je 2,21:2
Rainbow Island 1944,O 26,19:6
Princess and the Pirate, The 1945,F 10,16:2
Dillinger 1945,Ap 26,26:2
Flame of Barbary Coast 1945,My 28,22:2
Virginian, The 1946,Ap 18,22:2
Cloak and Dagger 1946,O 5,13:2
Unconquered 1947,O 11,11:2
Captain from Castile 1947,D 26,22:4
I Walk Alone 1948,Ja 22,36:3
Key Largo 1948,Jl 17,6:6
Jigsaw 1949,My 30,9:4
Calamity Jane and Sam Bass 1949,Jl 18,14:2
Black Hand 1950,Mr 13,15:2
Asphalt Jungle, The 1950,Je 9,29:3
Abbott and Costello in the Foreign Legion 1950,Ag 14,14:4

Lawrence, Marc— Cont
Desert Hawk, The 1950,Ag 26,9:2
My Favorite Spy 1951,D 26,19:3
Helen of Troy 1956,Ja 27,21:4
Johnny Cool 1963,O 3,31:1
Johnny Tiger 1966,Je 16,53:4
Custer of the West 1968,Jl 4,13:2
Lawrence, Margery H (Original Author)
Dangerous Woman, A 1929,My 20,22:6
Madonna of the Seven Moons 1946,My 23,18:4
Lawrence, Marjorie
Only Two Can Play 1962,Mr 21,33:2
Lawrence, Marjorie (Original Author)
Interrupted Melody 1955,My 6,18:1
Lawrence, Mark (Producer)
Vali 1967,Je 2,34:2
Lawrence, Martin
Hand in Hand 1961,F 7,41:3
Lawrence, Mary
Stratton Story, The 1949,My 13,29:1
Night Into Morning 1951,Je 11,20:7
Lady Says No, The 1952,Ja 7,14:3
Back Street 1961,O 13,27:1
Best Man, The 1964,Ap 7,29:1
Lawrence, Mittie
Funny Girl 1968,S 20,42:1
Lawrence, Muriel
Dream of Jeanie, I 1952,Je 26,26:2
Lawrence, Quentin (Director)
Crawling Eye, The 1959,Ja 1,38:1
Cash on Demand 1962,My 17,31:1
Lawrence, Raymond
Interference 1928,N 17,23:1
Lawrence, Reginald (Original Author)
Men Must Fight 1933,Mr 11,18:3
Lawrence, Richard
Betrayal, The 1948,Je 26,10:5
Lawrence, Robert L (Producer)
Harvey Middleman, Fireman 1965,Jl 13,39:1
Lawrence, Rosina
Your Uncle Dudley 1935,D 12,33:4
Charlie Chan's Secret 1936,Ja 18,19:4
Way out West 1937,My 4,29:1
Nobody's Baby 1937,My 20,17:3
Pick a Star 1937,My 28,17:2
Lawrence, Sarah
Browning Version, The 1951,O 30,33:2
Lawrence, Shirley
Secret Door, The 1964,Je 4,28:1
Lawrence, Terry
Trooper Hook 1957,Jl 13,11:2
Lawrence, Vincent (Original Author)
Scandal Sheet 1931,F 9,25:3
Men Call it Love 1931,Je 20,20:4
Let's Try Again 1934,Je 22,24:1
Lawrence, Vincent (Screenwriter)
Behold My Wife 1935,F 18,19:3
Hands Across the Table 1935,N 2,13:2
Peter Ibbetson 1935,N 8,18:2
One Way Ticket 1936,Ja 1,35:2
John Meade's Woman 1937,F 18,19:1
Man-Proof 1938,Ja 14,21:1
Test Pilot 1938,Ap 16,17:1
Lucky Night 1939,My 5,29:3
Moon Over Miami 1941,Jl 5,14:2
Gentleman Jim 1942,N 26,40:3
Adventure 1946,F 8,23:2
Sea of Grass, The 1947,F 28,27:2
Lawrence, William
Hell Bound 1931,My 9,15:4
Best of Enemies 1933,Jl 17,19:5
Lawson, Barbara
Visit to a Small Planet 1960,Ap 14,34:1
Lawson, Eleanor
Merton of the Movies 1924,S 8,15:3
Lights of Old Broadway 1925,N 2,20:1
Lawson, Elsie
Twenty-One 1924,F 18,13:1
Dancing Mothers 1926,F 18,21:1
Social Celebrity, A 1926,Ap 19,24:3
Lawson, Gerald
Becket 1964,Mr 12,40:2
Lawson, Glyn
Gay Adventure, The 1954,S 16,35:7
Lawson, John Howard (Original Author)
Bachelor Apartment 1931,My 16,13:3
Success at any Price 1934,My 4,24:2
Lawson, John Howard (Screenwriter)
Blockade 1938,Je 17,25:1
Algiers 1938,Jl 15,13:2
They Shall Have Music 1939,Jl 26,17:2
Earthbound 1940,Je 7,27:4
Four Sons 1940,Je 8,18:4
Action in the North Atlantic 1943,My 22,10:2
Sahara 1943,N 12,25:2
Counter-Attack 1945,My 17,15:2
Smash-Up, The Story of a Woman
1947,Ap 11,31:2
Lawson, Kate
Girl From God's Country 1940,S 9,18:5
Song of my Heart 1948,Mr 5,17:3
Bride of Vengeance 1949,Ap 7,38:2
Thelma Jordon 1950,Ja 19,35:2
Rock Island Trail 1950,Je 5,19:3

Lawson, Linda
Night Tide 1963,Je 7,37:1
Let's Kill Uncle 1966,N 19,26:1
Lawson, Mary
Scrooge 1935,D 14,11:1
Trouble Ahead 1936,S 21,26:5
Lawson, Priscilla
Rose Bowl 1936,D 2,35:2
Double Wedding 1937,O 22,27:2
Girl of the Golden West, The 1938,Mr 25,15:2
Test Pilot 1938,Ap 16,17:1
Lawson, Russell (Composer)
Blockade 1938,Je 17,25:1
Lawson, Sarah
Both Sides of the Law 1954,Ja 12,19:2
Devil's Bride, The 1968,D 19,60:1
Lawson, Ted W Capt (Original Author)
Thirty Seconds Over Tokyo 1944,N 16,19:1
Lawson, Wilfrid
Ladies in Love 1936,O 29,31:1
White Hunter 1936,N 26,39:2
Pygmalion 1938,D 8,34:2
Stolen Life 1939,Je 15,27:2
Allegheny Uprising 1939,N 10,27:3
Pastor Hall 1940,S 21,13:2
Long Voyage Home, The 1940,O 9,30:2 (In
Addenda)
It Happened to One Man 1941,F 24,11:6
Tower of Terror 1942,Je 29,11:4
Great Mr Handel, The 1943,S 10,29:3
Jeannie 1943,S 13,14:2
Man of Evil 1948,Mr 26,26:2
Prisoner, The 1955,D 12,37:1
Make Me an Offer 1956,F 29,35:2
War and Peace 1956,Ag 22,26:2
Alligator Named Daisy, An 1957,O 7,23:2
Expresso Bongo 1960,Ap 13,44:1
Naked Edge 1961,Jl 1,9:1
Tom Jones 1963,O 8,48:1
Wrong Box 1966,Jl 20,46:1
Lawton, Alma
My Cousin Rachel 1952,D 26,20:2
Mary Poppins 1964,S 25,34:1
Lawton, Frank
Young Woodley 1930,S 27,21:3
Perfect Alibi, The 1931,Ap 20,16:3
Skin Game, The 1931,Je 20,20:4
Michael and Mary 1932,Mr 5,11:2
Cavalcade 1933,Ja 6,23:2
Charming Deceiver, The 1933,D 9,18:3
Friday the 13th 1934,My 15,18:1
One More River 1934,Ag 10,21:1
David Copperfield 1935,Ja 19,8:1
Invisible Ray, The 1936,Ja 11,9:3
Devil Doll, The 1936,Ag 8,5:2
Mill On the Floss, The 1939,N 15,19:3
Secret Four, The 1940,Ap 22,13:2
48 Hours 1944,Je 26,21:2
Winslow Boy, The 1950,Je 7,34:4
Rising of the Moon, The (1921); 1921 (The Rising
of the Moon) 1957,Jl 10,23:1
A Night to Remember 1958,D 17,2:7
Gideon of Scotland Yard 1959,My 20,38:2
Lawton, Thais
Battle Cry for Peace, The 1915,Ag 7,8:3
Lax, Abe
Power of Life 1938,Ap 29,17:2
Americaner Shadchen; American Matchmaker
1940,My 7,31:3
Catskill Honeymoon 1950,Ja 28,10:3
Lax, Frances
Family Jewels, The 1965,Ag 12,30:4
Lax, Robert (Screenwriter)
Siren of Atlantis 1949,Ag 22,13:1
Lax, Weintraub
Apartment, The 1960,Je 16,37:2
Laxalt, Pedro
Dark River 1956,F 27,19:4
Lay, Beirne Jr (Original Author)
I Wanted Wings 1941,Mr 27,29:4
Twelve O'Clock High 1950,Ja 28,10:2
Strategic Air Command 1955,Ap 21,33:1
Lay, Beirne Jr (Screenwriter)
I Wanted Wings 1941,Mr 27,29:4
Twelve O'Clock High 1950,Ja 28,10:2
Above and Beyond 1953,Ja 31,10:6
Strategic Air Command 1955,Ap 21,33:1
Toward the Unknown 1956,S 28,24:4
Gallant Hours, The 1960,Je 23,19:4
Lay, Ubaldo
Monte Cassino 1948,N 25,47:3
Layde, Patrick
Home Is the Hero 1961,Ja 26,32:1
Layden, Elmer
Spirit of Notre Dame, The 1931,O 16,27:1
Laydu, Claude
Voyage to America 1952,O 20,18:2
Diary of a Country Priest 1954,Ap 6,35:2
We Are all Murderers 1957,Ja 9,27:2
Attila 1958,My 19,19:4
Laye, Dilys
Gay Lady, The 1951,Ap 16,21:2
Doctor at Large 1957,Jl 29,15:5

Laye, Dilys— Cont
Bridal Path, The 1959,D 21,34:2
Please Turn Over 1961,Ap 29,12:2
Laye, Evelyn
One Heavenly Night 1931,Ja 10,19:2
Waltz Time 1933,S 29,24:2
Evensong 1934,N 17,12:1
Night is Young, The 1935,Ja 14,11:2
Princess Charming 1935,Je 22,18:5
Layson, Lorena
I Loved a Woman 1933,S 22,14:2
Layson Brothers, The
Carolina Blues 1944,D 8,26:6
Layton, Dorothy
Pick Up 1933,Mr 25,13:4
Lazaga, Pedro (Director)
Gladiators Seven 1964,My 7,31:2
Lazar, Joan
Undercover Man, The 1949,Ap 21,30:2
Lazar, Lajos (Director)
Key Balvany, A 1933,Ap 18,13:6
Kek Balvany, A; Blue Idol, The 1933,Ap 18,13:6
Lazar, Maria
Az uj Foeldesur 1936,S 22,30:5
Harom Sarkany 1936,D 22,32:3
Pusztai Szel; Beauty of the Pusta 1938,Ja 10,13:4
111-es Szobaban; In Room 111 1938,Ap 2,18:2
Megvedten Egy Asszony; I Defended a Woman
1939,O 14,13:3
Lazarus, Erna (Original Author)
Atlantic Flight 1937,N 1,24:5
He Married his Wife 1940,Ja 20,11:2
Meet Me After the Show 1951,Ag 16,23:2
Lazarus, Erna (Screenwriter)
Atlantic Flight 1937,N 1,24:5
Moonlight in Hawaii 1941,O 10,26:6
Body Disappears, The 1942,Ja 31,13:2
Hollywood or Bust 1956,D 24,8:1
Lazarus, Jeff (Producer)
Give Me a Sailor 1938,Ag 11,31:1
Ride a Crooked Mile 1938,D 29,15:2
St Louis Blues 1939,F 9,17:2
Cafe Society 1939,F 23,19:2
Lady's From Kentucky, The 1939,Ap 27,31:1
Honeymoon in Bali 1939,S 21,21:1
Lazarus, Sidney (Screenwriter)
Dough Boys 1930,S 30,23:1
Lazer, Peter
Hombre 1967,Mr 22,41:1
Lazic, Dragoslav (Director)
Feverish Years, The 1967,S 22,57:2
Lazo, Maria Elena (Screenwriter)
Roots, The (The Filly); Filly, The (The Roots)
1957,S 3,23:2
Roots, The (The Cows); Cows, The (The Roots)
1957,S 3,23:2
Roots, The (The One-Eyed Boy); One-Eyed Boy,
The (The Roots) 1957,S 3,23:2
Roots, The (Our Lady); Our Lady (The Roots)
1957,S 3,23:2
Lazzarini, Guido
Carnevale di Venezia, Il; Carnival of Venice, The
1940,O 11,25:2
Lazzarino, Tony (Producer)
X-15 1962,Ap 5,30:2
Lazzarino, Tony (Screenwriter)
X-15 1962,Ap 5,30:2
Lazzaro, Sofia
Favorita, La 1953,O 30,27:4
Lazzeri, Tony
Slide, Kelly, Slide 1927,Mr 23,19:2
Le Beal, Robert
Sword and the Rose, The 1953,Ag 20,18:3
Le Blanc, Lionel
Louisiana Story 1948,S 29,36:2
Le Blanc, Maurice (Original Author)
Arsene Lupin 1932,F 27,22:1
Arsene Lupin Returns 1938,Mr 9,21:1
Enter Arsene Lupin 1944,D 2,17:6
Le Borgy
Madame Recamier 1928,Jl 15,VIII,3:3
Le Breton, Flora
I Am the Man 1925,Mr 6,23:1
White Monkey, The 1925,Je 9,16:3
Charley's Aunt 1930,D 26,18:4
Le Breton, Jacques
Lola 1962,O 15,32:2
Le Carre, John (Original Author)
Spy Who Came in From the Cold, The
1965,D 24,24:1
Deadly Affair, The 1967,Ja 27,31:1
Le Chanois, Jean-Paul (Director)
Passion for Life 1951,D 21,21:4
Mama, Papa, the Maid and I 1956,Ag 28,31:1
Case of Dr Laurent, The 1958,Je 26,23:2
Love and the Frenchwoman; (Francaise et
l'Amour, La) 1961,F 28,38:2
Le Chanois, Jean-Paul (Miscellaneous)
Mama, Papa, the Maid and I 1956,Ag 28,31:1
Le Chanois, Jean-Paul (Original Author)
Passion for Life 1951,D 21,21:4
Le Chanois, Jean-Paul (Screenwriter)
Carnival of Sinners 1947,Ap 8,34:2
Taxi 1953,Ja 22,20:3

Le Chanois, Jean-Paul (Screenwriter) — Cont

Case of Dr Laurent, The 1958,Je 26,23:2
Le Clair, Blanche
Jealousy 1929,S 14,17:1
Le Faure, G (Original Author)
Soul of France, The 1929,O 12,11:1
le Feuvre, Guy
Man of Evil 1948,Mr 26,26:2
Le Flon, Robert
Zero de Conduite 1947,Je 23,14:5
Le Francois, W S Capt USMC (Original Author)
Gung Ho! 1944,Ja 26,23:2
Le Gallienne, Eva
Prince of Players 1955,Ja 12,24:2
Devil's Disciple, The 1959,Ag 21,12:1
Le Goffic, Charles (Original Author)
Morgane, the Enchantress 1929,Je 21,17:2
Le Gon, Jeni
Hooray for Love 1935,Jl 13,16:2
Ali Baba Goes to Town 1937,O 23,14:1
Fools for Scandal 1938,Mr 25,15:3
Arabian Nights 1942,D 26,15:1
I Walked with a Zombie 1943,Ap 22,31:5
Easter Parade 1948,Jl 1,19:3
I Shot Jesse James 1949,Ap 2,12:2
Le Haneff, Rene (Director)
Colonel Chabert 1947,Je 21,11:2
Hoboes in Paradise 1950,O 9,21:5
Le Maire, William
Only the Brave 1930,Mr 8,21:1
Light of Western Stars, The 1930,Ap 26,11:1
Painted Desert, The 1931,Mr 9,19:1
Cabin in the Cotton 1932,S 30,17:3
I Am a Fugitive From a Chain Gang 1932,N 11,17:2
20,000 Years in Sing Sing 1933,Ja 10,26:2
Captured 1933,Ag 18,18:3
le Marchand, Lucienne
Mysteres de Paris, Les 1937,Ja 30,21:2
Le Massena, William
Carousel 1956,F 17,13:1
Le Mesurier, James
Pink Panther, The 1964,Ap 24,25:1
Le Mesurier, John
Brothers in Law 1957,Ag 20,22:1
Law and Disorder 1958,Ag 6,20:1
Too Many Crooks 1959,Ap 25,14:2
Happy is the Bride 1959,Je 30,27:2
Jack the Ripper 1960,F 18,37:4
Touch of Larceny, A 1960,Mr 17,28:1
I'm All Right Jack 1960,Ap 26,40:2
Man in a Cocked Hat 1960,Je 15,50:2
School for Scoundrels 1960,Jl 12,39:1
Day They Robbed the Bank of England, The 1960,S 5,11:2
Follow a Star 1961,Ap 26,34:1
Call Me Genius 1961,O 17,47:1
Invasion Quartet 1961,D 11,41:2
I Like Money 1962,My 19,18:2
Coming-Out Party, A 1962,Jl 31,19:2
Mouse on the Moon, The 1963,Je 18,32:1
Main Attraction, The 1963,Je 27,23:3
Moonspinners, The 1964,N 4,47:1
Where the Spies Are 1966,Ja 27,29:1
Bang, Bang, You're Dead 1967,Ja 19,41:2
Salt and Pepper 1968,S 19,62:3
Le Moyne, Charles
Riders of the Purple Sage 1925,Ap 15,16:1
Le Paul, Paul
Eternally Yours 1939,O 7,11:2
Le Roy, George
Man to Men 1949,F 21,20:2
Le Royer, Michel
Lafayette 1963,Ap 11,29:1
Chateau en Suede; Castle in Switzerland 1964,O 14,51:1
Le Saint, Edward
For the Defense 1930,Jl 19,7:5
Last Parade, The 1931,Mr 2,19:1
Night of June 13th, The 1932,S 17,18:4
Last Man, The 1932,S 17,18:4
Central Park 1932,D 7,29:3
No More Orchids 1933,Ja 2,29:2
Tomorrow at Seven 1933,Jl 3,14:6
Frontier Marshal 1934,Ja 31,20:3
George White's Scandals 1934,Mr 16,24:2
Once to Every Woman 1934,Mr 26,22:3
Lemon Drop Kid, The 1934,O 27,20:2
Thunder Mountain 1935,O 2,27:2
Trail of the Lonesome Pine, The 1936,F 20,23:5
Witness Chair, The 1936,Ap 18,19:2
Legion of Terror 1936,N 2,24:2
Counterfeit Lady 1937,Ja 11,15:6
College Swing 1938,Ap 28,27:2
Jesse James 1939,Ja 14,13:1
Le-Van-Kim
Merlusse 1938,Mr 17,17:2
Le Vasseur, Lloyd
Anatomy of a Murder 1959,Jl 3,10:1
Le Vien, Jack (Producer)
Finest Hours, The 1964,N 11,38:1
King's Story, A 1967,My 25,57:2

Le Vigan
It Happened at the Inn; Goupi Mains Rouge 1945,D 22,16:2
Le Vigan, Robert
Sous la Lune du Maroc 1933,Ja 23,9:2
Dr Knock 1937,My 1,16:4
Lower Depths, The 1937,S 11,20:1
Late Mathias Pascal, The 1937,N 18,27:2
Helene 1938,Ja 22,19:1
Escape From Yesterday 1939,My 3,27:2
Harvest 1939,O 3,19:4
Port of Shadows 1939,O 30,13:2
Citadel of Silence, The 1939,D 25,29:1
Louise 1940,F 3,9:4
Charrette Fantome, La 1940,My 28,29:2
Four Flights to Love 1942,Ap 13,12:2
Heart of a Nation, The 1943,Ap 8,27:2
Queen and the Cardinal, The 1944,Je 1,17:3
Who Killed Santa Claus? 1948,Ap 21,33:2
Le Vignan, Robert
Boys' School 1939,Je 6,26:2
Le Vino, Albert Shelby (Original Author)
Night Life 1927,D 20,33:2
Hold 'Em Navy 1937,N 6,14:2
Le Vino, Albert Shelby (Screenwriter)
While Satan Sleeps 1922,Je 26,16:2
Mr Billings Spends his Dime 1923,Mr 5,15:3
Le Vitte, Jean (Original Author)
Devil's Daughter 1949,F 26,11:2
Lea, Andrea
Dolwyn 1949,Ag 30,18:4
Lea, Barbara
Rebellion in Cuba 1961,Jl 1,9:1
Lea, China
Troublemaker, The 1964,Je 23,25:1
Lea, Fanny Heaslip (Original Author)
Man-Proof 1938,Ja 14,21:1
Lea, Tom
Wonderful Country, The 1959,N 5,39:7
Lea, Tom (Original Author)
Brave Bulls, The 1951,Ap 19,39:2
Wonderful Country, The 1959,N 5,39:7
Lea, William De Dane (Miscellaneous)
Michael Strogoff 1960,My 21,15:1
LEACH
See LEECH
Leachman, Cloris
Rack, The 1956,N 6,30:1
Chapman Report, The 1962,O 18,49:2
Leacock, Philip (Director)
Brave Don't Cry, The 1952,N 6,37:2
Little Kidnappers, The 1954,S 2,18:1
Escapade 1957,Ag 6,30:2
Spanish Gardner, The 1957,S 9,21:2
Rabbit Trap, The 1959,O 15,48:1
Let no Man Write my Epitaph 1960,N 11,36:2
Hand in Hand 1961,F 7,41:3
Take a Giant Step 1961,Mr 6,28:2
13 West Street 1962,Je 7,31:2
War Lover, The 1963,Mr 7,8:5
Reach for Glory 1963,S 10,46:1
Tamahine 1964,Jl 16,23:1
Leacock, Philip (Producer)
Firecreek 1968,F 22,36:2
Leacock, Richard (Cinematographer)
Monterey Pop 1968,D 27,44:1
Leacock, Richard (Miscellaneous)
Journey to Jerusalem, A 1968,N 18,59:1
Leader, Anton M (Director)
Children of the Damned 1964,Ja 30,24:2
Leader, Anton M (Producer)
Go, Man, Go 1954,Mr 10,29:5
Leaf, Allen
Act One 1963,D 27,17:2
Leaf, Paul (Director)
Last Mohican, The 1966,S 13,51:2
Leahy, Agnes Brand (Original Author)
Sky Bride 1932,Ap 23,11:5
Forgotten Commandments 1932,Je 2,25:2
Leahy, Eugene
Prince of Lovers, The 1927,N 29,31:1
Love From a Stranger 1937,Ap 19,27:2
Leak, Jennifer
Yours, Mine and Ours 1968,Ap 25,53:1
Leake, Barbara
Dead of Night 1946,Je 29,22:6
Saraband 1949,Je 13,16:3
Kind Hearts and Coronets 1950,Je 15,41:2
His Excellency 1956,F 2,19:3
Uncle, The 1966,Jl 19,34:1
Leake, Grace Sothcote (Original Author)
Bondage 1933,Ap 24,11:3
Leal, Milagros
Nail, The 1949,Jl 1,14:6
Lealand, Princess
Tracked in the Snow Country 1925,Jl 20,19:2
Lean, David (Director)
In Which We Serve 1942,D 24,18:1
Blithe Spirit 1945,O 4,27:2
Brief Encounter 1946,Ag 26,21:2
This Happy Breed 1947,Ap 14,24:2
Great Expectations 1947,My 23,31:1
One Woman's Story 1949,My 18,33:2

Lean, David (Director) — Cont

Madeleine 1950,S 1,17:2
Oliver Twist 1951,Jl 31,17:2
Breaking Through the Sound Barrier 1952,N 7,19:1
Hobson's Choice 1954,Je 15,37:1
Summertime 1955,Je 22,25:1
Bridge on the River Kwai 1957,D 19,39:1
Lawrence of Arabia 1962,D 17,5:6
Doctor Zhivago 1965,D 23,21:1
Lean, David (Producer)
Breaking Through the Sound Barrier 1952,N 7,19:1
Hobson's Choice 1954,Je 15,37:1
Lean, David (Screenwriter)
Blithe Spirit 1945,O 4,27:2
This Happy Breed 1947,Ap 14,24:2
Great Expectations 1947,My 23,31:1
One Woman's Story 1949,My 18,33:2
Oliver Twist 1951,Jl 31,17:2
Hobson's Choice 1954,Je 15,37:1
Summertime 1955,Je 22,25:1
Leander, Zarah
Zu neven Ufern; To new Shores 1938,Ja 29,12:1
Heimt ruft, Die; Home Is Calling 1938,Jl 9,10:3
Magda 1938,S 10,20:2
Blaufuchs; Blue Fox 1939,Mr 4,18:5
Lied der Wuste, Das; Desert Song 1940,F 3,9:3
Lear, Norman (Producer)
Come Blow Your Horn 1963,Je 7,37:1
Never too Late 1965,N 5,28:1
Divorce American Style 1967,Jl 20,30:2
Night They Raided Minsky's, The 1968,D 23,43:1
Lear, Norman (Screenwriter)
Come Blow Your Horn 1963,Je 7,37:1
Divorce American Style 1967,Jl 20,30:2
Night They Raided Minsky's, The 1968,D 23,43:1
Leary, Helen (Original Author)
Make Way for Tomorrow 1937,My 10,23:1
Leary, Nolan
Ten North Frederick 1958,My 23,29:2
Pollyanna 1960,My 20,26:1
Make Way for Tomorrow 1937,My 10,23:1
Lease, Rex
Last Edition, The 1925,N 11,27:3
Clancy's Kosher Wedding 1927,S 7,35:2
College Hero, The 1927,N 22,32:2
Troopers Three 1930,F 17,17:6
Sunny Skies 1930,My 17,21:2
Heroes of the Alamo 1938,Ap 2,18:2
Flame of Barbary Coast 1945,My 28,22:2
Time of Their Lives, The 1946,N 28,40:2
Ma and Pa Kettle 1949,Ag 12,13:2
Singing Guns 1950,Je 5,19:3
Curtain Call at Cactus Creek 1950,S 22,35:4
Leasor, James (Original Author)
Where the Spies Are 1966,Ja 27,29:1
Leaud, Jean-Pierre
400 Blows, The; (Les Quatre Cents Coups) 1959,N 17,41:1
Testament of Orpheus 1962,Ap 10,48:1
Love at Twenty 1963,F 7,5:6
Masculine Feminine 1966,S 19,57:1
Depart, Le 1967,S 23,20:3
Made in U S A 1967,S 28,58:2
Chinoise, La 1968,Ap 4,58:2
Weekend 1968,S 28,36:1
Leaver, Philip
Lady Vanishes, The 1938,D 26,29:1
Smiling Along 1939,F 20,13:2
This Man Is News 1939,Jl 20,16:4
Silver Fleet, The 1945,Mr 24,22:6
Tales of Hoffmann 1951,Ap 5,34:2
Martin Luther 1953,S 10,22:1
Leavitt, Douglas
You Were Never Lovelier 1942,D 4,31:1
Reveille With Beverly 1943,Ap 24,17:2
Murder in Times Square 1943,My 31,13:2
Two Senoritas From Chicago 1943,Ag 6,10:4
Leavitt, Norman
Harvey Girls, The 1946,Ja 25,26:2
Spider Woman Strikes Back, The 1946,Mr 23,8:3
Slattery's Hurricane 1949,Ag 13,6:6
Inspector General, The 1949,D 31,9:2
Stars and Stripes Forever 1952,D 23,17:2
Off Limits 1953,Mr 30,25:5
Inside Detroit 1956,Ja 28,10:5
Jumbo 1962,D 7,49:1
LeBaire, Dorothy
Man Who Played God, The 1932,F 11,16:1
Lebar, John (Original Author)
Enchanted Forest, The 1945,D 17,17:2
Lebar, John (Screenwriter)
Enchanted Forest, The 1945,D 17,17:2
LeBaron, Eddie
Innocent Affair, An 1948,S 29,36:2
Third Voice, The 1960,Mr 7,24:5
LeBaron, Eddie and his Continental Orchestra
Perilous Holiday 1946,Je 1,10:4
LeBaron, William (Original Author)
Lovin' the Ladies 1930,Mr 22,22:6

LeBaron, William (Producer)
It's a Gift 1935,Ja 5,20:2
Rumba 1935,F 25,13:2
All the King's Horses 1935,Mr 9,19:1
Goin' to Town 1935,My 11,21:2
Man on the Flying Trapeze 1935,Ag 3,16:2
Here Comes Cookie 1935,O 12,12:2
Coronado 1935,D 19,33:4
Rose of the Rancho 1936,Ja 9,25:2
Klondike Annie 1936,Mr 12,18:2
Give Us This Night 1936,Ap 6,18:1
Poppy 1936,Je 18,19:1
Rhythm on the River 1940,Ag 29,23:2
Las Vegas Nights 1941,Mr 20,25:2
Week-End in Havana 1941,N 8,11:2
Song of the Islands 1942,Mr 12,24:4
Footlight Serenade 1942,S 10,30:3
Orchestra Wives 1942,S 24,23:2
Iceland 1942,O 15,27:1
Springtime in the Rockies 1942,N 12,30:2
Stormy Weather 1943,Jl 22,15:1
Wintertime 1943,S 30,27:2
Gang's All Here, The 1943,D 23,26:4
Pin Up Girl 1944,My 11,25:6
Greenwich Village 1944,S 28,26:2
Sweet and Low Down 1944,O 19,19:2
Don Juan Quilligan 1945,Jl 30,16:2
Carnegie Hall 1947,My 3,10:2
LeBaron, William (Screenwriter)
Marika 1953,F 18,27:2
Lebeau, Madeleine
Hold Back the Dawn 1941,O 2,29:1
Casablanca 1942,N 27,27:1
Paris After Dark 1943,O 23,11:1
Music for Millions 1944,D 22,12:4
Case of Gold 1952,Ja 19,13:3
Cage of Gold 1952,Ja 19,13:3
Sins of Paris 1954,Ja 30,9:6
Parisienne, La 1958,Jl 31,27:1
Eight and One Half 1963,Je 26,36:1
Lebedeff, Ivan
Sorrows of Satan, The 1926,O 13,21:1
Forbidden Woman, The 1927,O 31,22:1
Angel of Broadway 1927,N 1,21:1 (In Addenda)
Let 'Er go, Galleher 1928,Ja 16,24:1
Walking Back 1928,Je 12,33:3
One Woman Idea, The 1929,Je 10,23:1
Street Girl 1929,Jl 31,17:3
They Had to See Paris 1929,O 12,11:1
Cuckoos, The 1930,Ap 26,11:1
Midnight Mystery 1930,Je 2,25:4
Bachelor Apartment 1931,My 16,13:3
Gay Diplomat, The 1931,O 10,20:4
Sweepings 1933,Mr 24,22:3
Made on Broadway 1933,Jl 8,14:5
Laughing at Life 1933,Jl 15,14:2
Bombshell 1933,O 21,11:2
Moulin Rouge 1934,F 8,14:4
Kansas City Princess 1934,N 5,23:1
Goin' to Town 1935,My 11,21:2
China Seas 1935,Ag 10,16:4
Golden Arrow, The 1936,My 4,16:1
Pepper 1936,Ag 24,11:2
Love on the Run 1936,N 28,13:3
History Is Made at Night 1937,Mr 29,14:2
Atlantic Flight 1937,N 1,24:5
Conquest 1937,N 5,19:1
Wise Girl 1938,Ja 10,13:3
Straight, Place and Show 1938,O 1,10:2
Hotel for Women 1939,Ag 26,20:2
Passport to Alcatraz 1940,Je 15,12:2
Public Deb No 1 1940,S 18,19:2
Shanghai Gesture, The 1941,D 26,21:2
Are These our Parents? 1944,Ag 23,16:2
Lebedev, A (Cinematographer)
Circus Festival 1958,Mr 17,21:4
Lebedev, Oleg (Director)
Cinerama's Russian Adventure 1966,Ap 14,42:1
Lebedev, V
Othello 1960,My 16,39:1
Lebedev-Kumach, V I (Composer)
Volga-Volga 1941,My 17,19:2
Spring 1948,Mr 15,26:2
Lebedev-Kumach, V I (Miscellaneous)
Country Bride 1938,Je 4,18:2
Lebel, Serge
Face to the Wind 1951,Ja 16,34:2
Lebiush, Zalman
Hill 24 Doesn't Answer 1955,N 3,37:1
Lebon, Lisset
Voyage to America 1952,O 20,18:2
Lebon, Yvette
Abused Confidence 1938,D 1,29:1
It Happened in Gibraltar 1943,N 16,27:1
Mlle Desiree 1948,N 19,35:2
Girl on the Third Floor, The; (Sophie et le Crime)
1958,O 11,47:1 (Incorrect in this edition; use
1958,O 11,18:4 elsewhere)
Viscount, The 1967,My 11,50:1
LeBorg, Reginald (Director)
Calling Dr Death 1944,F 12,11:3
Adventure in Music 1944,Mr 6,17:3
Weird Woman 1944,Ap 1,11:1

Mummy's Ghost, The 1944,Jl 1,10:7
Jungle Woman 1944,Jl 15,19:6
Dead Man's Eyes 1944,O 7,11:2
San Diego, I Love You 1944,N 10,25:1
Destiny 1945,F 3,16:5
Joe Palooka, Champ 1946,Ap 6,10:6
Wyoming Mail 1950,O 23,26:5
Models, Inc 1952,My 26,18:4
Sins of Jezebel 1954,Ja 9,12:2
Diary of a Madman 1963,Je 6,39:1
Eyes of Annie Jones, The 1964,My 14,39:1
LEBOWITZ
See LIEBOWITZ
LeBreton, Auguste (Original Author)
Speaking of Murder 1959,O 12,14:1
LeBreton, Auguste (Screenwriter)
Speaking of Murder 1959,O 12,14:1
Leccia, Francois
This Special Friendship 1967,N 8,56:1
Lechner, Billy
Penrod and Sam 1937,Mr 29,14:3
Lechtenbrink, Volker
Bridge, The; (Bruecke, Die) 1961,My 2,42:1
Leciere, Ginette
Easiest Profession, The 1960,Mr 26,15:7
Leclainche, Charles
Man Escaped, A 1957,Ag 27,33:2
Leclair, Sophie
Face to the Wind 1951,Ja 16,34:2
Leclair, Turk
Flower Thief, The 1962,Jl 14,11:5
Leclerc, Ginette
Late Mathias Pascal, The 1937,N 18,27:2
Louise 1939,F 3,9:4
Baker's Wife, The 1940,F 27,17:2
Two Women 1940,N 2,19:3
Corbeau, Le; Raven, The 1948,F 24,21:1
Plaisir, Le (The House of Madame Tellier); House
of Madame Tellier (Le Plaisir)
1954,My 20,38:1
Lover's Net 1957,Jl 23,23:1
Money, Money, Money 1962,Jl 18,20:1
Leclerc, Martine
Therese and Isabelle 1968,My 15,41:4
Lecointe, Serge
Face to the Wind 1951,Ja 16,34:2
Perfectionist, The 1952,My 2,21:3
Lecomte, Josiane
Game of Love, The 1954,D 15,41:1
Lecourtois, Daniel
Madame Borary 1934,N 19,13:2
Adorable Creatures 1956,Ja 11,36:2
Possessors, The 1959,Jl 21,24:1
Lecuona, Ernesto (Composer)
Carnival in Costa Rica 1947,Mr 29,21:2
Lecuyer, Rene (Miscellaneous)
Farrebique 1948,F 24,21:2
LeDeaux, Marie
Saboteur 1942,My 8,27:2
Ledebur, Frederick
Great Sinner, The 1949,Je 30,19:2
Alexander the Great 1956,Mr 29,23:1
Moby Dick 1956,Jl 5,18:1
Roots of Heaven, The 1958,O 16,46:1
Breath of Scandal, A 1960,D 17,19:1
Oedipus the King 1968,S 19,62:2
Ledebur, Leopold von
Blonde Nachtigall, Die 1931,Ag 22,7:5
Alte Kameraden 1936,Ap 27,19:3
Leder, Herbert J (Director)
Pretty Boy Floyd 1960,N 3,49:2
It 1967,N 16,58:1
Frozen Dead, The 1967,N 16,58:1
Leder, Herbert J (Producer)
Frozen Dead, The 1967,N 16,58:1
It 1967,N 16,58:1
Leder, Herbert J (Screenwriter)
Fiend Without a Face 1958,Jl 4,15:3
Pretty Boy Floyd 1960,N 3,49:2
Frozen Dead, The 1967,N 16,58:1
It 1967,N 16,58:1
Leder, Robert (Producer)
Revolution 1968,Ag 8,27:2
Lederer, Charles (Director)
Fingers at the Window 1942,Ap 23,27:3
Never Steal Anything Small 1959,F 12,23:1
Lederer, Charles (Original Author)
Red, Hot and Blue 1949,O 20,39:2
Never Steal Anything Small 1959,F 12,23:1
Lederer, Charles (Screenwriter)
Cock of the Air 1932,Ja 25,20:3
Mountain Music 1937,Je 24,30:3
Double or Nothing 1937,S 2,17:3
Within the Law 1939,Ap 6,31:2
Broadway Serenade 1939,Ap 7,25:2
I Love You Again 1940,Ag 16,11:2
Comrade X 1940,D 26,23:1
Love Crazy 1941,Je 6,25:5
Slightly Dangerous 1943,Ap 2,17:2
Youngest Profession, The 1943,Je 25,13:3
Kiss of Death 1947,Ag 28,28:2
Ride the Pink Horse 1947,O 9,32:3
Her Husband's Affairs 1947,N 14,29:2

Lederer, Charles (Screenwriter) — Cont
I Was a Male War Bride 1949,Ag 27,7:2
Wabash Avenue 1950,Ap 29,8:3
Thing, The 1951,My 3,34:4
Monkey Business 1952,S 6,12:6
Gentlemen Prefer Blondes 1953,Jl 16,17:2
Kismet 1955,D 9,32:2
Gaby 1956,My 10,26:3
Spirit of St Louis, The 1957,F 22,25:1
Tip on a Dead Jockey 1957,S 7,12:7
Never Steal Anything Small 1959,F 12,23:1
It Started With a Kiss 1959,Ag 20,14:2
Can-Can 1960,Mr 10,36:1
Ocean's Eleven 1960,Ag 11,19:1
Follow That Dream 1962,Ag 9,17:7
Mutiny on the Bounty 1962,N 9,31:2
Global Affair, A 1964,My 7,31:2
Lederer, Francis
Pandora's Box 1929,D 2,28:2
Wonderful Lies of Nova Petrova, The
1930,Je 30,27:2
Susanne Macht Ordnung 1931,O 12,28:2
Ihre Majestaet die Liebe 1933,F 7,23:4
Das Schicksal der Renate Langen 1933,N 4,18:4
Man of Two Worlds 1934,Ja 12,29:2
Pursuit of Happiness, The 1934,O 26,25:1
Romance in Manhattan 1935,Ja 18,29:2
Gay Deception, The 1935,O 11,31:1
One Rainy Afternoon 1936,My 14,29:2
My American Wife 1936,Ag 21,12:3
It's all Yours 1938,Ja 7,15:3
Lone Wolf in Paris, The 1938,My 23,21:2
Midnight 1939,Ap 6,31:1
Confessions of a Nazi Spy 1939,Ap 29,13:2
Man I Married, The 1940,Ag 3,9:2
Bridge of San Luis Rey, The 1944,Mr 4,11:1
Voice in the Wind 1944,Mr 16,17:2
Diary of a Chambermaid, The 1946,Je 23,28:2
Woman of Distinction, A 1950,Mr 17,28:2
Captain Carey U S A 1950,Mr 30,40:5
Surrender 1950,O 9,21:5
Ambassador's Daughter, The 1956,Ag 30,19:1
Lisbon 1956,Ag 30,19:2
Terror is a Man 1960,Jl 14,23:1
Lederer, Joe (Screenwriter)
Drei Tage Liebe; Three Days of Love
1931,Mr 15,IX,6:1
Lederer, Otto
Forget Me Not 1922,Jl 24,10:2
Hungry Hearts 1922,N 27,18:1
Black Oxen 1924,Ja 7,23:1
Worldly Goods 1924,N 3,20:1
Sweet Rosie O'Grady 1926,D 9,33:1
Jazz Singer, The 1927,O 7,24:4
Chicago 1927,D 24,9:1
Lederer, Pepi
Cardboard Lover, The 1928,S 3,14:2
Lederer, William J (Original Author)
Skipper Surprised his Wife, The 1950,Je 30,18:2
Ugly American, The 1963,Ap 12,30:2
Lederman, D
Dybbuk, The 1938,Ja 28,17:2
Lederman, D Ross (Director)
Man Hunter, The 1930,Ap 5,23:3
State Trooper 1933,Mr 27,13:6
Soldiers of the Storm 1933,My 17,15:3
Murder in the Clouds 1934,D 26,18:1
Red Hot Tires 1935,Mr 1,16:3
Case of the Missing Man, The 1935,N 23,23:2
Panic on the Air 1936,Ap 20,17:1
Pride of the Marines 1936,Ap 27,19:2
Final Hour, The 1936,Ag 1,16:3
Come Closer, Folks 1936,N 23,17:3
Counterfeit Lady 1937,Ja 11,15:6
I Promise to Pay 1937,Ap 26,15:2
Frame-Up 1937,Ag 9,23:2 (In Addenda)
Tarzan's Revenge 1938,Ja 10,13:3
Juvenile Court 1938,S 12,13:2
Adventure in Sahara 1938,D 19,19:2
Racketeers of the Range 1939,Je 8,31:4
Military Academy 1940,Ag 5,10:4
Glamour for Sale 1940,N 5,33:2
Father's Son 1941,F 13,25:3
Strange Alibi 1941,Ap 28,11:2
Body Disappears, The 1942,Ja 31,13:2
Bullet Scars 1942,Ap 24,21:4
I Was Framed 1942,Je 12,16:6
Busses Roar 1942,S 25,25:4
Escape From Crime 1942,O 12,12:3
Gorilla Man, The 1943,Ja 15,21:4
Key Witness 1947,Jl 30,27:6
Ledesma, Amanda
Dancing, El 1935,Ja 28,10:6
Ultimo Encventro, El; Last Meeting, The
1939,Ag 26,20:3
Ledi, Lotte
Tomorrow Is my Turn 1962,F 2,24:2
Young Torless 1968,Jl 23,27:2
Heidi 1968,S 23,42:4
Ledoux, Fernand
Youth in Revolt 1939,My 16,27:3
S O S Mediterranean 1940,Ja 1,29:2
Human Beast, The 1940,F 20,17:2
Heart of a Nation, The 1943,Ap 8,27:2

Ledoux, Fernand — Cont
It Happened at the Inn; Goupi Mains Rouge 1945,D 22,16:2
Stormy Waters 1946,Je 17,32:2
Her First Affair; (Children of Paradise) 1947,F 20,32:3
Bellman, The 1947,Ap 7,20:5
Devil's Own Envoy, The 1947,Ag 30,8:6
Volpone 1947,D 27,9:3
Who Killed Santa Claus? 1948,Ap 21,33:2
Devil's Daughter 1949,F 26,11:2
Act of Love 1954,F 12,20:5
Doctors, The 1956,Ag 7,19:2
Mama, Papa, the Maid and I 1956,Ag 28,31:1
He Who Must Die 1958,D 29,21:1
Freud 1962,D 13,37:1
I Spit on Your Grave 1963,Je 29,13:5
Up From the Beach 1965,Je 10,38:1

Ledoyen, Germaine
Devil in the Flesh 1949,My 10,29:2

Ledrov, D B (Screenwriter)
Shuttered Room, The 1968,F 15,47:1

Leduc, Jean
Girl on a Motorcycle, The 1968,N 28,66:5

Leduc, Violette (Original Author)
Therese and Isabelle 1968,My 15,41:4

Ledyakh, Gennady
Cinderella 1961,D 19,39:1

Lee
I Live for Love 1935,O 19,21:2
King of Burlesque 1936,Ja 16,25:2
Ready, Willing and Able 1937,Mr 15,27:1
King and the Chorus Girl, The 1937,Mr 29,14:4

Lee, Ah
Devil Tiger 1934,F 9,23:2

Lee, Anna
First a Girl 1936,Ja 4,19:1
Passing of the Third Floor Back, The 1936,Ap 29,19:2
Man Who Lived Again, The 1936,D 16,35:4
You're in the Army Now 1937,Ap 16,27:2
King Solomon's Mines 1937,Jl 3,18:1
Non-Stop New York 1937,N 29,19:2
Secret Four, The 1940,Ap 22,13:2
Seven Sinners 1940,N 18,23:2
How Green Was my Valley 1941,O 29,27:2
My Life With Caroline 1941,O 30,27:1
Flying Tigers 1942,O 23,25:2
Hangmen Also Die 1943,Ap 16,24:2
Flesh and Fantasy 1943,N 18,29:1
Young Man's Fancy, A 1943,D 4,11:2
Summer Storm 1944,O 23,14:3
Bedlam 1946,Ap 20,16:4
Ghost and Mrs Muir, The 1947,Je 27,17:2
Fort Apache 1948,Je 25,26:2
Prison Warden 1949,O 21,31:2
Boots Malone 1952,Mr 13,26:2
Commandos Strike at Dawn 1954,Ja 14,25:1
Last Hurrah, The 1958,O 24,40:1
Gideon of Scotland Yard 1959,My 20,38:2
Horse Soldiers, The 1959,Je 26,13:1
Earth Is Mine, The 1959,Je 27,13:1
Big Night, The 1960,F 18,37:4
What Ever Happened to Baby Jane? 1962,N 7,48:1
For Those Who Think Young 1964,Jl 9,27:1
Sound of Music, The 1965,Mr 3,34:1
7 Women 1966,My 5,59:1
In Like Flint 1967,Mr 16,53:2

Lee, Auriol
Suspicion 1941,N 21,23:2

Lee, Barbara
Betrayal, The 1948,Je 26,10:5

Lee, Belinda
Blackout 1954,My 22,8:2
Runaway Bus, The 1954,O 25,30:7
Footsteps of the Fog 1955,S 15,39:2
Dangerous Exile 1958,O 11,18:3
Elephant Gun 1959,Je 20,11:2
Chasers, The; Draguers, Les 1960,My 3,43:1
Nights of Lucretia Borgia, The 1960,O 6,51:4
Story of Joseph and his Brethern, The 1962,D 1,17:1
Constantine and the Cross 1963,Mr 14,8:2

Lee, Bernard
Let George Do It 1940,O 14,25:5
Quartet (The Kite); Kite, The (Quartet) 1949,Mr 29,30:3
Fallen Idol, The 1949,N 16,39:2
Third Man, The 1950,F 3,29:2
Last Holiday 1950,N 14,39:4
Blue Lamp, The 1951,Ja 9,25:1
Operation Disaster 1951,Ja 15,13:1
Odette 1951,Mr 28,33:2
Case of Gold 1952,Ja 19,13:3
Cage of Gold 1952,Ja 19,13:3
Island Rescue 1952,Jl 1,19:4
White Corridors 1952,Jl 16,21:1
Glory at Sea 1953,Mr 11,36:7
Mr Denning Drives North 1953,S 2,20:1
Sailor of the King 1953,S 3,15:2
Beat the Devil 1954,Mr 13,11:2
Yellow Balloon, The 1954,O 13,28:2
Detective, The 1954,N 2,25:2

Crest of the Wave 1954,N 11,43:2
Purple Plain, The 1955,Ap 11,29:1
Ship That Died of Shame, The 1956,Ag 21,33:2
Fire Down Below 1957,Ag 9,11:2
Spanish Gardner, The 1957,S 9,21:2
Across the Bridge 1957,O 30,24:1
Pursuit of the Graf Spee 1957,D 27,33:2
Key, The 1958,Jl 2,23:3
Dunkirk 1958,S 11,42:2
Man Upstairs, The 1959,Ag 11,23:2
Kidnapped 1960,My 19,44:3
Breakout 1960,My 19,44:3
Angry Silence, The 1960,D 13,25:2
Trouble in the Sky 1961,Jl 13,26:3
Whistle Down the Wind 1962,Ag 23,34:2
L-Shaped Room, The 1963,My 28,32:1
Dr No 1963,My 30,20:1
From Russia with Love 1964,Ap 9,25:1
Ring of Treason 1964,My 28,40:3 (Incorrect in this edition; use 1964,My 29,15:1 elsewhere)
Goldfinger 1964,D 22,36:1
Thunderball 1965,D 22,23:1
You Only Live Twice 1967,Je 14,40:1
Operation Kid Brother 1967,N 23,58:2

Lee, Betsy
Night Bird, The 1928,O 2,23:5

Lee, Billy
Wagon Wheels 1934,O 4,19:1
Silk Hat Kid 1935,Ag 7,22:5
Two Fisted 1935,O 5,18:3
Sky Parade, The 1936,Ap 20,17:1
Sudden Death, And 1936,Jl 18,18:2
Three Cheers for Love 1936,Ag 1,16:2
Make a Wish 1937,S 23,33:1
Thunder Trail 1938,F 5,19:3
Cocoanut Grove 1938,Je 16,21:2
Sons of the Legion 1938,S 30,24:3
Say It in French 1938,D 1,29:1
Biscuit Eater, The 1940,My 23,28:5
Power Dive 1941,My 29,15:4
Reluctant Dragon, The 1941,Jl 25,12:2
Hold Back the Dawn 1941,O 2,29:1
Road to Happiness 1942,Mr 27,27:4
Eyes of the Underworld 1942,O 5,15:2

Lee, Canada
Lifeboat 1944,Ja 13,17:1
Body and Soul 1947,N 10,21:2
Lost Boundaries 1949,Jl 1,14:4
Cry, the Beloved Country 1952,Ja 24,23:2

Lee, Canada (Narrator)
Roosevelt Story, The 1947,Ag 22,11:2

Lee, Candace
Love Is a Many-Splendored Thing 1955,Ag 19,10:1
South Pacific 1958,Mr 20,33:1

Lee, Carl
Connection, The 1962,O 4,44:1
Cool World, The 1964,Ap 21,42:1

Lee, Carl (Screenwriter)
Cool World, The 1964,Ap 21,42:1

Lee, Carolyn
Honeymoon in Bali 1939,S 21,21:1
Virginia 1941,Ja 29,21:2
Birth of the Blues 1941,D 11,39:1

Lee, Celeste
Temple of Venus, The 1923,N 1,24:3

Lee, Cherylene
Donovan's Reef 1963,Jl 25,14:1

Lee, China
Good Times 1967,Ag 3,26:4

Lee, Ching Wah
Good Earth, The 1937,F 3,27:1
Daughter of Shanghai 1937,D 24,21:2
China 1943,Ap 22,31:2

Lee, Christopher
One Night With You 1949,F 21,20:2
Corridor of Mirrors 1949,Mr 23,35:3
Crimson Pirate, The 1952,Ag 28,21:2
Cockleshell Heroes, The 1956,Je 4,25:2
Storm over the Nile 1956,Je 9,14:2
Beyond Mombasa 1957,My 31,14:2
Curse of Frankenstein, The 1957,Ag 8,15:5
Horror of Dracula 1958,My 29,24:4
Tale of Two Cities, A 1958,Ag 5,23:1
Hounds of the Baskervilles, The 1959,Jl 4,9:4
Mummy, The 1959,D 17,51:4
Scream of Fear 1961,Ag 23,29:1
House of Fright 1961,Ag 24,25:4
Corridors of Blood 1963,Je 6,39:1
Horror Hotel 1963,Je 20,29:1
She 1965,S 2,36:1
Face of Fu Manchu, The 1965,N 11,58:3
Vengeance of Fu Manchu, The 1968,F 15,47:1
Devil's Bride, The 1968,D 19,60:1

Lee, Connie (Original Author)
Return of October, The 1949,F 23,31:2

Lee, Davey
Singing Fool, The 1928,S 20,33:2
Sonny Boy 1929,Mr 9,24:3
Say It With Songs 1929,Ag 7,29:2
Squealer, The 1930,S 8,17:1

Lee, Dick
School for Wives 1925,Ap 1,21:3

Lee, Dixie
William Fox Movietone Follies of 1929 1929,My 27,22:1
Why Leave Home 1929,S 16,30:1
Happy Days 1930,F 14,20:1
Let's Go Places 1930,Mr 1,23:1
No Limit 1931,Ja 17,23:1
Love in Bloom 1935,Ap 20,16:2

Lee, Donivee
Great Moment, The 1944,N 13,15:2

Lee, Donna
Body Snatcher, The 1945,My 26,18:3

Lee, Doris
Girl Dodger, The 1919,F 24,11:3
Hay Foot, Straw Foot 1919,Je 23,10:3

Lee, Dorothy
Syncopation 1929,Ap 8,32:1
Rio Rita 1929,O 7,22:1
Cuckoos, The 1930,Ap 26,11:1
Dixiana 1930,S 5,21:1
Half Shot at Sunrise 1930,O 11,21:3
Hook, Line and Sinker 1930,D 25,31:5
Laugh and get Rich 1931,Mr 28,15:3
Cracked Nuts 1931,Ap 6,24:1
Too Many Cooks 1931,Ag 17,18:2
Caught Plastered 1931,S 12,15:4
Local Boy Makes Good 1931,N 27,29:3
Peach O'Reno 1931,D 24,20:8
Girl Crazy 1932,Mr 25,23:3
Take a Chance 1933,N 27,20:3
Hips, Hips, Hooray 1934,F 24,18:3
Cockeyed Cavaliers 1934,Jl 25,22:2
Rainmakers, The 1935,N 2,13:2
Silly Billies 1936,Ap 6,18:1
Twelve Crowded Hours 1939,F 24,15:2
S O S Tidal Wave 1939,Je 22,19:3

Lee, Duke
Tony Runs Wild 1926,Ap 28,28:3
Circus Ace, The 1927,Jl 6,23:2

Lee, Earl
Five 1951,Ap 26,34:2
Story of Will Rogers, The 1952,Jl 18,10:5

Lee, Eddie
Panic on the Air 1936,Ap 20,17:1
West of Shanghai 1937,O 29,19:2
To the Ends of the Earth 1948,F 13,26:2

Lee, Edna L (Original Author)
Queen Bee 1955,N 23,18:2
All That Heaven Allows 1956,F 29,35:1

Lee, Etta
Toll of the Sea, The 1922,N 27,18:1
Thief of Bagdad, The 1924,Mr 19,19:1
Thief in Paradise, A 1925,Ja 26,14:1
Recompense 1925,Ap 20,22:1
Trouble With Wives, The 1925,Ag 5,12:4
Camille 1927,Ap 22,19:1
Chinese Parrot, The 1928,Ja 2,28:1

Lee, Florence
City Lights 1931,F 7,11:1

Lee, Frances
Chicken a la King 1928,Je 11,27:1
Carnation Kid, The 1929,F 25,16:1
These Thirty Years 1934,My 24,28:3

Lee, Frankie
Westerners, The 1919,Ag 4,8:3
Bonds of Love 1919,N 3,13:3
Judy of Rogues Harbor 1920,Mr 1,16:2
Nurse Marjorie 1920,My 24,20:3
Old Fashioned Boy, An 1920,N 1,13:2
Borderland 1922,Jl 24,10:2
Third Alarm, The 1923,Ja 10,28:5
Barefoot Boy, The 1923,N 11,6:1
Unknown Purple, The 1924,Mr 24,13:1
Poisoned Paradise 1924,Ag 11,16:1
Code of the West 1925,Ap 13,24:1

Lee, George
Fort Ti 1953,My 30,7:1

Lee, Georgia
Good News 1947,D 5,33:2

Lee, Gerald
Guerrilla Girl 1953,Jl 7,23:7

Lee, Gwen
His Secretary 1925,D 21,27:2
Upstage 1926,N 15,19:1
Orchids and Ermine 1927,Ap 19,24:4
Adam and Evil 1927,Ag 10,21:4
After Midnight 1927,Ag 16,31:2
Sharp Shooters 1928,Ja 23,18:3
Her Wild Oat 1928,F 6,12:3
Laugh, Clown, Laugh 1928,My 28,23:2
Actress, The 1928,Jl 9,25:1
Show Girl 1928,N 5,26:1
Lady of Chance, A 1929,Ja 14,20:1
Lucky Boy 1929,F 25,16:1
Man and the Moment, The 1929,Ag 5,25:2
Fast Company 1929,O 5,22:5
Untamed 1929,N 30,23:1
Lord Byron of Broadway 1930,Mr 8,21:1
Free and Easy 1930,Ap 19,15:1
Extravagance 1930,D 9,31:3
Paid 1931,Ja 3,21:2

Lee, Gwen— Cont
Inspiration 1931,F 9,25:3
Lawless Woman, The 1931,Je 8,21:1
Traveling Husbands 1931,Ag 8,16:3
Corruption 1933,Je 20,22:7

Lee, Gypsy Rose
Stage Door Canteen 1943,Je 25,13:2
Belle of the Yukon 1945,Mr 30,18:4
Babes in Bagdad 1954,Ap 5,21:3
Screaming Mimi 1958,Je 26,23:3
Wind Across the Everglades 1958,S 12,21:1
Stripper, The 1963,Je 20,29:1
Trouble With Angels, The 1966,Ap 7,45:1

Lee, Gypsy Rose (Original Author)
Lady of Burlesque 1943,My 14,17:2

Lee, Hans
Kill a Dragon 1967,D 7,60:2

Lee, Harper (Original Author)
To Kill a Mockingbird 1963,F 15,10:2

Lee, Harry
Men of Steel 1926,Jl 12,24:4
Sunny Skies 1930,My 17,21:2

Lee, Harry (Original Author)
All That Heaven Allows 1956,F 29,35:1

Lee, Irving
Newspaper Boys, The 1937,N 6,14:3

Lee, Jack
Appointment in Berlin 1943,Jl 17,8:2
Broken Arrow 1950,Jl 21,15:2
Two Flags West 1950,O 13,23:2

Lee, Jack (Director)
Children on Trial 1947,N 10,21:3
Woman in the Hall, The 1949,Ja 24,16:2
Wooden Horse, The 1951,Ag 29,20:2
Undersea Raider 1953,F 11,33:7
Turn the Key Softly 1954,F 4,21:6
Golden Mask, The 1954,Mr 20,10:5
Town Like Alice, A 1958,S 22,27:1
Captain's Table, The 1960,S 27,40:1
Circle of Deception 1961,F 18,12:2

Lee, Jack (Original Author)
Children on Trial 1947,N 10,21:3
Undersea Raider 1953,F 11,33:7

Lee, Jack (Screenwriter)
Woman in the Hall, The 1949,Ja 24,16:2
Turn the Key Softly 1954,F 4,21:6

Lee, James
Kennell Murder Case, The 1933,O 30,14:2

Lee, James (Original Author)
Career 1959,O 9,24:1

Lee, James (Screenwriter)
Career 1959,O 9,24:1
Adventures of Huckleberry Fin, The 1960,Ag 4,17:1
Banning 1967,D 14,62:2
Counterpoint 1968,Mr 14,51:2

Lee, Jocelyn
Campus Flirt, The 1926,S 22,31:1
Everybody's Acting 1926,N 8,19:2
Kiss in a Taxi, A 1927,Mr 15,29:2
Afraid to Love 1927,Ap 12,25:3
Love Thrill, The 1927,My 10,24:5
Ten Modern Commandments 1927,Jl 11,23:4
Shanghai Bound 1927,N 7,26:4
Night Bird, The 1928,O 2,23:5
Dry Martini 1928,N 5,26:5 (In Addenda)
Twin Beds 1929,Jl 15,25:1
Young Nowheres 1929,O 2,28:4
Marriage Playground, The 1929,D 14,22:4
No, No, Nanette 1930,Ja 4,21:1

Lee, John
Dr Crippen 1964,F 15,14:1

Lee, Johnny
Stormy Weather 1943,Jl 22,15:1

Lee, Katherine
Side Show of Life, The 1924,Jl 22,9:1

Lee, Kendall
Sin Takes a Holliday 1930,N 28,23:1
Rain 1932,O 13,22:3
Secrets of the French Police 1932,D 12,18:4
Lady is Willing, The 1934,Ag 11,16:5

Lee, Laura
Top Speed 1930,Ag 30,7:4
Maybe It's Love 1930,O 18,23:2
Going Wild 1931,Ja 26,21:1
Jesse James' Women 1954,S 29,23:4

Lee, Laurie (Screenwriter)
Before the Raid 1944,F 26,10:3

Lee, Leon (Original Author)
Ladies at Ease 1927,O 5,31:1

Lee, Leonard (Original Author)
Bomber's Moon 1943,Jl 31,8:2
Time, The Place And The Girl, The 1946,D 27,14:3
Fat Man, The 1951,My 25,31:2

Lee, Leonard (Screenwriter)
Sinner Take All 1937,F 3,27:1
Espionage 1937,Mr 9,27:3
Beg, Borrow or Steal 1937,D 10,33:2
Street of Missing Men 1939,Je 1,31:3
Adventure in Diamonds 1940,Ap 4,27:2
Chocolate Soldier, The 1941,N 1,20:2
Pursuit to Algiers 1945,O 27,12:2
This Love of Ours 1945,N 1,20:2

Dressed to Kill 1946,My 25,12:4
Whispering City 1948,My 10,25:5
Spy Hunt 1950,S 8,25:2
Wyoming Mail 1950,O 23,26:5
Smuggler's Island 1951,My 24,47:2
Fat Man, The 1951,My 25,31:2
Glass Web, The 1953,N 12,37:5
Never Say Goodbye 1956,Ap 14,20:1

Lee, Lester (Composer)
Slightly French 1949,My 27,25:3
Double Crossbones 1951,Ap 27,19:2
Three for the Show 1955,F 25,16:1

Lee, Lila
Cruise of the Make-Believe, The 1918,S 2,7:1
Such a Little Pirate 1918,O 7,11:3
Lottery Man, The 1919,N 17,20:1
Hawthorne of the U.S.A. 1919,N 17,20:1
Male and Female 1919,N 24,13:1
Midsummer Madness 1920,D 6,19:1
Easy Road, The 1921,F 20,VI,2:2 (In Addenda)
One Glorious Day 1922,Ja 30,16:2
Is Matrimony a Failure 1922,Ap 17,22:3
Dictator, The 1922,Jl 3,8:6
Blood and Sand 1922,Ag 7,14:2
Ghost Breaker, The 1922,S 11,20:2
Ebb Tide 1922,N 20,21:3
Back Home and Broke 1922,D 25,21:1
Ne'er Do-Well, The 1923,My 1,24:3
Homeward Bound 1923,Jl 31,12:4
Woman Proof 1923,O 30,16:1
Love's Whirlpool 1924,Mr 11,16:2
Coming Through 1925,F 18,17:3
Old Home Week 1925,My 25,21:3
Broken Hearts 1926,Mr 3,26:1
New Klondike, The 1926,Mr 22,16:1
United States Smith 1928,Jl 24,13:3
Just Married 1928,Ag 13,23:2
Queen of the Night Clubs 1929,Mr 18,30:6
Honky Tonk 1929,Je 5,32:3
Drag 1929,Je 21,17:2
Argyle Case, The 1929,Ag 31,13:4
Flight 1929,S 14,17:1
Love, Live and Laugh 1929,N 2,14:6
Show of Shows 1929,N 21,24:5
Sacred Flame, The 1929,N 23,18:5
Second Wife 1930,F 10,20:4
Murder Will Out 1930,Ap 14,24:2
Double Cross Roads 1930,Ap 29,31:1
Unholy Three, The 1930,Jl 5,17:4
Those Who Dance 1930,Jl 7,22:3
Gorilla, The 1931,F 23,20:3
Woman Hungry 1931,Mr 23,24:7
Radio Patrol 1932,Jl 14,24:2
War Correspondent 1932,Ag 13,18:6
Night of June 13th, The 1932,S 17,18:4
False Faces 1932,N 25,19:2
Iron Master, The 1933,F 4,11:3
Face in the Sky 1933,F 20,11:5
Whirlpool 1934,My 5,22:3
In Love With Life 1934,My 12,12:3
People's Enemy, The 1935,Ap 30,13:7
Ex-Mrs Bradford, The 1936,My 28,19:2

Lee, Lily
Fight to the Last 1938,D 22,25:3

Lee, Lisa
Blue Murder at St Trinian's 1958,My 27,27:1

Lee, Lora
Holiday Inn 1942,Ag 5,16:1

Lee, Manfred (Original Author)
Closed Gates 1927,Je 1,25:2

Lee, Margaret
Casanova 1965,Jl 21,43:1
Bang, Bang, You're Dead 1967,Ja 19,41:2
Violent Four, The 1968,Ag 15,46:2

Lee, Margaret (Original Author)
Ever Since Eve 1937,Je 25,25:2

Lee, Mary
Melody Ranch 1940,D 26,23:3

Lee, May
Rose Tattoo, The 1955,D 13,55:1

Lee, Michele
How to Succeed in Business Without Really Trying 1967,Mr 10,30:1

Lee, Nancy
Second to Hell 1959,Jl 18,6:3

Lee, Norman (Director)
Bulldog Drummond at Bay 1937,O 25,23:2
Kathleen 1938,Ja 24,17:1

Lee, Owen
Chasing Rainbows 1930,F 22,13:1

Lee, Palmer
Francis Goes to West Point 1952,Ag 23,10:2
Raiders, The 1952,D 13,19:2
Redhead From Wyoming, The 1953,Ja 9,17:4
Veils of Bagdad, The 1953,N 27,99:9

Lee, Pami
Move Over Darling 1963,D 26,33:1

Lee, Peggy
Mr Music 1950,D 21,34:3
Jazz Singer, The 1953,Ja 14,27:3
Pete Kelly's Blues 1955,Ag 19,10:1

Lee, Peggy (Composer)
Jazz Singer, The 1953,Ja 14,27:3
Lady and the Tramp 1955,Je 24,17:1
Tom Thumb 1958,D 24,00:0

Lee, Pinky
Lady of Burlesque 1943,My 14,17:2
Earl Carroll Vanities 1945,Ap 2,15:6

Lee, Raymond
Long Live the King 1923,D 4,24:1
Bread 1924,Jl 21,14:4

Lee, Robert
World of Suzie Wong, The 1960,N 11,36:1
Satan Never Sleeps 1962,F 22,20:1

Lee, Robert (Miscellaneous)
Great Gabbo, The 1929,S 13,33:1

Lee, Robert E (Miscellaneous)
Auntie Mame 1958,D 5,39:1

Lee, Robert E (Original Author)
Inherit the Wind 1960,O 13,41:1

Lee, Robert N (Original Author)
Mighty, The 1929,D 30,16:4
From Headquarters 1933,N 17,22:4
Captain Kidd 1945,N 23,26:3

Lee, Robert N (Screenwriter)
While the Patient Slept 1935,Mr 2,18:2
Armored Car 1937,Jl 26,15:2
Dark Sands 1938,Ag 17,23:4
Tower of London 1939,D 12,37:2

Lee, Robert W
Peking Express 1951,Jl 19,20:2

Lee, Rohama (Original Author)
Tonight We Raid Calais 1943,Ap 15,20:2

Lee, Roland
Woman in the Suitcase, The 1920,Ja 12,7:1

Lee, Rowland V (Director)
Dust Flower, The 1922,Jl 3,8:6
Man Without a Country, The 1925,F 12,16:1
Whirlwind of Youth, The 1927,Je 6,27:2
Barbed Wire 1927,Ag 8,10:3
Secret Hour, The 1928,Mr 12,26:1
Doomsday 1928,Ap 2,25:1
Three Sinners 1928,Ap 23,20:2
First Kiss, The 1928,Ag 20,21:3
Wolf of Wall Street, The 1929,Ja 28,21:1
Dangerous Woman, A 1929,My 20,22:6
New Adventures of Dr Fu Manchu, The 1930,My 3,23:1
Ladies Love Brutes 1930,My 16,20:4
Derelict 1930,N 22,21:3
Ruling Voice, The 1931,N 5,29:3
Guilty Generation, The 1931,N 21,20:4
Zoo in Budapest 1933,Ap 28,15:2
I Am Suzanne 1934,Ja 19,24:3
Count of Monte Cristo, The 1934,S 27,25:2
Gambling 1934,D 4,22:3
Cardinal Richelieu 1935,Ap 19,24:2
Three Musketeers, The 1935,N 1,25:1
One Rainy Afternoon 1936,My 14,29:2
Love From a Stranger 1937,Ap 19,27:2
Toast of New York, The 1937,Jl 23,16:2
Mother Carey's Chickens 1938,Ag 5,11:1
Service de Luxe 1938,O 24,13:2
Son of Frankenstein 1939,Ja 30,9:2
Sun Never Sets, The 1939,Je 9,26:2
Tower of London 1939,D 12,37:2
Son of Monte Cristo, The 1940,D 5,33:1
Powder Town 1942,Je 8,11:2
Bridge of San Luis Rey, The 1944,Mr 4,11:1
Captain Kidd 1945,N 23,26:3

Lee, Rowland V (Original Author)
Ruling Voice, The 1931,N 5,29:3
I Am Suzanne 1934,Ja 19,24:3

Lee, Rowland V (Producer)
Service de Luxe 1938,O 24,13:2
Son of Frankenstein 1939,Ja 30,9:2
Sun Never Sets, The 1939,Je 9,26:2
Tower of London 1939,D 12,37:2

Lee, Rowland V (Screenwriter)
Three Musketeers, The 1935,N 1,25:1
Big Fisherman, The 1959,Ag 6,18:1

Lee, Rudy
Skipper Surprised his Wife, The 1950,Je 30,18:2
Something to Live For 1952,Mr 8,11:2

Lee, Russell
Once a Thief 1965,S 9,36:1

Lee, Ruta
Gaby 1956,My 10,26:3
Funny Face 1957,Mr 29,16:1
Witness for the Prosecution 1958,F 7,16:1
Marjorie Morningstar 1958,Ap 25,32:2
Operation Eichmann 1961,My 4,40:7
Sergeants 3 1962,F 12,28:2

Lee, Ruth
Sensations of 1945 1944,Jl 7,13:2
Whirlpool 1950,Ja 14,9:2

Lee, Sammy
Gracie Allen Murder Case, The 1939,Je 8,31:3

Lee, Sammy (Miscellaneous)
Hollywood Revue, The 1929,Ag 15,20:5
New Faces of 1937 1937,Jl 2,25:1

Lee, Samuel
Last Express, The 1938,O 11,24:4

Lee, Senor
Littlest Outlaw, The 1955,D 27,31:1
Lee, Sung
Samurai 1945,Ag 25,7:5
Lee, Sylvan
Cocoanuts, The 1929,My 25,17:3
Lee, Tommy
Sand Pebbles, The 1966,D 21,48:1
Lee, Virginia
Jack and the Beanstalk 1917,Jl 31,7:2
D O A 1950,My 1,18:2
Lee, Waveney
Touch of Larceny, A 1960,Mr 17,28:1
Lee, Weaver
Satan Never Sleeps 1962,F 22,20:1
Lee, Will
Almost Married 1942,Je 5,23:2
Casbah 1948,My 3,27:4
Little Fugitive 1953,O 7,35:1
Lee, William A
Edge of the City 1957,Ja 30,33:2
Lee, Woitried
Great British Train Robbery, The 1967,Ap 6,45:2
Leech, Richard
Lease of Life 1956,F 10,18:1
Third Key, The 1957,Je 3,30:2
Time Without Pity 1957,N 23,11:2
Horse's Mouth, The 1958,N 12,41:1
A Night to Remember 1958,D 17,2:7
Wind Cannot Read, The 1960,Mr 10,36:1
Tunes of Glory 1960,D 21,38:2
Desert Attack 1961,Mr 23,28:1
I Thank a Fool 1962,S 15,15:1
Leech, Steve
Big Country, The 1958,O 2,44:1
Leeds, Andrea
Come and Get It 1936,N 12,31:1
Stage Door 1937,O 8,27:2
Goldwyn Follies, The 1938,F 21,15:1
Letter of Introduction 1938,S 1,17:1
Youth Takes a Fling 1938,O 17,12:1
They Shall Have Music 1939,Jl 26,17:2
Real Glory, The 1939,S 15,26:2
Swanee River 1939,D 30,9:2
Earthbound 1940,Je 7,27:4
Leeds, Herbert I (Director)
Mr Moto in Danger Island 1938,Mr 20,13:3
Island in the Sky 1938,My 14,18:1
Keep Smiling 1938,Ag 10,15:2
Five of a Kind 1938,O 31,12:2
Return of the Cisco Kid, The 1939,Ap 29,13:2
Charlie Chan in City in Darkness 1939,D 18,29:2
Cisco Kid and the Lady, The 1939,D 25,29:2
Romance of the Rio Grande 1940,D 25,33:4
Ride on Vaquero 1941,Ap 19,20:2
Man Who Wouldn't Die, The 1942,Ap 28,25:5
Just off Broadway 1942,Ag 29,18:4
Manila Calling 1942,S 28,13:1
Time to Kill 1942,D 25,15:4
It Shouldn't Happen to a Dog 1946,S 7,11:2
Leeds, Howard
Sherlock Holmes 1932,N 12,20:5
Vanessa: Her Love Story 1935,Ap 13,11:3
Leeds, Lila
Lady in the Lake 1947,Ja 24,18:3
Show-Off, The 1947,Mr 20,38:2
Moonrise 1949,Mr 7,17:2
She Shoulda Said No 1957,Ja 31,21:1
Leeds, Peter
Treat 'Em Rough 1942,Ja 19,21:3
Ma and Pa Kettle Back on the Farm
1951,My 11,32:3
Frogmen, The 1951,Je 30,8:6
Last Time I saw Paris, The 1954,N 19,20:2
Tight Spot 1955,Mr 19,11:7
Interrupted Melody 1955,My 6,18:1
Love Me or Leave Me 1955,My 27,14:1
I'll Cry Tomorrow 1956,Ja 13,18:1
Facts of Life, The 1961,F 11,27:1
Leeds, Thelma
New Faces of 1937 1937,Jl 2,25:1
Toast of New York, The 1937,Jl 23,16:2
Leedy, Glenn
Song of the South 1946,N 28,40:2
Leela
Vagabond, The 1956,Ap 16,30:4
Lees, Hannah (Original Author)
Shadow on the Wall 1950,My 19,31:3
Lees, Paul
Beyond Glory 1948,Ag 4,18:2
Sealed Verdict 1948,N 3,36:2
Sorrowful Jones 1949,Je 6,15:2
Chicago Deadline 1949,N 3,37:2
Captain Carey U S A 1950,Mr 30,40:5
Union Station 1950,O 5,38:3
Copper Canyon 1950,N 16,39:2
Great Missouri Raid, The 1951,Ap 9,31:2
Appointment With Danger 1951,My 10,38:2
Lees, Robert (Original Author)
Hold That Ghost 1941,Ag 8,13:3
No Time for Love 1943,D 2,30:1

Lees, Robert (Screenwriter)
Invisible Woman, The 1941,Ja 9,27:2
Black Cat, The 1941,Ap 26,20:3
Hold That Ghost 1941,Ag 8,13:3
Juke Box Jenny 1942,Ap 17,21:3
Hit the Ice 1943,S 23,27:2
Crazy House 1943,D 16,33:3
Buck Privates Come Home 1947,Ap 12,11:3
Wistful Widow of Wagon Gap, The
1947,N 21,36:2
Abbott and Costello Meet Frankenstein
1948,Jl 29,17:2
Holiday in Havana 1949,O 14,33:5
Abbott and Costello Meet the Invisible Man
1951,Ap 13,18:6
Comin' Round the Mountain 1951,Jl 27,15:2
Jumping Jacks 1952,Jl 24,30:2
Lees, Tamara
Beautiful but Dangerous 1958,F 6,24:1
Leeson, Lois (Original Author)
Bright Lights 1935,Ag 15,15:2
Leet, Marjorie
Big Trail, The 1930,O 25,20:3
Leete, Carole
Man to Remember, A 1938,N 7,23:2
Leewood, Jack (Director)
20,000 Eyes 1961,Je 19,30:1
Leewood, Jack (Producer)
Young Jesse James 1960,Ag 25,25:1
20,000 Eyes 1961,Je 19,30:1
Swingin' Along 1962,Ag 27,18:1
We'll Bury You 1962,O 25,48:3
LeFanu, Joseph Sheridan (Original Author)
Inheritance, The 1951,F 12,19:2
Blood and Roses 1961,O 12,41:4
Lefaur, Andre
Bal, Le 1932,S 28,22:5
With a Smile 1939,F 6,8:4
King, The 1941,O 23,29:3
Nine Bachelors 1942,F 9,19:2
32 Rue de Montmartre 1944,S 28,26:3
Lefebre, Hans
Martin Luther 1953,S 10,22:1
Lefebure, Annie
Army Game, The; Tire Au Flanc
1963,Ap 24,40:1
Lefebvre, Jean
And God Created Woman 1957,O 22,41:1
Back to the Wall; (Dos au Mur) 1959,S 8,43:2
Port of Desire 1960,N 3,49:2
Gigot 1962,S 28,26:1
Lefebvre, Rene
Million, Le 1931,My 21,33:2
Million, The 1931,Jl 19,VIII,4:3
Jean de la Lune 1932,Mr 12,19:5
Sous la Lune du Maroc 1933,Ja 23,9:2
Lefebvre, Rolf
Count Five and Die 1958,My 15,25:1
Happy is the Bride 1959,Je 30,27:2
Lefebvre, Yves
Marriage Came Tumbling Down, The
1968,N 6,32:3
Lefeuvre, Guy
Bonnie Prince Charlie 1952,Ja 7,14:3
Lefevre
Atalante, L' 1947,Je 23,14:5
Lefevre, Pierre
Martin Luther 1953,S 10,22:1
Lefevre, Rene
Musiciens du Ciel 1945,Mr 1,26:6
They Are not Angels 1948,My 22,8:3
He Who Must Die 1958,D 29,21:1
Doulos-The Finger Man 1964,Mr 3,31:1
Crime of Monsieur Lange, The 1964,Ap 4,15:5
Lefevre, Rene (Original Author)
Musiciens du Ciel 1945,Mr 1,26:6
Rue de Paris 1960,D 23,14:3
Lefevre, Rene (Screenwriter)
Musiciens du Ciel 1945,Mr 1,26:6
Under the Paris Sky 1952,My 6,35:1
Lefferty, Jean
Matinee Ladies 1927,Ap 13,29:4
Lefondal, Henri
Big Sky, The 1952,Ag 20,21:1
Lefour, Andre
Entente Cordiale 1939,D 26,23:2
LeFranc, Guy (Director)
Dr Knock 1955,O 10,31:2
LeFranc, Guy (Screenwriter)
Dr Knock 1955,O 10,31:2
Lefranc, Guy (Screenwriter)
Elusive Corporal, The 1963,F 19,5:1
Leftwich, Alexander
Swing It, Sailor 1937,D 13,23:5
Juarez 1939,Ap 26,27:1
Legaffre, Roland
Adulteress, The 1958,Ja 14,42:1
Legal, Ernst
Kater Lampe 1938,Ap 23,19:3
Unsterbliche Herz, Das; Immortal Heart, The
1939,O 21,12:2
Marriage of Figaro 1950,N 3,31:2

Legare, Ovila
Thirteenth Letter, The 1951,F 22,27:2
I Confess 1953,Mr 23,28:2
Luck of Ginger Coffey, The 1964,S 22,44:1
Legay, Gilbert
Student Prince, The 1954,Je 16,18:2
Lege, Reg
Wrong Arm of the Law, The 1963,Ap 3,39:1
Leger, Fernand (Miscellaneous)
New Enchantment, The 1926,Mr 15,18:3
Dreams that Money can Buy 1948,Ap 24,11:2
Leger, Lucy
Open Road, The 1940,O 5,20:2
Legeshin, Vladimir (Director)
Military Secret 1945,Ag 2,16:2
Legg, Stuart (Miscellaneous)
Queen in Australia, The 1954,Je 16,37:3
Legg, Stuart (Producer)
Monkey Into Man 1941,My 31,14:1
Legg, Stuart (Screenwriter)
World in Action 1945,Jl 1,II,3:1
Now the Peace; World in Action 1945,Jl 1,II,3:1
War Clouds in the Pacific; World in Action
1945,Jl 11,3:1
Leggatt, Alison
This Happy Breed 1947,Ap 14,24:2
Waterloo Road 1948,D 25,10:3
Encore (The Ant and the Grasshopper); Ant and
the Grasshopper, The (Encore) 1952,Ap 3,45:1
Promoter, The 1952,O 29,36:2
Touch and go 1956,Mr 20,13:2
Day of the Triffids 1963,My 11,15:2
One Way Pendulum 1965,Mr 3,34:3
LeGlay, Maurice (Original Author)
Itto 1936,Ja 29,15:5
Legoff, Jean
Abysses, Les 1964,N 24,44:1
Legoshin, V (Director)
Pesnya O Stchasti 1935,Ap 8,23:4
Lonely White Sail 1938,My 7,18:1
Legoshin, Vladimir (Director)
Military Secret 1945,Ag 2,16:2
Legouve, Ernest (Original Author)
Devil May Care 1929,D 23,18:2
Legrand, Georges (Producer)
Ruy Blas 1948,O 4,14:2
Wench, The 1949,Mr 14,15:5
Legrand, H Andre (Screenwriter)
Kreutzer Sonata, The 1938,D 20,30:2
Shop-Girls of Paris; Au Bonheur de Dames
1947,Je 23,14:4
Symphonie Fantastique, La 1947,D 8,35:2
Forbidden Love 1948,Ag 26,16:4
Secret Document-Vienna 1954,Mr 29,22:4
Miracle of Saint Therese 1959,F 10,38:4 (In
Addenda)
Legrand, Martha
Games Men Play, The 1968,Mr 15,30:1
Legrand, Michel
Cleo From 5 to 7 1962,S 5,43:4
Legrand, Michel (Composer)
Umbrellas of Cherbourg, The; Parpapluis de
Cherbourg, Les 1964,D 17,50:1
Le Joli Mai 1966,Je 10,54:2
LeGrand, Richard
Gildersleeve's Bad Day 1943,Je 11,23:1
Legrange, Jacques (Screenwriter)
My Uncle 1958,N 4,30:2
Legras, Jacques
Belle Americaine, La 1961,D 18,42:1
Legris, Roger
Song of the Street 1939,S 5,21:2
Port of Shadows 1939,O 30,13:2
Dame de Pique, La 1944,O 19,19:2
Three Hours 1944,O 30,16:5
Lehar, Franz (Composer)
Friederike 1933,F 27,11:3
Noches de Gloria; Glorious Nights
1938,Ap 23,19:3
Merry Widow, The 1952,S 25,38:1
Lehar, Franz (Miscellaneous)
Merry Widow, The 1934,O 12,33:1
Lehar, Franz (Original Author)
Rogue Song, The 1930,Ja 29,26:4
World's in Love, The 1937,My 19,27:2
Lehman, Claude
Ordonnance, L'; Orderly, The 1935,Jl 1,22:3
Dark Eyes 1938,Ap 19,24:5
Friend Will come Tonight, A; Ami Viendra Ce
Soir, Un 1948,Jl 12,11:2
Lehman, Ernest (Original Author)
Sweet Smell of Success 1957,Je 28,29:2
Lehman, Ernest (Producer)
Who's Afraid of Virginia Woolf? 1966,Je 30,28:1
Lehman, Ernest (Screenwriter)
Executive Suite 1954,My 7,19:1
Sabrina 1954,S 23,43:2
King and I, The 1956,Je 29,15:6
Somebody up There Likes Me 1956,Jl 6,16:1
Sweet Smell of Success 1957,Je 28,29:2
North by Northwest 1959,Ag 7,28:1
From the Terrace 1960,Jl 16,10:1
West Side Story 1961,O 19,39:3

Lehman, Ernest (Screenwriter) — Cont
Prize, The 1964,Ja 24,21:1
Sound of Music, The 1965,Mr 3,34:1
Who's Afraid of Virginia Woolf? 1966,Je 30,28:1
Who's Afraid of Virginia Woolf? 1966,Jl 10,II,1:5
Lehman, Gladys (Original Author)
There's That Woman Again 1939,Ja 6,25:4
Lehman, Gladys (Screenwriter)
Out all Night 1927,S 27,31:1
Red Hot Speed 1929,F 5,26:3
Enter Madame 1935,Ja 12,12:1
County Chairman, The 1935,Ja 19,8:1
Old Kentucky, In 1935,N 29,24:1
Captain January 1936,Ap 25,21:1
Poor Little Rich Girl, The 1936,Je 26,16:1
Reunion 1936,N 27,27:1
Slave Ship 1937,Je 17,19:2
Midnight Madonna 1937,Jl 17,18:1
She Married an Artist 1938,F 25,15:2
There's Always a Woman 1938,Ap 29,17:2
Good Girls Go to Paris 1939,Je 23,23:1
Those High Grey Walls 1939,O 19,27:2
Hired Wife 1940,S 14,11:2
Nice Girl 1941,Mr 27,29:6
Rio Rita 1942,My 8,27:3
Presenting Lily Mars 1943,Ap 30,25:3
Two Girls and a Sailor 1944,Je 15,16:1
Thrill of a Romance 1945,My 25,22:2
Her Highness and the Bellboy 1945,S 28,16:2
This Time for Keeps 1947,D 5,33:4
Luxury Liner 1948,S 10,19:2
Golden Girl 1951,N 21,20:3
Lehman, Leo
Troublemaker, The 1964,Je 23,25:1
Lehman, Milton (Original Author)
Killer That Stalked New York, The
  1951,Ja 5,17:2
LEHMANN
See Also LEHMAN
Lehmann, Beatrix
Passing of the Third Floor Back, The
  1936,Ap 29,19:2
Strangers on a Honeymoon 1937,Mr 13,23:2
Rat, The 1938,F 28,19:1
Key, The 1958,Jl 2,23:3
Psyche 39 1964,Ap 30,30:1
Spy Who Came in From the Cold, The
  1965,D 24,24:1
Lehmann, Carla
Flying Fortress 1942,D 19,22:2
Candlelight in Algeria 1944,Jl 31,10:2
Facts of Love, The 1949,O 31,20:2
Fame Is the Spur 1948,N 8,34:2
Lehmann, Fritz
Unsterblicher Walzer; Immortal Waltz
  1939,N 18,22:6
Lehmann, Lotte
Big City 1948,My 17,23:3
Lehmann, Maurice (Director)
Courier of Lyons, The 1938,Je 3,17:1
Fric-Frac 1948,My 29,8:6
Lehmann, Maurice (Producer)
Pasteur 1936,Ja 30,14:3
Fric-Frac 1948,My 29,8:6
Lehmann, Siegfried Dr (Director)
Tomorrow's a Wonderful Day 1949,Ap 11,29:4
Lehmann, Walter (Producer)
Merry Wives of Windsor, The 1952,S 22,19:2
Lehotay, Arpad
Tokaji Rapszodia 1938,N 7,23:5
Tiszavirag; Flower of the Tisza 1939,D 30,9:3
Vadroza; Wild Rose 1940,Ja 29,11:6
Oeroek Titok, Az; Eternal Secret, The
  1940,Mr 9,19:3
Treasured Earth 1950,D 14,51:3
Lehr, Anna
Yellow Ticket, The 1918,My 27,11:3
Laughing Bill Hyde 1918,S 23,7:1
Ruggles of Red Gap 1923,S 10,15:4
Lehr, Lew (Miscellaneous)
First World War, The 1934,N 8,27:1
Baboona 1935,Ja 23,21:2
Lehr, Lew (Narrator)
Borneo 1937,S 4,8:3
Lehrer, Shifra
God, Man and Devil 1950,Ja 23,16:2
Lehrman, Henry (Director)
Reported Missing 1922,Ap 24,18:3
Why Sailors Go Wrong 1928,Ap 9,18:2
Chicken a la King 1928,Je 11,27:1
Lehrman, Henry (Miscellaneous)
Show Them no Mercy 1935,D 9,25:2
Lehrman, Henry (Screenwriter)
Reported Missing 1922,Ap 24,18:3
Lei, Chao
Empress Wu 1965,Mr 16,42:2
Leibelt, Hans
Morgenrot 1933,My 16,15:2
Freundin Eines Grossen Mannes, Die
  1934,S 11,24:5
Toerichte Jungfrau, Die 1935,S 9,24:3
Hoehere Befehl, Der 1936,Mr 31,17:3
Thunder, Lightening and Sunshine
  1937,N 13,11:2

Meadehen von Gestern Nacht, Das; Girl of Last
  Night, The 1938,Je 18,18:2
Razzia 1948,Je 14,19:2
Marriage in the Shadows 1948,S 17,28:3
Palace Scandal 1949,Je 6,15:5
Somewhere in Berlin 1949,Ag 16,19:3
Leibeneiner, Wolfgang
Freut Euch des Lebens 1934,N 3,20:3
Liebelei 1936,F 28,18:2
Leiber, Fritz
Cleopatra 1917,O 15,11:2
If I Were King 1920,Ag 10,10:3
Queen of Sheba 1921,Ap 11,9:1
Tale of Two Cities, A 1935,D 26,21:2
Story of Louis Pasteur, The 1936,F 10,15:1
Under Two Flags 1936,My 1,19:1
Sins of Man 1936,Je 19,17:2
Down Under the Sea 1936,Ag 10,10:2
Anthony Adverse 1936,Ag 27,16:1
Champagne Waltz 1937,F 4,17:2
Prince and the Pauper, The 1937,My 6,23:1
Great Garrick, The 1937,O 25,23:1
Flight Into Nowhere 1938,My 2,13:3
Gateway 1938,Ag 8,9:2
They Made Her a Spy 1939,Mr 29,21:4
Nurse Edith Cavell 1939,S 22,27:4
Pack up Your Troubles 1939,O 27,27:2
Hunchback of Notre Dame, The 1940,Ja 1,29:2
All This and Heaven, Too 1940,Jl 5,10:2
Sea Hawk, The 1940,Ag 10,16:2
Lady With red Hair 1940,D 6,28:2
Aloma of the South Seas 1941,Ag 28,23:4
Crossroads 1942,Jl 27,18:2
First Comes Courage 1943,S 3,15:3
Phantom of the Opera, The 1943,O 15,15:2
Cry of the Werewolf, The 1944,Ag 12,16:5
This Love of Ours 1945,N 1,20:2
Spanish Main, The 1945,N 7,20:2
Scandal In Paris, A 1946,S 16,9:7
Angel on my Shoulder 1946,O 21,27:2
Humoresque 1946,D 26,28:1
Web, The 1947,Je 5,32:1
To the Ends of the Earth 1948,F 13,26:2
Adventures of Casanova 1948,Mr 22,18:3
Another Part of the Forest 1948,My 19,30:2
Bride of Vengeance 1949,Ap 7,38:2
Song of India 1949,Je 10,32:3
Bagdad 1949,D 24,11:4
Devil's Doorway 1950,N 10,35:1
Leiber, Fritz (Original Author)
Burn, Witch, Burn 1962,Jl 5,21:2 (In Addenda)
Leiber, Fritz Jr
Camille 1937,Ja 23,13:1
Leiber, Fritz Jr (Original Author)
Weird Woman 1944,Ap 1,11:1
Leibl, Marianne
Steppe, The 1963,O 1,33:1
Leicester, Frederick
Crimson Pirate, The 1952,Ag 28,21:2
Leicester, James (Screenwriter)
Black Shadows 1949,N 7,33:2
River's Edge, The 1957,Ap 12,20:2
From the Earth to the Moon 1958,N 27,52:2
Most Dangerous Man Alive 1961,Jl 5,29:2
Leicester, William
Operation Secret 1952,N 6,37:2
Finger Man 1955,Jl 16,12:4
Beyond a Reasonable Doubt 1956,S 14,27:2
Leidmann, Eva (Screenwriter)
Kreutzer Sonata 1937,Mr 14,XI,4:6 (In Addenda)
Leidtke, Harry
Bohemian Dancer 1928,D 3,30:5 (In Addenda)
Leigh, Adele
Beggar's Opera, The 1953,Ag 25,18:2
Leigh, Andrew
Run for Your Money, A 1950,Ap 10,15:3
Leigh, Frank
Nurse Marjorie 1920,My 24,20:3
One Hour Before Dawn 1920,Jl 12,12:4
Bob Hampton of Placer 1921,My 2,12:1
Ashes of Vengeance 1923,Ag 7,20:2
Rosita 1923,S 4,14:1
Hill Billy, The 1924,Mr 12,19:4
Reckless Age, The 1924,Je 10,24:4
Breath of Scandal, The 1924,N 26,17:3
As Man Desires 1925,F 10,20:1
His Majesty Bunker Bean 1925,S 15,12:1
Flaming Forest, The 1926,N 22,28:3
Soft Cushions 1927,S 12,29:1
Night of Mystery, A 1928,Ap 16,20:5
Ten Nights in a Barroom 1931,F 28,15:2
Woman From Monte Carlo, The 1931,D 31,17:6
Black Swan, The 1942,D 24,18:3
Leigh, Fred W (Composer)
Cover Girl 1944,Mr 31,26:1
Leigh, George
Champagne for Caesar 1950,My 12,33:2
Dial M for Murder 1954,My 29,13:2
Leigh, Janet
Romance of Rosy Ridge, The 1947,S 12,18:3
If Winter Comes 1948,Ja 23,28:4
Hills of Home 1948,N 26,32:2
Words and Music 1948,D 10,34:2

Leigh, Janet — Cont
Act of Violence 1949,Ja 24,16:2
Little Women 1949,Mr 11,33:2
Doctor and the Girl, The 1949,O 31,20:2
That Forsyte Woman 1949,N 11,31:2
Holiday Affair 1949,N 24,48:2
Red Danube, The 1949,D 9,37:3
Strictly Dishonorable 1951,Jl 12,21:6
Angels in the Outfield 1951,O 18,32:1
Two Tickets to Broadway 1951,N 22,47:2
It's a big Country 1952,Ja 9,25:2
Just This Once 1952,Mr 18,22:3
Scaramouche 1952,My 9,20:2
Vikings, The 1952,Je 12,35:2
Naked Spur, The 1953,Mr 26,37:3
Houdini 1953,Jl 3,10:2
Walking my Baby Back Home 1954,Ja 16,10:5
Prince Valiant 1954,Ap 7,40:2
Living It Up 1954,Jl 24,6:6
Rogue Cop 1954,S 18,12:2
Black Shield of Falworth, The 1954,O 7,16:2
Pete Kelly's Blues 1955,Ag 19,10:1
My Sister Eileen 1955,S 23,21:1
Safari 1956,Je 21,35:2
Jet Pilot 1957,O 5,8:6
Touch of Evil 1958,My 22,25:2
Perfect Furlough, The 1959,Ja 22,27:4
Who Was That Lady? 1960,Ap 16,10:1
Psycho 1960,Je 17,37:1
Pepe 1960,D 22,18:1
Manchurian Candidate, The 1962,O 25,48:3
Bye Bye Birdie 1963,Ap 5,27:3
Wives and Lovers 1963,Ag 29,36:1
Kid Rodelo 1966,F 23,46:1
Harper 1966,Mr 31,43:1
3 on a Couch 1966,Jl 7,30:1
American Dream, An 1966,S 1,28:2
Grand Slam 1968,F 21,60:4
Leigh, Julian (Composer)
New Gulliver, The 1935,N 4,24:4
Leigh, Julian (Miscellaneous)
Mayor's Dilemma, The 1940,Ap 23,19:2
Leigh, Nelson
Barbary Pirate 1949,O 28,29:3
First Texan, The 1956,Je 23,20:2
Gunfight at the O K Corral 1957,My 30,23:2
Bombers B-52 1957,N 23,11:2
Gathering of Eagles, A 1963,Jl 11,21:2
Leigh, Rowland (Miscellaneous)
Heartbeat 1946,My 11,22:4
Leigh, Rowland (Screenwriter)
Charge of the Light Brigade, The 1936,N 2,24:1
First Lady 1937,D 23,25:1
Secrets of an Actress 1938,O 8,10:2
Vigil in the Night 1940,Mr 9,19:2
Knickerbocker Holiday 1944,Ap 20,22:7
Summer Storm 1944,O 23,14:3
Master Race, The 1944,N 2,22:1
Tarzan and the Huntress 1947,Ap 7,20:4
Siren of Atlantis 1949,Ag 22,13:1
Her Wonderful Lie 1950,Jl 17,15:2
Leigh, Suzanna
Boeing Boeing 1965,D 24,24:4
Pleasure Girls, The 1966,Ap 21,43:1
Paradise, Hawaiian Style 1966,Je 16,15:3
Deadlier Than the Male 1967,F 22,21:1
Deadly Bees, The 1967,My 20,39:2
Lost Continent, The 1968,Je 20,50:2
Leigh, Vivien
Fire Over England 1937,Mr 5,16:2
Dark Journey 1937,Ag 23,22:1
Yank at Oxford, A 1938,F 25,15:1
Storm in a Teacup 1938,Mr 22,18:4
Gone With the Wind 1939,D 20,31:2
Sidewalks of London 1940,F 15,15:1
Waterloo Bridge 1940,My 17,23:2
21 Days Together 1940,My 23,28:4
That Hamilton Woman 1941,Ap 4,25:1
Caesar and Cleopatra 1944,Jl 16,II,3:4
Caesar and Cleopatra 1946,S 6,18:2
Anna Karenina 1948,Ap 28,32:2
Streetcar Named Desire, A 1951,S 30,27:1
Deep Blue Sea, The 1955,O 13,35:2
Roman Spring of Mrs Stone, The 1961,D 29,11:1
Ship of Fools 1965,Jl 29,18:1
Gone With the Wind 1967,O 11,41:1
Leigh, Walter (Composer)
Song of Ceylon 1937,Ag 16,15:1
Leigh-Fermor, Patrick (Screenwriter)
Roots of Heaven, The 1958,O 16,46:1
Leigh-Hunt, Barbara
Midsummer Night's Dream, A 1961,D 19,39:1
Leigh-Hunt, Ronald
Oscar Wilde 1960,Je 21,28:2
Leighton, Donrue
Oh, Doctor 1937,Je 19,20:3
Leighton, Frank
It's in the Air 1940,D 10,33:2
Leighton, Isabel (Original Author)
Fight for Your Lady 1937,N 20,21:2
Leighton, Lillian
Ruggles of Red Gap 1923,S 10,15:4
Call of the Canyon, The 1923,D 17,23:1
Bedroom Window, The 1924,Je 9,14:3

Leighton, Lillian — Cont

Contraband 1925,Mr 24,20:6
Code of the West 1925,Ap 13,24:1
In the Name of Love 1925,Ag 27,14:1
Go Straight 1925,O 6,30:1
Tumbleweeds 1925,D 21,27:2
Ibanez's Torrent 1926,F 22,14:1
Lovers 1927,Ap 19,24:4
Fair Co-ed, The 1927,O 24,24:3
Feet First 1930,O 31,20:1
Subway Express 1931,My 2,23:4
Sweepstakes 1931,Je 25,23:5
Whipsaw 1936,Ja 25,18:4

Leighton, Margaret

Under Capricorn 1949,S 9,28:3
Astonished Heart, The 1950,F 15,23:2
Winslow Boy, The 1950,Je 7,34:4
Bonnie Prince Charlie 1952,Ja 7,14:3
Murder on Monday 1953,O 7,35:2
Holly and the Ivy, The 1954,F 5,16:1
Fighting Pimpernel, The 1954,Ap 19,19:1
Court Martial 1955,Ag 2,17:1
Teckman Mystery, The 1955,Ag 22,18:2
Constant Husband, The 1955,N 7,55:1
Constant Husband, The 1957,Jl 26,10:3
Novel Affair, A 1957,Ag 28,22:1
Sound and the Fury, The 1959,Mr 28,11:1
Waltz of the Toreadors 1962,Ag 14,34:1
Best Man, The 1964,Ap 7,29:1
Loved One, The 1965,O 12,57:1
7 Women 1966,My 5,59:1

Leighton, Michael (Original Author)

Appointment With Crime 1951,F 19,19:3

Leila

From Russia with Love 1964,Ap 9,25:1

Leiler, Lou (Director)

Su Ultimo Amor 1933,Ag 19,14:5

Leinster, Murray (Original Author)

Murder Will Out 1930,Ap 14,24:2
Torchy Blane in Chinatown 1939,F 3,13:2

Leipnitz, Harald

That Woman 1968,Jl 19,30:3

Leisen, Mitchell

Hold Back the Dawn 1941,O 2,29:1

Leisen, Mitchell (Director)

Cradle Song 1933,N 20,18:2
Death Takes a Holiday 1934,F 24,18:4
Murder at the Vanities 1934,My 21,20:2
Behold My Wife 1935,F 18,19:3
Four Hours to Kill 1935,Ap 11,27:3
Hands Across the Table 1935,N 2,13:2
13 Hours by Air 1936,Ap 30,17:2
Big Broadcast of 1937, The 1936,O 22,31:1
Swing High, Swing Low 1937,Ap 15,19:1
Easy Living 1937,Jl 8,20:1
Big Broadcast of 1938, The 1938,Mr 10,16:2
Artists and Models Abroad 1938,D 22,25:3
Midnight 1939,Ap 6,31:1
Remember the Night 1940,Ja 18,27:2
Arise my Love 1940,O 17,33:2
I Wanted Wings 1941,Mr 27,29:4
Hold Back the Dawn 1941,O 2,29:1
Lady is Willing, The 1942,Ap 24,21:2
Take a Letter Darling 1942,My 28,13:2
No Time for Love 1943,D 2,30:1
Lady in the Dark 1944,F 23,17:1
Frenchman's Creek 1944,S 21,26:2
Practically Yours 1945,Mr 29,18:2
Masquerade in Mexico 1945,N 29,27:2
Kitty 1946,Ap 1,23:1
To Each his Own 1946,My 24,15:2
Suddenly It's Spring 1947,F 27,26:2
Golden Earrings 1947,D 4,41:3
Dream Girl 1948,Je 17,29:2
Bride of Vengeance 1949,Ap 7,38:2
Captain Carey U S A 1950,Mr 30,40:5
No Man of her Own 1950,My 4,32:3
Mating Season, The 1951,Ap 12,41:2
Darling, How Could You! 1951,N 9,22:4
Young Man With Ideas 1952,Je 7,22:6
Tonight We Sing 1953,F 13,17:2
Bedevilled 1955,Ap 23,23:1
Girl Most Likely, The 1958,O 9,47:1
Spree 1967,N 30,59:2

Leisen, Mitchell (Producer)

No Time for Love 1943,D 2,30:1
Practically Yours 1945,Mr 29,18:2
Kitty 1946,Ap 1,23:1
Flame and the Fire 1966,Mr 29,37:1
Round Trip 1967,Jl 20,30:2

Leiser, Erwin (Miscellaneous)

Mein Kampf 1961,Ap 22,18:1

Leiser, Erwin (Screenwriter)

Mein Kampf 1961,Ap 22,18:1

Leister, Frederick

Dreyfus Case, The 1931,Ag 31,11:5
Iron Duke, The 1935,Ja 25,27:2
King Solomon's Mines 1937,Jl 3,18:1
Dinner at the Ritz 1937,D 4,21:1
Sixty Glorious Years 1938,N 18,25:2
Goodbye Mr Chips 1939,My 16,27:2
Outsider, The 1940,Mr 18,13:2
Mozart 1940,O 4,29:2
Prime Minister, The 1942,F 4,23:2

Next of Kin 1943,My 6,25:2
Randolph Family 1945,Mr 13,19:4
Captive Heart, The 1947,Ap 28,27:2
So Well Remembered 1947,N 5,34:3
Escape 1948,Ag 16,12:2
Quartet (The Kite); Kite, The (Quartet)
    1949,Mr 29,30:3
Agitator, The 1949,Ag 19,12:5
Mrs Fitzherbert 1950,My 11,37:2
For Them that Trespass 1950,S 27,37:2
Landfall 1953,My 11,25:2
End of the Affair, The 1955,Ap 29,28:2

Leitgeb, Willey

William Tell 1925,My 20,26:2

Leith, Virginia

Fear and Desire 1953,Ap 1,35:2
Black Widow 1954,O 28,46:6
Violent Saturday 1955,My 12,32:2
On the Threshold of Space 1956,Mr 30,10:5
Toward the Unknown 1956,S 28,24:4

Leitner, Hermann (Director)

Mediterannean Holiday 1964,D 16,51:1

Leitzbach, Adeline (Screenwriter)

Success 1923,Jl 10,22:5

Leiviush, Zalman

My Father's House 1947,S 26,28:3

Lejdey, E

Frigid Sea, The 1955,N 21,23:4

Lejtes, Jozef

Krawa Roza; Red Rose 1938,O 13,29:2

Lejtes, Jozef (Director)

Mlody Las 1935,D 3,32:7
Love or a Kingdom 1937,D 4,21:1
Dziewczeta z Nowolipek; Girls of Nowolipek
    1938,N 25,19:2
Kosciuszki 1938,D 27,13:2

Lekain, Tony (Producer)

Collier de la Reine, Le; Queen's Necklace, The
    1929,D 8,X,7:1

Leland, David

Hour Before the Dawn, The 1944,My 11,25:6
Nothing but Trouble 1945,Mr 10,14:1

Leland, Fiona

It Happened Here 1966,Ag 9,29:2

Lele, Indu

Householder, The 1963,O 22,43:2

Lella

Khartoum 1966,Jl 14,28:1

Lellie, Dudley (Screenwriter)

River of Unrest 1937,N 27,21:2

Lelouch, Claude (Director)

Man and a Woman, A; Homme et une Femme,
    Un 1966,Jl 13,35:1
To be a Crook 1967,F 7,33:2
Live for Life 1967,D 19,59:1
Far From Vietnam 1968,Je 7,32:1

Lelouch, Claude (Narrator)

Far from Vietnam 1967,O 2,58:1

Lelouch, Claude (Screenwriter)

Man and a Woman, A; Homme et une Femme,
    Un 1966,Jl 13,35:1
To be a Crook 1967,F 7,33:2
Live for Life 1967,D 19,59:1

Lemac, Karl (Director)

Landstreicher, Die; Hoboes, The 1938,N 26,18:1

Lemaine, Charlotte (Miscellaneous)

High Sign, The 1922,Mr 20,10:3

Lemaire, Martine

Diary of a Country Priest 1954,Ap 6,35:2

Lemaire, Philippe

Singing Taxi Driver 1953,My 16,10:1
Strange Deception 1953,My 27,28:2
Naked Heart, The 1955,Mr 9,22:4
Tempest in the Flesh 1957,Ja 19,12:2
Fire Under Her Skin 1958,Je 28,13:6
Cartouche 1964,Jl 22,39:1
Vice and Virtue 1965,Mr 18,25:1

Lemaitre, Jean

Love Is a Ball 1963,Ap 25,38:1

Leman, Juda (Director)

Land of Promise, The 1935,N 21,27:2

Lemarde, Goffredo (Producer)

Four Days of Naples, The 1963,Mr 20,5:1

LeMay, Alan (Director)

High Lonesome 1950,D 8,40:4

LeMay, Alan (Original Author)

Along Came Jones 1945,Jl 19,8:7
Rocky Mountain 1950,N 4,13:2
Flight Nurse 1954,Ja 30,9:6
Searchers, The 1956,My 31,21:4
Unforgiven, The 1960,Ap 7,46:1

LeMay, Alan (Producer)

Sundowners, The 1950,My 5,17:2
Quebec 1951,Mr 16,34:2

LeMay, Alan (Screenwriter)

North West Mounted Police 1940,N 7,33:2
Reap the Wild Wind 1942,Mr 27,27:2
Adventures of Mark Twain, The 1944,My 4,25:5
Story of Dr Wassell, The 1944,Je 7,13:2
San Antonio 1945,D 29,19:5
Cheyenne 1947,Je 7,9:2

LeMay, Alan (Screenwriter) — Cont

Gunfighters 1947,Jl 25,12:5
Tap Roots 1948,Ag 26,16:3
Sundowners, The 1950,My 5,17:2
Rocky Mountain 1950,N 4,13:2
High Lonesome 1950,D 8,40:4
Quebec 1951,Mr 16,34:2
Dream of Jeanie, I 1952,Je 26,26:2
Blackbeard the Pirate 1952,D 26,20:3

LeMay, Howard

Teenage Mother 1968,S 19,62:4

Lembach, Hedde

S A Mann Brand 1934,My 28,16:2

Lembeck, Harvey

U S S Teakettle 1951,F 24,11:2
Frogmen, The 1951,Je 30,8:6
Just Across the Street 1952,Je 28,12:4
Girls in the Night 1953,Ja 16,19:3
Stalag 17 1953,Jl 2,19:2
Mission Over Korea 1953,S 19,7:2
Command, The 1954,Ja 16,10:5
Between Heaven and Hell 1956,O 12,33:2
Last Time I Saw Archie, The 1961,My 29,9:6
View From the Bridge, A 1962,Ja 23,36:1
Sail a Crooked Ship 1962,F 3,12:6
Beach Party 1963,S 26,40:2
Love With the Proper Stranger 1963,D 26,33:1
Unsinkable Molly Brown, The 1964,Jl 17,15:1
Fireball 500 1966,N 24,65:4

Lembessl, Koula

Astero 1960,Ap 25,32:2

Lemeshev, Sergei

Moscow Music Hall 1946,S 9,20:1

Lemetayer, Huguette

Thirst of Men, The 1952,O 28,37:1

Lemkow, Tutte

Captain's Paradise, The 1953,S 29,25:5
I Am a Camera 1955,Ag 9,29:1
Guns of Navarone, The 1961,Je 23,19:1
Victors, The 1963,D 20,21:2

Lemmon, Jack

It Should Happen to You 1954,Ja 16,10:5
Phffft 1954,N 11,43:2
Three for the Show 1955,F 25,16:1
Mister Roberts 1955,Jl 15,14:1
My Sister Eileen 1955,S 23,21:1
Fire Down Below 1957,Ag 9,11:2
Operation Mad Ball 1957,N 21,38:1
Cowboy 1958,F 20,29:5
Bell, Book and Candle 1958,D 27,2:7
Some Like It Hot 1959,Mr 30,23:1
It Happened to Jane 1959,Ag 6,18:3
Apartment, The 1960,Je 16,37:2
Pepe 1960,D 22,18:1
Wackiest Ship in the Army, The 1961,F 9,36:1
Notorious Landlady, The 1962,Jl 27,15:2
Days of Wine and Roses 1963,Ja 18,7:2
Irma la Douce 1963,Je 6,39:1
Under the Yum Yum Tree 1963,N 21,43:2
Good Neighbor Sam 1964,Jl 23,19:1
How to Murder Your Wife 1965,Ja 27,26:1
Great Race, The 1965,S 16,00:0
Fortune Cookie, The 1966,O 20,52:1
Luv 1967,Jl 27,29:1
Odd Couple, The 1968,My 3,42:1

Lemmon, Jack (Narrator)

Stowaway in the Sky 1962,Je 19,28:1

Lemnitz, Tiana

Marriage of Figaro 1950,N 3,31:2

Lemoine, Michele

Testament of Orpheus 1962,Ap 10,48:1

Lemonnier, Meg

Il est Charmant; He is Charming
    1932,Mr 27,VIII,6:2
Il est Charmant 1932,Ap 9,18:1
Soir de Reveillon 1935,Ja 19,8:2
Green Glove, The 1952,Ap 24,38:1

Lemont, John (Director)

Shakedown, The 1961,Mr 16,44:2
Konga 1961,S 16,9:1

Lemont, John (Screenwriter)

Shakedown, The 1961,Mr 16,44:2

Lemontier, Charles

Francis the First 1947,N 20,38:4
Mr Orchid; Pere Tranquille, Le 1948,Mr 29,17:3
Room Upstairs, The 1948,S 4,8:6
Ruy Blas 1948,O 4,14:2

Lempell, Millard (Screenwriter)

Escape from East Berlin 1962,D 6,55:3

Lemus, Conchita

Apache Rose 1947,Jl 23,19:3

Lenack, Marcia

Three Russian Girls 1944,F 5,13:2

Lenard, Grace

Girls of the Road 1940,Jl 22,20:2
Paris Calling 1942,Ja 19,21:2

Lenas, Francois

Song of the Street 1939,S 5,21:2

Lenauer, Jean H (Miscellaneous)

Passion for Life 1951,D 21,21:4
Triorama 1953,F 11,33:6

Lencret, Simone

Grandeur et Decadence 1937,My 31,11:3

Lender, Mary Lou
Professor Beware 1938,Jl 14,17:1
Lengnich, Charles (Cinematographer)
Black Shadows 1949,N 7,33:2
Lengyel, Emil (Screenwriter)
World in Revolt, The 1934,Je 9,18:2
Lengyel, Gizi
Urilany Szobat Keres; Lady Seeks Room 1938,Mr 19,11:2
Lengyel, Ivan (Director)
Clouds Over Israel 1966,My 10,48:6
Lengyel, Melchior (Miscellaneous)
Angel 1937,N 4,29:1
Lengyel, Melchior (Original Author)
Caravan 1934,S 28,27:1
Ninotchka 1939,N 10,27:2
To Be or not to Be 1942,Mr 7,13:2
Days of Glory 1944,Je 17,10:2
Royal Scandal, A 1945,Ap 12,19:2
Silk Stockings 1957,Jl 19,11:1
Lengyel, Melchior (Screenwriter)
Strange Cargo 1929,F 18,28:1
Catherine the Great 1934,F 15,15:6
Lenhart, Bill
Under-Pup, The 1939,S 5,21:2
In the Navy 1941,Je 12,29:2
Leni, Paul (Director)
Cat and the Canary, The 1927,S 10,9:4
Chinese Parrot, The 1928,Ja 2,28:1
Man Who Laughs, The 1928,Ap 28,12:3
Last Warning, The 1929,Ja 7,36:2
Leni, Paul (Producer)
Three Way Works, The 1926,Mr 19,25:1
Lenier, Christiane
Under the Paris Sky 1952,My 6,35:1
Lenier, Christine
Religieuse, La 1968,S 23,42:3
Lenihan, Winifred
Jigsaw 1949,My 30,9:4
Lenin, Nadezhda K
Soviets on Parade 1933,Mr 6,16:7
Lenis, Maria
Lorenzino de Medici 1936,Ap 14,19:3
Lenkeffy, Ica
Othello 1923,F 26,15:1
Lennart, Isobel (Original Author)
Funny Girl 1968,S 20,42:1
Lennart, Isobel (Screenwriter)
Lost Angel 1944,Ap 10,14:1
Anchors Aweigh 1945,Jl 20,15:2
Holiday in Mexico 1946,Ag 16,19:3
It Happened in Brooklyn 1947,Mr 14,28:5
Kissing Bandit, The 1948,N 19,35:2
Holiday Affair 1949,N 24,48:2
East Side, West Side 1949,D 23,17:2
Life of her Own, A 1950,O 12,43:2
It's a big Country 1952,Ja 9,25:2
Skirts Ahoy! 1952,My 29,17:2
My Wife's Best Friend 1952,O 11,17:2
Latin Lovers 1953,Ag 13,17:2
Girl Next Door, The 1953,S 5,7:4
Love Me or Leave Me 1955,My 27,14:1
Meet Me in Las Vegas 1956,Mr 14,39:2
This Could be the Night 1957,My 15,39:1
Merry Andrews 1958,Mr 21,17:1
Inn of the Sixth Happiness, The 1958,D 14,2:7
Please Don't Eat the Daisies 1960,Ap 1,37:1
Sundowners, The 1960,D 9,39:1
Period of Adjustment 1962,N 1,34:1
Two for the Seesaw 1962,N 22,43:1
Fitzwilly 1967,D 21,45:1
Funny Girl 1968,S 20,42:1
Lennart, Rena
Prince of Foxes 1949,D 24,11:2
Lennertz, Elizabeth
Hell on Earth 1934,Ja 29,10:2
Ihr Erstes Erlebnis; Her First Experience 1940,Je 8,18:3
Lennie, Angus
Great Escape, The 1963,Ag 8,19:1
Lennen, John
Hard Day's Night, A 1964,Ag 12,41:1
Help! 1965,Ag 24,25:1
How I Won the War 1967,N 9,56:1
Lennon, John (Composer)
Yellow Submarine 1968,N 14,56:1
Lennon, Thomas (Miscellaneous)
Knickerbocker Holiday 1944,Ap 20,22:7
Lennon, Thomas (Original Author)
Silly Billies 1936,Ap 6,18:1
Grand Jury 1936,Ag 1,16:3
Killer McCoy 1948,F 12,31:2
Lennon, Thomas (Screenwriter)
Murder on a Bridle Path 1936,Ap 11,19:2
Special Investigator 1936,Ap 25,21:1
Second Wife 1936,Ag 29,16:3
Criminal Lawyer 1937,Ja 27,17:3
Man Who Found Himself, The 1937,Ap 9,19:3
Crowd Roars, The 1938,Ag 5,11:1
Secrets of a Nurse 1938,D 12,26:2
Spellbinder, The 1939,Ag 24,17:3
Jacare 1942,D 28,23:2
Killer McCoy 1948,F 12,31:2

Lennox, Helen
Knack...and how to get it, The 1965,Je 30,42:1
Lennox, Michael (Original Author)
Whispering City 1948,My 10,25:5
Lennox, Vera
How He Lied to her Husband 1931,Ja 17,23:1
Song of the Road 1940,My 6,13:2
Lenoir, Jean (Composer)
Sacrifice d'Honneur 1938,D 2,27:2
Moulin Rouge 1944,N 23,38:2
Lenoir, Leon
Brazil 1944,N 20,25:2
To the Ends of the Earth 1948,F 13,26:2
Stranger on the Prowl 1953,N 10,38:1
Man From Cairo, The 1953,D 17,52:4
LeNoire, Rosetta
Anna Lucasta 1959,Ja 15,27:1
Lenov, Nikolai
Hello, Moscow! 1946,Je 15,24:4
Lenoy, Andre
Venus of Venice 1927,My 3,25:1
Lenskaya, O G
Rivals 1933,Ap 5,22:6
Lensky, Lieb
Bye Bye Braverman 1968,F 22,36:1
Lenya, Lotte
Dreigroschenoper, Die; Beggar's Opera, The 1931,My 18,21:2
Threepenny Opera, The 1960,Jl 11,24:4
Roman Spring of Mrs Stone, The 1961,D 29,11:1
From Russia with Love 1964,Ap 9,25:1
Lenz, Rudolf
Story of Vickie, The 1958,Ja 30,19:2
Lenzer, Don (Cinematographer)
Have You Heard of the San Francisco Mime Troup? 1968,Je 28,37:1
Lenzer, Don (Director)
Have You Heard of the San Francisco Mime Troup? 1968,Je 28,37:1
Lenzer, Don (Miscellaneous)
Have You Heard of the San Francisco Mime Troup? 1968,Je 28,37:1
Lenzer, Don (Producer)
Have You Heard of the San Francisco Mime Troup? 1968,Je 28,37:1
Lenzi, Umberto (Director)
Samson and the Slave Queen 1964,Mr 5,36:2
Lenzi, Umberto (Screenwriter)
Samson and the Slave Queen 1964,Mr 5,36:2
Leo, Gordon
New Interns, The 1964,Ag 20,34:2
Leo, Maurice (Original Author)
Hollywood Hotel 1938,Ja 13,17:3
Leo, Maurice (Screenwriter)
Hollywood Hotel 1938,Ja 13,17:3
Swing Your Lady 1938,Ja 27,17:2
Hard To Get 1938,N 14,15:2
Going Places 1939,Ja 7,6:1
Flight Angels 1940,My 27,23:2
Hit Parade of 1941 1940,D 5,33:2
Leo, Richard
Girl Named Tamiku, A 1963,Mr 15,8:2
Leo (Lion)
Sunshine Dad 1916,Ap 17,9:3
LEON
See Also LEONE
Leon, Anne
Reach for the Sky 1957,My 1,40:1
Leon, Connie
Clive of India 1935,Ja 18,29:1
Singapore Woman 1941,My 12,13:6
Mrs Miniver 1942,Je 3,23:1
Bombs Over Burma 1942,Ag 10,15:2
Thunder Birds 1942,O 29,19:2
And Now Tomorrow 1944,N 23,38:2
Hangover Square 1945,F 8,15:2
Anna and the King of Siam 1946,Je 21,20:2
That Brennan Girl 1946,D 9,34:3
Leon, Gary
Dante's Inferno 1935,Ag 1,15:1
Leon, Joseph
Sweet Smell of Success 1957,Je 28,29:2
Act One 1963,D 27,17:2
Leon, Victor (Composer)
Merry Widow, The 1952,S 25,38:1
Leon, Victor (Original Author)
Merry Widow, The 1934,O 12,33:1
Leonard, Ada
Meet the Missus 1937,Jl 2,25:2
Forty Naughty Girls 1937,S 18,15:3
Music for Madame 1937,O 23,14:1
My Dream Is Yours 1949,Ap 16,11:3
Leonard, Archie
Mrs Mike 1950,F 9,36:5
Leonard, Audrey
Love, Honor and Behave 1938,Mr 21,18:2
Leonard, Barbara
Ladies of the Night Club 1928,Jl 17,15:3
Drake Case, The 1929,S 16,30:1
One Romantic Night 1930,My 31,19:4
Scotland Yard 1930,O 20,28:2
One Hour with You 1932,Mr 24,17:5
Crash, The 1932,S 9,17:5

Leonard, Barbara— Cont
Successful Calamity, A 1932,S 23,22:2
Desirable 1934,S 15,20:5
Senor Casada Necesita Marido 1935,F 11,14:3
Folies Bergere 1935,F 25,13:2
White Angel, The 1936,Je 25,24:1
Charlie Chan in City in Darkness 1939,D 18,29:2
Leonard, Charles (Original Author)
Lucky Jordan 1943,Ja 25,10:8
Leonard, David
Victims of Persecution 1933,Je 17,16:6
Song of my Heart 1948,Mr 5,17:3
Sword of the Avenger 1948,Ag 26,16:4
Adventures of Don Juan 1948,D 25,10:1
Captain Carey U S A 1950,Mr 30,40:5
Lust for Life 1956,S 18,39:1
Leonard, David (Original Author)
Victims of Persecution 1933,Je 17,16:6
Leonard, Eddie
Melody Lane 1929,Jl 16,23:5
If I Had my Way 1940,My 6,13:2
Leonard, Elmore (Original Author)
3:10 to Yuma 1957,Ag 29,22:1
Hombre 1967,Mr 22,41:1
Leonard, Grace
Red Planet Mars 1952,Je 16,15:2
Leonard, Gus
Girl I Loved, The 1923,My 14,18:2
When a Feller Needs a Friend 1932,My 14,11:5
Leonard, Herbert
Murder in the Old Red Barn 1936,Ag 19,18:3
Leonard, Herbert P (Director)
Perils of Pauline, The 1967,Ag 3,26:3
Leonard, Herbert P (Producer)
Perils of Pauline, The 1967,Ag 3,26:3
Leonard, Hugh (Original Author)
Broth of a Boy 1959,D 28,18:1
Leonard, Hugh (Screenwriter)
Interlude 1968,Jl 3,26:1
Leonard, Jack
Doulos-The Finger Man 1964,Mr 3,31:1
Leonard, Jack (Original Author)
Hell's Island 1955,My 7,10:2
Leonard, Jack (Screenwriter)
His Kind of Woman 1951,Ag 30,20:2
My Man and I 1952,S 6,12:6
Man in the Dark 1953,Ap 9,31:5
Leonard, Jack E
Three Sailors and a Girl 1953,N 23,32:2
Leonard, James
All Abroad 1927,Ap 19,24:4
Leonard, L P (Producer)
Headin' East 1938,Ja 15,19:2
Leonard, Marian (Director)
Treasure, The 1951,Mr 29,24:4
Leonard, Mark
Greatest Story Ever Told, The 1965,F 16,40:2
Leonard, Murray
In Society 1944,Ag 17,20:2
Lost in a Harem 1944,N 9,23:2
Leonard, Queenie
Moonlight Sonata 1938,My 10,17:2
Ladies in Retirement 1941,N 7,27:1
Confirm or Deny 1941,D 19,35:2
This Above All 1942,My 13,14:3
Lodger, The 1944,Ja 20,15:3
Molly and Me 1945,My 26,18:2
And Then There Were None 1945,N 1,20:2
My Name is Julia Ross 1945,N 9,16:3
Cluny Brown 1946,Je 3,27:3
Locket, The 1947,Mr 20,38:2
Life With Father 1947,Ag 16,6:6
Lone Wolf in London, The 1947,N 22,10:3
Thunder on the Hill 1951,O 18,32:3
Narrow Margin, The 1952,My 5,18:7
Leonard, Robert Z (Director)
Restless Sex, The 1920,S 13,12:1
Gilded Lily, The 1921,Mr 7,8:1
Heedless Moths 1921,Je 4,14:2
Jazzmania 1923,Mr 12,18:1
French Doll, The 1923,S 5,15:3
Fashion Row 1924,Ja 28,12:1
Mademoiselle Midnight 1924,My 27,14:1
Circe the Enchantress 1924,D 9,23:3
Love's Wilderness 1924,D 22,20:2
Cheaper to Marry 1925,F 2,14:1
Bright Lights 1925,N 18,27:4
Time, the Comedian 1925,D 14,18:2
Dance Madness 1926,Ja 25,21:2
Mlle Modiste 1926,Ap 26,25:1
Waning Sex, The 1926,S 21,33:1
Little Journey, A 1927,Ja 4,21:1
Adam and Evil 1927,Ag 10,21:4
Tea For Three 1927,O 31,22:1
Baby Mine 1928,Ja 9,20:1
Cardboard Lover, The 1928,S 3,14:2
Lady of Chance, A 1929,Ja 14,20:1
Marianne 1929,O 19,22:6
Divorcee, The 1930,My 10,25:3
In Gay Madrid 1930,Je 7,10:4
Bachelor Father, The 1931,F 2,23:1
It's a Wise Child 1931,My 16,13:3
Five and Ten 1931,Jl 11,7:6
Susan Lenox; Her Fall and Rise 1931,O 17,20:1

Leonard, Robert Z (Director) — Cont

Lovers Courageous 1932,F 20,11:2
Strange Interlude 1932,S 1,24:3
Peg o'my Heart 1933,My 20,11:4
Dancing Lady 1933,D 1,23:2
Outcast Lady 1934,N 3,20:3
After Office Hours 1935,Mr 9,19:1
Escapade 1935,Jl 6,16:2
Great Ziegfeld, The 1936,Ap 9,21:2
Piccadilly Jim 1936,Ag 31,19:1
Maytime 1937,Mr 19,27:1
Firefly, The 1937,S 2,17:2
Girl of the Golden West, The 1938,Mr 25,15:2
Broadway Serenade 1939,Ap 7,25:2
New Moon 1940,Jl 19,22:2
Pride and Prejudice 1940,Ag 9,19:1
Third Finger, Left Hand 1940,D 12,37:2
Ziegfeld Girl 1941,Ap 25,17:2
When Ladies Meet 1941,S 5,19:2
We Were Dancing 1942,My 1,23:2
Stand by for Action 1943,Mr 12,12:2
Man From Down Under, The 1943,S 27,23:2
Marriage Is a Private Affair 1944,O 27,17:7
Week-End at the Waldorf 1945,O 5,27:2
Secret Heart, The 1946,D 26,28:2
Cynthia 1947,S 19,27:2
B F's Daughter 1948,Mr 25,35:2
Bribe, The 1949,F 4,31:2
In the Good Old Summertime 1949,Ag 5,23:2
Nancy Goes to Rio 1950,Ap 7,22:2
Duchess of Idaho 1950,Jl 21,15:3
Grounds for Marriage 1951,Ja 12,24:6
Too Young to Kiss 1951,N 23,32:2
Everything I Have is Yours 1952,O 30,40:5
Clown, The 1953,Ja 29,25:1
Her Twelve Men 1954,Ag 12,23:2
King's Thief, The 1955,Ag 13,7:2
Beautiful but Dangerous 1958,F 6,24:1

Leonard, Robert Z (Producer)

Broadway Serenade 1939,Ap 7,25:2
New Moon 1940,Jl 19,22:2
When Ladies Meet 1941,S 5,19:2
We Were Dancing 1942,My 1,23:2
Stand by for Action 1943,Mr 12,12:2
Man From Down Under, The 1943,S 27,23:2

Leonard, Sheldon

Another Thin Man 1939,N 24,29:1
Tall, Dark and Handsome 1941,Ja 24,15:2
Private Nurse 1941,Ag 29,13:3
Married Bachelor 1941,O 16,25:3
Buy Me That Town 1941,O 23,27:2
Week-End in Havana 1941,N 8,11:2
Rise and Shine 1941,D 6,14:3
Born to Sing 1942,F 19,23:2
Tortilla Flat 1942,My 22,27:1
Pierre of the Plains 1942,Jl 30,17:3
Street Of Chance 1942,N 19,31:3
Lucky Jordan 1943,Ja 25,10:8
Taxi, Mister 1943,Ap 15,20:2
Hit the Ice 1943,S 23,27:2
Uncertain Glory 1944,Ap 8,9:2
To Have and Have Not 1944,O 12,24:1
Falcon in Hollywood, The 1944,D 9,21:2
Zombies on Broadway 1945,Ap 27,23:2
Crime Incorporated 1945,Je 23,9:7
Why Girls Leave Home 1945,Ag 4,7:3
Radio Stars on Parade 1945,S 22,14:2
River Gang 1945,O 6,9:7
Captain Kidd 1945,N 23,26:3
Frontier Gal 1945,D 15,14:2
Her Kind of Man 1946,My 4,10:6
Somewhere in the Night 1946,Je 13,24:2
Last Crooked Mile, The 1946,S 14,10:8
Decoy 1946,N 2,12:2
It's a Wonderful Life 1946,D 23,19:2
Sinbad the Sailor 1947,Ja 23,31:2
Violence 1947,My 10,8:5
Gangster, The 1947,O 31,29:3
Open Secret 1948,F 2,15:2
If You Knew Susie 1948,F 23,19:2
My Dream Is Yours 1949,Ap 16,11:3
Take one False Step 1949,Je 23,33:2
Iroquois Trail, The 1950,O 27,24:4
Abbott and Costello Meet the Invisible Man 1951,Ap 13,18:6
Behave Yourself 1951,N 8,35:2
Come Fill the Cup 1951,N 22,47:2
Young Man With Ideas 1952,Je 7,22:6
Stop, You're Killing Me 1952,D 11,45:3
Diamond Queen, The 1954,Ja 27,24:2
Money From Home 1954,F 27,11:3
Guys and Dolls 1955,N 5,26:1
Pocketful of Miracles 1961,D 19,39:1

Leoncavallo (Composer)

Love of a Clown (Pagliacci) 1950,Ap 17,18:5

LEONE

See Also LEON

Leone, Henry

My Cousin 1918,N 25,11:3

Leone, Sergio (Director)

Colossus of Rhodes, The 1961,D 14,55:6
Fistful of Dollars, A 1967,F 2,29:1
For a Few Dollars More 1967,Jl 4,23:1
Good, The Bad and the Ugly, The 1968,Ja 25,33:1

Leone, Sergio (Original Author)

Good, The Bad and the Ugly, The 1968,Ja 25,33:1

Leone, Sergio (Screenwriter)

Sign of the Gladiator 1959,D 3,46:1
Last Days of Pompeii, The 1960,Ag 11,19:1
Colossus of Rhodes, The 1961,D 14,55:6
Duel of the Titans 1963,Ag 8,19:1
Good, The Bad and the Ugly, The 1968,Ja 25,33:1

Leonetti, Francesco

Gospel According to St Matthew, The 1966,F 18,23:1

Leong, James

Devil Dancer, The 1927,D 19,30:1
Shanghai Lady 1929,N 11,20:2
Shadows of the Orient 1937,O 11,26:6
West of Shanghai 1937,O 29,19:2
South of Pago-Pago 1940,Ag 2,12:2
Remember Pearl Harbor 1942,Je 4,22:4

Leoni, G (Screenwriter)

Ring Around the Clock 1953,My 19,36:2

Leoni, Harry

Prunelia 1918,Je 3,9:3

Leonidov, Leon

Czar Ivan the Terrible 1928,Mr 12,26:1
Seeds of Freedom 1929,S 9,30:2
Red and White 1932,N 29,23:5
Marionettes 1934,My 8,28:6

Leonidov, Leonid

Gobsek 1937,Jl 16,22:1

Leonidov, Y

Mussorgsky 1951,Ag 20,14:3
Sadko 1953,Je 1,18:6
House With an Attic 1964,D 21,42:5

Leonis, Charito

Verbena de la Paloma, La 1938,O 25,19:2

Leoniv, A (Director)

Chekhov 1954,D 27,22:7

Leonnardt, Roger

Married Woman, The; Femme Mariee, La 1965,Ag 17,39:1

Leonotiev, Serge

Ukrainian Festival 1965,N 1,57:1

Leonov, Vladimir

Dark Is The Night 1946,Mr 18,24:3
Heroes of Shipka 1956,S 3,10:5

Leonova, Kira

Khovanschina 1960,S 19,41:2

Leontovich, Eugenie

Four Sons 1940,Je 8,18:4
Men In her Life, The 1941,D 12,35:1
Anything Can Happen 1952,Ap 4,21:1
World in His Arms, The 1952,O 10,21:2
Rains of Ranchipur, The 1955,D 16,38:2
Homicidal 1961,Jl 27,23:4

Leontovitsch, Maria

Divided Heart, The 1955,Ag 4,16:1

Leovalli, Emilia

Cantante de Napoles, El; Singer of Naples, The 1935,F 25,13:4

Lepage, Henry (Director)

Sins of Paris 1954,Ja 30,9:6

Lepanova, Katya

In the Name of Life 1947,O 20,29:2

Lepe, Rosita

Jalisco Nunca Pierde; Jalisco Never Loses 1937,N 20,21:3
Guadalajara 1943,Je 12,9:3

Lepere, Paul

They Knew What They Wanted 1940,O 11,25:2

LePerson, Paul

Thief of Paris, The 1967,Ag 24,43:2

Lepeshinsky, Volodya

Village Teacher 1948,Jl 5,8:4

Lepko, Victoria

Lullaby, The 1961,My 15,35:2

Leporace, Enrique

Terrace, The 1964,N 25,45:1

LePore, Richard

Gathering of Eagles, A 1963,Jl 11,21:2
In Harm's Way 1965,Ap 7,36:1

Lepvrier, Denise

Landru 1963,Ap 10,31:1

Leray

Battle of the Rails; (Bataille Du Rail) 1949,D 27,27:2

Lerch, Fred Louis

Student Sein 1931,My 4,15:3
Walzerkoenig, Der 1932,D 5,21:2

Lerch, Louis

Carmen 1928,My 7,29:1
Whirl of Life, The 1929,Mr 25,32:2
Doctor's Women, The 1929,Je 3,27:2

Lerczynska, Severine

Boudu Saved From Drowning; Boudu Sauve Des Eaux 1967,F 24,26:2

Lerdorff, Preben

Day of Wrath 1948,Ap 26,27:2

Leriche, Irenee (Producer)

Frantic 1961,Je 12,34:1

Lermontov, Mikhail Yurevich (Original Author)

Masquerade 1943,My 17,11:2

Lerner

Soir de Rafle, Un 1931,O 16,27:1

Lerner, Alan Jay (Composer)

Gigi 1958,My 16,21:1

Lerner, Alan Jay (Original Author)

Brigadoon 1954,S 17,18:2
My Fair Lady 1964,O 22,41:1
Camelot 1967,O 26,54:1

Lerner, Alan Jay (Screenwriter)

Royal Wedding 1951,Mr 9,30:2
American in Paris, An 1951,O 5,24:2
Brigadoon 1954,S 17,18:2
Gigi 1958,My 16,21:1
My Fair Lady 1964,O 22,41:1
Camelot 1967,O 26,54:1

Lerner, Carl (Director)

Black Like Me 1964,My 21,42:1

Lerner, Carl (Screenwriter)

Black Like Me 1964,My 21,42:1

Lerner, Diki

Li'l Abner 1959,D 12,19:2
Irma la Douce 1963,Je 6,39:1

Lerner, Geraldine (Miscellaneous)

Kings of the Olympics 1948,Ap 23,28:3

Lerner, Gerda (Screenwriter)

Black Like Me 1964,My 21,42:1

Lerner, Irma

Salome of the Tenements 1925,F 24,17:3

Lerner, Irving (Director)

Suicide Attack 1951,Jl 14,7:2
Studs Lonigan 1960,D 15,59:1
Cry of Battle 1963,O 12,27:2

Lerner, Irving (Producer)

Hymn of the Nations 1946,Ap 22,26:2
Custer of the West 1968,Jl 4,13:2

Lerner, Jacques

Monkey Talks, The 1927,Ap 5,30:7

Lerner, Joseph (Director)

C-Man 1949,My 28,11:4
Guilty Bystander 1950,Ap 21,18:2
Mr Universe 1951,Mr 23,16:2

Lerner, Joseph (Producer)

C-Man 1949,My 28,11:4
Mr Universe 1951,Mr 23,16:2

Lerner, Murray (Cinematographer)

Secrets of the Reef 1956,Jl 24,19:2
Festival 1967,O 24,53:2

Lerner, Murray (Director)

Secrets of the Reef 1956,Jl 24,19:2
Festival 1967,O 24,53:2

Lerner, Murray (Producer)

Festival 1967,O 24,53:2

Lerner, Murray (Screenwriter)

Secrets of the Reef 1956,Jl 24,19:2

Lerner, Sam (Composer)

Gangway 1937,Ag 21,7:3
Golden Girl 1951,N 21,20:3

Leroux, Gaston (Original Author)

Phantom of the Opera, The 1925,S 7,15:3
Wizard, The 1927,N 28,18:5
Phantom of the Opera 1930,F 10,20:4
Mystere de la Chambre Jaune, Le 1931,My 26,33:2
Phantom of Paris, The 1931,N 14,15:3
Phantom of the Opera, The 1943,O 15,15:2
Phantom of the Opera, The 1962,Ag 23,25:2

Leroux, Xavier (Original Author)

Open Road, The 1940,O 5,20:2

LeRoy, Baby

Bedtime Story, A 1933,Ap 20,20:3
Torch Singer 1933,O 7,18:5
Tillie and Gus 1933,N 13,21:1
Miss Fane's Baby is Stolen 1934,Ja 20,12:2
Old-Fashioned Way 1934,Jl 14,16:5
Lemon Drop Kid, The 1934,O 27,20:2
It's a Gift 1935,Ja 5,20:2

LeRoy, Dickie

Mask of the Avenger 1951,Je 27,25:2

Leroy, Eddie

Vicious Circle, The 1948,Jl 22,27:2

LeRoy, Hal

Wonder Bar 1934,Mr 1,23:2
Start Cheering 1938,Mr 17,17:3
Too Many Girls 1940,N 21,43:1

LeRoy, Kenneth

Back Door to Heaven 1939,Ap 20,21:2

LeRoy, Mervyn

Little Johnny Jones 1923,Ag 13,16:1
Going Up 1923,O 10,16:2
Broadway After Dark 1924,My 20,15:2

LeRoy, Mervyn (Director)

Flying Romeos 1928,Ap 3,33:2
Harold Teen 1928,Ag 14,15:4
Oh, Kay! 1928,Ag 27,23:1
Naughty Baby 1929,F 5,26:3
Hot Stuff 1929,My 13,27:2
Playing Around 1930,Mr 31,24:3
Show Girl in Hollywood 1930,My 5,27:3
Numbered Men 1930,Je 9,23:3
Top Speed 1930,Ag 30,7:4
Little Casear 1931,Ja 10,19:2

LeRoy, Mervyn (Director) — Cont

Too Young to Marry 1931,My 4,15:3
Gentleman's Fate 1931,Je 27,20:3
Broad Minded 1931,Jl 6,24:4
Five Star Final 1931,S 11,24:2
Local Boy Makes Good 1931,N 27,29:3
Tonight or Never 1931,D 18,29:2
High Pressure 1932,F 1,22:3
Heart of New York, The 1932,Mr 2,15:3
Two Seconds 1932,My 19,25:3
Big City Blues 1932,S 10,18:5
Three on a Match 1932,O 29,18:4
I Am a Fugitive From a Chain Gang
  1932,N 11,17:2
Hard to Handle 1933,F 2,21:5
Elmer the Great 1933,My 26,24:2
Gold Diggers of 1933 1933,Je 8,22:3
Tugboat Annie 1933,Ag 12,14:2
World Changes, The 1933,O 27,22:3
Hi, Nellie! 1934,F 1,15:5
Heat Lightning 1934,Mr 8,23:2
Happiness Ahead 1934,O 11,28:2
Sweet Adeline 1935,Ja 7,13:2
Oil for the Lamps of China 1935,Je 6,25:2
Page Miss Glory 1935,Ag 29,25:2
I Found Stella Parish 1935,N 4,24:4
Anthony Adverse 1936,Ag 27,16:1
Three Men on a Horse 1936,N 26,39:1
King and the Chorus Girl, The 1937,Mr 29,14:4
They Won't Forget 1937,Jl 15,16:1
Fools for Scandal 1938,Mr 25,15:3
Waterloo Bridge 1940,My 17,23:2
Escape 1940,N 1,33:1
Blossoms in the Dust 1941,Je 27,14:4
Unholy Partners 1941,D 29,21:4
Johnny Eager 1942,F 20,21:2
Random Harvest 1942,D 18,36:6
Madame Curie 1943,D 17,23:1
Madame Curie 1944,Ja 9,II,3:1
Thirty Seconds Over Tokyo 1944,N 16,19:1
Without Reservations 1946,Je 8,17:2
Homecoming 1948,Ap 30,28:4
Little Women 1949,Mr 11,33:2
Any Number Can Play 1949,Jl 1,14:4
East Side, West Side 1949,D 23,17:2
Quo Vadis 1951,N 9,22:2
Lovely to Look At 1952,My 30,11:2
Million Dollar Mermaid 1952,D 5,35:2
Latin Lovers 1953,Ag 13,17:2
Rose Marie 1954,Ap 2,22:2
Strange Lady in Town 1955,My 21,11:1
Mister Roberts 1955,Jl 15,14:1
Bad Seed, The 1956,S 13,39:6
Toward the Unknown 1956,S 28,24:4
No Time for Sergeants 1958,My 30,13:2
Home Before Dark 1958,N 7,23:1
F B I Story, The 1959,S 25,23:1
Wake Me When It's Over 1960,Ap 9,17:2
Devil at 4 O'Clock, The 1961,O 19,39:3
Majority of One, A 1962,Ja 12,29:2
Gypsy 1962,N 2,24:1
Mary, Mary 1963,O 25,38:2
Moment to Moment 1966,Mr 3,28:1

LeRoy, Mervyn (Miscellaneous)

Great Garrick, The 1937,O 25,23:1

LeRoy, Mervyn (Producer)

King and the Chorus Girl, The 1937,Mr 29,14:4
They Won't Forget 1937,Jl 15,16:1
Fools for Scandal 1938,Mr 25,15:3
Dramatic School 1938,D 9,31:2
Stand up and Fight 1939,Ja 27,17:2
Wizard of Oz, The 1939,Ag 18,16:2
At the Circus 1939,N 17,17:2
Escape 1940,N 1,33:1
Little Women 1949,Mr 11,33:2
Bad Seed, The 1956,S 13,39:6
Toward the Unknown 1956,S 28,24:4
Home Before Dark 1958,N 7,23:1
F B I Story, The 1959,S 25,23:1
Wake Me When It's Over 1960,Ap 9,17:2
Gypsy 1962,N 2,24:1
Mary, Mary 1963,O 25,38:2
Moment to Moment 1966,Mr 3,28:1

Leroy, Philippe

Night Watch, The; Trou, Le 1964,My 27,46:1
White Voices; Voci Blanche 1965,Ap 13,32:2
Married Woman, The; Femme Mariee, La
  1965,Ag 17,39:1
Mandragola 1966,Je 7,50:2
Love and Marriage (Saturday, July 18); Saturday,
  July 18 (Love and Marriage) 1966,Ag 5,20:1
Wild Eye, The 1968,Ag 22,47:1

Lerski, Helmar (Cinematographer)

Tomorrow's a Wonderful Day 1949,Ap 11,29:4

Lesaffre, Roland

To Catch a Thief 1955,Ag 5,14:2
Crime and Punishment 1958,S 16,23:2

Lesczynski, J

Border Street 1950,Ap 26,35:2

Leshin, E D (Producer)

Salty O'Rourke 1945,Ap 26,26:2
Murder, He Says 1945,Je 25,20:3

Leshschenko, N (Screenwriter)

Conquests of Peter The Great, The
  1939,Ag 24,17:2

Lesiewicz, Witold (Miscellaneous)

Passenger 1964,S 21,37:3

Lesile, Dudley (Screenwriter)

Housemaster 1939,Ap 10,13:2

Leskov, Nicolai (Original Author)

Fury is a Woman 1964,S 28,19:1

Lesley, Carole

Woman in a Dressing Gown 1957,S 13,15:2
Three on a Spree 1961,Ag 31,22:3
Doctor in Love 1962,Ap 27,27:2

Leslie, Aleen (Original Author)

Doctor Takes a Wife, The 1940,Je 15,12:2
Affectionaly Yours 1941,My 24,18:2
It Comes up Love 1943,Ja 22,25:3
Date with Judy, A 1948,Ag 7,8:2

Leslie, Aleen (Screenwriter)

Father Was a Fullback 1949,O 13,33:3
Father Is a Bachelor 1950,F 23,33:3

Leslie, Alfred (Miscellaneous)

Pull my Daisy 1960,Ap 10,II,1:8 (In Addenda)

Leslie, Bethel

Rabbit Trap, The 1959,O 15,48:1
Captain Newman, MD 1964,F 21,36:1
Rage to Live, A 1965,O 21,57:1

Leslie, Colin

Ghost Goes West, The 1936,Ja 11,9:2

Leslie, Dudley (Screenwriter)

Black Limelight 1939,Je 26,12:2
Outsider, The 1940,Mr 18,13:2
Hell's Cargo 1940,S 16,15:2
Portrait of a Sinner 1961,D 7,52:1

Leslie, Eddy

Follow a Star 1961,Ap 26,34:1

Leslie, Edgar (Composer)

Tin Pan Alley 1940,N 22,27:3
For Me and My Gal 1942,O 22,25:1

Leslie, Edith

Green Dolphin Street 1947,O 16,34:2

Leslie, Frank

King of Jazz 1930,My 3,23:1

Leslie, Hubert

Adventures of Tartu, The 1943,S 24,26:1

Leslie, Joan

High Sierra 1941,Ja 25,11:2
Wagons Roll at Night, The 1941,My 10,20:4
Sergeant York 1941,Jl 3,15:1
Male Animal, The 1942,Mr 28,11:1
Yankee Doodle Dandy 1942,My 30,9:1
Hard Way, The 1943,Mr 13,9:2
This Is the Army 1943,Jl 29,11:6
Sky's the Limit, The 1943,S 3,15:2
Thank Your Lucky Stars 1943,O 2,19:2
Hollywood Canteen 1944,D 16,19:2
Where Do We Go From Here? 1945,Je 7,25:2
Rhapsody in Blue 1945,Je 28,22:2
Too Young to Know 1945,D 8,21:2
Cinderella Jones 1946,Mr 16,9:6
Janie Gets Married 1946,Je 15,24:2
Two Guys From Milwaukee 1946,Jl 27,12:5
Repeat Performance 1947,Jl 2,19:2
Northwest Stampede 1948,D 10,34:3
Skipper Surprised his Wife, The 1950,Je 30,18:2
Born to be Bad 1950,S 29,31:5
Flight Nurse 1954,Ja 30,9:6
Jubilee Trail 1954,My 1,13:3
Hell's Outpost 1955,F 26,13:3
Revolt of Mamie Stover, The 1956,My 12,12:7

Leslie, June

War Is a Racket 1934,D 10,16:2

Leslie, Katherine

My Life With Caroline 1941,O 30,27:1

Leslie, Lawrence

Gentlemen of the Press 1929,My 13,27:2
Why Bring That Up? 1929,O 5,22:5

Leslie, Lila

Why Men Leave Home 1924,My 12,14:4
Being Respectable 1924,Ag 4,16:3
Last Edition, The 1925,N 11,27:3
Forever After 1926,N 9,31:1
Getting Gertie's Garter 1927,F 9,17:3
Secret Studio, The 1927,Je 15,31:4

Leslie, Maude

King's Vacation, The 1933,Ja 20,21:2
Captain Blood 1935,D 27,14:1

Leslie, Nan

Devil Thumbs a Ride, The 1947,Mr 22,10:2
Woman on the Beach, The 1947,Je 9,26:6

Leslie, Vilma Ann

Too Many Crooks 1959,Ap 25,14:2

Leslie, William

Long Gray Line, The 1955,F 11,19:2
Queen Bee 1955,N 23,18:2
Operation Mad Ball 1957,N 21,38:1
Last Hurrah, The 1958,O 24,40:1
Andy Hardy Comes Home 1958,D 24,00:0
Up Periscope 1959,Mr 5,35:4
Couch, The 1962,F 22,20:3

Lesnevich, Gus

Requiem for a Heavyweight 1962,O 17,35:1

Lesou, Pierre (Original Author)

Doulos-The Finger Man 1964,Mr 3,31:1

Lesser, Arthur (Producer)

Belle Americaine, La 1961,D 18,42:1

Lesser, Julian (Producer)

Massacre River 1949,Jl 15,17:2
Jungle Headhunters 1951,D 6,42:5

Lesser, Len

Shack out on 101 1956,Ja 10,26:2
Crime and Punishment, U S A 1959,Je 17,39:3

Lesser, Sol (Miscellaneous)

When a Man's a Man 1935,F 22,27:2

Lesser, Sol (Producer)

Blame the Woman 1932,O 25,24:5
When a Man's a Man 1935,F 22,27:2
Hard Rock Harrigan 1935,Jl 30,16:2
Thunder Mountain 1935,O 2,27:2
Whispering Smith Speaks 1936,F 17,21:1
O'Malley of the Mounted 1936,Ap 6,18:1
Let's Sing Again 1936,My 9,11:2
Border Patrolman 1936,Je 29,11:2
King of the Royal Mounted 1936,S 29,35:2
Rainbow on the River 1936,D 18,31:4
Secret Valley 1937,Ja 25,22:2
It Happened Out West 1937,Je 7,22:3
Make a Wish 1937,S 23,33:1
Tarzan's Revenge 1938,Ja 10,13:3
Rawhide 1938,Ap 25,19:2
Breaking the Ice 1938,S 23,35:3
Peck's bad Boy With the Circus 1939,Ja 11,17:4
Fisherman's Wharf 1939,F 24,15:2
Way Down South 1939,Ag 18,16:4
Everything's on Ice 1939,O 6,31:1
Tuttles of Tahiti, The 1942,Ap 30,14:1
Tarzan Triumphs 1943,F 5,16:3
Stage Door Canteen 1943,Je 25,13:2
Tarzan's Desert Mystery 1943,D 27,23:3
3 Is a Family 1944,D 20,20:3
Tarzan and the Amazons 1945,Ap 30,13:4
Tarzan and the Leopard Woman 1946,F 11,25:2
Red House, The 1947,Mr 17,27:2
Tarzan and the Huntress 1947,Ap 7,20:4
Tarzan and the Mermaids 1948,Mr 30,26:4
Tarzan's Magic Fountain 1949,F 7,15:2
Tarzan and the Slave Girl 1950,Je 24,7:3
Tarzan's Fight for Life 1958,Ag 16,10:2

Lesser, Ted (Miscellaneous)

College Swing 1938,Ap 28,27:2

Lesser, Ted (Original Author)

Souls at Sea 1937,Ag 10,23:2

Lessey, George

Silent Command, The 1923,S 5,15:3
Fool, The 1925,Ap 13,24:1
Dr Kildare's Strange Case 1940,Ap 12,19:2
Edison the Man 1940,Je 7,27:2
Sporting Blood 1940,Jl 22,20:2
Andy Hardy Meets Debutante 1940,Ag 2,12:2
Boom Town 1940,S 6,25:2
Strike up the Band 1940,S 30,13:2
Golden Fleecing, The 1940,N 7,33:4
Sky Murder 1940,N 14,28:3
Go West 1941,F 21,16:2
Men of Boys Town 1941,Ap 11,24:6
Blossoms in the Dust 1941,Je 27,14:4
Moon Over Miami 1941,Jl 5,14:2
Roxie Hart 1942,F 20,21:1
Rings on her Fingers 1942,Ap 24,21:4
Gay Sisters, The 1942,Ag 15,14:2
Pistol Packin' Mama 1943,D 20,27:4
None Shall Escape 1944,Ap 7,23:2
Buffalo Bill 1944,Ap 20,22:6

Lessing, Marion

Seas Beneath 1931,Ja 31,15:1
Downstairs 1932,O 8,15:4
Red-Haired Alibi 1932,O 24,18:5

Lessing, Norman (Original Author)

Artists and Models 1955,D 22,20:1

Lessing, Norman (Screenwriter)

Joy in the Morning 1965,Je 10,38:1

Lesslie, Colin (Producer)

No Resting Place 1952,My 5,18:5
Horse's Mouth, The 1954,Ja 20,33:4
Breakout 1960,My 19,44:3
Tunes of Glory 1960,D 21,38:2

Lesslie, Colin (Screenwriter)

No Resting Place 1952,My 5,18:5
Breakout 1960,My 19,44:3

Lessor, James (Original Author)

One That Got Away, The 1958,Ap 23,40:2

Lessy, Ben

Thousands Cheer 1943,S 14,27:1
Music for Millions 1944,D 22,12:4
Dark Delusion 1947,Je 26,19:2
Pirate, The 1948,My 21,19:2
Jackie Robinson Story, The 1950,My 17,36:1
Just for You 1952,O 9,40:6
Gypsy 1962,N 2,24:1

Lestelly, Rene

Crise est Finie, La 1935,Mr 14,18:1

Lester, Bruce

Boy Meets Girl 1938,Ag 27,7:2
If I Were King 1938,S 29,31:1
Witness Vanishes, The 1939,O 23,15:2

Lester, Bruce— Cont
British Intelligence 1940,F 12,14:2
My Son, My Son! 1940,My 10,26:6
Pride and Prejudice 1940,Ag 9,19:1
Letter, The 1940,N 23,12:6
Singapore Woman 1941,My 12,13:6
Shining Victory 1941,My 31,14:1
Yank in the R A F, A 1941,S 27,11:3
Desperate Journey 1942,S 26,11:2
Mysterious Doctor, The 1943,My 20,26:4
Above Suspicion 1943,Ag 6,10:3
Golden Earrings 1947,D 4,41:3
Lester, Buddy
Ocean's Eleven 1960,Ag 11,19:1
Sergeants 3 1962,F 12,28:2
3 on a Couch 1966,Jl 7,30:1
Big Mouth, The 1967,Jl 13,30:2
Party, The 1968,Ap 5,56:2
Lester, Elliott (Original Author)
Two Seconds 1932,My 19,25:3
Lester, Henry E (Producer)
Study in Terror, A 1966,N 3,45:3
Lester, Jack
No Orchids for Miss Blandish 1951,F 23,33:2
Lester, Jerry
Rookie, The 1960,Mr 17,28:1
Lester, Kate
Man and his Money, A 1919,Ap 14,11:4
Bonds of Love 1919,N 3,13:3
Paliser Case, The 1920,F 16,8:1
Remembrance 1922,O 2,21:2
Gimme 1923,Ja 15,18:3
Black Oxen 1924,Ja 7,23:1
Goldfish, The 1924,My 20,15:2
Wife of the Centaur, The 1925,Ja 7,33:5
Price of Pleasure, The 1925,My 26,24:2
Lester, Leoni
Man and Maid 1925,Ap 7,17:3
Lester, Mark
Seven Sinners 1936,Ag 22,6:1
Our Mother's House 1967,O 10,56:1
Oliver! 1968,D 11,57:1
Lester, Neil
Ghost Goes West, The 1936,Ja 11,9:2
Lester, Richard (Director)
Mouse on the Moon, The 1963,Je 18,32:1
Hard Day's Night, A 1964,Ag 12,41:1
Knack...and how to get it, The 1965,Je 30,42:1
Help! 1965,Ag 24,25:1
Funny Thing Happened on the Way to the Forum,
  A 1966,O 17,48:1
How I Won the War 1967,N 9,56:1
Petulia 1968,Je 11,54:4
Lester, Richard (Producer)
How I Won the War 1967,N 9,56:1
Lester, Roy
Ringside Maisie 1941,Ag 1,11:2
Lester, Seeleg (Original Author)
Winning Team, The 1952,Je 21,12:2
Sergeant Ryker 1968,Mr 21,56:2
Lester, Seeleg (Screenwriter)
Winning Team, The 1952,Je 21,12:2
Sergeant Ryker 1968,Mr 21,56:2
Lester, Sue
Cyanamide 1954,Mr 26,17:6
Lester, Vicki
Patient in Room 18, The 1938,Ap 22,15:6
Sky Giant 1938,Jl 20,22:2
Mad Miss Manton, The 1938,O 21,27:2
Great Plane Robbery, The 1940,N 15,25:2
Tom, Dick and Harry 1941,Jl 18,22:2
Lester, William
Bad Boy 1949,Mr 23,35:2
Above and Beyond 1953,Ja 31,10:6
Lestina, Adolph
Girl Who Stayed Home, The 1919,Mr 24,11:3
Scarlet Days 1919,N 10,18:2
L'Estrange, Dick (Director)
Teen Age 1944,Je 19,17:1
Lestringuez, Pierre (Screenwriter)
Clandestine 1948,My 24,23:2
Of Love and Bandits 1953,Ja 17,12:4
Leszczynski, Jerzy
Halka 1938,Ja 17,11:3
Leterrier, Francois
Man Escaped, A 1957,Ag 27,33:2
Leterrier, Francois (Director)
Naked Autumn 1963,N 15,25:3
Letichevsky, Alik
Rainbow, The 1944,O 23,14:3
Letlani, Dione
Pagan Love Song 1950,D 26,19:1
Letondal, Henri
Razor's Edge, The 1946,N 20,42:2
Apartment for Peggy 1948,O 16,9:2
Come to the Stable 1949,Jl 28,19:1
Please Believe Me 1950,Je 12,19:4
Royal Wedding 1951,Mr 9,30:2
On the Riviera 1951,My 24,47:1
Kind Lady 1951,Ag 8,21:2
Across the Wide Missouri 1951,N 7,35:4
What Price Glory 1952,Ag 23,10:2
Monkey Business 1952,S 6,12:6
South Sea Woman 1953,Je 4,33:6

Dangerous When Wet 1953,Je 19,18:1
Little Boy Lost 1953,S 22,38:2
Gambler From Natchez, The 1954,Ag 14,8:2
Lettieri, Alfredo
Bobo, The 1967,S 29,53:1
Lettieri, Felicia
Two Cents Worth of Hope 1952,D 16,44:2
Lettieri, Louis
Hollywood Story 1951,Je 7,40:6
Stop, You're Killing Me 1952,D 11,45:3
Lettinger
Luther 1929,Je 24,27:1
Letts, Barry
Frieda 1947,Ag 15,12:3
Letts, Pauline
Pink String and Sealing Wax 1950,O 4,38:2
Leuchaire, Corinne
Prison Without Bars 1939,Ap 10,13:2
Leudesdorff, Ernest
Mit versiegelter Order; Under Sealed Orders
  1938,Jl 30,10:2
Leurini, Gino
Heart and Soul 1950,Je 15,41:3
Tomorrow is too Late 1952,Ap 14,22:2
Queen of Sheba, The 1953,N 4,29:3
Anita Garibaldi 1954,Mr 19,19:4
Leuthge, B E (Original Author)
Der Schrecken der Garnison 1932,Je 1,19:5
Leutzinger, Eric
Bible, The 1966,S 29,60:1
Leuwerik, Ruth
Portrait of an Unknown Woman 1958,Ap 26,14:6
Taiga 1959,Mr 17,42:4
Trapp Family, The 1961,Ag 31,22:4
Leux, Leo (Composer)
Maria, Die Magd 1937,My 22,19:2
Lev, Maurice (Miscellaneous)
One Inch From Victory 1944,Ap 27,18:5
Levant, Oscar
Dance of Life, The 1929,Ag 16,18:6
Rhythm on the River 1940,Ag 29,23:2
Kiss the Boys Goodbye 1941,Ag 14,21:2
Rhapsody in Blue 1945,Je 28,22:2
Humoresque 1946,D 26,28:1
You Were Meant for Me 1948,Ja 29,27:5
Romance on the High Seas 1948,Je 26,10:5
Barkleys of Broadway, The 1949,My 5,34:2
American in Paris, An 1951,O 5,24:2
Band Wagon, The 1953,Jl 10,10:2
Cobweb, The 1955,Ag 6,13:3
Levant, Oscar (Composer)
In Person 1935,D 13,31:5
Levant, Oscar (Miscellaneous)
Black Sheep 1935,Je 28,34:1
Levashev, Vladimir
Swan Lake 1960,Ja 26,25:2
Bolshoi Ballet 67 1966,S 30,54:1
Levay, Harry (Producer)
Around the World With Burton Holmes
  1922,Ap 25,14:3 (In Addenda)
LEVE
See Also LEVI, LEVY
Leve, Paolo (Screenwriter)
Wife for a Night 1958,Je 12,35:2
Leven, Edward (Producer)
Second Face, The 1951,Mr 2,21:3
Basketball Fix, the 1951,S 14,21:2
Leven, Mel (Composer)
Babes in Toyland 1961,D 15,49:1
LEVENE
See Also LEVIEN, LEVIN, LEVINE, LAVINE
Levene, Sam
Three Men on a Horse 1936,N 26,39:1
After the Thin Man 1936,D 25,19:2
Yellow Jack 1938,My 20,17:2
Shopworn Angel, The 1938,Jl 8,11:2
Mad Miss Manton, The 1938,O 21,27:2
Golden Boy 1939,S 8,28:2
Married Bachelor 1941,O 16,25:3
Shadow of the Thin Man 1941,N 21,23:2
Sunday Punch 1942,My 11,19:2
Sing Your Worries Away 1942,My 15,25:2
Grand Central Murder 1942,My 23,8:8
Big Street, The 1942,Ag 14,13:1
Destination Unknown 1942,O 29,19:3
Action in the North Atlantic 1943,My 22,10:2
I Dood It 1943,N 11,29:1
Gung Ho! 1944,Ja 26,23:2
Purple Heart, The 1944,Mr 9,15:2
Whistling in Brooklyn 1944,Mr 24,17:3
Killers, The 1946,Ag 29,24:2
Boomerang 1947,Mr 6,36:2
Brute Force 1947,Jl 17,16:2
Crossfire 1947,Jl 23,19:2
Killer McCoy 1948,F 12,31:2
Babe Ruth Story, The 1948,Jl 29,17:2
Guilty Bystander 1950,Ap 21,18:2
With These Hands 1950,Je 16,28:4
Dial 1119 1950,D 4,32:6
Three Sailors and a Girl 1953,N 23,32:2
Opposite Sex, The 1956,N 16,23:2
Designing Woman 1957,My 17,20:2
Sweet Smell of Success 1957,Je 28,29:2

Levene, Sam— Cont
Slaughter on Tenth Avenue 1957,N 6,43:1
Kathy O' 1958,S 25,29:2
Act One 1963,D 27,17:2
Leventhal, J F (Director)
Arabian Duet 1922,My 15,20:3
Leverett, Lewis
Boomerang 1947,Mr 6,36:2
Levering, Joseph
Sporting Chance 1931,N 28,20:4
Levering, Joseph (Director)
Cheating Blondes 1933,My 20,11:4
Leverson, Loretta
Playground, The 1965,O 4,00:0
Levert, J (Miscellaneous)
Toni 1968,S 19,62:2
Levert, J (Original Author)
Toni 1968,S 19,62:2
Levesque, Marcel
Crime of Monsieur Lange, The 1964,Ap 4,15:5
Levett, Harold
East Side, West Side 1927,O 18,33:2
LEVEY
See LEVI, LEVY, LEVE
LEVI
See Also LEVY, LEVE
Levi, Juda
Faithful City 1952,Ap 8,35:2
Levi, Shaika
Sallah 1965,O 13,39:1
Clouds Over Israel 1966,My 10,48:6
Levi, Yona
Impossible on Saturday 1966,F 17,29:1
LEVIEN
See Also LEVIN, LEVINE, LAVINE, LEVENE
Levien, Sonya (Original Author)
Top of New York, The 1922,Je 19,10:3
Snow Bride, The 1923,Je 12,22:2
She Wanted a Millionaire 1932,F 20,11:2
Here's to Romance 1935,O 3,29:2
Amazing Mrs Holliday, The 1943,F 22,20:2
Rhapsody in Blue 1945,Je 28,22:2
Pepe 1960,D 22,18:1
Levien, Sonya (Screenwriter)
Exciters, The 1923,Je 4,13:3
White Parade, The 1934,N 10,19:1
Country Doctor, The 1936,Mr 13,32:2 (Incorrect
  in this edition; use 1936,Mr 13,27:2 elsewhere)
Reunion 1936,N 27,27:1
In Old Chicago 1938,Ja 7,15:2
Four Men and a Prayer 1938,My 7,18:1
Kidnapped 1938,My 28,9:2
Cowboy and the Lady, The 1938,N 25,19:3
Drums Along the Mohawk 1939,N 4,11:2
Hunchback of Notre Dame, The 1940,Ja 1,29:2
Ziegfeld Girl 1941,Ap 25,17:2
Valley of Decision, The 1945,My 4,23:2
State Fair 1945,Ag 31,14:3
Green Years, The 1946,Ap 5,21:2
Cass Timberlane 1947,N 7,20:2
Three Daring Daughters 1948,F 13,26:3
Great Caruso, The 1951,My 11,32:2
Quo Vadis 1951,N 9,22:2
Merry Widow, The 1952,S 25,38:1
Student Prince, The 1954,Je 16,18:2
Hit the Deck 1955,Mr 4,17:1
Interrupted Melody 1955,My 6,18:1
Oklahoma! 1955,O 11,49:1
Bhowani Junction 1956,My 25,26:1
Jeanne Eagels 1957,Ag 31,19:1
State Fair 1962,Ap 12,41:4
Leville, Jean (Screenwriter)
My Wife's Husband 1965,Ja 27,26:1
LEVIN
See Also LEVINE, LAVINE, LEVENE,
  LEVIEN
Levin, Chane
Brivele der Mamen, A; Little Letter to Mother, A
  1939,S 15,26:4
Levin, Henry (Director)
Cry of the Werewolf, The 1944,Ag 12,16:5
Fighting Guardsman, The 1945,O 6,9:6
Bandit of Sherwood Forest, The 1946,Mr 23,8:4
Night Editor 1946,Mr 30,11:2
Unknown, The 1946,Jl 20,10:3
Return of Monte Cristo, The 1947,Ja 3,16:4
Guilt of Janet Ames, The 1947,My 23,31:2
Corpse came C O D, The 1947,Ag 19,27:2
Mating of Millie, The 1948,Mr 13,12:2
Gallant Blade 1948,O 13,31:3
Man From Colorado 1949,Ja 21,24:3
Jolson Sings Again 1949,Ag 18,16:6
And Baby Makes Three 1949,D 23,17:3
Petty Girl, The 1950,Ag 18,17:2
Flying Missile, The 1950,D 25,25:1
Two of a Kind 1951,Je 30,8:6
Belles on Their Toes 1952,My 3,17:5
President's Lady, The 1953,My 22,31:1
Farmer Takes a Wife, The 1953,Je 13,11:2
Mister Scoutmaster 1953,Ag 29,10:1
Three Young Texans 1954,Ap 17,8:2
Gambler From Natchez, The 1954,Ag 14,8:2
Warriors, The 1955,S 10,11:2
Let's Be Happy 1957,My 25,25:1

Levin, Henry (Director) — Cont

Bernardine 1957,Jl 25,28:1
April Love 1957,N 28,57:2
Nice Little Bank That Should Be Robbed, A 1958,D 11,17:4
Remarkable Mr Pennypacker, The 1959,F 21,25:2
Holiday for Lovers 1959,Jl 25,10:2
Where the Boys Are 1961,Ja 20,22:1
Wonders of Aladdin, The 1961,D 23,16:1
Wonderful World of the Brothers Grimm, The 1962,Ag 8,35:1
Wonderful World of the Brothers Grimm, The (The Dancing Princess) 1962,Ag 8,35:1
Wonderful World of the Brothers Grimm, The (The Singing Bone) 1962,Ag 8,35:1
Wonderful World of the Brothers Grimm, The (The Cobbler and the Elves) 1962,Ag 8,35:1
If a Man Answers 1962,N 22,43:1
Come Fly With Me 1963,My 2,40:2
Honeymoon Hotel 1964,Je 4,28:1
Genghis Khan 1965,Je 24,28:2
Murderers' Row 1966,D 22,40:3
Kiss the Girls and Make Them Die 1967,Ja 26,25:1
Ambushers, The 1967,D 23,29:1

Levin, Henry (Miscellaneous)

Journey to the Center of the Earth 1959,D 17,51:1

Levin, Ira (Original Author)

No Time for Sergeants 1958,My 30,13:2
Critic's Choice 1963,My 2,40:2
Rosemary's Baby 1968,Je 13,57:1

Levin, Irving H (Producer)

Hell to Eternity 1960,O 13,41:1

Levin, Meyer (Director)

Illegals, The 1948,Jl 15,26:2

Levin, Meyer (Original Author)

My Father's House 1947,S 26,28:3
Compulsion 1959,Ap 2,26:2

Levin, Meyer (Producer)

My Father's House 1947,S 26,28:3
Illegals, The 1948,Jl 15,26:2

Levin, Meyer (Screenwriter)

Illegals, The 1948,Jl 15,26:2

Levin, Moissei (Director)

Poet and Tsar 1938,Ag 25,15:1
Amangeldy 1939,Je 16,27:4

Levin, Yiola

Loerdagskvaellar 1936,F 13,25:3

LEVINE

See Also LAVINE, LEVENE, LEVIEN, LEVIN

Levine, Helen

Frisco Sally Levy 1927,Ap 13,29:4

Levine, Isaac Don (Screenwriter)

Jack London 1944,Mr 3,19:3

Levine, Joseph E (Producer)

Carpetbaggers, The 1964,Jl 2,24:4
Where Love Has Gone 1964,N 3,26:1
Casanova 1965,Jl 21,43:1
Harlow 1965,Jl 22,24:1
Sands of the Kalahari 1965,N 25,64:5
Spy With a Cold Nose, The 1966,D 20,58:2
Woman Times Seven 1967,Je 28,38:1
Tiger and the Pussycat, The 1967,S 21,56:4
Shoot Loud, Louder... I Don't Understand 1967,S 21,56:4
Robbery 1967,S 28,58:2
Producers, The 1968,Mr 19,38:1
Lion in Winter, The 1968,O 31,54:1

LeVine, Margaret (Screenwriter)

Confession 1937,Ag 19,23:1

Levine, Martin (Producer)

Roosevelt Story, The 1947,Ag 22,11:2

Levine, Michel (Composer)

Lie of Nina Petrovna, The 1938,Mr 30,19:2

Levine, Nat (Miscellaneous)

Laughing at Life 1933,Jl 15,14:2

Levine, Nat (Producer)

House of a Thousand Candles, The 1936,Ap 2,29:2
President's Mystery, The 1936,O 19,22:1
Follow Your Heart 1936,O 22,31:1
Hit Parade, The 1937,My 31,11:2
Four Girls in White 1939,F 23,19:3

Levine, Saul

Green Fields 1937,O 12,31:4

Levine, Susan

Private Buckaroo 1942,Je 25,27:4

Levingstone, Jerry (Composer)

Cinderella 1950,F 23,33:1

Levinnes, Carl

Twin Beds 1929,Jl 15,25:1

Levino, Margaret P (Original Author)

Queen Christina 1933,D 27,23:3

Levinson, Arthur (Original Author)

Face Behind the Mask, The 1941,F 7,23:2

Levison, Charles

Blonde Crazy 1931,D 4,28:2
My Woman 1933,O 16,20:3
Advice to the Lovelorn 1933,D 14,28:2
20th Century 1934,My 4,24:2
I'll Fix It 1934,N 12,17:3
Broadway Bill 1934,N 30,22:2

Levitow, Abe (Director)

Gay Purr--ee 1962,D 6,55:3

Levitt, Alfred Lewis (Miscellaneous)

My Outlaw Brother 1951,Ag 23,19:2

Levitt, Alfred Lewis (Screenwriter)

Boy With Green Hair, The 1949,Ja 13,26:2
Mrs Mike 1950,F 9,36:5
Shakedown 1950,S 4,11:2
Dream Wife 1953,Jl 30,20:1

Levitt, Gene (Original Author)

Foreign Intrigue 1956,Jl 13,23:2

Levitt, Gene (Screenwriter)

Beyond Mombasa 1957,My 31,14:2

Levitt, Helen (Producer)

Affair of the Skin, An 1963,N 21,43:2

Levitt, Helen (Screenwriter)

Quiet One, The 1949,F 14,15:2

Levitt, Saul (Miscellaneous)

Strange Victory 1948,S 27,27:2

Levitt, Saul (Screenwriter)

Covenant with Death, A 1967,F 16,32:3

Levka, Uta

Carmen Baby 1967,O 11,41:2

Levoy, Albert E (Producer)

Portia on Trial 1937,D 3,29:2
Sporting Blood 1940,Jl 22,20:2

Levsly, Cecila

36 Hours 1965,Ja 29,25:2

Levu-Corti, Pierre (Screenwriter)

My Wife's Husband 1965,Ja 27,26:1

LEVY

See Also LEVE, LEVI

Levy, Benn W (Miscellaneous)

Unfinished Symphony 1935,Ja 14,11:2

Levy, Benn W (Original Author)

Evergreen 1935,Ja 11,29:1

Levy, Benn W (Screenwriter)

Gay Diplomat, The 1931,O 10,20:4
Loves of a Dictator 1935,Je 1,18:2

Levy, David S (Screenwriter)

Gold Racket, The 1937,Ag 2,10:3

Levy, J (Screenwriter)

Traitors, The 1963,Je 27,23:4

Levy, Jules (Producer)

Boys From Syracuse, The 1940,Ag 1,25:2
Hellzapoppin 1941,D 26,21:4
Hairy Ape, The 1944,Jl 3,8:3
Abilene Town 1946,Mr 4,16:5
New Orleans 1947,Je 20,25:6
Vice Squad 1953,Ag 26,23:2
Down Three Dark Streets 1954,S 4,6:4
Clambake 1967,D 14,62:3
Scalphunters, The 1968,Ap 3,40:1

Levy, Julien

8 X 8 1957,Mr 16,13:2

Levy, Leon (Miscellaneous)

Spain Fights on 1939,F 13,13:2

Levy, Melvin (Original Author)

Hideaway 1937,S 25,10:2

Levy, Melvin (Screenwriter)

Robin Hood of El Dorado, The 1936,Mr 14,10:1
Hitler's Madman 1943,Ag 28,15:1
First Comes Courage 1943,S 3,15:3
Sunday Dinner for a Soldier 1945,Ja 25,16:2
Bandit of Sherwood Forest, The 1946,Mr 23,8:4
Renegades 1946,Jl 11,18:2
Calamity Jane and Sam Bass 1949,Jl 18,14:2
Great Sioux Uprising, The 1953,Jl 18,6:2

Levy, Newman (Screenwriter)

Jury's Secret, The 1938,F 4,17:2

Levy, Oliver (Miscellaneous)

Merlusse 1938,Mr 17,17:2

Levy, Parke (Original Author)

Hit Parade of 1947 1947,My 5,32:8

Levy, Parke (Screenwriter)

Having Wonderful Crime 1945,Ap 13,15:2
George White's Scandals 1945,O 11,26:2
Earl Carroll Sketchbook 1946,Ag 30,13:2
My Friend Irma 1949,S 29,39:2
My Friend Irma Goes West 1950,Ag 3,20:2

Levy, Paul (Screenwriter)

Operation Kid Brother 1967,N 23,58:2

Levy, Ralph (Director)

Bedtime Story 1964,Je 11,27:1
Do Not Disturb 1965,D 25,17:2

Levy, Raoul J

Two or Three Things I Know About Her 1968,S 26,60:1

Levy, Raoul J (Director)

Defector, The 1966,N 17,55:1

Levy, Raoul J (Original Author)

Babette Goes to War 1960,Je 8,46:1
Marco the Magnificent 1966,D 15,60:1

Levy, Raoul J (Producer)

And God Created Woman 1957,O 22,41:1
Love Is my Profession 1959,Ap 28,41:1
Babette Goes to War 1960,Je 8,46:1
Truth, The 1961,Je 27,23:2
Moderato Cantabile 1964,Ja 7,24:1
Defector, The 1966,N 17,55:1

Levy, Raoul J (Screenwriter)

And God Created Woman 1957,O 22,41:1
Defector, The 1966,N 17,55:1

Levy, Raoul J (Screenwriter) — Cont

Marco the Magnificent 1966,D 15,60:1

Levy, Reuben (Miscellaneous)

Babes in Bagdad 1954,Ap 5,21:3

Levy, Weaver

Prisoner of War 1954,My 10,20:2

Levy-Corti, Pierre (Original Author)

Impossible on Saturday 1966,F 17,29:1

Levy-Corti, Pierre (Screenwriter)

Impossible on Saturday 1966,F 17,29:1

Levyush, Salman

Khamishia-Five Tales From Israel 1954,My 7,19:3

Lew, Shirley

Behind the Rising Sun 1943,O 14,26:2

Lewbel, Bunny

I'll See You in my Dreams 1951,D 7,35:1

Lewenstein, Oscar (Producer)

Knack...and how to get it, The 1965,Je 30,42:1
Mademoiselle 1966,Ag 2,23:1
Sailor From Gibraltar, The 1967,Ap 25,38:2

Lewin, Albert (Director)

Moon and Sixpence, The 1942,O 28,26:4
Picture of Dorian Gray, The 1945,Mr 2,15:2
Private Affairs of Bel Ami, The 1947,Je 16,25:4
Pandora and the Flying Dutchman 1951,D 7,35:2
Living Idol, The 1957,My 3,18:1

Lewin, Albert (Original Author)

Pandora and the Flying Dutchman 1951,D 7,35:2

Lewin, Albert (Producer)

Good Earth, The 1937,F 3,27:1
True Confession 1937,D 16,35:2
Spawn of the North 1938,S 8,27:1
Zaza 1939,Ja 5,17:1
So Ends our Night 1941,F 28,17:2
Pandora and the Flying Dutchman 1951,D 7,35:2
Living Idol, The 1957,My 3,18:1

Lewin, Albert (Screenwriter)

Moon and Sixpence, The 1942,O 28,26:4
Picture of Dorian Gray, The 1945,Mr 2,15:2
Private Affairs of Bel Ami, The 1947,Je 16,25:4
Call Me Mister 1951,F 1,21:2
Alice in Wonderland 1951,Jl 27,15:2
Pandora and the Flying Dutchman 1951,D 7,35:2
Down Among the Sheltering Palms 1953,Je 13,11:2
Saadia 1954,Mr 20,10:5
Living Idol, The 1957,My 3,18:1
Boy, Did I Get a Wrong Number! 1966,Je 9,54:2
Eight on the Lam 1967,Ap 27,52:1
Wicked Dreams of Paula Schultz, The 1968,Ja 4,28:1

Lewin, C

Yiddle With his Fiddle 1937,Ja 2,15:1

Lewin, Robert (Screenwriter)

Bold and the Brave, The 1956,My 26,15:2

Lewin, Stuart

Love Among the Millionaires 1930,Jl 5,17:4

LEWIS

See Also LOUIS

Lewis, Al

World of Henry Orient, The 1964,Mr 20,27:2
Munster, Go Home 1966,Je 16,53:4

Lewis, Al (Composer)

Life Begins In College 1937,O 9,16:1
Listen, Darling 1938,N 24,37:2

Lewis, Al (Screenwriter)

Ma and Pa Kettle 1949,Ag 12,13:2

Lewis, Albert (Director)

Saadia 1954,Mr 20,10:5

Lewis, Albert (Original Author)

Golden Girl 1951,N 21,20:3

Lewis, Albert (Producer)

Gilded Lily, The 1935,F 9,11:2
Stolen Harmony 1935,Ap 20,16:2
Men Without Names 1935,Je 29,16:2
Till We Meet Again 1936,My 9,11:2
Florida Special 1936,My 29,15:2
My American Wife 1936,Ag 21,12:3
Son Comes Home, A 1936,S 5,7:1
Woman I Love, The 1937,Ap 16,27:2
Meet the Missus 1937,Jl 2,25:2
Fight for Your Lady 1937,N 20,21:2
there Goes The Groom 1937,D 25,10:6
She's Got Everything 1938,Ja 14,21:3
Show-Off, The 1947,Mr 20,38:2
Merton of the Movies 1947,N 7,20:3
Saadia 1954,Mr 20,10:5

Lewis, Albert (Screenwriter)

Oh, You Beautiful Doll 1949,N 12,8:4

Lewis, Alfred (Screenwriter)

Rose of Wolfville 1918,O 21,15:1

Lewis, Ann

In the French Style 1963,S 19,23:1

Lewis, Anthony (Original Author)

Three Brave Men 1957,Mr 16,13:2

Lewis, Art

Pickup 1951,Ag 31,12:2
What Did You Do in the War, Daddy? 1966,S 1,28:1

Lewis, Arthur (Original Author)

Golden Girl 1951,N 21,20:3

Lewis, Arthur (Screenwriter)
  Oh, You Beautiful Doll 1949,N 12,8:4
Lewis, Ben
  You're a Sweetheart 1937,D 25,10:5
Lewis, Blayney
  Escape in the Desert 1945,My 12,10:2
Lewis, Bobo
  Way...Way Out 1966,O 27,55:1
Lewis, Catherine
  Kid Glove Killer 1942,Ap 17,21:4
Lewis, Cathy
  Story of Molly X, The 1949,D 2,35:4
  Devil at 4 O'Clock, The 1961,O 19,39:3
Lewis, Cecil (Director)
  How He Lied to her Husband 1931,Ja 17,23:1
  Carmen; Gipsy Blood 1931,N 22,VIII,6:1
Lewis, Cecil (Screenwriter)
  Pygmalion 1938,D 8,34:2
Lewis, Cordella (Screenwriter)
  Face of War, The 1963,N 1,30:2
Lewis, D B Wyndham (Original Author)
  Man Who Knew too Much, The 1935,Mr 23,11:2
  Man Who Knew too Much, The 1956,My 17,37:1
Lewis, David
  That Certain Felling 1956,Je 21,35:2
  Apartment, The 1960,Je 16,37:2
  Kid Galahad 1963,Mr 7,8:5
  Honeymoon Hotel 1964,Je 4,28:1
  John Goldfarb, Please Come Home 1965,Mr 25,42:4
Lewis, David (Producer)
  It's a Pleasure 1945,My 4,23:3
  Tomorrow Is Forever 1946,F 22,21:2
  Other Love, The 1947,My 15,32:4
  Arch of Triumph 1948,Ap 21,33:2
  End of the Affair, The 1955,Ap 29,28:2
  Seventh Sin, The 1957,Je 29,10:6
  Raintree County 1957,D 21,22:1
Lewis, Diana
  Forty Little Mothers 1940,Ap 19,25:2
  Andy Hardy Meets Debutante 1940,Ag 2,12:2
  Bitter Sweet 1940,N 22,27:1
  Go West 1941,F 21,16:2
  People vs Dr Kildare, The 1941,My 8,21:1
  Johnny Eager 1942,F 20,21:2
  Seven Sweethearts 1942,N 13,28:1
  Whistling in Dixie 1942,D 31,20:4
  Cry Havoc 1943,N 24,16:2
Lewis, DiDaDna
  It's a Gift 1935,Ja 5,20:2
Lewis, Dora
  Chu Chin Chow 1925,F 11,19:4
Lewis, Dorothy
  Ice-Capades 1941,S 25,29:1
Lewis, Ed (Strangler)
  That Nazty Nuisance 1943,My 29,10:3
  Bodyhold 1949,D 12,29:4
Lewis, Edgar (Director)
  Ladies in Love 1930,Je 14,9:4
Lewis, Edgar P
  Wives of Men 1918,Ag 26,9:1 (In Addenda)
Lewis, Edward (Producer)
  Careless Years, The 1957,N 28,57:3
  Spartacus 1960,O 7,28:1
  Last Sunset, The 1961,Je 15,51:1
  Lonely are the Brave 1962,Je 28,21:2
  List of Adrian Messenger, The 1963,My 30,20:1
  Seven Days in May 1964,F 20,22:1
  Seconds 1966,O 6,56:1
  Grand-Prix 1966,D 22,40:1
  Fixer, The 1968,D 9,59:1
Lewis, Edward (Screenwriter)
  Careless Years, The 1957,N 28,57:3
Lewis, Elliott
  Story of Molly X, The 1949,D 2,35:4
  Saturday's Hero 1951,S 12,37:2
Lewis, Eva
  Hunchback of Notre Dame, The 1923,S 3,9:3
Lewis, Fiona
  Fearless Vampire Killers, The, or Pardon Me but
    Your Teeth are in my Neck 1967,N 14,52:1
Lewis, Forrest
  It Grows on Trees 1952,N 29,11:2
  Spoilers, The 1955,D 24,10:2
  Absent-Minded Professor, The 1961,Mr 16,44:2
  Man's Favorite Sport? 1964,F 20,22:1
Lewis, Fred
  Enemy to the King, An 1916,N 27,9:1
Lewis, Frederick
  Moral Sinner, The 1924,Ap 7,15:3
Lewis, Gary
  Rock-a-Bye Baby 1958,Jl 24,18:1
Lewis, Gene
  Honeymoon Lane 1931,Ag 1,16:4
Lewis, Gene (Screenwriter)
  Cobra Woman 1944,My 18,17:2
  Gypsy Wildcat 1944,O 5,18:6
  Trail Street 1947,Ap 10,35:2
  Albuquerque 1948,Mr 1,17:2
Lewis, George
  Captain Blood 1924,S 9,19:1
  Proud Heart 1925,N 3,25:4
  Devil's Island 1926,Ag 2,21:2

Fourflusher, The 1928,Ja 16,24:1
13 Washington Square 1928,Ja 30,18:1
We Americans 1928,Mr 29,25:3
Give and Take 1928,D 27,27:1
College Love 1929,S 25:2
Lazy River 1934,Ap 4,26:2
Back Door to Heaven 1939,Ap 20,21:2
Di que me Quieres; Say That You Love Me
  1939,Ap 24,13:2
Outside the Three-Mile Limit 1940,Ap 8,15:2
Falcon's Brother, The 1942,O 3,9:5
Lulu Belle 1948,Je 21,18:3
When my Baby Smiles at Me 1948,N 24,20:2
Captain Carey U S A 1950,Mr 30,40:5
One Way Street 1950,My 12,33:3
Short Grass 1951,Ja 13,10:4
Iron Mistress, The 1952,N 20,39:2
Saskatchewan 1954,Mr 11,26:2
Drum Beat 1954,N 18,42:1
Lewis, George J
  Beware, Spooks 1939,N 3,17:4
  Tarzan and the Leopard Woman 1946,F 11,25:2
  Blackmail 1947,Ag 5,26:3
  Appointment With Danger 1951,My 10,38:2
  Devil's Canyon 1953,O 3,14:2
  Santiago 1956,Jl 14,13:2
  Sign of Zorro, The 1961,S 5,37:6
Lewis, Gillian
  Ring of Treason 1964,My 28,40:3 (Incorrect in
    this edition; use 1964,My 29,15:1 elsewhere)
  Fahrenheit 451 1966,N 15,53:1
Lewis, Harold (Composer)
  Eight Girls in a Boat 1934,Ja 13,16:3
Lewis, Harry
  Always in my Heart 1942,Mr 14,19:2
  Winged Victory 1944,D 21,16:2
  Her Kind of Man 1946,My 4,10:6
  Unsuspected, The 1947,O 4,9:2
  Key Largo 1948,Jl 17,6:6
  Gun Crazy 1950,Ag 25,17:5
  Fat Man, The 1951,My 25,31:2
Lewis, Henry B Major
  Classmates 1924,D 30,15:3
Lewis, Herbert Clyde (Original Author)
  Don Juan Quilligan 1945,Jl 30,16:2
  It Happened on Fifth Avenue 1947,Je 11,33:2
  One Last Fling 1949,Jl 1,14:6
Lewis, Herbert Clyde (Screenwriter)
  Fisherman's Wharf 1939,F 24,15:2
Lewis, Hilda (Original Author)
  Story of Mandy, The 1953,F 24,21:3
Lewis, Ida
  Sinners in the Sun 1932,My 14,11:5
Lewis, Idris (Miscellaneous)
  Heart's Desire 1937,Jl 12,20:4
Lewis, Jack (Director)
  Malamondo 1964,N 19,49:1
Lewis, Jack (Original Author)
  Yank in Vietnam, A 1964,F 6,36:4
Lewis, Jack (Screenwriter)
  Amazing Transparent Man, The 1961,Mr 30,24:2
  Yank in Vietnam, A 1964,F 6,36:4
  Malamondo 1964,N 19,49:1
Lewis, James
  Magnetic Monster, The 1953,My 14,32:5
Lewis, Jarma
  River of no Return 1954,My 1,13:2
  Cobweb, The 1955,Ag 6,13:3
  Tender Trap, The 1955,N 11,29:6
  It's a Dog's Life 1955,D 23,14:3
  Raintree County 1957,D 21,22:1
Lewis, Jay (Director)
  Baby and the Battleship, The 1957,O 1,37:2
  Invasion Quartet 1961,D 11,41:2
Lewis, Jay (Producer)
  Operation Disaster 1951,Ja 15,13:1
  Front Page Story 1955,Ap 19,28:1
Lewis, Jay (Screenwriter)
  Front Page Story 1955,Ap 19,28:1
  Baby and the Battleship, The 1957,O 1,37:2
Lewis, Jeffrey Mrs
  Regular Girl, A 1919,N 11,13:3
Lewis, Jera
  Only Thing, The 1925,N 23,25:4
Lewis, Jerry
  My Friend Irma 1949,S 29,39:2
  My Friend Irma Goes West 1950,Ag 3,20:2
  At War With the Army 1951,Ja 25,21:5
  That's My Boy 1951,Ag 2,18:1
  Sailor Beware 1952,F 1,17:1
  Jumping Jacks 1952,Jl 24,30:2
  Stooge, The 1953,F 5,19:2
  Scared Stiff 1953,Jl 3,10:2
  Caddy, The 1953,S 18,16:6
  Money From Home 1954,F 27,11:3
  Living It Up 1954,Jl 24,6:6
  Three Ring Circus 1954,D 25,7:2
  You're Never too Young 1955,Ag 26,10:2
  Artists and Models 1955,D 22,20:1
  Pardners 1956,Jl 26,20:2
  Hollywood or Bust 1956,D 24,8:1
  Delicate Delinquent, The 1957,Jl 4,16:1
  Sad Sack, The 1957,N 28,57:1

Lewis, Jerry — Cont
  Rock-a-Bye Baby 1958,Jl 24,18:1
  Geisha Boy, The 1958,D 24,00:0
  Don't Give up the Ship 1959,Jl 9,22:1
  Visit to a Small Planet 1960,Ap 14,34:1
  Bellboy, The 1960,Jl 21,17:1
  Cinderfella 1960,D 17,19:2
  Ladies Man, The 1961,Jl 13,26:3
  It's Only Money 1962,N 22,43:1
  Nutty Professor, The 1963,Jl 18,15:2
  It's a Mad, Mad, Mad, Mad World
    1963,N 19,47:1
  Who's Minding the Store? 1963,N 29,67:6
    (Incorrect in this edition; use 1963,N 28,67:6
    elsewhere)
  Patsy, The 1964,Ag 13,24:2
  Disorderly Orderly, The 1964,D 24,8:3
  Family Jewels, The 1965,Ag 12,30:4
  Boeing Boeing 1965,D 24,24:4
  3 on a Couch 1966,Jl 7,30:1
  Way...Way Out 1966,O 27,55:1
  Big Mouth, The 1967,Jl 13,30:2
  Don't Raise the Bridge, Lower the River
    1968,Jl 13,18:1
Lewis, Jerry (Director)
  Bellboy, The 1960,Jl 21,17:1
  Ladies Man, The 1961,Jl 13,26:3
  Errand Boy, The 1962,F 8,25:1
  Nutty Professor, The 1963,Jl 18,15:2
  Patsy, The 1964,Ag 13,24:2
  Family Jewels, The 1965,Ag 12,30:4
  3 on a Couch 1966,Jl 7,30:1
  Big Mouth, The 1967,Jl 13,30:2
Lewis, Jerry (Producer)
  Delicate Delinquent, The 1957,Jl 4,16:1
  Rock-a-Bye Baby 1958,Jl 24,18:1
  Geisha Boy, The 1958,D 24,00:0
  Bellboy, The 1960,Jl 21,17:1
  Cinderfella 1960,D 17,19:2
  Ladies Man, The 1961,Jl 13,26:3
  Family Jewels, The 1965,Ag 12,30:4
  3 on a Couch 1966,Jl 7,30:1
  Big Mouth, The 1967,Jl 13,30:2
Lewis, Jerry (Screenwriter)
  Bellboy, The 1960,Jl 21,17:1
  Ladies Man, The 1961,Jl 13,26:3
  Errand Boy, The 1962,F 8,25:1
  Nutty Professor, The 1963,Jl 18,15:2
  Patsy, The 1964,Ag 13,24:2
  Family Jewels, The 1965,Ag 12,30:4
  Big Mouth, The 1967,Jl 13,30:2
Lewis, Jerry Lee
  High School Confidential 1958,My 31,6:6
Lewis, Joe
  Private Number 1936,Je 12,19:1
  Holy Terror, The 1937,Ja 30,21:2
Lewis, Joe (Director)
  Ghost Creeps, The 1940,Ag 19,13:3
Lewis, Joe E
  Private Buckaroo 1942,Je 25,27:4
Lewis, Joseph H (Director)
  Spy Ring, The 1938,Ja 15,19:1
  Pride of the Bowery 1941,Ja 24,15:2
  Invisible Ghost, The 1941,My 8,21:2
  Mad Doctor of Market Street, The 1942,Ja 5,21:5
  Bombs Over Burma 1942,Ag 10,15:2
  Minstrel Man 1944,Jl 17,18:5
  Falcon in San Francisco, The 1945,Jl 21,7:2
  My Name is Julia Ross 1945,N 9,16:3
  So Dark the Night 1946,D 7,16:2
  Swordsman, The 1947,O 17,18:4
  Return of October, The 1949,F 23,31:2
  Undercover Man, The 1949,Ap 21,30:2
  Lady Without Passport, A 1950,Ag 4,13:2
  Gun Crazy 1950,Ag 25,17:5
  Retreat Hell! 1952,F 20,26:2
  Big Combo, The 1955,Mr 26,13:2
Lewis, Joseph H (Screenwriter)
  Bombs Over Burma 1942,Ag 10,15:2
Lewis, Katherine
  Recompense 1925,Ap 20,22:1
Lewis, Lalage
  Man on the Run 1952,F 27,22:5
Lewis, Mabel Terry
  Stolen Life 1939,Je 15,27:2
  Jamaica Inn 1939,O 12,33:1
  Adventures of Tartu, The 1943,S 24,26:1
Lewis, Martin J (Miscellaneous)
  Maternelle, La 1935,O 15,19:1
  Golem, The 1937,Mr 22,27:2
  Curtain Rises, The 1939,Ap 22,15:2
  Schubert's Serenade 1940,S 3,21:2
Lewis, Maxine
  East Side Kids 1940,F 19,21:6
Lewis, Meade Lux
  New Orleans 1947,Je 20,25:6
Lewis, Mitchell
  Safe for Democracy 1918,N 4,11:3
  At the End of the World 1921,Ag 15,14:3
  On the High Seas 1922,O 8,VI,3:1 (In Addenda)
  Salome 1923,Ja 1,18:1
  Spoilers, The 1923,Ag 6,14:2
  Three Weeks 1924,Ap 1,19:3
  Red Lily, The 1924,S 29,10:1

Lewis, Mitchell— Cont

Flaming Love 1925,Ja 19,14:1
Crimson Runner, The 1925,My 27,26:2
Tracked in the Snow Country 1925,Jl 20,19:2
Mystic, The 1925,Ag 31,19:3
Ben Hur 1925,D 31,10:5 (In Addenda)
Eagle of the Sea, The 1926,N 17,21:6
Tell It to the Marines 1926,D 24,18:2
Hard-Boiled Haggerty 1927,Ag 23,29:4
Back to God's Country 1927,O 24,24:3
Beau Sabreur 1928,Ja 23,18:3
Tenderloin 1928,Mr 15,28:3
Hawk's Nest, The 1928,Je 25,27:1
Docks of New York, The 1928,S 17,28:2
Leatherneck, The 1929,Ap 22,23:1
Madame X 1929,Ap 25,32:3
Bridge of San Luis Rey, The 1929,My 20,22:6
Mammy 1930,Mr 27,24:5
Cuckoos, The 1930,Ap 26,11:1
Bad One, The 1930,Je 13,28:3
Beau Bandit 1930,Je 14,9:4
See America Thirst 1930,D 12,35:3
Never the Twain Shall Meet 1931,Je 6,15:5
Son of India 1931,Jl 25,11:6
Squaw Man, The 1931,S 19,10:2
Ben Hur 1931,D 4,28:2
World and the Flesh, The 1932,My 7,11:5
New Morals for Old 1932,Je 24,15:3
Kongo 1932,N 17,22:5
Secret of Madame Blanche, The 1933,F 4,11:3
Ann Vickers 1933,S 29,24:1
Count of Monte Cristo, The 1934,S 27,25:2
Tale of Two Cities, A 1935,D 26,21:2
Sutter's Gold 1936,Mr 27,25:2
Dancing Pirate 1936,Je 18,19:1
Espionage 1937,Mr 9,27:3
Waikiki Wedding 1937,Mr 25,29:1
Mysterious Mr Moto of Devil's Island
  1938,S 19,16:2
I'll Wait for You 1941,Je 2,13:6
Billy the Kid 1941,Je 20,28:2
Rio Rita 1942,My 8,27:3
Courage of Lassie 1946,Jl 25,18:5
Man With a Cloak, The 1951,N 28,37:2
All the Brothers Were Valiant 1953,D 29,19:2

Lewis, Monica

Inside Straight 1951,Mr 16,34:2
Excuse my Dust 1951,Je 28,21:2
Everything I Have is Yours 1952,O 30,40:5
Affair With a Stranger 1953,Jl 11,8:2
D I, The 1957,Je 6,35:2

Lewis, Morgan (Composer)

Unconquered, The; (Helen Keller in Her Story)
  1954,Je 16,37:1

Lewis, Peter

Lady Gambles, The 1949,My 21,9:2

Lewis, Ralph

Eyes of Youth 1919,D 1,9:3
Prisoners of Love 1921,Ja 17,9:1
Private Scandal, A 1921,Je 13,16:1
Conquering Power, The 1921,Jl 10,VI,2:1 (In
  Addenda)
In the Name of the Law 1922,Jl 10,9:5
Sin Flood, The 1922,O 30,11:1
Birth of a Nation, The 1922,D 5,24:3
Third Alarm, The 1923,Ja 10,28:5
Man Who Came Back, The 1924,S 1,9:1
Dante's Inferno 1924,S 30,27:3
East of Broadway 1924,N 12,13:1
Bridge of Sighs, The 1925,Mr 23,14:2
Last Edition, The 1925,N 11,27:3
Fascinating Youth 1926,My 10,19:1
Outside the Law 1926,My 12,31:1
Bigger Than Barnum's 1926,Jl 13,19:3
Shield of Honor 1927,D 13,33:2
Crooks Can't Win 1928,My 29,17:2
Bad One, The 1930,Je 13,28:3
Birth of a Nation, The 1930,D 22,16:2
Sucker Money 1933,Ap 7,22:5
Lost City, The 1935,F 21,23:3
Dillinger 1945,Ap 26,26:2

Lewis, Randolph C (Screenwriter)

Without Benefit of Clergy 1921,Je 20,17:2

Lewis, Ray (Original Author)

Girl in the Street 1938,My 26,31:2

Lewis, Richard (Producer)

Lovely Way to Die, A 1968,Jl 13,18:1

Lewis, Robert

Tonight We Raid Calais 1943,Ap 15,20:2
Paris After Dark 1943,O 23,11:1
Dragon Seed 1944,Jl 21,16:4
Son of Lassie 1945,Je 11,12:1
Ziegfeld Follies 1946,Mr 23,8:3

Lewis, Robert (Director)

Anything Goes 1956,Mr 22,38:1

Lewis, Robert Q

Affair to Remember, An 1957,Jl 20,8:5
Good Neighbor Sam 1964,Jl 23,19:1
Ski Party 1965,O 23,17:3
Ride Beyond Vengance 1966,S 29,60:1
How to Succeed in Business Without Really
  Trying 1967,Mr 10,30:1

Lewis, Roger (Composer)

In the Navy 1941,Je 12,29:2

Lewis, Roger (Producer)

Swimmer, The 1968,My 16,53:1

Lewis, Roger H (Producer)

Pawnbroker, The 1965,Ap 21,51:1

Lewis, Ronald

Beachcomber, The 1955,Ja 17,27:5
Prisoner, The 1955,D 12,37:1
Storm over the Nile 1956,Je 9,14:2
Panic in the Parlor 1957,D 18,45:1
Wind Cannot Read, The 1960,Mr 10,36:1
Conspiracy of Hearts 1960,Ap 8,24:1
Stop Me Before I Kill 1961,Je 22,23:4
Scream of Fear 1961,Ag 23,29:1
Mr Sardonicus 1961,O 19,39:3
Billy Budd 1962,O 31,32:1

Lewis, Ronnie Trio

Big Circus, The 1959,Jl 18,6:1

Lewis, Sheldon

Darling of New York, The 1924,Ja 18,20:1
Enemy Sex, The 1924,Jl 1,21:4
Top of the World, The 1925,F 17,18:1
New Lives for Old 1925,F 25,16:7
Silent Sanderson 1925,Je 11,14:3
Sporting Chance, The 1925,Je 24,14:3
Red Kimono, The 1926,F 3,23:1
Bride of the Storm 1926,Ap 5,24:1
Two-Gun Man, The 1926,Jl 13,19:3
Senor Daredevil 1926,Ag 17,15:3

Lewis, Sinclair (Miscellaneous)

Love of a Clown (Pagliacci) 1950,Ap 17,18:5

Lewis, Sinclair (Original Author)

Main Street 1923,Je 12,22:2
Babbitt 1924,Jl 15,9:4
Mantrap 1926,Jl 12,24:4
Newly Rich 1931,Jl 3,22:1
Arrowsmith 1931,D 8,36:4
Ann Vickers 1933,S 29,24:1
Babbitt 1934,D 17,24:2
I Married a Doctor 1936,Ap 20,17:1
Dodsworth 1936,S 24,29:1
Untamed 1940,Jl 25,14:3
This is the Life 1944,Ap 28,23:3
Cass Timberlane 1947,N 7,20:2
Elmer Gantry 1960,Jl 8,16:1

Lewis, Stephen (Original Author)

Sparrows Don't Sing 1963,My 7,46:2

Lewis, Stephen (Screenwriter)

Sparrows Don't Sing 1963,My 7,46:2

Lewis, Steven

Negatives 1968,O 15,40:1

Lewis, Sybil

Miracle in Harlem 1949,O 24,19:4

Lewis, Sylvia

Lieutenant Wore Skirts, The 1956,Ja 12,22:1

Lewis, Ted

Is Everybody Happy? 1929,N 2,14:6
Show of Shows 1929,N 21,24:5
Follow the Boys 1944,Ap 26,24:6

Lewis, Ted (Composer)

Hold That Ghost 1941,Ag 8,13:3

Lewis, Ted and his entertainers

Hold That Ghost 1941,Ag 8,13:3

Lewis, Ted and orchestra

Manhattan Merry-Go-Round 1937,D 31,9:3

Lewis, Therese (Screenwriter)

What a Woman 1943,D 3,27:2

Lewis, Tom

Passers By 1920,Je 21,13:1
Go-Getter 1923,Ap 9,14:3 (In Addenda)
Marriage Morals 1923,Ag 14,10:3
Great White Way, The 1924,Ja 4,10:1
Steamboat Bill, Jr 1928,My 15,17:3

Lewis, Tom (Producer)

Cause for Alarm 1951,Mr 30,28:5

Lewis, Tom (Screenwriter)

Cause for Alarm 1951,Mr 30,28:5

Lewis, Tommy

Teresa 1951,Ap 6,31:2

Lewis, Vance (Director)

Stranger in Town, A 1968,Ap 25,53:4
Stranger Returns, The 1968,S 12,54:3

Lewis, Vera

Mother and the Law, The 1919,Ag 19,10:1
Nurse Marjorie 1920,My 24,20:3
Peg o'my Heart 1923,Ja 22,10:1
Long Live the King 1923,D 4,24:1
Broadway After Dark 1924,My 20,15:2
Black Swan, The 1924,N 25,26:1
Enticement 1925,Mr 21,16:3
Eve's Secret 1925,Jl 11,14:3
Stella Dallas 1925,N 17,30:2
Ella Cinders 1926,Je 7,23:2
Take It From Me 1926,N 2,35:1
Resurrection 1927,My 17,27:2
Ramona 1928,My 15,17:3
Home Towners, The 1928,O 24,26:4
Iron Mask, The 1929,F 22,18:6
Night Nurse 1931,Jl 17,23:4
Man on the Flying Trapeze 1935,Ag 3,16:2
Way Down East 1935,O 31,16:2
Paddy O'Day 1936,F 8,19:2

Lewis, Vera— Cont

Dancing Pirate 1936,Je 18,19:1
Four Daughters 1938,Ag 19,13:3
Comet over Broadway 1938,D 16,33:3
Naughty but Nice 1939,Je 23,23:2
Hell's Kitchen 1939,Jl 3,10:5
Roaring Twenties, The 1939,N 11,12:1
Return Of Doctor X, The 1939,N 23,38:5
Four Wives 1939,D 23,9:1
Courageous Dr Christian, The 1940,Mr 29,25:3
Four Mothers 1941,Ja 11,12:7
She Couldn't Say No 1941,Ja 17,21:3
Nine Loves Are not Enough 1941,O 30,27:2
Lady Gangster 1942,Jl 10,13:2
Cat Creeps, The 1946,My 18,12:4

Lewis, Walter P

Three Miles Out 1924,Ja 1,20:1
Beware of Blondes 1928,Ag 21,27:4
Arizona Kid, The 1930,My 17,21:2

Lewton, Val (Producer)

Cat People 1942,D 7,22:2
I Walked With a Zombie 1943,Ap 22,31:5
Leopard Man, The 1943,My 20,26:4
Seventh Victim, The 1943,S 18,11:3
Ghost Ship, The 1943,D 25,19:4
Curse of the Cat People, The 1944,Mr 4,11:1
Youth Runs Wild 1944,S 2,17:2
Body Snatcher, The 1945,My 26,18:3
Isle of the Dead 1945,S 8,12:2
Bedlam 1946,Ap 20,16:4
My Own True Love 1949,F 3,27:3
Please Believe Me 1950,Je 12,19:4
Apache Drums 1951,My 7,22:2

Lex, Lee (Producer)

Awful Dr Orlof, The 1964,D 3,58:3

Lexy, Edward

Troopship 1938,Ap 26,18:2
South Riding 1938,Ag 2,15:2
This Man Is News 1939,Jl 20,16:4
Larceny Street 1941,Ja 6,11:2
Convoy 1941,Ja 17,21:2
Queen of Crime 1941,F 19,25:2
Proud Valley 1941,My 17,19:2
Captain Boycott 1947,D 6,11:2
Blanche Fury 1948,N 24,20:2
Girl in a Million, A 1950,Jl 24,15:2
Miss Robin Hood 1953,Je 27,7:2
Gay Adventure, The 1954,S 16,35:7

Ley, Fritz

Ich Geh' aus und Du Bleibst da 1932,N 21,21:1

Ley, Grita

Berlin After Dark 1929,My 28,36:2

Ley, Willy (Original Author)

Conquest of Space 1955,My 28,7:6

Leyba, Claire

Anna Lucasta 1959,Ja 15,27:1

Leyden, Leo

Mask, The 1961,O 28,12:4
Luck of Ginger Coffey, The 1964,S 22,44:1

Leymarie, Pierre

Pickpocket 1963,My 22,36:2

Leyon, J

Flame of Love, The 1930,N 3,19:3

Leyssac, Paul

Head Over Heels in Love 1937,F 13,9:1
Victoria the Great 1937,O 29,19:1
Paris Calling 1942,Ja 19,21:2

Leytes, Josef (Director)

Faithful City 1952,Ap 8,35:2

Leytes, Josef (Original Author)

Passion 1954,D 11,11:1

Leytes, Josef (Producer)

Faithful City 1952,Ap 8,35:2

Leytes, Josef (Screenwriter)

Faithful City 1952,Ap 8,35:2
Passion 1954,D 11,11:1

Leyton, Drue

Change of Heart 1934,My 11,24:2
Charlie Chan's Courage 1934,Ag 25,16:6
Charlie Chan in London 1934,S 13,26:1
Charlie Chan at the Circus 1936,Mr 19,22:4

Leyton, John

Guns at Batasi 1964,N 17,47:1
Von Ryan's Express 1965,Je 24,28:1
Idol, The 1966,Ag 11,27:1

Lezama, Luis (Director)

Cemetario de las Aquilas, El; Eagles' Cementery,
  The 1939,S 2,20:1
Viejo Amor, Un; Old Love, An 1940,Ja 29,11:6

Lezana, Sara

Tarantos, Los 1964,Je 30,22:1

Lezar, Maria

A Ferfi Mind Oeruelt; All Men Are Crazy
  1937,D 11,22:3

Lezard, Cecile

Native Son 1951,Je 18,19:2

Lezhava, Zurab

Last Hill, The 1945,Je 26,13:2

Lherbay, Mme

End of a Day, The 1939,S 12,28:4

L'Herbier, Marcel (Director)

Living Dead Man, The 1927,Mr 7,16:3
Argent, L' 1929,Mr 3,VII,7:2 (Incorrect in this
  edition; use 1929,Mr 3,VIII,8:5 in film)

L'Herbier, Marcel (Director)— Cont
Mystere de la Chambre Jaune, Le 1931,My 26,33:2
Donna D'una Notte, La 1933,Mr 10,19:4
Bonheur, Le 1936,F 28,18:2
Sacrifice d'Honneur 1938,D 2,27:2
Rasputin 1939,O 17,31:4
Entente Cordiale 1939,D 26,23:2
Living Corpse, The 1940,S 23,21:4
Amoureux, Les 1940,D 9,23:3
Great Temptation, The 1942,Jl 10,13:3
Queen's Necklace, The 1947,My 17,8:5
Vie de Boheme, La 1947,N 28,37:4
Foolish Husbands 1948,O 11,27:2
Savage Brigade 1948,D 3,33:4
Stolen Affections 1951,Mr 12,20:2
Argent, L' 1968,S 23,42:5
L'Herbier, Marcel (Screenwriter)
Sacrifice d'Honneur 1938,D 2,27:2
Living Corpse, The 1940,S 23,21:4
Amoureux, Les 1940,D 9,23:3
Great Temptation, The 1942,Jl 10,13:3
Stolen Affections 1951,Mr 12,20:2
Argent, L' 1968,S 23,42:5
Li-Den-Ten
In the Far East 1937,O 20,27:3
Li-Hua, Li
Empress Wu 1965,Mr 16,42:2
Grand Substitution, The 1965,N 25,64:5
Li-Iun-Shen
Igdenbu 1930,D 9,31:3
Liabel
Frochard et les Deux Orphelines, La 1934,F 7,16:2
Lianeza, Luis
Dos Mujeres y un Don Juan 1934,Je 4,12:4
Lianos, Theo
Forty Thousand Horsemen 1941,Ag 15,13:2
Liarov, M
Nazar Stodolya 1937,Ag 7,7:2
Lonely White Sail 1938,My 7,18:1
Liashenko, L I
Mother and Sons 1938,S 15,29:2
Libaire, Dorothy
Confessions of a Co-Ed 1931,Je 20,20:4
Madame Butterfly 1932,D 26,26:2
Bondage 1933,Ap 24,11:3
Zoo in Budapest 1933,Ap 28,15:2
Jennie Gerhardt 1933,Je 9,20:2
Affairs of a Gentleman 1934,Je 23,16:7
Baby, Take a Bow 1934,Je 30,18:6
Murder on a Honeymoon 1935,Mr 4,12:2
Perfect Clue, The 1935,Mr 14,18:1
Libassi, Renato (Producer)
Crazy Desire 1964,Jl 3,13:2
Fascist, The 1965,Je 18,28:3
Hours of Love, The 1965,S 4,11:5
Libbey, J Aldrich
Greed 1924,D 5,28:1
Libbott, Robert (Screenwriter)
Stage to Tucson 1951,My 5,14:2
Libby, Fred
Captain from Castile 1947,D 26,22:4
Belle Star's Daughter 1949,Ja 10,19:2
Wagonmaster 1950,Je 19,17:2
What Price Glory 1952,Ag 23,10:2
Sergeant Rutledge 1960,My 26,37:1
Libeau, Gustave
Nine Bachelors 1942,F 9,19:2
Libeneiner, Wolfgang
Nacht an der Donau, Eine; Night on the Danube, A 1938,N 19,9:3
Liberace
South Sea Sinner 1950,Ja 16,18:4
Sincerely Yours 1955,N 3,37:1
Loved One, The 1965,O 12,57:1
Liberaki, Margarita (Screenwriter)
Phaedra 1962,O 19,24:1
Liberatore, Ugo (Original Author)
300 Spartans, The 1962,S 20,29:2
Idol, The 1966,Ag 11,27:1
Minute to Pray, A Second to Die, A 1968,My 23,56:2
Liberatore, Ugo (Screenwriter)
Pharaohs' Woman, The 1962,Ap 19,35:2
Arturo Island 1962,D 22,5:2
Empty Canvas, The 1964,My 16,21:1 (Incorrect in this edition; use 1964,My 16,12:1 elsewhere)
Tramplers, The 1966,D 8,64:1
Minute to Pray, A Second to Die, A 1968,My 23,56:2
Libgold, L
Dybbuk, The 1938,Ja 28,17:2
Libin, Z (Original Author)
Broken Hearts 1926,Mr 3,26:1
Libman, M
Dybbuk, The 1938,Ja 28,17:2
Libora, Jan (Producer)
Capricious Summer 1968,S 18,50:2
Libott, Robert (Screenwriter)
Barbary Pirate 1949,O 28,29:3
Chinatown at Midnight 1949,N 18,35:3
Fortunes of Captain Blood 1950,Je 10,11:3
Groom Wore Spurs, The 1951,Mr 14,41:2

Liburn, James
Quiet Man, The 1952,Ag 22,13:1
Licalzi, Lawrence
Boy of Mine 1923,D 24,12:1 (In Addenda)
Licata, Vincenzo
Seduced and Abandoned 1964,Jl 16,23:1
Liceaga, Antonio
Madre Querida 1935,D 23,15:5
Desheredados, Los 1936,Mr 23,22:6
Irma la Mala 1936,O 6,28:7
Tras la Reja 1937,Ja 11,15:7
Eterna Martir 1938,Ja 3,16:3
Suprema Ley; Supreme Law 1938,Ja 15,19:2
Lichine, David
Sensations of 1945 1944,Jl 7,13:2
Licho, A E
Loves of Jeanne Ney, The 1928,Jl 10,17:3
1914: The Last Days Before the War 1932,S 5,9:6
Licho, Edgar
Days of Glory 1944,Je 17,10:2
Licho, Ernst (Director)
His Late Excellency 1929,Je 11,27:2
Lichtman, Al (Producer)
Young Lions, The 1958,Ap 3,23:1
Licudi, Gabriella
Fall of the Roman Empire, The 1964,Mr 27,14:2
Liquidator, The 1966,O 29,34:1
Casino Royale 1967,Ap 29,25:1
Jokers, The 1967,My 16,50:1
Liddell, Jane
Rogue River 1951,F 16,21:4
Liddell, Laura
Shakespeare Wallah 1966,Mr 23,40:2
Liddi, Francesca
Sensualita 1954,Ap 29,40:2
Lider, Ann
For Singles Only 1968,Je 6,54:1
Lidonni, Ferdinando
Madame Butterfly 1956,Ap 24,26:2
Lieb, Robert
Somebody up There Likes Me 1956,Jl 6,16:1
Lieban, Fritz-Albert
Annemarie, Die Braut der Kompanie 1934,D 8,18:6
Liebeneiner, Wolfgang
Liebelei; Light Love 1933,Jl 2,IX,2:2
Was Bin Ich Ohne dich? 1935,D 14,11:2
Alle Tage Ist Kein Sonntag 1936,Jl 11,11:4
Selige Exzellenz, Die 1937,Je 15,26:2
Blonde Carmen, Die 1939,O 7,11:3
Liebeneiner, Wolfgang (Director)
Promise Me Nothing 1937,N 13,11:3
Mustergatte, Der; Model Husband 1938,Mr 19,11:3
Ziel den Wolken; Goal in the Clouds 1939,My 27,13:3
Florentiner Hut, Der; Leghorn Hat, The 1939,Je 3,11:3
April 1, 2000 1954,F 17,27:2
Dancing Heart, The 1958,Ja 18,10:3
Taiga 1959,Mr 17,42:4
Trapp Family, The 1961,Ag 31,22:4
Liebeneiner, Wolfgang (Screenwriter)
Dancing Heart, The 1958,Ja 18,10:3
Lieberman, Art (Producer)
Hippie Revolt, The 1967,D 20,53:1
Lieberman, Frank
Dutchman 1967,F 28,32:1
Lieberman, Leo (Miscellaneous)
Mad Dog Coll 1961,My 13,10:1
Lieberman, Leo (Original Author)
Yank in Korea, A 1951,Ap 2,29:2
Lieberson, Goddard (Original Author)
3 for Bedroom C 1952,Je 27,18:3
Liebert, Yakof
Mass Struggle 1934,S 17,20:3
Liebgold, L
Yiddle With his Fiddle 1937,Ja 2,15:1
Liebgold, Leon
Tevya 1939,D 22,15:3
Liebler, Theodore A Jr (Screenwriter)
Success 1923,Jl 10,22:5
Liebman, Max (Composer)
Kid From Brooklyn, The 1946,Ap 19,25:2
Liebmann, Robert (Original Author)
Stuerme der Leidenschaft 1932,Mr 16,17:3
Congress Dances 1932,My 12,23:2
Heart Song 1934,Je 6,24:6
Liebmann, Robert (Screenwriter)
Blue Angel, The 1959,S 5,11:4
Liebowitz, Francis
Unstrap Me 1968,N 21,41:2
Liebst, Padre Agostinho
Amazon Trader, The 1956,N 17,17:6
Lieck, Lotte
Marriage in the Shadows 1948,S 17,28:3
Liedtke, Harry
Gypsy Blood 1921,My 9,16:2
Madame Wants no Children 1927,Je 21,23:3
Love Is A Lie 1928,Je 26,29:1
Forbidden Love 1929,Ja 14,20:1

Liedtke, Harry— Cont
Nie Wieder Liebe; No More Love 1931,O 4,VIII,7:1
Nie Wieder Liebe 1932,Ja 16,13:1
I Kiss Your Hand, Madame 1932,Ag 29,9:2
Korvettenkapitaen, Der 1933,Mr 20,18:3
Eine Liebesnacht 1933,My 15,16:2
Liebe in Uniform 1934,O 9,17:2
Page vom Dalmasse-Hotel, Der 1935,Mr 25,12:3
Wenn am Sonntagabend die Dorfmusik Spielt 1935,D 9,25:3
Zwichen Zwei Herzen; Between Two Hearts 1936,Ja 28,15:3
Liebesleute 1936,O 3,21:2
Liedtke, Henry
Last Payment, The 1922,Ja 22,VI,3:2 (In Addenda)
Loves of Pharaoh 1922,F 22,13:3 (In Addenda)
Lief, J O (Original Author)
Two for Tonight 1935,Ag 31,16:2
Lief, Max (Original Author)
Two for Tonight 1935,Ag 31,16:2
Lieferant, Henry (Original Author)
Doctors' Wives 1931,Ap 25,23:4
Lieferant, Sylvia (Original Author)
Doctors' Wives 1931,Ap 25,23:4
Lieffen, Karl
One, Two, Three 1961,D 22,17:1
Jack of Diamonds 1967,N 11,26:3
Lieren, Albert
Hotel Sahara 1952,Ja 1,21:4
Lieske, Trude
Two Neckties; Zwei Kravatten 1930,N 30,IX,6:5
Rendez-Vous 1932,Ap 30,19:3
Liebling von Wien, Der 1933,Je 10,16:5
Liessem, Vera
S A Mann Brand 1934,My 28,16:2
Zwischen Himmel und Erde; Between Heaven and Earth 1935,Ja 21,19:3
Zwei im Sonnenschein 1937,Jl 31,6:2
Lietten, Karl
Defector, The 1966,N 17,55:1
Lieu, Maurice
Waikiki Wedding 1937,Mr 25,29:1
Lieven, Albert
Krach um Iolanthe 1935,My 11,21:3
Die vom Niederrhein; Lower Rhine Folks 1935,My 20,20:6
Fraeulein Liselott 1935,My 27,20:7
Fraulein Liselott 1935,My 27,20:7
Hermine und die Sieben Aufrechten 1935,S 21,18:2
Reifende Jugend 1936,Ja 4,19:1
Glueckspilze 1936,O 26,21:1
Frau Ohne Bedeutung, Ein 1938,Ap 16,17:2
Kater Lampe 1938,Ap 23,19:3
Convoy 1941,Ja 17,21:2
Young Mr Pitt, The 1943,Mr 11,17:1
Jeannie 1943,S 13,14:2
Yellow Canary, The 1944,Ap 14,24:7
Life and Death of Colonel Blimp, The 1945,Mr 30,18:2
Seventh Veil, The 1945,D 26,15:1
Frieda 1947,Ag 15,12:3
Beware of Pity 1947,N 1,11:2
Sleeping Car to Trieste 1949,Ap 18,18:6
Her Man Gilbey 1949,Je 9,35:2
Desperate Moment 1953,S 1,19:4
Devil's General, The 1957,Ap 16,38:2
House of Intrigue, The 1960,Mr 10,36:3
Conspiracy of Hearts 1960,Ap 8,24:1
Foxhole in Cairo 1961,F 16,25:2
Guns of Navarone, The 1961,Je 23,19:1
Victors, The 1963,D 20,21:2
Lieven, Domenic
Town Like Alice, A 1958,S 22,27:1
Liewehr, Fred
Jana, Das Maedchen aus dem Boehmerwald 1936,Je 20,22:3
Unsterblicher Walzer; Immortal Waltz 1939,N 18,22:6
Marika 1953,F 18,27:2
Story of Vickie, The 1958,Ja 30,19:2
Embezzled Heaven 1959,Ap 24,23:1
Lifanoff, B
In old Siberia 1929,Jl 22,17:1
Lifar, Serge
Testament of Orpheus 1962,Ap 10,48:1
Lifar, Serge (Miscellaneous)
Ballerina 1938,N 15,27:1
Lifshitz, Ammon
Faithful City 1952,Ap 8,35:2
Ligeri, Bruno
Cyanamide 1954,Mr 26,17:6
Ligero, Miguel
Nobleza Baturra; Rustic Chivalry 1938,Mr 28,19:3
Morena Clara 1938,Je 18,18:3
Verbena de la Paloma, La 1938,O 25,19:2
Vida Bohemia, La 1939,F 6,8:5
Rumbo al Cairo; Bound for Cairo 1940,Je 8,18:3
Ligeti, Juliska D
Melody of The Heart 1930,S 1,16:1

Liggon, Grover
Father's Son 1931,F 21,15:2
Light, Robert
Gentlemen are Born 1934,N 22,27:2
Murder in the Clouds 1934,D 26,18:1
Reckless 1935,Ap 20,16:1
Shipmates Forever 1935,O 17,29:3
Ceiling Zero 1936,Ja 20,22:2
My Man Godfrey 1936,S 19,18:1 (Incorrect in this edition; use 1936,S 18,18:1 elsewhere)
Lightner, Frances (Original Author)
Puppets 1926,Je 21,17:2
Lightner, Fred
Babe Ruth Story, The 1948,Jl 29,17:2
Lightner, Winnie
Gold Diggers of Broadway, The 1929,Ag 31,13:4
Show of Shows 1929,N 21,24:5
She Couldn't Say No 1930,F 16,III,8:1
Hold Everything 1930,Ap 23,24:1
Life of the Party, The 1930,N 10,16:2
Sit Tight 1931,F 19,20:4
Gold Dust Gertie 1931,My 30,9:2
Side Show 1931,S 19,10:2
Manhattan Parade 1931,D 25,29:2
Play Girl 1932,Mr 19,11:2
She Had to Say Yes 1933,Jl 29,14:2
Dancing Lady 1933,D 1,23:2
I'll Fix It 1934,N 12,17:3
Lightning (Dog)
White Fang 1936,Jl 18,18:2
Renfrew of the Royal Mounted 1937,N 3,29:4
Lighton, Louis D (Producer)
College Rhythm 1934,N 24,19:1
Here is my Heart 1934,D 22,21:1
Lives of a Bengal Lancer, The 1935,Ja 12,12:2
Peter Ibbetson 1935,N 8,18:2
Collegiate 1936,Ja 23,25:2
Trouble for Two 1936,My 30,7:2
Captains Courageous 1937,My 12,27:1
Man-Proof 1938,Ja 14,21:1
Test Pilot 1938,Ap 16,17:1
Lucky Night 1939,My 5,29:3
Tree Grows in Brooklyn, A 1945,Mr 1,25:5
Bell for Adano, A 1945,Jl 6,8:3
Anna and the King of Siam 1946,Je 21,20:2
Home Sweet Homicide 1946,S 12,5:7
Down to the Sea in Ships 1949,F 23,31:2
No Highway in the Sky 1951,S 22,8:6
Lightstone, Leonard (Producer)
Idol, The 1966,Ag 11,27:1
Spy With a Cold Nose, The 1966,D 20,58:2
Ligneres, Laurence
Suitor, The; Soupirant, Le 1963,S 18,35:1
Liguisos, Mitsos
Never on Sunday 1960,O 19,54:1
Liguoro, Eugenio di
Lost-a Wife 1925,Je 22,10:2
Liguoro, Rina de
Quo Vadis 1925,F 16,24:1
Liijeback, Synnove
Dear John 1966,Mr 9,46:1
Likashevitch, T (Director)
Sound of Life, The 1962,F 12,28:2
Lilburn, James
Titanic 1953,My 28,27:5
Fire over Africa 1954,N 22,29:5
Lilburn, Jim
Suddenly 1954,O 8,27:2
Liliana, Lill
Dybbuk, The 1938,Ja 28,17:2
Lilien, Kurt
Bockbierfest 1931,Mr 31,25:3
Lumpenball 1931,Ap 27,25:1
Drei von der Kavallerie 1935,Ap 13,11:4
Lilina, E
On his Own 1939,S 13,31:3
Liljedahl, Marie
Inga 1968,N 21,41:2
Liljencrantz, Ottilie A (Original Author)
Viking, The 1928,N 29,32:4
Lillard, Tom
Brig, The 1964,S 21,37:4
Lillen, Kurt
Zwei Herzen und ein Schlag 1932,S 9,17:5
Lilley, Clark (Original Author)
Ladies' Day 1943,Mr 26,14:3
Lilley, Joseph J (Composer)
Riding High 1943,D 23,26:4
Lillie, Beatrice
Show of Shows 1929,N 21,24:5
Doctor Rhythm 1938,My 19,25:2
On Approval 1945,Ja 29,17:1
Around the World in 80 Days 1956,O 18,37:1
Thoroughly Modern Millie 1967,Mr 23,25:1
Lilliecrona, Torsten
Of Love and Lust (Doll's House, A); Doll's House, A (Of Love and Lust) 1959,My 26,31:2
Lesson in Love, A 1960,Mr 15,46:1
Lillmore, Clyde
Devil's Pass Key, The 1920,Ag 9,6:3
Lilly Brothers
Festival 1967,O 24,53:2

Limbaugh, Conrad (Cinematographer)
Hunters of the Deep 1954,D 17,37:4
Limburg, Olga
Apaches of Paris 1928,D 11,35:3
Der Schrecken der Garnison 1932,Je 1,19:5
Luegen auf Ruegen 1934,Ja 1,28:2
Rosen aus dem Sueden; Roses from the South 1935,Ap 23,24:5
Schwarzwaldmaedel 1935,O 12,12:3
Ich Kenn' Dich Nicht und Liebe Dich; I Don't Know You, but I Love You 1935,N 18,20:1
Lied vom Glueck, Das; Song of Happiness, The 1935,N 30,12:7
Selige Exzellenz, Die 1937,Je 15,26:2
Fraeulein Frau 1937,Jl 3,18:2
Peter, Paul und Nanette 1940,My 25,20:1
Hurra! Ich bin Papa; Hurrah! I'm a Papa 1940,Je 1,12:3
Lime, Yvonne
Rainmaker, The 1956,D 13,51:1
Untamed Youth 1957,My 11,24:6
Limon, Jose
Dance Of Life, The 1951,F 28,33:2
Linaker, Kay
Murder of Dr Harrigan, The 1936,Ja 21,27:5
Road Gang 1936,F 24,14:1
Crack-Up 1937,Ja 4,20:4
Outer Gate, The 1937,N 22,15:2
Charlie Chan at Monte Carlo 1937,D 18,18:1
Personal Secretary 1938,O 5,20:2
Last Warning, The 1938,D 8,34:4
Trade Winds 1939,Ja 13,17:2
Charlie Chan in Reno 1939,My 31,27:2
Young Mr Lincoln 1939,Je 3,11:2
Man About Town 1939,Je 29,19:1
Drums Along the Mohawk 1939,N 4,11:2
Free, Blonde and 21 1940,Ap 5,25:2
Buck Benny Rides Again 1940,Ap 25,28:4
Mystery Sea Raider 1940,Ag 26,11:4
Kitty Foyle 1941,Ja 9,27:2
They Dare not Love 1941,My 16,21:4
Private Nurse 1941,Ag 29,13:3
Night Before the Divorce, The 1942,Ap 10,21:3
Men of Texas 1942,Jl 13,18:3 (In Addenda)
Let's Face It 1943,Ag 5,18:1
Lady in the Dark 1944,F 23,17:1
Lincke, Anna Mueller
O Alte Burschenherrlichkeit 1932,Je 18,9:2
Lincoln, Abbey
Girl Can't Help It, The 1957,F 9,12:7
Nothing but a Man 1964,S 21,37:2
For Love of Ivy 1968,Jl 18,26:1
Lincoln, Caryl
Girl in Every Port, A 1928,F 20,14:1
Lincoln, Eimo
Tarzan of the Apes 1918,Ja 28,13:2
Romance of Tarzan, The 1918,O 14,15:1
Lafayette, We Come 1918,N 4,11:3
Greatest Thing in Life, The 1918,D 23,9:1
Quincy Adams Sawyer 1922,D 18,22:2
Rupert of Hentzau 1923,Jl 9,8:4
Fashion Row 1924,Ja 28,12:1
Lind, Charles
Adam Had Four Sons 1941,Mr 28,26:6
Adventure in Washington 1941,Ag 1,11:3
Lind, Della
Swiss Miss 1938,Je 4,18:2
Lind, Georgia
Lumpenball 1931,Ap 27,25:1
Wie Sag' Ich's Meinem Mann? 1934,Ja 23,22:4
Kalte Mamsell, Die 1935,Ja 12,12:2
Beiden Seehunde, Die 1935,Mr 9,19:2
Lind, Gillian
Condemned to Death 1932,Jl 14,24:2
Horse's Mouth, The 1954,Ja 20,33:4
Lind, Jenny
Deliverance 1919,Ag 19,10:1
Lind, Lars
Swedish Wedding Night 1965,N 15,48:1
491 1967,D 21,45:1
Obession 1968,Ag 29,46:3
Lind, Laurie
Alimony 1949,Jl 22,16:3
Lind, Sarah
Deliverance 1919,Ag 19,10:1
Lindahl, Anna
Under Falsk Flagg 1937,Ja 20,18:5
Frustration 1949,Ag 27,7:3
Sunshine Follows Rain 1949,S 29,39:2
Lindau, Paul (Original Author)
Andere, Der 1932,Ja 15,24:4
Lindberg, Lennart
Matter of Morals, A 1961,Je 1,31:1-
Lindberg, Sven
Dreams; Kvinnodrom 1960,Je 1,42:1
Lindbergh, Charles A (Original Author)
Spirit of St Louis, The 1957,F 22,25:1
Lindblad, Arne
Sun Over Klara 1944,My 1,20:8
Lesson in Love, A 1960,Mr 15,46:1
Lindblom, Gunnel
Seventh Seal 1958,O 14,44:1
Wild Strawberries 1959,Je 23,37:1

Lindblom, Gunnel — Cont
Virgin Spring, The; Jungfrukallan 1960,N 15,46:1
Winter Light 1963,My 14,32:1
Silence, The 1964,F 4,28:1
Rapture 1965,Ag 24,25:3
Hunger 1966,S 14,53:2
Loving Couples 1966,S 20,38:1
Hunger 1968,Ag 13,45:2
Lindegren, Sven
Haelsingar 1934,S 25,25:2
Lindemann, Mitch (Screenwriter)
Way West, The 1967,My 25,54:1
Linden, Eric
Are These our Children 1931,N 14,15:3
Crowd Roars, The 1932,Mr 23,25:4
Love Starved 1932,Ap 15,23:1
Roadhouse Murder 1932,Ap 29,13:4
Life Begins 1932,Ag 26,20:3
Age of Consent, The 1932,S 3,16:2
Big City Blues 1932,S 10,18:5
Afraid to Talk 1932,D 19,19:5
No Other Woman 1933,Ja 30,9:4 (In Addenda)
Sweepings 1933,Mr 24,22:3
Past of Mary Holmes, The 1933,My 1,10:3
Silver Cord, The 1933,My 5,18:1
Flying Devils 1933,Ag 26,14:3
I Give my Love 1934,Jl 17,24:2
Let 'Em Have It 1935,My 30,21:1
Ah, Wilderness! 1935,D 25,30:2
Voice of Bugle Ann, The 1936,F 27,23:1
Robin Hood of El Dorado, The 1936,Mr 14,10:1
In His Steps 1936,O 29,31:1
Old Hutch 1936,D 7,27:4
Family Affair, A 1937,Ap 20,29:2
Good Old Soak 1937,Ap 20,25:3
Everything's on Ice 1939,O 6,31:1
Linden, Jennie
Nightmare 1964,Je 18,29:2
Linden, Liane
Lasse-Maja 1943,Mr 22,15:4
Linden, Marta
Yank at Eton, A 1942,O 16,23:1
Random Harvest 1942,D 18,36:6
Stand by for Action 1943,Mr 12,12:2
Three Hearts for Julia 1943,My 21,22:4
Youngest Profession, The 1943,Je 25,13:3
Swing Shift Maisie 1943,S 10,29:2
See Here Private Hargrove 1944,Mr 22,17:2
Andy Hardy's Blonde Trouble 1944,My 5,17:3
Maisie Goes to Reno 1944,S 29,18:1
Keep Your Powder Dry 1945,Mr 12,22:6
Linden, Nat (Screenwriter)
Yellowback 1957,Ap 5,24:2
Lindenbaum, Elaine
One-Way Ticket to Hell 1955,D 8,45:1
Linder, Alfred
House on Ninety-Second Street, The 1945,S 27,24:7
13 Rue Madeleine 1947,Ja 16,30:2
Brasher Doubloon, The 1947,My 22,34:5
Canon City 1948,Jl 8,19:2
I Was a Male War Bride 1949,Ag 27,7:2
Guilty of Treason 1950,Ap 11,26:2
Girl in the Kremlin, The 1957,My 22,29:2
Linder, Cec
S O S Pacific 1960,O 13,41:3
Goldfinger 1964,D 22,36:1
Linder, Max
Max Comes Across 1917,F 19,9:3
Three Must-Get-Theres, The 1922,Ag 28,14:1
Lindforff, Henny
Girls are Willing, The 1959,My 11,30:1
Lindfors, Viveca
To the Victor 1948,Ap 17,11:2
Adventures of Don Juan 1948,D 25,10:1
Interlude 1949,Ja 3,19:2
Night Unto Night 1949,Je 11,11:2
Backfire 1950,Ja 27,29:2
No Sad Songs for Me 1950,Ap 28,26:2
This Side of the Law 1950,Jl 7,15:2
Dark City 1950,O 19,40:5
Flying Missile, The 1950,D 25,25:1
Four in a Jeep 1951,Je 12,35:2
Journey Into Light 1951,O 5,24:4
Raiders, The 1952,D 13,19:2
No Time for Flowers 1952,D 26,20:3
Run for Cover 1955,Ap 30,10:6
Moonfleet 1955,Je 25,9:2
I Accuse! 1958,Mr 6,32:1
Tempest 1959,Mr 27,19:2
Story of Ruth, The 1960,Je 18,12:3
Weddings and Babies 1960,O 6,51:3
King of Kings 1961,O 12,41:2
No Exit 1962,D 6,55:2
Affair of the Skin, An 1963,N 21,43:2
Sylvia 1965,F 11,45:1
Brainstorm 1965,Je 10,38:1
These Are the Damned 1965,Jl 8,35:1
Lindfors, Viveca (Narrator)
Witness, The 1967,N 7,47:1
Lindgen, Sten
Berslagsfolk 1938,Mr 12,13:3

Lindgren, Goran (Producer)
My Sister, My Love 1967,F 20,45:2
Puss and Kram 1967,S 25,56:1
Hugs and Kisses 1968,Ag 19,44:1
Hugo and Josephine 1968,S 30,60:1
Lindgren, Lars Magnus (Director)
Dear John 1966,Mr 9,46:1
Lindgren, Lars Magnus (Screenwriter)
Dear John 1966,Mr 9,46:1
Lindgren, Orley
Great Lover, The 1949,N 26,48:2
Young Man With a Horn 1950,F 10,18:4
Under my Skin 1950,Mr 18,9:2
Japanese War Bride 1952,Ja 30,22:6
Red Planet Mars 1952,Je 16,15:2
Mister Scoutmaster 1953,Ag 29,10:1
Lindgren, Sien
Froeken Blir Piga 1937,Je 12,8:3
Sunshine Follows Rain 1949,S 29,39:2
Surf, The 1949,D 17,15:2
Lindholm, Britt Maj
Vicious Breed, The 1958,My 23,29:2
Lindlberg, Leopold (Director)
Marie-Louise 1945,N 13,24:2
Lindley, Bert
Dixie Handicap, The 1924,D 30,15:3
Are We Civilized? 1934,Je 14,28:5
Lindner, Robert (Original Author)
Pressure Point 1962,O 11,49:3
Lindo, Olga
Last Journey, The 1936,Je 8,22:4
Stars Look Down, The 1941,Jl 24,15:2
Adventures, The 1947,Ap 4,19:2
Hidden Room, The 1950,Ja 9,19:2
Inspector Calls, An 1954,N 26,24:4
Blonde Sinner 1957,Ja 24,34:1
Raising a Riot 1957,My 8,44:1
Sapphire 1959,N 3,27:1
Dr Crippen 1964,F 15,14:1
Lindoff, Anita
Flamboyant Sex, The 1963,Ag 13,25:1
Lindop, Audrey Erskine (Original Author)
Singer not the Song, The 1962,My 3,25:4
Lindop, Audrey Erskine (Screenwriter)
Blanche Fury 1948,N 24,20:2
Frightened Bride, The 1953,Ag 20,18:5
Lindroth, Helen
Unseeing Eyes 1923,O 22,17:1
Humming Bird, The 1924,Ja 14,2:1
Confidence Man, The 1924,Ap 15,24:1
Unguarded Women 1924,Je 24,18:2
Swan, The 1925,Mr 2,14:1
Song and Dance Man, The 1926,F 1,16:1
LINDSAY
See Also LINDSEY
Lindsay, Fred Colonel
Rough Riders, The 1927,Mr 16,28:2
Lindsay, Helen
Darling 1965,Ag 4,20:1
Lindsay, Herald
Soldiers of Fortune 1919,N 24,13:1
Lindsay, Howard (Miscellaneous)
Anything Goes 1936,F 6,23:3
Big Broadcast of 1938, The 1938,Mr 10,16:2
Anything Goes 1956,Mr 22,38:1
Lindsay, Howard (Original Author)
Love, Honor and Oh, Baby! 1933,O 28,20:3
She Loves Me Not 1934,S 8,18:5
Your Uncle Dudley 1935,D 12,33:4
Slight Case of Murder, A 1938,F 28,19:1
Artists and Models Abroad 1938,D 22,25:3
True to the Army 1942,Je 15,15:4
Life With Father 1947,Ag 16,6:6
State of the Union 1948,Ap 23,28:1
Stop, You're Killing Me 1952,D 11,45:3
Call Me Madam 1953,Mr 26,37:1
How to be Very, Very Popular 1955,Jl 23,10:1
Tall Story 1960,Ap 7,46:1
Sound of Music, The 1965,Mr 3,34:1
Lindsay, Howard (Producer)
She Loves Me Not 1933,N 26,IX,1:1 (In Addenda)
Lindsay, Howard (Screenwriter)
Swing Time 1936,Ag 28,21:2
Artists and Models Abroad 1938,D 22,25:3
Lindsay, Lara
Sweet Ride, The 1968,Je 13,57:2
Lindsay, Lex
Sob Sister 1931,O 3,20:2
Lindsay, Margaret
Okay America 1932,S 10,18:5
Cavalcade 1933,Ja 6,23:2
West of Singapore 1933,Ap 1,18:3
Baby Face 1933,Je 24,16:2
Private Detective 62 1933,Jl 7,20:2
Captured 1933,Ag 18,18:3
Voltaire 1933,Ag 23,21:2
Paddy, the Next Best Thing 1933,Ag 25,12:2
World Changes, The 1933,O 27,22:3
From Headquarters 1933,N 17,22:4
House on 56th Street, The 1933,D 2,9:3
Lady Killer 1934,Ja 1,28:2
Fog over Frisco 1934,Je 7,26:2

Dragon Murder Case, The 1934,Ag 23,13:3
Gentlemen are Born 1934,N 22,27:2
Bordertown 1935,Ja 24,22:5
Devil Dogs of the Air 1935,F 7,23:2
Case of the Curious Bride, The 1935,Ap 5,21:3
Florentine Dagger, The 1935,Ap 27,20:6
G Men 1935,My 2,17:1
Frisco Kid 1935,N 25,22:1
Dangerous 1935,D 27,14:1
Lady Consents, The 1936,F 6,23:4
Law in her Hands, The 1936,Je 6,21:2
Public Enemy's Wife 1936,Jl 9,17:2
Sinner Take All 1937,F 3,27:1
Green Light 1937,F 13,9:1
Slim 1937,Je 24,30:2
Back in Circulation 1937,O 4,17:1
Gold Is Where You Find It 1938,F 14,20:6
Jezebel 1938,Mr 11,15:2
When Were You Born? 1938,Je 9,27:2
Garden of the Moon 1938,S 24,13:1
Broadway Musketeers 1938,O 14,27:1
There's That Woman Again 1939,Ja 6,25:4
On Trial 1939,Ap 5,31:2
Hell's Kitchen 1939,Jl 3,10:5
Under-Pup, The 1939,S 5,21:2
20,000 Men a Year 1939,O 28,11:2
British Intelligence 1940,F 12,14:2
Honeymoon Deferred 1940,F 16,23:4
Double Alibi 1940,Mr 11,11:2
House of the Seven Gables, The 1940,Ap 15,21:3
Meet the Wildcat 1940,O 23,27:2
Ellery Queen, Master Detective 1940,D 19,33:1
Ellery Queen's Penthouse Mystery 1941,Mr 7,17:2
There's Magic in Music 1941,Je 5,27:2
Ellery Queen and the Perfect Crime 1941,Ag 11,17:3
Ellery Queen and the Murder Ring 1941,O 21,29:4
Spoilers, The 1942,My 22,27:2
Enemy Agents meet Ellery Queen 1942,Ag 22,16:2
Crime Doctor 1943,Jl 5,11:4
Scarlet Street 1946,F 15,29:2
Her Sister's Secret 1947,Ja 23,31:3
Vigilantes Return, The 1947,Jl 1,30:2
Cass Timberlane 1947,N 7,20:2
B F's Daughter 1948,Mr 25,35:2
Bottom of the Bottle, The 1956,F 2,19:2
Please Don't Eat the Daisies 1960,Ap 1,37:1
Tammy and the Doctor 1963,Je 27,23:2
Lindsay, Mary
Pamela, Pamela You Are.... 1968,D 21,49:4
Lindsay, Norman (Original Author)
Adventures of Sadie, The 1955,My 18,35:2
Lindsay, Philip (Screenwriter)
Under the Red Robe 1937,Je 1,27:2
Lindsay, Rosemary
Royal Ballet, The (The Firebird); Firebird, The (The Royal Ballet) 1960,O 5,45:2
Lindsay-Hoff, Michael (Miscellaneous)
Stop the World-I Want to Get Off 1966,My 12,54:2
Lindsell, R Stuart
Young Mr Pitt, The 1943,Mr 11,17:1
Man of Evil 1948,Mr 26,26:2
Broken Journey 1949,My 26,34:3
Blue Lagoon, The 1949,O 3,13:2
Passport to Pimlico 1949,O 27,35:2
High Treason 1952,My 21,23:3
LINDSEY
See Also LINDSAY
Lindsey, Ben Judge
Soul of Youth, The 1920,Ag 16,8:2
One Mile From Heaven 1937,Ag 19,23:1
Lindsey, Enid
Prison Without Bars 1939,Ap 10,13:2
Lindstrom, Jorgen
Silence, The 1964,F 4,28:1
Night Games 1966,D 20,58:1
Persona 1967,Mr 7,46:2
Lindstrom, Lasse
I Am With You 1949,Mr 1,30:5
Lindstrom, Pia
Marriage Italian Style 1964,D 21,42:1
Lindstrom, Rune
Himlaspelet 1944,O 9,17:3
I Am With You 1949,Mr 1,30:5
Sorciere, La 1956,D 28,17:2
Lindstrom, Rune (Screenwriter)
Himlaspelet 1944,O 9,17:3
I Am With You 1949,Mr 1,30:5
Affairs of a Model 1952,Ag 7,12:8
Lindt, Ilsa de
Crimson Runner, The 1925,My 27,26:2
Lindt, Karl Ludwig
Dangerous Crossing 1953,S 30,37:2
One, Two, Three 1961,D 22,17:1
Lindtberg, Leopold (Director)
Last Chance, The 1945,N 28,21:6
Four in a Jeep 1951,Je 12,35:2
Village, The 1953,S 23,37:2

Lindtberg, Leopold (Miscellaneous)
Village, The 1953,S 23,37:2
Lindtberg, Leopold (Screenwriter)
Four Days' Leave 1950,Je 9,29:4
Line, Bruce
Newly Rich 1931,Jl 3,22:1
No Greater Glory 1934,My 5,22:2
Linehan, Rosaleen
Ulysses 1967,Mr 14,55:1
Linel, Francis
Wild Oat, The 1956,Je 28,33:2
Lines, David
It Always Rains on Sunday 1949,F 14,15:5
Lines, Graham
Ulysses 1967,Mr 14,55:1
Linford, Dee (Original Author)
Man Without a Star 1955,Mr 25,19:3
Ling, Bo
Calling Philo Vance 1940,F 9,15:3
Ling, Eugene (Screenwriter)
Fighting Lady, The 1945,Ja 16,17:2
Within These Walls 1945,Jl 16,8:4
Shock 1946,Mr 9,10:2
It Shouldn't Happen to a Dog 1946,S 7,11:2
Lost Boundaries 1949,Jl 1,14:4
Port of New York 1950,F 3,29:2
Between Midnight and Dawn 1950,O 2,19:2
Scandal Sheet 1952,Ja 17,23:1
Lone Shark 1952,My 12,21:2
Mission Over Korea 1953,S 19,7:2
Man From Cairo, The 1953,D 17,52:4
Ling, F
Fight to the Last 1938,D 22,25:3
Ling, Jow Guen
Fortune Hunters, The 1953,S 16,35:6
Ling, Mai
Call Me Bwana 1963,Jl 4,9:1
Ling, Mei
Song of China 1936,N 10,31:3
Ling, Nien Son
Survival 1930,Ja 13,21:1
Lingen, Theo
Dolly Macht Karriere 1931,Jl 18,16:6
M 1933,Ap 3,13:3
Eine Stadt Steht Kopf 1934,Ja 29,10:2
Waltz Time in Vienna 1934,N 19,13:2
Liebe Dumme Mama; Stupid Mama 1935,Mr 2,18:3
Konjunkturritter 1935,Ap 29,12:4
Lied vom Glueck, Das; Song of Happiness, The 1935,N 30,12:7
Keine Angst vor Liebe 1936,Ja 21,27:6
Ich Sehne Mich Nach Dir 1936,S 9,32:4
Einmaleins der Liebe, Das 1937,Ja 2,15:2
Falscher Fuffziger, Ein 1937,F 13,9:1
Thank You, Madame 1937,Ap 27,18:2
Grosse Bluff, Der; Big Bluff, The 1937,S 6,20:2
Charm of la Boheme, The 1938,Mr 19,11:2
Abduction, The 1938,Je 11,9:2
Alles Fuer Veronika 1939,F 4,11:2
Dingehort mein Herz; My Heart Belongs to Thee 1939,Mr 25,19:2
Verkannte Lebemann, Der; Unrecognized Man of the World, The 1939,S 16,20:2
Das Erlebnis Geht Weiter; Another Experience 1940,F 3,9:3
Walzerlange; Waltz Melodies 1940,Ap 27,9:3
Opernball; Opera Ball 1940,O 15,29:2
Vienna Blood 1951,F 22,27:4
Heidi 1953,D 21,27:2
Heidi and Peter 1955,D 13,55:2
Tonio Kroger 1968,Ja 16,24:1
Linghelm, Emil A (Director)
Sun Over Klara 1944,My 1,20:8
Pimpernel Svensson 1953,F 6,16:4
Lingin, S (Screenwriter)
Welcome Kostya! 1965,N 22,48:2
Lingren, Hans
Children, The 1949,D 23,17:1
Linh-Nam
drame De Shanghai; Shanghai Drama, The 1945,Ja 11,19:2
Linkers, Eduard
Krakatit 1951,Ap 30,16:2
Farewell to Arms, A 1958,Ja 25,14:1
Matter of Who, A 1962,Jl 25,29:2
Jack of Diamonds 1967,N 11,26:3
Linklater, Eric (Original Author)
Scotch on the Rocks 1954,Je 14,18:2
Linkletter, Art
People Are Funny 1946,Ja 28,15:6
Champagne for Caesar 1950,My 12,33:2
Linkmann, Ludwig
Glass Tower, The; (Glaserne Turm, Der) 1959,Ag 27,24:4
Linley, Betty
Heiress, The 1949,O 7,35:2
Linlow, Ivan
Rackety Rax 1932,N 5,12:5
Linn, Bambi
Oklahoma! 1955,O 11,49:1

Linn-Po, Ivy
Love Eterne, The; Liang Shan Po and Chu
Ying-lai 1965,Ja 16,14:1
Linnane, Joe
Woman in Question, The 1952,F 19,24:2
Angel Who Pawned her Harp, The
1956,F 29,35:2
Linnanposki, Johannes (Original Author)
Milkmaid, The 1959,My 2,14:5
Linow, Ivan
Zaza 1923,S 17,18:2
Three Miles Out 1924,Ja 1,20:1
Wages of Virtue 1924,N 24,15:3
Red Dance, The 1928,Je 26,29:1
Plastered in Paris 1928,S 24,25:1
River, The 1928,D 24,11:1
In old Arizona 1929,Ja 21,18:4
Cock Eyed World, The 1929,Ag 5,25:2
Ship From Shanghai, The 1930,Ap 26,11:1
Song of the Flame 1930,My 7,24:5
Temple Tower 1930,My 10,25:3
Numbered Men 1930,Je 9,23:3
Unholy Three, The 1930,Jl 5,17:4
Silver Horde, The 1930,O 25,20:6
Just Imagine 1930,N 22,21:3
Madonna of the Streets 1930,N 29,21:4
It's Tough to be Famous 1932,Ap 9,18:1
Jewel Robbery 1932,Jl 23,6:6
Scarlet Dawn 1932,N 4,25:4
Linow, Joyzelle
Just Imagine 1930,N 22,21:3
Linville, Albert
Damn Yankees 1958,S 27,12:7
Linville, Joan
Goddess, The 1958,Je 25,24:1
LION
See Also LYON
Lion, Leon M
Man With 100 Faces 1938,N 1,27:2
Lion, Margo
Ich Geh' aus und Du Bleibst da 1932,N 21,21:1
Und Wer Kuesst Mich? 1935,Ja 28,10:5
Alibi, L' 1939,Ap 10,13:3
Escape From Yesterday 1939,My 3,27:2
Claudine 1940,Ap 1,15:2
Room Upstairs, The 1948,S 4,8:6
Devil and the Angel, The 1949,D 3,8:6
Lola 1962,O 15,32:2
Julie the Redhead 1963,O 15,44:1
Lion, Roger (Screenwriter)
Venenosa, La 1928,D 16,IX,8:2
Lion Cub
Her Jungle Love 1938,Ap 14,27:2
Lionello, Albero
Birds, the Bees and the Italians, The
1967,Ag 8,33:2
Lions, Louis
Panic 1947,N 27,50:2
Lipchitz, Philippe (Producer)
Chronicle of a Summer; Chronique d'un Ete
1965,My 7,34:1
Lipham Four
Song of the Open Road 1944,Je 7,13:3
Lipinska, Marta
Salto 1966,O 4,50:1
Lipkowitz, Joe (Cinematographer)
Unconquered, The; (Helen Keller in Her Story)
1954,Je 16,37:1
LIPMAN
See Also LIPPMAN
Lipman, Harry
Lost at the Front 1927,Je 14,33:2
Lipman, M
Tkies Khaf; (Vow, The) 1938,S 15,29:3
Lipman, Maureen
Up the Junction 1968,Mr 14,51:1
Lipman, William R (Original Author)
Double Cross Roads 1930,Ap 29,31:1
Broadway Bad 1933,Mr 6,16:6
Good Dame 1934,Mr 17,11:4
Yours for the Asking 1936,Ag 20,14:2
Love Is News 1937,Mr 6,10:1
Texas Rangers Ride Again 1941,Ja 9,27:4
Sweet Rosie O'Grady 1943,O 21,30:2
Barbary Coast Gent 1944,S 29,18:2
That Wonderful Urge 1948,D 22,29:6
Lipman, William R (Screenwriter)
On Such a Night 1937,S 17,29:2
Love Is a Headache 1938,Ja 28,17:3
Dangerous to Know 1938,Mr 11,15:4
Hunted Men 1938,My 21,9:2
Persons in Hiding 1939,Mr 2,19:2
Undercover Doctor 1939,Je 1,31:2
Island of Lost Men 1939,Ag 17,16:3
Parole Fixer 1940,Ap 18,28:5
Women Without Names 1940,My 9,26:4
Phantom Raiders 1940,Je 24,19:5
Queen of the Mob 1940,Jl 1,23:2
Sky Murder 1940,N 14,28:3
Gallant Sons 1940,D 12,37:2
Texas Rangers Ride Again 1941,Ja 9,27:4
Tarzan's New York Adventure 1942,Ag 7,13:2
Rationing 1944,Ap 10,14:2

Barbary Coast Gent 1944,S 29,18:2
Bad Bascomb 1946,My 23,18:4
Mighty McGurk, The 1947,Ap 4,19:4
Lippe, Jonathan
Act One 1963,D 27,17:2
Lippert, Albert
Schlussakkord 1936,S 10,29:4
Lippert, Gerhart
Town Without Pity 1961,O 11,53:1
Lippert, Robert L (Producer)
Yellow Canary, The 1963,My 16,42:1
Night Train to Paris 1964,D 3,58:2
Return of Mr Moto 1965,D 2,48:1
Murder Game, The 1966,Mr 31,43:2
Lippert, Robert L Jr (Producer)
Massacre 1956,Je 2,13:5
LIPPMAN
See Also LIPMAN
Lippman, Julia M (Original Author)
Hoodlum, The 1919,S 1,5:6
Lipscomb, W P (Miscellaneous)
Cardinal Richelieu 1935,Ap 19,24:2
Lipscomb, W P (Original Author)
Channel Crossing 1934,My 24,28:3
Woman in Command, The 1934,My 29,22:2
Clive of India 1935,Ja 18,29:1
Forever and a Day 1943,Mr 13,9:2
Lipscomb, W P (Producer)
Beware of Pity 1947,N 1,11:2
Make Me an Offer 1956,F 29,35:2
Lipscomb, W P (Screenwriter)
Clive of India 1935,Ja 18,29:1
Miserables, Les 1935,Ap 22,14:2
Tale of Two Cities, A 1935,D 26,21:2
Message to Garcia, A 1936,Ap 10,27:1
Under Two Flags 1936,My 1,19:1
Garden of Allah, The 1936,N 20,27:2
Sun Never Sets, The 1939,Je 9,26:2
Moon Over Burma 1940,D 12,37:4
Pacific Blackout 1942,Ja 15,25:2
Beware of Pity 1947,N 1,11:2
Ivory Hunter 1952,Ag 19,19:1
Make Me an Offer 1956,F 29,35:2
Seven Wonders of the World 1956,Ap 11,29:1
Dunkirk 1958,S 11,42:2
Town Like Alice, A 1958,S 22,27:1
Lipscombe, W P (Screenwriter)
Pygmalion 1938,D 8,34:2
Lipscott, Alan (Screenwriter)
Snow Queen, The 1960,Ap 14,34:1
Lipsius, Morris (Original Author)
Finger Man 1955,Jl 16,12:4
Lipska, Olga (Miscellaneous)
Pictura 1952,Ap 8,35:3
Lipskerova, Lydia
Great Glinka, The 1947,D 22,30:2
Lipsky, Eleazar (Original Author)
Kiss of Death 1947,Ag 28,28:2
People Against O'Hara, The 1951,S 6,39:3
Lipsky, Oldrich (Director)
Lemonade Joe 1967,N 21,53:1
Happy End 1968,Je 11,54:4
Lipsky, Oldrich (Screenwriter)
Lemonade Joe 1967,N 21,53:1
Happy End 1968,Je 11,54:4
Lipson, Arthur
Struggle, The 1931,D 11,35:1
Lipton, Albert
Mirele Efros 1939,O 21,12:2
Lipton, Celia
This Was a Woman 1949,Ja 5,22:2
Lipton, Gene
Brig, The 1964,S 21,37:4
Lipton, Jimmy (Narrator)
Tomorrow's a Wonderful Day 1949,Ap 11,29:4
Lipton, Lawrence (Screenwriter)
Alimony 1949,Jl 22,16:3
Lipton, Lew (Original Author)
Frisco Sally Levy 1927,Ap 13,29:4
Sweepstakes 1931,Je 25,23:5
Hold 'Em Jail! 1932,Ag 20,7:4
It's in the Air 1935,N 8,18:2
Broadway Serenade 1939,Ap 7,25:2
Lipton, Lew (Screenwriter)
Spite Marriage 1929,Mr 25,32:2
It's in the Air 1935,N 8,18:2
Lipton, Robert
Blue 1968,My 11.28:1
Liqueres, Laurence
My Wife's Husband 1965,Ja 27,26:1
Lira, Miguel N (Original Author)
Tierra de Pasiones 1944,N 7,24:3
Liron, Georges
Married Woman, The; Femme Mariee, La
1965,Ag 17,39:1
Lisa, Mona
To Please one Woman 1920,D 20,11:2
Lisandrini, Antonio Rev O F M (Screenwriter)
Flowers of St Francis 1952,O 7,26:2
Lisene, Mme
Edmund Kean, Prince Among Lovers
1927,Je 1,25:2

Lisi, Virna
Duel of the Titans 1963,Ag 8,19:1
Don't Tempt the Devil 1964,Ap 28,43:1
How to Murder Your Wife 1965,Ja 27,26:1
Eva 1965,Je 5,21:2
Bambole; Dolls, The (The Telephone Call);
Telephone Call, The (The Dolls)
1965,Je 29,26:1
Casanova 1965,Jl 21,43:1
Assault on a Queen 1966,Jl 28,23:3
Not With my Wife, You Don't! 1966,N 3,45:2
25th Hour, The 1967,F 17,45:1
Made in Italy 1967,My 1,44:2
Birds, the Bees and the Italians, The
1967,Ag 8,33:2
Girl and the General, The 1967,D 7,60:1
Kiss the Other Sheik 1968,Jl 30,33:1
Lisitsian, Pavel (Composer)
Yolanta 1964,D 23,22:3
Lisle, David (Original Author)
Impossible Mrs Bellew, The 1922,O 23,10:1
L'Isle, Marie de
Jeanne Dore 1928,Ja 2,28:3 (In Addenda)
Liss, Zvi
Dream no More 1950,Ja 6,25:2
Lissek, Leon
Persecution and Assassination of Jean-Paul Marat
as Performed by the Inmates of the Asylum of
Charenton Under the Direction of the Marquis
De Sade, The 1967,F 23,41:1
Lissenko, Nathalie
Sea-Fever 1929,O 28,20:1
Hurrah I'm Alive 1930,Je 16,25:3
Lissianskaya,a, Anastasia
Girl No 217 1945,S 3,17:2
List, Eugene
Bachelor's Daughters, The 1946,O 7,23:2
List, Inge
Prinzessin, Turandot 1935,Ja 16,21:2
Csardasfuerstin 1935,Ap 25,18:3
Krach und Glueckum Kuennemann; Row and Joy
About Kuennemann 1938,S 17,20:3
Alle stehen Kopf; General Confusion
1940,Je 22,18:4
Lister, Bruce
Ourselves Alone 1937,Jl 31,6:2
Tenth Man, The 1937,N 15,15:2
Crime Over London 1938,Jl 28,23:2
Lister, Francis
Mystery at the Villa Rose 1930,Je 2,25:4
Atlantic 1930,O 6,21:1
Night and Day 1933,My 29,22:2
Clive of India 1935,Ja 18,29:1
Cardinal Richelieu 1935,Ap 19,24:2
Return of the Scarlet Pimpernel, The
1938,Ap 11,12:2
Henry V 1946,Je 18,30:2
Wicked Lady, The 1946,D 23,19:5
Christopher Columbus 1949,O 13,33:2
Lister, Frederick
Fugitive, The 1940,Jl 23,22:2
Lister, Margot
Prince and the Showgirl 1957,Je 14,22:2
Lister, Moira
Lady Surrenders, A 1947,Je 20,25:6
So Evil my Love 1948,Jl 22,27:2
Agitator, The 1949,Ag 19,12:5
Run for Your Money, A 1950,Ap 10,15:3
Another Shore 1951,F 12,19:3
Pool of London 1951,N 28,37:2
White Corridors 1952,Jl 16,21:1
Cruel Sea, The 1953,Ag 11,18:5
Something Money Can't Buy 1953,O 1,34:3
Deep Blue Sea, The 1955,O 13,35:2
Trouble in Store 1956,Ja 14,13:2
Abandon Ship 1957,Ap 18,35:1
John and Julie 1957,My 7,40:1
Yellow Rolls-Royce, The 1965,My 14,42:2
Double Man, The 1968,My 2,57:1
Listuzzi, Giorgio
Roof, The 1959,My 13,43:4
Lisyanskava, A
Twelfth Night 1956,Mr 5,21:1
Lisyanskaya, Anna
Rainbow, The 1944,O 23,14:3
Days and Nights 1946,Ap 29,24:4
Litel, John
On the Border 1930,F 3,17:1
Wayward 1932,F 15,13:1
Fugitive in the Sky 1937,Ja 16,21:1
Black Legion 1937,Ja 18,21:1
Midnight Court 1937,Mr 4,27:3
Marked Woman 1937,Ap 12,15:2
Slim 1937,Je 24,30:2
Life of Emile Zola, The 1937,Ag 12,14:2
Back in Circulation 1937,O 4,17:1
Alcatraz Island 1937,O 14,22:2
Missing Witness 1937,D 10,33:3
Gold Is Where You Find It 1938,F 14,20:6
Slight Case of Murder, A 1938,F 28,19:1
Jezebel 1938,Mr 11,15:2
Love, Honor and Behave 1938,Mr 21,18:2
Over the Wall 1938,Mr 28,19:2

Litel, John— Cont

My Bill 1938,Jl 7,22:4
Amazing Dr Clitterhouse, The 1938,Jl 21,14:2
Valley of the Giants 1938,S 10,20:2
Broadway Musketeers 1938,O 14,27:1
Comet over Broadway 1938,D 16,33:3
Wings of the Navy 1939,F 4,11:1
Secret Service of the Air 1939,Mr 2,19:2
You Can't Get Away With Murder
  1939,Mr 25,19:2
On Trial 1939,Ap 5,31:2
Dodge City 1939,Ap 8,19:1
Dust Be my Destiny 1939,O 7,11:2
Dress Parade 1939,O 28,11:2
One Hour to Live 1939,N 4,11:3
Return Of Doctor X, The 1939,N 23,38:5
Child Is Born, A 1940,Ja 11,19:2
Fighting 69th, The 1940,Ja 27,9:2
Castle on the Hudson 1940,Mr 4,11:2
It all Came True 1940,Ap 6,13:2
Angel From Texas, An 1940,My 10,26:7
Men Without Souls 1940,My 13,21:2
Flight Angels 1940,My 27,23:2
Man Who Talked too Much, The 1940,Je 29,12:2
Murder in the Air 1940,Jl 4,12:2
They Drive by Night 1940,Jl 27,17:5
Money and the Woman 1940,Ag 4,29:2
Lady With red Hair 1940,D 6,28:2
Santa Fe Trail 1940,D 21,21:2
Father's Son 1941,F 13,25:3
Trial of Mary Dugan, The 1941,Mr 6,25:4
Henry Aldrich for President 1941,O 18,22:2
They Died With Their Boots On 1941,N 21,23:3
Kid Glove Killer 1942,Ap 17,21:4
Mystery of Marie Roget, The 1942,My 5,17:3
Men of Texas 1942,Jl 13,18:3 (In Addenda)
Invisible Agent 1942,Ag 6,23:2
Murder in Times Square 1943,My 31,13:2
Crime Doctor 1943,Jl 5,11:4
Where Are Your Children? 1944,Ja 17,14:5
Murder in the Blue Room 1944,O 28,12:2
Lake Placid Serenade 1944,D 25,15:6
Brewster's Millions 1945,Ap 27,23:2
Salome, Where She Danced 1945,My 3,27:1
Daltons Ride Again, The 1945,D 8,21:2
Enchanted Forest, The 1945,D 17,17:2
San Antonio 1945,D 29,19:5
Night in Paradise 1946,Je 6,16:3
She Wrote the Book 1946,Je 20,20:3
Sister Kenny 1946,S 30,21:2
Swell Guy 1947,Ja 27,17:2
Easy Come, Easy Go 1947,F 6,29:2
Beginning or the End, The 1947,F 21,15:1
Guilty, The 1947,My 19,27:2
Cass Timberlane 1947,N 7,20:2
Heaven Only Knows 1947,N 14,29:3
Christmas Eve 1947,N 28,30:2
I, Jane Doe 1948,Jl 5,8:4
Pitfall 1948,Ag 25,31:2
Outpost in Morocco 1949,Mr 25,28:3
Mary Ryan, Detective 1949,N 4,33:3
Woman in Hiding 1950,F 23,33:2
Sundowners, The 1950,My 5,17:2
Kiss Tomorrow Goodbye 1950,Ag 5,9:2
Groom Wore Spurs, The 1951,Mr 14,41:2
Texas Rangers, The 1951,Jl 14,7:2
Take Care of my Little Girl 1951,Jl 19,20:2
Scaramouche 1952,My 9,20:2
Montana Belle 1952,N 8,9:2
Jack Slade 1953,O 29,42:6
Sitting Bull 1954,N 26,24:4
Kentuckian, The 1955,S 2,13:2
Voyage to the Bottom of the Sea 1961,Jl 20,32:2
Pocketful of Miracles 1961,D 19,39:1

Litovsky, V
Young Pushkin 1937,D 16,35:3

Litson, Mason N (Director)
Edgar's Little Saw 1920,D 27,11:3

Littl, A I (Director)
Schimmelkrieg von Holledau, Der 1938,Jl 19,15:4

Little, Ann
Believe Me, Xantippe 1918,Je 3,9:3
Firefly of France, The 1918,Jl 8,9:4
Squaw Man, The 1918,D 30,7:3
Cradle of Courage, The 1920,S 20,13:1

Little, Arthur Jr
Hard, Fast and Beautiful 1951,Jl 2,16:6

Little, Herbert Jr (Screenwriter)
Trooper Hook 1957,Jl 13,11:2

Little, Little Jack (Composer)
Lullaby of Broadway 1951,Mr 27,35:2

Little Fred's Football Dogs
Around the World 1943,N 25,39:2

Little Richard and His Band
Girl Can't Help It, The 1957,F 9,12:7

Little Singers of the Wooden Cross
Cage aux Rossignols, La; (Cage of Nightingales,
  A) 1947,Ap 3,31:2

Little Sky, Eddie
Sergeants 3 1962,F 12,28:2

Little Tough Guys
East Side Kids 1940,F 19,21:6

Littlefield, Jack
Blackjack Ketchum Desperado 1956,Ap 5,26:2

Littlefield, Lucien
Too Much Speed 1921,Je 6,16:4
French Doll, The 1923,S 5,15:3
In the Palace of the King 1923,D 3,14:1
Name the Man 1924,F 4,23:3
True as Steel 1924,Je 17,22:4
Babbitt 1924,Jl 15,9:4
Deadwood Coach, The 1925,Ja 21,19:3
Charley's Aunt 1925,F 9,15:3
Rainbow Trail, The 1925,Je 3,26:4
Tumbleweeds 1925,D 21,27:2
Soul Mates 1926,Ja 4,16:1
Ibanez's Torrent 1926,F 22,14:1
Tony Runs Wild 1926,Ap 28,28:3
Take It From Me 1926,N 2,35:1
Twinkletoes 1926,D 27,20:3
Taxi, Taxi 1927,F 15,23:1
Cat and the Canary, The 1927,S 10,9:4
Uncle Tom's Cabin 1927,N 5,16:2
My Best Girl 1927,N 7,26:4
Cheating Cheaters 1927,D 6,27:1
Texas Steer, A 1928,Ja 2,28:1
Harold Teen 1928,Ag 14,15:4
Heart to Heart 1928,S 10,29:2
Mother Knows Best 1928,S 17,27:1
Clear the Decks 1929,Ap 1,22:1
Saturday's Children 1929,Ap 29,29:2
This Is Heaven 1929,My 27,22:1
Drag 1929,Je 21,17:2
Seven Keys to Baldpate 1929,D 26,21:1
No, No, Nanette 1930,Ja 4,21:1
Great Divide, The 1930,F 17,17:6
High Society Blues 1930,Ap 19,15:1
Clancy in Wall Street 1930,My 3,23:1
She's my Weakness 1930,Je 21,20:5
Tom Sawyer 1930,D 20,20:6
Reducing 1931,Ja 17,23:1
Scandal Sheet 1931,F 9,25:3
Pays to Advertise, It 1931,F 21,15:2
It Pays to Advertise 1931,F 21,15:2
Young as You Feel 1931,Ag 3,16:3
Man I Killed, The 1932,Ja 20,17:4
High Pressure 1932,F 1,22:3
Strangers in Love 1932,Mr 5,11:2
Shopworn 1932,Ap 4,13:6
Strangers of the Evening 1932,Je 4,9:2
Miss Pinkerton 1932,Jl 9,7:5
Downstairs 1932,O 8,15:4
Evenings for Sale 1932,N 12,20:5
That's my Boy 1932,N 21,21:1
If I Had a Million 1932,D 3,21:4
Bitter Tea of General Yen, The 1933,Ja 12,20:6
Big Pay-Off, The 1933,Ja 17,22:7
Sailor's Luck 1933,Mr 17,21:2
Sweepings 1933,Mr 24,22:3
Professional Sweetheart 1933,Jl 14,15:3
Chance at Heaven 1933,D 26,19:3
Sons of the Desert 1934,Ja 12,29:3
Mandalay 1934,F 15,15:6
Thirty Day Princess 1934,My 12,12:3
Kiss and Make-Up 1934,Je 29,17:1
Ruggles of Red Gap 1935,Mr 7,26:1
Murder Man, The 1935,Jl 27,16:2
Man on the Flying Trapeze 1935,Ag 3,16:2
Return of Peter Grimm, The 1935,O 4,25:2
I Dream too Much 1935,N 29,24:1
Magnificent Obsession 1935,D 31,11:2
Rose Marie 1936,F 1,9:2
Let's Sing Again 1936,My 9,11:2
Moon's our Home, The 1936,My 13,29:2
Early to Bed 1936,Jl 16,20:2
High, Wide and Handsome 1937,Jl 22,15:1
Souls at Sea 1937,Ag 10,23:2
Bulldog Drummond's Revenge 1937,D 17,33:2
Wells Fargo 1937,D 30,15:2
Scandal Street 1938,F 5,19:2 (In Addenda)
Stadium Murders, The 1938,Ap 9,11:2
Wide Open Faces 1938,Ap 15,23:2
Gladiator, The 1938,Ag 29,10:2
What a Life 1939,O 12,33:1
Sabotage 1939,N 16,29:5
Those Were the Days 1940,Jl 15,18:4
Great American Broadcast, The 1941,My 2,25:2
Little Foxes, The 1941,Ag 22,19:2
Man at Large 1941,O 11,21:4
Henry Aldrich for President 1941,O 18,22:2
Mr and Mrs North 1942,Ja 22,13:2
Whistling in Dixie 1942,D 31,20:4
One Body too Many 1944,N 25,21:2
Rendezvous With Annie 1946,S 23,29:3
That Brennan Girl 1946,D 9,34:3

Littlefield, Lucien (Original Author)
Early to Bed 1936,Jl 16,20:2

Littlefield, Robert
Infernal Machine 1933,Ap 8,16:3

Littleton, Scott (Original Author)
Night Editor 1946,Mr 30,11:2

Littlewood, Joan (Producer)
Sparrows Don't Sing 1963,My 7,46:2

Littlewood, Joan (Screenwriter)
Sparrows Don't Sing 1963,My 7,46:2

Littmen, Gordon
Red Shoes, The 1948,O 23,9:2

Litvak, Anatole (Director)
Dolly Macht Karriere; Dolly's Way to Stardom
  1930,N 23,IX,6:2
Dolly Macht Karriere 1931,Jl 18,16:6
Nie Wieder Liebe; No More Love
  1931,O 4,VIII,7:1
Nie Wieder Liebe 1932,Ja 16,13:1
Be Mine Tonight 1933,Ap 14,22:5
Cette Vieille Canaille 1935,Ja 12,12:2
Celle Vieille Canaille 1935,Ja 12,12:2
Woman I Love, The 1937,Ap 16,27:2
Mayerling 1937,S 14,27:1
Tovarich 1937,D 31,9:2
Amazing Dr Clitterhouse, The 1938,Jl 21,14:2
Flight Into Darkness (L'Equipage)
  1938,O 17,12:1
Confessions of a Nazi Spy 1939,Ap 29,13:2
Castle on the Hudson 1940,Mr 4,11:2
All This and Heaven, Too 1940,Jl 5,10:2
City for Conquest 1940,S 28,9:2
Out of the Fog 1941,Je 21,20:2
Blues in the Night 1941,D 12,35:2
This Above All 1942,My 13,14:3
Battle of Russia, The 1943,N 15,23:3
Long Night, The 1947,S 17,31:2
Sorry, Wrong Number 1948,S 2,18:2
Snake Pit, the 1948,N 5,29:2
Decision Before Dawn 1951,D 22,12:2
Act of Love 1954,F 12,20:5
Deep Blue Sea, The 1955,O 13,35:2
Anastasia 1956,D 14,35:6
Journey, The 1959,F 20,19:1
Goodbye Again 1961,Je 30,32:2
Five Miles to Midnight 1963,Mr 21,8:6
Night of the Generals, The 1967,F 3,38:1

Litvak, Anatole (Producer)
Amazing Dr Clitterhouse, The 1938,Jl 21,14:2
Sisters, The 1938,O 15,21:3
All This and Heaven, Too 1940,Jl 5,10:2
City for Conquest 1940,S 28,9:2
Long Night, The 1947,S 17,31:2
Sorry, Wrong Number 1948,S 2,18:2
Snake Pit, the 1948,N 5,29:2
Decision Before Dawn 1951,D 22,12:2
Act of Love 1954,F 12,20:5
Deep Blue Sea, The 1955,O 13,35:2
Journey, The 1959,F 20,19:1
Goodbye Again 1961,Je 30,32:2
Five Miles to Midnight 1963,Mr 21,8:6
10:30 PM Summer 1966,O 20,52:1

Litvak, Anatole (Screenwriter)
Flight Into Darkness (L'Equipage)
  1938,O 17,12:1

Litvinenko-Volgemut, M
Cossack Beyond the Danube, A 1954,F 8,18:5

Litvinoff, Si (Producer)
Queen, The 1968,Je 18,37:1

Litvinov, Alyosha
Flying Carpet, The 1960,F 28,31:1

Litvinov, N
Peter the First 1937,D 25,10:4

Litwhiler, Danny
Safe at Home 1941,N 26,31:2

Litwina, Berta
Purimspieler, Der 1937,D 6,19:2
Tkies Khaf; (Vow, The) 1938,S 15,29:3
Long Is the Road 1948,N 12,30:5

Litzie, Ann
Roaring Road, The 1919,Ap 14,11:4

Liu, Dan
Big Jim McLain 1952,S 18,35:2

Liu, Kalen
Welcome to Hard Times 1967,My 2,56:1

Liu, Lotus
Waikiki Wedding 1937,Mr 25,29:1
China Passage 1937,Ap 16,27:2
Adventures of Marco Polo, The 1965,Ap 8,17:2

Liu, Maurice
Daughter of Shanghai 1937,D 24,21:2

Liubashevski, L S
Lenin in 1918 1939,Je 27,27:2

Liubeshkin, P
Lad From our Town 1943,O 7,26:2

Liubimov, V
Train Goes East, The 1949,S 5,13:3

Liubimov, Yuri
Days and Nights 1946,Ap 29,24:4
Life in Bloom 1949,My 9,20:4

Livanof, MM
Enemies of Progress 1934,Ja 11,19:2

Livanov, Boris
Deserter 1934,O 13,10:1
Peter Vinogradof 1935,Je 28,24:1
Dubrovsky 1936,Mr 30,17:6
Baltic Deputy 1937,S 4,8:2
Men of the Sea 1938,Je 20,11:2
Great Glinka, The 1947,D 22,30:2
First Front, The 1949,N 14,19:2
Admiral Ushakov 1954,Ja 18,19:2

Livanov, Boris — Cont
Poem of the Sea 1959,D 21,34:4
Livanov, Vasili
Victors and the Vanquished, The 1950,My 1,18:2
Sound of Life, The 1962,F 12,28:2
Letter That Was Never Sent, The 1962,N 19,39:2
Lively, Robert (Original Author)
Great Victor Herbert, The 1939,D 7,35:1
East Side Kids 1940,F 19,21:6
There's Magic in Music 1941,Je 5,27:2
Lively, Robert (Screenwriter)
Girl Said No, The 1937,O 18,14:1
Personal Secretary 1938,O 5,20:2
Great Victor Herbert, The 1939,D 7,35:1
East Side Kids 1940,F 19,21:6
Isle of Destiny 1940,Ap 8,15:2
Lively, William (Original Author)
Ghost Creeps, The 1940,Ag 19,13:3
Lively, William (Screenwriter)
Ghost Creeps, The 1940,Ag 19,13:3
Livermore, Paul
At War With the Army 1951,Ja 25,21:5
Livernoin, Richard
Don't Gamble With Love 1936,Mr 2,13:3
Livesey, Barrie
Mr Cohen Takes a Walk 1936,F 13,25:2
They Were Sisters 1946,Jl 24,24:2
Livesey, Jack
Wandering Jew, The 1935,Ja 14,11:3
Passing of the Third Floor Back, The 1936,Ap 29,19:2
That Touch of Mink 1962,Je 15,16:2
Livesey, Roger
Drums 1938,S 30,24:4
Smiling Along 1939,F 20,13:2
Spies of the Air 1940,Jl 4,12:3
Girl in the News, The 1941,My 5,13:2
Life and Death of Colonel Blimp, The 1945,Mr 30,18:2
Stairway to Heaven 1946,D 26,28:1
I Know Where I'm Going 1947,Ag 20,25:2
If This Be Sin 1950,Jl 1,9:2
Master of Ballantrae, The 1953,Ag 6,16:2
It Happened in Broad Daylight 1960,S 30,33:1
Entertainer, The 1960,O 4,49:2
League of Gentlemen, The 1961,Ja 25,30:4
No, My Darling Daughter 1964,Mr 28,13:5
Of Human Bondage 1964,S 24,46:2
Oedipus the King 1968,S 19,62:2
Livesey, Sam
Young Woodley 1930,S 27,21:3
Dreyfus Case, The 1931,Ag 31,11:5
Man Who Won, The 1933,F 27,11:2
Private Life of Henry VIII, The 1933,O 13,25:2
Rembrandt 1936,D 3,31:1
Wings of the Morning 1937,Mr 12,19:1
Dark Journey 1937,Ag 23,22:1
Mill On the Floss, The 1939,N 15,19:3
Livien, Albert
Confession of Ina Kahn, The 1958,Ja 1,31:4
Livikou, Ilya
Germans Strike Again, The 1949,Ap 14,29:4
Mademoiselle-Age 39 1956,Mr 26,34:2
Santa Chikita 1959,My 11,30:1
Counterfeit Coin 1960,My 16,39:1
Livikou, Lila
Antigone 1962,S 19,30:1
LIVINGSTON
See Also LIVINGSTONE
Livingston, Bob
Call the Mesquiteers 1938,Mr 19,11:2
Arson Racket Squad 1938,Je 18,18:2
Livingston, Harold (Original Author)
Hell With Heroes, The 1968,S 3,54:2
Livingston, Harold (Screenwriter)
Hell With Heroes, The 1968,S 3,54:2
Livingston, Hazel (Screenwriter)
Secret Studio, The 1927,Je 15,31:4
Livingston, Jay
Sunset Boulevard 1950,Ag 11,15:2
Livingston, Jay (Composer)
Private's Affair, A 1959,Ag 15,8:7
Livingston, Jerry (Composer)
At War With the Army 1951,Ja 25,21:5
Livingston, Jock
Zero in the Universe 1966,O 12,36:3
Livingston, Jock (Producer)
Zero in the Universe 1966,O 12,36:3
Livingston, Jock (Screenwriter)
Zero in the Universe 1966,O 12,36:3
Livingston, Mae (Original Author)
Without Reservations 1946,Je 8,17:2
Livingston, Margaret
Divorce 1923,Je 26,14:2
Love's Whirlpool 1924,Mr 11,16:2
Capital Punishment 1925,F 5,23:3
Up the Ladder 1925,My 12,26:2
I'll Show You the Town 1925,Je 8,19:1
Best People 1925,O 21,21:3
Yankee Senor, The 1926,Ja 28,14:4
First Year, The 1926,Mr 8,17:1
Slaves of Beauty 1927,Je 8,23:3
Secret Studio, The 1927,Je 15,31:4
Sunrise 1927,S 24,15:3 (In Addenda)

American Beauty 1927,O 11,27:1
Streets of Shanghai 1928,F 21,19:3
Mad Hour, The 1928,Ap 16,20:5
Wheels of Chance 1928,Jl 2,11:2
His Private Life 1928,N 12,18:2
Last Warning, The 1929,Ja 7,36:2
Bellamy Trial, The 1929,Ja 24,30:5
Charlatan, The 1929,Ap 15,22:6
Innocents of Paris 1929,Ap 27,16:5
Tonight at Twelve 1929,S 23,24:3
Seven Keys to Baldpate 1929,D 26,21:1
What a Widow 1930,O 4,15:2
Big Money 1930,N 22,21:3
Kiki 1931,Mr 6,16:1
God's Gift to Women 1931,Ap 18,17:3
Smart Money 1931,Je 19,21:1
Livingston, Robert
Death on the Diamond 1934,S 24,14:1
Band Plays on, The 1934,D 22,21:2
West Point of the Air 1935,Ap 6,10:1
Three Godfathers, The 1936,Mr 9,20:2
Absolute Quiet 1936,My 2,11:1
Federal Man-Hunt 1939,F 2,17:3
Pistol Packin' Mama 1943,D 20,27:4
Storm Over Lisbon 1944,S 11,14:1
Brazil 1944,N 20,25:2
Lake Placid Serenade 1944,D 25,15:6
Big Bonanza, The 1945,F 26,14:5
Cheaters, The 1945,Jl 21,7:2
Dakota 1945,D 17,17:2
Livingston, Sandy
Certain Smile, A 1958,Ag 1,13:2
Livingston, Stanley
Rally Round the Flag Boys! 1958,D 24,2:7
Please Don't Eat the Daisies 1960,Ap 1,37:1
X-15 1962,Ap 5,30:2
LIVINGSTONE
See Also LIVINGSTON
Livingstone, Mary
This Way Please 1937,O 8,27:2
Livingstone, Pickies
Things to Come 1936,Ap 18,19:2
Liwanag, Vincente
No Man is an Island 1962,O 11,49:2
Lix, Germaine
Daybreak 1940,Jl 30,16:2
Lizengevich, Luda
Taras Family, The 1946,D 9,34:4
Lizter, Francis
Mutiny on the Bounty 1935,N 9,19:2
Lizzani, Carlo
Outcry 1949,Mr 14,15:5
Lizzani, Carlo (Director)
Behind the Great Wall 1959,D 10,51:6
Violent Four, The 1968,Ag 15,46:2
Lizzani, Carlo (Original Author)
Tragic Hunt 1948,O 22,30:2
Bitter Rice 1950,S 19,39:2
Lizzani, Carlo (Screenwriter)
Outcry 1949,Mr 14,15:5
Bitter Rice 1950,S 19,39:2
Under the Olive Tree 1951,O 5,24:4
Violent Four, The 1968,Ag 15,46:2
Lizzio, Marlene
Cinerama-South Seas Adventure 1958,Jl 16,26:1
Ljung, Oscar
Folket Pa Hogbogarden; People of the Hogbo Farm, The 1940,F 24,9:3
Magician, The 1959,Ag 28,27:1
Virgin Spring, The; Jungfrukallan 1960,N 15,46:1
Ljunquist, Walter (Screenwriter)
Interlude 1949,Ja 3,19:2
Llewellyn, Doris
Menace 1934,N 22,27:2
Llewellyn, Fewlass
This Freedom 1923,N 28,15:1
Llewellyn, Richard (Original Author)
How Green Was my Valley 1941,O 29,27:2
None but the Lonely Heart 1944,N 18,16:6
None but the Lonely Heart 1944,D 3,II,1:8
Llewellyn, Richard (Screenwriter)
Tale of Five Women, A 1953,Ja 16,19:2
Llewelyn, Desmond
Thunderball 1965,D 22,23:1
You Only Live Twice 1967,Je 14,40:1
Llopis, Francisco
Virgin of Guadalupe, The 1943,My 15,13:3
Lloyd, Alma
Jimmy and Sally 1933,D 16,12:3
Fish 1936,Ja 25,18:5
Freshman Love 1936,Ja 25,18:5
Song of the Saddle 1936,Mr 21,13:3
Brides are Like That 1936,Mr 23,22:5
I Married a Doctor 1936,Ap 20,17:1
White Angel, The 1936,Je 25,24:1
Big Noise, The 1936,Jl 4,18:3
If I Were King 1938,S 29,31:1
Lloyd, Doris
Lady, The 1925,Ja 27,11:2
Black Bird, The 1926,F 1,16:1
Is Zat So? 1927,My 17,27:2
Lonesome Ladies 1927,Ag 2,19:2
Two Girls Wanted 1927,N 14,26:1

Lloyd, Doris — Cont
Come to My House 1928,Ja 16,24:1
Drake Case, The 1929,S 16,30:1
Disraeli 1929,O 3,27:5
Sarah and Son 1930,Mr 13,22:4
Way for a Sailor 1930,D 13,22:2
Charley's Aunt 1930,D 26,18:4
Bachelor Father, The 1931,F 2,23:1
Transgression 1931,Je 15,23:3
Bought 1931,Ag 15,18:3
Waterloo Bridge 1931,S 5,7:4
Devotion 1931,O 3,20:2
Once a Lady 1931,N 9,22:4
Tarzan, The Ape Man 1932,Mr 28,11:2
Back Street 1932,Ag 29,9:2
Secrets 1933,Mr 16,21:2
Oliver Twist 1933,Ap 13,15:3
Looking Forward 1933,My 1,10:2
Peg o'my Heart 1933,My 20,11:4
Study in Scarlet, A 1933,Je 1,15:3
Voltaire 1933,Ag 23,21:2
Tarzan and his Mate 1934,Ap 21,12:1
Glamour 1934,My 12,12:3
Sisters Under the Skin 1934,Je 8,18:1
Kiss and Make-Up 1934,Je 29,17:1
She Was a Lady 1934,Ag 22,21:2
British Agent 1934,S 20,20:1
Clive of India 1935,Ja 18,29:1
Woman in Red, The 1935,Mr 23,11:3
Shot in the Dark, A 1935,My 22,23:2
Becky Sharp 1935,Je 14,27:2
Peter Ibbetson 1935,N 8,18:2
Perfect Gentleman, The 1935,D 19,33:4
Don't Get Personal 1936,F 22,12:1
Mary of Scotland 1936,Jl 31,22:2
Plough and the Stars, The 1937,Ja 29,15:1
Soldier and the Lady, The 1937,Ap 10,11:1
Alcatraz Island 1937,O 14,22:2
Tovarich 1937,D 31,9:2
I'm From Missouri 1939,Mr 23,27:1
Under-Pup, The 1939,S 5,21:2
Barricade 1939,D 9,18:2
Vigil in the Night 1940,Mr 9,19:2
Great Plane Robbery, The 1940,N 15,25:2
Letter, The 1940,N 23,12:6
Shining Victory 1941,My 31,14:1
Ghost of Frankenstein, The 1942,Ap 4,19:2
Night Monster 1942,N 30,18:5
Journey for Margaret 1942,D 18,36:7
Mission to Moscow 1943,Ap 30,25:2
Constant Nymph, The 1943,Jl 24,8:2
Lodger, The 1944,Ja 20,15:3
Phantom Lady 1944,F 18,15:2
Molly and Me 1945,My 26,18:2
My Name is Julia Ross 1945,N 9,16:3
Devotion 1946,Ap 6,10:5
Holiday in Mexico 1946,Ag 16,19:3
Secret Life of Walter Mitty, The 1947,Ag 15,12:2
Sign of the Ram, The 1948,Mr 4,30:2
Kind Lady 1951,Ag 8,21:2
Young Bess 1953,My 22,31:1
Swan, The 1956,Ap 27,21:5
Time Machine, The 1960,Ag 18,19:1
Midnight Lace 1960,O 14,27:1
Notorious Landlady, The 1962,Jl 27,15:2
Sound of Music, The 1965,Mr 3,34:1
Lloyd, E James (Screenwriter)
Born Losers, The 1967,Ag 19,16:2
Lloyd, Euan (Producer)
Shalako 1968,N 6,32:1
Lloyd, Frank (Director)
Madame X 1920,S 27,18:1
Tale of Two Worlds, A 1921,Mr 14,9:2
Voice in the Dark, A 1921,Je 6,16:4
Man From Lost River, The 1922,Ja 16,18:3
Eternal Flame, The 1922,S 18,14:2
Oliver Twist 1922,O 30,11:1
Sin Flood, The 1922,O 30,11:1
Voice From the Minaret, The 1923,F 5,18:2
Within the Law 1923,Ap 30,11:2
Ashes of Vengeance 1923,Ag 7,20:2
Black Oxen 1924,Ja 7,23:1
Sea Hawk, The 1924,Je 3,22:1
Silent Watcher, The 1924,O 26,VIII,5:1 (In Addenda)
Splendid Road, The 1926,Je 13,31:1
Eagle of the Sea, The 1926,N 17,21:6
Children of Divorce 1927,Ap 26,33:3
Adoration 1929,Ja 14,20:1
Weary River 1929,Ja 25,20:6
Divine Lady, The 1929,Mr 23,22:4
Drag 1929,Je 21,17:2
Young Nowheres 1929,O 2,28:4
Son of the Gods 1930,Ja 31,24:1
Way of all Men, The 1930,S 20,15:4
Lash, The 1931,Ja 1,31:3
East Lynne 1931,F 21,15:2
Right of Way, The 1931,Mr 24,31:2
Age for Love, The 1931,N 13,27:2
Passport to Hell, A 1932,Ag 27,13:4
Cavalcade 1933,Ja 6,23:2
Berkeley Square 1933,S 14,26:2
Hoopla 1933,D 1,23:3
Servants' Entrance 1934,S 27,25:2

Lloyd, Frank (Director) — Cont
Mutiny on the Bounty 1935,N 9,19:2
Under Two Flags 1936,My 1,19:1
Maid of Salem 1937,Mr 4,27:2
Wells Fargo 1937,D 30,15:2
If I Were King 1938,S 29,31:1
Rulers of the Sea 1939,N 9,27:1
Howards of Virginia, The 1940,S 27,27:1
Lady From Cheyenne, The 1941,Ap 18,18:2
This Woman Is Mine 1941,O 13,21:2
Forever and a Day 1943,Mr 13,9:2
Blood on the Sun 1945,Je 29,12:2
Shanghai Story, The 1954,S 25,10:7

Lloyd, Frank (Miscellaneous)
Wells Fargo 1938,Ja 16,X,5:1 (In Addenda)

Lloyd, Frank (Original Author)
Man Hunter, The 1919,Mr 3,11:2

Lloyd, Frank (Producer)
Maid of Salem 1937,Mr 4,27:2
Wells Fargo 1937,D 30,15:2
If I Were King 1938,S 29,31:1
Rulers of the Sea 1939,N 9,27:1
Howards of Virginia, The 1940,S 27,27:1
Lady From Cheyenne, The 1941,Ap 18,18:2
This Woman Is Mine 1941,O 13,21:2
Spoilers, The 1942,My 22,27:2
Forever and a Day 1943,Mr 13,9:2

Lloyd, Frank (Screenwriter)
Oliver Twist 1922,O 30,11:1

Lloyd, Frederick
Battle of Gallipoli, The 1931,D 7,16:1
Sleepless Nights 1933,Jl 22,14:2
April Romance 1937,Ja 27,17:4
21 Days Together 1940,My 23,28:4
Oliver Twist 1951,Jl 31,17:2

Lloyd, George
Men Without Names 1935,Je 29,16:2
Smart Blonde 1937,Ja 9,21:1
Smashing the Rackets 1938,Ag 9,22:5
Mr Wong, Detective 1938,N 21,14:4
Waterfront 1939,Jl 17,10:2
Behind Prison Gates 1939,Ag 21,9:3
Florian 1940,Je 6,33:2
Fugitive From Justice, A 1940,Jl 8,13:3
Devil's Island 1940,Jl 12,11:4
They Drive by Night 1940,Jl 27,17:5
City for Conquest 1940,S 28,9:2
Father's Son 1941,F 13,25:3
Blues in the Night 1941,D 12,35:2
Hello, Frisco, Hello 1943,Mr 25,25:1
Dancing Masters, The 1943,D 2,30:2
Whistler, The 1944,Ap 29,12:2
Since You Went Away 1944,Jl 21,16:2
Frisco Sal 1945,F 17,11:2
Singapore 1947,S 17,31:2

Lloyd, George H
Bodyhold 1949,D 12,29:4

Lloyd, Gerrit J (Original Author)
Drums of Love 1928,Ja 25,20:4

Lloyd, Gladys
Five Star Final 1931,S 11,24:2

Lloyd, Gloria
Temptation 1946,D 25,33:6

Lloyd, Gwyneth
Are You a Mason? 1934,O 30,23:5

Lloyd, Harold
Be my Wife 1919,Ag 18,9:2
Now or Never 1921,My 6,20:2
Among Those Present 1921,Jl 4,10:2
I Do 1921,S 12,16:1
Grandma's Boy 1922,S 4,14:4
Doctor Jack 1922,D 31,VII,2:2 (In Addenda)
Safety Last 1923,Ap 2,22:1
Why Worry? 1923,S 3,9:3
Sailor-Made Man, A 1923,N 6,23:3
Girl Shy 1924,Ap 21,21:4
Hot Water 1924,O 27,27:1
Freshman, The 1925,S 21,12:4
For Heaven's Sake 1926,Ap 5,24:1
Kid Brother, The 1927,Ja 24,14:1
Speedy 1928,Ap 7,20:4
Welcome Danger 1929,O 21,30:1
Feet First 1930,O 31,20:1
Movie Crazy 1932,S 15,19:3
Cat's Paw, The 1934,Ag 17,12:2
Milky Way, The 1936,Mr 26,27:2
Professor Beware 1938,Jl 14,17:1
Mad Wednesday 1951,Ja 25,21:5
Freshman, The 1953,Ap 28,31:6

Lloyd, Harold (Director)
Feet First 1930,O 31,20:1

Lloyd, Harold (Miscellaneous)
Harold Lloyd's World of Comedy 1962,Je 5,36:4

Lloyd, Harold (Narrator)
Harold Lloyd's World of Comedy 1962,Je 5,36:4

Lloyd, Harold (Original Author)
Freshman, The 1953,Ap 28,31:6

Lloyd, Harold (Producer)
Get Out and Get Under 1920,S 13,12:1
High and Dizzy 1922,N 20,21:3
Professor Beware 1938,Jl 14,17:1
Girl, a Guy and a Gob, A 1941,Ap 24,25:3
My Favorite Spy 1942,My 29,13:4
Harold Lloyd's World of Comedy 1962,Je 5,36:4

Lloyd, Harold Jr
Frankenstein's Daughter 1958,N 17,37:2

Lloyd, James
Love-Ins, The 1967,Ag 19,16:1

Lloyd, Jeremy
Coming-Out Party, A 1962,Jl 31,19:2
Smashing Time 1967,D 21,44:1

Lloyd, Jimmy
Story of G I Joe 1945,O 6,9:6
Snafu 1945,D 26,15:2
Gallant Journey 1946,O 10,33:2
Key Witness 1947,Jl 30,27:6
Walk a Crooked Mile 1948,O 13,31:2
Beauty on Parade 1950,Ag 18,17:2
Touch of Larceny, A 1960,Mr 17,28:1

Lloyd, John
Last Journey, The 1936,Je 8,22:4

Lloyd, Norman
Saboteur 1942,My 8,27:2
Unseen, The 1945,My 14,20:5
Within These Walls 1945,Jl 16,8:4
Southerner, The 1945,Ag 27,22:3
Spellbound 1945,N 2,22:2
Walk in the Sun, A 1946,Ja 12,10:6
Green Years, The 1946,Ap 5,21:2
Letter for Evie, A 1946,Je 28,17:4
Young Widow 1946,Jl 29,12:8
Beginning or the End, The 1947,F 21,15:1
No Minor Vices 1949,F 26,11:2
Calamity Jane and Sam Bass 1949,Jl 18,14:2
Scene of the Crime 1949,Jl 29,12:2
Black Book, The 1949,O 17,18:2
Buccaneer's Girl 1950,Mr 27,19:2
Flame and the Arrow, The 1950,Jl 8,7:2
M 1951,Je 11,20:7
He Ran all the Way 1951,Je 21,24:2
Light Touch, The 1952,Ja 17,23:1
Limelight 1952,O 24,27:2

Lloyd, Richard
Hercules, Samson and Ulysses 1965,N 4,57:2

Lloyd, Robert
Persecution and Assassination of Jean-Paul Marat
   as Performed by the Inmates of the Asylum of
   Charenton Under the Direction of the Marquis
   De Sade, The 1967,F 23,41:1

Lloyd, Rollo
Prestige 1932,F 5,25:2
Okay America 1932,S 10,18:5
Strictly Personal 1933,Mr 20,18:2
Destination Unknown 1933,Ap 8,16:2
Out all Night 1933,Ap 8,16:2
Today We Live 1933,Ap 15,16:2
Madame Spy 1934,F 10,20:1
Private Scandal 1934,Je 15,26:2
Whom the Gods Destroy 1934,Jl 13,14:2
Man Who Reclaimed his Head, The
   1935,Ja 9,22:1
Lives of a Bengal Lancer, The 1935,Ja 12,12:2
Murder on a Honeymoon 1935,Mr 4,12:2
Barbary Coast 1935,O 14,21:1
Devil Doll, The 1936,Ag 8,5:2
Anthony Adverse 1936,Ag 27,16:1
Man I Marry, The 1936,O 31,24:3
Come and Get It 1936,N 12,31:1
Seventh Heaven 1937,Mr 26,25:1
Armored Car 1937,Jl 26,15:2
Westland Case, The 1937,O 23,14:2
Arsene Lupin Returns 1938,Mr 9,21:1
Lady in the Morgue, The 1938,My 9,13:3
Goodbye Broadway 1938,My 14,18:1

Lloyd, Rollo (Screenwriter)
Revolt of the Zombies 1936,Je 5,17:2

Lloyd, Sherman
Pamela, Pamela You Are.... 1968,D 21,49:4

Lloyd, Sue
Ipcress File, The 1965,Ag 3,35:1
Return of Mr Moto 1965,D 2,48:1
Champagne Murders, The 1968,Ap 25,53:1
Attack on the Iron Coast 1968,Je 6,54:2
Corruption 1968,D 5,59:1

Lloyd, Ted (Producer)
Week-End With Lulu, A 1962,My 24,29:2

Lloyd, Ted (Screenwriter)
Week-End With Lulu, A 1962,My 24,29:2

Lloyd, Warren
Naval Academy 1941,Je 5,27:3

Lloyd-Jones, Beti
Mikado, The 1967,Mr 15,53:1

Llyon, Richard
Headless Ghost, The 1959,Ap 30,37:2

Lo Briglio, Francesco
Mafioso 1964,Jl 1,42:1

Lo Nigro, Antonio
Shoe-Shine 1947,Ag 27,19:2

Lo-Van, Margaret
Married Woman, The; Femme Mariee, La
   1965,Ag 17,39:1

Loach, Kenneth (Director)
Poor Cow 1968,F 1,28:2

Loach, Kenneth (Screenwriter)
Poor Cow 1968,F 1,28:2

Loan, H H Van (Original Author)
I'd Give my Life 1936,Ag 17,9:1

Lobel, Bruni
Big Lift, The 1950,Ap 27,37:2
Almost Angels 1962,N 1,34:2
City of Secrets 1963,Jl 27,10:2

Loblov, Bela
Reunion in Vienna 1933,Ap 29,14:2

Locatelii, Alfredo
Under the Sun of Rome 1949,O 6,40:4

Locchi, Pino
One Hundred Days of Napoleon 1936,S 14,25:1

Locher, Charles
Charlie Chan in Shanghai 1935,O 14,21:1

Lock, Gerry
Compulsion 1959,Ap 2,26:2

Locke, Charles O (Composer)
Let's Sing Again 1936,My 9,11:2

Locke, Charles O (Original Author)
From Hell to Texas 1958,Je 5,39:2

Locke, Edward (Original Author)
Case of Becky, The 1921,O 10,16:1
Climax, The 1944,D 14,28:5

Locke, Harry
Treasure Island 1950,Ag 16,24:2
Carry on Nurse 1960,S 10,11:1

Locke, Katherine
Seventh Cross, The 1944,S 29,18:1
Snake Pit, the 1948,N 5,29:2
Try and Get Me 1951,My 7,22:2
People Will Talk 1951,Ag 30,20:1
Flesh and Fury 1952,Mr 28,27:4
Certain Smile, A 1958,Ag 1,13:2

Locke, Shamus
Hungry Hill 1947,O 11,11:2
You Can't Fool an Irishman 1950,D 7,45:4

Locke, Sharyl
Father Goose 1964,D 11,55:1
I Saw What You Did 1965,Jl 22,24:2

Locke, Sondra
Heart is a Lonely Hunter, The 1968,Ag 1,24:1

Locke, Tammy
Once a Thief 1965,S 9,36:1

Locke, William J
Tragedy of the East Side, A 1920,Ag 24,6:2

Locke, William J (Original Author)
Oath, The 1921,Ap 11,9:1
Side Show of Life, The 1924,Jl 22,9:1
Coming of Amos, The 1925,S 8,29:1
Simon the Jester 1925,N 19,22:1
Strangers in Love 1932,Mr 5,11:2
Morals of Marcus, The 1936,Ja 13,14:2
Beloved Vagabond, The 1937,F 8,12:5

Locker, Felix
Thunder in the Sun 1959,Ap 9,37:2

Lockerbee, Beth
Incredible Journey, The 1963,N 21,43:2

Lockhart, Anne
Clean Heart, The 1924,S 15,28:1

Lockhart, Calvin
Joanna 1968,N 25,54:1

Lockhart, Gene
Star of Midnight 1935,Ap 12,26:5
Crime and Punishment 1935,N 22,18:2
Garden Murder Case, The 1936,Mr 2,13:2
Brides are Like That 1936,Mr 23,22:5
Times Square Playboy 1936,My 2,11:2
Gorgeous Hussy, The 1936,S 5,7:1
Devil is a Sissy, The 1936,O 17,21:2
Wedding Present 1936,N 19,31:3
Come Closer, Folks 1936,N 23,17:3
Make Way for Tomorrow 1937,My 10,23:1
Something to Sing About 1937,S 21,29:4
Of Human Hearts 1938,F 18,23:1
Sinners in Paradise 1938,My 20,17:2
Men Are Such Fools 1938,Je 17,25:1
Algiers 1938,Jl 15,13:2
Meet the Girls 1938,S 3,16:6
Listen, Darling 1938,N 24,37:2
Blondie 1938,D 22,25:4
Christmas Carol, A 1938,D 23,16:2
Sweethearts 1938,D 23,16:2
I'm From Missouri 1939,Mr 23,27:1
Story of Alexander Graham Bell, The
   1939,Ap 1,17:2
Hotel Imperial 1939,My 11,31:3
Bridal Suite 1939,My 26,20:2
Tell no Tales 1939,Je 2,27:3
Our Leading Citizen 1939,Ag 24,17:1
Blackmail 1939,S 16,26:3
His Girl Friday 1940,Ja 12,13:2
Geronimo 1940,F 8,18:3
Abe Lincoln in Illinois 1940,F 23,19:2
Edison the Man 1940,Je 7,27:2
South of Pago-Pago 1940,Ag 2,12:2
We Who Are Young 1940,S 13,27:2
Dr Kildare Goes Home 1940,S 19,27:4
Dispatch From Reuters, A 1940,D 12,37:2
Meet John Doe 1941,Mr 13,25:2
Sea Wolf, The 1941,Mr 26,27:3
Billy the Kid 1941,Je 20,28:2
All That Money Can Buy 1941,O 17,27:2
International Lady 1941,N 11,29:2

Lockhart, Gene— Cont

One Foot in Heaven 1941,N 14,28:3
Juke Girl 1942,Je 20,9:2
Gay Sisters, The 1942,Ag 15,14:2
You Can't Escape Forever 1942,O 17,11:1
Hangmen Also Die 1943,Ap 16,24:2
Mission to Moscow 1943,Ap 30,25:2
Northern Pursuit 1943,N 26,29:2
Desert Song, The 1943,D 18,10:6
Action in Arabia 1944,F 19,18:7
Man From Frisco 1944,Je 16,14:7
That's the Spirit 1945,Je 2,11:2
House on Ninety-Second Street, The
  1945,S 27,24:7
Leave Her to Heaven 1945,D 26,15:1
Scandal In Paris, A 1946,S 16,9:7
Shocking Miss Pilgrim, The 1947,F 12,34:2
Strange Woman, The 1947,F 24,16:4
Honeymoon 1947,My 19,27:2
Miracle on 34th Street 1947,Je 5,32:1
Cynthia 1947,S 19,27:2
Foxes of Harrow, The 1947,S 25,35:4
Her Husband's Affairs 1947,N 14,29:2
I, Jane Doe 1948,Jl 5,8:4
Apartment for Peggy 1948,O 16,9:2
Joan of Arc 1948,N 12,30:5
That Wonderful Urge 1948,D 22,29:6
Down to the Sea in Ships 1949,F 23,31:2
Madame Bovary 1949,Ag 26,15:2
Inspector General, The 1949,D 31,9:2
Red Light 1950,Ja 16,18:4
Riding High 1950,Ap 11,26:2
Big Hangover, The 1950,My 26,20:3
I'd Climb the Highest Mountain 1951,My 10,38:1
Rhubarb 1951,Ag 31,12:2
Girl in Every Port, A 1952,F 14,23:1
Hoodlum Empire 1952,Mr 6,25:6
Secret Sharer, The 1953,Ja 14,27:2
Androcles and the Lion 1953,Ja 15,23:2
Lady Wants Mink, The 1953,Ap 6,24:2
Down Among the Sheltering Palms
  1953,Je 13,11:2
World for Ransom 1954,Je 5,11:2
Carousel 1956,F 17,13:1
Man in the Gray Flannel Suit, The
  1956,Ap 13,21:1

Lockhart, Gene (Composer)
Mrs Miniver 1942,Je 5,23:1

Lockhart, Gene (Original Author)
Forever and a Day 1943,Mr 13,9:2

Lockhart, Harry
One That Got Away, The 1958,Ap 23,40:2
Once More With Feeling 1960,F 12,22:2

Lockhart, June
All This and Heaven, Too 1940,Jl 5,10:2
Adam Had Four Sons 1941,Mr 28,26:6
Sergeant York 1941,Jl 3,15:1
White Cliffs of Dover, The 1944,My 12,15:2
Meet Me in St Louis 1944,N 29,20:2
Keep Your Powder Dry 1945,Mr 12,22:6
Son of Lassie 1945,Je 11,12:1
She Wolf of London 1946,Ap 6,10:6
Easy to Wed 1946,Jl 12,14:2
Yearling, The 1947,Ja 24,18:2
Bury Me Dead 1947,O 25,13:3
T-Men 1948,Ja 23,28:3
Time Limit 1957,O 24,37:2

Lockhart, Kathleen
Brides are Like That 1936,Mr 23,22:5
Times Square Playboy 1936,My 2,11:2
Devil is a Sissy, The 1936,O 17,21:2
Something to Sing About 1937,S 21,29:4
Men Are Such Fools 1938,Je 17,25:1
Give Me a Sailor 1938,Ag 11,31:1
Blondie 1938,D 22,25:4
Christmas Carol, A 1938,D 23,16:2
Sweethearts 1938,D 23,16:2
Man of Conquest 1939,Ap 28,31:2
Our Leading Citizen 1939,Ag 24,17:1
What a Life 1939,O 12,33:1
Are Husbands Necessary? 1942,Jl 9,17:2
Mission to Moscow 1943,Ap 30,25:2
Lost Angel 1944,Ap 10,14:1
Roughly Speaking 1945,F 1,18:4
Bewitched 1945,Ag 17,20:3
Lady in the Lake 1947,Ja 24,18:3
Mother Wore Tights 1947,Ag 21,33:2
Gentleman's Agreement 1947,N 12,36:2
I'd Climb the Highest Mountain 1951,My 10,38:1
Walking my Baby Back Home 1954,Ja 16,10:5
Glenn Miller Story, the 1954,F 11,33:2

Lockhart, R H Bruce (Original Author)
British Agent 1934,S 20,20:1

Locklear, Lieutenant
Great Air Robbery, The 1920,F 16,8:1

Lockney, J P
String Beans 1918,D 30,7:3
Greased Lightning 1919,Ap 28,13:2
Hay Foot, Straw Foot 1919,Je 23,10:3
Egg Crate Wallop, The 1919,S 29,16:1
Dixie Handicap, The 1924,D 30,15:3
Barriers Burned Away 1925,Mr 12,17:2

Lockridge, Frances (Original Author)
Mr and Mrs North 1942,Ja 22,13:2

Lockridge, Richard (Original Author)
Mr and Mrs North 1942,Ja 22,13:2

Lockridge, Ross Jr (Original Author)
Raintree County 1957,D 21,22:1

Lockwood, Alexander
Flight From Destiny 1941,Mr 28,26:7
Just off Broadway 1942,Ag 29,18:4
Jigsaw 1949,My 30,9:4
Tattered Dress, The 1957,Mr 15,22:3
Tarnished Angels, The 1958,Ja 7,31:1

Lockwood, Alyn
Blondie Hits the Jackpot 1949,S 9,28:3

Lockwood, Gary
Wild in the Country 1961,Je 10,12:2
Splendor in the Grass 1961,O 11,53:1
It Happened at the World's Fair 1963,My 30,20:1
Firecreek 1968,F 22,36:2
2001 A Space Odyssey 1968,Ap 4,58:1

Lockwood, Julia
Please Turn Over 1961,Ap 29,12:2

Lockwood, Margaret
Amateur Gentleman, The 1936,Ap 27,19:2
Beloved Vagabond, The 1937,F 8,12:5
Dr Syn 1937,N 15,15:1
To the Victor 1938,Ap 13,21:2
Lady Vanishes, The 1938,D 26,29:1
Susannah of the Mounties 1939,Je 24,13:2
Rulers of the Sea 1939,N 9,27:1
Night Train 1940,D 30,21:1
Girl in the News, The 1941,My 5,13:2
Stars Look Down, The 1941,Jl 24,15:2
Quiet Wedding 1941,D 29,27:4
Girl Must Live, A 1942,Mr 24,25:2
Randolph Family 1945,Mr 13,19:4
Man in Grey, The 1945,N 30,18:6
Wicked Lady, The 1946,D 23,19:5
Bedelia 1947,F 8,10:2
Lady Surrenders, A 1947,Je 20,25:6
Hungry Hill 1947,O 11,11:2
Jassy 1948,F 20,19:2
Bad Sister 1948,Je 11,27:3
Place of One's Own, A 1949,F 8,30:2
Madness of the Heart 1950,O 12,43:2
Trent's Last Case 1953,N 27,99:9
Laughing Anne 1954,My 8,15:2
Trouble in the Glen 1955,Ap 11,29:2
Cast a Dark Shadow 1957,N 28,57:1

Lockwood, Roy (Director)
Mutiny of the Elsinore, The 1939,F 16,17:2

Lockwood, Toots
Bad Sister 1948,Je 11,27:3

Lodato, Carlo (Miscellaneous)
Suicide Attack 1951,Jl 14,7:2

Loddi, Loris
Cleopatra 1963,Je 13,29:1

Loden, Barbara
Wild River 1960,My 27,22:1
Splendor in the Grass 1961,O 11,53:1

Loder, John
Doctor's Secret, The 1929,F 4,20:1
Racketeer, The 1930,Ja 6,30:8
Her Private Affair 1930,Ja 11,21:3
Man Hunter, The 1930,Ap 5,23:3
Second Story Murder, The 1930,My 3,23:1
One Night at Susie's 1930,N 24,26:5
Seas Beneath 1931,Ja 31,15:1
Private Life of Henry VIII, The 1933,O 13,25:2
You Made Me Love You 1934,My 30,14:3
Battle, The 1934,N 23,23:2
Java Head 1935,Jl 31,21:4
Man Who Lived Again, The 1936,D 16,35:4
Woman Alone, The 1937,F 27,9:2
King Solomon's Mines 1937,Jl 3,18:1
Ourselves Alone 1937,Jl 31,6:2
Dr Syn 1937,N 15,15:1
River of Unrest 1937,N 27,21:2
Non-Stop New York 1937,N 29,19:2
To the Victor 1938,Ap 13,21:2
Katia 1939,D 23,9:2
Adventure in Diamonds 1940,Ap 4,27:2
Mozart 1940,O 4,29:2
Diamond Frontiers 1940,O 4,29:2
Tin Pan Alley 1940,N 22,27:3
Scotland Yard 1941,Ap 9,33:3
One Night in Lisbon 1941,Je 12,29:3
How Green Was my Valley 1941,O 29,27:2
Confirm or Deny 1941,D 19,35:2
Continental Express 1942,Ap 7,26:3
Eagle Squadron 1942,Jl 3,12:5
Now, Voyager 1942,O 23,25:3
Gentleman Jim 1942,N 26,40:3
Gorilla Man, The 1943,Ja 15,21:4
Mysterious Doctor, The 1943,My 20,26:4
Old Acquaintance 1943,N 3,20:2
Passage to Marseille 1944,F 17,12:5
Hairy Ape, The 1944,Jl 3,8:3
Abroad With two Yanks 1944,O 26,19:7
Brighton Strangler, The 1945,My 19,15:2
Fighting Guardsman, The 1945,O 6,9:6
Game of Death, A 1945,N 24,22:4
Wife of Monte Cristo, The 1946,Ap 8,31:2

Loder, John— Cont

One More Tomorrow 1946,My 25,12:2
Dishonored Lady 1947,My 24,10:5
Story of Esther Costello, The 1957,N 6,43:1
Gideon of Scotland Yard 1959,My 20,38:2

Loder, Lotti
Sit Tight 1931,F 19,20:4
Soldiers Plaything, A 1931,My 2,23:4

Loder, Sydney
Massacre Hill 1950,D 14,51:3

Loder, Ted
Lilies of the Field 1930,F 22,13:1

Lodge, David
Cockleshell Heroes, The 1956,Je 4,25:2
Two-Way Stretch 1961,Ja 24,20:3
League of Gentlemen, The 1961,Ja 25,30:4
Kill or Cure 1962,N 13,43:4
Trial and Error 1962,N 17,17:2
Never Let Go 1963,Je 15,10:2
Shot in the Dark, A 1964,Je 24,28:1
Guns at Batasi 1964,N 17,47:1
Having a Wild Weekend 1965,Ag 19,35:1

Lodge, Jean
White Corridors 1952,Jl 16,21:1
Brandy for the Parson 1952,Ag 18,13:4
Black Knight, The 1954,O 29,27:2

Lodge, John
Woman Accused, The 1933,Mr 13,18:2
Murders in the Zoo 1933,Ap 3,13:4
Scralet Empress, The 1934,S 15,20:2
Menace 1934,N 22,27:2
Little Colonel, The 1935,Mr 22,26:2
Ourselves Alone 1937,Jl 31,6:2
Bulldog Drummond at Bay 1937,O 25,23:2
Tenth Man, The 1937,N 15,15:2
River of Unrest 1937,N 27,21:2
Mayerling to Sarajevo 1940,O 30,27:6
Pasha's Wives, The 1942,Ap 6,19:2

Lodge, John Davis
Little Women 1933,N 17,22:3

Lodi, Theodore
They Had to See Paris 1929,O 12,11:1
Once a Sinner 1931,Ja 17,23:1
Down to Earth 1932,S 2,19:2

Lodijensky, General
Her Love Story 1924,O 7,26:1
Swan, The 1925,Mr 2,14:1

Lodwick, Peter
Mikado, The 1967,Mr 15,53:1

Loeb, Janice (Producer)
Quiet One, The 1949,F 14,15:2

Loeb, Janice (Screenwriter)
Quiet One, The 1949,F 14,15:2

Loeb, Lee (Original Author)
Case of the Missing Man, The 1935,N 23,23:2
Don't Gamble With Love 1936,Mr 2,13:3
Shall We Dance 1937,My 14,21:1
Devil is Driving, The 1937,Jl 16,22:1
It Can't Last Forever 1937,Jl 30,22:5
Three Loves Has Nancy 1938,S 2,21:2

Loeb, Lee (Screenwriter)
Case of the Missing Man, The 1935,N 23,23:2
Don't Gamble With Love 1936,Mr 2,13:3
Trapped by Television 1936,Je 15,24:3
Come Closer, Folks 1936,N 23,17:3
It Can't Last Forever 1937,Jl 30,22:5
Counsel for Crime 1937,O 9,16:1
Main Event, The 1938,Je 20,11:3
Hawaiian Nights 1939,S 29,19:4
Gentleman at Heart, A 1942,F 23,25:2
It Happened in Flatbush 1942,Jl 3,12:8
Dixie Dugan 1943,Ap 9,25:5
Love, Honor and Goodbye 1945,S 8,12:2
Undertow 1949,D 16,37:2

Loeb, Philip
Room Service 1938,S 22,27:1
Double Life, A 1948,F 20,19:1
Molly 1951,Mr 8,37:2

Loebell, Marc
Great Commandment, The 1942,O 17,11:1

Loebinger, Lottie
Kampf, Der 1936,S 11,29:3

Loeck, Carsta
Doppelbraeutigam, Der; Double Fiance, The
  1935,Mr 23,11:3
Krach um Iolanthe 1935,My 11,21:3
Wenn am Sonntagabend die Dorfmusik Spielt
  1935,D 9,25:3
Alles um Eine Frau 1935,D 21,11:1
Reifende Jugend 1936,Ja 4,19:1
Wenn der Hahn Kraeht 1936,N 14,23:3
Mutige Seefahrer, Der 1936,N 21,21:5
Pour le Merite 1939,Ap 8,19:2

Loefgren, Marianne
Froeken Blir Piga 1937,Je 12,8:3
Med Folket Foer Fosterlandet 1939,F 21,14:2
Rena Rama Sanningen; Nothing but the Truth
  1939,O 7,11:2

Loehr, Dolly
There's Magic in Music 1941,Je 5,27:2

Loehr, Hans
Emil und die Detektive 1931,D 21,28:4

Loesser, Frank
  Red, Hot and Blue 1949,O 20,39:2
Loesser, Frank (Composer)
  Vogues of 1938 1937,Ag 20,21:1
  College Swing 1938,Ap 28,27:2
  Sing You Sinners 1938,Ag 18,23:1
  Man About Town 1939,Je 29,19:1
  Las Vegas Nights 1941,Mr 20,25:2
  Kiss the Boys Goodbye 1941,Ag 14,21:2
  Mr Bug Goes to Town 1942,F 20,21:3
  Priorities on Parade 1942,Jl 23,19:2
  Seven Days' Leave 1942,D 11,33:2
  Happy Go Lucky 1943,Mr 25,25:1
  Roseanna McCoy 1949,O 13,33:2
  Let's Dance 1950,N 30,42:2
  Hans Christian Andersen 1952,N 26,20:2
  Guys and Dolls 1955,N 5,26:1
Loesser, Frank (Miscellaneous)
  Blossoms On Broadway 1937,D 3,29:2
  Hawaiian Nights 1939,S 29,19:4
Loesser, Frank (Screenwriter)
  Priorities on Parade 1942,Jl 23,19:2
Loesser Frank (Composer)
  Thank Your Lucky Stars 1943,O 2,19:2
LOEW
  See Also LOEWE, LOWE
Loew, Arthur M Jr (Original Author)
  Arena 1953,Jl 23,20:2
Loew, Arthur M Jr (Producer)
  Teresa 1951,Ap 6,31:2
  Arena 1953,Jl 23,20:2
  Rack, The 1956,N 6,30:1
  Penelope 1966,N 11,36:6
Loew, David L (Producer)
  Riding on Air 1937,Je 26,20:2 (In Addenda)
  Fit for a King 1937,O 15,18:5
  Wide Open Faces 1938,Ap 15,23:2
  Gladiator, The 1938,Ag 29,10:2
  Flirting With Fate 1938,D 15,35:3
  So Ends our Night 1941,F 28,17:2
  Moon and Sixpence 1942,O 28,26:4
  Southerner, The 1945,Ag 27,22:3
  Night in Casablanca, A 1946,Ag 12,17:2
  Private Affairs of Bel Ami, The 1947,Je 16,25:4
LOEWE
  See Also LOEW, LOWE
Loewe, Frederick (Composer)
  Gigi 1958,My 16,21:1
Loewe, Frederick (Original Author)
  My Fair Lady 1964,O 22,41:1
Loewenadler, Holger
  Skaergaards-Flirt 1936,Ap 8,26:3
Loewenbein, Richard (Director)
  Tenderness 1950,Jl 27,VIII,4:2 (In Addenda)
Lof, Arthur
  Who Killed Gail Preston? 1938,My 6,27:2
Loff, Jeanette
  At Yale 1928,Jl 30,21:2
  Man Made Women 1928,S 18,33:2
  Sophomore, The 1929,Ag 24,11:5
  Party Girl 1930,Ja 2,28:2
  Racketeer, The 1930,Ja 6,30:8
  King of Jazz 1930,My 3,23:1
  Boudoir Diplomat, The 1930,D 8,26:1
  Million Dollar Baby 1935,My 6,22:3
Loffredo, G (Original Author)
  Genoese Dragnet 1954,F 12,20:5
Loffredo, G (Screenwriter)
  Genoese Dragnet 1954,F 12,20:5
Lofgren, Marianne
  En Enda Natt 1942,D 7,22:2
  Incorrigible 1949,Jl 2,8:2
  Affairs of a Model 1952,Ag 7,12:8
  Time of Desire 1959,N 21,26:5
  Devil's Wanton, The 1962,Jl 5,21:2
Loft, Arthur
  Alimony Madness 1933,My 5,18:1
  King of the Royal Mounted 1936,S 29,35:2
  Legion of Terror 1936,N 2,24:2
  Without Orders 1936,N 4,41:3
  Night Waitress 1936,D 18,31:5
  It Happened in Hollywood 1937,O 2,18:1
  Paid to Dance 1937,D 6,19:1
  Shadow, The 1937,D 17,33:3
  No Time to Marry 1938,F 23,27:2
  Women in Prison 1938,Mr 1,19:3
  Start Cheering 1938,Mr 17,17:3
  Rawhide 1938,Ap 25,19:2
  Main Event, The 1938,Je 20,11:3
  City Streets 1938,Jl 25,18:2
  Highway Patrol 1938,Ag 4,15:2
  I Am the Law 1938,Ag 26,14:2
  Risky Business 1939,Mr 23,27:2
  Hell's Kitchen 1939,Jl 3,10:5
  Woman Is the Judge, A 1939,S 28,29:5
  Street of Missing Women 1940,Ja 8,11:2
  Crooked Road, The 1940,Je 11,33:4
  Caught in the Draft 1941,Je 26,27:3
  Dr Broadway 1942,Je 25,27:3
  Magnificent Dope, The 1942,Jl 3,12:5
  Priorities on Parade 1942,Jl 23,19:2
  Glass Key, The 1942,O 16,23:1
  Man in the Trunk, The 1942,O 23,25:1

Street Of Chance 1942,N 19,31:3
Meanest Man in the World, The 1943,F 25,27:3
Happy Go Lucky 1943,Mr 25,25:1
My Friend Flicka 1943,My 27,21:4
Let's Face It 1943,Ag 5,18:1
Frontier Badmen 1943,Ag 14,12:8
Hitler Gang, The 1944,My 8,15:2
Woman in the Window, The 1945,Ja 26,16:4
It's a Pleasure 1945,My 4,23:3
Along Came Jones 1945,Jl 19,8:7
Men in her Diary 1945,S 24,16:5
Scarlet Street 1946,F 15,29:2
To Each his Own 1946,My 24,15:2
Lofts, Norah (Original Author)
  Jassy 1948,F 20,19:2
  7 Women 1966,My 5,59:1
Loftus, Cecilia
  East Lynne 1931,F 21,15:2
  Doctors' Wives 1931,Ap 25,23:4
  Young Sinners 1931,My 9,15:4
  Once in a Blue Moon 1936,D 2,35:1
  Old Maid, The 1939,Ag 12,16:2
  Blue Bird, The 1940,Ja 20,11:2
  It's a Date 1940,Mr 23,16:2
  Lucky Partners 1940,S 6,25:2
  Black Cat, The 1941,Ap 26,20:3
Loftus, Cissie
  Dress Parade 1939,O 28,11:2
Logan, Annabelle
  Presenting Lily Mars 1943,Ap 30,25:3
Logan, Ella
  Flying Hostess 1936,D 14,29:4
  Top of the Town 1937,Mr 27,19:2
  Woman Chases Man 1937,Je 11,26:2
  52d Street 1937,N 15,15:1
  Goldwyn Follies, The 1938,F 21,15:1
Logan, Gwendolyn
  Disraeli 1929,O 3,27:5
  Alexander Hamilton 1931,S 17,21:4
  Once a Lady 1931,N 9,22:4
  Christopher Strong 1933,Mr 10,19:2
  We Live Again 1934,N 2,27:2
Logan, Helen (Original Author)
  Off to the Races 1937,F 6,15:2
  Charlie Chan on Broadway 1937,S 20,19:1
  Charlie Chan at Monte Carlo 1937,D 18,18:1
  Tin Pan Alley 1940,N 22,27:3
  I'll Get by 1950,N 2,39:3
Logan, Helen (Screenwriter)
  Charlie Chan in Egypt 1935,Je 24,12:2
  Charlie Chan's Secret 1936,Ja 18,19:4
  Charlie Chan at the Circus 1936,Mr 19,22:4
  Charlie Chan at the Race Track 1936,Ag 15,6:2
  Off to the Races 1937,F 6,15:2
  Charlie Chan at the Olympics 1937,My 24,23:1
  Big Business 1937,Je 1,27:2
  Born Reckless 1937,Jl 30,22:6
  Big Town Girl 1937,D 13,23:4
  Rascals 1938,My 27,12:2
  Trip to Paris, A 1938,Je 10,18:2
  Speed to Burn 1938,S 9,25:1
  Sharpshooters 1938,D 5,19:2
  Susannah of the Mounties 1939,Je 24,13:2
  Escape, The 1939,N 3,17:4
  Charlie Chan in City in Darkness 1939,D 18,29:2
  Man Who Wouldn't Talk, The 1940,Ja 12,13:3
  Star Dust 1940,My 4,13:1
  Lucky Cisco Kid 1940,Je 24,19:5
  Great American Broadcast, The 1941,My 2,25:2
  Sun Valley Serenade 1941,S 6,20:1
  Song of the Islands 1942,Mr 12,24:4
  Footlight Serenade 1942,S 10,30:3
  Iceland 1942,O 15,27:1
  Hello, Frisco, Hello 1943,Mr 25,25:1
  Four Jills in a Jeep 1944,Ap 6,27:2
  Pin Up Girl 1944,My 11,25:6
  Something for the Boys 1944,N 30,19:1
  Do You Love Me 1946,My 25,12:2
  If I'm Lucky 1946,S 20,41:3
  Three Little Girls in Blue 1946,S 26,32:3
Logan, Jacqueline
  Ebb Tide 1922,N 20,21:3
  Blind Bargain, A 1922,D 4,20:2
  Mr Billings Spends his Dime 1923,Mr 5,15:3
  Sixty Cents an Hour 1923,My 15,22:1
  Salomy Jane 1923,S 9,9:3
  Light That Failed, The 1923,N 27,11:2
  Flaming Barriers 1924,Ja 29,16:1
  Dawn of a Tomorrow, The 1924,Mr 26,19:2
  Manhattan 1924,O 29,18:1
  Man Must Live, A 1925,Ja 29,12:2
  Playing With Souls 1925,Ap 20,18:1 (Incorrect in
    this edition; use 1925,Ap 28,18:1 elsewhere)
  If Marriage Fails 1925,Je 2,16:3
  Thank You 1925,O 6,30:1
  Tony Runs Wild 1926,Ap 28,28:3
  Footloose Windows 1926,Je 22,21:2
  King of Kings, The 1927,Ap 20,29:2
  Blood Ship, The 1927,Jl 19,27:2
  Wise Wife 1927,N 1,21:1 (In Addenda)
  Leopard Lady, The 1928,F 27,16:2
  Stocks and Blondes 1928,O 23,33:1
  Cop, The 1928,N 6,35:1

Logan, Jacqueline— Cont
  Power 1928,N 27,34:1
  General Crack 1929,D 4,36:6
  Middle Watch, The 1930,D 20,20:6
Logan, James
  Blonde Savage 1947,O 4,9:2
  Mr Peabody and the Mermaid 1948,Ag 14,6:5
Logan, Janice
  Undercover Doctor 1939,Je 1,31:2
  What a Life 1939,O 12,33:1
  Dr Cyclops 1940,Ap 11,32:3
Logan, Joshua
  Main Street to Broadway 1953,O 14,34:1
Logan, Joshua (Composer)
  South Pacific 1958,Mr 20,33:1
Logan, Joshua (Director)
  I Met my Love Again 1938,Ja 15,19:1
  Picnic 1956,F 17,13:3
  Bus Stop 1956,S 1,19:2
  Soyonara 1957,D 6,39:4
  Sayonara 1957,D 6,39:4
  South Pacific 1958,Mr 20,33:1
  Tall Story 1960,Ap 7,46:1
  Fanny 1961,Jl 7,16:1
  Ensign Pulver 1964,Ag 1,13:2
  Camelot 1967,O 26,54:1
Logan, Joshua (Original Author)
  Higher and Higher 1944,Ja 22,8:4
  Mister Roberts 1955,Jl 15,14:1
Logan, Joshua (Producer)
  Tall Story 1960,Ap 7,46:1
  Fanny 1961,Jl 7,16:1
  Ensign Pulver 1964,Ag 1,13:2
Logan, Joshua (Screenwriter)
  Mister Roberts 1955,Jl 15,14:1
  Ensign Pulver 1964,Ag 1,13:2
Logan, M (Original Author)
  Loves of a Dictator 1935,Je 1,18:2
  Some Like It Hot 1959,Mr 30,23:1
Logan, Stanley
  We Are not Alone 1939,D 1,27:1
  My Son, My Son! 1940,My 10,26:6
  Women in War 1940,My 30,21:2
  Submarine Zone; (Escape To Glory)
    1941,Ap 7,13:2
  Singapore Woman 1941,My 12,13:6
  Counter-Espionage 1942,S 28,13:2
  Nightmare 1942,D 4,31:2
  Wilson 1944,Ag 2,18:1
  Three Strangers 1946,F 23,20:2
  Home Sweet Homicide 1946,S 12,5:7
  Sword in the Desert 1949,Ag 25,20:2
  Double Crossbones 1951,Ap 27,19:2
  With a Song in my Heart 1952,Ap 5,20:2
Logan, Stanley (Director)
  First Lady 1937,D 23,25:1
  Love, Honor and Behave 1938,Mr 21,18:2
  Women Are Like That 1938,Ap 11,12:2
  Falcon's Brother, The 1942,O 3,9:5
Logan, Tex
  Festival 1967,O 24,53:2
Logardt, Bengt
  Unmarried Mothers 1956,F 23,32:5
  Unmarried Mothers 1956,F 23,32:5
Logardt, Bengt (Producer)
  Unmarried Mothers 1956,F 23,32:5
Logardt, Bengt (Screenwriter)
  Unmarried Mothers 1956,F 23,32:5
Logathetidi, Basil
  Germans Strike Again, The 1949,Ap 14,29:4
Logereau, Edouard (Director)
  Paris Secret 1965,S 4,11:5
Loggia, Robert
  Somebody up There Likes Me 1956,Jl 6,16:1
  Garment Jungle, The 1957,My 16,28:2
  Cop Hater 1958,O 2,44:3
Logis, Ronald
  Helen of Troy 1956,Ja 27,21:4
Logothetides, Vasilis
  Trouble for Father 1958,Ja 6,26:4
  Counterfeit Coin 1960,My 16,39:1
Logothetidis, Basil
  Mademoiselle-Age 39 1956,Mr 26,34:2
  Santa Chikita 1959,My 11,30:1
Logue, Charles (Miscellaneous)
  Sing Sing Nights 1935,Ja 26,13:2
  Home on the Range 1935,F 13,24:4
Logue, Charles (Original Author)
  Flame of the Desert 1919,O 27,9:3
  Clash of the Wolves, The 1925,N 18,27:4
  Shakedown, The 1929,Ap 8,32:1
Logue, Charles (Screenwriter)
  Drake Case, The 1929,S 16,30:1
  Make a Million 1935,N 9,19:3
  Conflict 1937,Ja 18,21:2
  Renfrew of the Royal Mounted 1937,N 3,29:4
  Crime Takes a Holiday 1938,N 28,11:2
Logue, Charles A (Original Author)
  Below the Line 1925,S 21,12:4
Logue, Elizabeth
  New Faces 1954,F 20,8:7
  Nude Odyssey 1962,O 27,14:6
  Hawaii 1966,O 11,54:1

Lohde, Sigurd
Theodor Koerner 1933,My 6,11:2
Frau Lehmann's Toechter 1933,O 27,22:3
Tannenberg 1934,Ap 3,26:6
Lohkamp, Emil
Horst Wessel; Hans Westmar 1934,F 4,IX,4:4
Lohner, Fritz (Screenwriter)
Student's Romance, The 1936,O 12,23:2
Lohner, Helmut
Spessart Inn, The 1961,F 18,12:3
Lohnisky, Vaclav
Transport From Paradise 1967,F 8,22:1
Lohr, Marie
Aren't We All? 1932,Jl 1,19:3
My Heart Is Calling 1935,Ap 15,16:3
South Riding 1938,Ag 2,15:2
Pygmalion 1938,D 8,34:2
Mozart 1940,O 4,29:2
Major Barbara 1941,My 15,27:1
48 Hours 1944,Je 26,21:2
Notorious Gentleman 1946,N 14,39:3
Magic Bow, The 1947,Jl 7,13:2
Anna Karenina 1948,Ap 28,32:2
Silent Dust 1949,D 30,13:2
Winslow Boy, The 1950,Je 7,34:4
Devil's Plot 1953,Je 19,18:1
Always a Bride 1954,My 28,19:2
Abandon Ship 1957,Ap 18,35:1
Escapade 1957,Ag 6,30:2
Town Like Alice, A 1958,S 22,27:1
Man in a Cocked Hat 1960,Je 15,50:2
Loibner, Eduard
Four in a Jeep 1951,Je 12,35:2
Loin, Herbert
Mr Denning Drives North 1953,S 2,20:1
Loja, Maria
Finanzen des Grossherzogs, Die; Grand Duke's
Finances, The 1935,Ap 6,10:3
Lokshin, Aleksandr (Composer)
Cinerama's Russian Adventure 1966,Ap 14,42:1
Loktov, Alexei
Farewell, Doves 1962,Mr 19,38:3
Meet Me in Moscow 1966,My 3,51:1
Lola
Pan-Americana 1945,Mr 23,13:2
Lolli, Albert C
Monte Cassino 1948,N 25,47:3
Lollier, George
Hold 'Em Navy 1937,N 6,14:2
Lollobrigida, Gina
Mad About Opera 1950,Ap 6,33:2
Love of a Clown (Pagliacci) 1950,Ap 17,18:5
Miss Italy 1952,My 10,16:2
White Line, The 1952,D 6,17:2
Tale of Five Women, A 1953,Ja 16,19:2
Fanfan the Tulip 1953,My 5,34:2
Young Caruso, The 1953,O 13,34:4
Times Gone By (The Trial of Frine); Trial of
Frine, The (Times Gone By) 1953,D 30,16:2
Beat the Devil 1954,Mr 13,11:2
Beauties of the Night 1954,Mr 23,23:5
Bread, Love and Dreams 1954,S 21,24:1
Wayward Wife, The 1955,Ap 11,29:3
Frisky 1955,O 25,37:3
Trapeze 1956,Je 5,39:2
Woman of Rome 1956,N 6,30:1
Hunchback of Notre Dame, The 1957,D 12,35:1
Beautiful but Dangerous 1958,F 6,24:1
Wife for a Night 1958,Je 12,35:2
Solomon and Sheba 1959,D 26,7:2
Never so Few 1960,Ja 22,15:2
Fast and Sexy 1960,O 6,51:2
Where the Hot Wind Blows 1960,N 12,15:1
Go Naked in the World 1961,Mr 11,15:1
Come September 1961,S 8,34:1
Woman of Straw 1964,O 1,30:6
Strange Bedfellows 1965,Mr 11,38:1
Bambole; Dolls, The (Monsignor Cupid);
Monsignor Cupid (The Dolls) 1965,Je 29,26:1
Hotel Paradiso 1966,O 15,34:2
Private Navy of Sgt O'Farrell, The
1968,My 9,54:1
Lom, Herbert
Young Mr Pitt, The 1943,Mr 11,17:1
Seventh Veil, The 1945,D 26,15:1
Snowbound 1949,F 21,20:2
Girl in the Painting, The 1949,Ag 22,13:1
Night and the City 1950,Je 10,11:2
Black Rose, The 1950,S 2,11:2
Good Time Girl 1950,S 25,18:5
State Secret 1950,O 5,38:2
Appointment With Crime 1951,F 19,19:3
Golden Salamander 1951,Mr 24,8:3
Case of Gold 1952,Ja 19,13:3
Cage of Gold 1952,Ja 19,13:3
Paris Express, The 1953,Je 6,8:6
Project M 7 1953,N 27,22:5
Ladykillers 1956,F 21,37:2
Star of India 1956,Ap 28,11:1
War and Peace 1956,Ag 22,26:2
Fire Down Below 1957,Ag 9,11:2
Action of the Tiger 1957,N 14,41:1
I Accuse! 1958,Mr 6,32:1

Chase a Crooked Shadow 1958,Mr 25,28:4
Roots of Heaven, The 1958,O 16,46:1
Intent to Kill 1959,Ap 1,43:2
Big Fisherman, The 1959,Ag 6,18:1
Third Man on the Mountain 1959,N 12,27:1
Room 43 1959,D 3,46:1
Flame Over India 1960,Ap 30,14:1
Spartacus 1960,O 7,28:1
I Aim at the Stars 1960,O 20,42:2
Cid, El 1961,D 15,49:1
Mysterious Island 1961,D 21,30:6
I Like Money 1962,My 19,18:2
Phantom of the Opera, The 1962,Ag 23,25:2
Tiara Tahiti 1963,N 6,32:1
Shot in the Dark, A 1964,Je 24,28:1
Return From the Ashes 1965,N 17,53:1
Gambit 1966,D 22,40:2
Bang, Bang, You're Dead 1967,Ja 19,41:2
Villa Rides 1968,Jl 18,26:3
Lomas, Herbert
Missing Rembrandt, The 1932,Mr 26,17:2
Sign of the Four, The 1932,Ag 20,7:4
Java Head 1935,Jl 31,21:4
Ghost Goes West, The 1936,Ja 11,9:2
Rembrandt 1936,D 3,31:1
Knight Without Armor 1937,Jl 9,18:1
South Riding 1938,Ag 2,15:2
Jamaica Inn 1939,O 12,33:1
Courageous Mr Penn 1943,D 23,26:5
Smugglers, The 1948,Mr 29,17:1
Guinea Pig, The 1949,My 2,20:2
Master of Bankdam 1949,O 17,18:2
Bonnie Prince Charlie 1952,Ja 7,14:3
Lomas, Jack
April in Paris 1952,D 25,34:5
Lomax, Harry
Othello 1966,F 2,24:1
Lombard, Carol
White Woman 1933,D 3,IX,9:4 (In Addenda)
Lombard, Carole
Me, Gangster 1928,O 22,29:1
Power 1928,N 27,34:1
Show Folks 1928,D 10,25:1
Ned McCobb's Daughter 1929,F 18,28:1
Big News 1929,O 7,22:1
Racketeer, The 1930,Ja 6,30:8
Arizona Kid, The 1930,My 17,21:2
Safety in Numbers 1930,My 31,19:4
Fast and Loose 1930,D 1,21:1
Pays to Advertise, It 1931,F 21,15:2
It Pays to Advertise 1931,F 21,15:2
Man of the World 1931,Mr 21,15:1
Ladies' Man 1931,My 1,30:3
Up Pops the Devil 1931,My 16,13:3
I Take This Woman 1931,Je 13,20:4
No One Man 1932,Ja 23,18:4
Sinners in the Sun 1932,My 14,11:5
Virtue 1932,O 25,24:5
No Man of her Own 1932,D 31,10:1
No More Orchids 1933,Ja 2,29:2
From Hell to Heaven 1933,Mr 18,9:3
Supernatural 1933,Ap 22,16:3
Eagle and the Hawk, The 1933,My 13,16:2
Brief Moment 1933,S 30,18:5
White Woman 1933,N 18,18:5
Bolero 1934,F 17,20:3
We're not Dressing 1934,Ap 26,27:2
20th Century 1934,My 4,24:2
Now and Forever 1934,O 13,10:1
Lady by Choice 1934,N 17,12:1
Gay Bride, The 1934,D 19,27:2
Rumba 1935,F 25,13:2
Hands Across the Table 1935,N 2,13:2
Love Before Breakfast 1936,Mr 14,10:1
Princess Comes Across, The 1936,Je 4,27:2
My Man Godfrey 1936,S 19,18:1 (Incorrect in
this edition; use 1936,S 18,18:1 elsewhere)
Swing High, Swing Low 1937,Ap 15,19:1
Nothing Sacred 1937,N 26,27:2
True Confession 1937,D 16,35:2
Fools for Scandal 1938,Mr 25,15:3
Made for Each Other 1939,F 17,17:2
In Name Only 1939,Ag 4,11:3
Vigil in the Night 1940,Mr 9,19:2
They Knew What They Wanted 1940,O 11,25:2
Mr and Mrs Smith 1941,F 21,16:3
To Be or not to Be 1942,Mr 7,13:2
Lombard, Robert
Pantaloons 1956,D 26,34:1
Dog, a Mouse and a Sputnik, A; Pied, a Cheval et
un Sputnik, A 1960,N 1,46:2
Lombard, Yvonne
Lesson in Love, A 1960,Mr 15,46:1
Swedish Wedding Night 1965,N 15,48:1
Lombardi, Carlo
Richiamo del Cuore, Il; Appeal of the Heart, The
1931,Mr 2,19:1
Amore e Dolore 1937,My 13,31:4
Scipio Africanus 1939,S 23,22:2
Stella del Mare; Star of the Sea 1940,My 3,17:6
Moglie in Pericolo, Una; Wife in Danger, A
1940,Je 7,27:3
Lost One, The; La Traviata 1948,Mr 30,26:2

Lombardi, Dillo
Strange Case of Captain Ramper, The
1928,Je 4,13:2
Lombardi, Rodolfo (Screenwriter)
Voice in Your Heart, A 1952,F 23,7:5
Lombardi, Vincent
Paper Lion 1968,O 24,54:1
Lombardo, Carmen (Composer)
Thrill of a Lifetime 1937,D 9,30:2
Lombardo, Goffredo (Producer)
Naked Maja, The 1959,Je 11,36:2
Angel Wore Red, The 1960,S 29,32:1
Sodom and Gomorrah 1963,Ja 24,5:3
Leopard, The 1963,Ag 13,25:1
Malamondo 1964,N 19,49:1
Lombardo, Guy
Many Happy Returns 1934,Je 9,18:2
Lombardo, Guy and orchestra
No Leave, No Love 1946,O 18,29:2
Lombardo, Guy, Band
Stage Door Canteen 1943,Je 25,13:2
Lombos
Wajan 1938,Ap 18,11:1
Lominicki, Tadeusz
Eroica (Second Episode) 1966,F 2,24:1
Lommel, Ulli
Fanny Hill 1965,D 2,48:1
Lomnicki, Tadeusz
Five From Barska Street 1955,Mr 14,29:4
Eighth Day of the Week, The 1959,Mr 24,45:2
Barrier 1967,S 27,39:3
Lomond, Britt
Tonka 1959,Mr 26,27:1
Sign of Zorro, The 1961,S 5,37:6
Lon, Audrey
Cavalry Scout 1951,Je 8,32:2
Lonardos, Urylee
No Sad Songs for Me 1950,Ap 28,26:2
Loncar, Bebe
Long Ships, The 1964,Je 25,25:1
Boy Cried Murder, The 1966,Ap 14,42:3
Birds, the Bees and the Italians, The
1967,Ag 8,33:2
Sucker, The 1967,O 9,61:1
Loncar, Desanka
Ninth Circle, The 1961,S 15,30:3
London, Babe
All Abroad 1927,Ap 19,24:4
Fortune Hunter, The 1928,Ja 10,28:4
London, Barbara
Pad, The (And How to Use It) 1966,Ag 18,27:2
London, Charmian (Original Author)
Jack London 1944,Mr 3,19:3
London, Cherry
Blanche Fury 1948,N 24,20:2
London, Jack (Original Author)
Abysmal Brute, The 1923,Ap 18,24:5
Adventure 1925,Ap 15,16:1
Haunted Ship, The 1928,Ja 23,18:3
Burning Daylight 1928,Ap 23,20:2
Sea Wolf, The 1930,O 6,21:1
Call of the Wild 1935,Ag 15,15:2
White Fang 1936,Jl 18,18:2
Conflict 1937,Ja 18,21:2
Mutiny of the Elsinore, The 1939,F 16,17:2
Romance of the Redwoods 1939,Ap 24,13:2
Sea Wolf, The 1941,Mr 26,27:3
North to the Klondike 1942,Mr 12,24:3
Adventures of Martin Eden 1942,Mr 16,19:2
London, Julie
Red House, The 1947,Mr 17,27:2
Tap Roots 1948,Ag 26,16:3
Task Force 1949,O 1,8:6
Return of the Frontiersman 1950,Je 10,11:3
Fat Man, The 1951,My 25,31:2
Great Man, The 1957,Ja 2,28:2
Girl Can't Help It, The 1957,F 9,12:7
Saddle the Wind 1958,Mr 21,17:1
Voice in the Mirror 1958,Ag 14,23:2
Man of the West 1958,O 2,44:3
Night of the Quarter Moon 1959,Mr 5,35:5
Wonderful Country, The 1959,N 5,39:7
Third Voice, The 1960,Mr 7,24:5
Question of Adultery, A 1961,Jl 6,18:2
George Raft Story, The 1962,Mr 22,40:1
London, Mark
Privilege 1967,Jl 25,30:2
London, Pauline (Original Author)
Tell no Tales 1939,Je 2,27:3
London, Steve
Zero Hour 1957,N 14,41:1
London, Tom
Winds of Chance 1925,Ag 17,10:3
Troopers Three 1930,F 17,17:6
Iron Master, The 1933,F 4,11:3
O'Malley of the Mounted 1936,Ap 6,18:1
Lawless Nineties, The 1936,Je 29,11:1
Roaring Timber 1937,Ag 19,23:1
Renegade Ranger, The 1939,F 17,17:3
Santa Fe Stampede 1939,Ap 26,27:3
Romance of the Rio Grande 1940,D 25,33:4
Sand 1949,Ag 5,23:2
High Noon 1952,Jl 25,14:2

London Symphony Orchestra (Miscellaneous)
Mikado, The 1939,Je 2,27:2
Londone, Avice
Alligator Named Daisy, An 1957,O 7,23:2
Lonehill, Ed
Last Hunt, The 1956,Mr 1,37:2
Lonergan, Lenore
Tom, Dick and Harry 1941,Jl 18,22:2
Whistle at Eaton Falls, The 1951,O 11,49:2
Westward the Women 1952,Ja 1,21:2
Lady Says No, The 1952,Ja 7,14:3
Lonergan, Lester
Seven Faces 1929,N 16,25:2
Boomerang 1947,Mr 6,36:2
Long, Amelia Reynolds (Original Author)
Fiend Without a Face 1958,Jl 4,15:3
Long, Audrey
Night of Adventure, A 1944,Je 3,10:4
Tall in the Saddle 1944,D 15,25:3
Pan-Americana 1945,Mr 23,13:2
Wanderer of the Wasteland 1945,S 29,12:2
Game of Death, A 1945,N 24,22:4
Perilous Holiday 1946,Je 1,10:4
Born to Kill 1947,My 1,34:2
Song of my Heart 1948,Mr 5,17:3
Miraculous Journey 1948,S 20,21:2
Petty Girl, The 1950,Ag 18,17:2
Long, Avon
Centennial Summer 1946,Jl 18,20:2
Long, Bobby
It Happened in Brooklyn 1947,Mr 14,28:5
Long, Dwight (Cinematographer)
Tanga Tika 1953,O 6,34:4
Long, Dwight (Director)
Tanga Tika 1953,O 6,34:4
Long, Dwight (Producer)
Tanga Tika 1953,O 6,34:4
Long, Frederick
Lost Patrol, The 1929,D 16,34:2
Long, Hal (Miscellaneous)
Stanley and Livingstone 1939,Ag 5,18:2
Long, Hal (Original Author)
Blood Money 1933,N 16,30:5
Bad Guy 1937,Ag 26,25:2
Johnny Apollo 1940,Ap 13,21:2
Fabulous Texan, The 1947,D 26,22:5
Long, Hal (Screenwriter)
Folies Bergere 1935,F 25,13:2
White Fang 1936,Jl 18,18:2
Nancy Steele is Missing 1937,Mr 8,22:1
Viva Cisco Kid 1940,Mr 22,23:4
That Night in Rio 1941,Mr 10,21:2
Long, John Luther (Original Author)
Madame Butterfly 1915,N 8,13:5
Madame Butterfly 1932,D 26,26:2
Long, Johnny, and his Orchestra
Hit the Ice 1943,S 23,27:2
Long, Lily
Old Curiosity Shop, The 1935,D 23,15:5
Long, Lotus
Sing Sing Nights 1935,Ja 26,13:2
Mysterious Mr Wong, The 1935,Mr 7,26:1
China Passage 1937,Ap 16,27:2
Think Fast, Mr Moto 1937,Ag 16,15:3
Mister Wong in Chinatown 1939,Jl 31,9:2 (In Addenda)
Long, Nick
Shore Leave 1925,S 14,16:1
Long, Nick Jr
Broadway Melody of 1936 1935,S 19,28:1
King of Burlesque 1936,Ja 16,25:2
Long, Richard
Tomorrow Is Forever 1946,F 22,21:2
Stranger, The 1946,Jl 11,18:2
Dark Mirror, The 1946,O 19,15:2
Egg and I, The 1947,Ap 25,29:2
Tap Roots 1948,Ag 26,16:3
Criss Cross 1949,Mr 12,10:2
Life of Riley, The 1949,Ap 18,18:4
Ma and Pa Kettle 1949,Ag 12,13:2
Kansas Raiders 1951,Ja 26,19:2
Air Cadet 1951,My 11,32:3
Ma and Pa Kettle Back on the Farm 1951,My 11,32:3
All I Desire 1953,Ag 29,10:1
Saskatchewan 1954,Mr 11,26:2
Playgirl 1954,My 15,13:3
House on Haunted Hill 1959,Mr 12,27:5
Follow the Boys 1963,F 28,8:2
Make Like a Thief 1967,Ap 6,45:2
Long, Ronald
Two Loves 1961,Je 22,23:2
Notorious Landlady, The 1962,Jl 27,15:2
Long, Sally
Cock O' the Walk 1930,Ap 12,23:1
Long, Soo
Soldier of Fortune 1955,My 28,7:4
Long, Sumner Arthur (Original Author)
Never too Late 1965,N 5,28:1
Long, Sumner Arthur (Screenwriter)
Never too Late 1965,N 5,28:1

Long, Victor
King Kong 1933,Mr 3,12:1
Long, Walter
Mother and the Law, The 1919,Ag 19,10:1
Scarlet Days 1919,N 10,18:2
Fighting Shepherdess, The 1920,Mr 29,18:1
Go and Get It 1920,Jl 19,16:3
Moran of the Lady Letty 1922,F 6,9:1
Dictator, The 1922,Jl 3,8:6
Blood and Sand 1922,Ag 7,14:2
Birth of a Nation, The 1922,D 5,24:3
Beautiful and Damned, The 1922,D 11,22:1
Kick In 1922,D 18,22:2
Isle of Lost Ships, The 1923,My 14,18:2
Broken Wing, The 1923,O 9,17:4
Lady, The 1925,Ja 27,11:2
Soul Fire 1925,My 6,26:3
Shock Punch, The 1925,My 11,14:3
Bobbed Hair 1925,N 4,17:4
Steel Preferred 1925,D 22,13:1
Red Dice 1926,Ap 16,20:3
Jim, The Conqueror 1926,D 28,17:1
Yankee Clipper, The 1927,My 3,25:1
Back to God's Country 1927,O 24,24:3
Gang War 1928,N 19,16:7
Black Watch, The 1929,My 23,26:3
Beau Bandit 1930,Je 14,9:4
Moby Dick 1930,Ag 15,20:5
Birth of a Nation, The 1930,D 22,16:2
Other Men's Women 1931,Ap 20,16:3
Maltese Falcon, The 1931,My 29,26:5
Pardon Us 1931,Ag 22,7:5
Escapade 1932,My 28,18:2
Six of a Kind 1934,Mr 10,18:3
Operator 13 1934,Je 23,16:5
Pick a Star 1937,My 28,17:2
Long, Walter (Director)
Cock O' the Walk 1930,Ap 12,23:1
Long, Walter B
Broadway Rhythm 1944,Ap 14,24:6
Long Lance, Chief
Silent Enemy, The 1930,My 20,32:3
Longa, Remy
Therese and Isabelle 1968,My 15,41:4
Longarini, Renee
Dolce Vita, La 1961,Ap 20,30:1
Climax, The 1967,S 12,55:1
Longden, John
Blackmail 1929,O 7,22:1
Flame of Love, The 1930,Mr 23,IX,6:1
Juno and the Paycock 1930,Je 30,22:6
Atlantic 1930,O 6,21:1
Flame of Love, The 1930,N 3,19:3
Two Worlds 1930,N 22,21:3
Children of Chance 1931,Ja 24,15:1
Skin Game, The 1931,Je 20,20:4
Ringer, The 1932,Je 2,25:2
Girl Was Young, The 1938,F 11,27:2
Clouds Over Europe 1939,Je 16,27:2
Tower of Terror 1942,Je 29,11:4
Silver Fleet, The 1945,Mr 24,22:6
Pool of London 1951,N 28,37:2
Ship That Died of Shame, The 1956,Ag 21,33:2
Longden, Terence
Simon and Laura 1956,Jl 3,17:2
Another Time Another Place 1958,My 3,10:4
Carry on Sergeant 1959,O 28,40:5
Ben Hur 1959,N 19,50:2
Carry on Nurse 1960,S 10,11:1
Longet, Claudine
McHale's Navy 1964,Jl 11,15:2
Party, The 1968,Ap 5,56:2
Longfellow, Henry Wadsworth (Original Author)
Evangeline 1919,Ag 20,12:3
Village Blacksmith, The 1922,N 3,17:5
Wreck of the Hesperus, The 1927,N 28,18:5
Evangeline 1929,Jl 29,23:3
Hiawatha 1952,D 26,20:4
Longhi, Otto (Original Author)
Thank You, Madame 1937,Ap 27,18:2
Longhurst, Henry
Man With 100 Faces 1938,N 1,27:2
Long Dark Hall, The 1951,My 10,38:3
His Excellency 1956,F 2,19:3
Touch and go 1956,Mr 20,13:2
Brothers in Law 1957,Ag 20,22:1
Murder Ahoy 1964,S 23,55:3
Longmire, Adele
Bullet Scars 1942,Ap 24,21:4
People Will Talk 1951,Ag 30,20:1
Turning Point, The 1952,N 15,15:2
Battle Circus 1953,My 28,27:5
Longstreet, Stephen (Miscellaneous)
Impostor, The 1944,Mr 27,17:2
Longstreet, Stephen (Original Author)
Gay Sisters, The 1942,Ag 15,14:2
Stallion Road 1947,Ap 5,12:5
Silver River 1948,My 22,8:3
Untamed Youth 1957,My 11,24:6
Secret Door, The 1964,Je 4,28:1

Longstreet, Stephen (Screenwriter)
Uncle Harry 1945,Ag 24,14:5
Jolson Story, The 1946,O 11,28:2
Stallion Road 1947,Ap 5,12:5
Silver River 1948,My 22,8:3
Helen Morgan Story, The 1957,O 3,33:2
Lono, James
Call of the Yukon 1938,My 6,27:1
Lonsdale, Eric
Smilin' Through 1941,D 5,29:2
Lonsdale, Frederick (Original Author)
Fast Set, The 1924,N 18,22:1
Kiss in the Dark, A 1925,Ap 7,17:3
Last of Mrs Cheyney, The 1929,Ag 12,22:2
Lady of Scandal, The 1930,Je 14,9:4
Aren't We All? 1932,Jl 1,19:3
Just Smith 1934,Ap 23,20:2
Private Life of Don Juan, The 1934,D 10,16:2
Last of Mrs Cheyney, The 1937,F 19,15:1
Forever and a Day 1943,Mr 13,9:2
On Approval 1945,Ja 29,17:1
Law and the Lady, The 1951,Ag 16,23:2
Lonsdale, Frederick (Screenwriter)
Devil to Pay, The 1930,D 19,30:1
Lovers Courageous 1932,F 20,14:2
Lonsdale, Michel
Trial, The 1963,F 21,5:1
Bride Wore Black, The 1968,Je 26,42:1
Lontoc, Leon
I Was an American Spy 1951,Jl 4,13:2
Gallant Hours, The 1960,Je 23,19:4
Loo, Angela
Love Is a Many-Splendored Thing 1955,Ag 19,10:1
Loo, Anita
Experiment in Terror 1962,Ap 14,14:1
Loo, Bessie
Mister Wong in Chinatown 1939,Jl 31,9:2 (In Addenda)
Loo, Richard
Bitter Tea of General Yen, The 1933,Ja 12,20:6
West of Shanghai 1937,O 29,19:2
Shadows Over Shanghai 1938,D 1,29:2
Mister Wong in Chinatown 1939,Jl 31,9:2 (In Addenda)
Bombs Over Burma 1942,Ag 10,15:2
Falcon Strikes Back, The 1943,Ap 2,17:4
Flight for Freedom 1943,Ap 16,24:2
China 1943,Ap 22,31:2
Purple Heart, The 1944,Mr 9,15:2
Story of Dr Wassell, The 1944,Je 7,13:2
God is my Co-Pilot 1945,Mr 24,22:6
Betrayal From the East 1945,Ap 25,27:2
China Sky 1945,My 25,22:3
Back to Bataan 1945,S 13,26:3
First Yank into Tokyo 1945,O 25,18:2
Woman in the Night 1948,Ja 10,16:2
Rogues' Regiment 1948,D 20,31:2
State Department-File 649 1949,F 21,20:2
Malaya 1950,F 23,33:1
Steel Helmet, The 1951,Ja 25,21:5
I Was an American Spy 1951,Jl 4,13:2
Hell and High Water 1954,F 2,20:6
Soldier of Fortune 1955,My 28,7:4
Love Is a Many-Splendored Thing 1955,Ag 19,10:1
Conqueror, The 1956,Mr 31,13:3
Battle Hymn 1957,F 16,14:1
Quiet American, The 1958,F 6,24:1
Sand Pebbles, The 1966,D 21,48:1
Loomis, Frederic M Dr (Original Author)
Paid in Full 1950,F 16,28:2
Loomis, Margaret
Why Smith Left Home 1919,O 13,16:3
Conrad in Quest of his Youth 1920,N 8,20:2
Law of the Lawless, The 1923,Je 19,22:4
Loomis, Virginia
Babbitt 1924,Jl 15,9:4
Loor, Friedl
Eternal Waltz, The; (Ewiger Walzer) 1959,Jl 9,22:1
LOOS
See Also LUCE
Loos, Anita (Director)
Mamma's Affair 1921,Ja 24,16:2
Loos, Anita (Miscellaneous)
Woman's Place 1921,O 23,VI,4:1 (In Addenda)
Loos, Anita (Original Author)
Temperamental Wife, A 1919,S 15,16:3
Publicity Madness 1927,D 12,30:6
Gentlemen Prefer Blondes 1928,Ja 16,24:1
Struggle, The 1931,D 11,35:1
Hold Your Man 1933,Jl 1,16:6
Midnight Mary 1933,Jl 15,14:2
Girl From Missouri, The 1934,Ag 4,14:6
Saratoga 1937,Jl 23,16:3
Gentlemen Prefer Blondes 1953,Jl 16,17:2
Loos, Anita (Producer)
Temperamental Wife, A 1919,S 15,16:3
Virtuous Vamp, A 1919,N 17,20:1
In Search of a Sinner 1920,Mr 8,9:5

Loos, Anita (Producer)— Cont
In Search of a Sinner 1920,Mr 8,9:6

Loos, Anita (Screenwriter)
Let's Get a Divorce 1918,Ap 29,11:1
Come on In 1918,S 23,7:1
Come On In 1918,S 23,7:1
Isle of Conquest, The 1919,O 27,9:3
Red Hot Romance 1922,Ja 23,11:4
Learning to Love 1925,F 23,24:1
Biography of a Bachelor Girl 1935,Mr 2,18:2
Riffraff 1936,Ja 13,14:2
San Francisco 1936,Je 27,21:1
Saratoga 1937,Jl 23,16:3
Women, The 1939,S 22,27:2
Susan and God 1940,Jl 12,11:2
Blossoms in the Dust 1941,Je 27,14:4
They Met in Bombay 1941,Jl 4,17:1
When Ladies Meet 1941,S 5,19:2
I Married an Angel 1942,Jl 10,13:2

Loos, Anne
Jam Session 1944,My 3,25:3
Over 21 1945,Ag 17,20:2
Solid Gold Cadillac, The 1956,O 25,40:3

Loos, Mary
Student Tour 1934,O 31,17:3

Loos, Mary (Original Author)
Rendezvous With Annie 1946,S 23,29:3

Loos, Mary (Screenwriter)
Rendezvous With Annie 1946,S 23,29:3
Hit Parade of 1947 1947,My 5,32:8
Mother is a Freshman 1949,Mr 12,10:2
Mr Belvedere Goes to College 1949,Ap 16,11:2
Father Was a Fullback 1949,O 13,33:3
When Willie Comes Marching Home
  1950,F 18,9:2
Ticket to Tomahawk, A 1950,My 20,8:6
I'll Get by 1950,N 2,39:3
Meet Me After the Show 1951,Ag 16,23:2
Let's Do It Again 1953,O 14,34:3
French Line, The 1954,My 15,13:2
Woman's World 1954,S 29,23:4
Gentlemen Marry Brunettes 1955,O 31,31:5

Loos, Theodor
Siegfried 1925,Ag 24,17:3
Manon Lescaut 1926,N 30,27:1
Metropolis 1927,Mr 7,16:3
Kriemhild's Revenge 1928,O 16,29:1
Weavers, The 1929,O 7,22:1
Grosse Sehnsucht, Die 1931,O 8,22:6
In Geheimdienst; In the Employ of the Secret
  Service 1931,O 25,VIII,6:1
Fall des Oberst Redl, Der 1932,Ag 18,23:3
1914: The Last Days Before the War 1932,S 5,9:6
Ich Geh' aus und Du Bleibst da 1932,N 21,21:1
Yorck 1932,N 24,35:2
Holzapfel Weiss Alles 1933,Ja 7,11:3
M 1933,Ap 3,13:3
Tod Ueber Schanghai 1933,D 16,12:4
Die Blonde Christl 1934,F 23,23:3
Trenck 1934,Ap 7,19:2
Freundin Eines Grossen Mannes, Die
  1934,S 11,24:5
Schuss im Morgengrauen 1934,S 29,12:3
Maedchen Johanna, Das 1935,O 9,27:2 (In
  Addenda)
Gruen ist die Heide 1935,O 14,21:2
Schlussakkord 1936,S 10,29:4
Abenteurer von Paris, Der 1937,My 29,20:3
Weisse Sklaven 1937,Jl 31,6:2
Maulkorb, Der 1938,Ap 9,11:3
Kamera den auf See; Comrades at Sea
  1939,Ap 22,15:3
Glaserne Kugel, Die; Glass Ball, The
  1939,Je 17,12:3

Lopashinsky, Faust (Director)
False Uniforms 1932,N 19,20:2

Loper, Don
Thousands Cheer 1943,S 14,27:1
Lady in the Dark 1944,F 23,17:1
It's a Pleasure 1945,My 4,23:3

Lopert, Ilya (Producer)
Summertime 1955,Je 22,25:1

Lopert, Tanya
My Son, The Hero 1963,S 19,23:1
Young World, A 1966,My 17,52:1
Lady L 1966,My 19,51:1
Navajo Joe 1967,D 7,60:2

Lopez, Al
Safe at Home 1941,N 26,31:2

Lopez, Augustina
Redskin 1929,Ja 28,21:1
Wolf Song 1929,F 25,16:1

Lopez, Carlos
Cielito Lindo 1936,N 9,22:5
Baul Macabro, El; Macabre Trunk, The
  1937,N 30,26:3
Ave sin Rumbo; Wandering Bird 1938,Ja 24,17:2
Millones de Chaflan, Los 1938,S 13,28:3
Rancho Grande 1938,D 2,27:2
Indio, El 1939,My 13,11:5

Lopez, Carmen
Great Flamario, The 1945,Ja 15,15:5

Lopez, Cecilia
Walls of Hell, The 1965,N 18,55:3

Lopez, Chel
Que Hago con la Criatura? 1936,Mr 17,25:6
My Outlaw Brother 1951,Ag 23,19:2
Adventures of Robinson Crusoe, The
  1954,Ag 6,10:5

Lopez, Julio
Creature from the Black Lagoon 1954,My 1,13:4

Lopez, Lina
Sheep Has Five Legs, The 1955,Ag 10,19:2

Lopez, Marga
Nazarin 1968,Je 21,48:1

Lopez, Mary
Bestia Negra, La; Black Beast, The 1940,Je 3,11:2

Lopez, Paul
Arizona 1941,F 7,23:3

Lopez, Pepe
Brave Bulls, The 1951,Ap 19,39:2

Lopez, Perry
Drum Beat 1954,N 18,42:1
Battle Cry 1955,F 3,18:1
Mister Roberts 1955,Jl 15,14:1
I Died a Thousand Times 1955,N 10,45:2
Hell on Frisco Bay 1956,Ja 7,21:1
Lone Ranger, The 1956,F 11,12:1
Steel Jungle, The 1956,Mr 10,9:5
Cry Tough 1959,S 17,48:4
Flaming Star 1960,D 17,19:1
Taras Bulba 1962,D 26,5:2
McLintock 1963,N 14,41:3

Lopez, Rafael
Young Savages, The 1961,My 25,31:1
Dime With a Halo 1963,Je 27,23:3
Reward, The 1965,S 16,55:1

Lopez, Raymond
Girl from Havana, The 1929,S 2,16:1

Lopez, Sylvia
Hercules Unchained 1960,Jl 14,23:1

Lopez, Trini
Dirty Dozen, The 1967,Je 16,36:1
Poppy is Also a Flower, The 1967,D 14,62:4

Loraine, Oscar
Rhapsody in Blue 1945,Je 28,22:2

Loraine, Philip (Original Author)
Eye of the Devil 1967,D 7,60:1

Loraine, Robert
Perfect Alibi, The 1931,Ap 20,16:3
Outcast Lady 1934,N 3,20:3
Marie Galante 1934,N 21,23:4
Limehouse Blues 1934,D 12,28:2

Lorand, Auric
Beachcomber, The 1955,Ja 17,27:5

Lorca, Frederico Garcia (Original Author)
Bodas de Sangre; Bloody Wedding
  1939,N 13,15:3

Lorch, Louis
Sealed Lips 1928,Ap 17,27:2

Lorch, Theodore
Sea Hawk, The 1924,Je 3,22:1
Man on the Box, The 1925,S 28,24:1
Tracked by the Police 1927,Ap 27,22:5
Grip of the Yukon, The 1928,Jl 10,17:3
Show Boat 1929,Ap 18,32:3
Hold 'Em Yale 1935,Ap 27,20:6

Lord, Anthony
You Said a Mouthful 1932,N 18,23:2

Lord, Billy
Penrod and Sam 1931,S 26,25:3

Lord, Del (Director)
Lost at the Front 1927,Je 14,33:2
Topsy and Eva 1927,Ag 8,10:3
Trapped by Television 1936,Je 15,24:3
What Price Vengeance 1937,My 26,30:3
Rough, Tough and Ready 1945,Mr 24,22:7

Lord, Fred (Miscellaneous)
Loose Ends 1930,O 18,23:2

Lord, Grace
Death Valley 1927,N 22,32:2

Lord, Jack
Court-Martial of Billy Mitchell, The
  1955,D 23,14:2
Vagabond King, The 1956,S 13,39:6
Tip on a Dead Jockey 1957,S 7,12:7
God's Little Acre 1958,Ag 14,23:2
Man of the West 1958,O 2,44:3
Walk Like a Dragon 1960,S 16,24:1
Dr No 1963,My 30,20:1
Name of the Game Is Kill, The 1968,Je 6,54:1

Lord, Justine
Tamahine 1964,Jl 16,23:1

Lord, Marian
Broadway 1929,My 28,36:2
One Heavenly Night 1931,Ja 10,19:2

Lord, Marjorie
Forty Naughty Girls 1937,S 18,15:3
On Again-Off Again 1937,S 18,15:3
Hideaway 1937,S 25,10:2
Johnny Come Lately 1943,S 24,26:1
Flesh and Fantasy 1943,N 18,29:1
New Orleans 1947,Je 20,25:6
Riding High 1950,Ap 11,26:2
Port of Hell 1954,D 18,12:2

Lord, Marjorie— Cont
Boy, Did I Get a Wrong Number! 1966,Je 9,54:2

Lord, Martha (Original Author)
Love's Whirlpool 1924,Mr 11,16:2

Lord, Mindred (Original Author)
Alias Nick Beal 1949,Mr 10,35:2

Lord, Mindred (Screenwriter)
Sainted Sisters, The 1948,My 20,35:2
Virgin Queen, The 1955,Ag 6,13:2

Lord, Pauline
Mrs Wiggs of the Cabbage Patch 1934,O 29,14:2
Feather in her Hat, A 1935,O 25,24:5

Lord, Phillips
Way Back Home 1932,Ja 16,13:1

Lord, Phillips H (Original Author)
Mr District Attorney 1941,Ap 17,29:3
Mr District Attorney 1947,F 28,27:3

Lord, Phillips Mrs
Way Back Home 1932,Ja 16,13:1

Lord, Robert (Original Author)
Lucky Horseshoe, The 1925,Ag 18,14:3
Fireman, Save My Child 1932,F 18,25:3
One Way Passage 1932,O 14,23:2
Little Giant, The 1933,My 27,11:5
Heroes for Sale 1933,Jl 22,14:3
He Was her Man 1934,My 17,28:2
Housewife 1934,Ag 10,21:2
Dames 1934,Ag 16,20:2
Bordertown 1935,Ja 24,22:5
Gold Diggers of 1935 1935,Mr 15,25:2
Colleen 1936,Mr 9,20:2
Singing Kid, The 1936,Ap 4,11:1
Stage Struck 1936,S 28,14:4
Black Legion 1937,Ja 18,21:1
'Til We Meet Again 1940,Ap 14,14:2

Lord, Robert (Producer)
High Wall 1947,D 26,22:2
Knock on any Door 1949,F 23,31:2
Tokyo Joe 1949,O 27,35:2
And Baby Makes Three 1949,D 23,17:3
In a Lonely Place 1950,My 18,37:2
Sirocco 1951,Je 14,31:2

Lord, Robert (Screenwriter)
Page Miss Glory 1935,Ag 29,25:2
Dr Socrates 1935,O 3,29:2

Lord, Walter (Original Author)
A Night to Remember 1958,D 17,2:7

Loren, Sophia
Aida 1954,N 12,17:1
Too Bad She's Bad 1955,D 26,23:2
Gold of Naples (Pizza on Credit); Pizza on Credit
  (Gold of Naples) 1957,F 12,30:1
Boy on a Dolphin 1957,Ap 20,21:2
Miller's Beautiful Wife, The 1957,Je 12,40:2
Scandal in Sorrento 1957,Je 13,37:1
Pride and the Passion, The 1957,Je 29,10:6
Legend of the Lost 1957,D 23,18:2
Desire Under the Elms 1958,Mr 13,24:2
Attila 1958,My 19,19:4
Key, The 1958,Jl 2,23:3
Houseboat 1958,N 14,24:1
Black Orchid, The 1959,F 13,33:2
That Kind of Woman 1959,S 12,12:2
Anatomy of Love 1959,S 29,46:2
Heller in Pink Tights 1960,Mr 17,28:1
It Started in Naples 1960,S 3,7:6
Breath of Scandal, A 1960,D 17,19:1
Millionairess, The 1961,F 10,19:1
Two Women; (Ciociara, La) 1961,My 9,43:2
Neapolitan Carousel 1961,O 12,41:3
Cid, El 1961,D 15,49:1
Boccaccio '70 (The Raffle); Raffle, The (Boccaccio
  '70) 1962,Je 27,40:1
Madame 1963,Mr 21,8:6
Five Miles to Midnight 1963,Mr 21,8:6
Day in Court, A 1963,My 11,15:2
Condemned of Altona, The 1963,O 31,26:1
Yesterday, Today and Tomorrow (Part 1-Adelina
  Naples); Adelina Naples (Yesterday, Today and
  Tomorrow) 1964,Mr 18,46:1
Yesterday, Today, and Tomorrow (Part III-Mara
  Rome); Mara Rome (Yesterday, Today and
  Tomorrow) 1964,Mr 18,46:1
Yesterday, Today and Tomorrow (Part II-Anna
  Milan); Anna Milan (Yesterday, Today and
  Tomorrow) 1964,Mr 18,46:1
Fall of the Roman Empire, The 1964,Mr 27,14:2
Marriage Italian Style 1964,D 21,42:1
Operation Crossbow 1965,Ap 2,29:1
Judith 1966,Ja 21,22:1
Arabesque 1966,My 6,54:1
Lady L 1966,My 19,51:1
Countess from Hong Kong, A 1967,Mr 17,35:1
More Than a Miracle 1967,N 2,58:2

Lorena, Linda
Where Words Fail; Donde Mueren las Palabraso
  1948,Ag 19,18:4

Lorentowicz, Malgorzata
Barrier 1967,S 27,39:3

Lorentz, Pare (Director)
River, The 1938,F 5,19:2 (In Addenda)
Fight for Life, The 1940,Mr 7,19:2

Lorentz, Pare (Producer)
Fight for Life, The   1940,Mr 7,19:2
Lorentz, Pare (Screenwriter)
River, The   1938,F 5,19:2 (In Addenda)
Fight for Life, The   1940,Mr 7,19:2
LORENTZEN
See LORENZEN
Lorenz, Margo
Out of the Clouds   1957,Ag 1,20:4
Lorenzen, Henry
Geschichten aus dem Wienerwald; Tales From the
Vienna Woods   1935,N 2,13:3
Lorenzon, Livio
Goliath and the Barbarians   1960,Ja 7,24:6
Gladiators Seven   1964,My 7,31:2
Loridan, Marceline (Miscellaneous)
17th Parallel: Vietnam in War   1968,S 27,36:1
Lorimer, Glennis
Orders Is Orders   1934,My 7,20:2
It's Love Again   1936,My 23,12:1
Lorimer, Graeme (Original Author)
June Bride   1948,O 30,10:2
Lorimer, James
Mating Season, The   1951,Ap 12,41:2
Girl in the Red Velvet Swing, The
1955,O 20,41:2
Lorimer, Louise
Gangster's Boy   1938,N 7,23:6
Flying Cadets   1941,O 14,29:2
Gentleman's Agreement   1947,N 12,36:2
Glass Menagerie, The   1950,S 29,31:5
Sun Sets at Dawn, The   1951,Ja 15,13:1
Prowler, The   1951,Jl 2,16:6
People Against O'Hara, The   1951,S 6,39:3
Japanese War Bride   1952,Ja 30,22:6
Night Without Sleep   1952,S 27,13:2
Compulsion   1959,Ap 2,26:2
30   1959,N 12,27:1
Impossible Years, The   1968,D 6,54:1
Lorimer, Wright (Original Author)
Shepherd King, The   1923,D 11,26:2
Lorin, Gerard
Last Year at Marienbad   1962,Mr 8,26:1
Lorin, Leon
Nous, La Liberte, A   1932,My 18,25:2
Loring, Ann
Robin Hood of El Dorado, The   1936,Mr 14,10:1
Absolute Quiet   1936,My 2,11:1
Loring, Eugene
National Velvet   1944,D 15,25:2
Torch Song   1953,O 13,34:2
Loring, John (Screenwriter)
Gorgo   1961,Mr 30,24:2
Loring, Lynn
Splendor in the Grass   1961,O 11,53:1
Loring, Michael
Flying Hostess   1936,D 14,29:4
Breezing Home   1937,Mr 20,23:5
Loring, Phillis
Middle Watch, The   1930,D 20,20:6
Loring, Richard (Composer)
Snow Queen, The   1960,Ap 14,34:1
Loring, Teala
Allotment Wives   1945,N 22,39:3
Black Market Babies   1946,Ap 1,23:1
Loring, Thomas Z (Director)
Who Is Hope Schuyler   1942,My 22,27:1
He Hired the Boss   1943,Je 4,17:4
Loris, Fabien
Youth in Revolt   1939,My 16,27:3
Enfants du Paradis, Les   1947,F 20,32:2
Loriskin, V
Resurrection   1963,O 7,35:2
Lorne, Constance
Curtain Up   1953,F 2,17:3
Lorne, Marion
Strangers on a Train   1951,Jl 4,13:2
Graduate, The   1967,D 22,44:4
Lorraine
Fleet's In, The   1942,Mr 12,24:2
Lorraine, Betty
Bedtime Story, A   1933,Ap 20,20:3
Lorraine, Guido
One Woman's Story   1949,My 18,33:2
Hotel Sahara   1952,Ja 1,21:4
Encore (Gigolo and Gigolette); Gigolo and
Gigolette (Encore)   1952,Ap 3,45:1
Village, The   1953,S 23,37:2
Gentlemen Marry Brunettes   1955,O 31,31:5
Blue Murder at St Trinian's   1958,My 27,27:1
Lorraine, Harry
Slave of Desire   1923,D 11,26:2
Shooting of Dan McGrew, The   1924,Je 9,14:3
Siege   1925,Je 16,24:1
Lorraine, Jean
Wild Party, The   1929,Ap 2,28:4
Lorraine, Leota
Infatuation   1926,Ja 4,16:1
Ruggles of Red Gap   1935,Mr 7,26:1

Lorraine, Louise
Rookies   1927,Ap 25,20:4
Legionnaires in Paris   1927,D 26,26:6
Baby Mine   1928,Ja 9,20:1
Circus Rookies   1928,My 14,25:1
Lorraine, Ola
Woman's Vengeance, A   1948,Ja 30,19:2
My Cousin Rachel   1952,D 26,20:2
Lorre, Peter
M   1933,Ap 3,13:3
Was Frauen Traeumen; What Women Dream
1933,Jl 2,IX,2:2
Schuss im Morgengrauen   1934,S 29,12:3
Man Who Knew too Much, The   1935,Mr 23,11:2
Mad Love   1935,Ag 5,20:2
Crime and Punishment   1935,N 22,18:2
Secret Agent   1936,Je 13,13:1
Crack-Up   1937,Ja 4,20:4
Nancy Steele is Missing   1937,Mr 8,22:1
Think Fast, Mr Moto   1937,Ag 16,15:3
Lancer Spy   1937,N 4,29:1
Thank You, Mr Moto   1938,Ja 3,16:2
Mr Moto in Danger Island   1938,Mr 20,13:3
Mr Moto's Gamble   1938,Ap 8,17:2
Mr Moto Takes a Chance   1938,Je 13,15:4
I'll Give a Million   1938,Jl 16,7:2
Mysterious Mr Moto of Devil's Island
1938,S 19,16:2
Mr Moto's Last Warning   1939,Ja 27,17:3
Mr Moto Takes a Vacation   1939,Je 19,12:6
Strange Cargo   1940,Ap 26,25:2
I Was an Adventuress   1940,My 20,13:2
Island Of Doomed Men   1940,Je 10,21:2
Stranger on the Third Floor   1940,S 2,19:2
You'll Find Out   1940,N 15,25:2
Face Behind the Mask, The   1941,F 7,23:2
Mr District Attorney   1941,Ap 17,29:3
They Met in Bombay   1941,Jl 4,17:1
Maltese Falcon, The   1941,O 4,18:2
All Through the Night   1942,Ja 24,13:2
Invisible Agent   1942,Ag 6,23:2
Boogie Man Will Get You, The   1942,O 12,12:4
Casablanca   1942,N 27,27:1
Background to Danger   1943,Jl 3,11:2
Constant Nymph, The   1943,Jl 24,8:2
Cross of Lorraine, The   1943,D 3,27:4
Passage to Marseille   1944,F 17,12:5
Mask of Dimitrios, The   1944,Je 24,16:2
Arsenic and old Lace   1944,S 2,17:2
Conspirators, The   1944,O 21,15:2
Hollywood Canteen   1944,D 16,19:2
Hotel Berlin   1945,Mr 3,11:2
Confidential Agent   1945,N 3,11:2
Three Strangers   1946,F 23,20:2
Black Angel   1946,S 26,32:4
Chase, The   1946,N 18,31:2
Verdict, The   1946,D 13,29:4
Beast With Five Fingers, The   1946,D 26,28:3
My Favorite Brunette   1947,Mr 20,38:2
Casbah   1948,My 3,27:4
Rope of Sand   1949,Ag 4,19:2
Quicksand   1950,Je 16,28:4
Double Confession   1953,My 1,17:2
Beat the Devil   1954,Mr 13,11:2
20,000 Leagues Under the Sea   1954,D 24,7:2
Congo Crossing   1956,Jl 14,13:2
Around the World in 80 Days   1956,O 18,37:1
Buster Keaton Story, The   1957,Ap 22,31:6
Silk Stockings   1957,Jl 19,11:1
Story of Mankind, The   1957,N 9,31:2
Sad Sack, The   1957,N 28,57:1
Big Circus, The   1959,Jl 18,6:1
Scent of Mystery   1960,F 19,23:1
Voyage to the Bottom of the Sea   1961,Jl 20,32:2
Tales of Terror   1962,Jl 5,21:2 (In Addenda)
Five Weeks in a Balloon   1962,Ag 27,18:1
Raven, The   1963,Ja 26,5:8
Comedy of Terrors, The   1964,Ja 23,26:2
Muscle Beach Party   1964,My 28,40:1
Patsy, The   1964,Ag 13,24:2
Torn Curtain   1966,Jl 28,23:1
Lorring, Joan
Bridge of San Luis Rey, The   1944,Mr 4,11:1
Corn is Green, The   1945,Mr 30,18:2
Three Strangers   1946,F 23,20:2
Verdict, The   1946,D 13,29:4
Other Love, The   1947,My 15,32:4
Gangster, The   1947,O 31,29:3
Lost Moment, The   1947,N 22,10:2
Good Sam   1948,S 17,28:2
Big Night, The   1952,Mr 20,37:5
Stranger on the Prowl   1953,N 10,38:1
Lorring, Lotte
Johannisnact   1935,F 25,13:4
Ich Sing Mich in Dein Herz Hinein
1935,Je 3,22:3
Schwarzwaldmaedel   1935,O 12,12:3
Lory, Jacques
Fools for Scandal   1938,Mr 25,15:3
Suez   1938,O 15,21:2
Bulldog Drummond's Bride   1939,Jl 13,17:2

Lory, Jeanne
Orage   1938,D 12,26:2
Bizarre, Bizarre   1939,Mr 21,27:2
Lory, Robin
Gidget Goes Hawaiian   1961,Ag 10,17:4
Lorys, Dany
Ignace   1950,S 19,39:4
Lorys, Denise
Madame Sans Gene   1925,Ap 18,19:1
Lorys, Diana
Backfire   1965,Ap 27,27:1
Gunfighters of Casa Grande   1965,S 2,36:1
Losby, Donald
Mating Game, The   1959,Ap 30,37:1
How Sweet It Is   1968,Ag 22,47:1
Losch, Tilly
Garden of Allah, The   1936,N 20,27:2
Good Earth, The   1937,F 3,27:1
Duel in the Sun   1947,My 8,30:2
Loschilin, Lev
Ballet of Romeo and Juliet, The   1956,Ap 3,31:2
Losciavo, G E (Original Author)
Mafia; (In Nome Della Legge)   1950,Mr 2,33:2
Losee, Frank
Old Homestead, The   1915,D 27,9:1
Song of Songs, The   1918,F 19,11:2
In Pursuit of Polly   1918,S 2,7:1
His Parisian Wife   1919,Ja 20,13:2
Here Comes the Bride   1919,F 3,13:2
Lady Rose's Daughter   1920,Ag 30,12:3
False Fronts   1922,Je 5,16:2
Unguarded Women   1924,Je 24,18:2
Speed Spook, The   1924,O 21,21:3
Losee, Harry (Miscellaneous)
Thin Ice   1937,S 4,8:2
My Lucky Star   1938,S 10,20:2
Ice-Capades   1941,S 25,29:1
Loseff, Mary
Liebeskommando   1932,Ap 27,13:6
Losenko, N
May Night   1953,Jl 13,22:4
Stars of the Ukraine   1953,Jl 13,22:4
Loser, Kaspar (Screenwriter)
Lysistrata   1948,Je 19,19:2
Losey, Joseph (Director)
Boy With Green Hair, The   1949,Ja 13,26:2
Lawless, The   1950,Je 23,29:2
M   1951,Je 11,20:7
Prowler, The   1951,Jl 2,16:6
Big Night, The   1952,Mr 20,37:5
Time Without Pity   1957,N 23,11:2
Chance Meeting   1960,O 27,45:2
Servant, The   1964,Mr 17,30:2
King and Country   1964,S 24,46:2
Eva   1965,Je 5,21:2
These Are the Damned   1965,Jl 8,35:1
King and Country   1966,Ja 28,20:4
Modesty Blaise   1966,Ag 11,27:1
Accident   1967,Ap 18,33:1
Boom!   1968,My 27,56:1
Secret Ceremony   1968,O 24,55:1
Losey, Joseph (Producer)
Servant, The   1964,Mr 17,30:2
King and Country   1964,S 24,46:2
King and Country   1966,Ja 28,20:4
Modesty Blaise   1966,Ag 11,27:1
Accident   1967,Ap 18,33:1
Losey, Joseph (Screenwriter)
Big Night, The   1952,Mr 20,37:5
Losfgren, Marianne
Paa Solsidan   1936,Ag 26,16:3
Losley, Dudley (Miscellaneous)
Golden Madonna, The   1949,S 5,13:4
Lossen, Lena
Trial of Donald Westhof, The   1928,F 18,11:2
Lot-Dupont, Ilse (Screenwriter)
Scampolo   1959,Ag 6,18:4
Loth, Pauline (Narrator)
Mr Bug Goes to Town   1942,F 20,21:3
Lothar, Ernst (Original Author)
Little Friend   1934,O 20,20:2
Clairvoyant, The   1935,Je 8,12:2
Live Today for Tomorrow   1948,D 6,29:2
Lothar, Hanns
One, Two, Three   1961,D 22,17:1
Lothar, Ralph
Girls Behind Bars   1950,My 10,41:2
Guitars of Love   1958,Jl 12,18:1
Lothar, Rudolph (Original Author)
For Wives Only   1926,D 1,24:5
Magic Flame, The   1927,S 19,30:3
That Night in Rio   1941,Mr 10,21:2
On the Riviera   1951,My 24,47:1
Loti, Peter (Original Author)
Ramuntcho   1953,Mr 2,19:2
Loti, Pierre (Original Author)
Ramuntcho   1953,Mr 2,19:2
Lotis, Dennis
Horror Hotel   1963,Je 20,29:1
Lotsenko, Lesha
Summer to Remember, A; (Seryozha)
1961,N 7,38:1

Lott, Milton (Original Author)
Last Hunt, The 1956,Mr 1,37:2
Lottanzi, Tina
Loyalty of Love 1937,Mr 1,15:1
Lotti, Mariella
Marco Visconti 1947,S 20,12:4
Pirates of Capri, The 1949,D 26,33:5
Life of Donizetti, The 1952,Ap 26,19:2
What Price Innocence? 1953,My 2,13:3
His Last Twelve Hours 1953,N 13,24:7
Lotti, Maso
His Last Twelve Hours 1953,N 13,24:7
Lotting, Hugh (Original Author)
Doctor Dolittle 1967,D 20,55:1
Lou, Marie
That They May Live 1939,N 7,31:2
Loubignac, Jean (Director)
Barber of Seville 1949,Jl 21,21:2
Loudan, Colin
Malta Story 1954,Jl 17,7:2
Louden, Thomas
Our Leading Citizen 1939,Ag 24,17:1
Safari 1940,Je 20,29:2
Ministry of Fear 1945,F 8,15:2
Corn is Green, The 1945,Mr 30,18:2
Louden, Thomas (Original Author)
World's Champion, The 1922,F 27,13:4
Loughery, Jackie
Veils of Bagdad, The 1953,N 27,99:9
Pardners 1956,Jl 26,20:2
D I, The 1957,Je 6,35:2
Eighteen and Anxious 1957,D 14,16:6
Louie, Ducky
China Sky 1945,My 25,22:3
Back to Bataan 1945,S 13,26:3
Black Gold 1947,S 5,16:4
Smuggler's Island 1951,My 24,47:2
LOUIS
See Also LEWIS
Louis, Alyce
Harpoon 1948,D 9,48:8
Louis, Joe
Spirit of Youth 1938,F 28,19:1
This Is the Army 1943,Jl 29,11:6
Square Jungle, The 1955,D 31,17:2
Louis, Pierre
Kameradschaft 1932,N 9,28:5
Heroes of the Marne; (Famille Lefrancois, Le)
  1939,Ap 24,13:2
They Are not Angels 1948,My 22,8:3
Strollers, The 1952,Jl 22,22:7
Razzi 1957,N 19,39:4
Cow and I, The 1961,Je 6,42:2
Louis, Viola
King of Kings, The 1927,Ap 20,29:2
Louis, Willard
Madame X 1920,S 27,18:1
Robin Hood 1922,O 31,15:4 (In Addenda)
Vanity Fair 1923,My 7,19:3
French Doll, The 1923,S 5,15:3
Daddies 1924,F 11,18:3
Beau Brummell 1924,Mr 31,20:1
Broadway After Dark 1924,My 20,15:2
Babbitt 1924,Jl 15,9:4
Three Women 1924,O 6,25:1
Lover of Camille, The 1924,N 11,14:1
Eve's Lover 1925,Jl 27,17:3
Kiss Me Again 1925,Ag 3,10:1
Limited Mail, The 1925,S 1,18:2
Love Hour, The 1925,S 2,21:3
Hogan's Alley 1925,N 24,28:4
His Secretary 1925,D 21,27:2
Mlle Modiste 1926,Ap 26,25:1
Don Juan 1926,Ag 7,6:1 (In Addenda)
Louise, Anita
Marriage Playground, The 1929,D 14,22:4
What a Man 1930,Jl 21,20:3
Millie 1931,F 7,11:1
Great Meadow, The 1931,Mr 14,23:2
Everything's Rosie 1931,My 22,28:5
Woman Between, The 1931,O 24,20:3
Heaven on Earth 1931,D 19,16:4
Mississippi 1931,D 27,VIII,5:4 (In Addenda)
Phantom of Crestwood, The 1932,O 17,18:3
Our Betters 1933,F 24,13:2
Are We Civilized? 1934,Je 14,28:5
I Give my Love 1934,Jl 17,24:2
Judge Priest 1934,O 12,33:1
Madame Du Barry 1934,O 25,26:2
Firebird, The 1934,N 15,25:2
Lady Tubbs 1935,Jl 22,20:2
Here's to Romance 1935,O 3,29:2
Midsummer Night's Dream, A 1935,O 10,31:1
Story of Louis Pasteur, The 1936,F 10,15:1
Brides are Like That 1936,Mr 23,22:5
Anthony Adverse 1936,Ag 27,16:1
Green Light 1937,F 13,9:1
Call it a Day 1937,My 7,29:2
Go Getter, The 1937,Je 4,27:2
That Certain Woman 1937,S 16,29:1
First Lady 1937,D 23,25:1
Tovarich 1937,D 31,9:2
My Bill 1938,Jl 7,22:4

Marie Antoinette 1938,Ag 17,23:2
Sisters, The 1938,O 15,21:3
Going Places 1939,Ja 7,6:1
Little Princess, The 1939,Mr 11,21:1
Gorilla, The 1939,My 28,6:2
These Glamour Girls 1939,Ag 31,14:2
Main Street Lawyer 1939,N 9,27:2
Reno 1939,D 21,29:2
Wagons Westward 1940,Jl 8,13:2
Phantom Submarine, The 1941,F 12,25:3
Harmon of Michigan 1941,O 2,29:2
Casanova Brown 1944,S 15,16:1
Love Letters 1945,Ag 27,22:3
Fighting Guardsman, The 1945,O 6,9:6
Bandit of Sherwood Forest, The 1946,Mr 23,8:4
Retreat Hell! 1952,F 20,26:2
Louise, Tina
God's Little Acre 1958,Ag 14,23:2
Trap, The 1959,Ja 29,18:4
Warrior Empress, The 1961,Ag 10,17:4
Armored Command 1961,O 7,14:3
Siege of Syracuse, The 1962,Ag 9,17:8
For Those Who Think Young 1964,Jl 9,27:1
Louise, Viola
Chicago 1927,D 24,9:1
Loukes, Nicholas
Doctor Faustus 1968,F 7,38:1
Loureira, Oswaldo
Rose for Everyone, A 1967,Je 30,30:1
LOURIE
See Also LOWREY, LOWRY, LAURIE
Lourie, Eugene (Director)
Beast From 20,000 Fathoms, The 1953,Je 25,23:1
Gorgo 1961,Mr 30,24:2
Lourie, Norman (Producer)
Dream no More 1950,Ja 6,25:2
Loury, Jeanne
Topaze 1935,F 16,9:2
Crise est Finie, La 1935,Mr 14,18:1
Kiss of Fire, The 1940,N 20,27:4
Louvigny
Symphonie Pastorale 1948,S 14,34:3
Twilight 1949,D 30,13:2
Souvenir 1950,O 3,34:4
My First Love 1951,Je 11,20:7
Louys, Pierre (Original Author)
Devil is a Woman, The 1935,My 4,17:2
Female, The 1960,Ap 28,29:1
Lovatt, Grant
He Who Rides a Tiger 1968,S 10,39:1
Love, Bessie
Reggie Mixes In 1916,My 29,9:2
Hell-to-Pay Austin 1916,Ag 7,9:5
Sister of Six 1916,O 9,12:1
Forget Me Not 1922,Jl 24,10:2
Village Blacksmith, The 1922,N 3,17:5
Human Wreckage 1923,Je 28,10:2
Eternal Three, The 1923,O 12,7:2 (Incorrect in
  this edition; use 1927,O 1,7:2 elsewhere)
Slave of Desire 1923,D 11,26:2
Woman on the Jury, The 1924,My 19,14:2
Those Who Dance 1924,Je 30,16:1
Sundown 1924,D 1,17:3
Tongues of Flame 1924,D 16,28:1
Lost World, The 1925,F 9,15:3
Soul Fire 1925,My 6,26:3
Son of his Father, A 1925,S 29,31:3
King on Main Street, The 1925,O 26,25:2
New Brooms 1925,N 4,17:4
Song and Dance Man, The 1926,F 1,16:1
Lovey Mary 1926,Je 21,17:2
Young April 1926,Ag 31,15:3
Rubber Tires 1927,Mr 9,29:1
Dress Parade 1927,O 31,22:1
Matinee Idol, The 1928,Ap 24,29:3
Sally of the Scandals 1928,Jl 3,19:3
Broadway Melody, The 1929,F 9,15:3
Idle Rich, The 1929,Je 17,29:1
Hollywood Revue, The 1929,Ag 15,20:5
Broadway Melody 1929,D 1,X,8:6
Chasing Rainbows 1930,F 22,13:1
Good News 1930,S 6,9:2
See America Thirst 1930,D 12,35:3
Morals for Women 1931,N 16,23:1
Journey Together 1946,Mr 4,16:5
Barefoot Contessa, The 1954,S 30,37:1
Touch and go 1956,Mr 20,13:2
Next to no Time 1960,My 28,13:2
Loss of Innocence 1961,N 22,27:1
Love, Dorothea
That Royle Girl 1926,Ja 4,33:1
Love, Edmund G (Original Author)
Destination Gobi 1953,My 30,7:1
Love, Geoff
Dream Maker, The 1964,Ap 23,34:1
Love, Lucinda
Unstrap Me 1968,N 21,41:2
Love, Montagu
Bought and Paid For 1916,N 9,11:4
Rasputin, The Black Monk 1917,S 13,11:4
World and his Wife, The 1920,Jl 19,16:3
Case of Becky, The 1921,O 10,16:1
Peter Ibbetson; (Forever) 1921,O 17,18:1

Secrets of Paris 1923,Ja 8,22:1
Eternal City, The 1924,Ja 21,20:1
Son of the Sahara, A 1924,My 27,14:1
Sinners in Heaven 1924,S 10,21:3
Ancient Highway, The 1925,N 11,27:3
Hands Up 1926,Ja 18,26:2
Social Highwayman, The 1926,Je 15,23:3
Son of the Sheik, The 1926,Jl 26,13:2
Don Juan 1926,Ag 7,6:1 (In Addenda)
Silent Lover, The 1926,N 15,19:1
Night of Love, The 1927,Ja 25,18:4
King of Kings 1927,Ap 20,29:2
Tender Hour, The 1927,Je 7,27:4
Rose of the Golden West 1927,S 26,27:1
Jesse James 1927,O 17,20:2
Good Time Charley 1927,N 21,20:1
Haunted Ship, The 1928,Ja 23,18:3
Noose, The 1928,Mr 19,26:4
Hawk's Nest, The 1928,Je 25,27:1
Wind, The 1928,N 5,26:1
Haunted House, The 1928,D 17,23:1
Last Warning, The 1929,Ja 7,36:2
Synthetic Sin 1929,Ja 7,36:2
Divine Lady, The 1929,Mr 23,22:4
Bulldog Drummond 1929,My 3,23:2
Charming Sinners 1929,Jl 8,17:3
Most Immoral Lady, A 1929,O 21,30:1
Mysterious Island, The 1929,D 21,17:1
Love Comes Along 1930,F 1,15:1
Notorious Affair, A 1930,Ap 26,11:1
Double Cross Roads 1930,Ap 29,31:1
Back Pay 1930,My 31,19:4
Inside the Lines 1930,Jl 5,17:4
Outward Bound 1930,S 18,28:3
Kismet 1930,O 31,20:1
Reno 1930,N 4,36:1
Cat Creeps, The 1930,N 8,21:3
Alexander Hamilton 1931,S 17,21:4
Silver Lining, The 1932,My 30,16:5
Midnight Lady, The 1932,Jl 1,19:3
His Double Life 1933,D 16,12:3
Limehouse Blues 1934,D 12,28:2
Clive of India 1935,Ja 18,29:1
Crusades, The 1935,Ag 22,21:3
Man Who Broke the Bank at Monte Carlo, The
  1935,N 15,20:2
Country Doctor, The 1936,Mr 13,32:2 (Incorrect
  in this edition; use 1936,Mr 13,27:2 elsewhere)
Sutter's Gold 1936,Mr 27,25:2
Champagne Charlie 1936,My 7,21:2
White Angel, The 1936,Je 25,24:1
Sing, Baby, Sing 1936,S 12,20:1
Lloyds of London 1936,N 26,39:1
Reunion 1936,N 27,27:1
One in a Million 1937,Ja 1,19:3
Prince and the Pauper, The 1937,My 6,23:1
Parnell 1937,Je 4,27:2
Life of Emile Zola, The 1937,Ag 12,14:2
London by Night 1937,Ag 13,13:1
Prisoner of Zenda, The 1937,S 3,12:1
Damsel in Distress, A 1937,N 25,37:1
Adventure's End 1937,D 20,23:2
Tovarich 1937,D 31,9:2
Buccaneer, The 1938,F 17,17:2
Adventures of Robin Hood, The 1938,My 13,17:2
Kidnapped 1938,My 28,9:2
Professor Beware 1938,Jl 14,17:1
If I Were King 1938,S 29,31:1
Gunga Din 1939,Ja 28,19:2
Juarez 1939,Ap 26,27:1
Man in the Iron Mask, The 1939,Jl 14,11:1
Rulers of the Sea 1939,N 9,27:1
We Are not Alone 1939,D 1,27:1
Lone Wolf Strikes, The 1940,F 5,13:2
Dr Ehrlich's Magic Bullet 1940,F 24,9:2
Northwest Passage 1940,Mr 8,25:1
All This and Heaven, Too 1940,Jl 5,10:2
Private Affairs 1940,Jl 5,10:3
Sea Hawk, The 1940,Ag 10,16:2
Mark of Zorro, The 1940,N 4,23:2
North West Mounted Police 1940,N 7,33:2
Son of Monte Cristo, The 1940,D 5,33:1
Dispatch From Reuters, A 1940,D 12,37:2
Hudson's Bay 1941,Ja 10,23:2
Devil and Miss Jones, The 1941,My 16,21:2
Shining Victory 1941,My 31,14:1
Lady for a Night 1942,F 12,27:2
Remarkable Andrew, The 1942,Mr 6,17:2
Sherlock Holmes and the Voice Of Terror
  1942,S 19,9:2
Tennessee Johnson 1943,Ja 13,18:2
Constant Nymph, The 1943,Jl 24,8:2
Holy Matrimony 1943,S 16,25:2
Devotion 1946,Ap 6,10:5
Love, Phyllis
Friendly Persuasion 1956,N 2,30:1
Young Doctors, The 1961,Ag 24,25:2
Love, Richard
Top Man 1943,O 29,23:2
Lovecraft, H P (Original Author)
Haunted Palace, The 1964,Ja 30,24:1
Shuttered Room, The 1968,F 15,47:1

Lovejoy, Arthur
Full of Life 1957,F 13,38:1
Lovejoy, Frank
Black Bart 1948,Mr 4,30:4
Home of the Brave 1949,My 13,29:1
South Sea Sinner 1950,Ja 16,18:4
In a Lonely Place 1950,My 18,37:2
Three Secrets 1950,O 21,10:6
Breakthrough 1950,N 18,10:2
I Was a Communist for the F B I 1951,My 3,34:4
Try and Get Me 1951,My 7,22:2
Goodbye, my Fancy 1951,My 30,14:2
Force of Arms 1951,Ag 14,20:2
I'll See You in my Dreams 1951,D 7,35:1
Starlift 1951,D 15,11:2
Retreat Hell! 1952,F 20,26:2
Winning Team, The 1952,Je 21,12:2
She's Back on Broadway 1953,Mr 12,24:2
House of Wax 1953,Ap 11,15:2
Hitch-Hiker, The 1953,Ap 30,39:3
System, The 1953,My 23,19:3
Charge at Feather River, The 1953,Jl 16,17:2
Beachhead 1954,Ap 17,8:2
Men of the Fighting Lady 1954,My 8,15:2
Americano, The 1955,Ja 20,35:1
Strategic Air Command 1955,Ap 21,33:1
Mad at the World 1955,My 14,10:8
Finger Man 1955,Jl 16,12:4
Crooked Web, The 1955,D 10,19:1
Shack out on 101 1956,Ja 10,26:2
Julie 1956,N 22,51:1
Three Brave Men 1957,Mr 16,13:2
Lovell, Nigel
Massacre Hill 1950,D 14,51:3
Wherever She Goes 1953,Ja 28,24:4
Lovell, Raymond
King of the Damned 1936,F 1,9:2
Blackout 1940,D 2,19:2
Invaders, The 1942,Mr 6,17:1
Young Mr Pitt, The 1943,Mr 11,17:1
Candlelight in Algeria 1944,Jl 31,10:2
Caesar and Cleopatra 1946,S 6,18:2
End of the River, The 1948,Je 21,18:2
So Evil my Love 1948,Jl 22,27:2
My Brothers Keeper 1949,F 14,15:3
Easy Money (Episode 4) 1949,F 14,15:3
Quartet (The Alien Corn); Alien Corn, The (Quartet) 1949,Mr 29,30:3
Blind Goddess, The 1949,Je 23,33:3
Madness of the Heart 1950,O 12,43:2
Mudlark, The 1950,D 25,25:1
Appointment With Crime 1951,F 19,19:3
Time, Gentlemen, Please 1953,S 24,39:2
Lovell, Roderick
So Evil my Love 1948,Jl 22,27:2
Ivanhoe 1952,Ag 1,8:2
Lovelock, Ray
Violent Four, The 1968,Ag 15,46:2
Lovely, Louise
Old Nest, The 1921,Je 29,10:3
Lovering, Otho (Director)
Sky Parade, The 1936,Ap 20,17:1
Border Flight 1936,Je 22,22:1
Lovering, Otho (Screenwriter)
Lady in a Jam 1942,S 11,25:2
Lovett, Dorothy
That's Right, You're Wrong 1939,N 30,25:3
Meet Doctor Christian 1939,D 1,27:2
Courageous Dr Christian, The 1940,Mr 29,25:3
Look Who's Laughing 1941,D 25,33:2
Call out the Marines 1942,Ja 26,18:3
Sing Your Worries Away 1942,My 15,25:2
Powder Town 1942,Je 8,11:2
Lovett, Helen
Street Scene 1931,Ag 27,22:5
Lovett, Josephine (Original Author)
Our Modern Maidens 1929,S 7,15:1
Lovett, Josephine (Screenwriter)
Sentimental Tommy 1921,My 9,16:2
Footlights 1921,S 9,IV,4:1
Annie Laurie 1927,My 12,24:3
Our Dancing Daughters 1928,O 8,14:2
What a Widow 1930,O 4,15:2
Lovsky, Celia
Sealed Verdict 1948,N 3,36:2
Captain Carey U S A 1950,Mr 30,40:5
Night Into Morning 1951,Je 11,20:7
Because You're Mine 1952,S 26,18:2
Rhapsody 1954,Mr 12,17:1
Last Time I saw Paris, The 1954,N 19,20:2
New York Confidential 1955,F 19,18:1
Foxfire 1955,Jl 14,19:1
Death of a Scoundrel 1956,N 6,30:1
Trooper Hook 1957,Jl 13,11:2
Man of a Thousand Faces 1957,Ag 14,21:1
Twilight for the Gods 1958,Ag 7,21:1
Me and the Colonel 1958,Ag 27,33:1
Gene Krupa Story, The 1959,D 26,7:1
LOWE
See Also LOEW, LOEWE
Lowe, Arthur
Kind Hearts and Coronets 1950,Je 15,41:2
This Sporting Life 1963,Jl 17,19:2

Lowe, Barry
Stowaway Girl 1957,N 6,43:3
Up the Creek 1958,N 11,26 2
Cash on Demand 1962,My 17,31:1
Lowe, Edmund
Spreading Dawn, The 1917,O 22,13:2
Eyes of Youth 1919,D 1,9:3
Devil, The 1921,Ja 17,9:1
Silent Command, The 1923,S 5,15:3
In the Palace of the King 1923,D 3,14:1
Nellie, the Beautiful Cloak Model 1924,Ap 14,14:1
East of Suez 1925,Ja 26,22:1
Fool, The 1925,Ap 13,24:1
Soul Mates 1926,Ja 4,16:1
What Price Glory 1926,N 24,26:4
Is Zat So? 1927,My 17,27:2
Wizard, The 1927,N 28,18:5
Publicity Madness 1927,D 12,30:6
Dressed to Kill 1928,Mr 12,26:1
Happiness Ahead 1928,Je 19,31:1
Outcast 1928,N 26,30:2
In old Arizona 1929,Ja 21,18:4
Thru Different Eyes 1929,Ap 15,22:6
Cock Eyed World, The 1929,Ag 5,25:2
This Thing Called Love 1929,D 14,22:4
Happy Days 1930,F 14,20:1
Born Reckless 1930,Je 7,10:4
Bad One, The 1930,Je 13,28:3
Good Intentions 1930,Jl 26,16:4
Scotland Yard 1930,O 20,28:2
Shepper - Newfounder, The 1930,D 25,31:5
Don't Bet on Women 1931,Mr 7,17:2
Women of all Nations 1931,My 30,9:2
Transatlantic 1931,Jl 31,15:2
Spider, The 1931,S 5,7:4
Cisco Kid, The 1931,O 24,20:3
Misleading Lady, The 1932,Ap 9,18:1
Attorney for the Defense 1932,My 28,18:2
Guilty as Hell 1932,Ag 6,14:5
Chandu the Magician 1932,O 1,10:4
Devil Is Driving, The 1932,D 16,25:5
Hot Pepper 1933,Ja 23,9:2
I Love That Man 1933,Jl 10,11:7
Her Bodyguard 1933,Ag 7,18:2
Dinner at Eight 1933,Ag 24,18:1
Bombay Mail 1934,Ja 6,18:2
Let's Fall in Love 1934,Ja 22,12:3
No More Women 1934,Mr 15,27:4
Gift of Gab 1934,S 26,17:6
Best Man Wins 1935,Ja 2,22:4
Under Pressure 1935,F 4,11:3
Great Hotel Murder, The 1935,F 28,17:4
Mr Dynamite 1935,My 25,12:1
Black Sheep 1935,Je 28,34:1
King Solomon of Broadway 1935,O 19,12:2
Grand Exit 1935,N 4,24:5
Great Impersonation, The 1935,D 14,11:1
Garden Murder Case, The 1936,Mr 2,13:2
Seven Sinners 1936,Ag 22,6:1
Girl on the Front Page, The 1936,N 7,15:2
Mad Holiday 1936,N 26,39:2
Under Cover of Night 1937,Ja 20,18:4
Espionage 1937,Mr 9,27:3
Murder on Diamond Row 1937,N 12,27:2
Every Day's a Holiday 1938,Ja 27,17:2
Secrets of a Nurse 1938,D 12,26:2
Newsboys' Home 1939,Ja 23,8:2
Witness Vanishes, The 1939,O 23,15:2
Our Neighbors-The Carters 1940,F 15,15:2
Honeymoon Deferred 1940,F 16,23:4
Wolf of New York 1940,Mr 7,19:3
Crooked Road, The 1940,Je 11,33:4
I Love You Again 1940,Ag 16,11:2
Men Against the Sky 1940,S 12,31:2
Flying Cadets 1941,O 14,29:2
Call out the Marines 1942,Ja 26,18:3
Murder in Times Square 1943,My 31,13:2
Dillinger 1945,Ap 26,26:2
Enchanted Forest, The 1945,D 17,17:2
Good Sam 1948,S 17,28:2
Around the World in 80 Days 1956,O 18,37:1
Wings of Eagles, The 1957,F 1,28:1
Heller in Pink Tights 1960,Mr 17,28:1
Lowe, Edward T (Original Author)
Other Women's Husbands 1926,Ap 27,23:2
Escapade 1932,My 28,18:2
Midnight Lady, The 1932,Jl 1,19:3
Vampire Bat, The 1933,Ja 23,9:1
World Gone Mad, The 1933,Ap 15,16:3
Charlie Chan in Shanghai 1935,O 14,21:1
Pirates of Monterey 1947,D 17,41:4
Lowe, Edward T (Producer)
Charlie Chan in Egypt 1935,Je 24,12:2
Champagne Charlie 1936,My 7,21:2
Lowe, Edward T (Screenwriter)
Charlie Chan in Paris 1935,Ja 22,23:2
Charlie Chan in Shanghai 1935,O 14,21:1
Educating Father 1936,Je 20,22:2
Charlie Chan at the Race Track 1936,Ag 15,6:2
Bulldog Drummond Comes Back 1937,S 4,8:3
Bulldog Drummond's Revenge 1937,D 17,33:2
Scattergood Baines 1941,Ap 4,25:2

Lowe, Edward T (Screenwriter) — Cont
Sherlock Holmes and the Secret Weapon 1943,Ja 5,15:2
Tarzan's Desert Mystery 1943,D 27,23:3
House of Frankenstein 1944,D 16,19:3
Rough, Tough and Ready 1945,Mr 24,22:7
House of Dracula 1945,D 22,16:3
Lowe, Ellen
Christopher Bean 1933,N 25,10:2
King of Burlesque 1936,Ja 16,25:2
Dancing Pirate 1936,Je 18,19:1
Beloved Brat 1938,My 2,13:2
You Belong to Me 1941,N 29,14:2
Hi Diddle Diddle 1943,S 24,26:2
Open Secret 1948,F 2,15:2
Black Book, The 1949,O 17,18:2
Lowe, Elmo
These Thirty Years 1934,My 24,28:3
Lowe, George (Cinematographer)
Conquest of Everest, The 1953,D 10,64:4
Antarctic Crossing 1959,My 11,30:1
Lowe, Harry Jr
Sequoia 1935,F 23,14:6
Lowe, Irma
Shanghai Lady 1929,N 11,20:2
Lowe, James B
Uncle Tom's Cabin 1927,N 5,16:2
Lowe, K Elmo
Kid From Cleveland, The 1949,S 5,13:2
Lowe, Olga
State Secret 1950,O 5,38:2
Hotel Sahara 1952,Ja 1,21:4
Lowe, Sherman (Original Author)
Dames Ahoy 1930,Mr 29,23:1
Lost Jungle, The 1934,Je 8,18:1
Crimson Romance 1934,O 13,10:1
Trapped by Television 1936,Je 15,24:3
Alimony 1949,Jl 22,16:3
Lowe, Sherman (Screenwriter)
Daredevil Drivers, The 1938,F 23,27:2
Mystery House 1938,Je 29,15:5
Everything's on Ice 1939,O 6,31:1
West of Carson City 1940,My 7,31:3
Catman of Paris, The 1946,Jl 13,12:2
Alimony 1949,Jl 22,16:3
Lowell, Bob
Mom and Dad 1957,Ja 31,21:1
Lowell, Helen
Isn't Life Wonderful? 1924,D 1,17:3
Midnight Alibi 1934,Jl 4,18:3
Side Streets 1934,Ag 15,13:5
Dragon Murder Case, The 1934,Ag 23,13:3
Case of the Howling Dog, The 1934,O 18,26:5
Madame Du Barry 1934,O 25,26:2
Big Hearted Herbert 1934,N 14,23:2
Devil Dogs of the Air 1935,F 7,23:2
Maybe It's Love 1935,F 11,14:2
Living on Velvet 1935,Mr 8,25:4
Transient Lady 1935,Mr 11,15:1
Page Miss Glory 1935,Ag 29,25:2
Goose and the Gander, The 1935,S 12,29:2
Dr Socrates 1935,O 3,29:2
Strike Me Pink 1936,Ja 17,15:2
Snowed Under 1936,Mr 30,17:5
I'd Give my Life 1936,Ag 17,9:1
High, Wide and Handsome 1937,Jl 22,15:1
Lowell, James B (Original Author)
They Asked for It 1939,Je 30,17:4
Lowell, Joan
Adventure Girl 1934,Ag 9,14:5
Lowell, Joan (Narrator)
Adventure Girl 1934,Ag 9,14:5
Lowell, Joan (Original Author)
Adventure Girl 1934,Ag 9,14:5
Lowell, Mark
Pickup 1951,Ag 31,12:2
Lowell, Robert
Too Young to Know 1945,D 8,21:2
Walk in the Sun, A 1946,Ja 12,10:6
Whiplash 1948,D 27,16:3
Lowell, Tom
Carpetbaggers, The 1964,Jl 2,24:4
That Darn Cat 1965,D 3,44:1
Gnome-Mobile, The 1967,Jl 20,30:2
Lowenadler, Holger
Himlaspelet 1944,O 9,17:3
Frustration 1949,Ag 27,7:3
Lowendahl, Walter (Producer)
Adventure in Music 1944,Mr 6,17:3
Medium, The 1951,S 6,39:2
Lowens, Curt
Francis of Assisi 1961,Jl 29,8:2
Werewolf in a Girls Dormitory 1963,Je 6,39:1
Lowenworth, Ann
Victims of Persecution 1933,Je 17,16:6
Lowery, Helen
Avalanche 1946,Jl 8,25:2
Lowery, Robert
Passport Husband 1938,Ag 5,11:2
Submarine Patrol 1938,N 19,9:2
Tail Spin 1939,F 11,13:2
Charlie Chan in Reno 1939,My 31,27:2
Young Mr Lincoln 1939,Je 3,11:2
Hollywood Cavalcade 1939,O 14,13:2

Lowery, Robert — Cont

Drums Along the Mohawk 1939,N 4,11:2
City of Chance 1940,Ja 22,11:3
Free, Blonde and 21 1940,Ap 5,25:2
Shooting High 1940,Ap 12,19:2
Charlie Chan's Murder Cruise 1940,My 3,17:5
Star Dust 1940,My 4,13:1
Four Sons 1940,Je 8,18:4
Mark of Zorro, The 1940,N 4,23:2
Ride on Vaquero 1941,Ap 19,20:2
Private Nurse 1941,Ag 29,13:3
Cadet Girl 1941,D 11,39:1
Who Is Hope Schuyler 1942,My 22,27:1
North Star, The 1943,N 5,23:1
Tarzan's Desert Mystery 1943,D 27,23:3
Mummy's Ghost, The 1944,Jl 1,10:7
House of Horrors 1946,F 23,20:3
Dalton Gang, The 1949,N 25,27:5
Crosswinds 1951,D 7,35:4
Rise and Fall of Legs' Diamond, The
    1960,F 4,34:1
Johnny Reno 1966,Mr 10,26:3

Lowery, William
Red Hot Tires 1925,O 20,28:1
Haunted Ship, The 1928,Ja 23,18:3

Lowitz, Siegfried
Sins of Rose Bernd, The 1959,Ja 24,13:4 (In
    Addenda)
It Happened in Broad Daylight 1960,S 30,33:1
Confess, Dr Corda 1960,O 24,25:5
Great British Train Robbery, The 1967,Ap 6,45:2

Lowler, Margaretha
Time of Desire 1959,N 21,26:5

Lowndes, Marie Belloc (Original Author)
Letty Lynton 1932,Ap 30,19:3
Phantom Fiend 1935,Ap 22,14:2
Ivy 1947,Je 26,19:1
Man in the Attic 1954,F 6,17:2

Lowney, Raymond
Awful Truth, The 1925,Jl 2,12:4

LOWREY
See Also LOWRY, LAURIE, LOURIE

Lowrey, Robert (Original Author)
That Kind of Woman 1959,S 12,12:2

LOWRY
See Also LAURIE, LOURIE, LOWREY

Lowry, Emily
As the Earth Turns 1934,Ap 12,27:2

Lowry, Judith
Ladybug, Ladybug 1963,D 24,9:1

Lowry, Morton
Dawn Patrol 1938,D 24,12:1
Hound of the Baskervilles, The 1939,Mr 25,19:2
Tarzan Finds a Son 1939,Je 15,27:2
Winter Carnival 1939,Jl 28,14:2
Hudson's Bay 1941,Ja 10,23:2
Charley's Aunt 1941,Ag 2,18:2
How Green Was my Valley 1941,O 29,27:2
Captains of the Clouds 1942,F 13,24:2
Loves of Edgar Allan Poe, The 1942,S 21,19:2
Counter-Espionage 1942,S 28,13:2
Immortal Sergeant 1943,F 4,29:2
No Time for Love 1943,D 2,30:1
Hour Before the Dawn, The 1944,My 11,25:6
Story of Dr Wassell, The 1944,Je 7,13:2
None but the Lonely Heart 1944,N 18,16:6
Man in Half Moon Street, The 1945,Ja 20,16:2
Picture of Dorian Gray, The 1945,Mr 2,15:2
Pursuit to Algiers 1945,O 27,12:2
Verdict, The 1946,D 13,29:4

Lowry, Roger (Screenwriter)
Negatives 1968,O 15,40:1

Loxley, D A (Original Author)
Bad Bascomb 1946,My 23,18:4

Loy, Myrna
Cave Man, The 1926,Mr 1,17:1
Why Girls Go Back Home 1926,My 18,28:2
Don Juan 1926,Ag 7,6:1 (In Addenda)
Climbers, The 1927,My 4,29:2
Girl From Chicago, The 1927,D 20,33:2
If I Were Single 1928,Mr 5,21:1
Beware of Married Men 1928,Ap 10,33:2
State Street Sadie 1928,S 3,14:2
Midnight Taxi, The 1928,O 29,29:1
Noah's Ark 1929,Mr 13,28:6
Desert Song, The 1929,My 2,20:6
Squall, The 1929,My 10,32:5
Black Watch, The 1929,My 23,26:3
Show of Shows 1929,N 21,24:5
Cameo Kirby 1930,F 8,12:5
Great Divide, The 1930,F 17,17:6
Isle of Escape 1930,Mr 31,24:3
Under a Texas Moon 1930,Ap 4,22:1
Cock O' the Walk 1930,Ap 12,23:1
Bride of the Regiment 1930,My 22,32:6
Last of the Duanes 1930,S 13,9:3
Renegades 1930,N 8,21:3
Truth About Youth, The 1930,D 13,22:2
Devil to Pay, The 1930,D 19,30:1
Body and Soul 1931,Mr 14,23:2
Naughty Flirt, The 1931,Ap 13,17:1
Connecticut Yankee, A 1931,Ap 13,17:1
Hush Money 1931,Jl 11,7:6
Transatlantic 1931,Jl 31,15:2

Rebound 1931,Ag 29,16:3
Skyline 1931,O 5,17:3
Consolation Marriage 1931,O 30,26:4
Arrowsmith 1931,D 8,36:4
Emma 1932,F 6,14:4
Wet Parade, The 1932,Ap 22,23:2
Woman in Room 13, The 1932,My 21,9:2
New Morals for Old 1932,Je 24,15:3
Love Me Tonight 1932,Ag 19,20:6
Thirteen Women 1932,O 15,13:1
Mask of Fu Manchu, The 1932,D 3,21:4
Animal Kingdom, The 1932,D 30,14:2
Topaze 1933,F 10,12:2
Barbarian, The 1933,My 13,16:2
When Ladies Meet 1933,Je 24,16:2
Penthouse 1933,S 9,9:2
Night Flight 1933,O 7,18:4
Prizefighter and the Lady, The 1933,N 11,11:3
Manhattan Melodrama 1934,My 5,22:2
Men in White 1934,Je 9,18:2
Thin Man, The 1934,Je 30,18:5
Stamboul Quest 1934,Jl 14,16:6
Evelyn Prentice 1934,N 10,19:1
Broadway Bill 1934,N 30,22:2
Wings in the Dark 1935,F 2,10:1
Whipsaw 1936,Ja 25,18:4
Wife vs Secretary 1936,F 29,11:1
Petticoat Fever 1936,Mr 21,13:2
Great Ziegfeld, The 1936,Ap 9,21:2
Connecticut Yankee at the Court of King Arthur,
    A 1936,My 4,16:1
To Mary-With Love 1936,Ag 27,16:1
Libeled Lady 1936,O 31,24:2
After the Thin Man 1936,D 25,19:2
Parnell 1937,Je 4,27:2
Double Wedding 1937,O 22,27:2
Man-Proof 1938,Ja 14,21:1
Test Pilot 1938,Ap 16,17:1
too Hot To Handle 1938,S 30,24:2
Lucky Night 1939,My 5,29:3
Rains Came, The 1939,S 9,11:2
Another Thin Man 1939,N 24,29:1
I Love You Again 1940,Ag 16,11:2
Third Finger, Left Hand 1940,D 12,37:2
Love Crazy 1941,Je 6,25:5
Shadow of the Thin Man 1941,N 21,23:2
Thin Man Goes Home, The 1945,Ja 26,16:5
So Goes my Love 1946,My 2,3:7
Best Years of our Lives, The 1946,N 22,27:2
Bachelor and the Bobby-Soxer, The
    1947,Jl 25,12:5
Song of the Thin Man 1947,Ag 29,14:2
Mr Blandings Builds his Dream House
    1948,Mr 26,26:2
Red Pony, The 1949,Mr 9,33:2
Cheaper by the Dozen 1950,Ap 1,12:2
If This Be Sin 1950,Jl 1,9:2
Belles on Their Toes 1952,My 3,17:5
Ambassador's Daughter, The 1956,Ag 30,19:1
Lonelyhearts 1959,Mr 5,35:3
From the Terrace 1960,Jl 16,10:1
Midnight Lace 1960,O 14,27:1

Loy, Nanni (Director)
Four Days of Naples, The 1963,Mr 20,5:1
Fiasco in Milan 1963,Ap 11,29:2
Made in Italy 1967,My 1,44:2

Loy, Nanni (Screenwriter)
Four Days of Naples, The 1963,Mr 20,5:1
Fiasco in Milan 1963,Ap 11,29:2
Made in Italy 1967,My 1,44:2

Loy, Sonny
Mr Wu 1927,My 16,24:2

Loyd, Alison
Corsair 1931,N 19,27:5

Loyd, Beverly
Utah 1945,Mr 12,22:7
Here Comes Trouble 1948,Ap 15,31:4

Loyer, Raymond
Crime Does Not Pay (The Man on the Avenue);
    Man on the Avenue, The (Crime Does Not
    Pay) 1962,O 17,35:2

Lozach
Battle of the Rails; (Bataille Du Rail)
    1949,D 27,27:2

Lozach, Pierre (Screenwriter)
Wild Oat, The 1956,Je 28,33:2

Lozano, Ada
El Rey de los Gitanos 1933,My 29,22:2
    (Incorrect in this edition; use 1933,My 29,16:5
    elsewhere)

Lozano, Margarita
Viridiana 1962,Mr 20,43:4
Lazarillo 1963,Ap 5,27:6
Tarantos, Los 1964,Je 30,22:1
Fistful of Dollars, A 1967,F 2,29:1

Lu, Lisa
Mountain Road, The 1960,Je 30,22:3

Lualdi, Antonella
Overcoat, The 1953,O 13,34:1
His Last Twelve Hours 1953,N 13,24:7
Three Forbidden Stories 1953,N 16,21:4
Cavalcade of Song 1954,D 27,22:8
Adorable Creatures 1956,Ja 11,36:2

Lualdi, Antonella — Cont
Rouge et Noir 1958,Ap 9,42:1
Young Girls Beware 1959,Ag 22,8:2
Wild Love; (Gli Inamorati) 1961,Ap 6,30:2
Leda 1961,Jl 19,33:1
Notte Brava, La 1962,Ja 25,25:2
End of Desire 1962,Jl 10,29:2
I Spit on Your Grave 1963,Je 29,13:5
Run With the Devil 1963,Jl 16,25:1
My Son, The Hero 1963,S 19,23:1
Disorder 1964,My 26,44:2
How to Seduce a Playboy 1968,My 16,53:2

Luans, Princess
Hawaiian Nights 1939,S 29,19:4

Luath (dog)
Incredible Journey, The 1963,N 21,43:2

Lubelska, Paula
Mothers of Today 1939,Mr 2,19:2
Tevya 1939,D 22,15:3

Luber, Bernard (Producer)
Of Men and Music 1951,F 15,27:2
Lone Shark 1952,My 12,21:2
Man From Cairo, The 1953,D 17,52:4
Sword of Lancelot 1963,O 10,49:2

Lubeznov, Ivan
Six PM 1946,Ja 28,15:5
Hello, Moscow! 1946,Je 15,24:4

Lubienska, Karolina
Dziesieciu z Pawiaka 1932,Ap 21,25:2
Ksiazatko; Lottery Prince, The 1937,D 27,11:2

Lubin, A Ronald (Producer)
Convicts 4 1962,O 4,44:2
Outrage, The 1964,O 8,48:2

Lubin, Arthur
Woman on the Jury, The 1924,My 19,14:2
Proud Heart 1925,N 3,25:4
Bardelys The Magnificent 1926,N 1,28:1 (In
    Addenda)
Afraid to Love 1927,Ap 12,25:3

Lubin, Arthur (Director)
Great God Gold 1935,My 6,22:3
House of a Thousand Candles, The
    1936,Ap 2,29:2
Mysterious Crossing 1937,F 2,20:5
I Cover the War 1937,Ag 2,10:2
Idol of the Crowd 1937,D 4,21:1
Adventure's End 1937,D 20,23:2
Beloved Brat 1938,My 2,13:2
Prison Break 1938,Jl 13,17:4
Secrets of a Nurse 1938,D 12,26:2
Risky Business 1939,Mr 23,27:2
Big Town Czar 1939,My 4,27:3
Mickey, the Kid 1939,Jl 6,27:1
Big Guy, The 1940,Ja 1,29:2
Black Friday 1940,Mr 22,23:3
Gangs of Chicago 1940,Je 13,29:2
Meet the Wildcat 1940,O 23,27:2
San Francisco Docks 1940,D 26,23:3
Buck Privates 1941,F 14,15:2
In the Navy 1941,Je 12,29:2
Hold That Ghost 1941,Ag 8,13:3
Keep 'Em Flying 1941,N 27,29:2
Ride 'Em Cowboy 1942,My 5,27:3
Eagle Squadron 1942,Jl 3,12:5
White Savage 1943,Ap 26,15:2
Phantom of the Opera, The 1943,O 15,15:2
Ali Baba and the Forty Thieves 1944,Mr 16,17:3
Delightfully Dangerous 1945,Je 9,17:3
Spider Woman Strikes Back, The 1946,Mr 23,8:3
Night in Paradise 1946,Je 6,16:3
New Orleans 1947,Je 20,25:6
Impact 1949,Mr 21,19:2
Francis 1950,Mr 16,40:2
Francis Goes to the Races 1951,Jl 25,19:2
Rhubarb 1951,Ag 31,12:2
Francis Goes to West Point 1952,Ag 23,10:2
It Grows on Trees 1952,N 29,11:2
South Sea Woman 1953,Je 4,33:6
Francis Joins the Wacs 1954,Jl 31,6:3
Francis in the Navy 1955,Ag 6,13:4
Footsteps of the Fog 1955,S 15,39:2
Lady Godiva 1955,D 3,13:3
Star of India 1956,Ap 28,11:1
Escapde in Japan 1957,D 24,11:1
Thief of Baghdad, The 1961,Ag 17,18:2
Incredible Mr Limpet, The 1964,Mr 26,40:4
Hold On! 1966,Je 23,29:4

Lubin, Arthur (Producer)
Escapde in Japan 1957,D 24,11:1

Lubin, Lou
Shadow of the Thin Man 1941,N 21,23:2
Johnny Eager 1942,F 20,21:2
A-Haunting We Will Go 1942,Ag 3,18:4
Hi 'Ya Chum 1943,F 26,17:4
Hard Way, The 1943,Mr 13,9:2
Scarlet Street 1945,F 15,29:2
Cry Danger 1951,F 22,27:3
Models, Inc 1952,My 26,18:4
Pat and Mike 1952,Je 19,32:6
Clown, The 1953,Ja 29,25:1

Lubin, Tibi
Prince and the Pauper, The 1922,Ag 14,12:4

Lubinsky, I (Director)
Chuk and Gek 1953,D 21,27:4
Lubitsch, Ernst
One Arabian Night 1921,O 3,16:2
Lubitsch, Ernst (Director)
Passion 1920,D 13,19:3
Deception 1921,Ap 18,8:1
Gypsy Blood 1921,My 9,16:2
One Arabian Night 1921,O 3,16:2
Loves of Pharaoh 1922,F 22,13:3 (In Addenda)
Passion 1923,Je 26,14:2
Rosita 1923,S 4,14:1
Marriage Circle, The 1924,F 4,23:3
Three Women 1924,O 6,25:1
Kiss Me Again 1925,Ag 3,10:1
Lady Windemere's Fan 1925,D 28,19:2
So This Is Paris 1926,Ag 16,10:1
Student Prince, The 1927,S 22,33:2
Patriot, The 1928,Ag 18,7:2 (In Addenda)
Eternal Love 1929,My 13,27:2
Love Parade, The 1929,N 20,32:6
Monte Carlo 1930,Ag 28,22:4
Smiling Lieutenant, The 1931,My 23,13:4
Man I Killed, The 1932,Ja 20,17:4
One Hour with You 1932,Mr 24,17:5
Trouble in Paradise 1932,N 9,28:5
If I Had a Million 1932,D 3,21:4
Design for Living 1933,N 23,24:2
Merry Widow, The 1934,O 12,33:1
Angel 1937,N 4,29:1
Bluebeard's Eighth Wife 1938,Mr 24,21:2
Ninotchka 1939,N 10,27:2
Shop Around the Corner, The 1940,Ja 26,13:2
That Uncertain Feeling 1941,My 2,25:1
To Be or not to Be 1942,Mr 7,13:2
Heaven Can Wait 1943,Ag 12,15:1
Cluny Brown 1946,Je 3,27:3
That Lady in Ermine 1948,Ag 25,31:2
Lubitsch, Ernst (Original Author)
To Be or not to Be 1942,Mr 7,13:2
Lubitsch, Ernst (Producer)
Desire 1936,Ap 13,15:1
Angel 1937,N 4,29:1
Bluebeard's Eighth Wife 1938,Mr 24,21:2
Shop Around the Corner, The 1940,Ja 26,13:2
That Uncertain Feeling 1941,My 2,25:1
To Be or not to Be 1942,Mr 7,13:2
Heaven Can Wait 1943,Ag 12,15:1
Royal Scandal, A 1945,Ap 12,19:2
Cluny Brown 1946,Je 3,27:3
That Lady in Ermine 1948,Ag 25,31:2
Lubitsch, Ernst (Screenwriter)
Three Women 1924,O 6,25:1
Lubosc, Gaston
Nine Bachelors 1942,F 9,19:2
Lubovsky, Igor (Screenwriter)
Admiral Nakhimov 1948,N 25,47:4
Luc, Jean-Bernard (Screenwriter)
Lafayette 1963,Ap 11,29:1
Lucantoni, Alberto
Bible, The 1966,S 29,60:1
Lucari, Gianna Hecht (Producer)
Queens, The (Queen Marta); Queen Marta (The Queens) 1968,Mr 11,49:1
Queens, The (Queen Armenia); Queen Armenia (The Queens) 1968,Mr 11,49:1
Queens, The (Queen Elena); Queen Elena (The Queens) 1968,Mr 11,49:1
Queens, The (Queen Sabina); Queen Sabina (The Queens) 1968,Mr 11,49:1
Lucari, Gianni Hecht (Producer)
Run With the Devil 1963,Jl 16,25:1
Bambole; Dolls, The (Monsignor Cupid); Monsignor Cupid (The Dolls) 1965,Je 29,26:1
Bambole; Dolls, The (Treatise on Eugenics); Treatise on Eugenics (The Dolls) 1965,Je 29,26:1
Bambole; Dolls, The (The Soup); Soup, The (The Dolls) 1965,Je 29,26:1
Bambole; Dolls, The (The Telephone Call); Telephone Call, The (The Dolls) 1965,Je 29,26:1
High Infidelity (Sin in the Afternoon); Sin in the Afternoon (High Infidelity) 1965,Jl 2,17:1
High Infidelity (Modern People); Modern People (High Infidelity) 1965,Jl 2,17:1
High Infidelity (The Victim); Victim, The (High Infidelity) 1965,Jl 2,17:1
High Infidelity (The Scandal); Scandal, The (High Infidelity) 1965,Jl 2,17:1
Made in Italy 1967,My 1,44:2
Lucas, Cleo (Original Author)
Merrily We Go to Hell 1932,Je 11,9:3
Lucas, Isobel
Lolita 1962,Je 14,23:2
Lucas, John Meredyth (Original Author)
My Blood Runs Cold 1965,Mr 25,42:4
Lucas, John Meredyth (Screenwriter)
Dark City 1950,O 19,40:5
Peking Express 1951,Jl 19,20:2
Red Mountain 1952,Ap 26,19:2
Sign of Zorro, The 1961,S 5,37:6

Lucas, Nick
Gold Diggers of Broadway, The 1929,Ag 31,13:4
Lucas, Paul
Hot News 1928,Jl 23,11:2
Lucas, Tom
Treasure Island 1950,Ag 16,24:2
Lucas, Victor
Under Capricorn 1949,S 9,28:3
Lucas, Wilfred
Hell-to-Pay Austin 1916,Ag 7,9:5
Westerners, The 1919,Ag 4,8:3
Girl of the Golden West, The 1923,My 21,12:2
Trilby 1923,Jl 30,11:4
Price She Paid, The 1925,Ja 13,16:1
Man Without a Country, The 1925,F 12,16:1
Riders of the Purple Sage 1925,Ap 15,16:1
How Baxter Buttered In 1925,Je 23,24:3
Wife Who Wasn't Wanted 1925,S 9,23:1
Cock O' the Walk 1930,Ap 12,23:1
Arizona Kid, The 1930,My 17,21:2
Those Who Dance 1930,Jl 7,22:3
Just Imagine 1930,N 22,21:3
Dishonored 1931,Mr 6,16:1
Donovan's Kid 1931,My 22,28:5
Pardon Us 1931,Ag 22,7:5
Cross Examination 1932,F 27,22:1
Tenderfoot, The 1932,My 23,18:4
Racetrack 1933,Mr 6,16:6
Big Cage, The 1933,My 9,20:5
I Cover the Waterfront 1933,My 18,17:3
Devil's Brother, The 1933,Je 10,16:4
Strange People 1933,Je 17,16:5
Count of Monte Cristo, The 1934,S 27,25:2
Mary of Scotland 1936,Jl 31,22:2
Criminal Lawyer 1937,Ja 27,17:3
Baroness and the Butler, The 1938,F 19,19:2
Chump at Oxford, A 1940,F 20,17:3
Sea Wolf, The 1941,Mr 26,27:3
Lucas, Wilfred (Miscellaneous)
Sweden, Land of the Vikings 1934,Ja 4,17:2
Lucas, William
Crack in the Mirror 1960,My 20,26:1
Sons and Lovers 1960,Ag 3,35:1
Shadow of the Cat, The 1961,Je 8,40:2
Payroll 1963,My 11,15:2
Lucas Philippine Folk Dancers
World Dances 1954,N 8,24:6
Lucchetti, Virginia
Shepherd King, The 1923,D 11,26:2
Lucci, Mike
Paper Lion 1968,O 24,54:1
Luccioni, Micheline
Gervaise 1957,N 12,46:1
Pot Bouille 1958,O 28,39:1
LUCE
See Also LOOS
Luce
Claudine 1940,Ap 1,15:2
Luce, Alethea (Original Author)
Young Rajah, The 1922,N 6,13:1
Luce, Alexis B
Chechahcos, The 1924,My 19,14:2
Luce, Claire
Up the River 1930,O 11,21:3
Luce, Clare Boothe (Original Author)
Come to the Stable 1949,Jl 28,19:1
Lucenay, A Martin de (Director)
A lo Macho; In Rough Style 1939,Je 3,11:3
Lucero, Enrique
Macario 1961,S 28,48:6
Love Has Many Faces 1965,F 25,24:1
Luchaire, Corinne
Affair Lafont, The; Conflit 1939,O 9,15:2
Three Hours 1944,O 30,16:5
Luchaire, Julien (Original Author)
Youth in Revolt 1939,My 16,27:3
Luchko, Katya
Cossacks of the Kuban 1950,O 30,22:4
Vasili's Return 1953,S 28,21:4
Big Family, A 1955,Je 6,24:1
Twelfth Night 1956,Mr 5,21:1
Luchkov, Clara
House on the Front Line, The 1963,S 2,18:1
Lucia
Roman Spring of Mrs Stone, The 1961,D 29,11:1
Luciardo, Tito
Vida es un Tango, La; Life is a Tango 1939,Jl 8,20:5
Lucisano, Fulvio (Producer)
Cobra, The 1968,Mr 28,52:3
Luck, James
Reach for Glory 1963,S 10,46:1
Lucke, Rosemarie
Tonio Kroger 1968,Ja 16,24:1
Luckey, Evelyn
Union Pacific 1939,My 11,31:2
Luckey, Susan
Carousel 1956,F 17,13:1
Music Man, The 1962,Ag 24,14:1
Luckham, Cyril
How to Murder a Rich Uncle 1957,O 26,19:2
Invasion Quartet 1961,D 11,41:2
Pumpkin Eater, The 1964,N 10,58:1

Luckham, Cyril — Cont
Alphabet Murders, The 1966,Jl 12,36:2
Lucot, M (Director)
Melbourne Rendezvous 1957,O 11,38:4
Lucot, Rene (Miscellaneous)
Melbourne Rendezvous 1957,O 11,38:4
Lucy, Arnold
In Search of a Sinner 1920,Mr 8,9:5
Ghost Talks, The 1929,F 18,28:1
One Woman Idea, The 1929,Je 10,23:1
All Quiet on The Western Front 1930,Ap 30,29:1
Manslaughter 1930,Jl 24,26:4
Princess and the Plumber, The 1930,D 23,25:1
Unfaithful 1931,Mr 7,17:2
Young Sinners 1931,My 9,15:4
Merely Mary Ann 1931,S 12,15:4
Dr Jekyll and Mr Hyde 1932,Ja 2,14:2
Lady With a Past 1932,F 22,23:2
Alias the Doctor 1932,Mr 3,22:3
Guilty as Hell 1932,Ag 6,14:5
Sherlock Holmes 1932,N 12,20:5
Loyalties 1934,O 26,25:1
Lud, Irene
Honorable Catherine, The 1948,Ag 23,13:3
Luddy, Barbara
Rose of the World 1925,N 10,25:3
Lude, Christian
Prize, The 1952,Ap 30,33:2
Letters From my Windmill (The Elixir of Father Gaucher); Elixir of Father Gaucher, The (Letters From my Windmill) 1955,D 19,33:1
Truth, The 1961,Je 27,23:2
Doulos-The Finger Man 1964,Mr 3,31:1
Thief of Paris, The 1967,Ag 24,43:2
Luden, Jack
Fascinating Youth 1926,My 10,19:1
It's the old Army Game 1926,Jl 5,6:4
Tell It to Sweeney 1927,O 17,20:2
Two Flaming Youths 1928,Ja 2,28:1
Partners in Crime 1928,Ap 30,18:3
Fools for Luck 1928,Je 12,33:5
Forgotten Faces 1928,Ag 6,15:2
Woman From Moscow, The 1928,N 5,26:1
Sins of the Fathers 1929,Ja 28,21:1
Wild Party, The 1929,Ap 2,28:4
Innocents of Paris 1929,Ap 27,16:5
Dangerous Curves 1929,Jl 15,25:1
Why Bring That Up? 1929,O 5,22:5
Young Eagles 1930,Mr 22,22:6
King of the Royal Mounted 1936,S 29,35:2
Susannah of the Mounties 1939,Je 24,13:2
Ludlow, Patrick
Evergreen 1935,Ja 11,29:1
Gangway 1937,Ag 21,7:3
Ludney, John (Miscellaneous)
Elizabeth is Queen 1953,Je 29,20:4
Ludovici, Carlo
Alpine Love 1936,Je 8,22:5
Ludovici, Cesare (Original Author)
Merchant of Slaves 1949,O 27,35:4
Margaret of Cortona 1957,Ja 21,20:4
Ludovisi, Vicky
Fiasco in Milan 1963,Ap 11,29:2
Ludwig, Arthur
Hoosier Schoolmaster, The 1924,Mr 18,25:2
Too Many Kisses 1925,Mr 3,20:1
Ludwig, Edward (Director)
They Just Had to Get Married 1933,F 13,11:4
Friends of Mr Sweeney 1934,Jl 31,20:4
Man Who Reclaimed his Head, The 1935,Ja 9,22:1
Age of Indiscretion 1935,My 18,21:2
Three Kids and a Queen 1935,N 9,19:2
Fatal Lady 1936,Jl 11,11:3
Adventure in Manhattan 1936,O 23,27:5
Her Husband Lies 1937,Mr 18,20:1
Last Gangster, The 1937,D 10,33:2
That Certain Age 1938,N 5,15:2
Coast Guard 1939,Ag 28,17:2
Swiss Family Robinson 1940,F 9,15:3
Born to Sing 1942,F 19,23:2
They Came to Blow up America 1943,My 15,13:2
Fighting Seabees, The 1944,Mr 20,14:2
3 Is a Family 1944,D 20,20:3
Fabulous Texan, The 1947,D 26,22:5
Wake of the Red Witch 1949,Ja 10,19:2
Smuggler's Island 1951,My 24,47:2
Big Jim McLain 1952,S 18,35:2
Sangaree 1953,Je 5,19:1
Jivaro 1954,F 13,11:5
Flame of the Islands 1956,F 25,12:4
Black Scorpion, The 1957,O 12,23:2
Ludwig, Emil (Original Author)
Hitler's Madman 1943,Ag 28,15:1
Ludwig, Fred
Naked Among the Wolves 1967,Ap 19,54:7
Ludwig, Ralph
Children of no Importance 1928,Ap 3,33:2
Ludwig, Salem
Never Love a Stranger 1958,N 22,27:4
America America 1963,D 16,44:1

Ludwig, Walter
St Matthew Passion 1952,Ja 29,17:4
Ludwig, William (Original Author)
Love Crazy 1941,Je 6,25:5
Athena 1954,D 22,28:2
Ten Thousand Bedrooms 1957,Ap 4,37:1
Ludwig, William (Screenwriter)
Out West With the Hardys 1938,D 9,31:2
Hardys Ride High, The 1939,Ap 14,28:2
Stronger Than Desire 1939,Je 30,17:3
Blackmail 1939,S 15,26:3
Love Crazy 1941,Je 6,25:5
Journey for Margaret 1942,D 18,36:7
Andy Hardy's Blonde Trouble 1944,My 5,17:3
American Romance, An 1944,N 24,19:1
Boy's Ranch 1946,Ag 9,12:2
Love Laughs at Andy Hardy 1947,Ja 8,28:2
Julia Misbehaves 1948,O 8,30:2
Hills of Home 1948,N 26,32:2
Sun comes up, The 1949,My 13,29:2
Challenge to Lassie 1950,Ap 7,22:3
Shadow on the Wall 1950,My 19,31:3
Great Caruso, The 1951,My 11,32:2
It's a big Country 1952,Ja 9,25:2
Merry Widow, The 1952,S 25,38:1
Student Prince, The 1954,Je 16,18:2
Hit the Deck 1955,Mr 4,17:1
Interrupted Melody 1955,My 6,18:1
Oklahoma! 1955,O 11,49:1
Gun Glory 1957,Jl 20,8:7
Back Street 1961,O 13,27:1
Ludy, Ken
Sioux City Sue 1947,Jl 23,19:3
Luedecke, Werner Joerg (Original Author)
Saboteur, The: Code Name-Mori Turi
1965,Ag 26,40:2
Luedecke, Werner Joerg (Screenwriter)
Devil Strikes at Night, The 1959,Ja 30,31:3
Journey to the Lost City 1960,D 8,43:3
Lueders, Else
Selige Exzellenz, Die 1937,Je 15,26:2
Lueders, Guenther
Fraeulein Liselott 1935,My 27,20:7
Dell Etappenhase 1938,Ja 1,11:3
Musketier Meier III 1938,D 31,7:2
Spessart Inn, The 1961,F 18,12:3
Luez, Laurette
D O A 1950,My 1,18:2
Kim 1950,D 8,40:4
Prehistoric Women 1950,D 29,15:5
Lufkin, Sam
Battling Orioles, The 1924,N 4,24:1
Shepper - Newfounder, The 1930,D 25,31:5
Luft, Sidney (Producer)
Star is Born, A 1954,O 12,23:1
Luft, Uriel
Nikki, Wild Dog of the North 1961,S 5,37:6
Lufteck, Alfonse (Cinematographer)
Seven Ravens, The 1953,Ap 3,20:6
Lugagne, Francoise
Paris Frills 1946,N 25,38:3
Landru 1963,Ap 10,31:1
Diary of a Chambermaid; Journal d'une Femme de
Chambre, Le 1964,S 22,44:1
Lughin, Irene
Rome, 11 O'Clock 1953,Ap 30,39:2
Lugon, Pierre
Song of the Street 1939,S 5,21:2
Lugosi, Bela
Silent Command, The 1923,S 5,15:3
Rejected Woman, The 1924,My 5,18:3
Such Men Are Dangerous 1930,Mr 8,21:1
Renegades 1930,N 8,21:3
Dracula 1931,F 13,21:3
Women of all Nations 1931,My 30,9:2
Black Camel, The 1931,Jl 4,11:5
Murders in the Rue Morgue 1932,F 11,16:1
White Zombie 1932,Jl 29,18:2
Chandu the Magician 1932,O 1,10:4
Island of Lost Souls 1933,Ja 13,19:2
Death Kiss, The 1933,F 5,IX,5:3
International House 1933,My 27,11:5
Black Cat, The 1934,My 19,18:4
Best Man Wins 1935,Ja 2,22:4
Mysterious Mr Wong, The 1935,Mr 7,26:1
Return of Chandu 1935,Ap 15,16:3
Mark of the Vampire 1935,My 3,23:4
Raven, The 1935,Jl 5,9:2
Invisible Ray, The 1936,Ja 11,9:3
Son of Frankenstein 1939,Ja 30,9:2
Gorilla, The 1939,My 28,6:2
Ninotchka 1939,N 10,27:2
Saint's Double Trouble, The 1940,F 13,27:2
Black Friday 1940,Mr 22,23:3
Human Monster, The 1940,Mr 25,11:2
You'll Find Out 1940,N 15,25:2
Black Cat, The 1941,Ap 26,20:3
Invisible Ghost, The 1941,My 8,21:2
Spooks Run Wild 1941,N 1,20:3
Wolf Man, The 1941,D 22,24:5
Ghost of Frankenstein, The 1942,Ap 4,19:2

Night Monster 1942,N 30,18:5
Frankenstein Meets the Wolf Man 1943,Mr 6,8:3
Return of the Vampire, The 1944,Ja 29,10:1
One Body too Many 1944,N 25,21:2
Zombies on Broadway 1945,Ap 27,23:2
Body Snatcher, The 1945,My 26,18:3
Abbott and Costello Meet Frankenstein
1948,Jl 29,17:2
Luguet, Andre
Si l'Empereur Savait Ca 1931,F 23,20:3
Mad Genius, The 1931,O 24,20:3
Man Who Played God, The 1932,F 11,16:1
Love Is a Racket 1932,Je 11,9:3
Jewel Robbery 1932,Jl 23,6:6
Dame de Pique, La 1944,O 19,19:2
Honorable Catherine, The 1948,Ag 23,13:3
French They Are a Funny Race, The
1957,My 21,41:1
Parisienne, La 1958,Jl 31,27:1
Roots of Heaven, The 1958,O 16,46:1
Young Girls Beware 1959,Ag 22,8:2
Paris Blues 1961,N 8,41:1
Male Companion 1966,F 15,33:2
Luguet, Rosine
Her First Affair; (Children of Paradise)
1947,F 20,32:3
Symphonie Pastorale 1948,S 14,34:3
Mademoiselle 1966,Ag 2,23:1
Lui, Kalen
Matter of Innocence, A 1968,F 22,36:1
Lui, Maurice
West of Shanghai 1937,O 29,19:2
Lui, Roland
Good Earth, The 1937,F 3,27:1
Lui, Wonci
Kismet 1955,D 9,32:2
Luibimov, Victor
Cossacks of the Kuban 1950,O 30,22:4
Luisetti (Hank)
Campus Confessions 1938,S 23,35:1
Luisiardo, Tito
Tango-Bar 1935,Jl 6,16:3
Dia que me Quieras, El; Day You Love Me, The
1935,Ag 27,23:3
Luistig, Arnost (Screenwriter)
Diamonds of the Night 1968,Mr 15,30:1
Luitz-Morat (Producer)
Vierge Folle, La 1929,Ja 13,VIII,7:4
Lukachy, Wolfgang
Affairs of Julie, The 1958,D 10,53:1
Lukacs, Margaret
Szegeny Gazdagok; Poor Plutocrats
1939,D 4,18:4
Lukas, James
Journey to the Beginning of Time 1967,F 11,20:1
Lukas, Karl
Onionhead 1958,O 2,44:1
Lukas, Kurt
Eine Tuer geht Auf 1933,F 6,11:5
Lukas, Paul
Two Lovers 1928,Mr 23,24:4
Three Sinners 1928,Ap 23,20:2
Loves of an Actress 1928,Jl 30,21:2
Night Watch, The 1928,O 8,14:2
Woman From Moscow, The 1928,N 5,26:1
Manhattan Cocktail 1928,N 26,30:2
Shopworn Angel, The 1929,Ja 1,60:1
Wolf of Wall Street, The 1929,Ja 28,21:1
Half Way to Heaven 1929,D 7,19:3
Behind the Makeup 1930,Ja 18,21:1
Slightly Scarlet 1930,Mr 1,23:1
Young Eagles 1930,Mr 22,22:6
Benson Murder Case, The 1930,Ap 12,23:1
Devil's Holiday, The 1930,My 10,25:3
Grumpy 1930,Ag 2,16:4
Anybody's Woman 1930,Ag 16,8:3
Right to Love, The 1931,Ja 2,25:1
Unfaithful 1931,Mr 7,17:2
City Streets 1931,Ap 18,17:3
Vice Squad, The 1931,Je 6,15:5
Women Love Once 1931,Je 27,20:3
Beloved Bachelor, The 1931,O 17,20:1
Strictly Dishonorable 1931,N 11,27:1
No One Man 1932,Ja 23,18:4
Tomorrow and Tomorrow 1932,Ja 30,13:2
Thunder Below 1932,Je 20,11:2
Passport to Hell, A 1932,Ag 27,13:4
Downstairs 1932,O 8,15:4
Rockabye 1932,D 5,21:2
Grand Slam 1933,F 22,25:2
Kiss Before the Mirror, The 1933,My 15,16:2
Sing Sinner Sing 1933,Ag 15,20:2
Captured 1933,Ag 18,18:3
Secret of the Blue Room, The 1933,S 13,22:1
Little Women 1933,N 17,22:3
By Candlelight 1934,Ja 6,18:2
Countess of Monte Cristo, The 1934,Ap 2,13:2
Glamour 1934,My 12,12:3
Affairs of a Gentleman 1934,Je 23,16:7
I Give my Love 1934,Jl 17,24:2
Fountain, The 1934,Ag 31,14:1
Casino Murder Case, The 1935,Ap 17,26:5
Age of Indiscretion 1935,My 18,21:2

Lukas, Paul— Cont
Three Musketeers, The 1935,N 1,25:1
I Found Stella Parish 1935,N 4,24:4
Dodsworth 1936,S 24,29:1
Ladies in Love 1936,O 29,31:1
Espionage 1937,Mr 9,27:3
Dinner at the Ritz 1937,D 4,21:1
Lady Vanishes, The 1938,D 26,29:1
Mutiny of the Elsinore, The 1939,F 16,17:2
Confessions of a Nazi Spy 1939,Ap 29,13:2
Captain Fury 1939,My 26,20:2
Strange Cargo 1940,Ap 26,25:2
Ghost Breakers, The 1940,Jl 4,12:2
Monster and the Girl, The 1941,Mr 20,25:3
Chinese Den 1941,Mr 26,27:3
They Dare not Love 1941,My 16,21:4
Lady in Distress 1942,F 16,21:2
Watch on the Rhine 1943,Ag 28,15:1
Hostages 1943,O 11,23:2
Uncertain Glory 1944,Ap 8,9:2
Address Unknown 1944,Ap 17,20:1
Experiment Perilous 1944,D 30,15:2
Deadline at Dawn 1946,Ap 4,33:2
Temptation 1946,D 25,33:6
Whispering City 1948,My 10,25:5
Berlin Express 1948,My 21,19:3
Kim 1950,D 8,40:4
20,000 Leagues Under the Sea 1954,D 24,7:2
Roots of Heaven, The 1958,O 16,46:1
Scent of Mystery 1960,F 19,23:1
Tender is the Night 1962,Ja 20,13:2
55 Days at Peking 1963,My 30,20:1
Fun in Acapulco 1964,F 20,22:4
Lord Jim 1965,F 26,18:1
Sol Madrid 1968,Je 14,43:1
Lukas, Paul (Narrator)
Capture of Budapest 1945,Ag 31,14:4
Lukashevich, T (Director)
Bride with a Dowry 1954,Ag 23,20:5
Problem Child 1955,Ja 24,20:5
Lukats, Nick
Sophie Lang Goes West 1937,S 30,19:2
Start Cheering 1938,Mr 17,17:3
Duke of West Point, The 1938,D 16,33:2
Lukavsky, Randovan
Girl With Three Camels, The 1968,Ag 13,45:2
Luke, Keye
Charlie Chan in Paris 1935,Ja 22,23:2
Oil for the Lamps of China 1935,Je 6,25:2
Shanghai 1935,Jl 20,16:2
Mad Love 1935,Ag 5,20:2
Here's to Romance 1935,O 3,29:2
Charlie Chan in Shanghai 1935,O 14,21:1
King of Burlesque 1936,Ja 16,25:2
Charlie Chan at the Circus 1936,Mr 19,22:4
Charlie Chan at the Race Track 1936,Ag 15,6:2
Charlie Chan at the Opera 1936,D 5,16:2
Good Earth, The 1937,F 3,27:1
Charlie Chan at the Olympics 1937,My 24,23:1
Charlie Chan on Broadway 1937,S 20,19:1
Charlie Chan at Monte Carlo 1937,D 18,18:1
International Settlement 1938,F 12,20:3
Mr Moto's Gamble 1938,Ap 8,17:2
Disputed Passage 1939,O 26,27:2
Barricade 1939,D 9,18:2
Sued for Libel 1940,Ja 19,15:3
Bowery Blitzkrieg 1941,O 1,24:5
Burma Convoy 1941,O 7,26:7
No Hands on the Clock 1941,D 22,24:6
Mr and Mrs North 1942,Ja 22,13:2
Yank on the Burma Road, A 1942,Ja 29,25:3
North to the Klondike 1942,Mr 12,24:3
Spy Ship 1942,Jl 11,8:2
Invisible Agent 1942,Ag 6,23:2
Across the Pacific 1942,S 5,9:2
Falcon's Brother, The 1942,O 3,9:5
Destination Unknown 1942,O 29,19:3
Salute to the Marines 1943,Ag 30,11:3
Andy Hardy's Blonde Trouble 1944,My 5,17:3
Three Men in White 1944,My 26,23:3
Between Two Women 1945,Mr 29,18:3
First Yank into Tokyo 1945,O 25,18:2
Dark Delusion 1947,Je 26,19:2
Sleep, My Love 1948,F 19,29:4
Hell's Half Acre 1954,F 27,11:3
World for Ransom 1954,Je 5,11:2
Battle Hell 1957,Ag 22,23:1
Nobody's Perfect 1968,Ap 4,58:3
Luke, Michael (Producer)
Oedipus the King 1968,S 19,62:2
Luke, Michael (Screenwriter)
Oedipus the King 1968,S 19,62:2
Lukianov, Sergei
Military Secret 1945,Ag 2,16:2
Cossacks of the Kuban 1950,O 30,22:4
Lukic, Sveta (Screenwriter)
Fury is a Woman 1964,S 28,19:1
Lukin, V
Peasants 1935,Ag 29,25:2
Defense of Volotchayevsk, The 1938,Ag 11,13:3
Man With the Gun, The 1939,Ja 30,9:3
Lukin, Y (Screenwriter)
Fate of Man 1961,Jl 11,28:1

Lukov, L (Director)
Two Soldiers 1944,Jl 27,14:2
Miners of the Don 1951,N 12,21:2
Mistress, The 1954,My 31,9:2
Lukov, L (Producer)
Miners of the Don 1951,N 12,21:2
Lukowski, Igor (Screenwriter)
Zygmunt Kolosowski 1947,N 13,13:3
Lukoye, Peter
Born Free 1966,Je 23,29:1
Lukschy, W
Fistful of Dollars, A 1967,F 2,29:1
Lukschy, Wolfgang
Christina 1951,Ja 15,13:1
Luksik, Karel
Bohemian Rapture 1948,F 16,16:2
Lukyanov, S
Twelfth Night 1956,Mr 5,21:1
Italiano Brava Gente 1966,F 4,20:1
Lukyanov, Sergei
Vasili's Return 1953,S 28,21:4
Big Family, A 1955,Je 6,24:1
Captain's Daughter, The 1959,N 23,41:3
Gordeyev Family, The 1961,O 16,33:6
Lulli, Folco
Tragic Hunt 1948,O 22,30:2
Bandit, The 1949,Je 7,26:3
Flight Into France 1949,Jl 22,16:2
Without Pity; (Senza Pieta) 1950,Mr 16,40:4
Under the Olive Tree 1951,O 5,24:4
Times Gone By (A Question of Property);
  Question of Property, A (Times Gone By)
  1953,D 30,16:2
Wages of Fear, The 1955,F 17,23:1
Sign of the Gladiator 1959,D 3,46:1
House of Intrigue, The 1960,Mr 10,36:3
Always Victorious 1960,Ap 7,46:1
Island Sinner, The 1960,S 5,11:2
Eye for an Eye, An 1961,F 10,19:1
Great War; (Grande Guerra, La) 1961,Ag 31,22:3
Neapolitan Carousel 1961,O 12,41:3
Tartars, The 1962,Je 21,26:2
Lafayette 1963,Ap 11,29:1
Organizer, The 1964,My 7,31:2
Variety Lights; Luci del Varieta 1965,My 7,34:1
Marco the Magnificent 1966,D 15,60:1
All the Other Girls Do! 1967,My 30,12:1
Lulli, Piero
Tragic Hunt 1948,O 22,30:2
Always Victorious 1960,Ap 7,46:1
Lumdin, Vic
Robinson Crusoe on Mars 1964,Ag 27,28:2
Lumet, Baruch
One Third of a Nation 1939,F 11,13:2
Pawnbroker, The 1965,Ap 21,51:1
Lumet, Sidney
One Third of a Nation 1939,F 11,13:2
Lumet, Sidney (Director)
12 Angry Men 1957,Ap 15,24:1
Stage Struck 1958,Ap 23,40:1
That Kind of Woman 1959,S 12,12:2
Fugitive Kind, The 1960,Ap 15,13:1
View From the Bridge, A 1962,Ja 23,36:1
Long Day's Journey Into Night 1962,O 10,57:2
Fail Safe 1964,S 16,36:1
Pawnbroker, The 1965,Ap 21,51:1
Hill, The 1965,O 4,00:0
Group, The 1966,Mr 17,35:1
Deadly Affair, The 1967,Ja 27,31:1
Bye Bye Braverman 1968,F 22,36:1
Sea Gull, The 1968,D 24,14:1
Lumet, Sidney (Producer)
Deadly Affair, The 1967,Ja 27,31:1
Bye Bye Braverman 1968,F 22,36:1
Sea Gull, The 1968,D 24,14:1
Lummis, Dayton
Man in the Dark 1953,Ap 9,31:5
Loophole 1954,Mr 13,11:3
Prince of Players 1955,Ja 12,24:2
Court-Martial of Billy Mitchell, The
  1955,D 23,14:2
Spoilers, The 1955,D 24,10:2
First Texan, The 1956,Je 23,20:2
Wrong Man, The 1956,D 24,8:1
Monkey on my Back 1957,My 30,23:2
Jack the Giant Killer 1962,Jl 26,17:1
Luna, Barbara
Cry Tough 1959,S 17,48:4
Devil at 4 O'Clock, The 1961,O 19,39:3
Five Weeks in a Balloon 1962,Ag 27,18:1
Dime With a Halo 1963,Je 27,23:3
Mail Order Bride 1964,Je 11,27:3
Synanon 1965,My 6,44:1
Ship of Fools 1965,Jl 29,18:1
Firecreek 1968,F 22,36:2
Luna, Charito
Steel Claw, The 1961,S 21,40:2
Luna, Manuel
Nobleza Baturra; Rustic Chivalry
  1938,Mr 28,19:3
Morena Clara 1938,Je 18,18:3
Carmen de la Triana 1940,Je 15,12:2
Mad Queen, The 1950,O 27,24:3

Loyola, The Soldier Saint 1952,Ap 25,19:2
Luna, Margarito
Treasure of Sierra Madre 1948,Ja 24,11:2
One Way Street 1950,My 12,33:3
Torch, The 1950,Ag 21,15:2
My Outlaw Brother 1951,Ag 23,19:2
Plunder of the Sun 1953,Ag 27,22:1
Littlest Outlaw, The 1955,D 27,31:1
Luna, Ricardo (Screenwriter)
Hand in the Trap 1963,Jl 2,16:2
Luna (Composer)
Molinos de Viento; Windmills 1940,F 26,11:2
Luna Boys, The
Sidewalks of London 1940,F 15,15:1
Lunardi, Lote
Before the Revolution; Prima della Revolutiona
  1964,S 25,32:1
Lunceford, Jimmy and his orchestra
Blues in the Night 1941,D 12,35:2
Lund, Annalena
Free, White and 21 1963,Je 20,29:3
Lund, John
To Each his Own 1946,My 24,15:2
Perils of Pauline, The 1947,Jl 10,17:2
Foreign Affair, A 1948,Jl 1,19:3
Night Has a Thousand Eyes 1948,O 14,38:3
Miss Tatlock's Millions 1948,N 25,47:2
Bride of Vengeance 1949,Ap 7,38:2
My Friend Irma 1949,S 29,39:2
No Man of her Own 1950,My 4,32:3
Duchess of Idaho 1950,Jl 21,15:3
My Friend Irma Goes West 1950,Ag 3,20:2
Mating Season, The 1951,Ap 12,41:2
Darling, How Could You! 1951,N 9,22:4
Battle at Apache Pass, The 1952,My 10,16:4
Steel Town 1952,My 10,16:4
Just Across the Street 1952,Je 28,12:4
Latin Lovers 1953,Ag 13,17:2
White Feather 1955,F 17,23:1
Chief Crazy Horse 1955,Ap 28,25:1
High Society 1956,Ag 10,9:2
Dakota Incident 1956,N 10,14:2
Wackiest Ship in the Army, The 1961,F 9,36:1
If a Man Answers 1962,N 22,43:1
Lund, Lucille
Saturday's Millions 1933,O 14,18:3
Black Cat, The 1934,My 19,18:4
Kiss and Make-Up 1934,Je 29,17:1
What Price Vengeance 1937,My 26,30:3
Fight to the Finish, A 1937,Je 26,20:2 (In
  Addenda)
Lund, Richard
Three Who Were Doomed, The 1928,Ja 10,28:4
Lund, Rickard
John Ericsson Victor of Hampton Roads
  1938,My 18,17:2
Lundberg, Dan (Original Author)
Raw Wind in Eden 1958,S 20,10:6
Lundberg, Sven
Wonderful Adventures of Nils, The
  1962,S 14,37:1
Lundell, Nils
Vaermlaenningarna 1932,N 18,23:2
Skaergaards-Flirt 1936,Ap 8,26:3
Raggen, Det Aer Jag Det 1936,My 22,19:1
Sun Over Sweden 1938,Ap 9,11:2
Skicka Hem Nr 7; Send Home No 7
  1939,My 9,29:2
Vi paa Solglantan; We at Solglantan
  1940,O 9,30:3
Lundequist, Gerda
Natt, En 1935,Ja 29,24:1
Of Love and Lust (On Payment); On Payment (Of
  Love and Lust) 1959,My 26,31:2
Lundigan, Ted
What Next Corporal Hargrove? 1945,D 26,15:2
Lundigan, William
Armored Car 1937,Jl 26,15:2
Black Doll, The 1938,F 7,10:2
Wives Under Suspicion 1938,Jl 1,22:3
Missing Guest, The 1938,S 7,30:7
Three Smart Girls Grow Up 1939,Mr 18,9:2
Dodge City 1939,Ap 8,19:1
They Asked for It 1939,Je 30,17:4
Forgotten Woman, The 1939,Ag 4,11:2
Old Maid, The 1939,Ag 12,16:2
Legion of Lost Flyers 1939,O 30,13:3
Fighting 69th, The 1940,Ja 27,9:2
Three Cheers for the Irish 1940,Mr 9,19:2
Man Who Talked too Much, The 1940,Je 29,12:2
Sea Hawk, The 1940,Ag 10,16:2
East of the River 1940,O 28,21:2
Santa Fe Trail 1940,D 21,21:2
Case of the Black Parrot, The 1941,Ja 10,23:3
Highway West 1941,Ag 8,13:4
International Squadron 1941,N 14,28:4
Bugle Sounds, The 1942,Ap 3,25:2
Courtship of Andy Hardy, The 1942,Ap 10,21:2
Sunday Punch 1942,My 11,19:2
Andy Hardy's Double Life 1943,Ja 12,23:3
Salute to the Marines 1943,Ag 30,11:3
Dishonored Lady 1947,My 24,10:5
Fabulous Dorseys, The 1947,My 30,25:3

Lundigan, William— Cont
State Department-File 649 1949,F 21,20:2
Follow Me Quietly 1949,Jl 8,14:5
Pinky 1949,S 30,28:2
Mother Didn't Tell Me 1950,Mr 4,11:2
I'll Get by 1950,N 2,39:3
I'd Climb the Highest Mountain 1951,My 10,38:1
House on Telegraph Hill, The 1951,My 14,29:1
Elopement 1951,D 21,21:3
Down Among the Sheltering Palms
  1953,Je 13,11:2
Inferno 1953,Ag 12,22:2
Riders to the Stars 1954,Mr 20,10:7
Lundor, Fritz (Miscellaneous)
Hampelmann, Der 1931,S 8,38:7
Lundquist, Goran
Wild Strawberries 1959,Je 23,37:1
Lung, Charles
Destination Unknown 1942,O 29,19:3
Flight for Freedom 1943,Ap 16,24:2
Thunder in the East 1953,F 4,32:2
Lung, Clarence
Dragon Seed 1944,Jl 21,16:4
Prisoner of War 1954,My 10,20:2
World for Ransom 1954,Je 5,11:2
Lunge, Romilly
Man of Affairs 1937,F 20,9:2
Two Who Dared 1937,Jl 10,18:2
Sidewalks of London 1940,F 15,15:1
Lunsford, Beverly
That Night 1957,O 15,39:3
Intruder, The 1962,My 15,48:1
Lunt, Alfred
Backbone 1923,Ap 30,11:2
Ragged Edge, The 1923,Je 5,24:5
Second Youth 1924,Ap 22,19:3
Lovers in Quarantine 1925,O 13,20:1
Guardsman, The 1931,S 10,22:4
Stage Door Canteen 1943,Je 25,13:2
Luong, Ham Chau
Game is Over, The 1967,Ja 10,34:1
Lupanov, B (Screenwriter)
Road to the Stars 1958,Je 5,39:2
Lupi, Mario
Bebo's Girl 1964,N 12,40:1
Lupi, Roldano
Flesh will Surrender 1950,O 26,38:7
Malia 1952,F 2,11:4
Man With the Grey Glove, The 1953,Ja 3,11:2
Devotion 1953,Ja 31,10:6
Duel Without Honor 1953,F 28,8:8
Times Gone By (The Vise); Vise, The (Times Gone
  By) 1953,D 30,16:2
House of Ricordi 1956,Mr 13,32:1
Ten Commandments, The 1958,Ap 7,26:1
Lupino, Ida
Search for Beauty 1934,F 10,20:2
Come on Marines 1934,Mr 24,20:3
Paris in Spring 1935,Jl 13,16:2
Peter Ibbetson 1935,N 8,18:2
Anything Goes 1936,F 6,23:3
One Rainy Afternoon 1936,My 14,29:2
Yours for the Asking 1936,Ag 20,14:2
Gay Desperado, The 1936,O 9,31:4
Sea Devils 1937,Mr 16,26:4
Artists and Models 1937,Ag 5,19:2
Fight for Your Lady 1937,N 20,21:2
Lone Wolf Spy Hunt, The 1939,Mr 6,11:3
Adventures of Sherlock Holmes, The
  1939,S 2,20:1
Light That Failed, The 1939,D 25,19:1
They Drive by Night 1940,Jl 27,17:5
High Sierra 1941,Ja 25,11:2
Sea Wolf, The 1941,Mr 26,27:3
Out of the Fog 1941,Je 21,20:2
Ladies in Retirement 1941,N 7,27:1
Moontide 1942,Ap 30,14:1
Life Begins at Eight-Thirty 1942,D 10,35:2
Forever and a Day 1943,Mr 13,9:2
Hard Way, The 1943,Mr 13,9:2
Thank Your Lucky Stars 1943,O 2,19:2
In our Time 1944,F 12,11:2
Hollywood Canteen 1944,D 16,19:2
Pillow to Post 1945,My 26,18:2
Devotion 1946,Ap 6,10:5
Man I Love, The 1947,Ja 25,12:2
Deep Valley 1947,Ag 23,7:2
Escape me Never 1947,N 8,11:2
Road House 1948,N 8,24:2
Lust for Gold 1949,Jl 4,9:2
Woman in Hiding 1950,F 23,33:2
On Dangerous Ground 1952,F 13,35:2
Beware my Lovely 1953,S 13,10:5
Bigamist, The 1953,D 26,10:4
Women's Prison 1955,F 3,18:5
Big Knife, The 1955,N 9,41:2
While the City Sleeps 1956,My 17,37:1
Lupino, Ida (Director)
Outrage 1950,O 16,30:5
Hard, Fast and Beautiful 1951,Jl 2,16:6
Hitch-Hiker, The 1953,Ap 30,39:3
Bigamist, The 1953,D 26,10:4
Trouble With Angels, The 1966,Ap 7,45:1

Lupino, Ida (Producer)
Not Wanted 1949,Jl 25,11:4
Lupino, Ida (Screenwriter)
Not Wanted 1949,Jl 25,11:4
Outrage 1950,O 16,30:5
Hitch-Hiker, The 1953,Ap 30,39:3
Private Hell 36 1954,S 4,6:4
Lupino, Richard
Rhapsody 1954,Mr 12,17:1
Never so Few 1960,Ja 22,15:2
Midnight Lace 1960,O 14,27:1
Lupino, Rita
Not Wanted 1949,Jl 25,11:4
Outrage 1950,O 16,30:5
Lupino, Stanley
Sleepless Nights 1933,Jl 22,14:2
You Made Me Love You 1934,My 30,14:3
Lupino, Stanley (Composer)
You Made Me Love You 1934,My 30,14:3
Lupino, Stanley (Original Author)
Sleepless Nights 1933,Jl 22,14:2
You Made Me Love You 1934,My 30,14:3
Lupino, Wallace
Man Who Could Work Miracles, The
1937,F 22,13:1
Lupo, Alberto
Minotaur, The 1961,N 8,41:1
Lupo, Michele (Director)
Goliath and the Sins of Babylon 1964,Mr 5,36:2
Lupovici
Pasha's Wives, The 1942,Ap 6,19:2
Lupovici, Marcel
Rififi 1956,Je 6,37:1
Lupton, John
Scandal at Scourie 1953,Je 16,24:2
All the Brothers Were Valiant 1953,D 29,19:2
Escape from Fort Bravo 1954,Ja 23,11:2
Prisoner of War 1954,My 10,20:2
Battle Cry 1955,F 3,18:1
Man With the Gun 1955,D 23,14:2
Diane 1956,Ja 13,18:1
Great Locomotive Chase, The 1956,Je 27,35:1
Man in the Net, The 1959,Je 11,36:2
Luquet, Andre
Spectre Vert, Le 1930,Je 8,IX,6:1
Luray, Doris
Grumpy 1930,Ag 2,16:4
Lurville, Armand
Passion Of Joan Of Arc, The 1929,Mr 29,21:1
Passion of Jeanne d'Arc, The 1929,Mr 31,VIII,7:1
Couturiere de Luneville, La 1932,O 14,23:2
Avec l'Assurance 1935,My 4,17:3
Open Road, The 1940,O 5,20:2
Ruy Blas 1948,O 4,14:2
Lurville, M
Amour Maitre des Choses, L' 1931,Mr 30,25:2
Luschik, Voloiya
Adventure in Odessa 1954,Je 21,19:6
Lusiardo, Tito
Idolos de la Radio 1935,Jl 2,24:5
Mujeres que Trabajan; Women Who Work
1940,Ja 1,29:4
Oro entre Barro; Gold in Clay 1940,Jl 1,23:2
Je Hatore 1940,Ag 27,17:2
Jettatore 1940,Ag 27,17:2
Lusicic, Andro (Screenwriter)
Seventh Continent, The 1968,Jl 30,33:2
Luske, Hamilton (Director)
Saludos Amigos 1943,F 13,8:2
Make Mine Music 1946,Ap 22,26:2
Melody Time 1948,My 28,28:2
Cinderella 1950,F 23,33:1
Peter Pan 1953,F 12,23:1
Lady and the Tramp 1955,Je 24,17:1
one Hundred and One Dalmations
1961,F 11,27:1
Luske, Hamilton (Miscellaneous)
Reluctant Dragon, The 1941,Jl 25,12:2
Luske, Jimmy
Reluctant Dragon, The 1941,Jl 25,12:2
Lussier, Dane (Miscellaneous)
Let's Dance 1950,N 30,42:2
Lussier, Dane (Screenwriter)
Ladies' Day 1943,Mr 26,14:3
Lady and the Monster, The 1944,Ap 8,9:2
Storm Over Lisbon 1944,S 11,14:1
Dick Tracy vs Cueball 1946,N 23,12:2
Family Honeymoon 1949,F 25,28:2
My Dream Is Yours 1949,Ap 16,11:3
Lady Wants Mink, The 1953,Ap 6,24:2
Lussier, Doris
Big Red 1962,S 3,11:2
Lustgarten, Edgar (Original Author)
Long Dark Hall, The 1951,My 10,38:3
Lustig, Arnost (Original Author)
Transport From Paradise 1967,F 8,22:1
Diamonds of the Night 1968,Mr 15,30:1
Lustig, Arnost (Screenwriter)
Transport From Paradise 1967,F 8,22:1
Lustig, H G (Miscellaneous)
Loves of a Dictator 1935,Je 1,18:2

Lustig, H G (Original Author)
Loves of a Dictator 1935,Je 1,18:2
Lustig, H G (Screenwriter)
Heart of Paris 1939,Ja 13,17:3
Lustig, Jan (Miscellaneous)
Town Without Pity 1961,O 11,53:1
Lustig, Jan (Screenwriter)
Orage 1938,D 12,26:2
Reunion in France 1943,Mr 5,20:3
White Cliffs of Dover, The 1944,My 12,15:2
Homecoming 1948,Ap 30,28:4
That Forsyte Woman 1949,N 11,31:2
Story of Three Loves, The (Equilibrium);
Equilibrium (The Story of Three Loves)
1953,Mr 6,29:2
Story of Three Loves, The (The Jealous Lover);
Jealous Lover, The (The Story of Three Loves)
1953,Mr 6,29:2
Story of Three Loves, The (Mademoiselle);
Mademoiselle (The Story of Three Loves)
1953,Mr 6,29:2
Equilibrium 1953,Mr 6,29:2
Story of Three Loves, The 1953,Mr 6,29:2
Young Bess 1953,My 22,31:1
Torch Song 1953,O 13,34:2
Knights of the Round Table 1954,Ja 8,17:2
Moonfleet 1955,Je 25,9:2
Situation Hopeless-But not Serious
1965,O 14,53:1
Lusty, Lou (Producer)
Fugitives for a Night 1938,S 21,30:4
Affairs of Annabel, The 1938,O 13,29:2
Annabel Takes a Tour 1938,D 29,15:3
Luterkort, Ingrid
Children, The 1949,D 23,17:1
Luther, Ann
Sinners in Silk 1924,S 8,15:3
Luther, Barbara (Original Author)
Ticklish Affair, A 1963,Ag 22,19:2
Luther, Lester
Red Menace, The 1949,Je 27,18:2
Luttazzi, Lelio
Avventura, L' 1961,Ap 5,30:1
Weekend, Italian Style 1968,My 23,56:2
Lutz, Catherine
Lola 1962,O 15,32:2
Lutz, Stuart J (Original Author)
Youngest of the Regiment, The
1931,S 27,VIII,7:1
Lutzkendorf, Felix (Screenwriter)
Third Sex, The 1959,Mr 26,27:1
Luxford, Nola
Successful Calamity, A 1932,S 23,22:2
Iron Master, The 1933,F 4,11:3
Luz, Dora
Three Caballeros, The 1945,F 5,20:1
Luz, Ernest (Miscellaneous)
Two Lovers 1928,Mr 23,24:4
Submarine 1928,Ag 31,23:3
Luzhina, Larisa
House on the Front Line, The 1963,S 2,18:1
Luzi, Enrico
Three Forbidden Stories 1953,N 16,21:4
Luzi, Maria Pia
Night, The; Notte, La 1962,F 20,29:4
Lvova, Ludmila
Young, The Evil and the Savage, The
1968,Ag 15,46:2
Lyanov, N
Jew at War, A 1931,Jl 25,11:6
Lyapina, G
Problem Child 1955,Ja 24,20:5
Lyarof, M
Simple Tailor, The 1934,F 19,18:3
Lyarsky, Alexei
On his Own 1939,S 13,31:3
Lyarsky, Alyosha
Childhood of Maxim Gorky 1938,S 28,29:3
Lyaudanskaya, E V
Gobsek 1937,Jl 16,22:1
Lybarger, Lee Francis (Original Author)
Democracy, The Vision Restored 1920,Ag 25,6:4
Lyberopoulos, E (Screenwriter)
Girl From Corfu, The 1957,My 20,28:2
Lycan, Georges
Tramplers, The 1966,D 8,64:1
Lydell, Al
Way Down East 1935,O 31,16:2
Angel's Holiday 1937,My 29,20:2
Lyden, Marlene
Miracle on 34th Street 1947,Je 5,32:1
Lyden, Robert
I'll See You in my Dreams 1951,D 7,35:1
Man of a Thousand Faces 1957,Ag 14,21:1
Lydon, Eithne
Playboy of the Western World, The
1963,Mr 19,8:2
Lydon, James
Back Door to Heaven 1939,Ap 20,21:2
Tom Brown's School Days 1940,Je 28,22:2
Little Men 1940,D 9,23:2
Naval Academy 1941,Je 5,27:3
Henry Aldrich for President 1941,O 18,22:2

Lydon, James— Cont
Aerial Gunner 1943,Je 26,10:2
Twice Blessed 1945,Jl 7,7:5
Life With Father 1947,Ag 16,6:6
Cynthia 1947,S 19,27:2
Time of your Life, The 1948,My 27,29:2
Bad Boy 1949,Mr 23,35:2
When Willie Comes Marching Home
1950,F 18,9:2
Magnificent Yankee, The 1951,Ja 19,21:2
September Affair 1951,F 2,19:2
Oh! Susanna 1951,Mr 30,28:5
Island in the Sky 1953,S 10,22:2
I Passed for White 1960,Ag 18,19:3
Last Time I Saw Archie, The 1961,My 29,9:6
Lyel, Viola
Patient Vanishes, The 1947,My 23,31:2
Mr Perrin and Mr Traill 1949,Ja 17,15:2
Little Hut, The 1957,My 4,25:1
Lyford, Richard (Director)
Island of Allah 1956,Je 27,35:1
Lyford, Richard (Miscellaneous)
Titan-Story of Michelangelo, The 1950,Ja 23,16:2
Lyford, Richard (Producer)
Island of Allah 1956,Je 27,35:1
Lygizos, Mitsos
Casablan 1964,D 14,50:1
Lykhin, S
Apartment in Moscow 1962,My 28,25:5
Lykkehus, Karen
Child of Man 1950,F 1,25:2
Lyle, Bessie
Littlest Rebel, The 1935,D 20,30:1
Lyle, Edythe
Deliverance 1919,Ag 19,10:1
Lyle, R C Capt
Wings of the Morning 1937,Mr 12,19:1
Lyles, A C (Original Author)
Johnny Reno 1966,Mr 10,26:3
Lyles, A C (Producer)
Black Spurs 1965,My 29,17:1
Johnny Reno 1966,Mr 10,26:3
Fort Utah 1967,My 25,54:3
Lyley, Gerard
Loose Ends 1930,O 18,23:2
Lyman, Abe (Producer)
Singing Guns 1950,Je 5,19:3
Lyman, Mel
Festival 1967,O 24,53:2
Lymon, Frankie and the Teenagers
Mister Rock and Roll 1957,O 17,42:2
Lymperopulus, D (Screenwriter)
Shepherd's Daughter, The 1956,My 14,23:3
Lyn, Jacquie
Pack up Your Troubles 1932,O 1,10:4
Prosperity 1932,N 26,11:4
Lynch, Alfred
Password Is Courage, The 1962,D 22,5:2
Operation Snafu 1965,My 22,18:1
Hill, The 1965,O 4,00:0
Taming of the Shrew, The 1967,Mr 9,43:1
Sea Gull, The 1968,D 24,14:1
Lynch, Brid
Poacher's Daughter, The 1960,F 16,31:2
Lynch, Christopher (Composer)
Hills of Ireland, The 1951,My 22,38:2
Lynch, Helen
Eternal Three, The 1923,O 12,7:2 (Incorrect in
this edition; use 1927,O 1,7:2 elsewhere)
Oh, Doctor! 1925,F 23,24:1
Smouldering Fires 1925,Mr 31,17:4
Fifth Avenue Models 1925,My 4,16:2
My Own Pal 1926,Mr 15,18:3
Underworld 1927,Ag 22,21:3
Love and Learn 1928,F 20,14:1
Showdown, The 1928,Mr 5,21:1
Ladies of the Mob 1928,Je 18,13:2
Romance of the Underworld 1929,Ja 7,36:2
Why Bring That Up? 1929,O 5,22:5
Elmer and Elsie 1934,Ag 4,14:5
Women Without Names 1940,My 9,26:4
Lynch, Joe
Ulysses 1967,Mr 14,55:1
Lynch, John
It's a Great Life 1920,Ag 30,12:3
Lynch, John (Screenwriter)
Pride of Palomar, The 1922,N 20,21:3
Enemies of Women 1923,Ap 1,5:4
Go-Getter 1923,Ap 9,14:3 (In Addenda)
Rejected Woman, The 1924,My 5,18:3
Miami 1924,Je 3,22:2
Lynch, Ken
Pork Chop Hill 1959,My 30,9:2
Anatomy of a Murder 1959,Jl 3,10:1
Walk on the Wild Side 1962,F 22,20:1
Dear Heart 1965,Mr 8,33:1
Mister Buddwing 1966,O 12,36:1
Hotel 1967,Ja 20,27:1
Lynch, Kenneth (Narrator)
Roosevelt Story, The 1947,Ag 22,11:2
Lynch, Sean
Kitchen, The 1961,N 2,42:1

Lynd, Helen
Melody in Spring 1934,Mr 31,8:2
Lone Wolf Spy Hunt, The 1939,Mr 6,11:3
Flight at Midnight 1939,S 7,29:2
Murder in the Air 1940,Jl 4,12:2
Lucky Partners 1940,S 6,25:2
Strawberry Blonde 1941,F 22,11:2
Great Man's Lady, The 1942,Ap 30,14:3

Lynd, Patty Lou
Ten Nights in a Barroom 1931,F 28,15:2

Lynde, Paul
New Faces 1954,F 20,8:7
Son of Flubber 1963,F 9,5:2
Bye Bye Birdie 1963,Ap 5,27:3
Under the Yum Yum Tree 1963,N 21,43:2
For Those Who Think Young 1964,Jl 9,27:1
Send Me no Flowers 1964,N 13,30:1
Glass Bottom Boat, The 1966,Je 10,54:1
How Sweet It Is 1968,Ag 22,47:1

Lynde, Paul (Screenwriter)
New Faces 1954,F 20,8:7

Lyndon, Barre (Original Author)
Amazing Dr Clitterhouse, The 1938,Jl 21,14:2
Sundown 1941,D 26,21:3
Man in Half Moon Street, The 1945,Ja 20,16:2

Lyndon, Barre (Screenwriter)
Sundown 1941,D 26,21:3
Lodger, The 1944,Ja 20,15:3
Hangover Square 1945,F 8,15:2
House on Ninety-Second Street, The
   1945,S 27,24:7
Night Has a Thousand Eyes 1948,O 14,38:3
To Please a Lady 1950,O 27,24:3
Greatest Show on Earth, The 1952,Ja 11,17:2
War of the Worlds, The 1953,Ag 14,10:2
Man in the Attic 1954,F 6,17:2
Sign of the Pagan 1955,F 14,24:2
Conquest of Space 1955,My 28,7:6
Omar Khayyam 1957,Ag 24,12:4
Dark Intruder 1965,Jl 22,24:2

Lyndon, Victor (Producer)
Station Six-Sahara 1964,N 12,40:2

Lynen, Robert
Poil de Carotte 1933,My 26,24:2
Sans Famille 1935,Je 4,26:5
Carnet de Bal, Un 1938,Mr 26,12:1
Man of the Hour, The 1940,N 21,43:2
Hatred 1941,Ja 27,11:2
Barge-Keeper's Daughter, The 1945,S 6,23:3

Lynley, Carol
Light in the Forest, The 1958,Jl 11,15:2
Holiday for Lovers 1959,Jl 25,10:2
Blue Denim 1959,Jl 31,21:1
Hound-Dog Man 1960,Ap 28,29:1
Return to Peyton Place 1961,My 6,26:1
Last Sunset, The 1961,Je 15,51:1
Stripper, The 1963,Je 20,29:1
Under the Yum Yum Tree 1963,N 21,43:2
Cardinal, The 1963,D 13,41:1
Shock Treatment 1964,Jl 23,19:1
Pleasure Seekers, The 1964,D 26,9:1
Harlow 1965,My 15,18:1
Bunny Lake is Missing 1965,O 4,00:0
Shuttered Room, The 1968,F 15,47:1
Danger Route 1968,Je 6,54:2

Lynn, Ann
Flame in the Streets 1962,S 13,32:1
Girl-Getters, The 1966,Ap 13,37:6
Uncle, The 1966,Jl 19,34:1
Separation 1968,Mr 26,41:2
I'll Never Forget What's 'Isname
   1968,Ap 15,51:1

Lynn, April
Body Is a Shell, The 1957,S 9,21:2

Lynn, Barbara
Tales of Manhattan 1942,S 25,25:1

Lynn, Betty
Sitting Pretty 1948,Mr 11,35:2
June Bride 1948,O 30,10:2
Mother is a Freshman 1949,Mr 12,10:2
Once Upon a Dream 1949,Jl 15,17:2
Father Was a Fullback 1949,O 13,33:3
Cheaper by the Dozen 1950,Ap 1,12:2
Payment on Demand 1951,F 16,21:2
Take Care of my Little Girl 1951,Jl 19,20:2
Meet Me in Las Vegas 1956,Mr 14,39:2
Gun for a Coward 1957,Ja 31,21:1

Lynn, Billy
Mr Belvedere Rings the Bell 1951,Ag 2,18:1
Outcasts of Poker Flat 1952,My 16,19:3

Lynn, Cynthia
Bedtime Story 1964,Je 11,27:1

Lynn, Dani
If a Man Answers 1962,N 22,43:1

Lynn, Diana
Major and the Minor, The 1942,S 17,21:3
Miracle of Morgan's Creek 1944,Ja 20,15:2
And the Angels Sing 1944,Jl 13,14:2
Our Hearts Were Young and Gay 1944,O 12,24:2
Out of This World 1945,Je 7,25:2
Duffy's Tavern 1945,S 6,23:3
Bride Wore Boots, The 1946,Je 6,16:3
Our Hearts Were Growing Up 1946,Ag 12,17:2

Easy Come, Easy Go 1947,F 6,29:2
Ruthless 1948,S 4,8:7
Every Girl Should be Married 1948,D 24,14:2
My Friend Irma 1949,S 29,39:2
Paid in Full 1950,F 16,28:2
Peggy 1950,Jl 21,15:4
My Friend Irma Goes West 1950,Ag 3,20:2
Bedtime for Bonzo 1951,Ap 6,31:4
People Against O'Hara, The 1951,S 6,39:3
Plunder of the Sun 1953,Ag 27,22:1
Track of the Cat 1954,D 2,38:2
Annapolis Story, An 1955,Ap 9,8:2
You're Never too Young 1955,Ag 26,10:2
Kentuckian, The 1955,S 2,13:2

Lynn, Eleanor
As Husbands Go 1934,Ja 26,20:3
You're Only Young Once 1938,Ja 3,16:2
Shopworn Angel, The 1938,Jl 8,11:2
Fugitives for a Night 1938,S 21,30:4

Lynn, Emmett
Frisco Lil 1942,F 12,27:2
In old California 1942,Je 18,25:3
Relentless 1948,Mr 6,17:3
Bait 1954,F 24,21:3

Lynn, Emmy
Sheik's Wife, The 1922,Mr 6,9:3
Living Image, The 1928,Je 4,13:2
Vierge Folle, La 1929,Ja 13,VIII,7:4
Frochard et les Deux Orphelines, La
   1934,F 7,16:2

Lynn, Florence
Portrait of a Woman 1946,Ap 22,26:2

Lynn, George
Sinner Take All 1937,F 3,27:1
Charlie Chan at Monte Carlo 1937,D 18,18:1
City Girl 1938,F 4,17:3
To Be or not to Be 1942,Mr 7,13:2
Grand Central Murder 1942,My 23,8:8
A-Haunting We Will Go 1942,Ag 3,18:4
Sudan 1945,Ap 19,22:8
Atomic City, The 1952,My 2,21:1
I Was a Teenage Frankenstein 1958,Ja 30,19:4

Lynn, Grafton
St Louis Blues 1939,F 9,17:2

Lynn, Henry (Director)
Youth of Russia, The 1934,N 10,19:3
Shir Hashirim 1935,O 11,31:1
Power of Life 1938,Ap 29,17:2
Mothers of Today 1939,Mr 2,19:2

Lynn, Henry (Original Author)
Youth of Russia, The 1934,N 10,19:3

Lynn, Henry (Producer)
Power of Life 1938,Ap 29,17:2

Lynn, Henry (Screenwriter)
Mothers of Today 1939,Mr 2,19:2

Lynn, Hilary (Original Author)
Hollywood Cavalcade 1939,O 14,13:2
Where Are Your Children? 1944,Ja 17,14:5
Are These our Parents? 1944,Ag 23,16:2

Lynn, Hilary (Screenwriter)
Great Profile, The 1940,O 18,25:1
Where Are Your Children? 1944,Ja 17,14:5

Lynn, Homer
Let Not Man Put Asunder 1924,Ja 15,16:1

Lynn, Jeffrey
When Were You Born? 1938,Je 9,27:2
Cowboy From Brooklyn 1938,Jl 14,17:1
Four Daughters 1938,Ag 19,13:3
Yes, My Darling Daughter 1939,F 27,11:2
Daughters Courageous 1939,Je 24,14:2
Espionage Agent 1939,S 23,22:2
Roaring Twenties, The 1939,N 11,12:1
Four Wives 1939,D 23,9:1
Child Is Born, A 1940,Ja 11,19:2
Fighting 69th, The 1940,Ja 27,9:2
It all Came True 1940,Ap 6,13:2
All This and Heaven, Too 1940,Jl 5,10:2
My Love Came Back 1940,Jl 13,16:5
Money and the Woman 1940,O 4,29:2
Four Mothers 1941,Ja 11,12:7
Flight From Destiny 1941,Mr 28,26:7
Million Dollar Baby 1941,Je 7,20:2
Underground 1941,Je 23,13:2
Law of the Tropics 1941,O 10,26:5
Body Disappears, The 1942,Ja 31,13:2
Black Bart 1948,Mr 4,30:4
For the Love of Mary 1948,S 23,37:2
Whiplash 1948,D 27,16:3
Letter to Three Wives, A 1949,Ja 21,24:2
Strange Bargain 1949,S 30,28:3
Captain China 1950,Mr 2,33:2
Up Front 1951,Mr 26,19:2
Butterfield 8 1960,N 17,46:1
Tony Rome 1967,N 16,58:1

Lynn, Jill
School for Wives 1925,Ap 1,21:3

Lynn, Judy
Top Banana 1954,F 20,8:6

Lynn, Kane W (Producer)
Walls of Hell, The 1965,N 18,55:3

Lynn, Leni
Babes in Arms 1939,O 20,27:2
Hullabaloo 1940,D 19,33:1

Lynn, Leni — Cont
Showtime 1948,My 20,35:3

Lynn, Mara
Prehistoric Women 1950,D 29,15:5
Let's Make Love 1960,S 9,36:1

Lynn, Mauri
Night Without Sleep 1952,S 27,13:2

Lynn, Peter
Time Out for Murder 1938,O 7,21:2
Cipher Bureau 1938,D 14,32:6
Let Us Live 1939,Mr 30,19:2
Lone Wolf Strikes, The 1940,F 5,13:2
Great Dictator, The 1940,O 16,29:1
Kit Carson 1940,N 15,25:3
Bombay Clipper 1942,Ja 12,23:3

Lynn, Peter George
Mister Wong in Chinatown 1939,Jl 31,9:2 (In
   Addenda)

Lynn, Ralph
Rookery-Nook 1930,Mr 23,IX,6:1
Chance of a Night Time, A 1931,Je 7,VIII,6:1

Lynn, Robert (Director)
Dr Crippen 1964,F 15,14:1
Code 7...Victim 5 1965,My 20,52:1
Mozambique 1966,F 10,33:1

Lynn, Royce and Vanya
Seven Days' Leave 1942,D 11,33:2

Lynn, Sharon
Clancy's Kosher Wedding 1927,S 7,35:2
Give and Take 1928,D 27,27:1
Speakeasy 1929,Mr 11,22:2
William Fox Movietone Follies of 1929
   1929,My 27,22:1
One Woman Idea, The 1929,Je 10,23:1
Sunny Side Up 1929,O 4,24:5
Happy Days 1930,F 14,20:1
Let's Go Places 1930,Mr 1,23:1
Wild Company 1930,Jl 19,7:5
Up the River 1930,O 11,21:3
Lightnin' 1930,N 29,21:4
Too Many Cooks 1931,Ag 17,18:2
Big Broadcast, The 1932,O 15,13:1
Enter Madame 1935,Ja 12,12:1
Go Into Your Dance 1935,My 4,17:2
Way out West 1937,My 4,29:1
West Point Widow 1941,S 11,21:5

Lynn, Sydney
Atlantic 1930,O 6,21:1

Lynn, William
Harvey 1950,D 22,19:1

Lynne, Eve
Flame of Barbary Coast 1945,My 28,22:2

Lynwood, Burt (Director)
Shadows of the Orient 1937,O 11,26:6

LYON
See Also LION

Lyon, Alice
Horror of Party Beach, The 1964,Ap 30,30:1

Lyon, Ben
Open Your Eyes 1919,Je 30,16:3
Potash and Perlmutter 1923,S 24,5:4
Flaming Youth 1923,N 26,15:6
Painted People 1924,Ja 29,16:1
White Moth, The 1924,Je 16,18:3
Wine of Youth 1924,Ag 11,16:1
Lily of the Dust 1924,Ag 25,16:2
Wages of Virtue 1924,N 24,15:3
So Big 1925,Ja 5,19:1
Winds of Chance 1925,Ag 17,10:3
New Commandment, The 1925,N 10,25:3
Bluebeard's Seven Wives 1925,D 28,19:2
Reckless Lady, The 1926,Ja 25,21:2
Great Deception, The 1926,Ag 9,10:3
Prince of Tempters, The 1926,O 18,18:1
Perfect Sap, The 1927,Ja 11,18:2
Tender Hour, The 1927,Je 7,27:4
Dance Magic 1927,Jl 13,21:2
For the Love of Mike 1927,Ag 24,27:5
Air Legion, The 1928,N 13,37:1
Lummox 1930,Mr 24,25:1
Alias French Gertie 1930,Ap 14,24:2
Hell's Angels 1930,Ag 16,8:3
My Past 1931,Mr 12,22:7
Hot Heiress, The 1931,Mr 14,23:2
Soldiers Plaything, A 1931,My 2,23:4
Indiscreet 1931,My 7,21:4
Night Nurse 1931,Jl 17,23:4
Bought 1931,Ag 15,18:3
Compromised 1931,N 7,16:5
Her Majesty, Love 1931,N 26,37:2
Lady With a Past 1932,F 22,23:2
Week Ends Only 1932,Je 18,9:2
Hat Check Girl 1932,O 8,15:4
Girl Missing 1933,Ap 1,18:2
I Cover the Waterfront 1933,My 18,17:3
Women in his Life, The 1934,Ja 27,9:3
Crimson Romance 1934,O 13,10:1
Dancing Feet 1936,Mr 28,11:2
Down Under the Sea 1936,Ag 10,10:2

Lyon, Dana (Original Author)
House on Telegraph Hill, The 1951,My 14,29:1

Lyon, Francis D (Director)
Bob Mathias Story, The 1954,O 16,14:6
Great Locomotive Chase, The 1956,Je 27,35:1

Lyon, Francis D (Director)— Cont
Oklahoman, The 1957,My 15,39:1
Bailout at 43,000 1957,Je 8,13:2
Cinerama-South Seas Adventure 1958,Jl 16,26:1
Lyon, Frank
Big Pond, The 1930,My 19,21:1
Paris After Dark 1943,O 23,11:1
Lyon, Frank A
Inside of the Cup, The 1921,Ja 16,VI,2:1 (In Addenda)
Lyon, Margo
Die Grosse Attraktion 1933,Jl 24,11:2
Lyon, Priscilla
Beloved Brat 1938,My 2,13:2
Lyon, Richard
Unseen, The 1945,My 14,20:5
Green Years, The 1946,Ap 5,21:2
Anna and the King of Siam 1946,Je 21,20:2
Boy With Green Hair, The 1949,Ja 13,26:2
Great Lover, The 1949,N 24,48:2
Lyon, Robert (Director)
Coast of Skeletons 1965,N 11,58:3
Lyon, Sue
Lolita 1962,Je 14,23:2
Night of the Iguana, The 1964,Jl 1,42:1
7 Women 1966,My 5,59:1
Flim Flam Man, The 1967,Ag 23,40:1
Tony Rome 1967,N 16,58:1
Lyon, Therese
Letter for Evie, A 1946,Je 28,17:4
Half Angel 1951,Je 16,9:2
Lyon, Wanda
Greatest Love of All, The 1924,N 11,14:1
Lyons, Arthur S (Producer)
Ruthless 1948,S 4,8:7
Lyons, Cliff
Lawless Nineties, The 1936,Je 29,11:1
She Wore a Yellow Ribbon 1949,N 18,35:2
Wagonmaster 1950,Je 19,17:2
Bend of the River 1952,Ap 10,37:1
Lyons, Collette
Dance Charlie Dance 1937,Ag 26,25:2
52d Street 1937,N 15,15:1
Frisco Sal 1945,F 17,11:2
Dolly Sisters, The 1945,N 15,24:6
Wabash Avenue 1950,Ap 29,8:3
Lyons, Eddie
Declassee 1925,Mr 23,14:2
Lyons, Frances
College Coquette, The 1929,Ag 26,17:1
Lyons, Gene
Young Don't Cry, The 1957,Jl 27,10:7
Lyons, H Agar
Little Lord Fauntleroy 1914,Je 23,11:3
Lyons, James Pvt MP USA
Tokyo File 212 1951,Je 1,20:7
Lyons, Richard E (Producer)
Ride the High Country 1962,Je 21,26:2
Mail Order Bride 1964,Je 11,27:3
Rounders, The 1965,Ap 29,40:2
Plainsman, The 1966,N 19,26:1
Coogan's Bluff 1968,O 3,56:1
Lyons, Ruth
Ladies of the Big House 1932,Ja 1,31:1
Okay America 1932,S 10,18:5
Lyons, Ted
Untitled-Baseball Technique 1941,Ja 17,11:3
Lys, Lya
Clear all Wires 1933,Mr 4,11:2
Jimmy and Sally 1933,D 16,12:3
Great Gambini, The 1937,Jl 12,20:4
Confessions of a Nazi Spy 1939,Ap 29,13:2
Return Of Doctor X, The 1939,N 23,38:5
Murder in the Air 1940,Jl 4,12:2
Age d'Or, L'; Golden Age, The 1964,S 22,44:1
Lysak, Anastasia
Six PM 1946,Ja 28,15:5
Lysenko, Olga
Dimka 1964,Mr 21,13:5
Lysianskaya, Anna
Lucky Bride, The 1948,Ja 26,15:2
Lytell, Bert
Alias Jimmy Valentine 1920,Ap 19,13:3
To Have and to Hold 1922,N 6,13:1
Kick In 1922,D 18,22:2
Rupert of Hentzau 1923,Jl 9,8:4
Eternal City, The 1924,Ja 21,20:1
Son of the Sahara, A 1924,My 27,14:1
Sandra 1924,D 22,20:2
Steele of the Royal Mounted 1925,Je 18,16:3
Boomerang, The 1925,Jl 1,16:1
Eve's Lover 1925,Jl 27,17:3
Never the Twain Shall Meet 1925,Jl 29,24:4
Lady Windemere's Fan 1925,D 28,19:2
Alias the Lone Wolf 1927,S 20,32:2
Women's Wares 1927,N 15,27:1
On Trial 1928,N 15,26:5
Lone Wolf's Daughter, The 1929,Mr 4,20:2
Brothers 1930,N 15,15:3
Single Sin, The 1931,Mr 17,34:3
Stolen Jools 1931,Ap 4,23:1
Stage Door Canteen 1943,Je 25,13:2

Lytell, Marjorie
Finishing School 1934,Ap 30,11:4
Lytell, Wilfred
Hellotrope 1920,N 29,20:3
Bluebeard's Seven Wives 1925,D 28,19:2
Lytess, Natasha
Comrade X 1940,D 26,23:1
Once Upon a Honeymoon 1942,N 13,28:1
House on Telegraph Hill, The 1951,My 14,29:1
Anything Can Happen 1952,Ap 4,21:1
Lyton, Robert
Regular Girl, A 1919,N 11,13:3
Lytton, Bart (Original Author)
Bowery to Broadway 1944,N 30,19:2
Lytton, Bart (Screenwriter)
Bowery to Broadway 1944,N 30,19:2
Lytton, Roger
Little Child Shall Lead Them, A 1922,S 2,10:4
Zaza 1923,S 17,18:2
Sainted Devil, A 1924,N 24,15:3
Lyubashevsky, L
New Horizons 1939,My 12,25:3
Lyubeznov, Ivan
Sailor From the Comet, The 1959,Ag 3,21:2
Idiot, The 1960,Jl 22,11:2
Lyvikou, Ilia
Trouble for Father 1958,Ja 6,26:4
Lyx, Al (Screenwriter)
Prisoner of the Volga 1960,Je 2,27:2

M

Maack, Alfred
Marriage in the Shadows 1948,S 17,28:3
Maas, Ernest (Original Author)
Shocking Miss Pilgrim, The 1947,F 12,34:2
Maas, Fredericka (Original Author)
Shocking Miss Pilgrim, The 1947,F 12,34:2
Maasdorp, Reinet
After You, Comrade 1967,Ap 11,54:1
Maazel, Marvine
Delicious 1931,D 26,15:5
Maben, Alvis
Unholy Four, The 1954,N 20,10:2
Mabery, Mary
Restless Youth 1929,Ja 1,60:1
McAfee, Mara
Pal Joey 1957,O 28,30:1
McAlinney, Patrick
She Didn't Say No 1963,Jl 30,18:1
McAlister, Mary
On the Level 1930,Jl 5,17:4
McAllister, Mary
Ashes of Vengeance 1923,Ag 7,20:2
Boomerang, The 1925,Jl 1,16:1
One Minute to Play 1926,S 6,16:2
Waning Sex, The 1926,S 21,33:1
Singed 1927,Jl 12,29:3
Loves of an Actress 1928,Jl 30,21:2
McAllister, Paul
Peter Ibbetson; (Forever) 1921,O 17,18:1
You Can't Fool Your Wife 1923,Ap 24,25:3
Yolanda 1924,F 20,23:1
Moral Sinner, The 1924,Ap 7,15:3
Lone Wolf, The 1924,My 7,19:4
Manhandled 1924,Jl 29,9:2
Winning of Barbara Worth, The 1926,N 29,16:3
Sorrell and Son 1927,N 14,26:1
She's a Shiek 1927,N 21,20:1
Big Killing, The 1928,Jl 2,11:2
Noah's Ark 1929,Mr 13,28:6
Evangeline 1929,Jl 29,23:3
Case of Sergeant Grischa, The 1930,Mr 8,21:1
Beau Ideal 1931,Ja 19,25:1
Inspiration 1931,F 9,25:3
Mary of Scotland 1936,Jl 31,22:2
Doctor Takes a Wife, The 1940,Je 15,12:2
McAlpin, Donald
Rosita 1923,S 4,14:1
Macaluso, Armando (Miscellaneous)
Dream of Butterfly 1941,F 13,25:2
Manon Lescaut 1941,Ap 14,23:5
King's Jester, The 1947,Je 26,19:3
McAnally, Ray
Naked Edge 1961,Jl 1,9:1
She Didn't Say No 1963,Jl 30,18:1
McAnnally, Ray
Billy Budd 1962,O 31,32:1
McAnnan, George Burr
White Zombie 1932,Jl 29,18:2
Macardie, Dorothy (Original Author)
Uninvited, The 1944,F 21,19:3
McArdle, Mackey
Father Was a Fullback 1949,O 13,33:3
MacArthur, Charles (Director)
Crime Without Passion 1934,S 1,16:2
Scoundrel, The 1935,My 3,23:2
Soak the Rich 1936,F 5,14:2
Once in a Blue Moon 1936,D 2,35:1

MacArthur, Charles (Original Author)
Front Page, The 1931,Mr 20,29:1
Unholy Garden, The 1931,O 29,27:1
Rasputin and the Empress 1932,D 24,11:4
20th Century 1934,My 4,24:2
Once in a Blue Moon 1936,D 2,35:1
Gunga Din 1939,Ja 28,19:2
His Girl Friday 1940,Ja 12,13:2
I Take This Woman 1940,F 16,23:3
Lulu Belle 1948,Je 21,18:3
Perfect Strangers 1950,Mr 11,8:2
Jumbo 1962,D 7,49:1
MacArthur, Charles (Producer)
Crime Without Passion 1934,S 1,16:2
Scoundrel, The 1935,My 3,23:2
Soak the Rich 1936,F 5,14:2
Once in a Blue Moon 1936,D 2,35:1
MacArthur, Charles (Screenwriter)
Crime Without Passion 1934,S 1,16:2
Scoundrel, The 1935,My 3,23:2
Barbary Coast 1935,O 14,21:1
Soak the Rich 1936,F 5,14:2
Wuthering Heights 1939,Ap 14,28:2
Senator Was Indiscreet, The 1947,D 27,9:2
McArthur, Harold
Hoosier Schoolmaster, The 1924,Mr 18,25:2
MacArthur, James
Young Stranger, The 1957,Ap 9,40:1
Light in the Forest, The 1958,Jl 11,15:2
Third Man on the Mountain 1959,N 12,27:1
Kidnapped 1960,My 19,44:3
Swiss Family Robinson 1960,D 24,8:4
Interns, The 1962,Ag 9,17:5
Spencer's Mountain 1963,My 17,26:6
Cry of Battle 1963,O 12,27:2
Truth About Spring, The 1965,Je 17,27:2
Bedford Incident, The 1965,N 3,43:1
Battle of the Bulge 1965,D 18,36:1
Ride Beyond Vengeance 1966,S 29,60:1
Love-Ins, The 1967,Ag 19,16:1
Hang 'Em High 1968,Ag 8,27:3
McArthur, James (Original Author)
Bonnie Brier Bush, The 1921,N 28,16:1
McAtee, Clyde
Percy 1925,Mr 25,24:2
Macateer, Alan
Jigsaw 1949,My 30,9:4
Macaulay, Joseph
Lottery Bride, The 1930,N 29,21:4
Macaulay, Richard (Miscellaneous)
Wings for the Eagle 1942,Ag 1,14:2
Macaulay, Richard (Original Author)
Front Page Woman 1935,Jl 12,15:1
Ready, Willing and Able 1937,Mr 15,27:1
Melody for Two 1937,My 21,19:5
Riding on Air 1937,Je 26,20:2 (In Addenda)
Gold Diggers in Paris 1938,Je 2,19:2
Flight Angels 1940,My 27,23:2
Buck Privates Come Home 1947,Ap 12,11:3
Macaulay, Richard (Screenwriter)
Earthworm Tractors 1936,Jl 25,16:1
Riding on Air 1937,Je 26,20:2 (In Addenda)
Varsity Show 1937,S 2,17:2
Hollywood Hotel 1938,Ja 13,17:3
Garden of the Moon 1938,S 24,13:1
Brother Rat 1938,N 5,15:2
Hard To Get 1938,N 14,15:2
Kid From Kokomo, The 1939,My 20,11:2
Naughty but Nice 1939,Je 23,23:2
On Your Toes 1939,O 21,12:2
Roaring Twenties, The 1939,N 11,12:1
Three Cheers for the Irish 1940,Mr 9,19:2
Torrid Zone 1940,My 18,11:3
They Drive by Night 1940,Jl 27,17:5
Million Dollar Baby 1941,Je 7,20:2
Out of the Fog 1941,Je 21,20:2
Manpower 1941,Jl 5,14:2
Navy Blues 1941,S 20,11:2
Captains of the Clouds 1942,F 13,24:2
Across the Pacific 1942,S 5,9:2
Hello, Frisco, Hello 1943,Mr 25,25:1
Tampico 1944,Je 2,21:2
Young Widow 1946,Jl 29,12:8
Born to Kill 1947,My 1,34:2
Macaulay, Tom
Adventures, The 1947,Ap 4,19:2
Amazing Mr Beecham, The 1949,D 26,33:4
Outpost in Malaya 1952,N 27,49:2
MCAVOY
See Also MCEVOY
McAvoy, Charles
Murder at the Vanities 1934,My 21,20:2
Strike Me Pink 1936,Ja 17,15:2
King of the Turf 1939,My 8,21:2
Strange Holiday 1945,O 20,8:2
McAvoy, May
Perfect Lady, A 1918,D 2,11:3
Sentimental Tommy 1921,My 9,16:2
Private Scandal, A 1921,Je 13,16:1
Top of New York, The 1922,Je 19,10:3
Clarence 1922,O 16,20:2
Kick In 1922,D 18,22:2
Grumpy 1923,Mr 26,16:2

McAvoy, May— Cont
Only 38 1923,Je 11,16:2
Hollywood 1923,Jl 30,11:4
West of the Water Tower 1923,D 31,9:3
Enchanted Cottage, The 1924,Ap 14,14:1
Bedroom Window, The 1924,Je 9,14:3
Three Women 1924,O 6,25:1
Tarnish 1924,O 13,21:1
Mad Whirl, The 1925,Jl 1,16:1
Lady Windemere's Fan 1925,D 28,19:2
Ben Hur 1925,D 31,10:5 (In Addenda)
Fire Brigade, The 1926,D 21,20:2
Matinee Ladies 1927,Ap 13,29:4
Jazz Singer, The 1927,O 7,24:4
If I Were Single 1928,Mr 5,21:1
Lion and the Mouse, The 1928,Je 16,11:4
Terror, The 1928,Ag 16,25:3
Caught in the Fog 1928,D 4,29:1
Ben Hur 1931,D 4,28:2
McBain, Alastair (Original Author)
Cloak and Dagger 1946,O 5,13:2
McBain, Diane
Ice Palace 1960,Je 30,22:1
Parrish 1961,My 5,22:1
Claudelle Inglish 1961,S 21,40:2
Caretakers, The 1963,Ag 22,19:2
Mary, Mary 1963,O 25,38:2
Distant Trumpet, A 1964,My 28,40:1
Spinout 1966,D 15,60:1
Thunder Valley 1967,S 14,55:1
Thunder Alley 1967,S 14,55:1
Maryjane 1968,Mr 14,51:4
Mini-Skirt Mob, The 1968,O 24,55:5
McBain, Ed (Original Author)
Cop Hater 1958,O 2,44:3
Mugger, The 1959,Je 25,20:7
High and Low 1963,N 27,30:1
McBan, Mickey
Temple of Venus, The 1923,N 1,24:3
Hot Water 1924,O 27,27:1
Splendid Crime, The 1925,D 17,27:1
Splendid Road, The 1926,Je 13,31:1
Sorrell and Son 1927,N 14,26:1
Father and Son 1929,Je 4,29:3
McBane, Roy
Emil 1938,Ap 15,23:2
MacBride, Donald
Misleading Lady, The 1932,Ap 9,18:1
Room Service 1938,S 22,27:1
Annabel Takes a Tour 1938,D 29,15:3
Great Man Votes, The 1939,Ja 20,15:2
Twelve Crowded Hours 1939,F 24,15:2
Story of Vernon and Irene Castle, The
  1939,Mr 31,19:2
Flying Irishman, The 1939,Ap 12,27:2
Gracie Allen Murder Case, The 1939,Je 8,31:3
Girl From Mexico, The 1939,Je 8,31:4
Girl and the Gambler, The 1939,Je 28,17:3
Charlie Chan at Treasure Island 1939,S 1,15:5
Amazing Mr Williams, The 1940,Ja 19,15:2
Saint's Double Trouble, The 1940,F 13,27:2
Northwest Passage 1940,Mr 8,25:1
Curtain Call 1940,Ap 19,25:2
My Favorite Wife 1940,My 31,15:2
Hit Parade of 1941 1940,D 5,33:2
Michael Shayne, Private Detective
  1940,D 19,33:2
High Sierra 1941,Ja 25,11:2
Topper Returns 1941,Mr 28,26:6
Love Crazy 1941,Je 6,25:5
Here Comes Mr Jordan 1941,Ag 8,13:2
You'll Never Get Rich 1941,O 24,27:2
Rise and Shine 1941,D 6,14:3
You're in the Army Now 1941,D 26,21:4
Louisiana Purchase 1942,Ja 1,37:1
Two Yanks in Trinidad 1942,Ap 6,19:4
Juke Girl 1942,Je 20,9:2
Mexican Spitfire Sees a Ghost 1942,Jl 31,11:2
My Sister Eileen 1942,O 23,15:1
Night to Remember, A 1943,Ja 1,27:2
They Got Me Covered 1943,Mr 5,20:2
Doughgirls, The 1944,Ag 31,14:1
Thin Man Goes Home, The 1945,Ja 26,16:5
She Gets her Man 1945,F 9,20:5
Out of This World 1945,Jl 25,5:2
Hold That Blonde 1945,N 8,17:2
Doll Face 1946,Mr 28,35:3
Little Giant 1946,My 9,37:5
Killers, The 1946,Ag 29,24:2
Time of Their Lives, The 1946,N 28,40:2
Buck Privates Come Home 1947,Ap 12,11:3
Egg and I, The 1947,Ap 25,29:2
Good News 1947,D 5,33:2
Texas Carnival 1951,O 13,9:1
Seven Year Itch, The 1955,Je 4,9:1
McBride, Patricia
Midsummer Night's Dream, A 1967,Ap 18,32:1
McBride, Sue
Betrayal, The 1948,Je 26,10:5
McCabe, Frank
Ramparts We Watch, The 1940,S 20,27:1
McCabe, Leo
Informer, The 1935,My 10,25:2
Beloved Enemy 1936,D 26,15:2

Quare Fellow 1963,F 20,6:1
McCall, George (Producer)
Street Corner 1948,D 4,9:4
McCall, June
Tattered Dress, The 1957,Mr 15,22:3
McCall, Mary C Jr (Original Author)
It's Tough to be Famous 1932,Ap 9,18:1
Scarlet Dawn 1932,N 4,25:4
Desirable 1934,S 15,20:5
McCall, Mary C Jr (Screenwriter)
Babbitt 1934,D 17,24:2
Secret Bride, The 1935,F 2,10:1
Woman in Red, The 1935,Mr 23,11:3
Dr Socrates 1935,O 3,29:2
Midsummer Night's Dream, A 1935,O 10,31:1
Craig's Wife 1936,O 2,29:3
Women of Glamour 1937,Mr 6,10:1
I Promise to Pay 1937,Ap 26,15:2
It's all Yours 1938,Ja 7,15:3
Breaking the Ice 1938,S 23,35:3
Dramatic School 1938,D 9,31:2
Maisie 1939,Je 23,23:1
Congo Maisie 1940,F 8,18:4
Gold Rush Maisie 1940,S 2,19:2
Maisie Was a Lady 1941,F 13,25:2
Ringside Maisie 1941,Ag 1,11:2
Kathleen 1941,D 19,35:3
Maisie Gets her Man 1942,Jl 16,23:2
Swing Shift Maisie 1943,S 10,29:2
Sullivans, The 1944,F 10,19:2
Maisie Goes to Reno 1944,S 29,18:1
Keep Your Powder Dry 1945,Mr 12,22:6
Mr Belvedere Goes to College 1949,Ap 16,11:2
Dancing in the Dark 1949,D 3,8:6
Thunderbirds 1953,Mr 12,24:4
McCall, Mitzi
You're Never too Young 1955,Ag 26,10:2
McCall, Sidney (Original Author)
Breath of the Gods, The 1920,Jl 26,9:5
McCallin, Clement
Stolen Life 1939,Je 15,27:2
Edward my Son 1949,Je 3,21:2
Murder in the Cathedral 1952,Mr 26,35:2
McCallion, James
Boy Slaves 1939,F 9,17:3
Vera Cruz 1954,D 27,22:4
PT 109 1963,Je 27,23:1
McCallister, Bud
Over my Dead Body 1942,D 26,15:2
McCallister, Lon
Stage Door Canteen 1943,Je 25,13:2
Home in Indiana 1944,Je 22,23:1
Winged Victory 1944,D 21,16:2
Red House, The 1947,Mr 17,27:2
Thunder in the Valley 1947,N 28,30:1
Scudda-Hoo! Scudda-Hay! 1948,Ap 15,31:1
Big Cat, The 1949,Jl 29,12:2
Story of Seabiscuit, The 1949,N 12,8:4
Yank in Korea, A 1951,Ap 2,29:2
McCallum, Clement
Story of Robin Hood, The 1952,Je 27,18:3
McCallum, David
Prelude to Fame 1950,N 10,35:3
Jungle Fighters 1962,Mr 15,28:2
Freud 1962,D 13,37:1
Great Escape, The 1963,Ag 8,19:1
Greatest Story Ever Told, The 1965,F 16,40:2
Around the World Under the Sea 1966,Jl 21,20:2
One Spy too Many 1966,D 8,64:1
Three Bites of the Apple 1967,My 25,54:2
Sol Madrid 1968,Je 14,43:1
McCallum, John
Bush Christmas 1947,N 27,50:4
It Always Rains on Sunday 1949,F 14,15:5
Miranda 1949,Ap 25,20:2
Woman in Question, The 1952,F 19,24:2
Valley of the Eagles 1952,Ap 11,19:2
Melba 1953,Je 25,23:1
Long Memory, The 1953,Jl 27,15:2
Trent's Last Case 1953,N 27,99:9
Trouble in the Glen 1955,Ap 11,29:2
McCallum, Neil
Devil's Disciple, The 1959,Ag 21,12:1
Lisa 1962,My 25,28:1
Woman Who Wouldn't Die, The 1965,Je 10,38:1
Lost Continent, The 1968,Je 20,50:2
McCambridge, Mercedes
All the King's Men 1949,N 9,37:2
Inside Straight 1951,Mr 16,34:2
Lightning Strikes Twice 1951,Ap 13,18:7
Screen, The 1951,Ap 23,21:2
Johnny Guitar 1954,My 28,19:2
Giant 1956,O 11,51:1
Farewell to Arms, A 1958,Ja 25,14:1
Suddenly, Last Summer 1959,D 23,22:1
Cimarron 1961,F 17,12:2
Angel Baby 1961,O 5,43:1
Maccan, Ruggero (Screenwriter)
Vista, La; Visit, The 1966,Ag 10,32:1
MacCandless, R H
Luck of the Irish, The 1937,Ja 16,21:1

McCann, Chuck
Heart is a Lonely Hunter, The 1968,Ag 1,24:1
McCann, Donal
Fighting Prince of Donegal, The 1966,N 10,64:1
McCann, Doreen
From This Day Forward 1946,Ap 20,16:2
Sister Kenny 1946,S 30,21:2
Guilt of Janet Ames, The 1947,My 23,31:2
Mary Ryan, Detective 1949,N 4,33:3
Love Is Better Than Ever 1952,Mr 4,23:2
McCann, Henry
No Time for Sergeants 1958,My 30,13:2
McCann, William (Director)
Frontier Badmen 1943,Ag 14,12:8
McCardle, Mickey
Fighter Squadron 1948,N 20,9:2
McCarey, Leo (Director)
Sophomore, The 1929,Ag 24,11:5
Let's Go Native 1930,Ag 30,7:4
Shepper - Newfounder, The 1930,D 25,31:5
Indiscreet 1931,My 7,21:4
Kid From Spain, The 1932,N 18,23:2
Duck Soup 1933,N 23,24:2
Six of a Kind 1934,Mr 10,18:3
Belle of the Nineties 1934,S 22,12:2
Ruggles of Red Gap 1935,Mr 7,26:1
Milky Way, The 1936,Mr 26,27:2
Make Way for Tomorrow 1937,My 10,23:1
Awful Truth, The 1937,N 5,19:3
Love Affair 1939,Mr 17,25:2
Once Upon a Honeymoon 1942,N 13,28:1
Going my Way 1944,My 3,25:2
Bells of St Mary's, The 1945,D 7,26:2
Good Sam 1948,S 17,28:2
My Son John 1952,Ap 9,27:1
Affair to Remember, An 1957,Jl 20,8:5
Rally Round the Flag Boys! 1958,D 24,2:7
Satan Never Sleeps 1962,F 22,20:1
McCarey, Leo (Original Author)
Cowboy and the Lady, The 1938,N 25,19:3
Love Affair 1939,Mr 17,25:2
My Favorite Wife 1940,My 31,15:2
Once Upon a Honeymoon 1942,N 13,28:1
Going my Way 1944,My 3,25:2
Good Sam 1948,S 17,28:2
My Son John 1952,Ap 9,27:1
Affair to Remember, An 1957,Jl 20,8:5
Move Over Darling 1963,D 26,33:1
McCarey, Leo (Producer)
Make Way for Tomorrow 1937,My 10,23:1
Love Affair 1939,Mr 17,25:2
Once Upon a Honeymoon 1942,N 13,28:1
Going my Way 1944,My 3,25:2
Bells of St Mary's, The 1945,D 7,26:2
Good Sam 1948,S 17,28:2
My Son John 1952,Ap 9,27:1
Rally Round the Flag Boys! 1958,D 24,2:7
Satan Never Sleeps 1962,F 22,20:1
McCarey, Leo (Screenwriter)
My Son John 1952,Ap 9,27:1
Affair to Remember, An 1957,Jl 20,8:5
Rally Round the Flag Boys! 1958,D 24,2:7
Satan Never Sleeps 1962,F 22,20:1
McCarey, Mary
Pillow Talk 1959,O 7,47:2
McCarey, Parnell
Bedazzled 1967,D 11,65:2
McCarey, Ray (Director)
Pack up Your Troubles 1932,O 1,10:4
Millions in the Air 1935,D 12,33:4
Three Cheers for Love 1936,Ag 1,16:2
Oh, Doctor 1937,Je 19,20:3
Goodbye Broadway 1938,My 14,18:1
Devil's Party, The 1938,My 31,8:3
You Can't Fool Your Wife 1940,My 24,23:4
Millionaires in Prison 1940,Jl 16,21:3
Cadet Girl 1941,D 11,39:1
Gentleman at Heart, A 1942,F 23,25:2
It Happened in Flatbush 1942,Jl 3,12:8
Atlantic City 1944,Ag 14,11:4
Falcon's Alibi, The 1946,Ap 13,23:2
Gay Intruders, The 1949,Je 28,33:4
McCarey, Ray (Original Author)
You Can't Fool Your Wife 1940,My 24,23:4
Gay Intruders, The 1949,Je 28,33:4
Maccari, Ruggero (Original Author)
Successo, Il 1965,Ap 29,40:2
Made in Italy 1967,My 1,44:2
Devil in Love, The 1968,Jl 4,13:2
Maccari, Ruggero (Screenwriter)
My Heart Sings 1954,Mr 5,15:5
Easy Life, The 1963,D 23,18:2
Let's Talk About Women 1964,S 29,52:5
Love a la Carte 1965,Ja 12,31:1
Magnificent Cuckold 1965,Ap 20,42:1
Successo, Il 1965,Ap 29,40:2
High Infidelity (The Victim); Victim, The (High
  Infidelity) 1965,Jl 2,17:1
High Infidelity (Modern People); Modern People
  (High Infidelity) 1965,Jl 2,17:1
High Infidelity (Sin in the Afternoon); Sin in the
  Afternoon (High Infidelity) 1965,Jl 2,17:1
High Infidelity (The Scandal); Scandal, The (High
  Infidelity) 1965,Jl 2,17:1

Maccari, Ruggero (Screenwriter) — Cont
Made in Italy 1967,My 1,44:2
Queens, The (Queen Sabina); Queen Sabina (The Queens) 1968,Mr 11,49:1
Devil in Love, The 1968,Jl 4,13:4
McCarron, Patricia
Sleeping Tiger, The 1954,O 9,8:7
McCarten, John (Miscellaneous)
Silken Affair, The 1957,O 31,41:1
McCarthy, Charlie
Goldwyn Follies, The 1938,F 21,15:1
Letter of Introduction 1938,S 1,17:1
You Can't Cheat an Honest Man 1939,F 20,13:2
Look Who's Laughing 1941,D 25,33:2
Here We Go Again 1942,O 12,12:3
Stage Door Canteen 1943,Je 25,13:2
Song of the Open Road 1944,Je 7,13:3
McCarthy, Cletus Rev (Narrator)
Life and Miracles of Blesses Mother Cabrini, The 1946,Jl 8,25:2
Citizen Saint 1948,My 28,28:2
McCarthy, Earl
Red Lips 1928,O 16,29:2 (In Addenda)
Sucker Money 1933,Ap 7,22:5
Cheating Blondes 1933,My 20,11:4
McCarthy, Frank (Producer)
Decision Before Dawn 1951,D 22,12:2
Sailor of the King 1953,S 3,15:2
Guide for the Married Man, A 1967,My 27,16:1
McCarthy, Gene
Last Time I Saw Archie, The 1961,My 29,9:6
McCarthy, Henry (Miscellaneous)
Song of Love, The 1929,N 14,24:3
McCarthy, Henry (Screenwriter)
Song of Love, The 1929,N 14,24:3
McCarthy, Jack (Narrator)
Spell of Ireland, The 1954,My 11,25:5
McCarthy, Joe
Safe at Home 1941,N 26,31:2
McCarthy, John (Original Author)
Conspiracy 1939,Ag 23,19:2
McCarthy, John P (Director)
Lovelorn, The 1927,D 19,30:1
MacCarthy, Johnny
Dawn Over Ireland 1938,F 19,19:2
McCarthy, Joseph (Composer)
New Movietone Follies of 1930, The 1930,Je 21,20:5
Listen, Darling 1938,N 24,37:2
Ziegfeld Girl 1941,Ap 25,17:2
Rio Rita 1942,My 8,27:3
McCarthy, Joseph (Original Author)
Irene 1940,My 24,23:3
McCarthy, Justin Huntly (Original Author)
If I Were King 1920,Ag 10,10:3
Vagabond King, The 1930,F 20,22:4
If I Were King 1930,Mr 2,IX,5:1
If I Were King 1938,S 29,31:1
Fighting O'Flynn, The 1949,F 28,16:2
Vagabond King, The 1956,S 13,39:6
McCarthy, Kevin
Death of a Salesman 1951,D 21,21:3
Drive a Crooked Road 1954,Ap 3,19:3
Gambler From Natchez, The 1954,Ag 14,8:2
Annapolis Story, An 1955,Ap 9,8:2
Nightmare 1956,My 12,12:7
Misfits, The 1961,F 2,24:2
Gathering of Eagles, A 1963,Jl 11,21:2
Affair of the Skin, An 1963,N 21,43:2
Prize, The 1964,Ja 24,21:1
Best Man, The 1964,Ap 7,29:1
Mirage 1965,My 27,28:1
Big Hand for the Little Lady, A 1966,Je 9,54:2
Hotel 1967,Ja 20,27:1
Hell With Heroes, The 1968,S 3,54:2
If He Hollers, Let Him Go 1968,O 10,59:7
McCarthy, Lin
Yellowback 1957,Ap 5,24:2
D I, The 1957,Je 6,35:2
McCarthy, Mary (Original Author)
Theodora Goes Wild 1936,N 13,27:4
Petty Girl, The 1950,Ag 18,17:2
Group, The 1966,Mr 17,35:1
McCarthy, Mary (Screenwriter)
Sister Kenny 1946,S 30,21:2
McCarthy, Michael (Director)
Operation Amsterdam 1960,Jl 7,26:1
McCarthy, Michael (Original Author)
Girl in the Canal, The 1947,O 9,32:3
McCarthy, Michael (Screenwriter)
Operation Amsterdam 1960,Jl 7,26:1
McCarthy, Molly
Great St Louis Bank Robbery, The 1960,F 4,34:1
Blast of Silence 1961,D 30,12:1
McCarthy, Myles
Day of Faith, The 1923,N 27,11:2
Captain Blood 1924,S 9,19:1
Lady, The 1925,Ja 27,11:2
McCarthy, Neil
Zulu 1964,Jl 8,38:1
McCarthy, Nobu
Geisha Boy, The 1958,D 24,00:0
Wake Me When It's Over 1960,Ap 9,17:2
Walk Like a Dragon 1960,S 16,24:1
Two Loves 1961,Je 22,23:2

McCarthy, Red
Ice-Capades 1941,S 25,29:1
McCarthy, Senator (Miscellaneous)
Point of Order 1964,Ja 15,27:2
McCartney, Paul
Hard Day's Night, A 1964,Ag 12,41:1
Help! 1965,Ag 24,25:1
McCartney, Paul (Composer)
Yellow Submarine 1968,N 14,56:1
McCarty, Henry (Screenwriter)
Great Guy 1937,Ja 1,19:2
23 1/2 Hours Leave 1937,My 17,23:2
McCarty, Mary
Rebecca of Sunnybrook Farm 1938,Mr 26,12:1
Keep Smiling 1938,Ag 10,15:2
Sullivans, The 1944,F 10,19:2
French Line, The 1954,My 15,13:2
Babes in Toyland 1961,D 15,49:1
My Six Loves 1963,Ap 4,58:4
McCash Twins, The
Winter Carnival 1939,Jl 28,14:2
McCaskill, Roddy
Sitting Pretty 1948,Mr 11,35:2
Cheaper by the Dozen 1950,Ap 1,12:2
McCay, Peggy
Uncle Vanya 1958,Ap 29,26:2
Lad: A Dog 1963,My 2,40:2
FBI Code 98 1964,Ap 9,25:6
McCay, Winson (Producer)
Dream of a Rarebit Fiend 1921,S 26,18:1
Macchi, Giulio (Director)
Defend my Love; (Difendo il Mio Amore) 1959,O 8,48:7
Macchi, Giulio (Screenwriter)
Golden Coach, The 1954,Ja 22,30:2
McClain, Billie Dr
Nagana 1933,F 16,23:2
McClain, Billy
Dimples 1936,O 10,21:2
McClain, John (Screenwriter)
Turnabout 1940,Jl 27,17:6
Lady Be Good 1941,S 19,27:1
Cairo 1942,N 6,27:2
McClaren, John
Chance Meeting 1955,Ap 20,38:1
McCleery, Albert (Screenwriter)
Lady is Willing, The 1942,Ap 24,21:2
McClintic, Guthrie
On Your Back 1930,S 15,29:3
McClintic, Guthrie (Director)
Once a Sinner 1931,Ja 17,23:1
Once a Lady 1931,N 9,22:4
McClintock, Libby
Luck of Ginger Coffey, The 1964,S 22,44:1
McClintock, Poley
Varsity Show 1937,S 2,17:2
McClory, Kevin (Original Author)
Thunderball 1965,D 22,23:1
McClory, Kevin (Producer)
Thunderball 1965,D 22,23:1
McClory, Sean
Daughter of Rosie O'Grady, The 1950,Mr 31,36:2
Lorna Doone 1951,S 21,19:4
Anne of the Indies 1951,O 25,36:3
Secret Sharer, The 1953,Ja 14,27:2
Niagara 1953,Ja 22,20:3
Plunder of the Sun 1953,Ag 27,22:1
Island in the Sky 1953,S 10,22:2
Them 1954,Je 17,36:2
Ring of Fear 1954,Jl 29,18:3
Long Gray Line, The 1955,F 11,19:2
Moonfleet 1955,Je 25,9:2
Diane 1956,Ja 13,18:1
Cheyenne Autumn 1964,D 24,8:1
Follow Me, Boys! 1966,D 2,46:1
Gnome-Mobile, The 1967,Jl 20,30:2
Bandolero 1968,Jl 18,26:2
McCloskey, Richard
Manhunt in the Jungle 1958,Ap 12,13:1
MacCloy, June
Reaching for the Moon 1930,D 30,24:2
June Moon 1931,Mr 14,23:2
Big Gamble, The 1931,S 21,20:2
Go West 1941,F 21,16:2
McClung, Robert
Toast of New York, The 1937,Jl 23,16:2
McClure, Doug
Enemy Below, The 1957,D 26,23:2
Unforgiven, The 1960,Ap 7,46:1
Lively Set, The 1964,O 15,54:1
Shenandoah 1965,Jl 29,18:3
Beau Geste 1966,S 8,43:1
Nobody's Perfect 1968,Ap 4,58:3
McClure, Greg
Great John L, The 1945,Jl 9,14:6
Bury Me Dead 1947,O 25,13:3
Lulu Belle 1948,Je 21,18:3
Breakthrough 1950,N 18,10:2
Emergency Wedding 1950,D 22,19:2
McCluskey, Joyce
Outrage 1950,O 16,30:5
Blueprint for Murder, A 1953,Jl 25,8:2
Night Holds Terror, The 1955,S 15,39:2

McCollough, Philo
Winds of Chance 1925,Ag 17,10:3
Warming Up 1928,Jl 16,25:3
Tarzan, The Fearless 1933,Ag 12,14:3
McCollum, Warren
Great Commandment, The 1942,O 17,11:1
McComas, Kendall
Daddy Long Legs 1931,Je 6,15:5
Spider, The 1931,S 5,7:4
McConnell, Fred (Original Author)
Swamp Woman 1941,D 27,15:2
McConnell, Gladys
Three's a Crowd 1927,O 3,20:1
Chaser, The 1928,Ap 10,33:2
Parade of the West 1930,Mr 3,18:4
McConnell, Gordon (Original Author)
When Thief Meets Thief 1937,Je 15,26:2
McConnell, Keith
Kind Lady 1951,Ag 8,21:2
Mutiny on the Bounty 1962,N 9,31:2
McConnell, Lulu
Stage Struck 1936,S 28,14:4
McConnor, Vincent (Screenwriter)
Jigsaw 1949,My 30,9:4
McConnville, Bernard (Original Author)
Trapped by G-Men 1937,N 4,29:1
McConville, Bernard (Original Author)
I Cover the War 1937,Ag 2,10:2
Call the Mesquiteers 1938,Mr 19,11:2
Racketeers of the Range 1939,Je 8,31:4
Cherokee Strip 1940,N 4,23:2
McConville, Bernard (Screenwriter)
Old Swimmin' Hole, The 1921,F 28,16:2
Connecticut Yankee in King Arthur's Court, A 1921,Mr 15,14:3
Shame 1921,Ag 1,8:3 (Incorrect in this edition; use 1921,Ag 1,6:4 elsewhere)
Monte Cristo 1922,Ag 15,20:3
Quincy Adams Sawyer 1922,D 18,22:2
Cherokee Strip 1940,N 4,23:2
McCoo, Arthur
Eetrayal, The 1948,Je 26,10:5
McCorkindale, Don
We're Going to Be Rich 1938,Jl 4,10:2
McCormack, Frank
Case of Becky, The 1921,O 10,16:1
Case of Sergeant Grischa, The 1930,Mr 8,21:1
Brothers 1930,N 15,15:3
McCormack, Hugh
Nix on Dames 1929,N 23,18:5
McCormack, John
Song O' my Heart 1930,Mr 12,32:6
Wings of the Morning 1937,Mr 12,19:1
MacCormack, Muriel
Sparrows 1926,S 20,21:3
King of Kings, The 1927,Ap 20,29:2
Dynamite 1929,D 28,11:1
McCormack, Patty
Bad Seed, The 1956,S 13,39:6
Kathy O' 1958,S 25,29:2
All Mine to Give 1959,Ag 4,32:5
Adventures of Huckleberry Fin, The 1960,Ag 4,17:1
Explosive Generation, The 1962,F 15,24:2
Young Runaways, The 1968,S 12,54:3
Mini-Skirt Mob, The 1968,O 24,55:5
Born Wild 1968,D 12,62:6
McCormack, Patty (Narrator)
Snow Queen, The 1960,Ap 14,34:1
McCormic, Mary
Paddy the Next Best Thing 1933,Ag 25,12:2
McCormick, Alyce
Reno 1930,N 4,36:1
McCormick, F J
Plough and the Stars, The 1937,Ja 29,15:1
Odd Man Out 1947,Ap 24,30:2
Hungry Hill 1947,O 11,11:2
McCormick, Frank
Untitled-Baseball Technique 1941,Ja 17,11:3
McCormick, Joe
On the Beach 1959,D 18,34:1
McCormick, John (Screenwriter)
Victim 1962,F 6,27:2
7 Women 1966,My 5,59:1
Walk in the Shadow 1966,S 12,52:5
McCormick, Langdon (Original Author)
Storm, The 1930,Ag 23,7:3
McCormick, Megan
Greetings 1968,D 16,61:2
McCormick, Merrill
Romance of Rio Grande 1929,N 9,22:5
New Adventures of Tarzan, The 1935,O 15,19:3
McCormick, Myron
Winterset 1936,D 4,31:1
One Third of a Nation 1939,F 11,13:2
Fight for Life, The 1940,Mr 7,19:2
China Girl 1943,Ja 21,27:2
Jigsaw 1949,My 30,9:4
Jolson Sings Again 1949,Ag 18,16:6
Three for the Show 1955,F 25,16:1
Not as a Stranger 1955,Je 29,24:1
No Time for Sergeants 1958,My 30,13:2
Man Who Understood, The 1959,O 3,14:7

McCormick, Myron— Cont
Hustler, The 1961,S 27,35:1
McCormick, S Barret (Original Author)
False Fronts 1922,Je 5,16:2
McCormick, William
Trail of the Lonesome Pine, The 1936,F 20,23:5
McCormick, William Merrill
Tundra 1930,D 3,31:2
McCowan, Alec
Cruel Sea, The 1953,Ag 11,18:5
Time Without Pity 1957,N 23,11:2
Midsummer Night's Dream, A 1961,D 19,39:1
Loneliness of the Long Distance Runner, The 1962,O 9,44:1
Devil's Own, The 1967,Mr 16,53:2
McCown, Frank
Bullfighters, The 1945,My 12,10:3
McCoy, D'Arcy
Flaming Forest, The 1926,N 22,28:3
McCoy, Frances
Wild Company 1930,Jl 19,7:5
McCoy, Homer (Narrator)
Cinerama's Russian Adventure 1966,Ap 14,42:1
McCoy, Horace (Miscellaneous)
Trail of the Lonesome Pine, The 1936,F 20,23:5
Great Guy 1937,Ja 1,19:2
McCoy, Horace (Original Author)
Parole 1936,Je 27,21:1
King of the Newsboys 1938,Ap 2,18:2
Flight for Freedom 1943,Ap 16,24:2
Kiss Tomorrow Goodbye 1950,Ag 5,9:2
Turning Point, The 1952,N 15,15:2
Bad for Each Other 1953,D 24,9:3
McCoy, Horace (Screenwriter)
Parole 1936,Je 27,21:1
Fatal Lady 1936,Jl 11,11:3
Dangerous to Know 1938,Mr 11,15:4
Hunted Men 1938,My 21,9:2
Persons in Hiding 1939,Mr 2,19:2
Undercover Doctor 1939,Je 1,31:2
Island of Lost Men 1939,Ag 17,16:3
Parole Fixer 1940,Ap 18,28:5
Women Without Names 1940,My 9,26:4
Queen of the Mob 1940,Jl 1,23:2
Texas Rangers Ride Again 1941,Ja 9,27:4
Wild Geese Calling 1941,Ag 30,10:2
Texas 1941,O 17,27:3
Valley of the Sun 1942,Mr 19,29:2
Gentleman Jim 1942,N 26,40:3
Appointment in Berlin 1943,Jl 17,8:2
Fabulous Texan, The 1947,D 26,22:5
Fireball, The 1950,N 10,35:4
Lusty Men, The 1952,O 25,12:6
Montana Belle 1952,N 8,9:2
Bad for Each Other 1953,D 24,9:3
Dangerous Mission 1954,Mr 6,13:5
McCoy, Ruby
Broadway 1929,My 28,36:2
McCoy, Tim
Around the World in 80 Days 1956,O 18,37:1
McCracken, Esther (Original Author)
Quiet Wedding 1941,D 29,27:4
Quiet Week-End 1948,Ag 20,13:2
Weaker Sex, The 1949,Jl 11,13:2
McCracken, Esther (Screenwriter)
Weaker Sex, The 1949,Jl 11,13:2
McCracken, Harold
Explorers of the World 1931,D 18,29:3
McCracken, Joan
Hollywood Canteen 1944,D 16,19:2
Good News 1947,D 5,33:2
MCCREA
See Also MACRAE, MCRAE
McCrea, Ann
Will Success Spoil Rock Hunter 1957,S 12,37:5
Kiss Them for Me 1957,N 9,31:2
China Doll 1958,D 4,52:1
McCrea, Jody
First Texan, The 1956,Je 23,20:2
Lafayette Escadrille 1958,Ap 19,10:4
Beach Party 1963,S 26,40:2
Muscle Beach Party 1964,My 28,40:1
Glory Stompers, The 1968,Mr 28,52:4
McCrea, Joel
Penrod and Sam 1923,Je 25,16:5
Jazz Age, The 1929,Ja 7,36:2
Dynamite 1929,D 28,11:1
Silver Horde, The 1930,O 25,20:6
Lightnin' 1930,N 29,21:4
Once a Sinner 1931,Ja 17,23:1
Kept Husbands 1931,Mr 24,31:2
Born to Love 1931,Ap 25,23:4
Common Law, The 1931,Jl 20,20:4
Girls About Town 1931,N 2,27:1
Business and Pleasure 1932,F 13,23:4
Lost Squadron, The 1932,Mr 11,15:4
Bird of Paradise 1932,S 10,18:5
Most Dangerous Game, The 1932,N 21,21:1
Rockabye 1932,D 5,21:2
Sport Parade, The 1932,D 17,22:3
Silver Cord, The 1933,My 5,18:1
Bed of Roses 1933,Je 30,20:3
One Man's Journey 1933,S 1,15:2
Chance at Heaven 1933,D 26,19:3

Gambling Lady 1934,Ap 5,25:2
Half a Sinner 1934,Je 23,16:5
Richest Girl in the World, The 1934,S 21,29:2
Private Worlds 1935,Mr 28,25:2
Our Little Girl 1935,Je 7,24:4
Barbary Coast 1935,O 14,21:1
Splendor 1935,N 23,23:2
These Three 1936,Mr 19,22:4
Two in a Crowd 1936,O 5,25:1
Adventure in Manhattan 1936,O 23,27:5
Come and Get It 1936,N 12,31:1
Banjo on My Knee 1936,D 12,15:1
Internes Can't Take Money 1937,My 6,23:2
Woman Chases Man 1937,Je 11,26:2
Dead End 1937,Ag 25,25:1
Wells Fargo 1937,D 30,15:2
Wells Fargo 1938,Ja 16,X,5:1 (In Addenda)
Three Blind Mice 1938,Je 18,18:2
Youth Takes a Fling 1938,O 17,12:1
Union Pacific 1939,My 11,31:2
They Shall Have Music 1939,Jl 26,17:2
Espionage Agent 1939,S 23,22:2
He Married his Wife 1940,Ja 20,11:2
Primrose Path 1940,Mr 23,16:2
Foreign Correspondent 1940,Ag 28,15:2
Reaching for the Sun 1941,My 8,21:1
Sullivan's Travels 1942,Ja 29,25:2
Great Man's Lady, The 1942,Ap 30,14:3
Palm Beach Story, The 1942,D 11,33:1
More the Merrier, The 1943,My 14,17:1
Buffalo Bill 1944,Ap 20,22:6
Great Moment, The 1944,N 13,15:2
Unseen, The 1945,My 14,20:5
Virginian, The 1946,My 18,22:2
Ramrod 1947,Je 30,25:6
Four Faces West 1948,Ag 4,18:3
South of St Louis 1949,Mr 7,17:2
Colorado Territory 1949,Je 25,8:6
Outriders, The 1950,Mr 9,25:2
Saddle Tramp 1950,N 24,31:4
Stars in my Crown 1950,D 22,19:1
Frenchie 1951,F 12,19:2
Cattle Drive 1951,Ag 9,17:5
San Francisco Story, The 1952,My 10,16:4
Lone Hand 1953,Je 27,7:2
First Texan, The 1956,Je 23,20:2
Oklahoman, The 1957,My 15,39:1
Trooper Hook 1957,Jl 13,11:2
Ride the High Country 1962,Je 21,26:2
McCrindle, Alex
I Believe in You 1953,My 5,34:3
McCullers, Carson (Original Author)
Member of the Wedding, The 1952,D 31,10:2
Reflections in a Golden Eye 1967,O 12,59:1
Heart is a Lonely Hunter, The 1968,Ag 1,24:1
McCulley, Johnston (Original Author)
Mark of Zorro, The 1920,N 29,20:3
Ice Flood, The 1926,O 19,26:2
Rose of the Rio Grande 1938,Jl 9,10:3
Mark of Zorro, The 1940,N 4,23:2
Mark of the Renegade 1951,S 7,24:2
Sign of Zorro, The 1961,S 5,37:6
McCullough, Philo
Soldiers of Fortune 1919,N 24,13:1
Trilby 1923,Jl 30,11:4
Daughters of Today 1924,Mr 4,17:1
Wife of the Centaur, The 1925,Ja 7,33:5
Dick Turpin 1925,Ja 26,14:1
Boomerang, The 1925,Jl 1,16:1
Everybody's Acting 1926,N 8,19:2
Ladies at Play 1926,N 16,25:3
Easy Pickings 1927,Mr 25,25:3
Smile, Brother, Smile 1927,Ag 29,21:1
We're all Gamblers 1927,O 12,30:6
Night Flyer, The 1928,Mr 13,23:3
Lost in the Arctic 1928,Jl 26,25:3
Leatherneck, The 1929,Ap 22,23:1
On the Border 1930,F 3,17:1
Sky Spider, The 1931,Ag 31,11:5
Lawless Nineties, The 1936,Je 29,11:1
MCCUNE
See Also MCEWEN
McCune, Hank (Director)
Wetbacks 1956,My 5,13:2
McCune, Hank (Producer)
Wetbacks 1956,My 5,13:2
McCurdy, Anna Marie
Crowning Experience, The 1960,O 24,25:3
McCurdy, Geoge
Crowning Experience, The 1960,O 24,25:3
McCurry, John
Last Mile, The 1959,F 19,27:1
Pawnbroker, The 1965,Ap 21,51:1
McCurry, Samuel J
Across the River 1965,Ap 27,27:1
McCutcheon, Bill
Santa Claus Conquers the Martians 1964,D 17,50:2
McCutcheon, Dick (Narrator)
North Vietnam-A Personal Report 1968,Ja 23,79:1

McCutcheon, George Barr (Original Author)
City of Masks, The 1920,Jl 12,12:4
Fast Worker, The 1924,N 12,13:1
Graustark 1925,S 28:2
Miss Brewster's Millions 1926,Mr 8,17:1
Beverly of Graustark 1926,Ap 19,24:3
Brewster's Millions 1945,Ap 27,23:2
McCutcheon, Wallace
Virtuous Vamp, A 1919,N 17,20:1
McDaniel, Etta
Lawless Nineties, The 1936,Je 29,11:1
Devil is a Sissy, The 1936,O 17,21:2
Magnificent Brute, The 1936,O 24,23:1
Keep Smiling 1938,Ag 10,15:2
Sergeant Madden 1939,Mr 24,27:2
Life With Henry 1941,F 6,25:2
Pittsburgh Kid, The 1941,S 23,27:4
Great Man's Lady, The 1942,Ap 30,14:3
American Empire 1943,Ja 14,25:4
Johnny Doughboy 1943,My 6,25:3
Son of Dracula 1943,N 6,16:4
McDaniel, George
Barefoot Boy, The 1923,N 11,6:1
McDaniel, Hattie
Judge Priest 1934,O 12,33:1
Little Colonel, The 1935,Mr 22,26:2
Alice Adams 1935,Ag 16,11:3
Gentle Julia 1936,Ap 11,19:1
Show Boat 1936,My 15,29:4
Hearts Divided 1936,Je 13,13:1
High Tension 1936,Jl 11,11:4
Star for a Night 1936,S 5,7:2
Valiant Is the Word for Carrie 1936,O 8,27:2
Crime Nobody Saw, The 1937,Ap 5,17:2
Saratoga 1937,Jl 23,16:3
Nothing Sacred 1937,N 26,27:2
45 Fathers 1937,D 11,22:2
True Confession 1937,D 16,35:2
Battle of Broadway 1938,Ap 25,19:2
Shopworn Angel, The 1938,Jl 8,11:2
Mad Miss Manton, The 1938,O 21,27:2
Shining Hour, The 1939,Ja 20,15:2
Zenobia 1939,My 15,15:2
Gone With the Wind 1939,D 20,31:2
Maryland 1940,Jl 13,16:5
Great Lie, The 1941,Ap 12,19:2
Affectionally Yours 1941,My 24,18:2
Male Animal, The 1942,Mr 28,11:1
In This our Life 1942,My 9,10:2
George Washington Slept Here 1942,O 31,11:1
Johnny Come Lately 1943,S 24,26:1
Thank Your Lucky Stars 1943,O 2,19:2
Since You Went Away 1944,Jl 21,16:2
Janie 1944,Ag 5,16:2
3 Is a Family 1944,D 20,20:3
Margie 1946,O 17,28:3
Never Say Goodbye 1946,N 23,12:2
Song of the South 1946,N 28,40:2
Flame, The 1948,F 20,19:2
Mickey 1948,Jl 19,11:2
Family Honeymoon 1949,F 25,28:2
McDaniel, Sam
Hearts Divided 1936,Je 13,13:1
Captains Courageous 1937,My 12,27:1
Gambling Ship 1939,Ja 21,19:2
Great Lie, The 1941,Ap 12,19:2
Broadway Limited 1941,Je 16,11:6
Bad Men of Missouri 1941,Ag 16,18:2
All Through the Night 1942,Ja 24,13:2
I Was Framed 1942,Je 12,16:6
Foxes of Harrow, The 1947,S 25,35:4
Flamingo Road 1949,My 7,10:2
McDaniels, Eda
House Across the Bay, The 1940,Mr 22,23:2
McDarby, John
You Can't Beat the Irish 1952,My 1,34:4
McDermott, Hugh
Revenge of General Ling, The 1938,F 21,15:1
Mister V 1942,F 13,24:4
Young Mr Pitt, The 1943,Mr 11,17:1
Seventh Veil, The 1945,D 26,15:1
Good Time Girl 1950,S 25,18:5
No Orchids for Miss Blandish 1951,F 23,33:2
Lilli Marlene 1952,Mr 29,19:2
Trent's Last Case 1953,N 27,99:9
Night People 1954,Mr 13,11:2
Fire over Africa 1954,N 22,29:5
McDermott, John (Original Author)
She's a Shiek 1927,N 21,20:1
McDermott, John (Screenwriter)
Senorita 1927,My 9,26:4
Cohens and the Kelleys In Scotland, The 1930,Mr 10,24:1
College Rhythm 1934,N 24,19:1
Three Wise Fools 1946,S 27,19:2
McDermott, John F (Director)
Her Temporary Husband 1924,Ja 1,20:1
McDermott, John W (Original Author)
Fast Workers 1933,Mr 20,18:2
McDermott, Marc
Tragedy of the East Side, A 1920,Ag 24,6:2
Footlights 1921,S 9,IV,4:1
Lucretia Lombard 1923,D 17,23:1
Three Miles Out 1924,Ja 1,20:1

McDermott, Marc— Cont

Sea Hawk, The 1924,Je 3,22:1
This Woman 1924,O 21,21:3
He Who Gets Slapped 1924,N 10,20:1
Lady, The 1925,Ja 27,11:2
Siege 1925,Je 16,24:1
Goose Woman, The 1925,Ag 4,14:3
Graustark 1925,S 8,29:1
Kiki 1926,Ap 6,26:4
Temptress, The 1926,O 11,18:1
Taxi Dancer, The 1927,Mr 8,18:4
Resurrection 1927,My 17,27:2
Road to Romance, The 1927,O 10,24:1
Man, Woman and Sin 1927,D 5,26:2
Glorious Betsy 1928,Ap 27,16:4
Yellow Lily, The 1928,My 21,25:1
Whip, The 1928,S 17,28:2

McDevitt, Ruth

Guy Who Came Back, The 1951,Ag 17,13:2
Parent Trap, The 1961,Je 22,23:1
Boys' Night Out 1962,Je 22,15:2
Birds, The 1963,Ap 1,5:5 (Incorrect in this
   edition; use 1963,Ap 1,54:1 elsewhere)
Love Is a Ball 1963,Ap 25,38:1
Dear Heart 1965,Mr 8,33:1
Shakiest Gun in the West, The 1968,Jl 11,30:1

MacDonald, Archer

Latin Lovers 1953,Ag 13,17:2
Three Sailors and a Girl 1953,N 23,32:2
Student Prince, The 1954,Je 16,18:2
Anything Goes 1956,Mr 22,38:1

MacDonald, Audrey

Naked Maja, The 1959,Je 11,36:2

MacDonald, Ballard (Composer)

Rose of Washington Square 1939,My 6,21:2
Lullaby of Broadway 1951,Mr 27,35:2

MacDonald, Betty (Original Author)

Egg and I, The 1947,Ap 25,29:2
Ma and Pa Kettle 1949,Ag 12,13:2

McDonald, Charles

Salvation Neil 1921,Je 27,16:3
Irish Luck 1925,N 24,28:4

MacDonald, David (Director)

This Man Is News 1939,Jl 20,16:4
Dead Men Tell no Tales 1939,Jl 24,9:2
Spies of the Air 1940,Jl 4,12:3
This England 1941,N 18,33:2
Desert Victory 1943,Ap 14,1:6
Brothers, The 1948,My 5,30:4
Snowbound 1949,F 21,20:2
Christopher Columbus 1949,O 13,33:2
Good Time Girl 1950,S 25,18:5
Bad Lord Byron, The 1952,Mr 20,37:5
Cairo Road 1952,N 1,17:2

MacDonald, David Lieut Col (Producer)

Burma Victory 1949,Ap 2,12:2

MacDonald, Donald

String Beans 1918,D 30,7:3
Woman in the Suitcase, The 1920,Ja 12,7:1
Village Sleuth 1920,S 13,12:1
Midnight Bell, A 1921,Ag 8,12:2
Lorna Doone 1922,D 4,20:2
If Marriage Fails 1925,Je 2,16:3
These Thirty Years 1934,My 24,28:3
Her Twelve Men 1954,Ag 12,23:2
Kentuckian, The 1955,S 2,13:2
Great Day in the Morning 1956,My 19,12:6

MacDonald, Donald (Director)

Season, The 1966,N 25,49:1

MacDonald, Edmund

Prison Break 1938,Jl 13,17:4
Black Friday 1940,Mr 22,23:3
Sailor's Lady 1940,Je 29,12:2
Gay Caballero, The 1940,O 25,25:3
Bride Wore Crutches, The 1941,My 26,15:3
Great Guns 1941,O 3,27:2
Texas 1941,O 17,27:3
To the Shores of Tripoli 1942,Mr 26,27:2
Strange Case of Dr Rx 1942,Mr 28,11:2
Whispering Ghosts 1942,My 18,19:4
Flying Tigers 1942,O 23,25:2
Who Done It 1942,D 3,35:2
Hi 'Ya Chum 1943,F 26,17:4
Corvette K-225 1943,O 21,30:1
Hold That Blonde 1945,N 8,17:2
Shoot to Kill 1947,My 17,8:5
That Lady in Ermine 1948,Ag 25,31:2
Red Canyon 1949,Ap 28,28:2

McDonald, Francis

Nomads of the North 1920,S 27,18:1
Monte Cristo 1922,Ag 15,20:3
Trilby 1923,Jl 30,11:4
Going Up 1923,O 10,16:2
East of Broadway 1924,N 12,13:1
So This Is Marriage 1924,D 23,16:2
Go Straight 1925,O 6,30:1
Satan in Sables 1925,O 15,27:3
Yankee Senor, The 1926,Ja 28,14:4
Puppets 1926,Je 21,17:2
Battling Butler 1926,Ag 23,9:1
Temptress, The 1926,O 11,18:1
Notorious Lady, The 1927,Ap 11,18:3
Girl in Every Port, A 1928,F 20,14:1
Legion of the Condemned, The 1928,Mr 19,26:2

Drag Net, The 1928,Je 4,13:2
Carnation Kid, The 1929,F 25,16:1
Burning Up 1930,F 8,12:5
Dangerous Paradise 1930,F 16,III,8:1
Runaway Bride 1930,My 17,21:2
Safety in Numbers 1930,My 31,19:4
Brothers 1930,N 15,15:3
Morocco 1930,N 17,29:1
Gang Buster, The 1931,Ja 24,15:1
Lawyer's Secret, The 1931,My 30,9:2
Woman From Monte Carlo, The 1931,D 31,17:6
Devil Is Driving, The 1932,D 16,25:5
Terror Trail 1933,F 11,11:3
Broadway Bad 1933,Mr 6,16:6
Trumpet Blows, The 1934,Ap 14,18:2
Star of Midnight 1935,Ap 12,26:5
Prisoner of Shark Island, The 1936,F 13,25:2
Robin Hood of El Dorado, The 1936,Mr 14,10:1
Under Two Flags 1936,My 1,19:1
Devil's Playground 1937,F 15,12:5
Parole Racket 1937,Mr 8,22:1
Born Reckless 1937,Jl 30,22:6
Love Under Fire 1937,Ag 28,8:2
Gun Law 1938,Je 24,15:1
Union Pacific 1939,My 11,31:2
Bad Lands 1939,Ag 9,15:2
Light That Failed, The 1939,D 25,19:1
Green Hell 1940,Ja 30,15:6
Sea Hawk, The 1940,Ag 10,16:2
North West Mounted Police 1940,N 7,33:2
Devil's Pipeline, The 1940,N 11,22:4
Sea Wolf, The 1941,Mr 26,27:3
Kid From Kansas, The 1941,D 2,29:4
Kansan, The 1943,O 1,15:3
Strange Confession 1945,N 8,17:3
Tangier 1946,Je 7,II,16:4
Perils of Pauline, The 1947,Jl 10,17:2
Live Today for Tomorrow 1948,D 6,29:2
Samson and Delilah 1949,D 22,29:2
Red Mountain 1952,Ap 26,19:2
Rancho Notorious 1952,My 15,39:5

McDonald, Frank (Director)

Broadway Hostess 1935,D 16,23:3
Murder of Dr Harrigan, The 1936,Ja 21,27:5
Boulder Dam 1936,Mr 30,17:5
Treachery Rides the Range 1936,My 30,7:3
Murder by an Aristocrat 1936,Je 13,13:2
Big Noise, The 1936,Jl 4,18:3
Love Begins at 20 1936,S 19,20:1
Smart Blonde 1937,Ja 9,21:1
Midnight Court 1937,Mr 4,27:3
Her Husband's Secretary 1937,Mr 20,23:6
Fly Away Baby 1937,Jl 9,18:2
Dance Charlie Dance 1937,Ag 26,25:2
Torchy Blane, The Adventurous Blonde
   1937,D 18,18:1

MacDonald, Frank (Director)

Over the Wall 1938,Mr 28,19:2

McDonald, Frank (Director)

Flirting With Fate 1938,D 15,35:3
They Asked for It 1939,Je 30,17:4
No Hands on the Clock 1941,D 22,24:6
One Body too Many 1944,N 25,21:2
Chicago Kid, The 1945,F 12,24:3
My Pal Trigger 1946,Ag 17,16:3
Hit Parade of 1947 1947,My 5,32:8
Sioux City Sue 1947,Jl 23,19:3
Ringside 1949,S 17,10:8
Purple Gang, The 1960,Ja 23,15:5

McDonald, George

Four Faces West 1948,Ag 4,18:3

McDonald, Gordon

Thirty Seconds Over Tokyo 1944,N 16,19:1

McDonald, Grace

What's Cookin' 1942,F 26,15:5
Give Out, Sisters 1942,Ag 28,22:3
It Ain't Hay 1943,Mr 11,17:3
Gals, Inc 1943,Ag 13,13:4
Flesh and Fantasy 1943,N 18,29:1
Crazy House 1943,D 16,33:3
Gung Ho! 1944,Ja 26,23:2
Follow the Boys 1944,Ap 26,24:6
Murder in the Blue Room 1944,O 28,12:2
Destiny 1944,F 3,16:5
See my Lawyer 1945,My 4,23:4

MacDonald, Grant

Convicted 1938,Ag 22,9:3

McDonald, Hugh

Union Pacific 1939,My 11,31:2

MacDonald, Ian

Swamp Woman 1941,D 27,15:2
Adventures of Martin Eden 1942,Mr 16,19:2
Ramrod 1947,Je 30,25:6
16 Fathoms Deep 1948,O 7,35:2
Road House 1948,N 8,24:2
Man From Colorado 1949,Ja 21,24:3
Whirlpool 1950,Ja 14,9:2
Montana 1950,F 4,9:2
Malaya 1950,F 23,33:1
Comanche Territory 1950,Ap 8,9:3
Colt 45 1950,My 6,8:6
Lawless, The 1950,Je 23,29:2
Texas Rangers, The 1951,Jl 14,7:2

Ten Tall Men 1951,O 27,10:5
This Woman is Dangerous 1952,F 28,23:2
High Noon 1952,Jl 25,14:2
Hiawatha 1952,D 26,20:4
Savage, The 1953,Ja 2,11:1
Blowing Wild 1953,O 8,37:5
Johnny Guitar 1954,My 28,19:2
Timberjack 1955,Mr 10,33:3

MacDonald, J Farrell

Drifting 1923,Ag 20,4:2
Mademoiselle Midnight 1924,My 27,14:1
Signal Tower, The 1924,Jl 21,14:4
Iron Horse, The 1924,Ag 29,6:1
Lightnin 1925,Jl 22,14:4
Lucky Horseshoe, The 1925,Ag 18,14:3
Thank You 1925,O 6,30:1
First Year, The 1926,Mr 8,17:1
Bertha, The Sewing Machine Girl 1927,Ja 4,21:1
Ankles Preferred 1927,Ap 18,21:2
Rich but Honest 1927,My 18,29:3
Cradle Snatchers 1927,My 31,25:2
Paid to Love 1927,Jl 25,25:3
Sunrise 1927,S 24,15:3 (In Addenda)
East Side, West Side 1927,O 18,33:2
Cohens and the Kellys In Paris, The
   1928,F 6,12:3
Bringing Up Father 1928,Mr 19,26:2
Abie's Irish Rose 1928,Ap 20,26:7
4 Devils 1928,O 4,26:3
Riley, The Cop 1928,D 4,29:1
In old Arizona 1929,Ja 21,18:4
Strong Boy 1929,Ap 1,22:1
South Sea Rose 1929,D 7,19:3
Men Without Women 1930,F 1,15:1
Song O' my Heart 1930,Mr 12,32:6
Girl of the Golden West, The 1930,O 27,17:1
Truth About Youth, The 1930,D 13,22:2
Easiest Way, The 1931,F 28,15:2
River's End 1931,Mr 7,17:2
Painted Desert, The 1931,Mr 9,19:1
Woman Hungry 1931,Mr 23,24:7
Millionaire, The 1931,Ap 9,30:5
Other Men's Women 1931,Ap 20,16:3
Too Young to Marry 1931,My 4,15:3
Maltese Falcon, The 1931,My 29,26:5
Sporting Blood 1931,Ag 15,18:3
Brat, The 1931,Ag 24,13:4
Squaw Man, The 1931,S 19,10:2
Spirit of Notre Dame, The 1931,O 16,27:1
Touchdown 1931,N 16,23:1
Under Eighteen 1931,D 26,15:5
Hotel Continental 1932,Mr 21,19:5
Scandal for Sale 1932,Ap 3,26:2
Week-End Marriage 1932,Je 4,9:2
70,000 Witnesses 1932,S 3,16:2
Phantom Express, The 1932,S 20,26:3
This Sporting Age 1932,O 1,10:4
Me and my Gal 1932,D 12,18:4
No Man of her Own 1932,D 31,10:1
Big Pay-Off, The 1933,Ja 17,22:7
Iron Master, The 1933,F 4,11:3
Heritage of the Desert 1933,Mr 11,18:3
Working Man, The 1933,Ap 21,20:3
Peg o'my Heart 1933,My 20,11:4
Power and the Glory, The 1933,Ag 17,13:2
I Loved a Woman 1933,S 22,14:2
Man of Two Worlds 1934,Ja 12,29:2
Myrt and Marge 1934,Ja 17,23:2
Once to Every Woman 1934,Mr 26,22:3
Crime Doctor, The 1934,My 11,24:3
Cat's Paw, The 1934,Ag 17,12:2
Best Man Wins 1935,Ja 2,22:4
Romance in Manhattan 1935,Ja 18,29:2
Maybe It's Love 1935,F 11,14:2
Whole Town's Talking, The 1935,Mr 1,16:2
Star of Midnight 1935,Ap 12,26:5
Let 'Em Have It 1935,My 30,21:1
Our Little Girl 1935,Je 7,24:4
Front Page Woman 1935,Jl 12,15:1
Irish in US, The 1935,Ag 1,15:1
Fighting Youth 1935,N 2,13:3
Riffraff 1936,Ja 13,14:2
Exclusive Story 1936,Ja 18,19:2
Show Boat 1936,My 15,29:4
Florida Special 1936,My 29,15:2
Mysterious Crossing 1937,F 2,20:5
Silent Barriers 1937,Mr 26,25:1
Hit Parade, The 1937,My 31,11:2
Slave Ship 1937,Je 17,19:2
Slim 1937,Je 24,30:2
Roaring Timber 1937,Ag 19,23:1
Topper 1937,Ag 20,21:2
Shadows of the Orient 1937,O 11,26:6
White Banners 1938,Je 23,27:1
Crowd Roars, The 1938,Ag 5,11:1
There Goes my Heart 1938,O 14,27:1
Submarine Patrol 1938,N 19,9:2
East Side of Heaven 1939,My 5,29:3
Zenobia 1939,My 15,15:2
Susannah of the Mounties 1939,Je 24,13:2
Mickey, the Kid 1939,Jl 6,27:1

MacDonald, J Farrell — Cont
Conspiracy 1939,Ag 23,19:2
Dark Command 1940,My 11,15:2
Untamed 1940,Jl 25,14:3
Meet John Doe 1941,Mr 13,25:2
Great Lie, The 1941,Ap 12,19:2
Broadway Limited 1941,Je 16,11:6
Captains of the Clouds 1942,F 13,24:2
Little Tokyo, USA 1942,Ag 7,13:2
Miracle of Morgan's Creek, The 1944,Ja 20,15:2
Great Moment, The 1944,N 13,15:2
Tree Grows in Brooklyn, A 1945,Mr 1,25:5
Johnny Angel 1945,D 28,12:2
Pillow of Death 1946,Ja 26,19:3
Smoky 1946,Je 27,29:1
My Darling Clementine 1946,D 4,44:5
Fury at Furnace Creek 1948,Jl 12,11:2
Belle Star's Daughter 1949,Ja 10,19:2
Whispering Smith 1949,F 15,28:2
Beautiful Blonde From Bashful Bend, The
   1949,My 28,11:2
Woman on the Run 1950,N 30,24:2
Mr Belvedere Rings the Bell 1951,Ag 2,18:1
Elopement 1951,D 21,21:3
McDonald, J K (Director)
Flaming Love 1925,Ja 19,14:1
McDonald, Jack
White Circle, The 1920,Ag 23,9:2
Great Redeemer, The 1920,O 25,18:1
Lorna Doone 1922,D 4,20:2
Don Q, Son of Zorro 1925,Je 16,24:1
13 Washington Square 1928,Ja 30,18:1
Burning Daylight 1928,Ap 23,20:2
Show Boat 1929,Ap 18,32:3
Ship From Shanghai, The 1930,Ap 26,11:1
MacDonald, Jeanette
Love Parade, The 1929,N 20,32:6
Vagabond King, The 1930,F 20,22:4
Vagabond King, The 1930,Mr 2,IX,5:1
Monte Carlo 1930,Ag 28,22:4
Let's Go Native 1930,Ag 30,7:4
Lottery Bride, The 1930,N 29,21:4
Don't Bet on Women 1931,Mr 7,17:2
Annabelle's Affairs 1931,Je 29,20:3
One Hour with You 1932,Mr 24,17:5
Love Me Tonight 1932,Ag 19,20:6
Cat and the Fiddle, The 1934,F 17,20:2
Merry Widow, The 1934,O 12,33:1
Naughty Marietta 1935,Mr 23,11:2
Rose Marie 1936,F 1,9:2
San Francisco 1936,Je 27,21:1
Maytime 1937,Mr 19,27:1
Firefly, The 1937,S 2,17:2
Girl of the Golden West, The 1938,Mr 25,15:2
Sweethearts 1938,D 23,16:2
Broadway Serenade 1939,Ap 7,25:2
New Moon 1940,Jl 19,22:2
Bitter Sweet 1940,N 22,27:1
Smilin' Through 1941,D 5,29:2
I Married an Angel 1942,Jl 10,13:2
Cairo 1942,N 6,27:2
Follow the Boys 1944,Ap 26,24:6
Three Daring Daughters 1948,F 13,26:3
Sun comes up, The 1949,My 13,29:2
MacDonald, John D (Original Author)
Man Trap 1961,N 30,40:4
Cape Fear 1962,Ap 19,35:2
McDonald, Joseph
Romance of the Rio Grande 1940,D 25,33:4
MacDonald, Katherine
Squaw Man, The 1918,D 30,7:3
Woman Thou Gavest Me, The 1919,Je 9,16:3
Beauty Market, The 1920,Ja 19,16:3
Old Loves and New 1926,Ap 20,24:7
MacDonald, Kenneth
Last Mile, The 1932,Ag 26,20:3
Island Of Doomed Men 1940,Je 10,21:2
Before I Hang 1940,O 3,31:3
Devil Commands, The 1941,F 14,15:3
Mystery Ship 1941,Ag 16,18:3
Confessions of Boston Blackie 1941,D 8,31:2
Belle Star's Daughter 1949,Ja 10,19:2
Southwest Passage 1954,S 11,11:2
Return to Peyton Place 1961,My 6,26:1
McDonald, Marie
Pardon my Sarong 1942,Ag 27,15:1
Lucky Jordan 1943,Ja 25,10:8
I Love a Soldier 1944,N 2,22:2
Guest in the House 1945,F 16,19:2
It's a Pleasure 1945,My 4,23:3
Getting Gertie's Garter 1946,F 4,21:2
Living in a Big Way 1947,O 10,31:4
Once a Thief 1951,Ja 19,21:3
Geisha Boy, The 1958,D 24,00:0
McDonald, Mark (Cinematographer)
Royal Tour of Queen Elizabeth and Philip, The
   1954,Je 22,24:2
MacDonald, Mary Monica
Beautiful Blonde From Bashful Bend, The
   1949,My 28,11:2
McDonald, May
Mr Perrin and Mr Traill 1949,Ja 17,15:2

McDonald, Melbourn
Behind the Front 1926,F 10,16:2
McDonald, Moira
Return to Paradise 1953,S 11,24:2
MacDonald, Philip (Miscellaneous)
Mask of the Avenger 1951,Je 27,25:2
MacDonald, Philip (Original Author)
Lost Patrol, The 1929,D 16,34:2
Mystery of Mr X, The 1934,F 26,21:3
Lost Patrol, The 1934,Ap 2,13:2
Charlie Chan in London 1934,S 13,26:1
Menace 1934,N 22,27:2
Charlie Chan in Paris 1935,Ja 22,23:2
Princess Comes Across, The 1936,Je 4,27:2
Mr Moto Takes a Vacation 1939,Je 19,12:6
Whispering Ghosts 1942,My 18,19:4
Sahara 1943,N 12,25:2
Hour of 13, The 1952,O 28,37:1
23 Paces to Baker Street 1956,My 19,12:6
List of Adrian Messenger, The 1963,My 30,20:1
MacDonald, Philip (Screenwriter)
Mystery Woman 1935,Ja 9,22:2
Last Outpost, The 1935,O 5,18:2
Yours for the Asking 1936,Ag 20,14:2
Mysterious Mr Moto of Devil's Island
   1938,S 19,16:2
Mr Moto's Last Warning 1939,Ja 27,17:3
Blind Alley 1939,My 23,27:2
Rebecca 1940,Mr 29,25:2
Action in Arabia 1944,F 19,18:7
Body Snatcher, The 1945,My 26,18:3
Love From a Stranger 1947,N 28,30:1
Dark Past, The 1948,D 23,25:2
Man Who Cheated Himself, The 1951,F 9,21:2
Circle of Danger 1951,Jl 12,21:6
Ring of Fear 1954,Jl 29,18:3
McDonald, Ray
Life Begins for Andy Hardy 1941,Ag 22,19:4
Babes on Broadway 1942,Ja 1,37:1
Born to Sing 1942,F 19,23:2
Presenting Lily Mars 1943,Ap 30,25:3
Till the Clouds Roll By 1946,D 6,27:4
Good News 1947,D 5,33:2
There's a Girl in my Heart 1950,Ja 20,29:2
McDonald, Robert J
Adventures of Martin Eden 1942,Mr 16,19:2
MacDonald, Ross (Original Author)
Harper 1966,Mr 31,43:1
McDonald, Sandy
Dutchman 1967,F 28,32:1
MacDonald, Wallace
Leave It to Susan 1919,My 26,19:4
Spoilers, The 1923,Ag 6,14:2
Day of Faith, The 1923,N 27,11:2
Thy Name Is Woman 1924,Mr 4,17:1
Maytime 1924,Je 2,14:3
Sea Hawk, The 1924,Je 3,22:1
Love and Glory 1924,Ag 5,10:2
Roaring Rails 1924,O 15,27:3
Lady, The 1925,Ja 27,11:2
Pampered Youth 1925,F 10,20:1
Learning to Love 1925,F 23,24:1
New Lives for Old 1925,F 25,16:7
Charmer, The 1925,Ap 6,17:3
Lightnin 1925,Jl 22,14:4
Sweetie 1929,O 26,15:1
Hit the Deck 1930,Ja 15,28:6
Rogue Song, The 1930,Ja 29,26:4
Fifty Fathoms Deep 1931,S 19,10:2
MacDonald, Wallace (Producer)
Island Of Doomed Men 1940,Je 10,21:2
Glamour for Sale 1940,N 5,33:2
Devil Commands, The 1941,F 14,15:3
Harmon of Michigan 1941,O 2,29:2
Parachute Nurse 1942,Jl 27,18:2
Two Senoritas From Chicago 1943,Ag 6,10:4
My Name is Julia Ross 1945,N 9,16:3
Girl's School 1950,F 3,29:2
Beauty on Parade 1950,Ag 18,17:2
Okinawa 1952,Ap 24,38:3
Man in the Dark 1953,Ap 9,31:5
Black Dakotas, The 1954,O 2,21:2
McDonald, William
Twinkletoes 1926,D 27,20:3
MacDonald, William Colt (Original Author)
Powdersmoke Range 1936,Mr 9,20:2
McDonel, Fergus (Director)
Prelude to Fame 1950,N 10,35:3
McDonell, Gordon (Original Author)
Shadow of a Doubt 1943,Ja 13,18:2
They Won't Believe Me 1947,Jl 17,16:2
McDonnell, A C (Original Author)
Mister V 1942,F 13,24:4
McDonnell, Arch
Luck of Ginger Coffey, The 1964,S 22,44:1
MacDonnell, Colonel
Dr Jekyll and Mr Hyde 1932,Ja 2,14:2
McDonnell, G L
White Black Sheep, The 1926,D 21,20:2
MacDonnell, Kyle
Taxi 1953,Ja 22,20:3

MacDonnell, Norman (Producer)
Ballad of Josie, The 1968,Mr 14,51:2
McDonough, Glenn (Composer)
Babes in Toyland 1961,D 15,49:1
McDonough, Glenn (Original Author)
Babes in Toyland 1934,D 13,28:2
McDonough, Tom
House on Telegraph Hill, The 1951,My 14,29:1
McDonough, W S
Those Who Dance 1924,Je 30,16:1
McDougal, Rex
Hound of the Baskervilles, The 1922,S 11,20:2
McDougal, Sandy
Sez O'Reilly to MacNab 1938,F 19,19:4
MacDougall, Allan Ross
Soak the Rich 1936,F 5,14:2
MacDougall, Ranald (Director)
Queen Bee 1955,N 23,18:2
Man on Fire 1957,Ag 23,10:1
World, The Flesh and the Devil, The
   1959,My 21,35:1
Subterraneans, The 1960,Jl 7,26:1
Go Naked in the World 1961,Mr 11,15:1
MacDougall, Ranald (Producer)
Decision of Christopher Blake, The
   1948,D 11,12:2
Jigsaw 1968,Je 6,54:2
MacDougall, Ranald (Screenwriter)
Objective Burma 1945,Ja 27,15:2
Mildred Pierce 1945,S 29,12:2
Possessed 1947,My 30,25:2
Unsuspected, The 1947,O 4,9:2
June Bride 1948,O 30,10:2
Decision of Christopher Blake, The
   1948,D 11,12:2
Hasty Heart, The 1950,Ja 21,10:5
Bright Leaf 1950,Je 17,7:2
Breaking Point, The 1950,O 7,10:6
Mr Belvedere Rings the Bell 1951,Ag 2,18:1
I'll Never Forget You 1951,D 8,9:2
Naked Jungle, The 1954,Ap 3,19:2
Secret of the Incas 1954,My 29,13:3
We're no Angels 1955,Jl 8,15:2
Queen Bee 1955,N 23,18:2
Mountain, The 1956,N 15,44:6
Man on Fire 1957,Ag 23,10:1
Go Naked in the World 1961,Mr 11,15:1
Cleopatra 1963,Je 13,29:1
Macdougall, Robin
Blue Bird, The 1918,Ap 1,9:3
MacDougall, Roger (Original Author)
Cash on Delivery 1956,S 1,19:3
Escapade 1957,Ag 6,30:2
MacDougall, Roger (Screenwriter)
Man in the White Suit, The 1952,Ap 1,35:2
Gentle Gunman, The 1953,O 1,34:3
Mouse That Roared, The 1959,O 27,40:1
Touch of Larceny, A 1960,Mr 17,28:1
McDowall, Betty
Jack the Ripper 1960,F 18,37:4
She Didn't Say No 1963,Jl 30,18:1
Blues for Lovers 1966,S 8,43:1
McDowall, Roddy
Man Hunt 1941,Je 14,20:2
How Green Was my Valley 1941,O 29,27:2
This England 1941,N 18,33:2
Confirm or Deny 1941,D 19,35:2
Son of Fury 1942,Ja 30,23:2
Pied Piper, The 1942,Ag 13,15:3
My Friend Flicka 1943,My 27,21:4
Lassie Come Home 1943,O 8,15:4
White Cliffs of Dover, The 1944,My 12,15:2
Keys of the Kingdom, The 1944,D 30,15:2
Thunderhead 1945,Mr 16,21:2
Molly and Me 1945,My 26,18:2
Holiday in Mexico 1946,Ag 16,19:3
Macbeth 1950,D 28,22:6
Subterraneans, The 1960,Jl 7,26:1
Midnight Lace 1960,O 14,27:1
Longest Day, The 1962,O 5,28:1
Cleopatra 1963,Je 13,29:1
Shock Treatment 1964,Jl 23,19:1
Greatest Story Ever Told, The 1965,F 16,40:2
Third Day, The 1965,Ag 5,15:3
Loved One, The 1965,O 12,57:1
That Darn Cat 1965,D 3,44:1
Inside Daisy Clover 1966,F 18,23:1
Lord Love a Duck 1966,F 22,14:6
Defector, The 1966,N 17,55:1
Adventures of Bullwhip Griffin, The
   1967,Mr 9,43:2
Cool Ones, The 1967,My 11,50:1
It 1967,N 16,58:1
Planet of the Apes 1968,F 9,55:2
5 Card Stud 1968,Ag 1,24:1
McDowall, Virginia
Fan, The 1949,Ap 2,12:2
McDowell, Allen (Producer)
George Washington Carver 1940,Ap 17,26:4
McDowell, Claire
Heart o' the Hills 1919,D 1,9:3
Woman in the Suitcase, The 1920,Ja 12,7:1
Prisoners of Love 1921,Ja 17,9:1

McDowell, Claire— Cont
In the Name of the Law 1922,Jl 10,9:5
Human Wreckage 1923,Je 28,10:2
Circus Days 1923,Ag 6,14:2
Ashes of Vengeance 1923,Ag 7,20:2
Ponjola 1923,N 19,19:3
Black Oxen 1924,Ja 7,23:1
Thy Name Is Woman 1924,Mr 4,17:1
Secrets 1924,Mr 25,25:2
Waking up the Town 1925,Mr 31,17:4
Tower of Lies, The 1925,S 28,24:1
Big Parade, The 1925,N 20,18:1 (In Addenda)
Ben Hur 1925,D 31,10:5 (In Addenda)
Devil's Circus, The 1926,Mr 29,24:3
Unknown Soldier, The 1926,My 31,10:2
Show-Off, The 1926,Ag 23,9:1
Flaming Forest, The 1926,N 22,28:3
Little Journey, A 1927,Ja 4,21:1
Taxi Dancer, The 1927,Mr 8,18:4
Tillie the Toiler 1927,Je 7,27:4
Shield of Honor 1927,D 13,33:2
Don't Marry 1928,My 21,25:1
4 Devils 1928,O 4,26:3
Marriage by Contract 1928,N 13,37:1
Viking, The 1928,N 29,32:4
Redemption 1930,My 3,23:1
Big House, The 1930,Je 25,31:2
Wild Company 1930,Jl 19,7:5
Brothers 1930,N 15,15:3
Mothers Cry 1930,D 6,21:3
American Tragedy, An 1931,Ag 6,22:5
Ben Hur 1931,D 4,28:2
Manhattan Parade 1931,D 25,29:2
It's Tough to be Famous 1932,Ap 9,18:1
Strange Love of Molly Louvain, The
   1932,My 9,19:5
Rebecca of Sunnybrook Farm 1932,Jl 30,16:5
Working Man, The 1933,Ap 21,20:3
Central Airport 1933,My 4,20:5
Paddy the Next Best Thing 1933,Ag 25,12:2
Wild Boys of the Road 1933,S 22,14:1
High, Wide and Handsome 1937,Jl 22,15:1
Teen Age 1944,Je 19,17:1
Are These our Parents? 1944,Ag 23,16:2
McDowell, Fred
Festival 1967,O 24,53:2
MacDowell, Melbourne
Nomads of the North 1920,S 27,18:1
Golden Snare, The 1921,Jl 11,9:3
Richard the Lion-Hearted 1923,O 22,17:1
What Happened to Jones 1926,F 9,22:1
Outside the Law 1926,My 12,31:1
Rainmaker, The 1926,My 18,28:2
Feel my Pulse 1928,F 27,16:2
McDowell, Nelson
Last of the Mohicans, The 1921,Ja 3,20:2
Girl of the Golden West, The 1923,My 21,12:2
Scaramouche 1923,O 12,7:2 (Incorrect in this
   edition; use 1927,O 1,7:2 elsewhere)
Pioneer Trails 1923,N 12,15:3
Shooting of Dan McGrew, The 1924,Je 9,14:3
Claw, The 1927,My 11,28:3
Kentucky Courage 1928,My 14,25:1
Billy the Kid 1930,O 18,23:2
Oliver Twist 1933,Ap 13,15:3
Mace, Borden (Screenwriter)
Animal Farm 1954,D 30,14:1
Mace, Patricia
Powers Girl, The 1943,Mr 26,14:2 (In Addenda)
Mace, Patsy
Our Neighbors-The Carters 1940,F 15,15:2
Macedo, Rita
Nazarin 1968,Je 21,48:1
McEdward, Gordon
Silent Command, The 1923,S 5,15:3
McElbern, James
Passionate Youth 1925,Je 30,14:3
McEldowney, Kenneth (Producer)
River, The 1951,S 11,33:2
McElhern, James
Courtship of Myles Standish, The 1923,D 31,9:3
Daddy's Gone A-Hunting 1925,F 24,17:3
Confessions of a Queen 1925,Mr 24,20:6
McEndrec, Maurice (Producer)
Shadows 1961,Mr 22,37:1
McEndree, Maurice (Producer)
Hollywood or Bust 1956,D 24,8:1
Faces 1968,S 23,42:4
Faces 1968,N 25,54:2
McEnery, John
Romeo and Juliet 1968,O 9,41:1
McEnery, Peter
Tunes of Glory 1960,D 21,38:2
Victim 1962,F 6,27:2
Moonspinners, The 1964,N 4,47:1
Fighting Prince of Donegal, The 1966,N 10,64:1
Game is Over, The 1967,Ja 10,34:1
Negatives 1968,O 15,40:1

McEnroe, Robert E (Original Author)
Mr Belvedere Rings the Bell 1951,Ag 2,18:1
McEveety, Bernard (Director)
Ride Beyond Vengance 1966,S 29,60:1
McEveety, Vincent (Director)
Firecreek 1968,F 22,36:2
McEvilly, Burton
Janice Meredith 1924,Ag 6,13:3
MCEVOY
See Also MCAVOY
McEvoy, Earl (Director)
Cargo to Capetown 1950,Mr 31,36:3
Killer That Stalked New York, The
   1951,Ja 5,17:2
McEvoy, J P (Original Author)
Potters, The 1927,Ja 18,23:1
Glorifying the American Girl 1930,Ja 11,21:3
Show Girl in Hollywood 1930,My 5,27:3
Woman Accused, The 1933,Mr 13,18:2
It's a Gift 1935,Ja 5,20:2
Artists and Models Abroad 1938,D 22,25:3
Dixie Dugan 1943,Ap 9,25:5
McEvoy, J P (Screenwriter)
It's the old Army Game 1926,Jl 5,6:4
Love in Bloom 1935,Ap 20,16:2
College Holiday 1936,D 24,21:2
Just Around the Corner 1938,D 3,11:2
McEvoy, Renny
Story of Dr Wassell, The 1944,Je 7,13:2
Wing and a Prayer 1944,Ag 31,14:1
Miss Susie Slagle's 1946,F 7,29:2
From This Day Forward 1946,Ap 20,16:2
Cry Danger 1951,F 22,27:3
Bigger Than Life 1956,Ag 3,11:2
McEwan, Jack
Q Ships 1928,S 17,27:1
MCEWEN
See Also MCCUNE
McEwen, Brian
Return to Paradise 1953,S 11,24:2
MacEwen, Walter (Producer)
Night Plane From Chungking 1943,My 31,13:2
Miracle of the Bells, The 1948,Mr 17,30:1
McFadden, Elizabeth (Original Author)
Double Door 1934,My 5,22:3
MacFadden, Hamilton
Touchdown Army 1938,O 28,27:2
Five of a Kind 1938,O 31,12:2
Tarnished Angel 1938,N 15,27:2
Sharpshooters 1938,D 5,19:2
Charlie Chan in Reno 1939,My 31,27:2
Shooting High 1940,Ap 12,19:2
Sleepers West 1941,Mr 20,25:3
Reluctant Dragon, The 1941,Jl 25,12:2
MacFadden, Hamilton (Director)
Charlie Chan Carries On 1931,Mr 21,15:1
Black Camel, The 1931,Jl 4,11:5
Riders of the Purple Sage 1931,S 26,25:3
Cheaters at Play 1932,F 27,22:1
Second Hand Wife 1933,Ja 14,8:4
Trick for Trick 1933,Je 10,16:4
Man Who Dared, The 1933,S 9,9:3
Charlie Chan's Greatest Case 1933,O 7,18:4
As Husbands Go 1934,Ja 26,20:3
Hold That Girl 1934,Mr 24,20:3
Stand up and Cheer 1934,Ap 20,17:1
She Was a Lady 1934,Ag 22,21:2
Fighting Youth 1935,N 2,13:3
Three Legionnaires 1937,Jl 10,18:2
It Can't Last Forever 1937,Jl 30,22:5
Sea Racketeers 1937,O 4,17:2
MacFadden, Hamilton (Screenwriter)
Fighting Youth 1935,N 2,13:3
Honeymoon's Over, The 1939,D 15,33:3
McFadden, Ira
Bride of the Storm 1926,Ap 5,24:1
McFadden, Ivor
Tides of Passion 1925,Ap 20,22:1
Two-Gun Man, The 1926,Jl 13,19:3
MacFarland, Frank
Winning Team, The 1952,Je 21,12:2
MacFarland, George
Varsity Show 1937,S 2,17:2
McFarland, Georgie
Miss Fane's Baby is Stolen 1934,Ja 20,12:2
McFarland, Spanky
Day of Reckoning 1933,N 4,18:2
Kentucky Kernels 1935,Ja 5,20:2
O'Shaughnessy's Boy 1935,O 5,18:2
Trail of the Lonesome Pine, The 1936,F 20,23:5
Peck's bad Boy With the Circus 1939,Ja 11,17:4
Johnny Doughboy 1943,My 6,25:3
MacFarlane, Bruce
Come on Leathernecks 1938,S 15,29:3
Macfarlane, Elsa
Co-Optimists, The 1930,F 5,27:2
MacFarlane, George
Nix on Dames 1929,N 23,18:5
South Sea Rose 1929,D 7,19:3
Happy Days 1930,F 14,20:1
Double Cross Roads 1930,Ap 29,31:1
Up the River 1930,O 11,21:3
Half Shot at Sunrise 1930,O 11,21:3

MacFarlane, George— Cont
Rich Man's Folly 1931,N 27,29:3
Taxi 1932,Ja 8,27:3
Union Depot 1932,Ja 15,24:4
Fireman, Save My Child 1932,F 18,25:3
Heart of New York, The 1932,Mr 2,15:3
MacFarlane, Louella (Screenwriter)
Guilt of Janet Ames, The 1947,My 23,31:2
Mating of Millie, The 1948,Mr 13,12:2
Macfarlane, Peter Clark (Original Author)
Tongues of Flame 1924,D 16,28:1
MacFric (Director)
Janosik 1936,D 25,19:3
McGann, William (Director)
On the Border 1930,F 3,17:1
I Like Your Nerve 1931,S 12,15:4
Buenaventura, La 1934,S 15,20:3
Maybe It's Love 1935,F 11,14:2
Night at the Ritz, A 1935,My 16,20:2
Man of Iron 1935,D 7,22:2
Fish 1936,Ja 25,18:5
Freshman Love 1936,Ja 25,18:5
Brides are Like That 1936,Mr 23,22:5
Times Square Playboy 1936,My 2,11:2
Hot Money 1936,Jl 25,16:2
Polo Joe 1936,N 5,35:1
Case of the Black Cat, The 1936,D 26,15:4
Penrod and Sam 1937,Mr 29,14:3
Marry the Girl 1937,Jl 31,6:2
Alcatraz Island 1937,O 14,22:2
Sh! The Octopus 1937,D 24,21:2
Penrod and his Twin Brother 1938,Ap 18,11:1
When Were You Born? 1938,Je 9,27:2
Girls on Probation 1938,O 21,27:3
Blackwell's Island 1939,Mr 2,19:1
Dr Christian Meets the Women 1940,Ag 2,12:2
Parson of Panamint, The 1941,Jl 26,18:2
Highway West 1941,Ag 8,13:4
In old California 1942,Je 18,25:3
Tombstone, The Town too Tough to Die
   1942,Jl 27,18:2
American Empire 1943,Ja 14,25:4
McGarrity, Everett
Hallelujah 1929,Ag 21,33:1
McGarvey, Cathal
Irish Destiny 1927,Mr 29,23:2 (In Addenda)
McGaugh, W F (Director)
New Adventures of Tarzan, The 1935,O 15,19:3
McGavin, Darren
Summertime 1955,Je 22,25:1
Man With the Golden Arm, The 1955,D 16,38:2
Court-Martial of Billy Mitchell, The
   1955,D 23,14:2
Beau James 1957,Je 27,21:1
Delicate Delinquent, The 1957,Jl 4,16:1
McGaw, William C
To Please a Lady 1950,O 27,24:3
MCGEE
See Also MAGEE, MCKEE
McGee, Roger
Stop, Look and Love 1939,S 8,28:5
Escape, The 1939,N 3,17:4
Forbidden Planet 1956,My 4,21:2
McGeehan, William O (Original Author)
Quarterback, The 1926,O 12,30:2
McGehee, Gloria
Child Is Waiting, A 1963,F 14,5:6
MacGerr, Pat (Original Author)
One Step to Eternity 1955,O 3,22:2
McGhee, Brownie
Festival 1967,O 24,53:2
MacGibbon, Harriet
Cry for Happy 1961,Mr 4,16:1
Majority of One, A 1962,Ja 12,29:2
4 Horsemen of the Apocalypse, The
   1962,Mr 10,10:2
McGibney, Donald (Screenwriter)
Two Arabian Knights 1927,O 24,24:3
Macgill, Moyna
Frenchman's Creek 1944,S 21,26:2
Picture of Dorian Gray, The 1945,Mr 2,15:2
Uncle Harry 1945,Ag 24,14:5
Black Beauty 1946,Ag 30,13:2
Green Dolphin Street 1947,O 16,34:2
Three Daring Daughters 1948,F 13,26:3
Kind Lady 1951,Ag 8,21:2
MacGill, Patrick (Original Author)
Suspense 1930,N 8,21:3
MacGill (Original Author)
Howling Success, A 1919,Jl 28,8:5
McGinley, Phyllis (Miscellaneous)
Emperor's Nightingale, The 1951,My 14,29:1
McGinnis, Joel
Bedside Manner 1945,Je 23,9:6
MacGinnis, Niall
Luck of the Irish, The 1937,Ja 16,21:1
Ourselves Alone 1937,Jl 31,6:2
River of Unrest 1937,N 27,21:2
Edge of the World, The 1938,S 12,13:2
Invaders, The 1942,Mr 6,17:1
Avengers, The 1942,N 25,18:2
Henry V 1946,Je 18,30:2
Tawny Pipit 1947,S 8,25:5
Captain Boycott 1947,D 6,11:2

MacGinnis, Niall — Cont
Anna Karenina 1948,Ap 28,32:2
Hamlet 1948,S 30,32:2
Christopher Columbus 1949,O 13,33:2
Chance of a Lifetime 1951,Mr 15,37:2
No Highway in the Sky 1951,S 22,8:6
Murder in the Cathedral 1952,Mr 26,35:2
You Can't Beat the Irish 1952,My 1,34:4
Martin Luther 1953,S 10,22:1
Knights of the Round Table 1954,Ja 8,17:2
Hell Below Zero 1954,Jl 17,7:3
Betrayed 1954,S 9,36:1
Fuss Over Feathers 1954,D 27,22:6
Helen of Troy 1956,Ja 27,21:4
Alexander the Great 1956,Mr 29,23:1
Lust for Life 1956,S 18,39:1
Nun's Story, The 1959,Je 19,30:1
Tarzan's Greatest Adventure 1959,Jl 9,22:1
Kidnapped 1960,My 19,44:3
Night Fighters, The 1960,D 15,59:1
Sword of Sherwood Forest 1961,Ja 26,32:3
Foxhole in Cairo 1961,F 16,25:2
Billy Budd 1962,O 31,32:1
Playboy of the Western World, The
  1963,Mr 19,8:2
She Didn't Say No 1963,Jl 30,18:1
Jason and the Argonauts 1963,Ag 8,19:1
Becket 1964,Mr 12,40:2
Truth About Spring, The 1965,Je 17,27:2
War Lord, The 1965,N 18,55:2
Johnny Nobody 1965,N 24,35:1
Man Could Get Killed, A 1966,My 12,54:2
McGinty
Bride of the Lake, The 1934,S 11,24:5
McGiveney, Maura
Twist Around the Clock 1962,Ja 27,13:4
Do Not Disturb 1965,D 25,17:2
McGiveney, Owen
If Winter Comes 1948,Ja 23,28:4
Show Boat 1951,Jl 20,14:1
Scaramouche 1952,My 9,20:2
Pat and Mike 1952,Je 19,32:6
Maze, The 1953,Jl 11,8:2
Brigadoon 1954,S 17,18:2
McGiver, John
Love in the Afternoon 1957,Ag 24,12:1
Man in the Raincoat, The 1958,Jl 15,21:2
Gazebo, The 1960,Ja 16,14:4
Love in a Goldfish Bowl 1961,Jl 13,26:3
Breakfast at Tiffany's 1961,O 6,28:1
Bachelor in Paradise 1961,N 17,41:2
Mr Hobbs Takes a Vacation 1962,Je 16,11:2
Manchurian Candidate, The 1962,O 25,48:3
Who's Got the Action? 1962,D 26,5:4
My Six Loves 1963,Ap 4,58:4
Hot Horse 1963,Jl 25,14:2
Take Her, She's Mine 1963,N 14,41:1
Who's Minding the Store? 1963,N 29,67:6
  (Incorrect in this edition; use 1963,N 28,67:6
  elsewhere)
Man's Favorite Sport? 1964,F 20,22:1
Marriage on the Rocks 1965,S 16,00:0
Made in Paris 1966,F 17,29:1
Glass Bottom Boat, The 1966,Je 10,54:1
Fitzwilly 1967,D 21,45:1
McGivern, Cecil (Screenwriter)
Blanche Fury 1948,N 24,20:2
McGivern, William P (Original Author)
Big Heat, The 1953,O 15,43:2
Rogue Cop 1954,S 18,12:2
Hell on Frisco Bay 1956,Ja 7,21:1
Odds Against Tomorrow 1959,O 16,27:1
Caper of the Golden Bulls, The 1967,Je 22,46:1
McGivern, William P (Screenwriter)
I Saw What You Did 1965,Jl 22,24:2
McGlory, Sean
Quiet Man, The 1952,Ag 22,13:1
McGlynn, Frank
America 1924,F 22,20:1
Judgment of the Hills 1927,Ag 2,19:2
Good News 1930,S 6,9:2
Min and Bill 1930,N 24,26:5
Secret Six, The 1931,My 2,23:4
Huckleberry Finn 1931,Ag 8,16:3
Riders of the Purple Sage 1931,S 26,25:3
No Man of her Own 1932,D 31,10:1
Frisco Jenny 1933,Ja 7,11:2
Face in the Sky 1933,F 20,11:5
Charlie Chan's Greatest Case 1933,O 7,18:4
Massacre 1934,Ja 18,19:2
Search for Beauty 1934,F 10,20:2
Little Miss Marker 1934,My 19,18:3
Are We Civilized? 1934,Je 14,28:5
Kentucky Kernels 1935,Ja 5,20:2
Folies Bergere 1935,F 25,13:2
Littlest Rebel, The 1935,D 20,30:1
Captain Blood 1935,D 27,14:1
Prisoner of Shark Island, The 1936,F 13,25:2
Trail of the Lonesome Pine, The 1936,F 20,23:5
Parole 1936,Je 27,21:1
Last of the Mohicans, The 1936,S 3,17:3
King of the Royal Mounted 1936,S 29,35:2
Plainsman, The 1937,Ja 14,16:2
Sing and Be Happy 1937,Je 19,20:2

Wells Fargo 1937,D 30,15:2
Kentucky Moonshine 1938,My 21,9:2
Mad Empress, The 1940,F 15,15:1
Girl, a Guy and a Gob, A 1941,Ap 24,25:3
Marry the Boss's Daughter 1941,D 4,33:4
McGoldrick, Rita C (Miscellaneous)
Through the Centuries 1933,D 2,9:8 (In
  Addenda)
McGoohan, Patrick
Elephant Gun 1959,Je 20,11:2
Quare Fellow 1963,F 20,6:1
Three Lives of Thomasina, The 1963,D 12,46:1
Walk in the Shadow 1966,S 12,52:5
Ice Station Zebra 1968,D 21,49:1
McGovern, James (Original Author)
Fraulein 1958,Je 9,27:2
McGovern, John
Splendor in the Grass 1961,O 11,53:1
McGovern, Johnny
Night Unto Night 1949,Je 11,11:2
McGowan, Bryan
Irish Destiny 1927,Mr 29,23:2 (In Addenda)
McGowan, Dorothy
Ghost Talks, The 1929,F 18,28:1
McGowan, Dorrell (Director)
Tokyo File 212 1951,Je 1,20:7
McGowan, Dorrell (Miscellaneous)
Stadium Murders, The 1938,Ap 9,11:2
McGowan, Dorrell (Original Author)
Sea Racketeers 1937,O 4,17:2
Missing Evidence 1939,N 17,17:3
Hellfire 1949,My 30,9:4
McGowan, Dorrell (Producer)
Tokyo File 212 1951,Je 1,20:7
McGowan, Dorrell (Screenwriter)
Under Western Stars 1938,Je 25,7:3
Come on Leathernecks 1938,S 15,29:3
Big Bonanza, The 1945,F 26,14:5
Singing Guns 1950,Je 5,19:3
Tokyo File 212 1951,Je 1,20:7
McGowan, J P
Senor Daredevil 1926,Ag 17,15:3
Red Raiders, The 1927,S 28,28:3
No More Women 1934,Mr 15,27:4
Wagon Wheels 1934,O 4,19:1
Fury and the Woman 1937,Je 22,26:2
McGowan, J P (Screenwriter)
What Price Vengeance 1937,My 26,30:3
McGowan, Jack (Original Author)
Born to Dance 1936,D 5,16:1
Broadway Melody of 1938 1937,S 3,12:1
Broadway Melody of 1940 1940,Mr 29,25:3
Lady Be Good 1941,S 19,27:1
Girl Crazy 1943,D 3,27:2
Broadway Rhythm 1944,Ap 14,24:6
McGowan, Jack (Screenwriter)
Broadway Melody of 1936 1935,S 19,28:1
Born to Dance 1936,D 5,16:1
Broadway Melody of 1938 1937,S 3,12:1
Babes in Arms 1939,O 20,27:2
Little Nellie Kelly 1940,D 25,33:2
Lady Be Good 1941,S 19,27:1
Panama Hattie 1942,O 2,31:2
McGowan, John (Original Author)
Excess Baggage 1928,S 24,25:1
Girl Crazy 1932,Mr 25,23:3
McGowan, John (Screenwriter)
Stork Club, The 1945,D 20,18:2
Macgowan, Kenneth (Producer)
Anne of Green Gables 1934,D 22,21:1
Murder on a Honeymoon 1935,Mr 4,12:2
Enchanted April 1935,Mr 9,19:1
Jalna 1935,S 14,8:4
Return of Peter Grimm, The 1935,O 4,25:2
This Is my Affair 1937,My 28,17:1
Love and Hisses 1938,Ja 1,11:1
Four Men and a Prayer 1938,My 7,18:1
Kentucky Moonshine 1938,My 21,9:2
Happy Land 1943,D 9,33:3
Lifeboat 1944,Ja 13,17:1
Easy Come, Easy Go 1947,F 6,29:2
McGowan, Oliver
Screaming Mimi 1958,Je 26,23:3
McGowan, Robert F (Original Author)
Sons of the Legion 1938,S 30,24:3
McGowan, Robert F (Screenwriter)
Sons of the Legion 1938,S 30,24:3
McGowan, Stuart (Director)
Tokyo File 212 1951,Je 1,20:7
McGowan, Stuart (Miscellaneous)
Stadium Murders, The 1938,Ap 9,11:2
McGowan, Stuart (Original Author)
Sea Racketeers 1937,O 4,17:2
Missing Evidence 1939,N 17,17:3
Hellfire 1949,My 30,9:4
McGowan, Stuart (Producer)
Tokyo File 212 1951,Je 1,20:7
McGowan, Stuart (Screenwriter)
Under Western Stars 1938,Je 25,7:3
Come on Leathernecks 1938,S 15,29:3
Big Bonanza, The 1945,F 26,14:5
Singing Guns 1950,Je 5,19:3
Tokyo File 212 1951,Je 1,20:7

McGowan, T M (Screenwriter)
Man With my Face, The 1951,Je 15,27:5
McGowan, Tom (Director)
Amazon Trader, The 1956,N 17,17:6
Manhunt in the Jungle 1958,Ap 12,13:1
Hound that Thought he was a Racoon, The
  1960,Ag 18,19:2
McGowan and Mack
Lake Placid Serenade 1944,D 25,15:6
MacGowran, Jack
No Resting Place 1952,My 5,18:5
Quiet Man, The 1952,Ag 22,13:1
Titfield Thunderbolt, The 1953,O 6,34:2
Rising of the Moon, The (The Majesty of the
  Law); Majesty of the Law, The (The Rising of
  the Moon) 1957,Jl 10,23:1
Stowaway Girl 1957,N 6,43:3
Rooney 1958,Je 6,29:2
Darby O'Gill and the Little People 1959,Jl 1,26:1
Chance Meeting 1960,O 27,45:2
She Didn't Say No 1963,Jl 30,18:1
Tom Jones 1963,O 8,48:1
Ceremony, The 1964,My 14,39:1
Lord Jim 1965,F 26,18:1
Young Cassidy 1965,Mr 23,35:1
Doctor Zhivago 1965,D 23,21:1
Cul de Sac 1966,N 8,44:2
How I Won the War 1967,N 9,56:1
Fearless Vampire Killers, The, or Pardon Me but
  Your Teeth are in my Neck 1967,N 14,52:1
McGrail, Walter
Suzanna 1923,Mr 26,16:2
Where the North Begins 1923,Ag 27,14:3
Eleventh Hour, The 1923,Ag 28,12:1
Bad Man, The 1923,O 9,17:4
Flaming Youth 1923,N 26,15:6
Son of the Sahara, A 1924,My 27,14:1
Unguarded Women 1924,Je 24,18:2
Dancers, The 1925,Ja 26,22:1
Adventure 1925,Ap 15,16:1
Teaser, The 1925,Je 15,10:1
Son of his Father, A 1925,S 29,31:3
Secret Studio, The 1927,Je 15,31:4
American Beauty 1927,O 11,27:1
Man Crazy 1927,D 19,30:1
Play Girl, The 1928,Ap 23,20:2
River of Romance, The 1929,Jl 29,23:3
Men Without Women 1930,F 1,15:1
Soldiers and Women 1930,My 12,27:3
Anybody's War 1930,Jl 11,22:1
Last of the Duanes 1930,S 13,9:3
Shepper - Newfounder, The 1930,D 25,31:5
Seas Beneath 1931,Ja 31,15:1
River's End 1931,Mr 7,17:2
Night Nurse 1931,Jl 17,23:4
Murder by the Clock 1931,Jl 18,16:6
Under Eighteen 1931,D 26,15:5
State Trooper 1933,Mr 27,13:6
Police Call 1933,Ag 22,20:3
World Moves On, The 1934,Je 30,18:5
All the King's Horses 1935,Mr 9,19:1
Shadow Strikes, The 1937,S 13,17:1
Calling All Marines 1939,O 26,27:2
McGranahan, Thomas (Miscellaneous)
High Sign, The 1922,Mr 20,10:3
McGranary, Al
Sunrise at Campobello 1960,S 29,32:1
McGrath, Frank
She Wore a Yellow Ribbon 1949,N 18,35:2
Shakiest Gun in the West, The 1968,Jl 11,30:1
McGrath, Harold (Original Author)
Mollycoddle, The 1920,Je 14,13:2
Ragged Edge, The 1923,Je 5,24:5
Man on the Box, The 1925,S 28,24:1
McGrath, John (Original Author)
Bofors Gun, The 1968,S 23,42:3
McGrath, John (Screenwriter)
Billion Dollar Brain 1967,D 23,29:1
Bofors Gun, The 1968,S 23,42:3
McGrath, Joseph (Director)
Casino Royale 1967,Ap 29,25:1
30 Is a Dangerous Age, Cynthia 1968,Mr 5,34:1
Bliss of Mrs Blossom, The 1968,D 12,62:6
McGrath, Joseph (Original Author)
30 Is a Dangerous Age, Cynthia 1968,Mr 5,34:1
McGrath, Joseph (Screenwriter)
30 Is a Dangerous Age, Cynthia 1968,Mr 5,34:1
McGrath, Larry
Knockout Reilly 1927,Ap 18,21:2
Arizona Kid, The 1930,My 17,21:2
Milky Way, The 1936,Mr 26,27:2
Jackie Robinson Story, The 1950,My 17,36:1
MacGrath, Leueen
Pygmalion 1938,D 8,34:2
Saint's Vacation, The 1941,Je 13,22:2
Edward my Son 1949,Je 3,21:2
Three Cases of Murder (In the Picture); In the
  Picture (Three Cases of Murder)
  1955,Mr 16,39:4

McGrath, Pat
Half-Way House 1945,Ag 13,22:4
McGrath, Paul
Parole Fixer 1940,Ap 18,28:5
This Thing Called Love 1941,F 14,15:2
Dead Men Tell 1941,Ap 17,29:3
No Time for Love 1943,D 2,30:1
Face in the Crowd, A 1957,My 29,33:1
Advise and Consent 1962,Je 7,31:2
McGratl, James
Fury and the Woman 1937,Je 22,26:2
McGraw, Charles
Mad Ghoul, The 1943,D 11,11:2
Impostor, The 1944,Mr 27,17:2
Killers, The 1946,Ag 29,24:2
Big Fix, The 1947,My 3,10:3
Long Night, The 1947,S 17,31:2
Gangster, The 1947,O 31,29:3
Roses Are Red 1947,N 15,11:2
T-Men 1948,Ja 23,28:3
Hazard 1948,Je 3,19:2
Blood on the Moon 1948,N 12,30:5
Once More, my Darling 1949,S 26,17:1
Black Book, The 1949,O 17,18:2
Border Incident 1949,N 21,29:2
Story of Molly X, The 1949,D 2,35:4
Threat, The 1949,D 2,35:4
Side Street 1950,Mr 24,29:2
Double Crossbones 1951,Ap 27,19:2
His Kind of Woman 1951,Ag 30,20:2
Narrow Margin, The 1952,My 5,18:7
One Minute to Zero 1952,S 20,13:2
Thunder Over the Plains 1953,D 10,64:4
Loophole 1954,Mr 13,11:3
Bridges at Toko-Ri, The 1955,Ja 21,20:2
Away all Boats 1956,Ag 17,14:2
Toward the Unknown 1956,S 28,24:4
Joe Butterfly 1957,My 30,23:2
Slaughter on Tenth Avenue 1957,N 6,43:1
Saddle the Wind 1958,Mr 21,17:1
Twilight for the Gods 1958,Ag 7,21:1
Defiant Ones, The 1958,S 25,29:1
Man in the Net, The 1959,Je 11,36:2
Wonderful Country, The 1959,N 5,39:7
Spartacus 1960,O 7,28:1
Cimarron 1961,F 17,12:2
Horizontal Lieutenant, The 1962,My 12,15:3
Birds, The 1963,Ap 1,5:5 (Incorrect in this edition; use 1963,Ap 1,54:1 elsewhere)
It's a Mad, Mad, Mad, Mad World 1963,N 19,47:1
Busy Body, The 1967,Je 8,52:2
In Cold Blood 1967,D 15,60:1
Hang 'Em High 1968,Ag 8,27:3
McGraw, Hugh (Producer)
Funnyman 1967,S 25,56:3
McGreevey, Mike
Way West, The 1967,My 25,54:1
Impossible Years, The 1968,D 6,54:1
MacGregor, Cathey
Strange Victory 1948,S 27,27:2
MacGregor, Doreen
Convicted 1938,Ag 22,9:3
McGregor, Harmon
Slave of Desire 1923,D 11,26:2
MacGregor, Hector
Hungry Hill 1947,O 11,11:2
Stage Fright 1950,F 24,27:2
MacGregor, Lee
Scudda-Hoo! Scudda-Hay! 1948,Ap 15,31:1
Slattery's Hurricane 1949,Ag 13,6:6
Twelve O'Clock High 1950,Ja 28,10:2
Sealed Cargo 1951,My 24,47:1
McGregor, Malcolm
Bedroom Window, The 1924,Je 9,14:3
Lady of the Night 1925,Mr 2,14:1
Smouldering Fires 1925,Mr 31,17:4
Happy Warrior, The 1925,Jl 7,24:2
Circle, The 1925,S 22,22:3
Vanishing American, The 1925,O 16,18:2
Infatuation 1926,Ja 4,16:1
It Must Be Love 1926,O 4,20:2
Matinee Ladies 1927,Ap 13,29:4
Buck Privates 1928,Ja 30,18:1
Port of Missing Girls, The 1928,Jl 31,13:4
Girl on the Barge, The 1929,F 26,31:1
Murder Will Out 1930,Ap 14,24:2
McGregor, Norval
Courtship of Myles Standish, The 1923,D 31,9:3
MacGregor, Warren
It Came From Outer Space 1953,Je 18,38:2
McGrill, George
Last Man, The 1932,S 17,18:4
MCGUINESS
See MCGUINNESS
McGuinn, Joe
Officer and the Lady, The 1941,Ag 11,17:4
Glass Key, The 1942,O 16,23:1
Ten North Frederick 1958,My 23,29:2

McGuinness, J K (Original Author)
Girl in Every Port, A 1928,F 20,14:1
Men Without Women 1930,F 1,15:1
Attorney for the Defense 1932,My 28,18:2
This Sporting Age 1932,O 1,10:4
Cocktail Hour 1933,Je 5,18:5
West Point of the Air 1935,Ap 6,10:1
Night at the Opera, A 1935,D 7,22:1
McGuinness, J K (Producer)
Madame X 1937,O 25,23:1
McGuinness, J K (Screenwriter)
China Seas 1935,Ag 10,16:4
Arsene Lupin Returns 1938,Mr 9,21:1
Lord Jeff 1938,Jl 1,22:2
I Take This Woman 1940,F 16,23:3
Florian 1940,Je 6,33:2
Men of Boys Town 1941,Ap 11,24:6
Rio Grande 1950,N 20,21:2
MCGUIRE
See Also MAGUIRE, MACGUIRE
MACGUIRE
See Also MAGUIRE, MCGUIRE
McGuire, Anne Tucker
Strangers on a Honeymoon 1937,Mr 13,23:2
McGuire, Barry
President's Analyst, The 1967,D 22,44:4
You Are What You Eat 1968,S 25,38:1
McGuire, Biff
Phenix City Story, The 1955,S 3,9:1
Station Six-Sahara 1964,N 12,40:2
Thomas Crown Affair, The 1968,Je 27,48:2
Heart is a Lonely Hunter, The 1968,Ag 1,24:1
McGuire, Billy
Thunder Birds 1942,O 29,19:2
McGuire, Don
Pride of the Marines 1945,Ag 25,7:3
Too Young to Know 1945,D 8,21:2
Humoresque 1946,D 26,28:1
Man I Love, The 1947,Ja 25,12:2
That Way With Women 1947,F 15,20:4
Love and Learn 1947,My 3,10:3
Always Together 1947,D 11,46:1
My Wild Irish Rose 1947,D 25,32:2
Fuller Brush Man, The 1948,My 15,18:2
Wallflower 1948,Je 12,8:5
Whiplash 1948,D 27,16:3
Threat, The 1949,D 2,35:4
Three Guys Named Mike 1951,Mr 2,21:2
Double Dynamite 1951,D 26,19:4
McGuire, Don (Director)
Johnny Concho 1956,Ag 16,30:1
Delicate Delinquent, The 1957,Jl 4,16:1
McGuire, Don (Original Author)
Dial 1119 1950,D 4,32:6
Meet Danny Wilson 1952,Mr 27,34:4
McGuire, Don (Screenwriter)
Meet Danny Wilson 1952,Mr 27,34:4
Walking my Baby Back Home 1954,Ja 16,10:5
Three Ring Circus 1954,D 25,7:2
Bad Day at Black Rock 1955,F 2,22:2
Artists and Models 1955,D 22,20:1
Johnny Concho 1956,Ag 16,30:1
Delicate Delinquent, The 1957,Jl 4,16:1
McGuire, Dorothy
Claudia 1943,N 5,23:2
Tree Grows in Brooklyn, A 1945,Mr 1,25:5
Enchanted Cottage, The 1945,Ap 28,19:2
Spiral Staircase, The 1946,F 7,29:3
Till the End of Time 1946,Jl 24,24:1
Claudia and David 1946,Ag 15,19:2
Gentleman's Agreement 1947,N 12,36:2
Mother Didn't Tell Me 1950,Mr 4,11:2
Mister 880 1950,S 30,13:2
Callaway Went Thataway 1951,D 6,42:1
I Want You 1951,D 24,9:1
Invitation 1952,Ja 30,22:6
Make Haste to Live 1954,Mr 26,16:2
Three Coins in the Fountain 1954,My 21,18:2
Trial 1955,O 14,21:2
Friendly Persuasion 1956,N 2,30:1
Old Yeller 1957,D 26,23:4
Remarkable Mr Pennypacker, The 1959,F 21,25:2
Earth Is Mine, The 1959,Je 27,13:1
Summer Place, A 1959,O 23,24:1
Khovanschina 1960,S 23,33:1
Swiss Family Robinson 1960,D 24,8:4
Susan Slade 1961,N 11,14:6
Summer Magic 1963,Ag 22,19:2
Greatest Story Ever Told, The 1965,F 16,40:2
McGuire, Harp
On the Beach 1959,D 18,34:1
Incident in an Alley 1962,My 17,31:1
McGuire, James P (Miscellaneous)
Call Northside 777 1948,F 19,29:2
McGuire, John
Steamboat Around the Bend 1935,S 20,17:2
Your Uncle Dudley 1935,D 12,33:4
Prisoner of Shark Island, The 1936,F 13,25:2
Charlie Chan at the Circus 1936,My 19,22:4
Wanted: Jane Turner 1936,N 30,24:7
Women Without Names 1940,My 9,26:4
Stranger on the Third Floor 1940,S 2,19:2
Invisible Ghost, The 1941,My 8,21:2

McGuire, John — Cont
Sands of Iwo Jima 1949,D 31,9:2
First Legion, The 1951,Ap 28,9:2
Tanks are Coming, The 1951,D 6,42:4
McGuire, Kathryn
Silent Call, The 1922,Ja 30,16:2
Crossroads of New York, The 1922,My 22,18:4
Shriek of Araby, The 1923,Je 11,16:2
Sherlock Jr 1924,My 26,21:1
Navigator, The 1924,O 13,21:1
Naughty but Nice 1927,Jl 5,19:2
Girl on the Pullman, The 1927,N 1,21:1 (In Addenda)
Lilac Time 1928,Ag 4,7:2
Synthetic Sin 1929,Ja 7,36:2
Long, Long Trail, The 1929,N 4,28:1
Lost Zeppelin, The 1930,F 3,17:1
McGuire, Marcy
Seven Days' Leave 1942,D 11,33:2
Around the World 1943,N 25,39:2
Higher and Higher 1944,Ja 22,8:4
Seven Days Ashore 1944,Ap 26,24:7
It Happened in Brooklyn 1947,Mr 14,28:5
You Gotta Stay Happy 1948,N 5,29:2
Jumping Jacks 1952,Jl 24,30:2
McGuire, Mickey
Once Upon a Time 1944,Je 30,17:2
McGuire, Tom
Spoilers, The 1923,Ag 6,14:2
Reckless Age, The 1924,Je 10,24:4
Captain Blood 1924,S 9,19:1
Red Hot Tires 1925,O 20,28:1
We Moderns 1925,D 8,28:5
My Own Pal 1926,Mr 15,18:3
Missing Link, The 1927,My 7,15:2
Shanghai Bound 1927,N 7,26:4
Steamboat Bill, Jr 1928,My 15,17:3
Lights of New York 1928,Jl 9,25:1
Sawdust Paradise, The 1928,Ag 27,23:1
Politics 1931,Ag 1,16:4
No Greater Love 1932,My 14,11:5
She Done Him Wrong 1933,F 10,12:3
Charlie Chan at the Opera 1936,D 5,16:2
McGuire, Tucker
Climbing High 1939,Je 5,20:3
Shipyard Sally 1940,Ja 18,27:3
McGuire, William Anthony (Original Author)
Tin Gods 1926,S 20,21:3
Twelve Miles Out 1927,Jl 26,17:1
Six Cylinder Love 1931,My 16,31:3
Disorderly Conduct 1932,Ap 11,19:2
King for a Night 1933,D 11,23:4
I Believed in You 1934,Ap 11,25:3
Rosalie 1937,D 31,9:2
Risky Business 1939,Mr 23,27:2
Ziegfeld Girl 1941,Ap 25,17:2
McGuire, William Anthony (Producer)
Girl of the Golden West, The 1938,Mr 25,15:2
McGuire, William Anthony (Screenwriter)
Don't Bet on Women 1931,Mr 7,17:2
Okay America 1932,S 10,18:5
Kid From Spain, The 1932,N 18,23:2
Great Ziegfeld, The 1936,Ap 9,21:2
Rosalie 1937,D 31,9:2
Lillian Russell 1940,My 18,11:2
MacGunigle, Robert (Screenwriter)
Whistling in the Dark 1941,Ag 28,23:2
McGurk, J W
Great White Way, The 1924,Ja 4,10:1
MACH
See Also MACK
Mach, Joseph (Screenwriter)
Thunder in the Hills 1947,My 24,10:5
Machacek, Miroslav
Devil's Trap, The 1964,Ag 14,16:1
Fifth Horseman is Fear, The 1968,My 7,52:1
McHale, Michael
Threat, The 1949,D 2,35:4
Machard, Alfred (Director)
Petits, Les 1936,D 30,17:2
Machard, Alfred (Original Author)
Trapeze 1932,My 3,25:2
Machard, Alfred (Screenwriter)
Tomorrow is too Late 1952,Ap 14,22:2
Macharen, Mary
Mysterious Mrs M, The 1917,Ja 22,9:1
MacHarg, William (Original Author)
Price of a Party, The 1924,N 26,17:3
McHarris, Lindsay
Two Kinds of Women 1932,Ja 16,13:1
Machaty, G (Producer)
Kreutzer Sonata, The 1928,S 10,29:3
Seduction 1929,N 17,IX,5:6
Machavarian, Alexei (Composer)
Ballet of Othello, The 1964,My 4,35:1
Machen, Yvonne
Betrayal, The 1948,Je 26,10:5
Macheret, A (Director)
Call to Arms 1937,My 3,23:3
Macheret, A (Screenwriter)
Men on Wings 1935,Je 11,24:5
Concentration Camp 1939,Mr 20,13:2

Machiavelli, Niccolo (Original Author)
Mandragola 1966,Je 7,50:2
Machiavelli, Nicoletta
Matchless 1967,N 11,26:3
Hills Run Red, The 1967,N 11,26:3
Navajo Joe 1967,D 7,60:2
Minute to Pray, A Second to Die, A
1968,My 23,56:2
Machida, Isako
Hiroshima 1955,My 17,32:1
Machika, Hiroko
Street of Shame 1959,Je 5,17:2
Machnik, Edwin
Paris Incident 1954,Ag 18,20:2
Machnik, Frances
Ramuntcho 1953,Mr 2,19:2
Machon, Max
Liebe im Ring 1930,Ag 11,13:1
Machover, Robert (Producer)
Edge, The 1968,Mr 28,52:1
Machowski, Ignacy
Ashes and Diamonds 1961,My 30,8:1
Eroica (First Episode) 1966,F 2,24:1
McHugh, Charles
Girl of the Golden West, The 1923,My 21,12:2
Lights of Old Broadway 1925,N 2,20:1
Golden Cocoon, The 1925,D 15,14:5
Waning Sex, The 1926,S 21,33:1
McHugh, Frank
Dawn Patrol, The 1930,Jl 11,22:1
Top Speed 1930,Ag 30,7:4
Widow From Chicago, The 1930,D 20,20:6
Kiss Me Again 1931,Ja 8,21:4
Going Wild 1931,Ja 26,21:1
Millie 1931,F 7,11:1
Bright Lights 1931,F 10,24:4
Front Page, The 1931,Mr 20,29:1
Up for Murder 1931,My 30,9:2
Traveling Husbands 1931,Ag 8,16:3
Bad Company 1931,N 7,16:5
Corsair 1931,N 19,27:5
Union Depot 1932,Ja 15,24:4
High Pressure 1932,F 1,22:3
Crowd Roars, The 1932,Mr 23,25:4
Strange Love of Molly Louvain, The
1932,My 9,19:5
Dark Horse, The 1932,Je 9,27:3
Life Begins 1932,Ag 26,20:3
Blessed Event 1932,S 3,16:2
One Way Passage 1932,O 14,23:2
Parachute Jumper 1933,Ja 26,12:2
Mystery of the Wax Museum, The
1933,F 18,13:3
Grand Slam 1933,F 22,25:2
Private Jones 1933,Mr 25,13:4
Ex-Lady 1933,My 15,16:2
Hold Me Tight 1933,My 22,18:6
Elmer the Great 1933,My 26,24:2
Lilly Turner 1933,Je 15,21:2
Tomorrow at Seven 1933,Jl 3,14:6
Professional Sweetheart 1933,Jl 14,15:3
Footlight Parade 1933,O 6,21:3
Havana Widows 1933,N 23,24:3
Son of a Sailor 1933,N 30,38:4
House on 56th Street, The 1933,D 2,9:3
Convention City 1933,D 25,28:2
Fashions of 1934 1934,Ja 20,12:2
Heat Lightning 1934,Mr 8,23:2
Return of the Terror 1934,Jl 11,20:2
Here Comes the Navy 1934,Jl 21,14:2
Happiness Ahead 1934,O 11,28:2
6-Day Bike Rider 1934,N 3,20:3
Devil Dogs of the Air 1935,F 7,23:2
Maybe It's Love 1935,F 11,14:2
Gold Diggers of 1935 1935,Mr 15,25:2
Irish in US, The 1935,Ag 1,15:1
Page Miss Glory 1935,Ag 29,25:2
Midsummer Night's Dream, A 1935,O 10,31:1
Stars Over Broadway 1935,N 14,17:3
Fish 1936,Ja 25,18:5
Freshman Love 1936,Ja 25,18:5
Moonlight Murder 1936,Mr 28,11:2
Snowed Under 1936,Mr 30,17:5
Bullets or Ballots 1936,My 27,27:1
Stage Struck 1936,S 28,14:4
Three Men on a Horse 1936,N 26,39:1
Ever Since Eve 1937,Je 25,25:2
Marry the Girl 1937,Jl 31,6:2
Mr Dodd Takes the Air 1937,Ag 12,14:2
Submarine D-1 1937,D 30,15:4
Swing Your Lady 1938,Ja 27,17:2
Four Daughters 1938,Ag 19,13:3
Boy Meets Girl 1938,Ag 27,7:2
Valley of the Giants 1938,S 10,20:2
Wings of the Navy 1939,F 4,11:1
Dodge City 1939,Ap 8,19:1
Daughters Courageous 1939,Je 24,14:2
Indianapolis Speedway 1939,Jl 15,8:2
Dust Be my Destiny 1939,O 7,11:2
On Your Toes 1939,O 21,12:2
Roaring Twenties, The 1939,N 11,12:1
Four Wives 1939,D 23,9:1
Fighting 69th, The 1940,Ja 27,9:2

'Til We Meet Again 1940,Ap 14,14:2
I Love You Again 1940,Ag 16,11:2
City for Conquest 1940,S 28,9:2
Four Mothers 1941,Ja 11,12:7
Back Street 1941,F 12,25:2
Manpower 1941,Jl 5,14:2
All Through the Night 1942,Ja 24,13:2
Her Cardboard Lover 1942,Jl 17,19:2
Going my Way 1944,My 3,25:2
Marine Raiders 1944,Jl 1,10:7
Bowery to Broadway 1944,N 30,19:2
Medal for Benny, A 1945,My 24,15:2
State Fair 1945,Ag 31,14:3
Runaround, The 1946,Je 7,16:3
Hoodlum Saint, The 1946,Je 27,29:1
Easy Come, Easy Go 1947,F 6,29:2
Carnegie Hall 1947,My 3,10:2
Velvet Touch, The 1948,Ag 26,16:2
Mighty Joe Young 1949,Jl 28,19:3
Paid in Full 1950,F 16,28:2
My Son John 1952,Ap 9,27:1
Lion Is in the Streets, A 1953,S 24,39:2
There's no Business Like Show Business
1954,D 17,37:3
Last Hurrah, The 1958,O 24,40:1
Say One for Me 1959,Je 20,11:2
Tiger Walks, A 1964,Ag 27,28:2
Easy Come, Easy Go 1967,Je 15,56:1
McHugh, Jack
Chinatown Nights 1929,Ap 1,22:1
McHugh, Jimmy
Helen Morgan Story, The 1957,O 3,33:2
McHugh, Jimmy (Composer)
Meet the Baron 1933,O 28,20:3
Dancing Lady 1933,D 1,23:2
King of Burlesque 1936,Ja 16,25:2
Let's Sing Again 1936,My 9,11:2
Top of the Town 1937,Mr 27,19:2
When Love Is Young 1937,Ap 17,15:1
Merry-Go-Round of 1938 1937,N 26,27:2
You're a Sweetheart 1937,D 25,10:5
Hitting a new High 1937,D 27,11:1
Mad About Music 1938,Mr 12,13:2
You're the One 1941,F 20,23:2
Dance Hall 1941,Jl 19,16:2
Seven Days' Leave 1942,D 11,33:2
Happy Go Lucky 1943,Mr 25,25:1
Hers to Hold 1943,Jl 22,15:1
Around the World 1943,N 25,39:2
Four Jills in a Jeep 1944,Ap 6,27:2
Something for the Boys 1944,N 30,19:1
Bring on the Girls 1945,Mr 1,25:5
Nob Hill 1945,Jl 4,10:3
Doll Face 1946,Mr 28,35:3
Do You Love Me 1946,My 25,12:2
Hit Parade of 1947 1947,My 5,32:8
If You Knew Susie 1948,F 23,19:2
Date with Judy, A 1948,Ag 7,8:2
Private's Affair, A 1959,Ag 15,8:7
McHugh, Jimmy (Miscellaneous)
Roberta 1935,Mr 8,25:2
Hooray for Love 1935,Jl 13,16:2
Every Night at Eight 1935,Ag 3,16:2
Dimples 1936,O 10,21:2
Banjo on My Knee 1936,D 12,15:1
McHugh, Kitty
Hollywood Boulevard 1936,S 21,26:4
Blonde Trouble 1937,Ag 7,7:2
On Again-Off Again 1937,S 18,15:3
Grapes of Wrath, The 1940,Ja 25,17:2
Magnificent Dope, The 1942,Jl 3,12:5
McHugh, Martin J (Miscellaneous)
Rising of the Moon, The (A Minute's Wait);
Minute's Wait, A (The Rising of the Moon)
1957,Jl 10,23:1
Rising of the Moon, The (1921); 1921 (The Rising
of the Moon) 1957,Jl 10,23:1
McHugh, Martin J (Original Author)
Rising of the Moon, The (The Majesty of the
Law); Majesty of the Law, The (The Rising of
the Moon) 1957,Jl 10,23:1
McHugh, Matt
Street Scene 1931,Ag 27,22:5
Woman From Monte Carlo, The 1931,D 31,17:6
Taxi 1932,Ja 8,27:3
Freaks 1932,Jl 9,7:5
Purchase Price, The 1932,Jl 16,5:5
Afraid to Talk 1932,D 19,19:5
Hypnotized 1933,Ja 16,13:3
Hard to Handle 1933,F 2,21:5
Devil's Brother, The 1933,Je 10,16:4
Man Who Dared, The 1933,S 9,9:3
Mad Game, The 1933,N 13,21:1
She Loves Me Not 1934,S 8,18:5
Wings in the Dark 1935,F 2,10:1
Murder on a Honeymoon 1935,Mr 4,12:2
Mr Dynamite 1935,My 25,12:1
Barbary Coast 1935,O 14,21:1
If You Could Only Cook 1935,D 26,21:4
Country Beyond, The 1936,Ap 30,17:3
Two in a Crowd 1936,O 5,25:1
Navy Blue and Gold 1937,D 24,21:2
No Time to Marry 1938,F 23,27:2

McHugh, Matt — Cont
Federal Man-Hunt 1939,F 2,17:3
$1,000 a Touchdown 1939,O 5,27:2
Escape, The 1939,N 3,17:4
Blues in the Night 1941,D 12,35:2
It Happened in Flatbush 1942,Jl 3,12:8
Man in the Trunk, The 1942,O 23,25:1
Flight for Freedom 1943,Ap 16,24:2
Secret Command 1944,Je 14,16:2
Salome, Where She Danced 1945,My 3,27:1
Dark Corner, The 1946,My 9,27:3
Deadline for Murder 1946,Je 29,22:7
Trouble With Women, The 1947,Jl 14,14:4
Give my Regards to Broadway 1948,Je 23,32:2
Innocent Affair, An 1948,S 29,36:2
Bodyhold 1949,D 12,29:4
Return of the Frontiersman 1950,Je 10,11:3
McHugh, Vincent (Original Author)
What's so bad About Feeling Good?
1968,My 25,27:1
Macia, Cheres
Payasada de la Vida; Tricks of Life
1935,Mr 18,14:5
Macias, Gaby
Circo Tragic, El; Tragic Circus, The
1939,Je 17,12:3
McIllwain, William
Passionate Youth 1925,Je 30,14:3
MacInnes, Helen (Original Author)
Assignment in Brittany 1943,Ap 22,31:2
Above Suspicion 1943,Ag 6,10:3
Venetian Affair, The 1967,Ja 19,41:2
McIntire, John
Call Northside 777 1948,F 19,29:2
Black Bart 1948,Mr 4,30:4
River Lady 1948,My 21,19:5
Street with no Name, The 1948,Jl 15,26:6
Live Today for Tomorrow 1948,D 6,29:2
Down to the Sea in Ships 1949,F 23,31:2
Red Canyon 1949,Ap 28,28:2
Scene of the Crime 1949,Jl 29,12:2
Top o' the Morning 1949,S 1,25:2
Johnny Stool Pigeon 1949,S 23,28:3
Ambush 1950,Ja 19,35:2
Francis 1950,Mr 16,40:2
No Sad Songs for Me 1950,Ap 28,26:2
Shadow on the Wall 1950,My 19,31:3
Winchester 73 1950,Je 8,38:2
Asphalt Jungle, The 1950,Je 9,29:3
Walk Softly Stranger 1950,O 16,30:5
Saddle Tramp 1950,N 24,31:4
Under the Gun 1951,F 23,33:2
U S S Teakettle 1951,F 24,11:2
That's My Boy 1951,Ag 2,18:1
Westward the Women 1952,Ja 1,21:2
World in His Arms, The 1952,O 10,21:2
Horizons West 1952,N 22,16:5
Mississippi Gambler, The 1953,Ja 30,25:1
President's Lady, The 1953,My 22,31:1
Lion Is in the Streets, A 1953,S 24,39:2
Apache 1954,Jl 10,7:2
Far Country, The 1955,F 14,24:2
Scarlet Coat, The 1955,Jl 30,14:2
Kentuckian, The 1955,S 2,13:2
Phenix City Story, The 1955,S 3,9:1
Spoilers, The 1955,D 24,10:2
World in my Corner 1956,F 18,12:5
Backlash 1956,Ap 21,11:2
I've Lived Before 1956,Ag 4,13:1
Away all Boats 1956,Ag 17,14:2
Tin Star, The 1957,O 24,37:2
Sing Boy Sing 1958,F 22,9:4
Mark of the Hawk, The 1958,Mr 6,32:1
Light in the Forest, The 1958,Jl 11,15:2
Who Was That Lady? 1960,Ap 16,10:1
Psycho 1960,Je 17,37:1
Elmer Gantry 1960,Jl 8,16:1
Flaming Star 1960,D 17,19:1
Seven Ways From Sundown 1960,D 22,18:4
Two Rode Together 1961,Jl 27,23:3
Summer and Smoke 1961,N 17,41:1
Rough Night in Jericho 1967,N 9,56:4
McIntire, Tim
Shenandoah 1965,Jl 29,18:3
MacIntosh, Alex
Boy Cried Murder, The 1966,Ap 14,42:3
McIntosh, Burr
Driven 1923,F 12,13:4
Exciters, The 1923,Je 4,13:3
On the Banks of the Wabash 1923,O 23,21:3
Virtuous Liars 1924,Mr 31,20:1
Wilderness Woman, The 1926,My 10,19:1
Taxi, Taxi 1927,F 15,23:1
See You in Jail 1927,Ap 4,30:5
Yankee Clipper, The 1927,My 3,25:1
Naughty but Nice 1927,Jl 5,19:2
Breakfast at Sunrise 1927,N 14,26:1
Silk Stockings 1927,N 29,31:1
Hero for a Night, A 1927,D 26,26:6
Fourflusher 1928,Ja 24,26:1
Sailors' Wives 1928,F 28,18:4
Racket, The 1928,Jl 9,25:1
Grip of the Yukon, The 1928,Jl 10,17:3
Lilac Time 1928,Ag 4,7:2

McIntosh, Burr— Cont

Me, Gangster 1928,O 22,29:1
Last Warning, The 1929,Ja 7,36:2
Skinner Steps Out 1929,D 7,19:3
Rogue Song, The 1930,Ja 29,26:4
Way Down East 1931,Mr 16,25:1
Sweetheart of Sigma Chi, The 1933,N 9,27:1
Richest Girl in the World, The 1934,S 21,29:2

McIntosh, David
Doctor Faustus 1968,F 7,38:1

McIntosh, Eileen
Walk in the Shadow 1966,S 12,52:5

McIntosh, Ellen
Stolen Hours 1963,O 17,39:1

MacIntosh, Fraser
Boy Cried Murder, The 1966,Ap 14,42:3

McIntosh, J T (Screenwriter)
Satellite in the Sky 1956,S 4,32:7

MacIntosh, Ken and his band
Alligator Named Daisy, An 1957,O 7,23:2

McIntosh, Morris
Girl on the Barge, The 1929,F 26,31:1

McIntyre, Francis A Rev
Pope Speaks, The 1933,Ap 17,13:3 (In Addenda)

McIntyre, Frank
Traveling Salesman, The 1916,D 18,9:3
Too Fat to Fight 1918,D 2,11:3

McIntyre, John
Command Decision 1949,Ja 20,34:2
Glory Alley 1952,Jl 30,20:8
Four Guns to the Border 1954,N 6,15:3

McIntyre, Leila
On the Level 1930,Jl 5,17:4
Pick a Star 1937,My 28,17:2
Housekeeper's Daughter, The 1939,D 2,21:4

McIntyre, Peggy
Syncopation 1942,My 29,13:3
Loves of Edgar Allan Poe, The 1942,S 21,19:2
I Remember Mama 1948,Mr 12,29:2
El Paso 1949,Mr 24,35:2

Macip, Jose
Cemetario de las Aquilas, El; Eagles' Cementery,
The 1939,S 2,20:1

MacIsaacs, Fred (Original Author)
Mysterious Crossing 1937,F 2,20:5

MACK
See Also MACH

Mack, Al
Hoodlum Priest, The 1961,Ap 3,28:5

Mack, Andrew
Bluebeard's Seven Wives 1925,D 28,19:2

Mack, Arthur
Return of Sherlock Holmes, The 1929,O 19,22:6

Mack, Baby
Ghost Talks, The 1929,F 18,28:1
Close Harmony 1929,Ap 29,29:2

Mack, Billy
Wave, A Wac and a Marine, A 1944,Ag 14,11:4

Mack, Bobby
Black Beauty 1921,F 21,16:1
Vanity Fair 1923,My 7,19:3
Girl From Montmarte, The 1926,F 25,26:2
Student Prince, The 1927,S 22,33:2
Road to Romance, The 1927,O 10,24:1
Evangeline 1929,Jl 29,23:3

Mack, Cactus
Racketeers of the Range 1939,Je 8,31:4

Mack, Charles Emmett
One Exciting Night 1922,O 24,17:3
Driven 1923,F 12,13:4
America 1924,F 22,20:1
Youth for Sale 1924,S 3,17:1
Bad Company 1925,Mr 16,16:1
White Monkey, The 1925,Je 9,16:3
Woman of the World, A 1925,D 14,18:2
Devil's Circus, The 1926,Mr 29,24:3
Unknown Soldier, The 1926,My 31,10:2
Rough Riders, The 1927,Mr 16,28:2
Old San Francisco 1927,Je 23,23:3
First Auto, The 1927,Je 28,28:4
Why Bring That Up? 1929,O 5,22:5
Hypnotized 1933,Ja 16,13:3

Mack, David (Composer)
At War With the Army 1951,Ja 25,21:5

Mack, E J
It's a Great Life 1920,Ag 30,12:3

Mack, Gunther
Yesterday Girl 1967,S 22,57:2

Mack, Helen
Struggle, The 1931,D 11,35:1
Silent Witness, The 1932,F 8,21:1
Sweepings 1933,Mr 24,22:3
Melody Cruise 1933,Je 23,15:2
Blind Adventure 1933,O 31,24:3
Christopher Bean 1933,N 25,10:2
Son of Kong 1933,D 30,9:2
All of Me 1934,F 5,19:2
Kiss and Make-Up 1934,Je 29,17:1
You Belong to Me 1934,S 13,26:1
Lemon Drop Kid, The 1934,O 27,20:2
College Rhythm 1934,N 24,19:1
Four Hours to Kill 1935,Ap 11,27:3
She 1935,Jl 26,18:2
Return of Peter Grimm, The 1935,O 4,25:2

Milky Way, The 1936,Mr 26,27:2
I Promise to Pay 1937,Ap 26,15:2
You Can't Buy Luck 1937,My 14,21:2
Last Train from Madrid, The 1937,Je 19,20:2
Fit for a King 1937,O 15,18:5
King of the Newsboys 1938,Ap 2,18:2
Secrets of a Nurse 1938,D 12,26:2
I Stand Accused 1939,Ja 5,17:1
Gambling Ship 1939,Ja 21,19:2
Calling All Marines 1939,O 26,27:2
His Girl Friday 1940,Ja 12,13:2
Girls of the Road 1940,Jl 22,20:2
Power Dive 1941,My 29,15:4
And Now Tomorrow 1944,N 23,38:2
Strange Holiday 1945,O 20,8:2

Mack, Hughie
Going Up 1923,O 10,16:2
Reno 1924,Ja 8,27:1
Greed 1924,D 5,28:1
Woman's Faith, A 1925,Jl 27,17:3
Merry Widow, The 1925,Ag 27,14:1
Four Sons 1928,F 14,27:1
Wedding March, The 1928,O 15,26:1

Mack, Jack
Lover Come Back 1931,Je 5,26:5
Redhead 1934,N 16,27:1
I Cover the War 1937,Ag 2,10:2

Mack, James T
Swim, Girl, Swim 1927,S 5,13:2
Women's Wares 1927,N 15,27:1
Home Towners, The 1928,O 24,26:4
Queen of the Night Clubs 1929,Mr 18,30:6
Anna Christie 1930,Mr 15,22:5
Arsene Lupin 1932,F 27,22:1
In Love With Life 1934,My 12,12:3

Mack, Joe
Finders Keepers 1928,Mr 5,21:3

Mack, Marian
General, The 1927,F 8,21:1

Mack, Max
You Belong to Me 1934,S 13,26:1

Mack, Max (Director)
Nur am Rhein 1931,S 25,28:7
Tausend Fuer Eine Nacht 1934,F 12,19:2

Mack, Max (Original Author)
Nur am Rhein 1931,S 25,28:7

Mack, Richard (Screenwriter)
Isle of Paradise 1932,Jl 21,15:2

Mack, Robert
Under Two Flags 1922,S 25,10:2

Mack, Russell (Director)
Second Wife 1930,F 10,20:4
Big Money 1930,N 22,21:3
Lonely Wives 1931,Mr 16,25:1
Spirit of Notre Dame, The 1931,O 16,27:1
Heaven on Earth 1931,D 19,16:4
Mississippi 1931,D 27,VIII,5:4 (In Addenda)
Scandal for Sale 1932,Ap 3,26:2
All American, The 1932,O 22,18:4
Once in a Lifetime 1932,O 29,18:4
Private Jones 1933,Mr 25,13:3
Band Plays on, The 1934,D 22,21:2

Mack, Stanley
Gun Smoke 1931,Ap 24,27:1

Mack, Tommy
New Faces of 1937 1937,Jl 2,25:1
Zenobia 1939,My 15,15:2

Mack, Wilbur
Argyle Case, The 1929,Ag 31,13:4
Czar of Broadway, The 1930,Je 30,22:6
Scarlet Pages 1930,D 6,21:3
Remote Control 1930,D 8,26:1
Annabelle's Affairs 1931,Je 29,20:3
Million Dollar Baby 1935,My 6,22:3

Mack, Willard
Voice of the City, The 1929,Ap 29,29:2
What Price Innocence? 1933,Je 26,16:3
Voice of the City, The 1929,Ap 29,29:2
What Price Innocence? 1933,Je 26,16:3
Broadway to Hollywood 1933,S 2,14:4

Mack, Willard (Original Author)
Kick In 1922,D 18,22:2
Dove, The 1928,Ja 3,28:2
Noose, The 1928,Mr 19,26:4
Tiger Rose 1929,D 25,23:1
Kick In 1931,My 25,17:1
Girl of the Rio 1932,Ja 9,21:1
What Price Innocence? 1933,Je 26,16:3
Broadway to Hollywood 1933,S 2,14:4
I'd Give my Life 1936,Ag 17,9:1
Girl and the Gambler, The 1939,Je 28,17:3

Mack, Willard (Screenwriter)
Little Robinson Crusoe 1924,S 3,17:1
Old Clothes 1925,N 25,5:1
Voice of the City, The 1929,Ap 29,29:2

Mack, William (Original Author)
Shadows 1919,F 10,11:3

Mack, William (Screenwriter)
One Week of Life 1919,My 19,20:5

Mack, William B
Hellotrope 1920,N 29,20:3
Backbone 1923,Ap 30,11:2
Steadfast Heart, The 1923,D 25,26:1

Mack, William B— Cont

American Venus, The 1926,Ja 26,25:2
Song and Dance Man, The 1926,F 1,16:1

Mackaill, Dorothy
Bits of Life 1921,O 17,18:1
Mighty Lak' a Rose 1923,Mr 20,24:3
Fighting Blade, The 1923,O 15,15:4
His Children's Children 1923,N 5,15:1
Twenty-One 1924,F 18,13:1
Man Who Came Back, The 1924,S 1,9:1
Bridge of Sighs, The 1925,Mr 23,14:2
Chickie 1925,Ap 27,15:2
Making of O'Malley 1925,Je 22,10:2
One Year to Live 1925,Jl 6,12:2
Shore Leave 1925,S 14,16:1
Joanna 1925,D 15,14:5
Dancers of Paris, The 1926,Mr 29,24:3
Ranson's Folly 1926,My 31,10:2
Subway Sadie 1926,S 13,18:1
Girl from Coney Island or Just Another Blonde
1926,D 13,27:1
Lunatic at Large, The 1927,F 1,25:1
Convoy 1927,My 9,26:4
Smile, Brother, Smile 1927,Ag 29,21:1
Crystal Cup, The 1927,O 25,33:3
Man Crazy 1927,D 19,30:1
Ladies' Night in a Turkish Bath 1928,Ap 9,18:2
Lady Be Good 1928,My 28,23:2
Whip, The 1928,S 17,28:2
Waterfront 1928,O 22,29:1
Barker, The 1928,D 6,35:1
Children of the Ritz 1929,Ap 2,28:4
His Captive Woman 1929,Ap 3,26:4
Two Weeks Off 1929,Je 24,27:1
Hard to Get 1929,S 28,17:3
Great Divide, The 1930,F 17,17:6
Strictly Modern 1930,My 3,23:1
Flirting Widow, The 1930,Ag 2,16:4
Office Wife, The 1930,S 27,21:3
Once a Sinner 1931,Ja 17,23:1
Bright Lights 1931,F 10,24:4
Kept Husbands 1931,Mr 24,31:2
Party Husband 1931,My 16,13:3
Reckless Hour, The 1931,Ag 1,16:4
Safe in Hell 1931,D 19,16:4
No Man of her Own 1932,D 31,10:1
Chief, The 1933,D 2,9:4
Cheaters 1934,My 12,12:4
Bulldog Drummond at Bay 1937,O 25,23:2

Mackay, Angus
Morgan! 1966,Ap 5,42:2

Mackay, Barry
Private Life of Don Juan, The 1934,D 10,16:2
Evergreen 1935,Ja 11,29:1
Born for Glory 1935,O 21,22:4
Great Barrier, The 1937,F 5,17:5
Silent Barriers 1937,Mr 26,25:1
Gangway 1937,Ag 21,7:3
Sailing Along 1938,Ap 16,17:1
Christmas Carol, A 1938,D 23,16:2

Mackay, Fulton
Brave Don't Cry, The 1952,N 6,37:2
Scotch on the Rocks 1954,Je 14,18:2

McKay, Gardner
Pleasure Seekers, The 1964,D 26,9:1

McKay, George
Case of the Missing Man, The 1935,N 23,23:2
One Way Ticket 1936,Ja 1,35:2
You may Be Next 1936,F 24,14:1
Don't Gamble With Love 1936,Mr 2,13:3
Pride of the Marines 1936,Ap 27,19:2
Counterfeit 1936,Jl 20,11:1
Final Hour, The 1936,Ag 1,16:3
Shakedown 1936,Ag 17,9:2
Two-Fisted Gentleman 1936,Ag 24,11:2
Killer at Large 1936,O 26,20:1
Come Closer, Folks 1936,N 23,17:3
Counterfeit Lady 1937,Ja 11,15:6
Devil's Playground 1937,F 15,12:5
Racketeers in Exile 1937,Ap 12,15:3
Fight to the Finish, A 1937,Je 26,20:2 (In
Addenda)
Frame-Up 1937,Ag 9,23:2 (In Addenda)
Murder in Greenwich Village 1937,O 30,22:2
It's all Yours 1938,Ja 7,15:3
Highway Patrol 1938,Ag 4,15:2
Convicted 1938,Ag 22,9:3
Illegal Traffic 1938,N 17,29:3
Duke of West Point, The 1938,D 16,33:2
King of the Turf 1939,My 8,21:2
Babes in Arms 1939,O 20,27:2
Big Guy, The 1940,Ja 1,29:2
Face Behind the Mask, The 1941,F 7,23:2
Canal Zone 1942,Mr 30,21:2
Sabotage Squad 1942,Ag 5,16:1
Boogie Man Will Get You, The 1942,O 12,12:4
Murder in Times Square 1943,My 31,13:2

McKay, James
Big Country, The 1958,O 2,44:1

McKay, James (Director)
Souls for Sables 1925,S 15,12:1 (Incorrect in this
edition; use 1925,S 15,29:1 elsewhere)

McKay, Jock
Brave Don't Cry, The 1952,N 6,37:2
McKay, John
Cuban Rebel Girls 1959,D 26,7:3
MacKay, Norman
Untamed Fury 1947,Ap 26,10:6
Frogmen, The 1951,Je 30,8:6
McKay, Scott
Thirty Seconds Over Tokyo 1944,N 16,19:1
Guest in the House 1945,F 16,19:2
Kiss and Tell 1945,O 26,16:2
Duel in the Sun 1947,My 8,30:2
McKay, Wanda
Corregidor 1943,My 28,19:2
McKay, Winsor
Great White Way, The 1924,Ja 4,10:1
Mackaye, Dorothy (Original Author)
Ladies They Talk About 1933,F 25,20:4
Lady Gangster 1942,Jl 10,13:2
MacKaye, Fred
Charlatan, The 1929,Ap 15,22:6
Last Performance, The 1929,N 4,28:1
MacKaye, Norman
Hoodlum Priest, The 1961,Ap 3,28:5
MacKaye, Percy (Original Author)
Puritan Passions 1923,O 15,15:4
McKechnie, Cromwell
Here is my Heart 1934,D 22,21:1
Mackechnie, Duncan Capt
I Know Where I'm Going 1947,Ag 20,25:2
McKechnie, James
Years Between, The 1947,Mr 10,25:2
Girl in the Canal, The 1947,O 9,32:3
Bond Street 1950,Mr 30,40:6
Madeleine 1950,S 1,17:2
Scott of the Antarctic 1951,F 26,20:2
MCKEE
See Also MCGEE, MAGEE
McKee, Donald
Whistle at Eaton Falls, The 1951,O 11,49:2
Goddess, The 1958,Je 25,24:1
McKee, Georgette
Ramparts We Watch, The 1940,S 20,27:1
McKee, John
House on Ninety-Second Street, The
  1945,S 27,24:7
Father Was a Fullback 1949,O 13,33:3
Angels in the Outfield 1951,O 18,32:1
Pride of St Louis, The 1952,My 3,17:5
Above and Beyond 1953,Ja 31,10:6
Strategic Air Command 1955,Ap 21,33:1
Gathering of Eagles, A 1963,Jl 11,21:2
McKee, Lafe
Terror Trail 1933,F 11,11:3
Quitter, The 1934,Mr 14,23:3
Keeper of the Bees, The 1935,Ag 17,18:5
Mystery of the Hooded Horsemen, The
  1937,Ag 13,13:2
Rawhide 1938,Ap 25,19:2
I'm From the City 1938,Ag 19,13:4
McKee, Pat
Straight, Place and Show 1938,O 1,10:2
McKee, Raymond
Spirit of the Red Cross, The 1918,Ap 21,IV,11:8
Blind Bargain, A 1922,D 4,20:2
Down to the Sea in Ships 1923,F 19,10:1
Babbitt 1924,Jl 15,9:4
Silent Accuser, The 1924,N 25,26:1
Contraband 1925,Mr 24,20:6
Compromise 1925,O 27,23:3
Heart to Heart 1928,S 10,29:2
McKee, Tom
Court-Martial of Billy Mitchell, The
  1955,D 23,14:2
MacKellar, Helen
Past of Mary Holmes, The 1933,My 1,10:3
High School Girl 1935,Mr 16,19:1
Federal Bullets 1937,D 27,11:1
Crime School 1938,My 11,17:2
Valley of the Giants 1938,S 10,20:2
Disbarred 1939,Ja 19,17:2
Dark Command 1940,My 11,15:2
Three Faces West 1940,Ag 19,13:2
Cheers for Miss Bishop 1941,Mr 14,17:2
Powers Girl, The 1943,Mr 26,14:2 (In Addenda)
McKelway, St Clair (Original Author)
Mister 880 1950,S 30,13:2
McKelway, St Clair (Screenwriter)
Sleep, My Love 1948,F 19,29:4
Mating of Millie, The 1948,Mr 13,12:2
Macken, Walter
Home Is the Hero 1961,Ja 26,32:1
Quare Fellow 1963,F 20,6:1
Macken, Walter (Original Author)
Home Is the Hero 1961,Ja 26,32:1
Mackendrick, Alexander (Director)
Tight Little Island 1949,D 26,33:2
Man in the White Suit, The 1952,Ap 1,35:2
Story of Mandy, The 1953,F 24,21:3
High and Dry 1954,Ag 31,25:5
Ladykillers 1956,F 21,37:2
Sweet Smell of Success 1957,Je 28,29:2

Boy Ten Feet Tall, A 1965,My 13,32:2
High Wind in Jamaica, A 1965,Je 17,27:2
Don't Make Waves 1967,Je 21,36:2
Mackendrick, Alexander (Original Author)
High and Dry 1954,Ag 31,25:5
Mackendrick, Alexander (Screenwriter)
Saraband 1949,Je 13,16:3
Man in the White Suit, The 1952,Ap 1,35:2
MacKenna, Kate
Bride Comes Home, The 1935,D 25,30:2
MacKenna, Kenneth
Miss Bluebeard 1925,Ja 28,14:1
Kiss in the Dark, A 1925,Ap 7,17:3
American Venus, The 1926,Ja 26,25:2
Lunatic at Large, The 1927,F 1,25:1
Pleasure Crazed 1929,Jl 15,25:1
Love, Live and Laugh 1929,N 2,14:6
South Sea Rose 1929,D 7,19:3
Men Without Women 1930,F 1,15:1
Temple Tower 1930,My 10,25:3
Sin Takes a Holliday 1930,N 28,23:1
Man Who Came Back, The 1931,Ja 3,21:2
High Time 1960,S 17,15:1
Judgment at Nuremberg 1961,D 20,36:1
13 West Street 1962,Je 7,31:2
MacKenna, Kenneth (Director)
Always Good-Bye 1931,My 23,13:4
Spider, The 1931,S 5,7:4
Good Sport 1931,D 12,23:3
Careless Lady 1932,Ap 18,19:2
Walls of Gold 1933,O 21,11:3
McKenna, Martha (Original Author)
I Was a Spy 1934,Ja 15,12:2
Lancer Spy 1937,N 4,29:1
McKenna, Richard (Original Author)
Sand Pebbles, The 1966,D 21,48:1
McKenna, Siobhan
Hungry Hill 1947,O 11,11:2
Lost People, The 1950,O 2,19:4
King of Kings 1961,O 12,41:2
Playboy of the Western World, The
  1963,Mr 19,8:2
Of Human Bondage 1964,S 24,46:2
Doctor Zhivago 1965,D 23,21:1
McKenna, T P
Girl With Green Eyes 1964,Ag 11,37:2
Young Cassidy 1965,Mr 23,35:1
Ulysses 1967,Mr 14,55:1
McKenna, Virginia
Cruel Sea, The 1953,Ag 11,18:5
Horse's Mouth, The 1954,Ja 20,33:4
Simba 1955,O 22,24:2
Ship That Died of Shame, The 1956,Ag 21,33:2
Barretts of Wimpole Street, The 1957,Ja 18,15:3
Smallest Show on Earth 1957,N 23,11:2
Town Like Alice, A 1958,S 22,27:1
Wreck of the Mary Deare, The 1959,N 7,27:1
Born Free 1966,Je 23,29:1
McKenney, Ruth (Original Author)
My Sister Eileen 1942,O 23,15:1
San Diego, I Love You 1944,N 10,25:1
Margie 1946,O 17,28:3
Trouble With Women, The 1947,Jl 14,14:4
McKennon, Dal
Tom Thumb 1958,D 24,00:0
Misadventures of Merlin Jones, The
  1964,Mr 26,40:4
McKenns, Philip
Flower Thief, The 1962,Jl 14,11:5
MacKenzie, Aeneas (Original Author)
Back to Bataan 1945,S 13,26:3
Spanish Main, The 1945,N 7,20:2
Black Book, The 1949,O 17,18:2
Against all Flags 1952,D 25,34:6
MacKenzie, Aeneas (Screenwriter)
Juarez 1939,Ap 26,27:1
Private Lives of Elizabeth and Essex, The
  1939,D 2,21:2
They Died With Their Boots On 1941,N 21,23:3
Navy Comes Through, The 1942,N 12,30:3
Woman of the Town, The 1944,Mr 6,17:2
Fighting Seabees, The 1944,Mr 20,14:2
Buffalo Bill 1944,Ap 20,22:6
Black Book, The 1949,O 17,18:2
Prince Who Was a Thief, The 1951,Jl 4,13:2
Captain Horatio Hornblower 1951,S 14,21:2
Ivanhoe 1952,Ag 1,8:2
Against all Flags 1952,D 25,34:6
Secret Sharer, The 1953,Ja 14,27:2
Ten Commandments, The 1956,N 9,35:2
Mackenzie, Alex
High and Dry 1954,Ag 31,25:5
Mad Little Island 1958,D 31,12:1
Bridal Path, The 1959,D 21,34:2
Battle of the Sexes, The 1960,Ap 19,40:4
Greyfriars' Bobby 1961,O 12,41:4
MacKenzie, Alice
Summer Holiday 1948,Je 12,8:5
McKenzie, Bob
Fifth Avenue Models 1925,My 4,16:2
Half-Naked Truth, The 1932,D 31,10:1
Bride Comes Home, The 1935,D 25,30:2
Hideaway 1937,S 25,10:2

McKenzie, Bob— Cont
Death of a Champion 1939,Ag 24,17:3
When the Daltons Rode 1940,Ag 23,13:3
In old California 1942,Je 18,25:3
Tall in the Saddle 1944,D 15,25:3
Mackenzie, Compton
Tight Little Island 1949,D 26,33:2
Chance of a Lifetime 1951,Mr 15,37:2
Mackenzie, Compton (Original Author)
Carnival 1931,N 22,VIII,6:1
Sylvia Scarlett 1936,Ja 10,16:2
Tight Little Island 1949,D 26,33:2
Mad Little Island 1958,D 31,12:1
Mackenzie, Compton (Screenwriter)
Tight Little Island 1949,D 26,33:2
MacKenzie, Donald
True Heaven 1929,F 11,26:3
Studio Murder Mystery, The 1929,Je 10,23:1
Insidious Dr Fu Manchu, The 1929,Jl 22,17:1
Fighting Caravans 1931,Ja 26,21:1
Unfaithful 1931,Mr 7,17:2
MacKenzie, Donald (Original Author)
Malaga 1962,F 22,20:3
McKenzie, Ella
Alice Adams 1935,Ag 16,11:3
McKenzie, Eva
Virtuous Husband 1931,My 8,30:2
McKenzie, Fay
Student Tour 1934,O 31,17:3
When the Daltons Rode 1940,Ag 23,13:3
Remember Pearl Harbor 1942,Je 4,22:4
Murder in the Music Hall 1946,Ap 15,22:2
Mackenzie, Gordon
Mikado, The 1967,Mr 15,53:1
McKenzie, Iona
How to be Very, Very Popular 1955,Jl 23,10:1
MacKenzie, Joyce
Twelve O'Clock High 1950,Ja 28,10:2
Mother Didn't Tell Me 1950,Mr 4,11:2
Broken Arrow 1950,Jl 21,15:2
Stella 1950,Ag 19,9:2
On the Riviera 1951,My 24,47:1
People Will Talk 1951,Ag 30,20:1
Racket, The 1951,D 13,44:2
Deadline U S A 1952,Mr 15,8:2
Wait Till the Sun Shines, Nellie 1952,Je 28,12:2
Night Without Sleep 1952,S 27,13:2
Rails Into Laramie 1954,My 13,34:2
French Line, The 1954,My 15,13:2
MacKenzie, Lewis
Native Son 1951,Je 18,19:2
MacKenzie, Mary
Blonde Sinner 1957,Ja 24,34:1
McKenzie, Melanie
Rocking Horse Winner, The 1950,Je 9,29:2
McKenzie, Robert
Tillie and Gus 1933,N 13,21:1
You're Telling Me 1934,Ap 7,19:1
Shot in the Dark, A 1935,My 22,23:2
Mackenzie, Will
Harvey Middleman, Fireman 1965,Jl 13,39:1
McKern, Leo
Murder in the Cathedral 1952,Mr 26,35:2
Time Without Pity 1957,N 23,11:2
Tale of Two Cities, A 1958,Ag 5,23:1
Mouse That Roared, The 1959,O 27,40:1
Scent of Mystery 1960,F 19,23:1
Yesterday's Enemy 1960,Mr 4,19:1
Day the Earth Caught Fire, The 1962,Mr 16,25:1
I Like Money 1962,My 19,18:2
Lisa 1962,My 25,28:1
They all Died Laughing 1964,Mr 16,37:2
King and Country 1964,S 24,46:2
Amorous Adventures of Moll Flanders, The
  1965,My 27,28:1
Agent 8 3/4 1965,O 14,53:1
King and Country 1966,Ja 28,20:4
Man for all Seasons, A 1966,D 13,60:1
Assignment K 1968,Jl 20,18:2
Shoes of the Fisherman, The 1968,N 15,40:3
McKernan, Kim
Greenwich Village Story 1963,Jl 12,14:3
Mackie, Richard
Ghost Goes West, The 1936,Ja 11,9:2
McKim, Josephine
Lady, Be Careful 1936,O 10,21:1
McKim, Robert
Brand, The 1919,Mr 17,13:2
Greased Lightning 1919,Ap 28,13:2
Westerners, The 1919,Ag 4,8:3
Her Kingdom of Dreams 1919,S 22,8:1
Riders of the Dawn 1920,My 3,18:1
Silver Horde, The 1920,My 10,18:2
Mark of Zorro, The 1920,N 29,20:3
Monte Cristo 1922,Ag 15,20:3
Human Wreckage 1923,Je 28,10:2
Spoilers, The 1923,Ag 6,14:2
Strangers of the Night 1923,O 8,20:1
Flaming Barriers 1924,Ja 29,16:1
Mademoiselle Midnight 1924,My 27,14:1
Maytime 1924,Je 2,14:3
Bat, The 1926,Mr 15,18:3
Strong Man, The 1926,S 7,44:2

McKim, Sammy
Little Men 1940,D 9,23:2
Father's Son 1941,F 13,25:3
McKimmon, Rodger
Strictly Confidential 1919,O 6,15:1
McKinley, J Edward
Thunder of Drums, A 1961,S 27,35:1
Impossible Years, The 1968,D 6,54:1
McKinnel, Herman
Fanny Hawthorn 1929,N 11,20:2
McKinnel, Norman
Sherlock Holmes's Fatal Hour 1931,Jl 13,13:5
White Face 1933,D 4,22:3
Criminal at Large 1933,D 20,27:2
McKinney, Florine
Miracle Man, The 1932,Ap 21,25:2
Horse Feathers 1932,Ag 11,12:2
Cynara 1932,D 26,26:2
Beauty for Sale 1933,S 16,9:3
Student Tour 1934,O 31,17:3
David Copperfield 1935,Ja 19,8:1
Night Life of the Gods 1935,F 23,14:6
Muss 'Em Up 1936,F 3,21:2
McKinney, Mira
Road to Reno, The 1938,O 3,11:2
Cafe Society 1939,F 23,19:2
Harriet Craig 1950,N 3,31:2
Groom Wore Spurs, The 1951,Mr 14,41:2
McKinney, Nina Mae
Hallelujah 1929,Ag 21,33:1
Safe in Hell 1931,D 19,16:4
Reckless 1935,Ap 20,16:1
Sanders of the River 1935,Je 27,16:1
Dark Waters 1944,N 22,25:2
Pinky 1949,S 30,28:2
Mackinnon, Allan (Screenwriter)
Sleeping Car to Trieste 1949,Ap 18,18:6
Mackintosh, Kenneth
Othello 1966,F 2,24:1
Mackintosh, Louise
Chickie 1925,Ap 27,15:2
Doctors' Wives 1931,Ap 25,23:4
Black Camel, The 1931,Jl 4,11:5
Compromised 1931,N 7,16:5
Down to Earth 1932,S 2,19:2
Phantom President, The 1932,O 1,10:4
Hard to Handle 1933,F 2,21:5
They Just Had to Get Married 1933,F 13,11:4
Little Giant, The 1933,My 27,11:5
Macklin, Clifton
Mark of the Hawk, The 1958,Mr 6,32:1
Macklin, David
Born Wild 1968,D 12,62:6
Macklin, Hughes
Bride of the Lake, The 1934,S 11,24:5
Macklin, James
Voice of Bugle Ann, The 1936,F 27,23:1
McKnaughton, Jack
Dulcimer Street 1948,N 8,24:2
McKnight, Tom (Producer)
Black Angel 1946,S 26,32:4
MACKS
See Also MAX
Macks, Helen
Success 1923,Jl 10,22:5
McKuen, Rod
Summer Love 1958,Je 26,23:4
McKutcheon, John
Thief, The 1952,O 16,37:1
MacLachlan, Janet
Up Tight 1968,D 19,62:1
MacLaghlen, Clifford
Fight for Matterhorn, The 1929,Jl 29,23:3
McLaglen, Andrew V (Director)
McLintock 1963,N 14,41:3
Shenandoah 1965,Jl 29,18:3
Rare Breed, The 1966,Ap 14,42:3
Monkeys Go Home 1967,Mr 30,55:1
Way West, The 1967,My 25,54:1
Ballad of Josie, The 1968,Mr 14,51:2
Devil's Brigade, The 1968,My 23,56:2
Bandolero 1968,Jl 18,26:2
McLaglen, Clifford
White Sheik, The 1929,D 9,32:5
Bride 68 1930,Ap 15,28:5
McLaglen, Cyril
Underground 1928,Ag 12,VII,4:3 (In Addenda)
Underground 1929,F 26,31:1
Lost Patrol, The 1929,D 16,34:2
Suspense 1930,N 8,21:3
Jaws of Hell 1931,Ja 5,21:3
Mary of Scotland 1936,Jl 31,22:2
Plough and the Stars, The 1937,Ja 29,15:1
Wee Willie Winkie 1937,Jl 24,12:1
Long Voyage Home, The 1940,O 9,30:2 (In Addenda)
Black Swan, The 1942,D 24,18:3
McLaglen, Victor
Beloved Brute, The 1924,N 10,20:1
Percy 1925,Mr 25,24:2
Unholy Three, The 1925,Ag 4,14:3

Winds of Chance 1925,Ag 17,10:3
Men of Steel 1926,Jl 12,24:4
Beau Geste 1926,Ag 26,17:3
What Price Glory 1926,N 24,26:4
Loves of Carmen 1927,S 27,31:1
Girl in Every Port, A 1928,F 20,14:1
Mother Machree 1928,Mr 6,20:3
Hangman's House 1928,My 14,25:1
River Pirate, The 1928,S 17,27:1
Captain Lash 1929,F 4,20:1
Strong Boy 1929,Ap 1,22:1
Black Watch, The 1929,My 23,26:3
Cock Eyed World, The 1929,Ag 5,25:2
Hot for Paris 1930,Ja 4,21:1
Happy Days 1930,F 14,20:1
Hot for Paris 1930,Mr 9,IX,6:1
On the Level 1930,Jl 5,17:4
Devil With Women, A 1930,O 20,28:2
Dishonored 1931,Mr 6,16:1
Three Rogues 1931,Ap 4,23:1
Women of all Nations 1931,My 30,9:2
Annabelle's Affairs 1931,Je 29,20:3
Wicked 1931,S 19,10:2
Gay Caballero, The 1932,Mr 26,17:2
Devil's Lottery 1932,Ap 2,13:2
Guilty as Hell 1932,Ag 6,14:5
Rackety Rax 1932,N 5,12:5
Hot Pepper 1933,Ja 23,9:2
Laughing at Life 1933,Jl 15,14:2
No More Women 1934,Mr 15,27:4
Lost Patrol, The 1934,Ap 2,13:2
Wharf Angel 1934,Ap 21,12:1
Murder at the Vanities 1934,My 21,20:2
Captain Hates the Sea, The 1934,N 29,33:2
Under Pressure 1935,F 4,11:3
Great Hotel Murder, The 1935,F 28,17:4
Informer, The 1935,My 10,25:2
Professional Soldier 1936,Ja 30,14:2
Klondike Annie 1936,Mr 12,18:2
Under Two Flags 1936,My 1,19:1
Magnificent Brute, The 1936,O 24,23:1
Nancy Steele is Missing 1937,Mr 8,22:1
Sea Devils 1937,Mr 16,26:4
This Is my Affair 1937,My 28,17:1
Wee Willie Winkie 1937,Jl 24,12:1
Battle of Broadway 1938,Ap 25,19:2
Devil's Party, The 1938,My 31,8:3
We're Going to Be Rich 1938,Jl 4,10:2
Pacific Liner 1939,Ja 18,17:3
Gunga Din 1939,Ja 28,19:2
Let Freedom Ring 1939,Mr 10,19:2
Ex-Champ 1939,My 12,25:3
Captain Fury 1939,My 26,20:2
Full Confession 1939,S 28,29:4
Rio 1939,O 27,27:2
Big Guy, The 1940,Ja 1,29:2
South of Pago-Pago 1940,Ag 2,12:2
Diamond Frontiers 1940,O 4,29:2
Broadway Limited 1941,Je 16,11:6
Call out the Marines 1942,Ja 26,18:3
Powder Town 1942,Je 8,11:2
China Girl 1943,Ja 21,27:2
Tampico 1944,Je 2,21:2
Roger Touhy, Gangster 1944,Je 5,14:7
Princess and the Pirate, The 1945,F 10,16:2
Rough, Tough and Ready 1945,Mr 24,22:7
Love, Honor and Goodbye 1945,S 8,12:2
Whistle Stop 1946,Mr 18,24:2
Michigan Kid 1947,F 22,16:3
Foxes of Harrow, The 1947,S 25,35:4
Fort Apache 1948,Je 25,26:2
She Wore a Yellow Ribbon 1949,N 18,35:2
Rio Grande 1950,N 20,21:2
Quiet Man, The 1952,Ag 22,13:1
Fair Wind to Java 1953,Ag 28,13:3
Prince Valiant 1954,Ap 7,40:2
Many Rivers to Cross 1955,F 24,21:2
Trouble in the Glen 1955,Ap 11,29:2
Bengazi 1955,O 8,13:4
Lady Godiva 1955,D 3,13:3
Around the World in 80 Days 1956,O 18,37:1
McLain, Billy
Undercurrent 1946,N 29,36:2
MacLaine, Shirley
Trouble With Harry, The 1955,O 18,46:2
Artists and Models 1955,D 22,20:1
Around the World in 80 Days 1956,O 18,37:1
Sheepman, The 1958,My 8,36:1
Matchmaker, The 1958,Ag 13,22:1
Hot Spell 1958,S 18,37:2
Some Came Running 1959,Ja 23,17:1
Ask any Girl 1959,My 22,32:1
Career 1959,O 9,24:1
Can-Can 1960,Mr 10,36:1
Apartment, The 1960,Je 16,37:2
All in a Nights Work 1961,Mr 23,28:1
Two Loves 1961,Je 22,23:2
Childrens Hour, The 1962,Mr 15,28:2
My Geisha 1962,Je 14,23:2
Two for the Seesaw 1962,N 22,43:1
Irma la Douce 1963,Je 6,39:1
What a Way to Go! 1964,My 15,44:1
John Goldfarb, Please Come Home 1965,Mr 25,42:4

MacLaine, Shirley — Cont
Yellow Rolls-Royce, The 1965,My 14,42:2
Gambit 1966,D 22,40:2
Woman Times Seven 1967,Je 28,38:1
Bliss of Mrs Blossom, The 1968,D 12,62:6
MCLANE
See Also MACLEAN, MCLEAN
MacLane, Barton
Tillie and Gus 1933,N 13,21:1
Last Round-Up, The 1934,My 10,25:2
Case of the Curious Bride, The 1935,Ap 5,21:3
Black Fury 1935,Ap 11,27:2
G Men 1935,My 2,17:1
Go Into Your Dance 1935,My 4,17:2
Stranded 1935,Je 20,16:2
Page Miss Glory 1935,Ag 29,25:2
Dr Socrates 1935,O 3,29:2
Case of the Lucky Legs, The 1935,N 1,25:1
I Found Stella Parish 1935,N 4,24:4
Frisco Kid 1935,N 25,22:1
Man of Iron 1935,D 7,22:2
Ceiling Zero 1936,Ja 20,22:2
Walking Dead, The 1936,Mr 2,13:2
Times Square Playboy 1936,My 2,11:2
Bullets or Ballots 1936,My 27,27:1
Bengal Tiger 1936,Jl 30,22:1
Jailbreak 1936,Ag 6,22:1
Smart Blonde 1937,Ja 9,21:1
God's Country and the Woman 1937,Ja 11,15:5
You Only Live Once 1937,F 1,15:2
Prince and the Pauper, The 1937,My 6,23:1
Ever Since Eve 1937,Je 25,25:2
Fly Away Baby 1937,Jl 9,18:2
Born Reckless 1937,Jl 30,22:6
San Quentin 1937,Ag 4,15:2
Torchy Blane, The Adventurous Blonde 1937,D 18,18:1
Kid Comes Back, The 1938,F 7,10:2
Gold Is Where You Find It 1938,F 14,20:6
You and Me 1938,Je 2,19:1
Prison Break 1938,Jl 13,17:4
Storm, The 1938,O 31,12:2
Torchy Gets her Man 1938,N 18,25:3
Stand up and Fight 1939,Ja 27,17:2
Torchy Blane in Chinatown 1939,F 3,13:2
I Was a Convict 1939,Mr 23,27:2
Big Town Czar 1939,My 4,27:3
Mutiny in the Big House 1939,D 11,26:2
Men Without Souls 1940,My 13,21:2
Gangs of Chicago 1940,Je 13,29:2
Secret Seven, The 1940,Ag 12,11:6
Melody Ranch 1940,D 26,23:3
High Sierra 1941,Ja 25,11:2
Western Union 1941,F 7,23:2
Come Live With Me 1941,F 28,17:3
Hit the Road 1941,Jl 3,15:3
Manpower 1941,Jl 5,14:2
Barnacle Bill 1941,Jl 25,12:4
Dr Jekyll and Mr Hyde 1941,Ag 13,13:2
Wild Geese Calling 1941,Ag 30,10:2
Maltese Falcon, The 1941,O 4,18:2
All Through the Night 1942,Ja 24,13:2
Big Street, The 1942,Ag 14,13:1
Bombardier 1943,Jl 2,15:2
Secret Command 1944,Je 14,16:2
Marine Raiders 1944,Jl 1,10:7
Mummy's Ghost, The 1944,Jl 1,10:7
Cry of the Werewolf, The 1944,Ag 12,16:5
Tarzan and the Amazons 1945,Ap 30,13:4
Gentle Annie 1945,My 5,11:5
Spanish Main, The 1945,N 7,20:2
San Quentin 1947,F 10,24:3
Tarzan and the Huntress 1947,Ap 7,20:4
Cheyenne 1947,Je 7,9:2
Treasure of Sierra Madre 1948,Ja 24,11:2
Relentless 1948,Mr 6,17:3
Silver River 1948,My 22,8:3
Walls of Jericho, The 1948,Ag 5,16:2
Unknown Island 1949,Ja 8,11:4
Red Light 1950,Ja 16,18:4
Kiss Tomorrow Goodbye 1950,Ag 5,9:2
Let's Dance 1950,N 30,42:2
Best of the Badmen 1951,Ag 10,13:2
Bugles in the Afternoon 1952,Mr 5,32:2
Half Breed, The 1952,Jl 5,7:2
Thunderbirds 1953,Mr 12,24:4
Jack Slade 1953,O 29,42:6
Glenn Miller Story, the 1954,F 11,33:2
Foxfire 1955,Jl 14,19:1
Backlash 1956,Ap 21,11:2
Wetbacks 1956,My 5,13:2
Three Violent People 1957,F 11,34:2
Geisha Boy, The 1958,D 24,00:0
Pocketful of Miracles 1961,D 19,39:1
Law of the Lawless 1964,Ag 27,28:2
McLane, Mary
Which Shall It Be? 1924,Ap 7,15:3
MacLaren, Ian
Under the Red Robe 1923,N 13,25:3
Yolanda 1924,F 20,23:1
Monsieur Beaucaire 1924,Ag 12,12:1 (In Addenda)
Journey's End 1930,Ap 9,25:1
Body and Soul 1931,Mr 14,23:2

MacLaren, Ian — Cont
Conquering Horde, The 1931,Mr 30,25:2
Prestige 1932,F 5,25:2
Afraid to Talk 1932,D 19,19:5
Cleopatra 1934,Ag 17,12:1
Miserables, Les 1935,Ap 22,14:2
House of Secrets 1937,F 22,13:1
Prisoner of Zenda, The 1937,S 3,12:1
Portia on Trial 1937,D 3,29:2
Invisible Enemy 1938,Ap 30,18:2
Man in the Iron Mask, The 1939,Jl 14,11:1

MacLaren, Ian (Original Author)
Bonnie Brier Bush, The 1921,N 28,16:1
Hills of Home 1948,N 26,32:2

McLaren, Ivor
Woman in Command, The 1934,My 29,22:2
Along Came Sally 1934,Je 16,20:3

Maclaren, Ivor
Evergreen 1935,Ja 11,29:1
Princess Charming 1935,Je 22,18:5

McLaren, Jack (Original Author)
Isle of Escape 1930,Mr 31,24:3

McLaren, Jean
Date with Judy, A 1948,Ag 7,8:2

MacLaren, Mary
Under the Red Robe 1923,N 13,25:3
Black Swan, The 1924,N 25,26:1

MacLaren-Rose, J (Narrator)
Great Adventure, The 1955,My 24,34:6

McLarnin, Jimmy
Joe Palooka, Champ 1946,Ap 6,10:6

McLaughlin, Betty
What a Life 1939,O 12,33:1
Those Were the Days 1940,Jl 15,18:4

McLaughlin, Gibb
White Sheik, The 1929,D 9,32:5
W Plan, The 1931,Mr 23,24:7
Congress Dances 1932,My 12,23:2
Magic Night 1932,N 3,25:3
Private Life of Henry VIII, The 1933,O 13,25:2
White Face 1933,D 4,22:3
Catherine the Great 1934,F 15,15:6
No Funny Business 1934,Mr 9,22:4
Friday the 13th 1934,My 15,18:1
Power 1934,O 5,29:3
Little Friend 1934,O 20,20:2
Iron Duke, The 1935,Ja 25,27:2
Alias Bulldog Drummond 1935,S 10,26:2
Old Curiosity Shop, The 1935,D 23,15:5
Broken Blossoms 1937,Ja 14,16:3
April Romance 1937,Ja 27,17:4
Juggernaut 1937,Jl 15,16:1
Loves of Madame Dubarry, The 1938,Ap 4,12:5
Inspector Hornleigh 1939,Je 15,27:3
Break the News 1941,Ja 2,24:2
Voice in the Night, The 1941,My 23,25:4
Courageous Mr Penn 1943,D 23,26:5
Black Rose, The 1950,S 2,11:2
Oliver Twist 1951,Jl 31,17:2
Lavender Hill Mob, The 1951,O 16,35:2
Promoter, The 1952,O 29,36:2
Hobson's Choice 1954,Je 15,37:1

McLaughlin, Jeff
Madame Pompadour 1927,Ag 2,19:2

McLaurin, Hamish (Screenwriter)
Greatest Gift, The 1918,D 16,13:3

McLaurin, Kate (Original Author)
Always Good-Bye 1931,My 23,13:4

MCLEAN
See Also MACLEAN, MCLANE

MACLEAN
See Also MCLANE, MCLEAN

MacLean, Alistair (Original Author)
Secret Ways, The 1961,My 25,31:1
Guns of Navarone, The 1961,Je 23,19:1
Ice Station Zebra 1968,D 21,49:1

McLean, Barbara (Producer)
Seven Cities of Gold 1955,O 8,13:2

McLean, D D
Beloved Brute, The 1924,N 10,20:1

McLean, David
Right Approach, The 1961,My 18,41:1
X-15 1962,Ap 5,30:2
Strangler, The 1964,Je 11,27:4

McLean, Doreen
Back Street 1961,O 13,27:1

MacLean, Douglas
Hun Within, The 1918,Ag 26,9:1
Fuss and Feathers 1918,D 9,11:4
Mirandy Smiles 1918,D 16,13:3
Captain Kidd, Jr 1919,Ap 21,13:4
Twenty-three and a Half Hours' Leave 1919,O 27,9:3
Mary's Ankle 1920,Mr 1,16:2
Let's Be Fashionable 1920,Je 14,13:2
Rookie's Return, The 1920,D 27,11:3
Hottentot, The 1923,F 19,10:1
Man of Action, A 1923,Je 4,13:3
Going Up 1923,O 10,16:2
Yankee Consul, The 1924,F 11,18:3
Introduce Me 1925,Mr 9,21:1
Seven Keys to Baldpate 1925,N 3,25:4
That's My Baby 1926,Ap 12,18:4
Hold That Lion 1926,S 6,16:2

Let It Rain 1927,Mr 9,29:1
Soft Cushions 1927,S 12,29:1
Carnation Kid, The 1929,F 25,16:1

MacLean, Douglas (Original Author)
Caught Plastered 1931,S 12,15:4
Mama Loves Papa 1933,Jl 24,11:2

MacLean, Douglas (Producer)
People Will Talk 1935,Je 17,20:2
Accent on Youth 1935,Ag 12,10:3
So Red the Rose 1935,N 28,39:1
Great Guy 1937,Ja 1,19:2
23 1/2 Hours Leave 1937,My 17,23:2

MacLean, Douglas (Screenwriter)
Laugh and get Rich 1931,Mr 28,15:3
Cracked Nuts 1931,Ap 6,24:1

McLean, Ian
Brewster's Millions 1935,Ap 8,23:3
Young Mr Pitt, The 1943,Mr 11,17:1

McLean, Jackie
Connection, The 1962,O 4,44:1

MacLean, Lorraine
If I Were Free 1934,Ja 5,25:2

MacLean, Peter
Playground, The 1965,O 4,00:0

McLean, R D
Cradle Song 1933,N 20,18:2

McLean, William
Fighter Squadron 1948,N 20,9:2

McLeay, Janet
Honor Among Lovers 1931,F 28,15:2
Calling All Marines 1939,O 26,27:2

MacLeish, Archibald (Narrator)
Grandma Moses 1950,O 24,34:6
Eleanor Roosevelt Story, The 1965,N 9,50:1

MacLeish, Archibald (Original Author)
Spanish Earth, The 1937,Ag 21,7:2

MacLeish, Archibald (Screenwriter)
Grandma Moses 1950,O 24,34:6
Eleanor Roosevelt Story, The 1965,N 9,50:1

McLellan, C M S (Original Author)
Moral Sinner, The 1924,Ap 7,15:3

McLennan, Andy
Black Bird, The 1926,F 1,16:1
Show, The 1927,Mr 14,16:1

McLennan, Rod
Tattooed Stranger, The 1950,F 10,18:6

McLennon, Rodney
Charley's Aunt 1930,D 26,18:4
Man I Killed, The 1932,Ja 20,17:4

MCLEOD
See Also MACLEOD

MACLEOD
See Also MCLEOD

McLeod, Catherine
Courage of Lassie 1946,Jl 25,18:5
I've Always Loved You 1946,S 7,11:1
That's my Man 1947,Ap 7,20:2
Fabulous Texan, The 1947,D 26,22:5
Old Los Angeles 1948,Jl 12,11:2
So Young, So Bad 1950,Jl 24,15:2
My Wife's Best Friend 1952,O 11,17:2
Blueprint for Murder, A 1953,Jl 25,8:2
Outcast, The 1954,Jl 3,9:2
Ride the Wild Surf 1964,D 24,8:4

MacLeod, E E Jr
Loves of Ricardo, The 1926,Ag 16,10:1

MacLeod, Gavin
I Want to Live 1958,N 19,45:1
Compulsion 1959,Ap 2,26:2
Operation Petticoat 1959,D 6,38:1
High Time 1960,S 17,15:1
War Hunt 1962,Ag 8,35:2
McHale's Navy 1964,Jl 11,15:2
Sand Pebbles, The 1966,D 21,48:1
Deathwatch 1967,Je 28,38:1
Party, The 1968,Ap 5,56:2

McLeod, Gordon
There Goes the Bride 1933,Mr 4,11:3
Victoria the Great 1937,O 29,19:1
Murder on Diamond Row 1937,N 12,27:2
Rat, The 1938,F 28,19:1
Sixty Glorious Years 1938,N 18,25:2
Clouds Over Europe 1939,Je 16,27:2
Saint in London, The 1939,Jl 19,23:3
Saint's Vacation, The 1941,Je 13,22:2
Spitfire 1943,Je 14,13:2
Patient Vanishes, The 1947,My 23,31:2
Easy Money (Episode 2) 1949,F 14,15:3
Corridor of Mirrors 1949,Mr 23,35:3
Chance of a Lifetime 1951,Mr 15,37:2

MacLeod, Janet
Win That Girl 1928,O 1,23:1
Take Me Home 1928,O 23,33:1
Alice Adams 1935,Ag 16,11:3

McLeod, Norman Z (Director)
Finn and Hattie 1931,Ja 31,15:1
Monkey Business 1931,O 8,22:6
Touchdown 1931,N 16,23:1
Miracle Man, The 1932,Ap 21,25:2
Horse Feathers 1932,Ag 11,12:2
If I Had a Million 1932,D 3,21:4

McLeod, Norman Z (Director) — Cont
Lady's Profession, A 1933,Mr 25,13:3
Mama Loves Papa 1933,Jl 24,11:2
Alice in Wonderland 1933,D 23,19:1
Melody in Spring 1934,Mr 31,8:2
Many Happy Returns 1934,Je 9,18:2
It's a Gift 1935,Ja 5,20:2
Here Comes Cookie 1935,O 12,12:2
Coronado 1935,D 19,33:4
Early to Bed 1936,Jl 16,20:2
Pennies From Heaven 1936,D 10,35:2
Topper 1937,Ag 20,21:2
Merrily We Live 1938,Mr 18,23:3
There Goes my Heart 1938,O 14,27:1
Topper Takes a Trip 1938,D 30,11:2
Remember? 1939,D 15,33:4
Little Men 1940,D 9,23:2
Trial of Mary Dugan, The 1941,Mr 6,25:4
Lady Be Good 1941,S 19,27:1
Jackass Mail 1942,Jl 2,25:2
Panama Hattie 1942,O 2,31:2
Powers Girl, The 1943,Mr 26,14:2 (In Addenda)
Swing Shift Maisie 1943,S 10,29:2
Kid From Brooklyn, The 1946,Ap 19,25:2
Secret Life of Walter Mitty, The 1947,Ag 15,12:2
Road to Rio 1948,F 19,29:3
Isn't It Romantic? 1948,O 7,35:2
Paleface, The 1948,D 16,41:2
Let's Dance 1950,N 30,42:2
My Favorite Spy 1951,D 26,19:3
Never Wave at a Wac 1953,Ap 24,30:2
Casanova's Big Night 1954,Ap 19,19:1
Public Pigeon No 1 1957,My 18,23:2
Alias Jesse James 1959,My 18,31:2

McLeod, Norman Z (Original Author)
Remember? 1939,D 15,33:4

MacLeod, Robert (Original Author)
Appaloosa, The 1966,S 15,51:1

McLeod, Victor (Screenwriter)
Horror Island 1941,Mr 31,11:3
Mutiny in the Arctic 1941,My 3,20:5

McLeon, Gordon
Talk of the Devil 1937,My 15,23:5

McLerie, Allyn
Where's Charley? 1952,Je 27,18:3
Desert Song, The 1953,My 21,39:2
Calamity Jane 1953,N 5,40:2
Phantom of the Rue Morgue 1954,Mr 20,10:5

McLiam, John
Cool Hand Luke 1967,N 2,58:1
In Cold Blood 1967,D 15,60:1

MacLiammoir, Michael
Othello 1955,S 13,27:1

MacMahon, Aline
Five Star Final 1931,S 11,24:2
Heart of New York, The 1932,Mr 2,15:3
Mouthpiece, The 1932,Ap 21,25:2
Week-End Marriage 1932,Je 4,9:2
Life Begins 1932,Ag 26,20:3
One Way Passage 1932,O 14,23:2
Once in a Lifetime 1932,O 29,18:4
Silver Dollar 1932,D 23,20:1
Gold Diggers of 1933 1933,Je 8,22:3
Life of Jimmy Dolan, The 1933,Je 14,22:3
Heroes for Sale 1933,Jl 22,14:3
World Changes, The 1933,O 27,22:3
Heat Lightning 1934,Mr 8,23:2
Side Streets 1934,Ag 15,13:5
Big Hearted Herbert 1934,N 14,23:2
Babbitt 1934,D 17,24:2
While the Patient Slept 1935,Mr 2,18:2
I Live my Life 1935,O 12,12:2
Ah, Wilderness! 1935,D 25,30:2
When You're in Love 1937,F 19,15:2
Back Door to Heaven 1939,Ap 20,21:2
Out of the Fog 1941,Je 21,20:2
Lady is Willing, The 1942,Ap 24,21:2
Tish 1942,S 18,25:2
Stage Door Canteen 1943,Je 25,13:2
Dragon Seed 1944,Jl 21,16:4
Guest in the House 1945,F 16,19:2
Mighty McGurk, The 1947,Ap 4,19:4
Search, The 1948,Mr 24,30:3
Roseanna McCoy 1949,O 13,33:2
Flame and the Arrow, The 1950,Jl 8,7:2
Eddie Cantor Story, The 1953,D 26,10:2
Man From Laramie, The 1955,S 1,20:2
Cimarron 1961,F 17,12:2
Young Doctors, The 1961,Ag 24,25:2
Diamond Head 1963,F 21,5:2
I Could go on Singing 1963,My 16,42:1
All the Way Home 1963,O 30,46:1

McMahon, David
I Was a Male War Bride 1949,Ag 27,7:2
Eight Iron Men 1953,Ja 2,11:1
Creature Walks among Us, The 1956,Ap 27,21:6
Operation Mad Ball 1957,N 21,38:1

McMahon, Ed
Incident, The 1967,N 6,65:1

MacMahon, Horace
Exclusive 1937,Jl 22,15:1
Girl With Ideas, A 1938,Ja 1,11:2
When G-Men Step In 1938,Mr 14,13:2
King of the Newsboys 1938,Ap 2,18:2

MacMahon, Horace— Cont

Fast Company 1938,Jl 6,21:2
Tenth Avenue Kid 1938,S 2,21:3
Broadway Musketeers 1938,O 14,27:1
Secrets of a Nurse 1938,D 12,26:2
Federal Man-Hunt 1939,F 2,17:3
I Was a Convict 1939,Mr 23,27:2
Sergeant Madden 1939,Mr 24,27:2
Big Town Czar 1939,My 4,27:3
Rose of Washington Square 1939,My 6,21:2
Gracie Allen Murder Case, The 1939,Je 8,31:3
Sabotage 1939,N 16,29:5
Dr Kildare's Strange Case 1940,Ap 12,19:2
Gangs of Chicago 1940,Je 13,29:2
Millionaires in Prison 1940,Jl 16,21:3
We Who Are Young 1940,S 13,27:2
Dr Kildare's Crisis 1940,D 19,33:1
Melody Ranch 1940,D 26,23:3
Come Live With Me 1941,F 28,17:3
Rookies on Parade 1941,My 22,25:2
Lady Scarface 1941,Ag 4,16:6
Buy Me That Town 1941,O 23,27:2
Birth of the Blues 1941,D 11,39:1
Jail House Blues 1942,F 6,23:2
Roger Touhy, Gangster 1944,Je 5,14:7
Detective Story 1951,N 7,35:2
Man in the Dark 1953,Ap 9,31:5
Duffy of San Quentin 1954,F 10,38:5
Susan Slept Here 1954,Jl 30,9:1
Blackboard Jungle 1955,Mr 21,21:5
My Sister Eileen 1955,S 23,21:1
Delicate Delinquent, The 1957,Jl 4,16:1
Never Steal Anything Small 1959,F 12,23:1
Swinger, The 1966,D 15,60:1
Detective, The 1968,My 29,20:3

MacMahon, Leo
Heart of Arizona 1938,Ap 16,17:1

McManmon, Al
Spirit of Notre Dame, The 1931,O 16,27:1

MacManus, Edward A (Producer)
Lost Battalion 1919,Jl 3,16:2

McManus, George
Great White Way, The 1924,Ja 4,10:1
Bringing Up Father 1946,N 22,27:3

McManus, George (Original Author)
Bringing Up Father 1928,Mr 19,26:2
Bringing Up Father 1946,N 22,27:3

McManus, Sharon
Bewitched 1945,Ag 17,20:3
Boy's Ranch 1946,Ag 9,12:2
This Time for Keeps 1947,D 5,33:4
No Minor Vices 1949,F 26,11:2
City Across the River 1949,Ap 8,31:3
It's a big Country 1952,Ja 9,25:2

McMartin, John
What's so bad About Feeling Good?
1968,My 25,27:1

McMaster, Andrew
Lost Patrol, The 1929,D 16,34:2

McMein, Neysa (Original Author)
Three Miles Out 1924,Ja 1,20:1

MacMichael, Florence
Woman Obsessed 1959,My 28,34:1

McMichen, Pappy Clayton
Festival 1967,O 24,53:2

McMillan, Roddy
Operation Disaster 1951,Ja 15,13:1
Scotch on the Rocks 1954,Je 14,18:2
Battle of the Sexes, The 1960,Ap 19,40:4
Mouse on the Moon, The 1963,Je 18,32:1

Macmillan, Tonie
Chalk Garden, The 1964,My 22,42:2

McMorrow, Thomas (Original Author)
Bits of Life 1921,O 17,18:1

McMullan, James
Shenandoah 1965,Jl 29,18:3

McMullen, Dennis
Fear Strikes Out 1957,Mr 21,37:2

McMullen, Doug
Back Door to Heaven 1939,Ap 20,21:2

McMullen, Virginia
Beyond Tomorrow 1940,S 27,27:1

McMurphy, Charles
Benson Murder Case, The 1930,Ap 12,23:1
Phantom Submarine, The 1941,F 12,25:3
Spoilers, The 1942,My 22,27:2

MacMurray, Fred
Gilded Lily, The 1935,F 9,11:2
Car 99 1935,F 23,14:7
Grand Old Girl 1935,F 26,16:4
Men Without Names 1935,Je 29,16:2
Alice Adams 1935,Ag 16,11:3
Hands Across the Table 1935,N 2,13:2
Bride Comes Home, The 1935,D 25,30:2
Trail of the Lonesome Pine, The 1936,F 20,23:5
13 Hours by Air 1936,Ap 30,17:2
Princess Comes Across, The 1936,Je 4,27:2
Texas Rangers, The 1936,S 24,29:1
Champagne Waltz 1937,F 4,17:2
Maid of Salem 1937,Mr 4,27:2
Swing High, Swing Low 1937,Ap 15,19:1
Exclusive 1937,Jl 22,15:1
True Confession 1937,D 16,35:2
Cocoanut Grove 1938,Je 16,21:2

Sing You Sinners 1938,Ag 18,23:1
Men With Wings 1938,O 27,27:2
Cafe Society 1939,F 23,19:2
Invitation to Happiness 1939,Je 8,31:2
Honeymoon in Bali 1939,S 21,21:1
Remember the Night 1940,Ja 18,27:2
Little Old New York 1940,F 3,9:2
Too Many Husbands 1940,Mr 8,25:2
Rangers of Fortune 1940,S 19,27:2
Virginia 1941,Ja 29,21:2
One Night in Lisbon 1941,Je 12,29:3
Dive Bomber 1941,Ag 30,10:2
New York Town 1941,N 13,35:2
Lady is Willing, The 1942,Ap 24,21:2
Take a Letter Darling 1942,My 28,13:2
Forest Rangers, The 1942,O 22,25:2
Star Spangled Rhythm 1942,D 31,20:1
Flight for Freedom 1943,Ap 16,24:2
Above Suspicion 1943,Ag 6,10:3
No Time for Love 1943,D 2,30:1
Standing Room Only 1944,F 23,17:2
And the Angels Sing 1944,Jl 13,14:2
Double Indemnity 1944,S 7,21:1
Practically Yours 1945,Mr 29,18:2
Where Do We Go From Here? 1945,Je 7,25:2
Murder, He Says 1945,Je 25,20:3
Captain Eddie 1945,Ag 9,24:2
Pardon my Past 1946,Ja 28,15:5
Smoky 1946,Je 27,29:1
Suddenly It's Spring 1947,F 27,26:2
Egg and I, The 1947,Ap 25,29:2
Singapore 1947,S 17,31:2
Miracle Can Happen, A 1948,F 4,28:4
Miracle of the Bells, The 1948,Mr 17,30:1
Innocent Affair, An 1948,S 29,36:2
Family Honeymoon 1949,F 25,28:2
Father Was a Fullback 1949,O 13,33:3
Borderline 1950,Mr 6,17:2
Never a Dull Moment 1950,N 22,20:2
Millionaire for Christy, A 1951,O 5,24:3
Callaway Went Thataway 1951,D 6,42:1
Fair Wind to Java 1953,Ag 28,13:3
Moonlighter, The 1953,S 23,37:2
Caine Mutiny, The 1954,Je 25,17:1
Pushover 1954,Jl 31,6:3
Woman's World 1954,S 29,23:4
Far Horizons, The 1955,My 21,11:1
Rains of Ranchipur, The 1955,D 16,38:2
There's Always Tomorrow 1956,Ja 21,18:2
At Gunpoint 1956,F 4,24:5
Gun for a Coward 1957,Ja 31,21:1
Quantez 1957,S 7,12:7
Day of the Badman 1958,Ja 30,19:2
Shaggy Dog, The 1959,Mr 20,26:2
Oregon Trail, The 1959,D 10,51:6
Apartment, The 1960,Je 16,37:2
Absent-Minded Professor, The 1961,Mr 16,44:2
Bon Voyage! 1962,My 18,34:2
Son of Flubber 1963,F 9,5:2
Kisses for my President 1964,Ag 22,13:1
Follow Me, Boys! 1966,D 2,46:1
Happiest Millionaire, The 1967,D 1,56:1

McMurray, Richard
David and Lisa 1962,D 27,5:5
Swimmer, The 1968,My 16,53:1

McMurty, Larry (Original Author)
Hud 1963,My 29,36:1

McNair, Barbara
If He Hollers, Let Him Go 1968,O 10,59:7

MacNair, Hugh (Original Author)
Fools First 1922,Jl 31,12:3

McNally, Ed
Time Limit 1957,O 24,37:2
Naked and the Dead, The 1958,Ag 7,21:1
Never Steal Anything Small 1959,F 12,23:1
Charly 1968,S 24,55:1

McNally, Horace
Grand Central Murder 1942,My 23,8:8
Eyes in the Night 1942,O 16,23:1
For Me and My Gal 1942,O 22,25:1
War Against Mrs Hadley, The 1942,N 26,40:2
Keeper of the Flame 1943,Mr 19,15:2
Air Raid Wardens 1943,Ap 5,15:5
Man From Down Under, The 1943,S 27,23:2
Thirty Seconds Over Tokyo 1944,N 16,19:1
American Romance, An 1944,N 24,19:1
Bewitched 1945,Ag 17,20:3
Harvey Girls, The 1946,Ja 25,26:2
Up Goes Maisie 1946,Ja 25,26:7
Magnificent Doll 1946,D 9,34:2

McNally, Stephen
Johnny Belinda 1948,O 2,11:2
Rogues' Regiment 1948,D 20,31:2
Criss Cross 1949,Mr 12,10:2
City Across the River 1949,Ap 8,31:3
Lady Gambles, The 1949,My 21,9:2
Sword in the Desert 1949,Ag 25,20:2
Woman in Hiding 1950,F 23,33:2
Winchester 73 1950,Je 8,38:2
No Way Out 1950,Ag 17,23:1
Wyoming Mail 1950,O 23,26:5
Apache Drums 1951,My 7,22:2
Air Cadet 1951,My 11,32:3

McNally, Stephen— Cont

Iron Man 1951,Ag 20,14:2
Diplomatic Courier 1952,Je 14,12:2
Duel at Silver Creek 1952,Ag 2,7:6
Battle Zone 1952,N 1,17:2
Black Castle, The 1952,D 26,20:4
Split Second 1953,My 13,34:2
Devil's Canyon 1953,O 3,14:2
Make Haste to Live 1954,Mr 26,16:2
Bullet is Waiting, A 1954,N 12,17:2
Violent Saturday 1955,My 12,32:2
Tribute to a Bad Man 1956,Mr 31,13:3
Hell's Five Hours 1957,Jl 24,18:1
Hell's Five Hours 1958,Jl 24,18:1

McNamara, Edward
Lucky in Love 1929,D 14,22:4
I Am a Fugitive From a Chain Gang
1932,N 11,17:2
20,000 Years in Sing Sing 1933,Ja 10,26:2
Great Guy 1937,Ja 1,19:2
Girl Overboard 1937,Mr 1,15:1
League of Frightened Men, The 1937,Jl 2,25:1
Strawberry Blonde 1941,F 22,11:2
Devil and Miss Jones, The 1941,My 16,21:2
Margin for Error 1943,Ja 25,10:7
Johnny Come Lately 1943,S 24,26:1
Arsenic and old Lace 1944,S 2,17:2

MacNamara, James H Major
Lady From Louisiana 1941,My 15,27:2

McNamara, John
Slaughter on Tenth Avenue 1957,N 6,43:1

McNamara, Maggie
Moon Is Blue, The 1953,Jl 9,18:3
Three Coins in the Fountain 1954,My 21,18:2
Prince of Players 1955,Ja 12,24:2
Cardinal, The 1963,D 13,41:1

McNamara, Richard
Three Forbidden Stories 1953,N 16,21:4
Campbell's Kingdom 1960,Ja 11,35:5

McNamara, Ted
Shore Leave 1925,S 14,16:1
What Price Glory 1926,N 24,26:4
Monkey Talks, The 1927,Ap 5,30:7
Rich but Honest 1927,My 18,29:3
Gay Retreat, The 1927,O 10,24:1
Gateway of the Moon, The 1928,Ja 9,20:1
Mother Machree 1928,Mr 6,20:3
Why Sailors Go Wrong 1928,Ap 9,18:2

Macnamara, Walter (Producer)
Ireland, A Nation 1914,S 24,11:6

Macnamara, Walter (Screenwriter)
Ireland, A Nation 1914,S 24,11:6

McNamee, Graham (Miscellaneous)
World in Revolt, The 1934,Je 9,18:2

Macnaty, Gustav (Director)
Ecstasy 1940,D 25,33:2

McNaught, Bob (Director)
Sea Wife 1957,D 5,45:2

McNaughton, Charles
Three Live Ghosts 1929,S 30,23:1
Bad One, The 1930,Je 13,28:3
Common Clay 1930,Ag 2,16:4
Single Sin, The 1931,Mr 17,34:3
Charlie Chan's Chance 1932,Ja 23,18:4
Treasure Island 1934,Ag 18,5:5
Fountain, The 1934,Ag 31,14:1
Lloyds of London 1936,N 26,39:1
Black Swan, The 1942,D 24,18:3
Moss Rose 1947,Jl 3,14:2

McNaughton, Gus
Charming Deceiver, The 1933,D 9,18:3
Storm in a Teacup 1938,Mr 22,18:4
Divorce of Lady X, The 1938,Ap 1,17:2
We're Going to Be Rich 1938,Jl 4,10:2
South Riding 1938,Ag 2,15:2
Clouds Over Europe 1939,Je 16,27:2
Sidewalks of London 1940,F 15,15:1
Courageous Mr Penn 1943,D 23,26:5
Place of One's Own, A 1949,F 8,30:2

McNaughton, Harry
Vagabond King, The 1956,S 13,39:6

McNaughton, Jack
High Treason 1952,My 21,23:3
Trent's Last Case 1953,N 27,99:9
Purple Plain, The 1955,Ap 11,29:1

McNear, Howard
Bell, Book and Candle 1958,D 27,2:7
Anatomy of a Murder 1959,Jl 3,10:1
Big Circus, The 1959,Jl 18,6:1
Voyage to the Bottom of the Sea 1961,Jl 20,32:2
Bachelor Flat 1962,Ja 13,14:1
Blue Hawaii 1962,F 22,20:2
Irma la Douce 1963,Je 6,39:1
Kiss Me, Stupid 1964,D 23,22:2

MacNee, Patrick
Girls, Les 1957,O 4,27:2

McNeely, Howard
Jackie Robinson Story, The 1950,My 17,36:1
Bright Road 1953,Ap 29,33:5

McNeely, Robert
Bright Road 1953,Ap 29,33:5

McNeer, Howard
Wheeler Dealers, The 1963,N 15,25:2

Macneice, Louis (Miscellaneous)
Conquest of Everest, The 1953,D 10,64:4
McNeil, Claudia
Last Angry Man, The 1959,O 23,24:1
Raisin in the Sun, A 1961,Mr 30,24:1
MacNeil, Jennie
Fist in his Pocket 1968,My 28,40:1
MacNeil, Mary
Tight Little Island 1949,D 26,33:2
McNeil, Steve (Screenwriter)
Man's Favorite Sport? 1964,F 20,22:1
McNeile, H C (Sapper) (Original Author)
Temple Tower 1930,My 10,25:3
Bulldog Drummond Strikes Back 1934,Ag 16,20:2
Bulldog Drummond Comes Back 1937,S 4,8:3
Bulldog Drummond's Revenge 1937,D 17,33:2
Bulldog Drummond's Peril 1938,Mr 18,23:2
Bulldog Drummond in Africa 1938,Ag 25,15:1
Arrest Bulldog Drummond 1939,Ja 12,23:2
Bulldog Drummond's Secret Police
1939,Mr 30,19:3
Bulldog Drummond's Bride 1939,Jl 13,17:2
McNiven, D
Uncivilized 1937,N 17,27:4
McNulty, Charles
Gay Intruders, The 1949,Je 28,33:4
McNulty, Dorothy
Good News 1930,S 6,9:2
Love in the Rough 1930,S 27,21:3
After the Thin Man 1936,D 25,19:2
Vogues of 1938 1937,Ag 20,21:1
Sea Racketeers 1937,O 4,17:2
McNulty, John (Original Author)
Easy Come, Easy Go 1947,F 6,29:2
Jackpot, The 1950,N 23,55:2
McNulty, John (Screenwriter)
Easy Come, Easy Go 1947,F 6,29:2
McNutt, Patterson (Original Author)
Jam Session 1944,My 3,25:3
Pardon my Past 1946,Ja 28,15:5
McNutt, Patterson (Producer)
This Thing Called Love 1941,F 14,15:2
McNutt, Patterson (Screenwriter)
George White's 1935 Scandals 1935,Ap 29,12:3
Curly Top 1935,Ag 2,22:3
Everybody's Old Man 1936,Mr 26,27:2
Return of Sophie Lang, The 1936,Jl 24,13:1
Vacation From Love 1938,N 10,33:2
Come Live With Me 1941,F 28,17:3
Gentleman After Dark, A 1942,Ap 17,21:2
McNutt, William Slavens (Director)
Hell and Highwater 1933,D 18,24:4
McNutt, William Slavens (Miscellaneous)
Quarterback, The 1926,O 12,30:2
Annapolis Farewell 1935,Ag 24,18:2
McNutt, William Slavens (Original Author)
Trifling With Honor 1923,My 30,10:4
Gun Smoke 1931,Ap 24,27:1
Lady and Gent 1932,Jl 16,5:5
McNutt, William Slavens (Screenwriter)
Dangerous Paradise 1930,Mr 2,IX,5:1
Derelict 1930,N 22,21:3
Lives of a Bengal Lancer, The 1935,Ja 12,12:2
Macoby, Irving (Producer)
Lonely Night, The 1954,Mr 29,22:2
Macollum, Barry
Hole in the Wall, The 1929,Ap 15,22:6
Internes Can't Take Money 1937,My 6,23:2
Murder in Greenwich Village 1937,O 30,22:2
If I Were King 1938,S 29,31:1
On the Waterfront 1954,Jl 29,18:1
Trouble With Harry, The 1955,O 18,46:2
MacOrlan, Pierre (Original Author)
Port of Shadows 1939,O 30,13:2
MacOrlan, Pierre (Screenwriter)
Francois Villon 1950,Jl 3,9:2
Macourek, Milos (Original Author)
Happy End 1968,Je 11,54:4
Macourek, Milos (Screenwriter)
Happy End 1968,Je 11,54:4
MacOwan, Norman
Tight Little Island 1949,D 26,33:2
Valley of the Eagles 1952,Ap 11,19:2
Macowan, Norman
Horror Hotel 1963,Je 20,29:1
McPartland, Jimmy and his Jazz Band
Jazz Dance 1954,S 21,24:1
McPartland, John (Original Author)
No Down Payment 1957,O 31,41:1
McPartland, John (Screenwriter)
Wild Party, The 1956,D 22,13:1
McPhail, Addie
Extravagance 1930,D 9,31:3
Girls Demand Excitement 1931,F 7,11:1
Corsair 1931,N 19,27:5
MacPhail, Angus (Miscellaneous)
Shrine of Victory 1943,Ag 20,13:2
MacPhail, Angus (Original Author)
Channel Crossing 1934,My 24,28:3
Dead of Night 1946,Je 29,22:6
MacPhail, Angus (Screenwriter)
Secret Four, The 1940,Ap 22,13:2
Let George Do It 1940,O 14,25:5

Haunted Honeymoon 1940,O 31,28:2
Three Cockeyed Sailors 1942,Ja 26,18:3
Next of Kin 1943,My 6,25:2
Somewhere in France 1943,Jl 12,11:2
48 Hours 1944,Je 26,21:2
Half-Way House 1945,Ag 13,22:4
Dead of Night 1946,Je 29,22:6
Captive Heart, The 1947,Ap 28,27:2
Frieda 1947,Ag 15,12:3
Champagne Charlie 1948,Ag 7,8:2
It Always Rains on Sunday 1949,F 14,15:5
Tight Little Island 1949,D 26,33:2
Train of Events 1952,My 26,18:4
Wrong Man, The 1956,D 24,8:1
McPhail, Douglas
Sweethearts 1938,D 23,16:2
Babes in Arms 1939,O 20,27:2
Broadway Melody of 1940 1940,Mr 29,25:3
Little Nellie Kelly 1940,D 25,33:2
Born to Sing 1942,F 19,23:2
MacPhail, Larry
Safe at Home 1941,N 26,31:2
Macpherson, Cameron (Composer)
Dawn to Dawn 1933,D 27,23:5
Macpherson, Cameron (Original Author)
Dawn to Dawn 1933,D 27,23:5
Macpherson, Cameron (Producer)
Dawn to Dawn 1933,D 27,23:5
MacPherson, Douglas
Let's Get Married 1926,Mr 2,22:1
MacPherson, J DuRocher (Original Author)
Evidence 1929,O 5,22:5
Washington Melodrama 1941,My 26,15:3
Macpherson, James (Screenwriter)
Young April 1926,Ag 31,15:3
Macpherson, Jeanie (Narrator)
Land of Liberty 1939,Je 16,27:3
Land of Liberty 1941,Ja 30,19:2
Macpherson, Jeanie (Original Author)
Something to Think About 1920,O 18,13:1
Forbidden Fruit 1921,Ja 24,16:2
Godless Girl, The 1929,Ap 1,22:1
Buccaneer, The 1938,F 17,17:2
Macpherson, Jeanie (Screenwriter)
Old Wives for New 1918,My 20,9:7
Affairs of Anatol, The 1921,S 12,16:1
King of Kings, The 1927,Ap 20,29:2
Dynamite 1929,D 28,11:1
Madam Satan 1930,O 6,21:1
Macpherson, Jeannie (Miscellaneous)
Buccaneer, The 1958,D 24,00:0
McPherson, Quinton
Ghost Goes West, The 1936,Ja 11,9:2
Murder in the Old Red Barn 1936,Ag 19,18:3
Talk of the Devil 1937,My 15,23:5
MacPherson, Quinton
Storm in a Teacup 1938,Mr 22,18:4
McPherson, Quinton
Forbidden Music 1938,D 27,13:2
McQuade, Arlene
Molly 1951,Mr 8,37:2
McQuade, Edward
Monster, The 1925,F 16,24:1
MacQuarrie, Albert
Hunchback of Notre Dame, The 1923,S 3,9:3
Don Q, Son of Zorro 1925,Je 16,24:1
Gaucho, The 1927,N 22,32:2
Viking, The 1928,N 29,32:4
MacQuarrie, George
Love Flower, The 1920,Ag 23,9:2
Uncle Sam of Freedom Ridge 1920,S 27,15:2
Ragged Edge, The 1923,Je 5,24:5
Rejected Woman, The 1924,My 5,18:3
Hole in the Wall, The 1929,Ap 15,22:6
Bedtime Story, A 1933,Ap 20,20:3
All the King's Horses 1935,Mr 9,19:1
Fourteen Hours 1951,Mr 7,43:2
McQuarrie, Murdock
Ashes of Vengeance 1923,Ag 7,20:2
Only Woman, The 1924,N 3,20:1
Captain of the Guard 1930,Mr 29,23:1
Stone of Silver Creek 1935,Ap 8,23:3
McQueen, Butterfly
Gone With the Wind 1939,D 20,31:2
Affectionately Yours 1941,My 24,18:2
Cabin in the Sky 1943,My 28,19:3
I Dood It 1943,N 11,29:1
Flame of Barbary Coast 1945,My 28,22:2
Mildred Pierce 1945,S 29,12:2
Duel in the Sun 1947,My 8,30:2
McQueen, Justus E
Battle Cry 1955,F 3,18:1
McQueen, Steve
Blob, The 1958,N 7,23:1
Never Love a Stranger 1958,N 22,27:4
Never so Few 1960,Ja 22,15:2
Great St Louis Bank Robbery, The 1960,F 4,34:1
Magnificent Seven, The 1960,N 24,48:3
Honeymoon Machine, The 1961,Ag 24,25:2
Hell is for Heroes 1962,Jl 12,19:3
War Lover, The 1962,N 7,8:5
Great Escape, The 1963,Ag 8,19:1
Soldier in the Rain 1963,N 29,67:6 (Incorrect in
this edition; use 1963,N 28,67:6 elsewhere)

McQueen, Steve— Cont
Love With the Proper Stranger 1963,D 26,33:1
Baby, the Rain Must Fall 1965,Ja 14,44:1
Cincinnati Kid, The 1965,O 28,48:1
Nevada Smith 1966,Je 24,28:1 (Incorrect in this
edition; use 1966,Je 30,28:1 elsewhere)
Sand Pebbles, The 1966,D 21,48:1
Thomas Crown Affair, The 1968,Je 27,48:2
Bullitt 1968,O 18,41:2
MacQuitty, William (Producer)
Mr Lord Says No! 1952,F 12,22:5
Both Sides of the Law 1954,Ja 12,19:2
Beachcomber, The 1955,Ja 17,27:5
Above Us the Waves 1957,Ap 18,35:2
A Night to Remember 1958,D 17,2:7
Underworld Informers 1965,O 14,53:1
MACRAE
See Also MCCREA, MCRAE
MCRAE
See Also MCCREA, MACRAE
Macrae, Arthur
Saint's Vacation, The 1941,Je 13,22:2
Horse's Mouth, The 1954,Ja 20,33:4
Macrae, Arthur (Screenwriter)
Gaiety Girls, The 1938,Mr 31,15:1
She Shall Have Music 1942,O 31,11:2
McRae, Bruce
Star Overnight, A 1919,N 17,20:1
McRae, Carmen
Subterraneans, The 1960,Jl 7,26:1
Hotel 1967,Ja 20,27:1
MacRae, Duncan
Brothers, The 1948,My 5,30:4
Tight Little Island 1949,D 26,33:2
Woman in Question, The 1952,F 19,24:2
Little Kidnappers, The 1954,S 2,18:1
Wee Geordie 1956,O 8,31:1
Mad Little Island 1958,D 31,12:1
Bridal Path, The 1959,D 21,34:2
Our Man in Havana 1960,Ja 28,26:1
Tunes of Glory 1960,D 21,38:2
Greyfriars' Bobby 1961,O 12,41:4
Best of Enemies, The 1962,Ag 7,35:2
They all Died Laughing 1964,Mr 16,37:2
Model Murder Case, The 1964,N 25,45:1
30 Is a Dangerous Age, Cynthia 1968,Mr 5,34:1
MacRae, Elizabeth
Everything's Ducky 1961,D 21,30:6
For Love or Money 1963,Ag 8,19:1
McRae, Ellen
For Those Who Think Young 1964,Jl 9,27:1
Goodbye, Charlie 1964,N 19,49:1
MacRae, Gordon
East Side, West Side 1927,O 18,33:2
Look for the Silver Lining 1949,Je 24,29:2
Backfire 1950,Ja 27,29:2
Daughter of Rosie O'Grady, The
1950,Mr 31,36:2
Return of the Frontiersman 1950,Je 10,11:3
Tea for Two 1950,S 2,11:2
West Point Story, The 1950,D 23,11:3
On Moonlight Bay 1951,Jl 27,15:2
Starlift 1951,D 15,11:2
About Face 1952,My 24,15:3
By the Light of the Silvery Moon
1953,Mr 27,28:2
Desert Song, The 1953,My 21,39:2
Three Sailors and a Girl 1953,N 23,32:2
Oklahoma! 1955,O 11,49:1
Carousel 1956,F 17,13:1
Best Things in Life are Free, The 1956,S 29,12:2
MacRae, Henry A (Director)
Price She Paid, The 1925,Ja 13,16:1
Macrea, Arthur
Horse's Mouth, The 1958,N 12,41:1
Macrea, Arthur (Screenwriter)
Encore (The Ant and the Grasshopper); Ant and
the Grasshopper, The (Encore) 1952,Ap 3,45:1
Encore (Gigolo and Gigolette); Gigolo and
Gigolette (Encore) 1952,Ap 3,45:1
Encore (Winter Cruise); Winter Cruise (Encore)
1952,Ap 3,45:1
Macready, George
Follow the Boys 1944,Ap 26,24:6
Soul of a Monster, The 1944,S 9,12:4
Seventh Cross, The 1944,S 29,18:1
Song to Remember, A 1945,Ja 26,16:4
Counter-Attack 1945,My 17,15:2
Don Juan Quilligan 1945,Jl 30,16:2
Fighting Guardsman, The 1945,O 6,9:6
My Name is Julia Ross 1945,N 9,16:3
Gilda 1946,Mr 15,27:2
Bandit of Sherwood Forest, The 1946,Mr 23,8:4
Walls Came Tumbling Down, The 1946,N 9,13:5
Return of Monte Cristo, The 1947,Ja 3,16:4
Down to Earth 1947,S 12,18:2
Swordsman, The 1947,O 17,18:4
Big Clock, The 1948,Ap 22,34:2
Beyond Glory 1948,Ag 4,18:2
Black Arrow, The 1948,O 4,14:2
Gallant Blade 1948,O 13,31:3
Knock on any Door 1949,F 23,31:2
Alias Nick Beal 1949,Mr 10,35:2
Johnny Allegro 1949,My 31,19:2

Macready, George — Cont

Nevadan, The 1950,Ja 13,19:4
Fortunes of Captain Blood 1950,Je 10,11:3
Lady Without Passport, A 1950,Ag 4,13:2
Desert Hawk, The 1950,Ag 26,9:2
Desert Fox, The 1951,O 18,32:1
Detective Story 1951,N 7,35:2
Green Glove, The 1952,Ap 24,38:1
Treasure of the Golden Condor 1953,My 23,19:2
Julius Caesar 1953,Je 5,19:1
Stranger Wore a Gun, The 1953,Jl 30,20:3
Commandos Strike at Dawn 1954,Ja 14,25:1
Duffy of San Quentin 1954,F 10,38:5
Vera Cruz 1954,D 27,22:4
Paths of Glory 1957,D 26,23:2
Taras Bulba 1962,D 26,5:2
Dead Ringer 1964,F 20,22:3
Seven Days in May 1964,F 20,22:1
Where Love Has Gone 1964,N 3,26:1
Great Race, The 1965,S 16,00:0

Macready, Renee
Lovin' the Ladies 1930,Mr 22,22:6

Macrorie, Alma
To Each his Own 1946,My 24,15:2
Emperor Waltz, The 1948,Je 18,19:2
Anything Goes 1956,Mr 22,38:1

McShane, Charles
Cry From the Streets, A 1959,F 24,32:2

McShane, Ian
Young and Willing 1964,F 27,28:1
Pleasure Girls, The 1966,Ap 21,43:1

McShane, Mark (Original Author)
Seance on a Wet Afternoon 1964,N 6,30:1

McStay, Michael
Robbery 1967,S 28,58:2
Battle Beneath the Earth 1968,S 12,54:3

MacSunday, Con
Smiling Lieutenant, The 1931,My 23,13:4
Soak the Rich 1936,F 5,14:2

McTaggart, Malcolm
Full Confession 1939,S 28,29:4
Flying Tigers 1942,O 23,25:2

Mactavish
Echoes of Silence 1967,Ap 7,32:2

McTurk, Joe
Guys and Dolls 1955,N 5,26:1

McVeagh, Eve
High Noon 1952,Jl 25,14:2
Tight Spot 1955,Mr 19,11:7
Crime and Punishment, U S A 1959,Je 17,39:3

MacVeigh, Sue (Original Author)
Grand Central Murder 1942,My 23,8:8

McVey, Pat
Pierre of the Plains 1942,Jl 30,17:3
Two Guys From Milwaukee 1946,Jl 27,12:5
Big Caper, The 1957,Mr 29,16:1
Party Girl 1958,O 29,30:1

McVey, Paul
Cocktail Hour 1933,Je 5,18:5
Show Them no Mercy 1935,D 9,25:2
Country Beyond, The 1936,Ap 30,17:3
Crime of Dr Forbes, The 1936,Jl 6,11:4
Sing, Baby, Sing 1936,S 12,20:1
Stowaway 1936,D 19,16:1
One Mile From Heaven 1937,Ag 19,23:1
Passport Husband 1938,Ag 5,11:2
Meet the Girls 1938,S 3,16:6
Safety in Numbers 1938,S 6,17:2
Drums Along the Mohawk 1939,N 4,11:2
Silver Skates 1943,Mr 19,15:3
Happy Go Lucky 1943,Mr 25,25:1
Force of Evil 1948,D 27,16:2
No Room for the Groom 1952,Je 14,12:2
Bwana Devil 1953,F 19,20:5
Shane 1953,Ap 24,30:3

McVey, Tyler
Day the Earth Stood Still, The 1951,S 19,37:1
Come on, The 1956,Ap 7,13:1

MacVicar, Martha
Captive Wild Woman 1943,Je 7,9:4
Marine Raiders 1944,Jl 1,10:7
Falcon in Mexico, The 1944,Ag 5,16:2

McVicker, Julius
Phantom President, The 1932,O 1,10:4

McWade, Edward
Big Shot, The 1932,Ja 2,14:2
Two Seconds 1932,My 19,25:3
Big City Blues 1932,S 10,18:5
Six Hours to Live 1932,O 22,18:4
Lawyer Man 1932,D 27,10:2
Murders in the Zoo 1933,Ap 3,13:4
Journal of a Crime 1934,Ap 28,11:3
Notorious Sophie Lang, The 1934,Jl 21,14:2
Lost Lady, A 1934,O 4,19:1
Girl From 10th Avenue, The 1935,My 27,20:6
Oil for the Lamps of China 1935,Je 6,25:2
Red Salute 1935,S 30,13:1
Dr Socrates 1935,O 3,29:2
Frisco Kid 1935,N 25,22:1
Calling of Dan Matthews, The 1936,Ja 25,18:4
Man I Marry, The 1936,O 31,24:3
They Won't Forget 1937,Jl 15,16:1
Patient in Room 18, The 1938,Ap 22,15:6
White Banners 1938,Je 23,27:1

Garden of the Moon 1938,S 24,13:1
They Asked for It 1939,Je 30,17:4
Indianapolis Speedway 1939,Jl 15,8:2
Magnificent Fraud, The 1939,Jl 20,16:2
Our Neighbors-The Carters 1940,F 15,15:2
Hot Steel 1940,Je 21,25:3
Return of Frank James, The 1940,Ag 10,16:4
Chad Hanna 1940,D 26,23:1
Lady in a Jam 1942,S 11,25:2
You Can't Escape Forever 1942,O 17,11:1
Crash Dive 1943,Ap 29,25:2
Arsenic and old Lace 1944,S 2,17:2

McWade, Margaret
Broken Barriers 1924,Ag 4,16:3
Sundown 1924,D 1,17:3
Lost World, The 1925,F 9,15:3
Theodora Goes Wild 1936,N 13,27:4
Wings Over Honolulu 1937,My 29,20:1
Danger-Love at Work 1937,D 11,22:2
Bishop's Wife, The 1947,D 10,44:2

McWade, Robert
Second Youth 1924,Ap 22,19:3
New Brooms 1925,N 4,17:4
Home Towners, The 1928,O 24,26:4
Good Intentions 1930,Jl 26,16:4
Feet First 1930,O 31,20:1
Cimarron 1931,Ja 27,20:5
Kept Husbands 1931,Mr 24,31:2
It's a Wise Child 1931,My 16,13:3
Too Many Cooks 1931,Ag 17,18:2
Skyline 1931,O 5,17:3
New Adventures of Get-Rich-Quick Wallingford 1931,O 10,20:4
Girls About Town 1931,N 2,27:1
Ladies of the Jury 1932,Ap 2,13:2
Grand Hotel 1932,Ap 13,23:2
Madame Racketeer 1932,Jl 23,6:6
First Year, The 1932,Ag 22,20:2
Back Street 1932,Ag 29,9:2
Movie Crazy 1932,S 15,19:3
Phantom of Crestwood, The 1932,O 17,18:3
Once in a Lifetime 1932,O 29,18:4
Match King, The 1932,D 8,25:3
Hard to Handle 1933,F 2,21:5
Ladies They Talk About 1933,F 25,20:4
42d Street 1933,Mr 10,19:3
Pick Up 1933,Mr 25,13:4
Big Cage, The 1933,My 9,20:5
I Loved a Woman 1933,S 22,14:2
Solitaire Man, The 1933,S 23,11:5
Kennell Murder Case, The 1933,O 30,14:2
Prizefighter and the Lady, The 1933,N 11,11:3
Cross Country Cruise 1934,Ja 20,12:3
Hold That Girl 1934,Mr 24,20:3
Countess of Monte Cristo, The 1934,Ap 2,13:2
Thirty Day Princess 1934,My 12,12:3
Operator 13 1934,Je 23,16:5
Midnight Alibi 1934,Jl 4,18:3
Dragon Murder Case, The 1934,Ag 23,13:3
Lemon Drop Kid, The 1934,O 27,20:2
College Rhythm 1934,N 24,19:1
President Vanishes, The 1934,D 8,18:5
County Chairman, The 1935,Ja 19,8:1
Society Doctor 1935,F 4,11:3
Diamond Jim 1935,Ag 24,18:2
His Night Out 1935,N 16,19:2
Frisco Kid 1935,N 25,22:1
Next Time We Love 1936,Ja 31,16:2
Anything Goes 1936,F 6,23:3
Moonlight Murder 1936,Mr 28,11:2
Bunker Bean 1936,Je 27,21:2
Big Noise, The 1936,Jl 4,18:3
High Tension 1936,Jl 11,11:4
Early to Bed 1936,Jl 16,20:2
Fifteen Maiden Lane 1936,O 17,21:3
Old Hutch 1936,D 7,27:4
We're on the Jury 1937,F 10,18:5
Good Old Soak 1937,Ap 20,25:3
Mountain Justice 1937,My 13,31:2
This Is my Affair 1937,My 28,17:1
On Such a Night 1937,S 17,29:2
Gold Is Where You Find It 1938,F 14,20:6
Of Human Hearts 1938,F 18,23:1

McWhorter, Mac
Tender is the Night 1962,Ja 20,13:2

McWhorter, Richard (Producer)
Doctor Faustus 1968,F 7,38:1

MacWilliams, Bill
Murder in the Blue Room 1944,O 28,12:2

McWilliams, Paul
Disputed Passage 1939,O 26,27:2

Macy, Ann Sullivan
Deliverance 1919,Ag 19,10:1

Macy, Carlton
Seven Keys to Baldpate 1929,D 26,21:1

Macy, Cora
Irene 1926,Mr 1,17:1

Macy, Dora (Original Author)
Night Nurse 1931,Jl 17,23:4

Madaras, Jozef
Red and the White, The 1968,S 21,26:1

Madd, Pierrette
Milady 1923,Ja 22,10:1

Maddax, William
Doctors' Wives 1931,Ap 25,23:4

Madden, Doreen
Rising of the Moon, The (1921); 1921 (The Rising of the Moon) 1957,Jl 10,23:1

Madden, Edward (Composer)
Tin Pan Alley 1940,N 22,27:3

Madden, Henry
Small Hours, The 1962,Ag 14,34:1

Madden, Jeanne
Stage Struck 1936,S 28,14:4
Talent Scout 1937,Ag 20,21:3
Sea Racketeers 1937,O 4,17:2

Madden, Jerry
Haunted Ship, The 1928,Ja 23,18:3
Penrod and Sam 1937,Mr 29,14:3
Penrod and his Twin Brother 1938,Ap 18,11:1

Madden, Peter
Fiend Without a Face 1958,Jl 4,15:3
Road to Hong Kong, The 1962,Je 28,21:1
Loneliness of the Long Distance Runner, The 1962,O 9,44:1
Nothing but the Best 1964,Jl 14,28:1
Woman of Straw 1964,O 1,30:6
He Who Rides a Tiger 1968,S 10,39:1

Madden, Tom
Running Wild 1927,Je 14,33:2

Madden, Tony
Small Hours, The 1962,Ag 14,34:1

Maddern, Victor
Operation Disaster 1951,Ja 15,13:1
Sailor of the King 1953,S 3,15:2
Court Martial 1955,Ag 2,17:1
Night my Number Came up, The 1955,D 20,39:5
His Excellency 1956,F 2,19:3
Cockleshell Heroes, The 1956,Je 4,25:2
Private's Progress 1956,Jl 24,19:2
Abandon Ship 1957,Ap 18,35:1
Saint Joan 1957,Je 27,21:1
All at Sea 1957,D 23,18:2
Dunkirk 1958,S 11,42:2
Happy is the Bride 1959,Je 30,27:2
I'm All Right Jack 1960,Ap 26,40:2
Exodus 1960,D 16,44:1
Damn the Defiant 1962,S 20,29:2
Rotten to the Core 1965,Jl 20,39:2
Carry on Cleo 1965,O 23,17:2

Maddow, Ben (Director)
Savage Eye, The 1960,Je 7,27:1
Affair of the Skin, An 1963,N 21,43:2

Maddow, Ben (Producer)
Affair of the Skin, An 1963,N 21,43:2

Maddow, Ben (Screenwriter)
Framed 1947,My 26,24:2
Kiss the Blood off my Hands 1948,O 30,10:1
Man From Colorado 1949,Ja 21,24:3
Intruder in the Dust 1949,N 23,19:1
Asphalt Jungle, The 1950,Je 9,29:3
Shadow in the Sky 1952,Jl 19,8:2
Unforgiven, The 1960,Ap 7,46:1
Savage Eye, The 1960,Je 7,27:1
Two Loves 1961,Je 22,23:2
Balcony, The 1963,Mr 22,7:1
Affair of the Skin, An 1963,N 21,43:2
Way West, The 1967,My 25,54:1

Maddox, Martha
Woman Proof 1923,O 30,16:1

Made, Mady
Curtain Rises, The 1939,Ap 22,15:2

Madeira, Humberto
Lisbon 1956,Ag 30,19:2

Madell, Rose (Miscellaneous)
Cavalcade of Russian Ballet and Dance 1965,My 31,8:1

Madelova, Rozina
Country Doctor, The 1953,F 16,16:2

Madhyma Lanka Mandala Dancers
Elephant Walk 1954,Ap 22,37:2

Madikisa, Linda
Magic Garden, The 1952,F 6,24:2

MADISON
See Also MADSEN

Madison, Cleo
Dangerous Age, The 1923,Ja 29,11:1
True as Steel 1924,Je 17,22:4
Roughneck, The 1924,D 3,14:1

Madison, Ellen
Goldstein 1965,My 8,19:7

Madison, Gloria
Native Son 1951,Je 18,19:2

Madison, Guy
Since You Went Away 1944,Jl 21,16:2
Till the End of Time 1946,Jl 24,24:1
Honeymoon 1947,My 19,27:2
Massacre River 1949,Jl 15,17:2
Charge at Feather River, The 1953,Jl 16,17:2
Command, The 1954,Ja 16,10:5
Five Against the House 1955,Je 11,8:7
Last Frontier, The 1955,D 8,45:1
On the Threshold of Space 1956,Mr 30,10:5
Hilda Crane 1956,My 3,35:2

Madison, Guy— Cont
Shatterhand 1968,Je 6,54:1
Payment in Blood 1968,D 5,59:1
Madison, Helene
Warrior's Husband, The 1933,My 12,20:4
Madison, Julian
Come on Marines 1934,Mr 24,20:3
It's a Gift 1935,Ja 5,20:2
Private Worlds 1935,Mr 28,25:2
Shot in the Dark, A 1935,My 22,23:2
Madison, Mae
Chances 1931,Je 12,27:1
Smart Money 1931,Je 19,21:1
Reckless Hour, The 1931,Ag 1,16:4
Bought 1931,Ag 15,18:3
Mad Genius, The 1931,O 24,20:3
Expensive Women 1931,N 14,15:3
Her Majesty, Love 1931,N 26,37:2
Union Depot 1932,Ja 15,24:4
Play Girl 1932,Mr 19,11:2
Mouthpiece, The 1932,Ap 21,25:2
So Big 1932,Ap 30,19:3
Tenderfoot, The 1932,My 23,18:4
Miss Pinkerton 1932,Jl 9,7:5
Madison, Martha
Miss Bluebeard 1925,Ja 28,14:1
Madison, Noel
Doorway to Hell, The 1930,N 1,23:2
Star Witness 1931,Ag 4,19:5
Hatchet Man, The 1932,F 4,25:2
Play Girl 1932,Mr 19,11:2
Symphony of Six Million 1932,Ap 15,23:1
Trial of Vivienne Ware, The 1932,Ap 30,19:3
Man About Town 1932,My 28,18:2
Last Mile, The 1932,Ag 26,20:3
Hat Check Girl 1932,O 8,15:4
Me and my Gal 1932,D 12,18:4
Laughter in Hell 1933,Ja 2,29:2
West of Singapore 1933,Ap 1,18:3
Destination Unknown 1933,Ap 8,16:2
Humanity 1933,Ap 22,16:3
House of Rothschild, The 1934,Mr 15,27:2
I Like It That Way 1934,Ap 18,23:3
Journal of a Crime 1934,Ap 28,11:3
Manhattan Melodrama 1934,My 5,22:2
Four Hours to Kill 1935,Ap 11,27:3
G Men 1935,My 2,17:1
Three Kids and a Queen 1935,N 9,19:2
Morals of Marcus, The 1936,Ja 13,14:2
Muss 'Em Up 1936,F 3,21:2
Champagne Charlie 1936,My 7,21:2
Missing Girls 1936,O 5,25:1
Our Relations 1936,N 11,55:1
House of Secrets 1937,F 22,13:1
Man of the People 1937,F 23,25:4
Gangway 1937,Ag 21,7:3
Sailing Along 1938,Ap 16,17:1
Man With 100 Faces 1938,N 1,27:2
Climbing High 1939,Je 5,20:3
Missing Evidence 1939,N 17,17:3
Charlie Chan in City in Darkness 1939,D 18,29:2
Great Plane Robbery, The 1940,N 15,25:2
Queen of Crime 1941,F 19,25:2
Ellery Queen's Penthouse Mystery
   1941,Mr 7,17:2
Footsteps in the Dark 1941,Mr 15,13:2
Highway West 1941,Ag 8,13:4
Secret Agent of Japan 1942,Mr 23,19:3
Joe Smith, American 1942,Ap 2,27:4
Bombs Over Burma 1942,Ag 10,15:2
Jitterbugs 1943,Je 5,12:2
Madison, Virginia
Everlasting Whisper, The 1925,O 12,19:3
First Year, The 1926,Mr 8,17:1
Heart of a Salome, The 1927,Je 6,27:2
Madoc, Philip
Berserk! 1968,Ja 11,42:2
Madrid, Francesco (Screenwriter)
Song of Dolores 1951,Je 16,9:2
Madriguera, Enric (Composer)
Thrill of Brazil, The 1946,S 6,18:3
Madriguera, Enric and His Orchestra
Thrill of Brazil, The 1946,S 6,18:3
MADSEN
See Also MADISON
Madsen, Holger (Director)
Sol Over Danmark 1937,Ap 14,31:6
Maertens, Gaston-Marie (Original Author)
Hoboes in Paradise 1950,O 9,21:5
Maertens, Willy
Seven Journeys 1951,Mr 12,20:2
MAES
See Also MAYES
Maes, Tove
Child of Man 1950,F 1,25:2
Maesso, J G (Producer)
Tarantos, Los 1964,Je 30,22:1
Maesso, Jose E Jr (Producer)
Ugly Ones, The 1968,D 12,62:5
Maesso, Jose E Jr (Screenwriter)
Ugly Ones, The 1968,D 12,62:5
Maestri, Anna
Bitter Rice 1950,S 19,39:2

Maeterlinck, Maurice (Original Author)
Blue Bird, The 1918,Ap 1,9:3
Monna Vanna 1923,S 25,8:2
Blue Bird, The 1940,Ja 20,11:2
Maetty, Marion
Merry Monahans, The 1944,O 13,16:2
Maetzig, Kurt (Director)
Marriage in the Shadows 1948,S 17,28:3
Maetzig, Kurt (Screenwriter)
Marriage in the Shadows 1948,S 17,28:3
Maffel, Marlo (Producer)
Mondo Pazzo 1965,Ap 1,30:3
Maffeo, Gianni
Boheme, La 1965,O 20,51:2
Maffet, Claire
Antoine and Antoinette 1948,Ap 16,29:2
Maga, Mickey
Diane 1956,Ja 13,18:1
Man in the Gray Flannel Suit, The
   1956,Ap 13,21:1
Eddy Duchin Story, The 1956,Je 22,15:1
Magallanes, Nicholas
Midsummer Night's Dream, A 1967,Ap 18,32:1
Magalona, Enrique
Hook, The 1963,F 16,5:6
Yank in Vietnam, A 1964,F 6,36:4
Magana, Angel
Viejo Doctor, El; Old Doctor, The
   1940,Ap 13,21:3
Games Men Play, The 1968,Mr 15,30:1
Magana, Delia
Cascarrabias 1933,O 30,14:2
Magarill, Sophie
Cities and Years 1931,Ap 4,23:1
Diary of a Revolutionist 1932,Je 10,22:3
Czar wants to Sleep, The 1934,D 10,16:3
Magda, Olty
Kiralyne Huszarja, A 1936,Ja 17,15:3
Mage, Jacques (Producer)
Riff Raff Girls 1962,O 20,13:5
Mage, Jacques (Screenwriter)
Riff Raff Girls 1962,O 20,13:5
MAGEE
See Also MCGEE, MCKEE
Magee, Anita
Back Door to Heaven 1939,Ap 20,21:2
Magee, Barney
Ireland, A Nation 1914,S 24,11:6
Magee, Patrick
Young Racers, The 1963,O 10,49:3
Dementia 13 1963,O 24,37:1
Servant, The 1964,Mr 17,30:2
Zulu 1964,Jl 8,38:1
Masque of the Red Death, The 1964,S 17,52:6
Persecution and Assassination of Jean-Paul Marat
   as Performed by the Inmates of the Asylum of
   Charenton Under the Direction of the Marquis
   De Sade, The 1967,F 23,41:1
Birthday Party, The 1968,D 10,54:1
Magee, Virginia
Bond Boy, The 1922,O 9,10:2
Mageean, Jimmy
Luck of the Irish, The 1937,Ja 16,21:1
Irish and Proud of It 1938,O 31,12:3
Macushla 1940,Ja 6,9:2
Magel, Anne
Innocent Affair, An 1948,S 29,36:2
Magello, Giovanni
Hell Raiders of the Deep 1954,Jl 3,9:2
Maggi, Ethel
Giovanni De Medici, The Leader 1940,Ja 5,15:4
Maggio, Angelo
Angelo in the Crowd 1952,O 4,15:2
Maggio, Dante
Woman Trouble 1949,My 26,34:2
Tombolo 1949,D 31,9:4
Under the Olive Tree 1951,O 5,24:4
Angelo in the Crowd 1952,O 4,15:2
Side Street Story 1954,Je 24,30:4
Variety Lights; Luci del Varieta 1965,My 7,34:1
Maggio, Pupella
Bible, The 1966,S 29,60:1
Maggiorani, Lamberto
Bicycle Thief, The 1949,D 13,44:2
Women Without Names 1951,Ag 7,22:2
Maghenzani, Giuseppe
Before the Revolution; Prima della Revoluziona
   1964,S 25,32:1
Maghier, Pierre
Schubert's Serenade 1940,S 3,21:2
Magidson, Herb (Composer)
Gay Divorcee, The 1934,N 16,27:1
Reckless 1935,Ap 20,16:1
George White's 1935 Scandals 1935,Ap 29,12:3
Here's to Romance 1935,O 3,29:2
King Solomon of Broadway 1935,O 19,12:2
Miss Pacific Fleet 1935,D 7,22:2
Life of the Party, The 1937,O 4,17:1
Priorities on Parade 1942,Jl 23,19:2
Hers to Hold 1943,Jl 22,15:1
Do You Love Me 1946,My 25,12:2

Magidson, Herb (Miscellaneous)
Great Ziegfeld, The 1936,Ap 9,21:2
I'd Give my Life 1936,Ag 17,9:1
Music for Madame 1937,O 23,14:1
Radio City Revels 1938,Mr 21,18:3
Magill, James
Canon City 1948,Jl 8,19:2
Magini, Gino (Screenwriter)
David and Goliath 1961,O 7,14:3
MAGINNIS
See MCGUINNESS
Maglione, Margherita (Screenwriter)
Doctor, Beware 1951,Ap 30,16:3
Magnan, Janine
To be a Crook 1967,F 7,33:2
Magnani, Anna
Tempo Massimo 1936,Mr 13,27:2
Cieca di Sorrento, La 1936,Ag 3,11:3
Open City; Citta Aperta 1946,F 26,21:2
Before Him all Rome Trembled 1947,F 22,16:2
Revenge 1947,N 28,37:4
Angelina 1948,Ap 6,27:2
Woman Trouble 1949,My 26,34:2
Bandit, The 1949,Je 7,26:3
Peddler and the Lady, The 1949,S 30,28:4
Peddlin' in Society 1950,F 23,33:3
Ways of Love (The Miracle); Miracle, The (Ways
   of Love) 1950,D 13,50:2
Doctor, Beware 1951,Ap 30,16:3
Scarred 1951,O 27,10:5
Bellissima 1953,My 18,26:2
Volcano 1953,Jl 21,19:2
Golden Coach, The 1954,Ja 22,30:2
Anita Garibaldi 1954,Mr 19,19:4
Rose Tattoo, The 1955,D 13,55:1
Wild Is the Wind 1957,D 12,35:1
Awakening, The 1958,Mr 3,24:6
Of Life and Love 1958,O 7,40:2
Fugitive Kind, The 1960,Ap 15,13:1
Made in Italy 1967,My 1,44:2
Magnani, Anna (Miscellaneous)
Of Life and Love 1958,O 7,40:2
Magnani, Anna (Screenwriter)
Angelina 1948,Ap 6,27:2
Magner, Don (Screenwriter)
Sailor From Gibraltar, The 1967,Ap 25,38:2
Magness, Annabelle
Lovey Mary 1926,Je 21,17:2
Magni, Eva
Canzione del Sole, La 1936,My 6,27:2
Serpente a Sonagli, Il 1936,Ag 17,9:2
Magni, Gianni
Taming of the Shrew, The 1967,Mr 9,43:1
Magni, Luigi (Screenwriter)
White Voices; Voci Blanche 1965,Ap 13,32:2
Bambole; Dolls, The (The Soup); Soup, The (The
   Dolls) 1965,Je 29,26:1
Mandragola 1966,Je 7,50:2
Queens, The (Queen Sabina); Queen Sabina (The
   Queens) 1968,Mr 11,49:1
Magnier, Claude (Original Author)
Where Were You When the Lights Went Out?
   1968,Ag 9,30:2
Magnier, Pierre
Cyrano de Bergerac 1925,Jl 6,12:2
Fra Diavolo 1931,N 23,22:1
Frochard et les Deux Orphelines, La
   1934,F 7,16:2
End of a Day, The 1939,S 12,28:4
Resistance; Peleton d'Execution 1946,Jl 5,15:3
Ruy Blas 1948,O 4,14:2
Naked Woman, The 1950,Ja 21,10:2
Ignace 1950,S 19,39:4
Rules of the Game, The 1961,Ja 19,26:1
Magnolia, Lou
Madison Square Garden 1932,O 12,26:5
Magnus, Annabelle
His Dog 1927,Ag 16,31:2
Magnuson, John (Producer)
Lenny Bruce 1967,Mr 20,26:4
Magnusson, Ingrid
Sunshine Follows Rain 1949,S 29,39:2
Magranville, Paul
Little Boy Lost 1953,S 22,38:2
Magre, Judith
Man in the Raincoat, The 1958,Jl 15,21:2
Lovers, The 1959,O 27,40:2
Magrill, George
Wild Horse Mesa 1925,Ag 10,8:2
Vanishing American, The 1925,O 16,18:2
Lord Jim 1925,N 16,19:4
Enchanted Hill, The 1925,D 29,19:2 (In
   Addenda)
Give Me a Sailor 1938,Ag 11,31:1
Meet Boston Blackie 1941,F 26,17:2
Magrini, Gitt
Night, The; Notte, La 1962,F 20,29:4
Magruder, Ann
Side Show 1931,S 19,10:2
MAGUIRE
See Also MACGUIRE, MCGUIRE

Maguire, John
Powder Town 1942,Je 8,11:2
Mexican Spitfire Sees a Ghost 1942,Jl 31,11:2
Navy Comes Through, The 1942,N 12,30:3
Maguire, Johnny
Dead of Night 1946,Je 29,22:6
Maguire, Kathleen
Edge of the City 1957,Ja 30,33:2
Flipper 1963,S 19,23:1
Maguire, Les
Ferry Cross the Mersey 1965,F 20,16:2
Maguire, Lupe
Man in Grey, The 1945,N 30,18:6
Maguire, Mary
That Man's Here Again 1937,My 6,23:3
Alcatraz Island 1937,O 14,22:2
Mysterious Mr Moto of Devil's Island
1938,S 19,16:2
Smiling Along 1939,F 20,13:2
Outsider, The 1940,Mr 18,13:2
Maguire, Nian (Miscellaneous)
Michael Strogoff 1960,My 21,15:1
Magy, Istvan Homoki Dr (Cinematographer)
Kingdom on the Waters, A 1954,Ag 2,12:3
Magy, Istvan Homoki Dr (Director)
Kingdom on the Waters, A 1954,Ag 2,12:3
Magy, Istvan Homoki Dr (Original Author)
Kingdom on the Waters, A 1954,Ag 2,12:3
Mahan, Billy
Every Saturday Night 1936,Mr 14,10:2
Educating Father 1936,Je 20,22:2
Off to the Races 1937,F 6,15:2
Big Business 1937,Je 1,27:2
Hot Water 1937,N 5,19:4
Trip to Paris, A 1938,Je 10,18:2
Safety in Numbers 1938,S 6,17:2
Young as You Feel 1940,Mr 8,25:3
Maharis, George
Sylvia 1965,F 11,45:1
Quick, Before it Melts 1965,Ap 1,30:2
Satan Bug, The 1965,Ap 15,38:1
Covenant with Death, A 1967,F 16,32:3
Happening, The 1967,My 18,56:3
Mahe (Miscellaneous)
Louise 1940,F 3,9:4
Mahen, J (Original Author)
Janosik 1936,D 25,19:3
MAHER
See Also MAYER, MEAGHER, MAIER
Maher, Marty Sgt (Original Author)
Long Gray Line, The 1955,F 11,19:2
Maher, Wally
23 1/2 Hours Leave 1937,My 17,23:2
Submarine D-1 1937,D 30,15:4
Nick Carter, Master Detective 1939,D 14,35:2
Strange Holiday 1945,O 20,8:2
Johnny Stool Pigeon 1949,S 23,28:3
Reformer and the Redhead, The 1950,Ap 10,15:2
Mystery Street 1950,Jl 28,12:5
Right Cross 1950,N 16,39:2
Mahike, Knut
Flying Classroom, The 1958,Je 28,13:7
Mahin, John Lee
Hell Below 1933,Ap 26,13:2
Mahin, John Lee (Miscellaneous)
My Son John 1952,Ap 9,27:1
Mahin, John Lee (Producer)
Horse Soldiers, The 1959,Je 26,13:1
Mahin, John Lee (Screenwriter)
Naughty Marietta 1935,Mr 23,11:2
Wife vs Secretary 1936,F 29,11:1
Small Town Girl 1936,Ap 11,19:1
Devil is a Sissy, The 1936,O 17,21:2
Love on the Run 1936,N 28,13:3
Captains Courageous 1937,My 12,27:1
Last Gangster, The 1937,D 10,33:2
too Hot To Handle 1938,S 30,24:2
Boom Town 1940,S 6,25:2
Dr Jekyll and Mr Hyde 1941,Ag 13,13:2
Johnny Eager 1942,F 20,21:2
Tortilla Flat 1942,My 22,27:1
Adventures of Tartu, The 1943,S 24,26:1
Down to the Sea in Ships 1949,F 23,31:2
Love That Brute 1950,My 27,10:6
Show Boat 1951,Jl 20,14:1
Quo Vadis 1951,N 9,22:2
Mogambo 1953,O 2,18:1
Elephant Walk 1954,Ap 22,37:2
Lucy Gallant 1955,O 21,30:1
Bad Seed, The 1956,S 13,39:6
Heaven Knows Mr Allison 1957,Mr 15,22:1
No Time for Sergeants 1958,My 30,13:2
Horse Soldiers, The 1959,Je 26,13:1
North to Alaska 1960,N 11,36:1
Spiral Road, The 1962,Ag 4,11:2
Moment to Moment 1966,Mr 3,28:1
Mahlich, Hans (Producer)
Naked Among the Wolves 1967,Ap 19,54:7
Mahlowe, David
Kind of Loving, A 1962,O 2,46:1
Mahomed, Ahmed Ben
Another Sky 1960,O 25,40:2

MAHON
See Also MANN
Mahon, Barry (Director)
Cuban Rebel Girls 1959,D 26,7:3
Mahon, Barry (Producer)
Cuban Rebel Girls 1959,D 26,7:3
Mahon, Clelle
Cuban Rebel Girls 1959,D 26,7:3
Mahoney, Francis X
Show Boat 1936,My 15,29:4
Mahoney, Jack (Composer)
Tin Pan Alley 1940,N 22,27:3
Mahoney, Jock
I've Lived Before 1956,Ag 4,13:1
Away all Boats 1956,Ag 17,14:2
Battle Hymn 1957,F 16,14:1
Time to Love and a Time to Die, A
1958,Jl 10,22:1
Tarzan the Magnificent 1960,Jl 21,17:1
Tarzan Goes to India 1962,S 6,37:2
Walls of Hell, The 1965,N 18,55:3
Glory Stompers, The 1968,Mr 28,52:4
Mahoney, Maggie
Blackjack Ketchum Desperado 1956,Ap 5,26:2
Desire in the Dust 1960,O 12,47:2
Mahoney, Mike
Father Was a Fullback 1949,O 13,33:3
Sailor Beware 1952,F 1,17:1
Off Limits 1953,Mr 30,25:5
Mahoney, Wilkie (Miscellaneous)
Caught in the Draft 1941,Je 26,27:3
Whistling in Dixie 1942,D 31,20:4
Du Barry Was a Lady 1943,Ag 20,13:1
Whistling in Brooklyn 1944,Mr 24,17:3
Doughgirls, The 1944,Ag 31,14:1
Mahoney, Wilkie (Screenwriter)
Some Like It Hot 1939,My 25,31:2
Panama Hattie 1942,O 2,31:2
Abroad With two Yanks 1944,O 26,19:7
Brewster's Millions 1945,Ap 27,23:2
Mahoney, Will
Lost in the Arctic 1928,Jl 26,25:3
Sez O'Reilly to MacNab 1938,F 19,19:4
Sound of Laughter, The 1963,D 18,44:2
Mahony, Jerry
Dawn Over Ireland 1938,F 19,19:2
Mahrt, Preben
I, A Woman 1966,O 12,36:3
Maiatian, Barbara
Power of Evil, The 1929,Ag 12,22:2
Maibaum, Richard (Original Author)
Gold Diggers of 1937 1936,D 25,19:2
Maibaum, Richard (Producer)
O S S 1946,My 27,15:5
Big Clock, The 1948,Ap 22,34:2
Sainted Sisters, The 1948,My 20,35:2
Bride of Vengeance 1949,Ap 7,38:2
Dear Wife 1950,F 2,31:2
No Man of her Own 1950,My 4,32:3
Battle at Bloody Beach, The 1961,Ag 17,18:2
Maibaum, Richard (Screenwriter)
We Went to College 1936,Jl 27,20:2
They Gave Him a Gun 1937,My 14,21:1
Live, Love and Learn 1937,N 19,27:2
Stablemates 1938,O 21,27:2
Coast Guard 1939,Ag 28,17:2
Amazing Mr Williams, The 1940,Ja 19,15:2
Twenty-Mule Team 1940,My 10,26:6
I Wanted Wings 1941,Mr 27,29:4
O S S 1946,My 27,15:5
Ransom 1956,Ja 25,28:3
Cockleshell Heroes, The 1956,Je 4,25:2
Bigger Than Life 1956,Ag 3,11:2
Zarak 1956,D 27,22:1
Battle at Bloody Beach, The 1961,Ag 17,18:2
From Russia with Love 1964,Ap 9,25:1
Maicon, Boris (Director)
Isla Maldita, La 1935,D 2,18:3
Infidelidad 1939,My 8,21:3
Maida and Ray
You're a Sweetheart 1937,D 25,10:5
Maidment, Kenneth L (Producer)
Village, The 1953,S 23,37:2
Maienatti, Malene (Producer)
Madame 1963,Mr 21,8:6
MAIER
See Also MAHER, MAYER, MEAGHER
Maier, William (Original Author)
Girls of Pleasure Island, The 1953,My 16,10:1
Maieroni, Achille
Loyalty of Love 1937,Mr 1,15:1
Conjugal Bed, The 1963,S 17,30:1
Maigne, Charles (Director)
Firing Line, The 1919,Jl 7,18:5
Copperhead, The 1920,F 9,10:3
Drums of Fate 1923,Ja 15,18:3
Trail of the Lonesome Pine, The 1923,Mr 20,24:3
Silent Partner, The 1923,Ag 20,4:2
Maigne, Liliane
Corbeau, Le; Raven, The 1948,F 24,21:1
Sins of Youth 1960,D 24,8:2

Maikut, Erich
Rosenkavalier, Der 1962,O 10,57:1
Mailer, Norman
Wild 90 1968,Ja 8,33:1
Beyond the Law 1968,S 30,60:4
Beyond the Law 1968,O 24,55:1
Mailer, Norman (Director)
Wild 90 1968,Ja 8,33:1
Beyond the Law 1968,S 30,60:4
Beyond the Law 1968,O 24,55:1
Mailer, Norman (Original Author)
Naked and the Dead, The 1958,Ag 7,21:1
American Dream, An 1966,S 1,28:2
Mailer, Norman (Producer)
Wild 90 1968,Ja 8,33:1
Beyond the Law 1968,S 30,60:4
Beyond the Law 1968,O 24,55:1
Mailes, Charles Hill
Red Hot Dollars 1919,D 29,7:2
Go and Get It 1920,Jl 19,16:3
Name the Man 1924,F 4,23:3
Find Your Man 1924,S 23,26:1
Lighthouse by the Sea, The 1924,D 29,11:4
Playing With Souls 1925,Ap 20,18:1 (Incorrect in
this edition; use 1925,Ap 28,18:1 elsewhere)
Crimson Runner, The 1925,My 27,26:2
Social Highwayman, The 1926,Je 15,23:3
Old Ironsides 1926,D 7,21:2
College Widow, The 1927,N 7,26:4
City Gone Wild, The 1927,D 6,27:1
Drums of Love 1928,Ja 25,20:4
What a Night! 1928,D 24,11:1
Give and Take 1928,D 27,27:1
Bellamy Trial, The 1929,Ja 24,30:5
Carnation Kid, The 1929,F 25,16:1
Unholy Garden, The 1931,O 29,27:1
Maillard, Henry
Passion Of Joan Of Arc, The 1929,Mr 29,21:1
Passion of Jeanne d'Arc, The 1929,Mr 31,VIII,7:1
Maillard, M
Miserables, Les 1926,Jl 9,17:1
Miserables, Les 1927,Ag 23,29:4
Maillard, Pierre
Twelve:Ten 1919,D 22,18:3
Maillot, Maurice
Whirlpool; (Remous) 1940,O 8,31:2
Last Will of Dr Mabuse, The 1943,Mr 20,11:1
Mailly
Miracle des Loups, Le 1930,Jl 28,22:1
Mailly, Fernand
Mare Nostrum 1926,F 16,22:4
Mails, Charles Hills
No More Orchids 1933,Ja 2,29:2
Mailshevsky, N
Sadko 1953,Je 1,18:6
Maiman, R (Director)
Red Tanks 1942,Je 6,9:2
Maiman, R (Screenwriter)
Red Tanks 1942,Je 6,9:2
Maimon, Alex (Screenwriter)
Casablan 1964,D 14,50:1
Main, Marjorie
Music in the Air 1934,D 14,29:3
Stella Dallas 1937,Ag 6,21:1
Dead End 1937,Ag 25,25:1
Shadow, The 1937,D 17,33:3
Boy of the Streets 1938,Ja 24,17:1
Penitentiary 1938,Mr 7,13:2
King of the Newsboys 1938,Ap 2,18:2
Test Pilot 1938,Ap 16,17:1
Prison Farm 1938,Jl 15,13:3
Little Tough Guy 1938,Ag 18,23:3
Girls' School 1938,N 3,27:1
Lucky Night 1939,My 5,29:3
They Shall Have Music 1939,Jl 26,17:2
Angels Wash Their Faces 1939,S 4,16:2
Women, The 1939,S 22,27:2
Another Thin Man 1939,N 24,29:1
I Take This Woman 1940,F 16,23:3
Women Without Names 1940,My 9,26:4
Dark Command 1940,My 11,15:2
Susan and God 1940,Jl 12,11:2
Turnabout 1940,Jl 27,17:6
Wyoming 1940,O 3,31:4
Trial of Mary Dugan, The 1941,Mr 6,25:4
Woman's Face, A 1941,My 16,21:2
Barnacle Bill 1941,Jl 25,12:4
Shepherd of the Hills, The 1941,Jl 31,13:2
Honky Tonk 1941,O 3,27:3
Bugle Sounds, The 1942,Ap 3,25:2
We Were Dancing 1942,My 1,23:2
Jackass Mail 1942,Jl 2,25:2
Tish 1942,S 18,25:2
Tennessee Johnson 1943,Ja 13,18:2
Heaven Can Wait 1943,Ag 12,15:1
Johnny Come Lately 1943,S 24,26:1
Rationing 1944,Ap 10,14:2
Meet Me in St Louis 1944,N 29,20:2
Gentle Annie 1945,My 5,11:5
Murder, He Says 1945,Je 25,20:3
Harvey Girls, The 1946,Ja 25,26:2
Bad Bascomb 1946,My 23,18:4
Undercurrent 1946,N 29,36:2

Main, Marjorie— Cont

Show-Off, The 1947,Mr 20,38:2
Egg and I, The 1947,Ap 25,29:2
Wistful Widow of Wagon Gap, The
1947,N 21,36:2
Big Jack 1949,My 23,27:4
Ma and Pa Kettle 1949,Ag 12,13:2
Summer Stock 1950,S 1,17:2
Mrs O'Malley and Mr Malone 1951,F 23,33:2
Ma and Pa Kettle Back on the Farm
1951,My 11,32:3
Law and the Lady, The 1951,Ag 16,23:2
Mr Imperium 1951,O 15,22:2
It's a big Country 1952,Ja 9,25:2
Belle of New York, The 1952,Mr 6,25:6
Ma and Pa Kettle at the Fair 1952,Jl 12,16:2
Long, Long Trailer, The 1954,F 19,24:3
Rose Marie 1954,Ap 2,22:2
Friendly Persuasion 1956,N 2,30:1

Mainati, Umberto
Canzione del Sole, La 1936,My 6,27:2

Mains, Marlene
Woman of the Town, The 1944,Mr 6,17:2

Mainwaring, Daniel (Screenwriter)
Phenix City Story, The 1955,S 3,9:1
Baby Face Nelson 1957,D 12,35:1
Walk Like a Dragon 1960,S 16,24:1
Atlantis the Lost Continent 1961,My 27,12:1
Minotaur, The 1961,N 8,41:1
Woman Who Wouldn't Die, The 1965,Je 10,38:1

Mainz, F A (Producer)
White Hell of Pitz Palu, The 1953,N 14,14:2

Maio, Gina
Bride of the Lake, The 1934,S 11,24:5

Mairesse, Guy
Tamango 1959,S 17,48:4

Mairos, Jorge
En un Burro Tres Baturros; Three Rustics on one
Donkey 1940,S 21,13:3

Mais, Suzet
Claudine 1940,Ap 1,15:2
Shop-Girls of Paris; Au Bonheur de Dames
1947,Je 23,14:4

Maisch, Herbert (Director)
Royal Waltz, The 1936,Ap 10,27:1
Boccaccio 1937,F 27,9:3
Andalusische Naechte; Nights in Andalusia
1938,S 24,13:2
Nanon 1938,N 26,18:2
Frau Sylvelin 1939,D 9,18:3
D III 88, Die neue deutsche Luftwaffe greift an; D
III 88, The New German Air Force Attacks
1940,F 17,9:3

Maisey, Susan
Mikado, The 1967,Mr 15,53:1

MAISON
See MASON, MASSON

Maistre, Aman
Maternelle, La 1935,O 15,19:1

Maistre, Francois
Love Game, The 1960,N 9,44:1
Joker, The; (Farceur, Le) 1961,Ag 8,32:2
Paris Belongs to Us 1962,N 6,38:1
Shameless Old Lady, The 1966,S 27,52:1

Maitland, Jules (Screenwriter)
Justice and Caryl Chessman 1960,Mr 3,24:5

Maitland, Marne
Outcast of the Islands 1952,My 16,19:2
Golden Mask, The 1954,Mr 20,10:5
Flame and the Flesh 1954,My 3,21:2
Detective, The 1954,N 2,25:2
Bhowani Junction 1956,My 25,26:1
Mark of the Hawk, The 1958,Mr 6,32:1
Camp on Blood Island, The 1958,S 18,37:2
Windom's Way 1958,O 1,45:1
Tiger Bay 1959,D 15,50:1
Wind Cannot Read, The 1960,Mr 10,36:1
I'm All Right Jack 1960,Ap 26,40:2
Man in a Cocked Hat 1960,Je 15,50:2
Nine Hours to Rama 1963,Ap 4,58:2
Cleopatra 1963,Je 13,29:1
Lord Jim 1965,F 26,18:1
Return of Mr Moto 1965,D 2,48:1
Khartoum 1966,Jl 14,28:1
Bobo, The 1967,S 29,53:1
Duffy 1968,S 17,50:3

Maitland, Richard
Is Zat So? 1927,My 17,27:2
Come to My House 1928,Ja 16,24:1

Maitland, Ruth
Heart Song 1934,Je 6,24:6

Maiuri, Dino (Original Author)
Kiss the Girls and Make Them Die
1967,Ja 26,25:1
Danger Diabolik 1968,D 12,62:6

Maiuri, Dino (Screenwriter)
Kiss the Girls and Make Them Die
1967,Ja 26,25:1
Violent Four, The 1968,Ag 15,46:2
Danger Diabolik 1968,D 12,62:6

Maizin, Azucena
Di que me Quieres; Say That You Love Me
1939,Ap 24,13:2

Majeroni, A
Wally, La 1939,Ja 2,28:3

Majeroni, Achille
Ape Woman, The 1964,S 23,55:1

Majeroni, Mario
Partners of the Night 1920,Mr 1,16:2
Snow Bride, The 1923,Je 12,22:2
Humming Bird, The 1924,Ja 14,2:1
Her Love Story 1924,O 7,26:1
Argentine Love 1924,D 23,16:2
Little French Girl, The 1925,Je 1,10:3
King on Main Street, The 1925,O 26,25:2
Rubber Heels 1927,Je 28,29:4

Major, Charles (Original Author)
When Knighthood Was in Flower 1922,S 15,17:2
(In Addenda)
Yolanda 1924,F 20,23:1
Sword and the Rose, The 1953,Ag 20,18:3

Majors, Lee
Will Penny 1968,Ap 11,51:2

Majuri, A (Screenwriter)
Side Street Story 1954,Je 24,30:4

Majuto
Man's Hope; (Sierra de Teruel) 1947,Ja 21,29:2

Makabuerza, Violet
Man of Africa 1956,O 11,51:1

Makagonova, Roza
No Ordinary Summer 1958,O 6,36:3

Makarcznski, Tadeusz (Screenwriter)
Good Times, Wonderful Times 1966,Jl 19,34:1

Makarenke, David
Tevya 1939,D 22,15:3

Makarenko, Daniel
Surrender 1927,O 11,27:1

Makaroff, V
Czar Ivan the Terrible 1928,Mr 12,26:1

Makarov, V
Immortal Garrison, The 1957,Mr 4,30:2

Makarova, Inna
Vasili's Return 1953,S 28,21:4
My Beloved 1959,Je 15,31:4
Marriage of Baezaminov, The 1966,Je 11,20:2

Makarova, Tamara
Deserter 1934,O 13,10:1
Seven Brave Men 1936,Je 15,24:2
City of Youth 1938,S 5,30:4
They Wanted Peace 1940,Ja 8,11:3
New Teacher, The 1941,Ap 7,13:3
Ural Front, The 1945,Je 7,25:3
Stone Flower 1946,D 30,15:2
Country Doctor, The 1953,F 16,16:2

Makasova, M
Sleeping Beauty, The 1966,My 4,50:1

Makavelev, Dusan (Director)
Affair of the Heart, An 1967,S 23,20:3
Love Affair, or the Case of the Missing
Switchboard Operator; Affair of the Heart, An
1968,F 7,38:3

Makavelev, Dusan (Original Author)
Love Affair, or the Case of the Missing
Switchboard Operator; Affair of the Heart, An
1968,F 7,38:3

Makavelev, Dusan (Screenwriter)
Affair of the Heart, An 1967,S 23,20:3

Makefa, Harry
Rhino! 1964,Ag 27,28:2

Makeham, Eliot
Rome Express 1933,F 27,11:2
Orders Is Orders 1934,My 7,20:2
Friday the 13th 1934,My 15,18:1
Unfinished Symphony 1935,Ja 14,11:2
Last Journey, The 1936,Je 8,22:4
Head Over Heels in Love 1937,F 13,9:1
Dark Journey 1937,Ag 23,22:1
Storm in a Teacup 1938,Mr 22,18:4
Troopship 1938,Ap 26,18:2
Beachcomber, The 1938,D 26,29:3
Inspector Hornleigh 1939,Je 15,27:3
Secret Four, The 1940,Ap 22,13:2
Pastor Hall 1940,S 21,13:2
Haunted Honeymoon 1940,O 31,28:2
Night Train 1940,D 30,21:1
Wings and the Woman 1942,O 8,31:1
Vacation From Marriage 1946,Mr 15,27:2
Frieda 1947,Ag 15,12:3
Canterbury Tale, A 1949,Ja 24,16:2
Daybreak 1949,Jl 4,9:2
Verger, The 1950,O 11,42:1
Crimson Pirate, The 1952,Ag 28,21:2

Makgoba, Paul
Dingaka 1965,Jl 1,34:1

Makharova, T
Vow, The 1947,Je 23,14:3

Maki, Tsjundo
Compliments of Mr Iflow 1941,F 17,10:7

Makin, William J (Original Author)
Return Of Doctor X, The 1939,N 23,38:5

Maklakiewicz, Zdzislaw
Salto 1966,O 4,50:1
Barrier 1967,S 27,39:3

Maklari, Zoltan
Key Balvany, A 1933,Ap 18,13:6
Kek Balvany, A; Blue Idol, The 1933,Ap 18,13:6

Maklyarsky, M (Screenwriter)
Secret Agent 1949,F 10,37:3

Mako
Sand Pebbles, The 1966,D 21,48:1
Private Navy of Sgt O'Farrell, The
1968,My 9,54:1

Makowska, Helen
Taras Bulba 1927,D 28,26:6

Makris, Orestis
Horse and Carriage 1958,Je 30,23:3
Counterfeit Coin 1960,My 16,39:1
Aunt From Chicago, The 1960,Je 6,33:6
House on Stournara Street, The 1960,O 17,33:4
Grouch, The 1961,F 27,23:2
Midwife, The 1961,S 25,41:2

Makumbi, Eseza
Kisenga, Man of Africa 1952,Mr 7,18:2

Mal, Rose
Hell on Earth 1934,Ja 29,10:2

Mala
Jungle Princess 1936,D 24,21:3
Call of the Yukon 1938,My 6,27:1
Mutiny on the Blackhawk 1939,Ag 2,17:2
Girl From God's Country 1940,S 9,18:5
Devil's Pipeline, The 1940,N 11,22:4

Mala, Ina
Crazy Quilt, The 1966,O 4,50:1

Mala, Ray
Green Hell 1940,Ja 30,15:6

Malalesta, Fred
Bardelys The Magnificent 1926,N 1,28:1 (In
Addenda)

Malamud, Bernard (Original Author)
Fixer, The 1968,D 9,59:1

Malandrinos, Andrea
Broken Melody, The 1934,O 31,17:3
Champagne Charlie 1948,Ag 7,8:2
Prince and the Showgirl 1957,Je 14,22:2

Malanga, Gerard
Illiac Passion, The 1968,Ap 19,40:1

Malanowicz, Zygmunt
Knife in the Water 1963,O 29,31:2
Barrier 1967,S 27,39:3

Malaparte, Curzio (Director)
Strange Deception 1953,My 27,28:2

Malaparte, Curzio (Screenwriter)
Strange Deception 1953,My 27,28:2

Malaschini, Ilario
Under the Sun of Rome 1949,O 6,40:4

Malasomma, Nunzio (Director)
Cieca di Sorrento, La 1936,Ag 3,11:3
I Tre Innamorati 1937,Je 17,19:2
Eravamo Sette Sorelle; We Were Seven Sisters
1939,Mr 3,21:3
Revolt of the Slaves, The 1961,N 8,41:1

Malatesta, Fern
$1,000 a Minute 1935,D 21,11:1

Malatesta, Fred
Little Lord Fauntleroy 1921,S 16,17:3
Reckless Age, The 1924,Je 10,24:4
Forbidden Paradise 1924,N 17,16:1
Farewell to Arms, A 1932,D 9,26:5

Malatesta, Guido (Screenwriter)
Head of a Tyrant 1962,Je 7,31:2
Samson and the Slave Queen 1964,Mr 5,36:2

Malbaum, Richard (Miscellaneous)
Day They Robbed the Bank of England, The
1960,S 5,11:2

Malbaum, Richard (Original Author)
See my Lawyer 1945,My 4,23:4

Malbaum, Richard (Producer)
Great Gatsby, The 1949,Jl 14,20:5
Captain Carey U S A 1950,Mr 30,40:5

Malbaum, Richard (Screenwriter)
Bad Man of Brimstone, The 1938,F 4,17:2
Ten Gentlemen From West Point 1942,Je 5,23:3
Great Gatsby, The 1949,Jl 14,20:5
Paratrooper 1953,D 31,9:3
Dr No 1963,My 30,20:1
Thunderball 1965,D 22,23:1

Malberg, Anna
Gertrud 1966,Je 3,33:1

Malberg, Henrik
Ordet 1957,D 16,33:6

Malchin, Edelweiss
Girls Behind Bars 1950,My 10,41:2
Man on a Tightrope 1953,Je 5,19:1

Malcolm, David (Screenwriter)
Wild Wild Winter 1966,Ja 6,20:2

Malcolm, Robert
To the Ends of the Earth 1948,F 13,26:2
Foreign Affair, A 1948,Jl 1,19:3
Hans Christian Andersen 1952,N 26,20:2

Malcomson, Ronald
Ireland's Border Line 1939,O 13,27:3

Malcon, Boris (Director)
Ojos Tapatios 1939,F 13,13:3
Novillero 1939,Mr 4,18:5

Maldacea, Francesco
Farewell to Love 1933,N 25,10:2

Maldanado, Bertha
Tundra 1936,D 3,31:2

Malden, Karl
They Knew What They Wanted 1940,O 11,25:2
Winged Victory 1944,D 21,16:2
Boomerang 1947,Mr 6,36:2
Kiss of Death 1947,Ag 28,28:2
Gunfighter, The 1950,Je 24,7:2
Where the Sidewalk Ends 1950,Jl 8,7:4
Halls of Montezuma, The 1951,Ja 6,9:6
Streetcar Named Desire, A 1951,S 30,27:1
Sellout, The 1952,My 31,12:7
Diplomatic Courier 1952,Je 14,12:2
Operation Secret 1952,N 6,37:2
Ruby Gentry 1952,D 26,20:2
I Confess 1953,Mr 23,28:2
Take the High Ground 1953,N 20,19:2
Phantom of the Rue Morgue 1954,Mr 20,10:5
On the Waterfront 1954,Jl 29,18:1
Baby Doll 1956,D 19,40:2
Fear Strikes Out 1957,Mr 21,37:2
Bombers B-52 1957,N 23,11:2
Hanging Tree, The 1959,F 12,23:1
Pollyanna 1960,My 20,26:1
Great Impostor, The 1961,Mr 30,24:1
One Eyed Jacks 1961,Mr 31,21:1
Parrish 1961,My 5,22:1
All Fall Down 1962,Ap 12,41:3
Birdman of Alcatraz 1962,Jl 19,19:2
Gypsy 1962,N 2,24:1
How the West Was Won 1963,Ap 1,54:1
Come Fly With Me 1963,My 2,40:2
Dead Ringer 1964,F 20,22:3
Cheyenne Autumn 1964,D 24,8:1
Cincinnati Kid, The 1965,O 28,48:1
Nevada Smith 1966,Je 24,28:1 (Incorrect in this edition; use 1966,Je 30,28:1 elsewhere)
Murderers' Row 1966,D 22,40:3
Hotel 1967,Ja 20,27:1
Adventures of Bullwhip Griffin, The 1967,Mr 9,43:2
Billion Dollar Brain 1967,D 23,29:1
Blue 1968,My 11,28:1
Hot Millions 1968,S 20,42:1
Malden, Karl (Director)
Time Limit 1957,O 24,37:2
Maldonado, Ruben
Hawaii Calls 1938,Ap 29,17:2
Malducce, Francesco
Die Singende Stadt 1932,My 10,25:4
Malena, Lena
Burning Heart, The 1930,My 12,27:3
Maleno (Director)
Slave Trade in the World Today 1964,N 24,44:1
Malenotti, Maleno (Original Author)
Beautiful but Dangerous 1958,F 6,24:1
Malenotti, Maleno (Producer)
Fear No Evil 1949,Mr 31,31:2
Young Caruso, The 1953,O 13,34:4
Life and Music of Giuseppe Verdi, The 1957,My 2,26:2
Beautiful but Dangerous 1958,F 6,24:1
Savage Innocents, The 1961,My 25,31:1
Malenotti, Maleno (Screenwriter)
Young Caruso, The 1953,O 13,34:4
Malentjew Sisters
World Dances 1954,N 8,24:6
Maler, Sigrid
G I Blues 1960,N 5,28:1
Malerba, Luigi (Screenwriter)
Lupa, La 1954,F 18,36:2
Matchless 1967,N 11,26:3
Girl and the General, The 1967,D 7,60:1
Malet, Arthur
Convicts 4 1962,O 4,44:2
Mary Poppins 1964,S 25,34:1
MALEY
See Also MALY
Maley, Laila
Littlest Outlaw, The 1955,D 27,31:1
Maley, Peggy
I Want You 1951,D 24,9:1
Lady Says No, The 1952,Ja 7,14:3
Bigamist, The 1953,D 26,10:4
Wild One, The 1953,D 31,9:2
Midnight Story, The 1957,Jl 5,14:2
Maleyef, Igor
Anna 1936,Jl 17,20:2
Malgarini, Pina
First Opera Film Festival 1948,My 31,12:7
Malgetso, Paco
Torero! 1957,My 22,29:2
Malia
Return to Paradise 1953,S 11,24:2
Malicka, Maria
Barrier 1967,S 27,39:3
Malies, Louis (Director)
Fire Within, The 1964,F 18,27:1
Malies, Louis (Screenwriter)
Fire Within, The 1964,F 18,27:1
Malieson, Miles
They all Died Laughing 1964,Mr 16,37:2
Malikoff, H
Spy of Madame de Pompadour, The 1929,S 10,27:1

Malikoff, Nicolai
Trial of Donald Westhof, The 1928,F 18,11:2
Malikoff, Nikolai
Apaches of Paris 1928,D 11,35:3
President, The 1929,Ja 21,18:4
Rasputin: The Holy Devil 1930,Ag 25,14:2
Malikoff, Nikolai (Director)
Apaches of Paris 1928,D 11,35:3
Malikov, Nicholas
Little Flower of Jesus, The 1938,D 13,31:2
Malin, Eddie
Hard Day's Night, A 1964,Ag 12,41:1
How to Steal a Million 1966,Jl 15,34:1
MALINA
See Also MOLINA
Malina, Luba
Mexican Hayride 1949,Ja 12,33:3
Malinda, Charles
Africa-Texas Style! 1967,Jl 13,30:2
Malinovskya, V S
Station Master, The 1928,Je 18,13:2
Malishevsky, Ivan
Military Secret 1945,Ag 2,16:2
Maliszewski, Josef
Ulan I Dziewczyna 1933,O 9,22:3
Maliughin, L (Screenwriter)
Train Goes East, The 1949,S 5,13:3
Maliutin, Y
Pugachev 1938,Jl 4,10:2
Professor Mamlock 1938,N 8,26:2
Malkiewicz, Irena
Tredowata 1936,D 31,21:2
Malko, O
Leningrad Symphony 1958,Je 23,19:6
Mall, Elick (Screenwriter)
You Were Meant for Me 1948,Ja 29,27:5
Mallalieu, Aubrey
21 Days Together 1940,My 23,28:4
Haunted Honeymoon 1940,O 31,28:2
Wings and the Woman 1942,O 8,31:1
Courageous Mr Penn 1943,D 23,26:5
Meet Me at Dawn 1948,My 18,26:2
Facts of Love, The 1949,O 31,20:2
Girl in a Million, A 1950,Jl 24,15:2
Malland, Alf
Nine Lives 1959,Ja 6,28:1
Mallbaum, Richard (Screenwriter)
Goldfinger 1964,D 22,36:1
Malle, Louis (Director)
Frantic 1961,Je 12,34:1
Zazie 1961,N 21,45:5
Very Private Affair, A 1962,S 29,15:1
Viva Maria 1965,D 20,48:2
Thief of Paris, The 1967,Ag 24,43:2
Malle, Louis (Miscellaneous)
Silent World, The 1956,S 25,30:1
Very Private Affair, A 1962,S 29,15:1
Malle, Louis (Producer)
Zazie 1961,N 21,45:5
Viva Maria 1965,D 20,48:2
Thief of Paris, The 1967,Ag 24,43:2
Malle, Louis (Screenwriter)
Frantic 1961,Je 12,34:1
Zazie 1961,N 21,45:5
Viva Maria 1965,D 20,48:2
Thief of Paris, The 1967,Ag 24,43:2
Malleson, Miles
Sign of the Four, The 1932,Ag 20,7:4
Nell Gwyn 1935,Je 20,16:2
Nine Days a Queen 1936,O 3,21:1
Knight Without Armor 1937,Jl 9,18:1
Thief of Bagdad, The 1940,D 6,28:2
Major Barbara 1941,My 15,27:1
Wings and the Woman 1942,O 8,31:1
Dead of Night 1946,Je 29,22:6
One Night With You 1949,F 21,20:2
Saraband 1949,Je 13,16:3
Stage Fright 1950,F 24,27:2
Kind Hearts and Coronets 1950,Je 15,41:2
While the Sun Shines 1950,Jl 1,9:2
Perfect Woman, The 1951,F 17,10:7
Golden Salamander 1951,Mr 24,8:3
Mr Lord Says No! 1952,F 12,22:5
Man in the White Suit, The 1952,Ap 1,35:2
Magic Box, The 1952,S 24,40:2
Importance of Being Earnest, The 1952,D 23,17:2
Assassin, The 1953,Ap 18,17:2
Captain's Paradise, The 1953,S 29,25:5
Trent's Last Case 1953,N 27,99:9
Folly to be Wise 1953,D 28,17:2
Woman's Angle, The 1954,Ag 27,11:6
Private's Progress 1956,Jl 24,19:2
Wee Geordie 1956,O 8,31:1
Brothers in Law 1957,Ag 20,22:1
Silken Affair, The 1957,O 31,41:1
Admirable Crichton, The 1957,D 15,45:4 (Incorrect in this edition; use 1957,D 17,45:4 elsewhere)
Horror of Dracula 1958,My 29,24:4
Your Past Is Showing 1958,Jl 1,36:2
Gideon of Scotland Yard 1959,My 20,38:2
Happy is the Bride 1959,Je 30,27:2
Hounds of the Baskervilles, The 1959,Jl 4,9:4

Malleson, Miles— Cont
3 Men in a Boat 1959,Jl 29,33:2
I'm All Right Jack 1960,Ap 26,40:2
Man in a Cocked Hat 1960,Je 15,50:2
Day They Robbed the Bank of England, The 1960,S 5,11:2
Brides of Dracula, The 1960,S 6,41:4
Captain's Table, The 1960,S 27,40:1
Heavens Above! 1963,My 21,28:2
Circus World 1964,Je 26,34:2
Murder Ahoy 1964,S 23,55:3
Malleson, Miles (Miscellaneous)
Nell Gwyn 1935,Je 20,16:2
Rhodes 1936,F 29,11:1
Malleson, Miles (Original Author)
Perfect Understanding 1933,F 23,20:2
Malleson, Miles (Screenwriter)
Peg of Old Drury 1936,Ap 13,15:1
Nine Days a Queen 1936,O 3,21:1
Victoria the Great 1937,O 29,19:1
Sixty Glorious Years 1938,N 18,25:2
Thief of Bagdad, The 1940,D 6,28:2
Wings and the Woman 1942,O 8,31:1
Spitfire 1943,Je 14,13:2
Yellow Canary, The 1944,Ap 14,24:7
Mallet, Robert (Original Author)
Valiant, The 1962,Je 14,23:4
Mallet, Tania
Goldfinger 1964,D 22,36:1
Mallett, Jack Arundel
Ivory Hunter 1952,Ag 19,19:1
Mallian, Jacqueline
Grand Maneuver, The 1956,O 2,39:1
Magnificent Tramp, The 1962,Ap 25,30:1
Mallinson, Rory
Pride of the Marines 1945,Ag 25,7:3
Cry Wolf 1947,Jl 19,10:2
Dark Passage 1947,S 6,11:2
Task Force 1949,O 1,8:6
Short Grass 1951,Ja 13,10:4
Cavalry Scout 1951,Je 8,32:2
Mallock (Original Author)
Devil's Maze, The 1929,N 10,X,6:7 (In Addenda)
Mallory, Boots
Handle with Care 1932,D 24,11:4
Humanity 1933,Ap 22,16:3
Hello Sister! 1933,My 6,11:2
Sing Sing Nights 1935,Ja 26,13:2
Powdersmoke Range 1936,Mr 9,20:2
Mallory, Drue
Three Came Home 1950,F 21,22:5
Please Believe Me 1950,Je 12,19:4
Mallory, Edward
Diamond Head 1963,F 21,5:2
Mallory, Jay (Joyce Carey) (Original Author)
Give Me your Heart 1936,S 17,18:2
Mallot, Yollande
Dark Streets of Cairo 1940,D 2,19:3
MALLOY
See Also MOLLOY
Malloy, Doris (Miscellaneous)
Diamond Jim 1935,Ag 24,18:2
King Solomon of Broadway 1935,O 19,12:2
Malloy, Doris (Original Author)
Mad Parade, The 1931,S 19,10:2
Shadows of Sing Sing 1934,F 21,23:2
Gambling Lady 1934,Ap 5,25:2
I am a Thief 1935,Ja 1,24:1
Corregidor 1943,My 28,19:2
Malloy, Doris (Screenwriter)
I am a Thief 1935,Ja 1,24:1
Princess O'Hara 1935,Ap 13,11:3
Mr Dynamite 1935,My 25,12:1
His Night Out 1935,N 16,19:2
Remember Last Night? 1935,N 21,27:2
Human Cargo 1936,My 16,11:2
Two in a Crowd 1936,O 5,25:1
Outcast 1937,Mr 3,27:2
Midnight Madonna 1937,Jl 17,18:1
On Such a Night 1937,S 17,29:2
Mickey, the Kid 1939,Jl 6,27:1
Corregidor 1943,My 28,19:2
Hitler's Madman 1943,Ag 28,15:1
Malloy, Francetta
Las Vegas Nights 1941,Mr 20,25:2
Malm, Mona
All These Women 1964,O 6,35:1
Malmen, Lennart
Elvira Madigan 1967,S 30,26:1
Malmsberg, Bertil (Screenwriter)
Crime and Punishment 1948,Mr 1,17:2
Blood and Fire 1950,Je 24,7:4
Malmsjo, Jan
Loving Couples 1966,S 20,38:1
Malmsten, Birger
Frustration 1949,Ag 27,7:3
Illicit Interlude 1954,O 27,32:6
Time of Desire 1959,N 21,26:5
Secrets of Woman 1961,Jl 12,36:1
Devil's Wanton, The 1962,Jl 5,21:2
Silence, The 1964,F 4,28:1
Malmstrom, O B (Producer)
Young Have no Time, The 1959,N 23,41:2

Malnati, Umberto
But It's Nothing Serious 1939,O 10,27:2
Malneck, Matty (Composer)
To Beat the Band 1935,N 23,23:2
Hit Parade, The 1937,My 31,11:2
Man About Town 1939,Je 29,19:1
Let's Make Music 1941,Ja 23,19:2
Do You Love Me 1946,My 25,12:2
Malneck, Matty (Miscellaneous)
Hawaiian Nights 1939,S 29,19:4
Malneck, Matty and his orchestra
St Louis Blues 1939,F 9,17:2
You're in the Army Now 1941,D 26,21:4
Malnick (Miscellaneous)
Transatlantic Merry-Go-Round 1934,N 1,25:2
Malo, Frank
Boy Slaves 1939,F 9,17:3
Malo, Gina
Magic Night 1932,N 3,25:3
Waltz Time 1933,S 29,24:2
In a Monastery Garden 1935,Mr 13,16:2
My Song For You 1935,My 27,20:6
Malo, Jesse (Original Author)
Star Dust 1940,My 4,13:1
Malone, Dorothy
One Mysterious Night 1944,O 21,15:3
Too Young to Know 1945,D 8,21:2
Janie Gets Married 1946,Je 15,24:2
Night and Day 1946,Jl 26,16:2
Big Sleep, The 1946,Ag 24,6:6
To the Victor 1948,Ap 17,11:2
Two Guys From Texas 1948,Ag 28,8:6
One Sunday Afternoon 1948,D 27,16:3
South of St Louis 1949,Mr 7,17:2
Colorado Territory 1949,Je 25,8:6
Nevadan, The 1950,Ja 13,19:4
Killer That Stalked New York, The
1951,Ja 5,17:2
Mrs O'Malley and Mr Malone 1951,F 23,33:2
Torpedo Valley 1952,D 20,15:3
Scared Stiff 1953,Jl 3,10:2
Jack Slade 1953,O 29,42:6
Loophole 1954,Mr 13,11:3
Pushover 1954,Jl 31,6:3
Young at Heart 1955,Ja 20,35:1
Battle Cry 1955,F 3,18:1
Sincerely Yours 1955,N 3,37:1
Artists and Models 1955,D 22,20:1
At Gunpoint 1956,F 4,24:5
Pillars of the Sky 1956,O 13,15:2
Written on the Wind 1957,Ja 12,12:6
Man of a Thousand Faces 1957,Ag 14,21:1
Tip on a Dead Jockey 1957,S 7,12:7
Quantez 1957,S 7,12:7
Tarnished Angels, The 1958,Ja 7,31:1
Too Much, Too Soon 1958,My 10,19:2
Warlock 1959,My 1,34:1
Last Voyage, The 1960,F 20,14:2
Last Sunset, The 1961,Je 15,51:1
Beach Party 1963,S 26,40:2
Malone, Dudley Field
Mission to Moscow 1943,Ap 30,25:2
Malone, Jessica
Uncivilized 1937,N 17,27:4
Malone, Joel (Screenwriter)
Big Fix, The 1947,My 3,10:3
Illegal Entry 1949,Je 11,11:2
Arctic Manhunt 1949,Ag 19,12:5
South Sea Sinner 1950,Ja 16,18:4
Just Across the Street 1952,Je 28,12:4
Malone, Molly
It's a Great Life 1920,Ag 30,12:3
Little Johnny Jones 1923,Ag 13,16:1
Malone, Nancy
Violators, The 1959,Ag 4,32:5
Affair of the Skin, An 1963,N 21,43:2
Malone, Ralph
Woman Trap 1936,Mr 7,11:4
Malone, Today
Revolution 1968,Ag 8,27:2
Maloney, Jim
Detective Story 1951,N 7,35:2
Wait Till the Sun Shines, Nellie 1952,Je 28,12:2
Mister Roberts 1955,Jl 15,14:1
Malory, Thomas Sir (Original Author)
Knights of the Round Table 1954,Ja 8,17:2
Malot, Hector (Original Author)
Sans Famille 1959,S 5,11:4
Malotte, Albert Hay (Composer)
Enchanted Forest, The 1945,D 17,17:2
Malou
Doll, The 1964,Ja 14,27:1
Malouf, Jacqueline
Donovan's Reef 1963,Jl 25,14:1
Malouf, Yusuf (Director)
Broken Wings, The 1968,Mr 16.34:1
Malouvier, J C
Wench, The 1949,Mr 14,15:5
Malraux, Andre (Director)
Man's Hope; (Sierra de Teruel) 1947,Ja 21,29:2
Malraux, Andre (Producer)
Man's Hope; (Sierra de Teruel) 1947,Ja 21,29:2

Malraux, Andre (Screenwriter)
Man's Hope; (Sierra de Teruel) 1947,Ja 21,29:2
Mals, Ray
Mad Doctor of Market Street, The 1942,Ja 5,21:5
Malsky, A
Polish Terror, The 1933,Mr 13,18:3
Maltby, H F
Trouble Ahead 1936,S 21,26:5
Girl Was Young, The 1938,F 11,27:2
To the Victor 1938,Ap 13,21:2
Malten, Fee
D-Zug 13 Hat Verspaetung 1931,Ag 10,18:3
Sein Liebeslied 1931,N 19,27:5
Der Falsche Feldmarschall 1932,Je 30,26:2
Das Nachtigall Maedel 1933,Ja 23,9:2
Schwebende Jungfrau, Die 1937,Ag 7,7:2
Malter, William
T-Men 1948,Ja 23,28:3
Malton, Felicitas
Mystic Mirror, The 1928,O 1,23:1
Maltox, Martha
Cat and the Canary, The 1927,S 10,9:4
Maltz, Albert (Miscellaneous)
Moscow Strikes Back 1942,Ag 17,19:2
Seeds of Freedom 1943,Ag 25,17:2
Maltz, Albert (Original Author)
Afraid to Talk 1932,D 19,19:5
Maltz, Albert (Screenwriter)
This Gun for Hire 1942,My 14,23:2
Destination Tokyo 1944,Ja 1,9:2
Pride of the Marines 1945,Ag 25,7:3
Cloak and Dagger 1946,O 5,13:2
Naked City, The 1948,Mr 5,17:2
Malvern, Paul (Producer)
Doomed to Die 1940,Jl 30,16:3
Ali Baba and the Forty Thieves 1944,Mr 16,17:3
House of Frankenstein 1944,D 16,19:3
Sudan 1945,Ap 19,22:8
House of Dracula 1945,D 22,16:3
Tangier 1946,Je 7,II,16:4
Pirates of Monterey 1947,D 17,41:4
Rock Island Trail 1950,Je 5,19:3
Malveyev, Yevgeni
Resurrection 1963,O 7,35:2
Malville, Marion
Twilight 1949,D 30,13:2
Malwitz, Gerda
Marriage in the Shadows 1948,S 17,28:3
MALY
See Also MALEY
Maly, Gero
Melody of The Heart 1930,S 1,16:1
Borcsa Amerikaben; Barbara in America
1939,F 11,13:2
Fekete Gyemantok; Black Diamonds
1939,Ap 24,13:2
Gyimesi Vadvirag; Wildflower of Gyimes
1939,O 21,12:3
Szegeny Gazdagok; Poor Plutocrats
1939,D 4,18:4
Uz Bence 1940,Ja 15,11:2
Rozmaring; Rosemary 1940,F 10,19:3
Sut a Nap (Sun Shines, The); Sun Shines, The
1940,Ap 6,13:3
Malyavina, V
My Name Is Ivan (Ivan's Childhood)
1963,Je 28,25:4
Malyon, Eily
His Greatest Gamble 1934,Jl 18,20:2
Little Minister, The 1934,D 28,25:1
Romance in Manhattan 1935,Ja 18,29:2
Clive of India 1935,Ja 18,29:1
Miserables, Les 1935,Ap 22,14:2
Florentine Dagger, The 1935,Ap 27,20:6
Flame Within, The 1935,Je 1,18:2
Melody Lingers on, The 1935,N 7,27:1
Tale of Two Cities, A 1935,D 26,21:2
One Rainy Afternoon 1936,My 14,29:2
Dracula's Daughter 1936,My 18,14:2
White Angel, The 1936,Je 25,24:1
Anthony Adverse 1936,Ag 27,16:1
Woman Rebels, A 1936,O 30,27:2
Three Men on a Horse 1936,N 26,39:1
Night Must Fall 1937,Ap 30,17:2
Rebecca of Sunnybrook Farm 1938,Mr 26,12:1
Kidnapped 1938,My 28,9:2
Young in Heart, The 1938,N 4,27:2
Little Princess, The 1939,Mr 11,21:1
Hound of the Baskervilles, The 1939,Mr 25,19:2
Confessions of a Nazi Spy 1939,Ap 29,13:2
On Borrowed Time 1939,Jl 7,13:2
We Are not Alone 1939,D 1,27:1
Barricade 1939,D 9,18:2
Young Tom Edison 1940,Mr 15,27:2
Untamed 1940,Jl 25,14:3
Foreign Correspondent 1940,Ag 28,15:2
Man Hunt 1941,Je 14,20:2
Man in the Trunk, The 1942,O 23,25:1
I Married a Witch 1942,N 20,27:2
Going my Way 1944,My 3,25:2
Seventh Cross, The 1944,S 29,18:1
Paris Underground 1945,O 20,8:2
She Wolf of London 1946,Ap 6,10:6

Malyon, Eily — Cont
Secret Heart, The 1946,D 26,28:2
Malyutin, Y
Secret Brigade 1951,Mr 19,23:2
Mamakos, Peter
Cargo to Capetown 1950,Mr 31,36:3
Adventures of Haji Baba, The 1954,O 9,8:7
Desert Sands 1955,N 19,22:7
Conqueror, The 1956,Mr 31,13:3
Mammi, Fulvia
I Cadetti di Guascogna 1952,O 6,22:2
Mamo
Mutiny on the Bounty 1935,N 9,19:2
Mamo, John
Girl Named Tamiku, A 1963,Mr 15,8:2
Mamoulian, Rouben (Director)
Applause 1929,O 8,24:5
City Streets 1931,Ap 18,17:3
Dr Jekyll and Mr Hyde 1932,Ja 2,14:2
Love Me Tonight 1932,Ag 19,20:6
Song of Songs 1933,Jl 20,22:2
Queen Christina 1933,D 27,23:3
We Live Again 1934,N 2,27:2
Becky Sharp 1935,Je 14,27:2
Gay Desperado, The 1936,O 9,31:4
High, Wide and Handsome 1937,Jl 22,15:1
Golden Boy 1939,S 8,28:2
Mark of Zorro, The 1940,N 4,23:2
Blood and Sand 1941,My 23,25:3
Rings on her Fingers 1942,Ap 24,21:4
Summer Holiday 1948,Je 12,8:5
Silk Stockings 1957,Jl 19,11:1
Applause 1967,O 2,58:2
Mamoulian, Rouben (Original Author)
Never Steal Anything Small 1959,F 12,23:1
Mamounah
Samarang 1933,Je 29,22:2
Mamporia, I
Caucasian Love 1929,D 3,28:4
Man o' War (Horse)
Race of the Age, The 1920,N 1,13:2
Managadze, S (Director)
Ballet Tales 1956,O 25,40:5
Manahan, Anna
Ulysses 1967,Mr 14,55:1
Manahan, Sheila
Saints and Sinners 1949,S 12,17:2
Seven Days to Noon 1950,D 19,41:3
Another Shore 1951,F 12,19:3
Abandon Ship 1957,Ap 18,35:1
Manakos, Peter
Merry Andrews 1958,Mr 21,17:1
Manara, Luciano
Little World of Don Camillo, The
1953,Ja 14,27:1
Manas, Alfredo (Screenwriter)
Tarantos, Los 1964,Je 30,22:1
Mance, Gina
Napoleon 1929,F 12,23:1
Manciet, Yves
Amazon Trader, The 1956,N 17,17:6
Mancini, Henry (Composer)
Great Race, The 1965,S 16,00:0
Mancini, Hugo
Way of a Gaucho 1952,N 5,36:2
Mancini, Liliana
Under the Sun of Rome 1949,O 6,40:4
Mandal, Gustav (Producer)
Flamboyant Sex, The 1963,Ag 13,25:1
MANDEL
See Also MENDEL
Mandel, Deryk (Miscellaneous)
Belles and Ballets 1960,N 15,45:3
Mandel, Frank (Composer)
New Moon 1930,D 25,18:6
Mandel, Frank (Original Author)
New Moon 1930,D 25,18:6
New Moon 1940,Jl 19,22:2
No, No, Nanette 1940,D 20,33:1
Desert Song, The 1943,D 18,10:6
Tea for Two 1950,S 2,11:2
Desert Song, The 1953,My 21,39:2
Mandel, Loring (Screenwriter)
Countdown 1968,My 2,57:3
Mander, Miles
First Born, The 1929,Ja 13,VIII,5:2 (In Addenda)
Doctor's Women, The 1929,Je 3,27:2
Loose Ends 1930,O 18,23:2
Murder 1930,O 25,20:6
Jaws of Hell 1931,Ja 5,21:3
Missing Rembrandt, The 1932,Mr 26,17:2
Bitter Sweet 1933,Ag 24,18:2
Private Life of Henry VIII, The 1933,O 13,25:2
Loyalties 1934,O 26,25:1
Battle, The 1934,N 23,23:2
Don Quixote 1934,D 24,17:1
Here's to Romance 1935,O 3,29:2
Three Musketeers, The 1935,N 1,25:1
Wake up and Live 1937,Ap 24,16:2
Slave Ship 1937,Je 17,19:2
Kidnapped 1938,My 28,9:2
Suez 1938,O 15,21:2
Mad Miss Manton, The 1938,O 21,27:2
Three Musketeers, The 1939,F 18,12:2

Mander, Miles— Cont

Little Princess, The 1939,Mr 11,21:1
Wuthering Heights 1939,Ap 14,28:2
Man in the Iron Mask, The 1939,Jl 14,11:1
Stanley and Livingstone 1939,Ag 5,18:2
Tower of London 1939,D 12,37:2
Primrose Path 1940,Mr 23,16:2
House of the Seven Gables, The 1940,Ap 15,21:3
Captain Caution 1940,O 21,21:3
South of Suez 1940,D 19,33:2
That Hamilton Woman 1941,Ap 4,25:1
Dr Kildare's Wedding Day 1941,S 18,31:1
To Be or not to Be 1942,Mr 7,13:2
Fingers at the Window 1942,Ap 23,27:3
This Above All 1942,My 13,14:3
Tarzan's New York Adventure 1942,Ag 7,13:2
War Against Mrs Hadley, The 1942,N 26,40:2
Assignment in Brittany 1943,Ap 22,31:2
Five Graves to Cairo 1943,My 27,21:2
Phantom of the Opera, The 1943,O 15,15:2
Guadalcanal Diary 1943,N 18,29:1
Return of the Vampire, The 1944,Ja 29,10:1
Four Jills in a Jeep 1944,Ap 6,27:2
Scarlet Claw, The 1944,My 19,12:1
Pearl of Death 1944,Ag 26,15:2
Enter Arsene Lupin 1944,D 2,17:6
Picture of Dorian Gray, The 1945,Mr 2,15:2
Murder, my Sweet 1945,Mr 9,16:2
Brighton Strangler, The 1945,My 19,15:2
Confidential Agent 1945,N 3,11:2
Walls Came Tumbling Down, The 1946,N 9,13:5
Imperfect Lady, The 1947,My 22,34:5

Mander, Miles (Director)
First Born, The 1929,Ja 13,VIII,5:2 (In Addenda)
Morals of Marcus, The 1936,Ja 13,14:2

Mander, Miles (Original Author)
First Born, The 1929,Ja 13,VIII,5:2 (In Addenda)

Mander, Miles (Screenwriter)
First Born, The 1929,Ja 13,VIII,5:2 (In Addenda)
Phantom Fiend 1935,Ap 22,14:2
Morals of Marcus, The 1936,Ja 13,14:2

Mandia, Ricardo
On the Avenue 1937,F 5,17:3

Mandlova, Adina
Merry Wives, The 1940,N 12,28:3

Mandy
Raising a Riot 1957,My 8,44:1

Mandy, Jerry
Underworld 1927,Ag 22,21:3
Gay Defender, The 1927,D 26,26:6
Love and Learn 1928,F 20,14:1
At Yale 1928,Jl 30,21:2
Love, Live and Laugh 1929,N 2,14:6
Doorway to Hell, The 1930,N 1,23:2
Girls Demand Excitement 1931,F 7,11:1
Sailor's Luck 1933,Mr 17,21:2
Strange People 1933,Je 17,16:5
It's a Gift 1935,Ja 5,20:2
McFadden's Flats 1935,Mr 13,16:2
Bride Comes Home, The 1935,D 25,30:2
King of Burlesque 1936,Ja 16,25:2
Spendthrift 1936,Jl 23,24:1
Hawaii Calls 1938,Ap 29,17:2
Ghost Creeps, The 1940,Ag 19,13:3

Manel, Ettore
Mademoiselle 1966,Ag 2,23:1

Manenti, Carlo
Man of Courage 1934,N 14,23:2

Manes, Gina
Postmaster's Daughter, The 1946,Ag 19,17:6

Manet, Elizabeth
Heroes and Sinners; (Heros Sont Fatigues, Les) 1959,My 12,38:2
Mirror Has two Faces, The 1959,My 27,31:1
Young Girls Beware 1959,Ag 22,8:2

Manet, Jeanne
Slightly French 1949,My 27,25:3
Operation Mad Ball 1957,N 21,38:1

Manetta, G D
Blame the Woman 1932,O 25,24:5

Manetti, Lido
Evening Clothes 1927,Mr 21,10:4

Manevic, I (Screenwriter)
Road to Life 1956,Je 11,26:6
Sound of Life, The 1962,F 12,28:2

Manford, Guy
Flesh Merchant, The 1956,My 19,12:6

Manfredi, Nino
Wild Love; (Gli Inamorati) 1961,Ap 6,30:2
Fiasco in Milan 1963,Ap 11,29:2
...And Suddenly It's Murder! 1964,Ja 24,21:1
Of Wayward Love (The Soldier); Soldier, The (Of Wayward Love) 1964,Mr 24,29:1
Not on Your Life; Verdugo, El 1965,Mr 30,52:1
Bambole; Dolls, The (The Telephone Call); Telephone Call, The (The Dolls) 1965,Je 29,26:1
High Infidelity (The Scandal); Scandal, The (High Infidelity) 1965,Jl 2,17:1
Made in Italy 1967,My 1,44:2
Rose for Everyone, A 1967,Je 30,30:1
Treasure of San Gennaro 1968,F 27,36:1

Manfredi, Nino (Director)
Of Wayward Love (The Women); Women, The (Of Wayward Love) 1964,Mr 24,29:1
Of Wayward Love (The Soldier); Soldier, The (Of Wayward Love) 1964,Mr 24,29:1
Of Wayward Love (The Serpent); Serpent, The (Of Wayward Love) 1964,Mr 24,29:1

Manfredi, Nino (Miscellaneous)
Rose for Everyone, A 1967,Je 30,30:1

Manfredi, Nino (Screenwriter)
Treasure of San Gennaro 1968,F 27,36:1

Mang, Jone (Screenwriter)
Stranger Returns, The 1968,S 12,54:3

Mangano, Natascia
Anna 1953,F 19,20:5

Mangano, Patrizia
Anna 1953,F 19,20:5
Ring Around the Clock 1953,My 19,36:2

Mangano, Roy
Barabbas 1962,O 11,49:1

Mangano, Silvana
Bitter Rice 1950,S 19,39:2
Anna 1953,F 19,20:5
Lure of the Sira 1953,D 26,10:7
Mambo 1955,Mr 31,23:3
Ulysses 1955,Ag 18,17:2
Gold of Naples (Theresa); Theresa (Gold of Naples) 1957,F 12,30:1
This Angry Age 1958,Je 26,23:3
Tempest 1959,Mr 27,19:2
Five Branded Women 1960,Je 2,27:2
Great War; (Grande Guerra, La) 1961,Ag 31,22:3
Barabbas 1962,O 11,49:1
...And Suddenly It's Murder! 1964,Ja 24,21:1

Mangiante, Juan
Canillita y la Dama, El; Newsie and the Lady, The 1939,F 18,12:2

Mangini, Alda
I Cadetti di Guascogna 1952,O 6,22:2
O K Nero 1953,Je 20,8:6
Wayward Wife, The 1955,Ap 11,29:3

Mangini, Gino (Screenwriter)
Goliath and the Barbarians 1960,Ja 7,24:6

Mangione, G (Screenwriter)
Sign of the Gladiator 1959,D 3,46:1
Eye of the Needle, The 1965,Je 22,25:2

Mangione, John (Screenwriter)
Stranger in Town, A 1968,Ap 25,53:4

Mangioneo, Giuseppi (Screenwriter)
Mighty Ursus, The 1962,Jl 26,17:1

Mangioni, Giuseppe (Screenwriter)
Mafia; (In Nome Della Legge) 1950,Mr 2,33:2

Mango, Alec
Captain Horatio Hornblower 1951,S 14,21:2
His Excellency 1956,F 2,19:3
Cosmic Monster, The 1959,Ja 1,38:1
Khartoum 1966,Jl 14,28:1

Mangoli, Carmelina
Paraninfo, Il; Matchmaker, The 1940,Ja 23,17:2

Mangrove, Guiseppe (Screenwriter)
Wild Love; (Gli Inamorati) 1961,Ap 6,30:2

Manheim, Emanuel (Original Author)
Gambling Ship 1939,Ja 21,19:2

Manisco, Girolamo
Hell Raiders of the Deep 1954,Jl 3,9:2

Mankiewicz, Don M (Original Author)
Trial 1955,O 14,21:2

Mankiewicz, Don M (Screenwriter)
Trial 1955,O 14,21:2
House of Numbers 1957,S 13,15:2
I Want to Live 1958,N 19,45:1
Chapman Report, The 1962,O 18,49:2

Mankiewicz, Herman H (Original Author)
Man of the World 1931,Mr 21,15:1

Mankiewicz, Herman J (Original Author)
Road to Mandalay, The 1926,Je 29,21:2
Man I Love, The 1929,My 28,36:2
Meet the Baron 1933,O 28,20:3
It's a Wonderful World 1939,My 19,27:2

Mankiewicz, Herman J (Screenwriter)
After Office Hours 1935,Mr 9,19:1
Escapade 1935,Jl 6,16:2
John Meade's Woman 1937,F 18,19:1
Citizen Kane 1941,My 2,25:1
Rise and Shine 1941,D 6,14:3
Pride of the Yankees, The 1942,Jl 16,23:1
Stand by for Action 1943,Mr 12,12:2
Christmas Holiday 1944,Je 29,16:1
Enchanted Cottage, The 1945,Ap 28,19:2
Spanish Main, The 1945,N 7,20:2
Pride of St Louis, The 1952,My 3,17:5

Mankiewicz, Joseph L
Woman Trap 1929,Ag 31,13:4

Mankiewicz, Joseph L (Director)
Dragonwyck 1946,Ap 11,35:2
Somewhere in the Night 1946,Je 13,24:2
Late George Apley, The 1947,Mr 21,29:2
Ghost and Mrs Muir, The 1947,Je 27,17:2
Escape 1948,Ag 16,12:2
Letter to Three Wives, A 1949,Ja 21,24:2
House of Strangers 1949,Jl 2,8:2
No Way Out 1950,Ag 17,23:1
All About Eve 1950,O 14,13:2

Mankiewicz, Joseph L (Director)— Cont
People Will Talk 1951,Ag 30,20:1
Five Fingers 1952,F 23,7:5
Julius Caesar 1953,Je 5,19:1
Barefoot Contessa, The 1954,S 30,37:1
Guys and Dolls 1955,N 5,26:1
Quiet American, The 1958,F 6,24:1
Suddenly, Last Summer 1959,D 23,22:1
Cleopatra 1963,Je 13,29:1
Honey Pot, The 1967,My 23,52:1

Mankiewicz, Joseph L (Original Author)
Sky Bride 1932,Ap 23,11:5
Diplomaniacs 1933,Ap 29,14:2
Too Much Harmony 1933,S 23,11:5

Mankiewicz, Joseph L (Producer)
Three Godfathers, The 1936,Mr 9,20:2
Fury 1936,Je 6,21:1
Gorgeous Hussy, The 1936,S 5,7:1
Love on the Run 1936,N 28,13:3
Bride Wore Red, The 1937,O 15,18:4
Double Wedding 1937,O 22,27:2
Mannequin 1938,Ja 21,15:2
Three Comrades 1938,Je 3,17:1
Shopworn Angel, The 1938,Jl 8,11:2
Christmas Carol, A 1938,D 23,16:2
Shining Hour, The 1939,Ja 20,15:2
Huckleberry Finn 1939,Mr 3,21:2
Strange Cargo 1940,Ap 26,25:2
Philadelphia Story, The 1940,D 27,22:2
Feminine Touch, The 1941,D 12,35:3
Woman of the Year 1942,F 6,23:2
Reunion in France 1943,Mr 5,20:3
Keys of the Kingdom, The 1944,D 30,15:2
Quiet American, The 1958,F 6,24:1

Mankiewicz, Joseph L (Screenwriter)
Million Dollar Legs 1932,Jl 9,7:5
Forsaking all Others 1934,D 21,18:1
I Live my Life 1935,O 12,12:2
Keys of the Kingdom, The 1944,D 30,15:2
Dragonwyck 1946,Ap 11,35:2
Somewhere in the Night 1946,Je 13,24:2
Letter to Three Wives, A 1949,Ja 21,24:2
No Way Out 1950,Ag 17,23:1
All About Eve 1950,O 14,13:2
People Will Talk 1951,Ag 30,20:1
Barefoot Contessa, The 1954,S 30,37:1
Guys and Dolls 1955,N 5,26:1
Quiet American, The 1958,F 6,24:1
Cleopatra 1963,Je 13,29:1
Honey Pot, The 1967,My 23,52:1

Mankiewicz, Tola
Moj Wujaszek Z Ameryki 1933,O 25,25:3
Parada Rezerwistow 1934,My 1,26:6
Sluby Ulanskie; Love in the Army 1935,F 22,27:3
Co Moj Maz Robi W Nocy?; What Is my Husband Doing Tonight? 1935,N 29,24:2
Manewry Milosne 1936,N 11,55:1

Mankiewicz, Tom (Screenwriter)
Sweet Ride, The 1968,Je 13,57:2

Mankowitz, Wolf (Miscellaneous)
Make Me an Offer 1956,F 29,35:2

Mankowitz, Wolf (Original Author)
Make Me an Offer 1956,F 29,35:2
Kid for two Farthings, A 1956,Ap 18,25:1

Mankowitz, Wolf (Screenwriter)
Kid for two Farthings, A 1956,Ap 18,25:1
Bespoke Overcoat, The 1956,O 8,31:1
Expresso Bongo 1960,Ap 13,44:1
Millionairess, The 1961,F 10,19:1
House of Fright 1961,Ag 24,25:4
Jungle Fighters 1962,Mr 15,28:2
Day the Earth Caught Fire, The 1962,Mr 16,25:1
Waltz of the Toreadors 1962,Ag 14,34:1
Where the Spies Are 1966,Ja 27,29:1
25th Hour, The 1967,F 17,45:1
Casino Royale 1967,Ap 29,25:1

Manley, Dave
Struggle, The 1931,D 11,35:1

Manley, William Ford (Original Author)
Big Broadcast, The 1932,O 15,13:1

Manly, J B
Through the Wrong Door 1919,Jl 21,12:3

MANN
See Also MAHON

Mann, Abby (Screenwriter)
Judgment at Nuremberg 1961,D 20,36:1
Child Is Waiting, A 1963,F 14,5:6
Condemned of Altona, The 1963,O 31,26:1
Ship of Fools 1965,Jl 29,18:1
Detective, The 1968,My 29,20:3

Mann, Adolph (Producer)
Without a Home 1939,Ap 1,17:3

Mann, Alice
West of the Water Tower 1923,D 31,9:3

Mann, Anthony (Director)
Dr Broadway 1942,Je 25,27:3
Great Flamario, The 1945,Ja 15,15:5
Two O'Clock Courage 1945,Ap 14,13:3
T-Men 1948,Ja 23,28:3
Raw Deal 1948,Jl 9,11:4
Black Book, The 1949,O 17,18:2
Border Incident 1949,N 21,29:2
Side Street 1950,Mr 24,29:2
Winchester 73 1950,Je 8,38:2

Mann, Anthony (Director) — Cont
Furies, The 1950,Ag 17,23:2
Devil's Doorway 1950,N 10,35:1
Tall Target, The 1951,S 28,26:2
Bend of the River 1952,Ap 10,37:1
Naked Spur, The 1953,Mr 26,37:3
Thunder Bay 1953,My 21,39:2
Glenn Miller Story, the 1954,F 11,33:2
Far Country, The 1955,F 14,24:2
Strategic Air Command 1955,Ap 21,33:1
Man From Laramie, The 1955,S 1,20:2
Last Frontier, The 1955,D 8,45:1
Serenade 1956,Mr 24,21:1 (Incorrect in this
    edition; use 1956,Mr 23,21:1 elsewhere)
Men in War 1957,Mr 20,32:4
Tin Star, The 1957,O 24,37:2
God's Little Acre 1958,Ag 14,23:2
Man of the West 1958,O 2,44:3
Cimarron 1961,F 17,12:2
Cid, El 1961,D 15,49:1
Fall of the Roman Empire, The 1964,Mr 27,14:2
Heroes of Telemark, The 1966,Mr 10,26:1
Dandy in Aspic, A 1968,Ap 3,40:1
Mann, Anthony (Original Author)
Follow Me Quietly 1949,Jl 8,14:5
Mann, Anthony (Producer)
Dandy in Aspic, A 1968,Ap 3,40:1
Mann, Arthur (Screenwriter)
Jackie Robinson Story, The 1950,My 17,36:1
Mann, Bertha
All Quiet on The Western Front 1930,Ap 30,29:1
Little Accident 1930,Ag 4,13:4
Free Love 1930,D 15,29:1
Father's Son 1931,F 21,15:2
Woman of Experience, A 1931,Jl 9,26:5
Final Edition, The 1932,F 22,23:2
Behind the Mask 1932,My 2,13:2
Mann, Claude
Bay of the Angels; Baie des Anges, La
    1964,N 24,44:1
Sleeping Car Murder, The 1966,Mr 8,45:1
Mann, Colin
Happy Road, The 1957,Je 21,20:2
Mann, Colin (Screenwriter)
Adventures of Scaramouche, The 1964,N 23,34:1
    (Incorrect in this edition; use 1964,N 21,34:1
    elsewhere)
Mann, Daniel (Director)
Come Back, Little Sheba 1952,D 24,13:2 (In Addenda)
About Mrs Leslie 1954,Je 28,16:2
I'll Cry Tomorrow 1956,Ja 13,18:1
Teahouse of the August Moon, The
    1956,N 30,19:1
Hot Spell 1958,S 18,37:2
Last Angry Man, The 1959,O 23,24:1
Mountain Road, The 1960,Je 30,22:3
Butterfield 8 1960,N 17,46:1
Ada 1961,Ag 26,15:1
Who's Got the Action? 1962,D 26,5:4
Who's Been Sleeping in My Bed? 1963,D 26,33:2
Judith 1966,Ja 21,22:1
Our Man Flint 1966,Ja 26,23:4
For Love of Ivy 1968,Jl 18,26:1
Mann, Delbert
Iron Horse, The 1924,Ag 29,6:1
Mann, Delbert (Director)
Marty 1955,Ap 12,25:3
Bachelor Party, The 1957,Ap 10,37:2
Desire Under the Elms 1958,Mr 13,24:2
Separate Tables 1958,D 19,2:7
Middle of the Night 1959,Je 18,36:1
Outsider, The 1962,F 8,25:1
Lover Come Back 1962,F 9,21:1
Five Finger Exercise 1962,Ap 20,20:2
That Touch of Mink 1962,Je 15,16:2
Gathering of Eagles, A 1963,Jl 11,21:2
Dear Heart 1965,Mr 8,33:1
Quick, Before it Melts 1965,Ap 1,30:2
Mister Buddwing 1966,O 12,36:1
Fitzwilly 1967,D 21,45:1
Pink Jungle, The 1968,O 17,52:1
Mann, Delbert (Producer)
Quick, Before it Melts 1965,Ap 1,30:2
Mister Buddwing 1966,O 12,36:1
Mann, E B (Original Author)
Stampede 1949,S 16,36:2
Mann, Elizabeth
Avengers, The 1942,N 25,18:2
Mann, Erika (Miscellaneous)
Confessions of Felix Krull, The 1958,Mr 5,38:1
Mann, Erika (Screenwriter)
Tonio Kroger 1968,Ja 16,24:1
Mann, Frankie
Passionate Pilgrim, The 1921,Ja 3,20:2
Barriers Burned Away 1925,Mr 12,17:2
Mann, George
Yearling, The 1947,Ja 24,18:2
Neptune's Daughter 1949,Je 10,32:2
Mann, Greta
Caught Short 1930,Je 21,20:5
Mann, Hank
Don't Marry for Money 1923,Ag 21,17:3
Empty Hands 1924,Ag 18,8:2
Sporting Venus, The 1925,My 11,14:3

Skyrocket, The 1926,Ja 26,25:2
Garden of Eden, The 1928,Mr 19,26:2
Donovan Affair, The 1929,Ap 29,29:2
Arizona Kid, The 1930,My 17,21:2
City Lights 1931,F 7,11:1
Annabelle's Affairs 1931,Je 29,20:3
Strange Love of Molly Louvain, The
    1932,My 9,19:5
Million Dollar Legs 1932,Jl 9,7:5
Smoky 1934,Ja 1,28:2
Modern Times 1936,F 6,23:2
Hollywood Cavalcade 1939,O 14,13:2
Great Dictator, The 1940,O 16,29:1
Bullets for O'Hara 1941,Jl 28,16:4
Bullet Scars 1942,Ap 24,21:4
Perils of Pauline, The 1947,Jl 10,17:2
Mann, Heinrich (Original Author)
Blue Angel, The 1930,Je 6,21:3
Blue Angel, The 1959,S 5,11:4
Mann, Helen
Employees' Entrance 1933,Ja 21,10:6
Ladies They Talk About 1933,F 25,20:4
Little Giant, The 1933,My 27,11:5
Mann, Iris
Room for One More 1952,Ja 16,21:2
Mann, Klaus (Screenwriter)
Paisan 1948,Mr 30,26:2
Mann, Larry D
Appaloosa, The 1966,S 15,51:1
Caprice 1967,Je 8,52:2
Mann, Lisa
Lilies of the Field 1963,O 2,51:1
Mann, Louis
Sins of the Children 1930,Jl 26,16:4
Mann, Louis (Producer)
Horrible Dr Hitchcock, The 1964,D 3,58:3
Mann, Margaret
Heart of Humanity, The 1918,D 22,17:3
Four Sons 1928,F 14,27:1
River, The 1928,D 24,11:1
Conflict 1937,Ja 18,21:2
Federal Man-Hunt 1939,F 2,17:3
Mann, Paul
America America 1963,D 16,44:1
Mann, Peter
Pocketful of Miracles 1961,D 19,39:1
Lively Set, The 1964,O 15,54:1
Greatest Story Ever Told, The 1965,F 16,40:2
Mann, Stanley (Screenwriter)
Another Time Another Place 1958,My 3,10:4
Mouse That Roared, The 1959,O 27,40:1
Mark, The 1961,O 3,46:2
Woman of Straw 1964,O 1,30:6
Up From the Beach 1965,Je 10,38:1
High Wind in Jamaica, A 1965,Je 17,27:2
Collector, The 1965,Je 18,28:1
Rapture 1965,Ag 24,25:3
Naked Runner, The 1967,Jl 20,30:2
Strange Affair, The 1968,Jl 25,26:2
Mann, Thomas (Original Author)
Confessions of Felix Krull, The 1958,Mr 5,38:1
Tonio Kroger 1968,Ja 16,24:1
Menne, Max (Miscellaneous)
Sound Your A 1919,Ag 25,8:5
Manne, Shelly
Five Pennies, The 1959,Je 19,30:1
Subterraneans, The 1960,Jl 7,26:1
Mannering, Cecil
Storm in a Teacup 1938,Mr 22,18:4
Manners, David
Journey's End 1930,Ap 9,25:1
He Knew Women 1930,Ap 23,24:1
Sweet Mamma 1930,Jl 12,16:4
Kismet 1930,O 31,20:1
Mothers Cry 1930,D 6,21:3
Truth About Youth, The 1930,D 13,22:2
Right to Love, The 1931,Ja 2,25:1
Dracula 1931,F 13,21:3
Millionaire, The 1931,Ap 9,30:5
Miracle Woman, The 1931,Ag 17,18:2
Last Flight, The 1931,Ag 20,17:4
Ruling Voice, The 1931,N 5,29:3
Greeks Had a Word for Them, The 1932,F 4,25:2
Lady With a Past 1932,F 22,23:2
Beauty and the Boss 1932,Ap 2,13:2
Man Wanted 1932,Ap 16,11:2
Stranger in Town 1932,Jl 8,22:5
Crooner 1932,Ag 20,7:4
Bill of Divorcement, A 1932,O 3,15:2
They Call It Sin 1932,O 21,25:4
Mummy, The 1933,Ja 7,11:2
Death Kiss, The 1933,F 5,IX,5:3
From Hell to Heaven 1933,Mr 18,9:3
Warrior's Husband, The 1933,My 12,20:4
Girl in 419 1933,My 20,11:5
Devil's in Love, The 1933,Jl 28,18:2
Torch Singer 1933,O 7,18:5
Roman Scandals 1933,D 25,28:2
Black Cat, The 1934,My 19,18:4
Great Flirtation, The 1934,Je 22,16:5
Perfect Clue, The 1935,Mr 14,18:1
Mystery of Edwin Drood, The 1935,Mr 21,27:1
Jalna 1935,S 14,8:4

Manners, David — Cont
Woman Rebels, A 1936,O 30,27:2
Manners, J Hartley (Original Author)
Peg o'my Heart 1923,Ja 22,10:1
Happiness 1924,Mr 11,16:2
Peg o'my Heart 1933,My 20,11:4
Manners, Marcia
Pays to Advertise, It 1931,F 21,15:2
It Pays to Advertise 1931,F 21,15:2
Manners J Hartley (Original Author)
Gay Divorcee, The 1934,N 16,27:1
Mannhardt, Renata
Big Show, The 1961,My 11,42:4
Mannheim, Lucie
Danton 1931,S 7,19:3
Madame Wuenscht Keine Kinder 1933,Je 2,22:4
Thirty-Nine Steps, The 1935,S 14,8:4
East Meets West 1936,O 31,24:2
Yellow Canary, The 1944,Ap 14,24:7
Tawny Pipit 1947,S 8,25:5
So Little Time 1953,Jl 28,23:2
Confess, Dr Corda 1960,O 24,25:5
Bunny Lake is Missing 1965,O 4,00:0
Mannheimer, Albert (Miscellaneous)
Billy the Kid 1941,Je 20,28:2
Mannheimer, Albert (Screenwriter)
Dancing Co-Ed 1939,N 10,27:3
Sporting Blood 1940,Jl 22,20:2
Dulcy 1940,N 28,28:2
Whistling in the Dark 1941,Ag 28,23:2
Song of the Open Road 1944,Je 7,13:3
Three Daring Daughters 1948,F 13,26:3
Born Yesterday 1950,D 27,30:2
Manni, Ettore
Lupa, La 1954,F 18,36:2
Attila 1958,My 19,19:4
Warrior and the Slave, The 1960,Mr 10,36:2
Legions of the Nile 1961,Mr 4,16:1
Revolt of the Slaves, The 1961,N 8,41:1
Valiant, The 1962,Je 14,23:4
Devil in Love, The 1968,Jl 4,13:4
Manni, Harold
Secrets of a Soul 1950,S 16,12:6
Last Illusion, The 1951,Mr 8,37:2
Manning, Ailean
Snob, The 1924,D 15,14:1
Enticement 1925,Mr 21,16:3
Bridge of Sighs, The 1925,Mr 23,14:2
Uncle Tom's Cabin 1927,N 5,16:2
Man, Woman and Sin 1927,D 5,26:2
Home James 1928,S 11,31:3
Sweetie 1929,O 26,15:1
Huckleberry Finn 1931,Ag 8,16:3
Manning, Bruce (Director)
Amazing Mrs Holliday, The 1943,F 22,20:2
Manning, Bruce (Original Author)
Private Scandal 1934,Je 15,26:2
Rage of Paris 1938,Jl 2,10:2
Service de Luxe 1938,O 24,13:2
Manning, Bruce (Producer)
Back Street 1941,F 12,25:2
Appointment for Love 1941,N 7,27:1
Broadway 1942,Je 5,23:2
Amazing Mrs Holliday, The 1943,F 22,20:2
So Goes my Love 1946,My 2,3:7
Magnificent Doll 1946,D 9,34:2
Manning, Bruce (Screenwriter)
Best Man Wins 1935,Ja 2,22:4
Grand Exit 1935,N 4,24:5
Lone Wolf Returns, The 1936,F 4,25:5
Devil's Squadron 1936,My 11,16:2
Meet Nero Wolfe 1936,Jl 16,20:1
Counterfeit 1936,Jl 20,11:1
100 Men and a Girl 1937,S 18,15:2
Girl With Ideas, A 1938,Ja 1,11:2
Mad About Music 1938,Mr 12,13:2
Rage of Paris 1938,Jl 2,10:2
That Certain Age 1938,N 5,15:2
Three Smart Girls Grow Up 1939,Mr 18,9:2
First Love 1939,N 9,27:3
Spring Parade 1940,O 4,29:2
Back Street 1941,F 12,25:2
Appointment for Love 1941,N 7,27:1
Broadway 1942,Je 5,23:2
Guest Wife 1945,O 18,21:2
This Love of Ours 1945,N 1,20:2
So Goes my Love 1946,My 2,3:7
That Midnight Kiss 1949,S 23,28:2
Bride for Sale 1949,N 21,29:4 (In Addenda)
Payment on Demand 1951,F 16,21:2
Hoodlum Empire 1952,Mr 6,25:6
Jubilee Trail 1954,My 1,13:3
Flame of the Islands 1956,F 25,12:4
Never Say Goodbye 1956,Ap 14,20:1
Manning, Dean
Chip off the Old Block 1944,Mr 17,14:2
Manning, Eileen
Heart to Heart 1928,S 10,29:2
Manning, Hallie
New Klondike, The 1926,Mr 22,16:1
Manning, Hugh
Midsummer Night's Dream, A 1961,D 19,39:1

Manning, Irene
Yankee Doodle Dandy 1942,My 30,9:1
Spy Ship 1942,Jl 11,8:2
Big Shot, The 1942,Jl 18,8:2
Desert Song, The 1943,D 18,10:6
Shine on Harvest Moon 1944,Mr 11,10:2
Make Your own Bed 1944,My 27,12:2
Doughgirls, The 1944,Ag 31,14:1
Hollywood Canteen 1944,D 16,19:2
Escape in the Desert 1945,My 12,10:2
Yank in London, A 1946,Ap 20,16:3
Manning, Jack
Walk East on Beacon 1952,My 29,17:2
Manning, Knox
Meet John Doe 1941,Mr 13,25:2
Cheers for Miss Bishop 1941,Mr 14,17:2
Tanks a Million 1941,O 9,27:2
Yank on the Burma Road, A 1942,Ja 29,25:3
Hit Parade of 1947 1947,My 5,32:8
Manning, Knox (Narrator)
Ravaged Earth 1942,N 27,27:3
Manning, Margery
Waterloo Bridge 1940,My 17,23:2
Manning, Mary (Original Author)
Passages From James Joyce's Finnegans Wake
1967,O 10,56:1
Manning, Mary (Screenwriter)
Passages From James Joyce's Finnegans Wake
1967,O 10,56:1
Manning, Mildred
Enemy to the King, An 1916,N 27,9:1
Westerners, The 1919,Ag 4,8:3
Manning, Philip Dr
F P 1 1933,S 16,9:3
Manning, Phillip
Monte Carlo Madness 1932,Je 4,9:2
Manning, Robert
Sign of the Cross, The 1932,D 1,25:1
Eagle and the Hawk, The 1933,My 13,16:2
Manning, T H
Street Scene 1931,Ag 27,22:5
Counsellor-At-Law 1933,D 8,31:2
Manning, Thelma
In Old Chicago 1938,Ja 7,15:2
Manning, Tom
Singing Kid, The 1936,Ap 4,11:1
Mannix, Dan P (Original Author)
Killers of Kilimanjaro 1960,Ap 7,46:1
Mannix, E J (Producer)
Mark of the Vampire 1935,My 3,23:4
Mannix, Roy Sergeant
Forty Thousand Horsemen 1941,Ag 15,13:2
Mannone, Wingy
Rhythm on the River 1940,Ag 29,23:2
Mannors, Sheila
Daddy Long Legs 1931,Je 6,15:5
Behind the Evidence 1935,Ja 26,13:2
Manoff, Arnold (Screenwriter)
Man From Frisco 1944,Je 16,14:7
Casbah 1948,My 3,27:4
No Minor Vices 1949,F 26,11:2
Manolete
Torero! 1957,My 22,29:2
Manon, Marcia
Test of Honor, The 1919,Ap 7,11:5
Ladies Must Live 1921,N 21,20:1
Masquerader, The 1922,Ag 14,12:4
Skin Deep 1922,O 23,10:1
Greater Glory, The 1926,My 4,31:1
They Had to See Paris 1929,O 12,11:1
Love, Live and Laugh 1929,N 2,14:6
Manoussakis, Costas (Director)
Fear, The 1967,O 10,56:3
Manoussakis, Costas (Screenwriter)
Fear, The 1967,O 10,56:3
Manoussi, Jean (Original Author)
Purple Mask, The 1955,Je 16,35:7
Manrique, Arturo
Abnegacion 1938,My 31,8:3
Mansard, Claude
Breathless 1961,F 8,26:1
Five Day Lover, The 1961,D 14,55:4
Shoot the Piano Player 1962,Jl 24,19:1
Landru 1963,Ap 10,31:1
Mansart, Marie
Snow Was Black, The 1956,O 16,36:5
Manse, Jean (Miscellaneous)
Fernandel the Dressmaker 1957,Jl 1,19:2
Manse, Jean (Original Author)
Cow and I, The 1961,Je 6,42:2
Manse, Jean (Screenwriter)
Wild Oat, The 1956,Je 28,33:2
Forbidden Fruit 1959,F 23,19:1
Big Chief, The 1960,Ap 27,32:1
Mansfield, Duncan
White Sister, The 1923,S 6,10:2
Mansfield, Jayne
Illegal 1955,O 29,12:6
Hell on Frisco Bay 1956,Ja 7,21:1
Girl Can't Help It, The 1957,F 9,12:7
Wayward Bus, The 1957,Je 6,35:2
Will Success Spoil Rock Hunter 1957,S 12,37:5
Kiss Them for Me 1957,N 9,31:2

Sheriff of Fractured Jaw, The 1959,Mr 14,27:4
George Raft Story, The 1962,Mr 22,40:1
It Happened in Athens 1962,N 15,46:2
It Takes a Thief 1963,Ag 15,24:7
Guide for the Married Man, A 1967,My 27,16:1
Mansfield, John
Man-Eater of Kumaon 1948,Jl 2,24:2
Naked Jungle, The 1954,Ap 3,19:2
Mansfield, Marian
Here is my Heart 1934,D 22,21:1
Love in Bloom 1935,Ap 20,16:2
Mansfield, Martha
Civilian Clothes 1920,S 6,10:5
Fog Bound 1923,My 29,10:3
Potash and Perlmutter 1923,S 24,5:4
Mansfield, Michael (Screenwriter)
Bridge, The; (Bruecke, Die) 1961,My 2,42:1
Mansfield, Sally
Forever Female 1954,Ja 13,26:2
Manson, Eddy (Composer)
Lovers and Lollipops 1956,Ap 19,35:1
Manson, Helena
Helene 1938,Ja 22,19:1
Corbeau, Le; Raven, The 1948,F 24,21:1
Who Killed Santa Claus? 1948,Ap 21,33:2
Eternal Husband, The 1949,Ja 10,19:2
Strangers in the House 1949,O 13,33:3
Adventures of Captain Fabian 1951,D 14,36:2
Stranger on the Prowl 1953,N 10,38:1
Women Are Weak 1959,Je 9,44:2
Nude in a White Car 1960,O 27,47:2
Eye for an Eye, An 1961,F 10,19:1
Manson, Maurice
Close-Up 1948,Ap 5,24:2
Creature Walks among Us, The 1956,Ap 27,21:6
Autumn Leaves 1956,Ag 2,21:2
Girl in the Kremlin, The 1957,My 22,29:2
Hell's Five Hours 1957,Jl 24,18:1
Hell's Five Hours 1958,Jl 24,18:1
Manstadt, Margit
Doctor's Women, The 1929,Je 3,27:2
Dream Waltz, The 1930,D 27,16:3
Mantania, Clelia
Angelo in the Crowd 1952,O 4,15:2
Mantasi, Martin Rodriguez (Screenwriter)
Casa del Angel, La 1960,Ag 30,25:1
Mantee, Paul
Robinson Crusoe on Mars 1964,Ag 27,28:2
Mantell, Joe
Barbary Pirate 1949,O 28,29:3
Marty 1955,Ap 12,25:3
Storm Center 1956,O 22,25:4
Beau James 1957,Je 27,21:1
Sad Sack, The 1957,N 28,57:1
Onionhead 1958,O 2,44:1
Crowded Sky, The 1961,F 11,27:2
Birds, The 1963,Ap 1,5:5 (Incorrect in this
edition; use 1963,Ap 1,54:1 elsewhere)
Mister Buddwing 1966,O 12,36:1
Mantell, Robert B
Under the Red Robe 1923,N 13,25:3
Mantell, Robert P
Blindness of Devotion, The 1915,N 8,13:5
Mantg, Paul (Director)
Seven Wonders of the World 1956,Ap 11,29:1
Mantheakis, Alexis
Oedipus the King 1968,S 19,62:2
Manthorpe, Raymond
She Didn't Say No 1963,Jl 30,18:1
Mantle, Burns (Screenwriter)
How Molly Made Good 1915,O 20,5:5
Silver King, The 1919,Ja 13,9:3
Lady Rose's Daughter 1920,Ag 30,12:3
Mantle, Mickey
Safe at Home 1962,Ap 14,14:1
Mantley, John (Original Author)
Woman Obsessed 1959,My 28,34:1
Mantley, John (Screenwriter)
My Blood Runs Cold 1965,Mr 25,42:4
Mantovani
Guitars of Love 1958,Jl 12,18:1
Manuel, Jacques (Director)
Just a big Simple Girl; Une Grande Fille Toute
Simple 1949,O 28,29:2
Manuel, Robert
Orage 1938,D 12,26:2
Paris Waltz, The 1950,Ag 23,35:2
Rififi 1956,Je 6,37:1
Deadlier Than the Male 1957,O 9,41:1
Crazy in the Noodle 1957,D 15,45:4 (Incorrect in
this edition; use 1957,D 17,45:4 elsewhere)
Would-Be Gentleman, The 1960,Mr 23,31:1
Night Affair 1961,O 13,27:1
How Not to Rob a Department Store
1965,D 29,23:1
Manuel, Roland (Composer)
Escape From Yesterday 1939,My 3,27:2
Manulis, Martin (Producer)
Dear Heart 1965,Mr 8,33:1
Luv 1967,Jl 27,29:1
Duffy 1968,S 17,50:3

Manunta, Vittorio
Never Take No for an Answer 1952,Ap 29,32:2
Stranger on the Prowl 1953,N 10,38:1
Manx, Kate
Private Property 1960,Ap 25,40:2
Many Treaties, Chief
Buffalo Bill 1944,Ap 20,22:6
Black Bart 1948,Mr 4,30:4
Manza, Ralph
Enemy Below, The 1957,D 26,23:2
Manzari, Nicola (Original Author)
Merchant of Slaves 1949,O 27,35:4
Lieutenant Craig-Missing 1951,My 19,9:4
Manzari, Nicola (Screenwriter)
Lieutenant Craig-Missing 1951,My 19,9:4
Of Love and Bandits 1953,Ja 17,12:4
Sword and the Cross, The 1960,Jl 7,26:1
Manzi, Homero (Screenwriter)
Where Words Fail; Donde Mueren las Palabraso
1948,Ag 19,18:4
Manzoni, Allessandro (Original Author)
Spirit and the Flesh, The 1948,N 1,28:2
Manzuleas, Natalia
Manhunt in the Jungle 1958,Ap 12,13:1
Mapes, Jacques (Producer)
Rosie 1968,F 8,36:1
Mapes, Victor (Original Author)
Boomerang, The 1925,Jl 1,16:1
Hottentot, The 1929,S 7,15:1
Going Places 1939,Ja 7,6:1
Maple City Four, The
Under Western Stars 1938,Je 25,7:3
Mapp, Neville
Silver Fleet, The 1945,Mr 24,22:6
Maquire, Charles (Producer)
I Love You Alice B Toklasi 1968,O 8,40:1
Mar, Anibal del
Aventura Peligrosa, Una; Dangerous Adventure,
The 1940,My 20,13:2
Mar, Henry
Moon of Israel 1927,Je 29,29:3
Mara, Adele
You Were Never Lovelier 1942,D 4,31:1
Reveille With Beverly 1943,Ap 24,17:2
Catman of Paris, The 1946,Jl 13,12:2
I've Always Loved You 1946,S 7,11:1
Last Crooked Mile, The 1946,S 14,10:8
Blackmail 1947,Ag 5,26:3
I, Jane Doe 1948,Jl 5,8:4
Wake of the Red Witch 1949,Ja 10,19:2
Sands of Iwo Jima 1949,D 31,9:2
Rock Island Trail 1950,Je 5,19:3
California Passage 1950,D 16,10:5
Count the Hours 1953,Je 24,30:4
Back From Eternity 1956,S 8,20:6
Big Circus, The 1959,Jl 18,6:1
Mara, Goesti Bagus
Legong 1935,O 2,27:1
Mara, Lya
Bohemian Dancer 1928,D 3,30:5 (In Addenda)
Crimson Circle, The 1929,D 28,11:1
Maragon, Julie
Big Country, The 1958,O 2,44:1
Marais, Jean
Carmen 1946,N 27,20:2
Beauty and the Beast 1947,D 24,12:2
Eternal Return, The; Eternel Retour, L'
1948,Ja 5,15:2
Ruy Blas 1948,O 4,14:2
Eagle with Two Heads 1948,D 30,24:2
Storm Within, The; (Parents Terribles, Les)
1950,Ap 24,21:2
Souvenir 1950,O 3,34:4
Orpheus 1950,N 30,42:2
Secret of Mayerling, The 1951,My 8,39:2
Inside a Girls' Dormitory 1956,F 6,27:7
Royal Affairs in Versailles 1957,Mr 9,16:1
Paris Does Strange Things 1957,Mr 30,13:2
Julietta 1957,Je 18,38:2
White Nights 1961,My 29,9:6
Testament of Orpheus 1962,Ap 10,48:1
Friend of the Family 1965,N 18,55:3
Marakova, Irene
Young Guard 1949,D 26,33:6
Marakova, Tamara
Young Guard 1949,D 26,33:6
MARAN
See Also MARIN, MORAN, MORIN
Maran, Francesco
Cantante de Napoles, El; Singer of Naples, The
1935,F 25,13:4
Melody Lingers on, The 1935,N 7,27:1
Maran, Francisco
Under a Texas Moon 1930,Ap 4,22:1
Mutiny on the Blackhawk 1939,Ag 2,17:2
Marandi, Evi
Francis of Assisi 1961,Jl 29,8:2
Maranne, Andre
Damn the Defiant 1962,S 20,29:2
Shot in the Dark, A 1964,Je 24,28:1
Night Train to Paris 1964,D 3,58:2

Marascaichi, Pietro
Best of Enemies, The 1962,Ag 7,35:2
Maraschal, Lance
Detective, The 1954,N 2,25:2
Green Scarf, The 1955,Ja 15,10:2
Maratini, Rosita
Shadows of Paris 1924,F 18,13:1
Maravidi, Mirella
Three Bites of the Apple 1967,My 25,54:2
Marba, Fred
Bardelys The Magnificent 1926,N 1,28:1 (In Addenda)
Marbeuf, Ginette
Generals Without Buttons 1938,Mr 8,23:2
Marble, Harry (Narrator)
Pictura 1952,Ap 8,35:3
Marboe, Ernst (Producer)
April 1, 2000 1954,F 17,27:2
Marboe, Ernst (Screenwriter)
April 1, 2000 1954,F 17,27:2
Marburgh, Bertram
Proud Heart 1925,N 3,25:4
Affair of the Follies, An 1927,F 28,22:3
For the Defense 1930,Jl 19,7:5
They Just Had to Get Married 1933,F 13,11:4
Before I Hang 1940,O 3,31:3
Crossroads 1942,Jl 27,18:2
Marbury, Jane
Mr Belvedere Rings the Bell 1951,Ag 2,18:1
Marc, Marie
Naked Childhood 1968,S 28,36:1
Marc, Ted
Good Morning, Miss Dove 1955,N 24,41:1
Marcacci, Augusto
One Hundred Days of Napoleon 1936,S 14,25:1
Giovanni De Medici, The Leader 1940,Ja 5,15:4
Marcangeli, Anna
First Opera Film Festival 1948,My 31,12:7
Marceau, Emily
Open Your Eyes 1919,Je 30,16:3
Marceau, Felicien (Original Author)
Bonne Soupe, La 1964,Mr 16,37:1
Marceau, Felicien (Screenwriter)
Love and the Frenchwoman; (Francaise et l'Amour, La) 1961,F 28,38:2
7 Capital Sins (Greed); Greed (7 Capital Sins) 1963,Ja 17,5:2
Marceau, Marcel
Barbarella 1968,O 12,43:1
Marceau, Michele
Great Spy Chase, The 1966,O 6,56:4
Marceau-Cocinor (Producer)
French Game 1963,S 21,13:5
Marcelli, Filippo Pompa
Ape Woman, The 1964,S 23,55:1
Marcellini, Romolo (Director)
Tale of Five Women, A 1953,Ja 16,19:2
Grand Olympics, The 1964,Ap 22,57:2
Taboos of the World 1965,My 20,52:4
Macarbo 1967,Mr 18,19:2
Marcerou, J (Screenwriter)
No Escape 1959,My 23,18:4
Marces, Joe
Elmer Gantry 1960,Jl 8,16:1
Marceuil, Colette
Three Sinners 1952,Jl 8,23:2
MARCH
See Also MARSH
March, Alex (Director)
Paper Lion 1968,O 24,54:1
March, Allen (Original Author)
Pirates of Tripoli 1955,F 24,21:2
March, Allen (Screenwriter)
Pirates of Tripoli 1955,F 24,21:2
March, Carol
Young Scarface 1951,N 8,35:2
March, Corinne
Lola 1962,O 15,32:2
March, Elspeth
Mr Emmanuel 1945,Ja 8,15:2
Quo Vadis 1951,N 9,22:2
His Excellency 1956,F 2,19:3
Miracle, The 1959,N 13,25:4
Playboy of the Western World, The 1963,Mr 19,8:2
Dr Crippen 1964,F 15,14:1
March, Eve
How Green Was my Valley 1941,O 29,27:2
Curse of the Cat People, The 1944,Mr 4,11:1
Killer McCoy 1948,F 12,31:2
Adam's Rib 1949,D 26,33:2
Sun Shines Bright, The 1954,Mr 17,25:2
March, Fredric
Dummy, The 1929,Mr 4,20:2
Wild Party, The 1929,Ap 2,28:4
Studio Murder Mystery, The 1929,Je 10,23:1
Jealousy 1929,S 14,17:1
Paris Bound 1929,S 21,17:1
Footlights and Fools 1929,N 9,22:5
Marriage Playground, The 1929,D 14,22:4
Sarah and Son 1930,Mr 13,22:4
Ladies Love Brutes 1930,My 16,20:4
True to the Navy 1930,My 24,21:2

Manslaughter 1930,Jl 24,26:4
Laughter 1930,N 15,15:3
Royal Family of Broadway, The 1930,D 23,25:1
Honor Among Lovers 1931,F 28,15:2
Night Angel, The 1931,Je 11,28:4
My Sin 1931,S 11,24:2
Dr Jekyll and Mr Hyde 1932,Ja 2,14:2
Strangers in Love 1932,Mr 5,11:2
Merrily We Go to Hell 1932,Je 11,9:3
Smilin' Through 1932,O 15,13:1
Sign of the Cross, The 1932,D 1,25:1
Tonight Is Ours 1933,Ja 21,10:6
Eagle and the Hawk, The 1933,My 13,16:2
Design for Living 1933,N 23,24:2
All of Me 1934,F 5,19:2
Death Takes a Holiday 1934,F 24,18:4
Good Dame 1934,Mr 17,11:4
Affairs of Cellini, The 1934,S 6,22:3
Barretts of Wimpole Street, The 1934,S 29,12:2
We Live Again 1934,N 2,27:2
Miserables, Les 1935,Ap 22,14:2
Anna Karenina 1935,Ag 31,16:2
Dark Angel, The 1935,S 6,12:2
Mary of Scotland 1936,Jl 31,22:2
Road to Glory, The 1936,Ag 6,22:1
Anthony Adverse 1936,Ag 27,16:1
Star Is Born, A 1937,Ap 23,25:1
Nothing Sacred 1937,N 26,27:2
Buccaneer, The 1938,F 17,17:2
There Goes my Heart 1938,O 14,27:1
Trade Winds 1939,Ja 13,17:2
Susan and God 1940,Jl 12,11:2
Victory 1940,D 23,23:2
So Ends our Night 1941,F 28,17:2
One Foot in Heaven 1941,N 14,28:3
Bedtime Story 1942,Mr 20,25:4
I Married a Witch 1942,N 20,27:2
Adventures of Mark Twain, The 1944,My 4,25:5
Tomorrow the World 1944,D 22,12:4
Best Years of our Lives, The 1946,N 22,27:2
Another Part of the Forest 1948,My 19,30:2
Live Today for Tomorrow 1948,D 6,29:2
Christopher Columbus 1949,O 13,33:2
Death of a Salesman 1951,D 21,21:3
It's a big Country 1952,Ja 9,25:2
Man on a Tightrope 1953,Je 5,19:1
Executive Suite 1954,My 7,19:1
Bridges at Toko-Ri, The 1955,Ja 21,20:2
Desperate Hours, The 1955,O 6,25:1
Alexander the Great 1956,Mr 29,23:1
Man in the Gray Flannel Suit, The 1956,Ap 13,21:1
Middle of the Night 1959,Je 18,36:1
Inherit the Wind 1960,O 13,41:1
Young Doctors, The 1961,Ag 24,25:2
Condemned of Altona, The 1963,O 31,26:1
Seven Days in May 1964,F 20,22:1
Hombre 1967,Mr 22,41:1
March, Fredric (Miscellaneous)
400,000,000, The 1939,Mr 8,19:2
Lights Out In Europe 1940,Ap 15,21:2
March, Fredric (Narrator)
Black Sea Fighters 1943,Jl 28,18:3
Titan-Story of Michelangelo, The 1950,Ja 23,16:2
Albert Schweitzer 1957,Ja 21,20:2
March, Hal
Outrage 1950,O 16,30:5
Eddie Cantor Story, The 1953,D 26,10:2
Yankee Pasha 1954,Ap 19,19:2
It's Always Fair Weather 1955,S 16,19:1
My Sister Eileen 1955,S 23,21:1
Send Me no Flowers 1964,N 13,30:1
Guide for the Married Man, A 1967,My 27,16:1
March, Joseph (Miscellaneous)
Liberation of Belgrade 1946,Jl 15,21:1
March, Joseph Moncure (Miscellaneous)
Transatlantic Merry-Go-Round 1934,N 1,25:2
March, Joseph Moncure (Original Author)
Hell's Angels 1930,Ag 16,8:3
Sky Devils 1932,Mr 4,17:3
Let 'Em Have It 1935,My 30,21:1
Set-Up, The 1949,Mr 30,31:2
March, Joseph Moncure (Screenwriter)
Sudden Death, And 1936,Jl 18,18:2
Hideaway Girl 1937,Ja 13,20:4
Her Jungle Love 1938,Ap 14,27:2
Flirting With Fate 1938,D 15,35:3
Woman Doctor 1939,Mr 24,27:3
Wagons Westward 1940,Jl 8,13:2
Three Faces West 1940,Ag 19,13:2
March, Lori
Ransom 1956,Ja 25,28:3
Lovers and Lollipops 1956,Ap 19,35:1
March, Nadine
Rat, The 1938,F 28,19:1
March, William (Original Author)
Bad Seed, The 1956,S 13,39:6
Marchal, Arlette
Madame Sans Gene 1925,Ap 18,19:1
Born to the West 1926,Je 30,18:1 (In Addenda)
Diplomacy 1926,S 13,18:1
Blonde or Brunette 1927,Ja 11,18:2
Moon of Israel 1927,Je 29,29:3

Marchal, Arlette — Cont
Wings 1927,Ag 13,10:4
Hula 1927,Ag 29,21:1
Gentleman of Paris, A 1927,O 3,20:1
Spotlight, The 1927,N 28,18:5
Figaro 1929,N 25,22:1
Entente Cordiale 1939,D 26,23:2
Marchal, Franck (Original Author)
Foxiest Girl in Paris 1958,S 20,10:6
Marchal, George
Royal Affairs in Versailles 1957,Mr 9,16:1
Sign of the Gladiator 1959,D 3,46:1
Marchal, Georges
Her First Affair; (Children of Paradise) 1947,F 20,32:3
Vautrin, the Thief 1949,N 11,31:2
Au Grand Balcon 1951,My 5,14:2
French Way, The 1952,S 6,12:6
Thirst of Men, The 1952,O 28,37:1
Theodora, Slave Empress 1955,Ja 12,24:2
Girls of the Night 1959,Mr 21,13:2
Warrior and the Slave, The 1960,Mr 10,36:2
Legions of the Nile 1961,Mr 4,16:1
Colossus of Rhodes, The 1961,D 14,55:6
Marchand, Colette
Moulin Rouge 1953,F 11,33:5
Marchand, Corinne
Cleo From 5 to 7 1962,S 5,43:4
7 Capital Sins (Lust); Lust (7 Capital Sins) 1963,Ja 17,5:2
Marchand, Henri
A Nous la Liberte 1932,Ja 10,VIII,5:1
Nous, La Liberte, A 1932,My 18,25:2
Paris Incident 1954,Ag 18,20:2
Marchand, Leopold (Original Author)
Love Me Tonight 1932,Ag 19,20:6
Three Waltzes 1939,Ap 25,19:2
Marchand, Leopold (Screenwriter)
Lucrezia Borgia 1937,O 13,27:2
Three Waltzes 1939,Ap 25,19:2
Faust and the Devil 1950,My 1,18:2
Marchand, Nancy
Bachelor Party, The 1957,Ap 10,37:2
Ladybug, Ladybug 1963,D 24,9:1
Marchant, William (Original Author)
Desk Set 1957,My 16,28:2
Marcharet, A (Director)
Concentration Camp 1939,Mr 20,13:2
Marchat, Jean
Stormy Waters 1946,Je 17,32:2
Tomorrow Is my Turn 1962,F 2,24:2
Dames du Bois de Boulogne, Les; Ladies of the Park 1964,Ap 4,15:5
Marchaty, Gustav (Director)
Within the Law 1939,Ap 6,31:2
Marchellier, Suzanne
Therese and Isabelle 1968,My 15,41:4
Marchenko, Liudmila
Home for Tanya, A 1961,Ag 14,28:5
Marchesi, Marcello (Original Author)
I Cadetti di Guascogna 1952,O 6,22:2
Marchesi, Marcello (Screenwriter)
I Cadetti di Guascogna 1952,O 6,22:2
Marchesi, Nino
Paolo and Francesca 1953,F 14,8:3
Marchetti, Giuli
Stranger on the Prowl 1953,N 10,38:1
Marchetti, Milo Jr
Fisherman's Wharf 1939,F 24,15:2
Marchetti, Nino
Giovanni De Medici, The Leader 1940,Ja 5,15:4
Marchi, Ruggero
Tailor's Maid, The; (Patri e Figli) 1959,S 2,35:4
Marchi, Virgilio (Screenwriter)
Iron Crown 1949,Je 11,11:2
Marchio, Fanny
Per Vomini Soli; For Men Only 1939,Ap 21,27:4
Variety Lights; Luci del Varieta 1965,My 7,34:1
Marchio, Gilda
Spirit and the Flesh, The 1948,N 1,28:2
Marci, Georges (Producer)
Wild Eye, The 1968,Ag 22,47:1
Marcillas, Raymond (Miscellaneous)
Melbourne Rendezvous 1957,O 11,38:4
Marcin, Max (Director)
Lawyer's Secret, The 1931,My 30,9:2
Silence 1931,Ag 15,18:3
Strange Case of Clara Deane, The 1932,My 6,15:3
King of the Jungle 1933,F 25,20:3
Gambling Ship 1933,Jl 13,17:5
Love Captive, The 1934,Je 8,18:1
Marcin, Max (Miscellaneous)
Cheating Cheaters 1919,Ja 27,11:4
Shadows in the Night 1944,Jl 29,16:2
Marcin, Max (Original Author)
Silence 1926,My 19,29:3
Love of Sunya, The 1927,Mr 12,12:2
Cheating Cheaters 1927,D 6,27:1
Ghost Talks, The 1929,F 18,28:1
Silence 1931,Ag 15,18:3
Woman in Room 13, The 1932,My 21,9:2
Love Captive, The 1934,Je 8,18:1
Jungle Princess 1936,D 24,21:3

Marcin, Max (Original Author) — Cont
Slightly Tempted 1940,N 1,33:1
Crime Doctor 1943,Jl 5,11:4

Marcin, Natalie (Original Author)
Anchors Aweigh 1945,Jl 20,15:2

Marco, Henry
Mara Maru 1952,Ap 24,38:1

Marco, Jose
Alexander the Great 1956,Mr 29,23:1

Marco, Joseph
Gladiators Seven 1964,My 7,31:2

Marco, Maria San
Sleep, My Love 1948,F 19,29:4

Marco, Raoul
Mysteres de Paris, Les 1937,Ja 30,21:2

Marco, Rossana San
Rose Tattoo, The 1955,D 13,55:1

Marco, Silvia
Man Who Wagged his Tail, The 1961,S 19,39:1

Marconi
Francis the First 1947,N 20,38:4

Marconi, Lana
Private Life of an Actor; En Scene 1948,S 7,21:3
Royal Affairs in Versailles 1957,Mr 9,16:1
Virtuous Scoundrel, The 1957,O 23,37:1

Marcos, Creta
Strangers in the City 1962,Jl 17,19:2

Marcoux, Vanni
Miracle of the Wolves, The 1925,F 24,17:3
Sans Famille 1935,Je 4,26:5

MARCUS
See Also MARKUS

Marcus, Bernie
Outrage 1950,O 16,30:5

Marcus, Ellen
Echoes of Silence 1967,Ap 7,32:2

Marcus, Frank (Original Author)
Killing of Sister George, The 1968,D 17,58:4

Marcus, James
Little Lord Fauntleroy 1921,S 16,17:3
Scaramouche 1923,O 12,7:2 (Incorrect in this edition; use 1927,O 1,7:2 elsewhere)
Beau Brummell 1924,Mr 31,20:1
Iron Horse, The 1924,Ag 29,6:1
Dick Turpin 1925,Ja 26,14:1
Goose Hangs High, The 1925,Mr 10,19:3
Eagle, The 1925,N 9,25:1
Hell-Bent for Heaven 1926,My 4,31:1
Scarlet Letter, The 1926,Ag 10,19:2
Eagle of the Sea, The 1926,N 17,21:6
Captain Salvation 1927,Je 27,25:2
Buck Privates 1928,Ja 30,18:1
Sadie Thompson 1928,F 6,12:3
Revenge 1928,D 10,25:1
In old Arizona 1929,Ja 21,18:4
Evangeline 1929,Jl 29,23:3
Captain of the Guard 1930,Mr 29,23:1
Texan, The 1930,My 17,21:2
Billy the Kid 1930,O 18,23:2
Fighting Caravans 1931,Ja 26,21:1
Arrowsmith 1931,D 8,36:4
Hell's House 1932,F 12,24:5
Wagon Wheels 1934,O 4,19:1

Marcus, Larry (Miscellaneous)
Witness for the Prosecution 1958,F 7,16:1

Marcus, Larry (Original Author)
Backfire 1950,Ja 27,29:2
Dark City 1950,O 19,40:5
Cause for Alarm 1951,Mr 30,28:5
Paula 1952,Jl 16,21:2

Marcus, Larry (Screenwriter)
Backfire 1950,Ja 27,29:2
Dark City 1950,O 19,40:5
Voice in the Mirror 1958,Ag 14,23:2
Covenant with Death, A 1967,F 16,32:3

Marcus, Lawrence B (Screenwriter)
Petulia 1968,Je 11,54:4

Marcus, Lee (Producer)
Love on a Bet 1936,Mr 5,25:2
Silly Billies 1936,Ap 6,18:1
Second Wife 1936,Ag 29,16:3
On Again-Off Again 1937,S 18,15:3
Stranger on the Third Floor 1940,S 2,19:2
Father takes a Wife 1941,S 5,19:3
They Came to Blow up America 1943,My 15,13:2
Dancing Masters, The 1943,D 2,30:2
Roger Touhy, Gangster 1944,Je 5,14:7
Lost Honeymoon 1947,Je 20,25:6

Marcus, Morris
Youth of Russia, The 1934,N 10,19:3

Marcus, Perle
Tevya 1939,D 22,15:3

Marcus, Raymond T (Screenwriter)
Earth vs the Flying Saucers 1956,Ag 2,21:2
Chicago Confidential 1957,Ag 31,19:1

Marcus, Vicki
Tevya 1939,D 22,15:3

Marcus, Vitina
Lost World, The 1960,Jl 14,23:1

Marcuse, Theodore
Tiger Walks, A 1964,Ag 27,28:2
Sands of Beersheba 1966,My 6,54:2
Last of the Secret Agents, The? 1966,Je 23,29:1

Marcy, George
Last Mile, The 1959,F 19,27:1

Mardayn, Christl
Stolz der 3 Kompagnie, Der 1932,Jl 21,15:2
Florentiner Hut, Der; Leghorn Hat, The 1939,Je 3,11:3
Kleine Nachtmusik, Eine 1940,Mr 2,9:5
Story of Vickie, The 1958,Ja 30,19:2
Last Waltz, The 1958,Ap 12,13:1

Mardayne, Christiane
drame De Shanghai; Shanghai Drama, The 1945,Ja 11,19:2

Marden, Adrienne
13 Hours by Air 1936,Ap 30,17:2
F-Man 1936,My 4,16:1
Star for a Night 1936,S 5,7:2
Dangerous Crossing 1953,S 30,37:2
Shrike, The 1955,Jl 8,15:2
Birdman of Alcatraz 1962,Jl 19,19:2
Kisses for my President 1964,Ag 22,13:1

Marden, Mabel
Madame Spy 1934,F 10,20:1

Marechal
Miquette 1951,F 5,18:2

Maren, Grete
Die Blumenfrau von Lindenau 1932,Jl 8,22:5

Maren, Jerry
When my Baby Smiles at Me 1948,N 24,20:2

Marena, Emma
Trial of Donald Westhof, The 1928,F 18,11:2

Marena, Mario
Asi es mi Tierra; Such Is my Country 1939,Mr 18,9:3

Marenbach, Leny
Jana, Das Maedchen aus dem Boehmerwald 1936,Je 20,22:3
If We All Were Angels 1937,O 9,16:2
Dell Etappenhase 1938,Ja 1,11:3
Mustergatte, Der; Model Husband 1938,Mr 19,11:3
Starker als die Liebe; Stronger Than Love 1939,My 6,21:3
Ziel den Wolken; Goal in the Clouds 1939,My 27,13:3
Fuenf Millionem suchen einen Erben; Five Millions Seek an Heir 1939,O 23,15:3

Marenghi, Jerry
At the Circus 1939,N 17,17:2

Marengo, Lina
Tomorrow is too Late 1952,Ap 14,22:2

Mares, Karel
Report on the Party and the Guests, A 1968,S 20,37:5
Report on the Party and the Guests, A 1968,S 28,37:1

Maresa, Franca
Lost Youth 1949,O 27,35:4

Marescat, Simone (Screenwriter)
Truth, The 1961,Je 27,23:2

Maresch, Harold D
Stalag 17 1953,Jl 2,19:2

Marese, Janie
Mam'zelle Nitouche 1933,N 20,18:3

Mareth, Glenville (Screenwriter)
Santa Claus Conquers the Martians 1964,D 17,50:2

Maretini, Rosita
Proud Flesh 1925,Ap 14,26:1

Maretskaya, Vera
Revolutionists 1936,D 26,15:3
Paris Commune 1937,Je 2,20:4
No Greater Love 1944,F 25,23:3
Marriage 1945,F 22,31:3
Village Teacher 1948,Jl 5,8:4
1905 1956,Jl 9,27:2
Ukrainian Festival 1965,N 1,57:1

Marette, Marcelle (Original Author)
Anastasia 1956,D 14,35:6

Mareuil, Philippe
Judex 1966,Ap 26,55:1

Mareuil, Simone
Juif Polonais, Le 1937,S 17,29:3

Mareze, Janie
Mam'zelle Nitouche 1932,Ja 10,VIII,5:1

Marfield, Dwight
Trouble With Harry, The 1955,O 18,46:2

Margadonna, E M (Original Author)
Frisky 1955,O 25,37:3

Margadonna, Ettore (Miscellaneous)
Scandal in Sorrento 1957,Je 13,37:1

Margadonna, Ettore (Original Author)
Two Cents Worth of Hope 1952,D 16,44:2
Bread, Love and Dreams 1954,S 21,24:1

Margadonna, Ettore (Screenwriter)
Bandit, The 1949,Je 7,26:3
Under the Sun of Rome 1949,O 6,40:4
Bread, Love and Dreams 1954,S 21,24:1
Scandal in Sorrento 1957,Je 13,37:1
Fast and Sexy 1960,O 6,51:4

Margarill, Dofie
New Babylon, The 1929,D 2,28:2

Margaritis, Gilles
Atalante, L' 1947,Je 23,14:5

Margelis, Charles
Merry Widow, The 1925,Ag 27,14:1

Margetson, Arthur
Little Friend 1934,O 20,20:2
Wanted Men 1936,Jl 8,15:2
Broken Blossoms 1937,Ja 14,16:3
Juggernaut 1937,Jl 15,16:1
Loves of Madame Dubarry, The 1938,Ap 4,12:5
Clown Must Laugh, A 1938,O 12,35:2
Larceny Street 1941,Ja 6,11:2
Random Harvest 1942,D 18,36:6
Sherlock Holmes Faces Death 1943,O 8,15:3
Commandos Strike at Dawn 1954,Ja 14,25:1

Margheriti, Anthony (Producer)
Wild, Wild Planet 1967,Ag 10,45:5

Margie, Baby
Chechahcos, The 1924,My 19,14:2

Margo
Crime Without Passion 1934,S 1,16:2
Rumba 1935,F 25,13:2
Robin Hood of El Dorado, The 1936,Mr 14,10:1
Winterset 1936,D 4,31:1
Lost Horizon 1937,Mr 4,27:1
Leopard Man, The 1943,My 20,26:4
Behind the Rising Sun 1943,O 14,26:2
Viva Zapata 1952,F 8,19:2
I'll Cry Tomorrow 1956,Ja 13,18:1
From Hell to Texas 1958,Je 5,39:2
Who's Got the Action? 1962,D 26,5:4

Margo, George
Windom's Way 1958,O 1,45:1
Mouse That Roared, The 1959,O 27,40:1

Margolese, E M
Pawnbroker, The 1965,Ap 21,51:1

Margolin, Janet
David and Lisa 1962,D 27,5:5
Greatest Story Ever Told, The 1965,F 16,40:2
Bus Riley's Back in Town 1965,Ap 8,45:2
Saboteur, The: Code Name-Mori Turi 1965,Ag 26,40:2
Nevada Smith 1966,Je 24,28:1 (Incorrect in this edition; use 1966,Je 30,28:1 elsewhere)
Eavesdropper, The 1966,S 15,51:1
Enter Laughing 1967,Ag 1,24:1

Margolis, Herbert (Original Author)
Smuggler's Island 1951,My 24,47:2
For Men Only 1952,Ja 16,21:2
Summer Love 1958,Je 26,23:4
Wackiest Ship in the Army, The 1961,F 9,36:1

Margolis, Herbert (Screenwriter)
Larceny 1948,S 4,8:6
Ma and Pa Kettle 1949,Ag 12,13:2
Francis in the Haunted House 1956,Jl 21,9:2

Margulies, Stan (Producer)
Those Magnificent Men in Their Flying Machines (Or How I Flew From London to Paris in 25 Hours and 11 Minutes) 1965,Je 17,27:1
Don't Just Stand There 1968,S 3,54:2
Pink Jungle, The 1968,O 17,52:1

Mari, Marisa
Mistress of the Mountains 1954,My 27,34:5

Maria, Norma
House of Fright 1961,Ag 24,25:4

Marian, David (Director)
In the Far East 1937,O 20,27:3

Marian, Ferdinand
Heimt ruft, Die; Home Is Calling 1938,Jl 9,10:3

Mariana, Nicholas
Unidentified Flying Objects 1956,Je 13,46:2

Mariane
Maternelle, La 1935,O 15,19:1

Mariani, Mario (Producer)
Fuga, La 1966,Mr 22,33:1

Marianna
Guerrilla Girl 1953,Jl 7,23:7

Mariano, Luis
Candide 1962,N 20,39:1

Mariari, Petri (Screenwriter)
15 From Rome 1968,Ap 11,51:3

Maricle, Leona
O'Shaughnessy's Boy 1935,O 5,18:2
Theodora Goes Wild 1936,N 13,27:4
Women of Glamour 1937,Mr 6,10:1
Parole Racket 1937,Mr 8,22:1
Woman Chases Man 1937,Je 11,26:2
Lone Wolf in Paris, The 1938,My 23,21:2
Mad Miss Manton, The 1938,O 21,27:2
Comet over Broadway 1938,D 16,33:3
Beauty for the Asking 1939,F 10,19:1
Judge Hardy and Son 1940,Ja 18,27:3 (In Addenda)
Curtain Call 1940,Ap 19,25:2
This Thing Called Love 1941,F 14,15:2
Hard Way, The 1943,Mr 13,9:2
My Pal, Wolf 1944,O 9,17:2
My Reputation 1946,Ja 26,19:2
Scandal In Paris, A 1946,S 16,9:7

Marie, Else
Girls are Willing, The 1959,My 11,30:1

Marie, Renaud
Bernadette of Lourdes 1962,Ja 30,20:2
Marie-France
Under the Paris Sky 1952,My 6,35:1
Moment of Truth, The 1954,Ap 27,36:2
Marie-Jose
Extenuating Circumstances; Circostances
Attenuantes 1946,S 24,41:3
Marie-Laurent, Jeanne
Call, The 1938,Mr 29,18:3
Marieau, Louise
Adolescents, The (Genevieve); Genevieve (The
Adolescents) 1967,Ap 14,33:1
Marielle, Jean-Paul
Weekend at Dunkirk 1966,My 19,51:2
Marielle, Jean-Pierre
Sweet and Sour 1964,D 28,34:2
Banana Peel; Peau de Banane 1965,Ja 19,29:1
Backfire 1965,Ap 27,27:1
How Not to Rob a Department Store
1965,D 29,23:1
Male Companion 1966,F 15,33:2
Tender Scoundrel 1967,N 16,58:2
Marier, Victor Captain (Miscellaneous)
Hearts of the World 1918,Ap 5,13:1
Marietto
It Started in Naples 1960,S 3,7:6
Pigeon That Took Rome, The 1962,Ag 23,25:1
Story of Joseph and his Brethern, The
1962,D 1,17:1
Marievsky, Joseph
Three Godfathers, The 1936,Mr 9,20:2
Marihugh, Tammy
Last Voyage, The 1960,F 20,14:2
Thunder of Drums, A 1961,S 27,35:1
Back Street 1961,O 13,27:1
Marika, Roekk
Csokolj Meg Edes 1932,N 25,19:2
Mariln-Sibirvak, D (Original Author)
Lust for Gold 1958,Jl 24,18:1
MARIN
See Also MORAN, MORIN, MARAN
Marin, Antoine
Lovers of Teruel, The 1962,D 15,5:1
Mademoiselle 1966,Ag 2,23:1
Marin, Arturo
Mad Queen, The 1950,O 27,24:3
Marin, Chinita
Pan-Americana 1945,Mr 23,13:2
Marin, Christian
Belle Americaine, La 1961,D 18,42:1
Story of a Three Day Pass, The 1968,Jl 9,31:1
Marin, Edwin L (Director)
Death Kiss, The 1933,F 5,IX,5:3
Study in Scarlet, A 1933,Je 1,15:3
Avenger, The 1933,O 3,28:3
Sweetheart of Sigma Chi, The 1933,N 9,27:1
Bombay Mail 1934,Ja 6,18:2
Affairs of a Gentleman 1934,Je 23,16:7
Paris Interlude 1934,Jl 28,16:5
Casino Murder Case, The 1935,Ap 17,26:5
Garden Murder Case, The 1936,Mr 2,13:2
Moonlight Murder 1936,Mr 28,11:2
Speed 1936,My 16,11:2
I'd Give my Life 1936,Ag 17,9:1
Sworn Enemy 1936,S 12,20:1
Man of the People 1937,F 23,25:4
Married Before Breakfast 1937,Jl 23,16:2
Everybody Sing 1938,Mr 11,15:3
Hold That Kiss 1938,Je 11,9:1
Chaser, The 1938,Ag 2,15:3
Listen, Darling 1938,N 24,37:2
Christmas Carol, A 1938,D 23,16:2
Fast and Loose 1939,Mr 9,18:1
Society Lawyer 1939,Mr 31,19:2
Maisie 1939,Je 23,23:1
Florian 1940,Je 6,33:2
Gold Rush Maisie 1940,S 2,19:2
Hullabaloo 1940,D 19,33:1
Maisie Was a Lady 1941,F 13,25:2
Ringside Maisie 1941,Ag 1,11:2
Gentleman After Dark, A 1942,Ap 17,21:2
Miss Annie Rooney 1942,Je 8,11:1
Two Tickets to London 1943,Jl 3,11:2
Show Business 1944,My 11,25:7
Tall in the Saddle 1944,D 15,25:3
Johnny Angel 1945,D 28,12:2
Abilene Town 1946,Mr 4,16:5
Young Widow 1946,Jl 29,12:8
Mr Ace 1946,S 30,21:3
Lady Luck 1946,O 31,22:3
Nocturne 1946,N 11,42:2
Christmas Eve 1947,N 28,30:2
Intrigue 1948,Ap 24,11:2
Race Street 1948,Ag 23,13:3
Canadian Pacific 1949,My 20,32:4
Younger Brothers, The 1949,My 28,11:2
Fighting Man of the Plains 1949,N 17,35:6
Colt 45 1950,My 6,8:6
Cariboo Trail, The 1950,S 1,17:2
Sugarfoot 1951,F 12,19:4
Raton Pass 1951,Ap 20,25:1
Fort Worth 1951,Jl 13,12:7

Marin, Edwin L (Producer)
Two Tickets to London 1943,Jl 3,11:2
Marin, Gloria
Casa del Ogro, La; House of the Ogre, The
1939,F 13,13:2
Muerto Murio, El; Dead Man Died, The
1939,Jl 29,18:3
Tia de las Muchachas, La; Girls' Aunt, The
1939,O 30,13:3
Silk, Blood and Sun 1943,Ja 30,10:6
Ay Jalisco no te Rajes 1943,Ap 24,17:3
El Conde de Monte Cristo 1943,N 9,26:2
Que Lindo es Michoacan 1944,Ap 22,8:7
Marin, Guillermo
Don Quixote 1949,My 13,29:3
Marin, Ivan
There Was an old Couple 1967,My 22,53:1
Marin, Jacques
Forbidden Games 1952,D 9,43:2
Gates of Paris 1958,Ja 15,24:1
Roots of Heaven, The 1958,O 16,46:1
Enemy General, The 1960,O 20,42:2
Big Gamble, The 1961,S 2,19:2
Gigot 1962,S 28,26:1
Tiara Tahiti 1963,N 6,32:1
Charade 1963,D 6,40:1
Train, The 1965,Mr 18,25:1
How to Steal a Million 1966,Jl 15,34:1
Lost Command 1966,S 15,51:1
Paris in the Month of August 1968,Ag 26,46:4
Girl on a Motorcycle, The 1968,N 28,66:5
Marin, Lily
Tia de las Muchachas, La; Girls' Aunt, The
1939,O 30,13:3
Marin, Luciano
Goliath and the Barbarians 1960,Ja 7,24:6
Tartars, The 1962,Je 21,26:2
Marin, Ned (Producer)
Band Plays on, The 1934,D 22,21:2
Garden Murder Case, The 1936,Mr 2,13:2
Moonlight Murder 1936,Mr 28,11:2
Under Cover of Night 1937,Ja 20,18:4
Marina
Pardon my French 1952,Mr 31,17:2
Marinelli, Lulu
Eredita dello Zio, L' 1935,Je 29,16:3
Marini, Ernest
One Hundred Days of Napoleon 1936,S 14,25:1
Marini, Pir
Shadows 1961,Mr 22,37:1
Marini, Tullio
Wild Eye, The 1968,Ag 22,47:1
Marinkovich, Marko
Magic Sword, The 1952,N 19,37:2
Marino, Flora
Lost One, The; La Traviata 1948,Mr 30,26:2
Marinoff, Fania
Rise of Jennie Cushing, The 1917,N 12,11:3
Marinucci, Vinicio (Composer)
Gran Varieta 1955,Ap 11,29:5
Marion, Charles (Original Author)
Spooks Run Wild 1941,N 1,20:3
Gals, Inc 1943,Ag 13,13:4
Marion, Charles (Screenwriter)
Spooks Run Wild 1941,N 1,20:3
Sarong Girl 1943,Je 18,16:6
Marion, Don
Golden Bed, The 1925,Ja 20,18:2
Percy 1925,Mr 25,24:2
Playing With Souls 1925,Ap 20,18:1 (Incorrect in
this edition; use 1925,Ap 28,18:1 elsewhere)
Golden Princess 1925,S 7,15:3
Courage 1930,My 23,21:1
Marion, Frances (Director)
Love Light, The 1921,Ja 10,9:1
Song of Love, The 1924,F 25,13:1
Marion, Frances (Original Author)
Toll of the Sea, The 1922,N 27,18:1
Awakening, The 1928,D 31,9:1
Champ, The 1931,N 10,29:4
Emma 1932,F 6,14:4
Prizefighter and the Lady, The 1933,N 11,11:3
Going Hollywood 1933,D 23,19:2
Riffraff 1936,Ja 13,14:2
Green Hell 1940,Ja 30,15:6
Molly and Me 1945,My 26,18:2
Clown, The 1953,Ja 29,25:1
Marion, Frances (Screenwriter)
Pollyanna 1920,Ja 19,16:3
Humoresque 1920,My 31,14:2
World and his Wife, The 1920,Jl 19,16:3
Love Light, The 1921,Ja 10,9:1
Back Pay 1922,F 13,10:1
Primitive Lover, The 1922,My 15,20:3
Sonny 1922,My 29,14:1
Voice From the Minaret, The 1923,F 5,18:2
Nth Commandment, The 1923,Ap 10,24:3
Famous Mrs Fair, The 1923,Ap 23,18:3
Dramatic Life of Abraham Lincoln, The
1924,Ja 22,17:3
Madame Pompadour 1927,Ag 2,19:2
Big House, The 1930,Je 25,31:2
Secret Six, The 1931,My 2,23:4

Marion, Frances (Screenwriter) — Cont
Blondie of the Follies 1932,S 2,19:2
Riffraff 1936,Ja 13,14:2
Camille 1937,Ja 23,13:1
Love From a Stranger 1937,Ap 19,27:2
Knight Without Armor 1937,Jl 9,18:1
Green Hell 1940,Ja 30,15:6
Marion, Frank
Wreck of the Hesperus, The 1927,N 28,18:5
Marion, George
Anna Christie 1923,D 10,20:1
White Monkey, The 1925,Je 9,16:3
Clothes Make the Pirate 1925,N 30,17:1
Tumbleweeds 1925,D 21,27:2
Texas Steer, A 1928,Ja 2,28:1
Evangeline 1929,Ja 29,23:3
Bishop-Murder Case, The 1930,F 1,15:1
Anna Christie 1930,Mr 15,22:5
Big House, The 1930,Je 25,31:2
Lady's Morals, A 1930,N 8,21:3
Pay-Off, The 1930,N 10,16:2
Hook, Line and Sinker 1930,D 25,31:5
Man to Man 1931,Ja 3,21:2
Laughing Sinners 1931,Jl 4,11:5
Safe in Hell 1931,D 19,16:4
Six Hours to Live 1932,O 22,18:4
Her First Mate 1933,S 2,14:5
Metropolitan 1935,O 18,27:4
Marion, George Jr (Composer)
Adorable 1933,My 19,20:2
Marion, George Jr (Miscellaneous)
Gladiator, The 1938,Ag 29,10:2
Marion, George Jr (Original Author)
Safety in Numbers 1930,My 31,19:4
Sea Legs 1930,N 11,29:1
No Limit 1931,Ja 17,23:1
College Rhythm 1934,N 24,19:1
To Beat the Band 1935,N 23,23:2
Three Cheers for Love 1936,Ag 1,16:2
Too Many Girls 1940,N 21,43:1
Marion, George Jr (Screenwriter)
Sweetie 1929,O 26,15:1
Let's Go Native 1930,Ag 30,7:4
Gay Divorcee, The 1934,N 16,27:1
Two for Tonight 1935,Ag 31,16:2
Metropolitan 1935,O 18,27:4
Fifty Roads to Town 1937,Je 5,21:1
Marion, Joan
Black Limelight 1939,Je 26,12:2
Spies of the Air 1940,Jl 4,12:3
Missing Ten Days 1941,Ap 21,15:5 (In Addenda)
Marion, Marty
Safe at Home 1941,N 26,31:2
Marion, Oscar
Taras Bulba 1927,D 28,26:6
Nie Wieder Liebe 1932,Ja 16,13:1
Zirkus Leben 1932,D 28,14:7
Marion, Paul
To Have and Have Not 1944,O 12,24:1
So Dark the Night 1946,D 7,16:2
Sword in the Desert 1949,Ag 25,20:2
Scared Stiff 1953,Jl 3,10:2
Green Fire 1954,D 25,7:1
Marion, Ruth
Old-Fashioned Way, The 1934,Jl 14,16:5
Servants' Entrance 1934,S 27,25:2
Marion-Crawford, Howard
Born for Glory 1935,O 21,22:4
Voice in the Night, The 1941,My 23,25:4
Mister Drake's Duck 1952,Ja 28,15:2
Gideon of Scotland Yard 1959,My 20,38:2
Next to no Time 1960,My 28,13:2
Mariotti
Francois Villon 1950,Jl 3,9:2
Mariotti, Frederick
Mare Nostrum 1926,F 16,22:4
Maris, Giannis (Screenwriter)
Lisa, Tosca of Athens 1961,Je 20,27:1
Maris, J (Screenwriter)
You Came too Late 1962,N 12,35:8
Maris, Mona
Bondage 1928,N 6,35:1
Spy of Madame de Pompadour, The
1929,S 10,27:1
Romance of Rio Grande 1929,N 9,22:5
Under a Texas Moon 1930,Ap 4,22:1
Arizona Kid, The 1930,My 17,21:2
One mad Kiss 1930,Jl 19,7:5
Devil With Women, A 1930,O 20,28:2
Man Called Back 1932,Jl 30,16:5
Once in a Lifetime 1932,O 29,18:4
Death Kiss, The 1933,F 5,IX,5:3
Secrets 1933,Mr 16,21:2
El Precio de un Beso 1933,Jl 25,17:3
Viuda Romantica, La 1933,S 4,9:6
Melodia Prohibida, La 1933,O 4,27:2
Quando el Amor Rie 1933,O 17,26:3
No Dejes la Puerta Abierta 1933,N 6,24:4
IO... TU... Y...; (I... Thou... and... She)
1933,D 5,31:6
White Heat 1934,Je 16,20:2
Kiss and Make-Up 1934,Je 29,17:1
Cuesta Abajo 1934,Ag 15,13:5
Tres Amores 1934,N 5,23:1

Maris, Mona — Cont

Cantante de Napoles, El; Singer of Naples, The 1935,F 25,13:4
Asegure a su Mujer; Insure Your Wife 1935,Mr 12,25:3
Flight From Destiny 1941,Mr 28,26:7
Underground 1941,Je 23,13:2
Law of the Tropics 1941,O 10,26:5
Date With the Falcon, A 1941,N 25,33:2
My Gal Sal 1942,My 1,23:1
Pacific Rendezvous 1942,Jl 8,27:4
I Married an Angel 1942,Jl 10,13:2
Berlin Correspondent 1942,S 4,19:2
Tampico 1944,Je 2,21:2
Falcon in Mexico, The 1944,Ag 5,16:2
Heartbeat 1946,My 11,22:4

Maris, Roger
Safe at Home 1962,Ap 14,14:1

Marischka, Ernst (Director)
St Matthew Passion 1952,Ja 29,17:4
Story of Vickie, The 1958,Ja 30,19:2
Embezzled Heaven 1959,Ap 24,23:1
Dreimaederlhaus, Das; (House of Three Girls, The) 1961,N 18,15:1
Forever My Love 1962,Mr 28,36:4
You Are the World for Me 1964,D 26,9:4

Marischka, Ernst (Original Author)
Ich Will Nicht Wissen Wer Du Bist 1933,F 16,23:2
My Heart Is Calling 1935,Ap 15,16:3
King Steps Out, The 1936,My 29,15:2
Spring Parade 1940,O 4,29:2
Song to Remember, A 1945,Ja 26,16:4
Eternal Melodies 1948,F 14,17:3
Her Wonderful Lie 1950,Jl 17,15:2
Forever My Love 1962,Mr 28,36:4

Marischka, Ernst (Producer)
St Matthew Passion 1952,Ja 29,17:4

Marischka, Ernst (Screenwriter)
Lied fur Dich, Ein; Song for You, A 1933,Jl 2,IX,2:2
Strauss's Great Waltz 1935,Ap 8,23:3
World's in Love, The 1937,My 19,27:2
Charm of la Boheme, The 1938,Mr 19,11:2
Her Wonderful Lie 1950,Jl 17,15:2
Story of Vickie, The 1958,Ja 30,19:2
Embezzled Heaven 1959,Ap 24,23:1
Dreimaederlhaus, Das; (House of Three Girls, The) 1961,N 18,15:1
You Are the World for Me 1964,D 26,9:4

Marischka, Hubert
Graefin Mariza 1935,Ja 26,13:3

Marischka, Hubert (Director)
Liebe im Dreiviertel Takt; Love in Waltz Time 1938,S 24,13:1
Fasching in Wien 1939,Mr 18,9:2

Marischka, Hubert (Original Author)
King Steps Out, The 1936,My 29,15:2

Marishige, Hisaya
Country Doctor, The 1963,Ag 14,28:1

Marito, Mike
They Call It Sin 1932,O 21,25:4

Maritza, Sari
Forgotten Commandments 1932,Je 2,25:2
Monte Carlo Madness 1932,Je 4,9:2
Evenings for Sale 1932,N 12,20:5
Lady's Profession, A 1933,Mr 25,13:3
International House 1933,My 27,11:5
Right to Romance, The 1933,D 15,28:2
Crimson Romance 1934,O 13,10:1

Marivale, Philip
Adventure 1946,F 8,23:2

Marjane
Paris Does Strange Things 1957,Mr 30,13:2

Mark, Flip
Please Don't Eat the Daisies 1960,Ap 1,37:1

Mark, John (Screenwriter)
Loves of a Greek in Paris 1960,Ag 15,19:7

Mark, Michael
Resurrection 1931,Ja 24,15:1
Frankenstein 1931,D 5,21:2
Missing Witness 1937,D 10,33:3
Ride a Crooked Mile 1938,D 29,15:2
Mummy's Hand, The 1940,S 20,27:2
House of Frankenstein 1944,D 16,19:3
Great Flamario, The 1945,Ja 15,15:5
Joe Palooka, Champ 1946,Ap 6,10:6
Once a Thief 1951,Ja 19,21:3

Markarova, Tamara
Masquerade 1943,My 17,11:2

Markart, Annie
Ungetreue Eckehart, Der 1932,Ja 23,18:4
Adjutant Seiner Hoheit, Der 1934,O 22,12:3
Unbekannte Gast, Der; Unknown Guest, The 1935,Je 1,18:3
Knock-Out 1936,F 29,11:2
Alle Tage Ist Kein Sonntag 1936,Jl 11,11:4
Idealer Gatte, Ein 1937,Ja 11,15:7

Marke, Maritta
Troette Teodor 1932,Ja 18,18:4

Marken, Jane
Confessions of a Rogue 1948,Mr 30,26:3
Eternal Husband, The 1949,Ja 10,19:2
Dedee 1949,Ap 9,9:2

Cheat, The 1950,O 2,19:3
Lady Paname 1951,Mr 20,35:4
Riptide 1951,Ap 7,9:2
Ma Pomme 1951,O 15,22:2
Sins of Paris 1954,Ja 30,9:6
Caroline Cherie 1954,My 25,23:1
Dr Knock 1955,O 10,31:2
And God Created Woman 1957,O 22,41:1
Pot Bouille 1958,O 28,39:1
Mirror Has two Faces, The 1959,My 27,31:1
Crazy for Love 1960,N 26,13:2
Bonne Soupe, La 1964,Mr 16,37:1
Friend of the Family 1965,N 18,55:3

Marken, Jeanne
Dame aux Camelias, La 1935,Mr 21,27:1
Open Road, The 1940,O 5,20:2
Enfants du Paradis, Les 1947,F 20,32:2
Eternal Return, The; Eternel Retour, L' 1948,Ja 5,15:2
Scandals of Clochemerle, The 1950,Mr 28,28:2
Ways of Love (A Day in the Country); Day in the Country, A (Ways of Love) 1950,D 13,50:2
Secret of Mayerling, The 1951,My 8,39:2
Marie du Port 1951,Jl 24,21:2
Companions of the Night 1954,N 25,44:2

Marker, Chris (Cinematographer)
Koumiko Mystery, The; Mystere Keumiko, Le 1967,Ap 7,32:2

Marker, Chris (Director)
Le Joli Mai 1966,Je 10,54:2
Jetee, La 1967,Ja 16,27:3
Koumiko Mystery, The; Mystere Keumiko, Le 1967,Ap 7,32:2

Marker, Chris (Miscellaneous)
Koumiko Mystery, The; Mystere Keumiko, Le 1967,Ap 7,32:2
Far From Vietnam 1968,Je 7,32:1

Marker, Chris (Narrator)
Le Joli Mai 1966,Je 10,54:2

Marker, Chris (Screenwriter)
Koumiko Mystery, The; Mystere Keumiko, Le 1967,Ap 7,32:2

Markert, Russell dancers
King of Jazz 1930,My 3,23:1

Markes, Larry (Screenwriter)
For Love or Money 1963,Ag 8,19:1
Wild and Wonderful 1964,Je 11,27:4

Markey, Alexander (Director)
Hei Tiki 1935,F 2,10:3

Markey, Alexander (Producer)
Hei Tiki 1935,F 2,10:3

Markey, Enid
Snafu 1945,D 26,15:2
Naked City, The 1948,Mr 5,17:2

Markey, Gene (Original Author)
Syncopation 1929,Ap 8,32:1
Close Harmony 1929,Ap 29,29:2
Mother's Boy 1929,My 8,34:6
Baby Face 1933,Je 24,16:2
Female 1933,N 4,18:3
White Hunter 1936,N 26,39:2
You're the One 1941,F 20,23:2

Markey, Gene (Producer)
Wee Willie Winkie 1937,Jl 24,12:1
Suez 1938,O 15,21:2
You're the One 1941,F 20,23:2
Moss Rose 1947,Jl 3,14:2

Markey, Gene (Screenwriter)
Lucky in Love 1929,D 14,22:4
Florodora Girl, The 1930,My 31,19:4
Let's Live Tonight 1935,Mr 18,14:4
King of Burlesque 1936,Ja 16,25:2
Private Number 1936,Je 12,19:1
Girls' Dormitory 1936,Ag 29,16:2
On the Avenue 1937,F 5,17:3
You're the One 1941,F 20,23:2
If This Be Sin 1950,Jl 1,9:2
Wonder Boy 1951,D 26,19:5

Markey, Melinda
Adventures of Haji Baba, The 1954,O 9,8:7

Markfield, Wallace (Original Author)
Bye Bye Braverman 1968,F 22,36:1

Markham, Harry
This Sporting Life 1963,Jl 17,19:2

Markham, Kyra (Director)
Forest Ring, The 1930,Ap 26,11:1

Markin, Vasili
She-Wolf, The 1963,S 2,18:1

Markland, Ted
Angels From Hell 1968,O 24,55:5

Markle, Fletcher (Director)
Jigsaw 1949,My 30,9:4
Night Into Morning 1951,Je 11,20:7
Man With a Cloak, The 1951,N 28,37:2
Incredible Journey, The 1963,N 21,43:2

Markle, Fletcher (Screenwriter)
Jigsaw 1949,My 30,9:4

Marko, Zekial
Once a Thief 1965,S 9,36:1

Marko, Zekial (Original Author)
Once a Thief 1965,S 9,36:1

Marko, Zekial (Screenwriter)
Once a Thief 1965,S 9,36:1

Markopoulos, Gregory
Illiac Passion, The 1968,Ap 19,40:1

Markopoulos, Gregory (Director)
Illiac Passion, The 1968,Ap 19,40:1

Markopoulos, Gregory (Producer)
Illiac Passion, The 1968,Ap 19,40:1

Markopoulos, Gregory (Screenwriter)
Illiac Passion, The 1968,Ap 19,40:1

Markos, Andreas
Kitchen, The 1961,N 2,42:1

Markov, V M
Lenin in 1918 1939,Je 27,27:2

Markovic, Olivera
Fury is a Woman 1964,S 28,19:1

Markovich, Rade
Magic Sword, The 1952,N 19,37:2

MARKS
See Also MARX

Marks, Alfred
Week-End With Lulu, A 1962,My 24,29:2

Marks, Barbara
One-Way Ticket to Hell 1955,D 8,45:1

Marks, Clarence (Original Author)
Swing It, Sailor 1937,D 13,23:5

Marks, Clarence (Screenwriter)
Don't Get Personal 1936,F 22,12:1
Wide Open Faces 1938,Ap 15,23:2
Taxi, Mister 1943,Ap 15,20:2
That Nazty Nuisance 1943,My 29,10:3

Marks, Eduard
Faust 1963,Ap 16,31:1

Marks, Jennifer
Mikado, The 1967,Mr 15,53:1

Marks, Joe E
Li'l Abner 1959,D 12,19:2

Marks, Leo (Screenwriter)
Guns at Batasi 1964,N 17,47:1
Sebastian 1968,Ja 25,33:2

Marks, Lou
Mister Rock and Roll 1957,O 17,42:2

Marks, Percy (Original Author)
Plastic Age, The 1926,Jl 19,13:1

Marks, William (Screenwriter)
Kill a Dragon 1967,D 7,60:2

Marks, Willis
Greased Lightning 1919,Ap 28,13:2
Dancin' Fool, The 1920,My 3,18:1
Dramatic Life of Abraham Lincoln, The 1924,Ja 22,17:3
Which Shall It Be? 1924,Ap 7,15:3
Unknown Soldier, The 1926,My 31,10:2
Rebecca of Sunnybrook Farm 1932,Jl 30,16:5

Markson, Ben (Miscellaneous)
Babbitt 1934,D 17,24:2

Markson, Ben (Original Author)
Is my Face red 1932,Je 11,9:3
Half-Naked Truth, The 1932,D 31,10:1
Here Comes the Navy 1934,Jl 21,14:2

Markson, Ben (Screenwriter)
White Cockatoo, The 1935,Ja 16,21:1
Bright Lights 1935,Ag 15,15:2
Case of the Lucky Legs, The 1935,N 1,25:1
Brides are Like That 1936,Mr 23,22:5
Woman Wise 1937,Ja 23,13:1
That I May Live 1937,My 10,23:2
Sing and Be Happy 1937,Je 19,20:2
Danger-Love at Work 1937,D 11,22:2
I Was a Convict 1939,Mr 23,27:2
He Hired the Boss 1943,Je 4,17:4
Falcon in San Francisco, The 1945,Jl 21,7:2
Mr District Attorney 1947,F 28,27:3

Markstein, George (Screenwriter)
Robbery 1967,S 28,58:2

MARKUS
See Also MARCUS

Markus, Emma P
Harom Sarkany 1936,D 22,32:3

Markus, Lajos
Nagymama 1935,D 30,15:1

Markus, Rachel
Faithful City 1952,Ap 8,35:2

Markus, Winnie
Mozart Story, The 1948,N 15,21:5
Seven Journeys 1951,Mr 12,20:2

Marla, Elvira
Su Ultimo Amor 1933,Ag 19,14:5

Marle, Arnold
One of our Aircraft Is Missing 1942,N 2,17:2
Mr Emmanuel 1945,Ja 8,15:2
Girl in the Painting, The 1949,Ag 22,13:1
Glass Mountain, The 1950,My 18,37:3
Kisenga, Man of Africa 1952,Mr 7,18:2

Marlen, Trude
Eines Prinzen Junge Liebe 1934,Mr 24,20:4
Spiel mit dem Feuer 1934,N 26,12:2
Ehestreik 1935,Ag 31,16:3
Schabernack 1937,Ag 14,16:5
Graue Dame, Die; Gray Lady, The 1938,D 17,10:4
Hummel-Hummel 1939,Mr 11,21:2
Verkannte Lebemann, Der; Unrecognized Man of the World, The 1939,S 16,20:2

Marlen, Trude— Cont

Favorit der Kaiserin, Der; Favorite of the Empress,
The 1939,D 25,29:3
Paradies der Junggesellen; Bachelors' Paradise
1940,Ap 13,21:3

Marley, John
My Six Convicts 1952,Mr 28,27:3
Joe Louis Story, The 1953,N 4,29:4
Square Jungle, The 1955,D 31,17:2
Timetable 1956,Mr 17,13:2
I Want to Live 1958,N 19,45:1
America America 1963,D 16,44:1
Cat Ballou 1965,Je 25,36:1
Faces 1968,S 23,42:4
Faces 1968,N 25,54:2

Marlieb, John
Native Land 1942,My 12,16:3

Marlier, Carla
Zazie 1961,N 21,45:5
Any Number Can Win 1963,O 9,47:2

Marlin, Edwin (Director)
Paris Calling 1942,Ja 19,21:2

Marlo, Mary
Second Greatest Sex, The 1956,F 11,12:2

Marlo, Steven
Buccaneer, The 1958,D 24,00:0
Slender Thread, The 1965,D 24,24:2

Marlow, Brian (Miscellaneous)
Road to Reno, The 1938,O 3,11:2

Marlow, Brian (Original Author)
My Woman 1933,O 16,20:3
Among the Living 1941,D 13,25:2
Jumping Jacks 1952,Jl 24,30:2

Marlow, Brian (Screenwriter)
Woman Trap 1936,Mr 7,11:4
Preview Murder Mystery, The 1936,Mr 21,13:2
Sky Parade, The 1936,Ap 20,17:1
Till We Meet Again 1936,My 9,11:2
Forgotten Faces 1936,Jl 4,18:2
Return of Sophie Lang, The 1936,Jl 24,13:1
Accusing Finger, The 1936,N 17,35:4
Sophie Lang Goes West 1937,S 30,19:2
Beware, Spooks 1939,N 3,17:4

Marlow, Jean
Little Ones, The 1965,S 16,55:2

Marlow, Lucy
Star is Born, A 1954,O 12,23:1
Tight Spot 1955,Mr 19,11:7
My Sister Eileen 1955,S 23,21:1
Queen Bee 1955,N 23,18:2

Marlow, Tony
Racket, The 1928,Jl 9,25:1
Mummy, The 1933,Ja 7,11:2

Marlowe, Alona
Argyle Case, The 1929,Ag 31,13:4

Marlowe, Anthony
Great Commandment, The 1942,O 17,11:1
Saadia 1954,Mr 20,10:5

Marlowe, Charles (Original Author)
When Knights Were Bold 1942,Mr 31,29:2

Marlowe, Christopher (Original Author)
Doctor Faustus 1968,F 7,38:1

Marlowe, Derek (Original Author)
Dandy in Aspic, A 1968,Ap 3,40:1

Marlowe, Derek (Screenwriter)
Dandy in Aspic, A 1968,Ap 3,40:1

Marlowe, Eleanor
Bimbo the Great 1961,Je 29,26:1

Marlowe, Faye
Hangover Square 1945,F 8,15:2
Junior Miss 1945,Je 18,15:4
Spider, The 1946,Je 21,20:3
Rendezvous With Annie 1946,S 23,29:3

Marlowe, Frank
Now I'll Tell 1934,My 26,12:2
Glass Key, The 1935,Je 15,20:2
Murder in the Blue Room 1944,O 28,12:2
Barricade 1950,Mr 25,8:6
Winning Team, The 1952,Je 21,12:2
Americano, The 1955,Ja 20,35:1
Square Jungle, The 1955,D 31,17:2

Marlowe, Gloria
Anything Can Happen 1952,Ap 4,21:1

Marlowe, Hugh
Married Before Breakfast 1937,Jl 23,16:2
Between Two Women 1937,Ag 6,21:1
Mrs Parkington 1944,O 13,16:1
Marriage Is a Private Affair 1944,O 27,17:7
Meet Me in St Louis 1944,N 29,20:2
Come to the Stable 1949,Jl 28,19:1
Twelve O'Clock High 1950,Ja 28,10:2
Night and the City 1950,Je 10,11:2
All About Eve 1950,O 14,13:2
Rawhide 1951,Mr 26,19:2
Mr Belvedere Rings the Bell 1951,Ag 2,18:1
Day the Earth Stood Still, The 1951,S 19,37:1
Bugles in the Afternoon 1952,Mr 5,32:2
Wait Till the Sun Shines, Nellie 1952,Je 28,12:2
Monkey Business 1952,S 6,12:6
Way of a Gaucho 1952,N 5,36:2
Casanova's Big Night 1954,Ap 19,19:1
Garden of Evil 1954,Jl 10,17:1
Illegal 1955,O 29,12:6
Earth vs the Flying Saucers 1956,Ag 2,21:2

Elmer Gantry 1960,Jl 8,16:1
Birdman of Alcatraz 1962,Jl 19,19:2
13 Frightened Girls 1963,S 12,32:2
Seven Days in May 1964,F 20,22:1

Marlowe, James
Back Home and Broke 1922,D 25,21:1

Marlowe, Jerry
Big Town Czar 1939,My 4,27:3
Legion of Lost Flyers 1939,O 30,13:3
Honeymoon Deferred 1940,F 16,23:4

Marlowe, Jo Ann
Mildred Pierce 1945,S 29,12:2
Scandal In Paris, A 1946,S 16,9:7

Marlowe, June
When a Man's a Man 1924,F 5,20:1
Find Your Man 1924,S 23,26:1
Tracked in the Snow Country 1925,Jl 20,19:2
Wife Who Wasn't Wanted, The 1925,S 9,23:1
Below the Line 1925,S 21,12:4
Clash of the Wolves, The 1925,N 18,27:4
Night Cry, The 1926,Ap 7,26:6
Don Juan 1926,Ag 7,6:1 (In Addenda)
Fourth Commandment, The 1927,Ap 6,25:1
Alias the Deacon 1927,Je 21,29:2
Life of Riley, The 1927,S 5,13:2
Foreign Legion, The 1928,Je 25,27:1
Grip of the Yukon, The 1928,Jl 10,17:3
Pardon Us 1931,Ag 22,7:5
Gente Bien 1939,O 9,15:2

Marlowe, Katherine
Phenix City Story, The 1955,S 3,9:1

Marlowe, Kathryn
Dodsworth 1936,S 24,29:1

Marlowe, Lilli
Private Hell 36 1954,S 4,6:4

Marlowe, Nora
Affair to Remember, An 1957,Jl 20,8:5
Brass Bottle, The 1964,My 21,42:1

Marlowe, Scott
Gaby 1956,My 10,26:3
Men in War 1957,Mr 20,32:4
Subterraneans, The 1960,Jl 7,26:1
Cold Wind in August, A 1961,Jl 27,23:2

Marlowe, William
Tunes of Glory 1960,D 21,38:2
Uncle, The 1966,Jl 19,34:1
Robbery 1967,S 28,58:2

Marly, Florence
Damned, The; Maudits, Les 1948,Ap 26,27:2
Sealed Verdict 1948,N 3,36:2
Tokyo Joe 1949,O 27,35:2
Krakatit 1951,Ap 30,16:2
Tokyo File 212 1951,Je 1,20:7

Marmont, Patricia
Front Page Story 1955,Ap 19,28:1
Suddenly, Last Summer 1959,D 23,22:1

Marmont, Percy
Turn of the Wheel 1918,S 2,7:1
Three Men and a Girl 1919,Mr 31,11:3
Branded Woman, The 1920,S 6,10:5
Marriage Cheat, The 1921,Je 2,14:3
If Winter Comes 1923,S 4,14:1
Light That Failed, The 1923,N 27,11:2
Shooting of Dan McGrew, The 1924,Je 9,14:3
Enemy Sex, The 1924,Jl 1,21:4
Clean Heart, The 1924,S 15,28:1
Unknown, The 1924,N 18,22:1
K-The Unknown 1924,N 18,22:1
Broken Laws 1925,Ja 21,19:3
Daddy's Gone A-Hunting 1925,F 24,17:3
Just a Woman 1925,My 26,24:2
Street of Forgotten Men, The 1925,Jl 21,26:2
Woman's Faith, A 1925,Jl 27,17:3
Fine Clothes 1925,O 20,28:1
Lord Jim 1925,N 16,19:4
Infatuation 1926,Ja 4,16:1
Aloma of the South Seas 1926,My 17,19:1
Mantrap 1926,Jl 12,24:4
San Francisco Nights 1928,Ja 31,29:1
Silver King, The 1929,S 2,16:1
Ariane 1934,Mr 7,23:4
Secret Agent 1936,Je 13,13:1
Girl Was Young, The 1938,F 11,27:2
Pearls of the Crown, The 1938,Ap 12,26:2
Courageous Mr Penn 1943,D 23,26:5
No Orchids for Miss Blandish 1951,F 23,33:2
Four Sided Triangle 1953,My 16,10:1
Lisbon 1956,Ag 30,19:2

Marmstedt, Lorens (Producer)
Crime and Punishment 1948,Mr 1,17:2
Frustration 1949,Ag 27,7:3
Devil's Wanton, The 1962,Jl 5,21:2
Night is my Future 1963,Ja 9,5:6
Doll, The 1964,Ja 14,27:1
Swedish Wedding Night 1965,N 15,48:1

Marnac, Jane
Paris-Beguin 1932,D 31,10:1

Marnay, Andre
Little Flower of Jesus, The 1938,D 13,31:2

Marnay, Marcelle
Uncivilized 1937,N 17,27:4

Marner, Richard
One That Got Away, The 1958,Ap 23,40:2
Touch of Larceny, A 1960,Mr 17,28:1
Password Is Courage, The 1962,D 22,5:2

Marney, Jacques
Madame Sans Gene 1925,Ap 18,19:1

Marnik, Burt (Original Author)
Cyanamide 1954,Mr 26,17:6

Marno, Marc
Majority of One, A 1962,Ja 12,29:2
Diamond Head 1963,F 21,5:2

Maro, Alexandra
Schlemihl, Der 1934,N 5,23:1

Maroff, Hilde
Mother Love 1931,F 16,17:1

Marokoff, M
Yellow Ticket, The 1928,D 10,25:1

Marold, Helga
Dreiland; Triad 1938,Jl 23,10:5

Maron, Eddie (Screenwriter)
Topper 1937,Ag 20,21:2

Maron, Francisco
Down Under the Sea 1936,Ag 10,10:2

Maros, Basil (Cinematographer)
Girl From Corfu, The 1957,My 20,28:2

Maros, Basil (Director)
Aegean Tragedy, The 1965,F 1,29:1

Maros, Basil (Producer)
Aegean Tragedy, The 1965,F 1,29:1

Maross, Joe
Run Silent, Run Deep 1958,Mr 28,29:1

Marotta, Giuseppe (Original Author)
Gold of Naples (The Gambler); Gambler, The
(Gold of Naples) 1957,F 12,30:1
Gold of Naples (Theresa); Theresa (Gold of
Naples) 1957,F 12,30:1
Gold of Naples (Pizza on Credit); Pizza on Credit
(Gold of Naples) 1957,F 12,30:1
Gold of Naples (The Racketeer); Racketeer, The
(Gold of Naples) 1957,F 12,30:1

Marotta, Giuseppe (Screenwriter)
Gold of Naples (Pizza on Credit); Pizza on Credit
(Gold of Naples) 1957,F 12,30:1
Gold of Naples (Theresa); Theresa (Gold of
Naples) 1957,F 12,30:1
Gold of Naples (The Gambler); Gambler, The
(Gold of Naples) 1957,F 12,30:1
Gold of Naples (The Racketeer); Racketeer, The
(Gold of Naples) 1957,F 12,30:1

Marow, Hilde
Gaesschen zum Paradies, Das 1937,Ag 21,7:3

Marples, Jim
Milky Way, The 1936,Mr 26,27:2

Marquand, Christian
Sins of the Borgias 1956,Mr 5,21:1
Doctors, The 1956,Ag 7,19:2
And God Created Woman 1957,O 22,41:1
No Sun in Venice 1958,Je 10,40:2
End of Desire 1962,Jl 10,29:2
Tales of Paris (The Tale of Antonio); Tale of
Antonio, The (Tales of Paris) 1962,Ag 27,18:1
Longest Day, The 1962,O 5,28:1
Crime Does Not Pay (The Fenayrou Case);
Fenayrou Case, The (Crime Does Not Pay)
1962,O 17,35:2
Temptation 1962,N 10,16:2
Playtime; Receation, La 1963,Ja 16,5:2
I Spit on Your Grave 1963,Je 29,13:5
Bonne Soupe, La 1964,Mr 16,37:1
Behold a Pale Horse 1964,Ag 14,16:1
Lord Jim 1965,F 26,18:1
Flight of the Phoenix, The 1966,F 1,26:1
Corrupt Ones, The 1967,F 23,41:3

Marquand, Christian (Director)
Candy 1968,D 18,54:2

Marquand, J P (Miscellaneous)
Mr Moto's Gamble 1938,Ap 8,17:2
Mr Moto Takes a Chance 1938,Je 13,15:4

Marquand, J P (Original Author)
Think Fast, Mr Moto 1937,Ag 16,15:3
Thank You, Mr Moto 1938,Ja 3,16:2
Mr Moto in Danger Island 1938,Mr 20,13:3
Mysterious Mr Moto of Devil's Island
1938,S 19,16:2
Mr Moto's Last Warning 1939,Ja 27,17:3
Mr Moto Takes a Vacation 1939,Je 19,12:6
H M Pulham, Esq 1941,D 19,35:1
Late George Apley, The 1947,Mr 21,29:2
B F's Daughter 1948,Mr 25,35:2
Top Secret Affair 1957,Ja 31,21:1
Stopover Tokyo 1957,D 27,23:4

Marquand, Serga
Vice and Virtue 1965,Mr 18,25:1

Marquand, Tina
Modesty Blaise 1966,Ag 11,27:1
Texas Across the River 1966,N 24,65:1
Game is Over, The 1967,Ja 10,34:1

Marquardt, Paul (Miscellaneous)
Girl of the Golden West, The 1938,Mr 25,15:2

Marquat, Mary
Vie de Chateau, La 1967,Mr 21,35:1

Marques, Gilberto
  Given Word, The 1964,Mr 25,47:1
Marques, Maria Elena
  Asi Se Quiere En Jalisco 1943,Ag 7,6:2
  Romeo and Juliet 1944,Je 17,10:3
  Pearl, The 1948,F 18,36:4
  Across the Wide Missouri 1951,N 7,35:4
  Doctors, The 1956,Ag 7,19:2
  Royal Affairs in Versailles 1957,Mr 9,16:1
  Maid in Paris 1957,Jl 13,11:1
  Landru 1963,Ap 10,31:1
  Marriage Came Tumbling Down, The
    1968,N 6,32:3
Marquet, Henri (Screenwriter)
  Jour de Fete 1952,F 20,26:4
  Mr Hulot's Holiday 1954,Je 17,36:2
Marquette, Doris (Original Author)
  Garden of Weeds, The 1924,N 4,24:1
MARQUEZ
  See Also MARQUIS
Marquez, Esteban
  Mexican Bus ride 1954,Jl 21,18:3
MARQUIS
  See Also MARQUEZ
Marquis, Don (Original Author)
  Good Old Soak 1937,Ap 20,25:3
Marquis, Margaret
  Penrod and Sam 1931,S 26,25:3
  Eight Girls in a Boat 1934,Ja 13,16:3
  Family Affair, A 1937,Ap 20,29:2
Marquis, Robert
  Crazy Quilt, The 1966,O 4,50:1
Marquis, Rosalind
  Gold Diggers of 1937 1936,D 25,19:2
  Marked Woman 1937,Ap 12,15:2
  Talent Scout 1937,Ag 20,21:3
Marqulies, Stan (Producer)
  40 Pounds of Trouble 1963,Ja 24,5:2
Marr, Edward
  Forty Naughty Girls 1937,S 18,15:3
  Mr Moto's Gamble 1938,Ap 8,17:2
  Time Out for Murder 1938,O 7,21:2
  Affairs of Annabel, The 1938,O 13,29:2
  Disbarred 1939,Ja 19,17:2
  Tail Spin 1939,F 11,13:2
  City of Chance 1940,Ja 22,11:3
  Our Neighbors-The Carters 1940,F 15,15:2
  Charlie Chan At the Wax Museum 1940,S 28,9:3
  Youth Will Be Served 1940,N 15,25:2
  Glass Key, The 1942,O 16,23:1
  Hi Diddle Diddle 1943,S 24,26:2
  Rhapsody in Blue 1945,Je 28,22:2
  Deadline for Murder 1946,Je 29,22:7
  On Moonlight Bay 1951,Jl 27,15:2
  Confidence Girl 1952,Je 21,12:2
  Steel Trap, The 1952,N 13,35:2
  Clown, The 1953,Ja 29,25:1
  20,000 Leagues Under the Sea 1954,D 24,7:2
Marr, Edwin
  Sky Giant 1938,Jl 20,22:2
Marr, Hans
  Legend of William Tell, The 1935,O 2,27:1
Marr, Joe
  Portland Expose 1957,S 27,16:6
Marr, Sadia
  Drifter, The 1967,My 25,54:1
Marra, Luciano della
  Aida 1954,N 12,17:1
Marracci, Livia
  Amore che non Torna; Love That Doesn't Return
    1938,Ag 15,11:2
Marrall, Mary
  Encore (Gigolo and Gigolette); Gigolo and
    Gigolette (Encore) 1952,Ap 3,45:1
Marrero, Sonia
  Rebellion in Cuba 1961,Jl 1,9:1
Marriner, John
  Java Head 1935,Jl 31,21:4
Marrio, J J (Original Author)
  Gideon of Scotland Yard 1959,My 20,38:2
Marriott, Crittenden (Original Author)
  Isle of Lost Ships, The 1923,My 14,18:2
  Isle of Lost Ships, The 1929,O 26,15:1
Marriott, John
  Little Foxes, The 1941,Ag 22,19:2
  Joe Louis Story, The 1953,N 4,29:4
  Cool World, The 1964,Ap 21,42:1
  Black Like Me 1964,My 21,42:1
Marriott, Moore
  Widecombe Fair 1929,O 28,20:1
  Man Who Won, The 1933,F 27,11:2
  As You Like It 1936,N 6,29:3
  Accused 1936,D 17,35:1
  Dreaming Lips 1937,My 20,17:1
  To the Victor 1938,Ap 13,21:2
  Girl Must Live, A 1942,Mr 24,25:2
  When Knights Were Bold 1942,Mr 31,29:2
  Green for Danger 1947,Ag 8,10:2
  Place of One's Own, A 1949,F 8,30:2
  Agitator, The 1949,Ag 19,12:5
  History of Mr Polly, The 1951,O 25,36:3

Marrone, Enrico
  Eredita dello Zio, L' 1935,Je 29,16:3
Marrosu, Arnaldo (Screenwriter)
  Legions of the Nile 1961,Mr 4,16:1
Marroudis, Tonis
  Santa Chikita 1959,My 11,30:1
Marrs, Mona
  Passionate Plumber, The 1932,Mr 12,19:5
Mars, Colette
  Souvenir 1950,O 3,34:4
Mars, Janice
  Up the Down Staircase 1967,Ag 18,36:2
Mars, Kenneth
  Producers, The 1968,Mr 19,38:1
Mars, Marjorie
  Crouching Beast, The 1936,Ag 22,6:1
  Spy of Napoleon 1939,Ag 19,18:4
  Take my Life 1949,Ja 19,34:2
Mars, Severin
  I Accuse; (J'Accuse) 1921,O 10,16:1
Marsac, Jean
  Edward and Caroline 1952,Ap 30,33:3
Marsac, Maurice
  ThIs is the Life 1944,Ap 28,23:3
  Happy Time, The 1952,O 31,30:2
  How to Marry a Millionaire 1953,N 11,37:1
  China Gate 1957,My 23,40:2
  Scent of Mystery 1960,F 19,23:1
  King of Kings 1961,O 12,41:2
  Werewolf in a Girls Dormitory 1963,Je 6,39:1
  What a Way to Go! 1964,My 15,44:1
  Pleasure Seekers, The 1964,D 26,9:1
  Clarence, the Cross-Eyed Lion 1965,Ag 5,15:3
  Gambit 1966,D 22,40:2
  Caprice 1967,Je 8,52:2
Marsach, Roberto
  Terror in the City 1966,N 9,43:4
Marsan, Jean (Original Author)
  Sheep Has Five Legs, The 1955,Ag 10,19:2
Marsan, Jean (Screenwriter)
  Fruits of Summer 1956,Jl 18,22:2
  Grand Maneuver, The 1956,O 2,39:1
Marsden, Berry
  Leather Boys, The 1965,N 9,50:1
Marsden, Betty
  Chance Meeting 1955,Ap 20,38:1
Marsden, Frances
  No Orchids for Miss Blandish 1951,F 23,33:2
Marsden, Fred
  Ferry Cross the Mersey 1965,F 20,16:2
Marsden, Gerry
  Ferry Cross the Mersey 1965,F 20,16:2
Marsden, John
  Count of Monte Cristo, The 1934,S 27,25:2
Marsdon, Trudi
  Dance Hall 1941,Jl 19,16:2
MARSH
  See Also MARCH
Marsh, Anthony
  Portia on Trial 1937,D 3,29:2
Marsh, Betty
  Cinerama Holiday 1955,F 9,31:1
Marsh, Carol
  Alice in Wonderland 1951,Jl 27,15:2
  Christmas Carol, A 1951,N 29,41:2
  Marry Me 1952,Mr 14,27:3
  Horror of Dracula 1958,My 29,24:4
Marsh, Charles
  Atlantic City 1944,Ag 14,11:4
  My Wild Irish Rose 1947,D 25,32:2
Marsh, Earle
  United States Smith 1928,Jl 24,13:3
Marsh, Eve
  Canon City 1948,Jl 8,19:2
Marsh, Garry
  Night Birds 1931,Ja 3,21:2
  Dreyfus Case, The 1931,Ag 31,11:5
  Man they Couldn't Arrest, The 1933,Mr 14,19:3
  Fires of Fate 1933,Ap 3,13:4
  Scrooge 1935,D 14,11:1
  This Man Is News 1939,Jl 20,16:4
  Secret Four, The 1940,Ap 22,13:2
  Let George Do It 1940,O 14,25:5
  It's in the Air 1940,D 10,33:2
  Break the News 1941,Ja 2,24:2
  When Knights Were Bold 1942,Mr 31,29:2
  Notorious Gentleman 1946,N 14,39:3
  Adventures, The 1947,Ap 4,19:2
  While the Sun Shines 1950,J 1,9:2
  Pink String and Sealing Wax 1950,O 4,38:2
  Murder Will Out 1953,Ap 6,24:2
  Camelot 1967,O 26,54:1
Marsh, Jean
  Cleopatra 1963,Je 13,29:1
Marsh, Joan
  All Quiet on The Western Front 1930,Ap 30,29:1
  Little Accident 1930,Ag 4,13:4
  Inspiration 1931,F 9,25:3
  Dance, Fools, Dance 1931,Mr 21,15:1
  Tailor-Made Man, A 1931,Ap 25,23:4
  Three Girls Lost 1931,My 2,23:4
  Shipmates 1931,My 23,13:4
  Politics 1931,Ag 1,16:4

Marsh, Joan— Cont
  Maker of Men 1931,D 19,16:4
  Wet Parade, The 1932,Ap 22,23:2
  Bachelor's Affairs 1932,Je 25,18:2
  Daring Daughters 1933,Mr 25,13:4
  High Gear 1933,Ap 15,16:2
  It's Great to be Alive 1933,Jl 8,14:6
  Three-Cornered Moon 1933,Ag 12,14:2
  Man Who Dared, The 1933,S 9,9:3
  You're Telling Me 1934,Ap 7,19:1
  Many Happy Returns 1934,Je 9,18:2
  We're Rich Again 1934,S 1,16:3
  Anna Karenina 1935,Ag 31,16:2
  Dancing Feet 1936,Mr 28,11:2
  Charlie Chan on Broadway 1937,S 20,19:1
  Life Begins In College 1937,O 9,16:1
  Hot Water 1937,N 5,19:4
  Idiot's Delight 1939,F 3,13:1
  Fast and Loose 1939,Mr 9,18:1
  Road to Zanzibar 1941,Ap 10,29:2
  Man in the Trunk, The 1942,O 23,25:1
Marsh, John
  Cinerama Holiday 1955,F 9,31:1
Marsh, Linda
  America America 1963,D 16,44:1
  Hamlet 1964,S 24,46:1
Marsh, Lucille
  Streets of Sorrow 1952,N 18,37:4
Marsh, Mae
  Marriage of Molly-O, The 1916,Jl 24,7:4
  Polly of the Circus 1917,S 10,11:3
  Face in the Dark, The 1918,Ap 15,13:3
  All Woman 1918,Je 10,9:3
  Mother and the Law, The 1919,Ag 19,10:1
  Birth of a Nation, The 1921,My 2,12:1
  Birth of a Nation, The 1922,D 5,24:3
  White Rose, The 1923,My 23,18:3
  Daddies 1924,F 11,18:3
  Tides of Passion 1925,Ap 20,22:1
  Birth of a Nation, The 1930,D 22,16:2
  Over the Hill 1931,N 21,20:4
  Rebecca of Sunnybrook Farm 1932,Jl 30,16:5
  That's my Boy 1932,N 21,21:1
  Alice in Wonderland 1933,D 23,19:1
  Little Man, What Now? 1934,Je 1,29:1
  Black Fury 1935,Ap 11,27:2
  Hollywood Boulevard 1936,S 21,26:4
  Man Who Wouldn't Talk, The 1940,Ja 12,13:3
  Young People 1940,Ag 24,16:2
  Great Guns 1941,O 3,27:2
  Tales of Manhattan 1942,S 25,25:1
  Jane Eyre 1944,F 4,12:5
  Deep Waters 1948,Jl 23,12:4
  Three Godfathers 1949,Mr 4,25:2
  Impact 1949,Mr 21,19:2
  Fighting Kentuckian, The 1949,S 19,18:3
  When Willie Comes Marching Home
    1950,F 18,9:2
  Gunfighter, The 1950,Je 24,7:2
  Night Without Sleep 1952,S 27,13:2
  While the City Sleeps 1956,My 17,37:1
  Two Rode Together 1961,Jl 27,23:3
Marsh, Marian
  Svengali 1931,My 1,30:3
  Five Star Final 1931,S 11,24:2
  Road to Singapore, The 1931,O 1,25:2
  Mad Genius, The 1931,O 24,20:3
  Under Eighteen 1931,D 26,15:5
  Alias the Doctor 1932,Mr 3,22:3
  Beauty and the Boss 1932,Ap 2,13:2
  Strange Justice 1932,O 20,24:2
  Sport Parade, The 1932,D 17,22:3
  Daring Daughters 1933,Mr 25,13:4
  I Like It That Way 1934,Ap 18,23:3
  Girl of the Limberlost, A 1934,N 9,24:6
  Crime and Punishment 1935,N 22,18:2
  Lady of Secrets 1936,F 22,12:1
  Counterfeit 1936,Jl 20,11:1
  Man Who Lived Twice, The 1936,O 12,23:2
  Come Closer, Folks 1936,N 23,17:3
  When's Your Birthday? 1937,Mr 19,27:2
  Great Gambini, The 1937,Jl 12,20:4
  Saturday's Heroes 1937,O 16,22:2
  Prison Nurse 1938,Mr 4,17:5
  Missing Daughters 1939,Je 12,14:5
  Prison Camp 1940,Ag 3,9:3
  Murder by Invitation 1941,Jl 23,15:4
Marsh, Mildred
  Country Flapper, The 1922,Jl 31,12:3
Marsh, Myra
  Gentle Julia 1936,Ap 11,19:1
  Rascals 1938,My 27,12:2
  Father's Son 1941,F 13,25:3
  Ruby Gentry 1952,D 26,20:2
Marsh, Tani
  Mad Doctor of Market Street, The 1942,Ja 5,21:5
Marsh, Vera
  Way out West 1930,Ag 18,24:1
Marsh, Yvonne
  Little Ballerina, The 1951,F 28,33:2
Marshal, Alan
  Garden of Allah, The 1936,N 20,27:2
  After the Thin Man 1936,D 25,19:2
  Robber Symphony 1937,Ja 27,17:2

Marshal, Alan — Cont

Night Must Fall 1937,Ap 30,17:2
Parnell 1937,Je 4,27:2
Conquest 1937,N 5,19:1
I Met my Love Again 1938,Ja 15,19:1
Invisible Enemy 1938,Ap 30,18:2
Road to Reno, The 1938,O 3,11:2
Dramatic School 1938,D 9,31:2
Four Girls in White 1939,F 23,19:3
Exile Express 1939,Ag 16,21:3
Adventures of Sherlock Holmes, The
  1939,S 2,20:1
Hunchback of Notre Dame, The 1940,Ja 1,29:2
Married and in Love 1940,F 2,13:2
Irene 1940,My 24,23:3
He Stayed for Breakfast 1940,Ag 31,16:2
Howards of Virginia, The 1940,S 27,27:1
Tom, Dick and Harry 1941,Jl 18,22:2
Lydia 1941,S 19,27:1
White Cliffs of Dover, The 1944,My 12,15:2
Bride by Mistake 1944,S 16,20:2
Opposite Sex, The 1956,N 16,23:2
House on Haunted Hill 1959,Mr 12,27:5

Marshal, Gary

Camelot 1967,O 26,54:1

Marshall, Armina (Original Author)

Pursuit of Happiness, The 1934,O 26,25:1

Marshall, Arthur

For Men Only 1952,Ja 16,21:2

Marshall, Bodie

Spinout 1966,D 15,60:1

Marshall, Brenda

Espionage Agent 1939,S 23,22:2
Man Who Talked too Much, The 1940,Je 29,12:2
Sea Hawk, The 1940,Ag 10,16:2
Money and the Woman 1940,O 4,29:2
East of the River 1940,O 28,21:2
South of Suez 1940,D 19,33:2
Footsteps in the Dark 1941,Mr 15,13:2
Singapore Woman 1941,My 12,13:6
Highway West 1941,Ag 8,13:4
Smiling Ghost, The 1941,S 26,26:5
Captains of the Clouds 1942,F 13,24:2
You Can't Escape Forever 1942,O 17,11:1
Background to Danger 1943,Jl 3,11:2
Constant Nymph, The 1943,Jl 24,8:2
Paris After Dark 1943,O 23,11:1
Whispering Smith 1949,F 15,28:2
Iroquois Trail, The 1950,O 27,24:4

Marshall, Bruce (Original Author)

Red Danube, The 1949,D 9,37:3

Marshall, Catherine (Original Author)

Man Called Peter, A 1955,Ap 1,22:1

Marshall, Charles (Red)

Wave, A Wac and a Marine, A 1944,Ag 14,11:4
Specter of the Rose 1946,S 2,12:4

Marshall, Clark

Voice of the City, The 1929,Ap 29,29:2
Criminal Code, The 1931,Ja 5,21:3
Polly of the Circus 1932,Mr 19,11:2

Marshall, Connie

Sunday Dinner for a Soldier 1945,Ja 25,16:2
Sentimental Journey 1946,Mr 7,33:2
Dragonwyck 1946,Ap 11,35:2
Home Sweet Homicide 1946,S 12,5:7
Wake up and Dream 1947,Ja 24,18:4
Mother Wore Tights 1947,Ag 21,33:2
Daisy Kenyon 1947,D 25,32:1
Mr Blandings Builds his Dream House
  1948,Mr 26,26:2
Green Promise, The 1949,Je 24,29:2
Kill the Umpire 1950,My 29,10:6

Marshall, Dodie

Easy Come, Easy Go 1967,Je 15,56:1

Marshall, E G

13 Rue Madeleine 1947,Ja 16,30:2
Untamed Fury 1947,Ap 26,10:6
Caine Mutiny, The 1954,Je 25,17:1
Broken Lance 1954,Jl 30,9:1
Pushover 1954,Jl 31,6:3
Silver Chalice, The 1954,D 27,22:5
Left Hand of God, The 1955,S 22,34:5
Mountain, The 1956,N 15,44:6
Bachelor Party, The 1957,Ap 10,37:2
12 Angry Men 1957,Ap 15,24:1
Man on Fire 1957,Ag 23,10:1
Buccaneer, The 1958,D 24,00:0
Journey, The 1959,F 20,19:1
Compulsion 1959,Ap 2,26:2
Cash McCall 1960,Ja 28,26:1
Town Without Pity 1961,O 11,53:1
Chase, The 1966,F 19,24:1
Poppy is Also a Flower, The 1967,D 14,62:4

Marshall, Edison (Original Author)

Son of Fury 1942,Ja 30,23:2
Vikings, The 1952,Je 12,35:2
Treasure of the Golden Condor 1953,My 23,19:2
Yankee Pasha 1954,Ap 19,19:2

Marshall, Edward (Original Author)

Gay Retreat, The 1927,O 10,24:1

Marshall, Ellye

Champagne for Caesar 1950,My 12,33:2
Rogue River 1951,F 16,21:4

Marshall, Everett

Dixiana 1930,S 5,21:1
I Live for Love 1935,O 19,21:2

Marshall, Gary (Producer)

How Sweet It Is 1968,Ag 22,47:1

Marshall, Gary (Screenwriter)

How Sweet It Is 1968,Ag 22,47:1

Marshall, George

Timberjack 1955,Mr 10,33:3

Marshall, George (Director)

Pack up Your Troubles 1932,O 1,10:4
Ever Since Eve 1934,Mr 28,27:5
Wild Gold 1934,Jl 24,20:2
She Learned About Sailors 1934,Jl 30,9:4
365 Nights in Hollywood 1934,N 7,32:1
Life Begins at 40 1935,Ap 5,21:3
Old Kentucky, In 1935,N 29,24:1
Show Them no Mercy 1935,D 9,25:2
Message to Garcia, A 1936,Ap 10,27:1
Crime of Dr Forbes, The 1936,Jl 6,11:4
Nancy Steele is Missing 1937,Mr 8,22:1
Love Under Fire 1937,Ag 28,8:2
Goldwyn Follies, The 1938,F 21,15:1
Battle of Broadway 1938,Ap 25,19:2
Hold That Co-ed 1938,S 24,13:1
You Can't Cheat an Honest Man 1939,F 20,13:2
Destry Rides Again 1939,N 30,25:1
Ghost Breakers, The 1940,Jl 4,12:2
When the Daltons Rode 1940,Ag 23,13:3
Pot o'Gold 1941,Ap 4,25:2
Texas 1941,O 17,27:3
Valley of the Sun 1942,Mr 19,29:2
Forest Rangers, The 1942,O 22,25:2
Star Spangled Rhythm 1942,D 31,20:1
True to Life 1943,O 14,26:1
Riding High 1943,D 23,26:4
And the Angels Sing 1944,Jl 13,14:2
Murder, He Says 1945,Je 25,20:3
Incendiary Blonde 1945,Jl 26,13:2
Hold That Blonde 1945,N 8,17:2
Blue Dahlia, The 1946,My 9,27:3
Monsieur Beaucaire 1946,S 5,23:1
Perils of Pauline, The 1947,Jl 10,17:2
Variety Girl 1947,O 16,34:4
Hazard 1948,Je 3,19:2
Tap Roots 1948,Ag 26,16:3
My Friend Irma 1949,S 29,39:2
Fancy Pants 1950,Ag 31,21:2
Never a Dull Moment 1950,N 22,20:2
Millionaire for Christy, A 1951,O 5,24:3
Savage, The 1953,Ja 2,11:1
Off Limits 1953,Mr 30,25:5
Houdini 1953,Jl 3,10:2
Scared Stiff 1953,Jl 3,10:2
Money From Home 1954,F 27,11:3
Red Garters 1954,Mr 27,13:5
Duel in the Jungle 1954,Ag 9,13:2
Second Greatest Sex, The 1956,F 11,12:2
Pillars of the Sky 1956,O 13,15:2
Beyond Mombasa 1957,My 31,14:2
Sad Sack, The 1957,N 28,57:1
Sheepman, The 1958,My 8,36:1
Imitation General 1958,Ag 21,22:2
Mating Game, The 1959,Ap 30,37:1
Gazebo, The 1960,Ja 16,14:4
Cry for Happy 1961,Mr 4,16:1
Happy Thieves, The 1962,F 5,19:4
Papa's Delicate Condition 1963,Mr 7,8:5
How the West Was Won 1963,Ap 1,54:1
Dark Purpose 1964,F 6,36:4
Advance to the Rear 1964,Je 11,27:3
Boy, Did I Get a Wrong Number! 1966,Je 9,54:2
Eight on the Lam 1967,Ap 27,52:1
Wicked Dreams of Paula Schultz, The
  1968,Ja 4,28:1

Marshall, George (Original Author)

Call it Luck 1934,Jl 10,24:5

Marshall, Gregory

That's my Man 1947,Ap 7,20:2
Adventure in Baltimore 1949,Ap 29,27:2
Washington Story 1952,Jl 2,22:3
Tanganyika 1954,Je 19,9:2

Marshall, Herbert

Letter, The 1929,Mr 8,30:1
Murder 1930,O 25,20:6
Secrets of a Secretary 1931,Ag 29,16:3
Calendar, The 1931,N 22,VIII,6:1
Michael and Mary 1932,Mr 5,11:2
Blonde Venus 1932,S 24,18:4
Trouble in Paradise 1932,N 9,28:5
Evenings for Sale 1932,N 12,20:5
Faithful Heart 1933,Ag 15,20:2
Solitaire Man, The 1933,S 23,11:5
I Was a Spy 1934,Ja 15,12:2
Four Frightened People 1934,Ja 27,9:2
Riptide 1934,Mr 31,8:2
Outcast Lady 1934,N 3,20:3
Painted Veil, The 1934,D 7,29:1
Good Fairy, The 1935,F 1,18:1
Flame Within, The 1935,Je 1,18:2
Accent on Youth 1935,Ag 12,10:3
Dark Angel, The 1935,S 6,12:2
If You Could Only Cook 1935,D 26,21:4

Marshall, Herbert — Cont

Lady Consents, The 1936,F 6,23:4
Till We Meet Again 1936,My 9,11:2
Forgotten Faces 1936,Jl 4,18:2
Girls' Dormitory 1936,Ag 29,16:2
Woman Rebels, A 1936,O 30,27:2
Make Way for a Lady 1936,D 12,15:1
Angel 1937,N 4,29:1
Breakfast for Two 1937,N 20,21:2
Mad About Music 1938,Mr 12,13:2
Always Goodbye 1938,Je 25,7:2
Woman Against Woman 1938,Ag 23,20:6
Zaza 1939,Ja 5,17:1
Bill of Divorcement, A 1940,Jl 12,11:2
Foreign Correspondent 1940,Ag 28,15:2
Letter, The 1940,N 23,12:6
Adventure in Washington 1941,Ag 1,11:3
Little Foxes, The 1941,Ag 22,19:2
When Ladies Meet 1941,S 5,19:2
Kathleen 1941,D 19,35:3
Moon and Sixpence, The 1942,O 28,26:4
Forever and a Day 1943,Mr 13,9:2
Flight for Freedom 1943,Ap 16,24:2
Andy Hardy's Blonde Trouble 1944,My 5,17:3
Enchanted Cottage, The 1945,Ap 28,19:2
Unseen, The 1945,My 14,20:5
Crack-Up 1946,S 7,11:1
Razor's Edge, The 1946,N 20,42:2
Duel in the Sun 1947,My 8,30:2
Ivy 1947,Je 26,19:1
High Wall 1947,D 26,22:2
Underworld Story, The 1950,Jl 27,29:4
Anne of the Indies 1951,O 25,36:3
Captain Black Jack 1952,O 22,31:3
Angel Face 1953,Ap 25,11:5
Riders to the Stars 1954,Mr 20,10:7
Gog 1954,Ag 14,8:2
Black Shield of Falworth, The 1954,O 7,16:2
Virgin Queen, The 1955,Ag 6,13:2
Stage Struck 1958,Ap 23,40:1
Fly, The 1958,Ag 30,6:6
College Confidential 1960,Ag 22,23:1
Midnight Lace 1960,O 14,27:1
Fever in the Blood 1961,Ap 20,30:4
Five Weeks in a Balloon 1962,Ag 27,18:1
List of Adrian Messenger, The 1963,My 30,20:1
Caretakers, The 1963,Ag 22,19:2
Third Day, The 1965,Ag 5,15:3

Marshall, Herbert (Original Author)

Proud Valley 1941,My 17,19:2

Marshall, James (Original Author)

Santa Fe 1951,My 4,31:2

Marshall, Joan

Tammy and the Doctor 1963,Je 27,23:2

Marshall, M T

Gunn 1967,Je 29,32:1

Marshall, Marion

Apartment for Peggy 1948,O 16,9:2
I Was a Male War Bride 1949,Ag 27,7:2
Love That Brute 1950,My 27,10:6
Stella 1950,Ag 19,9:2
I Can Get It for You Wholesale 1951,Ap 5,34:4
That's My Boy 1951,Ag 2,18:1
Sailor Beware 1952,F 17,1:1
Stooge, The 1953,F 5,19:2

Marshall, Mort

Go, Man, Go 1954,Mr 10,29:5
Silver Chalice, The 1954,D 27,22:5

Marshall, Nini

Mujeres que Trabajan; Women Who Work
  1940,Ja 1,29:4
Divorcio en Montevideo 1940,Ap 8,15:3

Marshall, Patricia

Good News 1947,D 5,33:2

Marshall, Perle

Wizard, The 1927,N 28,18:5

Marshall, Pete

Rookie, The 1960,Mr 17,28:1
Swingin' Along 1962,Ag 27,18:1

Marshall, Peter L

Cavern, The 1965,D 25,17:2

Marshall, Peter L (Screenwriter)

Maryjane 1968,Mr 14,51:4

Marshall, Rosamond (Original Author)

Kitty 1946,Ap 1,23:1
All the Fine Young Cannibals 1960,S 23,33:1

Marshall, S L A, USAR (Miscellaneous)

Pork Chop Hill 1959,My 30,9:2

Marshall, Sarah

Long, Hot Summer, The 1958,Ap 4,16:1
Wild and Wonderful 1964,Je 11,27:4

Marshall, Sidney (Screenwriter)

Mr District Attorney 1947,F 28,27:3

Marshall, Terry

Too Much Business 1922,My 1,20:3

Marshall, Trudy

Dancing Masters, The 1943,D 2,30:2
Sullivans, The 1944,F 10,19:2
Circumstantial Evidence 1945,Ap 21,18:3
Dolly Sisters, The 1945,N 15,24:6
Sentimental Journey 1946,Mr 7,33:2
Dragonwyck 1946,Ap 11,35:2
Key Witness 1947,Jl 30,27:6
Fuller Brush Man, The 1948,My 15,18:2

Marshall, Trudy— Cont

Barbary Pirate 1949,O 28,29:3
Mark of the Gorilla 1950,F 17,27:2
Full of Life 1957,F 13,38:1

Marshall, Tully

Sable Lorcha, The 1915,O 18,9:1
Oliver Twist 1916,D 11,7:3
Countess Charming 1917,S 17,11:3
We Can't Have Everything 1918,Jl 15,9:3
Too Many Millions 1918,D 9,11:4
Squaw Man, The 1918,D 30,7:3
Cheating Cheaters 1919,Ja 27,11:4
Girl Who Stayed Home, The 1919,Mr 24,11:3
Crimson Gardenia, The 1919,Je 16,11:2
Fall of Babylon, The 1919,Jl 22,10:2
Her Kingdom of Dreams 1919,S 22,8:1
Life Line, The 1919,S 29,16:1
Lottery Man, The 1919,N 17,20:1
Hawthorne of the U.S.A. 1919,N 17,20:1
Everywoman 1919,D 15,20:1
Double Speed 1920,F 2,10:1
Dancin' Fool, The 1920,My 3,18:1
Hail the Woman 1922,Ja 16,18:3
Penrod 1922,F 20,7:1
Is Matrimony a Failure 1922,Ap 17,22:3
Too Much Business 1922,My 1,20:3
Village Blacksmith, The 1922,N 3,17:5
Beautiful and Damned, The 1922,D 11,22:1
Law of the Lawless, The 1923,Je 19,22:4
Brass Bottle, The 1923,Jl 23,13:4
Hunchback of Notre Dame, The 1923,S 3,9:3
Richard the Lion-Hearted 1923,O 22,17:1
Barefoot Boy, The 1923,N 11,6:1
Ponjola 1923,N 19,19:3
Dangerous Maid, The 1923,D 11,26:2
Her Temporary Husband 1924,Ja 1,20:1
Stranger, The 1924,F 5,20:1
For Sale 1924,Jl 14,11:5
He Who Gets Slapped 1924,N 10,20:1
Smouldering Fires 1925,Mr 31,17:4
Talker, The 1925,My 12,26:2
Half-Way Girl, The 1925,Jl 29,24:4
Merry Widow, The 1925,Ag 27,14:1
Clothes Make the Pirate 1925,N 30,17:1
Ibanez's Torrent 1926,F 22,14:1
Old Loves and New 1926,Ap 20,24:7
Her big Night 1926,O 13,21:1
Twinkletoes 1926,D 27,20:3
Jim, The Conquerer 1926,D 28,17:1
Beware of Widows 1927,My 24,23:4
Cat and the Canary, The 1927,S 10,9:4
Gorilla, The 1927,N 21,20:1
Drums of Love 1928,Ja 25,20:4
Trail of '98, The 1928,Mr 21,30:3
Mad Hour, The 1928,Ap 16,20:5
Perfect Crime, The 1928,Ag 6,15:2
Alias Jimmy Valentine 1928,N 16,28:6
Redskin 1929,Ja 28,21:1
Conquest 1929,F 11,26:3
Bridge of San Luis Rey, The 1929,My 20,22:6
Thunderbolt 1929,Je 21,17:2
Insidious Dr Fu Manchu, The 1929,Jl 22,17:1
Skin Deep 1929,S 30,23:1
Show of Shows 1929,N 21,24:5
Tiger Rose 1929,D 25,23:1
Burning Up 1930,F 8,12:5
She Couldn't Say No 1930,F 16,III,8:1
Mammy 1930,Mr 27,24:5
Under a Texas Moon 1930,Ap 4,22:1
Murder Will Out 1930,Ap 14,24:2
Numbered Men 1930,Je 9,23:3
Common Clay 1930,Ag 2,16:4
Dancing Sweeties 1930,Ag 16,8:3
Big Trail, The 1930,O 25,20:3
One Night at Susie's 1930,N 24,26:5
Tom Sawyer 1930,D 20,20:6
Fighting Caravans 1931,Ja 26,21:1
Millionaire, The 1931,Ap 9,30:5
Virtuous Husband 1931,My 8,30:2
Unholy Garden 1931,O 29,27:1
Man I Killed, The 1932,Ja 20,17:4
Hatchet Man, The 1932,F 4,25:2
Arsene Lupin 1932,F 27,22:1
Beast of the City, The 1932,Mr 14,13:3
Scandal for Sale 1932,Ap 3,26:2
Grand Hotel 1932,Ap 13,23:2
Scarface, The Shame of the Nation
  1932,My 20,22:3
Night Court 1932,My 27,27:5
Strangers of the Evening 1932,Je 4,9:2
Cabin in the Cotton 1932,S 30,17:3
Red Dust 1932,N 5,12:5
Afraid to Talk 1932,D 19,19:5
Corruption 1933,Je 20,22:7
Murder on the Blackboard 1934,Je 20,24:2
Black Fury 1935,Ap 11,27:2
Diamond Jim 1935,Ag 24,18:2
Tale of Two Cities, A 1935,D 26,21:2
Souls at Sea 1937,Ag 10,23:2
Hold 'Em Navy 1937,N 6,14:2
Stand-In 1937,N 19,27:2
Yank at Oxford, A 1938,F 25,15:1
Arsene Lupin Returns 1938,Mr 9,21:1
Making the Headlines 1938,Ap 1,17:2

College Swing 1938,Ap 28,27:2
Invisible Stripes 1940,Ja 13,11:2
Brigham Young - Frontiersman 1940,S 21,13:2
Youth Will Be Served 1940,N 15,25:2
Chad Hanna 1940,D 26,23:1
Ball of Fire 1942,Ja 16,25:2
Moontide 1942,Ap 30,14:1
This Gun for Hire 1942,My 14,23:2
Ten Gentlemen From West Point 1942,Je 5,23:3
Hitler's Madman 1943,Ag 28,15:1

Marshall, Virginia

Daddy's Gone A-Hunting 1925,F 24,17:3
How Baxter Buttered In 1925,Je 23,24:3
My Own Pal 1926,Mr 15,18:3

Marshall, Vivian

Women's Prison 1955,F 3,18:5

Marshall, William

Flowing Gold 1940,S 2,19:3
Santa Fe Trail 1940,D 21,21:2
Belle of the Yukon 1945,Mr 30,18:4
State Fair 1945,Ag 31,14:3
Murder in the Music Hall 1946,Ap 15,22:2
Earl Carroll Sketchbook 1946,Ag 30,13:2
That Brennan Girl 1946,D 9,34:3
Blackmail 1947,Ag 5,26:3
Lydia Bailey 1952,My 31,12:5
Demetrius and the Gladiators 1954,Je 19,9:1
Something of Value 1957,My 11,24:6
Boston Strangler, The 1968,O 17,52:1

Marshall, William (Director)

Adventures of Captain Fabian 1951,D 14,36:2

Marshall, William (Producer)

Adventures of Captain Fabian 1951,D 14,36:2

Marshall, Zena

Snowbound 1949,F 21,20:2
Sleeping Car to Trieste 1949,Ap 18,18:6
Lost People, The 1950,O 2,19:4
So Long at the Fair 1951,Ja 22,14:2
Marry Me 1952,Mr 14,27:3
Caretaker's Daughter, The 1953,Ag 20,18:5
Let's Be Happy 1957,My 25,25:1
Dr No 1963,My 30,20:1

Marshe, Vera

Getting Gertie's Garter 1946,F 4,21:2
Hucksters, The 1947,Jl 18,21:2
Crimson Key, The 1947,O 18,9:2
Where There's Life 1947,D 25,32:1
You Gotta Stay Happy 1948,N 5,29:2
Davy Crockett, Indian Scout 1950,Mr 17,28:3

Marshman, D M Jr (Screenwriter)

Sunset Boulevard 1950,Ag 11,15:2
Taxi 1953,Ja 22,20:3

Marsland, James

Mikado, The 1967,Mr 15,53:1

Marson, Aileen

My Song For You 1935,My 27,20:6
Tenth Man, The 1937,N 15,15:2

Marstini, Rosita

Lover of Camille, The 1924,N 11,14:1
Redeeming Sin, The 1925,Ja 20,18:2
Big Parade, The 1925,N 20,18:1 (In Addenda)
We Americans 1928,Mr 29,25:3
Hot for Paris 1930,Ja 4,21:1
I Cover the Waterfront 1933,My 18,17:3
In Love With Life 1934,My 12,12:3
Holiday in Mexico 1946,Ag 16,19:3

Marston, Joel

There's a Girl in my Heart 1950,Ja 20,29:2
Last Voyage, The 1960,F 20,14:2
Ring of Fire 1961,Ag 17,18:2

Marston, John

Love Is a Racket 1932,Je 11,9:3
Skyscraper Souls 1932,Ag 5,11:2
Cabin in the Cotton 1932,S 30,17:3
Three on a Match 1932,O 29,18:4
Scarlet Dawn 1932,N 4,25:4
Silver Dollar 1932,D 23,20:1
Son of a Sailor 1933,N 30,38:4
Son of Kong 1933,D 30,9:2
All of Me 1934,F 5,19:2
Pursuit of Happiness, The 1934,O 26,25:1

Mart, Gin

Cleopatra 1963,Je 13,29:1

Martan, Nita

Lady Be Good 1928,My 28,23:2
Twin Beds 1929,Jl 15,25:1
Chasing Rainbows 1930,F 22,13:1

Martel, Arlene

Angels From Hell 1968,O 24,55:5

Martel, Christiane

So This Is Paris 1955,F 12,11:1

Martel, June

Front Page Woman 1935,Jl 12,15:1
Fighting Youth 1935,N 2,13:3
Her Husband Lies 1937,Mr 18,20:1
Santa Fe Stampede 1939,Ap 26,27:3

Martel, S Z

Gilda 1946,Mr 15,27:2

Martel, William

Red Menace, The 1949,Je 27,18:2

Martell, Alphonse

Night Bird, The 1928,O 2,23:5
Dream of Love 1928,D 24,11:1

Martell, Alphonse— Cont

Count of Monte Cristo, The 1934,S 27,25:2
Girl From Scotland Yard, The 1937,My 31,11:2
Doctor Rhythm 1938,My 19,25:2
Swingtime Johnny 1943,D 17,23:3
Enter Arsene Lupin 1944,D 2,17:6

Martell, Donna

Love Is a Many-Splendored Thing
  1955,Ag 19,10:1

Martell, Gregg

Red Menace, The 1949,Je 27,18:2
Undertow 1949,D 16,37:2
I Was a Shoplifter 1950,Ap 28,26:3
Winchester 73 1950,Je 8,38:2
Under the Gun 1951,F 23,33:2
Double Crossbones 1951,Ap 27,19:2
Affair in Trinidad 1952,Jl 31,14:2
Dinosaurusi 1960,S 9,36:4

Martell, Karl

Heimt ruft, Die; Home Is Calling 1938,Jl 9,10:3

Martell, Kurt

Steel Trap, The 1952,N 13,35:2

Martell, Kurt (Narrator)

One-Way Ticket to Hell 1955,D 8,45:1

Martell, Peter

Cobra, The 1968,Mr 28,52:3
Violent Four, The 1968,Ag 15,46:2

Martelli, Anna

Zappatore 1932,Mr 28,11:2

Marten, Felix

Frantic 1961,Je 12,34:1
Maxime 1962,O 25,48:3
Bonne Soupe, La 1964,Mr 16,37:1

Marten, Philip

Loneliness of the Long Distance Runner, The
  1962,O 9,44:1

Martenov, Anton

Wait for Me 1945,Mr 19,23:3

MARTENS

See Also MARTINS

Martens, Lena Von

Fall of the Roman Empire, The 1964,Mr 27,14:2

Martens, Paul

Stelldichein im Schwarzwald, Ein; Rendezvous in
  the Black Forest, A 1937,F 20,9:3

Martenson, Mona

Sealed Lips 1928,Ap 17,27:2

Marter, Ian

Doctor Faustus 1968,F 7,38:1

Marti, Alberto

Martin Garatuza 1935,S 30,13:1
Madre Querida 1935,D 23,15:5
Todo un Hombre 1936,Ja 6,20:5
Sor Juana Ines de la Cruz 1936,Je 6,21:2
Mujeres Sin Alma 1936,D 12,29:4
Don Juan Tenorio 1937,D 28,29:3
Noches de Gloria; Glorious Nights
  1938,Ap 23,19:3
A la Orilla de un Palmar; At the Edge of a Palm
  Grove 1938,D 17,10:4
Casa del Ogro, La; House of the Ogre, The
  1939,F 13,13:2
Cada Loco con su Tema; Every Madman to his
  Specialty 1939,Ap 29,13:3
Capitan Aventurero, El; Adventureous Captain,
  The 1939,O 3,19:5
Viejo Amor, Un; Old Love, An 1940,Ja 29,11:6
Perfidia; Perfidy 1940,F 17,9:3

Martial, J F

Panic 1947,N 27,50:2

MARTIN

See Also MARTON, MARTYN

Martin, Al (Original Author)

Lost Jungle, The 1934,Je 8,18:1
Crimson Romance 1934,O 13,10:1
Trapped by Television 1936,Je 15,24:3
Standing Room Only 1944,F 23,17:2

Martin, Al (Screenwriter)

Shadow Strikes, The 1937,S 13,17:1
Peck's bad Boy With the Circus 1939,Ja 11,17:4
Flying Wild 1941,Ap 12,19:3
Invisible Ghost, The 1941,My 8,21:2
Mad Doctor of Market Street, The 1942,Ja 5,21:5
Devil With Hitler, The 1942,O 19,15:2
Carolina Blues 1944,D 8,26:6
Amazon Quest 1949,My 14,9:3

Martin, Alexander

Without a Home 1939,Ap 1,17:3

Martin, Alexander (Director)

Without a Home 1939,Ap 1,17:3

Martin, Allen Jr

Johnny Holiday 1950,My 17,36:1

Martin, Allen Langdon (Original Author)

Smilin' Through 1922,Ap 17,22:3

Martin, Andra

Lady Takes a Flyer, The 1958,Ja 30,19:2
Big Beat, The 1958,Je 26,23:4
Thing That Couldn't Die, The 1958,Je 28,13:7
Up Periscope 1959,Mr 5,35:4
Fever in the Blood 1961,Ap 20,30:4

Martin, Antonio

Pandora and the Flying Dutchman 1951,D 7,35:2

Martin, Barney
Charly 1968,S 24,55:1
Martin, Bill
Saturday's Hero 1951,S 12,37:2
Martin, Bruce (Miscellaneous)
Journey to Jerusalem, A 1968,N 18,59:1
Martin, Buddy
David Copperfield 1923,N 6,23:3
Martin, Charles
Gentle Giant 1968,Ap 20,26:1
Martin, Charles (Director)
No Leave, No Love 1946,O 18,29:2
My Dear Secretary 1949,F 14,15:4
Death of a Scoundrel 1956,N 6,30:1
If He Hollers, Let Him Go 1968,O 10,59:7
Martin, Charles (Original Author)
I'll Be Seeing You 1945,Ap 6,20:6
On an Island With You 1948,Jl 30,13:2
Martin, Charles (Producer)
Death of a Scoundrel 1956,N 6,30:1
If He Hollers, Let Him Go 1968,O 10,59:7
Martin, Charles (Screenwriter)
Missing Guest, The 1938,S 7,30:7
No Leave, No Love 1946,O 18,29:2
On an Island With You 1948,Jl 30,13:2
My Dear Secretary 1949,F 14,15:4
Death of a Scoundrel 1956,N 6,30:1
Secret Door, The 1964,Je 4,28:1
If He Hollers, Let Him Go 1968,O 10,59:7
Martin, Chris-Pin
Cisco Kid, The 1931,O 24,20:3
Girl Crazy 1932,Mr 25,23:3
Painted Woman, The 1932,S 16,24:4
Four Frightened People 1934,Ja 27,9:2
Under the Pampas Moon 1935,My 31,11:1
Gay Desperado, The 1936,O 9,31:4
Tropic Holiday 1938,Je 30,21:2
Texans, The 1938,Jl 28,23:2
Stagecoach 1939,Mr 3,21:1
Return of the Cisco Kid, The 1939,Ap 29,13:2
Girl and the Gambler, The 1939,Je 28,17:3
Frontier Marshal 1939,Jl 29,18:2
Cisco Kid and the Lady, The 1939,D 25,29:2
Viva Cisco Kid 1940,Mr 22,23:4
Lucky Cisco Kid 1940,Je 24,19:5
Down Argentine Way 1940,O 18,25:1
Gay Caballero, The 1940,O 25,25:3
Mark of Zorro, The 1940,N 4,23:2
Romance of the Rio Grande 1940,D 25,33:4
Bad Man, The 1941,Ap 4,25:1
Ride on Vaquero 1941,Ap 19,20:2
Tombstone, The Town too Tough to Die
1942,Jl 27,18:2
American Empire 1943,Ja 14,25:4
Ox-Bow Incident, The 1943,My 10,15:2 (In
Addenda)
Ali Baba and the Forty Thieves 1944,Mr 16,17:3
Tampico 1944,Je 2,21:2
San Antonio 1945,D 29,19:5
Fugitive, The 1947,D 26,22:2
Belle Star's Daughter 1949,Ja 10,19:2
Mexican Hayride 1949,Ja 12,33:3
Beautiful Blonde From Bashful Bend, The
1949,My 28,11:2
Millionaire for Christy, A 1951,O 5,24:3
Martin, Christiane
Four Days' Leave 1950,Je 9,29:4
Martin, Christopher
Rescue, The 1929,Ja 14,20:1
Martin, Claude
Champs-Elysees 1939,F 28,17:2
Martin, Conrado S
Mad Queen, The 1950,O 27,24:3
Martin, Daniel
Tarantos, Los 1964,Je 30,22:1
Fistful of Dollars, A 1967,F 2,29:1
Martin, Dean
My Friend Irma 1949,S 29,39:2
My Friend Irma Goes West 1950,Ag 3,20:2
At War With the Army 1951,Ja 25,21:5
That's My Boy 1951,Ag 2,18:1
Sailor Beware 1952,F 1,17:1
Jumping Jacks 1952,Jl 24,30:2
Stooge, The 1953,F 5,19:2
Scared Stiff 1953,Jl 3,10:2
Caddy, The 1953,S 18,16:6
Money From Home 1954,F 27,11:3
Living It Up 1954,Jl 24,6:6
Three Ring Circus 1954,D 25,7:2
You're Never too Young 1955,Ag 26,10:2
Artists and Models 1955,D 22,20:1
Pardners 1956,Jl 26,20:2
Hollywood or Bust 1956,D 24,8:1
Ten Thousand Bedrooms 1957,Ap 4,37:1
Young Lions, The 1958,Ap 3,23:1
Some Came Running 1959,Ja 23,17:1
Rio Bravo 1959,Mr 19,40:2
Career 1959,O 9,24:1
Who Was That Lady? 1960,Ap 16,10:1
Bells Are Ringing 1960,Je 24,31:2
Ocean's Eleven 1960,Ag 11,19:1
All in a Nights Work 1961,Mr 23,28:1
Ada 1961,Ag 26,15:1

Sergeants 3 1962,F 12,28:2
Who's Got the Action? 1962,D 26,5:4
Toys in the Attic 1963,Ag 1,17:2
4 for Texas 1963,D 26,33:3
Who's Been Sleeping in My Bed? 1963,D 26,33:2
What a Way to Go! 1964,My 15,44:1
Robin and the 7 Hoods 1964,Ag 6,20:1
Kiss Me, Stupid 1964,D 23,22:2
Sons of Katie Elder, The 1965,Ag 26,40:3
Marriage on the Rocks 1965,S 16,00:0
Silencers, The 1966,Mr 17,35:1
Texas Across the River 1966,N 24,65:1
Murderers' Row 1966,D 22,40:3
Rough Night in Jericho 1967,N 9,56:4
Ambushers, The 1967,D 23,29:1
How to Save a Marriage - And Ruin Your Life
1968,Ja 19,30:1
Bandolero 1968,Jl 18,26:2
5 Card Stud 1968,Ag 1,24:1
Martin, Dewey
Kansas Raiders 1951,Ja 26,19:2
Thing, The 1951,My 3,34:4
Big Sky, The 1952,Ag 20,21:1
Men of the Fighting Lady 1954,My 8,15:2
Prisoner of War 1954,My 10,20:2
Land of the Pharaohs 1955,Jl 27,15:2
Desperate Hours, The 1955,O 6,25:1
Proud and Profane, The 1956,Je 14,41:2
Ten Thousand Bedrooms 1957,Ap 4,37:1
Martin, Dick
Hot Horse 1963,Jl 25,14:2
Glass Bottom Boat, The 1966,Je 10,54:1
Martin, Don (Original Author)
Shakedown 1950,S 4,11:2
Martin, Don (Screenwriter)
Pretender, The 1947,Ag 12,26:2
Arrow in the Dust 1954,My 1,13:2
Martin, Duke
City Gone Wild, The 1927,D 6,27:1
We're in the Air Now 1927,D 31,31:1
Fortune Hunter, The 1928,Ja 10,28:4
Flying Romeos 1928,Ap 3,33:2
Across to Singapore 1928,Ap 30,18:3
Danger Street 1928,S 25,29:4 (In Addenda)
Moran of the Marines 1928,O 15,16:1
Marriage by Contract 1928,N 13,37:1
True Heaven 1929,F 11,26:3
Lost Zeppelin, The 1930,F 3,17:1
Martin, Eddie
Place of One's Own, A 1949,F 8,30:2
Martin, Edie
Trooship 1938,Ap 26,18:2
Adventure for Two 1945,D 14,24:5
Lavender Hill Mob, The 1951,O 16,35:2
Man in the White Suit, The 1952,Ap 1,35:2
Time, Gentlemen, Please 1953,S 24,39:2
Titfield Thunderbolt, The 1953,O 6,34:2
Lease of Life 1956,F 10,18:1
Too Many Crooks 1959,Ap 25,14:2
Martin, Edwin L (Director)
Invisible Agent 1942,Ag 6,23:2
Martin, Ellen
Open the Door and See all the People
1964,Ap 2,28:1
Martin, Ernst (Director)
Heimatland; Homeland 1939,O 28,11:2
Martin, Ethel
On the Riviera 1951,My 24,47:1
Martin, Eugenio (Director)
Ugly Ones, The 1968,D 12,62:5
Martin, Eugenio (Screenwriter)
Ugly Ones, The 1968,D 12,62:5
Martin, Francis (Director)
Tillie and Gus 1933,N 13,21:1
Martin, Francis (Screenwriter)
College Rhythm 1934,N 24,19:1
Mississippi 1935,Ap 18,27:2
Big Broadcast of 1936, The 1935,S 16,15:2
Strike Me Pink 1936,Ja 17,15:2
Collegiate 1936,Ja 23,25:2
Princess Comes Across, The 1936,Je 4,27:2
Rhythm on the Range 1936,Jl 30,22:1
Big Broadcast of 1937, The 1936,O 22,31:1
Waikiki Wedding 1937,Mr 25,29:1
Artists and Models 1937,Ag 5,19:2
Big Broadcast of 1938, The 1938,Mr 10,16:2
College Swing 1938,Ap 28,27:2
One Night in the Tropics 1940,D 20,33:2
Unidentified Flying Objects 1956,Je 13,46:2
Martin, Freddy
Mayor of Forty-Fourth Street, The
1942,Je 11,27:4
What's Buzzin Cousin 1943,Jl 23,21:4
Martin, Freddy and Orchestra
Seven Days' Leave 1942,D 11,33:2
Hit Parade of 1943 1943,Ap 16,24:3
Stage Door Canteen 1943,Je 25,13:2
What's Buzzin Cousin 1943,Jl 23,21:4
Martin, George
On the Riviera 1951,My 24,47:1
Pistol for Ringo, A 1966,N 3,45:4

Martin, George Victor (Original Author)
Our Vines Have Tender Grapes 1945,S 7,21:2
Martin, Georges Andre
Robber Symphony 1937,Ja 27,17:2
Martin, Gloria
Odio; Hate 1940,Ap 6,13:2
Martin, Helen
Phenix City Story, The 1955,S 3,9:1
Martin, Helen (Screenwriter)
Invisible Ghost, The 1941,My 8,21:2
Martin, Helen R (Original Author)
Snob, The 1924,D 15,14:1
Parasite, The 1925,F 16,24:1
Martin, Herbert
Dawn Over Ireland 1938,F 19,19:2
Martin, Hugh (Composer)
Best Foot Forward 1943,Je 30,25:2
Meet Me in St Louis 1944,N 29,20:2
Ziegfeld Follies 1946,Mr 23,8:3
Grandma Moses 1950,O 24,34:6
Athena 1954,D 22,28:2
Martin, J Lockard
Lost in a Harem 1944,N 9,23:2
Martin, J S (Miscellaneous)
Spain Fights on 1939,F 13,13:2
Martin, J S (Screenwriter)
We Are the Marines 1942,D 14,19:2
Fighting Lady, The 1945,Ja 16,17:2
Martin, James
Babes in Toyland 1961,D 15,49:1
Martin, Janet
Lady and the Monster, The 1944,Ap 8,9:2
Martin, Jared
Murder a la Mod 1968,My 2,57:1
Martin, Jaye
Something to Shout About 1943,Ap 8,27:3
Martin, Jean
Last Chance, The 1945,N 28,21:6
Battle of Algiers, The 1967,S 21,56:1
Martin, John (Narrator)
George Washington Carver 1940,Ap 17,26:4
Monkey Into Man 1941,My 31,14:1
Martin, Jose Manuel
Spanish Affair 1958,F 6,24:1
Tarantos, Los 1964,Je 30,22:1
Martin, Karl Heinz (Director)
Paloma, La 1936,O 21,35:3
Abenteurer von Paris, Der 1937,My 29,20:3
Punks Kommt aus Amerika 1937,Je 12,8:2
Gluecklichste Ehe von Wien, Die; Happiest
Married Couple in Vienna, The 1938,O 8,10:2
Konzert in Tirol 1939,Ja 7,6:4
Du Bist mein Glueck; Thou Art my Joy
1940,Ja 6,9:2
Martin, Leonardo (Original Author)
Rocket From Calabuch 1958,O 8,41:1
Martin, Leonardo (Screenwriter)
Rocket From Calabuch 1958,O 8,41:1
Martin, Lewis
Three Guys Named Mike 1951,Mr 2,21:2
Ace in the Hole 1951,Je 30,8:6
Wild North, The 1952,My 12,21:2
Houdini 1953,Jl 3,10:2
War of the Worlds, The 1953,Ag 14,10:2
Arrowhead 1953,S 16,38:6
Caddy, The 1953,S 18,16:6
Witness to Murder 1954,Ap 16,16:4
Men of the Fighting Lady 1954,My 8,15:2
Cry Vengence 1955,F 19,18:3
Court Jester, The 1956,F 2,19:1
Slander 1957,Ja 17,34:4
Diary of a Madman 1963,Je 6,39:1
Martin, Lock
Day the Earth Stood Still, The 1951,S 19,37:1
Martin, Lori
Cape Fear 1962,Ap 19,35:2
Martin, Marcella
Gone With the Wind 1939,D 20,31:2
Martin, Margaret
Road to Singapore, The 1931,O 1,25:2
Siren of Atlantis 1949,Ag 22,13:1
Eagle and the Hawk, The 1950,Jl 6,31:2
Martin, Marguerite
One Way Street 1950,My 12,33:3
Men, The 1950,Jl 21,15:2
Martin, Marion
Sinners in Paradise 1938,My 20,17:2
Youth Takes a Fling 1938,O 17,12:1
Storm, The 1938,O 31,12:2
Sergeant Madden 1939,Mr 24,27:2
Invitation to Happiness 1939,Je 8,31:2
Man in the Iron Mask, The 1939,Jl 14,11:1
Boom Town 1940,S 6,25:2
Ellery Queen, Master Detective 1940,D 19,33:1
Tall, Dark and Handsome 1941,Ja 24,15:2
Lady From Cheyenne, The 1941,Ap 18,18:2
Big Store, The 1941,Je 27,14:4
Lady Scarface 1941,Ag 4,16:6
Week End for Three 1941,O 24,27:4
New Wine 1942,F 2,11:2
Powder Town 1942,Je 8,11:2
Mexican Spitfire at Sea 1942,Je 26,16:5
Big Street, The 1942,Ag 14,13:1

Martin, Marion— Cont
Mexican Spitfire's Elephant 1942,S 18,25:2
Tales of Manhattan 1942,S 25,25:1
They Got Me Covered 1943,Mr 5,20:2
Lady of Burlesque 1943,My 14,17:2
Swingtime Johnny 1943,D 17,23:3
Woman of the Town, The 1944,Mr 6,17:2
It Happened Tomorrow 1944,My 29,18:2
Deadline for Murder 1946,Je 29,22:7
Angel on my Shoulder 1946,O 21,27:2
That Brennan Girl 1946,D 9,34:3
Come to the Stable 1949,Jl 28,19:1
Mikado, The 1967,Mr 15,53:1
Martin, Mary
Great Victor Herbert, The 1939,D 7,35:1
Rhythm on the River 1940,Ag 29,23:2
Love Thy Neighbor 1940,D 18,32:5
Kiss the Boys Goodbye 1941,Ag 14,21:2
New York Town 1941,N 13,35:2
Birth of the Blues 1941,D 11,39:1
Star Spangled Rhythm 1942,D 31,20:1
Happy Go Lucky 1943,Mr 25,25:1
True to Life 1943,O 14,26:1
Night and Day 1946,Jl 26,16:2
Main Street to Broadway 1953,O 14,34:1
Martin, Maryse
Happy Road, The 1957,Je 21,20:2
Mitsou 1958,Ap 15,42:5
Martin, Melvyn
Strange Ones, The 1952,Jl 29,17:3
Martin, Millicent
Invasion Quartet 1961,D 11,41:2
Nothing but the Best 1964,Jl 14,28:1
Stop the World-I Want to Get Off
1966,My 12,54:2
Alfie 1966,Ag 25,42:1
Martin, Nan
Buster Keaton Story, The 1957,Ap 22,31:6
Mugger, The 1959,Je 25,20:7
Toys in the Attic 1963,Ag 1,17:2
For Love of Ivy 1968,Jl 18,26:1
Martin, Nell (Original Author)
Lord Byron of Broadway 1930,Mr 8,21:1
Martin, Nora
Hollywood Canteen 1944,D 16,19:2
Martin, Owen
Pajama Game, The 1957,Ag 30,12:2
Martin, Paul (Director)
Liebe Ist Liebe 1932,Je 2,25:2
Orient Express 1934,F 28,23:2
Glueckskinder 1937,Je 5,21:1
Untitled-Dance 1937,D 25,10:4
Sieben Ohrfeigen; Seven Slaps 1938,F 12,20:5
Lied der Wuste, Das; Desert Song 1940,F 3,9:3
Martin, Paul Anthony
Life at the Top 1965,D 15,53:1
Martin, Pete (Miscellaneous)
I Was a Communist for the F B I 1951,My 3,34:4
Martin, Philippe
Trial of Joan of Arc, The 1965,F 12,19:1
Martin, Quinn (Original Author)
Blondie Goes Latin 1941,F 26,17:3
Martin, Ray
Green Pastures, The 1936,Jl 17,20:1
Martin, Richard
Leopard Man, The 1943,My 20,26:4
Bombardier 1943,Jl 2,15:2
Falcon in Danger, The 1943,Jl 23,21:2
Iron Major, The 1943,N 1,12:5
Tender Comrade 1944,Je 2,21:2
Marine Raiders 1944,Jl 1,10:7
West of the Pecos 1945,Ag 11,14:6
Wanderer of the Wasteland 1945,S 29,12:2
Raiders, The 1952,D 13,19:2
Martin, Ross
Experiment in Terror 1962,Ap 14,14:1
Ceremony, The 1964,My 14,39:1
Great Race, The 1965,S 16,00:0
Martin, Sally
Timothy's Quest 1936,F 29,11:2
Jungle Princess 1936,D 24,21:3
Barrier, The 1937,N 27,21:2
Martin, Sheila
You Can't Fool an Irishman 1950,D 7,45:4
Martin, Skip
Masque of the Red Death, The 1964,S 17,52:6
Guess Who's Coming to Dinner 1967,D 12,56:1
Martin, Steve
Iron Man 1951,Ag 20,14:2
Martin, Strother
Attack! 1956,S 20,29:4
Sanctuary 1961,F 22,31:1
Deadly Companions, The 1962,Ap 12,41:7
Man Who Shot Liberty Valance, The
1962,My 24,29:2
Harper 1966,Mr 31,43:1
Flim Flam Man, The 1967,Ag 23,40:1
Cool Hand Luke 1967,N 2,58:1
Martin, Todd
Thomas Crown Affair, The 1968,Je 27,48:2
Martin, Tony
Sing, Baby, Sing 1936,S 12,20:1
Pigskin Parade 1936,N 14,23:3
Banjo on My Knee 1936,D 12,15:1

Holy Terror, The 1937,Ja 30,21:2
Sing and Be Happy 1937,Je 19,20:2
You Can't Have Everything 1937,Ag 4,15:2
Life Begins In College 1937,O 9,16:1
Ali Baba Goes to Town 1937,O 23,14:1
Sally, Irene and Mary 1938,F 26,9:2
Kentucky Moonshine 1938,My 21,9:2
Up the River 1938,D 3,11:2
Thanks For Everything 1938,D 10,13:2
Winner Take All 1939,Mr 31,19:3
Music in My Heart 1940,Ja 4,19:2
Ziegfeld Girl 1941,Ap 25,17:2
Big Store, The 1941,Je 27,14:4
Till the Clouds Roll By 1946,D 6,27:4
Casbah 1948,My 3,27:4
Two Tickets to Broadway 1951,N 22,47:2
Easy to Love 1953,N 27,99:9
Here Come the Girls 1953,D 26,10:1
Deep in my Heart 1954,D 10,35:2
Hit the Deck 1955,Mr 4,17:1
Let's Be Happy 1957,My 25,25:1
Martin, Townsend
Cradle Buster, The 1922,My 22,18:4
Martin, Townsend (Original Author)
American Venus, The 1926,Ja 26,25:2
Martin, Vivian
Unclaimed Goods 1918,Ap 15,13:3
Mirandy Smiles 1918,D 16,13:3
Louisiana 1919,Jl 21,12:3
Martin, Vivienne
Belles of St Trinian's, The 1954,D 23,13:4
Martin, W Thornton (Original Author)
Band Plays on, The 1934,D 22,21:2
Martin (Composer)
Broadway Rhythm 1944,Ap 14,24:6
Martin-Harvey, Michael
Robber Symphony 1937,Ja 27,17:2
Mutiny of the Elsinore, The 1939,F 16,17:2
Martindel, Edward
Clarence 1922,O 16,20:2
Day of Faith, The 1923,N 27,11:2
Love's Whirlpool 1924,Mr 11,16:2
Dixie Handicap, The 1924,D 30,15:3
Man Without a Country, The 1925,F 12,16:1
Sporting Venus, The 1925,My 11,14:3
Compromise 1925,O 27,23:3
Tony Runs Wild 1926,Ap 28,28:3
Duchess of Buffalo, The 1926,Ag 9,10:3
You'd Be Surprised 1926,S 27,27:3
Taxi, Taxi 1927,F 15,23:1
Fashions For Women 1927,Mr 28,26:4
Lovers 1927,Ap 19,24:4
Children of Divorce 1927,Ap 26,33:3
Venus of Venice 1927,My 3,25:1
Lonesome Ladies 1927,Ag 2,19:2
In old Kentucky 1927,N 21,20:1
Garden of Eden, The 1928,Mr 19,26:2
We Americans 1928,Mr 29,25:3
Singing Fool, The 1928,S 20,33:2
On Trial 1928,N 15,26:5
Desert Song, The 1929,My 2,20:6
Why Be Good? 1929,My 6,30:4
Aviator, The 1930,Ja 11,21:3
Song O' my Heart 1930,Mr 12,32:6
Rain or Shine 1930,Ag 8,11:1
Divorce Among Friends 1931,Ap 2,30:4
Gay Diplomat, The 1931,O 10,20:4
American Madness 1932,Ag 6,14:5
False Faces 1932,N 25,19:2
Afraid to Talk 1932,D 19,19:5
Martinelli, Alfredo
White Sister, The 1923,S 6,10:2
Romola 1924,D 2,13:2
Martinelli, Elsa
Indian Fighter, The 1955,D 22,20:1
Four Girls in Town 1957,Ja 17,34:5
Stowaway Girl 1957,N 6,43:3
Prisoner of the Volga 1960,Je 2,27:2
Blood and Roses 1961,O 12,41:4
Notte Brava, La 1962,Ja 25,25:2
Hatari 1962,Jl 12,19:1
Pigeon That Took Rome, The 1962,Ag 23,25:1
Trial, The 1963,F 21,5:1
V I P's, The 1963,S 20,29:1
Rampage 1963,O 17,39:2
10th Victim, The 1965,D 21,46:1
Marco the Magnificent 1966,D 15,60:1
Woman Times Seven 1967,Je 28,38:1
Oldest Profession, The (Roman Nights); Roman
Nights (The Oldest Profession) 1968,N 8,42:1
Martinelli, Frank
Date With the Falcon, A 1941,N 25,33:2
Martinelli, Jean
Frochard et les Deux Orphelines, La
1934,F 7,16:2
To Catch a Thief 1955,Ag 5,14:2
Rouge et Noir 1958,Ap 9,42:1
Martinet, Henri (Producer)
Nuestra Tierra de Paz; Our Land of Peace
1940,Je 1,12:3

Martinez, Elena
Texas Rangers, The 1936,S 24,29:1
Martinez, Elsa
Nuestra Tierra de Paz; Our Land of Peace
1940,Je 1,12:3
Martinez, J J
Cruz Diablo 1935,Ap 6,10:1
Martin Garatuza 1935,S 30,13:1
Martinez, Paco
Cruz Diablo 1935,Ap 6,10:1
Martinez, Tony
Barricade 1950,Mr 25,8:6
Martinez, Velia
Big Boodle, The 1957,Mr 12,38:1
Martini, Depi
Phaedra 1962,O 19,24:1
Martini, Emilia
Roof, The 1959,My 13,43:4
Martini, Giuseppe
Roof, The 1959,My 13,43:4
Martini, Lou
Hoodlum Priest, The 1961,Ap 3,28:5
Martini, Nino
Paramount on Parade 1930,Ap 21,20:4
Here's to Romance 1935,O 3,29:2
Gay Desperado, The 1936,O 9,31:4
Music for Madame 1937,O 23,14:1
One Night With You 1949,F 21,20:2
Martino, Adriana
Boheme, La 1965,O 20,51:2
Martino, Giovanni
Lady's Morals, A 1930,N 8,21:3
Martino, Luciano (Screenwriter)
Beautiful but Dangerous 1958,F 6,24:1
Warrior Empress, The 1961,Ag 10,17:4
Colossus of Rhodes, The 1961,D 14,55:6
Martino, vittorio (Producer)
Psycosissimo 1962,S 8,16:2
Martino, Vittorio (Screenwriter)
Dead Woman's Kiss, A 1951,O 6,16:4
Martino (Screenwriter)
Duel of the Titans 1963,Ag 8,19:1
Martinovich, Peter
Backfire 1965,Ap 27,27:1
MARTINS
See Also MARTENS
Martins, Orlando
Hasty Heart, The 1950,Ja 21,10:5
Good Time Girl 1950,S 25,18:5
American Guerrilla in the Philippines
1950,N 8,37:2
Kisenga, Man of Africa 1952,Mr 7,18:2
Ivory Hunter 1952,Ag 19,19:1
West of Zanzibar 1955,Ja 18,31:2
Simba 1955,O 22,24:2
Safari 1956,Je 21,35:2
Tarzan and the Lost Safari 1957,Ap 13,12:3
Abandon Ship 1957,Ap 18,35:1
Sapphire 1959,N 3,27:1
Call Me Bwana 1963,Jl 4,9:1
Mister Moses 1965,My 13,32:1
Martinson, Leslie H (Director)
Atomic Kid, The 1954,D 4,14:2
Lad: A Dog 1963,My 2,40:2
PT 109 1963,Je 27,23:1
FBI Code 98 1964,Ap 9,25:6
For Those Who Think Young 1964,Jl 9,27:1
Batman 1966,Ag 25,42:4
Fathom 1967,D 14,62:1
Martinson, S
Marionettes 1934,My 8,28:6
Golden Key, The 1939,D 21,29:3
Secret Agent 1949,F 10,37:3
Idiot, The 1960,Jl 22,11:2
Night Before Christmas, A 1963,D 16,44:4
Martinson, S A
Diary of a Revolutionist 1932,Je 10,22:3
Oppenheim Family, The 1939,My 24,29:2
Martinson, Sergei
Spring Song 1942,S 12,9:2
Marriage 1945,F 22,31:3
Martinson, Sovol
Sword and the Dragon, The 1960,N 17,46:3
Martinyunk, Griory
There Was an old Couple 1967,My 22,53:1
Martlew, Mary
Anna Karenina 1948,Ap 28,32:2
Quiet Week-End 1948,Ag 20,13:2
Forbidden Street, The 1949,My 14,9:2
MARTON
See Also MARTIN, MARTYN
Marton, Andrew (Director)
School for Husbands 1939,F 7,16:2
Little Bit of Heaven, A 1940,N 8,24:2
Secret of Stamboul, The 1941,My 31,14:1
Gentle Annie 1945,My 5,11:5
Gallant Bess 1946,D 6,27:6
King Solomon's Mines 1950,N 10,35:1
Wild North, The 1952,My 12,21:2
Devil Makes Three, The 1952,Ag 30,6:2
Mask of the Himalayas 1953,Ag 12,22:3
Men of the Fighting Lady 1954,My 8,15:2
Prisoner of War 1954,My 10,20:2

Marton, Andrew (Director)— Cont
 Green Fire 1954,D 25,7:1
 Seven Wonders of the World 1956,Ap 11,29:1
 It Happened in Athens 1962,N 15,46:2
 55 Days at Peking 1963,My 30,20:1
 Thin Red Line, The 1964,O 29,38:1
 Crack in the World 1965,My 13,32:2
 Clarence, the Cross-Eyed Lion 1965,Ag 5,15:3
 Around the World Under the Sea 1966,Jl 21,20:2
 Africa-Texas Style! 1967,Jl 13,30:2
Marton, Andrew (Miscellaneous)
 Longest Day, The 1962,O 5,28:1
Marton, Andrew (Producer)
 Around the World Under the Sea 1966,Jl 21,20:2
 Africa-Texas Style! 1967,Jl 13,30:2
Marton, Endre (Director)
 Elnoek Kisasszony 1935,O 12,12:3
Marton, George (Producer)
 Whispering City 1948,My 10,25:5
Marton, Jarmila
 Mask of the Himalayas 1953,Ag 12,22:3
Marton, Pierre (Screenwriter)
 Arabesque 1966,My 6,54:1
Martonffy, Emil (Director)
 Vasember 1935,D 9,25:3
 Okos Mama, Az 1936,Ap 13,15:2
 Rozmaring; Rosemary 1940,F 10,19:3
 Eb Ura Fako 1940,Mr 23,16:4
Martori, Ramon
 Goyescas 1944,My 29,18:3
 Nail, The 1949,Jl 1,14:6
Martsevich, Eduard
 Fathers and Sons 1960,D 26,27:2
Marty, Marthe
 Marseillaise 1939,N 6,20:2
Marty, Mme
 Poil de Carotte 1933,My 26,24:2
MARTYN
 See Also MARTIN, MARTON
Martyn, Gilbert (Miscellaneous)
 World in Flames, The 1940,O 24,31:2
Martyn, Marty
 Night after Night 1932,O 31,18:4
Martyn, Peter
 Folly to be Wise 1953,D 28,17:2
Marus, Gina
 Shadows of Fear 1928,N 6,35:1
Maruta, B
 On his Own 1939,S 13,31:3
Maruta, V
 University of Life 1941,F 26,17:1
Maruta, Vassaili
 Village Teacher 1948,Jl 5,8:4
Maruyama, Sadao
 Kimiko 1937,Ap 13,31:3
Maruzin, A
 Young Pushkin 1937,D 16,35:3
Maruzzi, Tom (Screenwriter)
 Sniper's Ridge 1961,Ag 24,25:3
Marvan, J
 Inspector General, The 1937,N 25,37:1
Marvell, Holt (Miscellaneous)
 Gay Desperado, The 1936,O 9,31:4
Marvell, Holt (Original Author)
 Invitation to the Waltz 1938,Jl 2,10:3
Marvell, Holt (Screenwriter)
 Magic Night 1932,N 3,25:3
Marvin, Albert (Original Author)
 Ugly Ones, The 1968,D 12,62:5
Marvin, Chris
 Boots and Saddles 1937,N 8,19:2
Marvin, Frankie
 Boots and Saddles 1937,N 8,19:2
 Under Western Stars 1938,Je 25,7:3
 Racketeers of the Range 1939,Je 8,31:4
Marvin, Grace
 Phantom of the Opera, The 1925,S 7,15:3
Marvin, Johnny (Composer)
 Under Western Stars 1938,Je 25,7:3
Marvin, Lee
 Duel at Silver Creek 1952,Ag 2,7:6
 Hangman's Knot 1952,Jl 11,45:3
 Eight Iron Men 1953,Ja 2,11:1
 Stranger Wore a Gun, The 1953,Jl 30,20:3
 Glory Brigade, The 1953,Ag 15,8:4
 Big Heat, The 1953,O 15,43:2
 Wild One, The 1953,D 31,9:2
 Gorilla at Large 1954,Je 12,13:2
 Caine Mutiny, The 1954,Je 25,17:1
 Raid, The 1954,Ag 21,10:4
 Bad Day at Black Rock 1955,F 2,22:2
 Violent Saturday 1955,My 12,32:2
 Not as a Stranger 1955,Je 29,24:1
 Life in the Balance, A 1955,Jl 14,19:1
 Pete Kelly's Blues 1955,Ag 19,10:1
 I Died a Thousand Times 1955,N 10,45:2
 Shack out on 101 1956,Ja 10,26:2
 Attack! 1956,S 20,29:4
 Pillars of the Sky 1956,O 13,15:2
 Rack, The 1956,N 6,30:1
 Raintree County 1957,D 21,22:1
 Comancheros, The 1961,N 2,42:1
 Man Who Shot Liberty Valance, The
  1962,My 24,29:2
 Donovan's Reef 1963,Jl 25,14:1
 Killers, The 1964,Jl 18,10:4
 Cat Ballou 1965,Je 25,36:1
 Ship of Fools 1965,Jl 29,18:1
 Professionals, The 1966,N 3,45:1
 Dirty Dozen, The 1967,Je 16,36:1
 Point Blank 1967,S 19,53:1
 London Scene, The (Tonite Let's All Make Love
  in London); Tonite Let's All Make Love in
  London (The London Scene) 1967,S 27,39:1
 Sergeant Ryker 1968,Mr 21,56:2
Marvin, Mia
 You Said a Mouthful 1932,N 18,23:2
MARX
 See Also MARKS
Marx, Arthur (Original Author)
 Impossible Years, The 1968,D 6,54:1
Marx, Arthur (Screenwriter)
 Global Affair, A 1964,My 7,31:2
 I'll Take Sweden 1965,Ag 12,30:4
 Eight on the Lam 1967,Ap 27,52:1
Marx, Chico
 Monkey Business 1931,O 8,22:6
 Horse Feathers 1932,Ag 11,12:2
 Duck Soup 1933,N 23,24:2
 Night at the Opera, A 1935,D 7,22:1
 Day at the Races, A 1937,Je 18,25:2
 Room Service 1938,S 22,27:1
 At the Circus 1939,N 17,17:2
 Go West 1941,F 21,16:2
 Big Store, The 1941,Je 27,14:4
 Night in Casablanca, A 1946,Ag 12,17:2
 Love Happy 1950,Ap 8,9:4
 Story of Mankind, The 1957,N 9,31:2
Marx, Chris
 Dark Odyssey 1961,Je 26,22:2
Marx, Groucho
 Monkey Business 1931,O 8,22:6
 Horse Feathers 1932,Ag 11,12:2
 Duck Soup 1933,N 23,24:2
 Night at the Opera, A 1935,D 7,22:1
 Day at the Races, A 1937,Je 18,25:2
 Room Service 1938,S 22,27:1
 At the Circus 1939,N 17,17:2
 Go West 1941,F 21,16:2
 Big Store, The 1941,Je 27,14:4
 Night in Casablanca, A 1946,Ag 12,17:2
 Copacabana 1947,Jl 12,7:2
 Love Happy 1950,Ap 8,9:4
 Mr Music 1950,D 21,34:3
 Double Dynamite 1951,D 26,19:4
 Girl in Every Port, A 1952,F 14,23:1
 Story of Mankind, The 1957,N 9,31:2
Marx, Groucho (Screenwriter)
 King and the Chorus Girl, The 1937,Mr 29,14:4
Marx, Harpo
 Too Many Kisses 1925,Mr 3,20:1
 Monkey Business 1931,O 8,22:6
 Horse Feathers 1932,Ag 11,12:2
 Duck Soup 1933,N 23,24:2
 Night at the Opera, A 1935,D 7,22:1
 Day at the Races, A 1937,Je 18,25:2
 Room Service 1938,S 22,27:1
 At the Circus 1939,N 17,17:2
 Go West 1941,F 21,16:2
 Big Store, The 1941,Je 27,14:4
 Stage Door Canteen 1943,Je 25,13:2
 Night in Casablanca, A 1946,Ag 12,17:2
 Love Happy 1950,Ap 8,9:4
 Story of Mankind, The 1957,N 9,31:2
Marx, Harpo (Original Author)
 Love Happy 1950,Ap 8,9:4
Marx, Samuel (Original Author)
 Night Mayor, The 1932,N 25,19:2
 Student Tour 1934,O 31,17:3
 Grounds for Marriage 1951,Ja 12,24:6
Marx, Samuel (Producer)
 Longest Night, The 1936,O 17,21:2
 Sinner Take All 1937,F 3,27:1
 Family Affair, A 1937,Ap 20,29:2
 Girls' School 1938,N 3,27:1
 Unholy Partners 1941,D 29,21:4
 Yank on the Burma Road, A 1942,Ja 29,25:3
 Lassie Come Home 1943,O 8,15:4
 This Man's Navy 1945,Ap 16,18:6
 Son of Lassie 1945,Je 11,12:1
 Beginning or the End, The 1947,F 21,15:1
 My Brother Talks to Horses 1947,Je 19,27:4
 Lady Without Passport, A 1950,Ag 4,13:2
 Grounds for Marriage 1951,Ja 12,24:6
 Assignment-Paris 1952,O 25,12:6
 Ain't Misbehavin' 1955,Jl 2,13:2
 Kiss of Fire 1955,S 24,11:2
Marx, Samuel (Screenwriter)
 Society Doctor 1935,F 4,11:3
 Duel in the Jungle 1954,Ag 9,13:2
Marx, Wilhelm
 Acht Tage Glueck 1931,Jl 24,22:1
Marx, Zeppo
 Monkey Business 1931,O 8,22:6
 Horse Feathers 1932,Ag 11,12:2
 Duck Soup 1933,N 23,24:2
Marx Brothers, Four
 Cocoanuts, The 1929,My 25,17:3
 Animal Crackers 1930,Ag 29,20:3
Mary
 Festival 1967,O 24,53:2
Mary, Felisa
 Asi es la Vida; Such Is Life 1940,Ag 6,15:1
Mary, Renaud
 Crime Does Not Pay (The Hugues Case)
  1962,O 17,35:2
Maryanenko, I
 Mass Struggle 1934,S 17,20:3
Maryanov, E (Screenwriter)
 Circus Festival 1958,Mr 17,21:4
Maryev, V
 Secret Brigade 1951,Mr 19,23:2
Marzi, Franca
 Pirates of Capri, The 1949,D 26,33:5
 Tombolo 1949,D 31,9:4
 Island of Procida, The 1952,Mr 15,8:2
 Streets of Sorrow 1952,N 18,37:4
 Devotion 1953,Ja 31,10:6
 Verginita 1953,Ap 18,17:2
 My Heart Sings 1954,Mr 5,15:5
 Cabiria 1957,O 29,34:2
 See Naples and Die 1959,Ag 31,16:2
 Psycosissimo 1962,S 8,16:2
Mas, Carlos
 Big Boodle, The 1957,Mr 12,38:1
Masa, Antonin (Director)
 Wandering 1967,Je 19,41:1
Masayeva, Nina
 Moscow Skies 1945,Ja 22,22:5
Mascagni, Pietro (Composer)
 Canzione del Sole, La 1936,My 6,27:2
 Cavalleria Rusticana 1953,D 28,17:2
Mascagni, Pietro (Miscellaneous)
 Traviata, La 1953,D 28,17:2
Mascagno, Bob
 Immortal Sergeant 1943,F 4,29:2
Mascetti, Gina
 Two Cents Worth of Hope 1952,D 16,44:2
 Variety Lights; Luci del Varieta 1965,My 7,34:1
Mascherini, Enzo
 Trovatore, Il 1950,F 9,36:7
Maschwitz, Eric (Composer)
 Showtime 1948,My 20,35:3
Maschwitz, Eric (Miscellaneous)
 Forbidden Music 1938,D 27,13:2
Maschwitz, Eric (Screenwriter)
 Goodbye Mr Chips 1939,My 16,27:2
 Balalaika 1939,D 15,33:2
Mascomeio, Jeddu
 Heroina 1965,N 11,58:2
Mascott, Laurence E (Producer)
 Look in any Window 1962,Mr 22,40:1
Mascott, Laurence E (Screenwriter)
 Look in any Window 1962,Mr 22,40:1
Mase, Marino
 Love and Marriage (One Moment Is Enough); One
  Moment Is Enough (Love and Marriage)
  1966,Ag 5,20:1
 Carabiniers, Les 1967,S 28,58:3
 Carabiniers, Les 1968,Ap 26,31:1
 Fist in his Pocket 1968,My 28,40:1
Maselli, Francesco (Director)
 Time of Indifference 1965,O 13,50:1
 Time of Indifference 1966,O 13,50:1
Maselli, Francesco (Screenwriter)
 Time of Indifference 1965,O 13,50:1
 Time of Indifference 1966,O 13,50:1
Masengale, Terry
 Happy Land 1943,D 9,33:3
Mash, Joan
 Moonlighting Wives 1968,My 9,54:4
Masheret, A V (Director)
 Peter Vinogradof 1935,Je 28,24:1
Mashimoto, Shinobu (Screenwriter)
 Rebellion 1967,S 25,56:4
Mashiyane, Spokes
 Festival 1967,O 24,53:2
Mashkara, E
 Train Goes to Kiev, The 1961,Ap 10,26:1
Masina, Giulietta
 Without Pity; (Senza Pieta) 1950,Mr 16,40:4
 Behind Closed Shutters 1952,Je 10,22:7
 Greatest Love, The 1954,Ja 12,19:2
 White Sheik, The 1956,Ap 26,37:4
 Strada, La 1956,Jl 17,19:2
 Angels of Darkness 1956,N 22,51:1
 Cabiria 1957,O 29,34:2
 Bidone, Il 1964,N 20,42:1
 Variety Lights; Luci del Varieta 1965,My 7,34:1
 Juliet of the Spirits 1965,N 4,57:1
Masing, Esther
 Young, The Evil and the Savage, The
  1968,Ag 15,46:2
Masini, Galliano
 Stella del Mare; Star of the Sea 1940,My 3,17:6
Masini, Tito
 Eight and One Half 1963,Je 26,36:1

Masiro, Lauretia
Gran Varieta 1955,Ap 11,29:5
Maskell, Virginia
Man Upstairs, The 1959,Ag 11,23:2
Virgin Island 1960,Mr 24,39:5
Risk, The 1961,S 25,41:2
Only Two Can Play 1962,Mr 21,33:2
Doctor in Love 1962,Ap 27,27:2
Young and Willing 1964,F 27,28:1
Interlude 1968,Jl 3,26:1
Maslennikov, Alexei
Khovanschina 1960,S 19,41:2
Maslow, Sophie
Strange Victory 1948,S 27,27:2
Maslow, Walter
Francis of Assisi 1961,Jl 29,8:2
Maslyukof, A (Director)
Childred of the Revolution 1936,Ap 6,18:2
Maslyukov, A (Director)
Road to Life 1956,Je 11,26:6
Maslyukov, A (Screenwriter)
Road to Life 1956,Je 11,26:6
Masokha, Peter
Soil 1930,O 21,34:4
Ivan 1933,F 27,11:3
Thirteen, The 1937,Je 19,20:2
Guerrilla Brigade 1942,Ap 14,17:2
Two Soldiers 1944,Jl 27,14:2
MASON
See Also MAISON, MASSON
Mason, A E W (Original Author)
Witness for the Defense, The 1919,S 15,16:3
Four Feathers, The 1929,Je 13,35:4
Flirting Widow, The 1930,Ag 2,16:4
Mystere de la Villa Rose, Le 1932,Ja 11,28:5
Widow From Monte Carlo, The 1936,Ja 23,25:2
Fire Over England 1937,Mr 5,16:2
Drums 1938,S 30,24:4
Four Feathers 1939,Ag 4,11:1
Storm over the Nile 1956,Je 9,14:2
Mason, Ann
Deliverance 1919,Ag 19,10:1
Mason, Bernice (Original Author)
Under Your Spell 1936,N 7,15:2
Mason, Bill
Yellowback 1957,Ap 5,24:2
Mason, Dan
Yellow Ticket, The 1918,My 27,11:3
Sally 1925,Mr 16,16:1
Fire Brigade, The 1926,D 21,20:2
Out all Night 1927,S 27,31:1
Chinese Parrot, The 1928,Ja 2,28:1
Mason, David (Cinematographer)
Zanzabuku 1956,Ag 16,30:3
Mason, Elliot
Ghost Goes West, The 1936,Ja 11,9:2
Black Limelight 1939,Je 26,12:2
21 Days Together 1940,My 23,28:4
On Approval 1945,Ja 29,17:1
Vacation From Marriage 1946,Mr 15,27:2
Agitator, The 1949,Ag 19,12:5
Mason, Grace Sartwell (Original Author)
Man Crazy 1927,D 19,30:1
Honeymoon in Bali 1939,S 21,21:1
Mason, Haddon
Triumph of the Scarlet Pimpernel, The
1929,Jl 8,17:3
Yellow Mask, The 1930,D 8,26:1
French Leave 1931,D 7,16:1
Under the Red Robe 1937,Je 1,27:2
Mason, Hal (Producer)
Boy Ten Feet Tall, A 1965,My 13,32:2
Mason, Harold (Producer)
John and Julie 1957,My 7,40:1
Mason, Helene
Mystere de la Villa Rose, Le 1932,Ja 11,28:5
Mason, Herbert (Director)
East Meets West 1936,O 31,24:2
Man of Affairs 1937,F 20,9:2
Lady in Distress 1942,F 16,21:2
Continental Express 1942,Ap 7,26:3
Mason, Herbert (Producer)
Edge of Divorce 1954,Jl 2,10:1
Fuss Over Feathers 1954,D 27,22:6
Cast a Dark Shadow 1957,N 28,57:1
Mason, James
Godless Men 1921,Ja 31,11:1
Old Homestead, The 1922,O 9,10:2
Scars of Jealousy 1923,My 7,19:3
Why Worry? 1923,S 3,9:3
Heritage of the Desert, The 1924,Ja 24,15:1
Wanderer of the Wasteland, The 1924,Jl 8,14:2
Barriers Burned Away 1925,Mr 12,17:2
Beggar on Horseback 1925,Je 6,9:2
Under the Rouge 1925,Jl 22,14:4
Old Clothes 1925,N 9,25:1
For Heaven's Sake 1926,Ap 5,24:1
Let It Rain 1927,Mr 9,29:1
King of Kings, The 1927,Ap 20,29:2
Alias the Lone Wolf 1927,S 20,32:2
Back to God's Country 1927,O 24,24:3
Chicago After Midnight 1928,Mr 6,20:3
Across to Singapore 1928,Ap 30,18:3

Long, Long Trail, The 1929,N 4,28:1
Last of the Duanes 1930,S 13,9:3
Story of Temple Drake, The 1933,My 6,11:2
Dude Ranger, The 1934,O 2,18:5
Mason, James (English)
Return of the Scarlet Pimpernel, The
1938,Ap 11,12:2
I Met a Murderer 1939,O 2,15:2
Mill On the Floss, The 1939,N 15,19:3
Secret of Stamboul, The 1941,My 31,14:1
Candlelight in Algeria 1944,Jl 31,10:2
Thunder Rock 1944,S 15,16:1
Man in Grey, The 1945,N 30,18:6
Seventh Veil, The 1945,D 26,15:1
They Were Sisters 1946,Jl 24,24:2
Wicked Lady, The 1946,D 23,19:5
Odd Man Out 1947,Ap 24,30:2
Patient Vanishes, The 1947,My 23,31:2
Upturned Glass, The 1947,N 5,34:4
Man of Evil 1948,Mr 26,26:2
Hatter's Castle 1948,Jl 3,8:6
Place of One's Own, A 1949,F 8,30:2
Caught 1949,F 18,26:4
Madame Bovary 1949,Ag 26,15:2
East Side, West Side 1949,D 23,17:2
Reckless Moment, The 1949,D 30,13:2
One Way Street 1950,My 12,33:3
Desert Fox, The 1951,O 18,32:1
Desert Fox, The 1951,O 28,II,1:8
Pandora and the Flying Dutchman 1951,D 7,35:2
Lady Possessed 1952,F 15,17:2
Five Fingers 1952,F 23,7:5
Prisoner of Zenda, The 1952,N 5,36:2
Secret Sharer, The 1953,Ja 14,27:2
Story of Three Loves, The (The Jealous Lover);
Jealous Lover, The (The Story of Three Loves)
1953,Mr 6,29:2
Desert Rats, The 1953,My 9,13:2
Julius Caesar 1953,Je 5,19:1
Botany Bay 1953,O 30,27:2
Man Between, The 1953,N 19,41:2
Prince Valiant 1954,Ap 7,40:2
Star is Born, A 1954,O 12,23:1
20,000 Leagues Under the Sea 1954,D 24,7:2
Forever, Darling 1956,F 10,18:1
Bigger Than Life 1956,Ag 3,11:2
Island in the Sun 1957,Je 13,37:1
Cry Terror 1958,My 15,25:1
Decks Ran Red, The 1958,O 11,18:2
North by Northwest 1959,Ag 7,28:1
Journey to the Center of the Earth
1959,D 17,51:1
Touch of Larceny, A 1960,Mr 17,28:1
Trials of Oscar Wilde, The 1960,Je 28,26:1
Marriage-Go-Round 1961,Ja 7,12:2
Lolita 1962,Je 14,23:2
Escape from Zahrain 1962,Jl 12,19:3
Tiara Tahiti 1963,N 6,32:1
Fall of the Roman Empire, The 1964,Mr 27,14:2
Pumpkin Eater, The 1964,N 10,58:1
Lord Jim 1965,F 26,18:1
Genghis Khan 1965,Je 24,28:2
Blue Max, The 1966,Je 22,38:1
Georgy Girl 1966,O 18,48:1
Deadly Affair, The 1967,Ja 27,31:1
Uninhibited, The 1968,Je 13,57:2
Duffy 1968,S 17,50:3
Sea Gull, The 1968,D 24,14:1
Mason, James (English) (Original Author)
I Met a Murderer 1939,O 2,15:2
Mason, James (English) (Producer)
Lady Possessed 1952,F 15,17:2
Bigger Than Life 1956,Ag 3,11:2
Mason, James (English) (Screenwriter)
Lady Possessed 1952,F 15,17:2
Mason, Jim
Renegade Ranger, The 1939,F 17,17:3
Mason, John Capt
Big Lift, The 1950,Ap 27,37:2
Mason, Kathleen
My Cousin Rachel 1952,D 26,20:2
Mason, LeRoy
Hit of the Show 1928,Jl 9,25:1
Viking, The 1928,N 29,32:4
Revenge 1928,D 10,25:1
See America Thirst 1930,D 12,35:3
Smoky 1934,Ja 1,28:2
Are We Civilized? 1934,Je 14,28:5
Dude Ranger, The 1934,O 2,18:5
Redhead 1934,N 16,27:1
It Happened Out West 1937,Je 7,22:3
Santa Fe Stampede 1939,Ap 26,27:3
Man Who Wouldn't Die, The 1942,Ap 28,25:5
It Happened in Flatbush 1942,Jl 3,12:8
Time to Kill 1942,D 25,15:4
Chetniks 1943,Mr 19,15:3
My Pal Trigger 1946,Ag 17,16:3
Apache Rose 1947,Jl 23,19:3
Mason, Louis
Spitfire 1934,Mr 9,22:3
This Man is Mine 1934,Ap 13,25:1
Kentucky Kernels 1935,Ja 5,20:2
In Person 1935,D 13,31:5

Mason, Louis— Cont
Banjo on My Knee 1936,D 12,15:1
Return of Frank James, The 1940,Ag 10,16:4
Gold Rush Maisie 1940,S 2,19:2
Sea Wolf, The 1941,Mr 26,27:3
Whistling in Dixie 1942,D 31,20:4
What's Buzzin Cousin 1943,Jl 23,21:4
Broadway Rhythm 1944,Ap 14,24:6
Mason, Martin
Shane 1953,Ap 24,30:3
Mason, Mary
Walls of Gold 1933,O 21,11:3
Mad Game, The 1933,N 13,21:1
Mason, Melissa
Radio City Revels 1938,Mr 21,18:3
Mason, Morgan
Sandpiper, The 1965,Jl 16,14:1
Mason, Paul (Screenwriter)
Angel Baby 1961,O 5,43:1
King Kong vs. Godzilla 1963,Je 27,23:4
Mason, Portland
Man in the Gray Flannel Suit, The
1956,Ap 13,21:1
Mason, Ralph
Mikado, The 1967,Mr 15,53:1
Mason, Reginald
Two Weeks 1920,Ja 26,16:1
Life Begins 1932,Ag 26,20:3
Topaze 1933,F 10,12:2
Bedtime Story, A 1933,Ap 20,20:3
Kiss Before the Mirror, The 1933,My 15,16:2
Emergency Call 1933,Je 24,16:2
Big Brain, The 1933,Ag 5,9:5
Shanghai Madness 1933,S 23,11:6
Brief Moment 1933,S 30,18:5
You Can't Buy Everything 1934,F 3,9:2
Call it Luck 1934,Jl 10,24:5
Suzy 1936,Jl 25,16:1
Mason, Richard (Original Author)
Wind Cannot Read, The 1960,Mr 10,36:1
World of Suzie Wong, The 1960,N 11,36:1
Mason, Richard (Screenwriter)
Town Like Alice, A 1958,S 22,27:1
Wind Cannot Read, The 1960,Mr 10,36:1
Mason, Roy
Border Patrolman 1936,Je 29,11:2
Spy Ring, The 1938,Ja 15,19:1
Mason, Sarah Y (Original Author)
Shopworn 1932,Ap 4,13:6
Mason, Sarah Y (Screenwriter)
Little Minister, The 1934,D 28,25:1
Break of Hearts 1935,My 17,24:3
Magnificent Obsession 1935,D 31,11:2
Golden Boy 1939,S 8,28:2
Little Women 1949,Mr 11,33:2
Magnificent Obsession 1954,Ag 5,18:4
Mason, Shirley
Come On In 1918,S 23,7:1
Treasure Island 1920,Ap 12,13:1
Eleventh Hour, The 1923,Ag 28,12:1
Talker, The 1925,My 12,26:2
What Fools Men 1925,S 29,31:3
Lord Jim 1925,N 16,19:4
Desert Gold 1926,Mr 23,24:5
Sweet Rosie O'Grady 1926,D 9,33:1
Let It Rain 1927,Mr 9,29:1
Show of Shows 1929,N 21,24:5
Mason, Sully
That's Right, You're Wrong 1939,N 30,25:3
You'll Find Out 1940,N 15,25:2
Playmates 1941,D 26,21:3
Around the World 1943,N 25,39:2
Mason, Sydney
Paula 1952,Jl 16,21:2
Creature from the Black Lagoon 1954,My 1,13:4
Blackjack Ketchum Desperado 1956,Ap 5,26:2
Mason, Walter
Black Like Me 1964,My 21,42:1
Masreliez, Curt
Devil's Wanton, The 1962,Jl 5,21:2
Mass, Vladimir (Screenwriter)
Song Over Moscow 1964,N 23,52:1
Massaini, Oswaldo (Producer)
Given Word, The 1964,Mr 25,47:1
Massalitinova, V O
Thunderstorm 1934,S 29,12:2
Childhood of Maxim Gorky 1938,S 28,29:3
Alexander Nevsky 1939,Mr 23,27:1
On his Own 1939,S 13,31:3
Massalsky, Augustus Pavel
Ivan the Terrible, Part II 1959,N 25,22:4
Massalsky, Pavel
Resurrection 1963,O 7,35:2
Massard, Yves
Lovemaker, The 1958,Mr 11,33:4
Massari, Lea
Avventura, L' 1961,Ap 5,30:1
From a Roman Balcony 1961,O 16,33:5
Colossus of Rhodes, The 1961,D 14,55:6
Paris Pick-Up 1963,Ag 29,36:2
Made in Italy 1967,My 1,44:2
Massen, Osa
Honeymoon in Bali 1939,S 21,21:1
Honeymoon for Three 1941,F 8,19:2

Massen, Osa— Cont

Woman's Face, A 1941,My 16,21:2
You'll Never Get Rich 1941,O 24,27:2
Iceland 1942,O 15,27:1
Background to Danger 1943,Jl 3,11:2
Jack London 1944,Mr 3,19:3
Cry of the Werewolf, The 1944,Ag 12,16:5
Master Race, The 1944,N 2,22:1
Deadline at Dawn 1946,Ap 4,33:2
Night Unto Night 1949,Je 11,11:2
Rocketship X-M 1950,My 27,10:6

Massey, Anna
Gideon of Scotland Yard 1959,My 20,38:2
Bunny Lake is Missing 1965,O 4,00:0

Massey, Chris (Original Author)
Love Letters 1945,Ag 27,22:3
Corridor of Mirrors 1949,Mr 23,35:3

Massey, Daniel
In Which We Serve 1942,D 24,18:1
Entertainer, The 1960,O 4,49:2
Upstairs and Downstairs 1960,D 2,53:4
Amorous Adventures of Moll Flanders, The 1965,My 27,28:1
Jokers, The 1967,My 16,50:1
Star! 1968,O 23,36:2

Massey, Darla
Miracle, The 1959,N 13,25:4

Massey, Emily
Without Love 1945,Mr 23,13:1

Massey, Ilona
Rosalie 1937,D 31,9:2
Balalaika 1939,D 15,33:2
International Lady 1941,N 11,29:2
New Wine 1942,F 2,11:2
Invisible Agent 1942,Ag 6,23:2
Frankenstein Meets the Wolf Man 1943,Mr 6,8:3
Holiday in Mexico 1946,Ag 16,19:3
Northwest Outpost 1947,Ag 8,10:2
Plunders, The 1948,N 1,28:2
Love Happy 1950,Ap 8,9:4
Jet Over the Atlantic 1960,Ja 7,24:6

Massey, Jane (Director)
Problems of Sleep 1948,D 27,16:4

Massey, Raymond
Speckled Band, The 1931,N 7,16:5
Old Dark House, The 1932,O 28,22:4
Scarlet Pimpernel, The 1935,F 8,27:2
Things to Come 1936,Ap 18,19:2
Fire Over England 1937,Mr 5,16:2
Dreaming Lips 1937,My 20,17:1
Under the Red Robe 1937,Je 1,27:2
Prisoner of Zenda, The 1937,S 3,12:1
Hurricane, The 1937,N 10,31:2
Drums 1938,S 30,24:4
Black Limelight 1939,Je 26,12:2
Abe Lincoln in Illinois 1940,F 23,19:2
Santa Fe Trail 1940,D 21,21:2
Invaders, The 1942,Mr 6,17:1
Reap the Wild Wind 1942,Mr 27,27:2
Dangerously They Live 1942,Ap 11,9:2
Desperate Journey 1942,S 26,11:2
Action in the North Atlantic 1943,My 22,10:2
Arsenic and old Lace 1944,S 2,17:2
Woman in the Window, The 1945,Ja 26,16:4
Hotel Berlin 1945,Mr 3,11:2
God is my Co-Pilot 1945,Mr 24,22:6
Stairway to Heaven 1946,D 26,28:1
Possessed 1947,My 30,25:2
Mourning Becomes Electra 1947,N 20,38:2
Fountainhead, The 1949,Jl 9,8:5
Roseanna McCoy 1949,O 13,33:2
Chain Lightning 1950,F 20,21:2
Barricade 1950,Mr 25,8:6
Dallas 1951,Ja 13,10:4
Sugarfoot 1951,F 12,19:4
David and Bathsheba 1951,Ag 15,23:2
Come Fill the Cup 1951,N 22,47:2
Carson City 1952,Je 14,12:2
Desert Song, The 1953,My 21,39:2
Prince of Players 1955,Ja 12,24:2
Battle Cry 1955,F 3,18:1
East of Eden 1955,Mr 10,33:1
Seven Angry Men 1955,Ap 2,15:2
Omar Khayyam 1957,Ag 24,12:4
Naked and the Dead, The 1958,Ag 7,21:1
Great Impostor, The 1961,Mr 30,24:1
Fiercest Heart, The 1961,Ag 3,13:5
How the West Was Won 1963,Ap 1,54:1

Massey, Raymond (Narrator)
Jacqueline Kennedy's Asian Journey 1962,D 26,5:2

Massica (Screenwriter)
Four Days of Naples, The 1963,Mr 20,5:1

Massie, Paul
Orders to Kill 1958,N 18,41:2
Libel 1959,O 24,12:4
Sapphire 1959,N 3,27:1
House of Fright 1961,Ag 24,25:4
Call Me Genius 1961,O 17,47:1

Massine, Leonide
Versailles 1929,N 16,25:2
Red Shoes, The 1948,O 23,9:2
Tales of Hoffmann 1951,Ap 5,34:2
Neapolitan Carousel 1961,O 12,41:3

Massini, Mia
Secret Invasion, The 1964,S 17,52:5

Massis, Louis
Crazy in the Noodle 1957,D 15,45:4 (Incorrect in this edition; use 1957,D 17,45:4 elsewhere)

MASSON
See Also MAISON, MASON

Masson, Jean (Cinematographer)
Wedding in Monaco, The 1956,My 18,19:3

Masson, Louis (Miscellaneous)
Life and Loves of Beethoven, The 1937,N 22,15:1

Masson, Viola
Ne Sirj Edesanyam 1936,N 24,35:4

Masson, Yvette
Head of a Tyrant 1962,Je 7,31:2

Massot, Claude
Suitor, The; Soupirant, Le 1963,S 18,35:1

Massot, Jose Luis
Virgin of Guadalupe, The 1943,My 15,13:3

Massow, Marjorie
Take It or Leave It 1944,Jl 13,14:2

Masters, John (Original Author)
Bhowani Junction 1956,My 25,26:1

Masters, Ruth
Bridge to the Sun 1961,O 18,50:1

Masterson, Edward
World Dances 1954,N 8,24:6

Masterson, Pete
Ambush Bay 1966,S 15,51:4

Masterson, Valerie
Mikado, The 1967,Mr 15,53:1

Masterson, Whit (Original Author)
Cry in the Night, A 1956,S 1,19:4
Touch of Evil 1958,My 22,25:2
Yellow Canary, The 1963,My 16,42:1

Mastrantoni, Augusto
Heart and Soul 1950,Je 15,41:3

Mastriani, Francesco (Original Author)
Dead Woman's Kiss, A 1951,O 6,16:4

Mastripietri, Augusto
Messalina 1924,Ag 25,16:2

Mastrocinque, Camillo
Mafia; (In Nome Della Legge) 1950,Mr 2,33:2

Mastrocinque, Camillo (Director)
Matrimonio Ideale, Un 1939,D 15,33:3
When Love Calls 1948,O 9,12:6
Lost in the Dark 1949,My 14,9:2
Life of Donizetti, The 1952,Ap 26,19:2
Man With the Grey Glove, The 1953,Ja 3,11:2
Duel Without Honor 1953,F 28,8:8
Tarantella Napoletana 1954,Ap 19,19:3

Mastrocinque, Camillo (Screenwriter)
Man With the Grey Glove, The 1953,Ja 3,11:2
Duel Without Honor 1953,F 28,8:8

Mastrocinque, Novarese (Screenwriter)
Life of Donizetti, The 1952,Ap 26,19:2

Mastroianni, Marcello
Three Girls From Rome 1953,O 14,34:2
Sensualita 1954,Ap 29,40:2
Too Bad She's Bad 1955,D 26,23:2
House of Ricordi 1956,Mr 13,32:1
Miller's Beautiful Wife, The 1957,Je 12,40:2
Bigamist, The 1958,My 12,25:1
Most Wonderful Moment, The 1959,Je 1,23:6
Anatomy of Love 1959,S 29,46:2
Where the Hot Wind Blows 1960,N 12,15:1
Big Deal on Madonna Street, The 1960,N 23,20:1
Dolce Vita, La 1961,Ap 20,30:1
White Nights 1961,My 29,9:6
Night, The; Notte, La 1962,F 20,29:4
Bell Antonio 1962,Ap 3,43:2
Divorce-Italian Style 1962,S 18,34:1
Very Private Affair, A 1962,S 29,15:1
Eight and One Half 1963,Je 26,36:1
Family Diary 1963,N 12,48:1
Yesterday, Today and Tomorrow (Part II-Anna Milan); Anna Milan (Yesterday, Today and Tomorrow) 1964,Mr 18,46:1
Yesterday, Today, and Tomorrow (Part III-Mara Rome); Mara Rome (Yesterday, Today and Tomorrow) 1964,Mr 18,46:1
Yesterday, Today and Tomorrow (Part 1-Adelina Naples); Adelina Naples (Yesterday, Today and Tomorrow) 1964,Mr 18,46:1
Organizer, The 1964,My 7,31:2
Marriage Italian Style 1964,D 21,42:1
Love a la Carte 1965,Ja 12,31:1
Casanova 1965,Jl 21,43:1
10th Victim, The 1965,D 21,46:1
Lady Killer From Rome, The 1966,Je 9,54:3
Shoot Loud, Louder... I Don't Understand 1967,S 21,56:4
Poppy is Also a Flower, The 1967,D 14,62:4
Stranger, The 1967,D 19,59:1
Man With the Balloons, The 1968,Je 25,33:2
Kiss the Other Sheik 1968,Jl 30,33:1

Mastroly, Frank R (Producer)
Great John L, The 1945,Jl 9,14:6

Masunder, Shanti
Gyandev of India 1943,Ap 10,12:5

Maszynski, Marjusz
Kazdemu Wolno Kochac 1933,My 24,24:3

Mata, Yama
Rivers End, The 1920,F 23,11:2

Mata and Hari
Meet The People 1944,S 8,16:2

Matahi
Tabu 1931,Mr 19,21:3

Mataion, Vivian
King and Country 1964,S 24,46:2

Mataka, Michael
Duel in the Jungle 1954,Ag 9,13:2

Matalon, Vivian
King and Country 1966,Ja 28,20:4

Matania, Celia
Cuore Napoletano; Neapolitan Heart 1940,O 8,31:2
Seven Hills of Rome 1958,Ja 28,24:2 (Incorrect in this edition; use 1958,Ja 31,24:2 elsewhere)
Neapolitan Carousel 1961,O 12,41:3
Five Golden Hours 1961,O 19,39:3

Matarazzo, Raffaello (Director)
Serpente a Sonagli, Il 1936,Ag 17,9:2
Lacrime e Sorrisi 1936,D 17,35:2
Sono Stato Io; It Was I 1940,My 10,26:7
Paolo and Francesca 1953,F 14,8:3
Tormento 1953,Ap 4,9:2
Life and Music of Giuseppe Verdi, The 1957,My 2,26:2

Matarazzo, Raffaello (Screenwriter)
Paolo and Francesca 1953,F 14,8:3

Mataumua, Mamea
Return to Paradise 1953,S 11,24:2

Matcheret, A (Director)
Men and Jobs 1933,Ja 3,19:3

Mate, Rudolph (Director)
It Had to be You 1947,D 8,35:2
Dark Past, The 1948,D 23,25:2
No Sad Songs for Me 1950,Ap 28,26:2
D O A 1950,My 1,18:2
Union Station 1950,O 5,38:3
Branded 1951,Ja 11,28:5
Prince Who Was a Thief, The 1951,Jl 4,13:2
When Worlds Collide 1952,F 7,30:2
Green Glove, The 1952,Ap 24,38:1
Paula 1952,Jl 16,21:2
Mississippi Gambler, The 1953,Ja 30,25:1
Forbidden 1954,Ja 23,11:2
Siege at Red River, The 1954,Ap 3,19:2
Black Shield of Falworth, The 1954,O 7,16:2
Violent Men, The 1955,Ja 27,17:2
Far Horizons, The 1955,My 21,11:1
Miracle in the Rain 1956,Ap 2,18:1
Rawhide Years, The 1956,Je 16,12:2
Port Afrique 1956,N 3,27:5
Three Violent People 1957,F 11,34:2
Deep Six, The 1958,Ja 16,32:1
For the First Time 1959,Ag 15,8:7
300 Spartans, The 1962,S 20,29:2

Mate, Rudolph (Original Author)
Second Chance 1953,Jl 23,20:2

Mate, Rudolph (Producer)
Return of October, The 1949,F 23,31:2
300 Spartans, The 1962,S 20,29:2

Mateos, Julian
Return of the Seven 1966,O 20,52:5
10:30 PM Summer 1966,O 20,52:1

Mathan, Mahdu
Children of the Damned 1964,Ja 30,24:2

Mathe, Edouard
Vampires, Les 1965,S 14,54:1

Matheos, Nicos
Anna of Rhodes 1950,Mr 23,34:2

Mather, Aubrey
Young Woodley 1930,S 27,21:3
Aren't We All? 1932,Jl 1,19:3
Woman in Chains 1932,N 21,21:1
Be Mine Tonight 1933,Ap 14,22:5
Man Who Changed his Name, The 1934,O 17,26:2
As You Like It 1936,N 6,29:3
No, No, Nanette 1940,D 20,33:1
Rage in Heaven 1941,Mr 21,19:2
Ball of Fire 1942,Ja 16,25:2
Wife Takes a Flyer, The 1942,Je 19,19:1
Random Harvest 1942,D 18,36:6
Heaven Can Wait 1943,Ag 12,15:1
Lodger, The 1944,Ja 20,15:3
Song of Bernadette, The 1944,Ja 27,15:2
Jane Eyre 1944,F 4,12:5
House of Fear, The 1945,Mr 19,23:3
Temptation 1946,D 25,33:6
It Happened in Brooklyn 1947,Mr 14,28:5
Mighty McGurk, The 1947,Ap 4,19:4
Hucksters, The 1947,Jl 18,21:2
Julia Misbehaves 1948,Ag 30,8:2
Adventures of Don Juan 1948,D 25,10:1
Everybody Does It 1949,O 26,32:2
That Forsyte Woman 1949,N 11,31:2
Importance of Being Earnest, The 1952,D 23,17:2
Golden Mask, The 1954,Mr 20,10:5

Mather, Berkely (Original Author)
Genghis Khan 1965,Je 24,28:2
Mather, Berkely (Screenwriter)
Long Ships, The 1964,Je 25,25:1
Mather, Berkley (Screenwriter)
Dr No 1963,My 30,20:1
Mather, George Edward
Blackjack Ketchum Desperado 1956,Ap 5,26:2
Mather, Jack
River of no Return 1954,My 1,13:2
Mather, John
Jungle Book 1942,Ap 6,19:1
Mather, John (Screenwriter)
Satellite in the Sky 1956,S 4,32:7
Mathers, Jerry
Trouble With Harry, The 1955,O 18,46:2
That Certain Felling 1956,Je 21,35:2
Mathers, Jimmy
Summer Magic 1963,Ag 22,19:2
New Interns, The 1964,Ag 20,34:2
Mathes, Marrisa
Ride Beyond Vengance 1966,S 29,60:1
Matheson, Ilsa
Ariane 1934,Mr 7,23:4
Matheson, Murray
Hurricane Smith 1952,O 4,15:2
Botany Bay 1953,O 30,27:2
King of the Khyber Rifles 1953,D 23,21:1
Love Is a Many-Splendored Thing
 1955,Ag 19,10:1
Wall of Noise 1963,S 5,27:1
Signpost to Murder 1965,My 20,52:2
Assault on a Queen 1966,Jl 28,23:3
How to Succeed in Business Without Really
 Trying 1967,Mr 10,30:1
Matheson, Richard (Original Author)
Incredible Shrinking Man, The 1957,F 23,13:1
Young Warriors, The 1968,F 8,36:1
Matheson, Richard (Screenwriter)
Incredible Shrinking Man, The 1957,F 23,13:1
Beat Generation, The 1959,O 22,47:4
House of Usher, The 1960,S 15,45:4
Pit and the Pendulum, The 1961,Ag 24,25:3
Master of the World 1961,S 16,9:1
Tales of Terror 1962,Jl 5,21:2 (In Addenda)
Burn, Witch, Burn 1962,Jl 5,21:2 (In Addenda)
Raven, The 1963,Ja 26,5:8
Comedy of Terrors, The 1964,Ja 23,26:2
Die! Die! My Darling 1965,My 20,52:1
Young Warriors, The 1968,F 8,36:1
Devil's Bride, The 1968,D 19,60:1
Mathet, Leon
Mystere de la Villa Rose, Le 1932,Ja 11,28:5
MATHEWS
See Also MATTHEWS
Mathews, Allen
Doctor Rhythm 1938,My 19,25:2
16 Fathoms Deep 1948,O 7,35:2
Force of Evil 1948,D 27,16:2
Mathews, Carole
Amazon Quest 1949,My 14,9:3
Great Gatsby, The 1949,Jl 14,20:5
Massacre River 1949,Jl 15,17:2
Special Agent 1949,Ag 22,13:1
No Man of her Own 1950,My 4,32:3
Man With my Face, The 1951,Je 15,27:5
City of Bad Men 1953,O 21,37:6
Port of Hell 1954,D 18,12:2
Tender is the Night 1962,Ja 20,13:2
Look in any Window 1962,Mr 22,40:1
Mathews, Dorothy
Girl in Every Port, A 1928,F 20,14:1
Doorway to Hell, The 1930,N 1,23:2
Mathews, George
Up in Arms 1944,Mr 3,19:2
Eve of St Mark, The 1944,My 31,22:2
Wing and a Prayer 1944,Ag 31,14:1
Great John L, The 1945,Jl 9,14:6
Pat and Mike 1952,Je 19,32:6
City Beneath the Sea 1953,Mr 12,24:3
Act of Love 1954,F 12,20:5
Man With the Golden Arm, The 1955,D 16,38:2
Proud Ones, The 1956,Ag 11,10:2
Last Wagon, The 1956,S 22,20:2
Gunfight at the O K Corral 1957,My 30,23:2
Buccaneer, The 1958,D 24,00:0
Heller in Pink Tights 1960,Mr 17,28:1
Mathews, Gisella
Golden Coach, The 1954,Ja 22,30:2
Mathews, Joyce
$1,000 a Touchdown 1939,O 5,27:2
Mathews, Kerwin
Five Against the House 1955,Je 11,8:7
Garment Jungle, The 1957,My 16,28:2
Seventh Voyage of Sinbad 1958,D 24,00:0
Last Blitzkrieg, The 1959,Ja 31,13:5
Man on a String 1960,My 21,15:1
Three Worlds of Gulliver, The 1960,D 17,19:3
Warrior Empress, The 1961,Ag 10,17:4
Devil at 4 O'Clock, The 1961,O 19,39:3
Jack the Giant Killer 1962,Jl 26,17:1
Maniac 1963,O 31,26:3
Viscount, The 1967,My 11,50:1

Battle Beneath the Earth 1968,S 12,54:3
Mathews, Lester
Sangaree 1953,Je 5,19:1
Mathews, Martin
Leather Boys, The 1965,N 9,50:1
Mathews, Mary Jo
Society Doctor 1935,F 4,11:3
Mathias, Bob
Bob Mathias Story, The 1954,O 16,14:6
China Doll 1958,D 4,52:1
Minotaur, The 1961,N 8,41:1
It Happened in Athens 1962,N 15,46:2
Mathias, Frank
For Men Only 1952,Ja 16,21:2
Mathias, Melba
Bob Mathias Story, The 1954,O 16,14:6
Mathieson, Muir
Seventh Veil, The 1945,D 26,15:1
Mathis, Alfunso
Cheaters, The; (Tricheurs, Les) 1961,Je 5,37:4
Mathis, Johnny
Certain Smile, A 1958,Ag 1,13:2
Mathis, June (Screenwriter)
Out of the Fog 1919,F 10,11:3
Old Lady 31 1920,My 24,20:3
Polly With a Past 1921,Ja 10,9:1
Conquering Power, The 1921,Jl 10,VI,2:1 (In
 Addenda)
Turn to the Right 1922,Ja 24,11:1
Blood and Sand 1922,Ag 7,14:2
Young Rajah, The 1922,N 6,13:1
Three Wise Fools 1923,Jl 23,13:4
Mathis, Milly
Crise est Finie, La 1935,Mr 14,18:1
Prenez Garde a la Peinture 1935,Ag 17,18:6
With a Smile 1939,F 6,8:4
Personal Column 1941,F 3,13:2
Well-Digger's Daughter, The 1946,S 30,21:4
Topaze 1952,O 28,37:1
Mathieu, Andre (Composer)
Whispering City 1948,My 10,25:5
Mathot, Leon
Daughter of Israel, A 1928,My 21,25:1
Appassionata 1929,Jl 8,17:3
Mathot, Leon (Director)
Thunder Over Paris 1940,Je 28,22:3
Mathur
Gyandev of India 1943,Ap 10,12:5
Matic, Ana
Feverish Years, The 1967,S 22,57:2
Matieson, Otto
Scaramouche 1923,O 12,7:2 (Incorrect in this
 edition; use 1927,O 1,7:2 elsewhere)
Dangerous Maid, The 1923,D 11,26:2
Revelation 1924,Je 24,18:2
Captain Blood 1924,S 9,19:1
Folly of Vanity 1925,Ja 28,14:1
Salvation Hunters, The 1925,F 2,14:1
Sackcloth and Scarlet 1925,Mr 25,24:2
Happy Warrior, The 1925,Jl 7,24:2
Bride of the Storm 1926,Ap 5,24:1
Beloved Rogue, The 1927,Mr 14,16:1
Road to Romance, The 1927,O 10,24:1
Surrender 1927,O 11,27:1
Last Moment, The 1928,Mr 12,26:1
Scarlet Lady, The 1928,Ag 15,19:4
Woman From Moscow, The 1928,N 5,26:1
Napoleon's Barber 1928,N 26,30:2
Strange Cargo 1929,F 18,28:1
Show of Shows 1929,N 21,24:5
General Crack 1929,D 4,36:6
Beau Ideal 1931,Ja 19,25:1
Soldiers Plaything, A 1931,My 2,23:4
Maltese Falcon, The 1931,My 29,26:5
Matisse, Jacqueline
8 X 8 1957,Mr 16,13:2
Matov, V
They Wanted Peace 1940,Ja 8,11:3
Matray, Maria (Original Author)
Murder in the Music Hall 1946,Ap 15,22:2
Matray, Maria (Screenwriter)
Tempestous Love 1958,N 22,27:4
Matrossov, K
Men of the Sea 1938,Je 20,11:2
Matsas, Artemis
Casablan 1964,D 14,50:1
Matson, Norman (Miscellaneous)
I Married a Witch 1942,N 20,27:2
Matsuda, Tommy
War Hunt 1962,Ag 8,35:2
Matsue, Yoichi
Wind Cannot Read, The 1960,Mr 10,36:1
Matsui
Hell and Highwater 1933,D 18,24:4
Matsui, Suisei
Tokyo File 212 1951,Je 1,20:7
Matsumoto, Kaoru
Rikisha Man, The 1960,My 4,57:1
Matsumoto, Koshiro
Chushingura 1963,O 4,26:1
Samurai Assassin 1965,Mr 19,27:5

Matsumoto, Susie
Japanese War Bride 1952,Ja 30,22:6
Matsumura, Tatsuo
Rebellion 1968,O 26,27:4
Matsura, Elsaku (Producer)
Island, The; Hadaka No Shima 1962,S 11,27:2
Matsuura, Kenro (Screenwriter)
Kojiro 1968,Ag 30,23:1
Matsuyama, Zenzo (Director)
Happiness of Us Alone 1963,Ap 10,31:5
My Hobo 1963,Jl 24,27:3
Could I but Live 1965,Ja 20,34:2
Matsuyama, Zenzo (Miscellaneous)
Human Condition, The 1959,D 16,56:1
Matsuyama, Zenzo (Screenwriter)
Human Condition, The 1959,D 16,56:1
Girl in the Mist 1959,D 23,22:1
Happiness of Us Alone 1963,Ap 10,31:5
My Hobo 1963,Jl 24,27:3
Different Sons 1964,F 13,25:1
Honolulu-Tokyo-Hong Kong 1964,S 2,33:3
Could I but Live 1965,Ja 20,34:2
Mattax, Martha
Oh, Doctor! 1925,F 23,24:1
Matter, Alex (Director)
Drifter, The 1967,My 25,54:1
Matter, Alex (Screenwriter)
Drifter, The 1967,My 25,54:1
Mattera, Gino
Lost One, The; La Traviata 1948,Mr 30,26:2
Lost One, The; La Traviata 1948,Mr 30,26:2
Faust and the Devil 1950,My 1,18:2
Matterstock, Albert
Stimme des Blutes; Blood Bond 1937,D 28,29:2
Ziel den Wolken; Goal in the Clouds
 1939,My 27,13:3
Solo per Danne 1939,My 30,13:3
Our Little Wife 1940,Ja 27,9:2
Matteucci, Guerrino
Grido, Il 1962,O 23,42:1
Matthau, Walter
Kentuckian, The 1955,S 2,13:2
Indian Fighter, The 1955,D 22,20:1
Bigger Than Life 1956,Ag 3,11:2
Face in the Crowd, A 1957,My 29,33:1
Slaughter on Tenth Avenue 1957,N 6,43:1
King Creole 1958,Jl 4,15:2
Voice in the Mirror 1958,Ag 14,23:2
Onionhead 1958,O 2,44:1
Strangers When we Meet 1960,Je 30,22:2
Lonely are the Brave 1962,Je 28,21:2
Who's Got the Action? 1962,D 26,5:4
Island of Love 1963,Je 13,30:4
Charade 1963,D 6,40:1
Ensign Pulver 1964,Ag 1,13:2
Fail Safe 1964,S 16,36:1
Goodbye, Charlie 1964,N 19,49:1
Mirage 1965,My 27,28:1
Fortune Cookie, The 1966,O 20,52:1
Guide for the Married Man, A 1967,My 27,16:1
Odd Couple, The 1968,My 3,42:1
Secret Life of an American Wife, The
 1968,Je 26,42:2
Candy 1968,D 18,54:2
MATTHEWS
See Also MATHEWS
Matthews, A E
Men Are not Gods 1937,Ja 19,28:1
Quiet Wedding 1941,D 29,27:4
Mister V 1942,F 13,24:4
Great Mr Handel, The 1943,S 10,29:3
They Came to a City 1945,F 19,21:3
Life and Death of Colonel Blimp, The
 1945,Mr 30,18:2
Piccadilly Incident 1948,Ag 5,16:2
Forbidden Street, The 1949,My 14,9:2
Amazing Mr Beecham, The 1949,D 26,33:4
Laughter in Paradise 1951,N 12,21:2
Galloping Major, The 1951,D 17,27:2
Mister Drake's Duck 1952,Ja 28,15:2
Castle in the Air 1953,Ja 5,19:2
Penny Princess 1953,Mr 25,37:3
Landfall 1953,My 11,25:2
Something Money Can't Buy 1953,O 1,34:3
Passionate Sentry, The 1953,N 12,37:5
Man With a Million 1954,Je 29,21:2
Tonight's the Night 1954,D 23,13:4
Around the World in 80 Days 1956,O 18,37:1
Doctor at Large 1957,Jl 29,15:5
Ship Was Loaded, The 1958,Ja 20,20:1
3 Men in a Boat 1959,Jl 29,33:2
Matthews, Adelaide (Original Author)
Scrambled Wives 1921,My 23,16:3
Matthews, Adelaide (Screenwriter)
Teaser, The 1925,Je 15,10:1
Matthews, Carmen
Butterfield 8 1960,N 17,46:1
Rage to Live, A 1965,O 21,57:1
Matthews, Dorcas
Woman in the Suitcase, The 1920,Ja 12,7:1
Matthews, Dorothy
Son of the Gods 1930,Ja 31,24:1
Truth About Youth, The 1930,D 13,22:2

Matthews, Francis
Bhowani Junction 1956,My 25,26:1
Murder Ahoy 1964,S 23,55:3
Matthews, James (Screenwriter)
Teckman Mystery, The 1955,Ag 22,18:2
Raising a Riot 1957,My 8,44:1
Matthews, Jessie
There Goes the Bride 1933,Mr 4,11:3
Good Companions, The 1933,O 10,24:1
Friday the 13th 1934,My 15,18:1
Evergreen 1935,Ja 11,29:1
Strauss's Great Waltz 1935,Ap 8,23:3
First a Girl 1936,Ja 4,19:1
It's Love Again 1936,My 23,12:1
Head Over Heels in Love 1937,F 13,9:1
Gangway 1937,Ag 21,7:3
Sailing Along 1938,Ap 16,17:1
Climbing High 1939,Je 5,20:3
Forever and a Day 1943,Mr 13,9:2
Tom Thumb 1958,D 24,00:0
Matthews, Junius
Black Angel 1946,S 26,32:4
Shocking Miss Pilgrim, The 1947,F 12,34:2
Chicken every Sunday 1949,Ja 19,34:2
Matthews, Lester
Fires of Fate 1933,Ap 3,13:4
Norah O'Neale 1934,O 25,26:3
Werewolf of London, The 1935,My 10,25:2
Raven, The 1935,Jl 5,9:2
Professional Soldier 1936,Ja 30,14:2
Spy 77 1936,F 10,15:1
Song and Dance Man 1936,Mr 12,18:2
Thank You, Jeeves 1936,O 5,25:1
Fifteen Maiden Lane 1936,O 17,21:3
Lloyds of London 1936,N 26,39:1
Crack-Up 1937,Ja 4,20:4
April Romance 1937,Ja 27,17:4
Prince and the Pauper, The 1937,My 6,23:1
Lancer Spy 1937,N 4,29:1
There's Always a Woman 1938,Ap 29,17:2
Adventures of Robin Hood, The 1938,My 13,17:2
Three Loves Has Nancy 1938,S 2,21:2
Mysterious Mr Moto of Devil's Island
1938,S 19,16:2
If I Were King 1938,S 29,31:1
Time Out for Murder 1938,O 7,21:2
Three Musketeers, The 1939,F 18,12:2
Susannah of the Mounties 1939,Je 24,13:2
Conspiracy 1939,Ag 23,19:2
Rulers of the Sea 1939,N 9,27:1
Everything Happens at Night 1939,D 16,12:6
British Intelligence 1940,F 12,14:2
Northwest Passage 1940,Mr 8,25:1
Biscuit Eater, The 1940,My 23,28:5
Women in War 1940,My 30,21:2
Lone Wolf Keeps a Date, The 1941,Ja 2,24:3
Yank in the R A F, A 1941,S 27,11:3
Son of Fury 1942,Ja 30,23:2
Pied Piper, The 1942,Ag 13,15:3
Across the Pacific 1942,S 5,9:2
Desperate Journey 1942,S 26,11:2
Manila Calling 1942,S 28,13:1
Mysterious Doctor, The 1943,My 20,26:4
Four Jills in a Jeep 1944,Ap 6,27:2
Between Two Worlds 1944,My 6,11:2
Story of Dr Wassell, The 1944,Je 7,13:2
Invisible Man's Revenge, The 1944,Je 10,12:2
Shadows in the Night 1944,Jl 29,16:2
Objective Burma 1945,Ja 27,15:2
Two O'Clock Courage 1945,Ap 14,13:3
Dark Delusion 1947,Je 26,19:2
Exile, The 1947,D 26,22:4
Fighting Father Dunne 1948,Je 25,26:2
Her Wonderful Lie 1950,Jl 17,15:2
Lorna Doone 1951,S 21,19:4
Lady in the Iron Mask 1952,Jl 5,7:2
Miserables, Les 1952,Ag 15,11:2
Operation Secret 1952,N 6,37:2
Stars and Stripes Forever 1952,D 23,17:2
Niagara 1953,Ja 22,20:3
Trouble Along the Way 1953,My 7,37:2
Young Bess 1953,My 22,31:1
Fort Ti 1953,My 30,7:1
Bad for Each Other 1953,D 24,9:3
Flame of the Islands 1956,F 25,12:4
Mary Poppins 1964,S 25,34:1
Matthews, Pamela
Secret Flight 1952,Jl 3,16:2
Matthews, Paul
Tom Brown's School Days 1940,Je 28,22:2
Little Men 1940,D 9,23:2
Matthieson, Timothy
Yours, Mine and Ours 1968,Ap 25,53:1
Mattia, Ettore
Overcoat, The 1953,O 13,34:1
Mattingly, Hedley
Thrill of it All, The 1963,Ag 2,15:3
Torn Curtain 1966,Jl 28,23:1
Mattingly, Phil
In Harm's Way 1965,Ap 7,36:1
Mattioli, Mario (Director)
Amo Te Sola 1936,Jl 20,11:2

Mattioli, Raf
Guendalina 1958,Je 30,23:2
Holiday Island; (Vacanzie a Izchia)
1959,S 22,46:1
Where the Hot Wind Blows 1960,N 12,15:1
Violent Summer 1961,My 20,12:1
Mattoli, Mario (Director)
Musica in Piazza 1936,My 7,21:3
Uomo Che Sorr'de, L' 1937,Ap 17,15:2
Destino, Il 1938,F 8,17:3
Trionfo dell'Amore, Il; Love's Triumph
1938,Mr 29,18:4
Eravamo Sette Vedove; We Were Seven Widows
1940,F 16,23:4
Al Vostri Ordini, Signora; At Your Orders,
Madame 1940,My 25,20:1
Dama Bianca, La; Lady in White, The
1940,My 31,15:3
Life Begins Anew; Vita Ricomincia, La
1947,Ap 7,20:5
Schoolgirl Diary 1947,O 18,9:2
Lady is Fickle, The 1948,F 7,10:4
Scarred 1951,O 27,10:5
I Cadetti di Guascogna 1952,O 6,22:2
Lucky Five, The 1953,N 27,22:5
My Heart Sings 1954,Mr 5,15:5
Mattoli, Mario (Original Author)
I Cadetti di Guascogna 1952,O 6,22:2
Mattoli, Mario (Producer)
Lady is Fickle, The 1948,F 7,10:4
Mattoli, Mario (Screenwriter)
Anything for a Song 1947,Ag 5,26:2
Schoolgirl Diary 1947,O 18,9:2
I Cadetti di Guascogna 1952,O 6,22:2
Matton, Brett
Jet Over the Atlantic 1960,Ja 7,24:6
Matton, Charles (Director)
Pomme, La 1968,Jl 19,30:1
Mattoni, Andre
Youth Astray 1928,My 29,17:2
Walzerlange; Waltz Melodies 1940,Ap 27,9:3
Mattos, Michael
Connection, The 1962,O 4,44:1
Mattox, Martha
Huckleberry Finn 1920,F 23,11:2
Maytime 1924,Je 2,14:3
Dangerous Innocence 1925,Je 8,19:1
I'll Show You the Town 1925,Je 8,19:1
Home Maker, The 1925,Ag 10,8:2
Keeper of the Bees, The 1925,O 28,29:2
Infatuation 1926,Ja 4,16:1
Yankee Senor, The 1926,Ja 28,14:4
Ibanez's Torrent 1926,F 22,14:1
Lovey Mary 1926,Je 21,17:2
Waning Sex, The 1926,S 21,33:1
Thirteenth Juror, The 1927,N 22,20:1
Love Me and the World Is Mine 1928,F 6,12:3
Her Wild Oat 1928,F 6,12:3
Kentucky Courage 1928,My 14,25:1
Fools for Luck 1928,Je 12,33:5
Born to Love 1931,Ap 25,23:4
Murder by the Clock 1931,Jl 18,16:6
Careless Lady 1932,Ap 18,19:2
No Greater Love 1932,My 14,11:5
Bitter Tea of General Yen, The 1933,Ja 12,20:6
Mattox, Matt
Seven Brides for Seven Brothers 1954,Jl 23,8:3
Pepe 1960,D 22,18:1
Mattraw, Scott
Two Lovers 1928,Mr 23,24:4
In Old Chicago 1938,Ja 7,15:2
Mattray, Ernest (Director)
Adventure in Music 1944,Mr 6,17:3
Matts, Frank
Thunder Over the Plains 1953,D 10,64:4
Mattsson, Arne (Director)
Incorrigible 1949,Jl 2,8:2
One Summer of Happiness 1955,Mr 22,35:2
Doll, The 1964,Ja 14,27:1
Mattsson, Sten
One Summer of Happiness 1955,Mr 22,35:2
Mattyasovsky, I
Paul Street Boys, The 1929,Jl 15,25:1
Mature, Victor
Housekeeper's Daughter, The 1939,D 2,21:4
One Million BC 1940,Ap 27,9:2
Captain Caution 1940,O 21,21:3
No, No, Nanette 1940,D 20,33:1
Shanghai Gesture, The 1941,D 26,21:2
I Wake up Screaming 1942,Ja 17,13:2
Song of the Islands 1942,Mr 12,24:4
My Gal Sal 1942,My 1,23:1
Footlight Serenade 1942,S 10,30:3
Seven Days' Leave 1942,D 11,33:2
My Darling Clementine 1946,D 4,44:5
Moss Rose 1947,Jl 3,14:2
Kiss of Death 1947,Ag 28,28:2
Fury at Furnace Creek 1948,Jl 12,11:2
Cry of the City 1948,S 30,32:4
Easy Living 1949,O 13,33:3
Red, Hot and Blue 1949,O 20,39:2
Samson and Delilah 1949,D 22,29:2
Wabash Avenue 1950,Ap 29,8:3

Mature, Victor — Cont
Stella 1950,Ag 19,9:2
Gambling House 1951,Mr 19,23:2
Las Vegas Story, The 1952,Ja 31,37:6
Something for the Birds 1952,N 15,15:2
Million Dollar Mermaid 1952,D 5,35:2
Androcles and the Lion 1953,Ja 15,23:2
Affair With a Stranger 1953,Jl 11,8:2
Glory Brigade, The 1953,Ag 15,8:4
Robe, The 1953,S 17,32:6
Veils of Bagdad, The 1953,N 27,99:9
Dangerous Mission 1954,Mr 6,13:5
Demetrius and the Gladiators 1954,Je 19,9:1
Egyptian, The 1954,Ag 25,23:1
Betrayed 1954,S 9,36:1
Chief Crazy Horse 1955,Ap 28,25:1
Violent Saturday 1955,My 12,32:2
Last Frontier, The 1955,D 8,45:1
Safari 1956,Je 21,35:2
Zarak 1956,D 27,22:1
China Doll 1958,D 4,52:1
Big Circus, The 1959,Jl 18,6:1
Hannibal 1960,Ag 4,17:1
Tartars, The 1962,Je 21,26:2
After the Fox 1966,D 24,11:1
Head 1968,N 7,51:1
Maturin, Eric
Sanders of the River 1935,Je 27,16:1
Life and Death of Colonel Blimp, The
1945,Mr 30,18:2
Last Holiday 1950,N 14,39:4
Matveyev, Ivan
Country Bride 1938,Je 4,18:2
Matveyev, V
Cossack Beyond the Danube, A 1954,F 8,18:5
Matz, Johanna
White Horse Inn, The 1957,D 4,50:3
Life and Loves of Mozart, The 1958,Ja 7,28:2
Dreimaederlhaus, Das; (House of Three Girls,
The) 1961,N 18,15:1
Matzenauer, Margaret
Mr Deeds Goes to Town 1936,Ap 17,17:2
Mauban, Maria
Case of Gold 1952,Ja 19,13:3
Cage of Gold 1952,Ja 19,13:3
Strollers, The 1952,Jl 22,22:7
Cairo Road 1952,N 1,17:2
Of Love and Bandits 1953,Ja 17,12:4
Easiest Profession, The 1960,Mr 26,15:7
Mauch, Billy
White Angel, The 1936,Je 25,24:1
Anthony Adverse 1936,Ag 27,16:1
Penrod and Sam 1937,Mr 29,14:3
Prince and the Pauper, The 1937,My 6,23:1
Penrod and his Twin Brother 1938,Ap 18,11:1
Street with no Name, The 1948,Jl 15,26:6
Roseanna McCoy 1949,O 13,33:2
Mauch, Bobby
Prince and the Pauper, The 1937,My 6,23:1
Penrod and his Twin Brother 1938,Ap 18,11:1
Mauclair, Jacques
Female, The 1960,Ap 28,29:1
Maude, Beatrice
Dodsworth 1936,S 24,29:1
Maude, Cyril
Peer Gynt 1915,S 20,9:1
Grumpy 1930,Ag 2,16:4
Orders Is Orders 1934,My 7,20:2
While the Sun Shines 1950,Jl 1,9:2
Maude, Joan
This Freedom 1923,N 28,15:1
Power 1934,O 5,29:3
Wandering Jew, The 1935,Ja 14,11:3
In a Monastery Garden 1935,Mr 13,16:2
Stairway to Heaven 1946,D 26,28:1
Corridor of Mirrors 1949,Mr 23,35:3
Maude, Margery
You're Never too Young 1955,Ag 26,10:2
Birds and the Bees, The 1956,Ap 23,22:1
Maugham, Robin (Miscellaneous)
Slave Trade in the World Today 1964,N 24,44:1
Maugham, Robin (Original Author)
Portrait of a Sinner 1961,D 7,52:1
Servant, The 1964,Mr 17,30:2
Maugham, Robin (Screenwriter)
Intruder, The 1955,Ja 26,22:1
Maugham, W Somerset (Original Author)
East of Suez 1925,Ja 26,22:1
Circle, The 1925,S 22,22:3
Infatuation 1926,Ja 4,16:1
Magician, The 1926,O 25,15:1
Canadian, The 1926,N 30,27:1
Sadie Thompson 1928,F 6,12:3
Letter, The 1929,Mr 8,30:1
Sacred Flame, The 1929,N 23,18:5
Our Betters 1933,F 24,13:2
Narrow Corner, The 1933,Jl 14,15:3
Of Human Bondage 1934,Je 29,17:1
Painted Veil, The 1934,D 7,29:1
Right to Live, The 1935,F 16,9:1
Secret Agent 1936,Je 13,13:1
Tenth Man, The 1937,N 15,15:2
Beachcomber, The 1938,D 26,29:3
Too Many Husbands 1940,Mr 8,25:2

Maugham, W Somerset (Original Author)— Cont
Letter, The 1940,N 23,12:6
Moon and Sixpence, The 1942,O 28,26:4
Hour Before the Dawn, The 1944,My 11,25:6
Christmas Holiday 1944,Je 29,16:1
Of Human Bondage 1946,Jl 6,11:2
Razor's Edge, The 1946,N 20,42:2
Quartet (The Kite); Kite, The (Quartet)
 1949,Mr 29,30:3
Quartet (The Colonel's Lady); Colonel's Lady, The
 (Quartet) 1949,Mr 29,30:3
Quartet (The Facts of Life); Facts of Life, The
 (Quartet) 1949,Mr 29,30:3
Quartet (The Alien Corn); Alien Corn, The
 (Quartet) 1949,Mr 29,30:3
Trio 1950,O 11,42:1
Encore (The Ant and the Grasshopper); Ant and
 the Grasshopper, The (Encore) 1952,Ap 3,45:1
Encore (Winter Cruise); Winter Cruise (Encore)
 1952,Ap 3,45:1
Encore (Gigolo and Gigolette); Gigolo and
 Gigolette (Encore) 1952,Ap 3,45:1
Miss Sadie Thompson 1953,D 24,9:1
Beachcomber, The 1955,Ja 17,27:5
Three for the Show 1955,F 25,16:1
Seventh Sin, The 1957,Je 29,10:6
Adorable Julia 1964,Ap 8,33:1
Of Human Bondage 1964,S 24,46:2
Of Human Bondage 1965,S 15,41:1
Maugham, W Somerset (Screenwriter)
Trio 1950,O 11,42:1
Maughan, Susan
Go Go Mania 1965,My 20,52:4
Mauldin, Bill
Teresa 1951,Ap 6,31:2
Red Badge of Courage, The 1951,O 19,22:2
Mauldin, Bill (Original Author)
Up Front 1951,Mr 26,19:2
Mauley, Georges
Si l'Empereur Savait Ca 1931,F 23,20:3
Mauloy, Georges
Fantomas 1934,Mr 13,27:4
Heritage 1940,N 5,33:2
Ces Dames aux Chapeaux Verts; Ladies in the
 Green Hats, The 1945,Ap 5,26:2
Her First Affair; (Children of Paradise)
 1947,F 20,32:3
Maunsell, David
Francis of Assisi 1961,Jl 29,8:2
Maupain
Miracle des Loups, Le 1930,Jl 28,22:1
Maupassant, Guy de (Original Author)
Shattered 1926,Ap 30,17:2
Ordonnance, L'; Orderly, The 1933,O 22,IX,4:2
He 1933,D 27,23:6
Puishka; Ball of Suet, A 1934,O 28,IX,4:2 (In
 Addenda)
Private Affairs of Bel Ami, The 1947,Je 16,25:4
Ways of Love (A Day in the Country); Day in the
 Country, A (Ways of Love) 1950,D 13,50:2
Prize, The 1952,Ap 30,33:2
Plaisir, Le (The House of Madame Tellier); House
 of Madame Tellier (Le Plaisir)
 1954,My 20,38:1
Plaisir, Le (The Mask); Mask, The (Le Plaisir)
 1954,My 20,38:1
Plaisir, Le (The Model); Model, The (Le Plaisir)
 1954,My 20,38:1
Boule de Suif 1958,My 5,24:1
End of Desire 1962,Jl 10,29:2
Inheritance, The; Herencia, La 1964,S 16,36:3
Maupi
Cesar 1948,O 28,36:2
Hoboes in Paradise 1950,O 9,21:5
Maupin, Ernest
Daughter of Israel, A 1928,My 21,25:1
Maupin, Georges
Miracle of the Wolves, The 1925,F 24,17:3
Maur, Meinhart
Rembrandt 1936,D 3,31:1
Dr Syn 1937,N 15,15:1
21 Days Together 1940,My 23,28:4
Candlelight in Algeria 1944,Jl 31,10:2
Never Let Me Go 1953,Je 11,37:2
Maurel, Raymond
Dixiana 1930,S 5,21:1
Maurer, Georges (Producer)
Green Glove, The 1952,Ap 24,38:1
Maurer, Norman (Director)
Three Stooges Go Around the World in a Daze,
 The 1963,D 19,40:2
Who's Minding the Mint? 1967,D 7,60:3
Maurer, Norman (Producer)
Angry Red Planet, The 1960,My 5,41:2
Three Stooges Meet Hercules, The
 1962,Ja 27,13:4
Three Stooges Go Around the World in a Daze,
 The 1963,D 19,40:2

Maurey, Nicole
Little Boy Lost 1953,S 22,38:2
Diary of a Country Priest 1954,Ap 6,35:2
Secret of the Incas 1954,My 29,13:3
Companions of the Night 1954,N 25,44:2
Bold and the Brave, The 1956,My 26,15:2
Constant Husband, The 1957,Jl 26,10:3
Me and the Colonel 1958,Ag 27,33:1
Scapegoat, The 1959,Ag 7,28:1
House of the Seven Hawks, The 1959,D 17,51:2
High Time 1960,S 17,15:1
Day of the Triffids 1963,My 11,15:2
Mauri, Glauco
China Is Near 1968,Ja 9,37:1
Mauriac, Claude (Original Author)
Therese 1963,N 13,35:2
Mauriac, Claude (Screenwriter)
7 Capital Sins (Envy); Envy (7 Capital Sins)
 1963,Ja 17,5:2
Therese 1963,N 13,35:2
Mauriac, Francois (Screenwriter)
Therese 1963,N 13,35:2
Maurice, Frank (Producer)
Bad Men of Tombstone 1949,Mr 5,10:2
Mauriello, Tami
On the Waterfront 1954,Jl 29,18:1
Maurier, Claire
Parisienne, La 1958,Jl 31,27:1
Back to the Wall; (Dos au Mur) 1959,S 8,43:2
400 Blows, The; (Les Quatre Cents Coups)
 1959,N 17,41:1
Mistress for the Summer, A 1964,Mr 28,13:5
My Wife's Husband 1965,Ja 27,26:1
Maurin, Dominque
Rififi 1956,Je 6,37:1
Maurin, J P
Amazing Monsieur Fabre, The 1952,S 9,21:2
Mauro, David
Beau Geste 1966,S 8,43:1
Ambushers, The 1967,D 23,29:1
Mauro, Jole
Francis of Assisi 1961,Jl 29,8:2
Everybody go Home!; Tutti a Casa 1962,N 6,38:1
Maurois, Andre (Original Author)
Entente Cordiale 1939,D 26,23:2
Maurstad, Alfred
Valley of the Eagles 1952,Ap 11,19:2
Maurus, Gerda
Spione; Spies 1928,My 20,VIII,8:5
Spies 1929,Mr 5,29:1
By Rocket to the Moon 1931,F 7,11:1
Tod Ueber Schanghai 1933,D 16,12:4
Prinzessin Sissy 1939,Ja 14,13:2
Maury, Alfred (Original Author)
Till We Meet Again 1944,Ag 30,15:1
Maury, Jacques
Man and his Wife, A 1939,Mr 28,20:1
Maury, Jacques (Screenwriter)
Generals Without Buttons 1938,Mr 8,23:2
Maury, Jean-Louis
Love Game, The 1960,N 9,44:1
Landru 1963,Ap 10,31:1
Mauu, Charles
Pagan Love Song 1950,D 26,19:1
Mavropoulou, Gelly
Aunt From Chicago, The 1960,Je 6,33:6
Mawby, Angella
Man From Blankley's, The 1930,Mr 29,23:1
Mawdesley, Robert
Loyalties 1934,O 26,25:1
Mawn, Marilyn
Captivation 1931,S 28,17:4
MAX
See Also MACKS
Max, Edwin
Stairway to Heaven 1946,D 26,28:1
Set-Up, The 1949,Mr 30,31:2
Follow Me Quietly 1949,Jl 8,14:5
Thieves' Highway 1949,S 24,8:6
Side Street 1950,Mr 24,29:2
Love That Brute 1950,My 27,10:6
Well, The 1951,S 27,37:2
Models, Inc 1952,My 26,18:4
Bloodhounds of Broadway 1952,N 15,15:2
Max, Jean
Paris-Beguin 1932,D 31,10:1
Pension Mimosas 1936,My 6,27:1
Dark Eyes 1938,Ap 19,24:5
That They May Live 1939,N 7,31:2
Max, Maximilienne
Maria Chapdelaine 1935,S 25,18:2
Maxellos, The
Bright Lights 1935,Ag 15,15:2
Incendiary Blonde 1945,Jl 26,13:2
Maxey, Paul
Till the Clouds Roll By 1946,D 6,27:4
Brasher Doubloon, The 1947,My 22,34:5
South of St Louis 1949,Mr 7,17:2
Bride for Sale 1949,N 21,29:4 (In Addenda)
Reformer and the Redhead, The 1950,Ap 10,15:2
Narrow Margin, The 1952,My 5,18:7
Stranger Wore a Gun, The 1953,Jl 30,20:3

Maxfield, Henry S (Original Author)
Double Man, The 1968,My 2,57:1
Maxim, Hiram (Original Author)
Virgin Paradise, A 1921,Ag 4,18:3
Maxim, Hiram Percy (Original Author)
So Goes my Love 1946,My 2,3:7
Maxim, Hudson (Original Author)
Battle Cry for Peace, The 1915,Ag 7,8:3
Maxim, Hudson (Screenwriter)
Battle Cry for Peace, The 1915,Ag 7,8:3
Maxime, Roger
Pecheurs d'Islande 1935,S 21,18:2
Maximilian, Max
Docks of Hamburg 1930,Jl 7,22:3
Maximilienne
Murderer Lives at Number 21, The
 1947,Ag 18,12:3
Scandals of Clochemerle, The 1950,Mr 28,28:2
Pardon my French 1952,Mr 31,17:2
Maximilienne, Mme
Liliom 1935,Mr 18,14:4
Maximov, E
Bountiful Summer 1951,D 24,9:1
Maximova, A
Paris Commune 1937,Je 2,20:4
Othello 1960,My 16,39:1
Maximova, A M
Heroes of the Sea 1941,Ap 28,11:2
Maximova, Antonina
Ballad of a Soldier 1960,D 27,22:1
Maximova, E
Village of Sin, The 1929,My 21,29:3
Pugachev 1938,Jl 4,10:2
Maximova, Ekaterina
Cinderella 1961,D 19,39:1
Maximova, Lyudmila
There Was an old Couple 1967,My 22,53:1
Maximova, Raia
Idiot, The 1960,Jl 22,11:2
Maxted, Stanley
Never Let Me Go 1953,Je 11,37:2
Final Test, The 1954,Ja 26,21:5
I Am a Camera 1955,Ag 9,29:1
Across the Bridge 1957,O 30,24:1
Fiend Without a Face 1958,Jl 4,15:3
Campbell's Kingdom 1960,Ja 11,35:5
Maxudian
Arab, The 1924,Jl 14,11:5
Venus 1929,O 14,20:2
Dark Eyes 1938,Ap 19,24:5
Three Waltzes 1939,Ap 25,19:2
Sextette (Part 3-The Key to Sin); Key to Sin, The
 (Sextette) 1953,Mr 2,19:2
Maxwell
I Want my Man 1925,Ap 6,17:3
Maxwell, Aymer (Producer)
Another Sky 1960,O 25,40:2
Maxwell, Edwin
Taming of the Shrew, The 1929,N 30,23:1
All Quiet on The Western Front 1930,Ap 30,29:1
Du Barry, Woman of Passion 1930,N 3,19:3
Inspiration 1931,F 9,25:3
Gorilla, The 1931,F 23,20:3
Kiki 1931,Mr 6,16:1
Daybreak 1931,Je 1,15:1
Daddy Long Legs 1931,Je 6,15:5
Ambassador Bill 1931,N 14,15:3
Two Kinds of Women 1932,Ja 16,13:1
Shopworn 1932,Ap 4,13:6
Grand Hotel 1932,Ap 13,23:2
Cohens and Kellys in Hollywood, The
 1932,Ap 22,23:2
Scarface, The Shame of the Nation
 1932,My 20,22:3
American Madness 1932,Ag 6,14:5
Blessed Event 1932,S 3,16:2
Six Hours to Live 1932,O 22,18:4
You Said a Mouthful 1932,N 18,23:2
Tonight Is Ours 1933,Ja 21,10:6
Mystery of the Wax Museum, The
 1933,F 18,13:3
State Trooper 1933,Mr 27,13:6
Emergency Call 1933,Je 24,16:2
Woman I Stole, The 1933,Je 28,24:3
Mayor of Hell, The 1933,Jl 1,16:5
Gambling Ship 1933,Jl 13,17:5
Dinner at Eight 1933,Ag 24,18:1
Duck Soup 1933,N 23,24:2
Miss Fane's Baby is Stolen 1934,Ja 20,12:2
Ninth Guest, The 1934,Mr 3,8:5
Dancing Man 1934,Jl 16,11:3
Cleopatra 1934,Ag 17,12:1
Cat's Paw, The 1934,Ag 17,12:2
Gift of Gab 1934,S 26,17:6
All the King's Horses 1935,Mr 9,19:1
Great God Gold 1935,My 6,22:3
Thanks a Million 1935,N 14,17:1
Panic on the Air 1936,Ap 20,17:1
Fury 1936,Je 6,21:1
Come and Get It 1936,N 12,31:1
Night Key 1937,Ap 19,27:2
Slave Ship 1937,Je 17,19:2
Road Back, The 1937,Je 18,25:2

Maxwell, Edwin — Cont

Love Takes Flight 1937,S 27,24:3
Young Mr Lincoln 1939,Je 3,11:2
Way Down South 1939,Ag 18,16:4
Drums Along the Mohawk 1939,N 4,11:2
Ninotchka 1939,N 10,27:2
His Girl Friday 1940,Ja 12,13:2
Blue Bird, The 1940,Ja 20,11:2
Kit Carson 1940,N 15,25:3
Ride on Vaquero 1941,Ap 19,20:2
Devil and Miss Jones, The 1941,My 16,21:2
Ten Gentlemen From West Point 1942,Je 5,23:3
I Live on Danger 1942,Ag 22,16:2
Holy Matrimony 1943,S 16,25:2
Wilson 1944,Ag 2,18:1
Great Moment, The 1944,N 13,15:2
Swamp Fire 1946,Ag 26,21:4
Jolson Story, The 1946,O 11,28:2
Gangster, The 1947,O 31,29:3
Vicious Circle, The 1948,Jl 22,27:2

Maxwell, Elsa
Hotel for Women 1939,Ag 26,20:2
Public Deb No 1 1940,S 18,19:2
Stage Door Canteen 1943,Je 25,13:2

Maxwell, Elsa (Original Author)
Hotel for Women 1939,Ag 26,20:2

Maxwell, Frank
Lonelyhearts 1959,Mr 5,35:3
By Love Possessed 1961,Jl 20,32:2
Ada 1961,Ag 26,15:1
Intruder, The 1962,My 15,48:1
Haunted Palace, The 1964,Ja 30,24:1

Maxwell, I R (Producer)
Bolshoi Ballet, The 1957,D 18,45:1

Maxwell, James
Traitors, The 1963,Je 27,23:4

Maxwell, Jenny
Blue Denim 1959,Jl 31,21:1
Blue Hawaii 1962,F 22,20:2

Maxwell, John
Flying Cadets 1941,O 14,29:2
Nine Loves Are not Enough 1941,O 30,27:2
You're in the Army Now 1941,D 26,21:4
Spy Ship 1942,Jl 11,8:2
Truck Busters 1943,Ja 29,23:5
Silver Skates 1943,Mr 19,15:3
Asphalt Jungle, The 1950,Je 9,29:3
Three Guys Named Mike 1951,Mr 2,21:2
Prowler, The 1951,Jl 2,16:6
Bigamist, The 1953,D 26,10:4

Maxwell, Lois
That Hagen Girl 1947,O 25,13:2
Decision of Christopher Blake, The
  1948,D 11,12:2
Dark Past, The 1948,D 23,25:2
Corridor of Mirrors 1949,Mr 23,35:3
Brief Rapture 1952,F 28,23:2
Tomorrow is too Late 1952,Ap 14,22:2
Woman's Angle, The 1954,Ag 27,11:6
Aida 1954,N 12,17:1
Satellite in the Sky 1956,S 4,32:7
Time Without Pity 1957,N 23,11:2
Lolita 1962,Je 14,23:2
Dr No 1963,My 30,20:1
Haunting, The 1963,S 19,23:1
From Russia with Love 1964,Ap 9,25:1
Goldfinger 1964,D 22,36:1
Thunderball 1965,D 22,23:1
You Only Live Twice 1967,Je 14,40:1
Operation Kid Brother 1967,N 23,58:2

Maxwell, Marilyn
Stand by for Action 1943,Mr 12,12:2
Salute to the Marines 1943,Ag 30,11:3
Thousands Cheer 1943,S 14,27:1
Swing Fever 1944,Ja 28,14:1
Three Men in White 1944,My 26,23:3
Lost in a Harem 1944,N 9,23:2
Between Two Women 1945,Mr 29,18:3
Show-Off, The 1947,Mr 20,38:2
High Barbaree 1947,Je 6,27:2
Summer Holiday 1948,Je 12,8:5
Race Street 1948,Ag 23,13:3
Champion 1949,Ap 11,29:2
Key to the City 1950,F 2,31:2
Outside the Wall 1950,Mr 15,34:8
Lemon Drop Kid, The 1951,Mr 22,41:2
New Mexico 1951,Jl 14,7:2
Off Limits 1953,Mr 30,25:5
New York Confidential 1955,F 19,18:1
Forever, Darling 1956,F 10,18:1
Rock-a-Bye Baby 1958,Jl 24,18:1
Critic's Choice 1963,My 2,40:2
Lively Set, The 1964,O 15,54:1

Maxwell, Milton
Blessed Event 1932,S 3,16:2

Maxwell, Norman
Forty Thousand Horsemen 1941,Ag 15,13:2

Maxwell, Paul
Man in the Middle 1964,Mr 5,36:1
25th Hour, The 1967,F 17,45:1
It 1967,N 16,58:1

Maxwell, Stacey
Eight on the Lam 1967,Ap 27,52:1

Maxwell, Tony
Dime With a Halo 1963,Je 27,23:3

Maxwell, W B (Original Author)
Madonna of the Streets 1930,N 29,21:4

Maxwell, William
Conqueror Worm, The 1968,Ag 15,46:2

Maxwell-Conover, Theresa
Age of Innocence, The 1934,O 19,27:1

May, Ada
Dance, Girl, Dance 1933,O 25,23:3

May, Ann
Peaceful Valley 1920,O 11,19:3
Dangerous Maid, The 1923,D 11,26:2
Waking up the Town 1925,Mr 31,17:4

May, Betty
Night Nurse 1931,Jl 17,23:4

May, Billy
Nightmare 1956,My 12,12:7

May, Claude
Generals Without Buttons 1938,Mr 8,23:2
Ignace 1950,S 19,39:4

May, Cynthia
I, A Man 1967,Ag 25,28:1

May, Donald
Crowded Sky, The 1961,F 11,27:2
Kisses for my President 1964,Ag 22,13:1
Follow Me, Boys! 1966,D 2,46:1

May, Doris
Twenty-three and a Half Hours' Leave
  1919,O 27,9:3
Mary's Ankle 1920,Mr 1,16:2
Let's Be Fashionable 1920,Je 14,13:2
Rookie's Return, The 1920,D 27,11:3
Common Law, The 1923,O 29,18:1
Deadwood Coach, The 1925,Ja 21,19:3

May, Edna
Salvation Joan 1916,Ap 10,11:3

May, Elaine
Luv 1967,Jl 27,29:1
Enter Laughing 1967,Ag 1,24:1

May, Hans (Composer)
Ein Burschenlied aus Heidelberg 1931,S 14,15:3
Waltz Time 1946,F 11,25:2

May, Hans (Miscellaneous)
Wien Du Stadt der Lieder; (Vienna City of Song)
  1931,Mr 20,29:1

May, Joe (Director)
Dragon's Claw, The 1922,Mr 6,9:3
Homecoming 1928,N 19,16:7
Asphalt 1930,My 6,33:4
Und das Ist die Hauptsache; That's All That
  Matters 1931,My 24,VIII,4:1
Paris-Mediterranee 1932,Mr 27,VIII,6:2
Ihre Majestaet die Liebe 1933,F 7,23:4
Eine Liebesnacht 1933,My 15,16:2
On Demande un Compaznon 1933,Je 5,18:5
Music in the Air 1934,D 14,29:3
Confession 1937,Ag 19,23:1
Invisible Man Returns, The 1940,Ja 16,19:2
House of the Seven Gables, The 1940,Ap 15,21:3
You're not so Tough 1940,Jl 9,25:3
Hit the Road 1941,Jl 3,15:3

May, Joe (Original Author)
Invisible Man Returns, The 1940,Ja 16,19:2
Invisible Woman, The 1941,Ja 9,27:2
Strange Death of Adolf Hitler, The 1943,O 9,11:5
Uncertain Glory 1944,Ap 8,9:2
Buccaneer's Girl 1950,Mr 27,19:2

May, Jules
Mistigri 1933,Ja 13,19:3

May, Mia
Dragon's Claw, The 1922,Mr 6,9:3

May, Pamela
Bride of the Lake, The 1934,S 11,24:5

May, Vincent
Fra Diavolo 1931,N 23,22:1

Mayall, Herschel
Money Corporal, The 1919,Ap 21,13:4
Thirty Days 1922,D 11,22:1
Wild Bill Hickok 1923,N 21,22:1
Fast and Loose 1930,D 1,21:1
Royal Family of Broadway, The 1930,D 23,25:1
His Woman 1931,D 5,21:2
War Is a Racket 1934,D 10,16:2

Maybach, Christine
Head, The 1963,Je 20,29:1

Maybelle, Big
Jazz on a Summer's Day 1960,Mr 29,46:2

Maybert, Ludwig
Counterfeit Traitor, The 1962,Ap 18,28:1

Mayble, Jackie
Emperor Jones, The 1933,S 20,26:2

Mayehoff, Eddie
That's My Boy 1951,Ag 2,18:1
Stooge, The 1953,F 5,19:2
Off Limits 1953,Mr 30,25:5
Artists and Models 1955,D 22,20:1
How to Murder Your Wife 1965,Ja 27,26:1
Luv 1967,Jl 27,29:1

Mayen, Harry
Enough Rope 1966,Jl 15,34:3

MAYER
See Also MEAGHER, MAIER, MAHER

Mayer, Arthur (Miscellaneous)
Eternal Mask, The 1937,Ja 13,20:3

Mayer, Carl (Original Author)
Cabinet of Dr Caligari, The 1921,Mr 20,VI,2:1
Last Laugh, The 1925,Ja 28,14:1

Mayer, Carl (Producer)
Berlin, A Symphony of a Big City
  1928,My 14,25:1

Mayer, Carl (Screenwriter)
Tartuffe 1927,Jl 25,25:3
Sunrise; Song of two Human Beings
  1928,Ja 29,VIII,6:2
Mann der den Mord Beging, Der; Man Who
  Committed the Murder, The 1931,F 22,VIII,6:2
Dreaming Lips 1937,My 20,17:1

Mayer, Carl Walter
Die Mutter der Kompagnie 1934,Mr 9,22:3

Mayer, Edwin Justus (Miscellaneous)
Peter Ibbetson 1935,N 8,18:2

Mayer, Edwin Justus (Original Author)
I Am Suzanne 1934,Ja 19,24:3
Affairs of Cellini, The 1934,S 6,22:3
Midnight 1939,Ap 6,31:1
Underground 1941,Je 23,13:2

Mayer, Edwin Justus (Screenwriter)
Here is my Heart 1934,D 22,21:1
Give Us This Night 1936,Ap 6,18:1
Desire 1936,Ap 13,15:1
Till We Meet Again 1936,My 9,11:2
Buccaneer, The 1938,F 17,17:2
Exile Express 1939,Ag 16,21:3
They Met in Bombay 1941,Jl 4,17:1
To Be or not to Be 1942,Mr 7,13:2
Royal Scandal, A 1945,Ap 12,19:2
Masquerade in Mexico 1945,N 29,27:2
Buccaneer, The 1958,D 24,00:0

Mayer, Emile
Taggart 1964,D 25,24:4

Mayer, Ferinando
Don Bosco 1936,My 27,27:3

Mayer, Gerald (Director)
Dial 1119 1950,D 4,32:6
Inside Straight 1951,Mr 16,34:2
Sellout, The 1952,My 31,12:7
Holiday for Sinners 1952,S 20,13:2
Bright Road 1953,Ap 29,33:5

Mayer, Harold (Director)
Inheritance, The 1964,N 9,42:2

Mayer, Harold (Producer)
Inheritance, The 1964,N 9,42:2

Mayer, Hy (Miscellaneous)
Such Is Life 'Mong the Children of France
  1922,My 1,20:3
Such Is Life 'Mong Alpine Sports 1922,Jl 10,9:5

Mayer, Hy (Producer)
Such Is Life in New York Uptown 1920,Ja 5,15:1
Such Is Life at Coney Island 1920,Jl 5,12:4
Such Is Life Behind the Scenes of a Circus
  1920,O 25,18:1

Mayer, Johannes (Director)
Gibt nur eine Liebe, Es 1937,Ja 23,23:2

Mayer, Ray
Young and Beautiful 1934,S 18,18:4
Arizonian, The 1935,Jl 27,16:2
To Beat the Band 1935,N 23,23:2
Seven Keys to Baldpate 1935,D 14,11:2
Follow the Fleet 1936,F 21,21:2
I Married a Doctor 1936,Ap 20,17:1
Special Investigator 1936,Ap 25,21:1
Last Outlaw, The 1936,Je 15,24:1
We Who Are About to Die 1937,Ja 2,15:1
Top of the Town 1937,Mr 27,19:2
Make Way for Tomorrow 1937,My 10,23:1
Meet the Missus 1937,Jl 2,25:2
Hideaway 1937,S 25,10:2
Swing It, Sailor 1937,D 13,23:5
Prison Nurse 1938,Mr 4,17:5
Comet over Broadway 1938,D 16,33:3
King of Chinatown 1939,Mr 16,27:2
Snafu 1945,D 26,15:2

Mayerhofer, Elfie
Hotel Sacher 1939,Je 10,14:2

Mayerova, Vojtova
Ecstasy of Young Love 1936,Mr 10,27:3

MAYES
See Also MAES

Mayes, Johnnie L Pvt
Cease Fire! 1953,N 25,17:1

Mayes, Mary (Screenwriter)
Freckles 1935,O 26,12:2

Mayes, Norman
You Can't Fool Your Wife 1940,My 24,23:4

Mayes, Wendell (Producer)
Hotel 1967,Ja 20,27:1

Mayes, Wendell (Screenwriter)
Spirit of St Louis, The 1957,F 22,25:1
Way to the Gold, The 1957,My 11,24:6
From Hell to Texas 1958,Je 5,39:2
Hunters, The 1958,Ag 27,33:1
Hanging Tree, The 1959,F 12,23:1
Anatomy of a Murder 1959,Jl 3,10:1

Mayes, Wendell (Screenwriter)— Cont
Advise and Consent 1962,Je 7,31:2
In Harm's Way 1965,Ap 7,36:1
Von Ryan's Express 1965,Je 24,28:1
Hotel 1967,Ja 20,27:1
Mayes, William (Screenwriter)
Enemy Below, The 1957,D 26,23:2
Mayeska, Irena
Incredible Journey, The 1963,N 21,43:2
Mayevsky, A (Director)
Road to Life 1956,Je 11,26:6
Mayfair, Mitzi
Four Jills in a Jeep 1944,Ap 6,27:2
Mayfair, Mitzi (Miscellaneous)
Four Jills in a Jeep 1944,Ap 6,27:2
Mayfield, Julian
Up Tight 1968,D 19,62:1
Mayfield, Julian (Screenwriter)
Up Tight 1968,D 19,62:1
Mayflower, Z (Director)
Ada, to Nie Wypada 1937,My 4,29:1
Mayhew, Kate
Tongues of Flame 1924,D 16,28:1
Maylia
Singapore 1947,S 17,31:2
To the Ends of the Earth 1948,F 13,26:2
Chinatown at Midnight 1949,N 18,35:3
Maynard, Audrey
Our Neighbors-The Carters 1940,F 15,15:2
Women Without Names 1940,My 9,26:4
Maynard, Claire
Over the Hill 1931,N 21,20:4
Good Sport 1931,D 12,23:3
Maynard, George (Producer)
Cosmic Monster, The 1959,Ja 1,38:1
Ferry to Hong Kong 1961,Ap 27,27:7
Maynard, Ken
Janice Meredith 1924,Ag 6,13:3
Senor Daredevil 1926,Ag 17,15:3
Red Raiders, The 1927,S 28,28:3
Parade of the West 1930,Mr 3,18:4
Branded Men 1931,D 12,23:3
Maynard, Kermit
Golden Girl 1951,N 21,20:3
Maynard, Theodore (Miscellaneous)
Citizen Saint 1948,My 28,28:2
Mayne, Eric
Suzanna 1923,Mr 26,16:2
Human Wreckage 1923,Je 28,10:2
Black Oxen 1924,Ja 7,23:1
Extra Girl, The 1924,Ja 21,20:1
Yankee Consul, The 1924,F 11,18:3
Goldfish, The 1924,My 20,15:2
Barriers Burned Away 1925,Mr 12,17:2
Black Bird, The 1926,F 1,16:1
Hangman's House 1928,My 14,25:1
East Lynne 1931,F 21,15:2
Rackety Rax 1932,N 5,12:5
All the King's Horses 1935,Mr 9,19:1
Mayne, Ferdy
Prelude to Fame 1950,N 10,35:3
Hotel Sahara 1952,Ja 1,21:4
Paris Express, The 1953,Je 6,8:6
Desperate Moment 1953,S 1,19:4
White Fire 1954,S 18,12:4
1954,S 18,12:4
Divided Heart, The 1955,Ag 4,16:1
Gentlemen Marry Brunettes 1955,O 31,31:5
Storm over the Nile 1956,Je 9,14:2
Abandon Ship 1957,Ap 18,35:1
Blue Murder at St Trinian's 1958,My 27,27:1
Third Man on the Mountain 1959,N 12,27:1
Bobo, The 1967,S 29,53:1
Fearless Vampire Killers, The, or Pardon Me but
  Your Teeth are in my Neck 1967,N 14,52:1
Mayniel, Juliette
Cousins, The (Les Cousins) 1959,N 24,44:1
Landru 1963,Ap 10,31:1
Maynor, Asa
Promise her Anything 1966,F 23,46:1
Mayo, Alfredo
Teacher and the Miracle, The 1961,Ap 24,36:4
Hunt, The 1967,Ap 25,38:1
Mayo, Archie (Director)
Money Talks 1926,My 11,24:3
Dearie 1927,Jl 4,20:3
College Widow, The 1927,N 7,26:4
Beware of Married Men 1928,Ap 10,33:2
State Street Sadie 1928,S 3,14:2
On Trial 1928,N 15,26:5
My Man 1928,D 22,14:3
Sonny Boy 1929,Mr 9,24:3
Is Everybody Happy? 1929,N 2,14:6
Sacred Flame, The 1929,N 23,18:5
Wide Open 1930,Mr 22,22:6
Courage 1930,My 23,21:1
Doorway to Hell, The 1930,N 1,23:2
Illicit 1931,Ja 19,25:1
Svengali 1931,My 1,30:3
Bought 1931,Ag 15,18:3
Under Eighteen 1931,D 26,15:5
Expert, The 1932,F 27,22:1
Street of Women 1932,My 30,16:5
Two Against the World 1932,Ag 19,20:6

Night after Night 1932,O 31,18:4
Life of Jimmy Dolan, The 1933,Je 14,22:3
Mayor of Hell, The 1933,Jl 1,16:5
Ever in my Heart 1933,O 13,25:3
Convention City 1933,D 25,28:2
Gambling Lady 1934,Ap 5,25:2
Man With two Faces, The 1934,Jl 12,20:2
Desirable 1934,S 15,20:5
Bordertown 1935,Ja 24,22:5
Go Into Your Dance 1935,My 4,17:2
Case of the Lucky Legs, The 1935,N 1,25:1
Petrified Forest, The 1936,F 7,14:2
I Married a Doctor 1936,Ap 20,17:1
Give Me your Heart 1936,S 17,18:2
Black Legion 1937,Ja 18,21:1
Call it a Day 1937,My 7,29:2
It's Love I'm After 1937,N 11,31:2
Youth Takes a Fling 1938,O 17,12:1
They Shall Have Music 1939,Jl 26,17:2
House Across the Bay, The 1940,Mr 22,23:2
Four Sons 1940,Je 8,18:4
Great American Broadcast, The 1941,My 2,25:2
Charley's Aunt 1941,Ag 2,18:2
Confirm or Deny 1941,D 19,35:2
Moontide 1942,Ap 30,14:1
Orchestra Wives 1942,S 24,23:2
Crash Dive 1943,Ap 29,25:2
Sweet and Low Down 1944,O 19,19:2
Night in Casablanca, A 1946,Ag 12,17:2
Angel on my Shoulder 1946,O 21,27:2
Adventures of Marco Polo, The 1965,Ap 8,17:2
Mayo, Christine
Don't Marry for Money 1923,Ag 21,17:3
For Sale 1924,Jl 14,11:5
Mayo, Frank
Mary Regan 1919,My 5,11:1
Souls for Sale 1923,Ap 9,14:3
Six Days 1923,S 24,5:4
Wild Oranges 1924,Mr 3,22:3
Woman on the Jury, The 1924,My 19,14:2
Perfect Flapper, The 1924,Je 23,22:4
If I Marry Again 1925,Ja 12,11:2
Price She Paid, The 1925,Ja 13,16:1
Barriers Burned Away 1925,Mr 12,17:2
Passionate Youth 1925,Je 30,14:3
Dough Boys 1930,S 30,23:1
Hollywood Boulevard 1936,S 21,26:4
Confessions of a Nazi Spy 1939,Ap 29,13:2
British Intelligence 1940,F 12,14:2
Torrid Zone 1940,My 18,11:3
Flowing Gold 1940,S 2,19:3
Male Animal, The 1942,Mr 28,11:1
Lady Gangster 1942,Jl 10,13:2
Gentleman Jim 1942,N 26,40:3
Gorilla Man, The 1943,Ja 15,21:4
Mayo, James (Original Author)
Hammerhead 1968,S 12,54:3
Mayo, Margaret (Original Author)
Polly of the Circus 1917,S 10,11:3
Twin Beds 1920,N 1,13:2
Baby Mine 1928,Ja 9,20:1
Polly of the Circus 1932,Mr 19,11:2
Twin Beds 1942,My 1,23:4
Mayo, Susana
No Exit 1962,D 6,55:2
Mayo, Virginia
Jack London 1944,Mr 3,19:3
Seven Days Ashore 1944,Ap 26,24:7
Princess and the Pirate, The 1945,F 10,16:2
Wonder Man 1945,Je 9,17:2
Kid From Brooklyn, The 1946,Ap 19,25:2
Best Years of our Lives, The 1946,N 22,27:2
Secret Life of Walter Mitty, The 1947,Ag 15,12:2
Song Is Born, A 1948,O 20,37:2
Colorado Territory 1949,Je 25,8:6
Girl from Jones Beach, The 1949,Jl 30,9:2
White Heat 1949,S 3,7:2
Always Leave Them Laughing 1949,N 24,48:2
Red Light 1950,Ja 16,18:4
Backfire 1950,Ja 27,29:2
Flame and the Arrow, The 1950,Jl 8,7:2
West Point Story, The 1950,D 23,11:3
Along the Great Divide 1951,My 17,38:3
Painting the Clouds With Sunshine 1951,S 1,9:6
Captain Horatio Hornblower 1951,S 14,21:2
Starlift 1951,D 15,11:2
She's Working her Way Through College
  1952,Jl 10,27:2
Iron Mistress, The 1952,N 20,39:2
She's Back on Broadway 1953,Mr 12,24:2
South Sea Woman 1953,Je 4,33:6
Devil's Canyon 1953,O 3,14:2
King Richard and the Crusaders 1954,Ag 23,20:5
Silver Chalice, The 1954,D 27,22:5
Pearl of the South Pacific 1955,S 17,12:2
Great Day in the Morning 1956,My 19,12:6
Congo Crossing 1956,Jl 14,13:2
Proud Ones, The 1956,Ag 11,10:2
Big Land, The 1957,Mr 2,18:2
Story of Mankind, The 1957,N 9,31:2
Fort Dobbs 1958,Ap 19,10:4
Jet Over the Atlantic 1960,Ja 7,24:6
Fort Utah 1967,My 25,54:3

Mayock, Peter
Ulysses 1967,Mr 14,55:1
Mayon, Helen
Hilda Crane 1956,My 3,35:2
Mayring, Lothar
Tanz Geht Weiter, Der 1931,Ja 6,25:1
Mayring, Philipp L (Director)
Schlacht von Bademuende, Die 1931,N 21,20:4
Maysles, Albert (Cinematographer)
Monterey Pop 1968,D 27,44:1
Maysles, Albert (Producer)
Meet Marlon Brando 1966,S 18,78:1
Maysles, David (Producer)
Meet Marlon Brando 1966,S 18,78:1
Maysles Brothers (Miscellaneous)
Journey to Jerusalem, A 1968,N 18,59:1
Mayura.
Chinese Den 1941,Mr 26,27:3
Maza, Armando Vargas de la (Director)
Indio, El 1939,My 13,11:5
Mazar, Richard
Uncivilized 1937,N 17,27:4
Mazarella, Piero
Violent Four, The 1968,Ag 15,46:2
Mazurki, Mike
Shanghai Gesture, The 1941,D 26,21:2
Taxi, Mister 1943,Ap 15,20:2
Behind the Rising Sun 1943,O 14,26:2
Murder, my Sweet 1945,Mr 9,16:2
Horn Blows at Midnight, The 1945,Ap 21,18:2
Spanish Main, The 1945,N 7,20:2
Abbott and Costello in Hollywood
  1945,N 23,26:2
Dakota 1945,D 17,17:2
Dick Tracy 1946,Ja 12,10:7
Sinbad the Sailor 1947,Ja 23,31:2
Nightmare Alley 1947,O 10,31:3
Unconquered 1947,O 11,11:2
I Walk Alone 1948,Ja 22,36:3
Relentless 1948,Mr 6,17:3
Noose Hangs High, The 1948,My 29,8:6
Neptune's Daughter 1949,Je 10,32:2
Come to the Stable 1949,Jl 28,19:1
Rope of Sand 1949,Ag 4,19:2
Abandoned Woman 1949,O 27,35:3
Night and the City 1950,Je 10,11:2
Dark City 1950,O 19,40:5
He's a Cockeyed Wonder 1950,O 20,32:4
Criminal Lawyer 1951,Ag 24,11:4
Ten Tall Men 1951,O 27,10:5
My Favorite Spy 1951,D 26,19:3
Light Touch, The 1952,Ja 17,23:1
New York Confidential 1955,F 19,18:1
New Orleans Uncensored 1955,Ap 30,10:8
Davy Crockett, King of the Wild Frontier
  1955,My 26,36:1
Blood Alley 1955,O 6,25:3
Kismet 1955,D 9,32:2
Around the World in 80 Days 1956,O 18,37:1
Some Like It Hot 1959,Mr 30,23:1
Facts of Life, The 1961,F 11,27:1
Pocketful of Miracles 1961,D 19,39:1
Five Weeks in a Balloon 1962,Ag 27,18:1
Donovan's Reef 1963,Jl 25,14:1
Cheyenne Autumn 1964,D 24,8:1
7 Women 1966,My 5,59:1
Adventures of Bullwhip Griffin, The
  1967,Mr 9,43:2
Mazurova, Yulia
When the Trees Were Tall 1965,F 22,14:1
Mazursky, Paul
Fear and Desire 1953,Ap 1,35:2
Blackboard Jungle 1955,Mr 21,21:5
Deathwatch 1967,Je 28,38:1
Mazursky, Paul (Producer)
I Love You Alice B Toklas! 1968,O 8,40:1
Mazursky, Paul (Screenwriter)
I Love You Alice B Toklas! 1968,O 8,40:1
Mazza, Mario
Ring Around the Clock 1953,My 19,36:2
Mazzacurati, Rosy
Night, The; Notte, La 1962,F 20,29:4
Mazzari, Amedeo
Poppy is Also a Flower, The 1967,D 14,62:4
Mazze, Francesco (Producer)
Ecco 1965,N 5,28:1
Mazziotti, Nino
Barber of Seville, The 1947,My 6,35:2
Mazziotti, P A (Original Author)
Sei tu l'Amore 1930,N 18,28:4
Mazzola, Frank
Rebel without a Cause 1955,O 27,28:3
Mazzone-Abbott Dancers
It's a Great Feeling 1949,Ag 13,6:6
Mazzoni, A (Director)
Signora Paradiso 1937,Jl 22,15:2
Mazzotti, Adrianna
Father's Dilemma 1952,S 23,25:1
Mazzullo, Gaetano (Screenwriter)
Favorita, La 1953,O 30,27:4
Mazzunchelli, Fausta
Stranger on the Prowl 1953,N 10,38:1

Mc
Names are filed as though spelled Mac.
Mdivani, Georgil (Screenwriter)
Apartment in Moscow 1962,My 28,25:5
Red and the White, The 1968,S 21,26:1
Meacham, Anne
Lilith 1964,S 21,37:2
Meacham, Michael
Adventures of Sadie, The 1955,My 18,35:2
Midsummer Night's Dream, A 1961,D 19,39:1
Sword of Lancelot 1963,O 10,49:2
Mead, Frank Lieut Commander (Screenwriter)
Great Impersonation, The 1935,D 14,11:1
Mead, Shepherd (Original Author)
How to Succeed in Business Without Really
Trying 1967,Mr 10,30:1
Mead, Taylor
Flower Thief, The 1962,Jl 14,11:5
Lemon Hearts 1962,Ag 3,14:2
Hallelujah the Hills 1963,D 17,49:1
Open the Door and See all the People
1964,Ap 2,28:1
Nude Restaurant, The 1967,N 14,52:1
Illiac Passion, The 1968,Ap 19,40:1
Meade, Claire
Unfaithful, The 1947,Je 28,10:2
Mother is a Freshman 1949,Mr 12,10:2
Meade, Julia
Pillow Talk 1959,O 7,47:2
Tammy Tell me True 1961,Jl 27,23:2
Zotz! 1962,O 4,44:3
Meade, Mary
T-Men 1948,Ja 23,28:3
Meade, Walter (Screenwriter)
Another Shore 1951,F 12,19:3
Scott of the Antarctic 1951,F 26,20:2
Meader, George
Courageous Dr Christian, The 1940,Mr 29,25:3
Life With Henry 1941,F 6,25:2
Man Made Monster 1941,Mr 19,25:4
Father takes a Wife 1941,S 5,19:3
Smiling Ghost, The 1941,S 26,26:5
Glass Key, The 1942,O 16,23:1
That Midnight Kiss 1949,S 23,28:2
On the Town 1949,D 9,37:2
Groom Wore Spurs, The 1951,Mr 14,41:2
She's Working her Way Through College
1952,Jl 10,27:2
Meader, William
Wild Harvest 1947,N 13,33:2
Meador, Josh (Director)
Make Mine Music 1946,Ap 22,26:2
Meadow, Edward (Producer)
Incident, The 1967,N 6,65:1
Meadow, Herb (Screenwriter)
Strange Woman, The 1947,F 24,16:4
Redhead From Wyoming, The 1953,Ja 9,17:4
Master of Ballantrae, The 1953,Ag 6,16:2
Highway Dragnet 1954,F 20,8:7
Lone Ranger, The 1956,F 11,12:1
Man Afraid 1957,Ap 5,24:2
Meadow, Noel (Miscellaneous)
One Inch From Victory 1944,Ap 27,18:5
Meadows, Audrey
That Touch of Mink 1962,Je 15,16:2
Take Her, She's Mine 1963,N 14,41:1
Rosie 1968,F 8,36:1
Meadows, George
Midnight Express, The 1924,N 19,19:3
Meadows, Jayne
Undercurrent 1946,N 29,36:2
Lady in the Lake 1947,Ja 24,18:3
Dark Delusion 1947,Je 26,19:2
Song of the Thin Man 1947,Ag 29,14:2
Luck of the Irish, The 1948,S 16,34:1
Enchantment 1948,D 27,16:2
Fat Man, The 1951,My 25,31:2
David and Bathsheba 1951,Ag 15,23:2
College Confidential 1960,Ag 22,23:1
Meadows, Leslie
Half a Sixpence 1968,F 21,60:3
Meadows, Stanley
Kaleidoscope 1966,S 23,45:1
MEAGHER
See Also MAIER, MAHER, MAYER
Meagher, Edward (Original Author)
Night Cry, The 1926,Ap 7,26:6
Meakin, Charles
Marriage Clause, The 1926,S 28,30:2
Upstage 1926,N 15,19:1
Meakin, Jack (Composer)
Hit Parade of 1947 1947,My 5,32:8
Mealand, Richard (Original Author)
Always Leave Them Laughing 1949,N 24,48:2
Means, Grant
16 Fathoms Deep 1948,O 7,35:2
Mear, H Fowler (Miscellaneous)
Morals of Marcus, The 1936,Ja 13,14:2

Mear, H Fowler (Original Author)
In a Monastery Garden 1935,Mr 13,16:2
Mear, H Fowler (Screenwriter)
Triumph of Sherlock Holmes, The
1935,My 27,20:6
Last Journey, The 1936,Je 8,22:4
Juggernaut 1937,Jl 15,16:1
She Shall Have Music 1942,O 31,11:2
Mears, Martha
Our Neighbors-The Carters 1940,F 15,15:2
My Foolish Heart 1950,Ja 20,29:2
Mears, Stannard (Original Author)
Seventeen 1940,F 29,15:2
Mearson, Lyon (Original Author)
Our Wife 1941,S 18,31:1
Measor, Beryl
Odd Man Out 1947,Ap 24,30:2
Meck, Donald
Whole Town's Talking, The 1935,Mr 1,16:2
Mecker, George
Emma 1932,F 6,14:4
Tarzan's Revenge 1938,Ja 10,13:3
Meckert, Jean (Miscellaneous)
Young Girls Beware 1959,Ag 22,8:2
Medak, Peter (Director)
Negatives 1968,O 15,40:1
Medard, Mimi
My Seven Little Sins 1956,My 2,27:1
Medbury, John (Miscellaneous)
Reported Missing 1922,Ap 24,18:3
Medbury, John P (Miscellaneous)
Love in Bloom 1935,Ap 20,16:2
What's Buzzin Cousin 1943,Jl 23,21:4
Medcraft, Russell G (Original Author)
Let's Face It 1943,Ag 5,18:1
Medcroft, Russell
Wild, Wild Susan 1925,Ag 5,12:4
Meddick, Lane
Purple Plain, The 1955,Ap 11,29:1
Medel, Manuel
Payasada de la Vida; Tricks of Life
1935,Mr 18,14:5
Asi es mi Tierra; Such Is my Country
1939,Mr 18,9:3
Medeolti, J (Director)
Gottes Muehlen mahlen Langsam; Mills of the
Gods, The 1939,F 18,12:4
Mederow, Paul
Brand in der Oper 1932,Jl 11,11:4
1914: The Last Days Before the War 1932,S 5,9:6
Medford, Harold (Narrator)
Marilyn 1963,Jl 18,15:1
Medford, Harold (Original Author)
Target Unknown 1951,Mr 5,24:2
Cinerama-South Seas Adventure 1958,Jl 16,26:1
Medford, Harold (Screenwriter)
Berlin Express 1948,My 21,19:3
Damned Don't Cry, The 1950,Ap 8,9:2
Operation Secret 1952,N 6,37:2
Phantom of the Rue Morgue 1954,Mr 20,10:5
Killer is Loose, The 1956,Mr 3,17:2
Incident in an Alley 1962,My 17,31:1
Fate Is the Hunter 1964,D 10,61:1
Medford, Jill
Blackout 1954,My 22,8:2
Will any Gentleman? 1955,S 28,70:6
Medford, Kay
Swing Shift Maisie 1943,S 10,29:2
Undercover Man, The 1949,Ap 21,30:2
Guilty Bystander 1950,Ap 21,18:2
Singing in the Dark 1956,Mr 8,32:5
Face in the Crowd, A 1957,My 29,33:1
Rat Race, The 1960,My 26,37:3
Girl of the Night 1960,N 12,15:1
Butterfield 8 1960,N 17,46:1
Two Tickets to Paris 1962,N 29,46:5
Ensign Pulver 1964,Ag 1,13:2
Busy Body, The 1967,Je 8,52:2
Funny Girl 1968,S 20,42:1
Medici, Nona
Eva 1965,Je 5,21:2
Medin, Harriette White
Blood and Black Lace 1965,N 11,58:3
Medina, Jesus
Yanco 1964,Je 18,29:2
Medina, Patricia
Avengers, The 1942,N 25,18:2
Waltz Time 1946,F 11,25:2
Secret Heart, The 1946,D 26,28:2
Moss Rose 1947,Jl 3,14:2
Foxes of Harrow, The 1947,S 25,35:4
Three Musketeers, The 1948,O 21,33:2
Don't Take it to Heart 1948,D 25,10:3
Fighting O'Flynn, The 1949,F 28,16:2
Francis 1950,Mr 16,40:2
Fortunes of Captain Blood 1950,Je 10,11:3
Abbott and Costello in the Foreign Legion
1950,Ag 14,14:4
Jackpot, The 1950,N 23,55:2
Valentino 1951,Ap 20,25:1
Lady in the Iron Mask 1952,Jl 5,7:2
Sangaree 1953,Je 5,19:1
Plunder of the Sun 1953,Ag 27,22:1

Medina, Patricia— Cont
Botany Bay 1953,O 30,27:2
Phantom of the Rue Morgue 1954,Mr 20,10:5
Drums of Tahiti 1954,Ap 24,14:5
Black Knight, The 1954,O 29,27:2
Pirates of Tripoli 1955,F 24,21:2
Count Your Blessings 1959,Ap 24,23:1
Snow White and the Three Stooges 1961,Jl 1,9:1
Mr Arkadin 1962,O 12,26:1
Killing of Sister George, The 1968,D 17,58:4
Medina, Rafael
Podoroso Caballero 1936,O 26,20:2
They Were Five 1938,Je 1,19:5
Medioll, Enrico (Screenwriter)
Rocco and his Brothers 1961,Je 28,40:2
Girl With a Suitcase 1961,S 12,36:2
Leopard, The 1963,Ag 13,25:1
Sandra 1966,Ja 17,32:1
Medland, Paul
Browning Version, The 1951,O 30,33:2
Medvedev, Peter
My Beloved 1959,Je 15,31:4
Medvedev, V
Lad From our Town 1943,O 7,26:2
Big Family, A 1955,Je 6,24:1
Twelfth Night 1956,Mr 5,21:1
Gadfly, The 1956,S 17,22:2
Sisters 1959,My 25,33:2
Eugene Onegin 1959,S 14,33:1
Hamlet 1964,S 15,32:1
Hamlet 1966,Mr 16,48:1
Medvedeva, N
Behind the Show Window 1957,Ap 17,37:1
Medvedeva, Natalya
Vasili's Return 1953,S 28,21:4
Medvedeva, Nina
Sword and the Dragon, The 1960,N 17,46:3
Medwick, Joe
Ninth Inning, The 1942,Ja 8,30:3
Medwin, Michael
For Them that Trespass 1950,S 27,37:2
Mr Know-All 1950,O 11,42:1
Another Shore 1951,F 12,19:3
Gay Lady, The 1951,Ap 16,21:2
Long Dark Hall, The 1951,My 10,38:3
Four in a Jeep 1951,Je 12,35:2
Kathy's Love Affair 1952,Jl 3,16:2
Curtain Up 1953,F 2,17:3
Miss Robin Hood 1953,Je 27,7:2
Caretaker's Daughter, The 1953,Ag 20,18:5
Both Sides of the Law 1954,Ja 12,19:2
Horse's Mouth, The 1954,Ja 20,33:4
Green Scarf, The 1955,Ja 15,10:2
Intruder, The 1955,Ja 26,22:1
Teckman Mystery, The 1955,Ag 22,18:2
Doctor at Sea 1956,Mr 1,37:3
Above Us the Waves 1957,Ap 18,35:2
Doctor at Large 1957,Jl 29,15:5
Checkpoint 1957,S 19,25:2
Wind Cannot Read, The 1960,Mr 10,36:1
Crooks Anonymous 1963,O 31,26:3
Night Must Fall 1964,Mr 19,28:1
Dream Maker, The 1964,Ap 23,34:1
Rattle of a Simple Man 1964,D 21,42:2
Countess from Hong Kong, A 1967,Mr 17,35:1
Medwin, Michael (Producer)
Charlie Bubbles 1968,F 12,47:2
Meehan, Danny
Blast of Silence 1961,D 30,12:1
Meehan, Elizabeth (Original Author)
Parachute Nurse 1942,Jl 27,18:2
Storm Over Lisbon 1944,S 11,14:1
Out of This World 1945,Je 7,25:2
Meehan, Elizabeth (Screenwriter)
Harmony Lane 1935,O 24,19:4
Harvester, The 1936,Jl 4,18:2
Girl From God's Country 1940,S 9,18:5
Northwest Outpost 1947,Ag 8,10:2
Meehan, James Leo (Director)
Keeper of the Bees, The 1925,O 28,29:2
Mother 1927,My 4,29:2
Judgment of the Hills 1927,Ag 2,19:2
Harvester, The 1927,N 7,33:1
Meehan, John (Miscellaneous)
Peter Ibbetson 1935,N 8,18:2
Meehan, John (Original Author)
Lady Lies, The 1929,S 7,15:1
Miracle Woman, The 1931,Ag 17,18:2
Wake up and Dream 1934,O 11,28:3
Meehan, John (Screenwriter)
Painted Veil, The 1934,D 7,29:1
His Brother's Wife 1936,Ag 15,6:2
When Thief Meets Thief 1937,Je 15,26:2
Madame X 1937,O 25,23:1
Boys Town 1938,S 9,25:1
Seven Sinners 1940,N 18,23:2
Nazi Agent 1942,Je 13,11:2
Destination Unknown 1942,O 29,19:3
Kismet 1944,Ag 23,16:1
Valley of Decision, The 1945,My 4,23:2
Story of the Pope, The 1946,D 20,31:3
Three Daring Daughters 1948,F 13,26:3

Meehan, John Jr (Screenwriter)
Missing Ten Days 1941,Ap 21,15:5 (In Addenda)
Meek, Donald
Hole in the Wall, The 1929,Ap 15,22:6
Girl Habit, The 1931,Jl 4,11:5
Personal Maid 1931,S 5,7:4
Love, Honor and Oh, Baby! 1933,O 28,20:3
College Coach 1933,N 11,10:4
Hi, Nellie! 1934,F 1,15:5
Bedside 1934,Mr 7,23:4
Murder at the Vanities 1934,My 21,20:2
Defense Rests, The 1934,Ag 16,20:3
Merry Widow, The 1934,O 12,33:1
Last Gentleman, The 1934,O 18,26:5
Mrs Wiggs of the Cabbage Patch 1934,O 29,14:2
Captain Hates the Sea, The 1934,N 29,33:2
Romance in Manhattan 1935,Ja 18,29:2
Society Doctor 1935,F 4,11:3
Gilded Lily, The 1935,F 9,11:2
Biography of a Bachelor Girl 1935,Mr 2,18:2
Mark of the Vampire 1935,My 3,23:4
Informer, The 1935,My 10,25:2
Accent on Youth 1935,Ag 12,10:3
Top Hat 1935,Ag 30,12:2
Return of Peter Grimm, The 1935,O 4,25:2
Barbary Coast 1935,O 14,21:1
She Couldn't Take It 1935,N 7,27:1
Peter Ibbetson 1935,N 8,18:2
Bride Comes Home, The 1935,D 25,30:2
Captain Blood 1935,D 27,14:1
Everybody's Old Man 1936,Mr 26,27:2
One Rainy Afternoon 1936,My 14,29:2
And So They Were Married 1936,My 14,29:3
Three Wise Guys, The 1936,My 23,12:2
Two in a Crowd 1936,O 5,25:1
Love on the Run 1936,N 28,13:3
Old Hutch 1936,D 7,27:4
Pennies From Heaven 1936,D 10,35:2
Maid of Salem 1937,Mr 4,27:2
Behind the Headlines 1937,Je 1,27:2
Parnell 1937,Je 4,27:2
Three Legionnaires 1937,Jl 10,18:2
Toast of New York, The 1937,Jl 23,16:2
Artists and Models 1937,Ag 5,19:2
Make a Wish 1937,S 23,33:1
Breakfast for Two 1937,N 20,21:2
You're a Sweetheart 1937,D 25,10:5
Double Danger 1938,F 10,17:5
Goodbye Broadway 1938,My 14,18:1
Having Wonderful Time 1938,Jl 8,11:2
Little Miss Broadway 1938,Jl 23,10:4
You Can't Take It With You 1938,S 2,21:2
Hold That Co-ed 1938,S 24,13:1
Jesse James 1939,Ja 14,13:1
Stagecoach 1939,Mr 3,21:1
Young Mr Lincoln 1939,Je 3,11:2
Hollywood Cavalcade 1939,O 14,13:2
Housekeeper's Daughter, The 1939,D 2,21:4
Nick Carter, Master Detective 1939,D 14,35:2
Man From Dakota, The 1940,F 22,29:2
Dr Ehrlich's Magic Bullet 1940,F 24,9:2
My Little Chickadee 1940,Mr 16,8:2
Star Dust 1940,My 4,13:1
Phantom Raiders 1940,Je 24,19:5
Turnabout 1940,Jl 27,17:6
Return of Frank James, The 1940,Ag 10,16:4
Sky Murder 1940,N 14,28:3
Third Finger, Left Hand 1940,D 12,37:2
Hullabaloo 1940,D 19,33:1
Come Live With Me 1941,F 28,17:3
Woman's Face, A 1941,My 16,21:2
Barnacle Bill 1941,Jl 25,12:4
Rise and Shine 1941,D 6,14:3
Feminine Touch, The 1941,D 12,35:3
Babes on Broadway 1942,Ja 1,37:1
Tortilla Flat 1942,My 22,27:1
Maisie Gets her Man 1942,Jl 16,23:2
Seven Sweethearts 1942,N 13,28:1
They Got Me Covered 1943,Mr 5,20:2
Keeper of the Flame 1943,Mr 19,15:2
Air Raid Wardens 1943,Ap 5,15:5
Du Barry Was a Lady 1943,Ag 20,13:1
Rationing 1944,Ap 10,14:2
Lost Angel 1944,Ap 10,14:1
Two Girls and a Sailor 1944,Je 15,16:1
Bathing Beauty 1944,Je 28,20:1
Maisie Goes to Reno 1944,S 29,18:1
Barbary Coast Gent 1944,S 29,18:2
Thin Man Goes Home, The 1945,Ja 26,16:5
State Fair 1945,Ag 31,14:3
Because of Him 1946,Ja 25,26:6
Colonel Effingham's Raid 1946,Ap 5,21:3
Janie Gets Married 1946,Je 15,24:2
Magic Town 1947,O 8,29:2
Meek, John
Tonight We Sing 1953,F 13,17:2
Meeker, George
Four Sons 1928,F 14,27:1
Escape, The 1928,My 7,29:1
Chicken a la King 1928,Je 11,27:1
Strictly Dishonorable 1931,N 11,27:1
Fireman, Save My Child 1932,F 18,25:3
Misleading Lady, The 1932,Ap 9,18:1

Famous Ferguson Case, The 1932,Ap 25,18:6
First Year, The 1932,Ag 22,20:2
Back Street 1932,Ag 29,9:2
Blessed Event 1932,S 3,16:2
Vanity Street 1932,O 15,13:1
Tess of the Storm Country 1932,N 19,20:2
Match King, The 1932,D 8,25:3
Afraid to Talk 1932,D 19,19:5
Sweepings 1933,Mr 24,22:3
Pick Up 1933,Mr 25,13:4
Life of Jimmy Dolan, The 1933,Je 14,22:3
Double Harness 1933,Jl 21,20:2
Only Yesterday 1933,N 10,25:1
King for a Night 1933,D 11,23:4
Chance at Heaven 1933,D 26,19:3
Hi, Nellie! 1934,F 1,15:5
Dark Hazard 1934,F 23,23:3
Hips, Hips, Hooray 1934,F 24,18:3
Ever Since Eve 1934,Mr 28,27:5
Melody in Spring 1934,Mr 31,8:2
I Believed in You 1934,Ap 11,25:3
Little Man, What Now? 1934,Je 1,29:1
Paris Interlude 1934,Jl 28,16:5
Dragon Murder Case, The 1934,Ag 23,13:3
Richest Girl in the World, The 1934,S 21,29:2
Broadway Bill 1934,N 30,22:2
Murder on a Honeymoon 1935,Mr 4,12:2
Wedding Night, The 1935,Mr 16,19:1
Oil for the Lamps of China 1935,Je 6,25:2
Rainmakers, The 1935,N 2,13:2
Remember Last Night? 1935,N 21,27:2
Don't Get Personal 1936,F 22,12:1
Country Doctor, The 1936,Mr 13,32:2 (Incorrect
  in this edition; use 1936,Mr 13,27:2 elsewhere)
Gentle Julia 1936,Ap 11,19:1
Walking on Air 1936,S 12,20:2
Wedding Present 1936,N 19,31:3
History Is Made at Night 1937,Mr 29,14:2
On Again-Off Again 1937,S 18,15:3
Westland Case, The 1937,O 23,14:2
Four's a Crowd 1938,Ag 12,11:1
Undercover Doctor 1939,Je 1,31:2
Everything's on Ice 1939,O 6,31:1
Roaring Twenties, The 1939,N 11,12:1
Swanee River 1939,D 30,9:2
Michael Shayne, Private Detective
  1940,D 19,33:2
Marry the Boss's Daughter 1941,D 4,33:4
You're in the Army Now 1941,D 26,21:4
Murder in the Big House 1942,My 8,27:3
Spy Ship 1942,Jl 11,8:2
Wings for the Eagle 1942,Ag 1,14:2
You Can't Escape Forever 1942,O 17,11:1
Secret Enemies 1943,Ja 1,27:3
Up in Arms 1944,Mr 3,19:2
Dead Man's Eyes 1944,O 7,11:2
Crime Incorporated 1945,Je 23,9:7
Black Market Babies 1946,Ap 1,23:1
Angel on my Shoulder 1946,O 21,27:2
Her Sister's Secret 1947,Ja 23,31:3
Smash-Up, The Story of a Woman
  1947,Ap 11,31:2
Apache Rose 1947,Jl 23,19:3
Meeker, Ralph
Teresa 1951,Ap 6,31:2
Four in a Jeep 1951,Je 12,35:2
Shadow in the Sky 1952,Jl 19,8:2
Glory Alley 1952,Jl 30,20:8
Somebody Loves Me 1952,S 25,38:1
Naked Spur, The 1953,Mr 26,37:3
Jeopardy 1953,Mr 31,36:2
Big House U S A 1955,Mr 12,11:6
Desert Sands 1955,N 19,22:7
Woman's Devotion, A 1957,Mr 22,26:1
Run of the Arrow 1957,Ag 3,8:6
Fuzzy Pink Nightgown, The 1957,O 31,41:1
Paths of Glory 1957,D 26,23:2
Ada 1961,Ag 26,15:1
Something Wild 1961,D 24,30:6
Wall of Noise 1963,S 5,27:1
Dirty Dozen, The 1967,Je 16,36:1
St Valentine's Day Massacre, The 1967,Jl 27,29:2
Gentle Giant 1968,Ap 20,26:1
Detective, The 1968,My 29,20:3
Meellish, Fuller Jr
Applause 1929,O 8,24:5
Meersman, Key
Young One, The 1961,Ja 19,26:1
Arturo Island 1962,D 22,5:2
Meersman, Peter
Naked Maja, The 1959,Je 11,36:2
Meftre, Armand
Shameless Old Lady, The 1966,S 27,52:1
Megian, Petti
Counterfeit Coin 1960,My 16,39:1
Megna, John
To Kill a Mockingbird 1963,F 15,10:2
Blindfold 1966,My 26,55:2
Megowan, Don
Davy Crockett, King of the Wild Frontier
  1955,My 26,36:1
Creature Walks among Us, The 1956,Ap 27,21:6
Great Locomotive Chase, The 1956,Je 27,35:1

Megrue, Roi Cooper (Miscellaneous)
Tea For Three 1927,O 31,22:1
Megrue, Roi Cooper (Original Author)
Under Cover 1916,Jl 24,7:4
Megrue, Roi Cooper (Screenwriter)
Seven Chances 1925,Mr 17,18:1
It Pays to Advertise 1931,F 21,15:2
Pays to Advertise, It 1931,F 21,15:2
Megrue (Original Author)
Fighting Odds 1917,O 1,14:2
Meguro, Sachiko
Golden Demon 1956,Ja 31,34:3
Mehaffey, Blanche
Battling Orioles, The 1924,N 4,24:1
Proud Heart 1925,N 3,25:4
Woman of the World, A 1925,D 14,18:2
Take It From Me 1926,N 2,35:1
Sky Spider, The 1931,Ag 31,11:5
Mehboob (Director)
Handful of Grain, A 1959,Jl 4,9:4
Meherin, Eleanore (Original Author)
Chickie 1925,Ap 27,15:2
Mehr, Gerald
Murder in Times Square 1943,My 31,13:2
Mehra, Lal Chand
Friends and Lovers 1931,N 7,16:5
Singapore 1947,S 17,31:2
Mei, Tsen Lady
Letter, The 1929,Mr 8,30:1
Meighan, Tho
Conquest of Canaan, The 1921,Jl 11,9:3
Meighan, Thomas
Heart of the Wilds 1918,Ag 19,7:1
Miracle Man, The 1919,Ag 27,9:5
Male and Female 1919,N 24,13:1
Why Change Your Wife 1920,Ap 26,18:1
Civilian Clothes 1920,S 6,10:5
Conrad in Quest of his Youth 1920,N 8,20:2
Easy Road, The 1921,F 20,VI,2:2 (In Addenda)
White and Unmarried 1921,My 30,12:5
Cappy Ricks 1921,Ag 22,13:6
Our Leading Citizen 1922,Je 12,16:2 (Incorrect in
  this edition; use 1922,Je 12,10:2 elsewhere)
Manslaughter 1922,S 18,14:2
Back Home and Broke 1922,D 25,21:1
Ne'er Do-Well, The 1923,My 1,24:3
Hollywood 1923,Jl 30,11:4
Homeward Bound 1923,Jl 31,12:4
Woman Proof 1923,O 30,16:1
Pied Piper Malone 1924,Ja 28,12:1
Confidence Man, The 1924,Ap 15,24:1
Alaskan, The 1924,S 15,28:1
Tongues of Flame 1924,D 16,28:1
Coming Through 1925,F 18,17:3
Old Home Week 1925,My 25,21:3
Man Who Found Himself, The 1925,Ag 24,17:3
Irish Luck 1925,N 24,28:4
New Klondike, The 1926,Mr 22,16:1
Tin Gods 1926,S 20,21:3
Canadian, The 1926,N 30,27:1
Blind Alleys 1927,Mr 1,31:1
We're all Gamblers 1927,O 12,30:6
City Gone Wild, The 1927,D 6,27:1
Racket, The 1928,Jl 9,25:1
Mating Call, The 1928,O 8,14:2
Argyle Case, The 1929,Ag 31,13:4
Young Sinners 1931,My 9,15:4
Skyline 1931,O 5,17:3
Cheaters at Play 1932,F 27,22:1
Madison Square Garden 1932,O 12,26:5
Peck's bad Boy 1934,O 6,20:1
Meihaner, Maria
Private Life of Louis XIV, The 1936,Ja 9,25:2
Meil, Marie
Thank You, Madame 1937,Ap 27,18:2
Meillon, John
On the Beach 1959,D 18,34:1
Sundowners, The 1960,D 9,39:1
Jungle Fighters 1962,Mr 15,28:2
Billy Budd 1962,O 31,32:1
633 Squadron 1964,Je 25,25:1
Guns at Batasi 1964,N 17,47:1
Meinard, Josef
Don Juan 1956,Mr 6,26:2
Forever My Love 1962,Mr 28,36:4
Meinardi, Helen (Original Author)
I Met Him in Paris 1937,Je 3,29:2
Meinardi, Helen (Screenwriter)
Next Time I Marry 1938,D 2,27:2
Meinati, Umberto
Passa L'Amore 1933,N 25,10:3
Meineche, Annelise (Director)
Eric Soya's 17 1967,Ja 25,37:1
Meineke, Eva Maria
Scampolo 1959,Ag 6,18:4
Yesterday Girl 1967,S 22,57:2
Meiners, Emil
Manhunt in the Jungle 1958,Ap 12,13:1
Meinert, M (Director)
Strange Case of District Attorney M, The
  1930,Mr 17,20:3

Meinert, Rudolf
Eleven Who Were Loyal 1929,My 20,22:6
Meinert, Rudolf (Director)
Marie Antoinette 1929,F 25,16:1
Eleven Who Were Loyal 1929,My 20,22:6
Meinhard, Carl
Gluecszylinder, Der 1934,Mr 10,18:4
Meinhardt, Edith
Voruntersuchung; Inquest 1931,My 24,VIII,4:1
Meinikov, Alexander
Beethoven Concerto 1937,Mr 24,29:1
Baltic Deputy 1937,S 4,8:2
Lonely White Sail 1938,My 7,18:1
Meinikova, E K
Men on Wings 1935,Je 11,24:5
Meinl, Michiko
Letzte Liebe; Last; Last Love 1938,Jl 19,15:4
Meinrad, Josef
April 1, 2000 1954,F 17,27:2
Trapp Family, The 1961,Ag 31,22:4
Cardinal, The 1963,D 13,41:1
Meins, Douglas
Dress Parade 1939,O 28,11:2
Meins, Gus (Director)
Babes in Toyland 1934,D 13,28:2
Kelly the Second 1936,O 3,21:2
Nobody's Baby 1937,My 20,17:3
Hit Parade, The 1937,My 31,11:2
Meis, Ellen
Miracolo Di Sant' Antonio, Il 1932,Ap 18,19:2
Meisel, Kurt
Klein Dorrit 1935,O 19,21:2
Nanon 1938,N 26,18:2
Ekel, Das; Grouch, The 1939,D 4,18:4
Kleine Nachtmusik, Eine 1940,Mr 2,9:5
Time to Love and a Time to Die, A
1958,Jl 10,22:1
Embezzled Heaven 1959,Ap 24,23:1
Meisel, Will (Composer)
Der Storch Streikt 1932,My 2,13:2
Meiser, Edith
Go West, Young Lady 1941,N 24,11:6
It Grows on Trees 1952,N 29,11:2
Middle of the Night 1959,Je 18,36:1
Meisiter, Ian (Original Author)
Mister Drake's Duck 1952,Ja 28,15:2
Meisler, Nathan
Sallah 1965,O 13,39:1
MEISNER
See Also MEISSNER
Meisner, Gunter
Quiller Memorandum, The 1966,D 16,59:1
Funeral in Berlin 1966,D 23,17:1
Meisner, Sanford
Story of Page One, The 1960,Ja 14,28:1
Tender is the Night 1962,Ja 20,13:2
MEISSNER
See Also MEISNER
Meissner, Emma
Vi Som Gar Koeksvaegen 1933,O 7,18:5
Sara Laer Sig Folkvett 1938,F 16,17:1
Meissner, Gante
Counterfeit Traitor, The 1962,Ap 18,28:1
Meissner, H O Dr (Original Author)
Angelika 1954,S 25,10:7
Meissner, Maria
Der Herr Buerovorsteher 1932,Je 17,24:1
Theodor Koerner 1933,My 6,11:2
Herr Kobin Geht auf Abenteuer; Mr Kobin Seeks
Adventure 1935,N 26,28:2
Koenigin der Liebe 1936,My 4,16:2
Meitzer, Lewis (Original Author)
Comanche Territory 1950,Ap 8,9:3
Meitzer, Lewis (Screenwriter)
Comanche Territory 1950,Ap 8,9:3
Jazz Singer, The 1953,Ja 14,27:3
New Orleans Uncensored 1955,Ap 30,10:8
Meixner, Karl
Last Will of Dr Mabuse, The 1943,Mr 20,11:1
Meizel, Kurt
Cat, The 1959,Ap 13,35:1
Mejano, Sy
World Dances 1954,N 8,24:6
Mejia, Al
Jim Thorpe - All American 1951,Ag 25,7:2
Mejia, Alfonso
Young and the Damned, The 1952,Mr 25,23:2
Mekas, Adolfas
Guns of the Trees 1964,F 29,12:2
Mekas, Adolfas (Director)
Hallelujah the Hills 1963,D 17,49:1
Windflowers 1968,F 23,43:1
Mekas, Adolfas (Screenwriter)
Hallelujah the Hills 1963,D 17,49:1
Windflowers 1968,F 23,43:1
Mekas, Jonas (Director)
Guns of the Trees 1964,F 29,12:2
Brig, The 1964,S 21,37:4
Mekas, Jonas (Producer)
Guns of the Trees 1964,F 29,12:2
Mekas, Jonas (Screenwriter)
Guns of the Trees 1964,F 29,12:2

Mekhraliev, F
Arshin Takes a Wife 1950,Jl 31,13:6
Mekler, Gene
Cyanamide 1954,Mr 26,17:6
Melamed, I
Othello 1960,My 16,39:1
Melano, Sy
She's Back on Broadway 1953,Mr 12,24:2
Melayia, Mayia
Madame X 1960,O 3,34:5
Melbourne, Mauricette
Bitter Sweet 1940,N 22,27:1
MELCHER
See Also MELCHIOR
Melcher, Martin (Producer)
Julie 1956,N 22,51:1
Tunnel of Love 1958,N 22,27:4
Pillow Talk 1959,O 7,47:2
Lover Come Back 1962,F 9,21:1
That Touch of Mink 1962,Je 15,16:2
Jumbo 1962,D 7,49:1
Thrill of it All, The 1963,Ag 2,15:3
Move Over Darling 1963,D 26,33:1
Do Not Disturb 1965,D 25,17:2
Glass Bottom Boat, The 1966,Je 10,54:1
Caprice 1967,Je 8,52:2
Ballad of Josie, The 1968,Mr 14,51:2
Where Were You When the Lights Went Out?
1968,Ag 9,30:2
With Six You Get Egg Roll 1968,O 10,59:6
MELCHIOR
See Also MELCHER
Melchior, Dauritz
Thrill of a Romance 1945,My 25,22:2
Melchior, Ib (Screenwriter)
Journey to the Seventh Planet 1962,My 25,28:3
Robinson Crusoe on Mars 1964,Ag 27,28:2
Melchior, Lauritz
Two Sisters From Boston 1946,Je 7,16:2
This Time for Keeps 1947,D 5,33:4
Luxury Liner 1948,S 10,19:2
Stars Are Singing, The 1953,Mr 12,24:2
Melchoir, Ib (Director)
Angry Red Planet, The 1960,My 5,41:2
Melchoir, Ib (Screenwriter)
Angry Red Planet, The 1960,My 5,41:2
Ambush Bay 1966,S 15,51:4
Mele, Antello
Shoe-Shine 1947,Ag 27,19:2
Melendez, Jeronimo Mitchell (Director)
Heroina 1965,N 11,58:2
Melendez, Jeronimo Mitchell (Original Author)
Heroina 1965,N 11,58:2
Melendez, Jeronimo Mitchell (Producer)
Heroina 1965,N 11,58:2
Melendez, Pamela
Johnny Tiger 1966,Je 16,53:4
Melentyeva, Elena
Girl From Leningrad 1941,D 20,25:2
Melesh, Alex
His Private Life 1928,N 12,18:2
Marquis Preferred 1929,Ja 21,18:4
Big Broadcast, The 1932,O 15,13:1
Artists and Models Abroad 1938,D 22,25:3
Paris Honeymoon 1939,Ja 26,17:1
On Your Toes 1939,O 21,12:2
Beyond Tomorrow 1940,S 27,27:1
Once Upon a Honeymoon 1942,N 13,28:1
Lady Takes a Chance, A 1943,S 16,25:2
Melesi, Alex
Girl Without a Room 1933,D 7,26:3
Melford, Austin (Miscellaneous)
My Song For You 1935,My 27,20:6
It's Love Again 1936,My 23,12:1
Seven Sinners 1936,Ag 22,6:1
Melford, Austin (Screenwriter)
Its a Boy 1933,Jl 23,IX,2:2 (In Addenda)
You're in the Army Now 1937,Ap 16,27:2
School for Husbands 1939,F 7,16:2
Mill On the Floss, The 1939,N 15,19:3
Let George Do It 1940,O 14,25:5
Three Cockeyed Sailors 1942,Ja 26,18:3
Ships With Wings 1942,My 25,11:2
Champagne Charlie 1948,Ag 7,8:2
Melford, Frank (Director)
Ljubav I Strast 1932,D 16,25:5
Melford, Frank (Producer)
Massacre River 1949,Jl 15,17:2
Rogue River 1951,F 16,21:4
Diamond Queen, The 1954,Ja 27,24:2
Black Scorpion, The 1957,O 12,23:2
Melford, George
Flying Cadets 1941,O 14,29:2
Miracle of Morgan's Creek, The 1944,Ja 20,15:2
Melford, George (Director)
Pettigrew's Girl 1919,Ap 14,11:4
Men, Women and Money 1919,Je 16,11:2
Sporting Chance, A 1919,Jl 14,12:2
Everywoman 1919,D 15,20:1
Behold my Wife 1920,O 11,19:3
Faith Healer, The 1921,Mr 14,9:2
Sheik, The 1921,N 7,20:1
Moran of the Lady Letty 1922,F 6,9:1

Melford, George (Director)— Cont
Ebb Tide 1922,N 20,21:3
You Can't Fool Your Wife 1923,Ap 24,25:3
Light That Failed, The 1923,N 27,11:2
Flaming Barriers 1924,Ja 29,16:1
Dawn of a Tomorrow, The 1924,Mr 26,19:2
Tiger Love 1924,Je 16,18:3
Top of the World, The 1925,F 17,18:1
Friendly Enemies 1925,My 5,24:2
Simon the Jester 1925,N 19,22:1
Man's Past, A 1927,O 4,34:2
Charlatan, The 1929,Ap 15,22:6
East of Borneo 1931,S 26,25:3
Homicide Squad 1931,O 19,28:1
Melford, Jack
When Thief Meets Thief 1937,Je 15,26:2
It's in the Air 1940,D 10,33:2
October Man, The 1948,Ap 16,29:2
No Room at the Inn 1949,D 26,33:4
Melford, Jill
Abandon Ship 1957,Ap 18,35:1
Vengance of She, The 1968,My 30,21:4
Melgares, Francisco
Morena Clara 1938,Je 18,18:3
Melghan, Thomas
Prince There Was 1921,N 14,18:1
Meli, Marinella
House of Ricordi 1956,Mr 13,32:1
Melia, Joe
Too Many Crooks 1959,Ap 25,14:2
Melichar, Alois (Composer)
Wenn die Musik Nicht Waer 1937,Ap 3,17:2
Maedchen Irene, Das 1937,My 22,19:3
Drei Maeoerl um Schubert 1937,Je 5,21:2
Nanon 1938,N 26,18:2
Titan-Story of Michelangelo, The 1950,Ja 23,16:2
Melik-Avakyan, G (Director)
Heart Sings, The 1958,Ag 18,15:2
Melik-Avakyan, G (Original Author)
Heart Sings, The 1958,Ag 18,15:2
Melinand, Monique
Between Eleven and Midnight 1950,F 23,33:3
Sinners, The 1950,N 11,11:2
Lady Paname 1951,Mr 20,35:4
Women Are Weak 1959,Je 9,44:2
Passion of Slow Fire, The 1962,O 12,26:1
Magnificent Sinner 1963,Ap 25,38:1
Meliskova, Anna
Sweet Light in a Dark Room 1966,Je 30,28:1
Melkle, Richard
On the Beach 1959,D 18,34:1
Mell, Marisa
Masquerade 1965,Ap 29,40:2
Casanova 1965,Jl 21,43:1
Danger Diabolik 1968,D 12,62:6
Mella, Joe
Follow a Star 1961,Ap 26,34:1
Mellas, Peter (Producer)
Girl From Corfu, The 1957,My 20,28:2
Mellen, Albert
Outrage 1950,O 16,30:5
MELLER
See Also MELLOR
Meller, Harro
Counter-Attack 1945,My 17,15:2
House on Ninety-Second Street, The
1945,S 27,24:7
Jewels of Brandenburg 1947,My 24,10:5
Meller, Raquel
Carmen 1928,My 7,29:1
Violette Imperiale 1928,Je 19,31:1
Venenosa, La 1928,D 16,IX,8:2
Oppressed, The 1929,Jl 15,25:1
Violetera, La 1935,Ja 14,11:3
Mellican, Jane
Life and Death of Colonel Blimp, The
1945,Mr 30,18:2
Mellinger, Michael
Beachcomber, The 1955,Ja 17,27:5
Mellinina, Ardita
Deliverance 1919,Ag 19,10:1
Mellish, Fuller Jr
Roadhouse Nights 1930,F 22,13:1
Sarah and Son 1930,Mr 13,22:4
Crime Without Passion 1934,S 1,16:2
Mello, Breno
Black Orpheus 1959,D 22,41:1
MELLOR
See Also MELLER
Mellor, Harro
Night in Casablanca, A 1946,Ag 12,17:2
Mellor, James
Persecution and Assassination of Jean-Paul Marat
as Performed by the Inmates of the Asylum of
Charenton Under the Direction of the Marquis
De Sade, The 1967,F 23,41:1
Mellor, Tom (Composer)
Mister Big 1943,Je 14,13:4
Mellot, Martha
Frochard et les Deux Orphelines, La
1934,F 7,16:2
Dernier Milliardaire, Le 1935,O 30,16:2

Melly, Andree
Novel Affair, A 1957,Ag 28,22:1
Melly, Audrey
Brides of Dracula, The 1960,S 6,41:4
Melly, George (Screenwriter)
Smashing Time 1967,D 21,44:1
Melnati, Umberto
Contessa di Parma, La 1938,F 24,23:2
Matrimonio Ideale, Un 1939,D 15,33:3
Too Bad She's Bad 1955,D 26,23:2
Melnyk, Stephania
Marusia 1938,D 12,26:2
Meloney, William Brown (Original Author)
Secret Heart, The 1946,D 26,28:2
Meloney, William Brown (Screenwriter)
Beloved Enemy 1936,D 26,15:2
Claudia and David 1946,Ag 15,19:2
Melsen, Christian
Love on a Pillow 1963,D 17,49:1
Melson, Charlie (Screenwriter)
Swiss Miss 1938,Je 4,18:2
Gladiator, The 1938,Ag 29,10:2
Flirting With Fate 1938,D 15,35:3
Melson, John (Screenwriter)
Battle of the Bulge 1965,D 18,36:1
Melton, Frank
State Fair 1933,Ja 27,13:2
David Harum 1934,Mr 2,23:2
World Moves On, The 1934,Je 30,18:5
Handy Andy 1934,Ag 4,14:5
Judge Priest 1934,O 12,33:1
365 Nights in Hollywood 1934,N 7,32:1
White Parade, The 1934,N 10,19:1
County Chairman, The 1935,Ja 19,8:1
Daring Young Man, The 1935,Jl 18,15:2
Wild and Woolly 1937,S 6,20:1
Marriage Forbidden 1938,Jl 16,7:2
Second Chorus 1941,Ja 16,25:2
Pot o'Gold 1941,Ap 4,25:2
Tanks a Million 1941,O 9,27:2
Loves of Edgar Allan Poe, The 1942,S 21,19:2
Melton, James
Stars Over Broadway 1935,N 14,17:3
Sing Me a Love Song 1936,D 26,15:2
Melody for Two 1937,My 21,19:5
Ziegfeld Follies 1946,Mr 23,8:3
Melton, Sid
Close-Up 1948,Ap 5,24:2
Steel Helmet, The 1951,Ja 25,21:5
Lemon Drop Kid, The 1951,Mr 22,41:2
Meltzer, Lewis (Original Author)
Texas 1941,O 17,27:3
Lady Gambles, The 1949,My 21,9:2
Meltzer, Lewis (Screenwriter)
Golden Boy 1939,S 8,28:2
Those High Grey Walls 1939,O 19,27:2
Lady in Question, The 1940,D 10,33:2
Texas 1941,O 17,27:3
New York Town 1941,N 13,35:2
Tuttles of Tahiti, The 1942,Ap 30,14:1
Destroyer 1943,S 2,15:3
First Comes Courage 1943,S 3,15:3
Once Upon a Time 1944,Je 30,17:2
Ladies' Man 1947,Ja 13,18:5
Man-Eater of Kumaon 1948,Jl 2,24:2
Along the Great Divide 1951,My 17,38:3
Desert Legion 1953,My 9,13:2
Man With the Golden Arm, The 1955,D 16,38:2
Autumn Leaves 1956,Ag 2,21:2
High School Confidential 1958,My 31,6:6
Beat Generation, The 1959,O 22,47:4
Meltzer, Robert
Journey Into Fear 1943,Mr 19,15:3
Melville, Alan (Original Author)
Simon and Laura 1956,Jl 3,17:2
Melville, Alan (Screenwriter)
Castle in the Air 1953,Ja 5,19:2
Melville, Emilie
Illusion 1929,S 28,17:3
Melville, Herman (Original Author)
Sea Hunt, The 1926,Ja 16,8:5
Sea Beast, The 1926,Ja 16,8:5
Moby Dick 1930,Ag 15,20:5
Moby Dick 1956,Jl 5,18:1
Billy Budd 1962,O 31,32:1
Melville, Jean-Paul
Breathless 1961,F 8,26:1
Melville, Jean-Pierre (Director)
Strange Ones, The 1952,Jl 29,17:3
Doulos-The Finger Man 1964,Mr 3,31:1
Melville, Jean-Pierre (Producer)
Strange Ones, The 1952,Jl 29,17:3
Melville, Jean-Pierre (Screenwriter)
Strange Ones, The 1952,Jl 29,17:3
Doulos-The Finger Man 1964,Mr 3,31:1
Melville, Rose (Original Author)
Sis 1919,Mr 3,11:2
Melville, Sam
Hour of the Gun 1967,N 2,58:4
Thomas Crown Affair, The 1968,Je 27,48:2
Melvin, Murray
Taste of Honey, A 1962,My 1,33:3
Damn the Defiant 1962,S 20,29:2

Sparrows Don't Sing 1963,My 7,46:2
Ceremony, The 1964,My 14,39:1
Alfie 1966,Ag 25,42:1
Kaleidoscope 1966,S 23,45:1
Membrives, Lola
Chrismosa, La; Gossiper, The 1940,Mr 30,11:2
Memirovsky, Irene (Original Author)
Operation X 1950,D 11,31:2
Menacker, Sam
Bodyhold 1949,D 12,29:4
Abbott and Costello in the Foreign Legion
1950,Ag 14,14:4
Menaco, James (Composer)
Dolly Sisters, The 1945,N 15,24:6
Menaker, A
Variety Stars 1955,F 21,16:7
Menaker, L (Director)
Leningrad Music Hall 1943,N 6,16:3
Menard, Jimmy
Wild River 1960,My 27,22:1
Menard, Wilmon (Original Author)
Six Thousand Enemies 1939,Je 9,26:2
Mencher, Murray (Composer)
Life Begins In College 1937,O 9,16:1
You're a Sweetheart 1937,D 25,10:5
Listen, Darling 1938,N 24,37:2
Mendaille, Daniel
Kameradschaft 1932,N 9,28:5
Maria Chapdelaine 1935,S 25,18:2
Porteuse de Pain, La 1936,Jl 1,29:5
Last Will of Dr Mabuse, The 1943,Mr 20,11:1
Heart of a Nation, The 1943,Ap 8,27:2
Mendaille, Danielle
Stolen Life 1939,Je 15,27:2
MENDEL
See Also MANDEL
Mendel, Charles Sir
Ivy 1947,Je 26,19:1
Mendelsohn, Jack (Screenwriter)
Yellow Submarine 1968,N 14,56:1
Mendelssohn, Eleonora
Black Hand 1950,Mr 13,15:2
Mendelssohn, Felix (Composer)
Midsummer Night's Dream, A 1967,Ap 18,32:1
MENDES
See Also MENDEZ
Mendes, Lothar (Director)
Love Makes Us Blind 1927,Ag 23,29:4
Night of Mystery, A 1928,Ap 16,20:5
Illusion 1929,S 28,17:3
Marriage Playground, The 1929,D 14,22:4
Ladies' Man 1931,My 1,30:3
Personal Maid 1931,S 5,7:4
Strangers in Love 1932,Mr 5,11:2
Payment Deferred 1932,N 8,26:3
Luxury Liner 1933,F 3,21:3
Power 1934,O 5,29:3
Man Who Could Work Miracles, The
1937,F 22,13:1
Moonlight Sonata 1938,My 10,17:2
International Squadron 1941,N 14,28:4
Flight for Freedom 1943,Ap 16,24:2
Tampico 1944,Je 2,21:2
Walls Came Tumbling Down, The 1946,N 9,13:5
Mendes, Lothar (Miscellaneous)
Interference 1928,N 17,23:1
Mendes, Lothar (Original Author)
Nazi Agent 1942,Je 13,11:2
Mendes, Lothar (Producer)
Four Feathers, The 1929,Je 13,35:4
Moonlight Sonata 1938,My 10,17:2
Mendes, Lother (Miscellaneous)
Prince of Tempters, The 1926,O 18,18:1
MENDEZ
See Also MENDES
Mendez, Gene
Big Circus, The 1959,Jl 18,6:1
Mendez, Hector
Where Words Fail; Donde Mueren las Palabraso
1948,Ag 19,18:4
Mendez, Jola
Chicago After Midnight 1928,Mr 6,20:3
Mendez, Lothar (Miscellaneous)
Moonlight Sonata 1937,Je 6,XI,4:4 (In Addenda)
Mendez, Lucila
Coney Island 1928,F 14,27:1 (In Addenda)
Mendez, Lucille
Bigger Than Barnum's 1926,Jl 13,19:3
Mendez, Ricardo Lopez (Composer)
Broadway Rhythm 1944,Ap 14,24:6
Mendl, Charles Sir
Notorious 1946,Ag 16,19:2
Mendoza, Alberto
Murio el Sargento Laprida; Sergeant Laprida Died
1939,Mr 20,13:2
Mendoza, Antonio Jr
Madres del Mundo 1936,Ag 17,9:3
Mendoza, David (Composer)
Ben Hur 1925,D 31,10:5 (In Addenda)
Fire Brigade, The 1926,D 21,20:2
Camille 1927,Ap 22,19:1
Trail of '98, The 1928,Mr 21,30:3

Mendoza, David (Miscellaneous)
Trail of '98, The 1928,Mr 21,30:3
Mendoza, George
Conquering Horde, The 1931,Mr 30,25:2
Mendoza, Victor Manuel
Ojos Tapatios 1939,F 13,13:3
Rosa de Xochimilco 1939,O 14,13:3
Ay Jalisco no te Rajes 1943,Ap 24,17:3
Que Lindo es Michoacan 1944,Ap 22,8:7
Garden of Evil 1954,Jl 10,17:1
Proud and the Beautiful, The 1956,My 29,32:2
Cowboy 1958,F 20,29:5
Wonderful Country, The 1959,N 5,39:7
Mendrek, William
At-War With the Army 1951,Ja 25,21:5
Meneaugh, Michael
Doctor Faustus 1968,F 7,38:1
Menedes, Jesus
Relicario, El; Reliquary, The 1935,D 31,11:3
Menendez, Juan Jose
Marcelino 1956,O 23,39:1
Lazarillo 1963,Ap 5,27:6
Menendez, Nilo and Orchestra
Music in Manhattan 1944,O 7,11:2
Menezes, Gloria
Given Word, The 1964,Mr 25,47:1
Menger, W H (Screenwriter)
Blindfold 1966,My 26,55:2
Menglet, Maya
Sailor From the Comet, The 1959,Ag 3,21:2
Menicacci, Bernardino
General Della Rovere 1960,N 22,41:1
Menichkova, Nina
Sons and Mothers 1967,O 2,58:1
Meniconi, Furio
Cleopatra 1963,Je 13,29:1
Menikof
Red Army Days 1935,O 21,22:4
Menjou, Adolphe
Faith Healer, The 1921,Mr 14,9:2
Marriage Cheat, The 1921,Je 2,14:3
Three Musketeers, The 1921,Ag 29,14:4
Fast Mail, The 1922,Jl 10,9:5
Bella Donna 1923,Ap 16,20:2
Rupert of Hentzau 1923,Jl 9,8:4
Woman of Paris, A 1923,O 2,7:2
Spanish Dancer, The 1923,O 8,20:1
Marriage Circle, The 1924,F 4,23:3
Shadows of Paris 1924,F 18,13:1
Broadway After Dark 1924,My 20,15:2
For Sale 1924,Jl 14,11:5
Broken Barriers 1924,Ag 4,16:3
Sinners in Silk 1924,S 8,15:3
Open all Night 1924,S 9,19:1
Forbidden Paradise 1924,N 17,16:1
Fast Set, The 1924,N 18,22:1
Swan, The 1925,Mr 2,14:1
Kiss in the Dark, A 1925,Ap 7,17:3
Are Parents People 1925,Je 9,16:3
Lost-a Wife 1925,Je 22,10:2
King on Main Street, The 1925,O 26,25:2
Grand Duchess and the Waiter, The
1926,F 9,22:1
Social Celebrity, A 1926,Ap 19,24:3
Sorrows of Satan, The 1926,O 13,21:1
Ace of Cads, The 1926,O 18,18:1 (In Addenda)
Blonde or Brunette 1927,Ja 11,18:2
Evening Clothes 1927,Mr 21,10:4
Service for Ladies 1927,Ag 15,22:5
Gentleman of Paris, A 1927,O 3,20:1
Serenade 1927,D 19,30:1
Night of Mystery, A 1928,Ap 16,20:5
His Tiger Lady 1928,My 28,23:2
Tiger Lady, The 1928,Je 3,VIII,5:1
His Private Life 1928,N 12,18:2
Marquis Preferred 1929,Ja 21,18:4
Fashions in Love 1929,Jl 1,31:2
Forbidden Paradise 1929,O 8,24:5
Mon Gosse de Pere 1930,Je 8,IX,6:1
Enigmatique Monsieur Parkes, L' 1930,S 2,19:3
Morocco 1930,N 17,29:1
New Moon 1930,D 25,18:6
Easiest Way, The 1931,F 28,15:2
Front Page, The 1931,Mr 20,29:1
Men Call it Love 1931,Je 20,20:4
Parisian, The 1931,Ag 22,7:5
Great Lover, The 1931,Ag 24,13:4
Friends and Lovers 1931,N 7,16:5
Forbidden 1932,Ja 11,28:5
Prestige 1932,F 5,25:2
Bachelor's Affairs 1932,Je 25,18:2
Night Club Lady, The 1932,Ag 27,13:4
Blame the Woman 1932,O 25,24:5
Farewell to Arms, A 1932,D 9,26:5
Circus Queen Murder, The 1933,My 9,20:5
Morning Glory 1933,Ag 18,18:2
Worst Woman in Paris, The 1933,N 25,10:3
Convention City 1933,D 25,28:2
Easy to Love 1934,Ja 15,12:2
Trumpet Blows, The 1934,Ap 14,18:2
Journal of a Crime 1934,Ap 28,11:3
Little Miss Marker 1934,My 19,18:3
Great Flirtation, The 1934,Je 22,16:5

Menjou, Adolphe— Cont

Human Side, The 1934,S 15,20:3
Mighty Barnum, The 1934,D 24,17:1
Gold Diggers of 1935 1935,Mr 15,25:2
Broadway Gondolier 1935,Jl 18,15:2
Milky Way, The 1936,Mr 26,27:2
Sing, Baby, Sing 1936,S 12,20:1
Wives Never Know 1936,O 31,24:2
One in a Million 1937,Ja 1,19:3
Star Is Born, A 1937,Ap 23,25:1
Cafe Metropole 1937,Ap 29,17:1
100 Men and a Girl 1937,S 18,15:2
Stage Door 1937,O 8,27:2
Goldwyn Follies, The 1938,F 21,15:1
Letter of Introduction 1938,S 1,17:1
Thanks For Everything 1938,D 10,13:2
King of the Turf 1939,My 8,21:2
Golden Boy 1939,S 8,28:2
That's Right, You're Wrong 1939,N 30,25:3
Housekeeper's Daughter, The 1939,D 2,21:4
Bill of Divorcement, A 1940,Jl 12,11:2
Turnabout 1940,Jl 27,17:6
Road Show 1941,F 19,25:2
Father takes a Wife 1941,S 5,19:3
Roxie Hart 1942,F 20,21:1
Syncopation 1942,My 29,13:3
You Were Never Lovelier 1942,D 4,31:1
Hi Diddle Diddle 1943,S 24,26:2
Sweet Rosie O'Grady 1943,O 21,30:2
Step Lively 1944,Jl 27,14:1
Man Alive 1945,N 17,14:5
Heartbeat 1946,My 11,22:4
Bachelor's Daughters, The 1946,O 7,23:2
I'll Be Yours 1947,F 22,16:2
Mr District Attorney 1947,F 28,27:3
Hucksters, The 1947,Jl 18,21:2
State of the Union 1948,Ap 23,28:1
My Dream Is Yours 1949,Ap 16,11:3
Dancing in the Dark 1949,D 3,8:6
To Please a Lady 1950,O 27,24:3
Tall Target, The 1951,S 28,26:2
Across the Wide Missouri 1951,N 7,35:4
Sniper, The 1952,My 10,16:3
Man on a Tightrope 1953,Je 5,19:1
Timberjack 1955,Mr 10,33:3
Ambassador's Daughter, The 1956,Ag 30,19:1
Bundle of Joy 1956,D 20,36:1
Fuzzy Pink Nightgown, The 1957,O 31,41:1
Paths of Glory 1957,D 26,23:2
I Married a Woman 1958,N 5,42:5
Pollyanna 1960,My 20,26:1

Menjou, Henri

Blonde or Brunette 1927,Ja 11,18:2

Menken, Helen

Stage Door Canteen 1943,Je 25,13:2

Menken, Shepard

Red Menace, The 1949,Je 27,18:2
Great Caruso, The 1951,My 11,32:2
Merry Widow, The 1952,S 25,38:1
Man in the Dark 1953,Ap 9,31:5
Juggler, The 1953,My 6,39:2
Benny Goodman Story 1956,F 22,22:1

Mennioz, Gori (Screenwriter)

Games Men Play, The 1968,Mr 15,30:1

Menotti, Gian-Carlo (Director)

Medium, The 1951,S 6,39:2

Menotti, Gian-Carlo (Original Author)

Medium, The 1951,S 6,39:2

Mensik, Vladimir

Happy End 1968,Je 11,54:4
Murder Czech Style 1968,Ag 20,33:1

Menta, Narciso Ibanez

Games Men Play, The 1968,Mr 15,30:1

Mentkowska, Steffie

Peasant's Wedding, The 1939,Ap 19,20:5

Mentz, Susan

Women Without Names 1951,Ag 7,22:2

Menuhin, Yehudi

Stage Door Canteen 1943,Je 25,13:2

Menzel, Gerhard (Original Author)

Morgenrot 1933,My 16,15:2
Sunderin 1954,D 24,7:2

Menzel, Jiri

Closely Watched Trains 1967,O 16,59:2
Capricious Summer 1968,S 18,50:2
Capricious Summer 1968,S 25,38:2

Menzel, Jiri (Director)

Closely Watched Trains; Diffucult Love, A
  1967,Je 19,41:1
Closely Watched Trains 1967,O 16,59:2
Capricious Summer 1968,S 18,50:2
Capricious Summer 1968,S 25,38:2

Menzel, Jiri (Screenwriter)

Closely Watched Trains 1967,O 16,59:2
Capricious Summer 1968,S 18,50:2
Capricious Summer 1968,S 25,38:2

Menzer, Ernest

Made in U S A 1967,S 28,58:2

Menzies, Heather

Sound of Music, The 1965,Mr 3,34:1
Hawaii 1966,O 11,54:1

Menzies, William Cameron (Director)

Spider, The 1931,S 5,7:4
Chandu the Magician 1932,O 1,10:4

I Loved You Wednesday 1933,Je 16,20:2
Wharf Angel 1934,Ap 21,12:1
Things to Come 1936,Ap 18,19:2
Address Unknown 1944,Ap 17,20:1
Green Cockatoo, The 1947,Jl 19,10:2
Invaders From Mars 1953,My 30,7:1
Maze, The 1953,Jl 11,8:2

Menzies, William Cameron (Miscellaneous)

Gone With the Wind 1939,D 20,31:2
Foreign Correspondent 1940,Ag 28,15:2
For Whom the Bell Tolls 1943,Jl 15,25:2

Menzies, William Cameron (Producer)

Address Unknown 1944,Ap 17,20:1
Black Book, The 1949,O 17,18:2

Meoe, Paul

Tanga Tika 1953,O 6,34:4

Mera, Edith

Culte de Beaute, Le 1931,Je 8,21:1
Soir de Rafle, Un 1931,O 16,27:1
Miche 1932,D 2,27:4
Trois Mousquetaires, Les 1933,My 1,10:2
Milady 1933,S 8,22:3
Mam'zelle Nitouche 1933,N 20,18:3
Criez-Le sur les Toits; Shout it From the
  Housetops 1935,Je 22,18:5
Grandeur et Decadence 1937,My 31,11:3

Merande, Doro

Our Town 1940,Je 14,25:3
Mr Belvedere Rings the Bell 1951,Ag 2,18:1
Whistle at Eaton Falls, The 1951,O 11,49:2
Seven Year Itch, The 1955,Je 4,9:1
Man With the Golden Arm, The 1955,D 16,38:2
Gazebo, The 1960,Ja 16,14:4
Cardinal, The 1963,D 13,41:1
Kiss Me, Stupid 1964,D 23,22:2

Mercader, Maria

Molinos de Viento; Windmills 1940,F 26,11:2
King's Jester, The 1947,Je 26,19:3
Man of the Sea 1948,Ja 24,11:2
Escape into Dreams 1950,Ap 13,34:5
Heart and Soul 1950,Je 15,41:3
Hello Elephant 1954,S 10,18:5

Mercadier, Marthe

Night is my Kingdom, The 1953,S 30,37:1
Act of Love 1954,F 12,20:5
Companions of the Night 1954,N 25,44:2

Mercanon, Louis (Director)

Jeanne Dore 1928,Ja 2,28:3 (In Addenda)

Mercante, Arthur

Requiem for a Heavyweight 1962,O 17,35:1

Mercanton, Jean

Venus 1929,O 14,20:2
Charrette Fantome, La 1940,My 28,29:2
Man Who Seeks the Truth, The 1941,O 7,26:6
Heart of a Nation, The 1943,Ap 8,27:2
Children of Chaos 1950,Ap 20,37:2

Mercanton, Louis (Director)

Miarka, The Daughter of the Bear
  1921,O 15,16:2
Gypsy Passion 1922,Mr 27,12:1
Venus 1929,O 14,20:2
Il est Charmant 1932,Ap 9,18:1
Cognasse 1935,Ag 15,16:4

MERCER

See Also MERCIER

Mercer, Beryl

Christian, The 1923,F 12,13:4
We Americans 1928,Mr 29,25:3
Mother's Boy 1929,My 8,34:6
Three Live Ghosts 1929,S 30,23:1
Seven Days' Leave 1930,Ja 25,13:2
All Quiet on The Western Front 1930,Ap 30,29:1
In Gay Madrid 1930,Je 7,10:4
Dumbbells in Ermine 1930,Jl 28,22:1
Common Clay 1930,Ag 2,16:4
Matrimonial Bed, The 1930,Ag 25,14:2
Outward Bound 1930,S 18,28:3
Inspiration 1931,F 9,25:3
East Lynne 1931,F 21,15:2
Public Enemy, The 1931,Ap 24,27:1
Man in Possession, The 1931,Jl 18,16:6
Miracle Woman, The 1931,Ag 17,18:2
Merely Mary Ann 1931,S 12,15:4
Are These our Children 1931,N 14,15:3
Lovers Courageous 1932,F 20,11:2
Devil's Lottery 1932,Ap 2,13:2
Young America 1932,My 7,11:5
No Greater Love 1932,My 14,11:5
Lena Rivers 1932,My 21,9:2
Smilin' Through 1932,O 15,13:1
Six Hours to Live 1932,O 22,18:4
Cavalcade 1933,Ja 6,23:2
Supernatural 1933,Ap 22,16:3
Berkeley Square 1933,S 14,26:2
Blind Adventure 1933,O 31,24:3
Broken Dreams 1933,N 21,23:3
Change of Heart 1934,My 11,24:2
Richest Girl in the World, The 1934,S 21,29:2
Little Minister, The 1934,D 28,25:1
Age of Indiscretion 1935,My 18,21:2
Magnificent Obsession 1935,D 31,11:2
Night Must Fall 1937,Ap 30,17:2
Call it a Day 1937,My 7,29:2

Mercer, Beryl— Cont

Little Princess, The 1939,Mr 11,21:1
Hound of the Baskervilles, The 1939,Mr 25,19:2
Woman Is the Judge, A 1939,S 28,29:5

Mercer, Charles (Original Author)

Sins of Rachel Cade, The 1961,Ap 6,30:3

Mercer, David (Screenwriter)

Morgan! 1966,Ap 5,42:2
90 Degrees in the Shade 1966,N 16,52:1

Mercer, Frances

Blind Alibi 1938,My 20,17:2
Vivacious Lady 1938,Je 3,17:3
Crime Ring 1938,Jl 22,10:3
Smashing the Rackets 1938,Ag 9,22:5
Mad Miss Manton, The 1938,O 21,27:2
Annabel Takes a Tour 1938,D 29,15:3
Beauty for the Asking 1939,F 10,19:1
Story of Vernon and Irene Castle, The
  1939,Mr 31,19:2
Society Lawyer 1939,Mr 31,19:2
Piccadilly Incident 1948,Ag 5,16:2

Mercer, Freddie

Loves of Edgar Allan Poe, The 1942,S 21,19:2
Great Gildersleeve, The 1942,D 18,36:8
Gildersleeve's Bad Day 1943,Je 11,23:1

Mercer, Jack (Narrator)

Mr Bug Goes to Town 1942,F 20,21:3

Mercer, Jane

Day of Faith, The 1923,N 27,11:2
Man and Maid 1925,Ap 7,17:3

Mercer, Johnny (Composer)

Transatlantic Merry-Go-Round 1934,N 1,25:2
To Beat the Band 1935,N 23,23:2
Ready, Willing and Able 1937,Mr 15,27:1
Varsity Show 1937,S 2,17:2
Hollywood Hotel 1938,Ja 13,17:3
Gold Diggers in Paris 1938,Je 2,19:2
Cowboy From Brooklyn 1938,Jl 14,17:1
Garden of the Moon 1938,S 24,13:1
Going Places 1939,Ja 7,6:1
Naughty but Nice 1939,Je 23,23:2
Second Chorus 1941,Ja 16,25:2
Let's Make Music 1941,Ja 23,19:2
You're the One 1941,F 20,23:2
Blues in the Night 1941,D 12,35:2
Fleet's In, The 1942,Mr 12,24:2
You Were Never Lovelier 1942,D 4,31:1
Star Spangled Rhythm 1942,D 31,20:1
Riding High 1943,D 23,26:4
Here Come the Waves 1944,D 28,25:2
Harvey Girls, The 1946,Ja 25,26:2
Dangerous When Wet 1953,Je 19,18:1
Seven Brides for Seven Brothers 1954,Jl 23,8:3
Daddy Long Legs 1955,My 6,17:5
Li'l Abner 1959,D 12,19:2
Great Race, The 1965,S 16,00:0

Mercer, Johnny (Miscellaneous)

Singing Marine, The 1937,Jl 1,33:2

Mercer, William (Original Author)

Velvet Touch, The 1948,Ag 26,16:2

Merchant, Ismail (Producer)

Householder, The 1963,O 22,43:2
Shakespeare Wallah 1966,Mr 23,40:2

Merchant, Vivien

Alfie 1966,Ag 25,42:1
Accident 1967,Ap 18,33:1

MERCIER

See Also MERCER

Mercier, Christine

That Man in Istanbul 1966,My 19,51:2

Mercier, Jocelyne

There's Always a Price Tag 1958,My 26,25:2

Mercier, Louis

Charlie Chan at Monte Carlo 1937,D 18,18:1
Bulldog Drummond's Bride 1939,Jl 13,17:2
Charlie Chan in City in Darkness 1939,D 18,29:2
This Woman Is Mine 1941,O 13,21:2
Sahara 1943,N 12,25:2
Passage to Marseille 1944,F 17,12:5
Conspirators, The 1944,O 21,15:2
So Dark the Night 1946,D 7,16:2
Jewels of Brandenburg 1947,My 24,10:5
Untamed 1955,Mr 12,11:6
Attack! 1956,S 20,29:4
Affair to Remember, An 1957,Jl 20,8:5
Will Success Spoil Rock Hunter 1957,S 12,37:5

Mercier, Michele

Nights of Lucretia Borgia, The 1960,O 6,51:4
Goodbye Again 1961,Je 30,32:2
Wonders of Aladdin, The 1961,D 23,16:1
Shoot the Piano Player 1962,Jl 24,19:1
Two Are Guilty 1964,F 29,12:1
Global Affair, A 1964,My 7,31:2
Symphony for a Massacre 1965,My 28,40:1
High Infidelity (Modern People); Modern People
  (High Infidelity) 1965,Jl 2,17:1
Casanova 1965,Jl 21,43:1
Love in 4 Dimensions 1965,S 16,00:0
Oldest Profession, The (Prehistoric Era);
  Prehistoric Era (The Oldest Profession)
  1968,N 8,42:1

Mercouri, Melina

Stella 1957,Je 11,40:1
He Who Must Die 1958,D 29,21:1

Mercouri, Melina — Cont
Never on Sunday 1960,O 19,54:1
Where the Hot Wind Blows 1960,N 12,15:1
Phaedra 1962,O 19,24:1
Victors, The 1963,D 20,21:2
Topkapi 1964,S 18,25:1
Man Could Get Killed, A 1966,My 12,54:2
10:30 PM Summer 1966,O 20,52:1
Uninhibited, The 1968,Je 13,57:2

Mercure, Jean
Skipper Next to God 1953,Ja 13,24:2
Sword and the Rose, The 1953,Ag 20,18:3
Rouge et Noir 1958,Ap 9,42:1
Dangerous Exile 1958,O 11,18:3

Mercure, Monique
Take it All; A Tout Prendre 1966,Ap 26,55:1

Mere, Charles (Original Author)
Three Masques, The 1929,N 24,X,8:4
Trois Masques, The 1929,N 24,X,8:4 (In Addenda)

Meredith, Bess (Screenwriter)
Mark of Zorro, The 1940,N 4,23:2

Meredith, Burgess
Winterset 1936,D 4,31:1
there Goes The Groom 1937,D 25,10:6
Spring Madness 1938,D 1,29:3
Idiot's Delight 1939,F 3,13:1
Of Mice and Men 1940,F 17,9:2
Castle on the Hudson 1940,Mr 4,11:2
San Francisco Docks 1940,D 26,23:3
Second Chorus 1941,Ja 16,25:2
That Uncertain Feeling 1941,My 2,25:1
Tom, Dick and Harry 1941,Jl 18,22:2
Street Of Chance 1942,N 19,31:3
Story of G I Joe 1945,O 6,9:6
Diary of a Chambermaid, The 1946,Je 23,28:2
Magnificent Doll 1946,D 9,34:2
Miracle Can Happen, A 1948,F 4,28:4
Mine Own Executioner 1949,Ja 19,34:2
Man on the Eiffel Tower, The 1950,Ja 30,12:2
Gay Adventure, The 1954,S 16,35:7
Joe Butterfly 1957,My 30,23:2
Advise and Consent 1962,Je 7,31:2
Cardinal, The 1963,D 13,41:1
In Harm's Way 1965,Ap 7,36:1
Madame X 1966,Ap 28,49:1
Big Hand for the Little Lady, A 1966,Je 9,54:2
Batman 1966,Ag 25,42:4
Crazy Quilt, The 1966,O 4,50:1
Hurry Sundown 1967,Mr 24,22:1
Torture Garden 1968,Jl 20,18:2

Meredith, Burgess (Director)
Man on the Eiffel Tower, The 1950,Ja 30,12:2

Meredith, Burgess (Narrator)
Forgotten Village, The 1941,N 19,26:3
Tunisian Victory 1944,Mr 24,17:2
Hymn of the Nations 1946,Ap 22,26:2
Albert Schweitzer 1957,Ja 21,20:2
Sorcerers' Village 1958,Jl 3,22:6

Meredith, Burgess (Original Author)
Yank Comes Back, A 1949,Ap 21,30:2

Meredith, Burgess (Producer)
Diary of a Chambermaid, The 1946,Je 23,28:2
Miracle Can Happen, A 1948,F 4,28:4

Meredith, Burgess (Screenwriter)
Diary of a Chambermaid, The 1946,Je 23,28:2

Meredith, Charles
In Hollywood with Potash and Perlmutter 1924,S 30,27:3
Daisy Kenyon 1947,D 25,32:1
Miracle of the Bells, The 1948,Mr 17,30:1
Foreign Affair, A 1948,Jl 1,19:3
For the Love of Mary 1948,S 23,37:2
Boy With Green Hair, The 1949,Ja 13,26:2
Lucky Stiff, The 1949,Ja 31,14:2
Tokyo Joe 1949,O 27,35:2
Lady Takes a Sailor, The 1949,D 17,15:2
Francis 1950,Mr 16,40:2
Sun Sets at Dawn, The 1951,Ja 15,13:1
Along the Great Divide 1951,My 17,38:3
Submarine Command 1952,Ja 19,13:2
Big Trees, The 1952,F 6,24:2

Meredith, Iris
Mystery of the Hooded Horsemen, The 1937,Ag 13,13:2
Those High Grey Walls 1939,O 19,27:2
Convicted Woman 1940,F 26,11:2

Meredith, Judith
Summer Love 1958,Je 26,23:4
Jack the Giant Killer 1962,Jl 26,17:1
Night Walker, The 1965,Ja 21,22:1
Dark Intruder 1965,Jl 22,24:2

Meredith, Lee
Producers, The 1968,Mr 19,38:1

Meredith, Lois
Headless Horseman, The 1922,D 25,21:1

Meredith, Madge
Falcon's Adventure, The 1946,D 14,19:2
Trail Street 1947,Ap 10,35:2

Meredith, Stanley (Cinematographer)
Festival 1967,O 24,53:2

Meredyth, Bess (Original Author)
Scarlet Lady, The 1928,Ag 15,19:4
Prodigal, The 1931,Je 27,20:3

Cuban Love Song, The 1931,D 5,21:2
Metropolitan 1935,O 18,27:4
Charlie Chan at the Opera 1936,D 5,16:2

Meredyth, Bess (Screenwriter)
One Clear Call 1922,Je 19,10:3
Love Hour, The 1925,S 2,21:3
Don Juan 1926,Ag 7,6:1 (In Addenda)
Chasing Rainbows 1930,F 22,13:1
Mighty Barnum, The 1934,D 24,17:1
Folies Bergere 1935,F 25,13:2
Metropolitan 1935,O 18,27:4
Half Angel 1936,My 30,7:3
Great Hospital Mystery, The 1937,Jl 16,22:2
That Night in Rio 1941,Mr 10,21:2
Unsuspected, The 1947,O 4,9:2

Merefield, Bernard
Man of Affairs 1937,F 20,9:2

Merelle, Claude
Milady 1923,Ja 22,10:1

Merello, Tita
Noches de Buenos Aires 1935,D 10,31:3
Noches de Buenos Aires; Buenos Aires Nights 1935,D 12,33:4

Meremblum, Peter California Junior Symphony /Orchestra
They Shall Have Music 1939,Jl 26,17:2

Mereno, Antonio
Alas sobre el Chaco; Wings Over the Chaco 1939,Mr 28,20:2

Mererda, Victor
Pardon my French 1952,Mr 31,17:2

Mergendahl, Charles (Original Author)
Bramble Bush, The 1960,F 25,34:2

Meriam, Charlotte (Original Author)
Code of the Wilderness, The 1924,Jl 1,21:4

Mericka, Marti
One Potato, Two Potato 1964,Jl 30,16:1

Merighi, Augusta
Rose Tattoo, The 1955,D 13,55:1
Catered Affair, The 1956,Je 15,32:4
Earth Is Mine, The 1959,Je 27,13:1

Meril, Macha
Love on a Pillow 1963,D 17,49:1
Who's Been Sleeping in My Bed? 1963,D 26,33:2
Anatomy of a Marriage; My Days With Jean Marc; My Nights With Francoise 1964,O 27,42:1
Married Woman, The; Femme Mariee, La 1965,Ag 17,39:1
Defector, The 1966,N 17,55:1
Belle de Jour 1968,Ap 11,51:1

Merimee, Prosper (Original Author)
Carmen 1915,N 1,11:1
Gypsy Blood 1921,My 9,16:2
Loves of Carmen 1927,S 27,31:1
Carmen 1928,My 7,29:1
Carmen; Gipsy Blood 1931,N 22,VIII,6:1
Carmen 1946,N 27,20:2
Loves of Carmen, The 1948,S 3,16:2
Vendetta 1950,D 26,19:1
Tamango 1959,S 17,48:4
Carmen Baby 1967,O 11,41:2

Meritz, Michele
Beau Serge, Le 1959,Ag 3,21:1
Cousins, The (Les Cousins) 1959,N 24,44:1
War of the Buttons, The 1963,D 19,40:2

Meritzis, T (Director)
Castle in Greece 1960,D 12,38:2

Merivale, Bernard (Original Author)
Wrecker, The 1929,Ag 13,23:2
Flying Fool 1931,O 19,28:1
Seven Sinners 1936,Ag 22,6:1
Footsteps in the Dark 1941,Mr 15,13:2

Merivale, John
A Night to Remember 1958,D 17,2:7
List of Adrian Messenger, The 1963,My 30,20:1
Arabesque 1966,My 6,54:1

Merivale, Philip
Give Us This Night 1936,Ap 6,18:1
Mr and Mrs Smith 1941,F 21,16:3
Rage in Heaven 1941,Mr 21,19:2
Pacific Blackout 1942,Ja 15,25:2
Lady for a Night 1942,F 12,27:2
This Above All 1942,My 13,14:3
Crossroads 1942,Jl 27,18:2
This Land Is Mine 1943,My 28,19:1
Lost Angel 1944,Ap 10,14:1
Hour Before the Dawn, The 1944,My 11,25:6
Nothing but Trouble 1945,Mr 10,14:1
Stranger, The 1946,Jl 11,18:2
Sister Kenny 1946,S 30,21:2

Meriwether, Lee
Batman 1966,Ag 25,42:4

Merk, Kaethe
Silence of the Forest, The; Schweigen im Walde, Das 1937,D 6,19:2

Merkel, Una
Eyes of the World 1930,Ag 15,20:5
Abraham Lincoln 1930,Ag 26,24:1
Bat Whispers, The 1931,Ja 16,27:1
Don't Bet on Women 1931,Mr 7,17:2
Six Cylinder Love 1931,My 16,31:3
Maltese Falcon, The 1931,My 29,26:5

Merkel, Una — Cont
Daddy Long Legs 1931,Je 6,15:5
Bargain, The 1931,S 5,7:4
Wicked 1931,S 19,10:2
Private Lives 1931,D 19,16:4
Secret Witness, The 1931,D 21,28:4
She Wanted a Millionaire 1932,F 20,11:2
Impatient Maiden, The 1932,Mr 4,17:3
Man Wanted 1932,Ap 16,11:2
Huddle 1932,Je 17,24:1
Red Headed Woman 1932,Jl 1,19:3
They Call It Sin 1932,O 21,25:4
Secret of Madame Blanche, The 1933,F 4,11:3
Whistling in the Dark 1933,F 5,IX,5:1
Clear all Wires 1933,Mr 4,11:2
42d Street 1933,Mr 10,19:3
Reunion in Vienna 1933,Ap 29,14:2
Midnight Mary 1933,Jl 15,14:2
Her First Mate 1933,S 2,14:5
Beauty for Sale 1933,S 16,9:3
Bombshell 1933,O 21,11:2
Day of Reckoning 1933,N 4,18:2
Women in his Life, The 1934,Ja 27,9:3
This Side of Heaven 1934,F 10,21:2
Paris Interlude 1934,Jl 28,16:5
Bulldog Drummond Strikes Back 1934,Ag 16,20:2
Cat's Paw, The 1934,Ag 17,12:2
Merry Widow, The 1934,O 12,33:1
Have a Heart 1934,O 20,20:2
Evelyn Prentice 1934,N 10,19:1
Night is Young, The 1935,Ja 14,11:2
Biography of a Bachelor Girl 1935,Mr 2,18:2
Murder in the Fleet 1935,Je 3,22:2
Broadway Melody of 1936 1935,S 19,28:1
It's in the Air 1935,N 8,18:2
Riffraff 1936,Ja 13,14:2
Speed 1936,My 16,11:2
We Went to College 1936,Jl 27,20:2
Born to Dance 1936,D 5,16:1
Don't Tell the Wife 1937,F 19,15:2
Good Old Soak 1937,Ap 20,25:3
Saratoga 1937,Jl 23,16:3
True Confession 1937,D 16,35:2
Four Girls in White 1939,F 23,19:3
Some Like It Hot 1939,My 25,31:2
On Borrowed Time 1939,Jl 7,13:2
Destry Rides Again 1939,N 30,25:1
Comin' Round the Mountain 1940,S 26,27:3
Bank Dick, The 1940,D 13,29:2
Road to Zanzibar 1941,Ap 10,29:2
Mad Doctor of Market Street, The 1942,Ja 5,21:5
Twin Beds 1942,My 1,23:4
This Is the Army 1943,Jl 29,11:6
Bride Goes Wild, The 1948,Je 4,27:2
Man From Texas 1948,Ag 12,16:5
Kill the Umpire 1950,My 29,10:6
My Blue Heaven 1950,S 16,12:6
Emergency Wedding 1950,D 22,19:2
Rich, Young and Pretty 1951,Jl 26,17:3
Millionaire for Christy, A 1951,O 5,24:3
Golden Girl 1951,N 21,20:3
With a Song in my Heart 1952,Ap 5,20:2
Merry Widow, The 1952,S 25,38:1
I Love Melvin 1953,Ap 10,18:4
Kentuckian, The 1955,S 2,13:2
Bundle of Joy 1956,D 20,36:1
Fuzzy Pink Nightgown, The 1957,O 31,41:1
Girl Most Likely, The 1958,O 9,47:1
Mating Game, The 1959,Ap 30,37:1
Parent Trap, The 1961,Je 22,23:1
Summer and Smoke 1961,N 17,41:1
Summer Magic 1963,Ag 22,19:2
Tiger Walks, A 1964,Ag 27,28:2
Spinout 1966,D 15,60:1

Merker, Philip
Illiac Passion, The 1968,Ap 19,40:1

Merkulov, M
Flames on the Volga 1958,Ja 27,21:7

Merkuriev, V
Professor Mamlock 1938,N 8,26:2
Red Tanks 1942,Je 6,9:2
Victors and the Vanquished, The 1950,My 1,18:2
Miners of the Don 1951,N 12,21:2
Twelfth Night 1956,Mr 5,21:1

Merkuriev, Vasili
Cranes are Flying, The 1960,Mr 22,31:2
Summer to Remember, A; (Seryozha) 1961,N 7,38:1
Song Over Moscow 1964,N 23,52:1

Merkuriev, Victor
Road Home, The 1947,My 2,28:3
Great Glinka, The 1947,D 22,30:2

Merkuryev, V
First Front, The 1949,N 14,19:2
True Friends 1954,N 15,33:2

Merkyl, John
Captain January 1924,Jl 7,10:4
Unholy Three, The 1925,Ag 4,14:3
Fine Clothes 1925,O 20,28:1

Merle, Robert (Original Author)
Weekend at Dunkirk 1966,My 19,51:2

Merlin, Dominique (Cinematographer)
Anderson Platoon, The 1967,D 18,70:4

Merlin, Jan
Six Bridges to Cross 1955,Ja 22,8:2
Illegal 1955,O 29,12:6
Running Wild 1955,N 12,23:2
Merlini, Elsa
Albero di Adamo, L'; Adam's Tree
1938,Ja 20,19:2
Diamante Porta-Fortuna, Il; Lucky Diamond, The
1938,S 29,31:1
Amicizia; Friendship 1940,Mr 1,17:3
Al Vostri Ordini, Signora; At Your Orders,
Madame 1940,My 25,20:1
Dama Bianca, La; Lady in White, The
1940,My 31,15:3
Merlini, Marisa
Bread, Love and Dreams 1954,S 21,24:1
Frisky 1955,O 25,37:3
Bigamist, The 1958,My 12,25:1
Most Wonderful Moment, The 1959,Je 1,23:6
Engagement Italiano 1966,Je 21,35:1
Merlo, Ismael
Hunt, The 1967,Ap 25,38:1
Merlo, Tony
Love Me Tonight 1932,Ag 19,20:6
Merman, Ethel
Follow the Leader 1930,D 6,21:3
We're not Dressing 1934,Ap 26,27:2
Kid Millions 1934,N 12,17:2
Strike Me Pink 1936,Ja 17,15:2
Anything Goes 1936,F 6,23:3
Happy Landing 1938,Ja 22,19:1
Alexander's Ragtime Band 1938,Ag 6,7:2
Straight, Place and Show 1938,O 1,10:2
Stage Door Canteen 1943,Je 25,13:2
Call Me Madam 1953,Mr 26,37:1
There's no Business Like Show Business
1954,D 17,37:3
It's a Mad, Mad, Mad, Mad World
1963,N 19,47:1
Art of Love, The 1965,Jl 1,34:1
Mernay, M (Director)
Face to the Wind 1951,Ja 16,34:2
Merola, A A
Under my Skin 1950,Mr 18,9:2
Merrall, Mary
Love on the Dole 1945,O 13,11:2
Dead of Night 1946,Je 29,22:6
Nicholas Nickleby 1947,D 1,27:2
For Them that Trespass 1950,S 27,37:2
Pink String and Sealing Wax 1950,O 4,38:2
Obsessed 1952,F 6,24:2
Tonight at 8:30 (Fumed Oak); Fumed Oak
(Tonight at 8:30) 1953,My 26,33:2
Pickwick Papers, The 1954,Ap 5,21:2
Duel in the Jungle 1954,Ag 9,13:2
Belles of St Trinian's, The 1954,D 23,13:4
It's Great to be Young 1957,D 26,23:3
Campbell's Kingdom 1960,Ja 11,35:5
Merriam, Charlotte
Nth Commandment, The 1923,Ap 10,24:3
Brass Bottle, The 1923,Jl 23,13:4
Painted People 1924,Ja 29,16:1
Captain Blood 1924,S 9,19:1
So Big 1924,Ja 5,19:1
Pampered Youth 1925,F 10,20:1
Steele of the Royal Mounted 1925,Je 18,16:3
Queen of the Night Clubs 1929,Mr 18,30:6
Pleasure Crazed 1929,Jl 15,25:1
Dumbbells in Ermine 1930,Jl 28,22:1
Night Nurse 1931,Jl 17,23:4
Crowd Roars, The 1932,Mr 23,25:4
Man Wanted 1932,Ap 16,11:2
Daring Daughters 1933,Mr 25,13:4
Alimony Madness 1933,My 5,18:1
Avenger, The 1933,O 3,28:3
Broken Dreams 1933,N 21,23:3
Dancing Man 1934,Jl 16,11:3
Damaged Lives 1937,Je 14,26:2
Merrick, Doris
Girl Trouble 1942,O 8,31:2
Time to Kill 1942,D 25,15:4
Big Noise, The 1944,S 23,16:1
Merrick, Fred V (Screenwriter)
Spy of Napoleon 1939,Ag 19,18:4
Merrick, George (Producer)
Swamp Woman 1941,D 27,15:2
Merrick, George W (Original Author)
Lost City, The 1935,F 21,23:3
Merrick, Leonard (Original Author)
Conrad in Quest of his Youth 1920,N 8,20:2
Fool's Paradise 1921,D 10,11:4
Magnificent Lie, The 1931,Jl 25,11:6
Merrick, Leonard (Screenwriter)
Thief in Paradise, A 1925,Ja 26,14:1
School for Wives 1925,Ap 1,21:3
Merrick, Lynn
Sis Hopkins 1941,My 1,27:5
Merrick, Marilyn
Flight Angels 1940,My 27,23:2
Merrill, Barbara
What Ever Happened to Baby Jane?
1962,N 7,48:1

Merrill, Blanche (Screenwriter)
Bluebeard's Seven Wives 1925,D 28,19:2
Merrill, Catherine
Edge, The 1968,Mr 28,52:1
Merrill, Dick
Atlantic Flight 1937,N 1,24:5
Merrill, Dina
Desk Set 1957,My 16,28:2
Nice Little Bank That Should Be Robbed, A
1958,D 11,17:4
Don't Give up the Ship 1959,Jl 9,22:1
Operation Petticoat 1959,D 6,38:1
Butterfield 8 1960,N 17,46:1
Sundowners, The 1960,D 9,39:1
Young Savages, The 1961,My 25,31:1
Courtship of Eddie's Father, The 1963,Mr 7,8:5
(Incorrect in this edition; use 1963,Mr 28,8:5
elsewhere)
I'll Take Sweden 1965,Ag 12,30:4
Merrill, Gary
Winged Victory 1944,D 21,16:2
Slattery's Hurricane 1949,Ag 13,6:6
Twelve O'Clock High 1950,Ja 28,10:2
Mother Didn't Tell Me 1950,Mr 4,11:2
Where the Sidewalk Ends 1950,Jl 8,7:4
All About Eve 1950,O 14,13:2
Frogmen, The 1951,Je 30,8:6
Decision Before Dawn 1951,D 22,12:2
Another Man's Poison 1952,Ja 7,14:3
Phone Call From a Stranger 1952,F 2,11:2
Girl in White, The 1952,My 31,12:5
Night Without Sleep 1952,S 27,13:2
Blueprint for Murder, A 1953,Jl 25,8:2
Witness to Murder 1954,Ap 16,16:4
Black Dakotas, The 1954,O 2,21:2
Human Jungle, The 1954,N 26,24:6
Wonderful Country, The 1959,N 5,39:7
Savage Eye, The 1960,Je 7,27:1
Great Impostor, The 1961,Mr 30,24:1
Pleasure of his Company, The 1961,Je 2,36:1
Mysterious Island 1961,D 21,30:6
Girl Named Tamiku, A 1963,Mr 15,8:2
Woman Who Wouldn't Die, The 1965,Je 10,38:1
Cast a Giant Shadow 1966,Mr 31,43:3
Around the World Under the Sea 1966,Jl 21,20:2
Ride Beyond Vengance 1966,S 29,60:1
Incident, The 1967,N 6,65:1
Clambake 1967,D 14,62:3
Last Challenge, The 1967,D 28,25:1
Power, The 1968,Mr 7,52:2
Merrill, Gary (Narrator)
Strange Victory 1948,S 27,27:2
Quiet One, The 1949,F 14,15:2
Merrill, Joan
Time Out for Rhythm 1941,Jl 10,16:3
Mayor of Forty-Fourth Street, The
1942,Je 11,27:4
Iceland 1942,O 15,27:1
Merrill, Louis
Tropic Fury 1939,S 8,28:4
Kit Carson 1940,N 15,25:3
Lady From Shanghai, The 1948,Je 10,28:2
Crooked Web, The 1955,D 10,19:1
Devil at 4 O'Clock, The 1961,O 19,39:3
Merrill, Martha
Living on Velvet 1935,Mr 8,25:4
Shipmates Forever 1935,O 17,29:3
Merrill, Robert
Aaron Slick From Punkin Crick 1952,Ap 19,18:6
Merrill, Toni
Crime and Punishment, U S A 1959,Je 17,39:3
Merrill, Walter
Office Wife, The 1930,S 27,21:3
Parlor, Bedroom and Bath 1931,Ap 4,23:1
Wanted by the Police 1938,S 26,13:2
Merriman, Charlotte
Code of the Wilderness, The 1924,Jl 1,21:4
Merritt, Abraham (Original Author)
Devil Doll, The 1936,Ag 8,5:2
Merritt, Arnold
Unforgiven, The 1960,Ap 7,46:1
Merritt, Bruce
Abie's Irish Rose 1946,D 23,19:4
Merritt, George
W Plan, The 1931,Mr 23,24:7
Dreyfus Case, The 1931,Ag 31,11:5
F P 1 1933,S 16,9:3
White Face 1933,D 4,22:3
I Was a Spy 1934,Ja 15,12:2
Power 1934,O 5,29:3
My Song For You 1935,My 27,20:6
Born for Glory 1935,O 21,22:4
Mr Cohen Takes a Walk 1936,F 13,25:2
Rembrandt 1936,D 3,31:1
Dr Syn 1937,N 15,15:1
Girl Was Young, The 1938,F 11,27:2
Rat, The 1938,F 28,19:1
Return of the Scarlet Pimpernel, The
1938,Ap 11,12:2
Emil 1938,Ap 15,23:2
Clouds Over Europe 1939,Je 16,27:2
Secret Four, The 1940,Ap 22,13:2
Frightened Lady 1941,N 10,21:3

Merritt, George — Cont
Lady in Distress 1942,F 16,21:2
Wings and the Woman 1942,O 8,31:1
Smugglers, The 1948,Mr 29,17:1
Hatter's Castle 1948,Jl 3,8:6
Quiet Week-End 1948,Ag 20,13:2
Don't Take it to Heart 1948,D 25,10:3
Canterbury Tale, A 1949,Ja 24,16:2
Merritt, Sybil
Song to Remember, A 1945,Ja 26,16:4
Easy to Wed 1946,Jl 12,14:2
Japanese War Bride 1952,Ja 30,22:6
Merrmann, Julius P
Fruehlingsmaerchen 1935,My 20,20:5
Merrow, Jane
Woman Who Wouldn't Die, The 1965,Je 10,38:1
Girl-Getters, The 1966,Ap 13,37:6
Lion in Winter, The 1968,O 31,54:1
Merry, Ila
Luc Aux Dames 1936,Ja 15,14:4
Pension Mimosas 1936,My 6,27:1
Merry Macs, The
Love Thy Neighbor 1940,D 18,32:5
Moonlight in Hamaii 1941,O 10,26:6
Ride 'Em Cowboy 1942,Mr 5,27:3
Mr Music 1950,D 21,34:3
Merry Meisters, The
Lake Placid Serenade 1944,D 25,15:6
Mers, Harold
Betrayal, The 1948,Je 26,10:5
Mersch, Mary
Top of the World, The 1925,F 17,18:1
Mersereau, Violet
Thunderclap 1921,Jl 31,22:4
Nero 1922,My 26,17:2
Shepherd King, The 1923,D 11,26:2
Merson, Marc (Producer)
Heart is a Lonely Hunter, The 1968,Ag 1,24:1
Merton, Colette
Clear the Decks 1929,Ap 1,22:1
Merton, Ivy
Gallant Lady 1934,Ja 22,12:3
Merton, John
Crusade Against Rackets 1937,Jl 26,15:3
Federal Bullets 1937,D 27,11:1
Female Fugitive 1938,Ap 11,12:3
Great Commandment, The 1942,O 17,11:1
Mervyn, William
Blue Lamp, The 1951,Ja 9,25:1
Third Key, The 1957,Je 3,30:2
Invasion Quartet 1961,D 11,41:2
Murder Ahoy 1964,S 23,55:3
Jokers, The 1967,My 16,50:1
Hammerhead 1968,S 12,54:3
Merwin, Sam Jr (Screenwriter)
Manhunt in the Jungle 1958,Ap 12,13:1
Merwin, Samuel (Original Author)
Passionate Pilgrim, The 1921,Ja 3,20:2
Mery, Arlette
Eternal Husband, The 1949,Ja 10,19:2
Mery, Christian
Crazy in the Noodle 1957,D 15,45:4 (Incorrect in
this edition; use 1957,D 17,45:4 elsewhere)
Merzbach, Paul (Director)
Invitation to the Waltz 1938,Jl 2,10:3
Merzbach, Paul (Miscellaneous)
Mimi 1936,Ja 10,16:3
Merzbach, Paul (Original Author)
Doctor's Women, The 1929,Je 3,27:2
For Her Sake 1930,N 11,29:1
Merzbach, Paul (Screenwriter)
Invitation to the Waltz 1938,Jl 2,10:3
It Happened to One Man 1941,F 24,11:6
Hatter's Castle 1948,Jl 3,8:6
Mesa, Gilbert
Way Out 1967,O 26,54:3
Meschke, Edmund
Germany Year Zero 1949,S 20,35:2
Meserow, Albert J (Original Author)
Great God Gold 1935,My 6,22:3
Meskill, Jack (Composer)
Folies Bergere 1935,F 25,13:2
Meskill, Katherine
House on Telegraph Hill, The 1951,My 14,29:1
Hollywood Story 1951,Je 7,40:6
Meskin, A
Chalutzim 1934,Ap 2,13:3
Messemer, Hannes
Sins of Rose Bernd, The 1959,Ja 24,13:4 (In
Addenda)
Devil Strikes at Night, The 1959,Ja 30,31:3
Taiga 1959,Mr 17,42:4
Glass Tower, The; (Glaserne Turm, Der)
1959,Ag 27,24:4
Babette Goes to War 1960,Je 8,46:1
General Della Rovere 1960,N 22,41:1
Great Escape, The 1963,Ag 8,19:1
Defector, The 1966,N 17,55:1
MESSENGER
See Also MESSINGER
Messenger, Buddy
Flirt, The 1922,D 31,VII,2:2 (In Addenda)

Messine, Monique
My Life to Live 1963,S 24,43:2
MESSINGER
See Also MESSENGER
Messinger, Buddy
Abysmal Brute, The 1923,Ap 18,24:5
Trifling With Honor 1923,My 30,10:4
Penrod and Sam 1923,Je 25,16:5
Lady of Chance, A 1929,Ja 14,20:1
Hot Stuff 1929,My 13,27:2
Messinger, Gertie
Barefoot Boy, The 1923,N 11,6:1
Messinger, Gertrude
Penrod and Sam 1923,Je 25,16:5
Jazz Age, The 1929,Ja 7,36:2
Two Weeks Off 1929,Je 24,27:1
Madame Racketeer 1932,Jl 23,6:6
Woman Accused, The 1933,Mr 13,18:2
Anne of Green Gables 1934,D 22,21:1
Messinger, M
Dybbuk, The 1938,Ja 28,17:2
Messiter, Eric
Kind Hearts and Coronets 1950,Je 15,41:2
Mestayer, Harry
Acquittal, The 1923,D 12,24:5
Black Oxen 1924,Ja 7,23:1
Locked Door, The 1930,Ja 20,21:1
Mestel, Jacob
Wandering Jew, The 1933,O 21,11:2
Mirele Efros 1939,O 21,12:2
Vilna Legend, A (American Cast) 1949,S 26,17:1
Mestel, Jacob (Miscellaneous)
Vilna Legend, A (American Cast) 1949,S 26,17:1
Vilna Legend, A (Russian-Jewish Cast)
1949,S 26,17:1
Mestral, Armand
Gervaise 1957,N 12,46:1
Morgan the Pirate 1961,Jl 20,32:2
Meszaros, Agi
Treasured Earth 1950,D 14,51:3
Metalious, Grace (Original Author)
Peyton Place 1957,D 13,35:1
Return to Peyton Place 1961,My 6,26:1
Metalnikov, Budimir (Screenwriter)
Home for Tanya, A 1961,Ag 14,28:5
Metaxa, Georges
Secrets of a Secretary 1931,Ag 29,16:3
Swing Time 1936,Ag 28,21:2
Doctor Takes a Wife, The 1940,Je 15,12:2
Paris Calling 1942,Ja 19,21:2
Hi Diddle Diddle 1943,S 24,26:2
Mask of Dimitrios, The 1944,Je 24,16:2
Metcalf, Arthur
If Winter Comes 1923,S 4,14:1
Soul Fire 1925,My 6,26:3
Shore Leave 1925,S 14,16:1
Seven Days' Leave 1930,Ja 25,13:2
Metcalf, Bradley
Gangster's Boy 1938,N 7,23:6
Metcalf, Earl
Tragedy of the East Side, A 1920,Ag 24,6:2
Silent Accuser, The 1924,N 25,26:1
Man Without a Country, The 1925,F 12,16:1
Partners Again, With Potash and Perlmutter
1926,F 15,16:4
Midnight Sun, The 1926,Ap 24,20:4
Notorious Lady, The 1927,Ap 11,18:3
Metcalf, Edward
Animal Crackers 1930,Ag 29,20:3
Metcalfe, Burt
Gidget 1959,Ap 23,27:4
Canadians, The 1961,Je 1,31:1
Metelitsin, Seryozha
Summer to Remember, A; (Seryozha)
1961,N 7,38:1
Meter, Harry von
Hunchback of Notre Dame, The 1923,S 3,9:3
Kid Boots 1926,O 11,18:2
Methling, Finn (Screenwriter)
Stranger Knocks, A 1965,Ap 1,30:1
Methot, Mayo
Corsair 1931,N 19,27:5
Night Club Lady, The 1932,Ag 27,13:4
Vanity Street 1932,O 15,13:1
Virtue 1932,O 25,24:5
Afraid to Talk 1932,D 19,19:5
Mind Reader, The 1933,Ap 7,22:4
Lilly Turner 1933,Je 15,21:2
Counsellor-At-Law 1933,D 8,31:2
Jimmy the Gent 1934,Mr 26,22:3
Side Streets 1934,Ag 15,13:5
Dr Socrates 1935,O 3,29:2
Mr Deeds Goes to Town 1936,Ap 17,17:2
Marked Woman 1937,Ap 12,15:2
Women in Prison 1938,Mr 1,19:3
Unexpected Father 1939,Ag 11,12:2
Woman Is the Judge, A 1939,S 28,29:5
Brother Rat and a Baby 1940,Ja 27,9:4
Metkovich, George
Three Little Words 1950,Ag 10,21:2
Metz, Vittorio (Miscellaneous)
Psycosissimo 1962,S 8,16:2

Metz, Vittorio (Original Author)
I Cadetti di Guascogna 1952,O 6,22:2
Metz, Vittorio (Screenwriter)
I Cadetti di Guascogna 1952,O 6,22:2
Metzger, Radley (Director)
Dark Odyssey 1961,Je 26,22:2
Carmen Baby 1967,O 11,41:2
Therese and Isabelle 1968,My 15,41:4
Metzger, Radley (Producer)
Dark Odyssey 1961,Je 26,22:2
Carmen Baby 1967,O 11,41:2
Therese and Isabelle 1968,My 15,41:4
Metzger, Radley (Screenwriter)
Dark Odyssey 1961,Je 26,22:2
Metzger (Cinematographer)
Sorciere, La 1956,D 28,17:2
Metzger (Producer)
Love and the Frenchwoman; (Francaise et
l'Amour, La) 1961,F 28,38:2
Metzler, Robert (Screenwriter)
Circumstantial Evidence 1945,Ap 21,18:3
Meunier, Raymond
Night Watch, The; Trou, Le 1964,My 27,46:1
Meur, Meinhart
Tales of Hoffmann 1951,Ap 5,34:2
Meurisse, Paul
Back Streets of Paris 1948,O 16,9:2
Red Angel, The 1950,N 4,13:2
Diabolique 1955,N 22,41:1
Marie Octobre 1960,Ag 16,25:2
Picnic on the Grass 1960,O 12,47:1
Love and the Frenchwoman; (Francaise et
l'Amour, La) 1961,F 28,38:2
Truth, The 1961,Je 27,23:2
Meusel, Bob
Slide, Kelly, Slide 1927,Mr 23,19:2
Pride of the Yankees, The 1942,Jl 16,23:1
Meusel, Irish
Slide, Kelly, Slide 1927,Mr 23,19:2
Mey, Anita
Heidi 1953,D 21,27:2
Heidi and Peter 1955,D 13,55:2
Meyburg, Ursula
Marriage of Figaro 1950,N 3,31:2
Meyen, Harry
Devil's General, The 1957,Ap 16,38:2
Is Paris Burning? 1966,N 11,36:1
Meyendorff, Irene
Verraeter 1937,Ja 23,13:1
Mozart Story, The 1948,N 15,21:5
Meyer, Andrew (Director)
Match Girl 1966,N 25,49:1
Meyer, Carl (Narrator)
Mr Bug Goes to Town 1942,F 20,21:3
Meyer, Carl (Screenwriter)
Mr Bug Goes to Town 1942,F 20,21:3
Meyer, Carl Walter
Schoen Ist die Manoeverzeit 1932,Ag 19,20:6
Meyer, Edwin Justus (Screenwriter)
So Red the Rose 1935,N 28,39:1
Meyer, Emile
Hurricane Smith 1952,O 4,15:2
Bloodhounds of Broadway 1952,N 15,15:2
Shane 1953,Ap 24,30:3
Riot in Cell Block 11 1954,F 19,24:5
Silver Lode 1954,Jl 24,6:6
Shield for Murder 1954,Ag 28,8:3
Human Jungle, The 1954,N 26,24:6
Blackboard Jungle 1955,Mr 21,21:5
Tall Men, The 1955,O 12,36:2
Man With the Golden Arm, The 1955,D 16,38:2
Man With the Gun 1955,D 23,14:2
Maverick Queen, the 1956,Je 4,25:2
Raw Edge 1956,Jl 28,10:7
Sweet Smell of Success 1957,Je 28,29:2
Paths of Glory 1957,D 26,23:2
Young Jesse James 1960,Ag 25,25:1
Meyer, Frank
Unstrap Me 1968,N 21,41:2
Meyer, George W (Composer)
For Me and My Gal 1942,O 22,25:1
Meyer, Greta
Tonight or Never 1931,D 18,29:2
Match King, The 1932,D 8,25:3
Flesh 1932,D 10,19:3
Nuisance, The 1933,My 29,22:2
Jennie Gerhardt 1933,Je 9,20:2
Let's Fall in Love 1934,Ja 22,12:3
Servants' Entrance 1934,S 27,25:2
Forsaking all Others 1934,D 21,18:1
Biography of a Bachelor Girl 1935,Mr 2,18:2
Naughty Marietta 1935,Mr 23,11:2
Laddie 1935,My 6,22:3
Mr Dynamite 1935,My 25,12:1
Return of Peter Grimm, The 1935,O 4,25:2
Spendthrift 1936,Jl 23,24:1
Suzy 1936,Jl 25,16:1
When Love Is Young 1937,Ap 17,15:1
Thin Ice 1937,S 4,8:2
Torchy Gets her Man 1938,N 18,25:3
Great Waltz, The 1938,N 25,19:1
When Tomorrow Comes 1939,Ag 17,16:2
Four Sons 1940,Je 8,18:4

Meyer, Greta— Cont
Come Live With Me 1941,F 28,17:3
Friendly Enemies 1942,Je 22,19:1
Meyer, Hyman
Saturday Night Kid, The 1929,N 16,25:2
Meyer, Jean
Between Eleven and Midnight 1950,F 23,33:3
Would-Be Gentleman, The 1960,Mr 23,31:1
Marriage of Figaro, The 1963,Ap 30,26:1
Meyer, Jean (Director)
Would-Be Gentleman, The 1960,Mr 23,31:1
Marriage of Figaro, The 1963,Ap 30,26:1
Meyer, Johannes
Hagbard and Signe 1968,My 17,56:1
Meyer, Johannes (Director)
Schuldig 1928,Mr 11,VIII,7:6 (In Addenda)
Tiger von Berlin, Der 1930,S 15,29:3
Blonde Nachtigall, Die 1931,Ag 22,7:5
Traum von Schoenbrunn 1933,Je 1,15:4
Aschermittwoch; Ash Wednesday
1935,Mr 11,15:2
Schwarzer Jaeger Johanna 1935,Ap 1,17:2
Fluechtling aus Chicago, Der 1936,Mr 16,21:4
Erbe in Pretoria, Das 1936,Ap 18,19:3
Kleine Schwindlerin, Die 1937,Mr 27,19:3
Kleine Schwindlerin, Die 1937,Mr 27,19:2
Gilgi Eine Von Uns 1937,Jl 10,18:2
Ihr Groesster Erfolg; Her Greatest Success
1939,F 12,20:4
Fridericus 1939,F 25,19:2
Diskretion-Ehrensache; Discretion with Honor
1939,Mr 13,12:3
Henker Fraven und Soldaten; Hangmen, Women
and Soldiers 1940,Ja 13,11:3
Meyer, Joseph (Composer)
George White's 1935 Scandals 1935,Ap 29,12:3
If You Knew Susie 1948,F 23,19:2
Meyer, Karl Walter
Herzblut 1932,O 3,15:2
Meyer, Pierre
Paris-Beguin 1932,D 31,10:1
Meyer, Ray
Call it Luck 1934,Jl 10,24:5
Meyer, Roberto
Mexican Bus ride 1954,Jl 21,18:3
Meyer, Russ (Cinematographer)
Good Morning and Goodbye! 1968,F 20,53:1
Meyer, Russ (Director)
Fanny Hill 1965,D 2,48:1
Good Morning and Goodbye! 1968,F 20,53:1
Meyer, Russ (Producer)
Good Morning and Goodbye! 1968,F 20,53:1
Meyer, Sam (Screenwriter)
Mask of the Himalayas 1953,Ag 12,22:3
Meyer, Stanley (Miscellaneous)
Fighting Youth 1935,N 2,13:3
Meyer, Stanley (Producer)
Dragnet 1954,Ag 21,10:2
Meyer, Torben
Viking, The 1928,N 29,32:4
Last Warning, The 1929,Ja 7,36:2
Crime of the Century, The 1933,Mr 13,18:2
Roberta 1935,Mr 8,25:2
Splendor 1935,N 23,23:2
Till We Meet Again 1936,My 9,11:2
King and the Chorus Girl, The 1937,Mr 29,14:4
Prisoner of Zenda, The 1937,S 3,12:1
Thin Ice 1937,S 4,8:2
Romance in the Dark 1938,Mr 21,18:2
First 100 Years, The 1938,My 13,17:2
Four Sons 1940,Je 8,18:4
Christmas in July 1940,N 6,35:2
Sunny 1941,Je 13,22:2
Sullivan's Travels 1942,Ja 29,25:2
Berlin Correspondent 1942,S 4,19:2
Palm Beach Story, The 1942,D 11,33:1
Edge of Darkness 1943,Ap 10,12:4
Miracle of Morgan's Creek, The 1944,Ja 20,15:2
Purple Heart, The 1944,Mr 9,15:2
Hail the Conquering Hero 1944,Ag 10,14:2
Great Moment, The 1944,N 13,15:2
Mighty McGurk, The 1947,Ap 4,19:4
Beautiful Blonde From Bashful Bend, The
1949,My 28,11:2
Mad Wednesday 1951,Ja 25,21:5
Matchmaker, The 1958,Ag 13,22:1
Meyer-Foerster, Wilhelm (Original Author)
Student Prince, The 1954,Je 16,18:2
Meyerbeer, Giacomo (Composer)
Rio Rita 1942,My 8,27:3
Meyerhofer, Elfie
Palace Scandal 1949,Je 6,15:5
Meyerhofer, Ferdinand
Orphan Boy of Vienna, An 1937,S 9,19:2
Meyerinck, Hubert von
Manon Lescaut 1926,N 30,27:1
Aftermath 1927,D 6,27:1
Rosenmontag 1931,Mr 28,15:3
Grosse Chance, Die 1935,My 6,22:4
Fruehlingsmaerchen 1935,My 20,20:5
Fluechtling aus Chicago, Der 1936,Mr 16,21:4
Falscher Fuffziger, Ein 1937,F 13,9:1
Unwiderst Ehliche, Der; Irresistable Man, The
1937,D 20,23:3

Meyerinck, Hubert von— Cont
Sie und die Drei; She and the Three
1938,D 10,13:3
Alles Fuer Veronika 1939,F 4,11:2
Original Sin, The 1950,Ag 21,15:2
Film Without a Name 1950,O 20,32:2
Portrait of an Unknown Woman 1958,Ap 26,14:6
Holiday Island; (Vacanzie a Izchia)
1959,S 22,46:1
Secret Ways, The 1961,My 25,31:1
One, Two, Three 1961,D 22,17:1
Meyerink, Victoria
Speedway 1968,Je 14,43:1
Meyerkhold, V
Lash of the Czar, The 1929,F 12,23:1
Meyerovitch, C
Sunny Youth 1935,Ag 19,18:2
Meyers, Sidney
Quiet One, The 1949,F 14,15:2
Meyers, Sidney (Director)
Quiet One, The 1949,F 14,15:2
Savage Eye, The 1960,Je 7,27:1
Meyers, Sidney (Miscellaneous)
Now Cinema! (Film); Film (Now Cinema!)
1968,Ap 9,56:1
Meyers, Sidney (Screenwriter)
Quiet One, The 1949,F 14,15:2
Meyn, J Wolfgang
Sunderin 1954,D 24,7:2
Meyn, Robert
Sunderin 1954,D 24,7:2
Last Bridge, The 1957,Ag 21,22:2
Meynard, Claire
Disorderly Conduct 1932,Ap 11,19:2
Meynard, Lesly
Pit of Loneliness 1954,Ap 9,19:2
Meynier, Geronimo
Woman in the Painting, The 1959,Ja 15,27:1
Love at Twenty 1963,F 7,5:6
Meyor, Torben
Judgment at Nuremberg 1961,D 20,36:1
Meyr, Robert
Rest Is Silence, The 1960,Ag 2,22:6
Meyran, Jacques
Antoine and Antoinette 1948,Ap 16,29:2
Meyring, Philip (Screenwriter)
Thank You, Madame 1937,Ap 27,18:2
Meza, Jose
Brave Bulls, The 1951,Ap 19,39:2
Mezey, Maria
120 Kilometers an Hour 1937,N 23,27:4
Mezhinsky, S
Professor Mamlock 1938,N 8,26:2
Concentration Camp 1939,Mr 20,13:2
Wings of Victory 1941,N 17,15:2
1812 1944,S 11,14:1
MgBaroyne, Joyce
Daybreak in Udi 1950,Je 2,26:2
Mgebrov, Alexander
Ivan the Terrible, Part II 1959,N 25,22:4
Miake, Bontaro
Yang Kwei Fei 1956,S 11,41:2
Street of Shame 1959,Je 5,17:2
Utamaro, Painter of Women 1964,D 2,57:1
Miao, Ching
Last Woman of Shang, The 1964,D 15,56:2
Love Eterne, The; Liang Shan Po and Chu
Ying-lai 1965,Ja 16,14:1
Miasnikova, Barbara
Fortress on the Volga 1942,D 25,15:3
Micall, Renato
Ring Around the Clock 1953,My 19,36:2
Micaud, Andre
Nous, La Liberte, A 1932,My 18,25:2
MICHAEL
See Also MICHEL
Michael, Charlotte
Both Sides of the Law 1954,Ja 12,19:2
Michael, Gertrude
Wayward 1932,F 15,13:1
Unashamed 1932,Jl 15,13:4
Sailor Be Good 1933,F 27,11:2
Bedtime Story, A 1933,Ap 20,20:3
Ann Vickers 1933,S 29,24:1
I'm no Angel 1933,O 14,18:2
Cradle Song 1933,N 20,18:2
Search for Beauty 1934,F 10,20:2
Bolero 1934,F 17,20:3
George White's Scandals 1934,Mr 16,24:2
Hold That Girl 1934,Mr 24,20:3
I Believed in You 1934,Ap 11,25:3
Witching Hour, The 1934,Ap 28,11:3
Murder at the Vanities 1934,My 21,20:2
Murder on the Blackboard 1934,Je 20,24:2
Notorious Sophie Lang, The 1934,Jl 21,14:2
Cleopatra 1934,Ag 17,12:1
Menace 1934,N 22,27:2
It Happened in New York 1935,Ap 6,10:1
Four Hours to Kill 1935,Ap 11,27:3
Last Outpost, The 1935,O 5,18:2
Woman Trap 1936,Mr 7,11:4
Till We Meet Again 1936,My 9,11:2
Forgotten Faces 1936,Jl 4,18:2
Return of Sophie Lang, The 1936,Jl 24,13:1

Second Wife 1936,Ag 29,16:3
Make Way for a Lady 1936,D 12,15:1
Mr Dodd Takes the Air 1937,Ag 12,14:2
Sophie Lang Goes West 1937,S 30,19:2
Hidden Power 1939,Jl 26,17:3
Farmer's Daughter, The 1940,F 16,23:4
Parole Fixer 1940,Ap 18,28:5
Slightly Tempted 1940,N 1,33:1
Where Are Your Children? 1944,Ja 17,14:5
Woman in Bondage 1944,Mr 27,17:2
Allotment Wives 1945,N 22,39:3
Flamingo Road 1949,My 7,10:2
Caged 1950,My 20,8:6
Bugles in the Afternoon 1952,Mr 5,32:2
Women's Prison 1955,F 3,18:5
Michael, Jean
Native Son 1951,Je 18,19:2
Michael, Joy
Wind Cannot Read, The 1960,Mr 10,36:1
Michael, Ludmilla
Voyage of Silence 1968,S 12,54:1
Michael, Marion
Liane, Jungle Goddess 1959,F 23,19:1
Michael, Mary
Violators, The 1959,Ag 4,32:5
In Like Flint 1967,Mr 16,53:2
Michael, Pierre
Love and the Frenchwoman; (Francaise et
l'Amour, La) 1961,F 28,38:2
Michael, Ralph
Dead of Night 1946,Je 29,22:6
Johnny Frenchman 1946,O 21,27:3
Hasty Heart, The 1950,Ja 21,10:5
Breaking Through the Sound Barrier
1952,N 7,19:1
Abandon Ship 1957,Ap 18,35:1
They all Died Laughing 1964,Mr 16,37:2
Murder Most Foul 1965,My 24,36:2
Heroes of Telemark, The 1966,Mr 10,26:1
Khartoum 1966,Jl 14,28:1
Michaelis, Dario
House of Intrigue, The 1960,Mr 10,36:3
Michaelis, Karin (Original Author)
Star for a Night 1936,S 5,7:2
Michaels, Bert
West Side Story 1961,O 19,39:3
Michaels, Beverly
East Side, West Side 1949,D 23,17:2
Pickup 1951,Ag 31,12:2
Wicked Woman 1954,Mr 27,13:6
Crashout 1955,Jl 9,9:2
Michaels, Captain
Private Hell 36 1954,S 4,6:4
Michaels, Dan
Victims of Persecution 1933,Je 17,16:6
Michaels, Dolores
Wayward Bus, The 1957,Je 6,35:2
Time Limit 1957,O 24,37:2
April Love 1957,N 28,57:2
Fraulein 1958,Je 9,27:2
Warlock 1959,My 1,34:1
Five Gates to Hell 1959,D 10,51:6
One Foot in Hell 1960,O 20,42:2
Battle at Bloody Beach, The 1961,Ag 17,18:2
Michaels, Nicola
Power and The Prize, the 1956,S 27,42:1
Michaels, Noreen
Farmer Takes a Wife, The 1953,Je 13,11:2
Michaels, Sidney (Screenwriter)
Key Witness 1960,N 12,15:1
Night They Raided Minsky's, The
1968,D 23,43:1
Michaels, Toby
Love in a Goldfish Bowl 1961,Jl 13,26:3
MICHAELSON
See MICHELSON
Michalesko, Michal
Power of Life 1938,Ap 29,17:2
God, Man and Devil 1950,Ja 23,16:2
Catskill Honeymoon 1950,Ja 28,10:3
Michaud, Jean
Gigot 1962,S 28,26:1
Michaux, Lightfoot Solomon Elder (Narrator)
We've Come a Long, Long Way 1944,Je 26,21:3
Micheaux, Oscar (Director)
Betrayal, The 1948,Je 26,10:5
Micheaux, Oscar (Original Author)
Betrayal, The 1948,Je 26,10:5
Micheaux, Oscar (Producer)
Betrayal, The 1948,Je 26,10:5
Micheaux, Oscar (Screenwriter)
Betrayal, The 1948,Je 26,10:5
MICHEL
See Also MICHAEL
Michel, Albert
Francois Villon 1950,Jl 3,9:2
Beauties of the Night 1954,Mr 23,23:5
Big Chief, The 1960,Ap 27,32:1
Five Day Lover, The 1961,D 14,55:4
Michel, Andre (Director)
Sorciere, La 1956,D 28,17:2
Sans Famille 1959,S 5,11:4
Your Shadow Is Mine 1963,My 15,32:1

Michel, Andre (Miscellaneous)
Sans Famille 1959,S 5,11:4
Michel, Andre (Screenwriter)
Sans Famille 1959,S 5,11:4
Michel, Germaine
Rothchild 1938,O 12,35:2
Song of the Street 1939,S 5,21:2
Paris Incident 1954,Ag 18,20:2
Michel, Jean-Claude
Story of Monte Cristo, The 1962,N 7,48:1
Michel, Lora Lee
Good Sam 1948,S 17,28:2
Snake Pit, the 1948,N 5,29:2
State Department-File 649 1949,F 21,20:2
Mighty Joe Young 1949,Jl 28,19:3
Tokyo Joe 1949,O 27,35:2
Between Midnight and Dawn 1950,O 2,19:2
Michel, Marc
Lola 1962,O 15,32:2
Night Watch, The; Trou, Le 1964,My 27,46:1
Bebo's Girl 1964,N 12,40:1
Umbrellas of Cherbourg, The; Parpapluis de
Cherbourg, Les 1964,D 17,50:1
Michel, Max
Lucrezia Borgia 1937,O 13,27:2
Michel (Screenwriter)
Horse Ate the Hat, The 1931,S 1,30:6
Michelin, Andre (Producer)
Alphaville 1965,O 26,49:1
Michell, Keith
Dangerous Exile 1958,O 11,18:3
Prudence and the Pill 1968,My 24,37:1
Michell, Yvonne
Divided Heart, The 1955,Ag 4,16:1
Michelle, Donna
One Spy too Many 1966,D 8,64:1
Michelle, Janee
Love-Ins, The 1967,Ag 19,16:1
Michels, Simone
Scandals of Clochemerle, The 1950,Mr 28,28:2
MICHELSON
See Also MICHAELSON
Michelson, Esther
McFadden's Flats 1935,Mr 13,16:2
Great Dictator, The 1940,O 16,29:1
Palm Beach Story, The 1942,D 11,33:1
Micheluzzi, Carl
Lady is Fickle, The 1948,F 7,10:4
Micheluzzi, Mafalda
Traviata, La 1968,F 28,43:2
Micheluzzi, Nino
Schoolgirl Diary 1947,O 18,9:2
Michenaud, Gerald
Big Hand for the Little Lady, A 1966,Je 9,54:2
Michener, James A (Original Author)
Return to Paradise 1953,S 11,24:2
Men of the Fighting Lady 1954,My 8,15:2
Bridges at Toko-Ri, The 1955,Ja 21,20:2
Until They Sail 1957,O 9,41:2
Soyonara 1957,D 6,39:4
Sayonara 1957,D 6,39:4
South Pacific 1958,Mr 20,33:1
Hawaii 1966,O 11,54:1
Michi, Maria
Open City; Citta Aperta 1946,F 26,21:2
Paisan 1948,Mr 30,26:2
Shamed 1949,O 13,33:3
Michie, Byron
Tokyo File 212 1951,Je 1,20:7
Michle, Brian
Battle for Music 1945,O 15,13:2
Michon, Pat
I Passed for White 1960,Ag 18,19:3
Michurin, G
Cities and Years 1931,Ap 4,23:1
Prisoners 1937,F 20,9:2
Road Home, The 1947,My 2,28:3
Secret Brigade 1951,Mr 19,23:2
Michurin, Nikolay
Transport of Fire 1931,Mr 24,31:2
Mici, Erdelyi
Hyppolit, A Lakaj 1933,Ja 4,22:6
Mici, Haraszti
Hyppolit, A Lakaj 1933,Ja 4,22:6
Mickelsen, Jerry
Emergency Wedding 1950,D 22,19:2
Micklewood, Eric
48 Hours 1944,Je 26,21:2
Mida, Massimo (Screenwriter)
Behind Closed Shutters 1952,Je 10,22:7
House of Intrigue, The 1960,Mr 10,36:3
Middlecoff, Cary Dr
Follow the Sun 1951,Ap 26,34:4
Middlemass, Robert
Air Hawks 1935,Je 4,26:5
Grand Exit 1935,N 4,24:5
One Way Ticket 1936,Ja 1,35:2
Muss 'Em Up 1936,F 3,21:2
Lone Wolf Returns, The 1936,F 4,25:5
You may Be Next 1936,F 24,14:1
F-Man 1936,My 4,16:1
Case of the Velvet Claws, The 1936,Ag 29,16:3
Son Comes Home, A 1936,S 5,7:1

Middlemass, Robert— Cont
Hideaway Girl 1937,Ja 13,20:4
Day at the Races, A 1937,Je 18,25:2
Navy Blue and Gold 1937,D 24,21:2
Highway Patrol 1938,Ag 4,15:2
I Am the Law 1938,Ag 26,14:2
While New York Sleeps 1938,D 22,25:3
Kentucky 1938,D 24,12:1
I Stand Accused 1939,Ja 5,17:1
Stand up and Fight 1939,Ja 27,17:2
Indianapolis Speedway 1939,Jl 15,8:2
Magnificent Fraud, The 1939,Jl 20,16:2
Stanley and Livingstone 1939,Ag 5,18:2
Little Old New York 1940,F 3,9:2
Saint Takes Over, The 1940,My 28,29:3
Pop Always Pays 1940,Ag 30,16:6
No Hands on the Clock 1941,D 22,24:6
Dolly Sisters, The 1945,N 15,24:6
Middlemass, Robert (Original Author)
Valiant, The 1929,My 13,27:2
Man Who Wouldn't Talk, The 1940,Ja 12,13:3
Middleton, Charles
Bellamy Trial, The 1929,Ja 24,30:5
Welcome Danger 1929,O 21,30:1
Beau Bandit 1930,Je 14,9:4
Way out West 1930,Ag 18,24:1
American Tragedy, An 1931,Ag 6,22:5
Miracle Woman, The 1931,Ag 17,18:2
Caught Plastered 1931,S 12,15:4
Alexander Hamilton 1931,S 17,21:4
Palmy Days 1931,S 24,21:2
Sob Sister 1931,O 3,20:2
Dangerous Affair, A 1931,N 23,22:1
Safe in Hell 1931,D 19,16:4
Manhattan Parade 1931,D 25,29:2
High Pressure 1932,F 1,22:3
Hatchet Man, The 1932,F 4,25:2
Strange Love of Molly Louvain, The
  1932,My 9,19:5
Mystery Ranch 1932,Je 30,26:2
Hell's Highway 1932,S 26,18:2
Pack up Your Troubles 1932,O 1,10:4
Silver Dollar 1932,D 23,20:1
Destination Unknown 1933,Ap 8,16:2
Disgraced 1933,Jl 15,14:2
This Day and Age 1933,S 1,15:4
White Woman 1933,N 18,18:5
David Harum 1934,Mr 2,23:2
Last Round-Up, The 1934,My 10,25:2
Murder at the Vanities 1934,My 21,20:2
Mrs Wiggs of the Cabbage Patch 1934,O 29,14:2
County Chairman, The 1935,Ja 19,8:1
Behold My Wife 1935,F 18,19:3
Road Gang 1936,F 24,14:1
Song of the Saddle 1936,Mr 21,13:3
Show Boat 1936,My 15,29:4
Jailbreak 1936,Ag 6,22:1
Son Comes Home, A 1936,S 5,7:1
We're on the Jury 1937,F 10,18:5
Hollywood Cowboy 1937,Jl 24,12:1
Mars Attacks the World 1938,N 8,26:3
Kentucky 1938,D 24,12:1
Jesse James 1939,Ja 14,13:1
Oklahoma Kid, The 1939,Mr 11,21:1
Captain Fury 1939,My 26,20:2
Way Down South 1939,Ag 18,16:4
Flying Deuces, The 1939,N 24,29:2
Thou Shalt Not Kill 1940,Ja 8,11:2
Grapes of Wrath, The 1940,Ja 25,17:2
Abe Lincoln in Illinois 1940,F 23,19:2
Shooting High 1940,Ap 12,19:2
Charlie Chan's Murder Cruise 1940,My 3,17:5
Island Of Doomed Men 1940,Je 10,21:2
Wild Geese Calling 1941,Ag 30,10:2
Belle Starr 1941,N 1,20:2
Pretender, The 1947,Ag 12,26:2
Last Bandit, The 1949,Mr 21,19:2
Middleton, Edgar (Original Author)
Captivation 1931,S 28,17:4
Middleton, Gabrielle
Two for the Road 1967,Ap 28,36:2
Middleton, George (Original Author)
Tempered Steel 1918,Je 24,9:1
Polly With a Past 1921,Ja 10,9:1
Once a Sinner 1931,Ja 17,23:1
Middleton, George (Screenwriter)
Sleeping Fires 1917,Ap 16,9:2
Middleton, Guy
Two Who Dared 1937,Jl 10,18:2
French Without Tears 1940,Ap 29,12:2
Suicide Squadron 1942,My 14,23:2
Half-Way House 1945,Ag 13,22:4
Adventure for Two 1945,D 14,24:5
Notorious Gentleman 1946,N 14,39:3
Captive Heart, The 1947,Ap 28,27:2
Bad Sister 1948,Je 11,27:3
Champagne Charlie 1948,Ag 7,8:2
Snowbound 1949,F 21,20:2
Man About the House, A 1949,Mr 9,33:2
Once Upon a Dream 1949,Jl 15,17:2
Facts of Love, The 1949,O 31,20:2
Happiest Days of Your Life, The 1950,S 18,19:2
No Place for Jennifer 1951,Jl 17,31:2
Laughter in Paradise 1951,N 12,21:2

Marry Me 1952,Mr 14,27:3
Young Wives' Tale 1952,N 4,33:1
Fire over Africa 1954,N 22,29:5
Gentlemen Marry Brunettes 1955,O 31,31:5
Let's Be Happy 1957,My 25,25:1
Doctor at Large 1957,Jl 29,15:5
Middleton, James
Synanon 1965,My 6,44:1
Middleton, Josephine
Lady Surrenders, A 1947,Je 20,25:6
Browning Version, The 1951,O 30,33:2
Middleton, Noelle
Tonight's the Night 1954,D 23,13:4
Court Martial 1955,Ag 2,17:1
Iron Petticoat, The 1957,F 2,12:2
John and Julie 1957,My 7,40:1
Circle, The 1959,Ap 16,29:2
3 Men in a Boat 1959,Jl 29,33:2
Middleton, Ray
Gangs of Chicago 1940,Je 13,29:2
Lady From Louisiana 1941,My 15,27:2
Lady for a Night 1942,F 12,27:2
Dream of Jeanie, I 1952,Je 26,26:2
Jubilee Trail 1954,My 1,13:3
Middleton, Robert
Silver Chalice, The 1954,D 27,22:5
Big Combo, The 1955,Mr 26,13:2
Desperate Hours, The 1955,O 6,25:1
Trial 1955,O 14,21:2
Court Jester, The 1956,F 2,19:1
Proud Ones, The 1956,Ag 11,10:2
Friendly Persuasion 1956,N 2,30:1
Love Me Tender 1956,N 16,23:1
Tarnished Angels, The 1958,Ja 7,31:1
Day of the Badman 1958,Ja 30,19:2
Law and Jake Wade, the 1958,Je 7,11:1
Career 1959,O 9,24:1
Great Impostor, The 1961,Mr 30,24:1
Gold of the Seven Saints 1961,Ap 6,30:3
For Those Who Think Young 1964,Jl 9,27:1
Big Hand for the Little Lady, A 1966,Je 9,54:2
Middleton, Tom
Twist Around the Clock 1962,Ja 27,13:4
Middleton, Wallace
American Tragedy, An 1931,Ag 6,22:5
Midgette, Allen
Before the Revolution; Prima della Revolutiona
  1964,S 25,32:1
Nude Restaurant, The 1967,N 14,52:1
**** 1967,D 17,94:5
Midgley, Fanny
Lottery Man, The 1919,O 6,15:1
Stephen Steps Out 1923,N 19,19:3
Greed 1924,D 5,28:1
Bridge of Sighs, The 1925,Mr 23,14:2
Harvester, The 1927,N 7,33:1
American Tragedy, An 1931,Ag 6,22:5
Midgley, Florence
Sadie Thompson 1928,F 6,12:3
Midwesterners, The
Second Greatest Sex, The 1956,F 11,12:2
Miedeske, George
Return to Paradise 1953,S 11,24:2
Miege, Francis
Picnic on the Grass 1960,O 12,47:1
Miele, Donald
Bright Victory 1951,Ag 1,19:2
Mierendorff, Hans
U-Boat 9 1929,Ja 22,23:1
Because I Loved You 1930,Ja 25,13:2
Mifune, Setsuko
Idiot, The 1963,My 1,35:1
Mifune, Toshiro
Rasho-Mon 1951,D 27,18:3
Samurai 1956,Ja 10,26:1
Magnificent Seven, The 1956,N 20,46:2
Sword for Hire 1957,S 5,32:1
Drunken Angel 1959,D 31,12:1
Rikisha Man, The 1960,My 4,57:1
Throne of Blood 1961,N 23,50:2
Hidden Fortress The 1962,Ja 24,24:2
Lower Depths, The 1962,F 10,12:5
Important Man, The; El Mayordoma
  1962,Je 26,25:2
Yojimbo 1962,O 16,34:1
Bad Sleep Well, The 1963,Ja 23,5:2
Idiot, The 1963,My 1,35:1
Sanjuro 1963,My 8,34:2
Chushingura 1963,O 4,26:1
High and Low 1963,N 27,30:1
Stray Dog 1964,Mr 4,32:7
Life of Oharu 1964,Ap 21,42:2
Saga of the Vagabonds 1964,O 7,31:1 (Incorrect
  in this edition; use 1964,O 7,51:1 elsewhere)
Samurai Assassin 1965,Mr 19,27:5
Grand-Prix 1966,D 22,40:1
I Live in Fear; Ikimono no Kiroku
  1967,Ja 26,25:1
Sword of Doom, The 1967,Ap 15,35:2
Rebellion 1967,S 25,56:4
Samurai (Part II) 1967,O 21,16:1
Secret Scrolls-Part I 1968,My 9,54:3
Secret Scrolls-Part II; Ninjitsu 1968,My 23,56:3

Mifune, Toshiro— Cont
Whirlwind 1968,Jl 27,15:1
Rebellion 1968,O 26,27:4
Red Beard 1968,D 20,60:4
Migale, Rosario
Gospel According to St Matthew, The
  1966,F 18,23:1
Might, Mary
**** 1967,D 17,94:5
Migliari, Armando
Destino, Il 1938,F 8,17:3
Trionfo dell'Amore, Il; Love's Triumph
  1938,Mr 29,18:4
Angelina 1948,Ap 6,27:2
Four Steps in the Clouds 1948,N 22,25:2
Heart and Soul 1950,Je 15,41:3
Tomorrow is too Late 1952,Ap 14,22:2
Streets of Sorrow 1952,N 18,37:4
Man With the Grey Glove, The 1953,Ja 3,11:2
Little World of Don Camillo, The
  1953,Ja 14,27:1
Miguelin, Miguel Mateo
Moment of Truth, The 1965,Ag 10,18:1
Mihalesco
Francis the First 1947,N 20,38:4
Mihashi, Tatsuya
Bad Sleep Well, The 1963,Ja 23,5:2
High and Low 1963,N 27,30:1
Challenge to Live 1964,Ap 8,33:1
None but the Brave 1965,F 25,24:1
Burmese Harp, The 1967,Ap 29,25:1
Kojiro 1968,Ag 30,23:1
Mihic, Goraidan (Screenwriter)
Feverish Years, The 1967,S 22,57:2
Mikael, Ludmila
Sergeant, The 1968,D 26,53:5
Mikell, George
One That Got Away, The 1958,Ap 23,40:2
Mikhailov, A
Devotion 1955,Ag 1,15:2
Wrestler and the Clown, The 1959,Ja 1,38:1
Mikhailov, Grigori
Girl No 217 1945,S 3,17:2
School of Courage 1957,S 9,21:2
Italiano Brava Gente 1966,F 4,20:1
Mikhailov, K
Adventures in Bokhara 1944,Ag 21,9:4
First Front, The 1949,N 14,19:2
Mikhailov, Mikhail
Christmas Slippers 1945,D 24,19:2
Great Glinka, The 1947,D 22,30:2
Boris Godunov 1956,Ja 23,21:4
Mikhalkov, Nikita
Meet Me in Moscow 1966,My 3,51:1
Mikhallov, Sergei (Screenwriter)
Girl From Leningrad 1941,D 20,25:2
Mikheev, I (Cinematographer)
Circus Festival 1958,Mr 17,21:4
Mikhelson, Andre
Desperate Moment 1953,S 1,19:4
To Paris With Love 1955,Mr 29,33:4
Divided Heart, The 1955,Ag 4,16:1
I Am a Camera 1955,Ag 9,29:1
Touch of Larceny, A 1960,Mr 17,28:1
Mikhin, B A (Director)
Eagle of the Caucasus, The 1932,S 17,18:4
Mikhoels, S M
Return of Nathan Becker, The 1933,Ap 15,16:3
Oppenheim Family, The 1939,My 24,29:2
Mikhurin, M
Golden Mountains 1932,Ap 14,25:3
Miki, George
Go for Broke 1951,My 25,31:2
Miki, Norehei
My Hobo 1963,Jl 24,27:3
Miklos, Hajmassy
Maga Lesz a Ferjem; You Will Be my Husband
  1938,O 12,35:3
Mikolaiewska, Krystyna
Red and the White, The 1968,S 21,26:1
Mikolajewski, Adam
First Start, The 1953,F 2,17:3
Adventure in Warsaw 1955,O 24,22:2
Mikulski, Stanislaw
First Start, The 1953,F 2,17:3
Kanal 1961,My 10,52:1
Eve Wants to Sleep 1961,Je 6,42:2
Mikuni, Rentaro
Samurai 1956,Ja 10,26:1
Sword for Hire 1957,S 5,32:1
Kwaidan (Black Hair); Black Hair (Kwaidan)
  1965,N 23,51:1
Burmese Harp, The 1967,Ap 29,25:1
Milagritos
Heroes del Barrio, Los 1936,D 28,12:4
Milaine, Amille
Loves of Ricardo, The 1926,Ag 16,10:1
Milan, Art
Man Who Cheated Himself, The 1951,F 9,21:2
Milan, Frank
Hollywood Cowboy 1937,Jl 24,12:1
Gold Racket, The 1937,Ag 2,10:3
Joy of Living 1938,My 6,27:1
And One Was Beautiful 1940,Ap 11,32:4

Milan, Lita
Violent Men, The 1955,Ja 27,17:2
Ride Back, The 1957,Ap 30,24:1
Left Handed Gun, The 1958,My 8,36:2
Never Love a Stranger 1958,N 22,27:4
Milani, Chef
Seventh Victim, The 1943,S 18,11:3
Milar, Adolph
Love's Wilderness 1924,D 22,20:2
Uncle Tom's Cabin 1927,N 5,16:2
Gateway of the Moon, The 1928,Ja 9,20:1
Clothes Make the Woman 1928,Je 5,21:1
Michigan Kid, The 1928,Jl 2,11:2
Bulldog Drummond 1929,My 3,23:2
Rain or Shine 1930,Ag 8,11:1
Tanz Geht Weiter, Der 1931,Ja 6,25:1
Honeymoon Lane 1931,Ag 1,16:4
Sons of Steel 1935,Ap 15,16:3
Paris Calling 1942,Ja 19,21:2
Milasch, Robert
Thank You 1925,O 6,30:1
Milash, Bib
Hero for a Night, A 1927,D 26,26:6
Milash, Robert
Captain Blood 1924,S 9,19:1
Milburn, Mollie Hartley
To Paris With Love 1955,Mr 29,33:4
Milechor, Georges
Ne Sirj Edesanyam 1936,N 24,35:4
Miler, Adolph
Back to God's Country 1927,O 24,24:3
Milerta, John
Night Flyer, The 1928,Mr 13,23:3
Miles, Art
Gorilla, The 1939,My 28,6:2
Spoilers, The 1942,My 22,27:2
Miles, Bernard
Pastor Hall 1940,S 21,13:2
Voice in the Night, The 1941,My 23,25:4
One of our Aircraft Is Missing 1942,N 2,17:2
Avengers, The 1942,N 25,18:2
In Which We Serve 1942,D 24,18:1
Great Expectations 1947,My 23,31:1
Tawny Pipit 1947,S 8,25:5
Nicholas Nickleby 1947,D 1,27:2
Guinea Pig, The 1949,My 2,20:2
Fame Is the Spur 1949,N 8,34:2
Chance of a Lifetime 1951,Mr 15,37:2
Magic Box, The 1952,S 24,40:2
Never Let Me Go 1953,Je 11,37:2
Man Who Knew too Much, The 1956,My 17,37:1
Moby Dick 1956,Jl 5,18:1
Zarak 1956,D 27,22:1
Saint Joan 1957,Je 27,21:1
Smallest Show on Earth, The 1957,N 23,11:2
Tom Thumb 1958,D 24,00:0
Sapphire 1959,N 3,27:1
Heavens Above! 1963,My 21,28:2
Miles, Bernard (Director)
Tawny Pipit 1947,S 8,25:5
Chance of a Lifetime 1951,Mr 15,37:2
Miles, Bernard (Narrator)
Tunisian Victory 1944,Mr 24,17:2
Miles, Bernard (Screenwriter)
Thunder Rock 1944,S 15,16:1
Tawny Pipit 1947,S 8,25:5
Guinea Pig, The 1949,My 2,20:2
Chance of a Lifetime 1951,Mr 15,37:2
Miles, Bob
Water Hole, The 1928,S 3,14:2
Miles, Buster
No Other Woman 1933,Ja 30,9:4 (In Addenda)
Miles, Carlton (Original Author)
Ladies They Talk About 1933,F 25,20:4
Lady Gangster 1942,Jl 10,13:2
Miles, H
Chechahcos, The 1924,My 19,14:2
Miles, John
Wing and a Prayer 1944,Ag 31,14:1
Too Young to Know 1945,D 8,21:2
Gunfighters 1947,Jl 25,12:5
Fabulous Texan, The 1947,D 26,22:5
Tattooed Stranger, The 1950,F 10,18:6
Miles, Lillian
Man Against Woman 1932,D 17,22:3
Moonlight and Pretzels 1933,Ag 23,21:2
Miles, Peter
Heaven Only Knows 1947,N 14,29:3
Enchantment 1948,D 27,16:2
Family Honeymoon 1949,F 25,28:2
Red Pony, The 1949,Mr 9,33:2
Roseanna McCoy 1949,O 13,33:2
Good Humor Man, The 1950,Jl 14,17:2
California Passage 1950,D 16,10:5
Quo Vadis 1951,N 9,22:2
Miles, Sarah
Term of Trial 1963,Ja 31,5:2
Servant, The 1964,Mr 17,30:2
Ceremony, The 1964,My 14,39:1
Those Magnificent Men in Their Flying Machines
(Or How I Flew From London to Paris in 25
Hours and 11 Minutes) 1965,Je 17,27:1
Time Lost and Time Remembered
1966,Ag 30,35:2

Blow-Up 1966,D 19,52:2
Miles, Sylvia
Parrish 1961,My 5,22:1
Terror in the City 1966,N 9,43:4
Miles, Vera
For Men Only 1952,Ja 16,21:2
Charge at Feather River, The 1953,Jl 16,17:2
23 Paces to Baker Street 1956,My 19,12:6
Searchers, The 1956,My 31,21:4
Autumn Leaves 1956,Ag 2,21:2
Wrong Man, The 1956,D 24,8:1
Beau James 1957,Je 27,21:1
F B I Story, The 1959,S 25,23:1
Touch of Larceny, A 1960,Mr 17,28:1
Five Branded Women 1960,Je 2,27:2
Psycho 1960,Je 17,37:1
Back Street 1961,O 13,27:1
Man Who Shot Liberty Valance, The
1962,My 24,29:2
Tiger Walks, A 1964,Ag 27,28:2
Those Calloways 1965,Ap 15,38:2
Follow Me, Boys! 1966,D 2,46:1
Sergeant Ryker 1968,Mr 21,56:2
Gentle Giant 1968,Ap 20,26:1
Milestone, Lewis (Director)
Cave Man, The 1926,Mr 1,17:1
New Klondike, The 1926,Mr 22,16:1
Two Arabian Knights 1927,O 24,24:3
Garden of Eden, The 1928,Mr 19,26:2
Betrayal 1929,My 6,30:4
All Quiet on The Western Front 1930,Ap 30,29:1
Front Page, The 1931,Mr 20,29:1
Rain 1932,O 13,22:3
Hallelujah, I'm a Bum 1933,F 9,15:2
Captain Hates the Sea, The 1934,N 29,33:2
Paris in Spring 1935,Jl 13,16:2
Anything Goes 1936,F 6,23:3
General Died at Dawn, The 1936,S 3,17:2
Night of Nights, The 1939,D 28,17:1
Of Mice and Men 1940,F 17,9:2
Lucky Partners 1940,S 6,25:2
My Life With Caroline 1941,O 30,27:1
Edge of Darkness 1943,Ap 10,12:4
North Star, The 1943,N 5,23:1
Purple Heart, The 1944,Mr 9,15:2
Walk in the Sun, A 1946,Ja 12,10:6
Strange Love of Martha Ivers, The
1946,Jl 25,18:4
Arch of Triumph 1948,Ap 21,33:2
No Minor Vices 1949,F 26,11:2
Red Pony, The 1949,Mr 9,33:2
Halls of Montezuma, The 1951,Ja 6,9:6
Kangaroo 1952,My 17,22:7
Miserables, Les 1952,Ag 15,11:2
Melba 1953,Je 25,23:1
Pork Chop Hill 1959,My 30,9:2
Ocean's Eleven 1960,Ag 11,19:1
Mutiny on the Bounty 1962,N 9,31:2
Milestone, Lewis (Miscellaneous)
Our Russian Front 1942,F 12,27:2
Milestone, Lewis (Producer)
Of Mice and Men 1940,F 17,9:2
My Life With Caroline 1941,O 30,27:1
Walk in the Sun, A 1946,Ja 12,10:6
No Minor Vices 1949,F 26,11:2
Red Pony, The 1949,Mr 9,33:2
Milestone, Lewis (Screenwriter)
Arch of Triumph 1948,Ap 21,33:2
Milestone, Louis (Director)
Seven Sinners 1925,D 8,28:5
Milestone, Louis (Screenwriter)
Seven Sinners 1925,D 8,28:5
Miley, Jerry
Easy Pickings 1927,Mr 25,25:3
Understanding Heart, The 1927,My 10,24:5
Joy Girl, The 1927,S 6,34:3
Pajamas 1927,N 7,26:4
Sally of the Scandals 1928,Jl 3,19:3
Sky Devils 1932,Mr 4,17:3
Milford, Gene (Miscellaneous)
World at War, The 1942,S 4,19:1
Milford, Nancy (Screenwriter)
Little Hut, The 1957,My 4,25:1
Milgram, Frieda
Cyanamide 1954,Mr 26,17:6
Milhalesco
Passion Of Joan Of Arc, The 1929,Mr 29,21:1
Passion of Jeanne d'Arc, The 1929,Mr 31,VIII,7:1
Milhaud, Darius (Composer)
Rasputin 1939,O 17,31:4
Citadel of Silence, The 1939,D 25,29:1
Mayor's Dilemma, The 1940,Ap 23,19:2
Hatred 1941,Ja 27,11:2
Man's Hope; (Sierra de Teruel) 1947,Ja 21,29:2
Milhollan, James
No Time for Sergeants 1958,My 30,13:2
Milian, Tomas
Notte Brava, La 1962,Ja 25,25:2
Bell Antonio 1962,Ap 3,43:2
Boccaccio '70 (The Job); Job, The (Boccaccio '70)
1962,Je 27,40:1
Disorder 1964,My 26,44:2
Agony and the Ecstasy, The 1965,O 9,5:6

Time of Indifference 1965,O 13,50:1
Time of Indifference 1966,O 13,50:1
Violent Four, The 1968,Ag 15,46:2
Big Gundown, The 1968,Ag 23,33:1
Ugly Ones, The 1968,D 12,62:5
Milian, Victor
Touch of Evil 1958,My 22,25:2
Milier, Dean
Dream Wife 1953,Jl 30,20:1
Milisavjevic, Mirko
Legends of Anika 1956,Ap 19,35:1
Miliutenko, Dmitri
Zygmunt Kolosowski 1947,N 13,13:3
Secret Agent 1949,F 10,37:3
Miljan, George
Obliging Young Lady 1942,F 13,24:4
Miljan, John
Sackcloth and Scarlet 1925,Mr 25,24:2
Silent Sanderson 1925,Je 11,14:3
Phantom of the Opera, The 1925,S 7,15:3
Devil's Circus, The 1926,Mr 29,24:3
Footloose Windows 1926,Je 22,21:2
Devil's Island 1926,Ag 2,21:2
Amateur Gentleman, The 1926,Ag 17,15:3
Wolf's Clothing 1927,Mr 28,26:4
Lovers 1927,Ap 19,24:4
Yankee Clipper, The 1927,My 3,25:1
Rough House Rosie 1927,My 23,27:2
Framed 1927,Je 20,25:3
Old San Francisco 1927,Je 23,23:3
Satin Woman, The 1927,Ag 10,21:4
Desired Woman, The 1927,Ag 30,21:3
Silver Slave, The 1928,Ja 3,28:2
Glorious Betsy 1928,Ap 27,16:4
Lady Be Good 1928,My 28,23:2
Terror, The 1928,Ag 16,25:3
Women They Talk About 1928,O 15,16:1
Home Towners, The 1928,O 24,26:4
Queen of the Night Clubs 1929,Mr 18,30:6
Innocents of Paris 1929,Ap 27,16:5
Voice of the City, The 1929,Ap 29,29:2
Desert Song, The 1929,My 2,20:6
Fashions in Love 1929,Jl 1,31:2
Speedway 1929,S 21,17:1
Untamed 1929,N 30,23:1
Devil May Care 1929,D 23,18:2
Free and Easy 1930,Ap 19,15:1
Show Girl in Hollywood 1930,My 5,27:3
Unholy Three, The 1930,Jl 5,17:4
Our Blushing Brides 1930,Ag 2,16:4
Remote Control 1930,D 8,26:1
Paid 1931,Ja 3,21:2
Inspiration 1931,F 9,25:3
Iron Man 1931,Ap 18,17:3
Secret Six, The 1931,My 2,23:4
Gentleman's Fate 1931,Je 27,20:3
Son of India 1931,Jl 25,11:6
Politics 1931,Ag 1,16:4
Susan Lenox; Her Fall and Rise 1931,O 17,20:1
Possessed 1931,N 28,20:4
Hell Divers 1931,D 23,27:3
Emma 1932,F 6,14:4
Arsene Lupin 1932,F 27,22:1
Beast of the City, The 1932,Mr 14,13:3
Wet Parade, The 1932,Ap 22,23:2
Rich are Always With Us, The 1932,My 16,19:5
Night Court 1932,My 27,27:5
Unashamed 1932,Jl 15,13:4
Kid From Spain, The 1932,N 18,23:2
Flesh 1932,D 10,19:3
Whistling in the Dark 1933,F 5,IX,5:1
What! No Beer? 1933,F 11,11:3
Nuisance, The 1933,My 29,22:2
Blind Adventure 1933,O 31,24:3
Way to Love, The 1933,N 11,10:3
Mad Game, The 1933,N 13,21:1
King for a Night 1933,D 11,23:4
Sin of Nora Moran, The 1933,D 13,29:3
Madame Spy 1934,F 10,20:1
Unknown Blonde 1934,Ap 24,27:2
Whirlpool 1934,My 5,22:3
Young and Beautiful 1934,S 18,18:4
Belle of the Nineties 1934,S 22,12:2
Charlie Chan in Paris 1935,Ja 22,23:2
Ghost Walks, The 1935,Mr 30,11:2
Mississippi 1935,Ap 18,27:2
Under the Pampas Moon 1935,My 31,11:1
Three Kids and a Queen 1935,N 9,19:2
Sutter's Gold 1936,Mr 27,25:2
Private Number 1936,Je 12,19:1
Plainsman, The 1937,Ja 14,16:2
Man-Proof 1938,Ja 14,21:1
If I Were King 1938,S 29,31:1
Ride a Crooked Mile 1938,D 29,15:2
Oklahoma Kid, The 1939,Mr 11,21:1
Juarez 1939,Ap 26,27:1
Fast And Furious 1939,O 12,33:3
Women Without Names 1940,My 9,26:4
New Moon 1940,Jl 19,22:2
Texas Rangers Ride Again 1941,Ja 9,27:4
True to the Army 1942,Je 15,15:4
Bombardier 1943,Jl 2,15:2
Fallen Sparrow, The 1943,Ag 20,13:1

Miljan, John — Cont

Bride by Mistake 1944,S 16,20:2
Merry Monahans, The 1944,O 13,16:2
Killers, The 1946,Ag 29,24:2
White Tie and Tails 1946,N 8,28:2
Sinbad the Sailor 1947,Ja 23,31:2
That's my Man 1947,Ap 7,20:2
Adventure in Baltimore 1949,Ap 29,27:2
Stampede 1949,S 16,36:2
Samson and Delilah 1949,D 22,29:2
Mrs Mike 1950,F 9,36:5
M 1951,Je 11,20:7
Pirates of Tripoli 1955,F 24,21:2
Run for Cover 1955,Ap 30,10:6

Millakowsky, Herman (Producer)
Woman in Bondage 1944,Mr 27,17:2

Millan, Victor
Giant 1956,O 11,51:1
Ride Back, The 1957,Ap 30,24:1
F B I Story, The 1959,S 25,23:1

Milland, Lynn
Canon City 1948,Jl 8,19:2

Milland, Ray
Bachelor Father, The 1931,F 2,23:1
Just a Gigolo 1931,Je 13,20:4
Bought 1931,Ag 15,18:3
Ambassador Bill 1931,N 14,15:3
Blonde Crazy 1931,D 4,28:2
Man Who Played God, The 1932,F 11,16:1
Payment Deferred 1932,N 8,26:3
Bolero 1934,F 17,20:3
We're not Dressing 1934,Ap 26,27:2
Orders Is Orders 1934,My 7,20:2
Many Happy Returns 1934,Je 9,18:2
Charlie Chan in London 1934,S 13,26:1
Menace 1934,N 22,27:2
Gilded Lily, The 1935,F 9,11:2
Four Hours to Kill 1935,Ap 11,27:3
Glass Key, The 1935,Je 15,20:2
Alias Mary Dow 1935,Je 29,16:2
Next Time We Love 1936,Ja 31,16:2
Return of Sophie Lang, The 1936,Jl 24,13:1
Big Broadcast of 1937, The 1936,O 22,31:1
Jungle Princess 1936,D 24,21:3
Three Smart Girls 1937,Ja 25,22:2
Wings Over Honolulu 1937,My 29,20:1
Easy Living 1937,Jl 8,20:1
Ebb Tide 1937,N 18,27:2
Wise Girl 1938,Ja 10,13:3
Her Jungle Love 1938,Ap 14,27:2
Tropic Holiday 1938,Je 30,21:2
Men With Wings 1938,O 27,27:2
Say It in French 1938,D 1,29:1
Hotel Imperial 1939,My 11,31:3
Beau Geste 1939,Ag 3,15:2
Everything Happens at Night 1939,D 16,12:6
French Without Tears 1940,Ap 29,12:2
Irene 1940,My 24,23:3
Doctor Takes a Wife, The 1940,Je 15,12:2
Untamed 1940,Jl 25,14:3
Arise my Love 1940,O 17,33:2
I Wanted Wings 1941,Mr 27,29:4
Skylark 1941,N 20,39:2
Lady Has Plans, The 1942,Mr 5,27:1
Reap the Wild Wind 1942,Mr 27,27:2
Are Husbands Necessary? 1942,Jl 9,17:2
Major and the Minor, The 1942,S 17,21:3
Star Spangled Rhythm 1942,D 31,20:1
Crystal Ball, The 1943,F 19,22:2
Forever and a Day 1943,Mr 13,9:2
Uninvited, The 1944,F 21,19:3
Lady in the Dark 1944,F 23,17:1
Till We Meet Again 1944,Ag 30,15:1
Ministry of Fear 1945,F 8,15:2
Lost Weekend, The 1945,D 3,17:2
Kitty 1946,Ap 1,23:1
Well Groomed Bride, The 1946,My 11,22:5
California 1947,Ja 15,31:2
Imperfect Lady, The 1947,My 22,34:5
Trouble With Women, The 1947,Jl 14,14:4
Golden Earrings 1947,D 4,41:3
Big Clock, The 1948,Ap 22,34:2
So Evil my Love 1948,Jl 22,27:2
Sealed Verdict 1948,N 3,36:2
Alias Nick Beal 1949,Mr 10,35:2
It Happens Every Spring 1949,Je 11,11:2
Woman of Distinction, A 1950,Mr 17,28:2
Life of her Own, A 1950,O 12,43:2
Copper Canyon 1950,N 16,39:2
Night Into Morning 1951,Je 11,20:7
Circle of Danger 1951,Jl 12,21:6
Rhubarb 1951,Ag 31,12:2
Bugles in the Afternoon 1952,Mr 5,32:2
Something to Live For 1952,Mr 8,11:2
Thief, The 1952,O 16,37:1
Let's Do It Again 1953,O 14,34:3
Dial M for Murder 1954,My 29,13:2
Girl in the Red Velvet Swing, The 1955,O 20,41:2
Lisbon 1956,Ag 30,19:2
Three Brave Men 1957,Mr 16,13:2
River's Edge, The 1957,Ap 12,20:2
Safecracker, The 1958,Mr 6,32:1
Premature Burial, The 1962,My 24,29:2

X - The Man With X-Ray Eyes 1963,O 24,37:1

Milland, Ray (Director)
Lisbon 1956,Ag 30,19:2
Safecracker, The 1958,Mr 6,32:1

MILLAR
See Also MILLER

Millar, Adelqui
Arab, The 1924,Jl 14,11:5
Moon of Israel 1927,Je 29,29:3

Millar, Adelqui (Director)
Toda una Vida 1933,O 23,18:3
Luci Sommerse 1936,Je 22,22:2

Millar, Marjie
Money From Home 1954,F 27,11:3
About Mrs Leslie 1954,Je 28,16:2

Millar, Norma
Mikado, The 1967,Mr 15,53:1

Millar, Ronald (Original Author)
Frieda 1947,Ag 15,12:3

Millar, Ronald (Screenwriter)
Frieda 1947,Ag 15,12:3
So Evil my Love 1948,Jl 22,27:2
Miniver Story, The 1950,O 27,24:2
Unknown Man, The 1951,N 17,9:5
Scaramouche 1952,My 9,20:2
Train of Events 1952,My 26,18:4
Never Let Me Go 1953,Je 11,37:2
Rose Marie 1954,Ap 2,22:2
Betrayed 1954,S 9,36:1

Millar, Stuart (Producer)
Young Stranger, The 1957,Ap 9,40:1
Stage Struck 1958,Ap 23,40:1
Young Doctors, The 1961,Ag 24,25:2
Birdman of Alcatraz 1962,Jl 19,19:2
I Could go on Singing 1963,My 16,42:1
Best Man, The 1964,Ap 7,29:1
Paper Lion 1968,O 24,54:1

Millard, Claude (Miscellaneous)
Arabian Duet 1922,My 15,20:3

Millard, Harry
Last Mile, The 1959,F 19,27:1

Millard, Helene
Their own Desire 1930,Ja 25,13:2
Divorcee, The 1930,My 10,25:3
Don't Bet on Women 1931,Mr 7,17:2
Doctors' Wives 1931,Ap 25,23:4
Ladies of the Jury 1932,Ap 2,13:2
Broadway Bill 1934,N 30,22:2
Break of Hearts 1935,My 17,24:3
Biscuit Eater, The 1940,My 23,28:5

Millard, Oscar (Original Author)
Frogmen, The 1951,Je 30,8:6
Conqueror, The 1956,Mr 31,13:3

Millard, Oscar (Screenwriter)
Come to the Stable 1949,Jl 28,19:1
No Highway in the Sky 1951,S 22,8:6
Angel Face 1953,Ap 25,11:5
Second Chance 1953,Jl 23,20:2
Song Without End 1960,Ag 12,10:2
Dead Ringer 1964,F 20,22:3

Millarde, Harry (Director)
Over the Hill to the Poor House 1920,S 18,16:2
Town That Forgot God, The 1922,N 1,16:3
If Winter Comes 1923,S 4,14:1
Fool, The 1925,Ap 13,24:1
Taxi Dancer, The 1927,Mr 8,18:4

Mille, Martyn
Man on the Run 1952,F 27,22:5

Millen, Al
Convoy 1941,Ja 17,21:2

Millen, Max
Friday the 13th 1934,My 15,18:1

MILLER
See Also MILLAR

Miller, Alan (Producer)
Appaloosa, The 1966,S 15,51:1

Miller, Alice Duer
Soak the Rich 1936,F 5,14:2

Miller, Alice Duer (Original Author)
Come out of the Kitchen 1919,My 12,11:4
Ladies Must Live 1921,N 21,20:1
Manslaughter 1922,S 18,14:2
Are Parents People 1925,Je 9,16:3
Princess and the Plumber, The 1930,D 23,25:1
Keyhole, The 1933,Mr 31,23:3
Disgraced 1933,Jl 15,14:2
Collegiate 1936,Ja 23,25:2
And One Was Beautiful 1940,Ap 11,32:4
White Cliffs of Dover, The 1944,My 12,15:2
Tangier 1946,Je 7,II,16:4
Spring in Park Lane 1949,S 21,38:2
Lovely to Look At 1952,My 30,11:2

Miller, Alice Duer (Screenwriter)
Valencia 1926,D 27,20:3
Rose Marie 1936,F 1,9:2
Wife vs Secretary 1936,F 29,11:1
Girl on the Front Page, The 1936,N 7,15:2
On Borrowed Time 1939,Jl 7,13:2
Irene 1940,My 24,23:3
Forever and a Day 1943,Mr 13,9:2

Miller, Allen C (Original Author)
Doctor X 1932,Ag 4,17:2

Miller, Ann
Life of the Party, The 1937,O 4,17:1
Stage Door 1937,O 8,27:2
Radio City Revels 1938,Mr 21,18:3
Having Wonderful Time 1938,Jl 8,11:2
You Can't Take It With You 1938,S 2,21:2
Room Service 1938,S 22,27:1
Tarnished Angel 1938,N 15,27:2
Too Many Girls 1940,N 21,43:1
Hit Parade of 1941 1940,D 5,33:2
Melody Ranch 1940,D 26,23:3
Time Out for Rhythm 1941,Jl 10,16:3
Go West, Young Lady 1941,N 24,11:6
True to the Army 1942,Je 15,15:4
Priorities on Parade 1942,Jl 23,19:2
Reveille With Beverly 1943,Ap 24,17:2
What's Buzzin Cousin 1943,Jl 23,21:4
Jam Session 1944,My 3,25:3
Carolina Blues 1944,D 8,26:6
Thrill of Brazil, The 1946,S 6,18:3
Easter Parade 1948,Jl 1,19:3
On the Town 1949,D 9,37:2
Watch the Birdie 1950,D 12,46:4
Texas Carnival 1951,O 13,9:1
Two Tickets to Broadway 1951,N 22,47:2
Lovely to Look At 1952,My 30,11:2
Small Town Girl 1953,My 7,37:2
Kiss Me Kate 1953,N 6,23:2
Deep in my Heart 1954,D 10,35:2
Hit the Deck 1955,Mr 4,17:1
Opposite Sex, The 1956,N 16,23:2

Miller, Arthur (Director)
Promise her Anything 1966,F 23,46:1

Miller, Arthur (Miscellaneous)
Difficult Years 1950,Ag 22,31:2

Miller, Arthur (Original Author)
All my Sons 1948,Mr 29,17:3
Death of a Salesman 1951,D 21,21:3
Witches of Salem 1958,D 9,54:2
View From the Bridge, A 1962,Ja 23,36:1

Miller, Arthur (Screenwriter)
Misfits, The 1961,F 2,24:2

Miller, Billie
Scent of Mystery 1960,F 19,23:1

Miller, Blaine (Original Author)
Canal Zone 1942,Mr 30,21:2

Miller, Bodil
Scarlet Angel 1952,Je 21,12:2

Miller, Brother
Man Who Came Back, The 1924,S 1,9:1

Miller, Carl
Mary Regan 1919,My 5,11:1
Woman of Paris, A 1923,O 2,7:2
Black Swan, The 1924,N 25,26:1
Redeeming Sin, The 1925,Ja 20,18:2
We Moderns 1925,D 8,28:5
Red Kimono, The 1926,F 3,23:1
Why Sailors Go Wrong 1928,Ap 9,18:2
Traveling Husbands 1931,Ag 8,16:3
Honor of the Family 1931,O 17,20:1

Miller, Charles
Night of Nights, The 1939,D 28,17:1

Miller, Charlotte (Original Author)
Sailor's Luck 1933,Mr 17,21:2

Miller, Cheryl
Clarence, the Cross-Eyed Lion 1965,Ag 5,15:3

Miller, Colleen
Las Vegas Story, The 1952,Ja 31,37:6
Playgirl 1954,My 15,13:3
Four Guns to the Border 1954,N 6,15:3
Purple Mask, The 1955,Je 16,35:7
Rawhide Years, The 1956,Je 16,12:2
Man With a Shadow 1958,Ja 23,24:3

Miller, David (Director)
Billy the Kid 1941,Je 20,28:2
Sunday Punch 1942,My 11,19:2
Flying Tigers 1942,O 23,25:2
Top o' the Morning 1949,S 1,25:2
Love Happy 1950,Ap 8,9:4
Our Very Own 1950,Jl 28,12:5
Saturday's Hero 1951,S 12,37:2
Sudden Fear 1952,Ag 8,9:2
Diane 1956,Ja 13,18:1
Opposite Sex, The 1956,N 16,23:2
Story of Esther Costello, The 1957,N 6,43:1
Happy Anniversary 1959,N 11,41:1
Midnight Lace 1960,O 14,27:1
Back Street 1961,O 13,27:1
Lonely are the Brave 1962,Je 28,21:2
Captain Newman, MD 1964,F 21,36:1
Hammerhead 1968,S 12,54:3

Miller, Dean
Skirts Ahoy! 1952,My 29,17:2
Because You're Mine 1952,S 26,18:2
Everything I Have is Yours 1952,O 30,40:5

Miller, Denny
Party, The 1968,Ap 5,56:2

Miller, Don
Spirit of Notre Dame, The 1931,O 16,27:1

Miller, Doris (Miscellaneous)
Pretender, The 1947,Ag 12,26:2

Miller, Eddie
Safe at Home 1941,N 26,31:2
Miller, Eddie and his Bob Cats
Mister Big 1943,Je 14,13:4
Miller, Elizabeth Lee
Sang d'un Poete, Le 1933,N 3,23:3
Miller, Ella
Fog Bound 1923,My 29,10:3
North of 36 1924,D 8,13:3
Miller, Ethel
Broadway After Dark 1924,My 20,15:2
Miller, Eve
Big Trees, The 1952,F 6,24:2
Winning Team, The 1952,Je 21,12:2
She's Working her Way Through College
1952,Jl 10,27:2
Story of Will Rogers, The 1952,Jl 18,10:5
April in Paris 1952,D 25,34:5
Miller, Flournoy E
Stormy Weather 1943,Jl 22,15:1
Miller, Francis Trevelyan (Original Author)
Deliverance 1919,Ag 19,10:1
Miller, Frank
2001 A Space Odyssey 1968,Ap 4,58:1
Miller, Frank (Original Author)
Father O'Flynn 1938,D 26,29:2
Miller, Frank (Screenwriter)
Scotland Yard Mystery, The 1936,Mr 16,21:4
Miller, Fred
Gambling 1934,D 4,22:3
Sophie Lang Goes West 1937,S 30,19:2
Miller, Geri
Flesh 1968,S 27,36:1
Miller, Gilbert (Director)
Lady is Willing, The 1934,Ag 11,16:5
Miller, Gilbert (Miscellaneous)
Ladies in Retirement 1941,N 7,27:1
Miller, Glenn
Sun Valley Serenade 1941,S 6,20:1
Orchestra Wives 1942,S 24,23:2
Miller, Glenn and Orchestra
Orchestra Wives 1942,S 24,23:2
Miller, Glenn Orchestra
Sun Valley Serenade 1941,S 6,20:1
Miller, Glenn, Singers
Crazy House 1943,D 16,33:3
Miller, Grant
Johnny in the Clouds 1945,N 16,16:2
Miller, H C
All the King's Men 1949,N 9,37:2
Miller, Helen Topping (Original Author)
Lover Come Back 1931,Je 5,26:5
Miller, Herman (Original Author)
Coogan's Bluff 1968,O 3,56:1
Miller, Herman (Screenwriter)
Coogan's Bluff 1968,O 3,56:1
Miller, Hope
Bwana Devil 1953,F 19,20:5
Miller, Howard
Big Beat, The 1958,Je 26,23:4
Miller, Hugh
Blind Alleys 1927,Mr 1,31:1
Bulldog Drummond at Bay 1937,O 25,23:2
Victoria the Great 1937,O 29,19:1
Rat, The 1938,F 28,19:1
Loves of Madame Dubarry, The 1938,Ap 4,12:5
Return of the Scarlet Pimpernel, The
1938,Ap 11,12:2
Miller, Ivan
Dr Socrates 1935,O 3,29:2
Mary Burns, Fugitive 1935,N 16,19:2
Charlie Chan's Secret 1936,Ja 18,19:4
Nobody's Fool 1936,Je 4,27:2
Fight to the Finish, A 1937,Je 26,20:2 (In
Addenda)
Call of the Yukon 1938,My 6,27:1
I Am the Law 1938,Ag 26,14:2
Geronimo 1940,F 8,18:3
Man With Nine Lives, The 1940,Ap 29,12:3
Man Made Monster 1941,Mr 19,25:4
Lady for a Night 1942,F 12,27:2
Miller, J P (Original Author)
Rabbit Trap, The 1959,O 15,48:1
Days of Wine and Roses 1963,Ja 18,7:2
Miller, J P (Screenwriter)
Rabbit Trap, The 1959,O 15,48:1
Young Savages, The 1961,My 25,31:1
Behold a Pale Horse 1964,Ag 14,16:1
Miller, Jan
Raising a Riot 1957,My 8,44:1
Miller, Janine
Savage Triangle 1952,S 30,38:2
Miller, Jean DuPont (Original Author)
Canal Zone 1942,Mr 30,21:2
Miller, Jim
Desirable 1934,S 15,20:5
Miller, Joan
Cry of the City 1948,S 30,32:4
Woman in the Hall, The 1949,Ja 24,16:2
Criss Cross 1949,Mr 12,10:2
Caged 1950,My 20,8:6
Jackpot, The 1950,N 23,55:2
Blonde Sinner 1957,Ja 24,34:1

Heavens Above! 1963,My 21,28:2
Miller, John
Gift of Gab 1934,S 26,17:6
We Who Are About to Die 1937,Ja 2,15:1
Jury's Secret, The 1938,F 4,17:2
Girl Was Young, The 1938,F 11,27:2
Johnny Come Lately 1943,S 24,26:1
Time of your Life, The 1948,My 27,29:2
Top o' the Morning 1949,S 1,25:2
Men, The 1950,Jl 21,15:2
Shane 1953,Ap 24,30:3
Fire Down Below 1957,Ag 9,11:2
Miller, John P (Miscellaneous)
Pinocchio 1940,F 8,18:3
Reluctant Dragon, The 1941,Jl 25,12:2
Miller, Jonathan
One Way Pendulum 1965,Mr 3,34:3
Miller, Ken
Buccaneer, The 1958,D 24,00:0
Miller, Kenny
Surf Party 1964,Mr 12,40:4
Miller, Kristine
Desert Fury 1947,S 25,35:4
I Walk Alone 1948,Ja 22,36:3
Too Late for Tears 1949,Ag 15,12:3
Paid in Full 1950,F 16,28:2
Shadow on the Wall 1950,My 19,31:3
High Lonesome 1950,D 8,40:4
From Here to Eternity 1953,Ag 6,16:2
Hell's Outpost 1955,F 26,13:3
Miller, Linda
King Kong Escapes 1968,Jl 11,30:1
Miller, Lorraine
Happy Go Lucky 1943,Mr 25,25:1
Between Two Women 1945,Mr 29,18:3
Men in her Diary 1945,S 24,16:5
Rapture 1950,D 14,51:3
Miller, Lu
Hunted Men 1938,My 21,9:2
Miller, Magda
House of Fright 1961,Ag 24,25:4
Miller, Mandy
Story of Mandy, The 1953,F 24,21:3
Edge of Divorce 1954,Jl 2,10:1
Dance Little Lady 1955,D 26,23:3
Snorkel, The 1958,S 18,37:2
Miller, Marilyn
Sally 1929,D 24,14:4
Sally 1930,Mr 23,IX,6:1
Sunny 1930,D 27,16:3
Her Majesty, Love 1931,N 26,37:2
Miller, Mark
Hook, The 1963,F 16,5:6
Youngblood Hawke 1964,N 6,30:1
Miller, Martin
Squadron Leader X 1943,Jl 23,21:2
Adventures of Tartu, The 1943,S 24,26:1
Frenzy 1946,Jl 20,10:3
Her Man Gilbey 1949,Je 9,35:2
Encore (Gigolo and Gigolette); Gigolo and
Gigolette (Encore) 1952,Ag 3,45:1
Where's Charley? 1952,Je 27,18:3
Front Page Story 1955,Ap 19,28:1
Exodus 1960,D 16,44:1
Phantom of the Opera, The 1962,Ag 23,25:2
V I P's, The 1963,S 20,29:1
Miller, Marvin
Johnny Angel 1945,D 28,12:2
Deadline at Dawn 1946,Ap 4,33:2
Night in Paradise 1946,Je 6,16:3
Dead Reckoning 1947,Ja 23,31:2
Brasher Doubloon, The 1947,My 22,34:5
Corpse came C O D, The 1947,Ag 19,27:2
Intrigue 1948,Ap 24,11:2
Smuggler's Island 1951,My 24,47:2
Prince Who Was a Thief, The 1951,Jl 4,13:2
Peking Express 1951,Jl 19,20:2
Hong Kong 1952,Ap 5,20:3
Red Planet Mars 1952,Je 16,15:2
Off Limits 1953,Mr 30,25:5
Forbidden 1954,Ja 23,11:2
Jivaro 1954,F 13,11:5
Shanghai Story, The 1954,S 25,10:7
Miller, Marvin (Narrator)
Malamondo 1964,N 19,49:1
Macabro 1967,Mr 18,19:2
Miller, Mary Louise
Night Cry, The 1926,Ap 7,26:6
Sparrows 1926,S 20,21:3
Third Degree, The 1927,F 15,23:1
Three Hours 1927,Mr 8,18:4
Miller, Max
Princess Charming 1935,Je 22,18:5
Miller, Max (Original Author)
I Cover the Waterfront 1933,My 18,17:3
Hell and Highwater 1933,D 18,24:4
Secret of Deep Harbor 1961,O 26,39:7
Miller, Merle (Screenwriter)
Rains of Ranchipur, The 1955,D 16,38:2
Kings Go Forth 1958,Jl 4,15:2
Miller, Michael
Men in War 1957,Mr 20,32:4

Miller, Mildred
Merry Wives of Windsor, The 1966,F 28,21:1
Miller, Mirtha
No Exit 1962,D 6,55:2
Miller, Morris
Stakeout on Dope Street 1958,Ap 24,38:1
Miller, Mrs
Cool Ones, The 1967,My 11,50:1
Miller, Patsy Ruth
Remembrance 1922,O 2,21:2
Girl I Loved, The 1923,My 14,18:2
Hunchback of Notre Dame, The 1923,S 3,9:3
Drivin' Fool, The 1923,O 29,18:1
My Man 1924,F 11,18:3
Yankee Consul, The 1924,F 11,18:3
Daughters of Today 1924,Mr 4,17:1
Fools in the Dark 1924,Ag 18,8:2
Breath of Scandal, The 1924,N 26,17:3
Red Hot Tires 1925,O 20,28:1
Rose of the World 1925,N 10,25:3
Hogan's Alley 1925,N 24,28:4
Oh! What a Nurse! 1926,F 22,14:1
Hell-Bent for Heaven 1926,My 4,31:1
Why Girls Go Back Home 1926,My 18,28:2
So This Is Paris 1926,Ag 16,10:1
Private Izzy Murphy 1926,N 10,25:1
White Black Sheep, The 1926,D 21,20:2
Wolf's Clothing 1927,Mr 28,26:4
First Auto, The 1927,Je 28,28:4
Painting the Town 1927,Ag 2,19:2
Shanghaied 1927,S 13,36:2
Hero for a Night, A 1927,D 26,26:6
South Sea Love 1928,F 7,30:3
We Americans 1928,Mr 29,25:3
Hot Heels 1928,My 22,19:3
Marriage by Contract 1928,N 13,37:1
Fall of Eve, The 1929,Je 18,29:4
Twin Beds 1929,Jl 15,25:1
Hottentot, The 1929,S 7,15:1
Show of Shows 1929,N 21,24:5
Aviator, The 1930,Ja 11,21:3
So Long Letty 1930,F 8,12:5
Wide Open 1930,Mr 22,22:6
Lonely Wives 1931,Mr 16,25:1
Quebec 1951,Mr 16,34:2
Miller, Peggy
Pursued 1947,Mr 8,10:2
Miller, Peter
Forbidden Planet 1956,My 4,21:2
Marines, Lets Go! 1961,Ag 16,37:2
Miller, Peter (Screenwriter)
Three on a Spree 1961,Ag 31,22:3
Man in the Dark 1965,Ja 21,22:1
Miller, Robert Ellis (Director)
Any Wednesday 1966,O 14,50:1
Sweet November 1968,F 9,55:1
Heart is a Lonely Hunter, The 1968,Ag 1,24:1
Miller, Robin (Screenwriter)
Psychomania 1964,F 15,14:3
Miller, Ron (Director)
Misadventures of Merlin Jones, The
1964,Mr 26,40:4
Miller, Ron (Producer)
Monkey's Uncle, The 1965,Ag 19,35:4
That Darn Cat 1965,D 3,44:1
Lt Robin Crusoe, USN 1966,Jl 14,28:1
Never a Dull Moment 1968,Ag 15,46:2
Miller, Ruby
Sorrell and Son 1934,My 29,22:1
Anna Karenina 1948,Ap 28,32:2
Miller, Ruth
Name the Man 1924,F 4,23:3
Singer Jim McKee 1924,Mr 24,13:1
Miller, Seton I (Original Author)
Murders in the Zoo 1933,Ap 3,13:4
Frisco Kid 1935,N 25,22:1
Bullets or Ballots 1936,My 27,27:1
Singapore 1947,S 17,31:2
Man Who Cheated Himself, The 1951,F 9,21:2
Mississippi Gambler, The 1953,Ja 30,25:1
Istanbul 1957,Ja 24,34:1
Miller, Seton I (Producer)
Ministry of Fear 1945,F 8,15:2
Bride Wore Boots, The 1946,Je 6,16:3
California 1947,Ja 15,31:2
Calcutta 1947,Ap 24,30:2
Fighter Squadron 1948,N 20,9:2
Miller, Seton I (Screenwriter)
St Louis Kid, The 1934,N 1,25:2
Murder on a Honeymoon 1935,Mr 4,12:2
It Happened in New York 1935,Ap 6,10:1
G Men 1935,My 2,17:1
Frisco Kid 1935,N 25,22:1
Two in the Dark 1936,F 1,9:2
Leathernecks Have Landed, The 1936,Mr 23,22:3
Bullets or Ballots 1936,My 27,27:1
Kid Galahad 1937,My 27,21:3
Penitentiary 1938,Mr 7,13:2
Adventures of Robin Hood, The 1938,My 13,17:3
Valley of the Giants 1938,S 10,20:2
Dawn Patrol 1938,D 24,12:1
Castle on the Hudson 1940,Mr 4,11:2
Sea Hawk, The 1940,Ag 10,16:2

Miller, Seton I (Screenwriter) — Cont
Here Comes Mr Jordan 1941,Ag 8,13:2
This Woman Is Mine 1941,O 13,21:2
My Gal Sal 1942,My 1,23:1
Black Swan, The 1942,D 24,18:3
Ministry of Fear 1945,F 8,15:2
Two Years Before the Mast 1946,S 25,39:2
Calcutta 1947,Ap 24,30:2
Singapore 1947,S 17,31:2
Fighter Squadron 1948,N 20,9:2
Man Who Cheated Himself, The 1951,F 9,21:2
Mississippi Gambler, The 1953,Ja 30,25:1
Shanghai Story, The 1954,S 25,10:7
Istanbul 1957,Ja 24,34:1
Last Mile, The 1959,F 19,27:1

Miller, Sidney
Mayor of Hell, The 1933,Jl 1,16:5
Hi, Nellie! 1934,F 1,15:5
Our Daily Bread 1934,O 3,25:2
Band Plays on, The 1934,D 22,21:2
Boys Town 1938,S 9,25:1
Streets of New York 1939,My 1,21:1
Andy Hardy Gets Spring Fever 1939,Jl 19,23:2
What a Life 1939,O 12,33:1
20,000 Men a Year 1939,O 28,11:2
Golden Gloves 1940,Ag 21,23:6
Men of Boys Town 1941,Ap 11,24:6
Lucky Stiff, The 1949,Ja 31,14:2
Sniper, The 1952,My 10,16:3

Miller, Sidney (Composer)
Patrick the Great 1945,Ap 13,15:2
Are You With It? 1948,Ap 15,31:2

Miller, Sidney (Director)
Get Yourself a College Girl 1965,Ap 29,40:2

Miller, Sonny (Composer)
Dance Band 1936,Ja 4,19:2

Miller, Sonny (Miscellaneous)
Dance Band 1936,Ja 4,19:2

Miller, Susan
Never Give a Sucker an Even Break 1941,O 27,21:2
Innocent Affair, An 1948,S 29,36:2

Miller, Sy (Composer)
Lullaby of Broadway 1951,Mr 27,35:2

Miller, Vernal (Buzz)
On the Riviera 1951,My 24,47:1

Miller, Wade (Original Author)
Guilty Bystander 1950,Ap 21,18:2
Kitten With a Whip 1964,N 5,50:4

Miller, Walter
Unseeing Eyes 1923,O 22,17:1
Manhattan Parade 1931,D 25,29:2
Three Wise Girls 1932,F 6,14:4
Famous Ferguson Case, The 1932,Ap 25,18:6
Without Orders 1936,N 4,41:3
Night Waitress 1936,D 18,31:5
Midnight Court 1937,Mr 4,27:3
Border Cafe 1937,Je 8,30:2
Slim 1937,Je 24,30:2
Flight From Glory 1937,S 11,20:1
Saturday's Heroes 1937,O 16,22:2
Danger Patrol 1937,N 19,27:3
Blind Alibi 1938,My 20,17:2
Crime Ring 1938,Jl 22,10:3
Smashing the Rackets 1938,Ag 9,22:5
Three Cheers for the Irish 1940,Mr 9,19:2

Miller, Warren (Director)
Ski on the Wild Side 1967,Ag 2,24:1

Miller, Warren (Narrator)
Ski on the Wild Side 1967,Ag 2,24:1

Miller, Warren (Original Author)
Cool World, The 1964,Ap 21,42:1

Miller, Warren (Producer)
Ski on the Wild Side 1967,Ag 2,24:1

Miller, Wilson
April in Paris 1952,D 25,34:5

Miller, Winston
Love Piker, The 1923,Jl 16,14:2
Light That Failed, The 1923,N 27,11:2
Secrets 1924,Mr 25,25:2
Iron Horse, The 1924,Ag 29,6:1
Man and Maid 1925,Ap 7,17:3
Stolen Bride, The 1927,Ag 10,21:4

Miller, Winston (Miscellaneous)
Fury at Furnace Creek 1948,Jl 12,11:2

Miller, Winston (Original Author)
Good Morning, Judge 1943,Ap 30,25:4
Tripoli 1950,N 10,35:2

Miller, Winston (Screenwriter)
Home in Indiana 1944,Je 22,23:1
One Body too Many 1944,N 25,21:2
My Darling Clementine 1946,D 4,44:5
Relentless 1948,Mr 6,17:3
Rocky Mountain 1950,N 4,13:2
Tripoli 1950,N 10,35:2
Last Outpost, The 1951,Je 22,16:3
Hong Kong 1952,Ap 5,20:3
Carson City 1952,Je 14,12:2
Jivaro 1954,F 13,11:5
Run for Cover 1955,Ap 30,10:6
Far Horizons, The 1955,My 21,11:1
Lucy Gallant 1955,O 21,30:1
April Love 1957,N 28,57:2
Escapde in Japan 1957,D 24,11:1

Mardi Gras 1958,N 19,45:2
Private's Affair, A 1959,Ag 15,8:7
Hound-Dog Man 1960,Ap 28,29:1

Milletaire, Carl
Black Hand 1950,Mr 13,15:2
711 Ocean Drive 1950,Jl 20,21:2
Great Caruso, The 1951,My 11,32:2
Young Man With Ideas 1952,Je 7,22:6
Miracle of Our Lady Fatima, The 1952,Ag 21,16:2

Millett, Arthur
Man of Action, A 1923,Je 4,13:3
Crimson Runner, The 1925,My 27,26:2
Two-Gun Man, The 1926,Jl 13,19:3
Wolf's Clothing 1927,Mr 28,26:4

Millette, Arthur
Bitter Tea of General Yen, The 1933,Ja 12,20:6

Millgate, Irving H (Screenwriter)
Blob, The 1958,N 7,23:1

Millhauser, Bertram (Original Author)
Girls Gone Wild 1929,Ap 22,23:1
Life of Jimmy Dolan, The 1933,Je 14,22:3
Ever in my Heart 1933,O 13,25:3
They Made Me a Criminal 1939,Ja 21,19:2
Nick Carter, Master Detective 1939,D 14,35:2
Sweater Girl 1942,Jl 13,18:3
Walk a Crooked Mile 1948,O 13,31:2

Millhauser, Bertram (Screenwriter)
Fools in the Dark 1924,Ag 18,8:2
Garden Murder Case, The 1936,Mr 2,13:2
Magnificent Brute, The 1936,O 24,23:1
Under Cover of Night 1937,Ja 20,18:4
Crime Nobody Saw, The 1937,Ap 5,17:2
Ebb Tide 1937,N 18,27:2
Scandal Street 1938,F 5,19:2 (In Addenda)
Texans, The 1938,Jl 28,23:2
Six Thousand Enemies 1939,Je 9,26:2
Nick Carter, Master Detective 1939,D 14,35:2
Angel From Texas, An 1940,My 10,26:7
River's End 1940,Ag 26,11:4
Big Shot, The 1942,Jl 18,8:2
Pierre of the Plains 1942,Jl 30,17:3
Sherlock Holmes Faces Death 1943,O 8,15:3
Spider Woman 1944,Ja 17,14:5
Invisible Man's Revenge, The 1944,Je 10,12:2
Pearl of Death 1944,Ag 26,15:2
Enter Arsene Lupin 1944,O 2,17:6
Suspect, The 1945,F 1,18:5
Patrick the Great 1945,Ap 13,15:2
Woman in Green, The 1945,Je 16,10:3
White Tie and Tails 1946,N 8,28:2
Web, The 1947,Je 5,32:1
Tokyo Joe 1949,O 27,35:2
Pay or Die 1960,My 27,22:2

Millholland, Ray (Original Author)
Submarine Patrol 1938,N 19,9:2
Girl From God's Country 1940,S 9,18:5

Milli, Robert
Curse of the Living Corpse, The 1964,Ap 30,30:1
Hamlet 1964,S 24,46:1

Milliar, G
Stars of the Ukraine 1953,Jl 13,22:4
May Night 1953,Jl 13,22:4

Millican, Fred
Winning Team, The 1952,Je 21,12:2

Millican, James
Who Killed Gail Preston? 1938,My 6,27:2
Star Spangled Rhythm 1942,D 31,20:1
Story of Dr Wassell, The 1944,Je 7,13:2
Sign of the Cross 1944,D 21,16:3
Rendezvous With Annie 1946,S 23,29:3
Trouble With Women, The 1947,Jl 14,14:4
Hazard 1948,Je 3,19:2
Rogues' Regiment 1948,D 20,31:2
Command Decision 1949,Ja 20,34:2
Man From Colorado 1949,Ja 21,24:3
Dalton Gang, The 1949,N 25,27:5
Winchester 73 1950,Je 8,38:2
Mister 880 1950,S 30,13:2
Devil's Doorway 1950,N 10,35:1
Fourteen Hours 1951,Mr 7,43:2
Rawhide 1951,Mr 26,19:2
Great Missouri Raid, The 1951,Ap 9,31:2
I Was a Communist for the F B I 1951,My 3,34:4
Al Jennings of Oklahoma 1951,My 18,34:6
Cavalry Scout 1951,Je 8,32:2
Warpath 1951,N 23,32:2
Scandal Sheet 1952,Ja 17,23:1
Bugles in the Afternoon 1952,Mr 5,32:2
Diplomatic Courier 1952,Je 14,12:2
Carson City 1952,Je 14,12:2
Winning Team, The 1952,Je 21,12:2
Springfield Rifle 1952,O 23,40:2
Torpedo Valley 1952,D 20,15:3
Lion Is in the Streets, A 1953,S 24,39:2
Riding Shotgun 1954,Ap 2,22:2
Strategic Air Command 1955,Ap 21,33:1
Chief Crazy Horse 1955,Ag 28,25:1
Las Vegas Shakedown 1955,Je 18,14:2
Man From Laramie, The 1955,S 1,20:2

Millichip, Roy (Producer)
Time Lost and Time Remembered 1966,Ag 30,35:2

Millichip, Roy (Producer) — Cont
Smashing Time 1967,D 21,44:1

Milligan, Spike
Risk, The 1961,S 25,41:2
Invasion Quartet 1961,D 11,41:2

Millin, Sarah Gertrude (Original Author)
Rhodes 1936,F 29,11:1

Millington, Rodney
Bella Donna 1935,F 26,16:4

Millison, Clifford
Christmas Carol, A 1951,N 29,41:2

MILLMAN
See Also MILMAN

Millman, Mort (Producer)
Shack out on 101 1956,Ja 10,26:2

Millman, William
Lost City, The 1935,F 21,23:3

Millnaire, Catherine
Poupee, La 1963,Ag 28,39:1

MILLNER
See Also MILNER

Millner, Marietta
We're all Gamblers 1927,O 12,30:6
City Gone Wild, The 1927,D 6,27:1
Magnificent Flirt, The 1928,Je 25,27:1

Millner, Martin
Long Gray Line, The 1955,F 11,19:2

Milloecker, Karl (Original Author)
Gasparone 1938,Mr 12,13:4

Millot, Charles
Train, The 1965,Mr 18,25:1
Great Spy Chase, The 1966,O 6,56:4
Trans-Europ-Express 1968,My 13,52:1

Millow, Patrick
Possessors, The 1959,Jl 21,24:1

Millowitsch, Cordy
Lustigen Weiber von Wien, Die 1931,Jl 10,22:2

Millowitsch, Willy
Fledermaus, Die 1964,F 8,15:2

Mills, Alyce
Too Many Kisses 1925,Mr 3,20:1
School for Wives 1925,Ap 1,21:3
Keeper of the Bees, The 1925,O 28,29:2
Say It Again 1926,Je 7,23:2
Whirlwind of Youth, The 1927,Je 6,27:2
Two Girls Wanted 1927,N 14,26:1

Mills, Donna
Incident, The 1967,N 6,65:1

Mills, Edith
Legion of Lost Flyers 1939,O 30,13:3

Mills, Edwin
Happy Land 1943,D 9,33:3

Mills, Evelyn
Alias Jimmy Valentine 1928,N 16,28:6

Mills, Frank
Wives of Men 1918,Ag 26,9:1 (In Addenda)
Chicago After Midnight 1928,Mr 6,20:3
Hit of the Show 1928,Jl 9,25:1
Danger Street 1928,S 25,29:4 (In Addenda)
Make Me a Star 1932,Jl 1,19:3
Parole 1936,Je 27,21:1

Mills, Freddie
Hundred Hour Hunt 1953,Je 17,32:2

Mills, Grace
Where the Sidewalk Ends 1950,Jl 8,7:4
Harvey 1950,D 22,19:1
Vengeance Valley 1951,F 16,21:2

Mills, Hayley
Tiger Bay 1959,D 15,50:1
Pollyanna 1960,My 20,26:1
Parent Trap, The 1961,Je 22,23:1
Whistle Down the Wind 1962,Ap 23,34:2
In Search of the Castaways 1962,D 22,5:2
Summer Magic 1963,Ag 22,19:2
Chalk Garden, The 1964,My 22,42:2
Moonspinners, The 1964,N 4,47:1
Truth About Spring, The 1965,Je 17,27:2
That Darn Cat 1965,D 3,44:1
Trouble With Angels, The 1966,Ap 7,45:1
Family Way, The 1967,Je 29,32:1
Matter of Innocence, A 1968,F 22,36:1

Mills, Hugh (Miscellaneous)
Lovers, Happy Lovers 1954,O 1,19:2

Mills, Hugh (Original Author)
Prudence and the Pill 1968,My 24,37:1

Mills, Hugh (Screenwriter)
Beloved Vagabond, The 1937,F 8,12:5
Personal Property 1937,Ap 11,27:2
So Long at the Fair 1951,Ja 22,14:2
Lovers, Happy Lovers 1954,O 1,19:2
Prudence and the Pill 1968,My 24,37:1

Mills, Joe
Love's Whirlpool 1924,Mr 11,16:2
Old-Fashioned Way, The 1934,Jl 14,16:5

Mills, John
Born for Glory 1935,O 21,22:4
Nine Days a Queen 1936,O 3,21:1
You're in the Army Now 1937,Ap 16,27:2
Goodbye Mr Chips 1939,My 16,27:2
In Which We Serve 1942,D 24,18:1
Young Mr Pitt, The 1943,Mr 11,17:1
Johnny in the Clouds 1945,N 16,16:2
This Happy Breed 1947,Ap 14,24:2
Great Expectations 1947,My 23,31:1

Mills, John— Cont

Green Cockatoo, The 1947,Jl 19,10:2
So Well Remembered 1947,N 5,34:3
October Man, The 1948,Ap 16,29:2
Waterloo Road 1948,D 25,10:3
Rocking Horse Winner, The 1950,Je 9,29:2
Operation Disaster 1951,Ja 15,13:1
Scott of the Antarctic 1951,F 26,20:2
History of Mr Polly, The 1951,O 25,36:3
Long Memory, The 1953,Jl 27,15:2
Mr Denning Drives North 1953,S 2,20:1
Gentle Gunman, The 1953,O 1,34:3
Hobson's Choice 1954,Je 15,37:1
End of the Affair, The 1955,Ap 29,28:2
War and Peace 1956,Ag 22,26:2
Around the World in 80 Days 1956,O 18,37:1
Above Us the Waves 1957,Ap 18,35:2
Escapade 1957,Ag 6,30:2
Baby and the Battleship, The 1957,O 1,37:2
Colditz Story, The 1957,O 25,23:2
It's Great to be Young 1957,D 26,23:3
Dunkirk 1958,S 11,42:2
Circle, The 1959,Ap 16,29:2
Tiger Bay 1959,D 15,50:1
Tunes of Glory 1960,D 21,38:2
Swiss Family Robinson 1960,D 24,8:4
Desert Attack 1961,Mr 23,28:1
Singer not the Song, The 1962,My 3,25:4
Valiant, The 1962,Je 14,23:4
Flame in the Streets 1962,S 13,32:1
Tiara Tahiti 1963,N 6,32:1
Chalk Garden, The 1964,My 22,42:2
Operation Crossbow 1965,Ap 2,29:1
Truth About Spring, The 1965,Je 17,27:2
King Rat 1965,O 28,48:1
Wrong Box 1966,Jl 20,46:1
Family Way, The 1967,Je 29,32:1
Africa-Texas Style! 1967,Jl 13,30:2
Chuka 1967,N 2,58:3

Mills, John (Producer)
Rocking Horse Winner, The 1950,Je 9,29:2
History of Mr Polly, The 1951,O 25,36:3

Mills, Juliet
So Well Remembered 1947,N 5,34:3
History of Mr Polly, The 1951,O 25,36:3
No, My Darling Daughter 1964,Mr 28,13:5
Rare Breed, The 1966,Ap 14,42:3

Mills, Mort
Affair in Trinidad 1952,Jl 31,14:2
Farmer Takes a Wife, The 1953,Je 13,11:2
Cry Vengence 1955,F 19,18:3
Desert Sands 1955,N 19,22:7
Name of the Game Is Kill, The 1968,Je 6,54:1

Mills, Paul (Original Author)
Operation Snatch 1962,S 25,31:4

Mills, Pierre (Original Author)
Frenzy 1946,Jl 20,10:3

Mills, Shirley
Under-Pup, The 1939,S 5,21:2
Grapes of Wrath, The 1940,Ja 25,17:2
Young People 1940,Ag 24,16:2
None Shall Escape 1944,Ap 7,23:2

Mills, Thomas
Guilty One, The 1924,Je 17,22:4
Tides of Passion 1925,Ap 20,22:1
Miserables, Les 1935,Ap 22,14:2
It's Love I'm After 1937,N 11,31:2

Mills Brothers, The
Broadway Gondolier 1935,Jl 18,15:2
He's my Guy 1943,Mr 12,12:3
Reveille With Beverly 1943,Ap 24,17:2
Chatterbox 1943,Jl 2,15:3

Millvojevic, Dragan
Ninth Circle, The 1961,S 15,30:3

Milly
Tempo Massimo 1936,Mr 13,27:2
Musica in Piazza 1936,My 7,21:3
Amo Te Sola 1936,Jl 20,11:2

MILMAN
See Also MILLMAN

Milman, R M (Director)
Return of Nathan Becker, The 1933,Ap 15,16:3

Milne, A A (Original Author)
Perfect Alibi, The 1931,Ap 20,16:3
Michael and Mary 1932,Mr 5,11:2
Where Sinners Meet 1934,My 25,25:2
Winnie the Pooh and the Honey Tree
1966,Ap 7,45:1

Milne, Ella
Green Scarf, The 1955,Ja 15,10:2

Milne, Peter (Miscellaneous)
Great Mail Robbery, The 1927,Jl 20,29:3

Milne, Peter (Original Author)
Convention City 1933,D 25,28:2
Gold Diggers of 1935 1935,Mr 15,25:2
White Savage 1943,Ap 26,15:2

Milne, Peter (Screenwriter)
Great Mail Robbery, The 1927,Jl 20,29:3
Gold Diggers of 1935 1935,Mr 15,25:2
Woman in Red, The 1935,Mr 23,11:3
Miss Pacific Fleet 1935,D 7,22:2
Murder of Dr Harrigan, The 1936,Ja 21,27:5
Walking Dead, The 1936,Mr 2,13:2
Colleen 1936,Mr 9,20:2

Polo Joe 1936,N 5,35:1
God's Country and the Woman 1937,Ja 11,15:5
San Quentin 1937,Ag 4,15:2
Mr Moto in Danger Island 1938,Mr 20,13:3
Private Affairs 1940,Jl 5,10:3
Step Lively 1944,Jl 27,14:1
Verdict, The 1946,D 13,29:4
April Showers 1948,Mr 27,10:2
Painting the Clouds With Sunshine 1951,S 1,9:6
About Face 1952,My 24,15:3
She's Working her Way Through College
1952,Jl 10,27:2

MILNER
See Also MILLNER

Milner, Martin
Life With Father 1947,Ag 16,6:6
Sands of Iwo Jima 1949,D 31,9:2
Our Very Own 1950,Jl 28,12:5
Louisa 1950,O 25,45:2
Halls of Montezuma, The 1951,Ja 6,9:6
Operation Pacific 1951,F 3,10:2
Fighting Coast Guard 1951,My 12,14:6
I Want You 1951,D 24,9:1
Captive City, The 1952,Mr 27,34:2
Belles on Their Toes 1952,My 3,17:5
Springfield Rifle 1952,O 23,40:2
Battle Zone 1952,N 1,17:2
Destination Gobi 1953,My 30,7:1
Mister Roberts 1955,Jl 15,14:1
Pete Kelly's Blues 1955,Ag 19,10:1
On the Threshold of Space 1956,Mr 30,10:5
Gunfight at the O K Corral 1957,My 30,23:2
Sweet Smell of Success 1957,Je 28,29:2
Marjorie Morningstar 1958,Ap 25,32:2
Too Much, Too Soon 1958,My 10,19:2
Compulsion 1959,Ap 2,26:2
13 Ghosts 1960,Ag 6,9:2
Valley of the Dolls 1967,D 16,51:1

Milner, Peter (Screenwriter)
God is my Co-Pilot 1945,Mr 24,22:6
Daughter of Rosie O'Grady, The
1950,Mr 31,36:2

Milner, Victor (Cinematographer)
Crusades, The 1935,Ag 22,21:3

Milo, Sandra
Mirror Has two Faces, The 1959,My 27,31:1
General Della Rovere 1960,N 22,41:1
Green Mare, The; Jument Verte, La
1961,O 24,41:2
Eight and One Half 1963,Je 26,36:1
Love a la Carte 1965,Ja 12,31:1
White Voices; Voci Blanche 1965,Ap 13,32:2
Juliet of the Spirits 1965,N 4,57:1
Male Companion 1966,F 15,33:2
Vista, La; Visit, The 1966,Ag 10,32:1
Weekend, Italian Style 1968,My 23,56:2

Milosevic, Mata
Legends of Anika 1956,Ap 19,35:1

Milotte, Alfred G (Cinematographer)
African Lion, The 1955,S 15,39:2

Milotte, Elma (Cinematographer)
African Lion, The 1955,S 15,39:2

Milovitch, Cordy
Peter the Great 1923,Je 25,16:5

Milowanoff, Sandra
Miserables, Les 1926,Jl 9,17:1
Miserables, Les 1927,Ag 23,29:4

Milski, Stanislaw
Ashes and Diamonds 1961,My 30,8:1

Milsoga, Laszlo
Eb Ura Fako 1940,Mr 23,16:4

Miltern, John
On With the Dance 1920,F 16,8:1
Tongues of Flame 1924,D 16,28:1
Coming Through 1925,F 18,17:3
Fine Manners 1926,Ag 30,10:3
East Side, West Side 1927,O 18,33:2
Dark Angel, The 1935,S 6,12:2
Give Us This Night 1936,Ap 6,18:1
Murder on a Bridle Path 1936,Ap 11,19:2
Sins of Man 1936,Je 19,17:2
Parole 1936,Je 27,21:1

Milton, Beaufoy (Screenwriter)
Mutiny of the Elsinore, The 1939,F 16,17:2

Milton, Billy
Young Woodley 1930,S 27,21:3
Man From Chicago, The 1931,Ja 16,27:1
Along Came Sally 1934,Je 16,20:3

Milton, Ernest
Scarlet Pimpernel, The 1935,F 8,27:2
It's Love Again 1936,My 23,12:1
Alice in Wonderland 1951,Jl 27,15:2

Milton, Georges
Roi des Resquilleurs, Le 1932,Je 13,19:3
Nu Comme un Ver; Naked as a Worm
1933,Jl 9,X,2:2 (In Addenda)
Queen and the Cardinal, The 1944,Je 1,17:3

Milton, Gerald
China Gate 1957,My 23,40:2
Underworld, U S A 1961,My 13,10:1

Milton, Julie
Run for Your Money, A 1950,Ap 10,15:3

Milton, Paul R (Original Author)
Search for Beauty 1934,F 10,20:2

Milton, Robert (Director)
Dummy, The 1929,Mr 4,20:2
Behind the Makeup 1930,Ja 18,21:1
Outward Bound 1930,S 18,28:3
Bargain, The 1931,S 5,7:4
Devotion 1931,O 3,20:2
Husband's Holiday 1931,D 25,29:2
Westward Passage 1932,Je 4,9:2
Bella Donna 1935,F 26,16:4

Milton, Robert (Screenwriter)
Sin Takes a Holliday 1930,N 28,23:1

Milward, Jo (Original Author)
Guilty Generation, The 1931,N 21,20:4

Milward, Jo (Screenwriter)
Devil is Driving, The 1937,Jl 16,22:1

Milyutenko, D
My Name Is Ivan (Ivan's Childhood)
1963,Je 28,25:4

Mimasu, Aiko
Street of Shame 1959,Je 5,17:2
Naked General, The 1964,D 16,51:2

Mimica, Vatroslav (Director)
Kaya 1968,S 25,39:1

Mimica, Vatroslav (Screenwriter)
Kaya 1968,S 25,39:1

Mimieux, Yvette
Platinum High School 1960,My 26,37:3
Time Machine, The 1960,Ag 18,19:1
Where the Boys Are 1961,Ja 20,22:1
Light in the Piazza 1962,F 8,25:1
4 Horsemen of the Apocalypse, The
1962,Mr 10,10:2
Wonderful World of the Brothers Grimm, The
(The Dancing Princess); Dancing Princess, The
(The Wonderful World of the Brothers Grimm)
1962,Ag 8,35:1
Diamond Head 1963,F 21,5:2
Toys in the Attic 1963,Ag 1,17:2
Joy in the Morning 1965,Je 10,38:1
Reward, The 1965,S 16,55:1
Monkeys Go Home 1967,Mr 30,55:1
Caper of the Golden Bulls, The 1967,Je 22,46:1
Dark of the Sun 1968,Jl 4,13:1

Mims, William
Sanctuary 1961,F 22,31:1
Wild in the Country 1961,Je 10,12:5
Day Mars Invaded Earth, The 1964,Ap 2,28:3

Mimyura, Shintaro (Screenwriter)
Rabble, The 1968,Mr 29,31:1

Min, Shen
Maid of Formosa 1949,Ag 8,10:5

Mina, Mina
Payasada de la Vida; Tricks of Life
1935,Mr 18,14:5

Minami, Yoshie
Ikiru; To Live 1960,Ja 30,13:5

Minamida, Yoko
Yang Kwei Fei 1956,S 11,41:2

Minardos, Nico
Holiday for Lovers 1959,Jl 25,10:2
Samar 1962,Ap 12,41:6
It Happened in Athens 1962,N 15,46:2
Day of the Evil Gun 1968,Ap 25,53:2

Minato, Tamotsu (Producer)
Onibaba 1965,F 10,44:3

Minciotti, Esther
Undercover Man, The 1949,Ap 21,30:2
House of Strangers 1949,Jl 2,8:2
Strictly Dishonorable 1951,Jl 12,21:6
Marty 1955,Ap 12,25:3
Wrong Man, The 1956,D 24,8:1
Full of Life 1957,F 13,38:1

Minciotti, Silvio
Deported 1950,N 2,39:3
Up Front 1951,Mr 26,19:2
Strictly Dishonorable 1951,Jl 12,21:6
Clash by Night 1952,Je 19,32:6
Serenade 1956,Mr 24,21:1 (Incorrect in this
edition; use 1956,Mr 23,21:1 elsewhere)
Full of Life 1957,F 13,38:1

Mincle, Pable
Last Bridge, The 1957,Ag 21,22:2

Mindenburg, Ben (Original Author)
Samurai 1945,Ag 25,7:5

Mindenburg, Ben (Producer)
Scorched Earth 1942,S 12,9:2
Samurai 1945,Ag 25,7:5

Mindlin, I
Simple Tailor, The 1934,F 19,18:3

Mindlin, Michael Jr (Director)
Journey to Jerusalem, A 1968,N 18,59:1

Mindlin, Michael Jr (Producer)
Journey to Jerusalem, A 1968,N 18,59:1

Mineau, Charlotte
Extra Girl, The 1924,Ja 21,20:1
Sparrows 1926,S 20,21:3
Further Perils of Laurel and Hardy, The
1968,Ap 1,56:6

Mineo, Sal
Six Bridges to Cross 1955,Ja 22,8:2
Private War of Major Benson, The
1955,Ag 3,27:2

Mineo, Sal — Cont
Rebel without a Cause 1955,O 27,28:3
Crime in the Streets 1956,My 24,27:4
Somebody up There Likes Me 1956,Jl 6,16:1
Giant 1956,O 11,51:1
Dino 1957,Je 22,9:2
Young Don't Cry, The 1957,Jl 27,10:7
Tonka 1959,Mr 26,27:1
Private's Affair, A 1959,Ag 15,8:7
Gene Krupa Story, The 1959,D 26,7:1
Exodus 1960,D 16,44:1
Escape from Zahrain 1962,Jl 12,19:3
Longest Day, The 1962,O 5,28:1
Cheyenne Autumn 1964,D 24,8:1
Greatest Story Ever Told, The 1965,F 16,40:2

MINER
See Also MINOR

Miner, Allen H (Cinematographer)
Naked Sea, The 1955,D 21,37:1

Miner, Allen H (Director)
Naked Sea, The 1955,D 21,37:1
Ride Back, The 1957,Ap 30,24:1
Black Patch 1958,Ap 24,38:1

Miner, Allen H (Producer)
Naked Sea, The 1955,D 21,37:1
Black Patch 1958,Ap 24,38:1

Miner, Worthington (Director)
Let's Try Again 1934,Je 22,24:1
Hat, Coat and Glove 1934,Jl 27,21:2

Minervini, Angela
Vista, La; Visit, The 1966,Ag 10,32:1

Minetti, Bernhard
Karamazof 1931,S 21,20:2
Berlin-Alexanderplatz 1933,My 11,14:1
Volk Will Leben, Ein; People Wants to Live, A 1939,Mr 27,11:2
Henker Fraven und Soldaten; Hangmen, Women and Soldiers 1940,Ja 13,11:3

Minevitch, Borrah
One in a Million 1937,Ja 1,19:3

Minevitch, Borrah (Miscellaneous)
Jour de Fete 1952,F 20,26:4

Minevitch, Borrah and His Gang
Love Under Fire 1937,Ag 28,8:2
Rascals 1938,My 27,12:2
Always in my Heart 1942,Mr 14,19:2

Ming, Chao
Lady General, The 1965,F 12,19:1

Ming, Moy
Bitter Tea of General Yen, The 1933,Ja 12,20:6

Ming, Yuu
Honolulu-Tokyo-Hong Kong 1964,S 2,33:3

Ming-Yau, Lo (Director)
Song of China 1936,N 10,31:3

Mingand, Pierre
Meet Miss Mozart 1937,N 27,21:3
Abused Confidence 1938,D 1,29:1
Champs-Elysees 1939,F 28,17:2
She Returned at Dawn; Retour a l'Aube 1947,Ag 1,21:5

Mingus, Charlie (Miscellaneous)
Mingus 1968,My 17,56:1

Miniati, Lillian
Island of Love 1963,Je 13,30:4

Minin, S
China Express, The 1930,Mr 10,24:1

Minjir, Charles
Fog over Frisco 1934,Je 7,26:2

Minjir, Harold
Daughter of the Dragon 1931,Ag 22,7:5
Beloved Bachelor, The 1931,O 17,20:1
Tomorrow and Tomorrow 1932,Ja 30,13:2
It's Tough to be Famous 1932,Ap 9,18:1
Jewel Robbery 1932,Jl 23,6:6
Successful Calamity, A 1932,S 23,22:2
Night Mayor, The 1932,N 25,19:2
No More Orchids 1933,Ja 2,29:2
King's Vacation, The 1933,Ja 20,21:2
Death Kiss, The 1933,F 5,IX,5:3
Servants' Entrance 1934,S 27,25:2
College Rhythm 1934,N 24,19:1
Hands Across the Table 1935,N 2,13:2
Doctor Rhythm 1938,My 19,25:2
Great Commandment, The 1942,O 17,11:1

Minkin, A (Director)
Conquerors of the Night 1933,Jl 31,16:3
Leningrad Music Hall 1943,N 6,16:3

Minkin, A (Screenwriter)
Professor Mamlock 1938,N 8,26:2

Minkin, Adolph (Director)
Professor Mamlock 1938,N 8,26:2

Minkwanazi, David
Magic Garden, The 1952,F 6,24:2

Minneau, Charlotta
Happiness 1924,Mr 11,16:2

Minnelli, Liza
Charlie Bubbles 1968,F 12,47:2

Minnelli, Vincente (Director)
Cabin in the Sky 1943,My 28,19:3
I Dood It 1943,N 11,29:1
Meet Me in St Louis 1944,N 29,20:2
Clock, The 1945,My 4,23:2

Yolanda and the Thief 1945,N 23,26:2
Ziegfeld Follies 1946,Mr 23,8:3
Undercurrent 1946,N 29,36:2
Pirate, The 1948,My 21,19:2
Madame Bovary 1949,Ag 26,15:2
Father of the Bride 1950,My 19,31:2
Father's Little Dividend 1951,Ap 13,18:5
American in Paris, An 1951,O 5,24:2
Bad and the Beautiful, The 1953,Ja 16,19:1
Story of Three Loves, The (Equilibrium);
  Equilibrium (The Story of Three Loves)
  1953,Mr 6,29:2
Story of Three Loves, The (Mademoiselle);
  Mademoiselle (The Story of Three Loves)
  1953,Mr 6,29:2
Story of Three Loves, The (The Jealous Lover);
  Jealous Lover, The (The Story of Three Loves)
  1953,Mr 6,29:2
Story of Three Loves, The 1953,Mr 6,29:2
Equilibrium 1953,Mr 6,29:2
Band Wagon, The 1953,Jl 10,10:2
Long, Long Trailer, The 1954,F 19,24:3
Brigadoon 1954,S 17,18:2
Cobweb, The 1955,Ag 6,13:3
Kismet 1955,D 9,32:2
Lust for Life 1956,S 18,39:1
Tea and Sympathy 1956,S 28,24:4
Designing Woman 1957,My 17,20:2
Gigi 1958,My 16,21:1
Reluctant Debutante, The 1958,Ag 15,17:1
Some Came Running 1959,Ja 23,17:1
Home from the Hill 1960,Mr 4,19:1
Bells Are Ringing 1960,Je 24,31:2
4 Horsemen of the Apocalypse, The 1962,Mr 10,10:2
Two Weeks in Another Town 1962,Ag 18,10:1
Courtship of Eddie's Father, The 1963,Mr 7,8:5
  (Incorrect in this edition; use 1963,Mr 28,8:5
  elsewhere)
Goodbye, Charlie 1964,N 19,49:1
Sandpiper, The 1965,Jl 16,14:1

Minney, R J (Original Author)
Clive of India 1935,Ja 18,29:1
Time, Gentlemen, Please 1953,S 24,39:2

Minney, R J (Producer)
Wicked Lady, The 1946,D 23,19:5
Magic Bow, The 1947,Jl 7,13:2
Place of One's Own, A 1949,F 8,30:2
Final Test, The 1954,Ja 26,21:5

Minney, R J (Screenwriter)
Clive of India 1935,Ja 18,29:1
Randolph Family 1945,Mr 13,19:4

Mino, Ching
Lady General, The 1965,F 12,19:1

Minoff, Lee (Original Author)
Yellow Submarine 1968,N 14,56:1

Minoff, Lee (Screenwriter)
Yellow Submarine 1968,N 14,56:1

MINOR
See Also MINER

Minor, Frank
Our Daily Bread 1934,O 3,25:2

Minoru, Nesheda
Shanghai Express 1932,F 18,25:3

Minot, Dominique
Charade 1963,D 6,40:1

Minotis, Alexis
Notorious 1946,Ag 16,19:2
Chase, The 1946,N 18,31:2
Siren of Atlantis 1949,Ag 22,13:1
Panic in the Streets 1950,Ag 5,9:2
Land of the Pharaohs 1955,Jl 27,15:2
Boy on a Dolphin 1957,Ap 20,21:2

Minouchkine, Alexandre (Producer)
Eagle with Two Heads 1948,D 30,24:2

Minoura, Jingo (Producer)
Rasho-Mon 1951,D 27,18:3

Minovitskaya, G L
Oppenheim Family, The 1939,My 24,29:2

Minter, George (Producer)
Adventures of Sadie, The 1955,My 18,35:2
Svengali 1955,S 26,18:2
Dance Little Lady 1955,D 26,23:3
Ship Was Loaded, The 1958,Ja 20,20:1
Portrait of a Sinner 1961,D 7,52:1

Minter, Mary Miles
Barbara Frietchie 1915,N 29,11:3
Dimples 1916,F 14,11:2
Anne of Green Gables 1919,D 22,18:3
Judy of Rogues Harbor 1920,Mr 1,16:2
Nurse Marjorie 1920,My 24,20:3
Jenny, Be Good 1920,Je 28,13:2
Drums of Fate 1923,Ja 15,18:3
Trail of the Lonesome Pine, The 1923,Mr 20,24:3

Minto, Dorothy
Children of Chance 1931,Ja 24,15:1

Mints, K (Screenwriter)
Tiger Girl 1955,S 5,8:2
Sailor From the Comet, The 1959,Ag 3,21:2

Mintz, Eli
Molly 1951,Mr 8,37:2
Proud Rebel, The 1958,Jl 2,23:4
Murder, Inc 1960,Je 29,26:6

Mintz, Sam (Original Author)
Daring Daughters 1933,Mr 25,13:4
Best of Enemies 1933,Jl 17,19:5
Here Comes Cookie 1935,O 12,12:2

Mintz, Sam (Screenwriter)
Rubber Heels 1927,Je 28,29:4
Man Power 1927,Jl 26,17:1
Anne of Green Gables 1934,D 22,21:1
Roberta 1935,Mr 8,25:2
Chatterbox 1936,F 15,18:6
Farmer in the Dell, The 1936,Mr 7,11:4
Crack-Up 1937,Ja 4,20:4

Minuti, Baldo
Black Hand 1950,Mr 13,15:2

Mioni, Fabrizio
Hercules 1959,Jl 23,32:2
Blue Angel, The 1959,S 5,11:4
Venetian Affair, The 1967,Ja 19,41:2

Mir, David
His Hour 1924,O 7,26:1
Man and Maid 1925,Ap 7,17:3
Time, the Comedian 1925,D 14,18:2
Boheme, La 1926,F 25,26:2
Diplomacy 1926,S 13,18:1
Dearie 1927,Jl 4,20:3
Breakfast at Sunrise 1927,N 14,26:1
Bringing Up Father 1928,Mr 19,26:2
Matinee Idol, The 1928,Ap 24,29:3
Cavalier, The 1928,O 31,28:4
Escapade 1932,My 28,18:2

Mira, Naranda Rath (Original Author)
Mahanagar; Big City, The 1964,S 28,19:1

Mirabel, Alfred (Producer)
Blood and Black Lace 1965,N 11,58:3

Miracle, Silas
Stark Love 1927,F 28,22:3

Mirafiore, Rosi
Flight Into France 1949,Jl 22,16:2

Miral, Nina
Coiffeur Pour Dames 1932,O 31,18:4

Miranda, Aurora
Brazil 1944,N 20,25:2
Three Caballeros, The 1945,F 5,20:1

Miranda, Carmen
Down Argentine Way 1940,O 18,25:1
That Night in Rio 1941,Mr 10,21:2
Week-End in Havana 1941,N 8,11:2
Springtime in the Rockies 1942,N 12,30:2
Gang's All Here, The 1943,D 23,26:4
Four Jills in a Jeep 1944,Ap 6,27:2
Greenwich Village 1944,S 28,26:2
Something for the Boys 1944,N 30,19:1
Doll Face 1946,Mr 28,35:3
If I'm Lucky 1946,S 20,41:3
Copacabana 1947,Jl 12,7:2
Date with Judy, A 1948,Ag 7,8:2
Nancy Goes to Rio 1950,Ap 7,22:2
Scared Stiff 1953,Jl 3,10:2

Miranda, Carmen Orchestra
That Night in Rio 1941,Mr 10,21:2

Miranda, Isa
Dopo una Notte d'Amore; After a Night of Love 1935,O 29,16:5
Signora di Tutti, La 1936,Mr 26,27:3
Passaporto Rosso 1936,S 2,18:2
Late Mathias Pascal, The 1937,N 18,27:2
Lie of Nina Petrovna, The 1938,Mr 30,19:2
Come le Foglie; Like the Leaves 1938,S 29,31:1
Hotel Imperial 1939,My 11,31:3
Scipio Africanus 1939,S 23,22:2
Du Bist mein Gluck; Thou Art my Joy 1940,Ja 6,9:2
Between Two Worlds 1940,F 9,15:2
Adventure in Diamonds 1940,Ap 4,27:2
Walls of Malapaga, The 1950,Mr 21,34:2
My Widow and I 1950,Ag 30,27:5
Seven Deadly Sins, The (Avarice and Anger);
  Avarice and Anger (The Seven Deadly Sins)
  1953,My 12,31:3
Ronde, La 1954,Mr 17,27:2
Summertime 1955,Je 22,25:1
What Price Murder 1958,N 11,26:1
Empty Canvas, The 1964,My 16,21:1 (Incorrect
  in this edition; use 1964,My 16,12:1 elsewhere)
Yellow Rolls-Royce, The 1965,My 14,42:2

Mirande, Yves (Director)
32 Rue de Montmartre 1944,S 28,26:3
Moulin Rouge 1944,N 23,38:2

Mirande, Yves (Miscellaneous)
Papa sans le Savoir; Father Without Knowing It,
  A 1932,My 1,VIII,4:1 (In Addenda)

Mirande, Yves (Original Author)
Evening Clothes 1927,Mr 21,10:4
Perle, La 1932,S 18,IX,4:4 (In Addenda)
Moulin Rouge 1944,N 23,38:2

Mirande, Yves (Screenwriter)
Chance, La 1932,My 28,18:2
32 Rue de Montmartre 1944,S 28,26:3
Symphonie d'Amour 1946,Mr 11,19:2
Mirandy
Comin' Round the Mountain 1940,S 26,27:3
Mirante, Francois
Cloportes 1966,Ap 19,36:1
Mirbach, Irene
Sunderin 1954,D 24,7:2
Mirbeau, Octave (Original Author)
Diary of a Chambermaid, The 1946,Je 23,28:2
Mirei, Nicole
7 Capital Sins (Laziness); Laziness (7 Capital Sins) 1963,Ja 17,5:2
Miric, Voja
Three 1967,Je 30,30:1
Mirisch, Walter (Producer)
Bomba, the Jungle Boy 1949,Ap 16,11:4
Cavalry Scout 1951,Je 8,32:2
Flat Top 1952,D 6,17:2
Hiawatha 1952,D 26,20:4
Annapolis Story, An 1955,Ap 9,8:2
Warriors, The 1955,S 10,11:2
First Texan, The 1956,Je 23,20:2
Oklahoman, The 1957,My 15,39:1
Man of the West 1958,O 2,44:3
Man in the Net, The 1959,Je 11,36:2
By Love Possessed 1961,Jl 20,32:2
Two for the Seesaw 1962,N 22,43:1
Toys in the Attic 1963,Ag 1,17:2
Hawaii 1966,O 11,54:1
In the Heat of the Night 1967,Ag 3,26:1
Fitzwilly 1967,D 21,45:1
Miro, Sergio (Director)
Cancion del Regreso, La; Home-Coming Song 1940,Je 22,18:4
Mironov, Andrei
Uncommon Thief, An 1967,D 1,56:2
Mironova, M
Variety Stars 1955,F 21,16:7
Mironova, V
Signal, The 1943,Mr 25,25:3
Miroslava
Adventures of Casanova 1948,Mr 22,18:3
Brave Bulls, The 1951,Ap 19,39:2
Mirouze, M (Miscellaneous)
Yellow Cruise, The 1936,N 18,31:3
Mirov, L
Variety Stars 1955,F 21,16:7
Mirska, Zosia
Ulica 1933,Ja 27,13:2
Prokurator 1934,My 22,28:4
Mirza, Vajahat (Miscellaneous)
Handful of Grain, A 1959,Jl 4,9:4
Mirzaharimova, M
Adventures in Bokhara 1944,Ag 21,9:4
Misch, Margot
Children of no Importance 1928,Ap 3,33:2
Mischel, Josef (Screenwriter)
Isle of the Dead 1945,S 8,12:2
Isn't It Romantic? 1948,O 7,35:2
My Own True Love 1949,F 3,27:3
Misener, Helen
A Night to Remember 1958,D 17,2:7
Mishima, Masao
Harakiri 1964,Ag 5,24:2
Rebellion 1968,O 26,27:4
Mishima, Yukio (Director)
Now Cinema! (Rite of Love and Death); Rite of Love and Death (Now Cinema!) 1968,Ap 9,56:1
Mishima, Yukio (Original Author)
Enjo 1964,S 23,54:1
School for Sea 1967,D 2,48:5
Mishima, Yukio (Producer)
Now Cinema! (Rite of Love and Death); Rite of Love and Death (Now Cinema!) 1968,Ap 9,56:1
Mishima, Yukio (Screenwriter)
Now Cinema! (Rite of Love and Death); Rite of Love and Death (Now Cinema!) 1968,Ap 9,56:1
Mishkin, William (Producer)
Tainted 1950,Ja 21,10:2
Mishkin, William (Screenwriter)
Violated 1953,D 12,23:8
Mishurin, A (Director)
Train Goes to Kiev, The 1961,Ap 10,26:1
Misiano, Fortunato (Producer)
Lost in the Dark 1949,My 14,9:2
Verginita 1953,Ap 18,17:2
What Price Innocence? 1953,My 2,13:3
Samson and the Slave Queen 1964,Mr 5,36:2
Miskovitch, Milorad
Dr Coppelius 1968,D 26,56:1
Misraki, Paul (Composer)
Bonnes Femmes, Les 1966,My 13,32:1
Miss Universe Beauties
Yankee Pasha 1954,Ap 19,19:2
Missirio, Cenica
Figaro 1929,N 25,22:1

Missiroll, Mario (Screenwriter)
Family Diary 1963,N 12,48:1
Mistral, Jorge
Mad Queen, The 1950,O 27,24:3
Boy on a Dolphin 1957,Ap 20,21:2
Sword and the Cross, The 1960,Jl 7,26:1
Gunfighters of Casa Grande 1965,S 2,36:1
Mistrik, Ivan
Sweet Light in a Dark Room 1966,Je 30,28:1
Misumi, Kenji (Director)
Buddha 1965,Je 17,27:4
Showdown for Zatoichi 1968,O 5,40:1
Mita, Ura
Devil Dancer, The 1927,D 19,30:1
Mita, Yoshiko
Bushido 1964,S 13,39:1
Mitagi, Chikako
Imposter, The 1955,Mr 23,27:1
Mitaishvill, Liana
Ballet of Othello, The 1964,My 4,35:1
Mitchell
Stand up and Cheer 1934,Ap 20,17:1
Mitchell, Arthur
Midsummer Night's Dream, A 1967,Ap 18,32:1
Day the Fish Came Out, The 1967,O 3,57:1
Mitchell, Barry
Sinbad the Sailor 1947,Ja 23,31:2
Mitchell, Basil John (Original Author)
Perfect Woman, The 1951,F 17,10:7
Mitchell, Belle
Flying Romeos 1928,Ap 3,33:2
Firefly, The 1937,S 2,17:2
Mark of Zorro, The 1940,N 4,23:2
That Lady in Ermine 1948,Ag 25,31:2
Mitchell, Bruce (Director)
Love's Whirlpool 1924,Mr 11,16:2
Mitchell, Cameron
They Were Expendable 1945,D 21,25:2
What Next Corporal Hargrove? 1945,D 26,15:2
Mighty McGurk, The 1947,Ap 4,19:4
High Barbaree 1947,Je 6,27:2
Cass Timberlane 1947,N 7,20:2
Homecoming 1948,Ap 30,28:4
Command Decision 1949,Ja 20,34:2
Death of a Salesman 1951,D 21,21:3
Japanese War Bride 1952,Ja 30,22:6
Okinawa 1952,Ap 24,38:3
Outcasts of Poker Flat 1952,My 16,19:3
Sellout, The 1952,My 31,12:7
Miserables, Les 1952,Ag 15,11:2
Pony Soldier 1952,D 20,15:2
Man on a Tightrope 1953,Je 5,19:1
Powder River 1953,Jl 4,7:2
How to Marry a Millionaire 1953,N 11,37:1
Hell and High Water 1954,F 2,20:6
Gorilla at Large 1954,Je 12,13:2
Garden of Evil 1954,Jl 10,17:1
Desiree 1954,N 18,42:1
Strange Lady in Town 1955,My 21,11:1
Love Me or Leave Me 1955,My 27,14:1
House of Bamboo 1955,Jl 2,13:2
Tall Men, The 1955,O 12,36:2
View From Pompey's Head, The 1955,N 5,22:5
Carousel 1956,F 17,13:1
Monkey on my Back 1957,My 30,23:2
No Down Payment 1957,O 31,41:1
Escapde in Japan 1957,D 24,11:1
All Mine to Give 1959,Ag 4,32:5
As the Sea Rages 1961,My 18,41:1
Last of the Vikings 1962,S 27,33:4
Blood and Black Lace 1965,N 11,58:3
Hombre 1967,Mr 22,41:1
Mitchell, Charles
Big Fix, The 1947,My 3,10:3
Mitchell, Charles (Composer)
Two Tickets to London 1943,Jl 3,11:2
Mitchell, Charlotte
Laughter in Paradise 1951,N 12,21:2
Curtain Up 1953,F 2,17:3
Mitchell, Didson (Original Author)
Road to Paradise, The 1931,Ja 20,21:3
Mitchell, Frank
She Learned About Sailors 1934,Jl 30,9:4
365 Nights in Hollywood 1934,N 7,32:1
Singing Kid, The 1936,Ap 4,11:1
Tropic Fury 1939,S 8,28:4
Double Alibi 1940,Mr 11,11:2
Six Lessons From Madame La Zonga 1941,F 19,25:2
Neptune's Daughter 1949,Je 10,32:2
Scaramouche 1952,My 9,20:2
Mitchell, Geneva
Son of the Gods 1930,Ja 31,24:1
Back Pay 1930,My 31,19:4
Safety in Numbers 1930,My 31,19:4
Her Wedding Night 1930,S 29,19:1
Millie 1931,F 7,11:1
Single Sin, The 1931,Mr 17,34:3
Big Gamble, The 1931,S 21,20:2
Disorderly Conduct 1932,Ap 11,19:2
Night World 1932,My 28,18:2
False Faces 1932,N 25,19:2
Devil Is Driving, The 1932,D 16,25:5

Mitchell, Geneva — Cont
World Gone Mad, The 1933,Ap 15,16:3
Morning Glory 1933,Ag 18,18:2
I Am Suzanne 1934,Ja 19,24:3
Blind Date 1934,S 1,16:3
Behind the Evidence 1935,Ja 26,13:2
Night Life of the Gods 1935,F 23,14:6
Air Hawks 1935,Je 4,26:5
Mitchell, George
Phenix City Story, The 1955,S 3,9:1
3:10 to Yuma 1957,Ag 29,22:1
Unsinkable Molly Brown, The 1964,Jl 17,15:1
Flim Flam Man, The 1967,Ag 23,40:1
Mitchell, Gordon
Reflections in a Golden Eye 1967,O 12,59:1
Mitchell, Grant
Man to Man 1931,Ja 3,21:2
Star Witness, The 1931,Ag 4,19:5
Famous Ferguson Case, The 1932,Ap 25,18:6
Week-End Marriage 1932,Je 4,9:2
Big City Blues 1932,S 10,18:5
Successful Calamity, A 1932,S 23,22:2
Three on a Match 1932,O 29,18:4
No Man of her Own 1932,D 31,10:1
20,000 Years in Sing Sing 1933,Ja 10,26:2
Our Betters 1933,F 24,13:2
Central Airport 1933,My 4,20:5
Lilly Turner 1933,Je 15,21:2
Tomorrow at Seven 1933,Jl 3,14:6
Heroes for Sale 1933,Jl 22,14:3
Stranger's Return, The 1933,Jl 28,18:2
Dinner at Eight 1933,Ag 24,18:1
Wild Boys of the Road 1933,S 22,14:1
Saturday's Millions 1933,O 14,18:3
Dancing Lady 1933,D 1,23:2
King for a Night 1933,D 11,23:4
Convention City 1933,D 25,28:2
Shadows of Sing Sing 1934,F 21,23:2
Show-Off, The 1934,Mr 17,11:3
20 Million Sweethearts 1934,Ap 27,25:1
Cat's Paw, The 1934,Ag 17,12:2
We're Rich Again 1934,S 1,16:3
Case of the Howling Dog, The 1934,O 18,26:5
365 Nights in Hollywood 1934,N 7,32:1
Secret Bride, The 1935,F 2,10:1
One More Spring 1935,F 22,27:1
Gold Diggers of 1935 1935,Mr 15,25:2
Traveling Saleslady 1935,Mr 29,26:2
Men Without Names 1935,Je 29,16:2
Broadway Gondolier 1935,Jl 18,15:2
Midsummer Night's Dream, A 1935,O 10,31:1
It's in the Air 1935,N 8,18:2
In Person 1935,D 13,31:5
Seven Keys to Baldpate 1935,D 14,11:2
Next Time We Love 1936,Ja 31,16:2
Garden Murder Case, The 1936,Mr 2,13:2
Moonlight Murder 1936,Mr 28,11:2
Ex-Mrs Bradford, The 1936,My 28,19:2
Parole 1936,Je 27,21:1
My American Wife 1936,Ag 21,12:3
Piccadilly Jim 1936,Ag 31,19:1
Devil is a Sissy, The 1936,O 17,21:2
Life of Emile Zola, The 1937,Ag 12,14:2
Music for Madame 1937,O 23,14:1
Last Gangster, The 1937,D 10,33:2
First Lady 1937,D 23,25:1
Hollywood Hotel 1938,Ja 13,17:3
Lady Behave 1938,Ja 28,17:3
Women Are Like That 1938,Ap 11,12:2
Reformatory 1938,Je 27,13:6
Youth Takes a Fling 1938,O 17,12:1
Peck's bad Boy With the Circus 1939,Ja 11,17:4
Six Thousand Enemies 1939,Je 9,26:2
Hell's Kitchen 1939,Jl 3,10:5
On Borrowed Time 1939,Jl 7,13:2
Mr Smith Goes to Washington 1939,O 20,27:2
Secret of Dr Kildare, The 1939,D 8,33:5
Grapes of Wrath, The 1940,Ja 25,17:2
It all Came True 1940,Ap 6,13:2
Edison the Man 1940,Je 7,27:2
My Love Came Back 1940,Jl 13,16:5
New Moon 1940,Jl 19,22:2
We Who Are Young 1940,S 13,27:2
Tobacco Road 1941,F 21,16:2
Footsteps in the Dark 1941,Mr 15,13:2
Penalty, The 1941,Ap 10,29:3
Great Lie, The 1941,Ap 12,19:2
Bride Wore Crutches, The 1941,My 26,15:3
Nothing but the Truth 1941,O 23,27:1
One Foot in Heaven 1941,N 14,28:3
Skylark 1941,N 20,39:2
Feminine Touch, The 1941,D 12,35:3
Man Who Came to Dinner, The 1942,Ja 2,25:2
Larceny, Inc 1942,Ap 25,9:1
Gay Sisters, The 1942,Ag 15,14:2
Orchestra Wives 1942,S 24,23:2
My Sister Eileen 1942,O 23,15:1
Cairo 1942,N 6,27:2
Amazing Mrs Holliday, The 1943,F 22,20:2
Dixie 1943,Je 24,26:2
All by Myself 1943,Jl 16,20:3
See Here, Private Hargrove 1944,Mr 22,17:2
Step Lively 1944,Jl 27,14:1
Arsenic and old Lace 1944,S 2,17:2

Mitchell, Grant — Cont
Impatient Years, The 1944,S 20,20:1
Laura 1944,O 12,24:1
And Now Tomorrow 1944,N 23,38:2
Bring on the Girls 1945,Mr 1,25:5
Medal for Benny, A 1945,My 24,15:2
Conflict 1945,Je 16,10:2
Bedside Manner 1945,Je 23,9:6
Crime Incorporated 1945,Je 23,9:7
Guest Wife 1945,O 18,21:2
Colonel Effingham's Raid 1946,Ap 5,21:3
Easy to Wed 1946,Jl 12,14:2
Honeymoon 1947,My 19,27:2
It Happened on Fifth Avenue 1947,Je 11,33:2
Corpse came C O D, The 1947,Ag 19,27:2
Mitchell, Guy
Those Redheads From Seattle 1953,O 1,34:2
Red Garters 1954,Mr 27,13:5
Mitchell, Howard
Prison Farm 1938,Jl 15,13:3
Mitchell, Irving
Manslaughter 1930,Jl 24,26:4
Mitchell, James
Colorado Territory 1949,Je 25,8:6
House Across the Street 1949,S 2,14:4
Border Incident 1949,N 21,29:2
Toast of New Orleans, The 1950,S 30,13:3
Devil's Doorway 1950,N 10,35:1
Stars in my Crown 1950,D 22,19:1
Band Wagon, The 1953,Jl 10,10:2
Deep in my Heart 1954,D 10,35:2
Prodigal, The 1955,My 14,10:7
Oklahoma! 1955,O 11,49:1
Mitchell, Joe (Screenwriter)
Navigator, The 1924,O 13,21:1
Love Thrill, The 1927,My 10,24:5
Mitchell, John
Navajo 1952,F 21,24:4
Mitchell, John Ames (Original Author)
Young Rajah, The 1922,N 6,13:1
Mitchell, Johnny
Pillow to Post 1945,My 26,18:2
Mitchell, Joseph (Original Author)
Regular Fellow, A 1925,O 5,25:2
Mitchell, Joseph (Screenwriter)
Sherlock Jr 1924,My 26,21:1
Seven Chances 1925,Mr 17,18:1
Mitchell, Julian (Screenwriter)
Arabesque 1966,My 6,54:1
Mitchell, Julien
Last Journey, The 1936,Je 8,22:4
Drums 1938,S 30,24:4
Vigil in the Night 1940,Mr 9,19:2
Sea Hawk, The 1940,Ag 10,16:2
It's in the Air 1940,D 10,33:2
Bedelia 1947,F 8,10:2
Magnet, The 1951,F 27,22:6
Chance of a Lifetime 1951,Mr 15,37:2
Galloping Major, The 1951,D 17,27:2
Hobson's Choice 1954,Je 15,37:1
Mitchell, Langdon (Original Author)
Becky Sharp 1935,Je 14,27:2
Mitchell, Laurie
That Touch of Mink 1962,Je 15,16:2
Mitchell, Margaret (Original Author)
Gone With the Wind 1939,D 20,31:2
Mitchell, Mary
Twist Around the Clock 1962,Ja 27,13:4
Dementia 13 1963,O 24,37:1
Mitchell, Michael
His Hour 1924,O 7,26:1
Mitchell, Millard
Mr and Mrs North 1942,Ja 22,13:2
Grand Central Murder 1942,My 23,8:8
Mayor of Forty-Fourth Street, The 1942,Je 11,27:4
Big Street, The 1942,Ag 14,13:1
Get Help to Love 1942,O 19,15:3
Slightly Dangerous 1943,Ap 2,17:2
Swell Guy 1947,Ja 27,17:2
Kiss of Death 1947,Ag 28,28:2
Double Life, A 1948,F 20,19:1
Foreign Affair, A 1948,Jl 1,19:3
Thieves' Highway 1949,S 24,8:6
Everybody Does It 1949,O 26,32:2
Twelve O'Clock High 1950,Ja 28,10:2
Winchester 73 1950,Je 8,38:2
Gunfighter, The 1950,Je 24,7:2
Mister 880 1950,S 30,13:2
U S S Teakettle 1951,F 24,11:2
Strictly Dishonorable 1951,Jl 12,21:6
Singin' in the Rain 1952,Mr 28,27:2
My Six Convicts 1952,Mr 28,27:3
Naked Spur, The 1953,Mr 26,37:3
Here Come the Girls 1953,D 26,10:1
Mitchell, Norma
Woman Accused, The 1933,Mr 13,18:2
Melody in Spring 1934,Mr 31,8:2
Susan and God 1940,Jl 12,11:2
Mitchell, Norma (Original Author)
Let's Face It 1943,Ag 5,18:1
Mitchell, Patric
Harriet Craig 1950,N 3,31:2
Something to Live For 1952,Mr 8,11:2

Mitchell, Patsy
Beloved Brat 1938,My 2,13:2
Mitchell, Red
Subterraneans, The 1960,Jl 7,26:1
Mitchell, Rhea
Money Corporal, The 1919,Ap 21,13:4
Mitchell, Robert
Mister Moses 1965,My 13,32:1
Mitchell, Robert Boy Choir
Joan of Paris 1942,Ja 26,18:2
Going my Way 1944,My 3,25:2
Mitchell, Ruth Comfort (Original Author)
Into her Kingdom 1926,Ag 10,19:2
Mitchell, Shirley
Mr Lord Says No! 1952,F 12,22:5
Mitchell, Sidney (Miscellaneous)
Laughing Irish Eyes 1936,Ap 4,11:2
Pigskin Parade 1936,N 14,23:3
Rebecca of Sunnybrook Farm 1938,Mr 26,12:1
Mitchell, Sidney D (Composer)
Wine, Women and Song 1934,Mr 21,24:3
Down to Their Last Yacht 1934,S 24,14:1
Captain January 1936,Ap 25,21:1
One in a Million 1937,Ja 1,19:3
Thin Ice 1937,S 4,8:2
Life Begins In College 1937,O 9,16:1
Love and Hisses 1938,Ja 1,11:1
In Old Chicago 1938,Ja 7,15:2
Rebecca of Sunnybrook Farm 1938,Mr 26,12:1
Kentucky Moonshine 1938,My 21,9:2
Three Blind Mice 1938,Je 18,18:2
We're Going to Be Rich 1938,Jl 4,10:2
Mitchell, Sidney D (Miscellaneous)
Sing, Baby, Sing 1936,S 12,20:1
Mitchell, Stephen (Producer)
Last Holiday 1950,N 14,39:4
Mr Denning Drives North 1953,S 2,20:1
Mitchell, Steve
It's Always Fair Weather 1955,S 16,19:1
China Doll 1958,D 4,52:1
Once a Thief 1965,S 9,36:1
Mitchell, Thomas
Craig's Wife 1936,O 2,29:3
Adventure in Manhattan 1936,O 23,27:5
Theodora Goes Wild 1936,N 13,27:4
When You're in Love 1937,F 19,15:2
Man of the People 1937,F 23,25:4
Lost Horizon 1937,Mr 4,27:1
I Promise to Pay 1937,Ap 26,15:2
Make Way for Tomorrow 1937,My 10,23:1
Hurricane, The 1937,N 10,31:2
Love, Honor and Behave 1938,Mr 21,18:2
Trade Winds 1939,Ja 13,17:2
Stagecoach 1939,Mr 3,21:1
Only Angels Have Wings 1939,My 12,25:2
Mr Smith Goes to Washington 1939,O 20,27:2
Gone With the Wind 1939,D 20,31:2
Hunchback of Notre Dame, The 1940,Ja 1,29:2
Swiss Family Robinson 1940,F 9,15:3
Three Cheers for the Irish 1940,Mr 9,19:2
Our Town 1940,Je 14,25:3
Long Voyage Home, The 1940,O 9,30:2 (In Addenda)
Angels Over Broadway 1940,N 18,23:2
Flight From Destiny 1941,Mr 28,26:7
Out of the Fog 1941,Je 21,20:2
Joan of Paris 1942,Ja 26,18:2
Song of the Islands 1942,Mr 12,24:4
Moontide 1942,Ap 30,14:1
This Above All 1942,My 13,14:3
Tales of Manhattan 1942,S 25,25:1
Black Swan, The 1942,D 24,18:3
Immortal Sergeant 1943,F 4,29:2
Bataan 1943,Je 4,17:2
Flesh and Fantasy 1943,N 18,29:1
Sullivans, The 1944,F 10,19:2
Buffalo Bill 1944,Ap 20,22:6
Wilson 1944,Ag 2,18:1
Dark Waters 1944,N 22,25:2
Keys of the Kingdom, The 1944,D 30,15:2
Within These Walls 1945,Jl 16,8:4
Captain Eddie 1945,Ag 9,24:2
Adventure 1946,F 8,23:2
Three Wise Fools 1946,S 27,19:2
Dark Mirror, The 1946,O 19,15:2
It's a Wonderful Life 1946,D 23,19:2
High Barbaree 1947,Je 6,27:2
Romance of Rosy Ridge, The 1947,S 12,18:3
Outlaw, The 1947,S 12,18:4
Silver River 1948,My 22,8:3
Alias Nick Beal 1949,Mr 10,35:2
Journey Into Light 1951,O 5,24:4
High Noon 1952,Jl 25,14:2
Secret of the Incas 1954,My 29,13:3
While the City Sleeps 1956,My 17,37:1
By Love Possessed 1961,Jl 20,32:2
Pocketful of Miracles 1961,D 19,39:1
Mitchell, Thomas (Original Author)
Casanova Brown 1944,S 15,16:1
Mitchell, Warren
Stowaway Girl 1957,N 6,43:3
Crawling Eye, The 1959,Ja 1,38:1
Surprise Package 1960,O 15,26:2

Mitchell, Warren — Cont
Boy Who Stole a Million, The 1960,D 22,18:3
Small World of Sammy Lee, The 1963,Ag 14,28:1
Arrivederci, Baby! 1966,D 29,22:1
Jokers, The 1967,My 16,50:1
Mitchell, Yvonne
Queen of Spades, The 1949,Jl 1,14:4
Turn the Key Softly 1954,F 4,21:6
Blonde Sinner 1957,Ja 24,34:1
Escapade 1957,Ag 6,30:2
Woman in a Dressing Gown 1957,S 13,15:2
Sapphire 1959,N 3,27:1
Tiger Bay 1959,D 15,50:1
Conspiracy of Hearts 1960,Ap 8,24:1
Trials of Oscar Wilde, The 1960,Je 28,26:1
Main Attraction, The 1963,Je 27,23:3
Johnny Nobody 1965,N 24,35:1
Mitchell (Miscellaneous)
William Fox Movietone Follies of 1929 1929,My 27,22:1
I Like It That Way 1934,Ap 18,23:3
Mitchum, James
Last Time I Saw Archie, The 1961,My 29,9:6
Victors, The 1963,D 20,21:2
Ride the Wild Surf 1964,D 24,8:4
In Harm's Way 1965,Ap 7,36:1
Ambush Bay 1966,S 15,51:4
Tramplers, The 1966,D 8,64:1
Mitchum, Jim
Beat Generation, The 1959,O 22,47:4
Mitchum, Robert
Human Comedy, The 1943,Mr 3,19:2
Corvette K-225 1943,O 21,30:1
Dancing Masters, The 1943,D 2,30:2
Gung Ho! 1944,Ja 26,23:2
Thirty Seconds Over Tokyo 1944,N 16,19:1
West of the Pecos 1945,Ag 11,14:6
Story of G I Joe 1945,O 6,9:6
Till the End of Time 1946,Jl 24,24:1
Undercurrent 1946,N 29,36:2
Pursued 1947,Mr 8,10:2
Locket, The 1947,Mr 20,38:2
Crossfire 1947,Jl 23,19:2
Desire Me 1947,S 26,28:3
Out of the Past 1947,N 26,18:2
Rachel and the Stranger 1948,S 20,21:2
Blood on the Moon 1948,N 12,30:5
Red Pony, The 1949,Mr 9,33:2
Big Steal, The 1949,Jl 11,13:2
Holiday Affair 1949,N 24,48:2
Where Danger Lives 1951,Ja 1,13:6
My Forbidden Past 1951,Ap 26,34:2
Racket, The 1951,D 13,44:2
Macao 1952,My 1,34:2
One Minute to Zero 1952,S 20,13:2
Lusty Men, The 1952,O 25,12:6
Angel Face 1953,Ap 25,11:5
White Witch Doctor 1953,Jl 2,19:3
Second Chance 1953,Jl 23,20:2
She Couldn't Say No 1954,F 27,11:3
River of no Return 1954,My 1,13:2
Track of the Cat 1954,D 2,38:2
Not as a Stranger 1955,Je 29,24:1
Night of the Hunter, The 1955,S 30,23:1
Man With the Gun 1955,D 23,14:2
Foreign Intrigue 1956,My 13,23:2
Heaven Knows Mr Allison 1957,Mr 15,22:1
Fire Down Below 1957,Ag 9,11:2
Enemy Below, The 1957,D 26,23:2
Hunters, The 1958,Ag 27,33:1
Angry Hills, The 1959,Jl 16,31:3
Wonderful Country, The 1959,N 5,39:7
Home from the Hill 1960,Mr 4,19:1
Sundowners, The 1960,D 9,39:1
Night Fighters, The 1960,D 15,59:1
Grass is Greener, The 1960,D 24,8:2
Last Time I Saw Archie, The 1961,My 29,9:6
Cape Fear 1962,Ap 19,35:2
Longest Day, The 1962,O 5,28:1
Two for the Seesaw 1962,N 22,43:1
List of Adrian Messenger, The 1963,My 30,20:1
Rampage 1963,O 17,39:2
Man in the Middle 1964,Mr 5,36:1
What a Way to Go! 1964,My 15,44:1
Way West, The 1967,My 25,54:1
Dorado, El 1967,Je 29,32:1
Villa Rides 1968,Jl 18,26:3
Anzio 1968,Jl 25,26:1
5 Card Stud 1968,Ag 1,24:1
Secret Ceremony 1968,O 24,55:1
Mitchurin, Gennady
Conquerors of the Night 1933,Jl 31,16:3
Miteff, Alex
Requiem for a Heavyweight 1962,O 17,35:1
Mitford, Nancy (Original Author)
Count Your Blessings 1959,Ap 24,23:1
Mito, Mitsuko
Ugetsu 1954,S 8,40:3
Samurai 1956,Ja 10,26:1
Golden Demon 1956,Ja 31,34:3
Mitra, Ajay
Aparajito 1959,Ap 29,30:1

Mitropoulos, Dimitri
Of Men and Music 1951,F 15,27:2
Mitrovich, Marta
Dark Mirror, The 1946,O 19,15:2
Unfaithful, The 1947,Je 28,10:2
I, Jane Doe 1948,Jl 5,8:4
Lady Without Passport, A 1950,Ag 4,13:2
Once a Thief 1951,Ja 19,21:3
Titanic 1953,My 28,27:5
Mitsik, Ira
Ukrainian Festival 1965,N 1,57:1
Mitsuda, Ken
Ballad of Narayama 1961,Je 20,27:1
Mitternayr, Gertraud
Heidi 1968,S 23,42:4
Mittersteiner, L
Fremd im Sudetenland; Strange to the Sudeten
Country 1938,N 5,15:3
Mittini, Vittorio
Angelina 1948,Ap 6,27:2
Mittler, Leo (Original Author)
Mayor's Dilemma, The 1940,Ap 23,19:2
Ghost Ship, The 1943,D 25,19:4
Song of Russia 1944,F 11,17:2
Mittler, Leo (Screenwriter)
Mayor's Dilemma, The 1940,Ap 23,19:2
Mitzi, Gloria
36 Hours to Live 1936,Ag 15,6:3
Mitzi, Little
Marriage Playground, The 1929,D 14,22:4
Mitzi (dolphin)
Flipper 1963,S 19,23:1
Miuffko, K
They Wanted Peace 1940,Ja 8,11:3
Mix, Art
Maisie 1939,Je 23,23:1
Mix, Ruth
Four Sons 1928,F 14,27:1
Mix, Tom
Just Tony 1922,Ag 7,14:2
Deadwood Coach, The 1925,Ja 21,19:3
Dick Turpin 1925,Ja 26,14:1
Riders of the Purple Sage 1925,Ap 15,16:1
Rainbow Trail, The 1925,Je 3,26:4
Lucky Horseshoe, The 1925,Ag 18,14:3
Everlasting Whisper, The 1925,O 12,19:3
Best Bad Man, The 1925,D 2,23:1
Yankee Senor, The 1926,Ja 28,14:4
My Own Pal 1926,Mr 15,18:3
Tony Runs Wild 1926,Ap 28,28:3
Last Trail, The 1927,Ja 26,17:1
Circus Ace, The 1927,Jl 6,23:2
Under a Texas Moon 1930,Ap 4,22:1
My Pal the King 1932,O 4,26:4
Terror Trail 1933,F 11,11:3
Miya, Joanne
West Side Story 1961,O 19,39:3
Miyagawa, Kazuo (Cinematographer)
Tokyo Olympiad 1966,N 17,55:1
Miyaguchi, Seiji
Magnificent Seven, The 1956,N 20,46:2
Human Condition, The 1959,D 16,56:1
Ballad of Narayama 1961,Je 20,27:1
Miyake, Bontaro
Phantom Horse, the 1956,Jl 25,16:1
Miyake, Kuniko
Escapde in Japan 1957,D 24,11:1
Ohayo; (Good Morning) 1966,F 2,24:1
Miyasaki, Jun
Golden Demon 1956,Ja 31,34:3
Miyashita
Ana-Ta-Han 1954,My 18,38:2
Miyoshi, Eiko
Samurai 1956,Ja 10,26:1
Prodigal Son 1964,Ja 30,24:3 (Incorrect in this
edition; use 1964,Ja 31,16:1 elsewhere)
I Live in Fear; Ikimono no Kiroku
1967,Ja 26,25:1
Miyosho, Juro (Screenwriter)
Saga of the Vagabonds 1964,O 7,31:1 (Incorrect
in this edition; use 1964,O 7,51:1 elsewhere)
Mizner, Alfred
Bloodhounds of Broadway 1952,N 15,15:2
Mizner, Wilson (Original Author)
Strictly Personal 1933,Mr 20,18:2
Heroes for Sale 1933,Jl 22,14:3
Mizoguchi, Kenji (Director)
Ugetsu 1954,S 8,40:3
Yang Kwei Fei 1956,S 11,41:2
Street of Shame 1959,Je 5,17:2
Life of Oharu 1964,Ap 21,42:2
Taira Clan, The; Shin Heike Monagatari
1964,S 21,37:4
Mizrahi, Toga (Director)
Dr Epameinondas 1938,Ap 5,19:6
Otan o Syzygos Taxeideyei; When the Husband
Travels 1939,N 13,15:3
Mizuki, Yoko (Screenwriter)
Angry Island 1960,F 28,31:1
Naked General, The 1964,D 16,51:2
Kwaidan (In the Cup of Tea); In the Cup of Tea
(Kwaidan) 1965,N 23,51:1

Kwaidan (Black Hair); Black Hair (Kwaidan)
1965,N 23,51:1
Kwaidan (Hoichi, The Earless); Hoichi, The
Earless (Kwaidan) 1965,N 23,51:1
Mizuno, Kumi
Whirlwind 1968,Jl 27,15:1
Mjong, Mjoman Mjoang
Legong 1935,O 2,27:1
Mladova, Milada
Night and Day 1946,Jl 26,16:2
Escape me Never 1947,N 8,11:2
Siren of Atlantis 1949,Ag 22,13:1
Her Wonderful Lie 1950,Jl 17,15:2
Prince Who Was a Thief, The 1951,Jl 4,13:2
Mlodnicki, Artur
Ashes and Diamonds 1961,My 30,8:1
Mme Etienne's French Dancers
World Dances 1954,N 8,24:6
Mnader, Miles
Lloyds of London 1936,N 26,39:1
Mnouchkine, Alexandre (Producer)
Storm Within, The; (Parents Terribles, Les)
1950,Ap 24,21:2
Sins of the Borgias 1956,Mr 5,21:1
Rue de Paris 1960,D 23,14:3
My Son, The Hero 1963,S 19,23:1
That Man From Rio 1964,Je 9,30:1
Up to his Ears 1966,My 18,37:1
Live for Life 1967,D 19,59:1
Mnouchkine, Arlane (Screenwriter)
That Man From Rio 1964,Je 9,30:1
Mo, Wong Chew
Fortune Hunters, The 1953,S 16,35:6
Moad, Rex
Panic in the Streets 1950,Ag 5,9:2
Moan, Henny
Nine Lives 1959,Ja 6,28:1
Moana, Tarvera
Invaders, The 1942,Mr 6,17:1
Moatt, Christine
Sea Hawk, The 1924,Je 3,22:1
Mobley, Mary Ann
Get Yourself a College Girl 1965,Ap 29,40:2
Young Dillinger 1965,My 13,32:3
Girl Happy 1965,My 27,28:1
Harum Scarum 1965,D 16,63:3
3 on a Couch 1966,Jl 7,30:1
For Singles Only 1968,Je 6,54:1
Mobley, Roger
Comancheros, The 1961,N 2,42:1
Jack the Giant Killer 1962,Jl 26,17:1
Dime With a Halo 1963,Je 27,23:3
Emil and the Detectives 1964,D 24,8:3
Mocadi, Amos
Pillar of Fire, The 1963,Ap 8,35:2
Moccia, Giuseppe (Screenwriter)
Little Nuns, The 1966,Ap 28,49:1
Moch, Joachim
Every Second Counts 1957,O 15,39:4
Mochizuki, Yuko
Carmen Comes Home 1959,D 23,22:1
Ballad of Narayama 1961,Je 20,27:1
Different Sons 1964,F 13,25:1
Mock, Alice
Wonder Man 1945,Je 9,17:2
Mock, Laurie
Hot Rods to Hell 1967,Ag 10,45:5
Mockridge, Cyril J (Composer)
Judge Priest 1934,O 12,33:1
Mockridge, Cyril J (Original Author)
How to be Very, Very Popular 1955,Jl 23,10:1
Mockridge, Cyril J (Producer)
Mother Didn't Tell Me 1950,Mr 4,11:2
Mocky, Jean-Pierre (Director)
Chasers, The; Draguers, Les 1960,My 3,43:1
Thank Heaven for Small Favors 1965,Ja 14,44:2
Mocky, Jean-Pierre (Screenwriter)
Chasers, The; Draguers, Les 1960,My 3,43:1
Thank Heaven for Small Favors 1965,Ja 14,44:2
Moctezuma, Carlos
Perjura 1939,Ja 16,11:2
Perfidia; Perfidy 1940,F 17,9:3
Odio; Hate 1940,Ap 6,13:2
Luna Criolla; Creole Moon 1940,Ap 8,15:3
Bestia Negra, La; Black Beast, The 1940,Je 3,11:2
En un Burro Tres Baturros; Three Rustics on one
Donkey 1940,S 21,13:3
Vivire Otra Vez; I Shall Live Again
1940,O 23,27:2
Life of Simon Bolivar, The 1943,Je 18,16:5
Asi Se Quiere En Jalisco 1943,Ag 7,6:2
El Conde de Monte Cristo 1943,N 9,26:2
Hidden River 1950,D 1,31:2
Proud and the Beautiful, The 1956,My 29,32:2
Empty Star, The; Estrella Vacia, La
1962,Mr 28,36:4
Moctezuma, Carlos Lopez
Muerto Murio, El; Dead Man Died, The
1939,Jl 29,18:3
Viva Maria 1965,D 20,48:2
Modak, Shahu
Gyandev of India 1943,Ap 10,12:5

Mode, Eulabelle
Horror of Party Beach, The 1964,Ap 30,30:1
Modeen, Thor
Kaera Slaekten 1934,My 14,20:4
Klart till Drabbning; Cleared for Action
1937,D 10,33:3
Kustens Glada Kavaljerer; Coast's Happy
Cavaliers, The 1939,My 23,27:2
Modernaires
Glenn Miller Story, the 1954,F 11,33:2
Modia, Yolanda
Made in Italy 1967,My 1,44:2
Stranger in Town, A 1968,Ap 25,53:4
Modiano, Rene (Producer)
Story of Monte Cristo, The 1962,N 7,48:1
Modio, Yolanda
Casanova 1965,Jl 21,43:1
Modisane, William Bloke (Screenwriter)
Come Back Africa 1960,Ap 5,45:1
Modot, Gaston
Miracle of the Wolves, The 1925,F 24,17:3
Carmen 1928,My 7,29:1
Miracle des Loups, Le 1930,Jl 28,22:1
Sous les Toits de Paris; (Under the Roofs of
Paris) 1930,D 16,34:4
Secrets of the Orient 1932,Ja 4,27:3
Fantomas 1934,Mr 13,27:4
Crainquebille 1934,D 10,16:3
Grand Illusion 1938,S 13,28:2
Escape From Yesterday 1939,My 3,27:2
End of a Day, The 1939,S 12,28:4
Devil Is an Empress, The 1939,D 4,18:4
Enfants du Paradis, Les 1947,F 20,32:2
Antoine and Antoinette 1948,Ap 16,29:2
Rules of the Game, The 1950,Ap 10,15:3
Passion for Life 1951,D 21,21:4
Casque D'Or 1952,Ag 19,19:1
Beauty and the Devil 1952,Ag 26,15:2
Lovers, The 1959,O 27,40:2
Rules of the Game, The 1961,Ja 19,26:1
Devil and the 10 Commandments, The (Episode
5) 1963,O 15,44:1
Age d'Or, L'; Golden Age, The 1964,S 22,44:1
Modot, Gaston (Screenwriter)
Portrait of Innocence 1948,Je 9,35:2
Modot, Hilero (Screenwriter)
Portrait of Innocence 1948,Je 9,35:2
Modugno, Domenico
Three Bites of the Apple 1967,My 25,54:2
Modugno, Lucia
General Della Rovere 1960,N 22,41:1
Navajo Joe 1967,D 7,60:2
Modzelewska, Marja
Sluby Ulanskie; Love in the Army 1935,F 22,27:3
Moe
Three Stooges Go Around the World in a Daze,
The 1963,D 19,40:2
Moebis, Hans Joachim
Comrades of 1918 1931,F 20,18:5
Moebius, Rolf
Untitled-Dance 1937,D 25,10:4
Urlaub auf Ehrenwort; Furlough on Word of
Honor 1938,Mr 28,19:2
Dreikland; Triad 1938,Jl 23,10:5
Spiel in Sommerwind; Play in the Summer
Breezes 1939,Ap 1,17:2
Heidi 1968,S 23,42:4
Moellendorf, Else
Ekel, Das; Grouch, The 1939,D 4,18:4
MOELLER
See Also MOLLER, MUELLER, MULLER
Moeller, Gunnar
Dancing Heart, The 1958,Ja 18,10:3
Moeller, Kai
Friesennot 1936,O 26,20:1
Moeller, Philip (Director)
Age of Innocence, The 1934,O 19,27:1
Break of Hearts 1935,My 17,24:3
Moes, Jerzy
Lotna 1966,My 27,33:1
Moessinger, David (Screenwriter)
Caper of the Golden Bulls, The 1967,Je 22,46:1
Moffa, Paolo (Producer)
Revolt of the Slaves, The 1961,N 8,41:1
MOFFAT
See Also MOFFATT, MOFFETT, MOFFITT
Moffat, Charles
Give Us This Day 1949,D 21,41:2
Lonely Night, The 1954,Mr 29,22:2
Moffat, Graham (Original Author)
Bunty Pulls the Strings 1921,Ja 9,VI,2:1 (In
Addenda)
Moffat, Ivan (Screenwriter)
Bhowani Junction 1956,My 25,26:1
D-Day, The Sixth of June 1956,My 30,13:1
Giant 1956,O 11,51:1
Boy on a Dolphin 1957,Ap 20,21:2
Wayward Bus, The 1957,Je 6,35:2
They Came to Cordura 1959,O 22,47:2
Tender is the Night 1962,Ja 20,13:2
Heroes of Telemark, The 1966,Mr 10,26:1

Moffat, John
Tom Jones 1963,O 8,48:1
Moffat, Margaret
Just Smith 1934,Ap 23,20:2
Troopship 1938,Ap 26,18:2
U-Boat 29 1939,O 6,31:3
Song of the Road 1940,My 6,13:2
Ringside Maisie 1941,Ag 1,11:2
MOFFAT
See Also MOFFETT, MOFFITT, MOFFAT
Moffatt, Donald
Rachel Rachel 1968,Ag 27,36:1
Moffatt, Graham
Gangway 1937,Ag 21,7:3
Dr Syn 1937,N 15,15:1
To the Victor 1938,Ap 13,21:2
I Know Where I'm Going 1947,Ag 20,25:2
MOFFETT
See Also MOFITT, MOFFAT, MOFFATT
Moffett, Frances
Secret Call, The 1931,Jl 13,13:5
No One Man 1932,Ja 23,18:4
Dancers in the Dark 1932,Mr 19,11:2
Sinners in the Sun 1932,My 14,11:5
Moffett, Gregory
Let's Dance 1950,N 30,42:2
Moffett, Sharyn
My Pal, Wolf 1944,O 9,17:2
Body Snatcher, The 1945,My 26,18:3
Falcon in San Francisco, The 1945,Jl 21,7:2
Locket, The 1947,Mr 20,38:2
Mr Blandings Builds his Dream House
1948,Mr 26,26:2
Judge Steps Out, The 1949,Je 3,21:4
Moffit, Peggy
Blow-Up 1966,D 19,52:2
MOFFITT
See Also MOFFAT, MOFFATT, MOFFETT
Moffitt, Jack (Miscellaneous)
Conspirators, The 1944,O 21,15:2
Moffitt, Jack (Original Author)
Central Airport 1933,My 4,20:5
Man Betrayed, A 1941,Mr 27,29:5
Murder, He Says 1945,Je 25,20:3
Moffitt, Jack (Screenwriter)
Melody Ranch 1940,D 26,23:3
Passage to Marseille 1944,F 17,12:5
Night and Day 1946,Jl 26,16:2
Ramrod 1947,Je 30,25:6
African Lion, The 1955,S 15,39:2
Moffitt, Jeff (Original Author)
Kelly the Second 1936,O 3,21:2
Always in Trouble 1938,N 3,27:1
Moffitt, John C (Original Author)
Exclusive 1937,Jl 22,15:1
Ride a Crooked Mile 1938,D 29,15:2
Moffitt, John C (Screenwriter)
Rhythm on the Range 1936,Jl 30,22:1
Murder With Pictures 1936,N 21,21:4
Mountain Music 1937,Je 24,30:3
Exclusive 1937,Jl 22,15:1
Double or Nothing 1937,S 2,17:3
Tropic Holiday 1938,Je 30,21:2
St Louis Blues 1939,F 9,17:2
I'm From Missouri 1939,Mr 23,27:1
Our Leading Citizen 1939,Ag 24,17:1
Story of Will Rogers, The 1952,Jl 18,10:5
Moffo, Anna
Traviata, La 1968,F 28,43:2
Mog, Aribert
Lied vom Leben, Das 1931,O 19,28:1
Fahrmann Maria; Ferryman Maria
1938,D 24,12:3
Ihr Groesster Erfolg; Her Greatest Success
1939,F 12,20:4
Ecstasy 1940,D 25,33:2
Mogilov, Lev
Vilna Legend, A (Russian-Jewish Cast)
1949,S 26,17:1
Moglia
Cyrano de Bergerac 1925,Jl 6,12:2
Moguy, Leonide (Director)
Forty Little Mothers 1938,D 23,16:3
Affair Lafont, The; Conflit 1939,O 9,15:2
Two Women 1940,N 2,19:3
Paris After Dark 1943,O 23,11:1
Action in Arabia 1944,F 19,18:7
Three Hours 1944,O 30,16:5
Whistle Stop 1946,Mr 18,24:2
Tomorrow is too Late 1952,Ap 14,22:2
Diary of a Bad Girl 1958,My 30,13:2
Moguy, Leonide (Original Author)
Diary of a Bad Girl 1958,My 30,13:2
Moguy, Leonide (Screenwriter)
Tomorrow is too Late 1952,Ap 14,22:2
Mohan, Chandra
Shakuntala 1947,D 26,22:3
Mohner, Carl
Rififi 1956,Je 6,37:1
Last Bridge, The 1957,Ag 21,22:2
Camp on Blood Island, The 1958,S 18,37:2
He Who Must Die 1958,D 29,21:1

Sink the Bismarck! 1960,F 12,22:3
Kitchen, The 1961,N 2,42:1
It Takes a Thief 1963,Ag 15,24:7
Carmen Baby 1967,O 11,41:2
MOHR
See Also MOORE, MORE
Mohr, Gerald
Monster and the Girl, The 1941,Mr 20,25:3
Lady Has Plans, The 1942,Mr 5,27:1
Gilda 1946,Mr 15,27:2
Catman of Paris, The 1946,Jl 13,12:2
Truth About Murder, The 1946,Jl 27,12:6
Heaven Only Knows 1947,N 14,29:3
Lone Wolf in London, The 1947,N 22,10:3
Two Guys From Texas 1948,Ag 28,8:6
Undercover Girl 1950,N 8,37:2
Sirocco 1951,Je 14,31:2
Ten Tall Men 1951,O 27,10:5
Detective Story 1951,N 7,35:2
Sniper, The 1952,My 10,16:3
Duel at Silver Creek 1952,Ag 2,7:6
Son of Ali Baba 1952,Ag 16,7:4
Invasion USA 1953,Ap 30,39:4
Eddie Cantor Story, The 1953,D 26,10:2
Money From Home 1954,F 27,11:3
This Rebel Breed 1960,My 5,41:2
Angry Red Planet, The 1960,My 5,41:2
Funny Girl 1968,S 20,42:1
Mohr, Hal (Cinematographer)
Midsummer Night's Dream, A 1935,O 10,31:1
Mohr, Hal (Director)
When Love Is Young 1937,Ap 17,15:1
Mohri, Kikue
Gate of Hell 1954,D 14,45:2
Mohyeddin, Zia
Deadlier Than the Male 1967,F 22,21:1
Moik, Lutz
Grapes are Ripe, The 1953,O 15,43:2
Moiseiwitsch, Benno
Battle for Music 1945,O 15,13:2
Moiseiwitsch, Maurice (Original Author)
Sleeping Tiger, The 1954,O 9,8:7
Moiseyev Ballet
I Love, You Love 1962,N 10,16:2
Moissi, Alexander
Royal Box, The 1929,D 15,X,8:6
Lorenzino de Medici 1936,Ap 14,19:3
Moissi, Bettina
Long Is the Road 1948,N 12,30:5
Original Sin, The 1950,Ag 21,15:2
Seven Journeys 1951,Mr 12,20:2
Moja, Hella
U-Boat 9 1929,Ja 22,23:1
Mojica, Jose
One mad Kiss 1930,Jl 19,7:5
El Rey de los Gitanos 1933,My 29,22:2
(Incorrect in this edition; use 1933,My 29,16:5
elsewhere)
Ley Del Haren, La 1933,Je 17,16:7
El Precio de un Beso 1933,Jl 25,17:3
Su Ultimo Amor 1933,Ag 19,14:5
Melodia Prohibida, La 1933,O 4,27:2
Quando el Amor Rie 1933,O 17,26:3
Cruz y la Espada, La 1934,F 5,19:3
Las Fronteras del Amor 1934,D 4,23:3
Capitan Aventurero, El; Adventureous Captain,
The 1939,O 3,19:5
Cancion del Milagro, La; Miracle Song, The
1940,My 11,15:2
Mokae, Zaeks
Comedians, The 1967,N 1,37:1
Mokrinsky, Misha
Adventure in Odessa 1954,Je 21,19:6
Molander, Arne
Richthofhen: The Red Knight of the Air
1929,S 2,16:1
Molander, Gustav (Director)
Discord 1928,F 7,30:3
Sealed Lips 1928,Ap 17,27:2
Doctor's Women, The 1929,Je 3,27:2
Charlotte Loewenskoeld 1932,F 22,23:2
Vi Som Gar Koeksvaegen 1933,O 7,18:5
Kaera Slaekten 1934,My 14,20:4
Natt, En 1935,Ja 29,24:1
Swedenhielms 1935,S 6,12:3
Ungkarlspappan 1936,Ja 4,19:1
Paa Solsidan 1936,Ag 26,16:3
Intermezzo 1937,D 25,10:6
Sara Laer Sig Folkvett 1938,F 16,17:1
En Enda Natt 1942,D 7,22:2
Affairs of a Model 1952,Ag 7,12:8
Molander, Gustav (Screenwriter)
Intermezzo, A Love Story 1939,O 6,31:1
Molander, Jan
Torment 1947,Ap 22,34:2
Frustration 1949,Ag 27,7:3
Molant, Jacques
Golden Mistress, The 1954,O 30,15:6
Moliere (Original Author)
Tartuffe 1927,Jl 25,25:3
Monsieur de Pourceaugnac 1932,N 6,IX,4:2
Would-Be Gentleman, The 1960,Mr 23,31:1

Molieri, Lillian
Creature Walks among Us, The 1956,Ap 27,21:6
MOLINA
See Also MALINA
Molina, Carmen
Adios, Nicanor 1938,Mr 14,13:2
Life of Simon Bolivar, The 1943,Je 18,16:5
Three Caballeros, The 1945,F 5,20:1
St Francis of Assisi 1947,Ap 5,12:5
Molina, Joe
Ebb Tide 1937,N 18,27:2
Molina, Timmy
Strangers When we Meet 1960,Je 30,22:2
Molina, Vincente
Corazon de Nino; Heart of a Child
1940,Ja 1,29:4
Molinaro, Edouard (Director)
Back to the Wall; (Dos au Mur) 1959,S 8,43:2
Passion of Slow Fire, The 1962,O 12,26:1
7 Capital Sins (Envy); Envy (7 Capital Sins)
1963,Ja 17,5:2
Mistress for the Summer, A 1964,Mr 28,13:5
Male Hunt; Chasse a l'Homme, La
1965,Ap 20,42:1
Molinaro, Edouard (Screenwriter)
Mistress for the Summer, A 1964,Mr 28,13:5
Molinas, Richard
Snowbound 1949,F 21,20:2
Port Afrique 1956,N 3,27:5
Molinier, Corniglion (Producer)
Bizarre, Bizarre 1939,Mr 21,27:2
Molino, Antonio
Lazarillo 1963,Ap 5,27:6
Moll, Elick (Original Author)
Night Without Sleep 1952,S 27,13:2
Moll, Elick (Screenwriter)
Wake up and Dream 1947,Ja 24,18:4
House on Telegraph Hill, The 1951,My 14,29:1
Night Without Sleep 1952,S 27,13:2
Storm Center 1956,O 22,25:4
Spring Reunion 1957,My 6,25:2
Moll, Georgia
Quiet American, The 1958,F 6,24:1
Cossacks, The 1960,S 6,41:4
White Warrior, The 1961,F 11,27:2
Thief of Baghdad, The 1961,Ag 17,18:2
Island of Love 1963,Je 13,30:4
Dark Purpose 1964,F 6,36:4
Contempt 1964,D 19,25:2
Devil in Love, The 1968,Jl 4,13:4
MOLLER
See Also MUELLER, MULLER, MOELLER
Moller, Gunnar
S O S Pacific 1960,O 13,41:3
Mollinaro, Edward
Season for Love, The 1963,My 9,40:2
Mollinger, Dolly
Beachcomber, The 1938,D 26,29:3
Youth in Revolt 1939,My 16,27:3
Mollison, Clifford
Jaws of Hell 1931,Ja 5,21:3
Almost a Honeymoon 1931,Ja 10,19:2
Mollison, Henry
Great Impersonation, The 1935,D 14,11:1
Lone Wolf Returns, The 1936,F 4,25:5
Music Goes 'Round, The 1936,F 22,12:1
Devil's Squadron 1936,My 11,16:2
Trapped by Television 1936,Je 15,24:3
Shakedown 1936,Ag 17,9:2
They Met in a Taxi 1936,S 7,20:5
Counterfeit Lady 1937,Ja 11,15:6
Hungry Hill 1947,O 11,11:2
Tight Little Island 1949,D 26,33:2
Man in the White Suit, The 1952,Ap 1,35:2
Mollo, Andrew (Director)
It Happened Here 1966,Ag 9,29:2
Mollo, Andrew (Producer)
It Happened Here 1966,Ag 9,29:2
Mollo, Andrew (Screenwriter)
It Happened Here 1966,Ag 9,29:2
Mollo, Cumersindo (Screenwriter)
Cobra, The 1968,Mr 28,52:3
Mollot, Yolande
Turnabout 1940,Jl 27,17:6
MOLLOY
See Also MALLOY
Molnar, Ferenc
Olympia 1930,D 7,IX,6:4
Molnar, Ferenc (Original Author)
Swan, The 1925,Mr 2,14:1
Fine Clothes 1925,O 20,28:1
Guardsman, The 1927,S 7,35:2
Paul Street Boys, The 1929,Jl 15,25:1
His Glorious Night 1929,O 5,22:5
One Romantic Night 1930,My 31,19:4
Liliom 1930,O 4,15:2
Si l'Empereur Savait Ca 1931,F 23,20:3
Guardsman, The 1931,S 10,22:4
No Greater Glory 1934,My 5,22:2
Good Fairy, The 1935,F 1,18:1
Bride Wore Red, The 1937,O 15,18:4
Double Wedding 1937,O 22,27:2
Chocolate Soldier, The 1941,N 1,20:2

Molnar, Ferenc (Original Author) — Cont
I'll Be Yours 1947,F 22,16:2
Swan, The 1956,Ap 27,21:5
Breath of Scandal, A 1960,D 17,19:1
One, Two, Three 1961,D 22,17:1
Molnar, Ferenc (Screenwriter)
Tales of Manhattan 1942,S 25,25:1
Molnar, Julius
Last Moment, The 1928,Mr 12,26:1
No Greater Glory 1934,My 5,22:2
Molnar, Laszlo
Igloi Diakok 1935,My 24,24:3
Szent Peter Esernyoeje 1936,Ja 8,22:2
Molnar, Lila
Pandora and the Flying Dutchman 1951,D 7,35:2
Molnar, Lilly
No Orchids for Miss Blandish 1951,F 23,33:2
Long Dark Hall, The 1951,My 10,38:3
Molnar, Tibor
Treasured Earth 1950,D 14,51:3
Molo, Trude von
Mann der den Mord Beging, Der; Man Who
    Committed the Murder, The 1931,F 22,VIII,6:2
Raub der Mona Lisa, Der; Theft of the Mona Lisa,
    The 1931,S 27,VIII,7:1
Molotof, Vyatcheslaf
Soviets on Parade 1933,Mr 6,16:7
Molte, William (Director)
Ahora Seremos Felices; Now We Shall Be Happy
    1940,Mr 16,8:2
Molteni, Ambrigio (Screenwriter)
David and Goliath 1961,O 7,14:3
Molteni, Giacinto
Four Steps in the Clouds 1948,N 22,25:2
Molyneaux, Patrick J
Angels in the Outfield 1951,O 18,32:1
Mom, Artuor S (Director)
Loco Lindo; Crazy Dandy 1938,Ja 11,27:4
Palermo 1938,O 22,14:2
Mom, Arturo S (Director)
Monte Criollo 1937,Mr 8,22:2
Nuestra Tierra de Paz; Our Land of Peace
    1940,Je 1,12:3
Mom, Arturo S (Original Author)
Cock O' the Walk 1930,Ap 12,23:1
Mom, Arturo S (Producer)
Via de Oro, La; Gold Route, The
    1932,Ja 3,VIII,6:6
Momai, Tetsu
Bulldog Drummond 1929,My 3,23:2
Momi-Cajano (Producer)
See Naples and Die 1959,Ag 31,16:2
Momo, Irene Saffo Countess
Retribution 1922,Je 7,22:3
Monaco, James (Composer)
Pin Up Girl 1944,My 11,25:6
Monaco, James V (Composer)
Doctor Rhythm 1938,My 19,25:2
Sing You Sinners 1938,Ag 18,23:1
East Side of Heaven 1939,My 5,29:3
Road to Singapore 1940,Mr 14,29:2
If I Had my Way 1940,My 6,13:2
Week-End in Havana 1941,N 8,11:2
Stage Door Canteen 1943,Je 25,13:2
Monad, Jacques
7 Capital Sins (Envy); Envy (7 Capital Sins)
    1963,Ja 17,5:2
MONAGHAN
See Also MONAHAN
Monaghan, Anne
Mark, The 1961,O 3,46:2
Monaghan, John P
Lady Possessed 1952,F 15,17:2
Monaghan, John P (Original Author)
Upturned Glass, The 1947,N 5,34:4
Bad Men of Tombstone 1949,Mr 5,10:2
Monaghan, John P (Screenwriter)
Upturned Glass, The 1947,N 5,34:4
MONAHAN
See Also MONAGHAN
Monahan, Richard
Breakthrough 1950,N 18,10:2
Steel Helmet, The 1951,Ja 25,21:5
Monakhof, N
Dubrovsky 1936,Mr 30,17:6
Monaldi, Gisella
Under the Sun of Rome 1949,O 6,40:4
Monash, Paul (Original Author)
Sing Boy Sing 1958,F 22,9:4
Monash, Paul (Producer)
Deadfall 1968,S 12,54:1
Monash, Paul (Screenwriter)
Bailout at 43,000 1957,Je 8,13:2
Safecracker, The 1958,Mr 6,32:1
Monaster, Benjamin (Director)
Goldstein 1965,My 8,19:7
Monaster, Benjamin (Screenwriter)
Goldstein 1965,My 8,19:7
Monaster, Nate (Screenwriter)
Sad Sack, The 1957,N 28,57:1
That Touch of Mink 1962,Je 15,16:2
Call Me Bwana 1963,Jl 4,9:1
Very Special Favor, A 1965,Ag 26,40:3
How to Save a Marriage - And Ruin Your Life
    1968,Ja 19,30:1

Moncion, Francisco
Midsummer Night's Dream, A 1967,Ap 18,32:1
Monciova, Felix
Heroina 1965,N 11,58:2
Moncorbier
Thirst of Men, The 1952,O 28,37:1
Moncorbier, Pierre
Fire Within, The 1964,F 18,27:1
Moncorge, Jean (Original Author)
Magnificent Tramp, The 1962,Ap 25,30:1
Monda, Richard
Eddie Cantor Story, The 1953,D 26,10:2
Midnight Story, The 1957,Jl 5,14:2
Mondaini, Giaci (Screenwriter)
I'll Give a Million 1938,Jl 16,7:2
Mondo, Peggy
Who's Minding the Store? 1963,N 29,67:6
    (Incorrect in this edition; use 1963,N 28,67:6
    elsewhere)
Mondy, Pierre
Demoniaque 1958,Mr 4,34:5
Folies Bergere 1958,My 28,37:2
Women Are Weak 1959,Je 9,44:2
Young Girls Beware 1959,Ag 22,8:2
Story of Monte Cristo, The 1962,N 7,48:1
Sleeping Car Murder, The 1966,Mr 8,45:1
Weekend at Dunkirk 1966,My 19,51:2
Monecelli, Mario (Screenwriter)
Fear No Evil 1949,Mr 31,31:2
Monet, Robert
Thunder Bay 1953,My 21,39:2
Moneta, Adriana
Dolce Vita, La 1961,Ap 20,30:1
Monfort, Sylvia
Eagle with Two Heads 1948,D 30,24:2
Angels of the Streets 1950,Ja 17,24:2
Case of Dr Laurent, The 1958,Je 26,23:2
Love and the Frenchwoman; (Francaise et
    l'Amour, La) 1961,F 28,38:2
Riff Raff Girls 1962,O 20,13:5
Mong, William V
Connecticut Yankee in King Arthur's Court, A
    1921,Mr 15,14:3
Ten-Dollar Raise, The 1921,Je 13,16:1
Shame 1921,Ag 1,8:3 (Incorrect in this edition;
    use 1921,Ag 1,6:4 elsewhere)
Monte Cristo 1922,Ag 15,20:3
Wandering Daughters 1923,Jl 2,16:2
Drifting 1923,Ag 20,4:2
In the Palace of the King 1923,D 3,14:1
Thy Name Is Woman 1924,Mr 4,17:1
Why Men Leave Home 1924,My 12,14:4
Welcome Stranger 1924,O 14,21:5
Excuse Me 1925,Ja 27,11:2
Oh, Doctor! 1925,F 23,24:1
Barriers Burned Away 1925,Mr 12,17:2
Fine Clothes 1925,O 20,28:1
Steel Preferred 1925,D 22,13:1
Strong Man, The 1926,S 7,44:2
Silent Lover, The 1926,N 15,19:1
What Price Glory 1926,N 24,26:4
Taxi, Taxi 1927,F 15,23:1
Alias the Lone Wolf 1927,S 20,32:2
Telling the World 1928,Jl 16,25:3
Haunted House, The 1928,D 17,23:1
Noah's Ark 1929,Mr 13,28:6
Girl Said No, The 1930,Ap 5,23:3
Double Cross Roads 1930,Ap 29,31:1
In Gay Madrid 1930,Je 7,10:4
Big Trail, The 1930,O 25,20:3
Gun Smoke 1931,Ap 24,27:1
Flood, The 1931,Ap 27,25:1
Bad Company 1931,N 7,16:5
Dangerous Affair, A 1931,N 23,22:1
Cross Examination 1932,F 27,22:1
Sign of the Cross, The 1932,D 1,25:1
No More Orchids 1933,Ja 2,29:2
Vampire Bat, The 1933,Ja 23,9:1
Narrow Corner, The 1933,Jl 14,15:3
I Loved a Woman 1933,S 22,14:2
Massacre 1934,Ja 18,19:2
Dark Hazard 1934,F 23,23:3
Treasure Island 1934,Ag 18,5:5
County Chairman, The 1935,Ja 19,8:1
Last Days of Pompeii, The 1935,O 17,29:2
Whispering Smith Speaks 1936,F 17,21:1
Dancing Pirate 1936,Je 18,19:1
Stand-In 1937,N 19,27:2
Painted Desert 1938,S 14,26:5
Moniceili (Screenwriter)
O K Nero 1953,Je 20,8:6
Monicelli, Emmanuele (Screenwriter)
Tailor's Maid, The; (Patri e Figli) 1959,S 2,35:4
Monicelli, Mario (Director)
Tailor's Maid, The; (Patri e Figli) 1959,S 2,35:4
Great War; (Grande Guerra, La) 1961,Ag 31,22:3
Organizer, The 1964,My 7,31:2
High Infidelity (Modern People); Modern People
    (High Infidelity) 1965,Jl 2,17:1
Casanova 1965,Jl 21,43:1
Queens, The (Queen Armenia); Queen Armenia
    (The Queens) 1968,Mr 11,49:1

Monicelli, Mario (Miscellaneous)
Great War; (Grande Guerra, La) 1961,Ag 31,22:3
Monicelli, Mario (Original Author)
Mad About Opera 1950,Ap 6,33:2
Monicelli, Mario (Screenwriter)
Beautiful but Dangerous 1958,F 6,24:1
Big Deal on Madonna Street, The 1960,N 23,20:1
Organizer, The 1964,My 7,31:2
Casanova 1965,Jl 21,43:1
Monicelli, Vincezoni (Screenwriter)
Great War; (Grande Guerra, La) 1961,Ag 31,22:3
Monicelli (Original Author)
O K Nero 1953,Je 20,8:6
Lure of the Sira 1953,D 26,10:7
Monin, Janine
Belles and Ballets 1960,N 15,45:3
Monisha
Kanchenjungha 1966,Jl 26,27:2
Moniuszko, Stanislaw (Original Author)
Halka 1938,Ja 17,11:3
MONK
See Also MUNK
Monk, Egon (Producer)
Great British Train Robbery, The 1967,Ap 6,45:2
Monk, Julius
Girl of the Night 1960,N 12,15:1
Monk, Marlyn
Gentleman's Agreement 1947,N 12,36:2
Monk, Thelonious
Jazz on a Summer's Day 1960,Mr 29,46:2
Monk, Thomas
Peter Ibbetson 1935,N 8,18:2
Monkhouse, Bob
Carry on Sergeant 1959,O 28,40:5
Week-End With Lulu, A 1962,My 24,29:2
Monkhouse, Joseph
Forbidden Music 1938,D 27,13:2
Monkman, Phyllis
Co-Optimists, The 1930,F 5,27:2
Monks, James
How Green Was my Valley 1941,O 29,27:2
Joan of Paris 1942,Ja 26,18:2
Monks, John Jr (Director)
No Man is an Island 1962,O 11,49:2
Monks, John Jr (Original Author)
Brother Rat 1938,N 5,15:2
About Face 1952,My 24,15:3
Monks, John Jr (Producer)
No Man is an Island 1962,O 11,49:2
Monks, John Jr (Screenwriter)
Brother Rat and a Baby 1940,Ja 27,9:4
Strike up the Band 1940,S 30,13:2
We Are the Marines 1942,D 14,19:2
House on Ninety-Second Street, The
    1945,S 27,24:7
13 Rue Madeleine 1947,Ja 16,30:2
Wild Harvest 1947,N 13,33:2
Knock on any Door 1949,F 23,31:2
Dial 1119 1950,D 4,32:6
West Point Story, The 1950,D 23,11:3
People Against O'Hara, The 1951,S 6,39:3
Where's Charley? 1952,Je 27,18:3
So This Is Love 1953,Ag 12,22:1
No Man is an Island 1962,O 11,49:2
Monks of Nccere Inferiore Monastery
Flowers of St Francis 1952,O 7,26:2
Monlaur, Yvonne
Circus of Horrors 1960,S 1,31:1
Brides of Dracula, The 1960,S 6,41:4
Monnet, Marguerite (Composer)
Jessica 1962,Ap 20,20:2
Monnier, Jackie
Tourmoi, Le 1929,Mr 3,VIII,7:2
Bled, Le 1929,Ag 25,VIII,5:1
Comrades of 1918 1931,F 20,18:5
David Golder 1932,O 20,24:2
Monnin, Nicole
Pardon my French 1952,Mr 31,17:2
Monnot, Marguerite (Composer)
Star Without Light; Etoile Sans Lumiere
    1947,Ag 4,14:2
Monod, Jacques
Passion of Slow Fire, The 1962,O 12,26:1
Game is Over, The 1967,Ja 10,34:1
Monod, Roland
Man Escaped, A 1957,Ag 27,33:2
Monohan, Richard
Fixed Bayonets 1951,N 21,20:2
Monro, Matt
Go Go Mania 1965,My 20,52:4
Monro, Robert (Original Author)
Crooked Way, The 1949,S 5,13:2
French Mistress, A 1960,D 19,34:2
MONROE
See Also MUNRO, MUNROE
Monroe, Craddock C
Mr Peek-A-Boo 1951,S 19,37:1
Monroe, Delbert
Voyage to the Bottom of the Sea 1961,Jl 20,32:2
Monroe, Ellen Hope
Ride Back, The 1957,Ap 30,24:1

Monroe, Marilyn
Love Happy 1950,Ap 8,9:4
Asphalt Jungle, The 1950,Je 9,29:3
All About Eve 1950,O 14,13:2
As Young as You Feel 1951,Ag 3,10:6
Let's Make It Legal 1951,N 7,35:3
Clash by Night 1952,Je 19,32:6
We're not Married 1952,Jl 12,16:2
Don't Bother to Knock 1952,Jl 19,8:2
Monkey Business 1952,S 6,12:6
O Henry's Full House (The Cop and the Anthem);
  Cop and the Anthem, The (O Henry's Full
  House) 1952,O 17,33:1
Niagara 1953,Ja 22,20:3
Gentlemen Prefer Blondes 1953,Jl 16,17:2
How to Marry a Millionaire 1953,N 11,37:1
River of no Return 1954,My 1,13:2
There's no Business Like Show Business
  1954,D 17,37:3
Seven Year Itch, The 1955,Je 4,9:1
Bus Stop 1956,S 1,19:2
Prince and the Showgirl 1957,Je 14,22:2
Some Like It Hot 1959,Mr 30,23:1
Let's Make Love 1960,S 9,36:1
Misfits, The 1961,F 2,24:2
Marilyn 1963,Jl 18,15:1
Monroe, Rudolph
Raisin in the Sun, A 1961,Mr 30,24:1
Monroe, Thomas (Original Author)
Ball of Fire 1942,Ja 16,25:2
Affairs of Susan, The 1945,Mr 29,18:2
Song Is Born, A 1948,O 20,37:2
Monroe, Thomas (Screenwriter)
Affairs of Susan, The 1945,Mr 29,18:2
Monroe, Vaughan and His Orchestra
Meet The People 1944,S 8,16:2
Monroe, Vaughn
Singing Guns 1950,Je 5,19:3
Monroe, Vaughn and his orchestra
Carnegie Hall 1947,My 3,10:2
Monsarrat, Nicholas (Original Author)
Cruel Sea, The 1953,Ag 11,18:5
Ship That Died of Shame, The 1956,Ag 21,33:2
Story of Esther Costello, The 1957,N 6,43:1
Monsarrat, Sam
Bird of Paradise 1951,Mr 15,37:2
Monson, Arch (Producer)
Tanga Tika 1953,O 6,34:4
Monsour, Nyra
Americano, The 1955,Ja 20,35:1
Mont, Christina
Rose of the Golden West 1927,S 26,27:1
Montagne, Edward J (Director)
Tattooed Stranger, The 1950,F 10,18:6
Man With my Face, The 1951,Je 15,27:5
McHale's Navy 1964,Jl 11,15:2
Montagne, Edward J (Original Author)
One Week of Love 1923,Ja 8,22:1
Shanghaied 1927,S 13,36:2
P J 1968,Mr 7,52:3
Montagne, Edward J (Producer)
McHale's Navy 1964,Jl 11,15:2
P J 1968,Mr 7,52:3
Shakiest Gun in the West, The 1968,Jl 11,30:1
Montagne, Edward J (Screenwriter)
Man With my Face, The 1951,Je 15,27:5
Montagne, Lawrence
Pillar of Fire, The 1963,Ap 8,35:2
Synanon 1965,My 6,44:1
Montagu, Elizabeth (Miscellaneous)
Four in a Jeep 1951,Je 12,35:2
Village, The 1953,S 23,37:2
Montagu, Ewen (Original Author)
Man Who Never Was, The 1956,Ap 4,24:1
Montague, C E (Screenwriter)
True Heaven 1929,F 11,26:3
Montague, Edward (Producer)
Ghost and Mr Chicken, The 1966,S 22,57:2
Montague, Ivor (Director)
Day Dreams 1930,F 4,28:3
Montague, Ivor (Screenwriter)
Scott of the Antarctic 1951,F 26,20:2
Montague, Lee
Moulin Rouge 1953,F 11,33:5
Another Sky 1960,O 25,40:2
Operation Snatch 1962,S 25,31:4
Billy Budd 1962,O 31,32:1
Deadlier Than the Male 1967,F 22,21:1
How I Won the War 1967,N 9,56:1
Montague, Margaret Prescott (Original Author)
Uncle Sam of Freedom Ridge 1920,S 27,15:2
Montague, Monte
Impatient Maiden, The 1932,Mr 4,17:3
Song of the Saddle 1936,Mr 21,13:3
Law West of Tombstone, The 1938,N 25,19:1
Renegade Ranger, The 1939,F 17,17:3
Racketeers of the Range 1939,Je 8,31:4
Allegheny Uprising 1939,N 10,27:3
Montalban, Carlos
Harder They Fall, The 1956,My 10,26:3
Crowded Paradise 1956,Je 22,15:1
Pepe 1960,D 22,18:1
Love Has Many Faces 1965,F 25,24:1

Montalban, Carlos (Miscellaneous)
Mysterians, The 1959,Jl 2,15:2
Montalban, Carlos (Narrator)
Green Magic 1955,My 17,32:1
Montalban, Jess
Walls of Hell, The 1965,N 18,55:3
Montalban, Ricardo
Fiesta 1947,Je 27,17:3
On an Island With You 1948,Jl 30,13:2
Neptune's Daughter 1949,Je 10,32:2
Battleground 1949,N 12,8:4
Border Incident 1949,N 21,29:2
Mystery Street 1950,Jl 28,12:5
Right Cross 1950,N 16,39:2
Two Weeks With Love 1950,N 24,31:2
Mark of the Renegade 1951,S 7,24:2
Across the Wide Missouri 1951,N 7,35:4
My Man and I 1952,S 6,12:6
Sombrero 1953,Ap 23,37:2
Latin Lovers 1953,Ag 13,17:2
Saracen Blade, The 1954,My 15,13:4
Life in the Balance, A 1955,Jl 14,19:1
Three for Jamie Dawn 1956,Jl 7,11:3
Soyonara 1957,D 6,39:4
Sayonara 1957,D 6,39:4
Let no Man Write my Epitaph 1960,N 11,36:2
Hemingway's Adventures of a Young Man
  1962,Jl 26,17:1
Reluctant Saint, The 1962,D 4,47:2
Love Is a Ball 1963,Ap 25,38:1
Cheyenne Autumn 1964,D 24,8:1
Singing Nun, The 1966,Mr 18,33:1
Madame X 1966,Ap 28,49:1
Money Trap, The 1966,My 5,59:1
Blue 1968,My 11,28:1
Sol Madrid 1968,Je 14,43:1
Montaldo, Giuliano (Director)
Grand Slam 1968,F 21,60:4
Montalenli, Indro (Screenwriter)
Tombolo 1949,D 31,9:4
Montalto, Irene
Gold of Naples (The Gambler); Gambler, The
  (Gold of Naples) 1957,F 12,30:1
Montalvan, Celia
Amours de Toni, Les 1936,N 5,35:1
Toni 1968,S 19,62:2
Montana, Bull
Brass Buttons 1919,Ap 7,11:5
Unpardonable Sin, The 1919,My 3,11:3
Victory 1919,D 28,4:4
Go and Get It 1920,Jl 19,16:3
Three Must-Get-Theres, The 1922,Ag 28,14:1
Painted People 1924,Ja 29,16:1
Dick Turpin 1925,Ja 26,14:1
Lost World, The 1925,F 9,15:3
Skyrocket, The 1926,Ja 26,25:2
Son of the Sheik, The 1926,Jl 26,13:2
How to Handle Women 1928,Je 18,13:2
Good Morning, Judge 1928,Je 26,29:1
Show of Shows 1929,N 21,24:5
Tiger Rose 1929,D 25,23:1
Montand, Yves
Star Without Light; Etoile Sans Lumiere
  1947,Ag 4,14:2
Gates of the Night 1950,Mr 16,40:2
Wages of Fear, The 1955,F 17,23:1
Premier May 1958,S 17,44:2
Witches of Salem 1958,D 9,54:2
Heroes and Sinners; (Heros Sont Fatigues, Les)
  1959,My 12,38:2
Let's Make Love 1960,S 9,36:1
Where the Hot Wind Blows 1960,N 12,15:1
Sanctuary 1961,F 22,31:1
My Geisha 1962,Je 14,23:2
Sleeping Car Murder, The 1966,Mr 8,45:1
Le Joli Mai 1966,Je 10,54:2
Guerre est Fini, La; War Is Over, The
  1966,S 23,43:1
Is Paris Burning? 1966,N 11,36:1
Grand-Prix 1966,D 22,40:1
Guerre est Fini, La; War Is Over, The
  1967,F 2,29:2
Live for Life 1967,D 19,59:1
Montanelli, Indro (Screenwriter)
General Della Rovere 1960,N 22,41:1
Montaner, Rita
Romance del Palmar, El 1939,My 1,21:2
Montano, Dedi
Schoolgirl Diary 1947,O 18,9:2
Montanye, Harold P (Original Author)
Wings of Youth 1925,Ap 20,18:1 (Incorrect in
  this edition; use 1925,Ap 28,18:1 elsewhere)
Montau, Michele
Hell is for Heroes 1962,Jl 12,19:3
Made in Paris 1966,F 17,29:1
Monte, Paul
We Were Strangers 1949,Ap 28,28:2
Monteilhet, Hubert (Original Author)
Return from the Ashes 1965,N 17,53:1
Montel, Blanche
Trois Mousquetaires, Les 1933,My 1,10:2
Milady 1933,S 8,22:3

Montell, Lisa
Pearl of the South Pacific 1955,S 17,12:2
Gaby 1956,My 10,26:3
Ten Thousand Bedrooms 1957,Ap 4,37:1
Montemayor, Miguel
Soy Chato, Pero las Huelo; I Am Snub-nosed but I
  Can Smell 1939,Jl 22,12:3
Montemuri, Davide
Last Year at Marienbad 1962,Mr 8,26:1
Montenegro, Conchita
Strangers May Kiss 1931,Ap 13,17:1
Never the Twain Shall Meet 1931,Je 6,15:5
Cisco Kid, The 1931,O 24,20:3
Gay Caballero, The 1932,Mr 26,17:2
Laughing at Life 1933,Jl 15,14:2
Dos Noches 1933,Jl 29,14:3
Melodia Prohibida, La 1933,O 4,27:2
Handy Andy 1934,Ag 4,14:5
Granaderos del Amor 1934,S 4,23:4
Hell in the Heavens 1934,D 12,28:2
Asegure a su Mujer; Insure Your Wife
  1935,Mr 12,25:3
Eternal Melodies 1948,F 14,17:3
Montenegro, Juanita
Heritage 1940,N 5,33:2
Monter, Rudolph (Producer)
Voice in the Wind 1944,Mr 16,17:2
Monterey, Carlotta
Soul Fire 1925,My 6,26:3
King on Main Street, The 1925,O 26,25:2
Montero, Germaine
Lady Paname 1951,Mr 20,35:4
Lovers, Happy Lovers 1954,O 1,19:2
Any Number Can Win 1963,O 9,47:2
Montero, Roberto (Director)
Cliff of Sin, The 1952,N 22,16:5
Monteros, Rosenda
Woman's Devotion, A 1957,Mr 22,26:1
Magnificent Seven, The 1960,N 24,48:3
Tiara Tahiti 1963,N 6,32:1
She 1965,S 2,36:1
Nazarin 1968,Je 21,48:1
Montes, Conchita
Roots, The (The Cows); Cows, The (The Roots)
  1957,S 3,23:2
Montes, Elisa
Return of the Seven 1966,O 20,52:5
Cobra, The 1968,Mr 28,52:3
Montes, Felipe
Love in Morocco 1933,Mr 20,18:3
Montes, Lina
Dama de las Camelias, La 1944,S 26,16:1
Montes, Lola
Lady and the Monster, The 1944,Ap 8,9:2
Montevecchi, Liliane
Glass Slipper, The 1955,Mr 25,19:2
Moonfleet 1955,Je 25,9:2
Meet Me in Las Vegas 1956,Mr 14,39:2
Living Idol, The 1957,My 3,18:1
Sad Sack, The 1957,N 28,57:1
Young Lions, The 1958,Ap 3,23:1
Me and the Colonel 1958,Ag 27,33:1
Montez, Manolo
Heroes and Sinners; (Heros Sont Fatigues, Les)
  1959,My 12,38:2
Montez, Maria
That Night in Rio 1941,Mr 10,21:2
Moonlight in Hawaii 1941,O 10,26:6
South of Tahiti 1941,N 10,21:3
Bombay Clipper 1942,Ja 12,23:3
Mystery of Marie Roget, The 1942,My 5,17:3
Arabian Nights 1942,D 26,15:1
White Savage 1943,Ap 26,15:2
Ali Baba and the Forty Thieves 1944,Mr 16,17:3
Cobra Woman 1944,My 18,17:2
Gypsy Wildcat 1944,O 5,18:6
Bowery to Broadway 1944,N 30,19:2
Sudan 1945,Ap 19,22:8
Tangier 1946,Je 7,II,16:4
Pirates of Monterey 1947,D 17,41:4
Exile, The 1947,D 26,22:4
Siren of Atlantis 1949,Ag 22,13:1
Thief of Venice, The 1952,N 28,22:7
Montez, Richard
Don't Raise the Bridge, Lower the River
  1968,Jl 13,18:1
Montfort, Sylvia
Secret of Mayerling, The 1951,My 8,39:2
Montgomery, Doreen (Miscellaneous)
Man in Grey, The 1945,N 30,18:6
Montgomery, Doreen (Screenwriter)
Lady Surrenders, A 1947,Je 20,25:6
Man of Evil 1948,Mr 26,26:2
Dance Little Lady 1955,D 26,23:3
Murder Reported 1960,Jl 12,39:1
Montgomery, Douglass
Little Women 1933,N 17,22:3
Eight Girls in a Boat 1934,Ja 13,16:3
Little Man, What Now? 1934,Je 1,29:1
Music in the Air 1934,D 14,29:3
Mystery of Edwin Drood, The 1935,Mr 21,27:1
Lady Tubbs 1935,Jl 22,20:2
Harmony Lane 1935,O 24,19:4

Montgomery, Douglass— Cont
Counsel for Crime 1937,O 9,16:1
Cat and the Canary, The 1939,N 23,38:5
Johnny in the Clouds 1945,N 16,16:2
Montgomery, Edward Poor (Original Author)
Double Harness 1933,Jl 21,20:2
Montgomery, Elizabeth
Court-Martial of Billy Mitchell, The
1955,D 23,14:2
Johnny Cool 1963,O 3,31:1
Who's Been Sleeping in My Bed? 1963,D 26,33:2
Montgomery, Frank
Sainted Devil, A 1924,N 24,15:3
Aloma of the South Seas 1926,My 17,19:1
So's Your Old Man 1926,N 1,28:2
Montgomery, George
Cisco Kid and the Lady, The 1939,D 25,29:2
Star Dust 1940,My 4,13:1
Young People 1940,Ag 24,16:2
Cadet Girl 1941,D 11,39:1
Roxie Hart 1942,F 20,21:1
Ten Gentlemen From West Point 1942,Je 5,23:3
Orchestra Wives 1942,S 24,23:2
China Girl 1943,Ja 21,27:2
Coney Island 1943,Je 17,17:2
Bomber's Moon 1943,Jl 31,8:2
Three Little Girls in Blue 1946,S 26,32:3
Brasher Doubloon, The 1947,My 22,34:5
Lulu Belle 1948,Je 21,18:3
Belle Star's Daughter 1949,Ja 10,19:2
Dakota Lil 1950,Mr 3,21:5
Davy Crockett, Indian Scout 1950,Mr 17,28:3
Iroquois Trail, The 1950,O 27,24:4
Sword of Monte Cristo, The 1951,Ap 23,21:2
Texas Rangers, The 1951,Jl 14,7:2
Fort Ti 1953,My 30,7:1
Gun Belt 1953,Ag 1,8:2
Huk! 1956,D 15,20:4
Black Patch 1958,Ap 24,38:1
Watusi 1959,Jl 2,15:2
Steel Claw, The 1961,S 21,40:2
Samar 1962,Ap 12,41:6
Battle of the Bulge 1965,D 18,36:1
Montgomery, George (Director)
Steel Claw, The 1961,S 21,40:2
Samar 1962,Ap 12,41:6
Montgomery, George (Producer)
Steel Claw, The 1961,S 21,40:2
Samar 1962,Ap 12,41:6
Montgomery, George (Screenwriter)
Steel Claw, The 1961,S 21,40:2
Samar 1962,Ap 12,41:6
Montgomery, Goodee
Up the River 1930,O 11,21:3
Lightnin' 1930,N 29,21:4
Charlie Chan Carries On 1931,Mr 21,15:1
Transatlantic 1931,Jl 31,15:2
Let's Talk It Over 1934,Je 16,20:2
Stolen Harmony 1935,Ap 20,16:2
Montgomery, James (Original Author)
Going Up 1923,O 10,16:2
Nothing but the Truth 1929,Ap 22,23:1
Aviator, The 1930,Ja 11,21:3
Nothing but the Truth 1941,O 23,27:1
Riding High 1943,D 23,26:4
Montgomery, L M (Original Author)
Anne of Green Gables 1919,D 22,18:3
Anne of Green Gables 1934,D 22,21:1
Anne of Windy Poplars 1940,Ag 23,13:3
Montgomery, Peggy
Sensation Seekers 1927,Mr 16,28:2
Eight Girls in a Boat 1934,Ja 13,16:3
Montgomery, Ray
Air Force 1943,F 4,29:1
Hard Way, The 1943,Mr 13,9:2
June Bride 1948,O 30,10:2
House Across the Street 1949,S 2,14:4
Task Force 1949,O 1,8:6
Las Vegas Story, The 1952,Ja 31,37:6
Montgomery, Robert
So This Is College 1929,N 9,22:5
Untamed 1929,N 30,23:1
Their own Desire 1930,Ja 25,13:2
Free and Easy 1930,Ap 19,15:1
Divorcee, The 1930,My 10,25:3
Big House, The 1930,Je 25,31:2
Sins of the Children 1930,Jl 26,16:4
Our Blushing Brides 1930,Ag 2,16:4
Love in the Rough 1930,S 27,21:3
War Nurse 1930,O 24,31:1
Inspiration 1931,F 9,25:3
Easiest Way, The 1931,F 28,15:2
Strangers May Kiss 1931,Ap 13,17:1
Shipmates 1931,My 23,13:4
Man in Possession, The 1931,Jl 18,16:6
Private Lives 1931,D 19,16:4
Lovers Courageous 1932,F 20,11:2
But the Flesh Is Weak 1932,Ap 16,11:2
Letty Lynton 1932,Ap 30,19:3
Blondie of the Follies 1932,S 2,19:2
Faithless 1932,N 19,20:2
Hell Below 1933,Ap 26,13:2
When Ladies Meet 1933,Je 24,16:2
Made on Broadway 1933,Jl 8,14:5

Another Language 1933,Ag 5,9:5
Night Flight 1933,O 7,18:4
Fugitive Lovers 1934,Ja 13,16:3
Mystery of Mr X, The 1934,F 26,21:3
Riptide 1934,Mr 31,8:2
Hide-Out 1934,Ag 25,16:5
Forsaking all Others 1934,D 21,18:1
Biography of a Bachelor Girl 1935,Mr 2,18:2
Vanessa: Her Love Story 1935,Ap 13,11:3
No More Ladies 1935,Je 22,18:5
Petticoat Fever 1936,Mr 21,13:2
Trouble for Two 1936,My 30,7:2
Piccadilly Jim 1936,Ag 31,19:1
Last of Mrs Cheyney, The 1937,F 19,15:1
Night Must Fall 1937,Ap 30,17:2
Ever Since Eve 1937,Je 25,25:2
Live, Love and Learn 1937,N 19,27:2
First 100 Years, The 1938,My 13,17:2
Yellow Jack 1938,My 20,17:2
Three Loves Has Nancy 1938,S 2,21:2
Fast and Loose 1939,Mr 9,18:1
Earl of Chicago, The 1940,Mr 14,29:3
Haunted Honeymoon 1940,O 31,28:2
Mr and Mrs Smith 1941,F 21,16:3
Rage in Heaven 1941,Mr 21,19:2
Here Comes Mr Jordan 1941,Ag 8,13:2
Unfinished Business 1941,S 2,20:2
They Were Expendable 1945,D 21,25:2
Lady in the Lake 1947,Ja 24,18:3
Ride the Pink Horse 1947,O 9,32:3
Saxon Charm, The 1948,S 30,32:3
June Bride 1948,O 30,10:2
Once More, my Darling 1949,S 26,17:1
Eye Witness 1950,Ag 28,13:2
Montgomery, Robert (Director)
Lady in the Lake 1947,Ja 24,18:3
Ride the Pink Horse 1947,O 9,32:3
Once More, my Darling 1949,S 26,17:1
Eye Witness 1950,Ag 28,13:2
Gallant Hours, The 1960,Je 23,19:4
Montgomery, Robert (Narrator)
Secret Land, The 1948,D 2,39:2
Montgomery, Robert (Producer)
Gallant Hours, The 1960,Je 23,19:4
Montgomery, Rutherford (Original Author)
Hound that Thought he was a Racoon, The
1960,Ag 18,19:2
Montgomery, Thomas (Director)
King Kong vs. Godzilla 1963,Je 27,23:4
Month, Christopher
Santa Claus Conquers the Martians
1964,D 17,50:2
Monthil, Marcelle
Trois Mousquetaires, Les 1933,My 1,10:2
Monti, Milli
Girl From Scotland Yard, The 1937,My 31,11:2
On Such a Night 1937,S 17,29:2
Monti, Mirella
To Live in Peace 1947,N 25,37:2
Montiel, Sarita
Don Quixote 1949,My 13,29:3
Mad Queen, The 1950,O 27,24:3
Vera Cruz 1954,D 27,22:4
Serenade 1956,Mr 24,21:1 (Incorrect in this
edition; use 1956,Mr 23,21:1 elsewhere)
Run of the Arrow 1957,Ag 3,8:6
Montigny
Francois Villon 1950,Jl 3,9:2
Montor, Max
Street Scene 1931,Ag 27,22:5
Montoro, Jorge
Manhunt in the Jungle 1958,Ap 12,13:1
Montoya, Alex
Golden Hawk, The 1952,O 18,16:4
Flight of the Phoenix, The 1966,F 1,26:1
Appaloosa, The 1966,S 15,51:1
Montoya, Julia
One Way Street 1950,My 12,33:3
Montoya, Maria Teresa
Perfidia; Perfidy 1940,F 17,9:3
Montrose, Helen
Mighty Lak' a Rose 1923,Mr 20,24:3
Montsoret, Roger
Two or Three Things I Know About Her
1968,S 26,60:1
Montuori, Vittorio (Screenwriter)
Paolo and Francesca 1953,F 14,8:3
Monty, Ole
Eric Soya's 17 1967,Ja 25,37:1
Moody, Mark L (Producer)
Ravaged Earth 1942,N 27,27:3
Moody, Ralph
Red Mountain 1952,Ap 26,19:2
Affair in Trinidad 1952,Jl 31,14:2
Road to Bali 1953,Ja 30,25:1
I Died a Thousand Times 1955,N 10,45:2
Last Hunt, The 1956,Mr 1,37:2
Toward the Unknown 1956,S 28,24:4
Outsider, The 1962,F 8,25:1
Moody, Ron
Follow a Star 1961,Ap 26,34:1
Mouse on the Moon, The 1963,Je 18,32:1
Ladies Who Do 1963,N 26,52:2

Pair of Briefs, A 1964,F 3,22:2
Murder Most Foul 1965,My 24,36:2
Oliver! 1968,D 11,57:1
Moody, William Vaughn (Original Author)
Faith Healer, The 1921,Mr 14,9:2
Great Divide, The 1925,F 11,19:4
Great Divide, The 1930,F 17,17:6
Woman Hungry 1931,Mr 23,24:7
Moody, William Vaughn Mrs (Screenwriter)
Faith Healer, The 1921,Mr 14,9:2
Mooers, De Sacia
Potash and Perlmutter 1923,S 24,5:4
Any Woman 1925,My 27,26:2
Arizona Kid, The 1930,My 17,21:2
Moog, Heinz
Magic Face, The 1951,O 1,19:2
Secret Ways, The 1961,My 25,31:1
Senso 1968,Jl 9,31:1
Moomaw, Lewis H (Director)
Chechahcos, The 1924,My 19,14:2
Under the Rouge 1925,Jl 22,14:4
Moomaw, Lewis H (Screenwriter)
Chechahcos, The 1924,My 19,14:2
Moon, Lee Sue
Marco the Magnificent 1966,D 15,60:1
Moon, Lorna (Original Author)
Don't Tell Everything 1921,D 12,20:2
Min and Bill 1930,N 24,26:5
Moon, Lynne Sue
55 Days at Peking 1963,My 30,20:1
13 Frightened Girls 1963,S 12,32:2
Moondog
Chappaqua 1967,N 6,65:2
Mooney, Art
Opposite Sex, The 1956,N 16,23:2
Mooney, Martin (Original Author)
Special Agent 1935,S 19,28:1
Exclusive Story 1936,Ja 18,19:2
Bullets or Ballots 1936,My 27,27:1
You Can't Buy Luck 1937,My 14,21:2
Mutiny in the Big House 1939,D 11,26:2
Convicted Woman 1940,F 26,11:2
Millionaires in Prison 1940,Jl 16,21:3
Gangs Incorporated 1941,Ag 4,16:6
Mr Wise Guy 1942,Mr 5,27:2
Minstrel Man 1944,Jl 17,18:5
Crime Incorporated 1945,Je 23,9:7
Mooney, Martin (Producer)
Criminal Court 1946,N 16,15:3
San Quentin 1947,F 10,24:3
Mooney, Martin (Screenwriter)
Missing Girls 1936,O 5,25:1
You Can't Buy Luck 1937,My 14,21:2
Gangs Incorporated 1941,Ag 4,16:6
Mooney, Tex
Jungle Jim 1949,Ja 1,9:2
Moor
Dr Knock 1937,My 1,16:4
MOORE
See Also MOHR, MORE
Moore, Adrienne
Patterns 1956,Mr 28,26:1
Moore, Alvy
Glory Brigade, The 1953,Ag 15,8:4
Riot in Cell Block 11 1954,F 19,24:5
Susan Slept Here 1954,Jl 30,9:1
Annapolis Story, An 1955,Ap 9,8:2
Five Against the House 1955,Je 11,8:7
Designing Woman 1957,My 17,20:2
Perfect Furlough, The 1959,Ja 22,27:4
Wackiest Ship in the Army, The 1961,F 9,36:1
Move Over Darling 1963,D 26,33:1
Moore, Archie
Adventures of Huckleberry Fin, The
1960,Ag 4,17:1
Carpetbaggers, The 1964,Jl 2,24:4
Fortune Cookie, The 1966,O 20,52:1
Moore, Brian (Screenwriter)
Luck of Ginger Coffey, The 1964,S 22,44:1
Torn Curtain 1966,Jl 28,23:1
Moore, Cameron
Town Like Alice, A 1958,S 22,27:1
Moore, Carlyle
What a Man 1930,Jl 21,20:3
Transatlantic Merry-Go-Round 1934,N 1,25:2
Shipmates Forever 1935,O 17,29:3
Moore, Carlyle (Original Author)
Unknown Purple, The 1924,Mr 24,13:1
Moore, Carlyle Jr
High School Girl 1935,Mr 16,19:1
Ceiling Zero 1936,Ja 20,22:2
Road Gang 1936,F 24,14:1
Treachery Rides the Range 1936,My 30,7:3
Bengal Tiger 1936,Jl 30,22:1
China Clipper 1936,Ag 12,14:3
Case of the Black Cat, The 1936,D 26,15:4
Fugitive in the Sky 1937,Ja 16,21:1
Midnight Court 1937,Mr 4,27:3
Slim 1937,Je 24,30:2
Moore, Carroll (Original Author)
Send Me no Flowers 1964,N 13,30:1

Moore, Charles
Trial of Mary Dugan, The 1929,Mr 29,21:1
I'll Fix It 1934,N 12,17:3
Doctor Rhythm 1938,My 19,25:2
Adventure in Sahara 1938,D 19,19:2
Moore, Charles R
Little Foxes, The 1941,Ag 22,19:2
Moore, Claude
Nana 1929,Jl 30,19:4
Moore, Clayton
Kit Carson 1940,N 15,25:3
Son of Monte Cristo, The 1940,D 5,33:1
International Lady 1941,N 11,29:2
Lone Ranger, The 1956,F 11,12:1
Moore, Cleo
Gambling House 1951,Mr 19,23:2
On Dangerous Ground 1952,F 13,35:2
Bait 1954,F 24,21:3
Women's Prison 1955,F 3,18:5
Moore, Cleve
We Moderns 1925,D 8,28:5
It Must Be Love 1926,O 4,20:2
Stolen Bride, The 1927,Ag 10,21:4
Lilac Time 1928,Ag 4,7:2
Moore, Colleen
Busher, The 1919,My 26,19:4
Egg Crate Wallop, The 1919,S 29,16:1
Dinty 1920,N 22,13:3
Sky Pilot, The 1921,Ap 18,8:1
Wall Flower, The 1922,Je 26,16:2
Nth Commandment, The 1923,Ap 10,24:3
Flaming Youth 1923,N 26,15:6
Through the Dark 1924,Ja 8,27:1
Painted People 1924,Ja 29,16:1
Perfect Flapper, The 1924,Je 23,22:4
Flirting With Love 1924,S 1,9:1
So Big 1925,Ja 5,19:1
Sally 1925,Mr 16,16:1
Desert Flower, The 1925,Je 1,10:3
We Moderns 1925,D 8,28:5
Irene 1926,Mr 1,17:1
Ella Cinders 1926,Je 7,23:2
It Must Be Love 1926,O 4,20:2
Twinkletoes 1926,D 27,20:3
Orchids and Ermine 1927,Ap 19,24:4
Naughty but Nice 1927,Jl 5,19:2
Her Wild Oat 1928,F 6,12:3
Happiness Ahead 1928,Je 19,31:1
Lilac Time 1928,Ag 4,7:2
Oh, Kay! 1928,Ag 27,23:1
Synthetic Sin 1929,Ja 7,36:2
Why Be Good? 1929,My 6,30:4
Smiling Irish Eyes 1929,Jl 24,23:2
Footlights and Fools 1929,N 9,22:5
Power and the Glory, The 1933,Ag 17,13:2
Success at any Price 1934,My 4,24:2
Moore, Constance
Crime of Dr Hallet, The 1938,Mr 24,21:3
Wives Under Suspicion 1938,Jl 1,22:3
Prison Break 1938,Jl 13,17:4
Missing Guest, The 1938,S 7,30:7
Swing That Cheer 1938,N 11,31:2
You Can't Cheat an Honest Man 1939,F 20,13:2
Ex-Champ 1939,My 12,25:3
Mutiny on the Blackhawk 1939,Ag 2,17:2
Hawaiian Nights 1939,S 29,19:4
Charlie McCarthy, Detective 1939,D 25,29:2
Conga Nights, La 1940,Je 5,33:5
Argentine Nights 1940,O 11,25:3
Las Vegas Nights 1941,Mr 20,25:2
I Wanted Wings 1941,Mr 27,29:4
Buy Me That Town 1941,O 23,27:2
Take a Letter Darling 1942,My 28,13:2
Show Business 1944,My 11,25:7
Atlantic City 1944,Ag 14,11:4
Earl Carroll Vanities 1945,Ap 2,15:6
Delightfully Dangerous 1945,Je 9,17:3
Mexicana 1945,N 17,14:6
In old Sacramento 1946,Ap 29,24:4
Earl Carroll Sketchbook 1946,Ag 30,13:2
Hit Parade of 1947 1947,My 5,32:8
Moore, Daniel (Original Author)
Storm, The 1938,O 31,12:2
Flight at Midnight 1939,S 7,29:2
Illegal Entry 1949,Je 11,11:2
Moore, Daniel (Screenwriter)
Last of the Mohicans, The 1936,S 3,17:3
Storm, The 1938,O 31,12:2
Moore, Del
Last Time I Saw Archie, The 1961,My 29,9:6
Nutty Professor, The 1963,Jl 18,15:2
Disorderly Orderly, The 1964,D 24,8:3
Big Mouth, The 1967,Jl 13,30:2
Moore, Dennie
Sylvia Scarlett 1936,Ja 10,16:2
Meet Nero Wolfe 1936,Jl 16,20:1
Perfect Specimen, The 1937,O 28,29:2
Angel 1937,N 4,29:1
Submarine D-1 1937,D 30,15:4
Mystery House 1938,Je 29,15:5
Cowboy From Brooklyn 1938,Jl 14,17:1
Boy Meets Girl 1938,Ag 27,7:2
Secrets of an Actress 1938,O 8,10:2

I'm From Missouri 1939,Mr 23,27:1
Bachelor Mother 1939,Je 30,17:2
Women, The 1939,S 22,27:2
Eternally Yours 1939,O 7,11:2
Saturday's Children 1940,My 4,13:1
Women in War 1940,My 30,21:2
Ghost Creeps, The 1940,Ag 19,13:3
Dive Bomber 1941,Ag 30,10:2
Anna Lucasta 1949,Ag 12,13:2
Model and the Marriage Broker, The 1952,Ja 12,10:6
Moore, Dennis
China Clipper 1936,Ag 12,14:3
Sing Me a Love Song 1936,D 26,15:2
Four's a Crowd 1938,Ag 12,11:1
Mutiny in the Big House 1939,D 11,26:2
East Side Kids 1940,F 19,21:6
Prison Camp 1940,Ag 3,9:3
Bombs Over Burma 1942,Ag 10,15:2
Impostor, The 1944,Mr 27,17:2
Crime Doctor's Courage, The 1945,Mr 3,11:3
Mummy's Curse, The 1945,Mr 31,16:1
Moore, Dickie
Passion Flower 1930,D 22,16:2
Star Witness, The 1931,Ag 4,19:5
Star Witness, The 1931,Ag 4,19:5
Squaw Man, The 1931,S 19,10:2
Manhattan Parade 1931,D 25,29:2
Husband's Holiday 1931,D 25,29:2
Union Depot 1932,Ja 15,24:4
Expert, The 1932,F 27,22:1
Disorderly Conduct 1932,Ap 11,19:2
So Big 1932,Ap 30,19:3
No Greater Love 1932,My 14,11:5
Winner Take All 1932,Je 18,9:2
Million Dollar Legs 1932,Jl 9,7:5
Blonde Venus 1932,S 24,18:4
Devil Is Driving, The 1932,D 16,25:5
Deception 1933,Ja 10,26:2
Obey the Law 1933,Mr 13,18:3
Gabriel Over the White House 1933,Ap 1,18:2
Oliver Twist 1933,Ap 13,15:3
Cradle Song 1933,N 20,18:2
Man's Castle 1933,D 30,9:2
Gallant Lady 1934,Ja 22,12:3
This Side of Heaven 1934,F 10,21:2
In Love With Life 1934,My 12,12:3
Upper World 1934,My 25,25:4
Human Side, The 1934,S 15,20:3
Little Men 1935,F 18,19:3
World Accuses, The 1935,Mr 21,27:2
Peter Ibbetson 1935,N 8,18:2
So Red the Rose 1935,N 28,39:1
Story of Louis Pasteur, The 1936,F 10,15:1
Timothy's Quest 1936,F 29,11:2
Star for a Night 1936,S 5,7:2
Life of Emile Zola, The 1937,Ag 12,14:2
Bride Wore Red, The 1937,O 15,18:4
Love, Honor and Behave 1938,Mr 21,18:2
My Bill 1938,Jl 7,22:4
Gladiator, The 1938,Ag 29,10:2
Arkansas Traveler, The 1938,N 17,29:2
Hidden Power 1939,Jl 26,17:3
Under-Pup, The 1939,S 5,21:2
Dispatch From Reuters, A 1940,D 12,37:2
Sergeant York 1941,Jl 3,15:1
Adventures of Martin Eden 1942,Mr 16,19:2
Miss Annie Rooney 1942,Je 8,11:1
Heaven Can Wait 1943,Ag 12,15:1
Happy Land 1943,D 9,33:3
Eve of St Mark, The 1944,My 31,22:2
Youth Runs Wild 1944,S 2,17:2
Sweet and Low Down 1944,O 19,19:2
Out of the Past 1947,N 26,18:2
16 Fathoms Deep 1948,O 7,35:2
Bad Boy 1949,Mr 23,35:2
Member of the Wedding, The 1952,D 31,10:2
Eight Iron Men 1953,Ja 2,11:1
Moore, Donna
Citizen Saint 1948,My 28,28:2
Moore, Dorothy
Big Shot, The 1937,Ag 13,13:1
Girls' School 1938,N 3,27:1
Blondie 1938,D 22,25:4
Blondie Meets the Boss 1939,Ap 27,31:1
Girl in 313 1940,Je 14,25:3
Broadway 1942,Je 5,23:2
Moore, Dudley
Wrong Box 1966,Jl 20,46:1
Bedazzled 1967,D 11,65:2
30 Is a Dangerous Age, Cynthia 1968,Mr 5,34:1
Moore, Dudley (Original Author)
Bedazzled 1967,D 11,65:2
30 Is a Dangerous Age, Cynthia 1968,Mr 5,34:1
Moore, Dudley (Screenwriter)
30 Is a Dangerous Age, Cynthia 1968,Mr 5,34:1
Moore, Eileen
Mr Lord Says No! 1952,F 12,22:5
Mr Denning Drives North 1953,S 2,20:1
Inspector Calls, An 1954,N 26,24:4
Green Man, The 1957,My 23,40:1
Town Like Alice, A 1958,S 22,27:1

Moore, Eleanor
Love Is a Many-Splendored Thing 1955,Ag 19,10:1
Moore, Emmett
Where the River Shannon Flows 1928,Ja 24,26:3
Moore, Erin O'Brien
His Greatest Gamble 1934,Jl 18,20:2
Destination Moon 1950,Je 28,32:2
Long Gray Line, The 1955,F 11,19:2
Moore, Eva
Chu Chin Chow 1925,F 11,19:4
But the Flesh Is Weak 1932,Ap 16,11:2
Old Dark House, The 1932,O 28,22:4
Just Smith 1934,Ap 23,20:2
Power 1934,O 5,29:3
Bandit of Sherwood Forest, The 1946,Mr 23,8:4
Of Human Bondage 1946,Jl 6,11:2
Moore, Gar
To Live in Peace 1947,N 25,37:2
Paisan 1948,Mr 30,26:2
Illegal Entry 1949,Je 11,11:2
Johnny Stool Pigeon 1949,S 23,28:3
Underworld Story, The 1950,Jl 27,29:4
Girl in White, The 1952,My 31,12:5
Moore, Garry (Narrator)
Crazy World of Laurel and Hardy, The 1967,D 22,35:3
Moore, Gerald
Gay Intruders, The 1946,Mr 18,24:2
Moore, Grace
Lady's Morals, A 1930,N 8,21:3
New Moon 1930,D 25,18:6
One Night of Love 1934,S 7,25:3
Love Me Forever 1935,Je 28,24:1
King Steps Out, The 1936,My 29,15:2
When You're in Love 1937,F 19,15:2
I'll Take Romance 1937,D 17,33:2
Louise 1940,F 3,9:4
Moore, Grace (Original Author)
So This Is Love 1953,Ag 12,22:1
Moore, Granville (Original Author)
Famous Ferguson Case, The 1932,Ap 25,18:6
Moore, Hilda
Jealousy 1929,S 14,17:1
Moore, Ida
Merry Widow, The 1925,Ag 27,14:1
Thank You 1925,O 6,30:1
Easy Come, Easy Go 1947,F 6,29:2
Egg and I, The 1947,Ap 25,29:2
Johnny Belinda 1948,O 2,11:2
Ma and Pa Kettle 1949,Ag 12,13:2
Backfire 1950,Ja 27,29:2
Mr Music 1950,D 21,34:3
Lemon Drop Kid, The 1951,Mr 22,41:2
Comin' Round the Mountain 1951,Jl 27,15:2
Scandal Sheet 1952,Ja 17,23:1
Scandal at Scourie 1953,Je 16,24:2
Country Girl, The 1954,D 16,51:2
Desk Set 1957,My 16,28:2
Rock-a-Bye Baby 1958,Jl 24,18:1
Moore, Jack
When Were You Born? 1938,Je 9,27:2
Texans, The 1938,Jl 28,23:2
Moore, Jacqueline
Love, Honor and Goodbye 1945,S 8,12:2
Moore, James (Director)
Secret Seven, The 1940,Ag 12,11:6
Moore, Joanna
Appointment With a Shadow 1959,Ja 8,24:2
Last Angry Man, The 1959,O 23,24:1
Walk on the Wild Side 1962,F 22,20:1
Son of Flubber 1963,F 9,5:2
Man From Galveston, The 1964,Ja 23,26:3
Countdown 1968,My 2,57:3
Never a Dull Moment 1968,Ag 15,46:2
Moore, Joanne
Follow That Dream 1962,Ag 9,17:7
Moore, Joe
Wages of Virtue 1924,N 24,15:3
Moore, Juanita
Lydia Bailey 1952,My 31,12:5
Affair in Trinidad 1952,Jl 31,14:2
Witness to Murder 1954,Ap 16,16:4
Women's Prison 1955,F 3,18:5
Ransom 1956,Ja 25,28:3
Girl Can't Help It, The 1957,F 9,12:7
Imitation of Life 1959,Ap 18,18:1
Walk on the Wild Side 1962,F 22,20:1
Singing Nun, The 1966,Mr 18,33:1
Rosie 1968,F 8,36:1
Up Tight 1968,D 19,62:1
Moore, Katharine Leslie (Original Author)
Pennies From Heaven 1936,D 10,35:2
Moore, Kieron
Anna Karenina 1948,Ap 28,32:2
Mine Own Executioner 1949,Ja 19,34:2
Man About the House, A 1949,Mr 9,33:2
Saints and Sinners 1949,S 12,17:2
David and Bathsheba 1951,Ag 15,23:2
Ten Tall Men 1951,O 27,10:5
Fuss Over Feathers 1954,D 27,22:6
Green Scarf, The 1955,Ja 15,10:2
Naked Heart, The 1955,Mr 9,22:4

Moore, Kieron — Cont

Satellite in the Sky 1956,S 4,32:7
Key, The 1958,Jl 2,23:3
Darby O'Gill and the Little People 1959,Jl 1,26:1
Angry Hills, The 1959,Jl 16,31:3
Day They Robbed the Bank of England, The
1960,S 5,11:2
League of Gentlemen, The 1961,Ja 25,30:4
I Thank a Fool 1962,S 15,15:1
300 Spartans, The 1962,S 20,29:2
Day of the Triffids 1963,My 11,15:2
Main Attraction, The 1963,Je 27,23:3
Hide and Seek 1964,Mr 12,40:3
Thin Red Line, The 1964,O 29,38:1
Model Murder Case, The 1964,N 25,45:1
Crack in the World 1965,My 13,32:2
Arabesque 1966,My 6,54:1
Custer of the West 1968,Jl 4,13:2

Moore, Larry

Samurai 1945,Ag 25,7:5

Moore, Lee

King of the Turf 1939,My 8,21:2
Gracie Allen Murder Case, The 1939,Je 8,31:3

Moore, Lela

Night at Earl Carroll's, A 1941,Ja 23,19:1

Moore, M

King of Kings, The 1927,Ap 20,29:2

Moore, Margo

Wake Me When It's Over 1960,Ap 9,17:2
Bachelor Flat 1962,Ja 13,14:1
George Raft Story, The 1962,Mr 22,40:1

Moore, Marjorie

Wine, Women and Song 1934,Mr 21,24:3

Moore, Mary Tyler

X-15 1962,Ap 5,30:2
Thoroughly Modern Millie 1967,Mr 23,25:1
What's so bad About Feeling Good?
1968,My 25,27:1
Don't Just Stand There 1968,S 3,54:2

Moore, Matt

Unpardonable Sin, The 1919,My 3,11:3
Sahara 1919,Je 30,16:3
Regular Girl, A 1919,N 11,13:3
Don't Ever Marry 1920,Ap 19,13:3
Hairpins 1920,Ag 2,12:2
Passionate Pilgrim, The 1921,Ja 3,20:2
Man's Home, A 1921,D 19,13:1
Back Pay 1922,F 13,10:1
Sisters 1922,Ap 4,15:3
Drifting 1923,Ag 20,4:2
Strangers of the Night 1923,O 8,20:1
Fools in the Dark 1924,Ag 18,8:2
Narrow Street, The 1925,Ja 5,19:1
Lost Lady, A 1925,Ja 19,14:1
Way of a Girl, The 1925,Mr 30,21:3
How Baxter Buttered In 1925,Je 23,24:3
Grounds for Divorce 1925,Je 29,8:2
Unholy Three, The 1925,Ag 4,14:3
His Majesty Bunker Bean 1925,S 15,12:1
Cave Man, The 1926,Mr 1,17:1
First Year, The 1926,Mr 8,17:1
Diplomacy 1926,S 13,18:1
Summer Bachelors 1926,D 20,28:3
Tillie the Toiler 1927,Je 7,27:4
Beware of Blondes 1928,Ag 21,27:4
Dry Martini 1928,N 5,26:5 (In Addenda)
Coquette 1929,Ap 6,14:4 (In Addenda)
Side Street 1929,S 9,30:2
Call of the West 1930,My 27,27:2
Squealer, The 1930,S 8,17:1
Front Page, The 1931,Mr 20,29:1
Penrod and Sam 1931,S 26,25:3
Consolation Marriage 1931,O 30,26:4
Cock of the Air 1932,Ja 25,20:3
Rain 1932,O 13,22:3
Big Pay-Off, The 1933,Ja 17,22:7
Deluge 1933,O 9,22:3
Anything Goes 1936,F 6,23:3
Absolute Quiet 1936,My 2,11:1
My Life With Caroline 1941,O 30,27:1
Hoodlum Saint, The 1946,Je 27,29:1
Good Sam 1948,S 17,28:2
Big Hangover, The 1950,My 26,20:3
Invitation 1952,Ja 30,22:6
Affair to Remember, An 1957,Jl 20,8:5

Moore, McElbert (Miscellaneous)

There's a Girl in my Heart 1950,Ja 20,29:2

Moore, Michael

Atomic City, The 1952,My 2,21:1
Pony Express 1953,Je 6,8:6
Stalag 17 1953,Jl 2,19:2
Little Boy Lost 1953,S 22,38:2
Sabre Jet 1953,N 3,34:1
Othello 1960,My 16,39:1

Moore, Michael (Director)

Paradise, Hawaiian Style 1966,Je 16,15:3
Kill a Dragon 1967,D 7,60:2
Fastest Guitar Alive, The 1968,F 15,47:1

Moore, Mickey

Oytherea 1924,My 26,21:1

Moore, Milton (Cinematographer)

Great Air Robbery, The 1920,F 16,8:1

Moore, Norma

Fear Strikes Out 1957,Mr 21,37:2

Moore, Olga (Original Author)

You Can't Beat Love 1937,Je 25,25:3

Moore, Owen

Little Meena's Romance 1916,Ap 3,11:4
Under Cover 1916,Jl 24,7:4
Crimson Gardenia, The 1919,Je 16,11:2
Reported Missing 1922,Ap 24,18:3
Hollywood 1923,Jl 30,11:4
Silent Partner, The 1923,Ag 20,4:2
Her Temporary Husband 1924,Ja 1,20:1
East of Broadway 1924,N 12,13:1
Parasite, The 1925,F 16,24:1
Code of the West 1925,Ap 13,24:1
Go Straight 1925,O 6,30:1
Skyrocket, The 1926,Ja 26,25:2
Black Bird, The 1926,F 1,16:1
Money Talks 1926,My 11,24:3
Road to Mandalay, The 1926,Je 29,21:2
Red Mill, The 1927,F 14,15:1
Taxi Dancer, The 1927,Mr 8,18:4
Tea For Three 1927,O 31,22:1
Actress, The 1928,Jl 9,25:1
Side Street 1929,S 9,30:2
Outside the Law 1930,S 1,16:1
What a Widow 1930,O 4,15:2
Extravagance 1930,D 9,31:3
Hush Money 1931,Jl 11,7:6
As You Desire Me 1932,Je 3,23:4
She Done Him Wrong 1933,F 10,12:3
Star Is Born, A 1937,Ap 23,25:1

Moore, Pat

Fires of Faith 1919,My 6,16:2
Sahara 1919,Je 30,16:3
Queen of Sheba 1921,Ap 11,9:1
Village Blacksmith, The 1922,N 3,17:5
Young Rajah, The 1922,N 6,13:1
Stephen Steps Out 1923,N 19,19:3
Broken Laws 1925,Ja 21,19:3

Moore, Pauline

Love Is News 1937,Mr 6,10:1
Charlie Chan at the Olympics 1937,My 24,23:1
Born Reckless 1937,Jl 30,22:6
Wild and Woolly 1937,S 6,20:1
Heidi 1937,N 6,14:2
Three Blind Mice 1938,Je 18,18:2
Passport Husband 1938,Ag 5,11:2
Five of a Kind 1938,O 31,12:2
Three Musketeers, The 1939,F 18,12:2
Charlie Chan in Reno 1939,My 31,27:2
Young Mr Lincoln 1939,Je 3,11:2
Charlie Chan at Treasure Island 1939,S 1,15:5

Moore, Percy

Shock Punch, The 1925,My 11,14:3

Moore, Peter

Invaders, The 1942,Mr 6,17:1

Moore, Peter (Producer)

Stranger's Hand, The 1955,F 16,24:5

Moore, Robin (Original Author)

Green Berets, The 1968,Je 20,49:1

Moore, Roger

Fuller Brush Man, The 1948,My 15,18:2
Last Time I saw Paris, The 1954,N 19,20:2
Interrupted Melody 1955,My 6,18:1
King's Thief, The 1955,Ag 13,7:2
Diane 1956,Ja 13,18:1
Miracle, The 1959,N 13,25:4
Sins of Rachel Cade, The 1961,Ap 6,30:3
Gold of the Seven Saints 1961,Ap 6,30:3

Moore, Ruth (Original Author)

Deep Waters 1948,Jl 23,12:4

Moore, Samuel Taylor (Miscellaneous)

Dead March, The 1937,S 20,19:1 (In Addenda)

Moore, Scott

Struggle, The 1931,D 11,35:1

Moore, Stella

Unfaithful 1931,Mr 7,17:2
Once a Lady 1931,N 9,22:4

Moore, Stephen

Midsummer Night's Dream, A 1961,D 19,39:1

Moore, Sue

Swing Your Lady 1938,Ja 27,17:2

Moore, Terrence

Ten Commandments, The 1923,D 22,8:1
Lover of Camille, The 1924,N 11,14:1

Moore, Terry

Safe at Home 1941,N 26,31:2
Return of October, The 1949,F 23,31:2
Mighty Joe Young 1949,Jl 28,19:3
Great Rupert, The 1950,Ap 14,27:2
He's a Cockeyed Wonder 1950,O 20,32:4
Gambling House 1951,Mr 19,23:2
Two of a Kind 1951,Je 30,8:6
Come Back, Little Sheba 1952,D 24,13:2 (In Addenda)
Man on a Tightrope 1953,Je 5,19:1
Beneath the 12-Mile Reef 1953,D 17,52:2
King of the Khyber Rifles 1953,D 23,21:1
Daddy Long Legs 1955,My 6,17:5
Shack out on 101 1956,Ja 10,26:2
Between Heaven and Hell 1956,O 12,33:2
Bernardine 1957,Jl 25,28:1
Peyton Place 1957,D 13,35:1

Moore, Terry — Cont

Private's Affair, A 1959,Ag 15,8:7
Platinum High School 1960,My 26,37:3
Why Must I Die? 1960,S 15,45:4
Black Spurs 1965,My 29,17:1

Moore, Tom

Kingdom of Youth, The 1918,O 7,11:3
Thirty a Week 1918,O 14,15:1
Man and his Money, A 1919,Ap 14,11:4
One of the Finest 1919,Je 2,20:4
City of Comrades, The 1919,Jl 14,12:2
Heartsease 1919,Ag 25,8:5
Lord and Lady Algy 1919,S 29,16:1
Toby's Bow 1919,D 15,20:1
Marriage Morals 1923,Ag 14,10:3
Big Brother 1923,D 24,12:1 (In Addenda)
Manhandled 1924,Jl 29,9:2
Dangerous Money 1924,O 14,21:5
On Thin Ice 1925,Mr 9,21:1
Adventure 1925,Ap 15,16:1
Pretty Ladies 1925,Jl 14,14:1
Under the Rouge 1925,Jl 22,14:4
Trouble With Wives 1925,Ag 5,12:4
Kiss for Cinderella, A 1925,D 26,11:2
Song and Dance Man, The 1926,F 1,16:1
Good and Naughty 1926,Je 14,24:1
Syncopating Sue 1926,N 2,35:1
Cabaret 1927,My 2,26:4
Love Thrill, The 1927,My 10,24:5
Wise Wife 1927,N 1,21:1 (In Addenda)
Side Street 1929,S 9,30:2
Costello Case, The 1930,N 4,36:1
Last Parade, The 1931,Mr 2,19:1
Trouble for Two 1936,My 30,7:2
Reunion 1936,N 27,27:1
Scudda-Hoo! Scudda-Hay! 1948,Ap 15,31:1
Fighting O'Flynn, The 1949,F 28,16:2
Redhead and the Cowboy, The 1951,Je 6,37:2

Moore, Vernetties

Betrayal, The 1948,Je 26,10:5

Moore, Victor

Chimmie Fadden Out West 1915,N 22,12:3
Clown, The 1916,Je 19,9:5 (In Addenda)
Man Who Found Himself, The 1925,Ag 24,17:3
Dangerous Nan McGrew 1930,Je 21,20:5
Heads Up 1930,O 13,31:1
Romance in the Rain 1934,S 8,18:5
Gift of Gab 1934,S 26,17:6
Swing Time 1936,Ag 28,21:2
Gold Diggers of 1937 1936,D 25,19:2
We're on the Jury 1937,F 10,18:5
Make Way for Tomorrow 1937,My 10,23:1
Meet the Missus 1937,Jl 2,25:2
Life of the Party, The 1937,O 4,17:1
She's Got Everything 1938,Ja 14,21:3
Radio City Revels 1938,Mr 21,18:3
Louisiana Purchase 1942,Ja 1,37:1
Star Spangled Rhythm 1942,D 31,20:1
True to Life 1943,O 14,26:1
Heat's on, The 1943,N 26,29:2
Riding High 1943,D 23,26:4
Carolina Blues 1944,D 8,26:6
It's in the Bag 1945,Je 11,12:1
Duffy's Tavern 1945,S 6,23:3
Ziegfeld Follies 1946,Mr 23,8:3
It Happened on Fifth Avenue 1947,Je 11,33:2
Miracle Can Happen, A 1948,F 4,28:4
Kiss in the Dark, A 1949,Mr 26,10:6
We're not Married 1952,Jl 12,16:2
Seven Year Itch, The 1955,Je 4,9:1

Moore, Vin (Director)

Virtuous Husband 1931,My 8,30:2

Moore, Viola

Thunder Birds 1942,O 29,19:2

Moore, Willfred G (Original Author)

Sky Parade, The 1936,Ap 20,17:1

Moore, William

Love Takes Flight 1937,S 27,24:3
International Crime 1938,My 16,14:4
Mutiny on the Blackhawk 1939,Ag 2,17:2

Moorefield, Olive

Montpi 1959,Ap 21,40:1

Moorehead, Agnes

Citizen Kane 1941,My 2,25:1
Magnificent Ambersons, The 1942,Ag 14,13:3
Big Street, The 1942,Ag 14,13:1
Journey Into Fear 1943,Mr 19,15:3
Youngest Profession, The 1943,Je 25,13:3
Government Girl 1944,Ja 7,13:2
Jane Eyre 1944,F 4,12:5
Since You Went Away 1944,Jl 21,16:2
Dragon Seed 1944,Jl 21,16:4
Seventh Cross, The 1944,S 29,18:1
Mrs Parkington 1944,O 13,16:1
Tomorrow the World 1944,D 22,12:4
Keep Your Powder Dry 1945,Mr 12,22:6
Our Vines Have Tender Grapes 1945,S 7,21:2
Her Highness and the Bellboy 1945,S 28,16:2
Dark Passage 1947,S 6,11:2
Lost Moment, The 1947,N 22,10:2
Woman in White, The 1948,My 8,12:2
Summer Holiday 1948,Je 12,8:5
Johnny Belinda 1948,O 2,11:2
Stratton Story, The 1949,My 13,29:1

Moorehead, Agnes— Cont

Great Sinner, The 1949,Je 30,19:2
Caged 1950,My 20,8:6
Without Honor 1950,Jl 3,9:2
Fourteen Hours 1951,Mr 7,43:2
Show Boat 1951,Jl 20,14:1
Adventures of Captain Fabian 1951,D 14,36:2
Captain Black Jack 1952,O 22,31:3
Story of Three Loves, The (The Jealous Lover);
    Jealous Lover, The (The Story of Three Loves)
    1953,Mr 6,29:2
Scandal at Scourie 1953,Je 16,24:2
Those Redheads From Seattle 1953,O 1,34:2
Main Street to Broadway 1953,O 14,34:1
Magnificent Obsession 1954,Ag 5,18:4
Untamed 1955,Mr 12,11:6
Left Hand of God, The 1955,S 22,34:5
All That Heaven Allows 1956,F 29,35:1
Meet Me in Las Vegas 1956,Mr 14,39:2
Conqueror, The 1956,Mr 31,13:3
Swan, The 1956,Ap 27,21:5
Revolt of Mamie Stover, The 1956,My 12,12:7
Pardners 1956,Jl 26,20:2
Opposite Sex, The 1956,N 16,23:2
True Story of Jesse James, The 1957,Mr 23,17:2
Jeanne Eagels 1957,Ag 31,19:1
Story of Mankind, The 1957,N 9,31:2
Raintree County 1957,D 21,22:1
Night of the Quarter Moon 1959,Mr 5,35:5
Tempest 1959,Mr 27,19:2
Bat, The 1959,D 17,51:4
Pollyanna 1960,My 20,26:1
Bachelor in Paradise 1961,N 17,41:2
Jessica 1962,Ap 20,20:2
How the West Was Won 1963,Ap 1,54:1
Who's Minding the Store? 1963,N 29,67:6
    (Incorrect in this edition; use 1963,N 28,67:6
    elsewhere)
Hush...Hush, Sweet Charlotte 1965,Mr 4,36:1
Singing Nun, The 1966,Mr 18,33:1

Moorehead, Alan (Original Author)
Thunder in the East 1953,F 4,32:2

Moorehouse, Marie
Old Nest, The 1921,Je 29,10:3

MOORHEAD
See Also MOREHEAD

Moorhead, Jean
Amazing Colossal Man, The 1957,O 26,19:2

Moorhead, Natalie
Thru Different Eyes 1929,Ap 15,22:6
Girl from Havana, The 1929,S 2,16:1
Unholy Night, The 1929,O 12,11:1
Benson Murder Case, The 1930,Ap 12,23:1
Furies, The 1930,Ap 19,15:1
Runaway Bride 1930,My 17,21:2
Shadow of the Law 1930,Je 7,10:4
Manslaughter 1930,Jl 24,26:4
Office Wife, The 1930,S 27,21:3
Hook, Line and Sinker 1930,D 25,31:5
Illicit 1931,Ja 19,25:1
My Past 1931,Mr 12,22:7
Dance, Fools, Dance 1931,Mr 21,15:1
Divorce Among Friends 1931,Ap 2,30:4
Parlor, Bedroom and Bath 1931,Ap 4,23:1
Captain Thunder 1931,My 11,15:4
Women Men Marry 1931,Jl 13,13:5
Strictly Dishonorable 1931,N 11,27:1
Phantom of Paris, The 1931,N 14,15:3
Morals for Women 1931,N 16,23:1
Deceiver, The 1931,N 23,22:1
Maker of Men 1931,D 19,16:4
Menace, The 1932,Ja 30,13:2
Three Wise Girls 1932,F 6,14:4
Cross Examination 1932,F 27,22:1
Stoker, The 1932,Jl 16,5:5
Mind Reader, The 1933,Ap 7,22:4
Corruption 1933,Je 20,22:7
Private Detective 62 1933,Jl 7,20:2
Only Yesterday 1933,N 10,25:1
Thin Man, The 1934,Je 30,18:5
Dancing Man 1934,Jl 16,11:3
Torchy Blane, The Adventurous Blonde
    1937,D 18,18:1
Heart of Arizona 1938,Ap 16,17:1
Beloved Brat 1938,My 2,13:2
Lady of the Tropics 1939,S 8,28:3
Flight Angels 1940,My 27,23:2

Moorse, George
Zero in the Universe 1966,O 12,36:3

Moorse, George (Director)
Zero in the Universe 1966,O 12,36:3

Moorse, George (Screenwriter)
Zero in the Universe 1966,O 12,36:3

Moorwood, Teddy
My Son, My Son! 1940,My 10,26:6

Mora, Bradley
Cause for Alarm 1951,Mr 30,28:5

Mora, Margarita
Alma Jarocha 1938,Ap 30,18:2
Cementario de las Aquilas, El; Eagles' Cementery,
    The 1939,S 2,20:1
Capitan Aventurero, El; Adventureous Captain,
    The 1939,O 3,19:5
Life of Simon Bolivar, The 1943,Je 18,16:5

Tierra de Pasiones 1944,N 7,24:3

Morahan, T H (Producer)
Circle of Deception 1961,F 18,12:2

Moraine, Lyle
China Clipper 1936,Ag 12,14:3
Midnight Court 1937,Mr 4,27:3
Federal Bullets 1937,D 27,11:1
Port of Missing Girls, The 1938,Ap 4,12:5

Morales, Carmen
Primrose Path 1940,Mr 23,16:2
Long Voyage Home, The 1940,O 9,30:2 (In
    Addenda)
Ladies' Day 1943,Mr 26,14:3

Morales, Esy
Criss Cross 1949,Mr 12,10:2

Morales, Jose Diaz (Director)
Loyola, The Soldier Saint 1952,Ap 25,19:2

Morales, Luisa Maria
Madre Querida 1935,D 23,15:5

Morales, Robert A (Producer)
Novillero 1939,Mr 4,18:5

Morales, Robert A (Screenwriter)
Alla en el Rancho Chico; Out on the Little Ranch
    1939,F 25,19:3

MORAN
See Also MORIN, MARAN, MARIN

Moran, Baby
Toll of the Sea, The 1922,N 27,18:1

Moran, Betty
Seventeen 1940,F 29,15:2

Moran, Dolores
Old Acquaintance 1943,N 3,20:2
To Have and Have Not 1944,O 12,24:1
Hollywood Canteen 1944,D 16,19:2
Horn Blows at Midnight, The 1945,Ap 21,18:2
Too Young to Know 1945,D 8,21:2
Man I Love, The 1947,Ja 25,12:2
Christmas Eve 1947,N 28,30:2
Johnny One-Eye 1950,N 17,31:2
Count the Hours 1953,Je 24,30:4
Silver Lode 1954,Jl 24,6:6

Moran, E Edwin (Screenwriter)
Powers Girl, The 1943,Mr 26,14:2 (In Addenda)

Moran, Eddie
Treasure Island 1950,Ag 16,24:2

Moran, Eddie (Screenwriter)
Merrily We Live 1938,Mr 18,23:3
There Goes my Heart 1938,O 14,27:1
Topper Takes a Trip 1938,D 30,11:2
Twin Beds 1942,My 1,23:4
Wintertime 1943,S 30,27:2
Wonder Man 1945,Je 9,17:2
Hold That Blonde 1945,N 8,17:2

Moran, Frank
Sailor's Luck 1933,Mr 17,21:2
No More Women 1934,Mr 15,27:4
World Moves On, The 1934,Je 30,18:5
Battle of Broadway 1938,Ap 25,19:2
Date With the Falcon, A 1941,N 25,33:2
Sullivan's Travels 1942,Ja 29,25:2
Butch Minds the Baby 1942,My 1,23:3
Miracle of Morgan's Creek, The 1944,Ja 20,15:2
Great Moment, The 1944,N 13,15:2
Miracle Can Happen, A 1948,F 4,28:4
Mad Wednesday 1951,Ja 25,21:5

Moran, George
Why Bring That Up? 1929,O 5,22:5
Hypnotized 1933,Ja 16,13:3
My Little Chickadee 1940,Mr 16,8:2
Bank Dick, The 1940,D 13,29:2

Moran, H W (Original Author)
Secret Service of the Air 1939,Mr 2,19:2

Moran, Jackie
And So They Were Married 1936,My 14,29:3
Valiant Is the Word for Carrie 1936,O 8,27:2
Outcast 1937,Mr 3,27:2
Adventures of Tom Sawyer, The 1938,F 18,23:1
Mad About Music 1938,Mr 12,13:2
Arson Racket Squad 1938,Je 18,18:2
Mother Carey's Chickens 1938,Ag 5,11:1
Spirit of Culver 1939,Mr 9,18:1
Meet Doctor Christian 1939,D 1,27:2
Anne of Windy Poplars 1940,Ag 23,13:3
Song of the Open Road 1944,Je 7,13:3
Since You Went Away 1944,Jl 21,16:2
Janie 1944,Ag 5,16:2

Moran, Jim
Specter of the Rose 1946,S 2,12:4

Moran, John E (Screenwriter)
Good Morning and Goodbye! 1968,F 20,53:1

Moran, Lee
Fast Worker, The 1924,N 12,13:1
Fifth Avenue Models 1925,My 4,16:2
After Business Hour 1925,Je 17,16:2
Where Was I 1925,Ag 19,14:4
Little Irish Girl, The 1926,My 11,24:3
Her big Night 1926,O 13,21:1
Syncopating Sue 1926,N 2,35:1
Take It From Me 1926,N 2,35:1
Wolf's Clothing 1927,Mr 28,26:4
Fast and Furious 1927,Ap 4,20:3
Spring Fever 1927,O 18,33:2
Irresistible Lover, The 1927,O 19,24:4

Moran, Lee— Cont

Thanks For The Buggy Ride 1928,Ja 23,18:3
Actress, The 1928,Jl 9,25:1
Racket, The 1928,Jl 9,25:1
Ladies of the Night Club 1928,Jl 17,15:3
Show Girl 1928,N 5,26:1
Outcast 1928,N 26,30:2
On With the Show 1929,My 29,28:6
Madonna of Avenue A 1929,Ag 12,22:2
Gold Diggers of Broadway, The 1929,Ag 31,13:4
Show of Shows 1929,N 21,24:5
Dance Hall 1929,D 16,34:2
Aviator, The 1930,Ja 11,21:3
Hide Out 1930,Ap 12,23:1
Sweet Mamma 1930,Jl 12,16:4
Golden Dawn 1930,Jl 26,16:4
Soldiers Plaything, A 1931,My 2,23:4
Uptown New York 1932,D 10,19:3
Death Kiss, The 1933,F 5,IX,5:3
Grand Slam 1933,F 22,25:2
Racetrack 1933,Mr 6,16:6
High Gear 1933,Ap 15,16:2
Goldie Gets Along 1933,Je 3,16:4

Moran, Lois
Stella Dallas 1925,N 17,30:2
Just Suppose 1926,Ja 18,26:2
Reckless Lady, The 1926,Ja 25,21:2
Road to Mandalay, The 1926,Je 29,21:2
Padlocked 1926,Ag 2,21:2
Prince of Tempters, The 1926,O 18,18:1
God Gave Me Twenty Cents 1926,N 20,3:2
Music Master, The 1927,Ja 17,12:4 (In Addenda)
Living Dead Man, The 1927,Mr 7,16:3
Whirlwind of Youth, The 1927,Je 6,27:2
Irresistible Lover, The 1927,O 19,24:4
Publicity Madness 1927,D 12,30:6
Sharp Shooters 1928,Ja 23,18:3
Love Hungry 1928,Ap 16,20:5
Don't Marry 1928,My 21,25:1
River Pirate, The 1928,S 17,27:1
True Heaven 1929,F 11,26:3
Behind That Curtain 1929,Jl 1,31:2
Mammy 1930,Mr 27,24:5
Not Damaged 1930,Je 9,23:3
Dancers, The 1930,N 15,15:3
Transatlantic 1931,Jl 31,15:2
Spider, The 1931,S 5,7:4
Men in her Life 1931,N 30,16:2

Moran, Manolo
Don Quixote 1949,My 13,29:3

Moran, Manuel
Goyescas 1944,My 29,18:3

Moran, Peggy
Girls' School 1938,N 3,27:1
Big Guy, The 1940,Ja 1,29:2
West of Carson City 1940,My 7,31:3
Alias the Deacon 1940,My 14,27:5
Hot Steel 1940,Je 21,25:3
Mummy's Hand, The 1940,S 20,27:2
Spring Parade 1940,O 4,29:2
Argentine Nights 1940,O 11,25:3
Slightly Tempted 1940,N 1,33:1
Trail of the Vigilantes 1940,D 7,13:2
One Night in the Tropics 1940,D 20,33:2
Horror Island 1941,Mr 31,11:3
Flying Cadets 1941,O 14,29:2
Treat 'Em Rough 1942,Ja 19,21:3
Drums of the Congo 1942,Jl 20,16:4
Seven Sweethearts 1942,N 13,28:1

Moran, Polly
Callahans and the Murphys, The 1927,Jl 12,29:3
Thirteenth Hour, The 1927,N 28,18:5
Enemy, The 1927,D 28,26:6
London After Midnight 1927,D 31,31:1
Divine Woman, The 1928,Ja 16,24:1
Rose-Marie 1928,F 13,16:2
Bringing Up Father 1928,Mr 19,26:2
Telling the World 1928,Jl 16,25:3
While the City Sleeps 1928,O 22,29:1
Show People 1928,N 12,18:2
Hollywood Revue, The 1929,Ag 15,20:5
Speedway 1929,S 21,17:1
Unholy Night, The 1929,O 12,11:1
So This Is College 1929,N 9,22:5
Hot for Paris 1930,Ja 4,21:1
Chasing Rainbows 1930,F 22,13:1
Girl Said No, The 1930,Ap 5,23:3
Caught Short 1930,Je 21,20:5
Way out West 1930,Ag 18,24:1
Remote Control 1930,D 8,26:1
Way for a Sailor 1930,D 13,22:2
Reducing 1931,Ja 17,23:1
It's a Wise Child 1931,My 16,13:3
Politics 1931,Ag 1,16:4
Guilty Hands 1931,Ag 29,16:3
Passionate Plumber, The 1932,Mr 12,19:5
Prosperity 1932,N 26,11:4
Alice in Wonderland 1933,D 23,19:1
Hollywood Party 1934,My 26,12:2
Down to Their Last Yacht 1934,S 24,14:1
Tom Brown's School Days 1940,Je 28,22:2
Adam's Rib 1949,D 26,33:2
Yellow Cab Man, The 1950,Mr 27,19:2
Show People 1967,O 2,58:2

Moran, Priscilla
Daddies 1924,F 11,18:3
Love and Glory 1924,Ag 5,10:2
Up the Ladder 1925,My 12,26:2
Hold 'Em Navy 1937,N 6,14:2
Moran, William
Drifting 1923,Ag 20,4:2
Dramatic Life of Abraham Lincoln, The
1924,Ja 22,17:3
Beloved Brute, The 1924,N 10,20:1
Moran and Mack
Anybody's War 1930,Jl 11,22:1
Morand, Paul (Composer)
Don Quixote 1934,D 24,17:1
Morand, Paul (Original Author)
Open all Night 1924,S 9,19:1
Ballerina 1938,N 15,27:1
Unfinished Dance, The 1947,O 31,29:2
Morandi, Fernando (Original Author)
Big Gundown, The 1968,Ag 23,33:1
Morandini, Morando
Before the Revolution; Prima della Revolutiona
1964,S 25,32:1
Morane, Jacqueline
Gervaise 1957,N 12,46:1
Picnic on the Grass 1960,O 12,47:1
Morant, Frederick
No Room at the Inn 1949,D 26,33:4
Morante, Elsa (Original Author)
Arturo Island 1962,D 22,5:2
Morante, Giacomo
Gospel According to St Matthew, The
1966,F 18,23:1
Morante, Marcello
Gospel According to St Matthew, The
1966,F 18,23:1
Moranti, Milburn
Lost City, The 1935,F 21,23:3
Morasi
Scarlet Spear, The 1954,Ap 10,11:4
Morassi, Mauro (Director)
Successo, Il 1965,Ap 29,40:2
Morat, Bibi
Love and the Frenchwoman; (Francaise et
l'Amour, La) 1961,F 28,38:2
Moravia, Alberto (Miscellaneous)
Wild Eye, The 1968,Ag 22,47:1
Moravia, Alberto (Original Author)
Wayward Wife, The 1955,Ap 11,29:3
Too Bad She's Bad 1955,D 26,23:2
Woman of Rome 1956,N 6,30:1
Two Women; (Ciociara, La) 1961,My 9,43:2
From a Roman Balcony 1961,O 16,33:5
Empty Canvas, The 1964,My 16,21:1 (Incorrect
in this edition; use 1964,My 16,12:1 elsewhere)
Contempt 1964,D 19,25:2
Time of Indifference 1965,O 13,50:1
Time of Indifference 1966,O 13,50:1
Moravia, Alberto (Screenwriter)
Lupa, La 1954,F 18,36:2
Sensualita 1954,Ap 29,40:2
Woman of Rome 1956,N 6,30:1
From a Roman Balcony 1961,O 16,33:5
Yesterday, Today, and Tomorrow (Part III-Mara
Rome); Mara Rome (Yesterday, Today and
Tomorrow) 1964,Mr 18,46:1
Yesterday, Today and Tomorrow (Part II-Anna
Milan); Anna Milan (Yesterday, Today and
Tomorrow) 1964,Mr 18,46:1
Yesterday, Today and Tomorrow (Part 1-Adelina
Naples); Adelina Naples (Yesterday, Today and
Tomorrow) 1964,Mr 18,46:1
Moravkova, Consuela
Joseph Kilian 1966,Jl 19,34:1
Moray, Antonio
Regina di Sparta, La 1931,F 23,20:3
Moray, Dean
Follow Me, Boys! 1966,D 2,46:1
Moray, Helga (Original Author)
Untamed 1955,Mr 12,11:6
Mordant, Edwin
Shadows Over Shanghai 1938,D 1,29:2
Mordente, Tony
West Side Story 1961,O 19,39:3
Mordero, Germaine
Three Feet in a Bed 1957,My 18,23:2
Mordvinov, Nikolai
Gypsies 1936,Jl 30,22:2
Masquerade 1943,My 17,11:2
Lad From our Town 1943,O 7,26:2
Horsemen, The 1951,Ja 29,14:5
Mordyukova, Nonna
Young Guard 1949,D 26,33:6
Home for Tanya, A 1961,Ag 14,28:5
Marriage of Baezaminov, The 1966,Je 11,20:2
MORE
See Also MOHO, MOORE
More, J Neil
Ghost Goes West, The 1936,Ja 11,9:2
More, Kenneth
Scott of the Antarctic 1951,F 26,20:2
Chance of a Lifetime 1951,Mr 15,37:2
No Highway in the Sky 1951,S 22,8:6

Clouded Yellow, The 1951,N 13,33:2
Galloping Major, The 1951,D 17,27:2
Island Rescue 1952,Jl 1,19:4
Brandy for the Parson 1952,Ag 18,13:4
Never Let Me Go 1953,Je 11,37:2
Genevieve 1954,F 16,30:2
Yellow Balloon, The 1954,O 13,28:2
Doctor in the House 1955,F 19,18:3
Adventures of Sadie, The 1955,My 18,35:2
Deep Blue Sea, The 1955,O 13,35:2
Reach for the Sky 1957,My 1,40:1
Raising a Riot 1957,My 8,44:1
Admirable Crichton, The 1957,D 15,45:4
(Incorrect in this edition; use 1957,D 17,45:4
elsewhere)
A Night to Remember 1958,D 17,2:7
Sheriff of Fractured Jaw, The 1959,Mr 14,27:4
Sink the Bismarck! 1960,F 12,22:3
Flame Over India 1960,Ap 30,14:1
Next to no Time 1960,My 28,13:2
39 Steps, The 1960,O 11,55:2
Man in the Moon 1961,Je 13,29:2
Loss of Innocence 1961,N 22,27:1
Longest Day, The 1962,O 5,28:1
Dark of the Sun 1968,Jl 4,13:1
More, Kenneth (Narrator)
Man Who Loved Redheads, The 1955,Jl 26,29:2
Morean, Richard F (Narrator)
Mating Urge, The 1960,Ja 18,30:2
Moreau, Emile (Original Author)
Madame Sans Gene 1925,Ap 18,19:1
Madame 1963,Mr 21,8:6
Moreau, Jeanne
Three Sinners 1952,Jl 8,23:2
Bed, The (The Billet); Billet, The (The Bed)
1955,Je 8,26:4
Inside a Girls' Dormitory 1956,F 6,27:7
Doctors, The 1956,Ag 7,19:2
Julietta 1957,Je 18,38:2
Demoniaque 1958,Mr 4,34:5
Grisbi 1959,Jl 13,23:1
Back to the Wall; (Dos au Mur) 1959,S 8,43:2
Lovers, The 1959,O 27,40:2
Five Branded Women 1960,Je 2,27:2
Frantic 1961,Je 12,34:1
Liaisons Dangereuses, Les 1961,D 19,39:1
Night, The; Notte, La 1962,F 20,29:4
Jules and Jim 1962,Ap 24,32:1
Trial, The 1963,F 21,5:1
Victors, The 1963,D 20,21:2
Moderato Cantabile 1964,Ja 7,24:1
Fire Within, The 1964,F 18,27:1
Diary of a Chambermaid; Journal d'une Femme de
Chambre, Le 1964,S 22,44:1
Bay of the Angels; Baie des Anges, La
1964,N 24,44:1
Banana Peel; Peau de Banane 1965,Ja 19,29:1
Train, The 1965,Mr 18,25:1
Yellow Rolls-Royce, The 1965,My 14,42:2
Eva 1965,Je 5,21:2
Viva Maria 1965,D 20,48:2
Mademoiselle 1966,Ag 2,23:1
Falstaff; Chimes at Midnight 1967,Mr 18,19:2
Sailor From Gibraltar, The 1967,Ap 25,38:2
Bride Wore Black, The 1968,Je 26,42:1
Immortal Story, The 1968,S 19,62:2
Oldest Profession, The (Mademoiselle Mimi);
Mademoiselle Mimi (The Oldest Profession)
1968,N 8,42:1
MOREHEAD
See Also MOORHEAD
Morehouse, Bert
You Said a Mouthful 1932,N 18,23:2
Morehouse, Ward (Original Author)
Gentlemen of the Press 1929,My 13,27:2
Big City Blues 1932,S 10,18:5
Central Park 1932,D 7,29:3
It Happened in New York 1935,Ap 6,10:1
MOREL
See Also MORELL, MORRELL
Morel
Francois Villon 1950,Jl 3,9:2
Morel, Dante V Capt
Big Lift, The 1950,Ap 27,37:2
Morel, Dene
Spy of Madame de Pompadour, The
1929,S 10,27:1
Morel, Genevieve
Man to Men 1949,F 21,20:2
Thirst of Men, The 1952,O 28,37:1
Dr Knock 1955,O 10,31:2
Morel, Gloria
Payasada de la Vida; Tricks of Life
1935,Mr 18,14:5
Que Hago con la Criatura? 1936,Mr 17,25:6
Rosario 1936,Ap 20,17:2
Don Juan Tenorio 1937,D 28,29:3
Suprema Ley; Supreme Law 1938,Ja 15,19:2
Huapango 1938,Je 11,9:1
Mientras Mexico Duerme; While Mexico Sleeps
1940,F 12,14:3
Reina del Rio, La; Queen of the River, The
1940,F 24,9:3

Morel, Hector
Mercedes 1935,My 14,17:5
Morel, Jacques
Between Eleven and Midnight 1950,F 23,33:3
Topaze 1952,O 28,37:1
Morel, Michel
Candlelight in Algeria 1944,Jl 31,10:2
Morel, Natasha
Adventure in Odessa 1954,Je 21,19:6
Moreland, Andria
Let's Face It 1943,Ag 5,18:1
Moreland, Mantan
Spirit of Youth 1938,F 28,19:1
Next Time I Marry 1938,D 2,27:2
Ellery Queen's Penthouse Mystery
1941,Mr 7,17:2
Treat 'Em Rough 1942,Ja 19,21:3
Strange Case of Dr Rx 1942,Mr 28,11:2
Mexican Spitfire Sees a Ghost 1942,Jl 31,11:2
Footlight Serenade 1942,S 10,30:3
Eyes in the Night 1942,O 16,23:1
Cabin in the Sky 1943,My 28,19:3
Sarong Girl 1943,Je 18,16:6
Bowery to Broadway 1944,N 30,19:2
Spider, The 1946,Je 21,20:3
MORELL
See Also MOREL, MORRELL
Morell, Andre
Missing Ten Days 1941,Ap 21,15:5 (In Addenda)
Stage Fright 1950,F 24,27:2
Madeleine 1950,S 1,17:2
Sanitorium 1950,O 11,42:1
Seven Days to Noon 1950,D 19,41:3
So Long at the Fair 1951,Ja 22,14:2
Clouded Yellow, The 1951,N 13,33:2
High Treason 1952,My 21,23:3
Frightened Bride, The 1953,Ag 20,18:5
His Majesty O'Keefe 1954,F 6,17:2
Black Knight, The 1954,O 29,27:2
Three Cases of Murder (Lord Mountdrago); Lord
Mountdrago (Three Cases of Murder)
1955,Mr 16,39:4
Summertime 1955,Je 22,25:1
Man Who Never Was, The 1956,Ap 4,24:1
Baby and the Battleship, The 1957,O 1,37:2
Bridge on the River Kwai 1957,D 19,39:1
Paris Holiday 1958,My 10,19:2
Camp on Blood Island, The 1958,S 18,37:2
Hounds of the Baskervilles, The 1959,Jl 4,9:4
Ben Hur 1959,N 19,50:2
Shadow of the Cat, The 1961,Je 8,40:2
Trouble in the Sky 1961,Jl 13,26:3
Cash on Demand 1962,My 17,31:1
She 1965,S 2,36:1
Judith 1966,Ja 21,22:1
Vengance of She, The 1968,My 30,21:4
Dark of the Sun 1968,Jl 4,13:1
Morell, George
Shot in the Dark, A 1935,My 22,23:2
Morell, Parker (Original Author)
Diamond Jim 1935,Ag 24,18:2
Morell, Sybil
Richthofhen: The Red Knight of the Air
1929,S 2,16:1
Morelli, Giuseppe (Composer)
Barber of Seville, The 1947,My 6,35:2
Love of a Clown (Pagliacci) 1950,Ap 17,18:5
Morelli, Rina
Avventura di Salvator Rosa, Un; Adventure of
Salvator Rosa, An 1940,S 20,27:3
Loves of Don Juan, The 1948,S 2,18:4
Iron Crown 1949,Je 11,11:2
Strange Deception 1953,My 27,28:2
Times Gone By (The Idyll); Idyll, The (Times
Gone By) 1953,D 30,16:2
Bell Antonio 1962,Ap 3,43:2
Leopard, The 1963,Ag 13,25:1
Morena, Antonio (Producer)
Amor con Amor se Paga; Love for Love
1940,Mr 16,8:2
Morena, Erna
Peak of Fate 1925,Je 13,10:5
Die vom Niederrhein; Lower Rhine Folks
1935,My 20,20:6
Zwichen Zwei Herzen; Between Two Hearts
1936,Ja 28,15:3
Moreno, Antonio
Lost and Found 1923,Mr 19,22:2
Trail of the Lonesome Pine, The 1923,Mr 20,24:3
Exciters, The 1923,Je 4,13:3
Spanish Dancer, The 1923,O 8,20:1
Flaming Barriers 1924,Ja 29,16:1
Bluff 1924,Ap 28,18:2
Tiger Love 1924,Je 16,18:3
Story Without a Name, The 1924,O 6,25:1
Learning to Love 1925,F 23,24:1
One Year to Live 1925,Jl 6,12:2
Mare Nostrum 1926,F 16,22:4
Beverly of Graustark 1926,Ap 19,24:3
Temptress, The 1926,O 11,18:1
Flaming Forest, The 1926,N 22,28:3
Venus of Venice 1927,My 3,25:1
Madame Pompadour 1927,Ag 2,19:2

Moreno, Antonio— Cont

Come to My House 1928,Ja 16,24:1
Whip Woman, The 1928,F 13,16:2
Midnight Taxi, The 1928,O 29,29:1
Air Legion, The 1928,N 13,37:1
Synthetic Sin 1929,Ja 7,36:2
Adoration 1929,Ja 14,20:1
Careers 1929,Je 10,23:1
Romance of Rio Grande 1929,N 9,22:5
Rough Romance 1930,Je 16,25:3
One mad Kiss 1930,Jl 19,7:5
Primavera en Otono 1933,My 18,17:3
El Precio de un Beso 1933,Jl 25,17:3
Ciudad de Carton, La 1934,F 28,23:3
Senor Casada Necesita Marido 1935,F 11,14:3
Asegure a su Mujer; Insure Your Wife
 1935,Mr 12,25:3
Rosa de Francia 1935,O 28,16:3
Bohemian Girl, The 1936,F 17,21:1
Rose of the Rio Grande 1938,Jl 9,10:3
Seven Sinners 1940,N 18,23:2
Kid From Kansas, The 1941,D 2,29:4
Valley of the Sun 1942,Mr 19,29:2
Spanish Main, The 1945,N 7,20:2
Captain from Castile 1947,D 26,22:4
Lust for Gold 1949,Jl 4,9:2
Crisis 1950,Jl 4,10:2
Dallas 1951,Ja 13,10:4
Mark of the Renegade 1951,S 7,24:2
Thunder Bay 1953,My 21,39:2
Wings of the Hawk 1953,Ag 27,22:1
Saskatchewan 1954,Mr 11,26:2
Creature from the Black Lagoon 1954,My 1,13:4
Searchers, The 1956,My 31,21:4

Moreno, Consuelo

Calvario de una Esposa, El 1936,S 26,11:2
Eterna Martir 1938,Ja 3,16:3
Derecho y el Deber, El 1938,Jl 9,10:4

Moreno, Dario

Female, The 1960,Ap 28,29:1
Come Dance With Me!; Voulez-Vous Danser Avec
 Moi 1960,N 8,32:6
Revolt of the Slaves, The 1961,N 8,41:1
Candide 1962,N 20,39:1
Hotel Paradiso 1966,O 15,34:2

Moreno, Hilda

Incertidumbre 1936,S 21,26:5
Podoroso Caballero 1936,O 26,20:2
My Outlaw Brother 1951,Ag 23,19:2

Moreno, Liza

Cry of Battle 1963,O 12,27:2

Moreno, Marguerite

Miche 1932,D 2,27:4
Mon Coeur Balance 1933,F 3,21:4
Chasseur de Chez Maxim's, Le 1935,F 4,11:4
Amphitryon 1937,Mr 24,29:1
Pearls of the Crown, The 1938,Ap 12,26:2
Story of a Cheat, The 1938,S 27,25:2
Nine Bachelors 1942,F 9,19:2
32 Rue de Montmartre 1944,S 28,26:3
Dame de Pique, La 1944,O 19,19:2
Ces Dames aux Chapeaux Verts; Ladies in the
 Green Hats, The 1945,Ap 5,26:2
Carmen 1946,N 27,20:2
Miserables, Les 1946,D 26,28:4
Lover's Return, A; Revenant, Le 1948,Ja 26,15:2
Idiot, The 1948,F 5,26:2
Chips Are Down, The 1949,F 2,36:1
Love Story 1949,Je 27,18:4
Naughty Martine 1953,Ap 13,32:4

Moreno, Mario

Wages of Fear, The 1955,F 17,23:1
Night Heaven Fell, The 1958,O 22,40:4

Moreno, Paco

Papa Soltero; Bachelor Father 1939,N 6,20:3

Moreno, Rita

Toast of New Orleans, The 1950,S 30,13:3
Pagan Love Song 1950,D 26,19:1
Singin' in the Rain 1952,Mr 28,27:2
Latin Lovers 1953,Ag 13,17:2
Jivaro 1954,F 13,11:5
Garden of Evil 1954,Jl 10,17:1
Untamed 1955,Mr 12,11:6
Seven Cities of Gold 1955,O 8,13:2
Lieutenant Wore Skirts, The 1956,Ja 12,22:1
King and I, The 1956,Je 29,15:6
Vagabond King, The 1956,S 13,39:6
This Rebel Breed 1960,My 5,41:2
West Side Story 1961,O 19,39:3
Summer and Smoke 1961,N 17,41:1
Cry of Battle 1963,O 12,27:2

Moreno, Robert (Miscellaneous)

Baboona 1935,Ja 23,21:2

Moreno, Rosita

Her Wedding Night 1930,S 29,19:1
Sante Fe Trail, The 1930,O 18,23:2
El Rey de los Gitanos 1933,My 29,22:2
 (Incorrect in this edition; use 1933,My 29,16:5
 elsewhere)
El Ultimo Varon Sobre la Tierra 1933,Je 12,20:4
El Principe Gondolero 1933,S 11,20:4
Gente Alegre 1933,S 19,26:4
Walls of Gold 1933,O 21,11:3
No Dejes la Puerta Abierta 1933,N 6,24:4

IO... TU... Y...; (I... Thou... and... She)
 1933,D 5,31:6
Ladies Should Listen 1934,Jl 28,16:6
Dos Mas Uno Dos 1934,O 27,20:3
Las Fronteras del Amor 1934,D 4,23:3
Scoundrel, The 1935,My 3,23:2
Tango-Bar 1935,Jl 6,16:3
Dia que me Quieras, El; Day You Love Me, The
 1935,Ag 27,23:3
Te Quiero con Locura; I'm Crazy About You
 1935,N 4,24:6
House of a Thousand Candles, The
 1936,Ap 2,29:2
Canillita y la Dama, El; Newsie and the Lady,
 The 1939,F 18,12:2
Medal for Benny, A 1945,My 24,15:2
So Young, So Bad 1950,Jl 24,15:2

Morens, Erna

Drei Kaiserjaeger 1935,Mr 16,19:1

Morera, Eduardo (Director)

Idolos de la Radio 1935,Jl 2,24:5
Buen Camino, Por 1936,Jl 4,18:3

Moret, Neil (Composer)

Young and Beautiful 1934,S 18,18:4
Mister Big 1943,Je 14,13:4

Moretti, Alfredo

Armata Azzurra, La; Blue Fleet, The
 1937,D 13,23:4

Moretti, Raoul (Composer)

Moulin Rouge 1944,N 23,38:2

Moretti, Raoul (Miscellaneous)

Il est Charmant; He is Charming
 1932,Mr 27,VIII,6:2
Il est Charmant 1932,Ap 9,18:1

Moretti, Ugo (Original Author)

Run With the Devil 1963,Jl 16,25:1

Moreuil, Francois (Director)

Playtime; Receation, La 1963,Ja 16,5:2

Moreuil, Francois (Screenwriter)

Playtime; Receation, La 1963,Ja 16,5:2

Morevsky, Joseph

Second Chorus 1941,Ja 16,25:2

Morewski, A

Al Khet; I Have Sinned 1937,S 9,19:2
Dybbuk, The 1938,Ja 28,17:2

Morey, Elaine

Moonlight in Hamaii 1941,O 10,26:6
Broadway 1942,Je 5,23:2
Pardon my Sarong 1942,Ag 27,15:1

Morey, Harry T

Courage of Silence, The 1917,Ja 29,11:2
Within the Law 1917,Ap 30,11:3
Man's Home, A 1921,D 19,13:1
Where the Pavement Ends 1923,Ap 2,22:1
Marriage Morals 1923,Ag 14,10:3
Green Goddess, The 1923,Ag 15,21:1
Captain January 1924,Jl 7,10:4
Roughneck, The 1924,D 3,14:1
Barriers Burned Away 1925,Mr 12,17:2
Heart of a Siren, The 1925,Ap 8,24:3
Aloma of the South Seas 1926,My 17,19:1
Return of Sherlock Holmes, The 1929,O 19,22:6

Morey, Larry (Composer)

Reluctant Dragon, The 1941,Jl 25,12:2

Morey, Larry (Miscellaneous)

Bambi 1942,Ag 14,13:1

Morey, Nicole

Why Bother to Knock 1965,F 4,24:2

Morey, Walt (Original Author)

Gentle Giant 1968,Ap 20,26:1

Morga, Russ

Mister Cory 1957,F 23,13:1

Morgan, Ainsworth (Original Author)

Man of Two Worlds 1934,Ja 12,29:2
South of Tahiti 1941,N 10,21:3

Morgan, Ainsworth (Screenwriter)

Gorgeous Hussy, The 1936,S 5,7:1
Espionage 1937,Mr 9,27:3

Morgan, Al (Original Author)

Great Man, The 1957,Ja 2,28:2

Morgan, Al (Screenwriter)

Great Man, The 1957,Ja 2,28:2

Morgan, Boyd

Violent Saturday 1955,My 12,32:2

Morgan, Bruce

Mystery Submarine 1951,F 2,19:2

Morgan, Byron (Original Author)

What's Your Hurry? 1920,Ag 16,8:2
Too Much Speed 1921,Je 6,16:4
Sporting Youth 1924,Ap 2,16:1
California Straight Ahead 1926,Ja 12,27:5
Man Power 1927,Jl 26,17:1
Smart Set, The 1928,Mr 5,21:1
Speedway 1929,S 21,17:1
It's a Great Life 1930,Ja 18,21:1
Sons of the Desert 1934,Ja 12,29:3
Band Plays on, The 1934,D 22,21:2
It's in the Air 1935,N 8,18:2

Morgan, Byron (Screenwriter)

Fascinating Youth 1926,My 10,19:1
Palm Beach Girl, The 1926,Jl 22,22:1
One Minute to Play 1926,S 6,16:2
Rookies 1927,Ap 25,20:4

Morgan, Byron (Screenwriter)— Cont

Flying Fleet, The 1929,F 11,26:3
Way out West 1930,Ag 18,24:1
Hell in the Heavens 1934,D 12,28:2
It's in the Air 1935,N 8,18:2
Sky Parade, The 1936,Ap 20,17:1
Wings for the Eagle 1942,Ag 1,14:2
Gallant Journey 1946,O 10,33:2

Morgan, Charles (Original Author)

Fountain, The 1934,Ag 31,14:1

Morgan, Claudia

Vanity Street 1932,O 15,13:1
Once in a Lifetime 1932,O 29,18:4
Stand up and Fight 1939,Ja 27,17:2

Morgan, Clive

Peter Ibbetson 1935,N 8,18:2
Booloo 1938,Jl 30,10:2
Rings on her Fingers 1942,Ap 24,21:4

Morgan, Dan

Charly 1968,S 24,55:1

Morgan, Dennis

Waterfront 1939,Jl 17,10:2
Return Of Doctor X, The 1939,N 23,38:5
Fighting 69th, The 1940,Ja 27,9:2
Three Cheers for the Irish 1940,Mr 9,19:2
Flight Angels 1940,My 27,23:2
Tear Gas Squad 1940,My 31,15:3
River's End 1940,Ag 26,11:4
Kitty Foyle 1941,Ja 9,27:2
Affectionaly Yours 1941,My 24,18:2
Bad Men of Missouri 1941,Ag 16,18:2
Captains of the Clouds 1942,F 13,24:2
In This our Life 1942,My 9,10:2
Wings for the Eagle 1942,Ag 1,14:2
Hard Way, The 1943,Mr 13,9:2
Thank Your Lucky Stars 1943,O 2,19:2
Desert Song, The 1943,D 18,10:6
Shine on Harvest Moon 1944,Mr 11,10:2
Very Thought of You, The 1944,N 18,16:7
Hollywood Canteen 1944,D 16,19:2
God is my Co-Pilot 1945,Mr 24,22:6
Christmas in Connecticut 1945,Jl 28,7:2
One More Tomorrow 1946,My 25,12:2
Two Guys From Milwaukee 1946,Jl 27,12:5
Time, The Place And The Girl, The
 1946,D 27,14:3
Cheyenne 1947,Je 7,9:2
My Wild Irish Rose 1947,D 25,32:2
To the Victor 1948,Ap 17,11:2
Two Guys From Texas 1948,Ag 28,8:6
One Sunday Afternoon 1948,D 27,16:3
It's a Great Feeling 1949,Ag 13,6:6
Lady Takes a Sailor, The 1949,D 17,15:2
Perfect Strangers 1950,Mr 11,8:2
Pretty Baby 1950,S 23,11:2
Raton Pass 1951,Ap 20,25:1
Painting the Clouds With Sunshine 1951,S 1,9:6
ThIs Woman is Dangerous 1952,F 28,23:2
Pearl of the South Pacific 1955,S 17,12:2

Morgan, Diana (Miscellaneous)

Run for Your Money, A 1950,Ap 10,15:3

Morgan, Diana (Screenwriter)

Ships With Wings 1942,My 25,11:2
48 Hours 1944,Je 26,21:2
Half-Way House 1945,Ag 13,22:4
Pink String and Sealing Wax 1950,O 4,38:2
Let's Be Happy 1957,My 25,25:1
Hand in Hand 1961,F 7,41:3

Morgan, Donald

Medium, The 1951,S 6,39:2

Morgan, Edward

Chances 1931,Je 12,27:1
Side Show 1931,S 19,10:2

Morgan, Eula

Great American Broadcast, The 1941,My 2,25:2
Song of Bernadette, The 1944,Ja 27,15:2
Oh, You Beautiful Doll 1949,N 12,8:4

Morgan, Frank

Manhandled 1924,Jl 29,9:2
Crowded Hour, The 1925,Ap 27,15:2
Man Who Found Himself, The 1925,Ag 24,17:3
Love's Greatest Mistake 1927,F 21,14:2
Dangerous Nan McGrew 1930,Je 21,20:5
Queen High 1930,Ag 9,16:5
Laughter 1930,N 15,15:3
Fast and Loose 1930,D 1,21:1
Secrets of the French Police 1932,D 12,18:4
Half-Naked Truth, The 1932,D 31,10:1
Billion Dollar Scandal, The 1933,Ja 9,23:1
Luxury Liner 1933,F 3,21:3
Hallelujah, I'm a Bum 1933,F 9,15:2
Reunion in Vienna 1933,Ap 29,14:2
Kiss Before the Mirror, The 1933,My 15,16:2
Nuisance, The 1933,My 29,22:2
When Ladies Meet 1933,Je 24,16:2
Best of Enemies 1933,Jl 17,19:5
Broadway to Hollywood 1933,S 2,14:4
Bombshell 1933,O 21,11:2
Cat and the Fiddle, The 1934,F 17,20:2
Success at any Price 1934,My 4,24:2
Sisters Under the Skin 1934,Je 8,18:1
Affairs of Cellini, The 1934,S 6,22:3
Lost Lady, A 1934,O 4,19:1
There's Always Tomorrow 1934,N 10,19:2

Morgan, Frank— Cont

Good Fairy, The 1935,F 1,18:1
Enchanted April 1935,Mr 9,19:1
Naughty Marietta 1935,Mr 23,11:2
Escapade 1935,Jl 6,16:2
I Live my Life 1935,O 12,12:2
Perfect Gentleman, The 1935,D 19,33:4
Great Ziegfeld, The 1936,Ap 9,21:2
Trouble for Two 1936,My 30,7:2
Dancing Pirate 1936,Je 18,19:1
Piccadilly Jim 1936,Ag 31,19:1
Dimples 1936,O 10,21:2
Last of Mrs Cheyney, The 1937,F 19,15:1
Emperor's Candlesticks, The 1937,Jl 9,18:1
Saratoga 1937,Jl 23,16:3
Beg, Borrow or Steal 1937,D 10,33:2
Rosalie 1937,D 31,9:2
Paradise for Three 1938,F 16,17:1
Port of Seven Seas 1938,Jl 15,13:2
Crowd Roars, The 1938,Ag 5,11:1
Sweethearts 1938,D 23,16:2
Broadway Serenade 1939,Ap 7,25:2
Wizard of Oz, The 1939,Ag 18,16:2
Balalaika 1939,D 15,33:2
Shop Around the Corner, The 1940,Ja 26,13:2
Broadway Melody of 1940 1940,Mr 29,25:3
Mortal Storm, The 1940,Je 21,25:2
Boom Town 1940,S 6,25:2
Hullabaloo 1940,D 19,33:1
Washington Melodrama 1941,My 26,15:3
Honky Tonk 1941,O 3,27:3
Tortilla Flat 1942,My 22,27:1
Vanishing Virginian, The 1942,My 28,13:3
White Cargo 1942,N 27,27:2
Night Monster 1942,N 30,18:5
Human Comedy, The 1943,Mr 3,19:2
Thousands Cheer 1943,S 14,27:1
White Cliffs of Dover, The 1944,My 12,15:2
Casanova Brown 1944,S 15,16:1
Yolanda and the Thief 1945,N 23,26:2
Courage of Lassie 1946,Jl 25,18:5
Cockeyed Miracle, The 1946,O 25,28:1
Lady Luck 1946,O 31,22:3
Green Dolphin Street 1947,O 16,34:2
Summer Holiday 1948,Je 12,8:5
Three Musketeers, The 1948,O 21,33:2
Stratton Story, The 1949,My 13,29:1
Great Sinner, The 1949,Je 30,19:2
Any Number Can Play 1949,Jl 1,14:4
Key to the City 1950,F 2,31:2

Morgan, Gary
Wait Until Dark 1967,O 27,48:1

Morgan, Gene
Night World 1932,My 28,18:2
Blonde Venus 1932,S 24,18:4
Song of the Eagle 1933,Ap 29,14:3
Elmer the Great 1933,My 26,24:2
If You Could Only Cook 1935,D 26,21:4
Music Goes 'Round, The 1936,F 22,12:1
You may Be Next 1936,F 24,14:1
Mr Deeds Goes to Town 1936,Ap 17,17:2
Panic on the Air 1936,Ap 20,17:1
Devil's Squadron 1936,My 11,16:2
Meet Nero Wolfe 1936,Jl 16,20:1
Counterfeit 1936,Jl 20,11:1
Shakedown 1936,Ag 17,9:2
Two-Fisted Gentleman 1936,Ag 24,11:2
Come Closer, Folks 1936,N 23,17:3
Lady From Nowhere 1936,D 21,19:2
Make Way for Tomorrow 1937,My 10,23:1
Counsel for Crime 1937,O 9,16:1
Murder in Greenwich Village 1937,O 30,22:2
When G-Men Step In 1938,Mr 14,13:2
Start Cheering 1938,Mr 17,17:3
Who Killed Gail Preston? 1938,My 6,27:2
Main Event, The 1938,Je 20,11:3
Federal Man-Hunt 1939,F 2,17:3
Homicide Bureau 1939,F 2,17:2
Housekeeper's Daughter, The 1939,D 2,21:4
Girl From God's Country 1940,S 9,18:5
Meet John Doe 1941,Mr 13,25:2

Morgan, George
Chafed Elbows 1967,Ja 5,30:1

Morgan, Guy (Original Author)
Devil's Plot 1953,Je 19,18:1

Morgan, Guy (Screenwriter)
Captive Heart, The 1947,Ap 28,27:2
Anna Karenina 1948,Ap 28,32:2
Her Panelled Door 1951,Ag 28,18:2
Front Page Story 1955,Ap 19,28:1
Eight O'Clock Walk 1955,Ap 30,10:6

Morgan, H A
Beggars of Life 1928,S 24,25:1
Rogue Song, The 1930,Ja 29,26:4

Morgan, Harry
Not as a Stranger 1955,Je 29,24:1
Backlash 1956,Ap 21,11:2
Inherit the Wind 1960,O 13,41:1
How the West Was Won 1963,Ap 1,54:1
John Goldfarb, Please Come Home
  1965,Mr 25,42:4
Frankie and Johnny 1966,Jl 21,20:2
What Did You Do in the War, Daddy?
  1966,S 1,28:1

Flim Flam Man, The 1967,Ag 23,40:1

Morgan, Harry Hays
My Name is Julia Ross 1945,N 9,16:3
Avalanche 1946,Jl 8,25:2
Abie's Irish Rose 1946,D 23,19:4

Morgan, Helen
Applause 1929,O 8,24:5
Roadhouse Nights 1930,F 22,13:1
Roadhouse Nights 1930,Mr 2,IX,5:1
You Belong to Me 1934,S 13,26:1
Marie Galante 1934,N 21,23:4
Sweet Music 1935,F 21,23:2
Go Into Your Dance 1935,My 4,17:2
Show Boat 1936,My 15,29:4
Frankie and Johnnie 1936,My 25,23:2
Applause 1967,O 2,58:2

Morgan, Henry
To the Shores of Tripoli 1942,Mr 26,27:2
Loves of Edgar Allan Poe, The 1942,S 21,19:2
Orchestra Wives 1942,S 24,23:2
Crash Dive 1943,Ap 29,25:2
Ox-Bow Incident, The 1943,My 10,15:2 (In
  Addenda)
Happy Land 1943,D 9,33:3
Eve of St Mark, The 1944,My 31,22:2
Roger Touhy, Gangster 1944,Je 5,14:7
Wing and a Prayer 1944,Ag 31,14:1
Gentle Annie 1945,My 5,11:5
Bell for Adano, A 1945,Jl 6,8:3
State Fair 1945,Ag 31,14:3
Dragonwyck 1946,Ap 11,35:2
From This Day Forward 1946,Ap 20,16:2
It Shouldn't Happen to a Dog 1946,S 7,11:2
Gangster, The 1947,O 31,29:3
All my Sons 1948,Mr 29,17:3
Big Clock, The 1948,Ap 22,34:2
Race Street 1948,Ag 23,13:3
Saxon Charm, The 1948,S 30,32:3
Yellow Sky 1949,F 2,36:1
Down to the Sea in Ships 1949,F 23,31:2
Moonrise 1949,Mr 7,17:2
Madame Bovary 1949,Ag 26,15:2
Strange Bargain 1949,S 30,28:3
Holiday Affair 1949,N 24,48:2
Red Light 1950,Ja 16,18:4
Outside the Wall 1950,Mr 15,34:8
Dark City 1950,O 19,40:5
Appointment With Danger 1951,My 10,38:2
Belle le Grand 1951,My 18,34:6
Well, The 1951,S 27,37:2
Blue Veil, The 1951,O 27,10:5
Scandal Sheet 1952,Ja 17,23:1
Boots Malone 1952,Mr 13,26:2
My Six Convicts 1952,Mr 28,27:3
Bend of the River 1952,Ap 10,37:1
High Noon 1952,Jl 25,14:2
What Price Glory 1952,Ag 23,10:2
Stop, You're Killing Me 1952,D 11,45:3
Thunder Bay 1953,My 21,39:2
Arena 1953,Jl 23,20:2
Torch Song 1953,O 13,34:2
Glenn Miller Story, the 1954,F 11,33:2
Prisoner of War 1954,My 10,20:2
About Mrs Leslie 1954,Je 28,16:2
Far Country, The 1955,F 14,24:2
Strategic Air Command 1955,Ap 21,33:1
Bottom of the Bottle, The 1956,F 2,19:2
It Started With a Kiss 1959,Ag 20,14:2
Murder, Inc 1960,Je 29,26:6
Mountain Road, The 1960,Je 30,22:3
Cimarron 1961,F 17,12:2

Morgan, Henry (Harry)
Teahouse of the August Moon, The
  1956,N 30,19:1

Morgan, Horace
Sherlock Jr 1924,My 26,21:1

Morgan, Jackie
Tornado, The 1924,D 15,14:1

Morgan, Jeanne
Great Mail Robbery, The 1927,Jl 20,29:3

Morgan, Joan
Woman Tempted, The 1928,Ap 24,29:3

Morgan, Joan (Original Author)
This Was a Woman 1949,Ja 5,22:2

Morgan, John
Big Fix, The 1947,My 3,10:3
Outrage 1950,O 16,30:5

Morgan, Kenneth
French Without Tears 1940,Ap 29,12:2

Morgan, Kewpie
Spieler, The 1929,F 25,16:1

Morgan, Loumell Trio
All by Myself 1943,Jl 16,20:3

Morgan, Manley
Return of Mr Moto 1965,D 2,48:1

Morgan, Margaret
Snow Bride, The 1923,Je 12,22:2

Morgan, Marilyn
Whoopee 1930,O 1,26:3

Morgan, Marion (Original Author)
Goin' to Town 1935,My 11,21:2
Klondike Annie 1936,Mr 12,18:2

Morgan, Michele
Orage 1938,D 12,26:2
Heart of Paris 1939,Ja 13,17:3
Port of Shadows 1939,O 30,13:2
Joan of Paris 1942,Je 26,18:2
Heart of a Nation, The 1943,Ap 8,27:2
Two Tickets to London 1943,Jl 3,11:2
Higher and Higher 1944,Ja 22,8:4
Passage to Marseille 1944,F 17,12:5
Musiciens du Ciel 1945,Mr 1,26:6
Stormy Waters 1946,Je 17,32:2
Chase, The 1946,N 18,31:2
Symphonie Pastorale 1948,S 14,34:3
Fallen Idol, The 1949,N 16,39:2
Souvenir 1950,O 3,34:4
Fabiola 1951,My 30,14:2
Moment of Truth, The 1954,Ap 27,36:2
Daughters of Destiny (Jeanne); Jeanne (Daughters
  of Destiny) 1954,Jl 6,19:1
Naked Heart, The 1955,Mr 9,22:4
Proud and the Beautiful, The 1956,My 29,32:2
Grand Maneuver, The 1956,O 2,39:1
Vintage, The 1957,My 9,36:5
There's Always a Price Tag 1958,My 26,25:2
Mirror Has two Faces, The 1959,My 27,31:1
Oasis 1960,Jl 7,26:1
Crime Does Not Pay (The Hugues Case); Hugues
  Case, The (Crime Does Not Pay)
  1962,O 17,35:2
Maxime 1962,O 25,48:3
Landru 1963,Ap 10,31:1
Lost Command 1966,S 15,51:1
Benjamin 1968,Mr 26,41:2

Morgan, Mike
Horse's Mouth, The 1958,N 12,41:1

Morgan, Miles (Miscellaneous)
Bullfight 1956,Jl 4,15:2

Morgan, Paddy
Men Are not Gods 1937,Ja 19,28:1

Morgan, Patti
Here Comes Trouble 1948,Ap 15,31:4

Morgan, Paul
Why Cry at Parting 1930,F 4,28:3
Zwei Hertzen in Drei-Viertel Takt
  1930,O 13,31:1
Wien Du Stadt der Lieder; (Vienna City of Song)
  1931,Mr 20,29:1
Kabinett des Dr. Larifari, Das 1931,S 11,24:2
Theaternaechte von Berlin 1932,Ja 11,28:5
Parlor, Bedroom and Bath 1932,F 14,VIII,6:1
Liebeskommando 1932,Ap 27,13:6
Holzapfel Weiss Alles 1933,Ja 7,11:3

Morgan, Paula
David and Bathsheba 1951,Ag 15,23:2

Morgan, Phalba
Girl in Every Port, A 1928,F 20,14:1

Morgan, Priscilla
Separate Tables 1958,D 19,2:7

Morgan, R R (Original Author)
Chandu the Magician 1932,O 1,10:4

Morgan, Ralph
Man Who Found Himself, The 1925,Ag 24,17:3
Honor Among Lovers 1931,F 28,15:2
Dance Team 1932,Ja 16,13:1
Charlie Chan's Chance 1932,Ja 23,18:4
Cheaters at Play 1932,F 27,22:1
Devil's Lottery 1932,Ap 2,13:2
Disorderly Conduct 1932,Ap 11,19:2
Strange Interlude 1932,S 1,24:3
Rasputin and the Empress 1932,D 24,11:4
Son-Daughter, The 1933,Ja 2,29:2
Humanity 1933,Ap 22,16:3
Trick for Trick 1933,Je 10,16:4
Power and the Glory, The 1933,Ag 17,13:2
Shanghai Madness 1933,S 23,11:6
Doctor Bull 1933,O 6,21:2
Walls of Gold 1933,O 21,11:3
Kennel Murder Case, The 1933,O 30,14:2
Mad Game, The 1933,N 13,21:1
Orient Express 1934,F 28,23:2
Stand up and Cheer 1934,Ap 20,17:1
No Greater Glory 1934,My 5,22:2
She Was a Lady 1934,Ag 22,21:2
Their big Moment 1934,S 6,22:4
Last Gentleman, The 1934,O 18,26:5
Transatlantic Merry-Go-Round 1934,N 1,25:2
Girl of the Limberlost, A 1934,N 9,24:6
Hell in the Heavens 1934,D 12,28:2
Little Men 1935,F 18,19:3
Star of Midnight 1935,Ap 12,26:5
Magnificent Obsession 1935,D 31,11:2
Muss 'Em Up 1936,F 3,21:2
Human Cargo 1936,My 16,11:2
Speed 1936,My 16,11:2
Ex-Mrs Bradford, The 1936,My 28,19:2
Little Miss Nobody 1936,Je 6,21:1
Anthony Adverse 1936,Ag 27,16:1
Crack-Up 1937,Ja 4,20:4
Exclusive 1937,Jl 22,15:1
Life of Emile Zola, The 1937,Ag 12,14:2
Man in Blue, The 1937,Ag 30,25:2
Outer Gate, The 1937,N 22,15:2
Wells Fargo 1937,D 30,15:2

Morgan, Ralph— Cont

Mannequin 1938,Ja 21,15:2
Love Is a Headache 1938,Ja 28,17:3
Wives Under Suspicion 1938,Jl 1,22:3
Mother Carey's Chickens 1938,Ag 5,11:1
Army Girl 1938,Ag 12,11:1
Shadows Over Shanghai 1938,D 1,29:2
Out West With the Hardys 1938,D 9,31:2
Lone Wolf Spy Hunt, The 1939,Mr 6,11:3
Fast and Loose 1939,Mr 9,18:1
Man of Conquest 1939,Ap 28,31:2
Way Down South 1939,Ag 18,16:4
Geronimo 1940,F 8,18:3
Forty Little Mothers 1940,Ap 19,25:2
Mad Doctor, The 1941,F 27,23:4
Adventure in Washington 1941,Ag 1,11:3
Stage Door Canteen 1943,Je 25,13:2
Hitler's Madman 1943,Ag 28,15:1
Jack London 1944,Mr 3,19:3
Impostor, The 1944,Mr 27,17:2
Weird Woman 1944,Ap 1,11:1
Enemy of Women 1944,S 12,23:6
This Love of Ours 1945,N 1,20:2
Black Market Babies 1946,Ap 1,23:1
Mr District Attorney 1947,F 28,27:3
Song of the Thin Man 1947,Ag 29,14:2
Sleep, My Love 1948,F 19,29:4
Sword of the Avenger 1948,Ag 26,16:4
Blue Grass of Kentucky 1950,Ja 27,29:2

Morgan, Ray (Narrator)
Congolaise 1950,My 22,17:4

Morgan, Read
Ask any Girl 1959,My 22,32:1

Morgan, Robin
Citizen Saint 1948,My 28,28:2

Morgan, Russ
Great Man, The 1957,Ja 2,28:2

Morgan, Sheila
I Met a Murderer 1939,O 2,15:2

Morgan, Sidney
Juno and the Paycock 1930,Je 30,22:6

Morgan, Tanya
Targets 1968,Ag 14,34:1

Morgan, Terence
Hamlet 1948,S 30,32:2
Captain Horatio Hornblower 1951,S 14,21:2
Encore (Gigolo and Gigolette); Gigolo and
  Gigolette (Encore) 1952,Ap 3,45:1
Story of Mandy, The 1953,F 24,21:3
It Started in Paradise 1953,Jl 25,8:2
Both Sides of the Law 1954,Ja 12,19:2
Turn the Key Softly 1954,F 4,21:6
Always a Bride 1954,My 28,19:2
Svengali 1955,S 26,18:2
Dance Little Lady 1955,D 26,23:3
Penthouse, The 1967,O 4,38:3

Morgan, Thelma
So This Is Marriage 1924,D 23,16:2

Morgan, Thomas Bruce (Miscellaneous)
Albert Schweitzer 1957,Ja 21,20:2

Morgan, Wallace
Sandra 1924,D 22,20:2

Morgan, Wesley
Lone Hand 1953,Je 27,7:2

Morgan, William (Director)
Mr District Attorney 1941,Ap 17,29:3

Morgensen, Grethe
Venum 1968,Ja 11,42:1

Morgillo, N
Ramuntcho 1953,Mr 2,19:2

Morhaim, Joseph (Screenwriter)
Happy Road, The 1957,Je 21,20:2

Morheim, Lou (Original Author)
Smuggler's Island 1951,My 24,47:2
For Men Only 1952,Ja 16,21:2

Morheim, Lou (Screenwriter)
Larceny 1948,S 4,8:6
Ma and Pa Kettle 1949,Ag 12,13:2
For Men Only 1952,Ja 16,21:2
Beast From 20,000 Fathoms, The 1953,Je 25,23:1
Last Blitzkrieg, The 1959,Ja 31,13:5

Mori, Claudia
Sodom and Gomorrah 1963,Ja 24,5:3

Mori, Hideo
Tokyo Joe 1949,O 27,35:2

Mori, Masayuki
Rasho-Mon 1951,D 27,18:3
Ugetsu 1954,S 8,40:3
Yang Kwei Fei 1956,S 11,41:2
Men Who Tread on the Tiger's Tail, The
  1960,Ja 11,35:7
Bad Sleep Well, The 1963,Ja 23,5:2
Idiot, The 1963,My 1,35:1
When a Woman Ascends the Stairs
  1963,Je 26,36:4
Challenge to Live 1964,Ap 8,33:1
Bushido 1964,S 13,39:1
Alone on the Pacific 1964,S 24,46:2

Mori, Ogai (Original Author)
Mistress, The 1959,F 3,36:2

Mori, Paola
Mr Arkadin 1962,O 12,26:1

Mori, Toshia
Hatchet Man, The 1932,F 4,25:2
Bitter Tea of General Yen, The 1933,Ja 12,20:6
Blondie Johnson 1933,F 27,11:2
Chinatown Squad 1935,My 30,21:1
Charlie Chan on Broadway 1937,S 20,19:1

Mori, Yuko
Utamaro, Painter of Women 1964,D 2,57:1

Moriarity
Ambush 1950,Ja 19,35:2

Moriarty, D A Dr (Original Author)
Dawn Over Ireland 1938,F 19,19:2

Moriarty, D A Dr (Screenwriter)
Dawn Over Ireland 1938,F 19,19:2

Moriarty, Jan
New Kind of Love, A 1963,O 31,26:2

Moriarty, Pat
Up Pops the Devil 1931,My 16,13:3
McFadden's Flats 1935,Mr 13,16:2
Black Fury 1935,Ap 11,27:2
Glass Key, The 1935,Je 15,20:2
Message to Garcia, A 1936,Ap 10,27:1
God's Country and the Woman 1937,Ja 11,15:5
Plainsman, The 1937,Ja 14,16:2
Mutiny in the Big House 1939,D 11,26:2
Arizona 1941,F 7,23:3
Texas 1941,O 17,27:3
Kings Row 1942,F 3,23:2
Son of Dracula 1943,N 6,16:4

Moriconi, Vito
Marriage Italian Style 1964,D 21,42:1

Moridis, T
Antigone 1962,S 19,30:1

Morillo, Amparo
Virgin of Guadalupe, The 1943,My 15,13:3

MORIN
See Also MARON, MARIN, MORAN

Morin, Alberto
Wings of the Navy 1939,F 4,11:1
Desert Song, The 1943,D 18,10:6
House of Strangers 1949,Jl 2,8:2
Gunfighter, The 1950,Je 24,7:2
Tripoli 1950,N 10,35:2
Rio Grande 1950,N 20,21:2
Mark of the Renegade 1951,S 7,24:2
My Sister Eileen 1955,S 23,21:1
Affair to Remember, An 1957,Jl 20,8:5
Will Success Spoil Rock Hunter 1957,S 12,37:5

Morin, Clementina
no Basta ser Madre; Motherhood Is Not Enough
  1938,Ja 31,15:2

Morin, Edgar (Director)
Chronicle of a Summer; Chronique d'un Ete
  1965,My 7,34:1

Morin, Jacques
Four Bags Full 1957,S 5,32:1

Morin, Nea (Miscellaneous)
Annapurna 1953,D 14,45:4

Morin, Pierre
Inside a Girls' Dormitory 1956,F 6,27:7

Morishige, Hisaya
This Madding Crowd 1964,Je 17,48:1

Morisi, Renzo
Peddler and the Lady, The 1949,S 30,28:4

MORISON
See Also MORRISON

Morison, Patricia
Persons in Hiding 1939,Mr 2,19:2
I'm From Missouri 1939,Mr 23,27:1
Magnificent Fraud, The 1939,Jl 20,16:2
Untamed 1940,Jl 25,14:3
Rangers of Fortune 1940,S 19,27:2
Romance of the Rio Grande 1940,D 25,33:4
Roundup, The 1941,Mr 13,25:4
One Night in Lisbon 1941,Je 12,29:3
Beyond the Blue Horizon 1942,Je 25,27:2
Night in New Orleans 1942,Jl 2,25:2
Are Husbands Necessary? 1942,Jl 9,17:2
Silver Skates 1943,Mr 19,15:3
Fallen Sparrow, The 1943,Ag 20,13:1
Hitler's Madman 1943,Ag 28,15:1
Where Are Your Children? 1944,Ja 17,14:5
Song of Bernadette, The 1944,Ja 27,15:2
Calling Dr Death 1944,F 12,11:3
Without Love 1945,Mr 23,13:1
Lady on a Train 1945,S 15,21:2
Dressed to Kill 1946,My 25,12:4
Tarzan and the Huntress 1947,Ap 7,20:4
Song of the Thin Man 1947,Ag 29,14:2
Sofia 1948,S 4,8:7
Song Without End 1960,Ag 12,10:2

Morita, Miki
Front Page Woman 1935,Jl 12,15:1
I Live for Love 1935,O 19,21:2
Spendthrift 1936,Jl 23,24:1
Bulldog Drummond's Revenge 1937,D 17,33:2
House Across the Bay, The 1940,Mr 22,23:2
Turnabout 1940,Jl 27,17:6

Morita, Pat
Thoroughly Modern Millie 1967,Mr 23,25:1

Morits, M
Nagana 1933,F 16,23:2

Moriyama, Rollin
Prisoner of War 1954,My 10,20:2

Morl, Claudia
Of Wayward Love (The Women); Women, The
  (Of Wayward Love) 1964,Mr 24,29:1

Morlacchi, Lucilla
Leopard, The 1963,Ag 13,25:1

Morlander, Gustaf (Director)
Under Falsk Flagg 1937,Ja 20,18:5

Morlay, Gaby
Nouveau Messieurs, Les; New Gentlemen, The
  1929,D 15,X,6:5
Scandale, Le 1934,Ag 12,IX,2:1
Bonheur, Le 1936,F 28,18:2
Kreutzer Sonata, The 1938,D 20,30:2
Entente Cordiale 1939,D 26,23:2
Life of Giuseppe Verdi 1940,Ap 3,19:2
Living Corpse, The 1940,S 23,21:4
King, The 1941,O 23,29:3
32 Rue de Montmartre 1944,S 28,26:3
Blue Veil, The 1947,O 2,32:6
Lover's Return, A; Revenant, Le 1948,Ja 26,15:2
Mlle Desiree 1948,N 19,35:2
Gigi 1950,Ja 31,20:2
Simple Case of Money, A 1952,F 2,11:2
Father's Dilemma 1952,S 23,25:1
Anna 1953,F 19,20:5
Plaisir, Le (The Mask); Mask, The (Le Plaisir)
  1954,My 20,38:1
Mama, Papa, the Maid and I 1956,Ag 28,31:1
Royal Affairs in Versailles 1957,Mr 9,16:1
Mitsou 1958,Ap 15,42:5

Morlet, Jane
Face to the Wind 1951,Ja 16,34:2
Voyage to America 1952,O 20,18:2

Morley, Annabel
Outcast of the Islands 1952,My 16,19:2

Morley, Christopher (Original Author)
Kitty Foyle 1941,Ja 9,27:2

Morley, J B
Battle for Music 1945,O 15,13:2

Morley, John
Chicago Confidential 1957,Ag 31,19:1

Morley, Karen
Inspiration 1931,F 9,25:3
Daybreak 1931,Je 1,15:1
Never the Twain Shall Meet 1931,Je 6,15:5
Politics 1931,Ag 1,16:4
Sin of Madelon Claudet, The 1931,O 31,22:2
Cuban Love Song, The 1931,D 5,21:2
Mata Hari 1932,Ja 1,31:1
Arsene Lupin 1932,F 27,22:1
Scarface, The Shame of the Nation
  1932,My 20,22:3
Man About Town 1932,My 28,18:2
Washington Masquerade, The 1932,Jl 22,18:2
Phantom of Crestwood, The 1932,O 17,18:3
Mask of Fu Manchu, The 1932,D 3,21:4
Flesh 1932,D 10,19:3
Gabriel Over the White House 1933,Ap 1,18:2
Dinner at Eight 1933,Ag 24,18:1
Crime Doctor, The 1934,My 11,24:3
Straight Is the Way 1934,Ag 29,13:2
Our Daily Bread 1934,O 3,25:2
Wednesday's Child 1934,D 15,9:3
Black Fury 1935,Ap 11,27:2
Littlest Rebel, The 1935,D 20,30:1
Devil's Squadron 1936,My 11,16:2
Beloved Enemy 1936,D 26,15:2
Outcast 1937,Mr 3,27:2
Girl From Scotland Yard, The 1937,My 31,11:2
Last Train from Madrid, The 1937,Je 19,20:2
On Such a Night 1937,S 17,29:2
Kentucky 1938,D 24,12:1
Pride and Prejudice 1940,Ag 9,19:1
Unknown, The 1946,Jl 20,10:3
Framed 1947,My 26,24:2
M 1951,Je 11,20:7

Morley, Robert
Marie Antoinette 1938,Ag 17,23:2
Major Barbara 1941,My 15,27:1
Young Mr Pitt, The 1943,Mr 11,17:1
Somewhere in France 1943,Jl 12,11:2
Yank in London, A 1946,Ap 20,16:3
Small Back Room, The 1952,F 2,11:3
African Queen, The 1952,F 21,24:3
Outcast of the Islands 1952,My 16,19:2
Curtain Up 1953,F 2,17:3
Melba 1953,Je 25,23:1
Gilbert and Sullivan 1953,O 28,36:3
Final Test, The 1954,Ja 26,21:5
Beat the Devil 1954,Mr 13,11:2
Beau Brummell 1954,O 21,31:5
Quentin Durward 1955,N 24,41:1
Around the World in 80 Days 1956,O 18,37:1
Law and Disorder 1958,Ag 6,20:1
Journey, The 1959,F 20,19:1
Sheriff of Fractured Jaw, The 1959,Mr 14,27:4
Libel 1959,O 24,12:4
Battle of the Sexes, The 1960,Ap 19,40:4
Oscar Wilde 1960,Je 21,28:2
Road to Hong Kong, The 1962,Je 28,21:1
Story of Joseph and his Brethern, The
  1962,D 1,17:1

Morley, Robert — Cont

Nine Hours to Rama 1963,Ap 4,58:2
Murder at the Gallop 1963,Je 25,23:2
Old Dark House, The 1963,O 31,26:3
Take Her, She's Mine 1963,N 14,41:1
Ladies Who Do 1963,N 26,52:2
Topkapi 1964,S 18,25:1
Of Human Bondage 1964,S 24,46:2
Those Magnificent Men in Their Flying Machines (Or How I Flew From London to Paris in 25 Hours and 11 Minutes) 1965,Je 17,27:1
Genghis Khan 1965,Je 24,28:2
Loved One, The 1965,O 12,57:1
Agent 8 3/4 1965,O 14,53:1
Life at the Top 1965,D 15,53:1
Alphabet Murders, The 1966,Jl 12,36:2
Hotel Paradiso 1966,O 15,34:2
Way...Way Out 1966,O 27,55:1
Study in Terror, A 1966,N 3,45:3
Woman Times Seven 1967,Je 28,38:1
Tender Scoundrel 1967,N 16,58:2
Hot Millions 1968,S 20,42:1

Morley, Robert (Original Author)
Edward my Son 1949,Je 3,21:2

Morlion, Felix Rev O P (Screenwriter)
Flowers of St Francis 1952,O 7,26:2

Morner, Stanley
Suzy 1936,Jl 25,16:1
Navy Blue and Gold 1937,D 24,21:2

Moroccans, The
Always Leave Them Laughing 1949,N 24,48:2

Moronelli, Nick
Las Vegas Nights 1941,Mr 20,25:2

Moroni, Fabrizio
Hours of Love, The 1965,S 4,11:5
Made in Italy 1967,My 1,44:2

Morono, Darío
Eye for an Eye, An 1961,F 10,19:1

Morosco, Walter (Director)
Silken Shackles 1926,My 25,25:1

Morosco, Walter (Producer)
Gay Caballero, The 1940,O 25,25:3
Moon Over her Shoulder 1941,N 5,31:2
Gentleman at Heart, A 1942,F 23,25:2
It Happened in Flatbush 1942,Jl 3,12:8
Man in the Trunk, The 1942,O 23,25:1
Over my Dead Body 1942,D 26,15:2
Dixie Dugan 1943,Ap 9,25:5
Wing and a Prayer 1944,Ag 31,14:1
Sunday Dinner for a Soldier 1945,Ja 25,16:2
Sentimental Journey 1946,Mr 7,33:2
Margie 1946,O 17,28:3
Wake up and Dream 1947,Ja 24,18:4
Scudda-Hoo! Scudda-Hay! 1948,Ap 15,31:1
Give my Regards to Broadway 1948,Je 23,32:2
Mother is a Freshman 1949,Mr 12,10:2

Moroso, John (Original Author)
For the Love of Mike 1927,Ag 24,27:5

Morosov, Alexander
Son of the Regiment 1948,Ap 29,27:3

Morquecho, Luis White (Screenwriter)
St Francis of Assisi 1947,Ap 5,12:5

Morrales, Joe T
Salt of the Earth 1954,Mr 15,20:2

MORRELL
See Also MOREL, MORELL

Morrell, Henry
Hell's Cargo 1940,S 16,15:2
Take my Life 1949,Ja 19,34:2

Morrell, Penny
Make Mine Mink 1960,D 20,43:4

Morresi, Giuseppe
Boheme, La 1965,O 20,51:2

Morriconi, Valeria
Wild Love; (Gli Inamorati) 1961,Ap 6,30:2

Morrie, Margaret
Welcome Home 1925,My 18,12:1

Morris, Adrian
Age for Love, The 1931,N 13,27:2
Me and my Gal 1932,D 12,18:4
Trick for Trick 1933,Je 10,16:4
Bureau of Missing Persons 1933,S 9,9:2
Big Shakedown, The 1934,F 12,19:2
Pursuit of Happiness, The 1934,O 26,25:1
Age of Indiscretion 1935,My 18,21:2
Dr Socrates 1935,O 3,29:2
Petrified Forest, The 1936,F 7,14:2
Powdersmoke Range 1936,Mr 9,20:2
Poppy 1936,Je 18,19:1
My American Wife 1936,Ag 21,12:3
Her Husband Lies 1937,Mr 18,20:1
Woman I Love, The 1937,Ap 16,27:2
there Goes The Groom 1937,D 25,10:6
If I Were King 1938,S 29,31:1
Angels With Dirty Faces 1938,N 26,18:1
Return of the Cisco Kid, The 1939,Ap 29,13:2
Six Thousand Enemies 1939,Je 9,26:2
Grapes of Wrath, The 1940,Ja 25,17:2

Morris, Arto
Strange Affair, The 1968,Jl 25,26:2

Morris, Charles
We're not Dressing 1934,Ap 26,27:2
Cleopatra 1934,Ag 17,12:1

Morris, Chester
Alibi 1929,Ap 9,29:1
Fast Life 1929,Ag 17,5:3
Woman Trap 1929,Ag 31,13:4
Show of Shows 1929,N 21,24:5
Second Choice 1930,Ja 4,21:1
She Couldn't Say No 1930,F 16,III,8:1
Case of Sergeant Grischa, The 1930,Mr 8,21:1
Playing Around 1930,Mr 31,24:3
Divorcee, The 1930,My 10,25:3
Big House, The 1930,Je 25,31:2
Bat Whispers, The 1931,Ja 16,27:1
Corsair 1931,N 19,27:5
Cock of the Air 1932,Ja 25,20:3
Miracle Man, The 1932,Ap 21,25:2
Sinners in the Sun 1932,My 14,11:5
Red Headed Woman 1932,Jl 1,19:3
Blondie Johnson 1933,F 27,11:2
Infernal Machine 1933,Ap 8,16:3
Tomorrow at Seven 1933,Jl 3,14:6
King for a Night 1933,D 11,23:4
Let's Talk It Over 1934,Je 16,20:2
Gay Bride, The 1934,D 19,27:2
Society Doctor 1935,F 4,11:3
Princess O'Hara 1935,Ap 13,11:3
Public Hero No 1 1935,Je 8,12:2
Three Godfathers, The 1936,Mr 9,20:2
Moonlight Murder 1936,Mr 28,11:2
Frankie and Johnnie 1936,My 25,23:2
Counterfeit 1936,Jl 20,11:1
They Met in a Taxi 1936,S 7,20:5
Devil's Playground 1937,F 15,12:5
I Promise to Pay 1937,Ap 26,15:2
Flight From Glory 1937,S 11,20:1
Law of the Underworld 1938,Ap 28,27:2
Sky Giant 1938,Jl 20,22:2
Smashing the Rackets 1938,Ag 9,22:5
Pacific Liner 1939,Ja 18,17:3
Blind Alley 1939,My 23,27:2
Five came Back 1939,Jl 5,20:2
Thunder Afloat 1939,O 13,27:2
Wagons Westward 1940,Jl 8,13:2
Girl From God's Country 1940,S 9,18:5
Meet Boston Blackie 1941,F 26,17:2
Confessions of Boston Blackie 1941,D 8,31:2
No Hands on the Clock 1941,D 22,24:6
Canal Zone 1942,Mr 30,21:2
I Live on Danger 1942,Ag 22,16:2
Aerial Gunner 1943,Je 26,10:2
Secret Command 1944,Je 14,16:2
One Mysterious Night 1944,O 21,15:3
Rough, Tough and Ready 1945,Mr 24,22:7
Unchained 1955,Ja 28,15:2

Morris, Corbet
Firefly, The 1937,S 2,17:2
Tarzan's Revenge 1938,Ja 10,13:3
Making the Headlines 1938,Ap 1,17:2

Morris, David
Tracked by the Police 1927,Ap 27,22:5
Juno and the Paycock 1930,Je 30,22:6
These Thirty Years 1934,My 24,28:3
Gambling 1934,D 4,22:3
Swamp Water 1941,N 17,15:2
Tingler, The 1960,Mr 10,36:2

Morris, Donald R (Original Author)
All Hands on Deck 1961,Ap 1,10:2

Morris, Dorothy
Seven Sweethearts 1942,N 13,28:1
War Against Mrs Hadley, The 1942,N 26,40:2
Human Comedy, The 1943,Mr 3,19:2
Youngest Profession, The 1943,Je 25,13:3
Cry Havoc 1943,N 24,16:2
None Shall Escape 1944,Ap 7,23:2
Rationing 1944,Ap 10,14:2
Main Street After Dark 1945,Ja 13,15:4
Our Vines Have Tender Grapes 1945,S 7,21:2
Macabre 1958,Jl 24,18:1

Morris, Edmund (Screenwriter)
Walk on the Wild Side 1962,F 22,20:1

Morris, Edna
Another Man's Poison 1952,Ja 7,14:3
Saturday Night and Sunday Morning 1961,Ap 4,44:2

Morris, Ernest (Director)
Telltale Heart, The 1963,My 16,42:1
Return of Mr Moto 1965,D 2,48:1

Morris, Frances
Thunder 1929,Jl 8,17:3
Our Leading Citizen 1939,Ag 24,17:1
Our Neighbors-The Carters 1940,F 15,15:2
Over my Dead Body 1942,D 26,15:2
Unfaithful, The 1947,Je 28,10:2
Mrs Mike 1950,F 9,36:5
This Side of the Law 1950,Jl 7,15:2
Edge of Doom 1950,Ag 4,13:2
Captive City, The 1952,Mr 27,34:2
Miracle of Our Lady Fatima, The 1952,Ag 21,16:2
Miss Sadie Thompson 1953,D 24,9:1

Morris, Geoffrey
Once Upon a Dream 1949,Jl 15,17:2

Morris, George (Original Author)
Black Market Babies 1946,Ap 1,23:1

Morris, Gladys
Star Overnight, A 1919,N 17,20:1

Morris, Glenn
Tarzan's Revenge 1938,Ja 10,13:3
Hold That Co-ed 1938,S 24,13:1

Morris, Gordon (Original Author)
Six Hours to Live 1932,O 22,18:4
Under the Pampas Moon 1935,My 31,11:1

Morris, Gouverneur (Original Author)
Behind the Door 1920,Ja 5,15:1
Penalty, The 1920,N 15,12:2
Tale of Two Worlds, A 1921,Mr 14,9:2
Yellow Men and Gold 1922,My 29,14:1
Man Who Played God, The 1922,O 2,21:2
Anybody's Woman 1930,Ag 16,8:3
Man Who Played God, The 1932,F 11,16:1

Morris, Gouverneur (Screenwriter)
Jungle Princess 1936,D 24,21:3

Morris, Greg
New Interns, The 1964,Ag 20,34:2

Morris, Howard
Boys' Night Out 1962,Je 22,15:2
40 Pounds of Trouble 1963,Ja 24,5:2
Fluffy 1965,O 21,57:2
Way...Way Out 1966,O 27,55:1

Morris, Howard (Director)
With Six You Get Egg Roll 1968,O 10,59:6

Morris, Howard (Producer)
Who's Minding the Mint? 1967,D 7,60:3

Morris, Joanna
Nothing but the Best 1964,Jl 14,28:1

Morris, Johnnie
Fifty-Fifty Girl, The 1928,My 14,25:1
Street of Sin, The 1928,My 28,23:2
Beggars of Life 1928,S 24,25:1
Innocents of Paris 1929,Ap 27,16:5
Once in a Lifetime 1932,O 29,18:4
Sons of the Legion 1938,S 30,24:3
Thanks for the Memory 1938,D 8,34:3

Morris, Kirk
Hercules, Samson and Ulysses 1965,N 4,57:2

Morris, Lana
Weaker Sex, The 1949,Jl 11,13:2
Spring in Park Lane 1949,S 21,38:2
Amazing Mr Beecham, The 1949,D 26,33:4
Verger, The 1950,O 11,42:1
Operation Disaster 1951,Ja 15,13:1
Gay Lady, The 1951,Ap 16,21:2
Reluctant Widow, The 1951,S 8,8:6
Woman in Question, The 1952,F 19,24:2
Tale of Five Women, A 1953,Ja 16,19:2
Trouble in Store 1956,Ja 14,13:2

Morris, Libby
Tiara Tahiti 1963,N 6,32:1

Morris, Margaret
Wild Horse Mesa 1925,Ag 10,8:2
Best People 1925,O 21,21:3
Womanhandled 1926,Ja 5,25:2
That's My Baby 1926,Ap 12,18:4
Born to the West 1926,Je 30,18:1 (In Addenda)

Morris, Marjorie
Birthright 1952,F 15,17:2

Morris, Mary
Double Door 1934,My 5,22:3
Victoria the Great 1937,O 29,19:1
Prison Without Bars 1939,Ap 10,13:2
U-Boat 29 1939,O 6,31:3
Thief of Bagdad, The 1940,D 6,28:2
Mister V 1942,F 13,24:4
Man From Morocco, The 1946,N 25,38:2
Agitator, The 1949,Ag 19,12:5
High Treason 1952,My 21,23:3
Train of Events 1952,My 26,18:4

Morris, Michael
Pier 13 1940,Ag 9,19:3
Christmas in July 1940,N 6,35:2
Blood and Sand 1941,My 23,25:3
Wild Geese Calling 1941,Ag 30,10:2

Morris, Michael (Screenwriter)
For Love or Money 1963,Ag 8,19:1
Wild and Wonderful 1964,Je 11,27:4

Morris, Oswald (Cinematographer)
Stop the World-I Want to Get Off 1966,My 12,54:2

Morris, Paula
No More Excuses 1968,My 22,53:1

Morris, Phillip
Super-Sleuth 1937,Jl 17,18:1

Morris, Phyllis
Prison Without Bars 1939,Ap 10,13:2
Adventures of Tartu, The 1943,S 24,26:1
Julia Misbehaves 1948,O 8,30:2
My Own True Love 1949,F 3,27:3
Three Came Home 1950,F 21,22:5
Black Hand 1950,Mr 13,15:2
Kind Lady 1951,Ag 8,21:2

Morris, Reginald (Original Author)
Regular Fellow, A 1925,O 5,25:2

Morris, Reginald (Screenwriter)
Ladies Must Dress 1927,D 31,31:1

Morris, Richard
  Third Alarm, The 1923,Ja 10,28:5
  Intruder, The 1955,Ja 26,22:1
Morris, Richard (Original Author)
  Unsinkable Molly Brown, The 1964,Jl 17,15:1
Morris, Richard (Screenwriter)
  Ma and Pa Kettle at the Fair 1952,Jl 12,16:2
  Take Me to Town 1953,Je 20,8:6
  If a Man Answers 1962,N 22,43:1
  Thoroughly Modern Millie 1967,Mr 23,25:1
Morris, Wayne
  China Clipper 1936,Ag 12,14:3
  Kid Galahad 1937,My 27,21:3
  Submarine D-1 1937,D 30,15:4
  Kid Comes Back, The 1938,F 7,10:2
  Love, Honor and Behave 1938,Mr 21,18:2
  Men Are Such Fools 1938,Je 17,25:1
  Valley of the Giants 1938,S 10,20:2
  Brother Rat 1938,N 5,15:2
  Kid From Kokomo, The 1939,My 20,11:2
  Return Of Doctor X, The 1939,N 23,38:5
  Brother Rat and a Baby 1940,Ja 27,9:4
  Double Alibi 1940,Mr 11,11:2
  Angel From Texas, An 1940,My 10,26:7
  Flight Angels 1940,My 27,23:2
  Ladies Must Live 1940,S 6,25:3
  Quarterback, The 1940,O 17,33:3
  I Wanted Wings 1941,Mr 27,29:4
  Bad Men of Missouri 1941,Ag 16,18:2
  Smiling Ghost, The 1941,S 26,26:5
  Deep Valley 1947,Ag 23,7:2
  Voice of the Turtle, The 1947,D 26,22:4
  Time of your Life, The 1948,My 27,29:2
  John Loves Mary 1949,F 5,11:2
  Kiss in the Dark, A 1949,Mr 26,10:6
  Younger Brothers, The 1949,My 28,11:2
  House Across the Street 1949,S 2,14:4
  Task Force 1949,O 1,8:6
  Johnny One-Eye 1950,N 17,31:2
  Stage to Tucson 1951,My 5,14:2
  Riding Shotgun 1954,Ap 2,22:2
  Port of Hell 1954,D 18,12:2
  Paths of Glory 1957,D 26,23:2
Morris, William
  Brothers 1930,N 15,15:3
  Gang Buster, The 1931,Ja 24,15:1
  Behind Office Doors 1931,Mr 21,15:1
  Washington Masquerade, The 1932,Jl 22,18:2
Morris, Wolfe
  Night Ambush 1958,Ap 25,32:4
  Camp on Blood Island, The 1958,S 18,37:2
  Nine Hours to Rama 1963,Ap 4,58:2
MORRISON
  See Also MORISON
Morrison, Adrienne (Miscellaneous)
  Forest Ring, The 1930,Ap 26,11:1
Morrison, Angus
  Angel Street 1952,N 11,25:2
Morrison, Ann
  Walls of Jericho, The 1948,Ag 5,16:2
  Caught 1949,F 18,26:4
  House of Strangers 1949,Jl 2,8:2
  People Will Talk 1951,Ag 30,20:1
  Battle Circus 1953,My 28,27:5
  Violent Saturday 1955,My 12,32:2
  Brothers Karamazov, The 1958,F 21,18:2
Morrison, Arthur
  Riders of the Purple Sage 1925,Ap 15,16:1
  Tony Runs Wild 1926,Ap 28,28:3
Morrison, Barbara
  From Here to Eternity 1953,Ag 6,16:2
  These Thousand Hills 1959,My 7,36:1
  Do Not Disturb 1965,D 25,17:2
Morrison, Brett (Narrator)
  Green Magic 1955,My 17,32:1
Morrison, Dorothy
  Hearts in Dixie 1929,F 28,30:3
Morrison, E G
  Last Chance, The 1945,N 28,21:6
Morrison, Ernest
  Prison Camp 1940,Ag 3,9:3
Morrison, Jack
  There Goes the Bride 1933,Mr 4,11:3
Morrison, James
  Black Beauty 1921,F 21,16:1
  Dangerous Age, The 1923,Ja 29,11:1
  Nth Commandment, The 1923,Ap 10,24:3
  Man Next Door, The 1923,My 29,10:3
  On the Banks of the Wabash 1923,O 23,21:3
  Unknown Purple, The 1924,Mr 24,13:1
  Wine of Youth 1924,Ag 11,16:1
  Captain Blood 1924,S 9,19:1
Morrison, Joe
  Old-Fashioned Way, The 1934,Jl 14,16:5
  Four Hours to Kill 1935,Ap 11,27:3
  Love in Bloom 1935,Ap 20,16:2
Morrison, Joseph
  Dixie Handicap, The 1924,D 30,15:3
Morrison, Louis
  Village Sleuth 1920,S 13,12:1
  Dangerous Maid, The 1923,D 11,26:2
  Sea Hawk, The 1924,Je 3,22:1
  Unholy Three, The 1925,Ag 4,14:3

Rescue, The 1929,Ja 14,20:1
Morrison, Murdo
  I Know Where I'm Going 1947,Ag 20,25:2
Morrison, Peter
  Chinatown Nights 1929,Ap 1,22:1
Morrison, Sunshine
  Flying Wild 1941,Ap 12,19:3
  Spooks Run Wild 1941,N 1,20:3
  Mr Wise Guy 1942,Mr 5,27:2
Morrison, T J (Screenwriter)
  Quiet Week-End 1948,Ag 20,13:2
  Duel in the Jungle 1954,Ag 9,13:2
  Desert Attack 1961,Mr 23,28:1
  She Didn't Say No 1963,Jl 30,18:1
Morrison, Vera
  Passport to Hell, A 1932,Ag 27,13:4
Morriss, Ann
  Chaser, The 1938,Ag 2,15:3
  Spring Madness 1938,D 1,29:3
  Honolulu 1939,F 23,19:2
  Society Lawyer 1939,Mr 31,19:2
  Within the Law 1939,Ap 6,31:2
  Women, The 1939,S 22,27:2
  Broadway Melody of 1940 1940,Mr 29,25:3
  And One Was Beautiful 1940,Ap 11,32:4
  Third Finger, Left Hand 1940,D 12,37:2
  Hullabaloo 1940,D 19,33:1
  Blossoms in the Dust 1941,Je 27,14:4
Morrissey, Betty
  Woman of Paris, A 1923,O 2,7:2
  Fast Worker, The 1924,N 12,13:1
  Lady of the Night 1925,Mr 2,14:1
  Skinner's Dress Suit 1926,My 3,27:1
Morrissey, Paul (Cinematographer)
  Flesh 1968,S 27,36:1
Morrissey, Paul (Director)
  Flesh 1968,S 27,36:1
Morrissey, Paul (Screenwriter)
  Flesh 1968,S 27,36:1
Morros, Boris (Composer)
  Land of Promise, The 1935,N 21,27:2
Morros, Boris (Miscellaneous)
  Big Broadcast of 1938, The 1938,Mr 10,16:2
Morros, Boris (Original Author)
  Man on a String 1960,My 21,15:1
Morros, Boris (Producer)
  Second Chorus 1941,Ja 16,25:2
  Tales of Manhattan 1942,S 25,25:1
  Carnegie Hall 1947,My 3,10:2
  Marika 1953,F 18,27:2
Morrow, Brad
  Toy Tiger 1956,Je 30,11:2
Morrow, Doretta
  Because You're Mine 1952,S 26,18:2
Morrow, Douglas
  Lady Luck 1946,O 31,22:3
Morrow, Douglas (Original Author)
  Stratton Story, The 1949,My 13,29:1
  Jim Thorpe - All American 1951,Ag 25,7:2
  Trouble Along the Way 1953,My 7,37:2
  Beyond a Reasonable Doubt 1956,S 14,27:2
Morrow, Douglas (Screenwriter)
  Stratton Story, The 1949,My 13,29:1
  Jim Thorpe - All American 1951,Ag 25,7:2
  Beyond a Reasonable Doubt 1956,S 14,27:2
Morrow, Honore (Original Author)
  Of Human Hearts 1938,F 18,23:1
Morrow, Jackie
  Little Miss Nobody 1936,Je 6,21:1
  Penrod and Sam 1937,Mr 29,14:3
  Penrod and his Twin Brother 1938,Ap 18,11:1
Morrow, Jeff
  Robe, The 1953,S 17,32:6
  Flight to Tangier 1953,N 26,50:4
  Siege at Red River, The 1954,Ap 3,19:2
  Tanganyika 1954,Je 19,9:2
  Sign of the Pagan 1955,F 14,24:2
  This Island Earth 1955,Je 11,8:7
  World in my Corner 1956,F 18,12:5
  Creature Walks among Us, The 1956,Ap 27,21:6
  First Texan, The 1956,Je 23,20:2
  Pardners 1956,Jl 26,20:2
  Kronos 1957,My 11,24:6
  Story of Ruth, The 1960,Je 18,12:3
  Harbor Lights 1964,F 13,25:3
Morrow, Jo
  Our Man in Havana 1960,Ja 28,26:1
  13 Ghosts 1960,Ag 6,9:2
  Three Worlds of Gulliver, The 1960,D 17,19:3
  Sunday in New York 1964,F 12,30:2
  He Rides Tall 1964,F 27,28:1
Morrow, Neyle
  Pirates of Monterey 1947,D 17,41:4
  Steel Helmet, The 1951,Ja 25,21:5
  Fixed Bayonets 1951,N 21,20:2
  Park Row 1952,D 22,20:2
  China Gate 1957,My 23,40:2
Morrow, Patricia
  Surf Party 1964,Mr 12,40:4
Morrow, Susan
  Savage, The 1953,Ja 2,11:1
  Cat-Women of the Moon 1954,Mr 20,10:7
  Macabre 1958,Jl 24,18:1

Morrow, Vic
  Blackboard Jungle 1955,Mr 21,21:5
  Tribute to a Bad Man 1956,Mr 31,13:3
  Men in War 1957,Mr 20,32:4
  Hell's Five Hours 1957,Jl 24,18:1
  King Creole 1958,Jl 4,15:2
  Hell's Five Hours 1958,Jl 24,18:1
  God's Little Acre 1958,Ag 14,23:2
  Cimarron 1961,F 17,12:2
  Portrait of a Mobster 1961,Ap 20,30:4
Morrow, Vic (Director)
  Deathwatch 1967,Je 28,38:1
Morrow, Vic (Producer)
  Deathwatch 1967,Je 28,38:1
Morrow, Vic (Screenwriter)
  Deathwatch 1967,Je 28,38:1
Morrow, William (Screenwriter)
  Buck Benny Rides Again 1940,Ap 25,28:4
  Love Thy Neighbor 1940,D 18,32:5
  Road to Bali 1953,Ja 30,25:1
Morse, Barry
  Mrs Fitzherbert 1950,My 11,37:2
  King of the Sun 1963,D 26,33:4
Morse, Ella Mae
  Ghost Catchers 1944,My 31,22:3
Morse, Grace
  Old Fashioned Boy, An 1920,N 1,13:2
Morse, Karl
  Underworld 1927,Ag 22,21:3
Morse, N Brewster (Original Author)
  Breaking the Ice 1938,S 23,35:3
Morse, N Brewster (Screenwriter)
  Perfect Specimen, The 1937,O 28,29:2
  Lady With red Hair 1940,D 6,28:2
Morse, Robert
  Matchmaker, The 1958,Ag 13,22:1
  Honeymoon Hotel 1964,Je 4,28:1
  Quick, Before it Melts 1965,Ap 1,30:2
  Loved One, The 1965,O 12,57:1
  Oh Dad, Poor Dad, Mamma's Hung You in the
    Closet and I'm Feeling so Sad 1967,F 16,32:1
  How to Succeed in Business Without Really
    Trying 1967,Mr 10,30:1
  Guide for the Married Man, A 1967,My 27,16:1
  Where Were You When the Lights Went Out?
    1968,Ag 9,30:2
Morse, Robin
  Marty 1955,Ap 12,25:3
Morse, Terry (Director)
  On Trial 1939,Ap 5,31:2
  Waterfront 1939,Jl 17,10:2
  Smashing the Money Ring 1939,N 17,17:2
  British Intelligence 1940,F 12,14:2
  Tear Gas Squad 1940,My 31,15:3
  Fugitive From Justice, A 1940,Jl 8,13:3
  Godzilla, King of the Monsters 1956,Ap 28,11:1
Morse, Terry O (Director)
  Young Dillinger 1965,My 13,32:3
Morseby-White, G H (Original Author)
  Friday the 13th 1934,My 15,18:1
Mort, Claudia
  Rocco and his Brothers 1961,Je 28,40:2
Mort, Ellay
  Lady in the Lake 1947,Ja 24,18:3
Mortimer, Chapman (Screenwriter)
  Reflections in a Golden Eye 1967,O 12,59:1
Mortimer, Charles
  Triumph of Sherlock Holmes, The
    1935,My 27,20:6
Mortimer, Ed
  It's Love I'm After 1937,N 11,31:2
Mortimer, John
  Bride of the Lake, The 1934,S 11,24:5
Mortimer, John (Original Author)
  Trial and Error 1962,N 17,17:2
Mortimer, John (Screenwriter)
  Guns of Darkness 1962,Ag 18,10:1
  I Thank a Fool 1962,S 15,15:1
  Running Man, The 1963,O 3,31:1
  Bunny Lake is Missing 1965,O 4,00:0
  Flea in her Ear, A 1968,N 28,66:1
Mortimer, Lee (Original Author)
  New York Confidential 1955,F 19,18:1
Mortimer, Penelope (Original Author)
  Pumpkin Eater, The 1964,N 10,58:1
Mortimer, Penelope (Screenwriter)
  Bunny Lake is Missing 1965,O 4,00:0
Morton
  Frochard et les Deux Orphelines, La
    1934,F 7,16:2
  Open Road, The 1940,O 5,20:2
Morton, Charles
  Four Sons 1928,F 14,27:1
  4 Devils 1929,O 4,26:3
  Christina 1929,Ap 1,22:1
  Cameo Kirby 1930,F 8,12:5
  Caught Short 1930,Je 21,20:5
  Check and Double Check 1930,N 1,23:1 (In
    Addenda)
  Goldie Gets Along 1933,Je 3,16:4
Morton, Clive
  Dead Men Tell no Tales 1939,Jl 24,9:2
  Jassy 1948,F 20,19:2

Morton, Clive — Cont

Mine Own Executioner 1949,Ja 19,34:2
Blind Goddess, The 1949,Je 23,33:3
Run for Your Money, A 1950,Ap 10,15:3
Kind Hearts and Coronets 1950,Je 15,41:2
While the Sun Shines 1950,Jl 1,9:2
Mr Know-All 1950,O 11,42:1
Blue Lamp, The 1951,Ja 9,25:1
Lavender Hill Mob, The 1951,O 16,35:2
Castle in the Air 1953,Ja 5,19:2
Night Without Stars 1953,Jl 14,19:4
Turn the Key Softly 1954,F 4,21:6
Court Martial 1955,Ag 2,17:1
His Excellency 1956,F 2,19:3
Richard III 1956,Mr 12,1:4
Abandon Ship 1957,Ap 18,35:1
Safecracker, The 1958,Mr 6,32:1
Lucky Jim 1958,S 1,8:6
Matter of Who, A 1962,Jl 25,29:2
I Thank a Fool 1962,S 15,15:1
Alphabet Murders, The 1966,Jl 12,36:2

Morton, Danny

Crime Incorporated 1945,Je 23,9:7

Morton, Edna

Three Miles Out 1924,Ja 1,20:1
Wildfire 1925,Je 10,18:2

Morton, Gregory

Vagabond King, The 1956,S 13,39:6
Bye Bye Birdie 1963,Ap 5,27:3
New Interns, The 1964,Ag 20,34:2
Synanon 1965,My 6,44:1

Morton, Guy (Original Author)

Texas Trail, The 1925,Jl 9,14:2

Morton, Hugh (Original Author)

Belle of New York, The 1952,Mr 6,25:6

Morton, James C

Follow the Leader 1930,D 6,21:3
Devil's Brother, The 1933,Je 10,16:4
Lady From Louisiana 1941,My 15,27:2
Wild Geese Calling 1941,Ag 30,10:2
Boogie Man Will Get You, The 1942,O 12,12:4

Morton, Marjorie

Unholy Three, The 1925,Ag 4,14:3

Morton, Michael (Original Author)

On With the Dance 1920,F 16,8:1
Woman to Woman 1924,Ap 1,19:3
Guilty One, The 1924,Je 17,22:4

Morton, Tom

Wait Till the Sun Shines, Nellie 1952,Je 28,12:2
Stars Are Singing, The 1953,Mr 12,24:2
Main Street to Broadway 1953,O 14,34:1

Morton, William (Screenwriter)

Scalphunters, The 1968,Ap 3,40:1

Morucci, Filippo

Love of a Clown (Pagliacci) 1950,Ap 17,18:5

Morum, William (Original Author)

Obsessed 1952,F 6,24:2

Morven, Myrette

Ireland's Border Line 1939,O 13,27:3

Morzan, Michele

Seven Deadly Sins (Pride); Pride (The Seven Deadly Sins) 1953,My 12,31:3

Mosbacher, Peter

Deadly Decision 1958,Ap 29,26:2

Moscane, A (Miscellaneous)

Ernst Thaelmann: Fighter Against Fascism 1934,S 20,20:3

Moschin, Gastone

Of Wayward Love (The Serpent); Serpent, The (Of Wayward Love) 1964,Mr 24,29:1
Successo, Il 1965,Ap 29,40:2
Vista, La; Visit, The 1966,Ag 10,32:1
Birds, the Bees and the Italians, The 1967,Ag 8,33:2
Queens, The (Queen Armenia); Queen Armenia (The Queens) 1968,Mr 11,49:1
Oldest Profession, The (Roman Nights); Roman Nights (The Oldest Profession) 1968,N 8,42:1

Moscovich, Maurice

Winterset 1936,D 4,31:1
Make Way for Tomorrow 1937,My 10,23:1
Lancer Spy 1937,N 4,29:1
Gateway 1938,Ag 8,9:2
Suez 1938,O 15,21:2
Love Affair 1939,Mr 17,25:2
Susannah of the Mounties 1939,Je 24,13:2
In Name Only 1939,Ag 4,11:3
Rio 1939,O 27,27:2
Everything Happens at Night 1939,D 16,12:6
South to Karanga 1940,Ag 9,19:1
Great Dictator, The 1940,O 16,29:1
Great Commandment, The 1942,O 17,11:1

Moscow, Bob (Miscellaneous)

Moonlighting Wives 1968,My 9,54:4

Moscrip, James

Big Game, The 1936,O 24,23:1

Mose, Arnold

Caper of the Golden Bulls, The 1967,Je 22,46:1

Mosel, Tad (Original Author)

All the Way Home 1963,O 30,46:1
Dear Heart 1965,Mr 8,33:1

Mosel, Tad (Screenwriter)

Dear Heart 1965,Mr 8,33:1
Up the Down Staircase 1967,Ag 18,36:2

MOSER

See Also MOSHER

Moser, George (Original Author)

Pirates of Capri, The 1949,D 26,33:5

Moser, Hans

Darling of the Gods; Liebling der Gotter 1930,N 30,IX,6:5
Grosse Tenor, Der 1931,My 29,26:5
Causa Kaiser; Kaiser Case, The 1932,F 14,VIII,6:1
Man Braucht Kein Geld 1932,N 16,15:3
Madame Wuenscht Keine Kinder 1933,Je 2,22:4
Polenblut; Polish Blood 1935,N 16,19:3
Himmel auf Erden, Der 1935,D 26,21:4
Winternachtstraum 1935,D 28,10:6
Frasquita 1936,Ja 18,19:4
Karneval und Liebe 1936,Ap 4,11:2
Fahrt in Die Jugend, Die 1936,Ag 31,19:2
Masquerade in Vienna 1937,Ja 26,16:4
World's in Love, The 1937,My 19,27:2
Endstation 1937,Jl 17,18:1
Schabernack 1937,Ag 14,16:5
Gaesschen zum Paradies, Das 1937,Ag 21,7:3
Vienna Burgtheater 1937,O 27,47:1
Eva, das Fabriksmaedel 1938,Ja 8,19:2
Only for Thee; Solo per To 1938,S 12,13:2
Gluecklichste Ehe von Wien, Die; Happiest Married Couple in Vienna, The 1938,O 8,10:2
Wir Sind vom K u K Infantrie-Regiment 1938,N 19,9:2
Alles Fuer Veronika 1939,F 4,11:2
Kleines Bezirksgericht; Little Country Court 1939,F 18,12:4
Fasching in Wien 1939,Mr 18,9:2
Hohe Schule; College 1939,Ap 8,19:3
Familie Schimek 1939,S 2,20:2
Ekel, Das; Grouch, The 1939,D 4,18:4
Walzerlange; Waltz Melodies 1940,Ap 27,9:3
Wiener Geschichten; Vienna Tales 1940,S 28,9:3
Opernball; Opera Ball 1940,O 15,29:2
State Secret 1950,O 5,38:2
Vienna Blood 1951,F 22,27:4

Moser, James E (Screenwriter)

Wings of the Hawk 1953,Ag 27,22:1

Moser, Sonia

Quiet American, The 1958,F 6,24:1

Moses, Marion

Dead Heat on a Merry-Go-Round 1966,O 13,50:1

Moses, R G Major

West Point 1928,Ja 2,28:1

Mosgrove, Gertrude

Break the News 1941,Ja 2,24:2

Moshe, Yehuda Ben

Dream no More 1950,Ja 6,25:2

Mosheim, Grete

Primanerliebe 1928,Mr 13,23:3
Dame Care 1928,My 20,VIII,8:3
Cyankali 1930,Jl 13,VIII,4:2
Yorck 1932,N 24,35:2
Dreyfus Case, The 1940,O 30,29:3

MOSHER

See Also MOSER

Mosher, Bob (Original Author)

Private War of Major Benson, The 1955,Ag 3,27:2

Mosher, Bob (Producer)

Munster, Go Home 1966,Je 16,53:4

Mosher, Bob (Screenwriter)

Munster, Go Home 1966,Je 16,53:4

Mosini, Odeardo

Last Chance, The 1945,N 28,21:6

Mosjoukine, Ivan

Living Dead Man, The 1927,Mr 7,16:3
Edmund Kean, Prince Among Lovers 1927,Je 1,25:2
Casanova 1927,Je 23,23:3
Surrender 1927,O 11,27:1
President, The 1929,Ja 21,18:4
Loves of Casanova, The 1929,Ap 30,33:2
White Devil, The 1931,Ag 28,20:1

Mosjoukine, Ivan (Director)

Casanova 1927,Je 23,23:3

Mosk, Bernice (Screenwriter)

Buccaneer, The 1958,D 24,00:0

Mosk, Fern (Miscellaneous)

Liberation of Belgrade 1946,Jl 15,21:1

Moskine, Ivan

Michael Strogoff 1926,D 6,28:3

Moskov, George (Producer)

Champagne for Caesar 1950,My 12,33:2

Moskov, George (Screenwriter)

Joe Palooka, Champ 1946,Ap 6,10:6

Moskowitz, Jennie

Mother's Boy 1929,My 8,34:6

Moskvin, I M (Director)

Station Master, The 1928,Je 18,13:2

Moskvin, Ivan

Polikushka 1927,Ja 17,12:4 (In Addenda)
Station Master, The 1928,Je 18,13:2
Hour With Tchekhof, An 1933,S 6,24:4

Mosley, Leonard (Original Author)

Foxhole in Cairo 1961,F 16,25:2

Mosley, Leonard (Screenwriter)

Foxhole in Cairo 1961,F 16,25:2

Mosquini, Marie

Good and Naughty 1926,Je 14,24:1
Seventh Heaven 1927,My 26,22:1
Two Girls Wanted 1927,N 14,26:1

Mosquiz, Carlos

Treasure of Pancho Villa, The 1955,N 25,38:2

Moss, Arnold

Temptation 1946,D 25,33:6
Loves of Carmen, The 1948,S 3,16:2
Black Book, The 1949,O 17,18:2
Border Incident 1949,N 21,29:2
Kim 1950,D 8,40:4
Quebec 1951,Mr 16,34:2
Mask of the Avenger 1951,Je 27,25:2
My Favorite Spy 1951,D 26,19:3
Viva Zapata 1952,F 8,19:2
Salome 1953,Mr 25,37:1
Casanova's Big Night 1954,Ap 19,19:1
Bengal Brigade 1954,N 13,13:2
Hell's Island 1955,My 7,10:2
Gambit 1966,D 22,40:2

Moss, Charlie

Little Fugitive 1953,O 7,35:1

Moss, Frank (Screenwriter)

Sangaree 1953,Je 5,19:1

Moss, Geoffrey C G Major (Original Author)

Isn't Life Wonderful? 1924,D 1,17:3

Moss, Jack

Journey Into Fear 1943,Mr 19,15:3

Moss, Jack (Director)

Snafu 1945,D 26,15:2

Moss, Jack (Producer)

Biscuit Eater, The 1940,My 23,28:5
Monster and the Girl, The 1941,Mr 20,25:3
Shepherd of the Hills, The 1941,Jl 31,13:2
Mr Winkle Goes to War 1944,Ag 3,16:1
Snafu 1945,D 26,15:2

Moss, Jimmy

Inside Job 1946,Je 15,24:3
Man-Eater of Kumaon 1948,Jl 2,24:2
Damned Don't Cry, The 1950,Ap 8,9:2
Jim Thorpe - All American 1951,Ag 25,7:2
Miserables, Les 1952,Ag 15,11:2
Mister Scoutmaster 1953,Ag 29,10:1

Moss, Paul F (Original Author)

20 Million Sweethearts 1934,Ap 27,25:1

Moss, Paul F (Producer)

Detective, The 1954,N 2,25:2

Moss, Stewart

In Harm's Way 1965,Ap 7,36:1

Moss, W Stanley (Original Author)

Night Ambush 1958,Ap 25,32:4

Moss, William

Canterville Ghost, The 1944,Jl 29,16:2
Bring on the Girls 1945,Mr 1,25:5
Badman's Territory 1946,My 31,27:2

Moss, William (Producer)

Big Cat, The 1949,Jl 29,12:2

Mossbacher, Peter

Liane, Jungle Goddess 1959,F 23,19:1

Mossinsohn, Igal (Original Author)

Casablan 1964,D 14,50:1

Mostel, Zero

Du Barry Was a Lady 1943,Ag 20,13:1
Panic in the Streets 1950,Ag 5,9:2
Enforcer, The 1951,Ja 26,19:2
Sirocco 1951,Je 14,31:2
Mr Belvedere Rings the Bell 1951,Ag 2,18:1
Guy Who Came Back, The 1951,Ag 17,13:2
Model and the Marriage Broker, The 1952,Ja 12,10:6
Funny Thing Happened on the Way to the Forum, A 1966,O 17,48:1
Producers, The 1968,Mr 19,38:1

Mosthav, Franz

Great British Train Robbery, The 1967,Ap 6,45:2

Mostovoy, Leonide

Since You Went Away 1944,Jl 21,16:2

Mota, Felipe

Brave Bulls, The 1951,Ap 19,39:2

Motiet, Alain

Fire Within, The 1964,F 18,27:1

Motley, Willard (Original Author)

Knock on any Door 1949,F 23,31:2
Let no Man Write my Epitaph 1960,N 11,36:2

Motoko, Sojiro (Producer)

Magnificent Seven, The 1956,N 20,46:2

Mott, Ernie

None but the Lonely Heart 1944,D 3,II,1:8

Mott, Joe

We're Going to Be Rich 1938,Jl 4,10:2
Smiling Along 1939,F 20,13:2

Motveyeva, A

City of Youth 1938,S 5,30:4

Motylef, Ilya (Director)

Cantor's Son, The 1937,D 27,11:1

Moucle, Henri

Face to the Wind 1951,Ja 16,34:2

Mouezy-Eon, Andre (Miscellaneous)
army Game, The; Tire Au Flanc 1963,Ap 24,40:1
Mouezy-Eon, Andre (Screenwriter)
Army Game, The; Tire Au Flanc
1963,Ap 24,40:1
Moulan, Frank
Girl Said No, The 1937,O 18,14:1
Moulieres, Jacques
Lover's Net 1957,Jl 23,23:1
Every Second Counts 1957,O 15,39:4
Sans Famille 1959,S 5,11:4
Moulin, Charles
Baker's Wife, The 1940,F 27,17:2
They Are not Angels 1948,My 22,8:3
Bernadette of Lourdes 1962,Ja 30,20:2
Moulinot, Jean-Paul
Fire Within, The 1964,F 18,27:1
Mouloudji, Marcel
Generals Without Buttons 1938,Mr 8,23:2
Boys' School 1939,Je 6,26:2
Claudine 1940,Ap 1,15:2
They Met on Skis 1940,D 23,23:2
They Are not Angels 1948,My 22,8:3
Chips Are Down, The 1949,F 2,36:1
Wench, The 1949,Mr 14,15:5
Bed, The (Riviera Express); Riviera Express (The
Bed) 1955,Je 8,26:4
We Are all Murderers 1957,Ja 9,27:2
Sinners of Paris 1959,Ap 24,23:1
Moulton, Herbert L (Miscellaneous)
Land of Liberty 1939,Je 16,27:3
Land of Liberty 1941,Ja 30,19:2
Moulton, Zita
Expert, The 1932,F 27,22:1
Sinners in the Sun 1932,My 14,11:5
Employees' Entrance 1933,Ja 21,10:6
Awful Truth, The 1937,N 5,19:3
Moultrie, Fred
Bright Road 1953,Ap 29,33:5
Mounet, Lily
Friend Will come Tonight, A; Ami Viendra Ce
Soir, Un 1948,Jl 12,11:2
Mouneyres, Martine
Club De Femmes 1937,O 20,27:2
Mount, Peggy
Panic in the Parlor 1957,D 18,45:1
Your Past Is Showing 1958,Jl 1,36:2
Ladies Who Do 1963,N 26,52:2
One Way Pendulum 1965,Mr 3,34:3
Hotel Paradiso 1966,O 15,34:2
Oliver! 1968,D 11,57:1
Mountain Dancers
World Dances 1954,N 8,24:6
Mouque, Georges (Composer)
Enfants du Paradis, Les 1947,F 20,32:2
Moury, Alain (Screenwriter)
Thank Heaven for Small Favors 1965,Ja 14,44:2
Mouse, Mickey
Hollywood Party 1934,My 26,12:2
Moussia
Il est Charmant; He is Charming
1932,Mr 27,VIII,6:2
Moussy, Marcel (Screenwriter)
400 Blows, The; (Les Quatre Cents Coups)
1959,N 17,41:1
Moustache
Paris Blues 1961,N 8,41:1
How to Steal a Million 1966,Jl 15,34:1
Moustakas, Sotiris
Zorba, The Greek 1964,D 18,25:1
Moustakus, Athanias
Shepherd's Daughter, The 1956,My 14,23:3
Mouton, Albert
Five Day Lover, The 1961,D 14,55:4
Movin, Lisbeth
Day of Wrath 1948,Ap 26,27:2
Red Meadows 1950,Ja 19,35:2
Hagbard and Signe 1968,My 17,56:1
Moving Star, Hall Singers
Festival 1967,O 24,53:2
Movita
Mutiny on the Bounty 1935,N 9,19:2
Rose of the Rio Grande 1938,Jl 9,10:3
Tower of Terror 1942,Je 29,11:4
Dream Wife 1953,Jl 30,20:1
Barbarian and the Geisha 1958,O 3,25:1
Mowbray, Alan
God's Gift to Women 1931,Ap 18,17:3
Man in Possession, The 1931,Jl 18,16:6
Guilty Hands 1931,Ag 29,16:3
Alexander Hamilton 1931,S 17,21:4
Honor of the Family 1931,O 17,20:1
Leftover Ladies 1931,N 9,22:4
Silent Witness, The 1932,F 8,21:1
Lovers Courageous 1932,F 20,11:2
Nice Women 1932,F 20,11:2
Hotel Continental 1932,Mr 21,19:5
World and the Flesh, The 1932,My 7,11:5
Man About Town 1932,My 28,18:2
Winner Take All 1932,Je 18,9:2
Man From Yesterday, The 1932,Je 25,18:2
Man Called Back, The 1932,Jl 30,16:5
Two Against the World 1932,Ag 19,20:6

Sherlock Holmes 1932,N 12,20:5
Our Betters 1933,F 24,13:2
Peg o'my Heart 1933,My 20,11:4
Study in Scarlet, A 1933,Je 1,15:3
Midnight Club 1933,Jl 29,14:2
Voltaire 1933,Ag 23,21:2
Berkeley Square 1933,S 14,26:2
World Changes, The 1933,O 27,22:3
Roman Scandals 1933,D 25,28:2
Long Lost Father 1934,F 19,18:2
House of Rothschild, The 1934,Mr 15,27:2
Cheaters 1934,My 12,12:4
Where Sinners Meet 1934,My 25,25:2
Little Man, What Now? 1934,Je 1,29:1
Girl From Missouri, The 1934,Ag 4,14:6
One More River 1934,Ag 10,21:1
Charlie Chan in London 1934,S 13,26:1
Night Life of the Gods 1935,F 23,14:6
Becky Sharp 1935,Je 14,27:2
Lady Tubbs 1935,Jl 22,20:2
Gay Deception, The 1935,O 11,31:1
She Couldn't Take It 1935,N 7,27:1
In Person 1935,D 13,31:5
Rose Marie 1936,F 1,9:2
Muss 'Em Up 1936,F 3,21:2
Give Us This Night 1936,Ap 6,18:1
Desire 1936,Ap 13,15:1
Case Against Mrs Ames, The 1936,My 28,19:2
Fatal Lady 1936,Jl 11,11:3
Mary of Scotland 1936,Jl 31,22:2
My Man Godfrey 1936,S 19,18:1 (Incorrect in
this edition; use 1936,S 18,18:1 elsewhere)
Ladies in Love 1936,O 29,31:1
Rainbow on the River 1936,D 18,31:4
On the Avenue 1937,F 5,17:3
King and the Chorus Girl, The 1937,Mr 29,14:4
As Good as Married 1937,My 22,19:2
Marry the Girl 1937,Jl 31,6:2
Topper 1937,Ag 20,21:2
Vogues of 1938 1937,Ag 20,21:1
On Such a Night 1937,S 17,29:2
Music for Madame 1937,O 23,14:1
Stand-In 1937,N 19,27:2
Hollywood Hotel 1938,Ja 13,17:3
Merrily We Live 1938,Mr 18,23:3
There Goes my Heart 1938,O 14,27:1
Topper Takes a Trip 1938,D 30,11:2
Never Say Die 1939,Mr 9,18:1
Way Down South 1939,Ag 18,16:4
Music in My Heart 1940,Ja 4,19:2
Curtain Call 1940,Ap 19,25:2
Boys From Syracuse, The 1940,Ag 1,25:2
Quarterback, The 1940,O 17,33:3
That Hamilton Woman 1941,Ap 4,25:1
That Uncertain Feeling 1941,My 2,25:1
Ice-Capades 1941,S 25,29:1
Moon Over her Shoulder 1941,N 5,31:2
I Wake up Screaming 1942,Ja 17,13:2
We Were Dancing 1942,My 1,23:2
Panama Hattie 1942,O 2,31:2
Yank at Eton, A 1942,O 16,23:1
Devil With Hitler, The 1942,O 19,15:2
Powers Girl, The 1943,Mr 26,14:2 (In Addenda)
Slightly Dangerous 1943,Ap 2,17:2
Stage Door Canteen 1943,Je 25,13:2
Holy Matrimony 1943,S 16,25:2
His Butler's Sister 1943,D 30,13:2
Doughgirls, The 1944,Ag 31,14:1
Bring on the Girls 1945,Mr 1,25:5
Earl Carroll Vanities 1945,Ap 2,15:6
Where Do We Go From Here? 1945,Je 7,25:2
Men in her Diary 1945,S 24,16:5
Terror by Night 1946,F 9,9:2
My Darling Clementine 1946,D 4,44:5
Lured 1947,Ag 29,14:4
Merton of the Movies 1947,N 7,20:3
Captain from Castile 1947,D 26,22:4
Innocent Affair, An 1948,S 29,36:2
Every Girl Should be Married 1948,D 24,14:2
My Dear Secretary 1949,F 14,15:4
You're my Everything 1949,Jl 23,7:2
Abbott and Costello Meet the Killer Boris Karloff
1949,S 19,18:3
Wagonmaster 1950,Je 19,17:2
Jackpot, The 1950,N 23,55:2
Crosswinds 1951,D 7,35:4
Just Across the Street 1952,Je 28,12:4
Blackbeard the Pirate 1952,D 26,20:3
Androcles and the Lion 1953,Ja 15,23:2
King's Thief, The 1955,Ag 13,7:2
Man Who Knew too Much, The 1956,My 17,37:1
King and I, The 1956,Je 29,15:6
Around the World in 80 Days 1956,O 18,37:1
Majority of One, A 1962,Ja 12,29:2
Mowbray, Henry
Pursuit of Happiness, The 1934,O 26,25:1
Mower, Jack
Uncle Tom's Cabin 1927,N 5,16:2
Sailors' Wives 1928,F 28,18:4
Water Hole, The 1928,S 3,14:2
Hollywood Boulevard 1936,S 21,26:4
Love Is on the Air 1937,N 12,27:3
Missing Witness 1937,D 10,33:3

Mower, Jack — Cont
Invisible Menace, The 1938,F 14,20:6
Penrod and his Twin Brother 1938,Ap 18,11:1
Crime School 1938,My 11,17:2
Hard To Get 1938,N 14,15:2
Confessions of a Nazi Spy 1939,Ap 29,13:2
Return Of Doctor X, The 1939,N 23,38:5
British Intelligence 1940,F 12,14:2
Torrid Zone 1940,My 18,11:3
Mower, Patrick
Devil's Bride, The 1968,D 19,60:1
Mowery, Helen
Key Witness 1947,Jl 30,27:6
Woman in the Night 1948,Ja 10,16:2
Mowery, William Byron (Original Author)
Heart of the North 1938,D 21,29:2
Moxey, Hugh
Night my Number Came up, The 1955,D 20,39:5
Time Without Pity 1957,N 23,11:2
Moxey, John (Director)
Foxhole in Cairo 1961,F 16,25:2
Horror Hotel 1963,Je 20,29:1
Moxie, Paul
It's Always Fair Weather 1955,S 16,19:1
Moxon, Tim
Dr No 1963,My 30,20:1
Moya, Robert
Tropic Holiday 1938,Je 30,21:2
Law West of Tombstone, The 1938,N 25,19:1
Moyes, Patricia (Screenwriter)
School for Scoundrels 1960,Jl 12,39:1
Moyheddin, Zia
Khartoum 1966,Jl 14,28:1
Sailor From Gibraltar, The 1967,Ap 25,38:2
Moylan, Catherine
Love in the Rough 1930,S 27,21:3
Moyzisch, I C (Original Author)
Five Fingers 1952,F 23,7:5
Mozart, Wolfgang Amadeus (Composer)
First Opera Film Festival 1948,My 31,12:7
Don Juan 1956,Mr 6,26:2
Don Giovanni 1956,D 27,22:1
Mozo, Hugo (Screenwriter)
Torero! 1957,My 22,29:2
Mozouri, Rita
Golfo-Girl of the Mountains 1958,My 19,19:5
Mozvon, A (Screenwriter)
Secret Brigade 1951,Mr 19,23:2
Mratinez, Luis Mgr (Miscellaneous)
Virgin of Guadalupe, The 1943,My 15,13:3
Mrazova, Eva
Sweet Light in a Dark Room 1966,Je 30,28:1
Mruwka, Gunther
I Aim at the Stars 1960,O 20,42:2
Mu, Chu
Lady General, The 1965,F 12,19:1
Shepherd Girl, The 1965,S 2,36:3
Mubarak, Nasir Ibu
Island of Allah 1956,Je 27,35:1
Mucci, Edulia
Romola 1924,D 2,13:2
Muclinger, J
Border Street 1950,Ap 26,35:2
Mudie, James
Charlie Chan's Murder Cruise 1940,My 3,17:5
Mudie, Leonard
Mummy, The 1933,Ja 7,11:2
Voltaire 1933,Ag 23,21:2
Mystery of Mr X, The 1934,F 26,21:3
House of Rothschild, The 1934,Mr 15,27:2
Cleopatra 1934,Ag 17,12:1
Clive of India 1935,Ja 18,29:1
Cardinal Richelieu 1935,Ap 19,24:2
Becky Sharp 1935,Je 14,27:2
Rendezvous 1935,O 26,12:2
Great Impersonation, The 1935,D 14,11:1
Captain Blood 1935,D 27,14:1
Magnificent Obsession 1935,D 31,11:2
Mary of Scotland 1936,Jl 31,22:2
His Brother's Wife 1936,Ag 15,6:2
Anthony Adverse 1936,Ag 27,16:1
Lloyds of London 1936,N 26,39:1
King and the Chorus Girl, The 1937,Mr 29,14:4
League of Frightened Men, The 1937,Jl 2,25:1
They Won't Forget 1937,Jl 15,16:1
London by Night 1937,Ag 13,13:1
Lancer Spy 1937,N 4,29:1
Jury's Secret, The 1938,F 4,17:2
Kidnapped 1938,My 28,9:2
When Were You Born? 1938,Je 9,27:2
Arrest Bulldog Drummond 1939,Ja 12,23:2
Dark Victory 1939,Ap 21,27:2
Man About Town 1939,Je 29,19:1
Tropic Fury 1939,S 8,28:4
Congo Maisie 1940,F 8,18:4
British Intelligence 1940,F 12,14:2
Devil's Island 1940,Jl 12,11:4
Shining Victory 1941,My 31,14:1
Nurse's Secret, The 1941,Je 6,25:7
Berlin Correspondent 1942,S 4,19:2
Appointment in Berlin 1943,Jl 17,8:2
My Name is Julia Ross 1945,N 9,16:3
Song of my Heart 1948,Mr 5,17:3
Magnetic Monster, The 1953,My 14,32:5

Mudie, Leonard— Cont

Autumn Leaves 1956,Ag 2,21:2
Big Fisherman, The 1959,Ag 6,18:1
MUELLER
See Also MULLER, MOELLER, MOLLER
Mueller, Anneliese
Marriage of Figaro 1950,N 3,31:2
Mueller, Elisabeth
Power and The Prize, the 1956,S 27,42:1
Confession of Ina Kahn, The 1958,Ja 1,31:4
Ballerina 1958,My 10,19:2
Corinna Darling 1958,Je 14,14:3
Angry Hills, The 1959,Jl 16,31:3
Confess, Dr Corda 1960,O 24,25:5
Mueller, H K
Luther 1929,Je 24,27:1
Mueller, Hans (Original Author)
Monte Carlo 1930,Ag 28,22:4
Smiling Lieutenant, The 1931,My 23,13:4
Stuerme der Leidenschaft 1932,Mr 16,17:3
Monte Carlo Madness 1932,Je 4,9:2
White Horse Inn, The 1957,D 4,50:3
Mueller, Hans (Screenwriter)
Three Waltzes 1939,Ap 25,19:2
Mueller, Jane
World Dances 1954,N 8,24:6
Mueller, Renate
Liebe im Ring 1930,Ag 11,13:1
Darling of the Gods; Liebling der Gotter
1930,N 30,IX,6:5
Grosse Tenor, Der 1931,My 29,26:5
Floetenkonzert von Sanssouci, Das
1931,O 17,20:1
Kleine Seitensprung, Der 1932,Ja 1,31:1
Office Girl 1932,Je 27,20:7
Die Blumenfrau von Lindenau 1932,Jl 8,22:5
Herzblut 1932,O 3,15:2
Sohn der Weissen Berge, Der 1933,O 23,18:3
Wenn die Liebe Mode Macht 1933,O 30,14:3
Saison in Kairo 1933,D 25,28:2
Wie Sag' Ich's Meinem Mann? 1934,Ja 23,22:4
Waltz Time in Vienna 1934,N 19,13:2
Viktor und Viktoria 1935,Ja 28,10:5
Private Life of Louis XIV, The 1936,Ja 9,25:2
Liebesleute 1936,O 3,21:2
Togger 1937,Mr 14,XI,4:5 (In Addenda)
For Her Country's Sake 1937,N 27,21:3
Mueller, Walter
White Horse Inn, The 1957,D 4,50:3
Mueller-Stahl, Armin
Naked Among the Wolves 1967,Ap 19,54:7
Muethel, Lola
Judge and the Sinner, The 1964,Je 6,14:2
Muethel, Lothar
Yorck 1932,N 24,35:2
Muggeridge, Malcolm
I'm All Right Jack 1960,Ap 26,40:2
Muggeridge, Malcolm (Miscellaneous)
Heavens Above! 1963,My 21,28:2
Mugica, Rene
Where Words Fail; Donde Mueren las Palabraso
1948,Ag 19,18:4
Muhssin, Ertugrul
Ankara Postassi; Courier of Angora, The
1929,N 17,IX,7:1 (In Addenda)
Muhssin, Ertugrul (Director)
Ankara Postassi; Courier of Angora, The
1929,N 17,IX,7:1 (In Addenda)
Muhssin, Ertugrul (Screenwriter)
Ankara Postassi; Courier of Angora, The
1929,N 17,IX,7:1 (In Addenda)
Muino, Enrique
Viento Norte; North Wind 1939,S 16,20:3
Viejo Doctor, El; Old Doctor, The
1940,Ap 13,21:3
Alas de mi Patria; My Country's Wingo
1940,Je 4,19:4
Asi es la Vida; Such Is Life 1940,Ag 6,15:1
Huella; Trial 1940,O 22,27:3
Where Words Fail; Donde Mueren las Palabraso
1948,Ag 19,18:4
Muir, Augustus (Original Author)
Phantom Submarine, The 1941,F 12,25:3
Muir, Douglas
Breaking Through the Sound Barrier
1952,N 7,19:1
Muir, Esther
Dangerous Affair, A 1931,N 23,22:1
Sailor's Luck 1933,Mr 17,21:2
So This Is Africa! 1933,Ap 24,11:3
Wine, Women and Song 1934,Mr 21,24:3
Day at the Races, A 1937,Je 18,25:2
On Again-Off Again 1937,S 18,15:3
I'll Take Romance 1937,D 17,33:2
Under Suspicion 1937,D 20,23:2 (In Addenda)
City Girl 1938,F 4,17:3
Romance in the Dark 1938,Mr 21,18:2
Battle of Broadway 1938,Ap 25,19:2
Law West of Tombstone, The 1938,N 25,19:1
Girl and the Gambler, The 1939,Je 28,17:3
Muir, Florabel (Screenwriter)
Fighting Youth 1935,N 2,13:3

Muir, Gavin
Half Angel 1936,My 30,7:3
Mary of Scotland 1936,Jl 31,22:2
Charlie Chan at the Race Track 1936,Ag 15,6:2
Lloyds of London 1936,N 26,39:1
Holy Terror, The 1937,Ja 30,21:2
Wee Willie Winkie 1937,Jl 24,12:1
Nightmare 1942,D 4,31:2
Hitler's Children 1943,F 25,27:1
Sherlock Holmes Faces Death 1943,O 8,15:3
Merry Monahans, The 1944,O 13,16:2
Master Race, The 1944,N 2,22:1
Tonight and Every Night 1945,Mr 9,16:2
Patrick the Great 1945,Ap 13,15:2
Salome, Where She Danced 1945,My 3,27:1
O S S 1946,My 27,15:5
California 1947,Ja 15,31:2
Calcutta 1947,Ap 24,30:2
Ivy 1947,Je 26,19:1
Unconquered 1947,O 11,11:2
Chicago Deadline 1949,N 3,37:2
Abbott and Costello Meet the Invisible Man
1951,Ap 13,18:6
Thunder on the Hill 1951,O 18,32:3
Night Tide 1963,Je 7,37:1
Muir, Graeme
Meet Me at Dawn 1948,My 18,26:2
Showtime 1948,My 20,35:3
Muir, Helen
Strictly Confidential 1919,O 6,15:1
Muir, Jean
World Changes, The 1933,O 27,22:3
Son of a Sailor 1933,N 30,38:4
Bedside 1934,Mr 7,23:4
As the Earth Turns 1934,Ap 12,27:2
Modern Hero, A 1934,Ap 20,17:1
Dr Monica 1934,Je 21,28:2
Desirable 1934,S 15,20:5
Gentlemen are Born 1934,N 22,27:2
White Cockatoo, The 1935,Ja 16,21:1
Oil for the Lamps of China 1935,Je 6,25:2
Orchids to You 1935,Ag 10,16:4
Midsummer Night's Dream, A 1935,O 10,31:1
Stars Over Broadway 1935,N 14,17:3
White Fang 1936,Jl 18,18:2
Fugitive in the Sky 1937,Ja 16,21:1
Her Husband's Secretary 1937,Mr 20,23:6
Outcasts of Poker Flat, The 1937,Ap 27,18:3
White Bondage 1937,Ag 6,21:3
Dance Charlie Dance 1937,Ag 26,25:2
And One Was Beautiful 1940,Ap 11,32:4
Lone Wolf Meets a Lady, The 1940,Je 17,19:2
Constant Nymph, The 1943,Jl 24,8:2
Muir, Jean (Original Author)
Northwest Stampede 1948,D 10,34:3
Muiton, Roger
Girl on a Motorcycle, The 1968,N 28,66:5
Mujica, Alba
Inheritance, The; Herencia, La 1964,S 16,36:3
Mujica, Barbara
Casa del Angel, La 1960,Ag 30,25:1
Mujica, Francisco (Director)
Asi es la Vida; Such Is Life 1940,Ag 6,15:1
Mukerjee, Suprova
River, The 1951,S 11,33:2
Mukherjee, Arun
Kanchenjungha 1966,Jl 26,27:2
Mukherjee, Madhabi
Mahanagar; Big City, The 1964,S 28,19:1
Charulata 1965,S 11,16:1
Big City, The; Mahanager 1967,Je 30,30:1
Mukherjee, Prabhat Kumar (Original Author)
Devi 1962,O 8,19:1
Mukherjee, Purnendu
Devi 1962,O 8,19:1
Mukherjee, Sailen
Charulata 1965,S 11,16:1
Mukherji, Swapan
World of Apu; Apur Sansar 1960,O 5,45:1
Mukhutinov, K
Pugachev 1938,Jl 4,10:2
Mulcaster, G H
Iron Duke, The 1935,Ja 25,27:2
Patient Vanishes, The 1947,My 23,31:2
Under Capricorn 1949,S 9,28:3
Spring in Park Lane 1949,S 21,38:2
If This Be Sin 1950,Jl 1,9:2
Mulcaster, Michael
Naked Heart, The 1955,Mr 9,22:4
Muldaur, Diana
Swimmer, The 1968,My 16,53:1
Mule, Francesco
Psycosissimo 1962,S 8,16:2
Biggest Bundle of Them All, The 1968,Ja 18,46:1
Mulford, Clarence E (Original Author)
Deadwood Coach, The 1925,Ja 21,19:3
Three on the Trail 1936,My 5,26:5
Hopalong Rides Again 1938,Ja 22,19:1
Partners of the Plains 1938,F 12,20:4
Heart of Arizona 1938,Ap 16,17:1
Mulhall, Jack
Should a Woman Tell? 1920,Ja 5,15:1
You Never Can Tell 1920,O 4,14:3

Mulhall, Jack— Cont

Turn to the Right 1922,Ja 24,11:1
Within the Law 1923,Ap 30,11:2
Dulcy 1923,S 17,18:2
Bad Man, The 1923,O 9,17:4
Goldfish, The 1924,My 20,15:2
Into the Net 1924,Ag 23,10:2
Breath of Scandal, The 1924,N 26,17:3
Folly of Vanity 1925,Ja 28,14:1
Friendly Enemies 1925,My 5,24:2
Mad Whirl, The 1925,Jl 1,16:1
Classified 1925,N 2,20:1
We Moderns 1925,D 8,28:5
Joanna 1925,D 15,14:5
Silence 1926,My 19,29:3
Sweet Daddies 1926,Je 23,28:1
Subway Sadie 1926,S 13,18:1
Girl from Coney Island or Just Another Blonde
1926,D 13,27:1
See You in Jail 1927,Ap 4,30:5
Orchids and Ermine 1927,Ap 19,24:4
Poor Nut, The 1927,Jl 19,27:2
Smile, Brother, Smile 1927,Ag 29,21:1
Crystal Cup, The 1927,O 25,33:3
Man Crazy 1927,D 19,30:1
Ladies' Night in a Turkish Bath 1928,Ap 9,18:2
Lady Be Good 1928,My 28,23:2
Butter and Egg Man, The 1928,Ag 28,27:4
Waterfront 1928,O 22,29:1
Naughty Baby 1929,F 5,26:3
Children of the Ritz 1929,Ap 2,28:4
Two Weeks Off 1929,Je 24,27:1
Twin Beds 1929,Jl 15,25:1
Show of Shows 1929,N 21,24:5
Second Choice 1930,Ja 4,21:1
In the Next Room 1930,Ap 7,21:1
Murder Will Out 1930,Ap 14,24:2
Her Golden Calf 1930,My 5,27:3
Show Girl in Hollywood 1930,My 5,27:3
Fall Guy, The 1930,My 27,27:2
Road to Paradise 1930,S 30,23:1
Reaching for the Moon 1930,D 30,24:2
Road to Paradise, The 1931,Ja 20,21:3
Lover Come Back 1931,Je 5,26:5
Old-Fashioned Way, The 1934,Jl 14,16:5
Sweet Adeline 1935,Ja 7,13:2
Burn 'Em Up Barnes 1935,Mr 30,11:2
Big Broadcast of 1936, The 1935,S 16,15:2
Preview Murder Mystery, The 1936,Mr 21,13:2
13 Hours by Air 1936,Ap 30,17:2
Hollywood Boulevard 1936,S 21,26:4
Beloved Enemy 1936,D 26,15:2
Secret Valley 1937,Ja 25,22:2
100 Men and a Girl 1937,S 18,15:2
Spy Ring, The 1938,Ja 15,19:1
Crime Ring 1938,Jl 22,10:3
Chaser, The 1938,Ag 2,15:3
Storm, The 1938,O 31,12:2
First Love 1939,N 9,27:3
Black Friday 1940,Mr 22,23:3
Son of Monte Cristo, The 1940,D 5,33:1
Cheers for Miss Bishop 1941,Mr 14,17:2
Invisible Ghost, The 1941,My 8,21:2
Bowery Blitzkrieg 1941,O 1,24:5
Sin Town 1942,O 17,11:2
Mulhall, Rosalie (Original Author)
Hold That Lion 1926,S 6,16:2
Mulhare, Edward
Hill 24 Doesn't Answer 1955,N 3,37:1
Signpost to Murder 1965,My 20,52:2
Von Ryan's Express 1965,Je 24,28:1
Our Man Flint 1966,Ja 26,23:4
Caprice 1967,Je 8,52:2
Eye of the Devil 1967,D 7,60:1
Mulhauser, James (Screenwriter)
100 Men and a Girl 1937,S 18,15:2
Gladiator, The 1938,Ag 29,10:2
Mulholland, Gordon
Treasure Island 1950,Ag 16,24:2
Mullally, Don (Original Author)
Desert Flower, The 1925,Je 1,10:3
Mullally, Donn (Screenwriter)
Flying Fontaines, The 1959,D 24,13:6
Mullaly, Don (Original Author)
Girl Missing 1933,Ap 1,18:2
Mullaly, Donn (Original Author)
Wanted by the Police 1938,S 26,13:2
Mullaney, Jack
Young Stranger, The 1957,Ap 9,40:1
Vintage, The 1957,My 9,36:5
Kiss Them for Me 1957,N 9,31:2
South Pacific 1958,Mr 20,33:1
All the Fine Young Cannibals 1960,S 23,33:1
Honeymoon Machine, The 1961,Ag 24,25:2
Seven Days in May 1964,F 20,22:1
Tickle Me 1965,Je 24,28:3
Dr Goldfoot and the Bikini Machine
1966,F 17,29:3
Spinout 1966,D 15,60:1
Mullard, Arthur
Loneliness of the Long Distance Runner, The
1962,O 9,44:1
Morgan! 1966,Ap 5,42:2
Counterfeit Constable, The 1966,N 22,32:2

Mullard, Arthur— Cont
Smashing Time 1967,D 21,44:1

MULLEN
See Also MULLIN

Mullen, Barbara
Jeannie 1943,S 13,14:2
Thunder Rock 1944,S 15,16:1
Place of One's Own, A 1949,F 8,30:2
Corridor of Mirrors 1949,Mr 23,35:3
You Can't Beat the Irish 1952,My 1,34:4
So Little Time 1953,Jl 28,23:2
Gentle Gunman, The 1953,O 1,34:3
It Takes a Thief 1963,Ag 15,24:7

Mullen, Virginia
Lust for Gold 1949,Jl 4,9:2
For Men Only 1952,Ja 16,21:2

MULLER
See Also MOELLER, MOLLER, MUELLER

Muller, Cri-Cri
Scandals of Clochemerle, The 1950,Mr 28,28:2

Muller, Hella
Maternite 1937,Je 8,30:2

Muller, Paul
Invisible Army, The 1950,Je 26,17:3
Dead Woman's Kiss, A 1951,O 6,16:4
Hell Raiders of the Deep 1954,Jl 3,9:2
Checkpoint 1957,S 19,25:2
Queen of the Pirates 1961,Jl 27,23:4
Francis of Assisi 1961,Jl 29,8:2

Muller, Ray
Panic in the Streets 1950,Ag 5,9:2

Muller, Robert (Screenwriter)
Woman of Straw 1964,O 1,30:6

Muller, Steven
Adam Had Four Sons 1941,Mr 28,26:6
Seventh Cross, The 1944,S 29,18:1

Muller-Graf, Kurt
Head, The 1963,Je 20,29:1

Muller-Linke, Anna
Wahre Jakob, Der 1931,Ag 7,20:2

Mulliar, Fritz
Marika 1953,F 18,27:2

Mulligan, Gerry
Jazz on a Summer's Day 1960,Mr 29,46:2
Rat Race, The 1960,My 26,37:3
Subterraneans, The 1960,Jl 7,26:1

Mulligan, Richard
One Potato, Two Potato 1964,Jl 30,16:1
Group, The 1966,Mr 17,35:1

Mulligan, Robert (Director)
Fear Strikes Out 1957,Mr 21,37:2
Rat Race, The 1960,My 26,37:3
Great Impostor, The 1961,Mr 30,24:1
Come September 1961,S 8,34:1
Spiral Road, The 1962,Ag 4,11:2
To Kill a Mockingbird 1963,F 15,10:2
Love With the Proper Stranger 1963,D 26,33:1
Baby, the Rain Must Fall 1965,Ja 14,44:1
Inside Daisy Clover 1966,F 18,23:1
Up the Down Staircase 1967,Ag 18,36:2

Mullikin, Bill
New Faces 1954,F 20,8:7

MULLIN
See Also MULLEN

Mullin, Eugene (Screenwriter)
Lane That had no Turning, The 1922,Ja 9,15:2

Mullin, Virginia
Not Wanted 1949,Jl 25,11:4

Mullinor, Arthur
Sun Never Sets, The 1939,Je 9,26:2

Mullins, Moon
Spirit of Notre Dame, The 1931,O 16,27:1

Mullins, Peter
Mr Emmanuel 1945,Ja 8,15:2

Mulock, Al
Tarzan's Greatest Adventure 1959,Jl 9,22:1
Hellions, The 1962,Mr 15,28:2
Call Me Bwana 1963,Jl 4,9:1
Battle Beneath the Earth 1968,S 12,54:3

Mulqueen, Kathleen
Japanese War Bride 1952,Ja 30,22:6

Mulvihill, William (Original Author)
Sands of the Kalahari 1965,N 25,64:5

Mumblit, Gregory (Screenwriter)
Spring Song 1942,S 12,9:2

Mumford, Ethel Watts (Original Author)
After Business Hour 1925,Je 17,16:2

Mummert, Danny
Blondie 1938,D 22,25:4
Blondie Meets the Boss 1939,Ap 27,31:1
Blondie Goes Latin 1941,F 26,17:3
Blondie Hits the Jackpot 1949,S 9,28:3
Member of the Wedding, The 1952,D 31,10:2

Mummery, Browning
Evensong 1934,N 17,12:1

Mumy, Bill
Palm Springs Weekend 1963,N 6,32:1

Mumy, Billy
Ticklish Affair, A 1963,Ag 22,19:2
Dear Brigitte 1965,Ja 28,20:1

Munch, Richard
Visit, The 1964,O 22,44:1
Train, The 1965,Mr 18,25:1

MUNDAY
See Also MUNDY

Munday, Helen
Stark Love 1927,F 28,22:3

Mundin, Herbert
Silent Witness, The 1932,F 8,21:1
Devil's Lottery 1932,Ap 2,13:2
Trial of Vivienne Ware, The 1932,Ap 30,19:3
Bachelor's Affairs 1932,Je 25,18:2
Love Me Tonight 1932,Ag 19,20:6
Life Begins 1932,Ag 26,20:3
Chandu the Magician 1932,O 1,10:4
One Way Passage 1932,O 14,23:2
Sherlock Holmes 1932,N 12,20:5
Cavalcade 1933,Ja 6,23:2
Dangerously Yours 1933,F 23,20:3
Pleasure Cruise 1933,Ap 3,13:3
Adorable 1933,My 19,20:2
It's Great to be Alive 1933,Jl 8,14:6
Arizona to Broadway 1933,Jl 22,14:3
Devil's in Love, The 1933,Jl 28,18:2
Shanghai Madness 1933,S 23,11:6
Hoopla 1933,D 1,23:3
Orient Express 1934,F 28,23:2
Bottoms Up 1934,Mr 23,29:2
Ever Since Eve 1934,Mr 28,27:5
Such Women Are Dangerous 1934,Je 9,18:3
Call it Luck 1934,Jl 10,24:5
Hell in the Heavens 1934,D 12,28:2
David Copperfield 1935,Ja 19,8:1
Black Sheep 1935,Je 28,34:1
Mutiny on the Bounty 1935,N 9,19:2
Perfect Gentleman, The 1935,D 19,33:4
Charlie Chan's Secret 1936,Ja 18,19:4
Message to Garcia, A 1936,Ap 10,27:1
Under Two Flags 1936,My 1,19:1
Champagne Charlie 1936,My 7,21:2
Tarzan Escapes 1936,N 20,27:2
Another Dawn 1937,Je 18,25:3
You Can't Beat Love 1937,Je 25,25:3
Angel 1937,N 4,29:1
Invisible Enemy 1938,Ap 30,18:2
Adventures of Robin Hood, The 1938,My 13,17:2
Lord Jeff 1938,Jl 1,22:2
Exposed 1938,N 21,14:5
Society Lawyer 1939,Mr 31,19:2

MUNDY
See Also MUNDAY

Mundy, Edward
Chad Hanna 1940,D 26,23:1

Mundy, Talbot (Original Author)
Black Watch, The 1929,My 23,26:3
King of the Khyber Rifles 1953,D 23,21:1

Muni, Bella (Original Author)
Deceiver, The 1931,N 23,22:1

Muni, Paul
Valiant, The 1929,My 13,27:2
Seven Faces 1929,N 16,25:2
Scarface, The Shame of the Nation 1932,My 20,22:3
I Am a Fugitive From a Chain Gang 1932,N 11,17:2
I Am a Fugitive from a Chain Gang 1933,My 28,IX,2:5 (In Addenda)
World Changes, The 1933,O 27,22:3
Hi, Nellie! 1934,F 1,15:5
Bordertown 1935,Ja 24,22:5
Black Fury 1935,Ap 11,27:2
Dr Socrates 1935,O 3,29:2
Story of Louis Pasteur, The 1936,F 10,15:1
Good Earth, The 1937,F 3,27:1
Woman I Love, The 1937,Ap 16,27:2
Life of Emile Zola, The 1937,Ag 12,14:2
Juarez 1939,Ap 26,27:1
We Are not Alone 1939,D 1,27:1
Hudson's Bay 1941,Ja 10,23:2
Stage Door Canteen 1943,Je 25,13:2
Song to Remember, A 1945,Ja 26,16:4
Counter-Attack 1945,My 17,15:2
Angel on my Shoulder 1946,O 21,27:2
Stranger on the Prowl 1953,N 10,38:1
Commandos Strike at Dawn 1954,Ja 14,25:1
Last Angry Man, The 1959,O 23,24:1

Munier, Charlotte
Forty Little Mothers 1940,Ap 19,25:2

Munier, Ferdinand
Broken Wing, The 1923,O 9,17:4
Ambassador Bill 1931,N 14,15:3
Stepping Sisters 1932,Ja 9,21:1
After Tomorrow 1932,Mr 7,13:5
Woman I Stole, The 1933,Je 28,24:3
Queen Christina 1933,D 27,23:3
Count of Monte Cristo, The 1934,S 27,25:2
Barretts of Wimpole Street, The 1934,S 29,12:2
Babes in Toyland 1934,D 13,28:2
Clive of India 1935,Ja 18,29:1
Gilded Lily, The 1935,F 9,11:2
Folies Bergere 1935,F 25,13:2
Roberta 1935,Mr 8,25:2
Hands Across the Table 1935,N 2,13:2
One Rainy Afternoon 1936,My 14,29:2
White Angel, The 1936,Je 25,24:1
Tovarich 1937,D 31,9:2

Munier, Ferdinand— Cont
Marriage Forbidden 1938,Jl 16,7:2
Midnight 1939,Ap 6,31:1
Everything Happens at Night 1939,D 16,12:6
Model Wife 1941,Ap 24,25:3
Claudia 1943,N 5,23:2
Commandos Strike at Dawn 1954,Ja 14,25:1

Munier, Fred
Parachute Jumper 1933,Ja 26,12:2
Bowery, The 1933,O 5,24:2

Munj
Gyandev of India 1943,Ap 10,12:5

MUNK
See Also MONK

Munk, Andrzel (Director)
Passenger 1964,S 21,37:3
Eroica (Second Episode) 1966,F 2,24:1
Eroica (First Episode) 1966,F 2,24:1

Munk, Andrzel (Screenwriter)
Passenger 1964,S 21,37:3

Munk, Kaj (Original Author)
Ordet 1957,D 16,33:6

Munkacsi, Martin (Cinematographer)
Hansel and Gretel 1954,O 11,33:1

Munks, Mollie
On Approval 1945,Ja 29,17:1

Muno, Enrique
Cadetes de San Martin 1939,Jl 3,10:6

Munoz, Evita
Ay Jalisco no te Rajes 1943,Ap 24,17:3
Que Lindo es Michoacan 1944,Ap 22,8:7

Munoz, Jose
Massacre 1956,Je 2,13:5

Munoz, Marilou
Cry of Battle 1963,O 12,27:2

Munoz, Pepita
Ley que Olvidaron, La; Law They Forgot, The 1940,Ja 13,11:3

Munoz, Pilar
Nobleza Baturra; Rustic Chivalry 1938,Mr 28,19:3

MUNRO
See Also MONROE, MUNROE

Munro, Janet
Crawling Eye, The 1959,Ja 1,38:1
Darby O'Gill and the Little People 1959,Jl 1,26:1
Third Man on the Mountain 1959,N 12,27:1
Swiss Family Robinson 1960,D 24,8:4
Day the Earth Caught Fire, The 1962,Mr 16,25:1
Hide and Seek 1964,Mr 12,40:3
They all Died Laughing 1964,Mr 16,37:2
Walk in the Shadow 1966,S 12,52:5
Sebastian 1968,Ja 25,33:2

Munro, Nan
Morgan! 1966,Ap 5,42:2

Munro, Wendy
Wild Innocence 1938,N 11,31:2

MUNROE
See Also MONROE, MUNRO

Munroe, Bill (Composer)
Hold That Ghost 1941,Ag 8,13:3

Munsel, Patrice
Melba 1953,Je 25,23:1

Munshin, Jules
Easter Parade 1948,Jl 1,19:3
Take Me Out to the Ball Game 1949,Mr 10,35:2
That Midnight Kiss 1949,S 23,28:2
On the Town 1949,D 9,37:2
Monte Carlo Baby 1954,My 29,13:4
Ten Thousand Bedrooms 1957,Ap 4,37:1
Silk Stockings 1957,Jl 19,11:1
Monkeys Go Home 1967,Mr 30,55:1

Munson, Audrey
Purity 1916,Jl 24,7:4

Munson, Byron
Folly of Vanity 1925,Ja 28,14:1
Learning to Love 1925,F 23,24:1
Teaser, The 1925,Je 15,10:1
Publicity Madness 1927,D 12,30:6

Munson, Ona
Going Wild 1931,Ja 26,21:1
Hot Heiress, The 1931,Mr 14,23:2
Broad Minded 1931,Jl 6,24:4
Five Star Final 1931,S 11,24:2
Legion of Lost Flyers 1939,O 30,13:3
Gone With the Wind 1939,D 20,31:2
Big Guy, The 1940,Ja 1,29:2
Wagons Westward 1940,Jl 8,13:2
Lady From Louisiana 1941,My 15,27:2
Wild Geese Calling 1941,Ag 30,10:2
Shanghai Gesture, The 1941,D 26,21:2
Drums of the Congo 1942,Jl 20,16:4
Cheaters, The 1945,Jl 21,7:2
Dakota 1945,D 17,17:2
Red House, The 1947,Mr 17,27:2

Munzer, Michael
Carmen Baby 1967,O 11,41:2

Mura, Corinna
Call out the Marines 1942,Ja 26,18:3
Casablanca 1942,N 27,27:1
Honeymoon 1947,My 19,27:2

Muradian, Gregory
Strange Confession 1945,N 8,17:3
House of Dracula 1945,D 22,16:3

Muradian, Gregory— Cont
Bride Wore Boots, The 1946,Je 6,16:3
Murakami, Genzo (Original Author)
Kojiro 1968,Ag 30,23:1
Murano, Lia
Angelo in the Crowd 1952,O 4,15:2
Muranyi, Laszlo
Age of Illusions 1967,Mr 30,55:1
Muraoka, Kumiko
Koumiko Mystery, The; Mystere Keumiko, Le 1967,Ap 7,32:2
Murase, Hiromi
Hiroshima 1955,My 17,32:1
Murat
On Demande un Compaznon 1933,Je 5,18:5
Murat, Jean
Carmen 1928,My 7,29:1
Legion of Honor, The 1928,Jl 20,8:4
Eau du Nil, L' 1928,D 16,IX,8:2
Escaped From Hell 1929,Ja 29,27:1
Soul of France, The 1929,O 12,11:1
Venus 1929,O 14,20:2
Nuit est a Nous, La; (Night is Ours, The) 1931,F 21,15:2
Paris-Mediterranee 1932,Mr 27,VIII,6:2
Second Bureau 1936,F 17,21:2
Kermesse Heroique, La 1936,S 23,29:1
Generals Without Buttons 1938,Mr 8,23:2
Flight Into Darkness (L'Equipage) 1938,O 17,12:1
Eternal Return, The; Eternel Retour, L' 1948,Ja 5,15:2
Wench, The 1949,Mr 14,15:5
On the Riviera 1951,My 24,47:1
Rich, Young and Pretty 1951,Jl 26,17:3
Lady Chatterley's Lover 1959,Jl 11,11:1
Possessors, The 1959,Jl 21,24:1
7 Capital Sins (Envy); Envy (7 Capital Sins) 1963,Ja 17,5:2
Murat, Miranda
Island of Love 1963,Je 13,30:4
Murata, Takeo (Screenwriter)
Godzilla, King of the Monsters 1956,Ap 28,11:1
Murati, Lili
Elnoek Kisasszony 1935,O 12,12:3
Csunya Lany, A 1935,O 18,27:4
Fizessen Nagysag 1937,Je 4,27:3
120 Kilometers an Hour 1937,N 23,27:4
Muratore, Lucien
Manon Lescaut 1914,Je 14,15:1
Muratov, Alex (Director)
She-Wolf, The 1963,S 2,18:1
Muratov, Alex (Producer)
She-Wolf, The 1963,S 2,18:1
Muratov, Kira (Director)
She-Wolf, The 1963,S 2,18:1
Muratov, Kira (Producer)
She-Wolf, The 1963,S 2,18:1
Muratov, S
Concentration Camp 1939,Mr 20,13:2
Muraviev, V
Idiot, The 1960,Jl 22,11:2
Murayama, Noe
Nazarin 1968,Je 21,48:1
Murcell, George
Campbell's Kingdom 1960,Ja 11,35:5
MURDOCH
See Also MURDOCK
Murdoch, Henry
Overlanders, The 1946,D 20,31:2
Kangaroo 1952,My 17,22:7
Murdoch, Janet
Terror by Night 1946,F 9,9:2
Smash-Up, The Story of a Woman 1947,Ap 11,31:2
Murdoch, Richard
Gay Adventure, The 1954,S 16,35:7
MURDOCK
See Also MURDOCH
Murdock, Frank
Regular Girl, A 1919,N 11,13:3
Murdock, Kermit
In the Heat of the Night 1967,Ag 3,26:1
Murdock, Kermit (Narrator)
Farewell to Yesterday 1950,D 1,31:2
Murdock, Tim
Thirty Seconds Over Tokyo 1944,N 16,19:1
They Were Expendable 1945,D 21,25:2
Murepov, G (Screenwriter)
Amangeldy 1939,Je 16,27:4
Murfin, Jane (Original Author)
Lilac Time 1928,Ag 4,7:2
Way Back Home 1932,Ja 16,13:1
Smilin' Through 1932,O 15,13:1
After Tonight 1933,N 3,23:2
That Girl From Paris 1937,Ja 1,19:1
Smilin' Through 1941,D 5,29:2
Murfin, Jane (Screenwriter)
Silent Call, The 1922,Ja 30,16:2
Little Minister, The 1934,D 28,25:1
Romance in Manhattan 1935,Ja 18,29:2
Roberta 1935,Mr 8,25:2
Alice Adams 1935,Ag 16,11:3
Come and Get It 1936,N 12,31:1

I'll Take Romance 1937,D 17,33:2
Shining Hour, The 1939,Ja 20,15:2
Stand up and Fight 1939,Ja 27,17:2
Women, The 1939,S 22,27:2
Pride and Prejudice 1940,Ag 9,19:1
Andy Hardy's Private Secretary 1941,Mr 7,17:2
Flight for Freedom 1943,Ap 16,24:2
Dragon Seed 1944,Jl 21,16:4
Murger, Henri (Original Author)
Mimi 1936,Ja 10,16:3
Vie de Boheme, La 1947,N 28,37:4
Her Wonderful Lie 1950,Jl 17,15:2
Boheme, La 1965,O 20,51:2
Murgia, Tiberio
Big Deal on Madonna Street, The 1960,N 23,20:1
Fiasco in Milan 1963,Ap 11,29:2
Muria Tribe of India, The
Flute and the Arrow, The 1960,O 11,55:1
Muriel, Emilio Gomez (Director)
Empty Star, The; Estrella Vacia, La 1962,Mr 28,36:4
Muriel, Emilio Gomez (Producer)
Empty Star, The; Estrella Vacia, La 1962,Mr 28,36:4
Muriel, Emilio Gomez (Screenwriter)
Empty Star, The; Estrella Vacia, La 1962,Mr 28,36:4
Muriel, Gomez (Director)
Wave, The 1937,Ap 21,18:1
Muriel, Roel
Rose of the Golden West 1927,S 26,27:1
Murillo, Mary (Screenwriter)
Other Man's Wife, The 1919,Je 9,16:3
Murkland, Ted (Original Author)
Open Secret 1948,F 2,15:2
Murnau, F W (Director)
Last Laugh, The 1925,Ja 28,14:1
Faust 1926,D 7,21:2
Tartuffe 1927,Jl 25,25:3
Sunrise 1927,S 24,15:3 (In Addenda)
Sunrise; Song of two Human Beings 1928,Ja 29,VIII,8:2
4 Devils 1928,O 4,26:3
Nosferatu the Vampire 1929,Je 4,29:3
Murnau, F W (Original Author)
Tabu 1931,Mr 19,21:3
Murnau, F W (Producer)
Tabu 1931,Mr 19,21:3
Muro, Eloisa
Goyescas 1944,My 29,18:3
Muro, Klaus (Screenwriter)
How to Seduce a Playboy 1968,My 16,53:2
Murolo, Roberto
Tormento 1953,Ap 4,9:2
Murowa, Irena
Zygmunt Kolosowski 1947,N 13,13:3
Murphy, Al
Flame of Barbary Coast 1945,My 28,22:2
Murphy, Althea
Untamed Fury 1947,Ap 26,10:6
Murphy, Audie
Beyond Glory 1948,Ag 4,18:2
Bad Boy 1949,Mr 23,35:2
Kid From Texas, The 1950,Je 2,26:2
Sierra 1950,S 15,31:2
Kansas Raiders 1951,Ja 26,19:2
Red Badge of Courage, The 1951,O 19,22:2
Duel at Silver Creek 1952,Ag 2,7:6
To Hell and Back 1955,S 23,21:2
World in my Corner 1956,F 18,12:5
Walk the Proud Land 1956,S 8,20:6 (In Addenda)
Joe Butterfly 1957,My 30,23:2
Night Passage 1957,Jl 25,28:1
Quiet American, The 1958,F 6,24:1
Unforgiven, The 1960,Ap 7,46:1
Seven Ways From Sundown 1960,D 22,18:4
Battle at Bloody Beach, The 1961,Ag 17,18:2
6 Black Horses 1962,Ap 25,30:1
Trunk to Cairo 1966,D 29,22:1
Murphy, Audie (Original Author)
To Hell and Back 1955,S 23,21:2
Murphy, Ben
Yours, Mine and Ours 1968,Ap 25,53:1
Murphy, Bob
Broadway Gondolier 1935,Jl 18,15:2
Two in a Crowd 1936,O 5,25:1
You're a Sweetheart 1937,D 25,10:5
Girl of the Golden West, The 1938,Mr 25,15:2
Murphy, Catherine
Within the Law 1923,Ap 30,11:2
Murphy, Charles
Road to Reno, The 1938,O 3,11:2
Murphy, Charles B
Red Lights 1923,S 10,15:4
Murphy, Charles Bernard Jr
Price of Pleasure, The 1925,My 26,24:2
Murphy, Daisy
Men of Ireland 1938,S 30,24:2
Murphy, Dean
Broadway Rhythm 1944,Ap 14,24:6

Murphy, Dennis (Original Author)
Sergeant, The 1968,D 26,53:5
Murphy, Dennis (Screenwriter)
Eye of the Devil 1967,D 7,60:1
Sergeant, The 1968,D 26,53:5
Murphy, Donald
Shack out on 101 1956,Ja 10,26:2
On the Threshold of Space 1956,Mr 30,10:5
Frankenstein's Daughter 1958,N 17,37:2
Murphy, Dudley (Cinematographer)
Soul of Cypress, The 1921,Jl 11,9:3
Murphy, Dudley (Director)
Confessions of a Co-Ed 1931,Je 20,20:4
Sport Parade, The 1932,D 17,22:3
Emperor Jones, The 1933,S 20,26:2
Night is Young, The 1935,Ja 14,11:2
Don't Gamble With Love 1936,Mr 2,13:3
One Third of a Nation 1939,F 11,13:2
Main Street Lawyer 1939,N 9,27:2
Murphy, Dudley (Original Author)
Skyscraper 1928,Ap 9,18:2
Jazz Heaven 1929,O 30,29:2
Murphy, Dudley (Screenwriter)
One Third of a Nation 1939,F 11,13:2
Murphy, Edna
Over the Hill to the Poor House 1920,S 18,16:2
North Wind's Malice, The 1920,O 18,13:1
Going Up 1923,O 10,16:2
Daughters of Today 1924,Mr 4,17:1
White Moth, The 1924,Je 16,18:3
Into the Net 1924,Ag 23,10:2
Man Must Live, A 1925,Ja 29,12:2
Wildfire 1925,Je 10,18:2
Lying Wives 1925,Je 17,16:2
Clothes Make the Pirate 1925,N 30,17:1
All Abroad 1927,Ap 19,24:4
Dearie 1927,Jl 4,20:3
My Man 1928,D 22,14:3
Second Choice 1930,Ja 4,21:1
Little Johnny Jones 1930,F 1,15:1
Lummox 1930,Mr 24,25:1
Dancing Sweeties 1930,Ag 16,8:3
Behind Office Doors 1931,Mr 21,15:1
Girl of the Rio 1932,Ja 9,21:1
Laurel and Hardy's Laughing 20's 1965,N 18,55:2
Murphy, Emmett (Miscellaneous)
Walk East on Beacon 1952,My 29,17:2
Murphy, Frank
In Love and War 1958,N 1,14:2
Murphy, George
Kid Millions 1934,N 12,17:2
I'll Love You Always 1935,Mr 30,11:2
Woman Trap 1936,Mr 7,11:4
Top of the Town 1937,Mr 27,19:2
London by Night 1937,Ag 13,13:1
Broadway Melody of 1938 1937,S 3,12:1
You're a Sweetheart 1937,D 25,10:5
Little Miss Broadway 1938,Jl 23,10:4
Letter of Introduction 1938,S 1,17:1
Hold That Co-ed 1938,S 24,13:1
Risky Business 1939,Mr 23,27:2
Broadway Melody of 1940 1940,Mr 29,25:3
Two Girls on Broadway 1940,Ap 25,28:4
Public Deb No 1 1940,S 18,19:2
Little Nellie Kelly 1940,D 25,33:2
Girl, a Guy and a Gob, A 1941,Ap 24,25:3
Tom, Dick and Harry 1941,Jl 18,22:2
Ringside Maisie 1941,Ag 1,11:2
Rise and Shine 1941,D 6,14:3
Mayor of Forty-Fourth Street, The 1942,Je 11,27:4
For Me and My Gal 1942,O 22,25:1
Navy Comes Through, The 1942,N 12,30:3
Powers Girl, The 1943,Mr 26,14:2 (In Addenda)
Bataan 1943,Je 4,17:2
This Is the Army 1943,Jl 29,11:6
Broadway Rhythm 1944,Ap 14,24:6
Show Business 1944,My 11,25:7
Step Lively 1944,Jl 27,14:1
Having Wonderful Crime 1945,Ap 13,15:2
Up Goes Maisie 1946,Ja 25,26:7
Arnelo Affair, The 1947,S 13,8:5
Cynthia 1947,S 19,27:2
Big City 1948,My 17,23:3
Battleground 1949,N 12,8:4
Border Incident 1949,N 21,29:2
No Questions Asked 1951,Ag 10,13:2
It's a big Country 1952,Ja 9,25:2
Walk East on Beacon 1952,My 29,17:2
Murphy, Horace
Mine With the Iron Door, The 1936,Jl 11,11:3
Frame-Up 1937,Ag 9,23:2 (In Addenda)
Mystery of the Hooded Horsemen, The 1937,Ag 13,13:2
Girl Said No, The 1937,O 18,14:1
Frontier Town 1938,Mr 12,13:3
Wide Open Faces 1938,Ap 15,23:2
Stolen Heaven 1938,My 12,27:2
Boom Town 1940,S 6,25:2
Murphy, Jack
Name the Man 1924,F 4,23:3
Peter Pan 1924,D 29,11:4
Tumbleweeds 1925,D 21,27:2

Murphy, Jim
Mister Roberts 1955,Jl 15,14:1
Wall of Noise 1963,S 5,27:1
Murphy, John D
Icebound 1924,Mr 3,22:3 (In Addenda)
Murphy, John Daly
You Can't Fool Your Wife 1923,Ap 24,25:3
Murphy, Mary
When Worlds Collide 1952,F 7,30:2
Carrie 1952,Jl 17,20:2
Off Limits 1953,Mr 30,25:5
Main Street to Broadway 1953,O 14,34:1
Wild One, The 1953,D 31,9:2
Make Haste to Live 1954,Mr 26,16:2
Beachhead 1954,Ap 17,8:2
Mad Magician, The 1954,My 20,38:2
Sitting Bull 1954,N 26,24:4
Hell's Island 1955,My 7,10:2
Desperate Hours, The 1955,O 6,25:1
Maverick Queen, the 1956,Je 4,25:2
Crime and Punishment, U S A 1959,Je 17,39:3
Two Before Zero 1962,N 1,34:1
40 Pounds of Trouble 1963,Ja 24,5:2
Murphy, Matt
Harder They Fall, The 1956,My 10,26:3
Murphy, Maura
Mister Roberts 1955,Jl 15,14:1
Toward the Unknown 1956,S 28,24:4
Murphy, Maurice
Last Man on Earth, The 1924,D 13,12:4
Home Maker, The 1925,Ag 10,8:2
Thank You 1925,O 6,30:1
Alias the Deacon 1927,Je 21,29:2
Shepherd of the Hills, The 1928,F 20,14:1
Michigan Kid, The 1928,Jl 2,11:2
Women Go on Forever 1931,O 19,28:1
Divorce in the Family 1932,O 31,18:4
Faithless 1932,N 19,20:2
Pilgrimage 1933,Jl 13,17:5
Found Alive 1934,F 12,19:2
There's Always Tomorrow 1934,N 10,19:2
Private Worlds 1935,Mr 28,25:2
Curly Top 1935,Ag 2,22:3
Gentle Julia 1936,Ap 11,19:1
Down Under the Sea 1936,Ag 10,10:2
Romeo and Juliet 1936,Ag 21,12:2
Road Back, The 1937,Je 18,25:2
Under Suspicion 1937,D 20,23:2 (In Addenda)
Tovarich 1937,D 31,9:2
Nurse From Brooklyn 1938,My 13,17:3
My Bill 1938,Jl 7,22:4
Career 1939,Jl 28,14:2
Abe Lincoln in Illinois 1940,F 23,19:2
Reluctant Dragon, The 1941,Jl 25,12:2
Murphy, Michael
Last Illusion, The 1951,Mr 8,37:2
Legend of Lylah Clare, The 1968,Ag 23,33:1
Murphy, Morris
College Coquette, The 1929,Ag 26,17:1
Murphy, Ralph
Star Spangled Rhythm 1942,D 31,20:1
Murphy, Ralph (Director)
Big Shot, The 1932,Ja 2,14:2
Panama Flo 1932,Ja 20,17:4
70,000 Witnesses 1932,S 3,16:2
Strictly Personal 1933,Mr 20,18:2
Song of the Eagle 1933,Ap 29,14:3
Girl Without a Room 1933,D 7,26:3
She Made her Bed 1934,Ap 27,25:1
Private Scandal 1934,Je 15,26:2
Great Flirtation, The 1934,Je 22,16:5
Menace 1934,N 22,27:2
McFadden's Flats 1935,Mr 13,16:2
Men Without Names 1935,Je 29,16:2
Collegiate 1936,Ja 23,25:2
Florida Special 1936,My 29,15:2
Man I Marry, The 1936,O 31,24:3
Top of the Town 1937,Mr 27,19:2
Night Club Scandal 1937,N 12,27:2
Our Neighbors-The Carters 1940,F 15,15:2
I Want a Divorce 1940,O 3,31:2
You're the One 1941,F 20,23:2
Las Vegas Nights 1941,Mr 20,25:2
Pacific Blackout 1942,Ja 15,25:2
Night Plane From Chungking 1943,My 31,13:2
Rainbow Island 1944,O 26,19:6
Man in Half Moon Street, The 1945,Ja 20,16:2
Spirit of West Point 1947,O 3,31:2
Mickey 1948,Jl 19,11:2
Red Stallion in the Rockies 1949,Ag 26,15:2
Stage to Tucson 1951,My 5,14:2
Never Trust a Gambler 1951,Jl 20,14:2
Lady in the Iron Mask 1952,Jl 5,7:2
Murphy, Ralph (Original Author)
Sh! The Octopus 1937,D 24,21:2
Murphy, Ray Livingston (Original Author)
Private's Affair, A 1959,Ag 15,8:7
Murphy, Richard (Director)
Three Stripes in the Sun 1955,N 24,41:2
Wackiest Ship in the Army, The 1961,F 9,36:1
Murphy, Richard (Screenwriter)
I Live on Danger 1942,Ag 22,16:2
Boomerang 1947,Mr 6,36:2

Deep Waters 1948,Jl 23,12:4
Cry of the City 1948,S 30,32:4
Slattery's Hurricane 1949,Ag 13,6:6
Panic in the Streets 1950,Ag 5,9:2
U S S Teakettle 1951,F 24,11:2
Miserables, Les 1952,Ag 15,11:2
Desert Rats, The 1953,My 9,13:2
Broken Lance 1954,Jl 30,9:1
Three Stripes in the Sun 1955,N 24,41:2
Compulsion 1959,Ap 2,26:2
Last Angry Man, The 1959,O 23,24:1
Wackiest Ship in the Army, The 1961,F 9,36:1
Murphy, Robert Cushman Dr (Narrator)
Bottom of the World, The 1930,Jl 14,17:5
Murphy, Roger (Cinematographer)
Monterey Pop 1968,D 27,44:1
Murphy, Rose
Wave, A Wac and a Marine, A 1944,Ag 14,11:4
George White's Scandals 1945,O 11,26:2
Murphy, Rosemary
Last Illusion, The 1951,Mr 8,37:2
That Night 1957,O 15,39:3
To Kill a Mockingbird 1963,F 15,10:2
Any Wednesday 1966,O 14,50:1
Murphy, Steve
Circus, The 1928,Ja 9,20:1
Murphy, William
Story of G I Joe 1945,O 6,9:6
Young Widow 1946,Jl 29,12:8
Foreign Affair, A 1948,Jl 1,19:3
It Happens Every Spring 1949,Je 11,11:2
Sands of Iwo Jima 1949,D 31,9:2
Dear Wife 1950,F 2,31:2
Fighting Coast Guard 1951,My 12,14:6
Place in the Sun, A 1951,Ag 29,20:1
Six Bridges to Cross 1955,Ja 22,8:2
Murray, Al
Catskill Honeymoon 1950,Ja 28,10:3
Murray, Alena
Three Faces of Eve, The 1957,S 27,16:6
Say One for Me 1959,Je 20,11:2
Murray, Anita
Hot for Paris 1930,Ja 4,21:1
Murray, B
Little Lord Fauntleroy 1914,Je 23,11:3
Murray, Barbara
Passport to Pimlico 1949,O 27,35:2
Tony Draws a Horse 1951,My 15,38:6
Another Man's Poison 1952,Ja 7,14:3
Both Sides of the Law 1954,Ja 12,19:2
Doctor at Large 1957,Jl 29,15:5
Cry From the Streets, A 1959,F 24,32:2
Campbell's Kingdom 1960,Ja 11,35:5
Doctor in Distress 1964,Jl 8,38:2
Murray, Bert (Original Author)
Port of New York 1950,F 3,29:2
Murray, Brian
Angry Silence, The 1960,D 13,25:2
Murray, Charles
Small Town Idol, A 1921,Ap 17,VI,2:1 (In
    Addenda)
Painted People 1924,Ja 29,16:1
Lilies of the Field 1924,Mr 17,19:1
Sundown 1924,D 1,17:3
Percy 1925,Mr 25,24:2
Wizard of Oz, The 1925,Ap 14,26:1
Classified 1925,N 2,20:1
Steel Preferred 1925,D 22,13:1
Mike 1926,Ja 11,33:1
Reckless Lady, The 1926,Ja 25,21:2
Cohens and the Kellys, The 1926,F 23,26:5
Irene 1926,Mr 1,17:1
Sweet Daddies 1926,Je 23,28:1
Subway Sadie 1926,S 13,18:1
Paradise 1926,O 4,20:2
Silent Lover, The 1926,N 15,19:1
McFadden's Flats 1927,F 13,VII,7:2 (In
    Addenda)
Lost at the Front 1927,Je 14,33:2
Poor Nut, The 1927,Jl 19,27:2
Life of Riley, The 1927,S 5,13:2
Life of Riley, The 1927,S 11,VIII,5:1
Gorilla, The 1927,N 21,20:1
Flying Romeos 1928,Ap 3,33:2
Cohens and the Kelleys In Scotland, The
    1930,Mr 10,24:1
Clancy in Wall Street 1930,My 3,23:1
Cohens and Kellys in Africa, The 1930,D 20,20:6
Cohens and Kellys in Hollywood, The
    1932,Ap 22,23:2
Hypnotized 1933,Ja 16,13:3
Cohens and Kellys in Trouble, The
    1933,Ap 17,16:4
Dangerous Waters 1936,Ja 22,15:5
Breaking the Ice 1938,S 23,35:3
Murray, Don
Blood on the Moon 1948,N 12,30:5
Dallas 1951,Ja 13,10:4
Bus Stop 1956,S 1,19:2
Bachelor Party, The 1957,Ap 10,37:2
Hatful of Rain, A 1957,Jl 18,19:2
From Hell to Texas 1958,Je 5,39:2
These Thousand Hills 1959,My 7,36:1

Murray, Don — Cont
Shake Hands With the Devil 1959,Je 25,20:7
One Foot in Hell 1960,O 20,42:2
Hoodlum Priest, The 1961,Ap 3,28:5
Advise and Consent 1962,Je 7,31:2
Escape from East Berlin 1962,D 6,55:3
One Man's Way 1964,Mr 12,40:3
Baby, the Rain Must Fall 1965,Ja 14,44:1
Kid Rodelo 1966,F 23,46:1
Plainsman, The 1966,N 19,26:1
Sweet Love, Bitter 1967,Ja 31,50:1
Murray, Don (Producer)
Hoodlum Priest, The 1961,Ap 3,28:5
Murray, Edwin
Three Faces of Eve, The 1957,S 27,16:6
Murray, Elizabeth
Little Old New York 1923,Ag 2,10:3
Bachelor Father, The 1931,F 2,23:1
Murray, Forbes
Chump at Oxford, A 1940,F 20,17:3
Flight Command 1941,Ja 17,21:2
Dark Corner, The 1946,My 9,27:3
Yankee Pasha 1954,Ap 19,19:2
Murray, Hugh
Fan, The 1949,Ap 2,12:2
Murray, Ian
Virgin Queen, The 1955,Ag 6,13:2
Murray, J Harold
Married in Hollywood 1929,S 23,24:3
Cameo Kirby 1930,F 8,12:5
Happy Days 1930,F 14,20:1
Women Everywhere 1930,Je 23,15:1
Murray, James
In old Kentucky 1927,N 21,20:1
Lovelorn, The 1927,D 19,30:1
Rose-Marie 1928,F 13,16:2
Crowd, The 1928,F 20,14:1
Big City, The 1928,Mr 26,26:2
Little Wildcat, The 1929,Ja 21,18:4
Shakedown, The 1929,Ap 8,32:1
Thunder 1929,Jl 8,17:3
Shanghai Lady 1929,N 11,20:2
Hide Out 1930,Ap 12,23:1
Bright Lights 1931,F 10,24:4
Kick In 1931,My 25,17:1
Frisco Jenny 1933,Ja 7,11:2
Air Hostess 1933,Ja 23,9:2
High Gear 1933,Ap 15,16:2
Central Airport 1933,My 4,20:5
Baby Face 1933,Je 24,16:2
Murray, Jan
Busy Body, The 1967,Je 8,52:2
Thunder Valley 1967,S 14,55:1
Thunder Alley 1967,S 14,55:1
Murray, Jeanne
Mister Roberts 1955,Jl 15,14:1
Murray, John (Original Author)
Room Service 1938,S 22,27:1
Step Lively 1944,Jl 27,14:1
Murray, John Fenton (Original Author)
Man From the Diners' Club, The
    1963,Ap 18,39:1
Murray, John Fenton (Screenwriter)
Atomic Kid, The 1954,D 4,14:2
Everything's Ducky 1961,D 21,30:6
It's Only Money 1962,N 22,43:1
Man's Favorite Sport? 1964,F 20,22:1
Murray, John T
Madonna of the Streets 1924,O 28,23:4
Sally 1925,Mr 16,16:1
Stop Flirting 1925,Je 18,16:3
Winds of Chance 1925,Ag 17,10:3
Joanna 1925,D 15,14:5
Bardelys The Magnificent 1926,N 1,28:1 (In
    Addenda)
Fazil 1928,Je 5,21:1
Sonny Boy 1929,Mr 9,24:3
Honky Tonk 1929,Je 5,32:3
Charlie Chan Carries On 1931,Mr 21,15:1
Young as You Feel 1931,Ag 8,16:3
Alexander Hamilton 1931,S 17,21:4
Man Called Back, The 1932,Jl 30,16:5
Great God Gold 1935,My 6,22:3
Ever Since Eve 1937,Je 25,25:2
True Confession 1937,D 16,35:2
Hardys Ride High, The 1939,Ap 14,28:2
Andy Hardy Gets Spring Fever 1939,Jl 19,23:2
Murray, Ken
Half Marriage 1929,Ag 19,22:1
Leathernecking 1930,S 13,9:3
Ladies of the Jury 1932,Ap 2,13:2
Crooner 1932,Ag 20,7:4
Disgraced 1933,Jl 15,14:2
From Headquarters 1933,N 17,22:4
You're a Sweetheart 1937,D 25,10:5
Night at Earl Carroll's, A 1941,Ja 23,19:1
Juke Box Jenny 1942,Ap 17,21:3
Man Who Shot Liberty Valance, The
    1962,My 24,29:2
Son of Flubber 1963,F 9,5:2
Follow Me, Boys! 1966,D 2,46:1
Power, The 1968,Mr 7,52:2

Murray, Ken (Miscellaneous)
Ken Murray's Hollywood 1965,My 11,34:2
Murray, Ken (Producer)
Bill and Coo 1948,Mr 29,17:4
Murray, Mae
To Have and to Hold 1916,Mr 6,11:1
Sweet Kitty Bellairs 1916,My 22,20:4
Honor Thy Name 1916,Jl 17,9:4
On With the Dance 1920,F 16,8:1
Right to Love, The 1920,Ag 23,9:2
Idols of Clay 1920,N 21,VI,2:3
Gilded Lily, The 1921,Mr 7,8:1
Jazzmania 1923,Mr 12,18:1
French Doll, The 1923,S 5,15:3
Fashion Row 1924,Ja 28,12:1
Mademoiselle Midnight 1924,My 27,14:1
Circe the Enchantress 1924,D 9,23:3
Merry Widow, The 1925,Ag 27,14:1
Masked Bride, The 1925,N 30,17:1
Valencia 1926,D 27,20:3
Bachelor Apartment 1931,My 16,13:3
Murray, Marion
Paris Calling 1942,Ja 19,21:2
Pirate, The 1948,My 21,19:2
Murray, Pauline
It Happened Here 1966,Ag 9,29:2
Murray, Peggy
Illiac Passion, The 1968,Ap 19,40:1
Murray, Peter
Hungry Hill 1947,O 11,11:2
Caravan 1949,Ap 21,30:4
Murray, Rickey
Mating Game, The 1959,Ap 30,37:1
Murray, Rob
Man in the Raincoat, The 1958,Jl 15,21:2
Murray, Rosaleen
Blow-Up 1966,D 19,52:2
Murray, Roseanne
Magnificent Dope, The 1942,Jl 3,12:5
Girl Trouble 1942,O 8,31:2
Powers Girl, The 1943,Mr 26,14:2 (In Addenda)
Murray, Stephen
Prime Minister, The 1942,F 4,23:2
Next of Kin 1943,My 6,25:2
Dulcimer Street 1948,N 8,24:2
My Brother Jonathan 1949,Je 29,34:4
Master of Bankdam 1949,O 17,18:2
Silent Dust 1949,D 30,13:2
For Them that Trespass 1950,S 27,37:2
Magnet, The 1951,F 27,22:6
Alice in Wonderland 1951,Jl 27,15:2
Four Sided Triangle 1953,My 16,10:1
Stranger's Hand, The 1955,F 16,24:5
End of the Affair, The 1955,Ap 29,28:2
Tale of Two Cities, A 1958,Ag 5,23:1
Nun's Story, The 1959,Je 19,30:1
Master Spy 1964,Ag 20,34:2
Door in the Wall 1965,Ja 22,21:2
Murray, Tom
Gold Rush, The 1925,Ag 17,10:3
Tramp, Tramp, Tramp 1926,My 24,24:3
Into her Kingdom 1926,Ag 10,19:2
Private Izzy Murphy 1926,N 10,25:1
Murray, William (Original Author)
Sweet Ride, The 1968,Je 13,57:2
Murrell, Alys
Temptress, The 1926,O 11,18:1
Murrow, Edward R
Around the World in 80 Days 1956,O 18,37:1
Murrow, Edward R (Narrator)
Siege of Leningrad 1943,F 11,22:4
Satchmo the Great 1958,Mr 1,12:1
Murrow, Edward R (Producer)
Satchmo the Great 1958,Mr 1,12:1
Mursky, Alexander
Doctor's Women, The 1929,Je 3,27:2
Luther 1929,Je 24,27:1
Hungarian Nights 1930,Je 10,32:2
Fall des Oberst Redl, Der 1932,Ag 18,23:3
Murton, Lionel
Night People 1954,Mr 13,11:2
Pickwick Papers, The 1954,Ap 5,21:2
Adventures of Sadie, The 1955,My 18,35:2
Raising a Riot 1957,My 8,44:1
Pursuit of the Graf Spee 1957,D 27,33:2
Ship Was Loaded, The 1958,Ja 20,20:1
Up the Creek 1958,N 11,26:2
Surprise Package 1960,O 15,26:2
Murua, Alfredo P (Producer)
Ley que Olvidaron, La; Law They Forgot, The 1940,Ja 13,11:3
Murua, Lautaro
Casa del Angel, La 1960,Ag 30,25:1
Murzayeva, Elena
Four Hearts 1946,F 25,21:5
Murzayeva, I
Anna Cross, The 1954,O 25,30:7
Murzayeva, Irina
Twins 1947,Jl 28,12:2
Murzeau, Robert
Royal Affair, A; (Roi, Le) 1950,Mr 9,25:2
Souvenir 1950,O 3,34:4

Musaleyskaya, A
Woman's World 1933,Ja 23,9:2
Musante, Tony
Once a Thief 1965,S 9,36:1
Incident, The 1967,N 6,65:1
Detective, The 1968,My 29,20:3
Musco, Angelo
Eredita dello Zio, L' 1935,Je 29,16:3
Fiat Voluntas Dei 1936,Jl 6,11:5
Aria del Continente, L'; Continental Atmosphere 1939,N 17,17:3
Re di Danari; Money King 1939,D 22,15:2
Lo Smemorato 1940,F 20,17:4
Pensaci Giacomino; Think It Over, Jack 1940,Mr 25,11:3
Muse, Charles
Prestige 1932,F 5,25:2
Muse, Clarence
Hearts in Dixie 1929,F 28,30:3
Guilty 1930,Ap 7,21:1
Rain or Shine 1930,Ag 8,11:1
Last Parade, The 1931,Mr 2,19:1
Dirigible 1931,Ap 6,24:1
Huckleberry Finn 1931,Ag 8,16:3
Safe in Hell 1931,D 19,16:4
Wet Parade, The 1932,Ap 22,23:2
Lena Rivers 1932,My 21,9:2
Attorney for the Defense 1932,My 28,18:2
Night World 1932,My 28,18:2
Is my Face red 1932,Je 11,9:3
Winner Take All 1932,Je 18,9:2
White Zombie 1932,Jl 29,18:2
Hell's Highway 1932,S 26,18:2
Washington Merry-Go-Round 1932,O 24,18:5
Man Against Woman 1932,D 17,22:3
Laughter in Hell 1933,Ja 2,29:2
From Hell to Heaven 1933,Mr 18,9:3
Mind Reader, The 1933,Ap 7,22:4
Massacre 1934,Ja 18,19:2
Black Moon 1934,Je 28,26:2
Personality Kid, The 1934,Ag 1,14:2
Count of Monte Cristo, The 1934,S 27,25:2
Broadway Bill 1934,N 30,22:2
Alias Mary Dow 1935,Je 29,16:2
O'Shaughnessy's Boy 1935,O 5,18:2
Harmony Lane 1935,O 24,19:4
So Red the Rose 1935,N 28,39:1
Muss 'Em Up 1936,F 3,21:2
Laughing Irish Eyes 1936,Ap 4,11:2
Show Boat 1936,My 15,29:4
Follow Your Heart 1936,O 22,31:1
Daniel Boone 1936,O 24,23:2
Mysterious Crossing 1937,F 2,20:5
Spirit of Youth 1938,F 28,19:1
Toy Wife, The 1938,Je 24,15:1
Secrets of a Nurse 1938,D 12,26:2
Way Down South 1939,Ag 18,16:4
Zanzibar 1940,Ap 1,15:3
Maryland 1940,Jl 13,16:5
Sporting Blood 1940,Jl 22,20:2
Flame of New Orleans, The 1941,Ap 26,20:2
Invisible Ghost, The 1941,My 8,21:2
Tales of Manhattan 1942,S 25,25:1
Black Swan, The 1942,D 24,18:3
Shadow of a Doubt 1943,Ja 13,18:2
Heaven Can Wait 1943,Ag 12,15:1
Flesh and Fantasy 1943,N 18,29:1
Jam Session 1944,My 3,25:3
Two Smart People 1947,F 15,20:4
Live Today for Tomorrow 1948,D 6,29:2
Great Dan Patch, The 1949,N 9,37:2
Riding High 1950,Ap 11,26:2
My Forbidden Past 1951,Ap 26,34:2
Apache Drums 1951,My 7,22:2
Porgy and Bess 1959,Je 25,20:3
Muse, Clarence (Original Author)
Way Down South 1939,Ag 18,16:4
Muse, Clarence (Screenwriter)
Way Down South 1939,Ag 18,16:4
Musel, Robert (Screenwriter)
Circle of Deception 1961,F 18,12:2
Muser, Ernest
World Dances 1954,N 8,24:6
Musgrove, Gertrude
Scarlet Pimpernel, The 1935,F 8,27:2
Girl From Maxim's, The 1936,S 16,29:1
Man Who Could Work Miracles, The 1937,F 22,13:1
Divorce of Lady X, The 1938,Ap 1,17:2
Troopship 1938,Ap 26,18:2
Fugitive, The 1940,Jl 23,22:2
Lady in Distress 1942,F 16,21:2
Mushkadiani, T
Scrapper, The 1959,D 14,42:2
Music Maids
Hit Parade of 1943 1943,Ap 16,24:3
Musidora
Vampires, Les 1965,S 14,54:1
Musil, Robert (Original Author)
Young Torless 1967,S 25,56:2
Musmanno, M A (Original Author)
Black Fury 1935,Ap 11,27:2
Last ten Days, The 1956,Ap 12,26:1

Musnikova, L
Night Before Christmas, A 1963,D 16,44:4
Musolino, Vincenzo
Two Cents Worth of Hope 1952,D 16,44:2
Musquiz, Carlos
Torch, The 1950,Ag 21,15:2
Musselman, M M (Original Author)
She Had to Eat 1937,Jl 24,12:1
Kentucky Moonshine 1938,My 21,9:2
Bride Came C O D, The 1941,Jl 26,18:2
Playmates 1941,D 26,21:3
Get Help to Love 1942,O 19,15:3
Bathing Beauty 1944,Je 28,20:1
Carolina Blues 1944,D 8,26:6
Musselman, M M (Screenwriter)
Kentucky Moonshine 1938,My 21,9:2
Straight, Place and Show 1938,O 1,10:2
Three Musketeers, The 1939,F 18,12:2
Shady Lady 1945,O 11,26:2
Tangier 1946,Je 7,II,16:4
Mussey, Francine
Ronde des Heures, La 1932,Ja 25,20:3
Musso, Carlo (Screenwriter)
Flight Into France 1949,Jl 22,16:2
Musso, Jeff (Director)
Last Desire 1939,D 22,15:2
Mussolini, Benito
Liberation of Europe, The 1968,S 29,IV,7:1
Mussolini, Benito (Original Author)
Man of Courage 1934,N 14,23:2
Musson, Bernard
Cow and I, The 1961,Je 6,42:2
Mussorgsky, Modest (Composer)
Boris Godunov 1956,Ja 23,21:4
Khovanschina 1960,S 19,41:2
Mustafayava, R
Arshin Takes a Wife 1950,Jl 31,13:6
Mustin, Burt
Detective Story 1951,N 7,35:2
Lusty Men, The 1952,O 25,12:6
Thrill of it All, The 1963,Ag 2,15:3
Musu, Jone Salinas
Fuga, La 1966,Mr 22,33:1
Musuraca, Nick (Miscellaneous)
Sing and Like It 1934,Ap 14,18:2
Musy, Gianni
Jessica 1962,Ap 20,20:2
Musy, Louis
Barber of Seville 1949,Jl 21,21:2
Muthel, Lola
Spiel in Sommerwind; Play in the Summer Breezes 1939,Ap 1,17:2
Mutio, Ricardo
Nobleza Ranchero; Rural Chivalry 1939,F 20,13:3
Muto, Anthony (Director)
Holy Year 1950 1950,Ag 16,24:3
Muto, Anthony (Producer)
Nice Little Bank That Should Be Robbed, A 1958,D 11,17:4
Mutt
Peg o'my Heart 1933,My 20,11:4
Muxeneder, Franz
Good Soldier Schweik, The 1963,Ag 21,38:1
Muzaferila, Zaim
Kaya 1968,S 25,39:1
Muzalevsky, G V
Diary of a Revolutionist 1932,Je 10,22:3
Muzikant, R (Director)
Ski Battalion 1938,Mr 14,13:1
Muzikant, R (Screenwriter)
Ski Battalion 1938,Mr 14,13:1
Muzikant, Y (Director)
Ski Battalion 1938,Mr 14,13:1
Muzikant, Y (Screenwriter)
Ski Battalion 1938,Mr 14,13:1
Muzil, E N
Lenin in 1918 1939,Je 27,27:2
Muzio, Lando
Giovanni De Medici, The Leader 1940,Ja 5,15:4
Without Pity; (Senza Pieta) 1950,Mr 16,40:4
Muzquiz, Carlos
Hidden River 1950,D 1,31:2
My Outlaw Brother 1951,Ag 23,19:2
Life in the Balance, A 1955,Jl 14,19:1
Sun Also Rises, The 1957,Ag 24,12:2
Black Scorpion, The 1957,O 12,23:2
Myasnikova, Barbara
Tchapayef 1935,Ja 15,22:1
Defense of Volotchayevsk, The 1938,Ag 11,13:3
Mycroft, Walter C (Director)
Black Limelight 1939,Je 26,12:2
Mycroft, Walter C (Producer)
Hell's Cargo 1940,S 16,15:2
Woman's Angle, The 1954,Ag 27,11:6
Myerberg, Michael (Producer)
Patterns 1956,Mr 28,26:1
Myerink, Hubert V
Traum vom Rhein, Der 1935,D 9,25:2
Myers, Carmel
Famous Mrs Fair, The 1923,Ap 23,18:3
Slave of Desire 1923,D 11,26:2
Reno 1924,Ja 8,27:1

Myers, Carmel— Cont
Beau Brummell 1924,Mr 31,20:1
Broadway After Dark 1924,My 20,15:2
Babbitt 1924,Jl 15,9:4
Poisoned Paradise 1924,Ag 11.16:1
Ben Hur 1925,D 31,10:5 (In Addenda)
Devil's Circus, The 1926,Mr 29,24:3
Tell It to the Marines 1926,D 24,18:2
Understanding Heart, The 1927,My 10,24:5
Sorrell and Son 1927,N 14,26:1
Certain Young Man, A 1928,Je 11,27:1
Four Walls 1928,Ag 20,21:3
Dream of Love 1928,D 24,11:1
Ghost Talks, The 1929,F 18,28:1
Careers 1929,Je 10,23:1
Careless Age, The 1929,S 21,17:1
Broadway Scandals 1929,O 29,35:1
Show of Shows 1929,N 21,24:5
Ship From Shanghai, The 1930,Ap 26,11:1
Svengali 1931,My 1,30:3
Mad Genius, The 1931,O 24,20:3
Ben Hur 1931,D 4,28:2
Nice Women 1932,F 20,11:2
Countess of Monte Cristo, The 1934,Ap 2,13:2
Lady for a Night 1942,F 12,27:2

Myers, Greta
Young and Beautiful 1934,S 18,18:4

Myers, Harry
Peaceful Valley 1920,O 11,19:3
Turn to the Right 1922,Ja 24,11:1
Beautiful and Damned, The 1922,D 11,22:1
Brass 1923,Mr 12,18:1
Main Street 1923,Je 12,22:2
Brass Bottle, The 1923,Jl 23,13:4
Bad Man, The 1923,O 9,17:4
Common Law, The 1923,O 29,18:1
Stephen Steps Out 1923,N 19,19:3
Marriage Circle, The 1924,F 4,23:3
Daddies 1924,F 11,18:3
Behold This Woman 1924,Jl 22,9:1
Tarnish 1924,O 13,21:1
Zander the Great 1925,My 4,16:2
Grounds for Divorce 1925,Je 29,8:2
Up in Mabel's Room 1926,Je 29,21:2
Getting Gertie's Garter 1927,F 9,17:3
Girl on the Pullman, The 1927,N 1,21:1 (In Addenda)
Dove, The 1928,Ja 3,28:2
Dream of Love 1928,D 24,11:1
Wonder of Women 1929,Jl 22,17:1
City Lights 1931,F 7,11:1
Police Call 1933,Ag 22,20:3
Mississippi 1935,Ap 18,27:2
Hollywood Boulevard 1936,S 21,26:4
Damaged Lives 1937,Je 14,26:2

Myers, Harry C
Connecticut Yankee in King Arthur's Court, A 1921,Mr 15,14:3

Myers, Henry (Composer)
Heat's on, The 1943,N 26,29:2

Myers, Henry (Original Author)
Merry-Go-Round of 1938 1937,N 26,27:2

Myers, Henry (Screenwriter)
Luckiest Girl in the World, The 1936,D 5,16:3
College Holiday 1936,D 24,21:2
Destry Rides Again 1939,N 30,25:1
Alice in Wonderland 1951,Jl 27,15:2

Myers, Kathleen
Babbitt 1924,Jl 15,9:4
Dick Turpin 1925,Ja 26,14:1
Go West 1925,O 26,25:2
Kosher Kitty Kelly 1926,S 28,30:2
Fourth Commandment, The 1927,Ap 6,25:1

Myers, Kathlyn
His Supreme Moment 1925,Ap 13,24:1

Myers, Pauline
Take a Giant Step 1961,Mr 6,28:2
Shock Treatment 1964,Jl 23,19:1

Myers, Peter
Reluctant Debutante, The 1958,Ag 15,17:1

Myers, Peter (Screenwriter)
Snorkel, The 1958,S 18,37:2

Myers, Richard (Composer)
I Dood It 1943,N 11,29:1

Myers, Tommy
Skipper Surprised his Wife, The 1950,Je 30,18:2

Myers, Truett
All the King's Men 1949,N 9,37:2

Myers, Zion (Original Author)
Buck Benny Rides Again 1940,Ap 25,28:4

Myers, Zion (Producer)
Make Way for a Lady 1936,D 12,15:1
Something to Sing About 1937,S 21,29:4

Myers, Zion (Screenwriter)
Here Come the Waves 1944,D 28,25:2

Myhers, John
Weddings and Babies 1960,O 6,51:3
How to Succeed in Business Without Really Trying 1967,Mr 10,30:1
Private Navy of Sgt O'Farrell, The 1968,My 9,54:1

Myles, Meg
Satan in High Heels 1962,Mr 24,15:6

Mylong-Muenz, Jack
Bockbierfest 1931,Mr 31,25:3
Der Falsche Feldmarschall 1932,Je 30,26:2
Holzapfel Weiss Alles 1933,Ja 7,11:3
Kadetten 1933,D 26,19:3
Overture to Glory 1940,F 12,14:2
Crossroads 1942,Jl 27,18:2
For Whom the Bell Tolls 1943,Jl 15,25:2
Strange Death of Adolf Hitler, The 1943,O 9,11:5
Hostages 1943,O 11,23:2
Falcon in San Francisco, The 1945,Jl 21,7:2
Crooked Web, The 1955,D 10,19:1
Eddy Duchin Story, The 1956,Je 22,15:1

Mynhardt, Patrick
Naked Prey, The 1966,Je 15,40:1

Myral, Nina
Prince Jean, Le 1936,D 12,15:2
Prize, The 1952,Ap 30,33:2

Myrer, Anton (Original Author)
In Love and War 1958,N 1,14:2

Myrge, Mlle
Jade Casket, The 1929,Je 24,27:1

Myrian (Miscellaneous)
Bullfight 1956,Jl 4,15:2

Myrick, Susan (Miscellaneous)
Gone With the Wind 1939,D 20,31:2

Myron, Fred (Screenwriter)
Blood Ship, The 1927,Jl 19,27:2

Myron, Ron
Ring of Fire 1961,Ag 17,18:2

Myrow, Josef (Composer)
If I'm Lucky 1946,S 20,41:3
Three Little Girls in Blue 1946,S 26,32:3
Mother Wore Tights 1947,Ag 21,33:2

Myrrs, Vali (Miscellaneous)
Vali 1967,Je 2,34:2

Myrrs, Vali (Narrator)
Vali 1967,Je 2,34:2

Myrtil, Odette
Dodsworth 1936,S 24,29:1
Girl From Scotland Yard, The 1937,My 31,11:2
Kitty Foyle 1941,Ja 9,27:2
Out of the Fog 1941,Je 21,20:2
Yankee Doodle Dandy 1942,My 30,9:1
Reunion in France 1943,Mr 5,20:3
Assignment in Brittany 1943,Ap 22,31:2
Uncertain Glory 1944,Ap 8,9:2
Dark Waters 1944,N 22,25:2
Devotion 1946,Ap 6,10:5
Fighting Kentuckian, The 1949,S 19,18:3
Lady Possessed 1952,F 15,17:2

Mysels, Sammy (Composer)
Let's Make Music 1941,Ja 23,19:2

Myshkova, E
Sadko 1953,Je 1,18:6

Myshkova, Eva
House I Live in, The 1959,Ap 20,34:2

Myshkova, Nelly
House With an Attic 1964,D 21,42:5

Myshkova, Ninel
Sword and the Dragon, The 1960,N 17,46:3

Myskova, Alexandra
Fifth Horseman is Fear, The 1968,My 7,52:1

Myslikova, Mila
Capricious Summer 1968,S 18,50:2
Capricious Summer 1968,S 25,38:2

Myton, Fred (Original Author)
White Eagle 1932,S 24,18:4

Myton, Fred (Screenwriter)
Miraculous Journey 1948,S 20,21:2

Mzamo, Jonathan
Magic Garden, The 1952,F 6,24:2

N

Naaz, Baby
Boot Polish 1958,Ag 18,15:2

Nabatov
Vow, The 1947,Je 23,14:3

Nabilsy, Abed Salam
Little Miss Devil 1951,D 8,9:2

Nablo, James Benson (Original Author)
Drive a Crooked Road 1954,Ag 3,19:3
Bullet for Joey, A 1955,Ap 16,12:1
Raw Edge 1956,Jl 28,10:7
China Doll 1958,D 4,52:1

Nabokov, Vladimir (Original Author)
Lolita 1962,Je 14,23:2

Nabokov, Vladimir (Screenwriter)
Lolita 1962,Je 14,23:2

Nace, Anthony
Son Comes Home, A 1936,S 5,7:1
Murder With Pictures 1936,N 21,21:4
Riding on Air 1937,Je 26,20:2 (In Addenda)
Between Two Women 1937,Ag 6,21:1

Nachbaur, Ernest
Berlin After Dark 1929,My 28,36:2

Nachmann, Kurt (Screenwriter)
Hippodrome 1962,Mr 12,36:1

Nadal, Michele
Belles and Ballets 1960,N 15,45:3

Nadasdy, Kalman (Director)
Gul Baba 1940,O 26,18:8
Goose Boy, The 1951,O 13,9:2

Nadasi, Laszo (Screenwriter)
Merry Go-Round 1958,Ap 3,23:3

Naday, Marta
Elnoek Kisasszony 1935,O 12,12:3

Nadejin, Nicholas
Men Are not Gods 1937,Ja 19,28:1

Nadel, Arthur (Director)
Clambake 1967,D 14,62:3

Nadel, Eli
Womanhandled 1926,Ja 5,25:2

Nadell, Bernard
Exposed 1938,N 21,14:5

Nademski, M E
Nazar Stodolya 1937,Ag 7,7:2

Nademsky, A
Jew at War, A 1931,Jl 25,11:6

Nademsky, N Z
Clown George 1932,Ag 24,21:4

Nader, George
Monsoon 1953,S 26,15:2
Sins of Jezebel 1954,Ja 9,12:2
Carnival Story 1954,Ap 17,8:2
Four Guns to the Border 1954,N 6,15:3
Six Bridges to Cross 1955,Ja 22,8:2
Lady Godiva 1955,D 3,13:3
Second Greatest Sex, The 1956,F 11,12:2
Congo Crossing 1956,Jl 14,13:2
Away all Boats 1956,Ag 17,14:2
Four Girls in Town 1957,Ja 17,34:5
Man Afraid 1957,Ap 5,24:2
Joe Butterfly 1957,My 30,23:2
Female Animal, The 1958,Ja 23,24:3
Appointment With a Shadow 1959,Ja 8,24:2
House of 1,000 Dolls 1968,Mr 14,51:4

Nader, Saladin
Broken Wings, The 1968,Mr 16,34:1

Nadevin, Eugen
Demon of the Steppes 1930,Ja 18,21:1

Nadeznina, N (Miscellaneous)
Springtime on the Volga 1961,D 25,27:4

Nadi, Aldo
Tourmoi, Le 1929,Mr 3,VIII,7:2
To Have and Have Not 1944,O 12,24:1

Nadina, Sylvia
Resurrection 1931,Ja 24,15:1

Nadja
Unholy Garden, The 1931,O 29,27:1

Nadler, Alexander
Doctor's Women, The 1929,Je 3,27:2

Nadler, Max
Verkaufte Braut, Die 1934,Ap 27,25:2

Naefe, Jester
Confession of Ina Kahn, The 1958,Ja 1,31:4

Nag, Harimoran
Pather Panchali 1958,S 23,37:2

Nagala, Masaichi (Producer)
Enjo 1964,S 23,54:1

Nagalo, Hiroyuki
Insect Woman, The; Nippon Konchuki 1964,Jl 1,42:1

Nagano, Juichi (Cinematographer)
Tokyo Olympiad 1966,N 17,55:1

Nagata, Masaichi (Producer)
Ugetsu 1954,S 8,40:3
Gate of Hell 1954,D 14,45:2
Phantom Horse, the 1956,Jl 25,16:1
Yang Kwei Fei 1956,S 11,41:2
Mistress, The 1959,F 3,36:2
Odd Obsession 1961,D 27,16:1
Taira Clan, The; Shin Heike Monagatari 1964,S 21,37:4
Utamaro, Painter of Women 1964,D 2,57:1
Buddha 1965,Je 17,27:4
Majin 1968,Ag 10,15:5

Nagata, Massaichi (Producer)
Golden Demon 1956,Ja 31,34:3
Street of Shame 1959,Je 5,17:2
Fires on the Plain 1963,S 25,39:1

Nagato, Hiroyuki
Young Swordsman 1964,O 30,29:1

NAGEL
See Also NAGLE

Nagel, Anne
Hot Money 1936,Jl 25,16:2
China Clipper 1936,Ag 12,14:3
Love Begins at 20 1936,S 19,20:1
Here Comes Carter 1936,N 14,23:3
Three Legionnaires 1937,Jl 10,18:2
Footloose Heiress 1937,O 9,16:2
Torchy Blane, The Adventurous Blonde 1937,D 18,18:1
Mystery House 1938,Je 29,15:5
Unexpected Father 1939,Ag 11,12:2
Legion of Lost Flyers 1939,O 30,13:3
My Little Chickadee 1940,Mr 16,8:2
Black Friday 1940,Mr 22,23:3
Hot Steel 1940,Je 21,25:3
Diamond Frontiers 1940,O 4,29:2
Argentine Nights 1940,O 11,25:3
Meet the Chump 1941,F 27,23:4

Nagel, Anne— Cont

Man Made Monster 1941,Mr 19,25:4
Mutiny in the Arctic 1941,My 3,20:5
Never Give a Sucker an Even Break
1941,O 27,21:2
Mad Doctor of Market Street, The 1942,Ja 5,21:5
Woman in Bondage 1944,Mr 27,17:2
Spirit of West Point 1947,O 3,31:2

Nagel, Conrad

Midsummer Madness 1920,D 6,19:1
Lost Romance, The 1921,My 9,16:2
Fool's Paradise 1921,D 10,11:4
Impossible Mrs Bellew, The 1922,O 23,10:1
Grumpy 1923,Mr 26,16:2
Bella Donna 1923,Ap 16,20:2
Lawful Larceny 1923,Jl 24,14:3 (In Addenda)
Name the Man 1924,F 4,23:3
Three Weeks 1924,Ap 1,19:3
Rejected Woman, The 1924,My 5,18:3
Tess of the D'Urbervilles 1924,Jl 28,12:2
Sinners in Silk 1924,S 8,15:3
Married Flirts 1924,N 19,19:3
Snob, The 1924,D 15,14:1
So This Is Marriage 1924,D 23,16:2
Excuse Me 1925,Ja 27,11:2
Cheaper to Marry 1925,F 2,14:1
Pretty Ladies 1925,Jl 14,14:1
Sun Up 1925,Ag 18,14:3
Lights of Old Broadway 1925,N 2,20:1
Only Thing, The 1925,N 23,25:4
Dance Madness 1926,Ja 25,21:2
Memory Lane 1926,F 2,20:4
Waning Sex, The 1926,S 21,33:1
Tin Hats 1926,N 29,16:3
Quality Street 1927,N 2,24:5
Girl From Chicago, The 1927,D 20,33:2
London After Midnight 1927,D 31,31:1
If I Were Single 1928,Mr 5,21:1
Tenderloin 1928,Mr 15,28:3
Glorious Betsy 1928,Ap 27,16:4
Michigan Kid, The 1928,Jl 2,11:2
Mysterious Lady, The 1928,Ag 6,15:2
State Street Sadie 1928,S 3,14:2
Caught in the Fog 1928,D 4,29:1
Redeeming Sin, The 1929,F 16,14:6
Idle Rich, The 1929,Je 17,29:1
Kiss, The 1929,N 16,25:2
Sacred Flame, The 1929,N 23,18:5
Dynamite 1929,D 28,11:1
Second Wife 1930,F 10,20:4
Ship From Shanghai, The 1930,Ap 26,11:1
Redemption 1930,My 3,23:1
Divorcee, The 1930,My 10,25:3
One Romantic Night 1930,My 31,19:4
Numbered Men 1930,Je 9,23:3
Lady Surrenders, A 1930,O 4,15:2
Du Barry, Woman of Passion 1930,N 3,19:3
Today 1930,N 17,29:1
Free Love 1930,D 15,29:1
East Lynne 1931,F 21,15:2
Right of Way, The 1931,Mr 24,31:2
Bad Sister 1931,Mr 30,25:2
Son of India 1931,Jl 25,11:6
Reckless Hour, The 1931,Ag 1,16:4
Pagan Lady 1931,S 21,20:2
Hell Divers 1931,D 23,27:3
Man Called Back, The 1932,Jl 30,16:5
Divorce in the Family 1932,O 31,18:4
Kongo 1932,N 17,22:5
Fast Life 1932,D 24,11:4
Ann Vickers 1933,S 29,24:1
Marines are Coming, The 1935,F 23,14:7
Wedding Present 1936,N 19,31:3
Navy Spy 1937,Mr 22,27:3
Gold Racket, The 1937,Ag 2,10:3
Mad Empress, The 1940,F 15,15:1
One Million BC 1940,Ap 27,9:2
I Want a Divorce 1940,O 3,31:2
Vicious Circle, The 1948,Jl 22,27:2
All That Heaven Allows 1956,F 29,35:1
Stranger in my Arms 1959,Mr 4,34:2
Man Who Understood, The 1959,O 3,14:7

Nagel, Conrad (Director)

Love Takes Flight 1937,S 27,24:3

Nagel, Conrad (Narrator)

Dangerous Journey 1944,O 2,22:2

Nagel, Rolf

Great British Train Robbery, The 1967,Ap 6,45:2

NAGLE

See Also NAGEL

Nagorny, Semyon (Screenwriter)

At Your Doorstep 1964,Mr 15,9:1

Nagy, Alice

Eb Ura Fako 1940,Mr 23,16:4
Sut a Nap (Sun Shines, The); Sun Shines, The
1940,Ap 6,13:3

Nagy, Bill

Across the Bridge 1957,O 30,24:1
Boy Who Stole a Million, The 1960,D 22,18:3
Goldfinger 1964,D 22,36:1
Countess from Hong Kong, A 1967,Mr 17,35:1

Nagy, George

Lila Akac 1935,My 15,26:3
Magdat Kicsapjak; Magda Is Expelled
1938,S 26,13:2

Nagy, Kaethe von

Ihre Hoheit Befiehlt 1931,N 7,16:5
Andere, Der 1932,Ja 15,24:4
Meine Frau, Die Hochstaplerin 1932,F 6,14:4
Ronny 1932,Ap 14,25:3
Sieger, Der; Victor, The 1932,My 15,VIII,4:4 (In
Addenda)
Liebe Ist Liebe 1932,Je 2,25:2
Das Schoene Abenteuer 1932,D 8,25:3
Ihre Majestaet die Liebe 1933,F 7,23:4
Freundin Eines Grossen Mannes, Die
1934,S 11,24:5
Fluechtlinge 1934,O 15,20:5
Einmal Eine Grosse Dame Sein 1934,O 27,20:3
Prinzessin, Turandot 1935,Ja 16,21:2
Liebe, Tod und Teufel 1935,My 25,12:2
Ave Maria 1937,O 2,18:1
Pompadour, Die 1939,F 27,11:3
Volk Will Leben, Ein; People Wants to Live, A
1939,Mr 27,11:2
Solo per Danne 1939,My 30,13:3
Our Little Wife 1940,Ja 27,9:2

Nah-Shuk

Igloo 1932,Jl 21,15:2

Nahon, Philippe

Doulos-The Finger Man 1964,Mr 3,31:1

Nahum, Jacques (Miscellaneous)

Life Begins Tomorrow 1952,N 18,37:2

Naider, Reggie

Man Who Knew too Much, The 1956,My 17,37:1

Naidoo, Bobby

Nine Hours to Rama 1963,Ap 4,58:2

Naidu, Leela

Householder, The 1963,O 22,43:2

Nails, Shirley

Riders of the Purple Sage 1931,S 26,25:3

Nainby, Robert

Student's Romance, The 1936,O 12,23:2
We're Going to Be Rich 1938,Jl 4,10:2
Forbidden Music 1938,D 27,13:2

Nairnes, Carey

Lovely Way to Die, A 1968,Jl 13,18:1

Naish, J Carroll

Good Intentions 1930,Jl 26,16:4
Royal Bed, The 1931,Ja 31,15:1
Gun Smoke 1931,Ap 24,27:1
Homicide Squad 1931,O 19,28:1
Hatchet Man, The 1932,F 4,25:2
Beast of the City, The 1932,Mr 14,13:3
It's Tough to be Famous 1932,Ap 9,18:1
Mouthpiece, The 1932,Ap 21,25:2
Famous Ferguson Case, The 1932,Ap 25,18:6
Two Seconds 1932,My 19,25:3
Week-End Marriage 1932,Je 4,9:2
Crooner 1932,Ag 20,7:4
Tiger Shark 1932,S 23,22:2
Kid From Spain, The 1932,N 18,23:2
Frisco Jenny 1933,Ja 7,11:2
No Other Woman 1933,Ja 30,9:4 (In Addenda)
Infernal Machine 1933,Ap 8,16:3
World Gone Mad, The 1933,Ap 15,16:3
Past of Mary Holmes, The 1933,My 1,10:3
Elmer the Great 1933,My 26,24:2
Arizona to Broadway 1933,Jl 22,14:3
Devil's in Love, The 1933,Jl 28,18:2
Captured 1933,Ag 18,18:3
Avenger, The 1933,O 3,28:3
Mad Game, The 1933,N 13,21:1
Murder in Trinidad 1934,My 16,22:2
Upper World 1934,My 25,25:4
Hell Cat, The 1934,Jl 7,16:5
Return of the Terror 1934,Jl 11,20:2
British Agent 1934,S 20,20:1
Hell in the Heavens 1934,D 12,28:2
Lives of a Bengal Lancer, The 1935,Ja 12,12:2
Black Fury 1935,Ap 11,27:2
Under the Pampas Moon 1935,My 31,11:1
Front Page Woman 1935,Jl 12,15:1
Special Agent 1935,S 19,28:1
Little Big Shot 1935,O 7,11:2
Captain Blood 1935,D 27,14:1
Exclusive Story 1936,Ja 18,19:2
Robin Hood of El Dorado, The 1936,Mr 14,10:1
Charlie Chan at the Circus 1936,Mr 19,22:4
Leathernecks Have Landed, The 1936,Mr 23,22:5
Moonlight Murder 1936,Mr 28,11:2
Special Investigator 1936,Ap 25,21:1
Absolute Quiet 1936,My 2,11:1
Anthony Adverse 1936,Ag 27,16:1
Ramona 1936,O 7,32:4
Charge of the Light Brigade, The 1936,N 2,24:1
We Who Are About to Die 1937,Ja 2,15:1
Crack-Up 1937,Ja 4,20:4
Border Cafe 1937,Je 8,30:2
Think Fast, Mr Moto 1937,Ag 16,15:3
Bulldog Drummond Comes Back 1937,S 4,8:3
Hideaway 1937,S 25,10:2
Sea Racketeers 1937,O 4,17:2
Night Club Scandal 1937,N 12,27:2
Daughter of Shanghai 1937,D 24,21:2
Thunder Trail 1938,F 5,19:3
Tip-Off Girls 1938,Mr 25,15:3

Naish, J Carroll— Cont

Her Jungle Love 1938,Ap 14,27:2
Hunted Men 1938,My 21,9:2
Prison Farm 1938,Jl 15,13:3
Bulldog Drummond in Africa 1938,Ag 25,15:1
King of Alcatraz 1938,O 7,21:2
Illegal Traffic 1938,N 17,29:3
Persons in Hiding 1939,Mr 2,19:2
King of Chinatown 1939,Mr 16,27:2
Hotel Imperial 1939,My 11,31:3
Undercover Doctor 1939,Je 1,31:2
Beau Geste 1939,Ag 3,15:2
Typhoon 1940,My 23,28:4
Queen of the Mob 1940,Jl 1,23:2
Golden Gloves 1940,Ag 21,23:6
Down Argentine Way 1940,O 18,25:1
Night at Earl Carroll's, A 1941,Ja 23,19:1
That Night in Rio 1941,Mr 10,21:2
Mr Dynamite 1941,Mr 13,25:2
Blood and Sand 1941,My 23,25:3
Birth of the Blues 1941,D 11,39:1
Corsican Brothers, The 1942,Ja 16,25:4
Gentleman at Heart, A 1942,F 23,25:2
Sunday Punch 1942,My 11,19:2
Dr Broadway 1942,Je 25,27:3
Jackass Mail 1942,Jl 2,25:2
Pied Piper, The 1942,Ag 13,15:3
Tales of Manhattan 1942,S 25,25:1
Man in the Trunk, The 1942,O 23,25:1
Good Morning, Judge 1943,Ap 30,25:4
Behind the Rising Sun 1943,O 14,26:2
Sahara 1943,N 12,25:2
Gung Ho! 1944,Ja 26,23:2
Calling Dr Death 1944,F 12,11:3
Voice in the Wind 1944,Mr 16,17:2
Whistler, The 1944,Ap 29,12:2
Jungle Woman 1944,Jl 15,19:6
Dragon Seed 1944,Jl 21,16:4
Enter Arsene Lupin 1944,D 2,17:6
House of Frankenstein 1944,D 16,19:3
Medal for Benny, A 1945,My 24,15:2
Southerner, The 1945,Ag 27,22:3
Strange Confession 1945,N 8,17:3
Getting Gertie's Garter 1946,F 4,21:2
Bad Bascomb 1946,My 23,18:4
Beast With Five Fingers, The 1946,D 26,28:3
Humoresque 1946,D 26,28:1
Carnival in Costa Rica 1947,Mr 29,21:2
Fugitive, The 1947,D 26,22:2
Joan of Arc 1948,N 12,30:5
Kissing Bandit, The 1948,N 19,35:2
Canadian Pacific 1949,My 20,32:4
That Midnight Kiss 1949,S 23,28:2
Black Hand 1950,Mr 13,15:2
Annie Get Your Gun 1950,My 18,37:1
Please Believe Me 1950,Je 12,19:4
Toast of New Orleans, The 1950,S 30,13:3
Rio Grande 1950,N 20,21:2
Mark of the Renegade 1951,S 7,24:2
Across the Wide Missouri 1951,N 7,35:4
Denver and Rio Grande, The 1952,My 17,22:7
Clash by Night 1952,Je 19,32:6
Woman of the North Country 1952,Ag 30,6:2
Beneath the 12-Mile Reef 1953,D 17,52:2
Saskatchewan 1954,Mr 11,26:2
Sitting Bull 1954,N 26,24:4
New York Confidential 1955,F 19,18:1
Hit the Deck 1955,Mr 4,17:1
Violent Saturday 1955,My 12,32:2
Desert Sands 1955,N 19,22:7
This Could be the Night 1957,My 15,39:1
Young Don't Cry, The 1957,Jl 27,10:7

Naismith, Laurence

Happiest Days of Your Life, The 1950,S 18,19:2
High Treason 1952,My 21,23:3
Penny Princess 1953,Mr 25,37:3
I Believe in You 1953,My 5,34:3
Mogambo 1953,O 2,18:1
Court Martial 1955,Ag 2,17:1
His Excellency 1956,F 2,19:3
Richard III 1956,Mr 12,1:4
Man Who Never Was, The 1956,Ap 4,24:1
Lust for Life 1956,S 18,39:1
Barretts of Wimpole Street, The 1957,Ja 18,15:3
Abandon Ship 1957,Ap 18,35:1
Boy on a Dolphin 1957,Ap 20,21:2
Naked Earth 1958,Ag 29,18:1
A Night to Remember 1958,D 17,2:7
Two-Headed Spy, The 1959,Mr 3,38:4
Tempest 1959,Mr 27,19:2
Gideon of Scotland Yard 1959,My 20,38:2
Third Man on the Mountain 1959,N 12,27:1
Solomon and Sheba 1959,D 26,7:2
Sink the Bismarck! 1960,F 12,22:3
Trials of Oscar Wilde, The 1960,Je 28,26:1
World of Suzie Wong, The 1960,N 11,36:1
Village of the Damned 1960,D 8,43:3
Angry Silence, The 1960,D 13,25:2
Greyfriars' Bobby 1961,O 12,41:4
Singer not the Song, The 1962,My 3,25:4
Jason and the Argonauts 1963,Ag 8,19:1
Three Lives of Thomasina, The 1963,D 12,46:1
Deadlier Than the Male 1967,F 22,21:1
Camelot 1967,O 26,54:1

Naismith, Laurence — Cont
Long Duel, The 1967,N 2,58:3
Fitzwilly 1967,D 21,45:1
Naismith, Paddy
Iron Duke, The 1935,Ja 25,27:2
Naissiet, Henri
Bernadette of Lourdes 1962,Ja 30,20:2
Nakada, Yasuko
Utamaro, Painter of Women 1964,D 2,57:1
Naked General, The 1964,D 16,51:2
Nakadai, Tatsuya
Human Condition, The 1959,D 16,56:1
Odd Obsession 1961,D 27,16:1
Yojimbo 1962,O 16,34:1
Sanjuro 1963,My 8,34:2
When a Woman Ascends the Stairs
  1963,Je 26,36:4
High and Low 1963,N 27,30:1
Harakiri 1964,Ag 5,24:2
Enjo 1964,S 23,54:1
Blue Beast, The 1965,Ja 30,18:2
Sword of Doom, The 1967,Ap 15,35:2
Rebellion 1968,O 26,27:4
Illusion of Blood 1968,N 28,66:5
Nakadal, Tatsuya
Kojiro 1968,Ag 30,23:1
Nakagawa, Roger
Escapde in Japan 1957,D 24,11:1
Nakahara, Hitomi
Girl in the Mist 1959,D 23,22:1
Nakai, Akira (Producer)
Alone on the Pacific 1964,S 24,46:2
Nakakita, Chieko
Drunken Angel 1959,D 31,12:1
Nakamura, Ganjiro
Odd Obsession 1961,D 27,16:1
Lower Depths, The 1962,F 10,12:5
Prodigal Son 1964,Ja 30,24:3 (Incorrect in this
  edition; use 1964,Ja 31,16:1 elsewhere)
Enjo 1964,S 23,54:1
Great Wall, The 1965,D 16,63:2
Nakamura, Henry
Go for Broke 1951,My 25,31:2
Westward the Women 1952,Ja 1,21:2
Athena 1954,D 22,28:2
Unchained 1955,Ja 28,15:2
Blood Alley 1955,O 6,25:3
Nakamura, Kanyemon
Kwaidan (In the Cup of Tea); In the Cup of Tea
  (Kwaidan) 1965,N 23,51:1
Nakamura, Kanzaburo
Illusion of Blood 1968,N 28,66:5
Nakamura, Katsuo
Kwaidan (Hoichi, The Earless); Hoichi, The
  Earless (Kwaidan) 1965,N 23,51:1
Nakamura, Kinji (Cinematographer)
Tokyo Olympiad 1966,N 17,55:1
Nakamura, Kinnosuke
Bushido 1964,S 13,39:1
Nakamura, Meiko
This Madding Crowd 1964,Je 17,48:1
Nakamura, Satoshi
Tokyo File 212 1951,Je 1,20:7
Madame Butterfly 1956,Ap 24,26:2
Nakamura, Senjaku
Prodigal Son 1964,Ja 30,24:3 (Incorrect in this
  edition; use 1964,Ja 31,16:1 elsewhere)
Nakamura, Tamao
Three Stripes in the Sun 1955,N 24,41:2
Enjo 1964,S 23,54:1
Buddha 1965,Je 17,27:4
Nakamura, Yutaka
Zatoichi 1968,Je 28,37:1
Nakano, Lane
Go for Broke 1951,My 25,31:2
Japanese War Bride 1952,Ja 30,22:6
Nakano, Masataka (Miscellaneous)
New Japanese Cinema, The (One, Two, Three,
  Four-Shi-Death); One, Two, Three,
  Four-Shi-Death (The New Japanese Cinema)
  1968,My 3,42:1
Nakano, Minoru (Original Author)
Kimiko 1937,Ap 13,31:3
Nakara, Ichiro
Harakiri 1964,Ag 5,24:2
Nakarenko, Dan
Bigger Than Barnum's 1926,Jl 13,19:3
Nakaya, Ichiro
Blue Beast, The 1965,Ja 30,18:2
Nakaya, Noboru
Kwaidan (In the Cup of Tea); In the Cup of Tea
  (Kwaidan) 1965,N 23,51:1
Nakayama
Ana-Ta-Han 1954,My 18,38:2
Nakazato, Kazan (Original Author)
Sword of Doom, The 1967,Ap 15,35:2
Nakhapetov, Rodion
Sons and Mothers 1967,O 2,58:1
Nakhashkief, Z
City of Youth 1938,S 5,30:4
Nakopoulou, Aspa
Casablan 1964,D 14,50:1

Nalder, Reggie
Liane, Jungle Goddess 1959,F 23,19:1
Naldi, Enrico
Along Came Sally 1934,Je 16,20:3
Naldi, Neda
Tears of Blood 1952,Ja 19,13:2
Naldi, Nita
Blood and Sand 1922,Ag 7,14:2
Glimpses of the Moon 1923,Ap 3,23:4
You Can't Fool Your Wife 1923,Ap 24,25:3
Lawful Larceny 1923,Jl 24,14:3 (In Addenda)
Hollywood 1923,Jl 30,11:4
Don't Call it Love 1923,D 25,26:1
Sainted Devil, A 1924,N 24,15:3
Lady Who Lied, The 1925,Jl 7,24:2
Marriage Whirl, The 1925,Jl 15,22:3
Clothes Make the Pirate 1925,N 30,17:1
Cobra 1925,D 7,19:1
Naldi, Rino
Amore che non Torna; Love That Doesn't Return
  1938,Ag 15,11:2
Nalis, Antun
Kaya 1968,S 25,39:1
Namara
Peter Ibbetson 1935,N 8,18:2
Namara, Marguerite
Thirty Day Princess 1934,My 12,12:3
Nambara, Shinil
Human Condition, The 1959,D 16,56:1
Nambu, K
Thief of Bagdad, The 1924,Mr 19,19:1
Nanio, Nario (Original Author)
Bushido 1964,S 13,39:1
Naniwa, Chicko
Throne of Blood 1961,N 23,50:2
Nann, Daniel (Director)
Rose Tattoo, The 1955,D 13,55:1
Nannicini, Ernesto
Giovanni De Medici, The Leader 1940,Ja 5,15:4
Nanovich, Volslav (Director)
Magic Sword, The 1952,N 19,37:2
Nanovich, Volslav (Screenwriter)
Magic Sword, The 1952,N 19,37:2
Naon, Sebastian M (Director)
Nobleza Gaucha; Gaucho Chivalry
  1938,Ap 2,18:2
Napier, Alan
Loyalties 1934,O 26,25:1
In a Monastery Garden 1935,Mr 13,16:2
Revenge of General Ling, The 1938,F 21,15:1
We Are not Alone 1939,D 1,27:1
Invisible Man Returns, The 1940,Ja 16,19:2
House of the Seven Gables, The 1940,Ap 15,21:3
Secret Four, The 1940,Ap 22,13:2
Confirm or Deny 1941,D 19,35:2
Yank at Eton, A 1942,O 16,23:1
Cat People 1942,D 7,22:2
Random Harvest 1942,D 18,36:6
Assignment in Brittany 1943,Ap 22,31:2
Appointment in Berlin 1943,Jl 17,8:2
Lassie Come Home 1943,O 8,15:4
Song of Bernadette, The 1944,Ja 27,15:2
Action in Arabia 1944,F 19,18:7
Uninvited, The 1944,F 21,19:3
Lost Angel 1944,Ap 10,14:1
Hairy Ape, The 1944,Jl 3,8:3
Dark Waters 1944,N 22,25:2
Hangover Square 1945,F 8,15:2
Ministry of Fear 1945,F 8,15:2
Isle of the Dead 1945,S 8,12:2
House of Horrors 1946,F 23,20:3
Three Strangers 1946,F 23,20:2
Scandal In Paris, A 1946,S 16,9:7
Sinbad the Sailor 1947,Ja 23,31:2
Strange Woman, The 1947,F 24,16:4
Ivy 1947,Je 26,19:1
Fiesta 1947,Je 27,17:3
Unconquered 1947,O 11,11:2
Adventure Island 1947,O 20,29:2
Forever Amber 1947,O 23,31:2
Lone Wolf in London, The 1947,N 22,10:3
Joan of Arc 1948,N 12,30:5
Hills of Home 1948,N 26,32:2
My Own True Love 1949,F 3,27:3
Tarzan's Magic Fountain 1949,F 7,15:2
Criss Cross 1949,Mr 12,10:2
Connecticut Yankee in King Arthur's Court, A
  1949,Ap 8,31:2
Manhandled 1949,My 26,34:2
Red Danube, The 1949,D 9,37:3
Challenge to Lassie 1950,Ap 7,22:3
Tripoli 1950,N 10,35:2
Macbeth 1950,D 28,22:6
Double Crossbones 1951,Ap 27,19:2
Great Caruso, The 1951,My 11,32:2
Across the Wide Missouri 1951,N 7,35:4
Strange Door, The 1951,D 10,34:6
Big Jim McLain 1952,S 18,35:2
Young Bess 1953,My 22,31:1
Julius Caesar 1953,Je 5,19:1
Desiree 1954,N 18,42:1
Moonfleet 1955,Je 25,9:2
Court Jester, The 1956,F 2,19:1

Napier, Alan — Cont
Until They Sail 1957,O 9,41:2
Journey to the Center of the Earth
  1959,D 17,51:1
Premature Burial, The 1962,My 24,29:2
Marnie 1964,Je 23,19:1
36 Hours 1965,Ja 29,25:2
Loved One, The 1965,O 12,57:1
Napier, Diana
Catherine the Great 1934,F 15,15:6
Mimi 1936,Ja 10,16:3
Heart's Desire 1937,Jl 12,20:4
Clown Must Laugh, A 1938,O 12,35:2
Forbidden Music 1938,D 27,13:2
Napier, John
Slender Thread, The 1965,D 24,24:2
Napier, Paul
Secret Life of an American Wife, The
  1968,Je 26,42:2
Napier, Russell
Unholy Four, The 1954,N 20,10:2
Angry Silence, The 1960,D 13,25:2
Francis of Assisi 1961,Jl 29,8:2
Mark, The 1961,O 3,46:2
Napoleon, Art (Director)
Too Much, Too Soon 1958,My 10,19:2
Napoleon, Art (Producer)
Ride the Wild Surf 1964,D 24,8:4
Napoleon, Art (Screenwriter)
Too Much, Too Soon 1958,My 10,19:2
Ride the Wild Surf 1964,D 24,8:4
Napoleon, Jo (Producer)
Ride the Wild Surf 1964,D 24,8:4
Napoleon, Jo (Screenwriter)
Too Much, Too Soon 1958,My 10,19:2
Ride the Wild Surf 1964,D 24,8:4
Napoleon (Dog)
Thirteenth Hour, The 1927,N 28,18:5
Napoli, Nicholas (Miscellaneous)
Treasured Earth 1950,D 14,51:3
Napolitano, G G (Director)
Green Magic 1955,My 17,32:1
Napolitano, G G (Original Author)
Passaporto Rosso 1936,S 2,18:2
Narako, N
Grain 1936,Ja 16,25:2
Narayan, R K (Original Author)
Guide, The 1965,F 10,44:2
Narbekova, O
Village of Sin, The 1929,My 21,29:3
Narbonne, Roberta
Seduced and Abandoned 1964,Jl 16,23:1
Narcejac, Thomas (Original Author)
Diabolique 1955,N 22,41:1
Demoniaque 1958,Mr 4,34:5
Vertigo 1958,My 29,24:2
Narcejac, Thomas (Screenwriter)
Demoniaque 1958,Mr 4,34:5
Narciso, Grazia
Black Hand 1950,Mr 13,15:2
Between Midnight and Dawn 1950,O 2,19:2
September Affair 1951,F 2,19:2
Up Front 1951,Mr 26,19:2
Narcisse, Andre
Golden Mistress, The 1954,O 30,15:6
Narcisse, Joseph C
White Witch Doctor 1953,Jl 2,19:3
Nardelli, George
Cocktail Hour 1933,Je 5,18:5
Nardi, Corrado
Sensualita 1954,Ap 29,40:2
Nardi, Dino
Deported 1950,N 2,39:3
When in Rome 1952,My 12,21:2
Nardi, Pietro (Screenwriter)
Voice in Your Heart, A 1952,F 23,7:5
Nardini, Tom
Cat Ballou 1965,Je 25,36:1
Africa-Texas Style! 1967,Jl 13,30:2
Born Wild 1968,D 12,62:6
Nares, Owen
Loose Ends 1930,O 18,23:2
Middle Watch, The 1930,D 20,20:6
Office Girl 1932,Je 27,20:7
Aren't We All? 1932,Jl 1,19:3
Woman in Chains 1932,N 21,21:1
There Goes the Bride 1933,Mr 4,11:3
Loves of Madame Dubarry, The 1938,Ap 4,12:5
Prime Minister, The 1942,F 4,23:2
Nargis
Vagabond, The 1956,Ap 16,30:4
Handful of Grain, A 1959,Jl 4,9:4
Journey Beyond Three Seas 1960,Ap 11,42:6
Narisawa, Masashige (Screenwriter)
Yang Kwei Fei 1956,S 11,41:2
Narita, Mikio
Showdown for Zatoichi 1968,O 5,40:1
Narizzano, Silvio (Director)
Die! Die! My Darling 1965,My 20,52:1
Georgy Girl 1966,O 18,48:1
Blue 1968,My 11,28:1
Narlay, R
Passion Of Joan Of Arc, The 1929,Mr 29,21:1
Passion of Jeanne d'Arc, The 1929,Mr 31,VIII,7:1

Naroditsky, Arcady (Director)
Young Pushkin 1937,D 16,35:3
Narokof, M
Man From the Restaurant, The 1930,Ja 6,30:5
Narokov, M
Break-Up, The 1930,N 29,21:4
Narusawa, Masashige (Screenwriter)
Mistress, The 1959,F 3,36:2
Street of Shame 1959,Je 5,17:2
Taira Clan, The; Shin Heike Monogatari
1964,S 21,37:4
Naruse, Mikio (Director)
Kimiko 1937,Ap 13,31:3
When a Woman Ascends the Stairs
1963,Je 26,36:4
Nascimbene, Mario (Composer)
Jessica 1962,Ap 20,20:2
Nash, Alden (Original Author)
We're Rich Again 1934,S 1,16:3
Sainted Sisters, The 1948,My 20,35:2
Nash, Alden (Screenwriter)
Man-Eater of Kumaon 1948,Jl 2,24:2
Nash, Brian
Thrill of it All, The 1963,Ag 2,15:3
Nash, Clarence
Reluctant Dragon, The 1941,Jl 25,12:2
Three Caballeros, The 1945,F 5,20:1
Nash, Florence
Women, The 1939,S 22,27:2
Nash, George
When Knighthood Was in Flower 1922,S 15,17:2
(In Addenda)
Under the Red Robe 1923,N 13,25:3
Confidence Man, The 1924,Ap 15,24:1
Janice Meredith 1924,Ag 6,13:3
Man Must Live, A 1925,Ja 29,12:2
Song and Dance Man, The 1926,F 1,16:1
Great Gatsby, The 1926,N 22,28:3
Oliver Twist 1933,Ap 13,15:3
Sixteen Fathoms Deep 1934,Ja 19,24:3
Nash, J E (Screenwriter)
World's Champion, The 1922,F 27,13:4
Nash, Jacqueline
They Shall Have Music 1939,Jl 26,17:2
Nash, John E
Illusion 1929,S 28,17:3
Nash, Johnny
Key Witness 1960,N 12,15:1
Take a Giant Step 1961,Mr 6,28:2
Nash, June
Strange Cargo 1929,F 18,28:1
Dynamite 1929,D 28,11:1
Their own Desire 1930,Ja 25,13:2
Two Kinds of Women 1932,Ja 16,13:1
Nash, Kenneth
Cleopatra 1963,Je 13,29:1
Nash, Mary
Come and Get It 1936,N 12,31:1
King and the Chorus Girl, The 1937,Mr 29,14:4
Easy Living 1937,Jl 8,20:1
Heidi 1937,N 6,14:2
Wells Fargo 1937,D 30,15:2
Little Princess, The 1939,Mr 11,21:1
Rains Came, The 1939,S 9,11:2
Sailor's Lady 1940,Je 29,12:2
Gold Rush Maisie 1940,S 2,19:2
Philadelphia Story, The 1940,D 27,22:2
Men of Boys Town 1941,Ap 11,24:6
Calling Dr Gillespie 1942,Jl 9,17:4
Human Comedy, The 1943,Mr 3,19:2
Lady and the Monster, The 1944,Ap 8,9:2
Cobra Woman 1944,My 18,17:2
Monsieur Beaucaire 1946,S 5,23:1
Till the Clouds Roll By 1946,D 6,27:4
Swell Guy 1947,Ja 27,17:2
Nash, Maybelle
Sand Castle, The 1961,Ag 16,37:2
Open the Door and See all the People
1964,Ap 2,28:1
Nash, Michael (Screenwriter)
Lost Continent, The 1968,Je 20,50:2
Nash, N Richard (Original Author)
Flying Missile, The 1950,D 25,25:1
Nash, N Richard (Screenwriter)
Nora Prentiss 1947,F 22,16:2
Welcome Stranger 1947,Ag 7,15:2
Sainted Sisters, The 1948,My 20,35:2
Dear Wife 1950,F 2,31:2
Molly 1951,Mr 8,37:2
Mara Maru 1952,Ap 24,38:1
Rainmaker, The 1956,D 13,51:1
Nash, Nancy
Rich but Honest 1927,My 18,29:3
Loves of Carmen 1927,S 27,31:1
Nash, Noreen
Big Fix, The 1947,My 3,10:3
Red Stallion 1947,N 27,50:3
Adventures of Casanova 1948,Mr 22,18:3
Wake Me When It's Over 1960,Ap 9,17:2
Nash, Ogden (Original Author)
One Touch of Venus 1948,O 29,29:5

Nash, Ogden (Screenwriter)
Firefly, The 1937,S 2,17:2
Shining Hour, The 1939,Ja 20,15:2
Feminine Touch, The 1941,D 12,35:3
Nash, Richard (Screenwriter)
Porgy and Bess 1959,Je 25,20:3
Nasht, John (Producer)
S O S Pacific 1960,O 13,41:3
Nashville Teens, The
Go Go Mania 1965,My 20,52:4
Nasil, Lurville
Lover's Return, A; Revenant, Le 1948,Ja 26,15:2
Nasil, Maurice
Eagle with Two Heads 1948,D 30,24:2
Cow and I, The 1961,Je 6,42:2
Nasri, Husain (Miscellaneous)
Gyandev of India 1943,Ap 10,12:5
Nasser, James (Producer)
Lured 1947,Ag 29,14:4
Innocent Affair, An 1948,S 29,36:2
Nassiet, Henri
Bouquets From Nicholas 1939,Mr 2,19:1
Fire in the Straw 1943,Jl 2,15:2
They Are not Angels 1948,My 22,8:3
Michael Strogoff 1960,My 21,15:1
Nassonof, K
Ballad of Cossack Gloota, The 1938,F 28,19:1
Nassour, Edward (Producer)
Africa Screams 1949,My 5,34:2
Nast, Ilse
Rheinlandmaedel, Das 1931,S 18,29:1
Naswell, Ara
Crusader, The 1932,O 8,15:4
Nat, Lucien
Tender Enemy, The 1938,Mr 31,15:2 (In
Addenda)
Heart of a Nation, The 1943,Ap 8,27:2
Paris Waltz, The 1950,Ag 23,35:2
This Special Friendship 1967,N 8,56:1
Nat, Marie-Jose
Rue de Paris 1960,D 23,14:3
Love and the Frenchwoman; (Francaise et
l'Amour, La) 1961,F 28,38:2
Truth, The 1961,Je 27,23:2
7 Capital Sins (Anger); Anger (7Capital Sins)
1963,Ja 17,5:2
Anatomy of a Marriage; My Days With Jean
Marc; My Nights With Francoise
1964,O 27,42:2
Natan, Emile (Producer)
Cheat, The 1950,O 2,19:3
Natanson, Jacques (Director)
Grandeur et Decadence 1937,My 31,11:3
Natanson, Jacques (Miscellaneous)
Dark Eyes 1938,Ap 19,24:5
Moscow Nights 1938,My 3,19:3
Mayerling to Sarajevo 1940,O 30,27:6
Natanson, Jacques (Screenwriter)
Ronde, La 1954,Mr 17,27:2
Plaisir, Le (The House of Madame Tellier); House
of Madame Tellier (Le Plaisir)
1954,My 20,38:1
Plaisir, Le (The Mask); Mask, The (Le Plaisir)
1954,My 20,38:1
Plaisir, Le (The Model); Model, The (Le Plaisir)
1954,My 20,38:1
Natas, Alec (Producer)
Casablan 1964,D 14,50:1
Nathaeux, Louis
Secret Six, The 1931,My 2,23:4
Nathan, Mischa
Long Is the Road 1948,N 12,30:5
Nathan, Robert (Miscellaneous)
White Cliffs of Dover, The 1944,My 12,15:2
Nathan, Robert (Original Author)
One More Spring 1935,F 22,27:1
Wake up and Dream 1947,Ja 24,18:4
Bishop's Wife, The 1947,D 10,44:2
Portrait of Jennie 1949,Mr 30,31:2
Nathan, Robert (Screenwriter)
Clock, The 1945,My 4,23:2
Pagan Love Song 1950,D 26,19:1
Nathan, Vivian
Teacher's Pet 1958,Mr 20,33:1
Young Savages, The 1961,My 25,31:1
Outsider, The 1962,F 8,25:1
Nathanael, Helena
Fear, The 1967,O 10,56:3
Nathaniel, Violet
Bird of Paradise 1951,Mr 15,37:2
Nathanson, Charles
Broken Hearts 1926,Mr 3,26:1
Nathanson, E M (Original Author)
Dirty Dozen, The 1967,Je 16,36:1
Nathanson, George
Native Son 1951,Je 18,19:2
Natheaux, Louis
Fast Set, The 1924,N 18,22:1
Risky Business 1926,S 8,19:3
Man Bait 1927,Ja 19,21:1
Fighting Love 1927,My 23,27:2
Dress Parade 1927,O 31,22:1
Stand and Deliver 1928,Ap 2,25:1

Natheaux, Louis— Cont
Four Walls 1928,Ag 20,21:3
Tenth Avenue 1928,O 9,35:1
Cop, The 1928,N 6,35:1
Weary River 1929,Ja 25,20:6
Ned McCobb's Daughter 1929,F 18,28:1
Girls Gone Wild 1929,Ap 22,23:1
This mad World 1930,Jl 21,20:3
Street Scene 1931,Ag 27,22:5
Reckless Living 1931,D 5,21:2
Modern Times 1936,F 6,23:2
Yours for the Asking 1936,Ag 20,14:2
Missing Witness 1937,D 10,33:3
National Jitterbug Champions
Naughty but Nice 1939,Je 23,23:2
Natorp, Arthur
Lasse-Maja 1943,Mr 22,15:4
Natsukawa, Shizue
Golden Demon 1956,Ja 31,34:3
Natsuki, Yosuke
Country Doctor, The 1963,Ag 14,28:1
Bandits on the Wind 1964,Ja 15,27:3
Ghidrah, The Three-Headed Monster
1965,D 16,63:3
Natteau, Jacques (Producer)
Champagne Murders, The 1968,Ap 25,53:1
Birds in Peru 1968,N 7,51:2
Natteford, Jack (Original Author)
Women Men Marry 1931,Jl 13,13:5
Boots and Saddles 1937,N 8,19:2
Black Bart 1948,Mr 4,30:4
Last Bandit, The 1949,Mr 21,19:2
Natteford, Jack (Screenwriter)
Streets of Shanghai 1928,F 21,19:3
Lost Zeppelin, The 1930,F 3,17:1
$1,000 a Minute 1935,D 21,11:1
Ticket to Paradise 1936,Ag 8,5:3
Boots and Saddles 1937,N 8,19:2
International Crime 1938,My 16,14:4
Badman's Territory 1946,My 31,27:2
Black Bart 1948,Mr 4,30:4
Return of the Badmen 1948,Ag 5,16:2
Cattle Drive 1951,Ag 9,17:5
Blackjack Ketchum Desperado 1956,Ap 5,26:2
Kid Rodelo 1966,F 23,46:1
Nattier, Nathalie
Idiot, The 1948,F 5,26:2
Gates of the Night 1950,Mr 16,40:2
Secret Document-Vienna 1954,Mr 29,22:4
Nattoli, Mario (Director)
Tempo Massimo 1936,Mr 13,27:2
Nattova, Natacha and Company
Hollywood Revue, The 1929,Ag 15,20:5
Natwanov, Mikhail
Hamlet 1964,S 15,32:1
Natwick, Mildred
Long Voyage Home, The 1940,O 9,30:2 (In
Addenda)
Enchanted Cottage, The 1945,Ap 28,19:2
Yolanda and the Thief 1945,N 23,26:2
Late George Apley, The 1947,Mr 21,29:2
Woman's Vengeance, A 1948,Ja 30,19:2
Kissing Bandit, The 1948,N 19,35:2
Three Godfathers 1949,Mr 4,25:2
She Wore a Yellow Ribbon 1949,N 18,35:2
Cheaper by the Dozen 1950,Ap 1,12:2
Quiet Man, The 1952,Ag 22,13:1
Against all Flags 1952,D 25,34:6
Trouble With Harry, The 1955,O 18,46:2
Court Jester, The 1956,F 2,19:1
Teenage Rebel 1956,N 17,17:6
Tammy and the Bachelor 1957,Je 15,10:7
Barefoot in the Park 1967,My 26,51:1
Natzler, Grete
Wien Du Stadt der Lieder; (Vienna City of Song)
1931,Mr 20,29:1
Dolly Macht Karriere 1931,Jl 18,16:6
Eine Nacht im Paradies 1933,F 20,11:6
Scotland Yard Mystery, The 1936,Mr 16,21:4
Student's Romance, The 1936,O 12,23:2
Natzler, Lizzi
Es War Einmal ein Walzer 1934,O 15,20:5
Tolle Bomberg, Der 1935,O 26,12:2
Nauckhoff, Rolf V
Liane, Jungle Goddess 1959,F 23,19:1
Naud, Tom (Original Author)
Safe at Home 1962,Ap 14,14:1
Naud, Tom (Producer)
Safe at Home 1962,Ap 14,14:1
Naughton, Bill (Original Author)
Alfie 1966,Ag 25,42:1
Family Way, The 1967,Je 29,32:1
Naughton, Bill (Screenwriter)
Alfie 1966,Ag 25,42:1
Family Way, The 1967,Je 29,32:1
Naumov, Vladimir (Director)
Peace to Him Who Enters 1963,N 25,23:5
Naumov, Vladimir (Producer)
Peace to Him Who Enters 1963,N 25,23:5
Naumov, Vladimir (Screenwriter)
Peace to Him Who Enters 1963,N 25,23:5
Naumov-Straj, N (Cinematographer)
We Are From Kronstadt 1936,My 2,11:1

Naumu, Nohili
White Heat 1934,Je 16,20:2
Nava, Conchita
Professor, My Son 1949,Ap 18,18:4
Nava, Diana
Professor, My Son 1949,Ap 18,18:4
Nava, Lisetta
Professor, My Son 1949,Ap 18,18:4
Navara, Ernie
Fabulous World of Jules Verne, The
1961,Je 29,26:1
Navarra, Franco
Path of Hope, The (Il Cammino Della Speranza)
1952,Ag 5,15:5
Navarre, Armande
Man in the Raincoat, The 1958,Jl 15,21:2
Foxiest Girl in Paris 1958,S 20,10:6
Devil and the 10 Commandments, The (Episode
7) 1963,O 15,44:1
Navarro, Amparo
Two Girls and a Sailor 1944,Je 15,16:1
Navarro, Carlos
Brave One, The 1957,Mr 22,26:1
Navarro, Carlos (Director)
Amor con Amor se Paga; Love for Love
1940,Mr 16,8:2
Navarro, George
Americano, The 1955,Ja 20,35:1
Navarro, Jesus
Young and the Damned, The 1952,Mr 25,23:2
Navarro, Mieves
Pistol for Ringo, A 1966,N 3,45:4
Big Gundown, The 1968,Ag 23,33:1
Navarro, Nicolas
Agua en el Suelo, El 1935,F 4,11:4
Navarro, Pedro
Walls of Hell, The 1965,N 18,55:3
Navarro, Ruben C (Director)
Corazones en Derrota 1934,O 10,21:4
Navon, Mordehay (Producer)
Pillar of Fire, The 1963,Ap 8,35:2
Navy Blues Sextette, The
You're in the Army Now 1941,D 26,21:4
Nawroski, Zygmunt (Director)
Zygmunt Kolosowski 1947,N 13,13:3
Nay, Pierre
Thirteen Days of Love 1942,N 6,27:3
Nayfack, Nicholas (Producer)
Border Incident 1949,N 21,29:2
Devil's Doorway 1950,N 10,35:1
No Questions Asked 1951,Ag 10,13:2
Glory Alley 1952,Jl 30,20:8
Escape from Fort Bravo 1954,Ja 23,11:2
Rogue Cop 1954,S 18,12:2
Scarlet Coat, The 1955,Jl 30,14:2
Ransom 1956,Ja 25,28:3
Forbidden Planet 1956,My 4,21:2
Power and The Prize, the 1956,S 27,42:1
Gun Glory 1957,Jl 20,8:7
Naylor, Billy
Reducing 1931,Ja 17,23:1
Naylor, Kathleen
Mikado, The 1939,Je 2,27:2
Naylor, Mary
Man in Grey, The 1945,N 30,18:6
Naylor, Tom
Horror Hotel 1963,Je 20,29:1
Naytack, Nicholas (Producer)
Sellout, The 1952,My 31,12:7
Nazarenko, K G
Prisoners 1937,F 20,9:2
Nazarov
Last Game, The 1964,O 25,41:5 (Incorrect in this
edition; use 1964,O 26,41:5 elsewhere)
Nazarov, I
Friends 1939,Ja 2,28:3
New Teacher, The 1941,Ap 7,13:3
Nazarov, Yuri
Italiano Brava Gente 1966,F 4,20:1
Nazarri, Amedeo
Tormento 1953,Ap 4,9:2
Nazarro, Cliff
St Louis Blues 1939,F 9,17:2
King of the Turf 1939,My 8,21:2
Arise my Love 1940,O 17,33:2
Mr Dynamite 1941,Mr 13,25:2
Rookies on Parade 1941,My 22,25:2
World Premiere 1941,Ag 21,15:2
Dive Bomber 1941,Ag 30,10:2
You'll Never Get Rich 1941,O 24,27:2
Nazarro, Ray (Director)
Al Jennings of Oklahoma 1951,My 18,34:6
Gun Belt 1953,Ag 1,8:2
Southwest Passage 1954,S 11,11:2
Black Dakotas, The 1954,O 2,21:2
Nazarro, Ray (Original Author)
Jimmy the Gent 1934,Mr 26,22:3
Bullfighter and the Lady, The 1951,Ap 27,19:2
Nazimova
Eye for Eye 1918,D 23,9:1
Nazimova, Alla
War Brides 1916,N 13,11:1
Revelation 1918,F 18,9:5

Toys of Fate 1918,My 13,11:3
Out of the Fog 1919,F 10,11:3
Red Lantern, The 1919,My 5,11:1
Brat, The 1919,N 3,13:3
Stronger Than Death 1920,Ja 12,7:1
Heart of a Child, The 1920,Ap 12,13:1
Madame Peacock 1920,O 25,18:1
Doll's House, A 1922,F 13,10:1
Salome 1923,Ja 1,18:1
Madonna of the Streets 1924,O 28,23:4
Redeeming Sin, The 1925,Ja 20,18:2
Escape 1940,N 1,33:1
Blood and Sand 1941,My 23,25:3
In our Time 1944,F 12,11:2
Bridge of San Luis Rey, The 1944,Mr 4,11:1
Since You Went Away 1944,Jl 21,16:2
Salome 1967,F 15,42:4
Nazimova, Alla (Screenwriter)
Madame Peacock 1920,O 25,18:1
Nazir, Phil
Unknown Island 1949,Ja 8,11:4
South Sea Sinner 1950,Ja 16,18:4
Nazvanov, Mikhail
Ivan the Terrible, Part I 1947,Mr 10,25:2
Man of Music 1953,My 11,25:2
Safety Match, The 1955,Mr 28,24:5
No Ordinary Summer 1958,O 6,36:3
Hamlet 1966,Mr 16,48:1
Nazvanov, Nikolai
Wait for Me 1945,Mr 19,23:3
Ivan the Terrible, Part II 1959,N 25,22:4
Nazy, Bill
Surprise Package 1960,O 15,26:2
Nazzari, Amadeo
Grande Luce, La; Great Light, The
1940,Mr 15,27:4
Bandit, The 1949,Je 7,26:3
Brief Rapture 1952,F 28,23:2
Life of Donizetti, The 1952,Ap 26,19:2
Of Love and Bandits 1953,Ja 17,12:4
Lure of the Sira 1953,D 26,10:7
Times Gone By (The Vise); Vise, The (Times Gone
By) 1953,D 30,16:2
Sensualita 1954,Ap 29,40:2
We Are all Murderers 1957,Ja 9,27:2
Cabiria 1957,O 29,34:2
Ten Commandments, The 1958,Ap 7,26:1
Naked Maja, The 1959,Je 11,36:2
Fast and Sexy 1960,O 6,51:4
Best of Enemies, The 1962,Ag 7,35:2
Little Nuns, The 1966,Ap 28,49:1
Nazzari, Amedeo
Lancieri di Savoia 1938,Mr 8,23:2
Neagle, Anna
Should a Doctor Tell 1931,Ag 22,7:5
Magic Night 1932,N 3,25:3
Bitter Sweet 1933,Ag 24,18:2
Nell Gwyn 1935,Je 20,16:2
Peg of Old Drury 1936,Ap 13,15:1
Victoria the Great 1937,O 29,19:1
Girl in the Street 1938,My 26,31:2
Sixty Glorious Years 1938,N 18,25:2
Nurse Edith Cavell 1939,S 22,27:4
Irene 1940,My 24,23:3
No, No, Nanette 1940,D 20,33:1
Sunny 1941,Je 13,22:2
Wings and the Woman 1942,O 8,31:1
Forever and a Day 1943,Mr 13,9:2
Yellow Canary, The 1944,Ap 14,24:7
Yank in London, A 1946,Ap 20,16:3
Piccadilly Incident 1948,Ag 5,16:2
Spring in Park Lane 1949,S 21,38:2
Odette 1951,Mr 28,33:2
Maytime in Mayfair 1952,Ap 23,23:5
Kathy's Love Affair 1952,Jl 3,16:2
NEAL
See Also NEIL, NEILL, NEALE
Neal, Ella
Sweater Girl 1942,Jl 13,18:3
Neal, Frances
Lady Scarface 1941,Ag 4,16:6
Powder Town 1942,Je 8,11:2
Neal, Lloyd
Too Young to Marry 1931,My 4,15:3
6-Day Bike Rider 1934,N 3,20:3
Neal, Pat
Inspector Calls, An 1954,N 26,24:4
Neal, Patricia
John Loves Mary 1949,F 5,11:2
Fountainhead, The 1949,Jl 9,8:5
Hasty Heart, The 1950,Ja 21,10:5
Bright Leaf 1950,Je 17,7:2
Breaking Point, The 1950,O 7,10:6
Three Secrets 1950,O 21,10:6
Operation Pacific 1951,F 3,10:2
Raton Pass 1951,Ap 20,25:1
Day the Earth Stood Still, The 1951,S 19,37:1
Diplomatic Courier 1952,Je 14,12:2
Washington Story 1952,Jl 2,22:3
Something for the Birds 1952,N 15,15:2
Face in the Crowd, A 1957,My 29,33:1
Breakfast at Tiffany's 1961,O 6,28:1
Hud 1963,My 29,36:1

Neal, Patricia — Cont
Psyche 39 1964,Ap 30,30:1
In Harm's Way 1965,Ap 7,36:1
Subject Was Roses, The 1968,O 14,53:2
Neal, Richard
Fighting Coward, The 1924,Mr 17,19:1
Neal, Tom
Out West With the Hardys 1938,D 9,31:2
Four Girls in White 1939,F 23,19:3
Within the Law 1939,Ap 6,31:2
Six Thousand Enemies 1939,Je 9,26:2
They all Come Out 1939,Ag 3,15:4
Another Thin Man 1939,N 24,29:1
Courageous Dr Christian, The 1940,Mr 29,25:3
Sky Murder 1940,N 14,28:3
Top Sergeant Mulligan 1941,N 12,31:3
Flying Tigers 1942,O 23,25:2
China Girl 1943,Ja 21,27:2
Behind the Rising Sun 1943,O 14,26:2
Crime Incorporated 1945,Je 23,9:7
First Yank into Tokyo 1945,O 25,18:2
Beyond Glory 1948,Ag 4,18:2
Amazon Quest 1949,My 14,9:3
NEALE
See Also NEAL, NEIL, NEILL
Neale, Ralph (Screenwriter)
Old Curiosity Shop, The 1935,D 23,15:5
Neame, Ronald (Director)
Take my Life 1949,Ja 19,34:2
Golden Salamander 1951,Mr 24,8:3
Promoter, The 1952,O 29,36:2
Man With a Million 1954,Je 29,21:2
Man Who Never Was, The 1956,Ap 4,24:1
Seventh Sin, The 1957,Je 29,10:6
Windom's Way 1958,O 1,45:1
Horse's Mouth, The 1958,N 12,41:1
Tunes of Glory 1960,D 21,38:2
Escape from Zahrain 1962,Jl 12,19:3
I Could go on Singing 1963,My 16,42:1
Chalk Garden, The 1964,My 22,42:2
Mister Moses 1965,My 13,32:1
Man Could Get Killed, A 1966,My 12,54:2
Gambit 1966,D 22,40:2
Neame, Ronald (Producer)
Great Expectations 1947,My 23,31:1
One Woman's Story 1949,My 18,33:2
Oliver Twist 1951,Mr 31,17:2
Magic Box, The 1952,S 24,40:2
Escape from Zahrain 1962,Jl 12,19:3
Neame, Ronald (Screenwriter)
Blithe Spirit 1945,O 4,27:2
This Happy Breed 1947,Ap 14,24:2
Great Expectations 1947,My 23,31:1
Golden Salamander 1951,Mr 24,8:3
Nearne, Jacqueline
School for Danger 1947,N 10,21:3
Neary, Nolan
Man of a Thousand Faces 1957,Ag 14,21:1
Neastelberger, Robert
Holzapfel Weiss Alles 1933,Ja 7,11:3
Nebel, Frederick (Miscellaneous)
Torchy Blane in Panama 1938,Ap 18,11:1
Nebel, Frederick (Original Author)
Smart Blonde 1937,Ja 9,21:1
Fifty Roads to Town 1937,Je 5,21:1
Torchy Blane in Chinatown 1939,F 3,13:2
Sleepers West 1941,Mr 20,25:3
Bribe, The 1949,F 4,31:2
Nebenzal, Seymour (Producer)
Betrayal 1939,S 16,20:2
Mayor's Dilemma, The 1940,Ap 23,19:2
We Who Are Young 1940,S 13,27:2
Hitler's Madman 1943,Ag 28,15:1
Summer Storm 1944,O 23,14:3
Whistle Stop 1946,Mr 18,24:2
Chase, The 1946,N 18,31:2
Heaven Only Knows 1947,N 14,29:3
Siren of Atlantis 1949,Ag 22,13:1
M 1951,Je 11,20:7
Nebi, Abd el
Stampede 1930,Ap 28,24:5
Nechipalio, Victor
Khovanschina 1960,S 19,41:2
Neckar, Vaclav
Closely Watched Trains 1967,O 16,59:2
Nedashkovskaya, Raissa
Tsar's Bride, The 1966,Mr 12,13:2
Nedbal, Milos
Sweet Light in a Dark Room 1966,Je 30,28:1
Nedell, Bernard
Silver King, The 1929,S 2,16:1
Man From Chicago, The 1931,Ja 16,27:1
Man Who Could Work Miracles, The
1937,F 22,13:1
Mr Moto's Gamble 1938,Ap 8,17:2
Secret Service of the Air 1939,Mr 2,19:2
Lucky Night 1939,My 5,29:3
Some Like It Hot 1939,My 25,31:2
They all Come Out 1939,Ag 3,15:4
Angels Wash Their Faces 1939,S 4,16:2
Fast And Furious 1939,O 12,33:3
Those High Grey Walls 1939,O 19,27:2
Strange Cargo 1940,Ap 26,25:2
Slightly Honorable 1940,My 17,23:4

Nedell, Bernard — Cont

Rangers of Fortune 1940,S 19,27:2
So You Won't Talk 1940,O 17,33:2
Ship Ahoy 1942,Je 26,16:5
Desperadoes, The 1943,My 13,17:2
Northern Pursuit 1943,N 26,29:2
Maisie Goes to Reno 1944,S 29,18:1
One Body too Many 1944,N 25,21:2
Allotment Wives 1945,N 22,39:3
Behind Green Lights 1946,F 16,10:2
Albuquerque 1948,Mr 1,17:2
Loves of Carmen, The 1948,S 3,16:2

Nedjar, Claude (Producer)
Shameless Old Lady, The 1966,S 27,52:1

Nedobrovo, Vladimir (Screenwriter)
Once There Was a Girl 1945,D 24,19:2

Nedosinska, Antonie
Merry Wives, The 1940,N 12,28:3

Needham-Clark, Wallace
Ivory Hunter 1952,Ag 19,19:1

Needs, Philip
Hand in Hand 1961,F 7,41:3

Neelemose, Karin
Livet paa Hegnsgaard; Life on the Hegn Farm
1939,N 13,15:2

Neeley, Neil
West Point 1928,Ja 2,28:1

Neergaard, Preben
Red Meadows 1950,Ja 19,35:2
Child of Man 1950,F 1,25:2

Neeson, Ruadhan
Ulysses 1967,Mr 14,55:1

Neff, Hildegarde
Film Without a Name 1950,O 20,32:2
Decision Before Dawn 1951,D 22,12:2
Diplomatic Courier 1952,Je 14,12:2
Snows of Kilimanjaro, The 1952,S 19,19:2
Night Without Sleep 1952,S 27,13:2
Man Between, The 1953,N 19,41:2
Sunderin 1954,D 24,7:2
Holiday for Henrietta 1955,Ja 25,21:1
Svengali 1955,S 26,18:2
Port of Desire 1960,N 3,49:2
Landru 1963,Ap 10,31:1
And so to Bed 1965,Jl 31,11:3
Mozambique 1966,F 10,33:1

Neff, Pauline
Let Not Man Put Asunder 1924,Ja 15,16:1
Man Without a Country, The 1925,F 12,16:1
Midshipman, The 1925,O 13,20:1
Masked Bride, The 1925,N 30,17:1
Ranson's Folly 1926,My 31,10:2
Claw, The 1927,My 11,28:3
Two Girls Wanted 1927,N 14,26:1

Neff, William
Foreign Affair, A 1948,Jl 1,19:3
I Was a Male War Bride 1949,Ag 27,7:2
Cop Hater 1958,O 2,44:3

Neft, Else
Naked Street, The 1955,O 1,11:2

Negami, Jun
Golden Demon 1956,Ja 31,34:3
Teahouse of the August Moon, The
1956,N 30,19:1

Negishi, Akemi
Ana-Ta-Han 1954,My 18,38:2

Negley, Howard
Dead March, The 1937,S 20,19:1 (In Addenda)
Smoky 1946,Je 27,29:1
Big Fix, The 1947,My 3,10:3
Gentleman's Agreement 1947,N 12,36:2
Are You With It? 1948,Ag 15,31:2
Breakthrough 1950,N 18,10:2
Mystery Submarine 1951,F 2,19:2
Man Who Cheated Himself, The 1951,F 9,21:2
Farmer Takes a Wife, The 1953,Je 13,11:2

Negrete, Jorge
Madrina del Diablo, La; Devil's Godmother, The
1938,F 21,15:2
Perjura 1939,Ja 16,11:2
Cemetario de las Aquilas, El; Eagles' Cementery,
The 1939,S 2,20:1
Juntos pero no Revueltos; United but not Mixed
1939,O 23,15:3
Silk, Blood and Sun 1943,Ja 30,10:6
Ay Jalisco no te Rajes 1943,Ap 24,17:3
Asi Se Quiere En Jalisco 1943,Ag 7,6:2
Tierra de Pasiones 1944,N 7,24:3

Negri, Blanca
Vida Hija del Panal, La; Warden's Daughter, The
1940,Ja 6,9:2

Negri, Pola
Passion 1920,D 13,19:3
Passion 1921,Ja 22,9:2
Passion 1921,Ja 30,VI,2:1 (In Addenda)
Gypsy Blood 1921,My 9,16:2
One Arabian Night 1921,O 3,16:2
Vendetta 1921,D 19,13:1
Last Payment, The 1922,Ja 22,VI,3:2 (In
Addenda)
Red Peacock, The 1922,Ap 3,18:2
Mad Love 1923,Mr 5,15:3
Bella Donna 1923,Ap 16,20:2
Passion 1923,Je 26,14:2

Cheat, The 1923,Ag 27,14:3
Spanish Dancer, The 1923,O 8,20:1
Shadows of Paris 1924,F 18,13:1
Men 1924,My 5,18:3
Lily of the Dust 1924,Ag 25,16:2
Forbidden Paradise 1924,N 17,16:1
East of Suez 1925,Ja 26,22:1
Charmer, The 1925,Ap 6,17:3
Flower of the Night 1925,O 19,26:1
Woman of the World, A 1925,D 14,18:2
Crown of Lies 1926,Mr 30,20:6
Good and Naughty 1926,Je 14,24:1
Hotel Imperial 1927,Ja 3,16:2
Barbed Wire 1927,Ag 8,10:3
Woman on Trial, The 1927,S 26,27:1
Secret Hour, The 1928,Mr 12,26:1
Three Sinners 1928,Ap 23,20:2
Loves of an Actress 1928,Jl 30,21:2
Woman From Moscow, The 1928,N 5,26:1
Forbidden Paradise 1929,O 8,24:5
Woman Commands, A 1932,Ja 28,13:2
Madame Bovary 1937,O 30,22:2
Hi Diddle Diddle 1943,S 24,26:2
Moonspinners, The 1964,N 4,47:1

Negro, Giorno
Night, The; Notte, La 1962,F 20,29:4

Negron, Miguel Angel
Roots, The (The One-Eyed Boy); One-Eyed Boy,
The (The Roots) 1957,S 3,23:2

Negroni, B Count (Director)
Little Corporal, The 1927,O 25,33:3

Negulesco, Dusty (Composer)
Jessica 1962,Ap 20,20:2

Negulesco, Jean (Director)
Singapore Woman 1941,My 12,13:6
Mask of Dimitrios, The 1944,Je 24,16:2
Conspirators, The 1944,O 21,15:2
Three Strangers 1946,F 23,20:2
Nobody Lives Forever 1946,N 2,12:2
Humoresque 1946,D 26,28:1
Deep Valley 1947,Ag 23,7:2
Johnny Belinda 1948,O 2,11:2
Road House 1948,N 8,24:2
Forbidden Street, The 1949,My 14,9:2
Three Came Home 1950,F 21,22:5
Under my Skin 1950,Mr 18,9:2
Mudlark, The 1950,D 25,25:1
Take Care of my Little Girl 1951,Jl 19,20:2
Phone Call From a Stranger 1952,F 2,11:2
Lydia Bailey 1952,My 31,12:5
Lure of the Wilderness 1952,O 4,15:2
O Henry's Full House (The Gift of the Magi); Gift
of the Magi, The (O Henry's Full House)
1952,O 17,33:1
O Henry's Full House (The Last Leaf
1952,O 17,33:1
O Henry's Full House (The Clarion Call); Clarion
Call, The (O Henry's Full House)
1952,O 17,33:1
O Henry's Full House (The Cop and the Anthem);
Cop and the Anthem, The (O Henry's Full
House) 1952,O 17,33:1
Titanic 1953,My 28,27:5
How to Marry a Millionaire 1953,N 11,37:1
Three Coins in the Fountain 1954,My 21,18:2
Woman's World 1954,S 29,23:4
Daddy Long Legs 1955,My 6,17:5
Rains of Ranchipur, The 1955,D 16,38:2
Boy on a Dolphin 1957,Ap 20,21:2
Gift of Love, The 1958,F 12,32:2
Certain Smile, A 1958,Ag 1,13:2
Count Your Blessings 1959,Ap 24,23:1
Best of Everything 1959,O 9,24:2
Jessica 1962,Ap 20,20:2
Pleasure Seekers, The 1964,D 26,9:1

Negulesco, Jean (Original Author)
Fight for Your Lady 1937,N 20,21:2
Beloved Brat 1938,My 2,13:2
Swiss Miss 1938,Je 4,18:2
Rio 1939,O 27,27:2

Negulesco, Jean (Producer)
Jessica 1962,Ap 20,20:2

Negulesco, Jean (Screenwriter)
Expensive Husbands 1938,Ja 8,19:3

Nehan, Dod
Operation X 1950,D 11,31:2

Neher, Carola
Dreigroschenoper, Die; Beggar's Opera, The
1931,My 18,21:2
Threepenny Opera, The 1960,Jl 11,24:4

Nehrebecki, Gustaw
Barrier 1967,S 27,39:3

Neibandov, Sergei (Screenwriter)
Secret Four, The 1940,Ap 22,13:2

Neiberg, Al (Composer)
Gulliver's Travels 1939,D 21,29:1

Neider, Charles (Original Author)
One Eyed Jacks 1961,Mr 31,21:1

Neider, Henri (Screenwriter)
Affaire, L' 1950,N 13,23:2

NEIL
See Also NEILL, NEALE, NEAL

Neil, Tony
Little Men 1940,D 9,23:2

Neil, William M
Frogmen, The 1951,Je 30,8:6

Neilan, Marshall
Face in the Crowd, A 1957,My 29,33:1

Neilan, Marshall (Director)
Three Men and a Girl 1919,Mr 31,11:3
Unpardonable Sin, The 1919,My 3,11:3
Daddy Long Legs 1919,My 12,11:4
Her Kingdom of Dreams 1919,S 22,8:1
Go and Get It 1920,Jl 19,16:3
Dinty 1920,N 22,13:3
Bits of Life 1921,O 17,18:1
Lotus Eater, The 1921,N 28,16:1
Penrod 1922,F 20,7:1
Fools First 1922,Jl 31,12:3
Stranger's Banquet, The 1923,Ja 1,18:1
Eternal Three, The 1923,O 12,7:2 (Incorrect in
this edition; use 1927,O 1,7:2 elsewhere)
Tess of the D'Urbervilles 1924,Jl 28,12:2
Sporting Venus, The 1925,My 11,14:3
Mike 1926,Ja 11,33:1
Skyrocket, The 1926,Ja 26,25:2
Diplomacy 1926,S 13,18:1
Everybody's Acting 1926,N 8,19:2
Her Wild Oat 1928,F 6,12:3
Take Me Home 1928,O 23,33:1
Vagabond Lover, The 1929,N 27,30:6
Tanned Legs 1929,D 2,28:2
Lemon Drop Kid, The 1934,O 27,20:2

Neilan, Marshall (Original Author)
Bits of Life 1921,O 17,18:1
Hell's Angels 1930,Ag 16,8:3

Neilan, Marshall (Producer)
Rivers End, The 1920,F 23,11:2
Bob Hampton of Placer 1921,My 2,12:1

Neilan, Marshall (Screenwriter)
Eternal Three, The 1923,O 12,7:2 (Incorrect in
this edition; use 1927,O 1,7:2 elsewhere)
Mike 1926,Ja 11,33:1
Venus of Venice 1927,My 3,25:1

Neilan, Marshall Jr (Original Author)
Watch the Birdie 1950,D 12,46:4

Neilendam, Sigrid
Day of Wrath 1948,Ap 26,27:2

Neilep, G
Boris Godunov 1956,Ja 23,21:4

NEILL
See Also NEALE, NEAL, NEIL

Neill, Angus
After You, Comrade 1967,Ap 11,54:1

Neill, James
Men, Women and Money 1919,Je 16,11:2
Everywoman 1919,D 15,20:1
Paliser Case, The 1920,F 16,8:1
Bits of Life 1921,O 17,18:1
Ten Commandments, The 1923,D 22,8:1
Any Woman 1925,My 27,26:2
Crimson Runner, The 1925,My 27,26:2
Thank You 1925,O 6,30:1
New Brooms 1925,N 4,17:4
King of Kings, The 1927,Ap 20,29:2
Love Hungry 1928,Ap 16,20:5
Idle Rich, The 1929,Je 17,29:1
Only the Brave 1930,Mr 8,21:1
Shooting Straight 1930,Jl 28,22:1

Neill, Noel
Are These our Parents? 1944,Ag 23,16:2
Here Come the Waves 1944,D 28,25:2

Neill, R William (Director)
Woman Gives, The 1920,Ap 12,13:1
Yes or No 1920,Jl 5,12:4
Something Different 1921,Ja 30,VI,2:1 (In
Addenda)
Conquest of Canaan, The 1921,Jl 11,9:3
Iron Trail, The 1921,O 31,19:3
Vanity's Price 1924,O 8,16:2
Broken Laws 1925,Ja 21,19:3
San Francisco Nights 1928,Ja 31,29:1
Viking, The 1928,N 29,32:4
Wall Street 1929,N 25,22:1
Good Bad Girl, The 1931,My 15,20:6

Neill, Richard
Born to the West 1926,Je 30,18:1 (In Addenda)

Neill, Richard R
Heritage of the Desert, The 1924,Ja 24,15:1
Wanderer of the Wasteland, The 1924,Jl 8,14:2
Percy 1925,Mr 25,24:2
Tumbleweeds 1925,D 21,27:2

Neill, Roy William (Director)
Career of Catherine Bush, The 1919,Ag 4,8:3
Fifty Fathoms Deep 1931,S 19,10:2
Menace, The 1932,Ja 30,13:2
That's my Boy 1932,N 21,21:1
Circus Queen Murder, The 1933,My 9,20:5
Ninth Guest, The 1934,Mr 3,8:5
Whirlpool 1934,My 5,22:3
Black Moon 1934,Je 28,26:2
Blind Date 1934,S 1,16:3
I'll Fix It 1934,N 12,17:3
Lone Wolf Returns, The 1936,F 4,25:5
Dr Syn 1937,N 15,15:1

Neill, Roy William (Director) — Cont
Eyes of the Underworld 1942,O 5,15:2
Sherlock Holmes and the Secret Weapon
  1943,Ja 5,15:2
Frankenstein Meets the Wolf Man 1943,Mr 6,8:3
Sherlock Holmes Faces Death 1943,O 8,15:3
Spider Woman 1944,Ja 17,14:5
Scarlet Claw, The 1944,My 19,12:1
Pearl of Death 1944,Ag 26,15:2
Gypsy Wildcat 1944,O 5,18:6
House of Fear, The 1945,Mr 19,23:3
Woman in Green, The 1945,Je 16,10:3
Pursuit to Algiers 1945,O 27,12:2
Terror by Night 1946,F 9,9:2
Dressed to Kill 1946,My 25,12:4
Black Angel 1946,S 26,32:4
Neill, Roy William (Original Author)
Two Tickets to London 1943,Jl 3,11:2
Neill, Roy William (Producer)
Sherlock Holmes Faces Death 1943,O 8,15:3
Scarlet Claw, The 1944,My 19,12:1
Pearl of Death 1944,Ag 26,15:2
House of Fear, The 1945,Mr 19,23:3
Terror by Night 1946,F 9,9:2
Dressed to Kill 1946,My 25,12:4
Black Angel 1946,S 26,32:4
Neill, Roy William (Screenwriter)
Scarlet Claw, The 1944,My 19,12:1
Neilsen, Inga
Funny Thing Happened on the Way to the Forum,
  A 1966,O 17,48:1
Neilson, James (Director)
Night Passage 1957,Jl 25,28:1
Moon Pilot 1962,Ap 6,30:2
Bon Voyage! 1962,My 18,34:2
Summer Magic 1963,Ag 22,19:2
Moonspinners, The 1964,N 4,47:1
Adventures of Bullwhip Griffin, The
  1967,Mr 9,43:2
Where Angels Go-Trouble Follows
  1968,Ap 11,51:1
Gentle Giant 1968,Ap 20,26:1
Neilson, Perlita
She Didn't Say No 1963,Jl 30,18:1
Neilson-Terry, Phyllis
Look Back in Anger 1959,S 16,45:1
Neiman, Hal
Footloose Heiress 1937,O 9,16:2
Idol of the Crowd 1937,D 4,21:1
Neise, George N
Experiment Perilous 1944,D 30,15:2
One Sunday Afternoon 1948,D 27,16:3
Three Stooges in Orbit, The 1962,Jl 12,19:4
Neisel, Edmund
Peaks of Destiny 1927,N 29,31:1
Nekritsch, Azriel
Dream no More 1950,Ja 6,25:2
Nell, Carlo
Lola 1962,O 15,32:2
Nelsen, Anny
Jules and Jim 1962,Ap 24,32:1
Nelson, Barbara
Maid of Salem 1937,Mr 4,27:2
Nelson, Barry
Shadow of the Thin Man 1941,N 21,23:2
Yank on the Burma Road, A 1942,Ja 29,25:3
Dr Kildare's Victory 1942,F 5,25:2
Johnny Eager 1942,F 20,21:2
Rio Rita 1942,My 8,27:3
Eyes in the Night 1942,O 16,23:1
Human Comedy, The 1943,Mr 3,19:2
Bataan 1943,Je 4,17:2
Guy Named Joe, A 1943,D 24,17:2
Winged Victory 1944,D 21,16:2
Beginning or the End, The 1947,F 21,15:1
Man With my Face, The 1951,Je 15,27:5
Mary, Mary 1963,O 25,38:2
Nelson, Bek
Pal Joey 1957,O 28,30:1
Bell, Book and Candle 1958,D 27,2:7
Nelson, Bill
Milkman, The 1951,Ja 1,13:6
12 Angry Men 1957,Ap 15,24:1
I Live on Danger 1942,Ag 22,16:2
Nelson, Bobby
Oliver Twist 1933,Ap 13,15:3
Black Fury 1935,Ap 11,27:2
Nelson, Byron
Anne of the Indies 1951,O 25,36:3
Nelson, Carine
Rasputin 1939,O 17,31:4
Nelson, Christine
Send Me no Flowers 1964,N 13,30:1
Nelson, David
Peyton Place 1957,D 13,35:1
Remarkable Mr Pennypacker, The 1959,F 21,25:2
Big Circus, The 1959,Jl 18,6:1
30 1959,N 12,27:1
Big Show, The 1961,My 11,42:4
Nelson, Dick
Great Guns 1941,O 3,27:2
Nelson, Ed
Soldier in the Rain 1963,N 29,67:6 (Incorrect in
  this edition; use 1963,N 28,67:6 elsewhere)

Nelson, Edgar
Get-Rich-Quick Wallingford 1921,D 5,20:1
Sandra 1924,D 22,20:2
Womanhandled 1926,Ja 5,25:2
Way Down East 1931,Mr 16,25:1
Misleading Lady, The 1932,Ap 9,18:1
Nelson, Frank
Gentleman of Leisure, A 1923,Jl 16,14:2
Stephen Steps Out 1923,N 19,19:3
Stranger, The 1924,F 5,20:1
Shadows of Paris 1924,F 18,13:1
Sea Hunt, The 1926,Ja 16,8:5
Sea Beast, The 1926,Ja 16,8:5
Great Mail Robbery, The 1927,Jl 20,29:3
Milkman, The 1951,Ja 1,13:6
Kiss Them for Me 1957,N 9,31:2
Nelson, Gene
I Wonder Who's Kissing Her Now
  1947,Jl 24,27:2
Daughter of Rosie O'Grady, The
  1950,Mr 31,36:2
Tea for Two 1950,S 2,11:2
West Point Story, The 1950,D 23,11:3
Lullaby of Broadway 1951,Mr 27,35:2
Painting the Clouds With Sunshine 1951,S 1,9:6
Starlift 1951,D 15,11:2
She's Working her Way Through College
  1952,Jl 10,27:2
She's Back on Broadway 1953,Mr 12,24:2
Three Sailors and a Girl 1953,N 23,32:2
Crime Wave 1954,Ja 13,26:2
So This Is Paris 1955,F 12,11:1
Oklahoma! 1955,O 11,49:1
20,000 Eyes 1961,Je 19,30:1
Nelson, Gene (Director)
Kissin' Cousins 1964,Ap 2,28:3
Your Cheatin' Heart 1965,My 20,52:2
Harum Scarum 1965,D 16,63:3
Cool Ones, The 1967,My 11,50:1
Nelson, Gene (Screenwriter)
Kissin' Cousins 1964,Ap 2,28:3
Cool Ones, The 1967,My 11,50:1
Nelson, Gordon
Groom Wore Spurs, The 1951,Mr 14,41:2
Iron Mistress, The 1952,N 20,39:2
Nelson, Gwen
Kind of Loving, A 1962,O 2,46:1
Stolen Hours 1963,O 17,39:1
Nelson, Kay Anne
There's a Girl in my Heart 1950,Ja 20,29:2
Nelson, Kristin
Love and Kisses 1965,D 23,21:4
Nelson, Lori
Bend of the River 1952,Ap 10,37:1
Ma and Pa Kettle at the Fair 1952,Jl 12,16:2
Francis Goes to West Point 1952,Ag 23,10:2
All I Desire 1953,Ag 29,10:1
Walking my Baby Back Home 1954,Ja 16,10:5
Underwater! 1955,F 10,27:2
Revenge of the Creature 1955,My 14,10:7
Sincerely Yours 1955,N 3,37:1
I Died a Thousand Times 1955,N 10,45:2
Pardners 1956,Jl 26,20:2
Untamed Youth 1957,My 11,24:6
Nelson, Marjorie
Slender Thread, The 1965,D 24,24:2
Nelson, Matthew
Barbary Pirate 1949,O 28,29:3
Nelson, Mimi
Doll, The 1964,Ja 14,27:1
Nelson, Miss
Little Lord Fauntleroy 1914,Je 23,11:3
Nelson, Norma Jean
Seventeen 1940,F 29,15:2
Typhoon 1940,My 23,28:4
Aloma of the South Seas 1941,Ag 28,23:4
Nelson, Otto
Black Oxen 1924,Ja 7,23:1
Nelson, Ozzie
People Are Funny 1946,Ja 28,15:6
Impossible Years, The 1968,D 6,54:1
Nelson, Ozzie (Director)
Love and Kisses 1965,D 23,21:4
Nelson, Ozzie (Producer)
Love and Kisses 1965,D 23,21:4
Nelson, Ozzie (Screenwriter)
Love and Kisses 1965,D 23,21:4
Nelson, Ozzie and his Orchestra
Letter, The 1940,N 23,12:6
Nelson, Portia
Sound of Music, The 1965,Mr 3,34:1
Doctor Dolittle 1967,D 20,55:1
Nelson, Ralph
Lilies of the Field 1963,O 2,51:1
Nelson, Ralph (Director)
Requiem for a Heavyweight 1962,O 17,35:1
Lilies of the Field 1963,O 2,51:1
Soldier in the Rain 1963,N 29,67:6 (Incorrect in
  this edition; use 1963,N 28,67:6 elsewhere)
Fate Is the Hunter 1964,D 10,61:1
Father Goose 1964,D 11,55:1
Once a Thief 1965,S 9,36:1

Nelson, Ralph (Director) — Cont
Duel at Diablo 1966,Je 16,53:1
Counterpoint 1968,Mr 14,51:2
Charly 1968,S 24,55:1
Nelson, Ralph (Producer)
Lilies of the Field 1963,O 2,51:1
Duel at Diablo 1966,Je 16,53:1
Charly 1968,S 24,55:1
Nelson, Richard
No Orchids for Miss Blandish 1951,F 23,33:2
Nelson, Ricky
Story of Three Loves, The (Mademoiselle);
  Mademoiselle (The Story of Three Loves)
  1953,Mr 6,29:2
Rio Bravo 1959,Mr 19,40:2
Wackiest Ship in the Army, The 1961,F 9,36:1
Love and Kisses 1965,D 23,21:4
Nelson, Rudolf (Composer)
Dolly Macht Karriere 1931,Jl 18,16:6
Nelson, Rudolf (Miscellaneous)
Theaternaechte von Berlin 1932,Ja 11,28:5
Nelson, Rudy (Screenwriter)
Way Out 1967,O 26,54:3
Nelson, Ruth
North Star, The 1943,N 5,23:1
None Shall Escape 1944,Ap 7,23:2
Eve of St Mark, The 1944,My 31,22:2
Wilson 1944,Ag 2,18:1
Keys of the Kingdom, The 1944,D 30,15:2
Tree Grows in Brooklyn, A 1945,Mr 1,25:5
Sentimental Journey 1946,Mr 7,33:2
Till the End of Time 1946,Jl 24,24:1
Humoresque 1946,D 26,28:1
Sea of Grass, The 1947,F 28,27:2
Mother Wore Tights 1947,Ag 21,33:2
Nelson, Sam
Crooks Can't Win 1928,My 29,17:2
Circus Kid, The 1928,D 17,23:1
Rio Rita 1929,O 7,22:1
Soldiers and Women 1930,My 12,27:3
Lady From Shanghai, The 1948,Je 10,28:2
Nelson, Sam (Director)
Parents on Trial 1939,S 18,15:5
Nelson, Shirley (Screenwriter)
Way Out 1967,O 26,54:3
Nelson, Tracy
Yours, Mine and Ours 1968,Ap 25,53:1
Nelsons, Three
Keep Smiling 1938,Ag 10,15:2
Nem, Nop
Dragon Sky 1964,Ag 25,28:2
Nemchenko, E
Great Citizen, The 1939,Ja 16,11:2
Nemec, Jan (Director)
Diamonds of the Night 1968,Mr 15,30:1
Report on the Party and the Guests, A
  1968,S 20,37:5
Report on the Party and the Guests, A
  1968,S 28,37:1
Oratorio for Prague 1968,S 30,60:1
Nemec, Jan (Screenwriter)
Diamonds of the Night 1968,Mr 15,30:1
Report on the Party and the Guests, A
  1968,S 20,37:5
Report on the Party and the Guests, A
  1968,S 28,37:1
Oratorio for Prague 1968,S 30,60:1
Nemec, Jiri
Report on the Party and the Guests, A
  1968,S 28,37:1
Nemeth, Maria
Hello Budapest 1935,N 14,17:4
Nemeth, Romola
Pokhalo 1938,My 7,18:2
Nemirovsky, Irene (Original Author)
Bal, Le 1932,S 28,22:5
David Golder 1932,O 20,24:2
Nemo, Henry
Song of the Thin Man 1947,Ag 29,14:2
Nemo, Henry (Composer)
Duchess of Idaho 1950,Jl 21,15:3
Nemolyneva, Svetlana
Eugene Onegin 1959,S 14,33:1
Neny, Michele (Miscellaneous)
Survival 1967 1968,Je 12,40:2
Neola, Princess
Barrier, The 1926,Mr 22,16:1
Nephew, Neil
Mad Dog Coll 1961,My 13,10:1
Young Savages, The 1961,My 25,31:1
Nepoty, Georges (Original Author)
Woman From Monte Carlo, The 1931,D 31,17:6
Nepoty, Lucien (Original Author)
Sacrifice d'Honneur 1938,D 2,27:2
Nerdorff, Preben
Red Meadows 1950,Ja 19,35:2
Neri, Donatelle
Kif Tebbi 1929,My 20,22:6
Neri, Fabio
White Line, The 1952,D 6,17:2
Neri, Giulio
Rigoletto 1949,N 10,41:4
Forza del Destino, La 1952,O 17,33:1
Aida 1954,N 12,17:1

Neri, Giulio— Cont
House of Ricordi 1956,Mr 13,32:1
Neri, Tommaso
Battle of Algiers, The 1967,S 21,56:1
Nero, Curtis
West of Zanzibar 1928,D 31,9:1
Kongo 1932,N 17,22:5
Nero, Franco
Bible, The 1966,S 29,60:1
Tramplers, The 1966,D 8,64:1
Hired Killer, The 1967,Mr 2,30:3
Wild, Wild Planet 1967,Ag 10,45:5
Camelot 1967,O 26,54:1
Nero, Line
It Happened at the Inn; Goupi Mains Rouge
1945,D 22,16:2
Neroni, Nicola Fausto (Director)
Miracolo Di Sant'Antonio, Il 1932,Ap 18,19:2
Nersesyan, Grachia
Heart Sings, The 1958,Ag 18,15:2
Nerval, Natalie
Law Is the Law, The 1959,Mr 11,41:2
Dog, a Mouse and a Sputnik, A; Pied, a Cheval et
un Sputnik, A 1960,N 1,46:2
Nery, Gerard
My First Love 1951,Je 11,20:7
Nes, Ole M
Skinner's big Idea 1928,Mr 27,30:4
Nesbit, Evelyn
Redemption 1917,My 22,11:3
Nesbit, Pinna
Partners of the Night 1920,Mr 1,16:2
Nesbitt, Catherine
Trouble Ahead 1936,S 21,26:5
Nesbitt, Cathleen
Criminal at Large 1933,D 20,27:2
Passing of the Third Floor Back, The
1936,Ap 29,19:2
Beloved Vagabond, The 1937,F 8,12:5
Jassy 1948,F 20,19:2
Man of Evil 1948,Mr 26,26:2
Agitator, The 1949,Ag 19,12:5
Madness of the Heart 1950,O 12,43:2
So Long at the Fair 1951,Ja 22,14:2
Three Coins in the Fountain 1954,My 21,18:2
Black Widow 1954,O 28,46:6
Desiree 1954,N 18,42:1
Affair to Remember, An 1957,Jl 20,8:5
Separate Tables 1958,D 19,2:7
Parent Trap, The 1961,Je 22,23:1
Promise her Anything 1966,F 23,46:1
Nesbitt, Derren
Kill or Cure 1962,N 13,43:4
Amorous Adventures of Moll Flanders, The
1965,My 27,28:1
Underworld Informers 1965,O 14,53:1
Naked Runner, The 1967,Jl 20,30:2
Neshiplenko, V
Under Sunny Skies 1950,D 26,19:3
Nesmith, Michael
Head 1968,N 7,51:1
Nesmith, Ottola
Becky Sharp 1935,Je 14,27:2
Three Men on a Horse 1936,N 26,39:1
Nobody's Baby 1937,My 20,17:3
Fools for Scandal 1938,Mr 25,15:3
Return of the Vampire, The 1944,Ja 29,10:1
My Name is Julia Ross 1945,N 9,16:3
Witness for the Prosecution 1958,F 7,16:1
Nesor, Al
Li'l Abner 1959,D 12,19:2
Andy 1965,Ja 22,21:2
Ness, Ole M
Chicago After Midnight 1928,Mr 6,20:3
Hit of the Show 1928,Jl 9,25:1
Danger Street 1928,S 25,29:4 (In Addenda)
Jazz Heaven 1929,O 30,29:2
Dawn to Dawn 1933,D 27,23:5
Nestell, Bob
Kid Galahad 1937,My 27,21:3
Nestler, Joel
Mrs Mike 1950,F 9,36:5
Nestore, Gloria
Foxhole in Cairo 1961,F 16,25:2
Nesvadba, Josef (Original Author)
Death of Tarzan, The 1968,Jl 4,13:2
Nesvadba, Josef (Screenwriter)
Death of Tarzan, The 1968,Jl 4,13:2
Netkins, Matthew
Synanon 1965,My 6,44:1
Netscher, Robin
No Room at the Inn 1949,D 26,33:4
Inheritance, The 1951,F 12,19:2
Nettleton, Lois
Period of Adjustment 1962,N 1,34:1
Come Fly With Me 1963,My 2,40:2
Mail Order Bride 1964,Je 11,27:3
Neubach, Ernst (Original Author)
Ein Burschenlied aus Heidelberg 1931,S 14,15:3
Neubach, Ernst (Screenwriter)
Wien Du Stadt der Lieder; (Vienna City of Song)
1931,Mr 20,29:1
Joseph Schmidt Story, The 1951,Mr 5,24:2

Neubauer, Leonard (Original Author)
Fugitive From Justice, A 1940,Jl 8,13:3
Lady Wants Mink, The 1953,Ap 6,24:2
Neuberger, Harold (Miscellaneous)
Curtain Rises, The 1939,Ap 22,15:2
Schubert's Serenade 1940,S 3,21:2
Neufeld, Massimo (Director)
Moglie in Pericolo, Una; Wife in Danger, A
1940,Je 7,27:3
Neufeld, Max (Director)
K und K Balletmaedel, Das; Royal Ballet Girl,
The 1928,Ja 15,VIII,7:6 (In Addenda)
Opern-Ball, Der; Opera Ball 1931,N 6,28:3
Purpur und Waschblau 1932,Jl 11,11:4
Drunter und Drueber 1932,D 19,19:5
Geld Regiert die Welt 1934,My 12,12:4
Canzione del Sole, La 1936,My 6,27:2
Orphan Boy of Vienna, An 1937,S 9,19:2
Revenge 1947,N 28,37:4
Neufeld, Max (Original Author)
Opern-Ball, Der; Opera Ball 1931,N 6,28:3
Neufeld, Sigmund (Producer)
Miraculous Journey 1948,S 20,21:2
State Department-File 649 1949,F 21,20:2
Sins of Jezebel 1954,Ja 9,12:2
Neufield, Max (Director)
Opernredoute; Opera ball 1931,O 4,VIII,7:1
Neufold, Max
Rasputin, The Holy Sinner 1929,Ja 15,22:4
Neugebauer, Alfred
Purpur und Waschblau 1932,Jl 11,11:4
Thank You, Madame 1937,Ap 27,18:2
World's in Love, The 1937,My 19,27:2
Operetta 1949,Je 6,15:4
Singing Angels 1952,Ja 16,21:2
Story of Vickie, The 1958,Ja 30,19:2
NEUHAUS
See Also NEWHOUSE
Neuhaus, Rodolpho
Monte Cassino 1948,N 25,47:3
Neuman, E Jack (Producer)
Venetian Affair, The 1967,Ja 19,41:2
Neuman, E Jack (Screenwriter)
Venetian Affair, The 1967,Ja 19,41:2
Neuman, Liese
Karamazof 1931,S 21,20:2
Neuman, Sam (Original Author)
Hitler-Dead or Alive 1943,Mr 31,23:3
Neuman, Sam (Screenwriter)
Hitler-Dead or Alive 1943,Mr 31,23:3
Hoodlum, The 1951,Jl 6,14:6
Neumann, Alfred (Original Author)
Patriot, The 1928,Ag 18,7:2 (In Addenda)
Rasputin 1939,O 17,31:4
Mad Emperor, The 1941,Mr 10,21:3
None Shall Escape 1944,Ap 7,23:2
Conflict 1945,Je 16,10:2
Neumann, Alfred (Screenwriter)
Mad Emperor, The 1941,Mr 10,21:3
Return of Monte Cristo, The 1947,Ja 3,16:4
Neumann, Dorothy
Sorry, Wrong Number 1948,S 2,18:2
Wabash Avenue 1950,Ap 29,8:3
Latin Lovers 1953,Ag 13,17:2
Anything Goes 1956,Mr 22,38:1
Neumann, Elisabeth
House on Ninety-Second Street, The
1945,S 27,24:7
Wonderful World of the Brothers Grimm, The
1962,Ag 8,35:1
Neumann, Gunter (Original Author)
Wonderful Times 1951,Ap 24,35:2
Neumann, Gunter (Producer)
Wonderful Times 1951,Ap 24,35:2
Neumann, Gunther (Screenwriter)
Berliner, The 1952,O 28,37:1
Aren't We Wonderful? 1959,O 16,27:1
Neumann, Kurt (Director)
My Pal the King 1932,O 4,26:4
Big Cage, The 1933,My 9,20:5
Secret of the Blue Room, The 1933,S 13,22:1
King for a Night 1933,D 11,23:4
Let's Talk It Over 1934,Je 15,20:2
Half a Sinner 1934,Je 23,16:5
Wake up and Dream 1934,O 11,28:3
Alias Mary Dow 1935,Je 29,16:2
Let's Sing Again 1936,My 9,11:2
Rainbow on the River 1936,D 18,31:4
Espionage 1937,Mr 9,27:3
Make a Wish 1937,S 23,33:1
Hold 'Em Navy 1937,N 6,14:2
Wide Open Faces 1938,Ap 15,23:2
Touchdown Army 1938,O 28,27:2
Ambush 1939,F 9,17:2
Island of Lost Men 1939,Ag 17,16:3
Ellery Queen, Master Detective 1940,D 19,33:1
Night at Earl Carroll's, A 1941,Ja 23,19:1
Taxi, Mister 1943,Ap 15,20:2
Fall In 1943,My 15,13:3
Tarzan and the Amazons 1945,Ap 30,13:4
Tarzan and the Leopard Woman 1946,F 11,25:2
Tarzan and the Huntress 1947,Ap 7,20:4
Bad Men of Tombstone 1949,Mr 5,10:2

Neumann, Kurt (Director)— Cont
Bad Boy 1949,Mr 23,35:2
Rocketship X-M 1950,My 27,10:6
Kid From Texas, The 1950,Je 2,26:2
Cattle Drive 1951,Ag 9,17:5
Son of Ali Baba 1952,Ag 16,7:4
Hiawatha 1952,D 26,20:4
Carnival Story 1954,Ap 17,8:2
Kronos 1957,My 11,24:6
Circus of Love 1958,Ag 16,10:2
Fly, The 1958,Ag 30,6:6
Watusi 1959,Jl 2,15:2
Neumann, Kurt (Miscellaneous)
Return of the Vampire, The 1944,Ja 29,10:1
Neumann, Kurt (Producer)
Rocketship X-M 1950,My 27,10:6
Kronos 1957,My 11,24:6
Fly, The 1958,Ag 30,6:6
Angels From Hell 1968,O 24,55:5
Neumann, Kurt (Screenwriter)
Rocketship X-M 1950,My 27,10:6
Carnival Story 1954,Ap 17,8:2
Circus of Love 1958,Ag 16,10:2
Neumann, Robert (Original Author)
Abdul the Damned 1936,My 11,16:2
Neuner, Heiga
Dreimaederlhaus, Das; (House of Three Girls,
The) 1961,N 18,15:1
Neury, Roger
I Walk Alone 1948,Ja 22,36:3
Neutze, Gunther
Great British Train Robbery, The 1967,Ap 6,45:2
Neuville, Ernest (Screenwriter)
Personal Column 1941,F 3,13:2
It Happened in Gibraltar 1943,N 16,27:1
Neuwirth, Bob
Don't Look Back 1967,S 7,50:2
Nevalainen, Juho (Screenwriter)
Milkmaid, The 1959,My 2,14:5
Nevens, Norma
Rhapsody 1954,Mr 12,17:1
Neveux, Georges (Screenwriter)
Street of Shadows 1948,N 20,9:2
Souvenir 1950,O 3,34:4
Neville, Edgar (Director)
Flamenco 1954,My 24,24:2
Neville, Edgar (Producer)
Flamenco 1954,My 24,24:2
Neville, George
Way Down East 1931,Mr 16,25:1
Neville, Grace (Screenwriter)
Air Hawks 1935,Je 4,26:5
Shakedown 1936,Ag 17,9:2
Counsel for Crime 1937,O 9,16:1
Neville, John
Oscar Wilde 1960,Je 21,28:2
I Like Money 1962,My 19,18:2
Billy Budd 1962,O 31,32:1
Study in Terror, A 1966,N 3,45:3
Neville, John T (Original Author)
Flood, The 1931,Ap 27,25:1
Her mad Night 1932,N 15,24:5
Alimony Madness 1933,My 5,18:1
Female Fugitive 1938,Ap 11,12:3
Neville, John T (Screenwriter)
Desert Nights 1929,My 6,30:4
Female Fugitive 1938,Ap 11,12:3
Never Give a Sucker an Even Break
1941,O 27,21:2
Neville, Robert (Miscellaneous)
Peck's bad Boy With the Circus 1939,Ja 11,17:4
Neville, Robert (Screenwriter)
Peck's bad Boy With the Circus 1939,Ja 11,17:4
Black Cat, The 1941,Ap 26,20:3
Nevinny
Last Game, The 1964,O 25,41:5 (Incorrect in this
edition; use 1964,O 26,41:5 elsewhere)
Nevins, Claudette
Mask, The 1961,O 28,12:4
Nevins, Frank J (Original Author)
Rock Island Trail 1950,Je 5,19:3
Nevinson, Nancy
Othello 1960,My 16,39:1
Light in the Piazza 1962,F 8,25:1
Nevola, Eduardo
Teacher and the Miracle, The 1961,Ap 24,36:4
World in my Pocket, The 1962,My 10,30:2
Railroad Man, The; Ferroviere, II 1965,O 25,46:2
New York Philharmonic Quintet
Carnegie Hall 1947,My 3,10:2
New York Philharmonic Symphony Orchestra
Of Men and Music 1951,F 15,27:2
Newark, Derek
Little Ones, The 1965,S 16,55:2
Newberger, Ad (Producer)
Revolt of the Toymakers, The 1918,D 23,9:1
Newbrook, Peter (Producer)
Corruption 1968,D 5,59:1
Newburg, Frank
Home Maker, The 1925,Ag 10,8:2
Newcomb, Herbert
Johnny Holiday 1950,My 17,36:1

Newcombe, Grace
Once More With Feeling 1960,F 12,22:2
Newcombe, Jessica
One Body too Many 1944,N 25,21:2
Newcombe, Warren A (Producer)
Enchanted City, The 1922,F 6,9:1
Newell, Billy
Wife vs Secretary 1936,F 29,11:1
Newell, David
Dangerous Curves 1929,Jl 15,25:1
Marriage Playground, The 1929,D 14,22:4
Kibitzer, The 1929,D 21,17:1
Runaway Bride 1930,My 17,21:2
Let's Go Native 1930,Ag 30,7:4
Woman Hungry 1931,Mr 23,24:7
Flood, The 1931,Ap 27,25:1
New Morals for Old 1932,Je 24,15:3
Hell Below 1933,Ap 26,13:2
Made on Broadway 1933,Jl 8,14:5
White Heat 1934,Je 16,20:2
Educating Father 1936,Je 20,22:2
Polo Joe 1936,N 5,35:1
Newell, David M (Producer)
Matto Grosso 1933,Ja 14,8:5
Newell, Joan
Stolen Hours 1963,O 17,39:1
Newell, William
Voice of Bugle Ann, The 1936,F 27,23:1
Libeled Lady 1936,O 31,24:2
Ride a Crooked Mile 1938,D 29,15:2
Slightly Tempted 1940,N 1,33:1
Who Is Hope Schuyler 1942,My 22,27:1
Key Witness 1947,Jl 30,27:6
Second Chance 1947,S 20,12:4
Song of my Heart 1948,Mr 5,17:3
Traveling Saleswoman 1950,Ja 6,25:3
Newfield, Samuel (Director)
Jungle Siren 1942,O 10,11:3
Outlaw Woman 1952,Ap 5,20:3
Newhall, Mayo
That Lady in Ermine 1948,Ag 25,31:2
Newhart, Bob
Hell is for Heroes 1962,Jl 12,19:3
Hot Millions 1968,S 20,42:1
NEWHOUSE
See Also NEUHAUS
Newhouse, David (Screenwriter)
Point Blank 1967,S 19,53:1
Newhouse, Delbert C
Unidentified Flying Objects 1956,Je 13,46:2
Newhouse, Edward (Original Author)
I Want You 1951,D 24,9:1
Shadow in the Sky 1952,Jl 19,8:2
Newhouse, Rafe (Screenwriter)
Point Blank 1967,S 19,53:1
Newick, Kathleen
Return to Paradise 1953,S 11,24:2
Newill, James
Something to Sing About 1937,S 21,29:4
Renfrew of the Royal Mounted 1937,N 3,29:4
Great American Broadcast, The 1941,My 2,25:2
Falcon's Brother, The 1942,O 3,9:5
Bombardier 1943,Jl 2,15:2
Newlan, Paul
David and Bathsheba 1951,Ag 15,23:2
Captive City, The 1952,Mr 27,34:2
Against all Flags 1952,D 25,34:6
Pirates of Tripoli 1955,F 24,21:2
Americanization of Emily, The 1964,O 28,51:1
Slender Thread, The 1965,D 24,24:2
Newlan, Tiny
Gracie Allen Murder Case, The 1939,Je 8,31:3
Newland, Douglass
Sunday Punch 1942,My 11,19:2
Vanishing Virginian, The 1942,My 28,13:3
Newland, John
Gentleman's Agreement 1947,N 12,36:2
Newland, John (Director)
That Night 1957,O 15,39:3
Violators, The 1959,Ag 4,32:5
Newlands, Anthony
Hysteria 1965,S 9,36:3
Newley, Anthony
Guinea Pig, The 1949,My 2,20:2
Little Ballerina, The 1951,F 28,33:2
Oliver Twist 1951,Jl 31,17:2
Cockleshell Heroes, The 1956,Je 4,25:2
Port Afrique 1956,N 3,27:5
Fire Down Below 1957,Ag 9,11:2
How to Murder a Rich Uncle 1957,O 26,19:2
Man Inside, The 1959,F 5,24:7
Killers of Kilimanjaro 1960,Ap 7,46:1
Small World of Sammy Lee, The 1963,Ag 14,28:1
Doctor Dolittle 1967,D 20,55:1
Sweet November 1968,F 9,55:1
Newley, Anthony (Composer)
Stop the World-I Want to Get Off
1966,My 12,54:2
Newley, Anthony (Original Author)
Stop the World-I Want to Get Off
1966,My 12,54:2

Newman, Alfred
They Shall Have Music 1939,Jl 26,17:2
Newman, Alfred (Composer)
Mr Robinson Crusoe 1932,S 22,25:4
Kid Millions 1934,N 12,17:2
Mighty Barnum, The 1934,D 24,17:1
Clive of India 1935,Ja 18,29:1
Hurricane, The 1937,N 10,31:2
Hunchback of Notre Dame, The 1940,Ja 1,29:2
Blue Bird, The 1940,Ja 20,11:2
Grapes of Wrath, The 1940,Ja 25,17:2
Lillian Russell 1940,My 18,11:2
How Green Was my Valley 1941,O 29,27:2
Newman, Alfred (Miscellaneous)
Ramona 1936,O 7,32:4
Newman, Anne
Thrill of it All, The 1963,Ag 2,15:3
Best Man, The 1964,Ap 7,29:1
Newman, Barry
Pretty Boy Floyd 1960,N 3,49:2
Newman, Charles (Composer)
That's Right, You're Wrong 1939,N 30,25:3
Jitterbugs 1943,Je 5,12:2
Newman, Charles (Original Author)
Zombies on Broadway 1945,Ap 27,23:2
Newman, David (Producer)
He Who Rides a Tiger 1968,S 10,39:1
Newman, David (Screenwriter)
Bonnie and Clyde 1967,Ag 14,36:1
Newman, Hisparmery Sergio (Producer)
Awful Dr Orlof, The 1964,D 3,58:3
Newman, Joe (Director)
Abandoned Woman 1949,O 27,35:3
Great Dan Patch, The 1949,N 9,37:2
Newman, John Henry (Composer)
Two Tickets to London 1943,Jl 3,11:2
Newman, John K
Greatest Love of All, The 1924,N 11,14:1
Newman, Joseph (Director)
Guy Who Came Back, The 1951,Ag 17,13:2
This Island Earth 1955,Je 11,8:7
Thunder of Drums, A 1961,S 27,35:1
King of the Roaring Twenties 1961,O 5,43:1
Newman, Joseph H (Director)
711 Ocean Drive 1950,Jl 20,21:2
Newman, Joseph M (Director)
Lucky Nick Cain 1951,Ap 23,21:2
Smoke Jumpers 1952,Mr 22,9:6
Outcasts of Poker Flat 1952,My 16,19:3
Pony Soldier 1952,D 20,15:2
Dangerous Crossing 1953,S 30,37:2
Human Jungle, The 1954,N 26,24:6
Kiss of Fire 1955,S 24,11:2
Flight to Hong Kong 1957,Ja 3,28:2
Big Circus, The 1959,Jl 18,6:1
George Raft Story, The 1962,Mr 22,40:1
Newman, Joseph M (Producer)
Flight to Hong Kong 1957,Ja 3,28:2
Newman, Lionel (Composer)
Do You Love Me 1946,My 25,12:2
Bill and Coo 1948,Mr 29,17:4
Golden Girl 1951,N 21,20:3
Newman, Martin
Shrike, The 1955,Jl 8,15:2
Newman, Nanette
Wrong Arm of the Law, The 1963,Ap 3,39:1
Of Human Bondage 1964,S 24,46:2
Seance on a Wet Afternoon 1964,N 6,30:1
Wrong Box 1966,Jl 20,46:1
Whisperers, The 1967,Ag 1,24:1
Deadfall 1968,S 12,54:1
Newman, Paul
Silver Chalice, The 1954,D 27,22:5
Somebody up There Likes Me 1956,Jl 6,16:1
Rack, The 1956,N 6,30:1
Helen Morgan Story, The 1957,O 3,33:2
Until They Sail 1957,O 9,41:2
Long, Hot Summer, The 1958,Ap 4,16:1
Left Handed Gun, The 1958,My 8,36:2
Cat on a Hot Tin Roof 1958,S 19,24:1
Rally Round the Flag Boys! 1958,D 24,2:1
Young Philadelphians, The 1959,My 22,32:1
From the Terrace 1960,Jl 16,10:1
Exodus 1960,D 16,44:1
Hustler, The 1961,S 27,35:1
Paris Blues 1961,N 8,41:1
Sweet Bird of Youth 1962,Mr 29,28:2
Hemingway's Adventures of a Young Man
1962,Jl 26,17:1
Hud 1963,My 29,36:1
New Kind of Love, A 1963,O 31,26:2
Prize, The 1964,Ja 24,21:1
What a Way to Go! 1964,My 15,44:1
Outrage, The 1964,O 8,48:2
Harper 1966,Mr 31,43:1
Lady L 1966,My 19,51:1
Torn Curtain 1966,Jl 28,23:1
Hombre 1967,Mr 22,41:1
Cool Hand Luke 1967,N 2,58:1
Secret War of Harry Frigg, The 1968,Mr 5,34:5
Newman, Paul (Director)
Rachel Rachel 1968,Ag 27,36:1

Newman, Paul (Producer)
Rachel Rachel 1968,Ag 27,36:1
Newman, Peter R (Screenwriter)
Yesterday's Enemy 1960,Mr 4,19:1
Newman, Phyllis
Picnic 1956,F 17,13:3
Bye Bye Braverman 1968,F 22,36:1
Newman, Samuel (Miscellaneous)
Stampede 1949,S 16,36:2
Newman, Samuel (Original Author)
Wizard of Baghdad, The 1961,Mr 4,16:1
Newman, Walter (Screenwriter)
Ace in the Hole 1951,Je 30,8:6
Underwater! 1955,F 10,27:2
Man With the Golden Arm, The 1955,D 16,38:2
True Story of Jesse James, The 1957,Mr 23,17:2
Crime and Punishment, U S A 1959,Je 17,39:3
Interns, The 1962,Ag 9,17:5
Cat Ballou 1965,Je 25,36:1
Newmar, Julie
Li'l Abner 1959,D 12,19:2
Rookie, The 1960,Mr 17,28:1
Marriage-Go-Round 1961,Ja 7,12:2
For Love or Money 1963,Ag 8,19:1
Newmark, Lucille (Screenwriter)
Miss Pacific Fleet 1935,D 7,22:2
Newmeyer, Fred (Director)
Safety Last 1923,Ap 2,22:1
Girl Shy 1924,Ap 21,21:4
Freshman, The 1925,S 21,12:4
Seven Keys to Baldpate 1925,N 3,25:4
Quarterback, The 1926,O 12,30:2
Potters, The 1927,Ja 18,23:1
Lunatic at Large, The 1927,F 1,25:1
On Your Toes 1928,Ja 9,20:1
That's my Daddy 1928,F 13,16:2
Rainbow Man, The 1929,Ap 17,30:6
Sailor's Holiday 1929,O 21,30:1
Grand Parade, The 1930,F 1,15:1
Queen High 1930,Ag 9,16:5
Fast and Loose 1930,D 1,21:1
Subway Express 1931,My 2,23:4
They Never Come Back 1932,Je 4,9:2
Newmeyer, Fred (Screenwriter)
Hot Water 1924,O 27,27:1
Newmeyer, Julie
Seven Brides for Seven Brothers 1954,Jl 23,8:3
Newmeyer, Peter
Address Unknown 1944,Ap 17,20:1
Newsom, J D (Original Author)
Trouble in Morocco 1937,Mr 15,27:1
Newson, Buck
Untitled-Baseball Technique 1941,Ja 17,11:3
Newton, Charles
In the Palace of the King 1923,D 3,14:1
Vanity's Price 1924,O 8,16:2
Riders of the Purple Sage 1925,Ap 15,16:1
Newton, Christopher
Romeo and Juliet 1966,O 6,55:1
Newton, Daphne
Murder Will Out 1953,Ap 6,24:2
Newton, Dodo
Big Trail, The 1930,O 25,20:3
Newton, Joan
Bedlam 1946,Ap 20,16:4
Newton, Mary
Seventh Victim, The 1943,S 18,11:3
Tomorrow the World 1944,D 22,12:4
Spirit of West Point 1947,O 3,31:2
Bad Men of Tombstone 1949,Mr 5,10:2
Newton, Robert
Fire Over England 1937,Mr 5,16:2
Murder on Diamond Row 1937,N 12,27:2
Troopship 1938,Ap 26,18:2
Beachcomber, The 1938,D 26,29:3
Jamaica Inn 1939,O 12,33:1
21 Days Together 1940,My 23,28:4
Hell's Cargo 1940,S 16,15:2
Haunted Honeymoon 1940,O 31,28:2
Major Barbara 1941,My 15,27:1
Wings and the Woman 1942,O 8,31:1
Henry V 1946,Je 18,30:2
This Happy Breed 1947,Ap 14,24:2
Odd Man Out 1947,Ap 24,30:2
Green Cockatoo, The 1947,Jl 19,10:2
Hatter's Castle 1948,Jl 3,8:6
Kiss the Blood off my Hands 1948,O 30,10:2
Snowbound 1949,F 21,20:2
Temptation Harbor 1949,My 11,34:7
Hidden Room, The 1950,Ja 9,19:2
Treasure Island 1950,Ag 16,24:2
Soldiers Three 1951,Mr 30,28:5
Oliver Twist 1951,Jl 31,17:2
Tom Brown's School Days 1952,Ja 8,23:5
Miserables, Les 1952,Ag 15,11:2
Angel Street 1952,N 11,25:2
Blackbeard the Pirate 1952,D 26,20:3
Androcles and the Lion 1953,Ja 15,23:2
Desert Rats, The 1953,My 9,13:2
High and the Mighty, The 1954,Jl 1,21:2
Beachcomber, The 1955,Ja 17,27:5
Long John Silver 1955,Ap 7,24:1
Around the World in 80 Days 1956,O 18,37:1

Newton, Theodore
Working Man, The 1933,Ap 21,20:3
Sphinx, The 1933,Jl 6,26:5
Voltaire 1933,Ag 23,21:2
World Changes, The 1933,O 27,22:3
Ace of Aces 1933,N 11,10:4
From Headquarters 1933,N 17,22:4
Heat Lightning 1934,Mr 8,23:2
Modern Hero, A 1934,Ap 20,17:1
Upper World 1934,My 25,25:4
Now I'll Tell 1934,My 26,12:2
Let's Try Again 1934,Je 22,24:1
Blind Date 1934,S 1,16:3
Gambling 1934,D 4,22:3
Jalna 1935,S 14,8:4
Miss Susie Slagle's 1946,F 7,29:2
Two Years Before the Mast 1946,S 25,39:2
Come on, The 1956,Ap 7,13:1
Proud and Profane, The 1956,Je 14,41:2
Somebody up There Likes Me 1956,Jl 6,16:1
Friendly Persuasion 1956,N 2,30:1
Newton, W Douglas (Original Author)
Brute, The 1927,Ap 21,25:1
Nex, Andre
Daughter of Israel, A 1928,My 21,25:1
Nexo, Martin Anderson (Original Author)
Child of Man 1950,F 1,25:2
Ney, Marie
Escape 1930,N 1,23:2
Wandering Jew, The 1935,Ja 14,11:3
Scrooge 1935,D 14,11:1
Jamaica Inn 1939,O 12,33:1
Conspirator 1950,Ap 28,26:2
Simba 1955,O 22,24:2
Ney, Richard
Mrs Miniver 1942,Je 5,23:1
War Against Mrs Hadley, The 1942,N 26,40:2
Late George Apley, The 1947,Mr 21,29:2
Ivy 1947,Je 26,19:1
Joan of Arc 1948,N 12,30:5
Fan, The 1949,Ap 2,12:2
Miss Italy 1952,My 10,16:2
Babes in Bagdad 1954,Ap 5,21:3
Midnight Lace 1960,O 14,27:1
Premature Burial, The 1962,My 24,29:2
Nezer, Christopher
Youth of Athens 1949,O 31,20:4
Ngakane, Lionel
Cry, the Beloved Country 1952,Ja 24,23:2
Safari 1956,Je 21,35:2
Elephant Gun 1959,Je 20,11:2
Ngcobo, Reginald
Cry, the Beloved Country 1952,Ja 24,23:2
Ngebrof, A
Young Pushkin 1937,D 16,35:3
N'Gel, Paul
Ivory Hunter 1952,Ag 19,19:1
Nghiep, Phuong Thi
Quiet American, The 1958,F 6,24:1
Niall, Ian (Original Author)
No Resting Place 1952,My 5,18:5
Tiger Walks, A 1964,Ag 27,28:2
Nibert, Terry
Little Foxes, The 1941,Ag 22,19:2
Nibley, Sloan (Original Author)
Carson City 1952,Je 14,12:2
Springfield Rifle 1952,O 23,40:2
Nibley, Sloan (Screenwriter)
Surrender 1950,O 9,21:5
Carson City 1952,Je 14,12:2
Niblo, Fred
Free and Easy 1930,Ap 19,15:1
I'm Still Alive 1940,O 11,25:4
Ellery Queen, Master Detective 1940,D 19,33:1
Life With Henry 1941,F 6,25:2
Niblo, Fred (Director)
Fuss and Feathers 1918,D 9,11:4
Stepping Out 1919,S 22,8:1
Woman in the Suitcase, The 1920,Ja 12,7:1
Hairpins 1920,Ag 2,12:2
Mark of Zorro, The 1920,N 29,20:3
Blood and Sand 1922,Ag 7,14:2
Famous Mrs Fair, The 1923,Ap 23,18:3
Strangers of the Night 1923,O 8,20:1
Thy Name Is Woman 1924,Mr 4,17:1
Red Lily, The 1924,S 29,10:1
Ben Hur 1925,D 31,10:5 (In Addenda)
Temptress, The 1926,O 11,18:1
Camille 1927,Ap 22,19:1
Devil Dancer, The 1927,D 19,30:1
Enemy, The 1927,D 28,26:6
Two Lovers 1928,Mr 23,24:4
Mysterious Lady, The 1928,Ag 6,15:2
Dream of Love 1928,D 24,11:1
Redemption 1930,My 3,23:1
Way out West 1930,Ag 18,24:1
Donovan's Kid 1931,My 22,28:5
Big Gamble, The 1931,S 21,20:2
Ben Hur 1931,D 4,28:2
Blame the Woman 1932,O 25,24:5

Niblo, Fred Jr (Original Author)
Four Jills in a Jeep 1944,Ap 6,27:2
Niblo, Fred Jr (Screenwriter)
Escape from Devil's Island 1935,N 25,22:2
You may Be Next 1936,F 24,14:1
Man Who Lived Twice, The 1936,O 12,23:2
Lady From Nowhere 1936,D 21,19:2
Counsel for Crime 1937,O 9,16:1
Penitentiary 1938,Mr 7,13:2
City Streets 1938,Jl 25,18:2
Hell's Kitchen 1939,Jl 3,10:5
Fighting 69th, The 1940,Ja 27,9:2
Angel From Texas, An 1940,My 10,26:7
East of the River 1940,O 28,21:2
Father's Son 1941,F 13,25:3
Wagons Roll at Night, The 1941,My 10,20:4
Nine Loves Are not Enough 1941,O 30,27:2
You Can't Escape Forever 1942,O 17,11:1
Falcon in Danger, The 1943,Jl 23,21:2
Tampico 1944,Je 2,21:2
Nicaud, Philippe
Monelle 1950,F 3,29:2
Miquette 1951,F 5,18:2
Dream Ballerina 1951,Ap 16,21:2
Three Sinners 1952,Jl 8,23:2
Back to the Wall; (Dos au Mur) 1959,S 8,43:2
Come Dance With Me!; Voulez-Vous Danser Avec
Moi 1960,N 8,32:6
Magnificent Cuckold 1965,Ap 20,42:1
Nichel, Germaine
Au Grand Balcon 1951,My 5,14:2
Nichi, Carlo
Tears of Blood 1952,Ja 19,13:2
Constantine and the Cross 1963,Mr 14,8:2
Nichlisch, Fritz
Big Lift, The 1950,Ap 27,37:2
Nicholai, Boris
Anthony Adverse 1936,Ag 27,16:1
Nicholas, Fayard
Big Broadcast of 1936, The 1935,S 16,15:2
Nicholas, Harold
Big Broadcast of 1936, The 1935,S 16,15:2
Carolina Blues 1944,D 8,26:6
Nicholas Brothers
Down Argentine Way 1940,O 18,25:1
Great American Broadcast, The 1941,My 2,25:2
Sun Valley Serenade 1941,S 6,20:1
Orchestra Wives 1942,S 24,23:2
Stormy Weather 1943,Jl 22,15:1
Pirate, The 1948,My 21,19:2
Nicholas Brothers, The
Tin Pan Alley 1940,N 22,27:3
Nicholis, Anthony
Burn, Witch, Burn 1962,Jl 5,21:2 (In Addenda)
Nicholls, Anthony
Guinea Pig, The 1949,My 2,20:2
Hasty Heart, The 1950,Ja 21,10:5
Dancing Years, The 1951,Ja 29,14:4
No Place for Jennifer 1951,Jl 17,31:2
High Treason 1952,My 21,23:3
Franchise Affair, The 1952,Je 6,19:2
Both Sides of the Law 1954,Ja 12,19:2
Tonight's the Night 1954,D 23,13:4
Make Me an Offer 1956,F 29,35:2
Dunkirk 1958,S 11,42:2
Victim 1962,F 6,27:2
Othello 1966,F 2,24:1
Nicholls, George Jr (Director)
Finishing School 1934,Ap 30,11:4
Anne of Green Gables 1934,D 22,21:1
Return of Peter Grimm, The 1935,O 4,25:2
Chatterbox 1936,F 15,18:6
Witness Chair, The 1936,Ap 18,19:2
M'liss 1936,Ag 8,5:2
Big Game, The 1936,O 24,23:1
Soldier and the Lady, The 1937,Ap 10,11:1
Portia on Trial 1937,D 3,29:2
Army Girl 1938,Ag 12,11:1
Man of Conquest 1939,Ap 28,31:2
Marines Fly High, The 1940,Mr 5,19:2
Nicholls, Sarah
Our Mother's House 1967,O 10,56:1
Nicholls, Thomas
Romeo and Juliet 1954,D 22,28:1
Nichols, Anne (Original Author)
Abie's Irish Rose 1928,Ap 20,26:7
Just Married 1928,Ag 13,23:2
Give Me a Sailor 1938,Ag 11,31:1
Nichols, Anne (Screenwriter)
Abie's Irish Rose 1946,D 23,19:4
Nichols, Barbara
Miracle in the Rain 1956,Ap 2,18:1
Beyond a Reasonable Doubt 1956,S 14,27:2
King and Four Queens, The 1956,D 22,13:7
Sweet Smell of Success 1957,Je 28,29:2
Pajama Game, The 1957,Ag 30,12:2
Pal Joey 1957,O 28,30:1
Ten North Frederick 1958,My 23,29:2
Naked and the Dead, The 1958,Ag 7,21:1
Woman Obsessed 1959,My 28,34:1
That Kind of Woman 1959,S 12,12:2
Who Was That Lady? 1960,Ap 16,10:1
Where the Boys Are 1961,Ja 20,22:1

Nichols, Barbara — Cont
George Raft Story, The 1962,Mr 22,40:1
House of Women 1962,Ap 12,41:6
Dear Heart 1965,Mr 8,33:1
Power, The 1968,Mr 7,52:2
Nichols, Beverley (Original Author)
Evensong 1934,N 17,12:1
Nichols, Dandy
Fallen Idol, The 1949,N 16,39:2
Winslow Boy, The 1950,Je 7,34:4
Tony Draws a Horse 1951,My 15,38:6
Mr Lord Says No! 1952,F 12,22:5
Deep Blue Sea, The 1955,O 13,35:2
Blonde Sinner 1957,Ja 24,34:1
Ladies Who Do 1963,N 26,52:2
Georgy Girl 1966,O 18,48:1
Birthday Party, The 1968,D 10,54:1
Nichols, Dudley (Composer)
Judge Priest 1934,O 12,33:1
Nichols, Dudley (Director)
Government Girl 1944,Ja 7,13:2
Sister Kenny 1946,S 30,21:2
Mourning Becomes Electra 1947,N 20,38:2
Nichols, Dudley (Miscellaneous)
She 1935,Jl 26,18:2
400,000,000, The 1939,Mr 8,19:2
Nichols, Dudley (Original Author)
Hot Pepper 1933,Ja 23,9:2
Man Who Dared, The 1933,S 9,9:3
You Can't Buy Everything 1934,F 3,9:2
Hold That Girl 1934,Mr 24,20:3
Call it Luck 1934,Jl 10,24:5
Wild Gold 1934,Jl 24,20:2
Mystery Woman 1935,Ja 9,22:2
Arizonian, The 1935,Jl 27,16:2
Carefree 1938,S 23,35:1
Nichols, Dudley (Producer)
Government Girl 1944,Ja 7,13:2
Sister Kenny 1946,S 30,21:2
Mourning Becomes Electra 1947,N 20,38:2
Nichols, Dudley (Screenwriter)
Devil With Women, A 1930,O 20,28:2
Informer, The 1935,My 10,25:2
Arizonian, The 1935,Jl 27,16:2
Crusades, The 1935,Ag 22,21:3
Steamboat Around the Bend 1935,S 20,17:2
Three Musketeers, The 1935,N 1,25:1
Mary of Scotland 1936,Jl 31,22:2
Plough and the Stars, The 1937,Ja 29,15:1
Toast of New York, The 1937,Jl 23,16:2
Hurricane, The 1937,N 10,31:2
Bringing Up Baby 1938,Mr 4,17:5
Stagecoach 1939,Mr 3,21:1
Long Voyage Home, The 1940,O 9,30:2 (In
Addenda)
Man Hunt 1941,Je 14,20:2
Swamp Water 1941,N 17,15:2
Air Force 1943,F 4,29:1
This Land Is Mine 1943,My 28,19:1
For Whom the Bell Tolls 1943,Jl 15,25:2
Government Girl 1944,Ja 7,13:2
It Happened Tomorrow 1944,My 29,18:2
Sign of the Cross 1944,D 21,16:3
And Then There Were None 1945,N 1,20:2
Bells of St Mary's, The 1945,D 7,26:2
Scarlet Street 1946,F 15,29:2
Sister Kenny 1946,S 30,21:2
Mourning Becomes Electra 1947,N 20,38:2
Fugitive, The 1947,D 26,22:2
Pinky 1949,S 30,28:2
Rawhide 1951,Mr 26,19:2
Return of the Texan 1952,F 14,23:1
Big Sky, The 1952,Ag 20,21:1
Prince Valiant 1954,Ap 7,40:2
Run for the Sun 1956,Ag 25,7:2
Tin Star, The 1957,O 24,37:2
Heller in Pink Tights 1960,Mr 17,28:1
Stagecoach 1966,Je 16,53:1
Nichols, George
Turn in the Road, The 1919,Mr 30,IV,6:1
Greatest Question, The 1919,D 29,7:2
Shame 1921,Ag 1,8:3 (Incorrect in this edition;
use 1921,Ag 1,6:4 elsewhere)
Pride of Palomar, The 1922,N 20,21:3
Flirt, The 1922,D 31,VII,2:2 (In Addenda)
Suzanna 1923,Mr 26,16:2
Don't Marry for Money 1923,Ag 21,17:3
Country Kid, The 1923,O 30,16:1
Extra Girl, The 1924,Ja 21,20:1
Daughters of Today 1924,Mr 4,17:1
Secrets 1924,Mr 25,25:2
Red Lily, The 1924,S 29,10:1
East of Broadway 1924,N 12,13:1
Midnight Express, The 1924,N 19,19:3
Capital Punishment 1925,F 5,23:3
Proud Flesh 1925,Ap 14,26:1
Light of the Western Stars, The 1925,Je 24,14:3
Goose Woman, The 1925,Ag 4,14:3
His Majesty Bunker Bean 1925,S 15,12:1
Eagle, The 1925,N 9,25:1
Sea Horses 1926,F 23,26:5
Rolling Home 1926,Je 8,22:1
Senor Daredevil 1926,Ag 17,15:3
Gigolo 1926,O 5,27:1

Nichols, George— Cont

White Flannels 1927,Mr 22,31:2
White Gold 1927,Ap 11,18:3
Ritzy 1927,Je 20,25:3
Wedding March, The 1928,O 15,26:1

Nichols, Joy
Pacific Adventure 1947,N 26,18:2

Nichols, Loring (Red) (Miscellaneous)
Five Pennies, The 1959,Je 19,30:1

Nichols, Mike
Bed of Grass 1957,D 28,9:2

Nichols, Mike (Director)
Who's Afraid of Virginia Woolf? 1966,Je 30,28:1
Who's Afraid of Virginia Woolf? 1966,Jl 10,II,1:5
Graduate, The 1967,D 22,44:4

Nichols, Nellie V
Playing Around 1930,Mr 31,24:3
Women Go on Forever 1931,O 19,28:1
Manhattan Merry-Go-Round 1937,D 31,9:3

Nichols, Nichelle
Mister Buddwing 1966,O 12,36:1

Nichols, Peter (Screenwriter)
Having a Wild Weekend 1965,Ag 19,35:1
Georgy Girl 1966,O 18,48:1

Nichols, Richard
All This and Heaven, Too 1940,Jl 5,10:2
Little Men 1940,D 9,23:2
Dispatch From Reuters, A 1940,D 12,37:2
Kitty Foyle 1941,Ja 9,27:2
Woman's Face, A 1941,My 16,21:2
Blossoms in the Dust 1941,Je 27,14:4

Nichols, Robert
Thing, The 1951,My 3,34:4
Eight Iron Men 1953,Ja 2,11:1
Command, The 1954,Ja 16,10:5
Giant 1956,O 11,51:1
Don't Go Near the Water 1957,N 15,37:1
Follow the Boys 1963,F 28,8:2
Call Me Bwana 1963,Jl 4,9:1
Man in the Middle 1964,Mr 5,36:1

Nichols, Tad (Cinematographer)
Living Desert, The 1953,N 10,38:1

Nicholson, Ivy
I, A Man 1967,Ag 25,28:1

Nicholson, Jack
Studs Lonigan 1960,D 15,59:1
Raven, The 1963,Ja 26,5:8
Hells Angels on Wheels 1967,Jl 29,29:3
Psych-Out 1968,Mr 28,52:1

Nicholson, Jack (Original Author)
Head 1968,N 7,51:1

Nicholson, Jack (Producer)
Head 1968,N 7,51:1

Nicholson, Jack (Screenwriter)
Trip, The 1967,Ag 24,43:1

Nicholson, James H (Producer)
Master of the World 1961,S 16,9:1
Beach Party 1963,S 26,40:2
Comedy of Terrors, The 1964,Ja 23,26:2
Muscle Beach Party 1964,My 28,40:1
Bikini Beach 1964,S 17,52:6
Sergeant Deadhead 1965,O 23,17:3
Dr Goldfoot and the Bikini Machine 1966,F 17,29:3
Fireball 500 1966,N 24,65:4
How to Stuff a Wild Bikini 1967,Ja 12,48:1
Wild in the Streets 1968,My 30,21:1

Nicholson, Kenyon (Miscellaneous)
13 Hours by Air 1936,Ap 30,17:2

Nicholson, Kenyon (Original Author)
Barker, The 1928,D 6,35:1
Two Weeks Off 1929,Je 24,27:1
Laughing Sinners 1931,Jl 4,11:5
Hoopla 1933,D 1,23:3
Lady, Be Careful 1936,O 10,21:1
Swing Your Lady 1938,Ja 27,17:2
Waterfront 1939,Jl 17,10:2
Fleet's In, The 1942,Mr 12,24:2
Billy Rose's Diamond Horseshoe 1945,My 3,37:1
Sailor Beware 1952,F 1,17:1

Nicholson, Meredith (Original Author)
Broken Barriers 1924,Ag 4,16:3
House of a Thousand Candles, The 1936,Ap 2,29:2

Nicholson, Nora
Blue Lagoon, The 1949,O 3,13:2
Raising a Riot 1957,My 8,44:1
Town Like Alice, A 1958,S 22,27:1
Upstairs and Downstairs 1960,D 2,53:4

Nicholson, Paul
Married Flirts 1924,N 19,19:3
As Man Desires 1925,F 10,20:1
I Want my Man 1925,Ap 6,17:3
Chickie 1925,Ap 27,15:2
Joanna 1925,D 15,14:5
Up in Mabel's Room 1926,Je 29,21:2
Nervous Wreck, The 1926,O 12,30:2
Bertha, The Sewing Machine Girl 1927,Ja 4,21:1
Brute, The 1927,Ap 21,25:1
Smart Set, The 1928,Mr 5,21:1
Port of Missing Girls, The 1928,Jl 31,13:4
Not Quite Decent 1929,My 6,30:4
New Movietone Follies of 1930, The 1930,Je 21,20:5

Silence 1931,Ag 15,18:3
Scandal for Sale 1932,Ap 3,26:2

Nick, Edmund (Composer)
Hofkonzert, Das 1937,Mr 27,19:3

Nicklaus, Thelma (Original Author)
Tamahine 1964,Jl 16,23:1

Nickle, Burr (Producer)
Wonders of the World 1925,Ap 1,21:3

Nicklisch, Franz
Stuerme der Leidenschaft; Storms of Passion 1932,F 14,VIII,6:1
Stuerme der Leidenschaft 1932,Mr 16,17:3
Pantoffelhelden 1935,O 21,22:5
Soldaten-Kameraden 1936,O 5,25:1

Nickstadt, Gerd (Screenwriter)
Mediterannean Holiday 1964,D 16,51:1

Nico
**** 1967,D 17,94:5

Nicodemi, Aldo
Miserables, Les 1952,Mr 25,23:2
Margaret of Cortona 1957,Ja 21,20:4

Nicodemus
Go West, Young Man 1936,N 19,31:3
Cabin in the Sky 1943,My 28,19:3
Stormy Weather 1943,Jl 22,15:1

Nicol, Alex
Sleeping City, The 1950,S 21,20:2
Tomahawk 1951,F 19,19:2
Target Unknown 1951,Mr 5,24:2
Air Cadet 1951,My 11,32:3
Meet Danny Wilson 1952,Mr 27,34:4
Red Ball Express 1952,My 30,11:2
Because of You 1952,D 4,47:3
Redhead From Wyoming, The 1953,Ja 9,17:4
Lone Hand 1953,Je 27,7:2
About Mrs Leslie 1954,Je 28,16:2
Dawn at Socorro 1954,Ag 28,8:2
Strategic Air Command 1955,Ap 21,33:1
Man From Laramie, The 1955,S 1,20:2
Sincerely Yours 1955,N 3,37:1
Great Day in the Morning 1956,My 19,12:6
Five Branded Women 1960,Je 2,27:2
Under ten Flags 1960,S 16,24:1
Look in any Window 1962,Mr 22,40:1
Matter of Who, A 1962,Jl 25,29:2
Everybody go Home!; Tutti a Casa 1962,N 6,38:1
Run With the Devil 1963,Jl 16,25:1
Gunfighters of Casa Grande 1965,S 2,36:1

Nicol, Tyron
Johnny in the Clouds 1945,N 16,16:2

Nicola, Jules
Paris Incident 1954,Ag 18,20:2

Nicolai, Bruno (Composer)
Christmas That Almost Wasn't 1966,N 24,65:2

Nicolai, Otto (Composer)
Merry Wives of Windsor, The 1952,S 22,19:2
Merry Wives of Windsor, The 1966,F 28,21:1

Nicolaidis, Dimitris
Day the Fish Came Out, The 1967,O 3,57:1

Nicoletti, Louis
Across the Wide Missouri 1951,N 7,35:4

Nicoletti, Susi
Mutterliebe; Mother Love 1940,Mr 16,8:3
Confessions of Felix Krull, The 1958,Mr 5,38:1

Nicolini, Natalia
Barber of Seville, The 1947,My 6,35:2

Nicolle, Andre
Adieux les Beaux Jours 1934,Ap 23,20:2
Personal Column 1941,F 3,13:2

Nicols, Rosemary
Pleasure Girls, The 1966,Ap 21,43:1

Nicot, Claude
Minne 1951,Ap 17,35:2
Fruits of Summer 1956,Jl 18,22:2

Nicotra, Antonio
Behind Closed Shutters 1952,Je 10,22:7
Of Life and Love 1958,O 7,40:2

Nicotra, Mario
Ring Around the Clock 1953,My 19,36:2

Nicova, Leda
Waterloo Bridge 1940,My 17,23:2

Niederberger, Max (Miscellaneous)
Acht Tage Glueck 1931,Jl 24,22:1

Niehaus, Ruth
No Way Back 1955,My 19,25:5
Rape on the Moor 1957,N 21,38:1

Niel, Henri
Miquette 1951,F 5,18:2

Nielo, Jose
Kid Rodelo 1966,F 23,46:1

Nielsen, Anna Henriques
Girls are Willing, The 1959,My 11,30:1

Nielsen, Asta
Hamlet 1921,N 9,20:3 (In Addenda)
Streets of Sorrow 1927,Jl 6,23:2
Vanina 1928,Mr 20,20:3
Women Without Men 1928,N 12,18:2
Small Town Sinners 1928,N 27,34:1
Crown of Thorns 1934,Mr 28,27:6

Nielsen, Erik
I Want You 1951,D 24,9:1

Nielsen, Gerda
Ordet 1957,D 16,33:6

Nielsen, Hans
Rote Orchideen; Red Orchids 1939,Ap 15,15:2
Aufruhr in Damaskus; Tumult in Damascus 1939,My 6,21:2
Palace Scandal 1949,Je 6,15:5
Keepers of the Night 1953,Je 9,24:2
Third Sex, The 1959,Mr 26,27:1
Confess, Dr Corda 1960,O 24,25:5
Town Without Pity 1961,O 11,53:1
Judge and the Sinner, The 1964,Je 6,14:2

Nielsen, Leslie
Ransom 1956,Ja 25,28:3
Forbidden Planet 1956,My 4,21:2
Vagabond King, The 1956,S 13,39:6
Opposite Sex, The 1956,N 16,23:2
Tammy and the Bachelor 1957,Je 15,10:7
Sheepman, The 1958,My 8,36:1
Night Train to Paris 1964,D 3,58:2
Dark Intruder 1965,Jl 22,24:2
Harlow 1965,Jl 22,24:1
Beau Geste 1966,S 8,43:1
Rosie 1968,F 8,36:1
Counterpoint 1968,Mr 14,51:2
Dayton's Devils 1968,O 3,56:4

Niemczyk, Leon
Knife in the Water 1963,O 29,31:2

Niepach, Robert (Producer)
Gruen ist die Heide 1935,O 14,21:2

Niese, George N
Three Stooges Meet Hercules, The 1962,Ja 27,13:4

Niese, Hansi
Die Grosse Liebe 1932,F 22,23:2
Die Blumenfrau von Lindenau 1932,Jl 8,22:5
Purpur und Waschblau 1932,Jl 11,11:4
Frau Lehmann's Toechter 1933,O 27,22:3
Tante Gusti Kommandiert 1934,My 4,24:4
Hochzeit am Wolfgangsee 1934,N 17,12:2
Kaiserwalzer 1934,D 29,11:2
Grosse Chance, Die 1935,My 6,22:4
Mein Liebster ist ein Jaegersmann 1936,S 15,37:6

Niesen, Gertrude
Top of the Town 1937,Mr 27,19:2
Start Cheering 1938,Mr 17,17:3
Rookies on Parade 1941,My 22,25:2
He's my Guy 1943,Mr 12,12:3
This Is the Army 1943,Jl 29,11:6
Babe Ruth Story, The 1948,Jl 29,17:2

Nieto, Jose
Mama 1933,Jl 8,14:6
Captain Black Jack 1952,O 22,31:3
Alexander the Great 1956,Mr 29,23:1
Marcelino 1956,O 23,39:1
Pride and the Passion, The 1957,Je 29,10:6
Farewell to Arms, A 1958,Ja 25,14:1
Solomon and Sheba 1959,D 26,7:2

Nieto, Pepe
Night Heaven Fell, The 1958,O 22,40:4

Nifontov, Gleb (Director)
Hunting in Siberia 1962,Jl 2,22:2

Nifontova, R
Flames on the Volga 1958,Ja 27,21:7
Sisters 1959,My 25,33:2

Nigg, Sepp
White Horse Inn, The 1957,D 4,50:3

Niggli, Josefina (Original Author)
Sombrero 1953,Ap 23,37:2

Niggli, Josefina (Screenwriter)
Sombrero 1953,Ap 23,37:2

Nigh, Jane
Whistle Stop 1946,Mr 18,24:2
Dragonwyck 1946,Ap 11,35:2
Unconquered 1947,O 11,11:2
Give my Regards to Broadway 1948,Je 23,32:2
Red, Hot and Blue 1949,O 20,39:2
Zamba 1949,N 7,33:2
Fighting Man of the Plains 1949,N 17,35:6
Blue Grass of Kentucky 1950,Ja 27,29:2
Captain Carey U S A 1950,Mr 30,40:5

Nigh, William
Democracy, The Vision Restored 1920,Ag 25,6:4

Nigh, William (Director)
Fighting Roosevelts, The 1919,Ja 20,13:2
Democracy, The Vision Restored 1920,Ag 25,6:4
Marriage Morals 1923,Ag 14,10:3
Fire Brigade, The 1926,D 21,20:2
Mr Wu 1927,My 16,24:2
Across to Singapore 1928,Ap 30,18:3
Four Walls 1928,Ag 20,21:3
Desert Nights 1929,My 6,30:4
Lord Byron of Broadway 1930,Mr 8,21:1
Single Sin, The 1931,Mr 17,34:3
Mysterious Mr Wong, The 1935,Mr 7,26:1
His Night Out 1935,N 16,19:2
Don't Get Personal 1936,F 22,12:1
Crash Donovan 1936,Ag 10,10:3
Atlantic Flight 1937,N 1,24:5
Thirteenth Man, The 1938,Ja 1,11:2
Boy of the Streets 1938,Ja 24,17:1
Female Fugitive 1938,Ap 11,12:3
Rose of the Rio Grande 1938,Jl 9,10:3

Nigh, William (Director) — Cont
Gangster's Boy 1938,N 7,23:6
Mr Wong, Detective 1938,N 21,14:4
Streets of New York 1939,My 1,21:1
Mister Wong in Chinatown 1939,Jl 31,9:2 (In Addenda)
Mutiny in the Big House 1939,D 11,26:2
Doomed to Die 1940,Jl 30,16:3
Ape, The 1940,N 28,28:3
No Greater Sin 1941,Ag 29,18:2
Mob Town 1941,N 20,39:3
Kid From Kansas, The 1941,D 2,29:4
Mr Wise Guy 1942,Mr 5,27:2
Strange Case of Dr Rx 1942,Mr 28,11:2
Corregidor 1943,My 28,19:2
Where Are Your Children? 1944,Ja 17,14:5
Are These our Parents? 1944,Ag 23,16:2
Allotment Wives 1945,N 22,39:3
Nigh, William (Screenwriter)
Marriage Morals 1923,Ag 14,10:3
Nijinska (Miscellaneous)
Midsummer Night's Dream, A 1935,O 10,31:1
Nikashin, Sergei
Fortress on the Volga 1942,D 25,15:3
Niki, Terumi
Red Beard 1968,D 20,60:4
Nikitich, N
Ladies 1955,Je 27,18:2
Nikitin, F
Fragment of an Empire, A 1930,Ja 27,18:4
Lonely White Sail 1938,My 7,18:1
Ivan Pavlov 1950,F 13,15:2
Rimsky-Korsakov 1954,Mr 1,16:3
Yolanta 1964,D 23,22:3
Nikitin, Konstantin
Cranes are Flying, The 1960,Mr 22,31:2
Nikitina, E
Professor Mamlock 1938,N 8,26:2
Nikitina, N
Shors 1939,N 21,19:4
Nikkatsu (Producer)
God of our Times 1932,Jl 3,IX,2:2
Heroine of Shanghai, A 1932,Jl 3,IX,2:2
Nikolaidis, Dimitrios
Trouble for Father 1958,Ja 6,26:4
Nikolajeva, Genia
Quick, Koenig der Clowns 1933,D 9,18:3
Schuss im Morgengrauen 1934,S 29,12:3
Liebe und die Erste Eisenbahn, Die; Love and the First Railroad 1935,F 18,19:4
Pantoffelhelden 1935,O 21,22:5
Die Privatsekretaerin Heiratet 1936,D 5,16:4
Einmaleins der Liebe, Das 1937,Ja 2,15:2
Blinde Passagier; Stowaways 1937,Mr 6,10:1
Ride a Crooked Mile 1938,D 29,15:2
Adventure in Diamonds 1940,Ap 4,27:2
Lady Has Plans, The 1942,Mr 5,27:1
Nikolavef, F
Golden Mountains 1932,Ap 14,25:3
Nikolayeva, Galina (Original Author)
Vasili's Return 1953,S 28,21:4
Nikolinakos, Michel
Loves of a Greek in Paris 1960,Ag 15,19:7
Nikolovich, Galina (Screenwriter)
Vasili's Return 1953,S 28,21:4
Nikosa, V (Director)
Indonesia Today 1955,N 3,37:1
Nikosa, V (Screenwriter)
Indonesia Today 1955,N 3,37:1
Nikulin, Yuri
When the Trees Were Tall 1965,F 22,14:1
Niles, Blair (Original Author)
Condemned 1929,N 4,28:1
Niles, Denny
Mister Roberts 1955,Jl 15,14:1
Niles, Doris (Miscellaneous)
High Sign, The 1922,Mr 20,10:3
Niles, Fred A (Producer)
Two Before Zero 1962,N 1,34:1
Niles, Ken
Hollywood Hotel 1938,Ja 13,17:3
Kid Comes Back, The 1938,F 7,10:2
Out of the Past 1947,N 26,18:2
Niles, Mary Ann
Unsinkable Molly Brown, The 1964,Jl 17,15:1
Niles, Wendell
Three Faces West 1940,Ag 19,13:2
Sensations of 1945 1944,Jl 7,13:2
Hitch-Hiker, The 1953,Ap 30,39:3
NILSEN
See Also NILSON, NILSSON
Nilsen, Pairin
King of the White Elephant, The 1941,Ap 5,12:7
Nilsen, Suvat
King of the White Elephant, The 1941,Ap 5,12:7
NILSON
See Also NILSEN, NILSSON
Nilson, Anna Q
Winds of Chance 1925,Ag 17,10:3
Nilson, Tim
Seven Days 1925,Ag 31,19:3
NILSSON
See Also NILSEN, NILSON

Nilsson, Anna Q
Love Burglar, The 1919,Jl 28,8:5
Her Kingdom of Dreams 1919,S 22,8:1
Soldiers of Fortune 1919,N 24,13:1
Toll Gate, The 1920,Ap 19,13:3
Without Limit 1921,Mr 21,11:3
Oath, The 1921,Ap 11,9:1
Three Live Ghosts 1922,Ja 2,20:1
Man From Home, The 1922,My 1,20:3
Pink Gods 1922,S 25,10:2
Rustle of Silk, The 1923,My 8,22:4
Isle of Lost Ships, The 1923,My 14,18:2
Hollywood 1923,Jl 30,11:4
Spoilers, The 1923,Ag 6,14:2
Ponjola 1923,N 19,19:3
Painted People 1924,Ja 29,16:1
Flowing Gold 1924,Mr 10,18:2
Between Friends 1924,My 12,14:4
Broadway After Dark 1924,My 20,15:2
Side Show of Life, The 1924,Jl 22,9:1
Vanity's Price 1924,O 8,16:2
Inez From Hollywood 1924,D 16,28:1
If I Marry Again 1925,Ja 12,11:2
Top of the World, The 1925,F 17,18:1
Talker, The 1925,My 12,26:2
Greater Glory, The 1926,My 4,31:1
Splendid Road, The 1926,Je 13,31:1
Midnight Lovers 1926,O 26,23:1
Easy Pickings 1927,Mr 25,25:3
Lonesome Ladies 1927,Ag 2,19:2
Sorrell and Son 1927,N 14,26:1
Thirteenth Juror, The 1927,N 22,20:1
Whip, The 1928,S 17,28:2
World Changes, The 1933,O 27,22:3
Prison Farm 1938,Jl 15,13:3
Great Man's Lady, The 1942,Ap 30,14:3
Farmer's Daughter, The 1947,Mr 26,31:2
Cynthia 1947,S 19,27:2
Fighting Father Dunne 1948,Je 25,26:2
Sunset Boulevard 1950,Ag 11,15:2
Nilsson, Birgit
Rhapsody 1954,Mr 12,17:1
Nilsson, Helena
Dear John 1966,Mr 9,46:1
Nilsson, Leopoldo Torre (Director)
Casa del Angel, La 1960,Ag 30,25:1
Summerskin 1962,My 29,22:2
Hand in the Trap 1963,Jl 2,16:2
Terrace, The 1964,N 25,45:1
Eavesdropper, The 1966,S 15,51:1
Nilsson, Leopoldo Torre (Producer)
Summerskin 1962,My 29,22:2
Nilsson, Leopoldo Torre (Screenwriter)
Casa del Angel, La 1960,Ag 30,25:1
Hand in the Trap 1963,Jl 2,16:2
Eavesdropper, The 1966,S 15,51:1
Nilsson, Norma Jean
Actress, The 1953,O 13,34:1
Nilsson, Tommy
Swedish Wedding Night 1965,N 15,48:1
Nilsson, Vera
Brokiga Blad 1931,N 30,16:2
Nimbalkar
Shakuntala 1947,D 26,22:3
Nimier, Roger (Original Author)
Time Out for Love 1963,Ap 23,31:2
Nimier, Roger (Screenwriter)
Frantic 1961,Je 12,34:1
Time Out for Love 1963,Ap 23,31:2
Nimmo, Derek
Tamahine 1964,Jl 16,23:1
Murder Ahoy 1964,S 23,55:3
Nimoy, Leonard
Rhubarb 1951,Ag 31,12:2
Balcony, The 1963,Mr 22,7:1
Deathwatch 1967,Je 28,38:1
Nimoy, Leonard (Producer)
Deathwatch 1967,Je 28,38:1
Ninchi
Angelina 1948,Ap 6,27:2
Ninchi, Annibale
Scipio Africanus 1939,S 23,22:2
Dolce Vita, La 1961,Ap 20,30:1
Time Out for Love 1963,Ap 23,31:2
Eight and One Half 1963,Je 26,36:1
Ninchi, Ave
To Live in Peace 1947,N 25,37:2
Walls of Malapaga, The 1950,Mr 21,34:2
Escape into Dreams 1950,Ap 13,34:5
Heart and Soul 1950,Je 15,41:3
Difficult Years 1950,Ag 22,31:2
Flesh will Surrender 1950,O 26,38:7
Teresa 1951,Ap 6,31:2
Tomorrow is too Late 1952,Ap 14,22:2
Duel Without Honor 1953,F 28,8:8
Three Girls From Rome 1953,O 14,34:2
Mademoiselle Gobette 1955,F 5,13:3
Bigamist, The 1958,My 12,25:1
Purple Noon 1961,S 1,12:1
Ninchi, Carlo
Terra Madre 1931,O 31,22:2
Wally, La 1939,Ja 2,28:3
Scipio Africanus 1939,S 23,22:2

Ninchi, Carlo — Cont
King's Jester, The 1947,Je 26,19:3
Marco Visconti 1947,S 20,12:4
Cavalleria Rusticana 1947,D 20,21:2
Spirit and the Flesh, The 1948,N 1,28:2
Earth Cries Out, The; Grido Della Terra, Il 1949,Ag 31,26:2
Woman 1950,F 9,36:6
Bullet for Stefano 1950,O 26,38:7
Island of Procida, The 1952,Mr 15,8:2
Beauty and the Devil 1952,Ag 26,15:2
Anita Garibaldi 1954,Mr 19,19:4
Side Street Story 1954,Je 24,30:4
Ten Commandments, The 1958,Ap 7,26:1
Ninchi, Carol
Amo Te Sola 1936,Jl 20,11:2
Ninette
They Were Ten; (Heym Hayu Assara) 1961,Ap 18,44:2
Ning, Ting
Empress Wu 1965,Mr 16,42:2
Nipora, Maja
Vitelloni 1956,O 24,43:1
Nirdlinger, Charles Frederic (Original Author)
Lovers 1927,Ap 19,24:4
Nirvanas, Paul (Original Author)
Astero 1960,Ap 25,32:2
Nishida, Minoru
Four Frightened People 1934,Ja 27,9:2
Teahouse of the August Moon, The 1956,N 30,19:1
Nishimura, Akira
Bad Sleep Well, The 1963,Ja 23,5:2
Unholy Desire 1964,N 18,54:1
Niss, Stanley (Producer)
FBI Code 98 1964,Ap 9,25:6
Niss, Stanley (Screenwriter)
FBI Code 98 1964,Ap 9,25:6
Nissemson, Hugh (Screenwriter)
Pillar of Fire, The 1963,Ap 8,35:2
Nissen, Aud Egede
Peter the Pirate 1927,Ja 7,14:4
Slums of Berlin 1927,Ja 26,17:1
Nissen, Aude Egede
Dr Nabuse 1927,Ag 10,21:4
Nissen, Brian
They Were Sisters 1946,Jl 24,24:2
Nissen, Egede
Street, The 1927,S 6,34:3
Nissen, Goerril Egede
En Glad Gutt 1933,N 24,25:7
Nissen, Greta
Lost-a Wife 1925,Je 22,10:2
Wanderer, The 1925,Ag 20,22:1
In the Name of Love 1925,Ag 27,14:1
King on Main Street, The 1925,O 26,25:2
Popular Sin, The 1926,D 20,28:3
Blonde or Brunette 1927,Ja 11,18:2
Blind Alleys 1927,Mr 1,31:1
Fazil 1928,Je 5,21:1
Butter and Egg Man, The 1928,Ag 28,27:4
Women of all Nations 1931,My 30,9:2
Transatlantic 1931,Jl 31,15:2
Ambassador Bill 1931,N 14,15:3
Good Sport 1931,D 12,23:3
Silent Witness, The 1932,F 8,21:1
Rackety Rax 1932,N 5,12:5
Circus Queen Murder, The 1933,My 9,20:5
Melody Cruise 1933,Je 23,15:2
Best of Enemies 1933,Jl 17,19:5
Spy 77 1936,F 10,15:1
Red Wagon 1936,Je 22,22:1
Nisson, Aud Egede
Zwischen Nacht und Morgen 1931,O 25,VIII,6:1
Nissotti, Arys (Producer)
Under the Paris Sky 1952,My 6,35:1
Nitkin, A
False Uniforms 1932,N 19,20:2
Niven, David
Splendor 1935,N 23,23:2
Rose Marie 1936,F 1,9:2
Dodsworth 1936,S 24,29:1
Thank You, Jeeves 1936,O 5,25:1
Charge of the Light Brigade, The 1936,N 2,24:1
Beloved Enemy 1936,D 26,15:2
We Have our Moments 1937,Ap 30,17:3
Prisoner of Zenda, The 1937,S 3,12:1
Dinner at the Ritz 1937,D 4,21:1
Bluebeard's Eighth Wife 1938,Mr 24,21:2
Four Men and a Prayer 1938,My 7,18:1
Three Blind Mice 1938,Je 18,18:2
Dawn Patrol 1938,D 24,12:1
Wuthering Heights 1939,Ap 14,28:2
Bachelor Mother 1939,Je 30,17:2
Real Glory, The 1939,S 15,26:2
Eternally Yours 1939,O 7,11:2
Raffles 1940,Ja 13,11:2
Spitfire 1943,Je 14,13:2
Way Ahead, The 1944,Jl 16,II,3:4
Way Ahead, The 1945,Je 4,22:3
Magnificent Doll 1946,D 9,34:2
Stairway to Heaven 1946,D 26,28:1
Perfect Marriage, The 1947,Ja 16,30:3
Other Love, The 1947,My 15,32:4

Niven, David— Cont

Bishop's Wife, The 1947,D 10,44:2
Enchantment 1948,D 27,16:2
Kiss in the Dark, A 1949,Mr 26,10:6
Toast of New Orleans, The 1950,S 30,13:3
Soldiers Three 1951,Mr 30,28:5
Happy Go Lovely 1951,Jl 26,17:2
Lady Says No, The 1952,Ja 7,14:3
Bonnie Prince Charlie 1952,Ja 7,14:3
Island Rescue 1952,Jl 1,19:4
Moon Is Blue, The 1953,Jl 9,18:3
Fighting Pimpernel, The 1954,Ap 19,19:1
Tonight's the Night 1954,D 23,13:4
Court Martial 1955,Ag 2,17:1
King's Thief, The 1955,Ag 13,7:2
Birds and the Bees, The 1956,Ap 23,22:1
Around the World in 80 Days 1956,O 18,37:1
Oh Men! Oh Women! 1957,F 22,25:2
Little Hut, The 1957,My 4,25:1
My Man Godfrey 1957,O 12,23:1
Silken Affair, The 1957,O 31,41:1
Bonjour Tristesse 1958,Ja 16,32:1
Separate Tables 1958,D 19,2:7
Ask any Girl 1959,My 22,32:1
Happy Anniversary 1959,N 11,41:1
Please Don't Eat the Daisies 1960,Ap 1,37:1
Guns of Navarone, The 1961,Je 23,19:1
Best of Enemies, The 1962,Ag 7,35:2
Guns of Darkness 1962,Ag 18,10:1
55 Days at Peking 1963,My 30,20:1
Pink Panther, The 1964,Ap 24,25:1
Bedtime Story 1964,Je 11,27:1
Where the Spies Are 1966,Ja 27,29:1
Lady L 1966,My 19,51:1
Casino Royale 1967,Ap 29,25:1
Eye of the Devil 1967,D 7,60:1
Prudence and the Pill 1968,My 24,37:1
Impossible Years, The 1968,D 6,54:1

Niver, Kemp
Groom Wore Spurs, The 1951,Mr 14,41:2

Niwa, Matasaburo
Zatoichi 1968,Je 28,37:1

Nixon, Allan
Siren of Atlantis 1949,Ag 22,13:1
Prehistoric Women 1950,D 29,15:5
Pickup 1951,Ag 31,12:2
Outlaw Woman 1952,Ap 5,20:3

Nixon, Marian
Riders of the Purple Sage 1925,Ap 15,16:1
I'll Show You the Town 1925,Je 8,19:1
Where Was I 1925,Ag 19,14:4
What Happened to Jones 1926,F 9,22:1
Rolling Home 1926,Je 8,22:1
Devil's Island 1926,Ag 2,21:2
Taxi, Taxi 1927,F 15,23:1
Out all Night 1927,S 27,31:1
Chinese Parrot, The 1928,Ja 2,28:1
Fourflusher, The 1928,Ja 16,24:1
How to Handle Women 1928,Je 18,13:2
Out of the Ruins 1928,Ag 20,21:3
Red Lips 1928,O 16,29:2 (In Addenda)
Geraldine 1929,Mr 4,20:2
Rainbow Man, The 1929,Ap 17,30:6
Say It With Songs 1929,Ag 7,29:2
Young Nowheres 1929,O 2,28:4
Show of Shows 1929,N 21,24:5
General Crack 1929,D 4,36:6
Courage 1930,My 23,21:1
Pay-Off, The 1930,N 10,16:2
College Lovers 1930,N 28,23:1
Scarlet Pages 1930,D 6,21:3
Lash, The 1931,Ja 1,31:3
Ex-Flame 1931,Ja 24,15:1
Sweepstakes 1931,Je 25,23:5
Women Go on Forever 1931,O 19,28:1
Charlie Chan's Chance 1932,Ja 23,18:4
After Tomorrow 1932,Mr 7,13:5
Amateur Daddy 1932,Ap 23,11:5
Winner Take All 1932,Je 18,9:2
Rebecca of Sunnybrook Farm 1932,Jl 30,16:5
Madison Square Garden 1932,O 12,26:5
Too Busy to Work 1932,D 3,21:4
Face in the Sky 1933,F 20,11:5
Pilgrimage 1933,Jl 13,17:5
Best of Enemies 1933,Jl 17,19:5
Doctor Bull 1933,O 6,21:2
Chance at Heaven 1933,D 26,19:3
Strictly Dynamite 1934,Jl 4,18:2
We're Rich Again 1934,S 1,16:3

Nixon, Marion
Hands Up 1926,Ja 18,26:2
Man, Woman and Wife 1928,N 5,26:5 (In Addenda)

Nixon, Marni
Sound of Music, The 1965,Mr 3,34:1

Nixon, Marni (Miscellaneous)
Dementia 1955,D 23,14:4

Nizzard, Joyce
Hole in the Head, A 1959,Jl 16,31:2

Nintsky
Prince of Foxes 1949,D 24,11:2

N'Kosi, Lewis (Screenwriter)
Come Back Africa 1960,Ap 5,45:1

Noa, Manfred (Director)
Lady From Paris, The 1927,S 28,28:3
Wrath of the Seas, The 1929,Ag 19,22:1
Survival 1930,Ja 13,21:1
Walzerkoenig, Der 1932,D 5,21:2

Noah, Mary
Yolanda and the Thief 1945,N 23,26:2

Nobile, Umberto General
Conquerors of the Night 1933,Jl 31,16:3

Nobis, Alain
Razzi 1957,N 19,39:4

Noble, Hollister (Original Author)
Mutiny 1952,Mr 20,37:5
Mara Maru 1952,Ap 24,38:1

Noble, John W (Director)
Cardigan 1922,F 20,7:1

Noble, Leighton
Gift of Gab 1934,S 26,17:6
It Ain't Hay 1943,Mr 11,17:3
Crazy House 1943,D 16,33:3

Noble, Leighton and His Orchestra
It Ain't Hay 1943,Mr 11,17:3

Noble, Ray
Damsel in Distress, A 1937,N 25,37:1
Here We Go Again 1942,O 12,12:3

Noble, Ray (Composer)
Brewster's Millions 1935,Ap 8,23:3
Princess Charming 1935,Je 22,18:5
Big Broadcast of 1936, The 1935,S 16,15:2
Fun and Fancy Free 1947,S 29,17:2 (In Addenda)

Noble, Robert
Adventures of Robin Hood, The 1938,My 13,17:2
Witness Vanishes, The 1939,O 23,15:2

Noble, Shaun
Black Narcissus 1947,Ag 14,29:2

Noble, William (Original Author)
Blue Denim 1959,Jl 31,21:1

Nobriga, Ted
Hawaii 1966,O 11,54:1

Nocher, Francois
Love and the Frenchwoman; (Francaise et l'Amour, La) 1961,F 28,38:2

Noda, Koga (Screenwriter)
Ohayo; (Good Morning) 1966,F 2,24:1

Nodalsky, Sonia
East Side, West Side 1927,O 18,33:2

Nodell, Sonya
Salome of the Tenements 1925,F 24,17:3

Noe, Robert
Jigsaw 1949,My 30,9:4

Noe, Yvan (Director)
Meet Miss Mozart 1937,N 27,21:3

Noe, Yvan (Producer)
Meet Miss Mozart 1937,N 27,21:3

Noeile, Kate
Jules and Jim 1962,Ap 24,32:1

Noel, Andre
Courier of Lyons, The 1938,Je 3,17:1

Noel, Bernard
Fire Within, The 1964,F 18,27:1
Circle of Love 1965,Mr 25,42:4
Married Woman, The; Femme Mariee, La 1965,Ag 17,39:1

Noel, Chris
Soldier in the Rain 1963,N 29,67:6 (Incorrect in this edition; use 1963,N 28,67:6 elsewhere)
Honeymoon Hotel 1964,Je 4,28:1
Wild Wild Winter 1966,Ja 6,20:2
Glory Stompers, The 1968,Mr 28,52:4
For Singles Only 1968,Je 6,54:1

Noel, Danielle
Bedazzled 1967,D 11,65:2

Noel, Denise
Francois Villon 1950,Jl 3,9:2

Noel, Hattie
Our Leading Citizen 1939,Ag 24,17:1
Married and in Love 1940,F 2,13:2
Lady for a Night 1942,F 12,27:2

Noel, Hubert
Enemy General, The 1960,O 20,42:2
Season for Love, The 1963,My 9,40:2

Noel, J B L (Cinematographer)
Epic of Everest 1927,Mr 17,VII,7:3

Noel, Magali
Rififi 1956,Je 6,37:1
Grand Maneuver, The 1956,O 2,39:1
Passionate Summer 1957,Jl 22,15:5
Razzi 1957,N 19,39:4
Lovers and Thieves 1958,Ag 5,23:2
No Escape 1959,My 23,18:4
Dolce Vita, La 1961,Ap 20,30:1
Temptation 1962,N 10,16:2
All the Other Girls Do! 1967,My 30,12:1

Noel, Sterling (Original Author)
To Paris With Love 1955,Mr 29,33:4

Noel, Wendy
Brave Don't Cry, The 1952,N 6,37:2

Noel, Yves
Premier May 1958,S 17,44:2

Noel-Noel
Papa sans le Savoir; Father Without Knowing It, A 1932,My 1,VIII,4:1 (In Addenda)

Noel-Noel— Cont

Bouquets From Nicholas 1939,Mr 2,19:1
Cage aux Rossignols, La; (Cage of Nightingales, A) 1947,Ap 3,31:2
Mr Orchid; Pere Tranquille, Le 1948,Mr 29,17:3
Seven Deadly Sins, The (Sloth); Sloth (The Seven Deadly Sins) 1953,My 12,31:3
Spice of Life, The 1953,D 29,19:3
French They Are a Funny Race, The 1957,My 21,41:1
Dog, a Mouse and a Sputnik, A; Pied, a Cheval et un Sputnik, A 1960,N 1,46:2
Jessica 1962,Ap 20,20:2

Noel-Noel, Janine
Bouquets From Nicholas 1939,Mr 2,19:1

Noel-Noel, L
Mistigri 1933,Ja 13,19:3
Mon Coeur Balance 1933,F 3,21:4

Noel-Noel (Miscellaneous)
Mr Orchid; Pere Tranquille, Le 1948,Mr 29,17:3

Noel-Noel (Narrator)
Spice of Life, The 1953,D 29,19:3

Noel-Noel (Original Author)
Bouquets From Nicholas 1939,Mr 2,19:1

Noel-Noel (Screenwriter)
Cage aux Rossignols, La; (Cage of Nightingales, A) 1947,Ap 3,31:2
Mr Orchid; Pere Tranquille, Le 1948,Mr 29,17:3
Spice of Life, The 1953,D 29,19:3

Noelle, Jacqueline
Sins of Paris 1954,Ja 30,9:6
Lady Chatterley's Lover 1959,Jl 11,11:1

Noemi, Lea
Green Fields 1937,O 12,31:4
Singing Blacksmith, The 1938,N 3,27:1

Nofal, Emil
After You, Comrade 1967,Ap 11,54:1

Noflier, Claude
Loss of Innocence 1961,N 22,27:1

Nogauza, Grinsell
Magic Garden, The 1952,F 6,24:2

Noguero
On Demande un Compaznon 1933,Je 5,18:5

Noguero, Jose
Paris-Mediterranee 1932,Mr 27,VIII,6:2
Dernier Milliardaire, Le 1935,O 30,16:2
French Touch, The 1954,S 2,18:2

Nohain, Jean
Portrait of a Woman 1946,Ap 22,26:2

Nohain, Jean (Screenwriter)
Vierge Folle, La 1938,D 30,11:3

Noice, Harold
Explorers of the World 1931,D 18,29:3

Noice, Harold (Cinematographer)
Red Majesty 1929,My 6,30:4

Noice, Harold (Director)
Explorers of the World 1931,D 18,29:3

Noiret, Philippe
Zazie 1961,N 21,45:5
Crime Does Not Pay (The Hugues Case); Hugues Case, The (Crime Does Not Pay) 1962,O 17,35:2
Therese 1963,N 13,35:2
Cyrano and D'Artagnan 1964,S 26,16:1
Lady L 1966,My 19,51:1
Night of the Generals, The 1967,F 3,38:1
Vie de Chateau, La 1967,Mr 21,35:1
Other One, The 1967,S 29,53:1
Tender Scoundrel 1967,N 16,58:2

Nokes, George
Song of the South 1946,N 28,40:2
State of the Union 1948,Ap 23,28:1

Nolan, Andrew
This Sporting Life 1963,Jl 17,19:2

Nolan, Bob (Composer)
Utah 1945,Mr 12,22:7

Nolan, Bob and the Sons of the Pioneers
Utah 1945,Mr 12,22:7
Hit Parade of 1947 1947,My 5,32:8
Apache Rose 1947,Jl 23,19:3

Nolan, Dani Sue
Breakthrough 1950,N 18,10:2
Sniper, The 1952,My 10,16:3

Nolan, Doris
Man I Marry, The 1936,O 31,24:3
Top of the Town 1937,Mr 27,19:2
As Good as Married 1937,My 22,19:2
Holiday 1938,Je 24,15:1
One Hour to Live 1939,N 4,11:3
Irene 1940,My 24,23:3
Moon Over Burma 1940,D 12,37:4

Nolan, James F
Rogues' Regiment 1948,D 20,31:2

Nolan, Jeanette
Words and Music 1948,D 10,34:2
Abandoned Woman 1949,O 27,35:3
No Sad Songs for Me 1950,Ap 28,26:2
Saddle Tramp 1950,N 24,31:4
Macbeth 1950,D 28,22:6
Happy Time, The 1952,O 31,30:2
Hangman's Knot 1952,D 11,45:3
Big Heat, The 1953,O 15,43:2
Tribute to a Bad Man 1956,Mr 31,13:3
April Love 1957,N 28,57:2

Nolan, Jeanette— Cont
Great Impostor, The 1961,Mr 30,24:1
Two Rode Together 1961,Jl 27,23:3
Man Who Shot Liberty Valance, The
1962,My 24,29:2
Twilight of Honor 1963,N 14,41:2
My Blood Runs Cold 1965,Mr 25,42:4
Nolan, Jeannette Covert (Original Author)
Isn't It Romantic? 1948,O 7,35:2
Nolan, Jim
Miracle of the Bells, The 1948,Mr 17,30:1
Fighting Father Dunne 1948,Je 25,26:2
Race Street 1948,Ag 23,13:3
Nolan, John
Last Time I Saw Archie, The 1961,My 29,9:6
Nolan, Lloyd
Stolen Harmony 1935,Ap 20,16:2
She Couldn't Take It 1935,N 7,27:1
One Way Ticket 1936,Ja 1,35:2
Lady of Secrets 1936,F 22,12:1
You may Be Next 1936,F 24,14:1
Big Brown Eyes 1936,My 2,11:1
Devil's Squadron 1936,My 11,16:2
Counterfeit 1936,Jl 20,11:1
Texas Rangers, The 1936,S 24,29:1
Fifteen Maiden Lane 1936,O 17,21:3
Internes Can't Take Money 1937,My 6,23:2
King of Gamblers 1937,Jl 3,18:1
Exclusive 1937,Jl 22,15:1
Ebb Tide 1937,N 18,27:2
Wells Fargo 1937,D 30,15:2
Every Day's a Holiday 1938,Ja 27,17:2
Dangerous to Know 1938,Mr 11,15:4
Tip-Off Girls 1938,Mr 25,15:3
Hunted Men 1938,My 21,9:2
Prison Farm 1938,Jl 15,13:3
King of Alcatraz 1938,O 7,21:2
St Louis Blues 1939,F 9,17:2
Ambush 1939,F 9,17:2
Undercover Doctor 1939,Je 1,31:2
Magnificent Fraud, The 1939,Jl 20,16:2
Man Who Wouldn't Talk, The 1940,Ja 12,13:3
House Across the Bay, The 1940,Mr 22,23:2
Johnny Apollo 1940,Ap 13,21:2
Gangs of Chicago 1940,Je 13,29:2
Man I Married, The 1940,Ag 3,9:2
Pier 13 1940,Ag 9,19:3
Golden Fleecing, The 1940,N 7,33:4
Michael Shayne, Private Detective
1940,D 19,33:2
Behind the News 1941,Ja 16,25:3
Mr Dynamite 1941,Mr 13,25:2
Sleepers West 1941,Mr 20,25:3
Dressed to Kill 1941,Ag 22,19:3
Buy Me That Town 1941,O 23,27:2
Blues in the Night 1941,D 12,35:2
Man Who Wouldn't Die, The 1942,Ap 28,25:5
It Happened in Flatbush 1942,Jl 3,12:8
Just off Broadway 1942,Ag 29,18:4
Manila Calling 1942,S 28,13:1
Time to Kill 1942,D 25,15:4
Bataan 1943,Je 4,17:2
Guadalcanal Diary 1943,N 18,29:1
Tree Grows in Brooklyn, A 1945,Mr 1,25:5
Circumstantial Evidence 1945,Ap 21,18:3
Captain Eddie 1945,Ag 9,24:2
House on Ninety-Second Street, The
1945,S 27,24:7
Somewhere in the Night 1946,Je 13,24:2
Lady in the Lake 1947,Ja 24,18:3
Two Smart People 1947,F 15,20:4
Wild Harvest 1947,N 13,33:2
Green Grass of Wyoming 1948,Je 10,28:3
Street with no Name, The 1948,Jl 15,26:6
Bad Boy 1949,Mr 23,35:2
Sun comes up, The 1949,My 13,29:2
Easy Living 1949,O 13,33:3
Lemon Drop Kid, The 1951,Mr 22,41:2
Island in the Sky 1953,S 10,22:2
Last Hunt, The 1956,Mr 1,37:2
Santiago 1956,Jl 14,13:2
Toward the Unknown 1956,S 28,24:4
Abandon Ship 1957,Ap 18,35:1
Hatful of Rain, A 1957,Jl 18,19:2
Peyton Place 1957,D 13,35:1
Portrait in Black 1960,Jl 28,19:1
Girl of the Night 1960,N 12,15:1
Susan Slade 1961,N 11,14:6
Circus World 1964,Je 26,34:2
Never too Late 1965,N 5,28:1
American Dream, An 1966,S 1,28:2
Sergeant Ryker 1968,Mr 21,56:2
Double Man, The 1968,My 2,57:1
Ice Station Zebra 1968,D 21,49:1
Nolan, Margaret
Don't Raise the Bridge, Lower the River
1968,Jl 13,18:1
Nolan, Mary
Sorrell and Son 1927,N 14,26:1
Foreign Legion, The 1928,Je 25,27:1
Good Morning, Judge 1928,Je 26,29:1
Uneasy Money 1928,D 11,35:3
West of Zanzibar 1928,D 31,9:1
Desert Nights 1929,My 6,30:4

Eleven Who Were Loyal 1929,My 20,22:6
Charming Sinners 1929,Jl 8,17:3
Shanghai Lady 1929,N 11,20:2
Undertow 1930,Mr 1,23:1
Outside the Law 1930,S 1,16:1
Enemies of the Law 1931,Jl 13,13:5
X Marks the Spot 1931,D 7,16:1
Big Shot, The 1932,Ja 2,14:2
File No 113 1932,F 20,11:2
Midnight Patrol, The 1932,My 7,11:5
Nolan, O'Neill
East of the River 1940,O 28,21:2
Nolan, Tommy
Kiss Me, Stupid 1964,D 23,22:2
Nolan, William
Intruder, The 1962,My 15,48:1
Noland, Robert
Revolt of the Zombies 1936,Je 5,17:2
Noland, Valora
War Wagon, The 1967,Ag 3,26:3
Nolbandov, Sergei (Director)
Ships With Wings 1942,My 25,11:2
Nolbandov, Sergei (Producer)
Little Kidnappers, The 1954,S 2,18:1
Value for Money 1957,Ag 1,20:4
She Didn't Say No 1963,Jl 30,18:1
Nolbandov, Sergei (Screenwriter)
Fire Over England 1937,Mr 5,16:2
Ships With Wings 1942,My 25,11:2
Noll, Greg
Surfari 1967,Jl 19,26:2
Nolley, Edmonia
One Third of a Nation 1939,F 11,13:2
Nollier, Claude
Moulin Rouge 1953,F 11,33:5
Justice Is Done 1953,Mr 3,23:2
Dirty Hands 1954,My 11,25:5
Pot Bouille 1958,O 28,39:1
Forbidden Fruit 1959,F 23,19:1
Fidelio 1961,My 13,10:1
Devil and the 10 Commandments, The (Episode
1) 1963,O 15,44:1
Nomaz, Joseph
Lemonade Joe 1967,N 21,53:1
Nomis, Leo
California Straight Ahead 1926,Ja 12,27:5
Lost Squadron, The 1932,Mr 11,15:4
Crowd Roars, The 1932,Mr 23,25:4
Nondonk
Wajan 1938,Ap 18,11:1
Noni, Geula
Sallah 1965,O 13,39:1
Impossible on Saturday 1966,F 17,29:1
Nonin, Roland (Producer)
Joker, The; (Farceur, Le) 1961,Ag 8,32:2
Noon, Paisley
Night World 1932,My 28,18:2
Noonan, Pat
Bride of the Lake, The 1934,S 11,24:5
Ourselves Alone 1937,Jl 31,6:2
Kathleen 1938,Ja 24,17:1
Mutiny of the Elsinore, The 1939,F 16,17:2
Noonan, Tommy
Truth About Murder, The 1946,Jl 27,12:6
Big Fix, The 1947,My 3,10:3
I Shot Jesse James 1949,Ap 2,12:2
Gentlemen Prefer Blondes 1953,Jl 16,17:2
Star is Born, A 1954,O 12,23:1
Violent Saturday 1955,My 12,32:2
How to be Very, Very Popular 1955,Jl 23,10:1
Ambassador's Daughter, The 1956,Ag 30,19:1
Best Things in Life are Free, The 1956,S 29,12:2
Bundle of Joy 1956,D 20,36:1
Girl Most Likely, The 1958,O 9,47:1
Rookie, The 1960,Mr 17,28:1
Swingin' Along 1962,Ag 27,18:1
Rookie, The 1960,Mr 17,28:1
Noonan, Tommy (Screenwriter)
Rookie, The 1960,Mr 17,28:1
Noone, Peter Blair
Hold On! 1966,Je 23,29:4
Norberg, Inger
Miss Julie 1952,Ap 8,35:2
Norberg, Sven-Bertil
Interlude 1949,Ja 3,19:2
Norborg, Anders
Great Adventure, The 1955,My 24,34:6
Norby, Ghita
Young Have no Time, The 1959,N 23,41:2
Crazy Paradise 1965,Ag 11,41:2
Eric Sóya's 17 1967,Ja 25,37:1
Nord, Pierre (Original Author)
Crime in the Maginot Line 1939,My 8,21:2
Resistance; Peleton d'Execution 1946,Jl 5,15:3
Norden, Christine
Ideal Husband, An 1948,Ja 15,28:2
Mine Own Executioner 1949,Ja 19,34:2
Saints and Sinners 1949,S 12,17:2
Interrupted Journey 1951,My 29,20:2
Norden, Denis (Screenwriter)
Bliss of Mrs Blossom, The 1968,D 12,62:6

Norden, Tommy
Five Miles to Midnight 1963,Mr 21,8:6
Nordey, Veronique
Chasers, The; Draguers, Les 1960,My 3,43:1
Nordhoff, Charles (Original Author)
Mutiny on the Bounty 1935,N 9,19:2
Hurricane, The 1937,N 10,31:2
Tuttles of Tahiti, The 1942,Ap 30,14:1
Passage to Marseille 1944,F 17,12:5
High Barbaree 1947,Je 6,27:2
Botany Bay 1953,O 30,27:2
Mutiny on the Bounty 1962,N 9,31:2
Nordine, Ingrid
Picnic on the Grass 1960,O 12,47:1
Nordle, Ruth (Miscellaneous)
Young Widow 1946,Jl 29,12:8
Nordli, Stephanie (Screenwriter)
Journey Into Light 1951,O 5,24:4
Nordstrom, Clarence
Crooner 1932,Ag 20,7:4
42d Street 1933,Mr 10,19:3
Gold Diggers of 1933 1933,Je 8,22:3
Nordstrom, Frances (Original Author)
One Woman to Another 1927,S 19,30:3
Nordwall
Wild Strawberries 1959,Je 23,37:1
Noree, Eva
Wild Strawberries 1959,Je 23,37:1
Nores, Thielly (Original Author)
Diary of a Chambermaid, The 1946,Je 23,28:2
Norfolk, Edgar
Sign of the Four, The 1932,Ag 20,7:4
Mine Own Executioner 1949,Ja 19,34:2
Silent Dust 1949,D 30,13:2
Noriega, Eduardo
El Paso 1949,Mr 24,35:2
Plunder of the Sun 1953,Ag 27,22:1
Hell's Island 1955,My 7,10:2
Magnificent Matador, The 1955,My 25,38:1
Seven Cities of Gold 1955,O 8,13:2
Serenade 1956,Mr 24,21:1 (Incorrect in this
edition; use 1956,Mr 23,21:1 elsewhere)
Living Idol, The 1957,My 3,18:1
Of Love and Desire 1963,S 12,32:1
Noriega, Felix
To Hell and Back 1955,S 23,21:2
Noriega, Manolo
Muertos Hablan, Los; Dead Speak, The
1935,N 25,22:2
Malditas Sean las Mujeres 1936,Ag 29,16:3
Asi es la Mujer 1936,O 21,35:3
El Misterio del Rostro Palido 1937,Ja 4,20:5
Baul Macabro, El; Macabre Trunk, The
1937,N 30,26:3
Ave sin Rumbo; Wandering Bird 1938,Ja 24,17:2
Traidor, El 1938,Ap 9,11:3
Huapango 1938,Je 11,9:1
Rancho Grande 1938,D 2,27:2
Ojos Tapatios 1939,F 13,13:3
Estrellita; Starlet 1939,Ap 12,27:3
Odio; Hate 1940,Ap 6,13:2
Vivire Otra Vez; I Shall Live Again
1940,O 23,27:2
Noriegi, Inigo de Martino (Screenwriter)
Torch, The 1950,Ag 21,15:2
Norin, Guli-Maj
Karl Fredrik Reigns 1938,F 2,15:2
Noris, Assia
I Tre Innamorati 1937,Je 17,19:2
Commedia Fra I Pazzi, Una 1937,Jl 8,20:2
Signor Max, Il; Mr Max 1939,O 6,31:4
But It's Nothing Serious 1939,O 10,27:2
Matrimonio Ideale, Un 1939,D 15,33:3
Between Two Worlds 1940,F 9,15:2
Ten Commandments, The 1958,Ap 7,26:1
Norlega, Eduardo
Eagle and the Hawk, The 1950,Jl 6,31:2
Norlund, Evy
Flying Fontaines, The 1959,D 24,13:6
Normah, Jack
Black Gold 1947,S 5,16:4
Norman, Al
52d Street 1937,N 15,15:1
Norman, Amber
Drake Case, The 1929,S 16,30:1
Norman, Ann
Blow-Up 1966,D 19,52:2
Norman, Bart
Candlelight in Algeria 1944,Jl 31,10:2
No Orchids for Miss Blandish 1951,F 23,33:2
Norman, Charles (Original Author)
Wise Girl 1938,Ja 10,13:3
Norman, D G
Gunfighter, The 1950,Je 24,7:2
Norman, Gertrude
Widow by Proxy 1919,S 22,8:1
Strictly Confidential 1919,O 6,15:1
Greene Murder Case, The 1929,Ag 10,11:3
Cradle Song 1933,N 20,18:2
Trumpet Blows, The 1934,Ap 14,18:2
Norman, Jay
West Side Story 1961,O 19,39:3

Norman, Josephine
Road to Yesterday, The 1925,D 1,22:4
King of Kings, The 1927,Ap 20,29:2
Forbidden Woman, The 1927,O 31,22:1
Wreck of the Hesperus, The 1927,N 28,18:5
Norman, Leslie (Director)
Night my Number Came up, The 1955,D 20,39:5
Dunkirk 1958,S 11,42:2
Season of Passion 1962,F 5,19:4
Jungle Fighters 1962,Mr 15,28:2
Norman, Leslie (Producer)
Cruel Sea, The 1953,Ag 11,18:5
West of Zanzibar 1955,Ja 18,31:2
Season of Passion 1962,F 5,19:4
Norman, Leslie (Screenwriter)
Run for Your Money, A 1950,Ap 10,15:3
Ivory Hunter 1952,Ag 19,19:1
Norman, Lucille
For Me and My Gal 1942,O 22,25:1
Painting the Clouds With Sunshine 1951,S 1,9:6
Starlift 1951,D 15,11:2
Carson City 1952,Je 14,12:2
Norman, Maidie
Burning Cross, The 1948,F 20,19:1
Well, The 1951,S 27,37:2
Bright Road 1953,Ap 29,33:5
About Mrs Leslie 1954,Je 28,16:2
What Ever Happened to Baby Jane? 1962,N 7,48:1
Norman, Noelle
Loves of Casanova 1948,S 18,11:4
Wandering Jew, The 1949,Mr 11,33:2
Paris Waltz, The 1950,Ag 23,35:2
Big Chief, The 1960,Ap 27,32:1
Norman, Peggy
Der Herr Finanzdirektor 1932,Je 25,18:2
Norman, Robert
One-Way Ticket to Hell 1955,D 8,45:1
Men in War 1957,Mr 20,32:4
Norman, Roger von (Director)
Spiel in Sommerwind; Play in the Summer Breezes 1939,Ap 1,17:2
Norman, Rolla
Etoile Disparait, Une; Star Disappears, A 1935,F 9,11:3
Norman, Vera
Lady Paname 1951,Mr 20,35:4
Ma Pomme 1951,O 15,22:2
Snow Was Black, The 1956,O 16,36:5
Normand, Mabel
Venus Model, The 1918,Je 17,11:3
Fatty and Mabel Adrift 1918,Jl 8,9:4
Back to the Woods 1918,Jl 22,9:1
Sis 1919,Mr 3,11:2
Sis Hopkins 1919,Mr 3,11:2
Upstairs 1919,Ag 18,9:2
Molly O 1921,N 21,20:1
Suzanna 1923,Mr 26,16:2
Extra Girl, The 1924,Ja 21,20:1
When Comedy Was King 1960,Mr 30,42:1
Days of Thrills and Laughter 1961,Mr 22,37:1
Normington, John
Inadmissible Evidence 1968,Je 24,44:1
Noro, Line
Serment, Le 1934,Mr 14,23:2
Pepe le Moko 1941,Mr 4,20:2
Well-Digger's Daughter, The 1946,S 30,21:4
Blind Desire 1948,Je 10,28:4
Symphonie Pastorale 1948,S 14,34:3
Vautrin, the Thief 1949,N 11,31:2
Three Sinners 1952,Jl 8,23:2
Ramuntcho 1953,Mr 2,19:2
Inside a Girls' Dormitory 1956,F 6,27:7
We Are all Murderers 1957,Ja 9,27:2
Norring, Ava
Snows of Kilimanjaro, The 1952,S 19,19:2
Norris, Charles G (Original Author)
Brass 1923,Mr 12,18:1
Bread 1924,Jl 21,14:4
Seed 1931,My 15,20:6
Norris, Edward
Show Them no Mercy 1935,D 9,25:2
Magnificent Brute, The 1936,O 24,23:1
They Won't Forget 1937,Jl 15,16:1
Between Two Women 1937,Ag 6,21:1
Bad Guy 1937,Ag 26,25:2
Boys Town 1938,S 9,25:1
Newsboys' Home 1939,Ja 23,8:2
Tail Spin 1939,F 11,13:2
On Trial 1939,Ap 5,31:2
Gorilla, The 1939,My 28,6:2
Frontier Marshal 1939,Jl 29,18:2
Here I Am a Stranger 1939,S 30,11:2
Escape, The 1939,N 3,17:4
Dr Ehrlich's Magic Bullet 1940,F 24,9:2
Ski Patrol 1940,My 21,29:4
Lady in Question, The 1940,D 10,33:2
Road Show 1941,F 19,25:2
Lady Has Plans, The 1942,Mr 5,27:1
Mystery of Marie Roget, The 1942,My 5,17:3
Sabotage Squad 1942,Ag 5,16:1
I Live on Danger 1942,Ag 22,16:2
Shadows in the Night 1944,Jl 29,16:2

Murder in the Music Hall 1946,Ap 15,22:2
Truth About Murder, The 1946,Jl 27,12:6
Decoy 1946,N 2,12:2
Surrender 1950,O 9,21:5
Breakthrough 1950,N 18,10:2
Highway 301 1950,D 9,13:2
I Was a Communist for the F B I 1951,My 3,34:4
Inside the Walls of Folsom Prison 1951,My 28,17:4
Kentuckian, The 1955,S 2,13:2
Norris, Frank (Original Author)
Moran of the Lady Letty 1922,F 6,9:1
Greed 1924,D 5,28:1
Norris, Jan
Middle of the Night 1959,Je 18,36:1
Splendor in the Grass 1961,O 11,53:1
Norris, Jay
Fighting Seabees, The 1944,Mr 20,14:2
Well Groomed Bride, The 1946,My 11,22:5
Woman on the Beach, The 1947,Je 9,26:6
Norris, Karen
Bachelor Party, The 1957,Ap 10,37:2
Back Street 1961,O 13,27:1
Lover Come Back 1962,F 9,21:1
Impossible Years, The 1968,D 6,54:1
Norris, Kathleen (Original Author)
Sisters 1922,Ap 4,15:3
Lucretia Lombard 1923,D 17,23:1
Christine of the Hungry Heart 1924,D 8,13:3
Rose of the World 1925,N 10,25:3
Mother 1927,My 4,29:2
Callahans and the Murphys, The 1927,Jl 12,29:3
My Best Girl 1927,N 7,26:4
Passion Flower 1930,D 22,16:2
Second Hand Wife 1933,Ja 14,8:4
Walls of Gold 1933,O 21,11:3
Change of Heart 1934,My 11,24:2
Norris, Richard
Next of Kin 1943,My 6,25:2
Abie's Irish Rose 1946,D 23,19:4
Sealed Cargo 1951,My 24,47:1
Last Voyage, The 1960,F 20,14:2
Norris, William
When Knighthood Was in Flower 1922,S 15,17:2 (In Addenda)
Go-Getter 1923,Ap 9,14:3 (In Addenda)
Love Piker, The 1923,Jl 16,14:2
Eternal Three, The 1923,O 12,7:2 (Incorrect in this edition; use 1927,O 1,7:2 elsewhere)
My Man 1924,F 11,18:3
Maytime 1924,Je 2,14:3
Joy Girl, The 1927,S 6,34:3
Norrman, John
Swedish Wedding Night 1965,N 15,48:1
Nort, Nathalie
Therese and Isabelle 1968,My 15,41:4
Norta, Yrjo
Jumalen Tuomio; Judgement of God, The 1939,O 27,27:2
North, Alex (Composer)
Daddy Long Legs 1955,My 6,17:5
Outrage, The 1964,O 8,48:2
North, Edmund H (Original Author)
I'm Still Alive 1940,O 11,25:4
Lady Takes a Flyer, The 1958,Ja 30,19:2
North, Edmund H (Screenwriter)
I Dream too Much 1935,N 29,24:1
Murder on a Bridle Path 1936,Ap 11,19:2
Bunker Bean 1936,Je 27,21:2
I'm Still Alive 1940,O 11,25:4
Dishonored Lady 1947,My 24,10:5
Colorado Territory 1949,Je 25,8:6
Young Man With a Horn 1950,F 10,18:4
In a Lonely Place 1950,My 18,37:2
Only the Valiant 1951,Ap 14,9:6
Day the Earth Stood Still, The 1951,S 19,37:1
Outcasts of Poker Flat 1952,My 16,19:3
Far Horizons, The 1955,My 21,11:1
Proud Ones, The 1956,Ag 11,10:2
Cowboy 1958,F 20,29:5
Sink the Bismarck! 1960,F 12,22:3
Fiercest Heart, The 1961,Ag 3,13:5
Damn the Defiant 1962,S 20,29:2
North, Jay
Pepe 1960,D 22,18:1
Maya 1966,Je 23,29:4
North, Joe
Ladies Should Listen 1934,Jl 28,16:6
North, John Ringling
Greatest Show on Earth, The 1952,Ja 11,17:2
North, Joseph
Ex-Flame 1931,Ja 24,15:1
Paris in Spring 1935,Jl 13,16:2
North, Leslie
Young Girls of Rochefort, The 1968,Ap 12,50:1
North, Michael
Unsuspected, The 1947,O 4,9:2
North, Neil
Winslow Boy, The 1950,Je 7,34:4
North, Robert
Green Years, The 1946,Ap 5,21:2

North, Robert (Producer)
Paris 1929,N 8,31:2
North, Robert G (Original Author)
Jewels of Brandenburg 1947,My 24,10:5
North, Robert G (Screenwriter)
Dangerous Millions 1947,Mr 15,10:3
North, Sheree
Living It Up 1954,Jl 24,6:6
How to be Very, Very Popular 1955,Jl 23,10:1
Lieutenant Wore Skirts, The 1956,Ja 12,22:1
Best Things in Life are Free, The 1956,S 29,12:2
Way to the Gold, The 1957,My 11,24:6
No Down Payment 1957,O 31,41:1
In Love and War 1958,N 1,14:2
Mardi Gras 1958,N 19,45:2
Madigan 1968,Mr 30,22:2
North, Sterling (Original Author)
So Dear to my Heart 1949,Ja 31,14:2
North, Ted
Chad Hanna 1940,D 26,23:1
Bride Wore Crutches, The 1941,My 26,15:3
To the Shores of Tripoli 1942,Mr 26,27:2
Syncopation 1942,My 29,13:3
Manila Calling 1942,S 28,13:1
Girl Trouble 1942,O 8,31:2
Thunder Birds 1942,O 29,19:2
Margin for Error 1943,Ja 25,10:7
Ox-Bow Incident, The 1943,My 10,15:2 (In Addenda)
Devil Thumbs a Ride, The 1947,Mr 22,10:2
North, Virginia
Long Duel, The 1967,N 2,58:3
North, Wilfred
Drivin' Fool, The 1923,O 29,18:1
Captain Blood 1924,S 9,19:1
Beloved Brute, The 1924,N 10,20:1
On Thin Ice 1925,Mr 9,21:1
Happy Warrior, The 1925,Jl 7,24:2
Hell-Bent for Heaven 1926,My 4,31:1
Tracked by the Police 1927,Ap 27,22:5
Fourflusher, The 1928,Ja 16,24:1
Trial of Mary Dugan, The 1929,Mr 29,21:1
Unashamed 1932,Jl 15,13:4
North, Wilfred (Director)
Mind-the-Paint Girl, The 1919,N 24,13:1
North, Zeme
Zotz! 1962,O 4,44:3
Palm Springs Weekend 1963,N 6,32:1
Northpole, John
Wharf Angel 1934,Ap 21,12:1
Northrup, Harry
White Circle, The 1920,Ag 23,9:2
Devil's Island 1926,Ag 2,21:2
Burning Daylight 1928,Ap 23,20:2
Last Warning, The 1929,Ja 7,36:2
Party Girl 1930,Ja 2,28:2
Men Call it Love 1931,Je 20,20:4
Squaw Man, The 1931,S 19,10:2
Nortier, Nadine
Mouchette 1968,S 21,26:1
Norton, Angie
Scandal for Sale 1932,Ap 3,26:2
One Rainy Afternoon 1936,My 14,29:2
Norton, Barry
What Price Glory 1926,N 24,26:4
Ankles Preferred 1927,Ap 18,21:2
Heart of a Salome, The 1927,Je 6,27:2
Wizard, The 1927,N 28,18:5
Legion of the Condemned, The 1928,Mr 19,26:2
Mother Knows Best 1928,S 17,27:1
4 Devils 1928,O 4,26:3
Sins of the Fathers 1929,Ja 28,21:1
Dishonored 1931,Mr 6,16:1
Cocktail Hour 1933,Je 5,18:5
Lady for a Day 1933,S 8,22:2
Cascarrabias 1933,O 30,14:2
Only Yesterday 1933,N 10,25:1
Unknown Blonde 1934,Ap 24,27:2
World Moves On, The 1934,Je 30,18:5
Grand Canary 1934,Jl 20,11:1
Diablo Del Mar, El 1936,Ap 1,29:2
Asi es la Mujer 1936,O 21,35:3
I'll Take Romance 1937,D 17,33:2
Traidor, El 1938,Ap 9,11:3
Pasado Acusa, El; Accusing Past, The 1938,O 15,21:4
Papa Soltero; Bachelor Father 1939,N 6,20:3
Norton, Dennis Val
Evensong 1934,N 17,12:1
Norton, Edgar
Woman Proof 1923,O 30,16:1
Men 1924,My 5,18:3
Broadway After Dark 1924,My 20,15:2
Tiger Love 1924,Je 16,18:3
Fast Set, The 1924,N 18,22:1
Learning to Love 1925,F 23,24:1
Enticement 1925,Mr 21,16:3
Lost-a Wife 1925,Je 22,10:2
Regular Fellow, A 1925,O 5,25:2
King on Main Street, The 1925,O 26,25:2
Fast and Furious 1927,Jl 4,20:3
Singed 1927,Jl 12,29:3
Student Prince, The 1927,S 22,33:2

Norton, Edgar— Cont

Man Who Laughs, The 1928,Ap 28,12:3
Oh, Kay! 1928,Ag 27,23:1
Love Parade, The 1929,N 20,32:6
Man From Blankley's, The 1930,Mr 29,23:1
Runaway Bride 1930,My 17,21:2
One Romantic Night 1930,My 31,19:4
Lady of Scandal, The 1930,Je 14,9:4
Monte Carlo 1930,Ag 28,22:4
East Is West 1930,N 1,23:2
Du Barry, Woman of Passion 1930,N 3,19:3
Bachelor Father, The 1931,F 2,23:1
Compromised 1931,N 7,16:5
Dr Jekyll and Mr Hyde 1932,Ja 2,14:2
Love Me Tonight 1932,Ag 19,20:6
Lady's Profession, A 1933,Mr 25,13:3
Thirty Day Princess 1934,My 12,12:3
Million Dollar Ransom 1934,S 19,15:2
Richest Girl in the World, The 1934,S 21,29:2
We Live Again 1934,N 2,27:2
When a Man's a Man 1935,F 22,27:2
You Can't Buy Luck 1937,My 14,21:2
Son of Frankenstein 1939,Ja 30,9:2
Captain Fury 1939,My 26,20:2
House of the Seven Gables, The 1940,Ap 15,21:3
Are These our Parents? 1944,Ag 23,16:2
Thunder in the Valley 1947,N 28,30:1

Norton, Fletcher

Big House, The 1930,Je 25,31:2
Secret Six, The 1931,My 2,23:4
Is my Face red 1932,Je 11,9:3
Sucker Money 1933,Ap 7,22:5
Bowery, The 1933,O 5,24:2

Norton, Frederic (Composer)

Chu Chin Chow 1934,S 22,12:2

Norton, Grace (Miscellaneous)

Beauty for the Asking 1939,F 10,19:1

Norton, Grace (Original Author)

Sporting Blood 1940,Jl 22,20:2

Norton, Jack

Cockeyed Cavaliers 1934,Jl 25,22:2
Stolen Harmony 1935,Ap 20,16:2
Don't Bet on Blondes 1935,Jl 20,16:2
Meet the Girls 1938,S 3,16:6
Thanks for the Memory 1938,D 8,34:3
Joe and Ethel Turp Call on the President 1940,Ja 4,19:2
Farmer's Daughter, The 1940,F 16,23:4
Bank Dick, The 1940,D 13,29:2
Night at Earl Carroll's, A 1941,Ja 23,19:1
Road Show 1941,F 19,25:2
Fleet's In, The 1942,Mr 12,24:2
Spoilers, The 1942,My 22,27:2
Palm Beach Story, The 1942,D 11,33:1
Taxi, Mister 1943,Ap 15,20:2
Prairie Chickens 1943,Jl 9,21:6
Hail the Conquering Hero 1944,Ag 10,14:2
Flame of Barbary Coast 1945,My 28,22:2
Strange Confession 1945,N 8,17:3
Man Alive 1945,N 17,14:5
Bringing Up Father 1946,N 22,27:3
Mad Wednesday 1951,Ja 25,21:5

Norton, Margo

Murder a la Mod 1968,My 2,57:1

Norvello, Jay

Atlantis the Lost Continent 1961,My 27,12:1
Harum Scarum 1965,D 16,63:3

Norvo, Red

Screaming Mimi 1958,Je 26,23:3

Norvo, Red Trio

Texas Carnival 1951,O 13,9:1

Norwick, Natalie

23 Paces to Baker Street 1956,My 19,12:6

Norwood, Elle

Hound of the Baskervilles, The 1922,S 11,20:2

Norwood, Lily

Something to Shout About 1943,Ap 8,27:3

Norwood, Ralph

Eternally Yours 1939,O 7,11:2

Norworth, Jack

Queen of the Night Clubs 1929,Mr 18,30:6
Southerner, The 1945,Ag 27,22:3

Nosova, T

Dream of a Cossack 1952,F 18,15:2
Inspector General, The 1954,My 3,21:2
Safety Match, The 1955,Mr 28,24:5
Carnival in Moscow 1957,N 4,40:1
Marriage of Baezaminov, The 1966,Je 11,20:2

Noss, Rudolf von der (Director)

Aufforderung zum Tanz; Invitation to the Dance 1935,N 23,23:3

Nosseck, Max (Director)

Overture to Glory 1940,F 12,14:2
Girls Under 21 1940,N 11,22:4
Dillinger 1945,Ap 26,26:2
Brighton Strangler, The 1945,My 19,15:2
Black Beauty 1946,Ag 30,13:2
Hoodlum, The 1951,Jl 6,14:6
Singing in the Dark 1956,Mr 8,32:5
Garden of Eden 1957,D 18,45:3

Nosseck, Max (Original Author)

Singing in the Dark 1956,Mr 8,32:5

Nosseck, Max (Screenwriter)

Brighton Strangler, The 1945,My 19,15:2
Garden of Eden 1957,D 18,45:3

Nossek, Max (Director)

Einmal Moecht' Ich Keine Sorgen Haben 1933,My 25,24:4
Schlemihl, Der 1934,N 5,23:1
Semana de Felicidad, Una; One Week of Happiness 1935,Je 15,20:3
Podoroso Caballero 1936,O 26,20:2

Nossen, Bram

Go, Man, Go 1954,Mr 10,29:5

Notara, Sapho

Windfall in Athens 1956,O 1,31:1

Notari, Guido

Before Him all Rome Trembled 1947,F 22,16:2

Notarianni, Pietro (Producer)

Engagement Italiano 1966,Je 21,35:1
Shoot Loud, Louder... I Don't Understand 1967,S 21,56:4

Noti, Karl (Miscellaneous)

Top Hat 1935,Ag 30,12:2

Noti, Karl (Screenwriter)

Man Braucht Kein Geld 1932,N 16,15:3
Girl Downstairs, The 1939,Ja 26,17:1

Noto, Setsuo (Producer)

Onibaba 1965,F 10,44:3

Nourse, Allen

Pushover 1954,Jl 31,6:3
Tight Spot 1955,Mr 19,11:7
Phenix City Story, The 1955,S 3,9:1

Nourse, Dorothy

Fascinating Youth 1926,My 10,19:1

Nova, Hedda

Crimson Gardenia, The 1919,Je 16,11:2
My Own Pal 1926,Mr 15,18:3

Nova, Lou

Swing Fever 1944,Ja 28,14:1
Joe Palooka, Champ 1946,Ap 6,10:6
Somewhere in the Night 1946,Je 13,24:2
Love and Learn 1947,My 3,10:3
World for Ransom 1954,Je 5,11:2
Leather Saint, The 1956,Je 16,12:2
What a Way to Go! 1964,My 15,44:1
Thoroughly Modern Millie 1967,Mr 23,25:1

Novak, Eva

O'Malley of the Mounted 1921,F 7,8:2
Tiger's Claw, The 1923,Mr 19,22:2
Sally 1925,Mr 16,16:1
Irene 1926,Mr 1,17:1
Blackmail 1947,Ag 5,26:3
Four Faces West 1948,Ag 4,18:3

Novak, Jane

String Beans 1918,D 30,7:3
Money Corporal, The 1919,Ap 21,13:4
Behind the Door 1920,Ja 5,15:1
Rivers End, The 1920,F 23,11:2
Isobel, or the Trail's End 1920,D 20,11:2
Divorce 1923,Je 26,14:2
Closed Gates 1927,Je 1,25:2
Redskin 1929,Ja 28,21:1
Hollywood Boulevard 1936,S 21,26:4
Foreign Correspondent 1940,Ag 28,15:2
Desert Fury 1947,S 25,35:4
Thelma Jordon 1950,Ja 19,35:2

Novak, Kim

Pushover 1954,Jl 31,6:3
Phffft 1954,N 11,43:2
Five Against the House 1955,Je 11,8:7
Man With the Golden Arm, The 1955,D 16,38:2
Picnic 1956,F 17,13:3
Eddy Duchin Story, The 1956,Je 22,15:1
Jeanne Eagels 1957,Ag 31,19:1
Pal Joey 1957,O 28,30:1
Vertigo 1958,My 29,24:2
Bell, Book and Candle 1958,D 27,2:7
Middle of the Night 1959,Je 18,36:1
Strangers When we Meet 1960,Je 30,22:2
Pepe 1960,D 22,18:1
Boys' Night Out 1962,Je 22,15:2
Notorious Landlady, The 1962,Jl 27,15:2
Of Human Bondage 1964,S 24,46:2
Kiss Me, Stupid 1964,D 23,22:2
Amorous Adventures of Moll Flanders, The 1965,My 27,28:1
Legend of Lylah Clare, The 1968,Ag 23,33:1

Novak, Mickell (Screenwriter)

One Million BC 1940,Ap 27,9:2
Turnabout 1940,Jl 27,17:6
Road Show 1941,F 19,25:2

Novak, Peggy

Sailing Along 1938,Ap 16,17:1
South Riding 1938,Ag 2,15:2
Ware Case, The 1939,Jl 22,12:2

Novakova, Jana

Loves of a Blonde 1966,O 27,55:1

Novakova, M

Fall of Berlin 1952,Je 9,19:2

Novara, Medea

Mad Empress, The 1940,F 15,15:1

Novara, Medea de

Tribu 1935,Je 10,14:7
Paloma, La 1938,F 26,9:4

Novara, Medea de— Cont

Sonadores de la Gloria; Dreamers of Glory 1938,D 10,13:3
Golondrina, La; Swallow, The 1939,Jl 31,9:3

Novarese, Vittorio Nino (Original Author)

Wild Is the Wind 1957,D 12,35:1

Novarese, Vittorio Nino (Screenwriter)

Rossini 1948,Ja 31,14:2
When Love Calls 1948,O 9,12:6
Miserables, Les 1952,Mr 25,23:2
Miss Italy 1952,My 10,16:2
Of Love and Bandits 1953,Ja 17,12:4
Paolo and Francesca 1953,F 14,8:3
Queen of Sheba, The 1953,N 4,29:3
House of Ricordi 1956,Mr 13,32:1

Novarro, Ramon

Prisoner of Zenda, The 1922,Ag 1,14:3
Trifling Women 1922,O 4,23:4
Where the Pavement Ends 1923,Ap 2,22:1
Scaramouche 1923,O 12,7:2 (Incorrect in this edition; use 1927,O 1,7:2 elsewhere)
Thy Name Is Woman 1924,Mr 4,17:1
Arab, The 1924,Jl 14,11:5
Red Lily, The 1924,S 29,10:1
Midshipman, The 1925,O 13.20:1
Ben Hur 1925,D 31,10:5 (In Addenda)
Lovers 1927,Ap 19,24:4
Student Prince, The 1927,S 22,33:2
Road to Romance, The 1927,O 10,24:1
Across to Singapore 1928,Ap 30,18:3
Certain Young Man, A 1928,Je 11,27:1
Forbidden Hours 1928,Jl 23,11:2
Flying Fleet, The 1929,F 11,26:3
Pagan, The 1929,My 14,29:1
Devil May Care 1929,D 23,18:2
In Gay Madrid 1930,Je 7,10:4
Call of the Flesh 1930,S 13,9:3
Daybreak 1931,Je 1,15:1
Son of India 1931,Jl 25,11:6
Ben Hur 1931,D 4,28:2
Mata Hari 1932,Ja 1,31:1
Huddle 1932,Je 17,24:1
Son-Daughter, The 1933,Ja 2,29:2
Barbarian, The 1933,My 13,16:2
Cat and the Fiddle, The 1934,F 17,20:2
Night is Young, The 1935,Ja 14,11:2
We Were Strangers 1949,Ap 28,28:2
Big Steal, The 1949,Jl 11,13:2
Outriders, The 1950,Mr 9,25:2
Crisis 1950,Jl 4,10:2
Heller in Pink Tights 1960,Mr 17,28:1

Novarro, Ramon (Director)

Contra la Corriente 1936,Mr 10,27:3

Novarro, Ramon (Screenwriter)

Contra la Corriente 1936,Mr 10,27:3

Novelli, Anthony

Julius Caesar 1922,F 12,VI,3:1 (In Addenda)

Novello, Ivor

Carnival 1921,Je 27,16:3
White Rose, The 1923,My 23,18:3
Case of Jonathan Drew, The 1928,Je 11,27:1
Vortex, The 1928,Ag 27,23:1
Constant Nymph, The 1929,Je 10,23:1
Once a Lady 1931,N 9,22:4
Autumn Crocus 1934,O 25,26:2
Phantom Fiend 1935,Ap 22,14:2

Novello, Ivor (Original Author)

But the Flesh Is Weak 1932,Ap 16,11:2
Rat, The 1938,F 28,19:1
Free and Easy 1941,Ap 3,29:4
Dancing Years, The 1951,Ja 29,14:4

Novello, Jay

Tenth Avenue Kid 1938,S 2,21:3
Calling All Marines 1939,O 26,27:2
They Met in Bombay 1941,Jl 4,17:1
Swamp Woman 1941,D 27,15:2
Chicago Kid, The 1945,F 12,24:3
Perilous Holiday 1946,Je 1,10:4
Kiss the Blood off my Hands 1948,O 30,10:2
Smuggler's Island 1951,My 24,47:2
Sniper, The 1952,My 10,16:3
Miracle of Our Lady Fatima, The 1952,Ag 21,16:2
Operation Secret 1952,N 6,37:2
Iron Mistress, The 1952,N 20,39:2
Beneath the 12-Mile Reef 1953,D 17,52:2
Crime Wave 1954,Ja 13,26:2
Diamond Queen, The 1954,Ja 27,24:2
Mad Magician, The 1954,My 20,38:2
Gambler From Natchez, The 1954,Ag 14,8:2
Son of Sinbad 1955,Jl 28,18:2
Lisbon 1956,Ag 30,19:2
Pride and the Passion, The 1957,Je 29,10:6
Perfect Furlough, The 1959,Ja 22,27:4
Lost World, The 1960,Jl 14,23:1
Pocketful of Miracles 1961,D 19,39:1
Very Special Favor, A 1965,Ag 26,40:3
What Did You Do in the War, Daddy? 1966,S 1,28:1

Novikoff, Lou

Safe at Home 1941,N 26,31:2

Novikov

Last Game, The 1964,O 25,41:5 (Incorrect in this edition; use 1964,O 26,41:5 elsewhere)

Novikov, V K
Childhood of Maxim Gorky 1938,S 28,29:3
Alexander Nevsky 1939,Mr 23,27:1
On his Own 1939,S 13,31:3
Noville Bros
You're a Sweetheart 1937,D 25,10:5
Novis, Donald
Monte Carlo 1930,Ag 28,22:4
Novis, Julieta
Music in My Heart 1940,Ja 4,19:2
Novitsky, M
Variety Stars 1955,F 21,16:7
Novliansky, Nikolai
Home for Tanya, A 1961,Ag 14,28:5
Novodtna, Jarmila
Brand in der Oper; Fire in the Opera House
1930,N 23,IX,6:2
Novoseltzev, I
Golden Taiga 1935,Ag 2,22:3
Seven Brave Men 1936,Je 15,24:2
Thirteen, The 1937,Je 19,20:2
City of Youth 1938,S 5,30:4
Novotna, Jarmila
Bettelstudent, Der 1933,O 14,18:3
Verkaufte Braut, Die 1934,Ap 27,25:2
Frasquita 1936,Ja 18,19:4
Night of the Great Love, The 1937,O 1,19:5
Song of the Lark 1937,N 15,15:3
Search, The 1948,Mr 24,30:3
Great Caruso, The 1951,My 11,32:2
Novytsky, Slavko
Across the River 1965,Ap 27,27:1
Nowak, Irmgard
Junge Graf, Der 1936,D 14,15:2
Nowak, Josef
Eroica (Second Episode) 1966,F 2,24:1
Nowak, Leopold
First Start, The 1953,F 2,17:3
Nowell, Wedgewood
Don't Marry for Money 1923,Ag 21,17:3
To Mary-With Love 1936,Ag 27,16:1
Stolen Holiday 1937,F 1,15:3
Calling Philo Vance 1940,F 9,15:3
Nowina-Przybylski, Jan (Director)
Przysięgłas 1932,My 16,19:5
Maryjka 1934,D 3,15:2
Manewry Milosne 1936,N 11,55:1
Yiddle With his Fiddle 1937,Ja 2,15:1
Nowka, Lilo
Marriage in the Shadows 1948,S 17,28:3
Nowotna, Jarmila
Brand in der Oper 1932,Jl 11,11:4
Nox, Andre
Jolly Peasant, The 1929,Jl 1,31:2
That They May Live 1939,N 7,31:2
Noy, Wilfred
Janice Meredith 1924,Ag 6,13:3
Interference 1928,N 17,23:1
Doctor's Secret, The 1929,F 4,20:1
Let Us Be Gay 1930,Jl 12,16:4
Flirting Widow, The 1930,Ag 2,16:4
Emma 1932,F 6,14:4
Noy, Wilfred (Director)
Father O'Flynn 1938,D 26,29:2
Nozoe, Hitomi
Utamaro, Painter of Women 1964,D 2,57:1
Nubret, Serge
My Son, The Hero 1963,S 19,23:1
Nucci, Laura
Giovanni De Medici, The Leader 1940,Ja 5,15:4
Eravamo Sette Vedove; We Were Seven Widows
1940,F 16,23:4
We Still Kill the Old Way 1968,F 29,28:1
Nugent, Carol
Secret Command 1944,Je 14,16:2
Cheaper by the Dozen 1950,Ap 1,12:2
Lusty Men, The 1952,O 25,12:6
Nugent, Eddie
Duke Steps Out, The 1929,Ap 15,22:6
Vagabond Lover, The 1929,N 27,30:6
Girls Demand Excitement 1931,F 7,11:1
Bright Lights 1931,F 10,24:4
Young Sinners 1931,My 9,15:4
Crooner 1932,Ag 20,7:4
This Day and Age 1933,S 1,15:4
Beauty for Sale 1933,S 16,9:3
This Side of Heaven 1934,F 10,21:2
Fighting Youth 1935,N 2,13:3
Dancing Feet 1936,Mr 28,11:2
Harvester, The 1936,Jl 4,18:2
Pigskin Parade 1936,N 14,23:3
Nugent, Edward
Our Dancing Daughters 1928,O 8,14:2
Bellamy Trial, The 1929,Ja 24,30:5
Flying Fleet, The 1929,F 11,26:3
Our Modern Maidens 1929,S 7,15:1
Untamed 1929,N 30,23:1
Clancy in Wall Street 1930,My 3,23:1
War Nurse 1930,O 24,31:1
Remote Control 1930,D 8,26:1
Shipmates 1931,My 23,13:4
Night Nurse 1931,Jl 17,23:4
Star Witness, The 1931,Ag 4,19:5

Past of Mary Holmes, The 1933,My 1,10:3
Dance, Girl, Dance 1933,O 25,23:3
She Loves Me Not 1934,S 8,18:5
Girl of the Limberlost, A 1934,N 9,24:6
Ah, Wilderness! 1935,D 25,30:2
Bunker Bean 1936,Je 27,21:2
Big Game, The 1936,O 24,23:1
Man of the People 1937,F 23,25:4
Nugent, Edward J
Up Pops the Devil 1931,My 16,13:3
Bought 1931,Ag 15,18:3
Local Boy Makes Good 1931,N 27,29:3
42d Street 1933,Mr 10,19:3
Nugent, Elliott
So This Is College 1929,N 9,22:5
Not so Dumb 1930,F 8,12:5
Unholy Three, The 1930,Jl 5,17:4
Sins of the Children 1930,Jl 26,16:4
Romance 1930,Ag 23,7:3
Virtuous Husband 1931,My 8,30:2
Last Flight, The 1931,Ag 20,17:4
Stage Door Canteen 1943,Je 25,13:2
My Outlaw Brother 1951,Ag 23,19:2
Nugent, Elliott (Director)
Mouthpiece, The 1932,Ap 21,25:2
Whistling in the Dark 1933,F 5,IX,5:1
Three-Cornered Moon 1933,Ag 12,14:2
If I Were Free 1934,Ja 5,25:2
Strictly Dynamite 1934,Jl 4,18:2
She Loves Me Not 1934,S 8,18:5
Enter Madame 1935,Ja 12,12:1
Love in Bloom 1935,Ap 20,16:2
Splendor 1935,N 23,23:2
And So They Were Married 1936,My 14,29:3
Wives Never Know 1936,O 31,24:2
It's all Yours 1938,Ja 7,15:3
Professor Beware 1938,Jl 14,17:1
Give Me a Sailor 1938,Ag 11,31:1
Never Say Die 1939,Mr 9,18:1
Cat and the Canary, The 1939,N 23,38:5
Nothing but the Truth 1941,O 23,27:1
Male Animal, The 1942,Mr 28,11:1
Crystal Ball, The 1943,F 19,22:2
Up in Arms 1944,Mr 3,19:2
My Favorite Brunette 1947,Mr 20,38:2
Welcome Stranger 1947,Ag 7,15:2
My Girl Tisa 1948,F 21,9:2
Mr Belvedere Goes to College 1949,Ap 16,11:2
Great Gatsby, The 1949,Jl 14,20:5
Skipper Surprised his Wife, The 1950,Je 30,18:2
My Outlaw Brother 1951,Ag 23,19:2
Just for You 1952,O 9,40:6
Nugent, Elliott (Original Author)
Poor Nut, The 1927,Jl 19,27:2
Sins of the Children 1930,Jl 26,16:4
Local Boy Makes Good 1931,N 27,29:3
Male Animal, The 1942,Mr 28,11:1
She's Working her Way Through College
1952,Jl 10,27:2
Nugent, Frank (Original Author)
Wagonmaster 1950,Je 19,17:2
Two Flags West 1950,O 13,23:2
Nugent, Frank (Screenwriter)
Fort Apache 1948,Je 25,26:2
Three Godfathers 1949,Mr 4,25:2
Tulsa 1949,My 27,25:2
She Wore a Yellow Ribbon 1949,N 18,35:2
Quiet Man, The 1952,Ag 22,13:1
Angel Face 1953,Ap 25,11:5
Paratrooper 1953,D 31,9:3
Trouble in the Glen 1955,Ap 11,29:2
Mister Roberts 1955,Jl 15,14:1
Tall Men, The 1955,O 12,36:2
Searchers, The 1956,My 31,21:4
Rising of the Moon, The (1921); 1921 (The Rising
of the Moon) 1957,Jl 10,23:1
Rising of the Moon, The (The Majesty of the
Law); Majesty of the Law, The (The Rising of
the Moon) 1957,Jl 10,23:1
Rising of the Moon, The (A Minute's Wait);
Minute's Wait, A (The Rising of the Moon)
1957,Jl 10,23:1
Last Hurrah, The 1958,O 24,40:1
Two Rode Together 1961,Jl 27,23:3
Donovan's Reef 1963,Jl 25,14:1
Nugent, J C
Navy Blues 1930,Ja 11,21:3
Big House, The 1930,Je 25,31:2
Love in the Rough 1930,S 27,21:3
Remote Control 1930,D 8,26:1
Millionaire, The 1931,Ap 9,30:5
Virtuous Husband 1931,My 8,30:2
Love in Bloom 1935,Ap 20,16:2
Men Without Names 1935,Je 29,16:2
Star Is Born, A 1937,Ap 23,25:1
This is my Affair 1937,My 28,17:1
Life Begins In College 1937,O 9,16:1
Stand-In 1937,N 19,27:2
It's all Yours 1938,Ja 7,15:3
Give Me a Sailor 1938,Ag 11,31:1

Nugent, J C (Original Author)
Poor Nut, The 1927,Jl 19,27:2
Sins of the Children 1930,Jl 26,16:4
Local Boy Makes Good 1931,N 27,29:3
Nugent, Judy
There's Always Tomorrow 1956,Ja 21,18:2
Girl Most Likely, The 1958,O 9,47:1
Nugent, Richard
Sahara 1943,N 12,25:2
Pearl of Death 1944,Ag 26,15:2
Master Race, The 1944,N 2,22:1
Of Human Bondage 1946,Jl 6,11:2
Nulli, Edoardo (Screenwriter)
Margaret of Cortona 1957,Ja 21,20:4
Numata, Yoichi
Happiness of Us Alone 1963,Ap 10,31:5
Numkena, Anthony Earl
Pony Soldier 1952,D 20,15:2
Destination Gobi 1953,My 30,7:1
Strange Lady in Town 1955,My 21,11:1
Numkena, Ronald Alan
Naked Jungle, The 1954,Ap 3,19:2
Nunberg, Siegmund
Horst Wessel; Hans Westmar 1934,F 4,IX,4:4
Nunes, Robert (Producer)
Port of Hell 1954,D 18,12:2
Nunez, Fernando
Se ha Fugado un Preso 1935,My 21,22:3
Nunez, Ricardo
Susana Tiene un Secreto 1935,Je 5,22:2
Rumbo al Cairo; Bound for Cairo 1940,Je 8,18:3
Nunke, Margit
Hippodrome 1962,Mr 12,36:1
Nunn, Larry
Strike up the Band 1940,S 30,13:2
Men of Boys Town 1941,Ap 11,24:6
Born to Sing 1942,F 19,23:2
Major and the Minor, The 1942,S 17,21:3
Nunn, Wayne
One Third of a Nation 1939,F 11,13:2
Nureyev, Rudolf
Evening With the Royal Ballet, An 1965,D 9,60:1
Romeo and Juliet 1966,O 6,55:1
Nurney, Fred
Five Graves to Cairo 1943,My 27,21:2
Hitler Gang, The 1944,My 8,15:2
Scandal In Paris, A 1946,S 16,9:7
B F's Daughter 1948,Mr 25,35:2
South Sea Sinner 1950,Ja 16,18:4
Abbott and Costello in the Foreign Legion
1950,Ag 14,14:4
Mystery Submarine 1951,F 2,19:2
Nusciak, Loredana
Gladiators Seven 1964,My 7,31:2
Nusinov, I (Screenwriter)
Welcome Kostya! 1965,N 22,48:2
Nussbaum, Morris
Reunion in Vienna 1933,Ap 29,14:2
Nussgruber, Rudolph (Director)
Mediterannean Holiday 1964,D 16,51:1
Nutter, Nancy
David and Lisa 1962,D 27,5:5
Nuyen, France
South Pacific 1958,Mr 20,33:1
In Love and War 1958,N 1,14:2
Last Time I Saw Archie, The 1961,My 29,9:6
Satan Never Sleeps 1962,F 22,20:1
Diamond Head 1963,F 21,5:2
Girl Named Tamiku, A 1963,Mr 15,8:2
Man in the Middle 1964,Mr 5,36:1
Nuzzo, Ferruccio
Gospel According to St Matthew, The
1966,F 18,23:1
Nyberg, Borie (Director)
I, A Lover 1968,My 4,46:2
Nyby, Christian (Director)
Thing, The 1951,My 3,34:4
First to Fight 1967,Mr 30,55:1
Nye, Carrie
Group, The 1966,Mr 17,35:1
Nye, Carrol
Her Honor the Governor 1926,Jl 20,17:3
Silver Slave, The 1928,Ja 3,28:2
Powder my Back 1928,Ag 7,25:4
Nye, Carroll
Classified 1925,N 2,20:1
Kosher Kitty Kelly 1926,S 28,30:2
Brute, The 1927,Ap 21,25:1
Death Valley 1927,N 22,32:2
Girl From Chicago, The 1927,D 20,33:2
While the City Sleeps 1928,O 22,29:1
Craig's Wife 1928,D 4,29:1
Flying Fleet, The 1929,F 11,26:3
Madame X 1929,Ap 25,32:3
Squall, The 1929,My 10,32:5
Bishop Murder Case, The 1930,F 1,15:1
Lottery Bride, The 1930,N 29,21:4
Lawless Woman, The 1931,Je 8,21:1
Traveling Saleslady 1935,Mr 29,26:2
Rebecca of Sunnybrook Farm 1938,Mr 26,12:1
Gone With the Wind 1939,D 20,31:2

Nye, G R
Queen of Sheba 1921,Ap 11,9:1
Nye, G Raymond
Tiger Love 1924,Je 16,18:3
Tenderloin 1928,Mr 15,28:3
Nye, Louis
Facts of Life, The 1961,F 11,27:1
Last Time I Saw Archie, The 1961,My 29,9:6
Stripper, The 1963,Je 20,29:1
Wheeler Dealers, The 1963,N 15,25:2
Who's Been Sleeping in My Bed? 1963,D 26,33:2
Good Neighbor Sam 1964,Jl 23,19:1
Guide for the Married Man, A 1967,My 27,16:1
Nye, Pay
Mr Perrin and Mr Traill 1949,Ja 17,15:2
Nyikonyenko, Sergei
Red and the White, The 1968,S 21,26:1
Nylander, Marie
I, A Lover 1968,My 4,46:2
Nyltray, Emil (Original Author)
No, No, Nanette 1940,D 20,33:1
Tea for Two 1950,S 2,11:2
Nyman, Lena
491 1967,D 21,45:1
Nymark, Leif
491 1967,D 21,45:1
Nystrom, Anders
Torment 1947,Ap 22,34:2
Children, The 1949,D 23,17:1
Nyvit, Vaclav (Screenwriter)
Capricious Summer 1968,S 25,38:2
Nzyfack, Nicholas (Producer)
Vengeance Valley 1951,F 16,21:2

O

Oakes, Sue
West Side Story 1961,O 19,39:3
Oakie, Evelyn
Too Much Harmony 1933,S 23,11:5
Oakie, Jack
Fleet's In, The 1928,O 1,23:1
Some One to Love 1928,D 4,29:1
Dummy, The 1929,Mr 4,20:2
Chinatown Nights 1929,Ap 1,22:1
Wild Party, The 1929,Ap 2,28:4
Close Harmony 1929,Ap 29,29:2
Man I Love, The 1929,My 28,36:2
Street Girl 1929,Jl 31,17:3
Hard to Get 1929,S 28,17:3
Fast Company 1929,O 5,22:5
Sweetie 1929,O 26,15:1
Hit the Deck 1930,Ja 15,28:6
Paramount on Parade 1930,Ap 21,20:4
Social Lion, The 1930,Je 14,9:4
Sap From Syracuse, The 1930,Jl 26,16:4
Let's Go Native 1930,Ag 30,7:4
Sea Legs 1930,N 11,29:1
Gang Buster, The 1931,Ja 24,15:1
June Moon 1931,Mr 14,23:2
Dude Ranch 1931,Ap 25,23:4
Touchdown 1931,N 16,23:1
Dancers in the Dark 1932,Mr 19,11:2
Sky Bride 1932,Ap 23,11:5
Million Dollar Legs 1932,Jl 9,7:5
Madison Square Garden 1932,O 12,26:5
Once in a Lifetime 1932,O 29,18:4
If I Had a Million 1932,D 3,21:4
Uptown New York 1932,D 10,19:3
Sailor Be Good 1933,F 27,11:2
From Hell to Heaven 1933,Mr 18,9:3
Eagle and the Hawk, The 1933,My 13,16:2
College Humor 1933,Je 23,15:4
Too Much Harmony 1933,S 23,11:5
Sitting Pretty 1933,D 2,9:3
Alice in Wonderland 1933,D 23,19:1
Looking for Trouble 1934,Ap 12,27:2
Murder at the Vanities 1934,My 21,20:2
Shoot the Works 1934,Jl 7,16:5
College Rhythm 1934,N 24,19:1
Call of the Wild 1935,Ag 15,15:2
Big Broadcast of 1936, The 1935,S 16,15:2
King of Burlesque 1936,Ja 16,25:2
Collegiate 1936,Ja 23,25:2
Colleen 1936,Mr 9,20:2
Florida Special 1936,My 29,15:2
Texas Rangers, The 1936,S 24,29:1
That Girl From Paris 1937,Ja 1,19:1
Champagne Waltz 1937,F 4,17:2
Super-Sleuth 1937,Jl 17,18:1
Toast of New York, The 1937,Jl 23,16:2
Fight for Your Lady 1937,N 20,21:2
Hitting a new High 1937,D 27,11:1
Radio City Revels 1938,Mr 21,18:3
Affairs of Annabel, The 1938,O 13,29:2
Thanks For Everything 1938,D 10,13:2
Annabel Takes a Tour 1938,D 29,15:3
Young People 1940,Ag 24,16:2
Great Dictator, The 1940,O 16,29:1
Tin Pan Alley 1940,N 22,27:3
Little Men 1940,D 9,23:2
Great American Broadcast, The 1941,My 2,25:2

Navy Blues 1941,S 20,11:2
Rise and Shine 1941,D 6,14:3
Song of the Islands 1942,Mr 12,24:4
Iceland 1942,O 15,27:1
Hello, Frisco, Hello 1943,Mr 25,25:1
Something to Shout About 1943,Ap 8,27:3
Wintertime 1943,S 30,27:2
It Happened Tomorrow 1944,My 29,18:2
Merry Monahans, The 1944,O 13,16:2
Sweet and Low Down 1944,O 19,19:2
Bowery to Broadway 1944,N 30,19:2
That's the Spirit 1945,Je 2,11:2
She Wrote the Book 1946,Je 20,20:3
When my Baby Smiles at Me 1948,N 24,20:2
Northwest Stampede 1948,D 10,34:3
Thieves' Highway 1949,S 24,8:6
Last of the Buccaneers 1950,D 15,43:2
Tomahawk 1951,F 19,19:2
Around the World in 80 Days 1956,O 18,37:1
Wonderful Country, The 1959,N 5,39:7
Rat Race, The 1960,My 26,37:3
Lover Come Back 1962,F 9,21:1
Oakland, Ben (Composer)
Life of the Party, The 1937,O 4,17:1
Awful Truth, The 1937,N 5,19:3
Big Store, The 1941,Je 27,14:4
Oakland, Ben (Miscellaneous)
I'll Take Romance 1937,D 17,33:2
Oakland, Dagmar
Stolen Heaven 1931,F 14,11:4
Oakland, Simon
Brothers Karamazov, The 1958,F 21,18:2
I Want to Live 1958,N 19,45:1
Rise and Fall of Legs' Diamond, The
1960,F 4,34:1
Psycho 1960,Je 17,37:1
Murder, Inc 1960,Je 29,26:6
West Side Story 1961,O 19,39:3
Hemingway's Adventures of a Young Man
1962,Jl 26,17:1
Follow That Dream 1962,Ag 9,17:7
Wall of Noise 1963,S 5,27:1
Sand Pebbles, The 1966,D 21,48:1
Tony Rome 1967,N 16,58:1
Bullitt 1968,O 18,41:2
Oakland, Vivian
Madonna of the Streets 1924,O 28,23:4
Rainbow Trail, The 1925,Je 3,26:4
Teaser, The 1925,Je 15,10:1
Tony Runs Wild 1926,Ap 28,28:3
Wedding Bills 1927,Je 29,29:3
Uncle Tom's Cabin 1927,N 5,16:2
Time, The Place and the Girl, The 1929,Jl 8,17:3
Florodora Girl, The 1930,My 31,19:4
Matrimonial Bed, The 1930,Ag 25,14:2
Gold Dust Gertie 1931,My 30,9:2
House Divided, A 1932,Ja 9,21:1
Cock of the Air 1932,Ja 25,20:3
Tenderfoot, The 1932,My 23,18:4
They Just Had to Get Married 1933,F 13,11:4
Star of Midnight 1935,Ap 12,26:5
Way out West 1937,My 4,29:1
Double Danger 1938,F 10,17:5
Man in the Trunk, The 1942,O 23,25:1
Utah 1945,Mr 12,22:7
Laurel and Hardy's Laughing 20's 1965,N 18,55:2
Oakley, Patricia
They Knew What They Wanted 1940,O 11,25:2
Oakley, Robert
Hawaii 1966,O 11,54:1
Oakman, Wheeler
Virgin of Stamboul, The 1920,Mr 28,V,9:1
Outside the Law 1926,My 12,31:1
Out all Night 1927,S 27,31:1
Lights of New York 1928,Jl 9,25:1
While the City Sleeps 1928,O 22,29:1
Good-Bye Kiss, The 1928,N 12,18:2
What a Night! 1928,D 24,11:1
Shakedown, The 1929,Ap 8,32:1
Donovan Affair, The 1929,Ap 29,29:2
On With the Show 1929,My 29,28:6
Father and Son 1929,Je 4,29:3
Shanghai Lady 1929,N 11,20:2
Show of Shows 1929,N 21,24:5
Girl From Woolworth's, The 1929,D 21,17:1
Little Johnny Jones 1930,F 1,15:1
Big Fight, The 1930,Je 28,9:2
Costello Case, The 1931,My 15,20:6
Good Bad Girl, The 1931,My 15,20:6
Lawless Woman, The 1931,Je 8,21:1
Soldiers of the Storm 1933,My 17,15:3
Lost Jungle, The 1934,Je 8,18:1
Crusade Against Rackets 1937,Jl 26,15:3
Mars Attacks the World 1938,N 8,26:3
Mutiny in the Big House 1939,D 11,26:2
Teen Age 1944,Je 19,17:1
Oaks, Theresa (Original Author)
Lady From Cheyenne, The 1941,Ap 18,18:2
Oates, Cicely
Man Who Knew too Much, The 1935,Mr 23,11:2
Oates, Warren
Private Property 1960,Ap 25,40:2
Ride the High Country 1962,Je 21,26:2

Oates, Warren— Cont
Mail Order Bride 1964,Je 11,27:3
Return of the Seven 1966,O 20,52:5
Welcome to Hard Times 1967,My 2,56:1
In the Heat of the Night 1967,Ag 3,26:1
Split, The 1968,N 5,55:2
Obal, Max (Director)
Reserve Hat Ruh 1932,Ap 11,19:2
Die Lustigen Musikanten 1933,My 27,11:6
Zwel Gute Kameraden 1933,D 4,22:3
Die vom Niederrhein; Lower Rhine Folks
1935,My 20,20:6
Klosterjaeger, Der 1936,Ja 3,13:7
Annette in Paradise 1936,Mr 7,11:4
Schloss Vogeloed 1936,My 9,11:2
Fahrt ins Gruene, Die 1936,My 23,12:2
Slalom 1936,D 16,35:3
Jede Frau Hat ein Geheimnis 1937,Mr 15,27:2
O'Beck, Fred
Patent Leather Kid, The 1927,Ag 16,31:2
Oh, Kay! 1928,Ag 27,23:1
Obelensky, W
End of St Petersberg, The 1928,My 31,21:2 (In
Addenda)
Ober, Dillon
Every Night at Eight 1935,Ag 3,16:2
Ober, Harry L (Miscellaneous)
Francis the First 1947,N 20,38:4
Ober, Philip
Secret Fury, The 1950,Je 22,34:2
Never a Dull Moment 1950,N 22,20:2
Magnificent Yankee, The 1951,Ja 19,21:2
Washington Story 1952,Jl 2,22:3
Come Back,Little Sheba 1952,D 24,13:2 (In Addenda)
Clown, The 1953,Ja 29,25:1
Girls of Pleasure Island, The 1953,My 16,10:1
Scandal at Scourie 1953,Je 16,24:2
From Here to Eternity 1953,Ag 6,16:2
About Mrs Leslie 1954,Je 28,16:2
Broken Lance 1954,Jl 30,9:1
Tammy and the Bachelor 1957,Je 15,10:7
Escapde in Japan 1957,D 24,11:1
High Cost of Loving, The 1958,My 17,12:1
Ten North Frederick 1958,My 23,29:2
Torpedo Run 1958,O 25,16:2
Mating Game, The 1959,Ap 30,37:1
North by Northwest 1959,Ag 7,28:1
Beloved Infidel 1959,N 18,46:1
Elmer Gantry 1960,Jl 8,16:1
Let no Man Write my Epitaph 1960,N 11,36:2
Facts of Life, The 1961,F 11,27:1
Go Naked in the World 1961,Mr 11,15:1
Ugly American, The 1963,Ap 12,30:2
Brass Bottle, The 1964,My 21,42:1
Ghost and Mr Chicken, The 1966,S 22,57:2
Ober, Robert
Introduce Me 1925,Mr 9,21:1
Mystic, The 1925,Ag 31,19:3
Souls for Sables 1925,S 15,12:1 (Incorrect in this
edition; use 1925 15,29:1 elsewhere)
Big Parade, The 1925,N 20,18:1 (In Addenda)
Time, the Comedian 1925,D 14,18:2
Butterflies in the Rain 1926,D 25,10:5
Idle Rich, The 1929,Je 17,29:1
Oberg, Gustav
Peak of Fate 1925,Je 13,10:5
Obermaierova, Jarnslava
Happy End 1968,Je 11,54:4
Oberon, Merle
Private Life of Henry VIII, The 1933,O 13,25:2
Broken Melody, The 1934,O 31,17:3
Battle, The 1934,N 23,23:2
Private Life of Don Juan, The 1934,D 10,16:2
Scarlet Pimpernel, The 1935,F 8,27:2
Folies Bergere 1935,F 25,13:2
Men of Tomorrow 1935,Ap 16,27:2
Dark Angel, The 1935,S 6,12:2
These Three 1936,Mr 19,22:4
Beloved Enemy 1936,D 26,15:2
Divorce of Lady X, The 1938,Ap 1,17:2
Cowboy and the Lady, The 1938,N 25,19:3
Wuthering Heights 1939,Ap 14,28:2
Lion Has Wings, The 1939,N 19,X,4:1 (In
Addenda)
Lion Has Wings, The 1940,Ja 22,11:2
'Til We Meet Again 1940,Ap 14,14:2
That Uncertain Feeling 1941,My 2,25:1
Affectionaly Yours 1941,My 24,18:2
Lydia 1941,S 19,27:1
Forever and a Day 1943,Mr 13,9:2
Stage Door Canteen 1943,Je 25,13:2
First Comes Courage 1943,S 3,15:3
Lodger, The 1944,Ja 20,15:3
Dark Waters 1944,N 22,25:2
Song to Remember, A 1945,Ja 26,16:4
This Love of Ours 1945,N 1,20:2
Night in Paradise 1946,Je 6,16:3
Temptation 1946,D 25,33:6
Night Song 1948,Ja 29,27:5
Berlin Express 1948,My 21,19:3
Pardon my French 1952,Mr 31,17:2
Desiree 1954,N 18,42:1
Deep in my Heart 1954,D 10,35:2
Of Love and Desire 1963,S 12,32:1

Oberon, Merle— Cont

Hotel 1967,Ja 20,27:1

Oberth, Hermann Prof (Miscellaneous)

By Rocket to the Moon 1931,F 7,11:1

Obey, Andre (Narrator)

He Who Must Die 1958,D 29,21:1

Obey, Andre (Screenwriter)

Hoboes in Paradise 1950,O 9,21:5

Oboler, Arch (Director)

Bewitched 1945,Ag 17,20:3
Strange Holiday 1945,O 20,8:2
Arnelo Affair, The 1947,S 13,8:5
Five 1951,Ap 26,34:2
Bwana Devil 1953,F 19,20:5
1 ∎ 1 1961,N 8,41:1

Oboler, Arch (Original Author)

Miracle Can Happen, A 1948,F 4,28:4
Five 1951,Ap 26,34:2
Bwana Devil 1953,F 19,20:5
1 ∎ 1 1961,N 8,41:1

Oboler, Arch (Producer)

Strange Holiday 1945,O 20,8:2
Five 1951,Ap 26,34:2
Bwana Devil 1953,F 19,20:5
1 ∎ 1 1961,N 8,41:1

Oboler, Arch (Screenwriter)

Escape 1940,N 1,33:1
Bewitched 1945,Ag 17,20:3
Strange Holiday 1945,O 20,8:2
Arnelo Affair, The 1947,S 13,8:5
1 ∎ 1 1961,N 8,41:1

O'Brady

Mr Peek-A-Boo 1951,S 19,37:1
Julie the Redhead 1963,O 15,44:1

O'Brady, Frederick

Foreign Intrigue 1956,Jl 13,23:2
Picnic on the Grass 1960,O 12,47:1

O'Brady, Jim

Treasure Island 1950,Ag 16,24:2

Obrazov and his Puppets Theater

I Love, You Love 1962,N 10,16:2

O'Brian, Hugh

Rocketship X-M 1950,My 27,10:6
Vengeance Valley 1951,F 16,21:2
Fighting Coast Guard 1951,My 12,14:6
Little Big Horn 1951,Jl 27,15:2
Red Ball Express 1952,My 30,11:2
Son of Ali Baba 1952,Ag 16,7:4
Raiders, The 1952,D 13,19:2
Man From the Alamo, The 1953,S 12,13:2
Saskatchewan 1954,Mr 11,26:2
Broken Lance 1954,Jl 30,9:1
There's no Business Like Show Business
  1954,D 17,37:3
White Feather 1955,F 17,23:1
Come Fly With Me 1963,My 2,40:2
Love Has Many Faces 1965,F 25,24:1
Ten Little Indians 1966,F 10,33:1
Ambush Bay 1966,S 15,51:4
Africa-Texas Style! 1967,Jl 13,30:2

O'Brian, Michael

Playboy of the Western World, The
  1963,Mr 19,8:2

O'Brien, Barry

Ireland, A Nation 1914,S 24,11:6

O'Brien, Bill

Let Us Be Gay 1930,Jl 12,16:4
Hell Bound 1931,My 9,15:4
Power and the Glory, The 1933,Ag 17,13:2

O'Brien, Chris

Private Hell 36 1954,S 4,6:4

O'Brien, Daniel J

Little Robinson Crusoe 1924,S 3,17:1

O'Brien, Dave

Jennie Gerhardt 1933,Je 9,20:2
Mutiny in the Big House 1939,D 11,26:2
East Side Kids 1940,F 19,21:6
Ghost Creeps, The 1940,Ag 19,13:3
Flying Wild 1941,Ap 12,19:3
Spooks Run Wild 1941,N 1,20:3
Kiss Me Kate 1953,N 6,23:2

O'Brien, Edmond

Hunchback of Notre Dame, The 1940,Ja 1,29:2
Girl, a Guy and a Gob, A 1941,Ap 24,25:3
Parachute Battalion 1941,Ag 29,13:2
Obliging Young Lady 1942,F 13,24:4
Powder Town 1942,Je 8,11:2
Amazing Mrs Holliday, The 1943,F 22,20:2
Winged Victory 1944,D 21,16:2
Killers, The 1946,Ag 29,24:2
Web, The 1947,Je 5,32:1
Double Life, A 1948,F 20,19:1
Another Part of the Forest 1948,My 19,30:2
For the Love of Mary 1948,S 23,37:2
Fighter Squadron 1948,N 20,9:2
Live Today for Tomorrow 1948,D 6,29:2
White Heat 1949,S 3,7:2
Backfire 1950,Ja 27,29:2
D O A 1950,My 1,18:2
711 Ocean Drive 1950,Jl 20,21:2
Between Midnight and Dawn 1950,O 2,19:2
Admiral Was a Lady, The 1950,O 13,23:3
Redhead and the Cowboy, The 1951,Je 6,37:2
Two of a Kind 1951,Je 30,8:6

Warpath 1951,N 23,32:2
Denver and Rio Grande, The 1952,My 17,22:7
Turning Point, The 1952,N 15,15:2
Man in the Dark 1953,Ap 9,31:5
Hitch-Hiker, The 1953,Ap 30,39:3
Julius Caesar 1953,Je 5,19:1
Bigamist, The 1953,D 26,10:4
Shield for Murder 1954,Ag 28,8:3
Shanghai Story, The 1954,S 25,10:7
Barefoot Contessa, The 1954,S 30,37:1
Pete Kelly's Blues 1955,Ag 19,10:1
D-Day, The Sixth of June 1956,My 30,13:1
Cry in the Night, A 1956,S 1,19:4
1984 1956,O 1,31:1
Rack, The 1956,N 6,30:1
Girl Can't Help It, The 1957,F 9,12:7
Big Land, The 1957,Mr 2,18:2
Stopover Tokyo 1957,D 27,23:4
Sing Boy Sing 1958,F 22,9:4
Up Periscope 1959,Mr 5,35:4
Last Voyage, The 1960,F 20,14:2
Third Voice, The 1960,Mr 7,24:5
Great Impostor, The 1961,Mr 30,24:1
Moon Pilot 1962,Ap 6,30:2
Man Who Shot Liberty Valance, The
  1962,My 24,29:2
Birdman of Alcatraz 1962,Jl 19,19:2
Longest Day, The 1962,O 5,28:1
Seven Days in May 1964,F 20,22:1
Rio Conchos 1964,O 29,38:1
Sylvia 1965,F 11,45:1
Synanon 1965,My 6,44:1
Fantastic Voyage 1966,S 8,43:1
Viscount, The 1967,My 11,50:1

O'Brien, Edmond (Director)

Shield for Murder 1954,Ag 28,8:3
Man Trap 1961,N 30,40:4

O'Brien, Edmond (Producer)

Man Trap 1961,N 30,40:4

O'Brien, Edna

London Scene, The (Tonite Let's All Make Love
  in London) 1967,S 27,39:1

O'Brien, Edna (Original Author)

Girl With Green Eyes 1964,Ag 11,37:2
Time Lost and Time Remembered
  1966,Ag 30,35:2

O'Brien, Edna (Screenwriter)

Girl With Green Eyes 1964,Ag 11,37:2
Time Lost and Time Remembered
  1966,Ag 30,35:2

O'Brien, Erin

Onionhead 1958,O 2,44:1
John Paul Jones 1959,Je 17,39:1

O'Brien, Eugene

Poor Little Peppina 1916,F 21,9:2
Fires of Faith 1919,My 6,16:2
Come out of the Kitchen 1919,My 12,11:4
Voice From the Minaret, The 1923,F 5,18:2
Secrets 1924,Mr 25,25:2
Only Woman, The 1924,N 3,20:1
Flaming Love 1925,Ja 19,14:1
Dangerous Innocence 1925,Je 8,19:1
Siege 1925,Je 16,24:1
Graustark 1925,S 8,29:1
Souls for Sables 1925,S 15,12:1 (Incorrect in this
  edition; use 1925,S 15,29:1 elsewhere)
Simon the Jester 1925,N 19,22:1
Fine Manners 1926,Ag 30,10:3

O'Brien, Frank

Wait Until Dark 1967,O 27,48:1

O'Brien, Frederick (Original Author)

White Shadows of the South Seas 1928,Ag 1,13:3

O'Brien, George

Ne'er Do-Well, The 1923,My 1,24:3
Woman Proof 1923,O 30,16:1
Shadows of Paris 1924,F 18,13:1
Iron Horse, The 1924,Ag 29,6:1
Man Who Came Back, The 1924,S 1,9:1
Roughneck, The 1925,Ja 26,22:1
Dancers, The 1925,Ja 26,22:1
Thank You 1925,O 6,30:1
Is Zat So? 1927,My 17,27:2
Paid to Love 1927,Jl 25,25:3
Sunrise 1927,S 24,15:3 (In Addenda)
East Side, West Side 1927,O 18,33:2
Sharp Shooters 1928,Ja 23,18:3
Sunrise; Song of two Human Beings
  1928,Ja 29,VIII,6:2
Honor Bound 1928,Ap 30,18:3
True Heaven 1929,F 11,26:3
Noah's Ark 1929,Mr 13,28:6
Salute 1929,O 5,22:5
Rough Romance 1930,Je 16,25:3
Last of the Duanes 1930,S 13,9:3
Seas Beneath 1931,Ja 31,15:1
Holy Terror, A 1931,Jl 20,20:4
Riders of the Purple Sage 1931,S 26,25:3
Rainbow Trail, The 1932,Ja 30,13:2
Gay Caballero, The 1932,Mr 26,17:2
Mystery Ranch 1932,Je 30,26:2
Frontier Marshal 1934,Ja 31,20:3
Ever Since Eve 1934,Mr 28,27:5
Dude Ranger, The 1934,O 2,18:5

O'Brien, George— Cont

When a Man's a Man 1935,F 22,27:2
Hard Rock Harrigan 1935,Jl 30,16:2
Thunder Mountain 1935,O 2,27:2
Whispering Smith Speaks 1936,F 17,21:1
O'Malley of the Mounted 1936,Ap 6,18:1
Border Patrolman 1936,Je 29,11:2
Daniel Boone 1936,O 24,23:2
Hollywood Cowboy 1937,Jl 24,12:1
Gun Law 1938,Je 24,15:1
Painted Desert 1938,S 14,26:5
Renegade Ranger, The 1939,F 17,17:3
Racketeers of the Range 1939,Je 8,31:4
My Wild Irish Rose 1947,D 25,32:2
Fort Apache 1948,S 25,26:2
She Wore a Yellow Ribbon 1949,N 18,35:2
Cheyenne Autumn 1964,D 24,8:1

O'Brien, Gypsy

Master Mind, The 1920,S 13,12:1
Salvation Neil 1921,Je 27,16:3
Little Old New York 1923,Ag 2,10:3

O'Brien, Holly

Yours, Mine and Ours 1968,Ap 25,53:1

O'Brien, Hortense

Black Oxen 1924,Ja 7,23:1

O'Brien, Jack

Iron Horse, The 1924,Ag 29,6:1

O'Brien, Jimmy

Luck of the Irish, The 1948,S 16,34:1

O'Brien, Joan

Operation Petticoat 1959,D 6,38:1
Alamo, The 1960,O 27,45:1
Comancheros, The 1961,N 2,42:1
Samar 1962,Ap 12,41:6
6 Black Horses 1962,Ap 25,30:1
It's Only Money 1962,N 22,43:1
It Happened at the World's Fair 1963,My 30,20:1
Get Yourself a College Girl 1965,Ap 29,40:2

O'Brien, John

Spirit of Notre Dame, The 1931,O 16,27:1
Top o' the Morning 1949,S 1,25:2

O'Brien, Kate (Original Author)

That Lady 1955,Je 11,8:7

O'Brien, Liam (Original Author)

Here Comes the Groom 1951,S 21,19:2
Remarkable Mr Pennypacker, The 1959,F 21,25:2

O'Brien, Liam (Screenwriter)

Chain Lightning 1950,F 20,21:2
Of Men and Music 1951,F 15,27:2
Redhead and the Cowboy, The 1951,Je 6,37:2
Here Comes the Groom 1951,S 21,19:2
Diplomatic Courier 1952,Je 14,12:2
Stars Are Singing, The 1953,Mr 12,24:2
Young at Heart 1955,Ja 20,35:1
Trapeze 1956,Je 5,39:2
Great Impostor, The 1961,Mr 30,24:1
Devil at 4 O'Clock, The 1961,O 19,39:3

O'Brien, Lois

Mister Rock and Roll 1957,O 17,42:2

O'Brien, Margaret

Journey for Margaret 1942,D 18,36:7
Thousands Cheer 1943,S 14,27:1
Madame Curie 1943,D 17,23:1
Jane Eyre 1944,F 4,12:5
Lost Angel 1944,Ap 10,14:1
Canterville Ghost, The 1944,Jl 29,16:2
Meet Me in St Louis 1944,N 29,20:2
Music for Millions 1944,D 22,12:4
Our Vines Have Tender Grapes 1945,S 7,21:2
Bad Bascomb 1946,My 23,18:4
Three Wise Fools 1946,S 27,19:2
Unfinished Dance, The 1947,O 31,29:2
Big City 1948,My 17,23:3
Little Women 1949,Mr 11,33:2
Heller in Pink Tights 1960,Mr 17,28:1

O'Brien, Marianne

Very Thought of You, The 1944,N 18,16:7

O'Brien, Mary

It Must Be Love 1926,O 4,20:2

O'Brien, Pat

Honor Among Lovers 1931,F 28,15:2
Front Page, The 1931,Mr 20,29:1
Personal Maid 1931,S 5,7:4
Consolation Marriage 1931,O 30,26:4
Flying High 1931,D 12,23:3
Hell's House 1932,F 12,24:5
Final Edition, The 1932,F 22,23:2
Scandal for Sale 1932,Ap 3,26:2
Strange Case of Clara Deane, The
  1932,My 6,15:3
American Madness 1932,Ag 6,14:5
Hollywood Speaks 1932,Ag 12,18:2
Virtue 1932,O 25,24:5
Air Mail 1932,N 7,20:3
Laughter in Hell 1933,Ja 2,29:2
Destination Unknown 1933,Ag 8,16:2
World Gone Mad, The 1933,Ap 15,16:3
Bureau of Missing Persons 1933,S 9,9:2
Bombshell 1933,O 21,11:2
College Coach 1933,N 11,10:4
I've Got Your Number 1934,F 3,9:3
Gambling Lady 1934,Ap 5,25:2
20 Million Sweethearts 1934,Ap 27,25:1
Here Comes the Navy 1934,Jl 21,14:2

O'Brien, Pat— Cont

Personality Kid, The 1934,Ag 1,14:2
Flirtation Walk 1934,N 29,33:1
I Sell Anything 1934,D 27,25:2
Devil Dogs of the Air 1935,F 7,23:2
Oil for the Lamps of China 1935,Je 6,25:2
In Caliente 1935,Je 27,16:1
Irish in US, The 1935,Ag 1,15:1
Page Miss Glory 1935,Ag 29,25:2
Stars Over Broadway 1935,N 14,17:3
Ceiling Zero 1936,Ja 20,22:2
I Married a Doctor 1936,Ap 20,17:1
Public Enemy's Wife 1936,Jl 9,17:2
China Clipper 1936,Ag 12,14:3
Great O'Malley, The 1937,Mr 6,10:1
Slim 1937,Je 24,30:2
San Quentin 1937,Ag 4,15:2
Back in Circulation 1937,O 4,17:1
Submarine D-1 1937,D 30,15:4
Women Are Like That 1938,Ap 11,12:2
Cowboy From Brooklyn 1938,Jl 14,17:1
Boy Meets Girl 1938,Ag 27,7:2
Garden of the Moon 1938,S 24,13:1
Angels With Dirty Faces 1938,N 26,18:1
Off the Record 1939,F 18,12:2
Kid From Kokomo, The 1939,My 20,11:2
Indianapolis Speedway 1939,Jl 15,8:2
Night of Nights, The 1939,D 28,17:1
Fighting 69th, The 1940,Ja 27,9:2
Castle on the Hudson 1940,Mr 4,11:2
'Til We Meet Again 1940,Ap 14,14:2
Slightly Honorable 1940,My 17,23:4
Torrid Zone 1940,My 18,11:3
Flowing Gold 1940,S 2,19:3
Knute Rockne-All American 1940,O 19,21:2
Submarine Zone; (Escape To Glory)
1941,Ap 7,13:2
Two Yanks in Trinidad 1942,Ap 6,19:4
Broadway 1942,Je 5,23:2
Flight Lieutenant 1942,Jl 31,11:1
Navy Comes Through, The 1942,N 12,30:3
Bombardier 1943,Jl 2,15:2
Iron Major, The 1943,N 1,12:5
His Butler's Sister 1943,D 30,13:2
Secret Command 1944,Je 14,16:2
Marine Raiders 1944,Jl 1,10:7
Tonight and Every Night 1945,Mr 9,16:2
Having Wonderful Crime 1945,Ap 13,15:2
Man Alive 1945,N 17,14:5
Perilous Holiday 1946,Je 1,10:4
Crack-Up 1946,S 7,11:1
Riff-Raff 1947,Je 30,25:7
Fighting Father Dunne 1948,Je 25,26:2
Boy With Green Hair, The 1949,Ja 13,26:2
Dangerous Profession, A 1949,D 12,29:4
Fireball, The 1950,N 10,35:4
Johnny One-Eye 1950,N 17,31:2
Criminal Lawyer 1951,Ag 24,11:4
People Against O'Hara 1951,S 6,39:3
Okinawa 1952,Ap 24,38:3
Jubilee Trail 1954,My 1,13:3
Ring of Fear 1954,Jl 29,18:3
Inside Detroit 1956,Ja 28,10:5
Last Hurrah, The 1958,O 24,40:1
Some Like It Hot 1959,Mr 30,23:1

O'Brien, Pat (Narrator)

Hills of Ireland, The 1951,My 22,38:2

O'Brien, Robert (Screenwriter)

Lady on a Train 1945,S 15,21:2
Fancy Pants 1950,Ag 31,21:2
Lemon Drop Kid, The 1951,Mr 22,41:2
Belle of New York, The 1952,Mr 6,25:6
By the Light of the Silvery Moon
1953,Mr 27,28:2
Lucky Me 1954,Ap 10,11:2
Say One for Me 1959,Je 20,11:2

O'Brien, Tom

So This Is Marriage 1924,D 23,16:2
Big Parade, The 1925,N 20,18:1 (In Addenda)
Poker Faces 1926,S 14,25:4
Take It From Me 1926,N 2,35:1
Flaming Forest, The 1926,N 22,28:3
Tin Hats 1926,N 29,16:3
Fire Brigade, The 1926,D 21,20:2
Rookies 1927,Ap 25,20:4
Twelve Miles Out 1927,Jl 26,17:1
Private Life of Helen of Troy, The
1927,D 10,14:7
San Francisco Nights 1928,Ja 31,29:1
That's my Daddy 1928,F 13,16:2
Last Warning, The 1929,Ja 7,36:2
Smiling Irish Eyes 1929,Jl 24,23:2
Untamed 1929,N 30,23:1
Dance Hall 1929,D 16,34:2
Call of the West 1930,My 27,27:2
Moby Dick 1930,Ag 15,20:5
Night Mayor, The 1932,N 25,19:2

O'Brien, Vince

Hoodlum Priest, The 1961,Ap 3,28:5

O'Brien, Virginia

Hullabaloo 1940,D 19,33:1
Big Store, The 1941,Je 27,14:4
Ringside Maisie 1941,Ag 1,11:2
Lady Be Good 1941,S 19,27:1

Ship Ahoy 1942,Je 26,16:5
Panama Hattie 1942,O 2,31:2
Du Barry Was a Lady 1943,Ag 20,13:1
Thousands Cheer 1943,S 14,27:1
Two Girls and a Sailor 1944,Je 15,16:1
Meet The People 1944,S 8,16:2
Harvey Girls, The 1946,Ja 25,26:2
Ziegfeld Follies 1946,Mr 23,8:3
Till the Clouds Roll By 1946,D 6,27:4
Show-Off, The 1947,Mr 20,38:2
Merton of the Movies 1947,N 7,20:3

O'Brien, Willie H (Director)

Lost World, The 1925,F 9,15:3

O'Brien, Willis (Miscellaneous)

Mighty Joe Young 1949,Jl 28,19:3
Animal World, The 1956,My 31,21:6

O'Brien-Moore, Erin

Little Men 1935,F 18,19:3
Our Little Girl 1935,Je 7,24:4
Seven Keys to Baldpate 1935,D 14,11:2
Two in the Dark 1936,F 1,9:2
Ex-Mrs Bradford, The 1936,My 28,19:2
Black Legion 1937,Ja 18,21:1
Plough and the Stars, The 1937,Ja 29,15:1
Green Light 1937,F 13,9:1
Life of Emile Zola, The 1937,Ag 12,14:2
Phantom of the Rue Morgue 1954,Mr 20,10:5
Peyton Place 1957,D 13,35:1

Obukhova, V

Mistress, The 1954,My 31,9:2

O'Byrne, Patsy

Outcast 1928,N 26,30:2
Nice Women 1932,F 20,11:2
Doctor Bull 1933,O 6,21:2
Alice in Wonderland 1933,D 23,19:1
It's a Gift 1935,Ja 5,20:2
You Can't Fool Your Wife 1940,My 24,23:4

O'Cahill, Donal

Dawn Over Ireland 1938,F 19,19:2

O'Cahill, Donal (Original Author)

Dawn Over Ireland 1938,F 19,19:2

O'Cahill, Donal (Screenwriter)

Dawn Over Ireland 1938,F 19,19:2

O'Callaghan, Edward G (Original Author)

Flight to Hong Kong 1957,Ja 3,28:2

O'Callaghan, Edward G (Screenwriter)

This Island Earth 1955,Je 11,8:7
Flight to Hong Kong 1957,Ja 3,28:2

O'Callaghan, Richard

Bofors Gun, The 1968,S 23,42:3

O'Callaghan, Sean (Original Author)

Slave Trade in the World Today 1964,N 24,44:1

Ocasek, Viktor

Distant Journey 1950,Ag 28,13:3

O'Casey, Ronan

Give Us This Day 1949,D 21,41:2
Mudlark, The 1950,D 25,25:1
You Can't Beat the Irish 1952,My 1,34:4
1954,S 18,12:4
White Fire 1954,S 18,12:4
1984 1956,O 1,31:1

O'Casey, Sean (Original Author)

Plough and the Stars, The 1937,Ja 29,15:1
Young Cassidy 1965,Mr 23,35:1

Occhini, Haria

Damon and Pythias 1962,S 6,37:2
Tramplers, The 1966,D 8,64:1

Occhini, Ilaria

Carthage in Flames 1961,Ja 26,32:3
Almost a Man 1966,S 23,43:1

Ocenasek, Ladislav

Do You Keep a Lion at Home? 1966,S 18,78:1

Ochman, Martin

Sangen Till Henne; Song to Her, The
1935,F 22,27:3

Ochos, Fernando

Noches de Buenos Aires 1935,D 10,31:3
Noches de Buenos Aires; Buenos Aires Nights
1935,D 12,33:4

Ocko, Dan

Mission to Moscow 1943,Ap 30,25:2
Background to Danger 1943,Jl 3,11:2
Stage Struck 1958,Ap 23,40:1

O'Connell, Arthur

Open Secret 1948,F 2,15:2
Whistle at Eaton Falls, The 1951,O 11,49:2
Picnic 1956,F 17,13:3
Man in the Gray Flannel Suit, The
1956,Ap 13,21:1
Proud Ones, The 1956,Ag 11,10:2
Bus Stop 1956,S 1,19:2
Solid Gold Cadillac, The 1956,O 25,40:3
Operation Mad Ball 1957,N 21,38:1
April Love 1957,N 28,57:2
Monte Carlo Story, The 1958,F 13,23:2
Voice in the Mirror 1958,Ag 14,23:2
Man of the West 1958,O 2,44:3
Gidget 1959,Ap 23,27:4
Anatomy of a Murder 1959,Jl 3,10:1
Violators, The 1959,Ag 4,32:5
Operation Petticoat 1959,D 6,38:1
Hound-Dog Man 1960,Ap 28,29:1
Cimarron 1961,F 17,12:2

O'Connell, Arthur— Cont

Great Impostor, The 1961,Mr 30,24:1
Misty 1961,Jl 18,33:2
Thunder of Drums, A 1961,S 27,35:1
Pocketful of Miracles 1961,D 19,39:1
Follow That Dream 1962,Ag 9,17:7
Kissin' Cousins 1964,Ap 2,28:3
7 Faces of Dr Lao 1964,Jl 23,19:1
Your Cheatin' Heart 1965,My 20,52:2
Third Day, The 1965,Ag 5,15:3
Monkey's Uncle, The 1965,Ag 19,35:4
Great Race, The 1965,S 16,00:0
Silencers, The 1966,Mr 17,35:1
Fantastic Voyage 1966,S 8,43:1
Ride Beyond Vengance 1966,S 29,60:1
Power, The 1968,Mr 7,52:2
If He Hollers, Let Him Go 1968,O 10,59:7

O'Connell, Bob

Strangers in the City 1962,Jl 17,19:2

O'Connell, Helen

I Dood It 1943,N 11,29:1

O'Connell, Hugh

Smiling Lieutenant, The 1931,My 23,13:4
Secrets of a Secretary 1931,Ag 29,16:3
Personal Maid 1931,S 5,7:4
Broadway Thru a Keyhole 1933,N 2,18:3
Gift of Gab 1934,S 26,17:6
Man Who Reclaimed his Head, The
1935,Ja 9,22:1
Good Fairy, The 1935,F 1,18:1
It Happened in New York 1935,Ap 6,10:1
Chinatown Squad 1935,My 30,21:1
Diamond Jim 1935,Ag 24,18:2
Ready, Willing and Able 1937,Mr 15,27:1
Fly Away Baby 1937,Jl 9,18:2
Marry the Girl 1937,Jl 31,6:2
That Certain Woman 1937,S 16,29:1
Perfect Specimen, The 1937,O 28,29:2
Swing Your Lady 1938,Ja 27,17:2
Women Are Like That 1938,Ap 11,12:2
Torchy Blane in Panama 1938,Ap 18,11:1
Accidents Will Happen 1938,Ap 25,19:2
Mystery House 1938,Je 29,15:5
My Favorite Wife 1940,My 31,15:2
Lucky Partners 1940,S 6,25:2
Mad Doctor, The 1941,F 27,23:4
My Life With Caroline 1941,O 30,27:1

O'Connell, Jack (Director)

Greenwich Village Story 1963,Jl 12,14:3
Revolution 1968,Ag 8,27:2

O'Connell, Jack (Producer)

Greenwich Village Story 1963,Jl 12,14:3
Revolution 1968,Ag 8,27:2

O'Connell, Jack (Screenwriter)

Greenwich Village Story 1963,Jl 12,14:3

O'Connell, Marian

Dawn Over Ireland 1938,F 19,19:2

O'Connell, Michael

Jailbreakers, The 1961,Ja 5,27:2

O'Connell, Paddy

Quiet Man, The 1952,Ag 22,13:1

O'Connell, Pierre (Producer)

Under the Paris Sky 1952,My 6,35:1

O'Connell, Thomas Edward (Original Author)

Face Behind the Mask, The 1941,F 7,23:2

O'Connell, William

Way...Way Out 1966,O 27,55:1

O'Conner, Bill

No Orchids for Miss Blandish 1951,F 23,33:2

O'Connolly, J (Director)

Little Ones, The 1965,S 16,55:2
Berserk! 1968,Ja 11,42:2

O'Connolly, J (Producer)

Traitors, The 1963,Je 27,23:4

O'Connolly, J (Screenwriter)

Traitors, The 1963,Je 27,23:4
Little Ones, The 1965,S 16,55:2

O'Connor, Blueboy

Emperor Jones, The 1933,S 20,26:2

O'Connor, Bucky

Spirit of Notre Dame, The 1931,O 16,27:1

O'Connor, Carroll

By Love Possessed 1961,Jl 20,32:2
Belle Sommers 1962,My 31,23:2
Lonely are the Brave 1962,Je 28,21:2
Lad: A Dog 1963,My 2,40:2
Cleopatra 1963,Je 13,29:1
In Harm's Way 1965,Ap 7,36:1
What Did You Do in the War, Daddy?
1966,S 1,28:1
Hawaii 1966,O 11,54:1
Not With my Wife, You Don't! 1966,N 3,45:2
Point Blank 1967,S 19,53:1
Waterhole #3 1967,O 11,41:4
Devil's Brigade, The 1968,My 23,56:2
For Love of Ivy 1968,Jl 18,26:1

O'Connor, Donald

Sing You Sinners 1938,Ag 18,23:1
Sons of the Legion 1938,S 30,24:3
Men With Wings 1938,O 27,27:2
Beau Geste 1939,Ag 3,15:2
Death of a Champion 1939,Ag 24,17:3
On Your Toes 1939,O 21,12:2
What's Cookin' 1942,F 26,15:5

O'Connor, Donald — Cont

Private Buckaroo 1942,Je 25,27:4
Give Out, Sisters 1942,Ag 28,22:3
Get Help to Love 1942,O 19,15:3
It Comes up Love 1943,Ja 22,25:3
When Johnny Comes Marching Home
  1943,Mr 5,20:4
Mister Big 1943,Je 14,13:4
Top Man 1943,O 29,23:2
Chip off the Old Block 1944,Mr 17,14:2
Follow the Boys 1944,Ap 26,24:6
This is the Life 1944,Ap 28,23:3
Merry Monahans, The 1944,O 13,16:2
Patrick the Great 1945,Ap 13,15:2
Something in the Wind 1947,Ag 29,14:3
Are You With It? 1948,Ap 15,31:2
Yes Sir, That's my Baby 1949,N 11,31:2
Francis 1950,Mr 16,40:2
Curtain Call at Cactus Creek 1950,S 22,35:4
Milkman, The 1951,Ja 1,13:6
Double Crossbones 1951,Ap 27,19:2
Francis Goes to the Races 1951,Jl 25,19:2
Singin' in the Rain 1952,Mr 28,27:2
Francis Goes to West Point 1952,Ag 23,10:2
Call Me Madam 1953,Mr 26,37:1
I Love Melvin 1953,Ap 10,18:4
Walking my Baby Back Home 1954,Ja 16,10:5
Francis Joins the Wacs 1954,Jl 31,6:3
There's no Business Like Show Business
  1954,D 17,37:3
Francis in the Navy 1955,Ag 6,13:4
Anything Goes 1956,Mr 22,38:1
Buster Keaton Story, The 1957,Ap 22,31:6
Cry for Happy 1961,Mr 4,16:1
Wonders of Aladdin, The 1961,D 23,16:1
That Funny Feeling 1965,O 21,57:2

O'Connor, Edward

Dangerous Money 1924,O 14,21:5

O'Connor, Edwin (Original Author)

Last Hurrah, The 1958,O 24,40:1

O'Connor, Elsa

Vida de Carlos Gardel, A 1940,Ja 6,9:2
Loco Serenata, El; Crazy Musician, The
  1940,Ap 22,13:2

O'Connor, Frank

Handle with Care 1932,D 24,11:4
As Husbands Go 1934,Ja 26,20:3
Night Club Scandal 1937,N 12,27:2
Our Neighbors-The Carters 1940,F 15,15:2
Man Made Monster 1941,Mr 19,25:4

O'Connor, Frank (Director)

Penrod 1922,F 20,7:1
Go Straight 1925,O 6,30:1

O'Connor, Frank (Original Author)

Devil's Island 1926,Ag 2,21:2
Adventure in Diamonds 1940,Ap 4,27:2
Rising of the Moon, The (The Majesty of the
  Law); Majesty of the Law, The (The Rising of
  the Moon) 1957,Jl 10,23:1
Rising of the Moon, The (1921); 1921 (The Rising
  of the Moon) 1957,Jl 10,23:1
Rising of the Moon, The (A Minute's Wait);
  Minute's Wait, A (The Rising of the Moon)
  1957,Jl 10,23:1

O'Connor, Frank (Screenwriter)

Why Sailors Go Wrong 1928,Ap 9,18:2

O'Connor, Hugh

Footloose Heiress 1937,O 9,16:2

O'Connor, John Rev (Miscellaneous)

Story of the Pope, The 1946,D 20,31:3

O'Connor, Kathleen

Old Homestead, The 1922,O 9,10:2
Wild Bill Hickok 1923,N 21,22:1

O'Connor, Ken (Miscellaneous)

Fun and Fancy Free 1947,S 29,17:2 (In
  Addenda)

O'Connor, L J

Sporting Youth 1924,Ap 2,16:1

O'Connor, Manning (Screenwriter)

Michael Shayne, Private Detective
  1940,D 19,33:2
Dressed to Kill 1941,Ag 22,19:3

O'Connor, Maureen

Boy of the Streets 1938,Ja 24,17:1

O'Connor, Patsy

too Hot To Handle 1938,S 30,24:2
It Ain't Hay 1943,Mr 11,17:3
Quicksand 1950,Je 16,28:4

O'Connor, Robert Emmett

Tin Gods 1926,S 20,21:3
Dressed to Kill 1928,Mr 12,26:1
Four Walls 1928,Ag 20,21:3
Singing Fool, The 1928,S 20,33:2
Smiling Irish Eyes 1929,Jl 24,23:2
Isle of Lost Ships, The 1929,O 26,15:1
Framed 1930,Mr 29,23:1
In the Next Room 1930,Ap 7,21:1
Alias French Gertie 1930,Ap 14,24:2
Big House, The 1930,Je 25,31:2

Shooting Straight 1930,Jl 28,22:1
Paid 1931,Ja 3,21:2
Single Sin. The 1931,Mr 17,34:3
Public Enemy, The 1931,Ap 24,27:1
Fanny Foley Herself 1931,O 26,22:1
Reckless Living 1931,D 5,21:2
Two Kinds of Women 1932,Ja 16,13:1
Night World 1932,My 28,18:2
Dark Horse, The 1932,Je 9,27:3
American Madness 1932,Ag 6,14:5
Blonde Venus 1932,S 24,18:4
Kid From Spain, The 1932,N 18,23:2
Frisco Jenny 1933,Ja 7,11:2
Great Jasper, The 1933,F 17,5:3
Picture Snatcher 1933,My 20,3
Don't Bet on Love 1933,Jl 31,16:2
Lady for a Day 1933,S 8,22:2
Penthouse 1933,S 9,9:2
Big Shakedown, The 1934,F 12,19:2
Bottoms Up 1934,Mr 23,29:2
Return of the Terror 1934,Jl 11,20:2
Mysterious Mr Wong, The 1935,Mr 7,26:1
Star of Midnight 1935,Ap 12,26:5
Stolen Harmony 1935,Ap 20,16:2
Let 'Em Have It 1935,My 30,21:1
Night at the Opera, A 1935,D 7,22:1
Lone Wolf Returns, The 1936,F 4,25:5
Sing Me a Love Song 1936,D 26,15:2
We Who Are About to Die 1937,Ja 2,15:1
Girl Overboard 1937,Mr 1,15:1
Crime Nobody Saw, The 1937,Ap 5,17:2
Super-Sleuth 1937,Jl 17,18:1
Frame-Up 1937,Ag 9,23:2 (In Addenda)
Trapped by G-Men 1937,N 4,29:1
Wells Fargo 1937,D 30,15:2
Boy of the Streets 1938,Ja 24,17:1
Streets of New York 1939,My 1,21:1
Double Alibi 1940,Mr 11,11:2
Hot Steel 1940,Je 21,25:3
Fugitive From Justice, A 1940,Jl 8,13:3
No Time for Comedy 1940,S 7,9:2
Tight Shoes 1941,Je 19,25:2
Air Raid Wardens 1943,Ap 5,15:5
Whistling in Brooklyn 1944,Mr 24,17:3
Boy's Ranch 1946,Ag 9,12:2

O'Connor, T (Miscellaneous)

My Heart Is Calling 1935,Ap 15,16:3

O'Connor, Una

Cavalcade 1933,Ja 6,23:2
Pleasure Cruise 1933,Ap 3,13:3
Mary Stevens, M D 1933,Ag 5,9:6
Invisible Man, The 1933,N 18,18:4
Orient Express 1934,F 28,23:2
Stingaree 1934,My 18,27:1
Chained 1934,S 1,16:2
Barretts of Wimpole Street, The 1934,S 29,12:2
David Copperfield 1935,Ja 19,8:1
Informer, The 1935,My 10,25:2
Bride of Frankenstein, The 1935,My 11,21:2
Perfect Gentleman, The 1935,D 19,33:4
Rose Marie 1936,F 1,9:2
Little Lord Fauntleroy 1936,Ap 3,27:1
Suzy 1936,Jl 25,16:1
Lloyds of London 1936,N 26,39:1
Plough and the Stars, The 1937,Ja 29,15:1
Personal Property 1937,Ap 11,27:2
Call it a Day 1937,My 7,29:2
Adventures of Robin Hood, The 1938,My 13,17:2
We Are not Alone 1939,D 1,27:1
It all Came True 1940,Ap 6,13:2
Lillian Russell 1940,My 18,11:2
Sea Hawk, The 1940,Ag 10,16:2
He Stayed for Breakfast 1940,Ag 31,16:2
Strawberry Blonde 1941,F 22,11:2
Always in my Heart 1942,Mr 14,19:2
My Favorite Spy 1942,My 29,13:4
Random Harvest 1942,D 18,36:6
This Land Is Mine 1943,My 28,19:1
Holy Matrimony 1943,S 16,25:2
Government Girl 1944,Ja 7,13:2
Canterville Ghost, The 1944,Jl 29,16:2
My Pal, Wolf 1944,O 9,17:2
Christmas in Connecticut 1945,Jl 28,7:2
Bells of St Mary's, The 1945,D 7,26:2
Cluny Brown 1946,Je 3,27:3
Return of Monte Cristo, The 1947,Ja 3,16:4

O'Connor, Una — Cont

Lost Honeymoon 1947,Je 20,25:6
Ivy 1947,Je 26,19:1
Corpse came C O D, The 1947,Ag 19,27:2
Fighting Father Dunne 1948,Je 25,26:2
Adventures of Don Juan 1948,D 25,10:1
Witness for the Prosecution 1958,F 7,16:1

O'Conor, Joseph

Oliver! 1968,D 11,57:1

O'Crotty, Peter (Screenwriter)

Vendetta 1950,D 26,19:1

Oda, Masao

Angry Island 1960,F 28,31:1

Odagiri, Miki

Ikiru; To Live 1960,Ja 30,13:5

O'Dare, Eileen

Where the River Shannon Flows 1928,Ja 24,26:3

O'Davoren, Vesey

Clive of India 1935,Ja 18,29:1
Ladies in Love 1936,O 29,31:1
Raffles 1940,Ja 13,11:2

O'DAY

See Also O'DEA

O'Day, Alice

Suicide Legion 1940,My 6,13:3

O'Day, Anita

Jazz on a Summer's Day 1960,Mr 29,46:2

O'Day, Dawn

Spanish Dancer, The 1923,O 8,20:1
Man Who Fights Alone, The 1924,Jl 28,12:2
Fast Set, The 1924,N 18,22:1
Riders of the Purple Sage 1925,Ap 15,16:1
4 Devils 1928,O 4,26:3
Sins of the Fathers 1929,Ja 28,21:1
Gun Smoke 1931,Ap 24,27:1
Rich Man's Folly 1931,N 27,29:3
So Big 1932,Ap 30,19:3
Young America 1932,My 7,11:5
Purchase Price, The 1932,Jl 16,5:5
Life of Jimmy Dolan, The 1933,Je 14,22:3
Finishing School 1934,Ap 30,11:4
Key, The 1934,My 30,14:3

O'Day, Molly

Patent Leather Kid, The 1927,Ag 16,31:2
Hard-Boiled Haggerty 1927,Ag 23,29:4
Lovelorn, The 1927,D 19,30:1
Shepherd of the Hills, The 1928,F 20,14:1
Kentucky Courage 1928,My 14,25:1
Sob Sister 1931,O 3,20:2
Life of Vergie Winters, The 1934,Je 15,26:1

O'Day, Nell

Rackety Rax 1932,N 5,12:5
Road to Ruin, The 1934,F 21,23:2
Flight Angels 1940,My 27,23:2
Back Street 1941,F 12,25:2
Never Give a Sucker an Even Break
  1941,O 27,21:2
Mystery of Marie Roget, The 1942,My 5,17:3

Oddo, Jerry

From Hell to Texas 1958,Je 5,39:2

Ode, Eric

Ja, Treu Ist die Soldatenliebe 1934,Ap 28,11:4
Jungfrau Gegen Moench; Maiden vs Monk
  1935,Mr 16,19:2
Zigeunerblut 1935,Ap 8,23:5

Ode, Eric (Director)

Wonderful Times 1951,Ap 24,35:2

O'DEA

See Also O'DAY

O'Dea, Denis

Plough and the Stars, The 1937,Ja 29,15:1
Odd Man Out 1947,Ap 24,30:2
Under Capricorn 1949,S 9,28:3
Fallen Idol, The 1949,N 16,39:2
Treasure Island 1950,Ag 16,24:2
Long Dark Hall, The 1951,My 10,38:3
Captain Horatio Hornblower 1951,S 14,21:2
Marry Me 1952,Mr 14,27:3
Never Take No for an Answer 1952,Ap 29,32:2
Niagara 1953,Ja 22,20:3
Landfall 1953,My 11,25:2
Sea Devils 1953,Jl 31,11:5
Mogambo 1953,O 2,18:1
Rising of the Moon, The (1921) 1957,Jl 10,23:1
Rising of the Moon, The (The Majesty of the
  Law) 1957,Jl 10,23:1
Darby O'Gill and the Little People 1959,Jl 1,26:1
Esther and the King 1960,N 19,13:4

O'Dea, Jimmy

Ireland's Border Line 1939,O 13,27:3
Rising of the Moon, The (A Minute's Wait)
  1957,Jl 10,23:1
Darby O'Gill and the Little People 1959,Jl 1,26:1
Johnny Nobody 1965,N 24,35:1

O'Dea, John (Screenwriter)

Admiral Was a Lady, The 1950,O 13,23:3
Fugitive Lady 1951,Ag 25,7:2

O'Dea, Joseph

Quiet Man, The 1952,Ag 22,13:1
Rising of the Moon, The (1921) 1957,Jl 10,23:1

O'Dea, Judith
Night of the Living Dead 1968,D 5,59:2
O'Dea, Ken
Safe at Home 1941,N 26,31:2
O'Dea, Sunnie
Strike Me Pink 1936,Ja 17,15:2
Show Boat 1936,My 15,29:4
Moonlight in Hamaii 1941,O 10,26:6
O'Dell, Denis (Producer)
Playboy of the Western World, The
1963,Mr 19,8:2
O'Dell, Janette
Spirit of Youth 1938,F 28,19:1
O'Dell, Scott (Original Author)
Island of the Blue Dolphins 1964,Jl 4,8:2
Odemar, Franz
Skandal Um Eva 1931,Ap 21,35:2
Odemar, Fritz
Das Lied ist Aus 1932,Ja 29,13:2
Raub der Mona Lisa, Der 1932,Mr 30,15:2
Liebeskommando 1932,Ap 27,13:6
1914: The Last Days Before the War 1932,S 5,9:6
Eine Tuer geht Auf 1933,F 6,11:5
Ich Will Nicht Wissen Wer Du Bist
1933,F 16,23:2
Hertha's Erwachen 1933,Mr 14,18:3 (Incorrect in
this edition; use 1933,Mr 14,19:2 elsewhere)
M 1933,Ap 3,13:3
Toller Einfall, Ein 1934,My 21,20:3
Roman Einer Nacht 1934,Je 22,24:2
Schuss im Morgengrauen 1934,S 29,12:3
Frau wie Du, Eine 1934,D 24,17:3
Viktor und Viktoria 1935,Ja 28,10:5
Ich Sing Mich in Dein Herz Hinein
1935,Je 3,22:3
Gruen ist die Heide 1935,O 14,21:2
Herr Kobin Geht auf Abenteuer; Mr Kobin Seeks
Adventure 1935,N 26,28:2
Zwichen Zwei Herzen; Between Two Hearts
1936,Ja 28,15:3
Knock-Out 1936,F 29,11:2
Junge Graf, Der 1936,D 14,15:2
Gross Reinemachen; General Housecleaning
1938,Je 23,27:2
Teufelskerl, Ein; Devil of a Fellow, A
1938,O 1,10:3
Familie Schimek 1939,S 2,20:2
Arme Millionar, Der; Poor Millionaire, The
1939,D 30,9:2
Film Without a Name 1950,O 20,32:2
Oden, Elisabeth
Doll, The 1964,Ja 14,27:1
Odets, Clifford (Director)
None but the Lonely Heart 1944,N 18,16:6
Story of Page One, The 1960,Ja 14,28:1
Odets, Clifford (Original Author)
Golden Boy 1939,S 8,28:2
Clash by Night 1952,Je 19,32:6
Country Girl, The 1954,D 16,51:2
Big Knife, The 1955,N 9,41:2
Odets, Clifford (Screenwriter)
General Died at Dawn, The 1936,S 3,17:2
Black Sea Fighters 1943,Jl 28,18:3
None but the Lonely Heart 1944,N 18,16:6
Deadline at Dawn 1946,Ap 4,33:2
Humoresque 1946,D 26,28:1
Sweet Smell of Success 1957,Je 28,29:2
Story of Page One, The 1960,Ja 14,28:1
Wild in the Country 1961,Je 10,12:2
Odetta
Last Time I saw Paris, The 1954,N 19,20:2
Sanctuary 1961,F 22,31:1
Festival 1967,O 24,53:2
Odette, Mary
Edmund Kean, Prince Among Lovers
1927,Je 1,25:2
Odin, Susan
Girls in the Night 1953,Ja 16,19:3
Eddie Cantor Story, The 1953,D 26,10:2
Odlum, Bruce (Producer)
Spanish Affair 1958,F 6,24:1
Odlum, Jerome (Original Author)
Each Dawn I Die 1939,Jl 22,12:2
Dust Be my Destiny 1939,O 7,11:2
Nine Lives Are not Enough 1941,O 30,27:2
I Was Framed 1942,Je 12,16:6
In old Sacramento 1946,Ap 29,24:4
Song of India 1949,Je 10,32:3
Never Trust a Gambler 1951,Jl 20,14:2
Odlum, Jerome (Screenwriter)
Crime Doctor 1943,Jl 5,11:4
Never Trust a Gambler 1951,Jl 20,14:2
Highway Dragnet 1954,F 20,8:7
O'Doherty, Mignon
There Goes the Bride 1933,Mr 4,11:3
Faithful Heart 1933,Ag 15,20:2
Autumn Crocus 1934,O 25,26:2
O'Donavan, Harry (Director)
Ireland's Border Line 1939,O 13,27:3
O'Donavan, Harry (Producer)
Ireland's Border Line 1939,O 13,27:3

O'Donnell, Cathy
Best Years of our Lives, The 1946,N 22,27:2
Bury Me Dead 1947,O 25,13:3
They Live by Night 1949,N 4,33:2
Side Street 1950,Mr 24,29:2
Miniver Story, The 1950,O 27,24:2
Never Trust a Gambler 1951,Jl 20,14:2
Detective Story 1951,N 7,35:2
Woman's Angle, The 1954,Ag 27,11:6
Eight O'Clock Walk 1955,Ap 30,10:6
Mad at the World 1955,My 14,10:8
Man From Laramie, The 1955,S 1,20:2
Story of Mankind, The 1957,N 9,31:2
Ben Hur 1959,N 19,50:2
O'Donnell, Erin
Saintly Sinners 1962,Mr 29,28:2
Incident in an Alley 1962,My 17,31:1
O'Donnell, Gene
Ape, The 1940,N 28,28:3
Corvette K-225 1943,O 21,30:1
O'Donnell, Jack (Screenwriter)
Silver Streak, The 1935,Ja 16,21:1
O'Donnell, Jacklyn
Young Jesse James 1960,Ag 25,25:1
O'Donnell, James (Screenwriter)
Two-Headed Spy, The 1959,Mr 3,38:4
O'Donnell, Jean
Flight Angels 1940,My 27,23:2
O'Donnell, Maire
Home Is the Hero 1961,Ja 26,32:1
O'Donnell, Peggy
Stage Door 1937,O 8,27:2
O'Donnell, Peter (Original Author)
Modesty Blaise 1966,Ag 11,27:1
O'Donnell, Peter (Screenwriter)
Vengance of She, The 1968,My 30,21:4
O'Donnell, Spec
Country Kid, The 1923,O 30,16:1
Dressmaker from Paris, The 1925,Mr 18,19:2
Little Annie Rooney 1925,O 19,26:1
Sparrows 1926,S 20,21:3
Private Izzy Murphy 1926,N 10,25:1
Casey at the Bat 1927,Ap 4,30:5
We're all Gamblers 1927,O 12,30:6
Danger Street 1928,S 25,29:4 (In Addenda)
Sophomore, The 1929,Ag 24,11:5
Young America 1932,My 7,11:5
Big Broadcast, The 1932,O 15,13:1
Fish 1936,Ja 25,18:5
Freshman Love 1936,Ja 25,18:5
Love Is on the Air 1937,N 12,27:3
Accidents Will Happen 1938,Ap 25,19:2
Always Leave Them Laughing 1949,N 24,48:2
Laurel and Hardy's Laughing 20's 1965,N 18,55:2
O'Donohue, J T (Screenwriter)
Kindred of the Dust 1922,Ag 28,14:1
O'Donovan, Elizabeth
Doctor Faustus 1968,F 7,38:1
O'Donovan, Fred
Another Shore 1951,F 12,19:3
O'Dowd, Mike
On the Waterfront 1954,Jl 29,18:1
O'Driscoll, Martha
Secret of Dr Kildare, The 1939,D 8,33:5
Judge Hardy and Son 1940,Ja 18,27:3 (In
Addenda)
Forty Little Mothers 1940,Ap 19,25:2
Lady Eve, The 1941,F 26,17:1
Henry Aldrich for President 1941,O 18,22:2
Pacific Blackout 1942,Ja 15,25:2
Reap the Wild Wind 1942,Mr 27,27:2
We've Never Been Licked 1943,Ag 19,23:1
Fallen Sparrow, The 1943,Ag 20,13:1
Crazy House 1943,D 16,33:3
Follow the Boys 1944,Ap 26,24:6
Ghost Catchers 1944,My 31,22:3
Here Come the Co-Eds 1945,F 19,21:1
Shady Lady 1945,O 11,26:2
Daltons Ride Again, The 1945,D 8,21:2
House of Dracula 1945,D 22,16:3
Criminal Court 1946,N 16,15:3
Carnegie Hall 1947,My 3,10:2
Oehmen, Rita
Gun Law 1938,Je 24,15:1
Oerdog, Sari
Vadroza; Wild Rose 1940,Ja 29,11:6
Oerlemans, Jacques
Man Escaped, A 1957,Ag 27,33:2
Oertel, Curt (Director)
Schimmelreiter, Der; Rider of the White Horse,
The 1935,F 25,13:3
Oertel, Curt (Miscellaneous)
Titan-Story of Michelangelo, The 1950,Ja 23,16:2
Oertl, Eva
Artists Under the Big Top Perplexed
1968,S 27,34:1
Oesterreicher, R (Original Author)
Garden of Eden, The 1928,Mr 19,26:2
Once a Lady 1931,N 9,22:4
Her Majesty, Love 1931,N 26,37:2
Ihre Majestaet die Liebe 1933,F 7,23:4

O'Farrell, Bernadette
Captain Boycott 1947,D 6,11:2
Happiest Days of Your Life, The 1950,S 18,19:2
Gilbert and Sullivan 1953,O 28,36:3
Bridal Path, The 1959,D 21,34:2
O'Farrell, Broderick
What Happened to Jones 1926,F 9,22:1
No More Orchids 1933,Ja 2,29:2
Shot in the Dark, A 1935,My 22,23:2
O'Farrell, William (Original Author)
Repeat Performance 1947,Jl 2,19:2
O'Farril, Alberta
No Mataras; Thou Shalt not Kill 1935,N 11,20:2
O'Ferrall, George More (Director)
Holly and the Ivy, The 1954,F 5,16:1
Angels One Five 1954,Ap 30,28:2
Heart of the Matter, The 1954,N 19,20:2
Green Scarf, The 1955,Ja 15,10:2
Three Cases of Murder (Lord Mountdrago); Lord
Mountdrago (Three Cases of Murder)
1955,Mr 16,39:4
Three Cases of Murder (You Killed Elizabeth);
You Killed Elizabeth (Three Cases of Murder)
1955,Mr 16,39:4
Three Cases of Murder (In the Picture); In the
Picture (Three Cases of Murder)
1955,Mr 16,39:4
Offenbach, Jacques (Composer)
Affairs of Maupassant, The 1938,F 12,20:2
Offenbach, Jacques (Original Author)
Tales of Hoffmann 1951,Ap 5,34:2
Offenbach, Joseph
Montpi 1959,Ap 21,40:1
Offer, Harold
Smiling Faces 1932,Ag 31,12:3
Offerman, George
Girl on the Barge, The 1929,F 26,31:1
Mayor of Hell, The 1933,Jl 1,16:5
Action in the North Atlantic 1943,My 22,10:2
People Will Talk 1951,Ag 30,20:1
With a Song in my Heart 1952,Ap 5,20:2
Offerman, George Jr
Grand Old Girl 1935,F 26,16:4
Black Fury 1935,Ap 11,27:2
Jalna 1935,S 14,8:4
Chatterbox 1936,F 15,18:6
Scandal Street 1938,F 5,19:2 (In Addenda)
Crime School 1938,My 11,17:2
Calling Dr Kildare 1939,My 12,25:4
Prison Camp 1940,Ag 3,9:3
See Here Private Hargrove 1944,Mr 22,17:2
Walk in the Sun, A 1946,Ja 12,10:6
Offley, Hilda
Miracle in Harlem 1949,O 24,19:4
Offner, Mortimer (Screenwriter)
Alice Adams 1935,Ag 16,11:3
Sylvia Scarlett 1936,Ja 10,16:2
Quality Street 1937,Ap 9,19:2
Soldier and the Lady, The 1937,Ap 10,11:1
Radio City Revels 1938,Mr 21,18:3
Saint in New York, The 1938,My 26,31:2
Little Tough Guys in Society 1938,N 21,14:4
Family Next Door, The 1939,Ap 28,31:2
O'Flaherty, Liam (Original Author)
Informer, The 1935,My 10,25:2
Last Desire 1939,D 22,15:2
Up Tight 1968,D 19,62:1
O'Flaherty, Liam (Screenwriter)
Devil's Playground 1937,F 15,12:5
Last Desire 1939,D 22,15:2
O'Flynn, Damian
Marked Woman 1937,Ap 12,15:2
Lady Scarface 1941,Ag 4,16:6
Great Man's Lady, The 1942,Ap 30,14:3
Broadway 1942,Je 5,23:2
Powder Town 1942,Je 8,11:2
Wake Island 1942,S 2,19:2
Flight for Freedom 1943,Ap 16,24:2
Sarong Girl 1943,Je 18,16:6
Crack-Up 1946,S 7,11:1
Bachelor's Daughters, The 1946,O 7,23:2
Snake Pit, the 1948,N 5,29:2
Outpost in Morocco 1949,Mr 25,28:3
Gambling House 1951,Mr 19,23:2
Inside the Walls of Folsom Prison
1951,My 28,17:4
Miami Story, The 1954,My 15,13:2
Eighteen and Anxious 1957,D 14,16:6
O'Flynn, Philip
Rooney 1958,Je 6,29:2
Broth of a Boy 1959,D 28,18:1
Poacher's Daughter, The 1960,F 16,31:2
Home Is the Hero 1961,Ja 26,32:1
Young Cassidy 1965,Mr 23,35:1
Oganesyan, G (Director)
Ladies 1955,Je 27,18:2
Springtime on the Volga 1961,D 25,27:4
Oganesyan, G (Screenwriter)
Ladies 1955,Je 27,18:2

Ogasawara, Kelko
Ballad of Narayama 1961,Je 20,27:1
O'Gatty, Jimmy
East of the River 1940,O 28,21:2
Ogawa, Toranosuke
Street of Shame 1959,Je 5,17:2
Ogawa, Y
Slums of Tokyo 1930,Jl 7,22:3
Lost Sex 1968,Jl 23,27:2
Ogden, Edward
Dr Crippen 1964,F 15,14:1
Ogden, George Washington (Original Author)
Bond Boy, The 1922,O 9,10:2
Ogden, Vivia
Mrs Wiggs of the Cabbage Patch 1919,F 17,11:3
Denial, The 1925,Mr 10,19:3
Slave of Fashion, A 1925,Jl 21,26:2
Thank You 1925,O 6,30:1
Lovey Mary 1926,Je 21,17:2
Fire Brigade, The 1926,D 21,20:2
Way Down East 1931,Mr 16,25:1
Ogden, Vivien
Unguarded Hour, The 1926,Ja 5,25:2 (In Addenda)
Oger, Claudine
Testament of Orpheus 1962,Ap 10,48:1
Ogg, Sammy
Miracle of Our Lady Fatima, The 1952,Ag 21,16:2
Mister Scoutmaster 1953,Ag 29,10:1
Ogilvy, Ian
Day the Fish Came Out, The 1967,O 3,57:1
Conqueror Worm, The 1968,Ag 15,46:2
Ogle, Charles
Too Many Millions 1918,D 9,11:4
Squaw Man, The 1918,D 30,7:3
Lottery Man, The 1919,N 17,20:1
Hawthorne of the U.S.A. 1919,N 17,20:1
Treasure Island 1920,Ap 12,13:1
Conrad in Quest of his Youth 1920,N 8,20:2
Affairs of Anatol, The 1921,S 12,16:1
Miss Lulu Bett 1921,D 25,VI,2:1
Young Rajah, The 1922,N 6,13:1
Thirty Days 1922,D 11,22:1
Sixty Cents an Hour 1923,My 15,22:1
Garrison's Finish 1923,My 28,18:2
Ruggles of Red Gap 1923,S 10,15:4
Flaming Barriers 1924,Ja 29,16:1
Secrets 1924,Mr 25,25:2
Triumph 1924,Ap 21,21:4
Bedroom Window, The 1924,Je 9,14:3
Merton of the Movies 1924,S 8,15:3
Alaskan, The 1924,S 15,28:1
Garden of Weeds, The 1924,N 4,24:1
Golden Bed, The 1925,Ja 20,18:2
Contraband 1925,Mr 24,20:6
Code of the West 1925,Ap 13,24:1
One Minute to Play 1926,S 6,16:2
Flaming Forest, The 1926,N 22,28:3
Ognivisev, A
Rimsky-Korsakov 1954,Mr 1,16:3
O'Gorman, W
Adventures, The 1947,Ap 4,19:2
O'Grady, Monty
Sparrows 1926,S 20,21:3
O'Grady, Rohan (Original Author)
Let's Kill Uncle 1966,N 19,26:1
Oguni, Hideo (Screenwriter)
Magnificent Seven, The 1956,N 20,46:2
Ikiru; To Live 1960,Ja 30,13:5
Throne of Blood 1961,N 23,50:2
Hidden Fortress The 1962,Ja 24,24:2
Lower Depths, The 1962,F 10,12:5
Bad Sleep Well, The 1963,Ja 23,5:2
Sanjuro 1963,My 8,34:2
I Live in Fear; Ikimono no Kiroku 1967,Ja 26,25:1
Red Beard 1968,D 20,60:4
O'Hanlon, George
New Wine 1942,F 2,11:2
Spirit of West Point 1947,O 3,31:1
Are You With It? 1948,Ap 15,31:2
June Bride 1948,O 30,10:2
Zamba 1949,N 7,33:2
Tanks are Coming, The 1951,D 6,42:4
Lion and the Horse, The 1952,My 19,12:2
Park Row 1952,D 22,20:2
Kronos 1957,My 11,24:6
O'Hanlon, George (Director)
Rookie, The 1960,Mr 17,28:1
O'Hanlon, George (Screenwriter)
Rookie, The 1960,Mr 17,28:1
For Those Who Think Young 1964,Jl 9,27:1
O'Hanlon, James (Miscellaneous)
Two Sisters From Boston 1946,Je 7,16:2
Song of the Thin Man 1947,Ag 29,14:2
Great Rupert, The 1950,Ap 14,27:2
O'Hanlon, James (Original Author)
Over my Dead Body 1942,D 26,15:2
Maisie Goes to Reno 1944,S 29,18:1
Lucky Me 1954,Ap 10,11:2

O'Hanlon, James (Screenwriter)
Sahara 1943,N 12,25:2
Harvey Girls, The 1946,Ja 25,26:2
Three Wise Fools 1946,S 27,19:2
Destination Moon 1950,Je 28,32:2
Milkman, The 1951,Ja 1,13:6
Miracle of Our Lady Fatima, The 1952,Ag 21,16:2
Stop, You're Killing Me 1952,D 11,45:3
Calamity Jane 1953,N 5,40:2
Lucky Me 1954,Ap 10,11:2
Conquest of Space 1955,My 28,7:6
For Those Who Think Young 1964,Jl 9,27:1
O'Hara, Barry
World Dances 1954,N 8,24:6
Chuka 1967,N 2,58:3
O'Hara, Fiske
Paddy the Next Best Thing 1933,Ag 25,12:2
Change of Heart 1934,My 11,24:2
O'Hara, Geoffrey (Composer)
Tin Pan Alley 1940,N 22,27:3
O'Hara, George
Crossroads of New York, The 1922,My 22,18:4
Sea Hunt, The 1926,Ja 16,8:5
Sea Beast, The 1926,Ja 16,8:5
Why Girls Go Back Home 1926,My 18,28:2
Bigger Than Barnum's 1926,Jl 13,19:3
O'Hara, Gerry (Director)
Pleasure Girls, The 1966,Ap 21,43:1
O'Hara, Gerry (Screenwriter)
Pleasure Girls, The 1966,Ap 21,43:1
O'Hara, Henry
Gentleman Jim 1942,N 26,40:3
O'Hara, Jim
Garden of Eden 1957,D 18,45:3
Deadly Companions, The 1962,Ap 12,41:7
O'Hara, Joan
Home Is the Hero 1961,Ja 26,32:1
O'Hara, John
Too Busy to Work 1932,D 3,21:4
General Died at Dawn, The 1936,S 3,17:2
O'Hara, John (Miscellaneous)
Miracle Can Happen, A 1948,F 4,28:4
O'Hara, John (Original Author)
Best Things in Life are Free, The 1956,S 29,12:2
Pal Joey 1957,O 28,30:1
Ten North Frederick 1958,My 23,29:2
From the Terrace 1960,Jl 16,10:1
Butterfield 8 1960,N 17,46:1
Rage to Live, A 1965,O 21,57:1
O'Hara, John (Screenwriter)
I Was an Adventuress 1940,My 20,13:2
Moontide 1942,Ap 30,14:1
O'Hara, Kareen
Any Gun Can Play 1968,S 14,34:2
O'Hara, Mary (Original Author)
My Friend Flicka 1943,My 27,21:4
Thunderhead 1945,Mr 16,21:2
Green Grass of Wyoming 1948,Je 10,28:3
O'Hara, Mary (Screenwriter)
Turn to the Right 1922,Ja 24,11:1
Prisoner of Zenda, The 1922,Ag 1,14:3
O'Hara, Maureen
Jamaica Inn 1939,O 12,33:1
Hunchback of Notre Dame, The 1940,Ja 1,29:2
Bill of Divorcement, A 1940,Jl 12,11:2
Dance, Girl, Dance 1940,O 11,25:2
How Green Was my Valley 1941,O 29,27:2
To the Shores of Tripoli 1942,Mr 26,27:2
Ten Gentlemen From West Point 1942,Je 5,23:3
Black Swan, The 1942,D 24,18:3
Immortal Sergeant 1943,F 4,29:2
This Land Is Mine 1943,My 28,19:1
Fallen Sparrow, The 1943,Ag 20,13:1
Buffalo Bill 1944,Ap 20,22:6
Spanish Main, The 1945,N 7,20:2
Sentimental Journey 1946,Mr 7,33:2
Do You Love Me 1946,My 25,12:2
Sinbad the Sailor 1947,Ja 23,31:2
Homestretch, The 1947,Ap 24,30:2
Miracle on 34th Street 1947,Je 5,32:1
Foxes of Harrow, The 1947,S 25,35:4
Sitting Pretty 1948,Mr 11,35:2
Forbidden Street, The 1949,My 14,9:2
Father Was a Fullback 1949,O 13,33:3
Bagdad 1949,D 24,11:4
Comanche Territory 1950,Ap 8,9:3
Tripoli 1950,N 10,35:2
Rio Grande 1950,N 20,21:2
Flame of Araby 1951,D 20,41:7
At Swords Point 1952,Ap 10,37:1
Kangaroo 1952,My 17,22:7
Quiet Man, The 1952,Ag 22,13:1
Against all Flags 1952,D 25,34:6
Redhead From Wyoming, The 1953,Ja 9,17:4
Fire over Africa 1954,N 22,29:5
Long Gray Line, The 1955,F 11,19:2
Magnificent Matador, The 1955,My 25,38:1
Lady Godiva 1955,D 3,13:3
Lisbon 1956,Ag 30,19:2
Wings of Eagles, The 1957,F 1,28:1
Our Man in Havana 1960,Ja 28,26:1
Parent Trap, The 1961,Je 22,23:1

O'Hara, Maureen — Cont
Deadly Companions, The 1962,Ap 12,41:7
Mr Hobbs Takes a Vacation 1962,Je 16,11:2
Spencer's Mountain 1963,My 17,26:6
McLintock 1963,N 14,41:3
Battle of the Villa Fiorita, The 1965,My 27,28:1
Rare Breed, The 1966,Ap 14,42:3
O'Hara, Michael (Screenwriter)
Summer Storm 1944,O 23,14:3
O'Hara, Shirley
Gentleman of Paris, A 1927,O 3,20:1
Wild Party, The 1929,Ap 2,28:4
Tarzan and the Amazons 1945,Ap 30,13:4
Chase, The 1946,N 18,31:2
Ohberg, Ake
En Saga 1938,Ja 8,19:2
Fram for Framgang; Head for Success 1938,N 28,11:3
O'Hearn, Eileen
Parachute Nurse 1942,Jl 27,18:2
O'Herlihy, Dan
Odd Man Out 1947,Ap 24,30:2
Hungry Hill 1947,O 11,11:2
Larceny 1948,S 4,8:6
Macbeth 1950,D 28,22:6
Soldiers Three 1951,Mr 30,28:5
At Swords Point 1952,Ap 10,37:1
Actors and Sin; (Actor's Blood) 1952,My 30,11:3
Operation Secret 1952,N 6,37:2
Invasion USA 1953,Ap 30,39:4
Adventures of Robinson Crusoe, The 1954,Ag 6,10:5
Black Shield of Falworth, The 1954,O 7,16:2
Bengal Brigade 1954,N 13,13:2
Purple Mask, The 1955,Je 16,35:7
Virgin Queen, The 1955,Ag 6,13:2
Home Before Dark 1958,N 7,23:1
Imitation of Life 1959,Ap 18,18:1
One Foot in Hell 1960,O 20,42:2
Night Fighters, The 1960,D 15,59:1
King of the Roaring Twenties 1961,O 5,43:1
Cabinet of Caligari, The 1962,My 26,13:5
Fail Safe 1964,S 16,36:1
O'Herlihy, Dan (Narrator)
Hunters of the Deep 1954,D 17,37:4
O'Herlihy, Michael (Director)
Fighting Prince of Donegal, The 1966,N 10,64:1
One and Only Genuine Original Family Band, The 1968,Mr 22,55:1
Ohi, Fumio (Miscellaneous)
New Japanese Cinema, The (Folk Mithology); Folk Mithology (The New Japanese Cinema) 1968,My 3,42:1
O'Higgins, Brian
No Resting Place 1952,My 5,18:5
O'Higgins, Harvey (Miscellaneous)
I Married a Doctor 1936,Ap 20,17:1
O'Higgins, Harvey J (Original Author)
Dummy, The 1929,Mr 4,20:2
Argyle Case, The 1929,Ag 31,13:4
Make Your own Bed 1944,My 27,12:2
Ohilippi, Charles (Miscellaneous)
Pinocchio 1940,F 8,18:3
Ohimarks, Ake (Screenwriter)
Pimpernel Svensson 1953,F 6,16:4
Ohlason, Henning (Original Author)
Surf, The 1949,D 17,15:2
Ohlin, Anna
Raggen, Det Aer Jag Det 1936,My 22,19:1
Ohlin, Nils
Flickorna Fran Gamla Stan 1934,D 27,25:4
Ohlschager, Werner
Berliner, The 1952,O 28,37:1
Ohlsson, Bertil (Producer)
Hunger 1968,Ag 13,45:2
Ohlsson, Henning
Haelsingar 1934,S 25,25:2
Ohman, Marie
Hugo and Josephine 1968,S 30,60:1
Ohmart, Carol
Wild Party, The 1956,D 22,13:1
House on Haunted Hill 1959,Mr 12,27:5
One Man's Way 1964,Mr 12,40:3
Ohnet, Georges (Original Author)
Iron Master, The 1933,F 4,11:3
Ohono, Tadashi (Producer)
Woman in the Dunes; Suno no Onna 1964,S 17,52:1
Ohtani, Ryuzo (Producer)
Ballad of Narayama 1961,Je 20,27:1
Ohtsuki, Masako
Beach Red 1967,Ag 4,18:1
Ohya, Ichijobo
Temptress and the Monk, The 1963,My 28,32:1
Oikononmou, Parazkeur
Dr Epameinondas 1938,Ap 5,19:6
Oine (Producer)
One Body too Many 1944,N 25,21:2
Ojeda, Manuel R (Director)
Judas 1937,Ap 26,15:2
Circo Tragic, El; Tragic Circus, The 1939,Je 17,12:3

Okabe, Michio (Miscellaneous)
New Japanese Cinema, The (The Doctrine of
Creation); Doctrine of Creation, The (The New
Japanese Cimema) 1968,My 3,42:1
Okada, Eiji
Hiroshima 1955,My 17,32:1
Hiroshima, Mon Amour 1960,My 17,43:1
Ugly American, The 1963,Ap 12,30:2
Woman in the Dunes; Suno no Onna
1964,S 17,52:1
She and He 1964,S 26,16:1
Okada, Mariko
Samurai 1956,Ja 10,26:1
Samurai (Part II) 1967,O 21,16:1
Secret Scrolls-Part II; Ninjitsu 1968,My 23,56:3
Illusion of Blood 1968,N 28,66:5
Okami, Jojiro (Original Author)
Mysterians, The 1959,Jl 2,15:2
Okami, Jotaro (Original Author)
Battle in Outer Space 1960,Jl 9,10:5
Okamoto, Ken K
Go for Broke 1951,My 25,31:2
Okamoto, Kibachi (Director)
Samurai Assassin 1965,Mr 19,27:5
Sword of Doom, The 1967,Ap 15,35:2
Okawa, Henry
Three Stripes in the Sun 1955,N 24,41:2
Bridge on the River Kwai 1957,D 19,39:1
Wind Cannot Read, The 1960,Mr 10,36:1
Okawa, Hiroshi (Producer)
Magic Boy 1963,D 23,18:2
Okawa, Hoirachiro
Tokyo File 212 1951,Je 1,20:7
Okazaki, Bob
Girl Named Tamiku, A 1963,Mr 15,8:2
O'Keefe, Dennis
Bad Man of Brimstone, The 1938,F 4,17:2
Hold That Kiss 1938,Je 11,9:1
Chaser, The 1938,Ag 2,15:3
Vacation From Love 1938,N 10,33:2
Unexpected Father 1939,Ag 11,12:2
That's Right, You're Wrong 1939,N 30,25:3
Alias the Deacon 1940,My 14,27:5
Conga Nights, La 1940,Je 5,33:5
Pop Always Pays 1940,Ag 30,16:6
Arise my Love 1940,O 17,33:2
You'll Find Out 1940,N 15,25:2
Topper Returns 1941,Mr 28,26:6
Mr District Attorney 1941,Ap 17,29:3
Broadway Limited 1941,Je 16,11:6
Lady Scarface 1941,Ag 4,16:6
Week End for Three 1941,O 24,27:4
Hangmen Also Die 1943,Ap 16,24:2
Good Morning, Judge 1943,Ap 30,25:4
Tahiti Honey 1943,My 13,17:2
Leopard Man, The 1943,My 20,26:4
Hi Diddle Diddle 1943,S 24,26:2
Fighting Seabees, The 1944,Mr 20,14:2
Up in Mabel's Room 1944,Ap 22,8:6
Story of Dr Wassell, The 1944,Je 7,13:2
Sensations of 1945 1944,Jl 7,13:2
Abroad With two Yanks 1944,O 26,19:7
Affairs of Susan, The 1945,Mr 29,18:2
Earl Carroll Vanities, 1945,Ap 2,15:6
Brewster's Millions 1945,Ap 27,23:2
Getting Gertie's Garter 1946,F 4,21:2
Doll Face 1946,Mr 28,35:3
Mr District Attorney 1947,F 28,27:3
Dishonored Lady 1947,My 24,10:5
T-Men 1948,Ja 23,28:3
Raw Deal 1948,Jl 9,11:4
Walk a Crooked Mile 1948,O 13,31:2
Siren of Atlantis 1949,Ag 22,13:1
Abandoned Woman 1949,O 27,35:3
Great Dan Patch, The 1949,N 9,37:2
Eagle and the Hawk, The 1950,Jl 6,31:2
Woman on the Run 1950,N 30,24:2
Company She Keeps, The 1951,Ja 29,14:4
Follow the Sun 1951,Ap 26,34:4
Passage West 1951,Ag 31,12:2
Everything I Have is Yours 1952,O 30,40:5
Lady Wants Mink, The 1953,Ap 6,24:2
Drums of Tahiti 1954,Ap 24,14:5
Diamond Wizard, The 1954,Jl 17,7:4
Angela 1955,Je 4,9:2
Las Vegas Shakedown 1955,Je 18,14:2
Chicago Syndicate 1955,Je 21,37:1
Inside Detroit 1956,Ja 28,10:5
Dragoon Wells Massacre 1957,My 6,25:2
All Hands on Deck 1961,Ap 1,10:2
O'Keefe, Dennis (Director)
Diamond Wizard, The 1954,Jl 17,7:4
Angela 1955,Je 4,9:2
O'Keefe, Dennis (Miscellaneous)
Black Knight, The 1954,O 29,27:2
O'Keeffe, Walter (Original Author)
Go Chase Yourself 1938,Je 15,27:1
O'Kelly, Erin
Close-Up 1948,Ap 5,24:2
O'Kelly, Tim
Targets 1968,Ag 14,34:1

Okhlopkov, N
Men and Jobs 1933,Ja 3,19:3
Lenin in October 1938,Ap 2,18:1
Alexander Nevsky 1939,Mr 23,27:1
Lenin in 1918 1939,Je 27,27:2
1812 1944,S 11,14:1
Far for Moscow 1951,Jl 2,16:6
Oki, Minoru
Imposter, The 1955,Mr 23,27:1
Okochi, Denjiro
Men Who Tread on the Tiger's Tail, The
1960,Ja 11,35:7
Secret Scrolls-Part II; Ninjitsu 1968,My 23,56:3
Okuda, Kikumaru (Original Author)
None but the Brave 1965,F 25,24:1
Okumura, Teruo (Miscellaneous)
New Japanese Cinema, The (The Reprieve, Or a Man
Possessed of his Shadow); Reprieve, Or a Man
Possessed of his Shadow (The New Japanese
Cinema) 1968,My 3,42:1
Okunevskaya, T
Red Army Days 1935,O 21,22:4
Last Night, The 1937,Ap 28,18:3
Okuyama, Nagaharu (Screenwriter)
Walleyed Nippon 1963,S 3,36:1
Olaf, Pierre
Wild and Wonderful 1964,Je 11,27:4
Art of Love, The 1965,Jl 1,34:1
Counterfeit Constable, The 1966,N 22,32:2
Camelot 1967,O 26,54:1
Olaguivel, Juan
Scent of Mystery 1960,F 19,23:1
Oland, Warner
Yellow Ticket, The 1918,My 27,11:3
Avalanche, The 1919,Je 30,16:3
Witness for the Defense, The 1919,S 15,16:3
His Children's Children 1923,N 5,15:1
Fighting American, The 1924,My 13,24:1
So This Is Marriage 1924,D 23,16:2
Riders of the Purple Sage 1925,Ap 15,16:1
Don Q, Son of Zorro 1925,Je 16,24:1
Flower of the Night 1925,O 19,26:1
Infatuation 1926,Ja 4,16:1
Don Juan 1926,Ag 7,6:1 (In Addenda)
Marriage Clause, The 1926,S 28,30:2
Tell It to the Marines 1926,D 24,18:2
Twinkletoes 1926,D 27,20:3
When a Man Loves 1927,F 4,16:6
Million Bid, A 1927,My 31,25:2
Old San Francisco 1927,Je 23,23:3
Good Time Charley 1927,N 21,20:1
Stand and Deliver 1928,Ap 2,25:1
Wheels of Chance 1928,Jl 2,11:2
Scarlet Lady, The 1928,Ag 15,19:4
Dream of Love 1928,D 24,11:1
Chinatown Nights 1929,Ap 1,22:1
Studio Murder Mystery, The 1929,Je 10,23:1
Insidious Dr Fu Manchu, The 1929,Jl 22,17:1
Mysterious Dr Fu Manchu, The
1929,Jl 28,VIII,3:7 (In Addenda)
Mighty, The 1929,D 30,16:4
Dangerous Paradise 1930,F 16,III,8:1
Vagabond King, The 1930,F 20,22:4
Vagabond King, The 1930,Mr 2,IX,5:1
New Adventures of Dr Fu Manchu, The
1930,My 3,23:1
Dishonored 1931,Mr 6,16:1
Charlie Chan Carries On 1931,Mr 21,15:1
Black Camel, The 1931,Jl 4,11:5
Daughter of the Dragon 1931,Ag 22,7:5
Big Gamble, The 1931,S 21,20:2
Charlie Chan's Chance 1932,Ja 23,18:4
Shanghai Express 1932,F 18,25:3
Passport to Hell, A 1932,Ag 27,13:4
Son-Daughter, The 1933,Ja 2,29:2
Charlie Chan's Greatest Case 1933,O 7,18:4
Before Dawn 1933,O 17,26:2
As Husbands Go 1934,Ja 26,20:3
Mandalay 1934,F 15,15:6
Bulldog Drummond Strikes Back 1934,Ag 16,20:2
Charlie Chan's Courage 1934,Ag 25,16:6
Charlie Chan in London 1934,S 13,26:1
Painted Veil, The 1934,D 7,29:1
Werewolf of London, The 1935,My 10,25:2
Charlie Chan in Egypt 1935,Je 24,12:2
Shanghai 1935,Jl 20,16:2
Charlie Chan in Shanghai 1935,O 14,21:1
Charlie Chan's Secret 1936,Ja 18,19:4
Charlie Chan at the Circus 1936,Mr 19,22:4
Charlie Chan at the Race Track 1936,Ag 15,6:2
Charlie Chan at the Opera 1936,D 5,16:2
Charlie Chan at the Olympics 1937,My 24,23:1
Charlie Chan on Broadway 1937,S 20,19:1
Charlie Chan at Monte Carlo 1937,D 18,18:1
Days of Thrills and Laughter 1961,Mr 22,37:1
Olarra, Jose
Chrismosa, La; Gossiper, The 1940,Mr 30,11:2
Olasz, Janos
Sut a Nap (Sun Shines, The); Sun Shines, The
1940,Ap 6,13:3
Olcott, Chancey (Miscellaneous)
My Wild Irish Rose 1947,D 25,32:2

Olcott, Rita (Original Author)
My Wild Irish Rose 1947,D 25,32:2
Olcott, Sidney (Director)
Scratch my Back 1920,Je 5,19:3
Little Old New York 1923,Ag 2,10:3
Green Goddess, The 1923,Ag 15,21:1
Humming Bird, The 1924,Ja 14,2:1
Monsieur Beaucaire 1924,Ag 12,12:1 (In
Addenda)
Only Woman, The 1924,N 3,20:1
Salome of the Tenements 1925,F 24,17:3
Charmer, The 1925,Ap 6,17:3
Not so Long Ago 1925,Jl 28,24:4
Best People 1925,O 21,21:3
Ranson's Folly 1926,My 31,10:2
Amateur Gentleman, The 1926,Ag 17,15:3
White Black Sheep, The 1926,D 21,20:2
Claw, The 1927,My 11,28:3
Olden, Hans
Csardas, Ihre Tollste Nacht 1937,Je 21,15:3
Orphan Boy of Vienna, An 1937,S 9,19:2
Prater, Wiener 1938,D 3,11:3
Wiener Prater 1938,D 3,11:3
Manner Mussen so Sein; Men Are That Way
1939,My 13,11:6
Olden, Henry (Director)
Great British Train Robbery, The 1967,Ap 6,45:2
Oldfield, Barney
First Auto, The 1927,Je 28,28:4
First Auto, The 1927,Jl 3,VII,3:3
Oldham, Andrew Loog
London Scene, The (Tonite Let's All Make Love
in London); Tonite Let's All Make Love in
London (The London Scene) 1967,S 27,39:1
Oldham, Vera M (Original Author)
Chandu the Magician 1932,O 1,10:4
Oldridge, Alfred
Mikado, The 1967,Mr 15,53:1
O'Leary, William
Wistful Widow of Wagon Gap, The
1947,N 21,36:2
South Sea Woman 1953,Je 4,33:6
Olegario, Frank
Harry Black and the Tiger 1958,S 19,24:4
Oleinichenko, Galina
Tsar's Bride, The 1966,Mr 12,13:2
Oleinichenko, Galina (Composer)
Yolanta 1964,D 23,22:3
Oleinikov, P
Seven Brave Men 1936,Je 15,24:2
Olenev, P
Prisoners 1937,F 20,9:2
Volga-Volga 1941,My 17,19:2
Village Teacher 1948,Jl 5,8:4
Olenina, Iraida
Ballet of Romeo and Juliet, The 1956,Ap 3,31:2
Olenn, Johnny
Girl Can't Help It, The 1957,F 9,12:7
Olesenko, C
Hamlet 1964,S 15,32:1
Hamlet 1966,Mr 16,48:1
Oliansky, Joel (Screenwriter)
Counterpoint 1968,Mr 14,51:2
Olicova, Karla
Skeleton on Horseback 1940,F 5,13:3
Olin, Stig
Torment 1947,Ap 22,34:2
Incorrigible 1949,Jl 2,8:2
Illicit Interlude 1954,O 27,32:6
Devil's Wanton, The 1962,Jl 5,21:2
Oliva, Esther
Cuban Rebel Girls 1959,D 26,7:3
Olivari, Carlos (Original Author)
You Were Never Lovelier 1942,D 4,31:1
Romance on the High Seas 1948,Je 26,10:5
Olive, Philippe
Sins of Paris 1954,Ja 30,9:6
Oliveira, Jose
Three Caballeros, The 1945,F 5,20:1
OLIVER
See Also OLIVIER
Oliver, Anthony
Magnet, The 1951,F 27,22:6
Glory at Sea 1953,Mr 11,36:7
Penny Princess 1953,Mr 25,37:3
Both Sides of the Law 1954,Ja 12,19:2
Runaway Bus, The 1954,O 25,30:7
Tears for Simon 1957,Ap 18,35:2
Checkpoint 1957,S 19,25:2
Oliver, Charles
Drums 1938,S 30,24:4
Lady Vanishes, The 1938,D 26,29:1
Green Cockatoo, The 1947,Jl 19,10:2
Oliver, David
Girl on the Front Page, The 1936,N 7,15:2
Girl Overboard 1937,Mr 1,15:1
When Love Is Young 1937,Ap 17,15:1
Night Key 1937,Ap 19,27:2
As Good as Married 1937,My 22,19:2
Armored Car 1937,Jl 26,15:2
You're a Sweetheart 1937,D 25,10:5
Nurse From Brooklyn 1938,My 13,17:3
Devil's Party, The 1938,My 31,8:3

Oliver, David — Cont
Road to Reno, The 1938,O 3,11:2
Swing That Cheer 1938,N 11,31:2
Little Tough Guys in Society 1938,N 21,14:4
Exposed 1938,N 21,14:5
Secrets of a Nurse 1938,D 12,26:2
Little Bit of Heaven, A 1940,N 8,24:2
Oliver, Eddie
Easy to Love 1953,N 27,99:9
Oliver, Edna May
Icebound 1924,Mr 3,22:3 (In Addenda)
Manhattan 1924,O 29,18:1
Lady Who Lied, The 1925,Jl 7,24:2
Lucky Devil, The 1925,Jl 8,12:4
Lovers in Quarantine 1925,O 13,20:1
American Venus, The 1926,Ja 26,25:2
Let's Get Married 1926,Mr 2,22:1
Saturday Night Kid, The 1929,N 16,25:2
Half Shot at Sunrise 1930,O 11,21:3
Cimarron 1931,Ja 27,20:5
Laugh and get Rich 1931,Mr 28,15:3
Cracked Nuts 1931,Ap 6,24:1
Newly Rich 1931,Jl 3,22:1
Fanny Foley Herself 1931,O 26,22:1
Ladies of the Jury 1932,Ap 2,13:2
Hold 'Em Jail! 1932,Ag 20,7:4
Conquerors, The 1932,N 21,21:1
Great Jasper, The 1933,F 17,5:3
It's Great to be Alive 1933,Jl 8,14:6
Ann Vickers 1933,S 29,24:1
Meet the Baron 1933,O 28,20:3
Only Yesterday 1933,N 10,25:1
Little Women 1933,N 17,22:3
Alice in Wonderland 1933,D 23,19:1
Murder on the Blackboard 1934,Je 20,24:2
We're Rich Again 1934,S 1,16:3
Last Gentleman, The 1934,O 18,26:5
David Copperfield 1935,Ja 19,8:1
Murder on a Honeymoon 1935,Mr 4,12:2
No More Ladies 1935,Je 22,18:5
Tale of Two Cities, A 1935,D 26,21:2
Romeo and Juliet 1936,Ag 21,12:2
Parnell 1937,Je 4,27:2
Rosalie 1937,D 31,9:2
Paradise for Three 1938,F 16,17:1
Little Miss Broadway 1938,Jl 23,10:4
Story of Vernon and Irene Castle, The
  1939,Mr 31,19:2
Second Fiddle 1939,Jl 1,11:2
Nurse Edith Cavell 1939,S 22,27:4
Drums Along the Mohawk 1939,N 4,11:2
Pride and Prejudice 1940,Ag 9,19:1
Lydia 1941,S 19,27:1
Oliver, Fenwick
Enticement 1925,Mr 21,16:3
Oliver, Gordon
Fugitive in the Sky 1937,Ja 16,21:1
Fly Away Baby 1937,Jl 9,18:2
White Bondage 1937,Ag 6,21:3
Alcatraz Island 1937,O 14,22:2
Over the Goal 1937,O 16,22:2
West of Shanghai 1937,O 29,19:2
Expensive Husbands 1938,Ja 8,19:3
Daredevil Drivers, The 1938,F 23,27:2
Jezebel 1938,Mr 11,15:2
Women Are Like That 1938,Ap 11,12:2
Brother Rat 1938,N 5,15:2
Blondie 1938,D 22,25:4
There's That Woman Again 1939,Ja 6,25:4
Romance of the Redwoods 1939,Ap 24,13:2
Woman Is the Judge, A 1939,S 28,29:5
Sabotage 1939,N 16,29:5
Seven Days Ashore 1944,Ap 26,24:7
Heavenly Days 1944,O 21,15:2
Spiral Staircase, The 1946,F 7,29:3
My Forbidden Past 1951,Ap 26,34:2
Las Vegas Story, The 1952,Ja 31,37:6
Oliver, Guy
Secret Service 1919,Je 23,10:3
Lottery Man, The 1919,N 17,20:1
Hawthorne of the U.S.A. 1919,N 17,20:1
Prince There Was 1921,N 14,18:1
Woman With Four Faces, The 1923,Je 18,13:5
Cheat, The 1923,Ag 27,14:3
To the Last Man 1923,Ag 28,12:1
Dawn of a Tomorrow, The 1924,Mr 26,19:2
Bedroom Window, The 1924,Je 9,14:3
North of 36 1924,D 8,13:3
Air Mail, The 1925,Mr 17,18:1
Vanishing American, The 1925,O 16,18:2
Woman of the World, A 1925,D 14,18:2
Eagle of the Sea, The 1926,N 17,21:6
Easy Come, Easy Go 1928,My 8,25:3
Docks of New York, The 1928,S 17,28:2
Three Week Ends 1928,D 10,25:1
Studio Murder Mystery, The 1929,Je 10,23:1
Woman Trap 1929,Ag 31,13:4
Half Way to Heaven 1929,D 7,19:3
Kibitzer, The 1929,D 21,17:1
Light of Western Stars, The 1930,Ap 26,11:1
Skippy 1931,Ap 4,23:1
Gun Smoke 1931,Ap 24,27:1
Dude Ranch 1931,Ap 25,23:4
Up Pops the Devil 1931,My 16,13:3

Huckleberry Finn 1931,Ag 8,16:3
Beloved Bachelor, The 1931,O 17,20:1
Rich Man's Folly 1931,N 27,29:3
Sooky 1931,D 21,28:4
Oliver, James
Hells Angels on Wheels 1967,Jl 29,29:3
Oliver, Joe
Cool World, The 1964,Ap 21,42:1
Oliver, Larry
Born Yesterday 1950,D 27,30:2
Oliver, Shirling
Victims of Persecution 1933,Je 17,16:6
Oliver, Stephanie
Yours, Mine and Ours 1968,Ap 25,53:1
Oliver, Stephen
Angels From Hell 1968,O 24,55:5
Oliver, Susan
Gene Krupa Story, The 1959,D 26,7:1
Butterfield 8 1960,N 17,46:1
Caretakers, The 1963,Ag 22,19:2
Disorderly Orderly, The 1964,D 24,8:3
Your Cheatin' Heart 1965,My 20,52:2
Love-Ins, The 1967,Ag 19,16:1
Oliver, Ted
We're not Dressing 1934,Ap 26,27:2
Klondike Annie 1936,Mr 12,18:2
Border Flight 1936,Je 22,22:1
Return of Sophie Lang, The 1936,Jl 24,13:1
Frame-Up 1937,Ag 9,23:2 (In Addenda)
She Loved a Fireman 1938,Ja 21,15:3
Oliver, Thelma
Black Like Me 1964,My 21,42:1
Pawnbroker, The 1965,Ap 21,51:1
Oliver, William Elwell (Screenwriter)
Fighting American, The 1924,My 13,24:1
Oliver-Smith, Gerald
Bachelor Mother 1939,Je 30,17:2
Olivera, Hector (Producer)
No Exit 1962,D 6,55:2
Olivette, Nina
Queen High 1930,Ag 9,16:5
Olivia, Marie-Claire
Pit of Loneliness 1954,Ap 9,19:2
Red Inn, The 1954,Je 8,25:2
Olivia, Marie-Claire (Original Author)
Pit of Loneliness 1954,Ap 9,19:2
OLIVIER
See Also OLIVER
Olivier, Claire
Mr Orchid; Pere Tranquille, Le 1948,Mr 29,17:3
Olivier, Laurence
Murder for Sale 1930,Ag 3,4:1
Yellow Ticket, The 1931,O 31,22:2
Friends and Lovers 1931,N 7,16:5
Westward Passage 1932,Je 4,9:2
Perfect Understanding 1933,F 23,20:2
No Funny Business 1934,Mr 9,22:4
I Stand Condemned 1936,Jl 2,27:2
As You Like It 1936,N 6,29:3
Fire Over England 1937,Mr 5,16:2
Divorce of Lady X, The 1938,Ap 1,17:2
Wuthering Heights 1939,Ap 14,28:2
Clouds Over Europe 1939,Je 16,27:2
Rebecca 1940,Mr 29,25:2
21 Days Together 1940,My 23,28:4
Pride and Prejudice 1940,Ag 9,19:1
That Hamilton Woman 1941,Ap 4,25:1
Invaders, The 1942,Mr 6,17:1
Adventure for Two 1945,D 14,24:5
Henry V 1946,Je 18,30:2
Henry V 1946,Je 18,30:3
Hamlet 1948,S 30,32:2
Carrie 1952,Jl 17,20:2
Magic Box, The 1952,S 24,40:2
Beggar's Opera, The 1953,Ag 25,18:2
Richard III 1956,Mr 12,1:4
Prince and the Showgirl 1957,Je 14,22:2
Devil's Disciple, The 1959,Ag 21,12:1
Entertainer, The 1960,O 4,49:2
Spartacus 1960,O 7,28:1
Term of Trial 1963,Ja 31,5:2
Bunny Lake is Missing 1965,O 4,00:0
Othello 1966,F 2,24:1
Khartoum 1966,Jl 14,28:1
Shoes of the Fisherman, The 1968,N 15,40:3
Olivier, Laurence (Director)
Henry V 1946,Je 18,30:2
Henry V 1946,Je 18,30:3
Hamlet 1948,S 30,32:2
Richard III 1956,Mr 12,1:4
Prince and the Showgirl 1957,Je 14,22:2
Olivier, Laurence (Miscellaneous)
Henry V 1946,Je 18,30:2
Olivier, Laurence (Narrator)
Queen is Crowned, A 1953,Je 8,26:2
Olivier, Laurence (Producer)
Henry V 1946,Je 18,30:2
Hamlet 1948,S 30,32:2
Beggar's Opera, The 1953,Ag 25,18:2
Richard III 1956,Mr 12,1:4
Prince and the Showgirl 1957,Je 14,22:2

Olivier, Laurence (Screenwriter)
Richard III 1956,Mr 12,1:4
Olivier, Paul
Sous les Toits de Paris; (Under the Roofs of
  Paris) 1930,D 16,34:4
Million, Le 1931,My 21,33:2
Horse Ate the Hat, The 1931,S 1,30:6
A Nous la Liberte 1932,Ja 10,VIII,5:1
Nous, La Liberte, A 1932,My 18,25:2
Quatorez Juillet 1933,O 20,14:2
Dernier Milliardaire, Le 1935,O 30,16:2
Lie of Nina Petrovna, The 1938,Mr 30,19:2
Man About Town 1947,O 22,37:1
Olivier, Torquin
Two Tickets to London 1943,Jl 3,11:2
Olivieri, Egisto
Outcry 1949,Mr 14,15:5
Carmela 1949,My 14,9:2
Olivieri, Enrico
Flight Into France 1949,Jl 22,16:2
Black Sunday 1961,Mr 9,23:1
Oliviero, Carmelo
Mafioso 1964,Jl 1,42:1
Ollendorf, Julian (Producer)
Seeing Greenwich Village 1921,Ja 24,16:2
Ollestad, Norman
Cheaper by the Dozen 1950,Ap 1,12:2
Ollivant, Alfred (Original Author)
To the Victor 1938,Ap 13,21:2
Thunder in the Valley 1947,N 28,30:1
Olmer, Vit
Devil's Trap, The 1964,Ag 14,16:1
Olmi, Corrado
Easy Life, The 1963,D 23,18:2
Olmi, Ermanno (Director)
Sound of Trumpets, The 1963,O 23,36:1
Fiances, The 1964,Ja 29,23:1
And There Came a Man 1968,Ap 5,56:4
Olmi, Ermanno (Screenwriter)
Sound of Trumpets, The 1963,O 23,36:1
Fiances, The 1964,Ja 29,23:1
And There Came a Man 1968,Ap 5,56:4
Olmos, Sabina
Divorcio en Montevideo 1940,Ap 8,15:3
Apuros de Claudina, Los; Claudina's Troubles
  1940,Je 8,18:3
Asi es la Vida; Such Is Life 1940,Ag 6,15:1
Olmos, Sarita
Besos Brujos; Bewitching Kisses 1939,O 21,12:3
OLMSTEAD
See Also OLMSTED
Olmstead, Edwin (Screenwriter)
Crime of Dr Crespi, The 1936,Ja 13,14:3
Olmstead, Gertrude
Babbitt 1924,Jl 15,9:4
Empty Hands 1924,Ag 18,8:2
Monster, The 1925,F 16,24:1
Cobra 1925,D 7,19:1
Time, the Comedian 1925,D 14,18:2
California Straight Ahead 1926,Ja 12,27:5
Ibanez's Torrent 1926,F 22,14:1
Puppets 1926,Je 21,17:2
Cheerful Fraud, The 1926,D 28,17:1
Mr Wu 1927,My 16,24:2
Callahans and the Murphys, The 1927,Jl 12,29:3
Sporting Goods 1928,F 13,16:2
Bringing Up Father 1928,Mr 19,26:2
Hit of the Show 1928,Jl 9,25:1
Lone Wolf's Daughter, The 1929,Mr 4,20:2
Sonny Boy 1929,Mr 9,24:3
Time, The Place and the Girl, The 1929,Jl 8,17:3
Show of Shows 1929,N 21,24:5
OLMSTED
See Also OLMSTEAD
Olof, Karl
Vicious Breed, The 1958,My 23,29:2
Olos, Sara
Canillita y la Dama, El; Newsie and the Lady,
  The 1939,F 18,12:2
O'Loughlin, Gerald
Lovers and Lollipops 1956,Ap 19,35:1
Hatful of Rain, A 1957,Jl 18,19:2
Cop Hater 1958,O 2,44:3
Ensign Pulver 1964,Ag 1,13:2
In Cold Blood 1967,D 15,60:1
Olrich, April
Room at the Top 1959,Mr 31,26:1
OLSEN
See Also OLSON
Olsen, Christopher
Iron Curtain, The 1948,My 13,31:2
I'll See You in my Dreams 1951,D 7,35:1
Marrying Kind, The 1952,Mr 14,27:1
Above and Beyond 1953,Ja 31,10:6
Man Who Knew too Much, The 1956,My 17,37:1
Fastest Gun Alive, The 1956,Jl 13,23:3
Bigger Than Life 1956,Ag 3,11:2
Tarnished Angels, The 1958,Ja 7,31:1
Olsen, Ed
Cinerama-South Seas Adventure 1958,Jl 16,26:1
Olsen, George
Happy Days 1930,F 14,20:1

Olsen, John
Smugglers, The 1948,Mr 29,17:1
Olsen, Larry
Happy-Land 1943,D 9,33:3
Address Unknown 1944,Ap 17,20:1
Sitting Pretty 1948,Mr 11,35:2
Isn't It Romantic? 1948,O 7,35:2
Room for One More 1952,Ja 16,21:2
Olsen, Mononi
Mildred Pierce 1945,S 29,12:2
Task Force 1949,O 1,8:6
Samson and Delilah 1949,D 22,29:2
Olsen, Moroni
Three Musketeers, The 1935,N 1,25:1
Seven Keys to Baldpate 1935,D 14,11:2
Annie Oakley 1935,D 24,10:5
We're Only Human 1936,Ja 18,19:2
Yellow Dust 1936,F 24,14:1
Farmer in the Dell, The 1936,Mr 7,11:4
Witness Chair, The 1936,Ap 18,19:2
Two in Revolt 1936,Ap 25,21:1
Mary of Scotland 1936,Jl 31,22:2
Grand Jury 1936,Ag 1,16:3
M'liss 1936,Ag 8,5:2
Plough and the Stars, The 1937,Ja 29,15:1
Adventure's End 1937,D 20,23:2
Manhattan Merry-Go-Round 1937,D 31,9:3
Gold Is Where You Find It 1938,F 14,20:6
Kidnapped 1938,My 28,9:2
Submarine Patrol 1938,N 19,9:2
Kentucky 1938,D 24,12:1
Homicide Bureau 1939,F 2,17:2
Three Musketeers, The 1939,F 18,12:2
Rose of Washington Square 1939,My 6,21:2
Susannah of the Mounties 1939,Je 24,13:2
Dust Be my Destiny 1939,O 7,11:2
Allegheny Uprising 1939,N 10,27:3
That's Right, You're Wrong 1939,N 30,25:3
Barricade 1939,D 9,18:2
Invisible Stripes 1940,Ja 13,11:2
Brother Rat and a Baby 1940,Ja 27,9:4
If I Had my Way 1940,My 6,13:2
Brigham Young - Frontiersman 1940,S 21,13:2
East of the River 1940,O 28,21:2
Santa Fe Trail 1940,D 21,21:2
Life With Henry 1941,F 6,25:2
Dive Bomber 1941,Ag 30,10:2
One Foot in Heaven 1941,N 14,28:3
Dangerously They Live 1942,Ap 11,9:2
My Favorite Spy 1942,My 29,13:4
Nazi Agent 1942,Je 13,11:2
Glass Key, The 1942,O 16,23:1
Air Force 1943,F 4,29:1
Reunion in France 1943,Mr 5,20:3
Mission to Moscow 1943,Ap 30,25:2
Song of Bernadette, The 1944,Ja 27,15:2
Ali Baba and the Forty Thieves 1944,Mr 16,17:3
Buffalo Bill 1944,Ap 20,22:6
Cobra Woman 1944,My 18,17:2
Roger Touhy, Gangster 1944,Je 5,14:7
Pride of the Marines 1945,Ag 25,7:3
Night in Paradise 1946,Je 6,16:3
Boy's Ranch 1946,Ag 9,12:2
Notorious 1946,Ag 16,19:2
Walls Came Tumbling Down, The 1946,N 9,13:5
Beginning or the End, The 1947,F 21,15:1
Strange Woman, The 1947,F 24,16:4
Possessed 1947,My 30,25:2
Life With Father 1947,Ag 16,6:6
Black Gold 1947,S 5,16:4
Long Night, The 1947,S 17,31:2
That Hagen Girl 1947,O 25,13:2
High Wall 1947,D 26,22:2
Call Northside 777 1948,F 19,29:2
Up in Central Park 1948,My 27,29:3
Command Decision 1949,Ja 20,34:2
Fountainhead, The 1949,Jl 9,8:5
Father of the Bride 1950,My 19,31:2
Father's Little Dividend 1951,Ap 13,18:5
No Questions Asked 1951,Ag 10,13:2
Submarine Command 1952,Ja 19,13:2
Lone Star 1952,F 2,11:4
Washington Story 1952,Jl 2,22:3
So This Is Love 1953,Ag 12,22:1
Long, Long Trailer, The 1954,F 19,24:3
Olsen, Olaf
Sixty Glorious Years 1938,N 18,25:2
Olsen, Ole
Fifty Million Frenchmen 1931,Mr 26,31:2
Gold Dust Gertie 1931,My 30,9:2
Hellzapoppin 1941,D 26,21:4
Crazy House 1943,D 16,33:3
See my Lawyer 1945,My 4,23:4
Olsen, Ole (Miscellaneous)
Hellzapoppin 1941,D 26,21:4
Olsen, Rolf (Screenwriter)
Singing Angels 1952,Ja 16,21:2
Olsen and Johnson
Ghost Catchers 1944,My 31,22:3
Olshanetsky, Alexander (Composer)
Overture to Glory 1940,F 12,14:2

Olshensky, I (Screenwriter)
Day the War Ended, The 1961,Ja 30,17:2
OLSON
See Also OLSEN
Olson, James
Strange One, The 1957,Ap 13,12:3
Rachel Rachel 1968,Ag 27,36:1
Olson, Nancy
Canadian Pacific 1949,My 20,32:4
Sunset Boulevard 1950,Ag 11,15:2
Union Station 1950,O 5,38:3
Mr Music 1950,D 21,34:3
Force of Arms 1951,Ag 14,20:2
Submarine Command 1952,Ja 19,13:2
Big Jim McLain 1952,S 18,35:2
So Big 1953,O 22,34:2
Battle Cry 1955,F 3,18:1
Pollyanna 1960,My 20,26:1
Absent-Minded Professor, The 1961,Mr 16,44:2
Son of Flubber 1963,F 9,5:2
Olson, Olive
Dance Charlie Dance 1937,Ag 26,25:2
Olsson, Bror
Surf, The 1949,D 17,15:2
Olsson, Dagmar
Doll, The 1964,Ja 14,27:1
Olsson, Gunnar
Seventh Seal 1958,O 14,44:1
Olsson, Gunnar (Director)
Berslagsfolk 1938,Mr 12,13:3
Du Gamla, Du Fria; Thou old, Tho Free
1939,Mr 21,27:2
Vi paa Solglantan; We at Solglantan
1940,O 9,30:3
Lasse-Maja 1943,Mr 22,15:4
Olsza, T
Jego Wielka Milosc 1936,Mr 24,27:5
Olty, Magda
Nagymama 1935,D 30,15:1
Olvedy, Zsofia
Falu Rossza, A; Village Rogue, The
1938,Ap 18,11:2
Tiszavirag; Flower of the Tisza 1939,D 30,9:3
Olvis, William
Deep in my Heart 1954,D 10,35:2
O'Madden, Lawrence
Silver Fleet, The 1945,Mr 24,22:6
Mrs Fitzherbert 1950,My 11,37:2
Lisbon Story, The 1951,S 6,39:4
Guilt is my Shadow 1954,Mr 25,36:4
O'Madigan, Isabel
Smiling Faces 1932,Ag 31,12:3
Egg and I, The 1947,Ap 25,29:2
Ma and Pa Kettle 1949,Ag 12,13:2
O'Mahoney, Nora
Darby O'Gill and the Little People 1959,Jl 1,26:1
Holiday for Lovers 1959,Jl 25,10:2
O'Maille, Kit
Irish Destiny 1927,Mr 29,23:2 (In Addenda)
O'Malley, Charles
Iron Horse, The 1924,Ag 29,6:1
Only Woman, The 1924,N 3,20:1
O'Malley, David (Miscellaneous)
Shepherd of the Seven Hills, The 1933,Ag 8,22:7
O'Malley, James
Winds of Chance 1925,Ag 17,10:3
O'Malley, Kathleen
Down to Earth 1947,S 12,18:2
Wagonmaster 1950,Je 19,17:2
Mister Roberts 1955,Jl 15,14:1
O'Malley, Pat
Blooming Angel, The 1920,F 9,10:3
Go and Get It 1920,Jl 19,16:3
Brothers Under the Skin 1922,N 13,12:1
Wandering Daughters 1923,Jl 2,16:2
Eternal Struggle, The 1923,O 16,21:3
Man From Brodney's, The 1923,D 18,16:3
Happiness 1924,Mr 11,16:2
Fighting American, The 1924,My 13,24:1
Bread 1924,Jl 21,14:4
Worldly Goods 1924,N 3,20:1
Tomorrow's Love 1925,Ja 7,33:5
Proud Flesh 1925,Ap 14,26:1
Teaser, The 1925,Je 15,10:1
White Desert, The 1925,Jl 8,12:4
Midnight Sun, The 1926,Ap 24,20:4
Alibi 1929,Ap 9,29:1
Man I Love, The 1929,My 28,36:2
Fall Guy, The 1930,My 27,27:2
Mothers Cry 1930,D 6,21:3
Sky Spider, The 1931,Ag 31,11:5
Frisco Jenny 1933,Ja 7,11:2
Behind the Evidence 1935,Ja 26,13:2
Perfect Clue, The 1935,Mr 14,18:1
Hollywood Boulevard 1936,S 21,26:4
Beloved Enemy 1936,D 26,15:2
Romance of the Redwoods 1939,Ap 24,13:2
Frontier Marshal 1939,Jl 29,18:2
Night of Nights, The 1939,D 28,17:1
Captain Caution 1940,O 21,21:3
Little Bit of Heaven, A 1940,N 8,24:2

Meet Boston Blackie 1941,F 26,17:2
Paris Calling 1942,Ja 19,21:2
Over my Dead Body 1942,D 26,15:2
Lassie Come Home 1943,O 8,15:4
Rugged O'Riordans, The 1950,Ja 6,25:2
Kind Lady 1951,Ag 8,21:2
Blackjack Ketchum Desperado 1956,Ap 5,26:2
Long, Hot Summer, The 1958,Ap 4,16:1
Blueprint for Robbery 1961,F 2,24:3
Cabinet of Caligari, The 1962,My 26,13:5
House is not a Home, A 1964,S 2,33:1
Gunn 1967,Je 29,32:1
O'Malley, Pat (Miscellaneous)
Adventures of Ichabod and Mr Toad, The
1949,O 10,18:2
O'Malley, Rex
Camille 1937,Ja 23,13:1
Zaza 1939,Ja 5,17:1
Midnight 1939,Ap 6,31:1
Thief, The 1952,O 16,37:1
Oman, Paul
Frenchman's Creek 1944,S 21,26:2
O'Mara, Ellen
Up the Down Staircase 1967,Ag 18,36:2
Omen, Seena (Original Author)
Aloma of the South Seas 1941,Ag 28,23:4
Omens, Estelle
Secret Cinema, The 1968,My 2,57:1
Omi, Teruko
Three Stripes in the Sun 1955,N 24,41:2
Omitsu
Daughter of Two Fathers, A 1929,Mr 12,26:3
O'Mohoney, J W Major (Director)
Race of the Age, The 1920,N 1,13:2
Omoolu, Mutia
Trader Horn 1931,F 4,21:3
O'Moore, Pat
Smilin' Through 1941,D 5,29:2
Captains of the Clouds 1942,F 13,24:2
Desperate Journey 1942,S 26,11:2
Stage Door Canteen 1943,Je 25,13:2
Sahara 1943,N 12,25:2
Between Two Worlds 1944,My 6,11:2
Molly and Me 1945,My 26,18:2
Conflict 1945,Je 16,10:2
Two Mrs Carrolls, The 1947,Ap 7,20:1
Moss Rose 1947,Jl 3,14:2
Fighting O'Flynn, The 1949,F 28,16:2
Kind Lady 1951,Ag 8,21:2
Thunder on the Hill 1951,O 18,32:3
Bwana Devil 1953,F 19,20:5
Khyber Patrol 1954,S 20,19:2
O'Moore, Patrick
Evensong 1934,N 17,12:1
O'Morrison, Kenny
Dear Ruth 1947,Je 11,33:3
Set-Up, The 1949,Mr 30,31:2
On, Lev
Beachcomber, The 1938,D 26,29:3
Black Narcissus 1947,Ag 14,29:2
Ondine
**** 1967,D 17,94:5
Ondra, Anny
Blackmail 1929,Jl 14,IX,4:5
Blackmail 1929,O 7,22:1
Manxman, The 1929,D 17,28:7
Versuchen Sie Meine Schwester 1931,Je 20,20:4
Eine Freundin so Goldig wie Du 1931,O 24,20:3
Die vom Rummelplatz 1932,Ja 2,14:2
Eine Nacht im Paradies 1933,F 20,11:6
Tochter des Regiments, Die 1934,Mr 31,8:3
Klein Dorrit 1935,O 19,21:2
Polenblut; Polish Blood 1935,N 16,19:3
Knock-Out 1936,F 29,11:2
Donogoo Tonka 1936,Ap 13,15:2
Junge Graf, Der 1936,D 14,15:2
Unwiderst Ehliche, Der; Irresistable Man, The
1937,D 20,23:3
Gross Reinemachen; General Housecleaning
1938,Je 23,27:2
Ondrouchova, Zuzana
Girl With Three Camels, The 1968,Ag 13,45:2
O'Neal, Anne
In old California 1942,Je 18,25:3
In old Oklahoma 1943,D 6,21:1
Bishop's Wife, The 1947,D 10,44:2
Open Secret 1948,F 2,15:2
Black Bart 1948,Mr 4,30:4
O'Neal, Charles (Original Author)
Seventh Victim, The 1943,S 18,11:3
Something in the Wind 1947,Ag 29,14:3
O'Neal, Charles (Screenwriter)
Cry of the Werewolf, The 1944,Ag 12,16:5
Return of the Badmen 1948,Ag 5,16:2
Montana 1950,F 4,9:2
Golden Girl 1951,N 21,20:3
O'Neal, Frederick
Pinky 1949,S 30,28:2
Something of Value 1957,My 11,24:6
Anna Lucasta 1959,Ja 15,27:1

O'Neal, Frederick — Cont
Take a Giant Step 1961,Mr 6,28:2
Sins of Rachel Cade, The 1961,Ap 6,30:3
Free, White and 21 1963,Je 20,29:3
O'Neal, Patrick
Mad Magician, The 1954,My 20,38:2
Black Shield of Falworth, The 1954,O 7,16:2
From the Terrace 1960,Jl 16,10:1
Matter of Morals, A 1961,Je 1,31:1
In Harm's Way 1965,Ap 7,36:1
King Rat 1965,O 28,48:1
Fine Madness, A 1966,Je 30,28:2
Chamber of Horrors 1966,O 20,52:5
Alvarez Kelly 1966,N 17,55:2
Matchless 1967,N 11,26:3
Secret Life of an American Wife, The
1968,Je 26,42:2
Where Were You When the Lights Went Out?
1968,Ag 9,30:2
O'Neil, Barbara
Stella Dallas 1937,Ag 6,21:1
Love, Honor and Behave 1938,Mr 21,18:2
Toy Wife, The 1938,Je 24,15:1
I Am the Law 1938,Ag 26,14:2
Sun Never Sets, The 1939,Je 9,26:2
When Tomorrow Comes 1939,Ag 17,16:2
Tower of London 1939,D 12,37:2
Gone With the Wind 1939,D 20,31:2
All This and Heaven, Too 1940,Jl 5,10:2
Shining Victory 1941,My 31,14:1
Secret Beyond the Door 1948,Ja 16,25:4
I Remember Mama 1948,Mr 12,29:2
Whirlpool 1950,Ja 14,9:2
Angel Face 1953,Ap 25,11:5
Flame of the Islands 1956,F 25,12:4
Nun's Story, The 1959,Je 19,30:1
O'Neil, Dennis
Kathleen 1938,Ja 24,17:1
Father O'Flynn 1938,D 26,29:2
O'Neil, Eileen
Kiss Me, Stupid 1964,D 23,22:2
O'Neil, Frank (Screenwriter)
On Borrowed Time 1939,Jl 7,13:2
O'Neil, George
Magnificent Obsession 1935,D 31,11:2
High, Wide and Handsome 1937,Jl 22,15:1
O'Neil, George (Original Author)
Yellow Dust 1936,F 24,14:1
O'Neil, George (Screenwriter)
Sutter's Gold 1936,Mr 27,25:2
I'd Give my Life 1936,Ag 17,9:1
Intermezzo, A Love Story 1939,O 6,31:1
O'Neil, Kitty
Back Street 1941,F 12,25:2
O'Neil, Nance
His Glorious Night 1929,O 5,22:5
Rogue Song, The 1930,Ja 29,26:4
Ladies of Leisure 1930,My 24,21:2
Florodora Girl, The 1930,My 31,19:4
Lady of Scandal, The 1930,Je 14,9:4
Eyes of the World 1930,Ag 15,20:5
Call of the Flesh 1930,S 13,9:3
Resurrection 1931,Ja 24,15:1
Cimarron 1931,Ja 27,20:5
Royal Bed, The 1931,Ja 31,15:1
Good Bad Girl, The 1931,My 15,20:6
Transgression 1931,Je 15,23:3
Woman of Experience, A 1931,Jl 9,26:5
Secret Service 1931,D 14,16:3
Okay America 1932,S 10,18:5
False Faces 1932,N 25,19:2
Jack Ahoy 1935,F 9,11:2
Brewster's Millions 1935,Ap 8,23:3
O'Neil, Robert
Dr Strangelove or: How I Learned to Stop
Worrying and Love the Bomb 1964,Ja 31,16:1
(Incorrect in this edition; use 1964,Ja 30,24:1
elsewhere)
O'Neil, Sally
Sally, Irene and Mary 1925,D 7,19:1
Mike 1926,Ja 11,33:1
Auction Block, The 1926,F 15,16:4
Battling Butler 1926,Ag 23,9:1
Slide, Kelly, Slide 1927,Mr 23,19:2
Frisco Sally Levy 1927,Ap 13,29:4
Callahans and the Murphys, The 1927,Jl 12,29:3
Lovelorn, The 1927,D 19,30:1
Mad Hour, The 1928,Ap 16,20:5
Battle of The Sexes, The 1928,O 15,16:1
Girl on the Barge, The 1929,F 26,31:1
On With the Show 1929,My 29,28:6
Sophomore, The 1929,Ag 24,11:5
Broadway Scandals 1929,O 29,35:1
Jazz Heaven 1929,O 30,29:2
Show of Shows 1929,N 21,24:5
Hold Everything 1930,Ap 23,24:1
Salvation Nell 1931,Jl 6,24:4
Murder by the Clock 1931,Jl 18,16:6
Brat, The 1931,Ag 24,13:4
Sixteen Fathoms Deep 1934,Ja 19,24:3
Kathleen 1938,Ja 24,17:1
O'Neil, Zelma
Follow Thru 1930,S 13,9:3
Peach O'Reno 1931,D 24,20:8

O'Neill, Dick
Pretty Poison 1968,O 25,55:1
O'Neill, Eugene (Original Author)
Anna Christie 1923,D 10,20:1
Anna Christie 1928,D 23,VIII,7:1
Anna Christie 1930,Mr 15,22:5
Strange Interlude 1932,S 1,24:3
Emperor Jones, The 1933,S 20,26:2
Ah, Wilderness! 1935,D 25,30:2
Long Voyage Home, The 1940,O 9,30:2 (In
Addenda)
Hairy Ape, The 1944,Jl 3,8:3
Mourning Becomes Electra 1947,N 20,38:2
Summer Holiday 1948,Je 12,8:5
Desire Under the Elms 1958,Mr 13,24:2
Long Day's Journey Into Night 1962,O 10,57:2
O'Neill, Frank
Enigmatique Monsieur Parkes, L' 1930,S 2,19:3
O'Neill, Harry
America 1924,F 22,20:1
O'Neill, Henry
I Loved a Woman 1933,S 22,14:2
World Changes, The 1933,O 27,22:3
Kennell Murder Case, The 1933,O 30,14:2
From Headquarters 1933,N 17,22:4
House on 56th Street, The 1933,D 2,9:3
Lady Killer 1934,Ja 1,28:2
Massacre 1934,Ja 18,19:2
Fashions of 1934 1934,Ja 20,12:2
I've Got Your Number 1934,F 3,9:3
Big Shakedown, The 1934,F 12,19:2
Wonder Bar 1934,Mr 1,23:2
Bedside 1934,Mr 7,23:4
Midnight 1934,Mr 10,18:3
20 Million Sweethearts 1934,Ap 27,25:1
Journal of a Crime 1934,Ap 28,11:3
Upper World 1934,My 25,25:4
Now I'll Tell 1934,My 26,12:2
Key, The 1934,My 30,14:3
Midnight Alibi 1934,Jl 4,18:3
Man With two Faces, The 1934,Jl 12,20:2
Personality Kid, The 1934,Ag 1,14:2
Side Streets 1934,Ag 15,13:5
Madame Du Barry 1934,O 25,26:2
Big Hearted Herbert 1934,N 14,23:2
Gentlemen are Born 1934,N 22,27:2
Flirtation Walk 1934,N 29,33:1
Murder in the Clouds 1934,D 26,18:1
Man Who Reclaimed his Head, The
1935,Ja 9,22:1
Bordertown 1935,Ja 24,22:5
Secret Bride, The 1935,F 2,10:1
Sweet Music 1935,F 21,23:2
Great Hotel Murder, The 1935,F 28,17:4
While the Patient Slept 1935,Mr 2,18:2
Living on Velvet 1935,Mr 8,25:4
Black Fury 1935,Ap 11,27:2
Florentine Dagger, The 1935,Ap 27,20:6
Oil for the Lamps of China 1935,Je 6,25:2
Stranded 1935,Je 20,16:2
Alias Mary Dow 1935,Je 29,16:2
Bright Lights 1935,Ag 15,15:2
Special Agent 1935,S 19,28:1
Dr Socrates 1935,O 3,29:2
Case of the Lucky Legs, The 1935,N 1,25:1
Fish 1936,Ja 25,18:5
Freshman Love 1936,Ja 25,18:5
Story of Louis Pasteur, The 1936,F 10,15:1
Road Gang 1936,F 24,14:1
Walking Dead, The 1936,Mr 2,13:2
Boulder Dam 1936,Mr 30,17:5
Golden Arrow, The 1936,My 4,16:1
Bullets or Ballots 1936,My 27,27:1
White Angel, The 1936,Je 25,24:1
Big Noise, The 1936,Jl 4,18:3
Anthony Adverse 1936,Ag 27,16:1
Rainbow on the River 1936,D 18,31:4
Green Light 1937,F 13,9:1
Great O'Malley, The 1937,Mr 6,10:1
Marked Woman 1937,Ap 12,15:2
Go Getter, The 1937,Je 4,27:2
Singing Marine, The 1937,Jl 1,33:2
Mr Dodd Takes the Air 1937,Ag 12,14:2
Life of Emile Zola, The 1937,Ag 12,14:2
First Lady 1937,D 23,25:1
Submarine D-1 1937,D 30,15:4
Wells Fargo 1937,D 30,15:2
Gold Is Where You Find It 1938,F 14,20:6
Jezebel 1938,Mr 11,15:2
Yellow Jack 1938,My 20,17:2
White Banners 1938,Je 23,27:1
Amazing Dr Clitterhouse, The 1938,Jl 21,14:2
Chaser, The 1938,Ag 2,15:3
Racket Busters 1938,Ag 11,13:1
Girls on Probation 1938,O 21,27:3
Brother Rat 1938,N 5,15:2
Torchy Blane in Chinatown 1939,F 3,13:2
Wings of the Navy 1939,F 4,11:1
Dodge City 1939,Ap 8,19:1
Juarez 1939,Ap 26,27:1
Confessions of a Nazi Spy 1939,Ap 29,13:2
Lucky Night 1939,My 5,29:3

O'Neill, Henry — Cont
Angels Wash Their Faces 1939,S 4,16:2
Four Wives 1939,D 23,9:1
Child Is Born, A 1940,Ja 11,19:2
Invisible Stripes 1940,Ja 13,11:2
Fighting 69th, The 1940,Ja 27,9:2
Calling Philo Vance 1940,F 9,15:3
Dr Ehrlich's Magic Bullet 1940,F 24,9:2
Castle on the Hudson 1940,Mr 4,11:2
'Til We Meet Again 1940,Ap 14,14:2
Money and the Woman 1940,O 4,29:2
Santa Fe Trail 1940,D 21,21:2
Trial of Mary Dugan, The 1941,Mr 6,25:4
Men of Boys Town 1941,Ap 11,24:6
Billy the Kid 1941,Je 20,28:2
Blossoms in the Dust 1941,Je 27,14:4
Get-Away, The 1941,Jl 17,23:4
Whistling in the Dark 1941,Ag 28,23:2
Honky Tonk 1941,O 3,27:3
Shadow of the Thin Man 1941,N 21,23:2
Born to Sing 1942,F 19,23:2
Johnny Eager 1942,F 20,21:2
Bugle Sounds, The 1942,Ap 3,25:2
Tortilla Flat 1942,My 22,27:1
White Cargo 1942,N 27,27:2
Human Comedy, The 1943,Mr 3,19:2
Stand by for Action 1943,Mr 12,12:2
Air Raid Wardens 1943,Ap 5,15:5
Best Foot Forward 1943,Je 30,25:2
Girl Crazy 1943,D 3,27:2
Guy Named Joe, A 1943,D 24,17:2
Heavenly Body, The 1944,Mr 24,17:3
Whistling in Brooklyn 1944,Mr 24,17:3
Rationing 1944,Ap 10,14:2
Lost Angel 1944,Ap 10,14:1
Two Girls and a Sailor 1944,Je 15,16:1
Barbary Coast Gent 1944,S 29,18:2
Nothing but Trouble 1945,Mr 10,14:1
This Man's Navy 1945,Ap 16,18:6
Dangerous Partners 1945,N 2,22:4
Green Years, The 1946,Ap 5,21:2
Virginian, The 1946,Ap 18,22:2
Bad Bascomb 1946,My 23,18:4
Hoodlum Saint, The 1946,Je 27,29:1
Three Wise Fools 1946,S 27,19:2
Beginning or the End, The 1947,F 21,15:1
Return of October, The 1949,F 23,31:2
Alias Nick Beal 1949,Mr 10,35:2
You're my Everything 1949,Jl 23,7:2
Strange Bargain 1949,S 30,28:3
Holiday Affair 1949,N 24,48:2
Reckless Moment, The 1949,D 30,13:2
No Man of her Own 1950,My 4,32:3
Flying Missile, The 1950,D 25,25:1
Milkman, The 1951,Ja 1,13:6
Second Woman, The 1951,F 2,19:2
Scandal Sheet 1952,Ja 17,23:1
Untamed 1955,Mr 12,11:6
Wings of Eagles, The 1957,F 1,28:1
O'Neill, Marie
Juno and the Paycock 1930,Je 30,22:6
Peg of Old Drury 1936,Ap 13,15:1
Ourselves Alone 1937,Jl 31,6:2
Bulldog Drummond at Bay 1937,O 25,23:2
River of Unrest 1937,N 27,21:2
Troopship 1938,Ap 26,18:2
Sidewalks of London 1940,F 15,15:1
Courageous Mr Penn 1943,D 23,26:5
Love on the Dole 1945,O 13,11:2
Murder in Reverse 1946,Ja 11,23:5
Showtime 1948,My 20,35:3
Piccadilly Incident 1948,Ag 5,16:2
Saints and Sinners 1949,S 12,17:2
Horse's Mouth, The 1954,Ja 20,33:4
O'Neill, Peggy
Song of the Open Road 1944,Je 7,13:3
It's a Pleasure 1945,My 4,23:3
O'Neill (Original Author)
Anna Christie 1931,Ja 6,25:1
Onep, Fedor (Director)
Mirages De Paris 1933,D 25,28:3
Ongley, Byron (Original Author)
Brewster's Millions 1935,Ap 8,23:3
Brewster's Millions 1945,Ap 27,23:2
O'Nil, Moussia
Il est Charmant 1932,Ap 9,18:1
O'Nil, Suzette
Il est Charmant 1932,Ap 9,18:1
Onions, Eileen
Prince of Lovers, The 1927,N 29,31:1
Onna, Ferdinand
Moon of Israel 1927,Je 29,29:3
Onoe, Kikunosuke
Kojiro 1968,Ag 30,23:1
Onoe, Kuroemon
Samurai 1956,Ja 10,26:1
Onofri, Guglielmo
Amore e Morte; (Love and Death) 1932,O 4,26:4
Onyx, Narda
Gaby 1956,My 10,26:3
Ooi, K C
Clouded Yellow, The 1951,N 13,33:2

Ooka, Shohei (Original Author)
Fires on the Plain 1963,S 25,39:1
Ookawa, Heihachiro
Kimiko 1937,Ap 13,31:3
Opalinski, Kazimeriz
Guests are Coming; Jada Goscie Jada 1967,Ja 13,15:1
Opatoshu, David
Light Ahead, The 1939,S 23,22:3
Thieves' Highway 1949,S 24,8:6
Molly 1951,Mr 8,37:2
Crowded Paradise 1956,Je 22,15:1
Brothers Karamazov, The 1958,F 21,18:2
Party Girl 1958,O 29,30:1
Exodus 1960,D 16,44:1
Cimarron 1961,F 17,12:2
Best of Enemies, The 1962,Ag 7,35:2
Guns of Darkness 1962,Ag 18,10:1
Sands of Beersheba 1966,My 6,54:2
Defector, The 1966,N 17,55:1
One Spy too Many 1966,D 8,64:1
Tarzan and the Valley of Gold 1967,Mr 30,55:1
Enter Laughing 1967,Ag 1,24:1
Opert, Sylvia
Happy Go Lucky 1943,Mr 25,25:1
Desert Song, The 1943,D 18,10:6
Ophif, Shy
Tel Aviv Taxi 1956,D 31,10:7
Ophuls, Marcel
Love at Twenty 1963,F 7,5:6
Ophuls, Marcel (Director)
Banana Peel; Peau de Banane 1965,Ja 19,29:1
Ophuls, Marcel (Screenwriter)
Banana Peel; Peau de Banane 1965,Ja 19,29:1
Ophuls, Max (Director)
Bartered Bride, The 1932,N 13,IX,4:2
Liebelei; Light Love 1933,Jl 2,IX,2:2
Lachende Erben 1933,N 18,18:6
Verkaufte Braut, Die 1934,Ap 27,25:2
Liebelei 1936,F 28,18:2
Signora di Tutti, La 1936,Mr 26,27:3
Tender Enemy, The 1938,Mr 31,15:2 (In Addenda)
Mayerling to Sarajevo 1940,O 30,27:6
Exile, The 1947,D 26,22:4
Letters From an Unknown Woman 1948,Ap 29,20:6
Caught 1949,F 18,26:4
Reckless Moment, The 1949,D 30,13:2
Ronde, La 1954,Mr 17,27:2
Plaisir, Le (The Model); Model, The (Le Plaisir) 1954,My 20,38:1
Plaisir, Le (The House of Madame Tellier); House of Madame Tellier (Le Plaisir) 1954,My 20,38:1
Plaisir, Le (The Mask); Mask, The (Le Plaisir) 1954,My 20,38:1
Earrings of Madame De, The 1954,Jl 20,15:5
Lola Montes 1968,S 23,42:6
Ophuls, Max (Screenwriter)
Tender Enemy, The 1938,Mr 31,15:2 (In Addenda)
Ronde, La 1954,Mr 17,27:2
Plaisir, Le (The Mask); Mask, The (Le Plaisir) 1954,My 20,38:1
Plaisir, Le (The Model); Model, The (Le Plaisir) 1954,My 20,38:1
Plaisir, Le (The House of Madame Tellier); House of Madame Tellier (Le Plaisir) 1954,My 20,38:1
Earrings of Madame De, The 1954,Jl 20,15:5
Modigliani of Montparnasse 1961,Mr 1,27:3
Lola Montes 1968,S 23,42:6
Opoien, Lydia
Nine Lives 1959,Ja 6,28:1
Oppenheim, Dave (Composer)
Silver Skates 1943,Mr 19,15:3
Oppenheim, E Phillips (Original Author)
Test of Honor, The 1919,Ap 7,11:5
Behold This Woman 1924,Jl 22,9:1
Prince of Tempters, The 1926,O 18,18:1
Midnight Club 1933,Jl 29,14:2
Great Impersonation, The 1935,D 14,11:1
Oppenheim, M
Tkies Khaf; (Vow, The) 1938,S 15,29:3
Oppenheimer, George (Miscellaneous)
Born to be Bad 1950,S 29,31:5
Oppenheimer, George (Original Author)
We Went to College 1936,Jl 27,20:2
Yank at Eton, A 1942,O 16,23:1
Easy to Wed 1946,Jl 12,14:2
Killer McCoy 1948,F 12,31:2
Oppenheimer, George (Screenwriter)
Rendezvous 1935,O 26,12:2
Libeled Lady 1936,O 31,24:2
Day at the Races, A 1937,Je 18,25:2
Married Before Breakfast 1937,Jl 23,16:2
London by Night 1937,Ag 13,13:1
I'll Take Romance 1937,D 17,33:2
Man-Proof 1938,Ja 14,21:1
Paradise for Three 1938,F 16,17:1
Yank at Oxford, A 1938,F 25,15:1
Crowd Roars, The 1938,Ag 5,11:1

Three Loves Has Nancy 1938,S 2,21:2
Broadway Melody of 1940 1940,Mr 29,25:3
I Love You Again 1940,Ag 16,11:2
Feminine Touch, The 1941,D 12,35:3
Two Faced Woman 1942,Ja 1,37:2
Pacific Rendezvous 1942,Jl 8,27:4
Yank at Eton, A 1942,O 16,23:1
War Against Mrs Hadley, The 1942,N 26,40:2
Slightly Dangerous 1943,Ap 2,17:2
Youngest Profession, The 1943,Je 25,13:3
Killer McCoy 1948,F 12,31:2
Adventures of Don Juan 1948,D 25,10:1
Perfect Strangers 1950,Mr 11,8:2
Anything Can Happen 1952,Ap 4,21:1
Tonight We Sing 1953,F 13,17:2
Decameron Nights 1953,N 17,38:2
Oppenheimer, Hans (Producer)
Stop Train 349 1964,N 12,40:2
Optal, Bernard
Pension Mimosas 1936,My 6,27:1
O'Quigley, R (Director)
Cielito Lindo 1936,N 9,22:5
Ave sin Rumbo; Wandering Bird 1938,Ja 24,17:2
Padre de Mas de Cuatro; Father of More Than, Four 1939,Ap 24,13:3
O'Quinn, Catherine
Mad Miss Manton, The 1938,O 21,27:2
O'Rahilly, Ronan (Producer)
Girl on a Motorcycle, The 1968,N 28,66:5
Orain, Fred (Producer)
Jour de Fete 1952,F 20,26:4
Mr Hulot's Holiday 1954,Je 17,36:2
Winner's Circle, The 1957,My 6,25:2
Orana, Vincente
Rapsodia Mexicana 1938,N 26,18:2
Oransky, V A (Composer)
Diary of a Revolutionist 1932,Je 10,22:3
Orbach, Jerry
Mad Dog Coll 1961,My 13,10:1
John Goldfarb, Please Come Home 1965,Mr 25,42:4
Orbal
Twilight 1949,D 30,13:2
Scandals of Clochemerle, The 1950,Mr 28,28:2
Orbison, Roy
Fastest Guitar Alive, The 1968,F 15,47:1
Orbok, Attila (Original Author)
My Lips Betray 1933,N 4,18:3
Thin Ice 1937,S 4,8:2
Orchard, John
I Believe in You 1953,My 5,34:3
Thomas Crown Affair, The 1968,Je 27,48:2
Orchestra , of the Opera Comique, Paris
Barber of Seville 1949,Jl 21,21:2
Orchestra, S F (Composer)
John Ericsson Victor of Hampton Roads 1938,My 18,17:2
Orczy, Baroness (Original Author)
Two Lovers 1928,Mr 23,24:4
Scarlet Pimpernel, The 1935,F 8,27:2
Emperor's Candlesticks, The 1937,Jl 9,18:1
Return of the Scarlet Pimpernel, The 1938,Ap 11,12:2
Spy of Napoleon 1939,Ag 19,18:4
Fighting Pimpernel, The 1954,Ap 19,19:1
Ordeyne, Liane
Gangway 1937,Ag 21,7:3
Ordinsky, Vladimir (Director)
If Your Home Is Dear to You 1967,O 24,27:1
Ordonowna, Hanka
Szpieg 1934,Mr 5,19:3
Orduna, Juan de
Nobleza Baturra; Rustic Chivalry 1938,Mr 28,19:3
Ordway, Peter (Original Author)
Congolaise 1950,My 22,17:4
Ordynski, Richard
In our Time 1944,F 12,11:2
Ordynski, Richard (Director)
Dziesieciu z Pawiaka 1932,Ap 21,25:2
Zycie J Pilsudskiego 1935,My 31,11:1
Ordynsky, Vasily (Director)
At Your Doorstep 1964,Mr 15,9:1
O'Rear, James
Criss Cross 1949,Mr 12,10:2
Mister Buddwing 1966,O 12,36:1
Oreck, Don
Target Zero 1955,N 16,43:2
O'Regan, Kathleen
Juno and the Paycock 1930,Je 30,22:6
Fires of Fate 1933,Ap 3,13:4
O'Reilly, E S (Original Author)
Shanghai Bound 1927,N 7,26:4
O'Reilly, Rosemary
New Faces 1954,F 20,8:7
Orell, Felix
William Tell 1925,My 20,26:2
Orellana, Carlos
Llorona, La 1935,Jl 20,16:2
No te Enganes, Corazon; Don't Fool Thyself, Heart 1937,D 14,33:6
no Basta ser Madre; Motherhood Is Not Enough 1938,Ja 31,15:2

Orellana, Carlos— Cont
Hotel de los Chiflados, El 1939,Ag 28,17:2
Capitan Aventurero, El; Adventureous Captain, The 1939,O 3,19:5
Cancion del Milagro, La; Miracle Song, The 1940,My 11,15:2
En un Burro Tres Baturros; Three Rustics on one Donkey 1940,S 21,13:3
Life of Simon Bolivar, The 1943,Je 18,16:5
Tierra de Pasiones 1944,N 7,24:3
Orena, Vicenta Jr (Screenwriter)
Important Man, The; El Mayordoma 1962,Je 26,25:2
Orengo, Joe
Safe at Home 1941,N 26,31:2
Orez, Claire de
Cobra 1925,D 7,19:1
Orfei, Liana
Tartars, The 1962,Je 21,26:2
Damon and Pythias 1962,S 6,37:2
Casanova 1965,Jl 21,43:1
Hercules, Samson and Ulysses 1965,N 4,57:2
Devil in Love, The 1968,Jl 4,13:4
Orfei, Moira
Mighty Ursus, The 1962,Jl 26,17:1
Samson and the Slave Queen 1964,Mr 5,36:2
Casanova 1965,Jl 21,43:1
Orgaz, Elena d'
Gran Cruz, La; Heavy Cross, The 1937,D 7,31:6
Latigo, El; Whip, The 1939,Jl 1,11:3
Orico, Vanja
Cangaceiro 1954,S 3,13:2
Variety Lights; Luci del Varieta 1965,My 7,34:1
Oringer, Barry (Original Author)
Synanon 1965,My 6,44:1
Oringer, Harry (Screenwriter)
Damon and Pythias 1962,S 6,37:2
Orinvic, Mica
Marco the Magnificent 1966,D 15,60:1
Orkan, Sen
Topkapi 1964,S 18,25:1
Orkin, Ruth (Director)
Little Fugitive 1953,O 7,35:1
Lovers and Lollipops 1956,Ap 19,35:1
Orkin, Ruth (Original Author)
Lovers and Lollipops 1956,Ap 19,35:1
Orkin, Ruth (Producer)
Little Fugitive 1953,O 7,35:1
Lovers and Lollipops 1956,Ap 19,35:1
Orkin, Ruth (Screenwriter)
Little Fugitive 1953,O 7,35:1
Orko, Risto (Director)
Jaakarin Morsian; Soldiers' Bride 1939,D 18,29:3
Orkow, B (Screenwriter)
Boy Slaves 1939,F 9,17:3
Wings for the Eagle 1942,Ag 1,14:2
Orla, Nina
One Night in the Tropics 1940,D 20,33:2
Orlamond, William
Eternal Three, The 1923,O 12,7:2 (Incorrect in this edition; use 1927,O 1,7:2 elsewhere)
Slave of Desire 1923,D 11,26:2
Reno 1924,Ja 8,27:1
Name the Man 1924,F 4,23:3
Nellie, the Beautiful Cloak Model 1924,Ap 14,14:1
White Moth, The 1924,Je 16,18:3
True as Steel 1924,Je 17,22:4
Dixie Handicap, The 1924,D 30,15:3
Wife of the Centaur, The 1925,Ja 7,33:5
Great Divide, The 1925,F 11,19:4
Seven Keys to Baldpate 1925,N 3,25:4
Kiki 1926,Ap 6,26:4
That's My Baby 1926,Ap 12,18:4
Up in Mabel's Room 1926,Je 29,21:2
Mantrap 1926,Jl 12,24:4
Flesh and the Devil 1927,Ja 10,20:2
Getting Gertie's Garter 1927,F 9,17:3
Red Mill, The 1927,F 14,15:1
Taxi Dancer, The 1927,Mr 8,18:4
Fashions For Women 1927,Mr 28,26:4
See You in Jail 1927,Ap 4,30:5
Texas Steer, A 1928,Ja 2,28:1
Rose-Marie 1928,F 13,16:2
While the City Sleeps 1928,O 22,29:1
Wind, The 1928,N 5,26:1
Awakening, The 1928,D 31,9:1
Her Private Affair 1930,Ja 11,21:3
Cimarron 1931,Ja 27,20:5
Are These our Children 1931,N 14,15:3
Roar of the Dragon 1932,Jl 25,11:2
Orland, Warner
Jazz Singer, The 1927,O 7,24:4
Orland, William
Skinner's big Idea 1928,Mr 27,30:4
Orlandi, Felice
Harder They Fall, The 1956,My 10,26:3
Orlando, Don
Fixed Bayonets 1951,N 21,20:2
Park Row 1952,D 22,20:2
Hell and High Water 1954,F 2,20:6
Orlando, Orazio
Bambole; Dolls, The (The Soup); Soup, The (The Dolls) 1965,Je 29,26:1

Orlean, Will
Heaven Only Knows 1947,N 14,29:3
Orlenko, Helen
Cossacks in Exile 1939,Ja 28,19:2
Orlik, Stanislav
Zygmunt Kolosowski 1947,N 13,13:3
Orlob, Harold (Composer)
Citizen Saint 1948,My 28,28:2
Orlob, Harold (Original Author)
Citizen Saint 1948,My 28,28:2
Orlob, Harold (Producer)
One Third of a Nation 1939,F 11,13:2
Orlob, Harold (Screenwriter)
Citizen Saint 1948,My 28,28:2
Orloff, Arthur (Original Author)
Lone Wolf in London, The 1947,N 22,10:3
Gun Belt 1953,Ag 1,8:2
Orloff, Arthur (Screenwriter)
Lone Wolf in London, The 1947,N 22,10:3
Orloff, Arthur E (Original Author)
Beauty on Parade 1950,Ag 18,17:2
Orloff, Arthur E (Screenwriter)
Beauty on Parade 1950,Ag 18,17:2
Orloff, Nicholas
Dream Ballerina 1951,Ap 16,21:2
Orlov
Peter the First 1937,D 25,10:4
Orlov, A
Spring Song 1942,S 12,9:2
Tiger Girl 1955,S 5,8:2
Orlov, D N
Alexander Nevsky 1939,Mr 23,27:1
Lenin in 1918 1939,Je 27,27:2
Orlov, I
Red Tanks 1942,Je 6,9:2
Orlov, N
Guerrilla Brigade 1942,Ap 14,17:2
Orlov, V A
Lower Depths, The 1947,D 1,27:2
Orlova, Lubov
Petersburg Nights 1934,S 10,20:4
Moscow Laughs 1935,Mr 25,12:2
Volga-Volga 1941,My 17,19:2
Tanya 1942,Mr 5,27:1
Spring 1948,Mr 15,26:2
Mussorgsky 1951,Ag 20,14:3
Man of Music 1953,My 11,25:2
Orlova, Vera
Twins 1947,Jl 28,12:2
Ormandy, Eugene
Night Song 1948,Ja 29,27:5
Orme, Geoffrey (Screenwriter)
Long Duel, The 1967,N 2,58:3
Ormond, Czenzi (Screenwriter)
Strangers on a Train 1951,Jl 4,13:2
Ormond, Ron (Producer)
Ringside 1949,S 17,10:8
Dalton Gang, The 1949,N 25,27:5
Outlaw Woman 1952,Ap 5,20:3
Ornas, Barbro Hiorf Af
Shame 1968,D 24,14:1
Ornas, Barbro Hjort of
All These Women 1964,O 6,35:1
Ornitz, Samuel (Original Author)
Case of Lena Smith, The 1929,Ja 15,22:4
Chinatown Nights 1929,Ap 1,22:1
Secrets of the French Police 1932,D 12,18:4
King of the Newsboys 1938,Ap 2,18:2
Ornitz, Samuel (Screenwriter)
Hell's Highway 1932,S 26,18:2
Man Who Reclaimed his Head, The
  1935,Ja 9,22:1
Three Kids and a Queen 1935,N 9,19:2
Fatal Lady 1936,Jl 11,11:3
Follow Your Heart 1936,O 22,31:1
Hit Parade, The 1937,My 31,11:2
Portia on Trial 1937,D 3,29:2
Army Girl 1938,Ag 12,11:1
Three Faces West 1940,Ag 19,13:2
Circumstantial Evidence 1945,Ap 21,18:3
Oro, Juan Bustillo (Director)
Malditas Sean las Mujeres 1936,Ag 29,16:3
El Misterio del Rostro Palido 1937,Ja 4,20:5
El Rosal Bendito 1937,F 6,15:2
Nostradamus 1937,S 6,20:1
Huapango 1938,Je 11,9:1
Cada Loco con su Tema; Every Madman to his
  Specialty 1939,Ap 29,13:3
Tia de las Muchachas, La; Girls' Aunt, The
  1939,O 30,13:3
Caballo a Caballo; Horse for Horse
  1940,F 10,19:2
Oro, Juan Bustillo (Producer)
Tia de las Muchachas, La; Girls' Aunt, The
  1939,O 30,13:3
Orol, Juan
Calvario de una Esposa, El 1936,S 26,11:2
Mujeres Sin Alma 1936,D 12,29:4
Derecho y el Deber, El 1938,Jl 9,10:4
Orol, Juan (Director)
Madre Querida 1935,D 23,15:5
Calvario de una Esposa, El 1936,S 26,11:2
Honraras a tus Padres 1937,Ap 3,17:2

Eterna Martir 1938,Ja 3,16:3
Derecho y el Deber, El 1938,Jl 9,10:4
Orona, Vicente
Cruz Diablo 1935,Ap 6,10:1
Mater Nostra 1936,S 9,32:4
Abnegacion 1938,My 31,8:3
Guadalupe la Chinaca 1938,S 12,13:3
A la Orilla de un Palmar; At the Edge of a Palm
  Grove 1938,D 17,10:4
Luna Criolla; Creole Moon 1940,Ap 8,15:3
O'Rorke, Peggy
Irish Destiny 1927,Mr 29,23:2 (In Addenda)
Orosco, Teresa
Amor con Amor se Paga; Love for Love
  1940,Mr 16,8:2
O'Rourke, Brefni
Wings and the Woman 1942,O 8,31:1
Waltz Time 1946,F 11,25:2
Vacation From Marriage 1946,Mr 15,27:2
They Were Sisters 1946,Jl 24,24:2
Murder in Reverse 1947,Ja 11,23:5
Adventures, The 1947,Ap 4,19:2
Patient Vanishes, The 1947,My 23,31:2
Tawny Pipit 1947,S 8,25:5
Upturned Glass, The 1947,N 5,34:4
Hatter's Castle 1948,Jl 3,8:6
Don't Take it to Heart 1948,D 25,10:3
O'Rourke, Frank (Original Author)
Bravados, The 1958,Je 26,23:2
Professionals, The 1966,N 3,45:1
O'Rourke, J A
Blarney Kiss, The 1933,Ag 19,14:4
O'Rourke, Patricia
Jungle Book 1942,Ap 6,19:1
Orr, Althea
Battle of the Sexes, The 1960,Ap 19,40:4
Orr, Clifford (Original Author)
Shot in the Dark, A 1935,My 22,23:2
Orr, David
Crest of the Wave 1954,N 11,43:2
Night my Number Came up, The 1955,D 20,39:5
Orr, Forrest
Rainbow Island 1944,O 26,19:6
Orr, Gertrude (Miscellaneous)
Little Men 1935,F 18,19:3
Orr, Gertrude (Original Author)
Mad Parade, The 1931,S 19,10:2
Orr, Gertrude (Screenwriter)
Singed 1927,Jl 12,29:3
Little Men 1935,F 18,19:3
Harvester, The 1936,Jl 4,18:2
Call of the Yukon 1938,My 6,27:1
Orr, Mary (Original Author)
Wallflower 1948,Je 12,8:5
All About Eve 1950,O 14,13:2
Orr, William
Hardys Ride High, The 1939,Ap 14,28:2
Mortal Storm, The 1940,Je 21,25:2
My Love Came Back 1940,Jl 13,16:5
Honeymoon for Three 1941,F 8,19:2
Navy Blues 1941,S 20,11:2
Unholy Partners 1941,D 29,21:4
Big Street, The 1942,Ag 14,13:1
Gay Sisters, The 1942,Ag 15,14:2
He Hired the Boss 1943,Je 4,17:4
Orr, William T (Producer)
Sex and the Single Girl 1964,D 26,9:2
Orrick, David
Blackjack Ketchum Desperado 1956,Ap 5,26:2
Orrison, Jack
Never Steal Anything Small 1959,F 12,23:1
Orrom, Michael (Screenwriter)
No Resting Place 1952,My 5,18:5
Orsatti, Frank (Miscellaneous)
Irish in US, The 1935,Ag 1,15:1
Orsay, Lawrence d'
Miss Bluebeard 1925,Ja 28,14:1
Orsenwald, Francis (Original Author)
Red Stallion in the Rockies 1949,Ag 26,15:2
Orseray, Madeleine
Ramuntcho 1953,Mr 2,19:2
Orsini, Umberto
Don't Tempt the Devil 1964,Ap 28,43:1
Mademoiselle 1966,Ag 2,23:1
Sailor From Gibraltar, The 1967,Ap 25,38:2
Girl and the General, The 1967,D 7,60:1
That Woman 1968,Jl 19,30:3
Orsino, Silvio
Zappatore 1932,Mr 28,11:2
Orso, Anna Maria
Bible, The 1966,S 29,60:1
Ortalan, Riz (Composer)
Ecco 1965,N 5,28:1
Ortas, Casimiro
Podoroso Caballero 1936,O 26,20:2
Ortega, Eva
Di que me Quieres; Say That You Love Me
  1939,Ap 24,13:2
Ortego, Artie
King of the Royal Mounted 1936,S 29,35:2
Ortego, Sophie
Revenge 1928,D 10,25:1
Bird of Paradise 1932,S 10,18:5

Ortegosa, Berta
Casa del Angel, La 1960,Ag 30,25:1
Hand in the Trap 1963,Jl 2,16:2
Ortensi, Bruno
Shoe-Shine 1947,Ag 27,19:2
Orth, Frank
Hot Money 1936,Jl 25,16:2
Polo Joe 1936,N 5,35:1
Footloose Heiress 1937,O 9,16:2
Patient in Room 18, The 1938,Ap 22,15:6
Fast And Furious 1939,O 12,33:3
Secret of Dr Kildare, The 1939,D 8,33:5
His Girl Friday 1940,Ja 12,13:2
Dr Kildare's Strange Case 1940,Ap 12,19:2
'Til We Meet Again 1940,Ap 14,14:2
Conga Nights, La 1940,Je 5,33:5
Pier 13 1940,Ag 9,19:3
Gold Rush Maisie 1940,S 2,19:2
Dr Kildare's Crisis 1940,D 19,33:1
Strawberry Blonde 1941,F 22,11:2
Come Live With Me 1941,F 28,17:3
People vs Dr Kildare, The 1941,My 8,21:1
Dr Kildare's Wedding Day 1941,S 18,31:1
I Wake up Screaming 1942,Ja 17,13:2
Dr Kildare's Victory 1942,F 5,25:2
To the Shores of Tripoli 1942,Mr 26,27:2
Rings on her Fingers 1942,Ap 24,21:4
My Gal Sal 1942,My 1,23:1
Magnificent Dope, The 1942,Jl 3,12:5
Little Tokyo, USA 1942,Ag 7,13:2
Footlight Serenade 1942,S 10,30:3
Orchestra Wives 1942,S 24,23:2
Tales of Manhattan 1942,S 25,25:1
Springtime in the Rockies 1942,N 12,30:2
Over my Dead Body 1942,D 26,15:2
Hello, Frisco, Hello 1943,Mr 25,25:1
Ox-Bow Incident, The 1943,My 10,15:2 (In
  Addenda)
Coney Island 1943,Je 17,17:2
Sweet Rosie O'Grady 1943,O 21,30:2
Buffalo Bill 1944,Ap 20,22:6
Storm Over Lisbon 1944,S 11,14:1
Impatient Years, The 1944,S 20,20:1
Greenwich Village 1944,S 28,26:2
Pillow to Post 1945,My 26,18:2
Dolly Sisters, The 1945,N 15,24:6
Lost Weekend, The 1945,D 3,17:2
She Went to the Races 1946,F 1,29:2
Doll Face 1946,Mr 28,35:3
Murder in the Music Hall 1946,Ap 15,22:2
Strange Love of Martha Ivers, The
  1946,Jl 25,18:4
Guilt of Janet Ames, The 1947,My 23,31:2
Mother Wore Tights 1947,Ag 21,33:2
It Had to be You 1947,D 8,35:2
Fury at Furnace Creek 1948,Jl 12,11:2
Red Light 1950,Ja 16,18:4
Cheaper by the Dozen 1950,Ap 1,12:2
Great Rupert, The 1950,Ap 14,27:2
Father of the Bride 1950,My 19,31:2
Petty Girl, The 1950,Ag 18,17:2
Something to Live For 1952,Mr 8,11:2
Here Come the Girls 1953,D 26,10:1
Orth, Marion (Original Author)
To Please one Woman 1920,D 20,11:2
Orth, Marion (Screenwriter)
Sing Sing Nights 1935,Ja 26,13:2
Dr Christian Meets the Women 1940,Ag 2,12:2
Six Lessons From Madame La Zonga
  1941,F 19,25:2
Orthmann, Helmuth (Original Author)
Slalom 1936,D 16,35:3
Ortigoza, Carlos
Littlest Outlaw, The 1955,D 27,31:1
Ortin, Chato
Alla en el Rancho Chico; Out on the Little Ranch
  1939,F 25,19:3
Muerto Murio, El; Dead Man Died, The
  1939,Jl 29,18:3
Caballo a Caballo; Horse for Horse
  1940,F 10,19:2
Ortin, Leopoldino
Nostradamus 1937,S 6,20:1
Guadalupe la Chinaca 1938,S 12,13:3
Adelita, La 1938,O 12,35:2
Soy Chato, Pero las Huelo; I Am Snub-nosed but I
  Can Smell 1939,Jl 22,12:3
Ortin, Leopoldo
Martin Garatuza 1935,S 30,13:1
Que Hago con la Criatura? 1936,Mr 17,25:6
Malditas Sean las Mujeres 1936,Ag 29,16:3
Silencio Sublime 1937,Ja 16,21:2
Obligation to Assassinate, The 1937,O 19,29:6
Alma Jarocha 1938,Ap 30,18:2
Padre de Mas de Cuatro; Father of More Than
  Four 1939,Ap 24,13:3
Luces de Barriada; Neighborhood Lights
  1940,S 2,19:2
Ortin, Leopoldo Jr
Luces de Barriada; Neighborhood Lights
  1940,S 2,19:2

Ortiz, Alicia
Obligation to Assassinate, The 1937,O 19,29:6
Tierra del Mariachi, La; Country of the Mariachi, The 1938,D 3,11:2
China Hilaria, La 1939,Ag 12,16:3
Rosa de Xochimilco 1939,O 14,13:3
Ortiz, Ella
St Francis of Assisi 1947,Ap 5,12:5
Ortiz, Mecha
Que Tiempos Aquellos; Those Were the Days 1938,Mr 7,13:2
Mujeres que Trabajan; Women Who Work 1940,Ja 1,29:4
Con las Alas Rotas; With Broken Rings 1940,Mr 23,00:0
Maestro Leuita, El 1940,Je 10,21:2
Ortiz, Medea
Melgarejo 1937,S 20,19:2
Ortiz, Natalia
El Misterio del Rostro Palido 1937,Ja 4,20:5
No te Enganes, Corazon; Don't Fool Thyself, Heart 1937,D 14,33:6
Rapsodia Mexicana 1938,N 26,18:2
Casa del Ogro, La; House of the Ogre, The 1939,F 13,13:2
Ortiz, Natalie
Cada Loco con su Tema; Every Madman to his Specialty 1939,Ap 29,13:3
Ortiz, Pepe
Tigre de Yautepec, El 1934,O 20,20:3
Cielito Lindo 1936,N 9,22:5
Golondrina, La; Swallow, The 1939,Jl 31,9:3
Silk, Blood and Sun 1943,Ja 30,10:6
Marvels of the Bull Ring 1943,Jl 3,11:3
Littlest Outlaw, The 1955,D 27,31:1
Ortiz, Pepe (Original Author)
Marvels of the Bull Ring 1943,Jl 3,11:3
Ortiz, Peter
Rio Grande 1950,N 20,21:2
Sirocco 1951,Je 14,31:2
Ortiz, Peter (Miscellaneous)
Operation Secret 1952,N 6,37:2
Ortiz, Rosario
Tarantos, Los 1964,Je 30,22:1
Ortner, Hermann Heinz (Original Author)
Orphan Boy of Vienna, An 1937,S 9,19:2
Orton, J (Original Author)
After the Ball 1933,Mr 20,18:3
Woman in Command, The 1934,My 29,22:2
Jack Ahoy 1935,F 9,11:2
Orton, J (Screenwriter)
Born for Glory 1935,O 21,22:4
Non-Stop New York 1937,N 29,19:2
Orton, J O C (Screenwriter)
Alias Bulldog Drummond 1935,S 10,26:2
Orvantzov, Leo (Original Author)
Her Private Affair 1930,Ja 11,21:3
Orwell, George (Original Author)
Animal Farm 1954,D 30,14:1
1984 1956,O 1,31:1
Orwid, Joseph
Kazdemu Wolno Kochac 1933,My 24,24:3
Dodek na Froncie 1936,Mr 30,17:6
Pietro Wyzej; Apartment Above 1938,Ja 10,13:4
Neighbors; Shekhonim 1938,D 9,31:3
Ory, Edward (Kid)
New Orleans 1947,Je 20,25:6
Benny Goodman Story 1956,F 22,22:1
Orzazewski, Kasia
Call Northside 777 1948,F 19,29:2
Red Danube, The 1949,D 9,37:3
Deadline U S A 1952,Mr 15,8:2
Osato, Sono
Kissing Bandit, The 1948,N 19,35:2
OSBORN
See Also OSBORNE
Osborn, Andrew
Angels One Five 1954,Ap 30,28:2
Blackout 1954,My 22,8:2
Osborn, David (Screenwriter)
Chase a Crooked Shadow 1958,Mr 25,28:4
Malaga 1962,F 22,20:3
Follow the Boys 1963,F 28,8:2
Deadlier Than the Male 1967,F 22,21:1
Osborn, Lynn
Amazing Colossal Man, The 1957,O 26,19:2
Osborn, Mavis
Royal Ballet, The (Swan Lake Act II); Swan Lake Act II (The Royal Ballet) 1960,O 5,45:2
Osborn, Paul (Original Author)
Should Ladies Behave? 1933,D 18,24:3
On Borrowed Time 1939,Jl 7,13:2
World of Suzie Wong, The 1960,N 11,36:1
Osborn, Paul (Screenwriter)
Young in Heart, The 1938,N 4,27:2
Cry Havoc 1943,N 24,16:2
Madame Curie 1943,D 17,23:1
Yearling, The 1947,Ja 24,18:2
Homecoming 1948,Ap 30,28:4
Portrait of Jennie 1949,Mr 30,31:2
Invitation 1952,Ja 30,22:6
East of Eden 1955,Mr 10,33:1
Soyanara 1957,D 6,39:4

Sayonara 1957,D 6,39:4
South Pacific 1958,Mr 20,33:1
Wild River 1960,My 27,22:1
Osborn, Ralph 3d
Rally Round the Flag Boys! 1958,D 24,2:7
OSBORNE
See Also OSBORN
Osborne, Billy
Keeper of the Bees, The 1925,O 28,29:2
Osborne, Bud
Boots and Saddles 1937,N 8,19:2
Racketeers of the Range 1939,Je 8,31:4
Spoilers, The 1942,My 22,27:2
Blood on the Moon 1948,N 12,30:5
Osborne, Frances
I, The Jury 1953,Ag 22,8:2
Osborne, Hubert (Original Author)
Shore Leave 1925,S 14,16:1
Follow the Fleet 1936,F 21,21:2
Hit the Deck 1955,Mr 4,17:1
Osborne, John (Original Author)
Look Back in Anger 1959,S 16,45:1
Entertainer, The 1960,O 4,49:2
Inadmissible Evidence 1968,Je 24,44:1
Osborne, John (Screenwriter)
Entertainer, The 1960,O 4,49:2
Tom Jones 1963,O 8,48:1
Inadmissible Evidence 1968,Je 24,44:1
Osborne, Lee (Cinematographer)
Mingus 1968,My 17,56:1
Osborne, Lloyd (Original Author)
Ebb Tide 1922,N 20,21:3
Ebb Tide 1937,N 18,27:2
Adventure Island 1947,O 20,29:2
Wrong Box 1966,Jl 20,46:1
Osborne, Ted
Girl With Ideas, A 1938,Ja 1,11:2
Jury's Secret, The 1938,F 4,17:2
Road to Reno, The 1938,O 3,11:2
Isle of Destiny 1940,Ap 8,15:2
Charlie Chan At the Wax Museum 1940,S 28,9:3
Osborne, Vivienne
Over the Hill to the Poor House 1920,S 18,16:2
Beloved Bachelor, The 1931,O 17,20:1
Husband's Holiday 1931,D 25,29:2
Two Kinds of Women 1932,Ja 16,13:1
Famous Ferguson Case, The 1932,Ap 25,18:6
Two Seconds 1932,My 19,25:3
Week-End Marriage 1932,Je 4,9:2
Dark Horse, The 1932,Je 9,27:3
Life Begins 1932,Ag 26,20:3
Luxury Liner 1933,F 3,21:3
Sailor Be Good 1933,F 27,11:2
Supernatural 1933,Ap 22,16:3
Tomorrow at Seven 1933,Jl 3,14:6
Devil's in Love, The 1933,Jl 28,18:2
Phantom Broadcast, The 1933,Jl 31,16:2
No More Ladies 1935,Je 22,18:5
Let's Sing Again 1936,My 9,11:2
Follow Your Heart 1936,O 22,31:1
Wives Never Know 1936,O 31,24:2
Sinner Take All 1937,F 3,27:1
Champagne Waltz 1937,F 4,17:2
Crime Nobody Saw, The 1937,Ap 5,17:2
Primrose Path 1940,Mr 23,16:2
So You Won't Talk 1940,O 17,33:2
Captain Caution 1940,O 21,21:3
Dragonwyck 1946,Ap 11,35:2
Osborne, Will, and Orchestra
Blues in the Night 1941,D 12,35:2
Osborne Brothers
Festival 1967,O 24,53:2
Oscar, Henry
Transatlantic Tunnel 1935,O 28,16:2
Seven Sinners 1936,Ag 22,6:1
Fire Over England 1937,Mr 5,16:2
Return of the Scarlet Pimpernel, The 1938,Ap 11,12:2
Father O'Flynn 1938,D 26,29:2
Black Limelight 1939,Je 26,12:2
Saint in London, The 1939,Jl 19,23:3
Four Feathers 1939,Ag 4,11:1
Spy of Napoleon 1939,Ag 19,18:4
Spies of the Air 1940,Jl 4,12:3
Fugitive, The 1940,Jl 23,22:2
Hell's Cargo 1940,S 16,15:2
Avengers, The 1942,N 25,18:2
Squadron Leader X 1943,Jl 23,21:2
Courageous Mr Penn 1943,D 23,26:5
Upturned Glass, The 1947,N 5,34:4
Hatter's Castle 1948,Jl 3,8:6
Mrs Fitzherbert 1950,My 11,37:2
Black Rose, The 1950,S 2,11:2
Prelude to Fame 1950,N 10,35:3
Bonnie Prince Charlie 1952,Ja 7,14:3
Beau Brummell 1954,O 21,31:5
Little Hut, The 1957,My 4,25:1
Oscar Wilde 1960,Je 21,28:2
Brides of Dracula, The 1960,S 6,41:4
Murder Ahoy 1964,S 23,55:3
Oscar (Elephant)
Soul of the Beast, The 1923,My 22,14:4

Oscar and Elmer
Hit Parade, The 1937,My 31,11:2
Oscard, Miko
Brothers Karamazov, The 1958,F 21,18:2
Oscarsson, Per
Doll, The 1964,Ja 14,27:1
Hunger 1966,S 14,53:2
My Sister, My Love 1967,F 20,45:2
Dandy in Aspic, A 1968,Ap 3,40:1
Hunger 1968,Ag 13,45:2
Here's Your Life 1968,D 20,60:1
Oser, Jean (Miscellaneous)
Will It Happen Again 1948,My 17,23:4
Osgood, Bob and his Hill Billies
World Dances 1954,N 8,24:6
O'Shannon, Finola
Poacher's Daughter, The 1960,F 16,31:2
Playboy of the Western World, The 1963,Mr 19,8:2
O'Shaughnessy, Charles
Kitty 1929,Je 11,27:2
O'Shaughnessy, Edith (Original Author)
Greater Glory, The 1926,My 4,31:1
O'Shaughnessy, John (Director)
Sound of Laughter, The 1963,D 18,44:2
O'Shea, Danny
Manhattan Cocktail 1928,N 26,30:2
Vagabond Lover, The 1929,N 27,30:6
O'Shea, Denis
Irish Destiny 1927,Mr 29,23:2 (In Addenda)
O'Shea, Kevin
Purple Heart, The 1944,Mr 9,15:2
Wing and a Prayer 1944,Ag 31,14:1
O'Shea, Michael
Lady of Burlesque 1943,My 14,17:2
Jack London 1944,Mr 3,19:3
Eve of St Mark, The 1944,My 31,22:2
Man From Frisco 1944,Je 16,14:7
Something for the Boys 1944,N 30,19:1
Circumstantial Evidence 1945,Ap 21,18:3
It's a Pleasure 1945,My 4,23:3
Mr District Attorney 1947,F 28,27:3
Violence 1947,My 10,8:5
Last of the Redmen 1947,Ag 30,8:6
Threat, The 1949,D 2,35:4
Captain China 1950,Mr 2,33:2
Underworld Story, The 1950,Jl 27,29:4
Fixed Bayonets 1951,N 21,20:2
Model and the Marriage Broker, The 1952,Ja 12,10:6
Bloodhounds of Broadway 1952,N 15,15:2
It Should Happen to You 1954,Ja 16,10:5
O'Shea, Milo
You Can't Beat the Irish 1952,My 1,34:4
Ulysses 1967,Mr 14,55:1
Romeo and Juliet 1968,O 9,41:1
Barbarella 1968,O 12,43:1
O'Shea, Oscar
Captains Courageous 1937,My 12,27:1
Big City 1937,S 17,29:2
Rosalie 1937,D 31,9:2
Man-Proof 1938,Ja 14,21:1
Mannequin 1938,Ja 21,15:2
King of the Newsboys 1938,Ap 2,18:2
International Crime 1938,My 16,14:4
Main Event, The 1938,Je 20,11:3
Racket Busters 1938,Ag 11,13:1
Youth Takes a Fling 1938,O 17,12:1
Stablemates 1938,O 21,27:2
Shining Hour, The 1939,Ja 20,15:2
Big Town Czar 1939,My 4,27:3
Lucky Night 1939,My 5,29:3
King of the Turf 1939,My 8,21:2
Tell no Tales 1939,Je 2,27:3
Invitation to Happiness 1939,Je 8,31:2
S O S Tidal Wave 1939,Je 22,19:3
Those High Grey Walls 1939,O 19,27:2
Missing Evidence 1939,N 17,17:3
Night of Nights, The 1939,D 28,17:1
Of Mice and Men 1940,F 17,9:2
Zanzibar 1940,Ap 1,15:3
Twenty-Mule Team 1940,My 10,26:6
You Can't Fool Your Wife 1940,My 24,23:4
Pier 13 1940,Ag 9,19:3
Always a Bride 1940,N 21,43:3
Phantom Submarine, The 1941,F 12,25:3
Sleepers West 1941,Mr 20,25:3
Mutiny in the Arctic 1941,My 3,20:5
Ringside Maisie 1941,Ag 1,11:2
Officer and the Lady, The 1941,Ag 11,17:4
Harmon of Michigan 1941,O 2,29:2
I Was Framed 1942,Je 12,16:6
Just off Broadway 1942,Ag 29,18:4
Good Morning, Judge 1943,Ap 30,25:4
Two Tickets to London 1943,Jl 3,11:2
Corvette K-225 1943,O 21,30:1
Her Primitive Man 1944,Ap 1,11:1
Mummy's Ghost, The 1944,Jl 1,10:7
Bewitched 1945,Ag 17,20:3
My Wild Irish Rose 1947,D 25,32:2
One Sunday Afternoon 1948,D 27,16:3

O'Shea, Tessie
Russians are Coming the Russians are Coming, The 1966,My 26,55:1
O'Shiel, Fiona
Harriet Craig 1950,N 3,31:2
Oshins, Julie
This Is the Army 1943,Jl 29,11:6
I'll See You in my Dreams 1951,D 7,35:1
Oshurkoff (Producer)
Sixty-Ninth Parallel 1942,D 13,29:1
Oshurkov, I (Cinematographer)
In the Circus Arena 1952,Ap 14,22:3
Oshurkov, M (Cinematographer)
Circus Festival 1958,Mr 17,21:4
Osieli, David
Ivory Hunter 1952,Ag 19,19:1
West of Zanzibar 1955,Ja 18,31:2
Saint Joan 1957,Je 27,21:1
Osipenko, Alla
Bolshoi Ballet 67 1966,S 30,54:1
Osipets, Y
Childred of the Revolution 1936,Ap 6,18:2
Osipov, Valery (Screenwriter)
Letter That Was Never Sent, The 1962,N 19,39:2
Osmond, Cliff
Irma la Douce 1963,Je 6,39:1
Kiss Me, Stupid 1964,D 23,22:2
Fortune Cookie, The 1966,O 20,52:1
Osmond, Hal
Story of Robin Hood, The 1952,Je 27,18:3
Cash on Delivery 1956,S 1,19:3
Osmond, Henry (Original Author)
Truth About Youth, The 1930,D 13,22:2
Osmond, Lesley
This Was a Woman 1949,Ja 5,22:2
Osmond, Marion (Original Author)
Chinese Den 1941,Mr 26,27:3
Osmond, V Miss
Little Lord Fauntleroy 1914,Je 23,11:3
Osmyalovskaya, Elena
Taras Family, The 1946,D 9,34:4
Osmyalovskaya, K
Natalka-Poltavka 1936,D 25,19:4
Osone, Tatsuo (Director)
Imposter, The 1955,Mr 23,27:1
Oss, Edith
Alles Weg'n Dem Hund 1936,Mr 31,17:3
Osten, Franz (Director)
Shiraz 1928,O 7,IX,7:7
Shiraz 1929,Mr 19,37:2
Throw of the Dice 1930,Ja 6,30:5
Judas von Tirol, Der 1935,Ap 27,20:7
Zu Strassburg auf der Schanz; At the Strassburg 1936,F 15,18:7
Fuerst Sepp'l 1937,Jl 17,18:1
Osten-Sacken, Maria von (Screenwriter)
Reaching for the Stars 1958,My 24,18:2
Ostenso, Martha (Original Author)
Wild Geese 1927,D 5,26:2
Sister Kenny 1946,S 30,21:2
Oster, Fred
Last Blitzkrieg, The 1959,Ja 31,13:5
Osterholm, Jens
Weekend 1964,Ap 27,24:1
Osterloh, Robert
Dark Past, The 1948,D 23,25:2
City Across the River 1949,Ap 8,31:3
Undercover Man, The 1949,Ap 21,30:2
White Heat 1949,S 3,7:2
711 Ocean Drive 1950,Jl 20,21:2
Lady Without Passport, A 1950,Ag 4,13:2
Southside 1-1000 1950,N 3,31:2
Great Missouri Raid, The 1951,Ap 9,31:2
Fat Man, The 1951,My 25,31:2
Prowler, The 1951,Jl 2,16:6
Day the Earth Stood Still, The 1951,S 19,37:1
One Minute to Zero 1952,S 20,13:2
Wild One, The 1953,D 31,9:2
Riot in Cell Block 11 1954,F 19,24:5
Wicked Woman 1954,Mr 27,13:6
Violent Saturday 1955,My 12,32:2
Man With the Gun 1955,D 23,14:2
Osterman, Jack
Wanted Men 1936,Jl 8,15:2
Ostermann, Willy (Composer)
Rheinlandmaedel, Das 1931,S 18,29:1
Ostermayr, Peter (Director)
Youth Astray 1928,My 29,17:2
Edelweisskoenig, Der 1939,F 4,11:2
Ostermayr, Peter (Producer)
Heilige und Ihr Narr, Die; Saint and Her Fool, The 1935,N 29,24:2
Waldrausch; Forest Fever 1940,Ja 20,11:3
Osterwald, Bibi
Parrish 1961,My 5,22:1
World of Henry Orient, The 1964,Mr 20,27:2
Tiger Makes Out, The 1967,S 19,53:1
Ostrer, Bertram (Producer)
Green Scarf, The 1955,Ja 15,10:2
Nearly a Nasty Accident 1962,Je 28,21:2
Ostrer, Pamela
Power 1934,O 5,29:3

Ostroumof, S M
Mother and Sons 1938,S 15,29:2
Ostrovsky, A (Original Author)
Without Dowry 1946,Ap 15,22:2
Snegurochka; Snow Maiden, The 1953,S 7,15:2
Marriage of Baezaminov, The 1966,Je 11,20:2
Ostrovsky, Ben
Cuban Rebel Girls 1959,D 26,7:3
Ostrovsky, Nikolai (Original Author)
Heroes Are Made 1944,Mr 11,10:2
Ostyn, Berthe
Versuchen Sie Meine Schwester 1931,Je 20,20:4
Blonde Nachtigall, Die 1931,Ag 22,7:5
Grosse Sehnsucht, Die 1931,O 8,22:6
Dienst Ist Dienst 1932,Je 6,18:5
Ich Geh' aus und Du Bleibst da 1932,N 21,21:1
Schuetzen Koenig, Der 1933,My 3,15:5 (In Addenda)
Sohn der Weissen Berge, Der 1933,O 23,18:3
Eine Stadt Steht Kopf 1934,Ja 29,10:2
Fahrt ins Gruene, Die 1936,My 23,12:2
O'Sullivan, Arthur
Quare Fellow 1963,F 20,6:1
Girl With Green Eyes 1964,Ag 11,37:2
O'Sullivan, Brian
Dawn Over Ireland 1938,F 19,19:2
Men of Ireland 1938,S 30,24:2
O'Sullivan, Jerry
Pickup on South Street 1953,Je 18,38:2
O'Sullivan, Lawrence
Delicious 1931,D 26,15:5
O'Sullivan, Maureen
Song O' my Heart 1930,Mr 12,32:6
So This Is London 1930,My 24,21:2
Just Imagine 1930,N 22,21:3
Princess and the Plumber, The 1930,D 23,25:1
Connecticut Yankee, A 1931,Ap 13,17:1
Skyline 1931,O 5,17:3
Big Shot, The 1932,Ja 2,14:2
Tarzan, The Ape Man 1932,Mr 28,11:2
Silver Lining, The 1932,My 30,16:5
Skyscraper Souls 1932,Ag 5,11:2
Strange Interlude 1932,S 1,24:3
Okay America 1932,S 10,18:5
Payment Deferred 1932,N 8,26:3
Cohens and Kellys in Trouble, The 1933,Ap 17,16:4
Tugboat Annie 1933,Ag 12,14:2
Stage Mother 1933,S 30,18:5
Tarzan and his Mate 1934,Ap 21,12:1
Thin Man, The 1934,Je 30,18:5
Hide-Out 1934,Ag 25,16:5
Barretts of Wimpole Street, The 1934,S 29,12:2
David Copperfield 1935,Ja 19,8:1
West Point of the Air 1935,Ap 6,10:1
Cardinal Richelieu 1935,Ap 19,24:2
Flame Within, The 1935,Je 1,18:2
Anna Karenina 1935,Ag 31,16:2
Voice of Bugle Ann, The 1936,F 27,23:1
Connecticut Yankee at the Court of King Arthur, A 1936,My 4,16:1
Devil Doll, The 1936,Ag 8,5:2
Tarzan Escapes 1936,N 20,27:2
Day at the Races, A 1937,Je 18,25:2
Emperor's Candlesticks, The 1937,Jl 9,18:1
Between Two Women 1937,Ag 6,21:1
Yank at Oxford, A 1938,F 25,15:1
Hold That Kiss 1938,Je 11,9:1
Port of Seven Seas 1938,Jl 15,13:2
Crowd Roars, The 1938,Ag 5,11:1
Spring Madness 1938,D 1,29:3
Let Us Live 1939,Mr 30,19:2
Tarzan Finds a Son 1939,Je 15,27:2
Sporting Blood 1940,Jl 22,20:2
Pride and Prejudice 1940,Ag 9,19:1
Maisie Was a Lady 1941,F 13,25:2
Tarzan's Secret Treasure 1941,D 25,33:1
Tarzan's New York Adventure 1942,Ag 7,13:2
Big Clock, The 1948,Ap 22,34:2
Where Danger Lives 1951,Ja 1,13:6
No Resting Place 1952,My 5,18:5
All I Desire 1953,Ag 29,10:1
Mission Over Korea 1953,S 19,7:2
Duffy of San Quentin 1954,F 10,38:5
Never too Late 1965,N 5,28:1
O'Sullivan, Michael
You're a Big Boy Now 1967,Mr 21,35:3
O'Sullivan, Richard
Green Scarf, The 1955,Ja 15,10:2
Stranger's Hand, The 1955,F 16,24:5
It's Great to be Young 1957,D 26,23:3
Dangerous Exile 1958,O 11,18:3
Cleopatra 1963,Je 13,29:1
O'Sullivan, Sheila
Ulysses 1967,Mr 14,55:1
O'Sullivan, William J (Producer)
Hellfire 1949,My 30,9:4
Osvetzimsky, V
Heroes of the Sea 1941,Ap 28,11:2
Guerrilla Brigade 1942,Ap 14,17:2
Oswald
You're a Sweetheart 1937,D 25,10:5

Oswald, Gerd (Director)
Crime of Passion 1957,Ja 10,25:1
Fury at Showdown 1957,Ap 20,21:3
Paris Holiday 1958,My 10,19:2
Screaming Mimi 1958,Je 26,23:3
Agent for H.A.R.M 1966,Ja 6,20:2
Oswald, Gerd (Producer)
Oasis 1960,Jl 7,26:1
Oswald, Marianne
Lovers of Verona, The 1951,Mr 12,20:2
Sans Famille 1959,S 5,11:4
Modigliani of Montparnasse 1961,Mr 1,27:3
Oswald, Richard (Director)
Lucrecia Borgia 1928,D 25,31:3
Wien Du Stadt der Lieder; (Vienna City of Song) 1931,Mr 20,29:1
Hauptmann von Koepenick, Der; Captain of Koepenick, The 1932,F 28,VIII,6:1
Schubert's Fruehlingstraum 1932,Je 22,19:4
1914: The Last Days Before the War 1932,S 5,9:6
Hauptmann von Koepenick, Der 1933,Ja 17,22:6
Viktoria und Ihr Husar 1933,Ap 10,8:3
Alraune 1934,My 5,22:4
Graefin Mariza 1935,Ja 26,13:3
Ein Lied Geht um die Welt 1936,S 25,20:3
Dreyfus Case, The 1940,O 30,29:3
Living Dead, The 1940,D 17,33:2
Joseph Schmidt Story, The 1951,Mr 5,24:2
Oswald, Richard (Producer)
Dreyfus Case, The 1940,O 30,29:3
Joseph Schmidt Story, The 1951,Mr 5,24:2
Oswald, Richard (Screenwriter)
Living Dead, The 1940,D 17,33:2
Joseph Schmidt Story, The 1951,Mr 5,24:2
Oswalda, Ossi
Stern von Valencia, Der 1934,Ap 21,12:2
Osward, Mario
Ungkarlspappan 1936,Ja 4,19:1
Oswietsimski, Waclaw
Zygmunt Kolosowski 1947,N 13,13:3
Otani, Reiko
Tokyo File 212 1951,Je 1,20:7
Otawa, Nobuko
Onibaba 1965,F 10,44:3
Otcenasek, Jan (Original Author)
Murder Czech Style 1968,Ag 20,33:1
Otcenasek, Jan (Screenwriter)
Sweet Light in a Dark Room 1966,Je 30,28:1
Murder Czech Style 1968,Ag 20,33:1
Otero, Blanca Rosa
Gavilan, El; Hawk, The 1940,Ja 22,11:2
Dama de las Camelias, La 1944,S 26,16:1
Otero, Luis
Dark River 1956,F 27,19:4
Otho, Henry
Red Salute 1935,S 30,13:1
Treachery Rides the Range 1936,My 30,7:3
Murder by an Aristocrat 1936,Je 13,13:2
Love Begins at 20 1936,S 19,20:1
Slim 1937,Je 24,30:2
Othon, Yvonne
West Side Story 1961,O 19,39:3
Oti, Manuel Mur (Director)
Fedra, the Devil's Daughter 1957,O 26,19:2
Oti, Manuel Mur (Producer)
Fedra, the Devil's Daughter 1957,O 26,19:2
Oti, Manuel Mur (Screenwriter)
Fedra, the Devil's Daughter 1957,O 26,19:2
Otis, James (Original Author)
Circus Days 1923,Ag 6,14:2
Otis, Ted
Best of Everything 1959,O 9,24:2
Otis, William R
Goose Hangs High, The 1925,Mr 10,19:3
Otlosen, Carl
Journey to the Seventh Planet 1962,My 25,28:3
O'Toole, Peter
Kidnapped 1960,My 19,44:3
Day They Robbed the Bank of England, The 1960,S 5,11:2
Savage Innocents, The 1961,My 25,31:1
Lawrence of Arabia 1962,D 17,5:6
Becket 1964,Mr 12,40:2
Lord Jim 1965,F 26,18:1
What's New Pussycat? 1965,Je 23,49:1
How to Steal a Million 1966,Jl 15,34:1
Bible, The 1966,S 29,60:1
Night of the Generals, The 1967,F 3,38:1
Lion in Winter, The 1968,O 31,54:1
Otowa, Nobuko
Island, The; Hadaka No Shima 1962,S 11,27:2
This Madding Crowd 1964,Je 17,48:1
Lost Sex 1968,Jl 23,27:2
Otsuka, Michiko
Rebellion 1967,S 25,56:4
Rebellion 1968,O 26,9:4
Otsuka, Yawara (Miscellaneous)
Insect Woman, The; Nippon Konchuki 1964,Jl 1,42:1
Ott, Warrene
If a Man Answers 1962,N 22,43:1

Ottaviano, Roberto
Quo Vadis 1951,N 9,22:2
Otten, Karl (Screenwriter)
Kameradschaft 1932,N 9,28:5
Otterman, George Jr
Sullivans, The 1944,F 10,19:2
Ottesen, Pasmus
Child of Man 1950,F 1,25:2
Ottiano, Rafaela
Grand Hotel 1932,Ap 13,23:2
As You Desire Me 1932,Je 3,23:4
Washington Masquerade, The 1932,Jl 22,18:2
She Done Him Wrong 1933,F 10,12:3
Bondage 1933,Ap 24,11:3
Ann Vickers 1933,S 29,24:1
Female 1933,N 4,18:3
Mandalay 1934,F 15,15:6
Lost Lady, A 1934,O 4,19:1
Last Gentleman, The 1934,O 18,26:5
Enchanted April 1935,Mr 9,19:1
Florentine Dagger, The 1935,Ap 27,20:6
Curly Top 1935,Ag 2,22:3
Remember Last Night? 1935,N 21,27:2
We're Only Human 1936,Ja 18,19:2
Devil Doll, The 1936,Ag 8,5:2
Anthony Adverse 1936,Ag 27,16:1
Mad Holiday 1936,N 26,39:2
That Girl From Paris 1937,Ja 1,19:1
Maytime 1937,Mr 19,27:1
Seventh Heaven 1937,Mr 26,25:1
League of Frightened Men, The 1937,Jl 2,25:1
Suez 1938,O 15,21:2
Paris Honeymoon 1939,Ja 26,17:1
Long Voyage Home, The 1940,O 9,30:2 (In Addenda)
Victory 1940,D 23,23:2
Topper Returns 1941,Mr 28,26:6
Adventures of Martin Eden 1942,Mr 16,19:2
Otto, Frank
Kid Comes Back, The 1938,F 7,10:2
Crime School 1938,My 11,17:2
Born Yesterday 1950,D 27,30:2
Otto, Hans Dr (Director)
Life of Beethoven, The 1929,Mr 12,26:3
Otto, Henry
Iron Mask, The 1929,F 22,18:6
Otto, Henry (Director)
Willow Tree, The 1920,F 2,10:1
Temple of Venus, The 1923,N 1,24:3
Dante's Inferno 1924,S 30,27:3
Folly of Vanity 1925,Ja 28,14:1
Otto, Paul
Tradition 1921,Jl 1,8:1
Shattered 1921,D 11,VI,3:1 (In Addenda)
Trial of Donald Westhof, The 1928,F 18,11:2
Sajenko, The Soviet 1929,Ja 15,22:4
Sein Liebeslied 1931,N 19,27:5
Elisabeth von Oesterreich 1931,D 11,35:1
Die Blumenfrau von Lindenau 1932,Jl 8,22:5
Barberina, Die Taenzerin Von Sans-Souci 1932,O 26,15:4
Hauptmann von Koepenick, Der 1933,Ja 17,22:6
Drei Tage Mittelarrest 1933,My 18,17:4
Es Wird Schon Wieder Besser 1934,Ja 24,21:3
Ja, Treu Ist die Soldatenliebe 1934,Ap 28,11:4
Roman Einer Nacht 1934,Je 22,24:2
Die-oder Keine 1934,O 29,14:3
Choral von Leuthen, Der 1935,Ja 21,19:4
Liebelei 1936,F 28,18:2
Madonna, Wo Bist Du? 1936,Mr 21,13:3
Ein Liebesroman im Hause Habsburg 1936,O 12,23:2
Kleines Bezirksgericht; Little Country Court 1939,F 18,12:4
Pour le Merite 1939,Ap 8,19:2
Aufruhr in Damaskus; Tumult in Damascus 1939,My 6,21:2
Leidenschaft; Passion 1940,S 24,26:6
Otto, Paul (Director)
Tradition 1921,Jl 1,8:1
Otto, Paul (Original Author)
Tradition 1921,Jl 1,8:1
Otto, Ted (Miscellaneous)
Rosenkavalier, Der 1962,O 10,57:1
Otvos, A Dorian (Original Author)
Flirting With Fate 1938,D 15,35:3
Otvos, A Dorian (Screenwriter)
Goodbye Broadway 1938,My 14,18:1
Otzak, Nico
Dolce Vita, La 1961,Ap 20,30:1
Ouby, Joseph
Nine Hours to Rama 1963,Ap 4,58:2
Oudart, Felix
Maternite 1937,Je 8,30:2
Schubert's Serenade 1940,S 3,21:2
Back Streets of Paris 1948,O 16,9:2
Scandals of Clochemerle, The 1950,Mr 28,28:2
Oughton, Winifred
There Goes the Bride 1933,Mr 4,11:3
Ouhayour, Meyer
Last Outpost, The 1935,O 5,18:2

Ouida (Original Author)
Boy of Flanders, A 1924,Ap 15,24:1
Under Two Flags 1936,My 1,19:1
Dog of Flanders, A 1960,Ap 1,37:1
Oulton, Brian
Castle in the Air 1953,Ja 5,19:2
Man With a Million 1954,Je 29,21:2
Will any Gentleman? 1955,S 28,70:6
39 Steps, The 1960,O 11,55:2
Oumansky, Alexander (Miscellaneous)
High Sign, The 1922,Mr 20,10:3
Oumansky, Andre
Truth, The 1961,Je 27,23:2
Sundays and Cybele 1962,N 13,43:3
Joy House 1965,F 18,29:1
OUR
See Also AUER
Oursler, Fulton (Original Author)
Second Wife 1930,F 10,20:4
Spider, The 1931,S 5,7:4
Great Jasper, The 1933,F 17,5:3
Second Wife 1936,Ag 29,16:3
Spider, The 1946,Je 21,20:3
Oury, Gerard
Antoine and Antoinette 1948,Ap 16,29:2
Sea Devils 1953,Jl 31,11:5
Sword and the Rose, The 1953,Ag 20,18:3
Night is my Kingdom, The 1953,S 30,37:1
Detective, The 1954,N 2,25:2
Heart of the Matter, The 1954,N 19,20:2
Journey, The 1959,F 20,19:1
Heroes and Sinners; (Heros Sont Fatigues, Les) 1959,My 12,38:2
Mirror Has two Faces, The 1959,My 27,31:1
Young Girls Beware 1959,Ag 22,8:2
Back to the Wall; (Dos au Mur) 1959,S 8,43:2
Prize, The 1964,Ja 24,21:1
Oury, Gerard (Director)
Crime Does Not Pay (The Man on the Avenue);
Man on the Avenue, The (Crime Does Not Pay) 1962,O 17,35:2
Crime Does Not Pay (The Fenayrou Case);
Fenayrou Case, The (Crime Does Not Pay) 1962,O 17,35:2
Crime Does Not Pay (The Mask); Mask, The (Crime Does Not Pay) 1962,O 17,35:2
Crime Does Not Pay (The Hugues Case); Hugues Case, The (Crime Does Not Pay) 1962,O 17,35:2
Sucker, The 1967,O 9,61:1
Oury, Gerard (Original Author)
Babette Goes to War 1960,Je 8,46:1
Oury, Gerard (Screenwriter)
Mirror Has two Faces, The 1959,My 27,31:1
Crime Does Not Pay (The Man on the Avenue);
Man on the Avenue, The (Crime Does Not Pay) 1962,O 17,35:2
Crime Does Not Pay (The Mask); Mask, The (Crime Does Not Pay) 1962,O 17,35:2
Crime Does Not Pay (The Fenayrou Case);
Fenayrou Case, The (Crime Does Not Pay) 1962,O 17,35:2
Crime Does Not Pay (The Hugues Case); Hugues Case, The (Crime Does Not Pay) 1962,O 17,35:2
Sucker, The 1967,O 9,61:1
Ouspenskaya, Maria
Dodsworth 1936,S 24,29:1
Conquest 1937,N 5,19:1
Love Affair 1939,Mr 17,25:2
Rains Came, The 1939,S 9,11:2
Judge Hardy and Son 1940,Ja 18,27:3 (In Addenda)
Dr Ehrlich's Magic Bullet 1940,F 24,9:2
Waterloo Bridge 1940,My 17,23:2
Mortal Storm, The 1940,Je 21,25:2
Man I Married, The 1940,Ag 3,9:2
Beyond Tomorrow 1940,S 27,27:1
Dance, Girl, Dance 1940,O 11,25:2
Wolf Man, The 1941,D 22,24:5
Shanghai Gesture, The 1941,D 26,21:2
Kings Row 1942,F 3,23:2
Mystery of Marie Roget, The 1942,My 5,17:3
Frankenstein Meets the Wolf Man 1943,Mr 6,8:3
Tarzan and the Amazons 1945,Ap 30,13:4
I've Always Loved You 1946,S 7,11:1
Wyoming 1947,Jl 25,12:5
Kiss in the Dark, A 1949,Mr 26,10:6
Outing (Producer)
Mountaineering Memory, A 1918,My 13,11:3
Coorial on the Orinoco, A 1918,My 20,11:3
Untitled-Travel, Patamona 1918,My 27,11:3
Zuni Kicking Race, A 1918,Je 24,9:1
Dam Catastrophe, A 1918,Jl 1,9:3
Unblazed Trail, The 1918,Jl 15,9:3
Pin Feather Picitaninnies 1918,Ag 19,7:1
Finest on Four Feet 1918,S 16,9:3
Ballahooing on the Anarika 1919,Mr 17,13:2
Wasmanipae Week-End, A 1919,Ap 7,11:5
Up in the Air After Alligators 1919,Ap 14,11:4
Camering Through Africa 1919,Ap 21,13:4
Mr Outing Floats a Dream 1919,My 5,11:1
Itasca Makes Her Bow 1919,My 19,20:5

Outing (Producer) — Cont
Wrangling Dudes 1919,Je 9,16:3
Mr Outing Climbs Aboard 1919,Je 30,16:3
Getting the Cassiar's Goat 1919,Jl 7,18:5
Haitian Night Tale 1919,Jl 21,12:3
Put Your Cares on Ice 1919,Jl 28,8:5
Japanese Study, A 1919,Ag 11,9:1
Pigs and Kava 1920,My 24,20:3
Some More Samoa 1920,Jl 26,9:5
Ovanesova, Arsha (Screenwriter)
World Youth Festival 1950,Jl 10,18:4
Ovchinnikova, L
Day the War Ended, The 1961,Ja 30,17:2
Home for Tanya, A 1961,Ag 14,28:5
Springtime on the Volga 1961,D 25,27:4
Oved, Margalit
Hill 24 Doesn't Answer 1955,N 3,37:1
Overlander, Web
Quiet Man, The 1952,Ag 22,13:1
Return to Paradise 1953,S 11,24:2
Overman, Jack
Runaround, The 1946,Je 7,16:3
Brasher Doubloon, The 1947,My 22,34:5
Brute Force 1947,Jl 17,16:2
T-Men 1948,Ja 23,28:3
Noose Hangs High, The 1948,My 29,8:6
Force of Evil 1948,D 27,16:2
Overman, Lynne
Midnight 1934,Mr 10,18:3
Little Miss Marker 1934,My 19,18:3
Great Flirtation, The 1934,Je 22,16:5
She Loves Me Not 1934,S 8,18:5
You Belong to Me 1934,S 13,26:1
Broadway Bill 1934,N 30,22:2
Enter Madame 1935,Ja 12,12:1
Rumba 1935,F 25,13:2
Men Without Names 1935,Je 29,16:2
Paris in Spring 1935,Jl 13,16:2
Two for Tonight 1935,Ag 31,16:2
Collegiate 1936,Ja 23,25:2
Poppy 1936,Je 18,19:1
Yours for the Asking 1936,Ag 20,14:2
Jungle Princess 1936,D 24,21:3
Don't Tell the Wife 1937,F 19,15:2
Nobody's Baby 1937,My 20,17:3
Blonde Trouble 1937,Ag 7,7:2
Night Club Scandal 1937,N 12,27:2
True Confession 1937,D 16,35:2
Big Broadcast of 1938, The 1938,Mr 10,16:2
Her Jungle Love 1938,Ap 14,27:2
Hunted Men 1938,My 21,9:2
Spawn of the North 1938,S 8,27:1
Sons of the Legion 1938,S 30,24:3
Men With Wings 1938,O 27,27:2
Ride a Crooked Mile 1938,D 29,15:2
Persons in Hiding 1939,Mr 2,19:2
Union Pacific 1939,My 11,31:2
Death of a Champion 1939,Ag 24,17:3
Typhoon 1940,My 23,28:4
Edison the Man 1940,Je 7,27:2
Safari 1940,Je 20,29:2
North West Mounted Police 1940,N 7,33:2
There's Magic in Music 1941,Je 5,27:2
Caught in the Draft 1941,Je 26,27:3
Aloma of the South Seas 1941,Ag 28,23:4
New York Town 1941,N 13,35:2
Roxie Hart 1942,F 20,21:1
Reap the Wild Wind 1942,Mr 27,27:2
Forest Rangers, The 1942,O 22,25:2
Star Spangled Rhythm 1942,D 31,20:1
Silver Queen 1943,Ja 11,18:4
Dixie 1943,Je 24,26:2
Desert Song, The 1943,D 18,10:6
Overseas Press Club of America (Original Author)
Guilty of Treason 1950,Ap 11,26:2
Overton, Frank
Desire Under the Elms 1958,Mr 13,24:2
Last Mile, The 1959,F 19,27:1
Lonelyhearts 1959,Mr 5,35:3
Wild River 1960,My 27,22:1
Khovanschina 1960,S 23,33:1
Claudelle Inglish 1961,S 21,40:2
To Kill a Mockingbird 1963,F 15,10:2
Fail Safe 1964,S 16,36:1
Ovey, George
Yankee Clipper, The 1927,My 3,25:1
Hit the Deck 1930,Ja 15,28:6
Night Ride 1930,Ja 20,21:1
Ow, Anita Von
It Happened in Broad Daylight 1960,S 30,33:1
Owe, Baard
Gertrud 1966,Je 3,33:1
Owen, Alun
Servant, The 1964,Mr 17,30:2
Owen, Alun (Screenwriter)
Hard Day's Night, A 1964,Ag 12,41:1
Owen, Arthur E
Human Monster, The 1940,Mr 25,11:2
Owen, Bill
My Brothers Keeper 1949,F 14,15:3
Easy Money (Episode 3) 1949,F 14,15:3
Daybreak 1949,Jl 4,9:2
Weaker Sex, The 1949,Jl 11,13:2
Gay Lady, The 1951,Ap 16,21:2

Owen, Bill — Cont

Hotel Sahara 1952,Ja 1,21:4
Story of Robin Hood, The 1952,Je 27,18:3
Ship That Died of Shame, The 1956,Ag 21,33:2
Carry on Sergeant 1959,O 28,40:5
Carry on Nurse 1960,S 10,11:1
Georgy Girl 1966,O 18,48:1

Owen, Catherine Dale

His Glorious Night 1929,O 5,22:5
Rogue Song, The 1930,Ja 29,26:4
Such Men Are Dangerous 1930,Mr 8,21:1
Born Reckless 1930,Je 7,10:4
Today 1930,N 17,29:1
Behind Office Doors 1931,Mr 21,15:1

Owen, Charlie W Cpl

Cease Fire! 1953,N 25,17:1

Owen, Cliff (Director)

Wrong Arm of the Law, The 1963,Ap 3,39:1
Man Could Get Killed, A 1966,My 12,54:2
Vengance of She, The 1968,My 30,21:4

Owen, Don (Original Author)

Nobody Waved Goodbye 1964,S 17,52:1

Owen, Don (Producer)

Nobody Waved Goodbye 1964,S 17,52:1

Owen, Don (Screenwriter)

Nobody Waved Goodbye 1964,S 17,52:1

Owen, Frank (Miscellaneous)

Shrine of Victory 1943,Ag 20,13:2

Owen, Frank (Original Author)

Avengers, The 1942,N 25,18:2
Triple Cross 1967,Jl 20,20:2

Owen, Garry

Child of Manhattan 1933,F 13,11:4
Hold Your Man 1933,Jl 1,16:6
Son of a Sailor 1933,N 30,38:4
Little Miss Marker 1934,My 19,18:3
Hold 'Em Yale 1935,Ap 27,20:6
Ceiling Zero 1936,Ja 20,22:2
Return of Sophie Lang, The 1936,Jl 24,13:1
Case of the Black Cat, The 1936,D 26,15:4
Racketeers in Exile 1937,Ap 12,15:3
San Quentin 1937,Ag 4,15:2
True Confession 1937,D 16,35:2
Call of the Yukon 1938,My 6,27:1
Heart of the North 1938,D 21,29:2
Meet John Doe 1941,Mr 13,25:2
Arsenic and old Lace 1944,S 2,17:2
Killers, The 1946,Ag 29,24:2
Dark Mirror, The 1946,O 19,15:2
Flying Saucer, The 1950,Ja 5,28:3
Admiral Was a Lady, The 1950,O 13,23:3
Milkman, The 1951,Ja 1,13:6

Owen, George

French Leave 1931,D 7,16:1

Owen, George (Original Author)

Pittsburgh 1943,F 25,27:2

Owen, George (Screenwriter)

Something to Shout About 1943,Ap 8,27:3

Owen, Gillian

Prince and the Showgirl 1957,Je 14,22:2

Owen, Glyn

Attack on the Iron Coast 1968,Je 6,54:2

Owen, Granville

Torchy Blane, The Adventurous Blonde
 1937,D 18,18:1
Great Plane Robbery, The 1940,N 15,25:2

Owen, Guy (Original Author)

Flim Flam Man, The 1967,Ag 23,40:1

Owen, Jack (Miscellaneous)

Manhattan Merry-Go-Round 1937,D 31,9:3

Owen, LeRoy (Original Author)

Aloma of the South Seas 1941,Ag 28,23:4

Owen, Mary

You Belong to Me 1934,S 13,26:1

Owen, Mickey

Ninth Inning, The 1942,Ja 8,30:3

Owen, Milton

Great Garrick, The 1937,O 25,23:1
Exile, The 1947,D 26,22:4

Owen, Myrtle

Where the North Begins 1923,Ag 27,14:3

Owen, Paul

War Is a Racket 1934,D 10,16:2

Owen, Reginald

Letter, The 1929,Mr 8,30:1
Man in Possession, The 1931,Jl 18,16:6
Platinum Blonde 1931,O 31,22:2
Woman Commands, A 1932,Ja 28,13:2
Lovers Courageous 1932,F 20,11:2
Man Called Back, The 1932,Jl 30,16:5
Downstairs 1932,O 8,15:4
Sherlock Holmes 1932,N 12,20:5
Study in Scarlet, A 1933,Je 1,15:3
Narrow Corner, The 1933,Jl 14,15:3
Double Harness 1933,Jl 21,20:2
Big Brain, The 1933,Ag 5,9:5
Voltaire 1933,Ag 23,21:2
Queen Christina 1933,D 27,23:3
Fashions of 1934 1934,Ja 20,12:2
Nana 1934,F 2,20:3
Mandalay 1934,F 15,15:6
House of Rothschild, The 1934,Mr 15,27:2
Countess of Monte Cristo, The 1934,Ap 2,13:2
Stingaree 1934,My 18,27:1

Where Sinners Meet 1934,My 25,25:2
Of Human Bondage 1934,Je 29,17:1
Human Side, The 1934,S 15,20:3
Madame Du Barry 1934,O 25,26:2
Music in the Air 1934,D 14,29:3
Here is my Heart 1934,D 22,21:1
Good Fairy, The 1935,F 1,18:1
Enchanted April 1935,Mr 9,19:1
Escapade 1935,Jl 6,16:2
Call of the Wild 1935,Ag 15,15:2
Anna Karenina 1935,Ag 31,16:2
Tale of Two Cities, A 1935,D 26,21:2
Rose Marie 1936,F 1,9:2
Petticoat Fever 1936,Mr 21,13:2
Great Ziegfeld, The 1936,Ap 9,21:2
Trouble for Two 1936,My 30,7:2
Yours for the Asking 1936,Ag 20,14:2
Adventure in Manhattan 1936,O 23,27:5
Girl on the Front Page, The 1936,N 7,15:2
Love on the Run 1936,N 28,13:3
Dangerous Number 1937,Mr 12,19:2
Personal Property 1937,Ap 11,27:2
Bride Wore Red, The 1937,O 15,18:4
Madame X 1937,O 25,23:1
Conquest 1937,N 5,19:1
Rosalie 1937,D 31,9:2
Paradise for Three 1938,F 16,17:1
Everybody Sing 1938,Mr 11,15:3
Kidnapped 1938,My 28,9:2
Three Loves Has Nancy 1938,S 2,21:2
Vacation From Love 1938,N 10,33:2
Christmas Carol, A 1938,D 23,16:2
Girl Downstairs, The 1939,Ja 26,17:1
Fast and Loose 1939,Mr 9,18:1
Hotel Imperial 1939,My 11,31:3
Bridal Suite 1939,My 26,20:2
Real Glory, The 1939,S 15,26:2
Remember? 1939,D 15,33:4
Earl of Chicago, The 1940,Mr 14,29:3
Florian 1940,Je 6,33:2
Hullabaloo 1940,D 19,33:1
Free and Easy 1941,Ap 3,29:4
Woman's Face, A 1941,My 16,21:2
They Met in Bombay 1941,Jl 4,17:1
Charley's Aunt 1941,Ag 2,18:2
Lady Be Good 1941,S 19,27:1
Tarzan's Secret Treasure 1941,D 25,33:1
Woman of the Year 1942,F 6,23:2
We Were Dancing 1942,My 1,23:2
Mrs Miniver 1942,Je 5,23:1
I Married an Angel 1942,Jl 10,13:2
Pierre of the Plains 1942,Jl 30,17:3
Somewhere I'll Find You 1942,Ag 28,22:4
Cairo 1942,N 6,27:2
White Cargo 1942,N 27,27:2
Random Harvest 1942,D 18,36:6
Reunion in France 1943,Mr 5,20:3
Assignment in Brittany 1943,Ap 22,31:2
Three Hearts for Julia 1943,My 21,22:4
Above Suspicion 1943,Ag 6,10:3
Salute to the Marines 1943,Ag 30,11:3
Madame Curie 1943,D 17,23:1
Canterville Ghost, The 1944,Jl 29,16:2
National Velvet 1944,D 15,25:2
Valley of Decision, The 1945,My 4,23:2
Captain Kidd 1945,N 23,26:3
She Went to the Races 1946,F 1,29:2
Sailor Takes a Wife, The 1946,Mr 1,17:2
Kitty 1946,Ap 1,23:1
Cluny Brown 1946,Je 3,27:3
Diary of a Chambermaid, The 1946,Je 23,28:2
Monsieur Beaucaire 1946,S 5,23:1
Imperfect Lady, The 1947,My 22,34:5
Green Dolphin Street 1947,O 16,34:2
Thunder in the Valley 1947,N 28,30:1
If Winter Comes 1948,Ja 23,28:4
Pirate, The 1948,My 21,19:2
Piccadilly Incident 1948,Ag 5,16:2
Julia Misbehaves 1948,O 8,30:2
Three Musketeers, The 1948,O 21,33:2
Hills of Home 1948,N 26,32:2
Challenge to Lassie 1950,Ap 7,22:3
Miniver Story, The 1950,O 27,24:2
Kim 1950,D 8,40:4
Grounds for Marriage 1951,Ja 12,24:6
Red Garters 1954,Mr 27,13:5
Five Weeks in a Balloon 1962,Ag 27,18:1
Tammy and the Doctor 1963,Je 27,23:2
Thrill of it All, The 1963,Ag 2,15:3
Voice of the Hurricane 1964,Je 3,36:4
Mary Poppins 1964,S 25,34:1
Rosie 1968,F 8,36:1

Owen, Reginald (Original Author)

Stablemates 1938,O 21,27:2

Owen, Sally

Holly and the Ivy, The 1954,F 5,16:1

Owen, Seena

Sheriff's Son, The 1919,Mr 31,11:3
Man and his Money, A 1919,Ap 14,11:4
Fall of Babylon, The 1919,Jl 22,10:2
Life Line, The 1919,S 29,16:1
Victory 1919,D 28,4:4
Back Pay 1922,F 13,10:1

Owen, Seena — Cont

Sisters 1922,Ap 4,15:3
Go-Getter 1923,Ap 9,14:3 (In Addenda)
Unseeing Eyes 1923,O 22,17:1
I Am the Man 1925,Mr 6,23:1
Rush Hour, The 1928,Ja 31,29:1
Blue Danube, The 1928,Ap 30,18:3
Man Made Women 1928,S 18,33:2
Sinners in Love 1928,N 19,16:7
Marriage Playground, The 1929,D 14,22:4

Owen, Seena (Original Author)

Rumba 1935,F 25,13:2
Great Man's Lady, The 1942,Ap 30,14:3
Rainbow Island 1944,O 26,19:6
Carnegie Hall 1947,My 3,10:2

Owen, Seena (Screenwriter)

This Way Please 1937,O 8,27:2
Thrill of a Lifetime 1937,D 9,30:2
Aloma of the South Seas 1941,Ag 28,23:4

Owen, Tony (Producer)

Traveling Saleswoman 1950,Ja 6,25:3
Duel in the Jungle 1954,Ag 9,13:2
Beyond Mombasa 1957,My 31,14:2

Owen, Tudor

Bride of the Storm 1926,Ap 5,24:1
Top o' the Morning 1949,S 1,25:2
When in Rome 1952,My 12,21:2
My Cousin Rachel 1952,D 26,20:2
Dangerous When Wet 1953,Je 19,18:1
Houdini 1953,Jl 3,10:2
How to Marry a Millionaire 1953,N 11,37:1
Yankee Pasha 1954,Ap 19,19:2
Arrow in the Dust 1954,My 1,13:2
Brigadoon 1954,S 17,18:2
Most Dangerous Man Alive 1961,Jl 5,29:2

Owen, Yvonne

Seventh Veil, The 1945,D 26,15:1
Years Between, The 1947,Mr 10,25:2
Holiday Camp 1948,Ja 24,11:2
Easy Money (Episode 1) 1949,F 14,15:3
My Brothers Keeper 1949,F 14,15:3
Miranda 1949,Ap 25,20:2
Silent Dust 1949,Jl 30,13:2
Girl in a Million, A 1950,Jl 24,15:2

Owens, Freeman H (Cinematographer)

Flying with the Marines 1918,Je 24,9:1

Owens, Harry

Cocoanut Grove 1938,Je 16,21:2

Owens, Harry (Composer)

Waikiki Wedding 1937,Mr 25,29:1
Cocoanut Grove 1938,Je 16,21:2
Song of the Islands 1942,Mr 12,24:4

Owens, Harry and his Royal Hawaiians

It's a Date 1940,Mr 23,16:2
Lake Placid Serenade 1944,D 25,15:6

Owens, Patricia

Happiest Days of Your Life, The 1950,S 18,19:2
Island in the Sun 1957,Je 13,37:1
No Down Payment 1957,O 31,41:1
Soyonara 1957,D 6,39:4
Sayonara 1957,D 6,39:4
Law and Jake Wade, the 1958,Je 7,11:1
Fly, The 1958,Ag 30,6:6
These Thousand Hills 1959,My 7,36:1
Five Gates to Hell 1959,D 10,51:6
Hell to Eternity 1960,O 13,41:1
Seven Women From Hell 1962,F 1,22:2
X-15 1962,Ap 5,30:2
Black Spurs 1965,My 29,17:1

Owers, John

Girl in the Canal, The 1947,O 9,32:3

Owiklinska, M

Border Street 1950,Ap 26,35:2

Owin, Rita

Love Me Tonight 1932,Ag 19,20:6
Our Little Girl 1935,Je 7,24:4

Owsley, Monroe

First Kiss, The 1928,Ag 20,21:3
Holiday 1930,Jl 3,25:4
Free Love 1930,D 15,29:1
Honor Among Lovers 1931,F 28,15:2
Ten Cents a Dance 1931,Mr 7,17:2
Indiscreet 1931,My 7,21:4
This Modern Age 1931,S 7,19:3
Unashamed 1932,Jl 15,13:4
Hat Check Girl 1932,O 8,15:4
Call Her Savage 1932,N 25,19:2
Keyhold, The 1933,Mr 31,23:3
Ex-Lady 1933,My 15,16:2
Brief Moment 1933,S 30,18:5
Little Man, What Now? 1934,Je 1,29:1
Wild Gold 1934,Jl 24,20:2
She Was a Lady 1934,Ag 22,21:2
Behold My Wife 1935,F 18,19:3
Rumba 1935,F 25,13:2
Goin' to Town 1935,My 11,21:2
Remember Last Night? 1935,N 21,27:2
Private Number 1936,Je 12,19:1
Hideaway Girl 1937,Ja 13,20:4
Hit Parade, The 1937,My 31,11:2

Oxenham, John (Original Author)

Hearts in Exile 1929,N 29,25:1

Oxford, Earl
Riptide 1934,Mr 31,8:2
Sadie McKee 1934,My 18,18:3 (Incorrect in this
edition; use 1934,My 19,18:3 elsewhere)
Oxley, David
Bonjour Tristesse 1958,Ja 16,32:1
Night Ambush 1958,Ap 25,32:4
Yesterday's Enemy 1960,Mr 4,19:1
Oyama, Reiko
Stopover Tokyo 1957,D 27,23:4
Oyasato, Henry
Go for Broke 1951,My 25,31:2
Oysher, Moishe
Singing Blacksmith, The 1938,N 3,27:1
Overture to Glory 1940,F 12,14:2
Singing in the Dark 1956,Mr 8,32:5
Oysher, Moishe (Original Author)
Singing in the Dark 1956,Mr 8,32:5
Ozanire, Robert
Extenuating Circumstances; Circostances
Attenuantes 1946,S 24,41:3
Ozanne, Robert
Lower Depths, The 1937,S 11,20:1
They Were Five 1938,Je 1,19:5
Ozawa, Sakae
Ugetsu 1954,S 8,40:3
Yang Kwei Fei 1956,S 11,41:2
Ozawa, Shoichi
Insect Woman, The; Nippon Konchuki
1964,Jl 1,42:1
Ozenne, Jean
Cheat, The 1950,O 2,19:3
Possessors, The 1959,Jl 21,24:1
Julie the Redhead 1963,O 15,44:1
Diary of a Chambermaid; Journal d'une Femme de
Chambre, Le 1964,S 22,44:1
Ozep, Fedor (Director)
Yellow Ticket, The 1928,D 10,25:1
Living Corpse, The 1931,Ja 4,27:2
Murderer Dimitri Karamasoff, The
1931,Mr 1,VIII,6:7 (In Addenda)
Karamazof 1931,S 21,20:2
Betrayal 1939,S 16,20:2
It Happened in Gibraltar 1943,N 16,27:1
Three Russian Girls 1944,F 5,13:2
Dame de Pique, La 1944,O 19,19:2
Whispering City 1948,My 10,25:5
Ozep, Fedor (Original Author)
Two Who Dared 1937,Jl 10,18:2
Ozeray, Madeleine
Liliom 1935,Mr 18,14:4
Crime et Chatiment; Crime and Punishment
1935,N 13,25:3
Mysteres de Paris, Les 1937,Ja 30,21:2
Dr Knock 1937,My 1,16:4
Song of the Street 1939,S 5,21:2
End of a Day, The 1939,S 12,28:4
Dame de Pique, La 1944,O 19,19:2
Ozerov, Igor
Eugene Onegin 1959,S 14,33:1
Garnet Bracelet, The 1966,My 28,11:6
Ozerov, Yuri (Director)
Daring Circus Youth 1953,D 21,27:4
Ozerov, Yuri (Screenwriter)
Daring Circus Youth 1953,D 21,27:4
Ozora, Mayumi
Kojiro 1968,Ag 30,23:1
Ozu, Yasujiro (Director)
Ohayo; (Good Morning) 1966,F 2,24:1
Ozu, Yasujiro (Screenwriter)
Ohayo; (Good Morning) 1966,F 2,24:1

P

Pa, Solomon
Bird of Paradise 1951,Mr 15,37:2
Paal, Alexander (Producer)
Four Sided Triangle 1953,My 16,10:1
Paal, Elizabeth
My Wife, The Miss 1934,S 13,26:2
Paananen, Tuulikki
Jaakarin Morsian; Soldiers' Bride 1939,D 18,29:3
Paar, Jack
Easy Living 1949,O 13,33:3
Walk Softly Stranger 1950,O 16,30:5
Down Among the Sheltering Palms
1953,Je 13,11:2
Pabst, G W (Director)
Secrets of the Soul 1927,Ap 25,20:4
Streets of Sorrow 1927,Jl 6,23:2
Love of Jeanne Ney, The 1928,Ja 15,VIII,7:5
Pandora's Box 1929,D 2,28:2
Western Front 1918, The 1930,Je 22,VIII,4:2
White Hell of Pitz Palu, The 1930,S 27,21:3
Comrades of 1918 1931,F 20,18:5
Skandal Um Eva 1931,Ap 21,35:2
Dreigroschenoper, Die; Beggar's Opera, The
1931,My 18,21:2
Kameradschaft; Comradeship 1931,D 27,VIII,7:1
Kameradschaft 1932,N 9,28:5
Opera de Quat' Sous, L' 1933,D 9,18:4
Modern Hero, A 1934,Ap 20,17:1

Don Quixote 1934,D 24,17:1
drame De Shanghai; Shanghai Drama, The
1945,Ja 11,19:2
Street of Shadows 1948,N 20,9:2
Trial, The 1952,Mr 15,8:2
Last ten Days, The 1956,Ap 12,26:1
Confession of Ina Kahn, The 1958,Ja 1,31:4
Ballerina 1958,My 10,19:2
Threepenny Opera, The 1960,Jl 11,24:4
Pabst, G W (Producer)
Atlantide, L' 1932,Ag 7,IX,2:1
Don Quichotte 1933,Ap 23,X,4:1
Pacaud, Jacqueline
Youth in Revolt 1939,My 16,27:3
Pacci, Leone
Laugh Pagliacci 1948,Ja 31,14:2
Pace, Diane
Gypsy 1962,N 2,24:1
Pack, Charles Lloyd
High Treason 1952,My 21,23:3
Horror of Dracula 1958,My 29,24:4
Three Worlds of Gulliver, The 1960,D 17,19:3
Kitchen, The 1961,N 2,42:1
Victim 1962,F 6,27:2
Pack, Norman
Publicity Madness 1927,D 12,30:6
Packara, Clayton
King of Kings, The 1927,Ap 20,29:2
Packard, Frank L (Original Author)
Miracle Man, The 1919,Ag 27,9:5
Sin That Was His, The 1920,D 6,19:1
Miracle Man, The 1932,Ap 21,25:2
Packer, Doris
Perils of Pauline, The 1967,Ag 3,26:3
Packer, Joy (Original Author)
Elephant Gun 1959,Je 20,11:2
Packer, Netta
Condemned Woman 1938,Ap 22,15:5
Good Sam 1948,S 17,28:2
It Started With a Kiss 1959,Ag 20,14:2
Pacome, Maria
Love Game, The 1960,N 9,44:1
Up to his Ears 1966,My 18,37:1
Tender Scoundrel 1967,N 16,58:2
Pacovsky, Joseph
My Father's House 1947,S 26,28:3
Padavani, Lea
Anatomy of Love 1959,S 29,46:2
Padden, Sarah
Wonder of Women 1929,Jl 22,17:1
Sophomore, The 1929,Ag 24,11:5
Today 1930,N 17,29:1
Great Meadow, The 1931,Mr 14,23:2
Sob Sister 1931,O 3,20:2
Yellow Ticket, The 1931,O 31,22:2
Cross Examination 1932,F 27,22:1
Young America 1932,My 7,11:5
Midnight Lady, The 1932,Jl 1,19:3
Rebecca of Sunnybrook Farm 1932,Jl 30,16:5
Blondie of the Follies 1932,S 2,19:2
Tess of the Storm Country 1932,N 19,20:2
Face in the Sky 1933,F 20,11:5
Power and the Glory, The 1933,Ag 17,13:2
Sin of Nora Moran, The 1933,D 13,29:3
Man of Two Worlds 1934,Ja 12,29:2
David Harum 1934,Mr 2,23:2
As the Earth Turns 1934,Ap 12,27:2
He Was her Man 1934,My 17,28:2
Little Man, What Now? 1934,Je 1,29:1
Defense Rests, The 1934,Ag 16,20:3
Anna Karenina 1935,Ag 31,16:2
Women in Prison 1938,Mr 1,19:3
Rich Man, Poor Girl 1938,Ag 19,13:3
Woman Against Woman 1938,Ag 23,20:6
Let Freedom Ring 1939,Mr 10,19:2
Chad Hanna 1940,D 26,23:1
Woman's Face, A 1941,My 16,21:2
Tight Shoes 1941,Je 19,25:2
Murder by Invitation 1941,Jl 23,15:4
Assignment in Brittany 1943,Ap 22,31:2
Dakota 1945,D 17,17:2
Joe Palooka, Champ 1946,Ap 6,10:6
Angel on my Shoulder 1946,O 21,27:2
That Brennan Girl 1946,D 9,34:3
Ramrod 1947,Je 30,25:6
House by the River 1950,My 2,25:2
Padden, Tom
Frontier Badmen 1943,Ag 14,12:8
Paddick, Hugh
School for Scoundrels 1960,Jl 12,39:1
Killing of Sister George, The 1968,D 17,58:4
Paddock, Charles
Campus Flirt, The 1926,S 22,31:1
High School Hero 1927,O 24,24:3
College Hero, The 1927,N 22,32:2
Paderewski
Moonlight Sonata 1937,Je 6,XI,4:4 (In Addenda)
Padilla, Manuel
Dime With a Halo 1963,Je 27,23:3
Tarzan and the Valley of Gold 1967,Mr 30,55:1
Padilla, Miguel (Original Author)
Passion 1954,D 11,11:1

Padilla, Ruben
Bullfighter and the Lady, The 1951,Ap 27,19:2
Padilla Sisters
Pan-Americana 1945,Mr 23,13:2
Padjan, John
Iron Horse, The 1924,Ag 29,6:1
Tony Runs Wild 1926,Ap 28,28:3
Padmini
Journey Beyond Three Seas 1960,Ap 11,42:6
Padoa, Clara
Scipio Africanus 1939,S 23,22:2
Matrimonio Ideale, Un 1939,D 15,33:3
Cuore Napoletano; Neapolitan Heart
1940,O 8,31:2
Padoan, A Maria
Fear No Evil 1949,Mr 31,31:2
Padovani, Kathleen
Give Us This Day 1949,D 21,41:2
Padovani, Lea
Outcry 1949,Mr 14,15:5
Three Steps North 1951,Je 29,14:2
Rome, 11 O'Clock 1953,Ap 30,39:2
Gran Varieta 1955,Ap 11,29:5
Angels of Darkness 1956,N 22,51:1
Scandal in Sorrento 1957,Je 13,37:1
Naked Maja, The 1959,Je 11,36:2
Eye for an Eye, An 1961,F 10,19:1
Reluctant Saint, The 1962,D 4,47:2
Empty Canvas, The 1964,My 16,21:1 (Incorrect
in this edition; use 1964,My 16,12:1 elsewhere)
Padovano, John
Foreign Intrigue 1956,Jl 13,23:2
Padula, Marguerita
Hit the Deck 1930,Ja 15,28:6
Cuckoos, The 1930,Ap 26,11:1
Billy the Kid 1930,O 18,23:2
Lady of the Tropics 1939,S 8,28:3
Padula, Vicente
Cuesta Abajo 1934,Ag 15,13:5
Tango en Broadway, El 1934,D 29,11:3
Three Coins in the Fountain 1954,My 21,18:2
Padwa, Jack (Producer)
Hill 24 Doesn't Answer 1955,N 3,37:1
Paeger, Frederick
One That Got Away, The 1958,Ap 23,40:2
Pagan, Peter
Overlanders, The 1946,D 20,31:2
Paganelli, Guiseppe
Modesty Blaise 1966,Ag 11,27:1
Pagani, Ernesto
Warrior, The 1917,Jl 17,7:6
Cabiria 1921,Jl 4,10:2
Pagano, Bartolomeo
Maciste in Hell 1931,Je 29,20:3
Pagano, Ernest (Producer)
Her Primitive Man 1944,Ap 1,11:1
Merry Monahans 1944,O 13,16:2
San Diego, I Love You 1944,N 10,25:1
That's the Spirit 1945,Je 2,11:2
That Night With You 1945,N 9,16:2
Frontier Gal 1945,D 15,14:2
Lover Come Back 1946,Je 20,20:3
Slave Girl 1947,Jl 18,21:3
Pagano, Ernest (Screenwriter)
Shall We Dance 1937,My 14,21:1
Super-Sleuth 1937,Jl 17,18:1
Fight for Your Lady 1937,N 20,21:2
Damsel in Distress, A 1937,N 25,37:1
Vivacious Lady 1938,Je 3,17:3
Carefree 1938,S 23,35:1
Flying Irishman, The 1939,Ap 12,27:2
Forty Little Mothers 1940,Ap 19,25:2
Las Vegas Nights 1941,Mr 20,25:2
You'll Never Get Rich 1941,O 24,27:2
You Were Never Lovelier 1942,D 4,31:1
Fired Wife 1943,O 1,15:2
Her Primitive Man 1944,Ap 1,11:1
Greenwich Village 1944,S 28,26:2
Merry Monahans 1944,O 13,16:2
San Diego, I Love You 1944,N 10,25:1
That's the Spirit 1945,Je 2,11:2
That Night With You 1945,N 9,16:2
Frontier Gal 1945,D 15,14:2
Lover Come Back 1946,Je 20,20:3
Slave Girl 1947,Jl 18,21:3
Pagano, Jo (Original Author)
Try and Get Me 1951,My 7,22:2
Pagano, Jo (Screenwriter)
Tarnished Angel 1938,N 15,27:2
They Made Her a Spy 1939,Mr 29,21:4
Hotel Berlin 1945,Mr 3,11:2
Too Young to Know 1945,D 8,21:2
Man I Love, The 1947,Ja 25,12:2
Try and Get Me 1951,My 7,22:2
Pagay, Sophie
Because I Loved You 1930,Ja 25,13:2
Das Lockende Ziel 1933,Je 19,18:2
Sonne Geht auf, Die 1935,F 18,19:4
PAGE
See Also PAIGE
Page, Anita
Telling the World 1928,Jl 16,25:3
Our Dancing Daughters 1928,O 8,14:2

Page, Anita— Cont

While the City Sleeps 1928,O 22,29:1
Broadway Melody, The 1929,F 9,15:3
Flying Fleet, The 1929,F 11,26:3
Hollywood Revue, The 1929,Ag 15,20:5
Our Modern Maidens 1929,S 7,15:1
Speedway 1929,S 21,17:1
Broadway Melody 1929,D 1,X,8:6
Navy Blues 1930,Ja 11,21:3
Free and Easy 1930,Ap 19,15:1
Caught Short 1930,Je 21,20:5
Our Blushing Brides 1930,Ag 2,16:4
Little Accident 1930,Ag 4,13:4
War Nurse 1930,O 24,31:1
Reducing 1931,Ja 17,23:1
Easiest Way, The 1931,F 28,15:2
Gentleman's Fate 1931,Je 27,20:3
Under Eighteen 1931,D 26,15:5
Night Court 1932,My 27,27:5
Skyscraper Souls 1932,Ag 5,11:2
Prosperity 1932,N 26,11:4
Big Cage, The 1933,My 9,20:5
Jungle Bride 1933,My 13,16:3
Soldiers of the Storm 1933,My 17,15:3
I Have Lived 1933,S 6,24:4

Page, Anthony (Director)

Inadmissible Evidence 1968,Je 24,44:1

Page, Arthur

Winning Team, The 1952,Je 21,12:2

Page, Bradley

Final Edition, The 1932,F 22,23:2
Attorney for the Defense 1932,My 28,18:2
Night after Night 1932,O 31,18:4
From Hell to Heaven 1933,Mr 18,9:3
Goldie Gets Along 1933,Je 3,16:4
This Day and Age 1933,S 1,15:4
Chief, The 1933,D 2,9:4
Before Midnight 1934,Ja 10,24:3
Shadows of Sing Sing 1934,F 21,23:2
Six of a Kind 1934,Mr 10,18:3
Good Dame 1934,Mr 17,11:4
He Was her Man 1934,My 17,28:2
Million Dollar Ransom 1934,S 19,15:2
Gentlemen are Born 1934,N 22,27:2
Red Hot Tires 1935,Mr 1,16:3
Shadow of Doubt 1935,Mr 11,15:1
Nut Farm, The 1935,Ap 8,23:3
Mr Dynamite 1935,My 25,12:1
Chinatown Squad 1935,My 30,21:1
King Solomon of Broadway 1935,O 19,12:2
Woman Trap 1936,Mr 7,11:4
Princess Comes Across, The 1936,Je 4,27:2
Two in a Crowd 1936,O 5,25:1
Trouble in Morocco 1937,Mr 15,27:1
Her Husband Lies 1937,Mr 18,20:1
Outcasts of Poker Flat, The 1937,Ap 27,18:3
Fifty Roads to Town 1937,Je 5,21:1
There Goes my Girl 1937,Je 12,8:2
You Can't Beat Love 1937,Je 25,25:3
Super-Sleuth 1937,Jl 17,18:1
Hideaway 1937,S 25,10:2
Music for Madame 1937,O 23,14:1
Crashing Hollywood 1938,Ja 8,19:2
Go Chase Yourself 1938,Je 15,27:1
Crime Ring 1938,Jl 22,10:3
Fugitives for a Night 1938,S 21,30:4
Affairs of Annabel, The 1938,O 13,29:2
Law West of Tombstone, The 1938,N 25,19:1
Annabel Takes a Tour 1938,D 29,15:3
Twelve Crowded Hours 1939,F 24,15:2
Fixer Dugan 1939,My 6,21:2
Street of Missing Women 1940,Ja 8,11:2
Enemy Agent 1940,Ap 22,13:3
Scattergood Baines 1941,Ap 4,25:2
Big Store, The 1941,Je 27,14:4
Badlands of Dakota 1941,S 9,27:6
What's Buzzin Cousin 1943,Jl 23,21:4

Page, Dominique

Young Girls Beware 1959,Ag 22,8:2
Rue de Paris 1960,D 23,14:3

Page, Dorothy

King Solomon of Broadway 1935,O 19,12:2

Page, Elizabeth (Original Author)

Howards of Virginia, The 1940,S 27,27:1

Page, Gale

Crime School 1938,My 11,17:2
Amazing Dr Clitterhouse, The 1938,Jl 21,14:2
Four Daughters 1938,Ag 19,13:3
Heart of the North 1938,D 21,29:2
You Can't Get Away With Murder
 1939,Mr 25,19:2
Naughty but Nice 1939,Je 23,23:2
Daughters Courageous 1939,Je 24,14:2
Indianapolis Speedway 1939,Jl 15,8:2
Four Wives 1939,D 23,9:1
Child Is Born, A 1940,Ja 11,19:2
They Drive by Night 1940,Jl 27,17:5
Knute Rockne-All American 1940,O 19,21:2
Four Mothers 1941,Ja 11,12:7
Time of Your Life, The 1948,My 27,29:2
Anna Lucasta 1949,Ag 12,13:2
About Mrs Leslie 1954,Je 28,16:2

Page, Genevieve

Fanfan the Tulip 1953,My 5,34:2
Foreign Intrigue 1956,Jl 13,23:2
Silken Affair, The 1957,O 31,41:1
Michael Strogoff 1960,My 21,15:1
Song Without End 1960,Ag 12,10:2
Cid, El 1961,D 15,49:1
Day and the Hour, The 1964,F 20,22:2
Youngblood Hawke 1964,N 6,30:1
Grand-Prix 1966,D 22,40:1
Tender Scoundrel 1967,N 16,58:2
Belle de Jour 1968,Ap 11,51:1

Page, Geraldine

Hondo 1953,N 27,99:9
Summer and Smoke 1961,N 17,41:1
Sweet Bird of Youth 1962,Mr 29,28:2
Toys in the Attic 1963,Ag 1,17:2
Dear Heart 1965,Mr 8,33:1
You're a Big Boy Now 1967,Mr 21,35:3
Happiest Millionaire, The 1967,D 1,56:1

Page, Gertrude (Original Author)

Paddy the Next Best Thing 1933,Ag 25,12:2

Page, Helen

Playing With Souls 1925,Ap 20,18:1 (Incorrect in
 this edition; use 1925,Ap 28,18:1 elsewhere)

Page, James E

Charley's Aunt 1925,F 9,15:3

Page, Joy

Casablanca 1942,N 27,27:1
Kismet 1944,Ag 23,16:1
Man-Eater of Kumaon 1948,Jl 2,24:2
Bullfighter and the Lady, The 1951,Ap 27,19:2
Shrike, The 1955,Jl 8,15:2
Tonka 1959,Mr 26,27:1

Page, Mann (Original Author)

Lonesome 1928,O 2,23:5
Crashing Hollywood 1938,Ja 8,19:2

Page, Marco (Original Author)

Fast Company 1938,Jl 6,21:2

Page, Marco (Screenwriter)

Fast Company 1938,Jl 6,21:2

Page, Patti

Elmer Gantry 1960,Jl 8,16:1
Boys' Night Out 1962,Je 22,15:2

Page, Paul

Speakeasy 1929,Mr 11,22:2
Girl from Havana, The 1929,S 2,16:1
Men Without Women 1930,F 1,15:1
Happy Days 1930,F 14,20:1
Her Golden Calf 1930,My 5,27:3
Born Reckless 1930,Je 7,10:4
Naughty Flirt, The 1931,Ap 13,17:1
Palmy Days 1931,S 24,21:2
Women Go on Forever 1931,O 19,28:1
70,000 Witnesses 1932,S 3,16:2
Below the Sea 1933,Je 3,16:4
Phantom Broadcast, The 1933,Jl 31,16:2
Road to Ruin, The 1934,F 21,23:2
Countess of Monte Cristo, The 1934,Ap 2,13:2
Have a Heart 1934,O 20,20:2
Kentucky Kernels 1935,Ja 5,20:2

Page, Rita

Aren't We All? 1932,Jl 1,19:3
Vigil in the Night 1940,Mr 9,19:2
Little Nellie Kelly 1940,D 25,33:2

Page, Tilsa

Edward my Son 1949,Je 3,21:2

Page, William

Abandoned Woman 1949,O 27,35:3

Page Cavanaugh Trio

Song Is Born, A 1948,O 20,37:2
Lullaby of Broadway 1951,Mr 27,35:2

Pager, Antal

Piri Mindont Tud 1933,Ja 26,12:3
Huszarszerelem 1935,Ap 23,24:5
Koeszoenoem Hogy Elgazolt 1935,My 7,28:2
Edes Mostoha 1935,N 21,27:2
Salary, 200 a Month 1937,Ja 15,17:3
Hotel Sunrise 1937,O 30,22:3
Pesti Mese; Tales of Budapest 1938,Ja 3,16:3
Az Ember Neha Teved; Man Sometimes Errs
 1938,Mr 28,19:3
Edes a Bosszu; Sweet Revenge 1938,S 10,20:3
Doentoe Pillanat, A; Crucial Moment, The
 1938,S 17,20:3
Magdat Kicsapjak; Magda Is Expelled
 1938,S 26,13:2
Sziuel Szivert; Heart for Heart 1939,Ja 16,11:3
Rad Bizom a Felesegem; I Entrust my Wife to
 You 1939,My 6,21:3
Fehervari Huszarok; Hussars of Fehervari
 1939,S 16,20:3
Keseru Mezeshetek; Bitter Honeymoon
 1939,O 9,15:3
Megvedten Egy Asszony; I Defended a Woman
 1939,O 14,13:3
Pentek Rezi; Friday Rose 1939,D 23,9:2
Rozmaring; Rosemary 1940,F 10,19:3

Pages, Jean (Director)

Story of the Vatican, The 1941,S 20,11:3

Paget, Alfred

Fall of Babylon, The 1919,Jl 22,10:2

Paget, David

Sleeping Partners 1930,D 13,22:2

Paget, Debra

Cry of the City 1948,S 30,32:4
House of Strangers 1949,Jl 2,8:2
Broken Arrow 1950,Jl 21,15:2
Fourteen Hours 1951,Mr 7,43:2
Bird of Paradise 1951,Mr 15,37:2
Anne of the Indies 1951,O 25,36:3
Belles on Their Toes 1952,My 3,17:5
Miserables, Les 1952,Ag 15,11:2
Stars and Stripes Forever 1952,D 23,17:2
Prince Valiant 1954,Ap 7,40:2
Princess of the Nile 1954,Je 12,13:2
Demetrius and the Gladiators 1954,Je 19,9:1
Gambler From Natchez, The 1954,Ag 14,8:2
White Feather 1955,F 17,23:1
Seven Angry Men 1955,Ap 2,15:2
Last Hunt, The 1956,Mr 1,37:2
Ten Commandments, The 1956,N 9,35:2
Love Me Tender 1956,N 16,23:1
River's Edge, The 1957,Ap 12,20:2
Omar Khayyam 1957,Ag 24,12:4
From the Earth to the Moon 1958,N 27,52:2
Why Must I Die? 1960,S 15,45:4
Journey to the Lost City 1960,D 8,43:3
Most Dangerous Man Alive 1961,Jl 5,29:2
Tales of Terror 1962,Jl 5,21:2 (In Addenda)
Haunted Palace, The 1964,Ja 30,24:1

Paget-Bowman, Cicely

Conspirator 1950,Ap 28,26:2
Miniver Story, The 1950,O 27,24:2
Trials of Oscar Wilde, The 1960,Je 28,26:1

Pagett, Gary

Good Morning, Miss Dove 1955,N 24,41:1

Pagliero, Marcel

Open City; Citta Aperta 1946,F 26,21:2
Chips Are Down, The 1949,F 2,36:1
Dedee 1949,Ap 9,9:2
Your Shadow Is Mine 1963,My 15,32:1
Naked Autumn 1963,N 15,25:3

Pagliero, Marcel (Director)

Woman 1950,F 9,36:6
Daughters of Destiny (Elizabeth); Elizabeth
 (Daughters of Destiny) 1954,Jl 6,19:1
Respectful Prostitute, The 1957,Jl 11,21:1

Pagliero, Marcel (Screenwriter)

Paisan 1948,Mr 30,26:2

Pagliughi, Lina

Rigoletto 1949,N 10,41:4

Pagnani, Andreina

Serpente a Sonagli, Il 1936,Ag 17,9:2
Maestrina, La; Little School Mistress, The
 1938,Ap 29,17:2

Pagniez, Regis (Miscellaneous)

Chappaqua 1967,N 6,65:2

Pagnol, Jacqueline

Nais 1948,Je 16,37:2
Prize, The 1952,Ap 30,33:2
Topaze 1952,O 28,37:1

Pagnol, Marcel (Director)

Merlusse 1938,Mr 17,17:2
Heartbeat 1939,S 5,21:3
Harvest 1939,O 3,19:4
Baker's Wife, The 1940,F 27,17:2
Well-Digger's Daughter, The 1946,S 30,21:4
Cesar 1948,O 28,36:2
Belle Meuniere, La 1948,N 24,19:2
Ways of Love (Jofroi); Jofroi (Ways of Love)
 1950,D 13,50:2
Topaze 1952,O 28,37:1
Letters From my Windmill (The Three Low
 Masses); Three Low Masses, The (Letters From
 my Windmill) 1955,D 19,33:1
Letters From my Windmill (The Secret of Master
 Cornille); Secret of Master Cornille, The (Letters
 From my Windmill) 1955,D 19,33:1
Letters From my Windmill (The Elixir of Father
 Gaucher); Elixir of Father Gaucher, The (Letters
 From my Windmill) 1955,D 19,33:1

Pagnol, Marcel (Original Author)

Topaze 1933,F 10,12:2
Port of Seven Seas 1938,Jl 15,13:2
Well-Digger's Daughter, The 1946,S 30,21:4
Fanny 1961,Jl 7,16:1
I Like Money 1962,My 19,18:2

Pagnol, Marcel (Producer)

Amours de Toni, Les 1936,N 5,35:1
Merlusse 1938,Mr 17,17:2
Heartbeat 1939,S 5,21:3
Harvest 1939,O 3,19:4
Well-Digger's Daughter, The 1946,S 30,21:4
Fanny 1948,F 13,26:2
Nais 1948,Je 16,37:2
Cesar 1948,O 28,36:2
Belle Meuniere, La 1948,N 24,19:2
Topaze 1952,O 28,37:1
Letters From my Windmill (The Elixir of Father
 Gaucher); Elixir of Father Gaucher, The (Letters
 From my Windmill) 1955,D 19,33:1
Letters From my Windmill (The Secret of Master
 Cornille); Secret of Master Cornille, The (Letters
 From my Windmill) 1955,D 19,33:1

Pagnol, Marcel (Producer) — Cont

Letters From my Windmill (The Three Low
Masses); Three Low Masses, The (Letters From
my Windmill) 1955,D 19,33:1

Pagnol, Marcel (Screenwriter)

Merlusse 1938,Mr 17,17:2
Heartbeat 1939,S 5,21:3
Harvest 1939,O 3,19:4
Baker's Wife, The 1940,F 27,17:2
Fanny 1948,F 13,26:2
Nais 1948,Je 16,37:2
Cesar 1948,O 28,36:2
Prize, The 1952,Ap 30,33:2
Topaze 1952,O 28,37:1
Letters From my Windmill (The Secret of Master
Cornille); Secret of Master Cornille, The (Letters
From my Windmill) 1955,D 19,33:1
Letters From my Windmill (The Elixir of Father
Gaucher); Elixir of Father Gaucher, The (Letters
From my Windmill) 1955,D 19,33:1
Letters From my Windmill (The Three Low
Masses); Three Low Masses, The (Letters From
my Windmill) 1955,D 19,33:1

Pagodin, Nikolai (Screenwriter)

Wrestler and the Clown, The 1959,Ja 1,38:1

Paguin, Nicole

Woman Is a Woman, A 1964,S 19,19:1

Pahlen, Victor (Miscellaneous)

Damned, The; Maudits, Les 1948,Ap 26,27:2
Pirates of Capri, The 1949,D 26,33:5

PAIGE

See Also PAGE

Paige, Carol

You and Me 1938,Je 2,19:1

Paige, David

Catskill Honeymoon 1950,Ja 28,10:3

Paige, Dorothy

Catskill Honeymoon 1950,Ja 28,10:3

Paige, Janis

Hollywood Canteen 1944,D 16,19:2
Her Kind of Man 1946,My 4,10:6
Of Human Bondage 1946,Jl 6,11:2
Two Guys From Milwaukee 1946,Jl 27,12:5
Time, The Place And The Girl, The
1946,D 27,14:3
Love and Learn 1947,My 3,10:3
Cheyenne 1947,Je 7,9:2
Winter Meeting 1948,Ap 8,31:2
Wallflower 1948,Je 12,8:5
Romance on the High Seas 1948,Je 26,10:5
One Sunday Afternoon 1948,D 27,16:3
Younger Brothers, The 1949,My 28,11:2
House Across the Street 1949,S 2,14:4
This Side of the Law 1950,Jl 7,15:2
Mr Universe 1951,Mr 23,16:2
Fugitive Lady 1951,Ag 25,7:2
Silk Stockings 1957,Jl 19,11:1
Please Don't Eat the Daisies 1960,Ap 1,37:1
Bachelor in Paradise 1961,N 17,41:2
Follow the Boys 1963,F 28,8:2
Caretakers, The 1963,Ag 22,19:2
Welcome to Hard Times 1967,My 2,56:1

Paige, Jean

Black Beauty 1921,F 21,16:1
Prodigal Judge, The 1922,F 5,VI,3:1 (In
Addenda)
Captain Blood 1924,S 9,19:1

Paige, Leroy (Satchel)

Wonderful Country, The 1959,N 5,39:7

Paige, Mabel

Lucky Jordan 1943,Ja 25,10:8
Crystal Ball, The 1943,F 19,22:2
Happy Go Lucky 1943,Mr 25,25:1
True to Life 1943,O 14,26:1
Out of This World 1945,Je 7,25:2
Murder, He Says 1945,Je 25,20:3
Dangerous Partners 1945,N 2,22:4
She Wouldn't Say Yes 1946,Ja 12,10:7
Behind Green Lights 1946,F 16,10:2
Nocturne 1946,N 11,42:2
Johnny O'Clock 1947,Mr 27,39:2
Her Husband's Affairs 1947,N 14,29:2
If You Knew Susie 1948,F 23,19:2
Mating of Millie, The 1948,Mr 13,12:2
Canon City 1948,Jl 8,19:2
Johnny Belinda 1948,O 2,11:2
Hollow Triumph 1948,O 29,29:5
Roseanna McCoy 1949,O 13,33:2
Edge of Doom 1950,Ag 4,13:2
Petty Girl, The 1950,Ag 18,17:2
Sniper, The 1952,My 10,16:3
Houdini 1953,Jl 3,10:2

Paige, Nina

Two Tickets to Paris 1962,N 29,46:5

Paige, Raymond

Hawaii Calls 1938,Ap 29,17:2

Paige, Raymond, and his Orchestra

Hollywood Hotel 1938,Ja 13,17:3

Paige, Robert

Battling Orioles, The 1924,N 4,24:1
When G-Men Step In 1938,Mr 14,13:2
There's Always a Woman 1938,Ap 29,17:2
Who Killed Gail Preston? 1938,My 6,27:2
Main Event, The 1938,Je 20,11:3

Highway Patrol 1938,Ag 4,15:2
Last Warning, The 1938,D 8,34:4
I Stand Accused 1939,Ja 5,17:1
Homicide Bureau 1939,F 2,17:2
Death of a Champion 1939,Ag 24,17:3
Parole Fixer 1940,Ap 18,28:5
Women Without Names 1940,My 9,26:4
Golden Gloves 1940,Ag 21,23:6
Monster and the Girl, The 1941,Mr 20,25:3
Hellzapoppin 1941,D 26,21:4
Jail House Blues 1942,F 6,23:2
What's Cookin' 1942,F 26,15:5
Almost Married 1942,Je 5,23:2
Pardon my Sarong 1942,Ag 27,15:1
Get Help to Love 1942,O 19,15:3
Hi 'Ya Chum 1943,F 26,17:4
Cowboy in Manhattan 1943,My 28,19:2
Mister Big 1943,Je 14,13:4
Frontier Badmen 1943,Ag 14,12:8
Fired Wife 1943,O 1,15:2
Son of Dracula 1943,N 6,16:4
Her Primitive Man 1944,Ap 1,11:1
Can't Help Singing 1944,D 26,22:4
Shady Lady 1945,O 11,26:2
Tangier 1946,Je 7,II,16:4
Red Stallion 1947,N 27,50:3
Flame, The 1948,F 20,19:2
Green Promise, The 1949,Je 24,29:2
Split Second 1953,My 13,34:2
Marriage-Go-Round 1961,Ja 7,12:2
Bye Bye Birdie 1963,Ap 5,27:3

Paige, Robert (Producer)

Green Promise, The 1949,Je 24,29:2

Paige, Ronnie

Sons of the Legion 1938,S 30,24:3
Fisherman's Wharf 1939,F 24,15:2

Pail, Edward

Boots 1919,Mr 10,9:3

Pailenberg, Anita

Barbarella 1968,O 12,43:1

Pain, Barry (Original Author)

Blind Bargain, A 1922,D 4,20:2

Pain, Bunty

This'll Make You Whistle 1938,N 1,27:2

Pain, Matty

Boy of the Streets 1938,Ja 24,17:1

PAINE

See Also PAYNE

Paine, Harry

Trade Winds 1939,Ja 13,17:2

Painleve, Jean (Producer)

Oursin 1930,Ja 5,VIII,5:1

Painter, Jack (Cinematographer)

This Is Your Army 1954,D 15,41:1

Paishikar, Nana

Maya 1966,Je 23,29:4

Paiva, Nestor

Magnificent Fraud, The 1939,Jl 20,16:2
Hold Back the Dawn 1941,O 2,29:1
Kid From Kansas, The 1941,D 2,29:4
Broadway 1942,Je 5,23:2
Crystal Ball, The 1943,F 19,22:2
Pittsburgh 1943,F 25,27:2
Hard Way, The 1943,Mr 13,9:2
Dancing Masters, The 1943,D 2,30:2
Purple Heart, The 1944,Mr 9,15:2
Falcon in Mexico, The 1944,Ag 5,16:2
Salome, Where She Danced 1945,My 3,27:1
Thousand and one Nights, A 1945,Jl 12,8:2
Southerner, The 1945,Ag 27,22:3
Road to Utopia 1946,F 28,20:2
Badman's Territory 1946,My 31,27:2
Last Crooked Mile, The 1946,S 14,10:8
Carnival in Costa Rica 1947,Mr 29,21:2
Shoot to Kill 1947,My 17,8:5
Ramrod 1947,Je 30,25:6
Road to Rio 1948,F 19,29:3
Adventures of Casanova 1948,Mr 22,18:3
Alias Nick Beal 1949,Mr 10,35:2
Follow Me Quietly 1949,Jl 8,14:5
Mighty Joe Young 1949,Jl 28,19:3
Oh, You Beautiful Doll 1949,N 12,8:4
Inspector General, The 1949,D 31,9:2
Young Man With a Horn 1950,F 10,18:4
Great Caruso, The 1951,My 11,32:2
Jim Thorpe - All American 1951,Ag 25,7:2
Millionaire for Christy, A 1951,O 5,24:3
Double Dynamite 1951,D 26,19:4
Mara Maru 1952,Ap 24,38:1
Call Me Madam 1953,Mr 26,37:1
Creature from the Black Lagoon 1954,My 1,13:4
Revenge of the Creature 1955,My 14,10:7
Hell on Frisco Bay 1956,Ja 7,21:1
Lady Takes a Flyer, The 1958,Ja 30,19:2
Can-Can 1960,Mr 10,36:1
4 Horsemen of the Apocalypse, The
1962,Mr 10,10:2

Pak, Norman

Beach Red 1967,Ag 4,18:1

Pakula, Alan J (Producer)

Fear Strikes Out 1957,Mr 21,37:2
To Kill a Mockingbird 1963,F 15,10:2
Love With the Proper Stranger 1963,D 26,33:1

Pakula, Alan J (Producer) — Cont

Baby, the Rain Must Fall 1965,Ja 14,44:1
Inside Daisy Clover 1966,F 18,23:1
Up the Down Staircase 1967,Ag 18,36:2

Pal, George (Director)

Tom Thumb 1958,D 24,00:0
Time Machine, The 1960,Ag 18,19:1
Atlantis the Lost Continent 1961,My 27,12:1
Wonderful World of the Brothers Grimm, The
(The Cobbler and the Elves); Cobbler and the
Elves, The (The Wonderful World of the
Brothers Grimm) 1962,Ag 8,35:1
Wonderful World of the Brothers Grimm, The
(The Singing Bone); Singing Bone, The (The
Wonderful World of the Brothers Grimm)
1962,Ag 8,35:1
Wonderful World of the Brothers Grimm, The
1962,Ag 8,35:1
Wonderful World of the Brothers Grimm, The
(The Dancing Princess); Dancing Princess, The
(The Wonderful World of the Brothers Grimm)
1962,Ag 8,35:1
7 Faces of Dr Lao 1964,Jl 23,19:1

Pal, George (Producer)

Great Rupert, The 1950,Ap 14,27:2
Destination Moon 1950,Je 28,32:2
When Worlds Collide 1952,F 7,30:2
Houdini 1953,Jl 3,10:2
War of the Worlds, The 1953,Ag 14,10:2
Naked Jungle, The 1954,Ap 3,19:2
Conquest of Space 1955,My 28,7:6
Tom Thumb 1958,D 24,00:0
Time Machine, The 1960,Ag 18,19:1
Atlantis the Lost Continent 1961,My 27,12:1
Wonderful World of the Brothers Grimm, The
(The Singing Bone); Singing Bone, The (The
Wonderful World of the Brothers Grimm)
1962,Ag 8,35:1
Wonderful World of the Brothers Grimm, The
(The Cobbler and the Elves); Cobbler and the
Elves, The (The Wonderful World of the
Brothers Grimm) 1962,Ag 8,35:1
Wonderful World of the Brothers Grimm, The
(The Dancing Princess); Dancing Princess, The
(The Wonderful World of the Brothers Grimm)
1962,Ag 8,35:1
Wonderful World of the Brothers Grimm, The
1962,Ag 8,35:1
7 Faces of Dr Lao 1964,Jl 23,19:1
Power, The 1968,Mr 7,52:2

Pal, George, Puppetoons

Wonderful World of the Brothers Grimm, The
(The Cobbler and the Elves); Cobbler and the
Elves, The (The Wonderful World of the
Brothers Grimm) 1962,Ag 8,35:1

Pal, Javor

Hyppolit, A Lakaj 1933,Ja 4,22:6

Pala, Guido (Original Author)

Lieutenant Craig-Missing 1951,My 19,9:4

Pala, Guido (Screenwriter)

Lieutenant Craig-Missing 1951,My 19,9:4

Palacios, Adele

Run, Appaloosa, Run! 1966,Jl 14,28:1

Palacios, Alicia

Loyola, The Soldier Saint 1952,Ap 25,19:2

Palacios, Antonio

Dona Francisquita 1935,Ap 27,20:6
Semana de Felicidad, Una; One Week of
Happiness 1935,Je 15,20:3

Palance, Jack

Sudden Fear 1952,Ag 8,9:2
Shane 1953,Ap 24,30:3
Second Chance 1953,Jl 23,20:2
Arrowhead 1953,S 16,38:6
Flight to Tangier 1953,N 26,50:4
Man in the Attic 1954,F 6,17:2
Silver Chalice, The 1954,D 27,22:5
Sign of the Pagan 1955,F 14,24:2
Kiss of Fire 1955,S 24,11:2
Big Knife, The 1955,N 9,41:2
I Died a Thousand Times 1955,N 10,45:2
Attack! 1956,S 20,29:4
House of Numbers 1957,S 13,15:2
Man Inside, The 1959,F 5,24:7
Second to Hell 1959,Jl 18,6:3
Barabbas 1962,O 11,49:1
Contempt 1964,D 19,25:2
Once a Thief 1965,S 9,36:1
Professionals, The 1966,N 3,45:1
Kill a Dragon 1967,D 7,60:2
Torture Garden 1968,Jl 20,18:2

Palance, Walter (Jack)

Panic in the Streets 1950,Ag 5,9:2
Halls of Montezuma, The 1951,Ja 6,9:6

Palange, Inez

Sei tu l'Amore 1930,N 18,28:4
Scarface, The Shame of the Nation
1932,My 20,22:3
Melody Lingers on, The 1935,N 7,27:1
Woman Rebels, A 1936,O 30,27:2
Speed to Burn 1938,S 9,25:1
One Million BC 1940,Ap 27,9:2
I Was an Adventuress 1940,My 20,13:2
Romance of the Rio Grande 1940,D 25,33:4

Palange, Inez— Cont
Life Begins at Eight-Thirty 1942,D 10,35:2
Palasthy, A
Stand and Deliver 1928,Ap 2,25:1
Palasty, Irene
Married in Hollywood 1929,S 23,24:3
Palau
Dr Knock 1937,My 1,16:4
Rasputin 1939,O 17,31:4
Charrette Fantome, La 1940,My 28,29:2
Dame de Pique, La 1944,O 19,19:2
Angel and Sinner 1947,F 24,16:5
Carnival of Sinners 1947,Ap 8,34:2
Corbeau, Le; Raven, The 1948,F 24,21:1
Rumors 1949,Mr 19,10:7
Devil in the Flesh 1949,My 10,29:2
Beauties of the Night 1954,Mr 23,23:5
Joker, The; (Farceur, Le) 1961,Ag 8,32:2
Palau, Genin
Jericho 1946,D 16,31:2
Palau, Pierre
Enfants du Paradis, Les 1947,F 20,32:2
Queen's Necklace, The 1947,My 17,8:5
Nana 1957,Ap 13,12:3
Palav, Diana
Coiffeur Pour Dames 1932,O 31,18:4
Palavicini, Julieta
Sueno de Amor 1936,Ja 11,9:3
Mi Madrecita; My Little Mother 1940,S 24,26:6
Pale, Michael
Thunder on the Hill 1951,O 18,32:3
Julius Caesar 1953,Je 5,19:1
Major Dundee 1965,Ap 8,45:1
Palella, Orste
Seduced and Abandoned 1964,Jl 16,23:1
Palemi, Amleto (Director)
Corsaro Nero, Il; Black Corsair, The
1939,My 8,21:3
Palen, Anna von
Zu Strassburg auf der Schanz; At the Strassburg
1936,F 15,18:7
Palermi, Amleto (Director)
Vecchia Signora, La 1932,D 10,19:3
Passa L'Amore 1933,N 25,10:3
Eredita dello Zio, L' 1935,Je 29,16:3
Fiat Voluntas Dei 1936,Jl 6,11:5
Amore in Quarantena; Love in Quarantine
1938,D 13,31:2
Paraninfo, Il; Matchmaker, The 1940,Ja 23,17:2
Napoli che mon Muore; Naples That Never Dies
1940,Mr 4,11:3
Due Madri, Le; Two Mothers, The
1940,My 17,23:3
Cuore Napoletano; Neapolitan Heart
1940,O 8,31:2
Cavalleria Rusticana 1947,D 20,21:2
Palermi, Amleto (Miscellaneous)
Delitto di Mastrovanni, Il 1935,Jl 30,16:2
Palermini, Piero
To Live in Peace 1947,N 25,37:2
O K Nero 1953,Je 20,8:6
Paley, Jackie
Caribbean Mystery, The 1945,Ag 20,22:4
Paley, Natalie
Sylvia Scarlett 1936,Ja 10,16:2
Homme des Folies Bergere, L' 1936,Ap 18,19:3
Prince Jean, Le 1936,D 12,15:2
Amoureux, Les 1940,D 9,23:3
Paley, Susan
Death of a Champion 1939,Ag 24,17:3
Palfi, Lotte
Underground 1941,Je 23,13:2
Above Suspicion 1943,Ag 6,10:3
In our Time 1944,F 12,11:2
Walk East on Beacon 1952,My 29,17:2
Palitos, Pablo
Alas de mi Patria; My Country's Wingo
1940,Je 4,19:4
Palk, Anna
Play it Cool 1963,Jl 18,15:3
Frozen Dead, The 1967,N 16,58:1
Pallais, Dorita
Kid From Texas, The 1950,Je 2,26:2
Pallavicini, Sandro (Producer)
Sins of Casanova 1957,O 7,23:2
Palleja, Juan (Miscellaneous)
Fury Over Spain 1937,Jl 21,19:2
Pallenberg, Max
Brave Suender, Der; Upright Sinner, The
1931,N 22,VIII,6:6
Brave Suender, Der 1933,Mr 29,13:2
Pallenberg Bears
Sensations of 1945 1944,Jl 7,13:2
Palletier, Louis (Screenwriter)
Follow Me, Boys! 1966,D 2,46:1
Pallette, Eugene
Alias Jimmy Valentine 1920,Ap 19,13:3
Three Musketeers, The 1921,Ag 29,14:4
To the Last Man 1923,Ag 28,12:1
Light of the Western Stars, The 1925,Je 24,14:3
Mantrap 1926,Jl 12,24:4
Chicago 1927,D 24,9:1
Lights of New York 1928,Jl 9,25:1
Out of the Ruins 1928,Ag 20,21:3

Red Mark, The 1928,O 30,27:3
His Private Life 1928,N 12,18:2
Good-Bye Kiss, The 1928,N 12,18:2
Dummy, The 1929,Mr 4,20:2
Canary Murder Case, The 1929,Mr 11,22:2
Studio Murder Mystery, The 1929,Je 10,23:1
Greene Murder Case, The 1929,Ag 10,11:3
Love Parade, The 1929,N 20,32:6
Virginian, The 1929,D 23,18:2
Pointed Heels 1929,D 28,11:1
Slightly Scarlet 1930,Mr 1,23:1
Benson Murder Case, The 1930,Ap 12,23:1
Border Legion, The 1930,Je 30,22:6
Let's Go Native 1930,Ag 30,7:4
Sea God, The 1930,S 6,9:2
Follow Thru 1930,S 13,9:3
Sante Fe Trail, The 1930,O 18,23:2
Playboy of Paris 1930,N 1,23:2
Sea Legs 1930,N 11,29:1
Fighting Caravans 1931,Ja 26,21:1
Pays to Advertise, It 1931,F 21,15:2
It Pays to Advertise 1931,F 21,15:2
Gun Smoke 1931,Ap 24,27:1
Dude Ranch 1931,Ap 25,23:4
Huckleberry Finn 1931,Ag 8,16:3
Girls About Town 1931,N 2,27:1
Shanghai Express 1932,F 18,25:3
Dancers in the Dark 1932,Mr 19,11:2
Strangers of the Evening 1932,Je 4,9:2
Thunder Below 1932,Je 20,11:2
Night Mayor, The 1932,N 25,19:2
Half-Naked Truth, The 1932,D 31,10:1
Hell Below 1933,Ap 26,13:2
Made on Broadway 1933,Jl 8,14:5
Storm at Daybreak 1933,Jl 22,14:2
Shanghai Madness 1933,S 23,11:6
Kennel Murder Case, The 1933,O 30,14:2
From Headquarters 1933,N 17,22:4
Mr Skitch 1933,D 23,19:1
Cross Country Cruise 1934,Ja 20,12:3
I've Got Your Number 1934,F 3,9:3
Strictly Dynamite 1934,Jl 4,18:2
Friends of Mr Sweeney 1934,Jl 31,20:4
Dragon Murder Case, The 1934,Ag 23,13:3
Caravan 1934,S 28,27:1
Bordertown 1935,Ja 24,22:5
All the King's Horses 1935,Mr 9,19:1
Black Sheep 1935,Je 28,34:1
Steamboat Around the Bend 1935,S 20,17:2
Ghost Goes West, The 1935,D 18,33:8
Ghost Goes West, The 1936,Ja 11,9:2
Golden Arrow, The 1936,My 4,16:1
My Man Godfrey 1936,S 19,18:1 (Incorrect in
this edition; use 1936,S 18,18:1 elsewhere)
Luckiest Girl in the World, The 1936,D 5,16:3
Stowaway 1936,D 19,16:1
Crime Nobody Saw, The 1937,Ap 5,17:2
She Had to Eat 1937,Jl 24,12:1
Topper 1937,Ag 20,21:2
100 Men and a Girl 1937,S 18,15:2
Adventures of Robin Hood, The 1938,My 13,17:2
There Goes my Heart 1938,O 14,27:2
Wife, Husband and Friend 1939,F 25,19:2
Mr Smith Goes to Washington 1939,O 20,27:2
First Love 1939,N 9,27:3
Young Tom Edison 1940,Mr 15,27:2
It's a Date 1940,Mr 23,16:2
Sandy Is a Lady 1940,Je 28,22:2
He Stayed for Breakfast 1940,Ag 31,16:2
Mark of Zorro, The 1940,N 4,23:2
Little Bit of Heaven, A 1940,N 8,24:2
Lady Eve, The 1941,F 26,17:1
Bride Came C O D, The 1941,Jl 26,18:2
World Premiere 1941,Ag 21,15:2
Unfinished Business 1941,S 2,20:2
Appointment for Love 1941,N 7,27:1
Swamp Water 1941,N 17,15:2
Male Animal, The 1942,Mr 28,11:1
Almost Married 1942,Je 5,23:2
Are Husbands Necessary? 1942,Jl 9,17:2
Big Street, The 1942,Ag 14,13:1
Lady in a Jam 1942,S 11,25:2
Tales of Manhattan 1942,S 25,25:1
Forest Rangers, The 1942,O 22,25:2
Silver Queen 1943,Ja 11,18:4
It Ain't Hay 1943,Mr 11,17:3
Slightly Dangerous 1943,Ap 2,17:2
Heaven Can Wait 1943,Ag 12,15:1
Kansan, The 1943,O 1,15:3
Gang's All Here, The 1943,D 23,26:4
Pin Up Girl 1944,My 11,25:6
Sensations of 1945 1944,Jl 7,13:2
Step Lively 1944,Jl 27,14:1
Heavenly Days 1944,O 21,15:2
Lake Placid Serenade 1944,D 25,15:6
Cheaters, The 1945,Jl 21,7:2
In old Sacramento 1946,Ap 29,24:4
Suspense 1946,Jl 5,15:3
Pallin, Ingemar
Incorrigible 1949,Jl 2,8:2
Pallis, Byron
Golfo-Girl of the Mountains 1958,My 19,19:5
Antigone 1962,S 19,30:1

Pallis, Byron— Cont
Stefania 1968,N 29,56:1
Pallos, Steven (Producer)
Diamond Wizard, The 1954,Jl 17,7:4
Angela 1955,Je 4,9:2
They all Died Laughing 1964,Mr 16,37:2
Pallotta, Gabriella
Roof, The 1959,My 13,43:4
Pigeon That Took Rome, The 1962,Ag 23,25:1
Viaccia, La 1962,S 21,35:1
Grido, Il 1962,O 23,42:1
Madame 1963,Mr 21,8:6
Bible, The 1966,S 29,60:1
Sailor From Gibraltar, The 1967,Ap 25,38:2
Pallu, Georges (Director)
Ne Sirj Edesanyam 1936,N 24,35:4
Pally
Orage 1938,D 12,26:2
Janos Vitez; John, The Hero 1939,Ap 8,19:2
Confessions of a Rogue 1948,Mr 30,26:3
Honorable Catherine, The 1948,Ag 23,13:3
Palm, Dick
Michigan Kid, The 1928,Jl 2,11:2
Palm, Walter
Hoosier Schoolmaster, The 1924,Mr 18,25:2
Palma, Andrea
Ultima Cita, La 1936,Ja 22,15:6
Sor Juana Ines de la Cruz 1936,Je 6,21:2
Mujer del Puerto, La 1936,Ag 24,11:3
Ave sin Rumbo; Wandering Bird 1938,Ja 24,17:2
Senor Alcalde, El; Mayor, The 1939,My 20,11:2
Tarzan and the Mermaids 1948,Mr 30,26:4
Palma, Enriqueta
Dos Mujeres y un Don Juan 1934,Je 4,12:4
Palma, Joe
Brasher Doubloon, The 1947,My 22,34:5
Palma, Mona
Fascinating Youth 1926,My 10,19:1
Cabaret 1927,My 2,26:4
Palmara, Mimmo
Hercules 1959,Jl 23,32:2
Last Days of Pompeii, The 1960,Ag 11,19:1
Palmarini, Alberto
Lorenzino de Medici 1936,Ap 14,19:3
Palme, Ulf
Sunshine Follows Rain 1949,S 29,39:2
Miss Julie 1952,Ap 8,35:2
Sorciere, La 1956,D 28,17:2
Dreams; Kvinnodrom 1960,Je 1,42:1
Counterfeit Traitor, The 1962,Ap 18,28:1
To Bed...Or not to Bed 1963,D 23,18:2
Here's Your Life 1968,D 20,60:1
Palmer, Arnold
Call Me Bwana 1963,Jl 4,9:1
Palmer, Bert
Kind of Loving, A 1962,O 2,46:1
Palmer, Betsy
Long Gray Line, The 1955,F 11,19:2
Mister Roberts 1955,Jl 15,14:1
Queen Bee 1955,N 23,13:2
Tin Star, The 1957,O 24,37:2
Last Angry Man, The 1959,O 23,24:1
Palmer, Bob (Composer)
Utah 1945,Mr 12,22:7
Palmer, Byron
Tonight We Sing 1953,F 13,17:2
Man in the Attic 1954,F 6,17:2
Palmer, Charles (Screenwriter)
Lost Boundaries 1949,Jl 1,14:4
Sellout, The 1952,My 31,12:7
Palmer, Christene
Mikado, The 1967,Mr 15,53:1
Palmer, Conway
Quiet Week-End 1948,Ag 20,13:2
Palmer, Corliss
Man's Past, A 1927,O 4,34:2
Honeymoon Hate 1927,D 31,31:1
Clothes Make the Woman 1928,Je 5,21:1
Night Bird, The 1928,O 2,23:5
Honeymoon Lane 1931,Ag 1,16:4
Palmer, Effie
Way Back Home 1932,Ja 16,13:1
Palmer, Ernest (Cinematographer)
Edge of the World, The 1938,S 12,13:2
Palmer, Frederick (Original Author)
New Commandment, The 1925,N 10,25:3
Palmer, Gregg
Playgirl 1954,My 15,13:3
Magnificent Obsession 1954,Ag 5,18:4
To Hell and Back 1955,S 23,21:2
Creature Walks among Us, The 1956,Ap 27,21:6
Hilda Crane 1956,My 3,35:2
Most Dangerous Man Alive 1961,Jl 5,29:2
Palmer, Henning
Hagbard and Signe 1968,My 17,56:1
Palmer, Kiki
Marcia Nuziale, La 1936,F 27,23:2
Palmer, Leslie
Unfaithful 1931,Mr 7,17:2
Strangers in Love 1932,Mr 5,11:2
Palmer, Lilli
Secret Agent 1936,Je 13,13:1
Great Barrier, The 1937,F 5,17:5
Silent Barriers 1937,Mr 26,25:1

Palmer, Lilli — Cont

Man With 100 Faces 1938,N 1,27:2
Suicide Legion 1940,My 6,13:3
Girl Must Live, A 1942,Mr 24,25:2
Thunder Rock 1944,S 15,16:1
Cloak and Dagger 1946,O 5,13:2
Notorious Gentleman 1946,N 14,39:3
Beware of Pity 1947,N 1,11:2
Body and Soul 1947,N 10,21:2
My Girl Tisa 1948,F 21,9:2
No Minor Vices 1949,F 26,11:2
Her Man Gilbey 1949,Je 9,35:2
Long Dark Hall, The 1951,My 10,38:3
Four Poster, The 1952,O 16,37:1
Main Street to Broadway 1953,O 14,34:1
Tempestous Love 1958,N 22,27:4
Glass Tower, The; (Glaserne Turm, Der)
    1959,Ag 27,24:4
But Not for Me 1959,O 3,14:6
Conspiracy of Hearts 1960,Ap 8,24:1
Modigliani of Montparnasse 1961,Mr 1,27:3
Pleasure of his Company, The 1961,Je 2,36:1
Counterfeit Traitor, The 1962,Ap 18,28:1
Miracle of the White Stallions 1963,My 23,31:2
Of Wayward Love (The Serpent); Serpent, The (Of
    Wayward Love) 1964,Mr 24,29:1
Adorable Julia 1964,Ap 8,33:1
Operation Crossbow 1965,Ap 2,29:1
Amorous Adventures of Moll Flanders, The
    1965,My 27,28:1
And so to Bed 1965,Jl 31,11:3
Madchen in Uniform 1965,Ag 18,41:2
Sebastian 1968,Ja 25,33:2
Oedipus the King 1968,S 19,62:2
High Commissioner, The 1968,D 12,62:5

Palmer, Lilli (Narrator)

Pictura 1952,Ap 8,35:3

Palmer, Maria

Mission to Moscow 1943,Ap 30,25:2
Days of Glory 1944,Je 17,10:2
Lady on a Train 1945,S 15,21:2
Other Love, The 1947,My 15,32:4
Web, The 1947,Je 5,32:1
Surrender 1950,O 9,21:5
Strictly Dishonorable 1951,Jl 12,21:6
By the Light of the Silvery Moon
    1953,Mr 27,28:2
Three for Jamie Dawn 1956,Jl 7,11:3

Palmer, Max

Sniper, The 1952,My 10,16:3

Palmer, Mona

Quarterback, The 1926,O 12,30:2
Canadian, The 1926,N 30,27:1

Palmer, Patricia

Money Corporal, The 1919,Ap 21,13:4
To the Ladies 1923,N 26,15:6

Palmer, Peter

Li'l Abner 1959,D 12,19:2

Palmer, Richard

French Mistress, A 1960,D 19,34:2

Palmer, Shirley

Magic Flame, The 1927,S 19,30:3
Marriage by Contract 1928,N 13,37:1
This Sporting Age 1932,O 1,10:4

Palmer, Stuart (Miscellaneous)

Stadium Murders, The 1938,Ap 9,11:2

Palmer, Stuart (Original Author)

Penguin Pool Murder, The 1932,D 26,26:2
Murder on the Blackboard 1934,Je 20,24:2
Murder on a Honeymoon 1935,Mr 4,12:2
Murder on a Bridle Path 1936,Ap 11,19:2
Plot Thickens, The 1936,D 9,35:2
Forty Naughty Girls 1937,S 18,15:3
Stadium Murders, The 1938,Ap 9,11:2
Smiling Ghost, The 1941,S 26,26:5
Falcon Strikes Back, The 1943,Ap 2,17:4
Murder in Times Square 1943,My 31,13:2
Mrs O'Malley and Mr Malone 1951,F 23,33:2

Palmer, Stuart (Screenwriter)

Bulldog Drummond's Peril 1938,Mr 18,23:2
Arrest Bulldog Drummond 1939,Ja 12,23:2
Bulldog Drummond's Bride 1939,Jl 13,17:2
Death of a Champion 1939,Ag 24,17:3
Seventeen 1940,F 29,15:2
Smiling Ghost, The 1941,S 26,26:5
Falcon's Brother, The 1942,O 3,9:5
Step by Step 1946,Ag 24,6:7

Palmer, Thomas

Life and Death of Colonel Blimp, The
    1945,Mr 30,18:2

Palmer, Toni

Smashing Time 1967,D 21,44:1

Palmer, Violet

My Man 1924,F 11,18:3
Dearie 1927,Jl 4,20:3

Palmeri, Mimi

Ragged Edge, The 1923,Je 5,24:5
Second Youth 1924,Ap 22,19:3

Palmgren, Aurore

Pimpernel Svensson 1953,F 6,16:4

Palmgren, Helena

Winter Light 1963,My 14,32:1

Palmieri, F (Screenwriter)

Miss Italy 1952,My 10,16:2
Streets of Sorrow 1952,N 18,37:4
What Price Innocence? 1953,My 2,13:3
Cinderella 1953,My 15,20:2
Young Caruso, The 1953,O 13,34:4

Palmieri, Sandro

Casta Oiva 1937,O 5,29:2

Palnikof, N N

Clown George 1932,Ag 24,21:4

Palo, Janno

Milkmaid, The 1959,My 2,14:5

Palo, Tauno

Niskavvoren Naiset; Women of Niskavuori
    1938,N 21,14:5
Jumalen Tuomio; Judgement of God, The
    1939,O 27,27:2

Palomera, Lupita

Padre Mercader; Merchant Father 1939,Jl 15,8:3

Palou, Matilde

Juarez y Maximiliano 1935,F 16,9:2
Beso Mortal, El; Fatal Kiss, The 1939,Ja 21,19:3
Creo en Dios 1943,Jl 17,8:3

Palsa, Nani

White Heat 1934,Je 16,20:2

Palsson-Wettergren, Gertrud

Charlotte Loewenskoeld 1932,F 22,23:2

Paluzzi, Luciana

Return to Peyton Place 1961,My 6,26:1
Muscle Beach Party 1964,My 28,40:1
Vice and Virtue 1965,Mr 18,25:1
Thunderball 1965,D 22,23:1
Venetian Affair, The 1967,Ja 19,41:2
Chuka 1967,N 2,58:3

Pameschikov, Eugene (Screenwriter)

Symphony of Life 1948,D 28,19:7

Pamolli, Colombo

Hell Raiders of the Deep 1954,Jl 3,9:2

Pampanini, Silvana

When Love Calls 1948,O 9,12:6
Anthony of Padua 1952,Mr 29,19:2
O K Nero 1953,Je 20,8:6
Half a Century of Songs 1954,O 30,15:6
Cavalcade of Song 1954,D 27,22:8
Mademoiselle Gobette 1955,F 5,13:3
Island Sinner, The 1960,S 5,11:2
Day in Court, A 1963,My 11,15:2

Pan, Hermes

Life of her Own, A 1950,O 12,43:2

Pan, Hermes (Miscellaneous)

Three Little Words 1950,Ag 10,21:2
Can-Can 1960,Mr 10,36:1

Pan, Ingrid

White Horse Inn, The 1957,D 4,50:3
Aren't We Wonderful? 1959,O 16,27:1

Panalle, Juan

Specter of the Rose 1946,S 2,12:4

Panama, Norman (Director)

Reformer and the Redhead, The 1950,Ap 10,15:2
Strictly Dishonorable 1951,Jl 12,21:6
Callaway Went Thataway 1951,D 6,42:1
Above and Beyond 1953,Ja 31,10:6
Knock on Wood 1954,Ap 15,34:2
Court Jester, The 1956,F 2,19:1
That Certain Felling 1956,Je 21,35:2
Trap, The 1959,Ja 29,18:4
Road to Hong Kong, The 1962,Je 28,21:1
Not With my Wife, You Don't! 1966,N 3,45:2

Panama, Norman (Original Author)

My Favorite Blonde 1942,Ap 2,27:2
Southern Yankee, A 1948,N 25,47:2
Callaway Went Thataway 1951,D 6,42:1
Knock on Wood 1954,Ap 15,34:2
Li'l Abner 1959,D 12,19:2
Strange Bedfellows 1965,Mr 11,38:1
Not With my Wife, You Don't! 1966,N 3,45:2

Panama, Norman (Producer)

Mr Blandings Builds his Dream House
    1948,Mr 26,26:2
Reformer and the Redhead, The 1950,Ap 10,15:2
Strictly Dishonorable 1951,Jl 12,21:6
Callaway Went Thataway 1951,D 6,42:1
Above and Beyond 1953,Ja 31,10:6
Knock on Wood 1954,Ap 15,34:2
Court Jester, The 1956,F 2,19:1
That Certain Felling 1956,Je 21,35:2
Trap, The 1959,Ja 29,18:4
Li'l Abner 1959,D 12,19:2
Facts of Life, The 1961,F 11,27:1
Not With my Wife, You Don't! 1966,N 3,45:2

Panama, Norman (Screenwriter)

Happy Go Lucky 1943,Mr 25,25:1
Thank Your Lucky Stars 1943,O 2,19:2
And the Angels Sing 1944,Jl 13,14:2
Duffy's Tavern 1945,S 6,23:3
Road to Utopia 1946,F 28,20:2
Our Hearts Were Growing Up 1946,Ag 12,17:2
Monsieur Beaucaire 1946,S 5,23:1
It Had to be You 1947,D 8,35:2
Mr Blandings Builds his Dream House
    1948,Mr 26,26:2
Return of October, The 1949,F 23,31:2
Reformer and the Redhead, The 1950,Ap 10,15:2

Panama, Norman (Screenwriter) — Cont

Strictly Dishonorable 1951,Jl 12,21:6
Above and Beyond 1953,Ja 31,10:6
White Christmas 1954,O 15,16:3
Court Jester, The 1956,F 2,19:1
That Certain Felling 1956,Je 21,35:2
Trap, The 1959,Ja 29,18:4
Li'l Abner 1959,D 12,19:2
Facts of Life, The 1961,F 11,27:1
Road to Hong Kong, The 1962,Je 28,21:1
Not With my Wife, You Don't! 1966,N 3,45:2

Panaro, Alessandro

Poor but Beautiful 1958,Je 11,39:4
Rocco and his Brothers 1961,Je 28,40:2

Pancewicz, Leokadja

Love or a Kingdom 1937,D 4,21:1

Pandey, K S

Aparajito 1959,Ap 29,30:1

Pandolfi, Elio

Times Gone By (A Pot-Pourri of Songs);
    Pot-Pourri of Songs, A (Times Gone By)
    1953,D 30,16:2

Pandolfini, Turi

Of Life and Love 1958,O 7,40:2

Panerai, Rolando

Boheme, La 1965,O 20,51:2

Pangborn, Franklin

Getting Gertie's Garter 1927,F 9,17:3
Night Bride, The 1927,Mr 30,22:6
Cradle Snatchers 1927,My 31,25:2
Girl on the Pullman, The 1927,N 1,21:1 (In
    Addenda)
On Trial 1928,N 15,26:5
Not so Dumb 1930,F 8,12:5
Woman of Experience, A 1931,Jl 9,26:5
International House 1933,My 27,11:5
Professional Sweetheart 1933,Jl 14,15:3
Headline Shooters 1933,O 23,18:3
Only Yesterday 1933,N 10,25:1
Design for Living 1933,N 23,24:2
Many Happy Returns 1934,Je 9,18:2
Cockeyed Cavaliers 1934,Jl 25,22:2
Young and Beautiful 1934,S 18,18:4
College Rhythm 1934,N 24,19:1
$1,000 a Minute 1935,D 21,11:1
Don't Gamble With Love 1936,Mr 2,13:3
To Mary-With Love 1936,Ag 27,16:1
My Man Godfrey 1936,S 19,18:1 (Incorrect in
    this edition; use 1936,S 18,18:1 elsewhere)
Step Lively, Jeeves 1937,Ap 2,19:6
Swing High, Swing Low 1937,Ap 15,19:1
Star Is Born, A 1937,Ap 23,25:1
Turn off the Moon 1937,My 20,17:2
Easy Living 1937,Jl 8,20:1
She Had to Eat 1937,Jl 24,12:1
It Happened in Hollywood 1937,O 2,18:1
Life of the Party, The 1937,O 4,17:1
Stage Door 1937,O 8,27:2
Thrill of a Lifetime 1937,D 9,30:2
She Married an Artist 1938,F 25,15:2
Mad About Music 1938,Mr 12,13:2
Bluebeard's Eighth Wife 1938,Mr 24,21:2
Rebecca of Sunnybrook Farm 1938,Mr 26,12:1
Joy of Living 1938,My 6,27:1
Doctor Rhythm 1938,My 19,25:2
Vivacious Lady 1938,Je 3,17:3
Three Blind Mice 1938,Je 18,18:2
Always Goodbye 1938,Je 25,7:2
Four's a Crowd 1938,Ag 12,11:1
Carefree 1938,S 23,35:1
Just Around the Corner 1938,D 3,11:2
Topper Takes a Trip 1938,D 30,11:2
Girl Downstairs, The 1939,Ja 26,17:1
Broadway Serenade 1939,Ap 7,25:2
Fifth Avenue Girl 1939,Ag 25,12:2
Turnabout 1940,Jl 27,17:6
Public Deb No 1 1940,S 18,19:2
Spring Parade 1940,O 4,29:2
Christmas in July 1940,N 6,35:2
Hit Parade of 1941 1940,D 5,33:2
Bank Dick, The 1940,D 13,29:2
Girl, a Guy and a Gob, A 1941,Ap 24,25:3
Flame of New Orleans, The 1941,Ap 26,20:2
Week End for Three 1941,O 24,27:4
Never Give a Sucker an Even Break
    1941,O 27,21:2
Call out the Marines 1942,Ja 26,18:3
Sullivan's Travels 1942,Ja 29,25:2
Obliging Young Lady 1942,F 13,24:4
What's Cookin' 1942,F 26,15:5
Now, Voyager 1942,O 23,25:3
George Washington Slept Here 1942,O 31,11:1
Palm Beach Story, The 1942,D 11,33:1
Reveille With Beverly 1943,Ap 24,17:2
Stage Door Canteen 1943,Je 25,13:2
Holy Matrimony 1943,S 16,25:2
Crazy House 1943,D 16,33:3
Hail the Conquering Hero 1944,Ag 10,14:2
Great Moment, The 1944,N 13,15:2
Horn Blows at Midnight, The 1945,Ap 21,18:2
See my Lawyer 1945,My 4,23:4
You Came Along 1945,Jl 5,17:2
Lover Come Back 1946,Je 20,20:3
Two Guys From Milwaukee 1946,Jl 27,12:5

Pangborn, Franklin — Cont
I'll Be Yours 1947,F 22,16:2
Romance on the High Seas 1948,Je 26,10:5
My Dream Is Yours 1949,Ap 16,11:3
Her Wonderful Lie 1950,Jl 17,15:2
Mad Wednesday 1951,Ja 25,21:5
Oh Men! Oh Women! 1957,F 22,25:2

Pani, Corrado
Rocco and his Brothers 1961,Je 28,40:2
Girl With a Suitcase 1961,S 12,36:2
Run With the Devil 1963,Jl 16,25:1

Panich, Y
Road to Life 1956,Je 11,26:6

Pankratova, D
Mashenka 1942,N 21,10:7

Pannunzio, Mario (Screenwriter)
Greatest Love, The 1954,Ja 12,19:2

Panou, Katy
Anna of Rhodes 1950,Mr 23,34:2

Panov, V
Sleeping Beauty, The 1966,My 4,50:1

Panova, Alexandra
Lucky Bride, The 1948,Ja 26,15:2

Panova, Vera (Original Author)
Summer to Remember, A; (Seryozha)
1961,N 7,38:1

Panova, Vera (Screenwriter)
Summer to Remember, A; (Seryozha)
1961,N 7,38:1

Panzer, Paul
Unseeing Eyes 1923,O 22,17:1
Son of the Sahara, A 1924,My 27,14:1
Wages of Virtue 1924,N 24,15:3
Too Many Kisses 1925,Mr 3,20:1
Fool, The 1925,Ap 13,24:1
Shock Punch, The 1925,My 11,14:3
Best Bad Man, The 1925,D 2,23:1
Girl From Chicago, The 1927,D 20,33:2
Glorious Betsy 1928,Ap 27,16:4
Tanz Geht Weiter, Der 1931,Ja 6,25:1
Bedtime Story, A 1933,Ap 20,20:3
Perils of Pauline, The 1947,Jl 10,17:2

Panzeri, Sandro
Sound of Trumpets, The 1963,O 23,36:1

Pao-shu, Kao
Love Eterne, The; Liang Shan Po and Chu
Ying-lai 1965,Ja 16,14:1

Paola, Dria
Cieca di Sorrento, La 1936,Ag 3,11:3
Amore e Dolore 1937,My 13,31:4
Albero di Adamo, L'; Adam's Tree
1938,Ja 20,19:2
Pensaci Giacomino; Think It Over, Jack
1940,Mr 25,11:3

Paolella, Domenico (Director)
Half a Century of Songs 1954,O 30,15:6
Cavalcade of Song 1954,D 27,22:8
Gran Varieta 1955,Ap 11,29:5

Paolella, Domenico (Screenwriter)
Half a Century of Songs 1954,O 30,15:6

Paoletti, Marco
Teacher and the Miracle, The 1961,Ap 24,36:4
Lazarillo 1963,Ap 5,27:6

Paoli, Evelina
Miracolo Di Sant' Antonio, Il 1932,Ap 18,19:2

Paoli, Giulio
I Tre Innamorati 1937,Je 17,19:2

Paoli, Raoul
Beau Sabreur 1928,Ja 23,18:3
Night of Mystery, A 1928,Ap 16,20:5

Paolieri, Germana
Lorenzino de Medici 1936,Ap 14,19:3
Armata Azzurra, La; Blue Fleet, The
1937,D 13,23:4
Wally, La 1939,Ja 2,28:3
Life of Giuseppe Verdi 1940,Ap 3,19:2
Tutta la Vita in una Notte; All of Life in one
Night 1940,My 2,29:6
Dream of Butterfly, The 1941,F 13,25:2
Two Orphans, The 1950,O 19,40:6

Paolinelli, Bruno (Original Author)
Angels of Darkness 1956,N 22,51:1

Paoloni, Elvira
Ape Woman, The 1964,S 23,55:1

Paoloni, Omero
Under the Sun of Rome 1949,O 6,40:4

Paolos, Steven (Producer)
Foxhole in Cairo 1961,F 16,25:2

Paolucci, Giovanni (Director)
Shamed 1949,O 13,33:3

Paolucci, Giovanni (Screenwriter)
Monte Cassino 1948,N 25,47:3

Paoluzzi, Luciana
My Seven Little Sins 1956,My 2,27:1
Man in a Cocked Hat 1960,Je 15,50:2

Papadakis, Michael
Mademoiselle-Age 39 1956,Mr 26,34:2

Papadatou, Niki
Aunt From Chicago, The 1960,Je 6,33:6

Papadouka, Olympia
Phaedra 1962,O 19,24:1

Papageorgiou, Margarita
Aunt From Chicago, The 1960,Je 6,33:6

Papagianopoulos, D
Lisa, Tosca of Athens 1961,Je 20,27:1
You Came too Late 1962,N 12,35:8
Policeman of the 16th Precinct, The
1963,Ap 22,23:2

Papaloukas, P (Screenwriter)
Anna of Rhodes 1950,Mr 23,34:2

Papamichael, Dimitrios
Astero 1960,Ap 25,32:2
Aunt From Chicago, The 1960,Je 6,33:6
Never on Sunday 1960,O 19,54:1
Midwife, The 1961,S 25,41:2
Red Lanterns 1965,Ap 1,30:1

Papas, Irene
Man From Cairo, The 1953,D 17,52:4
Theodora, Slave Empress 1955,Ja 12,24:2
Tribute to a Bad Man 1956,Mr 31,13:3
Attila 1958,My 19,19:4
Guns of Navarone, The 1961,Je 23,19:1
Antigone 1962,S 19,30:1
Electra 1962,D 18,5:2
Moonspinners, The 1964,N 4,47:1
Zorba, The Greek 1964,D 18,25:1
We Still Kill the Old Way 1968,F 29,28:1

Papashvily, George (Original Author)
Anything Can Happen 1952,Ap 4,21:1

Papashvily, Helen (Original Author)
Anything Can Happen 1952,Ap 4,21:1

Papatikas, Nico (Director)
Abysses, Les 1964,N 24,44:1

Papava, M (Screenwriter)
Ivan Pavlov 1950,F 13,15:2
Far for Moscow 1951,Jl 2,16:6
Skanderbeg 1954,Jl 5,6:4
My Name Is Ivan (Ivan's Childhood)
1963,Je 28,25:4

Papayannopoule, D
Stella 1957,Je 11,40:1

Papazyan, Vagram
Heart Sings, The 1958,Ag 18,15:2

Pape, Lionel
Man Who Broke the Bank at Monte Carlo, The
1935,N 15,20:2
Mary of Scotland 1936,Jl 31,22:2
Beloved Enemy 1936,D 26,15:2
King and the Chorus Girl, The 1937,Mr 29,14:4
Prince and the Pauper, The 1937,My 6,23:1
Wee Willie Winkie 1937,Jl 24,12:1
Angel 1937,N 4,29:1
Big Broadcast of 1938, The 1938,Mr 10,16:2
Bluebeard's Eighth Wife 1938,Mr 24,21:2
Booloo 1938,Jl 30,10:2
Young in Heart, The 1938,N 4,27:2
Midnight 1939,Ap 6,31:1
Eternally Yours 1939,O 7,11:2
Drums Along the Mohawk 1939,N 4,11:2
Rulers of the Sea 1939,N 9,27:1
Raffles 1940,Ja 13,11:2
Congo Maisie 1940,F 8,18:4
Long Voyage Home, The 1940,O 9,30:2 (In
Addenda)
Arise my Love 1940,O 17,33:2
Tin Pan Alley 1940,N 22,27:3
Philadelphia Story, The 1940,D 27,22:2
Hudson's Bay 1941,Ja 10,23:2
Scotland Yard 1941,Ap 9,33:3
Charley's Aunt 1941,Ag 2,18:2
How Green Was my Valley 1941,O 29,27:2

Paper, David
Invaders, The 1942,Mr 6,17:1

Papi, George (Producer)
Fistful of Dollars, A 1967,F 2,29:1
Grand Slam 1968,F 21,60:4

Papouf
Big Chief, The 1960,Ap 27,32:1

Papousek, Jaroslav (Screenwriter)
Loves of a Blonde 1966,O 27,55:1
Firemen's Ball, The 1968,S 30,60:1

Papov, S
Heroes of Shipka 1956,S 3,10:5

Pappas, George
Windfall in Athens 1956,O 1,31:1
Madame X 1960,O 3,34:5

Papst (Director)
Scandal About Eva 1930,Jl 27,VIII,4:2 (In
Addenda)

Paquerette
Mare Nostrum 1926,F 16,22:4
Garden of Allah, The 1927,S 3,13:5
Modigliani of Montparnasse 1961,Mr 1,27:3

Paquet, Felix
Royal Affair, A; (Roi, Le) 1950,Mr 9,25:2
Ma Pomme 1951,O 15,22:2

Paquette, Pauline
Bluff 1924,Ap 28,18:2

Paqui, Felix
Mayor's Dilemma, The 1940,Ap 23,19:2

Parades, Jean
Vie de Boheme, La 1947,N 28,37:4

Paradis, Marjorie Bartholomew (Original Author)
This Side of Heaven 1934,F 10,21:2

Paradova, Joaquin
Cada Loco con su Tema; Every Madman to his
Specialty 1939,Ap 29,13:3

Parain, Brice
My Life to Live 1963,S 24,43:2

Paramof, L
Young Pushkin 1937,D 16,35:3

Paramonov, I
Italiano Brava Gente 1966,F 4,20:1

Paramore, E E (Original Author)
Mystery Woman 1935,Ja 9,22:2
Oklahoma Kid, The 1939,Mr 11,21:1
Crooked Road, The 1940,Je 11,33:4

Paramore, E E (Screenwriter)
Three Godfathers, The 1936,Mr 9,20:2
Trouble for Two 1936,My 30,7:2
Three Comrades 1938,Je 3,17:1
Oklahoma Kid, The 1939,Mr 11,21:1
Man of Conquest 1939,Ap 28,31:2
Twenty-Mule Team 1940,My 10,26:6
Mystery Sea Raider 1940,Ag 26,11:4
Chetniks 1943,Mr 19,15:3

Paraz, Albert (Screenwriter)
Noah's Ark 1950,Ag 21,15:1

Parbs, Margarete
Schloss Hubertus 1935,F 9,11:3

Parcell, Emory
Colonel Effingham's Raid 1946,Ap 5,21:3

Pardave, Joaquin
Zandunga, La 1938,My 14,18:2
Millones de Chaflan, Los 1938,S 13,28:3
Cancion del Alma; Song of the Soul
1938,O 11,20:4
Tierra Brava 1938,O 29,15:6
Mi Candidato; My Candidate 1938,O 31,12:3
Bajo el Cielo de Mexico; Beneath the Sky of
Mexico 1938,D 31,7:3
Senor Alcalde, El; Mayor, The 1939,My 20,11:2
Tia de las Muchachas, La; Girls' Aunt, The
1939,O 30,13:3
Caballo a Caballo; Horse for Horse
1940,F 10,19:2
Luna Criolla; Creole Moon 1940,Ap 8,15:3
En un Burro Tres Baturros; Three Rustics on one
Donkey 1940,S 21,13:3
Vivire Otra Vez; I Shall Live Again
1940,O 23,27:2
Guadalajara 1943,Je 12,9:3

Pardi, Mirabella
Destino, Il 1938,F 8,17:3

Pardo, Maria
Ahora Seremos Felices; Now We Shall Be Happy
1940,Mr 16,8:2

Paredes, Jean
Who Killed Santa Claus? 1948,Ap 21,33:2
Fanfan the Tulip 1953,My 5,34:2
Beauties of the Night 1954,Mr 23,23:5
French-Cancan 1956,Ap 17,26:2
Michael Strogoff 1960,My 21,15:1
Love Is a Ball 1963,Ap 25,38:1

Parely, Mila
Champs-Elysees 1939,F 28,17:2
They Met on Skis 1940,D 23,23:2
Pasha's Wives, The 1942,Ap 6,19:2
drame De Shanghai; Shanghai Drama, The
1945,Ja 11,19:2
Star Without Light; Etoile Sans Lumiere
1947,Ag 4,14:2
Beauty and the Beast 1947,D 24,12:2
Snowbound 1949,F 21,20:2
Angels of the Streets 1950,Ja 17,24:2
Rules of the Game, The 1950,Ap 10,15:3
Plaisir, Le (The House of Madame Tellier); House
of Madame Tellier (Le Plaisir)
1954,My 20,38:1
Dreams of Love 1954,Je 5,11:2
Rules of the Game, The 1961,Ja 19,26:1

Parera, Valentin
Granaderos del Amor 1934,S 4,23:4
Dos Mas Uno Dos 1934,O 27,20:3

Parfenov, Nikolai
Son of the Regiment 1948,Ap 29,27:3

Parfitt, Judy
Hide and Seek 1964,Mr 12,40:3

Parios, Gus
Close Harmony 1929,Ap 29,29:2

Paris, Dany
Bebo's Girl 1964,N 12,40:1

Paris, Franca
Scampolo 1959,Ag 6,18:4

Paris, Jerry
Outrage 1950,O 16,30:5
Cyrano De Bergerac 1950,N 17,31:2
Flying Missile, The 1950,D 25,25:1
Call Me Mister 1951,F 1,21:2
Sabre Jet 1953,N 3,34:1
Prisoner of War 1954,My 10,20:2
Caine Mutiny, The 1954,Je 25,17:1
Unchained 1955,Ja 28,15:2
Marty 1955,Ap 12,25:3
Naked Street, The 1955,O 1,11:2
View From Pompey's Head, The 1955,N 5,22:5
Good Morning, Miss Dove 1955,N 24,41:1

Paris, Jerry— Cont

D-Day, The Sixth of June 1956,My 30,13:1
I've Lived Before 1956,Ag 4,13:1
Zero Hour 1957,N 14,41:1
Female Animal, The 1958,Ja 23,24:3
Lady Takes a Flyer, The 1958,Ja 30,19:2
Sing Boy Sing 1958,F 22,9:4
Naked and the Dead, The 1958,Ag 7,21:1
Great Impostor, The 1961,Mr 30,24:1

Paris, Jerry (Director)

Don't Raise the Bridge, Lower the River
1968,Jl 13,18:1
Never a Dull Moment 1968,Ag 15,46:2
How Sweet It Is 1968,Ag 22,47:1

Paris, Jerry (Screenwriter)

Caretakers, The 1963,Ag 22,19:2

Paris, John

Way of a Gaucho 1952,N 5,36:2

Paris, Lucien

Song of the Street 1939,S 5,21:2
Panic 1947,N 27,50:2

Paris, Manuel

Odio 1935,Je 24,12:3

Paris, Maria

Tarantella Napoletana 1954,Ap 19,19:3

Paris, Simone

Minne 1951,Ap 17,35:2
Pantaloons 1956,D 26,34:1
Man and a Woman, A; Homme et une Femme,
Un 1966,Jl 13,35:1
Therese and Isabelle 1968,My 15,41:4

Paris Ski Club

They Met on Skis 1940,D 23,23:2

Parise, Goffredo (Original Author)

Kiss the Other Sheik 1968,Jl 30,33:1

Parise, Goffredo (Screenwriter)

Kiss the Other Sheik 1968,Jl 30,33:1

Pariset, Cristina

Before the Revolution; Prima della Revolutiona
1964,S 25,32:1

Parisi, Le Sozelle

I Cadetti di Guascogna 1952,O 6,22:2

Parisy, Andrea

Cheaters, The; (Tricheurs, Les) 1961,Je 5,37:4
Greed in the Sun 1965,Ag 19,35:3

PARK

See Also PARKE

Park, E L

Behind That Curtain 1929,Jl 1,31:2

Park, John (Director)

Private Life of Mussolini, The 1938,Je 24,15:2

Park, Marvin (Original Author)

Gallant Bess 1946,D 6,27:6

Park, Richard

Target Zero 1955,N 16,43:2

Park, William (Director)

Paliser Case, The 1920,F 16,8:1

Park, William C (Screenwriter)

World in Flames, The 1940,O 24,31:2
Secret Land, The 1948,D 2,39:2

PARKE

See Also PARK

Parke, MacDonald

Shipyard Sally 1940,Ja 18,27:3
Candlelight in Algeria 1944,Jl 31,10:2
No Orchids for Miss Blandish 1951,F 23,33:2
Penny Princess 1953,Mr 25,37:3
Paris Express, The 1953,Je 6,8:6
Babes in Bagdad 1954,Ap 5,21:3
Summertime 1955,Je 22,25:1
Mouse That Roared, The 1959,O 27,40:1
Battle of the Sexes, The 1960,Ap 19,40:4

Parker, Abe

High and Dry 1954,Ag 31,25:5

Parker, Albert (Director)

Knickerbocker Buckaroo, The 1919,My 26,19:4
Love's Redemption 1922,Ja 9,15:2
Sherlock Holmes 1922,My 8,14:3
Second Youth 1924,Ap 22,19:3
Rejected Woman, The 1924,My 5,18:3
Black Pirate, The 1926,Mr 9,21:4
Love of Sunya, The 1927,Mr 12,12:2

Parker, Alison

Mikado, The 1967,Mr 15,53:1

Parker, Austin (Original Author)

Honor Among Lovers 1931,F 28,15:2

Parker, Austin (Screenwriter)

Girl on the Front Page, The 1936,N 7,15:2
Something to Sing About 1937,S 21,29:4
When Knights Were Bold 1942,Mr 31,29:2

Parker, Barnett

President's Mystery, The 1936,O 19,22:1
Born to Dance 1936,D 5,16:1
We Who Are About to Die 1937,Ja 2,15:1
Last of Mrs Cheyney, The 1937,F 19,15:1
Espionage 1937,Mr 9,27:3
Dangerous Number 1937,Mr 12,19:2
Personal Property 1937,Ap 11,27:2
Wake up and Live 1937,Ap 24,16:2
Emperor's Candlesticks, The 1937,Jl 9,18:1
Married Before Breakfast 1937,Jl 23,16:2
Broadway Melody of 1938 1937,S 3,12:1
Double Wedding 1937,O 22,27:2
Navy Blue and Gold 1937,D 24,21:2

Love Is a Headache 1938,Ja 28,17:3
Sally, Irene and Mary 1938,F 26,9:2
Hold That Kiss 1938,Je 11,9:1
Marie Antoinette 1938,Ag 17,23:2
Listen, Darling 1938,N 24,37:2
Girl Downstairs, The 1939,Ja 26,17:1
Babes in Arms 1939,O 20,27:2
At the Circus 1939,N 17,17:2
He Married his Wife 1940,Ja 20,11:2
Conga Nights, La 1940,Je 5,33:5
Hit Parade of 1941 1940,D 5,33:2
Love Thy Neighbor 1940,D 18,32:5
Tall, Dark and Handsome 1941,Ja 24,15:2
Man Betrayed, A 1941,Mr 27,29:5
Reluctant Dragon, The 1941,Jl 25,12:2
New Wine 1942,F 2,11:2

Parker, Ben (Director)

George Washington Carver 1940,Ap 17,26:4

Parker, Ben (Screenwriter)

Guerrilla Girl 1953,Jl 7,23:7

Parker, Carol

Give Me a Sailor 1938,Ag 11,31:1

Parker, Cecil

Man Who Lived Again, The 1936,D 16,35:4
Storm in a Teacup 1938,Mr 22,18:4
Citadel, The 1938,N 4,27:2
Lady Vanishes, The 1938,D 26,29:1
Housemaster 1939,Ap 10,13:2
Saint's Vacation, The 1941,Je 13,22:2
Stars Look Down, The 1941,Jl 24,15:2
Suicide Squadron 1942,My 14,23:2
Ships With Wings 1942,My 25,11:2
Caesar and Cleopatra 1946,S 6,18:2
Magic Bow, The 1947,Jl 7,13:2
Hungry Hill 1947,O 11,11:2
Captain Boycott 1947,D 6,11:2
Woman in the Hall, The 1949,Ja 24,16:2
Quartet (The Colonel's Lady); Colonel's Lady, The
(Quartet) 1949,Mr 29,30:3
Weaker Sex, The 1949,Jl 11,13:2
Under Capricorn 1949,S 9,28:3
Amazing Mr Beecham, The 1949,D 26,33:4
Dear Mr Prohack 1950,Jl 15,7:2
Tony Draws a Horse 1951,My 15,38:6
Man in the White Suit, The 1952,Ap 1,35:2
Magic Box, The 1952,S 24,40:2
I Believe in You 1953,My 5,34:3
Detective, The 1954,N 2,25:2
Court Jester, The 1956,F 2,19:1
His Excellency 1956,F 2,19:3
Ladykillers 1956,F 21,37:2
23 Paces to Baker Street 1956,My 19,12:6
Constant Husband, The 1957,Jl 26,10:3
Admirable Crichton, The 1957,D 15,45:4
(Incorrect in this edition; use 1957,D 17,45:4
elsewhere)
It's Great to be Young 1957,D 26,23:3
Indiscreet 1958,Je 27,18:2
Tale of Two Cities, A 1958,Ag 5,23:1
Happy is the Bride 1959,Je 30,27:2
Wreck of the Mary Deare, The 1959,N 7,27:1
Under ten Flags 1960,S 16,24:1
French Mistress, A 1960,D 19,34:2
Swiss Family Robinson 1960,D 24,8:4
Pure Hell of St Trinian's, The 1961,S 26,31:1
Heavens Above! 1963,My 21,28:2
Swingin' Maiden, The 1964,Ja 1,16:2
Guns at Batasi 1964,N 17,47:1
Operation Snafu 1965,My 22,18:1
Amorous Adventures of Moll Flanders, The
1965,My 27,28:1
Man Could Get Killed, A 1966,My 12,54:2
Lady L 1966,My 19,51:1
Study in Terror, A 1966,N 3,45:3

Parker, Cecilia

Rainbow Trail, The 1932,Ja 30,13:2
Mystery Ranch 1932,Je 30,26:2
Man Trailer, The 1934,My 23,22:3
Lost Jungle, The 1934,Je 8,18:1
Painted Veil, The 1934,D 7,29:1
Here is my Heart 1934,D 22,21:1
Enter Madame 1935,Ja 12,12:1
High School Girl 1935,Mr 16,19:1
Naughty Marietta 1935,Mr 23,11:2
Ah, Wilderness! 1935,D 25,30:2
Mine With the Iron Door, The 1936,Jl 11,11:3
In His Steps 1936,O 29,31:1
Old Hutch 1936,D 7,27:4
Family Affair, A 1937,Ap 20,29:2
Damaged Lives 1937,Je 14,26:2
Hollywood Cowboy 1937,Jl 24,12:1
You're Only Young Once 1938,Ja 3,16:2
Judge Hardy's Children 1938,Ap 8,17:2
Love Finds Andy Hardy 1938,Jl 22,10:2
Out West With the Hardys 1938,D 9,31:2
Hardys Ride High, The 1939,Ap 14,28:2
Andy Hardy Gets Spring Fever 1939,Jl 19,23:2
Judge Hardy and Son 1940,Ja 18,27:3 (In
Addenda)
Andy Hardy Meets Debutante 1940,Ag 2,12:2
Courtship of Andy Hardy, The 1942,Ap 10,21:2
Grand Central Murder 1942,My 23,8:8
Seven Sweethearts 1942,N 13,28:1

Parker, Cecilia— Cont

Andy Hardy's Double Life 1943,Ja 12,23:3
Andy Hardy Comes Home 1958,D 24,00:0

Parker, Charlie

Drag 1929,Je 21,17:2

Parker, Dorian Leigh

Naked Autumn 1963,N 15,25:3

Parker, Dorothy (Composer)

Big Broadcast of 1936, The 1935,S 16,15:2

Parker, Dorothy (Miscellaneous)

Moon's our Home, The 1936,My 13,29:2
Little Foxes, The 1941,Ag 22,19:2

Parker, Dorothy (Original Author)

Smash-Up, The Story of a Woman
1947,Ap 11,31:2

Parker, Dorothy (Screenwriter)

Suzy 1936,Jl 25,16:1
Lady, Be Careful 1936,O 10,21:1
Star Is Born, A 1937,Ap 23,25:1
Woman Chases Man 1937,Je 11,26:2
Sweethearts 1938,D 23,16:2
Trade Winds 1939,Ja 13,17:2
Week End for Three 1941,O 24,27:4
Saboteur 1942,My 8,27:2
Fan, The 1949,Ap 2,12:2
Star is Born, A 1954,O 12,23:1

Parker, Edwin

Pistol Packin' Mama 1943,D 20,27:4
Strange Door, The 1951,D 10,34:6

Parker, Eleanor

Busses Roar 1942,S 25,25:4
Mission to Moscow 1943,Ap 30,25:2
Mysterious Doctor, The 1943,My 20,26:4
Between Two Worlds 1944,My 6,11:2
Very Thought of You, The 1944,N 18,16:7
Hollywood Canteen 1944,D 16,19:2
Pride of the Marines 1945,Ag 25,7:3
Of Human Bondage 1946,Jl 6,11:2
Never Say Goodbye 1946,N 23,12:2
Escape me Never 1947,N 8,11:2
Voice of the Turtle, The 1947,D 26,22:4
Woman in White, The 1948,My 8,12:2
Chain Lightning 1950,F 20,21:2
Caged 1950,My 20,8:6
Three Secrets 1950,O 21,10:6
Valentino 1951,Ap 20,25:1
Millionaire for Christy, A 1951,O 5,24:3
Detective Story 1951,N 7,35:2
Scaramouche 1952,My 9,20:2
Above and Beyond 1953,Ja 31,10:6
Escape from Fort Bravo 1954,Ja 23,11:2
Naked Jungle, The 1954,Ap 3,19:2
Valley of the Kings 1954,Jl 22,15:2
Many Rivers to Cross 1955,F 24,21:2
Interrupted Melody 1955,My 6,18:1
Man With the Golden Arm, The 1955,D 16,38:2
King and Four Queens, The 1956,D 22,13:7
Lizzie 1957,Ap 5,24:2
Seventh Sin, The 1957,Je 29,10:6
Hole in the Head, A 1959,Jl 16,31:2
Home from the Hill 1960,Mr 4,19:1
Return to Peyton Place 1961,My 6,26:1
Madison Avenue 1962,Mr 29,28:2
Sound of Music, The 1965,Mr 3,34:1
Oscar, The 1966,Mr 5,16:1
American Dream, An 1966,S 1,28:2
Warning Shot 1967,Je 8,52:2
Tiger and the Pussycat, The 1967,S 21,56:4

Parker, Ellen

Cop Hater 1958,O 2,44:3

Parker, Faith

Dementia 1955,D 23,14:4

Parker, Fess

Kid From Left Field, The 1953,S 26,15:3
Thunder Over the Plains 1953,D 10,64:4
Them 1954,Je 17,36:2
Battle Cry 1955,F 3,18:1
Davy Crockett, King of the Wild Frontier
1955,My 26,36:1
Great Locomotive Chase, The 1956,Je 27,35:1
Old Yeller 1957,D 26,23:4
Light in the Forest, The 1958,Jl 11,15:2
Hell is for Heroes 1962,Jl 12,19:3

Parker, Franklin

Millie 1931,F 7,11:1
Two Seconds 1932,My 19,25:3
Frisco Jenny 1933,Ja 7,11:2
Past of Mary Holmes, The 1933,My 1,10:3
Transatlantic Merry-Go-Round 1934,N 1,25:2
Air Hawks 1935,Je 4,26:5
I Cover the War 1937,Ag 2,10:2
Give Me a Sailor 1938,Ag 11,31:1
Eternally Yours 1939,O 7,11:2
Spirit of West Point 1947,O 3,31:2

Parker, Gilbert Sir (Original Author)

Jordan Is a Hard Road 1915,N 15,11:1
Behold my Wife 1920,O 11,19:3
Lane That had no Turning, The 1922,Ja 9,15:2
Right of Way, The 1931,Mr 24,31:2
Behold My Wife 1935,F 18,19:3

Parker, Gudrun (Original Author)

Stratford Adventure, The 1954,Ag 3,14:2

Parker, Jack
4 Devils 1928,O 4,26:3
Parker, Jean
Divorce in the Family 1932,O 31,18:4
Secret of Madame Blanche, The 1933,F 4,11:3
Gabriel Over the White House 1933,Ap 1,18:2
What Price Innocence? 1933,Je 26,16:3
Made on Broadway 1933,Jl 8,14:5
Storm at Daybreak 1933,Jl 22,14:2
Lady for a Day 1933,S 8,22:2
Little Women 1933,N 17,22:3
You Can't Buy Everything 1934,F 3,9:2
Lazy River 1934,Ap 4,26:2
Operator 13 1934,Je 23,16:5
Caravan 1934,S 28,27:1
Have a Heart 1934,O 20,20:2
Limehouse Blues 1934,D 12,28:2
Wicked Woman, A 1935,Ja 1,24:1
Sequoia 1935,F 23,14:6
Princess O'Hara 1935,Ap 13,11:3
Murder in the Fleet 1935,Je 3,22:2
Ghost Goes West, The 1935,D 18,33:8
Ghost Goes West, The 1936,Ja 11,9:2
Farmer in the Dell, The 1936,Mr 7,11:4
Texas Rangers, The 1936,S 24,29:1
Barrier, The 1937,N 27,21:2
Penitentiary 1938,Mr 7,13:2
Arkansas Traveler, The 1938,N 17,29:2
Romance of the Redwoods 1939,Ap 24,13:2
Zenobia 1939,My 15,15:2
Flight at Midnight 1939,S 7,29:2
Parents on Trial 1939,S 18,15:5
Flying Deuces, The 1939,N 24,29:2
Beyond Tomorrow 1940,S 27,27:1
Power Dive 1941,My 29,15:4
Pittsburgh Kid, The 1941,S 23,27:4
No Hands on the Clock 1941,D 22,24:6
I Live on Danger 1942,Ag 22,16:2
Dead Man's Eyes 1944,O 7,11:2
One Body too Many 1944,N 25,21:2
Gunfighter, The 1950,Je 24,7:2
Those Redheads From Seattle 1953,O 1,34:2
Black Tuesday 1955,Ja 1,16:2
Parker, Jeff
Twist Around the Clock 1962,Ja 27,13:4
Parker, Jefferson (Miscellaneous)
Great God Gold 1935,My 6,22:3
Parker, Jefferson (Screenwriter)
Human Cargo 1936,My 16,11:2
Mysterious Crossing 1937,F 2,20:5
Under Suspicion 1937,D 20,23:2 (In Addenda)
Making the Headlines 1938,Ap 1,17:2
Flight Into Nowhere 1938,My 2,13:3
Crime Takes a Holiday 1938,N 28,11:2
Parker, Joe (Director)
Eighteen and Anxious 1957,D 14,16:6
Parker, John (Director)
Dementia 1955,D 23,14:4
Parker, John (Original Author)
Dementia 1955,D 23,14:4
Parker, John (Producer)
Dementia 1955,D 23,14:4
Parker, Kim
Fiend Without a Face 1958,Jl 4,15:3
Count Your Blessings 1959,Ap 24,23:1
Parker, Lew
Are You With It? 1948,Ap 15,31:2
Parker, Lottie Blair (Original Author)
Way Down East 1935,O 31,16:2
Parker, Louis N (Original Author)
Disraeli 1921,Ag 22,13:6
Disraeli 1929,O 3,27:5
Parker, Mary
St Louis Blues 1939,F 9,17:2
Lady in the Dark 1944,F 23,17:1
Music for Millions 1944,D 22,12:4
Parker, Morten (Director)
Stratford Adventure, The 1954,Ag 3,14:2
Parker, Norton S (Original Author)
Prison Break 1938,Jl 13,17:4
Parker, Norton S (Screenwriter)
Tundra 1936,D 3,31:2
Prison Break 1938,Jl 13,17:4
Parker, Penney
Khovanschina 1960,S 23,33:1
Parker, Raymond
Service de Luxe 1938,O 24,13:2
Swing That Cheer 1938,N 11,31:2
Last Warning, The 1938,D 8,34:4
Parker, Ross (Composer)
Mister Big 1943,Je 14,13:4
Parker, Steve (Producer)
My Geisha 1962,Je 14,23:2
John Goldfarb, Please Come Home
1965,Mr 25,42:4
Parker, Suzy
Funny Face 1957,Mr 29,16:1
Kiss Them for Me 1957,N 9,31:2
Ten North Frederick 1958,My 23,29:2
Best of Everything 1959,O 9,24:2
Circle of Deception 1961,F 18,12:2
Interns, The 1962,Ag 9,17:5
Flight From Ashiya 1964,Ap 23,34:1

Chamber of Horrors 1966,O 20,52:5
Parker, Warren
Hoodlum Priest, The 1961,Ap 3,28:5
Parker, Willard
Over the Goal 1937,O 16,22:2
Love Is on the Air 1937,N 12,27:3
Slight Case of Murder, A 1938,F 28,19:1
What a Woman 1943,D 3,27:2
Fighting Guardsman, The 1945,O 6,9:6
Renegades 1946,Jl 11,18:2
Relentless 1948,Mr 6,17:3
Mating of Millie, The 1948,Mr 13,12:2
You Gotta Stay Happy 1948,N 5,29:2
Slightly French 1949,My 27,25:3
Calamity Jane and Sam Bass 1949,Jl 18,14:2
Bodyhold 1949,D 12,29:4
Emergency Wedding 1950,D 22,19:2
Apache Drums 1951,My 7,22:2
Sangaree 1953,Je 5,19:1
Kiss Me Kate 1953,N 6,23:2
Young Jesse James 1960,Ag 25,25:1
Parkes, Clifford
Mikado, The 1967,Mr 15,53:1
Parkes, Gerard
Isabel 1968,Jl 24,47:1
Parkhill, Forbes (Original Author)
Stand up and Fight 1939,Ja 27,17:2
Parkhomenko, Leonid
Idiot, The 1960,Jl 22,11:2
Parkins, Barbara
Valley of the Dolls 1967,D 16,51:1
Parkinson, Cliff
Rawhide 1938,Ap 25,19:2
Parkinson, Georgina
Romeo and Juliet 1966,O 6,55:1
Parkinson, Roy (Producer)
Bluebeard's Ten Honeymoons 1960,N 8,32:6
Parks, Eddie
Avalanche 1946,Jl 8,25:2
Are You With It? 1948,Ap 15,31:2
Gunfighter, The 1950,Je 24,7:2
Parks, Harry
Strike Me Pink 1936,Ja 17,15:2
Parks, Hildy
Night Holds Terror, The 1955,S 15,39:2
Fail Safe 1964,S 16,36:1
Parks, John (Producer)
China Story, The: One-Fourth of Humanity
1968,O 3,56:4
Parks, Larry
Mystery Ship 1941,Ag 16,18:3
Harmon of Michigan 1941,O 2,29:2
Canal Zone 1942,Mr 30,21:2
Atlantic Convoy 1942,Jl 6,18:5
Flight Lieutenant 1942,Jl 31,11:1
Boogie Man Will Get You, The 1942,O 12,12:4
You Were Never Lovelier 1942,D 4,31:1
Reveille With Beverly 1943,Ap 24,17:2
Counter-Attack 1945,My 17,15:2
Renegades 1946,Jl 11,18:2
Jolson Story, The 1946,O 11,28:2
Down to Earth 1947,S 12,18:2
Swordsman, The 1947,O 17,18:4
Gallant Blade 1948,O 13,31:3
Jolson Sings Again 1949,Ag 18,16:6
Emergency Wedding 1950,D 22,19:2
Love Is Better Than Ever 1952,Mr 4,23:2
Freud 1962,D 13,37:1
Parks, Michael
Bus Riley's Back in Town 1965,Ap 8,45:2
Idol, The 1966,Ag 11,27:1
Bible, The 1966,S 29,60:1
Happening, The 1967,My 18,56:3
Parks, Nanette
Over 21 1945,Ag 17,20:2
Snafu 1945,D 26,15:2
Parks, Van Dyke
Swan, The 1956,Ap 27,21:5
Parkyakarkus
New Faces of 1937 1937,Jl 2,25:1
Life of the Party, The 1937,O 4,17:1
She's Got Everything 1938,Ja 14,21:3
Earl Carroll Vanities 1945,Ap 2,15:6
Out of This World 1945,Je 7,25:2
Parkyn, Leslie (Producer)
Little Kidnappers, The 1954,S 2,18:1
Coming-Out Party, A 1962,Jl 31,19:2
Crooks Anonymous 1963,O 31,26:3
Parlo, Dita
Homecoming 1928,N 19,16:7
Hungarian Rhapsody 1929,Ag 5,25:2
Melody of The Heart 1930,S 1,16:1
Honor of the Family 1931,O 17,20:1
Secrets of the Orient 1932,Ja 4,27:3
Mystic Mountain, The 1936,Mr 31,17:2
Courier of Lyons, The 1938,Je 3,17:1
Grand Illusion 1938,S 13,28:2
Ultimatum 1940,F 5,13:2
Atalante, L' 1947,Je 23,14:5
Street of Shadows 1948,N 20,9:2
Parma, Tula
Leopard Man, The 1943,My 20,26:4

Parnell, Emory
Call of the Yukon 1938,My 6,27:1
Doctor Rhythm 1938,My 19,25:2
Arson Racket Squad 1938,Je 18,18:2
King of Alcatraz 1938,O 7,21:2
Pacific Liner 1939,Ja 18,17:3
One Hour to Live 1939,N 4,11:3
Sued for Libel 1940,Ja 19,15:3
Case of the Black Parrot, The 1941,Ja 10,23:3
Unholy Partners 1941,D 29,21:4
They all Kissed the Bride 1942,Jl 31,11:1
Wings for the Eagle 1942,Ag 1,14:2
Arabian Nights 1942,D 26,15:1
Over my Dead Body 1942,D 26,15:2
That Nazty Nuisance 1943,My 29,10:3
Two Senoritas From Chicago 1943,Ag 6,10:4
Government Girl 1944,Ja 7,13:2
Miracle of Morgan's Creek, The 1944,Ja 20,15:2
Address Unknown 1944,Ap 17,20:1
Seven Days Ashore 1944,Ap 26,24:7
Night of Adventure, A 1944,Je 3,10:4
Falcon in Mexico, The 1944,Ag 5,16:2
Casanova Brown 1944,S 15,16:1
Falcon in Hollywood, The 1944,D 9,21:2
Tall in the Saddle 1944,D 15,25:3
Crime Doctor's Courage, The 1945,Mr 3,11:3
Two O'Clock Courage 1945,Ap 14,13:3
Falcon's Alibi, The 1946,Ap 13,23:2
Abie's Irish Rose 1946,D 23,19:4
Show-Off, The 1947,Mr 20,38:2
Violence 1947,My 10,8:5
Guilt of Janet Ames, The 1947,My 23,31:2
Outlaw, The 1947,S 12,18:4
Here Comes Trouble 1948,Ap 15,31:4
You Gotta Stay Happy 1948,N 5,29:2
Beautiful Blonde From Bashful Bend, The
1949,My 28,11:2
Hellfire 1949,My 30,9:4
Massacre River 1949,Jl 15,17:2
Ma and Pa Kettle 1949,Ag 12,13:2
Rock Island Trail 1950,Je 5,19:3
To Please a Lady 1950,O 27,24:3
Ma and Pa Kettle Back on the Farm
1951,My 11,32:3
Golden Girl 1951,N 21,20:3
When in Rome 1952,My 12,21:2
Ma and Pa Kettle at the Fair 1952,Jl 12,16:2
Call Me Madam 1953,Mr 26,37:1
Sabrina 1954,S 23,43:2
How to be Very, Very Popular 1955,Jl 23,10:1
Parneti, Franco
Shoot Loud, Louder... I Don't Understand
1967,S 21,56:4
Parodi, Nelly
Quien Mato a Eva 1934,D 22,21:2
Parola, Daniele
Razumov 1937,Mr 9,27:2
Paroldi, Cecilia
Friend Will come Tonight, A; Ami Viendra Ce
Soir, Un 1948,Jl 12,11:2
Paroll, Julienne
Game of Love, The 1954,D 15,41:1
Parr, Katherine
This Sporting Life 1963,Jl 17,19:2
Parr, Sally
Sun Sets at Dawn, The 1951,Ja 15,13:1
Parr-Davies, Harry (Composer)
It's in the Air 1940,D 10,33:2
Parr-Davies, Harry (Original Author)
Lisbon Story, The 1951,S 6,39:4
Parra, Alfonson
Silk, Blood and Sun 1943,Ja 30,10:6
Parra, Vincente
Fedra, the Devil's Daughter 1957,O 26,19:2
Parravicini, Florencio
Melgarejo 1937,S 20,19:2
Que Tiempos Aquellos; Those Were the Days
1938,Mr 7,13:2
Vida es un Tango, La; Life is a Tango
1939,Jl 8,20:5
Parravicini, Florencio (Director)
Melgarejo 1937,S 20,19:2
Parravicini, Florencio (Screenwriter)
Melgarejo 1937,S 20,19:2
Parrett, Suzanne
Wherever She Goes 1953,Ja 28,24:4
Parride, Jacques
Paris Incident 1954,Ag 18,20:2
Parrin, Nat (Screenwriter)
Dimples 1936,O 10,21:2
Parrinello, Geraldina
Times Gone By (The Idyll); Idyll, The (Times
Gone By) 1953,D 30,16:2
Parrish, Anne (Original Author)
Born to be Bad 1950,S 29,31:5
Parrish, Gigi
20th Century 1934,My 4,24:2
Down to Their Last Yacht 1934,S 24,14:1
Girl of the Limberlost, A 1934,N 9,24:6
Parrish, Helen
His First Command 1929,D 23,18:2
Big Trail, The 1930,O 25,20:3
Cimarron 1931,Ja 27,20:5

Parrish, Helen— Cont

X Marks the Spot 1931,D 7,16:1
When a Feller Needs a Friend 1932,My 14,11:5
There's Always Tomorrow 1934,N 10,19:2
Make Way for a Lady 1936,D 12,15:1
Mad About Music 1938,Mr 12,13:2
Little Tough Guy 1938,Ag 18,23:3
Little Tough Guys in Society 1938,N 21,14:4
Three Smart Girls Grow Up 1939,Mr 18,9:2
Winter Carnival 1939,Jl 28,14:2
First Love 1939,N 9,27:3
You'll Find Out 1940,N 15,25:2
Six Lessons From Madame La Zonga
  1941,F 19,25:2
In old California 1942,Je 18,25:3
They all Kissed the Bride 1942,Jl 31,11:1

Parrish, Imboden

American Tragedy, An 1931,Ag 6,22:5

Parrish, James (Screenwriter)

Bulldog Drummond at Bay 1937,O 25,23:2

Parrish, John

Four Faces West 1948,Ag 4,18:3
That Lady in Ermine 1948,Ag 25,31:2
Canadian Pacific 1949,My 20,32:4
Barefoot Contessa, The 1954,S 30,37:1
Kronos 1957,My 11,24:6

Parrish, Julia

Fireball 500 1966,N 24,65:4

Parrish, Leslie

Li'l Abner 1959,D 12,19:2
Portrait of a Mobster 1961,Ap 20,30:4
Manchurian Candidate, The 1962,O 25,48:3
For Love or Money 1963,Ag 8,19:1
Sex and the Single Girl 1964,D 26,9:2
3 on a Couch 1966,Jl 7,30:1

Parrish, Robert (Director)

Cry Danger 1951,F 22,27:3
Mob, The 1951,O 18,32:2
San Francisco Story, The 1952,My 10,16:4
Assignment-Paris 1952,O 25,12:6
Purple Plain, The 1955,Ap 11,29:1
Lucy Gallant 1955,O 21,30:1
Fire Down Below 1957,Ag 9,11:2
Saddle the Wind 1958,Mr 21,17:1
Wonderful Country, The 1959,N 5,39:7
In the French Style 1963,S 19,23:1
Up From the Beach 1965,Je 10,38:1
Casino Royale 1967,Ap 29,25:1
Bobo, The 1967,S 29,53:1
Duffy 1968,S 17,50:3

Parrish, Robert (Producer)

In the French Style 1963,S 19,23:1

Parritt, Clive

Simon and Laura 1956,Jl 3,17:2

Parrott, James (Original Author)

Block-Heads 1938,Ag 30,14:2

Parrott, James (Producer)

Pardon Us 1931,Ag 22,7:5

Parrott, James (Screenwriter)

Way out West 1937,My 4,29:1
Swiss Miss 1938,Je 4,18:2
Block-Heads 1938,Ag 30,14:2

Parrott, Ursula (Original Author)

Divorcee, The 1930,My 10,25:3
Strangers May Kiss' 1931,Ap 13,17:1
Gentleman's Fate 1931,Je 27,20:3
Leftover Ladies 1931,N 9,22:4
Woman Accused, The 1933,Mr 13,18:2
There's Always Tomorrow 1934,N 10,19:2
Next Time We Love 1936,Ja 31,16:2
There's Always Tomorrow 1956,Ja 21,18:2

Parry, Gordon (Director)

Bond Street 1950,Mr 30,40:6
Tom Brown's School Days 1952,Ja 8,23:5
Innocents in Paris 1955,Mr 5,9:6
Front Page Story 1955,Ap 19,28:1
Midnight Episode 1955,My 19,25:5
Panic in the Parlor 1957,D 18,45:1

Parry, Ivan

Red River 1948,O 1,31:2

Parry, Lee

Monna Vanna 1923,S 25,8:2
Love Is A Lie 1928,Je 26,29:1
Eau du Nil, L' 1928,D 16,IX,8:2
Lustigen Weiber von Wien, Die 1931,Jl 10,22:2
Wiener Blut 1933,N 13,21:2
Einmaleins der Liebe, Das 1937,Ja 2,15:2
Grosse Bluff, Der; Big Bluff, The 1937,S 6,20:2

Parry, Loretta

Hand in Hand 1961,F 7,41:3

Parry, Natasha

Dark Man, The 1952,My 26,18:4
Lovers, Happy Lovers 1954,O 1,19:2
Midnight Episode 1955,My 19,25:5
Windom's Way 1958,O 1,45:1
Midnight Lace 1960,O 14,27:1
Portrait of a Sinner 1961,D 7,52:1
Model Murder Case, The 1964,N 25,45:1
Romeo and Juliet 1968,O 9,41:1

Parshley, H M Dr (Miscellaneous)

Mystery of Life, The 1931,Jl 6,24:4

Parsley, Ruby

Marriage Playground, The 1929,D 14,22:4

Parson, J Palmer (Original Author)

White Gold 1927,Ap 11,18:3

Parsonnet, Marion (Miscellaneous)

Cover Girl 1944,Mr 31,26:1

Parsonnet, Marion (Original Author)

Live, Love and Learn 1937,N 19,27:2

Parsonnet, Marion (Producer)

Uncle Vanya 1958,Ap 29,26:2

Parsonnet, Marion (Screenwriter)

Thirteenth Chair, The 1937,Je 18,25:3
Between Two Women 1937,Ag 6,21:1
Beg, Borrow or Steal 1937,D 10,33:2
Love Is a Headache 1938,Ja 28,17:3
Miracles for Sale 1939,Ag 10,15:2
These Glamour Girls 1939,Ag 31,14:2
Golden Fleecing, The 1940,N 7,33:4
Gallant Sons 1940,D 12,37:2
Washington Melodrama 1941,My 26,15:3
Dangerously They Live 1942,Ap 11,9:2
I'll Be Seeing You 1945,Ap 6,20:6
Dangerous Partners 1945,N 2,22:4
Gilda 1946,Mr 15,27:2
My Forbidden Past 1951,Ap 26,34:2

Parsons, Billy

Matching Billy 1918,My 20,9:7

Parsons, Estelle

Ladybug, Ladybug 1963,D 24,9:1
Bonnie and Clyde 1967,Ag 14,36:1
Rachel Rachel 1968,Ag 27,36:1

Parsons, Harriet (Producer)

Enchanted Cottage, The 1945,Ap 28,19:2
Night Song 1948,Ja 29,27:5
Never a Dull Moment 1950,N 22,20:2
Clash by Night 1952,Je 19,32:6
Susan Slept Here 1954,Jl 30,9:1

Parsons, Jack (Producer)

Eyes of Annie Jones, The 1964,My 14,39:1
Night Train to Paris 1964,D 3,58:2
Woman Who Wouldn't Die, The 1965,Je 10,38:1
Return of Mr Moto 1965,D 2,48:1
Murder Game, The 1966,Mr 31,43:2

Parsons, Lindsley (Producer)

Top Sergeant Mulligan 1941,N 12,31:3
Silver Skates 1943,Mr 19,15:3
Torpedo Valley 1952,D 20,15:3
Jack Slade 1953,O 29,42:6
Loophole 1954,Mr 13,11:3
Cry Vengence 1955,F 19,18:3
Finger Man 1955,Jl 16,12:4
Return of Jack Slade, The 1955,N 24,41:3
Come on, The 1956,Ap 7,13:1
Dragoon Wells Massacre 1957,My 6,25:2
Portland Expose 1957,S 27,16:6
Purple Gang, The 1960,Ja 23,15:5
Good Times 1967,Ag 3,26:4

Parsons, Lindsley (Screenwriter)

Frontier Town 1938,Mr 12,13:3

Parsons, Louella

Hollywood Hotel 1938,Ja 13,17:3
Starlift 1951,D 15,11:2

Parsons, Michael

Cry of Battle 1963,O 12,27:2
Walls of Hell, The 1965,N 18,55:3

Parsons, Milton

When Tomorrow Comes 1939,Ag 17,16:2
Edison the Man 1940,Je 7,27:2
Sky Murder 1940,N 14,28:3
Behind the News 1941,Ja 16,25:3
Dead Men Tell 1941,Ap 17,29:3
Dressed to Kill 1941,Ag 22,19:3
Man at Large 1941,O 11,21:4
Roxie Hart 1942,F 20,21:1
Remarkable Andrew, The 1942,Mr 6,17:2
Great Man's Lady, The 1942,Ap 30,14:3
Whispering Ghosts 1942,My 18,19:4
Man in the Trunk, The 1942,O 23,25:1
Hidden Hand, The 1942,N 26,40:4
Life Begins at Eight-Thirty 1942,D 10,35:2
Over my Dead Body 1942,D 26,15:2
Cry of the Werewolf, The 1944,Ag 12,16:5
Lost in a Harem 1944,N 9,23:2
Dick Tracy 1946,Ja 12,10:7
Margie 1946,O 17,28:3
Dick Tracy vs Cueball 1946,N 23,12:2
Secret Life of Walter Mitty, The 1947,Ag 15,12:2
Bury Me Dead 1947,O 25,13:3
Senator Was Indiscreet, The 1947,D 27,9:2
Dancing in the Dark 1949,D 3,8:6
How to be Very, Very Popular 1955,Jl 23,10:1

Parsons, Nicholas

Master of Bankdam 1949,O 17,18:2
Brothers in Law 1957,Ag 20,22:1
Too Many Crooks 1959,Ap 25,14:2
Man in a Cocked Hat 1960,Je 15,50:2
Doctor in Love 1962,Ap 27,27:2
Don't Raise the Bridge, Lower the River
  1968,Jl 13,18:1

Parsons, Patsy Lee

Meet Doctor Christian 1939,D 1,27:2
Yankee Doodle Dandy 1942,My 30,9:1

Parsons, Percy

Suspense 1930,N 8,21:3
Sleepless Nights 1933,Jl 22,14:2

Parsons, Percy— Cont

Good Companions, The 1933,O 10,24:1
Criminal at Large 1933,D 20,27:2
Orders Is Orders 1934,My 7,20:2
King of the Damned 1936,F 1,9:2
Victoria the Great 1937,O 29,19:1
Citadel, The 1938,N 4,27:2
Suicide Squadron 1942,My 14,23:2
Flying Fortress 1942,D 19,22:2

Parsons, Ted (Screenwriter)

Hell in the Heavens 1934,D 12,28:2

Parten, Peter

And so to Bed 1965,Jl 31,11:3

Parton, Reg

Backlash 1956,Ap 21,11:2

Partos, Erzsi

Goose Boy, The 1951,O 13,9:2

Partos, Frank (Miscellaneous)

Rumba 1935,F 25,13:2

Partos, Frank (Original Author)

Honolulu 1939,F 23,19:2

Partos, Frank (Screenwriter)

Wings in the Dark 1935,F 2,10:1
Rose of the Rancho 1936,Ja 9,25:2
Great Gambini, The 1937,Jl 12,20:4
She's no Lady 1937,Ag 12,14:3
Romance in the Dark 1938,Mr 21,18:2
Honolulu 1939,F 23,19:2
Stranger on the Third Floor 1940,S 2,19:2
And Now Tomorrow 1944,N 23,38:2
House on Telegraph Hill, The 1951,My 14,29:1
Night Without Sleep 1952,S 27,13:2
Port Afrique 1956,N 3,27:5

Partos, G

Lonesome 1928,O 2,23:5
Night Watch, The 1928,O 8,14:2
Last Performance, The 1929,N 4,28:1
Elnoek Kisasszony 1935,O 12,12:3

Partos, Jack (Screenwriter)

Uninvited, The 1944,F 21,19:3

Parturier, Francoise (Original Author)

Five Day Lover, The 1961,D 14,55:4

Partwee, Michael (Screenwriter)

Laughter in Paradise 1951,N 12,21:2

Party, Gordon (Director)

Gay Adventure, The 1954,S 16,35:7

Parvo, Elli

Carmen 1946,N 27,20:2
King's Jester, The 1947,Je 26,19:3
Man of the Sea 1948,Ja 24,11:2
Loves of Don Juan, The 1948,S 2,18:4
Outcry 1949,Mr 14,15:5
Woman 1950,F 9,36:6
His Last Twelve Hours 1953,N 13,24:7

Paryda, Karl

Pfarrer von Kirchfeld, Der; Pastor of Kirchfeld,
  The 1939,Ap 22,15:3

Parys, Van (Composer)

Moulin Rouge 1944,N 23,38:2

Pasaric, Tomislav

Seventh Continent, The 1968,Jl 30,33:2

Pascal, Ernest (Original Author)

Black Swan, The 1924,N 25,26:1
Hell's Highroad 1925,Ag 26,14:2
Sensation Seekers 1927,Mr 16,28:2
Charlatan, The 1929,Ap 15,22:6
Wedding Rings 1930,My 10,25:3
Born to Love 1931,Ap 25,23:4
Age for Love, The 1931,N 13,27:2
Husband's Holiday 1931,D 25,29:2
King's Vacation, The 1933,Ja 20,21:2
Here's to Romance 1935,O 3,29:2

Pascal, Ernest (Screenwriter)

Last of the Duanes 1930,S 13,9:3
White Parade, The 1934,N 10,19:1
Under the Pampas Moon 1935,My 31,11:1
Here's to Romance 1935,O 3,29:2
Lloyds of London 1936,N 26,39:1
Wee Willie Winkie 1937,Jl 24,12:1
Love Under Fire 1937,Ag 28,8:2
Kidnapped 1938,My 28,9:2
Hound of the Baskervilles, The 1939,Mr 25,19:2
Hollywood Cavalcade 1939,O 14,13:2
Blue Bird, The 1940,Ja 20,11:2
Flesh and Fantasy 1943,N 18,29:1
Jack London 1944,Mr 3,19:3
Destiny 1945,F 3,16:5
Night in Paradise 1946,Je 6,16:3
Canyon Passage 1946,Ag 8,18:2

Pascal, Gabriel (Director)

Major Barbara 1941,My 15,27:1
Caesar and Cleopatra 1946,S 6,18:2

Pascal, Gabriel (Miscellaneous)

Devil's Disciple, The 1959,Ag 21,12:1

Pascal, Gabriel (Producer)

Pygmalion 1938,D 8,34:2
Living Dead, The 1940,D 17,33:2
Major Barbara 1941,My 15,27:1
Caesar and Cleopatra 1946,S 6,18:2
Androcles and the Lion 1953,Ja 15,23:2

Pascal, Giselle

Vie de Boheme, La 1947,N 28,37:4
Naked Woman, The 1950,Ja 21,10:2
Fire Under Her Skin 1958,Je 28,13:6

Pascal, J C
Perfectionist, The 1952,My 2,21:3
Poppy is Also a Flower, The 1967,D 14,62:4
Pascal, Jefferson (Screenwriter)
Sword of Lancelot 1963,O 10,49:2
Beach Red 1967,Ag 4,18:1
Pascal, Louis A (Screenwriter)
Temptation 1962,N 10,16:2
Pascali
Mademoiselle ma Mere 1939,S 19,29:2
Pascaud, Nathalie
Mr Hulot's Holiday 1954,Je 17,36:2
Pasch, Reginald
Free Love 1930,D 15,29:1
Man I Killed, The 1932,Ja 20,17:4
Man From Yesterday, The 1932,Je 25,18:2
Pursuit of Happiness, The 1934,O 26,25:1
Paschoff, Pavel
Kampf, Der 1936,S 11,29:3
Pasco, Richard
Yesterday's Enemy 1960,Mr 4,19:1
Sword of Sherwood Forest 1961,Ja 26,32:3
6 Black Horses 1962,Ap 25,30:1
Pasetti, John
Ring Around the Clock 1953,My 19,36:2
Pasha, Kalla
Thirty Days 1922,D 11,22:1
Silken Shackles 1926,My 25,25:1
Devil Dancer, The 1927,D 19,30:1
Dove, The 1928,Ja 3,28:2
West of Zanzibar 1928,D 31,9:1
Pashalishvili, S (Screenwriter)
Keto and Kote 1954,Ap 5,21:4
Pashennaya, Vera
Mistress, The 1954,My 31,9:2
Idiot, The 1960,Jl 22,11:2
Pashkova, G
Peter Vinogradof 1935,Je 28,24:1
Paskalyevich, Mihailo
Magic Sword, The 1952,N 19,37:2
Pasl, Alexander (Producer)
Tale of Five Women, A 1953,Ja 16,19:2
Pasolini, Pier Paolo (Director)
Gospel According to St Matthew, The
1965,Ag 1,IV,9:6
Gospel According to St Matthew, The
1966,F 18,23:1
Hawks and the Sparrows, The 1966,S 17,28:2
Accattone 1966,S 17,20:2
Hawks and the Sparrows, The; Uccellacci e
Uccellini 1967,Jl 28,15:3
Accattone! 1968,Ap 5,56:1
Pasolini, Pier Paolo (Original Author)
Commare Secca, La; Grim Reaper, The
1966,S 15,51:1
Hawks and the Sparrows, The 1966,S 17,28:2
Pasolini, Pier Paolo (Screenwriter)
From a Roman Balcony 1961,O 16,33:5
Notte Brava, La 1962,Ja 25,25:2
Bell Antonio 1962,Ap 3,43:2
Hawks and the Sparrows, The; Uccellacci e
Uccellini 1967,Jl 28,15:3
Accattone! 1968,Ap 5,56:1
Pasolini, Susanna
Gospel According to St Matthew, The
1966,F 18,23:1
Pasquali
Passion of St Francis, The 1932,D 17,22:3
Grandeur et Decadence 1937,My 31,11:3
Avocate d'Amour 1938,S 8,27:2
Rothchild 1938,O 12,35:2
Honorable Catherine, The 1948,Ag 23,13:3
My Seven Little Sins 1956,My 2,27:1
Fernandel the Dressmaker 1957,Jl 1,19:2
Pasquero, Margherita
Rose Tattoo, The 1955,D 13,55:1
Passalla, Antonio
Voyage of Silence 1968,S 12,54:1
Passante, Mario
Lupa, La 1954,F 18,36:2
Too Bad She's Bad 1955,D 26,23:2
Gold of Naples (The Gambler); Gambler, The
(Gold of Naples) 1957,F 12,30:1
No Sun in Venice 1958,Je 10,40:2
Passarelli, Edoardo
Open City; Citta Aperta 1946,F 26,21:2
Journey to Love 1953,O 9,32:8
Passer, Dirch
Crazy Paradise 1965,Ag 11,41:2
I, A Lover 1968,My 4,46:2
Passer, Ivan (Director)
Intimate Lighting 1966,S 19,57:1
Boring Afternoon, A 1968,Jl 4,13:2
Passer, Ivan (Original Author)
Audition 1968,Jl 4,13:2
Passer, Ivan (Screenwriter)
Loves of a Blonde 1966,O 27,55:1
Boring Afternoon, A 1968,Jl 4,13:2
Audition 1968,Jl 4,13:2
Firemen's Ball, The 1968,S 30,60:1
Passgard, Lars
Through a Glass Darkly 1962,Mr 14,45:1
Swedish Wedding Night 1965,N 15,48:1

Passos, John Dos (Screenwriter)
Devil is a Woman, The 1935,My 4,17:2
Pastell, George
Tiger Bay 1959,D 15,50:1
Maniac 1963,O 31,26:3
From Russia with Love 1964,Ap 9,25:1
Secret Door, The 1964,Je 4,28:1
2nd Best Secret Agent in the Whole Wide World,
The 1966,Ap 28,49:1
Khartoum 1966,Jl 14,28:1
Deadlier Than the Male 1967,F 22,21:1
Pastellides, Nino
Give Us This Day 1949,D 21,41:2
Pasternak, Boris (Cinematographer)
Hamlet 1964,S 15,32:1
Pasternak, Boris (Miscellaneous)
Hamlet 1966,Mr 16,48:1
Pasternak, Boris (Original Author)
Doctor Zhivago 1965,D 23,21:1
Pasternak, Joe (Producer)
Mad About Music 1938,Mr 12,13:2
Youth Takes a Fling 1938,O 17,12:1
That Certain Age 1938,N 5,15:2
Three Smart Girls Grow Up 1939,Mr 18,9:2
Under-Pup, The 1939,S 5,21:2
First Love 1939,N 9,27:3
Destry Rides Again 1939,N 30,25:1
It's a Date 1940,Mr 23,16:2
Spring Parade 1940,O 4,29:2
Little Bit of Heaven, A 1940,N 8,24:2
Seven Sinners 1940,N 18,23:2
Nice Girl 1941,Mr 27,29:6
Flame of New Orleans, The 1941,Ap 26,20:2
It Started With Eve 1941,O 3,27:1
Seven Sweethearts 1942,N 13,28:1
Presenting Lily Mars 1943,Ap 30,25:3
Thousands Cheer 1943,S 14,27:1
Song of Russia 1944,F 11,17:2
Two Girls and a Sailor 1944,Je 15,16:1
Music for Millions 1944,D 22,12:4
Thrill of a Romance 1945,My 25,22:2
Anchors Aweigh 1945,Jl 20,15:2
Two Sisters From Boston 1946,Je 7,16:2
Holiday in Mexico 1946,Ag 16,19:3
No Leave, No Love 1946,O 18,29:2
Unfinished Dance, The 1947,O 31,29:2
This Time for Keeps 1947,D 5,33:4
Three Daring Daughters 1948,F 13,26:3
Big City 1948,My 17,23:3
On an Island With You 1948,Jl 30,13:2
Date with Judy, A 1948,Ag 7,8:2
Luxury Liner 1948,S 10,19:2
Kissing Bandit, The 1948,N 19,35:2
In the Good Old Summertime 1949,Ag 5,23:2
That Midnight Kiss 1949,S 23,28:2
Nancy Goes to Rio 1950,Ap 7,22:2
Duchess of Idaho 1950,Jl 21,15:3
Summer Stock 1950,S 1,17:2
Toast of New Orleans, The 1950,S 30,13:3
Great Caruso, The 1951,My 11,32:2
Rich, Young and Pretty 1951,Jl 26,17:3
Skirts Ahoy! 1952,My 29,17:2
Merry Widow, The 1952,S 25,38:1
Because You're Mine 1952,S 26,18:2
Small Town Girl 1953,My 7,37:2
Latin Lovers 1953,Ag 13,17:2
Easy to Love 1953,N 27,99:9
Flame and the Flesh 1954,My 3,21:2
Student Prince, The 1954,Je 16,18:2
Athena 1954,D 22,28:2
Hit the Deck 1955,Mr 4,17:1
Love Me or Leave Me 1955,My 27,14:1
Meet Me in Las Vegas 1956,Mr 14,39:2
Opposite Sex, The 1956,N 16,23:2
Ten Thousand Bedrooms 1957,Ap 4,37:1
This Could Be the Night 1957,My 15,39:1
Party Girl 1958,O 29,30:1
Ask any Girl 1959,My 22,32:1
Please Don't Eat the Daisies 1960,Ap 1,37:1
Where the Boys Are 1961,Ja 20,22:1
Horizontal Lieutenant, The 1962,My 12,15:3
Jumbo 1962,D 7,49:1
Courtship of Eddie's Father, The 1963,Mr 7,8:5
(Incorrect in this edition; use 1963,Mr 28,8:5
elsewhere)
Ticklish Affair, A 1963,Ag 22,19:2
Girl Happy 1965,My 27,28:1
Made in Paris 1966,F 17,29:1
Spinout 1966,D 15,60:1
Sweet Ride, The 1968,Je 13,57:2
Pastina, Giorgio (Director)
Streets of Sorrow 1952,N 18,37:4
Journey to Love 1953,O 9,32:8
Of Life and Love 1958,O 7,40:2
Pastina, Giorgio (Screenwriter)
Streets of Sorrow 1952,N 18,37:4
Pastore, Piero
Delitto di Mastrovanni, Il 1935,Jl 30,16:2
Pastorino, Franco
French-Cancan 1956,Ap 17,26:2
Pastorino, Malvina
Games Men Play, The 1968,Mr 15,30:1

Pastrone, Giovanni (Director)
Outwitting the Hun 1918,Jl 1,9:3
Pastukhova, Marina
Last Hill, The 1945,Je 26,13:2
Pasut, Franca
Accattone! 1968,Ap 5,56:1
Pasztor, Bela (Director)
Sarga Csiko 1937,Ja 29,15:2
Falu Rossza, A; Village Rogue, The
1938,Ap 18,11:2
Piros Bugyellaris; Red Purse 1939,Mr 11,21:2
Pasztor, Bela (Producer)
Piros Bugyellaris; Red Purse 1939,Mr 11,21:2
Pat
Maedchenraeuber 1936,Ag 15,6:3
Pat, Jacob (Screenwriter)
Children Must Laugh; Mir Kumen an
1938,Mr 26,12:2
Patachou
Maedchenraeuber 1936,Ag 15,6:3
Song of the Street 1939,S 5,21:2
French-Cancan 1956,Ap 17,26:2
Pataky, Jeno
Mami 1938,F 19,19:5
Majd a Zsuzsi 1938,O 22,14:3
Tokaji Rapszodia 1938,N 7,23:5
Eb Ura Fako 1940,Mr 23,16:4
Pataky, Veronica
Miracle of the Bells, The 1948,Mr 17,30:1
Patane, Giuseppe (Miscellaneous)
Traviata, La 1968,F 28,43:2
Patch, Wally
Jaws of Hell 1931,Ja 5,21:3
Battle of Gallipoli, The 1931,D 7,16:1
Sorrell and Son 1934,My 29,22:1
Don Quixote 1934,D 24,17:1
Scotland Yard Mystery, The 1936,Mr 16,21:4
Men Are not Gods 1937,Ja 19,28:1
Man Who Could Work Miracles, The
1937,F 22,13:1
Dr Syn 1937,N 15,15:1
Troopship 1938,Ap 26,18:2
Inspector Hornleigh 1939,Je 15,27:3
Ware Case, The 1939,Jl 22,12:2
Jeannie 1943,S 13,14:2
Guinea Pig, The 1949,My 2,20:2
Your Past Is Showing 1958,Jl 1,36:2
Pate, Michael
Rugged O'Riordans, The 1950,Ja 6,25:2
Strange Door, The 1951,D 10,34:6
Five Fingers 1952,F 23,7:5
Secret Sharer, The 1953,Ja 14,27:2
Scandal at Scourie 1953,Je 16,24:2
Houdini 1953,Jl 3,10:2
Hondo 1953,N 27,99:9
All the Brothers Were Valiant 1953,D 29,19:2
Secret of the Incas 1954,My 29,13:3
King Richard and the Crusaders 1954,Ag 23,20:5
Silver Chalice, The 1954,D 27,22:5
Court Jester, The 1956,F 2,19:1
Killer is Loose, The 1956,Mr 3,17:2
Revolt of Mamie Stover, The 1956,My 12,12:7
Congo Crossing 1956,Jl 14,13:2
Something of Value 1957,My 11,24:6
Oklahoman, The 1957,My 15,39:1
Green Mansions 1959,Mr 20,26:1
Walk Like a Dragon 1960,S 16,24:1
Canadians, The 1961,Je 1,31:1
Sergeants 3 1962,F 12,28:2
PT 109 1963,Je 27,23:1
McLintock 1963,N 14,41:3
Pate, Michael (Original Author)
Escape from Fort Bravo 1954,Ja 23,11:2
Most Dangerous Man Alive 1961,Jl 5,29:2
Patel, Surya
Born Free 1966,Je 23,29:1
Patelliere, Denys de la (Director)
There's Always a Price Tag 1958,My 26,25:2
Patelliere, Denys de la (Screenwriter)
There's Always a Price Tag 1958,My 26,25:2
Pateraki, Chris
Windfall in Athens 1956,O 1,31:1
Paternostro, Alessi (Original Author)
Angelo in the Crowd 1952,O 4,15:2
PATERSON
See Also PATTERSON
Paterson, Neil (Original Author)
Man on a Tightrope 1953,Je 5,19:1
Paterson, Neil (Screenwriter)
Little Kidnappers, The 1954,S 2,18:1
Spiral Road, The 1962,Ag 4,11:2
Paterson, Pat
Bitter Sweet 1933,Ag 24,18:2
Bottoms Up 1934,Mr 23,29:2
Call it Luck 1934,Jl 10,24:5
Charlie Chan in Egypt 1935,Je 24,12:2
Spendthrift 1936,Jl 23,24:1
52d Street 1937,N 15,15:1
Idiot's Delight 1939,F 3,13:1
Pathak, Madhusdan
Maya 1966,Je 23,29:4

Pathe, Arianne
Champs-Elysees 1939,F 28,17:2
Patisson, Danik
Diary of a Bad Girl 1958,My 30,13:2
Sinners of Paris 1959,Ap 24,23:1
Patjer, August
Nur am Rhein 1931,S 25,28:7
Patnaude, Ray
Run, Appaloosa, Run! 1966,Jl 14,28:1
Patoelf, Sacha
Is Paris Burning? 1966,N 11,36:1
PATON
See Also PATTEN, PATTON, PAYTON,
PEYTON
Paton, Alan (Original Author)
Cry, the Beloved Country 1952,Ja 24,23:2
Paton, Alan (Screenwriter)
Cry, the Beloved Country 1952,Ja 24,23:2
Paton, Charles
Blackmail 1929,O 7,22:1
Sherlock Holmes's Fatal Hour 1931,Jl 13,13:5
Paton, Stuart (Director)
Man to Man 1922,Mr 28,17:4
Patorni, Raphael
Blind Desire 1948,Je 10,28:4
Patorzhinsky, I
Cossack Beyond the Danube, A 1954,F 8,18:5
Patorzinsky, E
Natalka-Poltavka 1936,D 25,19:4
Patrache (dog)
Dog of Flanders, A 1960,Ap 1,37:1
Patrice, Francois
Devil's Daughter 1949,F 26,11:2
Patrick, Butch
Munster, Go Home 1966,Je 16,53:4
Patrick, Dorothy
Boy's Ranch 1946,Ag 9,12:2
Till the Clouds Roll By 1946,D 6,27:4
Mighty McGurk, The 1947,Ap 4,19:4
New Orleans 1947,Je 20,25:6
High Wall 1947,D 26,22:2
Follow Me Quietly 1949,Jl 8,14:5
Come to the Stable 1949,Jl 28,19:1
House by the River 1950,My 2,25:2
711 Ocean Drive 1950,Jl 20,21:2
Torch Song 1953,O 13,34:2
Las Vegas Shakedown 1955,Je 18,14:2
Patrick, Gail
Murders in the Zoo 1933,Ap 3,13:4
Phantom Broadcast, The 1933,Jl 31,16:2
Cradle Song 1933,N 20,18:2
Death Takes a Holiday 1934,F 24,18:4
Murder at the Vanities 1934,My 21,20:2
Wagon Wheels 1934,O 4,19:1
Rumba 1935,F 25,13:2
Mississippi 1935,Ap 18,27:2
No More Ladies 1935,Je 22,18:5
Doubting Thomas 1935,Jl 11,24:2
Two Fisted 1935,O 5,18:3
Two in the Dark 1936,F 1,9:2
Lone Wolf Returns, The 1936,F 4,25:5
Preview Murder Mystery, The 1936,Mr 21,13:2
Early to Bed 1936,Jl 16,20:2
My Man Godfrey 1936,S 19,18:1 (Incorrect in
this edition; use 1936,S 18,18:1 elsewhere)
Murder With Pictures 1936,N 21,21:4
White Hunter 1936,N 26,39:2
John Meade's Woman 1937,F 18,19:1
Her Husband Lies 1937,Mr 18,20:1
Artists and Models 1937,Ag 5,19:2
Stage Door 1937,O 8,27:2
Dangerous to Know 1938,Mr 11,15:4
Mad About Music 1938,Mr 12,13:2
Wives Under Suspicion 1938,Jl 1,22:3
King of Alcatraz 1938,O 7,21:2
Disbarred 1939,Ja 19,17:2
Man of Conquest 1939,Ap 28,31:2
Grand Jury Secrets 1939,Je 29,19:2
Reno 1939,D 21,29:2
My Favorite Wife 1940,My 31,15:2
Doctor Takes a Wife, The 1940,Je 15,12:2
Gallant Sons 1940,D 12,37:2
Love Crazy 1941,Je 6,25:5
Kathleen 1941,D 19,35:3
We Were Dancing 1942,My 1,23:2
Tales of Manhattan 1942,S 25,25:1
Quiet Please, Murder 1942,D 22,31:1
Hit Parade of 1943 1943,Ap 16,24:3
Woman in Bondage 1944,Mr 27,17:2
Up in Mabel's Room 1944,Ap 22,8:6
Brewster's Millions 1945,Ap 27,23:2
Twice Blessed 1945,Jl 7,7:5
Claudia and David 1946,Ag 15,19:2
Rendezvous With Annie 1946,S 23,29:3
Plainsman and the Lady, The 1946,N 4,33:1
Patrick, Jerome
Three Men and a Girl 1919,Mr 31,11:3
Patrick, John
Flaming Youth 1923,N 26,15:6
Her Temporary Husband 1924,Ja 1,20:1
Goldfish, The 1924,My 20,15:2
Sherlock Jr 1924,My 26,21:1
For Sale 1924,Jl 14,11:5

Single Wives 1924,Jl 29,9:2
Flirting With Love 1924,S 1,9:1
Sinners in Silk 1924,S 8,15:3
Black Swan, The 1924,N 25,26:1
So This Is Marriage 1924,D 23,16:2
Thief in Paradise, A 1925,Ja 26,14:1
Recompense 1925,Ap 20,22:1
After Business Hour 1925,Je 17,16:2
What Fools Men 1925,S 29,31:3
Seven Sinners 1925,D 8,28:5
Cave Man, The 1926,Mr 1,17:1
First Year, The 1926,Mr 8,17:1
Social Highwayman, The 1926,Je 15,23:3
Palm Beach Girl, The 1926,Je 22,21:2
Ladies at Play 1926,N 16,25:3
Rubber Tires 1927,Mr 9,29:1
Prince of Head-Waiters 1927,Jl 11,23:5
Love Hungry 1928,Ap 16,20:5
Patrick, John (Original Author)
Holy Terror, The 1937,Ja 30,21:2
Dangerously Yours 1937,O 18,14:2
Strange Love of Martha Ivers, The
1946,Jl 25,18:4
Framed 1947,My 26,24:2
Second Chance 1947,S 20,12:4
Hasty Heart, The 1950,Ja 21,10:5
Patrick, John (Producer)
Main Attraction, The 1963,Je 27,23:3
Patrick, John (Screenwriter)
Educating Father 1936,Je 20,22:2
36 Hours to Live 1936,Ag 15,6:3
Fifteen Maiden Lane 1936,O 17,21:3
Time Out for Romance 1937,Mr 13,23:2
Sing and Be Happy 1937,Je 19,20:2
Born Reckless 1937,Jl 30,22:6
One Mile From Heaven 1937,Ag 19,23:1
Big Town Girl 1937,D 13,23:4
International Settlement 1938,F 12,20:3
Battle of Broadway 1938,Ap 25,19:2
Mr Moto Takes a Chance 1938,Je 13,15:4
Five of a Kind 1938,O 31,12:2
Up the River 1938,D 3,11:2
Enchantment 1948,D 27,16:2
President's Lady, The 1953,My 22,31:1
Three Coins in the Fountain 1954,My 21,18:2
Love Is a Many-Splendored Thing
1955,Ag 19,10:1
High Society 1956,Ag 10,9:2
Teahouse of the August Moon, The
1956,N 30,19:1
Girls, Les 1957,O 4,27:2
Some Came Running 1959,Ja 23,17:1
World of Suzie Wong, The 1960,N 11,36:1
Gigot 1962,S 28,26:1
Main Attraction, The 1963,Je 27,23:3
Shoes of the Fisherman, The 1968,N 15,40:3
Patrick, Lee
Strange Cargo 1929,F 18,28:1
Border Cafe 1937,Je 8,30:2
Music for Madame 1937,O 23,14:1
Danger Patrol 1937,N 19,27:3
Crashing Hollywood 1938,Ja 8,19:2
Condemned Woman 1938,Ap 22,15:5
Law of the Underworld 1938,Ap 28,27:2
Sisters, The 1938,O 15,21:3
Fisherman's Wharf 1939,F 24,15:2
Invisible Stripes 1940,Ja 13,11:2
Saturday's Children 1940,My 4,13:1
Ladies Must Live 1940,S 6,25:3
City for Conquest 1940,S 28,9:2
Money and the Woman 1940,O 4,29:2
South of Suez 1940,D 19,33:2
Honeymoon for Three 1941,F 8,19:2
Footsteps in the Dark 1941,Mr 15,13:2
Nurse's Secret, The 1941,Je 6,25:7
Million Dollar Baby 1941,Je 7,20:2
Smiling Ghost, The 1941,S 26,26:5
Maltese Falcon, The 1941,O 4,18:2
Dangerously They Live 1942,Ap 11,9:2
In This our Life 1942,My 9,10:2
Somewhere I'll Find You 1942,Ag 28,22:4
Now, Voyager 1942,O 23,25:3
George Washington Slept Here 1942,O 31,11:1
Night to Remember, A 1943,Ja 1,27:2
Jitterbugs 1943,Je 5,12:2
Mrs Parkington 1944,O 13,16:1
Keep Your Powder Dry 1945,Mr 12,22:6
See my Lawyer 1945,My 4,23:4
Over 21 1945,Ag 17,20:2
Mildred Pierce 1945,S 29,12:2
Walls Came Tumbling Down, The 1946,N 9,13:5
Mother Wore Tights 1947,Ag 21,33:2
Snake Pit, the 1948,N 5,29:2
Caged 1950,My 20,8:6
Lawless, The 1950,Je 23,29:2
Fuller Brush Girl, The 1950,O 6,23:2
Tomorrow Is Another Day 1951,Ag 9,17:5
Take Me to Town 1953,Je 20,8:6
There's no Business Like Show Business
1954,D 17,37:3
Auntie Mame 1958,D 5,39:1
Pillow Talk 1959,O 7,47:2
Visit to a Small Planet 1960,Ap 14,34:1

Patrick, Lee — Cont
Goodbye Again 1961,Je 30,32:2
Summer and Smoke 1961,N 17,41:1
Girl Named Tamiku, A 1963,Mr 15,8:2
Wives and Lovers 1963,Ag 29,36:1
New Interns, The 1964,Ag 20,34:2
Patrick, Liliane
Senechal the Magnificent 1958,O 14,44:1
Julie the Redhead 1963,O 15,44:1
Patrick, Lory
Surf Party 1964,Mr 12,40:4
Patrick, Millicent
Man Without a Star 1955,Mr 25,19:3
Patrick, Nigel
Spring in Park Lane 1949,S 21,38:2
Silent Dust 1949,D 30,13:2
Mr Know-All 1950,O 11,42:1
Operation Disaster 1951,Ja 15,13:1
Perfect Woman, The 1951,F 17,10:7
Browning Version, The 1951,O 30,33:2
Pandora and the Flying Dutchman 1951,D 7,35:2
Encore (The Ant and the Grasshopper); Ant and
the Grasshopper, The (Encore) 1952,Ap 3,45:1
Young Wives' Tale 1952,N 4,33:1
Breaking Through the Sound Barrier
1952,N 7,19:1
Tonight at 8:30 (Ways and Means); Ways and
Means (Tonight at 8:30) 1953,My 26,33:2
Passionate Sentry, The 1953,N 12,37:5
Pickwick Papers, The 1954,Ap 5,21:2
Prize of Gold, A 1955,O 15,19:2
How to Murder a Rich Uncle 1957,O 26,19:2
Raintree County 1957,D 21,22:1
Count Five and Die 1958,My 15,25:1
Man Inside, The 1959,F 5,24:7
Sapphire 1959,N 3,27:1
Trials of Oscar Wilde, The 1960,Je 28,26:1
League of Gentlemen, The 1961,Ja 25,30:4
Underworld Informers 1965,O 14,53:1
Johnny Nobody 1965,N 24,35:1
Johnny Nobody 1965,N 24,35:1
Patrick, Nigel (Director)
How to Murder a Rich Uncle 1957,O 26,19:2
Patricola, Tom
Married in Hollywood 1929,S 23,24:3
Frozen Justice 1929,O 26,15:1
South Sea Rose 1929,D 7,19:3
Happy Days 1930,F 14,20:1
One mad Kiss 1930,Jl 19,7:5
Anybody's Woman 1930,Ag 16,8:3
Children of Dreams 1931,Jl 20,20:4
El Precio de un Beso 1933,Jl 25,17:3
Melodia Prohibida, La 1933,O 4,27:2
No Dejes la Puerta Abierta 1933,N 6,24:4
Rhapsody in Blue 1945,Je 28,22:2
Patroni, Giuseppe (Screenwriter)
Girl With a Suitcase 1961,S 12,36:2
Patston, Doris
Smiling Faces 1932,Ag 31,12:3
Patte, Jean-Marie
Rise of Louis XIV, The 1967,S 26,54:2
PATTEN
See Also PATTON, PAYTON, PEYTON,
PATON
Patten, Bob
Mr Belvedere Goes to College 1949,Ap 16,11:2
Sand 1949,Ag 5,23:2
Twelve O'Clock High 1950,Ja 28,10:2
American Guerrilla in the Philippines
1950,N 8,37:2
Frogmen, The 1951,Je 30,8:6
Patten, Dorothy
Botany Bay 1953,O 30,27:2
Patten, Luana
Song of the South 1946,N 28,40:2
So Dear to my Heart 1949,Ja 31,14:2
Johnny Tremain 1957,Jl 11,21:1
Home from the Hill 1960,Mr 4,19:1
Go Naked in the World 1961,Mr 11,15:1
Thunder of Drums, A 1961,S 27,35:1
Follow Me, Boys! 1966,D 2,46:1
PATTERSON
See Also PATERSON
Patterson, Colonel
Janice Meredith 1924,Ag 6,13:3
Patterson, Dick
Matter of Innocence, A 1968,F 22,36:1
Patterson, Elizabeth
South Sea Rose 1929,D 7,19:3
Cat Creeps, The 1930,N 8,21:3
Tarnished Lady 1931,Ap 30,29:3
Smiling Lieutenant, The 1931,My 23,13:4
Daddy Long Legs 1931,Je 6,15:5
Heaven on Earth 1931,D 19,16:4
Husband's Holiday 1931,D 25,29:2
Mississippi 1931,D 27,VIII,5:4 (In Addenda)
So Big 1932,Ap 30,19:3
New Morals for Old 1932,Je 24,15:3
Miss Pinkerton 1932,Jl 9,7:5
Guilty as Hell 1932,Ag 6,14:5
Love Me Tonight 1932,Ag 19,20:6
Life Begins 1932,Ag 26,20:3
Bill of Divorcement, A 1932,O 3,15:2
They Call It Sin 1932,O 21,25:4

Patterson, Elizabeth — Cont

No Man of her Own 1932,D 31,10:1
They Just Had to Get Married 1933,F 13,11:4
Infernal Machine 1933,Ap 8,16:3
Story of Temple Drake, The 1933,My 6,11:2
Hold Your Man 1933,Jl 1,16:6
Dinner at Eight 1933,Ag 24,18:1
Secret of the Blue Room, The 1933,S 13,22:1
Doctor Bull 1933,O 6,21:2
Hide-Out 1934,Ag 25,16:5
So Red the Rose 1935,N 28,39:1
Timothy's Quest 1936,F 29,11:2
Small Town Girl 1936,Ap 11,19:1
Return of Sophie Lang, The 1936,Jl 24,13:1
Three Cheers for Love 1936,Ag 1,16:2
Go West, Young Man 1936,N 19,31:3
Old Hutch 1936,D 7,27:4
High, Wide and Handsome 1937,Jl 22,15:1
Hold 'Em Navy 1937,N 6,14:2
Night Club Scandal 1937,N 12,27:2
Scandal Street 1938,F 5,19:2 (In Addenda)
Bulldog Drummond's Peril 1938,Mr 18,23:2
Bluebeard's Eighth Wife 1938,Mr 24,21:2
Sing You Sinners 1938,Ag 18,23:1
Sons of the Legion 1938,S 30,24:3
Bulldog Drummond's Secret Police
    1939,Mr 30,19:3
Story of Alexander Graham Bell, The
    1939,Ap 1,17:2
Bulldog Drummond's Bride 1939,Jl 13,17:2
Our Leading Citizen 1939,Ag 24,17:1
Cat and the Canary, The 1939,N 23,38:5
Remember the Night 1940,Ja 18,27:2
Adventure in Diamonds 1940,Ap 4,27:2
Earthbound 1940,Je 7,27:4
Anne of Windy Poplars 1940,Ag 23,13:3
Michael Shayne, Private Detective
    1940,D 19,33:2
Tobacco Road 1941,F 21,16:2
Kiss the Boys Goodbye 1941,Ag 14,21:2
Belle Starr 1941,N 1,20:2
Vanishing Virginian, The 1942,My 28,13:3
Almost Married 1942,Je 5,23:2
Beyond the Blue Horizon 1942,Je 25,27:2
Her Cardboard Lover 1942,Jl 17,19:2
My Sister Eileen 1942,O 23,15:1
I Married a Witch 1942,N 20,27:2
Sky's the Limit, The 1943,S 3,15:2
Follow the Boys 1944,Ap 26,24:6
Hail the Conquering Hero 1944,Ag 10,14:2
Together Again 1944,N 24,19:2
Lady on a Train 1945,S 15,21:2
Colonel Effingham's Raid 1946,Ap 5,21:3
I've Always Loved You 1946,S 7,11:1
Secret Heart, The 1946,D 26,28:2
Shocking Miss Pilgrim, The 1947,F 12,34:2
Welcome Stranger 1947,Ag 7,15:2
Miss Tatlock's Millions 1948,N 25,47:2
Little Women 1949,Mr 11,33:2
Intruder in the Dust 1949,N 23,19:1
Bright Leaf 1950,Je 17,7:2
Washington Story 1952,Jl 2,22:3
Las Vegas Shakedown 1955,Je 18,14:2
Pal Joey 1957,O 28,30:1
Oregon Trail, The 1959,D 10,51:6

Patterson, Hank

Abilene Town 1946,Mr 4,16:5
Relentless 1948,Mr 6,17:3
Gunfighter, The 1950,Je 24,7:2
Julie 1956,N 22,51:1
Amazing Colossal Man, The 1957,O 26,19:2
Decks Ran Red, The 1958,O 11,18:2

Patterson, James

Lilith 1964,S 21,37:2
In the Heat of the Night 1967,Ag 3,26:1

Patterson, Joe

Festival 1967,O 24,53:2

Patterson, John

Blonde Trouble 1937,Ag 7,7:2
Daughter of Shanghai 1937,D 24,21:2

Patterson, Kenneth

Outrage 1950,O 16,30:5
Hard, Fast and Beautiful 1951,Jl 2,16:6
Winning Team, The 1952,Je 21,12:2
Operation Secret 1952,N 6,37:2
Private Hell 36 1954,S 4,6:4

Patterson, Lee

Reach for the Sky 1957,My 1,40:1
Checkpoint 1957,S 19,25:2
Story of Esther Costello, The 1957,N 6,43:1
Third Man on the Mountain 1959,N 12,27:1
Jack the Ripper 1960,F 18,37:4
Three Worlds of Gulliver, The 1960,D 17,19:3
Ceremony, The 1964,My 14,39:1

Patterson, Neva

Taxi 1953,Ja 22,20:3
Solid Gold Cadillac, The 1956,O 25,40:3
Desk Set 1957,My 16,28:2
Affair to Remember, An 1957,Jl 20,8:5
Too Much, Too Soon 1958,My 10,19:2
Spiral Road, The 1962,Ag 4,11:2
David and Lisa 1962,D 27,5:5
Dear Heart 1965,Mr 8,33:1

Patterson, Robert (Original Author)

Brute Force 1947,Jl 17,16:2

Patterson, Russell (Personettes)

Artists and Models 1937,Ag 5,19:2

Patterson, Shirley

Parachute Nurse 1942,Jl 27,18:2
Between Two Women 1945,Mr 29,18:3

Patti, Ercole (Original Author)

Of Wayward Love (The Serpent); Serpent, The (Of
    Wayward Love) 1964,Mr 24,29:1
Of Wayward Love (The Soldier); Soldier, The (Of
    Wayward Love) 1964,Mr 24,29:1
Of Wayward Love (The Women); Women, The
    (Of Wayward Love) 1964,Mr 24,29:1

Patti, Ercole (Screenwriter)

It Happened in the Park 1957,Ag 13,23:2

Pattiero, Tino

Fra Diavolo 1931,N 23,22:1

PATTON

See Also PAYTON, PEYTON, PATON,
    PATTEN

Patton, Bart

Gidget Goes Hawaiian 1961,Ag 10,17:4
Dementia 13 1963,O 24,37:1

Patton, Bart (Producer)

Wild Wild Winter 1966,Ja 6,20:2

Patton, Dick Van

Charly 1968,S 24,55:1

Patton, Frances Gray (Original Author)

Good Morning, Miss Dove 1955,N 24,41:1

Patton, Malcolm

Kind of Loving, A 1962,O 2,46:1

Patton, Mary

Search, The 1948,Mr 24,30:3
Please Don't Eat the Daisies 1960,Ap 1,37:1
Marriage-Go-Round 1961,Ja 7,12:2
Outsider, The 1962,F 8,25:1

Patton, Robert

Riot in Cell Block 11 1954,F 19,24:5

Patton, Virginia

Janie 1944,Ag 5,16:2
It's a Wonderful Life 1946,D 23,19:2
Burning Cross, The 1948,F 20,19:1
Lucky Stiff, The 1949,Ja 31,14:2

Patullo, George (Original Author)

Private Affairs 1925,Jl 15,22:3

Paturel, Dominique

7 Capital Sins (Anger); Anger (7Capital Sins)
    1963,Ja 17,5:2

Patzak, Julius

Die Blonde Christl 1934,F 23,23:3

Pauck, Heinz (Screenwriter)

Affairs of Julie, The 1958,D 10,53:1
Aren't We Wonderful? 1959,O 16,27:1
Spessart Inn, The 1961,F 18,12:3
Shadows Grow Longer, The 1962,Je 11,36:4

Paudler, Maria

Ein Walzer vom Strauss 1932,F 11,16:1
Der Falsche Ehemann 1932,O 17,18:3
Korvettenkapitaen, Der 1933,Mr 20,18:3
Wenn am Sonntagabend die Dorfmusik Spielt
    1935,D 9,25:3
Unsterbliche Melodien; Immortal Melodies
    1938,Ap 23,19:3

PAUL

See Also PAULL

Paul

Festival 1967,O 24,53:2

Paul, Byron (Director)

Lt Robin Crusoe, USN 1966,Jl 14,28:1

Paul, Catherine

Spring in Park Lane 1949,S 21,38:2
Odette 1951,Mr 28,33:2

Paul, Charlotte

Guerrilla Girl 1953,Jl 7,23:7

Paul, Elliot (Original Author)

New Orleans 1947,Je 20,25:6

Paul, Elliot (Screenwriter)

Woman's Face, A 1941,My 16,21:2
Our Russian Front 1942,F 12,27:2
It's a Pleasure 1945,My 4,23:3
Rhapsody in Blue 1945,Je 28,22:2
New Orleans 1947,Je 20,25:6

Paul, Fred

Recoil, The 1924,Je 30,16:1

Paul, Heinz (Director)

U-Boat 9 1929,Ja 22,23:1
Student Sein 1931,My 4,15:3
Zirkus Leben 1932,D 28,14:7
Namensheirat 1933,Ja 9,23:1
Tannenberg 1934,Ap 3,26:6
Trenck 1934,Ap 7,19:2
Legend of William Tell, The 1935,O 2,27:1
Vier Musketiere, Die; Four Musketeers, The
    1935,N 9,19:3
Unsterbliche Melodien; Immortal Melodies
    1938,Ap 23,19:3
Kamera den auf See; Comrades at Sea
    1939,Ap 22,15:3

Paul, John

Countess from Hong Kong, A 1967,Mr 17,35:1

Paul, John (Director)

Hansel and Gretel 1954,O 11,33:1

Paul, Les Trio

Sensations of 1945 1944,Jl 7,13:2

Paul, Mimi

Midsummer Night's Dream, A 1967,Ap 18,32:1

Paul, Oscar (Screenwriter)

Once Upon a Time 1944,Je 30,17:2
Secret of Convict Lake, The 1951,Ag 4,7:2

Paul, Parveen

Shakespeare Wallah 1966,Mr 23,40:2

Paul, Rene

C-Man 1949,My 28,11:4

Paul, Val (Producer)

F-Man 1936,My 4,16:1

Paulais

Dark Eyes 1938,Ap 19,24:5
Rothchild 1938,O 12,35:2
Heroes of the Marne; (Famille Lefrancois, Le)
    1939,Ap 24,13:2
Postmaster's Daughter, The 1946,Ag 19,17:6

Pauleon

Battle of the Rails; (Bataille Du Rail)
    1949,D 27,27:2

Paulet, Reine

Escape From Yesterday 1939,My 3,27:2

Pauley

Topaze 1935,F 16,9:2
As du Turf, Les; Acres of Turf 1935,My 11,21:3
Criez-Le sur les Toits; Shout it From the
    Housetops 1935,Je 22,18:5
Life and Loves of Beethoven, The
    1937,N 22,15:1
Rothchild 1938,O 12,35:2

Paulig, Albert

It's Easy to Become a Father 1929,Je 24,27:1
Ein Burschenlied aus Heidelberg 1931,S 14,15:3
Susanne Macht Ordnung 1931,O 12,28:2
Ein Ausgekochter Junge 1932,My 3,25:5
Der Schrecken der Garnison 1932,Je 1,19:5
Hirsekorn Greift Ein 1932,Je 10,22:3
Schoen Ist die Manoeverzeit 1932,Ag 19,20:6
Drunter und Drueber 1932,D 19,19:5
Tanzhusar, Der 1933,Ap 10,8:4
Zu Befehl, Herr Unteroffizier 1934,Je 16,20:3
Es War Einmal ein Walzer 1934,O 15,20:5
Annemarie, Die Braut der Kompanie
    1934,D 8,18:6
Drei von der Kavallerie 1935,Ap 13,11:4

Paulin, Jean Paul (Director)

Femme Nue, La 1933,Ag 25,12:3

PAULL

See Also PAUL

Paull, Alan

Sunny Side Up 1929,O 4,24:5

Paull, Muriel

Captain Blood 1924,S 9,19:1

Paulot

Room Upstairs, The 1948,S 4,8:6

Paulsen, Albert

Manchurian Candidate, The 1962,O 25,48:3
Gunn 1967,Je 29,32:1

Paulsen, Arno

Razzia 1948,Je 14,19:2
Murderers Among Us 1948,Ag 17,19:6
Affair Blum, The 1949,O 18,35:2
Wozzeck 1962,Mr 3,13:1

Paulsen, Harald

Mein Leopold 1932,Ap 1,17:4
Die Blumenfrau von Lindenau 1932,Jl 8,22:5
Tausend Fuer Eine Nacht 1934,F 12,19:2
Alraune 1934,My 5,22:4
Ich Sing Mich in Dein Herz Hinein
    1935,Je 3,22:3
Frischer Wind aus Kanada 1935,S 21,18:2
Oberwachtmeister Schwenke 1936,My 5,26:7
Traumulus 1936,S 19,20:1
Mutige Seefahrer, Der 1936,N 21,21:5
Besuch am Abend 1937,Jl 3,18:2
If We All Were Angels 1937,O 9,16:2
For Her Country's Sake 1937,N 27,21:3
Lachende Dritte, Der 1938,Ap 9,11:2
Krach und Glueckum Kuennemann; Row and Joy
    About Kuennemann 1938,S 17,20:3
Sie und die Drei; She and the Three
    1938,D 10,13:3
1A in Oberbayern; 1A in Upper Bavaria
    1939,N 18,22:6
Living Dead, The 1940,D 17,33:2

Paulsen, Pat

Where Were You When the Lights Went Out?
    1968,Ag 9,30:2

Paulton, Edward (Original Author)

Her Temporary Husband 1924,Ja 1,20:1

Paulve, Andre (Producer)

Devil's Own Envoy, The 1947,Ag 30,8:6
Vie de Boheme, La 1947,N 28,37:4
Beauty and the Beast 1947,D 24,12:2
Eternal Return, The; Eternel Retour, L'
    1948,Ja 5,15:2
Damned, The; Maudits, Les 1948,Ap 26,27:2
Ruy Blas 1948,O 4,14:2
Perfectionist, The 1952,My 2,21:3

Pavan, Marisa
What Price Glory 1952,Ag 23,10:2
Down Three Dark Streets 1954,S 4,6:4
Drum Beat 1954,N 18,42:1
Rose Tattoo, The 1955,D 13,55:1
Diane 1956,Ja 13,18:1
Man in the Gray Flannel Suit, The
1956,Ap 13,21:1
Midnight Story, The 1957,Jl 5,14:2
John Paul Jones 1959,Je 17,39:1
Solomon and Sheba 1959,D 26,7:2
Pavanelli, Livio
Luther 1929,Je 24,27:1
Liebeskommando 1932,Ap 27,13:6
Fruehlingsmaerchen 1935,My 20,20:5
Canzione del Sole, La 1936,My 6,27:2
Amore e Dolore 1937,My 13,31:4
Pavaux, Paul (Producer)
Clandestine 1948,My 24,23:2
Pavese, Luigi
Re Burlone, Il 1936,Mr 28,11:3
Eternal Melodies 1948,F 14,17:3
His Young Wife 1949,Mr 12,10:2
Lost in the Dark 1949,My 14,9:2
Woman Trouble 1949,My 26,34:2
Mademoiselle Gobette 1955,F 5,13:3
Sword and the Cross, The 1960,Jl 7,26:1
Love and Larceny 1963,F 2,5:6
Pavese, Nino
Fear No Evil 1949,Mr 31,31:2
Mill on the Po, The 1951,O 23,35:2
Pavlenko, P
Inspector General, The 1954,My 3,21:2
Pavlenko, P (Director)
Alexander Nevsky 1939,Mr 23,27:1
Pavlenko, P (Original Author)
Soviet Border 1939,F 20,13:2
Pavlenko, P (Screenwriter)
In the Far East 1937,O 20,27:3
Vow, The 1947,Je 23,14:3
Fall of Berlin 1952,Je 9,19:2
Man of Music 1953,My 11,25:2
Pavlikov
Red Army Days 1935,O 21,22:4
Pugachev 1938,Jl 4,10:2
Pavlotzkaya, Trina
Spring Song 1942,S 12,9:2
Pavlov, D
Vow, The 1947,Je 23,14:3
Twins 1947,Jl 28,12:2
Village Teacher 1948,Jl 5,8:4
Chuk and Gek 1953,D 21,27:4
Pavlov, Muriel
It Started in Paradise 1953,Jl 25,8:2
Pavlova, Anna
Dumb Girl of Portici, The 1916,Ap 4,11:2
Pavlova, Soraya
Ukrainian Festival 1965,N 1,57:1
Pavlova, Tatiana
Signora di Tutti, La 1936,Mr 26,27:3
Pavlovsky, V (Screenwriter)
Guerrilla Brigade 1942,Ap 14,17:2
Pavlow, Muriel
Quiet Wedding 1941,D 29,27:4
Project M 7 1953,N 27,22:5
Malta Story 1954,Jl 17,7:2
Fuss Over Feathers 1954,D 27,22:6
Doctor in the House 1955,F 19,18:3
Simon and Laura 1956,Jl 3,17:2
Reach for the Sky 1957,My 1,40:1
Doctor at Large 1957,Jl 29,15:5
Rooney 1958,Je 6,29:2
Murder She Said 1962,Ja 8,27:2
Pavoni, Tatiana
Between Two Worlds 1940,F 9,15:2
Pawle, Lennox
Married in Hollywood 1929,S 23,24:3
Sky Hawk, The 1929,D 12,36:4
Hot for Paris 1930,Ja 4,21:1
Sin of Madelon Claudet, The 1931,O 31,22:2
David Copperfield 1935,Ja 19,8:1
Gay Deception, The 1935,O 11,31:1
Sylvia Scarlett 1936,Ja 10,16:2
Pawley, Edward
Thirteen Women 1932,O 15,13:1
Tess of the Storm Country 1932,N 19,20:2
Mississippi 1935,Ap 18,27:2
G Men 1935,My 2,17:1
King Solomon of Broadway 1935,O 19,12:2
Tough Guy 1936,Mr 14,10:1
Sworn Enemy 1936,S 12,20:1
Sinner Take All 1937,F 3,27:1
Mountain Justice 1937,My 13,31:2
It Can't Last Forever 1937,Jl 30,22:5
Dangerous to Know 1938,Mr 11,15:4
White Banners 1938,Je 23,27:1
Gun Law 1938,Je 24,15:1
Prison Break 1938,Jl 13,17:4
Smashing the Rackets 1938,Ag 9,22:5
Little Tough Guy 1938,Ag 18,23:3
Sons of the Legion 1938,S 30,24:3
Angels With Dirty Faces 1938,N 26,18:1
Oklahoma Kid, The 1939,Mr 11,21:1

Lady's From Kentucky, The 1939,Ap 27,31:1
Each Dawn I Die 1939,Jl 22,12:2
Big Guy, The 1940,Ja 1,29:2
Castle on the Hudson 1940,Mr 4,11:2
River's End 1940,Ag 26,11:4
Flowing Gold 1940,S 2,19:3
San Francisco Docks 1940,D 26,23:3
Hit the Road 1941,Jl 3,15:3
Treat 'Em Rough 1942,Ja 19,21:3
True to the Army 1942,Je 15,15:4
Flight Lieutenant 1942,Jl 31,11:1
Pawley, William
Bad Girl 1931,Ag 15,18:3
Spider, The 1931,S 5,7:4
Over the Hill 1931,N 21,20:4
Cheaters at Play 1932,F 27,22:1
After Tomorrow 1932,Mr 7,13:5
Careless Lady 1932,Ap 18,19:2
Amateur Daddy 1932,Ap 23,11:5
Trial of Vivienne Ware, The 1932,Ap 30,19:3
Letty Lynton 1932,Ap 30,19:3
Speak Easily 1932,Ag 19,20:6
Central Park 1932,D 7,29:3
Gabriel Over the White House 1933,Ap 1,18:2
Kentucky Kernels 1935,Ja 5,20:2
Stolen Harmony 1935,Ap 20,16:2
Daring Young Man, The 1935,Jl 18,15:2
Mary Burns, Fugitive 1935,N 16,19:2
Bullets or Ballots 1936,My 27,27:1
Public Enemy's Wife 1936,Jl 9,17:2
Born Reckless 1937,Jl 30,22:6
Trapped by G-Men 1937,N 4,29:1
International Crime 1938,My 16,14:4
White Banners 1938,Je 23,27:1
Crime Takes a Holiday 1938,N 28,11:2
Union Pacific 1939,My 11,31:2
Disputed Passage 1939,O 26,27:2
Grapes of Wrath, The 1940,Ja 25,17:2
Double Alibi 1940,Mr 11,11:2
Return of Frank James, The 1940,Ag 10,16:4
Great Profile, The 1940,O 18,25:1
Great American Broadcast, The 1941,My 2,25:2
Time to Kill 1942,D 25,15:4
Pawley, William Jr
Crowning Experience, The 1960,O 24,25:3
Voice of the Hurricane 1964,Je 3,36:4
Pawlikowski, Adam
Ashes and Diamonds 1961,My 30,8:1
Lotna 1966,My 27,33:1
Pawlo, Tolvo
Crime and Punishment 1948,Mr 1,17:2
Magician, The 1959,Ag 28,27:1
Pawlowski, Waclaw
Tredowata 1936,D 31,21:2
Pawn, Doris
Toby's Bow 1919,D 15,20:1
Shame 1921,Ag 1,8:3
Midnight Bell, A 1921,Ag 8,12:2
Paxinou, Katina
For Whom the Bell Tolls 1943,Jl 15,25:2
Hostages 1943,O 11,23:2
Confidential Agent 1945,N 3,11:2
Mourning Becomes Electra 1947,N 20,38:2
Prince of Foxes 1949,D 24,11:2
Inheritance, The 1951,F 12,19:2
Miracle, The 1959,N 13,25:4
Rocco and his Brothers 1961,Je 28,40:2
Mr Arkadin 1962,O 12,26:1
Zita 1968,Ag 12,40:2
Paxton, Dick
Iron Mistress, The 1952,N 20,39:2
Paxton, Guy (Original Author)
Caretaker's Daughter, The 1953,Ag 20,18:5
Paxton, John (Miscellaneous)
Rope of Sand 1949,Ag 4,19:2
Paxton, John (Producer)
How to Murder a Rich Uncle 1957,O 26,19:2
Paxton, John (Screenwriter)
My Pal, Wolf 1944,O 9,17:2
Murder, my Sweet 1945,Mr 9,16:2
Cornered 1945,D 26,15:1
Crack-Up 1946,S 7,11:1
Crossfire 1947,Jl 23,19:2
So Well Remembered 1947,N 5,34:3
Of Men and Music 1951,F 15,27:2
Fourteen Hours 1951,Mr 7,43:2
Wild One, The 1953,D 31,9:2
Cobweb, The 1955,Ag 6,13:3
Prize of Gold, A 1955,O 15,19:2
How to Murder a Rich Uncle 1957,O 26,19:2
On the Beach 1959,D 18,34:1
Paxton, Richard
Yank in Korea, A 1951,Ap 2,29:2
Paxton, Sidney
Old Home Week 1925,My 25,21:3
Paxton, Tom
Inheritance, The 1964,N 9,42:2
Payant, Gilles
Big Red 1962,S 3,11:2
Payer, Harry
Fidelio 1961,My 13,10:1

Payer, Ivo
David and Goliath 1961,O 7,14:3
Payn, Graham
Astonished Heart, The 1950,F 15,23:2
PAYNE
See Also PAINE
Payne, A W
Mill On the Floss, The 1939,N 15,19:3
Payne, Bruce
Little Boy Lost 1953,S 22,38:2
Payne, Douglas
Triumph of the Scarlet Pimpernel, The
1929,Jl 8,17:3
Payne, John
Dodsworth 1936,S 24,29:1
College Swing 1938,Ap 28,27:2
Garden of the Moon 1938,S 24,13:1
Wings of the Navy 1939,F 4,11:1
Indianapolis Speedway 1939,Jl 15,8:2
Kid Nightingale 1939,D 8,33:6
Star Dust 1940,My 4,13:1
Tear Gas Squad 1940,My 31,15:3
Maryland 1940,Jl 13,16:5
Great Profile, The 1940,O 18,25:1
Tin Pan Alley 1940,N 22,27:3
Great American Broadcast, The 1941,My 2,25:2
Sun Valley Serenade 1941,S 6,20:1
Week-End in Havana 1941,N 8,11:2
Remember the Day 1941,D 26,21:2
To the Shores of Tripoli 1942,Mr 26,27:2
Footlight Serenade 1942,S 10,30:3
Iceland 1942,O 15,27:1
Springtime in the Rockies 1942,N 12,30:2
Hello, Frisco, Hello 1943,Mr 25,25:1
Dolly Sisters, The 1945,N 15,24:6
Sentimental Journey 1946,Mr 7,33:2
Razor's Edge, The 1946,N 20,42:2
Wake up and Dream 1947,Ja 24,18:4
Miracle on 34th Street 1947,Je 5,32:1
Larceny 1948,S 4,8:6
Saxon Charm, The 1948,S 30,32:3
El Paso 1949,Mr 24,35:2
Crooked Way, The 1949,S 5,13:2
Captain China 1950,Mr 2,33:2
Eagle and the Hawk, The 1950,Jl 6,31:2
Tripoli 1950,N 10,35:2
Passage West 1951,Ag 31,12:2
Crosswinds 1951,D 7,35:4
Kansas City Confidential 1952,N 29,11:2
99 River Street 1953,O 3,14:2
Rails Into Laramie 1954,My 13,34:2
Silver Lode 1954,Jl 24,6:6
Hell's Island 1955,My 7,10:2
Tennessee's Partner 1955,N 5,22:8
Slightly Scarlet 1956,Mr 17,13:2
Bailout at 43,000 1957,Je 8,13:2
Payne, Julie
Island of the Blue Dolphins 1964,Jl 4,8:2
Payne, Laurence
Train of Events 1952,My 26,18:4
Night Ambush 1958,Ap 25,32:4
Crawling Eye, The 1959,Ja 1,38:1
Ben Hur 1959,N 19,50:2
Barabbas 1962,O 11,49:1
Telltale Heart, The 1963,My 16,42:1
Payne, Lou
Last Edition, The 1925,N 11,27:3
Payne, Louis
True as Steel 1924,Je 17,22:4
For Sale 1924,Jl 14,11:5
In Hollywood with Potash and Perlmutter
1924,S 30,27:3
As Man Desires 1925,F 10,20:1
Only Thing, The 1925,N 23,25:4
Blind Goddess 1926,Ap 6,26:4 (In Addenda)
Yankee Clipper, The 1927,My 3,25:1
Vanity 1927,Je 15,31:4
Whip, The 1928,S 17,28:2
Interference 1928,N 17,23:1
Evangeline 1929,Jl 29,23:3
Big News 1929,O 7,22:1
Shepper - Newfounder, The 1930,D 25,31:5
Saratoga Trunk 1945,N 22,39:2
Payne, Sally
Conga Nights, La 1940,Je 5,33:5
Payne, Sharyn
Smash-Up, The Story of a Woman
1947,Ap 11,31:2
Payne, Tom
We're Going to Be Rich 1938,Jl 4,10:2
Paynter, Elisabeth
Mikado, The 1939,Je 2,27:2
Paynter, Ernest (Original Author)
Shipmates 1931,My 23,13:4
Paysan, Catherine (Original Author)
Marriage Came Tumbling Down, The
1968,N 6,32:3
Payson, Blanche
Oh, Doctor! 1925,F 23,24:1
We Moderns 1925,D 8,28:5
Wicked 1931,S 19,10:2
Impatient Maiden, The 1932,Mr 4,17:3

PAYTON
See Also PEYTON, PATON, PATTEN, PATTON

Payton, Barbara
Trapped 1949,N 26,10:6
Kiss Tomorrow Goodbye 1950,Ag 5,9:2
Dallas 1951,Ja 13,10:4
Only the Valiant 1951,Ap 14,9:6
Four Sided Triangle 1953,My 16,10:1

Payton, Denis
Having a Wild Weekend 1965,Ag 19,35:1

Payton, Gloria
Where Lights Are Low 1921,Ag 1,8:3 (Incorrect in this edition; use 1921,Ag 1,6:4 elsewhere)

Payton, Lew
Valiant Is the Word for Carrie 1936,O 8,27:2
Jezebel 1938,Mr 11,15:2
Lady's From Kentucky, The 1939,Ap 27,31:1
Lady for a Night 1942,F 12,27:2

Paz, Miguel Caronatto (Director)
Apuros de Claudina, Los; Claudina's Troubles 1940,Je 8,18:3

Pazhitnov, Nikolai
Idiot, The 1960,Jl 22,11:2

Pazos, Felipe
Old Man and the Sea, The 1958,O 8,41:1

Peach, L du Garde (Miscellaneous)
Princess Charming 1935,Je 22,18:5
Transatlantic Tunnel 1935,O 28,16:2

Peach, L du Garde (Original Author)
Great Mr Handel, The 1943,S 10,29:3

Peach, L du Garde (Screenwriter)
Princess Charming 1935,Je 22,18:5
Seven Sinners 1936,Ag 22,6:1
Man Who Lived Again, The 1936,D 16,35:4
Man of Affairs 1937,F 20,9:2
Heart's Desire 1937,Jl 12,20:4
Forbidden Music 1938,D 27,13:2

Peach, Mary
Room at the Top 1959,Mr 31,26:1
No Love for Johnnie 1961,D 13,55:1
Gathering of Eagles, A 1963,Jl 11,21:2
Pair of Briefs, A 1964,F 3,22:2
Blues for Lovers 1966,S 8,43:1

Peacock, Kim
S O S Mediterranean 1940,Ja 1,29:2
Hell's Cargo 1940,S 16,15:2

Peacock, Trevor (Original Author)
He Who Rides a Tiger 1968,S 10,39:1

Peacock, Trevor (Screenwriter)
He Who Rides a Tiger 1968,S 10,39:1

PEARCE
See Also PEERCE, PIERCE

Pearce, Adele
Full Confession 1939,S 28,29:4
Three Sons 1939,N 24,29:3
One Crowded Night 1940,Ag 27,17:2
Pop Always Pays 1940,Ag 30,16:6
Mr and Mrs Smith 1941,F 21,16:3
No Greater Sin 1941,Ag 29,18:2

Pearce, Al
Hit Parade, The 1937,My 31,11:2

Pearce, Alice
On the Town 1949,D 9,37:2
Belle of New York, The 1952,Mr 6,25:6
How to be Very, Very Popular 1955,Jl 23,10:1
Opposite Sex, The 1956,N 16,23:2
My Six Loves 1963,Ap 4,58:4
Lad: A Dog 1963,My 2,40:2
Tammy and the Doctor 1963,Je 27,23:2
Kiss Me, Stupid 1964,D 23,22:2
Dear Heart 1965,Mr 8,33:1
Glass Bottom Boat, The 1966,Je 10,54:1

Pearce, Ann
Undertow 1949,D 16,37:2
Bagdad 1949,D 24,11:4
Desert Hawk, The 1950,Ag 26,9:2

Pearce, Bernard (Miscellaneous)
Road to Rio 1948,F 19,29:3

Pearce, Don (Original Author)
Cool Hand Luke 1967,N 2,58:1

Pearce, Don (Screenwriter)
Cool Hand Luke 1967,N 2,58:1

Pearce, George
Country Kid, The 1923,O 30,16:1
Narrow Street, The 1925,Ja 5,19:1
Wife Who Wasn't Wanted, The 1925,S 9,23:1
Social Highwayman, The 1926,Je 15,23:3
Hold That Lion 1926,S 6,16:2
Drop Kick, The 1927,S 20,32:2
Irresistible Lover, The 1927,O 19,24:4
Home James 1928,S 11,31:3
Valiant, The 1929,My 13,27:2
Right of Way, The 1931,Mr 24,31:2
This Reckless Age 1932,Ja 9,21:1
British Agent 1934,S 20,20:1
When You're in Love 1937,F 19,15:2

Pearce, Jacqueline
Don't Raise the Bridge, Lower the River 1968,Jl 13,18:1

Pearce, Leslie (Director)
Fall Guy, The 1930,My 27,27:2

Pearce, Perce (Director)
Victory Through Air Power 1943,Jl 19,13:1

Pearce, Perce (Miscellaneous)
Bambi 1942,Ag 14,13:1

Pearce, Perce (Producer)
Treasure Island 1950,Ag 16,24:2
Sword and the Rose, The 1953,Ag 20,18:3
Rob Roy 1954,F 4,21:5

Pearce, Peter (Producer)
Story of Robin Hood, The 1952,Je 27,18:3

Pearce, Vera
Nicholas Nickleby 1947,D 1,27:2

Pearl, Harold (Original Author)
Dumbo 1941,O 24,27:2

Pearl, Jack
Meet the Baron 1933,O 28,20:3
Hollywood Party 1934,My 26,12:2

Pearl, Lee (Composer)
Duchess of Idaho 1950,Jl 21,15:3

Pearl, Willa
Prince of Peace, The 1951,Mr 24,8:3

Pearl Twins
Ali Baba Goes to Town 1937,O 23,14:1

Pearlstein, Emma
Rainbow, The 1944,O 23,14:3

PEARSON
See Also PIERSON

Pearson, Beatrice
Force of Evil 1948,D 27,16:2
Lost Boundaries 1949,Jl 1,14:4

Pearson, Billy
Boots Malone 1952,Mr 13,26:2

Pearson, Brett
This Property is Condemned 1966,Ag 4,24:1

Pearson, Bud (Miscellaneous)
If You Knew Susie 1948,F 23,19:2

Pearson, Drew
Day the Earth Stood Still, The 1951,S 19,37:1

Pearson, Harry C (Cinematographer)
African Holiday 1937,Je 4,27:3

Pearson, Harry C (Producer)
African Holiday 1937,Je 4,27:3

Pearson, Harry C Mrs (Cinematographer)
African Holiday 1937,Je 4,27:3

Pearson, Humphrey (Original Author)
On With the Show 1929,My 29,28:6
Going Wild 1931,Ja 26,21:1
Bright Lights 1931,F 10,24:4
Traveling Husbands 1931,Ag 8,16:3
Red Salute 1935,S 30,13:1

Pearson, Humphrey (Screenwriter)
Ruggles of Red Gap 1935,Mr 7,26:1
Red Salute 1935,S 30,13:1

Pearson, Jesse
Bye Bye Birdie 1963,Ap 5,27:3

Pearson, John
Talent Scout 1937,Ag 20,21:3

Pearson, Lloyd
Kipps 1942,My 25,11:2
Mr Perrin and Mr Traill 1949,Ja 17,15:2

Pearson, Ted
You're Only Young Once 1938,Ja 3,16:2
Test Pilot 1938,Ap 16,17:1

Pearson, Virginia
Wizard of Oz, The 1925,Ap 14,26:1
Phantom of the Opera, The 1925,S 7,15:3
Red Kimono, The 1926,F 3,23:1
Silence 1926,My 19,29:3
Big City, The 1928,Mr 26,26:2
Actress, The 1928,Jl 9,25:1

Pearson, William (Original Author)
Fever in the Blood 1961,Ap 20,30:4

Peary, Harold
Comin' Round the Mountain 1940,S 26,27:3
Look Who's Laughing 1941,D 25,33:2
Here We Go Again 1942,O 12,12:3
Seven Days' Leave 1942,D 11,33:2
Great Gildersleeve, The 1942,D 18,36:8
Gildersleeve's Bad Day 1943,Je 11,23:1
Wetbacks 1956,My 5,13:2

Peasley, Dennis
Claudelle Inglish 1961,S 21,40:2

PEAT
See Also PEET

Peat, Harold R
Private Peat 1918,O 14,15:1

Peat, Harold R (Original Author)
Private Peat 1918,O 14,15:1

Peattie, Yvonne
Dangerous Crossing 1953,S 30,37:2
Private War of Major Benson, The 1955,Ag 3,27:2
Donovan's Reef 1963,Jl 25,14:1

Peche, S (Screenwriter)
Girl in the Bikini, The 1958,O 25,16:3

Peck, Charles
Dead End 1937,Ag 25,25:1
Of Human Hearts 1938,F 18,23:1
Mad About Music 1938,Mr 12,13:2
Andy Hardy Gets Spring Fever 1939,Jl 19,23:2

Peck, Charles Jr (Screenwriter)
Basketball Fix, the 1951,S 14,21:2

Peck, George W (Original Author)
Peck's bad Boy 1934,O 6,20:1
Peck's bad Boy With the Circus 1939,Ja 11,17:4

Peck, Gregory
Days of Glory 1944,Je 17,10:2
Keys of the Kingdom, The 1944,D 30,15:2
Valley of Decision, The 1945,My 4,23:2
Spellbound 1945,N 2,22:2
Yearling, The 1947,Ja 24,18:2
Macomber Affair, The 1947,Ap 21,21:2
Duel in the Sun 1947,My 8,30:2
Gentleman's Agreement 1947,N 12,36:2
Paradine Case, The 1948,Ja 9,26:2
Yellow Sky 1949,F 2,36:1
Great Sinner, The 1949,Je 30,19:2
Twelve O'Clock High 1950,Ja 28,10:2
Gunfighter, The 1950,Je 24,7:2
Only the Valiant 1951,Ap 14,9:6
David and Bathsheba 1951,Ag 15,23:2
Captain Horatio Hornblower 1951,S 14,21:2
Snows of Kilimanjaro, The 1952,S 19,19:2
World in His Arms, The 1952,O 10,21:2
Roman Holiday 1953,Ag 28,13:1
Night People 1954,Mr 13,11:2
Man With a Million 1954,Je 29,21:2
Purple Plain, The 1955,Ap 11,29:1
Man in the Gray Flannel Suit, The 1956,Ap 13,21:1
Moby Dick 1956,Jl 5,18:1
Designing Woman 1957,My 17,20:2
Bravados, The 1958,Je 26,23:2
Pork Chop Hill 1959,My 30,9:2
Beloved Infidel 1959,N 18,46:1
On the Beach 1959,D 18,34:1
Guns of Navarone, The 1961,Je 23,19:1
Cape Fear 1962,Ap 19,35:2
To Kill a Mockingbird 1963,F 15,10:2
How the West Was Won 1963,Ap 1,54:1
Captain Newman, MD 1964,F 21,36:1
Behold a Pale Horse 1964,Ag 14,16:1
Mirage 1965,My 27,28:1
Arabesque 1966,My 6,54:1

Peck, Gregory (Narrator)
Pictura 1952,Ap 8,35:3
John F Kennedy: Years of Lightning, Day of Drums 1966,Ap 11,41:1

Peck, Gregory (Producer)
Big Country, The 1958,O 2,44:1

Peck, Norman
Vagabond Lover, The 1929,N 27,30:6

Peck, Robert
Prep and Pep 1928,D 24,11:1

Peck, Robert (Miscellaneous)
Face of War, A 1968,My 11,28:1

Peck, Steven
Some Came Running 1959,Ja 23,17:1
House is not a Home, A 1964,S 2,33:1

Peckinpah, Sam (Director)
Deadly Companions, The 1962,Ap 12,41:7
Ride the High Country 1962,Je 21,26:2
Major Dundee 1965,Ap 8,45:1

Peckinpah, Sam (Screenwriter)
Major Dundee 1965,Ap 8,45:1
Villa Rides 1968,Jl 18,26:3

Peclet, Georges
Niemandsland; No Man's Land 1932,Ja 24,VIII,5:1
Sous la Lune du Maroc 1933,Ja 23,9:2
Hell on Earth 1934,Ja 29,10:2
Grand Illusion 1938,S 13,28:2
Heroes of the Marne; (Famille Lefrancois, Le) 1939,Ap 24,13:2
King, The 1941,O 23,29:3

Pecsi, Gizi
Edes Mostoha 1935,N 21,27:2
Tommy 1937,O 16,22:3

Pedelty, Donovan (Director)
Luck of the Irish, The 1937,Ja 16,21:1
Irish and Proud of It 1938,O 31,12:3

Pedelty, Donovan (Miscellaneous)
Brewster's Millions 1935,Ap 8,23:3

Pedelty, Donovan (Producer)
Luck of the Irish, The 1937,Ja 16,21:1
Irish and Proud of It 1938,O 31,12:3

Pedelty, Donovan (Screenwriter)
Brewster's Millions 1935,Ap 8,23:3

Pederson, Guy
Paris Blues 1961,N 8,41:1

Pederson, Harry (Cinematographer)
Hunters of the Deep 1954,D 17,37:4

Pederson, Maria
Thirteen Men and a Girl 1931,Ag 17,18:2

Pederson, Verne (Cinematographer)
Hunters of the Deep 1954,D 17,37:4

Pederzini, Gianna
Trovatore, Il 1950,F 9,36:7

Pedi, Tom
Native Land 1942,My 12,16:3
Naked City, The 1948,Mr 5,17:2
State of the Union 1948,Ap 23,28:1
Up in Central Park 1948,My 27,29:3
Criss Cross 1949,Mr 12,10:2
Sorrowful Jones 1949,Je 6,15:2

Pedinotti, Aldo
Always Victorious 1960,Ap 7,46:1
Pedler, Gertrude
Courtship of Myles Standish, The 1923,D 31,9:3
Pedoni, Anna
Shoe-Shine 1947,Ag 27,19:2
Pedroza, Alfonso
Buenaventura, La 1934,S 15,20:3
Cantante de Napoles, El; Singer of Naples, The 1935,F 25,13:4
Gay Desperado, The 1936,O 9,31:4
Pedrucho, Pedro Basauri
Moment of Truth, The 1965,Ag 10,18:1
Peebles, Melvin Van (Composer)
Story of a Three Day Pass, The 1968,Jl 9,31:1
Peebles, Melvin Van (Director)
Story of a Three Day Pass, The 1968,Jl 9,31:1
Peebles, Melvin Van (Screenwriter)
Story of a Three Day Pass, The 1968,Jl 9,31:1
Peel, David
Brides of Dracula, The 1960,S 6,41:4
Peel, Eileen
Bad Sister 1948,Je 11,27:3
Peel, Richard
Notorious Landlady, The 1962,Jl 27,15:2
Peelet, George
Mystere de la Villa Rose, Le 1932,Ja 11,28:5
Peeples, Samuel A (Screenwriter)
Advance to the Rear 1964,Je 11,27:3
PEERCE
See Also PEARCE, PIERCE
Peerce, Jan
Hymn of the Nations 1946,Ap 22,26:2
Carnegie Hall 1947,My 3,10:2
Something in the Wind 1947,Ag 29,14:3
Of Men and Music 1951,F 15,27:2
Peerce, Larry (Director)
One Potato, Two Potato 1964,Jl 30,16:1
Incident, The 1967,N 6,65:1
Peers, Joan
Applause 1929,O 8,24:5
Anybody's War 1930,Jl 11,22:1
Rain or Shine 1930,Ag 8,11:1
Tol'able David 1930,N 17,29:1
Parlor, Bedroom and Bath 1931,Ap 4,23:1
Tip Off, The 1931,O 26,22:1
Over the Hill 1931,N 21,20:4
PEET
See Also PEAT
Peet, Bill (Original Author)
Three Caballeros, The 1945,F 5,20:1
Peet, Bill (Screenwriter)
Cinderella 1950,F 23,33:1
one Hundred and One Dalmations 1961,F 11,27:1
Sword in the Stone, The 1963,D 26,33:3
Pegay, Sophie
Last Waltz, The 1927,N 14,26:1
Pegg, Barbara
To Sir, With Love 1967,Je 15,56:1
Peggy, Baby
Peggy Behave 1922,F 28,17:4
Hollywood 1923,Jl 30,11:4
Darling of New York, The 1924,Ja 18,20:1
Captain January 1924,Jl 7,10:4
Pegna, Vanna
Serpente a Sonagli, Il 1936,Ag 17,9:2
Pehrsson, Emil A (Director)
Baldvins Brollop; Baldwin's Wedding 1938,D 27,13:2
Skanor-Falsterbo 1939,Ap 17,13:2
Kalle paa Spaangen 1940,Ja 27,9:3
Peichev, S
Heroes of Shipka 1956,S 3,10:5
Peignot, Jo
Gervaise 1957,N 12,46:1
Demoniaque 1958,Mr 4,34:5
Peine, Josh
Mr Hobbs Takes a Vacation 1962,Je 16,11:2
Peisley, Frederick
Scotland Yard Mystery, The 1936,Mr 16,21:4
Pekalski, Aleksander (Director)
Cabman No 13 1937,N 1,24:6
Pekitillew, David
Shadows 1961,Mr 22,37:1
Pelayo, Sylvie
Fanfan the Tulip 1953,My 5,34:2
Pelegri, Jean
Pickpocket 1963,My 22,36:2
Olive Trees of Justice, The 1967,My 5,31:1
Pelegri, Jean (Original Author)
Olive Trees of Justice, The 1967,My 5,31:1
Pelegri, Jean (Screenwriter)
Olive Trees of Justice, The 1967,My 5,31:1
Pelegri, Pierre (Screenwriter)
Girl With the Golden Eyes, The 1962,Ag 21,36:2
Zita 1968,Ag 12,40:2
Pelella, Lucia
Condemned of Altona, The 1963,O 31,26:1
Pelevin, A
Frigid Sea, The 1955,N 21,23:4

Pelham, David M (Producer)
Rapture 1950,D 14,51:3
Pelham, David M (Screenwriter)
Rapture 1950,D 14,51:3
Peli, Afro
Lucia di Lammermoor 1947,N 1,11:3
Pelish, Thelma
Pajama Game, The 1957,Ag 30,12:2
Pelissier, Anthony (Director)
Rocking Horse Winner, The 1950,Je 9,29:2
History of Mr Polly, The 1951,O 25,36:3
Encore (The Ant and the Grasshopper); Ant and the Grasshopper, The (Encore) 1952,Ap 3,45:1
Encore (Winter Cruise); Winter Cruise (Encore) 1952,Ap 3,45:1
Encore (Gigolo and Gigolette); Gigolo and Gigolette (Encore) 1952,Ap 3,45:1
Tonight at 8:30 (Fumed Oak); Fumed Oak (Tonight at 8:30) 1953,My 26,33:2
Tonight at 8:30 (Ways and Means); Ways and Means (Tonight at 8:30) 1953,My 26,33:2
Night Without Stars 1953,Jl 14,19:4
Personal Affair 1954,O 23,13:2
Pelissier, Anthony (Screenwriter)
Vacation From Marriage 1946,Mr 15,27:2
Rocking Horse Winner, The 1950,Je 9,29:2
History of Mr Polly, The 1951,O 25,36:3
Pell, Edward
Dragon Painter, The 1919,O 5,IV,5:3 (In Addenda)
Pellati, Teresa
Greatest Love, The 1954,Ja 12,19:2
Pellegrin, Raymond
Nais 1948,Je 16,37:2
Companions of the Night 1954,N 25,44:2
Doctors, The 1956,Ag 7,19:2
Woman of Rome 1956,N 6,30:1
We Are all Murderers 1957,Ja 9,27:2
Tempest in the Flesh 1957,Ja 19,12:2
Light Across the Street, The; Lumiere d'en Face, La 1957,Jl 30,20:2
Fire Under Her Skin 1958,Je 28,13:6
View From the Bridge, A 1962,Ja 23,36:1
Bonne Soupe, La 1964,Mr 16,37:1
Behold a Pale Horse 1964,Ag 14,16:1
OSS 117-Mission for a Killer 1966,O 13,50:3
Pellegrini, Eugene
8 X 8 1957,Mr 16,13:2
Pellegrini, Glauco (Screenwriter)
Tombolo 1949,D 31,9:4
Most Wonderful Moment, The 1959,Je 1,23:6
Pellegrini, Hector
Terrace, The 1964,N 25,45:1
Pellegrini, Luis
Rose for Everyone, A 1967,Je 30,30:1
Pelletier, Alex (Screenwriter)
Adolescents, The (Genevieve); Genevieve (The Adolescents) 1967,Ap 14,33:1
Pelletier, Evon
Bride of the Storm 1926,Ap 5,24:1
Pelletier, Gilles
I Confess 1953,Mr 23,28:2
Pelletier, Louis (Original Author)
Two Guys From Texas 1948,Ag 28,8:6
Pelletier, Louis (Screenwriter)
Big Red 1962,S 3,11:2
Those Calloways 1965,Ap 15,38:2
Horse in the Gray Flannel Suit, The 1968,D 21,49:3
Pelletier, Louis Jr (Original Author)
Cowboy From Brooklyn 1938,Jl 14,17:1
Pelletier, Yvonne
Young Sinners 1931,My 9,15:4
Riders of the Purple Sage 1931,S 26,25:3
Cradle Song 1933,N 20,18:2
Pelletti, John
Outrage 1950,O 16,30:5
Pellevant, Antoinette (Screenwriter)
Marco Polo 1962,S 20,29:2
Pellicer, Pilar
Day of the Evil Gun 1968,Ap 25,53:2
Pellicer, Pina
One Eyed Jacks 1961,Mr 31,21:1
Macario 1961,S 28,48:6
Pellini, Liliana
Sky Is Red, The 1952,My 27,30:2
Pelly, Farrell
Darby O'Gill and the Little People 1959,Jl 1,26:1
Pelskova, Helena
Report on the Party and the Guests, A 1968,S 20,37:5
Report on the Party and the Guests, A 1968,S 28,37:1
Peltier, Kenout (Miscellaneous)
Chappaqua 1967,N 6,65:2
Peltser, I
Last Night, The 1937,Ap 28,18:3
Lonely White Sail 1938,My 7,18:1
No Greater Love 1944,F 25,23:3
Adventure in Odessa 1954,Je 21,19:6
Peltser, P
Private Ivan 1957,Ap 3,28:2

Peltser, T
Tiger Girl 1955,S 5,8:2
Apartment in Moscow 1962,My 28,25:5
Peluffo, A Luisa
Sword and the Cross, The 1960,Jl 7,26:1
Pelufo, Manuel
Dia que me Quieras, El; Day You Love Me, The 1935,Ag 27,23:3
Pelzer, George
If Winter Comes 1923,S 4,14:1
Hoosier Schoolmaster, The 1924,Mr 18,25:2
Peman, Jose Maria (Screenwriter)
Loyola, The Soldier Saint 1952,Ap 25,19:2
Pember, Clifford (Director)
Wanted Men 1936,Jl 8,15:2
Pemberton, Brock
Stage Door Canteen 1943,Je 25,13:2
Pembroke, George
Irish and Proud of It 1938,O 31,12:3
Flying Wild 1941,Ap 12,19:3
Invisible Ghost, The 1941,My 8,21:2
Gangs Incorporated 1941,Ag 4,16:6
Spooks Run Wild 1941,N 1,20:3
Pembroke, Scott (Original Author)
Lawless Nineties, The 1936,Je 29,11:1
Pena, Julio
Mama 1933,Jl 8,14:6
Angelita 1935,S 11,19:5
Rosa de Francia 1935,O 28,16:3
Cinco Advertencias de Satanas, Las; Satan's Five Warnings 1939,Ja 14,13:2
Alexander the Great 1956,Mr 29,23:1
Spanish Affair 1958,F 6,24:1
Solomon and Sheba 1959,D 26,7:2
Castilian, The 1963,O 3,31:1
Kid Rodelo 1966,F 23,46:1
Pena, Luis
Agua en el Suelo, El 1935,F 4,11:4
Pena, Pascual Garcia
Big Steal, The 1949,Jl 11,13:2
Torch, The 1950,Ag 21,15:2
My Man and I 1952,S 6,12:6
Jivaro 1954,F 13,11:5
Treasure of Pancho Villa, The 1955,N 25,38:2
Pena, Pastora
Cinco Advertencias de Satanas, Las; Satan's Five Warnings 1939,Ja 14,13:2
Penbroke, Clifford
Irish Destiny 1927,Mr 29,23:2 (In Addenda)
Pendleton, Diane
Around the World 1943,N 25,39:2
Pendleton, Gaylord
Success 1923,Jl 10,22:5
Manslaughter 1930,Jl 24,26:4
Up the River 1930,O 11,21:3
Seas Beneath 1931,Ja 31,15:1
Last Parade, The 1931,Mr 2,19:1
Young Sinners 1931,My 9,15:4
Informer, The 1935,My 10,25:2
Internes Can't Take Money 1937,My 6,23:2
Duke of West Point, The 1938,D 16,33:2
Geronimo 1940,F 8,18:3
One Crowded Night 1940,Ag 27,17:2
Untamed Fury 1947,Ap 26,10:6
Pendleton, Nat
Hoosier Schoolmaster, The 1924,Mr 18,25:2
Let's Get Married 1926,Mr 2,22:1
Laughing Lady, The 1930,Ja 4,21:1
Big Pond, The 1930,My 19,21:1
Last of the Duanes 1930,S 13,9:3
Liliom 1930,O 4,15:2
Sea Wolf, The 1930,O 6,21:1
Seas Beneath 1931,Ja 31,15:1
Mr Lemon of Orange 1931,Mr 28,15:3
Spirit of Notre Dame, The 1931,O 16,27:1
Blonde Crazy 1931,D 4,28:2
Secret Witness, The 1931,D 21,28:4
Manhattan Parade 1931,D 25,29:2
Taxi 1932,Ja 8,27:3
Play Girl 1932,Mr 19,11:2
Attorney for the Defense 1932,My 28,18:2
Horse Feathers 1932,Ag 11,12:2
Night Club Lady, The 1932,Ag 27,13:4
Sign of the Cross, The 1932,D 1,25:1
Deception 1933,Ja 10,26:2
Whistling in the Dark 1933,F 5,IX,5:1
Goldie Gets Along 1933,Je 3,16:4
Baby Face 1933,Je 24,16:2
Lady for a Day 1933,S 8,22:2
Penthouse 1933,S 9,9:2
I'm no Angel 1933,O 14,18:2
College Coach 1933,N 11,10:4
Chief, The 1933,D 2,9:4
Fugitive Lovers 1934,Ja 13,16:3
Lazy River 1934,Ap 4,26:2
Sing and Like It 1934,Ap 14,18:2
Manhattan Melodrama 1934,My 5,22:2
Thin Man, The 1934,Je 30,18:5
Girl From Missouri, The 1934,Ag 4,14:6
Defense Rests, The 1934,Ag 16,20:3
Cat's Paw, The 1934,Ag 17,12:2
Straight Is the Way 1934,Ag 29,13:2
Death on the Diamond 1934,S 24,14:1

Pendleton, Nat— Cont

Gay Bride, The 1934,D 19,27:2
Times Square Lady 1935,Mr 15,25:3
Reckless 1935,Ap 20,16:1
Murder in the Fleet 1935,Je 3,22:2
It's in the Air 1935,N 8,18:2
Garden Murder Case, The 1936,Mr 2,13:2
Great Ziegfeld, The 1936,Ap 9,21:2
Trapped by Television 1936,Je 15,24:3
Sworn Enemy 1936,S 12,20:1
Two in a Crowd 1936,O 5,25:1
Luckiest Girl in the World, The 1936,D 5,16:3
Sing Me a Love Song 1936,D 26,15:2
Under Cover of Night 1937,Ja 20,18:4
Gangway 1937,Ag 21,7:3
Life Begins In College 1937,O 9,16:1
Swing Your Lady 1938,Ja 27,17:2
Arsene Lupin Returns 1938,Mr 9,21:1
Fast Company 1938,Jl 6,21:2
Shopworn Angel, The 1938,Jl 8,11:2
Chaser, The 1938,Ag 2,15:3
Crowd Roars, The 1938,Ag 5,11:1
Young Doctor Kildare 1938,O 28,27:1
Calling Dr Kildare 1939,My 12,25:4
It's a Wonderful World 1939,My 19,27:2
Six Thousand Enemies 1939,Je 9,26:2
On Borrowed Time 1939,Jl 7,13:2
At the Circus 1939,N 17,17:2
Another Thin Man 1939,N 24,29:1
Secret of Dr Kildare, The 1939,D 8,33:5
Northwest Passage 1940,Mr 8,25:1
Dr Kildare's Strange Case 1940,Ap 12,19:2
Phantom Raiders 1940,Je 24,19:5
Dr Kildare Goes Home 1940,S 19,27:4
Golden Fleecing, The 1940,N 7,33:4
Dr Kildare's Crisis 1940,D 19,33:1
Flight Command 1941,Ja 17,21:2
Buck Privates 1941,F 14,15:2
Top Sergeant Mulligan 1941,N 12,31:3
Mad Doctor of Market Street, The 1942,Ja 5,21:5
Jail House Blues 1942,F 6,23:2
Calling Dr Gillespie 1942,Jl 9,17:4
Swing Fever 1944,Ja 28,14:1
Buck Privates Come Home 1947,Ap 12,11:3
Pendleton, Nat (Original Author)
Deception 1933,Ja 10,26:2
Pendleton, Steve
Beyond Glory 1948,Ag 4,18:2
Rio Grande 1950,N 20,21:2
Pendrell, Ernest (Screenwriter)
Violators, The 1959,Ag 4,32:5
Penella, Emma
Fedra, the Devil's Daughter 1957,O 26,19:2
Not on Your Life; Verdugo, El 1965,Mr 30,52:1
Penella, Manuel (Original Author)
Tiger Love 1924,Je 16,18:3
Penish, Leonard
Paisan 1948,Mr 30,26:2
Penkert, Rainer
Stefanie 1959,Je 18,36:1
Rest Is Silence, The 1960,Ag 2,22:6
Saboteur, The: Code Name-Mori Turi 1965,Ag 26,40:2
Penkovitch, N
Sunny Youth 1935,Ag 19,18:2
Penley, Derrick
Odette 1951,Mr 28,33:2
Penman, Lea
Stella 1950,Ag 19,9:2
Fancy Pants 1950,Ag 31,21:2
We're no Angels 1955,Jl 8,15:2
Portland Expose 1957,S 27,16:6
Penn, Arthur (Director)
Left Handed Gun, The 1958,My 8,36:2
Miracle Worker, The 1962,My 24,29:2
Mickey One 1965,S 9,36:1
Chase, The 1966,F 19,24:1
Bonnie and Clyde 1967,Ag 14,36:1
Penn, Beverly
Teen Age 1944,Je 19,17:1
Penn, Dena
Days of Glory 1944,Je 17,10:2
Penn, Leo
Undercover Man, The 1949,Ap 21,30:2
Not Wanted 1949,Jl 25,11:4
Story of Page One, The 1960,Ja 14,28:1
Birdman of Alcatraz 1962,Jl 19,19:2
Penn, Leo (Director)
Man Called Adam, A 1966,Ag 4,24:2
Penn, Leonard
Between Two Women 1937,Ag 6,21:1
Firefly, The 1937,S 2,17:2
Man-Proof 1938,Ja 14,21:1
Girl of the Golden West, The 1938,Mr 25,15:2
Judge Hardy's Children 1938,Ap 8,17:2
Toy Wife, The 1938,Je 24,15:1
Marie Antoinette 1938,Ag 17,23:2
Bachelor Mother 1939,Je 30,17:2
Penna, Tarva
Man With 100 Faces 1938,N 1,27:2
Pennberg, Jean-Marc
7 Capital Sins (Anger); Anger (7Capital Sins) 1963,Ja 17,5:2

Pennebaker, D A (Cinematographer)
Wild 90 1968,Ja 8,33:1
Monterey Pop 1968,D 27,44:1
Pennebaker, D A (Director)
Monterey Pop 1968,D 27,44:1
Pennell, Dan
You Can't Fool Your Wife 1923,Ap 24,25:3
Price of a Party, The 1924,N 26,17:3
Bluebeard's Seven Wives 1925,D 28,19:2
Pennell, Larry
Seven Angry Men 1955,Ap 2,15:2
Far Horizons, The 1955,My 21,11:1
F B I Story, The 1959,S 25,23:1
Pennell, Nicholas
Only When I Larf 1968,O 24,55:3
Pennell, R O
Dressed to Kill 1928,Mr 12,26:1
Clothes Make the Woman 1928,Je 5,21:1
On the Level 1930,Jl 5,17:4
Penner, Erdman (Miscellaneous)
Reluctant Dragon, The 1941,Jl 25,12:2
Penner, Erdman (Screenwriter)
Pinocchio 1940,F 8,18:3
Victory Through Air Power 1943,Jl 19,13:1
Adventures of Ichabod and Mr Toad, The 1949,O 10,18:2
Cinderella 1950,F 23,33:1
Lady and the Tramp 1955,Je 24,17:1
Sleeping Beauty 1959,F 18,36:1
Penner, Joe
College Rhythm 1934,N 24,19:1
Collegiate 1936,Ja 23,25:2
New Faces of 1937 1937,Jl 2,25:1
Life of the Party, The 1937,O 4,17:1
Go Chase Yourself 1938,Je 15,27:1
I'm From the City 1938,Ag 19,13:4
Mr Doodle Kicks Off 1938,S 28,29:4
Day the Bookies Wept, The 1939,S 14,18:2
Millionaire Playboy 1940,Mr 16,8:2
Boys From Syracuse, The 1940,Ag 1,25:2
Penner, Joe (Miscellaneous)
New Faces of 1937 1937,Jl 2,25:1
Penner, Walter
Woman Is the Judge, A 1939,S 28,29:5
PENNEY
See Also PENNY
Penney, Ralph
Devil Commands, The 1941,F 14,15:3
Pennick, Jack
Lone Eagle, The 1927,D 20,33:2
Four Sons 1928,F 14,27:1
Why Sailors Go Wrong 1928,Ap 9,18:2
Plastered in Paris 1928,S 24,25:1
Strong Boy 1929,Ap 1,22:1
Way out West 1930,Ag 18,24:1
Strange People 1933,Je 17,16:5
Tugboat Annie 1933,Ag 12,14:2
King of the Newsboys 1938,Ap 2,18:2
Submarine Patrol 1938,N 19,9:2
Drums Along the Mohawk 1939,N 4,11:2
Lady From Louisiana 1941,My 15,27:2
They Were Expendable 1945,D 21,25:2
Fort Apache 1948,Je 25,26:2
Three Godfathers 1949,Mr 4,25:2
Fighting Kentuckian, The 1949,S 19,18:3
When Willie Comes Marching Home 1950,F 18,9:2
Operation Pacific 1951,F 3,10:2
Beast From 20,000 Fathoms, The 1953,Je 25,23:1
Mister Roberts 1955,Jl 15,14:1
Pennings, Fred
Don Juan 1956,Mr 6,26:2
Pennington, Ann
Susie Snowflake 1916,Je 26,11:3
Rainbow Princess, The 1916,O 23,10:3
Kiss in the Dark, A 1925,Ap 7,17:3
Lucky Horseshoe, The 1925,Ag 18,14:3
Night Club 1929,Ag 12,22:2
Gold Diggers of Broadway, The 1929,Ag 31,13:4
Is Everybody Happy? 1929,N 2,14:6
Night Parade 1929,N 11,20:2
Tanned Legs 1929,D 2,28:2
Happy Days 1930,F 14,20:1
China Girl 1943,Ja 21,27:2
Pennington, Jon (Producer)
Shadow of the Cat, The 1961,Je 8,40:2
In the Wake of a Stranger 1961,Je 22,23:3
Valiant, The 1962,Je 14,23:4
Liquidator, The 1966,O 29,34:1
Pennington-Richards, C M (Director)
Magic Garden, The 1952,F 6,24:2
Double Bunk 1961,N 17,41:3
Ladies Who Do 1963,N 26,52:2
Pennington-Richards, C M (Miscellaneous)
Guns at Batasi 1964,N 17,47:1
Pennington-Richards, C M (Screenwriter)
Horse's Mouth, The 1954,Ja 20,33:4
Double Bunk 1961,N 17,41:3
PENNY
See Also PENNEY
Penny, Pat
Forty Thousand Horsemen 1941,Ag 15,13:2
Bush Christmas 1947,N 27,50:4

Penrose, Charles
Human Monster, The 1940,Mr 25,11:2
Penrose, John
Voice in the Night, The 1941,My 23,25:4
Adventures of Tartu, The 1943,S 24,26:1
Corridor of Mirrors 1949,Mr 23,35:3
Kind Hearts and Coronets 1950,Je 15,41:2
Penrose, Peter
Sorrell and Son 1934,My 29,22:1
Old Curiosity Shop, The 1935,D 23,15:5
Pentecost, Hugh (Original Author)
Appointment With a Shadow 1959,Ja 8,24:2
Penwarden, Duncan
Gentlemen of the Press 1929,My 13,27:2
Lady Lies, The 1929,S 7,15:1
Penz, Julio
Happy Thieves, The 1962,F 5,19:4
Penzer, Paul
Under the Red Robe 1923,N 13,25:3
Peon, Ramon (Director)
Sagrario 1934,Ja 22,12:3
Obre las Olas 1934,Mr 17,11:4
Sobre Las Olas 1934,Mr 17,11:4
Tiburon 1934,Ap 18,23:3
Oro y Plata 1934,Ag 29,13:2
Llorona, La 1935,Jl 20,16:2
Tierra, Amor y Dolor 1935,Ag 10,16:5
Todo un Hombre 1936,Ja 6,20:5
Mas Alla de la Muerta 1936,Mr 2,13:3
Que Hago con la Criatura? 1936,Mr 17,25:6
Sor Juana Ines de la Cruz 1936,Je 6,21:2
Mujeres de Hoy 1936,D 7,27:4
Mujeres Sin Alma 1936,D 12,29:4
Silencio Sublime 1937,Ja 16,21:2
Liaga, La; Torment, The 1937,O 4,17:2
Forgive Me, Son 1937,O 23,14:2
Newspaper Boys, The 1937,N 6,14:3
no Basta ser Madre; Motherhood Is Not Enough 1938,Ja 31,15:2
Madrina del Diablo, La; Devil's Godmother, The 1938,F 21,15:2
Mujer Mexicana, La; Mexican Woman, The 1938,Ap 18,11:2
Romance del Palmar, El 1939,My 1,21:2
Aventura Peligrosa, Una; Dangerous Adventure, The 1940,My 20,13:2
Pep, Willie
Requiem for a Heavyweight 1962,O 17,35:1
Pepe, Nico
Bitter Rice 1950,S 19,39:2
Pepere (dog)
Belle Americaine, La 1961,D 18,42:1
Pepito
Tropic Holiday 1938,Je 30,21:2
Annabel Takes a Tour 1938,D 29,15:3
Peple, Edward (Original Author)
Beloved Bachelor, The 1931,O 17,20:1
Littlest Rebel, The 1935,D 20,30:1
PEPPARD
See Also PEPPER
Peppard, George
Strange One, The 1957,Ap 13,12:3
Pork Chop Hill 1959,My 30,9:2
Home from the Hill 1960,Mr 4,19:1
Subterraneans, The 1960,Jl 7,26:1
Breakfast at Tiffany's 1961,O 6,28:1
How the West Was Won 1963,Ap 1,54:1
Victors, The 1963,D 20,21:2
Carpetbaggers, The 1964,Jl 2,24:4
Operation Crossbow 1965,Ap 2,29:1
Third Day, The 1965,Ag 5,15:3
Blue Max, The 1966,Je 22,38:1
Tobruk 1967,F 9,33:2
Rough Night in Jericho 1967,N 9,56:4
P J 1968,Mr 7,52:3
What's so bad About Feeling Good? 1968,My 25,27:1
PEPPER
See Also PEPPARD
Pepper, Art
Subterraneans, The 1960,Jl 7,26:1
Pepper, Barbara
Our Daily Bread 1934,O 3,25:2
M'liss 1936,Ag 8,5:2
Wanted: Jane Turner 1936,N 30,24:7
Winterset 1936,D 4,31:1
You Can't Beat Love 1937,Je 25,25:3
Big Shot, The 1937,Ag 13,13:1
Forty Naughty Girls 1937,S 18,15:3
Music for Madame 1937,O 23,14:1
Westland Case, The 1937,O 23,14:2
Portia on Trial 1937,D 3,29:2
Stadium Murders, The 1938,Ap 9,11:2
Wide Open Faces 1938,Ap 15,23:2
Lady in the Morgue, The 1938,My 9,13:3
Army Girl 1938,Ag 12,11:1
They Made Me a Criminal 1939,Ja 21,19:2
Magnificent Fraud, The 1939,Jl 20,16:2
Flight at Midnight 1939,S 7,29:2
Three Sons 1939,N 24,29:3
Castle on the Hudson 1940,Mr 4,11:2
Women in War 1940,My 30,21:2
Return of Frank James, The 1940,Ag 10,16:4

Pepper, Barbara— Cont
Manpower 1941,Jl 5,14:2
Man at Large 1941,O 11,21:4
Birth of the Blues 1941,D 11,39:1
Murder, He Says 1945,Je 25,20:3
Child Is Waiting, A 1963,F 14,5:6
Kiss Me, Stupid 1964,D 23,22:2
Pepper, Buddy
Streets of New York 1939,My 1,21:1
Seventeen 1940,F 29,15:2
Reluctant Dragon, The 1941,Jl 25,12:2
Pepper, Buddy (Composer)
Mister Big 1943,Je 14,13:4
Pepper, Cynthia
Kissin' Cousins 1964,Ap 2,28:3
Pepper, Dan (Original Author)
Enemy General, The 1960,O 20,42:2
Pepper, Dan (Screenwriter)
Enemy General, The 1960,O 20,42:2
Pepper, Harry
Co-Optimists, The 1930,F 5,27:2
Pepper, Harry S (Miscellaneous)
My Heart Is Calling 1935,Ap 15,16:3
Pepper, Jack
Stop, You're Killing Me 1952,D 11,45:3
Pepper, Sgt, Lonely Hearts Club Band
Yellow Submarine 1968,N 14,56:1
Peppler, Hans
Brand in der Oper 1932,Jl 11,11:4
1914: The Last Days Before the War 1932,S 5,9:6
Pepys, Samuel (Miscellaneous)
Nell Gwyn 1935,Je 20,16:2
Pera, Lisa
Do Not Disturb 1965,D 25,17:2
Perago, Didi
Vista, La; Visit, The 1966,Ag 10,32:1
Perakos, Sperie (Producer)
Antigone 1962,S 19,30:1
Perbellini, Dina
Cappello a Tre Punte, Il 1936,S 28,14:5
Perbellini, Dirce
Iron Crown 1949,Je 11,11:2
Perchicaut, Nicolas
Man of the Sea 1948,Ja 24,11:2
Night Heaven Fell, The 1958,O 22,40:4
Percival, Hugh (Producer)
Three Cases of Murder (Lord Mountdrago); Lord
Mountdrago (Three Cases of Murder)
1955,Mr 16,39:4
Three Cases of Murder (In the Picture); In the
Picture (Three Cases of Murder)
1955,Mr 16,39:4
Three Cases of Murder (You Killed Elizabeth);
You Killed Elizabeth (Three Cases of Murder)
1955,Mr 16,39:4
Raising a Riot 1957,My 8,44:1
Percival, Hugh (Screenwriter)
Raising a Riot 1957,My 8,44:1
Percival, Walter
Moral Sinner, The 1924,Ap 7,15:3
Big City, The 1928,Mr 26,26:2
Lights of New York 1928,Jl 9,25:1
Lightnin' 1930,N 29,21:4
Smart Money 1931,Je 19,21:1
Homicide Squad 1931,O 19,28:1
Blonde Crazy 1931,D 4,28:2
Carnival Boat 1932,Mr 21,19:5
Cabin in the Cotton 1932,S 30,17:3
Percy, David
William Fox Movietone Follies of 1929
1929,My 27,22:1
Monte Carlo 1930,Ag 28,22:4
Percy, Edward (Original Author)
Ladies in Retirement 1941,N 7,27:1
Percy, Edward (Screenwriter)
Brides of Dracula, The 1960,S 6,41:4
Percy, Eileen
Brass Buttons 1919,Ap 7,11:5
In Mizzoura 1919,O 13,16:3
Fast Mail, The 1922,Jl 10,9:5
Flirt, The 1922,D 31,VII,2:2 (In Addenda)
Within the Law 1923,Ap 30,11:2
Children of Jazz 1923,Jl 9,8:4
Tongues of Flame 1924,D 16,28:1
Under the Rouge 1925,Jl 22,14:4
Souls for Sables 1925,S 15,12:1 (Incorrect in this
edition; use 1925,S 15,29:1 elsewhere)
Fine Clothes 1925,O 20,28:1
Cobra 1925,D 7,19:1
Lovey Mary 1926,Je 21,17:2
Twelve Miles Out 1927,Jl 26,17:1
Spring Fever 1927,O 18,33:2
Telling the World 1928,Jl 16,25:3
Wicked 1931,S 19,10:2
Cohens and Kellys in Hollywood, The
1932,Ap 22,23:2
Percy, Esme
Murder 1930,O 25,20:6
Bitter Sweet 1933,Ag 24,18:2
Unfinished Symphony 1935,Ja 14,11:2
Nell Gwyn 1935,Je 20,16:2
Spy 77 1936,F 10,15:1
Amateur Gentleman, The 1936,Ap 27,19:2
Abdul the Damned 1936,My 11,16:2

Accused 1936,D 17,35:1
When Thief Meets Thief 1937,Je 15,26:2
Two Who Dared 1937,Jl 10,18:2
Return of the Scarlet Pimpernel, The
1938,Ap 11,12:2
Invitation to the Waltz 1938,Jl 2,10:3
Pygmalion 1938,D 8,34:2
Forbidden Music 1938,D 27,13:2
21 Days Together 1940,My 23,28:4
Percyval, T Wigney (Original Author)
Grumpy 1923,Mr 26,16:2
Perczel, Zita
Az Uj Rokon 1935,Mr 12,25:3
Perczell, Zita
As Uj Rokon; New Relative, The
1935,Mr 12,25:3
Budai Cukraszda 1936,Ja 2,21:5
Meseauto 1936,N 10,31:4
Affair of Honor, An 1937,S 20,19:1
Once a Week 1937,O 2,18:1
Marika 1938,N 19,9:3
Lovers and Thieves 1958,Ag 5,23:2
Perdriere, Helene
Roi des Resquilleurs, Le 1932,Je 13,19:3
Mon Coeur Balance 1933,F 3,21:4
Homme a Hommes D' 1948,Ag 30,14:8
Man to Men 1949,F 21,20:2
Topaze 1952,O 28,37:1
If all the Guys in the World 1957,Ap 23,34:1
Perdue, Derelys
Last Man on Earth, The 1924,D 13,12:4
Pereda, Ramon
Gente Alegre 1933,S 19,26:4
Cascarrabias 1933,O 30,14:2
Noche del Pecado, La 1933,D 26,19:4
Sagrario 1934,Ja 22,12:3
Payasada de la Vida; Tricks of Life
1935,Mr 18,14:5
Vuelo de la Muerte, El 1935,Ap 16,27:3
Llorona, La 1935,Jl 20,16:2
Heroe de Nacozari, El 1935,S 23,20:4
No Mataras; Thou Shalt not Kill 1935,N 11,20:2
Crimen de Media Noche, El 1936,F 22,12:3
Diablo Del Mar, El 1936,Ap 1,29:2
Malditas Sean las Mujeres 1936,Ag 29,16:3
Irma la Mala 1936,O 6,28:7
Mujeres de Hoy 1936,D 7,27:4
Cuatro Milpas, Las; Four Corn Patches, The
1937,S 13,17:2
Baul Macabro, El; Macabre Trunk, The
1937,N 30,26:3
Olvidados de Dios, Los; Those Forgotten by God
1940,Ja 15,11:2
Gavilan, El; Hawk, The 1940,Ja 22,11:2
Mexico Lindo 1940,F 10,19:2
Pereda, Ramon (Director)
Cuatro Milpas, Las; Four Corn Patches, The
1937,S 13,17:2
Mexico Lindo 1939,F 4,11:1
Olvidados de Dios, Los; Those Forgotten by God
1940,Ja 15,11:2
Gavilan, El; Hawk, The 1940,Ja 22,11:2
Pereda, Ramon (Producer)
Mexico Lindo 1939,F 4,11:1
Olvidados de Dios, Los; Those Forgotten by God
1940,Ja 15,11:2
Gavilan, El; Hawk, The 1940,Ja 22,11:2
Perego, Didi
Everybody go Home!; Tutti a Casa 1962,N 6,38:1
Little Nuns, The 1966,Ap 28,49:1
Perego, Maria (Screenwriter)
World of Topo Gigio 1965,N 27,34:1
Peregonjetz, A F
Aelita: The Revolt of the Robots
1929,Mr 26,34:1
Pereira, William (Producer)
From This Day Forward 1946,Ap 20,16:2
Perelli, Carlos
Besos Brujos; Bewitching Kisses 1939,O 21,12:3
Perelman, Laura (Original Author)
Paris Interlude 1934,Jl 28,16:5
Larceny, Inc 1942,Ap 25,9:1
Perelman, Laura (Screenwriter)
Florida Special 1936,My 29,15:2
Ambush 1939,F 9,17:2
Golden Fleecing, The 1940,N 7,33:4
Perelman, S J (Original Author)
Paris Interlude 1934,Jl 28,16:5
Larceny, Inc 1942,Ap 25,9:1
One Touch of Venus 1948,O 29,29:5
Perelman, S J (Screenwriter)
Monkey Business 1931,O 8,22:6
Horse Feathers 1932,Ag 11,12:2
Florida Special 1936,My 29,15:2
Ambush 1939,F 9,17:2
Golden Fleecing, The 1940,N 7,33:4
Around the World in 80 Days 1956,O 18,37:1
Perelshtein, R (Miscellaneous)
University of Life 1941,F 26,17:1
Perenyi, Laszlo
Nagymama 1935,D 30,15:1
Budai Cukraszda 1936,Ja 2,21:5
Kiralyne Huszarja, A 1936,Ja 17,15:3

Perenyi, Laszlo— Cont
Erik/a/Buzakalasz; Wheat Ripens, The
1939,S 11,15:2
Vadroza; Wild Rose 1940,Ja 29,11:6
Peres, Marcel
It Happened at the Inn; Goupi Mains Rouge
1945,D 22,16:2
Panic 1947,N 27,50:2
Justice Is Done 1953,Mr 3,23:2
We Are all Murderers 1957,Ja 9,27:2
Parisienne, La 1958,Jl 31,27:1
Perestiani, I
They Wanted Peace 1940,Ja 8,11:3
Perestiani, Ivan (Director)
Scandal? 1929,O 28,20:1
Anush 1932,N 7,20:3
Peretti, Pio
Lone Wolf in Paris, The 1938,My 23,21:2
Perevertsev, Ilya
Winner, The 1947,D 1,27:2
Pereverzev, I
Dream of a Cossack 1952,F 18,15:2
Admiral Ushakov 1954,Ja 18,19:2
Attack From the Sea 1954,Ap 19,19:4
Conflict 1955,D 26,23:4
Heroes of Shipka 1956,S 3,10:5
Lust for Gold 1958,Jl 24,18:1
Perez
Port of Shadows 1939,O 30,13:2
Louise 1940,F 3,9:4
Human Beast, The 1940,F 20,17:2
Daybreak 1940,Jl 30,16:2
Perez, Angos
Lydia Bailey 1952,My 31,12:5
Perez, Barbara
No Man is an Island 1962,O 11,49:2
Perez, Ben
Huk! 1956,D 15,20:4
Perez, Isabel Maria
10:30 PM Summer 1966,O 20,52:1
Perez, Ismael
Bullfighter and the Lady, The 1951,Ap 27,19:2
Perez, Jaquelin
Loves of a Greek in Paris 1960,Ag 15,19:7
Perez, Jeanne
Devil in the Flesh 1949,My 10,29:2
Love Game, The 1960,N 9,44:1
Perez, Jose
We Were Strangers 1949,Ap 28,28:2
Life in the Balance, A 1955,Jl 14,19:1
Young Savages, The 1961,My 25,31:1
Perez, Jose Eduardo
Mujer de Nadie, La; Nobody's Wife
1938,F 7,10:3
Perez, Paul (Original Author)
Hotel Continental 1932,Mr 21,19:5
Perez, Paul (Screenwriter)
Last of the Mohicans, The 1936,S 3,17:3
Missing Guest, The 1938,S 7,30:7
Perfitt, Frank
Night Birds 1931,Ja 3,21:2
Pergantis, E (Producer)
Youth of Athens 1949,O 31,20:4
Pergaud, Louis (Original Author)
Generals Without Buttons 1938,Mr 8,23:2
War of the Buttons, The 1963,D 19,40:2
Pergialis, Notis
Girl in Black, A 1957,S 17,39:2
Peridsky, Rodja
Pimpernel Svensson 1953,F 6,16:4
Perier, Etienne (Director)
Bridge to the Sun 1961,O 18,50:1
Swordsman of Siena 1962,D 6,55:3
Perier, Francois
Man About Town 1947,O 22,37:1
Lover's Return, A; Revenant, Le 1948,Ja 26,15:2
Loves of Colette 1949,D 3,8:6
Sylvie and the Phantom 1950,O 16,30:5
Orpheus 1950,N 30,42:2
Bed, The (The Pompadour Bed); Pompadour Bed,
The (The Bed) 1955,Je 8,26:4
It Happened in the Park 1957,Ag 13,23:2
Cabiria 1957,O 29,34:2
Gervaise 1957,N 12,46:1
Demoniaque 1958,Mr 4,34:5
Love and the Frenchwoman; (Francaise et
l'Amour, La) 1961,F 28,38:2
Five Day Lover, The 1961,D 14,55:4
Testament of Orpheus 1962,Ap 10,48:1
Organizer, The 1964,My 7,31:2
Sweet and Sour 1964,D 28,34:2
Vista, La; Visit, The 1966,Ag 10,32:1
Perier, Francois (Narrator)
Melbourne Rendezvous 1957,O 11,38:4
Perier, Jean
Pasteur 1936,Ja 30,14:3
Forty Little Mothers 1938,D 23,16:3
Three Waltzes 1939,Ap 25,19:2
Entente Cordiale 1939,D 26,23:2
Perilli, Ivo (Original Author)
Anna 1953,F 19,20:5
Three Forbidden Stories 1953,N 16,21:4

Perilli, Ivo (Screenwriter)
Anna 1953,F 19,20:5
Greatest Love, The 1954,Ja 12,19:2
Mambo 1955,Mr 31,23:3
Ulysses 1955,Ag 18,17:2
War and Peace 1956,Ag 22,26:2
Five Branded Women 1960,Je 2,27:2
Periolat, George
Rosita 1923,S 4,14:1
Slave of Desire 1923,D 11,26:2
Yankee Consul, The 1924,F 11,18:3
Red Lily, The 1924,S 29,10:1
Any Woman 1925,My 27,26:2
Butterflies in the Rain 1926,D 25,10:5
Secret Hour, The 1928,Mr 12,26:1
Night Watch, The 1928,O 8,14:2
Periquet, Fernando (Original Author)
Goyescas 1944,My 29,18:3
Peris, Frank
Lust for Life 1956,S 18,39:1
Perist-Petrenko, V
Heroes Are Made 1944,Mr 11,10:2
Perkins, Al (Screenwriter)
Girl on the Front Page, The 1936,N 7,15:2
Reluctant Dragon, The 1941,Jl 25,12:2
Perkins, Anthony
Actress, The 1953,O 13,34:1
Friendly Persuasion 1956,N 2,30:1
Fear Strikes Out 1957,Mr 21,37:2
Tin Star, The 1957,O 24,37:2
Desire Under the Elms 1958,Mr 13,24:2
This Angry Age 1958,Je 26,23:3
Matchmaker, The 1958,Ag 13,22:1
Green Mansions 1959,Mr 20,26:1
On the Beach 1959,D 18,34:1
Tall Story 1960,Ap 7,46:1
Psycho 1960,Je 17,37:1
Goodbye Again 1961,Je 30,32:2
Phaedra 1962,O 19,24:1
Trial, The 1963,F 21,5:1
Five Miles to Midnight 1963,Mr 21,8:6
Two Are Guilty 1964,F 29,12:1
Is Paris Burning? 1966,N 11,36:1
Champagne Murders, The 1968,Ap 25,53:1
Pretty Poison 1968,O 25,55:1
Perkins, Caroline
Old Hutch 1936,D 7,27:4
Perkins, Gil
Hans Christian Andersen 1952,N 26,20:2
Perkins, Grace (Original Author)
Personal Maid 1931,S 5,7:4
No More Orchids 1933,Ja 2,29:2
Air Hostess 1933,Ja 23,9:2
Torch Singer 1933,O 7,18:5
Perkins, Julia
Old Hutch 1936,D 7,27:4
Perkins, Kenneth (Original Author)
Beloved Brute, The 1924,N 10,20:1
Relentless 1948,Mr 6,17:3
Riding Shotgun 1954,Ap 2,22:2
Perkins, Kenneth (Screenwriter)
Song of India 1949,Je 10,32:3
Perkins, Millie
Diary of Anne Frank, The 1959,Mr 19,40:1
Wild in the Country 1961,Je 10,12:2
Ensign Pulver 1964,Ag 1,13:2
Wild in the Streets 1968,My 30,21:1
Perkins, Osgood
Cradle Buster, The 1922,My 22,18:4
Puritan Passions 1923,O 15,15:4
Wild, Wild Susan 1925,Ag 5,12:4
Love 'Em and Leave 'Em 1926,D 8,24:3
Knockout Reilly 1927,Ap 18,21:2
Syncopation 1929,Ap 8,32:1
Mother's Boy 1929,My 8,34:6
Tarnished Lady 1931,Ap 30,29:3
Scarface, The Shame of the Nation
1932,My 20,22:3
Madame Du Barry 1934,O 25,26:2
Kansas City Princess 1934,N 5,23:1
President Vanishes, The 1934,D 8,18:5
I Dream too Much 1935,N 29,24:1
Gold Diggers of 1937 1936,D 25,19:2
Perkins, Sydney
Phone Call From a Stranger 1952,F 2,11:2
Perkins, Valentine
Rock Island Trail 1950,Je 5,19:3
Perkins, Voltaire
Man Called Peter, A 1955,Ap 1,22:1
Macabre 1958,Jl 24,18:1
Compulsion 1959,Ap 2,26:2
Perkins, Walter
Bill Henry 1919,Ag 18,9:2
Peaceful Valley 1920,O 11,19:3
Perkins, William R
Subterraneans, The 1960,Jl 7,26:1
Perl, Alan
Toy Wife, The 1938,Je 24,15:1
Perl, Arnold (Screenwriter)
Jazz on a Summer's Day 1960,Mr 29,46:2
Perlberg, William (Producer)
Doctor Takes a Wife, The 1940,Je 15,12:2
Charley's Aunt 1941,Ag 2,18:2

Remember the Day 1941,D 26,21:2
Ten Gentlemen From West Point 1942,Je 5,23:3
Magnificent Dope, The 1942,Jl 3,12:5
Meanest Man in the World, The 1943,F 25,27:3
Coney Island 1943,Je 17,17:2
Sweet Rosie O'Grady 1943,O 21,30:2
Claudia 1943,N 5,23:2
Song of Bernadette, The 1944,Ja 27,15:2
Eve of St Mark, The 1944,My 31,22:2
Billy Rose's Diamond Horseshoe 1945,My 3,37:1
Where Do We Go From Here? 1945,Je 7,25:2
Junior Miss 1945,Je 18,15:4
State Fair 1945,Ag 31,14:3
Claudia and David 1946,Ag 15,19:2
Shocking Miss Pilgrim, The 1947,F 12,34:2
Miracle on 34th Street 1947,Je 5,32:1
Forever Amber 1947,O 23,31:2
Escape 1948,Ag 16,12:2
Apartment for Peggy 1948,O 16,9:2
Chicken every Sunday 1949,Ja 19,34:2
Forbidden Street, The 1949,My 14,9:2
It Happens Every Spring 1949,Je 11,11:2
Slattery's Hurricane 1949,Ag 13,6:6
Big Lift, The 1950,Ap 27,37:2
Wabash Avenue 1950,Ap 29,8:3
I'll Get by 1950,N 2,39:3
For Heaven's Sake 1950,D 16,10:5
Rhubarb 1951,Ag 31,12:2
Anything Can Happen 1952,Ap 4,21:1
Aaron Slick From Punkin Crick 1952,Ap 19,18:6
Somebody Loves Me 1952,S 25,38:1
Little Boy Lost 1953,S 22,38:2
Country Girl, The 1954,D 16,51:2
Bridges at Toko-Ri, The 1955,Ja 21,20:2
Proud and Profane, The 1956,Je 14,41:2
Tin Star, The 1957,O 24,37:2
Teacher's Pet 1958,Mr 20,33:1
But Not for Me 1959,O 3,14:6
Rat Race, The 1960,My 26,37:3
Pleasure of his Company, The 1961,Je 2,36:1
Counterfeit Traitor, The 1962,Ap 18,28:1
Hook, The 1963,F 16,5:6
Twilight of Honor 1963,N 14,41:2
36 Hours 1965,Ja 29,25:2
Perlman, E
Tkies Khaf; (Vow, The) 1938,S 15,29:3
Perlman, Milton (Producer)
Goddess, The 1958,Je 25,24:1
Pernerstorter, Alois
Rosenkavalier, Der 1962,O 10,57:1
Pernet, Andre
Ballerina 1938,N 15,27:1
Louise 1940,F 3,9:4
Pernice, Gino
Italiano Brava Gente 1966,F 4,20:1
Perojo, Benito (Director)
Mama 1933,Jl 8,14:6
Se ha Fugado un Preso 1935,My 21,22:3
Susana Tiene un Secreto 1935,Je 5,22:2
Hombre que se Reia del Amor, El 1935,Jl 18,15:3
Crisis Mundial; World Crisis 1937,F 15,12:6
Verbena de la Paloma, La 1938,O 25,19:2
Rumbo al Cairo; Bound for Cairo 1940,Je 8,18:3
Goyescas 1944,My 29,18:3
Song of Dolores 1951,Je 16,9:2
Perov, Yuri
Yolanta 1964,D 23,22:3
Perrault, Charles (Original Author)
Cinderella 1950,F 23,33:1
Sleeping Beauty 1959,F 18,36:1
Perrault, Louis
Mr Hulot's Holiday 1954,Je 17,36:2
Perrault, Pierre (Director)
Moontrap, The; Pour la Suite du Monde
1964,N 11,38:1
Perrault, Pierre (Screenwriter)
Moontrap, The; Pour la Suite du Monde
1964,N 11,38:1
Perrault, Serge
Tonight We Sing 1953,F 13,17:2
Folies Bergere 1958,My 28,37:2
Perreau, Gerald
San Diego, I Love You 1944,N 10,25:1
Possessed 1947,My 30,25:2
Perreau, Gigi
Mr Skeffington 1944,My 26,23:2
Song of Love 1947,O 10,31:2
Green Dolphin Street 1947,O 16,34:2
Enchantment 1948,D 27,16:2
Family Honeymoon 1949,F 25,28:2
Roseanna McCoy 1949,O 13,33:2
My Foolish Heart 1950,Ja 20,29:2
Shadow on the Wall 1950,My 19,31:3
Never a Dull Moment 1950,N 22,20:2
For Heaven's Sake 1950,D 16,10:5
Has Anybody Seen My Gal 1952,Jl 5,7:2
There's Always Tomorrow 1956,Ja 21,18:2
Man in the Gray Flannel Suit, The
1956,Ap 13,21:1
Dance With Me Henry 1956,D 24,8:2
Tammy Tell me True 1961,Jl 27,23:2
Look in any Window 1962,Mr 22,40:1

Perreau, Janine
Song of Love 1947,O 10,31:2
Red Danube, The 1949,D 9,37:3
Redhead and the Cowboy, The 1951,Je 6,37:2
M 1951,Je 11,20:7
3 for Bedroom C 1952,Je 27,18:3
Perreins, Michele (Screenwriter)
Truth, The 1961,Je 27,23:2
Perrer, Barbara
Big Game, The 1936,O 24,23:1
Perret, Jacques (Original Author)
Sheep Has Five Legs, The 1955,Ag 10,19:2
Elusive Corporal, The 1963,F 19,5:1
Perret, Leonce (Director)
Madame Sans Gene 1925,Ap 18,19:1
Morgane, the Enchantress 1929,Je 21,17:2
Culte de Beaute, Le 1931,Je 8,21:1
Perret, Leonce (Producer)
Lafayette, We Come 1918,N 4,11:3
Perrey, Mireille
Miquette 1951,F 5,18:2
Hotel Sahara 1952,Ja 1,21:4
Prize, The 1952,Ap 30,33:2
Three Sinners 1952,Jl 8,23:2
Dr Knock 1955,O 10,31:2
Green Mare, The; Jument Verte, La
1961,O 24,41:2
Umbrellas of Cherbourg, The; Parpapluis de
Cherbourg, Les 1964,D 17,50:1
Perri, John
Babes in Toyland 1961,D 15,49:1
Perri, Marko
Flesh Merchant, The 1956,My 19,12:6
Perrin, Jack
Those Who Dance 1924,Je 30,16:1
Water Hole, The 1928,S 3,14:2
Perrin, Jacques
Girl With a Suitcase 1961,S 12,36:2
Family Diary 1963,N 12,48:1
Sleeping Car Murder, The 1966,Mr 8,45:1
Almost a Man 1966,S 23,43:1
All the Other Girls Do! 1967,My 30,12:1
Young Girls of Rochefort, The 1968,Ap 12,50:1
Perrin, Nat (Original Author)
Pigskin Parade 1936,N 14,23:3
Big Store, The 1941,Je 27,14:4
Hellzapoppin 1941,D 26,21:4
Abbott and Costello in Hollywood
1945,N 23,26:2
Frankie and Johnny 1966,Jl 21,20:2
Perrin, Nat (Producer)
No Time to Marry 1938,F 23,27:2
Mighty McGurk, The 1947,Ap 4,19:4
Song of the Thin Man 1947,Ag 29,14:2
Petty Girl, The 1950,Ag 18,17:2
Emergency Wedding 1950,D 22,19:2
Perrin, Nat (Screenwriter)
Kid Millions 1934,N 12,17:2
Rose of the Rancho 1936,Ja 9,25:2
Stowaway 1936,D 19,16:1
Don't Tell the Wife 1937,F 19,15:2
New Faces of 1937 1937,Jl 2,25:1
On Again-Off Again 1937,S 18,15:3
Gracie Allen Murder Case, The 1939,Je 8,31:3
Alias the Deacon 1940,My 14,27:5
Hullabaloo 1940,D 19,33:1
Keep 'Em Flying 1941,N 27,29:2
Hellzapoppin 1941,D 26,21:4
Pardon my Sarong 1942,Ag 27,15:1
Whistling in Dixie 1942,D 31,20:4
Swing Fever 1944,Ag 28,14:1
Whistling in Brooklyn 1944,Mr 24,17:3
Abbott and Costello in Hollywood
1945,N 23,26:2
Song of the Thin Man 1947,Ag 29,14:2
Petty Girl, The 1950,Ag 18,17:2
Emergency Wedding 1950,D 22,19:2
I'll Take Sweden 1965,Ag 12,30:4
Wicked Dreams of Paula Schultz, The
1968,Ja 4,28:1
Perrin, Sam (Composer)
Are You With It? 1948,Ap 15,31:2
Perrin, Sam (Screenwriter)
Navy Blues 1941,S 20,11:2
Perrin, Victor
Forever Female 1954,Ja 13,26:2
Dragnet 1954,Ag 21,10:2
Black Tuesday 1955,Ja 1,16:2
Perring, Leslie
Triumph of Sherlock Holmes, The
1935,My 27,20:6
Perrins, Leslie
Sherlock Holmes's Fatal Hour 1931,Jl 13,13:5
White Face 1933,D 4,22:3
Just Smith 1934,Ap 23,20:2
Man Who Changed his Name, The
1934,O 17,26:2
Scotland Yard Mystery, The 1936,Mr 16,21:4
Nine Days a Queen 1936,O 3,21:1
High Treason 1937,Ja 27,17:3
Bulldog Drummond at Bay 1937,O 25,23:2
Run for Your Money, A 1950,Ap 10,15:3

Perrins, Stanley
Bride of the Lake, The 1934,S 11,24:5
Perris, Adriana
Laugh Pagliacci 1948,Ja 31,14:2
Perrone, Denise
Suitor, The; Soupirant, Le 1963,S 18,35:1
Perrot, Irma
Living Dead Man, The 1927,Mr 7,16:3
Perrott, William
Belle Star's Daughter 1949,Ja 10,19:2
Perry, Anthony (Original Author)
Simba 1955,O 22,24:2
Perry, Barbara
Counsellor-At-Law 1933,D 8,31:2
Perry, Bob
Light of the Western Stars, The 1925,Je 24,14:3
White Gold 1927,Ap 11,18:3
Fortune Hunter, The 1928,Ja 10,28:4
Dressed to Kill 1928,Mr 12,26:1
River Pirate, The 1928,S 17,27:1
Beggars of Life 1928,S 24,25:1
Me, Gangster 1928,O 22,29:1
Sea God, The 1930,S 6,9:2
Carnival Boat 1932,Mr 21,19:5
Hell's Highway 1932,S 26,18:2
Chief, The 1933,D 2,9:4
My Man Godfrey 1936,S 19,18:1 (Incorrect in this edition; use 1936,S 18,18:1 elsewhere)
Perry, Des
Ulysses 1967,Mr 14,55:1
Perry, Eleanor (Screenwriter)
David and Lisa 1962,D 27,5:5
Ladybug, Ladybug 1963,D 24,9:1
Swimmer, The 1968,My 16,53:1
Perry, Frank (Director)
David and Lisa 1962,D 27,5:5
Ladybug, Ladybug 1963,D 24,9:1
Swimmer, The 1968,My 16,53:1
Perry, Frank (Producer)
Ladybug, Ladybug 1963,D 24,9:1
Swimmer, The 1968,My 16,53:1
Perry, George Sessions (Original Author)
Southerner, The 1945,Ag 27,22:3
Perry, George Sessions (Screenwriter)
Arkansas Traveler, The 1938,N 17,29:2
Perry, Harvey
Winner Take All 1932,Je 18,9:2
Perry, Ida
Lindenwirtin vom Rhein, Die 1931,S 25,28:7
Elisabeth von Oesterreich 1931,D 11,35:1
Perry, Joan
Case of the Missing Man, The 1935,N 23,23:2
Meet Nero Wolfe 1936,Jl 16,20:1
Shakedown 1936,Ag 17,9:2
Counterfeit Lady 1937,Ja 11,15:6
Devil is Driving, The 1937,Jl 16,22:1
Start Cheering 1938,Mr 17,17:3
Blind Alley 1939,My 23,27:2
Good Girls Go to Paris 1939,Je 23,23:1
Lone Wolf Strikes, The 1940,F 5,13:2
Maisie Was a Lady 1941,F 13,25:2
Strange Alibi 1941,Ap 28,11:2
Bullets for O'Hara 1941,Jl 28,16:4
Nine Loves Are not Enough 1941,O 30,27:2
International Squadron 1941,N 14,28:4
Perry, John (Screenwriter)
Man About the House, A 1949,Mr 9,33:2
Perry, Julian (Screenwriter)
Horrible Dr Hitchcock, The 1964,D 3,58:3
Perry, Kathryn
Wings of Youth 1925,Ap 20,18:1
First Year, The 1926,Mr 8,17:1
Is Zat So? 1927,My 17,27:2
Side Street 1929,S 9,30:2
Call Her Savage 1932,N 25,19:2
Perry, Ken
China Doll 1958,D 4,52:1
Perry, Linda
Sing Me a Love Song 1936,D 26,15:2
They Won't Forget 1937,Jl 15,16:1
Mr Dodd Takes the Air 1937,Ag 12,14:2
Great Garrick, The 1937,O 25,23:1
Perry, Margaret
New Morals for Old 1932,Je 24,15:3
Go West, Young Man 1936,N 19,31:3
Perry, Marguerite
French Way, The 1952,S 6,12:6
Perry, Mary
Uncle Vanya 1958,Ap 29,26:2
Perry, Peter Jr (Screenwriter)
Flesh Merchant, The 1956,My 19,12:6
Perry, Roger
Follow the Boys 1963,F 28,8:2
Perry, Sara
Damned Don't Cry, The 1950,Ap 8,9:2
Perry, Stephen
Sound and the Fury, The 1959,Mr 28,11:1
Raisin in the Sun, A 1961,Mr 30,24:1
Perry, Susan
Knock on any Door 1949,F 23,31:2
Perry, Ty
At War With the Army 1951,Ja 25,21:5

Perry, Victor
Pickup on South Street 1953,Je 18,38:2
Perry, Walter
Love Master, The 1924,My 19,14:2
Unholy Three, The 1925,Ag 4,14:3
Foreign Legion, The 1928,Je 25,27:1
Troopers Three 1930,F 17,17:6
Perschy, Maria
Password Is Courage, The 1962,D 22,5:2
Man's Favorite Sport? 1964,F 20,22:1
633 Squadron 1964,Je 25,25:1
Pershing, Frank
When Willie Comes Marching Home 1950,F 18,9:2
Persoff, Nehemiah
Harder They Fall, The 1956,My 10,26:3
Wild Party, The 1956,D 22,13:1
Wrong Man, The 1956,D 24,8:1
Men in War 1957,Mr 20,32:4
This Angry Age 1958,Je 26,23:3
Badlanders, The 1958,S 4,33:1
Never Steal Anything Small 1959,F 12,23:1
Green Mansions 1959,Mr 20,26:1
Al Capone 1959,Mr 26,27:1
Some Like It Hot 1959,Mr 30,23:1
Big Show, The 1961,My 11,42:4
Comancheros, The 1961,N 2,42:1
Hook, The 1963,F 16,5:6
Fate Is the Hunter 1964,D 10,61:1
Greatest Story Ever Told, The 1965,F 16,40:2
Power, The 1968,Mr 7,52:2
PERSON
See Also PERSSON
Person, Tiny
Too Many Girls 1940,N 21,43:1
Personnel of the Royal Air Force
Journey Together 1946,Mr 4,16:5
Persse, Tom
It's a Great Life 1920,Ag 30,12:3
PERSSON
See Also PERSON
Persson, Edvard
Flickorna Fran Gamla Stan 1934,D 27,25:4
Tjocka Slaekten; Near Relatives 1935,My 20,20:5
Larsson I Andra Giftet 1935,O 19,21:3
Loerdagskvaellar 1936,F 13,25:3
Vaaran Pojke 1936,O 10,21:3
Soederkaakar 1936,D 19,16:2
Old Gods Still Live, The 1937,N 5,19:4
Baldvins Brollop; Baldwin's Wedding 1938,D 27,13:2
Skanor-Falsterbo 1939,Ap 17,13:2
Kalle paa Spaangen 1940,Ja 27,9:3
Kvinnorna Kring Larsson; Women Around Larsson, The 1940,My 18,11:3
Sun Over Klara 1944,My 1,20:8
Pimpernel Svensson 1953,F 6,16:4
Each Heart Has Its Own Story 1953,Mr 28,15:2
Persson, Essy
I, A Woman 1966,O 12,36:3
Therese and Isabelle 1968,My 15,41:4
Persson, Gene (Producer)
Dutchman 1967,F 28,32:1
Persson, Mim
Kalle paa Spaangen 1940,Ja 27,9:3
Persson, Sven (Producer)
Naked Prey, The 1966,Je 15,40:1
Pertos, Frank (Screenwriter)
Snake Pit, the 1948,N 5,29:2
Pertsovsky, M
Leningrad Symphony 1958,Je 23,19:6
Pertwee, Jon
Mister Drake's Duck 1952,Ja 28,15:2
Will any Gentleman? 1955,S 28,70:6
Pertwee, Michael (Original Author)
Silent Dust 1949,D 30,13:2
Interrupted Journey 1951,My 29,20:2
Thief of Venice, The 1952,N 28,22:7
Cavern, The 1965,D 25,17:2
Pertwee, Michael (Screenwriter)
Man With 100 Faces 1938,N 1,27:2
Against the Wind 1949,Je 27,18:3
Silent Dust 1949,D 30,13:2
Interrupted Journey 1951,My 29,20:2
Curtain Up 1953,F 2,17:3
Mr Potts Goes to Moscow 1953,S 3,15:2
Tonight's the Night 1954,D 23,13:4
Your Past Is Showing 1958,Jl 29,19:2
Too Many Crooks 1959,Ap 25,14:2
Make Mine Mink 1960,D 20,43:4
Mouse on the Moon, The 1963,Je 18,32:1
Ladies Who Do 1963,N 26,52:2
Strange Bedfellows 1965,Mr 11,38:1
Cavern, The 1965,D 25,17:2
Funny Thing Happened on the Way to the Forum, A 1966,O 17,48:1
Salt and Pepper 1968,S 19,62:3
Pertwee, Roland
Secret Four, The 1940,Ap 22,13:2
Mister V 1942,F 13,24:4
They Were Sisters 1946,Jl 24,24:2

Pertwee, Roland (Original Author)
Interference 1928,N 17,23:1
I Like Your Nerve 1931,S 12,15:4
Road to Singapore, The 1931,O 1,25:2
It Happened to One Man 1941,F 24,11:6
Silent Dust 1949,D 30,13:2
Pink String and Sealing Wax 1950,O 4,38:2
Pertwee, Roland (Screenwriter)
Non-Stop New York 1937,N 29,19:2
Dinner at the Ritz 1937,D 4,21:1
Secret Four, The 1940,Ap 22,13:2
Voice in the Night, The 1941,My 23,25:4
Jeannie 1943,S 13,14:2
Young Man's Fancy, A 1943,D 4,11:2
Madonna of the Seven Moons 1946,My 23,18:4
They Were Sisters 1946,Jl 24,24:2
Magic Bow, The 1947,Jl 7,13:2
Caravan 1949,Ap 21,30:4
Perugia, Luciano (Producer)
Girl and the General, The 1967,D 7,60:1
Perutz, Leo (Original Author)
Betrayal, The 1929,Ap 29,29:2
Perventsev, A (Screenwriter)
Heroes of Shipka 1956,S 3,10:5
Peryalis, Notis
Electra 1962,D 18,5:2
Peryalis, Notis (Screenwriter)
Bed of Grass 1957,D 28,9:2
Perzanowska, S (Director)
Jego Wielka Milosc 1936,Mr 24,27:5
Perzieff, Laurent
7 Capital Sins (Lust); Lust (7 Capital Sins) 1963,Ja 17,5:2
Pescatori, Olga
Passaporto Rosso 1936,S 2,18:2
Pesce, Franco
Mademoiselle Gobette 1955,F 5,13:3
Pesek, Ladislav
Merry Wives, The 1940,N 12,28:3
Transport From Paradise 1967,F 8,22:1
Peselev, A
Ladies 1955,Je 27,18:2
Peskay, Ben (Producer)
Top Banana 1954,F 20,8:6
Peskin, Dina
Faithful City 1952,Ap 8,35:2
Pessin, Leo
David and Bathsheba 1951,Ag 15,23:2
Petacci, Myriam
One Step to Eternity 1955,O 3,22:2
Petelle, Martha
Let Not Man Put Asunder 1924,Ja 15,16:1
Clean Heart, The 1924,S 15,28:1
Peter
Go Go Mania 1965,My 20,52:4
Festival 1967,O 24,53:2
Peter, M
Woman to Woman 1924,Ap 1,19:3
Peter, Sabine
Im Heidekrug 1934,D 31,9:7
Peter the Great (police dog)
Silent Accuser, The 1924,N 25,26:1
Peterka, Frantisek
Lady on the Tracks, The 1968,N 26,39:2
Peters, A D (Producer)
Last Holiday 1950,N 14,39:4
Inspector Calls, An 1954,N 26,24:4
Peters, Audrey
Middle of the Night 1959,Je 18,36:1
Peters, Brock
Porgy and Bess 1959,Je 25,20:3
To Kill a Mockingbird 1963,F 15,10:2
Heavens Above! 1963,My 21,28:2
L-Shaped Room, The 1963,My 28,32:1
Major Dundee 1965,Ap 8,45:1
Pawnbroker, The 1965,Ap 21,51:1
Incident, The 1967,N 6,65:1
P J 1968,Mr 7,52:3
Peters, Brooke L (Director)
World Dances 1954,N 8,24:6
Peters, Brooke L (Producer)
World Dances 1954,N 8,24:6
Peters, Denis
Dutchman 1967,F 28,32:1
Peters, Don (Screenwriter)
Naked Prey, The 1966,Je 15,40:1
Beach Red 1967,Ag 4,18:1
Peters, George
Teenage Mother 1968,S 19,62:4
Peters, Gordon
Lovely Way to Die, A 1968,Jl 13,18:1
Peters, House
Great Redeemer, The 1920,O 25,18:1
Isobel, or the Trail's End 1920,D 20,11:2
Lying Lips 1921,Mr 7,8:1
Man From Lost River, The 1922,Ja 16,18:3
Rich Men's Wives 1922,Ag 21,6:2
Lost and Found 1923,Mr 19,22:2
Don't Marry for Money 1923,Ag 21,17:3
Tornado, The 1924,D 15,14:1
Rose-Marie 1928,F 13,16:2

Peters, House Jr
Lion and the Horse, The 1952,My 19,12:2
Red Planet Mars 1952,Je 16,15:2
O Henry's Full House (The Clarion Call); Clarion Call, The (O Henry's Full House) 1952,O 17,33:1
Black Patch 1958,Ap 24,38:1
Peters, Ina
Spessart Inn, The 1961,F 18,12:3
Peters, J Baxter (Cinematographer)
Face of War, A 1968,My 11,28:1
Peters, Jean
Captain from Castile 1947,D 26,22:4
Deep Waters 1948,Jl 23,12:4
It Happens Every Spring 1949,Je 11,11:2
Love That Brute 1950,My 27,10:6
Take Care of my Little Girl 1951,Jl 19,20:2
As Young as You Feel 1951,Ag 3,10:6
Anne of the Indies 1951,O 25,36:3
Viva Zapata 1952,F 8,19:2
Wait Till the Sun Shines, Nellie 1952,Je 28,12:2
Lure of the Wilderness 1952,O 4,15:2
O Henry's Full House (The Last Leaf 1952,O 17,33:1
Niagara 1953,Ja 22,20:3
Pickup on South Street 1953,Je 18,38:2
Blueprint for Murder, A 1953,Jl 25,8:2
Vickie 1953,S 8,26:3
Three Coins in the Fountain 1954,My 21,18:2
Apache 1954,Jl 10,7:2
Broken Lance 1954,Jl 30,9:1
Man Called Peter, A 1955,Ap 1,22:1
Peters, John
Ranson's Folly 1926,My 31,10:2
Amateur Gentleman, The 1926,Ag 17,15:3
Student Prince, The 1927,S 22,33:2
Enemy, The 1927,D 28,26:6
Scarlet Lady, The 1928,Ag 15,19:4
White Zombie 1932,Jl 29,18:2
Beasts of Berlin 1939,N 20,15:6
Peters, Lauri
Mr Hobbs Takes a Vacation 1962,Je 16,11:2
For Love of Ivy 1968,Jl 18,26:1
Peters, Mammy
Lilies of the Field 1924,Mr 17,19:1
Peters, Mattie
Day of Faith, The 1923,N 27,11:2
Peters, Molly
Thunderball 1965,D 22,23:1
Peters, Petra
Girls Behind Bars 1950,My 10,41:2
Christina 1951,Ja 15,13:1
Peters, Ralph
Great Gambini, The 1937,Jl 12,20:4
Wanted by the Police 1938,S 26,13:2
You Belong to Me 1941,N 29,14:2
Ball of Fire 1942,Ja 16,25:2
Good Morning, Judge 1943,Ap 30,25:4
My Kingdom for a Cook 1943,O 15,15:3
See my Lawyer 1945,My 4,23:4
Radio Stars on Parade 1945,S 22,14:2
Hold That Blonde 1945,N 8,17:2
Nobody Lives Forever 1946,N 2,12:2
Millionaire for Christy, A 1951,O 5,24:3
Sniper, The 1952,My 10,16:3
While the City Sleeps 1956,My 17,37:1
Peters, Roberta
Tonight We Sing 1953,F 13,17:2
Peters, S J (Original Author)
High Pressure 1932,F 1,22:3
Peters, Sabine
Meine Frau, Die Schuetzenkoenigin 1935,Ja 7,13:3
Konjunkturritter 1935,Ap 29,12:4
Irene 1936,D 13,XI,6:6 (In Addenda)
Maedchen Irene, Das 1937,My 22,19:3
Glaserne Kugel, Die; Glass Ball, The 1939,Je 17,12:3
Biberpelz, Der; Beaver Coat, The 1939,S 9,11:3
Marriage of Figaro 1950,N 3,31:2
Peters, Scott
Canadians, The 1961,Je 1,31:1
Peters, Susan
Big Shot, The 1942,Jl 18,8:2
Tish 1942,S 18,25:2
Random Harvest 1942,D 18,36:6
Andy Hardy's Double Life 1943,Ja 12,23:3
Assignment in Brittany 1943,Ap 22,31:2
Song of Russia 1944,F 11,17:2
Keep Your Powder Dry 1945,Mr 12,22:6
Sign of the Ram, The 1948,Mr 4,30:2
Peters, Werner
Devil Strikes at Night, The 1959,Ja 30,31:3
Rosemary 1960,Ja 19,40:2
Roses for the Prosecutor; (Rosen fur den Staarsanwalt) 1961,O 10,38:2
Counterfeit Traitor, The 1962,Ap 18,28:1
36 Hours 1965,Ja 29,25:2
Battle of the Bulge 1965,D 18,36:1
Fine Madness, A 1966,Je 30,28:2
Corrupt Ones, The 1967,F 23,41:3
Secret War of Harry Frigg, The 1968,Mr 5,34:5

Peters, William Frederick (Composer)
Yolanda 1924,F 20,23:1
Peters Sisters
Ali Baba Goes to Town 1937,O 23,14:1
Love and Hisses 1938,Ja 1,11:1
Happy Landing 1938,Ja 22,19:1
Rebecca of Sunnybrook Farm 1938,Mr 26,12:1
PETERSEN
See Also PETERSON, PETTERSON
Petersen, Agnes
Secrets of the Orient 1932,Ja 4,27:3
Petersen, Colin
Cry From the Streets, A 1959,F 24,32:2
Petersen, Ernst
Peaks of Destiny 1927,N 29,31:1
Prisoners of the Mountain 1930,Ja 12,VIII,5:5 (In Addenda)
White Hell of Pitz Palu, The 1930,S 27,21:3
Avalanche 1932,Mr 26,17:2
Petersen, Hans
Crazy Paradise 1965,Ag 11,41:2
Eric Soya's 17 1967,Ja 25,37:1
Petersen, Kield
Crazy Paradise 1965,Ag 11,41:2
Petersen, Mogens Viggo
Girls are Willing, The 1959,My 11,30:1
Petersen, Paul
Houseboat 1958,N 14,24:1
Happiest Millionaire, The 1967,D 1,56:1
Petersen, Peter
Maskerade 1934,O 14,X,4:2 (In Addenda)
Eternal Mask, The 1937,Ja 13,20:3
Masquerade in Vienna 1937,Ja 26,16:4
Kreutzer Sonata 1937,Mr 14,XI,4:6 (In Addenda)
Kreutzer Sonata, The 1938,My 28,9:3
Spiegel des Lebens, Der; Life's Mirror 1940,F 17,9:3
PETERSON
See Also PETERSEN, PETTERSON
Peterson, Arthur
Targets 1968,Ag 14,34:1
Born Wild 1968,D 12,62:6
Peterson, Caleb
Till the Clouds Roll By 1946,D 6,27:4
Any Number Can Play 1949,Jl 1,14:4
Peterson, Carl O (Cinematographer)
Little America 1935,O 15,19:2
Peterson, Dorothy
Mothers Cry 1930,D 6,21:3
Party Husband 1931,My 16,13:3
Up for Murder 1931,My 30,9:2
Reckless Hour, The 1931,Ag 1,16:4
Traveling Husbands 1931,Ag 8,16:3
Bought 1931,Ag 15,18:3
Penrod and Sam 1931,S 26,25:3
Skyline 1931,O 5,17:3
Rich Man's Folly 1931,N 27,29:3
Forbidden 1932,Ja 11,28:5
Way Back Home 1932,Ja 16,13:1
Business and Pleasure 1932,F 13,23:4
She Wanted a Millionaire 1932,F 20,11:2
Beast of the City, The 1932,Mr 14,13:3
So Big 1932,Ap 30,19:3
When a Feller Needs a Friend 1932,My 14,11:5
Night World 1932,My 28,18:2
Attorney for the Defense 1932,My 28,18:2
Life Begins 1932,Ag 26,20:3
Cabin in the Cotton 1932,S 30,17:3
Payment Deferred 1932,N 8,26:3
Billion Dollar Scandal, The 1933,Ja 9,23:1
Hold Me Tight 1933,My 22,18:6
I'm no Angel 1933,O 14,18:2
Beloved 1934,Ja 27,9:3
As the Earth Turns 1934,Ap 12,27:2
Treasure Island 1934,Ag 18,5:5
Peck's bad Boy 1934,O 6,20:1
Society Doctor 1935,F 4,11:3
Laddie 1935,My 6,22:3
Freckles 1935,O 26,12:2
Man of Iron 1935,D 7,22:2
Country Doctor, The 1936,Mr 13,32:2 (Incorrect in this edition; use 1936,Mr 13,27:2 elsewhere)
Devil is a Sissy, The 1936,O 17,21:2
Reunion 1936,N 27,27:1
Under Cover of Night 1937,Ja 20,18:4
Her Husband Lies 1937,Mr 18,20:1
Confession 1937,Ag 19,23:1
52d Street 1937,N 15,15:1
Hunted Men 1938,My 21,9:2
Breaking the Ice 1938,S 23,35:3
Girls on Probation 1938,O 21,27:3
Flying Irishman, The 1939,Ap 12,27:2
Dark Victory 1939,Ap 21,27:2
Sabotage 1939,N 16,29:5
Too Many Husbands 1940,Mr 8,25:2
Lillian Russell 1940,My 18,11:2
Women in War 1940,My 30,21:2
Cheers for Miss Bishop 1941,Mr 14,17:2
Henry Aldrich for President 1941,O 18,22:2
Saboteur 1942,My 8,27:2
Man in the Trunk, The 1942,O 23,25:1
Air Force 1943,F 4,29:1
This Is the Army 1943,Jl 29,11:6

Peterson, Dorothy — Cont
ThIs is the Life 1944,Ap 28,23:3
Mr Skeffington 1944,My 26,23:2
Woman in the Window, The 1945,Ja 26,16:4
Canyon Passage 1946,Ag 8,18:2
Sister Kenny 1946,S 30,21:2
That Hagen Girl 1947,O 25,13:2
Peterson, Elsa
Madam Satan 1930,O 6,21:1
Expert, The 1932,F 27,22:1
Guilty as Hell 1932,Ag 6,14:5
Peterson, G H (Screenwriter)
Razzia 1948,Je 14,19:2
Peterson, Gene
Hiawatha 1952,D 26,20:4
Peterson, Gil
Cool Ones, The 1967,My 11,50:1
Peterson, Henry
Jack Ahoy 1935,F 9,11:2
Peterson, Jerry
Great White Way, The 1924,Ja 4,10:1
Peterson, John
Synanon 1965,My 6,44:1
Peterson, Lenka
Panic in the Streets 1950,Ag 5,9:2
Take Care of my Little Girl 1951,Jl 19,20:2
Phenix City Story, The 1955,S 3,9:1
Black Like Me 1964,My 21,42:1
Peterson, Louis (Original Author)
Take a Giant Step 1961,Mr 6,28:2
Peterson, Louis (Screenwriter)
Tempest 1959,Mr 27,19:2
Take a Giant Step 1961,Mr 6,28:2
Peterson, Margaret (Original Author)
Song of Love, The 1924,F 25,13:1
Peterson, Marjorie
Panama Flo 1932,Ja 20,17:4
Love Is a Racket 1932,Je 11,9:3
Peterson, Neil (Screenwriter)
Room at the Top 1959,Mr 31,26:1
Peterson, Ralph
Hoodlum Priest, The 1961,Ap 3,28:5
Peterson, Ruth
Charlie Chan in Paris 1935,Ja 22,23:2
Peterson, Sue
Surfari 1967,Jl 19,26:2
Pether, Henry E (Composer)
Cover Girl 1944,Mr 31,26:1
Pethes, Sandor
Key Balvany, A 1933,Ap 18,13:6
Kek Balvany, A; Blue Idol, The 1933,Ap 18,13:6
My Wife, The Miss 1934,S 13,26:2
Elnoek Kisasszony 1935,O 12,12:3
Zsivany Becsuelet 1935,O 30,16:3
Kiralyne Huszarja, A 1936,Ag 17,15:3
Szegeny Gazdagok; Poor Plutocrats 1939,D 4,18:4
Sut a Nap (Sun Shines, The); Sun Shines, The 1940,Ap 6,13:3
Petina, Irra
There's Magic in Music 1941,Je 5,27:2
Petipa, Marius (Miscellaneous)
Royal Ballet, The (Swan Lake Act II); Swan Lake Act II (The Royal Ballet) 1960,O 5,45:2
Sleeping Beauty, The 1966,My 4,50:1
Petit, Albert
Here is my Heart 1934,D 22,21:1
Petit, Michel
Marriage on the Rocks 1965,S 16,00:0
Petit, Pascale
Witches of Salem 1958,D 9,54:2
Women Are Weak 1959,Je 9,44:2
Cheaters, The; (Tricheurs, Les) 1961,Je 5,37:4
End of Desire 1962,Jl 10,29:2
Cross of the Living 1963,F 5,5:5
Julie the Redhead 1963,O 15,44:1
Mistress for the Summer, A 1964,Mr 28,13:5
Petit, Roland
Hans Christian Andersen 1952,N 26,20:2
Black Tights 1962,F 21,54:2
Petit, Roland (Miscellaneous)
Hans Christian Andersen 1952,N 26,20:2
Daddy Long Legs 1955,My 6,17:5
Petker, B
Spring 1948,Mr 15,26:2
Wrestler and the Clown, The 1959,Ja 1,38:1
Petkere, Bernice (Original Author)
Sabotage Squad 1942,Ag 5,16:1
Petkere, Bernice (Screenwriter)
Sabotage Squad 1942,Ag 5,16:1
Peto, Attila
Erik/a/Buzakalasz; Wheat Ripens, The 1939,S 11,15:2
Petofi, Alexander (Original Author)
Janos Vitez; John, The Hero 1939,Ap 8,19:2
Petra, Hortense
Love-Ins, The 1967,Ag 19,16:1
For Singles Only 1968,Je 6,54:1
Petracca, Joseph (Original Author)
Something for the Birds 1952,N 15,15:2
Petracca, Joseph (Screenwriter)
Proud Ones, The 1956,Ag 11,10:2
Proud Rebel, The 1958,Jl 2,23:4
Reluctant Saint, The 1962,D 4,47:2

Petrangeli, Carlo
Lacrime e Sorrisi 1936,D 17,35:2
Petransito, Luigi
Man of Courage 1934,N 14,23:2
Petrarca, Gerald
Goddess, The 1958,Je 25,24:1
Petre, Gio
Wild Strawberries 1959,Je 23,37:1
Doll, The 1964,Ja 14,27:1
Loving Couples 1966,S 20,38:1
PETRI
See Also PETRIE
Petri, Elio (Director)
High Infidelity (Sin in the Afternoon); Sin in the
Afternoon (High Infidelity) 1965,Jl 2,17:1
10th Victim, The 1965,D 21,46:1
Lady Killer From Rome, The 1966,Je 9,54:3
We Still Kill the Old Way 1968,F 29,28:1
Petri, Elio (Screenwriter)
10th Victim, The 1965,D 21,46:1
We Still Kill the Old Way 1968,F 29,28:1
Petri, Ilse
Raub der Sabinerinnen, Der 1937,Ja 16,21:1
Seltsamer Gast, Ein 1937,Jl 10,18:2
Thunder, Lightening and Sunshine
1937,N 13,11:2
PETRIE
See Also PETRI
Petrie, Daniel (Director)
Bramble Bush, The 1960,F 25,34:2
Raisin in the Sun, A 1961,Mr 30,24:1
Main Attraction, The 1963,Je 27,23:3
Stolen Hours 1963,O 17,39:1
Idol, The 1966,Ag 11,27:1
Spy With a Cold Nose, The 1966,D 20,58:2
Petrie, George
Winged Victory 1944,D 21,16:2
Four Days' Leave 1950,Je 9,29:4
Gypsy 1962,N 2,24:1
Hud 1963,My 29,36:1
Wall of Noise 1963,S 5,27:1
Petrie, Hay
Suspense 1930,N 8,21:3
Night Birds 1931,Ja 3,21:2
Old Curiosity Shop, The 1935,D 23,15:5
Ghost Goes West, The 1936,Ja 11,9:2
Peg of Old Drury 1936,Ap 13,15:1
I Stand Condemned 1936,Jl 2,27:2
Forever Yours 1937,Je 7,22:2
Knight Without Armor 1937,Jl 9,18:1
Loves of Madame Dubarry, The 1938,Ap 4,12:5
Smiling Along 1939,F 20,13:2
Clouds Over Europe 1939,Je 16,27:2
Four Feathers 1939,Ag 4,11:1
U-Boat 29 1939,O 6,31:3
Jamaica Inn 1939,O 12,33:1
21 Days Together 1940,My 23,28:4
Pastor Hall 1940,S 21,13:2
Blackout 1940,D 2,19:2
Thief of Bagdad, The 1940,D 6,28:2
Convoy 1941,Ja 17,21:2
Wings and the Woman 1942,O 8,31:1
One of our Aircraft Is Missing 1942,N 2,17:2
Great Mr Handel, The 1943,S 10,29:3
On Approval 1945,Ja 29,17:1
Battle for Music 1945,O 15,13:2
Waltz Time 1946,F 11,25:2
Great Expectations 1947,My 23,31:1
Canterbury Tale, A 1949,Ja 24,16:2
Guinea Pig, The 1949,My 2,20:2
Fallen Idol, The 1949,N 16,39:2
Petrie, Howard
Walk Softly Stranger 1950,O 16,30:5
Rocky Mountain 1950,N 4,13:2
No Questions Asked 1951,Ag 10,13:2
Bend of the River 1952,Ap 10,37:1
Carbine Williams 1952,My 8,37:2
Wild North, The 1952,My 12,21:2
Pony Soldier 1952,D 20,15:2
Fort Ti 1953,My 30,7:1
Veils of Bagdad, The 1953,N 27,99:9
Seven Brides for Seven Brothers 1954,Jl 23,8:3
Bob Mathias Story, The 1954,O 16,14:6
Timberjack 1955,Mr 10,33:3
How to be Very, Very Popular 1955,Jl 23,10:1
Return of Jack Slade, The 1955,N 24,41:3
Maverick Queen, the 1956,Je 4,25:2
Johnny Concho 1956,Ag 16,30:1
Tin Star, The 1957,O 24,37:2
Petrilli, Vittoriano (Screenwriter)
Island Sinner, The 1960,S 5,11:2
Under ten Flags 1960,S 16,24:1
Petrof, Vladimir (Director)
Thunderstorm 1934,S 29,12:2
Petroff, Paul
End of St Petersberg, The 1928,My 31,21:2 (In
Addenda)
Petronella, Peggy
Co-Optimists, The 1930,F 5,27:2
Petroni, Anna
Man of Courage 1934,N 14,23:2

Petroni, Filomena
Man of Courage 1934,N 14,23:2
Petropoulakis, J (Director)
Girl From Corfu, The 1957,My 20,28:2
Petrosino, Joaquin
Dark River 1956,F 27,19:4
Petrov, A
Peasants 1935,Ag 29,25:2
1905 1956,Jl 9,27:2
Petrov, Eugene (Screenwriter)
Spring Song 1942,S 12,9:2
Taxi to Heaven 1944,My 25,16:3
Petrov, G
Springtime on the Volga 1961,D 25,27:4
Petrov, Ivan
Eugene Onegin 1959,S 14,33:1
Petrov, Ivan (Composer)
Yolanta 1964,D 23,22:3
Petrov, S
Jew at War, A 1931,Jl 25,11:6
Heroes of the Sea 1941,Ap 28,11:2
Petrov, Vladimir
Khovanschina 1960,S 19,41:2
Petrov, Vladimir (Director)
Children of the New Day 1930,Je 30,22:6
Peter the First 1937,D 25,10:4
Conquests of Peter The Great, The
1939,Ag 24,17:2
1812 1944,S 11,14:1
Jubilee 1945,F 22,31:3
First Front, The 1949,N 14,19:2
Victors and the Vanquished, The 1950,My 1,18:2
Inspector General, The 1954,My 3,21:2
Petrov, Vladimir (Producer)
First Front, The 1949,N 14,19:2
Petrov, Vladimir (Screenwriter)
Peter the First 1937,D 25,10:4
Conquests of Peter The Great, The
1939,Ag 24,17:2
Jubilee 1945,F 22,31:3
Inspector General, The 1954,My 3,21:2
Petrov-Bytov, P (Director)
Cain and Artem 1930,Je 7,10:4
Miracles 1934,O 22,12:3
Pugachev 1938,Jl 4,10:2
Petrova, Mme
Life Mask, The 1918,My 13,11:3
Tempered Steel 1918,Je 24,9:1
Petrovic, Alexsander (Director)
Three 1967,Je 30,30:1
Three 1967,Je 30,30:1
I Even Met Happy Gypsies 1968,Mr 21,57:1
Petrovic, Alexsander (Screenwriter)
I Even Met Happy Gypsies 1968,Mr 21,57:1
Petrovic, Senka Veletanlic
Three 1967,Je 30,30:1
Petrovich, Ivan
Magician, The 1926,O 25,15:1
Garden of Allah, The 1927,S 3,13:5
Garden of Allah, The 1927,S 11,VIII,5:1
Alraune 1928,My 20,VIII,8:4
Morgane, the Enchantress 1929,Je 21,17:2
Opernredoute; Opera ball 1931,O 4,VIII,7:1
Opern-Ball, Der; Opera Ball 1931,N 6,28:3
Secrets of the Orient 1932,Ja 4,27:3
Holzapfel Weiss Alles 1933,Ja 7,11:3
Viktoria und Ihr Husar 1933,Ap 10,8:3
Feldherrnhuegel, Der 1934,Ap 20,17:2
Polenblut; Polish Blood 1935,N 16,19:3
Drei Maeoerl um Schubert 1937,Je 5,21:2
Herzenslieb; Heart Thief 1938,Jl 2,10:4
Ueber Alles die Treue 1939,F 13,13:3
Starker als die Liebe; Stronger Than Love
1939,My 6,21:3
Eroica; (The Beethoven Story) 1951,O 29,19:2
Frantic 1961,Je 12,34:1
Petrovich, Jans
Kreutzer Sonata, The 1928,S 10,29:3
Petrovich, Peter
End of St Petersberg, The 1928,My 31,21:2 (In
Addenda)
Petrovna, Natasia
Steppe, The 1963,O 1,33:1
Petrovsky, A
Lash of the Czar, The 1929,F 12,23:1
Man From the Restaurant, The 1930,Ja 6,30:5
Hour With Tchekhof, An 1933,S 6,24:4
Petrucci, Giovanni
Avventura, L' 1961,Ap 5,30:1
Petrunkin, M
Fall of Berlin 1952,Je 9,19:2
Petruzzi, Julian
Tenth Avenue Kid 1938,S 2,21:3
PETTERSON
See Also PETERSEN, PETERSON
Pettersson, Brigitta
Magician, The 1959,Ag 28,27:1
Virgin Spring, The; Jungfrukallan 1960,N 15,46:1
Creatures, Les 1966,S 16,31:2
Pettersson, Hjordis
Froeken Blir Piga 1937,Je 12,8:3
Lasse-Maja 1943,Mr 22,15:4
Frustration 1949,Ag 27,7:3

Pettersson, Hjordis — Cont
Of Love and Lust (Doll's House, A); Doll's House,
A (Of Love and Lust) 1959,My 26,31:2
Pettet, Joanna
Group, The 1966,Mr 17,35:1
Night of the Generals, The 1967,F 3,38:1
Casino Royale 1967,Ap 29,25:1
Robbery 1967,S 28,58:2
Blue 1968,My 11,28:1
Pettie, Graham
Westerners, The 1919,Ag 4,8:3
Pettingell, Frank
Good Companions, The 1933,O 10,24:1
In a Monastery Garden 1935,Mr 13,16:2
Amateur Gentleman, The 1936,Ap 27,19:2
Last Journey, The 1936,Je 8,22:4
Red Wagon 1936,Je 22,22:1
Sailing Along 1938,Ap 16,17:1
Haunted Honeymoon 1940,O 31,28:2
This England 1941,N 18,33:2
Ships With Wings 1942,My 25,11:2
Showtime 1948,My 20,35:3
Escape 1948,Ag 16,12:2
No Room at the Inn 1949,D 26,33:4
Crimson Pirate, The 1952,Ag 28,21:2
Promoter, The 1952,O 29,36:2
Angel Street 1952,N 11,25:2
Value for Money 1957,Ag 1,20:4
Trial and Error 1962,N 17,17:2
Term of Trial 1963,Ja 31,5:2
Pettit, E (Original Author)
Rich are Always With Us, The 1932,My 16,19:5
Pettit, Rosemary
Walk East on Beacon 1952,My 29,17:2
Pettitt, Frank
Saturday Night and Sunday Morning
1961,Ap 4,44:2
Kitchen, The 1961,N 2,42:1
Pettitt, Wilfrid (Miscellaneous)
Gallant Blade 1948,O 13,31:3
Pettitt, Wilfrid (Original Author)
Thousand and one Nights, A 1945,Jl 12,8:2
Pettitt, Wilfrid (Screenwriter)
Thousand and one Nights, A 1945,Jl 12,8:2
Bandit of Sherwood Forest, The 1946,Mr 23,8:4
Walls Came Tumbling Down, The 1946,N 9,13:5
Swordsman, The 1947,O 17,18:4
Petukhova, Anna
Road Home, The 1947,My 2,28:3
Petulengro, Gypsy
Caravan 1949,Ap 21,30:4
Peudovkine (Director)
Tempete sur l'Asie; Storm Over Asia
1929,N 17,IX,5:6
Peukert, Leo
Jolly Peasant, The 1929,Jl 1,31:2
Gretel and Liesel; (Kohlhiesel's Daughters)
1931,Ja 26,21:1
Die Mutter der Kompagnie 1934,Mr 9,22:3
Tante Gusti Kommandiert 1934,My 4,24:4
Gordian, Der Tyrann 1937,Je 21,15:3
Hotel Sacher 1939,Je 10,14:2
Ein Hoffnungsloser Fall 1939,S 18,15:5
Pevney, Joseph
Nocturne 1946,N 11,42:2
Body and Soul 1947,N 10,21:2
Street with no Name, The 1948,Jl 15,26:6
Thieves' Highway 1949,S 24,8:6
Outside the Wall 1950,Mr 15,34:8
Pevney, Joseph (Director)
Shakedown 1950,S 4,11:2
Undercover Girl 1950,N 8,37:2
Air Cadet 1951,My 11,32:3
Iron Man 1951,Ag 20,14:2
Strange Door, The 1951,D 10,34:6
Meet Danny Wilson 1952,Mr 27,34:4
Flesh and Fury 1952,Mr 28,27:4
Just Across the Street 1952,Je 28,12:4
Because of You 1952,D 4,47:3
Desert Legion 1953,My 9,13:2
Yankee Pasha 1954,Ap 19,19:2
Playgirl 1954,My 15,13:3
Three Ring Circus 1954,D 25,7:2
Six Bridges to Cross 1955,Ja 22,8:2
Foxfire 1955,Jl 14,19:1
Female on the Beach 1955,Ag 20,20:2
Congo Crossing 1956,Jl 14,13:2
Away all Boats 1956,Ag 17,14:2
Istanbul 1957,Ja 24,34:1
Tammy and the Bachelor 1957,Je 15,10:7
Midnight Story, The 1957,Jl 5,14:2
Man of a Thousand Faces 1957,Ag 14,21:1
Twilight for the Gods 1958,Ag 7,21:1
Torpedo Run 1958,O 25,16:2
Cash McCall 1960,Ja 28,26:1
Crowded Sky, The 1961,F 11,27:2
Portrait of a Mobster 1961,Ap 20,30:4
Night of the Grizzly, The 1966,Je 23,29:1
Pevtsof, I N
Tchapayef 1935,Ja 15,22:1
Peyof, I
Miracles 1934,O 22,12:3

Peyrefitte, Roger (Original Author)
  7 Capital Sins (Lust); Lust (7 Capital Sins)
    1963,Ja 17,5:2
  This Special Friendship 1967,N 8,56:1
Peyser, John (Director)
  Young Warriors, The 1968,F 8,36:1
Peyson, Casey
  Pretty Boy Floyd 1960,N 3,49:2
PEYTON
  See Also PATON, PATTEN, PATTON,
    PAYTON
Peyton, Robert
  Tokyo File 212 1951,Je 1,20:7
Peza, Graciela Munoz
  Profanacion 1934,Ja 31,20:4
Pezas, Alexis
  Phaedra 1962,O 19,24:1
Pezet, A W (Original Author)
  Broadway Bad 1933,Mr 6,16:6
Pezet, Juan (Producer)
  Cobarde, El; Coward, The 1939,Mr 27,11:2
Pfaff, Hanschen
  Befreite Hande; Freed Hans 1940,My 25,20:1
Pfaff, Joachim
  Reise Nach Tilsit, Die; Trip to Tilsit, The
    1940,F 10,19:2
Pfailzer, Marjorie (Screenwriter)
  3 Is a Family 1944,D 20,20:3
  Tarzan and the Amazons 1945,Ap 30,13:4
Pfalzgraf, Florence Leighton (Original Author)
  Our Little Girl 1935,Je 7,24:4
Pfaudler, Franz
  Mein Leben fuer Maria Isabell; My Life for Maria
    Isabell 1935,N 5,33:5
  Glueckspilze 1936,O 26,21:1
PFEIFER
  See Also PFEIFFER
Pfeifer, Henry
  Story of a Cheat, The 1938,S 27,25:2
PFEIFFER
  See Also PFEIFER
Pfeiffer, Hermann
  Guitars of Love 1958,Jl 12,18:1
Pfitzmann, Guenter
  Taiga 1959,Mr 17,42:4
Pfleghar, Michael (Director)
  How to Seduce a Playboy 1968,My 16,53:2
  Oldest Profession, The (Gay Nineties, The); Gay
    Nineties, The (The Oldest Profession)
    1968,N 8,42:1
Pfleghar, Michael (Screenwriter)
  How to Seduce a Playboy 1968,My 16,53:2
Pflug, Eva
  Confess, Dr Corda 1960,O 24,25:5
Pflunger, Paula
  Lysistrata 1948,Je 19,19:2
Phalin, Victor (Producer)
  Pirates of Capri, The 1949,D 26,33:5
Phares, Vera
  Generals Without Buttons 1938,Mr 8,23:2
Phat, Isabelle (Screenwriter)
  Tales of Paris (The Tale of Ella); Tale of Ella, The
    (Tales of Paris) 1962,Ag 27,18:1
Phelan, Brian
  Kitchen, The 1961,N 2,42:1
  Accident 1967,Ap 18,33:1
Phelan, Pat
  Miss Susie Slagle's 1946,F 7,29:2
Phelps, Buster
  Last Warning, The 1929,Ja 7,36:2
  Leftover Ladies 1931,N 9,22:4
  Scandal for Sale 1932,Ap 3,26:2
  Three on a Match 1932,O 29,18:4
  Handle with Care 1932,D 24,11:4
  Sailor's Luck 1933,Mr 17,21:2
  World Gone Mad, The 1933,Ap 15,16:3
  One Man's Journey 1933,S 1,15:2
  Broken Dreams 1933,N 21,23:3
  Servants' Entrance 1934,S 27,25:2
  Little Men 1935,F 18,19:3
  Anna Karenina 1935,Ag 31,16:2
  Blue Bird, The 1940,Ja 20,11:2
  Howards of Virginia, The 1940,S 27,27:1
Phelps, Eleanor
  Cleopatra 1934,Ag 17,12:1
  Count of Monte Cristo, The 1934,S 27,25:2
Phelps, George
  Kid From Left Field, The 1953,S 26,15:3
Phelps, Lee
  Anna Christie 1930,Mr 15,22:5
  Criminal Code, The 1931,Ja 5,21:3
  Cross Examination 1932,F 27,22:1
  Night Club Lady, The 1932,Ag 27,13:4
  Parole Girl 1933,Ap 10,8:2
  Woman I Stole, The 1933,Je 28,24:3
  Wings in the Dark 1935,F 2,10:1
  $1,000 a Minute 1935,D 21,11:1
  Gladiator, The 1938,Ag 29,10:2
  Kid Nightingale 1939,D 8,33:6
Phelps, Leroy (Cinematographer)
  Dangerous Journey 1944,O 2,22:2

Phelps, Marilee
  Arena 1953,Jl 23,20:2
Phil Spitalny and his all-girl orchestra
  When Johnny Comes Marching Home
    1943,Mr 5,20:4
Philbin, Mary
  Merry Go Round 1923,Jl 2,16:2
  Temple of Venus, The 1923,N 1,24:3
  Fifth Avenue Models 1925,My 4,16:2
  Phantom of the Opera, The 1925,S 7,15:3
  Surrender 1927,O 11,27:1
  Drums of Love 1928,Ja 25,20:4
  Love Me and the World Is Mine 1928,F 6,12:3
  Affairs of Hannerl 1928,F 12,VIII,7:2 (In
    Addenda)
  Man Who Laughs, The 1928,Ap 28,12:3
  Last Performance, The 1929,N 4,28:1
  Shannons of Broadway, The 1929,D 21,17:1
  Phantom of the Opera 1930,F 10,20:4
Philbrick, Will
  Whoopee 1930,O 1,26:3
  Gorilla, The 1931,F 23,20:3
Philbrook, James
  I Want to Live 1958,N 19,45:1
  Woman Obsessed 1959,My 28,34:1
  Thin Red Line, The 1964,O 29,38:1
Philharmonic-Symphony Orchestra of New York
  Carnegie Hall 1947,My 3,10:2
Philipe, Gerard
  Idiot, The 1948,F 5,26:2
  Devil in the Flesh 1949,My 10,29:2
  Riptide 1951,Ap 7,9:2
  Beauty and the Devil 1952,Ag 26,15:2
  Fanfan the Tulip 1953,My 5,34:2
  Seven Deadly Sins, The (The Eighth Sin); Eighth
    Sin, The (The Seven Deadly Sins)
    1953,My 12,31:3
  Ronde, La 1954,Mr 17,27:2
  Beauties of the Night 1954,Mr 23,23:5
  Lovers, Happy Lovers 1954,O 1,19:2
  Proud and the Beautiful, The 1956,My 29,32:2
  Grand Maneuver, The 1956,O 2,39:1
  Royal Affairs in Versailles 1957,Mr 9,16:1
  It Happened in the Park 1957,Ag 13,23:2
  Rouge et Noir 1958,Ap 9,42:1
  Pot Bouille 1958,O 28,39:1
  Modigliani of Montparnasse 1961,Mr 1,27:3
  Liaisons Dangereuses, Les 1961,D 19,39:1
  Knave of Hearts; Lovers, Happy Lovers
    1965,S 9,36:1
Philipidis, Andrew
  Youth of Athens 1949,O 31,20:4
Philipopoli, Nick
  Youth of Athens 1949,O 31,20:4
Philipov, Sergei
  Hello, Moscow! 1946,Je 15,24:4
Philipp, Gunther
  Beggar Student, The 1958,Ja 25,14:3
  Fledermaus, Die 1964,F 8,15:2
Philipp, Harold (Director)
  Bimbo the Great 1961,Je 29,26:1
Philipp, Harold (Screenwriter)
  Bimbo the Great 1961,Je 29,26:1
Philippe, Jean Lou
  What Price Murder 1958,N 11,26:1
Philippe, Little
  Forty Little Mothers 1938,D 23,16:3
Philippe, Michele
  Naked Woman, The 1950,Ja 21,10:2
  Hoboes in Paradise 1950,O 9,21:5
  Paris Hotel 1959,S 12,12:3
Philippe, Pierre
  Nana 1928,Ja 22,VIII,7:7
  Nana 1934,Jl 30,19:4
Philippi, Siegfried (Original Author)
  Lindenwirtin vom Rhein, Die 1931,S 25,28:7
Philippides, Andreas
  Phaedra 1962,O 19,24:1
Philippides, Manos
  Prosfygopoula; Girl Refugee, The 1938,S 27,25:3
  Otan o Syzygos Taxeideyei; When the Husband
    Travels 1939,N 13,15:3
Philippou, John (Director)
  Anna of Rhodes 1950,Mr 23,34:2
PHILIPS
  See Also PHILLIPS
Philips, Lee
  Peyton Place 1957,D 13,35:1
  Hunters, The 1958,Ag 27,33:1
  Middle of the Night 1959,Je 18,36:1
  Psychomania 1964,F 15,14:3
Philips, Mary
  Life Begins 1932,Ag 26,20:3
  Farewell to Arms, A 1932,D 9,26:5
  As Good as Married 1937,My 22,19:2
  Wings Over Honolulu 1937,My 29,20:1
  That Certain Woman 1937,S 16,29:1
  Bride Wore Red, The 1937,O 15,18:4
  Mannequin 1938,Ja 21,15:2
  Lady in the Dark 1944,F 23,17:1
  Incendiary Blonde 1945,Jl 26,13:2
  Captain Eddie 1945,Ag 9,24:2
  Kiss and Tell 1945,O 26,16:2

Philips, Mary— Cont
  Leave Her to Heaven 1945,D 26,15:1
  Dear Ruth 1947,Je 11,33:3
  Dear Wife 1950,F 2,31:2
  I Can Get It for You Wholesale 1951,Ap 5,34:4
  Dear Brat 1951,Jl 5,21:2
  Prince Valiant 1954,Ap 7,40:2
Philips, Wendell
  Close-Up 1948,Ap 5,24:2
Philipsen, Harriet
  Incorrigible 1949,Jl 2,8:2
Philliber, John
  Lady Takes a Chance, A 1943,S 16,25:2
  Impostor, The 1944,Mr 27,17:2
  It Happened Tomorrow 1944,My 29,18:2
  Summer Storm 1944,O 23,14:3
  3 Is a Family 1944,D 20,20:3
  Gentle Annie 1945,My 5,11:5
Phillip, Alice de
  Vivire Otra Vez; I Shall Live Again
    1940,O 23,27:2
Phillipi, Erich (Original Author)
  Secret of the Blue Room, The 1933,S 13,22:1
  Missing Guest, The 1938,S 7,30:7
  Murder in the Blue Room 1944,O 28,12:2
PHILLIPS
  See Also PHILIPS
Phillips, Alex (Director)
  Hoy Comienza la Vida 1936,Je 27,21:2
Phillips, Arnold (Original Author)
  Murder in the Music Hall 1946,Ap 15,22:2
  Return of Monte Cristo, The 1947,Ja 3,16:4
Phillips, Arnold (Screenwriter)
  Brighton Strangler, The 1945,My 19,15:2
  Time Out of Mind 1947,Ap 7,20:1
  Pickup 1951,Ag 31,12:2
Phillips, Arthur (Miscellaneous)
  Playmates 1941,D 26,21:3
Phillips, Arthur (Original Author)
  Limehouse Blues 1934,D 12,28:2
Phillips, Arthur (Screenwriter)
  Limehouse Blues 1934,D 12,28:2
  Last Outpost, The 1935,O 5,18:2
  Riding High 1943,D 23,26:4
  Rainbow Island 1944,O 26,19:6
  Out of This World 1945,Je 7,25:2
  Delightfully Dangerous 1945,Je 9,17:3
  Love, Honor and Goodbye 1945,S 8,12:2
Phillips, Augustus
  Toby's Bow 1919,D 15,20:1
Phillips, Barney
  Eight Iron Men 1953,Ja 2,11:1
  Blueprint for Murder, A 1953,Jl 25,8:2
  Square Jungle, The 1955,D 31,17:2
  Cry Terror 1958,My 15,25:1
  Decks Ran Red, The 1958,O 11,18:2
Phillips, Bernard
  Ruby Gentry 1952,D 26,20:2
Phillips, Carmen
  Ashes of Vengeance 1923,Ag 7,20:2
  Fighting Coward, The 1924,Mr 17,19:1
  Ask any Girl 1959,My 22,32:1
  It Started With a Kiss 1959,Ag 20,14:2
  Please Don't Eat the Daisies 1960,Ap 1,37:1
  Convicts 4 1962,O 4,44:2
Phillips, Claire (Original Author)
  I Was an American Spy 1951,Jl 4,13:2
Phillips, Conrad
  Sons and Lovers 1960,Ag 3,35:1
  Circus of Horrors 1960,S 1,31:1
  Shadow of the Cat, The 1961,Je 8,40:2
  Murder She Said 1962,Ja 8,27:2
  Murder Game, The 1966,Mr 31,43:2
Phillips, David Graham (Original Author)
  Old Wives for New 1918,My 20,9:7
  Souls for Sables 1925,S 15,12:1 (Incorrect in this
    edition; use 1925,S 15,29:1 elsewhere)
  Susan Lenox; Her Fall and Rise 1931,O 17,20:1
Phillips, David Graham (Screenwriter)
  Price She Paid, The 1925,Ja 13,16:1
Phillips, Dorothy
  Heart of Humanity, The 1918,D 22,17:3
  Right to Happiness, The 1919,S 1,5:6
  Paid in Advance 1919,D 1,9:3
  Man-Woman-Marriage 1921,Mr 28,11:4
  Slander the Woman 1923,My 28,18:2
  Sporting Chance, The 1925,Je 24,14:3
  Upstage 1926,N 15,19:1
  Cradle Snatchers 1927,My 31,25:2
Phillips, Eddie
  Love Light, The 1921,Ja 10,9:1
  Nth Commandment, The 1923,Ap 10,24:3
  Through the Dark 1924,Ja 8,27:1
  Women Who Give 1924,Je 3,22:1
  Capital Punishment 1925,F 5,23:3
  Fourflusher, The 1928,Ja 16,24:1
  Finders Keepers 1928,Mr 5,21:3
  We Americans 1928,Mr 29,25:3
  Lonesome 1928,O 2,23:5
  Scandal 1929,Ap 22,23:1
  College Love 1929,Ag 5,25:2
  Chasing Rainbows 1930,F 22,13:1
  Dancing Sweeties 1930,Ag 16,8:3
  Big Boy 1930,S 13,9:3

Phillips, Eddie— Cont
Night World 1932,My 28,18:2
Police Call 1933,Ag 22,20:3
Wild Boys of the Road 1933,S 22,14:1
Soak the Rich 1936,F 5,14:2
Federal Bullets 1937,D 27,11:1
Champagne Charlie 1948,Ag 7,8:2
Phillips, Eric
Touch and go 1956,Mr 20,13:2
Phillips, Gregory
I Could go on Singing 1963,My 16,42:1
Phillips, H I (Miscellaneous)
Reported Missing 1922,Ap 24,18:3
Phillips, Helena
Greene Murder Case, The 1929,Ag 10,11:3
Two Seconds 1932,My 19,25:3
Life Begins 1932,Ag 26,20:3
King's Vacation, The 1933,Ja 20,21:2
Voltaire 1933,Ag 23,21:2
Design for Living 1933,N 23,24:2
Phillips, Herbert O (Screenwriter)
Enemy of Women 1944,S 12,23:6
Phillips, Howard
Spider, The 1931,S 5,7:4
Sob Sister 1931,O 3,20:2
Surrender 1931,N 28,20:4
Stepping Sisters 1932,Ja 9,21:1
Careless Lady 1932,Ap 18,19:2
Trial of Vivienne Ware, The 1932,Ap 30,19:3
Last Mile, The 1932,Ag 26,20:3
Fugitive in the Sky 1937,Ja 16,21:1
Great Hospital Mystery, The 1937,Jl 16,22:2
White Bondage 1937,Ag 6,21:3
Gangs of New York 1938,My 28,9:2
Phillips, Irving (Original Author)
Song of the Open Road 1944,Je 7,13:3
Delightfully Dangerous 1945,Je 9,17:3
Phillips, Irving (Screenwriter)
Seven Days Ashore 1944,Ap 26,24:7
Phillips, Jean
Among the Living 1941,D 13,25:2
Dr Broadway 1942,Je 25,27:3
Night in New Orleans 1942,Jl 2,25:2
Phillips, Jimmy
Sally of the Scandals 1928,Jl 3,19:3
Queen of the Night Clubs 1929,Mr 18,30:6
Phillips, John
So Goes my Love 1946,My 2,3:7
Black Angel 1946,S 26,32:4
Richard III 1956,Mr 12,1:4
Village of the Damned 1960,D 8,43:3
Romanoff and Juliet 1961,Je 9,26:1
Man in the Moon 1961,Je 13,29:2
Mouse on the Moon, The 1963,Je 18,32:1
Phillips, Leo
Treasure Island 1950,Ag 16,24:2
Cruel Sea, The 1953,Ag 11,18:5
Phillips, Leslie
Pool of London 1951,N 28,37:2
Breaking Through the Sound Barrier 1952,N 7,19:1
Barretts of Wimpole Street, The 1957,Ja 18,15:3
Girls, Les 1957,O 4,27:2
Smallest Show on Earth, The 1957,N 23,11:2
Please Turn Over 1961,Ap 29,12:2
Doctor in Love 1962,Ap 27,27:2
Week-End With Lulu, A 1962,My 24,29:2
Coming-Out Party, A 1962,Jl 31,19:2
Crooks Anonymous 1963,O 31,26:3
Phillips, Margaret
Life of her Own, A 1950,O 12,43:2
Nun's Story, The 1959,Je 19,30:1
Phillips, Marilyn
Gentleman Jim 1942,N 26,40:3
Phillips, Michael J (Original Author)
Salome, Where She Danced 1945,My 3,27:1
Phillips, Minna
Male Animal, The 1942,Mr 28,11:1
Yank at Eton, A 1942,O 16,23:1
My Sister Eileen 1942,O 23,15:1
Gals, Inc 1943,Ag 13,13:4
Sherlock Holmes Faces Death 1943,O 8,15:3
Phillips, Nancy
City Gone Wild, The 1927,D 6,27:1
Phillips, Noreen
Secret Studio, The 1927,Je 15,31:4
Phillips, Norman Jr
Fifty Million Frenchmen 1931,Mr 26,31:2
Lovers Courageous 1932,F 20,11:2
Tom Brown of Culver 1932,Jl 30,16:5
Band Plays on, The 1934,D 22,21:2
Our Neighbors-The Carters 1940,F 15,15:2
Phillips, Paul
Brother Orchid 1940,Je 8,18:2
Strange Alibi 1941,Ap 28,11:2
Nine Lives Are not Enough 1941,O 30,27:2
Phillips, Redmond
Love Is a Ball 1963,Ap 25,38:1
Phillips, Robert Lieut
Unidentified Flying Objects 1956,Je 13,46:2
Phillips, Sian
Becket 1964,Mr 12,40:2
Young Cassidy 1965,Mr 23,35:1

Phillips, Thomas Hal (Screenwriter)
Tarzan's Fight for Life 1958,Ag 16,10:2
Phillips, Tita
Man in the Attic 1954,F 6,17:2
Phillips, William (Bill)
Lady Gangster 1942,Jl 10,13:2
Swingtime Johnny 1943,D 17,23:3
See Here Private Hargrove 1944,Mr 22,17:2
Thirty Seconds Over Tokyo 1944,N 16,19:1
What Next Corporal Hargrove? 1945,D 26,15:2
Harvey Girls, The 1946,Ja 25,26:2
Hoodlum Saint, The 1946,Je 27,29:1
Holiday in Mexico 1946,Ag 16,19:3
Till the Clouds Roll By 1946,D 6,27:4
Sea of Grass, The 1947,F 28,27:2
Living in a Big Way 1947,O 10,31:4
Man From Colorado 1949,Ja 21,24:3
Big Jack 1949,My 23,27:4
Johnny Allegro 1949,My 31,19:2
Mary Ryan, Detective 1949,N 4,33:3
He's a Cockeyed Wonder 1950,O 20,32:4
Yank in Korea, A 1951,Ap 2,29:2
Cavalry Scout 1951,Je 8,32:2
Detective Story 1951,N 7,35:2
High Noon 1952,Jl 25,14:2
Wicked Woman 1954,Mr 27,13:6
Phillott, Gordon
Battle of the Sexes, The 1960,Ap 19,40:4
Phillpotts, Ambrosine
Room at the Top 1959,Mr 31,26:1
Expresso Bongo 1960,Ap 13,44:1
Life at the Top 1965,D 15,53:1
Phillpotts, Eden (Original Author)
Widecombe Fair 1929,O 28,20:1
Farmer's Wife, The 1930,Ja 7,28:3
Philpotts, Eden (Original Author)
Widdicombe Fair 1929,Ja 13,VIII,5:2 (In Addenda)
Philpson, Harriet
Crime and Punishment 1948,Mr 1,17:2
Philson, Betty
Wise Girl 1938,Ja 10,13:3
Phipps, Nicholas
Spring in Park Lane 1949,S 21,38:2
Maytime in Mayfair 1952,Ap 23,23:5
Captain's Paradise, The 1953,S 29,25:5
Intruder, The 1955,Ja 26,22:1
Iron Petticoat, The 1957,F 2,12:2
Orders to Kill 1958,N 18,41:2
Pure Hell of St Trinian's, The 1961,S 26,31:1
Doctor in Love 1962,Ap 27,27:2
Pair of Briefs, A 1964,F 3,22:2
Phipps, Nicholas (Miscellaneous)
Adam and Evalyn 1950,My 12,33:4
I Believe in You 1953,My 5,34:3
Phipps, Nicholas (Screenwriter)
Piccadilly Incident 1948,Ag 5,16:2
Spring in Park Lane 1949,S 21,38:2
Madeleine 1950,S 1,17:2
Maytime in Mayfair 1952,Ap 23,23:5
Island Rescue 1952,Jl 1,19:4
Kathy's Love Affair 1952,Jl 3,16:2
Captain's Paradise, The 1953,S 29,25:5
Doctor in the House 1955,F 19,18:3
Doctor at Sea 1956,Mr 1,37:3
Doctor at Large 1957,Jl 29,15:5
Captain's Table, The 1960,S 27,40:1
No Love for Johnnie 1961,D 13,55:1
Doctor in Love 1962,Ap 27,27:2
Pair of Briefs, A 1964,F 3,22:2
Young and Willing 1964,F 27,28:1
Doctor in Distress 1964,Jl 8,38:2
Phipps, Sally
Bertha, The Sewing Machine Girl 1927,Ja 4,21:1
High School Hero 1927,O 24,24:3
Why Sailors Go Wrong 1928,Ap 9,18:2
News Parade, The 1928,My 29,17:2
One Woman Idea, The 1929,Je 10,23:1
Phipps, Thomas (Screenwriter)
Yank at Eton, A 1942,O 16,23:1
Phipps, William
Crossfire 1947,Jl 23,19:2
Belle Star's Daughter 1949,Ja 10,19:2
They Live by Night 1949,N 4,33:2
Man on the Eiffel Tower, The 1950,Ja 30,12:2
Five 1951,Ap 26,34:2
No Questions Asked 1951,Ag 10,13:2
Flat Top 1952,D 6,17:2
Julius Caesar 1953,Je 5,19:1
War of the Worlds, The 1953,Ag 14,10:2
Riot in Cell Block 11 1954,F 19,24:5
Cat-Women of the Moon 1954,Mr 20,10:7
Executive Suite 1954,My 7,19:1
Indian Fighter, The 1955,D 22,20:1
Lust for Life 1956,S 18,39:1
Phoenix, Nigel
Nine Hours to Rama 1963,Ap 4,58:2
Phoenix, Patricia
L-Shaped Room, The 1963,My 28,32:1
Pia, Isabella
Marianne of my Youth; (Marianne de ma Jeunesse) 1959,Ja 20,43:1

Piacenti, Enrico
Retribution 1922,Je 7,22:3
Piaf, Edith
Star Without Light; Etoile Sans Lumiere 1947,Ag 4,14:2
French-Cancan 1956,Ap 17,26:2
Royal Affairs in Versailles 1957,Mr 9,16:1
I Love, You Love 1962,N 10,16:2
Pialat, Maurice (Director)
Naked Childhood 1968,S 28,36:1
Pialat, Maurice (Screenwriter)
Naked Childhood 1968,S 28,36:1
Piaschkes, Otto (Producer)
Bofors Gun, The 1968,S 23,42:3
Piat, Jean
Would-Be Gentleman, The 1960,Mr 23,31:1
Marriage of Figaro, The 1963,Ap 30,26:1
Piatigorsky, Gregor
Carnegie Hall 1947,My 3,10:2
Piatnitsky Ensemble
Moscow Music Hall 1946,S 9,20:1
Piave, F M (Composer)
Lost One, The; La Traviata 1948,Mr 30,26:2
Piazza, Ben
No Exit 1962,D 6,55:2
Piazza, Fernando
Boom! 1968,My 27,56:1
Piazza, Zoro
Monte Cassino 1948,N 25,47:3
Peddlin' in Society 1950,F 23,33:3
Piazzatta, Enzo
Hotel Sahara 1952,Ja 1,21:4
Piazzi, Achille (Producer)
Goliath and the Dragon 1961,Ja 5,27:2
Of Wayward Love (The Women); Women, The (Of Wayward Love) 1964,Mr 24,29:1
Of Wayward Love (The Soldier); Soldier, The (Of Wayward Love) 1964,Mr 24,29:1
Of Wayward Love (The Serpent); Serpent, The (Of Wayward Love) 1964,Mr 24,29:1
Pibernat, Maruja
Riachuelo 1934,D 8,18:5
Pica, Tina
Guaglio 1949,My 19,35:2
Bread, Love and Dreams 1954,S 21,24:1
Frisky 1955,O 25,37:3
Scandal in Sorrento 1957,Je 13,37:1
Virtuous Bigamist, The 1959,My 28,34:3
Yesterday, Today, and Tomorrow (Part III-Mara Rome); Mara Rome (Yesterday, Today and Tomorrow) 1964,Mr 18,46:1
PICARD
See Also PICKARD
Picard, Andre (Original Author)
Evening Clothes 1927,Mr 21,10:4
Picard, Burt (Screenwriter)
Enemy General, The 1960,O 20,42:2
Picasso, Lamberto
One Hundred Days of Napoleon 1936,S 14,25:1
Tre Anni Senza Donne 1937,My 27,21:4
Al Buio Insieme 1937,Ag 6,21:3
Casta Oiva 1937,O 5,29:2
Scipio Africanus 1939,S 23,22:2
Dottor Antonio, Il 1939,D 7,35:1
Terra di Nessuno; Nobody's Land 1940,O 25,25:4
Manon Lescaut 1941,Ap 14,23:5
Rossini 1948,Ja 31,14:2
Life Begins Tomorrow 1952,N 18,37:2
Picasso, Mme
Testament of Orpheus 1962,Ap 10,48:1
Picasso, Pablo
Testament of Orpheus 1962,Ap 10,48:1
Picasso, Pablo (Screenwriter)
Picasso 1955,D 23,14:4
Picazo, Miguel (Director)
Tia Tula, A 1965,Je 3,24:1
Piccoli, Michel
Foxiest Girl in Paris 1958,S 20,10:6
Sinners of Paris 1959,Ap 24,23:1
Day and the Hour, The 1964,F 20,22:2
Doulos-The Finger Man 1964,Mr 3,31:1
Diary of a Chambermaid; Journal d'une Femme de Chambre, Le 1964,S 22,44:1
Contempt 1964,D 19,25:2
Masquerade 1965,Ap 29,40:2
Sleeping Car Murder, The 1966,Mr 8,45:1
Lady L 1966,My 19,51:1
Creatures, Les 1966,S 16,31:2
Is Paris Burning? 1966,N 11,36:1
Game is Over, The 1967,Ja 10,34:1
Guerre est Fini, La; War Is Over, The 1967,F 2,29:2
Benjamin 1968,Mr 26,41:2
Belle de Jour 1968,Ap 11,51:1
Young Girls of Rochefort, The 1968,Ap 12,50:1
Danger Diabolik 1968,D 12,62:6
Piccolo, Marco (Original Author)
Goliath and the Dragon 1961,Ja 5,27:2
Piccolo, Ottavia
Leopard, The 1963,Ag 13,25:1
Picerni, Paul
Breakthrough 1950,N 18,10:2
Operation Pacific 1951,F 3,10:2

Picerni, Paul— Cont
I Was a Communist for the F B I 1951,My 3,34:4
Inside the Walls of Folsom Prison
  1951,My 28,17:4
Force of Arms 1951,Ag 14,20:2
Tanks are Coming, The 1951,D 6,42:4
Mara Maru 1952,Ap 24,38:1
Operation Secret 1952,N 6,37:2
She's Back on Broadway 1953,Mr 12,24:2
House of Wax 1953,Ap 11,15:2
Desert Song, The 1953,My 21,39:2
System, The 1953,My 23,19:3
Adventures of Haji Baba, The 1954,O 9,8:7
Hell's Island 1955,My 7,10:2
To Hell and Back 1955,S 23,21:2
Miracle in the Rain 1956,Ap 2,18:1
Come on, The 1956,Ap 7,13:1
Flight to Hong Kong 1957,Ja 3,28:2
Big Caper, The 1957,Mr 29,16:1
Operation Mad Ball 1957,N 21,38:1
Marjorie Morningstar 1958,Ap 25,32:2
Torpedo Run 1958,O 25,16:2
Young Philadelphians, The 1959,My 22,32:1
Strangers When we Meet 1960,Je 30,22:2

Picha, Hermann
Women Without Men 1928,N 12,18:2
Small Town Sinners 1928,N 27,34:1
Weavers, The 1929,O 7,22:1
Because I Loved You 1930,Ja 25,13:2
Leutnant Warst Du Einst bei den Husaren
  1932,Mr 14,13:3
Ein Ausgekochter Junge 1932,My 3,25:5
Kyritz-Pyritz 1932,Ag 9,20:5
Die Lustigen Musikanten 1933,My 27,11:6
Gross Reinemachen; General Housecleaning
  1938,Je 23,27:2

Pichel, Irving
Right to Love, The 1931,Ja 2,25:1
Murder by the Clock 1931,Jl 18,16:6
American Tragedy, An 1931,Ag 6,22:5
Cheat, The 1931,D 12,23:3
Two Kinds of Women 1932,Ja 16,13:1
Miracle Man, The 1932,Ap 21,25:2
Forgotten Commandments 1932,Je 2,25:2
Westward Passage 1932,Je 4,9:2
Painted Woman, The 1932,S 16,24:4
Strange Justice 1932,O 20,24:2
Madame Butterfly 1932,D 26,26:2
Billion Dollar Scandal, The 1933,Ja 9,23:1
King of the Jungle 1933,F 25,20:3
Woman Accused, The 1933,Mr 13,18:2
Oliver Twist 1933,Ap 13,15:3
Story of Temple Drake, The 1933,My 6,11:2
I'm no Angel 1933,O 14,18:2
Right to Romance, The 1933,D 15,28:2
Fog over Frisco 1934,Je 7,26:2
Such Women Are Dangerous 1934,Je 9,18:3
Return of the Terror 1934,Jl 11,20:2
Cleopatra 1934,Ag 17,12:1
British Agent 1934,S 20,20:1
I am a Thief 1935,Ja 1,24:1
Silver Streak, The 1935,Ja 16,21:1
Special Agent 1935,S 19,28:1
Don't Gamble With Love 1936,Mr 2,13:3
House of a Thousand Candles, The
  1936,Ap 2,29:2
Dracula's Daughter 1936,My 18,14:2
Down Under the Sea 1936,Ag 10,10:2
High, Wide and Handsome 1937,Jl 22,15:1
Armored Car 1937,Jl 26,15:2
Jezebel 1938,Mr 11,15:2
There Goes my Heart 1938,O 14,27:1
Topper Takes a Trip 1938,D 30,11:2
Gambling Ship 1939,Ja 21,19:2
Newsboys' Home 1939,Ja 23,8:2
Juarez 1939,Ap 26,27:1
Exile Express 1939,Ag 16,21:3
Rio 1939,O 27,27:2
Moon Is Down, The 1943,Mr 27,8:6
Martin Luther 1953,S 10,22:1

Pichel, Irving (Director)
Most Dangerous Game, The 1932,N 21,21:1
Before Dawn 1933,O 17,26:2
She 1935,Jl 26,18:2
Earthbound 1940,Je 7,27:4
Man I Married, The 1940,Ag 3,9:2
Hudson's Bay 1941,Ja 10,23:2
Dance Hall 1941,Jl 19,16:2
Secret Agent of Japan 1942,Mr 23,19:3
Pied Piper, The 1942,Ag 13,15:3
Great Commandment, The 1942,O 17,11:1
Life Begins at Eight-Thirty 1942,D 10,35:2
Moon Is Down, The 1943,Mr 27,8:6
Happy Land 1943,D 9,33:3
And Now Tomorrow 1944,N 23,38:2
Medal for Benny, A 1945,My 24,15:2
Tomorrow Is Forever 1946,F 22,21:2
Colonel Effingham's Raid 1946,Ap 5,21:3
O S S 1946,My 27,15:5
Bride Wore Boots, The 1946,Je 6,16:3
Temptation 1946,D 25,33:6
They Won't Believe Me 1947,Jl 17,16:2
Something in the Wind 1947,Ag 29,14:3
Miracle of the Bells, The 1948,Mr 17,30:1

Mr Peabody and the Mermaid 1948,Ag 14,6:5
Great Rupert, The 1950,Ap 14,27:2
Quicksand 1950,Je 16,28:4
Destination Moon 1950,Je 28,32:2
Without Honor 1950,Jl 3,9:2
Santa Fe 1951,My 4,31:2
Martin Luther 1953,S 10,22:1

Pichel, Irving (Producer)
Swamp Water 1941,N 17,15:2

Pichelski, J
Kosciuszki 1938,D 27,13:2
Za Winy niepopelnione; For Crimes Not Theirs
  1939,F 20,13:3
Border Street 1950,Ap 26,35:2
Lotna 1966,My 27,33:1

Pichon, Jean-Charles (Screenwriter)
Chasers, The; Draguers, Les 1960,My 3,43:1

Pick, Lapu (Director)
Armored Vault 1928,N 13,37:2 (In Addenda)

Pick, Lepo (Director)
Shattered 1921,D 11,VI,3:1 (In Addenda)

Pick, Lupu
Spione; Spies 1928,My 20,VIII,8:5
Spies 1929,Mr 5,29:1

Pick and Pat
Hit Parade, The 1937,My 31,11:2

PICKARD
See Also PICARD

Pickard, Helena
Nell Gwyn 1935,Je 20,16:2
Let George Do It 1940,O 14,25:5
Lodger, The 1944,Ja 20,15:3

Pickard, John
Gunfighter, The 1950,Je 24,7:2
Oh! Susanna 1951,Mr 30,28:5
Stage to Tucson 1951,My 5,14:2
Flight to Tangier 1953,N 26,50:4
Human Desire 1954,Ag 7,7:2
Lone Ranger, The 1956,F 11,12:1
Oklahoman, The 1957,My 15,39:1
Gathering of Eagles, A 1963,Jl 11,21:2

Pickard, Lioni (Original Author)
Heart's Desire 1937,Jl 12,20:4

Pickard, Margaret
Dark Journey 1937,Ag 23,22:1

Pickens, Slim
Rocky Mountain 1950,N 4,13:2
Story of Will Rogers, The 1952,Jl 18,10:5
Outcast, The 1954,Jl 3,9:2
Sheepman, The 1958,My 8,36:1
One Eyed Jacks 1961,Mr 31,21:1
Thunder of Drums, A 1961,S 27,35:1
Dr Strangelove or: How I Learned to Stop
  Worrying and Love the Bomb 1964,Ja 31,16:1
  (Incorrect in this edition; use 1964,Ja 30,24:1
  elsewhere)
In Harm's Way 1965,Ap 7,36:1
Major Dundee 1965,Ap 8,45:1
Up From the Beach 1965,Je 10,38:1
Stagecoach 1966,Je 16,53:1
Flim Flam Man, The 1967,Ag 23,40:1
Rough Night in Jericho 1967,N 9,56:4
Will Penny 1968,Ap 11,51:2
Never a Dull Moment 1968,Ag 15,46:2

Picker, Leonard S (Producer)
Bandit of Sherwood Forest, The 1946,Mr 23,8:4
Adventures of Casanova 1948,Mr 22,18:3

Picker, Sylvia
Lucky Devils 1933,F 20,11:5

Pickering, Donald
Nothing but the Best 1964,Jl 14,28:1

Pickering, Robert
Let's Kill Uncle 1966,N 19,26:1

Pickett, Elizabeth (Screenwriter)
Redskin 1929,Ja 28,21:1

Pickford, Jack
Tom Sawyer 1917,D 3,13:4
Mile-a-Minute Kendall 1918,My 6,11:3
Sandy 1918,Jl 15,9:3
Just Out of College 1921,F 7,8:2
Garrison's Finish 1923,My 28,18:2
Hill Billy, The 1924,Mr 12,19:4
Waking up the Town 1925,Mr 31,17:4
Goose Woman, The 1925,Ag 4,14:3
Bat, The 1926,Mr 15,18:3
Brown of Harvard 1926,My 3,27:1
Gang War 1928,N 19,16:7

Pickford, Jack (Director)
Through the Back Door 1921,My 6,20:2
  (Incorrect in this edition; use 1921,My 16,20:2
  elsewhere)
Little Lord Fauntleroy 1921,S 16,17:3

Pickford, Lottie
Mile-a-Minute Kendall 1918,My 6,11:3

Pickford, Mary
Madame Butterfly 1915,N 8,13:5
Poor Little Peppina 1916,F 21,9:2
Eternal Grind, The 1916,Ap 10,11:3
Hulda from Holland 1916,Jl 31,6:5
Less Than the Dust 1916,N 6,9:2
Pride of the Clan, The 1917,Ja 8,9:2
Poor Little Rich Girl, The 1917,Mr 5,9:3
Romance of the Redwoods, A 1917,My 14,9:3

Pickford, Mary— Cont
Little Princess, The 1917,N 12,11:3
M'liss 1918,My 6,11:3
How Could You, Jean? 1918,Jl 1,9:3
Johanna Enlists 1918,S 16,9:3
Captain Kidd, Jr 1919,Ap 21,13:4
Daddy Long Legs 1919,My 12,11:4
Hoodlum, The 1919,S 1,5:6
Heart o' the Hills 1919,D 1,9:3
Pollyanna 1920,Ja 19,16:3
Suds 1920,Je 28,13:2
Love Light, The 1921,Ja 10,9:1
Little Lord Fauntleroy 1921,S 16,17:3
Going Straight 1922,Mr 28,17:4
Tess of the Storm Country 1922,N 13,12:1
Rosita 1923,S 4,14:1
Little Annie Rooney 1925,O 19,26:1
Sparrows 1926,S 20,21:3
My Best Girl 1927,N 7,26:4
Coquette 1929,Ap 6,14:4 (In Addenda)
Taming of the Shrew, The 1929,N 30,23:1
Kiki 1931,Mr 6,16:1
Secrets 1933,Mr 16,21:2

Pickles, Wilfred
Billy Liar 1963,D 17,49:1
Family Way, The 1967,Je 29,32:1

Pickow, George (Cinematographer)
Festival 1967,O 24,53:2

Pico, Marc
Voyage of Silence 1968,S 12,54:1

Picon, Molly
Yiddle With his Fiddle 1937,Ja 2,15:1
Mamele; Little Mothers 1938,D 26,29:1
Come Blow Your Horn 1963,Je 7,37:1

Picorri, John
Down Under the Sea 1936,Ag 10,10:2

Picozzi, Luciano
General Della Rovere 1960,N 22,41:1

Picton, Mac
Brave Don't Cry, The 1952,N 6,37:2

Pidgeon, Walter
Mannequinn 1926,Ja 12,27:5
Old Loves and New 1926,Ap 20,24:7
Heart of a Salome, The 1927,Je 6,27:2
Gorilla, The 1927,N 21,20:1
Thirteenth Juror, The 1927,N 22,20:1
Gateway of the Moon, The 1928,Ja 9,20:1
Clothes Make the Woman 1928,Je 5,21:1
Melody of Love 1928,O 22,29:1
Most Immoral Lady, A 1929,O 21,30:1
Bride of the Regiment 1930,My 22,32:6
Sweet Kitty Bellairs 1930,S 6,9:2
Viennese Nights 1930,N 27,32:5
Kiss Me Again 1931,Ja 8,21:4
Going Wild 1931,Ja 26,21:1
Gorilla, The 1931,F 23,20:3
Hot Heiress, The 1931,Mr 14,23:2
Rockabye 1932,D 5,21:2
Kiss Before the Mirror, The 1933,My 15,16:2
Journal of a Crime 1934,Ap 28,11:3
Big Brown Eyes 1936,My 2,11:1
Fatal Lady 1936,Jl 11,11:3
Girl Overboard 1937,Mr 1,15:1
As Good as Married 1937,My 22,19:2
Saratoga 1937,Jl 23,16:3
Girl With Ideas, A 1938,Ja 1,11:2
Man-Proof 1938,Ja 14,21:1
Girl of the Golden West, The 1938,Mr 25,15:2
Shopworn Angel, The 1938,Jl 8,11:2
too Hot To Handle 1938,S 30,24:2
Listen, Darling 1938,N 24,37:2
Society Lawyer 1939,Mr 31,19:2
Six Thousand Enemies 1939,Je 9,26:2
Stronger Than Desire 1939,Je 30,17:3
Nick Carter, Master Detective 1939,D 14,35:2
House Across the Bay, The 1940,Mr 22,23:2
It's a Date 1940,Mr 23,16:2
Dark Command 1940,My 11,15:2
Phantom Raiders 1940,Je 24,19:5
Sky Murder 1940,N 14,28:3
Flight Command 1941,Ja 17,21:2
Man Hunt 1941,Je 14,20:2
Blossoms in the Dust 1941,Je 27,14:4
How Green Was my Valley 1941,O 29,27:2
Design for Scandal 1942,F 6,23:3
Mrs Miniver 1942,Je 5,23:1
White Cargo 1942,N 27,27:2
Youngest Profession, The 1943,Je 25,13:3
Madame Curie 1943,D 17,23:1
Madame Curie 1944,Ja 9,II,3:1
Mrs Parkington 1944,O 13,16:1
Week-End at the Waldorf 1945,O 5,27:2
Holiday in Mexico 1946,Ag 16,19:3
Secret Heart, The 1946,D 26,28:2
If Winter Comes 1948,Ja 23,28:4
Julia Misbehaves 1948,O 8,30:2
Command Decision 1949,Ja 20,34:2
That Forsyte Woman 1949,N 11,31:2
Red Danube, The 1949,D 9,37:3
Miniver Story, The 1950,O 27,24:2
Soldiers Three 1951,Mr 30,28:5
Unknown Man, The 1951,N 17,9:5
Sellout, The 1952,My 31,12:7
Million Dollar Mermaid 1952,D 5,35:2

Pidgeon, Walter— Cont
Bad and the Beautiful, The 1953,Ja 16,19:1
Scandal at Scourie 1953,Je 16,24:2
Dream Wife 1953,Jl 30,20:1
Executive Suite 1954,My 7,19:1
Men of the Fighting Lady 1954,My 8,15:2
Last Time I saw Paris, The 1954,N 19,20:2
Deep in my Heart 1954,D 10,35:2
Hit the Deck 1955,Mr 4,17:1
Forbidden Planet 1956,My 4,21:2
These Wilder Years 1956,Ag 18,11:2
Rack, The 1956,N 6,30:1
Voyage to the Bottom of the Sea 1961,Jl 20,32:2
Advise and Consent 1962,Je 7,31:2
Big Red 1962,S 3,11:2
Warning Shot 1967,Je 8,52:2
Funny Girl 1968,S 20,42:1

Pidgin, Charles Felton (Original Author)
Quincy Adams Sawyer 1922,D 18,22:2

Piebani, Alberto
Juliet of the Spirits 1965,N 4,57:1

Pied Pipers
Gals, Inc 1943,Ag 13,13:4
Jam Session 1944,My 3,25:3
Luxury Liner 1948,S 10,19:2

Piedra, Emiliano (Producer)
Falstaff; Chimes at Midnight 1967,Mr 18,19:2

Piel, Edward
Broken Blossoms 1919,My 14,15:5
Isobel, or the Trail's End 1920,D 20,11:2
Iron Horse, The 1924,Ag 29,6:1
Man Who Came Back, The 1924,S 1,9:1
Man Without a Country, The 1925,F 12,16:1
Wife Who Wasn't Wanted, The 1925,S 9,23:1
Girl From Montmarte, The 1926,F 25,26:2
Framed 1927,Je 20,25:3
Cock O' the Walk 1930,Ap 12,23:1
Charlie Chan's Chance 1932,Ja 23,18:4
Hatchet Man, The 1932,F 4,25:2
Big Cage, The 1933,My 9,20:5
Pursuit of Happiness, The 1934,O 26,25:1
Mysterious Mr Wong, The 1935,Mr 7,26:1
Million Dollar Baby 1935,My 6,22:3
Heroes of the Alamo 1938,Ap 2,18:2

Piel, Edward Jr
Goose Hangs High, The 1925,Mr 10,19:3
Rose of the World 1925,N 10,25:3
College Coquette, The 1929,Ag 26,17:1

Piel, Harry
Sein bester Freund; His Best Friend 1938,Jl 2,10:4

Piel, Harry (Director)
Herr Der Welt, Der 1935,D 16,23:3
Dschungel Ruft, Der 1937,Ap 26,15:3
Sein bester Freund; His Best Friend 1938,Jl 2,10:4

Pieltrangeli, Carlo
Between Two Worlds 1940,F 9,15:2

Pienne, Yvette
Pearls of the Crown, The 1938,Ap 12,26:2

Pierade, M
Charlemagne 1935,Ag 24,18:3

Pieral
Eternal Return, The; Eternel Retour, L' 1948,Ja 5,15:2
Voyage Surprise 1948,F 14,17:3
Sins of the Borgias 1956,Mr 5,21:1

PIERCE
See Also PEARCE, PEERCE

Pierce, Barbara
Grand Duchess and the Waiter, The 1926,F 9,22:1

Pierce, Betty
Alias French Gertie 1930,Ap 14,24:2

Pierce, Charlotte
Peaceful Valley 1920,O 11,19:3
Courtship of Myles Standish, The 1923,D 31,9:3

Pierce, Evelyn
Tenderloin 1928,Mr 15,28:3
American Tragedy, An 1931,Ag 6,22:5
Monkey Business 1931,O 8,22:6

Pierce, James
Jesse James 1927,O 17,20:2
Ladies of the Mob 1928,Je 18,13:2
Horse Feathers 1932,Ag 11,12:2

Pierce, Lonnie
Mister Roberts 1955,Jl 15,14:1

Pierce, Maggie
Tales of Terror 1962,Jl 5,21:2 (In Addenda)
Fastest Guitar Alive, The 1968,F 15,47:1

Pierce, Noel (Screenwriter)
Under Pressure 1935,F 4,11:3

Pierce, Norman
48 Hours 1944,Je 26,21:2
Mr Emmanuel 1945,Ja 8,15:2
Life and Death of Colonel Blimp, The 1945,Mr 30,18:2
Chance of a Lifetime 1951,Mr 15,37:2
Angels One Five 1954,Ap 30,28:2
It's Great to be Young 1957,D 26,23:3
Brides of Dracula, The 1960,S 6,41:4

Pierce, Ted (Narrator)
Mr Bug Goes to Town 1942,F 20,21:3

Pierce, Ted (Original Author)
Mr Bug Goes to Town 1942,F 20,21:3

Pierce, Ted (Screenwriter)
Gulliver's Travels 1939,D 21,29:1
Mr Bug Goes to Town 1942,F 20,21:3

Pierce, William (Original Author)
Night Key 1937,Ap 19,27:2
Armored Car 1937,Jl 26,15:2
Star Maker, The 1939,Ag 31,14:2

Pierce, William A (Original Author)
Powers Girl, The 1943,Mr 26,14:2 (In Addenda)

Piergentili, Enrico
Variety Lights; Luci del Varieta 1965,My 7,34:1

Pieris, Miriam
Drums 1938,S 30,24:4

Pierlot, Francis
Strike up the Band 1940,S 30,13:2
Always a Bride 1940,N 21,43:3
Trial of Mary Dugan, The 1941,Mr 6,25:4
Submarine Zone; (Escape To Glory) 1941,Ap 7,13:2
International Lady 1941,N 11,29:2
Remember the Day 1941,D 26,21:2
Gentleman at Heart, A 1942,F 23,25:2
Just off Broadway 1942,Ag 29,18:4
Night Monster 1942,N 30,18:5
Uncertain Glory 1944,Ap 8,9:2
Doughgirls, The 1944,Ag 31,14:1
Very Thought of You, The 1944,N 18,16:7
Bewitched 1945,Ag 17,20:3
Catman of Paris, The 1946,Jl 13,12:2
Two Guys From Milwaukee 1946,Jl 27,12:5
Second Chance 1947,S 20,12:4
Senator Was Indiscreet, The 1947,D 27,9:2
I, Jane Doe 1948,Jl 5,8:4
That Wonderful Urge 1948,D 22,29:6
Bad Boy 1949,Mr 23,35:2
Take one False Step 1949,Je 23,33:2
Flame and the Arrow, The 1950,Jl 8,7:2
Copper Canyon 1950,N 16,39:2
Lemon Drop Kid, The 1951,Mr 22,41:2
That's My Boy 1951,Ag 2,18:1
Anne of the Indies 1951,O 25,36:3
Prisoner of Zenda, The 1952,N 5,36:2

Piermonte, Enzo
Grand-Prix 1966,D 22,40:1

Pierotti, Piero (Screenwriter)
Beautiful but Dangerous 1958,F 6,24:1
Marco Polo 1962,S 20,29:2

Pierozzi, G
Cappello a Tre Punte, Il 1936,S 28,14:5
Documento Fatale, Il 1940,S 26,27:3

Pierpont, Laura
My Blue Heaven 1950,S 16,12:6

Pierrauld, Guy
Light Across the Street, The; Lumiere d'en Face, La 1957,Jl 30,20:2

Pierre, Carlos
Deadfall 1968,S 12,54:1

Pierre, Jacques
Passion of Slow Fire, The 1962,O 12,26:1

Pierre, Roger
Sans Famille 1959,S 5,11:4
Belle Americaine, La 1961,D 18,42:1

Pierre-Louis
Counter Investigation 1949,D 30,13:2
Sins of Paris 1954,Ja 30,9:6

Pierreux, Jacqueline
Noah's Ark 1950,Ag 21,15:1
Of Love and Bandits 1953,Ja 17,12:4

Pierry, Marguerite
Bal, Le 1932,S 28,22:5
He 1933,D 27,23:6
Nine Bachelors 1942,F 9,19:2
Private Life of an Actor; En Scene 1948,S 7,21:3
Counter Investigation 1949,D 30,13:2
Dr Knock 1955,O 10,31:2
Nana 1957,Ap 13,12:3
Virtuous Scoundrel, The 1957,O 23,37:1
Ostrich Has two Eggs, The 1960,S 27,40:1

Piersall, James A (Original Author)
Fear Strikes Out 1957,Mr 21,37:2

PIERSON
See Also PEARSON

Pierson, Arthur
No One Man 1932,Ja 23,18:4
Tomorrow and Tomorrow 1932,Ja 30,13:2
Strange Case of Clara Deane, The 1932,My 6,15:3
Bachelor's Affairs 1932,Je 25,18:2
Hat Check Girl 1932,O 8,15:4
Rackety Rax 1932,N 5,12:5
Air Hostess 1933,Ja 23,9:2
Ann Carver's Profession 1933,Je 9,20:2
Devil's Brother, The 1933,Je 10,16:4
Way to Love, The 1933,N 11,10:3
Before Midnight 1934,Ja 10,24:3
You Belong to Me 1934,S 13,26:1
Murder in the Clouds 1934,D 26,18:1

Pierson, Arthur (Director)
Fighting O'Flynn, The 1949,F 28,16:2

Pierson, Frank R (Screenwriter)
Cat Ballou 1965,Je 25,36:1
Happening, The 1967,My 18,56:3
Cool Hand Luke 1967,N 2,58:1

Pierson, Ketty
Claudine 1940,Ap 1,15:2

Pierson, Louise Randall (Original Author)
Roughly Speaking 1945,F 1,18:4

Pierson, Louise Randall (Screenwriter)
Roughly Speaking 1945,F 1,18:4

Pierson, Suzy
6 1/2 x 11 1929,Ag 13,23:2

Pierson, William
Stalag 17 1953,Jl 2,19:2

Pietrangeli, Antonio (Director)
Love a la Carte 1965,Ja 12,31:1
Magnificent Cuckold 1965,Ap 20,42:1
Vista, La; Visit, The 1966,Ag 10,32:1
Queens, The (Queen Marta); Queen Marta (The Queens) 1968,Mr 11,49:1

Pietrangeli, Antonio (Screenwriter)
Lupa, La 1954,F 18,36:2
Love a la Carte 1965,Ja 12,31:1
Vista, La; Visit, The 1966,Ag 10,32:1

Pietrasskiewicz, Jerzy
First Start, The 1953,F 2,17:3

Pietro, Donald
Mrs Mike 1950,F 9,36:5

Pietruski, Ryszard
Guests are Coming; Jada Goscie Jada 1967,Ja 13,15:1
Barrier 1967,S 27,39:3

Piffle, John
Friendly Enemies 1942,Je 22,19:1

Pigaut, Roger
Bellman, The 1947,Ap 7,20:5
Antoine and Antoinette 1948,Ap 16,29:2
Wench, The 1949,Mr 14,15:5
Love Story 1949,Je 27,18:4
Light Across the Street, The; Lumiere d'en Face, La 1957,Jl 30,20:2

Pigott, Mildred (Original Author)
Fruits of Faith 1923,Ja 15,18:3

Pigott, Tempe
Dawn of a Tomorrow, The 1924,Mr 26,19:2
Narrow Street, The 1925,Ja 5,19:1
Black Pirate, The 1926,Mr 9,21:4
Seven Days' Leave 1930,Ja 25,13:2
Devotion 1931,O 3,20:2
Dr Jekyll and Mr Hyde 1932,Ja 2,14:2
Cavalcade 1933,Ja 6,23:2
Oliver Twist 1933,Ap 13,15:3
Study in Scarlet, A 1933,Je 1,15:3
Doctor Bull 1933,O 6,21:2
If I Were Free 1934,Ja 5,25:2
Long Lost Father 1934,F 19,18:2
One More River 1934,Ag 10,21:1
Limehouse Blues 1934,D 12,28:2
Devil is a Woman, The 1935,My 4,17:2
Bride of Frankenstein, The 1935,My 11,21:2
Becky Sharp 1935,Je 14,27:2
White Angel, The 1936,Je 25,24:1
Fools for Scandal 1938,Mr 25,15:3

Pigott, William (Original Author)
Fruits of Faith 1923,Ja 15,18:3

Pigulovitch, Zinaida
False Uniforms 1932,N 19,20:2

Pigurenko, Lida
Lullaby, The 1961,My 15,35:2

Pike, John
Reach for Glory 1963,S 10,46:1

Pike, Nita
Great Dictator, The 1940,O 16,29:1

Pike, Peter
It Takes a Thief 1963,Ag 15,24:7

Pike, Robert L (Original Author)
Bullitt 1968,O 18,41:2

Pilafian, Peter (Miscellaneous)
Chappaqua 1967,N 6,65:2

Pilbeam, Nova
Little Friend 1934,O 20,20:2
Man Who Knew too Much, The 1935,Mr 23,11:2
Tudor Rose 1936,My 24,IX,3:8 (In Addenda)
Nine Days a Queen 1936,O 3,21:1
Girl Was Young, The 1938,F 11,27:2
Pastor Hall 1940,S 21,13:2
Next of Kin 1943,My 6,25:2
Yellow Canary, The 1944,Ap 14,24:7
Devil's Plot 1953,Je 19,18:1

Pilchowski, Robert (Miscellaneous)
Third Sex, The 1959,Mr 26,27:1

Pilchowski, Robert (Original Author)
Corinna Darling 1958,Je 14,14:3

Piletskaya, T
1905 1956,Jl 9,27:2

Pilkington, Tom
Enter Arsene Lupin 1944,D 2,17:6

Pillina, La
Pandora and the Flying Dutchman 1951,D 7,35:2

Piloeff, Sacha
Prize, The 1964,Ja 24,21:1

Pilot, Andre
Because I Loved You 1930,Ja 25,13:2
Maedel von der Reeperbahn, Das 1931,Ja 31,15:1
Foresterchristl, Die 1931,Ap 27,25:1
Versuchen Sie Meine Schwester 1931,Je 20,20:4
Eine Freundin so Goldig wie Du 1931,O 24,20:3
Pilot, Bernice
Hearts in Dixie 1929,F 28,30:3
Penrod and Sam 1937,Mr 29,14:3
Penrod and his Twin Brother 1938,Ap 18,11:1
Beloved Brat 1938,My 2,13:2
My Bill 1938,Jl 7,22:4
Fugitive From Justice, A 1940,Jl 8,13:3
Father's Son 1941,F 13,25:3
Pilotto, Camillo
Passa L'Amore 1933,N 25,10:3
Delitto di Mastrovanni, Il 1935,Jl 30,16:2
Tempo Massimo 1936,Mr 13,27:2
Lorenzino de Medici 1936,Ap 14,19:3
Alpine Love 1936,Je 8,22:5
Padre delle Patria, Il; Father of his Country, The 1938,Ag 30,14:2
Amore in Quarantena; Love in Quarantine 1938,D 13,31:2
Grande Appello, Il; Last Roll-Call, The 1939,Ap 11,18:6
Scipio Africanus 1939,S 23,22:2
Paraninfo, Il; Matchmaker, The 1940,Ja 23,17:2
Tutta la Vita in una Notte; All of Life in one Night 1940,My 2,29:6
Foria 1948,Ja 21,30:2
Furia 1948,Ja 21,30:2
Rossini 1948,Ja 31,14:2
Thief of Venice, The 1952,N 28,22:7
Mistress of the Mountains 1954,My 27,34:5
Marco Polo 1962,S 20,29:2
Piltz, George
Ebb Tide 1937,N 18,27:2
Pinajeff, Elizabeth
Mother Love 1931,F 16,17:1
Pinal, Silvia
Viridiana 1962,Mr 20,43:4
Simon of the Desert 1966,S 21,42:2
Exterminating Angel, The 1967,Ag 22,33:1
Guns for San Sebastian 1968,Mr 21,57:2
Pinchon, Edgcumb (Original Author)
Viva Villa! 1934,Ap 11,25:2
Daniel Boone 1936,O 24,23:2
Viva Zapata 1952,F 8,19:2
Pinchot, Gifford
South Seas 1930,My 24,21:2
Pinchot, Rosamond
Three Musketeers, The 1935,N 1,25:1
Pinchot Family
South Seas 1930,My 24,21:2
Pincus, David (Director)
These Thirty Years 1934,My 24,28:3
PINE
See Also PYNE
Pine, Howard (Producer)
Private War of Major Benson, The 1955,Ag 3,27:2
Running Wild 1955,N 12,23:2
Big Caper, The 1957,Mr 29,16:1
Bailout at 43,000 1957,Je 8,13:2
Pine, Les (Screenwriter)
Man Called Adam, A 1966,Ag 4,24:2
Pine, Phillip
Set-Up, The 1949,Mr 30,31:2
Red Light 1950,Ja 16,18:4
My Foolish Heart 1950,Ja 20,29:2
Under the Gun 1951,F 23,33:2
Wild Blue Yonder, The 1952,Ja 2,20:1
Hoodlum Empire 1952,Mr 6,25:6
Men in War 1957,Mr 20,32:4
Dead Heat on a Merry-Go-Round 1966,O 13,50:1
Pine, Robert
Munster, Go Home 1966,Je 16,53:4
Young Warriors, The 1968,F 8,36:1
Pine, Virginia
Dr Monica 1934,Je 21,28:2
Pine, William H (Director)
Aerial Gunner 1943,Je 26,10:2
Swamp Fire 1946,Ag 26,21:4
Crosswinds 1951,D 7,35:4
Pine, William H (Miscellaneous)
Land of Liberty 1939,Je 16,27:3
Land of Liberty 1941,Ja 30,19:2
Pine, William H (Producer)
I Live on Danger 1942,Ag 22,16:2
Aerial Gunner 1943,Je 26,10:2
Midnight Manhunt 1945,Ag 18,12:5
Fear in the Night 1947,Ap 19,11:3
Adventure Island 1947,O 20,29:2
Albuquerque 1948,Mr 1,17:2
El Paso 1949,Mr 24,35:2
Manhandled 1949,My 26,34:2
Special Agent 1949,Ag 22,13:1
Captain China 1950,Mr 2,33:2
Lawless, The 1950,Je 23,29:2
Eagle and the Hawk, The 1950,Jl 6,31:2
Tripoli 1950,N 10,35:2

Last Outpost, The 1951,Je 22,16:3
Passage West 1951,Ag 31,12:2
Crosswinds 1951,D 7,35:4
Hong Kong 1952,Ap 5,20:3
Sangaree 1953,Je 5,19:1
Those Redheads From Seattle 1953,O 1,34:2
Jivaro 1954,F 13,11:5
Run for Cover 1955,Ap 30,10:6
Hell's Island 1955,My 7,10:2
Far Horizons, The 1955,My 21,11:1
Lucy Gallant 1955,O 21,30:1
Pinegin, N
Conquerors of the Night 1933,Jl 31,16:3
Pinelli, P (Screenwriter)
Bullet for Stefano 1950,O 26,38:7
Pinelli, Sandrino
Conjugal Bed, The 1963,S 17,30:1
Pinelli, Tullio (Miscellaneous)
Strada, La 1956,Jl 17,19:2
Pinelli, Tullio (Original Author)
Vitelloni 1956,O 24,43:1
Bidone, Il 1964,N 20,42:1
Juliet of the Spirits 1965,N 4,57:1
Pinelli, Tullio (Screenwriter)
Without Pity; (Senza Pieta) 1950,Mr 16,40:4
Ways of Love (The Miracle); Miracle, The (Ways of Love) 1950,D 13,50:2
Mill on the Po, The 1951,O 23,35:2
Path of Hope, The (Il Cammino Della Speranza) 1952,Ag 5,15:5
Strada, La 1956,Jl 17,19:2
Cabiria 1957,O 29,34:2
Dolce Vita, La 1961,Ap 20,30:1
Boccaccio '70 (The Tempation of Dr Antonio); Temptation of Dr Antonio, The (Boccaccio '70) 1962,Je 27,40:1
Eight and One Half 1963,Je 26,36:1
Steppe, The 1963,O 1,33:1
Bidone, Il 1964,N 20,42:1
Love a la Carte 1965,Ja 12,31:1
Variety Lights; Luci del Varieta 1965,My 7,34:1
Juliet of the Spirits 1965,N 4,57:1
Climax, The 1967,S 12,55:1
Pinero, Arthur Wing Sir (Original Author)
His House in Order 1920,Mr 8,9:6
His House in Order 1920,Mr 8,9:5
Enchanted Cottage, The 1924,Ap 14,14:1
Enchanted Cottage, The 1945,Ap 28,19:2
Pinero, Federico
Romance del Palmar, El 1939,My 1,21:2
Ultima Melodia, La; Last Melody, The 1939,Ag 5,18:3
Pines, Romain (Producer)
Sundays and Cybele 1962,N 13,43:3
Ping, Ho
Lady General, The 1965,F 12,19:1
Ping, Yeh
Fight to the Last 1938,D 22,25:3
Pingault, Claude (Composer)
Coiffeur Pour Dames 1932,O 31,18:4
Pingree, Earl
Holy Terror, A 1931,Jl 20,20:4
Guilty as Hell 1932,Ag 6,14:5
Pinheiro, Julie
Signs of Life; Lebenszeichen 1968,S 26,60:1
Pinikova, E
Jew at War, A 1931,Jl 25,11:6
Pink, Albert (Producer)
Man to Men 1949,F 21,20:2
Pink, Sid (Director)
Journey to the Seventh Planet 1962,My 25,28:3
Pink, Sid (Original Author)
Angry Red Planet, The 1960,My 5,41:2
Pink, Sid (Producer)
Angry Red Planet, The 1960,My 5,41:2
Journey to the Seventh Planet 1962,My 25,28:3
Pink, Sid (Screenwriter)
Angry Red Planet, The 1960,My 5,41:2
Journey to the Seventh Planet 1962,My 25,28:3
Pink, Sidney T
Are We Civilized? 1934,Je 14,28:5
Pinsent, Gordon
Thomas Crown Affair, The 1968,Je 27,48:2
Pinski, David (Original Author)
Singing Blacksmith, The 1938,N 3,27:1
Pinson, David
Babes in Toyland 1961,D 15,49:1
Pinter, Harold
Servant, The 1964,Mr 17,30:2
Accident 1967,Ap 18,33:1
Pinter, Harold (Original Author)
Guest, The 1964,Ja 21,25:2
Birthday Party, The 1968,D 10,54:1
Pinter, Harold (Screenwriter)
Guest, The 1964,Ja 21,25:2
Servant, The 1964,Mr 17,30:2
Pumpkin Eater, The 1964,N 10,58:1
Accident 1967,Ap 18,33:1
Birthday Party, The 1968,D 10,54:1

Pinter, Howard (Screenwriter)
Quiller Memorandum, The 1966,D 16,59:1
Pinto, Mercedes (Original Author)
This Strange Passion 1955,D 5,34:2
Pintoff, Ernest (Director)
Harvey Middleman, Fireman 1965,Jl 13,39:1
Pintoff, Ernest (Screenwriter)
Harvey Middleman, Fireman 1965,Jl 13,39:1
Pinza, Ezio
Carnegie Hall 1947,My 3,10:2
Strictly Dishonorable 1951,Jl 12,21:6
Mr Imperium 1951,O 15,22:2
Tonight We Sing 1953,F 13,17:2
Pinzon, Nathan
Inheritance, The; Herencia, La 1964,S 16,36:3
Pious, Minerva
It's in the Bag 1945,Je 11,12:1
Joe Macbeth 1956,Ap 7,13:1
Piovani, Pino
Woman of Rome 1956,N 6,30:1
Piovene, Guido (Screenwriter)
Mambo 1955,Mr 31,23:3
Piper, Evelyn (Original Author)
Bunny Lake is Missing 1965,O 4,00:0
Nanny, The 1965,N 4,57:2
Piper, Frederick
Jamaica Inn 1939,O 12,33:1
October Man, The 1948,Ap 16,29:2
Champagne Charlie 1948,Ag 7,8:2
Escape 1948,Ag 16,12:2
Easy Money (Episode 3) 1949,F 14,15:3
My Brothers Keeper 1949,F 14,15:3
Pink String and Sealing Wax 1950,O 4,38:2
Lavender Hill Mob, The 1951,O 16,35:2
Brandy for the Parson 1952,Ag 18,13:4
Stranger in Between, The 1952,Ag 20,21:3
Murder on Monday 1953,O 7,35:2
Novel Affair, A 1957,Ag 28,22:1
Piper, James
Hue and Cry 1951,Ja 9,25:2
Pipinic, Hermina
Steppe, The 1963,O 1,33:1
Seventh Continent, The 1968,Jl 30,33:2
Pipitone, Nino Jr
Song of Bernadette, The 1944,Ja 27,15:2
Pipolo, Castellano (Screenwriter)
Fascist, The 1965,Je 18,28:3
Pipolo (Giuseppe Moccia) (Screenwriter)
Crazy Desire 1964,Jl 3,13:2
Pipolo (Original Author)
Hours of Love, The 1965,S 4,11:5
Pipolo (Screenwriter)
Hours of Love, The 1965,S 4,11:5
Pipon, Lucien (Composer)
Moulin Rouge 1944,N 23,38:2
Piquer, V Saiso (Producer)
En un Burro Tres Baturros; Three Rustics on one Donkey 1940,S 21,13:3
Pirandello, Luigi (Miscellaneous)
Very Handy Man, A 1966,D 15,60:1
Pirandello, Luigi (Original Author)
Living Dead Man, The 1927,Mr 7,16:3
As You Desire Me 1932,Je 3,23:4
Herzblut 1932,O 3,15:2
Late Mathias Pascal, The 1937,N 18,27:2
But It's Nothing Serious 1939,O 10,27:2
Pensaci Giacomino; Think It Over, Jack 1940,Mr 25,11:3
Terra di Nessuno; Nobody's Land 1940,O 25,25:4
This Love of Ours 1945,N 1,20:2
Never Say Goodbye 1956,Ap 14,20:1
Of Life and Love 1958,O 7,40:2
Piretti, Katiuscia
Mafioso 1964,Jl 1,42:1
Piri, Vaszari
Csokolj Meg Edes 1932,N 25,19:2
Piriev, Ivan (Director)
Country Bride 1938,Je 4,18:2
We Will Come Back 1943,O 15,15:2
They Met in Moscow 1944,Je 7,13:2
Six PM 1946,Ja 28,15:5
Symphony of Life 1948,D 28,19:7
Cossacks of the Kuban 1950,O 30,22:4
World Festival of Song and Dance 1952,N 24,19:2
Piriev, Ivan (Producer)
They Met in Moscow 1944,Je 7,13:2
Cossacks of the Kuban 1950,O 30,22:4
Pirogov, Alexander
Boris Godunov 1956,Ja 23,21:4
Pirogov, Lev
Hello, Moscow! 1946,Je 15,24:4
Pirosh, Robert (Director)
Go for Broke 1951,My 25,31:2
Washington Story 1952,Jl 2,22:3
Valley of the Kings 1954,Jl 22,15:2
Spring Reunion 1957,My 6,25:2
Pirosh, Robert (Original Author)
Winning Ticket, The 1935,F 11,14:2
Day at the Races, A 1937,Je 18,25:2
Rings on her Fingers 1942,Ap 24,21:4
Battleground 1949,N 12,8:4
Hell is for Heroes 1962,Jl 12,19:3

Pirosh, Robert (Screenwriter)
Day at the Races, A 1937,Je 18,25:2
Quarterback, The 1940,O 17,33:3
Night of January 16th, The 1941,D 19,35:1
Song of the Islands 1942,Mr 12,24:4
I Married a Witch 1942,N 20,27:2
Up in Arms 1944,Mr 3,19:2
Battleground 1949,N 12,8:4
Go for Broke 1951,My 25,31:2
Washington Story 1952,Jl 2,22:3
Valley of the Kings 1954,Jl 22,15:2
Spring Reunion 1957,My 6,25:2
Gathering of Eagles, A 1963,Jl 11,21:2
What's so bad About Feeling Good?
  1968,My 25,27:1

Pirrie, James
Non-Stop New York 1937,N 29,19:2

Pirro, Ugo (Original Author)
Five Branded Women 1960,Je 2,27:2
Navajo Joe 1967,D 7,60:2

Pirro, Ugo (Screenwriter)
Most Wonderful Moment, The 1959,Je 1,23:6
We Still Kill the Old Way 1968,F 29,28:1

Pirrone, John
Penrod and his Twin Brother 1938,Ap 18,11:1
Speed to Burn 1938,S 9,25:1

Piryof, I (Director)
Anna 1936,Jl 17,20:2

Pisacane, Carlo
Big Deal on Madonna Street, The 1960,N 23,20:1
Fiasco in Milan 1963,Ap 11,29:2

Pisano, Rosita
Anna 1953,F 19,20:5

Pisano, Vittorina
Bandits of Orgosolo 1964,Ap 14,32:1

Pisetta, Friedel
Viktor und Viktoria 1935,Ja 28,10:5

Pisier, Marie-France
Love at Twenty 1963,F 7,5:6
Trans-Europ-Express 1968,My 13,52:1

Pistek, Doris
Carmen Baby 1967,O 11,41:2

Pistek, Theodor
Merry Wives, The 1940,N 12,28:3

Pistilli, Luigi
For a Few Dollars More 1967,Jl 4,23:1
We Still Kill the Old Way 1968,F 29,28:1

Pisu, Mario
Re Burlone, Il 1936,Mr 28,11:3
Passaporto Rosso 1936,S 2,18:2
Re di Danari; Money King 1939,D 22,15:2
Professor, My Son 1949,Ap 18,18:4
Margaret of Cortona 1957,Ja 21,20:4
Juliet of the Spirits 1965,N 4,57:1

Pisu, Raffaele
Italiano Brava Gente 1966,F 4,20:1
Weekend, Italian Style 1968,My 23,56:2

Pita, Aurora
Big Boodle, The 1957,Mr 12,38:1

Pitagora, Paola
Fist in his Pocket 1968,My 28,40:1

Pitaks, Vaivit V
King of the White Elephant, The 1941,Ap 5,12:7

Pitanga, Antonio
Tropics 1968,S 24,52:1

Pitcairn, Jack
In the Palace of the King 1923,D 3,14:1
Journey's End 1930,Ap 9,25:1

Pitcher, George (Producer)
Day of the Triffids 1963,My 11,15:2

Pithey, Wensley
Guilt is my Shadow 1954,Mr 25,36:4

Pitkin, Waldo
Panic in the Streets 1950,Ag 5,9:2

Pitkin, Walter B (Original Author)
Life Begins at 40 1935,Ap 5,21:3

Pitlik, Noam
Hallelujah Trail, The 1965,Jl 2,17:1

Pitman, Donald
Emil 1938,Ap 15,23:2

Pitoeff, Sacha
Anastasia 1956,D 14,35:6
Last Year at Marienbad 1962,Mr 8,26:1
Poupee, La 1963,Ag 28,39:1

Pitoeff, Svetlana
Abused Confidence 1938,D 1,29:1

Pitouto
Crise est Finie, La 1935,Mr 14,18:1
Mexican Bus ride 1954,Jl 21,18:3

Pitt, Dale (Miscellaneous)
Conspiracy of Hearts 1960,Ap 8,24:1

Pitt, Henna
Gluecklichste Ehe von Wien, Die; Happiest
  Married Couple in Vienna, The 1938,O 8,10:2
Verliebte Herzen; Hearts in Love 1939,Je 10,14:2

Pittard, Robert
Andy Hardy's Double Life 1943,Ja 12,23:3

Pittas, Elsie
Electra 1962,D 18,5:2

Pittcock, Michael (Screenwriter)
Where the Bullets Fly 1967,S 7,50:4

Pitti, Giuliana
Schoolgirl Diary 1947,O 18,9:2

Pittman, Montgomery (Screenwriter)
Tarzan and the Lost Safari 1957,Ap 13,12:3

Pittman, Tom
Black Patch 1958,Ap 24,38:1
Proud Rebel, The 1958,Jl 2,23:4
Verboten 1960,Jl 12,39:1

Pitts, Zasu
Is Matrimony a Failure 1922,Ap 17,22:3
Poor Men's Wives 1923,Ja 29,11:1
West of the Water Tower 1923,D 31,9:3
Daughters of Today 1924,Mr 4,17:1
Triumph 1924,Ap 21,21:4
Goldfish, The 1924,My 20,15:2
Changing Husbands 1924,Je 23,22:4
Wine of Youth 1924,Ag 11,16:1
Fast Set, The 1924,N 18,22:1
Greed 1924,D 5,28:1
Great Divide, The 1925,F 11,19:4
Pretty Ladies 1925,Jl 14,14:1
Woman's Faith, A 1925,Jl 27,17:3
Mannequinn 1926,Ja 12,27:5
What Happened to Jones 1926,F 9,22:1
Risky Business 1926,S 8,19:3
Her big Night 1926,O 13,21:1
Casey at the Bat 1927,Ap 4,30:5
Wife Savers 1928,Ja 17,23:2
Buck Privates 1928,Ja 30,18:1
13 Washington Square 1928,Ja 30,18:1
Wedding March, The 1928,O 15,26:1
Sins of the Fathers 1929,Ja 28,21:1
Dummy, The 1929,Mr 4,20:2
Squall, The 1929,My 10,32:5
Twin Beds 1929,Jl 15,25:1
Argyle Case, The 1929,Ag 31,13:4
Paris 1929,N 8,31:2
This Thing Called Love 1929,D 14,22:4
No, No, Nanette 1930,Ja 4,21:1
Locked Door, The 1930,Ja 20,21:1
Honey 1930,Mr 29,23:1
Devil's Holiday, The 1930,My 10,25:3
Little Accident 1930,Ag 4,13:4
Monte Carlo 1930,Ag 28,22:4
Squealer, The 1930,S 8,17:1
War Nurse 1930,O 24,31:1
Sin Takes a Holliday 1930,N 28,23:1
Lottery Bride, The 1930,N 29,21:4
Passion Flower 1930,D 22,16:2
Finn and Hattie 1931,Ja 31,15:1
River's End 1931,Mr 7,17:2
Bad Sister 1931,Mr 30,25:2
Beyond Victory 1931,Ap 6,24:1
Seed 1931,My 15,20:6
Woman of Experience, A 1931,Jl 9,26:5
Guardsman, The 1931,S 10,22:4
Big Gamble, The 1931,S 21,20:2
Penrod and Sam 1931,S 26,25:3
Secret Witness, The 1931,D 21,28:4
Man I Killed, The 1932,Ja 20,17:4
Shopworn 1932,Ap 4,13:6
Trial of Vivienne Ware, The 1932,Ap 30,19:3
Strangers of the Evening 1932,Je 4,9:2
Westward Passage 1932,Je 4,9:2
Is my Face red 1932,Je 11,9:3
Make Me a Star 1932,Jl 1,19:3
Roar of the Dragon 1932,Jl 25,11:2
Back Street 1932,Ag 29,9:2
Blondie of the Follies 1932,S 2,19:2
Madison Square Garden 1932,O 12,26:5
Once in a Lifetime 1932,O 29,18:4
They Just Had to Get Married 1933,F 13,11:4
Out all Night 1933,Ap 8,16:2
Hello Sister! 1933,My 6,11:2
Professional Sweetheart 1933,Jl 14,15:3
Her First Mate 1933,S 2,14:5
Aggie Appleby, Maker of Men 1933,O 20,14:2
Meet the Baron 1933,O 28,20:3
Love, Honor and Oh, Baby! 1933,O 28,20:3
Mr Skitch 1933,D 23,19:1
Sing and Like It 1934,Ap 14,18:2
Private Scandal 1934,Je 15,26:2
Dames 1934,Ag 16,20:2
Their big Moment 1934,S 6,22:4
Mrs Wiggs of the Cabbage Patch 1934,O 29,14:2
Gay Bride, The 1934,D 19,27:2
Ruggles of Red Gap 1935,Mr 7,26:1
13 Hours by Air 1936,Ap 30,17:2
Mad Holiday 1936,N 26,39:2
Plot Thickens, The 1936,D 9,35:2
Sing Me a Love Song 1936,D 26,15:2
Forty Naughty Girls 1937,S 18,15:3
52d Street 1937,N 15,15:1
Naughty but Nice 1939,Je 23,23:2
Mickey, the Kid 1939,Jl 6,27:1
Nurse Edith Cavell 1939,S 22,27:4
Eternally Yours 1939,O 7,11:2
It all Came True 1940,Ap 6,13:2
No, No, Nanette 1940,D 20,33:1
Broadway Limited 1941,Je 16,11:6
Week End for Three 1941,O 24,27:4
Mexican Spitfire at Sea 1942,Je 26,16:5
Tish 1942,S 18,25:2

Pitts, Zasu— Cont
Let's Face It 1943,Ag 5,18:1
Breakfast in Hollywood 1946,Jl 15,21:1
Perfect Marriage, The 1947,Ja 16,30:3
Life With Father 1947,Ag 16,6:6
Francis 1950,Mr 16,40:2
Denver and Rio Grande, The 1952,My 17,22:7
Francis Joins the Wacs 1954,Jl 31,6:3
This Could Be the Night 1957,My 15,39:1
Teenage Millionaire 1962,Ja 12,29:2
Thrill of it All, The 1963,Ag 2,15:3

Pittschau, Ernst
Germany Year Zero 1949,S 20,35:2

Pittschau, Werner
Women Without Men 1928,N 12,18:2

Pivar, Ben (Original Author)
Legion of Lost Flyers 1939,O 30,13:3

Pivar, Ben (Producer)
Mutiny on the Blackhawk 1939,Ag 2,17:2
Enemy Agent 1940,Ap 22,13:3
Horror Island 1941,Mr 31,11:3
Mummy's Tomb, The 1942,O 26,19:2
Mummy's Ghost, The 1944,Jl 1,10:7
Strange Confession 1945,N 8,17:3
Pillow of Death 1946,Ja 26,19:3
House of Horrors 1946,F 23,20:3
She Wolf of London 1946,Ap 6,10:6

Pivar, Maurice (Original Author)
Captive Wild Woman 1943,Je 7,9:4

Piver, Ben (Original Author)
Tropic Fury 1939,S 8,28:4

Pivneko, V
Forty-Nine Days 1964,Ja 27,19:1

Piyaff, Rostislav
Spring 1948,Mr 15,26:2

Pizani, Robert
Champs-Elysees 1939,F 28,17:2
Entente Cordiale 1939,D 26,23:2
S O S Mediterranean 1940,Ja 1,29:2
Man of the Hour, The 1940,N 21,43:2
Man About Town 1947,O 22,37:1
Fernandel the Dressmaker 1957,Jl 1,19:2
Deadlier Than the Male 1957,O 9,41:1
Parisienne, La 1958,Jl 31,27:1
Premier May 1958,S 17,44:2
Senechal the Magnificent 1958,O 14,44:1

Pizella, Stephanie (Screenwriter)
Children of Chaos 1950,Ap 20,37:2

Pizhova, O
Lonely White Sail 1938,My 7,18:1

Pizor, William M (Miscellaneous)
Virgins of Bali 1932,D 12,18:4

Pizzi, Nilla
Mandragola 1966,Je 7,50:2

Pizzuttio, Antonio
Revenge 1947,N 28,37:4

Pkhor, B R (Screenwriter)
Beethoven Concerto 1937,Mr 24,29:1

Place, Graham (Miscellaneous)
Mr Bug Goes to Town 1942,F 20,21:3

Place, Graham (Screenwriter)
Mr Bug Goes to Town 1942,F 20,21:3

Pladner, Milou
Winner, The 1965,Jl 1,34:1

Plane, Carlo Della
Ring Around the Clock 1953,My 19,36:2
No Sun in Venice 1958,Je 10,40:2

Planer, Lillian (Original Author)
Wave, A Wac and a Marine, A 1944,Ag 14,11:4

Plank, Melinda
Greenwich Village Story 1963,Jl 12,14:3

Plantier, Albert
Winner's Circle, The 1957,My 6,25:2

Plaschkes, Otto (Producer)
Georgy Girl 1966,O 18,48:1

Plashy, Jiri
Emperor and the Golem, The 1955,Ja 10,27:4

Plateados, Los
Silk, Blood and Sun 1943,Ja 30,10:6

Platen, Flockina von
Heimatland; Homeland 1939,O 28,11:2

Platen, Karl
Between Worlds 1924,Jl 7,10:4
Luther 1929,Je 24,27:1
Because I Loved You 1930,Ja 25,13:2
Lumpenball 1931,Ap 27,25:1
Lindenwirtin vom Rhein, Die 1931,S 25,28:7
M 1933,Ap 3,13:3
Junge Graf, Der 1936,D 14,15:2

Platonof, M
Natalka-Poltavka 1936,D 25,19:4

Platov, V
Flames on the Volga 1958,Ja 27,21:7

Platt, Alma
Johnny Holiday 1950,My 17,36:1

Platt, Billy
Face in the Sky 1933,F 20,11:5

Platt, Edward
Shrike, The 1955,Jl 8,15:2
Private War of Major Benson, The
  1955,Ag 3,27:2
Rebel without a Cause 1955,O 27,28:3
Illegal 1955,O 29,12:6
Sincerely Yours 1955,N 3,37:1

Platt, Edward — Cont

Lieutenant Wore Skirts, The 1956,Ja 12,22:1
Serenade 1956,Mr 24,21:1 (Incorrect in this
edition; use 1956,Mr 23,21:1 elsewhere)
Backlash 1956,Ap 21,11:2
Proud Ones, The 1956,Ag 11,10:2
Storm Center 1956,O 22,25:4
Great Man, The 1957,Ja 2,28:2
Written on the Wind 1957,Ja 12,12:6
Tattered Dress, The 1957,Mr 15,22:3
Designing Woman 1957,My 17,20:2
House of Numbers 1957,S 13,15:2
Helen Morgan Story, The 1957,O 3,33:2
Gift of Love, The 1958,F 12,32:2
High Cost of Loving, The 1958,My 17,12:1
Summer Love 1958,Je 26,23:4
North by Northwest 1959,Ag 7,28:1
They Came to Cordura 1959,O 22,47:2
Pollyanna 1960,My 20,26:1
Atlantis the Lost Continent 1961,My 27,12:1
Ticklish Affair, A 1963,Ag 22,19:2

Platt, George Foster (Director)
Deliverance 1919,Ag 19,10:1

Platt, Louise
I Met my Love Again 1938,Ja 15,19:1
Spawn of the North 1938,S 8,27:1
Stagecoach 1939,Mr 3,21:1
Tell no Tales 1939,Je 2,27:3
Captain Caution 1940,O 21,21:3
Street Of Chance 1942,N 19,31:3

Platt, Marc
Tonight and Every Night 1945,Mr 9,16:2
Tars and Spars 1946,F 15,29:2
Down to Earth 1947,S 12,18:2
Swordsman, The 1947,O 17,18:4
Her Wonderful Lie 1950,Jl 17,15:2
Seven Brides for Seven Brothers 1954,Jl 23,8:3
Oklahoma! 1955,O 11,49:1

Platt, Polly (Original Author)
Targets 1968,Ag 14,34:1

Platt, William
Simon the Jester 1925,N 19,22:1
Mother Machree 1928,Mr 6,20:3

Platte, Rudolf
Sonne Geht auf, Die 1935,F 18,19:4
Schuechterne Felix, Der 1935,S 7,19:5
Zigeunerbaron 1935,S 14,8:5
Pantoffelhelden 1935,O 21,22:5
Was Bin Ich Ohne dich? 1935,D 14,11:2
Einer zu viel an Bord 1936,Ja 25,18:5
Vetter aus Dingsda, Der 1936,F 1,9:3
Donogoo Tonka 1936,Ap 13,15:2
Koenigin der Liebe 1936,My 4,16:2
Blinde Passagier; Stowaways 1937,Mr 6,10:1
Meadehen von Gestern Nacht, Das; Girl of Last
Night, The 1938,Je 18,18:2
Landstreicher, Die; Hoboes, The 1938,N 26,18:1
Lustige Witwenball, Der; Merry Widows' Ball,
The 1939,My 1,21:2
Solo per Danne 1939,My 30,13:3
Our Little Wife 1940,Ja 27,9:2
Affairs of Julie, The 1958,D 10,53:1

Platters, The
Girl Can't Help It, The 1957,F 9,12:7

Plau, Mario
Cossacks, The 1960,S 6,41:4

Plaugher, Wilbur
Run, Appaloosa, Run! 1966,Jl 14,28:1

Playboys, The Four
You're a Sweetheart 1937,D 25,10:5

Playfair, Nigel Sir
Perfect Understanding 1933,F 23,20:2
Lady is Willing, The 1934,Ag 11,16:5

Playter, Wellington
Golden Snare, The 1921,Jl 11,9:3

Pleasence, Donald
Beachcomber, The 1955,Ja 17,27:5
1984 1956,O 1,31:1
Stowaway Girl 1957,N 6,43:3
Tale of Two Cities, A 1958,Ag 5,23:1
Two-Headed Spy, The 1959,Mr 3,38:4
Look Back in Anger 1959,S 16,45:1
Wind Cannot Read, The 1960,Mr 10,36:1
Battle of the Sexes, The 1960,Ap 19,40:4
Sons and Lovers 1960,Ag 3,35:1
Circus of Horrors 1960,S 1,31:1
Hell is a City 1961,Ja 19,26:3
Risk, The 1961,S 25,41:2
No Love for Johnnie 1961,D 13,55:1
Lisa 1962,My 25,28:1
No Place Like Homicide 1962,S 13,32:1
Great Escape, The 1963,Ag 8,19:1
Guest, The 1964,Ja 21,25:2
Dr Crippen 1964,F 15,14:1
Greatest Story Ever Told, The 1965,F 16,40:2
Hallelujah Trail, The 1965,Jl 2,17:1
Fantastic Voyage 1966,S 8,43:1
Cul de Sac 1966,N 8,44:2
Night of the Generals, The 1967,F 3,38:1
You Only Live Twice 1967,Je 14,40:1
Matchless 1967,N 11,26:3
Eye of the Devil 1967,D 7,60:1
Will Penny 1968,Ap 11,51:2

Plemic, Ivan
Ljubav I Strast 1932,D 16,25:5

Pleschkoff, Michael
Into her Kingdom 1926,Ag 10,19:2

Pleshette, Suzanne
Geisha Boy, The 1958,D 24,00:0
Rome Adventure 1962,Mr 16,25:1
40 Pounds of Trouble 1963,Ja 24,5:2
Birds, The 1963,Ap 1,5:5 (Incorrect in this
edition; use 1963,Ap 1,54:1 elsewhere)
Wall of Noise 1963,S 5,27:1
Distant Trumpet, A 1964,My 28,40:1
Youngblood Hawke 1964,N 6,30:1
Fate Is the Hunter 1964,D 10,61:1
Rage to Live, A 1965,O 21,57:1
Ugly Dachshund, The 1966,Ap 7,45:1
Nevada Smith 1966,Je 24,28:1 (Incorrect in this
edition; use 1966,Je 30,28:1 elsewhere)
Mister Buddwing 1966,O 12,36:1
Adventures of Bullwhip Griffin, The
1967,Mr 9,43:2
Power, The 1968,Mr 7,52:2
Blackbeard's Ghost 1968,Ap 11,51:3

Pless, George
Rheinlandmaedel, Das 1931,S 18,29:1

Pless, Henry
Tannenberg 1934,Ap 3,26:6

Plessis, Jacqueline
Lost in the Dark 1949,My 14,9:2
Seven Deadly Sins, The (Sloth); Sloth (The Seven
Deadly Sins) 1953,My 12,31:3

Pliatt, Roman
Zoya 1945,Ap 16,18:6
Village Teacher 1948,Jl 5,8:4

Pliego, Eduardo Gonzales
Mujer de Nadie, La; Nobody's Wife
1938,F 7,10:3

Plimpton, George
Beyond the Law 1968,S 30,60:4
Beyond the Law 1968,O 24,55:1

Plimpton, George (Original Author)
Paper Lion 1968,O 24,54:1

Plimpton, George (Producer)
Vali 1967,Je 2,34:2

Plisetskaya, Maya
Stars of the Russian Ballet (The Fountain of
Bakhchisarai); Fountain of Bakhchisarai (Stars of
the Russian Ballet) 1954,S 6,9:2
Swan Lake 1960,Ja 26,25:2
Khovanschina 1960,S 19,41:2
Little Humpbacked Horse, The 1962,O 8,19:1

Plisnier, Charles (Original Author)
Three Sinners 1952,Jl 8,23:2

Plisnier, Charles (Screenwriter)
Three Sinners 1952,Jl 8,23:2

Plivanoff, M I
Nazar Stodolya 1937,Ag 7,7:2

Ploquin, Raoul (Director)
Avocate d'Amour 1938,S 8,27:2

Ploquin, Raoul (Original Author)
Sheep Has Five Legs, The 1955,Ag 10,19:2

Ploquin, Raoul (Producer)
Avocate d'Amour 1938,S 8,27:2
Sheep Has Five Legs, The 1955,Ag 10,19:2
Maxime 1962,O 25,48:3

Ploski, Joe
Li'l Abner 1959,D 12,19:2

Plotnicki, Boleslaw
Naked Among the Wolves 1967,Ap 19,54:7

Plotnikov, N
Grain 1936,Ja 16,25:2
Revolutionists 1936,D 26,15:3
Paris Commune 1937,Je 2,20:4
Lonely White Sail 1938,My 7,18:1
Oppenheim Family, The 1939,My 24,29:2
Lenin in 1918 1939,Je 27,27:2
On his Own 1939,S 13,31:3
University of Life 1941,F 26,17:1
Vow, The 1947,Je 23,14:3
Ivan Pavlov 1950,F 13,15:2
Nine Days of one Year 1964,D 29,19:1

Plotnikov, Sergei
Farewell, Doves 1962,Mr 19,38:3

Plowden, Roger
Five Fingers 1952,F 23,7:5

Plowman, Melinda
Carrie 1952,Jl 17,20:2

Plowright, Hilda
Partners of the Plains 1938,F 12,20:4
Cafe Society 1939,F 23,19:2
Raffles 1940,Ja 13,11:2
Separate Tables 1958,D 19,2:7

Plowright, Joan
Time Without Pity 1957,N 23,11:2
Entertainer, The 1960,O 4,49:2

Ployardt, John (Miscellaneous)
Adventures of Ichabod and Mr Toad, The
1949,O 10,18:2

Plumb, Edward (Composer)
Bambi 1942,Ag 14,13:1
Victory Through Air Power 1943,Jl 19,13:1

Plumb, Hay
Orders Is Orders 1934,My 7,20:2

Plummer, Christopher
Stage Struck 1958,Ap 23,40:1
Wind Across the Everglades 1958,S 12,21:1
Fall of the Roman Empire, The 1964,Mr 27,14:2
Sound of Music, The 1965,Mr 3,34:1
Inside Daisy Clover 1966,F 18,23:1
Night of the Generals, The 1967,F 3,38:1
Triple Cross 1967,Jl 20,20:2
Oedipus the King 1968,S 19,62:2
High Commissioner, The 1968,D 12,62:5

Plummer, Elmer (Original Author)
Three Caballeros, The 1945,F 5,20:1

Plummer, Lincoln
Ten-Dollar Raise, The 1921,Je 13,16:1
Within the Law 1923,Ap 30,11:2
Dangerous Maid, The 1923,D 11,26:2
Regular Fellow, A 1925,O 5,25:2
Alias the Deacon 1927,Je 21,29:2

Plunkett, Joseph (Miscellaneous)
Sea Hawk, The 1924,Je 3,22:1
Lost World, The 1925,F 9,15:3

Plunkett, Patricia
It Always Rains on Sunday 1949,F 14,15:5
Bond Street 1950,Mr 30,40:6
For Them that Trespass 1950,S 27,37:2
Murder Without Crime 1951,D 26,19:6
Story of Mandy, The 1953,F 24,21:3
Landfall 1953,My 11,25:2
Dunkirk 1958,S 11,42:2

Plunkett, Walter (Miscellaneous)
Gone With the Wind 1939,D 20,31:2

Plush, Gail Capt
Big Lift, The 1950,Ap 27,37:2

Plutarch (Miscellaneous)
Cleopatra 1963,Je 13,29:1

Pluzhnik, G
Heroes of the Sea 1941,Ap 28,11:2
Son of the Regiment 1948,Ap 29,27:3

Plympton, George (Screenwriter)
Pride of the Bowery 1941,Ja 24,15:2
Last of the Redmen 1947,Ag 30,8:6

Plyta, Mary (Director)
Moment of Passion 1960,N 21,34:1

Po, Ivy Ling
Lady General, The 1965,F 12,19:1
Grand Substitution, The 1965,N 25,64:5

Poalieri, Germana
Stella del Mare; Star of the Sea 1940,My 3,17:6

Podelsnaya, Oxana
Demon of the Steppes 1930,Ja 18,21:1

Podesta, Antonio
Idolos de la Radio 1935,Jl 2,24:5

Podesta, Rossana
Ulysses 1955,Ag 18,17:2
Helen of Troy 1956,Ja 27,21:4
Rosanna 1956,My 17,37:2
Santiago 1956,Jl 14,13:2
Raw Wind in Eden 1958,S 20,10:6
Temptation 1962,N 10,16:2
Sodom and Gomorrah 1963,Ja 24,5:3

Podesto, Maria Esther
Escuadron Azul, El; Blue Squadron, The
1938,Je 4,18:3

Podgorny, Boris
Zoya 1945,Ap 16,18:6

Podgorny, N A
House of Death 1932,Ag 13,18:6

Podgorny, Nikita
Idiot, The 1960,Jl 22,11:2

Podhajsky, Alois Col (Original Author)
Miracle of the White Stallions 1963,My 23,31:2

Podorozhny, L
False Uniforms 1932,N 19,20:2

Podrecca Puppets
Where Words Fail; Donde Mueren las Palabraso
1948,Ag 19,18:4

Poe, Edgar Allan (Original Author)
Murders in the Rue Morgue 1932,F 11,16:1
Black Cat, The 1934,My 19,18:4
Tell-Tale Heart, The 1934,Je 15,26:3
Raven, The 1935,Jl 5,9:2
Living Dead, The 1940,D 17,33:2
Black Cat, The 1941,Ap 26,20:3
Mystery of Marie Roget, The 1942,My 5,17:3
Phantom of the Rue Morgue 1954,Mr 20,10:5
House of Usher, The 1960,S 15,45:4
Pit and the Pendulum, The 1961,Ag 24,25:3
Tales of Terror 1962,Jl 5,21:2 (In Addenda)
Raven, The 1963,Ja 26,5:8
Telltale Heart, The 1963,My 16,42:1
Haunted Palace, The 1964,Ja 30,24:1
Tomb of Ligeia 1965,My 6,44:1

Poe, Edgar Allen (Miscellaneous)
Crime of Dr Crespi, The 1936,Ja 13,14:3

Poe, Evelyn
To Beat the Band 1935,N 23,23:2

Poe, Fernando Jr
Walls of Hell, The 1965,N 18,55:3

Poe, James
Paula 1952,Jl 16,21:2

Poe, James (Original Author)
Close-Up 1948,Ap 5,24:2
Poe, James (Screenwriter)
Without Honor 1950,Jl 3,9:2
Scandal Sheet 1952,Ja 17,23:1
Big Knife, The 1955,N 9,41:2
Attack! 1956,S 20,29:4
Hot Spell 1958,S 18,37:2
Cat on a Hot Tin Roof 1958,S 19,24:1
Last Train from Gun Hill 1959,Jl 30,31:2
Sanctuary 1961,F 22,31:1
Summer and Smoke 1961,N 17,41:1
Toys in the Attic 1963,Ag 1,17:2
Lilies of the Field 1963,O 2,51:1
Bedford Incident, The 1965,N 3,43:1
Poe, Lugne
Dame aux Camelias, La 1935,Mr 21,27:1
Poeui, Mayor
Tanga Tika 1953,O 6,34:4
Poff, Lon
Village Blacksmith, The 1922,N 3,17:5
Dante's Inferno 1924,S 30,27:3
Greed 1924,D 5,28:1
Thief in Paradise, A 1925,Ja 26,14:1
Iron Mask, The 1929,F 22,18:6
Pogacic, Vladimir (Director)
Legends of Anika 1956,Ap 19,35:1
Pogacic, Vladimir (Screenwriter)
Legends of Anika 1956,Ap 19,35:1
Poggi, Gianni
House of Ricordi 1956,Mr 13,32:1
Poggi, Grace
Roman Scandals 1933,D 25,28:2
Melody Lingers on, The 1935,N 7,27:1
Poggi, Hugette
Olive Trees of Justice, The 1967,My 5,31:1
Poggi, Ottavio (Original Author)
Hannibal 1960,Ag 4,17:1
Poggi, Ottavio (Producer)
Hannibal 1960,Ag 4,17:1
Queen of the Pirates 1961,Jl 27,23:4
Mighty Crusaders, The 1961,S 23,17:1
Pogodin, N F (Original Author)
Prisoners 1937,F 20,9:2
Pogodin, Nikolai (Screenwriter)
Man With the Gun, The 1939,Ja 30,9:3
Cossacks of the Kuban 1950,O 30,22:4
Pogorzelska, Zula
Kocha, Lubi, Szanuje 1934,N 3,20:4
Pogostin, S Lee (Original Author)
Synanon 1965,My 6,44:1
Pogostin, S Lee (Screenwriter)
Pressure Point 1962,O 11,49:3
Synanon 1965,My 6,44:1
Pogson, N A (Original Author)
Adventures of Marco Polo, The 1965,Ap 8,17:2
Pogue, Mel
Fixed Bayonets 1951,N 21,20:2
Farmer Takes a Wife, The 1953,Je 13,11:2
Pogue, Thomas
I Married a Doctor 1936,Ap 20,17:1
Stage Struck 1936,S 28,14:4
Lloyds of London 1936,N 26,39:1
It's Love I'm After 1937,N 11,31:2
Poh, Richard (Director)
Sable Cicada 1939,Ja 14,13:1
POHL
See Also POLL
Pohl, Klaus
By Rocket to the Moon 1931,F 7,11:1
Pohl, Max
Monna Vanna 1923,S 25,8:2
Karamazof 1931,S 21,20:2
Pohle, Lawrence (Original Author)
Big Shot, The 1937,Ag 13,13:1
Pohlmann, Eric
State Secret 1950,O 5,38:2
Chance of a Lifetime 1951,Mr 15,37:2
Long Dark Hall, The 1951,My 10,38:3
Clouded Yellow, The 1951,N 13,33:2
Hundred Hour Hunt 1953,Je 17,32:2
Monsoon 1953,S 26,15:2
Mogambo 1953,O 2,18:1
Rob Roy 1954,F 4,21:5
Flame and the Flesh 1954,My 3,21:2
Belles of St Trinian's, The 1954,D 23,13:4
Prize of Gold, A 1955,O 15,19:2
Gentlemen Marry Brunettes 1955,O 31,31:5
Quentin Durward 1955,N 24,41:1
His Excellency 1956,F 2,19:3
Lust for Life 1956,S 18,39:1
Constant Husband, The 1957,Jl 26,10:3
Fire Down Below 1957,Ag 9,11:2
Triple Deception 1957,O 7,23:2
Across the Bridge 1957,O 30,24:1
Tale of Two Cities, A 1958,Ag 5,23:1
Elephant Gun 1959,Je 20,11:2
House of the Seven Hawks, The 1959,D 17,51:2
Expresso Bongo 1960,Ap 13,44:1
Surprise Package 1960,O 15,26:2
Kitchen, The 1961,N 2,42:1
Singer not the Song, The 1962,My 3,25:4
Follow the Boys 1963,F 28,8:2

Night Train to Paris 1964,D 3,58:2
Where the Spies Are 1966,Ja 27,29:1
Pointer, Sidney
Blue Lamp, The 1951,Ja 9,25:1
Pointner, Anton
That Murder in Berlin 1929,Mr 12,26:2
Those Who Dance; Tanz Geht Weiter, Der 1930,D 7,IX,6:4
Tanz Geht Weiter, Der 1931,Ja 6,25:1
Stuerme der Leidenschaft 1932,Mr 16,17:3
Raub der Mona Lisa, Der 1932,Mr 30,15:2
Liebeskommando 1932,Ap 27,13:6
Week-End Im Paradies 1932,O 24,18:5
Holzapfel Weiss Alles 1933,Ja 7,11:3
Frau Lehmann's Toechter 1933,O 27,22:3
Wiener Blut 1933,N 13,21:2
Saison in Kairo 1933,D 25,28:2
Frechdachs, Der 1934,Ja 6,18:3
Trenck 1934,Ap 7,19:2
Tante Gusti Kommandiert 1934,My 4,24:4
Graefin Mariza 1935,Ja 26,13:3
Drei von der Kavallerie 1935,Ap 13,11:4
Aufforderung zum Tanz; Invitation to the Dance 1935,N 23,23:3
Royal Waltz, The 1936,Ap 10,27:1
Ein Lied, Ein Kuss, Ein Maeder 1936,D 12,29:4
Thank You, Madame 1937,Ap 27,18:2
Fraeulein Frau 1937,Jl 3,18:2
Favorit der Kaiserin, Der; Favorite of the Empress, The 1939,D 25,29:3
Schatten der Vergangeheit; Shadows of the Past 1940,Ap 20,14:2
Poirault, Suzanne (Original Author)
Thirst of Men, The 1952,O 28,37:1
Poire, Alain (Producer)
French They Are a Funny Race, The 1957,My 21,41:1
Man Escaped, A 1957,Ag 27,33:2
Two Are Guilty 1964,F 29,12:1
Greed in the Sun 1965,Ag 19,35:3
Poire, Jacques Barand Alsin (Producer)
Speaking of Murder 1959,O 12,14:1
Poiret, Jean
Lovers and Thieves 1958,Ag 5,23:2
Tales of Paris (The Tale of Antonio); Tale of Antonio, The (Tales of Paris) 1962,Ag 27,18:1
Candide 1962,N 20,39:1
Three Fables of Love (The Fox and the Crow); Fox and the Crow, The (Three Fables of Love) 1963,Ag 21,38:1
Thank Heaven for Small Favors 1965,Ja 14,44:2
Poirier, Arlette
French Touch, The 1954,S 2,18:2
Modigliani of Montparnasse 1961,Mr 1,27:3
Poirier, Leon (Director)
Jade Casket, The 1929,Je 24,27:1
Cain 1932,Ja 18,18:4
Call, The 1938,Mr 29,18:3
Poirier, Leon (Miscellaneous)
Yellow Cruise, The 1936,N 18,31:3
Poirier, Leon (Producer)
Verdun, Visions d'Histoire 1929,Ja 13,VIII,7:4
Call, The 1938,Mr 29,18:3
Poirier, Leon (Screenwriter)
Cain 1932,Ja 18,18:4
Call, The 1938,Mr 29,18:3
Poiter, Kurt
General Della Rovere 1960,N 22,41:1
Poitier, Sidney
No Way Out 1950,Ag 17,23:1
Cry, the Beloved Country 1952,Ja 24,23:2
Red Ball Express 1952,My 30,11:2
Go, Man, Go 1954,Mr 10,29:5
Blackboard Jungle 1955,Mr 21,21:5
Edge of the City 1957,Ja 30,33:2
Something of Value 1957,My 11,24:6
Band of Angels 1957,Jl 11,21:1
Mark of the Hawk, The 1958,Mr 6,32:1
Defiant Ones, The 1958,S 25,29:1
Porgy and Bess 1959,Je 25,20:3
Virgin Island 1960,Mr 24,39:5
All the Young Men 1960,Ag 27,8:6
Raisin in the Sun, A 1961,Mr 30,24:1
Paris Blues 1961,N 8,41:1
Pressure Point 1962,O 11,49:3
Lilies of the Field 1963,O 2,51:1
Long Ships, The 1964,Je 25,25:1
Greatest Story Ever Told, The 1965,F 16,40:2
Bedford Incident, The 1965,N 3,43:1
Patch of Blue, A 1965,D 16,63:1
Slender Thread, The 1965,D 24,24:2
Duel at Diablo 1966,Je 16,53:1
To Sir, With Love 1967,Je 15,56:1
In the Heat of the Night 1967,Ag 3,26:1
Guess Who's Coming to Dinner 1967,D 12,56:1
For Love of Ivy 1968,Jl 18,26:1
Poitier, Sidney (Original Author)
For Love of Ivy 1968,Jl 18,26:1
Poitrenaud, Jacques (Director)
Tales of Paris (The Tale of Ella); Tale of Ella, The (Tales of Paris) 1962,Ag 27,18:1
Marriage Came Tumbling Down, The 1968,N 6,32:3

Poitrenaud, Jacques (Screenwriter)
Tales of Paris (The Tale of Ella); Tale of Ella, The (Tales of Paris) 1962,Ag 27,18:1
Marriage Came Tumbling Down, The 1968,N 6,32:3
Poivre, Annette
Voyage Surprise 1948,F 14,17:3
Confessions of a Rogue 1948,Mr 30,26:3
Antoine and Antoinette 1948,Ap 16,29:2
Rumors 1949,Mr 19,10:7
Gates of Paris 1958,Ja 15,24:1
Pokorny, Leo
Climbing High 1939,Je 5,20:3
Pokrass, Brothers (Composer)
If War Comes Tomorrow 1938,Jl 14,17:2
Pokrass, Daniel (Composer)
Red Tanks 1942,Je 6,9:2
Pokrass, Samuel (Composer)
Let's Sing Again 1936,My 9,11:2
Happy Landing 1938,Ja 22,19:1
Rebecca of Sunnybrook Farm 1938,Mr 26,12:1
Three Musketeers, The 1939,F 18,12:2
Wife, Husband and Friend 1939,F 25,19:2
Pokrass, Samuel (Miscellaneous)
Life Begins In College 1937,O 9,16:1
Pokrovski, V A
Lenin in October 1938,Ap 2,18:1
Pol, Talitha
Return From the Ashes 1965,N 17,53:1
Pola, Andre
Casbah 1948,My 3,27:4
Pola, Eddie (Composer)
Lullaby of Broadway 1951,Mr 27,35:2
Pola, Isa
Terra Madre 1931,O 31,22:2
Alpine Love 1936,Je 8,22:5
Sono Stato Io; It Was I 1940,My 10,26:7
Cavalleria Rusticana 1947,D 20,21:2
Foria 1948,Ja 21,30:2
Furia 1948,Ja 21,30:2
Angelo in the Crowd 1952,O 4,15:2
Queen of Sheba, The 1953,N 4,29:3
Three Forbidden Stories 1953,N 16,21:4
Margaret of Cortona 1957,Ja 21,20:4
Polack, Emilio Guitierrez
Hunt, The 1967,Ap 25,38:1
Polack, Fernando Sanchez
Hunt, The 1967,Ap 25,38:1
Polaire, Pauline
Maciste in Hell 1931,Je 29,20:3
POLAK
See Also POLLACK, POLLOCK
Polan, Lou
Across the River 1965,Ap 27,27:1
Poland, Joseph (Original Author)
Lawless Nineties, The 1936,Je 29,11:1
Poland, Joseph (Screenwriter)
Lawless Nineties, The 1936,Je 29,11:1
Polanski, Roman
Fearless Vampire Killers, The, or Pardon Me but Your Teeth are in my Neck 1967,N 14,52:1
Polanski, Roman (Director)
Knife in the Water 1963,O 29,31:2
Repulsion 1965,O 4,7:6
Cul de Sac 1966,N 8,44:2
Fearless Vampire Killers, The, or Pardon Me but Your Teeth are in my Neck 1967,N 14,52:1
Rosemary's Baby 1968,Je 13,57:1
Polanski, Roman (Screenwriter)
Knife in the Water 1963,O 29,31:2
Cul de Sac 1966,N 8,44:2
Fearless Vampire Killers, The, or Pardon Me but Your Teeth are in my Neck 1967,N 14,52:1
Rosemary's Baby 1968,Je 13,57:1
Polbentiva, Maria
Song Over Moscow 1964,N 23,52:1
Polesello, Franca
Successo, Il 1965,Ap 29,40:2
Navajo Joe 1967,D 7,60:2
Polesie, Herbert (Original Author)
East Side of Heaven 1939,My 5,29:3
Polevitskaya, Yelena
Mumu 1961,Je 5,37:4
Queen of Spades 1961,S 4,10:1
Polgar, Alfred (Screenwriter)
Brave Suender, Der; Upright Sinner, The 1931,N 22,VIII,6:6
Poli, Afro
Love of a Clown (Pagliacci) 1950,Ap 17,18:5
Cinderella 1953,My 15,20:2
Aida 1954,N 12,17:1
Tosca 1958,O 24,40:3
Polibin, A
Great Citizen, The 1939,Ja 16,11:2
Polidor
Dolce Vita, La 1961,Ap 20,30:1
Polidori, Gianni (Screenwriter)
Bambole; Dolls, The (The Telephone Call); Telephone Call, The (The Dolls) 1965,Je 29,26:1
Polidoro, Gian Luigi (Director)
To Bed...Or not to Bed 1963,D 23,18:2

Polidoro, Igi
  Conjugal Bed, The 1963,S 17,30:1
Polimer, Richard K (Original Author)
  Big Guy, The 1940,Ja 1,29:2
Politseimako, Vassili
  Road Home, The 1947,My 2,28:3
Poljakov, Vladimir (Screenwriter)
  Carnival in Moscow 1957,N 4,40:1
Polk, Brigitte
  Nude Restaurant, The 1967,N 14,52:1
Polk, Gordon
  Inherit the Wind 1960,O 13,41:1
Polk, Oscar
  Green Pastures, The 1936,Jl 17,20:1
  Gone With the Wind 1939,D 20,31:2
  White Cargo 1942,N 27,27:2
  Cabin in the Sky 1943,My 28,19:3
Polk, Rudolph (Producer)
  Adventure in Music 1944,Mr 6,17:3
  Of Men and Music 1951,F 15,27:2
POLL
  See Also POHL
Poll, Martin (Producer)
  Love Is a Ball 1963,Ap 25,38:1
  Sylvia 1965,F 11,45:1
  Lion in Winter, The 1968,O 31,54:1
Poll, Mimmi
  After You, Comrade 1967,Ap 11,54:1
POLLACK
  See Also POLAK, POLLOCK
Pollack, Andre
  Merlusse 1938,Mr 17,17:2
Pollack, Ben
  Glenn Miller Story, the 1954,F 11,33:2
  Benny Goodman Story 1956,F 22,22:1
Pollack, Ben (Composer)
  New Faces of 1937 1937,Jl 2,25:1
Pollack, Eileen (Original Author)
  Gri-Gri 1956,S 29,12:2
Pollack, Ellen
  Non-Stop New York 1937,N 29,19:2
Pollack, Lew (Composer)
  Under the Pampas Moon 1935,My 31,11:1
  Bad Boy 1935,O 28,16:3
  King of Burlesque 1936,Ja 16,25:2
  Song and Dance Man 1936,Mr 12,18:2
  Captain January 1936,Ap 25,21:1
  One in a Million 1937,Ja 1,19:3
  Thin Ice 1937,S 4,8:2
  Life Begins In College 1937,O 9,16:1
  Love and Hisses 1938,Ja 1,11:1
  In Old Chicago 1938,Ja 7,15:2
  Rebecca of Sunnybrook Farm 1938,Mr 26,12:1
  Kentucky Moonshine 1938,My 21,9:2
  Three Blind Mice 1938,Je 18,18:2
  We're Going to Be Rich 1938,Jl 4,10:2
  Hold That Co-ed 1938,S 24,13:1
  Straight, Place and Show 1938,O 1,10:2
  Jitterbugs 1943,Je 5,12:2
  Seven Days Ashore 1944,Ap 26,24:7
Pollack, Lew (Miscellaneous)
  Captain January 1936,Ap 25,21:1
  Sing, Baby, Sing 1936,S 12,20:1
  Pigskin Parade 1936,N 14,23:3
  Rebecca of Sunnybrook Farm 1938,Mr 26,12:1
Pollack, Mimi
  Illicit Interlude 1954,O 27,32:6
Pollack, Stanley (Director)
  This Property is Condemned 1966,Ag 4,24:1
Pollack, Sydney
  War Hunt 1962,Ag 8,35:2
Pollack, Sydney (Director)
  Slender Thread, The 1965,D 24,24:2
  Scalphunters, The 1968,Ap 3,40:1
Pollack, Teddy
  Benny Goodman Story 1956,F 22,22:1
Pollard, Alexander
  Cross Examination 1932,F 27,22:1
Pollard, Bud
  Victims of Persecution 1933,Je 17,16:6
Pollard, Bud (Director)
  Alice in Wonderland 1931,D 28,22:1
  Victims of Persecution 1933,Je 17,16:6
Pollard, Bud (Miscellaneous)
  Kukan 1941,Je 24,17:2
Pollard, Bud (Producer)
  Dead March, The 1937,S 20,19:1 (In Addenda)
Pollard, Daphne
  Hit of the Show 1928,Jl 9,25:1
  Sinners in Love 1928,N 19,16:7
  Big Time 1929,S 9,30:2
  South Sea Rose 1929,D 7,19:3
  Sky Hawk, The 1929,D 12,36:4
  Swing High 1930,Je 27,26:3
  What a Widow 1930,O 4,15:2
  Bright Lights 1931,F 10,24:4
  Our Relations 1936,N 11,55:1
  Dancing Masters, The 1943,D 2,30:2
Pollard, Harry (Director)
  Trifling With Honor 1923,My 30,10:4
  Reckless Age 1924,Je 10,24:4
  Unknown, The 1924,N 18,22:1
  K-The Unknown 1924,N 18,22:1

Oh, Doctor! 1925,F 23,24:1
I'll Show You the Town 1925,Je 8,19:1
California Straight Ahead 1926,Ja 12,27:5
Cohens and the Kellys, The 1926,F 23,26:5
Poker Faces 1926,S 14,25:4
Uncle Tom's Cabin 1927,N 5,16:2
Show Boat 1929,Ap 18,32:3
Tonight at Twelve 1929,S 23,24:3
Undertow 1930,Mr 1,23:1
Shipmates 1931,My 23,13:4
Prodigal, The 1931,Je 27,20:3
When a Feller Needs a Friend 1932,My 14,11:5
Fast Life 1932,D 24,11:4
Pollard, Harry (Original Author)
  California Straight Ahead 1926,Ja 12,27:5
Pollard, Michael J
  Hemingway's Adventures of a Young Man
    1962,Jl 26,17:1
  Stripper, The 1963,Je 20,29:1
  Summer Magic 1963,Ag 22,19:2
  Wild Angels, The 1966,D 22,40:4
  Caprice 1967,Je 8,52:2
  Enter Laughing 1967,Ag 1,24:1
  Bonnie and Clyde 1967,Ag 14,36:1
  Jigsaw 1968,Je 6,54:2
Pollard, Snub
  Ex-Flame 1931,Ja 24,15:1
  Purchase Price, The 1932,Jl 16,5:5
  Stingaree 1934,My 18,27:1
  Cockeyed Cavaliers 1934,Jl 25,22:2
  Frontier Town 1938,Mr 12,13:3
  Perils of Pauline, The 1947,Jl 10,17:2
  Crooked Way, The 1949,S 5,13:2
  When Comedy Was King 1960,Mr 30,42:1
  Days of Thrills and Laughter 1961,Mr 22,37:1
  30 Years of Fun 1963,D 26,33:4
  Further Perils of Laurel and Hardy, The
    1968,Ap 1,56:6
Pollet, Albert
  Under Two Flags 1922,S 25,10:2
  Mysterious Lady, The 1928,Ag 6,15:2
  Folies Bergere 1935,F 25,13:2
  Golden Hawk, The 1952,O 18,16:4
Pollet, Jean-Daniel (Director)
  Six in Paris 1965,S 16,54:2
Pollexfen, Jack (Original Author)
  Secret of Convict Lake, The 1951,Ag 4,7:2
Pollexfen, Jack (Screenwriter)
  Mister Big 1943,Je 14,13:4
  Desert Hawk, The 1950,Ag 26,9:2
  Man From Planet X, The 1951,Ap 9,31:2
  Lady in the Iron Mask 1952,Jl 5,7:2
  Son of Sinbad 1955,Jl 28,18:2
Pollina, Ferdinand
  Specter of the Rose 1946,S 2,12:4
Pollini, Joe
  Jessica 1962,Ap 20,20:2
POLLOCK
  See Also POLAK, POLLACK
Pollock, Channing
  Judex 1966,Ap 26,55:1
Pollock, Channing (Original Author)
  Little Gray Lady, The 1914,Jl 14,9:5
  Sign on the Door, The 1921,Jl 18,16:4 (In
    Addenda)
  Fool, The 1925,Ap 13,24:1
  Crowded Hour, The 1925,Ap 27,15:2
  Enemy, The 1927,D 28,26:6
  Locked Door, The 1930,Ja 20,21:1
Pollock, Channing (Screenwriter)
  Perfect Lady, A 1918,D 2,11:3
Pollock, Dee
  Beware my Lovely 1952,S 13,10:5
  It Grows on Trees 1952,N 29,11:2
  Park Row 1952,D 22,20:2
  Carousel 1956,F 17,13:1
  Wayward Bus, The 1957,Je 6,35:2
  Take a Giant Step 1961,Mr 6,28:2
Pollock, George (Director)
  Rooney 1958,Je 6,29:2
  Broth of a Boy 1959,D 28,18:1
  Poacher's Daughter, The 1960,F 16,31:2
  Murder She Said 1962,Ja 8,27:2
  Kill or Cure 1962,N 13,43:4
  Murder at the Gallop 1963,Je 25,23:2
  Murder Ahoy 1964,S 23,55:3
  Murder Most Foul 1965,My 24,36:2
  Ten Little Indians 1966,F 10,33:1
Pollock, Louis (Screenwriter)
  Suicide Attack 1951,Jl 14,7:2
Pollock, Nancy R
  Last Angry Man, The 1959,O 23,24:1
  Go Naked in the World 1961,Mr 11,15:1
  Pawnbroker, The 1965,Ap 21,51:1
Pollock, Robert Mason (Original Author)
  Gri-Gri 1956,S 29,12:2
Polo, Malvina
  Woman of Paris, A 1923,O 2,7:2
Polomska, Barbara
  Eighth Day of the Week, The 1959,Mr 24,45:2
  Eroica (First Episode) 1966,F 2,24:1

Polonskaya, Veronika
  Tovaristchi 1935,My 25,12:2
Polonsky, Abraham (Director)
  Force of Evil 1948,D 27,16:2
Polonsky, Abraham (Screenwriter)
  Body and Soul 1947,N 10,21:2
  Golden Earrings 1947,D 4,41:3
  Force of Evil 1948,D 27,16:2
  I Can Get It for You Wholesale 1951,Ap 5,34:4
  Madigan 1968,Mr 30,22:2
Polotsky, S (Screenwriter)
  Vanka 1943,Mr 25,25:3
Polovikova, K
  Broken Shoes 1934,Mr 31,8:3
Polovikova, Klavdia
  Idiot, The 1960,Jl 22,11:2
Polskikh, Galina
  Meet Me in Moscow 1966,My 3,51:1
Poltras, Henri
  Whispering City 1948,My 10,25:5
Poltras, Lucie
  Whispering City 1948,My 10,25:5
Polverosi, Manfredi
  Lost One, The; La Traviata 1948,Mr 30,26:2
Polyakof, S
  Men and Jobs 1933,Ja 3,19:3
Polyakov, V (Screenwriter)
  Girl With the Guitar, The 1960,F 1,22:4
Polyvios, Nikos
  Madame X 1960,O 3,34:5
Pomerani, Alberto
  Anthony of Padua 1952,Mr 29,19:2
Pomerant, Vera
  New Teacher, The 1941,Ap 7,13:3
Pomerantseva, Vera
  New Teacher, The 1941,Ap 7,13:3
Pomeroy, Allen
  Cain and Mabel 1936,O 19,22:1
Pomeroy, Roy (Director)
  Interference 1928,N 17,23:1
  Inside the Lines 1930,Jl 5,17:4
Pomes, Felix de
  Cinco Advertencias de Satanas, Las; Satan's Five
    Warnings 1939,Ja 14,13:2
Pomeshchikov, E (Original Author)
  Under Sunny Skies 1950,D 26,19:3
Pomeshchikov, E (Screenwriter)
  Country Bride 1938,Je 4,18:2
  Magic Horse, The 1949,Je 20,14:7
  Bountiful Summer 1951,D 24,9:1
  Tiger Girl 1955,S 5,8:2
  Sailor From the Comet, The 1959,Ag 3,21:2
Pommer, Erich (Director)
  Barbed Wire 1927,Ag 8,10:3
  Blonder Tram, Ein; Blond Dream, A
    1932,N 13,IX,4:2
  Beachcomber, The 1938,D 26,29:3
Pommer, Erich (Miscellaneous)
  Asphalt 1930,My 6,33:4
  Blue Angel, The 1930,D 6,21:3
  Mann der Seinen Moerder Sucht, Der; Looking for
    His Murderer 1931,Mr 15,IX,6:1
Pommer, Erich (Original Author)
  Bomben auf Monte Carlo; Bombardment of Monte
    Carlo, The 1931,S 27,VIII,7:1
Pommer, Erich (Producer)
  Darling of the Gods; Liebling der Gotter
    1930,N 30,IX,6:5
  Liebeswalzer 1931,My 4,15:3
  Stuerme der Leidenschaft; Storms of Passion
    1932,F 14,VIII,6:1
  Music in the Air 1934,D 14,29:3
  Troopship 1938,Ap 26,18:2
  Sidewalks of London 1940,F 15,15:1
  Dance, Girl, Dance 1940,O 11,25:2
  They Knew What They Wanted 1940,O 11,25:2
Pommereulle, Daniel
  Weekend 1968,S 28,36:1
Ponazecki, Joe
  What's so bad About Feeling Good?
    1968,My 25,27:1
PONCE
  See Also PONS
Ponce, Manuel Barbachano (Producer)
  Torero! 1957,My 22,29:2
  Nazarin 1968,Je 21,48:1
Poncet, Pierre
  Great Temptation, The 1942,Jl 10,13:3
Poncin, Marcel
  One Woman's Story 1949,My 18,33:2
  Lost People, The 1950,O 2,19:4
  So Long at the Fair 1951,Ja 22,14:2
  Melba 1953,Je 25,23:1
  Saadia 1954,Mr 20,10:5
Ponomarenko, Eugene
  Taras Family, The 1946,D 9,34:4
Ponomariov, Vova
  Rainbow, The 1944,O 23,14:3
PONS
  See Also PONCE
Pons, Henri
  Stormy Waters 1946,Je 17,32:2

Pons, Lily
I Dream too Much 1935,N 29,24:1
That Girl From Paris 1937,Ja 1,19:1
Hitting a new High 1937,D 27,11:1
Carnegie Hall 1947,My 3,10:2
Ponsova, Y
Overcoat, The 1965,Mr 2,31:2
Ponte, Maria Luisa
Not on Your Life; Verdugo, El 1965,Mr 30,52:1
Pontecorvo, Gillo (Director)
Kapo 1964,Je 2,33:3
Battle of Algiers, The 1967,S 21,56:1
Pontecorvo, Gillo (Original Author)
Kapo 1964,Je 2,33:3
Pontecorvo, Gillo (Screenwriter)
Kapo 1964,Je 2,33:3
Battle of Algiers, The 1967,S 21,56:1
Ponti, Carlo (Producer)
To Live in Peace 1947,N 25,37:2
Lost Youth 1949,O 27,35:4
Without Pity; (Senza Pieta) 1950,Mr 16,40:4
Mill on the Po, The 1951,O 23,35:2
Miserables, Les 1952,Mr 25,23:2
White Line, The 1952,D 6,17:2
Mambo 1955,Mr 31,23:3
Strada, La 1956,Jl 17,19:2
Miller's Beautiful Wife, The 1957,Je 12,40:2
Guendalina 1958,Je 30,23:2
Black Orchid, The 1959,F 13,33:2
That Kind of Woman 1959,S 12,12:2
Heller in Pink Tights 1960,Mr 17,28:1
Breath of Scandal, A 1960,D 17,19:1
Two Women; (Ciociara, La) 1961,My 9,43:2
Lola 1962,O 15,32:2
Arturo Island 1962,D 22,5:2
Third Lover, The 1963,Je 25,23:3
Condemned of Altona, The 1963,O 31,26:1
Doulos-The Finger Man 1964,Mr 3,31:1
Yesterday, Today and Tomorrow (Part II-Anna
Milan); Anna Milan (Yesterday, Today and
Tomorrow) 1964,Mr 18,46:1
Yesterday, Today, and Tomorrow (Part III-Mara
Rome); Mara Rome (Yesterday, Today and
Tomorrow) 1964,Mr 18,46:1
Yesterday, Today and Tomorrow (Part 1-Adelina
Naples); Adelina Naples (Yesterday, Today and
Tomorrow) 1964,Mr 18,46:1
Empty Canvas, The 1964,My 16,21:1 (Incorrect
in this edition; use 1964,My 16,12:1 elsewhere)
Ape Woman, The 1964,S 23,55:1
Contempt 1964,D 19,25:2
Marriage Italian Style 1964,D 21,42:1
Operation Crossbow 1965,Ap 2,29:1
Casanova 1965,Jl 21,43:1
Railroad Man, The; Ferroviere, Il 1965,O 25,46:2
10th Victim, The 1965,D 21,46:1
Doctor Zhivago 1965,D 23,21:1
Lady L 1966,My 19,51:1
Blow-Up 1966,D 19,52:2
Daisies 1967,O 26,54:2
More Than a Miracle 1967,N 2,58:2
Girl and the General, The 1967,D 7,60:1
Smashing Time 1967,D 21,44:1
Carabiniers, Les 1968,Ap 26,31:1
Man With the Balloons, The 1968,Je 25,33:2
Kiss the Other Sheik 1968,Jl 30,33:1
Ponting, Herbert G (Miscellaneous)
At the South Pole 1929,F 21,31:1 (In Addenda)
Ponto, Erich
Maedchen Johanna, Das 1935,O 9,27:2 (In
Addenda)
Palace Scandal 1949,Je 6,15:5
Third Man, The 1950,F 3,29:2
Ballerina 1958,My 10,19:2
Flying Classroom, The 1958,Je 28,13:7
Sky Without Stars 1959,My 30,9:2
Ponty, Francoise
Rise of Louis XIV, The 1967,S 26,54:2
Pool, William Jr
Babes on Broadway 1942,Ja 1,37:1
Poole, David
Dance Little Lady 1955,D 26,23:3
Poole, Mabbie (Screenwriter)
Saints and Sinners 1949,S 12,17:2
Woman's Angle, The 1954,Ag 27,11:6
Poole, Roy
Experiment in Terror 1962,Ap 14,14:1
Up the Down Staircase 1967,Ag 18,36:2
Pooley, Olaf
Woman's Angle, The 1954,Ag 27,11:6
Windom's Way 1958,O 1,45:1
Poore, Robert (Producer)
Name of the Game Is Kill, The 1968,Je 6,54:1
Pope, Alexander
Hitler Gang, The 1944,My 8,15:2
Burning Cross, The 1948,F 20,19:1
Wabash Avenue 1950,Ap 29,8:3
Pope, Gloria
It's in the Bag 1945,Je 11,12:1
Pope, John
Echoes of Silence 1967,Ap 7,32:2

Pope Pius XI
Pope Speaks, The 1933,Ap 17,13:3 (In Addenda)
Popel, Mary Ellen
She Shoulda Said No 1957,Ja 31,21:1
Popesco, Elvire
Man of the Hour, The 1940,N 21,43:2
King, The 1941,O 23,29:3
Nine Bachelors 1942,F 9,19:2
Four Flights to Love 1942,Ap 13,12:2
32 Rue de Montmartre 1944,S 28,26:3
Barge-Keeper's Daughter, The 1945,S 6,23:3
Blue Veil, The 1947,O 2,32:6
Purple Noon 1961,S 1,12:1
Popisil, Vladimir
Girl With Three Camels, The 1968,Ag 13,45:2
Popkin, Harry M (Miscellaneous)
Thief, The 1952,O 16,37:1
Popkin, Leo (Director)
Well, The 1951,S 27,37:2
Popkin, Leo (Producer)
My Dear Secretary 1949,F 14,15:4
Impact 1949,Mr 21,19:2
D O A 1950,My 1,18:2
Well, The 1951,S 27,37:2
Poplavets, V
Road to Life 1956,Je 11,26:6
Popov, A
Mussorgsky 1951,Ag 20,14:3
Safety Match, The 1955,Mr 28,24:5
Othello 1960,My 16,39:1
Popov, V
In old Siberia 1929,Jl 22,17:1
Last Night, The 1937,Ap 28,18:3
Without Dowry 1946,Ap 15,22:2
Lower Depths, The 1947,D 1,27:2
Popova, V
Three Women 1936,F 12,25:4
Lower Depths, The 1947,D 1,27:2
Popovich, Joe
One-Way Ticket to Hell 1955,D 8,45:1
Popp, Lucia
Merry Wives of Windsor, The 1966,F 28,21:1
Poppe, Harry (Original Author)
Three Kids and a Queen 1935,N 9,19:2
Poppe, Nils
Devil's Eye, The 1961,O 31,27:4
Poppi, Giorgio
Tropics 1968,S 24,52:1
Pops and Louie
Hit Parade of 1943 1943,Ap 16,24:3
Porath, Ove
Virgin Spring, The; Jungfrukallan 1960,N 15,46:1
Porcasi, Paul
Say It Again 1926,Je 7,23:2
Broadway 1929,My 28,36:2
Born Reckless 1930,Je 7,10:4
Lady's Morals, A 1930,N 8,21:3
Morocco 1930,N 17,29:1
Criminal Code, The 1931,Ja 5,21:3
Doctors' Wives 1931,Ap 25,23:4
Svengali 1931,My 1,30:3
Good Bad Girl, The 1931,My 15,20:6
Party Husband 1931,My 16,13:3
Smart Money 1931,Je 19,21:1
Gentleman's Fate 1931,Je 27,20:3
Bought 1931,Ag 15,18:3
I Like Your Nerve 1931,S 12,15:4
Under Eighteen 1931,D 26,15:5
Man Who Played God, The 1932,F 11,16:1
Passionate Plumber, The 1932,Mr 12,19:5
Devil and the Deep 1932,Ag 20,7:4
Painted Woman, The 1932,S 16,24:4
Red-Haired Alibi 1932,O 24,18:5
Kid From Spain, The 1932,N 18,23:2
Under-Cover Man 1932,D 5,21:2
Cynara 1932,D 26,26:2
Grand Slam 1933,F 22,25:2
When Strangers Marry 1933,My 25,24:3
I Loved a Woman 1933,S 22,14:2
Devil's Mate 1933,S 23,11:7
Saturday's Millions 1933,O 14,18:3
Great Flirtation, The 1934,Je 22,16:5
British Agent 1934,S 20,20:1
Wake up and Dream 1934,O 11,28:3
Imitation of Life 1934,N 24,19:1
Enter Madame 1935,Ja 12,12:1
Florentine Dagger, The 1935,Ap 27,20:6
Million Dollar Baby 1935,My 6,22:3
Night at the Ritz, A 1935,My 16,20:2
Under the Pampas Moon 1935,My 31,11:1
Charlie Chan in Egypt 1935,Je 24,12:2
Muss 'Em Up 1936,F 3,21:2
Leathernecks Have Landed, The 1936,Mr 23,22:5
Down Under the Sea 1936,Ag 10,10:2
Crash Donovan 1936,Ag 10,10:3
Maytime 1937,Mr 19,27:1
Emperor's Candlesticks, The 1937,Jl 9,18:1
Bride Wore Red, The 1937,O 15,18:4
Crime School 1938,My 11,17:2
Vacation From Love 1938,N 10,33:2
Lady of the Tropics 1939,S 8,28:3
Everything Happens at Night 1939,D 16,12:6
Dr Kildare's Strange Case 1940,Ap 12,19:2

Porcasi, Paul— Cont
Torrid Zone 1940,My 18,11:3
I Was an Adventuress 1940,My 20,13:2
Argentine Nights 1940,O 11,25:3
Road to Happiness 1942,Mr 27,27:4
Hi Diddle Diddle 1943,S 24,26:2
Porchet, Arturo (Director)
Hogueras en la Noche 1937,Mr 15,27:2
Porchet-Marquet, A (Cinematographer)
Spain Fights on 1939,F 13,13:2
Porchetria, Adrien (Cinematographer)
Fury Over Spain 1937,Jl 21,19:2
Porchon, Tao
World Dances 1954,N 8,24:6
Porel, Jacqueline
Heroes of the Marne; (Famille Lefrancois, Le)
1939,Ap 24,13:2
Youth in Revolt 1939,My 16,27:3
Desperate Decision 1954,N 9,31:5
Razzi 1957,N 19,39:4
Young Girls Beware 1959,Ag 22,8:2
Truth, The 1961,Je 27,23:2
Love on a Pillow 1963,D 17,49:1
Anatomy of a Marriage; My Days With Jean
Marc; My Nights With Francoise
1964,O 27,42:2
Porelli, Giuseppi
Of Love and Bandits 1953,Ja 17,12:4
Holiday Island; (Vacanzie a Izchia)
1959,S 22,46:1
Porquerol, Elizabeth (Screenwriter)
Thirst of Men, The 1952,O 28,37:1
Porreau, Ghislaine
Master Race, The 1944,N 2,22:1
Portabella, Pedro (Miscellaneous)
Moment of Truth, The 1965,Ag 10,18:1
Portas, R (Director)
Bohemios 1935,S 16,15:3
Suprema Ley; Supreme Law 1938,Ja 15,19:2
Adios, Nicanor 1938,Mr 14,13:2
Domingo en la Tarde, Un; On a Sunday
Afternoon 1939,Ja 7,6:3
Porte, Robert
Doctors, The 1956,Ag 7,19:2
Eye for an Eye, An 1961,F 10,19:1
Portelatine, Raymond
World Without Sun 1964,D 23,22:1
Porten, Henny
Deception 1921,Ap 18,8:1
Backstairs 1926,Je 4,26:2
Scandal About Eva 1930,Jl 27,VIII,4:2 (In
Addenda)
Gretel and Liesel; (Kohlhiesel's Daughters)
1931,Ja 26,21:1
Mother Love 1931,F 16,17:1
Skandal Um Eva 1931,Ap 21,35:2
Luise, Koenigin von Preussen 1932,O 5,26:6
Crown of Thorns 1934,Mr 28,27:6
Mutter und Kind 1934,N 30,22:3
Trouble Back Stairs; Krach im Hinterhaus
1937,D 4,21:1
Porter, Arthur Gould
Frenchman's Creek 1944,S 21,26:2
Porter, Cole (Composer)
Gay Divorcee, The 1934,N 16,27:1
Anything Goes 1936,F 6,23:3
Rosalie 1937,D 31,9:2
Broadway Melody of 1940 1940,Mr 29,25:3
Love Thy Neighbor 1940,D 18,32:5
Break the News 1941,Ja 2,24:2
Andy Hardy's Private Secretary 1941,Mr 7,17:2
You'll Never Get Rich 1941,O 24,27:2
Panama Hattie 1942,O 2,31:2
Something to Shout About 1943,Ap 8,27:3
Hers to Hold 1943,Jl 22,15:1
Let's Face It 1943,Ag 5,18:1
Du Barry Was a Lady 1943,Ag 20,13:1
I Dood It 1943,N 11,29:1
Something for the Boys 1944,N 30,19:1
Pirate, The 1948,My 21,19:2
Lullaby of Broadway 1951,Mr 27,35:2
Anything Goes 1956,Mr 22,38:1
High Society 1956,Ag 10,9:2
Silk Stockings 1957,Jl 19,11:1
Girls, Les 1957,O 4,27:2
Can-Can 1960,Mr 10,36:1
Porter, Cole (Miscellaneous)
Born to Dance 1936,D 5,16:1
Porter, Cole (Original Author)
Let's Face It 1943,Ag 5,18:1
Night and Day 1946,Jl 26,16:2
Porter, Del
Born to Dance 1936,D 5,16:1
Porter, Don
Eyes of the Underworld 1942,O 5,15:2
Night Monster 1942,N 30,18:5
Who Done It 1942,D 3,35:2
She Wolf of London 1946,Ap 6,10:6
Buck Privates Come Home 1947,Ap 12,11:3
711 Ocean Drive 1950,Jl 20,21:2
My Friend Irma Goes West 1950,Ag 3,20:2
Racket, The 1951,D 13,44:2
Because You're Mine 1952,S 26,18:2
Savage, The 1953,Ja 2,11:1

Porter, Don — Cont
Bachelor in Paradise 1961,N 17,41:2
Youngblood Hawke 1964,N 6,30:1
Porter, Dorothy
This Time for Keeps 1947,D 5,33:4
Porter, Eleanor H (Original Author)
Pollyanna 1920,Ja 19,16:3
Has Anybody Seen My Gal 1952,Jl 5,7:2
Pollyanna 1960,My 20,26:1
Porter, Eric
Fall of the Roman Empire, The 1964,Mr 27,14:2
Pumpkin Eater, The 1964,N 10,58:1
Heroes of Telemark, The 1966,Mr 10,26:1
Kaleidoscope 1966,S 23,45:1
Lost Continent, The 1968,Je 20,50:2
Porter, Gene Stratton (Original Author)
Harvester, The 1927,N 7,33:1
Porter, J Robert
Firecreek 1968,F 22,36:2
Porter, Jean
Fall In 1943,My 15,13:3
That Nazty Nuisance 1943,My 29,10:3
Youngest Profession, The 1943,Je 25,13:3
Calaboose 1943,Jl 30,19:2
Andy Hardy's Blonde Trouble 1944,My 5,17:3
Bathing Beauty 1944,Je 28,20:1
Twice Blessed 1945,Jl 7,7:5
Abbott and Costello in Hollywood
  1945,N 23,26:2
What Next Corporal Hargrove? 1945,D 26,15:2
Till the End of Time 1946,Jl 24,24:1
That Hagen Girl 1947,O 25,13:2
Cry Danger 1951,F 22,27:3
Left Hand of God, The 1955,S 22,34:5
Porter, Katherine Anne (Original Author)
Ship of Fools 1965,Jl 29,18:1
Porter, Lew (Composer)
That's Right, You're Wrong 1939,N 30,25:3
Porter, Lillian
Josette 1938,Je 11,9:1
Stop, Look and Love 1939,S 8,28:5
Tin Pan Alley 1940,N 22,27:3
That Night in Rio 1941,Mr 10,21:2
Song of the Islands 1942,Mr 12,24:4
Porter, LuLu
Brass Bottle, The 1964,My 21,42:1
Porter, Paul
Into the Net 1924,Ag 23,10:2
Porter, Rose Albert (Original Author)
All of Me 1934,F 5,19:2
Porter, William Sydney (Original Author)
Cisco Kid and the Lady, The 1939,D 25,29:2
Porterat, Maurice
Marriage of Figaro, The 1963,Ap 30,26:1
Porterfield, Robert
Sergeant York 1941,Jl 3,15:1
Portet, Jacques
Cheaters, The; (Tricheurs, Les) 1961,Je 5,37:4
To be a Crook 1967,F 7,33:2
Live for Life 1967,D 19,59:1
Portia, Rosemary
Spooks Run Wild 1941,N 1,20:3
Portin, William (Cinematographer)
Hunters of the Deep 1954,D 17,37:4
Portman, Eric
Murder in the Old Red Barn 1936,Ag 19,18:3
Prince and the Pauper, The 1937,My 6,23:1
Moonlight Sonata 1938,My 10,17:2
Invaders, The 1942,Mr 6,17:1
One of our Aircraft Is Missing 1942,N 2,17:2
Squadron Leader X 1943,Jl 23,21:2
Wanted for Murder 1946,D 12,38:4
Dear Murderer 1948,My 8,12:2
Canterbury Tale, A 1949,Ja 24,16:2
Corridor of Mirrors 1949,Mr 23,35:3
Blind Goddess, The 1949,Je 23,33:3
Daybreak 1949,Jl 4,9:2
Kisenga, Man of Africa 1952,Mr 7,18:2
Spider and the Fly, The 1952,Jl 29,17:3
Magic Box, The 1952,S 24,40:2
Cairo Road 1952,N 1,17:2
Golden Mask, The 1954,Mr 20,10:5
Deep Blue Sea, The 1955,O 13,35:2
His Excellency 1956,F 2,19:3
Colditz Story, The 1957,O 25,23:2
Naked Edge 1961,Jl 1,9:1
Freud 1962,D 13,37:1
Bedford Incident, The 1965,N 3,43:1
Spy With a Cold Nose, The 1966,D 20,58:2
Whisperers, The 1967,Ag 1,24:1
Deadfall 1968,S 12,54:1
Posas, Enrique de
Angelita 1935,S 11,19:5
Poschmann, Agatha
Razzia 1948,Je 14,19:2
Poselli, Luisa
Revenge 1947,N 28,37:4
Poselsky, I (Director)
Spartakiada 1929,Jl 8,17:3
Soviets on Parade 1933,Mr 6,16:7
Soviet Frontiers on the Danube 1941,Je 30,13:3
Russia on Parade 1946,S 9,20:1
Song and Dance Over the Vistula 1956,Je 25,19:7
Day in Moscow, A 1957,D 23,18:2

Poselsky, I (Screenwriter)
Day in Moscow, A 1957,D 23,18:2
Poselsky, Y (Miscellaneous)
Conquerors of the Arctic 1937,N 22,15:2
Posford, George (Composer)
Good Night, Vienna 1932,My 1,VIII,5:4
Good Companions, The 1933,O 10,24:1
Invitation to the Waltz 1938,Jl 2,10:3
Balalaika 1939,D 15,33:2
Showtime 1948,My 20,35:3
Posford, George (Miscellaneous)
Gay Desperado, The 1936,O 9,31:4
Posford, George (Screenwriter)
Magic Night 1932,N 3,25:3
Poslavsky, B
Golden Mountains 1932,Ap 14,25:3
Pozor 1933,Mr 11,18:4
Peasants 1935,Ag 29,25:2
Three Women 1936,F 12,25:4
Great Citizen, The 1939,Ja 16,11:2
We Will Come Back 1943,O 15,15:2
Zoya 1945,Ap 16,18:6
Posner, Phil
Gunfighters of Casa Grande 1965,S 2,36:1
Posnysz-Piasecka, Zofia (Screenwriter)
Passenger 1964,S 21,37:3
Possamay, Luciana
Summerskin 1962,My 29,22:2
Post, Buddy
Tender Hour, The 1927,Je 7,27:4
Post, Charles
Wild Oranges 1924,Mr 3,22:3
Behold This Woman 1924,Ja 22,9:1
Top of the World, The 1925,F 17,18:1
Crown of Lies 1926,Mr 30,20:6
Diplomacy 1926,S 13,18:1
Post, Guy Bates
Masquerader, The 1922,Ag 14,12:4
Prestige 1932,F 5,25:2
Till We Meet Again 1936,My 9,11:2
Case Against Mrs Ames, The 1936,My 28,19:2
Trouble for Two 1936,My 30,7:2
Fatal Lady 1936,Jl 11,11:3
Champagne Waltz 1937,F 4,17:2
Maytime 1937,Mr 19,27:1
Daughter of Shanghai 1937,D 24,21:2
Mad Empress, The 1940,F 15,15:1
Crossroads 1942,Jl 27,18:2
Post, Ted (Director)
Hang 'Em High 1968,Ag 8,27:3
Post, Wiley
Air Hawks 1935,Je 4,26:5
Post, William H (Original Author)
Never Say Die 1939,Mr 9,18:1
Vagabond King, The 1956,S 13,39:6
Post, William Jr
Black Camel, The 1931,Jl 4,11:5
Secret Service 1931,D 14,16:3
Mr and Mrs North 1942,Ja 22,13:2
Ship Ahoy 1942,Je 26,16:5
Pacific Rendezvous 1942,Jl 8,27:4
Sherlock Holmes and the Secret Weapon
  1943,Ja 5,15:2
Moon Is Down, The 1943,Mr 27,8:6
Roger Touhy, Gangster 1944,Je 5,14:7
Bride by Mistake 1944,S 16,20:2
Experiment Perilous 1944,D 30,15:2
House on Ninety-Second Street, The
  1945,S 27,24:7
Post, William Jr (Narrator)
Farewell to Yesterday 1950,D 1,31:2
Posta, Adrienne
To Sir, With Love 1967,Je 15,56:1
Here We Go Around the Mulberry Bush
  1968,Mr 5,34:5
Up the Junction 1968,Mr 14,51:1
Poston, Tom
Zotz! 1962,O 4,44:3
Old Dark House, The 1963,O 31,26:3
Soldier in the Rain 1963,N 29,67:6 (Incorrect in
  this edition; use 1963,N 28,67:6 elsewhere)
Potap (The Bear)
New Number Comes to Moscow, A
  1959,Jl 6,23:1
Potechina, Lydia
Waltz Dream, The 1926,Jl 26,13:2
Manon Lescaut 1926,N 30,27:1
Potel, Victor
Captain Kidd, Jr 1919,Ap 21,13:4
Mary's Ankle 1920,Mr 1,16:2
Tailor Made Man, A 1922,O 16,20:2
Women Who Give 1924,Je 3,22:1
Lost Lady, A 1925,Ja 19,14:1
Contraband 1925,Mr 24,20:6
Below the Line 1925,S 21,12:4
Special Delivery 1927,Ap 26,33:3
Captain Swagger 1928,D 24,17:7
Virginian, The 1929,D 23,18:2
Call of the West 1930,My 27,27:2
Dough Boys 1930,S 30,23:1
Squaw Man, The 1931,S 19,10:2
Purchase Price, The 1932,Jl 16,5:5
Hard Rock Harrigan 1935,Jl 30,16:2

Potel, Victor — Cont
Whispering Smith Speaks 1936,F 17,21:1
Song of the Saddle 1936,Mr 21,13:3
O'Malley of the Mounted 1936,Ap 6,18:1
Down Under the Sea 1936,Ag 10,10:2
God's Country and the Woman 1937,Ja 11,15:5
Girl From God's Country 1940,S 9,18:5
Miracle of Morgan's Creek, The 1944,Ja 20,15:2
Hail the Conquering Hero 1944,Ag 10,14:2
Great Moment, The 1944,N 13,15:2
Egg and I, The 1947,Ap 25,29:2
Mad Wednesday 1951,Ja 25,21:5
Potker, B
Girl With the Guitar, The 1960,F 1,22:4
Pototsky (Composer)
Lucky Bride, The 1948,Ja 26,15:2
Stars of the Ukraine 1953,Jl 13,22:4
May Night 1953,Jl 13,22:4
Potter, Betty
Stairway to Heaven 1946,D 26,28:1
Potter, H C (Director)
Beloved Enemy 1936,D 26,15:2
Wings Over Honolulu 1937,My 29,20:1
Romance in the Dark 1938,Mr 21,18:2
Shopworn Angel, The 1938,Jl 8,11:2
Cowboy and the Lady, The 1938,N 25,19:3
Story of Vernon and Irene Castle, The
  1939,Mr 31,19:2
Blackmail 1939,S 15,26:3
Congo Maisie 1940,F 8,18:4
Second Chorus 1941,Ja 16,25:2
Hellzapoppin 1941,D 26,21:4
Victory Through Air Power 1943,Jl 19,13:1
Mr Lucky 1943,Jl 23,21:2
Farmer's Daughter, The 1947,Mr 26,31:2
Mr Blandings Builds his Dream House
  1948,Mr 26,26:2
Time of your Life, The 1948,My 27,29:2
You Gotta Stay Happy 1948,N 5,29:2
Miniver Story, The 1950,O 27,24:2
Three for the Show 1955,F 25,16:1
Top Secret Affair 1957,Ja 31,21:1
Potter, H C (Original Author)
Fixer Dugan 1939,My 6,21:2
Potter, Maureen
Rising of the Moon, The (A Minute's Wait);
  Minute's Wait, A (The Rising of the Moon)
  1957,Jl 10,23:1
Gideon of Scotland Yard 1959,My 20,38:2
Ulysses 1967,Mr 14,55:1
Potter, Paul M (Original Author)
Woman's Experience, A 1918,N 11,13:3
Potter, Philip
Mikado, The 1967,Mr 15,53:1
Potter, Stephen (Original Author)
School for Scoundrels 1960,Jl 12,39:1
Pottier, Richard (Director)
Three Sinners 1952,Jl 8,23:2
Caroline Cherie 1954,My 25,23:1
Three Feet in a Bed 1957,My 18,23:2
David and Goliath 1961,O 7,14:3
Potts, Nyanza
Little Colonel, The 1935,Mr 22,26:2
Pouget, Eugene
Hearts of the World 1918,Ap 5,13:1
Merry Widow, The 1925,Ag 27,14:1
Boheme, La 1926,F 25,26:2
Poujouly, Georges
Forbidden Games 1952,D 9,43:2
We Are all Murderers 1957,Ja 9,27:2
If all the Guys in the World 1957,Ap 23,34:1
Every Second Counts 1957,O 15,39:4
And God Created Woman 1957,O 22,41:1
Frantic 1961,Je 12,34:1
Mistress for the Summer, A 1964,Mr 28,13:5
Poulsen, Karen
Child of Man 1950,F 1,25:2
Poulsen, William A
Another Thin Man 1939,N 24,29:1
Poulson, Howard
Return to Paradise 1953,S 11,24:2
Poulton, A G
Should a Doctor Tell 1931,Ag 22,7:5
Poulton, Mabel
Palais de Danse 1928,Ag 19,VII,3:7
Not Quite a Lady 1928,Ag 19,VII,3:7
Constant Nymph, The 1929,Je 10,23:1
Escape 1930,N 1,23:2
Children of Chance 1931,Ja 24,15:1
Pounds, Louise
Farmer's Wife, The 1930,Ja 7,28:3
Poupon, Henri
Merlusse 1938,Mr 17,17:2
Heartbeat 1939,S 5,21:3
Harvest 1939,O 3,19:4
Stormy Waters 1946,Je 17,32:2
Nais 1948,Je 16,37:2
Room Upstairs, The 1948,S 4,8:6
Ways of Love (Jofroi); Jofroi (Ways of Love)
  1950,D 13,50:2
Passion for Life 1951,D 21,21:4
Povah, Phyllis
Women, The 1939,S 22,27:2
Let's Face It 1943,Ag 5,18:1

Povah, Phyllis— Cont

Marrying Kind, The 1952,Mr 14,27:1
Pat and Mike 1952,Je 19,32:6
Happy Anniversary 1959,N 11,41:1

Povolotski, M

On his Own 1939,S 13,31:3

Powell, Addison

Mating Game, The 1959,Ap 30,37:1
In the French Style 1963,S 19,23:1
Thomas Crown Affair, The 1968,Je 27,48:2

Powell, Bellendom

Prince of Lovers, The 1927,N 29,31:1

Powell, Bonney (Director)

Fury in the Pacific 1945,Mr 23,13:2

Powell, Bonney (Miscellaneous)

First World War, The 1934,N 8,27:1

Powell, Clive

Children of the Damned 1964,Ja 30,24:2

Powell, David

Gloria's Romance 1916,My 23,9:2
His Parisian Wife 1919,Ja 20,13:2
Firing Line, The 1919,Jl 7,18:5
On With the Dance 1920,F 16,8:1
Right to Love, The 1920,Ag 23,9:2
Lady Rose's Daughter 1920,Ag 30,12:3
Glimpses of the Moon 1923,Ap 3,23:4
Fog Bound 1923,My 29,10:3
Green Goddess, The 1923,Ag 15,21:1
Virtuous Liars 1924,Mr 31,20:1

Powell, Dawn (Original Author)

Hello Sister! 1933,My 6,11:2
Man of Iron 1935,D 7,22:2

Powell, Dick

Street Scene 1931,Ag 27,22:5
Blessed Event 1932,S 3,16:2
Too Busy to Work 1932,D 3,21:4
King's Vacation, The 1933,Ja 20,21:2
42d Street 1933,Mr 10,19:3
Gold Diggers of 1933 1933,Je 8,22:3
Footlight Parade 1933,O 6,21:3
College Coach 1933,N 11,10:4
Convention City 1933,D 25,28:2
Wonder Bar 1934,Mr 1,23:2
20 Million Sweethearts 1934,Ap 27,25:1
Dames 1934,Ag 16,20:2
Happiness Ahead 1934,O 11,28:2
Flirtation Walk 1934,N 29,33:1
Gold Diggers of 1935 1935,Mr 15,25:2
Wedding Night, The 1935,Mr 16,19:1
Broadway Gondolier 1935,Jl 18,15:2
Page Miss Glory 1935,Ag 29,25:2
Midsummer Night's Dream, A 1935,O 10,31:1
Shipmates Forever 1935,O 17,29:3
Thanks a Million 1935,N 14,17:1
If You Could Only Cook 1935,D 26,21:4
Colleen 1936,Mr 9,20:2
Hearts Divided 1936,Je 13,13:1
Yours for the Asking 1936,Ag 20,14:2
Hollywood Boulevard 1936,S 21,26:4
Stage Struck 1936,S 28,14:4
Gold Diggers of 1937 1936,D 25,19:2
On the Avenue 1937,F 5,17:3
Another Dawn 1937,Je 18,25:3
Singing Marine, The 1937,Jl 1,33:2
Varsity Show 1937,S 2,17:2
Hollywood Hotel 1938,Ja 13,17:3
Cowboy From Brooklyn 1938,Jl 14,17:1
Hard To Get 1938,N 14,15:2
Going Places 1939,Ja 7,6:1
Naughty but Nice 1939,Je 23,23:2
I Want a Divorce 1940,O 3,31:2
Christmas in July 1940,N 6,35:2
Model Wife 1941,Ap 24,25:3
In the Navy 1941,Je 12,29:2
Star Spangled Rhythm 1942,D 31,20:1
Happy Go Lucky 1943,Mr 25,25:1
True to Life 1943,O 14,26:1
Riding High 1943,D 23,26:4
It Happened Tomorrow 1944,My 29,18:2
Meet The People 1944,S 8,16:2
Murder, my Sweet 1945,Mr 9,16:2
Cornered 1945,D 26,15:1
Johnny O'Clock 1947,Mr 27,39:2
To the Ends of the Earth 1948,F 13,26:2
Pitfall 1948,Ag 25,31:2
Rogues' Regiment 1948,D 20,31:2
Mrs Mike 1950,F 9,36:5
Reformer and the Redhead, The 1950,Ap 10,15:2
Right Cross 1950,N 16,39:2
Cry Danger 1951,F 22,27:3
Tall Target, The 1951,S 28,26:2
Bad and the Beautiful, The 1953,Ja 16,19:1
Susan Slept Here 1954,Jl 30,9:1

Powell, Dick (Director)

Split Second 1953,My 13,34:2
Conqueror, The 1956,Mr 31,13:3
Enemy Below, The 1957,D 26,23:2
Hunters, The 1958,Ag 27,33:1

Powell, Dick (Producer)

Conqueror, The 1956,Mr 31,13:3
Enemy Below, The 1957,D 26,23:2
Hunters, The 1958,Ag 27,33:1

Powell, Eleanor

George White's 1935 Scandals 1935,Ap 29,12:3
Broadway Melody of 1936 1935,S 19,28:1
Born to Dance 1936,D 5,16:1
Broadway Melody of 1938 1937,S 3,12:1
Rosalie 1937,D 31,9:2
Honolulu 1939,F 23,19:2
Broadway Melody of 1940 1940,Mr 29,25:3
Lady Be Good 1941,S 19,27:1
Ship Ahoy 1942,Je 26,16:5
Thousands Cheer 1943,S 14,27:1
I Dood It 1943,N 11,29:1
Sensations of 1945 1944,Jl 7,13:2
Duchess of Idaho 1950,Jl 21,15:3

Powell, Jack

Here Comes Cookie 1935,O 12,12:2
East Side of Heaven 1939,My 5,29:3
Bitter Sweet 1940,N 22,27:1

Powell, Jane

Song of the Open Road 1944,Je 7,13:3
Delightfully Dangerous 1945,Je 9,17:3
Holiday in Mexico 1946,Ag 16,19:3
Three Daring Daughters 1948,F 13,26:3
Date with Judy, A 1948,Ag 7,8:2
Luxury Liner 1948,S 10,19:2
Nancy Goes to Rio 1950,Ap 7,22:2
Two Weeks With Love 1950,N 24,31:2
Royal Wedding 1951,Mr 9,30:2
Rich, Young and Pretty 1951,Jl 26,17:3
Small Town Girl 1953,My 7,37:2
Three Sailors and a Girl 1953,N 23,32:2
Seven Brides for Seven Brothers 1954,Jl 23,8:3
Deep in my Heart 1954,D 10,35:2
Athena 1954,D 22,28:2
Hit the Deck 1955,Mr 4,17:1
Female Animal, The 1958,Ja 23,24:3
Girl Most Likely, The 1958,O 9,47:1

Powell, Mel

Song Is Born, A 1948,O 20,37:2

Powell, Michael

Garden of Allah, The 1927,S 3,13:5

Powell, Michael (Director)

Edge of the World, The 1938,S 12,13:2
U-Boat 29 1939,O 6,31:3
Lion Has Wings, The 1940,Ja 22,11:2
Blackout 1940,D 2,19:2
Thief of Bagdad, The 1940,D 6,28:2
Invaders, The 1942,Mr 6,17:1
One of our Aircraft Is Missing 1942,N 2,17:2
Life and Death of Colonel Blimp, The
    1945,Mr 30,18:2
Stairway to Heaven 1946,D 26,28:1
Black Narcissus 1947,Ag 14,29:2
I Know Where I'm Going 1947,Ag 20,25:2
Red Shoes, The 1948,O 23,9:2
Canterbury Tale, A 1949,Ja 24,16:2
Tales of Hoffmann 1951,Ap 5,34:2
Small Back Room, The 1952,F 2,11:3
Wild Heart, The 1952,My 29,17:2
Fighting Pimpernel, The 1954,Ap 19,19:1
Pursuit of the Graf Spee 1957,D 27,33:2
Night Ambush 1958,Ap 25,32:4

Powell, Michael (Original Author)

Stairway to Heaven 1946,D 26,28:1
I Know Where I'm Going 1947,Ag 20,25:2

Powell, Michael (Producer)

Invaders, The 1942,Mr 6,17:1
One of our Aircraft Is Missing 1942,N 2,17:2
Silver Fleet, The 1945,Mr 24,22:6
Life and Death of Colonel Blimp, The
    1945,Mr 30,18:2
Stairway to Heaven 1946,D 26,28:1
Black Narcissus 1947,Ag 14,29:2
I Know Where I'm Going 1947,Ag 20,25:2
End of the River, The 1948,Je 21,18:2
Red Shoes, The 1948,O 23,9:2
Canterbury Tale, A 1949,Ja 24,16:2
Tales of Hoffmann 1951,Ap 5,34:2
Small Back Room, The 1952,F 2,11:3
Wild Heart, The 1952,My 29,17:2
Fighting Pimpernel, The 1954,Ap 19,19:1
Pursuit of the Graf Spee 1957,D 27,33:2
Night Ambush 1958,Ap 25,32:4
Sebastian 1968,Ja 25,33:2

Powell, Michael (Screenwriter)

Edge of the World, The 1938,S 12,13:2
Blackout 1940,D 2,19:2
One of our Aircraft Is Missing 1942,N 2,17:2
Life and Death of Colonel Blimp, The
    1945,Mr 30,18:2
Black Narcissus 1947,Ag 14,29:2
Red Shoes, The 1948,O 23,9:2
Canterbury Tale, A 1949,Ja 24,16:2
Tales of Hoffmann 1951,Ap 5,34:2
Wild Heart, The 1952,My 29,17:2
Fighting Pimpernel, The 1954,Ap 19,19:1
Pursuit of the Graf Spee 1957,D 27,33:2
Night Ambush 1958,Ap 25,32:4

Powell, Paul (Director)

Pollyanna 1920,Ja 19,16:3
Crimson Challenge, The 1922,Ap 10,18:2
Awful Truth, The 1925,Jl 2,12:4
Death Valley 1927,N 22,32:2

Powell, Richard (Original Author)

Young Philadelphians, The 1959,My 22,32:1
Follow That Dream 1962,Ag 9,17:7
Wild and Wonderful 1964,Je 11,27:4

Powell, Russell

Boy of Flanders, A 1924,Ap 15,24:1
Red Mill, The 1927,F 14,15:1
Soft Cushions 1927,S 12,29:1
Riley, The Cop 1928,D 4,29:1
Fashions in Love 1929,Jl 1,31:2
Love Parade, The 1929,N 20,32:6
Grand Parade, The 1930,F 1,15:1
Big Trail, The 1930,O 25,20:3
American Tragedy, An 1931,Ag 6,22:5
Sin of Madelon Claudet, The 1931,O 31,22:2
Mystery Ranch 1932,Je 30,26:2
Zoo in Budapest 1933,Ap 28,15:2
Count of Monte Cristo, The 1934,S 27,25:2
Night of Nights, The 1939,D 28,17:1

Powell, Teddy and orchestra

Jam Session 1944,My 3,25:3

Powell, Templar

His Children's Children 1923,N 5,15:1
Monsieur Beaucaire 1924,Ag 12,12:1 (In
    Addenda)

Powell, Violet E (Screenwriter)

White Black Sheep, The 1926,D 21,20:2

Powell, William

Bright Shawl, The 1923,Ap 23,18:3
Under the Red Robe 1923,N 13,25:3
Dangerous Money 1924,O 14,21:5
Too Many Kisses 1925,Mr 3,20:1
Beautiful City, The 1925,N 23,25:4
Sea Horses 1926,F 23,26:5
Desert Gold 1926,Mr 23,24:5
Runaway, The 1926,Ap 27,23:2
Aloma of the South Seas 1926,My 17,19:1
Beau Geste 1926,Ag 26,17:3
Tin Gods 1926,S 20,21:3
Great Gatsby, The 1926,N 22,28:3
New York 1927,Ja 31,13:1
Love's Greatest Mistake 1927,F 21,14:2
Special Delivery 1927,Ap 26,33:3
Senorita 1927,My 9,26:4
Time to Love 1927,Je 23,23:3
Paid to Love 1927,Jl 25,25:3
She's a Shiek 1927,N 21,20:1
Last Command, The 1928,Ja 23,18:3
Beau Sabreur 1928,Ja 23,18:3
Feel my Pulse 1928,F 27,16:2
Partners in Crime 1928,Ap 30,18:3
Drag Net, The 1928,Je 4,13:2
Forgotten Faces 1928,Ag 6,15:2
Interference 1928,N 17,23:1
Canary Murder Case, The 1929,Mr 11,22:2
Four Feathers, The 1929,Je 13,35:4
Charming Sinners 1929,Jl 8,17:3
Greene Murder Case, The 1929,Ag 10,11:3
Pointed Heels 1929,D 28,11:1
Behind the Makeup 1930,Ja 18,21:1
Street of Chance 1930,F 3,17:1
Benson Murder Case, The 1930,Ap 12,23:1
Paramount on Parade 1930,Ap 21,20:4
Shadow of the Law 1930,Je 7,10:4
For the Defense 1930,Jl 19,7:5
Dishonored 1931,Mr 6,16:1
Man of the World 1931,Mr 21,15:1
Ladies' Man 1931,My 1,30:3
Road to Singapore, The 1931,O 1,25:2
High Pressure 1932,F 1,22:3
Jewel Robbery 1932,Jl 23,6:6
One Way Passage 1932,O 14,23:2
Lawyer Man 1932,D 27,10:2
Private Detective 62 1933,Jl 7,20:2
Double Harness 1933,Jl 21,20:2
Kennel Murder Case, The 1933,O 30,14:2
Fashions of 1934 1934,Ja 20,12:2
Manhattan Melodrama 1934,My 5,22:2
Key, The 1934,My 30,14:3
Thin Man, The 1934,Je 30,18:5
Evelyn Prentice 1934,N 10,19:1
Star of Midnight 1935,Ap 12,26:5
Reckless 1935,Ap 20,16:1
Escapade 1935,Jl 6,16:2
Rendezvous 1935,O 26,12:2
Great Ziegfeld, The 1936,Ap 9,21:2
Ex-Mrs Bradford, The 1936,My 28,19:2
My Man Godfrey 1936,S 19,18:1 (Incorrect in
    this edition; use 1936,S 18,18:1 elsewhere)
Libeled Lady 1936,O 31,24:2
After the Thin Man 1936,D 25,19:2
Last of Mrs Cheyney, The 1937,F 19,15:1
Emperor's Candlesticks, The 1937,Jl 9,18:1
Double Wedding 1937,O 22,27:2
Baroness and the Butler, The 1938,F 19,19:2
Another Thin Man 1939,N 24,29:1
I Love You Again 1940,Ag 16,11:2
Love Crazy 1941,Je 6,25:5
Shadow of the Thin Man 1941,N 21,23:2
Crossroads 1942,Jl 27,18:2
Youngest Profession, The 1943,Je 25,13:3
Heavenly Body, The 1944,Mr 24,17:3
Thin Man Goes Home, The 1945,Ja 26,16:5

Powell, William— Cont
Ziegfeld Follies 1946,Mr 23,8:3
Hoodlum Saint, The 1946,Je 27,29:1
Life With Father 1947,Ag 16,6:6
Song of the Thin Man 1947,Ag 29,14:2
Senator Was Indiscreet, The 1947,D 27,9:2
Mr Peabody and the Mermaid 1948,Ag 14,6:5
Take one False Step 1949,Je 23,33:2
Dancing in the Dark 1949,D 3,8:6
It's a big Country 1952,Ja 9,25:2
How to Marry a Millionaire 1953,N 11,37:1
Mister Roberts 1955,Jl 15,14:1
Powell, William H
When Knighthood Was in Flower 1922,S 15,17:2
(In Addenda)
Romola 1924,D 2,13:2
Power, Hartley
Just Smith 1934,Ap 23,20:2
Along Came Sally 1934,Je 16,20:3
Evergreen 1935,Ja 11,29:1
Lady in Distress 1942,F 16,21:2
Johnny in the Clouds 1945,N 16,16:2
Dead of Night 1946,Je 29,22:6
Man From Morocco, The 1946,N 25,38:2
Girl in a Million, A 1950,Jl 24,15:2
Roman Holiday 1953,Ag 28,13:1
Man With a Million 1954,Je 29,21:2
Cash on Delivery 1956,S 1,19:3
Island in the Sun 1957,Je 13,37:1
Power, Jules
Gloria's Romance 1916,My 23,9:2
For Sale 1924,Jl 14,11:5
Power, Romina
24 Hours in a Woman's Life 1968,S 25,39:1
Power, Tyrone
Black Panther's Cub, The 1921,My 30,12:5
Foot Falls 1921,S 9,18:3
Day of Faith, The 1923,N 27,11:2
Lone Wolf, The 1924,My 7,19:4
Janice Meredith 1924,Ag 6,13:3
Story Without a Name, The 1924,O 6,25:1
Where Was I 1925,Ag 19,14:4
Wanderer, The 1925,Ag 20,22:1
Regular Fellow, A 1925,O 5,25:2
Red Kimono, The 1926,F 3,23:1
Bride of the Storm 1926,Ap 5,24:1
Big Trail, The 1930,O 25,20:3
Tom Brown of Culver 1932,Jl 30,16:5
Girls' Dormitory 1936,Ag 29,16:2
Ladies in Love 1936,O 29,31:1
Lloyds of London 1936,N 26,39:1
Love Is News 1937,Mr 6,10:1
Cafe Metropole 1937,Ap 29,17:1
Thin Ice 1937,S 4,8:2
Second Honeymoon 1937,N 13,11:2
In Old Chicago 1938,Ja 7,15:2
Alexander's Ragtime Band 1938,Ag 6,7:2
Marie Antoinette 1938,Ag 17,23:2
Suez 1938,O 15,21:2
Jesse James 1939,Ja 14,13:1
Rose of Washington Square 1939,My 6,21:2
Second Fiddle 1939,Jl 1,11:2
Rains Came, The 1939,S 9,11:2
Daytime Wife 1939,N 24,29:1
Johnny Apollo 1940,Ap 13,21:2
Brigham Young - Frontiersman 1940,S 21,13:2
Mark of Zorro, The 1940,N 4,23:2
Blood and Sand 1941,My 23,25:3
Yank in the R A F, A 1941,S 27,11:3
Son of Fury 1942,Ja 30,23:2
This Above All 1942,My 13,14:3
Black Swan, The 1942,D 24,18:3
Crash Dive 1943,Ap 29,25:2
Razor's Edge, The 1946,N 20,42:2
Nightmare Alley 1947,O 10,31:3
Captain from Castile 1947,D 26,22:4
Luck of the Irish, The 1948,S 16,34:1
That Wonderful Urge 1948,D 22,29:6
Prince of Foxes 1949,D 24,11:2
Black Rose, The 1950,S 2,11:2
American Guerrilla in the Philippines
1950,N 8,37:2
Rawhide 1951,Mr 26,19:2
I'll Never. Forget You 1951,D 8,9:2
Diplomatic Courier 1952,Je 14,12:2
Pony Soldier 1952,D 20,15:2
Mississippi Gambler, The 1953,Ja 30,25:1
King of the Khyber Rifles 1953,D 23,21:1
Long Gray Line, The 1955,F 11,19:2
Untamed 1955,Mr 12,11:6
Eddy Duchin Story, The 1956,Je 22,15:1
Abandon Ship 1957,Ap 18,35:1
Sun Also Rises, The 1957,Ag 24,12:2
Witness for the Prosecution 1958,F 7,16:1
Powers, Charles
Boy Slaves 1939,F 9,17:3
Powers, Francis
Iron Horse, The 1924,Ag 29,6:1
Man Without a Country, The 1925,F 12,16:1
Powers, Harry
Crazy House 1943,D 16,33:3
Powers, John
We Are not Alone 1939,D 1,27:1

Powers, Leona
Deep Waters 1948,Jl 23,12:4
Powers, Lucille
Marquis Preferred 1929,Ja 21,18:4
Man to Man 1931,Ja 3,21:2
Amateur Daddy 1932,Ap 23,11:5
Powers, Mala
Edge of Doom 1950,Ag 4,13:2
Outrage 1950,O 16,30:5
Cyrano De Bergerac 1950,N 17,31:2
City Beneath the Sea 1953,Mr 12,24:3
City That Never Sleeps 1953,Ag 8,14:2
Bengazi 1955,O 8,13:4
Tammy and the Bachelor 1957,Je 15,10:7
Flight of the Lost Balloon 1962,My 24,29:2
Powers, Marie
Medium, The 1951,S 6,39:2
Powers, Maurine
Democracy, The Vision Restored 1920,Ag 25,6:4
Powers, Richard
Up in Arms 1944,Mr 3,19:2
San Quentin 1947,F 10,24:3
Dick Tracy's Dilemma 1947,Jl 14,14:5
Crossfire 1947,Jl 23,19:2
Berlin Express 1948,My 21,19:3
Return of the Badmen 1948,Ag 5,16:2
Race Street 1948,Ag 23,13:3
Blood on the Moon 1948,N 12,30:5
Red Planet Mars 1952,Je 16,15:2
Powers, Stefanie
Experiment in Terror 1962,Ap 14,14:1
Interns, The 1962,Ag 9,17:5
If a Man Answers 1962,N 22,43:1
Palm Springs Weekend 1963,N 6,32:1
McLintock 1963,N 14,41:3
New Interns, The 1964,Ag 20,34:2
Love Has Many Faces 1965,F 25,24:1
Die! Die! My Darling 1965,My 20,52:1
Stagecoach 1966,Je 16,53:1
Warning Shot 1967,Je 8,52:2
Powers, Tom
Double Indemnity 1944,S 7,21:1
Chicago Kid, The 1945,F 12,24:3
Practically Yours 1945,Mr 29,18:2
Blue Dahlia, The 1946,My 9,27:3
Last Crooked Mile, The 1946,S 14,10:8
Two Years Before the Mast 1946,S 25,39:2
Angel and the Badman 1947,Mr 3,28:4
Farmer's Daughter, The 1947,Mr 26,31:2
They Won't Believe Me 1947,Jl 17,16:2
Up in Central Park 1948,My 27,29:3
Time of your Life, The 1948,My 27,29:2
Mexican Hayride 1949,Ja 12,33:3
Scene of the Crime 1949,Jl 29,12:2
Special Agent 1949,Ag 22,13:1
Chicago Deadline 1949,N 3,37:2
Chinatown at Midnight 1949,N 18,35:3
East Side, West Side 1949,D 23,17:2
Nevadan, The 1950,Ja 13,19:4
Destination Moon 1950,Je 28,32:2
Right Cross 1950,N 16,39:2
Well, The 1951,S 27,37:2
Phone Call From a Stranger 1952,F 2,11:2
Horizons West 1952,N 22,16:5
Julius Caesar 1953,Je 5,19:1
Scared Stiff 1953,Jl 3,10:2
Donovan's Brain 1953,Ja 21,28:2
Americano, The 1955,Ja 20,35:1
Powley, Bryan
Love From a Stranger 1937,Ap 19,27:2
Moonlight Sonata 1938,My 10,17:2
Powys, Stephen (Original Author)
Three Blind Mice 1938,Je 18,18:2
Moon Over Miami 1941,Jl 5,14:2
Three Little Girls in Blue 1946,S 26,32:3
Poynter, Beaulah (Original Author)
Dancing Man 1934,Jl 16,11:3
Pozas, Blanca
Vida Bohemia, La 1939,F 6,8:5
Pozhkov, P (Screenwriter)
Magic Horse, The 1949,Je 20,14:7
Poznanski, Dimitri (Director)
Her Way of Love 1929,Ag 19,22:1
Pozner, Vladimir (Original Author)
Dark Mirror, The 1946,O 19,15:2
Pozner, Vladimir (Screenwriter)
Conspirators, The 1944,O 21,15:2
Another Part of the Forest 1948,My 19,30:2
Daughters of Destiny (Elizabeth); Elizabeth
(Daughters of Destiny) 1954,Jl 6,19:1
Pozzi, Mrs
Side Show of Life, The 1924,Jl 22,9:1
Pracharova, Jana
Report on the Party and the Guests, A
1968,S 20,37:5
Report on the Party and the Guests, A
1968,S 28,37:1
Pracher, Ilya
Transport From Paradise 1967,F 8,22:1
Fifth Horseman is Fear, The 1968,My 7,52:1
Prack, Rudolf
Mutterliebe; Mother Love 1940,Mr 16,8:3

Prada, Jose
Marcelino 1956,O 23,39:1
Tia Tula, A 1965,Je 3,24:1
Hunt, The 1967,Ap 25,38:1
Prades, James (Producer)
Native Son 1951,Je 18,19:2
Pradier, Perrette
Crime Does Not Pay (The Man on the Avenue);
Man on the Avenue, The (Crime Does Not
Pay) 1962,O 17,35:2
Burning Court, The 1963,Ag 1,17:2
That Man in Istanbul 1966,My 19,51:2
Prado, Lilia
Mexican Bus ride 1954,Jl 21,18:3
Prado, Marisa
Cangaceiro 1954,S 3,13:2
Prador, Irene
No Orchids for Miss Blandish 1951,F 23,33:2
Lilli Marlene 1952,Mr 29,19:2
Pradot, Marcelle
Living Dead Man, The 1927,Mr 7,16:3
Prager, Stanley
Eve of St Mark, The 1944,My 31,22:2
Take It or Leave It 1944,Jl 13,14:2
Junior Miss 1945,Je 18,15:4
Bell for Adano, A 1945,Jl 6,8:3
Do You Love Me 1946,My 25,12:2
Shocking Miss Pilgrim, The 1947,F 12,34:2
Foreign Affair, A 1948,Jl 1,19:3
You Gotta Stay Happy 1948,N 5,29:2
Force of Evil 1948,D 27,16:2
Lady Takes a Sailor, The 1949,D 17,15:2
Gun Crazy 1950,Ag 25,17:5
Prager, Willy
Grosse Tenor, Der 1931,My 29,26:5
Marriage in the Shadows 1948,S 17,28:3
Praince, Marcelle
Katia 1939,D 23,9:2
Entente Cordiale 1939,D 26,23:2
Twilight 1949,D 30,13:2
Under the Paris Sky 1952,My 6,35:1
Seven Deadly Sins (Pride); Pride (The Seven
Deadly Sins) 1953,My 12,31:3
Pramoi, Kukrit
Ugly American, The 1963,Ap 12,30:2
Prasch, Auguste
Waterloo 1929,Ap 16,32:5
Praskins, Leonard (Original Author)
Charlatan, The 1929,Ap 15,22:6
Ice Follies of 1939 1939,Mr 17,25:2
Big Bonanza, The 1945,F 26,14:5
It Grows on Trees 1952,N 29,11:2
Three Violent People 1957,F 11,34:2
Praskins, Leonard (Screenwriter)
We Live Again 1934,N 2,27:2
O'Shaughnessy's Boy 1935,O 5,18:2
One in a Million 1937,Ja 1,19:3
Stablemates 1938,O 21,27:2
Ice Follies of 1939 1939,Mr 17,25:2
My Pal, Wolf 1944,O 9,17:2
Molly and Me 1945,My 26,18:2
Caribbean Mystery, The 1945,Ag 20,22:4
Doll Face 1946,Mr 28,35:3
Brasher Doubloon, The 1947,My 22,34:5
It Grows on Trees 1952,N 29,11:2
Clown, The 1953,Ja 29,25:1
Mister Scoutmaster 1953,Ag 29,10:1
Prat, Rene
Song of the Street 1939,S 5,21:2
Pratesi, Mario (Original Author)
Viaccia, La 1962,S 21,35:1
Prather, Lee
Homicide Bureau 1939,F 2,17:2
Pratolini, Vasco (Original Author)
Most Wonderful Moment, The 1959,Je 1,23:6
Rocco and his Brothers 1961,Je 28,40:2
Family Diary 1963,N 12,48:1
Pratolini, Vasco (Screenwriter)
Viaccia, La 1962,S 21,35:1
Pratt, Gil (Director)
Elmer and Elsie 1934,Ag 4,14:5
Pratt, Gil (Screenwriter)
Saps at Sea 1940,Ap 29,12:2
Pratt, Jack
Desert Song, The 1929,My 2,20:6
Pratt, James (Producer)
Tonka 1959,Mr 26,27:1
Pratt, John
Whispering City 1948,My 10,25:5
Pratt, Judson
I Confess 1953,Mr 23,28:2
Somebody up There Likes Me 1956,Jl 6,16:1
Man Afraid 1957,Ap 5,24:2
Sergeant Rutledge 1960,My 26,37:1
Ugly American, The 1963,Ap 12,30:2
Distant Trumpet, A 1964,My 28,40:1
Cheyenne Autumn 1964,D 24,8:1
Pratt, Purnell
Midnight Lovers 1926,O 26,23:1
Alibi 1929,Ap 9,29:1
Thru Different Eyes 1929,Ap 15,22:6
Fast Life 1929,Ag 17,5:3
Trespasser, The 1929,N 2,14:6

Pratt, Purnell — Cont

Is Everybody Happy? 1929,N 2,14:6
Puttin' on the Ritz 1930,F 15,15:1
Lawful Larceny 1930,Jl 12,16:4
Common Clay 1930,Ag 2,16:4
Road to Paradise 1930,S 30,23:1
Silver Horde, The 1930,O 25,20:6
Paid 1931,Ja 3,21:2
Road to Paradise, The 1931,Ja 20,21:3
Gorilla, The 1931,F 23,20:3
Dance, Fools, Dance 1931,Mr 21,15:1
Bachelor Apartment 1931,My 16,13:3
Up for Murder 1931,My 30,9:2
Prodigal, The 1931,Je 27,20:3
Public Defender, The 1931,Ag 1,16:4
Traveling Husbands 1931,Ag 8,16:3
Spider, The 1931,S 5,7:4
Five Star Final 1931,S 11,24:2
Gay Diplomat, The 1931,O 10,20:4
Secret Witness, The 1931,D 21,28:4
Ladies of the Big House 1932,Ja 1,31:1
Emma 1932,F 6,14:4
Grand Hotel 1932,Ap 13,23:2
Famous Ferguson Case, The 1932,Ap 25,18:6
Roadhouse Murder 1932,Ap 29,13:4
Scarface, The Shame of the Nation
  1932,My 20,22:3
Hat Check Girl 1932,O 8,15:4
Red-Haired Alibi 1932,O 24,18:5
False Faces 1932,N 25,19:2
Billion Dollar Scandal, The 1933,Ja 9,23:1
I Cover the Waterfront 1933,My 18,17:3
Shriek in the Night, A 1933,Jl 24,11:2
Headline Shooters 1933,O 23,18:3
Love, Honor and Oh, Baby! 1933,O 28,20:3
Midshipman Jack 1933,N 20,18:2
Son of a Sailor 1933,N 30,38:4
Chief, The 1933,D 2,9:4
Witching Hour, The 1934,Ap 28,11:3
Hell Cat, The 1934,Jl 7,16:5
Winning Ticket, The 1935,F 11,14:2
Black Fury 1935,Ap 11,27:2
Casino Murder Case, The 1935,Ap 17,26:5
Behind the Green Lights 1935,Ap 22,14:2
Diamond Jim 1935,Ag 24,18:2
Red Salute 1935,S 30,13:1
$1,000 a Minute 1935,D 21,11:1
Magnificent Obsession 1935,D 31,11:2
Dancing Feet 1936,Mr 28,11:2
Return of Sophie Lang, The 1936,Jl 24,13:1
Wives Never Know 1936,O 31,24:2
Wedding Present 1936,N 19,31:3
Plainsman, The 1937,Ja 14,16:2
King of Gamblers 1937,Jl 3,18:1
Under Suspicion 1937,D 20,23:2 (In Addenda)
Ringside Maisie 1941,Ag 1,11:2

Pratt, Theodore (Original Author)

Juke Girl 1942,Je 20,9:2
Mr Winkle Goes to War 1944,Ag 3,16:1
Incredible Mr Limpet, The 1964,Mr 26,40:4

Prausewetter, Hans

Kleine Seitensprung, Der 1932,Ja 1,31:1

Pravda, George

Reach for Glory 1963,S 10,46:1
Hide and Seek 1964,Mr 12,40:3

Pravov, I (Director)

Grain 1936,Ja 16,25:2
Lust for Gold 1958,Jl 24,18:1

Pravov, I (Screenwriter)

Lust for Gold 1958,Jl 24,18:1

Prawitz, Elsa

Doll, The 1964,Ja 14,27:1

Preach, Henry

Brig, The 1964,S 21,37:4

Prebble, John (Miscellaneous)

Zulu 1964,Jl 8,38:1

Prebble, John (Original Author)

White Feather 1955,F 17,23:1

Prebble, John (Screenwriter)

Mysterious Island 1961,D 21,30:6
Zulu 1964,Jl 8,38:1

Preboist, Paul

7 Capital Sins (Gluttony); Gluttony (7 Capital
  Sins) 1963,Ja 17,5:2
Two of Us, The 1968,F 20,53:1

Precheur, Denise

Moment of Truth, The 1954,Ap 27,36:2

Predtechenskaya, Y

Friends 1939,Ja 2,28:3

Preedy, George (Original Author)

General Crack 1929,D 4,36:6

Preer, Evelyn

Blonde Venus 1932,S 24,18:4

Preis, Hassa (Director)

Liebe und die Erste Eisenbahn, Die; Love and the
  First Railroad 1935,F 18,19:4

Preiss, Wolfgang

Deadly Decision 1958,Ap 29,26:2
Counterfeit Traitor, The 1962,Ap 18,28:1
Lafayette 1963,Ap 11,29:1
Train, The 1965,Mr 18,25:1
Backfire 1965,Ap 27,27:1
Von Ryan's Express 1965,Je 24,28:1
Is Paris Burning? 1966,N 11,36:1

Jack of Diamonds 1967,N 11,26:3

Preisser, June

Babes in Arms 1939,O 20,27:2
Dancing Co-Ed 1939,N 10,27:3
Judge Hardy and Son 1940,Ja 18,27:3 (In
  Addenda)
Strike up the Band 1940,S 30,13:2
Gallant Sons 1940,D 12,37:2
Henry Aldrich for President 1941,O 18,22:2
Sweater Girl 1942,Jl 13,18:3
Murder in the Blue Room 1944,O 28,12:2

Prejean, Albert

Sous les Toits de Paris; (Under the Roofs of
  Paris) 1930,D 16,34:4
Horse Ate the Hat, The 1931,S 1,30:6
Theodore et Cie; Theodore & Co 1933,Jl 9,X,2:2
  (In Addenda)
Opera de Quat' Sous, L' 1933,D 9,18:4
Paquebot Tenacity 1934,Ag 12,IX,2:1
Crise est Finie, La 1935,Mr 14,18:1
Alibi, L' 1939,Ap 10,13:3
Hatred 1941,Ja 27,11:2
Shop-Girls of Paris; Au Bonheur de Dames
  1947,Je 23,14:4

Prelia, Claire

Living Image, The 1928,Je 4,13:2

Prelle, Micheline

Under my Skin 1950,Mr 18,9:2
American Guerrilla in the Philippines
  1950,N 8,37:2
Adventures of Captain Fabian 1951,D 14,36:2
French Way, The 1952,S 6,12:6
House of Ricordi 1956,Mr 13,32:1

Preller, Hubert

Itto 1936,Ja 29,15:5
Heritage 1940,N 5,33:2

Preminger, Otto

Pied Piper, The 1942,Ag 13,15:3
Margin for Error 1943,Ja 25,10:7
They Got Me Covered 1943,Mr 5,20:2
Stalag 17 1953,Jl 2,19:2

Preminger, Otto (Director)

Die Grosse Liebe 1932,F 22,23:2
Under Your Spell 1936,N 7,15:2
Danger-Love at Work 1937,D 11,22:2
Margin for Error 1943,Ja 25,10:7
Laura 1944,O 12,24:1
Royal Scandal, A 1945,Ap 12,19:2
Fallen Angel 1946,F 7,29:4
Centennial Summer 1946,Jl 18,20:2
Forever Amber 1947,O 23,31:2
Daisy Kenyon 1947,D 25,32:1
Fan, The 1949,Ap 2,12:2
Whirlpool 1950,Ja 14,9:2
Where the Sidewalk Ends 1950,Jl 8,7:4
Thirteenth Letter, The 1951,F 22,27:2
Angel Face 1953,Ap 25,11:5
Moon Is Blue, The 1953,Jl 9,18:3
River of no Return 1954,My 1,13:2
Carmen Jones 1954,O 29,27:2
Man With the Golden Arm, The 1955,D 16,38:2
Court-Martial of Billy Mitchell, The
  1955,D 23,14:2
Saint Joan 1957,Je 27,21:1
Bonjour Tristesse 1958,Ja 16,32:1
Porgy and Bess 1959,Je 25,20:3
Anatomy of a Murder 1959,Jl 3,10:1
Exodus 1960,D 16,44:1
Advise and Consent 1962,Je 7,31:2
Cardinal, The 1963,D 13,41:1
In Harm's Way 1965,Ap 7,36:1
Bunny Lake is Missing 1965,O 4,00:0
Hurry Sundown 1967,Mr 24,22:1

Preminger, Otto (Producer)

Laura 1944,O 12,24:1
Fallen Angel 1946,F 7,29:4
Centennial Summer 1946,Jl 18,20:2
Daisy Kenyon 1947,D 25,32:1
Fan, The 1949,Ap 2,12:2
Whirlpool 1950,Ja 14,9:2
Where the Sidewalk Ends 1950,Jl 8,7:4
Thirteenth Letter, The 1951,F 22,27:2
Angel Face 1953,Ap 25,11:5
Moon Is Blue, The 1953,Jl 9,18:3
Carmen Jones 1954,O 29,27:2
Man With the Golden Arm, The 1955,D 16,38:2
Saint Joan 1957,Je 27,21:1
Bonjour Tristesse 1958,Ja 16,32:1
Anatomy of a Murder 1959,Jl 3,10:1
Exodus 1960,D 16,44:1
Advise and Consent 1962,Je 7,31:2
Cardinal, The 1963,D 13,41:1
In Harm's Way 1965,Ap 7,36:1
Bunny Lake is Missing 1965,O 4,00:0
Hurry Sundown 1967,Mr 24,22:1

Prendergast, Lester

Dr No 1963,My 30,20:1

Prendergast, Tessa

His Majesty O'Keefe 1954,F 6,17:2

Prendes, Luis

Dr Coppelius 1968,D 26,56:1

Prendes, Mercedes

Tu Hijo 1934,D 17,24:3

Prentiss, Ann

Any Wednesday 1966,O 14,50:1
If He Hollers, Let Him Go 1968,O 10,59:7

Prentiss, Ed

F B I Story, The 1959,S 25,23:1
Man on a String 1960,My 21,15:1

Prentiss, Paula

Where the Boys Are 1961,Ja 20,22:1
Honeymoon Machine, The 1961,Ag 24,25:2
Bachelor in Paradise 1961,N 17,41:2
Horizontal Lieutenant, The 1962,My 12,15:3
Follow the Boys 1963,F 28,8:2
Man's Favorite Sport? 1964,F 20,22:1
World of Henry Orient, The 1964,Mr 20,27:2
In Harm's Way 1965,Ap 7,36:1
What's New Pussycat? 1965,Je 23,49:1

Prenzel, Marianne

Girls Behind Bars 1950,My 10,41:2

Preobrazhenskaya, Olga (Director)

Village of Sin, The 1929,My 21,29:3
Cossacks of the Don 1932,Mr 19,11:2
Grain 1936,Ja 16,25:2

Preov, Evgeni

Last Hill, The 1945,Je 26,13:2

Presber, Rudolf (Original Author)

His Late Excellency 1929,Je 11,27:2

Presberg, Alan (Miscellaneous)

We'll Bury You 1962,O 25,48:3

Prescott, Ellen

Ramparts We Watch, The 1940,S 20,27:1

Prescott, Elsie

Thirteen Women 1932,O 15,13:1
Peter Ibbetson 1935,N 8,18:2
Thou Shalt Not Kill 1940,Ja 8,11:2

Prescott, Jean

Confirm or Deny 1941,D 19,35:2
Immortal Sergeant 1943,F 4,29:2
Thunder in the Valley 1947,N 28,30:1

Prescott, Kerrigan

Fiend Without a Face 1958,Jl 4,15:3

Prescott, Norm (Producer)

Pinnocchio in Outer Space 1965,D 23,21:4

Preses, Peter

Magic Face, The 1951,O 1,19:2
No Time for Flowers 1952,D 26,20:3

Presgott, Gina

Girls Behind Bars 1950,My 10,41:2

Preskins, Leonard (Screenwriter)

Gorilla at Large 1954,Je 12,13:2

Presle, Micheline

Four Flights to Love 1942,Ap 13,12:2
Paris Frills 1946,N 25,38:3
Angel and Sinner 1947,F 24,16:5
Foolish Husbands 1948,O 11,27:2
Chips Are Down, The 1949,F 2,36:1
Devil in the Flesh 1949,My 10,29:2
Twilight 1949,D 30,13:2
Royal Affairs in Versailles 1957,Mr 9,16:1
It Happened in the Park 1957,Ag 13,23:2
Bride Is Much too Beautiful, The 1958,Ja 21,35:1
Demoniaque 1958,Mr 4,34:5
Chance Meeting 1960,O 27,45:2
Five Day Lover, The 1961,D 14,55:4
If a Man Answers 1962,N 22,43:1
7 Capital Sins (Lust); Lust (7 Capital Sins)
  1963,Ja 17,5:2
Time Out for Love 1963,Ap 23,31:2
Devil and the 10 Commandments, The (Episode
  4) 1963,O 15,44:1
Prize, The 1964,Ja 24,21:1
Dark Purpose 1964,F 6,36:4
Mistress for the Summer, A 1964,Mr 28,13:5
Male Hunt; Chasse a l'Homme, La
  1965,Ap 20,42:1
Lady Killer From Rome, The 1966,Je 9,54:3
King of Hearts 1967,Je 20,34:1
Religieuse, La 1968,S 23,42:3

Presles, Henri

Maternite 1937,Je 8,30:2
They Met on Skis 1940,D 23,23:2

Presley, Elvis

Love Me Tender 1956,N 16,23:1
Loving You 1957,Jl 18,19:2
Jailhouse Rock 1957,N 14,41:1
King Creole 1958,Jl 4,15:2
G I Blues 1960,N 5,28:1
Flaming Star 1960,D 17,19:1
Wild in the Country 1961,Je 10,12:2
Blue Hawaii 1962,F 22,20:2
Follow That Dream 1962,Ag 9,17:7
Kid Galahad 1963,Mr 7,8:5
It Happened at the World's Fair 1963,My 30,20:1
Fun in Acapulco 1964,F 20,22:4
Kissin' Cousins 1964,Ap 2,28:3
Viva Las Vegas 1964,My 21,42:1
Roustabout 1964,N 11,38:1
Girl Happy 1965,My 27,28:1
Tickle Me 1965,Je 24,28:3
Harum Scarum 1965,D 16,63:3
Paradise, Hawaiian Style 1966,Je 16,15:3
Frankie and Johnny 1966,Jl 21,20:2

Presley, Elvis— Cont
Spinout 1966,D 15,60:1
Double Trouble 1967,My 25,54:2
Easy Come, Easy Go 1967,Je 15,56:1
Clambake 1967,D 14,62:3
Speedway 1968,Je 14,43:1
Presnell, F G (Original Author)
Slightly Honorable 1940,My 17,23:4
Presnell, Harve
Unsinkable Molly Brown, The 1964,Jl 17,15:1
When the Boys Meet the Girls 1966,Ja 20,29:1
Presnell, Robert (Director)
Attack! The Battle of New Britain 1944,Je 21,1:6
Presnell, Robert (Miscellaneous)
Michigan Kid 1947,F 22,16:3
Presnell, Robert (Original Author)
Meet John Doe 1941,Mr 13,25:2
Big Bonanza, The 1945,F 26,14:5
Presnell, Robert (Producer)
Sofia 1948,S 4,8:7
Presnell, Robert (Screenwriter)
Disbarred 1939,Ja 19,17:2
Real Glory, The 1939,S 15,26:2
Thou Shalt Not Kill 1940,Ja 8,11:2
Money and the Woman 1940,O 4,29:2
High Tide 1947,N 8,11:2
13 West Street 1962,Je 7,31:2
Presnell, Robert Jr (Screenwriter)
Guilty, The 1947,My 19,27:2
Man in the Attic 1954,F 6,17:2
Life in the Balance, A 1955,Jl 14,19:1
Rawhide Years, The 1956,Je 16,12:2
Legend of the Lost 1957,D 23,18:2
Conspiracy of Hearts 1960,Ap 8,24:1
Let no Man Write my Epitaph 1960,N 11,36:2
Third Day, The 1965,Ag 5,15:3
Pressburger, Arnold (Producer)
Shanghai Gesture, The 1941,D 26,21:2
It Happened Tomorrow 1944,My 29,18:2
Three Hours 1944,O 30,16:5
Scandal In Paris, A 1946,S 16,9:7
Pressburger, Emeric (Director)
Life and Death of Colonel Blimp, The
1945,Mr 30,18:2
Stairway to Heaven 1946,D 26,28:1
Black Narcissus 1947,Ag 14,29:2
I Know Where I'm Going 1947,Ag 20,25:2
Red Shoes, The 1948,O 23,9:2
Canterbury Tale, A 1949,Ja 24,16:2
Tales of Hoffmann 1951,Ap 5,34:2
Small Back Room, The 1952,F 2,11:3
Wild Heart, The 1952,My 29,17:2
Fighting Pimpernel, The 1954,Ap 19,19:1
Pursuit of the Graf Spee 1957,D 27,33:2
Night Ambush 1958,Ap 25,32:4
Pressburger, Emeric (Original Author)
One Rainy Afternoon 1936,My 14,29:2
Blackout 1940,D 2,19:2
Invaders, The 1942,Mr 6,17:1
Squadron Leader X 1943,Jl 23,21:2
Stairway to Heaven 1946,D 26,28:1
I Know Where I'm Going 1947,Ag 20,25:2
Behold a Pale Horse 1964,Ag 14,16:1
Pressburger, Emeric (Producer)
Silver Fleet, The 1945,Mr 24,22:6
Life and Death of Colonel Blimp, The
1945,Mr 30,18:2
Stairway to Heaven 1946,D 26,28:1
Black Narcissus 1947,Ag 14,29:2
I Know Where I'm Going 1947,Ag 20,25:2
End of the River, The 1948,Je 21,18:2
Red Shoes, The 1948,O 23,9:2
Canterbury Tale, A 1949,Ja 24,16:2
Tales of Hoffmann 1951,Ap 5,34:2
Small Back Room, The 1952,F 2,11:3
Wild Heart, The 1952,My 29,17:2
Fighting Pimpernel, The 1954,Ap 19,19:1
Pursuit of the Graf Spee 1957,D 27,33:2
Night Ambush 1958,Ap 25,32:4
Pressburger, Emeric (Screenwriter)
Challenge, The 1939,O 2,15:2
U-Boat 29 1939,O 6,31:3
Blackout 1940,D 2,19:2
Invaders, The 1942,Mr 6,17:1
One of our Aircraft Is Missing 1942,N 2,17:2
Life and Death of Colonel Blimp, The
1945,Mr 30,18:2
Wanted for Murder 1946,D 12,38:4
Black Narcissus 1947,Ag 14,29:2
Red Shoes, The 1948,O 23,9:2
Canterbury Tale, A 1949,Ja 24,16:2
Tales of Hoffmann 1951,Ap 5,34:2
Wild Heart, The 1952,My 29,17:2
Fighting Pimpernel, The 1954,Ap 19,19:1
Pursuit of the Graf Spee 1957,D 27,33:2
Night Ambush 1958,Ap 25,32:4
Pressburger, Fred (Director)
Crowded Paradise 1956,Je 22,15:1
Pressburger, Fred (Miscellaneous)
Fabiola 1951,My 30,14:2
Pressin, Leo B
Letters From an Unknown Woman
1948,Ap 29,20:6

Presson, Jay (Original Author)
Wives and Lovers 1963,Ag 29,36:1
Prest, Pat
Chetniks 1943,Mr 19,15:3
On Dangerous Ground 1952,F 13,35:2
Easy Come, Easy Go 1967,Je 15,56:1
Preston, Ann
Parole 1936,Je 27,21:1
Magnificent Brute, The 1936,O 24,23:1
Preston, Billy
St Louis Blues 1958,Ap 12,13:1
Preston, Joey
No Leave, No Love 1946,O 18,29:2
Fiesta 1947,Je 27,17:3
Preston, June
Anne of Green Gables 1934,D 22,21:1
Preston, Robert
King of Alcatraz 1938,O 7,21:2
Illegal Traffic 1938,N 17,29:3
Disbarred 1939,Ja 19,17:2
Union Pacific 1939,My 11,31:2
Beau Geste 1939,Ag 3,15:2
Typhoon 1940,My 23,28:4
North West Mounted Police 1940,N 7,33:2
Moon Over Burma 1940,D 12,37:4
Lady From Cheyenne, The 1941,Ap 18,18:2
Parachute Battalion 1941,Ag 29,13:2
New York Town 1941,N 13,35:2
Night of January 16th, The 1941,D 19,35:1
Pacific Blackout 1942,Ja 15,25:2
Reap the Wild Wind 1942,Mr 27,27:2
This Gun for Hire 1942,My 14,23:2
Wake Island 1942,S 2,19:2
Night Plane From Chungking 1943,My 31,13:2
Macomber Affair, The 1947,Ap 21,21:2
Wild Harvest 1947,N 13,33:2
Big City 1948,My 17,23:3
Blood on the Moon 1948,N 12,30:5
Whispering Smith 1949,F 15,28:2
Lady Gambles, The 1949,My 21,9:2
Tulsa 1949,My 27,25:2
Sundowners, The 1950,My 5,17:2
Best of the Badmen 1951,Ag 10,13:2
My Outlaw Brother 1951,Ag 23,19:2
Bride Comes to Yellow Sky, The 1953,Ja 14,27:2
Last Frontier, The 1955,D 8,45:1
Khovanschina 1960,S 23,33:1
Music Man, The 1962,Ag 24,14:1
How the West Was Won 1963,Ap 1,54:1
Island of Love 1963,Je 13,30:4
All the Way Home 1963,O 30,46:1
Preston, Stephen
Don't Knock the Twist 1962,Ap 14,14:2
Pretal, Camillus
Abie's Irish Rose 1928,Ap 20,26:7
Pretty, Arline
Barriers Burned Away 1925,Mr 12,17:3
Preuty, Olive Higgins (Original Author)
Stella Dallas 1925,N 17,30:2
Prevert, Jacques (Miscellaneous)
Gates of the Night 1950,Mr 16,40:2
Prevert, Jacques (Screenwriter)
Bizarre, Bizarre 1939,Mr 21,27:2
Port of Shadows 1939,O 30,13:2
Daybreak 1940,Jl 30,16:2
Stormy Waters 1946,Je 17,32:2
Enfants du Paradis, Les 1947,F 20,32:2
Bellman, The 1947,Ap 7,20:5
Devil's Own Envoy, The 1947,Ag 30,8:6
Voyage Surprise 1948,F 14,17:3
Gates of the Night 1950,Mr 16,40:2
Lovers of Verona, The 1951,Mr 12,20:2
Hunchback of Notre Dame, The 1957,D 12,35:1
Crime of Monsieur Lange, The 1964,Ap 4,15:5
Prevert, Pierre
Age d'Or, L'; Golden Age, The 1964,S 22,44:1
Prevert, Pierre (Director)
Voyage Surprise 1948,F 14,17:3
Prevert, Pierre (Screenwriter)
Voyage Surprise 1948,F 14,17:3
Preville, Giselle
Against the Wind 1949,Je 27,18:3
Counter Investigation 1949,D 30,13:2
Dancing Years, The 1951,Ja 29,14:4
Previn, Andre
Subterraneans, The 1960,Jl 7,26:1
Pepe 1960,D 22,18:1
Previn, Andre (Composer)
Invitation to the Dance (Ring Around the Rosy);
Ring Around the Rosy (Invitation to the
Dance) 1956,My 23,35:7
Invitation to the Dance (Sinbad the Sailor); Sinbad
the Sailor (Invitation to the Dance)
1956,My 23,35:7
Invitation to the Dance (Circus); Circus (Invitation
to the Dance) 1956,My 23,35:7
Previn, Charles
Little Bit of Heaven, A 1940,N 8,24:2
Previn, Charles (Composer)
Patrick the Great 1945,Ap 13,15:2
Previn, Steve (Director)
Almost Angels 1962,N 1,34:2

Prevost, Abbe (Original Author)
Manon Lescaut 1914,Je 14,15:1
When a Man Loves 1927,F 4,16:6
Manon Lescaut 1941,Ap 14,23:5
Manon 1950,D 26,19:1
Prevost, Francoise
Enemy General, The 1960,O 20,42:2
Bon Voyage! 1962,My 18,34:2
Girl With the Golden Eyes, The 1962,Ag 21,36:2
Paris Belongs to Us 1962,N 6,38:1
Playtime; Receation, La 1963,Ja 16,5:2
Time Out for Love 1963,Ap 23,31:2
Season for Love, The 1963,My 9,40:2
Payroll 1963,My 11,15:2
Condemned of Altona, The 1963,O 31,26:1
Galia 1966,D 20,50:4
Other One, The 1967,S 29,53:1
Prevost, Marie
Old Swimmin' Hole, The 1921,F 28,16:2
Moonlight Follies 1921,S 19,12:1
Beautiful and Damned, The 1922,D 11,22:1
Brass 1923,Mr 12,18:1
Red Lights 1923,S 10,15:4
Marriage Circle, The 1924,F 4,23:3
Being Respectable 1924,Ag 4,16:3
Three Women 1924,O 6,25:1
Tarnish 1924,O 13,21:1
Lover of Camille, The 1924,N 11,14:1
Black Swan, The 1924,N 25,26:1
Recompense 1925,Ap 20,22:1
Kiss Me Again 1925,Ag 3,10:1
Bobbed Hair 1925,N 4,17:4
Seven Sinners 1925,D 8,28:5
Cave Man, The 1926,Mr 1,17:1
Other Women's Husbands 1926,Ap 27,23:2
Other Men's Wives 1926,My 2,VIII,5:3 (In
Addenda)
Up in Mabel's Room 1926,Je 29,21:2
For Wives Only 1926,D 1,24:5
Man Bait 1927,Ja 19,21:1
Getting Gertie's Garter 1927,F 9,17:3
Night Bride, The 1927,Mr 30,22:6
Girl on the Pullman, The 1927,N 1,21:1 (In
Addenda)
Rush Hour, The 1928,Ja 31,29:1
Racket, The 1928,Jl 9,25:1
Godless Girl, The 1929,Ap 1,22:1
Party Girl 1930,Ja 2,28:2
Ladies of Leisure 1930,My 24,21:2
War Nurse 1930,O 24,31:1
Paid 1931,Ja 3,21:2
Good Bad Girl, The 1931,My 15,20:6
It's a Wise Child 1931,My 16,13:3
Gentleman's Fate 1931,Je 27,20:3
Run Around, The 1931,Ag 10,18:3
Sporting Blood 1931,Ag 15,18:3
Sin of Madelon Claudet, The 1931,O 31,22:2
Reckless Living 1931,D 5,21:2
Hell Divers 1931,D 23,27:3
Three Wise Girls 1932,F 6,14:4
Carnival Boat 1932,Mr 21,19:5
Parole Girl 1933,Ap 10,8:2
Only Yesterday 1933,N 10,25:1
Hands Across the Table 1935,N 2,13:2
13 Hours by Air 1936,Ap 30,17:2
Prevot, Jacqueline
Louise 1940,F 3,9:4
Priadilova, Svetlana
Lonely White Sail 1938,My 7,18:1
Price, Alonzo
Forgotten Faces 1936,Jl 4,18:2
Black Legion 1937,Ja 18,21:1
Slim 1937,Je 24,30:2
Price, Bamlet L Jr
One-Way Ticket to Hell 1955,D 8,45:1
Price, Bamlet L Jr (Director)
One-Way Ticket to Hell 1955,D 8,45:1
Price, Bamlet L Jr (Original Author)
One-Way Ticket to Hell 1955,D 8,45:1
Price, Bamlet L Jr (Producer)
One-Way Ticket to Hell 1955,D 8,45:1
Price, Bamlet L Sr
One-Way Ticket to Hell 1955,D 8,45:1
Price, Dennis
Magic Bow, The 1947,Jl 7,13:2
Hungry Hill 1947,O 11,11:2
Holiday Camp 1948,Ja 24,11:2
Jassy 1948,F 20,19:2
Dear Murderer 1948,My 8,12:2
Bad Sister 1948,Je 11,27:3
Canterbury Tale, A 1949,Ja 24,16:2
Place of One's Own, A 1949,F 8,30:2
Easy Money (Episode 3) 1949,F 14,15:3
Snowbound 1949,F 21,20:2
Caravan 1949,Ap 21,30:4
Master of Bankdam 1949,O 17,18:2
Kind Hearts and Coronets 1950,Je 15,41:2
Good Time Girl 1950,S 25,18:5
Lost People, The 1950,O 2,19:4
Dancing Years, The 1951,Ja 29,14:4
I'll Never Forget You 1951,D 8,9:2
Murder Without Crime 1951,D 26,19:6
Bad Lord Byron, The 1952,Mr 20,37:5

Price, Dennis — Cont

Intruder, The 1955,Ja 26,22:1
That Lady 1955,Je 11,8:7
Private's Progress 1956,Jl 24,19:2
Port Afrique 1956,N 3,27:5
Your Past Is Showing 1958,Jl 1,36:2
I'm All Right Jack 1960,Ap 26,40:2
Breakout 1960,My 19,44:3
Oscar Wilde 1960,Je 21,28:2
School for Scoundrels 1960,Jl 12,39:1
Tunes of Glory 1960,D 21,38:2
Millionairess, The 1961,F 10,19:1
Pure Hell of St Trinian's, The 1961,S 26,31:1
Call Me Genius 1961,O 17,47:1
Five Golden Hours 1961,O 19,39:3
Double Bunk 1961,N 17,41:3
No Love for Johnnie 1961,D 13,55:1
Victim 1962,F 6,27:2
No Place Like Homicide 1962,S 13,32:1
Kill or Cure 1962,N 13,43:4
Play it Cool 1963,Jl 18,15:3
V I P's, The 1963,S 20,29:1
They all Died Laughing 1964,Mr 16,37:2
Doctor in Distress 1964,Jl 8,38:2
Tamahine 1964,Jl 16,23:1
Murder Most Foul 1965,My 24,36:2
High Wind in Jamaica, A 1965,Je 17,27:2
Ten Little Indians 1966,F 10,33:1
Ten Little Indians 1966,F 10,33:1
Those Fantastic Flying Fools 1967,O 19,59:2

Price, Dick
Beggar Student, The 1958,Ja 25,14:3
Price, Edward
That Girl From Paris 1937,Ja 1,19:1
Price, Elwood G (Director)
Mau Mau 1955,Jl 14,19:1
Price, Ginger
Prince of Peace, The 1951,Mr 24,8:3
Price, Hal
Night Ride 1930,Ja 20,21:1
Last Man, The 1932,S 17,18:4
This Sporting Age 1932,O 1,10:4
Girl in 419 1933,My 20,11:5
Price, Howard
Elopement 1951,D 21,21:3
Price, Kate
Little Lord Fauntleroy 1921,S 16,17:3
Spoilers, The 1923,Ag 6,14:2
Dangerous Maid, The 1923,D 11,26:2
Sea Hawk, The 1924,Je 3,22:1
Tornado, The 1924,D 15,14:1
Wife of the Centaur, The 1925,Ja 7,33:5
Way of a Girl, The 1925,Mr 30,21:3
Sporting Venus, The 1925,My 11,14:3
Desert Flower, The 1925,Je 1,10:3
Proud Heart 1925,N 3,25:4
Sally, Irene and Mary 1925,D 7,19:1
Memory Lane 1926,F 2,20:4
Cohens and the Kellys, The 1926,F 23,26:5
Irene 1926,Mr 1,17:1
Paradise 1926,O 4,20:2
Third Degree, The 1927,F 15,23:1
Frisco Sally Levy 1927,Ap 13,29:4
Orchids and Ermine 1927,Ap 19,24:4
Quality Street 1927,N 2,24:5
Thanks For The Buggy Ride 1928,Ja 23,18:3
Cohens and the Kellys In Paris, The
   1928,F 6,12:3
Mad Hour, The 1928,Ap 16,20:5
Show Girl 1928,N 5,26:1
Cohens and the Kellys In Atlantic City, The
   1929,Mr 18,30:6
Two Weeks Off 1929,Je 24,27:1
Rogue Song, The 1930,Ja 29,26:4
Cohens and the Kelleys In Scotland, The
   1930,Mr 10,24:1
Dancing Sweeties 1930,Ag 16,8:3
Cohens and Kellys in Africa, The 1930,D 20,20:6
Ladies of the Jury 1932,Ap 2,13:2
Have a Heart 1934,O 20,20:2
Price, Lucile
One-Way Ticket to Hell 1955,D 8,45:1
Price, Monte (Screenwriter)
Fleet's In, The 1928,O 1,23:1
Price, Nancy
Doctor's Secret, The 1929,F 4,20:1
Three Live Ghosts 1929,S 30,23:1
In Gay Madrid 1930,Je 7,10:4
Caught Short 1930,Je 21,20:5
Speckled Band, The 1931,N 7,16:5
Stars Look Down, The 1941,Jl 24,15:2
Yank in London, A 1946,Ap 20,16:3
Madonna of the Seven Moons 1946,My 23,18:4
I Know Where I'm Going 1947,Ag 20,25:2
Master of Bankdam 1949,O 17,18:2
Story of Mandy, The 1953,F 24,21:3
Naked Heart, The 1955,Mr 9,22:4
Price, Peter
Love That Brute 1950,My 27,10:6
Great Caruso, The 1951,My 11,32:2
New Mexico 1951,Jl 14,7:2

Price, Sherwood
Man From Galveston, The 1964,Ja 23,26:3
Price, Stanley
Undercover Doctor 1939,Je 1,31:2
Seventeen 1940,F 29,15:2
Moon Over Burma 1940,D 12,37:4
Great Commandment, The 1942,O 17,11:1
Sundowners, The 1950,My 5,17:2
Price, Stanley (Screenwriter)
Arabesque 1966,My 6,54:1
Price, Tony
Seventh Dawn, The 1964,S 3,24:1
Price, Vincent
Service de Luxe 1938,O 24,13:2
Private Lives of Elizabeth and Essex, The
   1939,D 2,21:2
Tower of London 1939,D 12,37:2
Invisible Man Returns, The 1940,Ja 16,19:2
Green Hell 1940,Ja 30,15:6
House of the Seven Gables, The 1940,Ap 15,21:3
Brigham Young - Frontiersman 1940,S 21,13:2
Hudson's Bay 1941,Ja 10,23:2
Song of Bernadette, The 1944,Ja 27,15:2
Eve of St Mark, The 1944,My 31,22:2
Wilson 1944,Ag 2,18:1
Laura 1944,O 12,24:1
Keys of the Kingdom, The 1944,D 30,15:2
Royal Scandal, A 1945,Ap 12,19:2
Leave Her to Heaven 1945,D 26,15:1
Shock 1946,Mr 9,10:2
Dragonwyck 1946,Ap 11,35:2
Web, The 1947,Je 5,32:1
Moss Rose 1947,Jl 3,14:2
Long Night, The 1947,S 17,31:2
Up in Central Park 1948,My 27,29:3
Three Musketeers, The 1948,O 21,33:2
Rogues' Regiment 1948,D 20,31:2
Bribe, The 1949,F 4,31:2
Bagdad 1949,D 24,11:4
Champagne for Caesar 1950,My 12,33:2
Baron of Arizona, The 1950,Je 23,29:2
Curtain Call at Cactus Creek 1950,S 22,35:4
His Kind of Woman 1951,Ag 30,20:2
Adventures of Captain Fabian 1951,D 14,36:2
Las Vegas Story, The 1952,Ja 31,37:6
House of Wax 1953,Ap 11,15:2
Dangerous Mission 1954,Mr 6,13:5
Mad Magician, The 1954,My 20,38:2
Son of Sinbad 1955,Jl 28,18:2
Serenade 1956,Mr 24,21:1 (Incorrect in this
   edition; use 1956,Mr 23,21:1 elsewhere)
While the City Sleeps 1956,My 17,37:1
Ten Commandments, The 1956,N 9,35:2
Story of Mankind, The 1957,N 9,31:2
Fly, The 1958,Ag 30,6:6
House on Haunted Hill 1959,Mr 12,27:5
Big Circus, The 1959,Jl 18,6:1
Bat, The 1959,D 17,51:4
Tingler, The 1960,Mr 10,36:2
House of Usher, The 1960,S 15,45:4
Pit and the Pendulum, The 1961,Ag 24,25:3
Master of the World 1961,S 16,9:1
Tales of Terror 1962,Jl 5,21:2 (In Addenda)
Convicts 4 1962,O 4,44:2
Raven, The 1963,Ja 26,5:8
Diary of a Madman 1963,Je 6,39:1
Comedy of Terrors, The 1964,Ja 23,26:2
Haunted Palace, The 1964,Ja 30,24:1
Twice Told Tales (Dr Heidegger's Experiment); Dr
   Heidegger's Experiment (Twice Told Tales)
   1964,Mr 28,40:1
Twice Told Tales (Rappaccini's Daughter);
   Rappaccini's Daughter (Twice Told Tales)
   1964,Mr 28,40:1
Twice Told Tales (The House of the Seven
   Gables); House of the Seven Gables, The (Twice
   Told Tales) 1964,My 28,40:1
Masque of the Red Death, The 1964,S 17,52:6
Tomb of Ligeia 1965,My 6,44:1
War Gods of the Deep 1965,Je 3,24:3
Dr Goldfoot and the Bikini Machine
   1966,F 17,29:3
House of 1,000 Dolls 1968,Mr 14,51:4
Conqueror Worm, The 1968,Ag 15,46:2
Price, Vincent (Narrator)
Pictura 1952,Ap 8,35:3
Taboos of the World 1965,My 20,52:4
Price, Will (Director)
Strange Bargain 1949,S 30,28:3
Tripoli 1950,N 10,35:2
Price, Will (Miscellaneous)
Gone With the Wind 1939,D 20,31:2
Price, Will (Original Author)
Tripoli 1950,N 10,35:2
Prichard, H (Original Author)
Don Q, Son of Zorro 1925,Je 16,24:1
Don Q, Son of Zorro 1925,Je 16,24:1
Prickett, Maudie
Slattery's Hurricane 1949,Ag 13,6:6
Model and the Marriage Broker, The
   1952,Ja 12,10:6
Stars and Stripes Forever 1952,D 23,17:2

Prida, Yolanda
Alarma 1939,Ja 23,8:2
Priest, Dan
Black Like Me 1964,My 21,42:1
Priest, John
Everybody Does It 1949,O 26,32:2
Priestley, Bertha
Andy Hardy's Private Secretary 1941,Mr 7,17:2
Priestley, J B
Battle for Music 1945,O 15,13:2
Priestley, J B (Miscellaneous)
Jamaica Inn 1939,O 12,33:1
Priestley, J B (Original Author)
Old Dark House, The 1932,O 28,22:4
Good Companions, The 1933,O 10,24:1
Laburnum Grove 1941,D 2,29:2
Somewhere in France 1943,Jl 12,11:2
They Came to a City 1945,F 19,21:3
Inspector Calls, An 1954,N 26,24:4
Old Dark House, The 1963,O 31,26:3
Priestley, J B (Producer)
Last Holiday 1950,N 14,39:4
Priestley, J B (Screenwriter)
They Came to a City 1945,F 19,21:3
Last Holiday 1950,N 14,39:4
Prieto, Antonio
Tarantos, Los 1964,Je 30,22:1
Fistful of Dollars, A 1967,F 2,29:1
Prieto, Jose
Our Man in Havana 1960,Ja 28,26:1
Priggen, Norman (Producer)
Payroll 1963,My 11,15:2
Servant, The 1964,Mr 17,30:2
King and Country 1964,S 24,46:2
King and Country 1966,Ja 28,20:4
Accident 1967,Ap 18,33:1
Boom! 1968,My 27,56:1
Secret Ceremony 1968,O 24,55:1
Prihoda, Vasa
Between Two Worlds 1940,F 9,15:2
Prim, Suzy
Lower Depths, The 1937,S 11,20:1
Mayerling 1937,S 14,27:1
Crossroads 1939,Mr 14,17:5
Betrayal 1939,S 16,20:2
Betrayal 1939,S 16,20:2
Mad Emperor, The 1941,Mr 10,21:3
Heart of a Nation, The 1943,Ap 8,27:2
Shop-Girls of Paris; Au Bonheur de Dames
   1947,Je 23,14:4
Sinners, The 1950,N 11,11:2
Companions of the Night 1954,N 25,44:2
Prima, Louis
You Can't Have Everything 1937,Ag 4,15:2
Rose of Washington Square 1939,My 6,21:2
Hey Boy! Hey Girl! 1959,Ag 6,18:3
Prima, Louis and Band
Manhattan Merry-Go-Round 1937,D 31,9:3
Prima, Louis with his band
Start Cheering 1938,Mr 17,17:3
Primavera, Nanda
Wayward Wife, The 1955,Ap 11,29:3
Primm, Frances
Merry Widow, The 1925,Ag 27,14:1
Prince, John
Battling Orioles, The 1924,N 4,24:1
King of Kings, The 1927,Ap 20,29:2
Ramona 1928,My 15,17:3
Country Beyond, The 1936,Ap 30,17:3
Prince, William
Destination Tokyo 1944,Ja 1,9:2
Very Thought of You, The 1944,N 18,16:7
Hollywood Canteen 1944,D 16,19:2
Objective Burma 1945,Ja 27,15:2
Pillow to Post 1945,My 26,18:2
Cinderella Jones 1946,Mr 16,9:6
Dead Reckoning 1947,Ja 23,31:2
Carnegie Hall 1947,My 3,10:2
Snowbound 1949,F 21,20:2
Lust for Gold 1949,Jl 4,9:2
Cyrano De Bergerac 1950,N 17,31:2
Vagabond King, The 1956,S 13,39:6
Macabre 1958,Jl 24,18:1
Princet, Lliane
Mouchette 1968,S 21,26:1
Prindle, Don (Screenwriter)
Ugly Ones, The 1968,D 12,62:5
Prindle, James (Original Author)
Orchestra Wives 1942,S 24,23:2
Prine, Andrew
Miracle Worker, The 1962,My 24,29:2
Advance to the Rear 1964,Je 11,27:3
Texas Across the River 1966,N 24,65:1
Devil's Brigade, The 1968,My 23,56:2
Bandolero 1968,Jl 18,26:2
Prineas, Yannis
Anna of Rhodes 1950,Mr 23,34:2
Pring, Gerald
Betrayal, The 1929,Ap 29,29:2
Human Monster, The 1940,Mr 25,11:2
Pringle, Aileen
Tiger's Claw, The 1923,Mr 19,22:2
Don't Marry for Money 1923,Ag 21,17:3

Pringle, Aileen— Cont
In the Palace of the King 1923,D 3,14:1
Name the Man 1924,F 4,23:3
Three Weeks 1924,Ap 1,19:3
True as Steel 1924,Je 17,22:4
His Hour 1924,O 7,26:1
Wife of the Centaur, The 1925,Ja 7,33:5
Thief in Paradise, A 1925,Ja 26,14:1
Kiss in the Dark, A 1925,Ap 7,17:3
Wildfire 1925,Je 10,18:2
One Year to Live 1925,Jl 6,12:2
Mystic, The 1925,Ag 31,19:3
Soul Mates 1926,Ja 4,16:1
Wilderness Woman, The 1926,My 10,19:1
Great Deception, The 1926,Ag 9,10:3
Tin Gods 1926,S 20,21:3
Adam and Evil 1927,Ag 10,21:4
Tea For Three 1927,O 31,22:1
Body and Soul 1927,N 8,33:1
Beau Broadway 1928,Jl 30,21:2
Dream of Love 1928,D 24,11:1
Night Parade 1929,N 11,20:2
Wall Street 1929,N 25,22:1
Puttin' on the Ritz 1930,F 15,15:1
Soldiers and Women 1930,My 12,27:3
Subway Express 1931,My 2,23:4
Murder at Midnight 1931,O 5,17:3
Fame Street 1932,Ap 2,13:2
Age of Consent, The 1932,S 3,16:2
Phantom of Crestwood, The 1932,O 17,18:3
Sons of Steel 1935,Ap 15,16:3
Unguarded Hour, The 1936,Ap 4,11:1
Piccadilly Jim 1936,Ag 31,19:1
John Meade's Woman 1937,F 18,19:1
Last of Mrs Cheyney, The 1937,F 19,15:1
She's no Lady 1937,Ag 12,14:3
Hardys Ride High, The 1939,Ap 14,28:2
Night of Nights, The 1939,D 28,17:1
Pringle, Bryan
Saturday Night and Sunday Morning
1961,Ap 4,44:2
Pringle, Jessie
Handy Andy 1934,Ag 4,14:5
Printemps, Yvonne
Dame aux Camelias, La 1935,Mr 21,27:1
Three Waltzes 1939,Ap 25,19:2
Paris Waltz, The 1950,Ag 23,35:2
Voyage to America 1952,O 20,18:2
Printignant, Jean-Louis
7 Capital Sins (Lust); Lust (7 Capital Sins)
1963,Ja 17,5:2
Printzlau, Olga (Original Author)
Broken Dreams 1933,N 21,23:3
Printzlau, Olga (Screenwriter)
Why Change Your Wife 1920,Ap 26,18:1
Conrad in Quest of his Youth 1920,N 8,20:2
Midsummer Madness 1920,D 6,19:1
Beautiful and Damned, The 1922,D 11,22:1
Prinz, LeRoy (Composer)
Artists and Models 1937,Ag 5,19:2
Prinz, LeRoy (Miscellaneous)
Rumba 1935,F 25,13:2
Night and Day 1946,Jl 26,16:2
Prioli, Angelo
Miracle in Milan 1951,D 18,42:2
Priolo, Giuseppe
Path of Hope, The (Il Cammino Della Speranza)
1952,Ag 5,15:5
PRIOR
See Also PRYOR
Prior, Allan
Bride of the Regiment 1930,My 22,32:6
Prior, Beatrix
Stella Dallas 1925,N 17,30:2
Prior, Herbert
Stronger Than Death 1920,Ja 12,7:1
Slave of Desire 1923,D 11,26:2
Madonna of the Streets 1924,O 28,23:4
Waking up the Town 1925,Mr 31,17:4
Why Girls Go Back Home 1926,My 18,28:2
Caught Short 1930,Je 21,20:5
Prior, J Redmond (Original Author)
Chain Lightning 1950,F 20,21:2
Prior, Robert
Little Johnny Jones 1923,Ag 13,16:1
Priour, Georges
Volga Boatman, The 1938,Ap 15,23:3
Pris, Jerry
Submarine Command 1952,Ja 19,13:2
Prisco, Albert
Monte Cristo 1922,Ag 15,20:3
Song of Love, The 1924,F 25,13:1
Sea Hawk, The 1924,Je 3,22:1
Midnight Sun, The 1926,Ap 24,20:4
White Black Sheep, The 1926,D 21,20:2
Soft Cushions 1927,S 12,29:1
Pritchett, Paula
Chappaqua 1967,N 6,65:2
Prithvira
Vagabond, The 1956,Ap 16,30:4
Prival, Bert
Emperor Waltz, The 1948,Je 18,19:2

Prival, Lucien
Puppets 1926,Je 21,17:2
Great Deception, The 1926,Ag 9,10:3
Patent Leather Kid, The 1927,Ag 16,31:2
American Beauty 1927,O 11,27:1
Racket, The 1928,Jl 9,25:1
Adoration 1929,Ja 14,20:1
Party Girl 1930,Ja 2,28:2
In the Next Room 1930,Ap 7,21:1
Hell's Angels 1930,Ag 16,8:3
Princess and the Plumber, The 1930,D 23,25:1
Young Sinners 1931,My 9,15:4
Hollywood Speaks 1932,Ag 12,18:2
Sherlock Holmes 1932,N 12,20:5
Secrets of the French Police 1932,D 12,18:4
Grand Slam 1933,F 22,25:2
After Tonight 1933,N 3,23:2
Bride of Frankenstein, The 1935,My 11,21:2
History Is Made at Night 1937,Mr 29,14:2
Trapped by G-Men 1937,N 4,29:1
Every Day's a Holiday 1938,Ja 27,17:2
Mr Wong, Detective 1938,N 21,14:4
Confessions of a Nazi Spy 1939,Ap 29,13:2
Nurse Edith Cavell 1939,S 22,27:4
Beasts of Berlin 1939,N 20,15:6
Privaltsev, Vladimir
Father of a Soldier 1966,F 21,51:1
Proach, Henry
Connection, The 1962,O 4,44:1
Probert, George
Madame Peacock 1920,O 25,18:1
Prochazkova, Zdenka
Fifth Horseman is Fear, The 1968,My 7,52:1
Proclamer, Anna
Malia 1952,F 2,11:4
Procopio, Lou
Wild Angels, The 1966,D 22,40:4
Proctor, Catherine
Society Scandal, A 1924,Mr 10,18:2
Youth Takes a Fling 1938,O 17,12:1
Proctor, George Dubois (Screenwriter)
Passionate Pilgrim, The 1921,Ja 3,20:2
Proctor, John
Anna Lucasta 1959,Ja 15,27:1
Proctor, Lynn, Trio
Miracle in Harlem 1949,O 24,19:4
Proctor, Maurice (Original Author)
Hell is a City 1961,Ja 19,26:3
Procuna, Angel
Torero! 1957,My 22,29:2
Procuna, Luis
Torero! 1957,My 22,29:2
Procuna, Senora
Torero! 1957,My 22,29:2
Prodler, Parrette
7 Capital Sins (Anger); Anger (7 Capital Sins)
1963,Ja 17,5:2
Proferes, Nick (Cinematographer)
Monterey Pop 1968,D 27,44:1
Projean, Albert
Soir de Rafle, Un 1931,O 16,27:1
Prokhorenko, Shanna
Ballad of a Soldier 1960,D 27,22:1
Italiano Brava Gente 1966,F 4,20:1
Marriage of Baezaminov, The 1966,Je 11,20:2
Prokofieff, Sergei (Composer)
Alexander Nevsky 1939,Mr 23,27:1
Ivan the Terrible, Part I 1947,Mr 10,25:2
Ballet of Romeo and Juliet, The 1956,Ap 3,31:2
Cinderella 1961,D 19,39:1
Prokosch, Frederic (Original Author)
Conspirators, The 1944,O 21,15:2
Prola, Angelo (Producer)
Gioconda, La 1958,O 13,33:4
Prola, Gianni (Director)
Ecco 1965,N 5,28:1
Pron, Louis Da
Are You With It? 1948,Ap 15,31:2
Pronin, Vassili (Director)
Son of the Regiment 1948,Ap 29,27:3
Journey Beyond Three Seas 1960,Ap 11,42:6
Prosper, Guy (Screenwriter)
Jailhouse Rock 1957,N 14,41:1
Prosperi, Franco (Director)
Women of the World 1963,Jl 3,14:1
Mondo Pazzo 1965,Ap 1,30:3
Africa Addio 1967,Mr 13,47:3
Prosperi, Franco (Original Author)
Africa Addio 1967,Mr 13,47:3
Prosperi, Franco (Producer)
Africa Addio 1967,Mr 13,47:3
Prosperi, Giorgio (Original Author)
Verginita 1953,Ap 18,17:2
Prosperi, Giorgio (Screenwriter)
Verginita 1953,Ap 18,17:2
Genoese Dragnet 1954,F 12,20:5
Indiscretion of an American Wife 1954,Je 26,7:2
Seven Hills of Rome 1958,Ja 28,24:2 (Incorrect
in this edition; use 1958,Ja 31,24:2 elsewhere)
Naked Maja, The 1959,Je 11,36:2
Defend my Love; (Difendo il Mio Amore)
1959,O 8,48:7
Violent Summer 1961,My 20,12:1

Prosperi, Giorgio (Screenwriter)— Cont
Sodom and Gomorrah 1963,Ja 24,5:3
Prosser, David
Matter of Innocence, A 1968,F 22,36:1
Prosser, Hugh
Pardon my Past 1946,Ja 28,15:5
Prothon, Pierre
Olive Trees of Justice, The 1967,My 5,31:1
Protopapas, Evangelo
Mademoiselle-Age 39 1956,Mr 26,34:2
Trouble for Father 1958,Ja 6,26:4
Santa Chikita 1959,My 11,30:1
Protozanof, J A (Director)
Lash of the Czar, The 1929,F 12,23:1
Man From the Restaurant, The 1930,Ja 6,30:5
Sibirsky Patrul 1932,My 14,11:5
Hour With Tchekhof, An 1933,S 6,24:4
Three Thieves 1933,O 30,14:3
Marionettes 1934,My 8,28:6
Protozanov, Yuri (Director)
Adventures in Bokhara 1944,Ag 21,9:4
Without Dowry 1946,Ap 15,22:2
Protozanov, Yuri (Screenwriter)
Without Dowry 1946,Ap 15,22:2
Proud, Peter (Original Author)
Outpost in Malaya 1952,N 27,49:2
Proud, Peter (Screenwriter)
Outpost in Malaya 1952,N 27,49:2
Proudlock, Roger (Producer)
You Can't Fool an Irishman 1950,D 7,45:4
Prouse, Derek (Screenwriter)
Champagne Murders, The 1968,Ap 25,53:1
Prouty, Jed
Coast of Folly, The 1925,Ag 31,19:3
Knockout, The 1925,O 27,23:3
Unguarded Hour, The 1926,Ja 5,25:2 (In
Addenda)
Everybody's Acting 1926,N 8,19:2
Orchids and Ermine 1927,Ap 19,24:4
Broadway Melody, The 1929,F 9,15:3
Sonny Boy 1929,Mr 9,24:3
His Captive Woman 1929,Ap 3,26:4
Fall of Eve, The 1929,Je 18,29:4
Two Weeks Off 1929,Je 24,27:1
Why Leave Home 1929,S 16,30:1
It's a Great Life 1930,Ja 18,21:1
Devil's Holiday, The 1930,My 10,25:3
Florodora Girl 1930,My 31,19:4
Strangers May Kiss 1931,Ap 13,17:1
Annabelle's Affairs 1931,Je 29,20:3
Secret Call, The 1931,Jl 13,13:5
Business and Pleasure 1932,F 13,23:4
Jimmy and Sally 1933,D 16,12:3
I Believed in You 1934,Ap 11,25:3
Private Scandal 1934,Je 15,26:2
Music in the Air 1934,D 14,29:3
Black Sheep 1935,Je 28,34:1
Every Saturday Night 1936,Mr 14,10:2
Special Investigator 1936,Ap 25,21:1
Little Miss Nobody 1936,Je 6,21:1
Educating Father 1936,Je 20,22:2
His Brother's Wife 1936,Ag 15,6:2
Under Your Spell 1936,N 7,15:2
Off to the Races 1937,F 6,15:2
Crime Nobody Saw, The 1937,Ap 5,17:2
Big Business 1937,Je 1,27:2
You Can't Have Everything 1937,Ag 4,15:2
100 Men and a Girl 1937,S 18,15:2
Sophie Lang Goes West 1937,S 30,19:2
Life Begins In College 1937,O 9,16:1
Hot Water 1937,N 5,19:4
Goodbye Broadway 1938,My 14,18:1
Trip to Paris, A 1938,Je 10,18:2
Keep Smiling 1938,Ag 10,15:2
Safety in Numbers 1938,S 6,17:2
Duke of West Point, The 1938,D 16,33:2
Exile Express 1939,Ag 16,21:3
Hollywood Cavalcade 1939,O 14,13:2
Young as You Feel 1940,Mr 8,25:3
Lone Wolf Keeps a Date, The 1941,Ja 2,24:3
Pot o'Gold 1941,Ap 4,25:2
Unexpected Uncle 1941,S 25,29:1
Go West, Young Lady 1941,N 24,11:6
Look Who's Laughing 1941,D 25,33:2
Guilty Bystander 1950,Ap 21,18:2
Prouty, Olive Higgins (Original Author)
Stella Dallas 1937,Ag 6,21:1
Now, Voyager 1942,O 23,25:3
Provaznik, Ludwig
Mr Belvedere Rings the Bell 1951,Ag 2,18:1
Provaznik, William
Mr Belvedere Rings the Bell 1951,Ag 2,18:1
Provence, Denise
Paris Waltz, The 1950,Ag 23,35:2
Landru 1963,Ap 10,31:1
Provensen, Martin (Miscellaneous)
Pinocchio 1940,F 8,18:3
Provenzale, Enzo (Screenwriter)
Hands Over the City 1964,S 18,28:1
Salvatore Giuliano 1964,S 18,28:1
Provine, Dorothy
Wall of Noise 1963,S 5,27:1
It's a Mad, Mad, Mad, Mad World
1963,N 19,47:1

Provine, Dorothy— Cont

Good Neighbor Sam 1964,Jl 23,19:1
Great Race, The 1965,S 16,00:0
That Darn Cat 1965,D 3,44:1
One Spy too Many 1966,D 8,64:1
Kiss the Girls and Make Them Die
 1967,Ja 26,25:1
Who's Minding the Mint? 1967,D 7,60:3
Never a Dull Moment 1968,Ag 15,46:2

Provorov, Feodor (Cinematographer)
Stone Flower 1946,D 30,15:2

Provost, Jeanne
Katia 1939,D 23,9:2

Provost, Jon
Back From Eternity 1956,S 8,20:6
Escapde in Japan 1957,D 24,11:1
This Property is Condemned 1966,Ag 4,24:1

Prowse, David
Hammerhead 1968,S 12,54:3

Prowse, Juliet
Can-Can 1960,Mr 10,36:1
G I Blues 1960,N 5,28:1
Right Approach, The 1961,My 18,41:1
Fiercest Heart, The 1961,Ag 3,13:5
Second Time Around, The 1961,D 23,16:1
Dingaka 1965,Jl 1,34:1

Prucha, Jaroslav
Skeleton on Horseback 1940,F 5,13:3
Thunder in the Hills 1947,My 24,10:5

Pruchniewski, Edmund J Pfc
Cease Fire! 1953,N 25,17:1

Prud'homme, Cameron
Abraham Lincoln 1930,Ag 26,24:1
Back From Eternity 1956,S 8,20:6
Power and The Prize, the 1956,S 27,42:1
Rainmaker, The 1956,D 13,51:1
Cardinal, The 1963,D 13,41:1

Prud'homme, Emile
Avocate d'Amour 1938,S 8,27:2

Prumbs, Lucille S (Original Author)
My Girl Tisa 1948,F 21,9:2

Prumbs, Z (Miscellaneous)
Beyond Endurance 1946,My 20,18:8

Prunas, Pasquale (Director)
Blood on the Balcony 1964,Je 30,22:1

Prut, I (Screenwriter)
Springtime on the Volga 1961,D 25,27:4

Prut, Ivan (Original Author)
We Will Come Back 1943,O 15,15:2

Pruzelius, Gosta
Lesson in Love, A 1960,Mr 15,46:1

Prydatkevych, Roman (Composer)
Marusia 1938,D 12,26:2

Pryde, Anthony (Original Author)
Girl From Montmarte, The 1926,F 25,26:2

Prygunov, Lev
Italiano Brava Gente 1966,F 4,20:1

PRYOR
See Also PRIOR

Pryor, Ainslie
Ransom 1956,Ja 25,28:3
Last Hunt, The 1956,Mr 1,37:2
Onionhead 1958,O 2,44:1

Pryor, Maureen
Walk in the Shadow 1966,S 12,52:5
Passages From James Joyce's Finnegans Wake
 1967,O 10,56:1

Pryor, Richard
Wild in the Streets 1968,My 30,21:1

Pryor, Roger
Moonlight and Pretzels 1933,Ag 23,21:2
I Like It That Way 1934,Ap 18,23:3
I'll Tell the World 1934,Ap 21,12:2
Romance in the Rain 1934,S 8,18:5
Belle of the Nineties 1934,S 22,12:2
Wake up and Dream 1934,O 11,28:3
Lady by Choice 1934,N 17,12:1
Girl Friend, The 1935,S 28,12:2
To Beat the Band 1935,N 23,23:2
Case of the Missing Man, The 1935,N 23,23:2
$1,000 a Minute 1935,D 21,11:1
Ticket to Paradise 1936,Ag 8,5:3
Missing Girls 1936,O 5,25:1
Sued for Libel 1940,Ja 19,15:3
Man With Nine Lives, The 1940,Ap 29,12:3
Lone Wolf Meets a Lady, The 1940,Je 17,19:2
Fugitive From Justice, A 1940,Jl 8,13:3
Money and the Woman 1940,O 4,29:2
She Couldn't Say No 1941,Ja 17,21:3
Power Dive 1941,My 29,15:4
Bullets for O'Hara 1941,Jl 28,16:4
Officer and the Lady, The 1941,Ag 11,17:4
I Live on Danger 1942,Ag 22,16:2

Pryse, Hugh
Botany Bay 1953,O 30,27:2
Three Cases of Murder (In the Picture); In the
 Picture (Three Cases of Murder)
 1955,Mr 16,39:4

Prytz, Angela
Doll, The 1964,Ja 14,27:1

Przyblski, Jan Nowina (Director)
Purimspieler, Der 1937,D 6,19:2

Ptushko, Alexander (Director)
New Gulliver, The 1935,N 4,24:4
Stone Flower 1946,D 30,15:2
Sadko 1953,Je 1,18:6
Sword and the Dragon, The 1960,N 17,46:3

Ptushko, Alexander (Producer)
Sword and the Dragon, The 1960,N 17,46:3

Ptushko, Alexander (Screenwriter)
New Gulliver, The 1935,N 4,24:4

Puccini, Giacomo (Composer)
Mimi 1936,Ja 10,16:3
Manon Lescaut 1941,Ap 14,23:5
Before Him all Rome Trembled 1947,F 22,16:2
Vie de Boheme, La 1947,N 28,37:4
Story of Tosca, The 1947,D 19,34:2
Her Wonderful Lie 1950,Jl 17,15:2
Tosca 1958,O 24,40:3
Boheme, La 1965,O 20,51:2

Puccini, Gianni (Director)
Love and Marriage (The Last Resort); Last Resort,
 The (Love and Marriage) 1966,Ag 5,20:1
Love and Marriage (Saturday, July 18); Saturday,
 July 18 (Love and Marriage) 1966,Ag 5,20:1
Love and Marriage (The First Night); First Night,
 The (Love and Marriage) 1966,Ag 5,20:1
Love and Marriage (One Moment Is Enough); One
 Moment Is Enough (Love and Marriage)
 1966,Ag 5,20:1

Puccini, Gianni (Original Author)
Under the Olive Tree 1951,O 5,24:4

Puccini, Gianni (Screenwriter)
Bitter Rice 1950,S 19,39:2
Under the Olive Tree 1951,O 5,24:4
Behind Closed Shutters 1952,Je 10,22:7
Rome, 11 O'Clock 1953,Ap 30,39:2
Love and Marriage (The First Night); First Night,
 The (Love and Marriage) 1966,Ag 5,20:1
Love and Marriage (Saturday, July 18); Saturday,
 July 18 (Love and Marriage) 1966,Ag 5,20:1
Love and Marriage (The Last Resort); Last Resort,
 The (Love and Marriage) 1966,Ag 5,20:1
Love and Marriage (One Moment Is Enough); One
 Moment Is Enough (Love and Marriage)
 1966,Ag 5,20:1

Puchinsky, Charles
Pat and Mike 1952,Je 19,32:6
House of Wax 1953,Ap 11,15:2

Pucholt, Vladimir
Loves of a Blonde 1966,S 13,51:2
Loves of a Blonde 1966,O 27,55:1

Pucini, Maria
Piccolo Eroe 1937,Jl 1,33:2

Pudney, John (Original Author)
Project M 7 1953,N 27,22:5

Pudney, John (Screenwriter)
Fuss Over Feathers 1954,D 27,22:6

Pudoffstin, J
Aelita: The Revolt of the Robots
 1929,Mr 26,34:1

Pudovkin, V
Living Corpse, The 1931,Ja 4,27:2
Ivan the Terrible, Part I 1947,Mr 10,25:2
Admiral Nakhimov 1948,N 25,47:4

Pudovkin, V (Director)
Mother 1928,Ja 8,VIII,3:2
Storm Over Asla 1930,S 8,17:1
Life is Beautiful 1933,F 13,11:5
Mother, 1905 1934,My 30,14:4
Mother and Sons 1938,S 15,29:2
General Suvorov 1941,S 20,11:2
Admiral Nakhimov 1948,N 25,47:4
Vasili's Return 1953,S 28,21:4

Pudovkin, V I (Director)
Deserter 1934,O 13,10:1

Pudovkin, Vyesolod (Director)
End of St Petersberg, The 1928,My 31,21:2 (In
 Addenda)

Puente, Jesus
Cobra, The 1968,Mr 28,52:3

Puertolas, Benita
Oro entre Barro; Gold in Clay 1940,Jl 1,23:2

Puettjer, Gustav
Kameradschaft 1932,N 9,28:5
Threepenny Opera, The 1960,Jl 11,24:4

Puff, Henri
Naked Childhood 1968,S 28,36:1

Puff, Lon
Tom Sawyer 1930,D 20,20:6

Puffy, Charles
Open all Night 1924,S 9,19:1
Mockery 1927,Ag 22,21:3
Man's Past, A 1927,O 4,34:2
Private Life of Helen of Troy, The
 1927,D 10,14:7
Love Me and the World Is Mine 1928,F 6,12:3
Yellow Lily, The 1928,My 21,25:1

Pugg, Marshall (Screenwriter)
Guns at Batasi 1964,N 17,47:1

Pugh, Carl (Screenwriter)
Death of a Dream 1950,Jl 19,26:2

Pughe, George
Storm in a Teacup 1938,Mr 22,18:4

Puglia, Frank
Orphans of the Storm 1922,Ja 29,VI,2:1 (In
 Addenda)
Isn't Life Wonderful? 1924,D 1,17:3
Romola 1924,D 2,13:2
Beautiful City, The 1925,N 23,25:4
Viva Villa! 1934,Ap 11,25:2
Men in White 1934,Je 9,18:2
Melody Lingers on, The 1935,N 7,27:1
Gay Desperado, The 1936,O 9,31:4
Devil is a Sissy, The 1936,O 17,21:2
When You're in Love 1937,F 19,15:2
Bride Wore Red, The 1937,O 15,18:4
Bulldog Drummond's Revenge 1937,D 17,33:2
Rascals 1938,My 27,12:2
Tropic Holiday 1938,Je 30,21:2
Sharpshooters 1938,D 5,19:2
Dramatic School 1938,D 9,31:2
Maisie 1939,Je 23,23:1
Girl and the Gambler, The 1939,Je 28,17:3
Torrid Zone 1940,My 18,11:3
Arise my Love 1940,O 17,33:2
Down Argentine Way 1940,O 18,25:1
Meet the Wildcat 1940,O 23,27:2
Mark of Zorro, The 1940,N 4,23:2
That Night in Rio 1941,Mr 10,21:2
Billy the Kid 1941,Je 20,28:2
Parson of Panamint, The 1941,Jl 26,18:2
Law of the Tropics 1941,O 10,26:5
Always in my Heart 1942,Mr 14,19:2
Secret Agent of Japan 1942,Mr 23,19:3
Jungle Book 1942,Ap 6,19:1
Who Is Hope Schuyler 1942,My 22,27:1
Flight Lieutenant 1942,Jl 31,11:1
Boogie Man Will Get You, The 1942,O 12,12:4
Now, Voyager 1942,O 23,25:3
Casablanca 1942,N 27,27:1
Mission to Moscow 1943,Ap 30,25:2
Pilot No 5 1943,Je 25,13:4
Background to Danger 1943,Jl 3,11:2
For Whom the Bell Tolls 1943,Jl 15,25:2
Phantom of the Opera 1943,O 15,15:2
Princess O'Rourke 1943,N 6,16:2
Ali Baba and the Forty Thieves 1944,Mr 16,17:3
Brazil 1944,N 20,25:2
Together Again 1944,N 24,19:2
Tall in the Saddle 1944,D 15,25:3
Song to Remember, A 1945,Ja 26,16:4
Blood on the Sun 1945,Je 29,12:2
Without Reservations 1946,Je 8,17:2
My Favorite Brunette 1947,Mr 20,38:2
Stallion Road 1947,Ap 5,12:5
Fiesta 1947,Je 27,17:3
Brute Force 1947,Jl 17,16:2
Escape me Never 1947,N 8,11:2
Lost Moment, The 1947,N 22,10:2
Road to Rio 1948,F 19,29:3
Dream Girl 1948,Je 17,29:2
Colorado Territory 1949,Je 25,8:6
Special Agent 1949,Ag 22,13:1
Bagdad 1949,D 24,11:4
Black Hand 1950,Mr 13,15:2
Captain Carey U S A 1950,Mr 30,40:5
Walk Softly Stranger 1950,O 16,30:5
Caddy, The 1953,S 18,16:6
Casanova's Big Night 1954,Ap 19,19:1
Serenade 1956,Mr 24,21:1 (Incorrect in this
 edition; use 1956,Mr 23,21:1 elsewhere)
First Texan, The 1956,Je 23,20:2
Burning Hills, The 1956,Ag 24,15:2
Black Orchid, The 1959,F 13,33:2
Cry Tough 1959,S 17,48:4

Pugliese, Alberto (Producer)
Pistol for Ringo, A 1966,N 3,45:4

Pugliese, Sergio (Miscellaneous)
Love and Larceny 1963,F 2,5:6

Puglisi, Adlo
Seduced and Abandoned 1964,Jl 16,23:1

Puglisi, Aldo
Marriage Italian Style 1964,D 21,42:1

Puhlmann, Willi
Marriage of Figaro 1950,N 3,31:2

Puig, Eva
Romance of the Rio Grande 1940,D 25,33:4
Singapore Woman 1941,My 12,13:6
Hold Back the Dawn 1941,O 2,29:1
Rio Rita 1942,My 8,27:3
Snafu 1945,D 26,15:2

Pujol, Rene (Original Author)
One Rainy Afternoon 1936,My 14,29:2

Pujol, Rene (Screenwriter)
Frochard et les Deux Orphelines, La
 1934,F 7,16:2

Pukui
Bird of Paradise 1932,S 10,18:5

Pulager, Clu
...And Now Miguel 1966,S 8,43:1

Pulaski, Frank
Robe, The 1953,S 17,32:6

Puleo, Johnny
Trapeze 1956,Je 5,39:2

Pullen, William
Farmer Takes a Wife, The 1953,Je 13,11:2
Those Redheads From Seattle 1953,O 1,34:2
Pullian, Darcy
Therese and Isabelle 1968,My 15,41:4
Pully, B S
Four Jills in a Jeep 1944,Ap 6,27:2
Wing and a Prayer 1944,Ag 31,14:1
Greenwich Village 1944,S 28,26:2
Tree Grows in Brooklyn, A 1945,Mr 1,25:5
Nob Hill 1945,Jl 4,10:3
Within These Walls 1945,Jl 16,8:4
Don Juan Quilligan 1945,Jl 30,16:2
Do You Love Me 1946,My 25,12:2
Taxi 1953,Ja 22,20:3
Guys and Dolls 1955,N 5,26:1
Hole in the Head, A 1959,Jl 16,31:2
Pulman, Jack (Screenwriter)
Best of Enemies, The 1962,Ag 7,35:2
Kiss the Girls and Make Them Die
1967,Ja 26,25:1
Matchless 1967,N 11,26:3
Pulver, Enid
So Young, So Bad 1950,Jl 24,15:2
Pulver, Liselotte
White Hell of Pitz Palu, The 1953,N 14,14:2
Spessart Inn, The 1961,F 18,12:3
Arms and the Man 1962,F 24,21:7
Lafayette 1963,Ap 11,29:1
Religieuse, La 1968,S 23,42:3
Pulver, Liselotte (Lilo)
Confessions of Felix Krull, The 1958,Mr 5,38:1
Reaching for the Stars 1958,My 24,18:2
Time to Love and a Time to Die, A
1958,Jl 10,22:1
Affairs of Julie, The 1958,D 10,53:1
One, Two, Three 1961,D 22,17:1
Global Affair, A 1964,My 7,31:2
Pung-Peng-Cheng, Mme
Your Shadow Is Mine 1963,My 15,32:1
Punsley, Bernard
Dead End 1937,Ag 25,25:1
Crime School 1938,My 11,17:2
Little Tough Guy 1938,Ag 18,23:3
Angels With Dirty Faces 1938,N 26,18:1
They Made Me a Criminal 1939,Ja 21,19:2
Hell's Kitchen 1939,Jl 3,10:5
Angels Wash Their Faces 1939,S 4,16:2
Dress Parade 1939,O 28,11:2
You're not so Tough 1940,Jl 9,25:3
Give Us Wings 1940,N 21,43:3
Hit the Road 1941,Jl 3,15:3
Mob Town 1941,N 20,39:3
Puntas, Marisa
Wife for a Night 1958,Je 12,35:2
Punynchoti, Javanart
Bridge on the River Kwai 1957,D 19,39:1
Purcell, Dick
Ceiling Zero 1936,Ja 20,22:2
Brides are Like That 1936,Mr 23,22:5
Times Square Playboy 1936,My 2,11:2
Bullets or Ballots 1936,My 27,27:1
Law in her Hands, The 1936,Je 6,21:2
Public Enemy's Wife 1936,Jl 9,17:2
Bengal Tiger 1936,Jl 30,22:1
Jailbreak 1936,Ag 6,22:1
Case of the Velvet Claws, The 1936,Ag 29,16:3
Melody for Two 1937,My 21,19:5
Slim 1937,Je 24,30:2
Reported Missing 1937,S 3,12:2
Alcatraz Island 1937,O 14,22:2
Missing Witness 1937,D 10,33:3
Daredevil Drivers, The 1938,F 23,27:2
Over the Wall 1938,Mr 28,19:2
Accidents Will Happen 1938,Ap 25,19:2
Fiight Into Nowhere 1938,My 2,13:3
Mystery House 1938,Je 29,15:5
Valley of the Giants 1938,S 10,20:2
Garden of the Moon 1938,S 24,13:1
Broadway Musketeers 1938,O 14,27:1
Blackwell's Island 1939,Mr 2,19:1
Streets of New York 1939,My 1,21:1
Outside the Three-Mile Limit 1940,Ap 8,15:2
Private Affairs 1940,Jl 5,10:3
New Moon 1940,Jl 19,22:2
Arise my Love 1940,O 17,33:2
Bank Dick, The 1940,D 13,29:2
Flight Command 1941,Ja 17,21:2
Bullets for O'Hara 1941,Jl 28,16:4
Pittsburgh Kid, The 1941,S 23,27:4
No Hands on the Clock 1941,D 22,24:6
In old California 1942,Je 18,25:3
I Live on Danger 1942,Ag 22,16:2
Reveille With Beverly 1943,Ap 24,17:2
Aerial Gunner 1943,Je 26,10:2
Purcell, Gertrude (Screenwriter)
Girl Friend, The 1935,S 28,12:2
If You Could Only Cook 1935,D 26,21:4
Witness Chair, The 1936,Ap 18,19:2
Make Way for a Lady 1936,D 12,15:1
Super-Sleuth 1937,Jl 17,18:1
Stella Dallas 1937,Ag 6,21:1
Music for Madame 1937,O 23,14:1

Fight for Your Lady 1937,N 20,21:2
Hitting a new High 1937,D 27,11:1
Mother Carey's Chickens 1938,Ag 5,11:1
Service de Luxe 1938,O 24,13:2
Destry Rides Again 1939,N 30,25:1
Little Bit of Heaven, A 1940,N 8,24:2
One Night in the Tropics 1940,D 20,33:2
Invisible Woman, The 1941,Ja 9,27:2
Ellery Queen and the Murder Ring
1941,O 21,29:4
In old California 1942,Je 18,25:3
Follow the Boys 1944,Ap 26,24:6
Paris Underground 1945,O 20,8:2
Purcell, Harold (Original Author)
Lisbon Story, The 1951,S 6,39:4
Purcell, Irene
Just a Gigolo 1931,Je 13,20:4
Man in Possession, The 1931,Jl 18,16:6
Passionate Plumber, The 1932,Mr 12,19:5
Westward Passage 1932,Je 4,9:2
Bachelor's Affairs 1932,Je 25,18:2
Purcell, June
Viennese Nights 1930,N 27,32:5
Purcell, Noel
Ireland's Border Line 1939,O 13,27:3
Captain Boycott 1947,D 6,11:2
Saints and Sinners 1949,S 12,17:2
Blue Lagoon, The 1949,O 3,13:2
Encore (Winter Cruise); Winter Cruise (Encore)
1952,Ap 3,45:1
You Can't Beat the Irish 1952,My 1,34:4
No Resting Place 1952,My 5,18:5
Island Rescue 1952,Jl 1,19:4
Crimson Pirate, The 1952,Ag 28,21:2
Land of Fury 1955,My 3,37:4
Svengali 1955,S 26,18:2
Doctor at Sea 1956,Mr 1,37:3
Moby Dick 1956,Jl 5,18:1
Lust for Life 1956,S 18,39:1
Rising of the Moon, The (The Majesty of the
Law); Majesty of the Law, The (The Rising of
the Moon) 1957,Jl 10,23:1
Merry Andrews 1958,Mr 21,17:1
Rooney 1958,Je 6,29:2
Key, The 1958,Jl 2,23:3
Mad Little Island 1958,D 31,12:1
Make Mine Mink 1960,D 20,43:4
Millionairess, The 1961,F 10,19:1
Ferry to Hong Kong 1961,Ap 27,27:7
Mutiny on the Bounty 1962,N 9,31:2
Running Man, The 1963,O 3,31:1
Swingin' Maiden, The 1964,Ja 1,16:2
Ceremony, The 1964,My 14,39:1
Lord Jim 1965,F 26,18:1
Johnny Nobody 1965,N 24,35:1
Arrivederci, Baby! 1966,D 29,22:1
Purcell, Robert
Red Menace, The 1949,Je 27,18:2
Mark of the Gorilla 1950,F 17,27:2
Purdell, Reginald
Middle Watch, The 1930,D 20,20:6
Congress Dances 1932,My 12,23:2
Old Curiosity Shop, The 1935,D 23,15:5
Haunted Honeymoon 1940,O 31,28:2
Lady Surrenders, A 1947,Je 20,25:6
Purdom, Edmund
Titanic 1953,My 28,27:5
Student Prince, The 1954,Je 16,18:2
Egyptian, The 1954,Ag 25,23:1
Athena 1954,D 22,28:2
Prodigal, The 1955,My 14,10:7
King's Thief, The 1955,Ag 13,7:2
Cossacks, The 1960,S 6,41:4
Malaga 1962,F 22,20:3
Last of the Vikings 1962,S 27,33:4
Lafayette 1963,Ap 11,29:1
Yellow Rolls-Royce, The 1965,My 14,42:2
Purdy, Constance
White Savage 1943,Ap 26,15:2
Shocking Miss Pilgrim, The 1947,F 12,34:2
Pursall, David (Screenwriter)
Count Five and Die 1958,My 15,25:1
Murder She Said 1962,Ja 8,27:2
Longest Day, The 1962,O 5,28:1
Kill or Cure 1962,N 13,43:4
Murder at the Gallop 1963,Je 25,23:2
Murder Ahoy 1964,S 23,55:3
Murder Most Foul 1965,My 24,36:2
Blue Max, The 1966,Je 22,38:1
Alphabet Murders, The 1966,Jl 12,36:2
Purviance, Edna
Kid, The 1921,Ja 22,9:2
Pilgrim, The 1923,F 26,15:1
Woman of Paris, A 1923,O 2,7:2
30 Years of Fun 1963,D 26,33:4
Purvis, Henry
I Am a Camera 1955,Ag 9,29:1
Pusey, Arthur
Scandal In Paris, A 1929,Je 10,23:1
Pushkin, Alexander (Original Author)
Eagle, The 1925,N 9,25:1
Poet and Tsar 1938,Ag 25,15:1
Dame de Pique, La 1944,O 19,19:2

Pushkin, Alexander (Original Author) — Cont
Postmaster's Daughter, The 1946,Ag 19,17:6
Queen of Spades, The 1949,Jl 1,14:4
Alego 1954,D 27,22:7
Boris Godunov 1956,Ja 23,21:4
Tempest 1959,Mr 27,19:2
Eugene Onegin 1959,S 14,33:1
Captain's Daughter, The 1959,N 23,41:3
Pushkov, N V (Composer)
Wings of Victory 1941,N 17,15:2
Masquerade 1943,My 17,11:2
Puter, Alice Mildred
Crowd, The 1928,F 20,14:1
Putman, Eric
Moonlight Sonata 1937,Je 6,XI,4:4 (In Addenda)
Putnam, George
Fourteen Hours 1951,Mr 7,43:2
Putnam, Nina Wilcox (Original Author)
Slaves of Beauty 1927,Je 8,23:3
Mummy, The 1933,Ja 7,11:2
Lady's Profession, A 1933,Mr 25,13:3
Sitting Pretty 1933,D 2,9:3
Putnam, Nina Wilcox (Screenwriter)
Democracy, The Vision Restored 1920,Ag 25,6:4
Putti, Lya de
Variety 1926,Je 28,15:5
Sorrows of Satan, The 1926,O 13,21:1
Prince of Tempters, The 1926,O 18,18:1
Manon Lescaut 1926,N 30,27:1
Puttjen, Gustav
Comrades of 1918 1931,F 20,18:5
Putz, Hans
Four in a Jeep 1951,Je 12,35:2
Eternal Waltz, The; (Ewiger Walzer)
1959,Jl 9,22:1
Puvic, Henry John
Hue and Cry 1951,Ja 9,25:2
Puzhnaya, R
Village of Sin, The 1929,My 21,29:3
Cossacks of the Don 1932,Mr 19,11:2
Pyatko, Paulina
Mass Struggle 1934,S 17,20:3
Pyle, Denver
Man From Colorado 1949,Ja 21,24:3
Red Canyon 1949,Ap 28,28:2
Hellfire 1949,My 30,9:4
Flying Saucer, The 1950,Ja 5,28:3
To Hell and Back 1955,S 23,21:2
Jet Pilot 1957,O 5,8:6
Man Who Shot Liberty Valance, The
1962,My 24,29:2
Shenandoah 1965,Jl 29,18:3
Great Race, The 1965,S 16,00:0
Bonnie and Clyde 1967,Ag 14,36:1
Bandolero 1968,Jl 18,26:2
Pyle, Ernie (Miscellaneous)
Story of G I Joe 1945,O 6,9:6
Pyle, Howard (Original Author)
Black Shield of Falworth, The 1954,O 7,16:2
PYNE
See Also PINE
Pyne, Natasha
Taming of the Shrew, The 1967,Mr 9,43:1
Pyriev, Ivan (Director)
Idiot, The 1960,Jl 22,11:2
Pyriev, Ivan (Screenwriter)
Idiot, The 1960,Jl 22,11:2
Pyryev, K (Director)
Devotion 1955,Ag 1,15:2
Pyryev, K (Screenwriter)
Devotion 1955,Ag 1,15:2
Pyzhova, Olga
Without Dowry 1946,Ap 15,22:2
Pyzhova, Valentina
Without Dowry 1946,Ap 15,22:2

Q

Quackenbush, Stan (Miscellaneous)
Mr Bug Goes to Town 1942,F 20,21:3
Quadflieg, Will
Maulkorb, Der 1938,Ap 9,11:3
Faust 1963,Ap 16,31:1
Lola Montes 1968,S 23,42:6
Qualen, Frank
Woman on the Run 1950,N 30,24:2
Qualen, John
Street Scene 1931,Ag 27,22:5
Arrowsmith 1931,D 8,36:4
Counsellor-At-Law 1933,D 8,31:2
Sing and Like It 1934,Ap 14,18:2
He Was her Man 1934,My 17,28:2
Servants' Entrance 1934,S 27,25:2
Our Daily Bread 1934,O 3,25:2
365 Nights in Hollywood 1934,N 7,32:1
Charlie Chan in Paris 1935,Ja 22,23:2
One More Spring 1935,F 22,27:1
Great Hotel Murder, The 1935,F 28,17:4
Black Fury 1935,Ap 11,27:2
Doubting Thomas 1935,Jl 11,24:2
Silk Hat Kid 1935,Ag 7,22:5
Farmer Takes a Wife, The 1935,Ag 9,21:2
Orchids to You 1935,Ag 10,16:4

Qualen, John — Cont
Three Musketeers, The 1935,N 1,25:1
Man of Iron 1935,D 7,22:2
Whipsaw 1936,Ja 25,18:4
Country Doctor, The 1936,Mr 13,32:2 (Incorrect in this edition; use 1936,Mr 13,27:2 elsewhere)
Meet Nero Wolfe 1936,Jl 16,20:1
Road to Glory, The 1936,Ag 6,22:1
Girls' Dormitory 1936,Ag 29,16:2
Reunion 1936,N 27,27:1
Seventh Heaven 1937,Mr 26,25:1
Angel's Holiday 1937,My 29,20:2
Fifty Roads to Town 1937,Je 5,21:1
She Had to Eat 1937,Jl 24,12:1
Fit for a King 1937,O 15,18:5
Nothing Sacred 1937,N 26,27:2
Bad Man of Brimstone, The 1938,F 4,17:2
Joy of Living 1938,My 6,27:1
Chaser, The 1938,Ag 2,15:3
Mad Miss Manton, The 1938,O 21,27:2
Five of a Kind 1938,O 31,12:2
Stand up and Fight 1939,Ja 27,17:2
Mickey, the Kid 1939,Jl 6,27:1
Thunder Afloat 1939,O 13,27:2
Four Wives 1939,D 23,9:1
His Girl Friday 1940,Ja 12,13:2
Grapes of Wrath, The 1940,Ja 25,17:2
Ski Patrol 1940,My 21,29:4
Long Voyage Home, The 1940,O 9,30:2 (In Addenda)
Knute Rockne-All American 1940,O 19,21:2
Youth Will Be Served 1940,N 15,25:2
Angels Over Broadway 1940,N 18,23:2
Model Wife 1941,Ap 24,25:3
Million Dollar Baby 1941,Je 7,20:2
Out of the Fog 1941,Je 21,20:2
Shepherd of the Hills, The 1941,Jl 31,13:2
All That Money Can Buy 1941,O 17,27:2
New Wine 1942,F 2,11:2
Jungle Book 1942,Ap 6,19:1
Larceny, Inc 1942,Ap 25,9:1
Tortilla Flat 1942,My 22,27:1
Casablanca 1942,N 27,27:1
Arabian Nights 1942,D 26,15:1
Swing Shift Maisie 1943,S 10,29:2
Impostor, The 1944,Mr 27,17:2
Dark Waters 1944,N 22,25:2
American Romance, An 1944,N 24,19:1
Roughly Speaking 1945,F 1,18:4
River Gang 1945,O 6,9:7
Captain Kidd 1945,N 23,26:3
Adventure 1946,F 8,23:2
Song of Scheherazade 1947,F 27,26:2
Fugitive, The 1947,D 26,22:2
My Girl Tisa 1948,F 21,9:2
16 Fathoms Deep 1948,O 7,35:2
Hollow Triumph 1948,O 29,29:5
Big Steal, The 1949,Jl 11,13:2
Captain China 1950,Mr 2,33:2
Buccaneer's Girl 1950,Mr 27,19:2
Jackpot, The 1950,N 23,55:2
Flying Missile, The 1950,D 25,25:1
Belle le Grand 1951,My 18,34:6
Goodbye, my Fancy 1951,My 30,14:2
Hans Christian Andersen 1952,N 26,20:2
I, The Jury 1953,Ag 22,8:2
Student Prince, The 1954,Je 16,18:2
High and the Mighty, The 1954,Jl 1,21:2
Passion 1954,D 11,11:1
Unchained 1955,Ja 28,15:2
At Gunpoint 1956,F 4,24:5
Searchers, The 1956,My 31,21:4
Big Land, The 1957,Mr 2,18:2
Anatomy of a Murder 1959,Jl 3,10:1
North to Alaska 1960,N 11,36:1
Man Who Shot Liberty Valance, The 1962,My 24,29:2
Prize, The 1964,Ja 24,21:1
Patch of Blue, A 1965,D 16,63:1
Firecreek 1968,F 22,36:2
Quaranti, Gennaro
Life and Miracles of Blesses Mother Cabrini, The 1946,Jl 8,25:2
Quarberg, Lincoln (Original Author)
I'll Tell the World 1934,Ap 21,12:2
Quarrier, Laian
Fearless Vampire Killers, The, or Pardon Me but Your Teeth are in my Neck 1967,N 14,52:1
Quarrier, Lian
Cul de Sac 1966,N 8,44:2
Separation 1968,Mr 26,41:2
Quarry, Robert
House of Bamboo 1955,Jl 2,13:2
Quartaro, Nena
Red Mark, The 1928,O 30,27:3
Redeeming Sin, The 1929,F 16,14:6
Bachelor Father, The 1931,F 2,23:1
Men Are Like That 1931,Ag 17,18:2
Quartermaine, Charles
Bishop Murder Case, The 1930,F 1,15:1
Redemption 1930,My 3,23:1
Quartermaine, Leon
As You Like It 1936,N 6,29:3

Quartero, Nena
Devil's Brother, The 1933,Je 10,16:4
Quartucci, P
Dancing, El 1935,Ja 28,10:6
Caballo del Pueblo, El 1935,D 16,23:4
Quashie, Harry
Safari 1956,Je 21,35:2
Quattrini, Paola
What Price Innocence? 1953,My 2,13:3
Quayle, Anna
Hard Day's Night, A 1964,Ag 12,41:1
Arrivederci, Baby! 1966,D 29,22:1
Smashing Time 1967,D 21,44:1
Chitty Chitty Bang Bang 1968,D 19,64:4
Quayle, Anthony
Hamlet 1948,S 30,32:2
Saraband 1949,Je 13,16:3
Wrong Man, The 1956,D 24,8:1
Woman in a Dressing Gown 1957,S 13,15:2
Pursuit of the Graf Spee 1957,D 27,33:2
Tarzan's Greatest Adventure 1959,Jl 9,22:1
Desert Attack 1961,Mr 23,28:1
Guns of Navarone, The 1961,Je 23,19:1
Damn the Defiant 1962,S 20,29:2
Lawrence of Arabia 1962,D 17,5:6
It Takes a Thief 1963,Ag 15,24:7
Fall of the Roman Empire, The 1964,Mr 27,14:2
Operation Crossbow 1965,Ap 2,29:1
Study in Terror, A 1966,N 3,45:3
Poppy is Also a Flower, The 1967,D 14,62:4
Qubeka, Harriet
Magic Garden, The 1952,F 6,24:2
Queant, Gilles
Ruy Blas 1948,O 4,14:2
Eagle with Two Heads 1948,D 30,24:2
Faust and the Devil 1950,My 1,18:2
Odette 1951,Mr 28,33:2
Night Without Stars 1953,Jl 14,19:4
Last Year at Marienbad 1962,Mr 8,26:1
Quedens, Eunice
Song of Love, The 1929,N 14,24:3
Queen, Ellery (Original Author)
Crime Nobody Saw, The 1937,Ap 5,17:2
Ellery Queen, Master Detective 1940,D 19,33:1
Ellery Queen's Penthouse Mystery 1941,Mr 7,17:2
Ellery Queen and the Perfect Crime 1941,Ag 11,17:3
Ellery Queen and the Murder Ring 1941,O 21,29:4
Enemy Agents meet Ellery Queen 1942,Ag 22,16:2
Queffelec, Henri (Original Author)
God Needs Men 1951,Mr 27,35:1
Queffelec, Jacqueline
Ballerina 1938,N 15,27:1
Queneau, Raymomd (Original Author)
Zazie 1961,N 21,45:5
Quennell, Peter (Screenwriter)
Bad Lord Byron, The 1952,Mr 20,37:5
Quensel, Isa
Pettersson & Bendel 1934,F 22,25:2
Raggen, Det Aer Jag Det 1936,My 22,19:1
To Love; Att Alska 1964,S 23,45:3 (Incorrect in this edition; use 1964,S 23,54:1 elsewhere)
Swedish Wedding Night 1965,N 15,48:1
Quentin, Patrick (Original Author)
Black Widow 1954,O 28,46:6
Man in the Net, The 1959,Je 11,36:2
Quenzer, Arthur (Composer)
You're a Sweetheart 1937,D 25,10:5
Quenzer (Composer)
Fun and Fancy Free 1947,S 29,17:2 (In Addenda)
Querio, Isa
Three Forbidden Stories 1953,N 16,21:4
Quesada, Milo
10th Victim, The 1965,D 21,46:1
Quest, Hans
Taiga 1959,Mr 17,42:4
Questel, Mae
Majority of One, A 1962,Ja 12,29:2
It's Only Money 1962,N 22,43:1
Funny Girl 1968,S 20,42:1
Quevedo, Nino (Producer)
Tia Tula, A 1965,Je 3,24:1
Quezon, Manuel (Miscellaneous)
Pledge to Bataan 1943,Jl 2,15:2
Quianna
Arctic Manhunt 1949,Ag 19,12:5
Quick, Jean
Neapolitan Carousel 1961,O 12,41:3
Quickly, Tommy
Go Go Mania 1965,My 20,52:4
Quien, Kruno (Screenwriter)
Kaya 1968,S 25,39:1
Quigley, Charles
King of Burlesque 1936,Ja 16,25:2
Charlie Chan's Secret 1936,Ja 18,19:4
Sudden Death, And 1936,Jl 18,18:2
Lady From Nowhere 1936,D 21,19:2
Criminals of the Air 1937,O 28,29:2
Shadow, The 1937,D 17,33:3

Quigley, Charles — Cont
Convicted 1938,Ag 22,9:3
Men Against the Sky 1940,S 12,31:2
Mexican Spitfire out West 1940,O 30,29:3
Woman's Face, A 1941,My 16,21:2
Quigley, Godfrey
Rising of the Moon, The (A Minute's Wait); Minute's Wait, A (The Rising of the Moon) 1957,Jl 10,23:1
Rooney 1958,Je 6,29:2
Broth of a Boy 1959,D 28,18:1
Nothing but the Best 1964,Jl 14,28:1
Quigley, Juanita
Riffraff 1936,Ja 13,14:2
Devil Doll, The 1936,Ag 8,5:2
Born to Dance 1936,D 5,16:1
Hawaii Calls 1938,Ap 29,17:2
Devil's Party, The 1938,My 31,8:3
Having Wonderful Time 1938,Jl 8,11:2
Woman Against Woman 1938,Ag 23,20:6
Men With Wings 1938,O 27,27:2
That Certain Age 1938,N 5,15:2
Family Next Door, The 1939,Ap 28,31:2
Blue Bird, The 1940,Ja 20,11:2
Vanishing Virginian, The 1942,My 28,13:3
Yank at Eton, A 1942,O 16,23:1
Assignment in Brittany 1943,Ap 22,31:2
Lady and the Monster, The 1944,Ap 8,9:2
National Velvet 1944,D 15,25:2
Quigley, Rita
Susan and God 1940,Jl 12,11:2
Howards of Virginia, The 1940,S 27,27:1
Human Comedy, The 1943,Mr 3,19:2
Woman in Bondage 1944,Mr 27,17:2
Quigley, Robert (Director)
Luces de Barriada; Neighborhood Lights 1940,S 2,19:2
Quigley, Robert (Original Author)
Before Midnight 1934,Ja 10,24:3
Quilici, Folco (Director)
Last Paradise, The 1958,Mr 1,12:1
Quilici, Folco (Screenwriter)
Last Paradise, The 1958,Mr 1,12:1
Quillan, Baby Bobby
Swiss Family Robinson 1940,F 9,15:3
Quillan, Eddie
Show Folks 1928,D 10,25:1
Geraldine 1929,Mr 4,20:2
Godless Girl, The 1929,Ap 1,22:1
Sophomore, The 1929,Ag 24,11:5
Big Money 1930,N 22,21:3
Sweepstakes 1931,Je 25,23:5
Tip Off, The 1931,O 26,22:1
Big Shot, The 1932,Ja 2,14:2
Girl Crazy 1932,Mr 25,23:3
Strictly Personal 1933,Mr 20,18:2
Broadway to Hollywood 1933,S 2,14:4
Hollywood Party 1934,My 26,12:2
Mutiny on the Bounty 1935,N 9,19:2
London by Night 1937,Ag 13,13:1
Big City 1937,S 17,29:2
Made for Each Other 1939,F 17,17:2
Flying Irishman, The 1939,Ap 12,27:2
Family Next Door, The 1939,Ap 28,31:2
Young Mr Lincoln 1939,Je 3,11:2
Hawaiian Nights 1939,S 29,19:4
Allegheny Uprising 1939,N 10,27:3
Grapes of Wrath, The 1940,Ja 25,17:2
Conga Nights, La 1940,Je 5,33:5
Dark Streets of Cairo 1940,D 2,19:3
Six Lessons From Madame La Zonga 1941,F 19,25:2
Flame of New Orleans, The 1941,Ap 26,20:2
Kid Glove Killer 1942,Ap 17,21:4
Priorities on Parade 1942,Jl 23,19:2
It Ain't Hay 1943,Mr 11,17:3
Impostor, The 1944,Mr 27,17:2
This is the Life 1944,Ap 28,23:3
Brigadoon 1954,S 17,18:2
Move Over Darling 1963,D 26,33:1
Quillan, Joseph (Screenwriter)
Show Business 1944,My 11,25:7
Son of Paleface 1952,O 2,32:3
Quillen, Robert (Miscellaneous)
Life Begins at 40 1935,Ap 5,21:3
Quimby, Margaret
Teaser, The 1925,Je 15,10:1
What Happened to Jones 1926,F 9,22:1
New York 1927,Ja 31,13:1
Sally of the Scandals 1928,Jl 3,19:3
Lucky Boy 1929,F 25,16:1
Ladies Love Brutes 1930,My 16,20:4
Quine, Richard
Counsellor-At-Law 1933,D 8,31:2
Little Men 1935,F 18,19:3
Babes on Broadway 1942,Ja 1,37:1
Tish 1942,S 18,25:2
For Me and My Gal 1942,O 22,25:1
My Sister Eileen 1942,O 23,15:1
Stand by for Action 1943,Mr 12,12:2
We've Never Been Licked 1943,Ag 19,23:1
Cockeyed Miracle, The 1946,O 25,28:1
Command Decision 1949,Ja 20,34:2
No Sad Songs for Me 1950,Ap 28,26:2

Quine, Richard — Cont

Flying Missile, The 1950,D 25,25:1

Quine, Richard (Director)

Drive a Crooked Road 1954,Ap 3,19:3
Pushover 1954,Jl 31,6:3
So This Is Paris 1955,F 12,11:1
My Sister Eileen 1955,S 23,21:1
Solid Gold Cadillac, The 1956,O 25,40:3
Full of Life 1957,F 13,38:1
Operation Mad Ball 1957,N 21,38:1
Bell, Book and Candle 1958,D 27,2:7
It Happened to Jane 1959,Ag 6,18:3
Strangers When we Meet 1960,Je 30,22:2
World of Suzie Wong, The 1960,N 11,36:1
Notorious Landlady, The 1962,Jl 27,15:2
Paris When it Sizzles 1964,Ap 9,25:3
Sex and the Single Girl 1964,D 26,9:2
How to Murder Your Wife 1965,Ja 27,26:1
Synanon 1965,My 6,44:1
Hotel 1967,Ja 20,27:1
Oh Dad, Poor Dad, Mamma's Hung You in the Closet and I'm Feeling so Sad 1967,F 16,32:1

Quine, Richard (Producer)

It Happened to Jane 1959,Ag 6,18:3
Strangers When we Meet 1960,Je 30,22:2
Paris When it Sizzles 1964,Ap 9,25:3
Synanon 1965,My 6,44:1

Quine, Richard (Screenwriter)

Drive a Crooked Road 1954,Ap 3,19:3
My Sister Eileen 1955,S 23,21:1

Quinlivan, Charles

All the Young Men 1960,Ag 27,8:6

Quinn, Anthony

Parole 1936,Je 27,21:1
Waikiki Wedding 1937,Mr 25,29:1
Last Train from Madrid, The 1937,Je 19,20:2
Ourselves Alone 1937,Jl 31,6:2
River of Unrest 1937,N 27,21:2
Daughter of Shanghai 1937,D 24,21:2
Buccaneer, The 1938,F 17,17:2
Dangerous to Know 1938,Mr 11,15:4
Tip-Off Girls 1938,Mr 25,15:3
Hunted Men 1938,My 21,9:2
Bulldog Drummond in Africa 1938,Ag 25,15:1
King of Alcatraz 1938,O 7,21:2
King of Chinatown 1939,Mr 16,27:2
Union Pacific 1939,My 11,31:2
Road to Singapore 1940,Mr 14,29:2
Parole Fixer 1940,Ap 18,28:5
Ghost Breakers, The 1940,Jl 4,12:2
City for Conquest 1940,S 28,9:2
Texas Rangers Ride Again 1941,Ja 9,27:4
Blood and Sand 1941,My 23,25:3
Bullets for O'Hara 1941,Jl 28,16:4
They Died With Their Boots On 1941,N 21,23:3
Larceny, Inc 1942,Ap 25,9:1
Road to Morocco 1942,N 12,30:1
Black Swan, The 1942,D 24,18:3
Ox-Bow Incident, The 1943,My 10,15:2 (In Addenda)
Guadalcanal Diary 1943,N 18,29:1
Buffalo Bill 1944,Ap 20,22:6
Roger Touhy, Gangster 1944,Je 5,14:7
Irish Eyes Are Smiling 1944,N 8,27:1
China Sky 1945,My 25,22:3
Where Do We Go From Here? 1945,Je 7,25:2
Back to Bataan 1945,S 13,26:3
California 1947,Ja 15,31:2
Sinbad the Sailor 1947,Ja 23,31:2
Imperfect Lady, The 1947,My 22,34:5
Black Gold 1947,S 5,16:4
Hungry Hill 1947,O 11,11:2
Tycoon 1947,D 26,22:6
Brave Bulls, The 1951,Ap 19,39:2
Mask of the Avenger 1951,Je 27,25:2
Viva Zapata 1952,F 8,19:2
You Can't Beat the Irish 1952,My 1,34:4
Brigand, The 1952,Jl 26,9:2
World in His Arms, The 1952,O 10,21:2
Against all Flags 1952,D 25,34:6
City Beneath the Sea 1953,Mr 12,24:3
Ride Vaquero 1953,Jl 16,17:2
Blowing Wild 1953,O 8,37:5
Long Wait, The 1954,Jl 3,9:2
Beachcomber, The 1955,Ja 17,27:5
Magnificent Matador, The 1955,My 25,38:1
Ulysses 1955,Ag 18,17:2
Naked Street, The 1955,O 1,11:2
Seven Cities of Gold 1955,O 8,13:2
Strada, La 1956,Jl 17,19:2
Lust for Life 1956,S 18,39:1
Angels of Darkness 1956,N 22,51:1
Wild Party, The 1956,D 22,13:1
River's Edge, The 1957,Ap 12,20:2
Ride Back, The 1957,Ap 30,24:1
Rising of the Moon, The (A Minute's Wait);
  Minute's Wait, A (The Rising of the Moon)
  1957,Jl 10,23:1
Wild Is the Wind 1957,D 12,35:1
Hunchback of Notre Dame, The 1957,D 12,35:1
Attila 1958,My 19,19:4
Hot Spell 1958,S 18,37:2
Black Orchid, The 1959,F 13,33:2
Warlock 1959,My 1,34:1

Last Train from Gun Hill 1959,Jl 30,31:2
Heller in Pink Tights 1960,Mr 17,28:1
Portrait in Black 1960,Jl 28,19:1
Savage Innocents, The 1961,My 25,31:1
Guns of Navarone, The 1961,Je 23,19:1
Barabbas 1962,O 11,49:1
Requiem for a Heavyweight 1962,O 17,35:1
Lawrence of Arabia 1962,D 17,5:6
Behold a Pale Horse 1964,Ag 14,16:1
Murder Ahoy 1964,S 23,55:3
Visit, The 1964,O 22,44:1
Zorba, The Greek 1964,D 18,25:1
High Wind in Jamaica, A 1965,Je 17,27:2
Lost Command 1966,S 15,51:1
Marco the Magnificent 1966,D 15,60:1
25th Hour, The 1967,F 17,45:1
Happening, The 1967,My 18,56:3
Guns for San Sebastian 1968,Mr 21,57:2
Shoes of the Fisherman, The 1968,N 15,40:3
Magus, The 1968,D 11,57:1

Quinn, Anthony (Director)

Buccaneer, The 1958,D 24,00:0

Quinn, Derry (Screenwriter)

Operation Crossbow 1965,Ap 2,29:1

Quinn, Don (Original Author)

Public Pigeon No 1 1957,My 18,23:2

Quinn, Don (Screenwriter)

Heavenly Days 1944,O 21,15:2

Quinn, Jimmie

Broadway After Dark 1924,My 20,15:2
Dixie Handicap, The 1924,D 30,15:3
On Thin Ice 1925,Mr 9,21:1
Wife Who Wasn't Wanted, The 1925,S 9,23:1
Red Hot Tires 1925,O 20,28:1
Two Flaming Youths 1928,Ja 2,28:1
Spieler, The 1929,F 25,16:1
Dance of Life, The 1929,Ag 16,18:6
Argyle Case, The 1929,Ag 31,13:4
Hold Everything 1930,Ap 23,24:1

Quinn, Louis

Al Capone 1959,Mr 26,27:1
Gypsy 1962,N 2,24:1

Quinn, Regina

Humming Bird, The 1924,Ja 14,2:1

Quinn, Tom

Adventures, The 1947,Ap 4,19:2

Quinn, Vie

Alice in Wonderland 1931,D 28,22:1

Quinn, William J

Darling of New York, The 1924,Ja 18,20:1

Quintanilla, Baby

Forty Little Mothers 1940,Ap 19,25:2
Boom Town 1940,S 6,25:2

Quintanilla, Hector

Tres Berretines, Los 1935,Ja 7,13:3

Quintero, Jose (Director)

Roman Spring of Mrs Stone, The 1961,D 29,11:1

Quirk, Josephine L (Original Author)

Bluff 1924,Ap 28,18:2

Quirk, Robert

Are These our Children 1931,N 14,15:3

Quirk, William

Success 1923,Jl 10,22:5
Dixie Handicap, The 1924,D 30,15:3

Quiroga, Camila

Viento Norte; North Wind 1939,S 16,20:3

Quiroga, Professor (Composer)

Goyescas 1944,My 29,18:3

Quitak, Oscar

Guinea Pig, The 1949,My 2,20:2
Cairo Road 1952,N 1,17:2
So Little Time 1953,Jl 28,23:2

Quivey, Marvel

New Lives for Old 1925,F 25,16:7

Quo, Beulah

Seventh Dawn, The 1964,S 3,24:1
Sand Pebbles, The 1966,D 21,48:1

Quon, Marianne

China 1943,Ap 22,31:2

Quynh, Le

Quiet American, The 1958,F 6,24:1

Qvistgaard, Berthe

Young Have no Time, The 1959,N 23,41:2

R

Raab, Leonid (Miscellaneous)

Girl of the Golden West, The 1938,Mr 25,15:2

Raaf, Vici

Champagne for Caesar 1950,My 12,33:2
Second Woman, The 1951,F 2,19:2
Yellow Canary, The 1963,My 16,42:1

Raal, Prayag

Shakespeare Wallah, 1966,Mr 23,40:2

Raarova, Lyda

What Price Innocence? 1953,My 2,13:3

Rab, Rudolf

Mutterliebe; Mother Love 1940,Mr 16,8:3

Rabagliati, Alberto

Street Angel 1928,Ap 10,33:2
Sei tu l'Amore 1930,N 18,28:4
Escape into Dreams 1950,Ap 13,34:5

Rabagliati, Alberto — Cont

Barefoot Contessa, The 1954,S 30,37:1
Jessica 1962,Ap 20,20:2
Christmas That Almost Wasn't 1966,N 24,65:2

Rabal, Francisco

Mighty Crusaders, The 1961,S 23,17:1
Viridiana 1962,Mr 20,43:4
Eclipse 1962,D 21,5:1
Hand in the Trap 1963,Jl 2,16:2
Belle de Jour 1968,Ap 11,51:1
Nazarin 1968,Je 21,48:1
Religieuse, La 1968,S 23,42:3

Rabal, Teresa

Viridiana 1962,Mr 20,43:4

Rabaud, M (Composer)

Miracle of the Wolves, The 1925,F 24,17:3

Rabdan, Tseven

Son of Mongolia 1936,N 21,21:4

Rabenalt, Arthur Maria (Director)

Was Bin Ich Ohne dich? 1935,D 14,11:2
Pappi 1936,My 16,11:3
Manner Mussen so Sein; Men Are That Way 1939,My 13,11:6
Frauenparadies, Das; Woman's Paradise 1939,Je 24,14:3
Johannis fever; St Johns' Fire 1940,Ap 6,13:2
Alle stehen Kopf; General Confusion 1940,Je 22,18:4
Christina 1951,Ja 15,13:1
Last Waltz, The 1958,Ap 12,13:1
Gypsy Baron, The 1959,N 14,13:1
Hippodrome 1962,Mr 12,36:1

Rabenalt, Arthur Maria (Producer)

Hippodrome 1962,Mr 12,36:1

Rabilvongse, Pradab

King of the White Elephant, The 1941,Ap 5,12:7

Rabin, Jack (Producer)

Cat-Women of the Moon 1954,Mr 20,10:7

Rabinovitch, Gregor (Producer)

Episode 1937,My 17,23:2
Port of Shadows 1939,O 30,13:2
Three Russian Girls 1944,F 5,13:2
Lost One, The; La Traviata 1948,Mr 30,26:2
Faust and the Devil 1950,My 1,18:2

Rabinson, Artur (Director)

Fuerst Woronzeff 1934,N 17,12:2

Racca, Corrado

Cieca di Sorrento, La 1936,Ag 3,11:3
One Hundred Days of Napoleon 1936,S 14,25:1
Padre delle Patria, Il; Father of his Country, The 1938,Ag 30,14:2

Rachawalska, Barbara

Last Stop, The 1949,Mr 22,31:2

Rachmil, Lewis J (Producer)

Human Desire 1954,Ag 7,7:2
Violent Men, The 1955,Ja 27,17:2
Tight Spot 1955,Mr 19,11:7
Gidget 1959,Ap 23,27:4
King of the Sun 1963,D 26,33:4
Rage to Live, A 1965,O 21,57:1
Inspector Clouseau 1968,Jl 25,26:1

Rack, Lisa

Flesh Merchant, The 1956,My 19,12:6

Rackerby, Donald

Little Men 1940,D 9,23:2

Rackin, Martin (Miscellaneous)

Close-Up 1948,Ap 5,24:2

Rackin, Martin (Original Author)

Buy Me That Town 1941,O 23,27:2
Bombardier 1943,Jl 2,15:2
Marine Raiders 1944,Jl 1,10:7
Lone Shark 1952,My 12,21:2
Long John Silver 1955,Ap 7,24:1
Santiago 1956,Jl 14,13:2
Lisbon 1956,Ag 30,19:2

Rackin, Martin (Producer)

Santiago 1956,Jl 14,13:2
Top Secret Affair 1957,Ja 31,21:1
Helen Morgan Story, The 1957,O 3,33:2
Darby's Rangers 1958,F 13,23:2
Fort Dobbs 1958,Ap 19,10:4
Horse Soldiers, The 1959,Je 26,13:1
Stagecoach 1966,Je 16,53:1
Rough Night in Jericho 1967,N 9,56:4

Rackin, Martin (Screenwriter)

Air Raid Wardens 1943,Ap 5,15:5
Riff-Raff 1947,Je 30,25:7
Fighting Father Dunne 1948,Je 25,26:2
Race Street 1948,Ag 23,13:3
Dangerous Profession, A 1949,D 12,29:4
Three Secrets 1950,O 21,10:6
Enforcer, The 1951,Ja 26,19:2
Distant Drums 1951,D 26,19:3
Sailor Beware 1952,F 1,17:1
Lone Shark 1952,My 12,21:2
Clown, The 1953,Ja 29,25:1
Stooge, The 1953,F 5,19:2
Hell on Frisco Bay 1956,Ja 7,21:1
Santiago 1956,Jl 14,13:2
Big Land, The 1957,Mr 2,18:2
Deep Six, The 1958,Ja 16,32:1
Horse Soldiers, The 1959,Je 26,13:1
North to Alaska 1960,N 11,36:1

Racz, Uali
Toprini Nasz; Wedding in Toprin 1939,N 6,20:2
Raday, Imre
Trial of Donald Westhof, The 1928,F 18,11:2
At the Edge of the World 1929,Je 18,29:4
Strauss, The Waltz King 1929,Jl 22,17:1
Vasember 1935,D 9,25:3
Cimzett Ismeretlen 1936,F 7,14:2
Legy Jo Mindhalalig 1936,O 26,20:2
Tisztelet a Kivetelnek 1937,Je 14,26:3
Affair of Honor, An 1937,S 20,19:1
Szerelemboel Noesueltem; I Married for Love 1938,F 7,10:3
Az en Lanyom nem olyan; My Daughter Is Different 1938,Ap 30,18:2
Pokhalo 1938,My 7,18:2
Te Csak Pipalj Ladanyi; Keep On Smoking, Ladanyi 1938,My 18,9:3
Kolcsonkert Kastely; Borrowed Castle, The 1938,D 17,10:4
Radchenko, Irina
Dark Is The Night 1946,Mr 18,24:3
Radchenko, S
Bolshoi Ballet 67 1966,S 30,54:1
Radcliffe, Jack
Wee Geordie 1956,O 8,31:1
Radd, Ronald
Camp on Blood Island, The 1958,S 18,37:2
Where the Spies Are 1966,Ja 27,29:1
Sea Gull, The 1968,D 24,14:1
Raddatz, Carl
Verklungene Melodie; Dead Melody 1938,Je 25,7:2
Befreite Hande; Freed Hans 1940,My 25,20:1
Seven Journeys 1951,Mr 12,20:2
Rosemary 1960,Ja 19,40:2
Counterfeit Traitor, The 1962,Ap 18,28:1
Raddeley, Hermione
Quartet (The Kite); Kite, The (Quartet) 1949,Mr 29,30:3
Rader, Jack
Edge, The 1968,Mr 28,52:1
Radford, Arthur W (Director)
Fighting Lady, The 1944,D 28,12:2
Radford, Basil
There Goes the Bride 1933,Mr 4,11:3
When Thief Meets Thief 1937,Je 15,26:2
Lady Vanishes, The 1938,D 26,29:1
Climbing High 1939,Je 5,20:3
Night Train 1940,D 30,21:1
Girl in the News, The 1941,My 5,13:2
Flying Fortress 1942,D 19,22:2
Randolph Family 1945,Mr 13,19:4
Johnny in the Clouds 1945,N 16,16:2
Captive Heart, The 1947,Ap 28,27:2
Quartet (The Facts of Life); Facts of Life, The (Quartet) 1949,Mr 29,30:3
Passport to Pimlico 1949,O 27,35:2
Tight Little Island 1949,D 26,33:2
Winslow Boy, The 1950,Je 7,34:4
Girl in a Million, A 1950,Jl 24,15:2
Chance of a Lifetime 1951,Mr 15,37:2
Galloping Major, The 1951,D 17,27:2
White Corridors 1952,Jl 16,21:1
Radford, Basil (Original Author)
Galloping Major, The 1951,D 17,27:2
Radha
River, The 1951,S 11,33:2
Radico, Assunta
Path of Hope, The (Il Cammino Della Speranza) 1952,Ag 5,15:5
Radiguet, Raymond (Original Author)
Devil in the Flesh 1949,My 10,29:2
Radilack, Charles
Torn Curtain 1966,Jl 28,23:1
Radin, M
House of Death 1932,Ag 13,18:6
Marionettes 1934,My 8,28:6
Radio Rogues
Reveille With Beverly 1943,Ap 24,17:2
Radio Rogues, The
Blossoms On Broadway 1937,D 3,29:2
Radnay, Hilde
Modern du Barry, A 1928,Mr 19,26:2
Radnitz, Robert B (Producer)
Dog of Flanders, A 1960,Ap 1,37:1
Misty 1961,Jl 18,33:2
Island of the Blue Dolphins 1964,Jl 4,8:2
...And Now Miguel 1966,S 8,43:1
Rado, Istvan (Producer)
Urilany Szobat Keres; Lady Seeks Room 1938,Mr 19,11:2
Rado, Nelly
Key Balvany, A 1933,Ap 18,13:6
Kek Balvany, A; Blue Idol, The 1933,Ap 18,13:6
Rado, Sandor
Filleres Gyoers 1933,Mr 27,13:7
Radok, Alfred (Director)
Distant Journey 1950,Ag 28,13:3
Radok, Alfred (Screenwriter)
Distant Journey 1950,Ag 28,13:3

Radovich, Bill
World in His Arms, The 1952,O 10,21:2
Trouble Along the Way 1953,My 7,37:2
Radsina, Medea
Midnight Sun, The 1926,Ap 24,20:4
Radspieler, Charlotte
Klosterjaeger, Der 1936,Ja 3,13:7
Radunskaya, Victoria
My Daughter 1960,N 28,40:2
Radunsky, Alexander
Ballet of Romeo and Juliet, The 1956,Ap 3,31:2
Little Humpbacked Horse, The 1962,O 8,19:1
Radunsky, Alexander (Miscellaneous)
Little Humpbacked Horse, The 1962,O 8,19:1
Radunsky, Alexander (Producer)
Little Humpbacked Horse, The 1962,O 8,19:1
Radvanyi, Geza (Director)
It Happened in Europe 1949,O 4,32:4
Women Without Names 1951,Ag 7,22:2
Madchen in Uniform 1965,Ag 18,41:2
Radvanyi, Geza (Original Author)
Women Without Names 1951,Ag 7,22:2
Radvanyi, Geza (Producer)
It Happened in Europe 1949,O 4,32:4
Women Without Names 1951,Ag 7,22:2
Radvanyi, Geza (Screenwriter)
It Happened in Europe 1949,O 4,32:4
Radzin, Elsa
Hamlet 1966,Mr 16,48:1
Radzina, MEdea
Sea Hawk, The 1924,Je 3,22:1
Radzina, Medea
Bedroom Window, The 1924,Je 9,14:3
Radzinski, Semyon (Screenwriter)
In the Far East 1937,O 20,27:3
RAE
See Also REA, WRAY, REY
Rae, Claude
Nobody Waved Goodbye 1964,S 17,52:1
Rae, John
Brave Don't Cry, The 1952,N 6,37:2
Little Kidnappers, The 1954,S 2,18:1
Stowaway Girl 1957,N 6,43:3
Reach for Glory 1963,S 10,46:1
Morgan! 1966,Ap 5,42:2
Rae, John (Original Author)
Reach for Glory 1963,S 10,46:1
Rae, John (Screenwriter)
Reach for Glory 1963,S 10,46:1
Rae, Peggy
Strange Bedfellows 1965,Mr 11,38:1
Rae, Raida
Death Valley 1927,N 22,32:2
Wild Geese 1927,D 5,26:2
Craig's Wife 1928,D 4,29:1
Raeburn, Frances
Seven Sweethearts 1942,N 13,28:1
Raelets
Blues for Lovers 1966,S 8,43:1
Raepina, I
Wrestler and the Clown, The 1959,Ja 1,38:1
Rafal, Roger
Jour de Fete 1952,F 20,26:4
Winner's Circle, The 1957,My 6,25:2
Rafe
Big Country, The 1958,O 2,44:1
Rafel, Jerome
Hallelujah the Hills 1963,D 17,49:1
Rafelson, Bob (Director)
Head 1968,N 7,51:1
Rafelson, Bob (Original Author)
Head 1968,N 7,51:1
Rafelson, Bob (Producer)
Head 1968,N 7,51:1
Raffaelli, Giuliano
Blood and Black Lace 1965,N 11,58:3
Raffell, Anthony
Mikado, The 1967,Mr 15,53:1
Rafferty, Chips
Forty Thousand Horsemen 1941,Ag 15,13:2
Overlanders, The 1946,D 20,31:2
Bush Christmas 1947,N 27,50:4
Massacre Hill 1950,D 14,51:3
Rats of Tobruk, The 1951,My 24,47:3
Kangaroo 1952,My 17,22:7
Desert Rats, The 1953,My 9,13:2
Sundowners, The 1960,D 9,39:1
Wackiest Ship in the Army, The 1961,F 9,36:1
Mutiny on the Bounty 1962,N 9,31:2
Rafferty, Frances
Seven Sweethearts 1942,N 13,28:1
War Against Mrs Hadley, The 1942,N 26,40:2
Thousands Cheer 1943,S 14,27:1
Girl Crazy 1943,D 3,27:2
Dragon Seed 1944,Jl 21,16:4
Barbary Coast Gent 1944,S 29,18:2
Mrs Parkington 1944,O 13,16:1
Hidden Eye, The 1945,Ag 31,14:3
Abbott and Costello in Hollywood 1945,N 23,26:2
Bad Bascomb 1946,My 23,18:4
Lost Honeymoon 1947,Je 20,25:6

Raffetto, Michael
Pirates of Monterey 1947,D 17,41:4
Foreign Affair, A 1948,Jl 1,19:3
I Was a Shoplifter 1950,Ap 28,26:3
Storm Center 1956,O 22,25:4
Rafil, Giovanna
Fuga, La 1966,Mr 22,33:1
Rafkin, Alan (Director)
Ski Party 1965,O 23,17:3
Ghost and Mr Chicken, The 1966,S 22,57:2
Nobody's Perfect 1968,Ap 4,58:3
Shakiest Gun in the West, The 1968,Jl 11,30:1
Raft, George
Quick Millions 1931,Ap 18,17:3
Hush Money 1931,Jl 11,7:6
Palmy Days 1931,S 24,21:2
Dancers in the Dark 1932,Mr 19,11:2
Scarface, The Shame of the Nation 1932,My 20,22:3
Night World 1932,My 28,18:2
Madame Racketeer 1932,Jl 23,6:6
Night after Night 1932,O 31,18:4
If I Had a Million 1932,D 3,21:4
Under-Cover Man 1932,D 5,21:2
Pick Up 1933,Mr 25,13:4
Midnight Club 1933,Jl 29,14:2
Bowery, The 1933,O 5,24:2
All of Me 1934,F 5,19:2
Bolero 1934,F 17,20:3
Trumpet Blows, The 1934,Ap 14,18:2
Limehouse Blues 1934,D 12,28:2
Rumba 1935,F 25,13:2
Stolen Harmony 1935,Ap 20,16:2
Glass Key, The 1935,Je 15,20:2
Every Night at Eight 1935,Ag 3,16:2
She Couldn't Take It 1935,N 7,27:1
It Had to Happen 1936,F 15,18:6
Yours for the Asking 1936,Ag 20,14:2
Souls at Sea 1937,Ag 10,23:2
You and Me 1938,Je 2,19:1
Spawn of the North 1938,S 8,27:1
Each Dawn I Die 1939,Jl 22,12:2
I Stole a Million 1939,Ag 7,11:2
Invisible Stripes 1940,Ja 13,11:2
House Across the Bay, The 1940,Mr 22,23:2
They Drive by Night 1940,Jl 27,17:5
Manpower 1941,Jl 5,14:2
Broadway 1942,Je 5,23:2
Stage Door Canteen 1943,Je 25,13:2
Background to Danger 1943,Jl 3,11:2
Follow the Boys 1944,Ap 26,24:6
Nob Hill 1945,Jl 4,10:3
Johnny Angel 1945,D 28,12:2
Whistle Stop 1946,Mr 18,24:2
Mr Ace 1946,S 30,21:3
Nocturne 1946,N 11,42:2
Christmas Eve 1947,N 28,30:2
Intrigue 1948,Ap 24,11:2
Race Street 1948,Ag 23,13:3
Outpost in Morocco 1949,Mr 25,28:3
Johnny Allegro 1949,My 31,19:2
Dangerous Profession, A 1949,D 12,29:4
Red Light 1950,Ja 16,18:4
Lucky Nick Cain 1951,Ap 23,21:2
Lone Shark 1952,My 12,21:2
Man From Cairo, The 1953,D 17,52:4
Rogue Cop 1954,S 18,12:2
Black Widow 1954,O 28,46:6
Bullet for Joey, A 1955,Ap 16,12:1
Around the World in 80 Days 1956,O 18,37:1
Some Like It Hot 1959,Mr 30,23:1
Jet Over the Atlantic 1960,Ja 7,24:6
Ocean's Eleven 1960,Ag 11,19:1
Casino Royale 1967,Ap 29,25:1
Upper Hand, The 1967,Jl 29,29:3
Ragaky, Mohammed (Director)
Little Miss Devil 1951,D 8,9:2
Ragaway, Martin (Original Author)
Milkman, The 1951,Ja 1,13:6
Ragaway, Martin (Screenwriter)
Abbott and Costello in the Foreign Legion 1950,Ag 14,14:4
Milkman, The 1951,Ja 1,13:6
Ragazzi, Jusupoff
Conjugal Bed, The 1963,S 17,30:1
Ragland, Rags
Ringside Maisie 1941,Ag 1,11:2
Whistling in the Dark 1941,Ag 28,23:2
Born to Sing 1942,F 19,23:2
Sunday Punch 1942,My 11,19:2
Maisie Gets her Man 1942,Jl 16,23:2
Panama Hattie 1942,O 2,31:2
War Against Mrs Hadley, The 1942,N 26,40:2
Whistling in Dixie 1942,D 31,20:4
Du Barry Was a Lady 1943,Ag 20,13:1
Girl Crazy 1943,D 3,27:2
Whistling in Brooklyn 1944,Mr 24,17:3
Three Men in White 1944,My 26,23:3
Canterville Ghost, The 1944,Jl 29,16:2
Meet The People 1944,S 8,16:2
Anchors Aweigh 1945,Jl 20,15:2
Her Highness and the Bellboy 1945,S 28,16:2
Abbott and Costello in Hollywood 1945,N 23,26:2

Ragland, Rags— Cont
Hoodlum Saint, The 1946,Je 27,29:1
Ragneborn, Arne
Vicious Breed, The 1958,My 23,29:2
Ragneborn, Arne (Director)
Vicious Breed, The 1958,My 23,29:2
Ragoo, Nadiege
Young World, A 1966,My 17,52:1
Raguen, Ernesto
Viejo Doctor, El; Old Doctor, The 1940,Ap 13,21:3
Rahl, Mady
Blinde Passagier; Stowaways 1937,Mr 6,10:1
Truxa 1937,Jl 26,15:2
Gaesschen zum Paradies, Das 1937,Ag 21,7:3
Wenn Du eine Schwiegermutter hast; When You Have a Mother-in-Law 1938,Ja 29,12:1
Husaren Heraus 1938,Mr 19,11:3
Nacht im Mai, Eine; Night in May, A 1938,N 12,10:3
Zweimal zwei im Himmelbett; Twice Two in a Four-Post Bed 1939,F 5,19:3
Geheimnisvolle Mister X, Der; Mysterious Mr X, The 1939,Jl 1,11:2
Stefanie 1959,Je 18,36:1
Hippodrome 1962,Mr 12,36:1
Situation Hopeless-But not Serious 1965,O 14,53:1
Rahn, Bruno (Director)
Small Town Sinners 1928,N 27,34:1
Rai, Himansu
Light of Asia, The 1928,My 12,8:4
Shiraz 1929,Mr 19,37:2
Throw of the Dice 1930,Ja 6,30:5
Raimbourg, Lucien
He Who Must Die 1958,D 29,21:1
Elusive Corporal, The 1963,F 19,5:1
Cartouche 1964,Jl 22,39:1
Raimu
Marius 1933,Ap 14,22:5
Theodore et Cie; Theodore & Co 1933,Jl 9,X,2:2 (In Addenda)
Mam'zelle Nitouche 1933,N 20,18:3
Charlemagne 1935,Ag 24,18:3
Carnet de Bal, Un 1938,Mr 26,12:1
Heart of Paris 1939,Ja 13,17:3
Heroes of the Marne; (Famille Lefrancois, Le) 1939,Ap 24,13:2
Last Desire 1939,D 22,15:2
Baker's Wife, The 1940,F 27,17:2
Man Who Seeks the Truth, The 1941,O 7,26:6
King, The 1941,O 23,29:3
Heart of a Nation, The 1943,Ap 8,27:2
Dawn Over France 1945,Mr 17,17:2
Well-Digger's Daughter, The 1946,S 30,21:4
Colonel Chabert 1947,Je 21,11:2
Midnight in Paris 1947,O 9,32:3
Fanny 1948,F 13,26:2
Cesar 1948,O 28,36:2
Eternal Husband, The 1949,Ja 10,19:2
Strangers in the House 1949,O 13,33:3
Hoboes in Paradise 1950,O 9,21:5
Rain, Douglas
Oedipus Rex 1957,Ja 8,26:1
2001 A Space Odyssey 1968,Ap 4,58:1
Raine, Jack
Suspense 1930,N 8,21:3
Hate Ship, The 1930,N 15,15:3
Middle Watch, The 1930,D 20,20:6
Night Birds 1931,Ja 3,21:2
Fires of Fate 1933,Ap 3,13:4
Clairvoyant, The 1935,Je 8,12:2
Mine Own Executioner 1949,Ja 19,34:2
Easy Money (Episode 3) 1949,F 14,15:3
My Brothers Keeper 1949,F 14,15:3
Good Time Girl 1950,S 25,18:5
Happy Time, The 1952,O 31,30:2
Above and Beyond 1953,Ja 31,10:6
Julius Caesar 1953,Je 5,19:1
Dangerous When Wet 1953,Je 19,18:1
Rhapsody 1954,Mr 12,17:1
Prince of Players 1955,Ja 12,24:2
Not as a Stranger 1955,Je 29,24:1
Power and The Prize, the 1956,S 27,42:1
Woman Obsessed 1959,My 28,34:1
Raine, Norman Reilly (Original Author)
Tugboat Annie 1933,Ag 12,14:2
White Woman 1933,N 18,18:5
Island of Lost Men 1939,Ag 17,16:3
Tugboat Annie Sails Again 1940,N 9,20:2
We've Never Been Licked 1943,Ag 19,23:1
Ladies Courageous 1944,Mr 16,17:2
Raine, Norman Reilly (Screenwriter)
God's Country and the Woman 1937,Ja 11,15:5
Mountain Justice 1937,My 13,31:2
Life of Emile Zola, The 1937,Ag 12,14:2
Perfect Specimen, The 1937,O 28,29:2
Adventures of Robin Hood, The 1938,My 13,17:2
Men Are Such Fools 1938,Je 17,25:1
Each Dawn I Die 1939,Jl 22,12:2
Private Lives of Elizabeth and Essex, The 1939,D 2,21:2
Fighting 69th, The 1940,Ja 27,9:2
Captains of the Clouds 1942,F 13,24:2

Eagle Squadron 1942,Jl 3,12:5
We've Never Been Licked 1943,Ag 19,23:1
Ladies Courageous 1944,Mr 16,17:2
Nob Hill 1945,Jl 4,10:3
Bell for Adano, A 1945,Jl 6,8:3
Captain Kidd 1945,N 23,26:3
M 1951,Je 11,20:7
Woman of the North Country 1952,Ag 30,6:2
Raine, Patricia
Madeleine 1950,S 1,17:2
Pandora and the Flying Dutchman 1951,D 7,35:2
Encore (The Ant and the Grasshopper); Ant and the Grasshopper, The (Encore) 1952,Ap 3,45:1
Caretaker's Daughter, The 1953,Ag 20,18:5
Raine, William MacLeod (Original Author)
Three Young Texans 1954,Ap 17,8:2
Rainer, Kari
Fluechtlinge 1934,O 15,20:5
Rainer, Luise
Escapade 1935,Jl 6,16:2
Great Ziegfeld, The 1936,Ap 9,21:2
Good Earth, The 1937,F 3,27:1
Emperor's Candlesticks, The 1937,Jl 9,18:1
Big City 1937,S 17,29:2
Toy Wife, The 1938,Je 24,15:1
Great Waltz, The 1938,N 25,19:1
Dramatic School 1938,D 9,31:2
Hostages 1943,O 11,23:2
Rainer, Margrit
Heidi 1953,D 21,27:2
Heidi and Peter 1955,D 13,55:2
RAINES
See Also RAINS
Raines, Ella
Corvette K-225 1943,O 21,30:1
Cry Havoc 1943,N 24,16:2
Phantom Lady 1944,F 18,15:2
Hail the Conquering Hero 1944,Ag 10,14:2
Enter Arsene Lupin 1944,D 2,17:6
Tall in the Saddle 1944,D 15,25:3
Suspect, The 1945,F 1,18:5
Uncle Harry 1945,Ag 24,14:5
Runaround, The 1946,Je 7,16:3
White Tie and Tails 1946,N 8,28:2
Time Out of Mind 1947,Ap 7,20:1
Web, The 1947,Je 5,32:1
Brute Force 1947,Jl 17,16:2
Senator Was Indiscreet, The 1947,D 27,9:2
Impact 1949,Mr 21,19:2
Dangerous Profession, A 1949,D 12,29:4
Singing Guns 1950,Je 5,19:3
Second Face, The 1951,Mr 2,21:3
Fighting Coast Guard 1951,My 12,14:6
Rainey, Ford
White Heat 1949,S 3,7:2
3:10 to Yuma 1957,Ag 29,22:1
Badlanders, The 1958,S 4,33:1
Last Mile, The 1959,F 19,27:1
Flaming Star 1960,D 17,19:1
Ada 1961,Ag 26,15:1
Johnny Tiger 1966,Je 16,53:4
Sand Pebbles, The 1966,D 21,48:1
Rainger, Ralph (Composer)
International House 1933,My 27,11:5
Song of Songs 1933,Jl 20,22:2
Torch Singer 1933,O 7,18:5
Way to Love, The 1933,N 11,10:3
All of Me 1934,F 5,19:2
Search for Beauty 1934,F 10,20:2
Bolero 1934,F 17,20:3
Wharf Angel 1934,Ap 21,12:1
Little Miss Marker 1934,My 19,18:3
Kiss and Make-Up 1934,Je 29,17:1
Shoot the Works 1934,Jl 7,16:5
She Loves Me Not 1934,S 8,18:5
Here is my Heart 1934,D 22,21:1
Rumba 1935,F 25,13:2
Ruggles of Red Gap 1935,Mr 7,26:1
Four Hours to Kill 1935,Ap 11,27:3
Devil is a Woman, The 1935,My 4,17:2
Big Broadcast of 1936, The 1935,S 16,15:2
Millions in the Air 1935,D 12,33:4
Rose of the Rancho 1936,Ja 9,25:2
Waikiki Wedding 1937,Mr 25,29:1
Swing High, Swing Low 1937,Ap 15,19:1
Big Broadcast of 1938, The 1938,Mr 10,16:2
Romance in the Dark 1938,Mr 21,18:2
Artists and Models Abroad 1938,D 22,25:3
Paris Honeymoon 1939,Ja 26,17:1
Gulliver's Travels 1939,D 21,29:1
Tall, Dark and Handsome 1941,Ja 24,15:2
Rise and Shine 1941,D 6,14:3
My Gal Sal 1942,My 1,23:1
Footlight Serenade 1942,S 10,30:3
Tales of Manhattan 1942,S 25,25:1
Coney Island 1943,Je 17,17:2
Riding High 1943,D 23,26:4
Rainger, Ralph (Miscellaneous)
Bedtime Story, A 1933,Ap 20,20:3
Trumpet Blows, The 1934,Ap 14,18:2
Poppy 1936,Je 18,19:1
College Holiday 1936,D 24,21:2
Blossoms On Broadway 1937,D 3,29:2

Rainnie, Hedley
Jigsaw 1949,My 30,9:4
RAINS
See Also RAINES
Rains, Claude
Invisible Man, The 1933,N 18,18:4
Crime Without Passion 1934,S 1,16:2
Man Who Reclaimed his Head, The 1935,Ja 9,22:1
Mystery of Edwin Drood, The 1935,Mr 21,27:1
Clairvoyant, The 1935,Je 8,12:2
Last Outpost, The 1935,O 5,18:2
Hearts Divided 1936,Je 13,13:1
Anthony Adverse 1936,Ag 27,16:1
Stolen Holiday 1937,F 1,15:3
Prince and the Pauper, The 1937,My 6,23:1
They Won't Forget 1937,Jl 15,16:1
Gold Is Where You Find It 1938,F 14,20:6
Adventures of Robin Hood, The 1938,My 13,17:2
White Banners 1938,Je 23,27:1
Four Daughters 1938,Ag 19,13:3
They Made Me a Criminal 1939,Ja 21,19:2
Juarez 1939,Ap 26,27:1
Daughters Courageous 1939,Je 24,14:2
Mr Smith Goes to Washington 1939,O 20,27:2
Four Wives 1939,D 23,9:1
Saturday's Children 1940,My 4,13:1
Sea Hawk, The 1940,Ag 10,16:2
Lady With red Hair 1940,D 6,28:2
Four Mothers 1941,Ja 11,12:7
Here Comes Mr Jordan 1941,Ag 8,13:2
Wolf Man, The 1941,D 22,24:5
Kings Row 1942,F 3,23:2
Moontide 1942,Ap 30,14:1
Now, Voyager 1942,O 23,25:3
Casablanca 1942,N 27,27:1
Forever and a Day 1943,Mr 13,9:2
Phantom of the Opera, The 1943,O 15,15:2
Passage to Marseille 1944,F 17,12:5
Mr Skeffington 1944,My 26,23:2
Caesar and Cleopatra 1944,Jl 16,II,3:4
Strange Holiday 1945,O 20,8:2
This Love of Ours 1945,N 1,20:2
Notorious 1946,Ag 16,19:2
Caesar and Cleopatra 1946,S 6,18:2
Deception 1946,O 19,15:3
Angel on my Shoulder 1946,O 21,27:2
Unsuspected, The 1947,O 4,9:2
One Woman's Story 1949,My 18,33:2
Rope of Sand 1949,Ag 4,19:2
White Tower, The 1950,Jl 3,9:2
Where Danger Lives 1951,Ja 1,13:6
Sealed Cargo 1951,My 24,47:1
Paris Express, The 1953,Je 6,8:6
Lisbon 1956,Ag 30,19:2
Earth Is Mine, The 1959,Je 27,13:1
Lost World, The 1960,Jl 14,23:1
Lawrence of Arabia 1962,D 17,5:6
Twilight of Honor 1963,N 14,41:2
Greatest Story Ever Told, The 1965,F 16,40:2
Rairden, Wallace
Mystery Sea Raider 1940,Ag 26,11:4
Raiskaya-Dore, N
Great Citizen, The 1939,Ja 16,11:2
Raisman, Yuri (Director)
Men on Wings 1935,Je 11,24:5
Mashenka 1942,N 21,10:7
Train Goes East, The 1949,S 5,13:3
Dream of a Cossack 1952,F 18,15:2
Conflict 1955,D 26,23:4
Raison, Milton (Original Author)
Shadow, The 1937,D 17,33:3
West of Carson City 1940,My 7,31:3
Bombs Over Burma 1942,Ag 10,15:2
Jungle Siren 1942,O 10,11:3
State Department-File 649 1949,F 21,20:2
Special Agent 1949,Ag 22,13:1
Southside 1-1000 1950,N 3,31:2
Raison, Milton (Screenwriter)
West of Carson City 1940,My 7,31:3
Bombs Over Burma 1942,Ag 10,15:2
State Department-File 649 1949,F 21,20:2
Prince of Peace, The 1951,Mr 24,8:3
Raitt, John
Minstrel Man 1944,Jl 17,18:5
Pajama Game, The 1957,Ag 30,12:2
Raizman, D (Director)
Zemlya Zhazhdet 1932,My 6,15:3
Rajna, Alice
Sportszerelem; Love of Sport 1938,F 14,20:8
Rajnay, Gabor
My Wife, The Miss 1934,S 13,26:2
Huszarszerelem 1935,Ap 23,24:5
Harom Sarkany 1936,D 22,32:3
111-es Szobaban; In Room 111 1938,Ap 2,18:2
Az en Lanyom nem olyan; My Daughter Is Different 1938,Ap 30,18:2
Harapos Ferj; Biting Husbank 1939,Ja 28,19:2
Varju a Toronyoran; Crow on the Tower 1939,N 18,22:6
Pentek Rezi; Friday Rose 1939,D 23,9:2

Raker, Lorin
Six Cylinder Love 1931,My 16,31:3
Women Go on Forever 1931,O 19,28:1
My Woman 1933,O 16,20:3
Nut Farm, The 1935,Ap 8,23:3
Miserables, Les 1935,Ap 22,14:2
Chicken every Sunday 1949,Ja 19,34:2
Rakhmanov, Leonid (Original Author)
Baltic Deputy 1937,S 4,8:2
Rakhmanov, Leonid (Screenwriter)
Baltic Deputy 1937,S 4,8:2
Raki, Laya
Land of Fury 1955,My 3,37:4
Poppy is Also a Flower, The 1967,D 14,62:4
Rakoff, Alvin (Director)
Room 43 1959,D 3,46:1
World in my Pocket, The 1962,My 10,30:2
Raky, Hortense
Vienna Burgtheater 1937,O 27,47:1
Frauenparadies, Das; Woman's Paradise
  1939,Je 24,14:3
Rale, M W
Three Miles Out 1924,Ja 1,20:1
Raleigh, Saba
Prince of Lovers, The 1927,N 29,31:1
Ralhaus, Carl
Nur am Rhein 1931,S 25,28:7
Ralkes, Napier
Booloo 1938,Jl 30,10:2
Rall, Tommy
Kiss Me Kate 1953,N 6,23:2
My Sister Eileen 1955,S 23,21:1
Second Greatest Sex, The 1956,F 11,12:2
World in my Corner 1956,F 18,12:5
Walk the Proud Land 1956,S 8,20:6 (In
  Addenda)
Merry Andrews 1958,Mr 21,17:1
Ralli, Giovanna
It Happened in the Park 1957,Ag 13,23:2
Bigamist, The 1958,My 12,25:1
Most Wonderful Moment, The 1959,Je 1,23:6
General Della Rovere 1960,N 22,41:1
What Did You Do in the War, Daddy?
  1966,S 1,28:1
Very Handy Man, A 1966,D 15,60:1
Caper of the Golden Bulls, The 1967,Je 22,46:1
Deadfall 1968,S 12,54:1
Ralli, Patrizia
Guendalina 1958,Je 30,23:2
Ralli, Paul
Water Hole, The 1928,S 3,14:2
Married in Hollywood 1929,S 23,24:3
Rallis, Orestes
Boy on a Dolphin 1957,Ap 20,21:2
Ralmondi, Gianni
Boheme, La 1965,O 20,51:2
Ralmondi, Sergio
Wild Love; (GI! Inamorati) 1961,Ap 6,30:2
Ralph, Hanna
Siegfried 1925,Ag 24,17:3
Faust 1926,D 7,21:2
Power 1928,Jl 16,25:3
Letzte Rose 1936,O 10,21:3
Ralph, Jessie
Child of Manhattan 1933,F 13,11:4
Elmer the Great 1933,My 26,24:2
Cocktail Hour 1933,Je 5,18:5
Ann Carver's Profession 1933,Je 9,20:2
Nana 1934,F 2,20:3
Coming-Out Party 1934,Mr 17,11:3
Murder at the Vanities 1934,My 21,20:2
Affairs of Cellini, The 1934,S 6,22:3
One Night of Love 1934,S 7,25:3
We Live Again 1934,N 2,27:2
Evelyn Prentice 1934,N 10,19:1
David Copperfield 1935,Ja 19,8:1
Vanessa: Her Love Story 1935,Ap 13,11:3
Miserables, Les 1935,Ap 22,14:2
Mark of the Vampire 1935,My 3,23:4
Paris in Spring 1935,Jl 13,16:2
Jalna 1935,S 14,8:4
I Live my Life 1935,O 12,12:2
Metropolitan 1935,O 18,27:4
I Found Stella Parish 1935,N 4,24:4
Captain Blood 1935,D 27,14:1
Yellow Dust 1936,F 24,14:1
Garden Murder Case, The 1936,Mr 2,13:2
Little Lord Fauntleroy 1936,Ap 3,27:1
Unguarded Hour, The 1936,Ap 4,11:1
San Francisco 1936,Je 27,21:1
Bunker Bean 1936,Je 27,21:2
Walking on Air 1936,S 12,20:2
After the Thin Man 1936,D 25,19:2
Camille 1937,Ja 23,13:1
Good Earth, The 1937,F 3,27:1
Last of Mrs Cheyney, The 1937,F 19,15:1
Double Wedding 1937,O 22,27:2
Love Is a Headache 1938,Ja 28,17:3
Hold That Kiss 1938,Je 11,9:1
Port of Seven Seas 1938,Jl 15,13:2
St Louis Blues 1939,F 9,17:2
Four Girls in White 1939,F 23,19:3
Cafe Society 1939,F 23,19:2

Mickey, the Kid 1939,Jl 6,27:1
Drums Along the Mohawk 1939,N 4,11:2
Blue Bird, The 1940,Ja 20,11:2
Star Dust 1940,My 4,13:1
I Want a Divorce 1940,O 3,31:2
Bank Dick, The 1940,D 13,29:2
Lady From Cheyenne, The 1941,Ap 18,18:2
They Met in Bombay 1941,Jl 4,17:1
Ralph, Julia
So's Your Old Man 1926,N 1,28:2
Ralph, Louis
Russia-1908 1929,Ja 7,36:2
Spies 1929,Mr 5,29:1
Kreuzer Emden 1932,S 8,17:2
Ralph, Louis (Director)
Kreuzer Emden 1932,S 8,17:2
Ralph, Susi
Schoen Ist die Manoeverzeit 1932,Ag 19,20:6
Ralphaelson, Samson (Screenwriter)
Harvey Girls, The 1946,Ja 25,26:2
Ralston, Esther
Peter Pan 1924,D 29,11:4
Goose Hangs High, The 1925,Mr 10,19:3
Little French Girl, The 1925,Je 1,10:3
Beggar on Horseback 1925,Je 6,9:2
Lady Who Lied, The 1925,Jl 7,24:2
Lucky Devil, The 1925,Jl 8,12:4
Trouble With Wives, The 1925,Ag 5,12:4
Best People 1925,O 21,21:3
Kiss for Cinderella, A 1925,D 26,11:2
Womanhandled 1926,Ja 5,25:2
American Venus, The 1926,Ja 26,25:2
Blind Goddess 1926,Ap 6,26:4 (In Addenda)
Quarterback, The 1926,O 12,30:2
Old Ironsides 1926,D 7,21:2
Fashions For Women 1927,Mr 28,26:4
Children of Divorce 1927,Ap 26,33:3
Ten Modern Commandments 1927,Jl 11,23:4
Spotlight, The 1927,N 28,18:5
Love and Learn 1928,F 20,14:1
Something Always Happens 1928,My 21,25:1
Sawdust Paradise, The 1928,Ag 27,23:1
Case of Lena Smith, The 1929,Ja 15,22:4
Betrayal 1929,My 6,30:4
Wheel of Life, The 1929,Je 24,27:1
Mighty, The 1929,D 30,16:4
Lonely Wives 1931,Mr 16,25:1
Prodigal, The 1931,Je 27,20:3
Rome Express 1932,D 18,X,6:5
Rome Express 1933,F 27,11:2
After the Ball 1933,Mr 20,18:3
Sadie McKee 1934,My 18,18:3 (Incorrect in this
  edition; use 1934,My 19,18:3 elsewhere)
Romance in the Rain 1934,S 8,18:5
Marines are Coming, The 1935,F 23,14:7
Mr Dynamite 1935,My 25,12:1
Hollywood Boulevard 1936,S 21,26:4
Reunion 1936,N 27,27:1
As Good as Married 1937,My 22,19:2
Shadows of the Orient 1937,O 11,26:6
Tin Pan Alley 1940,N 22,27:3
San Francisco Docks 1940,D 26,23:3
Ralston, Harry
Khovanschina 1960,S 23,33:1
Ralston, Howard
Pollyanna 1920,Ja 19,16:3
Ralston, Jobyna
Three Must-Get-Theres, The 1922,Ag 28,14:1
Why Worry? 1923,S 3,9:3
Girl Shy 1924,Ap 21,21:4
Hot Water 1924,O 27,27:1
Freshman, The 1925,S 21,12:4
For Heaven's Sake 1926,Ap 5,24:1
Sweet Daddies 1926,Je 23,28:1
Gigolo 1926,O 5,27:1
Kid Brother, The 1927,Ja 24,14:1
Special Delivery 1927,Ap 26,33:3
Wings 1927,Ag 13,10:4
Night Flyer, The 1928,Mr 13,23:3
Count of Ten, The 1928,Mr 13,23:3
College Coquette, The 1929,Ag 26,17:1
Freshman, The 1953,Ap 28,31:6
Ralston, Marcia
Call it a Day 1937,My 7,29:2
Ever Since Eve 1937,Je 25,25:2
Singing Marine, The 1937,Jl 1,33:2
Fly Away Baby 1937,Jl 9,18:2
Sh! The Octopus 1937,D 24,21:2
Gold Is Where You Find It 1938,F 14,20:6
Fools for Scandal 1938,Mr 25,15:3
Men Are Such Fools 1938,Je 17,25:1
Crime Takes a Holiday 1938,N 28,11:2
Kid From Kansas, The 1941,D 2,29:4
Paris Calling 1942,Ja 19,21:2
Ralston, Vera
Lady and the Monster, The 1944,Ap 8,9:2
Plainsman and the Lady, The 1946,N 4,33:1
Wyoming 1947,Jl 25,12:5
Flame, The 1948,F 20,19:2
I, Jane Doe 1948,Jl 5,8:4
Angel on the Amazon 1948,D 27,16:4
Fighting Kentuckian, The 1949,S 19,18:3
Surrender 1950,O 9,21:5

Belle le Grand 1951,My 18,34:6
Wild Blue Yonder, The 1952,Ja 2,20:1
Hoodlum Empire 1952,Mr 6,25:6
Fair Wind to Java 1953,Ag 28,13:3
Jubilee Trail 1954,My 1,13:3
Timberjack 1955,Mr 10,33:3
Ralston, Vera Hruba
Storm Over Lisbon 1944,S 11,14:1
Lake Placid Serenade 1944,D 25,15:6
Dakota 1945,D 17,17:2
Murder in the Music Hall 1946,Ap 15,22:2
Rama, Rau E
Shiraz 1928,O 7,IX,7:7
Rama-Tahe
Cain 1932,Ja 18,18:4
Ramage, Cecil
King of the Damned 1936,F 1,9:2
Spy 77 1936,F 10,15:1
April Romance 1937,Ja 27,17:4
Yank in London, A 1946,Ap 20,16:3
Nicholas Nickleby 1947,D 1,27:2
Kind Hearts and Coronets 1950,Je 15,41:2
Ramati, Alexander (Director)
Sands of Beersheba 1966,My 6,54:2
Ramati, Alexander (Producer)
Sands of Beersheba 1966,My 6,54:2
Ramati, Alexander (Screenwriter)
Sands of Beersheba 1966,My 6,54:2
Trunk to Cairo 1966,D 29,22:1
Ramati, Didi
Sands of Beersheba 1966,My 6,54:2
Rambal, Enrique
Empty Star, The; Estrella Vacia, La
  1962,Mr 28,36:4
Rambal, Ricardo
Desaparecido, El 1936,Je 2,25:3
Rambeau, Marjorie
Fortune Teller, The 1920,My 10,18:2
Syncopating Sue 1926,N 2,35:1
Her Man 1930,O 4,15:2
Min and Bill 1930,N 24,26:5
Inspiration 1931,F 9,25:3
Easiest Way, The 1931,F 28,15:2
Strangers May Kiss 1931,Ap 13,17:1
Tailor-Made Man, A 1931,Ap 25,23:4
Secret Six, The 1931,My 2,23:4
Laughing Sinners 1931,Jl 4,11:5
Son of India 1931,Jl 25,11:6
Leftover Ladies 1931,N 9,22:4
Hell Divers 1931,D 23,27:3
Strictly Personal 1933,Mr 20,18:2
Warrior's Husband, The 1933,My 12,20:4
Man's Castle 1933,D 30,9:2
Palooka 1934,F 28,23:2
Modern Hero, A 1934,Ap 20,17:1
Grand Canary 1934,Jl 20,11:1
Under Pressure 1935,F 4,11:3
First Lady 1937,D 23,25:1
Merrily We Live 1938,Mr 18,23:3
Woman Against Woman 1938,Ag 23,20:6
Rains Came, The 1939,S 9,11:2
Primrose Path 1940,Mr 23,16:2
Twenty-Mule Team 1940,My 10,26:6
East of the River 1940,O 28,21:2
Tugboat Annie Sails Again 1940,N 9,20:2
Tobacco Road 1941,F 21,16:2
Broadway 1942,Je 5,23:2
In old Oklahoma 1943,D 6,21:1
Salome, Where She Danced 1945,My 3,27:1
Walls of Jericho, The 1948,Ag 5,16:2
Lucky Stiff, The 1949,Ja 31,14:2
Any Number Can Play 1949,Jl 1,14:4
Abandoned Woman 1949,O 27,35:3
Torch Song 1953,O 13,34:2
Bad for Each Other 1953,D 24,9:3
Forever Female 1954,Ja 13,26:2
Man Called Peter, A 1955,Ap 1,22:1
View From Pompey's Head, The 1955,N 5,22:5
Slander 1957,Ja 17,34:4
Man of a Thousand Faces 1957,Ag 14,21:1
Ramboux, Sylvianne
We Lived Through Buchenwald 1947,Jl 24,27:3
Rambova, Natasha (Miscellaneous)
Salome 1923,Ja 1,18:1
Salome 1967,F 15,42:4
Rameau, Emil
Monna Vanna 1923,S 25,8:2
Nur am Rhein 1931,S 25,28:7
Gaslight 1944,My 5,17:2
Greenwich Village 1944,S 28,26:2
So Dark the Night 1946,D 7,16:2
Time Out of Mind 1947,Ap 7,20:1
Rameau, Hans (Original Author)
Moonlight Sonata 1938,My 10,17:2
Rameau, Hans (Screenwriter)
Confession 1937,Ag 19,23:1
Rat, The 1938,F 28,19:1
Waterloo Bridge 1940,My 17,23:2
We Were Dancing 1942,My 1,23:2
Rameau, Odile
Ramuntcho 1953,Mr 2,19:2

Rameau, Paul H (Screenwriter)
Madame Curie 1943,D 17,23:1
Gaby 1956,My 10,26:3
Ramgord, Freda
Sapphire 1959,N 3,27:1
Ramhardt, Sylvia (Screenwriter)
Situation Hopeless-But not Serious
1965,O 14,53:1
Ramine
Cinerama-South Seas Adventure 1958,Jl 16,26:1
Ramirez
Roots, The (The Cows); Cows, The (The Roots)
1957,S 3,23:2
Ramirez, Carlos
Two Girls and a Sailor 1944,Je 15,16:1
Bathing Beauty 1944,Je 28,20:1
Where Do We Go From Here? 1945,Je 7,25:2
Anchors Aweigh 1945,Jl 20,15:2
Easy to Wed 1946,Jl 12,14:2
Night and Day 1946,Jl 26,16:2
Ramirez, Dario
Bullfighter and the Lady, The 1951,Ap 27,19:2
Ramirez, Rosita
Mare Nostrum 1926,F 16,22:4
Ramokgopa, Tommy
Magic Garden, The 1952,F 6,24:2
Ramon
Wind, The 1928,N 5,26:1
Gold Diggers of 1935 1935,Mr 15,25:2
Thanks a Million 1935,N 14,17:1
Big Country, The 1958,O 2,44:1
Ramond, Harald
Frenchman's Creek 1944,S 21,26:2
Ramos, Beatriz
Pecados de Amor 1934,Ap 24,27:2
Sangre Manda, La 1934,My 15,18:2
Oro y Plata 1934,Ag 29,13:2
Maria Elena 1936,F 18,27:1
El Misterio del Rostro Palido 1937,Ja 4,20:5
Maria Candelaria 1944,S 12,23:7
Mexican Bus ride 1954,Jl 21,18:3
Ramos, Ely Jr
Walls of Hell, The 1965,N 18,55:3
Ramos, Roberto Garcia
Divorcio en Montevideo 1940,Ap 8,15:3
Ramos, Trini
Tango en Broadway, El 1934,D 29,11:3
Rampling, Charlotte
Rotten to the Core 1965,Jl 20,39:2
Georgy Girl 1966,O 18,48:1
Long Duel, The 1967,N 2,58:3
Ramsden, Frances
Mad Wednesday 1951,Ja 25,21:5
Ramsen, Al
City Across the River 1949,Ap 8,31:3
Ramsey, Alicia (Original Author)
Prince of Lovers, The 1927,N 29,31:1
Ramsey, Allan
Juvenile Court 1938,S 12,13:2
Ramsey, Freddy
Walk in the Shadow 1966,S 12,52:5
Ramsey, Logan
Hoodlum Priest, The 1961,Ap 3,28:5
Head 1968,N 7,51:1
Ramsey, Quen
When the Daltons Rode 1940,Ag 23,13:3
Ramsey, Ward
Dinosaurusi 1960,S 9,36:4
Great Impostor, The 1961,Mr 30,24:1
Lover Come Back 1962,F 9,21:1
Ranalow, Frederick
Autumn Crocus 1934,O 25,26:2
Inheritance, The 1951,F 12,19:2
Ranant, Simone
Women Are Weak 1959,Je 9,44:2
Ranavent, George
Paris Calling 1942,Ja 19,21:2
Ranchi, Federica
Goliath and the Dragon 1961,Ja 5,27:2
Violent Summer 1961,My 20,12:1
Rancourt, Jules
His Tiger Lady 1928,My 28,23:2
Rand, Ayn (Original Author)
Night of January 16th, The 1941,D 19,35:1
Fountainhead, The 1949,Jl 9,8:5
Rand, Ayn (Screenwriter)
You Came Along 1945,Jl 5,7:2
Love Letters 1945,Ag 27,22:3
Fountainhead, The 1949,Jl 9,8:5
Rand, Ed
Rendezvous With Annie 1946,S 23,29:3
Crimson Key, The 1947,O 18,9:2
Return of the Frontiersman 1950,Je 10,11:3
Undercover Girl 1950,N 8,37:2
Those Redheads From Seattle 1953,O 1,34:2
Rand, John
Circus, The 1928,Ja 9,20:1
Rand, Michael
Meet Boston Blackie 1941,F 26,17:2
Rand, Sally
Man Bait 1927,Ja 19,21:1
Night of Love, The 1927,Ja 25,18:4
Getting Gertie's Garter 1927,F 9,17:3

His Dog 1927,Ag 16,31:2
Girl in Every Port, A 1928,F 20,14:1
Bolero 1934,F 17,20:3
Randa, Cestmir
Devil's Trap, The 1964,Ag 14,16:1
Transport From Paradise 1967,F 8,22:1
RANDAL
See Also RANDALL, RANDELL
Randal, George
Green Pastures, The 1936,Jl 17,20:1
Randal, Terry
Woman in the Hall, The 1949,Ja 24,16:2
RANDALL
See Also RANDAL, RANDELL
Randall, Addison
Follow the Fleet 1936,F 21,21:2
Love on a Bet 1936,Mr 5,25:2
Don't Turn 'em Loose 1936,S 25,20:2
Flying Hostess 1936,D 14,29:4
Randall, Andre
Amazing Monsieur Fabre, The 1952,S 9,21:2
Goodbye Again 1961,Je 30,32:2
Randall, Bernard
Master Mind, The 1920,S 13,42:1
French Doll, The 1923,S 5,15:3
Ponjola 1923,N 19,19:3
Pretty Ladies 1925,Jl 14,14:1
Classified 1925,N 2,20:1
Skyrocket, The 1926,Ja 26,25:2
Say It Again 1926,Je 7,23:2
Subway Sadie 1926,S 13,18:1
Show Girl 1928,N 5,26:1
Randall, Carl
Reckless 1935,Ap 20,16:1
Randall, Chris
Running Wild 1955,N 12,23:2
Randall, Dick (Producer)
Wild, Wild World 1965,N 22,48:2
Randall, Meg
Romance in the Dark 1938,Mr 21,18:2
You and Me 1938,Je 2,19:1
Criss Cross 1949,Mr 12,10:2
Life of Riley, The 1949,Ap 18,18:4
Ma and Pa Kettle 1949,Ag 12,13:2
Abandoned Woman 1949,O 27,35:3
Ma and Pa Kettle Back on the Farm
1951,My 11,32:3
Randall, Pamela
Women in War 1940,My 30,21:2
Lady in Distress 1942,F 16,21:2
Randall, Rebel
Happy Go Lucky 1943,Mr 25,25:1
Fall In 1943,My 15,13:3
Randall, Stuart
Tomahawk 1951,F 19,19:2
Tomorrow Is Another Day 1951,Ag 9,17:5
Pride of St Louis, The 1952,My 3,17:5
Carbine Williams 1952,My 8,37:2
Rancho Notorious 1952,My 15,39:5
Pony Soldier 1952,D 20,15:2
Park Row 1952,D 22,20:2
Hiawatha 1952,D 26,20:4
Destination Gobi 1953,My 30,7:1
Pony Express 1953,Je 6,8:6
Pickup on South Street 1953,Je 18,38:2
Arena 1953,Jl 23,20:2
Vickie 1953,S 8,26:3
Southwest Passage 1954,S 11,11:2
Female on the Beach 1955,Ag 20,20:2
Pardners 1956,Jl 26,20:2
Big Fisherman, The 1959,Ag 6,18:1
Randall, Sue
Desk Set 1957,My 16,28:2
Randall, Tony
Oh Men! Oh Women! 1957,F 22,25:2
Will Success Spoil Rock Hunter 1957,S 12,37:5
No Down Payment 1957,O 31,41:1
Mating Game, The 1959,Ap 30,37:1
Pillow Talk 1959,O 7,47:2
Adventures of Huckleberry Fin, The
1960,Ag 4,17:1
Let's Make Love 1960,S 9,36:1
Lover Come Back 1962,F 9,21:1
Boys' Night Out 1962,Je 22,15:2
Island of Love 1963,Je 13,30:4
Brass Bottle, The 1964,My 21,42:1
7 Faces of Dr Lao 1964,Jl 23,19:1
Send Me no Flowers 1964,N 13,30:1
Fluffy 1965,O 21,57:2
Alphabet Murders, The 1966,Jl 12,36:2
Bang, Bang, You're Dead 1967,Ja 19,41:2
Randazzo, Rosalia
Tormento 1953,Ap 4,9:2
Randazzo, Teddy
Mister Rock and Roll 1957,O 17,42:2
Hey, Lets Twist 1962,F 8,25:1
RANDELL
See Also RANDAL, RANDALL
Randell, Andreas (Composer)
Vaermlaenningarna 1932,N 18,23:2
Randell, Ron
Night of Nights, The 1939,D 28,17:1
Pacific Adventure 1947,N 26,18:2

Randell, Ron— Cont
It Had to be You 1947,D 8,35:2
Sign of the Ram, The 1948,Mr 4,30:2
Mating of Millie, The 1948,Mr 13,12:2
Loves of Carmen, The 1948,S 3,16:2
Lorna Doone 1951,S 21,19:4
Brigand, The 1952,Jl 26,9:2
Mississippi Gambler, The 1953,Ja 30,25:1
Kiss Me Kate 1953,N 6,23:2
I Am a Camera 1955,Ag 9,29:1
Desert Sands 1955,N 19,22:7
Beyond Mombasa 1957,My 31,14:2
Story of Esther Costello, The 1957,N 6,43:1
Most Dangerous Man Alive 1961,Jl 5,29:2
King of Kings 1961,O 12,41:2
Longest Day, The 1962,O 5,28:1
Follow the Boys 1963,F 28,8:2
Randels, Bella
Naked Prey, The 1966,Je 15,40:1
Randi, Ermanno
Tragic Hunt 1948,O 22,30:2
Brief Rapture 1952,F 28,23:2
Cliff of Sin, The 1952,N 22,16:5
Young Caruso, The 1953,O 13,34:4
Randi, Lori
Cinderella 1953,My 15,20:2
Randolf, Anders
Love Flower, The 1920,Ag 23,9:2
Mighty Lak' a Rose 1923,Mr 20,24:3
Bright Shawl, The 1923,Ap 23,18:3
Eternal Struggle, The 1923,O 16,21:3
Behold This Woman 1924,Jl 22,9:1
In Hollywood with Potash and Perlmutter
1924,S 30,27:3
Souls for Sables 1925,S 15,12:1 (Incorrect in this
edition; use 1925,S 15,29:1 elsewhere)
Seven Keys to Baldpate 1925,N 3,25:4
Black Pirate, The 1926,Mr 9,21:4
Ranson's Folly 1926,My 31,10:2
Climbers, The 1927,My 4,29:2
Old San Francisco 1927,Je 23,23:3
Dearie 1927,Jl 4,20:3
Jazz Singer, The 1927,O 7,24:4
College Widow, The 1927,N 7,26:4
Gateway of the Moon, The 1928,Ja 9,20:1
Three Sinners 1928,Ap 23,20:2
Big Killing, The 1928,Jl 2,11:2
Powder my Back 1928,Ag 7,25:4
Women They Talk About 1928,O 15,16:1
Me, Gangster 1928,O 22,29:1
Viking, The 1928,N 29,32:4
Noah's Ark 1929,Mr 13,28:6
Dangerous Curves 1929,Jl 15,25:1
Young Nowheres 1929,O 2,28:4
Last Performance, The 1929,N 4,28:1
Kiss, The 1929,N 16,25:2
Show of Shows 1929,N 21,24:5
Son of the Gods 1930,Ja 31,24:1
Way of all Men, The 1930,S 20,15:4
Maybe It's Love 1930,O 28,23:2
Going Wild 1931,Ja 26,21:1
Laurel and Hardy's Laughing 20's 1965,N 18,55:2
Randolf, Rold (Director)
Tod Ueber Schanghai 1933,D 16,12:4
Sporck'schen Jaeger, Die 1937,F 22,13:2
Randolf, Rolf (Director)
O Alte Burschenherrlichkeit 1932,Je 18,9:2
Randolph, Amanda
No Way Out 1950,Ag 17,23:1
She's Working her Way Through College
1952,Jl 10,27:2
Randolph, Donald
Bride of Vengeance 1949,Ap 7,38:2
Under the Gun 1951,F 23,33:2
Fourteen Hours 1951,Mr 7,43:2
Gambling House 1951,Mr 19,23:2
Prince Who Was a Thief, The 1951,Jl 4,13:2
Night Without Sleep 1952,S 27,13:2
Assignment-Paris 1952,O 25,12:6
Dream Wife 1953,Jl 30,20:1
Mad Magician, The 1954,My 20,38:2
Gambler From Natchez, The 1954,Ag 14,8:2
Khyber Patrol 1954,S 20,19:2
Adventures of Haji Baba, The 1954,O 9,8:7
Phffft 1954,N 11,43:2
Chief Crazy Horse 1955,Ap 28,25:1
Rawhide Years, The 1956,Je 16,12:2
Cowboy 1958,F 20,29:5
Randolph, Elsie
This'll Make You Whistle 1938,N 1,27:2
Larceny Street 1941,Ja 6,11:2
Randolph, Isabel
Look Who's Laughing 1941,D 25,33:2
Here We Go Again 1942,O 12,12:3
Standing Room Only 1944,F 17,17:2
Practically Yours 1945,Mr 29,18:2
Our Hearts Were Growing Up 1946,Ag 12,17:2
If You Knew Susie 1948,F 23,19:2
Randolph, Jane
Falcon's Brother, The 1942,O 3,9:5
Cat People 1942,D 7,22:2
Falcon Strikes Back, The 1943,Ap 2,17:4
Curse of the Cat People, The 1944,Mr 4,11:1
T-Men 1948,Ja 23,28:3

Randolph, Jane— Cont
Open Secret 1948,F 2,15:2
Abbott and Costello Meet Frankenstein 1948,Jl 29,17:2
Randolph, John
Seconds 1966,O 6,56:1
Pretty Poison 1968,O 25,55:1
Randolph, Lillian
Little Men 1940,D 9,23:2
West Point Widow 1941,S 11,21:5
Mexican Spitfire Sees a Ghost 1942,Jl 31,11:2
Great Gildersleeve, The 1942,D 18,36:8
Gildersleeve's Bad Day 1943,Je 11,23:1
It's a Wonderful Life 1946,D 23,19:2
Bachelor and the Bobby-Soxer, The 1947,Jl 25,12:5
Once More, my Darling 1949,S 26,17:1
Dear Brat 1951,Jl 5,21:2
That's My Boy 1951,Ag 2,18:1
Randolph, Marion
Oh! Susanna 1951,Mr 30,28:5
Random, Bob
This Property is Condemned 1966,Ag 4,24:1
Randone, B L (Director)
Man of the Sea 1948,Ja 24,11:2
Randone, Salvo
Family Diary 1963,N 12,48:1
Salvatore Giuliano 1964,S 18,28:1
Magnificent Cuckold 1965,Ap 20,42:1
10th Victim, The 1965,D 21,46:1
We Still Kill the Old Way 1968,F 29,28:1
Raner, Ali
Three 1967,Je 30,30:1
Raner, Jaroslav
Transport From Paradise 1967,F 8,22:1
Ranevskaya, F
Marriage 1945,F 22,31:3
Spring 1948,Mr 15,26:2
Boule de Suif 1958,My 5,24:1
Girl With the Guitar, The 1960,F 1,22:4
Ranft, Albert
For Her Sake 1930,N 11,29:1
Rangda
Wajan 1938,Ap 18,11:1
Rangel, Arturo Soto
Silk, Blood and Sun 1943,Ja 30,10:6
Virgin of Guadalupe, The 1943,My 15,13:3
Maria Candelaria 1944,S 12,23:7
St Francis of Assisi 1947,Ap 5,12:5
Treasure of Sierra Madre 1948,Ja 24,11:2
Ranger, Clark
New Faces 1954,F 20,8:7
Ranger, Ralph (Composer)
Moon Over Miami 1941,Jl 5,14:2
Rango (Orangutan)
Rango 1931,F 19,20:4
Rani, Paul
Show People 1928,N 12,18:2
Rankin, Arthur
Copperhead, The 1920,F 9,10:3
Call of the Canyon, The 1923,D 17,23:1
Vanity's Price 1924,O 8,16:2
Black Swan, The 1924,N 25,26:1
Broken Laws 1925,Ja 21,19:3
Sun Up 1925,Ag 18,14:3
Volga Boatman, The 1926,Ap 14,21:1
Old Loves and New 1926,Ap 20,24:7
Dearie 1927,Jl 4,20:3
Blood Ship, The 1927,Jl 19,27:2
Finders Keepers 1928,Mr 5,21:3
Submarine 1928,Ag 31,23:3
Wolf of Wall Street, The 1929,Ja 28,21:1
Glad Rag Doll, The 1929,Je 3,27:2
Fall of Eve, The 1929,Je 18,29:4
Terror Trail 1933,F 11,11:3
Case of the Missing Man, The 1935,N 23,23:2
Rankin, Caroline
Lottery Man, The 1919,O 6,15:1
Village Blacksmith, The 1922,N 3,17:5
Rankin, Catherine
Three Must-Get-Theres, The 1922,Ag 28,14:1
Rankin, Doris
Copperhead, The 1920,F 9,10:3
Night Angel, The 1931,Je 11,28:4
Rankin, William (Original Author)
I've Got Your Number 1934,F 3,9:3
Counterfeit 1936,Jl 20,11:1
Time Out for Romance 1937,Mr 13,23:2
Girl With Ideas, A 1938,Ja 1,11:2
St Louis Blues 1939,F 9,17:2
Street of Missing Men 1939,Je 1,31:3
Dixie 1943,Je 24,26:2
Fighting Father Dunne 1948,Je 25,26:2
South Sea Woman 1953,Je 4,33:6
Rankin, William (Screenwriter)
Counterfeit 1936,Jl 20,11:1
Ranshoff, Doris (Original Author)
Jacqueline Kennedy's Asian Journey 1962,D 26,5:2
Ransohoff, Martin (Original Author)
Sandpiper, The 1965,Jl 16,14:1
Ransohoff, Martin (Producer)
Boys' Night Out 1962,Je 22,15:2
Americanization of Emily, The 1964,O 28,51:1

Sandpiper, The 1965,Jl 16,14:1
Cincinnati Kid, The 1965,O 28,48:1
Don't Make Waves 1967,Je 21,36:2
Our Mother's House 1967,O 10,56:1
Eye of the Devil 1967,D 7,60:1
Ice Station Zebra 1968,D 21,49:1
Ransom, Edith
Lilies of the Field 1924,Mr 17,19:1
Ransom, Frank
Overlanders, The 1946,D 20,31:2
Kangaroo 1952,My 17,22:7
Ransom, Herbert
Sophie Lang Goes West 1937,S 30,19:2
Ransom, Suzanne
Prodigal, The 1931,Je 27,20:3
Ransome, Prunella
Far From the Madding Crowd 1967,O 19,59:1
Ransome, Stephen (Original Author)
Who Is Hope Schuyler 1942,My 22,27:1
Ranson, Lois
Cheers for Miss Bishop 1941,Mr 14,17:2
Pierre of the Plains 1942,Jl 30,17:3
Ranson, Marcelle
Naked Autumn 1963,N 15,25:3
Ransome, Mary C (Original Author)
No Greater Sin 1941,Ag 29,18:2
Rao, Enakshi Rama
Shiraz 1929,Mr 19,37:2
Rao, Uma
Maya 1966,Je 23,29:4
RAPAPORT
See Also RAPPAPORT
Rapaport, A
Hill 24 Doesn't Answer 1955,N 3,37:1
Tel Aviv Taxi 1956,D 31,10:7
Rapee, Erno (Composer)
Man Without a Country, The 1925,F 12,16:1
Film Record of the Eucharistic Congress 1926,N 9,31:1
Dead March, The 1937,S 20,19:1 (In Addenda)
Rapee, Erno (Director)
4 Devils 1928,O 4,26:3
Rapee, Erno (Miscellaneous)
Iron Horse, The 1924,Ag 29,6:1
Last Man on Earth, The 1924,D 13,12:4
Mother Machree 1928,Mr 6,20:3
Rapelye, Robert
Ramparts We Watch, The 1940,S 20,27:1
Rapf, Harry (Producer)
Hollywood Party 1934,My 26,12:2
Wicked Woman, A 1935,Ja 1,24:1
Night is Young, The 1935,Ja 14,11:2
Murder Man, The 1935,Jl 27,16:2
It's in the Air 1935,N 8,18:2
Whipsaw 1936,Ja 25,18:4
Tough Guy 1936,Mr 14,10:1
Three Wise Guys, The 1936,My 23,12:2
We Went to College 1936,Jl 27,20:2
Piccadilly Jim 1936,Ag 31,19:1
Mad Holiday 1936,N 26,39:2
Old Hutch 1936,D 7,27:4
Good Old Soak 1937,Ap 20,25:3
Live, Love and Learn 1937,N 19,27:2
Thoroughbreds Don't Cry 1937,N 26,27:4
Bad Man of Brimstone, The 1938,F 4,17:2
Everybody Sing 1938,Mr 11,15:3
Stablemates 1938,O 21,27:2
Let Freedom Ring 1939,Mr 10,19:2
Ice Follies of 1939 1939,Mr 17,25:2
Forty Little Mothers 1940,Ap 19,25:2
Gallant Bess 1946,D 6,27:6
Scene of the Crime 1949,Jl 29,12:2
Rapf, Matthew (Original Author)
Sellout, The 1952,My 31,12:7
Rapf, Maurice (Original Author)
Bad Man of Brimstone, The 1938,F 4,17:2
Sharpshooters 1938,D 5,19:2
Rapf, Maurice (Producer)
They Gave Him a Gun 1937,My 14,21:1
Rapf, Maurice (Screenwriter)
We Went to College 1936,Jl 27,20:2
They Gave Him a Gun 1937,My 14,21:1
Winter Carnival 1939,Jl 28,14:2
Song of the South 1946,N 28,40:2
So Dear to my Heart 1949,Ja 31,14:2
Raphael, Frederic (Screenwriter)
Nothing but the Best 1964,Jl 14,28:1
Why Bother to Knock 1965,F 4,24:2
Darling 1965,Ag 4,20:1
Two for the Road 1967,Ap 28,36:2
Far From the Madding Crowd 1967,O 19,59:1
Raphael, John Nathaniel (Original Author)
Peter Ibbetson 1935,N 8,18:2
Raphaelson, Samson (Original Author)
Jazz Singer, The 1927,O 7,24:4
Accent on Youth 1935,Ag 12,10:3
Skylark 1941,N 20,39:2
Perfect Marriage, The 1947,Ja 16,30:3
Mr Music 1950,D 21,34:3
Jazz Singer, The 1953,Ja 14,27:3
Hilda Crane 1956,My 3,35:2

Raphaelson, Samson (Screenwriter)
Last of Mrs Cheyney, The 1937,F 19,15:1
Angel 1937,N 4,29:1
Shop Around the Corner, The 1940,Ja 26,13:2
Suspicion 1941,N 21,23:2
Heaven Can Wait 1943,Ag 12,15:1
Green Dolphin Street 1947,O 16,34:2
That Lady in Ermine 1948,Ag 25,31:2
In the Good Old Summertime 1949,Ag 5,23:2
Main Street to Broadway 1953,O 14,34:1
Raphaelson, Samuel (Screenwriter)
Smiling Lieutenant, The 1931,My 23,13:4
Raphel, Jerome
Connection, The 1962,O 4,44:1
Cool World, The 1964,Ap 21,42:1
Rapp, Philip (Miscellaneous)
Strike Me Pink 1936,Ja 17,15:2
Rapp, Philip (Original Author)
Wild and Wonderful 1964,Je 11,27:4
Rapp, Philip (Screenwriter)
Wonder Man 1945,Je 9,17:2
Inspector General, The 1949,D 31,9:2
Ain't Misbehavin' 1955,Jl 2,13:2
Rapp, Richard
Midsummer Night's Dream, A 1967,Ap 18,32:1
RAPPAPORT
See Also RAPAPORT
Rappaport, G (Director)
Stars of the Russian Ballet (Swan Lake); Swan Lake (Stars of the Russian Ballet) 1954,S 6,9:2
Stars of the Russian Ballet (The Flames of Paris); Flames of Paris, The (Stars of the Russian Ballet) 1954,S 6,9:2
Stars of the Russian Ballet (The Fountain of Bakhchisarai); Fountain of Bakhchisarai (Stars of the Russian Ballet) 1954,S 6,9:2
Rappaport, H (Director)
Professor Mamlock 1938,N 8,26:2
Vanka 1943,Mr 25,25:3
Leningrad Music Hall 1943,N 6,16:3
Taxi to Heaven 1944,My 25,16:3
Concert of Stars 1953,Mr 2,19:4
Song Over Moscow 1964,N 23,52:1
Rappaport, H (Screenwriter)
Professor Mamlock 1938,N 8,26:2
Rappel, Malvina
Motel, The Operator 1940,Ja 16,19:3
Rappeneau, Jean-Paul (Director)
Vie de Chateau, La 1967,Mr 21,35:1
Rappeneau, Jean-Paul (Screenwriter)
Zazie 1961,N 21,45:5
Very Private Affair, A 1962,S 29,15:1
That Man From Rio 1964,Je 9,30:1
Marco the Magnificent 1966,D 15,60:1
Vie de Chateau, La 1967,Mr 21,35:1
Rapper, Irving (Director)
Shining Victory 1941,My 31,14:1
One Foot in Heaven 1941,N 14,28:3
Gay Sisters, The 1942,Ag 15,14:2
Now, Voyager 1942,O 23,25:3
Adventures of Mark Twain, The 1944,My 4,25:5
Corn is Green, The 1945,Mr 30,18:2
Rhapsody in Blue 1945,Je 28,22:2
Deception 1946,O 19,15:3
Voice of the Turtle, The 1947,D 26,22:4
Anna Lucasta 1949,Ag 12,13:2
Glass Menagerie, The 1950,S 29,31:5
Another Man's Poison 1952,Ja 7,14:3
Bad for Each Other 1953,D 24,9:3
Forever Female 1954,Ja 13,26:2
Brave One, The 1957,Mr 22,26:1
Marjorie Morningstar 1958,Ap 25,32:2
Miracle, The 1959,N 13,25:4
Story of Joseph and his Brethern, The 1962,D 1,17:1
Rappold, Rudi (Miscellaneous)
Vali 1967,Je 2,34:2
Rappold, Rudi (Narrator)
Vali 1967,Je 2,34:2
Rapport, Fred
Conspiracy 1939,Ag 23,19:2
Raqua, Charles
East of Suez 1925,Ja 26,22:1
Raquello, Edward
Charlie Chan at Monte Carlo 1937,D 18,18:1
Patient in Room 18, The 1938,Ap 22,15:6
Last Express, The 1938,O 11,24:4
Torchy Gets her Man 1938,N 18,25:3
Girl From Mexico, The 1939,Je 8,31:4
Missing Daughters 1939,Je 12,14:5
Girl and the Gambler, The 1939,Je 28,17:3
Calling Philo Vance 1940,F 9,15:3
Rarben, Joan
Man in the White Suit, The 1952,Ap 1,35:2
Rareuil, Colette
Mirages De Paris 1933,D 25,28:3
Rarkhoudian, P (Director)
Power of Evil, The 1929,Ag 12,22:2
Ras, Eva
Affair of the Heart, An 1967,S 23,20:3
Love Affair, or the Case of the Missing Switchboard Operator; Affair of the Heart, An 1968,F 7,38:3

Rasbotnik, Hans (Screenwriter)
Bimbo the Great 1961,Je 29,26:1

Rascel, Renato
Overcoat, The 1953,O 13,34:1
Half a Century of Songs 1954,O 30,15:6
Gran Varieta 1955,Ap 11,29:5
Seven Hills of Rome 1958,Ja 28,24:2 (Incorrect in this edition; use 1958,Ja 31,24:2 elsewhere)
Monte Carlo Story, The 1958,F 13,23:2

Rasch, Albertina (Miscellaneous)
Firefly, The 1937,S 2,17:2
Rosalie 1937,D 31,9:2
Girl of the Golden West, The 1938,Mr 25,15:2
Sweethearts 1938,D 23,16:2

Rasch, Albertina, Ballet
Hollywood Revue, The 1929,Ag 15,20:5

Raschig, Kraft
Threepenny Opera, The 1960,Jl 11,24:4

Rascovich, Mark (Original Author)
Bedford Incident, The 1965,N 3,43:1

Rashevskaya, N
Great Citizen, The 1939,Ja 16,11:2

Rashevskaya, Natalia (Director)
Fathers and Sons 1960,D 26,27:2

Rashevskaya, Natalia (Producer)
Fathers and Sons 1960,D 26,27:2

Rashevskaya, Natalia (Screenwriter)
Fathers and Sons 1960,D 26,27:2

Rasimi, Eddy
Night Watch, The; Trou, Le 1964,My 27,46:1

Raskie, Barney
Running Wild 1927,Je 14,33:2

Raskin, A (Screenwriter)
Spring 1948,Mr 15,26:2

Raskin, David (Composer)
Big Hand for the Little Lady, A 1966,Je 9,54:2

Raskin, Sherman
Take a Giant Step 1961,Mr 6,28:2

Rasmussen, Knud (Miscellaneous)
Bride of Palo 1934,My 27,X,4:2 (In Addenda)

Rasmussen, Knud (Producer)
Wedding of Palo, The 1937,Mr 2,17:1

Rasmussen, Knud (Screenwriter)
Wedding of Palo, The 1937,Mr 2,17:1

Rasp, Fritz
Last Waltz, The 1927,N 14,26:1
Loves of Jeanne Ney, The 1928,Jl 10,17:3
Mystic Mirror, The 1928,O 1,23:1
Spies 1929,Mr 5,29:1
Prince of Rogues, The 1929,Jl 30,19:4
By Rocket to the Moon 1931,F 7,11:1
Dreigroschenoper, Die; Beggar's Opera, The 1931,My 18,21:2
Karamazof 1931,S 21,20:2
Emil und die Detektive 1931,D 21,28:4
Lockvogel 1935,Ja 5,20:3
Judas von Tirol, Der 1935,Ap 27,20:7
Klein Dorrit 1935,O 19,21:2
Grenzfeuer 1936,D 19,16:1
Nanu, Sie Kennen Korff noch Nicht?; So, You Don't Know Korff Yet? 1939,My 22,15:3
Leidenschaft; Passion 1940,S 24,26:6
Somewhere in Berlin 1949,Ag 16,19:3
Threepenny Opera, The 1960,Jl 11,24:4

Raspor, Vicko (Screenwriter)
Legends of Anika 1956,Ap 19,35:1

Rassington, Norman
Hard Day's Night, A 1964,Ag 12,41:1

Rasson, Arthur (Director)
You'd Be Surprised 1926,S 27,27:3

Rasumng, Mikhail
Stars Are Singing, The 1953,Mr 12,24:2

Rasumny, Mikhail
Comrade X 1940,D 26,23:1
Hold Back the Dawn 1941,O 2,29:1
Shanghai Gesture, The 1941,D 26,21:2
This Gun for Hire 1942,My 14,23:2
Wake Island 1942,S 2,19:2
Road to Morocco 1942,N 12,30:1
For Whom the Bell Tolls 1943,Jl 15,25:2
Hostages 1943,O 11,23:2
And the Angels Sing 1944,Jl 13,14:2
Practically Yours 1945,Mr 29,18:2
Royal Scandal, A 1945,Ap 12,19:2
Unseen, The 1945,My 14,20:5
Medal for Benny, A 1945,My 24,15:2
Masquerade in Mexico 1945,N 29,27:2
Stork Club, The 1945,D 20,18:2
Heartbeat 1946,My 11,22:4
Anna and the King of Siam 1946,Je 21,20:2
Our Hearts Were Growing Up 1946,Ag 12,17:2
Holiday in Mexico 1946,Ag 16,19:3
Her Husband's Affairs 1947,N 14,29:2
Pirates of Monterey 1947,D 17,41:4
Song of my Heart 1948,Mr 5,17:3
Saigon 1948,Ap 1,30:5
Kissing Bandit, The 1948,N 19,35:2
Pirates of Capri, The 1949,D 26,33:5
Anything Can Happen 1952,Ap 4,21:1
Tonight We Sing 1953,F 13,17:2
Hot Blood 1956,Mr 24,14:2

Ratcliffe, E J
Disraeli 1921,Ag 22,13:6
Wine of Youth 1924,Ag 11,16:1
Sundown 1924,D 1,17:3
Introduce Me 1925,Mr 9,21:1
Man on the Box, The 1925,S 28,24:1
Black Pirate, The 1926,Mr 9,21:4
Skinner's Dress Suit 1926,My 3,27:1
Rolling Home 1926,Je 8,22:1
Winning of Barbara Worth, The 1926,N 29,16:3
Notorious Lady, The 1927,Ap 11,18:3
Framed 1927,Je 20,25:3
Prince of Head-Waiters 1927,Jl 11,23:5
Smile, Brother, Smile 1927,Ag 29,21:1
Cheating Cheaters 1927,D 6,27:1
Publicity Madness 1927,D 12,30:6
Jazz Age, The 1929,Ja 7,36:2
Four Feathers, The 1929,Je 13,35:4
Show of Shows 1929,N 21,24:5
Skinner Steps Out 1929,D 7,19:3
Sally 1929,D 24,14:4
Cohens and the Kelleys In Scotland, The 1930,Mr 10,24:1
I Loved a Woman 1933,S 22,14:2

Ratcliffe, Jane
Uncle, The 1966,Jl 19,34:1

Rath, E J (Original Author)
Clear the Decks 1929,Ap 1,22:1
Fast Life 1932,D 24,11:4

Rath, Fred (Original Author)
Give Out, Sisters 1942,Ag 28,22:3

Rathaus, Karol (Composer)
Murderer Dimitri Karamasoff, The 1931,Mr 1,VIII,6:7 (In Addenda)
Karamazof 1931,S 21,20:2
Koffer des Herrn O F, Die; Trunks of Mr O F, The 1932,Ja 17,VIII,6:1

Rathbone, Basil
Masked Bride, The 1925,N 30,17:1
Great Deception, The 1926,Ag 9,10:3
Last of Mrs Cheyney, The 1929,Ag 12,22:2
Bishop Murder Case, The 1930,F 1,15:1
Notorious Affair, A 1930,Ap 26,11:1
Lady of Scandal, The 1930,Je 14,9:4
This Mad World 1930,Jl 21,20:3
Flirting Widow, The 1930,Ag 2,16:4
Lady Surrenders, A 1930,O 4,15:2
Sin Takes a Holliday 1930,N 28,23:1
Woman Commands, A 1932,Ja 28,13:2
After the Ball 1933,Mr 20,18:3
Loyalties 1934,O 26,25:1
David Copperfield 1935,Ja 19,8:1
Anna Karenina 1935,Ag 31,16:2
Last Days of Pompeii, The 1935,O 17,29:2
Feather in her Hat, A 1935,O 25,24:5
Tale of Two Cities, A 1935,D 26,21:2
Captain Blood 1935,D 27,14:1
Private Number 1936,Je 12,19:1
Romeo and Juliet 1936,Ag 21,12:2
Garden of Allah, The 1936,N 20,27:2
Love From a Stranger 1937,Ap 19,27:2
Confession 1937,Ag 19,23:1
Make a Wish 1937,S 23,33:1
Tovarich 1937,D 31,9:2
Adventures of Robin Hood, The 1938,My 13,17:2
If I Were King 1938,S 29,31:1
Dawn Patrol 1938,D 24,12:1
Son of Frankenstein 1939,Ja 30,9:2
Hound of the Baskervilles, The 1939,Mr 25,19:2
Sun Never Sets, The 1939,Je 9,26:2
Adventures of Sherlock Holmes, The 1939,S 2,20:1
Rio 1939,O 27,27:2
Tower of London 1939,D 12,37:2
Rhythm on the River 1940,Ag 29,23:2
Mark of Zorro, The 1940,N 4,23:2
Mad Doctor, The 1941,F 27,23:4
Black Cat, The 1941,Ap 26,20:3
International Lady 1941,N 11,29:2
Paris Calling 1942,Ja 19,21:2
Fingers at the Window 1942,Ap 23,27:3
Crossroads 1942,Jl 27,18:2
Sherlock Holmes and the Voice Of Terror 1942,S 19,9:2
Sherlock Holmes and the Secret Weapon 1943,Ja 5,15:2
Above Suspicion 1943,Ag 6,10:3
Sherlock Holmes Faces Death 1943,O 8,15:3
Spider Woman 1944,Ja 17,14:5
Scarlet Claw, The 1944,My 19,12:1
Bathing Beauty 1944,Je 28,20:1
Pearl of Death 1944,Ag 26,15:2
Frenchman's Creek 1944,S 21,26:2
House of Fear, The 1945,Mr 19,23:3
Woman in Green, The 1945,Je 16,10:3
Pursuit to Algiers 1945,O 27,12:2
Terror by Night 1946,F 9,9:2
Heartbeat 1946,My 11,22:4
Dressed to Kill 1946,My 25,12:4
Casanova's Big Night 1954,Ap 19,19:1
We're no Angels 1955,Jl 8,15:2
Court Jester, The 1956,F 2,19:1
Last Hurrah, The 1958,O 24,40:1

Rathbone, Basil — Cont
Tales of Terror 1962,Jl 5,21:2 (In Addenda)
Two Before Zero 1962,N 1,34:1
Comedy of Terrors, The 1964,Ja 23,26:2
Adventures of Marco Polo, The 1965,Ap 8,17:2

Rathbone, Basil (Narrator)
Adventures of Ichabod and Mr Toad, The 1949,O 10,18:2

Rathebe, Dolly
Magic Garden, The 1952,F 6,24:2

Rathmell, John (Original Author)
Marines are Coming, The 1935,F 23,14:7

Rathmell, John (Screenwriter)
Painted Desert 1938,S 14,26:5

Rathnov, Willy
Weekend 1964,Ap 27,24:1

Rathonyi, A
Megvedten Egy Asszony; I Defended a Woman 1939,O 14,13:3

Rathonyi, A (Director)
Fizessen Nagysag 1937,Je 4,27:3
Gyimesi Vadvirag; Wildflower of Gyimes 1939,O 21,12:3

Rathonyi, August (Director)
Tisztelet a Kivetelnek 1937,Je 14,26:3

Rathvon, Helen H (Producer)
Sun Sets at Dawn, The 1951,Ja 15,13:1

Rathvon, N Peter (Producer)
1984 1956,O 1,31:1

Ratib, Gamil
Lawrence of Arabia 1962,D 17,5:6

Ratkay, Marton
Piri Mindont Tud 1933,Ja 26,12:3
Tisztelet a Kivetelnek 1937,Je 14,26:3

Ratoff, Gregory
Symphony of Six Million 1932,Ap 15,23:1
What Price Hollywood 1932,Jl 16,5:5
Skyscraper Souls 1932,Ag 5,11:2
Once in a Lifetime 1932,O 29,18:4
Under-Cover Man 1932,D 5,21:2
Secrets of the French Police 1932,D 12,18:4
Sweepings 1933,Mr 24,22:3
Professional Sweetheart 1933,Jl 14,15:3
I'm no Angel 1933,O 14,18:2
Headline Shooters 1933,O 23,18:3
Broadway Thru a Keyhole 1933,N 2,18:3
Sitting Pretty 1933,D 2,9:3
Girl Without a Room 1933,D 7,26:3
Let's Fall in Love 1934,Ja 22,12:3
George White's Scandals 1934,Mr 16,24:2
Remember Last Night? 1935,N 21,27:2
King of Burlesque 1936,Ja 16,25:2
Under Two Flags 1936,My 1,19:1
Road to Glory, The 1936,Ag 6,22:1
Sing, Baby, Sing 1936,S 12,20:1
Trouble Ahead 1936,S 21,26:5
Under Your Spell 1936,N 7,15:2
Seventh Heaven 1937,Mr 26,25:1
Top of the Town 1937,Mr 27,19:2
Cafe Metropole 1937,Ap 29,17:1
Sally, Irene and Mary 1938,F 26,9:2
Gateway 1938,Ag 8,9:2
Great Profile, The 1940,O 18,25:1
All About Eve 1950,O 14,13:2
Operation X 1950,D 11,31:2
O Henry's Full House (The Last Leaf 1952,O 17,33:1
Sun Also Rises, The 1957,Ag 24,12:2
Once More With Feeling 1960,F 12,22:2
Exodus 1960,D 16,44:1
Big Gamble, The 1961,S 2,19:2

Ratoff, Gregory (Director)
Sins of Man 1936,Je 19,17:2
Lancer Spy 1937,N 4,29:1
Wife, Husband and Friend 1939,F 25,19:2
Rose of Washington Square 1939,My 6,21:2
Hotel for Women 1939,Ag 26,20:2
Intermezzo, A Love Story 1939,O 6,31:1
Daytime Wife 1939,N 24,29:1
Barricade 1939,D 9,18:2
I Was an Adventuress 1940,My 20,13:2
Public Deb No 1 1940,S 18,19:2
Adam Had Four Sons 1941,Mr 28,26:6
Men In her Life, The 1941,D 12,35:1
Corsican Brothers, The 1942,Ja 16,25:4
Two Yanks in Trinidad 1942,Ap 6,19:4
Footlight Serenade 1942,S 10,30:3
Something to Shout About 1943,Ap 8,27:3
Heat's on, The 1943,N 26,29:2
Song of Russia 1944,F 11,17:2
Irish Eyes Are Smiling 1944,N 8,27:1
Where Do We Go From Here? 1945,Je 7,25:2
Paris Underground 1945,O 20,8:2
Do You Love Me 1946,My 25,12:2
Carnival in Costa Rica 1947,Mr 29,21:2
Moss Rose 1947,Jl 3,14:2
Black Magic 1949,N 9,37:2
If This Be Sin 1950,Jl 1,9:2
Operation X 1950,D 11,31:2
Taxi 1953,Ja 22,20:3
Oscar Wilde 1960,Je 21,28:2

Ratoff, Gregory (Original Author)
Great Flirtation, The 1934,Je 22,16:5
Cafe Metropole 1937,Ap 29,17:1

Ratoff, Gregory (Original Author) — Cont
You Can't Have Everything 1937,Ag 4,15:2
Ratoff, Gregory (Producer)
Men In her Life, The 1941,D 12,35:1
Something to Shout About 1943,Ap 8,27:3
Black Magic 1949,N 9,37:2
If This Be Sin 1950,Jl 1,9:2
Operation X 1950,D 11,31:2
Ratomsky, V
Dream of a Cossack 1952,F 18,15:2
Rattigan, Terence (Original Author)
French Without Tears 1940,Ap 29,12:2
Winslow Boy, The 1950,Je 7,34:4
While the Sun Shines 1950,Jl 1,9:2
Browning Version, The 1951,O 30,33:2
Breaking Through the Sound Barrier
1952,N 7,19:1
Man Who Loved Redheads, The 1955,Jl 26,29:2
Deep Blue Sea, The 1955,O 13,35:2
Prince and the Showgirl 1957,Je 14,22:2
Separate Tables 1958,D 19,2:7
Rattigan, Terence (Screenwriter)
Quiet Wedding 1941,D 29,27:4
Avengers, The 1942,N 25,18:2
Johnny in the Clouds 1945,N 16,16:2
Journey Together 1946,Mr 4,16:5
Her Man Gilbey 1949,Je 9,35:2
Bond Street 1950,Mr 30,40:6
Winslow Boy, The 1950,Je 7,34:4
While the Sun Shines 1950,Jl 1,9:2
Browning Version, The 1951,O 30,33:2
Young Scarface 1951,N 8,35:2
Breaking Through the Sound Barrier
1952,N 7,19:1
Final Test, The 1954,Ja 26,21:5
Man Who Loved Redheads, The 1955,Jl 26,29:2
Deep Blue Sea, The 1955,O 13,35:2
Prince and the Showgirl 1957,Je 14,22:2
Separate Tables 1958,D 19,2:7
V I P's, The 1963,S 20,29:1
Yellow Rolls-Royce, The 1965,My 14,42:2
Raucher, Herman (Screenwriter)
Sweet November 1968,F 9,55:1
Rauchwergher, M (Composer)
Lonely White Sail 1938,My 7,18:1
Morning Star 1962,Ag 20,18:2
Raucourt, Jules
Prunelia 1918,Je 3,9:3
Spectre Vert, Le 1930,Je 8,IX,6:1
Rauet
Passion Of Joan Of Arc, The 1929,Mr 29,21:1
Passion of Jeanne d'Arc, The 1929,Mr 31,VIII,7:1
Rauh, Stanley (Original Author)
Cross Country Cruise 1934,Ja 20,12:3
Hold That Kiss 1938,Je 11,9:1
Cisco Kid and the Lady, The 1939,D 25,29:2
Harmon of Michigan 1941,O 2,29:2
A-Haunting We Will Go 1942,Ag 3,18:4
Rauh, Stanley (Screenwriter)
Laughing Irish Eyes 1936,Ap 4,11:2
Hold That Kiss 1938,Je 11,9:1
Young as You Feel 1940,Mr 8,25:3
Pier 13 1940,Ag 9,19:3
Michael Shayne, Private Detective
1940,D 19,33:2
Sleepers West 1941,Mr 20,25:3
Dance Hall 1941,Jl 19,16:2
Dressed to Kill 1941,Ag 22,19:3
Cadet Girl 1941,D 11,39:1
Raum, Warren
Robby 1968,Ag 15,46:3
Rauody, Laszlo (Director)
Goose Boy, The 1951,O 13,9:2
Rauscher, Hans
City Without Jews, The 1928,Jl 9,25:1
Rauzena, Fernand
Man to Men 1949,F 21,20:2
Battle of the Rails; (Bataille Du Rail)
1949,D 27,27:2
Cheat, The 1950,O 2,19:3
Rave, Don (Composer)
I Dood It 1943,N 11,29:1
Ravel, Gaston (Director)
Figaro 1929,N 25,22:1
Ravel, Gaston (Producer)
Collier de la Reine, Le; Queen's Necklace, The
1929,D 8,X,7:1
Ravel, Sandra
Enigmatique Monsieur Parkes, L' 1930,S 2,19:3
Those Three French Girls 1930,O 11,21:3
Single Sin, The 1931,Mr 17,34:3
Etoile Disparait, Une; Star Disappears, A
1935,F 9,11:3
Tre Anni Senza Donne 1937,My 27,21:4
Al Buio Insieme 1937,Ag 6,21:3
Ravelle, Rex
Song of Scheherazade 1947,F 27,26:2
Raven, John
San Francisco Story, The 1952,My 10,16:4
Hot Blood 1956,Mr 24,14:2
Ravenskikh, B (Director)
Bride with a Dowry 1954,Ag 23,20:5

Raver, Henry (Producer)
Outwitting the Hun 1918,Jl 1,9:3
Ravetch, Irving (Original Author)
Outriders, The 1950,Mr 9,25:2
Lone Hand 1953,Je 27,7:2
Run for Cover 1955,Ap 30,10:6
Ravetch, Irving (Producer)
Hud 1963,My 29,36:1
Hombre 1967,Mr 22,41:1
Ravetch, Irving (Screenwriter)
Living in a Big Way 1947,O 10,31:4
Outriders, The 1950,Mr 9,25:2
Vengeance Valley 1951,F 16,21:2
Long, Hot Summer, The 1958,Ap 4,16:1
Sound and the Fury, The 1959,Mr 28,11:1
Home from the Hill 1960,Mr 4,19:1
Hud 1963,My 29,36:1
Hombre 1967,Mr 22,41:1
Ravid, Shoshana
Khamishia-Five Tales From Israel
1954,My 7,19:3
Ravof, E Dobron
Petersburg Nights 1934,S 10,20:4
Rawley, James
Creature Walks among Us, The 1956,Ap 27,21:6
Rawley, Monte
Miracle in Harlem 1949,O 24,19:4
Rawlingon, A R (Screenwriter)
King Solomon's Mines 1937,Jl 3,18:1
RAWLINGS
See Also RAWLINS, ROLLINS
Rawlings, Margaret
Roman Holiday 1953,Ag 28,13:1
Rawlings, Marjorie Kinnan (Original Author)
Yearling, The 1947,Ja 24,18:2
Sun comes up, The 1949,My 13,29:2
RAWLINS
See Also RAWLINGS, ROLLINS
Rawlins, John (Director)
Missing Guest, The 1938,S 7,30:7
Six Lessons From Madame La Zonga
1941,F 19,25:2
Dangerous Game, A 1941,Mr 4,20:3
Mr Dynamite 1941,Mr 13,25:2
Mutiny in the Arctic 1941,My 3,20:5
Bombay Clipper 1942,Ja 12,23:3
Sherlock Holmes and the Voice Of Terror
1942,S 19,9:2
Arabian Nights 1942,D 26,15:1
We've Never Been Licked 1943,Ag 19,23:1
Ladies Courageous 1944,Mr 16,17:2
Sudan 1945,Ap 19,22:8
Dick Tracy's Dilemma 1947,Jl 14,14:5
Dick Tracy and Gruesome 1947,S 27,11:2
Massacre River 1949,Jl 15,17:2
Rogue River 1951,F 16,21:4
Rawlinson, A R (Original Author)
Blarney Kiss, The 1933,Ag 19,14:4
This England 1941,N 18,33:2
Rawlinson, A R (Screenwriter)
Man Who Knew too Much, The 1935,Mr 23,11:2
King of the Damned 1936,F 1,9:2
Man With 100 Faces 1938,N 1,27:2
Spies of the Air 1940,Jl 4,12:3
Bad Sister 1948,Je 11,27:3
Angel Street 1952,N 11,25:2
Rawlinson, Gerald
Young Woodley 1930,S 27,21:3
Battle of Gallipoli, The 1931,D 7,16:1
Sleepless Nights 1933,Jl 22,14:2
You Made Me Love You 1934,My 30,14:3
Rawlinson, Herbert
Come Through 1917,Je 18,7:2
Back to the Woods 1918,Jl 22,9:1
Turn of the Wheel 1918,S 2,7:1
Good Gracious, Annabelle 1919,Mr 31,11:3
Passers By 1920,Je 21,13:1
Charge It 1921,Ag 29,14:4
Moonlight and Pretzels 1933,Ag 23,21:2
People's Enemy, The 1935,Ap 30,13:7
Men Without Names 1935,Je 29,16:2
Show Them no Mercy 1935,D 9,25:2
Dancing Feet 1936,Mr 28,11:2
Bullets or Ballots 1936,My 27,27:1
Son Comes Home, A 1936,S 5,7:1
Hollywood Boulevard 1936,S 21,26:4
Mad Holiday 1936,N 26,39:2
God's Country and the Woman 1937,Ja 11,15:5
Mysterious Crossing 1937,F 2,20:5
Nobody's Baby 1937,My 20,17:3
Go Getter, The 1937,Je 4,27:2
That Certain Woman 1937,S 16,29:1
Make a Wish 1937,S 23,33:1
Back in Circulation 1937,O 4,17:1
Over the Goal 1937,O 16,22:2
Love Is on the Air 1937,N 12,27:3
Kid Comes Back, The 1938,F 7,10:2
Women Are Like That 1938,Ap 11,12:2
Hawaii Calls 1938,Ap 29,17:2
Secrets of an Actress 1938,O 8,10:2
Torchy Gets her Man 1938,N 18,25:3
You Can't Get Away With Murder
1939,Mr 25,19:2

Rawlinson, Herbert — Cont
Dark Victory 1939,Ap 21,27:2
Swiss Family Robinson 1940,F 9,15:3
Free, Blonde and 21 1940,Ap 5,25:2
Seven Sinners 1940,N 18,23:2
Flying Wild 1941,Ap 12,19:3
Lady Gangster 1942,Jl 10,13:2
Woman of the Town, The 1944,Mr 6,17:2
Brimstone 1949,O 7,35:3
RAWSON
See Also ROSEN
Rawson, Clayton (Original Author)
Miracles for Sale 1939,Ag 10,15:2
Man Who Wouldn't Die, The 1942,Ap 28,25:5
Ray, Albert (Director)
Midnight Bell, A 1921,Ag 8,12:2
Rich but Honest 1927,My 18,29:3
Publicity Madness 1927,D 12,30:6
Call of the West 1930,My 27,27:2
West of Singapore 1933,Ap 1,18:3
Shriek in the Night, A 1933,Jl 24,11:2
Dancing Man 1934,Jl 16,11:3
Ray, Albert (Original Author)
Cheaters, The 1945,Jl 21,7:2
Ray, Albert (Screenwriter)
Tailor Made Man, A 1922,O 16,20:2
Girl I Loved, The 1923,My 14,18:2
45 Fathers 1937,D 11,22:2
Island in the Sky 1938,My 14,18:1
Keep Smiling 1938,Ag 10,15:2
While New York Sleeps 1938,D 22,25:3
Charlie Chan in Reno 1939,My 31,27:2
Ray, Aldo
Saturday's Hero 1951,S 12,37:2
Marrying Kind, The 1952,Mr 14,27:1
Pat and Mike 1952,Je 19,32:6
Let's Do It Again 1953,O 14,34:3
Miss Sadie Thompson 1953,D 24,9:1
Battle Cry 1955,F 3,18:1
We're no Angels 1955,Jl 8,15:2
Three Stripes in the Sun 1955,N 24,41:2
Nightfall 1957,Ja 24,34:1
Men in War 1957,Mr 20,32:4
Naked and the Dead, The 1958,Ag 7,21:1
God's Little Acre 1958,Ag 14,23:2
Day They Robbed the Bank of England, The
1960,S 5,11:2
Sylvia 1965,F 11,45:1
Johnny Nobody 1965,N 24,35:1
What Did You Do in the War, Daddy?
1966,S 1,28:1
Dead Heat on a Merry-Go-Round
1966,O 13,50:1
Welcome to Hard Times 1967,My 2,56:1
Kill a Dragon 1967,D 7,60:2
Power, The 1968,Mr 7,52:2
Green Berets, The 1968,Je 20,49:1
Ray, Andrew
Mudlark, The 1950,D 25,25:1
Yellow Balloon, The 1954,O 13,28:2
Prize of Gold, A 1955,O 15,19:2
Escapade 1957,Ag 6,30:2
Woman in a Dressing Gown 1957,S 13,15:2
Gideon of Scotland Yard 1959,My 20,38:2
Girl-Getters, The 1966,Ap 13,37:6
Ray, Anthony
Men in War 1957,Mr 20,32:4
Shadows 1961,Mr 22,37:1
War Hunt 1962,Ag 8,35:2
Ray, Bernard B (Director)
Ultima Cita, La 1936,Ja 22,15:6
Crimen de Media Noche, El 1936,F 22,12:3
Ray, Billy
Adam Had Four Sons 1941,Mr 28,26:6
Ray, Buddy
Flood, The 1931,Ap 27,25:1
Our Daily Bread 1934,O 3,25:2
Ray, Charles
Honor Thy Name 1916,Jl 17,9:4
Plain Jane 1916,Ag 28,7:5
Claws of the Hun, The 1918,Jl 1,9:3
Nine o'Clock Town, A 1918,Jl 29,9:3
Law of the North, The 1918,S 9,9:1
String Beans 1918,D 30,7:3
Girl Dodger, The 1919,F 24,11:3
Sheriff's Son, The 1919,Mr 31,11:3
Greased Lightning 1919,Ap 28,13:2
Busher, The 1919,My 26,19:4
Hay Foot, Straw Foot 1919,Je 23,10:3
Bill Henry 1919,Ag 18,9:2
Egg Crate Wallop, The 1919,S 29,16:1
Red Hot Dollars 1919,D 29,7:2
Alarm Clock Andy 1920,Mr 15,13:2
Homer Comes Home 1920,Je 28,13:2
Village Sleuth 1920,S 13,12:1
Peaceful Valley 1920,O 11,19:3
Old Fashioned Boy, An 1920,N 1,13:2
Nineteen and Phyllis 1920,D 27,11:3
Old Swimmin' Hole, The 1921,F 28,16:2
Midnight Bell, A 1921,Ag 8,12:2
Two Minutes to Go 1921,O 24,13:1
R. S. V. P. 1921,D 12,20:2
Tailor Made Man, A 1922,O 16,20:2
Girl I Loved, The 1923,My 14,18:2

Ray, Charles— Cont

Courtship of Myles Standish, The 1923,D 31,9:3
Percy 1925,Mr 25,24:2
Bright Lights 1925,N 18,27:4
Auction Block, The 1926,F 15,16:4
Paris 1926,Je 1,29:3
Fire Brigade, The 1926,D 21,20:2
Nobody's Widow 1927,Ja 13,29:1
Getting Gertie's Garter 1927,F 9,17:3
Vanity 1927,Je 15,31:4
Count of Ten, The 1928,Mr 13,23:3
Garden of Eden, The 1928,Mr 19,26:2
Ladies Should Listen 1934,Jl 28,16:6
Hollywood Boulevard 1936,S 21,26:4
Little Bit of Heaven, A 1940,N 8,24:2

Ray, Charles (Director)
Midnight Bell, A 1921,Ag 8,12:2
R. S. V. P. 1921,D 12,20:2

Ray, Cyril (Miscellaneous)
Edge of the World, The 1938,S 12,13:2

Ray, Ellen
On the Riviera 1951,My 24,47:1

Ray, Emma
Old-Fashioned Way, The 1934,Jl 14,16:5

Ray, Gdeh (Miscellaneous)
Wajan 1938,Ap 18,11:1

Ray, Jacki
In Like Flint 1967,Mr 16,53:2

Ray, Joey
Music in My Heart 1940,Ja 4,19:2
Seventeen 1940,F 29,15:2
Navy Comes Through, The 1942,N 12,30:3
Steel Trap, The 1952,N 13,35:2

Ray, Johnnie
There's no Business Like Show Business
1954,D 17,37:3

Ray, Kail Charan
Aparajito 1959,Ap 29,30:1

Ray, Leah
Bedtime Story, A 1933,Ap 20,20:3
One in a Million 1937,Ja 1,19:3
Holy Terror, The 1937,Ja 30,21:2
Wake up and Live 1937,Ap 24,16:2
Sing and Be Happy 1937,Je 19,20:2
Thin Ice 1937,S 4,8:2
Walking Down Broadway 1938,Ap 1,17:3

Ray, Man (Miscellaneous)
Dreams that Money can Buy 1948,Ap 24,11:2

Ray, Man (Original Author)
Mystery of the Chateau of the Dice, The
1930,Ja 5,VIII,5:1

Ray, Michel
Divided Heart, The 1955,Ag 4,16:1
Brave One, The 1957,Mr 22,26:1
Tin Star, The 1957,O 24,37:2
Lawrence of Arabia 1962,D 17,5:6

Ray, Mona
Uncle Tom's Cabin 1927,N 5,16:2

Ray, Nicholas (Director)
Knock on any Door 1949,F 23,31:2
They Live by Night 1949,N 4,33:2
In a Lonely Place 1950,My 18,37:2
Born to be Bad 1950,S 29,31:5
Flying Leathernecks 1951,S 20,37:1
On Dangerous Ground 1952,F 13,35:2
Lusty Men, The 1952,O 25,12:6
Johnny Guitar 1954,My 28,19:2
Run for Cover 1955,Ap 30,10:6
Rebel without a Cause 1955,O 27,28:3
Hot Blood 1956,Mr 24,14:2
Bigger Than Life 1956,Ag 3,11:2
True Story of Jesse James, The 1957,Mr 23,17:2
Wind Across the Everglades 1958,S 12,21:1
Party Girl 1958,O 29,30:1
Savage Innocents, The 1961,My 25,31:1
King of Kings 1961,O 12,41:2
55 Days at Peking 1963,My 30,20:1

Ray, Nicholas (Original Author)
Rebel without a Cause 1955,O 27,28:3
Circus World 1964,Je 26,34:2

Ray, Nicholas (Screenwriter)
Savage Innocents, The 1961,My 25,31:1

Ray, Phil
Troopship 1938,Ap 26,18:2

Ray, Rene
Passing of the Third Floor Back, The
1936,Ap 29,19:2
Man of Affairs 1937,F 20,9:2
Rat, The 1938,F 28,19:1
Troopship 1938,Ap 26,18:2
Crime Over London 1938,Jl 28,23:2
Housemaster 1939,Ap 10,13:2
Green Cockatoo, The 1947,Jl 19,10:2
If Winter Comes 1948,Ja 23,28:4
Galloping Major, The 1951,D 17,27:2
Circle, The 1959,Ap 16,29:2

Ray, Robert (Original Author)
Ambush 1939,F 9,17:2

Ray, Roger
Hoodlum Priest, The 1961,Ap 3,28:5

Ray, Satyajit (Composer)
Charulata 1965,S 11,16:1
Shakespeare Wallah 1966,Mr 23,40:2
Kanchenjungha 1966,Jl 26,27:2

Ray, Satyajit (Director)
Aparajito 1959,Ap 29,30:1
World of Apu; Apur Sansar 1960,O 5,45:1
Devi 1962,O 8,19:1
Two Daughters (The Conclusion); Conclusion, The
(Two Daughters) 1963,My 1,35:1
Two Daughters (The Postman); Postman, The
(Two Daughters) 1963,My 1,35:1
Music Room, The 1963,O 16,50:6
Mahanagar; Big City, The 1964,S 28,19:1
Charulata 1965,S 11,16:1
Kanchenjungha 1966,Jl 26,27:2
Big City, The; Mahanager 1967,Je 30,30:1

Ray, Satyajit (Original Author)
Kanchenjungha 1966,Jl 26,27:2

Ray, Satyajit (Producer)
World of Apu; Apur Sansar 1960,O 5,45:1
Devi 1962,O 8,19:1
Two Daughters (The Postman); Postman, The
(Two Daughters) 1963,My 1,35:1
Two Daughters (The Conclusion); Conclusion, The
(Two Daughters) 1963,My 1,35:1
Music Room, The 1963,O 16,50:6

Ray, Satyajit (Screenwriter)
Aparajito 1959,Ap 29,30:1
World of Apu; Apur Sansar 1960,O 5,45:1
Devi 1962,O 8,19:1
Two Daughters (The Postman); Postman, The
(Two Daughters) 1963,My 1,35:1
Two Daughters (The Conclusion); Conclusion, The
(Two Daughters) 1963,My 1,35:1
Music Room, The 1963,O 16,50:6
Mahanagar; Big City, The 1964,S 28,19:1
Charulata 1965,S 11,16:1
Kanchenjungha 1966,Jl 26,27:2

Ray, Sonny
Oliver Twist 1933,Ap 13,15:3

Ray, Sudpita
Aparajito 1959,Ap 29,30:1

Ray, Ted
Please Turn Over 1961,Ap 29,12:2

Ray, Terrance
Girls Demand Excitement 1931,F 7,11:1
Young as You Feel 1931,Ag 8,16:3
Two Kinds of Women 1932,Ja 16,13:1
It's Tough to be Famous 1932,Ap 9,18:1
Love Is a Racket 1932,Je 11,9:3
Life Begins 1932,Ag 26,20:3
Hello Sister! 1933,My 6,11:2

Ray, Wallace
Over the Hill to the Poor House 1920,S 18,16:2

Ray and Trent
Letter, The 1940,N 23,12:6

Ray McKinley and his orchestra
Hit Parade of 1943 1943,Ap 16,24:3

Ray Noble and his orchestra
Pride of the Yankees, The 1942,Jl 16,23:1
Lake Placid Serenade 1944,D 25,15:6

Raya, Nita
Entente Cordiale 1939,D 26,23:2
Ignace 1950,S 19,39:4

Rayazanov, Eldar (Director)
Ballad of a Hussar, The 1963,Jl 15,25:5

Raybas, Andre
Clandestine 1948,My 24,23:2

Raye, Carol
Waltz Time 1946,F 11,25:2

Raye, Don (Composer)
In the Navy 1941,Je 12,29:2
Two Tickets to London 1943,Jl 3,11:2
Crazy House 1943,D 16,33:3
Broadway Rhythm 1944,Ap 14,24:6
Date with Judy, A 1948,Ag 7,8:2
Adventures of Ichabod and Mr Toad, The
1949,O 10,18:2

Raye, Martha
Rhythm on the Range 1936,Jl 30,22:1
Big Broadcast of 1937, The 1936,O 22,31:1
College Holiday 1936,D 24,21:2
Hideaway Girl 1937,Ja 13,20:4
Waikiki Wedding 1937,Mr 25,29:1
Mountain Music 1937,Je 24,30:3
Artists and Models 1937,Ag 5,19:2
Double or Nothing 1937,S 2,17:3
Big Broadcast of 1938, The 1938,Mr 10,16:2
College Swing 1938,Ap 28,27:2
Tropic Holiday 1938,Je 30,21:2
Give Me a Sailor 1938,Ag 11,31:1
Never Say Die 1939,Mr 9,18:1
$1,000 a Touchdown 1939,O 5,27:2
Farmer's Daughter, The 1940,F 16,23:4
Boys From Syracuse, The 1940,Ag 1,25:2
Navy Blues 1941,S 20,11:2
Keep 'Em Flying 1941,N 27,29:2
Hellzapoppin 1941,D 26,21:4
Four Jills in a Jeep 1944,Ap 6,27:2
Pin Up Girl 1944,My 11,25:6
Jumbo 1962,D 7,49:1
Monsieur Verdoux 1964,Jl 4,8:2

Raye, Martha (Miscellaneous)
Four Jills in a Jeep 1944,Ap 6,27:2

Rayes, Billy
Men In her Life, The 1941,D 12,35:1

Rayfield, Curt
General Crack 1929,D 4,36:6

Raymaker, Herman (Director)
Tracked in the Snow Country 1925,Jl 20,19:2
Love Hour, The 1925,S 2,21:3
Below the Line 1925,S 21,12:4
Night Cry, The 1926,Ap 7,26:6
Trailing the Killer 1932,D 2,27:4
Adventure Girl 1934,Ag 9,14:5

Rayment, Billy
Man in a Cocked Hat 1960,Je 15,50:2

Raymond, Alex (Original Author)
Mars Attacks the World 1938,N 8,26:3

Raymond, Allen (Original Author)
Heart of a Salome, The 1927,Je 6,27:2

Raymond, Cyril
Condemned to Death 1932,Jl 14,24:2
Ghost Train, The 1933,F 18,13:3
Criminal at Large 1933,D 20,27:2
It's Love Again 1936,My 23,12:1
Accused 1936,D 17,35:1
Thunder in the City 1937,Ap 23,25:2
Dreaming Lips 1937,My 20,17:1
U-Boat 29 1939,O 6,31:3
Brief Encounter 1946,Ag 26,21:2
This Was a Woman 1949,Ja 5,22:2
Angels One Five 1954,Ap 30,28:2
Lease of Life 1956,F 10,18:1
Dunkirk 1958,S 11,42:2
Night Train to Paris 1964,D 3,58:2

Raymond, Dean
Crime of Dr Crespi, The 1936,Ja 13,14:3

Raymond, Ernest (Original Author)
Atlantic 1930,O 6,21:1
Tell England 1931,Ap 19,VIII,6:1
Battle of Gallipoli, The 1931,D 7,16:1
For Them that Trespass 1950,S 27,37:2

Raymond, Frances
Flirting With Love 1924,S 1,9:1
Satan in Sables 1925,O 15,27:3
What Happened to Jones 1926,F 9,22:1
Three's a Crowd 1927,O 3,20:1
Get Your Man 1927,D 5,26:2
Gay Defender, The 1927,D 26,26:6
Illusion 1929,S 28,17:3
Happy Go Lucky 1943,Mr 25,25:1

Raymond, Frankie
Seven Chances 1925,Mr 17,18:1

Raymond, Fred (Screenwriter)
There Goes the Bride 1933,Mr 4,11:3

Raymond, Gary
Look Back in Anger 1959,S 16,45:1
Suddenly, Last Summer 1959,D 23,22:1
Millionairess, The 1961,F 10,19:1
Cid, El 1961,D 15,49:1
Playboy of the Western World, The
1963,Mr 19,8:2
Jason and the Argonauts 1963,Ag 8,19:1
Greatest Story Ever Told, The 1965,F 16,40:2

Raymond, Gene
Personal Maid 1931,S 5,7:4
Ladies of the Big House 1932,Ja 1,31:1
Forgotten Commandments 1932,Je 2,25:2
Night of June 13th, The 1932,S 17,18:4
Red Dust 1932,N 5,12:5
If I Had a Million 1932,D 3,21:4
Zoo in Budapest 1933,Ap 28,15:2
Ex-Lady 1933,My 15,16:2
Ann Carver's Profession 1933,Je 9,20:2
Brief Moment 1933,S 30,18:5
House on 56th Street, The 1933,D 2,9:3
Flying Down to Rio 1933,D 22,25:2
I Am Suzanne 1934,Ja 19,24:3
Coming-Out Party 1934,Mr 17,11:3
Sadie McKee 1934,My 18,18:3 (Incorrect in this
edition; use 1934,My 19,18:3 elsewhere)
Transatlantic Merry-Go-Round 1934,N 1,25:2
Behold My Wife 1935,F 18,19:3
Transient Lady 1935,Mr 11,15:1
Woman in Red, The 1935,Mr 23,11:3
Hooray for Love 1935,Jl 13,16:2
Seven Keys to Baldpate 1935,D 14,11:2
Love on a Bet 1936,Mr 5,25:2
Walking on Air 1936,S 12,20:2
That Girl From Paris 1937,Ja 1,19:1
There Goes my Girl 1937,Je 12,8:2
Life of the Party, The 1937,O 4,17:1
She's Got Everything 1938,Ja 14,21:3
Stolen Heaven 1938,My 12,27:2
Cross Country Romance 1940,Jl 19,22:3
Mr and Mrs Smith 1941,F 21,16:3
Smilin' Through 1941,D 5,29:2
Locket, The 1947,Mr 20,38:2
Sofia 1948,S 4,8:7
Hit the Deck 1955,Mr 4,17:1
Best Man, The 1964,Ag 7,29:1
I'd Rather Be Rich 1964,S 3,24:2

Raymond, Guy
Sail a Crooked Ship 1962,F 3,12:6
Gypsy 1962,N 2,24:1
Ballad of Josie, The 1968,Mr 14,51:2

Raymond, Helen
Twin Beds 1920,N 1,13:2
Raymond, Jack
Lunatic at Large, The 1927,F 1,25:1
Thanks For The Buggy Ride 1928,Ja 23,18:3
Sally of the Scandals 1928,Jl 3,19:3
Three Week Ends 1928,D 10,25:1
Wild Party, The 1929,Ap 2,28:4
Preview Murder Mystery, The 1936,Mr 21,13:2
Abbott and Costello in the Foreign Legion
1950,Ag 14,14:4
Raymond, Jack (Director)
Speckled Band, The 1931,N 7,16:5
French Leave 1931,D 7,16:1
Sorrell and Son 1934,My 29,22:1
Rat, The 1938,F 28,19:1
When Knights Were Bold 1942,Mr 31,29:2
Raymond, Jean
French-Cancan 1956,Ap 17,26:2
Raymond, Jill
Woman in the Hall, The 1949,Ja 24,16:2
Raymond, Paula
Crisis 1950,Jl 4,10:2
Duchess of Idaho 1950,Jl 21,15:3
Devil's Doorway 1950,N 10,35:1
Grounds for Marriage 1951,Ja 12,24:6
Inside Straight 1951,Mr 16,34:2
Tall Target, The 1951,S 28,26:2
Texas Carnival 1951,O 13,9:1
Sellout, The 1952,My 31,12:7
Beast From 20,000 Fathoms, The 1953,Je 25,23:1
City That Never Sleeps 1953,Ag 8,14:2
King Richard and the Crusaders 1954,Ag 23,20:5
Human Jungle, The 1954,N 26,24:6
Raymond, Robin
Moontide 1942,Ap 30,14:1
Arabian Nights 1942,D 26,15:1
Are These our Parents? 1944,Ag 23,16:2
Men in her Diary 1945,S 24,16:5
Web, The 1947,Je 5,32:1
Wabash Avenue 1950,Ap 29,8:3
There's no Business Like Show Business
1954,D 17,37:3
Beyond a Reasonable Doubt 1956,S 14,27:2
Raymond, Royal
Red Menace, The 1949,Je 27,18:2
Raymonne
Dame de Pique, La 1944,O 19,19:2
Virtuous Bigamist, The 1959,My 28,34:3
Rayner, D A Comdr (Original Author)
Enemy Below, The 1957,D 26,23:2
Rayner, Minnie
Sherlock Holmes's Fatal Hour 1931,Jl 13,13:5
Missing Rembrandt, The 1932,Mr 26,17:2
Triumph of Sherlock Holmes, The
1935,My 27,20:6
Angel Street 1952,N 11,25:2
Raynham, Frederick
Hound of the Baskervilles, The 1922,S 11,20:2
Raynor, Hal (Miscellaneous)
New Faces of 1937 1937,Jl 2,25:1
Raynor, William (Original Author)
Summer Love 1958,Je 26,23:4
Wackiest Ship in the Army, The 1961,F 9,36:1
Raynor, William (Screenwriter)
Francis in the Haunted House 1956,Jl 21,9:2
Raynore, Edythe
Road to Glory, The 1936,Ag 6,22:1
Rayo, Mirra
Woman From Moscow, The 1928,N 5,26:1
Rayson, David
Mikado, The 1967,Mr 15,53:1
Raz, Mati (Producer)
Clouds Over Israel 1966,My 10,48:6
Raza, S Ali (Miscellaneous)
Handful of Grain, A 1959,Jl 4,9:4
Razaf, Andy (Composer)
Hit Parade of 1943 1943,Ap 16,24:3
Razumova, N
Golden Mountains 1932,Ap 14,25:3
Re, Gustavo
That Man in Istanbul 1966,My 19,51:2
REA
See Also WRAY, REY, RAE
Reach, John
Lizzie 1957,Ap 5,24:2
Silencers, The 1966,Mr 17,35:1
Reachi, Manuel (Producer)
Toast to Love 1951,N 7,35:5
Reachi, Manuel (Screenwriter)
Mexican Bus ride 1954,Jl 21,18:3
READ
See Also REED, REID, READE
Read, Barbara
Three Smart Girls 1937,Ja 25,22:2
Make Way for Tomorrow 1937,My 10,23:1
Road Back, The 1937,Je 18,25:2
Merry-Go-Round of 1938 1937,N 26,27:2
Crime of Dr Hallet, The 1938,Mr 24,21:3
Spellbinder, The 1939,Ag 24,17:3
Married and in Love 1940,F 2,13:2
Curtain Call 1940,Ap 19,25:2
Key Witness 1947,Jl 30,27:6

Read, David
Alice in Wonderland 1951,Jl 27,15:2
Read, Douglas
Game is Over, The 1967,Ja 10,34:1
Read, J Parker Jr (Original Author)
Trumpet Blows, The 1934,Ap 14,18:2
Read, J Parker Jr (Producer)
Sahara 1919,Je 30,16:3
Read, Jan (Original Author)
Both Sides of the Law 1954,Ja 12,19:2
Haunted Strangler, The 1958,Jl 4,15:3
Read, Jan (Screenwriter)
White Corridors 1952,Jl 16,21:1
Haunted Strangler, The 1958,Jl 4,15:3
Jason and the Argonauts 1963,Ag 8,19:1
First Men in the Moon 1964,N 26,52:2
Read, Opie (Original Author)
Almost a Husband 1919,O 13,16:3
READE
See Also READ, REED, REID
Reade, Charles (Original Author)
Masks and Faces 1918,My 6,11:3
Reade, Janet
Smiling Lieutenant, The 1931,My 23,13:4
Readick, Bobby
Canterville Ghost, The 1944,Jl 29,16:2
Readick, Frank
Journey Into Fear 1943,Mr 19,15:3
Reagan, Ray
Last Chance, The 1945,N 28,21:6
Reagan, Ronald
Love Is on the Air 1937,N 12,27:3
Swing Your Lady 1938,Ja 27,17:2
Accidents Will Happen 1938,Ap 25,19:2
Cowboy From Brooklyn 1938,Jl 14,17:1
Boy Meets Girl 1938,Ag 27,7:2
Girls on Probation 1938,O 21,27:3
Brother Rat 1938,N 5,15:2
Going Places 1939,Ja 7,6:1
Secret Service of the Air 1939,Mr 2,19:2
Dark Victory 1939,Ap 21,27:2
Naughty but Nice 1939,Je 23,23:2
Hell's Kitchen 1939,Jl 3,10:5
Angels Wash Their Faces 1939,S 4,16:2
Smashing the Money Ring 1939,N 17,17:2
Brother Rat and a Baby 1940,Ja 27,9:4
Angel From Texas, An 1940,My 10,26:7
Murder in the Air 1940,Jl 4,12:2
Knute Rockne-All American 1940,O 19,21:2
Tugboat Annie Sails Again 1940,N 9,20:2
Santa Fe Trail 1940,D 21,21:2
Bad Man, The 1941,Ap 4,25:1
Million Dollar Baby 1941,Je 7,20:2
Nine Loves Are not Enough 1941,O 30,27:2
International Squadron 1941,N 14,28:4
Kings Row 1942,F 3,23:2
Juke Girl 1942,Je 20,9:2
Desperate Journey 1942,S 26,11:2
This Is the Army 1943,Jl 29,11:6
Stallion Road 1947,Ap 5,12:5
That Hagen Girl 1947,O 25,13:2
Voice of the Turtle, The 1947,D 26,22:4
John Loves Mary 1949,F 5,11:2
Night Unto Night 1949,Je 11,11:2
Girl from Jones Beach, The 1949,Jl 30,9:2
Hasty Heart, The 1950,Ja 21,10:5
Louisa 1950,O 25,45:2
Storm Warning 1951,Mr 3,8:2
Bedtime for Bonzo 1951,Ap 6,31:4
Last Outpost, The 1951,Je 22,16:3
Hong Kong 1952,Ap 5,20:3
Winning Team, The 1952,Je 21,12:2
She's Working her Way Through College
1952,Jl 10,27:2
Prisoner of War 1954,My 10,20:2
Cattle Queen of Montana 1955,Ja 26,22:1
Tennessee's Partner 1955,N 5,22:8
Killers, The 1964,Jl 18,10:4
Real, Alma
Dancing Pirate 1936,Je 18,19:1
Real, Aurorita
Silencio Sublime 1937,Ja 16,21:2
Reale, Paolo
Path of Hope, The (Il Cammino Della Speranza)
1952,Ag 5,15:5
REARDON
See Also RIORDAN
Reardon, Basil (Screenwriter)
Let George Do It 1940,O 14,25:5
Reardon, Casper
You're a Sweetheart 1937,D 25,10:5
Reardon, Marjorie
Parachute Nurse 1942,Jl 27,18:2
ReArmament, Moral (Director)
Crowning Experience, The 1960,O 24,25:3
ReArmament, Moral (Producer)
Crowning Experience, The 1960,O 24,25:3
Reason, Rex
Salome 1953,Mr 25,37:1
Mask of the Himalayas 1953,Ag 12,22:3
Mission Over Korea 1953,S 19,7:2

Reason, Rex— Cont
This Island Earth 1955,Je 11,8:7
Kiss of Fire 1955,S 24,11:2
Lady Godiva 1955,D 3,13:3
Creature Walks among Us, The 1956,Ap 27,21:6
Raw Edge 1956,Jl 28,10:7
Band of Angels 1957,Jl 11,21:1
Reason, Rhodes
Big Fisherman, The 1959,Ag 6,18:1
Fever in the Blood 1961,Ap 20,30:4
King Kong Escapes 1968,Jl 11,30:1
Reaton, Eric (Director)
Wedding Bills 1927,Je 29,29:3
Rebbot, Saddy
My Life to Live 1963,S 24,43:2
Rebe, Martial
Rasputin 1939,O 17,31:4
Pardon my French 1952,Mr 31,17:2
Rebeggiani, Luciano
Gioconda, La 1958,O 13,33:4
Rebel, Bernard
Chance of a Lifetime 1951,Mr 15,37:2
Chance Meeting 1955,Ap 20,38:1
Rebia
Woman in Command, The 1934,My 29,22:2
Rebiero, Marcel (Cinematographer)
Story of the Vatican, The 1941,S 20,11:3
Rebner, Arthur (Composer)
Eight Girls in a Boat 1934,Ja 13,16:3
Reborek, Josef
Firemen's Ball, The 1968,S 30,60:1
Rebuas, Harry (Screenwriter)
Sing for Your Supper 1941,D 1,15:5
Rebuffat, Gaston (Miscellaneous)
Annapurna 1953,D 14,45:4
Reburn, Stewart
Second Fiddle 1939,Jl 1,11:2
Rechtzeit, Seymour
Shir Hashirim 1935,O 11,31:1
Recklaw, Betty
Win That Girl 1928,O 1,23:1
Rector, George
Every Day's a Holiday 1938,Ja 27,17:2
Red Army Ensemble
Moscow Music Hall 1946,S 9,20:1
Red Stallion (horse), The
Red Stallion in the Rockies 1949,Ag 26,15:2
Redd, Freddie
Connection, The 1962,O 4,44:1
Redd, Mary-Robin
Group, The 1966,Mr 17,35:1
Reddin, Kenneth (Original Author)
Another Shore 1951,F 12,19:3
Redecki, Anthony
Rhubarb 1951,Ag 31,12:2
Redeker, Quinn
Three Stooges Meet Hercules, The
1962,Ja 27,13:4
Redel, Anna
Moscow Music Hall 1946,S 9,20:1
Redfield, William
Back Door to Heaven 1939,Ap 20,21:2
Proud and Profane, The 1956,Je 14,41:2
I Married a Woman 1958,N 5,42:5
Connection, The 1962,O 4,44:1
Hamlet 1964,S 24,46:1
Saboteur, The: Code Name-Mori Turi
1965,Ag 26,40:2
Duel at Diablo 1966,Je 16,53:1
Fantastic Voyage 1966,S 8,43:1
Redford, Basil
Jamaica Inn 1939,O 12,33:1
Redford, Robert
War Hunt 1962,Ag 8,35:2
Situation Hopeless-But not Serious
1965,O 14,53:1
Inside Daisy Clover 1966,F 18,23:1
Chase, The 1966,F 19,24:1
This Property is Condemned 1966,Ag 4,24:1
Barefoot in the Park 1967,My 26,51:1
Redgie, Charles
Parisian, The 1931,Ag 22,7:5
Monte Carlo Madness 1932,Je 4,9:2
Dernier Milliardaire, Le 1935,O 30,16:2
Ignace 1950,S 19,39:4
Redgrave, Corin
Man for all Seasons, A 1966,D 13,60:1
Deadly Affair, The 1967,Ja 27,31:1
Redgrave, Lynn
Girl With Green Eyes 1964,Ag 11,37:2
Georgy Girl 1966,O 18,48:1
Deadly Affair, The 1967,Ja 27,31:1
Smashing Time 1967,D 21,44:1
Redgrave, Michael
Lady Vanishes, The 1938,D 26,29:1
Climbing High 1939,Je 5,20:3
Stolen Life 1939,Je 15,27:2
Stars Look Down, The 1941,Jl 24,15:2
Lady in Distress 1942,F 16,21:2
Kipps 1942,My 25,11:2
Jeannie 1943,S 13,14:2
Thunder Rock 1944,S 15,16:1
Johnny in the Clouds 1945,N 16,16:2
Dead of Night 1946,Je 29,22:6

Redgrave, Michael— Cont

Years Between, The 1947,Mr 10,25:2
Captive Heart, The 1947,Ap 28,27:2
Mourning Becomes Electra 1947,N 20,38:2
Secret Beyond the Door 1948,Ja 16,25:4
Smugglers, The 1948,Mr 29,17:1
Fame Is the Spur 1949,N 8,34:2
Browning Version, The 1951,O 30,33:2
Importance of Being Earnest, The 1952,D 23,17:2
Green Scarf, The 1955,Ja 15,10:2
Night my Number Came up, The 1955,D 20,39:5
1984 1956,O 1,31:1
Happy Road, The 1957,Je 21,20:2
Time Without Pity 1957,N 23,11:2
Quiet American, The 1958,F 6,24:1
Law and Disorder 1958,Ag 6,20:1
Shake Hands With the Devil 1959,Je 25,20:7
Wreck of the Mary Deare, The 1959,N 7,27:1
Innocents, The 1961,D 26,15:2
Loneliness of the Long Distance Runner, The
 1962,O 9,44:1
Mr Arkadin 1962,O 12,26:1
No, My Darling Daughter 1964,Mr 28,13:5
Young Cassidy 1965,Mr 23,35:1
Hill, The 1965,O 4,00:0
Heroes of Telemark, The 1966,Mr 10,26:1
25th Hour, The 1967,F 17,45:1
Assignment K 1968,Jl 20,18:2
Redgrave, Michael Sir (Narrator)
Palaces of a Queen 1967,Je 27,32:1
Redgrave, Vanessa
Morgan! 1966,Ap 5,42:2
Man for all Seasons, A 1966,D 13,60:1
Blow-Up 1966,D 19,52:2
Sailor From Gibraltar, The 1967,Ap 25,38:2
London Scene, The (Tonite Let's All Make Love
 in London); Tonite Let's All Make Love in
 London (The London Scene) 1967,S 27,39:1
Camelot 1967,O 26,54:1
Charge of the Light Brigade, The 1968,O 7,59:1
Sea Gull, The 1968,D 24,14:1
Redina, Maria
Russian Ballerina 1947,S 11,31:2
Reding, Juli
Why Must I Die? 1960,S 15,45:4
REDMAN
See Also REDMOND
Redman, Joyce
One of our Aircraft Is Missing 1942,N 2,17:2
Tom Jones 1963,O 8,48:1
Othello 1966,F 2,24:1
Prudence and the Pill 1968,My 24,37:1
REDMOND
See Also REDMAN
Redmond, Liam
Adventures, The 1947,Ap 4,19:2
Captain Boycott 1947,D 6,11:2
Sword in the Desert 1949,Ag 25,20:2
Saints and Sinners 1949,S 12,17:2
High Treason 1952,My 21,23:3
Cruel Sea, The 1953,Ag 11,18:5
Tonight's the Night 1954,D 23,13:4
Divided Heart, The 1955,Ag 4,16:1
23 Paces to Baker Street 1956,My 19,12:6
Safari 1956,Je 21,35:2
Rooney 1958,Je 6,29:2
Scent of Mystery 1960,F 19,23:1
Under ten Flags 1960,S 16,24:1
Desert Attack 1961,Mr 23,28:1
Valiant, The 1962,Je 14,23:4
Kid Galahad 1963,Mr 7,8:5
Luck of Ginger Coffey, The 1964,S 22,44:1
Ghost and Mr Chicken, The 1966,S 22,57:2
Tobruk 1967,F 9,33:2
Adventures of Bullwhip Griffin, The
 1967,Mr 9,43:2
Redmond, Lian
Playboy of the Western World, The
 1963,Mr 19,8:2
Redmond, Marge
Sanctuary 1961,F 22,31:1
Trouble With Angels, The 1966,Ap 7,45:1
Fortune Cookie, The 1966,O 20,52:1
Redmond, Moira
Doctor in Love 1962,Ap 27,27:2
Kill or Cure 1962,N 13,43:4
Nightmare 1964,Je 18,29:2
Redon, Jean
Battle of the Rails; (Bataille Du Rail)
 1949,D 27,27:2
Redon, Jean (Miscellaneous)
Back to the Wall; (Dos au Mur) 1959,S 8,43:2
Redon, Jean (Screenwriter)
Crazy in the Noodle 1957,D 15,45:4 (Incorrect in
 this edition; use 1957,D 17,45:4 elsewhere)
Back to the Wall; (Dos au Mur) 1959,S 8,43:2
Redwing, Rodd
Song of India 1949,Je 10,32:3
Rancho Notorious 1952,My 15,39:5
Creature from the Black Lagoon 1954,My 1,13:4
Cattle Queen of Montana 1955,Ja 26,22:1
Flaming Star 1960,D 17,19:1

Redwood, Vicky
Mahanagar; Big City, The 1964,S 28,19:1
Ree, Harry Capt
School for Danger 1947,N 10,21:3
Ree, Max (Miscellaneous)
Midsummer Night's Dream, A 1935,O 10,31:1
REECE
See Also REES, REESE, REIS, RICE
Reece, Brian
Wee Geordie 1956,O 8,31:1
Ship Was Loaded, The 1958,Ja 20,20:1
Reece, Kathryn
Animal Crackers 1930,Ag 29,20:3
REED
See Also REID, READE, READ
Reed, Alan
Days of Glory 1944,Je 17,10:2
Nob Hill 1945,Jl 4,10:3
Postman Always Rings Twice, The
 1946,My 3,15:3
Perfect Strangers 1950,Mr 11,8:2
Emergency Wedding 1950,D 22,19:2
Redhead and the Cowboy, The 1951,Je 6,37:2
Here Comes the Groom 1951,S 21,19:2
Viva Zapata 1952,F 8,19:2
Actors and Sin; (Woman of Sin) 1952,My 30,11:3
I, The Jury 1953,Ag 22,8:2
Woman's World 1954,S 29,23:4
Far Horizons, The 1955,My 21,11:1
Kiss of Fire 1955,S 24,11:2
Timetable 1956,Mr 17,13:2
Revolt of Mamie Stover, The 1956,My 12,12:7
Tarnished Angels, The 1958,Ja 31,31:1
Marjorie Morningstar 1958,Ap 25,32:2
Breakfast at Tiffany's 1961,O 6,28:1
Reed, Alan (Narrator)
Man Called Flintstone, The 1967,N 25,42:1
Reed, Bernard
Troublemaker, The 1964,Je 23,25:1
Reed, Billy
Crazy House 1943,D 16,33:3
Reed, Carol (Director)
Talk of the Devil 1937,My 15,23:5
Three on a Week-End 1938,Je 2,19:3
Climbing High 1939,Je 5,20:3
Night Train 1940,D 30,21:1
Girl in the News, The 1941,My 5,13:2
Stars Look Down, The 1941,Jl 24,15:2
Laburnum Grove 1941,D 2,29:2
Girl Must Live, A 1942,Mr 24,25:2
Kipps 1942,My 25,11:2
Young Mr Pitt, The 1943,Mr 11,17:1
Way Ahead, The 1945,Je 4,22:3
True Glory, The 1945,S 7,1:2
Odd Man Out 1947,Ap 24,30:2
Fallen Idol, The 1949,N 16,39:2
Third Man, The 1950,F 3,29:2
Outcast of the Islands 1952,My 16,19:2
Man Between, The 1953,N 19,41:2
Kid for two Farthings, A 1956,Ap 18,25:1
Key, The 1958,Jl 2,23:3
Our Man in Havana 1960,Ja 28,26:1
Mutiny on the Bounty 1962,N 9,31:2
Running Man, The 1963,O 3,31:1
Agony and the Ecstacy, The 1965,O 9,5:6
Oliver! 1968,D 11,57:1
Reed, Carol (Producer)
Way Ahead, The 1944,Jl 16,II,3:4
Odd Man Out 1947,Ap 24,30:2
Fallen Idol, The 1949,N 16,39:2
Third Man, The 1950,F 3,29:2
Outcast of the Islands 1952,My 16,19:2
Man Between, The 1953,N 19,41:2
Kid for two Farthings, A 1956,Ap 18,25:1
Our Man in Havana 1960,Ja 28,26:1
Running Man, The 1963,O 3,31:1
Reed, Carol (Screenwriter)
Talk of the Devil 1937,My 15,23:5
Reed, Donald
Convoy 1927,My 9,26:4
Naughty but Nice 1927,Jl 5,19:2
Mad Hour, The 1928,Ap 16,20:5
Night Watch, The 1928,O 8,14:2
Show Girl 1928,N 5,26:1
Evangeline 1929,Jl 29,23:3
Little Johnny Jones 1930,F 1,15:1
Texan, The 1930,My 17,21:2
Hollywood, Ciudad de Ensueno 1934,Ap 4,26:3
Crusade Against Rackets 1937,Jl 26,15:3
Renfrew of the Royal Mounted 1937,N 3,29:4
Reed, Donna
Get-Away, The 1941,Jl 17,23:4
Shadow of the Thin Man 1941,N 21,23:2
Bugle Sounds, The 1942,Ap 3,25:2
Courtship of Andy Hardy, The 1942,Ap 10,21:2
Calling Dr Gillespie 1942,Jl 9,17:4
Eyes in the Night 1942,O 16,23:1
Human Comedy, The 1943,Mr 3,19:2
Thousands Cheer 1943,S 14,27:1
Man From Down Under, The 1943,S 27,23:2
See Here Private Hargrove 1944,Mr 22,17:2
Picture of Dorian Gray, The 1945,Mr 2,15:2
Gentle Annie 1945,My 5,11:5

Reed, Donna— Cont

They Were Expendable 1945,D 21,25:2
It's a Wonderful Life 1946,D 23,19:2
Green Dolphin Street 1947,O 16,34:2
Beyond Glory 1948,Ag 4,18:2
Chicago Deadline 1949,N 3,37:2
Saturday's Hero 1951,S 12,37:2
Scandal Sheet 1952,Ja 17,23:1
Hangman's Knot 1952,D 11,45:3
Trouble Along the Way 1953,My 7,37:2
From Here to Eternity 1953,Ag 6,16:2
Caddy, The 1953,S 18,16:6
Three Hours to Kill 1954,S 4,6:4
Last Time I saw Paris, The 1954,N 19,20:2
Far Horizons, The 1955,My 21,11:1
Ransom 1956,Ja 25,28:3
Benny Goodman Story 1956,F 22,22:1
Backlash 1956,Ap 21,11:2
Beyond Mombasa 1957,My 31,14:2
Pepe 1960,D 22,18:1
Reed, Florence
Wives of Men 1918,Ag 26,9:1 (In Addenda)
Black Panther's Cub, The 1921,My 30,12:5
Reed, Gayle
Johnny One-Eye 1950,N 17,31:2
Because of You 1952,D 4,47:3
Reed, George
Huckleberry Finn 1920,F 23,11:2
All Abroad 1927,Ap 19,24:4
River of Romance, The 1929,Jl 29,23:3
Father's Son 1931,F 21,15:2
Hold Your Man 1933,Jl 1,16:6
Mrs Wiggs of the Cabbage Patch 1934,O 29,14:2
Green Pastures, The 1936,Jl 17,20:1
Kentucky 1938,D 24,12:1
Going Places 1939,Ja 7,6:1
Secret of Dr Kildare, The 1939,D 8,33:5
Swanee River 1939,D 30,9:2
Dr Kildare's Strange Case 1940,Ap 12,19:2
Tales of Manhattan 1942,S 25,25:1
Home in Indiana 1944,Je 22,23:1
Dark Delusion 1947,Je 26,19:2
Reed, George H
Sporting Blood 1940,Jl 22,20:2
People vs Dr Kildare, The 1941,My 8,21:1
Dr Kildare's Victory 1942,F 5,25:2
Three Men in White 1944,My 26,23:3
Reed, John
Mikado, The 1967,Mr 15,53:1
Mikado, The 1967,Mr 15,53:1
Reed, Luther (Director)
Ace of Cads, The 1926,O 18,18:1 (In Addenda)
New York 1927,Ja 31,13:1
Evening Clothes 1927,Mr 21,10:4
Shanghai Bound 1927,N 7,26:4
Honeymoon Hate 1927,D 31,31:1
Sawdust Paradise, The 1928,Ag 27,23:1
Rio Rita 1929,O 7,22:1
Hit the Deck 1930,Ja 15,28:6
Dixiana 1930,S 5,21:1
Reed, Luther (Original Author)
Below the Surface 1920,Je 7,20:3 (In Addenda)
Purple Highway, The 1923,Jl 24,14:3 (In
 Addenda)
Reed, Luther (Screenwriter)
Let's Be Fashionable 1920,Je 14,13:2
Beauty's Worth 1922,Mr 27,12:1
When Knighthood Was in Flower 1922,S 15,17:2
 (In Addenda)
Little Old New York 1923,Ag 2,10:3
Great White Way, The 1924,Ja 4,10:1
Yolanda 1924,F 20,23:1
Say It Again 1926,Je 7,23:2
Reed, Lydia
Seven Little Foys, The 1955,Je 30,18:2
High Society 1956,Ag 10,9:2
Reed, Mark (Original Author)
Petticoat Fever 1936,Mr 21,13:2
Yes, My Darling Daughter 1939,F 27,11:2
Reed, Marshall
Angel and the Badman 1947,Mr 3,28:4
Oh! Susanna 1951,Mr 30,28:5
Reed, Maxwell
Brothers, The 1948,My 5,30:4
Dear Murderer 1948,My 8,12:2
Daybreak 1949,Jl 4,9:2
Lost People, The 1950,O 2,19:4
Madness of the Heart 1950,O 12,43:2
Clouded Yellow, The 1951,N 13,33:2
Flame of Araby 1951,D 20,41:7
Wall of Death 1952,My 19,12:4
Dark Man, The 1952,My 26,18:4
Sea Devils 1953,Jl 31,11:5
Helen of Troy 1956,Ja 27,21:4
Notorious Landlady, The 1962,Jl 27,15:2
Picture Mommy Dead 1966,N 3,45:4
Reed, Myrtle
Cast a Dark Shadow 1957,N 28,57:1
Eyes of Annie Jones, The 1964,My 14,39:1
Reed, Oliver
Angry Silence, The 1960,D 13,25:2
Curse of the Werewolf, The 1961,Je 8,40:2
Paranoiac 1963,My 23,31:2
These Are the Damned 1965,Jl 8,35:1

Reed, Oliver— Cont

Girl-Getters, The 1966,Ap 13,37:6
Jokers, The 1967,My 16,50:1
Shuttered Room, The 1968,F 15,47:1
I'll Never Forget What's 'Isname
1968,Ap 15,51:1
Oliver! 1968,D 11,57:1

Reed, Philip

Female 1933,N 4,18:3
House on 56th Street, The 1933,D 2,9:3
Fashions of 1934 1934,Ja 20,12:2
Jimmy the Gent 1934,Mr 26,22:3
Gambling Lady 1934,Ap 5,25:2
Journal of a Crime 1934,Ap 28,11:3
Glamour 1934,My 12,12:3
Dr Monica 1934,Je 21,28:2
Affairs of a Gentleman 1934,Je 23,16:7
British Agent 1934,S 20,20:1
Lost Lady, A 1934,O 4,19:1
Big Hearted Herbert 1934,N 14,23:2
Maybe It's Love 1935,F 11,14:2
Sweet Music 1935,F 21,23:2
Woman in Red, The 1935,Mr 23,11:3
Case of the Curious Bride, The 1935,Ap 5,21:3
Girl From 10th Avenue, The 1935,My 27,20:6
Accent on Youth 1935,Ag 12,10:3
Murder of Dr Harrigan, The 1936,Ja 21,27:5
Klondike Annie 1936,Mr 12,18:2
Last of the Mohicans, The 1936,S 3,17:3
Luckiest Girl in the World, The 1936,D 5,16:3
Madame X 1937,O 25,23:1
Merrily We Live 1938,Mr 18,23:3
Aloma of the South Seas 1941,Ag 28,23:4
Week End for Three 1941,O 24,27:4
Gentleman After Dark, A 1942,Ap 17,21:2
Old Acquaintance 1943,N 3,20:2
People Are Funny 1946,Ja 28,15:6
Rendezvous With Annie 1946,S 23,29:3
Her Sister's Secret 1947,Ja 23,31:3
Song of Scheherazade 1947,F 27,26:2
Song of the Thin Man 1947,Ag 29,14:2
Pirates of Monterey 1947,D 17,41:4
Unknown Island 1949,Ja 8,11:4
Manhandled 1949,My 26,34:2
Davy Crockett, Indian Scout 1950,Mr 17,28:3
Tripoli 1950,N 10,35:2
Take Me to Town 1953,Je 20,8:6
Girl in the Red Velvet Swing, The
1955,O 20,41:2
Tattered Dress, The 1957,Mr 15,22:3

Reed, Ralph

Scandal Sheet 1952,Ja 17,23:1
Lone Star 1952,F 2,11:4
Because You're Mine 1952,S 26,18:2
Long, Hot Summer, The 1958,Ap 4,16:1

Reed, Ralph (Composer)

Double or Nothing 1937,S 2,17:3

Reed, Robbie

Troublemaker, The 1964,Je 23,25:1

Reed, Robert

Star! 1968,O 23,36:2

Reed, Roland D (Director)

House of Secrets 1937,F 22,13:1

Reed, Theodore (Director)

Lady, Be Careful 1936,O 10,21:1
Double or Nothing 1937,S 2,17:3
Tropic Holiday 1938,Je 30,21:2
I'm From Missouri 1939,Mr 23,27:1
What a Life 1939,O 12,33:1
Those Were the Days 1940,Jl 15,18:4
Life With Henry 1941,F 6,25:2

Reed, Theodore (Producer)

Those Were the Days 1940,Jl 15,18:4
Life With Henry 1941,F 6,25:2
Song of my Heart 1948,Mr 5,17:3

Reed, Tom (Original Author)

Radio Patrol 1932,Jl 14,24:2
Pittsburgh 1943,F 25,27:2
Light Touch, The 1952,Ja 17,23:1
Night People 1954,Mr 13,11:2

Reed, Tom (Producer)

Bad Guy 1937,Ag 26,25:2

Reed, Tom (Screenwriter)

Babbitt 1934,D 17,24:2
Case of the Curious Bride, The 1935,Ap 5,21:3
Florentine Dagger, The 1935,Ap 27,20:6
Case of the Velvet Claws, The 1936,Ag 29,16:3
Love Begins at 20 1936,S 19,20:1
Great O'Malley, The 1937,Mr 6,10:1
Marry the Girl 1937,Jl 31,6:2
Dress Parade 1939,O 28,11:2
Calling Philo Vance 1940,F 9,15:3
Spoilers, The 1942,My 22,27:2
Loves of Edgar Allan Poe, The 1942,S 21,19:2
Pittsburgh 1943,F 25,27:2
Two Tickets to London 1943,Jl 3,11:2
Up in Mabel's Room 1944,Ap 22,8:6
Moss Rose 1947,Jl 3,14:2
Spirit of West Point 1947,O 3,31:2
Red Stallion in the Rockies 1949,Ag 26,15:2
Soldiers Three 1951,Mr 30,28:5

Reed, Tracy

Dr Strangelove or: How I Learned to Stop
Worrying and Love the Bomb 1964,Ja 31,16:1
(Incorrect in this edition; use 1964,Ja 30,24:1
elsewhere)

Shot in the Dark, A 1964,Je 24,28:1

Reed, Walter

Mexican Spitfire's Elephant 1942,S 18,25:2
Army Surgeon 1942,N 5,35:2
Seven Days' Leave 1942,D 11,33:2
Bombardier 1943,Jl 2,15:2
Night Song 1948,Ja 29,27:5
Return of the Badmen 1948,Ag 5,16:2
Fighter Squadron 1948,N 20,9:2
Angel on the Amazon 1948,D 27,16:4
Young Man With a Horn 1950,F 10,18:4
Lawless, The 1950,Je 23,29:2
Eagle and the Hawk, The 1950,Jl 6,31:2
Torch, The 1950,Ag 21,15:2
Sun Sets at Dawn, The 1951,Ja 15,13:1
Clown, The 1953,Ja 29,25:1
Those Redheads From Seattle 1953,O 1,34:2
Dangerous Mission 1954,Mr 6,13:5
Hell's Island 1955,My 7,10:2
Summer Love 1958,Je 26,23:4
Where Love Has Gone 1964,N 3,26:1

Reehm, George

Heart Thief, The 1927,Ap 27,22:5

Reek, Edmund (Producer)

United We Stand 1942,Jl 3,12:8
Holy Year 1950 1950,Ag 16,24:3
This Is Your Army 1954,D 15,41:1

Reel, Frances Irene (Original Author)

Dangerous Age, The 1923,Ja 29,11:1

Reenberg, Holger

Livet paa Hegnsgaard; Life on the Hegn Farm
1939,N 13,15:2

Reenberg, Jorgen

I, A Woman 1966,O 12,36:3

REES

See Also REESE, REIS, RICE, REECE

Rees, Joan

Lady Surrenders, A 1947,Je 20,25:6
Bad Sister 1948,Je 11,27:3

Rees, John

Jungle Fighters 1962,Mr 15,28:2

Rees, Lanny

Time of your Life, The 1948,My 27,29:2
Life of Riley, The 1949,Ap 18,18:4

REESE

See Also REIS, RICE, REECE, REES

Reese, Peewee

Safe at Home 1941,N 26,31:2

Reese, Tom

Flaming Star 1960,D 17,19:1
Marines, Lets Go! 1961,Ag 16,37:2
Greatest Story Ever Told, The 1965,F 16,40:2
Murderers' Row 1966,D 22,40:3

Reesen, Emil (Composer)

Sol Over Danmark 1937,Ap 14,31:6

Reesen, Emil (Miscellaneous)

Wedding of Palo, The 1937,Mr 2,17:1

Reeve, Ada

They Came to a City 1945,F 19,21:3
Meet Me at Dawn 1948,My 18,26:2
Night and the City 1950,Je 10,11:2
I Believe in You 1953,My 5,34:3
Novel Affair, A 1957,Ag 28,22:1

Reeves, Arnold (Original Author)

Shepherd King, The 1923,D 11,26:2

Reeves, Benny

Fistful of Dollars, A 1967,F 2,29:1

Reeves, Bob

Our Daily Bread 1934,O 3,25:2

Reeves, Geoffrey (Screenwriter)

Tell Me Lies 1968,F 13,46:3

Reeves, George

Gone With the Wind 1939,D 20,31:2
'Til We Meet Again 1940,Ap 14,14:2
Torrid Zone 1940,My 18,11:3
Tear Gas Squad 1940,My 31,15:3
Ladies Must Live 1940,S 6,25:3
Argentine Nights 1940,O 11,25:3
Always a Bride 1940,N 21,43:3
Strawberry Blonde 1941,F 22,11:2
Dead Men Tell 1941,Ap 17,29:3
Blood and Sand 1941,My 23,25:3
Lydia 1941,S 19,27:1
Man at Large 1941,O 11,21:4
So Proudly We Hail 1943,S 10,29:1
Winged Victory 1944,D 21,16:2
Sainted Sisters, The 1948,My 20,35:2
Jungle Jim 1949,Ja 1,9:2
Special Agent 1949,Ag 22,13:1
Great Lover, The 1949,N 24,48:2
Good Humor Man, The 1950,Jl 14,17:2
Bugles in the Afternoon 1952,Mr 5,32:2
Rancho Notorious 1952,My 15,39:5
Blue Gardenia, The 1953,Ap 28,31:1
From Here to Eternity 1953,Ag 6,16:2
Forever Female 1954,Ja 13,26:2

Reeves, Harry (Original Author)

Saludos Amigos 1943,F 13,8:2

Reeves, Harry (Screenwriter)

Adventures of Ichabod and Mr Toad, The
1949,O 10,18:2
Cinderella 1950,F 23,33:1

Reeves, Kynaston

Sign of the Four, The 1932,Ag 20,7:4
Broken Melody, The 1934,O 31,17:3
Phantom Fiend 1935,Ap 22,14:2
Housemaster 1939,Ap 10,13:2
Outsider, The 1940,Mr 18,13:2
Murder in Reverse 1947,Ja 11,23:5
This Was a Woman 1949,Ja 5,22:2
Guinea Pig, The 1949,My 2,20:2
Weaker Sex, The 1949,Jl 11,13:2
Winslow Boy, The 1950,Je 7,34:4
Madeleine 1950,S 1,17:2
Tony Draws a Horse 1951,My 15,38:6
Penny Princess 1953,Mr 25,37:3
Scotch on the Rocks 1954,Je 14,18:2
Fiend Without a Face 1958,Jl 4,15:3
Man in a Cocked Hat 1960,Je 15,50:2
School for Scoundrels 1960,Jl 12,39:1

Reeves, Michael (Director)

Conqueror Worm, The 1968,Ag 15,46:2

Reeves, Michael (Screenwriter)

Conqueror Worm, The 1968,Ag 15,46:2

Reeves, Steve

Athena 1954,D 22,28:2
Hercules 1959,Jl 23,32:2
Goliath and the Barbarians 1960,Ja 7,24:6
Giant of Marathon, The 1960,My 26,37:3
Hercules Unchained 1960,Jl 14,23:1
Last Days of Pompeii, The 1960,Ag 11,19:1
White Warrior, The 1961,F 11,27:2
Morgan the Pirate 1961,Jl 20,32:2
Thief of Baghdad, The 1961,Ag 17,18:2
Slave, The 1963,My 30,20:1
Duel of the Titans 1963,Ag 8,19:1

Reeves, Theodore (Original Author)

Society Doctor 1935,F 4,11:3
Dangerous Waters 1936,Ja 22,15:5
Sudden Death, And 1936,Jl 18,18:2
Almost Married 1942,Je 5,23:2
Devotion 1946,Ap 6,10:5
I Walk Alone 1948,Ja 22,36:3

Reeves, Theodore (Screenwriter)

Internes Can't Take Money 1937,My 6,23:2
Blossoms On Broadway 1937,D 3,29:2
Night Plane From Chungking 1943,My 31,13:2
National Velvet 1944,D 15,25:2
Doctor and the Girl, The 1949,O 31,20:2
Bernardine 1957,Jl 25,28:1

Reeves-Smith, H

Three Weeks 1924,Ap 1,19:3
Return of Sherlock Holmes, The 1929,O 19,22:6

Regamey, Maurice

Village, The 1953,S 23,37:2

Regamey, Maurice (Director)

Crazy in the Noodle 1957,D 15,45:4 (Incorrect in
this edition; use 1957,D 17,45:4 elsewhere)

Regamey, Maurice (Screenwriter)

Crazy in the Noodle 1957,D 15,45:4 (Incorrect in
this edition; use 1957,D 17,45:4 elsewhere)

Regan, Jayne

One More Spring 1935,F 22,27:1
Stowaway 1936,D 19,16:1
Second Honeymoon 1937,N 13,11:2
Thank You, Mr Moto 1938,Ja 3,16:2
Walking Down Broadway 1938,Ap 1,17:3
Mr Moto's Gamble 1938,Ap 8,17:2
Booloo 1938,Jl 30,10:2

Regan, Paul

Meet The People 1944,S 8,16:2

Regan, Phil

Key, The 1934,My 30,14:3
Housewife 1934,Ag 10,21:2
Dames 1934,Ag 16,20:2
Student Tour 1934,O 31,17:3
Sweet Adeline 1935,Ja 7,13:2
Go Into Your Dance 1935,My 4,17:2
In Caliente 1935,Je 27,16:1
Broadway Hostess 1935,D 16,23:3
Laughing Irish Eyes 1936,Ap 4,11:2
Hit Parade, The 1937,My 31,11:2
Manhattan Merry-Go-Round 1937,D 31,9:3
Flight at Midnight 1939,S 7,29:2
Las Vegas Nights 1941,Mr 20,25:2
Sweet Rosie O'Grady 1943,O 21,30:2
Three Little Words 1950,Ag 10,21:2

Regas, George

Newly Rich 1931,Jl 3,22:1
Sixteen Fathoms Deep 1934,Ja 19,24:3
Viva Villa! 1934,Ap 11,25:2
Bulldog Drummond Strikes Back 1934,Ag 16,20:2
Marines are Coming, The 1935,F 23,14:7
Rose Marie 1936,F 1,9:2
Robin Hood of El Dorado, The 1936,Mr 14,10:1
Daniel Boone 1936,O 24,23:2
Charge of the Light Brigade, The 1936,N 2,24:1
Love Under Fire 1937,Ag 28,8:2
Mr Moto Takes a Chance 1938,Je 13,15:4
Arrest Bulldog Drummond 1939,Ja 12,23:2
Adventures of Sherlock Holmes, The
1939,S 2,20:1
Light That Failed, The 1939,D 25,19:1
Torrid Zone 1940,My 18,11:3
Mark of Zorro, The 1940,N 4,23:2

Regas, Pedro
Black Fury 1935,Ap 11,27:2
Only Angels Have Wings 1939,My 12,25:2
Perilous Holiday 1946,Je 1,10:4
Reggiani, Serge
Star Without Light; Etoile Sans Lumiere
1947,Ag 4,14:2
Gates of the Night 1950,Mr 16,40:2
Children of Chaos 1950,Ap 20,37:2
Francois Villon 1950,Jl 3,9:2
Sinners, The 1950,N 11,11:2
Manon 1950,D 26,19:1
Lovers of Verona, The 1951,Mr 12,20:2
Act of Love 1954,F 12,20:5
Ronde, La 1954,Mr 17,27:2
Anita Garibaldi 1954,Mr 19,19:4
Marie Octobre 1960,Ag 16,25:2
Paris Blues 1961,N 8,41:1
Everybody go Home!; Tutti a Casa 1962,N 6,38:1
Leopard, The 1963,Ag 13,25:1
Doulos-The Finger Man 1964,Mr 3,31:1
Regin, Nadja
From Russia with Love 1964,Ap 9,25:1
Regis, Colette
Three Waltzes 1939,Ap 25,19:2
Human Beast, The 1940,F 20,17:2
Caroline Cherie 1954,My 25,23:1
Bride Is Much too Beautiful, The 1958,Ja 21,35:1
Attila 1958,My 19,19:4
Tomorrow Is my Turn 1962,F 2,24:2
Moderato Cantabile 1964,Ja 7,24:1
Abysses, Les 1964,N 24,44:1
Regnart, Florence
East of Suez 1925,Ja 26,22:1
Regnier, Charles
Last Illusion, The 1951,Mr 8,37:2
Deadly Decision 1958,Ap 29,26:2
Time to Love and a Time to Die, A
1958,Jl 10,22:1
Rest Is Silence, The 1960,Ag 2,22:6
Secret Ways, The 1961,My 25,31:1
Counterfeit Traitor, The 1962,Ag 18,28:1
Miracle of the White Stallions 1963,My 23,31:2
Adorable Julia 1964,Ap 8,33:1
Regnier, Georges
Portrait of Innocence 1948,Je 9,35:2
Regnier, Marthe
Mayerling 1937,S 14,27:1
Regua, Charles
Son of the Sheik, The 1926,Jl 26,13:2
Reguen, Ernesto
Con las Alas Rotas; With Broken Rings
1940,Mr 23,00:0
Regulski, Stefek
Ulica 1933,Ja 27,13:2
Reh, Mony
Mademoiselle 1966,Ag 2,23:1
Rehak, Frantisek
Capricious Summer 1968,S 18,50:2
Capricious Summer 1968,S 25,38:2
Rehfeld, Kurt (Director)
Greater Glory, The 1926,My 4,31:1
Rehfisch, H J (Original Author)
Dreyfus Case, The 1931,Ag 31,11:5
Danton 1931,S 7,19:3
Rehkopf, Paul
Berlin After Dark 1929,My 28,36:2
Brand in der Oper 1932,Jl 11,11:4
Letzte Rose 1936,O 10,21:3
Rehman, Waheeda
Guide, The 1965,F 10,44:2
Rehmann, Hans
Floetenkonzert von Sanssouci, Das
1931,O 17,20:1
Yorck 1932,N 24,35:2
Storch Hat Uns Getraut, Der 1933,D 1,23:2
Reiber, Willy (Director)
Sonne Geht auf, Die 1935,F 18,19:4
Johannisnact 1935,F 25,13:4
Reich, Albert (Original Author)
Key to the City 1950,F 2,31:2
Reich, Walter (Screenwriter)
Zwei Hertzen in Drei-Viertel Takt
1930,O 13,31:1
REICHART
See Also RICHARD
Reichenbach, Francois (Director)
Winner, The 1965,Jl 1,34:1
Reicher, Ernest
Lady From Paris, The 1927,S 28,28:3
Reicher, Ernst
Armored Vault 1928,N 13,37:2 (In Addenda)
Reicher, Frank
Beau Sabreur 1928,Ja 23,18:3
Four Sons 1928,F 14,27:1
Blue Danube, The 1928,Ap 30,18:3
Masks of the Devil, The 1928,N 26,30:2
Napoleon's Barber 1928,N 26,30:2
Some One to Love 1928,D 4,29:1
Sins of the Fathers 1929,Ja 28,21:1
Strange Cargo 1929,F 18,28:1
His Captive Woman 1929,Ap 3,26:4
Her Private Affair 1930,Ja 11,21:3

Beyond Victory 1931,Ap 6,24:1
Gentleman's Fate 1931,Je 27,20:3
Suicide Fleet 1931,N 23,22:1
Mata Hari 1932,Ja 1,31:1
Woman Commands, A 1932,Ja 28,13:2
Scarlet Dawn 1932,N 4,25:4
Employees' Entrance 1933,Ja 21,10:6
Topaze 1933,F 10,12:2
King Kong 1933,Mr 3,12:1
Captured 1933,Ag 18,18:3
Before Dawn 1933,O 17,26:2
Son of Kong 1933,D 30,9:2
Hi, Nellie! 1934,F 1,15:5
Countess of Monte Cristo, The 1934,Ap 2,13:2
Journal of a Crime 1934,Ap 28,11:3
No Greater Glory 1934,My 5,22:2
Little Man, What Now? 1934,Je 1,29:1
Let's Talk It Over 1934,Je 16,20:2
Return of the Terror 1934,Jl 11,20:2
Fountain, The 1934,Ag 31,14:1
Case of the Howling Dog, The 1934,O 18,26:5
I am a Thief 1935,Ja 1,24:1
Star of Midnight 1935,Ap 12,26:5
Florentine Dagger, The 1935,Ap 27,20:6
Rendezvous 1935,O 26,12:2
Man Who Broke the Bank at Monte Carlo, The
1935,N 15,20:2
Great Impersonation, The 1935,D 14,11:1
Magnificent Obsession 1935,D 31,11:2
Murder of Dr Harrigan, The 1936,Ja 21,27:5
Story of Louis Pasteur, The 1936,F 10,15:1
Country Doctor, The 1936,Mr 13,32:2 (Incorrect
in this edition; use 1936,Mr 13,27:2 elsewhere)
Murder on a Bridle Path 1936,Ap 11,19:2
Under Two Flags 1936,My 1,19:1
Ex-Mrs Bradford, The 1936,My 28,19:2
Anthony Adverse 1936,Ag 27,16:1
Girls' Dormitory 1936,Ag 29,16:2
Second Wife 1936,Ag 29,16:3
Star for a Night 1936,S 5,7:2
Under Cover of Night 1937,Ja 20,18:4
Stolen Holiday 1937,F 1,15:3
Road Back, The 1937,Je 18,25:2
Emperor's Candlesticks, The 1937,Jl 9,18:1
Midnight Madonna 1937,Jl 17,18:1
Stage Door 1937,O 8,27:2
Fit for a King 1937,O 15,18:5
Lancer Spy 1937,N 4,29:1
Prison Nurse 1938,Mr 4,17:5
Rascals 1938,My 27,12:2
I'll Give a Million 1938,Jl 16,7:2
City Streets 1938,Jl 25,18:2
Suez 1938,O 15,21:2
Torchy Gets her Man 1938,N 18,25:3
Woman Doctor 1939,Mr 24,27:3
Juarez 1939,Ap 26,27:1
Magnificent Fraud, The 1939,Jl 20,16:2
Unexpected Father 1939,Ag 11,12:2
Escape, The 1939,N 3,17:4
Everything Happens at Night 1939,D 16,12:6
Our Neighbors-The Carters 1940,F 15,15:2
Typhoon 1940,My 23,28:4
Devil's Island 1940,Jl 12,11:4
Man I Married, The 1940,Ag 3,9:2
South to Karanga 1940,Ag 9,19:1
Sky Murder 1940,N 14,28:3
Lady in Question, The 1940,D 10,33:2
Flight From Destiny 1941,Mr 28,26:7
They Dare not Love 1941,My 16,21:4
Shining Victory 1941,My 31,14:1
Nurse's Secret, The 1941,Je 6,25:7
Underground 1941,Je 23,13:2
Dangerously They Live 1942,Ap 11,9:2
Mystery of Marie Roget, The 1942,My 5,17:3
Nazi Agent 1942,Je 13,11:2
Gay Sisters, The 1942,Ag 15,14:2
Night Monster 1942,N 30,18:5
Secret Enemies 1943,Ja 1,27:3
Mission to Moscow 1943,Ap 30,25:2
Address Unknown 1944,Ap 17,20:1
Mummy's Ghost, The 1944,Jl 1,10:7
Big Bonanza, The 1945,F 26,14:5
Hotel Berlin 1945,Mr 3,11:2
Mr District Attorney 1947,F 28,27:3
Violence 1947,My 10,8:5
Secret Life of Walter Mitty, The 1947,Ag 15,12:2
Escape me Never 1947,N 8,11:2
Barbary Pirate 1949,O 28,29:3
Cargo to Capetown 1950,Mr 31,36:3
Kiss Tomorrow Goodbye 1950,Ag 5,9:2
Reicher, Hedwiga
Leopard Lady, The 1928,F 27,16:2
True Heaven 1929,F 11,26:3
Lucky Star 1929,Jl 22,17:1
Beyond Victory 1931,Ap 6,24:1
Sporting Chance 1931,N 28,20:4
House of a Thousand Candles, The
1936,Ap 2,29:2
I Married a Doctor 1936,Ap 20,17:1
REICHERT
See Also RICHARD

Reichert, Heinz (Screenwriter)
Strauss's Great Waltz 1935,Ap 8,23:3
Reichez, Frank
House of Frankenstein 1944,D 16,19:3
Reichhardt, Poul
Red Meadows 1950,Ja 19,35:2
Invisible Army, The 1950,Je 26,17:3
Venum 1968,Ja 11,42:1
Reichman, Sid (Miscellaneous)
Journey to Jerusalem, A 1968,N 18,59:1
Reichman, Thomas (Director)
Mingus 1968,My 17,56:1
Reichman, Thomas (Producer)
Mingus 1968,My 17,56:1
Reichman, Willy
Jonas 1959,Ap 30,37:1
Reichmann, Max (Director)
Manege 1928,Mr 11,VIII,7:6 (In Addenda)
Strange Case of Captain Ramper, The
1928,Je 4,13:2
Das Lockende Ziel 1933,Je 19,18:2
Die Grosse Attraktion 1933,Jl 24,11:2
Ich Glaub' nie Mehr an Eine Frau
1933,O 13,25:4
Reichmann, Wolfgang
Religieuse, La 1968,S 23,42:3
Signs of Life; Lebenszeichent 1968,S 26,60:1
Reichow, Otto
Paris Calling 1942,Ja 19,21:2
My Favorite Blonde 1942,Ap 2,27:2
Seven Miles From Alcatraz 1942,N 19,31:3
Dangerous Millions 1947,Mr 15,10:3
Rogues' Regiment 1948,D 20,31:2
REID
See Also READE, READ, REED
Reid, Arnold (Narrator)
Russians at War 1943,Ap 24,17:2
Reid, Beryl
Belles of St Trinian's, The 1954,D 23,13:4
Trial and Error 1962,N 17,17:2
Inspector Clouseau 1968,Jl 25,26:1
Star! 1968,O 23,36:2
Killing of Sister George, The 1968,D 17,58:4
Reid, Carl Benton
Little Foxes, The 1941,Ag 22,19:2
Tennessee Johnson 1943,Ja 13,18:2
North Star, The 1943,N 5,23:1
In a Lonely Place 1950,My 18,37:2
Fuller Brush Girl, The 1950,O 6,23:2
Flying Missile, The 1950,D 25,25:1
Killer That Stalked New York, The
1951,Ja 5,17:2
Stage to Tucson 1951,My 5,14:2
Great Caruso, The 1951,My 11,32:2
Criminal Lawyer 1951,Ag 24,11:4
Lorna Doone 1951,S 21,19:4
Boots Malone 1952,Mr 13,26:2
Carbine Williams 1952,My 8,37:2
Story of Will Rogers, The 1952,Jl 18,10:5
Brigand, The 1952,Jl 26,9:2
Command, The 1954,Ja 16,10:5
Escape from Fort Bravo 1954,Ja 23,11:2
Broken Lance 1954,Jl 30,9:1
Egyptian, The 1954,Ag 25,23:1
Athena 1954,D 22,28:2
One Desire 1955,S 3,9:1
Left Hand of God, The 1955,S 22,34:5
Spoilers, The 1955,D 24,10:2
First Texan, The 1956,Je 23,20:2
Last Wagon, The 1956,S 22,20:2
Battle Hymn 1957,F 16,14:1
Time Limit 1957,O 24,37:2
Tarzan's Fight for Life 1958,Ag 16,10:2
Trap, The 1959,Ja 29,18:4
Bramble Bush, The 1960,F 25,34:2
Gallant Hours, The 1960,Je 23,19:4
Pressure Point 1962,O 11,49:3
Reid, Cliff (Director)
Wanted: Jane Turner 1936,N 30,24:7
Reid, Cliff (Producer)
Grand Old Girl 1935,F 26,16:4
Arizonian, The 1935,Jl 27,16:2
Three Musketeers, The 1935,N 1,25:1
Annie Oakley 1935,D 24,10:5
Yellow Dust 1936,F 24,14:1
Powdersmoke Range 1936,Mr 9,20:2
Witness Chair, The 1936,Ap 18,19:2
Special Investigator 1936,Ap 25,21:1
Without Orders 1936,N 4,41:3
Criminal Lawyer 1937,Ja 27,17:3
Plough and the Stars, The 1937,Ja 29,15:1
Man Who Found Himself, The 1937,Ap 9,19:3
China Passage 1937,Ap 16,27:2
Behind the Headlines 1937,Je 1,27:2
Hideaway 1937,S 25,10:2
Crashing Hollywood 1938,Ja 8,19:2
Blind Alibi 1938,My 20,17:2
Crime Ring 1938,Jl 22,10:3
Law West of Tombstone, The 1938,N 25,19:1
Next Time I Marry 1938,D 2,27:2
Great Man Votes, The 1939,Ja 20,15:2
Fixer Dugan 1939,My 6,21:2
Girl and the Gambler, The 1939,Je 28,17:3

Reid, Cliff (Producer)— Cont

Conspiracy 1939,Ag 23,19:2
Spellbinder, The 1939,Ag 24,17:3
Mexican Spitfire 1940,Ja 10,16:4
Saint's Double Trouble, The 1940,F 13,27:2
You Can't Fool Your Wife 1940,My 24,23:4
Cross Country Romance 1940,Jl 19,22:3
Anne of Windy Poplars 1940,Ag 23,13:3
One Crowded Night 1940,Ag 27,17:2
Mexican Spitfire out West 1940,O 30,29:3
Play Girl 1941,Ja 30,19:3
Lady Scarface 1941,Ag 4,16:6
Sing Your Worries Away 1942,My 15,25:2
Powder Town 1942,Je 8,11:2
Mayor of Forty-Fourth Street, The 1942,Je 11,27:4
Mexican Spitfire at Sea 1942,Je 26,16:5
Mexican Spitfire Sees a Ghost 1942,Jl 31,11:2
Hoodlum Saint, The 1946,Je 27,29:1

Reid, Dorothy (Director)
Sucker Money 1933,Ap 7,22:5

Reid, Dorothy (Miscellaneous)
Redhead 1934,N 16,27:1

Reid, Dorothy (Producer)
Terror in the City 1966,N 9,43:4

Reid, Dorothy (Screenwriter)
Prison Break 1938,Jl 13,17:4
Impact 1949,Mr 21,19:2
Rhubarb 1951,Ag 31,12:2
Footsteps of the Fog 1955,S 15,39:2

Reid, Elliott
Ramparts We Watch, The 1940,S 20,27:1
Story of Dr Wassell, The 1944,Je 7,13:2
Sierra 1950,S 15,31:2
Gentlemen Prefer Blondes 1953,Jl 16,17:2
Vickie 1953,S 8,26:3
Woman's World 1954,S 29,23:4
Inherit the Wind 1960,O 13,41:1
Absent-Minded Professor, The 1961,Mr 16,44:2
Thrill of it All, The 1963,Ag 2,15:3
Wheeler Dealers, The 1963,N 15,25:2
Move Over Darling 1963,D 26,33:1
Follow Me, Boys! 1966,D 2,46:1

Reid, Frances
Seconds 1966,O 6,56:1

Reid, Frances Whiting (Original Author)
Big Town Girl 1937,D 13,23:4

Reid, Kate
1 ∎ 1 1961,N 8,41:1
This Property is Condemned 1966,Ag 4,24:1

Reid, Marita
Crowded Paradise 1956,Je 22,15:1

Reid, Milton
Wonders of Aladdin, The 1961,D 23,16:1
Deadlier Than the Male 1967,F 22,21:1

Reid, P R Major (Original Author)
Colditz Story, The 1957,O 25,23:2

Reid, Paula
Somewhere in the Night 1946,Je 13,24:2

Reid, Sheila
Othello 1966,F 2,24:1

Reid, Virginia (Original Author)
Black Market Babies 1946,Ap 1,23:1

Reid, Wallace
To Have and to Hold 1916,Mr 6,11:1
Woman God Forgot, The 1917,O 29,11:2
Believe Me, Xantippe 1918,Je 3,9:3
Firefly of France, The 1918,Jl 8,9:4
Less Than Kin 1918,Jl 22,9:1
Source, The 1918,S 9,9:1
Too Many Millions 1918,D 9,11:4
Roaring Road, The 1919,Ap 14,11:4
You're Fired 1919,Je 16,11:2
Love Burglar, The 1919,Jl 28,8:5
Lottery Man, The 1919,O 6,15:1
Double Speed 1920,F 2,10:1
Dancin' Fool, The 1920,My 3,18:1
What's Your Hurry? 1920,Ag 16,8:2
Love Special, The 1921,Mr 21,11:3
Too Much Speed 1921,Je 6,16:4
Affairs of Anatol, The 1921,S 12,16:1
Peter Ibbetson; (Forever) 1921,O 17,18:1
Don't Tell Everything 1921,D 12,20:2
World's Champion, The 1922,F 27,13:4
Dictator, The 1922,Jl 3,8:6
Ghost Breaker, The 1922,S 11,20:2
Clarence 1922,O 16,20:2
Birth of a Nation, The 1922,D 5,24:3
Thirty Days 1922,D 11,22:1
Birth of a Nation, The 1930,D 22,16:2

Reid, Wallace (Miscellaneous)
Hawthorne of the U.S.A. 1919,N 17,20:1

Reid, Wallace (Producer)
Lottery Man, The 1919,N 17,20:1

Reid, Wallace Jr
Gold Rush Maisie 1940,S 2,19:2

Reid, Wallace Mrs
Human Wreckage 1923,Je 28,10:2
Broken Laws 1925,Ja 21,19:3
Satin Woman, The 1927,Ag 10,21:4
Hell-Ship Bronson 1928,Je 19,31:1

Reid, Wallace Mrs (Director)
Red Kimono, The 1926,F 3,23:1
Road to Ruin, The 1934,F 21,23:2

Reid, Wallace Mrs (Miscellaneous)
House of a Thousand Candles, The 1936,Ap 2,29:2

Reid, Wallace Mrs (Original Author)
Road to Ruin, The 1934,F 21,23:2

Reiff, Fritz
Katzensteg 1938,Ja 22,19:2

Reigbert, Claire
Wenn der Hahn Kraeht 1936,N 14,23:3
Spiel in Sommerwind; Play in the Summer Breezes 1939,Ap 1,17:2

Reignier, Therese
Maternite 1937,Je 8,30:2

Reiguera, Francisco
Viva Maria 1965,D 20,48:2

Reilly, Charles Nelson
Two Tickets to Paris 1962,N 29,46:5
Tiger Makes Out, The 1967,S 19,53:1

Reilly, Dominick
Ireland, A Nation 1914,S 24,11:6

Reilly, Hugh
Johnny Stool Pigeon 1949,S 23,28:3
Bright Victory 1951,Ag 1,19:2
Chuka 1967,N 2,58:3

Reilly, Jack
Thirty Seconds Over Tokyo 1944,N 16,19:1
Story of G I Joe 1945,O 6,9:6
Well Groomed Bride, The 1946,My 11,22:5

Reilly, Jane
Passages From James Joyce's Finnegans Wake 1967,O 10,56:1

Reilly, Patricia (Original Author)
Big Business Girl 1931,Je 12,27:1

Reilly, Robert T (Original Author)
Fighting Prince of Donegal, The 1966,N 10,64:1

Reilly, Walter (Original Author)
Velvet Touch, The 1948,Ag 26,16:2

Reim, Einer
Girls are Willing, The 1959,My 11,30:1

REIMAN
See Also REIMANN

Reiman, Eric
Forty Thousand Horsemen 1941,Ag 15,13:2
Long John Silver 1955,Ap 7,24:1
Cinerama-South Seas Adventure 1958,Jl 16,26:1

Reiman, Walter (Miscellaneous)
Cabinet of Dr Caligari, The 1921,Mr 20,VI,2:1

REIMANN
See Also REIMAN

Reimer, Birgitte
Lesson in Love, A 1960,Mr 15,46:1

Reimer, Johannes
City Without Jews, The 1928,Jl 9,25:1
Scandal In Paris, A 1929,Je 10,23:1

Reimers, George
Queen of Sin and the Spectacle of Sodom and Gomorrah 1923,Mr 27,24:3 (In Addenda)

Reinach, Edward
Man's Past, A 1927,O 4,34:2

Reincke, Heinz
Always Victorious 1960,Ap 7,46:1
Faust 1963,Ap 16,31:1

Reinecker, Herbert (Screenwriter)
Deadly Decision 1958,Ap 29,26:2
Taiga 1959,Mr 17,42:4
Scampolo 1959,Ag 6,18:4

Reiner, Anna (Screenwriter)
Pastor Hall 1940,S 21,13:2

Reiner, Carl
Happy Anniversary 1959,N 11,41:1
Gazebo, The 1960,Ja 16,14:4
Gidget Goes Hawaiian 1961,Ag 10,17:4
It's a Mad, Mad, Mad, Mad World 1963,N 19,47:1
Art of Love, The 1965,Jl 1,34:1
Russians are Coming the Russians are Coming, The 1966,My 26,55:1
Guide for the Married Man, A 1967,My 27,16:1

Reiner, Carl (Director)
Enter Laughing 1967,Ag 1,24:1

Reiner, Carl (Original Author)
Thrill of it All, The 1963,Ag 2,15:3
Enter Laughing 1967,Ag 1,24:1

Reiner, Carl (Producer)
Enter Laughing 1967,Ag 1,24:1

Reiner, Carl (Screenwriter)
Thrill of it All, The 1963,Ag 2,15:3
Art of Love, The 1965,Jl 1,34:1
Enter Laughing 1967,Ag 1,24:1

Reiner, Fritz
Carnegie Hall 1947,My 3,10:2

Reiner, Ivan (Screenwriter)
Wild, Wild Planet 1967,Ag 10,45:5

Reiner, Maxine
Charlie Chan at the Circus 1936,Mr 19,22:4
Sins of Man 1936,Je 19,17:2
Girl on the Front Page, The 1936,N 7,15:2
Flying Hostess 1936,D 14,29:4

Reiner, Thomas
Blood and Black Lace 1965,N 11,58:3

Reinert, E E (Director)
Affaire, L' 1950,N 13,23:2
Strollers, The 1952,Jl 22,22:7

Reinert, E E (Director)— Cont

Tale of Five Women, A 1953,Ja 16,19:2
Naughty Martine 1953,Ap 13,32:4

Reinert, E E (Screenwriter)
Strollers, The 1952,Jl 22,22:7

Reingaard, Sisse
Venum 1968,Ja 11,42:1

REINHARD
See Also RINEHART, REINHARDT, REINHART

REINHARDT
See Also RINEHART, REINHARD, REINHART

Reinhardt, Artur
Reiter von Deutsch-Ostafrika, Die 1935,Je 8,12:3

Reinhardt, Betty (Original Author)
Maisie Was a Lady 1941,F 13,25:2
Maisie Gets her Man 1942,Jl 16,23:2

Reinhardt, Betty (Screenwriter)
Gold Rush Maisie 1940,S 2,19:2
Maisie Was a Lady 1941,F 13,25:2
Maisie Gets her Man 1942,Jl 16,23:2
His Butler's Sister 1943,D 30,13:2
Laura 1944,O 12,24:1
Sentimental Journey 1946,Mr 7,33:2

Reinhardt, Elizabeth (Screenwriter)
Cluny Brown 1946,Je 3,27:3
Carnival in Costa Rica 1947,Mr 29,21:2
Give my Regards to Broadway 1948,Je 23,32:2
When my Baby Smiles at Me 1948,N 24,20:2

Reinhardt, Gottfried (Director)
Invitation 1952,Ja 30,22:6
Story of Three Loves, The (The Jealous Lover); Jealous Lover, The (The Story of Three Loves) 1953,Mr 6,29:2
Story of Three Loves, The (Equilibrium); Equilibrium (The Story of Three Loves) 1953,Mr 6,29:2
Story of Three Loves, The (Mademoiselle); Mademoiselle (The Story of Three Loves) 1953,Mr 6,29:2
Equilibrium 1953,Mr 6,29:2
Story of Three Loves, The 1953,Mr 6,29:2
Betrayed 1954,S 9,36:1
Town Without Pity 1961,O 11,53:1
Situation Hopeless-But not Serious 1965,O 14,53:1

Reinhardt, Gottfried (Original Author)
Great Waltz, The 1938,N 25,19:1
Bridal Suite 1939,My 26,20:2

Reinhardt, Gottfried (Producer)
Comrade X 1940,D 26,23:1
Rage in Heaven 1941,Mr 21,19:2
Two Faced Woman 1942,Ja 1,37:2
Big Jack 1949,My 23,27:4
Great Sinner, The 1949,Je 30,19:2
Red Badge of Courage, The 1951,O 19,22:2
Young Man With Ideas 1952,Je 7,22:6
Town Without Pity 1961,O 11,53:1
Situation Hopeless-But not Serious 1965,O 14,53:1

Reinhardt, John
Love, Live and Laugh 1929,N 2,14:6
Tanz Geht Weiter, Der 1931,Ja 6,25:1

Reinhardt, John (Director)
IO... TU... Y...; (I... Thou... and... She) 1933,D 5,31:6
Granaderos del Amor 1934,S 4,23:4
Dos Mas Uno Dos 1934,O 27,20:3
Tango-Bar 1935,Jl 6,16:3
Dia que me Quieras, El; Day You Love Me, The 1935,Ag 27,23:3
Guilty, The 1947,My 19,27:2
High Tide 1947,N 8,11:2
Open Secret 1948,F 2,15:2
Sofia 1948,S 4,8:7

Reinhardt, John (Original Author)
Mamba 1930,Mr 11,25:2
Mr Moto in Danger Island 1938,Mr 20,13:3

Reinhardt, John (Producer)
Sofia 1948,S 4,8:7

Reinhardt, John (Screenwriter)
Tower of Terror 1942,Je 29,11:4

Reinhardt, Max (Director)
Midsummer Night's Dream, A 1935,O 10,31:1

Reinhardt, Silvia (Screenwriter)
Town Without Pity 1961,O 11,53:1

Reinhardt, Wolfgang (Producer)
Caught 1949,F 18,26:4
Trapp Family, The 1961,Ag 31,22:4
Freud 1962,D 13,37:1

Reinhardt, Wolfgang (Screenwriter)
Juarez 1939,Ap 26,27:1
Freud 1962,D 13,37:1

REINHART
See Also RINEHART, REINHARD, REINHARDT

Reinheart, Alice
Lieutenant Wore Skirts, The 1956,Ja 12,22:1
Bachelor Flat 1962,Ja 13,14:1

Reiniger, Lotte (Miscellaneous)
Cinderella 1928,Ja 22,VIII,7:7
Adventures of Prince Achmed, The 1931,F 27,19:3

Reinwald, Greta
Whirl of Life, The 1929,Mr 25,32:2
Eleven Who Were Loyal 1929,My 20,22:6
Reinzimmer, A (Director)
Girl With the Guitar, The 1960,F 1,22:4
REIS
See Also RICE, REECE, REES, REESE
Reis, Irving (Director)
One Crowded Night 1940,Ag 27,17:2
I'm Still Alive 1940,O 11,25:4
Week End for Three 1941,O 24,27:4
Date With the Falcon, A 1941,N 25,33:2
Falcon takes Over, The 1942,My 30,9:2
Big Street, The 1942,Ag 14,13:1
Crack-Up 1946,S 7,11:1
Bachelor and the Bobby-Soxer, The
  1947,Jl 25,12:5
All my Sons 1948,Mr 29,17:3
Enchantment 1948,D 27,16:2
Roseanna McCoy 1949,O 13,33:2
Dancing in the Dark 1949,D 3,8:6
Of Men and Music 1951,F 15,27:2
Three Husbands 1951,Mr 9,30:2
New Mexico 1951,Jl 14,7:2
Four Poster, The 1952,O 16,37:1
Reis, Irving (Original Author)
King of Alcatraz 1938,O 7,21:2
Time Out for Murder 1938,O 7,21:2
Grand Jury Secrets 1939,Je 29,19:2
Reis, Irving (Screenwriter)
King of Alcatraz 1938,O 7,21:2
King of Chinatown 1939,Mr 16,27:2
Grand Jury Secrets 1939,Je 29,19:2
Reisch, Walter (Director)
Men Are not Gods 1937,Ja 19,28:1
Episode 1937,My 17,23:2
Song of Scheherazade 1947,F 27,26:2
Reisch, Walter (Original Author)
Graefin von Monte Christo, Die; Countess of
  Monte Christo, The 1932,My 15,VIII,4:2 (In
  Addenda)
F P 1 1933,S 16,9:3
Heart Song 1934,Je 6,24:6
Unfinished Symphony 1935,Ja 14,11:2
Men Are not Gods 1937,Ja 19,28:1
Gateway 1938,Ag 8,9:2
My Love Came Back 1940,Jl 13,16:5
Comrade X 1940,D 26,23:1
Niagara 1953,Ja 22,20:3
Reisch, Walter (Producer)
Stopover Tokyo 1957,D 27,23:4
Fraulein 1958,Je 9,27:2
Reisch, Walter (Screenwriter)
Because I Loved You 1930,Ja 25,13:2
Blonder Tram, Ein; Blond Dream, A
  1932,N 13,IX,4:2
Escapade 1935,Jl 6,16:2
Masquerade in Vienna 1937,Ja 26,16:4
Episode 1937,My 17,23:2
Great Waltz, The 1938,N 25,19:1
Ninotchka 1939,N 10,27:2
That Hamilton Woman 1941,Ap 4,25:1
That Uncertain Feeling 1941,My 2,25:1
Somewhere I'll Find You 1942,Ag 28,22:4
Seven Sweethearts 1942,N 13,28:1
Heavenly Body, The 1944,Mr 24,17:3
Gaslight 1944,My 5,17:2
Song of Scheherazade 1947,F 27,26:2
Fan, The 1949,Ap 2,12:2
Mating Season, The 1951,Ap 12,41:2
Model and the Marriage Broker, The
  1952,Ja 12,10:6
Titanic 1953,My 28,27:5
Girl in the Red Velvet Swing, The
  1955,O 20,41:2
Teenage Rebel 1956,N 17,17:6
Stopover Tokyo 1957,D 27,23:4
Remarkable Mr Pennypacker, The 1959,F 21,25:2
Journey to the Center of the Earth
  1959,D 17,51:1
Reisenberg, Felix (Original Author)
East Side, West Side 1927,O 18,33:2
Skyline 1931,O 5,17:3
Reisenhofer, Maria
Nur am Rhein 1931,S 25,28:7
Reiser, Hans
Great British Train Robbery, The 1967,Ap 6,45:2
Reiser, Pete
Safe at Home 1941,N 26,31:2
Reisfeld, Bert (Composer)
Kyritz-Pyritz 1932,Ag 9,20:5
Reisman, Phil Jr (Original Author)
P J 1968,Mr 7,52:3
Reisman, Phil Jr (Screenwriter)
Frank Buck's Jungle Cavalcade 1941,Jl 4,17:1
Tattooed Stranger, The 1950,F 10,18:6
All the Way Home 1963,O 30,46:1
P J 1968,Mr 7,52:3
Reisman, Yuri (Director)
Last Night, The 1937,Ap 28,18:3
Moscow Skies 1945,Ja 22,22:5

Reisman, Yuri (Miscellaneous)
Fall of Berlin, The 1945,S 28,16:4
Reisman, Yuri (Producer)
Fall of Berlin, The 1945,S 28,16:4
Reisman, Yuri (Screenwriter)
Last Night, The 1937,Ap 28,18:3
Reisner, Allen (Director)
St Louis Blues 1958,Ap 12,13:1
All Mine to Give 1959,Ag 4,32:5
Reisner, C Francis (Composer)
Tin Pan Alley 1940,N 22,27:3
Reissmann, Rolf Dr (Screenwriter)
Secrets of a Soul 1950,S 16,12:6
Reisz, Karel (Director)
Saturday Night and Sunday Morning
  1961,Ap 4,44:2
Night Must Fall 1964,Mr 19,28:1
Morgan! 1966,Ap 5,42:2
Reisz, Karel (Producer)
This Sporting Life 1963,Jl 17,19:2
Night Must Fall 1964,Mr 19,28:1
Reitherman, Wolfgang (Director)
one Hundred and One Dalmations
  1961,F 11,27:1
Sword in the Stone, The 1963,D 26,33:3
Jungle Book, The 1967,D 23,29:1
Reizen, Mark
Khovanschina 1960,S 19,41:2
Rejane, Gabrielle
Miarka, The Daughter of the Bear
  1921,O 15,16:2
Gypsy Passion 1922,Mr 27,12:1
Relin, Herma
Ekel, Das; Grouch, The 1939,D 4,18:4
Relli, Lilli
Phaedra 1962,O 19,24:1
Relli, Santa
Jericho 1946,D 16,31:2
Shop-Girls of Paris; Au Bonheur de Dames
  1947,Je 23,14:4
Jour de Fete 1952,F 20,26:4
Rells, Harry (Screenwriter)
Captain Sindbad 1963,Jl 4,9:1
Rellys
Merlusse 1938,Mr 17,17:2
Merlusse 1938,Mr 17,17:2
Letters From my Windmill (The Elixir of Father
  Gaucher); Elixir of Father Gaucher, The (Letters
  From my Windmill) 1955,D 19,33:1
Easiest Profession, The 1960,Mr 26,15:7
Relph, George
Nicholas Nickleby 1947,D 1,27:2
I Believe in You 1953,My 5,34:3
Titfield Thunderbolt, The 1953,O 6,34:2
Final Test, The 1954,Ja 26,21:5
Doctor at Large 1957,Jl 29,15:5
Ben Hur 1959,N 19,50:2
Relph, Michael (Director)
I Believe in You 1953,My 5,34:3
Gentle Gunman, The 1953,O 1,34:3
Ship That Died of Shame, The 1956,Ag 21,33:2
Out of the Clouds 1957,Ag 1,20:4
Mad Little Island 1958,D 31,12:1
Relph, Michael (Producer)
I Believe in You 1953,My 5,34:3
Gentle Gunman, The 1953,O 1,34:3
Ship That Died of Shame, The 1956,Ag 21,33:2
Out of the Clouds 1957,Ag 1,20:4
Smallest Show on Earth, The 1957,N 23,11:2
Sapphire 1959,N 3,27:1
League of Gentlemen, The 1961,Ja 25,30:4
Man in the Moon 1961,Je 13,29:2
Victim 1962,F 6,27:2
Mind Benders, The 1963,My 2,40:2
Woman of Straw 1964,O 1,30:6
Masquerade 1965,Ap 29,40:2
Walk in the Shadow 1966,S 12,52:5
Relph, Michael (Screenwriter)
I Believe in You 1953,My 5,34:3
Ship That Died of Shame, The 1956,Ag 21,33:2
Out of the Clouds 1957,Ag 1,20:4
Man in the Moon 1961,Je 13,29:2
Masquerade 1965,Ap 29,40:2
Remarque, Erich Maria
Time to Love and a Time to Die, A
  1958,Jl 10,22:1
Remarque, Erich Maria (Original Author)
All Quiet on The Western Front 1930,Ap 30,29:1
Road Back, The 1937,Je 18,25:2
Three Comrades 1938,Je 3,17:1
All Quiet on the Western Front 1939,O 9,15:2
So Ends our Night 1941,F 28,17:2
Other Love, The 1947,My 15,32:4
Arch of Triumph 1948,Ap 21,33:2
Time to Love and a Time to Die, A
  1958,Jl 10,22:1
Remarque, Erich Maria (Screenwriter)
Last ten Days, The 1956,Ap 12,26:1
Remberg, Erika
Circus of Horrors 1960,S 1,31:1
Remer, Rubye de
Glimpses of the Moon 1923,Ap 3,23:4

Remi, Juan-Francois
Guerre est Fini, La; War Is Over, The
  1967,F 2,29:2
Remick, Lee
Face in the Crowd, A 1957,My 29,33:1
Long, Hot Summer, The 1958,Ap 4,16:1
These Thousand Hills 1959,My 7,36:1
Anatomy of a Murder 1959,Jl 3,10:1
Wild River 1960,My 27,22:1
Sanctuary 1961,F 22,31:1
Experiment in Terror 1962,Ap 14,14:1
Days of Wine and Roses 1963,Ja 18,7:2
Running Man, The 1963,O 3,31:1
Wheeler Dealers, The 1963,N 15,25:2
Baby, the Rain Must Fall 1965,Ja 14,44:1
Hallelujah Trail, The 1965,Jl 2,17:1
No Way to Treat a Lady 1968,Mr 21,56:1
Detective, The 1968,My 29,20:3
Remley, Ralph
Double Door 1934,My 5,22:3
Behold My Wife 1935,F 18,19:3
Princess O'Hara 1935,Ap 13,11:3
Dr Socrates 1935,O 3,29:2
Robin Hood of El Dorado, The 1936,Mr 14,10:1
Bullets or Ballots 1936,My 27,27:1
Poppy 1936,Je 18,19:1
Yours for the Asking 1936,Ag 20,14:2
Make Way for Tomorrow 1937,My 10,23:1
Let Them Live 1937,Je 8,30:3
King of the Underworld 1939,Ja 7,6:2
Story of Alexander Graham Bell, The
  1939,Ap 1,17:2
Remo, Four
Go Go Mania 1965,My 20,52:4
Remsen, Bert
Moon Pilot 1962,Ap 6,30:2
Remy, Albert
It Happened at the Inn; Goupi Mains Rouge
  1945,D 22,16:2
Enfants du Paradis, Les 1947,F 20,32:2
Devil's Daughter 1949,F 26,11:2
Francois Villon 1950,Jl 3,9:2
French-Cancan 1956,Ap 17,26:2
Razzi 1957,N 19,39:4
Crime and Punishment 1958,S 16,23:2
400 Blows, The; (Les Quatre Cents Coups)
  1959,N 17,41:1
Cow and I, The 1961,Je 6,42:2
4 Horsemen of the Apocalypse, The
  1962,Mr 10,10:2
Shoot the Piano Player 1962,Jl 24,19:1
Gigot 1962,S 28,26:1
Lafayette 1963,Ap 11,29:1
Seventh Juror, The 1964,Ja 28,25:1
Train, The 1965,Mr 18,25:1
How Not to Rob a Department Store
  1965,D 29,23:1
Remy, Constant
Soir de Rafle, Un 1931,O 16,27:1
Jean de la Lune 1932,Mr 12,19:5
Femme Nue, La 1933,Ag 25,12:3
Agonie des Aigles, L' 1934,D 1,8:5
Etoile Disparait, Une; Star Disappears, A
  1935,F 9,11:3
Petits, Les 1936,D 30,17:2
Mysteres de Paris, Les 1937,Ja 30,21:2
Helene 1938,Ja 22,19:1
Clandestine 1948,My 24,23:2
Remy, Constant (Director)
Petits, Les 1936,D 30,17:2
Remy, Helene
Always Victorious 1960,Ap 7,46:1
Last of the Vikings 1962,S 27,33:4
Remy, Jacques (Original Author)
Secret of Mayerling, The 1951,My 8,39:2
If all the Guys in the World 1957,Ap 23,34:1
Cat, The 1959,Ap 13,35:1
Remy, Jacques (Screenwriter)
Damned, The; Maudits, Les 1948,Ap 26,27:2
Secret of Mayerling, The 1951,My 8,39:2
If all the Guys in the World 1957,Ap 23,34:1
Night Heaven Fell, The 1958,O 22,40:4
Cat, The 1959,Ap 13,35:1
Marco the Magnificent 1966,D 15,60:1
Remy, Maurice
Topaze 1935,F 16,9:2
Remy, Ronald
No Man is an Island 1962,O 11,49:2
Renaldi, Tina
Zappatore 1932,Mr 28,11:2
Renaldo, Duncan
Trader Horn 1931,F 4,21:3
Moonlight Murder 1936,Mr 28,11:2
Rose of the Rio Grande 1938,Jl 9,10:3
Spawn of the North 1938,S 8,27:1
For Whom the Bell Tolls 1943,Jl 15,25:2
Fighting Seabees, The 1944,Mr 20,14:2
Sword of the Avenger 1948,Ag 26,16:4
Capture, The 1950,My 20,8:6
Renaldo, Tito
Sunday Punch 1942,My 11,19:2
Adventure 1946,F 8,23:2
Anna and the King of Siam 1946,Je 21,20:2

Renaldo, Tito — Cont
Old Los Angeles 1948,Jl 12,11:2
Bribe, The 1949,F 4,31:2
Tension 1950,Ja 12,32:4
One Way Street 1950,My 12,33:3
Tarzan and the Slave Girl 1950,Je 24,7:3
Renant, Simone
Pearls of the Crown, The 1938,Ap 12,26:2
Jenny Lamour 1948,Mr 6,17:2
Bedevilled 1955,Ap 23,23:1
Ostrich Has two Eggs, The 1960,S 27,40:1
Liaisons Dangereuses, Les 1961,D 19,39:1
That Man From Rio 1964,Je 9,30:1
Renar, Helmuth
Waterloo 1929,Ap 16,32:5
Renard, Colette
Back to the Wall; (Dos au Mur) 1959,S 8,43:2
Renard, Ervin
Eagle of the Sea, The 1926,N 17,21:6
Captain of the Guard 1930,Mr 29,23:1
Renard, Jules (Original Author)
Poil de Carotte 1933,My 26,24:2
Renard, Kaye
Glorifying the American Girl 1930,Ja 11,21:3
Renard, Ken
Lydia Bailey 1952,My 31,12:5
Something of Value 1957,My 11,24:6
These Thousand Hills 1959,My 7,36:1
Home from the Hill 1960,Mr 4,19:1
Renard, Maurice (Original Author)
Hands of Orlac, The 1928,Je 5,21:1
Mad Love 1935,Ag 5,20:2
Renaud, Madeleine
Jean de la Lune 1932,Mr 12,19:5
Couturiere de Luneville, La 1932,O 14,23:2
Mistigri 1933,Ja 13,19:3
Maria Chapdelaine 1935,S 25,18:2
Maternelle, La 1935,O 15,19:1
Helene 1938,Ja 22,19:1
Stormy Waters 1946,Je 17,32:2
Woman Who Dared, The 1949,Mr 19,10:7
Plaisir, Le (The House of Madame Tellier); House of Madame Tellier (Le Plaisir) 1954,My 20,38:1
Longest Day, The 1962,O 5,28:1
Renault, Jack
Knockout Reilly 1927,Ap 18,21:2
Renavent, Georges
Rio Rita 1929,O 7,22:1
Scotland Yard 1930,O 20,28:2
East of Borneo 1931,S 26,25:3
Queen Christina 1933,D 27,23:3
Bombay Mail 1934,Ja 6,18:2
Moulin Rouge 1934,F 8,14:4
House of Rothschild, The 1934,Mr 15,27:2
Folies Bergere 1935,F 25,13:2
Front Page Woman 1935,Jl 12,15:1
Last Outpost, The 1935,O 5,18:2
Whipsaw 1936,Ja 25,18:4
Sky Parade, The 1936,Ap 20,17:1
Lloyds of London 1936,N 26,39:1
Seventh Heaven 1937,Mr 26,25:1
History Is Made at Night 1937,Mr 29,14:2
King and the Chorus Girl, The 1937,Mr 29,14:4
Cafe Metropole 1937,Ap 29,17:1
Love Under Fire 1937,Ag 28,8:2
Fight for Your Lady 1937,N 20,21:2
Charlie Chan at Monte Carlo 1937,D 18,18:1
Love and Hisses 1938,Ja 1,11:1
Jezebel 1938,Mr 11,15:2
Gold Diggers in Paris 1938,Je 2,19:2
I'll Give a Million 1938,Jl 16,7:2
Suez 1938,O 15,21:2
Artists and Models Abroad 1938,D 22,25:3
Pack up Your Troubles 1939,O 27,27:2
Turnabout 1940,Jl 27,17:6
Son of Monte Cristo, The 1940,D 5,33:1
Comrade X 1940,D 26,23:1
That Night in Rio 1941,Mr 10,21:2
Road to Zanzibar 1941,Ap 10,29:2
Night of January 16th, The 1941,D 19,35:1
Sullivan's Travels 1942,Ja 29,25:2
Our Hearts Were Young and Gay 1944,O 12,24:2
Ladies' Man 1947,Ja 13,18:5
Mara Maru 1952,Ap 24,38:1
Renay, Paul
Tales of Manhattan 1942,S 25,25:1
Rencher, Derek
Romeo and Juliet 1966,O 6,55:1
Rendel, Robert
Missing Ten Days 1941,Ap 21,15:5 (In Addenda)
Rendell, Robert
Babbitt 1924,Jl 15,9:4
Her Night of Romance 1925,Ja 13,16:1
Fire Over England 1937,Mr 5,16:2
Four Feathers 1939,Ag 4,11:1
U-Boat 29 1939,O 6,31:3
Rene, Fernand
Monelle 1950,F 3,29:2
Rene, Leon (Composer)
Let Freedom Ring 1939,Mr 10,19:2
Rene, Otis (Composer)
Let Freedom Ring 1939,Mr 10,19:2

Renee, Renate
Rasputin, The Holy Sinner 1929,Ja 15,22:4
Renella, Pat
Dayton's Devils 1968,O 3,56:4
Renick, Ruth
Conrad in Quest of his Youth 1920,N 8,20:2
Golden Snare, The 1921,Jl 11,9:3
From Rags to Riches 1922,S 25,10:2
Renick, Sammy
Wind Across the Everglades 1958,S 12,21:1
Renn, Adrianne
Revenge of General Ling, The 1938,F 21,15:1
Renn, Katharina
Rise of Louis XIV, The 1967,S 26,54:2
Rennick, John
Native Land 1942,My 12,16:3
Rennick, Nancy
Young Lovers, The 1965,F 11,45:1
Rennie, Guy
Grounds for Marriage 1951,Ja 12,24:6
Rennie, James
Dust Flower, The 1922,Jl 3,8:6
Mighty Lak' a Rose 1923,Mr 20,24:3
His Children's Children 1923,N 5,15:1
Moral Sinner, The 1924,Ap 7,15:3
Argentine Love 1924,D 23,16:2
Clothes Make the Pirate 1925,N 30,17:1
Bad Man, The 1930,S 27,21:3
Girl of the Golden West, The 1930,O 27,17:1
Lash, The 1931,Ja 1,31:3
Illicit 1931,Ja 19,25:1
Party Husband 1931,My 16,13:3
Skylark 1941,N 20,39:2
Crossroads 1942,Jl 27,18:2
Tales of Manhattan 1942,S 25,25:1
Now, Voyager 1942,O 23,25:3
Wilson 1944,Ag 2,18:1
Rennie, Michael
Ships With Wings 1942,My 25,11:2
Tower of Terror 1942,Je 29,11:4
Wicked Lady, The 1946,D 23,19:5
Golden Madonna, The 1949,S 5,13:4
Sanitorium 1950,O 11,42:1
Thirteenth Letter, The 1951,F 22,27:2
Day the Earth Stood Still, The 1951,S 19,37:1
I'll Never Forget You 1951,D 8,9:2
Phone Call From a Stranger 1952,F 2,11:2
Five Fingers 1952,F 23,7:5
Miserables, Les 1952,Ag 15,11:2
Sailor of the King 1953,S 3,15:2
Robe, The 1953,S 17,32:6
Dangerous Crossing 1953,S 30,37:2
King of the Khyber Rifles 1953,D 23,21:1
Princess of the Nile 1954,Je 12,13:2
Demetrius and the Gladiators 1954,Je 19,9:1
Desiree 1954,N 18,42:1
Mambo 1955,Mr 31,23:3
Soldier of Fortune 1955,My 28,7:4
Seven Cities of Gold 1955,O 8,13:2
Rains of Ranchipur, The 1955,D 16,38:2
Teenage Rebel 1956,N 17,17:6
Island in the Sun 1957,Je 13,37:1
Omar Khayyam 1957,Ag 24,12:4
Third Man on the Mountain 1959,N 12,27:1
Lost World, The 1960,Jl 14,23:1
Mary, Mary 1963,O 25,38:2
Ride Beyond Vengance 1966,S 29,60:1
Hotel 1967,Ja 20,27:1
Power, The 1968,Mr 7,52:2
Devil's Brigade, The 1968,My 23,56:2
Young, The Evil and the Savage, The 1968,Ag 15,46:2
Renno, Vincent
Frenchie 1951,F 12,19:2
Great Caruso, The 1951,My 11,32:2
Sirocco 1951,Je 14,31:2
Renoir, Claude (Producer)
Rules of the Game, The 1950,Ap 10,15:3
Renoir, Jean
Human Beast, The 1940,F 20,17:2
Rules of the Game, The 1950,Ap 10,15:3
Ways of Love (A Day in the Country); Day in the Country, A (Ways of Love) 1950,D 13,50:2
Rules of the Game, The 1961,Ja 19,26:1
Renoir, Jean (Director)
Bled, Le 1929,Ag 25,VIII,5:1
Nuit du Carrefour; Night at the Crossroads, The 1932,Je 5,X,10:4 (In Addenda)
Madame Borary 1934,N 19,13:2
Amours de Toni, Les 1936,N 5,35:1
Lower Depths, The 1937,S 11,20:1
People of France, The 1937,D 6,19:1
Grand Illusion 1938,S 13,28:2
Bete Humaine, La 1939,F 26,IX,5:6 (In Addenda)
Marseillaise 1939,N 6,20:2
Human Beast, The 1940,F 20,17:2
Swamp Water 1941,N 17,15:2
This Land Is Mine 1943,My 28,19:1
Southerner, The 1945,Ag 27,22:3
Diary of a Chambermaid, The 1946,Je 23,28:2
Woman on the Beach, The 1947,Je 9,26:6
Rules of the Game, The 1950,Ap 10,15:3
Ways of Love (A Day in the Country); Day in the Country, A (Ways of Love) 1950,D 13,50:2

Renoir, Jean (Director) — Cont
River, The 1951,S 11,33:2
Golden Coach, The 1954,Ja 22,30:2
French-Cancan 1956,Ap 17,26:2
Paris Does Strange Things 1957,Mr 30,13:2
Picnic on the Grass 1960,O 12,47:1
Rules of the Game, The 1961,Ja 19,26:1
Elusive Corporal, The 1963,F 19,5:1
Crime of Monsieur Lange, The 1964,Ap 4,15:5
Boudu Saved From Drowning; Boudu Sauve Des Eaux 1967,F 24,26:2
Toni 1968,S 19,62:2
Renoir, Jean (Miscellaneous)
Lower Depths, The 1937,S 11,20:1
Renoir, Jean (Original Author)
Grand Illusion 1938,S 13,28:2
Paris Does Strange Things 1957,Mr 30,13:2
Crime of Monsieur Lange, The 1964,Ap 4,15:5
Renoir, Jean (Producer)
Nana 1928,Ja 22,VIII,7:7
French-Cancan 1956,Ap 17,26:2
Picnic on the Grass 1960,O 12,47:1
Renoir, Jean (Screenwriter)
Amours de Toni, Les 1936,N 5,35:1
Grand Illusion 1938,S 13,28:2
Marseillaise 1939,N 6,20:2
Southerner, The 1945,Ag 27,22:3
Woman on the Beach, The 1947,Je 9,26:6
Rules of the Game, The 1950,Ap 10,15:3
River, The 1951,S 11,33:2
Golden Coach, The 1954,Ja 22,30:2
French-Cancan 1956,Ap 17,26:2
Picnic on the Grass 1960,O 12,47:1
Rules of the Game, The 1961,Ja 19,26:1
Elusive Corporal, The 1963,F 19,5:1
Boudu Saved From Drowning; Boudu Sauve Des Eaux 1967,F 24,26:2
Toni 1968,S 19,62:2
Renoir, Marguerite
Ways of Love (A Day in the Country); Day in the Country, A (Ways of Love) 1950,D 13,50:2
Renoir, Pierre
Nuit du Carrefour; Night at the Crossroads, The 1932,Je 5,X,10:4 (In Addenda)
Madame Borary 1934,N 19,13:2
Agonie des Aigles, L' 1934,D 1,8:5
Razumov 1937,Mr 9,27:2
Sacrifice d'Honneur 1938,D 2,27:2
Kreutzer Sonata, The 1938,D 20,30:2
Escape From Yesterday 1939,My 3,27:2
Marseillaise 1939,N 6,20:2
Citadel of Silence, The 1939,D 25,29:1
Hatred 1941,Ja 27,11:2
Personal Column 1941,F 3,13:2
Mad Emperor, The 1941,Mr 10,21:3
Resistance; Peleton d'Execution 1946,Jl 5,15:3
Sirocco 1946,Ag 12,17:3
Enfants du Paradis, Les 1947,F 20,32:2
Foolish Husbands 1948,O 11,27:2
Dr Knock 1955,O 10,31:2
Renoir, Rita
Sweet and Sour 1964,D 28,34:2
Red Desert 1965,F 9,43:1
Renoit-Levy, Jean (Screenwriter)
Ballerina 1938,N 15,27:1
Renor, Renee
Guys and Dolls 1955,N 5,26:1
Rentschler, Mickey
Modern Hero, A 1934,Ap 20,17:1
Black Fury 1935,Ap 11,27:2
Sins of Man 1936,Je 19,17:2
Follow Your Heart 1936,O 22,31:1
Adventures of Tom Sawyer, The 1938,F 18,23:1
Devil's Party, The 1938,My 31,8:3
Boys Town 1938,S 9,25:1
Peck's bad Boy With the Circus 1939,Ja 11,17:4
Renwick, Ruth
Long Live the King 1923,D 4,24:1
Renzelli, Gastone
Bellissima 1953,My 18,26:2
Roof, The 1959,My 13,43:4
Renzi, Eva
Funeral in Berlin 1966,D 23,17:1
That Woman 1968,Jl 19,30:3
Pink Jungle, The 1968,O 17,52:1
Renzi, Pina
Passa L'Amore 1933,N 25,10:3
Fiat Voluntas Dei 1936,Jl 6,11:5
Al Vostri Ordini, Signora; At Your Orders, Madame 1940,My 25,20:1
Renzi, R (Screenwriter)
Anita Garibaldi 1954,Mr 19,19:4
Reordan, William
World Dances 1954,N 8,24:6
Repa, Vladimir
Thunder in the Hills 1947,My 24,10:5
Repet, Jose Pena
Castillos en el Aire; Castles in the Air 1938,My 21,9:3
Repetti, Caria
Revenge 1947,N 28,37:4
Repinof, Alexander
Thirteen, The 1937,Je 19,20:2

Repnin, P P
  Clown George 1932,Ag 24,21:4
Repnin, R
  Boule de Suif 1958,My 5,24:1
Repp, Guy
  Young as You Feel 1940,Mr 8,25:3
Repp, Pierre
  Five Day Lover, The 1961,D 14,55:4
Repp, Stafford
  Hot Spell 1958,S 18,37:2
  I Want to Live 1958,N 19,45:1
  Very Special Favor, A 1965,Ag 26,40:3
Requa, Charles
  King of Kings, The 1927,Ap 20,29:2
  Are We Civilized? 1934,Je 14,28:5
  Yours for the Asking 1936,Ag 20,14:2
Requena, Manuel
  Goyescas 1944,My 29,18:3
  Don Quixote 1949,My 13,29:3
Rereda, Ramon
  Cruz Diablo 1935,Ap 6,10:1
Reri
  Tabu 1931,Mr 19,21:3
  Hurricane, The 1937,N 10,31:2
Resko, John (Original Author)
  Convicts 4 1962,O 4,44:2
Resnais, Alain (Director)
  Hiroshima, Mon Amour 1960,My 17,43:1
  Last Year at Marienbad 1962,Mr 8,26:1
  Muriel 1963,O 31,26:1
  Guerre est Fini, La; War Is Over, The
    1966,S 23,43:1
  Forward Voyager 1966,N 25,49:1
  Guerre est Fini, La; War Is Over, The
    1967,F 2,29:2
  Far From Vietnam 1968,Je 7,32:1
Resnais, Alain (Miscellaneous)
  Pictura 1952,Ap 8,35:3
Resnais, Alain (Narrator)
  Far from Vietnam 1967,O 2,58:1
Resnais, Alain (Producer)
  Hiroshima, Mon Amour 1960,My 17,43:1
Resnik, Muriel (Original Author)
  Any Wednesday 1966,O 14,50:1
  How Sweet It Is 1968,Ag 22,47:1
Ressel, Franco
  Blood and Black Lace 1965,N 11,58:3
Resson, Arthur (Director)
  Little Johnny Jones 1923,Ag 13,16:1
Retchin, Norman (Producer)
  Leather Saint, The 1956,Je 16,12:2
Retchin, Norman (Screenwriter)
  Leather Saint, The 1956,Je 16,12:2
Reties, Jill
  His Hour 1924,O 7,26:1
Rettig, Tommy
  Panic in the Streets 1950,Ag 5,9:2
  Jackpot, The 1950,N 23,55:2
  Two Weeks With Love 1950,N 24,31:2
  For Heaven's Sake 1950,D 16,10:5
  Elopement 1951,D 21,21:3
  Paula 1952,Jl 16,21:2
  Lady Wants Mink, The 1953,Ap 6,24:2
  5,000 Fingers of Dr T, The 1953,Je 20,8:6
  River of no Return 1954,My 1,13:2
  Raid, The 1954,Ag 21,10:4
  Egyptian, The 1954,Ag 25,23:1
  Cobweb, The 1955,Ag 6,13:3
  At Gunpoint 1956,F 4,24:5
  Last Wagon, The 1956,S 22,20:2
Retty, Wolf Albach
  Winternachtstraum 1935,D 28,10:6
  Mutterliebe; Mother Love 1940,Mr 16,8:3
Reufer-Eichberg, Adele
  Explosion 1927,D 13,33:2
Reusch, Hans (Original Author)
  Racers, The 1955,F 5,13:2
  Savage Innocents, The 1961,My 25,31:1
Reutner, George M (Producer)
  Mediterannean Holiday 1964,D 16,51:1
Reuver, Germaine
  Prize, The 1952,Ap 30,33:2
Reval, Else
  Student Sein 1931,My 4,15:3
  Ein Prinz Verliebt Sich 1932,Ap 29,13:4
  Pension Schoeller 1932,S 20,26:3
  Zapfenstreich am Rhein 1933,F 2,21:6
  Lustige Witwenball, Der; Merry Widows' Ball,
    The 1939,My 1,21:2
Revalles, Flora
  Earthbound 1920,Ag 11,9:4
Revel, Harry
  Sitting Pretty 1933,D 2,9:3
  Collegiate 1936,Ja 23,25:2
Revel, Harry (Composer)
  Smiling Faces 1932,Ag 31,12:3
  Broadway Thru a Keyhole 1933,N 2,18:3
  White Woman 1933,N 18,18:5
  Sitting Pretty 1933,D 2,9:3
  We're not Dressing 1934,Ap 26,27:2
  Shoot the Works 1934,Jl 7,16:5
  Old-Fashioned Way, The 1934,Jl 14,16:5
  She Loves Me Not 1934,S 8,18:5

Now and Forever 1934,O 13,10:1
Gay Divorcee, The 1934,N 16,27:1
College Rhythm 1934,N 24,19:1
Love in Bloom 1935,Ap 20,16:2
Stolen Harmony 1935,Ap 20,16:2
Big Broadcast of 1936, The 1935,S 16,15:2
Head Over Heels in Love 1937,F 13,9:1
Wake up and Live 1937,Ap 24,16:2
This Is my Affair 1937,My 28,17:1
Thin Ice 1937,S 4,8:2
Ali Baba Goes to Town 1937,O 23,14:1
Love and Hisses 1938,Ja 1,11:1
In Old Chicago 1938,Ja 7,15:2
Sally, Irene and Mary 1938,F 26,9:2
Rebecca of Sunnybrook Farm 1938,Mr 26,12:1
Josette 1938,Je 11,9:1
Love Finds Andy Hardy 1938,Jl 22,10:2
My Lucky Star 1938,S 10,20:2
Hold That Co-ed 1938,S 24,13:1
Thanks For Everything 1938,D 10,13:2
Rose of Washington Square 1939,My 6,21:2
Dance Hall 1941,Jl 19,16:2
Call out the Marines 1942,Ja 26,18:3
Sing Your Worries Away 1942,My 15,25:2
Hit the Ice 1943,S 23,27:2
Minstrel Man 1944,Jl 17,18:5
Revel, Harry (Miscellaneous)
  Paris in Spring 1935,Jl 13,16:2
  Two for Tonight 1935,Ag 31,16:2
  Collegiate 1936,Ja 23,25:2
  Poor Little Rich Girl, The 1936,Je 26,16:1
  Stowaway 1936,D 19,16:1
Revel, Jean-Marie
  Strange Ones, The 1952,Jl 29,17:3
Revel, Mack (Composer)
  You Can't Have Everything 1937,Ag 4,15:2
Revela, Rita
  Greed 1924,D 5,28:1
Revelle, Hamilton
  Thais 1917,D 31,5:2
  Star Overnight, A 1919,N 17,20:1
  Telephone Girl, The 1927,My 16,24:2
Revere, Anne
  Double Door 1934,My 5,22:3
  One Crowded Night 1940,Ag 27,17:2
  Howards of Virginia, The 1940,S 27,27:1
  Devil Commands, The 1941,F 14,15:3
  Men of Boys Town 1941,Ap 11,24:6
  Flame of New Orleans, The 1941,Ap 26,20:2
  Remember the Day 1941,D 26,21:2
  Falcon takes Over, The 1942,My 30,9:2
  Gay Sisters, The 1942,Ag 15,14:2
  Star Spangled Rhythm 1942,D 31,20:1
  Meanest Man in the World, The 1943,F 25,27:3
  Old Acquaintance 1943,N 3,20:2
  Song of Bernadette, The 1944,Ja 27,15:2
  Standing Room Only 1944,F 23,17:2
  Rainbow Island 1944,O 26,19:6
  National Velvet 1944,D 15,25:2
  Keys of the Kingdom, The 1944,D 30,15:2
  Sunday Dinner for a Soldier 1945,Ja 25,16:2
  Thin Man Goes Home, The 1945,Ja 26,16:5
  Don Juan Quilligan 1945,Jl 30,16:2
  Fallen Angel 1946,F 7,29:4
  Dragonwyck 1946,Ap 11,35:2
  Shocking Miss Pilgrim, The 1947,F 12,34:2
  Carnival in Costa Rica 1947,Mr 29,21:2
  Forever Amber 1947,O 23,31:2
  Body and Soul 1947,N 10,21:2
  Gentleman's Agreement 1947,N 12,36:2
  Secret Beyond the Door 1948,Ja 16,25:4
  Scudda-Hoo! Scudda-Hay! 1948,Ap 15,31:1
  Deep Waters 1948,Jl 23,12:4
  You're my Everything 1949,Jl 23,7:2
  Great Missouri Raid, The 1951,Ap 9,31:2
  Place in the Sun, A 1951,Ag 29,20:1
Revere, Carla
  Open City; Citta Aperta 1946,F 26,21:2
Revides, Alex
  Eva 1965,Je 5,21:2
Revier, Dorothy
  Just a Woman 1925,My 26,24:2
  Poker Faces 1926,S 14,25:4
  Drop Kick, The 1927,S 20,32:2
  Red Dance, The 1928,Je 26,29:1
  Beware of Blondes 1928,Ag 21,27:4
  Submarine 1928,Ag 31,23:3
  Iron Mask, The 1929,F 22,18:6
  Donovan Affair, The 1929,Ap 29,29:2
  Father and Son 1929,Je 4,29:3
  Dance of Life, The 1929,Ag 16,18:6
  Mighty, The 1929,D 30,16:4
  Hold Everything 1930,Ap 23,24:1
  Call of the West 1930,My 27,27:2
  Squealer, The 1930,S 8,17:1
  Way of all Men, The 1930,S 20,15:4
  Bad Man, The 1930,S 27,21:3
  Black Camel, The 1931,Jl 4,11:5
  Leftover Ladies 1931,N 9,22:4
  Night World 1932,My 28,18:2
  By Candlelight 1934,Ja 6,18:2
  Unknown Blonde 1934,Ap 24,27:2

Revier, Harry (Director)
  Challenge of Chance, The 1919,Je 19,9:4
  Lost City, The 1935,F 21,23:3
Revill, Clive
  Headless Ghost, The 1959,Ap 30,37:2
  Bunny Lake is Missing 1965,O 4,00:0
  Fine Madness, A 1966,Je 30,28:2
  Modesty Blaise 1966,Ag 11,27:1
  Kaleidoscope 1966,S 23,45:1
  Double Man, The 1968,My 2,57:1
Reville, Alma (Miscellaneous)
  Thirty-Nine Steps, The 1935,S 14,8:4
  Secret Agent 1936,Je 13,13:1
  Jamaica Inn 1939,O 12,33:1
  Stage Fright 1950,F 24,27:2
Reville, Alma (Screenwriter)
  Passing of the Third Floor Back, The
    1936,Ap 29,19:2
  Suspicion 1941,N 21,23:2
  Shadow of a Doubt 1943,Ja 13,18:2
  It's in the Bag 1945,Je 11,12:1
  Paradine Case, The 1948,Ja 9,26:2
Revnes, Maurice (Producer)
  Suzy 1936,Jl 25,16:1
Revol, Max
  Voyage Surprise 1948,F 14,17:3
  Simple Case of Money, A 1952,F 2,11:2
Revueltas, Rosaura
  Salt of the Earth 1954,Mr 15,20:2
  Salt of the Earth 1965,N 1,57:1
Revueltas, Sylvestre (Composer)
  Wave, The 1937,Ap 21,18:1
Revuers, The
  Greenwich Village 1944,S 28,26:2
Rex
  Death Valley 1927,N 22,32:2
  Woman Doctor 1939,Mr 24,27:3
Rex, Eugen
  Verklungene Traume 1930,D 9,31:3
  Lindenwirtin vom Rhein, Die 1931,S 25,28:7
  Congress Dances 1932,My 12,23:2
  Kyritz-Pyritz 1932,Ag 9,20:5
  Hochtourist, Der 1934,Ja 13,16:4
  Konjunkturritter 1935,Ap 29,12:4
  Schwarzwaldmaedel 1935,O 12,12:3
  Maedchenraeuber 1936,Ag 15,6:3
  Selige Exzellenz, Die 1937,Je 15,26:2
Rex, Roberta
  Children of the Damned 1964,Ja 30,24:2
Rex (horse)
  Black Cyclone 1925,My 19,24:2
Rexiane
  Carnival of Sinners 1947,Ap 8,34:2
REY
  See Also RAE, REA, WRAY
Rey, Alejandro
  Solomon and Sheba 1959,D 26,7:2
  Casa del Angel, La 1960,Ag 30,25:1
  Battle at Bloody Beach, The 1961,Ag 17,18:2
  Fun in Acapulco 1964,F 20,22:4
  Blindfold 1966,My 26,55:2
Rey, Alvino, and hid Orchestra
  Sing Your Worries Away 1942,My 15,25:2
  Jam Session 1944,My 3,25:3
Rey, Dolores
  Vanity Street 1932,O 15,13:1
Rey, Fernando
  Don Quixote 1949,My 13,29:3
  Mad Queen, The 1950,O 27,24:3
  Marcelino 1956,O 23,39:1
  Pantaloons 1956,D 26,34:1
  Last Days of Pompeii, The 1960,Ag 11,19:1
  Revolt of the Slaves, The 1961,N 8,41:1
  Viridiana 1962,Mr 20,43:4
  Running Man, The 1963,O 3,31:1
  Castilian, The 1963,O 3,31:1
  Ceremony, The 1964,My 14,39:1
  Backfire 1965,Ap 27,27:1
  Return of the Seven 1966,O 20,52:5
  Falstaff; Chimes at Midnight 1967,Mr 18,19:2
  Viscount, The 1967,My 11,50:1
  Greco, El 1967,My 24,52:2
  Navajo Joe 1967,D 7,60:2
Rey, Florian (Director)
  Hermana San Sulpicio, La 1937,Ap 19,27:3
  Nobleza Baturra; Rustic Chivalry
    1938,Mr 28,19:3
  Morena Clara 1938,Je 18,18:3
Rey, Gaston
  My Wife's Husband 1965,Ja 27,26:1
Rey, Henri Francois (Original Author)
  Uninhibited, The 1968,Je 13,57:2
Rey, Kathleen
  Man From Brodney's, The 1923,D 18,16:3
Rey, Lysiane
  Sins of Paris 1954,Ja 30,9:6
Rey, Marcela Lopez
  Terrace, The 1964,N 25,45:1
Rey, Roberto
  El Principe Gondolero 1933,S 11,20:4
  Gente Alegre 1933,S 19,26:4
  Verbena de la Paloma, La 1938,O 25,19:2
  Termina Siempre Asi; It Always Ends That Way
    1940,S 3,21:3

Rey, Rosa
Secret Beyond the Door 1948,Ja 16,25:4
Rose Tattoo, The 1955,D 13,55:1
Rey, Sylvia
Third Voice, The 1960,Mr 7,24:5
Reybaz, Andre
Shop-Girls of Paris; Au Bonheur de Dames 1947,Je 23,14:4
Strangers in the House 1949,O 13,33:3
We Are all Murderers 1957,Ja 9,27:2
Reyburn, Noel
Lawless, The 1950,Je 23,29:2
Reyer, Vera (Screenwriter)
Beggar Maid, The 1921,S 26,18:1
Reyer, Walter
Journey to the Lost City 1960,D 8,43:3
Third Lover, The 1963,Je 25,23:3
Reyes, Chuy, Orchestra
Pan-Americana 1945,Mr 23,13:2
Reyes, Lucha
Ay Jalisco no te Rajes 1943,Ap 24,17:3
Reyher, Ferdinand (Original Author)
Fugitive Lovers 1934,Ja 13,16:3
Stranded 1935,Je 20,16:2
You may Be Next 1936,F 24,14:1
Ride a Crooked Mile 1938,D 29,15:2
Wait Till the Sun Shines, Nellie 1952,Je 28,12:2
Reyher, Ferdinand (Screenwriter)
You may Be Next 1936,F 24,14:1
Special Investigator 1936,Ap 25,21:1
Two in Revolt 1936,Ap 25,21:1
Don't Turn 'em Loose 1936,S 25,20:2
World, The Flesh and the Devil, The 1959,My 21,35:1
Reymond, Dalton (Original Author)
Song of the South 1946,N 28,40:2
Reymond, Dalton (Screenwriter)
Song of the South 1946,N 28,40:2
Reyna, Maurice
Boy Who Stole a Million, The 1960,D 22,18:3
Reynall, Paul
Jedda the Uncivilized 1957,F 28,18:7
Reyner, Iza
Dr Knock 1937,My 1,16:4
Reyner, Socorro
Tras la Reja 1937,Ja 11,15:7
Reynold, Jean-Lou
Truth, The 1961,Je 27,23:2
Reynolds, Abe
Swing Time 1936,Ag 28,21:2
My Dear Secretary 1949,F 14,15:4
Reynolds, Adeline De Walt
Come Live With Me 1941,F 28,17:3
Tales of Manhattan 1942,S 25,25:1
Iceland 1942,O 15,27:1
Street Of Chance 1942,N 19,31:3
Human Comedy, The 1943,Mr 3,19:2
Behind the Rising Sun 1943,O 14,26:2
Son of Dracula 1943,N 6,16:4
Tree Grows in Brooklyn, A 1945,Mr 1,25:5
Here Comes the Groom 1951,S 21,19:2
Lydia Bailey 1952,My 31,12:5
Pony Soldier 1952,D 20,15:2
Witness to Murder 1954,Ap 16,16:4
Reynolds, Burt
Angel Baby 1961,O 5,43:1
Armored Command 1961,O 7,14:3
Navajo Joe 1967,D 7,60:2
Reynolds, Cecil
Study in Scarlet, A 1933,Je 1,15:3
Reynolds, Charles (Producer)
Scarlet Spear, The 1954,Ap 10,11:4
Battle Beneath the Earth 1968,S 12,54:3
Reynolds, Clarke
Viscount, The 1967,My 11,50:1
Reynolds, Clarke (Screenwriter)
Genghis Khan 1965,Je 24,28:2
Gunfighters of Casa Grande 1965,S 2,36:1
Reynolds, Craig
Case of the Lucky Legs, The 1935,N 1,25:1
Man of Iron 1935,D 7,22:2
Ceiling Zero 1936,Ja 20,22:2
Brides are Like That 1936,Mr 23,22:5
Times Square Playboy 1936,My 2,11:2
Golden Arrow, The 1936,My 4,16:1
Sons o'Guns 1936,My 14,29:2
Treachery Rides the Range 1936,My 30,7:3
Jailbreak 1936,Ag 6,22:1
Stage Struck 1936,S 28,14:4
Here Comes Carter 1936,N 14,23:3
Case of the Black Cat, The 1936,D 26,15:4
Smart Blonde 1937,Ja 9,21:1
Penrod and Sam 1937,Mr 29,14:3
Melody for Two 1937,My 21,19:5
Slim 1937,Je 24,30:2
Back in Circulation 1937,O 4,17:1
Footloose Heiress 1937,O 9,16:2
Great Garrick, The 1937,O 25,23:1
Under Suspicion 1937,D 20,23:2 (In Addenda)
Making the Headlines 1938,Ap 1,17:2
Female Fugitive 1938,Ap 11,12:3
Uncle Harry 1945,Ag 24,14:5
Man From Colorado 1949,Ja 21,24:3

Reynolds, Debbie
Daughter of Rosie O'Grady, The 1950,Mr 31,36:2
Three Little Words 1950,Ag 10,21:2
Two Weeks With Love 1950,N 24,31:2
Mr Imperium 1951,O 15,22:2
Singin' in the Rain 1952,Mr 28,27:2
I Love Melvin 1953,Ap 10,18:4
Susan Slept Here 1954,Jl 30,9:1
Athena 1954,D 22,28:2
Hit the Deck 1955,Mr 4,17:1
Tender Trap, The 1955,N 11,29:6
Catered Affair, The 1956,Je 15,32:4
Bundle of Joy 1956,D 20,36:1
Tammy and the Bachelor 1957,Je 15,10:7
This Happy Feeling 1958,Je 19,28:2
Mating Game, The 1959,Ap 30,37:1
Say One for Me 1959,Je 20,11:2
It Started With a Kiss 1959,Ag 20,14:2
Gazebo, The 1960,Ja 16,14:4
Rat Race, The 1960,My 26,37:3
Pepe 1960,D 22,18:1
Pleasure of his Company, The 1961,Je 2,36:1
Second Time Around, The 1961,D 23,16:1
How the West Was Won 1963,Ap 1,54:1
My Six Loves 1963,Ap 4,58:4
Mary, Mary 1963,O 25,38:2
Unsinkable Molly Brown, The 1964,Jl 17,15:1
Goodbye, Charlie 1964,N 19,49:1
Singing Nun, The 1966,Mr 18,33:1
Divorce American Style 1967,Jl 20,30:2
How Sweet It Is 1968,Ag 22,47:1
Reynolds, Gene
Sins of Man 1936,Je 19,17:2
Thank You, Jeeves 1936,O 5,25:1
In Old Chicago 1938,Ja 7,15:2
Of Human Hearts 1938,F 18,23:1
Love Finds Andy Hardy 1938,Jl 22,10:2
Crowd Roars, The 1938,Ag 5,11:1
Boys Town 1938,S 9,25:1
Spirit of Culver 1939,Mr 9,18:1
Flying Irishman, The 1939,Ap 12,27:2
They Shall Have Music 1939,Jl 26,17:2
Blue Bird, The 1940,Ja 20,11:2
Edison the Man 1940,Je 7,27:2
Mortal Storm, The 1940,Je 21,25:2
Gallant Sons 1940,D 12,37:2
Santa Fe Trail 1940,D 21,21:2
Andy Hardy's Private Secretary 1941,Mr 7,17:2
Penalty, The 1941,Ap 10,29:3
Adventure in Washington 1941,Ag 1,11:3
Tuttles of Tahiti, The 1942,Ap 30,14:1
Eagle Squadron 1942,Jl 3,12:5
Big Cat, The 1949,Jl 29,12:2
Down Three Dark Streets 1954,S 4,6:4
Country Girl, The 1954,D 16,51:2
Diane 1956,Ja 13,18:1
Reynolds, H
Daughter of the Dragon 1931,Ag 22,7:5
Road to Singapore, The 1931,O 1,25:2
Reynolds, Harry (Producer)
Double Confession 1953,My 1,17:2
Reynolds, Helene
Confirm or Deny 1941,D 19,35:2
Roxie Hart 1942,F 20,21:1
Man Who Wouldn't Die, The 1942,Ap 28,25:5
Moontide 1942,Ap 30,14:1
Tales of Manhattan 1942,S 25,25:1
Girl Trouble 1942,O 8,31:2
Meanest Man in the World, The 1943,F 25,27:3
Dixie Dugan 1943,Ap 9,25:5
Heaven Can Wait 1943,Ag 12,15:1
Wintertime 1943,S 30,27:2
Bermuda Mystery 1944,My 13,17:1
Reynolds, Jack
In a Lonely Place 1950,My 18,37:2
Sun Sets at Dawn, The 1951,Ja 15,13:1
Reynolds, John W
Country Girl, The 1954,D 16,51:2
Reynolds, Joy
Flesh Merchant, The 1956,My 19,12:6
Reynolds, Joyce
George Washington Slept Here 1942,O 31,11:1
Constant Nymph, The 1943,Jl 24,8:2
Thank Your Lucky Stars 1943,O 2,19:2
Adventures of Mark Twain, The 1944,My 4,25:5
Janie 1944,Ag 5,16:2
Hollywood Canteen 1944,D 16,19:2
Always Together 1947,D 11,46:1
Wallflower 1948,Je 12,8:5
Girl's School 1950,F 3,29:2
Reynolds, Kay
How to Succeed in Business Without Really Trying 1967,Mr 10,30:1
Reynolds, Lynn (Director)
Just Tony 1922,Ag 7,14:2
Deadwood Coach, The 1925,Ja 21,19:3
Riders of the Purple Sage 1925,Ap 15,16:1
Rainbow Trail, The 1925,Je 3,26:4
Reynolds, Lynn (Screenwriter)
Just Tony 1922,Ag 7,14:2

Reynolds, Marjorie
Murder in Greenwich Village 1937,O 30,22:2
Streets of New York 1939,My 1,21:1
Racketeers of the Range 1939,Je 8,31:4
Mister Wong in Chinatown 1939,Jl 31,9:2 (In Addenda)
Enemy Agent 1940,Ap 22,13:3
Doomed to Die 1940,Jl 30,16:3
Great Swindle, The 1941,My 14,25:4
Top Sergeant Mulligan 1941,N 12,31:3
Holiday Inn 1942,Ag 5,16:1
Star Spangled Rhythm 1942,D 31,20:1
Dixie 1943,Je 24,26:2
Up in Mabel's Room 1944,Ap 22,8:6
3 Is a Family 1944,D 20,20:3
Ministry of Fear 1945,F 8,15:2
Bring on the Girls 1945,Mr 1,25:5
Duffy's Tavern 1945,S 6,23:3
Monsieur Beaucaire 1946,S 5,23:1
Time of Their Lives, The 1946,N 28,40:2
Heaven Only Knows 1947,N 14,29:3
Bad Men of Tombstone 1949,Mr 5,10:2
That Midnight Kiss 1949,S 23,28:2
Great Jewel Robber, The 1950,Ag 4,13:2
His Kind of Woman 1951,Ag 30,20:2
Models, Inc 1952,My 26,18:4
Reynolds, Peter
Guinea Pig, The 1949,My 2,20:2
Adam and Evalyn 1950,My 12,33:4
Guilt is my Shadow 1954,Mr 25,36:4
Woman's Angle, The 1954,Ag 27,11:6
Reynolds, PEter
Silver Chalice, The 1954,D 27,22:5
Reynolds, Peter
It Takes a Thief 1963,Ag 15,24:7
Reynolds, Quentin
Golden Earrings 1947,D 4,41:3
Reynolds, Quentin (Director)
Death of a Dream 1950,Jl 19,26:2
Justice and Caryl Chessman 1960,Mr 3,24:5
Reynolds, Quentin (Miscellaneous)
Eagle Squadron 1942,Jl 3,12:5
Call Northside 777 1948,F 19,29:2
Reynolds, Quentin (Narrator)
One Day in Soviet Russia 1941,O 27,21:2
One Inch From Victory 1944,Ap 27,18:5
Death of a Dream 1950,Jl 19,26:2
Blood Brothers 1953,F 21,10:7
Mahatma Gandhi-Twentieth Century Prophet 1953,Ap 29,33:5
Reynolds, Quentin (Original Author)
Secrets of a Nurse 1938,D 12,26:2
Blood Brothers 1953,F 21,10:7
Reynolds, Quentin (Screenwriter)
One Day in Soviet Russia 1941,O 27,21:2
Miracle of the Bells, The 1948,Mr 17,30:1
Death of a Dream 1950,Jl 19,26:2
Reynolds, Sheldon (Director)
Foreign Intrigue 1956,Jl 13,23:2
Reynolds, Sheldon (Original Author)
Foreign Intrigue 1956,Jl 13,23:2
Reynolds, Sheldon (Producer)
Foreign Intrigue 1956,Jl 13,23:2
Reynolds, Sheldon (Screenwriter)
Foreign Intrigue 1956,Jl 13,23:2
Reynolds, Shirley
Children on Trial 1947,N 10,21:3
Reynolds, Valerie
Untamed Youth 1957,My 11,24:6
Reynolds, Vera
Prodigal Daughters 1923,Ap 17,26:3
Woman Proof 1923,O 30,16:1
Shadows of Paris 1924,F 18,13:1
Icebound 1924,Mr 3,22:3 (In Addenda)
For Sale 1924,Jl 14,11:5
Broken Barriers 1924,Ag 4,16:3
Feet of Clay 1924,S 22,16:1
Golden Bed, The 1925,Ja 20,18:2
Night Club, The 1925,My 5,24:2
Limited Mail, The 1925,S 1,18:2
Road to Yesterday, The 1925,D 1,22:4
Steel Preferred 1925,D 22,13:1
Silence 1926,My 19,29:3
Risky Business 1926,S 8,19:3
Corporal Kate 1926,D 15,30:4
Main Event, The 1927,O 31,22:1
Tonight at Twelve 1929,S 23,24:3
Lawless Woman, The 1931,Je 8,21:1
Reynolds, William
Dear Brat 1951,Jl 5,21:2
No Questions Asked 1951,Ag 10,13:2
Desert Fox, The 1951,O 18,32:1
Has Anybody Seen My Gal 1952,Jl 5,7:2
Carrie 1952,Jl 17,20:2
Son of Ali Baba 1952,Ag 16,7:4
Francis Goes to West Point 1952,Ag 23,10:2
Mississippi Gambler, The 1953,Ja 30,25:1
There's Always Tomorrow 1956,Ja 21,18:2
All That Heaven Allows 1956,F 29,35:1
Away all Boats 1956,Ag 17,14:2
Mister Cory 1957,F 23,13:1
Big Beat, The 1958,Je 26,23:4
Thing That Couldn't Die, The 1958,Je 28,13:7

Reynolds, William— Cont
FBI Code 98 1964,Ap 9,25:6
Distant Trumpet, A 1964,My 28,40:1
Follow Me, Boys! 1966,D 2,46:1
Reynolds, William (Producer)
Time Limit 1957,O 24,37:2
Rezzori, Hanna Axmann
Young Torless 1968,Jl 23,27:2
Rhazis, Phoebus
Electra 1962,D 18,5:2
Rhed, Joyce
Jesse James' Women 1954,S 29,23:4
Rhein, Alan
Ball of Fire 1942,Ja 16,25:2
Rhekopf, Paul
Isn't Life Wonderful? 1924,D 1,17:3
Rhett, Alicia
Gone With the Wind 1939,D 20,31:2
RHINE
See Also RYAN
Rhine, Larry (Original Author)
Six Lessons From Madame La Zonga
1941,F 19,25:2
Dangerous Game, A 1941,Mr 4,20:3
Rhine, Larry (Screenwriter)
Devil's Pipeline, The 1940,N 11,22:4
Six Lessons From Madame La Zonga
1941,F 19,25:2
Dangerous Game, A 1941,Mr 4,20:3
Rho, Stella
Broken Melody, The 1934,O 31,17:3
Murder in the Old Red Barn 1936,Ag 19,18:3
Rhoades, Arthur S (Miscellaneous)
Animal World, The 1956,My 31,21:6
Rhoades, Harrison (Original Author)
Willow Tree, The 1920,F 2,10:1
RHODE
See Also RODE
Rhodes, Barbara
Shakiest Gun in the West, The 1968,Jl 11,30:1
Don't Just Stand There 1968,S 3,54:2
Rhodes, Betty Jane
Forgotten Faces 1936,Jl 4,18:2
Life of the Party, The 1937,O 4,17:1
Stage Door 1937,O 8,27:2
Fleet's In, The 1942,Mr 12,24:2
Sweater Girl 1942,Jl 13,18:3
Priorities on Parade 1942,Jl 23,19:2
Star Spangled Rhythm 1942,D 31,20:1
Rhodes, Charles W (Producer)
Suicide Attack 1951,Jl 14,7:2
Rhodes, Christopher
Betrayed 1954,S 9,36:1
Colditz Story, The 1957,O 25,23:2
Naked Earth 1958,Ag 29,18:1
Cid, El 1961,D 15,49:1
Becket 1964,Mr 12,40:2
Rhodes, Elizabeth
When a Man's a Man 1924,F 5,20:1
Rhodes, Erik
Gay Divorcee, The 1934,N 16,27:1
Charlie Chan in Paris 1935,Ja 22,23:2
Night at the Ritz, A 1935,My 16,20:2
Top Hat 1935,Ag 30,12:2
Two in the Dark 1936,F 1,9:2
Chatterbox 1936,F 15,18:6
Special Investigator 1936,Ap 25,21:1
One Rainy Afternoon 1936,My 14,29:2
Second Wife 1936,Ag 29,16:3
Criminal Lawyer 1937,Ja 27,17:3
Abenteurer von Paris, Der 1937,My 29,20:3
Woman Chases Man 1937,Je 11,26:2
Music for Madame 1937,O 23,14:1
Fight for Your Lady 1937,N 20,21:2
Beg, Borrow or Steal 1937,D 10,33:2
Meet the Girls 1938,S 3,16:6
Mysterious Mr Moto of Devil's Island
1938,S 19,16:2
Say It in French 1938,D 1,29:1
Dramatic School 1938,D 9,31:2
On Your Toes 1939,O 21,12:2
Rhodes, Eugene Manlove (Original Author)
Four Faces West 1948,Ag 4,18:3
Rhodes, Frank
I Married a Doctor 1936,Ap 20,17:1
Rhodes, George
Man Called Adam, A 1966,Ag 4,24:2
Rhodes, Georgette
Road to Paradise, The 1931,Ja 20,21:3
Lonely Wives 1931,Mr 16,25:1
World Moves On, The 1934,Je 30,18:5
Rhodes, Gordon
Tripoli 1950,N 10,35:2
Rhodes, Grandon
Magnificent Doll 1946,D 9,34:2
Born to Kill 1947,My 1,34:2
Song of my Heart 1948,Mr 5,17:3
Road House 1948,N 8,24:2
Streets of Laredo 1949,My 12,28:2
Canadian Pacific 1949,My 20,32:4
All the King's Men 1949,N 9,37:2
And Baby Makes Three 1949,D 23,17:3
Flying Missile, The 1950,D 25,25:1
Born Yesterday 1950,D 27,30:2

Guy Who Came Back, The 1951,Ag 17,13:2
Detective Story 1951,N 7,35:2
Secret of the Incas 1954,My 29,13:3
Human Desire 1954,Ag 7,7:2
Revenge of the Creature 1955,My 14,10:7
Earth vs the Flying Saucers 1956,Ag 2,21:2
These Wilder Years 1956,Ag 18,11:2
Rhodes, Hari
Drums of Africa 1963,Jl 4,9:1
Shock Corridor 1963,S 12,32:1
Satan Bug, The 1965,Ap 15,38:1
Mirage 1965,My 27,28:1
Blindfold 1966,My 26,55:2
Rhodes, Ila
Secret Service of the Air 1939,Mr 2,19:2
Rhodes, Marion (Director)
Cavalleria Rusticana 1953,D 28,17:2
Traviata, La 1953,D 28,17:2
Rhodes, Marion (Producer)
Traviata, La 1953,D 28,17:2
Cavalleria Rusticana 1953,D 28,17:2
Rhodes, Marjorie
On Approval 1945,Ja 29,17:1
Love on the Dole 1945,O 13,11:2
Escape 1948,Ag 16,12:2
Enchantment 1948,D 27,16:2
This Was a Woman 1949,Ja 5,22:2
Inheritance, The 1951,F 12,19:2
Time, Gentlemen, Please 1953,S 24,39:2
Both Sides of the Law 1954,Ja 12,19:2
Family Way, The 1967,Je 29,32:1
Rhouma, Gypsy
White Cargo 1930,F 24,18:1
Rhue, Madlyn
Operation Petticoat 1959,D 6,38:1
Majority of One, A 1962,Ja 12,29:2
Escape from Zahrain 1962,Jl 12,19:3
He Rides Tall 1964,F 27,28:1
Rhys, Margot
Uncivilized 1937,N 17,27:4
Rhythmaires (Miscellaneous)
Adventures of Ichabod and Mr Toad, The
1949,O 10,18:2
Riabinkin, C
Great Citizen, The 1939,Ja 16,11:2
Riano, Renie
You're a Sweetheart 1937,D 25,10:5
Tovarich 1937,D 31,9:2
Men Are Such Fools 1938,Je 17,25:1
Four's a Crowd 1938,Ag 12,11:1
Road to Reno, The 1938,O 3,11:2
Spring Madness 1938,D 1,29:3
Thanks For Everything 1938,D 10,13:2
Disputed Passage 1939,O 26,27:2
Daytime Wife 1939,N 24,29:1
Man Who Wouldn't Talk, The 1940,Ja 12,13:3
Kit Carson 1940,N 15,25:3
You're the One 1941,F 20,23:2
Affectionaly Yours 1941,My 24,18:2
Ice-Capades 1941,S 25,29:1
You Belong to Me 1941,N 29,14:2
Whispering Ghosts 1942,My 18,19:4
Jam Session 1944,My 3,25:3
Take It or Leave It 1944,Jl 13,14:2
3 Is a Family 1944,D 20,20:3
So Goes my Love 1946,My 2,3:7
Bad Bascomb 1946,My 23,18:4
Bringing Up Father 1946,N 22,27:3
Time of your Life, The 1948,My 27,29:2
Family Jewels, The 1965,Ag 12,30:4
Riazanov, V
Sleeping Beauty, The 1966,My 4,50:1
Riba, Shayiwa
Cry, the Beloved Country 1952,Ja 24,23:2
Ribalta, J Carner (Screenwriter)
Cascarrabias 1933,O 30,14:2
Ribeiro, Milton
Cangaceiro 1954,S 3,13:2
That Man From Rio 1964,Je 9,30:1
Ribercolles, Jacques
Seventh Juror, The 1964,Ja 28,25:1
Riberman, Abner
Back to Bataan 1945,S 13,26:3
Ribero, Catherine
Carabiniers, Les 1967,S 28,58:3
Carabiniers, Les 1968,Ap 26,31:1
Ribero, Julian
Nada Mas Que Una Mujer 1934,N 26,12:2
Ribes, Christiane
Postmaster's Daughter, The 1946,Ag 19,17:6
Ribinson, Rad
St Louis Blues 1939,F 9,17:2
Ribnikov, N
Victors and the Vanquished, The 1950,My 1,18:2
Ribovska, Malka
Shameless Old Lady, The 1966,S 27,52:1
Other One, The 1967,S 29,53:1
Ribulsi, Enrico (Screenwriter)
Measure for Measure 1951,D 8,9:2
Rica, Ron (Director)
Flower Thief, The 1962,Jl 14,11:5

Rica, Ron (Miscellaneous)
Flower Thief, The 1962,Jl 14,11:5
Rica, Ron (Producer)
Flower Thief, The 1962,Jl 14,11:5
Rica, Ron (Screenwriter)
Flower Thief, The 1962,Jl 14,11:5
Ricard, Andre (Original Author)
Shadows of Paris 1924,F 18,13:1
Ricardel, Molly (Original Author)
I Loved You Wednesday 1933,Je 16,20:2
Riccardi, Joseph
My Cousin 1918,N 25,11:3
Riccardini, Michele
Great Dawn, The 1947,Ag 28,28:3
Tragic Hunt 1948,O 22,30:2
Under the Olive Tree 1951,O 5,24:4
Voice in Your Heart, A 1952,F 23,7:5
Riccardo, Lucia
Tomorrow is too Late 1952,Ap 14,22:2
Ricci, Edward T (Miscellaneous)
Sang d'un Poete, Le 1933,N 3,23:3
Ricci, Luigi (Composer)
Lost One, The; La Traviata 1948,Mr 30,26:2
Ricci, Nora
Birds, the Bees and the Italians, The
1967,Ag 8,33:2
Ricci, Paolo
Shoot Loud, Louder... I Don't Understand
1967,S 21,56:4
Ricci, Renzo
Coraggio Della Gioventu Mussoliniana, Il
1936,F 5,14:2
Wally, La 1939,Ja 2,28:3
Avventura, L' 1961,Ap 5,30:1
Sandra 1966,Ja 17,32:1
Ricciardi, Franco
Boheme, La 1965,O 20,51:2
Ricciardi, Mirella
Eclipse 1962,D 21,5:1
Ricciardi, William
Humming Bird, The 1924,Ja 14,2:1
Side Show of Life, The 1924,Jl 22,9:1
Man Must Live, A 1925,Ja 29,12:2
Heart of a Siren, The 1925,Ap 8,24:3
Say It Again 1926,Je 7,23:2
Puppets 1926,Je 21,17:2
Strictly Dishonorable 1931,N 11,27:1
As You Desire Me 1932,Je 3,23:4
Crooner 1932,Ag 20,7:4
Tiger Shark 1932,S 23,22:2
Scarlet Dawn 1932,N 4,25:4
Scoundrel, The 1935,My 3,23:2
Stars Over Broadway 1935,N 14,17:3
Under Two Flags 1936,My 1,19:1
San Francisco 1936,Je 27,21:1
Anthony Adverse 1936,Ag 27,16:1
Man of the People 1937,F 23,25:4
Riccio, Attilio (Producer)
Wayward Wife, The 1955,Ap 11,29:3
Riccio, Frederick
Teenage Mother 1968,S 19,62:4
RICE
See Also REECE, REES, REESE, REIS
Rice, Albert (Original Author)
Meet the Missus 1937,Jl 2,25:2
Rice, Alice Hegan (Original Author)
Lovey Mary 1926,Je 21,17:2
Mrs Wiggs of the Cabbage Patch 1934,O 29,14:2
Rice, Andy (Miscellaneous)
McFadden's Flats 1935,Mr 13,16:2
Rice, Andy (Original Author)
Plastered in Paris 1928,S 24,25:1
Rice, Craig (Original Author)
Home Sweet Homicide 1946,S 12,5:7
Lucky Stiff, The 1949,Ja 31,14:2
Underworld Story, The 1950,Jl 27,29:4
Mrs O'Malley and Mr Malone 1951,F 23,33:2
Rice, Craig (Screenwriter)
Falcon's Brother, The 1942,O 3,9:5
Falcon in Danger, The 1943,Jl 23,21:2
Rice, Don
Lady Luck 1946,O 31,22:3
Rice, Edward
Little Men 1940,D 9,23:2
Rice, Elmer (Original Author)
Doubling for Romeo 1921,O 24,13:1
Street Scene 1931,Ag 27,22:5
Counsellor-At-Law 1933,D 8,31:2
On Trial 1939,Ap 5,31:2
Dream Girl 1948,Je 17,29:2
Rice, Elmer (Screenwriter)
Holiday Inn 1942,Ag 5,16:1
Rice, Florence
Best Man Wins 1935,Ja 2,22:4
Under Pressure 1935,F 4,11:3
Carnival 1935,F 16,9:1
Escape from Devil's Island 1935,N 25,22:2
Panic on the Air 1936,Ap 20,17:1
Pride of the Marines 1936,Ap 27,19:2
Sworn Enemy 1936,S 12,20:1
Longest Night, The 1936,O 17,21:2
Under Cover of Night 1937,Ja 20,18:4
Man of the People 1937,F 23,25:4

Rice, Florence — Cont

Riding on Air 1937,Je 26,20:2 (In Addenda)
Married Before Breakfast 1937,Jl 23,16:2
Double Wedding 1937,O 22,27:2
Beg, Borrow or Steal 1937,D 10,33:2
Navy Blue and Gold 1937,D 24,21:2
Paradise for Three 1938,F 16,17:1
Fast Company 1938,Jl 6,21:2
Vacation From Love 1938,N 10,33:2
Sweethearts 1938,D 23,16:2
Stand up and Fight 1939,Ja 27,17:2
Four Girls in White 1939,F 23,19:3
Miracles for Sale 1939,Ag 10,15:2
At the Circus 1939,N 17,17:2
Little Accident 1939,N 24,29:3
Broadway Melody of 1940 1940,Mr 29,25:3
Girl in 313 1940,Je 14,25:3
Phantom Raiders 1940,Je 24,19:5
Secret Seven, The 1940,Ag 12,11:6
Cherokee Strip 1940,N 4,23:2
Mr District Attorney 1941,Ap 17,29:3
Father takes a Wife 1941,S 5,19:3

Rice, Frank

Parade of the West 1930,Mr 3,18:4
Conquering Horde, The 1931,Mr 30,25:2
Squaw Man, The 1931,S 19,10:2
Corsair 1931,N 19,27:5
Last Round-Up, The 1934,My 10,25:2
Ruggles of Red Gap 1935,Mr 7,26:1
Hard Rock Harrigan 1935,Jl 30,16:2

Rice, Grantland (Producer)

Untitled-Sports 1921,Ja 17,9:1
Leading a Dog's Life 1921,F 7,8:2
Happy Duffer, The 1921,Mr 7,8:1
Fish and Totem 1921,My 30,12:5
Speed 1921,O 24,13:1

Rice, Jack

Arson Racket Squad 1938,Je 18,18:2
Swingtime Johnny 1943,D 17,23:3

Rice, Joan

Story of Robin Hood, The 1952,Je 27,18:3
Curtain Up 1953,F 2,17:3
Glory at Sea 1953,Mr 11,36:7
His Majesty O'Keefe 1954,F 6,17:2

Rice, Mary Alice

Flying Hostess 1936,D 14,29:4

Rice, Norman

Miracle of Our Lady Fatima, The
1952,Ag 21,16:2

Ricet-Barrier

Army Game, The; Tire Au Flanc
1963,Ap 24,40:1

Rich, Claude

Mitsou 1958,Ap 15,42:5
Love and the Frenchwoman; (Francaise et
l'Amour, La) 1961,F 28,38:2
Elusive Corporal, The 1963,F 19,5:1
Burning Court, The 1963,Ag 1,17:2
Male Hunt; Chasse a l'Homme, La
1965,Ap 20,42:1
Is Paris Burning? 1966,N 11,36:1
Bride Wore Black, The 1968,Je 26,42:1

Rich, David Lowell (Director)

Hey Boy! Hey Girl! 1959,Ag 6,18:3
Madame X 1966,Ap 28,49:1
Plainsman, The 1966,N 19,26:1
Rosie 1968,F 8,36:1
Lovely Way to Die, A 1968,Jl 13,18:1

Rich, Dick

Headin' East 1938,Ja 15,19:2
Let Freedom Ring 1939,Mr 10,19:2
Angels Wash Their Faces 1939,S 4,16:2
Lucky Cisco Kid 1940,Je 24,19:5
Murder in the Air 1940,Jl 4,12:2
Western Union 1941,F 7,23:2
Strange Alibi 1941,Ap 28,11:2
Dressed to Kill 1941,Ag 22,19:3
Rise and Shine 1941,D 6,14:3
Rio Rita 1942,My 8,27:3
Ox-Bow Incident, The 1943,My 10,15:2 (In
Addenda)
Burning Cross, The 1948,F 20,19:1
Oh, You Beautiful Doll 1949,N 12,8:4
Outcasts of Poker Flat 1952,My 16,19:3
Seven Brides for Seven Brothers 1954,Jl 23,8:3
Ransom 1956,Ja 25,28:3
Inside Detroit 1956,Ja 28,10:5

Rich, Frances

Zoo in Budapest 1933,Ap 28,15:2
Pilgrimage 1933,Jl 13,17:5

Rich, Freddie and Orchestra

Wave, A Wac and a Marine, A 1944,Ag 14,11:4

Rich, Gloria

King of the Newsboys 1938,Ap 2,18:2

Rich, Irene

Jes' Call Me Jim 1920,My 24,20:3
Voice in the Dark, A 1921,Je 6,16:4
Brass 1923,Mr 12,18:1
Rosita 1923,S 4,14:1
Lucretia Lombard 1923,D 17,23:1
Boy of Mine 1923,D 24,12:1 (In Addenda)
Beau Brummell 1924,Mr 31,20:1
Oytherea 1924,My 26,21:1
Captain January 1924,Jl 7,10:4

Behold This Woman 1924,Jl 22,9:1
Being Respectable 1924,Ag 4,16:3
This Woman 1924,O 21,21:3
Lost Lady, A 1925,Ja 19,14:1
My Wife and I 1925,My 20,26:2
Eve's Lover 1925,Jl 27,17:3
Wife Who Wasn't Wanted, The 1925,S 9,23:1
Compromise 1925,O 27,23:3
Lady Windemere's Fan 1925,D 28,19:2
Silken Shackles 1926,My 25,25:1
Don't Tell the Wife 1927,F 22,23:2
Climbers, The 1927,My 4,29:2
Dearie 1927,Jl 4,20:3
Desired Woman, The 1927,Ag 30,21:3
Silver Slave, The 1928,Ja 3,28:2
Beware of Married Men 1928,Ap 10,33:2
Perfect Crime, The 1928,Ag 6,15:2
Powder my Back 1928,Ag 7,25:4
Women They Talk About 1928,O 15,16:1
Craig's Wife 1928,D 4,29:1
Ned McCobb's Daughter 1929,F 18,28:1
They Had to See Paris 1929,O 12,11:1
So This Is London 1930,My 24,21:2
On Your Back 1930,S 15,29:3
Beau Ideal 1931,Ja 19,25:1
Father's Son 1931,F 21,15:2
Strangers May Kiss 1931,Ap 13,17:1
Five and Ten 1931,Jl 11,7:6
Wicked 1931,S 19,10:2
Mad Parade, The 1931,S 19,10:2
Champ, The 1931,N 10,29:4
Down to Earth 1932,S 2,19:2
Her mad Night 1932,N 15,24:5
That Certain Age 1938,N 5,15:2
Mortal Storm, The 1940,Je 21,25:2
Lady in Question, The 1940,D 10,33:2
Angel and the Badman 1947,Mr 3,28:4
New Orleans 1947,Je 20,25:6
Fort Apache 1948,Je 25,26:2
Joan of Arc 1948,N 12,30:5

Rich, John (Director)

Wives and Lovers 1963,Ag 29,36:1
New Interns, The 1964,Ag 20,34:2
Roustabout 1964,N 11,38:1
Boeing Boeing 1965,D 24,24:4
Easy Come, Easy Go 1967,Je 15,56:1

Rich, Lillian

Love Master, The 1924,My 19,14:2
Golden Bed, The 1925,Ja 20,18:2
Kiss in the Dark, A 1925,Ap 7,17:3
Seven Days 1925,Ag 31,19:3
Simon the Jester 1925,N 19,22:1
That's my Daddy 1928,F 13,16:2
Once a Lady 1931,N 9,22:4

Rich, Milo

Amazing Mrs Holliday, The 1943,F 22,20:2

Rich, Robert (Original Author)

Brave One, The 1957,Mr 22,26:1

Rich, Ron

Fortune Cookie, The 1966,O 20,52:1

Rich, Vernon

War of the Worlds, The 1953,Ag 14,10:2

Rich, Vido

Amazing Mrs Holliday, The 1943,F 22,20:2

RICHARD

See Also REICHERT

Richard, Cliff

Expresso Bongo 1960,Ap 13,44:1

Richard, Colette

Loves of Colette 1949,D 3,8:6

Richard, Dawn

Legion of the Doomed 1959,Mr 12,27:5

Richard, Frieda

Peak of Fate 1925,Je 13,10:5
Manon Lescaut 1926,N 30,27:1
Faust 1926,D 7,21:2
Two Brothers, The 1928,Ag 21,27:4
Burning Heart, The 1929,My 12,27:3
Liebe im Ring 1930,Ag 11,13:1
Liebe Ist Liebe 1932,Je 2,25:2
Unfinished Symphony 1935,Ja 14,11:2
Affairs of Maupassant, The 1938,F 12,20:2

Richard, Fritz

Prince of Rogues, The 1929,Jl 30,19:4

Richard, Henri

Liliom 1935,Mr 18,14:4

Richard, J

Paris Does Strange Things 1957,Mr 30,13:2

Richard, Jacques

Cross of the Living 1963,F 5,5:5

Richard, Jean

Seven Deadly Sins, The (Gluttony); Gluttony (The
Seven Deadly Sins) 1953,My 12,31:3
Candide 1962,N 20,39:1
War of the Buttons, The 1963,D 19,40:2
Oldest Profession, The (Mademoiselle Mimi);
Mademoiselle Mimi (The Oldest Profession)
1968,N 8,42:1

Richard, Jean-Louis (Miscellaneous)

Bride Wore Black, The 1968,Je 26,42:1

Richard, Jean-Louis (Screenwriter)

Soft Skin, The; Peau Douce, La 1964,O 13,49:2
Fahrenheit 451 1966,N 15,53:1

Richard, Jean-Louis (Screenwriter) — Cont

Bride Wore Black, The 1968,Je 26,42:1

Richard, Little

Don't Knock the Rock 1957,F 23,13:1
Mister Rock and Roll 1957,O 17,42:2

Richard, Philippe

Fantomas 1934,Mr 13,27:4
Alibi, L' 1939,Ap 10,13:3

Richard, Viola

Laurel and Hardy's Laughing 20's 1965,N 18,55:2

Richard-Willm, Pierre

Prince Jean, Le 1936,D 12,15:2
Betrayal 1939,S 16,20:2
Entente Cordiale 1939,D 26,23:2
Amoureux, Les 1940,D 9,23:3

Richards, A J (Producer)

World in Flames, The 1940,O 24,31:2
Cassino to Korea 1950,O 4,38:2

Richards, Addison

British Agent 1934,S 20,20:1
Our Daily Bread 1934,O 3,25:2
Case of the Howling Dog, The 1934,O 18,26:5
St Louis Kid, The 1934,N 1,25:2
Gentlemen are Born 1934,N 22,27:2
White Cockatoo, The 1935,Ja 16,21:1
Society Doctor 1935,F 4,11:3
Home on the Range 1935,F 13,24:4
Sweet Music 1935,F 21,23:2
G Men 1935,My 2,17:1
Alias Mary Dow 1935,Je 29,16:2
Front Page Woman 1935,Jl 12,15:1
Little Big Shot 1935,O 7,11:2
Freckles 1935,O 26,12:2
Frisco Kid 1935,N 25,22:1
Ceiling Zero 1936,Ja 20,22:2
Man Hunt 1936,Ja 30,14:2
Road Gang 1936,F 24,14:1
Colleen 1936,Mr 9,20:2
Song of the Saddle 1936,Mr 21,13:3
Sutter's Gold 1936,Mr 27,25:2
Law in her Hands, The 1936,Je 6,21:2
Public Enemy's Wife 1936,Jl 9,17:2
Hot Money 1936,Jl 25,16:2
Jailbreak 1936,Ag 6,22:1
China Clipper 1936,Ag 12,14:3
Anthony Adverse 1936,Ag 27,16:1
Case of the Velvet Claws, The 1936,Ag 29,16:3
Smart Blonde 1937,Ja 9,21:1
God's Country and the Woman 1937,Ja 11,15:5
Black Legion 1937,Ja 18,21:1
Ready, Willing and Able 1937,Mr 15,27:1
Her Husband's Secretary 1937,Mr 20,23:6
Singing Marine, The 1937,Jl 1,33:2
White Bondage 1937,Ag 6,21:3
Dance Charlie Dance 1937,Ag 26,25:2
Alcatraz Island 1937,O 14,22:2
Love Is on the Air 1937,N 12,27:3
Barrier, The 1937,N 27,21:2
Black Doll, The 1938,F 7,10:2
Prison Nurse 1938,Mr 4,17:5
Accidents Will Happen 1938,Ap 25,19:2
Boys Town 1938,S 9,25:1
Valley of the Giants 1938,S 10,20:2
Last Express, The 1938,O 11,24:4
Off the Record 1939,F 18,12:2
Twelve Crowded Hours 1939,F 24,15:2
They Made Her a Spy 1939,Mr 29,21:4
Andy Hardy Gets Spring Fever 1939,Jl 19,23:2
They all Come Out 1939,Ag 3,15:4
Bad Lands 1939,Ag 9,15:2
Exile Express 1939,Ag 16,21:3
Espionage Agent 1939,S 23,22:2
Thunder Afloat 1939,O 13,27:2
Nick Carter, Master Detective 1939,D 14,35:2
Lone Wolf Strikes, The 1940,F 5,13:2
Geronimo 1940,F 8,18:3
Man From Dakota, The 1940,F 22,29:2
Northwest Passage 1940,Mr 8,25:1
Slightly Honorable 1940,My 17,23:4
Edison the Man 1940,Je 7,27:2
Gangs of Chicago 1940,Je 13,29:2
Andy Hardy Meets Debutante 1940,Ag 2,12:2
South to Karanga 1940,Ag 9,19:1
Cherokee Strip 1940,N 4,23:2
Moon Over Burma 1940,D 12,37:4
Flight Command 1941,Ja 17,21:2
Tall, Dark and Handsome 1941,Ja 24,15:2
Arizona 1941,F 7,23:3
Strawberry Blonde 1941,F 22,11:2
Trial of Mary Dugan, The 1941,Mr 6,25:4
Andy Hardy's Private Secretary 1941,Mr 7,17:2
I Wanted Wings 1941,Mr 27,29:4
Men of Boys Town 1941,Ap 11,24:6
Great Lie, The 1941,Ap 12,19:2
Mutiny in the Arctic 1941,My 3,20:5
Badlands of Dakota 1941,S 9,27:6
Texas 1941,O 17,27:3
Lady Has Plans, The 1942,Mr 5,27:1
Secret Agent of Japan 1942,Mr 23,19:3
Friendly Enemies 1942,Je 22,19:1
Pacific Rendezvous 1942,Jl 8,27:4
Pride of the Yankees, The 1942,Jl 16,23:1
A-Haunting We Will Go 1942,Ag 3,18:4
Flying Tigers 1942,O 23,25:2

Richards, Addison— Cont

Seven Days' Leave 1942,D 11,33:2
Secret Enemies 1943,Ja 1,27:3
Air Force 1943,F 4,29:1
Where Are Your Children? 1944,Ja 17,14:5
Fighting Seabees, The 1944,Mr 20,14:2
Night of Adventure, A 1944,Je 3,10:4
Are These our Parents? 1944,Ag 23,16:2
Barbary Coast Gent 1944,S 29,18:2
Chicago Kid, The 1945,F 12,24:3
Mummy's Curse, The 1945,Mr 31,16:1
Betrayal From the East 1945,Ap 25,27:2
Bewitched 1945,Ag 17,20:3
Men in her Diary 1945,S 24,16:5
Spellbound 1945,N 2,22:2
Strange Confession 1945,N 8,17:3
Danger Signal 1945,N 22,39:2
Black Market Babies 1946,Ap 1,23:1
Hoodlum Saint, The 1946,Je 27,29:1
Renegades 1946,Jl 11,18:2
Step by Step 1946,Ag 24,6:7
Angel on my Shoulder 1946,O 21,27:2
Criminal Court 1946,N 16,15:3
Love Laughs at Andy Hardy 1947,Ja 8,28:2
Lulu Belle 1948,Je 21,18:3
Davy Crockett, Indian Scout 1950,Mr 17,28:3
Illegal 1955,O 29,12:6
Walk the Proud Land 1956,S 8,20:6 (In
  Addenda)

Richards, Ann

Random Harvest 1942,D 18,36:6
American Romance, An 1944,N 24,19:1
Love Letters 1945,Ag 27,22:3
Badman's Territory 1946,My 31,27:2
Searching Wind, The 1946,Je 27,29:1
Lost Honeymoon 1947,Je 20,25:4
Love From a Stranger 1947,N 28,30:1
Sorry, Wrong Number 1948,S 2,18:2

Richards, Aubrey

Ipcress File, The 1965,Ag 3,35:1
It 1967,N 16,58:1

Richards, Beah

Take a Giant Step 1961,Mr 6,28:2
Miracle Worker, The 1962,My 24,29:2
Gone are the Days! 1963,S 24,43:2
Hurry Sundown 1967,Mr 24,22:1
In the Heat of the Night 1967,Ag 3,26:1
Guess Who's Coming to Dinner 1967,D 12,56:1

Richards, Cully

Stolen Harmony 1935,Ap 20,16:2
Sing, Baby, Sing 1936,S 12,20:1
Pick a Star 1937,My 28,17:2
Something to Sing About 1937,S 21,29:4
Swing It, Sailor 1937,D 13,23:5
Let's Face It 1943,Ag 5,18:1
Pirate, The 1948,My 21,19:2
Race Street 1948,Ag 23,13:3

Richards, Doreen

Little Ballerina, The 1951,F 28,33:2

Richards, Frank

Before I Hang 1940,O 3,31:3
Threat, The 1949,D 2,35:4
No Way Out 1950,Ag 17,23:1
Carbine Williams 1952,My 8,37:2
Pat and Mike 1952,Je 19,32:6
Savage, The 1953,Ja 2,11:1

Richards, Gordon

Kitty 1946,Ap 1,23:1
Imperfect Lady, The 1947,My 22,34:5
Woman in the Night 1948,Ja 10,16:2
Big Hangover, The 1950,My 26,20:3
Man Who Cheated Himself, The 1951,F 9,21:2
High Society 1956,Ag 10,9:2

Richards, Grant

On Such a Night 1937,S 17,29:2
Risky Business 1939,Mr 23,27:2
Isle of Destiny 1940,Ap 8,15:2
Just off Broadway 1942,Ag 29,18:4

Richards, Jackson (Original Author)

Trailing the Killer 1932,D 2,27:4

Richards, Jeff

Angels in the Outfield 1951,O 18,32:1
Above and Beyond 1953,Ja 31,10:6
Seven Brides for Seven Brothers 1954,Jl 23,8:3
Crest of the Wave 1954,N 11,43:2
Many Rivers to Cross 1955,F 24,21:2
It's a Dog's Life 1955,D 23,14:3
Opposite Sex, The 1956,N 16,23:2
Don't Go Near the Water 1957,N 15,37:1

Richards, Keith

Aerial Gunner 1943,Je 26,10:2
Captain China 1950,Mr 2,33:2
Untamed Youth 1957,My 11,24:6

Richards, Laura E (Original Author)

Captain January 1924,Jl 7,10:4
Captain January 1936,Ap 25,21:1

Richards, Lucien

Espionage Agent 1939,S 23,22:2

Richards, Mary

Rosenkavalier, Der 1962,O 10,57:1

Richards, Paul

Fixed Bayonets 1951,N 21,20:2
Phantom of the Rue Morgue 1954,Mr 20,10:5
Strange One, The 1957,Ap 13,12:3

Monkey on my Back 1957,My 30,23:2
All the Young Men 1960,Ag 27,8:6

Richards, Percy Lieutenant

Diana the Huntress 1916,Je 19,9:5 (In Addenda)

Richards, Robert L (Original Author)

Air Cadet 1951,My 11,32:3

Richards, Robert L (Screenwriter)

Ramparts We Watch, The 1940,S 20,27:1
One Sunday Afternoon 1948,D 27,16:3
Act of Violence 1949,Ja 24,16:2
Johnny Stool Pigeon 1949,S 23,28:3
Winchester 73 1950,Je 8,38:2
Kansas Raiders 1951,Ja 26,19:2
Air Cadet 1951,My 11,32:3

Richards, Rosa

Forbidden Love 1929,Ja 14,20:1

Richards, Silvia (Screenwriter)

Possessed 1947,My 30,25:2
Secret Beyond the Door 1948,Ja 16,25:4
Tomahawk 1951,F 19,19:2
Ruby Gentry 1952,D 26,20:2

Richards, Stephen

Passage to Marseille 1944,F 17,12:5
Doughgirls, The 1944,Ag 31,14:1
Objective Burma 1945,Ja 27,15:2
God is my Co-Pilot 1945,Mr 24,22:6
Pride of the Marines 1945,Ag 25,7:3

Richards, Susan

Rocking Horse Winner, The 1950,Je 9,29:2

Richards, Toby

Sergeant Rutledge 1960,My 26,37:1

Richards, Vincent

Hiawatha 1952,D 26,20:4

Richardson, Anna Steese (Original Author)

Man's Home, A 1921,D 19,13:1

Richardson, Anna Steese (Screenwriter)

Big Hearted Herbert 1934,N 14,23:2

Richardson, Charles

Cool World, The 1964,Ap 21,42:1

Richardson, Duncan

Three Secrets 1950,O 21,10:6
Glass Web, The 1953,N 12,37:5

Richardson, Emory

Lost Boundaries 1949,Jl 1,14:4
Fugitive Kind, The 1960,Ap 15,13:1

Richardson, Florence

Price of a Party, The 1924,N 26,17:3

Richardson, Frank

William Fox Movietone Follies of 1929
  1929,My 27,22:1
Sunny Side Up 1929,O 4,24:5
Happy Days 1930,F 14,20:1
Let's Go Places 1930,Mr 1,23:1
New Movietone Follies of 1930, The
  1930,Je 21,20:5

Richardson, Henry H (Original Author)

Rhapsody 1954,Mr 12,17:1

Richardson, Ian

Persecution and Assassination of Jean-Paul Marat
  as Performed by the Inmates of the Asylum of
  Charenton Under the Direction of the Marquis
  De Sade, The 1967,F 23,41:1

Richardson, Jack

Toll Gate, The 1920,Ap 19,13:3
Fog Bound 1923,My 29,10:3
Beau Brummell 1924,Mr 31,20:1
Love Master, The 1924,My 19,14:2
Midnight Express, The 1924,N 19,19:3
Free and Equal 1925,Ap 20,22:1
Rainmaker, The 1926,My 18,28:2
Partners in Crime 1928,Ap 30,18:3
Only Saps Work 1930,D 13,22:2
Unfaithful 1931,Mr 7,17:2
Scandal for Sale 1932,Ap 3,26:2
Last Man, The 1932,S 17,18:4
Perfect Clue, The 1935,Mr 14,18:1

Richardson, John

Black Sunday 1961,Mr 9,23:1
She 1965,S 2,36:1
One Million Years BC 1967,F 22,21:1
Vengance of She, The 1968,My 30,21:4

Richardson, Ralph

Ghoul, The 1934,Ja 27,9:2
Friday the 13th 1934,My 15,18:1
Alias Bulldog Drummond 1935,S 10,26:2
Things to Come 1936,Ap 18,19:2
Man Who Could Work Miracles, The
  1937,F 22,13:1
Thunder in the City 1937,Ap 23,25:2
Divorce of Lady X, The 1938,Ap 1,17:2
South Riding 1938,Ag 2,15:2
Citadel, The 1938,N 4,27:2
Clouds Over Europe 1939,Je 16,27:2
Four Feathers 1939,Ag 4,11:1
Lion Has Wings, The 1939,N 19,X,4:1 (In
  Addenda)
Lion Has Wings, The 1940,Ja 22,11:2
Fugitive, The 1940,Jl 23,22:2
Avengers, The 1942,N 25,18:2
Silver Fleet, The 1945,Mr 24,22:6
Anna Karenina 1948,Ap 28,32:2
Heiress, The 1949,O 7,35:2
Fallen Idol, The 1949,N 16,39:2

Richardson, Ralph— Cont

Outcast of the Islands 1952,My 16,19:2
Secret Flight 1952,Jl 3,16:2
Breaking Through the Sound Barrier
  1952,N 7,19:1
Murder on Monday 1953,O 7,35:2
Holly and the Ivy, The 1954,F 5,16:1
Richard III 1956,Mr 12,1:4
Novel Affair, A 1957,Ag 28,22:1
Our Man in Havana 1960,Ja 28,26:1
Oscar Wilde 1960,Je 21,28:2
Exodus 1960,D 16,44:1
300 Spartans, The 1962,S 20,29:2
Long Day's Journey Into Night 1962,O 10,57:2
Woman of Straw 1964,O 1,30:6
Doctor Zhivago 1965,D 23,21:1
Khartoum 1966,Jl 14,28:1
Wrong Box 1966,Jl 20,46:1

Richardson, Ralph (Director)

Murder on Monday 1953,O 7,35:2

Richardson, Ralph (Narrator)

Falstaff; Chimes at Midnight 1967,Mr 18,19:2

Richardson, Tony (Director)

Look Back in Anger 1959,S 16,45:1
Entertainer, The 1960,O 4,49:2
Sanctuary 1961,F 22,31:1
Taste of Honey, A 1962,My 1,33:3
Loneliness of the Long Distance Runner, The
  1962,O 9,44:1
Tom Jones 1963,O 8,48:1
Loved One, The 1965,O 12,57:1
Mademoiselle 1966,Ag 2,23:1
Sailor From Gibraltar, The 1967,Ap 25,38:2
Charge of the Light Brigade, The 1968,O 7,59:1

Richardson, Tony (Producer)

Saturday Night and Sunday Morning
  1961,Ap 4,44:2
Taste of Honey, A 1962,My 1,33:3
Loneliness of the Long Distance Runner, The
  1962,O 9,44:1
Tom Jones 1963,O 8,48:1
Girl With Green Eyes 1964,Ag 11,37:2

Richardson, Tony (Screenwriter)

Taste of Honey, A 1962,My 1,33:3
Sailor From Gibraltar, The 1967,Ap 25,38:2

Richardson, Virgil

Strange Victory 1948,S 27,27:2

Richebe, Roger (Director)

Agonie des Aigles, L' 1934,D 1,8:5

Richebe, Roger (Producer)

Agonie des Aigles, L' 1934,D 1,8:5
Midnight in Paris 1947,O 9,32:3
Girl on the Third Floor, The; (Sophie et le Crime)
  1958,O 11,47:1 (Incorrect in this edition; use
  1958,O 11,18:4 elsewhere)

Richelli, G (Director)

Commedia Fra I Pazzi, Una 1937,Jl 8,20:2

Richepin, Jean (Original Author)

Gypsy Passion 1922,Mr 27,12:1
Open Road, The 1940,O 5,20:2

Richepin, Jean (Screenwriter)

Mothers of France 1917,Mr 12,9:1

Richfield, Edwin

Up the Creek 1958,N 11,26:2

Richfield, George (Producer)

First Opera Film Festival 1948,My 31,12:7

Richler, Mordecai (Screenwriter)

No Love for Johnnie 1961,D 13,55:1
Young and Willing 1964,F 27,28:1
Life at the Top 1965,D 15,53:1

Richlin, Maurice (Original Author)

What Did You Do in the War, Daddy?
  1966,S 1,28:1

Richlin, Maurice (Screenwriter)

Pillow Talk 1959,O 7,47:2
Operation Petticoat 1959,D 6,38:1
All in a Nights Work 1961,Mr 23,28:1
Come September 1961,S 8,34:1
Pink Panther, The 1964,Ap 24,25:1

RICHMAN

See Also RICHMOND

Richman, Arthur (Miscellaneous)

Gay Deception, The 1935,O 11,31:1

Richman, Arthur (Original Author)

Awful Truth, The 1925,Jl 2,12:4
Not so Long Ago 1925,Jl 28,24:4
Reckless Hour, The 1931,Ag 1,16:4
Awful Truth, The 1937,N 5,19:3
Let's Do It Again 1953,O 14,34:3

Richman, Arthur (Screenwriter)

Here's to Romance 1935,O 3,29:2

Richman, Charles

Battle Cry for Peace, The 1915,Ag 7,8:3
Struggle, The 1931,D 11,35:1
Take a Chance 1933,N 27,20:3
His Double Life 1933,D 16,12:3
President Vanishes, The 1934,D 8,18:5
Biography of a Bachelor Girl 1935,Mr 2,18:2
After Office Hours 1935,Mr 9,19:1
Case of the Curious Bride, The 1935,Ap 5,21:3
George White's 1935 Scandals 1935,Ap 29,12:3
Becky Sharp 1935,Je 14,27:2
Glass Key, The 1935,Je 15,20:2
Thanks a Million 1935,N 14,17:1

Richman, Charles— Cont

Old Kentucky, In 1935,N 29,24:1
Ex-Mrs Bradford, The 1936,My 28,19:2
Parole 1936,Je 27,21:1
I'd Give my Life 1936,Ag 17,9:1
In His Steps 1936,O 29,31:1
Under Your Spell 1936,N 7,15:2
Sing Me a Love Song 1936,D 26,15:2
Life of Emile Zola, The 1937,Ag 12,14:2
Nothing Sacred 1937,N 26,27:2
Lady Behave 1938,Ja 28,17:3
Adventures of Tom Sawyer, The 1938,F 18,23:1
Cowboy and the Lady, The 1938,N 25,19:3
Dark Victory 1939,Ap 21,27:2
Exile Express 1939,Ag 16,21:3
Devil's Island 1940,Jl 12,11:4

Richman, Harry

Puttin' on the Ritz 1930,F 15,15:1
Music Goes 'Round, The 1936,F 22,12:1

Richman, Marian

Gog 1954,Ag 14,8:2

Richman, Mark

Friendly Persuasion 1956,N 2,30:1
Strange One, The 1957,Ap 13,12:3
Black Orchid, The 1959,F 13,33:2
Dark Intruder 1965,Jl 22,24:2
Agent for H.A.R.M 1966,Ja 6,20:2
For Singles Only 1968,Je 6,54:1

Richman, Maurice (Screenwriter)

Soldier in the Rain 1963,N 29,67:6 (Incorrect in this edition; use 1963,N 28,67:6 elsewhere)

RICHMOND

See Also RICHMAN

Richmond, Al

Courtship of Myles Standish, The 1923,D 31,9:3

Richmond, Bill

Bellboy, The 1960,Jl 21,17:1

Richmond, Bill (Original Author)

Big Mouth, The 1967,Jl 13,30:2

Richmond, Bill (Screenwriter)

Ladies Man, The 1961,Jl 13,26:3
Errand Boy, The 1962,F 8,25:1
Nutty Professor, The 1963,Jl 18,15:2
Patsy, The 1964,Ag 13,24:2
Family Jewels, The 1965,Ag 12,30:4
Big Mouth, The 1967,Jl 13,30:2

Richmond, Edna

Price of a Party, The 1924,N 26,17:3

Richmond, Irene

Saturday Night and Sunday Morning 1961,Ap 4,44:2
Nightmare 1964,Je 18,29:2

Richmond, Kane

Politics 1931,Ag 1,16:4
Huddle 1932,Je 17,24:1
Devil Tiger 1934,F 9,23:2
Lost City, The 1935,F 21,23:3
Mars Attacks the World 1938,N 8,26:3
Tail Spin 1939,F 11,13:2
Return of the Cisco Kid, The 1939,Ap 29,13:2
Charlie Chan in Reno 1939,My 31,27:2
20,000 Men a Year 1939,O 28,11:2
Escape, The 1939,N 3,17:4
Sailor's Lady 1940,Je 29,12:2
Play Girl 1941,Ja 30,19:3
Great Guns 1941,O 3,27:2
Action in the North Atlantic 1943,My 22,10:2
Three Russian Girls 1944,F 5,13:2
Ladies Courageous 1944,Mr 16,17:2
Black Market Babies 1946,Ap 1,23:1
Black Gold 1947,S 5,16:4

Richmond, Kenneth

Night and the City 1950,Je 10,11:2

Richmond, Peter

Tol'able David 1930,N 17,29:1
Heaven on Earth 1931,D 19,16:4
Forgotten Commandments 1932,Je 2,25:2

Richmond, Ted (Producer)

Soul of a Monster, The 1944,S 9,12:4
One Mysterious Night 1944,O 21,15:3
Night Editor 1946,Mr 30,11:2
So Dark the Night 1946,D 7,16:2
Lone Wolf in London, The 1947,N 22,10:3
Blondie Hits the Jackpot 1949,S 9,28:3
Holiday in Havana 1949,O 14,33:5
Shakedown 1950,S 4,11:2
Milkman, The 1951,Ja 1,13:6
Kansas Raiders 1951,Ja 26,19:2
Smuggler's Island 1951,My 24,47:2
Strange Door, The 1951,D 10,34:6
No Room for the Groom 1952,Je 14,12:2
Has Anybody Seen My Gal 1952,Jl 5,7:2
Mississippi Gambler, The 1953,Ja 30,25:1
Desert Legion 1953,My 9,13:2
Walking my Baby Back Home 1954,Ja 16,10:5
Forbidden 1954,Ja 23,11:2
Rails Into Laramie 1954,My 13,34:2
Francis Joins the Wacs 1954,Jl 31,6:3
Bengal Brigade 1954,N 13,13:2
Nightfall 1957,Ja 24,34:1
Abandon Ship 1957,Ap 18,35:1
Solomon and Sheba 1959,D 26,7:2
Bachelor in Paradise 1961,N 17,41:2

It Happened at the World's Fair 1963,My 30,20:1
Advance to the Rear 1964,Je 11,27:3
Return of the Seven 1966,O 20,52:5
Villa Rides 1968,Jl 18,26:3

Richmond, Warner

Sporting Life 1918,S 16,9:3
My Lady's Garter 1920,Mr 15,13:2
Speed Spook, The 1924,O 21,21:3
Crowded Hour, The 1925,Ap 27,15:2
Making of O'Malley 1925,Je 22,10:2
Good and Naughty 1926,Je 14,24:1
Fire Brigade, The 1926,D 21,20:2
White Flannels 1927,Mr 22,31:2
Slide, Kelly, Slide 1927,Mr 23,19:2
Chicago 1927,D 24,9:1
Redeeming Sin, The 1929,F 16,14:6
Strange Cargo 1929,F 18,28:1
Men Without Women 1930,F 1,15:1
Strictly Modern 1930,My 3,23:1
Billy the Kid 1930,O 18,23:2
Remote Control 1930,D 8,26:1
Quick Millions 1931,Ap 18,17:3
Huckleberry Finn 1931,Ag 8,16:3
Beast of the City, The 1932,Mr 14,13:3
Night Court 1932,My 27,27:5
Strangers of the Evening 1932,Je 4,9:2
Hell's Highway 1932,S 26,18:2
King of the Jungle 1933,F 25,20:3
Fast Workers 1933,Mr 20,18:2
Corruption 1933,Je 20,22:7
Police Call 1933,Ag 22,20:3
Lost Jungle, The 1934,Je 8,18:1
Gift of Gab 1934,S 26,17:6
Under Pressure 1935,F 4,11:3
So Red the Rose 1935,N 28,39:1
In His Steps 1936,O 29,31:1
Gold Racket, The 1937,Ag 2,10:3
Federal Bullets 1937,D 27,11:1

Richow, Otto

Jewels of Brandenburg 1947,My 24,10:5

Richter, Conrad (Original Author)

Sea of Grass, The 1947,F 28,27:2
One Desire 1955,S 3,9:1
Light in the Forest, The 1958,Jl 11,15:2

Richter, Dan

2001 A Space Odyssey 1968,Ap 4,58:1

Richter, Elise

Battle in Outer Space 1960,Jl 9,10:5

Richter, Ellen

Carnival Crime, The 1929,Jl 8,17:3
Ein Liebesroman im Hause Habsburg 1936,O 12,23:2

Richter, Frederic

Squadron Leader X 1943,Jl 23,21:2
Adventures of Tartu, The 1943,S 24,26:1
Mr Emmanuel 1945,Ja 8,15:2

Richter, George

Kriemhild's Revenge 1928,O 16,29:1

Richter, Hans

Emil und die Detektive 1931,D 21,28:4
Blaue Vom Himmel, Das 1934,S 8,18:6
Liebe Dumme Mama; Stupid Mama 1935,Mr 2,18:3
Page vom Dalmasse-Hotel, Der 1935,Mr 25,12:3
Fahrt ins Gruene, Die 1936,My 23,12:2
Die Ganze Welt Dreht Sich um Liebe 1936,N 27,27:2
Drei Blaue Jungs-Ein Blondes Maedel 1936,D 29,16:3
Freuhling im Wien 1937,F 6,15:2
Maedchen Irene, Das 1937,My 22,19:3
Schabernack 1937,Ag 14,16:5
Gross Reinemachen; General Housecleaning 1938,Je 23,27:2
Klapperstorchverband, Der; Stork Society, The 1938,O 29,15:3
Peter, Paul und Nanette 1940,My 25,20:1

Richter, Hans (Director)

Dreams that Money can Buy 1948,Ap 24,11:2
8 X 8 1957,Mr 16,13:2

Richter, Hans (Miscellaneous)

Dreams that Money can Buy 1948,Ap 24,11:2
8 X 8 1957,Mr 16,13:2

Richter, Hans (Original Author)

8 X 8 1957,Mr 16,13:2

Richter, Hans (Producer)

Dreams that Money can Buy 1948,Ap 24,11:2
8 X 8 1957,Mr 16,13:2

Richter, Hans (Screenwriter)

Dreams that Money can Buy 1948,Ap 24,11:2

Richter, John

Kriemhild's Revenge 1928,O 16,29:1

Richter, Kurt (Miscellaneous)

Loves of Pharaoh 1922,F 22,13:3 (In Addenda)

Richter, Paul

Siegfried 1925,Ag 24,17:3
Peter the Pirate 1927,Ja 7,14:4
Kriemhild's Revenge 1928,O 16,29:1
Forbidden Love 1929,Ja 14,20:1
Foresterchristl, Die 1931,Ap 27,25:1
Schloss Hubertus 1935,F 9,11:3
Jungfrau Gegen Moench; Maiden vs Monk 1935,Mr 16,19:2

Richter, Paul— Cont

Drei Kaiserjaeger 1935,Mr 16,19:1
Ehestreik 1935,Ag 31,16:3
Klosterjaeger, Der 1936,Ja 3,13:7
Frauen vom Tannhof, Die 1936,F 18,27:1
Wackere Schustermeister, Der 1936,Jl 7,22:4
Ein Liebesroman im Hause Habsburg 1936,O 12,23:2
Silence of the Forest, The; Schweigen im Walde, Das 1937,D 6,19:2
Edelweisskoenig, Der 1939,F 4,11:2
Starker als die Liebe; Stronger Than Love 1939,My 6,21:3
Frau Sylvelin 1939,D 9,18:3
Waldrausch; Forest Fever 1940,Ja 20,11:3

Richter, Rotraut

Kirschen in Nachbars Garten 1937,My 15,23:6
Trouble Back Stairs; Krach im Hinterhaus 1937,D 4,21:1
Veilchen vom Potsdamer Platz, La; Violet of Potsdam Square, The 1939,Ap 8,19:3
Biberpelz, Der; Beaver Coat, The 1939,S 9,11:3

Richter, S

Man of Music 1953,My 11,25:2

Richtin, Maurice (Miscellaneous)

Inspector Clouseau 1968,Jl 25,26:1

Rickard, Dick (Screenwriter)

Snow White and the Seven Dwarfs 1938,Ja 14,21:1 (In Addenda)

Rickard, Marilyn

Touchables, The 1968,N 21,41:1

Rickard, Tex

Great White Way, The 1924,Ja 4,10:1

Rickelt, Gustav

Alte Lied, Das 1931,S 11,24:2

Ricketts, Tom

Tailor Made Man, A 1922,O 16,20:2
Within the Law 1923,Ap 30,11:2
Strangers of the Night 1923,O 8,20:1
Dangerous Maid, The 1923,D 11,26:2
Black Oxen 1924,Ja 7,23:1
Circe the Enchantress 1924,D 9,23:3
Oh, Doctor! 1925,F 23,24:1
My Wife and I 1925,My 20,26:2
Poker Faces 1926,S 14,25:4
Stranded in Paris 1926,D 13,27:1
Children of Divorce 1927,Ap 26,33:3
Venus of Venice 1927,My 3,25:1
Just Married 1928,Ag 13,23:2
Dry Martini 1928,N 5,26:5 (In Addenda)
Red Hot Speed 1929,F 5,26:3
Glad Rag Doll, The 1929,Je 3,27:2
Vagabond King, The 1930,F 20,22:4
Sea Legs 1930,N 11,29:1
Man of the World 1931,Mr 21,15:1
Side Show 1931,S 19,10:2
Ambassador Bill 1931,N 14,15:3
Surrender 1931,N 28,20:4
Forbidden 1932,Ja 11,28:5
Farewell to Arms, A 1932,D 9,26:5
No Greater Glory 1934,My 5,22:2
In Love With Life 1934,My 12,12:3
Little Man, What Now? 1934,Je 1,29:1
Count of Monte Cristo, The 1934,S 27,25:2
Forsaking all Others 1934,D 21,18:1
Tale of Two Cities, A 1935,D 26,21:2
We Went to College 1936,Jl 27,20:2
Pennies From Heaven 1936,D 10,35:2
Maid of Salem 1937,Mr 4,27:2
Young in Heart, The 1938,N 4,27:2

Rickles, Don

Run Silent, Run Deep 1958,Mr 28,29:1
Rat Race, The 1960,My 26,37:3
X - The Man With X-Ray Eyes 1963,O 24,37:1
Muscle Beach Party 1964,My 28,40:1
Bikini Beach 1964,S 17,52:6
Enter Laughing 1967,Ag 1,24:1

Ricks, Archie

Long, Long Trail, The 1929,N 4,28:1

Ricksen, Lucille

Old Nest, The 1921,Je 29,10:3
Hill Billy, The 1924,Mr 12,19:4
Those Who Dance 1924,Je 30,16:1
Vanity's Price 1924,O 8,16:2
Denial, The 1925,Mr 10,19:3

Rickson, Joe

Pioneer Trails 1923,N 12,15:3
Code of the Wilderness, The 1924,Jl 1,21:4
Captain Blood 1924,S 9,19:1
Riders of the Purple Sage 1925,Ap 15,16:1
Baree, Son of Kazan 1925,My 19,24:2

Rico, Alicia

Romance del Palmar, El 1939,My 1,21:2
Ultima Melodia, La; Last Melody, The 1939,Ag 5,18:3
Cancion del Regreso, La; Home-Coming Song 1940,Je 22,18:4

Rico, Mona

Eternal Love 1929,My 13,27:2
Shanghai Lady 1929,N 11,20:2
Devil With Women, A 1930,O 20,28:2
Thunder Below 1932,Je 20,11:2
Goin' to Town 1935,My 11,21:2

Riddle, Almeda
Festival 1967,O 24,53:2
Riddle, Hal
Cop Hater 1958,O 2,44:3
Ridenour, Ruth (Miscellaneous)
Bolero 1934,F 17,20:3
Rideout, Bob
What Price Vengeance 1937,My 26,30:3
Fury and the Woman 1937,Je 22,26:2
Convicted 1938,Ag 22,9:3
Rider, Martin Good
Susannah of the Mounties 1939,Je 24,13:2
Ridgely, Cleo
Law and the Woman, The 1922,Ja 22,VI,3:1 (In Addenda)
Ridgely, John
Submarine D-1 1937,D 30,15:4
Invisible Menace, The 1938,F 14,20:6
Patient in Room 18, The 1938,Ap 22,15:6
White Banners 1938,Je 23,27:1
My Bill 1938,Jl 7,22:4
Cowboy From Brooklyn 1938,Jl 14,17:1
Hard To Get 1938,N 14,15:2
Torchy Gets her Man 1938,N 18,25:3
Going Places 1939,Ja 7,6:1
They Made Me a Criminal 1939,Ja 21,19:2
Wings of the Navy 1939,F 4,11:1
Secret Service of the Air 1939,Mr 2,19:2
You Can't Get Away With Murder 1939,Mr 25,19:2
Kid From Kokomo, The 1939,My 20,11:2
Indianapolis Speedway 1939,Jl 15,8:2
Kid Nightingale 1939,D 8,33:6
Torrid Zone 1940,My 18,11:3
Flight Angels 1940,My 27,23:2
They Drive by Night 1940,Jl 27,17:5
River's End 1940,Ag 26,11:4
Strange Alibi 1941,Ap 28,11:2
Wagons Roll at Night, The 1941,My 10,20:4
Million Dollar Baby 1941,Je 7,20:2
Highway West 1941,Ag 8,13:4
International Squadron 1941,N 14,28:4
Man Who Came to Dinner, The 1942,Ja 2,25:2
Bullet Scars 1942,Ap 24,21:4
Big Shot, The 1942,Jl 18,8:2
Secret Enemies 1943,Ja 1,27:3
Air Force 1943,F 4,29:1
Northern Pursuit 1943,N 26,29:2
Destination Tokyo 1944,Ja 1,9:2
Doughgirls, The 1944,Ag 31,14:1
Arsenic and old Lace 1944,S 2,17:2
Hollywood Canteen 1944,D 16,19:2
God is my Co-Pilot 1945,Mr 24,22:6
Pride of the Marines 1945,Ag 25,7:3
Danger Signal 1945,N 22,39:2
My Reputation 1946,Ja 26,19:2
Two Guys From Milwaukee 1946,Jl 27,12:5
Big Sleep, The 1946,Ag 24,6:6
Man I Love, The 1947,Ja 25,12:2
That Way With Women 1947,F 15,20:4
Nora Prentiss 1947,F 22,16:2
That's my Man 1947,Ap 7,20:2
Possessed 1947,My 30,25:2
Cheyenne 1947,Je 7,9:2
Cry Wolf 1947,Jl 19,10:2
High Wall 1947,D 26,22:2
Iron Curtain, The 1948,My 13,31:2
Luxury Liner 1948,S 10,19:2
Sealed Verdict 1948,N 3,36:2
Command Decision 1949,Ja 20,34:2
Once More, my Darling 1949,S 26,17:1
Task Force 1949,O 1,8:6
Border Incident 1949,N 21,29:2
South Sea Sinner 1950,Ja 16,18:4
Edge of Doom 1950,Ag 4,13:2
Petty Girl, The 1950,Ag 18,17:2
Beauty on Parade 1950,Ag 18,17:2
Half Angel 1951,Je 16,9:2
Last Outpost, The 1951,Je 22,16:3
Place in the Sun, A 1951,Ag 29,20:1
Greatest Show on Earth, The 1952,Ja 11,17:2
Room for One More 1952,Ja 16,21:2
Outcasts of Poker Flat 1952,My 16,19:3
Off Limits 1953,Mr 30,25:5
Ridges, John
Wings for the Eagle 1942,Ag 1,14:2
Ridges, Stanley
Success 1923,Jl 10,22:5
Crime Without Passion 1934,S 1,16:2
Scoundrel, The 1935,My 3,23:2
Winterset 1936,D 4,31:1
Sinner Take All 1937,F 3,27:1
Internes Can't Take Money 1937,My 6,23:2
Yellow Jack 1938,My 20,17:2
If I Were King 1938,S 29,31:1
Mad Miss Manton, The 1938,O 21,27:2
There's That Woman Again 1939,Ja 6,25:4
Let Us Live 1939,Mr 30,19:2
Union Pacific 1939,My 11,31:2
Each Dawn I Die 1939,Jl 22,12:2
Espionage Agent 1939,S 23,22:2
Dust Be my Destiny 1939,O 7,11:2

Nick Carter, Master Detective 1939,D 14,35:2
Black Friday 1940,Mr 22,23:3
Sea Wolf, The 1941,Mr 26,27:3
Mr District Attorney 1941,Ap 17,29:3
Sergeant York 1941,Jl 3,15:1
They Died With Their Boots On 1941,N 21,23:3
To Be or not to Be 1942,Mr 7,13:2
Lady is Willing, The 1942,Ap 24,21:2
Big Shot, The 1942,Jl 18,8:2
Eyes in the Night 1942,O 16,23:1
Air Force 1943,F 4,29:1
Tarzan Triumphs 1943,F 5,16:3
This Is the Army 1943,Jl 29,11:6
Story of Dr Wassell, The 1944,Je 7,13:2
Wilson 1944,Ag 2,18:1
Master Race, The 1944,N 2,22:1
Sign of the Cross 1944,D 21,16:3
Suspect, The 1945,F 1,18:5
God is my Co-Pilot 1945,Mr 24,22:6
Captain Eddie 1945,Ag 9,24:2
Because of Him 1946,Ja 25,26:6
Canyon Passage 1946,Ag 8,18:2
Mr Ace 1946,S 30,21:3
Possessed 1947,My 30,25:2
Live Today for Tomorrow 1948,D 6,29:2
Streets of Laredo 1949,My 12,28:2
You're my Everything 1949,Jl 23,7:2
Task Force 1949,O 1,8:6
Thelma Jordon 1950,Ja 19,35:2
Paid in Full 1950,F 16,28:2
No Way Out 1950,Ag 17,23:1
Groom Wore Spurs, The 1951,Mr 14,41:2
Ridgeway, Fred
Blueprint for Murder, A 1953,Jl 25,8:2
Ridgeway, Fritz
Judy of Rogues Harbor 1920,Mr 1,16:2
Old Homestead, The 1922,O 9,10:2
Nobody's Widow 1927,Ja 13,29:1
Getting Gertie's Garter 1927,F 9,17:3
Flying Romeos 1928,Ap 3,33:2
This Is Heaven 1929,My 27,22:1
Hell's Heroes 1929,D 28,11:1
Ridgeway, Fritzi
Trifling With Honor 1923,My 30,10:4
Ruggles of Red Gap 1923,S 10,15:4
Man Bait 1927,Ja 19,21:1
Enemy, The 1927,D 28,26:6
Red Hot Speed 1929,F 5,26:3
Mad Parade, The 1931,S 19,10:2
Ladies of the Big House 1932,Ja 1,31:1
We Live Again 1934,N 2,27:2
Ridgeweill, Audrey
His Double Life 1933,D 16,12:3
Ridley, Arnold (Original Author)
Wrecker, The 1929,Ag 13,23:2
Flying Fool 1931,O 19,28:1
Ghost Train, The 1933,F 18,13:3
Seven Sinners 1936,Ag 22,6:1
Ridley, Judith
Night of the Living Dead 1968,D 5,59:2
Ridolfi, Giovanni
Yesterday, Today, and Tomorrow (Part III-Mara Rome); Mara Rome (Yesterday, Today and Tomorrow) 1964,Mr 18,46:1
Marriage Italian Style 1964,D 21,42:1
Riebling, John Terry
Come Back Baby 1968,Je 14,43:1
Ried, Elisabeth
Meine Freundin Barbara; My Firend Barbara 1938,Je 4,18:3
Riedmann, Gerhard
Beggar Student, The 1958,Ja 25,14:3
Gypsy Baron, The 1959,N 14,13:1
Hippodrome 1962,Mr 12,36:1
Riefenstahl, Leni
Peaks of Destiny 1927,N 29,31:1
White Hell of Pitz Palu, The 1930,S 27,21:3
Sturme Uber dem Mont Blanc; Storms on Mont Blanc 1931,Mr 1,VIII,6:6 (In Addenda)
Weisse Rausch, Der; White Ecstasy, The 1932,Ja 24,VIII,5:1
Avalanche 1932,Mr 26,17:2
S O S Iceberg 1933,S 25,18:4
Blue Light, The 1934,My 9,23:4
Riefenstahl, Leni (Director)
Blue Light, The 1934,My 9,23:4
Olympia-Festival of the Nation's 1940,Mr 9,19:3
Olympia, Festival of the Nations 1940,Mr 30,11:2
Riefensthal, Leni
Prisoners of the Mountain 1930,Ja 12,VIII,5:5 (In Addenda)
Riegal, Charles
Heart Raider, The 1923,Je 6,24:5
Rieger, Jack (Producer)
Congolaise 1950,My 22,17:4

Riego, Olav
Torment 1947,Ap 22,34:2
Riehl, Kay
Red Menace, The 1949,Je 27,18:2
Star, The 1953,Ja 29,25:1
Riehl, Raimondo van
Manege 1928,Mr 11,VIII,7:6 (In Addenda)
Riekelt, Gustave
That Murder in Berlin 1929,Mr 12,26:2
Rieman, Johannes
Armored Vault 1928,N 13,37:2 (In Addenda)
Riemann, Johannes
Sein Scheidungsgrund 1932,F 20,11:2
Der Falsche Ehemann 1932,O 17,18:3
Drunter und Drueber 1932,D 19,19:5
Heute Nacht-Eventuell 1933,Je 24,16:3
Hellseher, Der 1933,S 11,20:4
Kadetten 1933,D 26,19:3
Fraeulein-Falsch Verbunden! 1934,Ja 15,12:2
Wenn Herzen Sich Finden 1934,N 12,17:3
Tag Nach der Scheidung, Der; Day After the Divorce, The 1940,Mr 2,9:5
Ihr Erstes Erlebnis; Her First Experience 1940,Je 8,18:3
Riemann, Johannes (Director)
Ich Sehne Mich Nach Dir 1936,S 9,32:4
Dr Engel, Child Specialist 1937,S 20,19:2
Ave Maria 1937,O 2,18:1
Eva, das Fabriksmaedel 1938,Ja 8,19:2
Riener, Charles (Director)
Chasing Rainbows 1930,F 22,13:1
Riento, Virgilio
Anything for a Song 1947,Ag 5,26:2
Peddlin' in Society 1950,F 23,33:3
Miracle in Milan 1951,D 18,42:2
I Cadetti di Guascogna 1952,O 6,22:2
Bread, Love and Dreams 1954,S 21,24:1
Frisky 1955,O 25,37:3
Poor but Beautiful 1958,Je 11,39:4
Rierney, Harry (Composer)
Dixiana 1930,S 5,21:1
Rieseberg, Harry E (Original Author)
City Beneath the Sea 1953,Mr 12,24:3
Riesenfeld, Hugo Dr (Composer)
Blue Bird, The 1918,Ap 1,9:3
Grass 1925,Mr 31,17:4
Flaming Frontier, The 1926,Ap 5,24:1
Volga Boatman, The 1926,Ap 14,21:1
Beau Geste 1926,Ag 26,17:3
Sorrows of Satan, The 1926,O 13,21:1
Old Ironsides 1926,D 7,21:2
Rough Riders, The 1927,Mr 16,28:2
Little Men 1935,F 18,19:3
Let's Sing Again 1936,My 9,11:2
Riesenfeld, Hugo Dr (Miscellaneous)
Tosca, La 1921,N 21,20:1
Miserables, Les 1927,Ag 23,29:4
Cat and the Canary, The 1927,S 10,9:4
Tempest 1928,My 18,27:3
Iron Mask, The 1929,F 22,18:6
ThIs is America 1933,Jl 20,22:2
Wandering Jew, The 1935,Ja 14,11:3
Riesner, Charles F
Her Temporary Husband 1924,Ja 1,20:1
Man on the Box, The 1925,S 28,24:1
Riesner, Charles F (Director)
Man on the Box, The 1925,S 28,24:1
Oh! What a Nurse! 1926,F 22,14:1
Missing Link, The 1927,My 7,15:2
Fortune Hunter, The 1928,Ja 10,28:4
Steamboat Bill, Jr 1928,My 15,17:3
Fools for Luck 1928,Je 12,33:5
Hollywood Revue, The 1929,Ag 15,20:5
Caught Short 1930,Je 21,20:5
Love in the Rough 1930,S 27,21:3
Reducing 1931,Ja 17,23:1
Politics 1931,Ag 1,16:4
Flying High 1931,D 12,23:3
Divorce in the Family 1932,O 31,18:4
Chief, The 1933,D 2,9:4
You Can't Buy Everything 1934,F 3,9:2
Show-Off, The 1934,Mr 17,11:3
Student Tour 1934,O 31,17:3
Winning Ticket, The 1935,F 11,14:2
It's in the Air 1935,N 8,18:2
Sophie Lang Goes West 1937,S 30,19:2
Manhattan Merry-Go-Round 1937,D 31,9:3
Winter Carnival 1939,Jl 28,14:2
Big Store, The 1941,Je 27,14:4
Meet The People 1944,S 8,16:2
Lost in a Harem 1944,N 9,23:2
Traveling Saleswoman 1950,Ja 6,25:3
Riesner, Charles F (Original Author)
Missing Link, The 1927,My 7,15:2
Tombstone, The Town too Tough to Die 1942,Jl 27,18:2
Riesner, Charles F (Producer)
Winning Ticket, The 1935,F 11,14:2
Bury Me Dead 1947,O 25,13:3
Riesner, Dean
Traveling Saleswoman 1950,Ja 6,25:3

Riesner, Dean (Director)
Bill and Coo 1948,Mr 29,17:4
Riesner, Dean (Screenwriter)
Bill and Coo 1948,Mr 29,17:4
Helen Morgan Story, The 1957,O 3,33:2
Paris Holiday 1958,My 10,19:2
Man From Galveston, The 1964,Ja 23,26:3
Coogan's Bluff 1968,O 3,56:1
Riethof, Peter (Miscellaneous)
Mysterians, The 1959,Jl 2,15:2
Rietti, V
Juggernaut 1937,Jl 15,16:1
Rietty, Robert
Emil 1938,Ap 15,23:2
Give Us This Day 1949,D 21,41:2
Prelude to Fame 1950,N 10,35:3
Story of Joseph and his Brethern, The
1962,D 1,17:1
Bible, The 1966,S 29,60:1
Rieux, Max de (Director)
Cousine Bette, La 1928,Ag 12,VII,3:4
Rifberg, Klaus (Screenwriter)
Weekend 1964,Ap 27,24:1
Riga
Flute and the Arrow, The 1960,O 11,55:1
Rigali, Al
Dead March, The 1937,S 20,19:1 (In Addenda)
Rigano, Evi
10th Victim, The 1965,D 21,46:1
Riganti, Franco (Original Author)
Doctor, Beware 1951,Ap 30,16:3
Rigas, George
Love Light, The 1921,Ja 10,9:1
Wanderer, The 1925,Ag 20,22:1
That Royle Girl 1926,Ja 4,33:1
Desert Gold 1926,Mr 23,24:5
Rescue, The 1929,Ja 14,20:1
Redskin 1929,Ja 28,21:1
Wolf Song 1929,F 25,16:1
Beau Ideal 1931,Ja 19,25:1
Destination Unknown 1933,Ap 8,16:2
Way to Love, The 1933,N 11,10:3
Rigaud, George
Fantomas 1334,Mr 13,27:4
Quatorez Juillet 1933,O 20,14:2
Ordonnance, L'; Orderly, The 1935,Jl 1,22:3
Living Corpse, The 1940,S 23,21:4
Paris Underground 1945,O 20,8:2
Masquerade in Mexico 1945,N 29,27:2
Postmaster's Daughter, The 1946,Ag 19,17:6
I Walk Alone 1948,Ja 22,36:3
Native Son 1951,Je 18,19:2
Colossus of Rhodes, The 1961,D 14,55:6
Happy Thieves, The 1962,F 5,19:4
Riff Raff Girls 1962,O 20,13:5
Place Called Glory, A 1966,Ag 11,27:4
Grand Slam 1968,F 21,60:4
Rigaux, Jean
Man in the Raincoat, The 1958,Jl 15,21:2
Rigby, Edward
Accused 1936,D 17,35:1
When Thief Meets Thief 1937,Je 15,26:2
Girl Was Young, The 1938,F 11,27:2
Yank at Oxford, A 1938,F 25,15:1
Forbidden Music 1938,D 27,13:2
Smiling Along 1939,F 20,13:2
Ware Case, The 1939,Jl 22,12:2
Convoy 1941,Ja 17,21:2
Proud Valley 1941,My 17,19:2
Stars Look Down, The 1941,Jl 24,15:2
Kipps 1942,My 25,11:2
Flying Fortress 1942,D 19,22:2
Young Man's Fancy, A 1943,D 4,11:2
Courageous Mr Penn 1943,D 23,26:5
48 Hours 1944,Ja 26,21:2
Vacation From Marriage 1946,Mr 15,27:2
Murder in Reverse 1947,Ja 11,23:5
Years Between, The 1947,Mr 10,25:2
Piccadilly Incident 1948,Ag 5,16:2
Quiet Week-End 1948,Ag 20,13:2
Don't Take it to Heart 1948,D 25,10:3
Canterbury Tale, A 1949,Ja 24,16:2
Easy Money (Episode 4) 1949,F 14,15:3
Temptation Harbor 1949,My 11,34:7
Daybreak 1949,Jl 4,9:2
Agitator, The 1949,Ag 19,12:5
Christopher Columbus 1949,O 13,33:2
Run for Your Money, A 1950,Ap 10,15:3
Happiest Days of Your Life, The 1950,S 18,19:2
Tony Draws a Horse 1951,My 15,38:6
Circle of Danger 1951,Jl 12,21:6
Man in the Dinghy 1951,N 1,34:2
Double Confession 1953,My 1,17:2
Rigby, Gordon (Original Author)
Orchids to You 1935,Ag 10,16:4
Reformatory 1938,Je 27,13:6
Rigby, Gordon (Screenwriter)
Flight Into Nowhere 1938,My 2,13:3
Reformatory 1938,Je 27,13:6
Hidden Power 1939,Jl 26,17:3
Naval Academy 1941,Je 5,27:3

Rigby, Harry
Open the Door and See all the People
1964,Ap 2,28:1
Rigby, Ray (Screenwriter)
Operation Crossbow 1965,Ap 2,29:1
Hill, The 1965,O 4,00:0
Rigby, Terence
Accident 1967,Ap 18,33:1
Rigdon, Gertrude (Original Author)
Hold Me Tight 1933,My 22,18:6
Rigel, Arturo (Screenwriter)
Adventures of Scaramouche, The 1964,N 23,34:1
(Incorrect in this edition; use 1964,N 21,34:1
elsewhere)
Riggs, Lynn (Original Author)
Oklahoma! 1955,O 11,49:1
Riggs, Lynn (Screenwriter)
Garden of Allah, The 1936,N 20,27:2
Plainsman, The 1937,Ja 14,16:2
Sherlock Holmes and the Voice Of Terror
1942,S 19,9:2
Destination Unknown 1942,O 29,19:3
Riggs, Ralph
Lost Boundaries 1949,Jl 1,14:4
Riggs, Sidney
Sap From Syracuse, The 1930,Jl 26,16:4
Riggs, Tommy and his Betty Lou
Goodbye Broadway 1938,My 14,18:1
Righe, Eileen (Original Author)
June Bride 1948,O 30,10:2
Righelli, G (Director)
Al Buio Insieme 1937,Ag 6,21:3
Signora Fortuna; Lady Luck 1937,N 29,19:3
Armata Azzurra, La; Blue Fleet, The
1937,D 13,23:4
Aria del Continente, L'; Continental Atmosphere
1939,N 17,17:3
Lo Smemorato 1940,F 20,17:4
Peddlin' in Society 1950,F 23,33:3
Right, Massimo
Blood and Black Lace 1965,N 11,58:3
Rignault, Alexandre
Ordonnance, L'; Orderly, The 1935,Jl 1,22:3
Maria Chapdelaine 1935,S 25,18:2
Crime et Chatiment; Crime and Punishment
1935,N 13,25:3
Robber Symphony 1937,Ja 27,17:2
Dr Knock 1937,My 1,16:4
Rasputin 1939,O 17,31:4
Citadel of Silence, The 1939,D 25,29:1
Schubert's Serenade 1940,S 3,21:2
Francis the First 1947,N 20,38:4
Volpone 1947,D 27,9:3
Eternal Return, The; Eternel Retour, L
1948,Ja 5,15:2
Ruy Blas 1948,O 4,14:2
Pardon my French 1952,Mr 31,17:2
Sextette (Part I-The Gun); Gun, The (Sextette)
1953,Mr 2,19:2
Holiday for Henrietta 1955,Ja 25,21:1
Return of Don Camillo, The 1956,Mr 27,41:1
Happy Road, The 1957,Je 21,20:2
Pot Bouille 1958,O 28,39:1
Witches of Salem 1958,D 9,54:2
Rigsby, Howard (Original Author)
Last Sunset, The 1961,Je 15,51:1
Rigsone, Giuditta
Al Vostri Ordini, Signora; At Your Orders,
Madame 1940,My 25,20:1
Riha, Bobby
One and Only Genuine Original Family Band,
The 1968,Mr 22,55:1
Rihai, Mansouren
Marco the Magnificent 1966,D 15,60:1
Rilchard, Frida
Peaks of Destiny 1927,N 29,31:1
Rilety, Anna
City Without Jews, The 1928,Jl 9,25:1
Riley, Elaine
Big Clock, The 1948,Ap 22,34:2
Riley, Eleanor
Turnabout 1940,Jl 27,17:6
Riley, George
Over my Dead Body 1942,D 26,15:2
Riley, James Whitcomb (Original Author)
Old Swimmin' Hole, The 1921,F 28,16:2
Girl I Loved, The 1923,My 14,18:2
Riley, Jeannina
Big Mouth, The 1967,Jl 13,30:2
Riley, Lawrence (Original Author)
Go West, Young Man 1936,N 19,31:3
Ever Since Eve 1937,Je 25,25:2
Riley, Lawrence (Screenwriter)
Perfect Specimen, The 1937,O 28,29:2
On Your Toes 1939,O 21,12:2
Riley, Michael
Music Goes 'Round, The 1936,F 22,12:1
Riley, W (Original Author)
Agitator, The 1949,Ag 19,12:5
Rilla, Walter
Sajenko, The Soviet 1929,Ja 15,22:4
Last Night, The 1930,Ja 27,18:4
Rendez-Vous 1932,Ap 30,19:3

Rilla, Walter— Cont
Zirkus Leben 1932,D 28,14:7
Namensheirat 1933,Ja 9,23:1
Voce del Sangue, La 1933,Ap 17,16:4
Ein Gewisser Herr Gran 1934,F 24,18:5
Scarlet Pimpernel, The 1935,F 8,27:2
Abdul the Damned 1936,My 11,16:2
Victoria the Great 1937,O 29,19:1
Sixty Glorious Years 1938,N 18,25:2
Hell's Cargo 1940,S 16,15:2
Adventures of Tartu, The 1943,S 24,26:1
Candlelight in Algeria 1944,Jl 31,10:2
Mr Emmanuel 1945,Ja 8,15:2
State Secret 1950,O 5,38:2
Operation X 1950,D 11,31:2
Golden Salamander 1951,Mr 24,8:3
Lucky Nick Cain 1951,Ap 23,21:2
Lisbon Story, The 1951,S 6,39:4
Assassin, The 1953,Ap 18,17:2
Desperate Moment 1953,S 1,19:4
Star of India 1956,Ap 28,11:1
Confessions of Felix Krull, The 1958,Mr 5,38:1
Song Without End 1960,Ag 12,10:2
Secret Ways, The 1961,My 25,31:1
Code 7...Victim 5 1965,My 20,52:1
Rilla, Wolf (Director)
Village of the Damned 1960,D 8,43:3
Rilla, Wolf (Screenwriter)
Village of the Damned 1960,D 8,43:3
Rillon, John T
Dry Martini 1928,N 5,26:5 (In Addenda)
Rilsky, M (Screenwriter)
Cossack Beyond the Danube, A 1954,F 8,18:5
Rim, Carlo (Director)
Cupboard was Bare, The; (Armoire Volante, L')
1952,N 4,33:1
Rim, Carlo (Screenwriter)
Dawn Over France 1945,Mr 17,17:2
Barge-Keeper's Daughter, The 1945,S 6,23:3
Cupboard was Bare, The; (Armoire Volante, L')
1952,N 4,33:1
Seven Deadly Sins, The (Sloth); Sloth (The Seven
Deadly Sins) 1953,My 12,31:3
Bed, The (The Pompadour Bed); Pompadour Bed,
The (The Bed) 1955,Je 8,26:4
Rimi, Walter
S O S Iceberg 1933,S 25,18:4
Rimmer, Shane
Dr Strangelove or: How I Learned to Stop
Worrying and Love the Bomb 1964,Ja 31,16:1
(Incorrect in this edition; use 1964,Ja 30,24:1
elsewhere)
Rimoldi, Adriano
Carmen 1946,N 27,20:2
Story of Tosca, The 1947,D 19,34:2
Loves of Don Juan, The 1948,S 2,18:4
Mistress of the Mountains 1954,My 27,34:5
Rimsky, Nicholas
Tales of 1,001 Nights 1927,Ja 24,14:1
Heart of Paris 1939,Ja 13,17:3
Rimsky-Korsakov (Composer)
Stars of the Ukraine 1953,Jl 13,22:4
May Night 1953,Jl 13,22:4
Snegurochka; Snow Maiden, The 1953,S 7,15:2
Invitation to the Dance (Ring Around the Rosy);
Ring Around the Rosy (Invitation to the
Dance) 1956,My 23,35:7
Invitation to the Dance (Circus); Circus (Invitation
to the Dance) 1956,My 23,35:7
Invitation to the Dance (Sinbad the Sailor); Sinbad
the Sailor (Invitation to the Dance)
1956,My 23,35:7
Rimsky-Korsakov (Original Author)
Sadko 1953,Je 1,18:6
Rin-Tin-Tin (Dog)
Where the North Begins 1923,Ag 27,14:3
Find Your Man 1924,S 23,26:1
Lighthouse by the Sea, The 1924,D 29,11:4
Tracked in the Snow Country 1925,Jl 20,19:2
Below the Line 1925,S 21,12:4
Clash of the Wolves, The 1925,N 18,27:4
Night Cry, The 1926,Ap 7,26:6
Hills of Kentucky 1927,Mr 2,29:3
Tracked by the Police 1927,Ap 27,22:5
Show of Shows 1929,N 21,24:5
Tiger Rose 1929,D 25,23:1
On the Border 1930,F 3,17:1
Man Hunter, The 1930,Ap 5,23:3
Rin-Tin-Tin Jr (Dog)
Big Pay-Off, The 1933,Ja 17,22:7
Tough Guy 1936,Mr 14,10:1
Rina, Ita
Walzerkoenig, Der 1932,D 5,21:2
Rinaldi, Joe (Screenwriter)
Adventures of Ichabod and Mr Toad, The
1949,O 10,18:2
Lady and the Tramp 1955,Je 24,17:1
Babes in Toyland 1961,D 15,49:1
Rinaldi, Manuela
Jessica 1962,Ap 20,20:2
Rinaldi, Tina C
Romola 1924,D 2,13:2

Rinaldi, William
Thank You 1925,O 6,30:1
Rinaldo, Duncan
Bridge of San Luis Rey, The 1929,My 20,22:6
Rinaldo, Fred (Original Author)
Hold That Ghost 1941,Ag 8,13:3
No Time for Love 1943,D 2,30:1
Rinaldo, Fred (Screenwriter)
Invisible Woman, The 1941,Ja 9,27:2
Black Cat, The 1941,Ap 26,20:3
Hold That Ghost 1941,Ag 8,13:3
Juke Box Jenny 1942,Ap 17,21:3
Hit the Ice 1943,S 23,27:2
Crazy House 1943,D 16,33:3
Buck Privates Come Home 1947,Ap 12,11:3
Wistful Widow of Wagon Gap, The
1947,N 21,36:2
Abbott and Costello Meet Frankenstein
1948,Jl 29,17:2
Holiday in Havana 1949,O 14,33:5
Abbott and Costello Meet the Invisible Man
1951,Ap 13,18:6
Comin' Round the Mountain 1951,Jl 27,15:2
Jumping Jacks 1952,Jl 24,30:2
Rinaldo, Tito
We Were Strangers 1949,Ap 28,28:2
Rinch-Smiles, Frank
Doctor's Secret, The 1929,F 4,20:1
RINEHART
See Also REINHARD, REINHARDT,
REINHART
Rinehart, Mary Roberts (Original Author)
Doctor and the Woman, The 1918,Ap 15,13:3
Twenty-three and a Half Hours' Leave
1919,O 27,9:3
It's a Great Life 1920,Ag 30,12:3
Glorious Fool, The 1922,Mr 20,10:3
Long Live the King 1923,D 4,24:1
Her Love Story 1924,O 7,26:1
Unknown, The 1924,N 18,22:1
K-The Unknown 1924,N 18,22:1
Seven Days 1925,Ag 31,19:3
Bat, The 1926,Mr 15,18:3
Finders Keepers 1928,Mr 5,21:3
I Take This Woman 1931,Je 13,20:4
Miss Pinkerton 1932,Jl 9,7:5
Mr Cohen Takes a Walk 1936,F 13,25:2
23 1/2 Hours Leave 1937,My 17,23:2
Nurse's Secret, The 1941,Je 6,25:7
Tish 1942,S 18,25:2
Bat, The 1959,D 17,51:4
Ring, Blanche
It's the old Army Game 1926,Jl 5,6:4
If I Had my Way 1940,My 6,13:2
Ring, Cyril
Exciters, The 1923,Je 4,13:3
Homeward Bound 1923,Jl 31,12:4
Pied Piper Malone 1924,Ja 28,12:1
Guilty One, The 1924,Je 17,22:4
Tongues of Flame 1924,D 16,28:1
News Parade, The 1928,My 29,17:2
Cocoanuts, The 1929,My 25,17:3
Social Lion, The 1930,Je 14,9:4
Business and Pleasure 1932,F 13,23:4
Border Patrolman 1936,Je 29,11:2
Army Surgeon 1942,N 5,35:2
Navy Comes Through, The 1942,N 12,30:3
Over my Dead Body 1942,D 26,15:2
Body and Soul 1947,N 10,21:2
Ringer, Claude
Carmen Baby 1967,O 11,41:2
Ringheim, Viking
Nar Rosorna Sla Ut 1931,F 10,24:4
Rinker, Al (Composer)
Duchess of Idaho 1950,Jl 21,15:3
Rinze, Albert
Paisan 1948,Mr 30,26:2
Rio, Carmen
Cantante de Napoles, El; Singer of Naples, The
1935,F 25,13:4
Rio, Pepe del
Cancion del Milagro, La; Miracle Song, The
1940,My 11,15:2
Rio, Pepito
Alla en el Rancho Chico; Out on the Little Ranch
1939,F 25,19:3
Rio, Rafael del
Corazon de Nino; Heart of a Child
1940,Ja 1,29:4
Rio, Rita
Strike Me Pink 1936,Ja 17,15:2
Rioli, Riccardo
Golden Coach, The 1954,Ja 22,30:2
RIORDAN
See Also REARDON
Riordan, Marjorie
Stage Door Canteen 1943,Je 25,13:2
Mr Skeffington 1944,My 26,23:2
Pursuit to Algiers 1945,O 27,12:2
Three Strangers 1946,F 23,20:2
Hoodlum, The 1951,Jl 6,14:6

Rios, Elvira
Tropic Holiday 1938,Je 30,21:2
Stagecoach 1939,Mr 3,21:1
Rios, Lalo
Lawless, The 1950,Je 23,29:2
City Beneath the Sea 1953,Mr 12,24:3
Rios, Rosita
Di que me Quieres; Say That You Love Me
1939,Ap 24,13:2
Rios, S Pondal (Original Author)
You Were Never Lovelier 1942,D 4,31:1
Romance on the High Seas 1948,Je 26,10:5
Ripa, Robert
Modigliani of Montparnasse 1961,Mr 1,27:3
Riper, Kay (Screenwriter)
Lady Be Good 1941,S 19,27:1
Riper, Kay Van (Screenwriter)
Out West With the Hardys 1938,D 9,31:2
Ripert, Colette
Chips Are Down, The 1949,F 2,36:1
My Seven Little Sins 1956,My 2,27:1
Ripley, Arthur (Director)
I Met my Love Again 1938,Ja 15,19:1
Voice in the Wind 1944,Mr 16,17:2
Chase, The 1946,N 18,31:2
Ripley, Arthur (Original Author)
Hypnotized 1933,Ja 16,13:3
Voice in the Wind 1944,Mr 16,17:2
Ripley, Arthur (Producer)
Voice in the Wind 1944,Mr 16,17:2
Ripley, Arthur (Screenwriter)
Long Pants 1927,Mr 29,23:2
His First Flame 1927,My 2,26:4
Hide Out 1930,Ap 12,23:1
Waterfront 1939,Jl 17,10:2
Ripley, Clements (Original Author)
Devil With Women, A 1930,O 20,28:2
Black Moon 1934,Je 28,26:2
Gold Is Where You Find It 1938,F 14,20:6
Old Los Angeles 1948,Jl 12,11:2
Ripley, Clements (Screenwriter)
Jezebel 1938,Mr 11,15:2
Love, Honor and Behave 1938,Mr 21,18:2
Buffalo Bill 1944,Ap 20,22:6
Old Los Angeles 1948,Jl 12,11:2
Ripley, Heather
Chitty Chitty Bang Bang 1968,D 19,64:4
Ripper, Michael
Eye Witness 1950,Ag 28,13:2
Gilbert and Sullivan 1953,O 28,36:3
Richard III 1956,Mr 12,1:4
1984 1956,O 1,31:1
Woman in a Dressing Gown 1957,S 13,15:2
Brides of Dracula, The 1960,S 6,41:4
Matter of Who, A 1962,Jl 25,29:2
Where the Bullets Fly 1967,S 7,50:4
Ripple, Jimmy
Untitled-Baseball Technique 1941,Ja 17,11:3
Ripuli, Enrico (Screenwriter)
Arturo Island 1962,D 22,5:2
Riquelme, Carlos
Woman's Devotion, A 1957,Mr 22,26:1
Risacher, Rene (Producer)
Heartbreak Ridge 1955,My 5,41:2
Riscoe, Arthur
Gaiety Girls, The 1938,Mr 31,15:1
Kipps 1942,My 25,11:2
Risdon, Elizabeth
Star Overnight, A 1919,N 17,20:1
Crime and Punishment 1935,N 22,18:2
Lady of Secrets 1936,F 22,12:1
Don't Gamble With Love 1936,Mr 2,13:3
King Steps Out, The 1936,My 29,15:2
Final Hour, The 1936,Ag 1,16:3
Craig's Wife 1936,O 2,29:3
Theodora Goes Wild 1936,N 13,27:4
Woman I Love, The 1937,Ap 16,27:2
Make Way for Tomorrow 1937,My 10,23:1
Mountain Justice 1937,My 13,31:2
They Won't Forget 1937,Jl 15,16:1
Dead End 1937,Ag 25,25:1
Mannequin 1938,Ja 21,15:2
Mad About Music 1938,Mr 12,13:2
My Bill 1938,Jl 7,22:4
Cowboy From Brooklyn 1938,Jl 14,17:1
Affairs of Annabel, The 1938,O 13,29:2
Girls on Probation 1938,O 21,27:3
Great Man Votes, The 1939,Ja 20,15:2
Huckleberry Finn 1939,Mr 3,21:2
Girl From Mexico, The 1939,Je 8,31:4
Five came Back 1939,Jl 5,20:2
Forgotten Woman, The 1939,Ag 4,11:2
Full Confession 1939,S 28,29:4
Disputed Passage 1939,O 26,27:2
Roaring Twenties, The 1939,N 11,12:1
Mexican Spitfire 1940,Ja 10,16:4
Man Who Wouldn't Talk, The 1940,Ja 12,13:3
Honeymoon Deferred 1940,F 16,23:4
Abe Lincoln in Illinois 1940,F 23,19:2
Saturday's Children 1940,My 4,13:1
Howards of Virginia, The 1940,S 27,27:1
Mexican Spitfire out West 1940,O 30,29:3
Slightly Tempted 1940,N 1,33:1

Risdon, Elizabeth — Cont
Let's Make Music 1941,Ja 23,19:2
High Sierra 1941,Ja 25,11:2
Mr Dynamite 1941,Mr 13,25:2
Nice Girl 1941,Mr 27,29:6
Paris Calling 1942,Ja 19,21:2
Jail House Blues 1942,F 6,23:2
Reap the Wild Wind 1942,Mr 27,27:2
Lady is Willing, The 1942,Ap 24,21:2
Mexican Spitfire at Sea 1942,Je 26,16:5
Are Husbands Necessary? 1942,Jl 9,17:2
Mexican Spitfire Sees a Ghost 1942,Jl 31,11:2
I Live on Danger 1942,Ag 22,16:2
Mexican Spitfire's Elephant 1942,S 18,25:2
Journey for Margaret 1942,D 18,36:7
Random Harvest 1942,D 18,36:6
Amazing Mrs Holliday, The 1943,F 22,20:2
Higher and Higher 1944,Ja 22,8:4
Weird Woman 1944,Ap 1,11:1
Lost Angel 1944,Ap 10,14:1
Tall in the Saddle 1944,D 15,25:3
Unseen, The 1945,My 14,20:5
Fighting Guardsman, The 1945,O 6,9:6
Lover Come Back 1946,Je 20,20:3
Walls Came Tumbling Down, The 1946,N 9,13:5
Shocking Miss Pilgrim, The 1947,F 12,34:2
Egg and I, The 1947,Ap 25,29:2
Life With Father 1947,Ag 16,6:6
Romance of Rosy Ridge, The 1947,S 12,18:3
Mourning Becomes Electra 1947,N 20,38:2
High Wall 1947,D 26,22:2
Bride Goes Wild, The 1948,Je 4,27:2
Sealed Verdict 1948,N 3,36:2
Every Girl Should be Married 1948,D 24,14:2
Guilty of Treason 1950,Ap 11,26:2
Secret Fury, The 1950,Je 22,34:2
Milkman, The 1951,Ja 1,13:6
Scaramouche 1952,My 9,20:2
Riselle, Miriam
Singing Blacksmith, The 1938,N 3,27:1
Tevya 1939,D 22,15:3
Risi, Dino (Director)
Scandal in Sorrento 1957,Je 13,37:1
Poor but Beautiful 1958,Je 11,39:4
Love and Larceny 1963,F 2,5:6
Easy Life, The 1963,D 23,18:2
Bambole; Dolls, The (The Telephone Call);
Telephone Call, The (The Dolls)
1965,Je 29,26:1
Tiger and the Pussycat, The 1967,S 21,56:4
Treasure of San Gennaro 1968,F 27,36:1
15 From Rome 1968,Ap 11,51:3
Risi, Dino (Original Author)
Anna 1953,F 19,20:5
Poor but Beautiful 1958,Je 11,39:4
Treasure of San Gennaro 1968,F 27,36:1
Weekend, Italian Style 1968,My 23,56:2
Risi, Dino (Screenwriter)
Anna 1953,F 19,20:5
Scandal in Sorrento 1957,Je 13,37:1
Poor but Beautiful 1958,Je 11,39:4
Treasure of San Gennaro 1968,F 27,36:1
Weekend, Italian Style 1968,My 23,56:2
Rising, Lawrence (Original Author)
Proud Flesh 1925,Ap 14,26:1
Riskin, Everett (Producer)
I'll Take Romance 1937,D 17,33:2
Holiday 1938,Je 24,15:1
Here Comes Mr Jordan 1941,Ag 8,13:2
Guy Named Joe, A 1943,D 24,17:2
Kismet 1944,Ag 23,16:1
High Barbaree 1947,Je 6,27:2
Julia Misbehaves 1948,O 8,30:2
Thunder in the East 1953,F 4,32:2
Riskin, Robert (Director)
When You're in Love 1937,F 19,15:2
Riskin, Robert (Original Author)
Illicit 1931,Ja 19,25:1
Miracle Woman, The 1931,Ag 17,18:2
American Madness 1932,Ag 6,14:5
Ex-Lady 1933,My 15,16:2
Ann Carver's Profession 1933,Je 9,20:2
Carnival 1935,F 16,9:1
Thin Man Goes Home, The 1945,Ja 26,16:5
Magic Town 1947,O 8,29:2
Here Comes the Groom 1951,S 21,19:2
Riskin, Robert (Producer)
Thin Man Goes Home, The 1945,Ja 26,16:5
Magic Town 1947,O 8,29:2
Riskin, Robert (Screenwriter)
Broadway Bill 1934,N 30,22:2
Carnival 1935,F 16,9:1
Whole Town's Talking, The 1935,Mr 1,16:2
Mr Deeds Goes to Town 1936,Ap 17,17:2
When You're in Love 1937,F 19,15:2
Lost Horizon 1937,Mr 4,27:1
You Can't Take It With You 1938,S 2,21:2
Meet John Doe 1941,Mr 13,25:2
Thin Man Goes Home, The 1945,Ja 26,16:5
Magic Town 1947,O 8,29:2
Riding High 1950,Ap 11,26:2
Mister 880 1950,S 30,13:2
Half Angel 1951,Je 16,9:2
Pocketful of Miracles 1961,D 19,39:1

Riss, Dan
Pinky 1949,S 30,28:2
Love That Brute 1950,My 27,10:6
Kiss Tomorrow Goodbye 1950,Ag 5,9:2
Panic in the Streets 1950,Ag 5,9:2
Wyoming Mail 1950,O 23,26:5
Only the Valiant 1951,Ap 14,9:6
Appointment With Danger 1951,My 10,38:2
Go for Broke 1951,My 25,31:2
Carbine Williams 1952,My 8,37:2
Confidence Girl 1952,Je 21,12:2
Washington Story 1952,Jl 2,22:3
Operation Secret 1952,N 6,37:2
Man in the Dark 1953,Ap 9,31:5
Vice Squad 1953,Ag 26,23:2
Three Young Texans 1954,Ap 17,8:2
Miami Story, The 1954,My 15,13:2
Man on Fire 1957,Ag 23,10:1

Risse, Germaine
Army Game, The; Tire Au Flanc
1963,Ap 24,40:1

Risso, John
Street of Chance 1930,F 3,17:1

Risso, Roberto
Bread, Love and Dreams 1954,S 21,24:1
One Step to Eternity 1955,O 3,22:2
Frisky 1955,O 25,37:3
Paris Hotel 1959,S 12,12:3
Breath of Scandal, A 1960,D 17,19:1
Valiant, The 1962,Je 14,23:4

Rissone, Checco
Tragic Hunt 1948,O 22,30:2
Woman Trouble 1949,My 26,34:2
Bitter Rice 1950,S 19,39:2

Rissone, Francesco
Miracle in Milan 1951,D 18,42:2
Eva 1965,Je 5,21:2

Rissone, Giuditta
Passa L'Amore 1933,N 25,10:3
Amo Te Sola 1936,Jl 20,11:2
Trionfo dell'Amore, Il; Love's Triumph
1938,Mr 29,18:4
Schoolgirl Diary 1947,O 18,9:2
Four Steps in the Clouds 1948,N 22,25:2
Tormento 1953,Ap 4,9:2
Eight and One Half 1963,Je 26,36:1

Rist, Sepp
Sturme Uber dem Mont Blanc; Storms on Mont
Blanc 1931,Mr 1,VIII,6:6 (In Addenda)
Avalanche 1932,Mr 26,17:2
S O S Iceberg 1933,S 25,18:4
Reiter von Deutsch-Ostafrika, Die 1935,Je 8,12:3
Lachende Dritte, Der 1938,Ap 9,11:2

Ristori, Dedi
Bitter Rice 1950,S 19,39:2
Paolo and Francesca 1953,F 14,8:3

Ritch, Steve (Original Author)
Safe at Home 1962,Ap 14,14:1

Ritch, Steven
Crooked Web, The 1955,D 10,19:1
Bailout at 43,000 1957,Je 8,13:2

Ritchard, Cyril
Piccadilly 1929,Jl 15,25:1
Blackmail 1929,O 7,22:1
Reserved for Ladies 1932,My 21,9:2
Half a Sixpence 1968,F 21,60:3

Ritchey, Bruce
Child Is Waiting, A 1963,F 14,5:6

Ritchey, Will (Original Author)
White and Unmarried 1921,My 30,12:5

Ritchey, Will (Screenwriter)
North of the Rio Grande 1922,My 15,20:3
Drums of Fate 1923,Ja 15,18:3
Trail of the Lonesome Pine, The 1923,Mr 20,24:3

Ritchie, Clint
St Valentine's Day Massacre, The 1967,Jl 27,29:2
Bandolero 1968,Jl 18,26:2

Ritchie, June
Kind of Loving, A 1962,O 2,46:1
Mouse on the Moon, The 1963,Je 18,32:1

Ritchie, Larry
Connection, The 1962,O 4,44:1

Ritoy, Theodore Von
Bardelys The Magnificent 1926,N 1,28:1 (In
Addenda)

Ritt, Martin
Winged Victory 1944,D 21,16:2

Ritt, Martin (Director)
Edge of the City 1957,Ja 30,33:2
No Down Payment 1957,O 31,41:1
Long, Hot Summer, The 1958,Ap 4,16:1
Black Orchid, The 1959,F 13,33:2
Sound and the Fury, The 1959,Mr 28,11:1
Five Branded Women 1960,Je 2,27:2
Paris Blues 1961,N 8,41:1
Hemingway's Adventures of a Young Man
1962,Jl 26,17:1
Hud 1963,My 29,36:1
Outrage, The 1964,O 8,48:2
Spy Who Came in From the Cold, The
1965,D 24,24:1
Hombre 1967,Mr 22,41:1

Ritt, Martin (Producer)
Hud 1963,My 29,36:1
Spy Who Came in From the Cold, The
1965,D 24,24:1
Hombre 1967,Mr 22,41:1

Ritter, Gottfried (Miscellaneous)
Verraeter; Traitors 1936,N 22,XI,4:2 (In
Addenda)

Ritter, Karl (Director)
Weiberregiment 1936,S 14,25:2
Verraeter 1937,Ja 23,13:1
Patriots 1937,S 18,15:3
Urlaub auf Ehrenwort; Furlough on Word of
Honor 1938,Ap 28,19:2
Unternehmen Michael; Private's Job, The
1938,My 14,18:2
Pour le Merite 1939,Ap 8,19:2
Hochzeitstreise, Die; Wedding Journey, The
1939,My 13,11:5

Ritter, Lloyd (Cinematographer)
Secrets of the Reef 1956,Jl 24,19:2

Ritter, Lloyd (Director)
Secrets of the Reef 1956,Jl 24,19:2

Ritter, Lloyd (Screenwriter)
Secrets of the Reef 1956,Jl 24,19:2

Ritter, Tex
Mystery of the Hooded Horsemen, The
1937,Ag 13,13:2
Frontier Town 1938,Mr 12,13:3
Frontier Badmen 1943,Ag 14,12:8

Ritter, Tex (Narrator)
Cowboy, The 1954,Ag 3,14:2

Ritter, Thelma
Miracle on 34th Street 1947,Je 5,32:1
Letter to Three Wives, A 1949,Ja 21,24:2
City Across the River 1949,Ap 8,31:3
Father Was a Fullback 1949,O 13,33:3
Perfect Strangers 1950,Mr 11,8:2
All About Eve 1950,O 14,13:2
I'll Get by 1950,N 2,39:3
Mating Season, The 1951,Ap 12,41:2
As Young as You Feel 1951,Ag 3,10:6
Model and the Marriage Broker, The
1952,Ja 12,10:6
With a Song in my Heart 1952,Ap 5,20:2
Titanic 1953,My 28,27:5
Farmer Takes a Wife, The 1953,Je 13,11:2
Pickup on South Street 1953,Je 18,38:2
Rear Window 1954,Ag 5,18:2
Daddy Long Legs 1955,My 6,17:5
Lucy Gallant 1955,O 21,30:1
Proud and Profane 1956,Je 14,41:2
Hole in the Head, A 1959,Jl 16,31:2
Pillow Talk 1959,O 7,47:2
Misfits, The 1961,F 2,24:2
Second Time Around, The 1961,D 23,16:1
Birdman of Alcatraz 1962,Jl 19,19:2
How the West Was Won 1963,Ap 1,54:1
For Love or Money 1963,Ag 8,19:1
New Kind of Love, A 1963,O 31,26:2
Move Over Darling 1963,D 26,33:1
Boeing Boeing 1965,D 24,24:4
Incident, The 1967,N 6,65:1

Rittner, Rudolf
At the Grey House 1927,N 8,33:1
When Duty Calls 1929,Ja 1,60:1
Meistersinger 1929,D 16,34:2

Ritz, Al
Gorilla, The 1939,My 28,6:2
Hi 'Ya Chum 1943,F 26,17:4

Ritz, Harry
Gorilla, The 1939,My 28,6:2
Hi 'Ya Chum 1943,F 26,17:4

Ritz, Jimmy
Gorilla, The 1939,My 28,6:2
Hi 'Ya Chum 1943,F 26,17:4

Ritz Brothers
One in a Million 1937,Ja 1,19:3
On the Avenue 1937,F 5,17:3
You Can't Have Everything 1937,Ag 4,15:2
Life Begins in College 1937,O 9,16:1
Goldwyn Follies, The 1938,F 21,15:1
Kentucky Moonshine 1938,My 21,9:2
Straight, Place and Show 1938,O 1,10:2
Three Musketeers, The 1939,F 18,12:2
Pack up Your Troubles 1939,O 27,27:2
Sound of Laughter, The 1963,D 18,44:2

Ritz Brothers, The
Sing, Baby, Sing 1936,S 12,20:1
Argentine Nights 1940,O 11,25:3

Riva, Emanuelle
Therese 1963,N 13,35:2
Hours of Love, The 1965,S 4,11:5
Thomas the Imposter 1965,S 13,42:1

Riva, Emmanuelle
Hiroshima, Mon Amour 1960,My 17,43:1
Kapo 1964,Je 2,33:3
Love a la Carte 1965,Ja 12,31:1

Riva, Isabella
Mill on the Po, The 1951,O 23,35:2

Riva, Mario
I Cadetti di Guascogna 1952,O 6,22:2
My Heart Sings 1954,Mr 5,15:5

Rivalta, Giorgio (Director)
Cossacks, The 1960,S 6,41:4

Rivas, Carlos
King and I, The 1956,Je 29,15:6
Big Boodle, The 1957,Mr 12,38:1
Black Scorpion, The 1957,O 12,23:2
Miracle, The 1959,N 13,25:4
Unforgiven, The 1960,Ap 7,46:1

Rivas, Gabry
Thunder Below 1932,Je 20,11:2

Rivas, J M Linares
Romance del Palmar, El 1939,My 1,21:2

Rivas, Rogelio Barriga (Original Author)
Important Man, The; El Mayordoma
1962,Je 26,25:2

Rivelin, Michel (Screenwriter)
Two of Us, The 1968,F 20,53:1

Rivelles, Amparito
Nail, The 1949,Jl 1,14:6

Rivelles, Rafael
Mama 1933,Jl 8,14:6
Hombre que se Reia del Amor, El 1935,Jl 18,15:3
Carmen de la Triana 1940,Je 15,12:2
Goyescas 1944,My 29,18:3
Don Quixote 1949,My 13,29:3
Marcelino 1956,O 23,39:1
Revolt of the Slaves, The 1961,N 8,41:1
Cyrano and D'Artagnan 1964,S 26,16:1

Rivelli, Luisa
Big Gundown, The 1968,Ag 23,33:1

River, W L (Screenwriter)
Reaching for the Sun 1941,My 8,21:1
Adventures of Martin Eden 1942,Mr 16,19:2
Great Man's Lady, The 1942,Ap 30,14:3

Rivera, Fermin
Brave One, The 1957,Mr 22,26:1

Rivero, Enrique
Sang d'un Poete, Le 1933,N 3,23:3

Rivero, Fernando
Profanacion 1934,Ja 31,20:4

Rivero, Fernando (Director)
Beso Mortal, El; Fatal Kiss, The 1939,Ja 21,19:3
Juntos pero no Revueltos; United but not Mixed
1939,O 23,15:3
Silk, Blood and Sun 1943,Ja 30,10:6
Miserables, Los 1944,O 24,17:2

Rivero, Fernando (Screenwriter)
Miserables, Los 1944,O 24,17:2

Rivero, Julian
Broken Wing, The 1932,Mr 26,17:2
Kid From Spain, The 1932,N 18,23:2
Dancing Pirate 1936,Je 18,19:1
Heroes of the Alamo 1938,Ap 2,18:2
Girl and the Gambler, The 1939,Je 28,17:3
That Night With You 1945,N 9,16:2
Outlaw, The 1947,S 12,18:4
Old Los Angeles 1948,Jl 12,11:2
Amazon Quest 1949,My 14,9:3
Reward, The 1965,S 16,55:1

Rivero, Lorraine
Ladies of the Mob 1928,Je 18,13:2
Redskin 1929,Ja 28,21:1

Rivers, Clarice
Round Trip 1967,Jl 20,30:2

Rivers, Fernand (Director)
Dame aux Camelias, La 1935,Mr 21,27:1
Open Road, The 1940,O 5,20:2
Dirty Hands 1954,My 11,25:5

Rivers, Fernand (Producer)
Pasteur 1936,Ja 30,14:3
Open Road, The 1940,O 5,20:2

Rivers, Fletcher
Cabin in the Sky 1943,My 28,19:3

Rivers, Joan
Swimmer, The 1968,My 16,53:1

Rivers, Larry
Round Trip 1967,Jl 20,30:2

Rivet, Marcel (Screenwriter)
Between Eleven and Midnight 1950,F 23,33:3
Night is my Kingdom, The 1953,S 30,37:1
Lover's Net 1957,Jl 23,23:1

Rivette, Jacques (Director)
Paris Belongs to Us 1962,N 6,38:1
Religieuse, La 1968,S 23,42:3

Rivette, Jacques (Screenwriter)
Paris Belongs to Us 1962,N 6,38:1
Religieuse, La 1968,S 23,42:3

Riveyre, Jean
Diary of a Country Priest 1954,Ap 6,35:2

Riviere, Anne
Two Are Guilty 1964,F 29,12:1

Riviere, Georges
John Paul Jones 1959,Je 17,39:1
Tomorrow Is my Turn 1962,F 2,24:2
Lafayette 1963,Ap 11,29:1
...And Suddenly It's Murder! 1964,Ja 24,21:1
Anatomy of a Marriage; My Days With Jean
Marc; My Nights With Francoise
1964,O 27,42:2

Riviere, Julian
Winner Take All 1932,Je 18,9:2

Riviere, Marie-France (Screenwriter)
24 Hours in a Woman's Life 1968,S 25,39:1
Rivkin, Allen (Miscellaneous)
My Dream Is Yours 1949,Ap 16,11:3
Rivkin, Allen (Original Author)
Night World 1932,My 28,18:2
Is my Face red 1932,Je 11,9:3
Behind the News 1941,Ja 16,25:3
Battle Circus 1953,My 28,27:5
Prisoner of War 1954,My 10,20:2
Rivkin, Allen (Screenwriter)
Our Little Girl 1935,Je 7,24:4
Black Sheep 1935,Je 28,34:1
Bad Boy 1935,O 28,16:3
Your Uncle Dudley 1935,D 12,33:4
Champagne Charlie 1936,My 7,21:2
This Is my Affair 1937,My 28,17:1
Love Under Fire 1937,Ag 28,8:2
Straight, Place and Show 1938,O 1,10:2
Let Us Live 1939,Mr 30,19:2
It Could Happen to You 1939,Je 9,26:3
Typhoon 1940,My 23,28:4
Singapore Woman 1941,My 12,13:6
Highway West 1941,Ag 8,13:4
Joe Smith, American 1942,Ap 2,27:4
Kid Glove Killer 1942,Ap 17,21:4
Sunday Punch 1942,My 11,19:2
Till the End of Time 1946,Jl 24,24:1
Thrill of Brazil, The 1946,S 6,18:3
Dead Reckoning 1947,Ja 23,31:2
Farmer's Daughter, The 1947,Mr 26,31:2
Guilt of Janet Ames, The 1947,My 23,31:2
Tension 1950,Ja 12,32:4
Grounds for Marriage 1951,Ja 12,24:6
Gambling House 1951,Mr 19,23:2
It's a big Country 1952,Ja 9,25:2
Timberjack 1955,Mr 10,33:3
Etérnal Sea, The 1955,Je 10,16:2
Rix, Alexander (Screenwriter)
Eternal Waltz, The; (Ewiger Walzer).
1959,Jl 9,22:1
Rix, Jonathan (Screenwriter)
Angela 1955,Je 4,9:2
Rizhov, G
Poet and Tsar 1938,Ag 25,15:1
Rizos, Nilos
Taxi Driver, The 1958,Mr 3,24:8
Rizzo, Alfredo
Roman Holiday 1953,Ag 28,13:1
Rizzo, Carlo
Deported 1950,N 2,39:3
When in Rome 1952,My 12,21:2
Rains of Ranchipur, The 1955,D 16,38:2
Seven Hills of Rome 1958,Ja 28,24:2 (Incorrect
in this edition; use 1958,Ja 31,24:2 elsewhere)
Naked Maja, The 1959,Je 11,36:2
Rizzo, Gianni
Three Steps North 1951,Je 29,14:2
Head of a Tyrant 1962,Je 7,31:2
Rizzoli, Angelo (Producer)
Flowers of St Francis 1952,O 7,26:2
Eight and One Half 1963,Je 26,36:1
Moment of Truth, The 1965,Ag 10,18:1
Rleming, Susan
Ladies of the Jury 1932,Ap 2,13:2
Roa, Joaquin
Nail, The 1949,Jl 1,14:6
Marcelino 1956,O 23,39:1
ROACH
See Also ROCHE
Roach, Bert
Excuse Me 1925,Ja 27,11:2
Denial, The 1925,Mr 10,19:3
Smouldering Fires 1925,Mr 31,17:4
Money Talks 1926,My 11,24:3
Flaming Forest, The 1926,N 22,28:3
Tin Hats 1926,N 29,16:3
Taxi Dancer, The 1927,Mr 8,18:4
Tillie the Toiler 1927,Je 7,27:4
Twelve Miles Out 1927,Jl 26,17:1
Crowd, The 1928,F 20,14:1
Latest From Paris, The 1928,F 27,16:2
Certain Young Man, A 1928,Je 11,27:1
Telling the World 1928,Jl 16,25:3
Last Warning, The 1929,Ja 7,36:2
Time, The Place and the Girl, The 1929,Jl 8,17:3
Twin Beds 1929,Jl 15,25:1
Argyle Case, The 1929,Ag 31,13:4
Young Nowheres 1929,O 2,28:4
Show of Shows 1929,N 21,24:5
No, No, Nanette 1930,Ja 4,21:1
So Long Letty 1930,F 8,12:5
Hold Everything 1930,Ap 23,24:1
Song of the Flame 1930,My 7,24:5
Liliom 1930,O 4,15:2
Viennese Nights 1930,N 27,32:5
Princess and the Plumber, The 1930,D 23,25:1
Bad Sister 1931,Mr 30,25:2
Captain Thunder 1931,My 11,15:4
Six Cylinder Love 1931,My 16,31:3
Compromised 1931,N 7,16:5
Arrowsmith 1931,D 8,36:4
Murders in the Rue Morgue 1932,F 11,16:1

Hotel Continental 1932,Mr 21,19:5
Night World 1932,My 28,18:2
Love Me Tonight 1932,Ag 19,20:6
Bird of Paradise 1932,S 10,18:5
Evenings for Sale 1932,N 12,20:5
Hallelujah, I'm a Bum 1933,F 9,15:2
Daring Daughters 1933,Mr 25,13:4
Half a Sinner 1934,Je 23,16:5
Paris Interlude 1934,Jl 28,16:5
Traveling Saleslady 1935,Mr 29,26:2
Love Before Breakfast 1936,Mr 14,10:1
San Francisco 1936,Je 27,21:1
Hollywood Boulevard 1936,S 21,26:4
God's Country and the Woman 1937,Ja 11,15:5
Emperor's Candlesticks, The 1937,Jl 9,18:1
Girl Said No, The 1937,O 18,14:1
Jury's Secret, The 1938,F 4,17:2
Stolen Heaven 1938,My 12,27:2
Algiers 1938,Jl 15,13:2
Great Waltz, The 1938,N 25,19:1
Man in the Iron Mask, The 1939,Jl 14,11:1
Nurse Edith Cavell 1939,S 22,27:4
Fingers at the Window 1942,Ap 23,27:3
Hi Diddle Diddle 1943,S 24,26:2
Sensations of 1945 1944,Jl 7,13:2
Perils of Pauline, The 1947,Jl 10,17:2
Roach, Hal (Director)
Why Worry? 1923,S 3,9:3
Battling Orioles, The 1924,N 4,24:1
Devil's Brother, The 1933,Je 10,16:4
Captain Fury 1939,My 26,20:2
Housekeeper's Daughter, The 1939,D 2,21:4
One Million BC 1940,Ap 27,9:2
Turnabout 1940,Jl 27,17:6
Road Show 1941,F 19,25:2
Roach, Hal (Producer)
Safety Last 1923,Ap 2,22:1
Pardon Us 1931,Ag 22,7:5
Kelly the Second 1936,O 3,21:2
Our Relations 1936,N 11,55:1
Nobody's Baby 1937,My 20,17:3
Topper 1937,Ag 20,21:2
Captain Fury 1939,My 26,20:2
Housekeeper's Daughter, The 1939,D 2,21:4
One Million BC 1940,Ap 27,9:2
Saps at Sea 1940,Ap 29,12:2
Turnabout 1940,Jl 27,17:6
Road Show 1941,F 19,25:2
Topper Returns 1941,Mr 28,26:6
Broadway Limited 1941,Je 16,11:6
Tanks a Million 1941,O 9,27:2
Crazy World of Laurel and Hardy, The
1967,D 22,35:3
Roach, Hal (Screenwriter)
Battling Orioles, The 1924,N 4,24:1
Black Cyclone 1925,My 19,24:2
Roach, Hal Jr (Director)
One Million BC 1940,Ap 27,9:2
Prairie Chickens 1943,Jl 9,21:6
Calaboose 1943,Jl 30,19:2
Roach, John
Lady With a Past 1932,F 22,23:2
Roach, Margaret
Captain Fury 1939,My 26,20:2
Fast And Furious 1939,O 12,33:3
Turnabout 1940,Jl 27,17:6
Road Show 1941,F 19,25:2
Roach, Walter
Forest Ring, The 1930,Ap 26,11:1
Roache, Viola
Harriet Craig 1950,N 3,31:2
Royal Wedding 1951,Mr 9,30:2
Goodbye, my Fancy 1951,My 30,14:2
Roadman, Betty
Man Who Came to Dinner, The 1942,Ja 2,25:2
Burning Cross, The 1948,F 20,19:1
Roanne, Andre
Oppressed, The 1929,Jl 15,25:1
Venus 1929,O 14,20:2
Cognasse 1935,Ap 15,16:4
It Happened in Gibraltar 1943,N 16,27:1
Back Streets of Paris 1948,O 16,9:2
What Price Murder 1958,N 11,26:1
Roark, Garland (Original Author)
Wake of the Red Witch 1949,Ja 10,19:2
Fair Wind to Java 1953,Ag 28,13:3
Roark, Robert
Force of Arms 1951,Ag 14,20:2
Mister Roberts 1955,Jl 15,14:1
Blackjack Ketchum Desperado 1956,Ap 5,26:2
Roarke, Adam
Hells Angels on Wheels 1967,Jl 29,29:3
Psych-Out 1968,Mr 28,52:1
Savage Seven, The 1968,Ag 22,47:1
Roaves, Maurice
Fighting Prince of Donegal, The 1966,N 10,64:1
Robards, Jason
Gilded Lily, The 1921,Mr 7,8:1
Cohens and the Kellys, The 1926,F 23,26:5
Third Degree, The 1927,F 15,23:1
Hills of Kentucky 1927,Mr 2,29:3
White Flannels 1927,Mr 22,31:2
Tracked by the Police 1927,Ap 27,22:5

Robards, Jason— Cont
Wild Geese 1927,D 5,26:2
Streets of Shanghai 1928,F 21,19:3
On Trial 1928,N 15,26:5
Gamblers, The 1929,Ag 24,11:5
Isle of Lost Ships, The 1929,O 26,15:1
Paris 1929,N 8,31:2
Abraham Lincoln 1930,Ag 26,24:1
Lightnin' 1930,N 29,21:4
Charlie Chan Carries On 1931,Mr 21,15:1
Subway Express 1931,My 2,23:4
Salvation Nell 1931,Jl 6,24:4
Caught Plastered 1931,S 12,15:4
White Eagle 1932,S 24,18:4
Corruption 1933,Je 20,22:7
Devil's Mate 1933,S 23,11:7
Way to Love, The 1933,N 11,10:3
Broadway Bill 1934,N 30,22:2
President Vanishes, The 1934,D 8,18:5
Damaged Lives 1937,Je 14,26:2
Cipher Bureau 1938,D 14,32:6
Mad Empress, The 1940,F 15,15:1
Master Race, The 1944,N 2,22:1
Betrayal From the East 1945,Ap 25,27:2
Isle of the Dead 1945,S 8,12:2
Wanderer of the Wasteland 1945,S 29,12:2
Man Alive 1945,N 17,14:5
Game of Death, A 1945,N 24,22:4
Falcon's Alibi, The 1946,Ap 13,23:2
Bedlam 1946,Ap 20,16:4
Step by Step 1946,Ag 24,6:7
Trail Street 1947,Ap 10,35:2
Riff-Raff 1947,Je 30,25:7
Mr Blandings Builds his Dream House
1948,Mr 26,26:2
Fighting Father Dunne 1948,Je 25,26:2
Second Woman, The 1951,F 2,19:2
Thousand Clowns, A 1965,D 14,54:2
Big Hand for the Little Lady, A 1966,Je 9,54:2
Any Wednesday 1966,O 14,50:1
Divorce American Style 1967,Jl 20,30:2
St Valentine's Day Massacre, The 1967,Jl 27,29:2
Hour of the Gun 1967,N 2,58:4
Night They Raided Minsky's, The
1968,D 23,43:1
Robards, Jason Jr
Journey, The 1959,F 20,19:1
By Love Possessed 1961,Jl 20,32:2
Tender is the Night 1962,Ja 20,13:2
Act One 1963,D 27,17:2
Robb, Lotus
Star is Born, A 1954,O 12,23:1
Robbe-Grillet, Alain
Trans-Europ-Express 1968,My 13,52:1
Robbe-Grillet, Alain (Director)
Trans-Europ-Express 1968,My 13,52:1
Robbe-Grillet, Alain (Screenwriter)
Last Year at Marienbad 1962,Mr 8,26:1
Trans-Europ-Express 1968,My 13,52:1
Robbe-Grillet, Catherine
Trans-Europ-Express 1968,My 13,52:1
Robbin, Tod (Original Author)
Freaks 1932,Jl 9,7:5
Robbing, James
Lady in the Morgue, The 1938,My 9,13:3
ROBBINS
See Also ROBINS
Robbins, Archie Cpl
Winged Victory 1944,D 21,16:2
Robbins, Barbara
Hat, Coat and Glove 1934,Jl 27,21:2
Robbins, C A (Original Author)
Unholy Three, The 1925,Ag 4,14:3
Robbins, Cindy
Earth Is Mine, The 1959,Je 27,13:1
Robbins, Gale
My Girl Tisa 1948,F 21,9:2
Race Street 1948,Ag 23,13:3
My Dear Secretary 1949,F 14,15:4
Barkleys of Broadway, The 1949,My 5,34:2
Oh, You Beautiful Doll 1949,N 12,8:4
Three Little Words 1950,Ag 10,21:2
Between Midnight and Dawn 1950,O 2,19:2
Fuller Brush Girl, The 1950,O 6,23:2
Strictly Dishonorable 1951,Jl 12,21:6
Belle of New York, The 1952,Mr 6,25:6
Brigand, The 1952,Jl 26,9:2
Calamity Jane 1953,N 5,40:2
Girl in the Red Velvet Swing, The
1955,O 20,41:2
Robbins, Harold (Original Author)
King Creole 1958,Jl 4,15:2
Never Love a Stranger 1958,N 22,27:4
Carpetbaggers, The 1964,Jl 2,24:4
Where Love Has Gone 1964,N 3,26:1
Robbins, Harold (Producer)
Never Love a Stranger 1958,N 22,27:4
Robbins, Harold (Screenwriter)
Never Love a Stranger 1958,N 22,27:4
Robbins, James
Slim 1937,Je 24,30:2
Singing Marine, The 1937,Jl 1,33:2
Kid Comes Back, The 1938,F 7,10:2
Barbarian and the Geisha 1958,O 3,25:1

Robbins, Jerome (Director)
West Side Story 1961,O 19,39:3
Robbins, Jess (Director)
Too Much Business 1922,My 1,20:3
Robbins, Jessie
Fearless Vampire Killers, The, or Pardon Me but
Your Teeth are in my Neck 1967,N 14,52:1
Robbins, Marc
Alias Jimmy Valentine 1920,Ap 19,13:3
Robbins, Michael
Rattle of a Simple Man 1964,D 21,42:2
Robbins, Peter
Ticklish Affair, A 1963,Ag 22,19:2
Moment to Moment 1966,Mr 3,28:1
...And Now Miguel 1966,S 8,43:1
Good Times 1967,Ag 3,26:4
Robbins, Richard
Wrong Man, The 1956,D 24,8:1
Robbins, Sheila
Suddenly, Last Summer 1959,D 23,22:1
Robbins, Walt
Shanghaied 1927,S 13,36:2
Robe, Yellow Chief
Silent Enemy, The 1930,My 20,32:3
Rober, Richard
April Showers 1948,Mr 27,10:2
Larceny 1948,S 4,8:6
Illegal Entry 1949,Je 11,11:2
Any Number Can Play 1949,Jl 1,14:4
Task Force 1949,O 1,8:6
Thelma Jordon 1950,Ja 19,35:2
Backfire 1950,Ja 27,29:2
Port of New York 1950,F 3,29:2
Woman on Pier 13, The 1950,Je 16,28:4
Sierra 1950,S 15,31:2
Deported 1950,N 2,39:3
Dial 1119 1950,D 4,32:6
Watch the Birdie 1950,D 12,46:4
Father's Little Dividend 1951,Ap 13,18:5
Passage West 1951,Ag 31,12:2
Well, The 1951,S 27,37:2
Tall Target, The 1951,S 28,26:2
Outlaw Woman 1952,Ap 5,20:3
Devil Makes Three, The 1952,Ag 30,6:2
O Henry's Full House (The Clarion Call); Clarion
Call, The (O Henry's Full House)
1952,O 17,33:1
Savage, The 1953,Ja 2,11:1
Jet Pilot 1957,O 5,8:6
Robers, Edith
Dangerous Age, The 1923,Ja 29,11:1
Robert, A
Ways of Love (Jofroi); Jofroi (Ways of Love)
1950,D 13,50:2
Robert, Alfredo
Richiamo del Cuore, Il; Appeal of the Heart, The
1931,Mr 2,19:1
Passion of St Francis, The 1932,D 17,22:3
Robert, H J
Daughters of Today 1924,Mr 4,17:1
Robert, Helene
Roi des Resquilleurs, Le 1932,Je 13,19:3
Barbier de Seville, Le 1936,S 23,29:2
Fric-Frac 1948,My 29,8:6
Robert, Jacques (Original Author)
Marie Octobre 1960,Ag 16,25:2
Night Affair 1961,O 13,27:1
Robert, Jacques (Screenwriter)
Defend my Love; (Difendo il Mio Amore)
1959,O 8,48:7
Marie Octobre 1960,Ag 16,25:2
Love and the Frenchwoman; (Francaise et
l'Amour, La) 1961,F 28,38:2
Night Affair 1961,O 13,27:1
Seventh Juror, The 1964,Ja 28,25:1
Robert, Muriel
Pepper 1936,Ag 24,11:2
Robert, T (Screenwriter)
Lie of Nina Petrovna, The 1938,Mr 30,19:2
Living Corpse, The 1940,S 23,21:4
Postmaster's Daughter, The 1946,Ag 19,17:6
Robert, Yves
Grand Maneuver, The 1956,O 2,39:1
Folies Bergere 1958,My 28,37:2
Green Mare, The; Jument Verte, La
1961,O 24,41:2
Robert, Yves (Director)
War of the Buttons, The 1963,D 19,40:2
Robert, Yves (Producer)
War of the Buttons, The 1963,D 19,40:2
Roberti, Lyda
Dancers in the Dark 1932,Mr 19,11:2
Million Dollar Legs 1932,Jl 9,7:5
Kid From Spain, The 1932,N 18,23:2
Three-Cornered Moon 1933,Ag 12,14:2
Torch Singer 1933,O 7,18:5
College Rhythm 1934,N 24,19:1
George White's 1935 Scandals 1935,Ap 29,12:3
Big Broadcast of 1936, The 1935,S 16,15:2
Nobody's Baby 1937,My 20,17:3
Pick a Star 1937,My 28,17:2
Wide Open Faces 1938,Ap 15,23:2

Roberti, Manya
Spider, The 1931,S 5,7:4
Delicious 1931,D 26,15:5
Roberto
Lovers of Teruel, The 1962,D 15,5:1
Roberts, Adelle
Over 21 1945,Ag 17,20:2
Roberts, Alan
Two Loves 1961,Je 22,23:2
Roberts, Alice
Pandora's Box 1929,D 2,28:2
Douceur D'Aimer, La 1931,D 14,16:3
Roberts, Allan (Composer)
That's Right, You're Wrong 1939,N 30,25:3
Thrill of Brazil, The 1946,S 6,18:3
Down to Earth 1947,S 12,18:2
Slightly French 1949,My 27,25:3
Roberts, Allene
Red House, The 1947,Mr 17,27:2
Sign of the Ram, The 1948,Mr 4,30:2
Knock on any Door 1949,F 23,31:2
Union Station 1950,O 5,38:3
Hoodlum, The 1951,Jl 6,14:6
Roberts, Bart
Yankee Pasha 1954,Ap 19,19:2
Roberts, Beatrice
Love Takes Flight 1937,S 27,24:3
Devil's Party, The 1938,My 31,8:3
Mars Attacks the World 1938,N 8,26:3
It Comes up Love 1943,Ja 22,25:3
Her Primitive Man 1944,Ap 1,11:1
Mr Peabody and the Mermaid 1948,Ag 14,6:5
Roberts, Ben (Original Author)
Glory at Sea 1953,Mr 11,36:7
Portrait in Black 1960,Jl 28,19:1
Roberts, Ben (Screenwriter)
White Heat 1949,S 3,7:2
Backfire 1950,Ja 27,29:2
Goodbye, my Fancy 1951,My 30,14:2
Captain Horatio Hornblower 1951,S 14,21:2
Come Fill the Cup 1951,N 22,47:2
O Henry's Full House (The Gift of the Magi); Gift
of the Magi, The (O Henry's Full House)
1952,O 17,33:1
O Henry's Full House (The Clarion Call); Clarion
Call, The (O Henry's Full House)
1952,O 17,33:1
O Henry's Full House (The Last Leaf
1952,O 17,33:1
O Henry's Full House (The Cop and the Anthem);
Cop and the Anthem, The (O Henry's Full
House) 1952,O 17,33:1
White Witch Doctor 1953,Jl 2,19:3
King of the Khyber Rifles 1953,D 23,21:1
Green Fire 1954,D 25,7:1
Serenade 1956,Mr 24,21:1 (Incorrect in this
edition; use 1956,Mr 23,21:1 elsewhere)
Band of Angels 1957,Jl 11,21:1
Man of a Thousand Faces 1957,Ag 14,21:1
Shake Hands With the Devil 1959,Je 25,20:7
Portrait in Black 1960,Jl 28,19:1
Midnight Lace 1960,O 14,27:1
Roberts, Bernice
Outlaws of the Orient 1937,S 25,10:2
Roberts, Beverly
Singing Kid, The 1936,Ap 4,11:1
Sons o'Guns 1936,My 14,29:2
Hot Money 1936,Jl 25,16:2
China Clipper 1936,Ag 12,14:3
God's Country and the Woman 1937,Ja 11,15:5
Her Husband's Secretary 1937,Mr 20,23:6
Perfect Specimen, The 1937,O 28,29:2
West of Shanghai 1937,O 29,19:2
Expensive Husbands 1938,Ja 8,19:3
Daredevil Drivers, The 1938,F 23,27:2
Making the Headlines 1938,Ap 1,17:2
Call of the Yukon 1938,My 6,27:1
Tenth Avenue Kid 1938,S 2,21:3
Flirting With Fate 1938,D 15,35:3
I Was a Convict 1939,Mr 23,27:2
Tropic Fury 1939,S 8,28:4
Main Street Lawyer 1939,N 9,27:2
Roberts, Bill (Director)
Saludos Amigos 1943,F 13,8:2
Roberts, Bill (Miscellaneous)
Three Caballeros, The 1945,F 5,20:1
Roberts, Bob
Stairway to Heaven 1946,D 26,28:1
Call Me Mister 1951,F 1,21:2
Roberts, Bob (Producer)
Body and Soul 1947,N 10,21:2
Force of Evil 1948,D 27,16:2
He Ran all the Way 1951,Je 21,24:2
Roberts, C Edwards (Director)
Corruption 1933,Je 20,22:7
Roberts, C Edwards (Original Author)
Corruption 1933,Je 20,22:7
Roberts, Charles E (Director)
Hurry, Charlie, Hurry 1941,N 12,31:3
Roberts, Charles E (Original Author)
Millionaire Playboy 1940,Mr 16,8:2
Mexican Spitfire out West 1940,O 30,29:3
Sing Your Worries Away 1942,My 15,25:2

Roberts, Charles E (Original Author) — Cont
Mexican Spitfire's Elephant 1942,S 18,25:2
Roberts, Charles E (Screenwriter)
Mexican Spitfire 1940,Ja 10,16:4
Pop Always Pays 1940,Ag 30,16:6
Mexican Spitfire out West 1940,O 30,29:3
Mexican Spitfire at Sea 1942,Je 26,16:5
Mexican Spitfire Sees a Ghost 1942,Jl 31,11:2
Mexican Spitfire's Elephant 1942,S 18,25:2
Ladies' Day 1943,Mr 26,14:3
Roberts, Christian
To Sir, With Love 1967,Je 15,56:1
Anniversary, The 1968,Mr 21,57:2
Roberts, Clete
Swinger, The 1966,D 15,60:1
Roberts, Cyril (Screenwriter)
Christopher Columbus 1949,O 13,33:2
Roberts, Davis
Hotel 1967,Ja 20,27:1
Roberts, Denys (Original Author)
Law and Disorder 1958,Ag 6,20:1
Roberts, Desmond
Royal Bed, The 1931,Ja 31,15:1
Squaw Man, The 1931,S 19,10:2
But the Flesh Is Weak 1932,Ap 16,11:2
Cavalcade 1933,Ja 6,23:2
King's Vacation, The 1933,Ja 20,21:2
Christopher Strong 1933,Mr 10,19:2
Blind Adventure 1933,O 31,24:3
Tarzan and his Mate 1934,Ap 21,12:1
Of Human Bondage 1934,Je 29,17:1
Grand Canary 1934,Jl 20,11:1
Fountain, The 1934,Ag 31,14:1
Count of Monte Cristo, The 1934,S 27,25:2
Menace 1934,N 22,27:2
Limehouse Blues 1934,D 12,28:2
Clive of India 1935,Ja 18,29:1
Under the Red Robe 1937,Je 1,27:2
Beau Brummell 1954,O 21,31:5
Roberts, Doris
No Way to Treat a Lady 1968,Mr 21,56:1
Lovely Way to Die, A 1968,Jl 13,18:1
Roberts, Eddie
Some Blondes Are Dangerous 1937,N 3,29:3
Roberts, Edith
Bill Henry 1919,Ag 18,9:2
Backbone 1923,Ap 30,11:2
Big Brother 1923,D 24,12:1 (In Addenda)
Thy Name Is Woman 1924,Mr 4,17:1
$20 a Week 1924,Je 10,24:4
Roaring Rails 1924,O 15,27:3
On Thin Ice 1925,Mr 9,21:1
Seven Keys to Baldpate 1925,N 3,25:4
Roberts, Edith (Original Author)
That Hagen Girl 1947,O 25,13:2
Roberts, Edward (Original Author)
Vanity Street 1932,O 15,13:1
Forsaking all Others 1934,D 21,18:1
Roberts, Elizabeth Madox (Original Author)
Great Meadow, The 1931,Mr 14,23:2
Roberts, Eric
Watch on the Rhine 1943,Ag 28,15:1
North Star, The 1943,N 5,23:1
Fighting Father Dunne 1948,Je 25,26:2
Roberts, Evelyn
Sorrell and Son 1934,My 29,22:1
Return of the Scarlet Pimpernel, The
1938,Ap 11,12:2
Winslow Boy, The 1950,Je 7,34:4
Heart of the Matter, The 1954,N 19,20:2
Roberts, Ewan
Castle in the Air 1953,Ja 5,19:2
Titfield Thunderbolt, The 1953,O 6,34:2
Day of the Triffids 1963,My 11,15:2
Traitors, The 1963,Je 27,23:4
Roberts, Florence
Kept Husbands 1931,Mr 24,31:2
Everything's Rosie 1931,My 22,28:5
Too Many Cooks 1931,Ag 17,18:2
Fanny Foley Herself 1931,O 26,22:1
Westward Passage 1932,Je 4,9:2
Make Me a Star 1932,Jl 1,19:3
Dangerously Yours 1933,F 23,20:3
Daring Daughters 1933,Mr 25,13:4
Melody Cruise 1933,Je 23,15:2
Torch Singer 1933,O 7,18:5
Ever in my Heart 1933,O 13,25:3
Hoopla 1933,D 1,23:3
Miss Fane's Baby is Stolen 1934,Ja 20,12:2
Babes in Toyland 1934,D 13,28:2
Nut Farm, The 1935,Ap 8,23:3
Sons of Steel 1935,Ap 15,16:3
Miserables, Les 1935,Ap 22,14:2
Accent on Youth 1935,Ag 12,10:3
Top Hat 1935,Ag 30,12:2
Harmony Lane 1935,O 24,19:4
Your Uncle Dudley 1935,D 12,33:4
Next Time We Love 1936,Ja 31,16:2
Every Saturday Night 1936,Mr 14,10:2
Nobody's Fool 1936,Je 4,27:2
Educating Father 1936,Je 20,22:2
Off to the Races 1937,F 6,15:2
Nobody's Baby 1937,My 20,17:3
Big Business 1937,Je 1,27:2

Roberts, Florence— Cont

Life of Emile Zola, The 1937,Ag 12,14:2
Hot Water 1937,N 5,19:4
Trip to Paris, A 1938,Je 10,18:2
Safety in Numbers 1938,S 6,17:2
Personal Secretary 1938,O 5,20:2
Storm, The 1938,O 31,12:2
Abe Lincoln in Illinois 1940,F 23,19:2
Young as You Feel 1940,Mr 8,25:3
Roberts, Florian (Director)
Lady Gangster 1942,Jl 10,13:2
Roberts, George
William Tell 1925,My 20,26:2
Roberts, Glen
Girls in the Night 1953,Ja 16,19:3
Roberts, Hi
Adventure in Diamonds 1940,Ap 4,27:2
Roberts, J H
White Face 1933,D 4,22:3
It's a Boy 1934,Je 8,18:2
Accused 1936,D 17,35:1
Juggernaut 1937,Jl 15,16:1
Girl Was Young, The 1938,F 11,27:2
Divorce of Lady X, The 1938,Ap 1,17:2
Troopship 1938,Ap 26,18:2
Suicide Squadron 1942,My 14,23:2
Spitfire 1943,Je 14,13:2
Courageous Mr Penn 1943,D 23,26:5
Blanche Fury 1948,N 24,20:2
Agitator, The 1949,Ag 19,12:5
Roberts, James
Mill On the Floss, The 1939,N 15,19:3
Roberts, Joseph
Our Hospitality 1923,D 10,20:1
Roberts, Joseph L (Producer)
Pilgrimage for Peace: Pope Paul VI Visits America,
A 1966,Jl 21,20:2
Roberts, Kenneth (Original Author)
Northwest Passage 1940,Mr 8,25:1
Captain Caution 1940,O 21,21:3
Lydia Bailey 1952,My 31,12:5
Roberts, Lee
Lion and the Horse, The 1952,My 19,12:2
Roberts, Leona
Border Cafe 1937,Je 8,30:2
there Goes The Groom 1937,D 25,10:6
Of Human Hearts 1938,F 18,23:1
Bringing Up Baby 1938,Mr 4,17:5
Condemned Woman 1938,Ap 22,15:5
Having Wonderful Time 1938,Jl 8,11:2
Crime Ring 1938,Jl 22,10:3
Affairs of Annabel, The 1938,O 13,29:2
Kentucky 1938,D 24,12:1
I Stand Accused 1939,Ja 5,17:1
Persons in Hiding 1939,Mr 2,19:2
Bachelor Mother 1939,Je 30,17:2
Escape, The 1939,N 3,17:4
Gone With the Wind 1939,D 20,31:2
Swanee River 1939,D 30,9:2
Thou Shalt Not Kill 1940,Ja 8,11:2
Sued for Libel 1940,Ja 19,15:3
Blue Bird, The 1940,Ja 20,11:2
Abe Lincoln in Illinois 1940,F 23,19:2
Flight Angels 1940,My 27,23:2
Gangs of Chicago 1940,Je 13,29:2
Comin' Round the Mountain 1940,S 26,27:3
Boomerang 1947,Mr 6,36:2
Roberts, Lynne
Call the Mesquiteers 1938,Mr 19,11:2
Stadium Murders, The 1938,Ap 9,11:2
Everything's on Ice 1939,O 6,31:1
Star Dust 1940,My 4,13:1
Romance of the Rio Grande 1940,D 25,33:4
Ride on Vaquero 1941,Ap 19,20:2
Bride Wore Crutches, The 1941,My 26,15:3
Moon Over Miami 1941,Jl 5,14:2
Man in the Trunk, The 1942,O 23,25:1
Quiet Please, Murder 1942,D 22,31:1
Chicago Kid, The 1945,F 12,24:3
Big Bonanza, The 1945,F 26,14:5
Sioux City Sue 1947,Jl 23,19:3
Because of You 1952,D 4,47:3
Roberts, Margaret
Cinerama-South Seas Adventure 1958,Jl 16,26:1
Roberts, Marguerite (Miscellaneous)
Diamond Head 1963,F 21,5:2
Roberts, Marguerite (Original Author)
Sailor's Luck 1933,Mr 17,21:2
Jimmy and Sally 1933,D 16,12:3
Roberts, Marguerite (Screenwriter)
Men Without Names 1935,Je 29,16:2
Last Outpost, The 1935,O 5,18:2
Florida Special 1936,My 29,15:2
Forgotten Faces 1936,Jl 4,18:2
Hollywood Boulevard 1936,S 21,26:4
Rose Bowl 1936,D 2,35:2
Turn off the Moon 1937,My 20,17:2
Meet the Girls 1938,S 3,16:6
Escape 1940,N 1,33:1
Ziegfeld Girl 1941,Ap 25,17:2
Honky Tonk 1941,O 3,27:3
Somewhere I'll Find You 1942,Ag 28,22:4
Dragon Seed 1944,Jl 21,16:4
Sea of Grass, The 1947,F 28,27:2

Desire Me 1947,S 26,28:3
If Winter Comes 1948,Ja 23,28:4
Bribe, The 1949,F 4,31:2
Ambush 1950,Ja 19,35:2
Soldiers Three 1951,Mr 30,28:5
Rampage 1963,O 17,39:2
Love Has Many Faces 1965,F 25,24:1
5 Card Stud 1968,Ag 1,24:1
Roberts, Mark
Taxi 1953,Ja 22,20:3
Onionhead 1958,O 2,44:1
Roberts, Meade (Screenwriter)
Fugitive Kind, The 1960,Ap 15,13:1
Summer and Smoke 1961,N 17,41:1
In the Cool of the Day 1963,My 30,20:1
Stripper, The 1963,Je 20,29:1
Blue 1968,My 11,28:1
Danger Route 1968,Je 6,54:2
Roberts, Nancy
Prison Without Bars 1939,Ap 10,13:2
Black Narcissus 1947,Ag 14,29:2
Roberts, Pascale
Sleeping Car Murder, The 1966,Mr 8,45:1
Roberts, Pauline (Miscellaneous)
Children on Trial 1947,N 10,21:3
Roberts, Pernell
Desire Under the Elms 1958,Mr 13,24:2
Sheepman, The 1958,My 8,36:1
Roberts, Rachel
Saturday Night and Sunday Morning
1961,Ap 4,44:2
This Sporting Life 1963,Jl 17,19:2
Flea in her Ear, A 1968,N 28,66:1
Roberts, Ralph A
Tradition 1921,Jl 1,8:1
Oberkellner, Der 1929,Jl 1,31:2
Two Neckties; Zwei Kravatten 1930,N 30,IX,6:5
Wahre Jakob, Der 1931,Ag 7,20:2
Ungetreue Eckehart, Der 1932,Ja 23,18:4
Rendez-Vous 1932,Ap 30,19:3
Dienst Ist Dienst 1932,Je 6,18:5
Hurra! Ein Junge! 1932,Je 21,19:6
Keine Feier Ohne Meyer 1932,O 29,18:4
Ihre Majestaet die Liebe 1933,F 7,23:4
Eine Nacht im Paradies 1933,F 20,11:6
Luegen auf Ruegen 1934,Ja 1,28:2
Frechdachs, Der 1934,Ja 6,18:3
Zu Befehl, Herr Unteroffizier 1934,Je 16,20:3
Im Heidekrug 1934,D 31,9:7
Meine Frau, Die Schuetzenkoenigin
1935,Ja 7,13:3
Zigeunerblut 1935,Ap 8,23:5
Unschuld vom Lande, Die 1935,My 13,18:6
Keine Angst vor Liebe 1936,Ja 21,27:6
Schoen Ist Es Verliebt zu Sein 1936,Ap 7,31:2
Alte Kameraden 1936,Ap 27,19:3
Soldaten-Kameraden 1936,O 5,25:1
Die Ganze Welt Dreht Sich um Liebe
1936,N 27,27:2
Gibt nur eine Liebe, Es 1937,Ja 23,23:2
Punks Kommt aus Amerika 1937,Je 12,8:2
Hilde Petersen, Postlagernd 1937,Je 26,20:3 (In
Addenda)
Wenn Du eine Schwiegermutter hast; When You
Have a Mother-in-Law 1938,Ja 29,12:1
Husaren Heraus 1938,Mr 19,11:3
Maulkorb, Der 1938,Ap 9,11:3
Diskretion-Ehrensache; Discretion with Honor
1939,Mr 13,12:3
Geheimnisvolle Mister X, Der; Mysterious Mr X,
The 1939,Jl 1,11:2
Verkannte Lebemann, Der; Unrecognized Man of
the World, The 1939,S 16,20:2
Gone are the Days! 1963,S 24,43:2
Roberts, Ralph A (Director)
Spiel mit dem Feuer 1934,N 26,12:2
Roberts, Richard (Original Author)
Last Frontier, The 1955,D 8,45:1
Second Time Around, The 1961,D 23,16:1
Roberts, Roy
Guadalcanal Diary 1943,N 18,29:1
Sullivans, The 1944,F 10,19:2
Circumstantial Evidence 1945,Ap 21,18:3
Bell for Adano, A 1945,Jl 6,8:3
Within These Walls 1945,Jl 16,8:4
Caribbean Mystery, The 1945,Ag 20,22:4
Behind Green Lights 1946,F 16,10:2
Smoky 1946,Je 27,29:1
It Shouldn't Happen to a Dog 1946,S 7,11:2
My Darling Clementine 1946,D 4,44:5
Shocking Miss Pilgrim, The 1947,F 12,34:2
Brasher Doubloon, The 1947,My 22,34:5
Foxes of Harrow, The 1947,S 25,35:4
Nightmare Alley 1947,O 10,31:3
Gentleman's Agreement 1947,N 12,36:2
Daisy Kenyon 1947,D 25,32:1
Captain from Castile 1947,D 26,22:4
Fury at Furnace Creek 1948,Jl 12,11:2
Force of Evil 1948,D 27,16:2
Chicken every Sunday 1949,Ja 19,34:2
He Walked by Night 1949,F 7,15:2
No Minor Vices 1949,F 26,11:2
Bodyhold 1949,D 12,29:4

Roberts, Roy— Cont

Reckless Moment, The 1949,D 30,13:2
Chain Lightning 1950,F 20,21:2
Borderline 1950,Mr 6,17:2
Wyoming Mail 1950,O 23,26:5
Enforcer, The 1951,Ja 26,19:2
Second Face, The 1951,Mr 2,21:3
I Was a Communist for the F B I 1951,My 3,34:4
Santa Fe 1951,My 4,31:2
Stage to Tucson 1951,My 5,14:2
Man With a Cloak, The 1951,N 28,37:2
Tanks are Coming, The 1951,D 6,42:4
Big Trees, The 1952,F 6,24:2
Hoodlum Empire 1952,Mr 6,25:6
Stars and Stripes Forever 1952,D 23,17:2
House of Wax 1953,Ap 11,15:2
Second Chance 1953,Jl 23,20:2
Glory Brigade, The 1953,Ag 15,8:4
Dawn at Socorro 1954,Ag 28,8:2
Big House U S A 1955,Mr 12,11:6
First Texan, The 1956,Je 23,20:2
King and Four Queens, The 1956,D 22,13:7
Chapman Report, The 1962,O 18,49:2
Hotel 1967,Ja 20,27:1
Roberts, Ruth
Native Son 1951,Je 18,19:2
Roberts, Stanley (Original Author)
Who Done It 1942,D 3,35:2
Song of the Thin Man 1947,Ag 29,14:2
Curtain Call at Cactus Creek 1950,S 22,35:4
Roberts, Stanley (Screenwriter)
What's Cookin' 1942,F 26,15:5
Who Done It 1942,D 3,35:2
Louisa 1950,O 25,45:2
Up Front 1951,Mr 26,19:2
Death of a Salesman 1951,D 21,21:3
Story of Will Rogers, The 1952,Jl 18,10:5
Caine Mutiny, The 1954,Je 25,17:1
Made in Paris 1966,F 17,29:1
Roberts, Stephen
Rogue River 1951,F 16,21:4
Gog 1954,Ag 14,8:2
Diary of a Madman 1963,Je 6,39:1
Roberts, Stephen (Director)
Sky Bride 1932,Ap 23,11:5
Lady and Gent 1932,Jl 16,5:5
Night of June 13th, The 1932,S 17,18:4
If I Had a Million 1932,D 3,21:4
Story of Temple Drake, The 1933,My 6,11:2
One Sunday Afternoon 1933,S 2,14:4
Trumpet Blows, The 1934,Ap 14,18:2
Romance in Manhattan 1935,Ja 18,29:2
Star of Midnight 1935,Ap 12,26:5
Man Who Broke the Bank at Monte Carlo, The
1935,N 15,20:2
Lady Consents, The 1936,F 6,23:4
Ex-Mrs Bradford, The 1936,My 28,19:2
Roberts, Theodore
Trail of the Lonesome Pine 1916,F 14,11:2
Honor Thy Name 1916,Jl 17,9:4
M'liss 1918,My 6,11:3
We Can't Have Everything 1918,Jl 15,9:3
Source, The 1918,S 9,9:1
Such a Little Pirate 1918,O 7,11:3
Squaw Man, The 1918,D 30,7:3
Don't Change Your Husband 1919,F 3,13:2
Roaring Road, The 1919,Ap 14,11:4
Fires of Faith 1919,My 6,16:2
Woman Thou Gavest Me, The 1919,Je 9,16:3
You're Fired 1919,Je 16,11:2
Secret Service 1919,Je 23,10:3
Lottery Man, The 1919,N 17,20:1
Hawthorne of the U.S.A. 1919,N 17,20:1
Male and Female 1919,N 24,13:1
Everywoman 1919,D 15,20:1
Double Speed 1920,F 2,10:1
Judy of Rogues Harbor 1920,Mr 1,16:2
Something to Think About 1920,O 18,13:1
Forbidden Fruit 1921,Ja 24,16:2
Love Special, The 1921,Mr 21,11:3
Sham 1921,My 6,20:2
Too Much Speed 1921,Je 6,16:4
Affairs of Anatol, The 1921,S 12,16:1
Miss Lulu Bett 1921,D 25,VI,2:1
Hail the Woman 1922,Ja 16,18:3
Old Homestead, The 1922,O 9,10:2
Grumpy 1923,Mr 26,16:2
Prodigal Daughters 1923,Ap 17,26:3
Stephen Steps Out 1923,N 19,19:3
To the Ladies 1923,N 26,15:6
Ten Commandments, The 1923,D 22,8:1
Locked Doors 1925,Ja 12,11:2
Forty Winks 1925,F 3,24:1
Masks of the Devil, The 1928,N 26,30:2
Ned McCobb's Daughter 1929,F 18,28:1
Roberts, Tracey
Actors and Sin; (Woman of Sin) 1952,My 30,11:3
Anything Goes 1956,Mr 22,38:1
Roberts, Wilfred
Light That Failed, The 1939,D 25,19:1
Roberts, William
Seven Sweethearts 1942,N 13,28:1
Lady in the Lake 1947,Ja 24,18:3

Roberts, William (Screenwriter)
You for Me 1952,S 25,38:3
Easy to Love 1953,N 27,99:9
Her Twelve Men 1954,Ag 12,23:2
Private War of Major Benson, The
  1955,Ag 3,27:2
Sheepman, The 1958,My 8,36:1
Mating Game, The 1959,Ap 30,37:1
Magnificent Seven, The 1960,N 24,48:3
Wonderful World of the Brothers Grimm, The
  (The Singing Bone); Singing Bone, The (The
  Wonderful World of the Brothers Grimm)
  1962,Ag 8,35:1
Wonderful World of the Brothers Grimm, The
  (The Cobbler and the Elves); Cobbler and the
  Elves, The (The Wonderful World of the
  Brothers Grimm) 1962,Ag 8,35:1
Wonderful World of the Brothers Grimm, The
  1962,Ag 8,35:1
Wonderful World of the Brothers Grimm, The
  (The Dancing Princess); Dancing Princess, The
  (The Wonderful World of the Brothers Grimm)
  1962,Ag 8,35:1
Come Fly With Me 1963,My 2,40:2
Devil's Brigade, The 1968,My 23,56:2
Roberts (Miscellaneous)
23 1/2 Hours Leave 1937,My 17,23:2
Robertshaw, Jerrold
Arab, The 1924,Jl 14,11:5
Betrayal, The 1929,Ap 29,29:2
Robertson, Andrew
Far From the Madding Crowd 1967,O 19,59:1
Robertson, Blair (Screenwriter)
Agent for H.A.R.M 1966,Ja 6,20:2
Robertson, Chuck
Shock Corridor 1963,S 12,32:1
Robertson, Cliff
Picnic 1956,F 17,13:3
Autumn Leaves 1956,Ag 2,21:2
Naked and the Dead, The 1958,Ag 7,21:1
Girl Most Likely, The 1958,O 9,47:1
Gidget 1959,Ap 23,27:4
All in a Nights Work 1961,Mr 23,28:1
Big Show, The 1961,My 11,42:4
Underworld, U S A 1961,My 13,10:1
As the Sea Rages 1961,My 18,41:1
Interns, The 1962,Ag 9,17:5
My Six Loves 1963,Ap 4,58:4
PT 109 1963,Je 27,23:1
Sunday in New York 1964,F 12,30:2
Best Man, The 1964,Ap 7,29:1
633 Squadron 1964,Je 25,25:1
Love Has Many Faces 1965,F 25,24:1
Masquerade 1965,Ap 29,40:2
Up From the Beach 1965,Je 10,38:1
Honey Pot, The 1967,My 23,52:1
Devil's Brigade, The 1968,My 23,56:2
Charly 1968,S 24,55:1
Robertson, Dale
Two Flags West 1950,O 13,23:2
Call Me Mister 1951,F 1,21:2
Take Care of my Little Girl 1951,Jl 19,20:2
Golden Girl 1951,N 21,20:3
Return of the Texan 1952,F 14,23:1
Outcasts of Poker Flat 1952,My 16,19:3
Lydia Bailey 1952,My 31,12:5
O Henry's Full House (The Clarion Call); Clarion
  Call, The (O Henry's Full House)
  1952,O 17,33:1
Farmer Takes a Wife, The 1953,Je 13,11:2
Devil's Canyon 1953,O 3,14:2
City of Bad Men 1953,O 21,37:6
Gambler From Natchez, The 1954,Ag 14,8:2
Sitting Bull 1954,N 26,24:4
Son of Sinbad 1955,Jl 28,18:2
Dakota Incident 1956,N 10,14:2
Fast and Sexy 1960,O 6,51:4
Law of the Lawless 1964,Ag 27,28:2
Coast of Skeletons 1965,N 11,58:3
Robertson, Dick (Composer)
Let's Make Music 1941,Ja 23,19:2
Robertson, E Arnot (Original Author)
Four Frightened People 1934,Ja 27,9:2
Robertson, Eck
Festival 1967,O 24,53:2
Robertson, Fred (Producer)
Little Ones, The 1965,S 16,55:2
Robertson, Imogene
Armored Vault 1928,N 13,37:2 (In Addenda)
Robertson, J Francis
Girl on the Barge, The 1929,F 26,31:1
Robertson, John
Enemy to the King, An 1916,N 27,9:1
Alaskan Adventures 1927,My 10,24:5
Robertson, John (Director)
Here Comes the Bride 1919,F 3,13:2
Come out of the Kitchen 1919,My 12,11:4
Sentimental Tommy 1921,My 9,16:2
Footlights 1921,S 9,IV,4:1
Tess of the Storm Country 1922,N 13,12:1
Bright Shawl, The 1923,Ap 23,18:3
Fighting Blade, The 1923,O 15,15:4
Twenty-One 1924,F 18,13:1

Enchanted Cottage, The 1924,Ap 14,14:1
Classmates 1924,D 30,15:3
New Toys 1925,F 17,18:1
Soul Fire 1925,My 6,26:3
Shore Leave 1925,S 14,16:1
Annie Laurie 1927,My 12,24:3
Captain Salvation 1927,Je 27,25:2
Road to Romance, The 1927,O 10,24:1
Shanghai Lady 1929,N 11,20:2
Night Ride 1930,Ja 20,21:1
Captain of the Guard 1930,Mr 29,23:1
Madonna of the Streets 1930,N 29,21:4
Beyond Victory 1931,Ap 6,24:1
Phantom of Paris, The 1931,N 14,15:3
One Man's Journey 1933,S 15,15:2
Crime Doctor, The 1934,My 11,24:3
His Greatest Gamble 1934,Jl 18,20:2
Wednesday's Child 1934,D 15,9:3
Grand Old Girl 1935,F 26,16:4
Our Little Girl 1935,Je 7,24:4
Robertson, Morgan (Original Author)
Masters of Men 1923,My 15,22:1
Robertson, Ralph
Big Broadcast, The 1932,O 15,13:1
Behind the Headlines 1937,Je 1,27:2
Robertson, Stuart
Peg of Old Drury 1936,Ap 13,15:1
Sixty Glorious Years 1938,N 18,25:2
Irene 1940,My 24,23:3
No, No, Nanette 1940,D 20,33:1
Confirm or Deny 1941,D 19,35:2
Black Swan, The 1942,D 24,18:3
Robertson, Wilbur
Saturday's Hero 1951,S 12,37:2
Robertson, Willard
Last of the Duanes 1930,S 13,9:3
Skippy 1931,Ap 4,23:1
Murder by the Clock 1931,Jl 18,16:6
Silence 1931,Ag 15,18:3
Cisco Kid, The 1931,O 24,20:3
Ruling Voice, The 1931,N 5,29:3
Sooky 1931,D 21,28:4
Gay Caballero, The 1932,Mr 26,17:2
Broken Wing, The 1932,Mr 26,17:2
Famous Ferguson Case, The 1932,Ap 25,18:6
So Big 1932,Ap 30,19:3
Behind the Mask 1932,My 2,13:2
Strange Love of Molly Louvain, The
  1932,My 9,19:5
Tom Brown of Culver 1932,Jl 30,16:5
Doctor X 1932,Ag 4,17:2
Guilty as Hell 1932,Ag 6,14:5
Call Her Savage 1932,N 25,19:2
Central Park 1932,D 7,29:3
Destination Unknown 1933,Ap 8,16:2
Central Airport 1933,My 4,20:5
Trick for Trick 1933,Je 10,16:4
Another Language 1933,Ag 5,9:5
Tugboat Annie 1933,Ag 12,14:2
World Changes, The 1933,O 27,22:3
Mad Game, The 1933,N 13,21:1
Lady Killer 1934,Ja 1,28:2
Dark Hazard 1934,F 23,23:3
Heat Lightning 1934,Mr 8,23:2
Gambling Lady 1934,Ap 5,25:2
I'll Tell the World 1934,Ap 21,12:2
Whirlpool 1934,My 5,22:3
Let's Talk It Over 1934,Je 16,20:2
Operator 13 1934,Je 23,16:5
Here Comes the Navy 1934,Jl 21,14:2
Housewife 1934,Ag 10,21:2
Death on the Diamond 1934,S 24,14:1
Have a Heart 1934,O 20,20:2
Secret Bride, The 1935,F 2,10:1
Biography of a Bachelor Girl 1935,Mr 2,18:2
Black Fury 1935,Ap 11,27:2
Million Dollar Baby 1935,My 6,22:3
Laddie 1935,My 6,22:3
Oil for the Lamps of China 1935,Je 6,25:2
Dante's Inferno 1935,Ag 1,15:1
O'Shaughnessy's Boy 1935,O 5,18:2
His Night Out 1935,N 16,19:2
Dangerous Waters 1936,Ja 22,15:5
I Married a Doctor 1936,Ap 20,17:1
Last of the Mohicans, The 1936,S 3,17:3
Gorgeous Hussy, The 1936,S 5,7:1
Man Who Lived Twice, The 1936,O 12,23:2
Wanted: Jane Turner 1936,N 30,24:7
Winterset 1936,D 4,31:1
That Girl From Paris 1937,Ja 1,19:1
This Is my Affair 1937,My 28,17:1
Go Getter, The 1937,Je 4,27:2
Exclusive 1937,Jl 22,15:1
Roaring Timber 1937,Ag 19,23:1
Hot Water 1937,N 5,19:4
Island in the Sky 1938,My 14,18:1
Gangs of New York 1938,My 28,9:2
You and Me 1938,Je 2,19:1
Men With Wings 1938,O 27,27:2
Torchy Gets her Man 1938,N 18,25:3
Kentucky 1938,D 24,12:1
Each Dawn I Die 1939,Jl 22,12:2
Main Street Lawyer 1939,N 9,27:2

Robertson, Willard— Cont
Cat and the Canary, The 1939,N 23,38:5
Remember the Night 1940,Ja 18,27:2
Castle on the Hudson 1940,Mr 4,11:2
My Little Chickadee 1940,Mr 16,8:2
Lucky Cisco Kid 1940,Je 24,19:5
Brigham Young - Frontiersman 1940,S 21,13:2
North West Mounted Police 1940,N 7,33:2
I Wanted Wings 1941,Mr 27,29:4
Texas 1941,O 17,27:3
Night of January 16th, The 1941,D 19,35:1
Juke Girl 1942,Je 20,9:2
Air Force 1943,F 4,29:1
Background to Danger 1943,Jl 3,11:2
No Time for Love 1943,D 2,30:1
Along Came Jones 1945,Jl 19,8:7
To Each his Own 1946,My 24,15:2
Perilous Holiday 1946,Je 1,10:4
Renegades 1946,Jl 11,18:2
Gallant Journey 1946,O 10,33:2
Deep Valley 1947,Ag 23,7:2
Fury at Furnace Creek 1948,Jl 12,11:2
Robertson, Willard (Original Author)
Moontide 1942,Ap 30,14:1
Robertson, William
Jesse James 1939,Ja 14,13:1
ROBESON
See Also ROBINSON, ROBISON, ROBSON
See Also ROBESON, ROBINSON, ROBISON
Robeson, Paul
Emperor Jones, The 1933,S 20,26:2
Sanders of the River 1935,Je 27,16:1
Show Boat 1936,My 15,29:4
King Solomon's Mines 1937,Jl 3,18:1
Dark Sands 1938,Ag 17,23:4
Proud Valley 1941,My 17,19:2
Native Land 1942,My 12,16:3
Tales of Manhattan 1942,S 25,25:1
Robey, George
Chu Chin Chow 1934,S 22,12:2
Don Quixote 1934,D 24,17:1
Girl Must Live, A 1942,Mr 24,25:2
Waltz Time 1946,F 11,25:2
Henry V 1946,Je 18,30:2
Pickwick Papers, The 1954,Ap 5,21:2
Robie, Earl
My Cousin Rachel 1952,D 26,20:2
Lady Wants Mink, The 1953,Ap 6,24:2
Robies, Emmanuel (Screenwriter)
Stranger, The 1967,D 19,59:1
Robin, Dany
Man About Town 1947,O 22,37:1
Monelle 1950,F 3,29:2
Gates of the Night 1950,Mr 16,40:2
Thirst of Men, The 1952,O 28,37:1
Naughty Martine 1953,Ap 13,32:4
Act of Love 1954,F 12,20:5
Holiday for Henrietta 1955,Ja 25,21:1
Julietta 1957,Je 18,38:2
Maid in Paris 1957,Jl 13,11:1
Chasers, The; Draguers, Les 1960,My 3,43:1
Love and the Frenchwoman; (Francaise et
  l'Amour, La) 1961,F 28,38:2
Waltz of the Toreadors 1962,Ag 14,34:1
Tales of Paris (The Tale of Antonio); Tale of
  Antonio, The (Tales of Paris) 1962,Ag 27,18:1
Follow the Boys 1963,F 28,8:2
Robin, Leo (Composer)
International House 1933,My 27,11:5
My Weakness 1933,S 22,14:1
Torch Singer 1933,O 7,18:5
Way to Love, The 1933,N 11,10:3
All of Me 1934,F 5,19:2
Search for Beauty 1934,F 10,20:2
Wharf Angel 1934,Ap 21,12:1
Little Miss Marker 1934,My 19,18:3
Kiss and Make-Up 1934,Je 29,17:1
Shoot the Works 1934,Jl 7,16:5
She Loves Me Not 1934,S 8,18:5
Here is my Heart 1934,D 22,21:1
Four Hours to Kill 1935,Ap 11,27:3
Devil is a Woman, The 1935,My 4,17:2
Big Broadcast of 1936, The 1935,S 16,15:2
Here Comes Cookie 1935,O 12,12:2
Millions in the Air 1935,D 12,33:4
Anything Goes 1936,F 6,23:3
Desire 1936,Ap 13,15:1
Champagne Waltz 1937,F 4,17:2
Waikiki Wedding 1937,Mr 25,29:1
Swing High, Swing Low 1937,Ap 15,19:1
Big Broadcast of 1938, The 1938,Mr 10,16:2
Romance in the Dark 1938,Mr 21,18:2
Artists and Models Abroad 1938,D 22,25:3
Paris Honeymoon 1939,Ja 26,17:1
Gulliver's Travels 1939,D 21,29:1
Moon Over Miami 1941,S 14,2:2
Rise and Shine 1941,D 6,14:3
My Gal Sal 1942,My 1,23:1
Footlight Serenade 1942,S 10,30:3
Tales of Manhattan 1942,S 25,25:1
Coney Island 1943,Je 17,17:2
Wintertime 1943,S 30,27:2
I Dood It 1943,N 11,29:1

Robin, Leo (Composer)— Cont
Riding High 1943,D 23,26:4
Gang's All Here, The 1943,D 23,26:4
Greenwich Village 1944,S 28,26:2
Something in the Wind 1947,Ag 29,14:3
Casbah 1948,My 3,27:4
That Lady in Ermine 1948,Ag 25,31:2
Hit the Deck 1955,Mr 4,17:1
Robin, Leo (Miscellaneous)
Bedtime Story, A 1933,Ap 20,20:3
Song of Songs 1933,Jl 20,22:2
Trumpet Blows, The 1934,Ap 14,18:2
Rose of the Rancho 1936,Ja 9,25:2
Poppy 1936,Je 18,19:1
College Holiday 1936,D 24,21:2
Artists and Models 1937,Ag 5,19:2
Blossoms On Broadway 1937,D 3,29:2
Latin Lovers 1953,Ag 13,17:2
Robinne, Gabrielle
Rasputin 1939,O 17,31:4
ROBINS
See Also ROBBINS
Robins, Denise (Original Author)
Road to Singapore, The 1931,O 1,25:2
Robins, Edward H
Meet the Missus 1937,Jl 2,25:2
Music for Madame 1937,O 23,14:1
Robins, Phyllis
Showtime 1948,My 20,35:3
Robins, Sam (Original Author)
Enemy Agent 1940,Ap 22,13:3
Black Diamonds 1940,S 10,26:6
Robins, Sam (Screenwriter)
Enemy Agent 1940,Ap 22,13:3
Black Diamonds 1940,S 10,26:6
Bowery Blitzkrieg 1941,O 1,24:5
Mr Wise Guy 1942,Mr 5,27:2
Jungle Siren 1942,O 10,11:3
Robins, Toby
Naked Runner, The 1967,Jl 20,30:2
ROBINSON
See Also ROBESON, ROBISON, ROBSON
Robinson, Ann
War of the Worlds, The 1953,Ag 14,10:2
Dragnet 1954,Ag 21,10:2
Julie 1956,N 22,51:1
Imitation of Life 1959,Ap 18,18:1
Robinson, Armin (Original Author)
Forbidden Music 1938,D 27,13:2
Robinson, Bartlett
Toward the Unknown 1956,S 28,24:4
Spirit of St Louis, The 1957,F 22,25:1
No Time for Sergeants 1958,My 30,13:2
I Want to Live 1958,N 19,45:1
Stranger in my Arms 1959,Mr 4,34:2
Warlock 1959,My 1,34:1
Distant Trumpet, A 1964,My 28,40:1
Where Love Has Gone 1964,N 3,26:1
Robinson, Bertrand (Original Author)
Love, Honor and Oh, Baby! 1933,O 28,20:3
Your Uncle Dudley 1935,D 12,33:4
Ladies' Day 1943,Mr 26,14:3
Robinson, Bill
Dixiana 1930,S 5,21:1
Little Colonel, The 1935,Mr 22,26:2
Hooray for Love 1935,Jl 13,16:2
Old Kentucky, In 1935,N 29,24:1
Littlest Rebel, The 1935,D 20,30:1
One Mile From Heaven 1937,Ag 19,23:1
Rebecca of Sunnybrook Farm 1938,Mr 26,12:1
Just Around the Corner 1938,D 3,11:2
Up the River 1938,D 3,11:2
Stormy Weather 1943,Jl 22,15:1
Robinson, Cardew
I'm All Right Jack 1960,Ap 26,40:2
Waltz of the Toreadors 1962,Ag 14,34:1
Time Lost and Time Remembered
  1966,Ag 30,35:2
Robinson, Casey (Original Author)
Last Parade, The 1931,Mr 2,19:1
Lucky Devils 1933,F 20,11:5
Robinson, Casey (Producer)
Days of Glory 1944,Je 17,10:2
Macomber Affair, The 1947,Ap 21,21:2
Mating of Millie, The 1948,Mr 13,12:2
Under my Skin 1950,Mr 18,9:2
Two Flags West 1950,O 13,23:2
Diplomatic Courier 1952,Je 14,12:2
Earth Is Mine, The 1959,Je 27,13:1
Robinson, Casey (Screenwriter)
McFadden's Flats 1935,Mr 13,16:2
I Found Stella Parish 1935,N 4,24:4
Captain Blood 1935,D 27,14:1
I Married a Doctor 1936,Ap 20,17:1
Hearts Divided 1936,Je 13,13:1
Give Me your Heart 1936,S 17,18:2
Stolen Holiday 1937,F 1,15:3
Call it a Day 1937,My 7,29:2
It's Love I'm After 1937,N 11,31:2
Tovarich 1937,D 31,9:2
Four's a Crowd 1938,Ag 12,11:1
Dark Victory 1939,Ap 21,27:2
Old Maid, The 1939,Ag 12,16:2
All This and Heaven, Too 1940,Jl 5,10:2

Million Dollar Baby 1941,Je 7,20:2
One Foot in Heaven 1941,N 14,28:3
Kings Row 1942,F 3,23:2
Now, Voyager 1942,O 23,25:3
This Is the Army 1943,Jl 29,11:6
Passage to Marseille 1944,F 17,12:5
Days of Glory 1944,Je 17,10:2
Corn is Green, The 1945,Mr 30,18:2
Saratoga Trunk 1945,N 22,39:2
Macomber Affair, The 1947,Ap 21,21:2
Desire Me 1947,S 26,28:3
Father Was a Fullback 1949,O 13,33:3
Under my Skin 1950,Mr 18,9:2
Two Flags West 1950,O 13,23:2
Diplomatic Courier 1952,Je 14,12:2
Snows of Kilimanjaro, The 1952,S 19,19:2
Egyptian, The 1954,Ag 25,23:1
Bullet is Waiting, A 1954,N 12,17:2
While the City Sleeps 1956,My 17,37:1
Earth Is Mine, The 1959,Je 27,13:1
Robinson, Charles
Dear Brigitte 1965,Ja 28,20:1
Shenandoah 1965,Jl 29,18:3
Sand Pebbles, The 1966,D 21,48:1
For Singles Only 1968,Je 6,54:1
Robinson, Charles (Original Author)
Lady, Be Careful 1936,O 10,21:1
Swing Your Lady 1938,Ja 27,17:2
Fleet's In, The 1942,Mr 12,24:2
Sailor Beware 1952,F 1,17:1
Robinson, Chris
Young Savages, The 1961,My 25,31:1
Robinson, David
Damn the Defiant 1962,S 20,29:2
Robinson, David (Screenwriter)
Monsoon 1953,S 26,15:2
Robinson, Dewey
Enemies of the Law 1931,Jl 13,13:5
Woman From Monte Carlo, The 1931,D 31,17:6
Cheaters at Play 1932,F 27,22:1
Law and Order 1932,F 29,21:3
Painted Woman, The 1932,S 16,24:4
Hat Check Girl 1932,O 8,15:4
Big Broadcast, The 1932,O 15,13:1
Six Hours to Live 1932,O 22,18:4
Scarlet Dawn 1932,N 4,25:4
She Done Him Wrong 1933,F 10,12:3
Lady's Profession, A 1933,Mr 25,13:3
Diplomaniacs 1933,Ap 29,14:2
Soldiers of the Storm 1933,My 17,15:3
Big Shakedown, The 1934,F 12,19:2
Shadows of Sing Sing 1934,F 21,23:2
Behold My Wife 1935,F 18,19:3
Midsummer Night's Dream, A 1935,O 10,31:1
Dangerous Waters 1936,Ja 22,15:5
Florida Special 1936,My 29,15:2
Poppy 1936,Je 18,19:1
Missing Girls 1936,O 5,25:1
New Faces of 1937 1937,Jl 2,25:1
Toast of New York, The 1937,Jl 23,16:2
Broadway Musketeers 1938,O 14,27:1
Ride a Crooked Mile 1938,D 29,15:2
Blue Bird, The 1940,Ja 20,11:2
Sing for Your Supper 1941,D 1,15:5
Jail House Blues 1942,F 6,23:2
Palm Beach Story, The 1942,D 11,33:1
Ghost Ship, The 1943,D 25,19:4
Woman of the Town, The 1944,Mr 6,17:2
Gangster, The 1947,O 31,29:3
Beautiful Blonde From Bashful Bend, The
  1949,My 28,11:2
Hellfire 1949,My 30,9:4
Buccaneer's Girl 1950,Mr 27,19:2
Robinson, Dorothy
Peg of Old Drury 1936,Ap 13,15:1
Robinson, Earl
Air Circus, The 1928,S 3,14:2
Robinson, Earl (Composer)
Born to Sing 1942,F 19,23:2
Walk in the Sun, A 1946,Ja 12,10:6
Roosevelt Story, The 1947,Ag 22,11:2
Romance of Rosy Ridge, The 1947,S 12,18:3
Robinson, Edward G
Bright Shawl, The 1923,Ap 23,18:3
Hole in the Wall, The 1929,Ap 15,22:6
Night Ride 1930,Ja 20,21:1
Lady to Love, A 1930,Mr 1,23:1
Outside the Law 1930,S 1,16:1
East Is West 1930,N 1,23:2
Widow From Chicago, The 1930,D 20,20:6
Little Caesar 1931,Ja 10,19:2
Smart Money 1931,Je 19,21:1
Five Star Final 1931,S 11,24:2
Hatchet Man, The 1932,F 4,25:2
Two Seconds 1932,My 19,25:3
Tiger Shark 1932,S 23,22:2
Silver Dollar 1932,D 23,20:1
Little Giant, The 1933,My 27,11:5
I Loved a Woman 1933,S 22,14:2
Dark Hazard 1934,F 23,23:3
Man With two Faces, The 1934,Jl 12,20:2
Whole Town's Talking, The 1935,Mr 1,16:2
Barbary Coast 1935,O 14,21:1

Robinson, Edward G— Cont
Bullets or Ballots 1936,My 27,27:1
Thunder in the City 1937,Ap 23,25:2
Kid Galahad 1937,My 27,21:3
Last Gangster, The 1937,D 10,33:2
Slight Case of Murder, A 1938,F 28,19:1
Amazing Dr Clitterhouse, The 1938,Jl 21,14:2
I Am the Law 1938,Ag 26,14:2
Confessions of a Nazi Spy 1939,Ap 29,13:2
Blackmail 1939,S 15,26:3
Dr Ehrlich's Magic Bullet 1940,F 24,9:2
Brother Orchid 1940,Je 8,18:2
Dispatch From Reuters, A 1940,D 12,37:2
Sea Wolf, The 1941,Mr 26,27:3
Manpower 1941,Jl 5,14:2
Unholy Partners 1941,D 29,21:4
Larceny, Inc 1942,Ap 25,9:1
Tales of Manhattan 1942,S 25,25:1
Destroyer 1943,S 2,15:3
Flesh and Fantasy 1943,N 18,29:1
Tampico 1944,Je 2,21:2
Mr Winkle Goes to War 1944,Ag 3,16:1
Double Indemnity 1944,S 7,21:1
Woman in the Window, The 1945,Ja 26,16:4
Our Vines Have Tender Grapes 1945,S 7,21:2
Scarlet Street 1946,F 15,29:2
Journey Together 1946,Mr 4,16:5
Stranger, The 1946,Jl 11,18:2
Red House, The 1947,Mr 17,27:2
All my Sons 1948,Mr 29,17:3
Key Largo 1948,Jl 17,6:6
Night Has a Thousand Eyes 1948,O 14,38:3
House of Strangers 1949,Jl 2,8:2
Operation X 1950,D 11,31:2
Actors and Sin; (Actor's Blood) 1952,My 30,11:3
Vice Squad 1953,Ag 26,23:2
Glass Web, The 1953,N 12,37:5
Black Tuesday 1955,Ja 1,16:2
Violent Men, The 1955,Ja 27,17:2
Tight Spot 1955,Mr 19,11:7
Bullet for Joey, A 1955,Ap 16,12:1
Illegal 1955,O 29,12:6
Hell on Frisco Bay 1956,Ja 7,21:1
Nightmare 1956,My 12,12:7
Ten Commandments, The 1956,N 9,35:2
Some Like It Hot 1959,Mr 30,23:1
Hole in the Head, A 1959,Jl 16,31:2
Seven Thieves 1960,Mr 12,14:5
Pepe 1960,D 22,18:1
My Geisha 1962,Je 14,23:2
Two Weeks in Another Town 1962,Ag 18,10:1
Prize, The 1964,Ja 24,21:1
Good Neighbor Sam 1964,Jl 23,19:1
Robin and the 7 Hoods 1964,Ag 6,20:1
Outrage, The 1964,O 8,48:2
Cheyenne Autumn 1964,D 24,8:1
Boy Ten Feet Tall, A 1965,My 13,32:2
Cincinnati Kid, The 1965,O 28,48:1
Biggest Bundle of Them All, The 1968,Ja 18,46:1
Grand Slam 1968,F 21,60:4
Never a Dull Moment 1968,Ag 15,46:2
Robinson, Edward G (Narrator)
Moscow Strikes Back 1942,Ag 17,19:2
Robinson, Forrest
Tess of the Storm Country 1922,N 13,12:1
Ashes of Vengeance 1923,Ag 7,20:2
When a Man's a Man 1924,F 5,20:1
Robinson, Frances
Service de Luxe 1938,O 24,13:2
Last Warning, The 1938,D 8,34:4
Secrets of a Nurse 1938,D 12,26:2
Risky Business 1939,Mr 23,27:2
Family Next Door, The 1939,Ap 28,31:2
Tower of London 1939,D 12,37:2
Invisible Man Returns, The 1940,Ja 16,19:2
So You Won't Talk 1940,O 17,33:2
Lone Wolf Keeps a Date, The 1941,Ja 2,24:3
Dr Jekyll and Mr Hyde 1941,Ag 13,13:2
Smilin' Through 1941,D 5,29:2
Suddenly It's Spring 1947,F 27,26:2
Backfire 1950,Ja 27,29:2
Bedtime Story 1964,Je 11,27:1
Robinson, Frank M (Original Author)
Power, The 1968,Mr 7,52:2
Robinson, Gertrude
On Thin Ice 1925,Mr 9,21:1
Robinson, Henry Morton (Original Author)
Cardinal, The 1963,D 13,41:1
Robinson, Hugh
Seventh Dawn, The 1964,S 3,24:1
Robinson, J Russel (Miscellaneous)
Margie 1946,O 17,28:3
Robinson, Jackie
Jackie Robinson Story, The 1950,My 17,36:1
Robinson, James
Penrod and Sam 1931,S 26,25:3
Mrs Wiggs of the Cabbage Patch 1934,O 29,14:2
Becky Sharp 1935,Je 14,27:2
Robinson, Jane
Pepe 1960,D 22,18:1
Robinson, Jay
Robe, The 1953,S 17,32:6
Demetrius and the Gladiators 1954,Je 19,9:1
Virgin Queen, The 1955,Ag 6,13:2

Robinson, Jay— Cont

Wild Party, The 1956,D 22,13:1
My Man Godfrey 1957,O 12,23:1

Robinson, Joe
Kid for two Farthings, A 1956,Ap 18,25:1
Loneliness of the Long Distance Runner, The 1962,O 9,44:1

Robinson, John
Hundred Hour Hunt 1953,Je 17,32:2
Doctor's Dilemma, A 1958,D 18,2:7

Robinson, John (Screenwriter)
Midnight Story, The 1957,Jl 5,14:2

Robinson, Joseph F (Producer)
Agent for H.A.R.M 1966,Ja 6,20:2

Robinson, Julie
Kismet 1955,D 9,32:2
Lust for Life 1956,S 18,39:1

Robinson, June
Sullivans, The 1944,F 10,19:2

Robinson, Larry
Molly 1951,Mr 8,37:2

Robinson, Louis
Fireman, Save My Child 1932,F 18,25:3

Robinson, Madeleine
Forty Little Mothers 1938,D 23,16:3
Bouquets From Nicholas 1939,Mr 2,19:1
Living Corpse, The 1940,S 23,21:4
Bellman, The 1947,Ap 7,20:5
Love Story 1949,Je 27,18:4
Between Eleven and Midnight 1950,F 23,33:3
God Needs Men 1951,Mr 27,35:1
Riptide 1951,Ap 7,9:2
Savage Triangle 1952,S 30,38:2
Passionate Summer 1957,Jl 22,15:5
Demoniaque 1958,Mr 4,34:5
Sins of Youth 1960,D 24,8:2
Leda 1961,Jl 19,33:1
Cross of the Living 1963,F 5,5:5
Trial, The 1963,F 21,5:1
Devil and the 10 Commandments, The (Episode 6) 1963,O 15,44:1

Robinson, Percy (Screenwriter)
Wanted for Murder 1946,D 12,38:4

Robinson, Roberta
Dangerous Nan McGrew 1930,Je 21,20:5
Half Shot at Sunrise 1930,O 11,21:3

Robinson, Ruth
Story of Louis Pasteur, The 1936,F 10,15:1
Sins of Man 1936,Je 19,17:2
China Clipper 1936,Ag 12,14:3
Case of the Velvet Claws, The 1936,Ag 29,16:3
Lone Wolf in Paris, The 1938,My 23,21:2
Delightfully Dangerous 1945,Je 9,17:3
Spider Woman Strikes Back, The 1946,Mr 23,8:3
Guilty, The 1947,My 19,27:2

Robinson, Seymour B (Original Author)
Stormy Weather 1943,Jl 22,15:1

Robinson, Shari
You're my Everything 1949,Jl 23,7:2
Molly 1951,Mr 8,37:2

Robinson, Stanford (Miscellaneous)
Heart's Desire 1937,Jl 12,20:4

Robinson, Sugar Ray
Paper Lion 1968,O 24,54:1

Robinson, Sugarchile
No Leave, No Love 1946,O 18,29:2

Robinson, Thelma (Original Author)
Because of You 1952,D 4,47:3

Robinson, Thelma (Screenwriter)
Up Goes Maisie 1946,Ja 25,26:7

ROBISON
See Also ROBESON, ROBINSON, ROBSON

Robison, Arthur (Director)
Manon Lescaut 1926,N 30,27:1
Peter the Pirate 1927,Ja 7,14:4
Warning Shadows 1927,Ag 10,21:4
Last Waltz, The 1927,N 14,26:1
Eines Prinzen Junge Liebe 1934,Mr 24,20:4

Robison, Harris (Composer)
Road Show 1941,F 19,25:2

Robles, Ana Maria
Infidelidad 1939,My 8,21:3

Robles, Elisa
Sangre Manda, La 1934,My 15,18:2

Robles, Richard
Union Pacific 1939,My 11,31:2

Robles, Rudy
Real Glory, The 1939,S 15,26:2
South of Pago-Pago 1940,Ag 2,12:2

Roblin, Louise
Cat, The 1959,Ap 13,35:1

Roblot, Antoine
Zazie 1961,N 21,45:5
Very Private Affair, A 1962,S 29,15:1
Naked Autumn 1963,N 15,25:3

Robotham, George
Great Locomotive Chase, The 1956,Je 27,35:1

Roboz, Emmerich (Screenwriter)
Trial, The 1952,Mr 15,8:2

Robsahn, Margreta
Young Racers, The 1963,O 10,49:3

Robson, Andrew
Upstairs and Down 1919,Je 16,11:2
Alarm Clock Andy 1920,Mr 15,13:2

Scratch my Back 1920,Je 5,19:3
Cupid, the Cowpuncher 1920,Jl 26,9:5

Robson, Campbell
Edge of the World, The 1938,S 12,13:2

Robson, Flora
Catherine the Great 1934,F 15,15:6
Fire Over England 1937,Mr 5,16:2
Troopship 1938,Ap 26,18:2
Wuthering Heights 1939,Ap 14,28:2
We Are not Alone 1939,D 1,27:1
Invisible Stripes 1940,Ja 13,11:2
Lion Has Wings, The 1940,Ja 22,11:2
Sea Hawk, The 1940,Ag 10,16:2
Bahama Passage 1942,F 19,23:2
Saratoga Trunk 1945,N 22,39:2
Caesar and Cleopatra 1946,S 6,18:2
Years Between, The 1947,Mr 10,25:2
Black Narcissus 1947,Ag 14,29:2
Frieda 1947,Ag 15,12:3
Holiday Camp 1948,Ja 24,11:2
Saraband 1949,Je 13,16:3
Good Time Girl 1950,S 25,18:5
Frightened Bride, The 1953,Ag 20,18:5
Malta Story 1954,Jl 17,7:2
Romeo and Juliet 1954,D 22,28:1
55 Days at Peking 1963,My 30,20:1
Murder at the Gallop 1963,Je 25,23:2
Guns at Batasi 1964,N 17,47:1
Young Cassidy 1965,Mr 23,35:1
Those Magnificent Men in Their Flying Machines (Or How I Flew From London to Paris in 25 Hours and 11 Minutes) 1965,Je 17,27:1
7 Women 1966,My 5,59:1
Eye of the Devil 1967,D 7,60:1
Shuttered Room, The 1968,F 15,47:1

Robson, Flora Dame (Narrator)
King's Story, A 1967,My 25,57:2

Robson, Mark (Director)
Seventh Victim, The 1943,S 18,11:3
Ghost Ship, The 1943,D 25,19:4
Youth Runs Wild 1944,S 2,17:2
Isle of the Dead 1945,S 8,12:2
Bedlam 1946,Ap 20,16:4
Champion 1949,Ap 11,29:2
Home of the Brave 1949,My 13,29:1
Roughshod 1949,Je 17,27:2
My Foolish Heart 1950,Ja 20,29:2
Edge of Doom 1950,Ag 4,13:2
Bright Victory 1951,Ag 1,19:2
I Want You 1951,D 24,9:1
Return to Paradise 1953,S 11,24:2
Phffft 1954,N 11,43:2
Bridges at Toko-Ri, The 1955,Ja 21,20:2
Trial 1955,O 14,21:2
Prize of Gold, A 1955,O 15,19:2
Harder They Fall, The 1956,My 10,26:3
Little Hut, The 1957,My 4,25:1
Peyton Place 1957,D 13,35:1
Inn of the Sixth Happiness, The 1958,D 14,2:7
From the Terrace 1960,Jl 16,10:1
Nine Hours to Rama 1963,Ap 4,58:2
Prize, The 1964,Ja 24,21:1
Von Ryan's Express 1965,Je 24,28:1
Lost Command 1966,S 15,51:1
Valley of the Dolls 1967,D 16,51:1

Robson, Mark (Original Author)
Hell Below Zero 1954,Jl 17,7:3

Robson, Mark (Producer)
Little Hut, The 1957,My 4,25:1
From the Terrace 1960,Jl 16,10:1
Lisa 1962,My 25,28:1
Nine Hours to Rama 1963,Ap 4,58:2
Lost Command 1966,S 15,51:1

Robson, Mark (Screenwriter)
Bedlam 1946,Ap 20,16:4

Robson, May
How Molly Made Good 1915,O 20,5:5
Pals in Paradise 1926,N 24,26:4
Rubber Tires 1927,Mr 9,29:1
King of Kings, The 1927,Ap 20,29:2
Rejuvenation of Aunt Mary, The 1927,Jl 27,27:4
Angel of Broadway 1927,N 1,21:1 (In Addenda)
Chicago 1927,D 24,9:1
Blue Danube, The 1928,Ap 30,18:3
She-Wolf 1931,My 28,30:6
Letty Lynton 1932,Ap 30,19:3
Red Headed Woman 1932,Jl 1,19:3
Strange Interlude 1932,S 1,24:3
If I Had a Million 1932,D 3,21:4
Men Must Fight 1933,Mr 11,18:3
White Sister, The 1933,Mr 18,9:3
Reunion in Vienna 1933,Ap 29,14:2
Dinner at Eight 1933,Ag 24,18:1
One Man's Journey 1933,S 1,15:2
Lady for a Day 1933,S 8,22:2
Beauty for Sale 1933,S 16,9:3
Solitaire Man, The 1933,S 23,11:5
Dancing Lady 1933,D 1,23:2
Alice in Wonderland 1933,D 23,19:1
You Can't Buy Everything 1934,F 3,9:2
Straight Is the Way 1934,Ag 29,13:2
Lady by Choice 1934,N 17,12:1
Grand Old Girl 1935,F 26,16:4

Robson, May— Cont

Vanessa: Her Love Story 1935,Ap 13,11:3
Reckless 1935,Ap 20,16:1
Age of Indiscretion 1935,My 18,21:2
Anna Karenina 1935,Ag 31,16:2
Three Kids and a Queen 1935,N 9,19:2
Wife vs Secretary 1936,F 29,11:1
Rainbow on the River 1936,D 18,31:4
Top of the Town 1937,Mr 27,19:2
Star Is Born, A 1937,Ap 23,25:1
Perfect Specimen, The 1937,O 28,29:2
Adventures of Tom Sawyer, The 1938,F 18,23:1
Bringing Up Baby 1938,Mr 4,17:5
Texans, The 1938,Jl 28,23:2
Four Daughters 1938,Ag 19,13:3
They Made Me a Criminal 1939,Ja 21,19:2
Yes, My Darling Daughter 1939,F 27,11:2
Kid From Kokomo, The 1939,My 20,11:2
Daughters Courageous 1939,Je 24,14:2
Nurse Edith Cavell 1939,S 22,27:4
That's Right, You're Wrong 1939,N 30,25:3
Four Wives 1939,D 23,9:1
Irene 1940,My 24,23:3
Texas Rangers Ride Again 1941,Ja 9,27:4
Four Mothers 1941,Ja 11,12:7
Million Dollar Baby 1941,Je 7,20:2
Playmates 1941,D 26,21:3
Joan of Paris 1942,Ja 26,18:2

Robyns, William
Expert, The 1932,F 27,22:1
Elmer and Elsie 1934,Ag 4,14:5

Roc, Patricia
Lady in Distress 1942,F 16,21:2
Madonna of the Seven Moons 1946,My 23,18:4
Canyon Passage 1946,Ag 8,18:2
Johnny Frenchman 1946,O 21,27:3
Wicked Lady, The 1946,D 23,19:5
Lady Surrenders, A 1947,Je 20,25:6
So Well Remembered 1947,N 5,34:3
Jassy 1948,F 20,19:2
Brothers, The 1948,My 5,30:4
One Night With You 1949,F 21,20:2
Man on the Eiffel Tower, The 1950,Ja 30,12:2
Perfect Woman, The 1951,F 17,10:7
Circle of Danger 1951,Jl 12,21:6
Captain Black Jack 1952,O 22,31:3
Something Money Can't Buy 1953,O 1,34:3
Bluebeard's Ten Honeymoons 1960,N 8,32:6

Rocca, Daniela
Giant of Marathon, The 1960,My 26,37:3
Esther and the King 1960,N 19,13:4
Divorce-Italian Style 1962,S 18,34:1
Empty Canvas, The 1964,My 16,21:1 (Incorrect in this edition; use 1964,My 16,12:1 elsewhere)
Behold a Pale Horse 1964,Ag 14,16:1
Symphony for a Massacre 1965,My 28,40:1
Sucker, The 1967,O 9,61:1

Roccardi, Albert
Inside of the Cup, The 1921,Ja 16,VI,2:1 (In Addenda)
Partners in Crime 1928,Ap 30,18:3
Romance of Rio Grande 1929,N 9,22:5
Love Parade, The 1929,N 20,32:6

Roccardi, Giovanni (Screenwriter)
Island Sinner, The 1960,S 5,11:2

Rocco, Gustavo
Action of the Tiger 1957,N 14,41:1

Rocco, Lyla
One Step to Eternity 1955,O 3,22:2
No Sun in Venice 1958,Je 10,40:2

Rocco, Maurice
Incendiary Blonde 1945,Jl 26,13:2

Rocco and Saulter
52d Street 1937,N 15,15:1

Roccuzzo, Mario
Love-Ins, The 1967,Ag 19,16:1

Rocha
That Man in Istanbul 1966,My 19,51:2

Rochard, Henri (Original Author)
I Was a Male War Bride 1949,Ag 27,7:2

Rochard, Jean
Carmen 1946,N 27,20:2

Rochay, Joe
Cock Eyed World, The 1929,Ag 5,25:2

ROCHE
See Also ROACH

Roche, Arthur Somers (Original Author)
Day of Faith, The 1923,N 27,11:2
Any Woman 1925,My 27,26:2
Wolf's Clothing 1927,Mr 28,26:4
Rich but Honest 1927,My 18,29:3
Wise Wife 1927,N 1,21:1 (In Addenda)
Come to My House 1928,Ja 16,24:1
Penthouse 1933,S 9,9:2
Shadow of Doubt 1935,Mr 11,15:1
Star of Midnight 1935,Ap 12,26:5
Case Against Mrs Ames, The 1936,My 28,19:2
Society Lawyer 1939,Mr 31,19:2

Roche, Barbara
  People Are Funny 1946,Ja 28,15:6
Roche, Charles de
  Law of the Lawless, The 1923,Je 19,22:4
  Cheat, The 1923,Ag 27,14:3
  Ten Commandments, The 1923,D 22,8:1
Roche, Clara Darley
  Miserables, Les 1926,Jl 9,17:1
Roche, Darcey
  Kreutzer Sonata, The 1938,D 20,30:2
Roche, France (Screenwriter)
  Love and the Frenchwoman; (Francaise et
    l'Amour, La) 1961,F 28,38:2
  Male Hunt; Chasse a l'Homme, La
    1965,Ap 20,42:1
Roche, Henri-Pierre (Original Author)
  Jules and Jim 1962,Ap 24,32:1
Roche, John
  Lucretia Lombard 1923,D 17,23:1
  Flowing Gold 1924,Mr 10,18:2
  Unknown, The 1924,N 18,22:1
  K-The Unknown 1924,N 18,22:1
  Lost Lady, A 1925,Ja 19,14:1
  Recompense 1925,Ap 20,22:1
  My Wife and I 1925,My 20,26:2
  Marry Me 1925,Jl 13,20:2
  Kiss Me Again 1925,Ag 3,10:1
  Love Hour, The 1925,S 2,21:3
  Bobbed Hair 1925,N 4,17:4
  Don Juan 1926,Ag 7,6:1 (In Addenda)
  Her big Night 1926,O 13,21:1
  Midnight Lovers 1926,O 26,23:1
  Uncle Tom's Cabin 1927,N 5,16:2
  Donovan Affair, The 1929,Ap 29,29:2
  This Thing Called Love 1929,D 14,22:4
  Monte Carlo 1930,Ag 28,22:4
  Sin Takes a Holliday 1930,N 28,23:1
  Cohens and Kellys in Hollywood, The
    1932,Ap 22,23:2
  Winner Take All 1932,Je 18,9:2
Roche, Marcel
  Abysses, Les 1964,N 24,44:1
Roche, Mary
  Heat's on, The 1943,N 26,29:2
Roche, Paul (Miscellaneous)
  Oedipus the King 1968,S 19,62:2
Rochefort, Christiane (Original Author)
  Love on a Pillow 1963,D 17,49:1
Rochefort, Christiane (Screenwriter)
  Truth, The 1961,Je 27,23:2
Rochefort, Jean
  Cartouche 1964,Jl 22,39:1
  Symphony for a Massacre 1965,My 28,40:1
  Up to his Ears 1966,My 18,37:1
Rochefort, N
  Peter the First 1937,D 25,10:4
Rochelle, Claire
  Missing Daughters 1939,Je 12,14:5
Rochemont, Louis de (Producer)
  Fighting Lady, The 1945,Ja 16,17:2
Rocher, Pierre (Screenwriter)
  Vierge Folle, La 1938,D 30,11:3
Rochetti, John (Composer)
  First World War, The 1934,N 8,27:1
Rochlin, Sheldon (Director)
  Vali 1967,Je 2,34:2
Rochlin, Sheldon (Producer)
  Vali 1967,Je 2,34:2
Rock, Charles
  Better 'Ole, The 1919,F 24,11:3
Rock, Felippa
  Moss Rose 1947,Jl 3,14:2
Rock, Joe (Producer)
  Mau Mau 1955,Jl 14,19:1
Rock, Phillip (Original Author)
  Escape from Fort Bravo 1954,Ja 23,11:2
  Most Dangerous Man Alive 1961,Jl 5,29:2
Rock, Phillip (Screenwriter)
  Most Dangerous Man Alive 1961,Jl 5,29:2
Rockett, Al (Producer)
  Hell in the Heavens 1934,D 12,28:2
Rockettes, Radio City Music Hall
  Bitter Sweet 1940,N 22,27:1
Rockey, Howard (Original Author)
  This Woman 1924,O 21,21:3
Rockland, Jeffrey
  Doctor Zhivago 1965,D 23,21:1
Rockne, Knute Mrs (Original Author)
  Knute Rockne-All American 1940,O 19,21:2
Rockwell, Jack
  Lawless Nineties, The 1936,Je 29,11:1
  Under Western Stars 1938,Je 25,7:3
  Cherokee Strip 1940,N 4,23:2
  Tombstone, The Town too Tough to Die
    1942,Jl 27,18:2
Rockwell, Robert
  You Gotta Stay Happy 1948,N 5,29:2
  Red Menace, The 1949,Je 27,18:2
  Frogmen, The 1951,Je 30,8:6
  War of the Worlds, The 1953,Ag 14,10:2
Rockwood, Roy (Original Author)
  Bomba, the Jungle Boy 1949,Ap 16,11:4

Rocque, Rod La
  Night Life of New York 1925,Jl 14,14:1
  Wild, Wild Susan 1925,Ag 5,12:4
Rod, Einar
  Witch Woman, The 1929,Ap 8,32:1
Roda, Roda
  Versuchen Sie Meine Schwester 1931,Je 20,20:4
  Raub der Mona Lisa, Der 1932,Mr 30,15:2
  Der Falsche Feldmarschall 1932,Je 30,26:2
  Feldherrnhuegel, Der 1934,Ap 20,17:2
Rodann, Ziva
  Last Train from Gun Hill 1959,Jl 30,31:2
  Story of Ruth, The 1960,Je 18,12:3
  College Confidential 1960,Ag 22,23:1
  Samar 1962,Ap 12,41:6
Roddy, Drew
  Sergeant Madden 1939,Mr 24,27:2
Rode, Ebbe
  Child of Man 1950,F 1,25:2
  Invisible Army, The 1950,Je 26,17:3
  Gertrud 1966,Je 3,33:1
Rode, Nina Pens
  Gertrud 1966,Je 3,33:1
Rode, Walter
  Johnny Allegro 1949,My 31,19:2
Roden, Molly
  Witness for the Prosecution 1958,F 7,16:1
Rodensky, Smuel
  Tel Aviv Taxi 1956,D 31,10:7
Roderick, George
  Rattle of a Simple Man 1964,D 21,42:2
  25th Hour, The 1967,F 17,45:1
Rodger, Sarah Elizabeth (Original Author)
  Girl Overboard 1937,Mr 1,15:1
RODGERS
  See Also ROGERS
Rodgers, Anton
  Rotten to the Core 1965,Jl 20,39:2
Rodgers, Douglas Fletcher
  Never Love a Stranger 1958,N 22,27:4
Rodgers, Gene
  Sensations of 1945 1944,Jl 7,13:2
Rodgers, Ilona
  Salt and Pepper 1968,S 19,62:3
Rodgers, Jimmie
  Jes' Call Me Jim 1920,My 24,20:3
Rodgers, Mark (Screenwriter)
  Let's Kill Uncle 1966,N 19,26:1
Rodgers, Richard
  Main Street to Broadway 1953,O 14,34:1
Rodgers, Richard (Composer)
  Dancing Lady 1933,D 1,23:2
  Manhattan Melodrama 1934,My 5,22:2
  Hollywood Party 1934,My 26,12:2
  Evergreen 1935,Ja 11,29:1
  Mississippi 1935,Ap 18,27:2
  Fools for Scandal 1938,Mr 25,15:3
  Babes in Arms 1939,O 20,27:2
  Too Many Girls 1940,N 21,43:1
  I Married an Angel 1942,Jl 10,13:2
  Stage Door Canteen 1943,Je 25,13:2
  Higher and Higher 1944,Ja 22,8:4
  State Fair 1945,Ag 31,14:3
  Victory at Sea 1954,Jl 14,33:2
  Oklahoma! 1955,O 11,49:1
  Carousel 1956,F 17,13:1
  King and I, The 1956,Je 29,15:6
  Pal Joey 1957,O 28,30:1
  South Pacific 1958,Mr 20,33:1
  Jumbo 1962,D 7,49:1
  Sound of Music, The 1965,Mr 3,34:1
Rodgers, Richard (Miscellaneous)
  Hot Heiress, The 1931,Mr 14,23:2
  Dancing Pirate 1936,Je 18,19:1
Rodgers, Richard (Original Author)
  Babes in Arms 1939,O 20,27:2
  On Your Toes 1939,O 21,12:2
  Boys From Syracuse, The 1940,Ag 1,25:2
  I Married an Angel 1942,Jl 10,13:2
Rodgers, Sondra
  Easy to Wed 1946,Jl 12,14:2
  Tap Roots 1948,Ag 26,16:3
Rodien, Lily
  Eine Tuer geht Auf 1933,F 6,11:5
Rodin, Gil (Composer)
  Let's Make Music 1941,Ja 23,19:2
Rodin, Merrill
  Pied Piper, The 1942,Ag 13,15:3
  American Empire 1943,Ja 14,25:4
  Chetniks 1943,Mr 19,15:3
  Strange Death of Adolf Hitler, The 1943,O 9,11:5
  Song of Bernadette, The 1944,Ja 27,15:2
  Master Race, The 1944,N 2,22:1
Rodin, Yvette
  Liebeskommando 1932,Ap 27,13:6
Rodion, John
  Tower of London 1939,D 12,37:2
Rodman, Howard (Screenwriter)
  Coogan's Bluff 1968,O 3,56:1
Rodney, Eugene B (Producer)
  Relentless 1948,Mr 6,17:3

Rodney, John
  Pursued 1947,Mr 8,10:2
  Key Largo 1948,Jl 17,6:6
  Fighter Squadron 1948,N 20,9:2
Rodney, John (Narrator)
  Gods of Bali 1952,O 13,26:3
Rodney, Mickey
  You're Only Young Once 1938,Ja 3,16:2
Rodojewska, Renata
  Pan Redaktor Szaleje; Mr Editor Is Crazy
    1938,Je 14,17:3
Rodon, Francois
  Pasteur 1936,Ja 30,14:3
  Mysteres de Paris, Les 1937,Ja 30,21:2
Rodrigo, Raquel
  Dona Francisquita 1935,Ap 27,20:6
  Semana de Felicidad, Una; One Week of
    Happiness 1935,Je 15,20:3
  Odio 1935,Je 24,12:3
  Verbena de la Paloma, La 1938,O 25,19:2
Rodrigues, Amalia
  Lover's Net 1957,Jl 23,23:1
Rodriguez, A (Composer)
  Sioux City Sue 1947,Jl 23,19:3
Rodriguez, A Endre (Director)
  Varju a Toronyoran; Crow on the Tower
    1939,N 18,22:6
Rodriguez, Alfred
  Madeleine 1950,S 1,17:2
Rodriguez, Carmen
  El Ultimo Varon Sobre la Tierra 1933,Je 12,20:4
  Quando el Amor Rie 1933,O 17,26:3
  Dos Mas Uno Dos 1934,O 27,20:3
  Nada Mas Que Una Mujer 1934,N 26,12:2
  Octavo Mandamiento, El; Eighth Commandment,
    The 1937,Mr 1,15:2
Rodriguez, Emilio
  Kid Rodelo 1966,F 23,46:1
Rodriguez, Estelita
  Mexicana 1945,N 17,14:6
  Old Los Angeles 1948,Jl 12,11:2
  California Passage 1950,D 16,10:5
  Rio Bravo 1959,Mr 19,40:2
Rodriguez, Frank
  Way Out 1967,O 26,54:3
Rodriguez, George
  Rebellion in Cuba 1961,Jl 1,9:1
Rodriguez, Ismael (Director)
  Que Lindo es Michoacan 1944,Ap 22,8:7
  Cucaracha, La 1961,N 2,42:1
  Important Man, The; El Mayordoma
    1962,Je 26,25:2
Rodriguez, Ismael (Producer)
  Cucaracha, La 1961,N 2,42:1
  Important Man, The; El Mayordoma
    1962,Je 26,25:2
Rodriguez, Ismael (Screenwriter)
  Cucaracha, La 1961,N 2,42:1
  Important Man, The; El Mayordoma
    1962,Je 26,25:2
Rodriguez, Jorge
  Romance Tropical 1934,O 15,20:5
Rodriguez, Jose
  Up the Down Staircase 1967,Ag 18,36:2
Rodriguez, Joselito (Director)
  Ay Jalisco no te Rajes 1943,Ap 24,17:3
Rodriguez, Mario Alberto
  Macario 1961,S 28,48:6
Rodriguez, Orlando
  Pillars of the Sky 1956,O 13,15:2
Rodriguez, Percy
  Heart is a Lonely Hunter, The 1968,Ag 1,24:1
Rodriguez, Roberto (Director)
  Vivire Otra Vez; I Shall Live Again
    1940,O 23,27:2
Rodriguez, Yolanda
  Cool World, The 1964,Ap 21,42:1
Rodriquez, Humberto
  Olvidados de Dios, Los; Those Forgotten by God
    1940,Ja 15,11:2
Rodriquez, Jose (Screenwriter)
  Victory Through Air Power 1943,Jl 19,13:1
Rodriquez, Milton
  Rose for Everyone, A 1967,Je 30,30:1
Rodriquez, Nicolas
  Man's Hope; (Sierra de Teruel) 1947,Ja 21,29:2
Rodway, Norman
  Falstaff; Chimes at Midnight 1967,Mr 18,19:2
  Penthouse, The 1967,O 4,38:3
  I'll Never Forget What's 'Isname
    1968,Ap 15,51:1
Rodzinski, Artur
  Carnegie Hall 1947,My 3,10:2
ROE
  See Also ROWE, ROUX
  See Also ROWE
Roe, E P (Original Author)
  Barriers Burned Away 1925,Mr 12,17:2
Roe, Patricia
  It Happened to One Man 1941,F 24,11:6
Roe, Raymond
  Back Door to Heaven 1939,Ap 20,21:2
  Major and the Minor, The 1942,S 17,21:3

Roe, Raymond — Cont
It Comes up Love 1943,Ja 22,25:3
Youngest Profession, The 1943,Je 25,13:3
True to Life 1943,O 14,26:1
Paris After Dark 1943,O 23,11:1
June Bride 1948,O 30,10:2
Strange Bargain 1949,S 30,28:3
Dear Wife 1950,F 2,31:2
Pretty Baby 1950,S 23,11:2
West Point Story, The 1950,D 23,11:3

Roe, Vingie E (Original Author)
Crimson Challenge, The 1922,Ap 10,18:2
North of the Rio Grande 1922,My 15,20:3
Splendid Road, The 1926,Je 13,31:1

Roebuck, Tiny
Straight, Place and Show 1938,O 1,10:2

Roeburt, John
Strangers in the City 1962,Jl 17,19:2

Roeburt, John (Miscellaneous)
Babes in Bagdad 1954,Ap 5,21:3

Roeburt, John (Original Author)
Jigsaw 1949,My 30,9:4

Roeca, Sam (Screenwriter)
I Was an American Spy 1951,Jl 4,13:2
Torpedo Valley 1952,D 20,15:3
Tall Texan, The 1953,Ap 13,32:4
Angel Baby 1961,O 5,43:1
Fluffy 1965,O 21,57:2

Roehn, Franz
Me and the Colonel 1958,Ag 27,33:1

Roekk, Marika
Leichte Kavallerie 1936,F 8,19:2
Heisses Blut 1936,S 26,11:2
Bettelstudent, Der 1936,D 28,12:3
Gasparone 1938,Mr 12,13:4
Nacht im Mai, Eine; Night in May, A
  1938,N 12,10:3
Es War eine Rauschende Ballnacht; It Was a Gay
  Ball Night 1939,N 4,11:3
Marika 1953,F 18,27:2
Fledermaus, Die 1946,F 8,15:2

Roemer, Michael (Director)
Nothing but a Man 1964,S 21,37:2

Roemer, Michael (Producer)
Nothing but a Man 1964,S 21,37:2

Roemer, Michael (Screenwriter)
Nothing but a Man 1964,S 21,37:2

Roeque, Rod la
Don't Call it Love 1923,D 25,26:1

Roero, Manoci
Fear No Evil 1949,Mr 31,31:2

Roes, Joanna
Patterns 1956,Mr 28,26:1

Roesborg, Nikolai
Janice Meredith 1924,Ag 6,13:3

Roesner, George
Union Depot 1932,Ja 15,24:4

Roesner, Willy
Klosterjaeger, Der 1936,Ja 3,13:7
Macht der Berge, Die; Power of the Mountains,
  The 1938,O 22,14:2

Roessi-Maidan, Hilde
Rosenkavalier, Der 1962,O 10,57:1

Roevers, Maurice
Ulysses 1967,Mr 14,55:1

Roffman, Julian (Director)
Mask, The 1961,O 28,12:4

Roffman, Julian (Producer)
Mask, The 1961,O 28,12:4

Rogan, Beth
Count Five and Die 1958,My 15,25:1
Mysterious Island 1961,D 21,30:6

Rogell, Ablert (Producer)
Northwest Stampede 1948,D 10,34:3
Song of India 1949,Je 10,32:3
Admiral Was a Lady, The 1950,O 13,23:3

Rogell, Al (Director)
Below the Sea 1933,Je 3,16:4

Rogell, Albert (Director)
Senor Daredevil 1926,Ag 17,15:3
Red Raiders, The 1927,S 28,28:3
Shepherd of the Hills, The 1928,F 20,14:1
Lone Wolf's Daughter, The 1929,Mr 4,20:2
Mamba 1930,Mr 11,25:2
Sweepstakes 1931,Je 25,23:5
Tip Off, The 1931,O 26,22:1
Suicide Fleet 1931,N 23,22:1
Carnival Boat 1932,Mr 21,19:5
Air Hostess 1933,Ja 23,9:2
Wrecker, The 1933,Ag 7,18:3
No More Women 1934,Mr 15,27:4
Hell Cat, The 1934,Jl 7,16:5
Air Hawks 1935,Je 4,26:5
Escape from Devil's Island 1935,N 25,22:2
You may Be Next 1936,F 24,14:1
Grand Jury 1936,Ag 1,16:3
Murder in Greenwich Village 1937,O 30,22:2
Start Cheering 1938,Mr 17,17:3
Lone Wolf in Paris, The 1938,My 23,21:2
City Streets 1938,Jl 25,18:2
Last Warning, The 1938,D 8,34:4
Hawaiian Nights 1939,S 29,19:4
Private Affairs 1940,Jl 5,10:3
Argentine Nights 1940,O 11,25:3

Black Cat, The 1941,Ap 26,20:3
Tight Shoes 1941,Je 19,25:2
Jail House Blues 1942,F 6,23:2
Butch Minds the Baby 1942,My 1,23:3
True to the Army 1942,Je 15,15:4
Priorities on Parade 1942,Jl 23,19:2
Hit Parade of 1943 1943,Ap 16,24:3
In old Oklahoma 1943,D 6,21:1
Love, Honor and Goodbye 1945,S 8,12:2
Earl Carroll Sketchbook 1946,Ag 30,13:2
Heaven Only Knows 1947,N 14,29:3
Northwest Stampede 1948,D 10,34:3
Song of India 1949,Je 10,32:3
Admiral Was a Lady, The 1950,O 13,23:3

Rogell, Albert (Original Author)
Wrecker, The 1933,Ag 7,18:3

Rogell, Sid (Producer)
Step by Step 1946,Ag 24,6:7
Strange Bargain 1949,S 30,28:3
White Tower, The 1950,Jl 3,9:2

Roger, Edens (Composer)
Ziegfeld Follies 1946,Mr 23,8:3

Roger, Odette
Harvest 1939,O 3,19:4
Ways of Love (Jofroi); Jofroi (Ways of Love)
  1950,D 13,50:2

Roger, Sandra
Lost Honeymoon 1947,Je 20,25:6

ROGERS
See Also RODGERS

Rogers, Allan
Girl Said No, The 1937,O 18,14:1

Rogers, Anthony
Camelot 1967,O 26,54:1

Rogers, Barbara
Picture Snatcher 1933,My 19,20:3
Dark Hazard 1934,F 23,23:3

Rogers, Bogart (Original Author)
13 Hours by Air 1936,Ap 30,17:2
Man From Down Under, The 1943,S 27,23:2

Rogers, Bogart (Producer)
Everybody's Old Man 1936,Mr 26,27:2

Rogers, Bogart (Screenwriter)
13 Hours by Air 1936,Ap 30,17:2

Rogers, Cameron (Original Author)
Belle Starr 1941,N 1,20:2

Rogers, Cameron (Screenwriter)
Cardinal Richelieu 1935,Ap 19,24:2
White Banners 1938,Je 23,27:1

Rogers, Cecile
Athena 1954,D 22,28:2

Rogers, Charles
Red Lips 1928,O 16,29:2 (In Addenda)

Rogers, Charles (Buddy)
Fascinating Youth 1926,My 10,19:1
So's Your Old Man 1926,N 1,28:2
Wings 1927,Ag 13,10:4
My Best Girl 1927,N 7,26:4
Get Your Man 1927,D 5,26:2
Abie's Irish Rose 1928,Ap 20,26:7
Varsity 1928,O 29,29:1
Some One to Love 1928,D 4,29:1
Close Harmony 1929,Ap 29,29:2
River of Romance, The 1929,Jl 29,23:3
Illusion 1929,S 28,17:3
Half Way to Heaven 1929,D 7,19:3
Young Eagles 1930,Mr 22,22:6
Safety in Numbers 1930,My 31,19:4
Follow Thru 1930,S 13,9:3
Heads Up 1930,O 13,31:1
Lawyer's Secret, The 1931,My 30,9:2
Road to Reno, The 1931,O 10,20:4
This Reckless Age 1932,Ja 9,21:1
Best of Enemies 1933,Jl 17,19:5
Take a Chance 1933,N 27,20:3
Dance Band 1936,Ja 4,19:2
This Way Please 1937,O 8,27:2
Sing for Your Supper 1941,D 1,15:5
Mexican Spitfire at Sea 1942,Je 26,16:5
Mexican Spitfire Sees a Ghost 1942,Jl 31,11:2
Dancing Masters, The 1943,D 2,30:2
Innocent Affair, An 1948,S 29,36:2
Further Perils of Laurel and Hardy, The
  1968,Ap 1,56:6

Rogers, Charles (Director)
Babes in Toyland 1934,D 13,28:2
Bohemian Girl, The 1936,F 17,21:1

Rogers, Charles (Miscellaneous)
Our Relations 1936,N 11,55:1

Rogers, Charles (Original Author)
Way out West 1937,My 4,29:1
Swiss Miss 1938,Je 4,18:2
Block-Heads 1938,Ag 30,14:2
Flying Deuces, The 1939,N 24,29:2
Chump at Oxford, A 1940,F 20,17:3
Saps at Sea 1940,Ap 29,12:2

Rogers, Charles (Producer)
Varsity 1928,D 23,VIII,7:1
Hold 'Em Yale 1935,Ap 27,20:6
When Love Is Young 1937,Ap 17,15:1
Merry-Go-Round of 1938 1937,N 26,27:2
Star Maker, The 1939,Ag 31,14:2
Our Neighbors-The Carters 1940,F 15,15:2

Rogers, Charles (Producer) — Cont
She Knew All the Answers 1941,Je 20,28:4
Adventure in Washington 1941,Ag 1,11:3
Song of the Open Road 1944,Je 7,13:3
Delightfully Dangerous 1945,Je 9,17:3
Angel on my Shoulder 1946,O 21,27:2
Fabulous Dorseys, The 1947,My 30,25:3
Sleep, My Love 1948,F 19,29:4

Rogers, Charles (Screenwriter)
Way out West 1937,My 4,29:1
Block-Heads 1938,Ag 30,14:2
Flying Deuces, The 1939,N 24,29:2
Chump at Oxford, A 1940,F 20,17:3
Saps at Sea 1940,Ap 29,12:2
Air Raid Wardens 1943,Ap 5,15:5
Abroad With two Yanks 1944,O 26,19:7
Brewster's Millions 1945,Ap 27,23:2

Rogers, Charles R (Producer)
Powers Girl, The 1943,Mr 26,14:2 (In Addenda)

Rogers, Doris
Gangway 1937,Ag 21,7:3
Maytime in Mayfair 1952,Ap 23,23:5

Rogers, Gerald
Grand Canary 1934,Jl 20,11:1
Bulldog Drummond's Secret Police
  1939,Mr 30,19:3
Chump at Oxford, A 1940,F 20,17:3
Adventure in Diamonds 1940,Ap 4,27:2

Rogers, Gilbert
Yours, Mine and Ours 1968,Ap 25,53:1

Rogers, Ginger
Young Man of Manhattan 1930,Ap 19,15:1
Sap From Syracuse, The 1930,Jl 26,16:4
Queen High 1930,Ag 9,16:5
Follow the Leader 1930,D 6,21:3
Honor Among Lovers 1931,F 28,15:2
Tip Off, The 1931,O 26,22:1
Suicide Fleet 1931,N 23,22:1
Carnival Boat 1932,Mr 21,19:5
Tenderfoot, The 1932,My 23,18:4
Hat Check Girl 1932,O 8,15:4
You Said a Mouthful 1932,N 18,23:2
Broadway Bad 1933,Mr 6,16:6
42d Street 1933,Mr 10,19:3
Gold Diggers of 1933 1933,Je 8,22:3
Professional Sweetheart 1933,Jl 14,15:3
Shriek in the Night, A 1933,Jl 24,11:2
Don't Bet on Love 1933,Jl 31,16:2
Sitting Pretty 1933,D 2,9:3
Flying Down to Rio 1933,D 22,25:2
Chance at Heaven 1933,D 26,19:3
20 Million Sweethearts 1934,Ap 27,25:1
Finishing School 1934,Ap 30,11:4
Change of Heart 1934,My 11,24:2
Upper World 1934,My 25,25:4
Gay Divorcee, The 1934,N 16,27:1
Romance in Manhattan 1935,Ja 18,29:2
Roberta 1935,Mr 8,25:2
Star of Midnight 1935,Ap 12,26:5
Top Hat 1935,Ag 30,12:2
In Person 1935,D 13,31:5
Follow the Fleet 1936,F 21,21:2
Swing Time 1936,Ag 28,21:2
Shall We Dance 1937,My 14,21:1
Stage Door 1937,O 8,27:2
Vivacious Lady 1938,Je 3,17:3
Having Wonderful Time 1938,Jl 8,11:2
Carefree 1938,S 23,35:1
Story of Vernon and Irene Castle, The
  1939,Mr 31,19:2
Bachelor Mother 1939,Je 30,17:2
Fifth Avenue Girl 1939,Ag 25,12:2
Primrose Path 1940,Mr 23,16:2
Lucky Partners 1940,S 6,25:2
Kitty Foyle 1941,Ja 9,27:2
Tom, Dick and Harry 1941,Jl 18,22:2
Roxie Hart 1942,F 20,21:1
Major and the Minor, The 1942,S 17,21:3
Tales of Manhattan 1942,S 25,25:1
Once Upon a Honeymoon 1942,N 13,28:1
Lady in the Dark 1944,F 23,17:1
Tender Comrade 1944,Je 2,21:2
I'll Be Seeing You 1945,Ap 6,20:6
Week-End at the Waldorf 1945,O 5,27:2
Heartbeat 1946,My 11,22:4
Magnificent Doll 1946,D 9,34:2
It Had to be You 1947,D 8,35:2
Barkleys of Broadway, The 1949,My 5,34:2
Perfect Strangers 1950,Mr 11,8:2
Storm Warning 1951,Mr 3,8:2
Groom Wore Spurs, The 1951,Mr 14,41:2
We're not Married 1952,Jl 12,16:2
Dreamboat 1952,Jl 26,9:2
Monkey Business 1952,S 6,12:6
Forever Female 1954,Ja 13,26:2
Black Widow 1954,O 28,46:6
Tight Spot 1955,Mr 19,11:7
Teenage Rebel 1956,N 17,17:6
Oh Men! Oh Women! 1957,F 22,25:2
Harlow 1965,My 15,18:1

Rogers, Gregory (Original Author)
Red Hot Tires 1925,O 20,28:1
Hogan's Alley 1925,N 24,28:4
Tracked by the Police 1927,Ap 27,22:5

Rogers, Gregory (Original Author)— Cont
G Men 1935,My 2,17:1
Rogers, Gregory (Screenwriter)
Midnight Taxi, The 1928,O 29,29:1
Rogers, Hazel
Eight and One Half 1963,Je 26,36:1
Rogers, Howard Emmett (Original Author)
Nuisance, The 1933,My 29,22:2
Whirlpool 1934,My 5,22:3
Bride Walks Out, The 1936,Jl 10,15:1
Chaser, The 1938,Ag 2,15:3
Billy the Kid 1941,Je 20,28:2
Crossroads 1942,Jl 27,18:2
For Me and My Gal 1942,O 22,25:1
Easy to Wed 1946,Jl 12,14:2
Rogers, Howard Emmett (Screenwriter)
Paradise for Two 1927,Ja 25,18:4
Whipsaw 1936,Ja 25,18:4
Unguarded Hour, The 1936,Ap 4,11:1
Libeled Lady 1936,O 31,24:2
Arsene Lupin Returns 1938,Mr 9,21:1
Eyes in the Night 1942,O 16,23:1
Assignment in Brittany 1943,Ap 22,31:2
Adventures of Tartu, The 1943,S 24,26:1
Hour of 13, The 1952,O 28,37:1
Rogers, Jaime
West Side Story 1961,O 19,39:3
Rogers, Jean
Conflict 1937,Ja 18,21:2
Mysterious Crossing 1937,F 2,20:5
When Love Is Young 1937,Ap 17,15:1
Night Key 1937,Ap 19,27:2
Reported Missing 1937,S 3,12:2
Time Out for Murder 1938,O 7,21:2
Always in Trouble 1938,N 3,27:1
Mars Attacks the World 1938,N 8,26:3
While New York Sleeps 1938,D 22,25:3
Hotel for Women 1939,Ag 26,20:2
Stop, Look and Love 1939,S 8,28:5
Man Who Wouldn't Talk, The 1940,Ja 12,13:3
Viva Cisco Kid 1940,Mr 22,23:4
Brigham Young - Frontiersman 1940,S 21,13:2
Let's Make Music 1941,Ja 23,19:2
Dr Kildare's Victory 1942,F 5,25:2
Design for Scandal 1942,F 6,23:3
Sunday Punch 1942,My 11,19:2
Pacific Rendezvous 1942,Jl 8,27:4
War Against Mrs Hadley, The 1942,N 26,40:2
Swing Shift Maisie 1943,S 10,29:2
Whistling in Brooklyn 1944,Mr 24,17:3
Rough, Tough and Ready 1945,Mr 24,22:7
Backlash 1947,My 24,10:5
Second Woman, The 1951,F 2,19:2
Rogers, Jean Scott (Screenwriter)
Corridors of Blood 1963,Je 6,39:1
Rogers, Jimmy
Prairie Chickens 1943,Jl 9,21:6
Calaboose 1943,Jl 30,19:2
Rogers, John
Behind That Curtain 1929,Jl 1,31:2
Raffles 1930,Jl 25,20:4
Sea Wolf, The 1930,O 6,21:1
Charlie Chan Carries On 1931,Mr 21,15:1
Murder by the Clock 1931,Jl 18,16:6
Wharf Angel 1934,Ap 21,12:1
Grand Canary 1934,Jl 20,11:1
Charlie Chan in London 1934,S 13,26:1
Limehouse Blues 1934,D 12,28:2
People Will Talk 1935,Je 17,20:2
Klondike Annie 1936,Mr 12,18:2
Charlie Chan at the Race Track 1936,Ag 15,6:2
Think Fast, Mr Moto 1937,Ag 16,15:3
Bulldog Drummond Comes Back 1937,S 4,8:3
Buccaneer, The 1938,F 17,17:2
Mysterious Mr Moto of Devil's Island 1938,S 19,16:2
Typhoon 1940,My 23,28:4
Lassie Come Home 1943,O 8,15:4
Moss Rose 1947,Jl 3,14:2
Thunder in the Valley 1947,N 28,30:1
Rogers, John W (Producer)
Spirit of West Point 1947,O 3,31:2
Rogers, Lambert
Street Scene 1931,Ag 27,22:5
Hold 'Em Navy 1937,N 6,14:2
Rogers, Lela
Major and the Minor, The 1942,S 17,21:3
Rogers, Lela (Screenwriter)
Tanga Tika 1953,O 6,34:4
Rogers, Lorraine
Psychomania 1964,F 15,14:3
Rogers, Marilyn
Ladybug, Ladybug 1963,D 24,9:1
Rogers, Mildred
Girl Said No, The 1937,O 18,14:1
Rogers, Molly
Livingstone in Africa 1929,Mr 25,32:2
Rogers, Paul
Murder in the Cathedral 1952,Mr 26,35:2
Beau Brummell 1954,O 21,31:5
Beachcomber, The 1955,Ja 17,27:5
Svengali 1955,S 26,18:2
Our Man in Havana 1960,Ja 28,26:1
Trials of Oscar Wilde, The 1960,Je 28,26:1

Circle of Deception 1961,F 18,12:2
Mark, The 1961,O 3,46:2
No Love for Johnnie 1961,D 13,55:1
Billy Budd 1962,O 31,32:1
Stolen Hours 1963,O 17,39:1
Young and Willing 1964,F 27,28:1
Third Secret, The 1964,Ap 29,27:1
Walk in the Shadow 1966,S 12,52:5
He Who Rides a Tiger 1968,S 10,39:1
Rogers, Peter (Producer)
Cash on Delivery 1956,S 1,19:3
Novel Affair, A 1957,Ag 28,22:1
Circle, The 1959,Ap 16,29:2
Carry on Sergeant 1959,O 28,40:5
Carry on Nurse 1960,S 10,11:1
Please Turn Over 1961,Ap 29,12:2
Swingin' Maiden, The 1964,Ja 1,16:2
Carry on Cleo 1965,O 23,17:2
Rogers, Peter (Screenwriter)
Holiday Camp 1948,Ja 24,11:2
Dear Murderer 1948,My 8,12:2
Here Come the Huggetts 1950,D 25,25:3
Cash on Delivery 1956,S 1,19:3
Rogers, Rod
Teen Age 1944,Je 19,17:1
Youth Runs Wild 1944,S 2,17:2
Crime Incorporated 1945,Je 23,9:7
Rogers, Roswell (Screenwriter)
Just Across the Street 1952,Je 28,12:4
Rogers, Roy
Under Western Stars 1938,Je 25,7:3
Dark Command 1940,My 11,15:2
Brazil 1944,N 20,25:2
Hollywood Canteen 1944,D 16,19:2
Lake Placid Serenade 1944,D 25,15:6
Utah 1945,Mr 12,22:7
My Pal Trigger 1946,Ag 17,16:3
Apache Rose 1947,Jl 23,19:3
Son of Paleface 1952,O 2,32:3
Rogers, Roy and Trigger
Hit Parade of 1947 1947,My 5,32:8
Rogers, Shorty, and his Giants (Composer)
Dementia 1955,D 23,14:4
Rogers, Victor
Thoroughly Modern Millie 1967,Mr 23,25:1
Rogers, Walter
Dramatic Life of Abraham Lincoln, The 1924,Ja 22,17:3
Iron Horse, The 1924,Ag 29,6:1
Flaming Frontier, The 1926,Ap 5,24:1
Wolf's Clothing 1927,Mr 28,26:4
Seven Faces 1929,N 16,25:2
All Quiet on The Western Front 1930,Ap 30,29:1
Silver Dollar 1932,D 23,20:1
Rogers, Warren
Flaming Barriers 1924,Ja 29,16:1
Dawn of a Tomorrow, The 1924,Mr 26,19:2
Rogers, Wayne
Odds Against Tomorrow 1959,O 16,27:1
Cool Hand Luke 1967,N 2,58:1
Rogers, Will
Laughing Bill Hyde 1918,S 23,7:1
Almost a Husband 1919,O 13,16:3
Jubilo 1919,D 8,20:4
Jes' Call Me Jim 1920,My 24,20:3
Cupid, the Cowpuncher 1920,Jl 26,9:5
Honest Hutch 1920,S 26,VI,2:1 (In Addenda)
Guile of Women 1921,F 28,16:2
Boys Will Be Boys 1921,My 6,20:2 (Incorrect in this edition; use 1921,My 16,20:2 elsewhere)
Doubling for Romeo 1921,O 24,13:1
One Glorious Day 1922,Ja 30,16:2
Headless Horseman, The 1922,D 25,21:1
Fruits of Faith 1923,Ja 15,18:3
Texas Steer, A 1928,Ja 2,28:1
They Had to See Paris 1929,O 12,11:1
Happy Days 1930,F 14,20:1
So This Is London 1930,My 24,21:2
Lightnin' 1930,N 29,21:4
Connecticut Yankee, A 1931,Ap 13,17:1
Young as You Feel 1931,Ag 8,16:3
Ambassador Bill 1931,N 14,15:3
Business and Pleasure 1932,F 13,23:4
Down to Earth 1932,S 2,19:2
Too Busy to Work 1932,D 3,21:4
State Fair 1933,Ja 27,13:2
Doctor Bull 1933,O 6,21:2
Mr Skitch 1933,D 23,19:1
David Harum 1934,Mr 2,23:2
Handy Andy 1934,Ag 4,14:5
Judge Priest 1934,O 12,33:1
County Chairman, The 1935,Ja 19,8:1
Life Begins at 40 1935,Ap 5,21:3
Doubting Thomas 1935,Jl 11,24:2
Steamboat Around the Bend 1935,S 20,17:2
Old Kentucky, In 1935,N 29,24:1
Connecticut Yankee at the Court of King Arthur, A 1936,My 4,16:1
Rogers, Will (Original Author)
Stand up and Cheer 1934,Ap 20,17:1
Rogers, Will (Screenwriter)
Two Wagons-Both Covered 1924,Ja 29,16:1

Rogers, Will Jr
Look for the Silver Lining 1949,Je 24,29:2
Story of Will Rogers, The 1952,Jl 18,10:5
Eddie Cantor Story, The 1953,D 26,10:2
Rogers, Will Mrs (Original Author)
Story of Will Rogers, The 1952,Jl 18,10:5
Rogers, William
Search, The 1948,Mr 24,30:3
Rogerson, Wanda
One Woman's Story 1949,My 18,33:2
Rogge, Bernhardt Admiral (Original Author)
Under ten Flags 1960,S 16,24:1
Rogger, Louis Lucien (Original Author)
Princess Comes Across, The 1936,Je 4,27:2
Rogier, Frank
Hansel and Gretel 1954,O 11,33:1
Rognoni
Generals Without Buttons 1938,Mr 8,23:2
Personal Column 1941,F 3,13:2
Fleet's In, The 1942,Mr 12,24:2
Rogosin, Lionel (Director)
On the Bowery 1957,Mr 19,44:1
Come Back Africa 1960,Ap 5,45:1
Good Times, Wonderful Times 1966,Jl 19,34:1
Rogosin, Lionel (Producer)
On the Bowery 1957,Mr 19,44:1
Come Back Africa 1960,Ap 5,45:1
Good Times, Wonderful Times 1966,Jl 19,34:1
Rogosin, Lionel (Screenwriter)
Come Back Africa 1960,Ap 5,45:1
Good Times, Wonderful Times 1966,Jl 19,34:1
Rogoz, Jaromir
Ecstasy 1940,D 25,33:2
Rogozhin, N A
Alexander Nevsky 1939,Mr 23,27:1
Rogulina, E
Life is Beautiful 1933,F 13,11:5
Gypsies 1936,Jl 30,22:2
Rohauer, Raymond (Producer)
Vicious Breed, The 1958,My 23,29:2
Rohkopf, Paul
Der Falsche Feldmarschall 1932,Je 30,26:2
Rohmer, Eric (Director)
Six in Paris 1965,S 16,54:2
Rohmer, Sax (Original Author)
New Adventures of Dr Fu Manchu, The 1930,My 3,23:1
Daughter of the Dragon 1931,Ag 22,7:5
Mask of Fu Manchu, The 1932,D 3,21:4
Face of Fu Manchu, The 1965,N 11,58:3
Vengeance of Fu Manchu, The 1968,F 15,47:1
Rohmer (Original Author)
Mysterious Dr Fu Manchu, The 1929,Jl 28,VIII,3:7 (In Addenda)
Rohrig, Walter (Miscellaneous)
Cabinet of Dr Caligari, The 1921,Mr 20,VI,2:1
Roig, Gonzale (Composer)
Sioux City Sue 1947,Jl 23,19:3
Roijas, Alfonso
Fedra, the Devil's Daughter 1957,O 26,19:2
Roitfeld, Jacques (Producer)
Folies Bergere 1958,My 28,37:2
Rojas, Carmen
Dr Coppelius 1968,D 26,56:1
Rojas, Manuel
Magnificent Matador, The 1955,My 25,38:1
Rojo, Gustavo
Tarzan and the Mermaids 1948,Mr 30,26:4
Alexander the Great 1956,Mr 29,23:1
It Started With a Kiss 1959,Ag 20,14:2
Miracle, The 1959,N 13,25:4
Rojo, Maria
Heroes del Barrio, Los 1936,D 28,12:4
Rojo, Ruben
Alexander the Great 1956,Mr 29,23:1
Sword and the Cross, The 1960,Jl 7,26:1
Rokneddine, Prince
Just Suppose 1926,Ja 18,26:2
Rokossovsky, Konstantin K
If Your Home Is Dear to You 1967,O 24,27:1
Rola, Joven E
Eve of St Mark, The 1944,My 31,22:2
ROLAND
See Also ROLLAND, ROWLAND
Roland, Eric
Criminal at Large 1933,D 20,27:2
Roland, Fredric
Rainmakers, The 1935,N 2,13:2
Roland, George (Director)
Wandering Jew, The 1933,O 21,11:2
I Want to Be a Mother 1937,F 27,9:2
Vilna Legend, A (American Cast) 1949,S 26,17:1
Vilna Legend, A (Russian-Jewish Cast) 1949,S 26,17:1
Roland, Gilbert
Plastic Age, The 1926,Jl 19,13:1
Campus Flirt, The 1926,S 22,31:1
Blonde Saint, The 1926,N 23,27:1
Camille 1927,Ap 22,19:1
Rose of the Golden West 1927,S 26,27:1
Love Mart, The 1927,D 26,16:6
Dove, The 1928,Ja 3,28:2
Woman Disputed, The 1928,N 10,20:8

Roland, Gilbert— Cont
New York Nights 1930,F 1,15:1
Passionate Plumber, The 1932,Mr 12,19:5
Woman in Room 13, The 1932,My 21,9:2
Life Begins - 1932,Ag 26,20:3
Call Her Savage 1932,N 25,19:2
She Done Him Wrong 1933,F 10,12:3
Our Betters 1933,F 24,13:2
Viuda Romantica, La 1933,S 4,9:6
After Tonight 1933,N 3,23:2
IO... TU... Y...; (I... Thou... and... She)
  1933,D 5,31:6
Mystery Woman 1935,Ja 9,22:2
Julieta Compra un Hijo; Julieta Buys a Baby
  1935,Mr 25,12:3
Last Train from Madrid, The 1937,Je 19,20:2
Thunder Trail 1938,F 5,19:3
Gateway 1938,Ag 8,9:2
Vida Bohemia, La 1939,F 6,8:5
Juarez 1939,Ap 26,27:1
Isle of Destiny 1940,Ap 8,15:2
Sea Hawk, The 1940,Ag 10,16:2
Rangers of Fortune 1940,S 19,27:2
My Life With Caroline 1941,O 30,27:1
Enemy Agents meet Ellery Queen
  1942,Ag 22,16:2
Captain Kidd 1945,N 23,26:3
Other Love, The 1947,My 15,32:4
Pirates of Monterey 1947,D 17,41:4
We Were Strangers 1949,Ap 28,28:2
Malaya 1950,F 23,33:1
Crisis 1950,Jl 4,10:2
Furies, The 1950,Ag 17,23:2
Torch, The 1950,Ag 21,15:2
Bullfighter and the Lady, The 1951,Ap 27,19:2
Mark of the Renegade 1951,S 7,24:2
Ten Tall Men 1951,O 27,10:5
My Six Convicts 1952,Mr 28,27:3
Glory Alley 1952,Jl 30,20:8
Miracle of Our Lady Fatima, The
  1952,Ag 21,16:2
Bad and the Beautiful, The 1953,Ja 16,19:1
Thunder Bay 1953,My 21,39:2
Beneath the 12-Mile Reef 1953,D 17,52:2
Diamond Queen, The 1954,Ja 27,24:2
French Line, The 1954,My 15,13:2
Racers, The 1955,F 5,13:2
Underwater! 1955,F 10,27:2
That Lady 1955,Je 11,8:7
Treasure of Pancho Villa, The 1955,N 25,38:2
Around the World in 80 Days 1956,O 18,37:1
Three Violent People 1957,F 11,34:2
Midnight Story, The 1957,Jl 5,14:2
Big Circus, The 1959,Jl 18,6:1
Samar 1962,Ap 12,41:6
Reward, The 1965,S 16,55:1
Poppy is Also a Flower, The 1967,D 14,62:4
Any Gun Can Play 1968,S 14,34:2
Roland, Jeanne
Salt and Pepper 1968,S 19,62:3
Roland, Marc (Composer)
Barberina, Die Taenzerin Von Sans-Souci
  1932,O 26,15:4
Roland, Paul
Depart, Le 1967,S 23,20:3
Roland, Ruth
Reno 1930,N 4,36:1
Days of Thrills and Laughter 1961,Mr 22,37:1
Rolane, Andree
Miserables, Les 1926,Jl 9,17:1
Miserables, Les 1927,Ag 23,29:4
Roldan, Emma
Prisionero 13, El 1934,Ap 30,11:4
Silencio Sublime 1937,Ja 16,21:2
Millones de Chaflan, Los 1938,S 13,28:3
Adelita, La 1938,O 12,35:2
Rancho Grande 1938,D 2,27:2
Sonadores de la Gloria; Dreamers of Glory
  1938,D 10,13:3
Ojos Tapatios 1939,F 13,13:3
Casa del Ogro, La; House of the Ogre, The
  1939,F 13,13:2
Guadalajara 1943,Je 12,9:3
Romeo and Juliet 1944,Je 17,10:3
Miserables, Los 1944,O 24,17:2
One Way Street 1950,My 12,33:3
Roldan, Enrique
Oro entre Barro; Gold in Clay 1940,Jl 1,23:2
Roldan, Luis G
Bohemios 1935,S 16,15:3
Rolf, Erik
Atlantic Convoy 1942,Jl 6,18:5
Eyes in the Night 1942,O 16,23:1
First Comes Courage 1943,S 3,15:3
None Shall Escape 1944,Ap 7,23:2
Secret Command 1944,Je 14,16:2
Soul of a Monster, The 1944,S 9,12:4
Counter-Attack 1945,My 17,15:2
Davy Crockett, Indian Scout 1950,Mr 17,28:3
Rolf, Tutta
Swedenhielms 1935,S 6,12:3
Under Falsk Flagg 1937,Ja 20,18:5
Sara Laer Sig Folkvett 1938,F 16,17:1

Rolfe, Charles
Invaders, The 1942,Mr 6,17:1
Tower of Terror 1942,Je 29,11:4
Smugglers, The 1948,Mr 29,17:1
Girl in a Million, A 1950,Jl 24,15:2
Rolfe, E A (Original Author)
Screen, The 1951,Ap 23,21:2
Rolfe, Guy
Easy Money (Episode 4) 1949,F 14,15:3
Broken Journey 1949,My 26,34:3
Girl in the Painting, The 1949,Ag 22,13:1
Prelude to Fame 1950,N 10,35:3
Inheritance, The 1951,F 12,19:2
Reluctant Widow, The 1951,S 8,8:6
Spider and the Fly, The 1952,Jl 29,17:3
Ivanhoe 1952,Ag 1,8:2
Young Bess 1953,My 22,31:1
Veils of Bagdad, The 1953,N 27,99:9
King of the Khyber Rifles 1953,D 23,21:1
Dance Little Lady 1955,D 26,23:3
Yesterday's Enemy 1960,Mr 4,19:1
Snow White and the Three Stooges 1961,Jl 1,9:1
Mr Sardonicus 1961,O 19,39:3
Taras Bulba 1962,D 26,5:2
Fall of the Roman Empire, The 1964,Mr 27,14:2
Alphabet Murders, The 1966,Jl 12,36:2
Rolfe, Sam (Original Author)
Naked Spur, The 1953,Mr 26,37:3
Bombers B-52 1957,N 23,11:2
Rolfe, Sam (Screenwriter)
McConnell Story, The 1955,S 30,23:1
Target Zero 1955,N 16,43:2
Pillars of the Sky 1956,O 13,15:2
Rolins, David
Riley, The Cop 1928,D 4,29:1
Roll, Mino (Screenwriter)
Grand Slam 1968,F 21,60:4
Roll, Phillip (Screenwriter)
Adventures of Robinson Crusoe, The
  1954,Ag 6,10:5
Rolla, Michelle
Mr Hulot's Holiday 1954,Je 17,36:2
Rollan, Henri
Milady 1933,S 8,22:3
Mysteres de Paris, Les 1937,Ja 30,21:2
Harvest 1939,O 3,19:4
Fanfan the Tulip 1953,My 5,34:2
ROLLAND
See Also ROLAND, ROWLAND
Rolland, Monique
Barbier de Seville, Le 1936,S 23,29:2
Four Flights to Love 1942,Ap 13,12:2
Last Will of Dr Mabuse, The 1943,Mr 20,11:1
Rollens, Jacques
My Own Pal 1926,Mr 15,18:3
Mother Machree 1928,Mr 6,20:3
Rollett, Raymond
Master of Bankdam 1949,O 17,18:2
Blue Murder at St Trinians 1958,My 27,27:1
Rollin, Georges
That They May Live 1939,N 7,31:2
Ultimatum 1940,F 5,13:2
Hitler's Madman 1943,Ag 28,15:1
It Happened at the Inn; Goupi Mains Rouge
  1945,D 22,16:2
Clandestine 1948,My 24,23:2
ROLLINS
See Also RAWLINGS, RAWLINS
Rollins, David
High School Hero 1927,O 24,24:3
Thanks For The Buggy Ride 1928,Ja 23,18:3
Air Circus, The 1928,S 3,14:2
Win That Girl 1928,O 1,23:1
Prep and Pep 1928,D 24,11:1
Black Watch, The 1929,My 23,26:3
William Fox Movietone Follies of 1929
  1929,My 27,22:1
Why Leave Home 1929,S 16,30:1
Love, Live and Laugh 1929,N 2,14:6
Happy Days 1930,F 14,20:1
Big Trail, The 1930,O 25,20:3
Young Sinners 1931,My 9,15:4
Morals for Women 1931,N 16,23:1
Phantom Express, The 1932,S 20,26:3
Rollins, Jean
Beachcomber, The 1955,Ja 17,27:5
Rollins, Lizabeth
Beachcomber, The 1955,Ja 17,27:5
Rollis, Robert
Belle Americaine, La 1961,D 18,42:1
Roma, Tina (Screenwriter)
Man Called Adam, A 1966,Ag 4,24:2
Romain, Claude
Marie du Port 1951,Jl 24,21:2
To Paris With Love 1955,Mr 29,33:4
Light Across the Street, The; Lumiere d'en Face,
  La 1957,Jl 30,20:2
Romain, George E
Sea Hawk, The 1924,Je 3,22:1
Romain, Ray
Smiling Faces 1932,Ag 31,12:3

Romain, Tom
Smiling Faces 1932,Ag 31,12:3
Romain, Yvonne
Curse of the Werewolf, The 1961,Je 8,40:2
Swinger, The 1966,D 15,60:1
Double Trouble 1967,My 25,54:2
Romains, Jules (Original Author)
Dr Knock 1937,My 1,16:4
Dr Knock 1955,O 10,31:2
Romains, Jules (Screenwriter)
Volpone 1947,D 27,9:3
Dr Knock 1955,O 10,31:2
Roman, Alita
Loco Serenata, El; Crazy Musician, The
  1940,Ap 22,13:2
Je Hatore 1940,Ag 27,17:2
Roman, Alito
Jettatore 1940,Ag 27,17:2
Roman, Barbro (Director)
Flamboyant Sex, The 1963,Ag 13,25:1
Roman, Barbro (Screenwriter)
Flamboyant Sex, The 1963,Ag 13,25:1
Roman, Greg
Naked and the Dead, The 1958,Ag 7,21:1
Roman, Grete
Schloss Hubertus 1935,F 9,11:3
Roman, Hugh
Show Girl 1928,N 5,26:1
Roman, Lawrence (Original Author)
Under the Yum Yum Tree 1963,N 21,43:2
Roman, Lawrence (Screenwriter)
Vice Squad 1953,Ag 26,23:2
Naked Alibi 1954,O 2,21:2
One Desire 1955,S 3,9:1
Slaughter on Tenth Avenue 1957,N 6,43:1
Day of the Badman 1958,Ja 30,19:2
Under the Yum Yum Tree 1963,N 21,43:2
Swinger, The 1966,D 15,60:1
Paper Lion 1968,O 24,54:1
Roman, Leticia
G I Blues 1960,N 5,28:1
Gold of the Seven Saints 1961,Ap 6,30:3
Fanny Hill 1965,D 2,48:1
Roman, Peter
You Gotta Stay Happy 1948,N 5,29:2
Roman, Ric
Lone Star 1952,F 2,11:4
Appointment in Honduras 1953,N 19,41:4
Lizzie 1957,Ap 5,24:2
Roman, Ruth
Good Sam 1948,S 17,28:2
Belle Star's Daughter 1949,Ja 10,19:2
Champion 1949,Ap 11,29:2
Window, The 1949,Ag 8,10:5
Beyond the Forest 1949,O 22,11:2
Always Leave Them Laughing 1949,N 24,48:2
Barricade 1950,Mr 25,8:6
Colt 45 1950,My 6,8:6
Three Secrets 1950,O 21,10:6
Dallas 1951,Ja 13,10:4
Lightning Strikes Twice 1951,Ap 13,18:7
Strangers on a Train 1951,Jl 4,13:2
Tomorrow Is Another Day 1951,Ag 9,17:5
Starlift 1951,D 15,11:2
Invitation 1952,Ja 30,22:6
Mara Maru 1952,Ap 24,38:1
Young Man With Ideas 1952,Je 7,22:6
Blowing Wild 1953,O 8,37:5
Tanganyika 1954,Je 19,9:2
Down Three Dark Streets 1954,S 4,6:4
Shanghai Story, The 1954,S 25,10:7
Far Country, The 1955,F 14,24:2
Bottom of the Bottle, The 1956,F 2,19:2
Joe Macbeth 1956,Ap 7,13:1
Great Day in the Morning 1956,My 19,12:6
Five Steps to Danger 1957,Ja 31,21:1
Look in any Window 1962,Mr 22,40:1
Love Has Many Faces 1965,F 25,24:1
Romance, Viviane
Dark Eyes 1938,Ap 19,24:5
They Were Five 1938,Je 1,19:5
Kiss of Fire, The 1940,N 20,27:4
Pasha's Wives, The 1942,Ap 6,19:2
It Happened in Gibraltar 1943,N 16,27:1
Sirocco 1946,Ag 12,17:3
Carmen 1946,N 27,20:2
Queen's Necklace, The 1947,My 17,8:5
Panic 1947,N 27,50:2
Street of Shadows 1948,N 20,9:2
Marked Girls 1949,Je 25,8:7
Seven Deadly Sins, The (Lust); Lust (The Seven
  Deadly Sins) 1953,My 12,31:3
Flesh and Desire 1958,N 27,52:4
Any Number Can Win 1963,O 9,47:2
Romaniello, Sgt
Three Stripes in the Sun 1955,N 24,41:2
Romano, Amelia
Native Land 1942,My 12,16:3
Romano, Carlo
Life Begins Anew; Vita Ricomincia, La
  1947,Ap 7,20:5
Anything for a Song 1947,Ag 5,26:2
Cavalleria Rusticana 1947,D 20,21:2

Romano, Carlo— Cont
Laugh Pagliacci 1948,Ja 31,14:2
When Love Calls 1948,O 9,12:6
Four Steps in the Clouds 1948,N 22,25:2
Tomorrow is too Late 1952,Ap 14,22:2
Streets of Sorrow 1952,N 18,37:4
Vitelloni 1956,O 24,43:1
Variety Lights; Luci del Varieta 1965,My 7,34:1
Romano, Carlo (Screenwriter)
Very Handy Man, A 1966,D 15,60:1
All the Other Girls Do! 1967,My 30,12:1
Romano, Dina
Anna 1953,F 19,20:5
Romano, Nina
What Happened to Jones 1926,F 9,22:1
Midnight Sun, The 1926,Ap 24,20:4
Lost at the Front 1927,Je 14,33:2
Romano, Renato
Minute to Pray, A Second to Die, A 1968,My 23,56:2
Romano, Tony
Radio Stars on Parade 1945,S 22,14:2
Romanoff, Constance
Tender Hour, The 1927,Je 7,27:4
Romanoff, Constantine
Kid Brother, The 1927,Ja 24,14:1
Private Life of Helen of Troy, The 1927,D 10,14:7
Wolf Song 1929,F 25,16:1
Gang Buster, The 1931,Ja 24,15:1
Too Busy to Work 1932,D 3,21:4
People Will Talk 1935,Je 17,20:2
Meet the Girls 1938,S 3,16:6
Long Voyage Home, The 1940,O 9,30:2 (In Addenda)
Romanoff, Michael
Arch of Triumph 1948,Ap 21,33:2
Innocent Affair, An 1948,S 29,36:2
Do Not Disturb 1965,D 25,17:2
Caprice 1967,Je 8,52:2
Romanov, G
Sailor From the Comet, The 1959,Ag 3,21:2
Romanov, G (Screenwriter)
Sailor From the Comet, The 1959,Ag 3,21:2
Romanov, M
Secret Agent 1949,F 10,37:3
Poem of the Sea 1959,D 21,34:4
Romanov, S
Young Guard 1949,D 26,33:6
Romanova, Vera
Flying Carpet, The 1960,F 28,31:1
Romanowsky, Richard
Winternachtstraum 1935,D 28,10:6
Die Ganze Welt Dreht Sich um Liebe 1936,N 27,27:2
Nacht mit dem Kaiser, Die 1937,Ag 14,16:5
Fasching in Wien 1939,Mr 18,9:2
Dingehort mein Herz; My Heart Belongs to Thee 1939,Mr 25,19:2
Das Erlebnis Geht Weiter; Another Experience 1940,F 3,9:3
You Are the World for Me 1964,D 26,9:4
Romantini, Joe
Cipher Bureau 1938,D 14,32:6
Romantsef, Igor
Childred of the Revolution 1936,Ap 6,18:2
Romatko, Carlo
Last Chance, The 1945,N 28,21:6
Romay, Lina
Heat's on, The 1943,N 26,29:2
Two Girls and a Sailor 1944,Je 15,16:1
Bathing Beauty 1944,Je 28,20:1
Week-End at the Waldorf 1945,O 5,27:2
Adventure 1946,F 8,23:2
Love Laughs at Andy Hardy 1947,Ja 8,28:2
Honeymoon 1947,My 19,27:2
Lady Takes a Sailor, The 1949,D 17,15:2
Romay, Pepito
Important Man, The; El Mayordoma 1962,Je 26,25:2
Romberg, Sigmund (Composer)
New Moon 1930,D 25,18:6
Night is Young, The 1935,Ja 14,11:2
Maytime 1937,Mr 19,27:1
Girl of the Golden West, The 1938,Mr 25,15:2
New Moon 1940,Jl 19,22:2
Romberg, Sigmund (Miscellaneous)
Desert Song, The 1953,My 21,39:2
Romberg, Sigmund (Original Author)
Viennese Nights 1930,N 27,32:5
Desert Song, The 1943,D 18,10:6
Romberg, Sigmund (Screenwriter)
Children of Dreams 1931,Jl 20,20:4
Rome, Bert
Forward Pass, The 1929,N 29,25:1
Rome, Harold (Composer)
Babes on Broadway 1942,Ja 1,37:1
Thousands Cheer 1943,S 14,27:1
Call Me Mister 1951,F 1,21:2
Rome, Stewart
Crimson Circle, The 1929,D 28,11:1
Wings of the Morning 1937,Mr 12,19:1

Murder on Diamond Row 1937,N 12,27:2
Dinner at the Ritz 1937,D 4,21:1
Rome, Tina
Baron of Arizona, The 1950,Je 23,29:2
Park Row 1952,D 22,20:2
Rome Opera House Orchestra
Trovatore, Il 1950,F 9,36:7
Romeo, Carmelina
Amore e Morte; (Love and Death) 1932,O 4,26:4
Romeo, Rosario
Amore e Morte; (Love and Death) 1932,O 4,26:4
Romeo, Rosario (Director)
Amore e Morte; (Love and Death) 1932,O 4,26:4
Romer, Jeanne
Saboteur 1942,My 8,27:2
Romer, Leila
Anne of Green Gables 1919,D 22,18:3
Romer, Lynn
Saboteur 1942,My 8,27:2
Romero, Carlos
They Came to Cordura 1959,O 22,47:2
Island of the Blue Dolphins 1964,Jl 4,8:2
Romero, Cesar
Thin Man, The 1934,Je 30,18:5
British Agent 1934,S 20,20:1
Clive of India 1935,Ja 18,29:1
Good Fairy, The 1935,F 1,18:1
Cardinal Richelieu 1935,Ap 19,24:2
Hold 'Em Yale 1935,Ap 27,20:6
Devil is a Woman, The 1935,My 4,17:2
Diamond Jim 1935,Ag 24,18:2
Metropolitan 1935,O 18,27:4
Rendezvous 1935,O 26,12:2
Show Them no Mercy 1935,D 9,25:2
Love Before Breakfast 1936,Mr 14,10:1
Nobody's Fool 1936,Je 4,27:2
Public Enemy's Wife 1936,Jl 9,17:2
Fifteen Maiden Lane 1936,O 17,21:3
Wee Willie Winkie 1937,Jl 24,12:1
Armored Car 1937,Jl 26,15:2
Dangerously Yours 1937,O 18,14:2
Happy Landing 1938,Ja 22,19:1
Always Goodbye 1938,Je 25,7:2
My Lucky Star 1938,S 10,20:2
Five of a Kind 1938,O 31,12:2
Wife, Husband and Friend 1939,F 25,19:2
Little Princess, The 1939,Mr 11,21:1
Return of the Cisco Kid, The 1939,Ap 29,13:2
Frontier Marshal 1939,Jl 29,18:2
Charlie Chan at Treasure Island 1939,S 1,15:5
Cisco Kid and the Lady, The 1939,D 25,29:2
He Married his Wife 1940,Ja 20,11:2
Viva Cisco Kid 1940,Mr 22,23:4
Lucky Cisco Kid 1940,Je 24,19:5
Gay Caballero, The 1940,O 25,25:3
Romance of the Rio Grande 1940,D 25,33:4
Tall, Dark and Handsome 1941,Ja 24,15:2
Ride on Vaquero 1941,Ap 19,20:2
Great American Broadcast, The 1941,My 2,25:2
Dance Hall 1941,Jl 19,16:2
Week-End in Havana 1941,N 8,11:2
Gentleman at Heart, A 1942,F 23,25:2
Orchestra Wives 1942,S 24,23:2
Tales of Manhattan 1942,S 25,25:1
Springtime in the Rockies 1942,N 12,30:2
Coney Island 1943,Je 17,17:2
Wintertime 1943,S 30,27:2
Carnival in Costa Rica 1947,Mr 29,21:2
Captain from Castile 1947,D 26,22:4
Deep Waters 1948,Jl 23,12:4
That Lady in Ermine 1948,Ag 25,31:2
Julia Misbehaves 1948,O 8,30:2
Beautiful Blonde From Bashful Bend, The 1949,My 28,11:2
Love That Brute 1950,My 27,10:6
Once a Thief 1951,Ja 19,21:3
Happy Go Lovely 1951,Jl 26,17:2
Jungle, The 1952,O 2,32:3
Vera Cruz 1954,D 27,22:4
Americano, The 1955,Ja 20,35:1
Racers, The 1955,F 5,13:2
Sword of Granada 1956,My 19,12:6
Leather Saint, The 1956,Je 16,12:2
Around the World in 80 Days 1956,O 18,37:1
Story of Mankind, The 1957,N 9,31:2
Villa 1958,D 24,00:0
Ocean's Eleven 1960,Ag 11,19:1
Pepe 1960,D 22,18:1
Seven Women From Hell 1962,F 1,22:2
If a Man Answers 1962,N 22,43:1
Donovan's Reef 1963,Jl 25,14:1
Castilian, The 1963,O 3,31:1
House is not a Home, A 1964,S 2,33:1
Two on a Guillotine 1965,Ja 14,44:3
Marriage on the Rocks 1965,S 16,00:0
Sergeant Deadhead 1965,O 23,17:3
Batman 1966,Ag 25,42:4
Hot Millions 1968,S 20,42:1
Romero, Eddie (Director)
Walls of Hell, The 1965,N 18,55:3
Romero, Eddie (Producer)
Walls of Hell, The 1965,N 18,55:3

Romero, Eddie (Screenwriter)
Walls of Hell, The 1965,N 18,55:3
Romero, George A (Director)
Night of the Living Dead 1968,D 5,59:2
Romero, Manuel (Director)
Caballo del Pueblo, El 1935,D 16,23:4
Radio Bar 1937,Ja 25,22:3
Que Tiempos Aquellos; Those Were the Days 1938,Mr 7,13:2
Vida es un Tango, La; Life is a Tango 1939,Jl 8,20:5
Gente Bien 1939,O 9,15:2
Mujeres que Trabajan; Women Who Work 1940,Ja 1,29:4
Divorcio en Montevideo 1940,Ap 8,15:3
Fuera de la Ley; Outside the Law 1940,My 13,21:2
Romero, Ramon (Screenwriter)
City Beneath the Sea 1953,Mr 12,24:3
Romine, Charles (Screenwriter)
Flame and the Fire 1966,Mr 29,37:1
Romm, Harry (Producer)
Hey Boy! Hey Girl! 1959,Ag 6,18:3
Stop! Look! and Laugh! 1961,F 9,36:1
Hey, Lets Twist 1962,F 8,25:1
Two Tickets to Paris 1962,N 29,46:5
Romm, Michael (Director)
Puishka; Ball of Suet, A 1934,O 28,IX,4:2 (In Addenda)
Romm, Mikhail (Director)
Thirteen, The 1937,Je 19,20:2
Lenin in October 1938,Ap 2,18:1
Lenin in 1918 1939,Je 27,27:2
Girl No 217 1945,S 3,17:2
Lenin 1950,Mr 13,15:2
Admiral Ushakov 1954,Ja 18,19:2
Attack From the Sea 1954,Ap 19,19:4
Boule de Suif 1958,My 5,24:1
Nine Days of one Year 1964,D 29,19:1
Triumph over Violence 1968,Jl 10,27:3
Romm, Mikhail (Producer)
Diary of a Nazi 1943,Mr 25,25:3
Romm, Mikhail (Screenwriter)
Girl No 217 1945,S 3,17:2
Lenin 1950,Mr 13,15:2
Boule de Suif 1958,My 5,24:1
Nine Days of one Year 1964,D 29,19:1
Triumph over Violence 1968,Jl 10,27:3
Rommer, Claire
Schlacht von Bademuende, Die 1931,N 21,20:4
Reserve Hat Ruh 1932,Ap 11,19:2
Week-End Im Paradies 1932,O 24,18:5
Walzerkoenig, Der 1932,D 5,21:2
Tausend Fuer Eine Nacht 1934,F 12,19:2
Aschermittwoch; Ash Wednesday 1935,Mr 11,15:2
Romney, Edana
Corridor of Mirrors 1949,Mr 23,35:3
Romney, Edana (Screenwriter)
Corridor of Mirrors 1949,Mr 23,35:3
Romodanov, S
Devotion 1955,Ag 1,15:2
Romulo, Rommy
Walls of Hell, The 1965,N 18,55:3
Ronald, James (Original Author)
Witness Vanishes, The 1939,O 23,15:2
Suspect, The 1945,F 1,18:5
Gay Intruders, The 1946,Mr 18,24:2
Ronane, John
Charlie Bubbles 1968,F 12,47:2
Touchables, The 1968,N 21,41:1
Ronant, Simone
Sans Famille 1959,S 5,11:4
Ronay, Edina
Night Train to Paris 1964,D 3,58:2
Study in Terror, A 1966,N 3,45:3
He Who Rides a Tiger 1968,S 10,39:1
Ronay, Mac
After the Fox 1966,D 24,11:1
Roncal, Oscar
Cry of Battle 1963,O 12,27:2
Walls of Hell, The 1965,N 18,55:3
Roncier, E
Petits, Les 1936,D 30,17:2
Roncoroni, J I (Miscellaneous)
Back to the Wall; (Dos au Mur) 1959,S 8,43:2
Roncoroni, J I (Screenwriter)
Back to the Wall; (Dos au Mur) 1959,S 8,43:2
Rondi, Brunello
Hours of Love, The 1965,S 4,11:5
Rondi, Brunello (Screenwriter)
Greatest Love, The 1954,Ja 12,19:2
Dolce Vita, La 1961,Ap 20,30:1
Eight and One Half 1963,Je 26,36:1
Juliet of the Spirits 1965,N 4,57:1
Rondi, Gian Luigi (Screenwriter)
Pepote 1958,D 2,46:1
Rondinella, Giacomo
Neapolitan Carousel 1961,O 12,41:3
Ronet, Maurice
Seven Deadly Sins, The (Lust); Lust (The Seven Deadly Sins) 1953,My 12,31:3
Desperate Decision 1954,N 9,31:5

Ronet, Maurice — Cont

Sins of the Borgias 1956,Mr 5,21:1
House of Ricordi 1956,Mr 13,32:1
Sorciere, La 1956,D 28,17:2
He Who Must Die 1958,D 29,21:1
Frantic 1961,Je 12,34:1
Purple Noon 1961,S 1,12:1
Time Out for Love 1963,Ap 23,31:2
Victors, The 1963,D 20,21:2
Fire Within, The 1964,F 18,27:1
Circle of Love 1965,Mr 25,42:4
Enough Rope 1966,Jl 15,34:3
Lost Command 1966,S 15,51:1
Champagne Murders, The 1968,Ap 25,53:1
How Sweet It Is 1968,Ag 22,47:1
Birds in Peru 1968,N 7,51:2

Ronnell, Ann (Composer)
Down to Their Last Yacht 1934,S 24,14:1
Blockade 1938,Je 17,25:1

Ronnell, Ann (Miscellaneous)
Champagne Waltz 1937,F 4,17:2

Ronnell, Ann (Original Author)
There's Magic in Music 1941,Je 5,27:2

Ronsard, Helene
Lover's Return, A; Revenant, Le 1948,Ja 26,15:2

Ronson, Peter
Journey to the Center of the Earth 1959,D 17,51:1

Rook, Heidi
One and Only Genuine Original Family Band, The 1968,Mr 22,55:1

Rooks, Conrad
Chappaqua 1967,N 6,65:2

Rooks, Conrad (Director)
Chappaqua 1967,N 6,65:2

Rooks, Conrad (Producer)
Chappaqua 1967,N 6,65:2

Rooks, Conrad (Screenwriter)
Chappaqua 1967,N 6,65:2

Rooks, Virginia (Original Author)
Mister Big 1943,Je 14,13:4

Room, Abram (Director)
Garnet Bracelet, The 1966,My 28,11:6

Room, Abram (Screenwriter)
Garnet Bracelet, The 1966,My 28,11:6

Roome, Alfred (Director)
My Brothers Keeper 1949,F 14,15:3

Rooner, Charles
Dama de las Camelias, La 1944,S 26,16:1
Pearl, The 1948,F 18,36:4
Sofia 1948,S 4,8:7
Plunder of the Sun 1953,Ag 27,22:1

Rooney, Frank (Original Author)
Wild One, The 1953,D 31,9:2

Rooney, Mickey
My Pal the King 1932,O 4,26:4
Big Cage, The 1933,My 9,20:5
Life of Jimmy Dolan, The 1933,Je 14,22:3
Broadway to Hollywood 1933,S 2,14:4
World Changes, The 1933,O 27,22:3
Chief, The 1933,D 2,9:4
Half a Sinner 1934,Je 23,16:5
Hide-Out 1934,Ag 25,16:5
Blind Date 1934,S 1,16:3
Death on the Diamond 1934,S 24,14:1
County Chairman, The 1935,Ja 19,8:1
Midsummer Night's Dream, A 1935,O 10,31:1
Ah, Wilderness! 1935,D 25,30:2
Riffraff 1936,Ja 13,14:2
Little Lord Fauntleroy 1936,Ap 3,27:1
Devil is a Sissy, The 1936,O 17,21:2
Family Affair, A 1937,Ap 20,29:2
Captains Courageous 1937,My 12,27:1
Slave Ship 1937,Je 17,19:2
Live, Love and Learn 1937,N 19,27:2
Thoroughbreds Don't Cry 1937,N 26,27:4
Love Is a Headache 1938,Ja 28,17:3
Judge Hardy's Children 1938,Ap 8,17:2
Hold That Kiss 1938,Je 11,9:1
Lord Jeff 1938,Jl 1,22:2
Love Finds Andy Hardy 1938,Jl 22,10:2
Boys Town 1938,S 9,25:1
Stablemates 1938,O 21,27:2
Out West With the Hardys 1938,D 9,31:2
Huckleberry Finn 1939,Mr 3,21:2
Hardys Ride High, The 1939,Ap 14,28:2
Andy Hardy Gets Spring Fever 1939,Jl 19,23:2
Babes in Arms 1939,O 20,27:2
Judge Hardy and Son 1940,Ja 18,27:3 (In Addenda)
Young Tom Edison 1940,Mr 15,27:2
Andy Hardy Meets Debutante 1940,Ag 2,12:2
Strike up the Band 1940,S 30,13:2
Andy Hardy's Private Secretary 1941,Mr 7,17:2
Men of Boys Town 1941,Ap 11,24:6
Life Begins for Andy Hardy 1941,Ag 22,19:4
Babes on Broadway 1942,Ja 1,37:1
Courtship of Andy Hardy, The 1942,Ap 10,21:2
Yank at Eton, A 1942,O 16,23:1
Andy Hardy's Double Life 1943,Ja 12,23:3
Human Comedy, The 1943,Mr 3,19:2
Thousands Cheer 1943,S 14,27:1
Girl Crazy 1943,D 3,27:2
Andy Hardy's Blonde Trouble 1944,My 5,17:3

National Velvet 1944,D 15,25:2
Love Laughs at Andy Hardy 1947,Ja 8,28:2
Killer McCoy 1948,F 12,31:2
Summer Holiday 1948,Je 12,8:5
Words and Music 1948,D 10,34:2
Quicksand 1950,Je 16,28:4
He's a Cockeyed Wonder 1950,O 20,32:4
Fireball, The 1950,N 10,35:4
My Outlaw Brother 1951,Ag 23,19:2
Off Limits 1953,Mr 30,25:5
Drive a Crooked Road 1954,Ap 3,19:3
Atomic Kid, The 1954,D 4,14:2
Bridges at Toko-Ri, The 1955,Ja 21,20:2
Bold and the Brave, The 1956,My 26,15:2
Francis in the Haunted House 1956,Jl 21,9:2
Operation Mad Ball 1957,N 21,38:1
Baby Face Nelson 1957,D 12,35:1
Andy Hardy Comes Home 1958,D 24,00:0
Last Mile, The 1959,F 19,27:1
Platinum High School 1960,My 26,37:3
King of the Roaring Twenties 1961,O 5,43:1
Breakfast at Tiffany's 1961,O 6,28:1
Everything's Ducky 1961,D 21,30:6
Requiem for a Heavyweight 1962,O 17,35:1
It's a Mad, Mad, Mad, Mad World 1963,N 19,47:1
Secret Invasion, The 1964,S 17,52:6
Secret Invasion, The 1964,S 17,52:5
Ambush Bay 1966,S 15,51:4
How to Stuff a Wild Bikini 1967,Ja 12,48:1
Devil in Love, The 1968,Jl 4,13:4

Rooney, Pat
Night Club 1929,Ag 12,22:2

Rooney, Philip (Original Author)
Captain Boycott 1947,D 6,11:2

Rooney, Teddy
Andy Hardy Comes Home 1958,D 24,00:0
It Happened to Jane 1959,Ag 6,18:3
Seven Ways From Sundown 1960,D 22,18:4

Roope, Fay
Frogmen, The 1951,Je 30,8:6
Day the Earth Stood Still, The 1951,S 19,37:1
Callaway Went Thataway 1951,D 6,42:1
Viva Zapata 1952,F 8,19:2
My Six Convicts 1952,Mr 28,27:3
Carbine Williams 1952,My 8,37:2
Washington Story 1952,Jl 2,22:3
Brigand, The 1952,Jl 26,9:2
Clown, The 1953,Ja 29,25:1
Charge at Feather River, The 1953,Jl 16,17:2
Alaska Seas 1954,Mr 6,13:5
Black Dakotas, The 1954,O 2,21:2
Naked Alibi 1954,O 2,21:2
Proud Ones, The 1956,Ag 11,10:2
Rack, The 1956,N 6,30:1
F B I Story, The 1959,S 25,23:1

Roope, Glover
Royal Ballet, The (Swan Lake Act II); Swan Lake Act II (The Royal Ballet) 1960,O 5,45:2

Roos, George
Native Son 1951,Je 18,19:2

Roos, Joanna
Splendor in the Grass 1961,O 11,53:1

Roos, Kelley (Original Author)
Night to Remember, A 1943,Ja 1,27:2
Scent of Mystery 1960,F 19,23:1
Come Dance With Me!; Voulez-Vous Danser Avec Moi 1960,N 8,32:6

Roos, William (Screenwriter)
Scent of Mystery 1960,F 19,23:1

Roose, Thirkild
Day of Wrath 1948,Ap 26,27:2

Roosevelt, Andre (Producer)
Goona Goona 1932,S 17,18:4

Roosevelt, Buddy
Way out West 1930,Ag 18,24:1

Roosevelt, Elliott (Miscellaneous)
Roosevelt Story, The 1947,Ag 22,11:2

Roosevelt, Franklin D
Liberation of Europe, The 1968,S 29,IV,7:1

Roosevelt, Franklin D (Original Author)
President's Mystery, The 1936,O 19,22:1

Roosevelt, James (Producer)
Pot o'Gold 1941,Ap 4,25:2

Roosevelt, Leila (Miscellaneous)
Dangerous Journey 1944,O 2,22:2

Roosevelt (Miscellaneous)
Dark Rapture 1938,O 10,14:3

Root, George Jr (Original Author)
Gang's All Here, The 1943,D 23,26:4

Root, Lynn (Miscellaneous)
Keep Smiling 1938,Ag 10,15:2

Root, Lynn (Original Author)
Milky Way, The 1936,Mr 26,27:2
Woman Chases Man 1937,Je 11,26:2
International Settlement 1938,F 12,20:3
While New York Sleeps 1938,D 22,25:3
Golden Fleecing, The 1940,N 7,33:4
Cabin in the Sky 1943,My 28,19:3
Kid From Brooklyn, The 1946,Ap 19,25:2

Root, Lynn (Screenwriter)
Step Lively, Jeeves 1937,Ap 2,19:6
Angel's Holiday 1937,My 29,20:2

Root, Lynn (Screenwriter) — Cont

Wild and Woolly 1937,S 6,20:1
Saint in London, The 1939,Jl 19,23:3
Saint Takes Over, The 1940,My 28,29:3
Millionaires in Prison 1940,Jl 16,21:3
Date With the Falcon, A 1941,N 25,33:2
Falcon takes Over, The 1942,My 30,9:2
Sky's the Limit, The 1943,S 3,15:2
Lady Luck 1946,O 31,22:3

Root, Wells (Original Author)
Prodigal, The 1931,Je 27,20:3
Racetrack 1933,Mr 6,16:6
Public Hero No 1 1935,Je 8,12:2
Prisoner of Zenda, The 1937,S 3,12:1
Man of Conquest 1939,Ap 28,31:2
Get-Away, The 1941,Jl 17,23:4

Root, Wells (Screenwriter)
Varsity 1928,O 29,29:1
Shadow of Doubt 1935,Mr 11,15:1
Public Hero No 1 1935,Je 8,12:2
Sworn Enemy 1936,S 12,20:1
Sergeant Madden 1939,Mr 24,27:2
Man of Conquest 1939,Ap 28,31:2
Thunder Afloat 1939,O 13,27:2
Flight Command 1941,Ja 17,21:2
Bad Man, The 1941,Ap 4,25:1
Get-Away, The 1941,Jl 17,23:4
Tennessee Johnson 1943,Ja 13,18:2
Salute to the Marines 1943,Ag 30,11:3
Man From Down Under, The 1943,S 27,23:2
Prisoner of Zenda, The 1952,N 5,36:2
Magnificent Obsession 1954,Ag 5,18:4
Secret of Deep Harbor 1961,O 26,39:7
Texas Across the River 1966,N 24,65:1

Rooten, Luis Van
Champion 1949,Ap 11,29:2

Roper, Brian
Naked Heart, The 1955,Mr 9,22:4

Roper, Jack
Red Mark, The 1928,O 30,27:3
Duke Steps Out, The 1929,Ap 15,22:6
Angels Over Broadway 1940,N 18,23:2
Pittsburgh Kid, The 1941,S 23,27:4
Swing Fever 1944,Ja 28,14:1

Ropes, Bradford (Original Author)
42d Street 1933,Mr 10,19:3
Stage Mother 1933,S 30,18:5
Go Into Your Dance 1935,My 4,17:2
Hit Parade, The 1937,My 31,11:2
Lord Jeff 1938,Jl 1,22:2
Hullabaloo 1940,D 19,33:1
Ship Ahoy 1942,Je 26,16:5
Buck Privates Come Home 1947,Ap 12,11:3
Pirates of Monterey 1947,D 17,41:4

Ropes, Bradford (Screenwriter)
Hit Parade, The 1937,My 31,11:2
Hit Parade of 1941 1940,D 5,33:2
True to the Army 1942,Je 15,15:4
Why Girls Leave Home 1945,Ag 4,7:3
Time of Their Lives, The 1946,N 28,40:2

Roquemore, Henry
Social Lion, The 1930,Je 14,9:4
Sporting Chance 1931,N 28,20:4
Love Takes Flight 1937,S 27,24:3
Goodbye Broadway 1938,My 14,18:1
Arkansas Traveler, The 1938,N 17,29:2
Exile Express 1939,Ag 16,21:3
Babes in Arms 1939,O 20,27:2
Pot o'Gold 1941,Ap 4,25:2
No Greater Sin 1941,Ag 29,18:2

Roquemore, Larry
West Side Story 1961,O 19,39:3

Roques, Emile
Three Waltzes 1939,Ap 25,19:2

Roquette, Susanne
Vengeance of Fu Manchu, The 1968,F 15,47:1

Roquevert, Noel
Mayor's Dilemma, The 1940,Ap 23,19:2
Carnival of Sinners 1947,Ap 8,34:2
Murderer Lives at Number 21, The 1947,Ag 18,12:3
Corbeau, Le; Raven, The 1948,F 24,21:1
Antoine and Antoinette 1948,Ap 16,29:2
Strangers in the House 1949,O 13,33:3
Justice Is Done 1953,Mr 3,23:2
Fanfan the Tulip 1953,My 5,34:2
Companions of the Night 1954,N 25,44:2
Sheep Has Five Legs, The 1955,Ag 10,19:2
Diabolique 1955,N 22,41:1
Inside a Girls' Dormitory 1956,F 6,27:7
Nana 1957,Ap 13,12:3
Parisienne, La 1958,Jl 31,27:1
Law Is the Law, The 1959,Mr 11,41:2
Women Are Weak 1959,Je 9,44:2
Babette Goes to War 1960,Je 8,46:1
Marie Octobre 1960,Ag 16,25:2
Dog, a Mouse and a Sputnik, A; Pied, a Cheval et un Sputnik, A 1960,N 1,46:2
Come Dance With Me!; Voulez-Vous Danser Avec Moi 1960,N 8,32:6
Crazy for Love 1960,N 26,13:2
Magnificent Tramp, The 1962,Ap 25,30:1
Devil and the 10 Commandments, The (Episode 7) 1963,O 15,44:1

Roquevert, Noel— Cont
Cartouche 1964,Jl 22,39:1
Rorick, Isabel Scott (Original Author)
Are Husbands Necessary? 1942,Jl 9,17:2
Rork, Al
Notorious Lady, The 1927,Ap 11,18:3
Rork, Ann
Old Loves and New 1926,Ap 20,24:7
Blonde Saint, The 1926,N 23,27:1
Prince of Head-Waiters 1927,Jl 11,23:5
Texas Steer, A 1928,Ja 2,28:1
RORKE
See Also ROURKE
Rorke, Hayden
Lust for Gold 1949,Jl 4,9:2
Sword in the Desert 1949,Ag 25,20:2
Father's Little Dividend 1951,Ap 13,18:5
Double Crossbones 1951,Ap 27,19:2
Prince Who Was a Thief, The 1951,Jl 4,13:2
Francis Goes to the Races 1951,Jl 25,19:2
Law and the Lady, The 1951,Ag 16,23:2
Starlift 1951,D 15,11:2
When Worlds Collide 1952,F 7,30:2
Above and Beyond 1953,Ja 31,10:6
South Sea Woman 1953,Je 4,33:6
Girl Next Door, The 1953,S 5,7:4
Lucky Me 1954,Ap 10,11:2
Drum Beat 1954,N 18,42:1
Eternal Sea, The 1955,Je 10,16:2
This Happy Feeling 1958,Je 19,28:2
Stranger in my Arms 1959,Mr 4,34:2
Parrish 1961,My 5,22:1
Back Street 1961,O 13,27:1
Unsinkable Molly Brown, The 1964,Jl 17,15:1
Night Walker, The 1965,Ja 21,22:1
Rorke, J F Lieutenant
Unbeliever, The 1918,F 12,9:2
Rory, Rossana
Big Boodle, The 1957,Mr 12,38:1
Angel Wore Red, The 1960,S 29,32:1
Big Deal on Madonna Street, The 1960,N 23,20:1
Come September 1961,S 8,34:1
Jessica 1962,Ap 20,20:2
Eclipse 1962,D 21,5:1
Roscher, Charles (Cinematographer)
Love Light, The 1921,Ja 10,9:1
Rosa, Enrique de
Tango-Bar 1935,Jl 6,16:3
Rosa, Giovanni
Stella del Mare; Star of the Sea 1940,My 3,17:6
Rosa, Ria
I due Gemelli; Twins, The 1938,Ag 15,11:2
Rosa, Salvatore
Up the Down Staircase 1967,Ag 18,36:2
Rosado, Rudy
Way Out 1967,O 26,54:3
Rosal, Rosa
Badjao 1962,S 21,35:1
Rosalean
Manhattan Merry-Go-Round 1937,D 31,9:3
Rosamond, Marion
I Married an Angel 1942,Jl 10,13:2
Rosanova, Rosa
Blood and Sand 1922,Ag 7,14:2
Hungry Hearts 1922,N 27,18:1
Fashion Row 1924,Ja 28,12:1
Lover of Camille, The 1924,N 11,14:1
Proud Heart 1925,N 3,25:4
Cobra 1925,D 7,19:1
Abie's Irish Rose 1928,Ap 20,26:7
Lucky Boy 1929,F 25,16:1
Rosar, Annie
Hirsekorn Greift Ein 1932,Je 10,22:3
World's in Love, The 1937,My 19,27:2
Liebe in Dreiviertel Takt; Love in Waltz Time 1938,S 24,13:1
Mozart Story, The 1948,N 15,21:5
Devil Makes Three, The 1952,Ag 30,6:2
Marika 1953,F 18,27:2
Corinna Darling 1958,Je 14,14:3
Embezzled Heaven 1959,Ap 24,23:1
Rosario
Ziegfeld Girl 1941,Ap 25,17:2
Pan-Americana 1945,Mr 23,13:2
Rosario and Antonio
Hollywood Canteen 1944,D 16,19:2
Rosas, Lilia
Enemigos 1934,Ag 18,5:6
Rosay, Francois
Papa sans le Savoir; Father Without Knowing It, A 1932,My 1,VIII,4:1 (In Addenda)
Rosay, Francoise
One Woman Idea, The 1929,Je 10,23:1
Si l'Empereur Savait Ca 1931,F 23,20:3
Magnificent Lie, The 1931,Jl 25,11:6
Chance, La 1932,My 28,18:2
He 1933,D 27,23:6
Pension Mimosas 1936,My 6,27:1
Porteuse de Pain, La 1936,Jl 1,29:5
Kermesse Heroique, La 1936,S 23,29:1
Maternite 1937,Je 8,30:2
Carnet de Bal, Un 1938,Mr 26,12:1
Bizarre, Bizarre 1939,Mr 21,27:2
Hochzeitsreise, Die; Wedding Journey, The 1939,My 13,11:5

Devil Is an Empress, The 1939,D 4,18:4
Whirlpool; (Remous) 1940,O 8,31:2
Half-Way House 1945,Ag 13,22:4
Portrait of a Woman 1946,Ap 22,26:2
Johnny Frenchman 1946,O 21,27:3
Back Streets of Paris 1948,O 16,9:2
Quartet (The Alien Corn); Alien Corn, The (Quartet) 1949,Mr 29,30:3
Saraband 1949,Je 13,16:3
September Affair 1951,F 2,19:2
Thirteenth Letter, The 1951,F 22,27:2
Women Without Names 1951,Ag 7,22:2
Ramuntcho 1953,Mr 2,19:2
Seven Deadly Sins (Pride); Pride (The Seven Deadly Sins) 1953,My 12,31:3
Red Inn, The 1954,Je 8,25:2
Naked Heart, The 1955,Mr 9,22:4
That Lady 1955,Je 11,8:7
Seventh Sin, The 1957,Je 29,10:6
Me and the Colonel 1958,Ag 27,33:1
Sound and the Fury, The 1959,Mr 28,11:1
Stop Me Before I Kill 1961,Je 22,23:4
Money, Money, Money 1962,Jl 18,20:1
Riff Raff Girls 1962,O 20,13:5
Up From the Beach 1965,Je 10,38:1
Cloportes 1966,Ap 19,36:1
Roscoe, Alan
Last of the Mohicans, The 1921,Ja 3,20:2
Spoilers, The 1923,Ag 6,14:2
Flirting With Love 1924,S 1,9:1
Long Pants 1927,Mr 29,23:2
Sawdust Paradise, The 1928,Ag 27,23:1
Mating Call, The 1928,O 8,14:2
Flight 1929,S 14,17:1
Vagabond Lover, The 1929,N 27,30:6
Seven Keys to Baldpate 1929,D 26,21:1
Call of the West 1930,My 27,27:2
Fall Guy, The 1930,My 27,27:2
Rain or Shine 1930,Ag 8,11:1
Half Shot at Sunrise 1930,O 11,21:3
Pay-Off, The 1930,N 10,16:2
Danger Lights 1930,D 15,29:1
Royal Bed, The 1931,Ja 31,15:1
Dirigible 1931,Ap 6,24:1
Subway Express 1931,My 2,23:4
Public Defender, The 1931,Ag 1,16:4
Hell Divers 1931,D 23,27:3
Ladies of the Jury 1932,Ap 2,13:2
Strangers of the Evening 1932,Je 4,9:2
Last Mile, The 1932,Ag 26,20:3
Last Man, The 1932,S 17,18:4
Death Kiss, The 1933,F 5,IX,5:3
Roscoe, Barbara
School for Scoundrels 1960,Jl 12,39:1
Roscoe, Lee
Beyond the Law 1968,S 30,60:4
Beyond the Law 1968,O 24,55:1
Rose, Alexander
Hustler, The 1961,S 27,35:1
Rose, Alexander (Original Author)
Who's Got the Action? 1962,D 26,5:4
Rose, Alexander (Producer)
Who's Got the Action? 1962,D 26,5:4
Rose, Anna Perrott (Original Author)
Room for One More 1952,Ja 16,21:2
Rose, Billy (Composer)
Take a Chance 1933,N 27,20:3
Hold That Ghost 1941,Ag 8,13:3
Rose, Clifford
Persecution and Assassination of Jean-Paul Marat as Performed by the Inmates of the Asylum of Charenton Under the Direction of the Marquis De Sade, The 1967,F 23,41:1
Rose, David
Headless Ghost, The 1959,Ap 30,37:2
Rose, David (Producer)
Sea Devils 1953,Jl 31,11:5
House of the Seven Hawks, The 1959,D 17,51:2
Rose, Edward (Miscellaneous)
Prisoner of Zenda, The 1922,Ag 1,14:3
Rose, Edward (Original Author)
Red Lights 1923,S 10,15:4
Prisoner of Zenda, The 1937,S 3,12:1
Prisoner of Zenda, The 1952,N 5,36:2
Rose, Fred (Composer)
Pot o'Gold 1941,Ap 4,25:2
Rose, Gene (Composer)
Crime of Dr Forbes, The 1936,Jl 6,11:4
Rose, George
Night my Number Came up, The 1955,D 20,39:5
Last Wagon, The 1956,S 22,20:2
Devil's Disciple, The 1959,Ag 21,12:1
Jack the Ripper 1960,F 18,37:4
Hamlet 1964,S 24,46:1
Hawaii 1966,O 11,54:1
Pink Jungle, The 1968,O 17,52:1
Rose, H (Screenwriter)
Slipper Episode, The 1938,My 19,25:2
Rose, Helen (Miscellaneous)
Designing Woman 1957,My 17,20:2
Rose, Jack (Miscellaneous)
Riding High 1950,Ap 11,26:2

Rose, Jack (Original Author)
Road to Rio 1948,F 19,29:3
I'll See You in my Dreams 1951,D 7,35:1
Rose, Jack (Producer)
Seven Little Foys, The 1955,Je 30,18:2
Beau James 1957,Je 27,21:1
Houseboat 1958,N 14,24:1
Five Pennies, The 1959,Je 19,30:1
It Started in Naples 1960,S 3,7:6
On the Double 1961,My 20,12:1
Papa's Delicate Condition 1963,Mr 7,8:5
Who's Been Sleeping in My Bed? 1963,D 26,33:2
Rose, Jack (Screenwriter)
Ladies' Man 1947,Ja 13,18:5
My Favorite Brunette 1947,Mr 20,38:2
Road to Rio 1948,F 19,29:3
Sorrowful Jones 1949,Je 6,15:2
It's a Great Feeling 1949,Ag 13,6:6
Always Leave Them Laughing 1949,N 24,48:2
Great Lover, The 1949,N 24,48:2
Daughter of Rosie O'Grady, The 1950,Mr 31,36:2
On Moonlight Bay 1951,Jl 27,15:2
Room for One More 1952,Ja 16,21:2
April in Paris 1952,D 25,34:5
Trouble Along the Way 1953,My 7,37:2
Living It Up 1954,Jl 24,6:6
Seven Little Foys, The 1955,Je 30,18:2
Beau James 1957,Je 27,21:1
Houseboat 1958,N 14,24:1
Five Pennies, The 1959,Je 19,30:1
It Started in Naples 1960,S 3,7:6
On the Double 1961,My 20,12:1
Who's Got the Action? 1962,D 26,5:4
Papa's Delicate Condition 1963,Mr 7,8:5
Who's Been Sleeping in My Bed? 1963,D 26,33:2
Rose, Jane
Summertime 1955,Je 22,25:1
Monte Carlo Story, The 1958,F 13,23:2
1 ∎ 1 1961,N 8,41:1
Rose, John C (Producer)
Incredible Mr Limpet, The 1964,Mr 26,40:4
Rose, John C (Screenwriter)
Incredible Mr Limpet, The 1964,Mr 26,40:4
Rose, Katherine
Games 1967,S 18,58:2
Rose, Norman (Narrator)
Legendary Champions, The 1968,O 29,54:1
Rose, Philip (Producer)
Raisin in the Sun, A 1961,Mr 30,24:1
Rose, Polly
Specter of the Rose 1946,S 2,12:4
Rose, Reginald (Original Author)
Dino 1957,Je 22,9:2
Rose, Reginald (Producer)
12 Angry Men 1957,Ap 15,24:1
Rose, Reginald (Screenwriter)
Crime in the Streets 1956,My 24,27:4
12 Angry Men 1957,Ap 15,24:1
Dino 1957,Je 22,9:2
Man of the West 1958,O 2,44:3
Man in the Net, The 1959,Je 11,36:2
Rose, Robert
Woman From Monte Carlo, The 1931,D 31,17:6
Lucky Devils 1933,F 20,11:5
Guadalcanal Diary 1943,N 18,29:1
Rogue River 1951,F 16,21:4
Torpedo Valley 1952,D 20,15:3
Rose, Robert (Original Author)
Lucky Devils 1933,F 20,11:5
Rose, Ruth (Original Author)
Blind Adventure 1933,O 31,24:3
Son of Kong 1933,D 30,9:2
Rose, Ruth (Screenwriter)
She 1935,Jl 26,18:2
Last Days of Pompeii, The 1935,O 17,29:2
Mighty Joe Young 1949,Jl 28,19:3
Rose, Si (Original Author)
McHale's Navy 1964,Jl 11,15:2
Rose, Si (Screenwriter)
It Happened at the World's Fair 1963,My 30,20:1
Rose, Tania (Original Author)
Touch and go 1956,Mr 20,13:2
It's a Mad, Mad, Mad, Mad World 1963,N 19,47:1
Rose, Tania (Screenwriter)
It's a Mad, Mad, Mad, Mad World 1963,N 19,47:1
Rose, Veronica
Just Smith 1934,Ap 23,20:2
Rose, Willi
Circus of Love 1958,Ag 16,10:2
Wozzeck 1962,Mr 3,13:1
Rose, William (Director)
Pamela, Pamela You Are.... 1968,D 21,49:4
Rose, William (Original Author)
Touch and go 1956,Mr 20,13:2
Smallest Show on Earth, The 1957,N 23,11:2
It's a Mad, Mad, Mad, Mad World 1963,N 19,47:1
Pamela, Pamela You Are.... 1968,D 21,49:4

Rose, William (Producer)
Pamela, Pamela You Are.... 1968,D 21,49:4
Rose, William (Screenwriter)
Operation X 1950,D 11,31:2
Lucky Nick Cain 1951,Ap 23,21:2
Glory at Sea 1953,Mr 11,36:7
Genevieve 1954,F 16,30:2
High and Dry 1954,Ag 31,25:5
Ladykillers 1956,F 21,37:2
Touch and go 1956,Mr 20,13:2
Smallest Show on Earth, The 1957,N 23,11:2
It's a Mad, Mad, Mad, Mad World
   1963,N 19,47:1
Russians are Coming the Russians are Coming,
   The 1966,My 26,55:1
Flim Flam Man, The 1967,Ag 23,40:1
Guess Who's Coming to Dinner 1967,D 12,56:1

Rose-Boliborn, Ilse
Selige Exzellenz, Die 1937,Je 15,26:2
Rose Marie
Top Banana 1954,F 20,8:6
Big Beat, The 1958,Je 26,23:4
Dead Heat on a Merry-Go-Round
   1966,O 13,50:1
Roselle, Rita
Black Camel, The 1931,Jl 4,11:5
Roselle, William
Gloria's Romance 1916,My 23,9:2
Avalanche, The 1919,Je 30,16:3
Roseman, Ben
Dementia 1955,D 23,14:4
Roseman, E
On the Banks of the Wabash 1923,O 23,21:3
America 1924,F 22,20:1
Running Wild 1927,Je 14,33:2
Rosemond, Clinton
Green Pastures, The 1936,Jl 17,20:1
They Won't Forget 1937,Jl 15,16:1
Toy Wife, The 1938,Je 24,15:1
Stand up and Fight 1939,Ja 27,17:2
Calling Dr Kildare 1939,My 12,25:4
Safari 1940,Je 20,29:2
Blossoms in the Dust 1941,Je 27,14:4
ROSEN
See Also RAWSON
Rosen, Emile
Song of the Street 1939,S 5,21:2
Rosen, Eric
John Ericsson Victor of Hampton Roads
   1938,My 18,17:2
Rosen, Herb
Synanon 1965,My 6,44:1
Rosen, Jimmy
Alice in Wonderland 1931,D 28,22:1
Rosen, Leo (Screenwriter)
Velvet Touch, The 1948,Ag 26,16:2
Rosen, Milt (Screenwriter)
Do Not Disturb 1965,D 25,17:2
Rosen, Milton (Composer)
Crazy House 1943,D 16,33:3
See my Lawyer 1945,My 4,23:4
Rosen, Paul (Director)
West of the Pecos 1934,D 29,11:2
Rosen, Phil (Director)
World's Champion, The 1922,F 27,13:4
Young Rajah, The 1922,N 6,13:1
Dramatic Life of Abraham Lincoln, The
   1924,Ja 22,17:3
Being Respectable 1924,Ag 4,16:3
This Woman 1924,O 21,21:3
Bridge of Sighs, The 1925,Mr 23,14:2
Heart of a Siren, The 1925,Ap 8,24:3
Closed Gates 1927,Je 1,25:2
Extravagance 1930,D 9,31:3
Branded Men 1931,D 12,23:3
Lena Rivers 1932,My 21,9:2
Sphinx, The 1933,Jl 6,26:5
Phantom Broadcast, The 1933,Jl 31,16:2
Devil's Mate 1933,S 23,11:7
Shadows of Sing Sing 1934,F 21,23:2
Beggars in Ermine 1934,Ap 25,25:3
Cheaters 1934,My 12,12:4
Little Men 1935,F 18,19:3
Calling of Dan Matthews 1936,Ja 25,18:4
Missing Girls 1936,O 5,25:1
President's Mystery, The 1936,O 19,22:1
Roaring Timber 1937,Ag 19,23:1
Ex-Champ 1939,My 12,25:3
Missing Evidence 1939,N 17,17:3
Double Alibi 1940,Mr 11,11:2
Crooked Road, The 1940,Je 11,33:4
Murder by Invitation 1941,Jl 23,15:4
Gangs Incorporated 1941,Ag 4,16:6
Road to Happiness 1942,Mr 27,27:4
Mystery of Marie Roget, The 1942,My 5,17:3
Step by Step 1946,Ag 24,6:7
Rosen, Phil (Producer)
Missing Evidence 1939,N 17,17:3
Rosen, Trude
Geld Regiert die Welt 1934,My 12,12:4

Rosenberg, Aaron (Producer)
Johnny Stool Pigeon 1949,S 23,28:3
Story of Molly X, The 1949,D 2,35:4
Outside the Wall 1950,Mr 15,34:8
Winchester 73 1950,Je 8,38:2
Air Cadet 1951,My 11,32:3
Cattle Drive 1951,Ag 9,17:5
Iron Man 1951,Ag 20,14:2
Bend of the River 1952,Ap 10,37:1
World in His Arms, The 1952,O 10,21:2
Thunder Bay 1953,My 21,39:2
Wings of the Hawk 1953,Ag 27,22:1
Man From the Alamo, The 1953,S 12,13:2
Glenn Miller Story, The 1954,F 11,33:2
Saskatchewan 1954,Mr 11,26:2
Six Bridges to Cross 1955,Ja 22,8:2
Far Country, The 1955,F 14,24:2
Man Without a Star 1955,Mr 25,19:3
Shrike, The 1955,Jl 8,15:2
Foxfire 1955,Jl 14,19:1
To Hell and Back 1955,S 23,21:2
World in my Corner 1956,F 18,12:5
Benny Goodman Story 1956,F 22,22:1
Backlash 1956,Ap 21,11:2
Walk the Proud Land 1956,S 8,20:6 (In
   Addenda)
Great Man, The 1957,Ja 2,28:2
Four Girls in Town 1957,Ja 17,34:5
Joe Butterfly 1957,My 30,23:2
Night Passage 1957,Jl 25,28:1
Badlanders, The 1958,S 4,33:1
Never Steal Anything Small 1959,F 12,23:1
It Started With a Kiss 1959,Ag 20,14:2
Go Naked in the World 1961,Mr 11,15:1
Mutiny on the Bounty 1962,N 9,31:2
Move Over Darling 1963,D 26,33:1
Shock Treatment 1964,Jl 23,19:1
Fate Is the Hunter 1964,D 10,61:1
Saboteur, The: Code Name-Mori Turi
   1965,Ag 26,40:2
Reward, The 1965,S 16,55:1
Do Not Disturb 1965,D 25,17:2
Caprice 1967,Je 8,52:2
Tony Rome 1967,N 16,58:1
Detective, The 1968,My 29,20:3
Lady in Cement 1968,N 21,41:1
Rosenberg, Frank P (Producer)
Man-Eater of Kumaon 1948,Jl 2,24:2
Secret of Convict Lake, The 1951,Ag 4,7:2
Return of the Texan 1952,F 14,23:1
Farmer Takes a Wife, The 1953,Je 13,11:2
King of the Khyber Rifles 1953,D 23,21:1
Illegal 1955,O 29,12:6
Miracle in the Rain 1956,Ap 2,18:1
Girl He Left Behind, The 1956,O 27,17:1
One Eyed Jacks 1961,Mr 31,21:1
Critic's Choice 1963,My 2,40:2
Madigan 1968,Mr 30,22:2
Rosenberg, Frank P (Screenwriter)
Where the Sidewalk Ends 1950,Jl 8,7:4
Rosenberg, Jerry
My Son 1939,My 10,28:2
Mirele Efros 1939,O 21,12:2
Rosenberg, Max J (Producer)
Last Mile, The 1959,F 19,27:1
Girl of the Night 1960,N 12,15:1
Lad: A Dog 1963,My 2,40:2
Psycopath, The 1966,S 29,60:1
Deadly Bees, The 1967,My 20,39:2
Danger Route 1968,Je 6,54:2
Torture Garden 1968,Jl 20,18:2
Birthday Party, The 1968,D 10,54:1
Rosenberg, Michael
Cantor's Son, The 1937,D 27,11:1
Two Sisters 1938,D 1,29:3
Mirele Efros 1939,O 21,12:2
Rosenberg, Mikhail (Screenwriter)
Girl From Leningrad 1941,D 20,25:2
Rosenberg, Philip R (Miscellaneous)
We'll Bury You 1962,O 25,48:3
Rosenberg, Stuart (Director)
Murder, Inc 1960,Je 29,26:6
Question 7 1961,S 29,30:2
Cool Hand Luke 1967,N 2,58:1
Rosenblatt, Joseph, Cantor
Jazz Singer, The 1927,O 7,24:4
Dream of My People, The 1934,F 26,21:4
Rosenblatt, Max
Mothers of Today 1939,Mr 2,19:2
ROSENBLOOM
See Also ROSENBLUM
Rosenbloom, Maxie
Muss 'Em Up 1936,F 3,21:2
Kelly the Second 1936,O 3,21:2
Nothing Sacred 1937,N 26,27:2
Kid Comes Back, The 1938,F 7,10:2
Mr Moto's Gamble 1938,Ap 8,17:2
Gangs of New York 1938,My 28,9:2
Amazing Dr Clitterhouse, The 1938,Jl 21,14:2
Submarine Patrol 1938,N 19,9:2
Women in the Wind 1939,Ap 13,27:2
Kid From Kokomo, The 1939,My 20,11:2
Naughty but Nice 1939,Je 23,23:2

Rosenbloom, Maxie— Cont
Each Dawn I Die 1939,Jl 22,12:2
20,000 Men a Year 1939,O 28,11:2
Passport to Alcatraz 1940,Je 15,12:2
Public Deb No 1 1940,S 18,19:2
Ringside Maisie 1941,Ag 1,11:2
Louisiana Purchase 1942,Ja 1,37:1
To the Shores of Tripoli 1942,Mr 26,27:2
Boogie Man Will Get You, The 1942,O 12,12:4
Swing Fever 1944,Ja 28,14:1
Follow the Boys 1944,Ap 26,24:6
Irish Eyes Are Smiling 1944,N 8,27:1
Men in her Diary 1945,S 24,16:5
Hazard 1948,Je 3,19:2
Hollywood or Bust 1956,D 24,8:1
ROSENBLUM
See Also ROSENBLOOM
Rosenblum, Charles
Last Blitzkrieg, The 1959,Ja 31,13:5
Rosendahl, Lise
Eric Soya's 17 1967,Ja 25,37:1
Rosener, George
Alias the Doctor 1932,Mr 3,22:3
Doctor X 1932,Ag 4,17:2
70,000 Witnesses 1932,S 3,16:2
Devil Is Driving, The 1932,D 16,25:5
Circus Queen Murder, The 1933,My 9,20:5
Case of the Black Cat, The 1936,D 26,15:4
House of Secrets 1937,F 22,13:1
New Faces of 1937 1937,Jl 2,25:1
Super-Sleuth 1937,Jl 17,18:1
Sh! The Octopus 1937,D 24,21:2
Confessions of a Nazi Spy 1939,Ap 29,13:2
Beasts of Berlin 1939,N 20,15:6
Abe Lincoln in Illinois 1940,F 23,19:2
Great Commandment, The 1942,O 17,11:1
Rosener, George (Original Author)
Speakeasy 1929,Mr 11,22:2
Rosenfield, Lulla (Screenwriter)
Paris Blues 1961,N 8,41:1
Rosengren, Birgit
Flickorna Fran Gamla Stan 1934,D 27,25:4
Larsson I Andra Giftet 1935,O 19,21:3
Skicka Hem Nr 7; Send Home No 7
   1939,My 9,29:2
Kvinnorna Kring Larsson; Women Around
   Larsson, The 1940,My 18,11:3
Rosenhayn, Paul (Original Author)
Careers 1929,Je 10,23:1
Rosenthal, Harry
Wife, Husband and Friend 1939,F 25,19:2
Johnny Apollo 1940,Ap 13,21:2
Great McGinty, The 1940,Ag 15,23:1
Christmas in July 1940,N 6,55:2
Birth of the Blues 1941,D 11,39:1
Great Moment, The 1944,N 13,15:2
Rosenwald, Francis (Original Author)
Follow Me Quietly 1949,Jl 8,14:5
Undercover Girl 1950,N 8,37:2
Rosenwald, Franz (Original Author)
Wife of Monte Cristo, The 1946,Ap 8,31:2
Rosetti, Franco (Screenwriter)
Constantine and the Cross 1963,Mr 14,8:2
Duel of the Titans 1963,Ag 8,19:1
Roshal, G (Director)
Seeds of Freedom 1929,S 9,30:2
Jew at War, A 1931,Jl 25,11:6
Petersburg Nights 1934,S 10,20:4
Paris Commune 1937,Je 2,20:4
Oppenheim Family, The 1939,My 24,29:2
Ivan Pavlov 1950,F 13,15:2
Mussorgsky 1951,Ag 20,14:3
Rimsky-Korsakov 1954,Mr 1,16:3
Flames on the Volga 1958,Je 27,21:7
Sisters 1959,My 25,33:2
Roshal, G (Producer)
Alego 1954,D 27,22:7
Roshal, G (Screenwriter)
New Gulliver, The 1935,N 4,24:4
Paris Commune 1937,Je 2,20:4
Mussorgsky 1951,Ag 20,14:3
Rimsky-Korsakov 1954,Mr 1,16:3
Alego 1954,D 27,22:7
Roshal, S (Screenwriter)
Jew at War, A 1931,Jl 25,11:6
Oppenheim Family, The 1939,My 24,29:2
Rosher, Charles (Cinematographer)
Little Lord Fauntleroy 1921,S 16,17:3
Atlantic 1930,Ja 26,VIII,6:2
Rosi, Francesco (Director)
Hands Over the City 1964,S 18,28:1
Salvatore Giuliano 1964,S 18,28:1
Moment of Truth, The 1965,Ag 10,18:1
More Than a Miracle 1967,N 2,58:2
Rosi, Francesco (Screenwriter)
Bellissima 1953,My 18,26:2
Hands Over the City 1964,S 18,28:1
Salvatore Giuliano 1964,S 18,28:1
Moment of Truth, The 1965,Ag 10,18:1
More Than a Miracle 1967,N 2,58:2
Rosi, Paolo
Requiem for a Heavyweight 1962,O 17,35:1

Rosi (Miscellaneous)
Bigamist, The 1958,My 12,25:1
Rosing, Bodil
Lights of Old Broadway 1925,N 2,20:1
It Must Be Love 1926,O 4,20:2
Sunrise 1927,S 24,15:3 (In Addenda)
Big Noise, The 1928,My 7,29:1
Ladies of the Mob 1928,Je 18,13:2
Wheels of Chance 1928,Jl 2,11:2
Out of the Ruins 1928,Ag 20,21:3
Betrayal 1929,My 6,30:4
Why Be Good? 1929,My 6,30:4
Eternal Love 1929,My 13,27:2
Bishop Murder Case, The 1930,F 1,15:1
All Quiet on The Western Front 1930,Ap 30,29:1
Lady's Morals, A 1930,N 8,21:3
Shepper - Newfounder, The 1930,D 25,31:5
Surrender 1931,N 28,20:4
Downstairs 1932,O 8,15:4
Match King, The 1932,D 8,25:3
Crime of the Century, The 1933,Mr 13,18:2
Reunion in Vienna 1933,Ap 29,14:2
Ex-Lady 1933,My 15,16:2
Little Man, What Now? 1934,Je 1,29:1
Crimson Romance 1934,O 13,10:1
Painted Veil, The 1934,D 7,29:1
Roberta 1935,Mr 8,25:2
Four Hours to Kill 1935,Ap 11,27:3
Night at the Ritz, A 1935,My 16,20:2
Let 'Em Have It 1935,My 30,21:1
First 100 Years, The 1938,My 13,17:2
You Can't Take It With You 1938,S 2,21:2
Nurse Edith Cavell 1939,S 22,27:4
Beasts of Berlin 1939,N 20,15:6
Reaching for the Sun 1941,My 8,21:1
No Greater Sin 1941,Ag 29,18:2
Man at Large 1941,O 11,21:4
Marry the Boss's Daughter 1941,D 4,33:4
Rosita
Rio Rita 1929,O 7,22:1
All the King's Horses 1935,Mr 9,19:1
Gold Diggers of 1935 1935,Mr 15,25:2
Rosland, Jean
Life Begins Tomorrow 1952,N 18,37:2
Rosley, Adrian
My Weakness 1933,S 22,14:1
Girl Without a Room 1933,D 7,26:3
Great Flirtation, The 1934,Je 22,16:5
Notorious Sophie Lang, The 1934,Jl 21,14:2
Enter Madame 1935,Ja 12,12:1
Roberta 1935,Mr 8,25:2
Girl From 10th Avenue, The 1935,My 27,20:6
Alibi Ike 1935,Jl 17,22:1
Here's to Romance 1935,O 3,29:2
Metropolitan 1935,O 18,27:4
Sins of Man 1936,Je 19,17:2
Gay Desperado, The 1936,O 9,31:4
Magnificent Brute, The 1936,O 24,23:1
Sing Me a Love Song 1936,D 26,15:2
Ready, Willing and Able 1937,Mr 15,27:1
King and the Chorus Girl, The 1937,Mr 29,14:4
Star Is Born, A 1937,Ap 23,25:1
Rosmer, Milton
W Plan, The 1931,Mr 23,24:7
South Riding 1938,Ag 2,15:2
Goodbye Mr Chips 1939,My 16,27:2
Stars Look Down, The 1941,Jl 24,15:2
Frieda 1947,Ag 15,12:3
Fame Is the Spur 1949,N 8,34:2
Small Back Room, The 1952,F 2,11:3
Rosmer, Milton (Director)
Jaws of Hell 1931,Ja 5,21:3
Dreyfus Case, The 1931,Ag 31,11:5
After the Ball 1933,Mr 20,18:3
Channel Crossing 1934,My 24,28:3
Mister Hobo 1936,F 8,19:2
Murder in the Old Red Barn 1936,Ag 19,18:3
Great Barrier, The 1937,F 5,17:5
Silent Barriers 1937,Mr 26,25:1
Emil 1938,Ap 15,23:2
Rosmer, Milton (Miscellaneous)
Silent Barriers 1937,Mr 26,25:1
Rosmer, Milton (Screenwriter)
Transatlantic Tunnel 1935,O 28,16:2
Silent Barriers 1937,Mr 26,25:1
Challenge, The 1939,O 2,15:2
Rosmino, Ernesta
Strange Deception 1953,My 27,28:2
Rosmino, Gian Paolo
Don Bosco 1936,My 27,27:3
Rosny, J H (Original Author)
Song of the Street 1939,S 5,21:2
Rosoff, Charles (Composer)
Under Western Stars 1938,Je 25,7:3
Rose of the Rio Grande 1938,Jl 9,10:3
Roson, Manuel
No Exit 1962,D 6,55:2
Rospigliosi, William (Original Author)
Ring Around the Clock 1953,My 19,36:2
Rosqui, Tom
Crazy Quilt, The 1966,O 4,50:1

Ross, Annabel (Original Author)
Velvet Touch, The 1948,Ag 26,16:2
Ross, Anthony
Kiss of Death 1947,Ag 28,28:2
Perfect Strangers 1950,Mr 11,8:2
Gunfighter, The 1950,Je 24,7:2
Skipper Surprised his Wife, The 1950,Je 30,18:2
Between Midnight and Dawn 1950,O 2,19:2
Flying Missile, The 1950,D 25,25:1
On Dangerous Ground 1952,F 13,35:2
Girls in the Night 1953,Ja 16,19:3
Taxi 1953,Ja 22,20:3
Rogue Cop 1954,S 18,12:2
Country Girl, The 1954,D 16,51:2
Ross, Arnold
Synanon 1965,My 6,44:1
Ross, Art (Narrator)
Harold Lloyd's World of Comedy 1962,Je 5,36:4
Ross, Arthur (Original Author)
Port of New York 1950,F 3,29:2
Okinawa 1952,Ap 24,38:3
Great Race, The 1965,S 16,00:0
Ross, Arthur (Screenwriter)
San Quentin 1947,F 10,24:3
Okinawa 1952,Ap 24,38:3
Creature from the Black Lagoon 1954,My 1,13:4
Creature Walks among Us, The 1956,Ap 27,21:6
Three Worlds of Gulliver, The 1960,D 17,19:3
Great Race, The 1965,S 16,00:0
Ross, Barney
Requiem for a Heavyweight 1962,O 17,35:1
Ross, Betty
Massacre Hill 1950,D 14,51:3
Ross, Bob (Screenwriter)
3 on a Couch 1966,Jl 7,30:1
Ross, Charles J
How Molly Made Good 1915,O 20,5:5
Ross, Chet
Safe at Home 1941,N 26,31:2
Ross, Churchill
College Hero, The 1927,N 22,32:2
Fourflusher, The 1928,Ja 16,24:1
College Love 1929,Ag 5,25:2
Ross, David (Narrator)
Isle of Paradise 1932,Jl 21,15:2
Fight for Peace, The 1938,My 14,18:1
Ross, Dennis
Return of the Texan 1952,F 14,23:1
Shadow in the Sky 1952,Jl 19,8:2
Ross, Diana
Ariane 1934,Mr 7,23:4
Ross, Dick
Good Sam 1948,S 17,28:2
Ross, Don
Anatomy of a Murder 1959,Jl 3,10:1
Ross, Donald
Broadway Hostess 1935,D 16,23:3
Ross, Edna
Deliverance 1919,Ag 19,10:1
Ross, Ellen
Pirate, The 1948,My 21,19:2
Ross, Fanya (Original Author)
Girls Under 21 1940,N 11,22:4
Affectionaly Yours 1941,My 24,18:2
Ross, Fanya (Screenwriter)
Girls Under 21 1940,N 11,22:4
Ross, Frank
Young Eagles 1930,Mr 22,22:6
Ross, Frank (Director)
Lady Says No, The 1952,Ja 7,14:3
Ross, Frank (Original Author)
More the Merrier, The 1943,My 14,17:1
Walk, Don't Run 1966,Ag 25,42:3
Ross, Frank (Producer)
Devil and Miss Jones, The 1941,My 16,21:2
Lady Takes a Chance, A 1943,S 16,25:2
Flame and the Arrow, The 1950,Jl 8,7:2
Lady Says No, The 1952,Ja 7,14:3
Robe, The 1953,S 17,32:6
Demetrius and the Gladiators 1954,Je 19,9:1
Rains of Ranchipur, The 1955,D 16,38:2
Kings Go Forth 1958,Jl 4,15:2
One Man's Way 1964,Mr 12,40:3
Mister Moses 1965,My 13,32:1
Ross, Frank (Screenwriter)
More the Merrier, The 1943,My 14,17:1
Ross, George (Original Author)
Big Fix, The 1947,My 3,10:3
Ross, Govind Raja
Flame Over India 1960,Ap 30,14:1
Ross, Hal
Jazz Singer, The 1953,Ja 14,27:3
Ross, Harry
Good Time Girl 1950,S 25,18:5
Ross, Helen
Julius Caesar 1952,N 25,33:5
Ross, Herbert
Skin Game, The 1931,Je 20,20:4
Ross, Jerry (Composer)
Damn Yankees 1958,S 27,12:7

Ross, Joe E
All Hands on Deck 1961,Ap 1,10:2
Ross, Julie
Young Cassidy 1965,Mr 23,35:1
Ross, Katharine
Shenandoah 1965,Jl 29,18:3
Singing Nun, The 1966,Mr 18,33:1
Mister Buddwing 1966,O 12,36:1
Graduate, The 1967,D 22,44:4
Ross, Lanny
Melody in Spring 1934,Mr 31,8:2
College Rhythm 1934,N 24,19:1
Stage Door Canteen 1943,Je 25,13:2
Ross, Lanny (Miscellaneous)
Gulliver's Travels 1939,D 21,29:1
Ross, Leonard Q (Leo C Rosten) (Original Author)
All Through the Night 1942,Ja 24,13:2
Ross, Leonard Q (Original Author)
They Got Me Covered 1943,Mr 5,20:2
Ross, Manning
Time Limit 1957,O 24,37:2
Ross, Marion
Forever Female 1954,Ja 13,26:2
Glenn Miller Story, the 1954,F 11,33:2
Secret of the Incas 1954,My 29,13:3
Proud and Profane, The 1956,Je 14,41:2
Lizzie 1957,Ap 5,24:2
Teacher's Pet 1958,Mr 20,33:1
Operation Petticoat 1959,D 6,38:1
Ross, Martin
Dancing Years, The 1951,Ja 29,14:4
Ross, Michael
D O A 1950,My 1,18:2
Golden Girl 1951,N 21,20:3
Don't Bother to Knock 1952,Jl 19,8:2
Against all Flags 1952,D 25,34:6
Those Redheads From Seattle 1953,O 1,34:2
Kiss Them for Me 1957,N 9,31:2
Ross, Milton
Dixie Handicap, The 1924,D 30,15:3
Street Corner 1948,D 4,9:4
Ross, Myrna
Swinger, The 1966,D 15,60:1
Ross, Nat (Director)
Stop That Man 1928,Ap 17,27:2
Ross, Peggy
Business and Pleasure 1932,F 13,23:4
Ross, Robert Lee
Blues for Lovers 1966,S 8,43:1
Ross, Rosalind (Original Author)
Savage Seven, The 1968,Ag 22,47:1
Ross, Sam (Original Author)
He Ran all the Way 1951,Je 21,24:2
Ross, Shirley
Age of Indiscretion 1935,My 18,21:2
Devil's Squadron 1936,My 11,16:2
San Francisco 1936,Je 27,21:1
Big Broadcast of 1937, The 1936,O 22,31:1
Hideaway Girl 1937,Ja 13,20:4
Waikiki Wedding 1937,Mr 25,29:1
Blossoms On Broadway 1937,D 3,29:2
Big Broadcast of 1938, The 1938,Mr 10,16:2
Prison Farm 1938,Jl 15,13:3
Thanks for the Memory 1938,D 8,34:3
Paris Honeymoon 1939,Ja 26,17:1
Cafe Society 1939,F 23,19:2
Some Like It Hot 1939,My 25,31:2
Unexpected Father 1939,Ag 11,12:2
Ross, Stan
Pretender, The 1947,Ag 12,26:2
Requiem for a Heavyweight 1962,O 17,35:1
Ross, Terry Ann
Three Faces of Eve, The 1957,S 27,16:6
All Mine to Give 1959,Ag 4,32:5
Ross, Thomas
Without Limit 1921,Mr 21,11:3
Remember the Night 1940,Ja 18,27:2
Saint's Double Trouble, The 1940,F 13,27:2
Seventeen 1940,F 29,15:2
Mortal Storm, The 1940,Je 21,25:2
Phantom Raiders 1940,Je 24,19:5
Kings Row 1942,F 3,23:2
Remarkable Andrew, The 1942,Mr 6,17:2
Ross, Vera
Girl Said No, The 1937,O 18,14:1
Ross Sisters
Broadway Rhythm 1944,Ap 14,24:6
Rosseau, Serge
Naked Autumn 1963,N 15,25:3
Rossellini, Renzo
Love at Twenty 1963,F 7,5:6
Rossellini, Roberto (Director)
Open City; Citta Aperta 1946,F 26,21:2
Paisan 1948,Mr 30,26:2
Germany Year Zero 1949,S 20,35:2
Woman 1950,F 9,36:6
Stromboli 1950,F 16,28:2
Ways of Love (The Miracle); Miracle, The (Ways of Love) 1950,D 13,50:2
Flowers of St Francis 1952,O 7,26:2
Seven Deadly Sins, The (Envy); Envy (The Seven Deadly Sins) 1953,My 12,31:3
Greatest Love, The 1954,Ja 12,19:2

Rossellini, Roberto (Director) — Cont
General Della Rovere 1960,N 22,41:1
Rise of Louis XIV, The 1967,S 26,54:2
Rossellini, Roberto (Original Author)
Stromboli 1950,F 16,28:2
Greatest Love, The 1954,Ja 12,19:2
Rossellini, Roberto (Producer)
Paisan 1948,Mr 30,26:2
Germany Year Zero 1949,S 20,35:2
Stromboli 1950,F 16,28:2
Greatest Love, The 1954,Ja 12,19:2
Blood on the Balcony 1964,Je 30,22:1
Rossellini, Roberto (Screenwriter)
Paisan 1948,Mr 30,26:2
Germany Year Zero 1949,S 20,35:2
Ways of Love (The Miracle); Miracle, The (Ways of Love) 1950,D 13,50:2
Flowers of St Francis 1952,O 7,26:2
Seven Deadly Sins, The (Envy); Envy (The Seven Deadly Sins) 1953,My 12,31:3
Greatest Love, The 1954,Ja 12,19:2
Carabiniers, Les 1967,S 28,58:3
Carabiniers, Les 1968,Ap 26,31:1
Rossen, Robert (Director)
Johnny O'Clock 1947,Mr 27,39:2
Body and Soul 1947,N 10,21:2
All the King's Men 1949,N 9,37:2
Brave Bulls, The 1951,Ap 19,39:2
Mambo 1955,Mr 31,23:3
Alexander the Great 1956,Mr 29,23:1
Island in the Sun 1957,Je 13,37:1
They Came to Cordura 1959,O 22,47:2
Hustler, The 1961,S 27,35:1
Lilith 1964,S 21,37:2
Rossen, Robert (Miscellaneous)
Unknown Soldier Speaks, The 1934,My 26,12:3
Rossen, Robert (Original Author)
Cool World, The 1964,Ap 21,42:1
Rossen, Robert (Producer)
All the King's Men 1949,N 9,37:2
Brave Bulls, The 1951,Ap 19,39:2
Alexander the Great 1956,Mr 29,23:1
Hustler, The 1961,S 27,35:1
Lilith 1964,S 21,37:2
Rossen, Robert (Screenwriter)
They Won't Forget 1937,Jl 15,16:1
Racket Busters 1938,Ag 11,13:1
Dust Be my Destiny 1939,O 7,11:2
Roaring Twenties, The 1939,N 11,12:1
Child Is Born, A 1940,Ja 11,19:2
Sea Wolf, The 1941,Mr 26,27:3
Out of the Fog 1941,Je 21,20:2
Blues in the Night 1941,D 12,35:2
Edge of Darkness 1943,Ap 10,12:4
Walk in the Sun, A 1946,Ja 12,10:6
Strange Love of Martha Ivers, The 1946,Jl 25,18:4
Johnny O'Clock 1947,Mr 27,39:2
Desert Fury 1947,S 25,35:4
All the King's Men 1949,N 9,37:2
Mambo 1955,Mr 31,23:3
Alexander the Great 1956,Mr 29,23:1
They Came to Cordura 1959,O 22,47:2
Hustler, The 1961,S 27,35:1
Lilith 1964,S 21,37:2
Rosser, John
Somebody up There Likes Me 1956,Jl 6,16:1
Rosset, Barnet L Jr (Producer)
Strange Victory 1948,S 27,27:2
Rossetti, Giuseppe
General Della Rovere 1960,N 22,41:1
Rossi, Aldo (Screenwriter)
Cinderella 1953,My 15,20:2
Rossi, Eleonora
Behind Closed Shutters 1952,Je 10,22:7
Rossi, Franco (Director)
Anita Garibaldi 1954,Mr 19,19:4
Woman in the Painting, The 1959,Ja 15,27:1
Nude Odyssey 1962,O 27,14:6
Bambole; Dolls, The (The Soup); Soup, The (The Dolls) 1965,Je 29,26:1
High Infidelity (The Scandal); Scandal, The (High Infidelity) 1965,Jl 2,17:1
Rose for Everyone, A 1967,Je 30,30:1
Rossi, Franco (Screenwriter)
Nude Odyssey 1962,O 27,14:6
Rose for Everyone, A 1967,Je 30,30:1
Rossi, Luisa
Last Chance, The 1945,N 28,21:6
Anything for a Song 1947,Ag 5,26:2
Stranger on the Prowl 1953,N 10,38:1
Lure of the Sira 1953,D 26,10:7
Awakening, The 1958,Mr 3,24:6
Rossi, Nello de
Piccoli Avventurieri; Little Adventures 1940,Ap 26,25:2
Rossi, Rita
Bandolero, The 1924,O 27,27:1
Soul Fire 1925,My 6,26:3
Rossi, Steve
Last of the Secret Agents, The? 1966,Je 23,29:1
Rossi, Tino
Moscow Nights 1938,My 3,19:3
Kiss of Fire, The 1940,N 20,27:4

Belle Meuniere, La 1948,N 24,19:2
Candide 1962,N 20,39:1
Rossi, Ugo
Ape Woman, The 1964,S 23,55:1
Rossi-Drago, Eleonora
Verginita 1953,Ap 18,17:2
Three Forbidden Stories 1953,N 16,21:4
Sensualita 1954,Ap 29,40:2
Hell Raiders of the Deep 1954,Jl 3,9:2
Daughters of Destiny (Elizabeth); Elizabeth (Daughters of Destiny) 1954,Jl 6,19:1
Awakening, The 1958,Mr 3,24:6
Under ten Flags 1960,S 16,24:1
Violent Summer 1961,My 20,12:1
David and Goliath 1961,O 7,14:3
Love at Twenty 1963,F 7,5:6
Let's Talk About Women 1964,S 29,52:5
Facts of Murder, The 1965,Jl 1,34:1
Love and Marriage (The Last Resort); Last Resort, The (Love and Marriage) 1966,Ag 5,20:1
Bible, The 1966,S 29,60:1
Rossif, Frederic (Director)
To Die in Madrid 1965,S 16,00:0
Rossif, Frederic (Miscellaneous)
Witness, The 1967,N 7,47:1
Rossing, Bod"
Woman From Moscow, The 1928,N 5,26:1
Rossington, Norman
Carry on Sergeant 1959,O 28,40:5
Saturday Night and Sunday Morning 1961,Ap 4,44:2
Tobruk 1967,F 9,33:2
Negatives 1968,O 15,40:1
Rossini, Gioacchino (Composer)
Barber of Seville 1949,Jl 21,21:2
Cinderella 1953,My 15,20:2
Rossini, Gioacchino (Original Author)
Barber of Seville, The 1947,My 6,35:2
First Opera Film Festival 1948,My 31,12:7
Rossini, Nino
Smiling Along 1939,F 20,13:2
End of the River, The 1948,Je 21,18:2
Rossiter, Leonard
This Sporting Life 1963,Jl 17,19:2
Billy Liar 1963,D 17,49:1
They all Died Laughing 1964,Mr 16,37:2
King Rat 1965,O 28,48:1
Hotel Paradiso 1966,O 15,34:2
Deadlier Than the Male 1967,F 22,21:1
Whisperers, The 1967,Ag 1,24:1
2001 A Space Odyssey 1968,Ap 4,58:1
Rossitto, Angelo
Beloved Rogue, The 1927,Mr 14,16:1
Old San Francisco 1927,Je 23,23:3
Rossler, Karl (Original Author)
Waltz Time 1946,F 11,25:2
Rossman, Earl (Producer)
Kivalina of the Ice Lands 1925,Je 23,24:2
Rossmann, Herman (Original Author)
Hell in the Heavens 1934,D 12,28:2
Rosson, Arthur (Director)
Prisoners of Love 1921,Ja 17,9:1
Garrison's Finish 1923,My 28,18:2
Wet Paint 1926,My 17,19:1
Stranded in Paris 1926,D 13,27:1
Silk Legs 1927,D 26,26:6
Play Girl, The 1928,Ap 23,20:2
Long, Long Trail, The 1929,N 4,28:1
Rosson, Richard (Director)
Fine Manners 1926,Ag 30,10:3
Blonde or Brunette 1927,Ja 11,18:2
Ritzy 1927,Je 20,25:3
Rolled Stockings 1927,Jl 19,27:2
Wizard, The 1927,N 28,18:5
Escape, The 1928,My 7,29:1
West Point of the Air 1935,Ap 6,10:1
Behind the Headlines 1937,Je 1,27:2
Hideaway 1937,S 25,10:2
Corvette K-225 1943,O 21,30:1
Rosson, Robert (Producer)
Undercover Man, The 1949,Ap 21,30:2
Rosson, Robert (Screenwriter)
Marked Woman 1937,Ap 12,15:2
Rostand, Edmond (Original Author)
Cyrano de Bergerac 1925,Jl 6,12:2
Cyrano De Bergerac 1950,N 17,31:2
Rostand, Maurice (Original Author)
Man I Killed, The 1932,Ja 20,17:4
Rosten, Leo (Original Author)
Dark Corner, The 1946,My 9,27:3
Sleep, My Love 1948,F 19,29:4
Where Danger Lives 1951,Ja 1,13:6
Double Dynamite 1951,D 26,19:4
Mister Cory 1957,F 23,13:1
Captain Newman, MD 1964,F 21,36:1
Rosten, Leo (Screenwriter)
Conspirators, The 1944,O 21,15:2
Lured 1947,Ag 29,14:4
Sleep, My Love 1948,F 19,29:4
Walk East on Beacon 1952,My 29,17:2
Rosten, Norman (Screenwriter)
View From the Bridge, A 1962,Ja 23,36:1

Rostotsky, Stanislav (Director)
House on the Front Line, The 1963,S 2,18:1
Rostotsky, Stanislav (Screenwriter)
House on the Front Line, The 1963,S 2,18:1
Rostovtsef, Z
Krasnaya Derevnya 1935,My 2,17:1
Rostsk, Anna
First Start, The 1953,F 2,17:3
Rosty, Estephen
Little Miss Devil 1951,D 8,9:2
Roswaenge, Helge
Letzte Rose 1936,O 10,21:3
Rota, Giovanni
Romeo and Juliet 1954,D 22,28:1
Roteler, Wade
O'Shaughnessy's Boy 1935,O 5,18:2
ROTH
See Also ROTHE
Roth, Arthur (Original Author)
Night Fighters, The 1960,D 15,59:1
Roth, Bosy
Give Me a Sailor 1938,Ag 11,31:1
Roth, Elliott
Merton of the Movies 1924,S 8,15:3
Guilty Generation, The 1931,N 21,20:4
Roth, Gene
Baron of Arizona, The 1950,Je 23,29:2
Red Planet Mars 1952,Je 16,15:2
Farmer Takes a Wife, The 1953,Je 13,11:2
Roth, Hans
Blue Angel, The 1930,D 6,21:3
Roth, Joseph (Original Author)
Sins of Man 1936,Je 19,17:2
Roth, Leon (Producer)
Luck of Ginger Coffey, The 1964,S 22,44:1
Roth, Lillian
Love Parade, The 1929,N 20,32:6
Vagabond King, The 1930,F 20,22:4
Vagabond King, The 1930,Mr 2,IX,5:1
Honey 1930,Mr 29,23:1
Animal Crackers 1930,Ag 29,20:3
Madam Satan 1930,O 6,21:1
Sea Legs 1930,N 11,29:1
Ladies They Talk About 1933,F 25,20:4
Take a Chance 1933,N 27,20:3
Roth, Lillian (Original Author)
I'll Cry Tomorrow 1956,Ja 13,18:1
Roth, Lois (Original Author)
Maya 1966,Je 23,29:4
Roth, Marta
Massacre 1956,Je 2,13:5
Roth, Mickey
Anna and the King of Siam 1946,Je 21,20:2
Magic Town 1947,O 8,29:2
Roth, Murray (Director)
Don't Bet on Love 1933,Jl 31,16:2
Million Dollar Ransom 1934,S 19,15:2
Chinatown Squad 1935,My 30,21:1
Flying Hostess 1936,D 14,29:4
Roth, Murray (Original Author)
Don't Bet on Love 1933,Jl 31,16:2
Roth, Nancy
Yours, Mine and Ours 1968,Ap 25,53:1
Roth, Noreen
Southerner, The 1945,Ag 27,22:3
Roth, Paul Edwin
City of Torment 1950,Je 10,11:4
Our Daily Bread 1950,O 9,21:6
Great British Train Robbery, The 1967,Ap 6,45:2
Roth, Rose Rene
Town Without Pity 1961,O 11,53:1
Roth, Sandy
Beast of the City, The 1932,Mr 14,13:3
Hell's Highway 1932,S 26,18:2
Rotha, Paul (Director)
No Resting Place 1952,My 5,18:5
Rotha, Paul (Screenwriter)
Phantom Fiend 1935,Ap 22,14:2
No Resting Place 1952,My 5,18:5
Rotha, Wanda
Mrs Fitzherbert 1950,My 11,37:2
Saadia 1954,Mr 20,10:5
Circus World 1964,Je 26,34:2
Rothafel, S L (Composer)
4 Devils 1928,O 4,26:3
Rothafel, S L (Miscellaneous)
Under Four Flags 1918,N 18,13:3
And Women Must Weep 1922,F 20,7:1
Mother Machree 1928,Mr 6,20:3
Rothapfel, S L (Miscellaneous)
Easiest Way, The 1917,Ap 9,13:4 (In Addenda)
Rothauser, Eduard
Manon Lescaut 1926,N 30,27:1
Hertha's Erwachen 1933,Mr 14,18:3 (Incorrect in this edition; use 1933,Mr 14,19:2 elsewhere)
Rothberg, Wolf v
Week-End Im Paradies 1932,O 24,18:5
ROTHE
See Also ROTH
Rothe, Bendt
Gertrud 1966,Je 3,33:1

Rothe, Frank
Wind Across the Everglades 1958,S 12,21:1
Rothenberg, Jacob (Miscellaneous)
8 X 8 1957,Mr 16,13:2
Rothenberger, Anneliese
Rosenkavalier, Der 1962,O 10,57:1
Rother, Arthur Prof (Composer)
Marriage of Figaro 1950,N 3,31:2
Rothier, Leon
Webb Singing Pictures 1917,Ja 15,7:1
Rothman, Benjamin (Director)
Last Chapter, The 1966,F 22,14:5
Rothman, Benjamin (Producer)
Last Chapter, The 1966,F 22,14:5
Rothman, Lawrence (Director)
Last Chapter, The 1966,F 22,14:5
Rothman, Lawrence (Producer)
Last Chapter, The 1966,F 22,14:5
Rothstein, Arnold Mrs (Screenwriter)
Now I'll Tell 1934,My 26,12:2
Rothwell, Talbot (Screenwriter)
Carry on Cleo 1965,O 23,17:2
Rotmund, Ernst
Aufforderung zum Tanz; Invitation to the Dance 1935,N 23,23:3
Rotov, P V (Miscellaneous)
Spartakiada 1929,Jl 8,17:3
Rotter, Fritz (Miscellaneous)
Affairs of Maupassant, The 1938,F 12,20:2
Rotter, Fritz (Original Author)
Something in the Wind 1947,Ag 29,14:3
September Affair 1951,F 2,19:2
Rou, Alexander (Director)
May Night 1953,Jl 13,22:4
Stars of the Ukraine 1953,Jl 13,22:4
Roubaud, Andre (Composer)
Collier de la Reine, Le; Queen's Necklace, The 1929,D 8,X,7:1
Roubert, Matty
Close Harmony 1929,Ap 29,29:2
Up Pops the Devil 1931,My 16,13:3
Roubicek, George
One That Got Away, The 1958,Ap 23,40:2
Rouch, Jean (Director)
Chronicle of a Summer; Chronique d'un Ete 1965,My 7,34:1
Six in Paris 1965,S 16,54:2
Adolescents, The (Marie-France and Veronica); Marie-France and Veronica (The Adolescents) 1967,Ap 14,33:1
Lion Hunters, The 1967,S 26,54:4
Rouch, Jean (Screenwriter)
Adolescents, The (Marie-France and Veronica); Marie-France and Veronica (The Adolescents) 1967,Ap 14,33:1
Lion Hunters, The 1967,S 26,54:4
Roude, Neil
Harvey Middleman, Fireman 1965,Jl 13,39:1
Roudenko, Vladimir
Napoleon 1929,F 12,23:1
Roueche, Berton (Original Author)
Bigger Than Life 1956,Ag 3,11:2
Rouer, Germaine
Cousine Bette, La 1928,Ag 12,VII,3:4
Rouff, Jean-Jacques (Miscellaneous)
Senechal the Magnificent 1958,O 14,44:1
Rouff, Jean-Jacques (Screenwriter)
Senechal the Magnificent 1958,O 14,44:1
Rouffaer, Senne
Man With the Shaven Head, The 1966,S 21,42:2
Rouffe, Alida
Marius 1933,Ap 14,22:5
Mam'zelle Nitouche 1933,N 20,18:3
Fanny 1948,F 13,26:2
Cesar 1948,O 28,36:2
Rougeul, Jean
Eight and One Half 1963,Je 26,36:1
Rouillard, Jacqueline
Two of Us, The 1968,F 20,53:1
Rouleau, Raymond
Femme Nue, La 1933,Ag 25,12:3
Affair Lafont, The; Conflit 1939,O 9,15:2
drame De Shanghai; Shanghai Drama, The 1945,Ja 11,19:2
Paris Frills 1946,N 25,38:3
Who Killed Santa Claus? 1948,Ap 21,33:2
Honorable Catherine, The 1948,Ag 23,13:3
Just a big Simple Girl; Une Grande Fille Toute Simple 1949,O 28,29:2
Witches of Salem 1958,D 9,54:2
Rouleau, Raymond (Director)
Witches of Salem 1958,D 9,54:2
Lovers of Teruel, The 1962,D 15,5:1
Rouleau, Raymond (Screenwriter)
Lovers of Teruel, The 1962,D 15,5:1
Roulien, Raul
Delicious 1931,D 26,15:5
Careless Lady 1932,Ap 18,19:2
State's Attorney 1932,My 6,15:3
Painted Woman, The 1932,S 16,24:4
Primavera en Otono 1933,My 18,17:3
El Ultimo Varon Sobre la Tierra 1933,Je 12,20:4
It's Great to be Alive 1933,Jl 8,14:6

No Dejes la Puerta Abierta 1933,N 6,24:4
Flying Down to Rio 1933,D 22,25:2
World Moves On, The 1934,Je 30,18:5
Granaderos del Amor 1934,S 4,23:4
Asegure a su Mujer; Insure Your Wife 1935,Mr 12,25:3
Roulien, Rosas, Enrique de
Te Quiero con Locura; I'm Crazy About You 1935,N 4,24:6
Rounitch, Joseph
Taras Bulba 1927,D 28,26:6
Rounseville, Robert
Tales of Hoffmann 1951,Ap 5,34:2
Carousel 1956,F 17,13:1
Rouquier, Georges (Miscellaneous)
Farrebique 1948,F 24,21:2
Rouquier, Georges (Producer)
Farrebique 1948,F 24,21:2
ROURKE
See Also RORKE
Rourke, Thomas (Original Author)
Thunder Below 1932,Je 20,11:2
Rouse, Russell (Director)
Well, The 1951,S 27,37:2
Thief, The 1952,O 16,37:1
Wicked Woman 1954,Mr 27,13:6
New York Confidential 1955,F 19,18:1
Fastest Gun Alive, The 1956,Jl 13,23:3
House of Numbers 1957,S 13,15:2
Thunder in the Sun 1959,Ap 9,37:2
House is not a Home, A 1964,S 2,33:1
Oscar, The 1966,Mr 5,16:1
Caper of the Golden Bulls, The 1967,Je 22,46:1
Rouse, Russell (Original Author)
Pillow Talk 1959,O 7,47:2
Rouse, Russell (Screenwriter)
Nothing but Trouble 1945,Mr 10,14:1
D O A 1950,My 1,18:2
Well, The 1951,S 27,37:2
Thief, The 1952,O 16,37:1
Wicked Woman 1954,Mr 27,13:6
New York Confidential 1955,F 19,18:1
Fastest Gun Alive, The 1956,Jl 13,23:3
House of Numbers 1957,S 13,15:2
Thunder in the Sun 1959,Ap 9,37:2
House is not a Home, A 1964,S 2,33:1
Oscar, The 1966,Mr 5,16:1
Rousil, Robert (Original Author)
Young Torless 1968,Jl 23,27:2
ROUSSEAU
See Also RUSSO
Rousseau, Louise (Original Author)
Rockin' in The Rockies 1945,Jl 5,7:2
Rousseau, Marcel
13 Rue Madeleine 1947,Ja 16,30:2
Rousseliere, Jean
Mam'zelle Nitouche 1933,N 20,18:3
Roussell, Henry
Nuit est a Nous, La; (Night is Ours, The) 1931,F 21,15:2
Roussell, Henry (Director)
Sheik's Wife, The 1922,Mr 6,9:3
Nuit est a Nous, La; (Night is Ours, The) 1931,F 21,15:2
Roussell, Henry (Screenwriter)
Sheik's Wife, The 1922,Mr 6,9:3
Rousset, Madeleine
Gigi 1950,Ja 31,20:2
Roussillon, Jean-Paul
Deadlier Than the Male 1957,O 9,41:1
Marriage of Figaro, The 1963,Ap 30,26:1
Roussin, Andre
Vie de Boheme, La 1947,N 28,37:4
Paris Waltz, The 1950,Ag 23,35:2
Ostrich Has two Eggs, The 1960,S 27,40:1
Roussin, Andre (Miscellaneous)
Ostrich Has two Eggs, The 1960,S 27,40:1
Roussin, Andre (Original Author)
Little Hut, The 1957,My 4,25:1
Ostrich Has two Eggs, The 1960,S 27,40:1
Roussin, Andre (Screenwriter)
Just a big Simple Girl; Une Grande Fille Toute Simple 1949,O 28,29:2
Roustang, Pierre (Producer)
Love at Twenty 1963,F 7,5:6
Paris Secret 1965,S 4,11:5
Routh, Jonathan
30 Is a Dangerous Age, Cynthia 1968,Mr 5,34:1
Routledge, Patricia
To Sir, With Love 1967,Je 15,56:1
Matter of Innocence, A 1968,F 22,36:1
30 Is a Dangerous Age, Cynthia 1968,Mr 5,34:1
Don't Raise the Bridge, Lower the River 1968,Jl 13,18:1
Rouve, Pierre (Producer)
Millionairess, The 1961,F 10,19:1
I Like Money 1962,My 19,18:2
Rouve, Pierre (Screenwriter)
I Like Money 1962,My 19,18:2
Rouvel, Catherine
Picnic on the Grass 1960,O 12,47:1
Landru 1963,Ap 10,31:1
Benjamin 1968,Mr 26,41:2

Rouverol, Aurania (Miscellaneous)
Love Finds Andy Hardy 1938,Jl 22,10:2
Out West With the Hardys 1938,D 9,31:2
Judge Hardy and Son 1940,Ja 18,27:3 (In Addenda)
Courtship of Andy Hardy, The 1942,Ap 10,21:2
Rouverol, Aurania (Original Author)
Family Affair, A 1937,Ap 20,29:2
You're Only Young Once 1938,Ja 3,16:2
Judge Hardy's Children 1938,Ap 8,17:2
Hardys Ride High, The 1939,Ap 14,28:2
Andy Hardy Gets Spring Fever 1939,Jl 19,23:2
Andy Hardy's Private Secretary 1941,Mr 7,17:2
Life Begins for Andy Hardy 1941,Ag 22,19:4
Andy Hardy's Double Life 1943,Ja 12,23:3
Andy Hardy's Blonde Trouble 1944,My 5,17:3
Love Laughs at Andy Hardy 1947,Ja 8,28:2
Rouverol, Aurania (Screenwriter)
Dance, Fools, Dance 1931,Mr 21,15:1
Rouverol, Jean
It's a Gift 1935,Ja 5,20:2
Private Worlds 1935,Mr 28,25:2
Fatal Lady 1936,Jl 11,11:3
Road Back, The 1937,Je 18,25:2
Stage Door 1937,O 8,27:2
Law West of Tombstone, The 1938,N 25,19:1
Annabel Takes a Tour 1938,D 29,15:3
Rouverol, Jean (Screenwriter)
So Young, So Bad 1950,Jl 24,15:2
Legend of Lylah Clare, The 1968,Ag 23,33:1
Rouviere, Simone
Avec l'Assurance 1935,My 4,17:3
ROUX
See Also ROWE, ROE
Roux, Carmen La
Hombre Peligroso, Un; Dangerous Man, A 1935,O 14,21:2
Roux, Jacques
List of Adrian Messenger, The 1963,My 30,20:1
Secret War of Harry Frigg, The 1968,Mr 5,34:5
Roux, Michel
Holiday for Henrietta 1955,Ja 25,21:1
Female, The 1960,Ap 28,29:1
Rouye, Pierre (Screenwriter)
Trial and Error 1962,N 17,17:2
Rouyer, Louis
Pecheurs d'Islande 1935,S 21,18:2
Rove, Billie
Adoration 1929,Ja 14,20:1
Rovelle, Camille
Nix on Dames 1929,N 23,18:5
Madame Du Barry 1934,O 25,26:2
Rovensky, J (Director)
Ecstasy of Young Love 1936,Mr 10,27:3
Rovera, Marcella
Strada, La 1956,Jl 17,19:2
Five Day Lover, The 1961,D 14,55:4
Rovere, Gina
Hercules 1959,Jl 23,32:2
Love a la Carte 1965,Ja 12,31:1
All the Other Girls Do! 1967,My 30,12:1
Rovere, Luigi (Producer)
Mafia; (In Nome Della Legge) 1950,Mr 2,33:2
Behind Closed Shutters 1952,Je 10,22:7
Path of Hope, The (Il Cammino Della Speranza) 1952,Ag 5,15:5
White Sheik, The 1956,Ap 26,37:4
Roversi, Ermanno
Passa L'Amore 1933,N 25,10:3
Musica in Piazza 1936,My 7,21:3
Rovinskaya, Valentina
False Uniforms 1932,N 19,20:2
Rovira-Beleta (Director)
Tarantos, Los 1964,Je 30,22:1
Rovira-Beleta (Screenwriter)
Tarantos, Los 1964,Je 30,22:1
Row, Alexander (Director)
Cinderella 1961,D 19,39:1
Night Before Christmas, A 1963,D 16,44:4
Row, Alexander (Producer)
Cinderella 1961,D 19,39:1
Row, Alexander (Screenwriter)
Cinderella 1961,D 19,39:1
Night Before Christmas, A 1963,D 16,44:4
Rowan, Andrew S Lieutenant (Original Author)
Message to Garcia, A 1936,Ap 10,27:1
Rowan, Dan
Hot Horse 1963,Jl 25,14:2
Rowan, Don
Whipsaw 1936,Ja 25,18:4
Sudden Death, And 1936,Jl 18,18:2
Return of Sophie Lang, The 1936,Jl 24,13:1
Devil's Playground 1937,F 15,12:5
When's Your Birthday? 1937,Mr 19,27:2
Racket Busters 1938,Ag 11,13:1
Wanted by the Police 1938,S 26,13:2
ROWE
See Also ROE, ROUX
See Also ROE
Rowe, Earl
Blob, The 1958,N 7,23:1

Rowe, Frances
They Came to a City 1945,F 19,21:3
Miss Robin Hood 1953,Je 27,7:2
Rowe, Tom (Screenwriter)
Paris Secret 1965,S 4,11:5
Rowell, Ross E Major
Unbeliever, The 1918,F 12,9:2
Rowensky, Josef
Maedel von der Reeperbahn, Das 1931,Ja 31,15:1
Rowina, H
Chalutzim 1934,Ap 2,13:3
ROWLAND
See Also ROLAND, ROLLAND
Rowland, E G (Director)
Payment in Blood 1968,D 5,59:1
Rowland, E G (Original Author)
Payment in Blood 1968,D 5,59:1
Rowland, E G (Screenwriter)
Payment in Blood 1968,D 5,59:1
Rowland, Helen
Making of O'Malley 1925,Je 22,10:2
Rowland, Henry
Berlin Correspondent 1942,S 4,19:2
Moon Is Down, The 1943,Mr 27,8:6
Paris After Dark 1943,O 23,11:1
Winged Victory 1944,D 21,16:2
To the Victor 1948,Ap 17,11:2
Rogues' Regiment 1948,D 20,31:2
Sealed Cargo 1951,My 24,47:1
All the Brothers Were Valiant 1953,D 29,19:2
Rowland, Richard (Director)
Careless Age, The 1929,S 21,17:1
Rowland, Richard (Producer)
I'd Give my Life 1936,Ag 17,9:1
Cheers for Miss Bishop 1941,Mr 14,17:2
Rowland, Roy (Director)
Lost Angel 1944,Ap 10,14:1
Our Vines Have Tender Grapes 1945,S 7,21:2
Boy's Ranch 1946,Ag 9,12:2
Romance of Rosy Ridge, The 1947,S 12,18:3
Killer McCoy 1948,F 12,31:2
Scene of the Crime 1949,Jl 29,12:2
Outriders, The 1950,Mr 9,25:2
Two Weeks With Love 1950,N 24,31:2
Excuse my Dust 1951,Je 28,21:2
Bugles in the Afternoon 1952,Mr 5,32:2
5,000 Fingers of Dr T, The 1953,Je 20,8:6
Affair With a Stranger 1953,Jl 11,8:2
Moonlighter, The 1953,S 23,37:2
Witness to Murder 1954,Ap 16,16:4
Rogue Cop 1954,S 18,12:2
Many Rivers to Cross 1955,F 24,21:2
Hit the Deck 1955,Mr 4,17:1
Meet Me in Las Vegas 1956,Mr 14,39:2
These Wilder Years 1956,Ag 18,11:2
Slander 1957,Ja 17,34:4
Gun Glory 1957,Jl 20,8:7
Seven Hills of Rome 1958,Ag 28,24:2 (Incorrect
in this edition; use 1958,Ja 31,24:2 elsewhere)
Gunfighters of Casa Grande 1965,S 2,36:1
Rowland, Steve
Student Prince, The 1954,Je 16,18:2
Gun Glory 1957,Jl 20,8:7
Gunfighters of Casa Grande 1965,S 2,36:1
Rowland, William (Director)
Perfidia; Perfidy 1940,F 17,9:3
Odio; Hate 1940,Ap 6,13:2
Woman in the Night 1948,Ja 10,16:2
Rowland, William (Original Author)
This Rebel Breed 1960,My 5,41:2
Rowland, William (Producer)
Di que me Quieres; Say That You Love Me
1939,Ap 24,13:2
Perfidia; Perfidy 1940,F 17,9:3
This Rebel Breed 1960,My 5,41:2
Rowlands, Gena
High Cost of Loving, The 1958,My 17,12:1
Lonely are the Brave 1962,Je 28,21:2
Spiral Road, The 1962,Ag 4,11:2
Child Is Waiting, A 1963,F 14,5:6
Tony Rome 1967,N 16,58:1
Faces 1968,S 23,42:4
Faces 1968,N 25,54:2
Rowlands, Patsy
Tom Jones 1963,O 8,48:1
Rowles, Jack (Original Author)
That Night 1957,O 15,39:3
Rowles, Jack (Screenwriter)
That Night 1957,O 15,39:3
Rowles, Polly
Wings Over Honolulu 1937,My 29,20:1
Vogues of 1938 1937,Ag 20,21:1
Some Blondes Are Dangerous 1937,N 3,29:3
Rowley, Douglas
These Thousand Hills 1959,My 7,36:1
Rowman, Lee
Up in Mabel's Room 1944,Ap 22,8:6
Rox, John (Composer)
Sioux City Sue 1947,Jl 23,19:3
Rox, Sydney (Screenwriter)
Beachcomber, The 1955,Ja 17,27:5

Roxanne
Seven Year Itch, The 1955,Je 4,9:1
Young Don't Cry, The 1957,Jl 27,10:7
Roy, Billy
Aloma of the South Seas 1941,Ag 28,23:4
Lydia 1941,S 19,27:1
Hangmen Also Die 1943,Ap 16,24:2
Cross of Lorraine, The 1943,D 3,27:4
Passage to Marseille 1944,F 17,12:5
Corn is Green, The 1945,Mr 30,18:2
It Happened in Brooklyn 1947,Mr 14,28:5
Roy, Charu
Shiraz 1929,Mr 19,37:2
Throw of the Dice 1930,Ja 6,30:5
Roy, Claude
Boys' School 1939,Je 6,26:2
Roy, Ernest (Producer)
Wall of Death 1952,My 19,12:4
Hundred Hour Hunt 1953,Je 17,32:2
Roy, Gloria
Hot Pepper 1933,Ja 23,9:2
Charlie Chan's Greatest Case 1933,O 7,18:4
Jimmy and Sally 1933,D 16,12:3
Charlie Chan's Secret 1936,Ja 18,19:4
Song and Dance Man 1936,Mr 12,18:2
Crack-Up 1937,Ja 4,20:4
Frontier Marshal 1939,Jl 29,18:2
Roy, Rosalie
Transatlantic 1931,Jl 31,15:2
Young as You Feel 1931,Ag 8,16:3
Roy, Satyajit (Director)
Pather Panchali 1958,S 23,37:2
Roy, Satyajit (Screenwriter)
Pather Panchali 1958,S 23,37:2
Roy, Shibsankar
Kanchenjungha 1966,Jl 26,27:2
Royal, Ballet members
Evening With the Royal Ballet, An 1965,D 9,60:1
Royal, Charles Francis (Screenwriter)
New Adventures of Tarzan, The 1935,O 15,19:3
Outlaws of the Orient 1937,S 25,10:2
Shadows of the Orient 1937,O 11,26:6
Gangs of New York 1938,My 28,9:2
Royal, Lloyd (Producer)
Jesse James' Women 1954,S 29,23:4
Royal Canadian Air Force
Journey Together 1946,Mr 4,16:5
Royal Cansinos, The
Dancing Pirate 1936,Je 18,19:1
Royal Indian Ballet and Opera
Vagabond, The 1956,Ap 16,30:4
Royce, John
Claudia 1943,N 5,23:2
Royce, Julian
Criminal at Large 1933,D 20,27:2
Royce, Lionel
Confessions of a Nazi Spy 1939,Ap 29,13:2
Six Thousand Enemies 1939,Je 9,26:2
Conspiracy 1939,Ag 23,19:2
Nurse Edith Cavell 1939,S 22,27:4
Pack up Your Troubles 1939,O 27,27:2
Four Sons 1940,Je 8,18:4
Man I Married, The 1940,Ag 3,9:2
Son of Monte Cristo, The 1940,D 5,33:1
Victory 1940,D 23,23:2
So Ends our Night 1941,F 28,17:2
Lady Has Plans, The 1942,Mr 5,27:1
My Favorite Blonde 1942,Ap 2,27:2
My Favorite Spy 1942,My 29,13:4
Bomber's Moon 1943,Jl 31,8:2
Hitler Gang, The 1944,My 8,15:2
Gilda 1946,Mr 15,27:2
Royce, Rita
Good Neighbor Sam 1964,Jl 23,19:1
Roye, Philip
Sergeant, The 1968,D 26,53:5
Royere, Richard (Miscellaneous)
Point of Order 1964,Ja 15,27:2
Royle, Edwin Milton (Original Author)
Squaw Man, The 1931,S 19,10:2
Royle, Selena
Misleading Lady, The 1932,Ap 9,18:1
Stage Door Canteen 1943,Je 25,13:2
Mrs Parkington 1944,O 13,16:1
Main Street After Dark 1945,Ja 13,15:4
This Man's Navy 1945,Ap 16,18:6
Harvey Girls, The 1946,Ja 25,26:2
Green Years, The 1946,Ap 5,21:2
Till the End of Time 1946,Jl 24,24:1
Courage of Lassie 1946,Jl 25,18:5
Night and Day 1946,Jl 26,16:2
Gallant Journey 1946,O 10,33:2
No Leave, No Love 1946,O 18,29:2
Romance of Rosy Ridge, The 1947,S 12,18:3
Cass Timberlane 1947,N 7,20:2
You Were Meant for Me 1948,Ja 29,27:5
Summer Holiday 1948,Je 12,8:5
Date with Judy, A 1948,Ag 7,8:2
Joan of Arc 1948,N 12,30:5
Moonrise 1949,Mr 7,17:2
Bad Boy 1949,Mr 23,35:2
My Dream Is Yours 1949,Ap 16,11:3
You're my Everything 1949,Jl 23,7:2

Royle, Selena— Cont
Heiress, The 1949,O 7,35:2
Damned Don't Cry, The 1950,Ap 8,9:2
Big Hangover, The 1950,My 26,20:3
Branded 1951,Ja 11,28:5
He Ran all the Way 1951,Je 21,24:2
Come Fill the Cup 1951,N 22,47:2
Royle, William
Hollywood Cowboy 1937,Jl 24,12:1
She's no Lady 1937,Ag 12,14:3
Renfrew of the Royal Mounted 1937,N 3,29:4
Renegade Ranger, The 1939,F 17,17:3
Man in the Iron Mask, The 1939,Jl 14,11:1
Mister Wong in Chinatown 1939,Jl 31,9:2 (In
Addenda)
Rains Came, The 1939,S 9,11:2
Mutiny in the Big House 1939,D 11,26:2
Lucky Cisco Kid 1940,Je 24,19:5
Royston, Gerald
Little Lord Fauntleroy 1914,Je 23,11:3
Royston, Roy
Smiling Faces 1932,Ag 31,12:3
Roza, Lita
Cast a Dark Shadow 1957,N 28,57:1
Rozakis, Gregory
America America 1963,D 16,44:1
Rozan, Dominique
Guerre est Fini, La; War Is Over, The
1967,F 2,29:2
Rozan, Micheline (Producer)
Immortal Story, The 1968,S 19,62:2
Rozanne, Annie
Kreutzer Sonata, The 1938,D 20,30:2
Rozemberg, Lucien
Life and Loves of Beethoven, The
1937,N 22,15:1
Rozen, Florence
Song of Scheherazade 1947,F 27,26:2
Rozen, S (Screenwriter)
School of Courage 1957,S 9,21:2
Rozet, M
Miserables, Les 1926,Jl 9,17:1
Miserables, Les 1927,Ag 23,29:4
Rozhkov, N (Original Author)
Under Sunny Skies 1950,D 26,19:3
Rozhkov, N (Screenwriter)
Symphony of Life 1948,D 28,19:7
Rozier, Willy (Director)
Girl in the Bikini, The 1958,O 25,16:3
Rozier, Willy (Producer)
Girl in the Bikini, The 1958,O 25,16:3
Rozov, Victor (Screenwriter)
Cranes are Flying, The 1960,Mr 22,31:2
Letter That Was Never Sent, The 1962,N 19,39:2
Rozsahegyi, Kalman
Buzavirag 1935,Ja 14,11:3
Sarga Csiko 1937,Ja 29,15:2
Tisztelet a Kivetelnek 1937,Je 14,26:3
Falu Rosssza, A; Village Rogue, The
1938,Ap 18,11:2
Te Csak Pipalj Ladanyi; Keep On Smoking,
Ladanyi 1938,My 18,9:3
Sziuel Szivert; Heart for Heart 1939,Ja 16,11:3
Vadroza; Wild Rose 1940,Ja 29,11:6
Sut a Nap (Sun Shines, The); Sun Shines, The
1940,Ap 6,13:3
Rozsival, Jaroslav
Transport From Paradise 1967,F 8,22:1
Rozzi, Fausto (Original Author)
Under the Sun of Rome 1949,O 6,40:4
Rozzi, Fausto (Screenwriter)
Under the Sun of Rome 1949,O 6,40:4
Ruanova, Lucha
Madres del Mundo 1936,Ag 17,9:3
Ruanova, Maria
Where Words Fail; Donde Mueren las Palabraso
1948,Ag 19,18:4
Ruark, Robert C (Narrator)
Africa Adventure 1954,S 29,23:4
Ruark, Robert C (Original Author)
Something of Value 1957,My 11,24:6
Ruark, Robert C (Screenwriter)
Africa Adventure 1954,S 29,23:4
Rub, Christian
Trial of Vivienne Ware, The 1932,Ap 30,19:3
Man From Yesterday, The 1932,Je 25,18:2
Secrets of the French Police 1932,D 12,18:4
Silver Dollar 1932,D 23,20:1
No Other Woman 1933,Ja 30,9:4 (In Addenda)
Humanity 1933,Ap 22,16:3
Man of Two Worlds 1934,Ja 12,29:2
No More Women 1934,Mr 15,27:4
No Greater Glory 1934,My 5,22:2
Little Man, What Now? 1934,Je 1,29:1
Fountain, The 1934,Ag 31,14:1
Romance in the Rain 1934,S 8,18:5
Music in the Air 1934,D 14,29:3
Stolen Harmony 1935,Ap 20,16:2
Oil for the Lamps of China 1935,Je 6,25:2
Metropolitan 1935,O 18,27:4
Peter Ibbetson 1935,N 8,18:2
We're Only Human 1936,Ja 18,19:2
Next Time We Love 1936,Ja 31,16:2
Murder on a Bridle Path 1936,Ap 11,19:2

Rub, Christian— Cont
Dracula's Daughter 1936,My 18,14:2
Sins of Man 1936,Je 19,17:2
Parole 1936,Je 27,21:1
Suzy 1936,Jl 25,16:1
Girls' Dormitory 1936,Ag 29,16:2
Outcast 1937,Mr 3,27:2
When Love Is Young 1937,Ap 17,15:1
Cafe Metropole 1937,Ap 29,17:1
100 Men and a Girl 1937,S 18,15:2
Heidi 1937,N 6,14:2
Mad About Music 1938,Mr 12,13:2
Professor Beware 1938,Jl 14,17:1
I'll Give a Million 1938,Jl 16,7:2
You Can't Take It With You 1938,S 2,21:2
Great Waltz, The 1938,N 25,19:1
Everything Happens at Night 1939,D 16,12:6
Swiss Family Robinson 1940,F 9,15:3
Earthbound 1940,Je 7,27:4
Four Sons 1940,Je 8,18:4
Father's Son 1941,F 13,25:3
Dangerously They Live 1942,Ap 11,9:2
Berlin Correspondent 1942,S 4,19:2
Tales of Manhattan 1942,S 25,25:1
3 Is a Family 1944,D 20,20:3
Strange Confession 1945,N 8,17:3
Something for the Birds 1952,N 15,15:2

RUBEN
See Also RUBIN

Ruben, Alex (Original Author)
Time Out for Rhythm 1941,Jl 10,16:3

Ruben, J Walter (Director)
Public Defender, The 1931,Ag 1,16:4
Secret Service 1931,D 14,16:3
Roadhouse Murder 1932,Ap 29,13:4
Phantom of Crestwood, The 1932,O 17,18:3
No Other Woman 1933,Ja 30,9:4 (In Addenda)
Great Jasper, The 1933,F 17,5:3
No Marriage Ties 1933,Ag 4,18:2
Ace of Aces 1933,N 11,10:4
Man of Two Worlds 1934,Ja 12,29:2
Success at any Price 1934,My 4,24:2
Where Sinners Meet 1934,My 25,25:2
Public Hero No 1 1935,Je 8,12:2
Java Head 1935,Jl 31,21:4
Riffraff 1936,Ja 13,14:2
Trouble for Two 1936,My 30,7:2
Old Hutch 1936,D 7,27:4
Good Old Soak 1937,Ap 20,25:3
Bad Man of Brimstone, The 1938,F 4,17:2

Ruben, J Walter (Original Author)
Racetrack 1933,Mr 6,16:6
Public Hero No 1 1935,Je 8,12:2
Thoroughbreds Don't Cry 1937,N 26,27:4
Bad Man of Brimstone, The 1938,F 4,17:2
Get-Away, The 1941,Jl 17,23:4
Fleet's In, The 1942,Mr 12,24:2

Ruben, J Walter (Producer)
Sergeant Madden 1939,Mr 24,27:2
Maisie 1939,Je 23,23:1
Thunder Afloat 1939,O 13,27:2
Twenty-Mule Team 1940,My 10,26:6
Flight Command 1941,Ja 17,21:2
Maisie Was a Lady 1941,F 13,25:2
Bad Man, The 1941,Ap 4,25:1
Get-Away, The 1941,Jl 17,23:4
Ringside Maisie 1941,Ag 1,11:2
Bugle Sounds, The 1942,Ap 3,25:2
Maisie Gets her Man 1942,Jl 16,23:2
Her Cardboard Lover 1942,Jl 17,19:2
Tennessee Johnson 1943,Ja 13,18:2
Assignment in Brittany 1943,Ap 22,31:2

Ruben, J Walter (Screenwriter)
Fleet's In, The 1928,O 1,23:1
Phantom of Crestwood, The 1932,O 17,18:3

Ruben, Jose
Salome of the Tenements 1925,F 24,17:3

Rubener, Ascka
Juliet of the Spirits 1965,N 4,57:1

Rubener, Sujata
Juliet of the Spirits 1965,N 4,57:1

Rubens, Alma
Humoresque 1920,My 31,14:2
World and his Wife, The 1920,Jl 19,16:3
Enemies of Women 1923,Ap 1,5:4
Under the Red Robe 1923,N 13,25:3
Rejected Woman, The 1924,My 5,18:3
Oytherea 1924,My 26,21:1
Price She Paid, The 1925,Ja 13,16:1
Dancers, The 1925,Ja 26,22:1
Woman's Faith, A 1925,Jl 27,17:3
Fine Clothes 1925,O 20,28:1
Heart of a Salome, The 1927,Je 6,27:2
Show Boat 1929,Ap 18,32:3
She Goes to War 1929,Je 10,23:1

Rubens, Peter Paul (Miscellaneous)
Rubens 1949,Ap 30,9:2

RUBENSTEIN
See Also RUBINSTEIN

Rubenstein, Ida
Ship, The 1927,O 19,24:4

Rubenstein, Roberto
Kid Rodelo 1966,F 23,46:1

Rubes, Jan
Incredible Journey, The 1963,N 21,43:2

RUBIN
See Also RUBEN

Rubin, Benny
Naughty Baby 1929,F 5,26:3
Marianne 1929,O 19,22:6
It's a Great Life 1930,Ja 18,21:1
Lord Byron of Broadway 1930,Mr 8,21:1
Montana Moon 1930,Ap 14,24:2
Sunny Skies 1930,My 17,21:2
Leathernecking 1930,S 13,9:3
Love in the Rough 1930,S 27,21:3
George White's 1935 Scandals 1935,Ap 29,12:3
Sunny 1941,Je 13,22:2
Here Comes Mr Jordan 1941,Ag 8,13:2
Mr Wise Guy 1942,Mr 5,27:2
Just This Once 1952,Mr 18,22:3
Torch Song 1953,O 13,34:2
Yankee Pasha 1954,Ap 19,19:2
Hole in the Head, A 1959,Jl 16,31:2
Pocketful of Miracles 1961,D 19,39:1
Thoroughly Modern Millie 1967,Mr 23,25:1

Rubin, Benny (Miscellaneous)
Traveling Saleslady 1935,Mr 29,26:2

Rubin, Benny (Screenwriter)
Bright Lights 1935,Ag 15,15:2
Girl Friend, The 1935,S 28,12:2
On Again-Off Again 1937,S 18,15:3

Rubin, Daniel N (Original Author)
Women Go on Forever 1931,O 19,28:1
Guilty as Hell 1932,Ag 6,14:5
Night Club Scandal 1937,N 12,27:2

Rubin, Dr Theodore Isaac (Original Author)
David and Lisa 1962,D 27,5:5

Rubin, Jack (Miscellaneous)
Undercover Man, The 1949,Ap 21,30:2

Rubin, Leo (Composer)
Tall, Dark and Handsome 1941,Ja 24,15:2

Rubin, Mann (Screenwriter)
Best of Everything 1959,O 9,24:2
Brainstorm 1965,Je 10,38:1
American Dream, An 1966,S 1,28:2
Warning Shot 1967,Je 8,52:2

Rubin, Robert (Producer)
Nothing but a Man 1964,S 21,37:2

Rubin, Ronald
Sergeant, The 1968,D 26,53:5

Rubin, Stanley (Producer)
Narrow Margin, The 1952,My 5,18:7
Destination Gobi 1953,My 30,7:1
River of no Return 1954,My 1,13:2
Francis in the Navy 1955,Ag 6,13:4
Rawhide Years, The 1956,Je 16,12:2
Girl Most Likely, The 1958,O 9,47:1
Promise her Anything 1966,F 23,46:1
Oh Dad, Poor Dad, Mamma's Hung You in the
    Closet and I'm Feeling so Sad 1967,F 16,32:1
President's Analyst, The 1967,D 22,44:4

Rubin, Stanley (Screenwriter)
South to Karanga 1940,Ag 9,19:1
Diamond Frontiers 1940,O 4,29:2
San Francisco Docks 1940,D 26,23:3
Six Lessons From Madame La Zonga
    1941,F 19,25:2
Mr Dynamite 1941,Mr 13,25:2
Burma Convoy 1941,O 7,26:7
Flying Cadets 1941,O 14,29:2
Bombay Clipper 1942,Ja 12,23:3
Two Senoritas From Chicago 1943,Ag 6,10:4
Decoy 1946,N 2,12:2
Violence 1947,My 10,8:5
Macao 1952,My 1,34:2

Rubinek, Saul (Narrator)
Slow Run 1968,O 11,39:1

Rubini, Giulia
It Happened in the Park 1957,Ag 13,23:2
Virtuous Bigamist, The 1959,My 28,34:3
Goliath and the Barbarians 1960,Ja 7,24:6

Rubinia, Fanta
My Son 1939,My 10,28:2

Rubinoff
Thanks a Million 1935,N 14,17:1
You Can't Have Everything 1937,Ag 4,15:2

RUBINSTEIN
See Also RUBENSTEIN

Rubinstein, Arthur
Follow the Boys 1944,Ap 26,24:6
Carnegie Hall 1947,My 3,10:2
Night Song 1948,Ja 29,27:5
Of Men and Music 1951,F 15,27:2

Rubinstein, Arthur (Composer)
I've Always Loved You 1946,S 7,11:1

Rubintshik, Yisrael
They Were Ten; (Heym Hayu Assara)
    1961,Ap 18,44:2

Rubio, Olallo Jr (Producer)
Massacre 1956,Je 2,13:5

Ruby, Ellaloo
Soul Fire 1925,My 6,26:3

Ruby, Harry (Composer)
Horse Feathers 1932,Ag 11,12:2
Kid From Spain, The 1932,N 18,23:2

Ruby, Harry (Composer)— Cont
Hips, Hips, Hooray 1934,F 24,18:3
Happiness Ahead 1934,O 11,28:2
Kentucky Kernels 1935,Ja 5,20:2
Thanks a Million 1935,N 14,17:1
Man Who Broke the Bank at Monte Carlo, The
    1935,N 15,20:2
Do You Love Me 1946,My 25,12:2
Wake up and Dream 1947,Ja 24,18:4

Ruby, Harry (Miscellaneous)
Bright Lights 1935,Ag 15,15:2
Carnival in Costa Rica 1947,Mr 29,21:2

Ruby, Harry (Original Author)
Animal Crackers 1930,Ag 29,20:3
Top Speed 1930,Ag 30,7:4
Broad Minded 1931,Jl 6,24:4
Duck Soup 1933,N 23,24:2
Hips, Hips, Hooray 1934,F 24,18:3
Circus Clown, The 1934,Je 30,18:6
Kentucky Kernels 1935,Ja 5,20:2
Maisie Goes to Reno 1944,S 29,18:1
Look for the Silver Lining 1949,Je 24,29:2
Three Little Words 1950,Ag 10,21:2

Ruby, Harry (Screenwriter)
Horse Feathers 1932,Ag 11,12:2
Kid From Spain, The 1932,N 18,23:2
Kentucky Kernels 1935,Ja 5,20:2
Bright Lights 1935,Ag 15,15:2
Walking on Air 1936,S 12,20:2
Life of the Party, The 1937,O 4,17:1
Lovely to Look At 1952,My 30,11:2

Ruby, Herman (Composer)
On Again-Off Again 1937,S 18,15:3

Ruby, Thelma
Invasion Quartet 1961,D 11,41:2

Rucker, Christiane
Carmen Baby 1967,O 11,41:2

Rucker, Douglas
Little Men 1940,D 9,23:2

Rucker, Hanna
Confession of Ina Kahn, The 1958,Ja 1,31:4

Rucker, Johnny
Safe at Home 1941,N 26,31:2

Rucker, Joseph T (Miscellaneous)
With Byrd at the South Pole 1930,Je 20,6:3

Rud, Anthony M (Screenwriter)
Scars of Jealousy 1923,My 7,19:3

Rud, Ove
Ordet 1957,D 16,33:6

Rudd, Enid
Crowded Paradise 1956,Je 22,15:1

Ruddick, Bruce MD (Screenwriter)
Feeling of Rejection, The 1948,D 27,16:4

Ruddock, John
Waltz Time 1946,F 11,25:2
Meet Me at Dawn 1948,My 18,26:2
Under Capricorn 1949,S 9,28:3
Fallen Idol, The 1949,N 16,39:2
Quo Vadis 1951,N 9,22:2
Ivanhoe 1952,Ag 1,8:2
Martin Luther 1953,S 10,22:1
Lust for Life 1956,S 18,39:1

Rudens, Dyk
Mystic Mountain, The 1936,Mr 31,17:2

Ruderman, Mikhail (Original Author)
Counter-Attack 1945,My 17,15:2

Rudhyar, Dane
Three Weeks 1924,Ap 1,19:3

Rudie, Evelyn
Gift of Love, The 1958,F 12,32:2

Rudina, Rima
World Dances 1954,N 8,24:6

Rudkin, Lev (Director)
Duel, The 1964,S 7,11:2

Rudkin, Lev (Producer)
Duel, The 1964,S 7,11:2

Rudley, Herbert
Abe Lincoln in Illinois 1940,F 23,19:2
Seventh Cross, The 1944,S 29,18:1
Marriage Is a Private Affair 1944,O 27,17:7
Master Race, The 1944,N 2,22:1
Brewster's Millions 1945,Ap 27,23:2
Rhapsody in Blue 1945,Je 28,22:2
Walk in the Sun, A 1946,Ja 12,10:6
Decoy 1946,N 2,12:2
Casbah 1948,My 3,27:4
Hollow Triumph 1948,O 29,29:5
Silver Chalice, The 1954,D 27,22:5
Artists and Models 1955,D 22,20:1
Court Jester, The 1956,F 2,19:1
That Certain Felling 1956,Je 21,35:2
Raw Edge 1956,Jl 28,10:7
Young Lions, The 1958,Ap 3,23:1
Bravados, The 1958,Je 26,23:2
Big Fisherman, The 1959,Ag 6,18:1
Beloved Infidel 1959,N 18,46:1
Great Impostor, The 1961,Mr 30,24:1

Rudnaya, Natalya
Yolanta 1964,D 23,22:3
Tsar's Bride, The 1966,Mr 12,13:2

Rudol, Victor
Train Goes to Kiev, The 1961,Ap 10,26:1

Rudolf, Carl
Kleines Bezirksgericht; Little Country Court 1939,F 18,12:4
Rudolph, Helmuth
Dahinten in der Heide; Back in the Country 1939,Ja 21,19:3
Hummel-Hummel 1939,Mr 11,21:2
Affair Blum, The 1949,O 18,35:2
Rudolph, Oscar
Little Annie Rooney 1925,O 19,26:1
So This Is College 1929,N 9,22:5
This Day and Age 1933,S 1,15:4
Rudolph, Oscar (Director)
Twist Around the Clock 1962,Ja 27,13:4
Don't Knock the Twist 1962,Ap 14,14:2
Rudski, Kazimierz
Eroica (Second Episode) 1966,F 2,24:1
Ruecker, Manuela
Funnyman 1967,S 25,56:3
Rueckert, Ernst
Eleven Who Were Loyal 1929,My 20,22:6
Rasputin 1929,O 21,30:1
Rueckert, Helma
S A Mann Brand 1934,My 28,16:2
Grobe Adele, Die 1937,My 15,23:5
Rueda, Jose
Bandolero, The 1924,O 27,27:1
Ruehmann, Heinz
Drei von ver Tankstelle, Die 1931,Je 20,20:4
Bomben auf Monte Carlo; Bombardment of Monte Carlo, The 1931,S 27,VIII,7:1
Meine Frau, Die Hochstaplerin 1932,F 6,14:4
Es Wird Schon Wieder Besser; Things Will Soon Get Better 1932,F 28,VIII,6:1
Man Braucht Kein Geld; You Don't Need any Money 1932,F 28,VIII,6:1
Stolz der 3 Kompagnie, Der 1932,Jl 21,15:2
Man Braucht Kein Geld 1932,N 16,15:3
Brave Suender, Der 1933,Mr 29,13:2
Lachende Erben 1933,N 18,18:6
Es Wird Schon Wieder Besser 1934,Ja 24,21:3
Strich Durch die Rechnung 1934,Mr 3,8:6
Finanzen des Grossherzogs, Die; Grand Duke's Finances, The 1935,Ap 6,10:3
Himmel auf Erden, Der 1935,D 26,21:4
Frasquita 1936,Ja 18,19:4
Ein Walzer fuer Dich 1936,S 29,35:2
Drei Blaue Jungs-Ein Blondes Maedel 1936,D 29,16:3
Gibt nur eine Liebe, Es 1937,Ja 23,23:2
If We All Were Angels 1937,O 9,16:2
Zwei lustige Abenteurer; Two Merry Adventures 1938,Ja 1,11:2
Eva, das Fabriksmaedel 1938,Ja 8,19:2
Mustergatte, Der; Model Husband 1938,Mr 19,11:3
Nanu, Sie Kennen Korff noch Nicht?; So, You Don't Know Korff Yet? 1939,My 22,15:3
Florentiner Hut, Der; Leghorn Hat, The 1939,Je 3,11:3
Fuenf Millionem suchen einen Erben; Five Millions Seek an Heir 1939,O 23,15:3
Paradies der Junggesellen; Bachelors' Paradise 1940,Ap 13,21:3
Hurra! Ich bin Papa; Hurrah! I'm a Papa 1940,Je 1,12:3
Captain from Koepenick, The 1958,Jl 26,6:1
It Happened in Broad Daylight 1960,S 30,33:1
Good Soldier Schweik, The 1963,Ag 21,38:1
Judge and the Sinner, The 1964,Je 6,14:2
Ship of Fools 1965,Jl 29,18:1
Ruel, Marta
Fantasma del Convento, El; Fantasy of the Monastery 1935,Ap 22,14:3
Ruenkoesdy, Auguste
Singing Angels 1952,Ja 16,21:2
Rueprecht, Albert
Song Without End 1960,Ag 12,10:2
Ruf, Anita
Women Are Weak 1959,Je 9,44:2
Ruffin, K von
Schwarzwaldmaedel 1935,O 12,12:3
Ruffini, Sandro
Schoolgirl Diary 1947,O 18,9:2
Secret Conclave, The 1953,My 16,10:1
Ruffino, Mercedes
Tortilla Flat 1942,My 22,27:1
Ruffo, Leonora
Queen of Sheba, The 1953,N 4,29:3
Vitelloni 1956;O 24,43:1
Goliath and the Dragon 1961,Ja 5,27:2
Rufo, Francine
Old Acquaintance 1943,N 3,20:2
Ruge, Jack (Original Author)
Joe Butterfly 1957,My 30,23:2
Rugette
Gates of Paris 1958,Ja 15,24:1
Ruggeri, Ada
Amore e Morte; (Love and Death) 1932,O 4,26:4
Ruggeri, Antonino
Amore e Morte; (Love and Death) 1932,O 4,26:4

Ruggeri, Ruggero
Donna D'una Notte, La 1933,Mr 10,19:4
Documento Fatale, Il 1940,S 26,27:3
Spirit and the Flesh, The 1948,N 1,28:2
Ruggero, Marcelo
Gente Bien 1939,O 9,15:2
Divòrcio en Montevideo 1940,Ap 8,15:3
Ruggieri, Francoise
Seconds 1966,O 6,56:1
Ruggles, Charles
Peer Gynt 1915,S 20,9:1
Heart Raider, The 1923,Je 6,24:5
Gentlemen of the Press 1929,My 13,27:2
Lady Lies, The 1929,S 7,15:1
Roadhouse Nights 1930,F 22,13:1
Roadhouse Nights 1930,Mr 2,IX,5:1
Young Man of Manhattan 1930,Ap 19,15:1
Queen High 1930,Ag 9,16:5
Her Wedding Night 1930,S 29,19:1
Charley's Aunt 1930,D 26,18:4
Honor Among Lovers 1931,F 28,15:2
Smiling Lieutenant, The 1931,My 23,13:4
Girl Habit, The 1931,Jl 4,11:5
Beloved Bachelor, The 1931,O 17,20:1
Husband's Holiday 1931,D 25,29:2
This Reckless Age 1932,Ja 9,21:1
One Hour with You 1932,Mr 24,17:5
This is the Night 1932,Ap 16,11:2
Love Me Tonight 1932,Ag 19,20:6
70,000 Witnesses 1932,S 3,16:2
Night of June 13th, The 1932,S 17,18:4
Trouble in Paradise 1932,N 9,28:5
Evenings for Sale 1932,N 12,20:5
If I Had a Million 1932,D 3,21:4
Madame Butterfly 1932,D 26,26:2
Murders in the Zoo 1933,Ap 3,13:4
Melody Cruise 1933,Je 23,15:2
Mama Loves Papa 1933,Jl 24,11:2
Girl Without a Room 1933,D 7,26:3
Alice in Wonderland 1933,D 23,19:1
Six of a Kind 1934,Mr 10,18:3
Melody in Spring 1934,Mr 31,8:2
Friends of Mr Sweeney 1934,Jl 31,20:4
Pursuit of Happiness, The 1934,O 26,25:1
Ruggles of Red Gap 1935,Mr 7,26:1
People Will Talk 1935,Je 17,20:2
No More Ladies 1935,Je 22,18:5
Anything Goes 1936,F 6,23:3
Hearts Divided 1936,Je 13,13:1
Early to Bed 1936,Jl 16,20:2
Wives Never Know 1936,O 31,24:2
Turn off the Moon 1937,My 20,17:2
Exclusive 1937,Jl 22,15:1
Bringing Up Baby 1938,Mr 4,17:5
Breaking the Ice 1938,S 23,35:3
Service de Luxe 1938,O 24,13:2
Invitation to Happiness 1939,Je 8,31:2
Balalaika 1939,D 15,33:2
Farmer's Daughter, The 1940,F 16,23:4
Maryland 1940,Jl 13,16:5
No Time for Comedy 1940,S 7,9:2
Public Deb No 1 1940,S 18,19:2
Invisible Woman, The 1941,Ja 9,27:2
Honeymoon for Three 1941,F 8,19:2
Model Wife 1941,Ap 24,25:3
Parson of Panamint, The 1941,Jl 26,18:2
Go West, Young Lady 1941,N 24,11:6
Friendly Enemies 1942,Je 22,19:1
Dixie Dugan 1943,Ap 9,25:5
Doughgirls, The 1944,Ag 31,14:1
Our Hearts Were Young and Gay 1944,O 12,24:2
3 Is a Family 1944,D 20,20:3
Bedside Manner 1945,Je 23,9:6
Incendiary Blonde 1945,Jl 26,13:2
Stolen Life, A 1946,My 2,27:4
Gallant Journey 1946,O 10,33:2
Perfect Marriage, The 1947,Ja 16,30:3
It Happened on Fifth Avenue 1947,Je 11,33:2
My Brother Talks to Horses 1947,Je 19,27:4
Ramrod 1947,Je 30,25:6
Give my Regards to Broadway 1948,Je 23,32:2
Look for the Silver Lining 1949,Je 24,29:2
All in a Nights Work 1961,Mr 23,28:1
Pleasure of his Company, The 1961,Je 2,36:1
Parent Trap, The 1961,Je 22,23:1
Son of Flubber 1963,F 9,5:2
Papa's Delicate Condition 1963,Mr 7,8:5
I'd Rather Be Rich 1964,S 3,24:2
Ugly Dachshund, The 1966,Ap 7,45:1
Follow Me, Boys! 1966,D 2,46:1
Ruggles, Eleanor (Original Author)
Prince of Players 1955,Ja 12,24:2
Ruggles, Wesley (Director)
Wild Honey 1922,F 28,17:4
Mr Billings Spends his Dime 1923,Mr 5,15:3
Plastic Age, The 1926,Jl 19,13:1
Beware of Widows 1927,My 24,23:4
Silk Stockings 1927,N 29,31:1
Fourflusher, The 1928,Ja 16,24:1
Finders Keepers 1928,Mr 5,21:3
Scandal 1929,Ap 22,23:1
Condemned 1929,N 4,28:1
Honey 1930,Mr 29,23:1

Ruggles, Wesley (Director) — Cont
Cimarron 1931,Ja 27,20:5
Are These our Children 1931,N 14,15:3
Roar of the Dragon 1932,Jl 25,11:2
No Man of her Own 1932,D 31,10:1
College Humor 1933,Je 23,15:4
I'm no Angel 1933,O 14,18:2
Bolero 1934,F 17,20:3
Shoot the Works 1934,Jl 7,16:5
Gilded Lily, The 1935,F 9,11:2
Accent on Youth 1935,Ag 12,10:3
Bride Comes Home, The 1935,D 25,30:2
Valiant Is the Word for Carrie 1936,O 8,27:2
I Met Him in Paris 1937,Je 3,29:2
True Confession 1937,D 16,35:2
Sing You Sinners 1938,Ag 18,23:1
Invitation to Happiness 1939,Je 8,31:2
Too Many Husbands 1940,Mr 8,25:2
Arizona 1941,F 7,23:3
You Belong to Me 1941,N 29,14:2
Somewhere I'll Find You 1942,Ag 28,22:4
Slightly Dangerous 1943,Ap 2,17:2
See Here Private Hargrove 1944,Mr 22,17:2
Ruggles, Wesley (Producer)
I Met Him in Paris 1937,Je 3,29:2
Sing You Sinners 1938,Ag 18,23:1
Invitation to Happiness 1939,Je 8,31:2
Too Many Husbands 1940,Mr 8,25:2
Arizona 1941,F 7,23:3
You Belong to Me 1941,N 29,14:2
Ruggles, Wesley (Screenwriter)
Are These our Children 1931,N 14,15:3
Rugiani, Carlo (Director)
Anything for a Song 1947,Ag 5,26:2
Ruhl, Michel
Your Shadow Is Mine 1963,My 15,32:1
Ruhl, William
Juke Box Jenny 1942,Ap 17,21:3
Song of my Heart 1948,Mr 5,17:3
Ruhmann, Heinz
Mann der Seinen Moerder Sucht, Der; Looking for His Murderer 1931,Mr 15,IX,6:1
Ich und die Kaiserin 1933,My 28,IX,2:5 (In Addenda)
Ruhr, Gerard
Gates of Paris 1958,Ja 15,24:1
Ruick, Barbara
Invitation 1952,Ja 30,22:6
You for Me 1952,S 25,38:3
Above and Beyond 1953,Ja 31,10:6
I Love Melvin 1953,Ap 10,18:4
Carousel 1956,F 17,13:1
Ruick, Mel
President's Mystery, The 1936,O 19,22:1
Moon Over Miami 1941,Jl 5,14:2
Ruick, Walter (Composer)
Ship Ahoy 1942,Je 26,16:5
Ruis, Eliza
Her First Affair; (Children of Paradise) 1947,F 20,32:3
Ruiz, Albert
Hit Parade of 1947 1947,My 5,32:8
Ruiz, Antonio
Long Duel, The 1967,N 2,58:3
Ruiz, Gabriel (Composer)
Broadway Rhythm 1944,Ap 14,24:6
Mexicana 1945,N 17,14:6
Ruiz, Mercedes
Doctor Zhivago 1965,D 23,21:1
Ruiz, Nicholas de
Slave of Desire 1923,D 11,26:2
Girl From Montmarte, The 1926,F 25,26:2
Ruiz, Nick de
His Supreme Moment 1925,Ap 13,24:1
Lord Jim 1925,N 16,19:4
Ruiz, Starr
Way Out 1967,O 26,54:3
Rule, A J (Miscellaneous)
Big Drive, The 1933,Ja 20,21:2
Rule, Janice
Goodbye, my Fancy 1951,My 30,14:2
Starlift 1951,D 15,11:2
Holiday for Sinners 1952,S 20,13:2
Gun for a Coward 1957,Ja 31,21:1
Woman's Devotion, A 1957,Mr 22,26:1
Bell, Book and Candle 1958,D 27,2:7
Subterraneans, The 1960,Jl 7,26:1
Invitation to a Gunfighter 1964,O 28,51:3
Chase, The 1966,F 19,24:1
Alvarez Kelly 1966,N 17,55:2
Welcome to Hard Times 1967,My 2,56:1
Ambushers, The 1967,D 23,29:1
Swimmer, The 1968,My 16,53:1
Rulka, Marian
Five From Barska Street 1955,Mr 14,29:4
Rumann, Sig
World Moves On, The 1934,Je 30,18:5
Servants' Entrance 1934,S 27,25:2
Marie Galante 1934,N 21,23:4
Under Pressure 1935,F 4,11:3
Wedding Night, The 1935,Mr 16,19:1
Farmer Takes a Wife, The 1935,Ag 9,21:2
Night at the Opera, A 1935,D 7,22:1
Princess Comes Across, The 1936,Je 4,27:2

Rumann, Sig— Cont

On the Avenue 1937,F 5,17:3
Maytime 1937,Mr 19,27:1
Seventh Heaven 1937,Mr 26,25:1
This Is my Affair 1937,My 28,17:1
Day at the Races, A 1937,Je 18,25:2
Great Hospital Mystery, The 1937,Jl 16,22:2
Think Fast, Mr Moto 1937,Ag 16,15:3
Love Under Fire 1937,Ag 28,8:2
Thin Ice 1937,S 4,8:2
Lancer Spy 1937,N 4,29:1
Heidi 1937,N 6,14:2
Nothing Sacred 1937,N 26,27:2
Thank You, Mr Moto 1938,Ja 3,16:2
Paradise for Three 1938,F 16,17:1
Saint in New York, The 1938,My 26,31:2
I'll Give a Million 1938,Jl 16,7:2
Suez 1938,O 15,21:2
Girls on Probation 1938,O 21,27:3
Great Waltz, The 1938,N 25,19:1
Honolulu 1939,F 23,19:2
Never Say Die 1939,Mr 9,18:1
Confessions of a Nazi Spy 1939,Ap 29,13:2
Only Angels Have Wings 1939,My 12,25:2
Ninotchka 1939,N 10,27:2
Remember? 1939,D 15,33:4
Dr Ehrlich's Magic Bullet 1940,F 24,9:2
Outside the Three-Mile Limit 1940,Ap 8,15:2
I Was an Adventuress 1940,My 20,13:2
Four Sons 1940,Je 8,18:4
Bitter Sweet 1940,N 22,27:1
Victory 1940,D 23,23:2
Comrade X 1940,D 26,23:1
So Ends our Night 1941,F 28,17:2
That Uncertain Feeling 1941,My 2,25:1
Wagons Roll at Night, The 1941,My 10,20:4
Shining Victory 1941,My 31,14:1
Love Crazy 1941,Je 6,25:5
World Premiere 1941,Ag 21,15:2
This Woman Is Mine 1941,O 13,21:2
To Be or not to Be 1942,Mr 7,13:2
Remember Pearl Harbor 1942,Je 4,22:4
Crossroads 1942,Jl 27,18:2
Enemy Agents meet Ellery Queen
1942,Ag 22,16:2
Berlin Correspondent 1942,S 4,19:2
Desperate Journey 1942,S 26,11:2
China Girl 1943,Ja 21,27:2
Tarzan Triumphs 1943,F 5,16:3
They Came to Blow up America
1943,My 15,13:2
Sweet Rosie O'Grady 1943,O 21,30:2
Song of Bernadette, The 1944,Ja 27,15:2
Hitler Gang, The 1944,My 8,15:2
It Happened Tomorrow 1944,My 29,18:2
Summer Storm 1944,O 23,14:3
House of Frankenstein 1944,D 16,19:3
Royal Scandal, A 1945,Ap 12,19:2
Men in her Diary 1945,S 24,16:5
Dolly Sisters, The 1945,N 15,24:6
She Went to the Races 1946,F 1,29:2
Night and Day 1946,Jl 26,16:2
Night in Casablanca, A 1946,Ag 12,17:2
Mother Wore Tights 1947,Ag 21,33:2
If You Knew Susie 1948,F 23,19:2
Emperor Waltz, The 1948,Je 18,19:2
Give my Regards to Broadway 1948,Je 23,32:2
Border Incident 1949,N 21,29:2
On the Riviera 1951,My 24,47:1
World in His Arms, The 1952,O 10,21:2
O Henry's Full House (The Gift of the Magi); Gift
of the Magi, The (O Henry's Full House)
1952,O 17,33:1
Stalag 17 1953,Jl 2,19:2
Houdini 1953,Jl 3,10:2
Glenn Miller Story, the 1954,F 11,33:2
Living It Up 1954,Jl 24,6:6
White Christmas 1954,O 15,16:3
Three Ring Circus 1954,D 25,7:2
Wings of Eagles, The 1957,F 1,28:1
Fortune Cookie, The 1966,O 20,52:1

Rumford, Basil
Spies of the Air 1940,Jl 4,12:3

Rumistrzewicz, Krystyna
Divided Heart, The 1955,Ag 4,16:1

Rummelster, Augusta
Greene Murder Case, The 1929,Ag 10,11:3

Rumshinsky, Joseph (Composer)
Shir Hashirim 1935,O 11,31:1

Rumyantseva, N
Mexican, The 1957,Ap 3,28:2
Marriage of Baezaminov, The 1966,Je 11,20:2

Run, Carlo (Director)
Seven Deadly Sins, The (Gluttony); Gluttony (The
Seven Deadly Sins) 1953,My 12,31:3

Run, Carlo (Screenwriter)
Seven Deadly Sins, The (Gluttony); Gluttony (The
Seven Deadly Sins) 1953,My 12,31:3

Rung, Margaret
If all the Guys in the World 1957,Ap 23,34:1
No Sun in Venice 1958,Je 10,40:2

Runghe, B
Lonely White Sail 1938,My 7,18:1
Signal, The 1943,Mr 25,25:3

Heroes Are Made 1944,Mr 11,10:2

Runyon, Damon
Great White Way, The 1924,Ja 4,10:1

Runyon, Damon (Original Author)
Lady for a Day 1933,S 8,22:2
Little Miss Marker 1934,My 19,18:3
Midnight Alibi 1934,Jl 4,18:3
Million Dollar Ransom 1934,S 19,15:2
Lemon Drop Kid, The 1934,O 27,20:2
Princess O'Hara 1935,Ap 13,11:3
Hold 'Em Yale 1935,Ap 27,20:6
Professional Soldier 1936,Ja 30,14:2
Three Wise Guys, The 1936,My 23,12:2
Slight Case of Murder, A 1938,F 28,19:1
Straight, Place and Show 1938,O 1,10:2
Joe and Ethel Turp Call on the President
1940,Ja 4,19:2
Tight Shoes 1941,Je 19,25:2
Butch Minds the Baby 1942,My 1,23:3
Big Street, The 1942,Ag 14,13:1
It Ain't Hay 1943,Mr 11,17:3
Sorrowful Jones 1949,Je 6,15:2
Johnny One-Eye 1950,N 17,31:2
Lemon Drop Kid, The 1951,Mr 22,41:2
Bloodhounds of Broadway 1952,N 15,15:2
Stop, You're Killing Me 1952,D 11,45:3
Money From Home 1954,F 27,11:3
Guys and Dolls 1955,N 5,26:1
Pocketful of Miracles 1961,D 19,39:1

Runyon, Damon (Producer)
Big Street, The 1942,Ag 14,13:1
Irish Eyes Are Smiling 1944,N 8,27:1

Rupp, S
Fistful of Dollars, A 1967,F 2,29:1

Rupp, Walter (Producer)
Crazy for Love 1960,N 26,13:2

Rurdalek, Georg (Screenwriter)
Trapp Family, The 1961,Ag 31,22:4

Ruric, Peter (Original Author)
Gambling Ship 1933,Jl 13,17:5
Twelve Crowded Hours 1939,F 24,15:2

Ruric, Peter (Screenwriter)
Dark Sands 1938,Ag 17,23:4
Grand Central Murder 1942,My 23,8:8

Ruschel, Alberto
Cangaceiro 1954,S 3,13:2

Rush, Barbara
Molly 1951,Mr 8,37:2
Quebec 1951,Mr 16,34:2
First Legion, The 1951,Ap 28,9:2
When Worlds Collide 1952,F 7,30:2
It Came From Outer Space 1953,Je 18,38:2
Magnificent Obsession 1954,Ag 5,18:4
Black Shield of Falworth, The 1954,O 7,16:2
Kiss of Fire 1955,S 24,11:2
World in my Corner 1956,F 18,12:5
Bigger Than Life 1956,Ag 3,11:2
Flight to Hong Kong 1957,Ja 3,28:2
Oh Men! Oh Women! 1957,F 22,25:2
No Down Payment 1957,O 31,41:1
Young Lions, The 1958,Ap 3,23:1
Harry Black and the Tiger 1958,S 19,24:4
Young Philadelphians, The 1959,My 22,32:1
Bramble Bush, The 1960,F 25,34:2
Strangers When we Meet 1960,Je 30,22:2
Come Blow Your Horn 1963,Je 7,37:1
Robin and the 7 Hoods 1964,Ag 6,20:1
Hombre 1967,Mr 22,41:1

Rush, Dennis
Man of a Thousand Faces 1957,Ag 14,21:1

Rush, Dick
Village Sleuth 1920,S 13,12:1
Benson Murder Case, The 1930,Ap 12,23:1
Donovan's Kid 1931,My 22,28:5
Six of a Kind 1934,Mr 10,18:3
Last Round-Up, The 1934,My 10,25:2
Super-Sleuth 1937,Jl 17,18:1
Jury's Secret, The 1938,F 4,17:2
Bulldog Drummond's Secret Police
1939,Mr 30,19:3
Santa Fe Stampede 1939,Ap 26,27:3

Rush, Louise
Open the Door and See all the People
1964,Ap 2,28:1

Rush, Philip
Operation Secret 1952,N 6,37:2

Rush, Philip (Screenwriter)
Virgin Island 1960,Mr 24,39:5

Rush, Richard (Director)
Of Love and Desire 1963,S 12,32:1
Hells Angels on Wheels 1967,Jl 29,29:3
Thunder Valley 1967,S 14,55:1
Thunder Alley 1967,S 14,55:1
Psych-Out 1968,Mr 28,52:1
Savage Seven, The 1968,Ag 22,47:1

Rush, Richard (Screenwriter)
Of Love and Desire 1963,S 12,32:1

Rushkin, Shimin
Body and Soul 1947,N 10,21:2

Rushton, William
Nothing but the Best 1964,Jl 14,28:1

Rusinel, M (Original Author)
First Start, The 1953,F 2,17:3

Rusinov, A
Rubicon 1931,S 21,20:2

Ruskin, Harry (Miscellaneous)
Rumba 1935,F 25,13:2
Glass Key, The 1935,Je 15,20:2
Two for Tonight 1935,Ag 31,16:2

Ruskin, Harry (Original Author)
Married Before Breakfast 1937,Jl 23,16:2
Girl in the Kremlin, The 1957,My 22,29:2

Ruskin, Harry (Producer)
Watch the Birdie 1950,D 12,46:4

Ruskin, Harry (Screenwriter)
Stolen Harmony 1935,Ap 20,16:2
Lady, Be Careful 1936,O 10,21:1
Great Guy 1937,Ja 1,19:2
23 1/2 Hours Leave 1937,My 17,23:2
Bad Guy 1937,Ag 26,25:2
Beg, Borrow or Steal 1937,D 10,33:2
Love Is a Headache 1938,Ja 28,17:3
Paradise for Three 1938,F 16,17:1
Chaser, The 1938,Ag 2,15:3
Young Doctor Kildare 1938,O 28,27:1
Calling Dr Kildare 1939,My 12,25:4
Miracles for Sale 1939,Ag 10,15:2
Secret of Dr Kildare, The 1939,D 8,33:5
Dr Kildare's Strange Case 1940,Ap 12,19:2
Dr Kildare Goes Home 1940,S 19,27:4
Dr Kildare's Crisis 1940,D 19,33:1
Andy Hardy's Private Secretary 1941,Mr 7,17:2
Penalty, The 1941,Ap 10,29:3
People vs Dr Kildare, The 1941,My 8,21:1
Dr Kildare's Wedding Day 1941,S 18,31:1
Dr Kildare's Victory 1942,F 5,25:2
Calling Dr Gillespie 1942,Jl 9,17:4
Tish 1942,S 18,25:2
Rationing 1944,Ap 10,14:2
Andy Hardy's Blonde Trouble 1944,My 5,17:3
Three Men in White 1944,My 26,23:3
Barbary Coast Gent 1944,S 29,18:2
Lost in a Harem 1944,N 9,23:2
Between Two Women 1945,Mr 29,18:3
Hidden Eye, The 1945,Ag 31,14:3
Postman Always Rings Twice, The
1946,My 3,15:3
Love Laughs at Andy Hardy 1947,Ja 8,28:2
Dark Delusion 1947,Je 26,19:2
Julia Misbehaves 1948,O 8,30:2
Watch the Birdie 1950,D 12,46:4
Lady Godiva 1955,D 3,13:3

Ruskin, Shimen
Beau Brummell 1924,Mr 31,20:1
Having Wonderful Time 1938,Jl 8,11:2
Lady From Louisiana 1941,My 15,27:2
Dance Hall 1941,Jl 19,16:2

Ruslanova, Lidia
Moscow Music Hall 1946,S 9,20:1

Rusoff, Lou (Producer)
Beach Party 1963,S 26,40:2

Rusoff, Lou (Screenwriter)
Beach Party 1963,S 26,40:2

Ruspoli, Esmeralda
Avventura, L' 1961,Ap 5,30:1
Adolescents, The (Flammetta); Flammetta (The
Adolescents) 1967,Ap 14,33:1

Russ, Dan
Johnny Concho 1956,Ag 16,30:1

Russ, Hertha
Stern von Valencia, Der 1934,Ap 21,12:2

Russ, Martin
Sand Castle, The 1961,Ag 16,37:2

Russell, A J (Screenwriter)
Lovely Way to Die, A 1968,Jl 13,18:1

Russell, Alice B
Betrayal, The 1948,Je 26,10:5

Russell, Andy
Stork Club, The 1945,D 20,18:2
Breakfast in Hollywood 1946,Jl 15,21:1
Copacabana 1947,Jl 12,7:2

Russell, Anna
Hansel and Gretel 1954,O 11,33:1

Russell, Autumn
Sweet Smell of Success 1957,Je 28,29:2

Russell, Bob (Composer)
Three for the Show 1955,F 25,16:1

Russell, Bryan
Babes in Toyland 1961,D 15,49:1
Safe at Home 1962,Ap 14,14:1
Ticklish Affair, A 1963,Ag 22,19:2
Emil and the Detectives 1964,D 24,8:3
Adventures of Bullwhip Griffin, The
1967,Mr 9,43:2

Russell, Byron
World and his Wife, The 1920,Jl 19,16:3
Janice Meredith 1924,Ag 6,13:3
Parnell 1937,Je 4,27:2
One Third of a Nation 1939,F 11,13:2

Russell, Charles
Bombardier 1943,Jl 2,15:2
Purple Heart, The 1944,Mr 9,15:2
Captain Eddie 1945,Ag 9,24:2
Behind Green Lights 1946,F 16,10:2

Russell, Charles— Cont
Wake up and Dream 1947,Ja 24,18:4
Late George Apley, The 1947,Mr 21,29:2
Give my Regards to Broadway 1948,Je 23,32:2
Canon City 1948,Jl 8,19:2
Chinatown at Midnight 1949,N 18,35:3
Russell, Connie
Lady Be Good 1941,S 19,27:1
Nightmare 1956,My 12,12:7
Russell, Del
Cleopatra 1963,Je 13,29:1
Russell, Elizabeth
Hideaway Girl 1937,Ja 13,20:4
Cat People 1942,D 7,22:2
Hitler's Madman 1943,Ag 28,15:1
Curse of the Cat People, The 1944,Mr 4,11:1
Weird Woman 1944,Ap 1,11:1
Youth Runs Wild 1944,S 2,17:2
Bedlam 1946,Ap 20,16:4
Russell, Gail
Uninvited, The 1944,F 21,19:3
Lady in the Dark 1944,F 23,17:1
Our Hearts Were Young and Gay 1944,O 12,24:2
Salty O'Rourke 1945,Ap 26,26:2
Unseen, The 1945,My 14,20:5
Our Hearts Were Growing Up 1946,Ag 12,17:2
Bachelor's Daughters, The 1946,O 7,23:2
Angel and the Badman 1947,Mr 3,28:4
Calcutta 1947,Ap 24,30:2
Night Has a Thousand Eyes 1948,O 14,38:3
Wake of the Red Witch 1949,Ja 10,19:2
Moonrise 1949,Mr 7,17:2
El Paso 1949,Mr 24,35:2
Song of India 1949,Je 10,32:3
Great Dan Patch, The 1949,N 9,37:2
Captain China 1950,Mr 2,33:2
Lawless, The 1950,Je 23,29:2
Air Cadet 1951,My 11,32:3
Tattered Dress, The 1957,Mr 15,22:3
Russell, George
Free, White and 21 1963,Je 20,29:3
Russell, Gilbert
Everybody Does It 1949,O 26,32:2
Russell, Harold
Best Years of our Lives, The 1946,N 22,27:2
Russell, Harriet
Crime of Dr Crespi, The 1936,Ja 13,14:3
Russell, Henry (Composer)
Pot o'Gold 1941,Ap 4,25:2
Russell, Howard
Street Scene 1931,Ag 27,22:5
Russell, J Gordon
Singer Jim McKee 1924,Mr 24,13:1
Tumbleweeds 1925,D 21,27:2
Claw, The 1927,My 11,28:3
Uncle Tom's Cabin 1927,N 5,16:2
Russell, Jack Golden (Original Author)
Ocean's Eleven 1960,Ag 11,19:1
Russell, Jackie
Guide for the Married Man, A 1967,My 27,16:1
Russell, Jamie
New Faces 1954,F 20,8:7
Hot Blood 1956,Mr 24,14:2
Russell, Jane
Young Widow 1946,Jl 29,12:8
Outlaw, The 1947,S 12,18:4
Paleface, The 1948,D 16,41:2
His Kind of Woman 1951,Ag 30,20:2
Double Dynamite 1951,D 26,19:4
Las Vegas Story, The 1952,Ja 31,37:6
Macao 1952,My 1,34:2
Son of Paleface 1952,O 2,32:3
Montana Belle 1952,N 8,9:2
Gentlemen Prefer Blondes 1953,Jl 16,17:2
French Line, The 1954,My 15,13:2
Underwater! 1955,F 10,27:2
Foxfire 1955,Jl 14,19:1
Tall Men, The 1955,O 12,36:2
Gentlemen Marry Brunettes 1955,O 31,31:5
Hot Blood 1956,Mr 24,14:2
Revolt of Mamie Stover, The 1956,My 12,12:7
Fuzzy Pink Nightgown, The 1957,O 31,41:1
Fate Is the Hunter 1964,D 10,61:1
Johnny Reno 1966,Mr 10,26:3
Born Losers, The 1967,Ag 19,16:2
Russell, John
Always Goodbye 1938,Je 25,7:2
Prison Break 1938,Jl 13,17:4
Five of a Kind 1938,O 31,12:2
Jesse James 1939,Ja 14,13:1
Sabotage 1939,N 16,29:5
Blue Bird, The 1940,Ja 20,11:2
Man I Married, The 1940,Ag 3,9:2
Lady With red Hair 1940,D 6,28:2
Within These Walls 1945,Jl 16,8:4
Don Juan Quilligan 1945,Jl 30,16:2
Forever Amber 1947,O 23,31:2
Sitting Pretty 1948,Mr 11,35:2
Yellow Sky 1949,F 2,36:1
Slattery's Hurricane 1949,Ag 13,6:6
Story of Molly X, The 1949,D 2,35:4
Undertow 1949,D 16,37:2
Saddle Tramp 1950,N 24,31:4
Frenchie 1951,F 12,19:2

Fighting Coast Guard 1951,My 12,14:6
Fat Man, The 1951,My 25,31:2
Hoodlum Empire 1952,Mr 6,25:6
Fair Wind to Java 1953,Ag 28,13:3
Sun Shines Bright, The 1954,Mr 17,25:2
Jubilee Trail 1954,My 1,13:3
Hell's Outpost 1955,F 26,13:3
Untamed Youth 1957,My 11,24:6
Rio Bravo 1959,Mr 19,40:2
Yellowstone Kelly 1959,N 12,27:1
Fort Utah 1967,My 25,54:3
If He Hollers, Let Him Go 1968,O 10,59:7
Russell, John (Original Author)
Where the Pavement Ends 1923,Ap 2,22:1
Red Mark, The 1928,O 30,27:3
Pagan, The 1929,My 14,29:1
Sea God, The 1930,S 6,9:2
Russell, John (Screenwriter)
Mademoiselle Midnight 1924,My 27,14:1
Iron Horse, The 1924,Ag 29,6:1
Beau Geste 1926,Ag 26,17:3
Russell, Ken (Director)
Billion Dollar Brain 1967,D 23,29:1
Russell, Kurt
Follow Me, Boys! 1966,D 2,46:1
One and Only Genuine Original Family Band,
The 1968,Mr 22,55:1
Horse in the Gray Flannel Suit, The
1968,D 21,49:3
Russell, Lewis
Molly and Me 1945,My 26,18:2
Hold That Blonde 1945,N 8,17:2
Lost Weekend, The 1945,D 3,17:2
She Wouldn't Say Yes 1946,Ja 12,10:7
She Wrote the Book 1946,Je 20,20:3
Night in Casablanca, A 1946,Ag 12,17:2
If I'm Lucky 1946,S 20,41:3
Cross my Heart 1946,D 19,42:3
Ladies' Man 1947,Ja 13,18:5
Jewels of Brandenburg 1947,My 24,10:5
Trouble With Women, The 1947,Jl 14,14:4
Kiss the Blood off my Hands 1948,O 30,10:2
Russell, Mary
Happiness Ahead 1934,O 11,28:2
Night at the Ritz, A 1935,My 16,20:2
Murder in Greenwich Village 1937,O 30,22:2
Women in Prison 1938,Mr 1,19:3
Russell, Pee Wee
Jazz Dance 1954,S 21,24:1
Russell, Ray (Original Author)
Mr Sardonicus 1961,O 19,39:3
Russell, Ray (Screenwriter)
Mr Sardonicus 1961,O 19,39:3
Zotz! 1962,O 4,44:3
X - The Man With X-Ray Eyes 1963,O 24,37:1
Russell, Robert
Bedazzled 1967,D 11,65:2
Conqueror Worm, The 1968,Ag 15,46:2
Russell, Robert (Original Author)
More the Merrier, The 1943,My 14,17:1
Well Groomed Bride, The 1946,My 11,22:5
Walk, Don't Run 1966,Ag 25,42:3
Russell, Robert (Screenwriter)
More the Merrier, The 1943,My 14,17:1
Well Groomed Bride, The 1946,My 11,22:5
Lady Says No, The 1952,Ja 7,14:3
Russell, Rosalind
Evelyn Prentice 1934,N 10,19:1
President Vanishes, The 1934,D 8,18:5
Forsaking all Others 1934,D 21,18:1
Night is Young, The 1935,Ja 14,11:2
West Point of the Air 1935,Ap 6,10:1
Casino Murder Case, The 1935,Ap 17,26:5
Reckless 1935,Ap 20,16:1
China Seas 1935,Ag 10,16:4
Rendezvous 1935,O 26,12:2
It Had to Happen 1936,F 15,18:6
Under Two Flags 1936,My 1,19:1
Trouble for Two 1936,My 30,7:2
Craig's Wife 1936,O 2,29:3
Night Must Fall 1937,Ap 30,17:2
Live, Love and Learn 1937,N 19,27:2
Man-Proof 1938,Ja 14,21:1
Four's a Crowd 1938,Ag 12,11:1
Citadel, The 1938,N 4,27:2
Fast and Loose 1939,Mr 9,18:1
Women, The 1939,S 22,27:2
His Girl Friday 1940,Ja 12,13:2
No Time for Comedy 1940,S 7,9:2
Hired Wife 1940,S 14,11:2
This Thing Called Love 1941,F 14,15:2
They Met in Bombay 1941,Jl 4,17:1
Feminine Touch, The 1941,D 12,35:3
Design for Scandal 1942,F 6,23:3
Take a Letter Darling 1942,My 28,13:2
My Sister Eileen 1942,O 23,15:1
Flight for Freedom 1943,Ap 16,24:2
What a Woman 1943,D 3,27:2
Roughly Speaking 1945,F 1,18:4
She Wouldn't Say Yes 1946,Ja 12,10:7
Sister Kenny 1946,S 30,21:2
Guilt of Janet Ames, The 1947,My 23,31:2
Mourning Becomes Electra 1947,N 20,38:2

Russell, Rosalind— Cont
Velvet Touch, The 1948,Ag 26,16:2
Woman of Distinction, A 1950,Mr 17,28:2
Never Wave at a Wac 1953,Ap 24,30:2
Picnic 1956,F 17,13:3
Auntie Mame 1958,D 5,39:1
Majority of One, A 1962,Ja 12,29:2
Five Finger Exercise 1962,Ap 20,20:2
Gypsy 1962,N 2,24:1
Trouble With Angels, The 1966,Ap 7,45:1
Oh Dad, Poor Dad, Mamma's Hung You in the
Closet and I'm Feeling so Sad 1967,F 16,32:1
Rosie 1968,F 8,36:1
Where Angels Go-Trouble Follows
1968,Ap 11,51:1
Russell, Roxie
School for Husbands 1939,F 7,16:2
Russell, Roy
Young and Beautiful 1934,S 18,18:4
Russell, Roy (Screenwriter)
Premature Burial, The 1962,My 24,29:2
Russell, Stanley (Original Author)
Together Again 1944,N 24,19:2
Russell, Thomas
Battle for Music 1945,O 15,13:2
Russell, Tony
War Is Hell 1964,Ja 23,26:1
Wild, Wild Planet 1967,Ag 10,45:5
Russell, Wally
Hot Blood 1956,Mr 24,14:2
Russell, William
Brass Buttons 1919,Ap 7,11:5
Anna Christie 1923,D 10,20:1
Beloved Brute, The 1924,N 10,20:1
On Thin Ice 1925,Mr 9,21:1
Way of a Girl, The 1925,Mr 30,21:3
Desired Woman, The 1927,Ag 30,21:3
Girl From Chicago, The 1927,D 20,33:2
Escape, The 1928,My 7,29:1
State Street Sadie 1928,S 3,14:2
Midnight Taxi, The 1928,O 29,29:1
Girls Gone Wild 1929,Ap 22,23:1
Biscuit Eater, The 1940,My 23,28:5
Julius Caesar 1952,N 25,33:5
Russell, William D (Director)
Our Hearts Were Growing Up 1946,Ag 12,17:2
Ladies' Man 1947,Ja 13,18:5
Dear Ruth 1947,Je 11,33:3
Sainted Sisters, The 1948,My 20,35:2
Green Promise, The 1949,Je 24,29:2
Bride for Sale 1949,N 21,29:4 (In Addenda)
Best of the Badmen 1951,Ag 10,13:2
Russinof, A
Rubicon 1934,Mr 19,13:3
Russinova, N
Ballad of Cossack Gloota, The 1938,F 28,19:1
RUSSO
See Also ROUSSEAU
Russo, Filomena
Two Cents Worth of Hope 1952,D 16,44:2
Russo, John A (Screenwriter)
Night of the Living Dead 1968,D 5,59:2
Russo, Mario
Guaglio 1949,My 19,35:2
Russo and the Samba Kings
Song Is Born, A 1948,O 20,37:2
Russon, Albert (Original Author)
We're no Angels 1955,Jl 8,15:2
Rust, Carla
Lachdoktor, Der; Laugh Doctor, The
1938,Mr 12,13:4
Liebesbriefe aus dem Engadin; Love Letters From
the Engadine 1938,D 24,12:2
Dingehort mein Herz; My Heart Belongs to Thee
1939,Mr 25,19:2
Frau Sylvelin 1939,D 9,18:3
Rust, Richard
This Rebel Breed 1960,My 5,41:2
Underworld, U S A 1961,My 13,10:1
Walk on the Wild Side 1962,F 22,20:1
Alvarez Kelly 1966,N 17,55:2
Rustori, Rudolfo (Screenwriter)
Tears of Blood 1952,Ja 19,13:2
Ruth, Babe
Headin' Home 1920,S 20,13:1
Ninth Inning, The 1942,Ja 8,30:3
Pride of the Yankees, The 1942,Jl 16,23:1
Ruth, Jean
Suddenly It's Spring 1947,F 27,26:2
Union Station 1950,O 5,38:3
At War With the Army 1951,Ja 25,21:5
Ruth, Marshall
Broadway Melody, The 1929,F 9,15:3
Nix on Dames 1929,N 23,18:5
Ruth, Mary
They Shall Have Music 1939,Jl 26,17:2
Ruth, Patsy
Name the Man 1924,F 4,23:3
Ruth, Phyllis
Always a Bride 1940,N 21,43:3
Caught in the Draft 1941,Je 26,27:3
Louisiana Purchase 1942,Ja 1,37:1
They Got Me Covered 1943,Mr 5,20:2

Ruth, Roy del (Director)
Eve's Lover 1925,Jl 27,17:3
Hogan's Alley 1925,N 24,28:4
Little Irish Girl, The 1926,My 11,24:3
First Auto, The 1927,Jl 3,VII,3:3
Three Sailors and a Girl 1953,N 23,32:2
Why Must I Die? 1960,S 15,45:4

Rutherford, Ann
Lawless Nineties, The 1936,Je 29,11:1
Harvester, The 1936,Jl 4,18:2
Down Under the Sea 1936,Ag 10,10:2
Devil is Driving, The 1937,Jl 16,22:1
You're Only Young Once 1938,Ja 3,16:2
Of Human Hearts 1938,F 18,23:1
Judge Hardy's Children 1938,Ap 8,17:2
Love Finds Andy Hardy 1938,Jl 22,10:2
Out West With the Hardys 1938,D 9,31:2
Dramatic School 1938,D 9,31:2
Christmas Carol, A 1938,D 23,16:2
Four Girls in White 1939,F 23,19:3
Hardys Ride High, The 1939,Ap 14,28:2
Andy Hardy Gets Spring Fever 1939,Jl 19,23:2
These Glamour Girls 1939,Ag 31,14:2
Dancing Co-Ed 1939,N 10,27:3
Gone With the Wind 1939,D 20,31:2
Judge Hardy and Son 1940,Ja 18,27:3 (In Addenda)
Andy Hardy Meets Debutante 1940,Ag 2,12:2
Pride and Prejudice 1940,Ag 9,19:1
Wyoming 1940,O 3,31:4
Andy Hardy's Private Secretary 1941,Mr 7,17:2
Washington Melodrama 1941,My 26,15:3
Life Begins for Andy Hardy 1941,Ag 22,19:4
Whistling in the Dark 1941,Ag 28,23:2
Badlands of Dakota 1941,S 9,27:6
Courtship of Andy Hardy, The 1942,Ap 10,21:2
Orchestra Wives 1942,S 24,23:2
Whistling in Dixie 1942,D 31,20:4
Andy Hardy's Double Life 1943,Ja 12,23:3
Happy Land 1943,D 9,33:3
Whistling in Brooklyn 1944,Mr 24,17:3
Bermuda Mystery 1944,My 13,17:1
Two O'Clock Courage 1945,Ap 14,13:3
Bedside Manner 1945,Je 23,9:6
Murder in the Music Hall 1946,Ap 15,22:2
Inside Job 1946,Je 15,24:3
Secret Life of Walter Mitty, The 1947,Ag 15,12:2
Adventures of Don Juan 1948,D 25,10:1

Rutherford, Charles
Genoese Dragnet 1954,F 12,20:5

Rutherford, John
Whoopee 1930,O 1,26:3
Half Shot at Sunrise 1930,O 11,21:3
Woman From Monte Carlo, The 1931,D 31,17:6
Roman Scandals 1933,D 25,28:2
Cleopatra 1934,Ag 17,12:1
Affairs of Cellini, The 1934,S 6,22:3
Three on the Trail 1936,My 5,26:5
Hopalong Rides Again 1938,Ja 22,19:1
Utah 1945,Mr 12,22:7
Untamed Fury 1947,Ap 26,10:6

Rutherford, Margaret
Yellow Canary, The 1944,Ap 14,24:7
Blithe Spirit 1945,O 4,27:2
Adventure for Two 1945,D 14,24:5
Meet Me at Dawn 1948,My 18,26:2
Miranda 1949,Ap 25,20:2
Her Man Gilbey 1949,Je 9,35:2
Passport to Pimlico 1949,O 27,35:2
While the Sun Shines 1950,Jl 1,9:2
Happiest Days of Your Life, The 1950,S 18,19:2
Importance of Being Earnest, The 1952,D 23,17:2
Castle in the Air 1953,Ja 5,19:2
Curtain Up 1953,F 2,17:3
Miss Robin Hood 1953,Je 27,7:2
Runaway Bus, The 1954,O 25,30:7
Innocents in Paris 1955,Mr 5,9:6
Trouble in Store 1956,Ja 14,13:2
Alligator Named Daisy, An 1957,O 7,23:2
Smallest Show on Earth, The 1957,N 23,11:2
I'm All Right Jack 1960,Ap 26,40:2
On the Double 1961,My 20,12:1
Murder She Said 1962,Ja 8,27:2
Mouse on the Moon, The 1963,Je 18,32:1
Murder at the Gallop 1963,Je 25,23:2
V I P's, The 1963,S 20,29:1
Murder Ahoy 1964,S 23,55:3
Murder Most Foul 1965,My 24,36:2
Countess from Hong Kong, A 1967,Mr 17,35:1
Falstaff; Chimes at Midnight 1967,Mr 18,19:2

Rutherfurd, Tom
Firefly, The 1937,S 2,17:2
Beg, Borrow or Steal 1937,D 10,33:2
Rosalie 1937,D 31,9:2
Vacation From Love 1938,N 10,33:2
Those Were the Days 1940,Jl 15,18:4
Virginia 1941,Ja 29,21:2

Ruthven, Madeleine (Original Author)
Sudden Death, And 1936,Jl 18,18:2

Ruthven, Madeleine (Screenwriter)
Accusing Finger, The 1936,N 17,35:4

Ruthven, Ormond (Miscellaneous)
Billy the Kid 1941,Je 20,28:2

Ruthven, Ormond (Original Author)
Dr Kildare's Wedding Day 1941,S 18,31:1

Rutkin, Jerry
Way Out 1967,O 26,54:3

Rutklewicz, Jan (Director)
Guests are Coming; Jada Goscie Jada 1967,Ja 13,15:1

Rutledge, P
Uncivilized 1937,N 17,27:4

Rutolo, Carla
Inheritance, The 1964,N 9,42:2

Rutting, Barbara
Last Bridge, The 1957,Ag 21,22:2
Deadly Decision 1958,Ap 29,26:2
Time to Love and a Time to Die, A 1958,Jl 10,22:1
Town Without Pity 1961,O 11,53:1
Shadows Grow Longer, The 1962,Je 11,36:4
Operation Crossbow 1965,Ap 2,29:1

Ruttkay, Eva
Goose Boy, The 1951,O 13,9:2

Ruttmann, Walter (Producer)
Berlin, A Symphony of a Big City 1928,My 14,25:1

Ruud, Sif
Wild Strawberries 1959,Je 23,37:1
Magician, The 1959,Ag 28,27:1

Ruysdael, Basil
Cocoanuts, The 1929,My 25,17:3
Colorado Territory 1949,Je 25,8:6
Come to the Stable 1949,Jl 28,19:1
Pinky 1949,S 30,28:2
Doctor and the Girl, The 1949,O 31,20:2
Thelma Jordon 1950,Ja 19,35:2
One Way Street 1950,My 12,33:3
Broken Arrow 1950,Jl 21,15:2
High Lonesome 1950,D 8,40:4
Gambling House 1951,Mr 19,23:2
Raton Pass 1951,Ap 20,25:1
Screen, The 1951,Ap 23,21:2
My Forbidden Past 1951,Ap 26,34:2
Half Angel 1951,Je 16,9:2
Boots Malone 1952,Mr 13,26:2
Carrie 1952,Jl 17,20:2
Prince Valiant 1954,Ap 7,40:2
Violent Men, The 1955,Ja 27,17:2
Blackboard Jungle 1955,Mr 21,21:5
Davy Crockett, King of the Wild Frontier 1955,My 26,36:1
Pearl of the South Pacific 1955,S 17,12:2
Jubal 1956,Ap 25,39:1
These Wilder Years 1956,Ag 18,11:2
Last Hurrah, The 1958,O 24,40:1
Horse Soldiers, The 1959,Je 26,13:1
Story of Ruth, The 1960,Je 18,12:3

Ruysdael, Basil (Narrator)
Dealers in Death 1934,D 15,9:3

Ruzek, Martin
Death of Tarzan, The 1968,Jl 4,13:2

Ruzickova, Helena
Happy End 1968,Je 11,54:4

Ryabinkina, Elena
Cinderella 1961,D 19,39:1

RYAN
See Also RHINE

Ryan, Abigail
Mikado, The 1967,Mr 15,53:1

Ryan, Annie
Claw, The 1927,My 11,28:3

Ryan, Anthony
Amazon Trader, The 1956,N 17,17:6

Ryan, Ben (Miscellaneous)
I'd Give my Life 1936,Ag 17,9:1

Ryan, Ben (Screenwriter)
Chinatown Squad 1935,My 30,21:1
Laughing Irish Eyes 1936,Ap 4,11:2

Ryan, Cornelius (Original Author)
Longest Day, The 1962,O 5,28:1

Ryan, Cornelius (Screenwriter)
Longest Day, The 1962,O 5,28:1

Ryan, Dick
Constant Nymph, The 1943,Jl 24,8:2
Mr Peabody and the Mermaid 1948,Ag 14,6:5
Chicken every Sunday 1949,Ja 19,34:2
Top o' the Morning 1949,S 1,25:2
Born to be Bad 1950,S 29,31:5
For Heaven's Sake 1950,D 16,10:5

Ryan, Don
Merry Widow, The 1925,Ag 27,14:1

Ryan, Don (Original Author)
Carnival Boat 1932,Mr 21,19:5

Ryan, Don (Screenwriter)
Smart Blonde 1937,Ja 9,21:1
Midnight Court 1937,Mr 4,27:3
Fly Away Baby 1937,Jl 9,18:2
Missing Witness 1937,D 10,33:3
Broadway Musketeers 1938,O 14,27:1
You Can't Get Away With Murder 1939,Mr 25,19:2
On Trial 1939,Ap 5,31:2
Tear Gas Squad 1940,My 31,15:3

Ryan, Don (Screenwriter) — Cont
Devil's Island 1940,Jl 12,11:4

Ryan, Eddie
Breakfast in Hollywood 1946,Jl 15,21:1
It Happened on Fifth Avenue 1947,Je 11,33:2

Ryan, Edmon
Crime Over London 1938,Jl 28,23:2
Human Monster, The 1940,Mr 25,11:2
Side Street 1950,Mr 24,29:2
Mystery Street 1950,Jl 28,12:5
Breaking Point, The 1950,O 7,10:6
Three Secrets 1950,O 21,10:6
Undercover Girl 1950,N 8,37:2
Highway 301 1950,D 9,13:2
Guy Who Came Back, The 1951,Ag 17,13:2
Go, Man, Go 1954,Mr 10,29:5
Two for the Seesaw 1962,N 22,43:1
Americanization of Emily, The 1964,O 28,51:1
Playground, The 1965,O 4,00:0

Ryan, Edward
Sullivans, The 1944,F 10,19:2
Take It or Leave It 1944,Jl 13,14:2
Within These Walls 1945,Jl 16,8:4
Caribbean Mystery, The 1945,Ag 20,22:4

Ryan, Elaine (Screenwriter)
Mr Dodd Takes the Air 1937,Ag 12,14:2
Listen, Darling 1938,N 24,37:2
Second Chorus 1941,Ja 16,25:2
Babes on Broadway 1942,Ja 1,37:1

Ryan, Frank (Director)
Call out the Marines 1942,Ja 26,18:3
Hers to Hold 1943,Jl 22,15:1
Can't Help Singing 1944,D 26,22:4
Patrick the Great 1945,Ap 13,15:2
So Goes my Love 1946,My 2,3:7

Ryan, Frank (Screenwriter)
Girl, a Guy and a Gob, A 1941,Ap 24,25:3
Call out the Marines 1942,Ja 26,18:3
Obliging Young Lady 1942,F 13,24:4
Mayor of Forty-Fourth Street, The 1942,Je 11,27:4
Amazing Mrs Holliday, The 1943,F 22,20:2
Can't Help Singing 1944,D 26,22:4

Ryan, Irene
Sarong Girl 1943,Je 18,16:6
San Diego, I Love You 1944,N 10,25:1
That's the Spirit 1945,Je 2,11:2
That Night With You 1945,N 9,16:2
Diary of a Chambermaid, The 1946,Je 23,28:2
Woman on the Beach, The 1947,Je 9,26:6
My Dear Secretary 1949,F 14,15:4
There's a Girl in my Heart 1950,Ja 20,29:2
Half Angel 1951,Je 16,9:2
Meet Me After the Show 1951,Ag 16,23:2
Blackbeard the Pirate 1952,D 26,20:3
Spring Reunion 1957,My 6,25:2

Ryan, James
Manhunt in the Jungle 1958,Ap 12,13:1

Ryan, Joe
Vanishing American, The 1925,O 16,18:2

Ryan, Joe (Miscellaneous)
Journey to Jerusalem, A 1968,N 18,59:1

Ryan, Kathleen
Odd Man Out 1947,Ap 24,30:2
Captain Boycott 1947,D 6,11:2
Christopher Columbus 1949,O 13,33:2
Prelude to Fame 1950,N 10,35:3
Try and Get Me 1951,My 7,22:2
Scotch on the Rocks 1954,Je 14,18:2
Yellow Balloon, The 1954,O 13,28:2

Ryan, Madge
Upstairs and Downstairs 1960,D 2,53:4
Tiara Tahiti 1963,N 6,32:1

Ryan, Marian
Dream Maker, The 1964,Ap 23,34:1

Ryan, Maurice
K-The Unknown 1924,N 18,22:1
Unknown, The 1924,N 18,22:1
Midshipman, The 1925,O 13,20:1
Poor Nut, The 1927,Jl 19,27:2
Dress Parade 1927,O 31,22:1

Ryan, Michael
Small Hours, The 1962,Ag 14,34:1

Ryan, Mildred
Little French Girl, The 1925,Je 1,10:3
Wild, Wild Susan 1925,Ag 5,12:4
Man Who Found Himself, The 1925,Ag 24,17:3

Ryan, Nancy
Nothing but the Truth 1929,Ap 22,23:1

Ryan, Patrick (Original Author)
How I Won the War 1967,N 9,56:1

Ryan, Peggy
Top of the Town 1937,Mr 27,19:2
Flying Irishman, The 1939,Ap 12,27:2
Miss Annie Rooney 1942,Je 8,11:1
Private Buckaroo 1942,Je 25,27:4
Give Out, Sisters 1942,Ag 28,22:3
Get Help to Love 1942,O 19,15:3
When Johnny Comes Marching Home 1943,Mr 5,20:4
Mister Big 1943,Je 14,13:4
Top Man 1943,O 29,23:2
Chip off the Old Block 1944,Mr 17,14:2
Follow the Boys 1944,Ap 26,24:6

Ryan, Peggy— Cont
ThIs is the Life 1944,Ap 28,23:3
Merry Monahans, The 1944,O 13,16:2
Here Come the Co-Eds 1945,F 19,21:1
Patrick the Great 1945,Ap 13,15:2
That's the Spirit 1945,Je 2,11:2
Men in her Diary 1945,S 24,16:5
There's a Girl in my Heart 1950,Ja 20,29:2
Ryan, Phil (Producer)
Secret Command 1944,Je 14,16:2
Perilous Holiday 1946,Je 1,10:4
Fighting Father Dunne 1948,Je 25,26:2
Ryan, Robert
College Widow, The 1927,N 7,26:4
Strong Boy 1929,Ap 1,22:1
Golden Gloves 1940,Ag 21,23:6
Bombardier 1943,Jl 2,15:2
Sky's the Limit, The 1943,S 3,15:2
Behind the Rising Sun 1943,O 14,26:2
Iron Major, The 1943,N 1,12:5
Tender Comrade 1944,Je 2,21:2
Marine Raiders 1944,Jl 1,10:7
Walls Came Tumbling Down, The 1946,N 9,13:5
Trail Street 1947,Ap 10,35:2
Woman on the Beach, The 1947,Je 9,26:6
Crossfire 1947,Jl 23,19:2
Berlin Express 1948,My 21,19:3
Return of the Badmen 1948,Ag 5,16:2
Boy With Green Hair, The 1949,Ja 13,26:2
Act of Violence 1949,Ja 24,16:2
Caught 1949,F 18,26:4
Set-Up, The 1949,Mr 30,31:2
Woman on Pier 13, The 1950,Je 16,28:4
Secret Fury, The 1950,Je 22,34:2
Born to be Bad 1950,S 29,31:5
Best of the Badmen 1951,Ag 10,13:2
Flying Leathernecks 1951,S 20,37:1
Racket, The 1951,D 13,44:2
On Dangerous Ground 1952,F 13,35:2
Clash by Night 1952,Je 19,32:6
Beware my Lovely 1952,S 13,10:5
Horizons West 1952,N 22,16:5
City Beneath the Sea 1953,Mr 12,24:3
Naked Spur, The 1953,Mr 26,37:3
Inferno 1953,Ag 12,22:2
Alaska Seas 1954,Mr 6,13:5
About Mrs Leslie 1954,Je 28,16:2
Her Twelve Men 1954,Ag 12,23:2
Bad Day at Black Rock 1955,F 2,22:2
Escape to Burma 1955,My 21,11:2
House of Bamboo 1955,Jl 2,13:2
Tall Men, The 1955,O 12,36:2
Proud Ones, The 1956,Ag 11,10:2
Back From Eternity 1956,S 8,20:6
Men in War 1957,Mr 20,32:4
God's Little Acre 1958,Ag 14,23:2
Lonelyhearts 1959,Mr 5,35:3
Odds Against Tomorrow 1959,O 16,27:1
Ice Palace 1960,Je 30,22:1
Canadians, The 1961,Je 1,31:1
King of Kings 1961,O 12,41:2
Longest Day, The 1962,O 5,28:1
Billy Budd 1962,O 31,32:1
Crooked Road, The 1965,F 4,24:2
Battle of the Bulge 1965,D 18,36:1
Professionals, The 1966,N 3,45:1
Busy Body, The 1967,Je 8,52:2
Dirty Dozen, The 1967,Je 16,36:1
Hour of the Gun 1967,N 2,58:4
Minute to Pray, A Second to Die, A
1968,My 23,56:2
Custer of the West 1968,Jl 4,13:2
Anzio 1968,Jl 25,26:1
Ryan, Robert (Narrator)
Inheritance, The 1964,N 9,42:2
Ryan, Sheila
Gay Caballero, The 1940,O 25,25:3
Dead Men Tell 1941,Ap 17,29:3
Dressed to Kill 1941,Ag 22,19:3
Great Guns 1941,O 3,27:2
Who Is Hope Schuyler 1942,My 22,27:1
A-Haunting We Will Go 1942,Ag 3,18:4
Gang's All Here, The 1943,D 23,26:4
Something for the Boys 1944,N 30,19:1
Caribbean Mystery, The 1945,Ag 20,22:4
Getting Gertie's Garter 1946,F 4,21:2
Deadline for Murder 1946,Je 29,22:7
Big Fix, The 1947,My 3,10:3
Ringside 1949,S 17,10:8
Ryan, Thomas C (Producer)
Heart is a Lonely Hunter, The 1968,Ag 1,24:1
Ryan, Thomas C (Screenwriter)
Pad, The (And How to Use It) 1966,Ag 18,27:2
Hurry Sundown 1967,Mr 24,22:1
Heart is a Lonely Hunter, The 1968,Ag 1,24:1
Ryan, Tim
Private Affairs 1940,Jl 5,10:3
Man Betrayed, A 1941,Mr 27,29:5
Ice-Capades 1941,S 25,29:1
Harmon of Michigan 1941,O 2,29:2
Bedtime Story 1942,Mr 20,25:4
Get Help to Love 1942,O 19,15:3
Man in the Trunk, The 1942,O 23,25:1
Stand by for Action 1943,Mr 12,12:2

Hit Parade of 1943 1943,Ap 16,24:3
Reveille With Beverly 1943,Ap 24,17:2
Sarong Girl 1943,Je 18,16:6
Swingtime Johnny 1943,D 17,23:3
Rockin' in The Rockies 1945,Jl 5,7:2
Bringing Up Father 1946,N 22,27:3
Body and Soul 1947,N 10,21:2
Force of Evil 1948,D 27,16:2
Petty Girl, The 1950,Ag 18,17:2
From Here to Eternity 1953,Ag 6,16:2
Ryan, Tommy
Tenth Avenue Kid 1938,S 2,21:3
Street of Missing Men 1939,Je 1,31:3
Mickey, the Kid 1939,Jl 6,27:1
Ryan, Vera
Mikado, The 1967,Mr 15,53:1
Ryazanof, P I
Twenty-Six Commissars 1933,Jl 1,16:6
Ryazanov, Eldar (Director)
Spring Voices 1956,O 25,40:5
Carnival in Moscow 1957,N 4,40:1
Watch out for the Automobile 1966,My 23,48:1
Uncommon Thief, An 1967,D 1,56:2
Ryazanov, Eldar (Producer)
Carnival in Moscow 1957,N 4,40:1
Ryazanov, Eldar (Screenwriter)
Ballad of a Hussar, The 1963,Jl 15,25:5
Watch out for the Automobile 1966,My 23,48:1
Rybnick, Harry (Producer)
Golden Mistress, The 1954,O 30,15:6
Rybnikov, N N
Last Night, The 1937,Ap 28,18:3
Rychman, Ladislav (Director)
Lady on the Tracks, The 1968,N 26,39:2
Rydeberg, Georg
Hour of the Wolf 1968,Ap 10,50:2
Rydell, Bobby
Bye Bye Birdie 1963,Ap 5,27:3
Rydell, Charles
Open the Door and See all the People
1964,Ap 2,28:1
Rydell, Mark
Crime in the Streets 1956,My 24,27:4
Rydell, Mark (Director)
Fox, The 1968,F 8,36:1
Ryder, A (Director)
Great Test, The 1928,Ap 27,8:2
Legion of Honor, The 1928,Jl 20,8:4
Soul of France, The 1929,O 12,11:1
Ronde des Heures, La 1932,Ja 25,20:3
Ryder, Alfred
Winged Victory 1944,D 21,16:2
T-Men 1948,Ja 23,28:3
Story of Page One, The 1960,Ja 14,28:1
Invitation to a Gunfighter 1964,O 28,51:3
Hotel 1967,Ja 20,27:1
Ryder, Eddie
Country Girl, The 1954,D 16,51:2
Young Stranger, The 1957,Ap 9,40:1
Not With my Wife, You Don't! 1966,N 3,45:2
Ryder, Paul (Screenwriter)
Cosmic Monster, The 1959,Ja 1,38:1
Ryder, Rene (Original Author)
Cosmic Monster, The 1959,Ja 1,38:1
Rydkvist, Viran
Pettersson & Bendel 1934,F 22,25:2
Rydquist, Oscar (Screenwriter)
Karl Fredrik Reigns 1938,F 2,15:2
John Ericsson Victor of Hampton Roads
1938,My 18,17:2
Rye, Jorgen
I, A Lover 1968,My 4,46:2
Rye, Preben Lerdorff
Ordet 1957,D 16,33:6
Stranger Knocks, A 1965,Ap 1,30:1
Ryen, Richard
Cross of Lorraine, The 1943,D 3,27:4
Hitler Gang, The 1944,My 8,15:2
Paris Underground 1945,O 20,8:2
Ryerson, Florence (Original Author)
Call of the West 1930,My 27,27:2
Notorious Gentleman, A 1935,F 16,9:1
Tough Guy 1936,Mr 14,10:1
Everybody Sing 1938,Mr 11,15:3
Ryerson, Florence (Screenwriter)
Adam and Evil 1927,Ag 10,21:4
Wicked Woman, A 1935,Ja 1,24:1
Casino Murder Case, The 1935,Ap 17,26:5
Tough Guy 1936,Mr 14,10:1
Moonlight Murder 1936,Mr 28,11:2
Mad Holiday 1936,N 26,39:2
Everybody Sing 1938,Mr 11,15:3
Ice Follies of 1939 1939,Mr 17,25:2
Wizard of Oz, The 1939,Ag 18,16:2
Ryjanov, A
Peter the First 1937,D 25,10:4
Ryland, Bon Corporal
Unbeliever, The 1918,F 12,9:2
Ryland, George
High Tide 1947,N 8,11:2
Ryle, Lawrence
Houdini 1953,Jl 3,10:2

Rymal, Reggie
House of Wax 1953,Ap 11,15:2
Rymowicz, K S (Director)
Destiny of Russia 1927,F 21,14:2
Ryrenforth, Harald
Mask of the Himalayas 1953,Ag 12,22:3
Ryskind, Morrie (Miscellaneous)
Palmy Days 1931,S 24,21:2
Louisiana Purchase 1942,Ja 1,37:1
My Man Godfrey 1957,O 12,23:1
Ryskind, Morrie (Original Author)
Animal Crackers 1930,Ag 29,20:3
Man About Town 1939,Je 29,19:1
Where Do We Go From Here? 1945,Je 7,25:2
Ryskind, Morrie (Screenwriter)
Palmy Days 1931,S 24,21:2
Night at the Opera, A 1935,D 7,22:1
My Man Godfrey 1936,S 19,18:1 (Incorrect in
this edition; use 1936,S 18,18:1 elsewhere)
Stage Door 1937,O 8,27:2
Room Service 1938,S 22,27:1
Man About Town 1939,Je 29,19:1
Penny Serenade 1941,My 23,25:2
Claudia 1943,N 5,23:2
Where Do We Go From Here? 1945,Je 7,25:2
Heartbeat 1946,My 11,22:4
Ryu, Chishu
Carmen Comes Home 1959,D 23,22:1
She Was Like a Wild Chrysanthemum
1960,Ja 22,15:2
Rikisha Man, The 1960,My 4,57:1
Bandits on the Wind 1964,Ja 15,27:3
Ohayo; (Good Morning) 1966,F 2,24:1
Ryzhoff, Nikolai
Zoya 1945,Ap 16,18:6
Ryzhov, Ivan
Mumu 1961,Je 5,37:4

S

Saad, Margit
Gypsy Baron, The 1959,N 14,13:1
Chasers, The; Draguers, Les 1960,My 3,43:1
Call Me Genius 1961,O 17,47:1
Saadi, Omar Ben
Siroco 1931,N 26,37:2
Saadi, Yacef
Battle of Algiers, The 1967,S 21,56:1
Saala, Fernande
He 1933,D 27,23:6
Saavedra, Angelo (Original Author)
Forza del Destino, La 1952,O 17,33:1
Sabatello, Dario (Producer)
Operation Kid Brother 1967,N 23,58:2
Sabatier, Pierre (Original Author)
Stolen Affections 1951,Mr 12,20:2
Sabatini, Danilo (Producer)
Place Called Glory, A 1966,Ag 11,27:4
Sabatini, Rafael (Original Author)
Scaramouche 1923,O 12,7:2 (Incorrect in this
edition; use 1927,O 1,7:2 elsewhere)
Captain Blood 1924,S 9,19:1
Bardelys The Magnificent 1926,N 1,28:1 (In
Addenda)
Captain Blood 1935,D 27,14:1
Black Swan, The 1942,D 24,18:3
Fortunes of Captain Blood 1950,Je 10,11:3
Scaramouche 1952,My 9,20:2
Adventures of Scaramouche, The 1964,N 23,34:1
(Incorrect in this edition; use 1964,N 21,34:1
elsewhere)
Sabatini, Rafael (Screenwriter)
Sea Hawk, The 1924,Je 3,22:1
Sabatler, William
Casque D'Or 1952,Ag 19,19:1
Sabato, Alfredo
River, The 1928,D 24,11:1
Sabato, Alfredo (Director)
Sei tu l'Amore 1930,N 18,28:4
Sabato, Antonio
Grand-Prix 1966,D 22,40:1
Sabba, Betty
Take Me Away, My Love 1962,Jl 30,15:5
Sabbagh, Isa
Island of Allah 1956,Je 27,35:1
Sabbatini, Ernesto
Come le Foglie; Like the Leaves 1938,S 29,31:1
Between Two Worlds 1940,F 9,15:2
Sabel, Virgilio (Screenwriter)
Monte Cassino 1948,N 25,47:3
Sabini, Frank
Blaze O' Glory 1929,D 31,15:1
Sablin, V Korsh (Director)
Secret Brigade 1951,Mr 19,23:2
Sablon, Germaine
Glory of Faith, The 1938,N 24,37:2

SABO
See Also SZABO
Sabo, Joseph (Screenwriter)
Pinocchio 1940,F 8,18:3
Sabo, Oscar
Hampelmann, Der 1931,S 8,38:7
Lindenwirtin vom Rhein, Die 1931,S 25,28:7
Schoen Ist die Manoeverzeit 1932,Ag 19,20:6
Gitta Entdeckt Ihr Herz 1932,S 30,17:3
Eine Nacht im Paradies 1933,F 20,11:6
Liebe Muss Verstanden Sein 1934,Mr 21,24:3
Rosen aus dem Sueden; Roses from the South
1935,Ap 23,24:5
Unschuld vom Lande, Die 1935,My 13,18:6
Geschichten aus dem Wienerwald; Tales From the
Vienna Woods 1935,N 2,13:3
Endstation 1937,Jl 17,18:1
Zwei im Sonnenschein 1937,Jl 31,6:2
Sabouret, Marie
Rififi 1956,Je 6,37:1
Would-Be Gentleman, The 1960,Mr 23,31:1
Sabrina
Blue Murder at St Trinian's 1958,My 27,27:1
Satan in High Heels 1962,Mr 24,15:6
Sabu
Elephant Boy 1937,Ap 6,20:2
Drums 1938,S 30,24:4
Thief of Bagdad, The 1940,D 6,28:2
Jungle Book 1942,Ap 6,19:1
Arabian Nights 1942,D 26,15:1
White Savage 1943,Ap 26,15:2
Cobra Woman 1944,My 18,17:2
Tangier 1946,Je 7,II,16:4
Black Narcissus 1947,Ag 14,29:2
End of the River, The 1948,Je 21,18:2
Man-Eater of Kumaon 1948,Jl 2,24:2
Song of India 1949,Je 10,32:3
Hello Elephant 1954,S 10,18:5
Rampage 1963,O 17,39:2
Tiger Walks, A 1964,Ag 27,28:2
Sacchetti, Antonio
Tosca 1958,O 24,40:3
Sacha, Orlando
No Exit 1962,D 6,55:2
Sachdev, Achia
Nine Hours to Rama 1963,Ap 4,58:2
Householder, The 1963,O 22,43:2
SACHS
See Also SAKS, SAX, SAXE
Sachs, Leonard
Gentlemen Marry Brunettes 1955,O 31,31:5
Oscar Wilde 1960,Je 21,28:2
Scream of Fear 1961,Ag 23,29:1
Sachse, Leopold
Interrupted Melody 1955,My 6,18:1
Sachsi, Salli
Trip, The 1967,Ag 24,43:1
Sachson, Monroe (Producer)
Pretty Boy Floyd 1960,N 3,49:2
Incident, The 1967,N 6,65:1
Sack, Erna
Nanon 1938,N 26,18:2
Blumen aus Nizza; Flowers From Nice
1939,Ap 1,17:3
Sackett, Janet
Mrs Mike 1950,F 9,36:5
Sackett, Judith
Mrs Mike 1950,F 9,36:5
Sackheim, Jerry (Screenwriter)
Night Before the Divorce, The 1942,Ap 10,21:3
Last Crooked Mile, The 1946,S 14,10:8
Strange Door, The 1951,D 10,34:6
Paula 1952,Jl 16,21:2
Black Castle, The 1952,D 26,20:4
Young Jesse James 1960,Ag 25,25:1
Boy and the Pirates, The 1960,N 24,48:3
Sackheim, William (Original Author)
Chicago Syndicate 1955,Je 21,37:1
Art of Love, The 1965,Jl 1,34:1
Sackheim, William (Producer)
Belle Sommers 1962,My 31,23:2
Sackheim, William (Screenwriter)
One Last Fling 1949,Jl 1,14:6
Barricade 1950,Mr 25,8:6
Yank in Korea, A 1951,Ap 2,29:2
Man in the Dark 1953,Ap 9,31:5
Forbidden 1954,Ja 23,11:2
Tanganyika 1954,Je 19,9:2
Human Jungle, The 1954,N 26,24:6
Sackin, Moe (Director)
Tres Amores 1934,N 5,23:1
Sackler, Howard (Director)
Midsummer Night's Dream, A 1961,D 19,39:1
Sackler, Howard (Miscellaneous)
Midsummer Night's Dream, A 1961,D 19,39:1
Sackler, Howard (Screenwriter)
Fear and Desire 1953,Ap 1,35:2
Sackville, Gordon
Snob, The 1924,D 15,14:1
Sacred Harp Singers
Festival 1967,O 24,53:2

Sacripanti, Umberto
Bertoldo, Bertoldino, Cacasenno 1937,D 22,32:3
Giovanni De Medici, The Leader 1940,Ja 5,15:4
Grande Luce, La; Great Light, The
1940,Mr 15,27:4
Tutta la Vita in una Notte; All of Life in one
Night 1940,My 2,29:6
Terra di Nessuno; Nobody's Land 1940,O 25,25:4
Four Steps in the Clouds 1948,N 22,25:2
Thief of Venice, The 1952,N 28,22:7
Farewell to Arms, A 1958,Ja 25,14:1
Sada, Keiji
Ohayo; (Good Morning) 1966,F 2,24:1
Sada, Yutaka
High and Low 1963,N 27,30:1
I Live in Fear; Ikimono no Kiroku
1967,Ja 26,25:1
Sadden, Jack (Screenwriter)
Longest Day, The 1962,O 5,28:1
Sadler, Barry
Dayton's Devils 1968,O 3,56:4
Sadler, Dudley
Boomerang 1947,Mr 6,36:2
Sadler Wells Ballet
Dance Little Lady 1955,D 26,23:3
Sadlette, Michael (Original Author)
Man of Evil 1948,Mr 26,26:2
Sadlier, Michael (Original Author)
Fanny by Gaslight 1944,Jl 16,II,3:4
Sadoff, Fred
Quiet American, The 1958,F 6,24:1
Sadour, Ben
Garden of Allah, The 1927,S 3,13:5
Sadovski, M
Gobsek 1937,Jl 16,22:1
Masquerade 1943,My 17,11:2
Saenz, Ignacio
This Woman Is Mine 1941,O 13,21:2
South of Tahiti 1941,N 10,21:3
Saffo, Eveline
I Cadetti di Guascogna 1952,O 6,22:2
Safonov, D
Optimistic Tragedy, The 1964,F 24,20:2
Safonova, M
Ivan Pavlov 1950,F 13,15:2
Lady With the Dog, The 1962,N 7,48:1
Safra, Josef
They Were Ten; (Heym Hayu Assara)
1961,Ap 18,44:2
Safra, Michel (Producer)
Damned, The; Maudits, Les 1948,Ap 26,27:2
Paris Hotel 1959,S 12,12:3
Safranova, N
Peter the First 1937,D 25,10:4
Safronov, V
Men of the Sea 1938,Je 20,11:2
Fortress on the Volga 1942,D 25,15:3
Sagagu, Charles
Home in Indiana 1944,Je 22,23:1
Sagal, Boris (Director)
Dime With a Halo 1963,Je 27,23:3
Twilight of Honor 1963,N 14,41:2
Girl Happy 1965,My 27,28:1
Made in Paris 1966,F 17,29:1
Sagal, D
Childhood of Maxim Gorky 1938,S 28,29:3
Heroes Are Made 1944,Mr 11,10:2
Mexican, The 1957,Ap 3,28:2
Sagal, Daniel
Taras Family, The 1946,D 9,34:4
Sons and Mothers 1967,O 2,58:1
Sagal, Dmitri
Days and Nights 1946,Ap 29,24:4
Village Teacher 1948,Jl 5,8:4
Sagan, Francoise (Original Author)
Bonjour Tristesse 1958,Ja 16,32:1
Certain Smile, A 1958,Ag 1,13:2
Goodbye Again 1961,Je 30,32:2
Playtime; Receation, La 1963,Ja 16,5:2
Chateau en Suede; Castle in Switzerland
1964,O 14,51:1
Sagan, Francoise (Screenwriter)
Landru 1963,Ap 10,31:1
Sagan, Leontine (Director)
Maedchen in Uniform 1932,S 21,25:4
Men of Tomorrow 1935,Ap 16,27:2
Sagardze, G
They Wanted Peace 1940,Ja 8,11:3
Vow, The 1947,Je 23,14:3
Sage, Byron
Into her Kingdom 1926,Ag 10,19:2
Clothes Make the Woman 1928,Je 5,21:1
Courage 1930,My 23,21:1
One Romantic Night 1930,My 31,19:4
Sage, Frances
Witness Chair, The 1936,Ap 18,19:2
Without Orders 1936,N 4,41:3
Sage, Michael
Miss Susie Slagle's 1946,F 7,29:2
Sage, Stuart
Fighting Blade, The 1923,O 15,15:4

Sage, Willard
Dragnet 1954,Ag 21,10:2
It's a Dog's Life 1955,D 23,14:3
That Touch of Mink 1962,Je 15,16:2
Saget, Roger
Happy Road, The 1957,Je 21,20:2
Saggau, Charles
Gang's All Here, The 1943,D 23,26:4
Saghy, Gyorgyi
Nem Elhetek Muzsikaszo Nelkuel 1936,F 21,21:2
Sagor, Frederica (Screenwriter)
Silk Legs 1927,D 26,26:6
Sagovsky, V (Miscellaneous)
King's People, The 1937,My 12,27:1
Sahara, Kenji
Mysterians, The 1959,Jl 2,15:2
Ghidrah, The Three-Headed Monster
1965,D 16,63:3
Sahl, Mort
In Love and War 1958,N 1,14:2
All the Young Men 1960,Ag 27,8:6
Johnny Cool 1963,O 3,31:1
Doctor, You've Got to be Kidding
1967,My 11,50:1
Don't Make Waves 1967,Je 21,36:2
Sahler, Willi
Marriage of Figaro 1950,N 3,31:2
Sahni, Sonia
Maya 1966,Je 23,29:4
Sahu, Kishore
Guide, The 1965,F 10,44:2
Sai-Yu
Samarang 1933,Je 29,22:2
Said, Hassan
Stanley and Livingstone 1939,Ag 5,18:2
Said, Joe
Up to his Ears 1966,My 18,37:1
Said, Si
Itto 1936,Ja 29,15:5
Saidou, Victorien (Original Author)
Diplomacy 1926,S 13,18:1
Saidy, Fred (Narrator)
Sound of Laughter, The 1963,D 18,44:2
Saidy, Fred (Original Author)
Finian's Rainbow 1968,O 10,59:5
Saidy, Fred (Screenwriter)
I Dood It 1943,N 11,29:1
Meet The People 1944,S 8,16:2
Finian's Rainbow 1968,O 10,59:5
Saillard, Georges
That They May Live 1939,N 7,31:2
Saillard, M G
Miserables, Les 1926,Jl 9,17:1
Miserables, Les 1927,Ag 23,29:4
Saillard, Nivette
Miserables, Les 1926,Jl 9,17:1
Miserables, Les 1927,Ag 23,29:4
Sainati, Bella
Furia 1948,Ja 21,30:2
Sainati, Bella Starace
Napoli che mon Muore; Naples That Never Dies
1940,Mr 4,11:3
Due Madri, Le; Two Mothers, The
1940,My 17,23:3
Cavalleria Rusticana 1947,D 20,21:2
Carmela 1949,My 14,9:2
Ten Commandments, The 1958,Ap 7,26:1
Sainpolis, John
Coquette 1929,Ap 6,14:4 (In Addenda)
Saint, Eva Marie
On the Waterfront 1954,Jl 29,18:1
That Certain Felling 1956,Je 21,35:2
Hatful of Rain, A 1957,Jl 18,19:2
Raintree County 1957,D 21,22:1
North by Northwest 1959,Ag 7,28:1
Exodus 1960,D 16,44:1
All Fall Down 1962,Ap 12,41:3
36 Hours 1965,Ja 29,25:2
Sandpiper, The 1965,Jl 16,14:1
Russians are Coming the Russians are Coming,
The 1966,My 26,55:1
Grand-Prix 1966,D 22,40:1
Saint-Allier
Queen and the Cardinal, The 1944,Je 1,17:3
St Andrie, Stella
Little Lord Fauntleroy 1914,Je 23,11:3
St Angel, Michael
Marine Raiders 1944,Jl 1,10:7
Bride by Mistake 1944,S 16,20:2
Brighton Strangler, The 1945,My 19,15:2
Truth About Murder, The 1946,Jl 27,12:6
French Line, The 1954,My 15,13:2
St Angelo, Robert
Subway Express 1931,My 2,23:4
Last Man, The 1932,S 17,18:4
St Aubrey, Robert (Original Author)
Alias Jesse James 1959,My 18,31:2
St Brendan Choristers
College Swing 1938,Ap 28,27:2
Angels With Dirty Faces 1938,N 26,18:1
St Clair, Ana
All the Young Men 1960,Ag 27,8:6
Caretakers, The 1963,Ag 22,19:2

St Clair, Eric
Find Your Man 1924,S 23,26:1
St Clair, Lydia
House on Ninety-Second Street, The
  1945,S 27,24:7
St Clair, Malcolm (Director)
Find Your Man 1924,S 23,26:1
Lighthouse by the Sea, The 1924,D 29,11:4
On Thin Ice 1925,Mr 9,21:1
After Business Hour 1925,Je 17,16:2
Trouble With Wives, The 1925,Ag 5,12:4
Woman of the World, A 1925,D 14,18:2
Grand Duchess and the Waiter, The
  1926,F 9,22:1
Social Celebrity, A 1926,Ap 19,24:3
Good and Naughty 1926,Je 14,24:1
Show-Off, The 1926,Ag 23,9:1
Popular Sin, The 1926,D 20,28:3
Knockout Reilly 1927,Ap 18,21:2
Breakfast at Sunrise 1927,N 14,26:1
Gentlemen Prefer Blondes 1928,Ja 16,24:1
Sporting Goods 1928,F 13,16:2
Fleet's In, The 1928,O 1,23:1
Canary Murder Case, The 1929,Mr 11,22:2
Side Street 1929,S 9,30:2
Night Parade 1929,N 11,20:2
Montana Moon 1930,Ap 14,24:2
Dangerous Nan McGrew 1930,Je 21,20:5
Remote Control 1930,D 8,26:1
Boudoir Diplomat, The 1930,D 8,26:1
Goldie Gets Along 1933,Je 3,16:4
Crack-Up 1937,Ja 4,20:4
Time Out for Romance 1937,Mr 13,23:2
She Had to Eat 1937,Jl 24,12:1
Born Reckless 1937,Jl 30,22:6
Dangerously Yours 1937,O 18,14:2
Trip to Paris, A 1938,Je 10,18:2
Safety in Numbers 1938,S 6,17:2
Hollywood Cavalcade 1939,O 14,13:2
Young as You Feel 1940,Mr 8,25:3
Man in the Trunk, The 1942,O 23,25:1
Over my Dead Body 1942,D 26,15:2
Jitterbugs 1943,Je 5,12:2
Dancing Masters, The 1943,D 2,30:2
Big Noise, The 1944,S 23,16:1
Bullfighters, The 1945,My 12,10:3
St Clair, Maurice
Black Angel 1946,S 26,32:4
St Clair, Michael
Von Ryan's Express 1965,Je 24,28:1
Thoroughly Modern Millie 1967,Mr 23,25:1
St Clair, Robert (Screenwriter)
I'm From the City 1938,Ag 19,13:4
St Clair, Sally
Shadow, The 1937,D 17,33:3
St Clair, Sue
Shadow, The 1937,D 17,33:3
St Cyr, Lili
Son of Sinbad 1955,Jl 28,18:2
Naked and the Dead, The 1958,Ag 7,21:1
Saint-Cyr, Renee
Frochard et les Deux Orphelines, La
  1934,F 7,16:2
Dernier Milliardaire, Le 1935,O 30,16:2
Pearls of the Crown, The 1938,Ap 12,26:2
Symphonie Fantastique, La 1947,D 8,35:2
Marked Girls 1949,Je 25,8:7
Secret Document-Vienna 1954,Mr 29,22:4
Lafayette 1963,Ap 11,29:1
St Denis, Ruth, Dancers
World Dances 1954,N 8,24:6
St Dennis, Madelon (Original Author)
Death Kiss, The 1933,F 5,IX,5:3
Saint-Exupery, Antoine de (Original Author)
Night Flight 1933,O 7,18:4
St George, George (Producer)
300 Spartans, The 1962,S 20,29:2
St George, George (Screenwriter)
300 Spartans, The 1962,S 20,29:2
Saint-Giniez, Juliette (Screenwriter)
Bride Is Much too Beautiful, The 1958,Ja 21,35:1
Saint-Granier
Avec l'Assurance 1935,My 4,17:3
St Helier, Ivy
Bitter Sweet 1933,Ag 24,18:2
Dulcimer Street 1948,N 8,24:2
Saint-Iles
Lower Depths, The 1937,S 11,20:1
St Jacques, Raymond
Pawnbroker, The 1965,Ap 21,51:1
Mister Moses 1965,My 13,32:1
Mister Buddwing 1966,O 12,36:1
Comedians, The 1967,N 1,37:1
Madigan 1968,Mr 30,22:2
Green Berets, The 1968,Je 20,49:1
If He Hollers, Let Him Go 1968,O 10,59:7
Up Tight 1968,D 19,62:1
Saint James, Susan
P J 1968,Mr 7,52:3
Saint Jean, Guy
Life Upside Down; Inside Out 1965,Ag 18,41:4

St John, Adela Rogers (Original Author)
Inez From Hollywood 1924,D 16,28:1
Lady of the Night 1925,Mr 2,14:1
Pretty Ladies 1925,Jl 14,14:1
Singed 1927,Jl 12,29:3
Scandal 1929,Ap 22,23:1
Wicked 1931,S 19,10:2
What Price Hollywood 1932,Jl 16,5:5
Great Man's Lady, The 1942,Ap 30,14:3
Government Girl 1944,Ja 7,13:2
That Brennan Girl 1946,D 9,34:3
St John, Al
Garden of Weeds, The 1924,N 4,24:1
American Beauty 1927,O 11,27:1
She Goes to War 1929,Je 10,23:1
Dance of Life, The 1929,Ag 16,18:6
Hell Harbor 1930,Mr 28,22:6
Painted Desert, The 1931,Mr 9,19:1
Fame Street 1932,Ap 2,13:2
Outcasts of Poker Flat, The 1937,Ap 27,18:3
Saturday's Heroes 1937,O 16,22:2
Call of the Yukon 1938,My 6,27:1
When Comedy Was King 1960,Mr 30,42:1
Days of Thrills and Laughter 1961,Mr 22,37:1
St John, Betta
Dream Wife 1953,Jl 30,20:1
Robe, The 1953,S 17,32:6
All the Brothers Were Valiant 1953,D 29,19:2
Dangerous Mission 1954,Mr 6,13:5
Saracen Blade, The 1954,My 15,13:4
Student Prince, The 1954,Je 16,18:2
Tarzan and the Lost Safari 1957,Ap 13,12:3
Snerkel, The 1958,S 18,37:2
Tarzan the Magnificent 1960,Jl 21,17:1
Corridors of Blood 1963,Je 7,37:1
Horror Hotel 1963,Je 20,29:1
St John, Howard
Undercover Man, The 1949,Ap 21,30:2
711 Ocean Drive 1950,Jl 20,21:2
Men, The 1950,Jl 21,15:2
Mister 880 1950,S 30,13:2
Born Yesterday 1950,D 27,30:2
Sun Sets at Dawn, The 1951,Ja 15,13:1
Goodbye, my Fancy 1951,My 30,14:2
Strangers on a Train 1951,Jl 4,13:2
Saturday's Hero 1951,S 12,37:2
Starlift 1951,D 15,11:2
Big Night, The 1952,Mr 20,37:5
Stop, You're Killing Me 1952,D 11,45:3
Three Coins in the Fountain 1954,My 21,18:2
Illegal 1955,O 29,12:6
I Died a Thousand Times 1955,N 10,45:2
Tender Trap, The 1955,N 11,29:6
World in my Corner 1956,F 18,12:5
Li'l Abner 1959,D 12,19:2
Sanctuary 1961,F 22,31:1
Cry for Happy 1961,Mr 4,16:1
One, Two, Three 1961,D 22,17:1
Lover Come Back 1962,F 9,21:1
Madison Avenue 1962,Mr 29,28:2
Lafayette 1963,Ap 11,29:1
Strait Jacket 1964,Ja 23,26:1
Strange Bedfellows 1965,Mr 11,38:1
Quick, Before it Melts 1965,Ap 1,30:2
Banning 1967,D 14,62:2
St John, Jill
Summer Love 1958,Je 26,23:4
Remarkable Mr Pennypacker, The 1959,F 21,25:2
Holiday for Lovers 1959,Jl 25,10:2
Lost World, The 1960,Jl 14,23:1
Roman Spring of Mrs Stone, The 1961,D 29,11:1
Tender is the Night 1962,Ja 20,13:2
Come Blow Your Horn 1963,Je 7,37:1
Who's Minding the Store? 1963,N 29,67:6
  (Incorrect in this edition; use 1963,N 28,67:6
  elsewhere)
Who's Been Sleeping in My Bed? 1963,D 26,33:2
Honeymoon Hotel 1964,Je 4,28:1
Oscar, The 1966,Mr 5,16:1
Liquidator, The 1966,O 29,34:1
Eight on the Lam 1967,Ap 27,52:1
Tony Rome 1967,N 16,58:1
Banning 1967,D 14,62:2
St John, Marguerite
Laughing Lady, The 1930,Ja 4,21:1
St John, Richard
Kisses for my President 1964,Ag 22,13:1
St John, Robert (Narrator)
Congolaise 1950,My 22,17:4
St John, Theodore (Original Author)
Greatest Show on Earth, The 1952,Ja 11,17:2
St John, Theodore (Screenwriter)
Greatest Show on Earth, The 1952,Ja 11,17:2
St Johns, Adela Rogers (Original Author)
Broken Laws 1925,Ja 21,19:3
Skyrocket, The 1926,Ja 26,25:2
Heart of a Follies Girl, The 1928,Mr 12,26:1
Free Soul, A 1931,Je 3,29:2
Back in Circulation 1937,O 4,17:1
I Want a Divorce 1940,O 3,31:2
St Joseph, Ellis (Original Author)
Reno 1939,D 21,29:2
Flesh and Fantasy 1943,N 18,29:1

St Joseph, Ellis (Original Author)— Cont
Barbarian and the Geisha 1958,O 3,25:1
St Joseph, Ellis (Screenwriter)
Joan of Paris 1942,Ja 26,18:2
Flesh and Fantasy 1943,N 18,29:1
In our Time 1944,F 12,11:2
Scandal In Paris, A 1946,S 16,9:7
St Laurent, Cecil (Original Author)
Caroline Cherie 1954,My 25,23:1
Girl on the Third Floor, The; (Sophie et le Crime)
  1958,O 11,47:1 (Incorrect in this edition; use
  1958,O 11,18:4 elsewhere)
Lola Montes 1968,S 23,42:6
St Laurent, Cecil (Screenwriter)
Sins of the Borgias 1956,Mr 5,21:1
Maid in Paris 1957,Jl 13,11:1
St Leo, Leonard
Chad Hanna 1940,D 26,23:1
St Louis, Albert (Director)
Edmund Kean, Prince Among Lovers
  1927,Je 1,25:2
St Luke's Choristers
Prince and the Pauper, The 1937,My 6,23:1
St Maur, Adele
Worst Woman in Paris, The 1933,N 25,10:3
Gay Deception, The 1935,O 11,31:1
History Is Made at Night 1937,Mr 29,14:2
Little Boy Lost 1953,S 22,38:2
St Maur, Denizens of
My Uncle 1958,N 4,30:2
St-Ober
Call, The 1938,Mr 29,18:3
St Polis, John
Three Wise Fools 1923,Jl 23,13:4
Woman Proof 1923,O 30,16:1
Three Weeks 1924,Ap 1,19:3
Mademoiselle Midnight 1924,My 27,14:1
Those Who Dance 1924,Je 30,16:1
Alaskan, The 1924,S 15,28:1
Dixie Handicap, The 1924,D 30,15:3
Folly of Vanity 1925,Ja 28,14:1
Phantom of the Opera, The 1925,S 7,15:3
Greater Glory, The 1926,My 4,31:1
Four Horsemen of the Apocalypse, The
  1926,S 27,27:3
Marriage by Contract 1928,N 13,37:1
Why Be Good? 1929,My 6,30:4
Fast Life 1929,Ag 17,5:3
Party Girl 1930,Ja 2,28:2
Phantom of the Opera 1930,F 10,20:4
Guilty 1930,Ap 7,21:1
In the Next Room 1930,Ap 7,21:1
Bad One, The 1930,Je 13,28:3
Devil With Women, A 1930,O 20,28:2
Kismet 1930,O 31,20:1
Doctors' Wives 1931,Ap 25,23:4
Captain Thunder 1931,My 11,15:4
Transgression 1931,Je 15,23:3
Heartbreak 1931,O 17,20:1
Alias the Doctor 1932,Mr 3,22:3
Lena Rivers 1932,My 21,9:2
Crusader, The 1932,O 8,15:4
Terror Trail 1933,F 11,11:3
World Gone Mad, The 1933,Ap 15,16:3
Three on the Trail 1936,My 5,26:5
Border Patrolman 1936,Je 29,11:2
Shadow Strikes, The 1937,S 13,17:1
International Crime 1938,My 16,14:4
Mr Wong, Detective 1938,N 21,14:4
They Shall Have Music 1939,Jl 26,17:2
St Rayner, Helen
I Married a Witch 1942,N 20,27:2
St Saens, Georges
Ways of Love (A Day in the Country); Day in the
  Country, A (Ways of Love) 1950,D 13,50:2
Saint-Simon, Lucile
Bonnes Femmes, Les 1966,My 13,32:1
Saint Val, Claude
Kermesse Heroique, La 1936,S 23,29:1
Sainte-Marie, Buffy
Festival 1967,O 24,53:2
Sainteve, Louis
Forbidden Games 1952,D 9,43:2
Saintoult, Claude
Green Mare, The; Jument Verte, La
  1961,O 24,41:2
Sainval, Claude
Youth in Revolt 1939,My 16,27:3
Paris Waltz, The 1950,Ag 23,35:2
Muriel 1963,O 31,26:1
Saire, David
Loss of Innocence 1961,N 22,27:1
Rattle of a Simple Man 1964,D 21,42:2
Sais, Marin
Enemy of Women 1944,S 12,23:6
Sais, Tatjana
Berliner, The 1952,O 28,37:1
Saito, Tatsuo
Tokyo File 212 1951,Je 1,20:7
Three Stripes in the Sun 1955,N 24,41:2
Escapade in Japan 1957,D 24,11:1
My Geisha 1962,Je 14,23:2
Lord Jim 1965,F 26,18:1

Sakai, Franky
Mothra 1962,Jl 12,19:4
This Madding Crowd 1964,Je 17,48:1
Sakai, Sachio
Godzilla, King of the Monsters 1956,Ap 28,11:1
Samurai (Part II) 1967,O 21,16:1
Sakaki, Sumie
Insect Woman, The; Nippon Konchuki
1964,Jl 1,42:1
Sakala, Harold
Poppy is Also a Flower, The 1967,D 14,62:4
Sakall, S Z
It's a Date 1940,Mr 23,16:2
Florian 1940,Je 6,33:2
My Love Came Back 1940,Jl 13,16:5
Spring Parade 1940,O 4,29:2
That Night in Rio 1941,Mr 10,21:2
Devil and Miss Jones, The 1941,My 16,21:2
Ball of Fire 1942,Ja 16,25:2
Yankee Doodle Dandy 1942,My 30,9:1
Broadway 1942,Je 5,23:2
Seven Sweethearts 1942,N 13,28:1
Casablanca 1942,N 27,27:1
Wintertime 1943,S 30,27:2
Thank Your Lucky Stars 1943,O 2,19:2
Shine on Harvest Moon 1944,Mr 11,10:2
Hollywood Canteen 1944,D 16,19:2
Wonder Man 1945,Je 9,17:2
Christmas in Connecticut 1945,Jl 28,7:2
Dolly Sisters, The 1945,N 15,24:6
San Antonio 1945,D 29,19:5
Cinderella Jones 1946,Mr 16,9:6
Two Guys From Milwaukee 1946,Jl 27,12:5
Never Say Goodbye 1946,N 23,12:2
Cynthia 1947,S 19,27:2
April Showers 1948,Mr 27,10:2
Romance on the High Seas 1948,Je 26,10:5
Whiplash 1948,D 27,16:3
My Dream Is Yours 1949,Ap 16,11:3
Look for the Silver Lining 1949,Je 24,29:2
In the Good Old Summertime 1949,Ag 5,23:2
Oh, You Beautiful Doll 1949,N 12,8:4
Montana 1950,F 4,9:2
Daughter of Rosie O'Grady, The
1950,Mr 31,36:2
Tea for Two 1950,S 2,11:2
Sugarfoot 1951,F 12,19:4
Lullaby of Broadway 1951,Mr 27,35:2
Painting the Clouds With Sunshine 1951,S 1,9:6
It's a big Country 1952,Ja 9,25:2
Small Town Girl 1953,My 7,37:2
Student Prince, The 1954,Je 16,18:2
Sakamoto, Takeshi
Carmen Comes Home 1959,D 23,22:1
Sakatyan, Wram
Arshin Mal Alan; Peddler, Lover, The
1937,Mr 8,22:2
Sakelarios, Alekos (Director)
Germans Strike Again, The 1949,Ap 14,29:4
Mademoiselle-Age 39 1956,Mr 26,34:2
Trouble for Father 1958,Ja 6,26:4
Hurdy Gurdy, The 1958,S 22,27:1
Santa Chikita 1959,My 11,30:1
Aunt From Chicago, The 1960,Je 6,33:6
Fortune Teller, The 1961,My 22,37:5
Midwife, The 1961,S 25,41:2
Policeman of the 16th Precinct, The
1963,Ap 22,23:2
Sakelarios, Alekos (Original Author)
Germans Strike Again, The 1949,Ap 14,29:4
Midwife, The 1961,S 25,41:2
Sakelarios, Alekos (Screenwriter)
Mademoiselle-Age 39 1956,Mr 26,34:2
Trouble for Father 1958,Ja 6,26:4
Hurdy Gurdy, The 1958,S 22,27:1
Santa Chikita 1959,My 11,30:1
Astero 1960,Ap 25,32:2
Aunt From Chicago, The 1960,Je 6,33:6
Fortune Teller, The 1961,My 22,37:5
Midwife, The 1961,S 25,41:2
Policeman of the 16th Precinct, The
1963,Ap 22,23:2
Saker, Ethel
Wild Innocence 1938,N 11,31:2
Sakhni, B
Journey Beyond Three Seas 1960,Ap 11,42:6
Sakhnowsky, Berthe
Last Chance, The 1945,N 28,21:6
Sakhnowsky, M
Last Chance, The 1945,N 28,21:6
SAKS
See Also SAX, SAXE, SACHS
Saks, Gene
Thousand Clowns, A 1965,D 14,54:2
Saks, Gene (Director)
Barefoot in the Park 1967,My 26,51:1
Odd Couple, The 1968,My 3,42:1
Saks, Sol (Screenwriter)
Walk, Don't Run 1966,Ag 25,42:3
Sala, Franz
Maciste in Hell 1931,Je 29,20:3

Salacrou, Armand (Miscellaneous)
Beauty and the Devil 1952,Ag 26,15:2
Salacrou, Armand (Screenwriter)
Foolish Husbands 1948,O 11,27:2
Salah, Rehba Ben
Garden of Allah, The 1927,S 3,13:5
Salamanca, J R (Original Author)
Wild in the Country 1961,Je 10,12:2
Lilith 1964,S 21,37:2
Salamon, Bela
Sportszerelem; Love of Sport 1938,F 14,20:8
Salamonic, Yucca
Ljubav I Strast 1932,D 16,25:5
Salata, Paul
Angels in the Outfield 1951,O 18,32:1
Kid From Left Field, The 1953,S 26,15:3
Salazar, Abel
El Conde de Monte Cristo 1943,N 9,26:2
Salazar, Carlos
Thunder Below 1932,Je 20,11:2
Salce, Luciano (Director)
Crazy Desire 1964,Jl 3,13:2
Fascist, The 1965,Je 18,28:3
High Infidelity (The Victim); Victim, The (High
Infidelity) 1965,Jl 2,17:1
Hours of Love, The 1965,S 4,11:5
Little Nuns, The 1966,Ap 28,49:1
Greco, El 1967,My 24,52:2
Queens, The (Queen Sabina); Queen Sabina (The
Queens) 1968,Mr 11,49:1
Kiss the Other Sheik 1968,Jl 30,33:1
Salce, Luciano (Original Author)
Hours of Love, The 1965,S 4,11:5
Kiss the Other Sheik 1968,Jl 30,33:1
Salce, Luciano (Screenwriter)
Crazy Desire 1964,Jl 3,13:2
Fascist, The 1965,Je 18,28:3
Hours of Love, The 1965,S 4,11:5
Kiss the Other Sheik 1968,Jl 30,33:1
Salce, Pipolo (Original Author)
Kiss the Other Sheik 1968,Jl 30,33:1
Salce, Pipolo (Screenwriter)
Kiss the Other Sheik 1968,Jl 30,33:1
Salcedo, Elvia
Adios, Nicanor 1938,Mr 14,13:2
Mujer Mexicana, La; Mexican Woman, The
1938,Ap 18,11:2
En un Burro Tres Baturros; Three Rustics on one
Donkey 1940,S 21,13:3
Salcedo, Leopoldo
Cry of Battle 1963,O 12,27:2
Sale, Charles (Chic)
Marching On 1929,F 11,26:3
Star Witness, The 1931,Ag 4,19:5
Star Witness, The 1931,Ag 4,19:5
Expert, The 1932,F 27,22:1
When a Feller Needs a Friend 1932,My 14,11:5
Stranger in Town 1932,Jl 8,22:5
Chief, The 1933,D 2,9:4
Treasure Island 1934,Ag 18,5:5
Man Hunt 1936,Ja 30,14:2
Man I Marry, The 1936,O 31,24:3
You Only Live Once 1937,F 1,15:2
Sale, Richard (Director)
Ticket to Tomahawk, A 1950,My 20,8:6
I'll Get by 1950,N 2,39:3
Half Angel 1951,Je 16,9:2
Meet Me After the Show 1951,Ag 16,23:2
Let's Make It Legal 1951,N 7,35:3
My Wife's Best Friend 1952,O 11,17:2
Girl Next Door, The 1953,S 5,7:4
Fire over Africa 1954,N 22,29:5
Gentlemen Marry Brunettes 1955,O 31,31:5
Abandon Ship 1957,Ap 18,35:1
Sale, Richard (Original Author)
Shadows Over Shanghai 1938,D 1,29:2
Strange Cargo 1940,Ap 26,25:2
Rendezvous With Annie 1946,S 23,29:3
This Side of the Law 1950,Jl 7,15:2
Abandon Ship 1957,Ap 18,35:1
Torpedo Run 1958,O 25,16:2
Oscar, The 1966,Mr 5,16:1
Sale, Richard (Producer)
Gentlemen Marry Brunettes 1955,O 31,31:5
Sale, Richard (Screenwriter)
Rendezvous With Annie 1946,S 23,29:3
Northwest Outpost 1947,Ag 8,10:2
Mother is a Freshman 1949,Mr 12,10:2
Mr Belvedere Goes to College 1949,Ap 16,11:2
Father Was a Fullback 1949,O 13,33:3
When Willie Comes Marching Home
1950,F 18,9:2
Ticket to Tomahawk, A 1950,My 20,8:6
I'll Get by 1950,N 2,39:3
Meet Me After the Show 1951,Ag 16,23:2
Let's Do It Again 1953,O 14,34:3
French Line, The 1954,My 15,13:2
Woman's World 1954,S 29,23:4
Suddenly 1954,O 8,27:2
Gentlemen Marry Brunettes 1955,O 31,31:5
Torpedo Run 1958,O 25,16:2

Sale, Virginia
Legionnaires in Paris 1927,D 26,26:6
Harold Teen 1928,Ag 14,15:4
Cohens and the Kellys In Atlantic City, The
1929,Mr 18,30:6
Lovin' the Ladies 1930,Mr 22,22:6
Show Girl in Hollywood 1930,My 5,27:3
Moby Dick 1930,Ag 15,20:5
My Past 1931,Mr 12,22:7
Too Young to Marry 1931,My 4,15:3
Gold Dust Gertie 1931,My 30,9:2
Big Business Girl 1931,Je 12,27:1
Compromised 1931,N 7,16:5
Union Depot 1932,Ja 15,24:4
Fireman, Save My Child 1932,F 18,25:3
Iron Master, The 1933,F 4,11:3
Oliver Twist 1933,Ap 13,15:3
Man With two Faces, The 1934,Jl 12,20:2
Madame Du Barry 1934,O 25,26:2
We Have our Moments 1937,Ap 30,17:3
Topper 1937,Ag 20,21:2
Jury's Secret, The 1938,F 4,17:2
Flowing Gold 1940,S 2,19:3
Gold Rush Maisie 1940,S 2,19:2
Big Shot, The 1942,Jl 18,8:2
She Gets her Man 1945,F 9,20:5
Danger Signal 1945,N 22,39:2
Badman's Territory 1946,My 31,27:2
Trail Street 1947,Ap 10,35:2
Salerni, Laura
Love in Morocco 1933,Mr 20,18:3
Salerno, Enrico Maria
Angel Wore Red, The 1960,S 29,32:1
Siege of Syracuse, The 1962,Ag 9,17:8
Nude Odyssey 1962,O 27,14:6
Of Wayward Love (The Women); Women, The
(Of Wayward Love) 1964,Mr 24,29:1
Backfire 1965,Ap 27,27:1
Casanova 1965,Jl 21,43:1
Fuga, La 1966,Mr 22,33:1
Queens, The (Queen Sabina); Queen Sabina (The
Queens) 1968,Mr 11,49:1
Weekend, Italian Style 1968,My 23,56:2
Oldest Profession, The (Prehistoric Era);
Prehistoric Era (The Oldest Profession)
1968,N 8,42:1
Salerno, Giambattista
Tiger and the Pussycat, The 1967,S 21,56:4
Salew, John
Lady in Distress 1942,F 16,21:2
Continental Express 1942,Ap 7,26:3
Young Mr Pitt, The 1943,Mr 11,17:1
Beware of Pity 1947,N 1,11:2
Anna Karenina 1948,Ap 28,32:2
Meet Me at Dawn 1948,My 18,26:2
All Over the Town 1949,My 26,34:4
Kind Hearts and Coronets 1950,Je 15,41:2
For Them that Trespass 1950,S 27,37:2
Inheritance, The 1951,F 12,19:2
Lavender Hill Mob, The 1951,O 16,35:2
Spider and the Fly, The 1952,Jl 29,17:3
Detective, The 1954,N 2,25:2
Three Cases of Murder (In the Picture); In the
Picture (Three Cases of Murder)
1955,Mr 16,39:4
His Excellency 1956,F 2,19:3
It's Great to be Young 1957,D 26,23:3
Salfner, Heinz
Sein Scheidungsgrund 1932,F 20,11:2
Schuss im Morgengrauen 1934,S 29,12:3
Drei Kaiserjaeger 1935,Mr 16,19:1
Die vom Niederrhein; Lower Rhine Folks
1935,My 20,20:6
Schabernack 1937,Ag 14,16:5
Gross Reinemachen; General Housecleaning
1938,Je 23,27:2
Dingehort mein Herz; My Heart Belongs to Thee
1939,Mr 25,19:2
Anton der Letzte; Anthony the Last
1940,Mr 30,11:2
Salgado, Maria Rosa
It Happened in Broad Daylight 1960,S 30,33:1
Salgari, Emilio (Original Author)
Carthage in Flames 1961,Ja 26,32:3
Salina, Michel
Angel and Sinner 1947,F 24,16:5
Queen's Necklace, The 1947,My 17,8:5
Battle of the Rails; (Bataille Du Rail)
1949,D 27,27:2
Salinas, Jone
Eternal Melodies 1948,F 14,17:3
Ruy Blas 1948,O 4,14:2
Man About the House, A 1949,Mr 9,33:2
Mafia; (In Nome Della Legge) 1950,Mr 2,33:2
Salinger, J D (Original Author)
My Foolish Heart 1950,Ja 20,29:2
Salisbury, Barbara
Give Me a Sailor 1938,Ag 11,31:1
Salisbury, Edward A Captain (Miscellaneous)
Gow 1933,D 2,9:4
Salisbury, Edward A Captain (Producer)
Gow, The Head Hunter 1928,D 25,31:3
Lost Empire, The 1929,Ja 22,23:1

Salisbury, Edward A Captain (Producer) — Cont
  Ra-Mu: Children of the Sun 1929,F 13,20:3
Salisbury, Monroe
  Ramona 1916,Ap 6,11:1
Saljo, Ayuko
  Imposter, The 1955,Mr 23,27:1
Salkow, Sidney (Director)
  Girl Overboard 1937,Mr 1,15:1
  Storm Over Bengal 1938,D 8,34:4
  Woman Doctor 1939,Mr 24,27:3
  Street of Missing Men 1939,Je 1,31:3
  Zero Hour, The 1939,Jl 5,20:3
  Flight at Midnight 1939,S 7,29:2
  Street of Missing Women 1940,Ja 8,11:2
  Lone Wolf Strikes, The 1940,F 5,13:2
  Lone Wolf Meets a Lady, The 1940,Je 17,19:2
  Girl From God's Country 1940,S 9,18:5
  Lone Wolf Keeps a Date, The 1941,Ja 2,24:3
  Lone Wolf Takes a Chance, The 1941,Ap 7,13:2
  Time Out for Rhythm 1941,Jl 10,16:3
  Adventures of Martin Eden 1942,Mr 16,19:2
  Flight Lieutenant 1942,Jl 31,11:1
  Sword of the Avenger 1948,Ag 26,16:4
  Fugitive Lady 1951,Ag 25,7:2
  Scarlet Angel 1952,Je 21,12:2
  Golden Hawk, The 1952,O 18,16:4
  Sitting Bull 1954,N 26,24:4
  Las Vegas Shakedown 1955,Je 18,14:2
  Chicago Confidential 1957,Ag 31,19:1
  Big Night, The 1960,F 18,37:4
  Twice Told Tales (Dr Heidegger's Experiment); Dr
    Heidegger's Experiment (Twice Told Tales)
    1964,Mr 28,40:1
  Twice Told Tales (Rappaccini's Daughter);
    Rappaccini's Daughter (Twice Told Tales)
    1964,Mr 28,40:1
  Twice Told Tales (The House of the Seven
    Gables); House of the Seven Gables, The (Twice
    Told Tales) 1964,My 28,40:1
  Murder Game, The 1966,Mr 31,43:2
Salkow, Sidney (Producer)
  Sword of the Avenger 1948,Ag 26,16:4
Salkow, Sidney (Screenwriter)
  Rhythm on the Range 1936,Jl 30,22:1
  Murder With Pictures 1936,N 21,21:4
  Exclusive 1937,Jl 22,15:1
  Prison Nurse 1938,Mr 4,17:5
  Come on Leathernecks 1938,S 15,29:3
  Lone Wolf Keeps a Date, The 1941,Ja 2,24:3
  Lone Wolf Takes a Chance, The 1941,Ap 7,13:2
  Admiral Was a Lady, The 1950,O 13,23:3
  Sitting Bull 1954,N 26,24:4
Salkowitz, Sy (Screenwriter)
  Thunder Valley 1967,S 14,55:1
  Thunder Alley 1967,S 14,55:1
  Biggest Bundle of Them All, The 1968,Ja 18,46:1
Sallas, Dennis
  Shadows 1961,Mr 22,37:1
Salling, Jackie
  Fisherman's Wharf 1939,F 24,15:2
Sallis, Peter
  Mouse on the Moon, The 1963,Je 18,32:1
  Inadmissible Evidence 1968,Je 24,44:1
Sallis, Zoe
  Bible, The 1966,S 29,60:1
Salloker, Algela
  Maedchen Johanna, Das 1935,O 9,27:2 (In
    Addenda)
Salloker, Angela
  Zerbrochene Krug, Der; Broken Jugi, The
    1938,Ja 15,19:2
  Hohe Schule; College 1939,Ap 8,19:3
  Hochzeitstreise, Die; Wedding Journey, The
    1939,My 13,11:5
Sallusto, Massimo
  Brief Rapture 1952,F 28,23:2
Salmenov, Rakhmetulla
  Amangeldy 1939,Je 16,27:4
Salmi, Albert
  Brothers Karamazov, The 1958,F 21,18:2
  Bravados, The 1958,Je 26,23:2
  Unforgiven, The 1960,Ap 7,46:1
  Wild River 1960,My 27,22:1
  Outrage, The 1964,O 8,48:2
  Flim Flam Man, The 1967,Ag 23,40:1
  Hour of the Gun 1967,N 2,58:4
  Ambushers, The 1967,D 23,29:1
Salminen, Sally (Original Author)
  Katrina 1949,N 18,35:3
Salmon, John (Screenwriter)
  Only When I Larf 1968,O 24,55:3
Salmonova, Lydia
  Monna Vanna 1923,S 25,8:2
  Lost Shadow, The 1928,Mr 20,20:3
Salo, Mario
  Maciste in Hell 1931,Je 29,20:3
SALOMON
  See Also SOLOMON
Salomon, Henry (Original Author)
  Victory at Sea 1954,Jl 14,33:2
Salomon, Henry (Producer)
  Victory at Sea 1954,Jl 14,33:2

Salomos, Alexis
  Never on Sunday 1960,O 19,54:1
Salou, Louis
  Enfants du Paradis, Les 1947,F 20,32:2
  Angel and Sinner 1947,F 24,16:5
  Vie de Boheme, La 1947,N 28,37:4
  Friend Will come Tonight, A; Ami Viendra Ce
    Soir, Un 1948,Jl 12,11:2
  Devil and the Angel, The 1949,D 3,8:6
  Loves of Colette 1949,D 3,8:6
  Counter Investigation 1949,D 30,13:2
  Sylvie and the Phantom 1950,O 16,30:5
  Lovers of Verona, The 1951,Mr 12,20:2
  Fabiola 1951,My 30,14:2
Salsano, Carlo (Producer)
  Bigamist, The 1958,My 12,25:1
Salt, Waldo (Miscellaneous)
  M 1951,Je 11,20:7
Salt, Waldo (Screenwriter)
  Shopworn Angel, The 1938,Jl 8,11:2
  Tonight We Raid Calais 1943,Ap 15,20:2
  Mr Winkle Goes to War 1944,Ag 3,16:1
  Rachel and the Stranger 1948,S 20,21:2
  Flame and the Arrow, The 1950,Jl 8,7:2
  Taras Bulba 1962,D 26,5:2
  Flight From Ashiya 1964,Ap 23,34:1
  Wild and Wonderful 1964,Je 11,27:4
Saltamerenda, Gino
  When Love Calls 1948,O 9,12:6
  Bicycle Thief, The 1949,D 13,44:2
Saltamerenda, Louis
  Shoe-Shine 1947,Ag 27,19:2
  Thief of Venice, The 1952,N 28,22:7
Salten, Felix (Miscellaneous)
  Heart Song 1934,Je 6,24:6
Salten, Felix (Original Author)
  Florian 1940,Je 6,33:2
  Bambi 1942,Ag 14,13:1
  Perri 1957,O 2,27:5
  Shaggy Dog, The 1959,Mr 20,26:2
Salter, Hal
  Red Raiders, The 1927,S 28,28:3
Salter, James (Original Author)
  Hunters, The 1958,Ag 27,33:1
Saltus, Edgar (Original Author)
  Daughters of the Rich 1923,Je 18,13:5
Saltykov, Nikolai
  Demon of the Steppes 1930,Ja 18,21:1
Saltzman, Esta
  I Want to Be a Mother 1937,F 27,9:2
  God, Man and Devil 1950,Ja 23,16:2
Saltzman, Harry (Original Author)
  Iron Petticoat, The 1957,F 2,12:2
Saltzman, Harry (Producer)
  Entertainer, The 1960,O 4,49:2
  Call Me Bwana 1963,Jl 4,9:1
  From Russia with Love 1964,Ap 9,25:1
  Goldfinger 1964,D 22,36:1
  Ipcress File, The 1965,Ag 3,35:1
  You Only Live Twice 1967,Je 14,40:1
  Billion Dollar Brain 1967,D 23,29:1
  And There Came a Man 1968,Ap 5,56:4
Salvador, Jaime (Director)
  Castillos en el Aire; Castles in the Air
    1938,My 21,9:3
  Ultima Melodia, La; Last Melody, The
    1939,Ag 5,18:3
Salvador, Jaime (Screenwriter)
  Romeo and Juliet 1944,Je 17,10:3
Salvador, Leroy
  Badjao 1962,S 21,35:1
Salvadore, Sal
  Jazz on a Summer's Day 1960,Mr 29,46:2
Salvatori, Albert (Producer)
  Earth Cries Out, The; Grido Della Terra, Il
    1949,Ag 31,26:2
Salvatori, Fausto (Original Author)
  Christus 1917,My 1,11:4
Salvatori, Fausto (Screenwriter)
  Retribution 1922,Je 7,22:3
Salvatori, Renato
  Three Girls From Rome 1953,O 14,34:2
  Poor but Beautiful 1958,Je 11,39:4
  Big Deal on Madonna Street, The 1960,N 23,20:1
  Two Women; (Ciociara, La) 1961,My 9,43:2
  Rocco and his Brothers 1961,Je 28,40:2
  Fiasco in Milan 1963,Ap 11,29:2
  Two Are Guilty 1964,F 29,12:1
  Organizer, The 1964,My 7,31:2
  Disorder 1964,My 26,44:2
  How to Seduce a Playboy 1968,My 16,53:2
Salver, Lianna
  Bluebeard's 8th Wife 1923,Ag 7,20:2
Salvi, Emimmo (Producer)
  Goliath and the Barbarians 1960,Ja 7,24:6
  David and Goliath 1961,O 7,14:3
Salvi, Emimmo (Screenwriter)
  David and Goliath 1961,O 7,14:3
Salvi, Lola
  Plastered in Paris 1928,S 24,25:1
  Thru Different Eyes 1929,Ap 15,22:6

Salvietti, Agostino
  Yesterday, Today and Tomorrow (Part 1-Adelina
    Naples); Adelina Naples (Yesterday, Today and
    Tomorrow) 1964,Mr 18,46:1
Salvini, Alessandro
  Nero 1922,My 26,17:2
  Richiamo del Cuore, Il; Appeal of the Heart, The
    1931,Mr 2,19:1
  Terra Madre 1931,O 31,22:2
Salvioni, Giorgio (Screenwriter)
  10th Victim, The 1965,D 21,46:1
  Queens, The (Queen Armenia); Queen Armenia
    (The Queens) 1968,Mr 11,49:1
Salviucci, G (Screenwriter)
  Aida 1954,N 12,17:1
Samada, Cornelio Cardenas (Producer)
  Night of the Mayas 1941,Ja 14,16:7
Samarin-Elsky, E
  Dubrovsky 1936,Mr 30,17:6
Samberg, Ajzyk
  Purimspieler, Der 1937,D 6,19:2
Samberg, R
  Dybbuk, The 1938,Ja 28,17:2
Samborski, Boguslaw
  Dziesieciu z Pawiaka 1932,Ap 21,25:2
  Szpieg 1934,Mr 5,19:3
  Prokurator 1934,My 22,28:4
Samborski, I I Koval
  Yellow Ticket, The 1928,D 10,25:1
Samborski, Koval
  Prince of Rogues, The 1929,Jl 30,19:4
Sambrel, Aldo
  For a Few Dollars More 1967,Jl 4,23:1
Sammarco, Gina
  Viaccia, La 1962,S 21,35:1
Sammartino, D Venanzio
  Man of Courage 1934,N 14,23:2
Sammy, Sunshine
  Ghost Creeps, The 1940,Ag 19,13:3
  Pride of the Bowery 1941,Ja 24,15:2
Sammy Kaye and his orchestra
  Iceland 1942,O 15,27:1
  Song of the Open Road 1944,Je 7,13:3
Samoilov, E
  Rubicon 1931,S 21,20:2
  Rubicon 1934,Mr 19,13:3
  Shors 1939,N 21,19:4
  Tanya 1942,Mr 5,27:1
  Six PM 1946,Ja 28,15:5
  Four Hearts 1946,F 25,21:5
  Admiral Nakhimov 1948,N 25,47:4
  Adventure in Odessa 1954,Je 21,19:6
  Heroes of Shipka 1956,S 3,10:5
Samoilova, Tatyana
  Mexican, The 1957,Ap 3,28:2
  Cranes are Flying, The 1960,Mr 22,31:2
  Letter That Was Never Sent, The 1962,N 19,39:2
  Italiano Brava Gente 1966,F 4,20:1
Samokhvalova, Maya
  Bolshoi Ballet 67 1966,S 30,54:1
Samosvat, Maria
  Taras Family, The 1946,D 9,34:4
Sampaio, Antonio L
  Given Word, The 1964,Mr 25,47:1
SAMPSON
  See Also SAMSON
Sampson, Robert
  Look in any Window 1962,Mr 22,40:1
Sampson, Teddy
  Bits of Life 1921,O 17,18:1
  Bad Man, The 1923,O 9,17:4
SAMSON
  See Also SAMPSON
Samson, Ivan
  Student's Romance, The 1936,O 12,23:2
  April Romance 1937,Ja 27,17:4
  Winslow Boy, The 1950,Je 7,34:4
  Browning Version, The 1951,O 30,33:2
Samson, Yvonne
  Great Dawn, The 1947,Ag 28,28:3
Samsonov, S (Director)
  Grasshopper, The 1956,Ap 23,22:1
  Behind the Show Window 1957,Ap 17,37:1
  Optimistic Tragedy, The 1964,F 24,20:2
Samsonov, S (Miscellaneous)
  Miles of Fire 1958,N 10,36:6 (In Addenda)
Samsonov, S (Screenwriter)
  Grasshopper, The 1956,Ap 23,22:1
  Optimistic Tragedy, The 1964,F 24,20:2
Samuel, Julie
  Ferry Cross the Mersey 1965,F 20,16:2
Samuels, Charles (Miscellaneous)
  Man on a String 1960,My 21,15:1
Samuels, Lesser (Miscellaneous)
  Sailing Along 1938,Ap 16,17:1
Samuels, Lesser (Original Author)
  Climbing High 1939,Je 5,20:3
  Adventure in Baltimore 1949,Ap 29,27:2
Samuels, Lesser (Producer)
  Long Wait, The 1954,Jl 3,9:2
Samuels, Lesser (Screenwriter)
  It's Love Again 1936,My 23,12:1
  You're in the Army Now 1937,Ap 16,27:2

Samuels, Lesser (Screenwriter) — Cont
Sailing Along 1938,Ap 16,17:1
Earl of Chicago, The 1940,Mr 14,29:3
Bitter Sweet 1940,N 22,27:1
Unholy Partners 1941,D 29,21:4
Hour Before the Dawn, The 1944,My 11,25:6
Tonight and Every Night 1945,Mr 9,16:2
No Way Out 1950,Ag 17,23:1
Ace in the Hole 1951,Je 30,8:6
Darling, How Could You! 1951,N 9,22:4
Long Wait, The 1954,Jl 3,9:2
Silver Chalice, The 1954,D 27,22:5
Great Day in the Morning 1956,My 19,12:6
Samuels, Maurice
Black Hand 1950,Mr 13,15:2
Samuels, Maurice (Narrator)
Land of Promise, The 1935,N 21,27:2
Samuels, Maurice (Original Author)
Wanderer, The 1925,Ag 20,22:1
Samuels, Walter (Composer)
Under the Pampas Moon 1935,My 31,11:1
Samuelson, G B (Director)
Cancion del Dia, La 1933,Ag 26,14:3
Samuylew, M B
Wandering Jew, The 1933,O 21,11:2
Samvelyan, L
Heart Sings, The 1958,Ag 18,15:2
San, King
Sable Cicada 1939,Ja 14,13:1
San Cristobal Marimba Band
Tropic Holiday 1938,Je 30,21:2
San Francisco Mime Troupe (Miscellaneous)
Have You Heard of the San Francisco Mime
  Troup? 1968,Je 28,37:1
San Juan, Aura
World Dances 1954,N 8,24:6
San Juan, Olga
Variety Girl 1947,O 16,34:4
Are You With It? 1948,Ap 15,31:2
One Touch of Venus 1948,O 29,29:5
Beautiful Blonde From Bashful Bend, The
  1949,My 28,11:2
San Juan, Olgan
Rainbow Island 1944,O 26,19:6
San Marco, Maria
Intrigue 1948,Ap 24,11:2
San Martin, Carlos
Marked Woman 1937,Ap 12,15:2
Sanayer, Vassily
Four Hearts 1946,F 25,21:5
Sanayev, V
Vasili's Return 1953,S 28,21:4
Optimistic Tragedy, The 1964,F 24,20:2
Sanborn, Fred
Crazy House 1943,D 16,33:3
Sanborn, Helen
Charge of the Light Brigade, The 1936,N 2,24:1
Sanbrell, Aldo
Navajo Joe 1967,D 7,60:2
Sanchez, Angela
Salt of the Earth 1954,Mr 15,20:2
Sanchez, Arthur (Director)
Molinos de Viento; Windmills 1940,F 26,11:2
Sanchez, Ben
Walls of Hell, The 1965,N 18,55:3
Sanchez, Elvira
Torrid Zone 1940,My 18,11:3
Sanchez, Fernando
Ceremony, The 1964,My 14,39:1
Sanchez, Jaime
David and Lisa 1962,D 27,5:5
Pawnbroker, The 1965,Ap 21,51:1
Heroina 1965,N 11,58:2
Beach Red 1967,Ag 4,18:1
Sanchez, Luis Pena
Mad Queen, The 1950,O 27,24:3
Sanchez, Pedro
Any Gun Can Play 1968,S 14,34:2
Sanchez, Porfiria
Morena Clara 1938,Je 18,18:3
Fedra, the Devil's Daughter 1957,O 26,19:2
Sanchez, Regnier
Cuban Rebel Girls 1959,D 26,7:3
Sanchez-Silva, Jose Maria (Screenwriter)
Marcelino 1956,O 23,39:1
Sancho, Fernando
Backfire 1965,Ap 27,27:1
Pistol for Ringo, A 1966,N 3,45:4
Big Gundown, The 1968,Ag 23,33:1
Sancrotti, Ezio
Violent Four, The 1968,Ag 15,46:2
Sand, Carlton (Screenwriter)
She Loved a Fireman 1938,Ja 21,15:3
Sand, Rebecca
Bedtime Story 1964,Je 11,27:1
Sandars, Clare
Mrs Miniver 1942,Je 5,23:1
Sandberg, A W (Director)
Last Night, The 1930,Ja 27,18:4
Sandberg, A W (Producer)
Heart of a Clown 1928,Ja 17,23:2
Sandberg, Valdis
Yolanta 1964,D 23,22:3

Sandborg, Olof
En Enda Natt 1942,D 7,22:2
Sandburg, Carl (Miscellaneous)
Greatest Story Ever Told, The 1965,F 16,40:2
Sande, Earle
Great White Way, The 1924,Ja 4,10:1
Sande, Walter
Arson Racket Squad 1938,Je 18,18:2
Tenth Avenue Kid 1938,S 2,21:3
You Can't Fool Your Wife 1940,My 24,23:4
Confessions of Boston Blackie 1941,D 8,31:2
Reveille With Beverly 1943,Ap 24,17:2
Corvette K-225 1943,O 21,30:1
To Have and Have Not 1944,O 12,24:1
I Love a Soldier 1944,N 2,22:2
Daltons Ride Again, The 1945,D 8,21:2
Blue Dahlia, The 1946,My 9,27:3
Spider, The 1946,Je 21,20:3
Nocturne 1946,N 11,42:2
Red House, The 1947,Mr 17,27:2
Woman on the Beach, The 1947,Je 9,26:6
Wild Harvest 1947,N 13,33:2
Christmas Eve 1947,N 28,30:2
Killer McCoy 1948,F 12,31:2
Bad Boy 1949,Mr 23,35:2
Canadian Pacific 1949,My 20,32:4
Strange Bargain 1949,S 30,28:3
Kid From Texas, The 1950,Je 2,26:2
Dark City 1950,O 19,40:5
Payment on Demand 1951,F 16,21:2
Tomorrow Is Another Day 1951,Ag 9,17:5
Place in the Sun, A 1951,Ag 29,20:1
Basketball Fix, the 1951,S 14,21:2
Racket, The 1951,D 13,44:2
I Want You 1951,D 24,9:1
Red Mountain 1952,Ap 26,19:2
Red Planet Mars 1952,Je 16,15:2
Duel at Silver Creek 1952,Ag 2,7:6
Great Sioux Uprising, The 1953,Jl 18,6:2
War of the Worlds, The 1953,Ag 14,10:2
Kid From Left Field, The 1953,S 26,15:3
Bad Day at Black Rock 1955,F 2,22:2
Anything Goes 1956,Mr 22,38:1
Maverick Queen, the 1956,Je 4,25:2
Johnny Tremain 1957,Jl 11,21:1
Gallant Hours, The 1960,Je 23,19:4
Sunrise at Campobello 1960,S 29,32:1
Sanden, John (Original Author)
Karl Fredrik Reigns 1938,F 2,15:2
SANDERS
See Also SAUNDERS
Sanders, Anita
10th Victim, The 1965,D 21,46:1
Sanders, Barbara Ann
Bright Road 1953,Ap 29,33:5
Sanders, Denis (Director)
Crime and Punishment, U S A 1959,Je 17,39:3
War Hunt 1962,Ag 8,35:2
One Man's Way 1964,Mr 12,40:3
Shock Treatment 1964,Jl 23,19:1
Sanders, Denis (Screenwriter)
Naked and the Dead, The 1958,Ag 7,21:1
Sanders, Dick
Belles and Ballets 1960,N 15,45:3
Sanders, Dick (Miscellaneous)
Belles and Ballets 1960,N 15,45:3
Sanders, Dirk
Very Private Affair, A 1962,S 29,15:1
Sanders, George
Lloyds of London 1936,N 26,39:1
Love Is News 1937,Mr 6,10:1
Slave Ship 1937,Je 17,19:2
Lancer Spy 1937,N 4,29:1
International Settlement 1938,F 12,20:3
Four Men and a Prayer 1938,My 7,18:1
Mr Moto's Last Warning 1939,Ja 27,17:3
Saint Strikes Back, The 1939,Mr 9,18:2
Confessions of a Nazi Spy 1939,Ap 29,13:2
Saint in London, The 1939,Jl 19,23:3
Nurse Edith Cavell 1939,S 22,27:4
Allegheny Uprising 1939,N 10,27:3
Green Hell 1940,Ja 30,15:6
Saint's Double Trouble, The 1940,F 13,27:2
Outsider, The 1940,Mr 18,13:2
Rebecca 1940,Mr 29,25:2
House of the Seven Gables, The 1940,Ap 15,21:3
Saint Takes Over, The 1940,My 28,29:3
Foreign Correspondent 1940,Ag 28,15:2
Bitter Sweet 1940,N 22,27:1
Son of Monte Cristo, The 1940,D 5,33:1
Saint in Palm Springs, The 1941,Ja 31,15:5
Rage in Heaven 1941,Mr 21,19:2
Man Hunt 1941,Je 14,20:2
Date With the Falcon, A 1941,N 25,33:2
Son of Fury 1942,Ja 30,23:2
Falcon takes Over, The 1942,My 30,9:2
Her Cardboard Lover 1942,Jl 17,19:2
Tales of Manhattan 1942,S 25,25:1
Falcon's Brother, The 1942,O 3,9:5
Moon and Sixpence, The 1942,O 28,26:4
Quiet Please, Murder 1942,D 22,31:1
Black Swan, The 1942,D 24,18:3
They Came to Blow up America
  1943,My 15,13:2

Sanders, George — Cont
This Land Is Mine 1943,My 28,19:1
Appointment in Berlin 1943,Jl 17,8:2
Paris After Dark 1943,O 23,11:1
Lodger, The 1944,Ja 20,15:3
Action in Arabia 1944,F 19,18:7
Summer Storm 1944,O 23,14:3
Hangover Square 1945,F 8,15:2
Picture of Dorian Gray, The 1945,Mr 2,15:2
Uncle Harry 1945,Ag 24,14:5
Scandal In Paris, A 1946,S 16,9:7
Strange Woman, The 1947,F 24,16:4
Private Affairs of Bel Ami, The 1947,Je 16,25:4
Ghost and Mrs Muir, The 1947,Je 27,17:2
Lured 1947,Ag 29,14:4
Forever Amber 1947,O 23,31:2
Fan, The 1949,Ap 2,12:2
Samson and Delilah 1949,D 22,29:2
All About Eve 1950,O 14,13:2
I Can Get It for You Wholesale 1951,Ap 5,34:4
Light Touch, The 1952,Ja 17,23:1
Ivanhoe 1952,Ag 1,8:2
Captain Black Jack 1952,O 22,31:3
Assignment-Paris 1952,O 25,12:6
Call Me Madam 1953,Mr 26,37:1
Witness to Murder 1954,Ap 16,16:4
King Richard and the Crusaders 1954,Ag 23,20:5
Jupiter's Darling 1955,F 18,18:4
Moonfleet 1955,Je 25,9:2
Scarlet Coat, The 1955,Jl 30,14:2
King's Thief, The 1955,Ag 13,7:2
Never Say Goodbye 1956,Ap 14,20:1
While the City Sleeps 1956,My 17,37:1
That Certain Felling 1956,Je 21,35:2
Death of a Scoundrel 1956,N 6,30:1
Seventh Sin, The 1957,Je 29,10:6
From the Earth to the Moon 1958,N 27,52:2
That Kind of Woman 1959,S 12,12:2
Solomon and Sheba 1959,D 26,7:2
Last Voyage, The 1960,F 20,14:2
Touch of Larceny, A 1960,Mr 17,28:1
Bluebeard's Ten Honeymoons 1960,N 8,32:6
Village of the Damned 1960,D 8,43:3
Trouble in the Sky 1961,Jl 13,26:3
Call Me Genius 1961,O 17,47:1
Five Golden Hours 1961,O 19,39:3
Operation Snatch 1962,S 25,31:4
In Search of the Castaways 1962,D 22,5:2
Dark Purpose 1964,F 6,36:4
Shot in the Dark, A 1964,Je 24,28:1
Amorous Adventures of Moll Flanders, The
  1965,My 27,28:1
Quiller Memorandum, The 1966,D 16,59:1
Trunk to Cairo 1966,D 29,22:1
Warning Shot 1967,Je 8,52:2
Good Times 1967,Ag 3,26:4
Sanders, George (Narrator)
Ecco 1965,N 5,28:1
Sanders, George (Original Author)
Unholy Four, The 1954,N 20,10:2
Sanders, H P
Appointment in Berlin 1943,Jl 17,8:2
Sanders, Hugh
Damned Don't Cry, The 1950,Ap 8,9:2
Great Rupert, The 1950,Ap 14,27:2
Mister 880 1950,S 30,13:2
Sugarfoot 1951,F 12,19:4
Three Guys Named Mike 1951,Mr 2,21:2
Storm Warning 1951,Mr 3,8:2
I Was a Communist for the F B I 1951,My 3,34:4
Along the Great Divide 1951,My 17,38:3
Strictly Dishonorable 1951,Jl 12,21:6
That's My Boy 1951,Ag 2,18:1
Tomorrow Is Another Day 1951,Ag 9,17:5
Boots Malone 1952,Mr 13,26:2
Pride of St Louis, The 1952,My 3,17:5
Fighter, The 1952,My 31,12:6
Winning Team, The 1952,Je 21,12:2
Something for the Birds 1952,N 15,15:2
Scared Stiff 1953,Jl 3,10:2
Glass Web, The 1953,N 12,37:5
Thunder Over the Plains 1953,D 10,64:4
Wild One, The 1953,D 31,9:2
Cattle Queen of Montana 1955,Ja 26,22:1
Careless Years, The 1957,N 28,57:3
Sanders, Nadine
Eight and One Half 1963,Je 26,36:1
Sanders, Stuart
Mouse That Roared, The 1959,O 27,40:1
Sanders, Terry (Producer)
Crime and Punishment, U S A 1959,Je 17,39:3
War Hunt 1962,Ag 8,35:2
Sanders, Terry (Screenwriter)
Naked and the Dead, The 1958,Ag 7,21:1
Sanders, Troy (Composer)
Paddy O'Day 1936,F 8,19:2
Sanderson, G B (Producer)
Collision 1932,F 21,VIII,5:2 (In Addenda)
Sanderson, Kent
Strong Boy 1929,Ap 1,22:1
Sanderson, Lora
Chickie 1925,Ap 27,15:2

Sanderson, Ruth
Abandoned Woman 1949,O 27,35:3
SANDFORD
See Also SANFORD
Sandford, Christopher
Half a Sixpence 1968,F 21,60:3
Sandford, Stanley
Iron Mask, The 1929,F 22,18:6
Warrior's Husband, The 1933,My 12,20:4
Modern Times 1936,F 6,23:2
Sandford, Tiny
Rio Rita 1929,O 7,22:1
Laurel and Hardy's Laughing 20's 1965,N 18,55:2
Sandler, Oscar (Composer)
Twins 1947,Jl 28,12:2
Sandlin, Sally (Original Author)
Off the Record 1939,F 18,12:2
Sandoe, Toralf
Boer Boerson Jr 1939,N 4,11:3
Sandoe, Toralf (Director)
Boer Boerson Jr 1939,N 4,11:3
Sandoval, Miguel (Miscellaneous)
Gay Desperado, The 1936,O 9,31:4
Sandoz, Marl (Original Author)
Cheyenne Autumn 1964,D 24,8:1
Sandoz, Maurice (Original Author)
Maze, The 1953,Jl 11,8:2
Sandra, Samuel
Escuadron Azul, El; Blue Squadron, The
1938,Je 4,18:3
Sandre, Gisele
Tales of Paris (The Tale of Sophie); Tale of Sophie,
The (Tales of Paris) 1962,Ag 27,18:1
Landru 1963,Ap 10,31:1
Sandrelli, Stefania
Divorce-Italian Style 1962,S 18,34:1
Seduced and Abandoned 1964,Jl 16,23:1
Fascist, The 1965,Je 18,28:3
Climax, The 1967,S 12,55:1
Tender Scoundrel 1967,N 16,58:2
Partner 1968,S 24,52:2
Sandri, Anna-Maria
Reaching for the Stars 1958,My 24,18:2
Sandri, Gia
Stranger in Town, A 1968,Ap 25,53:4
Sandrich, Mark (Director)
Melody Cruise 1933,Je 23,15:2
Aggie Appleby, Maker of Men 1933,O 20,14:2
Hips, Hips, Hooray 1934,F 24,18:3
Cockeyed Cavaliers 1934,Jl 25,22:2
Gay Divorcee, The 1934,N 16,27:1
Top Hat 1935,Ag 30,12:2
Follow the Fleet 1936,F 21,21:2
Woman Rebels, A 1936,O 30,27:2
Shall We Dance 1937,My 14,21:1
Carefree 1938,S 23,35:1
Man About Town 1939,Je 29,19:1
Love Thy Neighbor 1940,D 18,32:5
Skylark 1941,N 20,39:2
Holiday Inn 1942,Ag 5,16:1
So Proudly We Hail 1943,S 10,29:1
I Love a Soldier 1944,N 2,22:2
Here Come the Waves 1944,D 28,25:2
Sandrich, Mark (Original Author)
Melody Cruise 1933,Je 23,15:2
Sandrich, Mark (Producer)
Buck Benny Rides Again 1940,Ap 25,28:4
Love Thy Neighbor 1940,D 18,32:5
Skylark 1941,N 20,39:2
Holiday Inn 1942,Ag 5,16:1
So Proudly We Hail 1943,S 10,29:1
I Love a Soldier 1944,N 2,22:2
Here Come the Waves 1944,D 28,25:2
Sandrini, Luis
Riachuelo 1934,D 8,18:5
Tres Berretines, Los 1935,Ja 7,13:3
Loco Lindo; Crazy Dandy 1938,Ja 11,27:4
Canillita y la Dama, El; Newsie and the Lady,
The 1939,F 18,12:2
Games Men Play, The 1968,Mr 15,30:1
Sandro
Lost in the Dark 1949,My 14,9:2
Sandrock, Adele
Skandal Um Eva 1931,Ap 21,35:2
Foresterchristl, Die 1931,Ap 27,25:1
Schlacht von Bademuende, Die 1931,N 21,20:4
Der Schrecken der Garnison 1932,Je 1,19:5
Keine Feier Ohne Meyer 1932,O 29,18:4
Das Schoene Abenteuer 1932,D 8,25:3
Ihre Majestaet die Liebe 1933,F 7,23:4
Friederike 1933,F 27,11:3
Morgenrot 1933,My 16,15:2
Einmal Moecht' Ich Keine Sorgen Haben
1933,My 25,24:4
Glueckszylinder, Der 1934,Mr 10,18:4
Tochter des Regiments, Die 1934,Mr 31,8:3
Frau wie Du, Eine 1934,D 24,17:3
Zigeunerblut 1935,Ap 8,23:5
Ich Sing Mich in Dein Herz Hinein
1935,Je 3,22:3
Tolle Bomberg, Der 1935,O 26,12:2
Himmel auf Erden, Der 1935,D 26,21:4
Alle Tage Ist Kein Sonntag 1936,Jl 11,11:4

Schuechterne Casanova, Der 1936,Ag 22,6:2
Ich Sehne Mich Nach Dir 1936,S 9,32:4
Ein Walzer fuer Dich 1936,S 29,35:2
Falscher Fuffziger, Ein 1937,F 13,9:1
Kirschen in Nachbars Garten 1937,My 15,23:6
Grobe Adele, Die 1937,My 15,23:5
Eva, das Fabriksmaedel 1938,Ja 8,19:2
Rendezvous in Wien 1938,F 19,19:4
Teufelskerl, Ein; Devil of a Fellow, A
1938,O 1,10:3
Favorit der Kaiserin, Der; Favorite of the Empress,
The 1939,D 25,29:3
Sands, Billy
McHale's Navy 1964,Jl 11,15:2
Sands, Carol
Modigliani of Montparnasse 1961,Mr 1,27:3
Sands, Diana
Raisin in the Sun, A 1961,Mr 30,24:1
Affair of the Skin, An 1963,N 21,43:2
Sands, Johnny
Till the End of Time 1946,Jl 24,24:1
Blaze of Noon 1947,Mr 5,31:2
Bachelor and the Bobby-Soxer, The
1947,Jl 25,12:5
Fabulous Texan, The 1947,D 26,22:5
Adventure in Baltimore 1949,Ap 29,27:2
Massacre River 1949,Jl 15,17:2
Lawless, The 1950,Je 23,29:2
Two Flags West 1950,O 13,23:2
Admiral Was a Lady, The 1950,O 13,23:3
Target Unknown 1951,Mr 5,24:2
Basketball Fix, the 1951,S 14,21:2
Sands, Lee (Original Author)
Give Out, Sisters 1942,Ag 28,22:3
Sands, Leslie
Walk in the Shadow 1966,S 12,52:5
Sands, Leslie (Original Author)
Another Man's Poison 1952,Ja 7,14:3
Sands, Sonny
Bellboy, The 1960,Jl 21,17:1
Sands, Tommy
Sing Boy Sing 1958,F 22,9:4
Mardi Gras 1958,N 19,45:2
Love in a Goldfish Bowl 1961,Jl 13,26:3
Babes in Toyland 1961,D 15,49:1
Longest Day, The 1962,O 5,28:1
Ensign Pulver 1964,Ag 1,13:2
None but the Brave 1965,F 25,24:1
Sandstrom, Flora (Original Author)
Bad Sister 1948,Je 11,27:3
Madness of the Heart 1950,O 12,43:2
Jessica 1962,Ap 20,20:2
Sandy, Baby
East Side of Heaven 1939,My 5,29:3
Unexpected Father 1939,Ag 11,12:2
Little Accident 1939,N 24,29:3
Sandy Is a Lady 1940,Je 28,22:2
Johnny Doughboy 1943,My 6,25:3
SANFORD
See Also SANDFORD
Sanford, Erskine
Pop Always Pays 1940,Ag 30,16:6
Citizen Kane 1941,My 2,25:1
Wife Takes a Flyer, The 1942,Je 19,19:1
Magnificent Ambersons, The 1942,Ag 14,13:3
Enemy of Women 1944,S 12,23:6
Ministry of Fear 1945,F 8,15:2
Spellbound 1945,N 2,22:2
From This Day Forward 1946,Ap 20,16:2
Crack-Up 1946,S 7,11:1
Angel on my Shoulder 1946,O 21,27:2
Best Years of our Lives, The 1946,N 22,27:2
Possessed 1947,My 30,25:2
Mourning Becomes Electra 1947,N 20,38:2
Voice of the Turtle, The 1947,D 26,22:4
Letters From an Unknown Woman
1948,Ap 29,20:6
Lady From Shanghai, The 1948,Je 10,28:2
Wake of the Red Witch 1949,Ja 10,19:2
Impact 1949,Mr 21,19:2
Night Unto Night 1949,Je 11,11:2
Macbeth 1950,D 28,22:6
Sanford, Isabell,Christine, Virginia
Guess Who's Coming to Dinner 1967,D 12,56:1
Sanford, Jack
Women They Talk About 1928,O 15,16:1
Sanford, John (Screenwriter)
Honky Tonk 1941,O 3,27:3
Sanford, Ralph
Patient in Room 18, The 1938,Ap 22,15:6
Give Me a Sailor 1938,Ag 11,31:1
I Live on Danger 1942,Ag 22,16:2
Ladies' Day 1943,Mr 26,14:3
Aerial Gunner 1943,Je 26,10:2
Lost in a Harem 1944,N 9,23:2
Thunderhead 1945,Mr 16,21:2
Bullfighters, The 1945,My 12,10:3
Hit Parade of 1947 1947,My 5,32:8
Copacabana 1947,Jl 12,7:2
Sioux City Sue 1947,Jl 23,19:3
Champion 1949,Ap 11,29:2
Glass Menagerie, The 1950,S 29,31:5
Union Station 1950,O 5,38:3

Sanford, Ralph— Cont
Rogue River 1951,F 16,21:4
Behave Yourself 1951,N 8,35:2
Blackjack Ketchum Desperado 1956,Ap 5,26:2
Sanforth, Clifford (Producer)
Bandit of Sherwood Forest, The 1946,Mr 23,8:4
Sangiorgi, Luciano
I Cadetti di Guascogna 1952,O 6,22:2
Sangoli, Vittorio
Grisbi 1959,Jl 13,23:1
Sangor, Frederica (Original Author)
Rolled Stockings 1927,Jl 19,27:2
Sangro, Elena di
Quo Vadis 1925,F 16,24:1
Sangro, Helene
Maciste in Hell 1931,Je 29,20:3
Sangster, Alfred
Young Mr Pitt, The 1943,Mr 11,17:1
Sangster, Jimmy (Original Author)
Deadlier Than the Male 1967,F 22,21:1
Sangster, Jimmy (Producer)
Scream of Fear 1961,Ag 23,29:1
Maniac 1963,O 31,26:3
Nightmare 1964,Je 18,29:2
Hysteria 1965,S 9,36:3
Nanny, The 1965,N 4,57:2
Anniversary, The 1968,Mr 21,57:2
Sangster, Jimmy (Screenwriter)
Curse of Frankenstein, The 1957,Ag 8,15:5
Horror of Dracula 1958,My 29,24:4
Snorkel, The 1958,S 18,37:2
Crawling Eye, The 1959,Ja 1,38:1
Intent to Kill 1959,Ap 1,43:2
Mummy, The 1959,D 17,51:4
Jack the Ripper 1960,F 18,37:4
Brides of Dracula, The 1960,S 6,41:4
Scream of Fear 1961,Ag 23,29:1
Paranoiac 1963,My 23,31:2
Maniac 1963,O 31,26:3
Nightmare 1964,Je 18,29:2
Hysteria 1965,S 9,36:3
Nanny, The 1965,N 4,57:2
Deadlier Than the Male 1967,F 22,21:1
Anniversary, The 1968,Mr 21,57:2
Sanicola, Henry (Producer)
X-15 1962,Ap 5,30:2
Sanin, P
Gypsies 1936,Jl 30,22:2
Sanipoli, Vittorio
See Naples and Die 1959,Ag 31,16:2
Great War; (Grande Guerra, La) 1961,Ag 31,22:3
Organizer, The 1964,My 7,31:2
Sanishvila, N (Director)
Scrapper, The 1959,D 14,42:2
Sanjust, Filippo (Screenwriter)
Morgan the Pirate 1961,Jl 20,32:2
Thief of Baghdad, The 1961,Ag 17,18:2
Sanmartin, Conrado
Colossus of Rhodes, The 1961,D 14,55:6
Awful Dr Orlof, The 1964,D 3,58:3
Sannell, Bertha
Winter Light 1963,My 14,32:1
Sano, Asao
Fires on the Plain 1963,S 25,39:1
Sano, Shuji
Carmen Comes Home 1959,D 23,22:1
Sanof, N
Zemlya Zhazhdet 1932,My 6,15:3
Eagle of the Caucasus, The 1932,S 17,18:4
Mother and Sons 1938,S 15,29:2
Sansom, Robert
In Which We Serve 1942,D 24,18:1
Sansom, William (Miscellaneous)
Flute and the Arrow, The 1960,O 11,55:1
Sanson, Yvonne
Flesh will Surrender 1950,O 26,38:7
Tormento 1953,Ap 4,9:2
Overcoat, The 1953,O 13,34:1
Star of India 1956,Ap 28,11:1
We Are all Murderers 1957,Ja 9,27:2
Miller's Beautiful Wife, The 1957,Je 12,40:2
This Angry Age 1958,Je 26,23:3
We Have Only one Life 1963,Je 24,21:4
Sansone, Alfonso (Producer)
Conjugal Bed, The 1963,S 17,30:1
Magnificent Cuckold 1965,Ap 20,42:1
Santander, Alberto (Miscellaneous)
Virgin of Guadalupe, The 1943,My 15,13:3
Santangelo, Guglielma (Screenwriter)
Constantine and the Cross 1963,Mr 14,8:2
Sante, Jose Villa
Kid Rodelo 1966,F 23,46:1
Santell, Alfred (Director)
Fools in the Dark 1924,Ag 18,8:2
Parisian Nights 1925,Je 2,16:3
Marriage Whirl, The 1925,Jl 15,22:3
Classified 1925,N 2,20:1
Bluebeard's Seven Wives 1925,D 28,19:2
Dancers of Paris, The 1926,Mr 29,24:3
Sweet Daddies 1926,Je 23,28:1
Subway Sadie 1926,S 13,18:1
Girl from Coney Island or Just Another Blonde
1926,D 13,27:1
Orchids and Ermine 1927,Ap 19,24:4

Santell, Alfred (Director) — Cont

Patent Leather Kid, The 1927,Ag 16,31:2
Gorilla, The 1927,N 21,20:1
Show Girl 1928,N 5,26:1
This Is Heaven 1929,My 27,22:1
Arizona Kid, The 1930,My 17,21:2
Sea Wolf, The 1930,O 6,21:1
Body and Soul 1931,Mr 14,23:2
Daddy Long Legs 1931,Je 6,15:5
Sob Sister 1931,O 3,20:2
Polly of the Circus 1932,Mr 19,11:2
Rebecca of Sunnybrook Farm 1932,Jl 30,16:5
Tess of the Storm Country 1932,N 19,20:2
Bondage 1933,Ap 24,11:3
Right to Romance, The 1933,D 15,28:2
Life of Vergie Winters, The 1934,Je 15,26:1
People Will Talk 1935,Je 17,20:2
Feather in her Hat, A 1935,O 25,24:5
Winterset 1936,D 4,31:1
Internes Can't Take Money 1937,My 6,23:2
Breakfast for Two 1937,N 20,21:2
Cocoanut Grove 1938,Je 16,21:2
Having Wonderful Time 1938,Jl 8,11:2
Arkansas Traveler, The 1938,N 17,29:2
Our Leading Citizen 1939,Ag 24,17:1
Aloma of the South Seas 1941,Ag 28,23:4
Beyond the Blue Horizon 1942,Je 25,27:2
Jack London 1944,Mr 3,19:3
Hairy Ape, The 1944,Jl 3,8:3
Mexicana 1945,N 17,14:6
That Brennan Girl 1946,D 9,34:3

Santell, Alfred (Producer)

Mexicana 1945,N 17,14:6
That Brennan Girl 1946,D 9,34:3

Santelton, Frederick

Darling of New York, The 1924,Ja 18,20:1

Santesso, Walter

Dolce Vita, La 1961,Ap 20,30:1

Santi, Angelo

And so to Bed 1965,Jl 31,11:3

Santi, Lionelio (Producer)

Italiano Brava Gente 1966,F 4,20:1

Santiago, Emilio

Lazarillo 1963,Ap 5,27:6

Santiago, Janira

Tropics 1968,S 24,52:1

Santigini, Jose (Screenwriter)

Pepote 1958,D 2,46:1

Santilla, Alfonso

Manhunt in the Jungle 1958,Ap 12,13:1

Santilli, Lamberto (Screenwriter)

Sky Is Red, The 1952,My 27,30:2

Santina, Bruno Della

Pay or Die 1960,My 27,22:2

Santis, Joe De

I Want to Live 1958,N 19,45:1

Santley, Fred

She's Got Everything 1938,Ja 14,21:3

Santley, Frederic

Morning Glory 1933,Ag 18,18:2
Walls of Gold 1933,O 21,11:3

Santley, Joseph (Composer)

Million Dollar Baby 1935,My 6,22:3

Santley, Joseph (Director)

Cocoanuts, The 1929,My 25,17:3
Young and Beautiful 1934,S 18,18:4
Million Dollar Baby 1935,My 6,22:3
Harmony Lane 1935,O 24,19:4
Dancing Feet 1936,Mr 28,11:2
Laughing Irish Eyes 1936,Ap 4,11:2
Harvester, The 1936,Jl 4,18:2
We Went to College 1936,Jl 27,20:2
Walking on Air 1936,S 12,20:2
Meet the Missus 1937,Jl 2,25:2
there Goes The Groom 1937,D 25,10:6
She's Got Everything 1938,Ja 14,21:3
Always in Trouble 1938,N 3,27:1
Spirit of Culver 1939,Mr 9,18:1
Family Next Door, The 1939,Ap 28,31:2
Two Bright Boys 1939,S 22,27:3
Music in My Heart 1940,Ja 4,19:2
Melody Ranch 1940,D 26,23:3
Behind the News 1941,Ja 16,25:3
Sis Hopkins 1941,My 1,27:5
Rookies on Parade 1941,My 22,25:2
Ice-Capades 1941,S 25,29:1
Remember Pearl Harbor 1942,Je 4,22:4
Chatterbox 1943,Jl 2,15:3
Brazil 1944,N 20,25:2
Earl Carroll Vanities 1945,Ap 2,15:6

Santley, Joseph (Original Author)

House on 56th Street, The 1933,D 2,9:3
Young and Beautiful 1934,S 18,18:4
Million Dollar Baby 1935,My 6,22:3
Mad Holiday 1936,N 26,39:2
Life of the Party, The 1937,O 4,17:1

Santley, Joseph (Screenwriter)

Million Dollar Baby 1935,My 6,22:3
Harmony Lane 1935,O 24,19:4

Santon, Penny

Full of Life 1957,F 13,38:1
Dino 1957,Je 22,9:2
Cry Tough 1959,S 17,48:4
Love With the Proper Stranger 1963,D 26,33:1

Funny Girl 1968,S 20,42:1

Santoni, Reni

Enter Laughing 1967,Ag 1,24:1
Anzio 1968,Jl 25,26:1

Santony, Spartaco

Castilian, The 1963,O 3,31:1

Santoro, Aldo

Parlami d'Amore Mariu 1934,O 20,20:3

Santoro, Francesca

Little Men 1940,D 9,23:2

Santos, Jack

Tundra 1936,D 3,31:2

Santos, Lita

Dos Noches 1933,Jl 29,14:3
Buenaventura, La 1934,S 15,20:3

Santos, Tiki

Advise and Consent 1962,Je 7,31:2

Santos, Tony

Badjao 1962,S 21,35:1

Santoyo, Jack

Midnight Taxi, The 1928,O 29,29:1

Santpere, Jose

Mercedes 1935,My 14,17:5

Santschi, Tom

Hell Cat, The 1918,N 25,11:3
Shadows 1919,F 10,11:3
Stronger Vow, The 1919,Ap 28,13:2
Cradle of Courage, The 1920,S 20,13:1
North Wind's Malice, The 1920,O 18,13:1
Little Robinson Crusoe 1924,S 3,17:1
Flaming Love 1925,Ja 19,14:1
Barriers Burned Away 1925,Mr 12,17:2
Paths to Paradise 1925,Je 30,14:3
My Own Pal 1926,Mr 15,18:3
Her Honor the Governor 1926,Jl 20,17:3
Jim, The Conquerer 1926,D 28,17:1
When a Man Loves 1927,F 4,16:6
Third Degree, The 1927,F 15,23:1
Hills of Kentucky 1927,Mr 2,29:3
Tracked by the Police 1927,Ap 27,22:5
Haunted Ship, The 1928,Ja 23,18:3
Honor Bound 1928,Ap 30,18:3
Shannons of Broadway, The 1929,D 21,17:1
Ten Nights in a Barroom 1931,F 28,15:2
River's End 1931,Mr 7,17:2

Sanyal, Pahari

Kanchenjungha 1966,Jl 26,27:2

Sapelli, Domingo

Escuadron Azul, El; Blue Squadron, The
1938,Je 4,18:3

Saper, Jack (Producer)

Across the Pacific 1942,S 5,9:2

Saperstein, Henry G (Producer)

Gay Purr--ee 1962,D 6,55:3
What's Up, Tiger Lily? 1966,N 18,33:1

Sapienza, Goliarda

Behind Closed Shutters 1952,Je 10,22:7

Sapin, Louis (Screenwriter)

Chasers, The; Draguers, Les 1960,My 3,43:1
Anatomy of a Marriage; My Days With Jean
Marc; My Nights With Francoise
1964,O 27,42:2

Saplak, Mjoman

Legong 1935,O 2,27:1

Sapper (Original Author)

Woman in Chains 1932,N 21,21:1

Sarafian, Richard C (Director)

Andy 1965,Ja 22,21:2

Sarafian, Richard C (Producer)

Andy 1965,Ja 22,21:2

Sarafian, Richard C (Screenwriter)

Andy 1965,Ja 22,21:2

Sarantsev, Y

Road to Life 1956,Je 11,26:6

Sarapo, Theo

Judex 1966,Ap 26,55:1

Sarcey, Martine

Thief of Paris, The 1967,Ag 24,43:2

Sardi, Alberto

Those Magnificent Men in Their Flying Machines
(Or How I Flew From London to Paris in 25
Hours and 11 Minutes) 1965,Je 17,27:1

Sardo, Cosmo

Amazon Quest 1949,My 14,9:3

Sardou, Fernand

Savage Triangle 1952,S 30,38:2
Letters From my Windmill (The Elixir of Father
Gaucher); Elixir of Father Gaucher, The (Letters
From my Windmill) 1955,D 19,33:1
Wild Oat, The 1956,Je 28,33:2
Forbidden Fruit 1959,F 23,19:1
Picnic on the Grass 1960,O 12,47:1

Sardou, Victorien (Original Author)

Let's Get a Divorce 1918,Ap 29,11:1
Fedora 1918,Ag 5,7:1
Theodora 1921,O 15,16:2
Madame Sans Gene 1925,Ap 18,19:1
Night of Mystery, A 1928,Ap 16,20:5
Woman From Moscow, The 1928,N 5,26:1
Story of Tosca, The 1947,D 19,34:2
Tosca 1958,O 24,40:3
Madame 1963,Mr 21,8:6

Sarecky, Barney (Original Author)

Run Around, The 1931,Ag 10,18:3

Sarecky, Barney (Producer)

Missing Guest, The 1938,S 7,30:7
Mars Attacks the World 1938,N 8,26:3

Sarecky, Louis (Original Author)

Legionnaires in Paris 1927,D 26,26:6
Kept Husbands 1931,Mr 24,31:2

Sarecky, Louis (Screenwriter)

North to the Klondike 1942,Mr 12,24:3

Sarfati, Maurice

Hunchback of Notre Dame, The 1957,D 12,35:1
Journey, The 1959,F 20,19:1
Lost Command 1966,S 15,51:1

Sarg, Tony (Original Author)

Almanac 1921,My 9,16:2
Tooth Carpenter, The 1921,My 30,12:5

Sarg-Dawley (Producer)

Fireman, Save My Child 1921,S 12,16:1

Sargent, Alvin (Screenwriter)

Gambit 1966,D 22,40:2

Sargent, Anne

Naked City, The 1948,Mr 5,17:2
Three Guys Named Mike 1951,Mr 2,21:2

Sargent, Bill (Producer)

Stop the World-I Want to Get Off
1966,My 12,54:2

Sargent, Christopher (Cinematographer)

Face of War, A 1968,My 11,28:1

Sargent, Dick

Bernardine 1957,Jl 25,28:1
Mardi Gras 1958,N 19,45:2
Operation Petticoat 1959,D 6,38:1
Great Impostor, The 1961,Mr 30,24:1
That Touch of Mink 1962,Je 15,16:2
Captain Newman, MD 1964,F 21,36:1
Billie 1965,S 16,55:3
Ghost and Mr Chicken, The 1966,S 22,57:2
Private Navy of Sgt O'Farrell, The
1968,My 9,54:1
Young Runaways, The 1968,S 12,54:3

Sargent, Herbert (Screenwriter)

Bye Bye Braverman 1968,F 22,36:1

Sargent, Joseph (Director)

One Spy too Many 1966,D 8,64:1
Hell With Heroes, The 1968,S 3,54:2

Sargent, Lewis

Huckleberry Finn 1920,F 23,11:2
Soul of Youth, The 1920,Ag 16,8:2
New Adventures of Tarzan, The 1935,O 15,19:3

Sargent, Malcolm

Battle for Music 1945,O 15,13:2

Sargent, Michael

Touch of Evil 1958,My 22,25:2

Sari, Diana

Whirlpool; (Remous) 1940,O 8,31:2

Sari, Sirkka

Wajan 1938,Ap 18,11:1
Niskavvoren Naiset; Women of Niskavuori
1938,N 21,14:5

Saris, Georges

Phaedra 1962,O 19,24:1

Sarkadi, Imre (Original Author)

Merry Go-Round 1958,Ap 3,23:3

Sarkar, Kali

Devi 1962,O 8,19:1
Music Room, The 1963,O 16,50:6

Sarkar, Mohammed Ibn

Devi 1962,O 8,19:1

Sarkka, Tolvo

Jumalen Tuomio; Judgement of God, The
1939,O 27,27:2

Sarkka, Tolvo (Director)

Milkmaid, The 1959,My 2,14:5

Sarle, Regina

Nugget Nell 1919,Jl 28,8:5

Sarmell, Walter

Kalle paa Spaangen 1940,Ja 27,9:3

Sarment, Jean

Transatlantic Merry-Go-Round 1934,N 1,25:2

Sarment, Jean (Miscellaneous)

Carnet de Bal, Un 1938,Mr 26,12:1
Stolen Affections 1951,Mr 12,20:2

Sarne, Michael (Director)

Joanna 1968,N 25,54:1

Sarne, Michael (Screenwriter)

Joanna 1968,N 25,54:1

Sarner, A

Dreyfus Case, The 1931,Ag 31,11:5
Passing of the Third Floor Back, The
1936,Ap 29,19:2

Sarno, Hector V

Ashes of Vengeance 1923,Ag 7,20:2
Song of Love, The 1924,F 25,13:1
Sea Hawk, The 1924,Je 3,22:1
Temptress, The 1926,O 11,18:1
Red Hot Speed 1929,F 5,26:3
Lucky Star 1929,Jl 22,17:1
Death Takes a Holiday 1934,F 24,18:4
Wee Willie Winkie 1937,Jl 24,12:1
Flight Into Nowhere 1938,My 2,13:3

Sarno, Joe (Director)
Moonlighting Wives 1968,My 9,54:4
Sarno, Joe (Screenwriter)
Moonlighting Wives 1968,My 9,54:4
Sarno, Joseph W (Director)
Inga 1968,N 21,41:2
Sarno, Joseph W (Screenwriter)
Inga 1968,N 21,41:2
Sarno, Tom
As Man Desires 1925,F 10,20:1
Sarnow, Hedda
Somewhere in Berlin 1949,Ag 16,19:3
Saroglou, Bambis (Producer)
Moment of Passion 1960,N 21,34:1
Sarovan, Don
Blast of Silence 1961,D 30,12:1
Saroyan, William (Original Author)
Human Comedy, The 1943,Mr 3,19:2
Time of your Life, The 1948,My 27,29:2
Sarracino, Ernest
Strangers When we Meet 1960,Je 30,22:2
Sarrazin, Michael
Flim Flam Man, The 1967,Ag 23,40:1
Sweet Ride, The 1968,Je 13,57:2
Sarri, Marco
Outcry 1949,Mr 14,15:5
Sarrut, Andre (Producer)
Pardon my French 1952,Mr 31,17:2
Sarta, Mary
Madonna of the Sleeping Cars, The
1929,O 14,20:2
Sarti, Andre
Woman on Trial, The 1927,S 26,27:1
Sarton, May (Screenwriter)
Hymn of the Nations 1946,Ap 22,26:2
Sartre, Jean-Paul
Life Begins Tomorrow 1952,N 18,37:2
Sartre, Jean-Paul (Miscellaneous)
Chips Are Down, The 1949,F 2,36:1
Respectful Prostitute, The 1957,Jl 11,21:1
Sartre, Jean-Paul (Original Author)
Dirty Hands 1954,My 11,25:5
Proud and the Beautiful, The 1956,My 29,32:2
Respectful Prostitute, The 1957,Jl 11,21:1
No Exit 1962,D 6,55:2
Condemned of Altona, The 1963,O 31,26:1
Sartre, Jean-Paul (Screenwriter)
Chips Are Down, The 1949,F 2,36:1
Witches of Salem 1958,D 9,54:2
Sarumaru, Kichizaemon
Teahouse of the August Moon, The
1956,N 30,19:1
Sarver, Charles (Original Author)
Nero 1922,My 26,17:2
Sarvil, Rene
Letters From my Windmill (The Three Low
Masses); Three Low Masses, The (Letters From
my Windmill) 1955,D 19,33:1
Sarvis, David
Salt of the Earth 1954,Mr 15,20:2
Sasaki, Mitsuzo (Original Author)
Imposter, The 1955,Mr 23,27:1
Sasaki, Takamaru
Throne of Blood 1961,N 23,50:2
Sascha, Alexander
Rosenmontag 1931,Mr 28,15:3
Sascha (Producer)
Queen of Sin and the Spectacle of Sodom and
Gomorrah 1923,Mr 27,24:3 (In Addenda)
Sashin-Nikolsky, A
Anna Cross, The 1954,O 25,30:7
Saslavsky, Luis (Director)
Puerta Cerrada; Closed Door 1940,F 5,13:3
Loco Serenata, El; Crazy Musician, The
1940,Ap 22,13:2
Snow Was Black, The 1956,O 16,36:5
Demoniaque 1958,Mr 4,34:5
Premier May 1958,S 17,44:2
Saslavsky, Luis (Screenwriter)
Snow Was Black, The 1956,O 16,36:5
Demoniaque 1958,Mr 4,34:5
Premier May 1958,S 17,44:2
Sass, Herbert Ravenel (Original Author)
Anne of the Indies 1951,O 25,36:3
Sassard, Jacqueline
Guendalina 1958,Je 30,23:2
Women Are Weak 1959,Je 9,44:2
Violent Summer 1961,My 20,12:1
My Son, The Hero 1963,S 19,23:1
White Voices; Voci Blanche 1965,Ap 13,32:2
Accident 1967,Ap 18,33:1
Biches, Les 1968,S 27,34:1
Sassler, Robert (Producer)
My Wife's Best Friend 1952,O 11,17:2
Sasso, Ugo
Ten Commandments, The 1958,Ap 7,26:1
Sassoli, Dina
Loves of Don Juan, The 1948,S 2,18:4
Spirit and the Flesh, The 1948,N 1,28:2
Mill on the Po, The 1951,O 23,35:2
Life of Donizetti, The 1952,Ap 26,19:2

Sassoli, Pietro (Composer)
Herzblut 1932,O 3,15:2
Sassoon, William (Producer)
Her Man Gilbey 1949,Je 9,35:2
Girl on a Motorcycle, The 1968,N 28,66:5
Satchidananda, Samai
Chappaqua 1967,N 6,65:2
Satenstein, Frank (Producer)
Open Secret 1948,F 2,15:2
Close-Up 1948,Ap 5,24:2
Satirlou, Helen
Midwife, The 1961,S 25,41:2
Sato, Ichiro (Producer)
This Madding Crowd 1964,Je 17,48:1
Could I but Live 1965,Ja 20,34:2
Sato, Kei
Onibaba 1965,F 10,44:3
Sato, Makoto
Bandits on the Wind 1964,Ja 15,27:3
Sato, Masaru (Composer)
Sanjuro 1963,My 8,34:2
Sato, Reiko
Mother Didn't Tell Me 1950,Mr 4,11:2
Woman on the Run 1950,N 30,24:2
Kismet 1955,D 9,32:2
Flower Drum Song 1961,N 10,40:1
Ugly American, The 1963,Ap 12,30:2
Satoff, Paul
Crusades, The 1935,Ag 22,21:3
Satorres, Rafaela
Nail, The 1949,Jl 1,14:6
Satterlee, Bruce
Stella Dallas 1937,Ag 6,21:1
Satto, Shiko
Golden Demon 1956,Ja 31,34:3
Satton, Lon
For Love of Ivy 1968,Jl 18,26:1
Sauber, Harry (Original Author)
Obey the Law 1933,Mr 13,18:3
I Like It That Way 1934,Ap 18,23:3
Happiness Ahead 1934,O 11,28:2
Sing Me a Love Song 1936,D 26,15:2
Racketeers in Exile 1937,Ap 12,15:3
Love and Learn 1947,My 3,10:3
Sauber, Harry (Producer)
Manhattan Merry-Go-Round 1937,D 31,9:3
Sauber, Harry (Screenwriter)
Maybe It's Love 1935,F 11,14:2
Adventure in Manhattan 1936,O 23,27:5
Racketeers in Exile 1937,Ap 12,15:3
Manhattan Merry-Go-Round 1937,D 31,9:3
What's Buzzin Cousin 1943,Jl 23,21:4
Sauer, Fred (Director)
Stolz der 3 Kompagnie, Der 1932,Jl 21,15:2
Tanzhusar, Der 1933,Ap 10,8:4
Heimat am Rhein 1934,D 11,29:4
Beiden Seehunde, Die 1935,Mr 9,19:2
Pantoffelhelden 1935,O 21,22:5
Alles Weg'n Dem Hund 1936,Mr 31,17:3
Alte Kameraden 1936,Ap 27,19:3
Maedchenraeuber 1936,Ag 15,6:3
Gordian, Der Tyrann 1937,Je 21,15:3
Lachdoktor, Der; Laugh Doctor, The
1938,Mr 12,13:4
Sauers, Joseph
Forgotten Commandments 1932,Je 2,25:2
Huddle 1932,Je 17,24:1
Saturday's Millions 1933,O 14,18:3
Ace of Aces 1933,N 11,10:4
Son of a Sailor 1933,N 30,38:4
Looking for Trouble 1934,Ap 12,27:2
Death on the Diamond 1934,S 24,14:1
Band Plays on, The 1934,D 22,21:2
Car 99 1935,F 23,14:7
Informer, The 1935,My 10,25:2
Broadway Gondolier 1935,Jl 18,15:2
Arizonian, The 1935,Jl 27,16:2
Special Agent 1935,S 19,28:1
Sauguet, Henri (Composer)
Farrebique 1948,F 24,21:2
Saul, Beverly Jean
Youngest Profession, The 1943,Je 25,13:3
Saul, Oscar (Miscellaneous)
Once More, my Darling 1949,S 26,17:1
Saul, Oscar (Original Author)
Road House 1948,N 8,24:2
Lady Gambles, The 1949,My 21,9:2
Naked Maja, The 1959,Je 11,36:2
Saul, Oscar (Producer)
Let's Do It Again 1953,O 14,34:3
Saul, Oscar (Screenwriter)
Dark Past, The 1948,D 23,25:2
Woman in Hiding 1950,F 23,33:2
Streetcar Named Desire, A 1951,S 30,27:1
Affair in Trinidad 1952,Jl 31,14:2
Joker Is Wild, The 1957,S 27,16:6
Helen Morgan Story, The 1957,O 3,33:2
Second Time Around, The 1961,D 23,16:1
Major Dundee 1965,Ap 8,45:1
Silencers, The 1966,Mr 17,35:1
Sauli, Anneli
Milkmaid, The 1959,My 2,14:5

Saulieu, Emile
Frochard et les Deux Orphelines, La
1934,F 7,16:2
Saulmier, Tony (Cinematographer)
Gri-Gri 1956,S 29,12:2
Saum, Cliff
Bridge of Sighs, The 1925,Mr 23,14:2
Torchy Gets her Man 1938,N 18,25:3
Ladies Must Live 1940,S 6,25:3
Case of the Black Parrot, The 1941,Ja 10,23:3
SAUNDERS
See Also SANDERS
Saunders, Charles (Director)
Tawny Pipit 1947,S 8,25:5
Murder Reported 1960,Jl 12,39:1
Saunders, Gloria
O S S 1946,My 27,15:5
Cry Danger 1951,F 22,27:3
Saunders, Hilary St George (Original Author)
Paratrooper 1953,D 31,9:3
Saunders, Hugh
Man Trap 1961,N 30,40:4
Saunders, Jacqueline
Broken Laws 1925,Ja 21,19:3
Saunders, John Monk (Original Author)
Too Many Kisses 1925,Mr 3,20:1
Shock Punch, The 1925,My 11,14:3
Wings 1927,Ag 13,10:4
Legion of the Condemned, The 1928,Mr 19,26:2
Docks of New York; Damnees de l'Ocean, Les
1930,Ap 20,VIII,6:5
Last Flight, The 1931,Ag 20,17:4
Eagle and the Hawk, The 1933,My 13,16:2
Ace of Aces 1933,N 11,10:4
Devil Dogs of the Air 1935,F 7,23:2
West Point of the Air 1935,Ap 6,10:1
I Found Stella Parish 1935,N 4,24:4
Dawn Patrol 1938,D 24,12:1
Saunders, John Monk (Screenwriter)
Finger Points, The 1931,Mr 28,15:3
Saunders, Kenneth (Original Author)
Lady Who Dared, The 1931,Je 6,15:5
Saunders, Lawrence (Original Author)
Snowed Under 1936,Mr 30,17:5
Saunders, Mary Jane
Sorrowful Jones 1949,Je 6,15:2
Father Is a Bachelor 1950,F 23,33:3
Woman of Distinction, A 1950,Mr 17,28:2
Girl Next Door, The 1953,S 5,7:4
Saunders, Nancy
Lone Wolf in London, The 1947,N 22,10:3
Saunders, Neza
Bush Christmas 1947,N 27,50:4
Saunders, Rai
Lost Boundaries 1949,Jl 1,14:4
Saunders, Russ
College Lovers 1930,N 28,23:1
That's my Boy 1932,N 21,21:1
Saunders, Stuart
Court Martial 1955,Ag 2,17:1
Crawling Eye, The 1959,Ja 1,38:1
Saunders, Terry
King and I, The 1956,Je 29,15:6
Saura, Carlos (Director)
Hunt, The 1966,S 20,39:1
Hunt, The 1967,Ap 25,38:1
Saura, Carlos (Screenwriter)
Hunt, The 1967,Ap 25,38:1
Saurel, Georges
South Sea Woman 1953,Je 4,33:6
Saurel, Maurice (Director)
Devil's Daughter 1949,F 26,11:2
Saures, Joseph
Surrender 1931,N 28,20:4
Saury, Alain
Roots of Heaven, The 1958,O 16,46:1
Young Girls Beware 1959,Ag 22,8:2
Big Gamble, The 1961,S 2,19:2
Sauter-Sarto, Otto
Alles Weg'n Dem Hund 1936,Mr 31,17:3
Sautet, Claude (Screenwriter)
Banana Peel; Peau de Banane 1965,Ja 19,29:1
Symphony for a Massacre 1965,My 28,40:1
Vie de Chateau, La 1967,Mr 21,35:1
Sauvage, Andre (Director)
Yellow Cruise, The 1936,N 18,31:3
Sauvage, Arlette
Vitelloni 1956,O 24,43:1
Sauvajon, Marc-Gilbert (Director)
Royal Affair, A; (Roi, Le) 1950,Mr 9,25:2
Ma Pomme 1951,O 15,22:2
Sauvajon, Marc-Gilbert (Original Author)
Ma Pomme 1951,O 15,22:2
Sauvajon, Marc-Gilbert (Screenwriter)
Not Guilty 1948,Ap 23,28:2
Loves of Casanova 1948,S 18,11:4
Devil's Daughter 1949,F 26,11:2
Vautrin, the Thief 1949,N 11,31:2
Royal Affair, A; (Roi, Le) 1950,Mr 9,25:2
Adorable Julia 1964,Ap 8,33:1
Sauveneix, Helene
Francois Villon 1950,Jl 3,9:2

Sauvlon, Serge
Naked Autumn 1963,N 15,25:3
Savage, Ann
Two Senoritas From Chicago 1943,Ag 6,10:4
What a Woman 1943,D 3,27:2
Midnight Manhunt 1945,Ag 18,12:5
Last Crooked Mile, The 1946,S 14,10:8
Savage, Archie
His Majesty O'Keefe 1954,F 6,17:2
Vera Cruz 1954,D 27,22:4
South Pacific 1958,Mr 20,33:1
Savage, Ben
Cheating Blondes 1933,My 20,11:4
Savage, Carol
Moss Rose 1947,Jl 3,14:2
Three Came Home 1950,F 21,22:5
Please Believe Me 1950,Je 12,19:4
My Six Convicts 1952,Mr 28,27:3
Savage, Daniel Boone
Swing Your Lady 1938,Ja 27,17:2
Savage, Jack
Francis of Assisi 1961,Jl 29,8:2
Savage, Mildred (Original Author)
Parrish 1961,My 5,22:1
Savage, Nellie
Sorrows of Satan, The 1926,O 13,21:1
Hole in the Wall, The 1929,Ap 15,22:6
Savage, Paul
Untamed Fury 1947,Ap 26,10:6
Savage, Richard Henry (Original Author)
My Official Wife 1914,Jl 14,9:5
Savage, Turner
How Baxter Buttered In 1925,Je 23,24:3
Tumbleweeds 1925,D 21,27:2
Frisco Sally Levy 1927,Ap 13,29:4
Saval, Dany
Cheaters, The; (Tricheurs, Les) 1961,Je 5,37:4
Moon Pilot 1962,Ap 6,30:2
7 Capital Sins (Envy); Envy (7 Capital Sins) 1963,Ja 17,5:2
Devil and the 10 Commandments, The (Episode 2) 1963,O 15,44:1
Boeing Boeing 1965,D 24,24:4
Saval, Manolita
Capitan Aventurero, El; Adventureous Captain, The 1939,O 3,19:5
Miserables, Los 1944,O 24,17:2
Savalas, Telly
Mad Dog Coll 1961,My 13,10:1
Young Savages, The 1961,My 25,31:1
Cape Fear 1962,Ap 19,35:2
Birdman of Alcatraz 1962,Jl 19,19:2
Interns, The 1962,Ag 9,17:5
Man From the Diners' Club, The 1963,Ap 18,39:1
Love Is a Ball 1963,Ap 25,38:1
Johnny Cool 1963,O 3,31:1
New Interns, The 1964,Ag 20,34:2
Greatest Story Ever Told, The 1965,F 16,40:2
Genghis Khan 1965,Je 24,28:2
Battle of the Bulge 1965,D 18,36:1
Slender Thread, The 1965,D 24,24:2
Beau Geste 1966,S 8,43:1
Dirty Dozen, The 1967,Je 16,36:1
Scalphunters, The 1968,Ap 3,40:1
Sol Madrid 1968,Je 14,43:1
Savarese, Nino (Screenwriter)
Man With the Grey Glove, The 1953,Ja 3,11:2
Savary, Gilberte
Ronde des Heures, La 1932,Ja 25,20:3
Savchenko, Igor
Twenty-Six Commissars 1933,Jl 1,16:6
Savchenko, Igor (Director)
Ballad of Cossack Gloota, The 1938,F 28,19:1
Guerrilla Brigade 1942,Ap 14,17:2
Diary of a Nazi 1943,Mr 25,25:3
Lucky Bride, The 1948,Ja 26,15:2
Taras Shevchenko 1952,Jl 28,12:6
Savchenko, Igor (Screenwriter)
Lucky Bride, The 1948,Ja 26,15:2
Taras Shevchenko 1952,Jl 28,12:6
Saveliev, I
Village of Sin, The 1929,My 21,29:3
China Express, The 1930,Mr 10,24:1
Savelyev, N
Last Game, The 1964,O 25,41:5 (Incorrect in this edition; use 1964,O 26,41:5 elsewhere)
Savelyeva, Lyudmila
War and Peace 1968,Ap 29,50:5
Saver, Frem (Director)
Blinde Passagier; Stowaways 1937,Mr 6,10:1
Savidan, George
Design for Living 1933,N 23,24:2
Saville, George M (Screenwriter)
Kiss, The 1929,N 16,25:2
Saville, Gus
Light of Western Stars, The 1930,Ap 26,11:1
Saville, Philip (Director)
Stop the World-I Want to Get Off 1966,My 12,54:2
Oedipus the King 1968,S 19,62:2

Saville, Philip (Screenwriter)
Oedipus the King 1968,S 19,62:2
Saville, Victor (Director)
Woman in the Night, A 1929,Mr 11,22:2
Kitty 1929,Je 11,27:2
Fanny Hawthorn 1929,N 11,20:2
Woman to Woman 1929,N 12,34:4
W Plan, The 1931,Mr 23,24:7
Calendar, The 1931,N 22,VIII,6:1
Office Girl 1932,Je 27,20:7
Faithful Heart 1933,Ag 15,20:2
Good Companions, The 1933,O 10,24:1
I Was a Spy 1934,Ja 15,12:2
Friday the 13th 1934,My 15,18:1
Evensong 1934,N 17,12:1
Evergreen 1935,Ja 11,29:1
Iron Duke, The 1935,Ja 25,27:2
Loves of a Dictator 1935,Je 1,18:2
First a Girl 1936,Ja 4,19:1
It's Love Again 1936,My 23,12:1
Dark Journey 1937,Ag 23,22:1
Storm in a Teacup 1938,Mr 22,18:4
South Riding 1938,Ag 2,15:2
Forever and a Day 1943,Mr 13,9:2
Tonight and Every Night 1945,Mr 9,16:2
Green Years, The 1946,Ap 5,21:2
Green Dolphin Street 1947,O 16,34:2
If Winter Comes 1948,Ja 23,28:4
Conspirator 1950,Ap 28,26:2
Kim 1950,D 8,40:4
Long Wait, The 1954,Jl 3,9:2
Silver Chalice, The 1954,D 27,22:5
Saville, Victor (Producer)
Dark Journey 1937,Ag 23,22:1
Storm in a Teacup 1938,Mr 22,18:4
South Riding 1938,Ag 2,15:2
Citadel, The 1938,N 4,27:2
Goodbye Mr Chips 1939,My 16,27:2
Bitter Sweet 1940,N 22,27:1
Woman's Face, A 1941,My 16,21:2
Chocolate Soldier, The 1941,N 1,20:2
Smilin' Through 1941,D 5,29:2
White Cargo 1942,N 27,27:2
Forever and a Day 1943,Mr 13,9:2
Keeper of the Flame 1943,Mr 19,15:2
Above Suspicion 1943,Ag 6,10:3
Tonight and Every Night 1945,Mr 9,16:2
I, The Jury 1953,Ag 22,8:2
Loss of Innocence 1961,N 22,27:1
Savin, Lee (Producer)
T A M I Show, The 1965,Ja 28,20:1
Harlow 1965,My 15,18:1
Savinova, Elena
Cossacks of the Kuban 1950,O 30,22:4
Big Family, A 1955,Je 6,24:1
Savinova, Katy
Lullaby, The 1961,My 15,35:2
Savio, Clara
Glueckspilze 1936,O 26,21:1
Savitskaya, Helena
Six PM 1946,Ja 28,15:5
Symphony of Life 1948,D 28,19:7
Savitskaya, M
Sunny Youth 1935,Ag 19,18:2
Savitsky, V
Golden Taiga 1935,Ag 2,22:3
Savkin, Igor
Miles of Fire 1958,N 10,36:6 (In Addenda)
Savo, Jimmy
Once in a Blue Moon 1936,D 2,35:1
Merry-Go-Round of 1938 1937,N 26,27:2
Savoca, John
12 Angry Men 1957,Ap 15,24:1
Savoir, Alfred
Time to Love 1927,Je 23,23:3
Savoir, Alfred (Original Author)
Lost-a Wife 1925,Je 22,10:2
Grand Duchess and the Waiter, The 1926,F 9,22:1
His Tiger Lady 1928,My 28,23:2
Coutariere de Luneville, La; Dressmaker of Luneville, The 1932,Je 5,X,10:5 (In Addenda)
Ladies Should Listen 1934,Jl 28,16:6
Here is my Heart 1934,D 22,21:1
Bluebeard's Eighth Wife 1938,Mr 24,21:2
Savon, Beatriz
10:30 PM Summer 1966,O 20,52:1
Savoye, Renee
Parisian, The 1931,Ag 22,7:5
Savva, T
Variety Stars 1955,F 21,16:7
Savvina, Iya
Lady With the Dog, The 1962,N 7,48:1
Savyotova, Svetlana
Farewell, Doves 1962,Mr 19,38:3
Sawal, Keiko
Kojiro 1968,Ag 30,23:1
Sawamura, Ikio
Yojimbo 1962,O 16,34:1
Sawamura, Mitsuko
Ana-Ta-Han 1954,My 18,38:2
Meet Me in Las Vegas 1956,Mr 14,39:2
Teahouse of the August Moon, The 1956,N 30,19:1

Sawamura, Sonosuke
Utamaro, Painter of Women 1964,D 2,57:1
Zatoichi 1968,Je 28,37:1
Sawyer, Arthur H (Director)
Sandra 1924,D 22,20:2
Sawyer, Connie
Hole in the Head, A 1959,Jl 16,31:2
Ada 1961,Ag 26,15:1
Sawyer, Geneva (Miscellaneous)
Life Begins In College 1937,O 9,16:1
Just Around the Corner 1938,D 3,11:2
Swanee River 1939,D 30,9:2
Sawyer, Joe
Little Big Shot 1935,O 7,11:2
I Found Stella Parish 1935,N 4,24:4
Frisco Kid 1935,N 25,22:1
Man of Iron 1935,D 7,22:2
Fish 1936,Ja 25,18:5
Petrified Forest, The 1936,F 7,14:2
Walking Dead, The 1936,Mr 2,13:2
Special Investigator 1936,Ap 25,21:1
Pride of the Marines 1936,Ap 27,19:2
High Tension 1936,Jl 11,11:4
Sudden Death, And 1936,Jl 18,18:2
Great Guy 1937,Ja 1,19:2
Black Legion 1937,Ja 18,21:1
Slim 1937,Je 24,30:2
San Quentin 1937,Ag 4,15:2
Reported Missing 1937,S 3,12:2
Tarzan's Revenge 1938,Ja 10,13:3
Stolen Heaven 1938,My 12,27:2
Passport Husband 1938,Ag 5,11:2
Storm, The 1938,O 31,12:2
Always in Trouble 1938,N 3,27:1
Heart of the North 1938,D 21,29:2
Gambling Ship 1939,Ja 21,19:2
You Can't Get Away With Murder 1939,Mr 25,19:2
Confessions of a Nazi Spy 1939,Ap 29,13:2
Union Pacific 1939,My 11,31:2
Frontier Marshal 1939,Jl 29,18:2
I Stole a Million 1939,Ag 7,11:2
Roaring Twenties, The 1939,N 11,12:1
Sabotage 1939,N 16,29:5
Grapes of Wrath, The 1940,Ja 25,17:2
Dark Command 1940,My 11,15:2
Lucky Cisco Kid 1940,JE 24,19:5
Melody Ranch 1940,D 26,23:3
Lady From Cheyenne, The 1941,Ap 18,18:2
Sergeant York 1941,Jl 3,15:1
Tanks a Million 1941,O 9,27:2
Belle Starr 1941,N 1,20:2
Swamp Water 1941,N 17,15:2
They Died With Their Boots On 1941,N 21,23:3
You're in the Army Now 1941,D 26,21:4
Taxi, Mister 1943,Ap 15,20:2
Fall In 1943,My 15,13:3
Cowboy in Manhattan 1943,My 28,19:2
Prairie Chickens 1943,Jl 9,21:6
Let's Face It 1943,Ag 5,18:1
Hit the Ice 1943,S 23,27:2
Tarzan's Desert Mystery 1943,D 27,23:3
Brewster's Millions 1945,Ap 27,23:2
Naughty Nineties, The 1945,Je 21,16:2
Gilda 1946,Mr 15,27:2
Deadline at Dawn 1946,Ap 4,33:2
Joe Palooka, Champ 1946,Ap 6,10:6
Runaround, The 1946,Je 7,16:3
Inside Job 1946,Je 15,24:3
Outlaw, The 1947,S 12,18:4
Roses Are Red 1947,N 15,11:2
Christmas Eve 1947,N 28,30:2
Double Life, A 1948,F 20,19:1
If You Knew Susie 1948,F 23,19:2
Here Comes Trouble 1948,Ap 15,31:4
Fighting Father Dunne 1948,Je 25,26:2
Lucky Stiff, The 1949,Ja 31,14:2
Deputy Marshal 1949,N 11,31:3
And Baby Makes Three 1949,D 23,17:3
Traveling Saleswoman 1950,Ja 6,25:3
Curtain Call at Cactus Creek 1950,S 22,35:4
Flying Missile, The 1950,D 25,25:1
Comin' Round the Mountain 1951,Jl 27,15:2
Smoke Jumpers 1952,Mr 22,9:6
It Came From Outer Space 1953,Je 18,38:2
Riding Shotgun 1954,Ap 2,22:2
Killing, The 1956,My 21,20:1
North to Alaska 1960,N 11,36:1
Sawyer, Joseph
Freshman Love 1936,Ja 25,18:5
Long Voyage Home, The 1940,O 9,30:2 (In Addenda)
Sawyer, William
Adventure Girl 1934,Ag 9,14:5
SAX
See Also SAXE, SACHS, SAKS
Sax, Sam (Producer)
Why Girls Leave Home 1945,Ag 4,7:3
SAXE
See Also SACHS, SAKS, SAX
Saxe, Templar
Beau Brummell 1924,Mr 31,20:1
Captain Blood 1924,S 9,19:1

Saxe, Templar— Cont
   Her Night of Romance 1925,Ja 13,16:1
   Dancers, The 1925,Ja 26,22:1
   Time, the Comedian 1925,D 14,18:2
   White Black Sheep, The 1926,D 21,20:2
   When a Man Loves 1927,F 4,16:6
Saxon, Don
   Subject Was Roses, The 1968,O 14,53:2
Saxon, John
   Running Wild 1955,N 12,23:2
   This Happy Feeling 1958,Je 19,28:2
   Summer Love 1958,Je 26,23:4
   Reluctant Debutante, The 1958,Ag 15,17:1
   Big Fisherman, The 1959,Ag 6,18:1
   Cry Tough 1959,S 17,48:4
   Unforgiven, The 1960,Ap 7,46:1
   Portrait in Black 1960,Jl 28,19:1
   Mr Hobbs Takes a Vacation 1962,Je 16,11:2
   War Hunt 1962,Ag 8,35:2
   Cardinal, The 1963,D 13,41:1
   Cavern, The 1965,D 25,17:2
   Appaloosa, The 1966,S 15,51:1
   For Singles Only 1968,Je 6,54:1
Saxon, Lyle (Original Author)
   Buccaneer, The 1958,D 24,00:0
Saxton, Charles (Original Author)
   High Gear 1933,Ap 15,16:2
Saxtorph, Werner
   Smiling Lieutenant, The 1931,My 23,13:4
Sayani, Hamid
   Shakespeare Wallah 1966,Mr 23,40:2
SAYER
   See Also SAYRE
Sayer, Diane
   Strangler, The 1964,Je 11,27:4
   Kitten With a Whip 1964,N 5,50:4
Sayers, Dorothy L (Original Author)
   Haunted Honeymoon 1940,O 31,28:2
Sayers, Jo Ann
   Young Doctor Kildare 1938,O 28,27:1
   Honolulu 1939,F 23,19:2
   Huckleberry Finn 1939,Mr 3,21:2
   Fast and Loose 1939,Mr 9,18:1
   Within the Law 1939,Ap 6,31:2
   Man With Nine Lives, The 1940,Ap 29,12:3
Sayers, Loretta
   Lover Come Back 1931,Je 5,26:5
   Men Are Like That 1931,Ag 17,18:2
   Fifty Fathoms Deep 1931,S 19,10:2
Sayers, Michael (Screenwriter)
   Casino Royale 1967,Ap 29,25:1
Sayger, Anthony
   Loneliness of the Long Distance Runner, The
     1962,O 9,44:1
Sayles, Francis
   Strangers of the Evening 1932,Je 4,9:2
   Blonde Venus 1932,S 24,18:4
   Black Legion 1937,Ja 18,21:1
Saylor, Syd
   Border Legion, The 1930,Je 30,22:6
   Fighting Caravans 1931,Ja 26,21:1
   Unfaithful 1931,Mr 7,17:2
   Lawyer's Secret, The 1931,My 30,9:2
   Million Dollar Legs 1932,Jl 9,7:5
   Crusader, The 1932,O 8,15:4
   Nuisance, The 1933,My 29,22:2
   Lost Jungle, The 1934,Je 8,18:1
   Young and Beautiful 1934,S 18,18:4
   Dude Ranger, The 1934,O 2,18:5
   Sky Parade, The 1936,Ap 20,17:1
   Kelly the Second 1936,O 3,21:2
   Secret Valley 1937,Ja 25,22:2
   House of Secrets 1937,F 22,13:1
   Wild and Woolly 1937,S 6,20:1
   Sea Racketeers 1937,O 4,17:2
   Union Pacific 1939,My 11,31:2
   $1,000 a Touchdown 1939,O 5,27:2
   Geronimo 1940,F 8,18:3
   Abe Lincoln in Illinois 1940,F 23,19:2
   Arizona 1941,F 7,23:3
   Man in the Trunk, The 1942,O 23,25:1
   Time to Kill 1942,D 25,15:4
   Swingtime Johnny 1943,D 17,23:3
   Sitting Pretty 1948,Mr 11,35:2
   Big Jack 1949,My 23,27:4
   Dancing in the Dark 1949,D 3,8:6
   Cheaper by the Dozen 1950,Ap 1,12:2
   Jackpot, The 1950,N 23,55:2
   Tall Texan, The 1953,Ap 13,32:4
Saynor, Charles
   Blue Lamp, The 1951,Ja 9,25:1
SAYRE
   See Also SAYER
Sayre, Bigelow
   Union Station 1950,O 5,38:3
Sayre, George (Original Author)
   Flying Hostess 1936,D 14,29:4
   Jungle Siren 1942,O 10,11:3
Sayre, George (Screenwriter)
   Jungle Siren 1942,O 10,11:3
   Black Market Babies 1946,Ap 1,23:1
Sayre, Jeffery
   Mutiny in the Big House 1939,D 11,26:2

Sayre, Joel (Original Author)
   Rackety Rax 1932,N 5,12:5
   Parole 1936,Je 27,21:1
   Road to Glory, The 1936,Ag 6,22:1
   Fourteen Hours 1951,Mr 7,43:2
Sayre, Joel (Screenwriter)
   Pay-Off, The 1935,N 13,25:3
   Annie Oakley 1935,D 24,10:5
   Parole 1936,Je 27,21:1
   Road to Glory, The 1936,Ag 6,22:1
   Meet the Missus 1937,Jl 2,25:2
   Toast of New York, The 1937,Jl 23,16:2
   Gunga Din 1939,Ja 28,19:2
Sazanka, Kyu
   Yojimbo 1962,O 16,34:1
   Fires on the Plain 1963,S 25,39:1
   Utamaro, Painter of Women 1964,D 2,57:1
Sazarina, Maria
   Fraeulein Liselott 1935,My 27,20:7
   Fraulein Liselott 1935,My 27,20:7
   Ein Walzer fuer Dich 1936,S 29,35:2
   Freiheit und Liebe, Um; For Freedom and Love
     1938,F 5,19:3
Sazio, Carmela
   Paisan 1948,Mr 30,26:2
Sazon, Lyle (Original Author)
   Buccaneer, The 1938,F 17,17:2
Scaccia, Mario
   Too Bad She's Bad 1955,D 26,23:2
   We Still Kill the Old Way 1968,F 29,28:1
Scafa, Ciro
   Young Caruso, The 1953,O 13,34:4
Scaglione, Michele (Producer)
   Colossus of Rhodes, The 1961,D 14,55:6
Scal, Dolly
   Pickpocket 1963,My 22,36:2
Scala, Delia
   Lieutenant Craig-Missing 1951,My 19,9:4
   Cliff of Sin, The 1952,N 22,16:5
   Rome, 11 O'Clock 1953,Ap 30,39:2
   Side Street Story 1954,Je 24,30:4
   Gran Varieta 1955,Ap 11,29:5
   My Seven Little Sins 1956,My 2,27:1
Scala, Gia
   Four Girls in Town 1957,Ja 17,34:5
   Big Boodle, The 1957,Mr 12,38:1
   Garment Jungle, The 1957,My 16,28:2
   Tip on a Dead Jockey 1957,S 7,12:7
   Don't Go Near the Water 1957,N 15,37:1
   Tunnel of Love 1958,N 22,27:4
   Two-Headed Spy, The 1959,Mr 3,38:4
   Angry Hills, The 1959,Jl 16,31:3
   I Aim at the Stars 1960,O 20,42:2
   Guns of Navarone, The 1961,Je 23,19:1
Scalapino, Robert A (Narrator)
   North Vietnam-A Personal Report
     1968,Ja 23,79:1
Scaldaferri, Angelina
   Path of Hope, The (Il Cammino Della Speranza)
     1952,Ag 5,15:5
Scales, Prunella
   Scotch on the Rocks 1954,Je 14,18:2
   Hobson's Choice 1954,Je 15,37:1
   Waltz of the Toreadors 1962,Ag 14,34:1
Scammon, P A
   America 1924,F 22,20:1
Scandurra, Franco
   Spirit and the Flesh, The 1948,N 1,28:2
Scannell, Frank
   Hit Parade of 1947 1947,My 5,32:8
   Stranger Wore a Gun, The 1953,Jl 30,20:3
   Country Girl, The 1954,D 16,51:2
   Tattered Dress, The 1957,Mr 15,22:3
   High Time 1960,S 17,15:1
Scannell, Jack
   Shock Punch, The 1925,My 11,14:3
Scarano, Tecla
   Bellissima 1953,My 18,26:2
   Marriage Italian Style 1964,D 21,42:1
   Shoot Loud, Louder... I Don't Understand
     1967,S 21,56:4
Scarborough, Dorothy (Original Author)
   Wind, The 1928,N 5,26:1
Scarborough, George M (Original Author)
   Son-Daughter, The 1933,Ja 2,29:2
Scardamagali, Elio (Producer)
   Goliath and the Sins of Babylon 1964,Mr 5,36:2
Scardamagali, Francesco (Screenwriter)
   Goliath and the Sins of Babylon 1964,Mr 5,36:2
Scardon, Paul
   Lady From Louisiana 1941,My 15,27:2
   Sign of the Ram, The 1948,Mr 4,30:2
Scardon, Paul (Director)
   Partners of the Night 1920,Mr 1,16:2
Scari, Jackie
   Sooky 1931,D 21,28:4
   Fabulous Dorseys, The 1947,My 30,25:3
Scarpelli, Age (Original Author)
   Good, The Bad and the Ugly, The
     1968,Ja 25,33:1
Scarpelli, Age (Screenwriter)
   Tailor's Maid, The; (Patri e Figli) 1959,S 2,35:4
   Big Deal on Madonna Street, The 1960,N 23,20:1

Scarpelli, Age (Screenwriter)— Cont
   Great War; (Grande Guerra, La) 1961,Ag 31,22:3
   Best of Enemies, The 1962,Ag 7,35:2
   Everybody go Home!; Tutti a Casa 1962,N 6,38:1
   Fiasco in Milan 1963,Ap 11,29:2
   Organizer, The 1964,My 7,31:2
   Seduces and Abandoned 1964,Jl 16,23:1
Scarpelli, Ago (Screenwriter)
   15 From Rome 1968,Ap 11,51:3
Scarpelli, Furio (Original Author)
   I Cadetti di Guascogna 1952,O 6,22:2
Scarpelli, Furio (Screenwriter)
   I Cadetti di Guascogna 1952,O 6,22:2
   House of Ricordi 1956,Mr 13,32:1
   Casanova 1965,Jl 21,43:1
   Tiger and the Pussycat, The 1967,S 21,56:4
Scarpelli, Umberto (Director)
   Secret Conclave, The 1953,My 16,10:1
Scarpelli, Umberto (Screenwriter)
   David and Goliath 1961,O 7,14:3
Scarpelli (Miscellaneous)
   Bigamist, The 1958,My 12,25:1
Scarpelli (Screenwriter)
   O K Nero 1953,Je 20,8:6
   Mafioso 1964,Jl 1,42:1
   Birds, the Bees and the Italians, The
     1967,Ag 8,33:2
Scars, Fred F (Director)
   Miami Story, The 1954,My 15,13:2
Scars, Zelda
   Sadie McKee 1934,My 18,18:3 (Incorrect in this
     edition; use 1934,My 19,18:3 elsewhere)
Scase, Rosalie
   Taste of Honey, A 1962,My 1,33:3
Scastrom, Victor (Director)
   Tower of Lies, The 1925,S 28,24:1
Scatigna, Angelo
   Romola 1924,D 2,13:2
Scavran, Luigi
   Honey Pot, The 1967,My 23,52:1
Scay, James
   Way of all Flesh, The 1940,Je 6,33:2
Scelzo, Filippo
   Passaporto Rosso 1936,S 2,18:2
   Loyalty of Love 1937,Mr 1,15:1
   Earth Cries Out, The; Grido Della Terra, Il
     1949,Ag 31,26:2
   Secret Conclave, The 1953,My 16,10:1
   Successo, Il 1965,Ap 29,40:2
Scervini, F
   Revenge 1947,N 28,37:4
Schaak, Liselott
   Schlacht von Bademuende, Die 1931,N 21,20:4
   Wie Man Maenner Fesselt 1934,My 21,20:3
   Tolle Bomberg, Der 1935,O 26,12:2
   Vier Musketiere, Die; Four Musketeers, The
     1935,N 9,19:3
   Musketier Meier III 1938,D 31,7:2
Schaake, Catherine
   What's New Pussycat? 1965,Je 23,49:1
Schable, Robert
   Test of Honor, The 1919,Ap 7,11:5
   On With the Dance 1920,F 16,8:1
   Without Limit 1921,Mr 21,11:3
   Bella Donna 1923,Ap 16,20:2
   Silent Partner, The 1923,Ag 20,4:2
   Cheat, The 1923,Ag 27,14:3
   Stranger, The 1924,F 5,20:1
   Partners Again, With Potash and Perlmutter
     1926,F 15,16:4
   Silken Shackles 1926,My 25,25:1
   Sailors' Wives 1928,F 28,18:4
   Man and the Moment, The 1929,Ag 5,25:2
Schach, Max (Producer)
   Love From a Stranger 1937,Ap 19,27:2
Schachter, Leon
   God, Man and Devil 1950,Ja 23,16:2
Schade, Betty
   Deliverance 1919,Ag 19,10:1
   Village Sleuth 1920,S 13,12:1
SCHAEFER
   See Also SCHAEFFER, SCHAFER, SCHAFFER,
    SHAFER, SHAFFER
Schaefer, Ann
   City of Masks, The 1920,Jl 12,12:4
   Main Street 1923,Je 12,22:2
   Heritage of the Desert, The 1924,Ja 24,15:1
   Love's Wilderness 1924,D 22,20:2
   Goose Hangs High, The 1925,Mr 10,19:3
   Sparrows 1926,S 20,21:3
   Three Hours 1927,Mr 8,18:4
   Night Flyer, The 1928,Mr 13,23:3
   Wheels of Chance 1928,Jl 2,11:2
   Saturday's Children 1929,Ap 29,29:2
   Smiling Irish Eyes 1929,Jl 24,23:2
Schaefer, Armand (Director)
   Terror Trail 1933,F 11,11:3
   Sixteen Fathoms Deep 1934,Ja 19,24:3
   Lost Jungle, The 1934,Je 8,18:1
Schaefer, Gert
   Seven Journeys 1951,Mr 12,20:2
Schaefer, Jack (Original Author)
   Shane 1953,Ap 24,30:3
   Tribute to a Bad Man 1956,Mr 31,13:3

Schaefer, Jack (Original Author) — Cont
Trooper Hook 1957,Jl 13,11:2
Advance to the Rear 1964,Je 11,27:3
SCHAEFFER
See Also SCHAEFER, SCHAFER, SCHAFFER, SHAFER, SHAFFER
Schaeffer, Billy
Ice Flood, The 1926,O 19,26:2
Warming Up 1928,Jl 16,25:3
As Good as Married 1937,My 22,19:2
Schaeffer, Billy Kent
Home Maker, The 1925,Ag 10,8:2
Hills of Kentucky 1927,Mr 2,29:3
Enemy, The 1927,D 28,26:6
Schaeffer, Eddie
Bellboy, The 1960,Jl 21,17:1
Schaeffers, Willy
Spiel mit dem Feuer 1934,N 26,12:2
Prinzessin, Turandot 1935,Ja 16,21:2
Schaert, Wolfran
Great British Train Robbery, The 1967,Ap 6,45:2
SCHAFER
See Also SCHAEFFER, SCHAEFER, SCHAFFER, SHAFER, SHAFFER
Schafer, Bob (Composer)
Oh, You Beautiful Doll 1949,N 12,8:4
Schafer, Natalie
Marriage Is a Private Affair 1944,O 27,17:7
Keep Your Powder Dry 1945,Mr 12,22:6
Molly and Me 1945,My 26,18:2
Wonder Man 1945,Je 9,17:2
Masquerade in Mexico 1945,N 29,27:2
Other Love, The 1947,My 15,32:4
Dishonored Lady 1947,My 24,10:5
Repeat Performance 1947,Jl 2,19:2
Secret Beyond the Door 1948,Ja 16,25:4
Time of your Life, The 1948,My 27,29:2
Snake Pit, the 1948,N 5,29:2
Caught 1949,F 18,26:4
Take Care of my Little Girl 1951,Jl 19,20:2
Law and the Lady, The 1951,Ag 16,23:2
Callaway Went Thataway 1951,D 6,42:1
Just Across the Street 1952,Je 28,12:4
Girl Next Door, The 1953,S 5,7:4
Female on the Beach 1955,Ag 20,20:2
Forever, Darling 1956,F 10,18:1
Anastasia 1956,D 14,35:6
Bernardine 1957,Jl 25,28:1
Back Street 1961,O 13,27:1
Susan Slade 1961,N 11,14:6
Schafer, Rose
Devil Strikes at Night, The 1959,Ja 30,31:3
SCHAFFER
See Also SCHAEFFER, SCHAEFER, SCHAFER, SHAFER, SHAFFER
Schaffer, Peggy
Light That Failed, The 1923,N 27,11:2
Schaffner, Franklin (Director)
Stripper, The 1963,Je 20,29:1
Best Man, The 1964,Ap 7,29:1
War Lord, The 1965,N 18,55:2
Planet of the Apes 1968,F 9,55:2
Double Man, The 1968,My 2,57:1
Schaffner, Franklin (Producer)
Best Man, The 1964,Ap 7,29:1
Schafheitlin, Franz
Frasquita 1936,Ja 18,19:4
Eternal Mask, The 1937,Ja 13,20:3
Fiakerlied, Das; (Cabbie's Song, The) 1937,S 6,20:2
Orphan Boy of Vienna, An 1937,S 9,19:2
Ball im Metropol 1938,Mr 5,11:3
Nanu, Sie Kennen Korff noch Nicht?; So, You Don't Know Korff Yet? 1939,My 22,15:3
Seven Journeys 1951,Mr 12,20:2
Angelika 1954,S 25,10:7
Schagen, Riek
Ciske 1963,Ag 3,8:2
SCHALL
See Also SCHOLL
Schallert, William
Man From Planet X, The 1951,Ap 9,31:2
Flat Top 1952,D 6,17:2
Riot in Cell Block 11 1954,F 19,24:5
Gog 1954,Ag 14,8:2
Tattered Dress, The 1957,Mr 15,22:3
Girl in the Kremlin, The 1957,My 22,29:2
Blue Denim 1959,Jl 31,21:1
In the Heat of the Night 1967,Ag 3,26:1
Speedway 1968,Je 14,43:1
Schanecke, Ellen
Mad Idea, A; Toller Einfall, Ein 1932,Jl 31,IX,3:4
Schanzer, Rudolph (Original Author)
Lady in Ermine, The 1927,Ja 3,16:2
Madame Pompadour 1927,Ag 2,19:2
That Lady in Ermine 1948,Ag 25,31:2
Scharf, Heidi
City of Torment 1950,Je 10,11:4
Scharf, Sabrina
Hells Angels on Wheels 1967,Jl 29,29:3
Scharff, Lester
New York 1927,Ja 31,13:1
Man Who Wouldn't Talk, The 1940,Ja 12,13:3
Earthbound 1940,Je 7,27:4

Great Commandment, The 1942,O 17,11:1
Scharff, Lester (Miscellaneous)
War's End 1934,My 19,18:5
Schary, Dore (Director)
Act One 1963,D 27,17:2
Schary, Dore (Miscellaneous)
They Live by Night 1949,N 4,33:2
Schary, Dore (Original Author)
Let's Talk It Over 1934,Je 16,20:2
Murder in the Clouds 1934,D 26,18:1
Boys Town 1938,S 9,25:1
Broadway Melody of 1940 1940,Mr 29,25:3
Edison the Man 1940,Je 7,27:2
Behind the News 1941,Ja 16,25:3
Battle of Gettysburg, The 1956,My 18,19:3
Sunrise at Campobello 1960,S 29,32:1
Schary, Dore (Producer)
I'll Be Seeing You 1945,Ap 6,20:6
Spiral Staircase, The 1946,F 7,29:3
Till the End of Time 1946,Jl 24,24:1
Farmer's Daughter, The 1947,Mr 26,31:2
Bachelor and the Bobby-Soxer, The 1947,Jl 25,12:5
Battleground 1949,N 12,8:4
Next Voice You Hear, The 1950,Je 30,18:2
Go for Broke 1951,My 25,31:2
Westward the Women 1952,Ja 1,21:2
Washington Story 1952,Jl 2,22:3
Plymouth Adventure 1952,N 14,20:3
Dream Wife 1953,Jl 30,20:1
Take the High Ground 1953,N 20,19:2
Bad Day at Black Rock 1955,F 2,22:2
Last Hunt, The 1956,Mr 1,37:2
Swan, The 1956,Ap 27,21:5
Designing Woman 1957,My 17,20:2
Lonelyhearts 1959,Mr 5,35:3
Sunrise at Campobello 1960,S 29,32:1
Act One 1963,D 27,17:2
Schary, Dore (Screenwriter)
Murder in the Clouds 1934,D 26,18:1
Chinatown Squad 1935,My 30,21:1
Silk Hat Kid 1935,Ag 7,22:5
Your Uncle Dudley 1935,D 12,33:4
Outcast 1937,Mr 3,27:2
Girl From Scotland Yard, The 1937,My 31,11:2
Big City 1937,S 17,29:2
Boys Town 1938,S 9,25:1
Young Tom Edison 1940,Mr 15,27:2
Married Bachelor 1941,O 16,25:3
It's a big Country 1952,Ja 9,25:2
Battle of Gettysburg, The 1956,My 18,19:3
Lonelyhearts 1959,Mr 5,35:3
Sunrise at Campobello 1960,S 29,32:1
Act One 1963,D 27,17:2
Schastlivtseva, Elena
They Met in Moscow 1944,Je 7,13:2
Schatz, Marcel (Miscellaneous)
Annapurna 1953,D 14,45:4
Schaub, Olga
Klosterjaeger, Der 1936,Ja 3,13:7
Schauffler, Elsie T (Original Author)
Parnell 1937,Je 4,27:2
Schaufuss, H
Lindenwirtin vom Rhein, Die 1931,S 25,28:7
Emil und die Detektive 1931,D 21,28:4
Der Herr Finanzdirektor 1932,Je 25,18:2
Week-End Im Paradies 1932,O 24,18:5
Schuechterne Felix, Der 1935,S 19,19:5
Annette in Paradise 1936,Mr 7,11:4
Schaufuss, Hans Joachim
Burning Secret 1933,My 28,IX,2:5 (In Addenda)
Schautz, Maurice
Miquette 1951,F 5,18:2
Schayer, Richard (Miscellaneous)
Black Magic 1949,N 9,37:2
Schayer, Richard (Original Author)
Free and Easy 1930,Ap 19,15:1
Spirit of Notre Dame, The 1931,O 16,27:1
My Pal the King 1932,O 4,26:4
All American, The 1932,O 22,18:4
Mummy, The 1933,Ja 7,11:2
Private Jones 1933,Mr 25,13:3
Khyber Patrol 1954,S 20,19:2
Schayer, Richard (Screenwriter)
Tell It to the Marines 1926,D 24,18:2
Winning Ticket, The 1935,F 11,14:2
Dangerous Waters 1936,Ja 22,15:5
Devil is a Sissy, The 1936,O 17,21:2
Black Arrow, The 1948,O 4,14:2
Davy Crockett, Indian Scout 1950,Mr 17,28:3
Iroquois Trail, The 1950,O 27,24:4
Kim 1950,D 8,40:4
Texas Rangers, The 1951,Jl 14,7:2
Lorna Doone 1951,S 21,19:4
Gun Belt 1953,Ag 1,8:2
Sword of Lancelot 1963,O 10,49:2
Schechtman, Frank
Power of Life 1938,Ap 29,17:2
Schee, Tamara
House on Telegraph Hill, The 1951,My 14,29:1
Scheerer, Bobby
Mister Big 1943,Je 14,13:4

Scheffer, Leo (Director)
Demon of the Steppes 1930,Ja 18,21:1
Scheib, Hans (Cinematographer)
Wedding of Palo, The 1937,Mr 2,17:1
Scheicher, Raimund
Unsterbliche Herz, Das; Immortal Heart, The 1939,O 21,12:2
Robert Koch 1939,N 25,13:2
Scheinpflugova, Olga
Fifth Horseman is Fear, The 1968,My 7,52:1
Schekutiev, A (Cinematographer)
Circus Festival 1958,Mr 17,21:4
Schelderup, George
Silver Fleet, The 1945,Mr 24,22:6
Schell, Karl
Escape from East Berlin 1962,D 6,55:3
Werewolf in a Girls Dormitory 1963,Je 6,39:1
Schell, Maria
Angel With the Trumpet 1951,D 21,21:5
Magic Box, The 1952,S 24,40:2
So Little Time 1953,Jl 28,23:2
Angelika 1954,S 25,10:7
Heart of the Matter, The 1954,N 19,20:2
Last Bridge, The 1957,Ag 21,22:2
Gervaise 1957,N 12,46:1
Brothers Karamazov, The 1958,F 21,18:2
Dreaming Lips; (Traumende Mund, The) 1958,N 1,14:3
Sins of Rose Bernd, The 1959,Ja 24,13:4 (In Addenda)
Hanging Tree, The 1959,F 12,23:1
Cimarron 1961,F 17,12:2
As the Sea Rages 1961,My 18,41:1
White Nights 1961,My 29,9:6
Mark, The 1961,O 3,46:2
End of Desire 1962,Jl 10,29:2
Schell, Maximilian
Young Lions, The 1958,Ap 3,23:1
Judgment at Nuremberg 1961,D 20,36:1
Five Finger Exercise 1962,Ap 20,20:2
Reluctant Saint, The 1962,D 4,47:2
Condemned of Altona, The 1963,O 31,26:1
Topkapi 1964,S 18,25:1
Return From the Ashes 1965,N 17,53:1
Deadly Affair, The 1967,Ja 27,31:1
Counterpoint 1968,Mr 14,51:2
Schellhammer, Edmund
Operetta 1949,Je 6,15:4
Schellhorn, Charlotte
Maulkorb, Der 1938,Ap 9,11:3
Jugend von Heute; Youth of Today 1938,N 5,15:3
Schellow, Erich
Seven Journeys 1951,Mr 12,20:2
Portrait of an Unknown Woman 1958,Ap 26,14:6
Captain from Koepenick, The 1958,Jl 26,6:1
City of Secrets 1963,Jl 27,10:2
Schenck, Aubrey (Miscellaneous)
Three bad Sisters 1956,F 13,24:1
Schenck, Aubrey (Producer)
Shock 1946,Mr 9,10:2
Repeat Performance 1947,Jl 2,19:2
T-Men 1948,Ja 23,28:3
Mickey 1948,Jl 19,11:2
Red Stallion in the Rockies 1949,Ag 26,15:2
Port of New York 1950,F 3,29:2
Wyoming Mail 1950,O 23,26:5
Undercover Girl 1950,N 8,37:2
Target Unknown 1951,My 5,24:2
Fat Man, The 1951,My 25,31:2
Shield for Murder 1954,Ag 28,8:3
Big House U S A 1955,Mr 12,11:6
Untamed Youth 1957,My 11,24:6
Up Periscope 1959,Mr 5,35:4
Robinson Crusoe on Mars 1964,Ag 27,28:2
Schenck, Earl
Ashes of Vengeance 1923,Ag 7,20:2
Song of Love, The 1924,F 25,13:1
Mademoiselle Midnight 1924,My 27,14:1
Tides of Passion 1925,Ap 20,22:1
Abilene Town 1946,Mr 4,16:5
Schenck, George (Screenwriter)
Kill a Dragon 1967,D 7,60:2
Schenck, Harry (Director)
Beyond Bengal 1934,My 18,27:1
Schenck, Harry (Producer)
Beyond Bengal 1934,My 18,27:1
Schenck, Harry (Screenwriter)
Beyond Bengal 1934,My 18,27:1
Scheppan, Hilde
Maedchen Irene, Das 1937,My 22,19:3
Scherbinina, Anya
Little Humpbacked Horse, The 1962,O 8,19:1
Scherick, Edgar J (Producer)
For Love of Ivy 1968,Jl 18,26:1
Birthday Party, The 1968,D 10,54:1
Schermer, Jules (Original Author)
Sullivans, The 1944,F 10,19:2
Schermer, Jules (Producer)
Framed 1947,My 26,24:2
Man From Colorado 1949,Ja 21,24:3
Illegal Entry 1949,Je 11,11:2
Union Station 1950,O 5,38:3

Schermer, Jules (Producer)— Cont
Pride of St Louis, The 1952,My 3,17:5
Lydia Bailey 1952,My 31,12:5
Pushover 1954,Jl 31,6:3
These Wilder Years 1956,Ag 18,11:2
Onionhead 1958,O 2,44:1

Schertzinger, Victor (Composer)
My Woman 1933,O 16,20:3
Beloved 1934,Ja 27,9:3
Music Goes 'Round, The 1936,F 22,12:1
Something to Sing About 1937,S 21,29:4
Road to Singapore 1940,Mr 14,29:2
Kiss the Boys Goodbye 1941,Ag 14,21:2
Fleet's In, The 1942,Mr 12,24:2

Schertzinger, Victor (Director)
String Beans 1918,D 30,7:3
Peace of Roaring River, The 1919,Ag 11,9:1
Upstairs 1919,Ag 18,9:2
Blooming Angel, The 1920,F 9,10:3
Concert, The 1921,F 21,16:1
Man Next Door, The 1923,My 29,10:3
Long Live the King 1923,D 4,24:1
Boy of Flanders, A 1924,Ap 15,24:1
Bread 1924,Jl 21,14:4
Man and Maid 1925,Ap 7,17:3
Heart of a Salome, The 1927,Je 6,27:2
Secret Studio, The 1927,Je 15,31:4
Showdown, The 1928,Mr 5,21:1
Redskin 1929,Ja 28,21:1
Nothing but the Truth 1929,Ap 22,23:1
Wheel of Life, The 1929,Je 24,27:1
Laughing Lady, The 1930,Ja 4,21:1
Safety in Numbers 1930,My 31,19:4
Heads Up 1930,O 13,31:1
Woman Between, The 1931,O 24,20:3
Friends and Lovers 1931,N 7,16:5
Strange Justice 1932,O 20,24:2
Uptown New York 1932,D 10,19:3
Cocktail Hour 1933,Je 5,18:5
My Woman 1933,O 16,20:3
Beloved 1934,Ja 27,9:3
One Night of Love 1934,S 7,25:3
Let's Live Tonight 1935,Mr 18,14:4
Love Me Forever 1935,Je 28,24:1
Music Goes 'Round, The 1936,F 22,12:1
Something to Sing About 1937,S 21,29:4
Mikado, The 1939,Je 2,27:2
Road to Singapore 1940,Mr 14,29:2
Road to Zanzibar 1941,Ap 10,29:2
Kiss the Boys Goodbye 1941,Ag 14,21:2
Birth of the Blues 1941,D 11,39:1
Fleet's In, The 1942,Mr 12,24:2

Schertzinger, Victor (Miscellaneous)
One Night of Love 1934,S 7,25:3
Love Me Forever 1935,Je 28,24:1
Follow Your Heart 1936,O 22,31:1

Schertzinger, Victor (Original Author)
Love Me Forever 1935,Je 28,24:1
Something to Sing About 1937,S 21,29:4

Schertzinger, Victor (Screenwriter)
Betrayal 1929,My 6,30:4

Schertzinger, William (Director)
Rhythm on the River 1940,Ag 29,23:2

Schetting
Respectful Prostitute, The 1957,Jl 11,21:1

SCHEUER
See Also SCHUR

Scheuer, David
Joanna 1968,N 25,54:1

Scheunzel, Reinhold (Director)
Irene 1936,D 13,XI,6:6 (In Addenda)

Scheybal, Vlad
Billion Dollar Brain 1967,D 23,29:1

Schiaffino, Rosanna
Minotaur, The 1961,N 8,41:1
Notte Brava, La 1962,Ja 25,25:2
Two Weeks in Another Town 1962,Ag 18,10:1
Crime Does Not Pay (The Mask); Mask, The
(Crime Does Not Pay) 1962,O 17,35:2
Lafayette 1963,Ap 11,29:1
Victors, The 1963,D 20,21:2
Long Ships, The 1964,Je 25,25:1
Cavern, The 1965,D 25,17:2
Mandragola 1966,Je 7,50:2
Arrivederci, Baby! 1966,D 29,22:1
Greco, El 1967,My 24,52:2

Schich, Wilhelm
Mein Liebster Ist ein Jaegersmann 1936,S 15,37:6

Schiel, Hannes
Last ten Days, The 1956,Ap 12,26:1
Fidelio 1961,My 13,10:1

Schieske, Alfred
Affair Blum, The 1949,O 18,35:2
Odette 1951,Mr 28,33:2
Tomorrow Is my Turn 1962,F 2,24:2

Schiffrin, Simon (Director)
Ordonnance, L'; Orderly, The 1935,Jl 1,22:3

Schiffrin, Simon (Producer)
Black Tights 1962,F 21,54:2

Schildkraut, Joseph
Song of Love, The 1924,F 25,13:1
Road to Yesterday, The 1925,D 1,22:4
Young April 1926,Ag 31,15:3
King of Kings, The 1927,Ap 20,29:2

Heart Thief, The 1927,Ap 27,22:5
His Dog 1927,Ag 16,31:2
Forbidden Woman, The 1927,O 31,22:1
Blue Danube, The 1928,Ap 30,18:3
Tenth Avenue 1928,O 9,35:1
Show Boat 1929,Ag 18,32:3
Mississippi Gambler, The 1929,O 28,20:1
Night Ride 1930,Ja 20,21:1
Cock O' the Walk 1930,Ap 12,23:1
Carnival 1931,N 22,VIII,6:1
Viva Villa! 1934,Ap 11,25:2
Sisters Under the Skin 1934,Je 8,18:1
Cleopatra 1934,Ag 17,12:1
Blue Danube 1934,N 8,27:1
Crusades, The 1935,Ag 22,21:3
Garden of Allah, The 1936,N 20,27:2
Slave Ship 1937,Je 17,19:2
Souls at Sea 1937,Ag 10,23:2
Life of Emile Zola, The 1937,Ag 12,14:2
Lancer Spy 1937,N 4,29:1
Lady Behave 1938,Ja 28,17:3
Baroness and the Butler, The 1938,F 19,19:2
Marie Antoinette 1938,Ag 17,23:2
Suez 1938,O 15,21:2
Idiot's Delight 1939,F 3,13:1
Three Musketeers, The 1939,F 18,12:2
Mr Moto Takes a Vacation 1939,Je 19,12:6
Man in the Iron Mask, The 1939,Jl 14,11:1
Lady of the Tropics 1939,S 8,28:3
Rains Came, The 1939,S 9,11:2
Pack up Your Troubles 1939,O 27,27:2
Shop Around the Corner, The 1940,Ja 26,13:2
Phantom Raiders 1940,Je 24,19:5
Rangers of Fortune 1940,S 19,27:2
Meet the Wildcat 1940,O 23,27:2
Parson of Panamint, The 1941,Jl 26,18:2
Flame of Barbary Coast 1945,My 28,22:2
Cheaters, The 1945,Jl 21,7:2
Monsieur Beaucaire 1946,S 5,23:1
Plainsman and the Lady, The 1946,N 4,33:1
Northwest Outpost 1947,Ag 8,10:2
Old Los Angeles 1948,Jl 12,11:2
Diary of Anne Frank, The 1959,Mr 19,40:1
King of the Roaring Twenties 1961,O 5,43:1
Greatest Story Ever Told, The 1965,F 16,40:2

Schildkraut, Rudolph
Proud Heart 1925,N 3,25:4
Young April 1926,Ag 31,15:3
Pals in Paradise 1926,N 24,26:4
King of Kings, The 1927,Ap 20,29:2
Main Event, The 1927,O 31,22:1
Ship Comes in, A 1928,S 4,21:2
Christina 1929,Ap 1,22:1

Schildt, Henrik
Each Heart Has Its Own Story 1953,Mr 28,15:2
Each Heart Has Its Own Story 1953,Mr 28,15:2

Schilleci, John
Panic in the Streets 1950,Ag 5,9:2

Schiller, Alfred (Original Author)
Flying Deuces, The 1939,N 24,29:2

Schiller, Alfred (Screenwriter)
Flying Deuces, The 1939,N 24,29:2

Schiller, Fanny
Dama de las Camelias, La 1944,S 26,16:1
Treasure of Pancho Villa, The 1955,N 25,38:2
Woman's Devotion, A 1957,Mr 22,26:1
Love Has Many Faces 1965,F 25,24:1

Schiller, Fred (Original Author)
They Met on Skis 1940,D 23,23:2
Something to Shout About 1943,Ap 8,27:3

Schiller, Fred (Screenwriter)
Heat's on, The 1943,N 26,29:2
Pistol Packin' Mama 1943,D 20,27:4

Schiller, Frederick
Mr Emmanuel 1945,Ja 8,15:2
Captive Heart, The 1947,Ap 28,27:2
Crawling Eye, The 1959,Ja 1,38:1

Schiller, Friedrich (Original Author)
William Tell 1925,My 20,26:2
Maria Stuart 1928,Mr 11,VIII,5:1

Schiller, Norbert
Sealed Verdict 1948,N 3,36:2
Girl in the Kremlin, The 1957,My 22,29:2
Torn Curtain 1966,Jl 28,23:1

Schiller, Wilton (Screenwriter)
New Interns, The 1964,Ag 20,34:2

Schilling, Gus
Mexican Spitfire out West 1940,O 30,29:3
Citizen Kane 1941,My 2,25:1
Ice-Capades 1941,S 25,29:1
It Started With Eve 1941,O 3,27:1
Appointment for Love 1941,N 7,27:1
Dr Kildare's Victory 1942,F 5,25:2
Broadway 1942,Je 5,23:2
You Were Never Lovelier 1942,D 4,31:1
Amazing Mrs Holliday, The 1943,F 22,20:2
Chatterbox 1943,Jl 2,15:3
Hers to Hold 1943,Jl 22,15:1
It's a Pleasure 1945,My 4,23:3
See my Lawyer 1945,My 4,23:4
Thousand and one Nights, A 1945,Jl 12,8:2
River Gang 1945,O 6,9:7
Lady From Shanghai, The 1948,Je 10,28:2

Schilling, Gus— Cont
Angel on the Amazon 1948,D 27,16:4
Bride for Sale 1949,N 21,29:4 (In Addenda)
Our Very Own 1950,Jl 28,12:5
On Dangerous Ground 1952,F 13,35:2
Run for Cover 1955,Ap 30,10:6

Schilling, Margaret
Children of Dreams 1931,Jl 20,20:4

Schimmoler, Lauretta M
Parachute Nurse 1942,Jl 27,18:2

Schipa, Carlo
Sally 1925,Mr 16,16:1
Little Annie Rooney 1925,O 19,26:1
Strictly Dishonorable 1931,N 11,27:1

Schipa, Tito
Vivere; To Live 1938,N 15,27:2
Chi e'piu felice di me?; Who Is Happier Than I
1940,F 6,17:5
Life of Donizetti, The 1952,Ap 26,19:2

Schipper, Max
Schoen Ist die Manoeverzeit 1932,Ag 19,20:6

Schirato, Gemma
Figaro E La Sua Gran Giornata 1933,O 28,20:4

Schirokauer, Alfred (Original Author)
Careers 1929,Je 10,23:1

Schisgal, Murray (Original Author)
Luv 1967,Jl 27,29:1
Tiger Makes Out, The 1967,S 19,53:1

Schisgal, Murray (Screenwriter)
Tiger Makes Out, The 1967,S 19,53:1

Schisgall, Oscar (Original Author)
Man I Married, The 1940,Ag 3,9:2

Schiumsi (Dog)
Tingel Tangel 1932,Mr 16,17:3

Schlanger, Ben (Miscellaneous)
Williamsburg: The Story of a Patriot
1957,Ap 1,22:2

Schlegel, Margarete
Das Lied ist Aus 1932,Ja 29,13:2
Berlin-Alexanderplatz 1933,My 11,14:1
Blaue Vom Himmel, Das 1934,S 8,18:6

Schleiermacher, Annette
Keepers of the Night 1953,Je 9,24:2

Schlenck, Hans
Kreuzer Emden 1932,S 8,17:2
Heideschulmeister uwe Karsten 1934,Ap 14,18:3
Schloss Hubertus 1935,F 9,11:3
Liebe und die Erste Eisenbahn, Die; Love and the
First Railroad 1935,F 18,19:4
Maria, Die Magd 1937,My 22,19:2
Susanne im Bade; Susanna in the Bath
1937,S 11,20:1
Kampf mit dem Drachen, Der; Fight With the
Dragon, The 1939,N 6,20:3

Schlesinger, John (Director)
Kind of Loving, A 1962,O 2,46:1
Billy Liar 1963,D 17,49:1
Darling 1965,Ag 4,20:1
Far From the Madding Crowd 1967,O 19,59:1

Schlettow, H A von
Ja, Treu Ist die Soldatenliebe 1934,Ap 28,11:4

Schlettow, Hans
Schuldig 1928,Mr 11,VIII,7:6 (In Addenda)

Schlettow, Hans A
Siegfried 1925,Ag 24,17:3
Kriemhild's Revenge 1928,O 16,29:1
Shadows of Fear 1928,N 6,35:1
Small Town Sinners 1928,N 27,34:1
Escaped From Dartmoor 1930,Ap 12,23:1
Immortal Vagabond, The 1931,Ag 3,15:5
Der Unsterbliche Lump 1932,My 20,22:3
Volga, Volga 1933,D 15,28:3
Schloss Hubertus 1935,F 9,11:3
Tolle Bomberg, Der 1935,O 26,12:2
Waldrausch; Forest Fever 1940,Ja 20,11:3
Anton der Letzte; Anthony the Last
1940,Mr 30,11:2
Congo Express 1940,My 11,15:3

Schlettow, Hans von
Last Waltz, The 1927,N 14,26:1
Aftermath 1927,D 6,27:1
Maedel von der Reeperbahn, Das 1931,Ja 31,15:
Bockbierfest 1931,Mr 31,25:3
Schlemihl, Der 1934,N 5,23:1
Konjunkturritter 1935,Ap 29,12:4
Ich Sing Mich in Dein Herz Hinein
1935,Je 3,22:3
Alte Kameraden 1936,Ap 27,19:3

Schlichter, Hedwig
Maedchen in Uniform 1932,S 21,25:4
Hertha's Erwachen 1933,Mr 14,18:3 (Incorrect ir
this edition; use 1933,Mr 14,19:2 elsewhere)

Schlick, Frederick (Original Author)
Wharf Angel 1934,Ap 21,12:1

Schlom, Herman (Producer)
Seven Miles From Alcatraz 1942,N 19,31:3
Great Gildersleeve, The 1942,D 18,36:8
Gildersleeve's Bad Day 1943,Ja 23,13:1
Night of Adventure, A 1944,Je 3,10:4
Betrayal From the East 1945,Ap 25,27:2
Brighton Strangler, The 1945,My 19,15:2
West of the Pecos 1945,Ag 11,14:6

Schlom, Herman (Producer)
Wanderer of the Wasteland 1945,S 29,12:2
Schlom, Herman (Producer)
Game of Death, A 1945,N 24,22:4
Dick Tracy 1946,Ja 12,10:7
Truth About Murder, The 1946,Jl 27,12:6
Dick Tracy vs Cueball 1946,N 23,12:2
Falcon's Adventure, The 1946,D 14,19:2
Devil Thumbs a Ride, The 1947,Mr 22,10:2
Born to Kill 1947,My 1,34:2
Dick Tracy's Dilemma 1947,Jl 14,14:5
Follow Me Quietly 1949,Jl 8,14:5
Best of the Badmen 1951,Ag 10,13:2
Half Breed, The 1952,Jl 5,7:2
Schlondorff, Volker (Director)
Young Torless 1967,S 25,56:2
Young Torless 1968,Jl 23,27:2
Schlondorff, Volker (Screenwriter)
Young Torless 1967,S 25,56:2
Young Torless 1968,Jl 23,27:2
Schlueter, Gisela
Nacht im Mai, Eine; Night in May, A
1938,N 12,10:3
Schlumberger, E
My Life to Live 1963,S 24,43:2
Schlumberger, Giselle
My Life to Live 1963,S 24,43:2
Schluter, Henning
One, Two, Three 1961,D 22,17:1
Schmelef (Screenwriter)
Man From the Restaurant, The 1930,Ja 6,30:5
Schmeling, Max
Liebe im Ring 1930,Ag 11,13:1
Knock-Out 1936,F 29,11:2
SCHMID
See Also SCHMIDT, SCHMITT
Schmid, Helmut
Head, The 1963,Je 20,29:1
Schmid-Wildy, Ludwig
Gewitter im Mai; Storms in May 1938,Mr 5,11:3
Schmid-Wildy, Ludwig (Director)
Stosstrupp 1917 1935,F 4,11:4
Schmidhofer, Martin
Waldrausch; Forest Fever 1940,Ja 20,11:3
SCHMIDT
See Also SCHMID, SCHMITT
Schmidt, Alexandra
Fight for Matterhorn, The 1929,Jl 29,23:3
Mutter und Kind 1934,N 30,22:3
Schmidt, Carl
Scoundrel, The 1935,My 3,23:2
Schmidt, Jan (Director)
Joseph Kilian 1966,Jl 19,34:1
Schmidt, Joseph
Acht Tage Glueck 1931,Jl 24,22:1
Ein Lied Geht um die Welt 1936,S 25,20:3
Joseph Schmidt Story, The 1951,Mr 5,24:2
Paper Lion 1968,O 24,54:1
Schmidt, Kai
Mockery 1927,Ag 22,21:3
Schmidt, Leonhard
Man Escaped, A 1957,Ag 27,33:2
Schmidt, Lothar (Original Author)
Marriage Circle, The 1924,F 4,23:3
One Hour with You 1932,Mr 24,17:5
Schmidt, Paul
Playground, The 1965,O 4,00:0
Schmidt, Peer
Confessions of Felix Krull, The 1958,Mr 5,38:1
Gypsy Baron, The 1959,N 14,13:1
Schmidt, Roswita
Woman 1950,F 9,36:6
Schmidt, Stephen (Producer)
Funnyman 1967,S 25,56:3
Schmidt, Tadeusz
Adventure in Warsaw 1955,O 24,22:2
Schmidt, Walter Robert (Screenwriter)
Hell to Eternity 1960,O 13,41:1
Schmidt-Geitner, Willy (Director)
Wiener Prater 1938,D 3,11:3
Schmidt-Gentner, Willy (Composer)
Dolly Macht Karriere 1931,Jl 18,16:6
Masquerade in Vienna 1937,Ja 26,16:4
Episode 1937,My 17,23:2
Rendezvous in Wien 1938,F 19,19:4
Schmidt-Gentner, Willy (Director)
Prater, Wiener 1938,D 3,11:3
Pompadour, Die 1939,F 27,11:3
Schmidt-Gentner, Willy (Miscellaneous)
Unfinished Symphony 1935,Ja 14,11:2
World's in Love, The 1937,My 19,27:2
Schmidthof, V (Director)
Beethoven Concerto 1937,Mr 24,29:1
Schmidtmer, Christiane
Stop Train 349 1964,N 12,40:2
Fanny Hill 1965,D 2,48:1
Boeing Boeing 1965,D 24,24:4
Schmidtmer, Christinae
Ship of Fools 1965,Jl 29,18:1
Schmiedel, Hans Joachim
Stop Train 349 1964,N 12,40:2

Schmieder, Willy
Life of Beethoven, The 1929,Mr 12,26:3
Schmitsdorf, Bruno
Kampf, Der 1936,S 11,29:3
SCHMITT
See Also SCHMID, SCHMIDT
Schmitz, Hubert
Emil und die Detektive 1931,D 21,28:4
Schmitz, Ludwig
Maulkorb, Der 1938,Ap 9,11:3
Schmitz, Sybille
Herr Der Welt, Der 1935,D 16,23:3
Oberwachtmeister Schwenke 1936,My 5,26:7
Idealer Gatte, Ein 1937,Ja 11,15:7
Punks Kommt aus Amerika 1937,Je 12,8:2
Fahrmann Maria; Ferryman Maria
1938,D 24,12:3
Hotel Sacher 1939,Je 10,14:2
Schmitzer, Henrietta
Broken Hearts 1926,Mr 3,26:1
Schmoele, Otto
Last ten Days, The 1956,Ap 12,26:1
Schnabel, Ernest (Original Author)
Seven Journeys 1951,Mr 12,20:2
Schnabel, Stefan
Journey Into Fear 1943,Mr 19,15:3
Iron Curtain, The 1948,My 13,31:2
Barbary Pirate 1949,O 28,29:3
Diplomatic Courier 1952,Je 14,12:2
Houdini 1953,Jl 3,10:2
Crowded Paradise 1956,Je 22,15:1
Secret Ways, The 1961,My 25,31:1
Counterfeit Traitor, The 1962,Ap 18,28:1
Two Weeks in Another Town 1962,Ag 18,10:1
Ugly American, The 1963,Ap 12,30:2
Rampage 1963,O 17,39:2
Schnee, Charles (Miscellaneous)
From This Day Forward 1946,Ap 20,16:2
Cross my Heart 1946,D 19,42:3
Schnee, Charles (Producer)
Prodigal, The 1955,My 14,10:7
Trial 1955,O 14,21:2
Somebody up There Likes Me 1956,Jl 6,16:1
Wings of Eagles, The 1957,F 1,28:1
House of Numbers 1957,S 13,15:2
Until They Sail 1957,O 9,41:2
Schnee, Charles (Screenwriter)
I Walk Alone 1948,Ja 22,36:3
Bad and the Beautiful, The 1953,Ja 16,19:1
Butterfield 8 1960,N 17,46:1
Crowded Sky, The 1961,F 11,27:2
Two Weeks in Another Town 1962,Ag 18,10:1
Schnee, Thelma (Screenwriter)
Detective, The 1954,N 2,25:2
Schneeberger, M (Cinematographer)
Blue Light, The 1934,My 9,23:4
Schneer, Charles H (Producer)
Earth vs the Flying Saucers 1956,Ag 2,21:2
I Aim at the Stars 1960,O 20,42:2
Three Worlds of Gulliver, The 1960,D 17,19:3
Mysterious Island 1961,D 21,30:6
Jason and the Argonauts 1963,Ag 8,19:1
First Men in the Moon 1964,N 26,52:2
Half a Sixpence 1968,F 21,60:3
Schneevoigt, George (Director)
Pastor of Vejlby, The 1931,N 1,VIII,6:1
En Saga 1938,Ja 8,19:2
Schneevoigt, Siri
En Saga 1938,Ja 8,19:2
SCHNEIDER
See Also SNYDER
Schneider, Alan (Director)
Film 1965,S 15,41:1
Now Cinema! (Film); Film (Now Cinema!)
1968,Ap 9,56:1
Schneider, Betty
My Uncle 1958,N 4,30:2
No Escape 1959,My 23,18:4
Tomorrow Is my Turn 1962,F 2,24:2
Paris Belongs to Us 1962,N 6,38:1
Schneider, Clarence Jay (Original Author)
Flight Into Nowhere 1938,My 2,13:3
Schneider, Edith
Quiller Memorandum, The 1966,D 16,59:1
Schneider, Edwin
Song O' my Heart 1930,Mr 12,32:6
Schneider, Eugene (Director)
Gypsies 1936,Jl 30,22:2
In the Rear of the Enemy 1942,O 10,11:2
Schneider, Friedrich
Peaks of Destiny 1927,N 29,31:1
Schneider, Gerda (Screenwriter)
Last Stop, The 1949,Mr 22,31:2
Schneider, Hannes
Peak of Fate 1925,Je 13,10:5
Fight for Matterhorn, The 1929,Jl 29,23:3
Weisse Rausch, Der; White Ecstasy, The
1932,Ja 24,VIII,5:1
Schneider, Hilde
Grobe Adele, Die 1937,My 15,23:5
Zweimal zwei im Himmelbett; Twice Two in a
Four-Post Bed 1939,F 5,19:3
Familie Schimek 1939,S 2,20:2

Schneider, Hilde— Cont
Paradies der Junggesellen; Bachelors' Paradise
1940,Ap 13,21:3
Schneider, Ira (Director)
Lost in Cuddihy 1966,N 25,49:1
Schneider, Larry (Miscellaneous)
Crossroads 1939,Mr 14,17:5
Schneider, Magda
Sehnsucht 202; Longing 202 1932,N 13,IX,4:2
Be Mine Tonight 1933,Ap 14,22:5
Liebelei; Light Love 1933,Jl 2,IX,2:2
Fraeulein-Falsch Verbunden! 1934,Ja 15,12:2
Marion, Das Gehoert Sich Nicht 1934,D 15,9:4
Fraeulein Liselott 1935,My 27,20:7
Fraulein Liselott 1935,My 27,20:7
Geschichten aus dem Wienerwald; Tales From the
Vienna Woods 1935,N 2,13:3
Ich Kenn' Dich Nicht und Liebe Dich; I Don't
Know You, but I Love You 1935,N 18,20:1
Winternachtstraum 1935,D 28,10:6
Gluecklicke Reise 1936,Ja 20,22:3
Liebelei 1936,F 28,18:2
Stelldichein im Schwarzwald, Ein; Rendezvous in
the Black Forest, A 1937,F 20,9:3
Eva, das Fabriksmaedel 1938,Ja 8,19:2
Rendezvous in Wien 1938,F 19,19:4
Wiener Prater 1938,D 3,11:3
Recht auf Liebe, Das; Right to Love, The
1940,Je 15,12:3
Story of Vickie, The 1958,Ja 30,19:2
Dreimaederlhaus, Das; (House of Three Girls,
The) 1961,N 18,15:1
Schneider, Magna
Prater, Wiener 1938,D 3,11:3
Schneider, Romy
Story of Vickie, The 1958,Ja 30,19:2
Montpi 1959,Ap 21,40:1
Scampolo 1959,Ag 6,18:4
Forever My Love 1962,Mr 28,36:4
Boccaccio '70 (The Job); Job, The (Boccaccio '70)
1962,Je 27,40:1
Trial, The 1963,F 21,5:1
Magnificent Sinner 1963,Ap 25,38:1
Cardinal, The 1963,D 13,41:1
Victors, The 1963,D 20,21:2
Good Neighbor Sam 1964,Jl 23,19:1
What's New Pussycat? 1965,Je 23,49:1
Madchen in Uniform 1965,Ag 18,41:2
10:30 PM Summer 1966,O 20,52:1
Triple Cross 1967,Jl 20,20:2
Schneider-Edenkoben, Richard (Director)
Inkognito 1937,Ap 17,15:2
Schneiderhof, Vladimir (Director)
Al-Yemen 1931,Ja 12,24:3
Golden Taiga 1935,Ag 2,22:3
SCHNELL
See Also SNELL
Schnell, G
Flame of Love, The 1930,N 3,19:3
Ferien vom Ich 1935,Ap 1,17:2
Schnickelfritz Band
Gold Diggers in Paris 1938,Je 2,19:2
Schnitzer, Gerald (Original Author)
Naked Sea, The 1955,D 21,37:1
Schnitzler, Arthur (Original Author)
Daybreak 1931,Je 1,15:1
Liebelei; Light Love 1933,Jl 2,IX,2:2
Liebelei 1936,F 28,18:2
Ronde, La 1954,Mr 17,27:2
Circle of Love 1965,Mr 25,42:4
Schnker, Hans
Corinna Darling 1958,Je 14,14:3
Schnyder, Franz (Director)
Heidi and Peter 1955,D 13,55:2
Schoberova, Olga
Lemonade Joe 1967,N 21,53:1
Schock, Rudolf
Dreimaederlhaus, Das; (House of Three Girls,
The) 1961,N 18,15:1
You Are the World for Me 1964,D 26,9:4
Schoeberg, Eugen
En Glad Gutt 1933,N 24,25:7
Schoedsack, Ernest B (Cinematographer)
Gow, The Head Hunter 1928,D 25,31:3
Lost Empire, The 1929,Ja 22,23:1
Schoedsack, Ernest B (Director)
Rango 1931,F 19,20:4
Most Dangerous Game, The 1932,N 21,21:1
Blind Adventure 1933,O 31,24:3
Son of Kong 1933,D 30,9:2
Long Lost Father 1934,F 19,18:2
Last Days of Pompeii, The 1935,O 17,29:2
Trouble in Morocco 1937,Mr 15,27:1
Outlaws of the Orient 1937,S 25,10:2
Dr Cyclops 1940,Ap 11,32:3
Mighty Joe Young 1949,Jl 28,19:3
Schoedsack, Ernest B (Producer)
Grass 1925,Mr 31,17:4
Chang 1927,Ap 30,25:3 (In Addenda)
Four Feathers, The 1929,Je 13,35:4
Rango 1931,F 19,20:4
Schoeller, Ingrid
My Son, The Hero 1963,S 19,23:1

Schoen, Margarete
Siegfried 1925,Ag 24,17:3
Kriemhild's Revenge 1928,O 16,29:1
Schoenauer, Marianne
Eroica; (The Beethoven Story) 1951,O 29,19:2
Don Juan 1956,Mr 6,26:2
Schoenboeck, Karl
Maedchen Irene, Das 1937,My 22,19:3
Nacht im Mai, Eine; Night in May, A
1938,N 12,10:3
Blaufuchs; Blue Fox 1939,Mr 4,18:5
Schoenbrun, DAvid (Narrator)
North Vietnam-A Personal Report
1968,Ja 23,79:1
Schoendorffer, Pierre (Producer)
Anderson Platoon, The 1967,D 18,70:4
Schoene, Mary
Golden Princess 1925,S 7,15:3
Schoener, Inge
Chasers, The; Draguers, Les 1960,My 3,43:1
Cow and I, The 1961,Je 6,42:2
Love and Marriage (One Moment Is Enough); One
Moment Is Enough (Love and Marriage)
1966,Ag 5,20:1
Schoenfeld, Bernard C (Screenwriter)
Phantom Lady 1944,F 18,15:2
Dark Corner, The 1946,My 9,27:3
Caged 1950,My 20,8:6
Macao 1952,My 1,34:2
Down Three Dark Streets 1954,S 4,6:4
There's Always Tomorrow 1956,Ja 21,18:2
13 West Street 1962,Je 7,31:2
Schoenfelder, Erich (Director)
It's Easy to Become a Father 1929,Je 24,27:1
Ein Ausgekochter Junge 1932,My 3,25:5
Schoen Ist die Manoeverzeit 1932,Ag 19,20:6
In Wien Hab' Ich Einmal ein Maedel Geliebt
1934,My 26,12:3
Zu Befehl, Herr Unteroffizier 1934,Je 16,20:3
Schoengold, Joseph
Motel, The Operator 1940,Ja 16,19:3
Schoenhals, Albrecht
Fuerst Woronzeff 1934,N 17,12:2
Einer zu viel an Bord 1936,Ja 25,18:5
Stuetzen der Gesellschaft 1936,N 7,15:3
Boccaccio 1937,F 27,9:3
Kreutzer Sonata 1937,Mr 14,XI,4:6 (In Addenda)
Kreutzer Sonata, The 1938,My 28,9:3
Ihr Groesster Erfolg; Her Greatest Success
1939,F 12,20:4
Rote Orchideen; Red Orchids 1939,Ap 15,15:2
Glaserne Kugel, Die; Glass Ball, The
1939,Je 17,12:3
Portrait of an Unknown Woman 1958,Ap 26,14:6
Schoenherr, Dietmar
Code 7...Victim 5 1965,My 20,52:1
Mozambique 1966,F 10,33:1
Schoenherr, Karl (Original Author)
Thy Name Is Woman 1924,Mr 4,17:1
SCHOFIELD
See Also SCOFIELD
Schofield, Johnnie
Father O'Flynn 1938,D 26,29:2
Song of the Road 1940,My 6,13:2
48 Hours 1944,Je 26,21:2
Murder Will Out 1953,Ap 6,24:2
Schofield, Paul (Original Author)
Framed 1930,Mr 29,23:1
Jimmy and Sally 1933,D 16,12:3
Schofield, Paul (Screenwriter)
Bluebeard's Seven Wives 1925,D 28,19:2
Beau Geste 1926,Ag 26,17:3
Poor Nut, The 1927,Jl 19,27:2
Wells Fargo 1937,D 30,15:2
SCHOLL
See Also SCHALL
Scholl, Danny
Top Banana 1954,F 20,8:6
Scholl, Edward (Miscellaneous)
Napoleon 1927,Je 5,VII,5:6 (In Addenda)
Scholl, Jack (Composer)
Rainmakers, The 1935,N 2,13:2
Freshman Love 1936,Ja 25,18:5
Song of the Saddle 1936,Mr 21,13:3
Silly Billies 1936,Ap 6,18:1
Melody for Two 1937,My 21,19:5
Kid Galahad 1937,My 27,21:3
Dance Charlie Dance 1937,Ag 26,25:2
She Loved a Fireman 1938,Ja 21,15:3
Slight Case of Murder, A 1938,F 28,19:1
Over the Wall 1938,Mr 28,19:2
Love and Learn 1947,My 3,10:3
Scholl, Jack (Miscellaneous)
Fish 1936,Ja 25,18:5
Treachery Rides the Range 1936,My 30,7:3
Talent Scout 1937,Ag 20,21:3
Swing Your Lady 1938,Ja 27,17:2
Scholl, Jack (Original Author)
Music in Manhattan 1944,O 7,11:2
Schollin, Christina
Swedish Wedding Night 1965,N 15,48:1
Dear John 1966,Mr 9,46:1

Schollwer, Edith
Student Sein 1931,My 4,15:3
Gasparone 1938,Mr 12,13:4
Scholz, Eva-Ingeborg
Grapes are Ripe, The 1953,O 15,43:2
Devil's General, The 1957,Ap 16,38:2
City of Secrets 1963,Jl 27,10:2
Scholz, Robert
All for a Woman 1921,D 5,20:1
Isn't Life Wonderful? 1924,D 1,17:3
Schomberg, Hermann
Friesennot 1936,O 26,20:1
Veilchen vom Potsdamer Platz, La; Violet of
Potsdam Square, The 1939,Ap 8,19:3
Rape on the Moor 1957,N 21,38:1
Faust 1963,Ap 16,31:1
Schomer, Abraham (Original Author)
Today 1930,N 17,29:1
Schon, Kyra
Night of the Living Dead 1968,D 5,59:2
Schonberg, Alexander
They Shall Have Music 1939,Jl 26,17:2
Schonblock, Paul
Blumen aus Nizza; Flowers From Nice
1939,Ap 1,17:3
Schoner, Sonja
Fidelio 1961,My 13,10:1
Schonrath, Hans
Knock-Out 1936,F 29,11:2
Schooler, Dave
Dreams of Hawaii 1929,My 6,30:4
Schoolman, Ralph (Miscellaneous)
Kukan 1941,Je 24,17:2
Schoolman, Ralph (Narrator)
Pledge to Bataan 1943,Jl 2,15:2
SCHOR
See Also SCHORR, SHOR
Schor, Lou (Original Author)
Lady Wants Mink, The 1953,Ap 6,24:2
Schorlemmer, Heinz
Gasparone 1938,Mr 12,13:4
Schorm, Evald
Report on the Party and the Guests, A
1968,S 20,37:5
Report on the Party and the Guests, A
1968,S 28,37:1
SCHORR
See Also SCHOR, SHOR
Schorr, Moishe
Mirele Efros 1939,O 21,12:2
Schorr, William (Director)
Forgotten Commandments 1932,Je 2,25:2
Schorr, William (Producer)
Indian Fighter, The 1955,D 22,20:1
Schott, Werner
Danton 1931,S 7,19:3
Legend of William Tell, The 1935,O 2,27:1
Schouwenaar, R N N Lieut
Silver Fleet, The 1945,Mr 24,22:6
Schrader, Hugo
Schuetzen Koenig, Der 1933,My 3,15:5 (In
Addenda)
Hochzeit am Wolfgangsee 1934,N 17,12:2
Royal Waltz, The 1936,Ap 10,27:1
Schrank, Joseph (Original Author)
Page Miss Glory 1935,Ag 29,25:2
Hard To Get 1938,N 14,15:2
Rings on her Fingers 1942,Ap 24,21:4
Magnificent Dope, The 1942,Jl 3,12:5
Schrank, Joseph (Screenwriter)
Swing Your Lady 1938,Ja 27,17:2
Slight Case of Murder, A 1938,F 28,19:1
Song of the Islands 1942,Mr 12,24:4
Cabin in the Sky 1943,My 28,19:3
Bathing Beauty 1944,Je 28,20:1
Clock, The 1945,My 4,23:2
Schreck, Max
Strange Case of Captain Ramper, The
1928,Je 4,13:2
Nosferatu the Vampire 1929,Je 4,29:3
At the Edge of the World 1929,Je 18,29:4
Rasputin: The Holy Devil 1930,Ag 25,14:2
Roman Einer Nacht 1934,Je 22,24:2
Schrecker, Frederick
Foreign Intrigue 1956,Jl 13,23:2
Schreiber, Alfred
Prince and the Pauper, The 1922,Ag 14,12:4
Schreiber, Edward (Producer)
Mad Dog Coll 1961,My 13,10:1
Schreiber, Edward (Screenwriter)
Mad Dog Coll 1961,My 13,10:1
Schreiber, Karl Ludwig
Abel Mit Der Mundharmonika 1934,S 1,16:3
Schreiber, Paul
High Time 1960,S 17,15:1
Schreyvogel, Friedrich (Screenwriter)
Eternal Waltz, The; (Ewiger Walzer)
1959,Jl 9,22:1
Schricker, Henry F
Johnny Holiday 1950,My 17,36:1
Schrift, Ben (Producer)
Cash on Delivery 1956,S 1,19:3

Schrock, Raymond (Original Author)
Private Izzy Murphy 1926,N 10,25:1
Navy Blues 1930,Ja 11,21:3
Devil's Island 1940,Jl 12,11:4
Minstrel Man 1944,Jl 17,18:5
Schrock, Raymond (Screenwriter)
West Point 1928,Ja 2,28:1
Hard Rock Harrigan 1935,Jl 30,16:2
Secret Service of the Air 1939,Mr 2,19:2
Smashing the Money Ring 1939,N 17,17:2
Kid Nightingale 1939,D 8,33:6
Murder in the Air 1940,Jl 4,12:2
Bullets for O'Hara 1941,Jl 28,16:4
Wild Bill Hickok Rides 1942,F 7,13:5
Murder in the Big House 1942,My 8,27:3
Escape From Crime 1942,O 12,12:3
Hidden Hand, The 1942,N 26,40:4
Secret Enemies 1943,Ja 1,27:3
Truck Busters 1943,Ja 29,23:5
Crime Incorporated 1945,Je 23,9:7
Key Witness 1947,Jl 30,27:6
Schroder, Doris (Screenwriter)
Three on the Trail 1936,My 5,26:5
Schroder, Ernst
Last Illusion, The 1951,Mr 8,37:2
Man Between, The 1953,N 19,41:2
Counterfeit Traitor, The 1962,Ap 18,28:1
Visit, The 1964,O 22,44:1
Heidi 1968,S 23,42:4
Schroeder, Anne
West of the Water Tower 1923,D 31,9:3
Schroeder, Arnulf
Eternal Waltz, The; (Ewiger Walzer)
1959,Jl 9,22:1
Schroeder, Arthur
Tradition 1921,Jl 1,8:1
Schloss Hubertus 1935,F 9,11:3
Selige Exzellenz, Die 1937,Je 15,26:2
Schroeder-Schrom
Traum vom Rhein, Der 1935,D 9,25:2
Maedchenraeuber 1936,Ag 15,6:3
Gaesschen zum Paradies, Das 1937,Ag 21,7:3
Schroell, N
Copperhead, The 1920,F 9,10:3
Schroll, Chris
Open the Door and See all the People
1964,Ap 2,28:1
Schron, Cania
Coffin Maker, The 1928,O 9,35:1
Schrorg, Greti
Hippodrome 1962,Mr 12,36:1
Schroth, Carl Heinz (Director)
Reaching for the Stars 1958,My 24,18:2
Schroth, Hannelore
Spiel in Sommerwind; Play in the Summer
Breezes 1939,Ap 1,17:2
Gouverneur, Der 1939,S 11,15:2
Corinna Darling 1958,Je 14,14:3
Captain from Koepenick, The 1958,Jl 26,6:1
Schroth, Heinrich
President, The 1929,Ja 21,18:4
Carnival Crime, The 1929,Jl 8,17:3
Hauptmann von Koepenick, Der 1933,Ja 17,22:6
Liebesleute 1936,O 3,21:2
SCHUBERT
See Also SHUBERT
Schubert, Bernard (Miscellaneous)
Song of my Heart 1948,Mr 5,17:3
Schubert, Bernard (Original Author)
Mark of the Vampire 1935,My 3,23:4
Song of Love 1947,O 10,31:2
Schubert, Bernard (Screenwriter)
Band Plays on, The 1934,D 22,21:2
Mark of the Vampire 1935,My 3,23:4
Make a Wish 1937,S 23,33:1
Barrier, The 1937,N 27,21:2
Breaking the Ice 1938,S 23,35:3
Fisherman's Wharf 1939,F 24,15:2
Silver Queen 1943,Ja 11,18:4
Jungle Woman 1944,Jl 15,19:6
Mummy's Curse, The 1945,Mr 31,16:1
Frozen Ghost, The 1945,Jl 28,7:3
Schubert, Heinz
Emil and the Detectives 1964,D 24,8:3
Funeral in Berlin 1966,D 23,17:1
Schubert, Marina
British Agent 1934,S 20,20:1
Car 99 1935,F 23,14:7
All the King's Horses 1935,Mr 9,19:1
Schuefftan, Eugen (Director)
Das Ekel 1932,Ja 30,13:2
Schuenzel (Screenwriter)
Amphitryon 38 1935,O 13,IX,4:6 (In Addenda)
Schuetzendorf, Leo
Lindenwirtin vom Rhein, Die 1931,S 25,28:7
Schukin, V V
Men on Wings 1935,Je 11,24:5
Schukow, A
Flames on the Volga 1929,Ap 2,28:4
Schulberg, B P (Producer)
Behold My Wife 1935,F 18,19:3
Crime and Punishment 1935,N 22,18:2
One Way Ticket 1936,Ja 1,35:2

Schulberg, B P (Producer) — Cont
Lady of Secrets 1936,F 22,12:1
And So They Were Married 1936,My 14,29:3
Counterfeit 1936,Jl 20,11:1
Wedding Present 1936,N 19,31:3
Doctor's Diary, A 1937,F 17,16:4
John Meade's Woman 1937,F 18,19:1
Her Husband Lies 1937,Mr 18,20:1
Great Gambini, The 1937,Jl 12,20:4
She's no Lady 1937,Ag 12,14:3
He Stayed for Breakfast 1940,Ag 31,16:2
Bedtime Story 1942,Mr 20,25:4
Wife Takes a Flyer, The 1942,Je 19,19:1
Flight Lieutenant 1942,Jl 31,11:1

Schulberg, Budd (Original Author)
Winter Carnival 1939,Jl 28,14:2
Week End for Three 1941,O 24,27:4
On the Waterfront 1954,Jl 29,18:1
Harder They Fall, The 1956,My 10,26:3
Face in the Crowd, A 1957,My 29,33:1

Schulberg, Budd (Screenwriter)
Winter Carnival 1939,Jl 28,14:2
On the Waterfront 1954,Jl 29,18:1
Face in the Crowd, A 1957,My 29,33:1
Wind Across the Everglades 1958,S 12,21:1

Schulberg, Stuart (Producer)
No Way Back 1955,My 19,25:5
Wind Across the Everglades 1958,S 12,21:1

Schulenberg, Bob (Producer)
Secret Cinema, The 1968,My 2,57:1

SCHULMAN
See Also SHULMAN

Schulman, Arnold (Original Author)
Wild Is the Wind 1957,D 12,35:1

Schulman, Arnold (Screenwriter)
Wild Is the Wind 1957,D 12,35:1
Cimarron 1961,F 17,12:2
Love With the Proper Stranger 1963,D 26,33:1
Night They Raided Minsky's, The
1968,D 23,43:1

Schulman, Arnold(dp)Capra, Frank (Screenwriter)
Hole in the Head, A 1959,Jl 16,31:2

SCHULTZ
See Also SHULTZ

Schultz, Alan Brener (Original Author)
Behind Office Doors 1931,Mr 21,15:1

Schultz, Harry
Riley, The Cop 1928,D 4,29:1
Hypnotized 1933,Ja 16,13:3
One Sunday Afternoon 1933,S 2,14:4
Pursuit of Happiness, The 1934,O 26,25:1

Schultz, Raymond
Alice in Wonderland 1931,D 28,22:1

Schulz, Charlotte
Verwehte Spuren; Covered Tracks
1939,O 14,13:3

Schulz, Franz (Miscellaneous)
April Romance 1937,Ja 27,17:4

Schulz, Franz (Original Author)
Monte Carlo Madness 1932,Je 4,9:2
Office Girl 1932,Je 27,20:7
Midnight 1939,Ap 6,31:1

Schulz, Franz (Screenwriter)
Drei von ver Tankstelle, Die 1931,Je 20,20:4
Night is Young, The 1935,Ja 14,11:2
Paris in Spring 1935,Jl 13,16:2
April Romance 1937,Ja 27,17:4
Adventure in Diamonds 1940,Ap 4,27:2

Schulz, Fritz
Lindenwirtin vom Rhein, Die 1931,S 25,28:7
Schlacht von Bademuende, Die 1931,N 21,20:4
Theaternaechte von Berlin 1932,Ja 11,28:5
Ungetreue Eckehart, Der 1932,Ja 23,18:4
Rendez-Vous 1932,Ap 30,19:3
Der Storch Streikt 1932,My 2,13:2
Dienst Ist Dienst 1932,Je 6,18:5
Hurra! Ein Junge! 1932,Je 21,19:6
Pension Schoeller 1932,S 20,26:3
Drei Tage Mittelarrest 1933,My 18,17:4
Heute Nacht-Eventuell 1933,Je 24,16:3
Waltz Time 1933,S 29,24:2
Bettelstudent, Der 1933,O 14,18:3
Constant Nymph, The 1934,Ap 7,19:1
Ja, Treu Ist die Soldatenliebe 1934,Ap 28,11:4
Madonna, Wo Bist Du? 1936,Mr 21,13:3
Schwebende Jungfrau, Die 1937,Ag 7,7:2
Cabaret 1957,N 9,31:2 (Incorrect in this edition;
use 1957,N 7,43:4 elsewhere)

Schulz, Fritz (Director)
Jo as a Haznal; Father Knows Best 1935,F 5,22:4
Letzte Liebe; Last; Last Love 1938,Jl 19,15:4

Schulz, Fritz (Screenwriter)
Zwei Hertzen in Drei-Viertel Takt
1930,O 13,31:1

Schulz-Lichterfeld, Frau
Ich Glaub' nie Mehr an Eine Frau
1933,O 13,25:4

SCHUMAN
See Also SCHUMANN, SHUMAN

SCHUMANN
See Also SCHUMAN, SHUMAN

Schumann, Erik
Reaching for the Stars 1958,My 24,18:2
Two-Headed Spy, The 1959,Mr 3,38:4

Sky Without Stars 1959,My 30,9:2
Question 7 1961,S 29,30:2
Counterfeit Traitor, The 1962,Ap 18,28:1

Schumann-Heink, Ernestine Mme
Here's to Romance 1935,O 3,29:2

Schumann-Heink, Ferdinand
Four Sons 1928,F 14,27:1
Riley, The Cop 1928,D 4,29:1
Blaze O' Glory 1929,D 31,15:1
Hell's Angels 1930,Ag 16,8:3
Seas Beneath 1931,Ja 31,15:1
My Pal the King 1932,O 4,26:4
World Moves On, The 1934,Je 30,18:5
King and the Chorus Girl, The 1937,Mr 29,14:4

Schumann-Heink, Ferdinand (Original Author)
Mamba 1930,Mr 11,25:2

Schumberg, Alex
Our Daily Bread 1934,O 3,25:2

Schumm, Hans
Beasts of Berlin 1939,N 20,15:6
Four Sons 1940,Je 8,18:4
So Ends our Night 1941,F 28,17:2
Underground 1941,Je 23,13:2
All Through the Night 1942,Ja 24,13:2
Lady Has Plans, The 1942,Mr 5,27:1
Atlantic Convoy 1942,Jl 6,18:5
Berlin Correspondent 1942,S 4,19:2
Margin for Error 1943,Ja 25,10:7
Moon Is Down, The 1943,Mr 27,8:6
Sahara 1943,N 12,25:2
Voice in the Wind 1944,Mr 16,17:2
Escape in the Desert 1945,My 12,10:2
Third Sex, The 1959,Mr 26,27:1
I Aim at the Stars 1960,O 20,42:2

Schundler, Rudolf
Last Waltz, The 1958,Ap 12,13:1

Schunemann, E (Cinematographer)
Shiraz 1928,O 7,IX,7:7

Schunzel, Reinhold
Last Payment, The 1922,Ja 22,VI,3:2 (In
Addenda)
Fortune's Fool 1928,Ag 13,23:2
Dreigroschenoper, Die; Beggar's Opera, The
1931,My 18,21:2
Ihre Hoheit Befiehlt 1931,N 7,16:5
1914: The Last Days Before the War 1932,S 5,9:6
First Comes Courage 1943,S 3,15:3
Hitler Gang, The 1944,My 8,15:2
Man in Half Moon Street, The 1945,Ja 20,16:2
Dragonwyck 1946,Ap 11,35:2
Notorious 1946,Ag 16,19:2
Plainsman and the Lady, The 1946,N 4,33:1
Golden Earrings 1947,D 4,41:3
Berlin Express 1948,My 21,19:3
Vicious Circle, The 1948,Jl 22,27:2
Washington Story 1952,Jl 2,22:3
Threepenny Opera, The 1960,Jl 11,24:4

Schunzel, Reinhold (Director)
Fortune's Fool 1928,Ag 13,23:2
Ronny 1932,Ap 14,25:3
Das Schoene Abenteuer 1932,D 8,25:3
Saison in Kairo 1933,D 25,28:2
Wie Sag' Ich's Meinem Mann? 1934,Ja 23,22:4
Viktor und Viktoria 1935,Ja 28,10:5
Donogoo Tonka 1936,Ap 13,15:2
Amphitryon 1937,Mr 24,29:1
Maedchen Irene, Das 1937,My 22,19:3
Aus den Wolken Kommt das Glueck; Luck Comes
From the Clouds 1938,Ap 16,17:2
Rich Man, Poor Girl 1938,Ag 19,13:3
Ice Follies of 1939 1939,Mr 17,25:2
Balalaika 1939,D 15,33:2
New Wine 1942,F 2,11:2

Schunzel, Reinhold (Miscellaneous)
Kleine Seitensprung, Der 1932,Ja 1,31:1

Schunzel, Reinhold (Screenwriter)
Amphitryon 1937,Mr 24,29:1

SCHUR
See Also SCHEUER

Schur, Willi
Hauptmann von Koepenick, Der 1933,Ja 17,22:6
Pechmarie 1935,Ap 22,14:3
Krach um Iolanthe 1935,My 11,21:3
Fraeulein Liselott 1935,My 27,20:7
Alles um Eine Frau 1935,D 21,11:1
Wer Nimmt die Liebe Ernst? 1936,F 10,15:2
Gaesschen zum Paradies, Das 1937,Ag 21,7:3
Abduction, The 1938,Je 11,9:2
Congo Express 1940,My 11,15:3

Schurenberg, Siegfried
Herr Der Welt, Der 1935,D 16,23:3
Hoehere Befehl, Der 1936,Mr 31,17:3
Tempestous Love 1958,N 22,27:4
Journey, The 1959,F 20,19:1
Third Sex, The 1959,Mr 26,27:1
Town Without Pity 1961,O 11,53:1

Schurr, Willi
Fraulein Liselott 1935,My 27,20:7

Schuster, Friedel
Viktoria und Ihr Husar 1933,Ap 10,8:3
Heart Song 1934,Je 6,24:6

Schuster, Harold (Director)
Wings of the Morning 1937,Mr 12,19:1
Dinner at the Ritz 1937,D 4,21:1
Swing That Cheer 1938,N 11,31:2
Exposed 1938,N 21,14:5
One Hour to Live 1939,N 4,11:3
Zanzibar 1940,Ap 1,15:3
Ma! He's Making Eyes at Me 1940,Ap 26,25:2
South to Karanga 1940,Ag 9,19:1
Diamond Frontiers 1940,O 4,29:2
Girl Trouble 1942,O 8,31:2
My Friend Flicka 1943,My 27,21:4
Marine Raiders 1944,Jl 1,10:7
Breakfast in Hollywood 1946,Jl 15,21:1
Jack Slade 1953,O 29,42:6
Loophole 1954,Mr 13,11:3
Port of Hell 1954,D 18,12:2
Finger Man 1955,Jl 16,12:4
Return of Jack Slade, The 1955,N 24,41:3
Dragoon Wells Massacre 1957,My 6,25:2
Portland Expose 1957,S 27,16:6

Schuster, Hugo
Prelude to Fame 1950,N 10,35:3

Schutz, Ernst
Merry Wives of Windsor, The 1966,F 28,21:1

Schutz, Maurice
Passion Of Joan Of Arc, The 1929,Mr 29,21:1
Passion of Jeanne d'Arc, The 1929,Mr 31,VIII,7:1
Oppressed, The 1929,Jl 15,25:1
Fantomas 1934,Mr 13,27:4
Call, The 1938,Mr 29,18:3
Champs-Elysees 1939,F 28,17:2
Three Waltzes 1939,Ap 25,19:2
It Happened at the Inn; Goupi Mains Rouge
1945,D 22,16:2

Schvartz, Lev (Composer)
On his Own 1939,S 13,31:3
Golden Key, The 1939,D 21,29:3
University of Life 1941,F 26,17:1
Stone Flower 1946,D 30,15:2

Schwab, Lawrence (Composer)
New Moon 1930,D 25,18:6

Schwab, Lawrence (Director)
Follow Thru 1930,S 13,9:3
Take a Chance 1933,N 27,20:3

Schwab, Lawrence (Original Author)
New Moon 1930,D 25,18:6

Schwab, LAwrence (Original Author)
New Moon 1940,Jl 19,22:2

Schwab, Lawrence (Original Author)
Desert Song, The 1943,D 18,10:6
Desert Song, The 1953,My 21,39:2

Schwab, Lawrence (Producer)
Ali Baba Goes to Town 1937,O 23,14:1

Schwade, Sol
Playground, The 1965,O 4,00:0

Schwalb, Ben (Producer)
George Raft Story, The 1962,Mr 22,40:1
Tickle Me 1965,Je 24,28:3

Schwannecke, Ellen
Maedchen in Uniform 1932,S 21,25:4
Kadetten 1933,D 26,19:3
Toller Einfall, Ein 1934,My 21,20:3
Royal Waltz, The 1936,Ap 10,27:1
Kein Wort von Liebe; Not a Word About Love
1938,S 10,20:3
Sextanerin, Die; Erste Liebe; First Love
1938,S 12,13:3

Schwannecke, Victor
Liebeswalzer 1931,My 4,15:3
D-Zug 13 Hat Verspaetung 1931,Ag 10,18:3
Die vom Rummelplatz 1932,Ja 2,14:2

SCHWARTZ
See Also SCHWARZ

Schwartz, Arthur (Composer)
That Girl From Paris 1937,Ja 1,19:1
Cairo 1942,N 6,27:2
Thank Your Lucky Stars 1943,O 2,19:2
Dangerous When Wet 1953,Je 19,18:1
Band Wagon, The 1953,Jl 10,10:2
Torch Song 1953,O 13,34:2

Schwartz, Arthur (Miscellaneous)
Under Your Spell 1936,N 7,15:2

Schwartz, Arthur (Original Author)
Thank Your Lucky Stars 1943,O 2,19:2

Schwartz, Arthur (Producer)
Cover Girl 1944,Mr 31,26:1
Night and Day 1946,Jl 26,16:2

Schwartz, Bernard (Producer)
Shuttered Room, The 1968,F 15,47:1

Schwartz, David R (Original Author)
Bobo, The 1967,S 29,53:1

Schwartz, David R (Screenwriter)
Island of Love 1963,Je 13,30:4
Robin and the 7 Hoods 1964,Ag 6,20:1
Sex and the Single Girl 1964,D 26,9:2
That Funny Feeling 1965,O 21,57:2
Bobo, The 1967,S 29,53:1

Schwartz, Irwin (Screenwriter)
Stakeout on Dope Street 1958,Ap 24,38:1

Schwartz, Marvin (Producer)
Blindfold 1966,My 26,55:2
War Wagon, The 1967,Ag 3,26:3

Schwartz, Maurice
Broken Hearts 1926,Mr 3,26:1
Tevya 1939,D 22,15:3
Bird of Paradise 1951,Mr 15.37:2
Salome 1953,Mr 25,37:1
Schwartz, Maurice (Director)
Broken Hearts 1926,Mr 3,26:1
Tevya 1939,D 22,15:3
Schwartz, Robert
Last Chance, The 1945,N 28,21:6
Great Man, The 1957,Ja 2,28:2
Schwartz, Sid (Original Author)
Man Made Monster 1941,Mr 19,25:4
Schwartz, Victor
One-Way Ticket to Hell 1955,D 8,45:1
SCHWARZ
See Also SCHWARTZ
Schwarz, Fred
Juno and the Paycock 1930,Je 30,22:6
Schwarz, Hans (Director)
Wonderful Lies of Nova Petrova, The
1930,Je 30,27:2
Melody of The Heart 1930,S 1,16:1
Darling of the Gods; Liebling der Gotter
1930,N 30,IX,6:5
Grosse Tenor, Der 1931,My 29,26:5
Ihre Hoheit Befiehlt 1931,N 7,16:5
Monte Carlo Madness 1932,Je 4,9:2
Returr. of the Scarlet Pimpernel, The
1938,Ap 11,12:2
Schwarz, Jack (Producer)
Enchanted Forest, The 1945,D 17,17:2
Schwarzkopf, Elisabeth
St Matthew Passion 1952,Ja 29,17:4
Rosenkavalier, Der 1962,O 10,57:1
Schwarzwald, Milton (Producer)
Top Man 1943,O 29,23:2
Schweda, Walter
Mutterliebe; Mother Love 1940,Mr 16,8:3
Schweikert, Hans (Director)
Befreite Hande; Freed Hans 1940,My 25,20:1
SCHWEITZER
See Also SWITZER
Schweitzer, Albert Dr
Albert Schweitzer 1957,Ja 21,20:2
Schweitzer, Albert Dr (Miscellaneous)
Albert Schweitzer 1957,Ja 21,20:2
Schweitzer, Armin
Marie-Louise 1945,N 13,24:2
Schweitzer, Ilya (Composer)
Cinerama's Russian Adventure 1966,Ap 14,42:1
Schweitzer, Mikhail (Director)
Resurrection 1963,O 7,35:2
Schweitzer, Mikhail (Screenwriter)
Resurrection 1963,O 7,35:2
Schweizer, Richard (Original Author)
Search, The 1948,Mr 24,30:3
Four Days' Leave 1950,Je 9,29:4
Schweizer, Richard (Screenwriter)
Marie-Louise 1945,N 13,24:2
Last Chance, The 1945,N 28,21:6
Four Days' Leave 1950,Je 9,29:4
Four in a Jeep 1951,Je 12,35:2
Heidi 1953,D 21,27:2
Heidi and Peter 1955,D 13,55:2
Heidi 1968,S 23,42:4
Schwenzen, Per (Screenwriter)
Guitars of Love 1958,Jl 12,18:1
Schwerin, Herman (Producer)
Bridge, The; (Bruecke, Die) 1961,My 2,42:1
Schwiers, Ellen
Arms and the Man 1962,F 24,21:7
Schwind, Wolfgang V
1914: The Last Days Before the War 1932,S 5,9:6
Sciascia, Leonardo (Original Author)
We Still Kill the Old Way 1968,F 29,28:1
Scilla-Gabel
Modesty Blaise 1966,Ag 11,27:1
Scire, Andrea
Woman in the Painting, The 1959,Ja 15,27:1
Scitti, Sergio (Screenwriter)
Commare Secca, La; Grim Reaper, The
1966,S 15,51:1
Scob, Edith
Burning Court, The 1963,Ag 1,17:2
Therese 1963,N 13,35:2
Judex 1966,Ap 26,55:1
Scoble, Leslie
She Didn't Say No 1963,Jl 30,18:1
Scoble, Teresa
She Didn't Say No 1963,Jl 30,18:1
Scoffici, Mario (Director)
Viento Norte; North Wind 1939,S 16,20:3
SCOFIELD
See Also SCHOFIELD
Scofield, Paul
That Lady 1955,Je 11,8:7
Train, The 1965,Mr 18,25:1
Man for all Seasons, A 1966,D 13,60:1
Scoggins, C E (Original Author)
Tycoon 1947,D 26,22:6

Scola, Age (Screenwriter)
High Infidelity (The Victim); Victim, The (High
Infidelity) 1965,Jl 2,17:1
High Infidelity (Modern People); Modern People
(High Infidelity) 1965,Jl 2,17:1
High Infidelity (Sin in the Afternoon); Sin in the
Afternoon (High Infidelity) 1965,Jl 2,17:1
High Infidelity (The Scandal); Scandal, The (High
Infidelity) 1965,Jl 2,17:1
Scola, Ettore (Director)
Let's Talk About Women 1964,S 29,52:5
Devil in Love, The 1968,Jl 4,13:4
Scola, Ettore (Original Author)
Successo, Il 1965,Ap 29,40:2
Made in Italy 1967,My 1,44:2
Devil in Love, The 1968,Jl 4,13:4
Scola, Ettore (Screenwriter)
Easy Life, The 1963,D 23,18:2
Let's Talk About Women 1964,S 29,52:5
Love a la Carte 1965,Ja 12,31:1
Magnificent Cuckold 1965,Ap 20,42:1
Successo, Il 1965,Ap 29,40:2
Made in Italy 1967,My 1,44:2
Devil in Love, The 1968,Jl 4,13:4
Scola, Kathryn (Original Author)
Baby Face 1933,Je 24,16:2
Female 1933,N 4,18:3
Shadows of Sing Sing 1934,F 21,23:2
Hotel for Women 1939,Ag 26,20:2
Scola, Kathryn (Screenwriter)
Glass Key, The 1935,Je 15,20:2
It Had to Happen 1936,F 15,18:6
Wife, Doctor and Nurse 1937,O 11,26:5
Second Honeymoon 1937,N 13,11:2
Baroness and the Butler, The 1938,F 19,19:2
Always Goodbye 1938,Je 25,7:2
Alexander's Ragtime Band 1938,Ag 6,7:2
Hotel for Women 1939,Ag 26,20:2
House Across the Bay, The 1940,Mr 22,23:2
One Night in the Tropics 1940,D 20,33:2
Lady From Cheyenne, The 1941,Ap 18,18:2
Constant Nymph, The 1943,Jl 24,8:2
Happy Land 1943,D 9,33:3
Colonel Effingham's Raid 1946,Ap 5,21:3
Night Unto Night 1949,Je 11,11:2
Scola, Scarpelli (Screenwriter)
High Infidelity (Sin in the Afternoon); Sin in the
Afternoon (High Infidelity) 1965,Jl 2,17:1
High Infidelity (Modern People); Modern People
(High Infidelity) 1965,Jl 2,17:1
High Infidelity (The Victim); Victim, The (High
Infidelity) 1965,Jl 2,17:1
High Infidelity (The Scandal); Scandal, The (High
Infidelity) 1965,Jl 2,17:1
Scolaro, Nino (Screenwriter)
Margaret of Cortona 1957,Ja 21,20:4
Scollay, Fred J
Odds Against Tomorrow 1959,O 16,27:1
Scopani, Giuseppe (Screenwriter)
House of Intrigue, The 1960,Mr 10,36:3
Scordi, Jack
Do You Love Me 1946,My 25,12:2
Scorpelli, Agee (Original Author)
Love and Larceny 1963,F 2,5:6
Scotese, Guiseppe M (Director)
Great Dawn, The 1947,Ag 28,28:3
Fear No Evil 1949,Mr 31,31:2
Scotese, Guiseppe M (Screenwriter)
Fear No Evil 1949,Mr 31,31:2
Scott, A H
As You Like It 1936,N 6,29:3
Scott, Adrian (Producer)
My Pal, Wolf 1944,O 9,17:2
Murder, my Sweet 1945,Mr 9,16:2
Cornered 1945,D 26,15:1
Deadline at Dawn 1946,Ap 4,33:2
Crossfire 1947,Jl 23,19:2
So Well Remembered 1947,N 5,34:3
Scott, Adrian (Screenwriter)
Parson of Panamint, The 1941,Jl 26,18:2
Mr Lucky 1943,Jl 23,21:2
Miss Susie Slagle's 1946,F 7,29:2
Scott, Alan
Lola 1962,O 15,32:2
Paris in the Month of August 1968,Ag 26,46:4
Scott, Alex
Darling 1965,Ag 4,20:1
Fahrenheit 451 1966,N 15,53:1
Scott, Allan (Miscellaneous)
Roberta 1935,Mr 8,25:2
Wait Till the Sun Shines, Nellie 1952,Je 28,12:2
Scott, Allan (Original Author)
Good-Bye Again 1933,S 2,15:2
Wise Girl 1938,Ja 10,13:3
Man About Town 1939,Je 29,19:1
Honeymoon for Three 1941,F 8,19:2
So Proudly We Hail 1943,S 10,29:1

Scott, Allan (Screenwriter)
Top Hat 1935,Ag 30,12:2
In Person 1935,D 13,31:5
Follow the Fleet 1936,F 21,21:2
Swing Time 1936,Ag 28,21:2
Quality Street 1937,Ap 9,19:2
Shall We Dance 1937,My 14,21:1
Wise Girl 1938,Ja 10,13:3
Joy of Living 1938,My 6,27:1
Carefree 1938,S 23,35:1
Fifth Avenue Girl 1939,Ag 25,12:2
Primrose Path 1940,Mr 23,16:2
Lucky Partners 1940,S 6,25:2
Skylark 1941,N 20,39:2
Remember the Day 1941,D 26,21:2
So Proudly We Hail 1943,S 10,29:1
I Love a Soldier 1944,N 2,22:2
Here Come the Waves 1944,D 28,25:2
Blue Skies 1946,O 17,28:2
Let's Dance 1950,N 30,42:2
Guy Who Came Back, The 1951,Ag 17,13:2
Wait Till the Sun Shines, Nellie 1952,Je 28,12:2
Four Poster, The 1952,O 16,37:1
5,000 Fingers of Dr T, The 1953,Je 20,8:6
Top Secret Affair 1957,Ja 31,21:1
Imitation of Life 1959,Ap 18,18:1
Scott, Anthony
Spirit of Youth 1938,F 28,19:1
Scott, Ashmead
For Heaven's Sake 1950,D 16,10:5
House on Telegraph Hill, The 1951,My 14,29:1
Scott, Avis
Hundred Hour Hunt 1953,Je 17,32:2
Scott, Bill (Miscellaneous)
Crazy World of Laurel and Hardy, The
1967,D 22,35:3
Scott, Bill (Producer)
Crazy World of Laurel and Hardy, The
1967,D 22,35:3
Scott, Brenda
Johnny Tiger 1966,Je 16,53:4
Scott, Bud
New Orleans 1947,Je 20,25:6
Scott, Carrie
Manhandled 1924,Jl 29,9:2
Stage Struck 1925,N 16,19:4
Scott, Connie
Flipper 1963,S 19,23:1
Scott, Cyril
How Molly Made Good 1915,O 20,5:5
Scott, David
In Gay Madrid 1930,Je 7,10:4
Melody Lingers on, The 1935,N 7,27:1
Scott, Derek
Life With Father 1947,Ag 16,6:6
Scott, DeVallon (Original Author)
She Went to the Races 1946,F 1,29:2
Scott, DeVallon (Screenwriter)
Saracen Blade, The 1954,My 15,13:4
Black Dakotas, The 1954,O 2,21:2
Maverick Queen, the 1956,Je 4,25:2
Scott, Douglas
Strong Boy 1929,Ap 1,22:1
Reno 1930,N 4,36:1
Rango 1931,F 19,20:4
Devotion 1931,O 3,20:2
Ruling Voice, The 1931,N 5,29:3
Cavalcade 1933,Ja 6,23:2
Eagle and the Hawk, The 1933,My 13,16:2
And So They Were Married 1936,My 14,29:3
Lloyds of London 1936,N 26,39:1
Wee Willie Winkie 1937,Jl 24,12:1
Wild and Woolly 1937,S 6,20:1
Last Gangster, The 1937,D 10,33:2
Wuthering Heights 1939,Ap 14,28:2
Intermezzo, A Love Story 1939,O 6,31:1
We Are not Alone 1939,D 1,27:1
Naval Academy 1941,Je 5,27:3
Get Help to Love 1942,O 19,15:3
Scott, Evelyn
Wicked Woman 1954,Mr 27,13:6
Scott, Ewing (Director)
Igloo 1932,Jl 21,15:2
Hollywood Cowboy 1937,Jl 24,12:1
Headin' East 1938,Ja 15,19:2
Hollywood Round-Up 1938,Mr 5,11:2
Untamed Fury 1947,Ap 26,10:6
Harpoon 1948,D 9,48:8
Scott, Ewing (Original Author)
Border Flight 1936,Je 22,22:1
Untamed Fury 1947,Ap 26,10:6
Arctic Manhunt 1949,Ag 19,12:5
Scott, Ewing (Producer)
Untamed Fury 1947,Ap 26,10:6
Scott, Ewing (Screenwriter)
Igloo 1932,Jl 21,15:2
Hollywood Cowboy 1937,Jl 24,12:1
Harpoon 1948,D 9,48:8
Scott, Fred
Bride of the Storm 1926,Ap 5,24:1
Grand Parade, The 1930,F 1,15:1
Swing High 1930,Je 27,26:3
Beyond Victory 1931,Ap 6,24:1

Scott, Fred — Cont
  Last Outlaw, The 1936,Je 15,24:1
  Make a Wish 1937,S 23,33:1
Scott, George C
  Hanging Tree, The 1959,F 12,23:1
  Anatomy of a Murder 1959,Jl 3,10:1
  Hustler, The 1961,S 27,35:1
  List of Adrian Messenger, The 1963,My 30,20:1
  Dr Strangelove or: How I Learned to Stop
    Worrying and Love the Bomb 1964,Ja 31,16:1
    (Incorrect in this edition; use 1964,Ja 30,24:1
    elsewhere)
  Yellow Rolls-Royce, The 1965,My 14,42:2
  Bible, The 1966,S 29,60:1
  Not With my Wife, You Don't! 1966,N 3,45:2
  Flim Flam Man, The 1967,Ag 23,40:1
  Petulia 1968,Je 11,54:4
Scott, Glenn (Miscellaneous)
  Fun and Fancy Free 1947,S 29,17:2 (In
    Addenda)
Scott, Gordon
  Tarzan and the Lost Safari 1957,Ap 13,12:3
  Tarzan's Fight for Life 1958,Ag 16,10:2
  Tarzan's Greatest Adventure 1959,Jl 9,22:1
  Tarzan the Magnificent 1960,Jl 21,17:1
  Duel of the Titans 1963,Ag 8,19:1
  Tramplers, The 1966,D 8,64:1
Scott, Hampton J
  That's my Man 1947,Ap 7,20:2
Scott, Harold
  Man in Grey, The 1945,N 30,18:6
  Gay Lady, The 1951,Ap 16,21:2
  Spanish Gardner, The 1957,S 9,21:2
  Brides of Dracula, The 1960,S 6,41:4
Scott, Hazel
  Something to Shout About 1943,Ap 8,27:3
  I Dood It 1943,N 11,29:1
  Heat's on, The 1943,N 26,29:2
  Broadway Rhythm 1944,Ap 14,24:6
  Rhapsody in Blue 1945,Je 28,22:2
  Night Affair 1961,O 13,27:1
Scott, Helen (Miscellaneous)
  To Die in Madrid 1965,S 16,00:0
Scott, Henry
  Anna Lucasta 1959,Ja 15,27:1
Scott, Ivy
  Too Many Girls 1940,N 21,43:1
  Higher and Higher 1944,Ja 22,8:4
Scott, J M (Original Author)
  Sea Wife 1957,D 5,45:2
Scott, Jacqueline
  Macabre 1958,Jl 24,18:1
  Firecreek 1968,F 22,36:2
Scott, Janette
  Spellbound 1945,N 2,22:2
  No Place for Jennifer 1951,Jl 17,31:2
  No Highway in the Sky 1951,S 22,8:6
  Galloping Major, The 1951,D 17,27:2
  Edge of Divorce 1954,Jl 2,10:1
  Helen of Troy 1956,Ja 27,21:4
  Happy is the Bride 1959,Je 30,27:2
  Devil's Disciple, The 1959,Ag 21,12:1
  School for Scoundrels 1960,Jl 12,39:1
  Double Bunk 1961,N 17,41:3
  Day of the Triffids 1963,My 11,15:2
  Paranoiac 1963,My 23,31:2
  Old Dark House, The 1963,O 31,26:3
  Crack in the World 1965,My 13,32:2
Scott, Jeff
  Young Warriors, The 1968,F 8,36:1
Scott, Jerry
  Thrill of a Romance 1945,My 25,22:2
Scott, Jesse
  Champ, The 1931,N 10,29:4
  Madame Du Barry 1934,O 25,26:2
Scott, John
  Telltale Heart, The 1963,My 16,42:1
  Horror of Party Beach, The 1964,Ap 30,30:1
Scott, Kay
  Fear in the Night 1947,Ap 19,11:3
Scott, Ken
  Three Faces of Eve, The 1957,S 27,16:6
  Stopover Tokyo 1957,D 27,23:4
  From Hell to Texas 1958,Je 5,39:2
  Bravados, The 1958,Je 26,23:2
  Woman Obsessed 1959,My 28,34:1
  Earth Is Mine, The 1959,Je 27,13:1
  Beloved Infidel 1959,N 18,46:1
  Five Gates to Hell 1959,D 10,51:6
  Desire in the Dust 1960,O 12,47:2
  Fiercest Heart, The 1961,Ag 3,13:5
  Second Time Around, The 1961,D 23,16:1
  Naked Brigade, The 1965,Je 17,27:2
  Murder Game, The 1966,Mr 31,43:2
Scott, Lee
  Excuse my Dust 1951,Je 28,21:2
Scott, Leroy (Original Author)
  Partners of the Night 1920,Mr 1,16:2
  Flirting With Love 1924,S 1,9:1
  City That Never Sleeps, The 1924,S 29,10:1
  13 Washington Square 1928,Ja 30,18:1
  Lady of Chance, A 1929,Ja 14,20:1

Scott, Leslie
  Porgy and Bess 1959,Je 25,20:3
Scott, Linda
  Don't Knock the Twist 1962,Ap 14,14:2
Scott, Lizabeth
  Frightened Lady 1941,N 10,21:3
  You Came Along 1945,Jl 5,7:2
  Strange Love of Martha Ivers, The
    1946,Jl 25,18:4
  Dead Reckoning 1947,Ja 23,31:2
  Desert Fury 1947,S 25,35:4
  I Walk Alone 1948,Ja 22,36:3
  Pitfall 1948,Ag 25,31:2
  Too Late for Tears 1949,Ag 15,12:3
  Easy Living 1949,O 13,33:3
  Paid in Full 1950,F 16,28:2
  Dark City 1950,O 19,40:5
  Company She Keeps, The 1951,Ja 29,14:4
  Two of a Kind 1951,Je 30,8:6
  Racket, The 1951,D 13,44:2
  Red Mountain 1952,Ap 26,19:2
  Scared Stiff 1953,Jl 3,10:2
  Bad for Each Other 1953,D 24,9:3
  Silver Lode 1954,Jl 24,6:6
  Loving You 1957,Jl 18,19:2
Scott, Mabel Julienne
  Behold my Wife 1920,O 11,19:3
  Concert, The 1921,F 21,16:1
  Abysmal Brute, The 1923,Ap 18,24:5
  So This Is Marriage 1924,D 23,16:2
  Steele of the Royal Mounted 1925,Je 18,16:3
  Seven Days 1925,Ag 31,19:3
  Stranded in Paris 1926,D 13,27:1
  Mother 1927,My 4,29:2
Scott, Mansfield (Original Author)
  One Hour Before Dawn 1920,Jl 12,12:4
Scott, Margaretta
  Private Life of Don Juan, The 1934,D 10,16:2
  Things to Come 1936,Ap 18,19:2
  Return of the Scarlet Pimpernel, The
    1938,Ap 11,12:2
  Girl in the News, The 1941,My 5,13:2
  Quiet Wedding 1941,D 29,27:4
  Man From Morocco, The 1946,N 25,38:2
  Man of Evil 1948,Mr 26,26:2
  Mrs Fitzherbert 1950,My 11,37:2
  Where's Charley? 1952,Je 27,18:3
  Landfall 1953,My 11,25:2
  Devil's Plot 1953,Je 19,18:1
Scott, Martha
  Our Town 1940,Je 14,25:3
  Howards of Virginia, The 1940,S 27,27:1
  Cheers for Miss Bishop 1941,Mr 14,17:2
  They Dare not Love 1941,My 16,21:4
  One Foot in Heaven 1941,N 14,28:3
  Stage Door Canteen 1943,Je 25,13:2
  Hi Diddle Diddle 1943,S 24,26:2
  In old Oklahoma 1943,D 6,21:1
  So Well Remembered 1947,N 5,34:3
  Strange Bargain 1949,S 30,28:3
  Desperate Hours, The 1955,O 6,25:1
  Ten Commandments, The 1956,N 9,35:2
  Soyonara 1957,D 6,39:4
  Sayonara 1957,D 6,39:4
  Eighteen and Anxious 1957,D 14,16:6
  Ben Hur 1959,N 19,50:2
Scott, Nelson (Producer)
  Naked Heart, The 1955,Mr 9,22:4
Scott, Noel (Original Author)
  Ourselves Alone 1937,Jl 31,6:2
  River of Unrest 1937,N 27,21:2
Scott, Peter
  Tom Brown's School Days 1952,Ja 8,23:5
Scott, Pippa
  Auntie Mame 1958,D 5,39:1
  Petulia 1968,Je 11,54:4
Scott, Randolph
  Women Men Marry 1931,Jl 13,13:5
  Successful Calamity, A 1932,S 23,22:2
  Hot Saturday 1932,N 5,12:5
  Hello, Everybody 1933,Ja 30,9:4
  Heritage of the Desert 1933,Mr 11,18:3
  Murders in the Zoo 1933,Ap 3,13:4
  Supernatural 1933,Ap 22,16:3
  Cocktail Hour 1933,Je 5 18:5
  Broken Dreams 1933,N 21,23:3
  Last Round-Up, The 1934,My 10,25:2
  Wagon Wheels 1934,O 4,19:1
  Home on the Range 1935,F 13,24:4
  Roberta 1935,Mr 8,25:2
  She 1935,Jl 26,18:2
  So Red the Rose 1935,N 28,39:1
  Follow the Fleet 1936,F 21,21:2
  Sudden Death, And 1936,Jl 18,18:2
  Last of the Mohicans, The 1936,S 3,17:3
  Go West, Young Man 1936,N 19,31:3
  High, Wide and Handsome 1937,Jl 22,15:1
  Rebecca of Sunnybrook Farm 1938,Mr 26,12:1
  Texans, The 1938,Jl 28,23:2
  Road to Reno, The 1938,O 3,11:2
  Jesse James 1939,Ja 14,13:1
  Susannah of the Mounties 1939,Je 24,13:2
  Frontier Marshal 1939,Jl 29,18:2

Scott, Randolph— Cont
  20,000 Men a Year 1939,O 28,11:2
  My Favorite Wife 1940,My 31,15:2
  When the Daltons Rode 1940,Ag 23,13:3
  Western Union 1941,F 7,23:2
  Belle Starr 1941,N 1,20:2
  Paris Calling 1942,Ja 19,21:2
  To the Shores of Tripoli 1942,Mr 26,27:2
  Spoilers, The 1942,My 22,27:2
  Pittsburgh 1943,F 25,27:2
  Desperadoes, The 1943,My 13,17:2
  Bombardier 1943,Jl 2,15:2
  Corvette K-225 1943,O 21,30:1
  Gung Ho! 1944,Ja 26,23:2
  Belle of the Yukon 1945,Mr 30,18:4
  China Sky 1945,My 25,22:3
  Captain Kidd 1945,N 23,26:3
  Abilene Town 1946,Mr 4,16:5
  Badman's Territory 1946,My 31,27:2
  Home Sweet Homicide 1946,S 12,5:7
  Trail Street 1947,Ap 10,35:2
  Gunfighters 1947,Jl 25,12:5
  Christmas Eve 1947,N 28,30:2
  Albuquerque 1948,Mr 1,17:2
  Return of the Badmen 1948,Ag 5,16:2
  Canadian Pacific 1949,My 20,32:4
  Fighting Man of the Plains 1949,N 17,35:6
  Nevadan, The 1950,Ja 13,19:4
  Colt 45 1950,My 6,8:6
  Cariboo Trail, The 1950,S 1,17:2
  Sugarfoot 1951,F 12,19:4
  Santa Fe 1951,My 4,31:2
  Fort Worth 1951,Jl 13,12:7
  Starlift 1951,D 15,11:2
  Carson City 1952,Je 14,12:2
  Hangman's Knot 1952,D 11,45:3
  Stranger Wore a Gun, The 1953,Jl 30,20:3
  Thunder Over the Plains 1953,D 10,64:4
  Riding Shotgun 1954,Ap 2,22:2
  Ride the High Country 1962,Je 21,26:2
Scott, Raymond (Composer)
  Sally, Irene and Mary 1938,F 26,9:2
  Rebecca of Sunnybrook Farm 1938,Mr 26,12:1
Scott, Raymond (Miscellaneous)
  Ali Baba Goes to Town 1937,O 23,14:1
  Love and Hisses 1938,Ja 1,11:1
Scott, Raymond Quintet
  Ali Baba Goes to Town 1937,O 23,14:1
  Rebecca of Sunnybrook Farm 1938,Mr 26,12:1
Scott, Raymond, Quintet
  Love and Hisses 1938,Ja 1,11:1
  Happy Landing 1938,Ja 22,19:1
  Sally, Irene and Mary 1938,F 26,9:2
Scott, Rey (Miscellaneous)
  Kukan 1941,Je 24,17:2
Scott, Rey Capt (Cinematographer)
  Report From the Aleutians 1943,Jl 31,8:2
Scott, Robert
  One Mysterious Night 1944,O 21,15:3
  Crime Doctor's Courage, The 1945,Mr 3,11:3
  Gilda 1946,Mr 15,27:2
  Unknown, The 1946,Jl 20,10:3
Scott, Robert L Col (Original Author)
  God is my Co-Pilot 1945,Mr 24,22:6
Scott, Russell
  Eagle and the Hawk, The 1933,My 13,16:2
Scott, Sandra
  Incredible Journey, The 1963,N 21,43:2
Scott, Sherman (Director)
  Beasts of Berlin 1939,N 20,15:6
  She Shoulda Said No 1957,Ja 31,21:1
Scott, Simon
  Man of a Thousand Faces 1957,Ag 14,21:1
  Compulsion 1959,Ap 2,26:2
  Moon Pilot 1962,Ap 6,30:2
  Dead Heat on a Merry-Go-Round
    1966,O 13,50:1
Scott, Terry
  Murder Most Foul 1965,My 24,36:2
Scott, Thelma
  Rugged O'Riordans, The 1950,Ja 6,25:2
Scott, Treva
  High School Girl 1935,Mr 16,19:1
Scott, Wallace
  Tarzan and the Huntress 1947,Ap 7,20:4
  Vigilantes Return, The 1947,Jl 1,30:2
Scott, Walter Sir (Original Author)
  Richard the Lion-Hearted 1923,O 22,17:1
  King Richard and the Crusaders 1954,Ag 23,20:5
  Quentin Durward 1955,My 24,41:1
Scott, Will (Original Author)
  London by Night 1937,Ag 13,13:1
Scott, William
  Voice in the Dark, A 1921,Je 6,16:4
  Dante's Inferno 1924,S 30,27:3
  After Business Hour 1925,Je 17,16:2
  Light of the Western Stars, The 1925,Je 24,14:3
  Caught Plastered 1931,S 12,15:4
  Hotel Continental 1932,Mr 21,19:5
  Strangers of the Evening 1932,Je 4,9:2
  Last Mile, The 1932,Ag 26,20:3
Scott, Zachary
  Mask of Dimitrios, The 1944,Je 24,16:2
  Hollywood Canteen 1944,D 16,19:2

Scott, Zachary — Cont

Southerner, The 1945,Ag 27,22:3
Mildred Pierce 1945,S 29,12:2
Danger Signal 1945,N 22,39:2
Her Kind of Man 1946,My 4,10:6
Stallion Road 1947,Ap 5,12:5
Unfaithful, The 1947,Je 28,10:2
Cass Timberlane 1947,N 7,20:2
Ruthless 1948,S 4,8:7
Whiplash 1948,D 27,16:3
South of St Louis 1949,Mr 7,17:2
Flamingo Road 1949,My 7,10:2
One Last Fling 1949,Jl 1,14:6
Guilty Bystander 1950,Ap 21,18:2
Colt 45 1950,My 6,8:6
Shadow on the Wall 1950,My 19,31:3
Pretty Baby 1950,S 23,11:2
Born to be Bad 1950,S 29,31:5
Lightning Strikes Twice 1951,Ap 13,18:7
Secret of Convict Lake, The 1951,Ag 4,7:2
Let's Make It Legal 1951,N 7,35:3
Appointment in Honduras 1953,N 19,41:4
Flame of the Islands 1956,F 25,12:4
Young One, The 1961,Ja 19,26:1
It's Only Money 1962,N 22,43:1

Scottane, Lillane
Headless Ghost, The 1959,Ap 30,37:2

Scotti, Gino
Gioconda, La 1958,O 13,33:4

Scotti, Ottavio (Screenwriter)
Count of St Elmo, The 1953,Mr 14,13:2

Scotti, Tino
Before Him all Rome Trembled 1947,F 22,16:2
Anything for a Song 1947,Ag 5,26:2

Scotti, Tony
Valley of the Dolls 1967,D 16,51:1

Scotti, Vito
Where the Boys Are 1961,Ja 20,22:1
Captain Newman, MD 1964,F 21,36:1
Pleasure Seekers, The 1964,D 26,9:1
Von Ryan's Express 1965,Je 24,28:1
Blindfold 1966,My 26,55:2
Caper of the Golden Bulls, The 1967,Je 22,46:1
Secret War of Harry Frigg, The 1968,Mr 5,34:5
Head 1968,N 7,51:1

Scotto, Aubrey (Director)
$1,000 a Minute 1935,D 21,11:1
Ticket to Paradise 1936,Ag 8,5:3
Follow Your Heart 1936,O 22,31:1
Gambling Ship 1939,Ja 21,19:2
I Was a Convict 1939,Mr 23,27:2

Scotto, Giovanna
Coraggio Della Gioventu Mussoliniana, Il 1936,F 5,14:2

Scotto, Vincent
Ways of Love (Jofroi); Jofroi (Ways of Love) 1950,D 13,50:2

Scotto, Vincent (Composer)
Man of the Hour, The 1940,N 21,43:2
Pepe le Moko 1941,Mr 4,20:2

Scoular, Angela
Countess from Hong Kong, A 1967,Mr 17,35:1
Casino Royale 1967,Ap 29,25:1
Here We Go Around the Mulberry Bush 1968,Mr 5,34:5

Scourby, Alexander
With These Hands 1950,Je 16,28:4
Affair in Trinidad 1952,Jl 31,14:2
Because of You 1952,D 4,47:3
Redhead From Wyoming, The 1953,Ja 9,17:4
Glory Brigade, The 1953,Ag 15,8:4
Big Heat, The 1953,O 15,43:2
Silver Chalice, The 1954,D 27,22:5
Sign of the Pagan 1955,F 14,24:2
Ransom 1956,Ja 25,28:3
Giant 1956,O 11,51:1
Me and the Colonel 1958,Ag 27,33:1
Shaggy Dog, The 1959,Mr 20,26:2
Big Fisherman, The 1959,Ag 6,18:1
Seven Thieves 1960,Mr 12,14:5
Man on a String 1960,My 21,15:1
Devil at 4 O'Clock, The 1961,O 19,39:3

Scourby, Alexander (Narrator)
Victory at Sea 1954,Jl 14,33:2
China 1965,My 26,41:1

Scrano, Tecla
Alone in the Streets 1956,Je 28,33:2

Scraps, Aye
Big Red 1962,S 3,11:2

Scribe, Eugene (Original Author)
Devil May Care 1929,D 23,18:2

Scroggins, Bobbie
Woman in Question, The 1952,F 19,24:2

Scroggins, C E (Original Author)
Untamed 1929,N 30,23:1

Scruffy
It's in the Air 1940,D 10,33:2

Scruffy (Dog)
Storm in a Teacup 1938,Mr 22,18:4

Scullin, George (Miscellaneous)
Gunfight at the O K Corral 1957,My 30,23:2

Scully, Frank
All Through the Night 1942,Ja 24,13:2

Scully, Jean
Almost Angels 1962,N 1,34:2

Scutt, Avid
Master of Bankdam 1949,O 17,18:2

Seabrook, Edward E (Screenwriter)
Tanks a Million 1941,O 9,27:2
Fall In 1943,My 15,13:3
Abroad With two Yanks 1944,O 26,19:7
Here Comes Trouble 1948,Ap 15,31:4

Seabrook, Gay
Corsair 1931,N 19,27:5
Strictly Personal 1933,Mr 20,18:2
Half a Sinner 1934,Je 23,16:5
County Chairman, The 1935,Ja 19,8:1
Racketeers of the Range 1939,Je 8,31:4

Seabury, Forrest
Auction Block, The 1926,F 15,16:4
Ranson's Folly 1926,My 31,10:2

Seacombe, Dorothy
Yellow Mask, The 1930,D 8,26:1
Ware Case, The 1939,Jl 22,12:2

Seaforth, Susan
Billie 1965,S 16,55:3

Seagram, Lisa
House is not a Home, A 1964,S 2,33:1
Caprice 1967,Je 8,52:2

Seal, Elizabeth
Trouble in the Sky 1961,Jl 13,26:3

Seaman, Earl
Lawless Nineties, The 1936,Je 29,11:1

Seamark (Original Author)
Man they Couldn't Arrest, The 1933,Mr 14,19:3

Searl, Jackie
Tom Sawyer 1930,D 20,20:6
Finn and Hattie 1931,Ja 31,15:1
Skippy 1931,Ap 4,23:1
Daybreak 1931,Je 1,15:1
Newly Rich 1931,Jl 3,22:1
Huckleberry Finn 1931,Ag 8,16:3
Lovers Courageous 1932,F 20,11:2
Topaze 1933,F 10,12:2
High Gear 1933,Ap 15,16:2
World Changes, The 1933,O 27,22:3
Alice in Wonderland 1933,D 23,19:1
No Greater Glory 1934,My 5,22:2
Murder on the Blackboard 1934,Je 20,24:2
Peck's bad Boy 1934,O 6,20:1
Wicked Woman, A 1935,Ja 1,24:1
Ginger 1935,Jl 19,13:2
Little Lord Fauntleroy 1936,Ap 3,27:1
Gentle Julia 1936,Ap 11,19:1
Wild and Woolly 1937,S 6,20:1
Little Tough Guy 1938,Ag 18,23:3
That Certain Age 1938,N 5,15:2
Little Tough Guys in Society 1938,N 21,14:4
Angels Wash Their Faces 1939,S 4,16:2
Military Academy 1940,Ag 5,10:4
Paleface, The 1948,D 16,41:2

Searle, Francis (Director)
Girl in a Million, A 1950,Jl 24,15:2
Caretaker's Daughter, The 1953,Ag 20,18:5

Searle, Pamela
If a Man Answers 1962,N 22,43:1

Searle, Ronald (Original Author)
Belles of St Trinian's, The 1954,D 23,13:4
Blue Murder at St Trinian's 1958,My 27,27:1

Searles, Eddie
Phffft 1954,N 11,43:2

Searles, Jefferson
Delicate Delinquent, The 1957,Jl 4,16:1

Searls, Hank (Original Author)
Crowded Sky, The 1961,F 11,27:2
Countdown 1968,My 2,57:3

Sears, Allan
Judy of Rogues Harbor 1920,Mr 1,16:2
Long Live the King 1923,D 4,24:1
Secrets 1933,Mr 16,21:2

Sears, Ann
Bridge on the River Kwai 1957,D 19,39:1

Sears, Barbara
Sunday Dinner for a Soldier 1945,Ja 25,16:2
That Night With You 1945,N 9,16:2

Sears, Fred
Corpse came C O D, The 1947,Ag 19,27:2
Down to Earth 1947,S 12,18:2
Gallant Blade 1948,O 13,31:3

Sears, Fred (Director)
Mission Over Korea 1953,S 19,7:2
Chicago Syndicate 1955,Je 21,37:1
Inside Detroit 1956,Ja 28,10:5
Earth vs the Flying Saucers 1956,Ag 2,21:2
Don't Knock the Rock 1957,F 23,13:1

Sears, Heather
Story of Esther Costello, The 1957,N 6,43:1
Room at the Top 1959,Mr 31,26:1
Sons and Lovers 1960,Ag 3,35:1
Phantom of the Opera, The 1962,Ag 23,25:2

Sears, Ted (Original Author)
Three Caballeros, The 1945,F 5,20:1

Sears, Ted (Screenwriter)
Snow White and the Seven Dwarfs 1938,Ja 14,21:1 (In Addenda)
Pinocchio 1940,F 8,18:3

Sears, Ted (Screenwriter) — Cont
Reluctant Dragon, The 1941,Jl 25,12:2
So Dear to my Heart 1949,Ja 31,14:2
Adventures of Ichabod and Mr Toad, The 1949,O 10,18:2
Cinderella 1950,F 23,33:1
Living Desert, The 1953,N 10,38:1
Vanishing Prairie, The 1954,Ag 17,17:3
African Lion, The 1955,S 15,39:2

Sears, Zelda
Bishop Murder Case, The 1930,F 1,15:1
Divorcee, The 1930,My 10,25:3
Inspiration 1931,F 9,25:3
Wicked Woman, A 1935,Ja 1,24:1

Sears, Zelda (Original Author)
Politics 1931,Ag 1,16:4

Sears, Zelda (Screenwriter)
Rejuvenation of Aunt Mary, The 1927,Jl 27,27:4
Wicked Woman, A 1935,Ja 1,24:1

Sears, Ziggy
Safe at Home 1941,N 26,31:2

Seastrom, Dorothy
It Must Be Love 1926,O 4,20:2

Seastrom, Victor
Man There Was, A 1920,Ap 26,18:1
Stroke of Midnight, The 1922,Je 5,16:2
John Ericsson Victor of Hampton Roads 1938,My 18,17:2
I Am With You 1949,Mr 1,30:5

Seastrom, Victor (Director)
Man There Was, A 1920,Ap 26,18:1
Stroke of Midnight, The 1922,Je 5,16:2
Name the Man 1924,F 4,23:3
He Who Gets Slapped 1924,N 10,20:1
Confessions of a Queen 1925,Mr 24,20:6
Scarlet Letter, The 1926,Ag 10,19:2
Divine Woman, The 1928,Ja 16,24:1
Wind, The 1928,N 5,26:1
Masks of the Devil, The 1928,N 26,30:2
Lady to Love, A 1930,Mr 1,23:1
Charles XII 1933,Mr 31,23:3

Seastrom, Victor (Screenwriter)
Stroke of Midnight, The 1922,Je 5,16:2

Seastrom, Victor (Sjorstrom)
Wild Strawberries 1959,Je 23,37:1

Seaton, Arthur
Ghost Goes West, The 1936,Ja 11,9:2
Storm in a Teacup 1938,Mr 22,18:4

Seaton, George (Director)
Billy Rose's Diamond Horseshoe 1945,My 3,37:1
Junior Miss 1945,Je 18,15:4
Shocking Miss Pilgrim, The 1947,F 12,34:2
Miracle on 34th Street 1947,Je 5,32:1
Apartment for Peggy 1948,O 16,9:2
Chicken every Sunday 1949,Ja 19,34:2
Big Lift, The 1950,Ap 27,37:2
For Heaven's Sake 1950,D 16,10:5
Anything Can Happen 1952,Ap 4,21:1
Country Girl, The 1954,D 16,51:2
Proud and Profane, The 1956,Je 14,41:2
Williamsburg: The Story of a Patriot 1957,Ap 1,22:2
Teacher's Pet 1958,Mr 20,33:1
Pleasure of his Company, The 1961,Je 2,36:1
Counterfeit Traitor, The 1962,Ap 18,28:1
Hook, The 1963,F 16,5:6
36 Hours 1965,Ja 29,25:2
What's so bad About Feeling Good? 1968,My 25,27:1

Seaton, George (Original Author)
Student Tour 1934,O 31,17:3
Winning Ticket, The 1935,F 11,14:2
Day at the Races, A 1937,Je 18,25:2
Cockeyed Miracle, The 1946,O 25,28:1

Seaton, George (Producer)
Rhubarb 1951,Ag 31,12:2
Aaron Slick From Punkin Crick 1952,Ap 19,18:6
Somebody Loves Me 1952,S 25,38:1
Bridges at Toko-Ri, The 1955,Ja 21,20:2
Tin Star, The 1957,O 24,37:2
But Not for Me 1959,O 3,14:6
Rat Race, The 1960,My 26,37:3
Twilight of Honor 1963,N 14,41:2
36 Hours 1965,Ja 29,25:2
What's so bad About Feeling Good? 1968,My 25,27:1

Seaton, George (Screenwriter)
Day at the Races, A 1937,Je 18,25:2
Doctor Takes a Wife, The 1940,Je 15,12:2
This Thing Called Love 1941,F 14,15:2
That Night in Rio 1941,Mr 10,21:2
Moon Over Miami 1941,Jl 5,14:2
Charley's Aunt 1941,Ag 2,18:2
Ten Gentlemen From West Point 1942,Je 5,23:3
Magnificent Dope, The 1942,Jl 3,12:5
Meanest Man in the World, The 1943,F 25,27:3
Coney Island 1943,Je 17,17:2
Song of Bernadette, The 1944,Ja 27,15:2
Eve of St Mark, The 1944,My 31,22:2
Billy Rose's Diamond Horseshoe 1945,My 3,37:1
Junior Miss 1945,Je 18,15:4
Shocking Miss Pilgrim, The 1947,F 12,34:2
Miracle on 34th Street 1947,Je 5,32:1
Apartment for Peggy 1948,O 16,9:2

Seaton, George (Screenwriter)— Cont

Chicken every Sunday 1949,Ja 19,34:2
Big Lift, The 1950,Ap 27,37:2
For Heaven's Sake 1950,D 16,10:5
Anything Can Happen 1952,Ap 4,21:1
Little Boy Lost 1953,S 22,38:2
Country Girl, The 1954,D 16,51:2
Proud and Profane, The 1956,Je 14,41:2
Counterfeit Traitor, The 1962,Ap 18,28:1
36 Hours 1965,Ja 29,25:2
What's so bad About Feeling Good?
  1968,My 25,27:1

Seay, Billy

My Man 1928,D 22,14:3
Marriage Playground, The 1929,D 14,22:4

Seay, James

Women Without Names 1940,My 9,26:4
Queen of the Mob 1940,Jl 1,23:2
Golden Gloves 1940,Ag 21,23:6
Son of Monte Cristo, The 1940,D 5,33:1
Face Behind the Mask, The 1941,F 7,23:2
Kid From Kansas, The 1941,D 2,29:4
Enemy Agents meet Ellery Queen
  1942,Ag 22,16:2
Time to Kill 1942,D 25,15:4
Miracle on 34th Street 1947,Je 5,32:1
Secret Beyond the Door 1948,Ja 16,25:4
Innocent Affair, An 1948,S 29,36:2
Red Canyon 1949,Ap 28,28:2
Union Station 1950,O 5,38:3
Flying Missile, The 1950,D 25,25:1
Day the Earth Stood Still, The 1951,S 19,37:1
Models, Inc 1952,My 26,18:4
Fort Ti 1953,My 30,7:1
Vera Cruz 1954,D 27,22:4
Amazing Colossal Man, The 1957,O 26,19:2
Buccaneer, The 1958,D 24,00:0

Sebalt, Maria

Captain from Koepenick, The 1958,Jl 26,6:1
Affairs of Julie, The 1958,D 10,53:1
Gypsy Baron, The 1959,N 14,13:1

Sebanek, Josef

Loves of a Blonde 1966,S 13,51:2
Loves of a Blonde 1966,O 27,55:1
Firemen's Ball, The 1968,S 30,60:1

Sebaroff, Robert (Screenwriter)

Split, The 1968,N 5,55:2

Sebastian, Dorothy

Sackcloth and Scarlet 1925,Mr 25,24:2
Winds of Chance 1925,Ag 17,10:3
Bluebeard's Seven Wives 1925,D 28,19:2
You'd Be Surprised 1926,S 27,27:3
Tea For Three 1927,O 31,22:1
Haunted Ship, The 1928,Ja 23,18:3
Our Dancing Daughters 1928,O 8,14:2
Woman of Affairs, A 1929,Ja 21,18:4
Spite Marriage 1929,Mr 25,32:2
Single Standard, The 1929,Jl 29,23:3
Unholy Night, The 1929,O 12,11:1
His First Command 1929,D 23,18:2
Officer O'Brien 1930,F 24,18:1
Montana Moon 1930,Ap 14,24:2
Free and Easy 1930,Ap 19,15:1
Hell's Island 1930,Jl 19,7:5
Our Blushing Brides 1930,Ag 2,16:4
Brothers 1930,N 15,15:3
Big Gamble, The 1931,S 21,20:2
Deceiver, The 1931,N 23,22:1
They Never Come Back 1932,Je 4,9:2

Sebastian, John

Cry Tough 1959,S 17,48:4

Sebellus, Johanna (Screenwriter)

Arms and the Man 1962,F 24,21:7

Seberg, Jean

Saint Joan 1957,Je 27,21:1
Bonjour Tristesse 1958,Ja 16,32:1
Mouse That Roared, The 1959,O 27,40:1
Let no Man Write my Epitaph 1960,N 11,36:2
Breathless 1961,F 8,26:1
Five Day Lover, The 1961,D 14,55:4
Playtime; Receation, La 1963,Ja 16,5:2
Time Out for Love 1963,Ap 23,31:2
In the French Style 1963,S 19,23:1
Lilith 1964,S 21,37:2
Backfire 1965,Ap 27,27:1
Moment to Moment 1966,Mr 3,28:1
Fine Madness, A 1966,Je 30,28:2
Birds in Peru 1968,N 7,51:2

Seccia, Cesare (Screenwriter)

Colossus of Rhodes, The 1961,D 14,55:6

Seck, Abdoula

Comedians, The 1967,N 1,37:1
Seventh Continent, The 1968,Jl 30,33:2

Secombe, Harry

Svengali 1955,S 26,18:2
Oliver! 1968,D 11,57:1

Secondari, John H (Original Author)

Three Coins in the Fountain 1954,My 21,18:2
Pleasure Seekers, The 1964,D 26,9:1

Secter, David (Director)

Winter Kept Us Warm 1968,F 9,55:3

Secter, David (Producer)

Winter Kept Us Warm 1968,F 9,55:3

Secter, David (Screenwriter)

Winter Kept Us Warm 1968,F 9,55:3

Secunda, Sholem (Composer)

Tevya 1939,D 22,15:3

Sedan, Rolfe

Sporting Youth 1924,Ap 2,16:1
Iron Mask, The 1929,F 22,18:6
Love Me Tonight 1932,Ag 19,20:6
All the King's Horses 1935,Mr 9,19:1
$1,000 a Minute 1935,D 21,11:1
Anything Goes 1936,F 6,23:3
Bluebeard's Eighth Wife 1938,Mr 24,21:2
Stolen Heaven 1938,My 12,27:2
Story of Vernon and Irene Castle, The
  1939,Mr 31,19:2
Ninotchka 1939,N 10,27:2
Everything Happens at Night 1939,D 16,12:6
I Was an Adventuress 1940,My 20,13:2
Law of the Tropics 1941,O 10,26:5
Phantom of the Rue Morgue 1954,Mr 20,10:5

Seddon, Jack (Screenwriter)

Count Five and Die 1958,My 15,25:1
Murder She Said 1962,Ja 8,27:2
Kill or Cure 1962,N 13,43:4
Murder at the Gallop 1963,Je 25,23:2
Murder Ahoy 1964,S 23,55:3
Murder Most Foul 1965,My 24,36:2
Blue Max, The 1966,Je 22,38:1
Alphabet Murders, The 1966,Jl 12,36:2

Seddon, Margaret

Inside of the Cup, The 1921,Ja 16,VI,2:1 (In Addenda)
Case of Becky, The 1921,O 10,16:1
Bright Shawl, The 1923,Ap 23,18:3
Little Johnny Jones 1923,Ag 13,16:1
Through the Dark 1924,Ja 8,27:1
Confidence Man, The 1924,Ap 15,24:1
Women Who Give 1924,Je 3,22:1
Snob, The 1924,D 15,14:1
Lady, The 1925,Ja 27,11:2
New Lives for Old 1925,F 25,16:7
Proud Flesh 1925,Ap 14,26:1
Midshipman, The 1925,O 13,20:1
Golden Cocoon, The 1925,D 15,14:5
Rolling Home 1926,Je 8,22:1
Matinee Ladies 1927,Ap 13,29:4
Quality Street 1927,N 2,24:5
Home Made 1927,D 13,33:2
Silk Legs 1927,D 26,26:6
Gentlemen Prefer Blondes 1928,Ja 16,24:1
Actress, The 1928,Jl 9,25:1
Bellamy Trial, The 1929,Ja 24,30:5
She Goes to War 1929,Je 10,23:1
Dance Hall 1929,D 16,34:2
Divorce Among Friends 1931,Ap 2,30:4
Smilin' Through 1932,O 15,13:1
Broadway Bad 1933,Mr 6,16:6
Lilly Turner 1933,Je 15,21:2
Walls of Gold 1933,O 21,11:3
Midshipman Jack 1933,N 20,18:2
Worst Woman in Paris, The 1933,N 25,10:3
Flame Within, The 1935,Je 1,18:2
Girl Friend, The 1935,S 28,12:2
Mr Deeds Goes to Town 1936,Ap 17,17:2
Big Game, The 1936,O 24,23:1
Woman Rebels, A 1936,O 30,27:2
Danger-Love at Work 1937,D 11,22:2
Raffles 1940,Ja 13,11:2
Dr Kildare's Strange Case 1940,Ap 12,19:2
Meanest Man in the World, The 1943,F 25,27:3
House by the River 1950,My 2,25:2

Sedgwick, Anne Douglas (Original Author)

Little French Girl, The 1925,Je 1,10:3

Sedgwick, Charles

Charge of the Light Brigade, The 1936,N 2,24:1

Sedgwick, Ed

Checkers 1919,Ag 25,8:5

Sedgwick, Edna

You're a Sweetheart 1937,D 25,10:5

Sedgwick, Edward (Director)

Flaming Frontier, The 1926,Ap 5,24:1
Tin Hats 1926,N 29,16:3
Slide, Kelly, Slide 1927,Mr 23,19:2
Spring Fever 1927,O 18,33:2
West Point 1928,Ja 2,28:1
Circus Rookies 1928,My 14,25:1
Cameraman, The 1928,S 17,27:1
Spite Marriage 1929,Mr 25,32:2
Free and Easy 1930,Ap 19,15:1
Dough Boys 1930,S 30,23:1
Parlor, Bedroom and Bath 1931,Ap 4,23:1
Dangerous Affair, A 1931,N 23,22:1
Maker of Men 1931,D 19,16:4
Passionate Plumber, The 1932,Mr 12,19:5
Speak Easily 1932,Ag 19,20:6
What! No Beer? 1933,F 11,11:3
Saturday's Millions 1933,O 14,18:3
I'll Tell the World 1934,Ap 21,12:2
Here Comes the Groom 1934,Je 16,20:2
Death on the Diamond 1934,S 24,14:1
Murder in the Fleet 1935,Je 3,22:2
Pick a Star 1937,My 28,17:2
Riding on Air 1937,Je 26,20:2 (In Addenda)

Sedgwick, Edward (Director)— Cont

Fit for a King 1937,O 15,18:5
Gladiator, The 1938,Ag 29,10:2
Beware, Spooks 1939,N 3,17:4
So You Won't Talk 1940,O 17,33:2
Air Raid Wardens 1943,Ap 5,15:5
Southern Yankee, A 1948,N 25,47:2
Ma and Pa Kettle Back on the Farm
  1951,My 11,32:3

Sedgwick, Edward (Original Author)

Maker of Men 1931,D 19,16:4

Sedgwick, Edward (Screenwriter)

Flaming Frontier, The 1926,Ap 5,24:1
Murder in the Fleet 1935,Je 3,22:2

Sedgwick, Josei

Daddy 1923,Ap 16,20:2

Sedgwick, Josie

White Moth, The 1924,Je 16,18:3

Sedgwick, Russell

If Winter Comes 1923,S 4,14:1

Sedillo, Juan

Girl from Havana, The 1929,S 2,16:1

Sedky, Lola

Little Miss Devil 1951,D 8,9:2

Sedlacek, Jiri

Fidlovacka 1931,Jl 7,27:5

Sedlacek, O (Producer)

Thunder in the Hills 1947,My 24,10:5

Sedlak, Karlheinz

Jugend von Heute; Youth of Today
  1938,N 5,15:3

Sedley, Henry

Fool, The 1925,Ap 13,24:1
Blonde or Brunette 1927,Ja 11,18:2
Racket, The 1928,Jl 9,25:1
Ghost Talks, The 1929,F 18,28:1
Cockeyed Cavaliers 1934,Jl 25,22:2

Seeberg, Eva (Screenwriter)

Doll, The 1964,Ja 14,27:1

Seeberg, Peter (Screenwriter)

Hunger 1968,Ag 13,45:2

Seebohm, Allison

Murder Most Foul 1965,My 24,36:2

Seeboonreaung, Vilaiwan

Bridge on the River Kwai 1957,D 19,39:1

Seeck, Adelheid

Rest Is Silence, The 1960,Ag 2,22:6

Seegar, Miriam

Fashions in Love 1929,Jl 1,31:2
Love Doctor, The 1929,N 9,22:5
Seven Keys to Baldpate 1929,D 26,21:1
Clancy in Wall Street 1930,My 3,23:1
New Movietone Follies of 1930, The
  1930,Je 21,20:5
What a Man 1930,Jl 21,20:3
Big Money 1930,N 22,21:3
Woman Between, The 1931,O 24,20:3
Famous Ferguson Case, The 1932,Ap 25,18:6
Strangers of the Evening 1932,Je 4,9:2
False Faces 1932,N 25,19:2

Seegar, Sanford

Uncle Vanya 1958,Ap 29,26:2
Never Steal Anything Small 1959,F 12,23:1

Seegar, Sara

Dead Men Tell no Tales 1939,Jl 24,9:2

Seeger, Mike

Festival 1967,O 24,53:2

Seeger, Pete

Inheritance, The 1964,N 9,42:2
Festival 1967,O 24,53:2

Seel, Charles

Not Wanted 1949,Jl 25,11:4
Lady in a Cage 1964,Je 11,27:1
Mister Buddwing 1966,O 12,36:1

Seelen, Jerry (Composer)

Call Me Mister 1951,F 1,21:2
Lullaby of Broadway 1951,Mr 27,35:2
Jazz Singer, The 1953,Ja 14,27:3

SEELEY

See Also SEELY

Seeley, Blossom

Broadway Thru a Keyhole 1933,N 2,18:3

Seeley, Blossom (Miscellaneous)

Somebody Loves Me 1952,S 25,38:1

Seeley, Clinton (Original Author)

Storm Fear 1955,D 17,19:2

Seeley, Kay

Stolen Life 1939,Je 15,27:2
Continental Express 1942,Ap 7,26:3

Seeley, S K (Director)

Blonde Savage 1947,O 4,9:2
Amazon Quest 1949,My 14,9:3

SEELY

See Also SEELEY

Seely, Tim

Poacher's Daughter, The 1960,F 16,31:2
Please Turn Over 1961,Ap 29,12:2
Mutiny on the Bounty 1962,N 9,31:2

Seestrom, Victor (Director)

Under the Red Robe 1937,Je 1,27:2

Seff, Jo

Der Falsche Feldmarschall 1932,Je 30,26:2

Seff, Manuel (Miscellaneous)
Night at the Ritz, A 1935,My 16,20:2
Seff, Manuel (Original Author)
Blessed Event 1932,S 3,16:2
College Coach 1933,N 11,10:4
Bedside 1934,Mr 7,23:4
Slightly Tempted 1940,N 1,33:1
Married Bachelor 1941,O 16,25:3
Walk Softly Stranger 1950,O 16,30:5
Seff, Manuel (Screenwriter)
Footlight Parade 1933,O 6,21:3
Kansas City Princess 1934,N 5,23:1
Gold Diggers of 1935 1935,Mr 15,25:2
Traveling Saleslady 1935,Mr 29,26:2
Red Salute 1935,S 30,13:1
Three Godfathers, The 1936,Mr 9,20:2
Trouble for Two 1936,My 30,7:2
Love on the Run 1936,N 28,13:3
Espionage 1937,Mr 9,27:3
Breaking the Ice 1938,S 23,35:3
Jam Session 1944,My 3,25:3
Seffertitz, Gustav von
Flower of the Night 1925,O 19,26:1
Sparrows 1926,S 20,21:3
Sefton, Ernest
Broken Blossoms 1937,Ja 14,16:3
SEGAL
See Also SEGALL, SIEGAL, SIGAL
Segal, Alex (Director)
Ransom 1956,Ja 25,28:3
All the Way Home 1963,O 30,46:1
Harlow 1965,My 15,18:1
Joy in the Morning 1965,Je 10,38:1
Segal, D
Lonely White Sail 1938,My 7,18:1
University of Life 1941,F 26,17:1
Tel Aviv Taxi 1956,D 31,10:7
Segal, Erich (Screenwriter)
Yellow Submarine 1968,N 14,56:1
Segal, George
Act One 1963,D 27,17:2
New Interns, The 1964,Ag 20,34:2
Invitation to a Gunfighter 1964,O 28,51:3
Ship of Fools 1965,Jl 29,18:1
King Rat 1965,O 28,48:1
Who's Afraid of Virginia Woolf? 1966,Je 30,28:1
Who's Afraid of Virginia Woolf? 1966,Jl 10,II,1:5
Lost Command 1966,S 15,51:1
Quiller Memorandum, The 1966,D 16,59:1
St Valentine's Day Massacre, The 1967,Jl 27,29:2
Bye Bye Braverman 1968,F 22,36:1
No Way to Treat a Lady 1968,Mr 21,56:1
Unstrap Me 1968,N 21,41:2
Segal, Gilles
Topkapi 1964,S 18,25:1
Segal, Helen
Unstrap Me 1968,N 21,41:2
Segal, Jeffrey
Traitors, The 1963,Je 27,23:4
Segal, Vivienne
Song of the West 1930,F 28,20:7
Bride of the Regiment 1930,My 22,32:6
Golden Dawn 1930,Jl 26,16:4
Viennese Nights 1930,N 27,32:5
Cat and the Fiddle, The 1934,F 17,20:2
SEGALL
See Also SIEGAL, SIGEL, SEGAL
Segall, Colette
Poil de Carotte 1933,My 26,24:2
Segall, Harry (Miscellaneous)
Wife Takes a Flyer, The 1942,Je 19,19:1
Segall, Harry (Original Author)
Fatal Lady 1936,Jl 11,11:3
Super-Sleuth 1937,Jl 17,18:1
Here Comes Mr Jordan 1941,Ag 8,13:2
Bride Wore Boots, The 1946,Je 6,16:3
Angel on my Shoulder 1946,O 21,27:2
For Heaven's Sake 1950,D 16,10:5
Monkey Business 1952,S 6,12:6
Segall, Harry (Screenwriter)
Don't Turn 'em Loose 1936,S 25,20:2
Outcasts of Poker Flat, The 1937,Ap 27,18:3
There Goes my Girl 1937,Je 12,8:2
Fight for Your Lady 1937,N 20,21:2
She's Got Everything 1938,Ja 14,21:3
Blind Alibi 1938,My 20,17:2
Coast Guard 1939,Ag 28,17:2
Lone Wolf Strikes, The 1940,F 5,13:2
She Knew All the Answers 1941,Je 20,28:4
Two Yanks in Trinidad 1942,Ap 6,19:4
Powers Girl, The 1943,Mr 26,14:2 (In Addenda)
Angel on my Shoulder 1946,O 21,27:2
Segar, Lucia
Knockout Reilly 1927,Ap 18,21:2
Boomerang 1947,Mr 6,36:2
Segard, Raymond
32 Rue de Montmartre 1944,S 28,26:3
Segarra, Conseulo
Tigre de Yautepec, El 1934,O 20,20:3
Segarra, Estella
No Mataras; Thou Shalt not Kill 1935,N 11,20:2

Seghers, Anna (Original Author)
Seventh Cross, The 1944,S 29,18:1
Segnitz, Paul (Composer)
Slipper Episode, The 1938,My 19,25:2
Segovia, Rosita
Neapolitan Carousel 1961,O 12,41:3
Segri, Aldo (Screenwriter)
Nights of Lucretia Borgia, The 1960,O 6,51:4
Segueiro, Adela
Mujer de Nadie, La; Nobody's Wife 1938,F 7,10:3
Segui, Mario (Director)
Cobra, The 1968,Mr 28,52:3
Segura, Antonio
Morena Clara 1938,Je 18,18:3
Segurini, Antonio
Story of Joseph and his Brethern, The 1962,D 1,17:1
Seibalova, Jirina
Sweet Light in a Dark Room 1966,Je 30,28:1
Seickard, Joseph
Playing With Souls 1925,Ap 20,18:1 (Incorrect in this edition; use 1925,Ap 28,18:1 elsewhere)
Seidel, Louise
Forty Little Mothers 1940,Ap 19,25:2
Seidel, Tom
20,000 Men a Year 1939,O 28,11:2
Tahiti Honey 1943,My 13,17:2
Seiden, Joseph (Director)
My Son 1939,My 10,28:2
Motel, The Operator 1940,Ja 16,19:3
Seiden, Joseph (Producer)
Motel, The Operator 1940,Ja 16,19:3
Seidl, Lea
I Am a Camera 1955,Ag 9,29:1
War and Peace 1956,Ag 22,26:2
I Aim at the Stars 1960,O 20,42:2
Seidman, Arie
Hill 24 Doesn't Answer 1955,N 3,37:1
Seidner, Irene
We Who Are Young 1940,S 13,27:2
All Through the Night 1942,Ja 24,13:2
Miracle in the Rain 1956,Ap 2,18:1
Seidowsky, Marian
Young Torless 1967,S 25,56:2
Young Torless 1968,Jl 23,27:2
Seige, Kurt;Greco, Mary
General Della Rovere 1960,N 22,41:1
Seigner, Louis
Entente Cordiale 1939,D 26,23:2
S O S Mediterranean 1940,Ja 1,29:2
Lover's Return, A; Revenant, Le 1948,Ja 26,15:2
Corbeau, Le; Raven, The 1948,F 24,21:1
Homme a Hommes D' 1948,Ag 30,14:8
Eternal Husband, The 1949,Ja 10,19:2
Man to Men 1949,F 21,20:2
Vautrin, the Thief 1949,N 11,31:2
Angels of the Streets 1950,Ja 17,24:2
Miquette 1951,F 5,18:2
Seven Deadly Sins (Pride); Pride (The Seven Deadly Sins) 1953,My 12,31:3
Holiday for Henrietta 1955,Ja 25,21:1
Adorable Creatures 1956,Ja 11,36:2
Sins of the Borgias 1956,Mr 5,21:1
We Are all Murderers 1957,Ja 9,27:2
Foxiest Girl in Paris 1958,S 20,10:6
Possessors, The 1959,Jl 21,24:1
Paris Hotel 1959,S 12,12:3
Would-Be Gentleman, The 1960,Mr 23,31:1
Truth, The 1961,Je 27,23:2
Eclipse 1962,D 21,5:1
Marriage of Figaro, The 1963,Ap 30,26:1
This Special Friendship 1967,N 8,56:1
Seigneuret, Michele
Belles and Ballets 1960,N 15,45:3
Seiler, Conrad (Miscellaneous)
Scorched Earth 1942,S 12,9:2
Seiler, Friedel
William Tell 1925,My 20,26:2
Seiler, Lewis (Director)
Last Trail, The 1927,Ja 26,17:1
Air Circus, The 1928,S 3,14:2
Ghost Talks, The 1929,F 18,28:1
Girls Gone Wild 1929,Ap 22,23:1
No Greater Love 1932,My 14,11:5
Deception 1933,Ja 10,26:2
Ley Del Haren, La 1933,Je 17,16:7
Frontier Marshal 1934,Ja 31,20:3
Charlie Chan in Paris 1935,Ja 22,23:2
Asegure a su Mujer; Insure Your Wife 1935,Mr 12,25:3
Ginger 1935,Jl 19,13:2
Paddy O'Day 1936,F 8,19:2
Star for a Night 1936,S 5,7:2
Turn off the Moon 1937,My 20,17:2
Crime School 1938,My 11,17:2
Heart of the North 1938,D 21,29:2
King of the Underworld 1939,Ja 7,6:2
You Can't Get Away With Murder 1939,Mr 25,19:2
Kid From Kokomo, The 1939,My 20,11:2
Hell's Kitchen 1939,Jl 3,10:5
Dust Be my Destiny 1939,O 7,11:2

Seiler, Lewis (Director)— Cont
It all Came True 1940,Ap 6,13:2
Flight Angels 1940,My 27,23:2
Murder in the Air 1940,Jl 4,12:2
Tugboat Annie Sails Again 1940,N 9,20:2
South of Suez 1940,D 19,33:2
Smiling Ghost, The 1941,S 26,26:5
You're in the Army Now 1941,D 26,21:4
Big Shot, The 1942,Jl 18,8:2
Pittsburgh 1943,F 25,27:2
Guadalcanal Diary 1943,N 18,29:1
Something for the Boys 1944,N 30,19:1
Molly and Me 1945,My 26,18:2
Doll Face 1946,Mr 28,35:3
If I'm Lucky 1946,S 20,41:3
Whiplash 1948,D 27,16:3
Breakthrough 1950,N 18,10:2
Tanks are Coming, The 1951,D 6,42:4
Winning Team, The 1952,Je 21,12:2
Operation Secret 1952,N 6,37:2
System, The 1953,My 23,19:3
Women's Prison 1955,F 3,18:5
Seilers, Heinrich (Original Author)
Hippodrome 1962,Mr 12,36:1
Seilinger, Carol
Johnny Tiger 1966,Je 16,53:4
Seinati, Bella
Foria 1948,Ja 21,30:2
Seingalt, Giovanni Jacobo Casanova de (Original /Author)
Avventura di Giacomo Casanova 1938,D 2,27:3
Seirgaakar, Bal
Bwana Devil 1953,F 19,20:5
Seiter, Bob
Out all Night 1927,S 27,31:1
Chicago After Midnight 1928,Mr 6,20:3
Seiter, Robert
Red Lips 1928,O 16,29:2 (In Addenda)
Seiter, William A (Director)
Beautiful and Damned, The 1922,D 11,22:1
Daddies 1924,F 11,18:3
Fast Worker, The 1924,N 12,13:1
Dangerous Innocence 1925,Je 8,19:1
Teaser, The 1925,Je 15,10:1
Mad Whirl, The 1925,Jl 1,16:1
Where Was I 1925,Ag 19,14:4
What Happened to Jones 1926,F 9,22:1
Skinner's Dress Suit 1926,My 3,27:1
Rolling Home 1926,Je 8,22:1
Take It From Me 1926,N 2,35:1
Cheerful Fraud, The 1926,D 28,17:1
Out all Night 1927,S 27,31:1
Thanks For The Buggy Ride 1928,Ja 23,18:3
Waterfront 1928,O 22,29:1
Synthetic Sin 1929,Ja 7,36:2
Why Be Good? 1929,My 6,30:4
Footlights and Fools 1929,N 9,22:5
Strictly Modern 1930,My 3,23:1
Back Pay 1930,My 31,19:4
Flirting Widow, The 1930,Ag 2,16:4
Truth About Youth, The 1930,D 13,22:2
Sunny 1930,D 27,16:3
Kiss Me Again 1931,Ja 8,21:4
Going Wild 1931,Ja 26,21:1
Big Business Girl 1931,Je 12,27:1
Too Many Cooks 1931,Ag 17,18:2
Caught Plastered 1931,S 12,15:4
Peach O'Reno 1931,D 24,20:8
Way Back Home 1932,Ja 16,13:1
Girl Crazy 1932,Mr 25,23:3
Love Starved 1932,Ap 15,23:1
Is my Face red 1932,Je 11,9:3
Hot Saturday 1932,N 5,12:5
If I Had a Million 1932,D 3,21:4
Hello, Everybody 1933,Ja 30,9:4
Diplomaniacs 1933,Ap 29,14:2
Professional Sweetheart 1933,Jl 14,15:3
Chance at Heaven 1933,D 26,19:3
Sons of the Desert 1934,Ja 12,29:3
Sing and Like It 1934,Ap 14,18:2
We're Rich Again 1934,S 1,16:3
Richest Girl in the World, The 1934,S 21,29:2
Roberta 1935,Mr 8,25:2
Daring Young Man, The 1935,Jl 18,15:2
Orchids to You 1935,Ag 10,16:4
In Person 1935,D 13,31:5
If You Could Only Cook 1935,D 26,21:4
Moon's our Home, The 1936,My 13,29:2
Case Against Mrs Ames, The 1936,My 28,19:2
Dimples 1936,O 10,21:2
Stowaway 1936,D 19,16:1
This Is my Affair 1937,My 28,17:1
Life of the Party, The 1937,O 4,17:1
Life Begins In College 1937,O 9,16:1
Sally, Irene and Mary 1938,F 26,9:2
Three Blind Mice 1938,Je 18,18:2
Room Service 1938,S 22,27:1
Thanks For Everything 1938,D 10,13:2
Susannah of the Mounties 1939,Je 24,13:2
Allegheny Uprising 1939,N 10,27:3
It's a Date 1940,Mr 23,16:2
Hired Wife 1940,S 14,11:2
Nice Girl 1941,Mr 27,29:6
Appointment for Love 1941,N 7,27:1

Seiter, William A (Director) — Cont
Broadway 1942,Je 5,23:2
You Were Never Lovelier 1942,D 4,31:1
Destroyer 1943,S 2,15:3
Lady Takes a Chance, A 1943,S 16,25:2
Four Jills in a Jeep 1944,Ap 6,27:2
Affairs of Susan, The 1945,Mr 29,18:2
Belle of the Yukon 1945,Mr 30,18:4
It's a Pleasure 1945,My 4,23:3
That Night With You 1945,N 9,16:2
Little Giant 1946,My 9,27:5
Lover Come Back 1946,Je 20,20:3
I'll Be Yours 1947,F 22,16:2
Up in Central Park 1948,My 27,29:3
One Touch of Venus 1948,O 29,29:5
Borderline 1950,Mr 6,17:2
Dear Brat 1951,Jl 5,21:2
Lady Wants Mink, The 1953,Ap 6,24:2
Make Haste to Live 1954,Mr 26,16:2
Seiter, William A (Producer)
Hired Wife 1940,S 14,11:2
Belle of the Yukon 1945,Mr 30,18:4
Make Haste to Live 1954,Mr 26,16:2
Seitz, Anny
Gewitter im Mai; Storms in May 1938,Mr 5,11:3
Seitz, Chris
Come September 1961,S 8,34:1
Seitz, Dran
I, The Jury 1953,Ag 22,8:2
Seitz, Franz (Director)
Meisterdetektiv, Der 1934,F 13,23:2
Die Blonde Christl 1934,F 23,23:3
Die Mutter der Kompagnie 1934,Mr 9,22:3
S A Mann Brand 1934,My 28,16:2
Mit dir Durch Dick und Duenn 1934,N 24,19:2
Bei der Blonden Kathrein 1934,D 3,15:2
Frauen vom Tannhof, Die 1936,F 18,27:1
Grobe Adele, Die 1937,My 15,23:5
Kampf mit dem Drachen, Der; Fight With the Dragon, The 1939,N 6,20:3
1A in Oberbayern; 1A in Upper Bavaria 1939,N 18,22:6
Seitz, Franz (Producer)
Young Torless 1967,S 25,56:2
Seitz, Franz (Screenwriter)
Schuetzen Koenig, Der 1933,My 3,15:5 (In Addenda)
Seitz, George B (Director)
Wild Horse Mesa 1925,Ag 10,8:2
Ice Flood, The 1926,O 19,26:2
Pals in Paradise 1926,N 24,26:4
Blood Ship, The 1927,Jl 19,27:2
Great Mail Robbery, The 1927,Jl 20,29:3
Beware of Blondes 1928,Ag 21,27:4
Circus Kid, The 1928,D 17,23:1
Guilty 1930,Ap 7,21:1
Midnight Mystery 1930,Je 2,25:4
Danger Lights 1930,D 15,29:1
Men Are Like That 1931,Ag 17,18:2
Women in his Life, The 1934,Ja 27,9:3
Lazy River 1934,Ap 4,26:2
Society Doctor 1935,F 4,11:3
Shadow of Doubt 1935,Mr 11,15:1
Times Square Lady 1935,Mr 15,25:3
Exclusive Story 1936,Ja 18,19:2
Absolute Quiet 1936,My 2,11:1
Three Wise Guys, The 1936,My 23,12:2
Last of the Mohicans, The 1936,S 3,17:3
Mad Holiday 1936,N 26,39:2
Under Cover of Night 1937,Ja 20,18:4
Family Affair, A 1937,Ap 20,29:2
Thirteenth Chair, The 1937,Je 18,25:3
Between Two Women 1937,Ag 6,21:1
You're Only Young Once 1938,Ja 3,16:2
Judge Hardy's Children 1938,Ap 8,17:2
Yellow Jack 1938,My 20,17:2
Love Finds Andy Hardy 1938,Jl 22,10:2
Out West With the Hardys 1938,D 9,31:2
Hardys Ride High, The 1939,Ap 14,28:2
Six Thousand Enemies 1939,Je 9,26:2
Thunder Afloat 1939,O 13,27:2
Judge Hardy and Son 1940,Ja 18,27:3 (In Addenda)
Andy Hardy Meets Debutante 1940,Ag 2,12:2
Sky Murder 1940,N 14,28:3
Kit Carson 1940,N 15,25:3
Gallant Sons 1940,D 12,37:2
Andy Hardy's Private Secretary 1941,Mr 7,17:2
Life Begins for Andy Hardy 1941,Ag 22,19:4
Yank on the Burma Road, A 1942,Ja 29,25:3
Courtship of Andy Hardy, The 1942,Ap 10,21:2
Pierre of the Plains 1942,Jl 30,17:3
Andy Hardy's Double Life 1943,Ja 12,23:3
Andy Hardy's Blonde Trouble 1944,My 5,17:3
Seitz, George B (Original Author)
Jim, The Conquerer 1926,D 28,17:1
Seitz, Tani
I, The Jury 1953,Ag 22,8:2
Greenwich Village Story 1963,Jl 12,14:3
Seitzer, Leo (Director)
Jacqueline Kennedy's Asian Journey 1962,D 26,5:2

Sekaryongo
King Solomon's Mines 1950,N 10,35:1
Sekely, Steve (Director)
Woman in Bondage 1944,Mr 27,17:2
Lake Placid Serenade 1944,D 25,15:6
Hollow Triumph 1948,O 29,29:5
Day of the Triffids 1963,My 11,15:2
Sekely, William (Miscellaneous)
Seeds of Freedom 1943,Ag 25,17:2
Sekely, William (Producer)
New Wine 1942,F 2,11:2
Sekerka, Martin
Mizici Svet; Vanishing World 1935,My 30,21:2
Sekh, Yaroslav
Bolshoi Ballet 67 1966,S 30,54:1
Seki, Kyoko
Ikiru; To Live 1960,Ja 30,13:5
Sekigawa, Hideo (Director)
Hiroshima 1955,My 17,32:1
Sekizawa, Schinichi (Screenwriter)
Ghidrah, The Three-Headed Monster 1965,D 16,63:3
Sekizawa, Shinichi (Screenwriter)
Battle in Outer Space 1960,Jl 9,10:5
Gozdilla vs the Thing 1964,N 26,52:2
Sekka, Johnny
Flame in the Streets 1962,S 13,32:1
Woman of Straw 1964,O 1,30:6
Khartoum 1966,Jl 14,28:1
Selander, Lesley (Director)
Barrier, The 1937,N 27,21:2
Hopalong Rides Again 1938,Ja 22,19:1
Partners of the Plains 1938,F 12,20:4
Heart of Arizona 1938,Ap 16,17:1
Cherokee Strip 1940,N 4,23:2
Roundup, The 1941,Mr 13,25:4
Catman of Paris, The 1946,Jl 13,12:2
Blackmail 1947,Ag 5,26:3
Red Stallion 1947,N 27,50:3
Belle Star's Daughter 1949,Ja 10,19:2
Stampede 1949,S 16,36:2
Dakota Lil 1950,Mr 3,21:5
Short Grass 1951,Ja 13,10:4
Cavalry Scout 1951,Je 8,32:2
I Was an American Spy 1951,Jl 4,13:2
Battle Zone 1952,N 1,17:2
Flat Top 1952,D 6,17:2
Raiders, The 1952,D 13,19:2
Arrow in the Dust 1954,My 1,13:2
Return From the Sea 1954,Jl 10,7:3
Desert Sands 1955,N 19,22:7
Fort Utah 1967,My 25,54:3
Selbie, Evelyn
Without Benefit of Clergy 1921,Je 20,17:2
Broken Wing, The 1923,O 9,17:4
Name the Man 1924,F 4,23:3
Mademoiselle Midnight 1924,My 27,14:1
Poisoned Paradise 1924,Ag 11,16:1
Cafe in Cairo, A 1925,Mr 18,19:2
Hell-Bent for Heaven 1926,My 4,31:1
Silken Shackles 1926,My 25,25:1
Into her Kingdom 1926,Ag 10,19:2
Camille 1927,Ap 22,19:1
Wild Geese 1927,D 5,26:2
Eternal Love 1929,My 13,27:2
Insidious Dr Fu Manchu, The 1929,Jl 22,17:1
Dangerous Paradise 1930,F 16,III,8:1
Hatchet Man, The 1932,F 4,25:2
Notorious Gentleman, A 1935,F 16,9:1
Selby, Sarah
San Diego, I Love You 1944,N 10,25:1
Iron Mistress, The 1952,N 20,39:2
McConnell Story, The 1955,S 30,23:1
Affair to Remember, An 1957,Jl 20,8:5
Stopover Tokyo 1957,D 27,23:4
Moon Pilot 1962,Ap 6,30:2
Selco, Arno
Act One 1963,D 27,17:2
Seldes, Gilbert (Miscellaneous)
ThIs is America 1933,Jl 20,22:2
Seldes, Marian
Lonely Night, The 1954,Mr 29,22:2
True Story of Jesse James, The 1957,Mr 23,17:2
Crime and Punishment, U S A 1959,Je 17,39:3
Big Fisherman, The 1959,Ag 6,18:1
Greatest Story Ever Told, The 1965,F 16,40:2
Seldow, Michel
Deadlier Than the Male 1957,O 9,41:1
Selena, Evelyne
My Wife's Husband 1965,Ja 27,26:1
Seleznef, Vitya
Ballad of Cossack Gloota, The 1938,F 28,19:1
Seleznev, F
We Are From Kronstadt 1936,My 2,11:1
On his Own 1939,S 13,31:3
Seleznev, Vassili
Hello, Moscow! 1946,Je 15,24:4
Self, William
Red River 1948,O 1,31:2
Father Was a Fullback 1949,O 13,33:3
Breakthrough 1950,N 18,10:2
Thing, The 1951,My 3,34:4
Pat and Mike 1952,Je 19,32:6

Selianin, I
Ski Battalion 1938,Mr 14,13:1
Seligman, Selig J (Producer)
Smashing Time 1967,D 21,44:1
Charly 1968,S 24,55:1
High Commissioner, The 1968,D 12,62:5
Candy 1968,D 18,54:2
Selinko, Annemarie (Original Author)
Desiree 1954,N 18,42:1
Selk, George
It Came From Outer Space 1953,Je 18,38:2
Sell, Bernie
Sunday Dinner for a Soldier 1945,Ja 25,16:2
Sellars, Elizabeth
Madeleine 1950,S 1,17:2
Stranger in Between, The 1952,Ag 20,21:3
Long Memory, The 1953,Jl 27,15:2
Gentle Gunman, The 1953,O 1,34:3
Guilt is my Shadow 1954,Mr 25,36:4
Barefoot Contessa, The 1954,S 30,37:1
Desiree 1954,N 18,42:1
Prince of Players 1955,Ja 12,24:2
Three Cases of Murder (You Killed Elizabeth); You Killed Elizabeth (Three Cases of Murder) 1955,Mr 16,39:4
Law and Disorder 1958,Ag 6,20:1
Day They Robbed the Bank of England, The 1960,S 5,11:2
55 Days at Peking 1963,My 30,20:1
Never Let Go 1963,Je 15,10:2
Chalk Garden, The 1964,My 22,42:2
Seller, Daniele
Caroline Cherie 1954,My 25,23:1
Seller, Robert
Personal Column 1941,F 3,13:2
Private Life of an Actor; En Scene 1948,S 7,21:3
Devil's Daughter 1949,F 26,11:2
Seller, Thomas (Screenwriter)
Andy Hardy Meets Debutante 1940,Ag 2,12:2
Tish 1942,S 18,25:2
Man From Down Under, The 1943,S 27,23:2
Black Arrow, The 1948,O 4,14:2
Sellers, Peter
Ladykillers 1956,F 21,37:2
Smallest Show on Earth, The 1957,N 23,11:2
Your Past Is Showing 1958,Jl 1,36:2
Up the Creek 1958,N 11,26:2
Tom Thumb 1958,D 24,00:0
Mouse That Roared, The 1959,O 27,40:1
Battle of the Sexes, The 1960,Ap 19,40:4
I'm All Right Jack 1960,Ap 26,40:2
Man in a Cocked Hat 1960,Je 15,50:2
Two-Way Stretch 1961,Ja 24,20:3
Millionairess, The 1961,F 10,19:1
Only Two Can Play 1962,Mr 21,33:2
I Like Money 1962,My 19,18:2
Lolita 1962,Je 14,23:2
Road to Hong Kong, The 1962,Je 28,21:1
Waltz of the Toreadors 1962,Ag 14,34:1
Trial and Error 1962,N 17,17:2
Wrong Arm of the Law, The 1963,Ap 3,39:1
Heavens Above! 1963,My 21,28:2
Never Let Go 1963,Je 15,10:2
Dr Strangelove or: How I Learned to Stop Worrying and Love the Bomb 1964,Ja 31,16:1 (Incorrect in this edition; use 1964,Ja 30,24:1 elsewhere)
World of Henry Orient, The 1964,Mr 20,27:2
Pink Panther, The 1964,Ap 24,25:1
Shot in the Dark, A 1964,Je 24,28:1
What's New Pussycat? 1965,Je 23,49:1
Wrong Box 1966,Jl 20,46:1
After the Fox 1966,D 24,11:1
Casino Royale 1967,Ap 29,25:1
Woman Times Seven 1967,Je 28,38:1
Bobo, The 1967,S 29,53:1
Party, The 1968,Ap 5,56:2
I Love You Alice B Toklas! 1968,O 8,40:1
Sellers, Peter (Director)
I Like Money 1962,My 19,18:2
Sellers, William (Screenwriter)
Gunfighter, The 1950,Je 24,7:2
Selling, Cal
Dr Coppelius 1968,D 26,56:1
Selling, Kenneth
Street Scene 1931,Ag 27,22:5
Nice Women 1932,F 20,11:2
Sellmer, Esna
Murderers Among Us 1948,Ag 17,19:6
Sellon, Charles
Bad Man, The 1923,O 9,17:4
Woman Proof 1923,O 30,16:1
Flowing Gold 1924,Mr 10,18:2
Merton of the Movies 1924,S 8,15:3
Roughneck, The 1924,D 3,14:1
Monster, The 1925,F 16,24:1
Old Home Week 1925,My 25,21:3
Tracked in the Snow Country 1925,Jl 20,19:2
Easy Pickings 1927,Mr 25,25:3
Valley of the Giants, The 1927,D 5,26:2
Love Me and the World Is Mine 1928,F 6,12:3
Feel my Pulse 1928,F 27,16:2
Count of Ten, The 1928,Mr 13,23:3

Sellon, Charles — Cont
Easy Come, Easy Go 1928,My 8,25:3
Something Always Happens 1928,My 21,25:1
Happiness Ahead 1928,Je 19,31:1
What a Night! 1928,D 24,11:1
Bulldog Drummond 1929,My 3,23:2
Hot Stuff 1929,My 13,27:2
Man and the Moment, The 1929,Ag 5,25:2
Gamblers, The 1929,Ag 24,11:5
Sweetie 1929,O 26,15:1
Saturday Night Kid, The 1929,N 16,25:2
Vagabond Lover, The 1929,N 27,30:6
Mighty, The 1929,D 30,16:4
Burning Up 1930,F 8,12:5
Honey 1930,Mr 29,23:1
Under a Texas Moon 1930,Ap 4,22:1
Social Lion, The 1930,Je 14,9:4
Love Among the Millionaires 1930,Jl 5,17:4
Let's Go Native 1930,Ag 30,7:4
Sea Legs 1930,N 11,29:1
Tom Sawyer 1930,D 20,20:6
Painted Desert, The 1931,Mr 9,19:1
Behind Office Doors 1931,Mr 21,15:1
Laugh and get Rich 1931,Mr 28,15:3
Dude Ranch 1931,Ap 25,23:4
Penrod and Sam 1931,S 26,25:3
Tip Off, The 1931,O 26,22:1
Carnival Boat 1932,Mr 21,19:5
Dark Horse, The 1932,Je 9,27:3
Make Me a Star 1932,Jl 1,19:3
Central Park 1932,D 7,29:3
Employees' Entrance 1933,Ja 21,10:6
Strictly Personal 1933,Mr 20,18:2
Central Airport 1933,My 4,20:5
Private Scandal 1934,Je 15,26:2
Elmer and Elsie 1934,Ag 4,14:5
Bright Eyes 1934,D 21,31:1
It's a Gift 1935,Ja 5,20:2
Life Begins at 40 1935,Ap 5,21:3
Casino Murder Case, The 1935,Ap 17,26:5
Diamond Jim 1935,Ag 24,18:2
Old Kentucky, In 1935,N 29,24:1
Selman, David (Director)
Shakedown 1936,Ag 17,9:2
Killer at Large 1936,O 26,20:1
Pasado Acusa, El; Accusing Past, The
1938,O 15,21:4
Selmar, Lia
Outcry 1949,Mr 14,15:5
Selpin, Herbert (Director)
Traum vom Rhein, Der 1935,D 9,25:2
Zwichen Zwei Herzen; Between Two Hearts
1936,Ja 28,15:3
Idealer Gatte, Ein 1937,Ja 11,15:7
Selsinger, Tess (Original Author)
Girls' School 1938,N 3,27:1
Selten, Morton
Ghost Goes West, The 1936,Ja 11,9:2
I Stand Condemned 1936,Jl 2,27:2
Fire Over England 1937,Mr 5,16:2
Juggernaut 1937,Jl 15,16:1
Yank at Oxford, A 1938,F 25,15:1
Divorce of Lady X, The 1938,Ap 1,17:2
Shipyard Sally 1940,Ja 18,27:3
Thief of Bagdad, The 1940,D 6,28:2
Seltzer, Frank N (Producer)
Gay Intruders, The 1949,Je 28,33:4
711 Ocean Drive 1950,Jl 20,21:2
Seltzer, Walter (Producer)
Naked Edge 1961,Jl 1,9:1
Paris Blues 1961,N 8,41:1
Man in the Middle 1964,Mr 5,36:1
War Lord, The 1965,N 18,55:2
Will Penny 1968,Ap 11,51:2
Selwart, Tonio
Edge of Darkness 1943,Ap 10,12:4
Hangmen Also Die 1943,Ap 16,24:2
North Star, The 1943,N 5,23:1
Cross of Lorraine, The 1943,D 3,27:4
Hitler Gang, The 1944,My 8,15:2
Tampico 1944,Je 2,21:2
Wilson 1944,Ag 2,18:1
My Favorite Spy 1951,D 26,19:3
Barefoot Contessa, The 1954,S 30,37:1
Congo Crossing 1956,Jl 14,13:2
Naked Maja, The 1959,Je 11,36:2
Selway, George
Tiger Bay 1959,D 15,50:1
Selwyn, Edgar (Director)
War Nurse 1930,O 24,31:1
Men Call it Love 1931,Je 20,20:4
Sin of Madelon Claudet, The 1931,O 31,22:2
Skyscraper Souls 1932,Ag 5,11:2
Men Must Fight 1933,Mr 11,18:3
Turn Back the Clock 1933,Ag 26,14:2
Mystery of Mr X, The 1934,F 26,21:3
Selwyn, Edgar (Original Author)
Heart of the Wilds 1918,Ag 19,7:1
Primitive Lover, The 1922,My 15,20:3
Arab, The 1924,Jl 14,11:5
Crowded Hour, The 1925,Ap 27,15:2
Dancing Mothers 1926,F 18,21:1
Possessed 1931,N 28,20:4
Barbarian, The 1933,My 13,16:2

Turn Back the Clock 1933,Ag 26,14:2
Chained 1934,S 1,16:2
Pierre of the Plains 1942,Jl 30,17:3
Selwyn, Edgar (Producer)
Bridal Suite 1939,My 26,20:2
Dancing Co-Ed 1939,N 10,27:3
Washington Melodrama 1941,My 26,15:3
Pierre of the Plains 1942,Jl 30,17:3
Selwyn, Ruth
Five and Ten 1931,Jl 11,7:6
Polly of the Circus 1932,Mr 19,11:2
Trial of Vivienne Ware, The 1932,Ap 30,19:3
New Morals for Old 1932,Je 24,15:3
Speak Easily 1932,Ag 19,20:6
Men Must Fight 1933,Mr 11,18:3
Fugitive Lovers 1934,Ja 13,16:3
Selwyn, William E (Producer)
Bob Mathias Story, The 1954,O 16,14:6
Selwynne, Clarissa
Black Oxen 1924,Ja 7,23:1
Secrets 1924,Mr 25,25:2
Beau Brummell 1924,Mr 31,20:1
Mademoiselle Midnight 1924,My 27,14:1
Fast Worker, The 1924,N 12,13:1
Last Man on Earth, The 1924,D 13,12:4
Sackcloth and Scarlet 1925,Mr 25,24:2
Lucky Horseshoe, The 1925,Ag 18,14:3
We Moderns 1925,D 8,28:5
Infatuation 1926,Ja 4,16:1
Resurrection 1927,My 17,27:2
Naughty but Nice 1927,Jl 5,19:2
Crystal Cup, The 1927,O 25,33:3
Devil Dancer, The 1927,D 19,30:1
Heart of a Follies Girl, The 1928,Mr 12,26:1
My Man 1928,D 22,14:3
Hard to Get 1929,S 28,17:3
My Pal the King 1932,O 4,26:4
Cynara 1932,D 26,26:2
Selzer, Milton
Young Savages, The 1961,My 25,31:1
Yellow Canary, The 1963,My 16,42:1
Legend of Lylah Clare, The 1968,Ag 23,33:1
Selznick, David O (Producer)
David Copperfield 1935,Ja 19,8:1
Vanessa: Her Love Story 1935,Ap 13,11:3
Reckless 1935,Ap 20,16:1
Anna Karenina 1935,Ag 31,16:2
Tale of Two Cities, A 1935,D 26,21:2
Little Lord Fauntleroy 1936,Ap 3,27:1
Star Is Born, A 1937,Ap 23,25:1
Prisoner of Zenda, The 1937,S 3,12:1
Nothing Sacred 1937,N 26,27:2
Adventures of Tom Sawyer, The 1938,F 18,23:1
Young in Heart, The 1938,N 4,27:2
Made for Each Other 1939,F 17,17:2
Gone With the Wind 1939,D 20,31:2
Since You Went Away 1944,Jl 21,16:2
Spellbound 1945,N 2,22:2
Duel in the Sun 1947,My 8,30:2
Paradine Case, The 1948,Ja 9,26:2
Portrait of Jennie 1949,Mr 30,31:2
Farewell to Arms, A 1958,Ja 25,14:1
Gone With the Wind 1967,O 11,41:1
Selznick, David O (Screenwriter)
Since You Went Away 1944,Jl 21,16:2
1947,My 8,30:2
Duel in the Sun 1947,My 8,30:2
Paradine Case, The 1948,Ja 9,26:2
Semels, Harry
America 1924,F 22,20:1
Beware of Blondes 1928,Ag 21,27:4
Subway Express 1931,My 2,23:4
Our Daily Bread 1934,O 3,25:2
Miserables, Les 1935,Ap 22,14:2
Last Outpost, The 1935,O 5,18:2
Under Two Flags 1936,My 1,19:1
Gay Desperado, The 1936,O 9,31:4
Semeniako, Michel
Chinoise, La 1968,Ap 4,58:2
Semenoff, Simon
Great John L, The 1945,Jl 9,14:6
Semenova, Ludmila
Fragment of an Empire, A 1930,Ja 27,18:4
Semien, Anita
Dialogue 1967,O 14,13:2
Semionov, G
Great Citizen, The 1939,Ja 16,11:2
Semitjov, W (Screenwriter)
One Summer of Happiness 1955,Mr 22,35:2
Semmler, Gustav
Eleven Who Were Loyal 1929,My 20,22:6
Semon, Larry
Wizard of Oz, The 1925,Ap 14,26:1
Underworld 1927,Ag 22,21:3
Semon, Larry (Director)
Wizard of Oz, The 1925,Ap 14,26:1
Semple, Elmer Jack
Margin for Error 1943,Ja 25,10:7
Semple, Lorenzo Jr (Original Author)
Honeymoon Machine, The 1961,Ag 24,25:2
Semple, Lorenzo Jr (Screenwriter)
Batman 1966,Ag 25,42:4
Fathom 1967,D 14,62:1

Semple, Lorenzo Jr (Screenwriter) — Cont
Pretty Poison 1968,O 25,55:1
Sempolinski, Ludwik
Treasure, The 1951,Mr 29,24:4
Semprun, Jorge
Guerre est Fini, La; War Is Over, The
1967,F 2,29:2
Semprun, Jorge (Screenwriter)
Guerre est Fini, La; War Is Over, The
1966,S 23,43:1
Guerre est Fini, La; War Is Over, The
1967,F 2,29:2
Semyonov, G
Poet and Tsar 1938,Ag 25,15:1
Semyonov, S (Cinematographer)
Pageant of Russia 1947,Ag 11,17:3
In the Circus Arena 1952,Ap 14,22:3
Sen, Pro
Householder, The 1963,O 22,43:2
Sen, Subrata
Kanchenjungha 1966,Jl 26,27:2
Sen-Elnikova, M D
Laughter Through Tears 1933,N 13,21:2
Sen Gupta, Pinaki
Music Room, The 1963,O 16,50:6
Senac, Renee
Paris Waltz, The 1950,Ag 23,35:2
Senaca (Original Author)
Fedra, the Devil's Daughter 1957,O 26,19:2
Senators
Wilson 1944,Ag 2,18:1
Senda, Koreya
Gate of Hell 1954,D 14,45:2
Phantom Horse, the 1956,Jl 25,16:1
Battle in Outer Space 1960,Jl 9,10:5
Blue Beast, The 1965,Ja 30,18:2
Senick, Don (Cinematographer)
Untitled-News, Battle of Tarawa, WWII
1943,D 7,31:3
Sennett, Bathing Beauties
Days of Thrills and Laughter 1961,Mr 22,37:1
Sennett, Mack
Hollywood Cavalcade 1939,O 14,13:2
Days of Thrills and Laughter 1961,Mr 22,37:1
Sennett, Mack (Director)
Good-Bye Kiss, The 1928,N 12,18:2
Hypnotized 1933,Ja 16,13:3
Sennett, Mack (Miscellaneous)
Hollywood Cavalcade 1939,O 14,13:2
Sennett, Mack (Original Author)
Suzanna 1923,Mr 26,16:2
Hypnotized 1933,Ja 16,13:3
Sennett, Mack (Producer)
No Mother to Guide Him 1919,Je 9,16:3
Submarine Pirate, The 1919,Je 9,16:3
Uncle Tom Without the Cabin 1919,S 22,8:1
Down on the Farm 1920,Ap 26,18:1
Molly O 1921,N 21,20:1
Crossroads of New York, The 1922,My 22,18:4
Sennett, Max (Producer)
Small Town Idol, A 1921,Ap 17,VI,2:1 (In
Addenda)
Sennett Girls
When Comedy Was King 1960,Mr 30,42:1
Senoret, Ottavio
Behind Closed Shutters 1952,Je 10,22:7
Sentis, Jose
Melodia de Arrabal 1933,Ag 5,9:5
Sentmeant, Ramon de
Octavo Mandamiento, El; Eighth Commandment,
The 1937,Mr 1,15:2
Seoane, Jose M
Don Quixote 1949,My 13,29:3
Seplin, Herbert (Director)
Reiter von Deutsch-Ostafrika, Die 1935,Je 8,12:3
Sequeiro, Adela
Mas Alla de la Muerta 1936,Mr 2,13:3
Sequeiro, Adela (Perlita) (Director)
Mujer de Nadie, La; Nobody's Wife
1938,F 7,10:3
Sequi, Mario (Director)
Island of Procida, The 1952,Mr 15,8:2
Serandrei, Mario (Miscellaneous)
Grand Olympics, The 1964,Ap 22,57:2
Serate, Rudolph
Pirates of Capri, The 1949,D 26,33:5
Serato, Massimo
Man of the Sea 1948,Ja 24,11:2
Lost One, The; La Traviata 1948,Mr 30,26:2
Outcry 1949,Mr 14,15:5
Fugitive Lady 1951,Ag 25,7:2
Thief of Venice, The 1952,N 28,22:7
Count of St Elmo, The 1953,Mr 14,13:2
Man From Cairo, The 1953,D 17,52:4
Sins of the Borgias 1956,Mr 5,21:1
Naked Maja, The 1959,Je 11,36:2
Queen of the Pirates 1961,Jl 27,23:4
David and Goliath 1961,O 7,14:3
Cid, El 1961,D 15,49:1
Constantine and the Cross 1963,Mr 14,8:2
Samson and the Slave Queen 1964,Mr 5,36:2
10th Victim, The 1965,D 21,46:1
Wild, Wild Planet 1967,Ag 10,45:5

Serda, Charlotte
Inge und die Millionen 1934,Ap 13,25:1
Serda, Julia
Modern du Barry, A 1928,Mr 19,26:2
Olympia 1930,D 7,IX,6:4
Living Corpse, The 1931,Ja 4,27:2
Liebeswalzer 1931,My 4,15:3
Ein Walzer vom Strauss 1932,F 11,16:1
Der Storch Streikt 1932,My 2,13:2
Der Herr Buerovorsteher 1932,Je 17,24:1
Zapfenstreich am Rhein 1933,F 2,21:6
Traum von Schoenbrunn 1933,Je 1,15:4
Liebe in Uniform 1934,O 9,17:2
Mein Leben fuer Maria Isabell; My Life for Maria
Isabell 1935,N 5,33:5
Alles Weg'n Dem Hund 1936,Mr 31,17:3
Liebesleute 1936,O 3,21:2
Masquerade in Vienna 1937,Ja 26,16:4
Drei Maeoerl um Schubert 1937,Je 5,21:2
Serdyik, L
Mass Struggle 1934,S 17,20:3
Nazar Stodolya 1937,Ag 7,7:2
Serel, Jean
Circle of Love 1965,Mr 25,42:4
Sereno, Gustavo
Zappatore 1932,Mr 28,11:2
Sereno, Gustavo (Director)
Zappatore 1932,Mr 28,11:2
Sereys, Jacques
Fire Within, The 1964,F 18,27:1
Sergava, Kathryn
Bedside 1934,Mr 7,23:4
Sergeant, Lewis
Oliver Twist 1922,O 30,11:1
Sergeev, Nikita
Nine Days of one Year 1964,D 29,19:1
Sergelius, Birgit
Charlotte Loewenskoeld 1932,F 22,23:2
Pettersson & Bendel 1934,F 22,25:2
Sergelva, Katya
Cock of the Air 1932,Ja 25,20:3
Sergeol
Thirst of Men, The 1952,O 28,37:1
Sergeyev, Konstantin (Director)
Sleeping Beauty, The 1966,My 4,50:1
Sergeyev, Konstantin (Miscellaneous)
Sleeping Beauty, The 1966,My 4,50:1
Sergeyev, Konstantin (Screenwriter)
Sleeping Beauty, The 1966,My 4,50:1
Sergeyev, N
Stars of the Russian Ballet (Swan Lake); Swan
Lake (Stars of the Russian Ballet) 1954,S 6,9:2
Big Family, A 1955,Je 6,24:1
Fathers and Sons 1960,D 26,27:2
Sun Shines for All 1961,Jl 10,25:3
Sergeyeva, G
Gobsek 1937,Jl 16,22:1
Boule de Suif 1958,My 5,24:1
Sergyl, Yvonne
Miracle of the Wolves, The 1925,F 24,17:3
Miracle des Loups, Le 1930,Jl 28,22:1
Serino, Franco (Director)
World of Topo Gigio 1965,N 27,34:1
Serling, Rod (Original Author)
Rack, The 1956,N 6,30:1
Incident in an Alley 1962,My 17,31:1
Requiem for a Heavyweight 1962,O 17,35:1
Serling, Rod (Screenwriter)
Saddle the Wind 1958,Mr 21,17:1
Requiem for a Heavyweight 1962,O 17,35:1
Yellow Canary, The 1963,My 16,42:1
Seven Days in May 1964,F 20,22:1
Assault on a Queen 1966,Jl 28,23:3
Planet of the Apes 1968,F 9,55:2
Sernas, Jacques
Lost Youth 1949,O 27,35:4
Golden Salamander 1951,Mr 24,8:3
Mill on the Po, The 1951,O 23,35:2
Sky Is Red, The 1952,My 27,30:2
Lure of the Sira 1953,D 26,10:7
Anita Garibaldi 1954,Mr 19,19:4
Helen of Troy 1956,Ja 27,21:4
Sign of the Gladiator 1959,D 3,46:1
Nights of Lucretia Borgia, The 1960,O 6,51:4
Dolce Vita, La 1961,Ap 20,30:1
Slave, The 1963,My 30,20:1
Duel of the Titans 1963,Ag 8,19:1
Serner, Hakan
Dear John 1966,Mr 9,46:1
Puss and Kram 1967,S 25,56:1
Hugs and Kisses 1968,Ag 19,44:1
Serof, Georgi
Volga, Volga 1933,D 15,28:3
Seroff, Muni
Two Sisters 1938,D 1,29:3
Two Senoritas From Chicago 1943,Ag 6,10:4
Serova, V
Wait for Me 1945,Mr 19,23:3
Four Hearts 1946,F 25,21:5
Great Glinka, The 1947,D 22,30:2
Immortal Garrison, The 1957,Mr 4,30:2

Serpe, Ralph (Producer)
Mister Rock and Roll 1957,O 17,42:2
Serpent, Hawk (Producer)
Unstrap Me 1968,N 21,41:2
Serpilli, Franco
To Live in Peace 1947,N 25,37:2
Serra, Domenicco
Maciste in Hell 1931,Je 29,20:3
Serra, Gianna
Our Man Flint 1966,Ja 26,23:4
Serra, Rodolfo de la
Murio el Sargento Laprida; Sergeant Laprida Died
1939,Mr 20,13:2
Serrano, Enrique
Noches de Buenos Aires 1935,D 10,31:3
Noches de Buenos Aires; Buenos Aires Nights
1935,D 12,33:4
Caballo del Pueblo, El 1935,D 16,23:4
Divorcio en Montevideo 1940,Ap 8,15:3
Asi es la Vida; Such Is Life 1940,Ag 6,15:1
Je Hatore 1940,Ag 27,17:2
Jettatore 1940,Ag 27,17:2
Games Men Play, The 1968,Mr 15,30:1
Serrano, Maria
Serenade 1956,Mr 24,21:1 (Incorrect in this
edition; use 1956,Mr 23,21:1 elsewhere)
Serrano, Vincent
Eyes of Youth 1919,D 1,9:3
Branded Woman, The 1920,S 6,10:5
Convoy 1927,My 9,26:4
Serrault, Michel
Diabolique 1955,N 22,41:1
Lovers and Thieves 1958,Ag 5,23:2
Belle Americaine, La 1961,D 18,42:1
Candide 1962,N 20,39:1
Three Fables of Love (The Fox and the Crow);
Fox and the Crow, The (Three Fables of Love)
1963,Ag 21,38:1
Love on a Pillow 1963,D 17,49:1
Male Hunt; Chasse a l'Homme, La
1965,Ap 20,42:1
How Not to Rob a Department Store
1965,D 29,23:1
King of Hearts 1967,Je 20,34:1
Serre, Henri
Jules and Jim 1962,Ap 24,32:1
Fire Within, The 1964,F 18,27:1
Serret, John
Scream of Fear 1961,Ag 23,29:1
Serret, Virginia
Mi Madrecita; My Little Mother 1940,S 24,26:6
Serrett, Jean
One Woman's Story 1949,My 18,33:2
Sert, Jose L
8 X 8 1957,Mr 16,13:2
Sertilange, Christiane
Thirst of Men, The 1952,O 28,37:1
Servaes, Dagney
Loves of Pharaoh 1922,F 22,13:3 (In Addenda)
Servaes, Dagny
Peter the Great 1923,Je 25,16:5
Fortune's Fool 1928,Ag 13,23:2
Nanon 1938,N 26,18:2
Laugh Pagliacci 1948,Ja 31,14:2
Eroica; (The Beethoven Story) 1951,O 29,19:2
You Are the World for Me 1964,D 26,9:4
Servais, Jean
Miserables, Les 1936,O 28,31:2
Heartbeat 1939,S 5,21:3
Miserables, Les 1946,D 26,28:4
Riptide 1951,Ap 7,9:2
Plaisir, Le (The Model); Model, The (Le Plaisir)
1954,My 20,38:1
Rififi 1956,Je 6,37:1
He Who Must Die 1958,D 29,21:1
Heroes and Sinners; (Heros Sont Fatigues, Les)
1959,My 12,38:2
Tamango 1959,S 17,48:4
World in my Pocket, The 1962,My 10,30:2
Crime Does Not Pay (The Hugues Case); Hugues
Case, The (Crime Does Not Pay)
1962,O 17,35:2
That Man From Rio 1964,Je 9,30:1
Lost Command 1966,S 15,51:1
Servanti, Luigi
President, The 1929,Ja 21,18:4
Servantie, Adrienne
My Uncle 1958,N 4,30:2
Women Are Weak 1959,Je 9,44:2
Servi, Helly
Marika 1953,F 18,27:2
Service, Robert W
Spoilers, The 1942,My 22,27:2
Service, Robert W (Original Author)
Shooting of Dan McGrew, The 1924,Je 9,14:3
Poisoned Paradise 1924,Ag 11,16:1
Roughneck, The 1924,D 3,14:1
Trail of '98, The 1928,Mr 21,30:3
Servin, Michel (Screenwriter)
Thank Heaven for Small Favors 1965,Ja 14,44:2
Servoss, Mary
Lone Wolf Keeps a Date, The 1941,Ja 2,24:3
In This our Life 1942,My 9,10:2

Servoss, Mary— Cont
So Proudly We Hail 1943,S 10,29:1
Four Jills in a Jeep 1944,Ap 6,27:2
Youth Runs Wild 1944,S 2,17:2
Mrs Parkington 1944,O 13,16:1
Summer Storm 1944,O 23,14:3
Experiment Perilous 1944,D 30,15:2
Conflict 1945,Je 16,10:2
Danger Signal 1945,N 22,39:2
Live Today for Tomorrow 1948,D 6,29:2
Sessak, Hilde
Schloss Vogeloed 1936,My 9,11:2
Raub der Sabinerinnen, Der 1937,Ja 16,21:1
Gleisdreieck 1938,Je 11,9:1
Verkannte Lebemann, Der; Unrecognized Man of
the World, The 1939,S 16,20:2
Man Between, The 1953,N 19,41:2
Sessions, Almira
Chad Hanna 1940,D 26,23:1
She Knew All the Answers 1941,Je 20,28:4
Sullivan's Travels 1942,Ja 29,25:2
My Kingdom for a Cook 1943,O 15,15:3
Heat's on, The 1943,N 26,29:2
Miracle of Morgan's Creek, The 1944,Ja 20,15:2
She Wouldn't Say Yes 1946,Ja 12,10:7
Diary of a Chambermaid, The 1946,Je 23,28:2
Apartment for Peggy 1948,O 16,9:2
Night Unto Night 1949,Je 11,11:2
Roseanna McCoy 1949,O 13,33:2
Sessions, Anne
Mikado, The 1967,Mr 15,53:1
Sestan, Mario
White Line, The 1952,D 6,17:2
Sestill, Otello
Gospel According to St Matthew, The
1966,F 18,23:1
Seta, Vittorio de (Director)
Almost a Man 1966,S 23,43:1
Seta, Vittorio de (Original Author)
Almost a Man 1966,S 23,43:1
Seta, Vittorio de (Producer)
Almost a Man 1966,S 23,43:1
Seth, S N
Nine Hours to Rama 1963,Ap 4,58:2
Setiz, George R (Director)
Vanishing American, The 1925,O 16,18:2
Setkina, Irina (Director)
August 14; One Day in the USSR
1948,Ag 16,12:2
New China, The 1952,Mr 10,18:4
Seto, Javier (Director)
Castilian, The 1963,O 3,31:1
Seto, Javier (Screenwriter)
Castilian, The 1963,O 3,31:1
Seton, Anya (Original Author)
Dragonwyck 1946,Ap 11,35:2
Foxfire 1955,Jl 14,19:1
Seton, Bruce
Love From a Stranger 1937,Ap 19,27:2
Song of the Road 1940,My 6,13:2
Green Cockatoo, The 1947,Jl 19,10:2
Tight Little Island 1949,D 26,33:2
Blue Lamp, The 1951,Ja 9,25:1
Cruel Sea, The 1953,Ag 11,18:5
Gorgo 1961,Mr 30,24:2
Seton, Graham (Original Author)
W Plan, The 1931,Mr 23,24:7
Seton, Joan
Frenzy 1946,Jl 20,10:3
Meet Me at Dawn 1948,My 18,26:2
Seton, Marie (Miscellaneous)
Time in the Sun 1940,O 1,29:2
Seton, Marie (Producer)
Time in the Sun 1940,O 1,29:2
Settle, Georgia Lee
Janie 1944,Ag 5,16:2
Very Thought of You, The 1944,N 18,16:7
Setton, Maxwell (Producer)
So Little Time 1953,Jl 28,23:2
Golden Mask, The 1954,Mr 20,10:5
Footsteps of the Fog 1955,S 15,39:2
Sety, Gerard
Inspector Maigret 1958,O 9,47:1
Lady Chatterley's Lover 1959,Jl 11,11:1
Modigliani of Montparnasse 1961,Mr 1,27:3
My Son, The Hero 1963,S 19,23:1
Setz, Val
Pirate, The 1948,My 21,19:2
Seurat, Pilar
Young Savages, The 1961,My 25,31:1
Seven Women From Hell 1962,F 1,22:2
Seuss, Dr (Screenwriter)
5,000 Fingers of Dr T, The 1953,Je 20,8:6
Sevareid, Eric (Narrator)
Eleanor Roosevelt Story, The 1965,N 9,50:1
Seven, Johnny
Last Mile, The 1959,F 19,27:1
Apartment, The 1960,Je 16,37:2
Sevening, Dora
Long Dark Hall, The 1951,My 10,38:3
Severac, Jacques (Director)
Siroco 1931,N 26,37:2

Severi, Gilberto
Monte Cassino 1948,N 25,47:3
Severin, Gaston
Maternelle, La 1935,O 15,19:1
Diary of a Country Priest 1954,Ap 6,35:2
Severin, Joschen (Miscellaneous)
Bridge, The; (Bruecke, Die) 1961,My 2,42:1
Severin-Mars
J'Accuse 1920,My 23,VI,2:2
Severn, Christopher
Mrs Miniver 1942,Je 5,23:1
Amazing Mrs Holliday, The 1943,F 22,20:2
Man From Down Under, The 1943,S 27,23:2
Cluny Brown 1946,Je 3,27:3
Severn, Clifford
Jalna 1935,S 14,8:4
Quality Street 1937,Ap 9,19:2
Man About Town 1939,Je 29,19:1
How Green Was my Valley 1941,O 29,27:2
Atlantic Convoy 1942,Jl 6,18:5
Severn, Ernest
Hour Before the Dawn, The 1944,My 11,25:6
Pursued 1947,Mr 8,10:2
Severn, Raymond
We Are not Alone 1939,D 1,27:1
Yank at Eton, A 1942,O 16,23:1
Hour Before the Dawn, The 1944,My 11,25:6
Suspect, The 1945,F 1,18:5
Severn, William (Billy)
Journey for Margaret 1942,D 18,36:7
Son of Lassie 1945,Je 11,12:1
Enchanted Forest, The 1945,D 17,17:2
Severn, Winston
Her Sister's Secret 1947,Ja 23,31:3
Lost Honeymoon 1947,Je 20,25:6
Severn, Yvonne
Amazing Mrs Holliday, The 1943,F 22,20:2
Sevffertitz, Gustav von
Seven Faces 1929,N 16,25:2
Sevilia, Antonio
Torero! 1957,My 22,29:2
Sevilla, Carmen
Pantaloons 1956,D 26,34:1
Spanish Affair 1958,F 6,24:1
King of Kings 1961,O 12,41:2
Sevilla, Rafael (Director)
Gran Cruz, La; Heavy Cross, The 1937,D 7,31:6
Sevilla, Raphael J (Director)
Almas Encontradas 1933,Je 27,13:5
Corazon Bandolero 1935,Mr 2,18:2
Maria Elena 1936,F 18,27:1
Irma la Mala 1936,O 6,28:7
113, El 1938,F 14,20:8
Guadalupe la Chinaca 1938,S 12,13:3
A la Orilla de un Palmar; At the Edge of a Palm
  Grove 1938,D 17,10:4
Perjura 1939,Ja 16,11:2
Luna Criolla; Creole Moon 1940,Ap 8,15:3
Marvels of the Bull Ring 1943,Jl 3,11:3
Sevilla, Raphael J (Producer)
Irma la Mala 1936,O 6,28:7
A la Orilla de un Palmar; At the Edge of a Palm
  Grove 1938,D 17,10:4
Luna Criolla; Creole Moon 1940,Ap 8,15:3
Sevillano, Jose Gomez
Moment of Truth, The 1965,Ag 10,18:1
Seville
Manhattan Merry-Go-Round 1937,D 31,9:3
Seville, Victor (Director)
Michael and Mary 1932,Mr 5,11:2
Sevolodov, V
Victors and the Vanquished, The 1950,My 1,18:2
Seward, Billie
Once to Every Woman 1934,Mr 26,22:3
20th Century 1934,My 4,24:2
Blind Date 1934,S 1,16:3
Air Hawks 1935,Je 4,26:5
Charlie Chan at Treasure Island 1939,S 1,15:5
One Crowded Night 1940,Ag 27,17:2
No Hands on the Clock 1941,D 22,24:6
Seward, Edmond (Miscellaneous)
Gulliver's Travels 1939,D 21,29:1
Seward, Edmond (Screenwriter)
Wild Innocence 1938,N 11,31:2
Gulliver's Travels 1939,D 21,29:1
Sewell, Anna (Original Author)
Black Beauty 1921,Mr 22,15:3
Black Beauty 1946,Ag 30,13:2
Sewell, George
Sparrows Don't Sing 1963,My 7,46:2
This Sporting Life 1963,Jl 17,19:2
Kaleidoscope 1966,S 23,45:1
Robbery 1967,S 28,58:2
Vengance of She, The 1968,My 30,21:4
Sewell, Vernon (Director)
Silver Fleet, The 1945,Mr 24,22:6
Frenzy 1946,Jl 20,10:3
Sewell, Vernon (Screenwriter)
Silver Fleet, The 1945,Mr 24,22:6
Frenzy 1946,Jl 20,10:3
Seyferth, Wilfried
Decision Before Dawn 1951,D 22,12:2
Devil Makes Three, The 1952,Ag 30,6:2

Grapes are Ripe, The 1953,O 15,43:2
Dancing Heart, The 1958,Ja 18,10:3
Golden Plaque, The 1963,Ag 10,8:6
Seyfferitz, Gustav von
Regular Fellow, A 1925,O 5,25:2
Seyffertitz, G Von
Safe in Hell 1931,D 19,16:4
Seyffertitz, Gustav von
Unseeing Eyes 1923,O 22,17:1
Under the Red Robe 1923,N 13,25:3
Grounds for Divorce 1925,Je 29,8:2
Goose Woman, The 1925,Ag 4,14:3
Diplomacy 1926,S 13,18:1
Private Izzy Murphy 1926,N 10,25:1
His Glorious Night 1929,O 5,22:5
Seyffertitz, Gustave von
Sherlock Holmes 1922,My 8,14:3
Seyfiertitz, Gustav von
Countess Charming 1917,S 17,11:3
Seyler, Athene
This Freedom 1923,N 28,15:1
Be Mine Tonight 1933,Ap 14,22:5
Private Life of Don Juan, The 1934,D 10,16:2
Scrooge 1935,D 14,11:1
It's Love Again 1936,My 23,12:1
I Stand Condemned 1936,Jl 2,27:2
High Treason 1937,Ja 27,17:3
April Romance 1937,Ja 27,17:4
Non-Stop New York 1937,N 29,19:2
Sailing Along 1938,Ap 16,17:1
Citadel, The 1938,N 4,27:2
Ware Case, The 1939,Jl 22,12:2
Mill On the Floss, The 1939,N 15,19:3
Quiet Wedding 1941,D 29,27:4
Randolph Family 1945,Mr 13,19:4
Nicholas Nickleby 1947,D 1,27:2
Franchise Affair, The 1952,Je 6,19:2
Young Wives' Tale 1952,N 4,33:1
Beggar's Opera, The 1953,Ag 25,18:2
Pickwick Papers, The 1954,Ap 5,21:2
Doctor at Large 1957,Jl 29,15:5
How to Murder a Rich Uncle 1957,O 26,19:2
Tale of Two Cities, A 1958,Ag 5,23:1
Inn of the Sixth Happiness, The 1958,D 14,2:7
Happy is the Bride 1959,Je 30,27:2
Campbell's Kingdom 1960,Ja 11,35:5
French Mistress, A 1960,D 19,34:2
Make Mine Mink 1960,D 20,43:4
Francis of Assisi 1961,Jl 29,8:2
Satan Never Sleeps 1962,F 22,20:1
I Thank a Fool 1962,S 15,15:1
Seymour
Way Down East 1935,O 31,16:2
Seymour, Al
Face Behind the Mask, The 1941,F 7,23:2
Seymour, Anne
All the King's Men 1949,N 9,37:2
Whistle at Eaton Falls, The 1951,O 11,49:2
Man on Fire 1957,Ag 23,10:1
Gift of Love, The 1958,F 12,32:2
Desire Under the Elms 1958,Mr 13,24:2
Home from the Hill 1960,Mr 4,19:1
Pollyanna 1960,My 20,26:1
Subterraneans, The 1960,Jl 7,26:1
Misty 1961,Jl 18,33:2
Good Neighbor Sam 1964,Jl 23,19:1
Where Love Has Gone 1964,N 3,26:1
Mirage 1965,My 27,28:1
Blindfold 1966,My 26,55:2
Fitzwilly 1967,D 21,45:1
Seymour, Anne (Miscellaneous)
Rainbow, The 1944,O 23,14:3
Seymour, Clarine
Girl Who Stayed Home, The 1919,Mr 24,11:3
True Heart Susie 1919,Je 2,20:4
Idol Dancer, The 1920,Mr 22,12:1
Seymour, Dan
Bombs Over Burma 1942,Ag 10,15:2
Casablanca 1942,N 27,27:1
Tahiti Honey 1943,My 13,17:2
To Have and Have Not 1944,O 12,24:1
Confidential Agent 1945,N 3,11:2
Searching Wind, The 1946,Je 27,29:1
Night in Casablanca, A 1946,Ag 12,17:2
Cloak and Dagger 1946,O 5,13:2
Slave Girl 1947,Jl 18,21:3
Intrigue 1948,Ap 24,11:2
Key Largo 1948,Jl 17,6:6
Johnny Belinda 1948,O 2,11:2
Mara Maru 1952,Ap 24,38:1
Rancho Notorious 1952,My 15,39:5
Glory Alley 1952,Jl 30,20:8
Bride Comes to Yellow Sky, The 1953,Ja 14,27:2
Second Chance 1953,Jl 23,20:2
Human Desire 1954,Ag 7,7:2
Moonfleet 1955,Je 25,9:2
Beyond a Reasonable Doubt 1956,S 14,27:2
Buster Keaton Story, The 1957,Ap 22,31:6
Watusi 1959,Jl 2,15:2
Seymour, Harry
Tenderfoot, The 1932,My 23,18:4
You Said a Mouthful 1932,N 18,23:2
Man Against Woman 1932,D 17,22:3

Seymour, Harry— Cont
Case of the Howling Dog, The 1934,O 18,26:5
6-Day Bike Rider 1934,N 3,20:3
Shipmates Forever 1935,O 17,29:3
Broadway Hostess 1935,D 16,23:3
Slight Case of Murder, A 1938,F 28,19:1
Boy Meets Girl 1938,Ag 27,7:2
Give my Regards to Broadway 1948,Je 23,32:2
Seymour, James
Phenix City Story, The 1955,S 3,9:1
Seymour, James (Miscellaneous)
Gold Diggers in Paris 1938,Je 2,19:2
Seymour, James (Screenwriter)
Footlight Parade 1933,O 6,21:3
King of Burlesque 1936,Ja 16,25:2
Meet Me at Dawn 1948,My 18,26:2
Seymour, Jane
Back Door to Heaven 1939,Ap 20,21:2
Tom, Dick and Harry 1941,Jl 18,22:2
Remember the Day 1941,D 26,21:2
Seymour, Jonah
King and Country 1966,Ja 28,20:4
Seymour, Madeline
Last of Mrs Cheyney, The 1929,Ag 12,22:2
His Glorious Night 1929,O 5,22:5
Seyn, Seyna
Casanova 1965,Jl 21,43:1
Seyrig, Delphine
Last Year at Marienbad 1962,Mr 8,26:1
Muriel 1963,O 31,26:1
Accident 1967,Ap 18,33:1
Sha-fei, Ouyang
Love Eterne, The; Liang Shan Po and Chu
  Ying-lai 1965,Ja 16,14:1
Shepherd Girl, The 1965,S 2,36:3
Shaarfenberg, Robert (Producer)
Kuhle Wampe 1933,Ap 24,11:4
Shabalina, L
Taxi to Heaven 1944,My 25,16:3
In the Name of Life 1947,O 20,29:2
Shabati-Tevet (Original Author)
Impossible on Saturday 1966,F 17,29:1
Shabati-Tevet (Screenwriter)
Impossible on Saturday 1966,F 17,29:1
Shackelford, Floyd
Black Fury 1935,Ap 11,27:2
Shackleton, Richard
Pony Soldier 1952,D 20,15:2
Shackleton, Robert
Wonder Boy 1951,D 26,19:5
Where's Charley? 1952,Je 27,18:3
SHAFER
See Also SCHAEFFER, SCHAEFER, SCHAFER,
  SCHAFFER, SHAFFER
Shafer, Robert
Damn Yankees 1958,S 27,12:7
Shaff, Monroe (Original Author)
Headin' East 1938,Ja 15,19:2
Hollywood Round-Up 1938,Mr 5,11:2
Shaff, Monroe (Producer)
Dealers in Death 1934,D 15,9:3
Shaff, Monroe (Screenwriter)
Hollywood Round-Up 1938,Mr 5,11:2
Cipher Bureau 1938,D 14,32:6
Shaff, Monty (Producer)
Man-Eater of Kumaon 1948,Jl 2,24:2
Never Trust a Gambler 1951,Jl 20,14:2
Shaffel, Josef (Original Author)
Biggest Bundle of Them All, The 1968,Ja 18,46:1
Shaffel, Josef (Producer)
Biggest Bundle of Them All, The 1968,Ja 18,46:1
SHAFFER
See Also SCHAEFFER, SCHAEFER, SCHAFER,
  SCHAFFER, SHAFER
Shaffer, Peter (Original Author)
Five Finger Exercise 1962,Ap 20,20:2
Pad, The (And How to Use It) 1966,Ag 18,27:2
Shaffer, Rosalind (Original Author)
Lady Killer 1934,Ja 1,28:2
Jesse James 1939,Ja 14,13:1
Shafi-Volina, M
Under Sunny Skies 1950,D 26,19:3
Shafron, A (Cinematographer)
Heroes of the Arctic 1935,My 24,24:2
Shaftel, Josef (Original Author)
Bliss of Mrs Blossom, The 1968,D 12,62:6
Shaftel, Josef (Producer)
Paris Express, The 1953,Je 6,8:6
Bliss of Mrs Blossom, The 1968,D 12,62:6
Shagaida, S
False Uniforms 1932,N 19,20:2
Frontier 1935,D 28,10:5
Shagalova, L
Young Guard 1949,D 26,33:6
True Friends 1954,N 15,33:2
Duel, The 1964,S 7,11:2
Marriage of Baezaminov, The 1966,Je 11,20:2
Shagin, A
Golden Key, The 1939,D 21,29:3
Shahdoodakian, Tatiezam
Honor 1929,S 10,27:1
Shaheen, John M Comdr (Miscellaneous)
O S S 1946,My 27,15:5

Shaid, Nick
  Private Worlds 1935,Mr 28,25:2
  Last Outpost, The 1935,O 5,18:2
Shaikevich, A (Screenwriter)
  Train Goes to Kiev, The 1961,Ap 10,26:1
Shaindlin, Jack (Composer)
  Days of Thrills and Laughter 1961,Mr 22,37:1
Shainov, Pavel
  House I Live in, The 1959,Ap 20,34:2
Shairp, Mordaunt (Miscellaneous)
  Barrier, The 1937,N 27,21:2
Shairp, Mordaunt (Screenwriter)
  Dark Angel, The 1935,S 6,12:2
  White Angel, The 1936,Je 25,24:1
Shakespeare, Co
  Tell Me Lies 1968,F 13,46:3
Shakespeare, Royal Co (Miscellaneous)
  London Scene, The (The Benefit of the Doubt);
    Benefit of the Doubt, The (The London Scene)
    1967,S 27,39:1
Shakespeare, William
  Big Game, The 1936,O 24,23:1
Shakespeare, William (Original Author)
  Macbeth 1916,Je 5,9:1
  Romeo and Juliet 1916,O 23,10:3
  Romeo and Juliet 1916,O 23,10:3
  Taming of the Shrew, The 1929,N 30,23:1
  Midsummer Night's Dream, A 1935,O 10,31:1
  Romeo and Juliet 1936,Ag 21,12:2
  As You Like It 1936,N 6,29:3
  Henry V 1946,Je 18,30:2
  Hamlet 1948,S 30,32:2
  Macbeth 1950,D 28,22:6
  Measure for Measure 1951,D 8,9:2
  Merry Wives of Windsor, The 1952,S 22,19:2
  Julius Caesar 1952,N 25,33:5
  Julius Caesar 1953,Je 5,19:1
  Romeo and Juliet 1954,D 22,28:1
  Othello 1955,S 13,27:1
  Twelfth Night 1956,Mr 5,21:1
  Richard III 1956,Mr 12,1:4
  Ballet of Romeo and Juliet, The 1956,Ap 3,31:2
  Throne of Blood 1961,N 23,50:2
  Midsummer Night's Dream, A 1961,D 19,39:1
  Ballet of Othello, The 1964,My 4,35:1
  Hamlet 1964,S 15,32:1
  Othello 1966,F 2,24:1
  Merry Wives of Windsor, The 1966,F 28,21:1
  Hamlet 1966,Mr 16,48:1 .
  Taming of the Shrew, The 1967,Mr 9,43:1
  Falstaff; Chimes at Midnight 1967,Mr 18,19:2
  Midsummer Night's Dream, A 1967,Ap 18,32:1
  Romeo and Juliet 1968,O 9,41:1
Shakhmagonov, F (Screenwriter)
  Fate of Man 1961,Jl 11,28:1
Shakhovskoi, G (Screenwriter)
  Paris Commune 1937,Je 2,20:4
Shale, Betty
  Evergreen 1935,Ja 11,29:1
Shaler, Virginia (Original Author)
  Walk East on Beacon 1952,My 29,17:2
Shaler, Virginia (Screenwriter)
  Lost Boundaries 1949,Jl 1,14:4
  Whistle at Eaton Falls, The 1951,O 11,49:2
  Man on a String 1960,My 21,15:1
Shall, Theo
  Olympia 1930,D 7,IX,6:4
  Anna Christie 1931,Ja 6,25:1
  Hochtourist, Der 1934,Ja 13,16:4
  Kirschen in Nachbars Garten 1937,My 15,23:6
  Graue Dame, Die; Gray Lady, The
    1938,D 17,10:4
Shallenbach, Frank
  Fireman, Save My Child 1932,F 18,25:3
Shamin, Pavel
  Life in Bloom 1949,My 9,20:4
Shamis, N
  Mistress, The 1954,My 31,9:2
Shan, Kwan
  Shepherd Girl, The 1965,S 2,36:3
Shand, Ian
  Life at the Top 1965,D 15,53:1
SHANE
  See Also SHAYNE
Shane, Maxwell (Director)
  Fear in the Night 1947,Ap 19,11:3
  City Across the River 1949,Ap 8,31:3
  Naked Street, The 1955,O 1,11:2
  Nightmare 1956,My 12,12:7
Shane, Maxwell (Miscellaneous)
  Wait Till the Sun Shines, Nellie 1952,Je 28,12:2
Shane, Maxwell (Original Author)
  This Way Please 1937,O 8,27:2
  Hitting a new High 1937,D 27,11:1
  Grand Jury Secrets 1939,Je 29,19:2
  Golden Gloves 1940,Ag 21,23:6
  Cowboy in Manhattan 1943,My 28,19:2
Shane, Maxwell (Producer)
  City Across the River 1949,Ap 8,31:3
Shane, Maxwell (Screenwriter)
  You Can't Beat Love 1937,Je 25,25:3
  You're a Sweetheart 1937,D 25,10:5
  She's Got Everything 1938,Ja 14,21:3

Tip-Off Girls 1938,Mr 25,15:3
Adventure in Sahara 1938,D 19,19:2
Federal Man-Hunt 1939,F 2,17:3
S O S Tidal Wave 1939,Je 22,19:3
Golden Gloves 1940,Ag 21,23:6
Mummy's Hand, The 1940,S 20,27:2
Comin' Round the Mountain 1940,S 26,27:3
Dangerous Game, A 1941,Mr 4,20:3
Power Dive 1941,My 29,15:4
No Hands on the Clock 1941,D 22,24:6
I Live on Danger 1942,Ag 22,16:2
Aerial Gunner 1943,Je 26,10:2
One Body too Many 1944,N 25,21:2
People Are Funny 1946,Ja 28,15:6
Fear in the Night 1947,Ap 19,11:3
Adventure Island 1947,O 20,29:2
City Across the River 1949,Ap 8,31:3
Hell's Island 1955,My 7,10:2
Naked Street, The 1955,O 1,11:2
Nightmare 1956,My 12,12:7
Shane, Michael
  One Potato, Two Potato 1964,Jl 30,16:1
Shane, Sara
  Magnificent Obsession 1954,Ag 5,18:4
  Daddy Long Legs 1955,My 6,17:5
  Three bad Sisters 1956,F 13,24:1
  King and Four Queens, The 1956,D 22,13:7
  Tarzan's Greatest Adventure 1959,Jl 9,22:1
Shank, Gregg
  Day Mars Invaded Earth, The 1964,Ap 2,28:3
Shank, Jon
  Thomas Crown Affair, The 1968,Je 27,48:2
Shankar, Ravi
  Kanchenjungha 1966,Jl 26,27:2
  Chappaqua 1967,N 6,65:2
Shankar, Ravi (Composer)
  Chappaqua 1967,N 6,65:2
Shanley, Robert Sgt
  This Is the Army 1943,Jl 29,11:6
Shannon, Cora
  Mr Belvedere Rings the Bell 1951,Ag 2,18:1
Shannon, Effie
  Mamma's Affair 1921,Ja 24,16:2
  Man Who Played God, The 1922,O 2,21:2
  Secrets of Paris 1923,Ja 8,22:1
  Side Show of Life, The 1924,Jl 22,9:1
  Sinners in Heaven 1924,S 10,21:3
  Soul Fire 1925,My 6,26:3
  New Commandment, The 1925,N 10,25:3
  Wiser Sex, The 1932,Mr 12,19:5
Shannon, Ethel
  Old Fashioned Boy, An 1920,N 1,13:2
  Daughters of the Rich 1923,Je 18,13:5
  Maytime 1924,Je 2,14:3
  Charley's Aunt 1925,F 9,15:3
  Stop Flirting 1925,Je 18,16:3
  Texas Trail, The 1925,Jl 9,14:2
  Oh Baby! 1926,Ag 11,25:2
Shannon, Frank
  Icebound 1924,Mr 3,22:3 (In Addenda)
  Monsieur Beaucaire 1924,Ag 12,12:1 (In
    Addenda)
  Men Without Names 1935,Je 29,16:2
  Prisoner of Shark Island, The 1936,F 13,25:2
  Texas Rangers, The 1936,S 24,29:1
  Torchy Blane, The Adventurous Blonde
    1937,D 18,18:1
  Mars Attacks the World 1938,N 8,26:3
  Torchy Gets her Man 1938,N 18,25:3
  Night of Nights, The 1939,D 28,17:1
  Return of Frank James, The 1940,Ag 10,16:4
Shannon, Frank (Director)
  Hired Killer, The 1967,Mr 2,30:3
Shannon, Frank (Screenwriter)
  Hired Killer, The 1967,Mr 2,30:3
Shannon, Harry
  Heads Up 1930,O 13,31:1
  City of Chance 1940,Ja 22,11:3
  Young as You Feel 1940,Mr 8,25:3
  Young Tom Edison 1940,Mr 15,27:2
  Tear Gas Squad 1940,My 31,15:3
  Sailor's Lady 1940,Je 29,12:2
  Tugboat Annie Sails Again 1940,N 9,20:2
  Too Many Girls 1940,N 21,43:1
  Saint in Palm Springs, The 1941,Ja 31,15:5
  Citizen Kane 1941,My 2,25:1
  Lady is Willing, The 1942,Ap 24,21:2
  Falcon takes Over, The 1942,My 30,9:2
  In old California 1942,Je 18,25:3
  Big Street, The 1942,Ag 14,13:1
  Once Upon a Honeymoon 1942,N 13,28:1
  Powers Girl, The 1943,Mr 26,14:2 (In Addenda)
  True to Life 1943,O 14,26:1
  Eve of St Mark, The 1944,My 31,22:2
  Mummy's Ghost, The 1944,Jl 1,10:7
  Crime Incorporated 1945,Je 23,9:7
  Within These Walls 1945,Jl 16,8:4
  Night Editor 1946,Mr 30,11:2
  Last Crooked Mile, The 1946,S 14,10:8
  San Quentin 1947,F 10,24:3
  Red House, The 1947,Mr 17,27:2
  Farmer's Daughter, The 1947,Mr 26,31:2
  Time Out of Mind 1947,Ap 7,20:1

Shannon, Harry— Cont
  Invisible Wall, The 1947,N 1,11:2
  Mr Blandings Builds his Dream House
    1948,Mr 26,26:2
  Lady From Shanghai, The 1948,Je 10,28:2
  Fighting Father Dunne 1948,Je 25,26:2
  Champion 1949,Ap 11,29:2
  Tulsa 1949,My 27,25:2
  Mary Ryan, Detective 1949,N 4,33:3
  Singing Guns 1950,Je 5,19:3
  Underworld Story, The 1950,Jl 27,29:4
  Three Little Words 1950,Ag 10,21:2
  Curtain Call at Cactus Creek 1950,S 22,35:4
  Flying Missile, The 1950,D 25,25:1
  Where Danger Lives 1951,Ja 1,13:6
  Lemon Drop Kid, The 1951,Mr 22,41:2
  Screen, The 1951,Ap 23,21:2
  Outcasts of Poker Flat 1952,My 16,19:3
  High Noon 1952,Jl 25,14:2
  Lure of the Wilderness 1952,O 4,15:2
  Jack Slade 1953,O 29,42:6
  Witness to Murder 1954,Ap 16,16:4
  Executive Suite 1954,My 7,19:1
  Rails Into Laramie 1954,My 13,34:2
  Tall Men, The 1955,O 12,36:2
  Written on the Wind 1957,Ja 12,12:6
  Buccaneer, The 1958,D 24,00:0
  Gypsy 1962,N 2,24:1
Shannon, Peggy
  Secret Call, The 1931,Jl 13,13:5
  Silence 1931,Ag 15,18:3
  Road to Reno, The 1931,O 10,20:4
  Touchdown 1931,N 16,23:1
  This Reckless Age 1932,Ja 9,21:1
  Hotel Continental 1932,Mr 21,19:5
  Society Girl 1932,Je 10,22:3
  Painted Woman, The 1932,S 16,24:4
  False Faces 1932,N 25,19:2
  Girl Missing 1933,Ap 1,18:2
  Turn Back the Clock 1933,Ag 26,14:2
  Devil's Mate 1933,S 23,11:7
  Deluge 1933,O 9,22:3
  Night Life of the Gods 1935,F 23,14:6
  Case of the Lucky Legs, The 1935,N 1,25:1
  Man I Marry, The 1936,O 31,24:3
  Blackwell's Island 1939,Mr 2,19:1
  Fixer Dugan 1939,My 6,21:2
  Street of Missing Women 1940,Ja 8,11:2
  House Across the Bay, The 1940,Mr 22,23:2
Shannon, Richard
  Pony Express 1953,Je 6,8:6
  Houdini 1953,Jl 3,10:2
  Arrowhead 1953,S 16,38:6
  Flight to Tangier 1953,N 26,50:4
  Forever Female 1954,Ja 13,26:2
  Alaska Seas 1954,Mr 6,13:5
  White Christmas 1954,O 15,16:3
  Bridges at Toko-Ri, The 1955,Ja 21,20:2
  Strategic Air Command 1955,Ap 21,33:1
  Seven Little Foys, The 1955,Je 30,18:2
  Artists and Models 1955,D 22,20:1
  Proud and Profane, The 1956,Je 14,41:2
  Leather Saint, The 1956,Je 16,12:2
  Tin Star, The 1957,O 24,37:2
Shannon, Robert T (Original Author)
  Taxi Dancer, The 1927,Mr 8,18:4
  Strictly Personal 1933,Mr 20,18:2
  I Sell Anything 1934,D 27,25:2
  Times Square Lady 1935,Mr 15,25:3
  Night at the Ritz, A 1935,My 16,20:2
  King Solomon of Broadway 1935,O 19,12:2
  Moonlight Murder 1936,Mr 28,11:2
  Murder in Greenwich Village 1937,O 30,22:2
  Invisible Enemy 1938,Ap 30,18:2
  Flame, The 1948,F 20,19:2
  Unknown Island 1949,Ja 8,11:4
Shannon, Robert T (Screenwriter)
  Night at the Ritz, A 1935,My 16,20:2
  King Solomon of Broadway 1935,O 19,12:2
Shannon, robert T (Screenwriter)
  Racketeers in Exile 1937,Ap 12,15:3
Shannon, Robert T (Screenwriter)
  Girl With Ideas, A 1938,Ja 1,11:2
  Unknown Island 1949,Ja 8,11:4
Shantaram, V
  Shakuntala 1947,D 26,22:3
Shantaram, V (Director)
  Shakuntala 1947,D 26,22:3
Shao-fen, Lo
  Song of China 1936,N 10,31:3
Shao-Hua, Tong (Screenwriter)
  Maid of Formosa 1949,Ag 8,10:5
Shapalina, L
  New Teacher, The 1941,Ap 7,13:3
Shapir, Ziva
  Tattered Dress, The 1957,Mr 15,22:3
Shapiro, Dan (Composer)
  Double Crossbones 1951,Ap 27,19:2
Shapiro, Helen
  Play it Cool 1963,Jl 18,15:3
Shapiro, Irvin (Producer)
  We Accuse 1945,Je 4,22:4

Shapiro, Irwin
Echoes of Silence 1967,Ap 7,32:2
Shapiro, Josif (Screenwriter)
Sleeping Beauty, The 1966,My 4,50:1
Shapiro, Lionel (Original Author)
Sealed Verdict 1948,N 3,36:2
Deported 1950,N 2,39:3
D-Day, The Sixth of June 1956,My 30,13:1
Shapiro, Mikhail (Director)
Leningrad Music Hall 1943,N 6,16:3
Christmas Slippers 1945,D 24,19:2
Shapiro, Mikhail (Screenwriter)
Christmas Slippers 1945,D 24,19:2
Shapiro, Seelen and Lee (Composer)
Crazy House 1943,D 16,33:3
Shapiro, Stanley (Producer)
Lover Come Back 1962,F 9,21:1
That Touch of Mink 1962,Je 15,16:2
Bedtime Story 1964,Je 11,27:1
Very Special Favor, A 1965,Ag 26,40:3
How to Save a Marriage - And Ruin Your Life
1968,Ja 19,30:1
Shapiro, Stanley (Screenwriter)
South Sea Woman 1953,Je 4,33:6
Perfect Furlough, The 1959,Ja 22,27:4
Pillow Talk 1959,O 7,47:2
Operation Petticoat 1959,D 6,38:1
Come September 1961,S 8,34:1
Lover Come Back 1962,F 9,21:1
That Touch of Mink 1962,Je 15,16:2
Bedtime Story 1964,Je 11,27:1
Very Special Favor, A 1965,Ag 26,40:3
How to Save a Marriage - And Ruin Your Life
1968,Ja 19,30:1
Shapley, Harlow (Original Author)
Of Stars and Men 1964,Ap 29,47:1
Shaporenko, Lidiya
Peace to Him Who Enters 1963,N 25,23:5
Shaporin, Y A (Composer)
Three Songs About Lenin 1934,N 7,32:1
Prisoners 1937,F 20,9:2
Mother and Sons 1938,S 15,29:2
Shaps, Cyril
Little Ones, The 1965,S 16,55:2
Sharar, Diwan (Screenwriter)
Shakuntala 1947,D 26,22:3
Sharbutt, Del
Hit Parade of 1947 1947,My 5,32:8
Sharff, Stefan (Director)
Across the River 1965,Ap 27,27:1
Sharff, Stefan (Screenwriter)
Across the River 1965,Ap 27,27:1
Shari, William
Tiger Bay 1959,D 15,50:1
Brig, The 1964,S 21,37:4
Shariakhov, Victor
Sisters 1959,My 25,33:2
Sharif, Omar
Lawrence of Arabia 1962,D 17,5:6
Fall of the Roman Empire, The 1964,Mr 27,14:2
Behold a Pale Horse 1964,Ag 14,16:1
Yellow Rolls-Royce, The 1965,My 14,42:2
Genghis Khan 1965,Je 24,28:2
Doctor Zhivago 1965,D 23,21:1
Marco the Magnificent 1966,D 15,60:1
Night of the Generals, The 1967,F 3,38:1
More Than a Miracle 1967,N 2,58:2
Poppy is Also a Flower, The 1967,D 14,62:4
Funny Girl 1968,S 20,42:1
Sharif, Tarek
Doctor Zhivago 1965,D 23,21:1
Sharkey, Sailor
Good Morning, Judge 1928,Je 26,29:1
Sharland, Gus
Children of Chance 1931,Ja 24,15:1
Sharland, Reginald
Woman to Woman 1929,N 12,34:4
Born to Love 1931,Ap 25,23:4
Long Lost Father 1934,F 19,18:2
Sharma, Amar N
Road to Singapore, The 1931,O 1,25:2
Sharma, Partap
Shakespeare Wallah 1966,Mr 23,40:2
Sharoff, Pietro
Wandering Jew, The 1949,Mr 11,33:2
Sharon, Jean
Child Is Born, A 1940,Ja 11,19:2
Sharp, Don (Director)
Kiss of the Vampire 1963,O 10,49:2
Dream Maker, The 1964,Ap 23,34:1
Face of Fu Manchu, The 1965,N 11,58:3
Bang, Bang, You're Dead 1967,Ja 19,41:2
Those Fantastic Flying Fools 1967,O 19,59:2
Sharp, Don (Screenwriter)
Edge of Divorce 1954,Jl 2,10:1
Fuss Over Feathers 1954,D 27,22:6
Sharp, Henry
Singing in the Dark 1956,Mr 8,32:5
Face in the Crowd, A 1957,My 29,33:1
Violators, The 1959,Ag 4,32:5
Sharp, Margery (Original Author)
Cluny Brown 1946,Je 3,27:3
Julia Misbehaves 1948,O 8,30:2

Forbidden Street, The 1949,My 14,9:2
Notorious Landlady, The 1962,Jl 27,15:2
Sharp-Bolster, Anita
Love From a Stranger 1947,N 28,30:1
Woman in White, The 1948,My 8,12:2
Rising of the Moon, The (A Minute's Wait);
Minute's Wait, A (The Rising of the Moon)
1957,Jl 10,23:1
Boy Cried Murder, The 1966,Ap 14,42:3
Sharpe, Albert
Up in Central Park 1948,My 27,29:3
Return of October, The 1949,F 23,31:2
Portrait of Jennie 1949,Mr 30,31:2
Adventure in Baltimore 1949,Ap 29,27:2
Royal Wedding 1951,Mr 9,30:2
Secret Sharer, The 1953,Ja 14,27:2
Brigadoon 1954,S 17,18:2
Darby O'Gill and the Little People 1959,Jl 1,26:1
Day They Robbed the Bank of England, The
1960,S 5,11:2
Sharpe, Alex
Rocky Mountain 1950,N 4,13:2
Sharpe, Edith
Guinea Pig, The 1949,My 2,20:2
No Place for Jennifer 1951,Jl 17,31:2
Landfall 1953,My 11,25:2
Brothers in Law 1957,Ag 20,22:1
Happy is the Bride 1959,Je 30,27:2
French Mistress, A 1960,D 19,34:2
Francis of Assisi 1961,Jl 29,8:2
Satan Never Sleeps 1962,F 22,20:1
Cash on Demand 1962,My 17,31:1
Sharpe, Karen
Mad at the World 1955,My 14,10:8
Man With the Gun 1955,D 23,14:2
Disorderly Orderly, The 1964,D 24,8:3
Sharpe, Lester
Time to Kill 1942,D 25,15:4
Song of my Heart 1948,Mr 5,17:3
Amazon Quest 1949,My 14,9:3
I Was a Male War Bride 1949,Ag 27,7:2
Flying Saucer, The 1950,Ja 5,28:3
Carrie 1952,Jl 17,20:2
Sharples, Winston (Composer)
Gulliver's Travels 1939,D 21,29:1
Sharpsteen, Ben (Director)
Dumbo 1941,O 24,27:2
Sharpsteen, Ben (Miscellaneous)
Melody Time 1948,My 28,28:2
Adventures of Ichabod and Mr Toad, The
1949,O 10,18:2
Alice in Wonderland 1951,Jl 30,12:4
Sharpsteen, Ben (Producer)
Cinderella 1950,F 23,33:1
Secrets of Life 1956,N 21,20:1
White Wilderness 1958,Ag 13,22:1
Shaternikova, N
Czar wants to Sleep, The 1934,D 10,16:3
Professor Mamlock 1938,N 8,26:2
Ladies 1955,Je 27,18:2
Shatner, William
Brothers Karamazov, The 1958,F 21,18:2
Judgment at Nuremberg 1961,D 20,36:1
Explosive Generation, The 1962,F 15,24:2
Intruder, The 1962,My 15,48:1
Outrage, The 1964,O 8,48:2
Shatov, A P
Gobsek 1937,Jl 16,22:1
Lenin in 1918 1939,Je 27,27:2
Shatrova, E M
Lenin in October 1938,Ap 2,18:1
Shattuck, Truly
Rubber Heels 1927,Je 28,29:4
Shatunovsky, William
And Quiet Flows the Don 1960,My 25,45:2
Shauer, Mel (Producer)
This Way Please 1937,O 8,27:2
Shaughnessy, Alfred (Screenwriter)
Scotch on the Rocks 1954,Je 14,18:2
Shaughnessy, Mickey
Marrying Kind, The 1952,Mr 14,27:1
From Here to Eternity 1953,Ag 6,16:2
Conquest of Space 1955,My 28,7:6
Designing Woman 1957,My 17,20:2
Until They Sail 1957,O 9,41:2
Slaughter on Tenth Avenue 1957,N 6,43:1
Jailhouse Rock 1957,N 14,41:1
Don't Go Near the Water 1957,N 15,37:1
Sheepman, The 1958,My 8,36:1
Nice Little Bank That Should Be Robbed, A
1958,D 11,17:4
Don't Give up the Ship 1959,Jl 9,22:1
Edge of Eternity 1960,F 25,34:2
Adventures of Huckleberry Fin, The
1960,Ag 4,17:1
College Confidential 1960,Ag 22,23:1
North to Alaska 1960,N 11,36:1
King of the Roaring Twenties 1961,O 5,43:1
Pocketful of Miracles 1961,D 19,39:1
House is not a Home, A 1964,S 2,33:1
Never a Dull Moment 1968,Ag 15,46:2

Shavelson, Melville (Director)
Seven Little Foys, The 1955,Je 30,18:2
Beau James 1957,Je 27,21:1
Houseboat 1958,N 14,24:1
Five Pennies, The 1959,Je 19,30:1
It Started in Naples 1960,S 3,7:6
On the Double 1961,My 20,12:1
Pigeon That Took Rome, The 1962,Ag 23,25:1
New Kind of Love, A 1963,O 31,26:2
Cast a Giant Shadow 1966,Mr 31,43:3
Yours, Mine and Ours 1968,Ap 25,53:1
Shavelson, Melville (Miscellaneous)
Riding High 1950,Ap 11,26:2
Shavelson, Melville (Original Author)
Where There's Life 1947,D 25,32:1
I'll See You in my Dreams 1951,D 7,35:1
Shavelson, Melville (Producer)
Trouble Along the Way 1953,My 7,37:2
Pigeon That Took Rome, The 1962,Ag 23,25:1
New Kind of Love, A 1963,O 31,26:2
Cast a Giant Shadow 1966,Mr 31,43:3
Shavelson, Melville (Screenwriter)
Princess and the Pirate, The 1945,F 10,16:2
Wonder Man 1945,Je 9,17:2
Kid From Brooklyn, The 1946,Ap 19,25:2
Where There's Life 1947,D 25,32:1
Sorrowful Jones 1949,Je 6,15:2
It's a Great Feeling 1949,Ag 13,6:6
Great Lover, The 1949,N 24,48:2
Always Leave Them Laughing 1949,N 24,48:2
Daughter of Rosie O'Grady, The
1950,Mr 31,36:2
On Moonlight Bay 1951,Jl 27,15:2
Double Dynamite 1951,D 26,19:4
Room for One More 1952,Ja 16,21:2
April in Paris 1952,D 25,34:5
Trouble Along the Way 1953,My 7,37:2
Living It Up 1954,Jl 24,6:6
Seven Little Foys, The 1955,Je 30,18:2
Beau James 1957,Je 27,21:1
Houseboat 1958,N 14,24:1
Five Pennies, The 1959,Je 19,30:1
It Started in Naples 1960,S 3,7:6
On the Double 1961,My 20,12:1
Pigeon That Took Rome, The 1962,Ag 23,25:1
New Kind of Love, A 1963,O 31,26:2
Cast a Giant Shadow 1966,Mr 31,43:3
Yours, Mine and Ours 1968,Ap 25,53:1
Shavgulidze, G
They Wanted Peace 1940,Ja 8,11:3
Dragonfly, The 1955,Je 27,18:2
Shaw, Al
Last Express, The 1938,O 11,24:4
Gracie Allen Murder Case, The 1939,Je 8,31:3
Shaw, Anabel
Shock 1946,Mr 9,10:2
Home Sweet Homicide 1946,S 12,5:7
Mother Wore Tights 1947,Ag 21,33:2
High Tide 1947,N 8,11:2
Secret Beyond the Door 1948,Ja 16,25:4
City Across the River 1949,Ap 8,31:3
Gun Crazy 1950,Ag 25,17:5
Shaw, Ann
Cavalcade 1933,Ja 6,23:2
Clive of India 1935,Ja 18,29:1
Shaw, Anthony
Wings and the Woman 1942,O 8,31:1
Patient Vanishes, The 1947,My 23,31:2
How to Murder a Rich Uncle 1957,O 26,19:2
Shaw, Artie
Dancing Co-Ed 1939,N 10,27:3
Second Chorus 1941,Ja 16,25:2
Shaw, Artie (Composer)
Second Chorus 1941,Ja 16,25:2
Big Store, The 1941,Je 27,14:4
Shaw, Barbara
Pearls of the Crown, The 1938,Ap 12,26:2
Woman in the Hall, The 1949,Ja 24,16:2
Shaw, Brinsley
Enemy to the King, An 1916,N 27,9:1
Mary Regan 1919,My 5,11:1
Unknown Purple, The 1924,Mr 24,13:1
Four Horsemen of the Apocalypse, The
1926,S 27,27:3
Dove, The 1928,Ja 3,28:2
Shaw, Charles (Original Author)
Heaven Knows Mr Allison 1957,Mr 15,22:1
Shaw, Danny
Silver Skates 1943,Mr 19,15:3
Shaw, David (Original Author)
Foreign Affair, A 1948,Jl 1,19:3
Shaw, DAvid (Original Author)
Take one False Step 1949,Je 23,33:2
Shaw, David (Screenwriter)
Man Inside, The 1959,F 5,24:7
Shaw, Dennis
Misfits, The 1961,F 2,24:2
Shaw, George Bernard (Original Author)
How He Lied to her Husband 1931,Ja 17,23:1
Pygmalion 1938,D 8,34:2
Major Barbara 1941,My 15,27:1
Caesar and Cleopatra 1946,S 6,18:2
Androcles and the Lion 1953,Ja 15,23:2

Shaw, George Bernard (Original Author)— Cont
  Saint Joan 1957,Je 27,21:1
  Doctor's Dilemma, A 1958,D 18,2:7
  Devil's Disciple, The 1959,Ag 21,12:1
  Millionairess, The 1961,F 10,19:1
  Arms and the Man 1962,F 24,21:7
  My Fair Lady 1964,O 22,41:1
Shaw, George Bernard (Screenwriter)
  Pygmalion 1938,D 8,34:2
  Major Barbara 1941,My 15,27:1
Shaw, Glen Byam
  Look Back in Anger 1959,S 16,45:1
Shaw, Irwin (Miscellaneous)
  Tip on a Dead Jockey 1957,S 7,12:7
Shaw, Irwin (Original Author)
  Out of the Fog 1941,Je 21,20:2
  Take one False Step 1949,Je 23,33:2
  Easy Living 1949,O 13,33:3
  Young Lions, The 1958,Ap 3,23:1
  Two Weeks in Another Town 1962,Ag 18,10:1
  In the French Style 1963,S 19,23:1
Shaw, Irwin (Producer)
  In the French Style 1963,S 19,23:1
  Survival 1967 1968,Je 12,40:2
Shaw, Irwin (Screenwriter)
  Big Game, The 1936,O 24,23:1
  Talk of the Town, The 1942,Ag 28,22:3
  Take one False Step 1949,Je 23,33:2
  I Want You 1951,D 24,9:1
  Commandos Strike at Dawn 1954,Ja 14,25:1
  Act of Love 1954,F 12,20:5
  Ulysses 1955,Ag 18,17:2
  Fire Down Below 1957,Ag 9,11:2
  Desire Under the Elms 1958,Mr 13,24:2
  This Angry Age 1958,Je 26,23:3
  Big Gamble, The 1961,S 2,19:2
  In the French Style 1963,S 19,23:1
  Survival 1967 1968,Je 12,40:2
Shaw, Janet
  Jezebel 1938,Mr 11,15:2
  Accidents Will Happen 1938,Ap 25,19:2
  Sisters, The 1938,O 15,21:3
  Old Maid, The 1939,Ag 12,16:2
  Waterloo Bridge 1940,My 17,23:2
  Flight Angels 1940,My 27,23:2
  Night Monster 1942,N 30,18:5
  Shadow of a Doubt 1943,Ja 13,18:2
  Ladies Courageous 1944,Mr 16,17:2
  Time Out of Mind 1947,Ap 7,20:1
Shaw, Kerry (Original Author)
  Men in her Diary 1945,S 24,16:5
Shaw, Lewis
  Are You a Mason? 1934,O 30,23:5
  High Treason 1937,Ja 27,17:3
Shaw, Lyn
  Grido, Il 1962,O 23,42:1
Shaw, Mary
  Hurricane, The 1937,N 10,31:2
Shaw, Maxwell
  Once More With Feeling 1960,F 12,22:2
Shaw, Montague
  Water Hole, The 1928,S 3,14:2
  Behind That Curtain 1929,Jl 1,31:2
  Silent Witness, The 1932,F 8,21:1
  Pack up Your Troubles 1932,O 1,10:4
  Sherlock Holmes 1932,N 12,20:5
  Masquerader, The 1933,S 4,9:5
  Sisters Under the Skin 1934,Je 8,18:1
  I Live for Love 1935,O 19,21:2
  King of Burlesque 1936,Ja 16,25:2
  Parole Racket 1937,Mr 8,22:1
  Ready, Willing and Able 1937,Mr 15,27:1
  King and the Chorus Girl, The 1937,Mr 29,14:4
  Little Miss Broadway 1938,Jl 23,10:4
  Mars Attacks the World 1938,N 8,26:3
  Stanley and Livingstone 1939,Ag 5,18:2
  Rains Came, The 1939,S 9,11:2
  Gay Caballero, The 1940,O 25,25:3
  Charley's Aunt 1941,Ag 2,18:2
  Burma Convoy 1941,O 7,26:7
  Thunder Birds 1942,O 29,19:2
Shaw, Oscar
  Great White Way, The 1924,Ja 4,10:1
  King on Main Street, The 1925,O 26,25:2
  Upstage 1926,N 15,19:1
  Cocoanuts, The 1929,My 25,17:3
  Rhythm on the River 1940,Ag 29,23:2
Shaw, Peggy
  Little Child Shall Lead Them, A 1922,S 2,10:4
  In Hollywood with Potash and Perlmutter 1924,S 30,27:3
  Subway Sadie 1926,S 13,18:1
Shaw, Peter
  Clive of India 1935,Ja 18,29:1
Shaw, Reta
  Picnic 1956,F 17,13:3
  Man Afraid 1957,Ap 5,24:2
  Pajama Game, The 1957,Ag 30,12:2
  Lady Takes a Flyer, The 1958,Ja 30,19:2
  All Mine to Give 1959,Ag 4,32:5
  Pollyanna 1960,My 20,26:1
  Sanctuary 1961,F 22,31:1
  Bachelor in Paradise 1961,N 17,41:2
  Mary Poppins 1964,S 25,34:1

  Made in Paris 1966,F 17,29:1
  Ghost and Mr Chicken, The 1966,S 22,57:2
Shaw, Richard
  Caribbean Mystery, The 1945,Ag 20,22:4
Shaw, Robert
  20,000 Men a Year 1939,O 28,11:2
  Adam Had Four Sons 1941,Mr 28,26:6
  Ride on Vaquero 1941,Ap 19,20:2
  Valiant, The 1962,Je 14,23:4
  Guest, The 1964,Ja 21,25:2
  From Russia with Love 1964,Ap 9,25:1
  Luck of Ginger Coffey, The 1964,S 22,44:1
  Battle of the Bulge 1965,D 18,36:1
  Man for all Seasons, A 1966,D 13,60:1
  Custer of the West 1968,Jl 4,13:2
  Birthday Party, The 1968,D 10,54:1
Shaw, Robert (Original Author)
  Situation Hopeless-But not Serious 1965,O 14,53:1
Shaw, Run Run (Producer)
  Yang Kwei Fei 1956,S 11,41:2
  Last Woman of Shang, The 1964,D 15,56:2
  Love Eterne, The; Liang Shan Po and Chu Ying-lai 1965,Ja 16,14:1
  Lady General, The 1965,F 12,19:1
  Empress Wu 1965,Mr 16,42:2
  Empress Wu 1965,Mr 16,42:2
  Shepherd Girl, The 1965,S 2,36:3
  Grand Substitution, The 1965,N 25,64:5
  Sons of Good Earth 1967,S 16,37:5
Shaw, Sam (Producer)
  Paris Blues 1961,N 8,41:1
Shaw, Sebastian
  Brewster's Millions 1935,Ap 8,23:3
  Men Are not Gods 1937,Ja 19,28:1
  Murder on Diamond Row 1937,N 12,27:2
  Troopship 1938,Ap 26,18:2
  U-Boat 29 1939,O 6,31:3
  Glass Mountain, The 1950,My 18,37:3
  Scotch on the Rocks 1954,Je 14,18:2
  It Happened Here 1966,Ag 9,29:2
Shaw, Susan
  Upturned Glass, The 1947,N 5,34:4
  Holiday Camp 1948,Ja 24,11:2
  Dulcimer Street 1948,N 8,24:2
  My Brothers Keeper 1949,F 14,15:3
  It Always Rains on Sunday 1949,F 14,15:5
  Quartet (The Kite) 1949,Mr 29,30:3
  Here Come the Huggetts 1950,D 25,25:3
  Pool of London 1951,N 28,37:2
  Woman in Question, The 1952,F 19,24:2
  Marry Me 1952,Mr 14,27:3
  Wall of Death 1952,My 19,12:4
  Intruder, The 1955,Ja 26,22:1
Shaw, Sydney
  Always Rains on Sunday, It 1949,F 14,15:5
Shaw, Victoria
  Eddy Duchin Story, The 1956,Je 22,15:1
  Edge of Eternity 1960,F 25,34:2
  I Aim at the Stars 1960,O 20,42:2
  Alvarez Kelly 1966,N 17,55:2
Shaw, Winifred
  Million Dollar Ransom 1934,S 19,15:2
  Gift of Gab 1934,S 26,17:6
  Wake up and Dream 1934,O 11,28:3
  Sweet Adeline 1935,Ja 7,13:2
  Gold Diggers of 1935 1935,Mr 15,25:2
  Case of the Curious Bride, The 1935,Ap 5,21:3
  In Caliente 1935,Je 27,16:1
  Front Page Woman 1935,Jl 12,15:1
  Broadway Hostess 1935,D 16,23:3
  Singing Kid, The 1936,Ap 4,11:1
  Sons o'Guns 1936,My 14,29:2
  Satan Met a Lady 1936,Jl 23,24:2
  Case of the Velvet Claws, The 1936,Ag 29,16:3
  Smart Blonde 1937,Ja 9,21:1
  Fugitive in the Sky 1937,Ja 16,21:1
  Ready, Willing and Able 1937,Mr 15,27:1
  Melody for Two 1937,My 21,19:5
Shaw and Lee
  Young and Beautiful 1934,S 18,18:4
Shawa, Said
  Island of Allah 1956,Je 27,35:1
Shawhan, William
  Forgotten Commandments 1932,Je 2,25:2
Shawlee, Joan
  Prehistoric Women 1950,D 29,15:5
  Some Like It Hot 1959,Mr 30,23:1
  Apartment, The 1960,Je 16,37:2
  Irma la Douce 1963,Je 6,39:1
  Wild Angels, The 1966,D 22,40:4
Shawley, Robert
  Stalag 17 1953,Jl 2,19:2
Shawn, Dick
  Opposite Sex, The 1956,N 16,23:2
  Wake Me When It's Over 1960,Ap 9,17:2
  Wizard of Baghdad, The 1961,Mr 4,16:1
  It's a Mad, Mad, Mad, Mad World 1963,N 19,47:1
  Very Special Favor, A 1965,Ag 26,40:3
  What Did You Do in the War, Daddy? 1966,S 1,28:1
  Way...Way Out 1966,O 27,55:1

Shawn, Dick— Cont
  Penelope 1966,N 11,36:6
  Producers, The 1968,Mr 19,38:1
Shawn, Philip
  Sun Sets at Dawn, The 1951,Ja 15,13:1
Shawn, Ted (Miscellaneous)
  Arabian Duet 1922,My 15,20:3
Shawn, Woog A (Producer)
  Julie the Redhead 1963,O 15,44:1
Shawzin, Barry
  Duffy 1968,S 17,50:3
SHAY
  See Also SHEA
Shay, Dorothy
  Comin' Round the Mountain 1951,Jl 27,15:2
Shay, John
  Canal Zone 1942,Mr 30,21:2
  Iron Curtain, The 1948,My 13,31:2
Shay, Mildred
  Balalaika 1939,D 15,33:2
Shay, Patricia
  To Have and Have Not 1944,O 12,24:1
Shay, William E
  Telephone Girl, The 1927,My 16,24:2
SHAYNE
  See Also SHANE
Shayne, Konstantin
  Paris Honeymoon 1939,Ja 26,17:1
  Mission to Moscow 1943,Ap 30,25:2
  Five Graves to Cairo 1943,My 27,21:2
  For Whom the Bell Tolls 1943,Jl 15,25:2
  Song of Russia 1944,F 11,17:2
  Passage to Marseille 1944,F 17,12:5
  Till We Meet Again 1944,Ag 30,15:1
  Seventh Cross, The 1944,S 29,18:1
  None but the Lonely Heart 1944,N 18,16:6
  Falcon in Hollywood, The 1944,D 9,21:2
  Stranger, The 1946,Jl 11,18:2
  Dangerous Millions 1947,Mr 15,10:3
  Secret Life of Walter Mitty, The 1947,Ag 15,12:2
  Song of Love 1947,O 10,31:2
  Christmas Eve 1947,N 28,30:2
  To the Victor 1948,Ap 17,11:2
  Cry of the City 1948,S 30,32:4
  Red Danube, The 1949,D 9,37:3
  I Was a Communist for the F B I 1951,My 3,34:4
  Unknown Man, The 1951,N 17,9:5
  Treasure of the Golden Condor 1953,My 23,19:2
Shayne, Richard
  Let's Live a Little 1948,D 10,34:2
Shayne, Robert
  Wednesday's Child 1934,D 15,9:3
  Shine on Harvest Moon 1944,Mr 11,10:2
  Mr Skeffington 1944,My 26,23:2
  Make Your own Bed 1944,My 27,12:2
  Christmas in Connecticut 1945,Jl 28,7:2
  San Antonio 1945,D 29,19:5
  Three Strangers 1946,F 23,20:2
  Nobody Lives Forever 1946,N 2,12:2
  Smash-Up, The Story of a Woman 1947,Ap 11,31:2
  Backlash 1947,My 24,10:5
  Welcome Stranger 1947,Ag 7,15:2
  Spirit of West Point 1947,O 3,31:2
  Swordsman, The 1947,O 17,18:4
  Threat, The 1949,D 2,35:4
  Criminal Lawyer 1951,Ag 24,11:4
Shayne, Tamara
  Song of Russia 1944,F 11,17:2
  Jolson Story, The 1946,O 11,28:2
  It Happened in Brooklyn 1947,Mr 14,28:5
  Northwest Outpost 1947,Ag 8,10:2
  Pirates of Monterey 1947,D 17,41:4
  Jolson Sings Again 1949,Ag 18,16:6
  Thieves' Highway 1949,S 24,8:6
  Red Danube, The 1949,D 9,37:3
  Romanoff and Juliet 1961,Je 9,26:1
Shayon, Robert (Composer)
  Bohemian Girl, The 1936,F 17,21:1
Shchukin, B V
  Revolutionists 1936,D 26,15:3
  Lenin in October 1938,Ap 2,18:1
  Lenin in 1918 1939,Je 27,27:2
Shckelokov, Vladimir
  In the Far East 1937,O 20,27:3
Shdanoff, George
  Specter of the Rose 1946,S 2,12:4
SHEA
  See Also SHAY
Shea, Eric
  Yours, Mine and Ours 1968,Ap 25,53:1
Shea, Gloria
  Life Begins 1932,Ag 26,20:3
  Big City Blues 1932,S 10,18:5
  Night Mayor, The 1932,N 25,19:2
  Strange People 1933,Je 17,16:5
  Dance, Girl, Dance 1933,O 25,23:3
  Bolero 1934,F 17,20:3
  I Like It That Way 1934,Ap 18,23:3
  We're Rich Again 1934,S 1,16:3
  Laddie 1935,My 6,22:3
  Great God Gold 1935,My 6,22:3
  Last Days of Pompeii, The 1935,O 17,29:2
  One Way Ticket 1936,Ja 1,35:2

Shea, Jack (Director)
Dayton's Devils 1968,O 3,56:4
Shea, Mervyn
Stratton Story, The 1949,My 13,29:1
Shea, Olive
Glorifying the American Girl 1930,Ja 11,21:3
Shea, Oscar
Stranger on the Third Floor 1940,S 2,19:2
Shea, Timothy (Original Author)
Sarah and Son 1930,Mr 13,22:4
Shean, Al
Music in the Air 1934,D 14,29:3
Sweet Music 1935,F 21,23:2
Traveling Saleslady 1935,Mr 29,26:2
Page Miss Glory 1935,Ag 29,25:2
Law in her Hands, The 1936,Je 6,21:2
San Francisco 1936,Je 27,21:1
Road Back, The 1937,Je 18,25:2
Prisoner of Zenda, The 1937,S 3,12:1
52d Street 1937,N 15,15:1
Live, Love and Learn 1937,N 19,27:2
Great Waltz, The 1938,N 25,19:1
Broadway Serenade 1939,Ap 7,25:2
Blue Bird, The 1940,Ja 20,11:2
Ziegfeld Girl 1941,Ap 25,17:2
Tish 1942,S 18,25:2
Hitler's Madman 1943,Ag 28,15:1
Atlantic City 1944,Ag 14,11:4
Shean, Al (Composer)
Ziegfeld Girl 1941,Ap 25,17:2
SHEAR
See Also SHER, SHERR
Shear, Barry (Director)
Wild in the Streets 1968,My 30,21:1
Shearer, Moira
Red Shoes, The 1948,O 23,9:2
Tales of Hoffmann 1951,Ap 5,34:2
Story of Three Loves, The (The Jealous Lover);
Jealous Lover, The (The Story of Three Loves)
1953,Mr 6,29:2
Man Who Loved Redheads, The 1955,Jl 26,29:2
Black Tights 1962,F 21,54:2
Shearer, Norma
Lucretia Lombard 1923,D 17,23:1
Pleasure Mad 1924,Ja 7,23:1
Broadway After Dark 1924,My 20,15:2
Broken Barriers 1924,Ag 4,16:3
Empty Hands 1924,Ag 18,8:2
He Who Gets Slapped 1924,N 10,20:1
Snob, The 1924,D 15,14:1
Excuse Me 1925,Ja 27,11:2
Lady of the Night 1925,Mr 2,14:1
Waking up the Town 1925,Mr 31,17:4
Pretty Ladies 1925,Jl 14,14:1
Slave of Fashion, A 1925,Jl 21,26:2
Tower of Lies, The 1925,S 28,24:1
His Secretary 1925,D 21,27:2
Devil's Circus, The 1926,Mr 29,24:3
Waning Sex, The 1926,S 21,33:1
Upstage 1926,N 15,19:1
After Midnight 1927,Ag 16,31:2
Student Prince, The 1927,S 22,33:2
Latest From Paris, The 1928,F 27,16:2
Actress, The 1928,Jl 9,25:1
Lady of Chance, A 1929,Ja 14,20:1
Trial of Mary Dugan, The 1929,Mr 29,21:1
Last of Mrs Cheyney, The 1929,Ag 12,22:2
Hollywood Revue, The 1929,Ag 15,20:5
Their own Desire 1930,Ja 25,13:2
Divorcee, The 1930,My 10,25:3
Let Us Be Gay 1930,Jl 12,16:4
Stolen Jools 1931,Ap 4,23:1
Strangers May Kiss 1931,Ap 13,17:1
Free Soul, A 1931,Je 3,29:2
Private Lives 1931,D 19,16:4
Strange Interlude 1932,S 1,24:3
Smilin' Through 1932,O 15,13:1
Riptide 1934,Mr 31,8:2
Barretts of Wimpole Street, The 1934,S 29,12:2
Romeo and Juliet 1936,Ag 21,12:2
Marie Antoinette 1938,Ag 17,23:2
Idiot's Delight 1939,F 3,13:1
Women, The 1939,S 22,27:2
Escape 1940,N 1,33:1
We Were Dancing 1942,My 1,23:2
Her Cardboard Lover 1942,Jl 17,19:2
Shearing, George, Quintet
Jazz on a Summer's Day 1960,Mr 29,46:2
Shearing, Joseph (Original Author)
Moss Rose 1947,Jl 3,14:2
So Evil my Love 1948,Jl 22,27:2
Blanche Fury 1948,N 24,20:2
Shebalin, V Y (Miscellaneous)
Gobsek 1937,Jl 16,22:1
Shedio, Ronald (Producer)
Whisperers, The 1967,Ag 1,24:1
Sheean, Vincent (Miscellaneous)
Crisis 1939,Mr 13,12:2
Sheedren (Composer)
Little Humpbacked Horse, The 1962,O 8,19:1
Sheehan, John
Swing High 1930,Je 27,26:3
Kismet 1930,O 31,20:1

Criminal Code, The 1931,Ja 5,21:3
Hard to Handle 1933,F 2,21:5
Past of Mary Holmes, The 1933,My 1,10:3
Warrior's Husband, The 1933,My 12,20:4
Countess of Monte Cristo, The 1934,Ap 2,13:2
Little Miss Marker 1934,My 19,18:3
Goose and the Gander, The 1935,S 12,29:2
Ex-Mrs Bradford, The 1936,My 28,19:2
Ticket to Paradise 1936,Ag 8,5:3
Here Comes Carter 1936,N 14,23:3
Smart Blonde 1937,Ja 9,21:1
On the Avenue 1937,F 5,17:3
Midnight Court 1937,Mr 4,27:3
Love Takes Flight 1937,S 27,24:3
Night Club Scandal 1937,N 12,27:2
Young as You Feel 1940,Mr 8,25:3
Broadway Limited 1941,Je 16,11:6
Swingtime Johnny 1943,D 17,23:3
Stage to Tucson 1951,My 5,14:2
Sheehan, Perley Poore (Original Author)
Love and Glory 1924,Ag 5,10:2
Way of all Flesh, The 1927,Je 27,25:2
Sheehan, Perley Poore (Screenwriter)
Old Homestead, The 1922,O 9,10:2
Lost City, The 1935,F 21,23:3
Sheehan, Perry
Washington Story 1952,Jl 2,22:3
Battle Circus 1953,My 28,27:5
Long, Long Trailer, The 1954,F 19,24:3
Sheehan, Winfield (Producer)
Marie Galante 1934,N 21,23:4
One More Spring 1935,F 22,27:1
Curly Top 1935,Ag 2,22:3
Farmer Takes a Wife, The 1935,Ag 9,21:2
Way Down East 1935,O 31,16:2
Florian 1940,Je 6,33:2
Captain Eddie 1945,Ag 9,24:2
Sheekman, Arthur (Miscellaneous)
Welcome Stranger 1947,Ag 7,15:2
Sheekman, Arthur (Original Author)
Pigskin Parade 1936,N 14,23:3
Wonder Man 1945,Je 9,17:2
Sheekman, Arthur (Screenwriter)
Kid Millions 1934,N 12,17:2
Rose of the Rancho 1936,Ja 9,25:2
Dimples 1936,O 10,21:2
Stowaway 1936,D 19,16:1
Gladiator, The 1938,Ag 29,10:2
Blue Skies 1946,O 17,28:2
Blaze of Noon 1947,Mr 5,31:2
Dear Ruth 1947,Je 11,33:3
Trouble With Women, The 1947,Jl 14,14:4
Welcome Stranger 1947,Ag 7,15:2
Saigon 1948,Ap 1,30:5
Hazard 1948,Je 3,19:2
Dear Wife 1950,F 2,31:2
Mr Music 1950,D 21,34:3
Young Man With Ideas 1952,Je 7,22:6
Call Me Madam 1953,Mr 26,37:1
Bundle of Joy 1956,D 20,36:1
Some Came Running 1959,Ja 23,17:1
Ada 1961,Ag 26,15:1
Sheen, Fulton J Rev Mgr
Eternal Gift, The 1942,Ja 12,23:3
Sheen, Fulton J Rev Msgr (Narrator)
Story of the Pope, The 1946,D 20,31:3
Sheen, Martin
Incident, The 1967,N 6,65:1
Subject Was Roses, The 1968,O 14,53:2
Sheffield, Bill
Knute Rockne-All American 1940,O 19,21:2
Boy With Green Hair, The 1949,Ja 13,26:2
Sheffield, Flora
Charley's Aunt 1930,D 26,18:4
East Lynne 1931,F 21,15:2
Sheffield, Jay
Three Stooges Go Around the World in a Daze,
The 1963,D 19,40:2
Sheffield, Johnny
Tarzan Finds a Son 1939,Je 15,27:2
Babes in Arms 1939,O 20,27:2
Lucky Cisco Kid 1940,Je 24,19:5
Knute Rockne-All American 1940,O 19,21:2
Million Dollar Baby 1941,Je 7,20:2
Tarzan's Secret Treasure 1941,D 25,33:1
Tarzan's New York Adventure 1942,Ag 7,13:2
Tarzan Triumphs 1943,F 5,16:3
Tarzan's Desert Mystery 1943,D 27,23:3
Tarzan and the Amazons 1945,Ap 30,13:4
Tarzan and the Leopard Woman 1946,F 11,25:2
Tarzan and the Huntress 1947,Ap 7,20:4
Bomba, the Jungle Boy 1949,Ap 16,11:4
Sheffield, Reginald
Classmates 1924,D 30,15:3
Green Goddess, The 1930,F 14,20:1
Of Human Bondage 1934,Je 29,17:1
Cardinal Richelieu 1935,Ap 19,24:2
Splendor 1935,N 23,23:2
Another Dawn 1937,Je 18,25:3
Female Fugitive 1938,Ap 11,12:3
Earthbound 1940,Je 7,27:4
Suspicion 1941,N 21,23:2
Eyes in the Night 1942,O 16,23:1

Sheffield, Reginald— Cont
Tonight We Raid Calais 1943,Ap 15,20:2
Wilson 1944,Ag 2,18:1
Kiss the Blood off my Hands 1948,O 30,10:2
Prison Warden 1949,O 21,31:2
Second Chance 1953,Jl 23,20:2
Buccaneer, The 1958,D 24,00:0
Sheider, Roy R
Curse of the Living Corpse, The 1964,Ap 30,30:1
Sheiner, David
Greatest Story Ever Told, The 1965,F 16,40:2
One Spy too Many 1966,D 8,64:1
Odd Couple, The 1968,My 3,42:1
Shejbalova, Jirina
Merry Wives, The 1940,N 12,28:3
Shekhtman, Lenya
Ballad of Cossack Gloota, The 1938,F 28,19:1
Shekley, Robert (Original Author)
10th Victim, The 1965,D 21,46:1
Shelby, Margaret
Jenny, Be Good 1920,Je 28,13:2
Sheldon, Charles M Rev (Original Author)
In His Steps 1936,O 29,31:1
Sheldon, E L (Original Author)
Call of her People, The 1917,My 28,11:2
Song of Songs, The 1918,F 19,11:2
Romance 1920,My 17,19:3
Salvation Neil 1921,Je 27,16:3
Lily of the Dust 1924,Ag 25,16:2
Half-Way Girl, The 1925,Jl 29,24:4
Romance 1930,Ag 23,7:3
Salvation Nell 1931,Jl 6,24:4
Song of Songs 1933,Jl 20,22:2
International Lady 1941,N 11,29:2
Beyond the Blue Horizon 1942,Je 25,27:2
Dishonored Lady 1947,My 24,10:5
Lulu Belle 1948,Je 21,18:3
Sheldon, E L (Producer)
Glass Key, The 1935,Je 15,20:2
Last Outpost, The 1935,O 5,18:2
Hands Across the Table 1935,N 2,13:2
Milky Way, The 1936,Mr 26,27:2
13 Hours by Air 1936,Ap 30,17:2
Jungle Princess 1936,D 24,21:3
Sheldon, E L (Screenwriter)
If I Were King 1920,Ag 10,10:3
Glimpses of the Moon 1923,Ap 3,23:4
Law of the Lawless, The 1923,Je 19,22:4
Sheldon, Forrest (Director)
Haunted Ship, The 1928,Ja 23,18:3
Sheldon, Gene
Where Do We Go From Here? 1945,Je 7,25:2
Dolly Sisters, The 1945,N 15,24:6
Golden Girl 1951,N 21,20:3
Three Ring Circus 1954,D 25,7:2
Toby Tyler 1960,Ap 20,45:2
Sign of Zorro, The 1961,S 5,37:6
Babes in Toyland 1961,D 15,49:1
Sheldon, James
Over the Hill to the Poor House 1920,S 18,16:2
Sheldon, Kathryn
I'm From the City 1938,Ag 19,13:4
Our Leading Citizen 1939,Ag 24,17:1
Gold Rush Maisie 1940,S 2,19:2
Happy Time, The 1952,O 31,30:2
Sheldon, Ralph (Miscellaneous)
Queen in Australia, The 1954,Je 16,37:3
Sheldon, Sidney (Director)
Dream Wife 1953,Jl 30,20:1
Buster Keaton Story, The 1957,Ap 22,31:6
Sheldon, Sidney (Original Author)
Buster Keaton Story, The 1957,Ap 22,31:6
Sheldon, Sidney (Producer)
Buster Keaton Story, The 1957,Ap 22,31:6
Sheldon, Sidney (Screenwriter)
Bachelor and the Bobby-Soxer, The
1947,Jl 25,12:5
Easter Parade 1948,Jl 1,19:3
Nancy Goes to Rio 1950,Ap 7,22:2
Annie Get Your Gun 1950,My 18,37:1
Three Guys Named Mike 1951,Mr 2,21:2
Rich, Young and Pretty 1951,Jl 26,17:3
No Questions Asked 1951,Ag 10,13:2
Just This Once 1952,Mr 18,22:3
Dream Wife 1953,Jl 30,20:1
You're Never too Young 1955,Ag 26,10:2
Anything Goes 1956,Mr 22,38:1
Birds and the Bees, The 1956,Ap 23,22:1
Pardners 1956,Jl 26,20:2
Jumbo 1962,D 7,49:1
Sheldon, Terry
Crazy House 1943,D 16,33:3
Shelenkov, Alexander (Director)
Bolshoi Ballet 67 1966,S 30,54:1
Shelenkov, Alexander (Screenwriter)
Bolshoi Ballet 67 1966,S 30,54:1
Shelkovski, M
Professor Mamlock 1938,N 8,26:2
Shellabarger, Samuel (Original Author)
Captain from Castile 1947,D 26,22:4
Prince of Foxes 1949,D 24,11:2
Shelley, Barbara
Camp on Blood Island, The 1958,S 18,37:2
Village of the Damned 1960,D 8,43:3

Shelley, Barbara— Cont
Shadow of the Cat, The 1961,Je 8,40:2
Man in the Dark 1965,Ja 21,22:1
Five Million Years to Earth 1968,My 30,21:4
Shelley, Carole
It's Great to be Young 1957,D 26,23:3
Odd Couple, The 1968,My 3,42:1
Shelley, George
Forty Naughty Girls 1937,S 18,15:3
Music for Madame 1937,O 23,14:1
Danger Patrol 1937,N 19,27:3
Law of the Underworld 1938,Ap 28,27:2
Shelley, Joshua
City Across the River 1949,Ap 8,31:3
Yes Sir, That's my Baby 1949,N 11,31:2
Shelley, Joshua (Director)
Perils of Pauline, The 1967,Ag 3,26:3
Shelley, Mary Wollstonecraft (Original Author)
Frankenstein 1931,D 5,21:2
Bride of Frankenstein, The 1935,My 11,21:2
Shelley, Norman
Iron Duke, The 1935,Ja 25,27:2
Adventures, The 1947,Ap 4,19:2
Shelley, Norman (Miscellaneous)
Roman d'un Tricheur; Confessions of a Cheat
1942,Ja 31,13:2
Great Adventure, The 1955,My 24,34:6
Shelley, Norworth
They Came to a City 1945,F 19,21:3
Shelly, Jacques
A Nous la Liberte 1932,Ja 10,VIII,5:1
Nous, La Liberte, A 1932,My 18,25:2
Shelly, Maxine
Win That Girl 1928,O 1,23:1
Shellyuzhko, N
Cossack Beyond the Danube, A 1954,F 8,18:5
Shelton, Don
Mystery Street 1950,Jl 28,12:5
Command, The 1954,Ja 16,10:5
Them 1954,Je 17,36:2
Shelton, Eleanor
Little French Girl, The 1925,Je 1,10:3
Shelton, Elsie
Prison Without Bars 1939,Ap 10,13:2
Shelton, George
House on Ninety-Second Street, The
1945,S 27,24:7
Shelton, John
We Who Are Young 1940,S 13,27:2
Dr Kildare Goes Home 1940,S 19,27:4
Whispering Ghosts 1942,My 18,19:4
A-Haunting We Will Go 1942,Ag 3,18:4
Time of Their Lives, The 1946,N 28,40:2
Big Fix, The 1947,My 3,10:3
Sins of Jezebel 1954,Ja 9,12:2
Shelton, Joy
Waterloo Road 1948,D 25,10:3
No Room at the Inn 1949,D 26,33:4
Hundred Hour Hunt 1953,Je 17,32:2
Damn the Defiant 1962,S 20,29:2
Shelton, Maria
Society Scandal, A 1924,Mr 10,18:2
Flying Hostess 1936,D 14,29:4
Under Cover of Night 1937,Ja 20,18:4
Dangerous Number 1937,Mr 12,19:2
Personal Property 1937,Ap 11,27:2
There Goes my Girl 1937,Je 12,8:2
Vogues of 1938 1937,Ag 20,21:1
52d Street 1937,N 15,15:1
Stand-In 1937,N 19,27:2
Lone Wolf Meets a Lady, The 1940,Je 17,19:2
When Johnny Comes Marching Home
1943,Mr 5,20:4
Saratoga Trunk 1945,N 22,39:2
Shelton, Morton
Reserved for Ladies 1932,My 21,9:2
Shengalev, Georgi (Screenwriter)
Conflict 1955,D 26,23:4
Shengelaya, Ariadna
Eugene Onegin 1959,S 14,33:1
Garnet Bracelet, The 1966,My 28,11:6
Shengelaya, N (Director)
Caucasian Love 1929,D 3,28:4
Twenty-Six Commissars 1933,Jl 1,16:6
Shenson, Walter (Producer)
Mouse That Roared, The 1959,O 27,40:1
Matter of Who, A 1962,Jl 25,29:2
Mouse on the Moon, The 1963,Je 18,32:1
Hard Day's Night, A 1964,Ag 12,41:1
30 Is a Dangerous Age, Cynthia 1968,Mr 5,34:1
Don't Raise the Bridge, Lower the River
1968,Jl 13,18:1
Shentall, Susan
Romeo and Juliet 1954,D 22,28:1
Shenton, Thomas
Tell-Tale Heart, The 1934,Je 15,26:3
SHEPARD
See Also SHEPHERD, SHEPPARD
Shepard, Elaine
Topper 1937,Ag 20,21:2
You Can't Fool Your Wife 1940,My 24,23:4
Falcon in Danger, The 1943,Jl 23,21:2
Seven Days Ashore 1944,Ap 26,24:7

Shepard, Ernest H (Miscellaneous)
Winnie the Pooh and the Honey Tree
1966,Ap 7,45:1
Shepard, Jan
Sabre Jet 1953,N 3,34:1
King Creole 1958,Jl 4,15:2
Shepard, Kathleen (Original Author)
Human Cargo 1936,My 16,11:2
Bad Guy 1937,Ag 26,25:2
Shepheard, Jean
Thunder Rock 1944,S 15,16:1
Adventures of Don Juan 1948,D 25,10:1
Fame Is the Spur 1949,N 8,34:2
SHEPHERD
See Also SHEPARD, SHEPPARD
Shepherd, Elizabeth
Man in the Dark 1965,Ja 21,22:1
Tomb of Ligeia 1965,My 6,44:1
Shepherd, Leonard
Dreyfus Case, The 1931,Ag 31,11:5
Shepherd, Mary
Artists and Models 1937,Ag 5,19:2
Shepherd, Norma
Miracle in Harlem 1949,O 24,19:4
Shepherd, Pauline
I Like Money 1962,My 19,18:2
Shepherd, Richard (Producer)
Hanging Tree, The 1959,F 12,23:1
Fugitive Kind, The 1960,Ap 15,13:1
Love in a Goldfish Bowl 1961,Jl 13,26:3
Breakfast at Tiffany's 1961,O 6,28:1
Shepherd, Roger
Midsummer Night's Dream, A 1961,D 19,39:1
Shepherd, Sally
House of Fear, The 1945,Mr 19,23:3
Woman in Green, The 1945,Je 16,10:3
Shepley, Michael
Are You a Mason? 1934,O 30,23:5
Bella Donna 1935,F 26,16:4
Triumph of Sherlock Holmes, The
1935,My 27,20:6
High Treason 1937,Ja 27,17:3
Man With 100 Faces 1938,N 1,27:2
Housemaster 1939,Ap 10,13:2
It's in the Air 1940,D 10,33:2
Quiet Wedding 1941,D 29,27:4
Great Mr Handel, The 1943,S 10,29:3
Adventure for Two 1945,D 14,24:5
Henry V 1946,Je 18,30:2
Mine Own Executioner 1949,Ja 19,34:2
Place of One's Own, A 1949,F 8,30:2
Murder on Monday 1953,O 7,35:2
Tonight's the Night 1954,D 23,13:4
Doctor at Sea 1956,Mr 1,37:3
Novel Affair, A 1957,Ag 28,22:1
Alligator Named Daisy, An 1957,O 7,23:2
Sheplner, Stan (Producer)
Two Rode Together 1961,Jl 27,23:3
Shepodd, Jon
Return of Jack Slade, The 1955,N 24,41:3
Attack! 1956,S 20,29:4
SHEPPARD
See Also SHEPARD, SHEPHERD
Sheppard, Dave (Original Author)
Mau Mau 1955,Jl 14,19:1
Sheppard, David P (Screenwriter)
Black Arrow, The 1948,O 4,14:2
Sheppard, Morgan
Persecution and Assassination of Jean-Paul Marat
as Performed by the Inmates of the Asylum of
Charenton Under the Direction of the Marquis
De Sade, The 1967,F 23,41:1
Shepperd, John
Belle Starr 1941,N 1,20:2
Cadet Girl 1941,D 11,39:1
Men In her Life, The 1941,D 12,35:1
Remember the Day 1941,D 26,21:2
Rings on her Fingers 1942,Ap 24,21:4
Ten Gentlemen From West Point 1942,Je 5,23:3
Loves of Edgar Allan Poe, The 1942,S 21,19:2
Chetniks 1943,Mr 19,15:3
Home Sweet Homicide 1946,S 12,5:7
Shepridge, John C (Screenwriter)
Rapture 1950,D 14,51:3
SHER
See Also SHEAR, SHERR
Sher, Jack (Director)
Four Girls in Town 1957,Ja 17,34:5
Three Worlds of Gulliver, The 1960,D 17,19:3
Love in a Goldfish Bowl 1961,Jl 13,26:3
Sher, Jack (Miscellaneous)
Shane 1953,Ap 24,30:3
Sher, Jack (Original Author)
Off Limits 1953,Mr 30,25:5
World in my Corner 1956,F 18,12:5
Four Girls in Town 1957,Ja 17,34:5
Kathy O' 1958,S 25,29:2
Sher, Jack (Screenwriter)
My Favorite Spy 1951,D 26,19:3
Off Limits 1953,Mr 30,25:5
Kid From Left Field, The 1953,S 26,15:3
World in my Corner 1956,F 18,12:5
Walk the Proud Land 1956,S 8,20:6 (In
Addenda)

Sher, Jack (Screenwriter) — Cont
Joe Butterfly 1957,My 30,23:2
Kathy O' 1958,S 25,29:2
Three Worlds of Gulliver, The 1960,D 17,19:3
Love in a Goldfish Bowl 1961,Jl 13,26:3
Paris Blues 1961,N 8,41:1
Critic's Choice 1963,My 2,40:2
Move Over Darling 1963,D 26,33:1
Sherbakof, J
Hour With Tchekhof, An 1933,S 6,24:4
Sherbokov, P
Day the War Ended, The 1961,Ja 30,17:2
Sherdeman, Ted (Original Author)
McConnell Story, The 1955,S 30,23:1
Sherdeman, Ted (Producer)
Riding Shotgun 1954,Ap 2,22:2
Big Show, The 1961,My 11,42:4
Sherdeman, Ted (Screenwriter)
Lust for Gold 1949,Jl 4,9:2
Breakthrough 1950,N 18,10:2
Scandal Sheet 1952,Ja 17,23:1
Retreat Hell! 1952,F 20,26:2
Winning Team, The 1952,Je 21,12:2
Eddie Cantor Story, The 1953,D 26,10:2
Them 1954,Je 17,36:2
McConnell Story, The 1955,S 30,23:1
Toy Tiger 1956,Je 30,11:2
Away all Boats 1956,Ag 17,14:2
St Louis Blues 1958,Ap 12,13:1
Dog of Flanders, A 1960,Ap 1,37:1
Hell to Eternity 1960,O 13,41:1
Misty 1961,Jl 18,33:2
Island of the Blue Dolphins 1964,Jl 4,8:2
...And Now Miguel 1966,S 8,43:1
Sheremetieva, Elena
Horizon, The Wandering Jew 1933,My 12,20:4
Sheridan, Ann
Wedding Bills 1927,Je 29,29:3
Behold My Wife 1935,F 18,19:3
Car 99 1935,F 23,14:7
Fighting Youth 1935,N 2,13:3
Sing Me a Love Song 1936,D 26,15:2
Black Legion 1937,Ja 18,21:1
Great O'Malley, The 1937,Mr 6,10:1
San Quentin 1937,Ag 4,15:2
Footloose Heiress 1937,O 9,16:2
Alcatraz Island 1937,O 14,22:2
She Loved a Fireman 1938,Ja 21,15:3
Patient in Room 18, The 1938,Ap 22,15:6
Mystery House 1938,Je 29,15:5
Cowboy From Brooklyn 1938,Jl 14,17:1
Letter of Introduction 1938,S 1,17:1
Broadway Musketeers 1938,O 14,27:1
Angels With Dirty Faces 1938,N 26,18:1
They Made Me a Criminal 1939,Ja 21,19:2
Dodge City 1939,Ap 8,19:1
Naughty but Nice 1939,Je 23,23:2
Indianapolis Speedway 1939,Jl 15,8:2
Winter Carnival 1939,Jl 28,14:2
Angels Wash Their Faces 1939,S 4,16:2
Castle on the Hudson 1940,Mr 4,11:2
It all Came True 1940,Ap 6,13:2
Torrid Zone 1940,My 18,11:3
They Drive by Night 1940,Jl 27,17:5
City for Conquest 1940,S 28,9:2
Honeymoon for Three 1941,F 8,19:2
Navy Blues 1941,S 20,11:2
Man Who Came to Dinner, The 1942,Ja 2,25:2
Kings Row 1942,F 3,23:2
Juke Girl 1942,Je 20,9:2
Wings for the Eagle 1942,Ag 1,14:2
George Washington Slept Here 1942,O 31,11:1
Edge of Darkness 1943,Ap 10,12:4
Thank Your Lucky Stars 1943,O 2,19:2
Shine on Harvest Moon 1944,Mr 11,10:2
Doughgirls, The 1944,Ag 31,14:1
One More Tomorrow 1946,My 25,12:2
Nora Prentiss 1947,F 22,16:2
Unfaithful, The 1947,Je 28,10:2
Silver River 1948,My 22,8:3
Good Sam 1948,S 17,28:2
I Was a Male War Bride 1949,Ag 27,7:2
Stella 1950,Ag 19,9:2
Woman on the Run 1950,N 30,24:2
Steel Town 1952,My 10,16:4
Just Across the Street 1952,Je 28,12:4
Take Me to Town 1953,Je 20,8:6
Appointment in Honduras 1953,N 19,41:4
Opposite Sex, The 1956,N 16,23:2
Sheridan, Clara Lou
Come on Marines 1934,Mr 24,20:3
Ladies Should Listen 1934,Jl 28,16:6
Sheridan, Dan
Hell's Five Hours 1957,Jl 24,18:1
Hell's Five Hours 1958,Jl 24,18:1
Sheridan, Dinah
Irish and Proud of It 1938,O 31,12:3
Murder in Reverse 1947,Ja 11,23:5
Facts of Love, The 1949,O 31,20:2
Ivory Hunter 1952,Ag 19,19:1
Breaking Through the Sound Barrier
1952,N 7,19:1
Gilbert and Sullivan 1953,O 28,36:3
Genevieve 1954,F 16,30:2

Sheridan, Francey
Private Hell 36 1954,S 4,6:4
Sheridan, Frank
One Exciting Night 1922,O 24,17:3
Man Next Door, The 1923,My 29,10:3
Fast Life 1929,Ag 17,5:3
Side Street 1929,S 9,30:2
Danger Lights 1930,D 15,29:1
Flood, The 1931,Ap 27,25:1
Donovan's Kid 1931,My 22,28:5
Murder by the Clock 1931,Jl 18,16:6
Public Defender, The 1931,Ag 1,16:4
Silence 1931,Ag 15,18:3
Ladies of the Big House 1932,Ja 1,31:1
Man I Killed, The 1932,Ja 20,17:4
Last Mile, The 1932,Ag 26,20:3
Okay America 1932,S 10,18:5
Washington Merry-Go-Round 1932,O 24,18:5
Afraid to Talk 1932,D 19,19:5
Deception 1933,Ja 10,26:2
Woman Accused, The 1933,Mr 13,18:2
Man Who Dared, The 1933,S 9,9:3
Wharf Angel 1934,Ap 21,12:1
Witching Hour, The 1934,Ap 28,11:3
Cat's Paw, The 1934,Ag 17,12:2
Pay-Off, The 1935,N 13,25:3
Whispering Smith Speaks 1936,F 17,21:1
Conflict 1937,Ja 18,21:2
Great O'Malley, The 1937,Mr 6,10:1
Fight to the Finish, A 1937,Je 26,20:2 (In Addenda)
Life of Emile Zola, The 1937,Ag 12,14:2
City Streets 1938,Jl 25,18:2
Sheridan, Jack
Objective Burma 1945,Ja 27,15:2
Private Hell 36 1954,S 4,6:4
Sheridan, Jimmy
Close-Up 1948,Ap 5,24:2
Sheridan, Margaret
Thing, The 1951,My 3,34:4
One Minute to Zero 1952,S 20,13:2
I, The Jury 1953,Ag 22,8:2
Diamond Wizard, The 1954,Jl 17,7:4
Sheridan, Otis
Night Angel, The 1931,Je 11,28:4
Sheridan, Tommy
Red Pony, The 1949,Mr 9,33:2
Sheriff, Paul (Miscellaneous)
Henry V 1946,Je 18,30:2
Sherin, Ed (Screenwriter)
Across the River 1965,Ap 27,27:1
Sherkot, Leon
Dance Band 1936,Ja 4,19:2
Sherlock, Charles
Shakedown 1950,S 4,11:2
Sherman, Evelyn
Suzanna 1923,Mr 26,16:2
Proud Flesh 1925,Ap 14,26:1
Blonde or Brunette 1927,Ja 11,18:2
Sherman, Fred
Chain Lightning 1950,F 20,21:2
Sherman, George (Director)
Santa Fe Stampede 1939,Ap 26,27:3
Lady and the Monster, The 1944,Ap 8,9:2
Storm Over Lisbon 1944,S 11,14:1
Crime Doctor's Courage, The 1945,Mr 3,11:3
Bandit of Sherwood Forest, The 1946,Mr 23,8:4
Renegades 1946,Jl 11,18:2
Last of the Redmen 1947,Ag 30,8:6
Black Bart 1948,Mr 4,30:4
Relentless 1948,Mr 6,17:3
River Lady 1948,My 21,19:5
Larceny 1948,S 4,8:6
Red Canyon 1949,Ap 28,28:2
Calamity Jane and Sam Bass 1949,Jl 18,14:2
Sword in the Desert 1949,Ag 25,20:2
Yes Sir, That's my Baby 1949,N 11,31:2
Comanche Territory 1950,Ap 8,9:3
Spy Hunt 1950,S 8,25:2
Sleeping City, The 1950,S 21,20:2
Tomahawk 1951,F 19,19:2
Target Unknown 1951,Mr 5,24:2
Steel Town 1952,My 10,16:4
Battle at Apache Pass, The 1952,My 10,16:4
Against all Flags 1952,D 25,34:6
Lone Hand 1953,Je 27,7:2
Veils of Bagdad, The 1953,N 27,99:9
Johnny Dark 1954,Je 26,7:2
Dawn at Socorro 1954,Ag 28,8:2
Chief Crazy Horse 1955,Ap 28,25:1
Treasure of Pancho Villa, The 1955,N 25,38:2
Flying Fontaines, The 1959,D 24,13:6
Enemy General, The 1960,O 20,42:2
Wizard of Baghdad, The 1961,Mr 4,16:1
Fiercest Heart, The 1961,Ag 3,13:5
Sherman, George (Original Author)
Calamity Jane and Sam Bass 1949,Jl 18,14:2
Sherman, George (Producer)
Fiercest Heart, The 1961,Ag 3,13:5
Comancheros, The 1961,N 2,42:1
Sherman, Geraldine
Poor Cow 1968,F 1,28:2
Interlude 1968,Jl 3,26:1

Sherman, Harold (Original Author)
Are We Civilized? 1934,Je 14,28:5
Adventures of Mark Twain, The 1944,My 4,25:5
Sherman, Harold (Screenwriter)
Adventures of Mark Twain, The 1944,My 4,25:5
Sherman, Harry (Producer)
Three on the Trail 1936,My 5,26:5
Barrier, The 1937,N 27,21:2
Hopalong Rides Again 1938,Ja 22,19:1
Partners of the Plains 1938,F 12,20:4
Heart of Arizona 1938,Ap 16,17:1
Cherokee Strip 1940,N 4,23:2
Roundup, The 1941,Mr 13,25:4
Parson of Panamint, The 1941,Jl 26,18:2
Tombstone, The Town too Tough to Die 1942,Jl 27,18:2
Silver Queen 1943,Ja 11,18:4
Kansan, The 1943,O 1,15:3
Woman of the Town, The 1944,Mr 6,17:2
Buffalo Bill 1944,Ap 20,22:6
Ramrod 1947,Je 30,25:6
Four Faces West 1948,Ag 4,18:3
Sherman, Hiram
One Third of a Nation 1939,F 11,13:2
Solid Gold Cadillac, The 1956,O 25,40:3
Mary, Mary 1963,O 25,38:2
Oh Dad, Poor Dad, Mamma's Hung You in the Closet and I'm Feeling so Sad 1967,F 16,32:1
Sherman, Jane
Hunchback of Notre Dame, The 1923,S 3,9:3
Sherman, Joe (Screenwriter)
Murder in the Fleet 1935,Je 3,22:2
Sherman, John
Hasty Heart, The 1950,Ja 21,10:5
Sherman, Lenny
She's Back on Broadway 1953,Mr 12,24:2
Sherman, Lois
Reckless Lady, The 1926,Ja 25,21:2
Sherman, Lowell
Yes or No 1920,Jl 5,12:4
Gilded Lily, The 1921,Mr 7,8:1
Grand Larceny 1922,F 27,13:4
Monsieur Beaucaire 1924,Ag 12,12:1 (In Addenda)
Satan in Sables 1925,O 15,27:3
Wilderness Woman, The 1926,My 10,19:1
You Never Know Women 1926,Jl 27,15:5
Convoy 1927,My 9,26:4
Divine Woman, The 1928,Ja 16,24:1
Whip Woman, The 1928,F 13,16:2
Heart of a Follies Girl, The 1928,Mr 12,26:1
Garden of Eden, The 1928,Mr 19,26:2
Mad Hour, The 1928,Ap 16,20:5
Whip, The 1928,S 17,28:2
Lady of Chance, A 1929,Ja 14,20:1
Evidence 1929,O 5,22:5
General Crack 1929,D 4,36:6
Mammy 1930,Mr 27,24:5
He Knew Women 1930,Ap 23,24:1
Ladies of Leisure 1930,My 24,21:2
Midnight Mystery 1930,Je 2,25:4
Lawful Larceny 1930,Jl 12,16:4
Pay-Off, The 1930,N 10,16:2
Royal Bed, The 1931,Ja 31,15:1
Way Down East 1931,Mr 16,25:1
Bachelor Apartment 1931,My 16,13:3
Greeks Had a Word for Them, The 1932,F 4,25:2
What Price Hollywood 1932,Jl 16,5:5
False Faces 1932,N 25,19:2
Sherman, Lowell (Director)
Lawful Larceny 1930,Jl 12,16:4
Pay-Off, The 1930,N 10,16:2
Royal Bed, The 1931,Ja 31,15:1
Bachelor Apartment 1931,My 16,13:3
Greeks Had a Word for Them, The 1932,F 4,25:2
Ladies of the Jury 1932,Ap 2,13:2
False Faces 1932,N 25,19:2
She Done Him Wrong 1933,F 10,12:3
Morning Glory 1933,Ag 18,18:2
Broadway Thru a Keyhole 1933,N 2,18:3
Born to be Bad 1934,My 31,22:6
Night Life of the Gods 1935,F 23,14:6
Sherman, R Capt (Screenwriter)
Johnny in the Clouds 1945,N 16,16:2
Sherman, Ransom
Bachelor and the Bobby-Soxer, The 1947,Jl 25,12:5
Gentleman's Agreement 1947,N 12,36:2
Always Together 1947,D 11,46:1
Winter Meeting 1948,Ap 8,31:2
Are You With It? 1948,Ap 15,31:2
Whiplash 1948,D 27,16:3
One Last Fling 1949,Jl 1,14:6
Always Leave Them Laughing 1949,N 24,48:2
Pretty Baby 1950,S 23,11:2
Sherman, Reed
Sabre Jet 1953,N 3,34:1
Sherman, Richard (Director)
Legend of Lobo, The 1962,N 10,16:2
Sherman, Richard (Original Author)
To Mary-With Love 1936,Ag 27,16:1

Sherman, Richard (Producer)
Legend of Lobo, The 1962,N 10,16:2
Sherman, Richard (Screenwriter)
To Mary-With Love 1936,Ag 27,16:1
Four Men and a Prayer 1938,My 7,18:1
Alexander's Ragtime Band 1938,Ag 6,7:2
Girls' School 1938,N 3,27:1
Story of Vernon and Irene Castle, The 1939,Mr 31,19:2
In Name Only 1939,Ag 4,11:3
For Me and My Gal 1942,O 22,25:1
Sherman, Robert
For Men Only 1952,Ja 16,21:2
Sherman, Robert (Director)
Legend of Lobo, The 1962,N 10,16:2
Sherman, Robert (Producer)
Legend of Lobo, The 1962,N 10,16:2
Sherman, Robert (Screenwriter)
Picture Mommy Dead 1966,N 3,45:4
Sherman, Teddi (Screenwriter)
Four Faces West 1948,Ag 4,18:3
Tennessee's Partner 1955,N 5,22:8
Second to Hell 1959,Jl 18,6:3
4 for Texas 1963,D 26,33:3
Sherman, Vincent
Counsellor-At-Law 1933,D 8,31:2
Midnight Alibi 1934,Jl 4,18:3
Sherman, Vincent (Director)
Return Of Doctor X, The 1939,N 23,38:5
Saturday's Children 1940,My 4,13:1
Man Who Talked too Much, The 1940,Je 29,12:2
Flight From Destiny 1941,Mr 28,26:7
Underground 1941,Je 23,13:2
All Through the Night 1942,Ja 24,13:2
Hard Way, The 1943,Mr 13,9:2
Old Acquaintance 1943,N 3,20:2
In our Time 1944,F 12,11:2
Mr Skeffington 1944,My 26,23:2
Pillow to Post 1945,My 26,18:2
Janie Gets Married 1946,Je 15,24:2
Nora Prentiss 1947,F 22,16:2
Unfaithful, The 1947,Je 28,10:2
Adventures of Don Juan 1948,D 25,10:1
Hasty Heart, The 1950,Ja 21,10:5
Backfire 1950,Ja 27,29:2
Damned Don't Cry, The 1950,Ap 8,9:2
Harriet Craig 1950,N 3,31:2
Goodbye, my Fancy 1951,My 30,14:2
Lone Star 1952,F 2,11:4
Affair in Trinidad 1952,Jl 31,14:2
Garment Jungle, The 1957,My 16,28:2
Naked Earth 1958,Ag 29,18:1
Young Philadelphians, The 1959,My 22,32:1
Ice Palace 1960,Je 30,22:1
Fever in the Blood 1961,Ap 20,30:4
Second Time Around, The 1961,D 23,16:1
Sherman, Vincent (Producer)
Affair in Trinidad 1952,Jl 31,14:2
Sherman, Vincent (Screenwriter)
Crime School 1938,My 11,17:2
My Bill 1938,Jl 7,22:4
Heart of the North 1938,D 21,29:2
King of the Underworld 1939,Ja 7,6:2
Shermet, Hazel
Star is Born, A 1954,O 12,23:1
SHERR
See Also SHEAR, SHER
Sherr, Jack (Composer)
Sioux City Sue 1947,Jl 23,19:3
Sherriff, R C (Original Author)
Journey's End 1930,Ap 9,25:1
Stand by for Action 1943,Mr 12,12:2
Forever and a Day 1943,Mr 13,9:2
Murder on Monday 1953,O 7,35:2
Sherriff, R C (Screenwriter)
Road Back, The 1937,Je 18,25:2
Goodbye Mr Chips 1939,My 16,27:2
That Hamilton Woman 1941,Ap 4,25:1
This Above All 1942,My 13,14:3
Odd Man Out 1947,Ap 24,30:2
Quartet (The Alien Corn); Alien Corn, The (Quartet) 1949,Mr 29,30:3
Quartet (The Colonel's Lady); Colonel's Lady, The (Quartet) 1949,Mr 29,30:3
Quartet (The Kite); Kite, The (Quartet) 1949,Mr 29,30:3
Quartet (The Facts of Life); Facts of Life, The (Quartet) 1949,Mr 29,30:3
Trio 1950,O 11,42:1
No Highway in the Sky 1951,S 22,8:6
Night my Number Came up, The 1955,D 20,39:5
Storm over the Nile 1956,Je 9,14:2
Sherry, Craighall
Spies 1929,Mr 5,29:1
Sherry, Diane
Hawaii 1966,O 11,54:1
Sherry, Edna (Original Author)
Thru Different Eyes 1929,Ap 15,22:6
Sudden Fear 1952,Ag 8,9:2
Sherry, Gordeon (Screenwriter)
School for Husbands 1939,F 7,16:2

Sherry, J Barney
  Go and Get It 1920,Jl 19,16:3
  Dinty 1920,N 22,13:3
  White Sister, The 1923,S 6,10:2
  Miami 1924,Je 3,22:2
  Crackerjack, The 1925,My 18,12:1
  Lying Wives 1925,Je 17,16:2
  Brown Derby, The 1926,Je 14,24:1
  Prince of Tempters, The 1926,O 18,18:1
  White Sister, The 1928,My 21,25:1
  Broadway Scandals 1929,O 29,35:1
  Jazz Heaven 1929,O 30,29:2
Sherry, John (Original Author)
  Last Challenge, The 1967,D 28,25:1
Sherry, John (Screenwriter)
  Last Challenge, The 1967,D 28,25:1
Sherry, Robert A
  One-Way Ticket to Hell 1955,D 8,45:1
Shershneva, Vera
  Two Soldiers 1944,Jl 27,14:2
Sherwin, Louis (Original Author)
  Bonds of Love 1919,N 3,13:3
Sherwin, Manning (Composer)
  Vogues of 1938 1937,Ag 20,21:1
  College Swing 1938,Ap 28,27:2
Sherwin, Manning (Miscellaneous)
  Blossoms On Broadway 1937,D 3,29:2
Sherwood, Angela (Original Author)
  Paris Honeymoon 1939,Ja 26,17:1
Sherwood, Bobby
  Pal Joey 1957,O 28,30:1
Sherwood, C L
  Sporting Youth 1924,Ap 2,16:1
  Two Girls Wanted 1927,N 14,26:1
Sherwood, Gale
  Blonde Savage 1947,O 4,9:2
  Song of my Heart 1948,Mr 5,17:3
Sherwood, John (Director)
  Creature Walks among Us, The 1956,Ap 27,21:6
  Raw Edge 1956,Jl 28,10:7
Sherwood, Lydia
  Little Friend 1934,O 20,20:2
  Don Quixote 1934,D 24,17:1
  Secret Four, The 1940,Ap 22,13:2
  Romeo and Juliet 1954,D 22,28:1
  League of Gentlemen, The 1961,Ja 25,30:4
  Darling 1965,Ag 4,20:1
Sherwood, Madeleine
  Cat on a Hot Tin Roof 1958,S 19,24:1
  Parrish 1961,My 5,22:1
  Sweet Bird of Youth 1962,Mr 29,28:2
  Hurry Sundown 1967,Mr 24,22:1
Sherwood, Robert
  Three Guys Named Mike 1951,Mr 2,21:2
Sherwood, Robert (Miscellaneous)
  Tovarich 1937,D 31,9:2
Sherwood, Robert (Original Author)
  Oh! What a Nurse! 1926,F 22,14:1
  Royal Bed, The 1931,Ja 31,15:1
  Waterloo Bridge 1931,S 5,7:4
  Two Kinds of Women 1932,Ja 16,13:1
  Reunion in Vienna 1933,Ap 29,14:2
  Roman Scandals 1933,D 25,28:2
  Ghost Goes West, The 1935,D 18,33:8
  Petrified Forest, The 1936,F 7,14:2
  Idiot's Delight 1939,F 3,13:1
  Abe Lincoln in Illinois 1940,F 23,19:2
  Waterloo Bridge 1940,My 17,23:2
  Escape in the Desert 1945,My 12,10:2
  Main Street to Broadway 1953,O 14,34:1
  Jupiter's Darling 1955,F 18,18:4
  Gaby 1956,My 10,26:3
Sherwood, Robert (Producer)
  Adam Had Four Sons 1941,Mr 28,26:6
Sherwood, Robert (Screenwriter)
  Cock of the Air 1932,Ja 25,20:3
  Scarlet Pimpernel, The 1935,F 8,27:2
  Ghost Goes West, The 1936,Jl 9,2
  Thunder in the City 1937,Ap 23,25:2
  Divorce of Lady X, The 1938,Ap 1,17:2
  Idiot's Delight 1939,F 3,13:1
  Abe Lincoln in Illinois 1940,F 23,19:2
  Rebecca 1940,Mr 29,25:2
  Best Years of our Lives, The 1946,N 22,27:2
  Bishop's Wife, The 1947,D 10,44:2
  Man on a Tightrope 1953,Je 5,19:1
  Adventures of Marco Polo, The 1965,Ap 8,17:2
Sherwood, Roberta
  Courtship of Eddie's Father, The 1963,Mr 7,8:5
    (Incorrect in this edition; use 1963,Mr 28,8:5
    elsewhere)
Sherwood, Yorke
  Gentlemen Prefer Blondes 1928,Ja 16,24:1
  Man From Blankley's, The 1930,Mr 29,23:1
  Man in Possession, The 1931,Jl 18,16:6
  Lloyds of London 1936,N 26,39:1
  Jane Eyre 1944,F 4,12:5
Shestopalov, Sergei
  Sound of Life, The 1962,F 12,28:2
Sheva, Bas
  Catskill Honeymoon 1950,Ja 28,10:3

Shevchenko, Taras (Original Author)
  Nazar Stodolya 1937,Ag 7,7:2
Shevelove, Burt (Original Author)
  Funny Thing Happened on the Way to the Forum,
    A 1966,O 17,48:1
Shevelove, Burt (Screenwriter)
  Wrong Box 1966,Jl 20,46:1
Shevtsov, G
  Tsar's Bride, The 1966,Mr 12,13:2
Sheybal, Wladyslaw
  Kanal 1961,My 10,52:1
Sheynin, Leo (Screenwriter)
  Military Secret 1945,Ag 2,16:2
Shibanov, V
  Forty-Nine Days 1964,Ja 27,19:1
Shibata, George
  Pork Chop Hill 1959,My 30,9:2
  Hell to Eternity 1960,O 13,41:1
  Ugly American, The 1963,Ap 12,30:2
  Around the World Under the Sea 1966,Jl 21,20:2
Shibata, Teruo
  Angry Island 1960,F 28,31:1
Shiber, Etta (Original Author)
  Paris Underground 1945,O 20,8:2
Shidara, Koji
  Ohayo; (Good Morning) 1966,F 2,24:1
Shiel, Mathew Phipps (Original Author)
  World, The Flesh and the Devil, The
    1959,My 21,35:1
Shield, Fred
  Three Caballeros, The 1945,F 5,20:1
Shield, LeRoy (Composer)
  Devil's Brother, The 1933,Je 10,16:4
Shields, Arthur
  Plough and the Stars, The 1937,Ja 29,15:1
  Drums Along the Mohawk 1939,N 4,11:2
  Long Voyage Home, The 1940,O 9,30:2 (In
    Addenda)
  Little Nellie Kelly 1940,D 25,33:2
  Lady Scarface 1941,Ag 4,16:6
  How Green Was my Valley 1941,O 29,27:2
  Confirm or Deny 1941,D 19,35:2
  This Above All 1942,My 13,14:3
  Broadway 1942,Je 5,23:2
  Pacific Rendezvous 1942,Jl 8,27:4
  Gentleman Jim 1942,N 26,40:3
  Nightmare 1942,D 4,31:2
  Black Swan, The 1942,D 24,18:3
  Man From Down Under, The 1943,S 27,23:2
  Lassie Come Home 1943,O 8,15:4
  White Cliffs of Dover, The 1944,My 12,15:2
  Youth Runs Wild 1944,S 2,17:2
  National Velvet 1944,D 15,25:2
  Sign of the Cross 1944,D 21,16:3
  Keys of the Kingdom, The 1944,D 30,15:2
  Roughly Speaking 1945,F 1,18:4
  Corn is Green, The 1945,Mr 30,18:2
  Too Young to Know 1945,D 8,21:2
  Three Strangers 1946,F 23,20:2
  Gallant Journey 1946,O 10,33:2
  Verdict, The 1946,D 13,29:4
  Easy Come, Easy Go 1947,F 6,29:2
  Shocking Miss Pilgrim, The 1947,F 12,34:2
  Fabulous Dorseys, The 1947,My 30,25:3
  Fighting Father Dunne 1948,Je 25,26:2
  Tap Roots 1948,Ag 26,16:3
  My Own True Love 1949,F 3,27:3
  Fighting O'Flynn, The 1949,F 28,16:2
  She Wore a Yellow Ribbon 1949,N 18,35:2
  Red Light 1950,Ja 16,18:4
  Challenge to Lassie 1950,Ap 7,22:3
  Tarzan and the Slave Girl 1950,Je 24,7:3
  Apache Drums 1951,My 7,22:2
  Sealed Cargo 1951,My 24,47:1
  People Against O'Hara, The 1951,S 6,39:3
  River, The 1951,S 11,33:2
  Quiet Man, The 1952,Ag 22,13:1
  South Sea Woman 1953,Je 4,33:6
  Scandal at Scourie 1953,Je 16,24:2
  World for Ransom 1954,Je 5,11:2
  King and Four Queens, The 1956,D 22,13:7
  Night of the Quarter Moon 1959,Mr 5,35:5
  Pigeon That Took Rome, The 1962,Ag 23,25:1
Shields, Frank
  Murder in the Fleet 1935,Je 3,22:2
  Come and Get It 1936,N 12,31:1
Shields, George (Original Author)
  Poacher's Daughter, The 1960,F 16,31:2
Shields, Helen
  Whistle at Eaton Falls, The 1951,O 11,49:2
Shields, Maryanne
  Bimbo the Great 1961,Je 29,26:1
Shields, Russell (Miscellaneous)
  First World War, The 1934,N 8,27:1
  Baboona 1935,Ja 23,21:2
Shields, Wendell G (Miscellaneous)
  Human Adventure, The 1935,O 30,16:3
Shiels, Una
  Irish Destiny 1927,Mr 29,23:2 (In Addenda)
Shigeta, James
  Walk Like a Dragon 1960,S 16,24:1
  Cry for Happy 1961,Mr 4,16:1
  Bridge to the Sun 1961,O 18,50:1

Shigeta, James — Cont
  Flower Drum Song 1961,N 10,40:1
  Paradise, Hawaiian Style 1966,Je 16,15:3
  Nobody's Perfect 1968,Ap 4,58:3
Shih-Kan, Chung (Original Author)
  Song of China 1936,N 10,31:3
Shikari, Tengru
  Flute and the Arrow, The 1960,O 11,55:1
Shilkret, Nathaniel (Composer)
  Bohemian Girl, The 1936,F 17,21:1
  Soldier and the Lady, The 1937,Ap 10,11:1
Shilkret, Nathaniel (Miscellaneous)
  Toast of New York, The 1937,Jl 23,16:2
  Music for Madame 1937,O 23,14:1
Shilling, Marion
  Lord Byron of Broadway 1930,Mr 8,21:1
  Shadow of the Law 1930,Je 7,10:4
  On Your Back 1930,S 15,29:3
  Beyond Victory 1931,Ap 6,24:1
  Donovan's Kid 1931,My 22,28:5
  Common Law, The 1931,Jl 20,20:4
  Shot in the Dark, A 1935,My 22,23:2
  Keeper of the Bees, The 1935,Ag 17,18:5
Shillo, Michael
  Hill 24 Doesn't Answer 1955,N 3,37:1
  Dunkirk 1958,S 11,42:2
  Pillar of Fire, The 1963,Ap 8,35:2
  Cast a Giant Shadow 1966,Mr 31,43:3
Shilno, Hideyuki (Producer)
  My Hobo 1963,Jl 24,27:3
  This Madding Crowd 1964,Je 17,48:1
  Could I but Live 1965,Ja 20,34:2
Shima, Kaori
  Lost Sex 1968,Jl 23,27:2
Shima, Keiko
  Joe Butterfly 1957,My 30,23:2
Shima, Koji (Director)
  Golden Demon 1956,Ja 31,34:3
  Phantom Horse, the 1956,Jl 25,16:1
Shima, Koji (Screenwriter)
  Golden Demon 1956,Ja 31,34:3
  Phantom Horse, the 1956,Jl 25,16:1
Shima, Yvonne
  World of Suzie Wong, The 1960,N 11,36:1
Shimada, Ryuzo
  Zatoichi 1968,Je 28,37:1
Shimada, Teru
  Night Club Lady, The 1932,Ag 27,13:4
  Four Frightened People 1934,Ja 27,9:2
  Revolt of the Zombies 1936,Je 5,17:2
  Tokyo Joe 1949,O 27,35:2
  Emergency Wedding 1950,D 22,19:2
  Bridges at Toko-Ri, The 1955,Ja 21,20:2
  You Only Live Twice 1967,Je 14,40:1
Shimamura, Tatsuo (Miscellaneous)
  New Japanese Cinema, The (White City); White
    City (The New Japanese Cinema)
    1968,My 3,42:1
Shimanyuk, Anatoli
  Adventure in Odessa 1954,Je 21,19:6
Shimazu, Masahiko
  Ohayo; (Good Morning) 1966,F 2,24:1
Shimizu, Gen
  Tokyo File 212 1951,Je 1,20:7
  Gate of Hell 1954,D 14,45:2
Shimizu, Magao
  I Live in Fear; Ikimono no Kiroku
    1967,Ja 26,25:1
Shimkus, Joanna
  Boom! 1968,My 27,56:1
  Zita 1968,Ag 12,40:2
Shimoda, Yuki
  Auntie Mame 1958,D 5,39:1
  Majority of One, A 1962,Ja 12,29:2
  Horizontal Lieutenant, The 1962,My 12,15:3
  Once a Thief 1965,S 9,36:1
Shimozawa, Kam (Original Author)
  Zatoichi 1968,Je 28,37:1
  Showdown for Zatoichi 1968,O 5,40:1
Shimura, Takashi
  Rasho-Mon 1951,D 27,18:3
  Godzilla, King of the Monsters 1956,Ap 28,11:1
  Magnificent Seven, The 1956,N 20,46:2
  Mysterians, The 1959,Jl 2,15:2
  Drunken Angel 1959,D 31,12:1
  Men Who Tread on the Tiger's Tail, The
    1960,Ja 11,35:7
  Ikiru; To Live 1960,Ja 30,13:5
  Throne of Blood 1961,N 23,50:2
  Hidden Fortress The 1962,Ja 24,24:2
  Yojimbo 1962,O 16,34:1
  Bad Sleep Well, The 1963,Ja 23,5:2
  Idiot, The 1963,My 1,35:1
  Sanjuro 1963,My 8,34:2
  Stray Dog 1964,Mr 4,32:7
  Saga of the Vagabonds 1964,O 7,31:1 (Incorrect
    in this edition; use 1964,O 7,51:1 elsewhere)
  Kwaidan (Hoichi, The Earless); Hoichi, The
    Earless (Kwaidan) 1965,N 23,51:1
  Ghidrah, The Three-Headed Monster
    1965,D 16,63:3
Shin, Kinzo
  Golden Demon 1956,Ja 31,34:3
  Enjo 1964,S 23,54:1

Shindo, Eitaro
Yang Kwei Fei 1956,S 11,41:2
Street of Shame 1959,Je 5,17:2
Shindo, Kaneto (Director)
Island, The; Hadaka No Shima 1962,S 11,27:2
Onibaba 1965,F 10,44:3
Lost Sex 1968,Jl 23,27:2
Shindo, Kaneto (Producer)
Island, The; Hadaka No Shima 1962,S 11,27:2
Shindo, Kaneto (Screenwriter)
Island, The; Hadaka No Shima 1962,S 11,27:2
Challenge to Live 1964,Ap 8,33:1
This Madding Crowd 1964,Je 17,48:1
Onibaba 1965,F 10,44:3
Lost Sex 1968,Jl 23,27:2
Shine, Andy
Richard III 1956,Mr 12,1:4
Shine, Bill
Yellow Mask, The 1930,D 8,26:1
Troopship 1938,Ap 26,18:2
Wanted for Murder 1946,D 12,38:4
Champagne Charlie 1948,Ag 7,8:2
Under Capricorn 1949,S 9,28:3
Amazing Mr Beecham, The 1949,D 26,33:4
Caretaker's Daughter, The 1953,Ag 20,18:5
Shine, John L
Little Lady Eileen 1916,Ag 14,7:6
Shiner, Ronald
Dreaming Lips 1937,My 20,17:1
Dinner at the Ritz 1937,D 4,21:1
Frightened Lady 1941,N 10,21:3
Wings and the Woman 1942,O 8,31:1
Smugglers, The 1948,Mr 29,17:1
Laughing Anne 1954,My 8,15:2
Innocents in Paris 1955,Mr 5,9:6
Ship Was Loaded, The 1958,Ja 20,20:1
Shingler, Helen
Quiet Week-End 1948,Ag 20,13:2
Caretaker's Daughter, The 1953,Ag 20,18:5
Edge of Divorce 1954,Jl 2,10:1
Shipman, Gwyn
Prince of Peace, The 1951,Mr 24,8:3
Shipman, Harry (Original Author)
Shakedown 1936,Ag 17,9:2
Shipman, Helen
Christopher Bean 1933,N 25,10:2
Double Door 1934,My 5,22:3
Men Without Names 1935,Je 29,16:2
Shipman, Kenneth (Producer)
Girl-Getters, The 1966,Ap 13,37:6
Shipman, Mary Raymond (Original Author)
Unbeliever, The 1918,F 12,9:2
Shipman, Neil (Original Author)
Wings in the Dark 1935,F 2,10:1
Shipman, Nina
Say One for Me 1959,Je 20,11:2
Blue Denim 1959,Jl 31,21:1
High Time 1960,S 17,15:1
Shipman, Samuel (Miscellaneous)
Law of the Underworld 1938,Ap 28,27:2
Shipman, Samuel (Original Author)
Lawful Larceny 1923,Jl 24,14:3 (In Addenda)
Cheaper to Marry 1925,F 2,14:1
Friendly Enemies 1925,My 5,24:2
Slave of Fashion, A 1925,Jl 21,26:2
Fast Life 1929,Ag 17,5:3
Lawful Larceny 1930,Jl 12,16:4
East Is West 1930,N 1,23:2
Pay-Off, The 1930,N 10,16:2
Scarlet Pages 1930,D 6,21:3
Manhattan Parade 1931,D 25,29:2
Woman in Room 13, The 1932,My 21,9:2
Friendly Enemies 1942,Je 22,19:1
Shipper, Max
Wiener Blut 1933,N 13,21:2
Shipstad, Eddie
Ice Follies of 1939 1939,Mr 17,25:2
Shipstad, Roy
Ice Follies of 1939 1939,Mr 17,25:2
Shirakawa, Yumi
Mysterians, The 1959,Jl 2,15:2
Walleyed Nippon 1963,S 3,36:1
Different Sons 1964,F 13,25:1
Challenge to Live 1964,Ap 8,33:1
Shirasaka, Yoshio (Screenwriter)
Blue Beast, The 1965,Ja 30,18:2
Kojiro 1968,Ag 30,23:1
Shiraskawa, Yoshio (Narrator)
Tokyo Olympiad 1966,N 17,55:1
Shirer, William L
Magic Face, The 1951,O 1,19:2
Shirley, Anne
Anne of Green Gables 1934,D 22,21:1
Steamboat Around the Bend 1935,S 20,17:2
Chatterbox 1936,F 15,18:6
M'liss 1936,Ag 8,5:2
Make Way for a Lady 1936,D 12,15:1
Meet the Missus 1937,Jl 2,25:2
Stella Dallas 1937,Ag 6,21:1
Condemned Woman 1938,Ap 22,15:5
Law of the Underworld 1938,Ap 28,27:2
Mother Carey's Chickens 1938,Ag 5,11:1
Girls' School 1938,N 3,27:1

Man to Remember, A 1938,N 7,23:2
Boy Slaves 1939,F 9,17:3
Career 1939,Jl 28,14:2
Vigil in the Night 1940,Mr 9,19:2
Saturday's Children 1940,My 4,13:1
Anne of Windy Poplars 1940,Ag 23,13:3
West Point Widow 1941,S 11,21:5
Unexpected Uncle 1941,S 25,29:1
All That Money Can Buy 1941,O 17,27:2
Mayor of Forty-Fourth Street, The
1942,Je 11,27:4
Powers Girl, The 1943,Mr 26,14:2 (In Addenda)
Bombardier 1943,Jl 2,15:2
Government Girl 1944,Ja 7,13:2
Man From Frisco 1944,Je 16,14:7
Music in Manhattan 1944,O 7,11:2
Murder, my Sweet 1945,Mr 9,16:2
Shirley, Bill
Flying Tigers 1942,O 23,25:2
Dream of Jeanie, I 1952,Je 26,26:2
Shirley, Florence
Private Affairs 1940,Jl 5,10:3
We Were Dancing 1942,My 1,23:2
Stars and Stripes Forever 1952,D 23,17:2
Shirley, Jack (Composer)
Dance Band 1936,Ja 4,19:2
Shirley, Jack (Miscellaneous)
Dance Band 1936,Ja 4,19:2
Shirley, Peggy
Thomas Crown Affair, The 1968,Je 27,48:2
Shirokova, S
Concentration Camp 1939,Mr 20,13:2
Shirshov, Andrei
Hello, Moscow! 1946,Je 15,24:4
Shirvanzada, A (Director)
Honor 1929,S 10,27:1
Shishkin, Boris
Taxi to Heaven 1944,My 25,16:3
Shkurat, S
Soil 1930,O 21,34:4
Ivan 1933,F 27,11:3
Tchapayef 1935,Ja 15,22:1
Krasnaya Derevnya 1935,My 2,17:1
Frontier 1935,D 28,10:5
Natalka-Poltavka 1936,D 25,19:4
Guerrilla Brigade 1942,Ap 14,17:2
Shlifko, Ola
Mamele; Little Mothers 1938,D 26,29:1
Shlikhting, Boris
Sniper 1932,Ag 26,20:3
Shlovsky, V (Original Author)
Under Sunny Skies 1950,D 26,19:3
Shlovsky, V (Screenwriter)
Chuk and Gek 1953,D 21,27:4
Shmidt, L A
Greater Promise, A 1936,O 8,27:3
Shmyga, Tatyana
Ballad of a Hussar, The 1963,Jl 15,25:5
Shneiderman, S L (Screenwriter)
Last Chapter, The 1966,F 22,14:5
Sho-Sho, Li
Song of China 1936,N 10,31:3
Shochiku (Producer)
Carmen Comes Home 1959,D 23,22:1
Shockley, Marion
Stage Door Canteen 1943,Je 25,13:2
Shoemaker, Ann
Chance at Heaven 1933,D 26,19:3
Dr Monica 1934,Je 21,28:2
Alice Adams 1935,Ag 16,11:3
Sins of Man 1936,Je 19,17:2
Shall We Dance 1937,My 14,21:1
They Won't Forget 1937,Jl 15,16:1
Stella Dallas 1937,Ag 6,21:1
Life of the Party, The 1937,O 4,17:1
Romance of the Redwoods 1939,Ap 24,13:2
They all Come Out 1939,Ag 3,15:4
Babes in Arms 1939,O 20,27:2
Farmer's Daughter, The 1940,F 16,23:4
Seventeen 1940,F 29,15:2
Angel From Texas, An 1940,My 10,26:7
My Favorite Wife 1940,My 31,15:2
Strike up the Band 1940,S 30,13:2
Ellery Queen, Master Detective 1940,D 19,33:1
You'll Never Get Rich 1941,O 24,27:2
Above Suspicion 1943,Ag 6,10:3
Man From Frisco 1944,Je 16,14:7
Mr Winkle Goes to War 1944,Ag 3,16:1
Magic Town 1947,O 8,29:2
Wallflower 1948,Je 12,8:5
House by the River 1950,My 2,25:2
Sunrise at Campobello 1960,S 29,32:1
Fortune Cookie, The 1966,O 20,52:1
Sholem, Lee (Director)
Tarzan's Magic Fountain 1949,F 7,15:2
Tarzan and the Slave Girl 1950,Je 24,7:3
Redhead From Wyoming, The 1953,Ja 9,17:4
Sholkovsky, N
Golden Mountains 1932,Ap 14,25:3
Sholokov, Mikhail (Original Author)
Cossacks of the Don 1932,Mr 19,11:2
And Quiet Flows the Don 1960,My 25,45:2
Colt, The 1961,Je 5,37:4

Sholokov, Mikhail (Original Author)— Cont
Fate of Man 1961,Jl 11,28:1
Shon, Hazel
Love Is a Many-Splendored Thing
1955,Ag 19,10:1
Shonteff, Lindsay (Director)
2nd Best Secret Agent in the Whole Wide World,
The 1966,Ap 28,49:1
Shonteff, Lindsay (Screenwriter)
2nd Best Secret Agent in the Whole Wide World,
The 1966,Ap 28,49:1
Shope, Hedi
Wedding Night, The 1935,Mr 16,19:1
SHOR
See Also SCHOR, SCHORR
Shore, Dinah
Thank Your Lucky Stars 1943,O 2,19:2
Up in Arms 1944,Mr 3,19:2
Follow the Boys 1944,Ap 26,24:6
Belle of the Yukon 1945,Mr 30,18:4
Till the Clouds Roll By 1946,D 6,27:4
Aaron Slick From Punkin Crick 1952,Ap 19,18:6
Shore, Jean
Red Shoes, The 1948,O 23,9:2
Go, Man, Go 1954,Mr 10,29:5
Shore, Lois
Forest Ring, The 1930,Ap 26,11:1
Shore, Roberta
Shaggy Dog, The 1959,Mr 20,26:2
Blue Denim 1959,Jl 31,21:1
Strangers When we Meet 1960,Je 30,22:2
Lolita 1962,Je 14,23:2
Shore, Viola Brothers (Original Author)
Lucky Boy 1929,F 25,16:1
Sailor Be Good 1933,F 27,11:2
Shore, Viola Brothers (Screenwriter)
Life of the Party, The 1937,O 4,17:1
Breakfast for Two 1937,N 20,21:2
Arkansas Traveler, The 1938,N 17,29:2
Shores, Byron
Too Many Girls 1940,N 21,43:1
Mad Doctor of Market Street, The 1942,Ja 5,21::
Shores, Lynn (Director)
Skinner's big Idea 1928,Mr 27,30:4
Shadow Strikes, The 1937,S 13,17:1
Charlie Chan At the Wax Museum 1940,S 28,9:3
Shorokhova, Rimma
House I Live in, The 1959,Ap 20,34:2
Shorp, Mimi
Eva, das Fabriksmaedel 1938,Ja 8,19:2
Short, Antrim
O'Malley of the Mounted 1921,F 7,8:2
Classmates 1924,D 30,15:3
Wildfire 1925,Je 10,18:2
Short, Doris
Huckleberry Finn 1931,Ag 8,16:3
Short, Dorothy
Heart of Arizona 1938,Ap 16,17:1
Spooks Run Wild 1941,N 1,20:3
Short, Florence
Enchanted Cottage, The 1924,Ap 14,14:1
Way Down East 1931,Mr 16,25:1
Short, Gertrude
You Never Can Tell 1920,O 4,14:3
Narrow Street, The 1925,Ja 5,19:1
Code of the West 1925,Ap 13,24:1
Talker, The 1925,My 12,26:2
Beggar on Horseback 1925,Je 6,9:2
Show, The 1927,Mr 14,16:1
Tillie the Toiler 1927,Je 7,27:4
Adam and Evil 1927,Ag 10,21:4
Ladies at Ease 1927,O 5,31:1
Women's Wares 1927,N 15,27:1
Gold Diggers of Broadway, The 1929,Ag 31,13:4
Little Accident 1930,Ag 4,13:4
Laughing Sinners 1931,Jl 4,11:5
Girl in 419 1933,My 20,11:5
Key, The 1934,My 30,14:3
St Louis Kid, The 1934,N 1,25:2
Helldorado 1935,Ja 7,13:2
Stella Dallas 1937,Ag 6,21:1
Tip-Off Girls 1938,Mr 25,15:3
Short, Harry
Just Suppose 1926,Ja 18,26:2
Short, Hassard
Turn of the Wheel 1918,S 2,7:1
Stronger Vow, The 1919,Ap 28,13:2
Way of a Woman, The 1919,Jl 28,8:5
Woman's Place 1921,O 23,VI,4:1 (In Addenda)
Short, Lew
Big City, The 1928,Mr 26,26:2
Short, Luke (Original Author)
Hurry, Charlie, Hurry 1941,N 12,31:3
Ramrod 1947,Je 30,25:6
Albuquerque 1948,Mr 1,17:2
Blood on the Moon 1948,N 12,30:5
Ambush 1950,Ja 19,35:2
Vengeance Valley 1951,F 16,21:2
Hell's Outpost 1955,F 26,13:3
Short, Luke (Screenwriter)
Blood on the Moon 1948,N 12,30:5
Short, Paul (Original Author)
Bad Boy 1949,Mr 23,35:2

Short, Paul (Producer)
Bad Boy 1949,Mr 23,35:2
Kid From Texas, The 1950,Je 2,26:2
Short, Robin
Baron of Arizona, The 1950,Je 23,29:2
Short, William
Twelve O'Clock High 1950,Ja 28,10:2
Shortall, Betty
Lonely Night, The 1954,Mr 29,22:2
Shortall, Katherine
Lonely Night, The 1954,Mr 29,22:2
Shortall, Leonard
Lonely Night, The 1954,Mr 29,22:2
Shortall, Stephen
Lonely Night, The 1954,Mr 29,22:2
Shortall, Thomas
Lonely Night, The 1954,Mr 29,22:2
Shostakovich, Dmitri (Composer)
Alone 1932,My 25,23:6
Pozor 1933,Mr 11,18:4
Youth of Maxim, The 1935,Ap 20,16:1
Three Women 1936,F 12,25:4
Return of Maxim, The 1937,N 2,33:1
Defense of Volotchayevsk, The 1938,Ag 11,13:3
New Horizons 1939,My 12,25:3
Thousands Cheer 1943,S 14,27:1
Zoya 1945,Ap 16,18:6
Life in Bloom 1949,My 9,20:4
Hamlet 1966,Mr 16,48:1
Shostakovich, Dmitri (Miscellaneous)
Golden Mountains 1932,Ap 14,25:3
Shostakovich, Dmitri (Screenwriter)
Khovanschina 1960,S 19,41:2
Shotter, Winifred
Chance of a Night Time, A 1931,Je 7,VIII,6:1
Night and Day 1933,My 29,22:2
Sorrell and Son 1934,My 29,22:1
Petticoat Fever 1936,Mr 21,13:2
High Treason 1937,Ja 27,17:3
Shotwell, James T (Miscellaneous)
Land of Liberty 1939,Je 16,27:3
Land of Liberty 1941,Ja 30,19:4
Shotwell, Marie
Witching Hour, The 1916,D 11,7:3
Manicure Girl, The 1925,Je 15,10:1
Shore Leave 1925,S 14,16:1
Lovers in Quarantine 1925,O 13,20:1
Running Wild 1927,Je 14,33:2
One Woman to Another 1927,S 19,30:3
Shoup, D M
Sands of Iwo Jima 1949,D 31,9:2
Shovorin, Alexander
Cranes are Flying, The 1960,Mr 22,31:2
Show, Mercury Wonder
Follow the Boys 1944,Ap 26,24:6
Showalter, Max
Always Leave Them Laughing 1949,N 24,48:2
With a Song in my Heart 1952,Ap 5,20:2
My Six Loves 1963,Ap 4,58:4
Move Over Darling 1963,D 26,33:1
How to Murder Your Wife 1965,Ja 27,26:1
Shpalikov, Gennadi (Screenwriter)
Meet Me in Moscow 1966,My 3,51:1
Shpias, B V (Director)
Return of Nathan Becker, The 1933,Ap 15,16:3
Shpigel, G
Gadfly, The 1956,S 17,22:2
Shpinel, Isaac (Miscellaneous)
Ivan the Terrible, Part I 1947,Mr 10,25:2
Shpringfeld, Pavel
Twins 1947,Jl 28,12:2
Shram, Violet
Riders of the Dawn 1920,My 3,18:1
Shreve, Florence
Forgotten Commandments 1932,Je 2,25:2
Shrimpton, Jean
Privilege 1967,Jl 25,30:2
Shriner, Herb
Main Street to Broadway 1953,O 14,34:1
Shroder, Kurt (Miscellaneous)
Girl From Maxim's, The 1936,S 16,29:1
Shscherbachev, V (Composer)
Conquests of Peter The Great, The 1939,Ag 24,17:2
Shtein, A (Screenwriter)
Admiral Ushakov 1954,Ja 18,19:2
Shtela, Alexander (Original Author)
Men of the Sea 1938,Je 20,11:2
Shtraukh, M
Golden Mountains 1932,Ap 14,25:3
Man With the Gun, The 1939,Ja 30,9:3
New Horizons 1939,My 12,25:3
Vow, The 1947,Je 23,14:3
Lucky Bride, The 1948,Ja 26,15:2
Shtykan, Leda
Once There Was a Girl 1945,D 24,19:2
Shu-Hu
Veil of Happiness, The 1928,My 1,33:3
SHUBERT
See Also SCHUBERT
Shubert, Eddie
Case of the Howling Dog, The 1934,O 18,26:5
St Louis Kid, The 1934,N 1,25:2

While the Patient Slept 1935,Mr 2,18:2
Black Fury 1935,Ap 11,27:2
Alibi Ike 1935,Jl 17,22:1
Don't Bet on Blondes 1935,Jl 20,16:2
Goose and the Gander, The 1935,S 12,29:2
Pay-Off, The 1935,N 13,25:3
Road Gang 1936,F 24,14:1
Song of the Saddle 1936,Mr 21,13:3
Law in her Hands, The 1936,Je 6,21:2
Shubnaya, A
Sunny Youth 1935,Ag 19,18:2
Shuford, Andy
When a Feller Needs a Friend 1932,My 14,11:5
Shuken, Phillip (Screenwriter)
Doctor, You've Got to be Kidding 1967,My 11,50:1
Speedway 1968,Je 14,43:1
Shull, Richard B (Original Author)
Pamela, Pamela You Are.... 1968,D 21,49:4
Shull, Richard B (Screenwriter)
Pamela, Pamela You Are.... 1968,D 21,49:4
SHULMAN
See Also SCHULMAN
Shulman, Irving (Original Author)
City Across the River 1949,Ap 8,31:3
Baby Face Nelson 1957,D 12,35:1
Cry Tough 1959,S 17,48:4
Harlow 1965,Jl 22,24:1
Shulman, Irving (Screenwriter)
City Across the River 1949,Ap 8,31:3
Journey Into Light 1951,O 5,24:4
Rebel without a Cause 1955,O 27,28:3
Baby Face Nelson 1957,D 12,35:1
College Confidential 1960,Ag 22,23:1
Shulman, Max (Original Author)
Always Leave Them Laughing 1949,N 24,48:2
Tender Trap, The 1955,N 11,29:6
Rally Round the Flag Boys! 1958,D 24,2:7
SHULTZ
See Also SCHULTZ
Shumacher, J
Without a Home 1939,Ap 1,17:3
SHUMAN
See Also SCHUMAN, SCHUMANN
Shuman, Harry
Red Raiders, The 1927,S 28,28:3
Shuman, Roy
Goddess, The 1958,Je 25,24:1
Shumate, Harold (Original Author)
Behind the Evidence 1935,Ja 26,13:2
Final Hour, The 1936,Ag 1,16:3
Crash Donovan 1936,Ag 10,10:3
Fight to the Finish, A 1937,Je 26,20:2 (In Addenda)
Counsel for Crime 1937,O 9,16:1
Main Event, The 1938,Je 20,11:3
Man of Conquest 1939,Ap 28,31:2
Man With Nine Lives, The 1940,Ap 29,12:3
Badlands of Dakota 1941,S 9,27:6
Renegades 1946,Jl 11,18:2
Shumate, Harold (Screenwriter)
Circus Ace, The 1927,Jl 6,23:2
Panic on the Air 1936,Ap 20,17:1
Pride of the Marines 1936,Ap 27,19:2
Final Hour, The 1936,Ag 1,16:3
Killer at Large 1936,O 26,20:1
Parole Racket 1937,Mr 8,22:1
Fight to the Finish, A 1937,Je 26,20:2 (In Addenda)
Frame-Up 1937,Ag 9,23:2 (In Addenda)
Street of Missing Women 1940,Ja 8,11:2
My Son Is Guilty 1940,Ja 15,11:2
When the Daltons Rode 1940,Ag 23,13:3
Trail of the Vigilantes 1940,D 7,13:2
Roundup, The 1941,Mr 13,25:4
Parson of Panamint, The 1941,Jl 26,18:2
Ride 'Em Cowboy 1942,Mr 5,27:3
Men of Texas 1942,Jl 13,18:3 (In Addenda)
Forest Rangers, The 1942,O 22,25:2
Kansan, The 1943,O 1,15:3
Abilene Town 1946,Mr 4,16:5
Blood on the Moon 1948,N 12,30:5
Buccaneer's Girl 1950,Mr 27,19:2
Saddle Tramp 1950,N 24,31:4
Half Breed, The 1952,Jl 5,7:2
Shumlin, Herman (Director)
Watch on the Rhine 1943,Ag 28,15:1
Confidential Agent 1945,N 3,11:2
Shumsky, Y
First Front, The 1949,N 14,19:2
Victors and the Vanquished, The 1950,My 1,18:2
Shumway, Lee
Yankee Consul, The 1924,F 11,18:3
Introduce Me 1925,Mr 9,21:1
Air Mail, The 1925,Mr 17,18:1
One Minute to Play 1926,S 6,16:2
Last Trail, The 1927,Ja 26,17:1
Let It Rain 1927,Mr 9,29:1
Great Mail Robbery, The 1927,Jl 20,29:3
South Sea Love 1928,F 7,30:3
Hit of the Show 1928,Jl 9,25:1
Queen of the Night Clubs 1929,Mr 18,30:6
Evangeline 1929,Jl 29,23:3

Shumway, Lee — Cont
So This Is College 1929,N 9,22:5
Night Parade 1929,N 11,20:2
Show Girl in Hollywood 1930,My 5,27:3
Widow From Chicago, The 1930,D 20,20:6
Mysterious Mr Wong, The 1935,Mr 7,26:1
Million Dollar Baby 1935,My 6,22:3
Hard Rock Harrigan 1935,Jl 30,16:2
Preview Murder Mystery, The 1936,Mr 21,13:2
Hollywood Cowboy 1937,Jl 24,12:1
Rawhide 1938,Ap 25,19:2
Painted Desert 1938,S 14,26:5
No Greater Sin 1941,Ag 29,18:2
Shuranova, Antonina
War and Peace 1968,Ap 29,50:5
Shurr, Robert (Screenwriter)
George Washington Carver 1940,Ap 17,26:4
Shushinka, Miss
Scoundrel, The 1935,My 3,23:2
Shute, James (Miscellaneous)
Unconquered, The; (Helen Keller in Her Story) 1954,Je 16,37:1
Shute, James (Original Author)
Fools for Scandal 1938,Mr 25,15:3
Windjammer 1958,Ap 10,32:2
Shute, James (Screenwriter)
We Are the Marines 1942,D 14,19:2
Windjammer 1958,Ap 10,32:2
Shute, Nevil (Original Author)
Pied Piper, The 1942,Ag 13,15:3
No Highway in the Sky 1951,S 22,8:6
Landfall 1953,My 11,25:2
Town Like Alice, A 1958,S 22,27:1
On the Beach 1959,D 18,34:1
Shutta, Ethel
Whoopee 1930,O 1,26:3
Playground, The 1965,O 4,00:0
Shutta, Jack
Burning Cross, The 1948,F 20,19:1
Shuval, Menachem (Screenwriter)
They Were Ten; (Heym Hayu Assara) 1961,Ap 18,44:2
Shvachko, A (Director)
Land, The 1955,Ap 11,29:3
Shvachko, A (Screenwriter)
Land, The 1955,Ap 11,29:3
Shvets, Michael
Cossacks in Exile 1939,Ja 28,19:2
Shvetsova, Elena
Lucky Bride, The 1948,Ja 26,15:2
Shvily, Michael (Producer)
Six Days to Eternity 1968,O 31,54:3
Shvorin, Alexei
Sword and the Dragon, The 1960,N 17,46:3
Shwartz, E (Screenwriter)
Don Quixote 1961,Ja 21,18:1
Shy, Gus
Good News 1930,S 6,9:2
Lady's Morals, A 1930,N 8,21:3
New Moon 1930,D 25,18:6
I Sell Anything 1934,D 27,25:2
Shyer, Melville (Director)
Sucker Money 1933,Ap 7,22:5
Road to Ruin, The 1934,F 21,23:2
Siame, Made
Antoine and Antoinette 1948,Ap 16,29:2
Siani, Ryp
Robby 1968,Ag 15,46:3
Siawinska, Zofja
Ulica 1933,Ja 27,13:2
Sibal, Reyaldo
Walls of Hell, The 1965,N 18,55:3
Sibaldi, Stefano
Man With the Grey Glove, The 1953,Ja 3,11:2
Sibelious, Johanna (Screenwriter)
Dreaming Lips; (Traumende Mund, The) 1958,N 1,14:3
Sibelius, Ceilia
Confessions of a Nazi Spy 1939,Ap 29,13:2
Sibirskaia, Nadia
Mystic Mountain, The 1936,Mr 31,17:2
Marseillaise 1939,N 6,20:2
Crime of Monsieur Lange, The 1964,Ap 4,15:5
Sibley, Antoinette
Royal Ballet, The (Swan Lake Act II); Swan Lake Act II (The Royal Ballet) 1960,O 5,45:2
Sica, Vittorio de
Trionfo dell'Amore, Il; Love's Triumph 1938,Mr 29,18:4
Diamante Porta-Fortuna, Il; Lucky Diamond, The 1938,S 29,31:1
Signor Max, Il; Mr Max 1939,O 6,31:4
But It's Nothing Serious 1939,O 10,27:2
Love in old Naples 1940,Ja 26,13:3
Sica, Vittorio De
Al Vostri Ordini, Signora; At Your Orders, Madame 1940,My 25,20:1
Sica, Vittorio de
Termina Siempre Asi; It Always Ends That Way 1940,S 3,21:3
Cuore Napoletano; Neapolitan Heart 1940,O 8,31:2

Siciliano, Enzo
Gospel According to St Matthew, The
1966,F 18,23:1
Siddons, Harold
Glory at Sea 1953,Mr 11,36:7
Genevieve 1954,F 16,30:2
Malta Story 1954,Jl 17,7:2
Purple Plain, The 1955,Ap 11,29:1
Baby and the Battleship, The 1957,O 1,37:2
Sidelov, Sergei (Director)
Alego 1954,D 27,22:7
Siderman, Conrad
Are We Civilized? 1934,Je 14,28:5
Sidery, Sherban (Screenwriter)
Ostrich Has two Eggs, The 1960,S 27,40:1
SIDNEY
See Also SYDNEY
Sidney, Basil
Next of Kin 1943,My 6,25:2
Treasure Island 1950,Ag 16,24:2
Sidney, George
In Hollywood with Potash and Perlmutter
1924,S 30,27:3
Classified 1925,N 2,20:1
Partners Again, With Potash and Perlmutter
1926,F 15,16:4
Cohens and the Kellys, The 1926,F 23,26:5
Sweet Daddies 1926,Je 23,28:1
Lost at the Front 1927,Je 14,33:2
For the Love of Mike 1927,Ag 24,27:5
Life of Riley, The 1927,S 5,13:2
Clancy's Kosher Wedding 1927,S 7,35:2
Life of Riley, The 1927,S 11,VIII,5:1
Cohens and the Kellys In Paris, The
1928,F 6,12:3
Latest From Paris, The 1928,F 27,16:2
We Americans 1928,Mr 29,25:3
Flying Romeos 1928,Ap 3,33:2
Give and Take 1928,D 27,27:1
Cohens and the Kellys In Atlantic City, The
1929,Mr 18,30:6
Cohens and the Kelleys In Scotland, The
1930,Mr 10,24:1
Cohens and Kellys in Africa, The 1930,D 20,20:6
High Pressure 1932,F 1,22:3
Heart of New York, The 1932,Mr 2,15:3
Cohens and Kellys in Hollywood, The
1932,Ap 22,23:2
Cohens and Kellys in Trouble, The
1933,Ap 17,16:4
Manhattan Melodrama 1934,My 5,22:2
Diamond Jim 1935,Ag 24,18:2
Good Old Soak 1937,Ap 20,25:3
Sidney, George (Director)
Free and Easy 1941,Ap 3,29:4
Pacific Rendezvous 1942,Jl 8,27:4
Pilot No 5 1943,Je 25,13:4
Thousands Cheer 1943,S 14,27:1
Bathing Beauty 1944,Je 28,20:1
Anchors Aweigh 1945,Jl 20,15:2
Harvey Girls, The 1946,Ja 25,26:2
Holiday in Mexico 1946,Ag 16,19:3
Cass Timberlane 1947,N 7,20:2
Three Musketeers, The 1948,O 21,33:2
Red Danube, The 1949,D 9,37:3
Key to the City 1950,F 2,31:2
Annie Get Your Gun 1950,My 18,37:1
Show Boat 1951,Jl 20,14:1
Scaramouche 1952,My 9,20:2
Young Bess 1953,My 22,31:1
Kiss Me Kate 1953,N 6,23:2
Jupiter's Darling 1955,F 18,18:4
Eddy Duchin Story, The 1956,Je 22,15:1
Jeanne Eagels 1957,Ag 31,19:1
Pal Joey 1957,O 28,30:1
Who Was That Lady? 1960,Ap 16,10:1
Pepe 1960,D 22,18:1
Bye Bye Birdie 1963,Ap 5,27:3
Ticklish Affair, A 1963,Ag 22,19:2
Viva Las Vegas 1964,My 21,42:1
Swinger, The 1966,D 15,60:1
Half a Sixpence 1968,F 21,60:3
Sidney, George (Producer)
Jeanne Eagels 1957,Ag 31,19:1
Pepe 1960,D 22,18:1
Viva Las Vegas 1964,My 21,42:1
Swinger, The 1966,D 15,60:1
Half a Sixpence 1968,F 21,60:3
Sidney, Louis K (Producer)
Hullabaloo 1940,D 19,33:1
Big Store, The 1941,Je 27,14:4
Sidney, P J
Joe Louis Story, The 1953,N 4,29:4
Black Like Me 1964,My 21,42:1
Sidney, Scott (Director)
Charley's Aunt 1925,F 9,15:3
Stop Flirting 1925,Je 18,16:3
Seven Days 1925,Ag 31,19:3
Nervous Wreck, The 1926,O 12,30:2
Sidney, Steffi
Rebel without a Cause 1955,O 27,28:3

Sidney, Sylvia
Thru Different Eyes 1929,Ap 15,22:6
City Streets 1931,Ap 18,17:3
Confessions of a Co-Ed 1931,Je 20,20:4
American Tragedy, An 1931,Ag 6,22:5
Street Scene 1931,Ag 27,22:5
Ladies of the Big House 1932,Ja 1,31:1
Merrily We Go to Hell 1932,Je 11,9:3
Madame Butterfly 1932,D 26,26:2
Pick Up 1933,Mr 25,13:4
Jennie Gerhardt 1933,Je 9,20:2
Good Dame 1934,Mr 17,11:4
Thirty Day Princess 1934,My 12,12:3
Behold My Wife 1935,F 18,19:3
Accent on Youth 1935,Ag 12,10:3
Mary Burns, Fugitive 1935,N 16,19:2
Trail of the Lonesome Pine, The 1936,F 20,23:5
Fury 1936,Je 6,21:1
You Only Live Once 1937,F 1,15:2
Woman Alone, The 1937,F 27,9:2
Dead End 1937,Ag 25,25:1
You and Me 1938,Je 2,19:1
One Third of a Nation 1939,F 11,13:2
Wagons Roll at Night, The 1941,My 10,20:4
Blood on the Sun 1945,Je 29,12:2
Searching Wind, The 1946,Je 27,29:1
Mr Ace 1946,S 30,21:3
Love From a Stranger 1947,N 28,30:1
Miserables, Les 1952,Ag 15,11:2
Violent Saturday 1955,My 12,32:2
Sidorkin, Mikhail
Spring 1948,Mr 15,26:2
Sieber, Josef
Hummel-Hummel 1939,Mr 11,21:2
Du Bist mein Gluck; Thou Art my Joy
1940,Ja 6,9:2
Paradies der Junggesellen; Bachelors' Paradise
1940,Ap 13,21:3
Sieber, Maria
Scralet Empress, The 1934,S 15,20:2
Siebert, John
Mozart Story, The 1948,N 15,21:5
Siedel, Erhard
Vier Musketiere, Die; Four Musketeers, The
1935,N 9,19:3
Kater Lampe 1938,Ap 23,19:3
Sieff, Percy
Code 7...Victim 5 1965,My 20,52:1
SIEGAL
See Also SIGEL, SEGAL, SEGALL
Siegel, Al (Composer)
Moonlight and Pretzels 1933,Ag 23,21:2
Swing High, Swing Low 1937,Ag 15,19:1
Double or Nothing 1937,S 2,17:3
Siegel, Bernard
Crimson Runner, The 1925,My 27,26:2
Wild Horse Mesa 1925,Ag 10,8:2
Phantom of the Opera, The 1925,S 7,15:3
Vanishing American, The 1925,O 16,18:2
Desert Gold 1926,Mr 23,24:5
Stand and Deliver 1928,Ap 2,25:1
Laugh, Clown, Laugh 1928,My 28,23:2
Rescue, The 1929,Ja 14,20:1
Redskin 1929,Ja 28,21:1
Case of Sergeant Grischa, The 1930,Mr 8,21:1
Shadow of Doubt 1935,Mr 11,15:1
Wells Fargo 1937,D 30,15:2
Siegel, Don (Director)
Verdict, The 1946,D 13,29:4
Night Unto Night 1949,Je 11,11:2
Big Steal, The 1949,Jl 11,13:2
Duel at Silver Creek 1952,Ag 2,7:6
Count the Hours 1953,Je 24,30:4
Riot in Cell Block 11 1954,F 19,24:5
Private Hell 36 1954,S 4,6:4
Annapolis Story, An 1955,Ap 9,8:2
Crime in the Streets 1956,My 24,27:4
Baby Face Nelson 1957,D 12,35:1
Spanish Affair 1958,F 6,24:1
Edge of Eternity 1960,F 25,34:2
Hound-Dog Man 1960,Ap 28,29:1
Flaming Star 1960,D 17,19:1
Hell is for Heroes 1962,Jl 12,19:3
Killers, The 1964,Jl 18,10:4
Madigan 1968,Mr 30,22:2
Coogan's Bluff 1968,O 3,56:1
Siegel, Don (Producer)
Killers, The 1964,Jl 18,10:4
Coogan's Bluff 1968,O 3,56:1
Siegel, Max (Original Author)
We Americans 1928,Mr 29,25:3
Siegel, Rohama (Screenwriter)
We're Going to Be Rich 1938,Jl 4,10:2
Siegel, Sol C (Producer)
World Premiere 1941,Ag 21,15:2
West Point Widow 1941,S 11,21:5
Henry Aldrich for President 1941,O 18,22:2
Buy Me That Town 1941,O 23,27:2
Among the Living 1941,D 13,25:2
Night of January 16th, The 1941,D 19,35:1
Pacific Blackout 1942,Ja 15,25:2
Night in New Orleans 1942,Jl 2,25:2
Sweater Girl 1942,Jl 13,18:3

Siegel, Sol C (Producer) — Cont
Street Of Chance 1942,N 19,31:3
Hostages 1943,O 11,23:2
Kiss and Tell 1945,O 26,16:2
Blue Skies 1946,O 17,28:2
Perils of Pauline, The 1947,Jl 10,17:2
Welcome Stranger 1947,Ag 7,15:2
Iron Curtain, The 1948,My 13,31:2
Cry of the City 1948,S 30,32:4
Letter to Three Wives, A 1949,Ja 21,24:2
House of Strangers 1949,Jl 2,8:2
I Was a Maie War Bride 1949,Ag 27,7:2
Prince of Foxes 1949,D 24,11:2
Panic in the Streets 1950,Ag 5,9:2
Stella 1950,Ag 19,9:2
My Blue Heaven 1950,S 16,12:6
Fourteen Hours 1951,Mr 7,43:2
I Can Get It for You Wholesale 1951,Ap 5,34:4
On the Riviera 1951,My 24,47:1
I'll Never Forget You 1951,D 8,9:2
Deadline U S A 1952,Mr 15,8:2
Dreamboat 1952,Jl 26,9:2
What Price Glory 1952,Ag 23,10:2
Monkey Business 1952,S 6,12:6
Call Me Madam 1953,Mr 26,37:1
President's Lady, The 1953,My 22,31:1
Gentlemen Prefer Blondes 1953,Jl 16,17:2
Three Coins in the Fountain 1954,My 21,18:2
Broken Lance 1954,Jl 30,9:1
There's no Business Like Show Business
1954,D 17,37:3
High Society 1956,Ag 10,9:2
Merry Andrews 1958,Mr 21,17:1
Some Came Running 1959,Ja 23,17:1
Walk, Don't Run 1966,Ag 25,42:3
Alvarez Kelly 1966,N 17,55:2
No Way to Treat a Lady 1968,Mr 21,56:1
Siegel, Yakov (Director)
House I Live in, The 1959,Ap 20,34:2
Day the War Ended, The 1961,Ja 30,17:2
Farewell, Doves 1962,Mr 19,38:3
Siegel, Yakov (Screenwriter)
Farewell, Doves 1962,Mr 19,38:3
Siegler, Otto
Adventure Girl 1934,Ag 9,14:5
Siegmann, George
Great Love, The 1918,Ag 12,7:1
Fall of Babylon, The 1919,Jl 22,10:2
Little Miss Rebellion 1920,S 20,13:1
Connecticut Yankee in King Arthur's Court, A
1921,Mr 15,14:3
Queen of Sheba 1921,Ap 11,9:1
Birth of a Nation, The 1921,My 2,12:1
Shame 1921,Ag 1,8:3 (Incorrect in this edition;
use 1921,Ag 1,6:4 elsewhere)
Three Musketeers, The 1921,Ag 29,14:4
Fools First 1922,Jl 31,12:3
Monte Cristo 1922,Ag 15,20:3
Oliver Twist 1922,O 30,11:1
Hungry Hearts 1922,N 27,18:1
Birth of a Nation, The 1922,D 5,24:3
Lost and Found 1923,Mr 19,22:2
Slander the Woman 1923,My 28,18:2
Merry Go Round 1923,Jl 2,16:2
Scaramouche 1923,O 12,7:2 (Incorrect in this
edition; use 1927,O 1,7:2 elsewhere)
Singer Jim McKee 1924,Mr 24,13:1
Shooting of Dan McGrew, The 1924,Je 9,14:3
Guilty One, The 1924,Je 17,22:4
Revelation 1924,Je 24,18:2
Janice Meredith 1924,Ag 6,13:3
Manhattan 1924,O 29,18:1
Sainted Devil, A 1924,N 24,15:3
Recompense 1925,Ap 20,22:1
Zander the Great 1925,My 4,16:2
Midnight Sun, The 1926,Ap 24,20:4
Born to the West 1926,Je 30,18:1 (In Addenda)
Poker Faces 1926,S 14,25:4
Hotel Imperial 1927,Ja 3,16:2
Red Mill, The 1927,F 14,15:1
King of Kings, The 1927,Ap 20,29:2
Cat and the Canary, The 1927,S 10,9:4
Uncle Tom's Cabin 1927,N 5,16:2
Thirteenth Juror, The 1927,N 22,20:1
Love Me and the World Is Mine 1928,F 6,12:3
Stop That Man 1928,Ap 17,27:2
Man Who Laughs, The 1928,Ap 28,12:3
Birth of a Nation, The 1930,D 22,16:2
Sielanski, Stanislaw
Parada Rezerwistow 1934,My 1,26:6
Maryjka 1934,D 3,15:2
Manewry Milosne 1936,N 11,55:1
Cabman No 13 1937,N 1,24:6
Ksiazatko; Lottery Prince, The 1937,D 27,11:2
Krolowa Przedmiescia; Queen of the Market
Place 1937,D 29,17:2
Pan Redaktor Szaleje; Mr Editor Is Crazy
1938,Je 14,17:3
Sielisch, Ute
Berliner, The 1952,O 28,37:1
Sielmann, Heinz (Director)
Masters of the Congo Jungle 1960,My 5,41:2

Siemion, Wojciech
Eroica (Second Episode) 1966,F 2,24:1
Salto 1966,O 4,50:1
Sienckiewicz, Henry (Original Author)
Quo Vadis 1925,F 16,24:1
Quo Vadis 1951,N 9,22:2
Siepi, Cesare
Don Giovanni 1956,D 27,22:1
Siepmann, Eric (Screenwriter)
I Stand Condemned 1936,Jl 2,27:2
Sierck, Claus Detlef
Streitum den Knaben Jo; Strife Over the Boy Jo
1938,D 10,13:2
Recht auf Liebe, Das; Right to Love, The
1940,Je 15,12:3
Sierck, Detlef (Director)
Schlussakkord 1936,S 10,29:4
Stuetzen der Gesellschaft 1936,N 7,15:3
Hofkonzert, Das 1937,Mr 27,19:3
Zu neven Ufern; To new Shores 1938,Ja 29,12:1
Heimt ruft, Die; Home Is Calling 1938,Jl 9,10:3
Sierra, Dante (Original Author)
Games Men Play, The 1968,Mr 15,30:1
Sierra, G M Martinez (Original Author)
Cradle Song 1933,N 20,18:2
Sierra, Melissa
Only Angels Have Wings 1939,My 12,25:2
Sietof, S
Zemlya Zhazhdet 1932,My 6,15:3
Sifton, Claire (Original Author)
Midnight 1934,Mr 10,18:3
Sifton, Elizabeth
Flight Angels 1940,My 27,23:2
Sifton, Paul (Original Author)
Midnight 1934,Mr 10,18:3
Sigaloff, Eugene
Clear all Wires 1933,Mr 4,11:2
Mirele Efros 1939,O 21,12:2
SIGEL
See Also SEGAL, SEGALL, SIEGAL
Sigler, Maurice (Composer)
Sailing Along 1938,Ap 16,17:1
This'll Make You Whistle 1938,N 1,27:2
She Shall Have Music 1942,O 31,11:2
Sigman, Carl (Composer)
She's Back on Broadway 1953,Mr 12,24:2
Sigmund, Elsbeth
Heidi 1953,D 21,27:2
Heidi and Peter 1955,D 13,55:2
Signore, Sandro del
Eredita dello Zio, L' 1935,Je 29,16:3
Signoret, Simone
Sacrifice d'Honneur 1938,D 2,27:2
Living Corpse, The 1940,S 23,21:4
Symphonie d'Amour 1946,Mr 11,19:2
Back Streets of Paris 1948,O 16,9:2
Dedee 1949,Ap 9,9:2
Against the Wind 1949,Je 27,18:3
Four Days' Leave 1950,Je 9,29:4
Cheat, The 1950,O 2,19:3
Casque D'Or 1952,Ag 19,19:1
Ronde, La 1954,Mr 17,27:2
Diabolique 1955,N 22,41:1
Adulteress, The 1958,Ja 14,42:1
Witches of Salem 1958,D 9,54:2
Room at the Top 1959,Mr 31,26:1
Term of Trial 1963,Ja 31,5:2
Naked Autumn 1963,N 15,25:3
Day and the Hour, The 1964,F 20,22:2
Sweet and Sour 1964,D 28,34:2
Love a la Carte 1965,Ja 12,31:1
Ship of Fools 1965,Jl 29,18:1
Sleeping Car Murder, The 1966,Mr 8,45:1
Le Joli Mai 1966,Je 10,54:2
Is Paris Burning? 1966,N 11,36:1
Deadly Affair, The 1967,Ja 27,31:1
Games 1967,S 18,58:2
Sea Gull, The 1968,D 24,14:1
Signorini, Evaristo
Grosse Tenor, Der 1931,My 29,26:5
Sigurd, Jacques (Miscellaneous)
Dedee 1949,Ap 9,9:2
Sigurd, Jacques (Screenwriter)
Dedee 1949,Ap 9,9:2
Cheat, The 1950,O 2,19:3
Riptide 1951,Ap 7,9:2
Desperate Decision 1954,N 9,31:5
Sins of the Borgias 1956,Mr 5,21:1
Cheaters, The; (Tricheurs, Les) 1961,Je 5,37:4
Sikevitch, Vladimir
Cossacks in Exile 1939,Ja 28,19:2
Sikiewicz, Bazyli
Ulan I Dziewczyna 1933,O 9,22:3
Sikiewicz, Bazyli (Director)
Tajemnica Oskarzonej 1937,Ap 27,18:2
Siklosy, Eve
Igloi Diakok 1935,My 24,24:3
Silayan, Vic
Badjao 1962,S 21,35:1
Silberman, S J
Laughter Through Tears 1933,N 13,21:2

Silbert, Liza
Broken Hearts 1926,Mr 3,26:1
Silbert, Theodore
Broken Hearts 1926,Mr 3,26:1
Silenti, Vira
Monte Cassino 1948,N 25,47:3
Shamed 1949,O 13,33:3
Gioconda, La 1958,O 13,33:4
Son of Samson 1962,S 27,33:4
Story of Joseph and his Brethern, The
1962,D 1,17:1
Siletti, Mario
Black Hand 1950,Mr 13,15:2
Enforcer, The 1951,Ja 26,19:2
Man Who Cheated Himself, The 1951,F 9,21:2
Great Caruso, The 1951,My 11,32:2
House on Telegraph Hill, The 1951,My 14,29:1
Strictly Dishonorable 1951,Jl 12,21:6
Force of Arms 1951,Ag 14,20:2
Anne of the Indies 1951,O 25,36:3
When in Rome 1952,My 12,21:2
My Cousin Rachel 1952,D 26,20:2
Thunder Bay 1953,My 21,39:2
So This Is Love 1953,Ag 12,22:1
Theodora, Slave Empress 1955,Ja 12,24:2
East of Eden 1955,Mr 10,33:1
Serenade 1956,Mr 24,21:1 (Incorrect in this
edition; use 1956,Mr 23,21:1 elsewhere)
Man With a Shadow 1958,Ja 23,24:3
Silk, Lawrence (Miscellaneous)
Inheritance, The 1964,N 9,42:2
Silliphant, Stirling (Producer)
Joe Louis Story, The 1953,N 4,29:4
Five Against the House 1955,Je 11,8:7
Silliphant, Stirling (Screenwriter)
Five Against the House 1955,Je 11,8:7
Nightfall 1957,Ja 24,34:1
Village of the Damned 1960,D 8,43:3
Slender Thread, The 1965,D 24,24:2
In the Heat of the Night 1967,Ag 3,26:1
Charly 1968,S 24,55:1
Sillitoe, Alan (Original Author)
Saturday Night and Sunday Morning
1961,Ap 4,44:2
Loneliness of the Long Distance Runner, The
1962,O 9,44:1
Counterpoint 1968,Mr 14,51:2
Sillitoe, Alan (Screenwriter)
Saturday Night and Sunday Morning
1961,Ap 4,44:2
Loneliness of the Long Distance Runner, The
1962,O 9,44:1
Sills, Milton
Hell Cat, The 1918,N 25,11:3
Shadows 1919,F 10,11:3
Stronger Vow, The 1919,Ap 28,13:2
Woman Thou Gavest Me, The 1919,Je 9,16:3
Eyes of Youth 1919,D 1,9:3
Behold my Wife 1920,O 11,19:3
Faith Healer, The 1921,Mr 14,9:2
Great Moment, The 1921,Jl 25,8:3
At the End of the World 1921,Ag 15,14:3
Miss Lulu Bett 1921,D 25,VI,2:1
One Clear Call 1922,Je 19,10:3
Borderland 1922,Jl 24,10:2
Skin Deep 1922,O 23,10:1
Isle of Lost Ships, The 1923,My 14,18:2
Spoilers, The 1923,Ag 6,14:2
Flaming Youth 1923,N 26,15:6
Flowing Gold 1924,Mr 10,18:2
Sea Hawk, The 1924,Je 3,22:1
Single Wives 1924,Jl 29,9:2
Madonna of the Streets 1924,O 28,23:4
As Man Desires 1925,F 10,20:1
I Want my Man 1925,Ap 6,17:3
Making of O'Malley 1925,Je 22,10:2
Knockout, The 1925,O 27,23:3
Unguarded Hour, The 1926,Ja 5,25:2 (In
Addenda)
Puppets 1926,Je 21,17:2
Men of Steel 1926,Jl 12,24:4
Paradise 1926,O 4,20:2
Silent Lover, The 1926,N 15,19:1
Framed 1927,Je 20,25:3
Hard-Boiled Haggerty 1927,Ag 23,29:4
Valley of the Giants, The 1927,D 5,26:2
Burning Daylight 1928,Ap 23,20:2
Hawk's Nest, The 1928,Je 25,27:1
Barker, The 1928,D 6,35:1
His Captive Woman 1929,Ap 3,26:4
Sea Wolf, The 1930,O 6,21:1
Sills, Ted (Screenwriter)
Abroad With two Yanks 1944,O 26,19:7
Silo, Susan
Convicts 4 1962,O 4,44:2
Silva, David
Vivire Otra Vez; I Shall Live Again
1940,O 23,27:2
Passion Island 1943,My 1,11:2
Miserables, Los 1944,O 24,17:2
First Texan, The 1956,Je 23,20:2

Silva, Felisberto (Composer)
Blondie Goes Latin 1941,F 26,17:3
Silva, Franco
Queen of Sheba, The 1953,N 4,29:3
Hannibal 1960,Ag 4,17:1
Story of Monte Cristo, The 1962,N 7,48:1
Silva, Henry
Hatful of Rain, A 1957,Jl 18,19:2
Law and Jake Wade, the 1958,Je 7,11:1
Bravados, The 1958,Je 26,23:2
Green Mansions 1959,Mr 20,26:1
Ocean's Eleven 1960,Ag 11,19:1
Cinderfella 1960,D 17,19:2
Sergeants 3 1962,F 12,28:2
Manchurian Candidate, The 1962,O 25,48:3
Gathering of Eagles, A 1963,Jl 11,21:2
Johnny Cool 1963,O 3,31:1
Secret Invasion, The 1964,S 17,52:6
Reward, The 1965,S 16,55:1
Return of Mr Moto 1965,D 2,48:1
Matchless 1967,N 11,26:3
Hills Run Red, The 1967,N 11,26:3
Never a Dull Moment 1968,Ag 15,46:2
Silva, Mario
Ring Around the Clock 1953,My 19,36:2
Silva, Mario (Original Author)
Song of Love 1947,O 10,31:2
Silva, Simone
Desperate Moment 1953,S 1,19:4
Weak and the Wicked, The 1954,Ag 21,10:3
Silva, Uilani
Hawaii Calls 1938,Ap 29,17:2
Silvani, Aldo
Life Begins Anew; Vita Ricomincia, La
1947,Ap 7,20:5
Anything for a Song 1947,Ag 5,26:2
To Live in Peace 1947,N 25,37:2
Four Steps in the Clouds 1948,N 22,25:2
Carmela 1949,My 14,9:2
Golden Madonna, The 1949,S 5,13:4
Mad About Opera 1950,Ap 6,33:2
Difficult Years 1950,Ag 22,31:2
Teresa 1951,Ap 6,31:2
Measure for Measure 1951,D 8,9:2
When in Rome 1952,My 12,21:2
Thief of Venice, The 1952,N 28,22:7
Paolo and Francesca 1953,F 14,8:3
Stranger on the Prowl 1953,N 10,38:1
Valley of the Kings 1954,Jl 22,15:2
Strada, La 1956,Jl 17,19:2
Sodom and Gomorrah 1963,Ja 24,5:3
Rise of Louis XIV, The 1967,S 26,54:2
Silvani, Mario
Three Girls From Rome 1953,O 14,34:2
Silveira, M (Original Author)
Appointment in Honduras 1953,N 19,41:4
Story of Vickie, The 1958,Ja 30,19:2
Silveni, Edward
Uncivilized 1937,N 17,27:4
Silver, Christine
Dead Men Tell no Tales 1939,Jl 24,9:2
Silver, Jeff
Young Stranger, The 1957,Ap 9,40:1
Outsider, The 1962,F 8,25:1
Silver, Johnny
Guys and Dolls 1955,N 5,26:1
Thomas Crown Affair, The 1968,Je 27,48:2
Silver, Marcel (Director)
William Fox Movietone Follies of 1929
1929,My 27,22:1
Married in Hollywood 1929,S 23,24:3
One mad Kiss 1930,Jl 19,7:5
El Precio de un Beso 1933,Jl 25,17:3
Silver, Paolo
Favorita, La 1953,O 30,27:4
Silver, Pat (Screenwriter)
Wizard of Baghdad, The 1961,Mr 4,16:1
Seven Women From Hell 1962,F 1,22:2
Silver King (horse)
Two-Gun Man, The 1926,Jl 13,19:3
Silvera, Frank
Viva Zapata 1952,F 8,19:2
Fighter, The 1952,My 31,12:6
Miracle of Our Lady Fatima, The
1952,Ag 21,16:2
Fear and Desire 1953,Ap 1,35:2
Crowded Paradise 1956,Je 22,15:1
Crime and Punishment, U S A 1959,Je 17,39:3
Mountain Road, The 1960,Je 30,22:3
Key Witness 1960,N 12,15:1
Mutiny on the Bounty 1962,N 9,31:2
Toys in the Attic 1963,Ag 1,17:2
Greatest Story Ever Told, The 1965,F 16,40:2
Appaloosa, The 1966,S 15,51:1
Hombre 1967,Mr 22,41:1
St Valentine's Day Massacre, The 1967,Jl 27,29:2
Up Tight 1968,D 19,62:1
Silvera, Frank (Narrator)
Lonely Night, The 1954,Mr 29,22:2
Silverheels, Jay
Captain from Castile 1947,D 26,22:4
Key Largo 1948,Jl 17,6:6
Yellow Sky 1949,F 2,36:1

Silverheels, Jay— Cont
Lust for Gold 1949,Jl 4,9:2
Sand 1949,Ag 5,23:2
Broken Arrow 1950,Jl 21,15:2
Red Mountain 1952,Ap 26,19:2
Saskatchewan 1954,Mr 11,26:2
Lone Ranger, The 1956,F 11,12:1
Walk the Proud Land 1956,S 8,20:6 (In Addenda)
Silvern, Charles
Alice in Wonderland 1931,D 28,22:1
Silvers, Louis (Miscellaneous)
One Night of Love 1934,S 7,25:3
Silvers, Phil
Hit Parade of 1941 1940,D 5,33:2
Penalty, The 1941,Ap 10,29:3
Tom, Dick and Harry 1941,Jl 18,22:2
Lady Be Good 1941,S 19,27:1
Ice-Capades 1941,S 25,29:1
You're in the Army Now 1941,D 26,21:4
All Through the Night 1942,Ja 24,13:2
Roxie Hart 1942,F 20,21:1
My Gal Sal 1942,My 1,23:1
Just off Broadway 1942,Ag 29,18:4
Footlight Serenade 1942,S 10,30:3
Coney Island 1943,Je 17,17:2
Lady Takes a Chance, A 1943,S 16,25:2
Cover Girl 1944,Mr 31,26:1
Four Jills in a Jeep 1944,Ap 6,27:2
Take It or Leave It 1944,Jl 13,14:2
Something for the Boys 1944,N 30,19:1
Billy Rose's Diamond Horseshoe 1945,My 3,37:1
Thousand and one Nights, A 1945,Jl 12,8:2
Don Juan Quilligan 1945,Jl 30,16:2
If I'm Lucky 1946,S 20,41:3
Summer Stock 1950,S 1,17:2
Top Banana 1954,F 20,8:6
Lucky Me 1954,Ap 10,11:2
40 Pounds of Trouble 1963,Ja 24,5:2
It's a Mad, Mad, Mad, Mad World 1963,N 19,47:1
Funny Thing Happened on the Way to the Forum, A 1966,O 17,48:1
Guide for the Married Man, A 1967,My 27,16:1
Silvers, Sid
My Weakness 1933,S 22,14:1
Bottoms Up 1934,Mr 23,29:2
Transatlantic Merry-Go-Round 1934,N 1,25:2
Broadway Melody of 1936 1935,S 19,28:1
Born to Dance 1936,D 5,16:1
52d Street 1937,N 15,15:1
Mr Ace 1946,S 30,21:3
Silvers, Sid (Composer)
Mr Ace 1946,S 30,21:3
Silvers, Sid (Original Author)
Bottoms Up 1934,Mr 23,29:2
Born to Dance 1936,D 5,16:1
Broadway Melody of 1938 1937,S 3,12:1
Stooge, The 1953,F 5,19:2
Silvers, Sid (Screenwriter)
Broadway Melody of 1936 1935,S 19,28:1
Born to Dance 1936,D 5,16:1
Gorilla, The 1939,My 28,6:2
Fleet's In, The 1942,Mr 12,24:2
For Me and My Gal 1942,O 22,25:1
Two Tickets to Broadway 1951,N 22,47:2
Silverstein, David (Original Author)
Devil's Mate 1933,S 23,11:7
Ticket to Paradise 1936,Ag 8,5:3
Silverstein, David (Screenwriter)
Fifteen Maiden Lane 1936,O 17,21:3
You Can't Beat Love 1937,Je 25,25:3
Flight From Glory 1937,S 11,20:1
Saturday's Heroes 1937,O 16,22:2
Military Academy 1940,Ag 5,10:4
Naval Academy 1941,Je 5,27:3
Mystery Ship 1941,Ag 16,18:3
Kid From Kansas, The 1941,D 2,29:4
Sabotage Squad 1942,Ag 5,16:1
Silverstein, Elliot (Director)
Belle Sommers 1962,My 31,23:2
Cat Ballou 1965,Je 25,36:1
Happening, The 1967,My 18,56:3
Silvertones, Swan
Festival 1967,O 24,53:2
Silvestra, Fior
Important Man, The; El Mayordoma 1962,Je 26,25:2
Silvestre, Armando
Wyoming Mail 1950,O 23,26:5
Apache Drums 1951,My 7,22:2
Mark of the Renegade 1951,S 7,24:2
Hiawatha 1952,D 26,20:4
Rosanna 1956,My 17,37:2
Scalphunters, The 1968,Ap 3,40:1
Silvestri, Umberto
Theodora, Slave Empress 1955,Ja 12,24:2
Silvey, Ben (Producer)
Within These Walls 1945,Jl 16,8:4
Spider, The 1946,Je 21,20:3
Sim, Alastair
Gangway 1937,Ag 21,7:3
Murder on Diamond Row 1937,N 12,27:2
Sailing Along 1938,Ap 16,17:1

Climbing High 1939,Je 5,20:3
Inspector Hornleigh 1939,Je 15,27:3
This Man Is News 1939,Jl 20,16:4
Green for Danger 1947,Ag 8,10:2
Captain Boycott 1947,D 6,11:2
Dulcimer Street 1948,N 8,24:2
Waterloo Road 1948,D 25,10:3
Stage Fright 1950,F 24,27:2
Happiest Days of Your Life, The 1950,S 18,19:2
Hue and Cry 1951,Ja 9,25:2
Laughter in Paradise 1951,N 12,21:2
Christmas Carol, A 1951,N 29,41:2
Folly to be Wise 1953,D 28,17:2
Inspector Calls, An 1954,N 26,24:4
Belles of St Trinian's, The 1954,D 23,13:4
Innocents in Paris 1955,Mr 5,9:6
Wee Geordie 1956,O 8,31:1
Green Man, The 1957,My 23,40:1
Escapade 1957,Ag 6,30:2
Blue Murder at St Trinian's 1958,My 27,27:1
School for Scoundrels 1960,Jl 12,39:1
Millionairess, The 1961,F 10,19:1
Left, Right and Centre 1961,F 10,19:1
Sim, Gerald
L-Shaped Room, The 1963,My 28,32:1
Seance on a Wet Afternoon 1964,N 6,30:1
King Rat 1965,O 28,48:1
Murder Game, The 1966,Mr 31,43:2
Whisperers, The 1967,Ag 1,24:1
Sim, Sheila
Canterbury Tale, A 1949,Ja 24,16:2
Guinea Pig, The 1949,My 2,20:2
Dear Mr Prohack 1950,Jl 15,7:2
Pandora and the Flying Dutchman 1951,D 7,35:2
West of Zanzibar 1955,Ja 18,31:2
Night my Number Came up, The 1955,D 20,39:5
Sima, Oscar
Fraulein Liselott 1935,My 27,20:7
Sima, Oskar
Skandal Um Eva 1931,Ap 21,35:2
Grosse Tenor, Der 1931,My 29,26:5
Lustigen Weiber von Wien, Die 1931,Jl 10,22:2
Lindenwirtin vom Rhein, Die 1931,S 25,28:7
Schubert's Fruehlingstraum 1932,Je 22,19:4
Ich Geh' aus und Du Bleibst da 1932,N 21,21:1
Teilnehmer Antwortet Nicht 1932,N 30,23:6
Eine Tuer geht Auf 1933,F 6,11:5
Ein Maedel der Strasse 1933,Ap 6,22:5
Das Lockende Ziel 1933,Je 19,18:2
Es Wird Schon Wieder Besser 1934,Ja 24,21:3
Glueckszylinder, Der 1934,Mr 10,18:4
Stern von Valencia, Der 1934,Ap 21,12:2
Geld Regiert die Welt 1934,My 12,12:4
Im Heidekrug 1934,D 31,9:7
Lockvogel 1935,Ja 5,20:3
Meine Frau, Die Schuetzenkoenigin 1935,Ja 7,13:3
Fraeulein Liselott 1935,My 27,20:7
Unbekannte Gast, Der; Unknown Guest, The 1935,Je 1,18:3
Ehestreik 1935,Ag 31,16:3
Schuechterne Felix, Der 1935,S 7,19:5
So ein Maedel Vergisst Man nicht 1935,S 28,12:3
Donogoo Tonka 1936,Ap 13,15:2
Weiberregiment 1936,S 14,25:2
Glueckskinder 1937,Je 5,21:1
Punks Kommt aus Amerika 1937,Je 12,8:2
Gasparone 1938,Mr 12,13:4
Charm of la Boheme, The 1938,Mr 19,11:2
Lachende Dritte, Der 1938,Ap 9,11:2
Werf zum Graven Hecht, Die; Gray Pikes Wharf, The 1938,Ap 18,11:2
Wir Sind vom K u K Infantrie-Regiment 1938,N 19,9:2
Nanon 1938,N 26,18:2
Fuenf Millionem suchen einen Erben; Five Millions Seek an Heir 1939,O 23,15:3
Schatten der Vergangeheit; Shadows of the Past 1940,Ap 20,14:2
Wiener Geschichten; Vienna Tales 1940,S 28,9:3
Gypsy Baron, The 1959,N 14,13:1
Fledermaus, Die 1964,F 8,15:2
Simachev, A
Bolshoi Ballet 67 1966,S 30,54:1
Simenon, Georges (Original Author)
Midnight in Paris 1947,O 9,32:3
Temptation Harbor 1949,My 11,34:7
Strangers in the House 1949,O 13,33:3
Man on the Eiffel Tower, The 1950,Ja 30,12:2
Marie du Port 1951,Jl 24,21:2
Paris Express, The 1953,Je 6,8:6
Midnight Episode 1953,My 19,25:5
Life in the Balance, A 1955,Jl 14,19:1
Bottom of the Bottle, The 1956,F 2,19:2
Snow Was Black, The 1956,O 16,36:5
Inspector Maigret 1958,O 9,47:1
Forbidden Fruit 1959,F 23,19:1
Love Is my Profession 1959,Ap 28,41:1
Passion of Slow Fire, The 1962,O 12,26:1
Simeon
Heart of Paris 1939,Ja 13,17:3

Simeon, Virginia
Summertime 1955,Je 22,25:1
Simi
Tarzan Goes to India 1962,S 6,37:2
Simiani, Maria
Man About the House, A 1949,Mr 9,33:2
Simmel, Johannes Mario (Screenwriter)
Cabaret 1957,N 9,31:2 (Incorrect in this edition; use 1957,N 7,43:4 elsewhere)
SIMMONDS
See Also SIMMONS
Simmonds, Charles
Native Son 1951,Je 18,19:2
Simmonds, Kathay
Touchables, The 1968,N 21,41:1
SIMMONS
See Also SIMMONDS
Simmons, Anthony (Producer)
Time Without Pity 1957,N 23,11:2
Simmons, Beverly
Frontier Gal 1945,D 15,14:2
Buck Privates Come Home 1947,Ap 12,11:3
Simmons, Dick
Seven Sweethearts 1942,N 13,28:1
Stand by for Action 1943,Mr 12,12:2
Youngest Profession, The 1943,Je 25,13:3
Pilot No 5 1943,Je 25,13:4
Thousands Cheer 1943,S 14,27:1
Love Laughs at Andy Hardy 1947,Ja 8,28:2
Lady in the Lake 1947,Ja 24,18:3
This Time for Keeps 1947,D 5,33:4
On an Island With You 1948,Jl 30,13:2
Look for the Silver Lining 1949,Je 24,29:2
Duchess of Idaho 1950,Jl 21,15:3
Dial 1119 1950,D 4,32:6
No Questions Asked 1951,Ag 10,13:2
Above and Beyond 1953,Ja 31,10:6
Men of the Fighting Lady 1954,My 8,15:2
Simmons, Floyd
Tattered Dress, The 1957,Mr 15,22:3
South Pacific 1958,Mr 20,33:1
Twice Told Tales (The House of the Seven Gables); House of the Seven Gables, The (Twice Told Tales) 1964,My 28,40:1
Simmons, Georgia
Mountain Music 1937,Je 24,30:3
Eight and One Half 1963,Je 26,36:1
All the Way Home 1963,O 30,46:1
Baby, the Rain Must Fall 1965,Ja 14,44:1
Simmons, H C
Into her Kingdom 1926,Ag 10,19:2
Simmons, Jean
Great Expectations 1947,My 23,31:1
Black Narcissus 1947,Ag 14,29:2
Hungry Hill 1947,O 11,11:2
Hamlet 1948,S 30,32:2
Woman in the Hall, The 1949,Ja 24,16:2
Blue Lagoon, The 1949,O 3,13:2
Adam and Evalyn 1950,My 12,33:4
Sanitorium 1950,O 11,42:1
So Long at the Fair 1951,Ja 22,14:2
Inheritance, The 1951,F 12,19:2
Clouded Yellow, The 1951,N 13,33:2
Case of Gold 1952,Ja 19,13:3
Cage of Gold 1952,Ja 19,13:3
Androcles and the Lion 1953,Ja 15,23:2
Angel Face 1953,Ap 25,11:5
Young Bess 1953,My 22,31:1
Affair With a Stranger 1953,Jl 11,8:2
Robe, The 1953,S 17,32:6
Actress, The 1953,O 13,34:1
She Couldn't Say No 1954,F 27,11:3
Egyptian, The 1954,Ag 25,23:1
Bullet is Waiting, A 1954,N 12,17:2
Desiree 1954,N 18,42:1
Footsteps of the Fog 1955,S 15,39:2
Guys and Dolls 1955,N 5,26:1
Hilda Crane 1956,My 3,35:2
This Could Be the Night 1957,My 15,39:1
Until They Sail 1957,O 9,41:2
Home Before Dark 1958,N 7,23:1
Earth Is Mine, The 1959,Je 27,13:1
Elmer Gantry 1960,Jl 8,16:1
Spartacus 1960,O 7,28:1
Grass is Greener, The 1960,D 24,8:2
All the Way Home 1963,O 30,46:1
Life at the Top 1965,D 15,53:1
Mister Buddwing 1966,O 12,36:1
Divorce American Style 1967,Jl 20,30:2
Rough Night in Jericho 1967,N 9,56:4
Simmons, Maude
Portrait of Jennie 1949,Mr 30,31:2
No Way Out 1950,Ag 17,23:1
Simmons, Michael (Original Author)
Bowery, The 1933,O 5,24:2
Simmons, Michael (Screenwriter)
Murder in Greenwich Village 1937,O 30,22:2
Juvenile Court 1938,S 12,13:2
Romance of the Redwoods 1939,Ap 24,13:2
Missing Daughters 1939,Je 12,14:5
Mutiny on the Blackhawk 1939,Ag 2,17:2
Tropic Fury 1939,S 8,28:4
Scattergood Baines 1941,Ap 4,25:2

Simmons, Richard
Dream of Jeanie, I 1952,Je 26,26:2
Sergeants 3 1962,F 12,28:2
Simmons, Richard Alan (Original Author)
Art of Love, The 1965,Jl 1,34:1
Simmons, Richard Alan (Screenwriter)
Lady Wants Mink, The 1953,Ap 6,24:2
Beachhead 1954,Ap 17,8:2
Tanganyika 1954,Je 19,9:2
Shield for Murder 1954,Ag 28,8:3
Three Hours to Kill 1954,S 4,6:4
Bengal Brigade 1954,N 13,13:2
Private War of Major Benson, The
1955,Ag 3,27:2
Female on the Beach 1955,Ag 20,20:2
Congo Crossing 1956,Jl 14,13:2
King and Four Queens, The 1956,D 22,13:7
Istanbul 1957,Ja 24,34:1
Fuzzy Pink Nightgown, The 1957,O 31,41:1
Trap, The 1959,Ja 29,18:4
SIMMS
See Also SIMS
Simms, Eddie
Ringside Maisie 1941,Ag 1,11:2
Simms, Ginny
That's Right, You're Wrong 1939,N 30,25:3
You'll Find Out 1940,N 15,25:2
Playmates 1941,D 26,21:3
Here We Go Again 1942,O 12,12:3
Seven Days' Leave 1942,D 11,33:2
Hit the Ice 1943,S 23,27:2
Broadway Rhythm 1944,Ap 14,24:6
Shady Lady 1945,O 11,26:2
Night and Day 1946,Jl 26,16:2
Simms, Hilda
Joe Louis Story, The 1953,N 4,29:4
Black Widow 1954,O 28,46:6
Simms, Hilda (Narrator)
Day After Day 1943,N 6,16:3
Simms, Larry
Blondie 1938,D 22,25:4
Blondie Meets the Boss 1939,Ap 27,31:1
Blondie Goes Latin 1941,F 26,17:3
Gay Sisters, The 1942,Ag 15,14:2
It's a Wonderful Life 1946,D 23,19:2
Blondie Hits the Jackpot 1949,S 9,28:3
Simms, Marilyn
Three for Jamie Dawn 1956,Jl 7,11:3
Simo, Margaret
Tiszavirag; Flower of the Tisza 1939,D 30,9:3
SIMON
See Also SIMONE
Simon, Abe
On the Waterfront 1954,Jl 29,18:1
Singing in the Dark 1956,Mr 8,32:5
Requiem for a Heavyweight 1962,O 17,35:1
Simon, Charles (Original Author)
Zaza 1923,S 17,18:2
Zaza 1939,Ja 5,17:1
Simon, Christian
Gates of the Night 1950,Mr 16,40:2
Simon, Cricri
Face to the Wind 1951,Ja 16,34:2
Simon, Frank (Director)
Queen, The 1968,Je 18,37:1
Simon, James (Cinematographer)
Jungle Cat 1960,Ag 18,19:2
Simon, James R (Cinematographer)
White Wilderness 1958,Ag 13,22:1
Simon, Marcel
He 1933,D 27,23:6
With a Smile 1939,F 6,8:4
Mademoiselle ma Mere 1939,S 19,29:2
Katia 1939,D 23,9:2
32 Rue de Montmartre 1944,S 28,26:3
Angel and Sinner 1947,F 24,16:5
Simon, Marosa
Melody of The Heart 1930,S 1,16:1
Sarga Csiko 1937,Ja 29,15:2
Simon, Mayo (Screenwriter)
I Could go on Singing 1963,My 16,42:1
Simon, Michel
Passion Of Joan Of Arc, The 1929,Mr 29,21:1
Passion of Jeanne d'Arc, The 1929,Mr 31,VIII,7:1
Jean de la Lune 1932,Mr 12,19:5
Luc Aux Dames 1936,Ja 15,14:4
Bonheur, Le 1936,F 28,18:2
Razumov 1937,Mr 9,27:2
Bizarre, Bizarre 1939,Mr 21,27:2
Boys' School 1939,Je 6,26:2
End of a Day, The 1939,S 12,28:4
Port of Shadows 1939,O 30,13:2
Kiss of Fire, The 1940,N 20,27:4
32 Rue de Montmartre 1944,S 28,26:3
Musiciens du Ciel 1945,Mr 1,26:6
Extenuating Circumstances; Circostances
Attenuantes 1946,S 24,41:3
Atalante, L' 1947,Je 23,14:5
Shop-Girls of Paris; Au Bonheur de Dames
1947,Je 23,14:4
King's Jester, The 1947,Je 26,19:3
Panic 1947,N 27,50:2
Story of Tosca, The 1947,D 19,34:2

Not Guilty 1948,Ap 23,28:2
Fric-Frac 1948,My 29,8:6
Friend Will come Tonight, A; Ami Viendra Ce
Soir, Un 1948,Jl 12,11:2
Vautrin, the Thief 1949,N 11,31:2
Fabiola 1951,My 30,14:2
Beauty and the Devil 1952,Ag 26,15:2
Saadia 1954,Mr 20,10:5
Virtuous Scoundrel, The 1957,O 23,37:1
Anatomy of Love 1959,S 29,46:2
It Happened in Broad Daylight 1960,S 30,33:1
Candide 1962,N 20,39:1
Head, The 1963,Je 20,29:1
Devil and the 10 Commandments, The (Episode
1) 1963,O 15,44:1
Cyrano and D'Artagnan 1964,S 26,16:1
Train, The 1965,Mr 18,25:1
Boudu Saved From Drowning; Boudu Sauve Des
Eaux 1967,F 24,26:2
Two of Us, The 1968,F 20,53:1
Marriage Came Tumbling Down, The
1968,N 6,32:3
Simon, Michel (Producer)
Boudu Saved From Drowning; Boudu Sauve Des
Eaux 1967,F 24,26:2
Simon, Neil (Original Author)
Come Blow Your Horn 1963,Je 7,37:1
Barefoot in the Park 1967,My 26,51:1
Odd Couple, The 1968,My 3,42:1
Simon, Neil (Screenwriter)
After the Fox 1966,D 24,11:1
Barefoot in the Park 1967,My 26,51:1
Odd Couple, The 1968,My 3,42:1
Simon, Robert A (Original Author)
Strictly Dynamite 1934,Jl 4,18:2
Simon, Robert F
Where the Sidewalk Ends 1950,Jl 8,7:4
Rogue Cop 1954,S 18,12:2
Chief Crazy Horse 1955,Ap 28,25:1
Foxfire 1955,Jl 14,19:1
Benny Goodman Story 1956,F 22,22:1
Catered Affair, The 1956,Je 15,32:4
Bigger Than Life 1956,Ag 3,11:2
Rack, The 1956,N 6,30:1
Edge of the City 1957,Ja 30,33:2
Spring Reunion 1957,My 6,25:2
Buccaneer, The 1958,D 24,00:0
Compulsion 1959,Ap 2,26:2
Last Angry Man, The 1959,O 23,24:1
Operation Petticoat 1959,D 6,38:1
Pay or Die 1960,My 27,22:2
Facts of Life, The 1961,F 11,27:1
Ada 1961,Ag 26,15:1
Wall of Noise 1963,S 5,27:1
New Kind of Love, A 1963,O 31,26:2
Captain Newman, MD 1964,F 21,36:1
Across the River 1965,Ap 27,27:1
Simon, S J (Original Author)
Gay Lady, The 1951,Ap 16,21:2
Simon, S J (Screenwriter)
One Night With You 1949,F 21,20:2
Simon, S S
Barker, The 1928,D 6,35:1
Simon, S Sylvan (Director)
Girl With Ideas, A 1938,Ja 1,11:2
Crime of Dr Hallet, The 1938,Mr 24,21:3
Nurse From Brooklyn 1938,My 13,17:3
Road to Reno, The 1938,O 3,11:2
Spring Madness 1938,D 1,29:3
Four Girls in White 1939,F 23,19:3
These Glamour Girls 1939,Ag 31,14:2
Dancing Co-Ed 1939,N 10,27:3
Two Girls on Broadway 1940,Ap 25,28:4
Sporting Blood 1940,Jl 22,20:2
Dulcy 1940,N 28,28:2
Washington Melodrama 1941,My 26,15:3
Whistling in the Dark 1941,Ag 28,23:2
Bugle Sounds, The 1942,Ap 3,25:2
Rio Rita 1942,My 8,27:3
Grand Central Murder 1942,My 23,8:8
Tish 1942,S 18,25:2
Whistling in Dixie 1942,D 31,20:4
Salute to the Marines 1943,Ag 30,11:3
Whistling in Brooklyn 1944,Mr 24,17:3
Song of the Open Road 1944,Je 7,13:3
Son of Lassie 1945,Je 11,12:1
Abbott and Costello in Hollywood
1945,N 23,26:2
Bad Bascomb 1946,My 23,18:4
Thrill of Brazil, The 1946,S 6,18:3
Cockeyed Miracle, The 1946,O 25,28:1
Her Husband's Affairs 1947,N 14,29:2
Fuller Brush Man, The 1948,My 15,18:2
Lust for Gold 1949,Jl 4,9:2
Simon, S Sylvan (Producer)
Lust for Gold 1949,Jl 4,9:2
Good Humor Man, The 1950,Jl 14,17:2
Simon, Simone
Prenez Garde a la Peinture 1935,Ag 17,18:6
Luc Aux Dames 1936,Ja 15,14:4
Girls' Dormitory 1936,Ag 29,16:2
Ladies in Love 1936,O 29,31:1
Seventh Heaven 1937,Mr 26,25:1

Simon, Simone — Cont
Love and Hisses 1938,Ja 1,11:1
Dark Eyes 1938,Ap 19,24:5
Josette 1938,Je 11,9:1
Bete Humaine, La 1939,F 26,IX,5:6 (In Addenda)
Human Beast, The 1940,F 20,17:2
All That Money Can Buy 1941,O 17,27:2
Cat People 1942,D 7,22:2
Tahiti Honey 1943,My 13,17:2
Curse of the Cat People, The 1944,Mr 4,11:1
Temptation Harbor 1949,My 11,34:7
Women Without Names 1951,Ag 7,22:2
Ronde, La 1954,Mr 17,27:2
Pit of Loneliness 1954,Ap 9,19:2
Plaisir, Le (The Model); Model, The (Le Plaisir)
1954,My 20,38:1
Simon, Zsuzsa
Egy ej Velencebzn 1935,D 27,14:2
Simon-Girard, Aime
Milady 1923,Ja 22,10:1
Trois Mousquetaires, Les 1933,My 1,10:2
Milady 1933,S 8,22:3
SIMONE
See Also SIMON
Simone, Pierre
Ramuntcho 1953,Mr 2,19:2
Simone, Ralph
Citizen Saint 1948,My 28,28:2
Simonelli, George (Screenwriter)
That Man in Istanbul 1966,My 19,51:2
Simonelli, George C (Director)
Bertoldo, Bertoldino, Cacasenno 1937,D 22,32:3
Simonelli, John (Original Author)
Young, The Evil and the Savage, The
1968,Ag 15,46:2
Simonet, Pierrette
Paris Incident 1954,Ag 18,20:2
Simonin, Albert (Original Author)
Grisbi 1959,Jl 13,23:1
Money, Money, Money 1962,Jl 18,20:1
Male Hunt; Chasse a l'Homme, La
1965,Ap 20,42:1
Tender Scoundrel 1967,N 16,58:2
Simonin, Albert (Screenwriter)
Grisbi 1959,Jl 13,23:1
Money, Money, Money 1962,Jl 18,20:1
Candide 1962,N 20,39:1
Any Number Can Win 1963,O 9,47:2
Cloportes 1966,Ap 19,36:1
Great Spy Chase, The 1966,O 6,56:4
Tender Scoundrel 1967,N 16,58:2
Simonof, N
Red Army Days 1935,O 21,22:4
Simonov, Konstantin (Narrator)
Battle for China 1953,N 2,29:2
Simonov, Konstantin (Original Author)
Lad From our Town 1943,O 7,26:2
Wait for Me 1945,Mr 19,23:3
Days and Nights 1946,Ap 29,24:4
Simonov, Konstantin (Screenwriter)
Wait for Me 1945,Mr 19,23:3
Days and Nights 1946,Ap 29,24:4
Immortal Garrison, The 1957,Mr 4,30:2
If Your Home Is Dear to You 1967,O 24,27:1
Simonov, Nikolai
Cain and Artem 1930,Je 7,10:4
Miracles 1934,O 22,12:3
Peter the First 1937,D 25,10:4
Conquests of Peter The Great, The
1939,Ag 24,17:2
First Front, The 1949,N 14,19:2
Victors and the Vanquished, The 1950,My 1,18:2
Gadfly, The 1956,S 17,22:2
Simonov, R
Admiral Nakhimov 1948,N 25,47:4
Gadfly, The 1956,S 17,22:2
Simonova, Nina
Cinderella 1961,D 19,39:1
Simons, William
Ivory Hunter 1952,Ag 19,19:1
West of Zanzibar 1955,Ja 18,31:2
Simonton, Ida Vera (Original Author)
White Cargo 1942,N 27,27:2
Simonx, S S
Greed 1924,D 5,28:1
Simor, Erzebet
Ele serelt Ember; Changed Man 1939,F 25,19:3
Janos Vitez; John, The Hero 1939,Ap 8,19:2
Varju a Toronyoran; Crow on the Tower
1939,N 18,22:6
Simoun, Henri (Screenwriter)
Madigan 1968,Mr 30,22:2
Simpson, Alan (Original Author)
Call Me Genius 1961,O 17,47:1
Spy With a Cold Nose, The 1966,D 20,58:2
Simpson, Alan (Screenwriter)
Call Me Genius 1961,O 17,47:1
Spy With a Cold Nose, The 1966,D 20,58:2
Simpson, Allan
Exciters, The 1923,Je 4,13:3
Society Scandal, A 1924,Mr 10,18:2
School for Wives 1925,Ap 1,21:3
Sea Horses 1926,F 23,26:5
Padlocked 1926,Ag 2,21:2

Simpson, Allan— Cont
Bertha, The Sewing Machine Girl 1927,Ja 4,21:1
Simpson, Colin
Pink String and Sealing Wax 1950,O 4,38:2
Simpson, David
Hue and Cry 1951,Ja 9,25:2
Simpson, Dr
Cupid, the Cowpuncher 1920,Jl 26,9:5
Simpson, Frank
Fail Safe 1964,S 16,36:1
Simpson, Gertrude
Jungle Bride 1933,My 13,16:3
Simpson, Harold (Screenwriter)
Spy of Napoleon 1939,Ag 19,18:4
Simpson, Helen (Miscellaneous)
Woman Alone, The 1937,F 27,9:2
Simpson, Helen (Original Author)
Saraband 1949,Je 13,16:3
Under Capricorn 1949,S 9,28:3
Simpson, Ivan
Man Who Played God, The 1922,O 2,21:2
Green Goddess, The 1923,Ag 15,21:1
Twenty-One 1924,F 18,13:1
$20 a Week 1924,Je 10,24:4
Miss Bluebeard 1925,Ja 28,14:1
Wild, Wild Susan 1925,Ag 5,12:4
Lovers in Quarantine 1925,O 13,20:1
Womanhandled 1926,Ja 5,25:2
Disraeli 1929,O 3,27:5
Green Goddess, The 1930,F 14,20:1
Inside the Lines 1930,Jl 5,17:4
Manslaughter 1930,Jl 24,26:4
Sea God, The 1930,S 6,9:2
Way of all Men, The 1930,S 20,15:4
Millionaire, The 1931,Ap 9,30:5
Lady Who Dared, The 1931,Je 6,15:5
Reckless Hour, The 1931,Ag 1,16:4
I Like Your Nerve 1931,S 12,15:4
Safe in Hell 1931,D 19,16:4
Man Who Played God, The 1932,F 11,16:1
Passport to Hell, A 1932,Ag 27,13:4
Crash, The 1932,S 9,17:5
Phantom of Crestwood, The 1932,O 17,18:3
Past of Mary Holmes, The 1933,My 1,10:3
Silk Express, The 1933,Je 28,24:2
Midnight Mary 1933,Jl 15,14:2
Voltaire 1933,Ag 23,21:2
Charlie Chan's Greatest Case 1933,O 7,18:4
Blind Adventure 1933,O 31,24:3
Man of Two Worlds 1934,Ja 12,29:2
Mystery of Mr X, The 1934,F 26,21:3
House of Rothschild, The 1934,Mr 15,27:2
World Moves On, The 1934,Je 30,18:5
British Agent 1934,S 20,20:1
David Copperfield 1935,Ja 19,8:1
Shadow of Doubt 1935,Mr 11,15:1
Mark of the Vampire 1935,My 3,23:4
Mutiny on the Bounty 1935,N 9,19:2
Splendor 1935,N 23,23:2
Captain Blood 1935,D 27,14:1
Little Lord Fauntleroy 1936,Ap 3,27:1
Trouble for Two 1936,My 30,7:2
Mary of Scotland 1936,Jl 31,22:2
Lloyds of London 1936,N 26,39:1
Maid of Salem 1937,Mr 4,27:2
Prince and the Pauper, The 1937,My 6,23:1
London by Night 1937,Ag 13,13:1
Baroness and the Butler, The 1938,F 19,19:2
Invisible Enemy 1938,Ap 30,18:2
Adventures of Robin Hood, The 1938,My 13,17:2
Booloo 1938,Jl 30,10:2
Rulers of the Sea 1939,N 9,27:1
Invisible Man Returns, The 1940,Ja 16,19:2
New Moon 1940,Jl 19,22:2
Body Disappears, The 1942,Ja 31,13:2
Male Animal, The 1942,Mr 28,11:1
Nazi Agent 1942,Je 13,11:2
They all Kissed the Bride 1942,Jl 31,11:1
Random Harvest 1942,D 18,36:6
This Land Is Mine 1943,My 28,19:1
My Kingdom for a Cook 1943,O 15,15:3
Hour Before the Dawn, The 1944,My 11,25:6
Simpson, Lanny
There's a Girl in my Heart 1950,Ja 20,29:2
Simpson, Mickey
Song of Scheherazade 1947,F 27,26:2
Tarzan and the Huntress 1947,Ap 7,20:4
Fighting Kentuckian, The 1949,S 19,18:3
She Wore a Yellow Ribbon 1949,N 18,35:2
When Willie Comes Marching Home 1950,F 18,9:2
Wagonmaster 1950,Je 19,17:2
Surrender 1950,O 9,21:5
Lion Is in the Streets, A 1953,S 24,39:2
New York Confidential 1955,F 19,18:1
Giant 1956,O 11,51:1
Simpson, N F (Screenwriter)
One Way Pendulum 1965,Mr 3,34:3
Simpson, Napoleon
Abe Lincoln in Illinois 1940,F 23,19:2
Drums of the Congo 1942,Jl 20,16:4
Mummy's Curse, The 1945,Mr 31,16:1
Red Menace, The 1949,Je 27,18:2

Simpson, Peggy
Thirty-Nine Steps, The 1935,S 14,8:4
Simpson, Reginald (Original Author)
Man From Chicago, The 1931,Ja 16,27:1
Simpson, Ronald
Long Dark Hall, The 1951,My 10,38:3
Simpson, Russell
Brand, The 1919,Mr 17,13:2
Bunty Pulls the Strings 1921,Ja 9,VI,2:1 (In Addenda)
Godless Men 1921,Ja 31,11:1
Snowblind 1921,My 23,16:3
Peg o'my Heart 1923,Ja 22,10:1
Girl of the Golden West, The 1923,My 21,12:2
Circus Days 1923,Ag 6,14:2
Painted People 1924,Ja 29,16:1
Narrow Street, The 1925,Ja 5,19:1
Splendid Road, The 1926,Je 13,31:1
Social Highwayman, The 1926,Je 15,23:3
Lovey Mary 1926,Je 21,17:2
Annie Laurie 1927,My 12,24:3
First Auto, The 1927,Je 28,28:4
First Auto, The 1927,Jl 3,VII,3:3
Wild Geese 1927,D 5,26:2
We're in the Air Now 1927,D 31,31:1
Trail of '98, The 1928,Mr 21,30:3
Innocents of Paris 1929,Ap 27,16:5
Abraham Lincoln 1930,Ag 26,24:1
Billy the Kid 1930,O 18,23:2
Man to Man 1931,Ja 3,21:2
Great Meadow, The 1931,Mr 14,23:2
Susan Lenox; Her Fall and Rise 1931,O 17,20:1
Law and Order 1932,F 29,21:3
Lena Rivers 1932,My 21,9:2
Cabin in the Cotton 1932,S 30,17:3
Silver Dollar 1932,D 23,20:1
Hello, Everybody 1933,Ja 30,9:4
Face in the Sky 1933,F 20,11:5
Frontier Marshal 1934,Ja 31,20:3
Carolina 1934,F 16,17:2
Ever Since Eve 1934,Mr 28,27:5
World Moves On, The 1934,Je 30,18:5
County Chairman, The 1935,Ja 19,8:1
Way Down East 1935,O 31,16:2
Man Hunt 1936,Ja 30,14:2
Paddy O'Day 1936,F 8,19:2
San Francisco 1936,Je 27,21:1
Harvester, The 1936,Jl 4,18:2
Crime of Dr Forbes, The 1936,Jl 6,11:4
Ramona 1936,O 7,32:4
Green Light 1937,F 13,9:1
Mountain Justice 1937,My 13,31:2
Gold Is Where You Find It 1938,F 14,20:6
Valley of the Giants 1938,S 10,20:2
Heart of the North 1938,D 21,29:2
Dodge City 1939,Ap 8,19:1
Young Mr Lincoln 1939,Je 3,11:2
Drums Along the Mohawk 1939,N 4,11:2
Grapes of Wrath, The 1940,Ja 25,17:2
Geronimo 1940,F 8,18:3
Three Faces West 1940,Ag 19,13:2
Brigham Young - Frontiersman 1940,S 21,13:2
Santa Fe Trail 1940,D 21,21:2
Tobacco Road 1941,F 21,16:2
Meet John Doe 1941,Mr 13,25:2
Bad Men of Missouri 1941,Ag 16,18:2
Wild Geese Calling 1941,Ag 30,10:2
Swamp Water 1941,N 17,15:2
Wild Bill Hickok Rides 1942,F 7,13:5
Spoilers, The 1942,My 22,27:2
Tennessee Johnson 1943,Ja 13,18:2
Big Bonanza, The 1945,F 26,14:5
Along Came Jones 1945,Jl 19,8:7
They Were Expendable 1945,D 21,25:2
Bad Bascomb 1946,My 23,18:4
My Darling Clementine 1946,D 4,44:5
Romance of Rosy Ridge, The 1947,S 12,18:3
Fabulous Texan, The 1947,D 26,22:5
Albuquerque 1948,Mr 1,17:2
Tap Roots 1948,Ag 26,16:3
Beautiful Blonde From Bashful Bend, The 1949,My 28,11:2
Wagonmaster 1950,Je 19,17:2
Saddle Tramp 1950,N 24,31:4
Across the Wide Missouri 1951,N 7,35:4
Lone Star 1952,F 2,11:4
Ma and Pa Kettle at the Fair 1952,Jl 12,16:2
Sun Shines Bright, The 1954,Mr 17,25:2
Seven Brides for Seven Brothers 1954,Jl 23,8:3
Broken Lance 1954,Jl 30,9:1
Friendly Persuasion 1956,N 2,30:1
Horse Soldiers, The 1959,Je 26,13:1
Simpson-Little, George
Jedda the Uncivilized 1957,F 28,18:7
SIMS
See Also SIMMS
Sims, Dorothea Carolyn
I'd Climb the Highest Mountain 1951,My 10,38:1
Sims, Joan
Belles of St Trinian's, The 1954,D 23,13:4
Will any Gentleman? 1955,S 28,70:6

Sims, Joan— Cont
Trouble in Store 1956,Ja 14,13:2
Ship Was Loaded, The 1958,Ja 20,20:1
Your Past Is Showing 1958,Jl 1,36:2
Carry on Nurse 1960,S 10,11:1
Captain's Table, The 1960,S 27,40:1
Upstairs and Downstairs 1960,D 2,53:4
Please Turn Over 1961,Ap 29,12:2
Doctor in Love 1962,Ap 27,27:2
I Like Money 1962,My 19,18:2
Pair of Briefs, A 1964,F 3,22:2
Carry on Cleo 1965,O 23,17:2
Simukov, A (Screenwriter)
Chelkash 1964,Ja 27,19:1
Sinatra, Frank
Reveille With Beverly 1943,Ap 24,17:2
Higher and Higher 1944,Ja 22,8:4
Step Lively 1944,Jl 27,14:1
Anchors Aweigh 1945,Jl 20,15:2
Till the Clouds Roll By 1946,D 6,27:4
It Happened in Brooklyn 1947,Mr 14,28:5
Miracle of the Bells, The 1948,Mr 17,30:1
Kissing Bandit, The 1948,N 19,35:2
Take Me Out to the Ball Game 1949,Mr 10,35:2
On the Town 1949,D 9,37:2
Double Dynamite 1951,D 26,19:4
Meet Danny Wilson 1952,Mr 27,34:4
From Here to Eternity 1953,Ag 6,16:2
Suddenly 1954,O 8,27:2
Young at Heart 1955,Ja 20,35:1
Not as a Stranger 1955,Je 29,24:1
Guys and Dolls 1955,N 5,26:1
Tender Trap, The 1955,N 11,29:6
Man With the Golden Arm, The 1955,D 16,38:2
High Society 1956,Ag 10,9:2
Johnny Concho 1956,Ag 16,30:1
Around the World in 80 Days 1956,O 18,37:1
Pride and the Passion, The 1957,Je 29,10:6
Joker Is Wild, The 1957,S 27,16:6
Pal Joey 1957,O 28,30:1
Kings Go Forth 1958,Jl 4,15:2
Some Came Running 1959,Ja 23,17:1
Hole in the Head, A 1959,Jl 16,31:2
Never so Few 1960,Ja 22,15:2
Can-Can 1960,Mr 10,36:1
Ocean's Eleven 1960,Ag 11,19:1
Pepe 1960,D 22,18:1
Devil at 4 O'Clock, The 1961,O 19,39:3
Sergeants 3 1962,F 12,28:2
Manchurian Candidate, The 1962,O 25,48:3
List of Adrian Messenger, The 1963,My 30,20:1
Come Blow Your Horn 1963,Je 7,37:1
4 for Texas 1963,D 26,33:3
Robin and the 7 Hoods 1964,Ag 6,20:1
None but the Brave 1965,F 25,24:1
Von Ryan's Express 1965,Je 24,28:1
Marriage on the Rocks 1965,S 16,00:0
Cast a Giant Shadow 1966,Mr 31,43:3
Assault on a Queen 1966,Jl 28,23:3
Naked Runner, The 1967,Jl 20,30:2
Tony Rome 1967,N 16,58:1
Detective, The 1968,My 29,20:3
Lady in Cement 1968,N 21,41:1
Sinatra, Frank (Director)
None but the Brave 1965,F 25,24:1
Sinatra, Frank (Producer)
Sergeants 3 1962,F 12,28:2
Robin and the 7 Hoods 1964,Ag 6,20:1
None but the Brave 1965,F 25,24:1
Sinatra, Frank Jr
Man Called Adam, A 1966,Ag 4,24:2
Sinatra, Nancy
For Those Who Think Young 1964,Jl 9,27:1
Marriage on the Rocks 1965,S 16,00:0
Last of the Secret Agents, The? 1966,Je 23,29:1
Wild Angels, The 1966,D 22,40:4
Speedway 1968,Je 14,43:1
Sinaz, Guglielmo
Stella del Mare; Star of the Sea 1940,My 3,17:6
Before Him all Rome Trembled 1947,F 22,16:2
Great Dawn, The 1947,Ag 28,28:3
Sinclair, Arthur
Evensong 1934,N 17,12:1
Peg of Old Drury 1936,Ap 13,15:1
King Solomon's Mines 1937,Jl 3,18:1
Hungry Hill 1947,O 11,11:2
Sinclair, Barry
Tenth Man, The 1937,N 15,15:2
Sinclair, Betty
City Streets 1931,Ap 18,17:3
Sinclair, Carol
Go, Man, Go 1954,Mr 10,29:5
Sinclair, Charles (Screenwriter)
Chase a Crooked Shadow 1958,Mr 25,28:4
Sinclair, Diane
Washington Masquerade, The 1932,Jl 22,18:2
Cradle Song 1933,N 20,18:2
Damaged Lives 1937,Je 14,26:2
Sinclair, Edward
Tower of Terror 1942,Je 29,11:4
Saraband 1949,Je 13,16:3
Sinclair, Eleanor
Under the Red Robe 1923,N 13,25:3

Sinclair, Harold (Original Author)
Horse Soldiers, The 1959,Je 26,13:1
Sinclair, Horace
One Third of a Nation 1939,F 11,13:2
Sinclair, Hugh
Our Betters 1933,F 24,13:2
Escape me Never 1935,My 24,24:2
Strangers on a Honeymoon 1937,Mr 13,23:2
Secret Four, The 1940,Ap 22,13:2
Saint's Vacation, The 1941,Je 13,22:2
Girl Must Live, A 1942,Mr 24,25:2
At Dawn We Die 1943,My 8,19:2
They Were Sisters 1946,Jl 24,24:2
Corridor of Mirrors 1949,Mr 23,35:3
Rocking Horse Winner, The 1950,Je 9,29:2
Gay Lady, The 1951,Ap 16,21:2
Circle of Danger 1951,Jl 12,21:6
Sinclair, Irene (Original Author)
One Exciting Night 1922,O 24,17:3
Sinclair, John
Million Dollar Legs 1932,Jl 9,7:5
Sinclair, Mary
Arrowhead 1953,S 16,38:6
Sinclair, Patricia
Cosmic Monster, The 1959,Ja 1,38:1
Sinclair, Peter
Man From Morocco, The 1946,N 25,38:2
Sinclair, Robert B (Director)
Woman Against Woman 1938,Ag 23,20:6
Dramatic School 1938,D 9,31:2
Joe and Ethel Turp Call on the President 1940,Ja 4,19:2
And One Was Beautiful 1940,Ap 11,32:4
I'll Wait for You 1941,Je 2,13:6
Mr and Mrs North 1942,Ja 22,13:2
Mr District Attorney 1947,F 28,27:3
That Wonderful Urge 1948,D 22,29:6
Sinclair, Ronald
Thoroughbreds Don't Cry 1937,N 26,27:4
Christmas Carol, A 1938,D 23,16:2
Tower of London 1939,D 12,37:2
Light That Failed, The 1939,D 25,19:1
Earl of Chicago, The 1940,Mr 14,29:3
That Hamilton Woman 1941,Ap 4,25:1
Desperate Journey 1942,S 26,11:2
Sinclair, Ruth
Masquerader, The 1922,Ag 14,12:4
Sinclair, Upton (Original Author)
Wet Parade, The 1932,Ap 22,23:2
Jimmie Higgins 1933,F 22,25:3
Gnome-Mobile, The 1967,Jl 20,30:2
Sinclair, Upton (Screenwriter)
Marriage Forbidden 1938,Jl 16,7:2
Sinden, Donald
Cruel Sea, The 1953,Ag 11,18:5
Mogambo 1953,O 2,18:1
Beachcomber, The 1955,Ja 17,27:5
Doctor in the House 1955,F 19,18:3
Simba 1955,O 22,24:2
Above Us the Waves 1957,Ap 18,35:2
Doctor at Large 1957,Jl 29,15:5
Alligator Named Daisy, An 1957,O 7,23:2
Mad Little Island 1958,D 31,12:1
Captain's Table, The 1960,S 27,40:1
Sindici, C
Open City; Citta Aperta 1946,F 26,21:2
Sinelnikova, M
Gypsies 1936,Jl 30,22:2
Sinev, Vova
Son of the Regiment 1948,Ap 29,27:3
Singelow, Alexander (Cinematographer)
Nomadie 1931,Je 13,20:4
Singenberger, Otto (Composer)
Film Record of the Eucharistic Congress 1926,N 9,31:1
Singer, Alexander (Director)
Cold Wind in August, A 1961,Jl 27,23:2
Psyche 59 1964,Ap 30,30:1
Love Has Many Faces 1965,F 25,24:1
Singer, Campbell
Blue Lamp, The 1951,Ja 9,25:1
Murder on Monday 1953,O 7,35:2
Singer, Howard (Original Author)
Wake Me When It's Over 1960,Ap 9,17:2
Singer, Jerry
Stalag 17 1953,Jl 2,19:2
Singer, John
My Heart Is Calling 1935,Ap 15,16:3
Emil 1938,Ap 15,23:2
Singer, Julia (Original Author)
Great Betrayal, The 1947,Je 6,27:2
Singer, Lou (Composer)
Hold That Ghost 1941,Ag 8,13:3
Singer, Ray (Miscellaneous)
She Gets her Man 1945,F 9,20:5
Singer, Simon (Original Author)
Great Betrayal, The 1947,Je 6,27:2
Singer, Stuffy
Her Twelve Men 1954,Ag 12,23:2
Singer Midgets
Wizard of Oz, The 1939,Ag 18,16:2

Singerman, Berta
Nada Mas Que Una Mujer 1934,N 26,12:2
Singh, Bhagwan
Bwana Devil 1953,F 19,20:5
Singh, Indrani
Kanchenjungha 1966,Jl 26,27:2
Singh, K N
Guide, The 1965,F 10,44:2
Singh, Paul
Calcutta 1947,Ap 24,30:2
Singh, Ram
River, The 1951,S 11,33:2
Singh, Ranveer (Original Author)
Long Duel, The 1967,N 2,58:3
Singh, Vidya
Kanchenjungha 1966,Jl 26,27:2
Singhammer, Eva Maria
Heidi 1968,S 23,42:4
Singla, Antonio
Tarantos, Los 1964,Je 30,22:1
Singleton, Joseph
Toll Gate, The 1920,Ap 19,13:3
Great Redeemer, The 1920,O 25,18:1
Skin Deep 1922,O 23,10:1
Mad Whirl, The 1925,Jl 1,16:1
Singleton, Penny
Swing Your Lady 1938,Ja 27,17:2
Men Are Such Fools 1938,Je 17,25:1
Racket Busters 1938,Ag 11,13:1
Boy Meets Girl 1938,Ag 27,7:2
Garden of the Moon 1938,S 24,13:1
Secrets of an Actress 1938,O 8,10:2
Mad Miss Manton, The 1938,O 21,27:2
Hard To Get 1938,N 14,15:2
Blondie 1938,D 22,25:4
Blondie Meets the Boss 1939,Ap 27,31:1
Blondie Goes Latin 1941,F 26,17:3
Go West, Young Lady 1941,N 24,11:6
Young Widow 1946,Jl 29,12:8
Blondie Hits the Jackpot 1949,S 9,28:3
Best Man, The 1964,Ap 7,29:1
Singleton, Zutty
Stormy Weather 1943,Jl 22,15:1
New Orleans 1947,Je 20,25:6
Sini, Linda
Stranger on the Prowl 1953,N 10,38:1
Conjugal Bed, The 1963,S 17,30:1
Easy Life, The 1963,D 23,18:2
Sinigalia, Annie
Love and the Frenchwoman; (Francaise et l'Amour, La) 1961,F 28,38:2
Sinimberghi, Gino
Before Him all Rome Trembled 1947,F 22,16:2
This Wine of Love 1948,Ap 19,27:2
Trovatore, Il 1950,F 9,36:7
Forza del Destino, La 1952,O 17,33:1
Favorita, La 1953,O 30,27:4
Beautiful but Dangerous 1958,F 6,24:1
Sinjen, Sabine
Stefanie 1959,Je 18,36:1
Sinkovits, Imre
Dialogue 1967,O 14,13:2
Sinnigen, William
Last Illusion, The 1951,Mr 8,37:2
Sinoel
Dernier Milliardaire, Le 1935,O 30,16:2
Francis the First 1947,N 20,38:4
Vie de Boheme, La 1947,N 28,37:4
Voyage Surprise 1948,F 14,17:3
Sinoff, Pepi
Have a Heart 1934,O 20,20:2
Princess O'Hara 1935,Ap 13,11:3
Sioberg, Gunnar
Devil's Eye, The 1961,O 31,27:4
Sioberg, Tora (Director)
Face of War, The 1963,N 1,30:2
Siobiom, Ulla
Here's Your Life 1968,D 20,60:1
Siodmak, Curt (Director)
Magnetic Monster, The 1953,My 14,32:5
Siodmak, Curt (Original Author)
F P 1 1933,S 16,9:3
Crise est Finie, La 1935,Mr 14,18:1
Her Jungle Love 1938,Ap 14,27:2
Invisible Man Returns, The 1940,Ja 16,19:2
Invisible Woman, The 1941,Ja 9,27:2
Aloma of the South Seas 1941,Ag 28,23:4
Pacific Blackout 1942,Ja 15,25:2
Son of Dracula 1943,N 6,16:4
Lady and the Monster, The 1944,Ap 8,9:2
House of Frankenstein 1944,D 16,19:3
Return of Monte Cristo, The 1947,Ja 3,16:4
Berlin Express 1948,My 21,19:3
Donovan's Brain 1954,Ja 21,28:2
Earth vs the Flying Saucers 1956,Ag 2,21:2
Siodmak, Curt (Screenwriter)
Transatlantic Tunnel 1935,O 28,16:2
Invisible Man Returns, The 1940,Ja 16,19:2
Black Friday 1940,Mr 22,23:3
Ape, The 1940,N 28,28:3
Wolf Man, The 1941,D 22,24:5
Invisible Agent 1942,Ag 6,23:2
Frankenstein Meets the Wolf Man 1943,Mr 6,8:3

Siodmak, Curt (Screenwriter) — Cont
I Walked With a Zombie 1943,Ap 22,31:5
Climax, The 1944,D 14,28:5
Frisco Sal 1945,F 17,11:2
Shady Lady 1945,O 11,26:2
Beast With Five Fingers, The 1946,D 26,28:3
Tarzan's Magic Fountain 1949,F 7,15:2
Four Days' Leave 1950,Je 9,29:4
Magnetic Monster, The 1953,My 14,32:5
Riders to the Stars 1954,Mr 20,10:7
Siodmak, Robert (Director)
Mann der Seinen Moerder Sucht, Der; Looking for His Murderer 1931,Mr 15,IX,6:1
Voruntersuchung; Inquest 1931,My 24,VIII,4:1
Stuerme der Leidenschaft 1932,Mr 16,17:3
Quick, Koenig der Clowns 1933,D 9,18:3
Crise est Finie, La 1935,Mr 14,18:1
Hatred 1941,Ja 27,11:2
Personal Column 1941,F 3,13:2
Compliments of Mr Iflow 1941,F 17,10:7
West Point Widow 1941,S 11,21:5
Night Before the Divorce, The 1942,Ap 10,21:3
Son of Dracula 1943,N 6,16:4
Phantom Lady 1944,F 18,15:2
Cobra Woman 1944,My 18,17:2
Christmas Holiday 1944,Je 29,16:1
Suspect, The 1945,F 1,18:5
Uncle Harry 1945,Ag 24,14:5
Spiral Staircase, The 1946,F 7,29:3
Symphonie d'Amour 1946,Mr 11,19:2
Killers, The 1946,Ag 29,24:2
Dark Mirror, The 1946,O 19,15:2
Time Out of Mind 1947,Ap 7,20:1
Cry of the City 1948,S 30,32:4
Criss Cross 1949,Mr 12,10:2
Great Sinner, The 1949,Je 30,19:2
Thelma Jordon 1950,Ja 19,35:2
Deported 1950,N 2,39:3
Whistle at Eaton Falls, The 1951,O 11,49:2
Crimson Pirate, The 1952,Ag 28,21:2
Devil Strikes at Night, The 1959,Ja 30,31:3
Portrait of a Sinner 1961,D 7,52:1
Escape from East Berlin 1962,D 6,55:3
Magnificent Sinner 1963,Ap 25,38:1
Custer of the West 1968,Jl 4,13:2
Siodmak, Robert (Miscellaneous)
Burning Secret 1933,My 28,IX,2:5 (In Addenda)
Siodmak, Robert (Original Author)
Conflict 1945,Je 16,10:2
Siodmak, Robert (Producer)
Stuerme der Leidenschaft; Storms of Passion 1932,F 14,VIII,6:1
Time Out of Mind 1947,Ap 7,20:1
Devil Strikes at Night, The 1959,Ja 30,31:3
Sipavina, Eda
Wait for Me 1945,Mr 19,23:3
Sipperly, Ralph
Sunrise 1927,S 24,15:3 (In Addenda)
Sirago, Marie
Bon Voyage! 1962,My 18,34:2
Siras, John (Composer)
Lullaby of Broadway 1951,Mr 27,35:2
Sire, Antoine
Man and a Woman, A; Homme et une Femme, Un 1966,Jl 13,35:1
Sire, Gerard
To be a Crook 1967,F 7,33:2
Sirett, Jeffrey
Hue and Cry 1951,Ja 9,25:2
Sirgo, Otto
Heroina 1965,N 11,58:2
Siriaque
King Solomon's Mines 1950,N 10,35:1
Sirk, Douglas (Director)
Hitler's Madman 1943,Ag 28,15:1
Summer Storm 1944,O 23,14:3
Scandal in Paris, A 1946,S 16,9:7
Lured 1947,Ag 29,14:4
Sleep, My Love 1948,F 19,29:4
Slightly French 1949,My 27,25:3
Mystery Submarine 1951,F 2,19:2
First Legion, The 1951,Ap 28,9:2
Thunder on the Hill 1951,O 18,32:3
No Room for the Groom 1952,Je 14,12:2
Has Anybody Seen My Gal 1952,Jl 5,7:2
Take Me to Town 1953,Je 20,8:6
All I Desire 1953,Ag 29,10:1
Magnificent Obsession 1954,Ag 5,18:4
Sign of the Pagan 1955,F 14,24:2
There's Always Tomorrow 1956,Ja 21,18:2
All That Heaven Allows 1956,F 29,35:1
Written on the Wind 1957,Ja 12,12:6
Battle Hymn 1957,F 16,14:1
Tarnished Angels, The 1958,Ja 7,31:1
Time to Love and a Time to Die, A 1958,Jl 10,22:1
Imitation of Life 1959,Ap 18,18:1
Sirk, Douglas (Producer)
First Legion, The 1951,Ap 28,9:2
Sirk, Douglas (Screenwriter)
Summer Storm 1944,O 23,14:3
Sirola, Joseph
Strange Bedfellows 1965,Mr 11,38:1

Sirota, Gerson (Miscellaneous)
Dybbuk, The 1938,Ja 28,17:2
Siscart, Solango
Living Dead Man, The 1927,Mr 7,16:3
Sisk, Robert (Producer)
Chatterbox 1936,F 15,18:6
Farmer in the Dell, The 1936,Mr 7,11:4
Two in Revolt 1936,Ap 25,21:1
Last Outlaw, The 1936,Je 15,24:1
M'liss 1936,Ag 8,5:2
Don't Turn 'em Loose 1936,S 25,20:2
Plough and the Stars, The 1937,Ja 29,15:1
Don't Tell the Wife 1937,F 19,15:2
Outcasts of Poker Flat, The 1937,Ap 27,18:3
Border Cafe 1937,Je 8,30:2
You Can't Beat Love 1937,Je 25,25:3
Flight From Glory 1937,S 11,20:1
Annapolis Salute 1937,O 2,18:1
Condemned Woman 1938,Ap 22,15:5
Law of the Underworld 1938,Ap 28,27:2
Go Chase Yourself 1938,Je 15,27:1
Sky Giant 1938,Jl 20,22:2
Mr Doodle Kicks Off 1938,S 28,29:4
Man to Remember, A 1938,N 7,23:2
Pacific Liner 1939,Ja 18,17:3
Twelve Crowded Hours 1939,F 24,15:2
Saint Strikes Back, The 1939,Mr 9,18:2
They Made Her a Spy 1939,Mr 29,21:4
Girl From Mexico, The 1939,Je 8,31:4
Five came Back 1939,Jl 5,20:2
Career 1939,Jl 28,14:2
Bad Lands 1939,Ag 9,15:2
Day the Bookies Wept, The 1939,S 14,18:2
Full Confession 1939,S 28,29:4
Three Sons 1939,N 24,29:3
Reno 1939,D 21,29:2
Married and in Love 1940,F 2,13:2
Marines Fly High, The 1940,Mr 5,19:2
Millionaire Playboy 1940,Mr 16,8:2
Bill of Divorcement, A 1940,Jl 12,11:2
Tom, Dick and Harry 1941,Jl 18,22:2
Lost Angel 1944,Ap 10,14:1
Gentle Annie 1945,My 5,11:5
Hidden Eye, The 1945,Ag 31,14:3
Our Vines Have Tender Grapes 1945,S 7,21:2
Courage of Lassie 1946,Jl 25,18:5
Boy's Ranch 1946,Ag 9,12:2
Love Laughs at Andy Hardy 1947,Ja 8,28:2
Hills of Home 1948,N 26,32:2
Sun comes up, The 1949,My 13,29:2
Tension 1950,Ja 12,32:4
Challenge to Lassie 1950,Ap 7,22:3
Shadow on the Wall 1950,My 19,31:3
Across the Wide Missouri 1951,N 7,35:4
ThIs Woman is Dangerous 1952,F 28,23:2
Sissia, Duccio
See Naples and Die 1959,Ag 31,16:2
Sisson, Vera
Love 'Em and Leave 'Em 1926,D 8,24:3
Sisters, Paxton
King of Burlesque 1936,Ja 16,25:2
Every Saturday Night 1936,Mr 14,10:2
Sisters G
King of Jazz 1930,My 3,23:1
Kiss Me Again 1931,Ja 8,21:4
Sistine Chapel Choir
Story of the Pope, The 1946,D 20,31:3
Holy Year 1950 1950,Ag 16,24:3
Sistrom, Joseph (Producer)
Something in the Wind 1947,Ag 29,14:3
Saxon Charm, The 1948,S 30,32:3
Submarine Command 1952,Ja 19,13:2
Atomic City, The 1952,My 2,21:1
Botany Bay 1953,O 30,27:2
Sistrom, William (Producer)
Murder on a Bridle Path 1936,Ap 11,19:2
Plot Thickens, The 1936,D 9,35:2
There Goes my Girl 1937,Je 12,8:2
Forty Naughty Girls 1937,S 18,15:3
Saint in New York, The 1938,My 26,31:2
I'm From the City 1938,Ag 19,13:4
Saint in London, The 1939,Jl 19,23:3
Saint's Vacation, The 1941,Je 13,22:2
Suicide Squadron 1942,My 14,23:2
Mr Emmanuel 1945,Ja 8,15:2
Sitbebe, John
Dingaka 1965,Jl 1,34:1
Sitjar, Lisa
Two Loves 1961,Je 22,23:2
Sitka, Emil
Three Stooges in Orbit, The 1962,Jl 12,19:4
Sitkey, Irene
Igioi Diakok 1935,My 24,24:3
Sittoro, Maria
Roof, The 1959,My 13,43:4
Sitwell, Osbert Sir (Original Author)
Place of One's Own, A 1949,F 8,30:2
Siu, Ronald
Samurai 1945,Ag 25,7:5
Sivieri, Adriana
Bitter Rice 1950,S 19,39:2
Behind Closed Shutters 1952,Je 10,22:7

Six, Eva
Beach Party 1963,S 26,40:2
Six Hits and a Miss
Hit Parade of 1941 1940,D 5,33:2
Time Out for Rythm 1941,Jl 10,16:3
Call out the Marines 1942,Ja 26,18:3
Butch Minds the Baby 1942,My 1,23:3
Sizov, I
Pugachev 1938,Jl 4,10:2
Sizova, Alla
Sleeping Beauty, The 1966,My 4,50:1
Sjoberg, Alf (Director)
Himlaspelet 1944,O 9,17:3
Torment 1947,Ap 22,34:2
Miss Julie 1952,Ap 8,35:2
Sjoberg, Alf (Screenwriter)
Himlaspelet 1944,O 9,17:3
Miss Julie 1952,Ap 8,35:2
Sjoberg, Anne-Charlotte
To Bed...Or not to Bed 1963,D 23,18:2
Sjoberg, Gunnar
Children, The 1949,D 23,17:1
Wild Strawberries 1959,Je 23,37:1
Brink of Life; (Nara Livet) 1959,N 9,36:2
Sjoberg, Tore (Director)
Secrets of the Nazi Criminals 1962,O 4,44:3
Sjoberg, Tore (Producer)
Mein Kampf 1961,Ap 22,18:1
Secrets of the Nazi Criminals 1962,O 4,44:3
Swedish Wedding Night 1965,N 15,48:1
Sjobiom, Tekla
Crime and Punishment 1948,Mr 1,17:2
Sjoblom, Ulla
Magician, The 1959,Ag 28,27:1
Sjoestrand, Arnold
Klart till Drabbning; Cleared for Action
1937,D 10,33:3
Berslagsfolk 1938,Mr 12,13:3
Himlaspelet 1944,O 9,17:3
Sjosirand, Inger
To Bed...Or not to Bed 1963,D 23,18:2
Sjostrand, Per
Unmarried Mothers 1956,F 23,32:5
Wild Strawberries 1959,Je 23,37:1
Skaiek, Mary
Disputed Passage 1939,O 26,27:2
Skala, Lilia
Call Me Madam 1953,Mr 26,37:1
Lilies of the Field 1963,O 2,51:1
Ship of Fools 1965,Jl 29,18:1
Caprice 1967,Je 8,52:2
Charly 1968,S 24,55:1
Skarf, George
Champagne Murders, The 1968,Ap 25,53:1
Skarstad, Vance
Walls of Hell, The 1965,N 18,55:3
Skatine, Little
Dragon Sky 1964,Ag 25,28:2
Skating Vanities
Pin Up Girl 1944,My 11,25:6
Skelly, Hal
Dance of Life, The 1929,Ag 16,18:6
Woman Trap 1929,Ag 31,13:4
Behind the Makeup 1930,Ja 18,21:1
Struggle, The 1931,D 11,35:1
Skelton, Red
Flight Command 1941,Ja 17,21:2
People vs Dr Kildare, The 1941,My 8,21:1
Whistling in the Dark 1941,Ag 28,23:2
Dr Kildare's Wedding Day 1941,S 18,31:1
Lady Be Good 1941,S 19,27:1
Ship Ahoy 1942,Je 26,16:5
Maisie Gets her Man 1942,Jl 16,23:2
Panama Hattie 1942,O 2,31:2
Whistling in Dixie 1942,D 31,20:4
Du Barry Was a Lady 1943,Ag 20,13:1
Thousands Cheer 1943,S 14,27:1
I Dood It 1943,N 11,29:1
Whistling in Brooklyn 1944,Mr 24,17:3
Bathing Beauty 1944,Je 28,20:1
Ziegfeld Follies 1946,Mr 23,8:3
Show-Off, The 1947,Mr 20,38:2
Merton of the Movies 1947,N 7,20:3
Fuller Brush Man, The 1948,My 15,18:2
Southern Yankee, A 1948,N 25,47:2
Neptune's Daughter 1949,Je 10,32:2
Yellow Cab Man, The 1950,Mr 27,19:2
Duchess of Idaho 1950,Jl 21,15:3
Three Little Words 1950,Ag 10,21:2
Watch the Birdie 1950,D 12,46:4
Excuse my Dust 1951,Je 28,21:2
Texas Carnival 1951,O 13,9:1
Lovely to Look At 1952,My 30,11:2
Clown, The 1953,Ja 29,25:1
Around the World in 80 Days 1956,O 18,37:1
Public Pigeon No 1 1957,My 18,23:2
Ocean's Eleven 1960,Ag 11,19:1
Those Magnificent Men in Their Flying Machines
(Or How I Flew From London to Paris in 25
Hours and 11 Minutes) 1965,Je 17,27:1
Skelton, Richard
Having Wonderful Time 1938,Jl 8,11:2

Skerla, Lena
Fire Within, The 1964,F 18,27:1
24 Hours in a Woman's Life 1968,S 25,39:1
Skerritt, Tom
War Hunt 1962,Ag 8,35:2
Sketch, Bartholomew
Ivory Hunter 1952,Ag 19,19:1
Sketch, Bethlehem
West of Zanzibar 1955,Ja 18,31:2
Skillan, George
Dreyfus Case, The 1931,Ag 31,11:5
Spitfire 1943,Je 14,13:2
Skinner, Constance L (Original Author)
Green Temptation, The 1922,Mr 20,10:3
Skinner, Cornelia Otis
Stage Door Canteen 1943,Je 25,13:2
Uninvited, The 1944,F 21,19:3
Girl in the Red Velvet Swing, The
1955,O 20,41:2
Swimmer, The 1968,My 16,53:1
Skinner, Cornelia Otis (Original Author)
Our Hearts Were Young and Gay 1944,O 12,24:2
Skinner, Edna
Kissing Bandit, The 1948,N 19,35:2
Easy to Love 1953,N 27,99:9
Second Greatest Sex, The 1956,F 11,12:2
Friendly Persuasion 1956,N 2,30:1
Skinner, Frank (Composer)
Night in Paradise 1946,Je 6,16:3
Skinner, Keith
Mademoiselle 1966,Ag 2,23:1
Skinner, Marion
Stranger, The 1924,F 5,20:1
Skinner, Otis
Kismet 1920,N 15,12:2
Kismet 1930,O 31,20:1
Skinner, Otis Mrs (Original Author)
Ne'er to Return Road, The 1921,S 26,18:1
Skipper, William
Up in Central Park 1948,My 27,29:3
Skippy
Topper Takes a Trip 1938,D 30,11:2
Skippy (Dog)
Smiling Along 1939,F 20,13:2
Skipworth, Alison
Raffles 1930,Jl 25,20:4
Outward Bound 1930,S 18,28:3
Du Barry, Woman of Passion 1930,N 3,19:3
Virtuous Husband 1931,My 8,30:2
Night Angel, The 1931,Je 11,28:4
Road to Singapore, The 1931,O 1,25:2
Devotion 1931,O 3,20:2
Tonight or Never 1931,D 18,29:2
High Pressure 1932,F 1,22:3
Sinners in the Sun 1932,My 14,11:5
Madame Racketeer 1932,Jl 23,6:6
Night after Night 1932,O 31,18:4
If I Had a Million 1932,D 3,21:4
Tonight Is Ours 1933,Ja 21,10:6
Lady's Profession, A 1933,Mr 25,13:3
Song of Songs 1933,Jl 20,22:2
Midnight Club 1933,Jl 29,14:2
Tillie and Gus 1933,N 13,21:1
Six of a Kind 1934,Mr 10,18:3
Coming-Out Party 1934,Mr 17,11:3
Wharf Angel 1934,Ap 21,12:1
Shoot the Works 1934,Jl 7,16:5
Notorious Sophie Lang, The 1934,Jl 21,14:2
Captain Hates the Sea, The 1934,N 29,33:2
Here is my Heart 1934,D 22,21:1
Casino Murder Case, The 1935,Ap 17,26:5
Devil is a Woman, The 1935,My 4,17:2
Girl From 10th Avenue, The 1935,My 27,20:6
Becky Sharp 1935,Je 14,27:2
Doubting Thomas 1935,Jl 11,24:2
Shanghai 1935,Jl 20,16:2
Dangerous 1935,D 27,14:1
Princess Comes Across, The 1936,Je 4,27:2
Satan Met a Lady 1936,Jl 23,24:2
Gorgeous Hussy, The 1936,S 5,7:1
Two in a Crowd 1936,O 5,25:1
White Hunter 1936,N 26,39:2
Stolen Holiday 1937,F 1,15:3
King of the Newsboys 1938,Ap 2,18:2
Wide Open Faces 1938,Ap 15,23:2
Skirball, Jack H (Director)
Bride for Sale 1949,N 21,29:4 (In Addenda)
Skirball, Jack H (Producer)
Shadow of a Doubt 1943,Ja 13,18:2
It's in the Bag 1945,Je 11,12:1
Guest Wife 1945,O 18,21:2
So Goes my Love 1946,My 2,3:7
Magnificent Doll 1946,D 9,34:2
Secret Fury, The 1950,Je 22,34:2
Payment on Demand 1951,F 16,21:2
Skjaer, Henry
Ordet 1957,D 16,33:6
Sklar, George (Original Author)
Afraid to Talk 1932,D 19,19:5
Sklar, George (Screenwriter)
First Comes Courage 1943,S 3,15:3

Skobtseva, Irana
Othello 1960,My 16,39:1
Summer to Remember, A; (Seryozha)
1961,N 7,38:1
Skoczylas, Wlodzimierz
Five From Barska Street 1955,Mr 14,29:4
Skoda, Albin
Liebe, Tod und Teufel 1935,My 25,12:2
Last ten Days, The 1956,Ap 12,26:1
Skodler, Stefan
Story of Vickie, The 1958,Ja 30,19:2
Skofic, Milko (Producer)
Fast and Sexy 1960,O 6,51:4
Skoglund, Alice
Adolf Armstrong 1937,O 1,19:5
Skoglund, Bibi
Night is my Future 1963,Ja 9,5:6
Skogsberg, Per
Wild Strawberries 1959,Je 23,37:1
Skolimowski, Jerzy
Identification Marks:None 1965,S 13,42:1
Walkover 1965,S 13,42:1
Skolimowski, Jerzy (Director)
Identification Marks:None 1965,S 13,42:1
Walkover 1965,S 13,42:1
Depart, Le 1967,S 23,20:3
Barrier 1967,S 27,39:3
Skolimowski, Jerzy (Screenwriter)
Knife in the Water 1963,O 29,31:2
Depart, Le 1967,S 23,20:3
Barrier 1967,S 27,39:3
Skolsky, Sidney (Original Author)
Daring Young Man, The 1935,Jl 18,15:2
Eddie Cantor Story, The 1953,D 26,10:2
Skolsky, Sidney (Producer)
Jolson Story, The 1946,O 11,28:2
Eddie Cantor Story, The 1953,D 26,10:2
Skolsky, Sidney (Screenwriter)
Eddie Cantor Story, The 1953,D 26,10:2
Skonglund, Captain (Miscellaneous)
Mediteranncan Holiday 1964,D 16,51:1
Skonieczny, Czeslaw
Kazdemu Wolno Kochac 1933,My 24,24:3
Skorobogatov, K
Pugachev 1938,Jl 4,10:2
Skorochad, Piotr
Zygmunt Kolosowski 1947,N 13,13:3
Skot-Hansen, Morgens (Screenwriter)
Day of Wrath 1948,Ap 26,27:2
Skouen, Arne (Director)
Nine Lives 1959,Ja 6,28:1
Skouen, Arne (Screenwriter)
Nine Lives 1959,Ja 6,28:1
Skouras, Daphne
Grouch, The 1961,F 27,23:2
Skouras, Edith (Screenwriter)
Always Goodbye 1938,Je 25,7:2
Skouras, Plato (Producer)
Villa 1958,D 24,00:0
Francis of Assisi 1961,Jl 29,8:2
Skovortsova, Katia
Zoya 1945,Ap 16,18:6
Skraup, Karl
Vienna Burgtheater 1937,O 27,47:1
Skulme
Last Game, The 1964,O 25,41:5 (Incorrect in this
edition; use 1964,O 26,41:5 elsewhere)
Skuratov, I
Shors 1939,N 21,19:4
Skurkoy, Mary
Greatest Love of All, The 1924,N 11,14:1
Skutezky, Victor (Producer)
Temptation Harbor 1949,My 11,34:7
For Them that Trespass 1950,S 27,37:2
Murder Without Crime 1951,D 26,19:6
Young Wives' Tale 1952,N 4,33:1
Landfall 1953,My 11,25:2
Weak and the Wicked, The 1954,Ag 21,10:3
Yellow Balloon, The 1954,O 13,28:2
It's Great to be Young 1957,D 26,23:3
Skutezky, Victor (Screenwriter)
Quiet Week-End 1948,Ag 20,13:2
Temptation Harbor 1949,My 11,34:7
Skvorecka, Zdenka
Report on the Party and the Guests, A
1968,S 20,37:5
Report on the Party and the Guests, A
1968,S 28,37:1
Slack, Freddie
Follow the Boys 1944,Ap 26,24:6
Slack, Freddie and his orchestra
Reveille With Beverly 1943,Ap 24,17:2
Seven Days Ashore 1944,Ap 26,24:7
Slack, William
Operation Secret 1952,N 6,37:2
Slade, Mark
Voyage to the Bottom of the Sea 1961,Jl 20,32:2
Slade, Olga
Farmer's Wife, The 1930,Ja 7,28:3
Sladkopevtsev, B
Peasants 1935,Ag 29,25:2

Sladkopievtsev, V
Poet and Tsar 1938,Ag 25,15:1
Amangeldy 1939,Je 16,27:4
Sladkopyevatev, Ivan
Fortress on the Volga 1942,D 25,15:3
Slangus, Axel
Virgin Spring, The; Jungfrukallan 1960,N 15,46:1
Slaska, A
Last Stop, The 1949,Mr 22,31:2
Slaska, Aleksandra
Young Chopin 1952,D 25,34:7
Five From Barska Street 1955,Mr 14,29:4
Passenger 1964,S 21,37:3
Slate, Henry
Winged Victory 1944,D 21,16:2
U S S Teakettle 1951,F 24,11:2
Frogmen, The 1951,Je 30,8:6
Rhubarb 1951,Ag 31,12:2
Belle of New York, The 1952,Mr 6,25:6
Just This Once 1952,Mr 18,22:3
Lone Shark 1952,My 12,21:2
Somebody Loves Me 1952,S 25,38:1
Bloodhounds of Broadway 1952,N 15,15:2
Stop, You're Killing Me 1952,D 11,45:3
Miss Sadie Thompson 1953,D 24,9:1
Hit the Deck 1955,Mr 4,17:1
My Sister Eileen 1955,S 23,21:1
Bus Stop 1956,S 1,19:2
Slate, Jack Cpl
Winged Victory 1944,D 21,16:2
Slate, Jeremy
Wives and Lovers 1963,Ag 29,36:1
I'll Take Sweden 1965,Ag 12,30:4
Sons of Katie Elder, The 1965,Ag 26,40:3
Born Losers, The 1967,Ag 19,16:2
Mini-Skirt Mob, The 1968,O 24,55:5
Slate Brothers, The
College Swing 1938,Ap 28,27:2
Slater, Barbara
Holiday Inn 1942,Ag 5,16:1
Happy Go Lucky 1943,Mr 25,25:1
Powers Girl, The 1943,Mr 26,14:2 (In Addenda)
Slater, Barney (Original Author)
It Grows on Trees 1952,N 29,11:2
Three Violent People 1957,F 11,34:2
Tin Star, The 1957,O 24,37:2
Slater, Barney (Screenwriter)
It Grows on Trees 1952,N 29,11:2
Mister Scoutmaster 1953,Ag 29,10:1
Gorilla at Large 1954,Je 12,13:2
Slater, Bill (Narrator)
Kings of the Olympics 1948,Ap 23,28:3
Slater, Bob
Brown Derby, The 1926,Je 14,24:1
Slater, Daphne
Kathy's Love Affair 1952,Jl 3,16:2
Slater, Humphrey (Original Author)
Conspirator 1950,Ap 28,26:2
Slater, John
48 Hours 1944,Je 26,21:2
Murder in Reverse 1947,Ja 11,23:5
Escape 1948,Ag 16,12:2
It Always Rains on Sunday 1949,F 14,15:5
Against the Wind 1949,Je 27,18:3
Passport to Pimlico 1949,O 27,35:2
Prelude to Fame 1950,N 10,35:3
Faithful City 1952,Ap 8,35:2
Long Memory, The 1953,Jl 27,15:2
Man With a Million 1954,Je 29,21:2
Star of India 1956,Ap 28,11:1
Three on a Spree 1961,Ag 31,22:3
Slater, Montagu (Screenwriter)
Daybreak in Udi 1950,Je 2,26:2
Brave Don't Cry, The 1952,N 6,37:2
Man of Africa 1956,O 11,51:1
Slattery, Charles
Ragged Edge, The 1923,Je 5,24:5
Dangerous Money 1924,O 14,21:5
Lunatic at Large, The 1927,F 1,25:1
Slaughter, Frank G (Original Author)
Sangaree 1953,Je 5,19:1
Slaughter, Tod
Murder in the Old Red Barn 1936,Ag 19,18:3
Slavenska, Mia
Ballerina 1938,N 15,27:1
Slavenskaya, Mia (Director)
Great Battle of the Volga, The 1963,My 20,36:1
Slavin, Buster
Devil is a Sissy, The 1936,O 17,21:2
Slavin, George F (Miscellaneous)
Thunder Bay 1953,My 21,39:2
Slavin, George F (Original Author)
Intrigue 1948,Ap 24,11:2
Nevadan, The 1950,Ja 13,19:4
Woman on Pier 13, The 1950,Je 16,28:4
Slavin, George F (Screenwriter)
Intrigue 1948,Ap 24,11:2
Nevadan, The 1950,Ja 13,19:4
Peggy 1950,Jl 21,15:4
Mystery Submarine 1951,F 2,19:2
Red Mountain 1952,Ag 26,19:2
City of Bad Men 1953,O 21,37:6
Desert Sands 1955,N 19,22:7

Slavin, Jo Jo
Passages From James Joyce's Finnegans Wake
1967,O 10,56:1
Slavin, Leo (Screenwriter)
Son of Mongolia 1936,N 21,21:4
Return of Maxim, The 1937,N 2,33:1
Slavinsky, M (Director)
New China, The 1952,Mr 10,18:4
Slavski, Fedor
Transport of Fire 1931,Mr 24,31:2
Golden Mountains 1932,Ap 14,25:3
Sleeman, Philip
So This Is Marriage 1924,D 23,16:2
After Midnight 1927,Ag 16,31:2
Cop, The 1928,N 6,35:1
Cock O' the Walk 1930,Ap 12,23:1
Donovan's Kid 1931,My 22,28:5
Girl From Scotland Yard, The 1937,My 31,11:2
Prisoner of Zenda, The 1937,S 3,12:1
Sleep 'n' Eat
Up Pops the Devil 1931,My 16,13:3
Sleep-'n'-Eat
West of the Pecos 1934,D 29,11:2
Sleep 'n' Eat
Kentucky Kernels 1935,Ja 5,20:2
Murder on a Honeymoon 1935,Mr 4,12:2
Sleeper, Martha
Skinner's big Idea 1928,Mr 27,30:4
Danger Street 1928,S 25,29:4 (In Addenda)
Air Legion, The 1928,N 13,37:1
War Nurse 1930,O 24,31:1
Girls Demand Excitement 1931,F 7,11:1
Ten Cents a Dance 1931,Mr 7,17:2
Tailor-Made Man, A 1931,Ap 25,23:4
Confessions of a Co-Ed 1931,Je 20,20:4
Huddle 1932,Je 17,24:1
Penthouse 1933,S 9,9:2
Broken Dreams 1933,N 21,23:3
Spitfire 1934,Mr 9,22:3
West of the Pecos 1934,D 29,11:2
Scoundrel, The 1935,My 3,23:2
Great God Gold 1935,My 6,22:3
Bells of St Mary's, The 1945,D 7,26:2
Slegenberg, Kurt
Windom's Way 1958,O 1,45:1
Slesar, Henry (Original Author)
Eyes of Annie Jones, The 1964,My 14,39:1
Slesar, Henry (Screenwriter)
Two on a Guillotine 1965,Ja 14,44:3
Slesinger, Tess (Screenwriter)
Good Earth, The 1937,F 3,27:1
Bride Wore Red, The 1937,O 15,18:4
Girls' School 1938,N 3,27:1
Dance, Girl, Dance 1940,O 11,25:2
Remember the Day 1941,D 26,21:2
Tree Grows in Brooklyn, A 1945,Mr 1,25:5
Slezak, Leo
Mad Idea, A; Toller Einfall, Ein 1932,Jl 31,IX,3:4
Toller Einfall, Ein 1934,My 21,20:3
Freut Euch des Lebens 1934,N 3,20:3
Geschichten aus dem Wienerwald; Tales From the
Vienna Woods 1935,N 2,13:3
Tanzmusik 1936,My 26,27:2
Fahrt in Die Jugend, Die 1936,Ag 31,19:2
Mein Liebster Ist ein Jaegersmann 1936,S 15,37:6
Paloma, La 1936,O 21,35:3
Freuhling im Wien 1937,F 6,15:2
World's in Love, The 1937,My 19,27:2
Postillon of Lonjumeau, The 1937,N 20,21:3
Rendezvous in Wien 1938,F 19,19:4
Gasparone 1938,Mr 12,13:4
Husaren Heraus 1938,My 9,11:3
Unsterbliche Melodien; Immortal Melodies
1938,Ap 23,19:3
Magda 1938,S 10,20:2
Liebe im Dreiviertel Takt; Love in Waltz Time
1938,S 24,13:1
Gluecklichste Ehe von Wien, Die; Happiest
Married Couple in Vienna, The 1938,O 8,10:2
Nacht an der Donau, Eine; Night on the Danube,
A 1938,N 19,9:3
Ihr Groesster Erfolg; Her Greatest Success
1939,F 12,20:4
Pompadour, Die 1939,F 27,11:3
Herbst-Monoever; Fall Manoeuvres
1939,Mr 18,9:3
Fasching in Wien 1939,Mr 18,9:2
Blonde Carmen, Die 1939,O 7,11:3
Operetta 1949,Je 6,15:4
Slezak, Margaret
Man on a Tightrope 1953,Je 5,19:1
Slezak, Walter
Queen of Sin and the Spectacle of Sodom and
Gomorrah 1923,Mr 27,24:3 (In Addenda)
Chained 1926,D 15,30:4
Once Upon a Honeymoon 1942,N 13,28:1
This Land Is Mine 1943,My 28,19:1
Fallen Sparrow, The 1943,Ag 20,13:1
Lifeboat 1944,Ja 13,17:1
Step Lively 1944,Jl 27,14:1
Till We Meet Again 1944,Ag 30,15:1
Princess and the Pirate, The 1945,F 10,16:2
Salome, Where She Danced 1945,My 3,27:1

Slezak, Walter — Cont

Spanish Main, The 1945,N 7,20:2
Cornered 1945,D 26,15:1
Sinbad the Sailor 1947,Ja 23,31:2
Born to Kill 1947,My 1,34:2
Riff-Raff 1947,Je 30,25:7
Pirate, The 1948,My 21,19:2
Inspector General, The 1949,D 31,9:2
Yellow Cab Man, The 1950,Mr 27,19:2
Abbott and Costello in the Foreign Legion
   1950,Ag 14,14:4
Spy Hunt 1950,S 8,25:2
Bedtime for Bonzo 1951,Ap 6,31:4
People Will Talk 1951,Ag 30,20:1
Call Me Madam 1953,Mr 26,37:1
White Witch Doctor 1953,Jl 2,19:3
Ten Thousand Bedrooms 1957,Ap 4,37:1
Miracle, The 1959,N 13,25:4
Come September 1961,S 8,34:1
Wonderful World of the Brothers Grimm, The
   1962,Ag 8,35:1
Emil and the Detectives 1964,D 24,8:3
Very Special Favor, A 1965,Ag 26,40:3
Caper of the Golden Bulls, The 1967,Je 22,46:1
Dr Coppelius 1968,D 26,56:1
Slezak, Warner
Die Galavorstellung 1933,D 11,23:4
Slifer, Lizz
Careless Years, The 1957,N 28,57:3
Slim and Sam
Star Spangled Rhythm 1942,D 31,20:1
Slitr, Jrl
Audition 1968,Jl 4,13:2
Sliva, David
Toast to Love 1951,N 7,35:5
Slivkova, Hana
Shop on Main Street, The 1966,Ja 25,47:1
Sliwinski, Jerzy
Dzien Upragniony; Anticipated Day, The
   1939,Mr 13,12:3
Sloan, Brant (Producer)
Kinetia Art, The 1968,Jl 19,30:1
Sloan, Edward (Director)
Soldiers and Women 1930,My 12,27:3
Sloan, Estelle
Night and Day 1946,Jl 26,16:2
Sloan, John R (Director)
To Sir, With Love 1967,Je 15,56:1
Sloan, John R (Producer)
Port Afrique 1956,N 3,27:5
Abandon Ship 1957,Ap 18,35:1
Safecracker, The 1958,Mr 6,32:1
Killers of Kilimanjaro 1960,Ap 7,46:1
Johnny Nobody 1965,N 24,35:1
To Sir, With Love 1967,Je 15,56:1
Sloan, Tod
When Romance Rides 1922,Ap 10,18:2
Hot Heels 1928,My 22,19:3
Sloane, Allan (Screenwriter)
Martin Luther 1953,S 10,22:1
Question 7 1961,S 29,30:2
Sloane, Everett
Citizen Kane 1941,My 2,25:1
Journey Into Fear 1943,Mr 19,15:3
Lady From Shanghai, The 1948,Je 10,28:2
Prince of Foxes 1949,D 24,11:2
Men, The 1950,Jl 21,15:2
Enforcer, The 1951,Ja 26,19:2
Bird of Paradise 1951,Mr 15,37:2
Sirocco 1951,Je 14,31:2
Prince Who Was a Thief, The 1951,Jl 4,13:2
Desert Fox, The 1951,O 18,32:1
Blue Veil, The 1951,O 27,10:5
Sellout, The 1952,My 31,12:7
Way of a Gaucho 1952,N 5,36:2
Big Knife, The 1955,N 9,41:2
Patterns 1956,Mr 28,26:1
Somebody up There Likes Me 1956,Jl 6,16:1
Lust for Life 1956,S 18,39:1
Marjorie Morningstar 1958,Ap 25,32:2
Home from the Hill 1960,Mr 4,19:1
By Love Possessed 1961,Jl 20,32:2
Man From the Diners' Club, The
   1963,Ap 18,39:1
Patsy, The 1964,Ag 13,24:2
Disorderly Orderly, The 1964,D 24,8:3
Sloane, Everett (Narrator)
We Accuse 1945,Je 4,22:4
Sloane, Mike (Original Author)
Top Banana 1954,F 20,8:6
Sloane, Olive
Dreaming Lips 1937,My 20,17:1
Guinea Pig, The 1949,My 2,20:2
Under Capricorn 1949,S 9,28:3
Seven Days to Noon 1950,D 19,41:3
Curtain Up 1953,F 2,17:3
Weak and the Wicked, The 1954,Ag 21,10:3
Brothers in Law 1957,Ag 20,22:1
Sloane, Paul (Director)
Man Must Live, A 1925,Ja 29,12:2
Too Many Kisses 1925,Mr 3,20:1
Shock Punch, The 1925,My 11,14:3
Coming of Amos, The 1925,S 8,29:1
Corporal Kate 1926,D 15,30:4

Hearts in Dixie 1929,F 28,30:3
Cuckoos, The 1930,Ap 26,11:1
Half Shot at Sunrise 1930,O 11,21:3
Traveling Husbands 1931,Ag 8,16:3
Consolation Marriage 1931,O 30,26:4
War Correspondent 1932,Ag 13,18:6
Woman Accused, The 1933,Mr 13,18:2
Straight Is the Way 1934,Ag 29,13:2
Down to Their Last Yacht 1934,S 24,14:1
Geronimo 1940,F 8,18:3
Sun Sets at Dawn, The 1951,Ja 15,13:1
Sloane, Paul (Original Author)
Thunderclap 1921,Jl 31,22:4
Silver Wings 1922,My 18,14:4
Sloane, Paul (Producer)
Sun Sets at Dawn, The 1951,Ja 15,13:1
Sloane, Paul (Screenwriter)
Little Child Shall Lead Them, A 1922,S 2,10:4
Town That Forgot God, The 1922,N 1,16:3
Village Blacksmith, The 1922,N 3,17:5
Texans, The 1938,Jl 28,23:2
Geronimo 1940,F 8,18:3
Sun Sets at Dawn, The 1951,Ja 15,13:1
Sloane, Robert (Original Author)
Cowboy From Brooklyn 1938,Jl 14,17:1
Two Guys From Texas 1948,Ag 28,8:6
Sloboda, Carl (Original Author)
Tea For Three 1927,O 31,22:1
Infernal Machine 1933,Ap 8,16:3
Slobodsky, M (Screenwriter)
Spring 1948,Mr 15,26:2
Sloman, Edward (Director)
Westerners, The 1919,Ag 4,8:3
Ten-Dollar Raise, The 1921,Je 13,16:1
Backbone 1923,Ap 30,11:2
Up the Ladder 1925,My 12,26:2
Price of Pleasure, The 1925,My 26,24:2
Proud Heart 1925,N 3,25:4
Butterflies in the Rain 1926,D 25,10:5
Alias the Deacon 1927,Je 21,29:2
Surrender 1927,O 11,27:1
We Americans 1928,Mr 29,25:3
Girl on the Barge, The 1929,F 26,31:1
Kibitzer, The 1929,D 21,17:1
Lost Zeppelin, The 1930,F 3,17:1
Puttin' on the Ritz 1930,F 15,15:1
Hell's Island 1930,Jl 19,7:5
Conquering Horde, The 1931,Mr 30,25:2
Gun Smoke 1931,Ap 24,27:1
Murder by the Clock 1931,Jl 18,16:6
His Woman 1931,D 5,21:2
Wayward 1932,F 15,13:1
There's Always Tomorrow 1934,N 10,19:2
Sloman, Ted (Director)
Jury's Secret, The 1938,F 4,17:2
Sloman, Vilgot (Director)
My Sister, My Love 1967,F 20,45:2
491 1967,D 21,45:1
Sloman, Vilgot (Screenwriter)
My Sister, My Love 1967,F 20,45:2
Slott, Nate
Hit the Deck 1930,Ja 15,28:6
Sloux, Guy
Great Temptation, The 1942,Jl 10,13:3
Slovina, Vera
Taras Family, The 1946,D 9,34:4
Slutsky, Mikhail (Director)
One Day in Soviet Russia 1941,O 27,21:2
Day After Day 1943,N 6,16:3
Festival in Moscow 1958,F 17,19:1
Slyfield, C O (Miscellaneous)
Fantasia 1940,N 14,28:2
Smak, Luang
King of the White Elephant, The 1941,Ap 5,12:7
Small, Bernard (Producer)
Iroquois Trail, The 1950,O 27,24:4
Texas Rangers, The 1951,Jl 14,7:2
Small, Edward (Producer)
Transatlantic Merry-Go-Round 1934,N 1,25:2
Let 'Em Have It 1935,My 30,21:1
Bride Walks Out, The 1936,Jl 10,15:1
Last of the Mohicans 1936,S 3,17:3
Sea Devils 1937,Mr 16,26:4
New Faces of 1937 1937,Jl 2,25:1
Super-Sleuth 1937,Jl 17,18:1
Toast of New York, The 1937,Jl 23,16:2
Duke of West Point, The 1938,D 16,33:2
King of the Turf 1939,My 8,21:2
South of Pago-Pago 1940,Ag 2,12:2
Kit Carson 1940,N 15,25:3
Son of Monte Cristo, The 1940,D 5,33:1
International Lady 1941,N 11,29:2
Corsican Brothers, The 1942,Ja 16,25:4
Gentleman After Dark, A 1942,Ap 17,21:2
Twin Beds 1942,My 1,23:4
Miss Annie Rooney 1942,Je 8,11:1
Friendly Enemies 1942,Je 22,19:1
Up in Mabel's Room 1944,Ap 22,8:6
Abroad With two Yanks 1944,O 26,19:7
Brewster's Millions 1945,Ap 27,23:2
Getting Gertie's Garter 1946,F 4,21:2
Temptation 1946,D 25,33:6
Return of Monte Cristo, The 1947,Ja 3,16:4

Small, Edward (Producer) — Cont

Raw Deal 1948,Jl 9,11:4
Davy Crockett, Indian Scout 1950,Mr 17,28:3
Valentino 1951,Ap 20,25:1
Lorna Doone 1951,S 21,19:4
Scandal Sheet 1952,Ja 17,23:1
Kansas City Confidential 1952,N 29,11:2
Naked Street, The 1955,O 1,11:2
Monkey on my Back 1957,My 30,23:2
Jack the Giant Killer 1962,Jl 26,17:1
I'll Take Sweden 1965,Ag 12,30:4
Small, Louise
Crusade Against Rackets 1937,Jl 26,15:3
Smallens, Alexander (Miscellaneous)
Fight for Life, The 1940,Mr 7,19:2
World at War, The 1942,S 4,19:1
Smalley, Phillips
Flaming Youth 1923,N 26,15:6
Daughters of Today 1924,Mr 4,17:1
For Sale 1924,Jl 14,11:5
Single Wives 1924,Jl 29,9:2
Charley's Aunt 1925,F 9,15:3
Awful Truth, The 1925,Jl 2,12:4
Soul Mates 1926,Ja 4,16:1
Money Talks 1926,My 11,24:3
Sensation Seekers 1927,Mr 16,28:2
Irresistible Lover, The 1927,O 19,24:4
Tea For Three 1927,O 31,22:1
Man Crazy 1927,D 19,30:1
Sinners in Love 1928,N 19,16:7
True Heaven 1929,F 11,26:3
Charley's Aunt 1930,D 26,18:4
Greeks Had a Word for Them, The 1932,F 4,25:2
Escapade 1932,My 28,18:2
Cocktail Hour 1933,Je 5,18:5
Night Life of the Gods 1935,F 23,14:6
All the King's Horses 1935,Mr 9,19:1
Booloo 1938,Jl 30,10:2
Smallwood, Joe
Some Blondes Are Dangerous 1937,N 3,29:3
Smallwood, Ray C (Director)
Heart of a Child, The 1920,Ap 12,13:1
Best of Luck, The 1920,Jl 5,12:4
Madame Peacock 1920,O 25,18:1
Smart, J Scott
Kiss of Death 1947,Ag 28,28:2
Fat Man, The 1951,My 25,31:2
Smart, Jack
Girl Overboard 1937,Mr 1,15:1
Top of the Town 1937,Mr 27,19:2
When Love Is Young 1937,Ap 17,15:1
100 Men and a Girl 1937,S 18,15:2
Some Like It Hot 1939,My 25,31:2
Smart, Ralph (Director)
Bush Christmas 1947,N 27,50:4
Quartet (The Facts of Life); Facts of Life, The
   (Quartet) 1949,Mr 29,30:3
Never Take No for an Answer 1952,Ap 29,32:2
Curtain Up 1953,F 2,17:3
Always a Bride 1954,My 28,19:2
Smart, Ralph (Original Author)
Bush Christmas 1947,N 27,50:4
Smart, Ralph (Producer)
Bush Christmas 1947,N 27,50:4
Smart, Ralph (Screenwriter)
Ivory Hunter 1952,Ag 19,19:1
Always a Bride 1954,My 28,19:2
Smektunovsky, Innokenty
Watch out for the Automobile 1966,My 23,48:1
Smelick, Donald
Try and Get Me 1951,My 7,22:2
Smetana, Bedrich (Composer)
Bartered Bride, The 1932,N 13,IX,4:2
Smethurst, Jack
Kind of Loving, A 1962,O 2,46:1
Smiah, C C Col
Ranson's Folly 1926,My 31,10:2
Smialowski, I
Young Chopin 1952,D 25,34:7
Smidd, Gorm
David Copperfield 1923,N 6,23:3
Smidje, Ulla
To Bed...Or not to Bed 1963,D 23,18:2
Smight, Jack (Director)
I'd Rather Be Rich 1964,S 3,24:2
Third Day, The 1965,Ag 5,15:3
Harper 1966,Mr 31,43:1
Kaleidoscope 1966,S 23,45:1
Secret War of Harry Frigg, The 1968,Mr 5,34:5
No Way to Treat a Lady 1968,Mr 21,56:1
Smight, Jack (Producer)
Third Day, The 1965,Ag 5,15:3
Smiles, Finch
For Sale 1924,Jl 14,11:5
Lost World, The 1925,F 9,15:3
Teaser, The 1925,Je 15,10:1
Love Thrill, The 1927,My 10,24:5
Behind That Curtain 1929,Jl 1,31:2
Smiley, George
New Faces 1954,F 20,8:7
Smiley, Joseph
Old Home Week 1925,My 25,21:3
Wild, Wild Susan 1925,Ag 5,12:4
Untamed Lady, The 1926,Mr 16,22:5

Smiley, Joseph — Cont
Aloma of the South Seas 1926,My 17,19:1
Show-Off, The 1926,Ag 23,9:1
Potters, The 1927,Ja 18,23:1
Smiley, Ralph
My Favorite Spy 1951,D 26,19:3
Bullet for Joey, A 1955,Ap 16,12:1
Smirke, Charlie
Galloping Major, The 1951,D 17,27:2
Smirnaki, Maria
Germans Strike Again, The 1949,Ap 14,29:4
Smirnitsky, Valentin
Ballad of Love, A 1966,F 21,51:1
Smirnof, Igor
Childhood of Maxim Gorky 1938,S 28,29:3
Smirnov, Boris
Man of Music 1953,My 11,25:2
Smirnov, Nikolai
And Quiet Flows the Don 1960,My 25,45:2
Smirnov, Serghei (Screenwriter)
Italiano Brava Gente 1966,F 4,20:1
Smirnova, Anna
They Wanted Peace 1940,Ja 8,11:3
Lad From our Town 1943,O 7,26:2
No Greater Love 1944,F 25,23:3
Road Home, The 1947,My 2,28:3
Smirnova, D
Private Ivan 1957,Ap 3,28:2
Smirnova, Dina
Coffin Maker, The 1928,O 9,35:1
She Goes to War 1929,Je 10,23:1
Smirnova, L
Miners of the Don 1951,N 12,21:2
Smirnova, Lydia
Welcome Kostya! 1965,N 22,48:2
Marriage of Baezaminov, The 1966,Je 11,20:2
Smirnova, Maria (Screenwriter)
Village Teacher 1948,Jl 5,8:4
Country Doctor, The 1953,F 16,16:2
Journey Beyond Three Seas 1960,Ap 11,42:6
Smith, Al
Last Man, The 1932,S 17,18:4
Smith, Albert E (Director)
My Man 1924,F 11,18:3
Smith, Albert J
Last Mile, The 1932,Ag 26,20:3
Smith, Alexis
Dive Bomber 1941,Ag 30,10:2
Smiling Ghost, The 1941,S 26,26:5
Gentleman Jim 1942,N 26,40:3
Constant Nymph, The 1943,Jl 24,8:2
Thank Your Lucky Stars 1943,O 2,19:2
Adventures of Mark Twain, The 1944,My 4,25:5
Doughgirls, The 1944,Ag 31,14:1
Hollywood Canteen 1944,D 16,19:2
Horn Blows at Midnight, The 1945,Ap 21,18:2
Conflict 1945,Je 16,10:2
Rhapsody in Blue 1945,Je 28,22:2
San Antonio 1945,D 29,19:5
One More Tomorrow 1946,My 25,12:2
Of Human Bondage 1946,Jl 6,11:2
Night and Day 1946,Jl 26,16:2
Stallion Road 1947,Ap 5,12:5
Two Mrs Carrolls, The 1947,Ap 7,20:1
Woman in White, The 1948,My 8,12:2
Decision of Christopher Blake, The
    1948,D 11,12:2
Whiplash 1948,D 27,16:3
South of St Louis 1949,Mr 7,17:2
Any Number Can Play 1949,Jl 1,14:4
One Last Fling 1949,Jl 1,14:6
Montana 1950,F 4,9:2
Wyoming Mail 1950,O 23,26:5
Undercover Girl 1950,N 8,37:2
Here Comes the Groom 1951,S 21,19:2
Turning Point, The 1952,N 15,15:2
Split Second 1953,My 13,34:2
Sleeping Tiger, The 1954,O 9,8:7
Eternal Sea, The 1955,Je 10,16:2
Beau James 1957,Je 27,21:1
This Happy Feeling 1958,Je 19,28:2
Young Philadelphians, The 1959,My 22,32:1
Smith, Anderson
Darling of New York, The 1924,Ja 18,20:1
Smith, Ann
Tony Draws a Horse 1951,My 15,38:6
Smith, Archie
Across the River 1965,Ap 27,27:1
Smith, Art
Native Land 1942,My 12,16:3
Edge of Darkness 1943,Ap 10,12:4
None Shall Escape 1944,Ap 7,23:2
Uncertain Glory 1944,Ap 8,9:2
Mr Winkle Goes to War 1944,Ag 3,16:1
Tree Grows in Brooklyn, A 1945,Mr 1,25:5
Brute Force 1947,Jl 17,16:2
Ride the Pink Horse 1947,O 9,32:3
Body and Soul 1947,N 10,21:2
T-Men 1948,Ja 23,28:3
Double Life, A 1948,F 20,19:1
Letters From an Unknown Woman
    1948,Ap 29,20:6
Mr Peabody and the Mermaid 1948,Ag 14,6:5
Caught 1949,F 18,26:4

South of St Louis 1949,Mr 7,17:2
Manhandled 1949,My 26,34:2
Red, Hot and Blue 1949,O 20,39:2
South Sea Sinner 1950,Ja 16,18:4
In a Lonely Place 1950,My 18,37:2
Quicksand 1950,Je 16,28:4
Next Voice You Hear, The 1950,Je 30,18:2
Killer That Stalked New York, The
    1951,Ja 5,17:2
Try and Get Me 1951,My 7,22:2
Just for You 1952,O 9,40:6
Smith, Bernard (Producer)
How the West Was Won 1963,Ap 1,54:1
Cheyenne Autumn 1964,D 24,8:1
7 Women 1966,My 5,59:1
Smith, Betty (Original Author)
Tree Grows in Brooklyn, A 1945,Mr 1,25:5
Smith, Bill
Mating Game, The 1959,Ap 30,37:1
Atlantis the Lost Continent 1961,My 27,12:1
Smith, Brendan (Producer)
Playboy of the Western World, The
    1963,Mr 19,8:2
Smith, Brian
No Place for Jennifer 1951,Jl 17,31:2
Browning Version, The 1951,O 30,33:2
Betrayed 1954,S 9,36:1
Barretts of Wimpole Street, The 1957,Ja 18,15:3
It's Great to be Young 1957,D 26,23:3
Smith, Bruce Meredith
Cry, the Beloved Country 1952,Ja 24,23:2
Smith, Buddy
Roughneck, The 1924,D 3,14:1
Smith, C Aubrey
Witching Hour, The 1916,D 11,7:3
Bohemian Girl, The 1923,F 5,18:2
Rejected Woman, The 1924,My 5,18:3
Bachelor Father, The 1931,F 2,23:1
Perfect Alibi, The 1931,Ap 20,16:3
Daybreak 1931,Je 1,15:1
Never the Twain Shall Meet 1931,Je 6,15:5
Just a Gigolo 1931,Je 13,20:4
Man in Possession, The 1931,Jl 18,16:6
Son of India 1931,Jl 25,11:6
Guilty Hands 1931,Ag 29,16:3
Phantom of Paris, The 1931,N 14,15:3
Surrender 1931,N 28,20:4
Polly of the Circus 1932,Mr 19,11:2
Tarzan, the Ape Man 1932,Mr 28,11:2
But the Flesh Is Weak 1932,Ap 16,11:2
Love Me Tonight 1932,Ag 19,20:6
Trouble in Paradise 1932,N 9,28:5
No More Orchids 1933,Ja 2,29:2
Luxury Liner 1933,F 3,21:3
They Just Had to Get Married 1933,F 13,11:4
Secrets 1933,Mr 16,21:2
Barbarian, The 1933,My 13,16:2
Adorable 1933,My 19,20:2
Morning Glory 1933,Ag 18,18:2
Bombshell 1933,O 21,11:2
Queen Christina 1933,D 27,23:3
House of Rothschild, The 1934,Mr 15,27:2
Gambling Lady 1934,Ap 5,25:2
One More River 1934,Ag 10,21:1
Bulldog Drummond Strikes Back 1934,Ag 16,20:2
Cleopatra 1934,Ag 17,12:1
Scarlet Empress, The 1934,S 15,20:2
Caravan 1934,S 28,27:1
We Live Again 1934,N 2,27:2
Firebird, The 1934,N 15,25:2
Lives of a Bengal Lancer, The 1935,Ja 12,12:2
Clive of India 1935,Ja 18,29:1
Gilded Lily, The 1935,F 9,11:2
Right to Live, The 1935,F 16,9:1
Florentine Dagger, The 1935,Ap 27,20:6
China Seas 1935,Ag 10,16:4
Crusades, The 1935,Ag 22,21:3
Jalna 1935,S 14,8:4
Transatlantic Tunnel 1935,O 28,16:2
Little Lord Fauntleroy 1936,Ap 3,27:1
Romeo and Juliet 1936,Ag 21,12:2
Garden of Allah, The 1936,N 20,27:2
Lloyds of London 1936,N 26,39:1
Wee Willie Winkie 1937,Jl 24,12:1
Prisoner of Zenda, The 1937,S 3,12:1
Hurricane, The 1937,N 10,31:2
Thoroughbreds Don't Cry 1937,N 26,27:4
Four Men and a Prayer 1938,My 7,18:1
Kidnapped 1938,My 28,9:2
Sixty Glorious Years 1938,N 18,25:2
East Side of Heaven 1939,My 5,29:3
Sun Never Sets, The 1939,Je 9,26:2
Five came Back 1939,Jl 5,20:2
Four Feathers 1939,Ag 4,11:1
Under-Pup, The 1939,S 5,21:2
Eternally Yours 1939,O 7,11:2
Another Thin Man 1939,N 24,29:1
Balalaika 1939,D 15,33:2
City of Chance 1940,Ja 22,11:3
Rebecca 1940,Mr 29,25:2
Waterloo Bridge 1940,My 17,23:2
Bill of Divorcement, A 1940,Jl 12,11:2
Beyond Tomorrow 1940,S 27,27:1

Smith, C Aubrey — Cont
Little Bit of Heaven, A 1940,N 8,24:2
Maisie Was a Lady 1941,F 13,25:2
Free and Easy 1941,Ap 3,29:4
Dr Jekyll and Mr Hyde 1941,Ag 13,13:2
Forever and a Day 1943,Mr 13,9:2
Two Tickets to London 1943,Jl 3,11:2
Flesh and Fantasy 1943,N 18,29:1
Madame Curie 1943,D 17,23:1
Adventures of Mark Twain, The 1944,My 4,25:5
White Cliffs of Dover, The 1944,My 12,15:2
Sensations of 1945 1944,Jl 7,13:2
And Then There Were None 1945,N 1,20:2
Cluny Brown 1946,Je 3,27:3
Rendezvous With Annie 1946,S 23,29:3
Unconquered 1947,O 11,11:2
Ideal Husband, An 1948,Ja 15,28:2
Little Women 1949,Mr 11,33:2
Smith, Charles
General, The 1927,F 8,21:1
Tom Brown's School Days 1940,Je 28,22:2
Adventure in Washington 1941,Ag 1,11:3
Henry Aldrich for President 1941,O 18,22:2
Major and the Minor, The 1942,S 17,21:3
Guy Named Joe, A 1943,D 24,17:2
God is my Co-Pilot 1945,Mr 24,22:6
Out of This World 1945,Je 7,25:2
Three Little Girls in Blue 1946,S 26,32:3
Trouble With Women, The 1947,Jl 14,14:4
Adventure in Baltimore 1949,Ap 29,27:2
Two Weeks With Love 1950,N 24,31:2
Smith, Clifford (Director)
Wild Bill Hickok 1923,N 21,22:1
Smith, Constance
Mudlark, The 1950,D 25,25:1
Thirteenth Letter, The 1951,F 22,27:2
Lucky Nick Cain 1951,Ap 23,21:2
Smoke Jumpers 1952,Mr 22,9:6
Lure of the Wilderness 1952,O 4,15:2
Taxi 1953,Ja 22,20:3
Treasure of the Golden Condor 1953,My 23,19:2
Man in the Attic 1954,F 6,17:2
Smith, Cyril
Good Companions, The 1933,O 10,24:1
Friday the 13th 1934,My 15,18:1
Alias Bulldog Drummond 1935,S 10,26:2
Born for Glory 1935,O 21,22:4
Storm in a Teacup 1938,Mr 22,18:4
Challenge, The 1939,O 2,15:2
Sidewalks of London 1940,F 15,15:1
Conspirator 1950,Ap 28,26:2
Rocking Horse Winner, The 1950,Je 9,29:2
Appointment With Crime 1951,F 19,19:3
Panic in the Parlor 1957,D 18,45:1
Smith, D A Clarke
White Face 1933,D 4,22:3
Man Who Knew too Much, The 1935,Mr 23,11:2
Smith, David (Director)
Black Beauty 1921,F 21,16:1
Masters of Men 1923,My 15,22:1
Pioneer Trails 1923,N 12,15:3
Captain Blood 1924,S 9,19:1
Pampered Youth 1925,F 10,20:1
Baree, Son of Kazan 1925,My 19,24:2
Steele of the Royal Mounted 1925,Je 18,16:3
Smith, Debbie
One and Only Genuine Original Family Band,
    The 1968,Mr 22,55:1
Smith, Dodie (Original Author)
Call it a Day 1937,My 7,29:2
Randolph Family 1945,Mr 13,19:4
one Hundred and One Dalmations
    1961,F 11,27:1
Smith, Dodie (Screenwriter)
Uninvited, The 1944,F 21,19:3
Darling, How Could You! 1951,N 9,22:4
Smith, Donald
Marriage Playground, The 1929,D 14,22:4
Smith, Dudley
Circus Ace, The 1927,Jl 6,23:2
Smith, Earl
Macomber Affair, The 1947,Ap 21,21:2
Smith, Edward
Pacific Adventure 1947,N 26,18:2
Smith, Eleanor Lady (Original Author)
Red Wagon 1936,Je 22,22:1
Men In her Life, The 1941,D 12,35:1
Man in Grey, The 1945,N 30,18:6
Caravan 1949,Ap 21,30:4
Smith, Emmett
To Have and Have Not 1944,O 12,24:1
Jackie Robinson Story, The 1950,My 17,36:1
Snows of Kilimanjaro, The 1952,S 19,19:2
Smith, Ethel
Bathing Beauty 1944,Je 28,20:1
George White's Scandals 1945,O 11,26:2
Easy to Wed 1946,Jl 12,14:2
C'mon Let's Live a Little 1967,My 4,34:1
Smith, Frank Leon (Original Author)
Melody in Spring 1934,Mr 31,8:2
Smith, Frederick E (Original Author)
633 Squadron 1964,Je 25,25:1

Smith, G Albert
Stolen Heaven 1931,F 14,11:4
Smith, Garret (Original Author)
Old Hutch 1936,D 7,27:4
Smith, Gerald Oliver
School for Wives 1925,Ap 1,21:3
Man I Marry, The 1936,O 31,24:3
When You're in Love 1937,F 19,15:2
Girl Overboard 1937,Mr 1,15:1
Top of the Town 1937,Mr 27,19:2
100 Men and a Girl 1937,S 18,15:2
Invisible Enemy 1938,Ap 30,18:2
Gateway 1938,Ag 8,9:2
Tish 1942,S 18,25:2
Sailor Takes a Wife, The 1946,Mr 1,17:2
That Forsyte Woman 1949,N 11,31:2
Smith, Geraldine
Flesh 1968,S 27,36:1
Smith, Gunboat
Manhattan 1924,O 29,18:1
Shock Punch, The 1925,My 11,14:3
Let's Get Married 1926,Mr 2,22:1
Say It Again 1926,Je 7,23:2
Great Gatsby, The 1926,N 22,28:3
Wings 1927,Ag 13,10:4
We're all Gamblers 1927,O 12,30:6
Smith, H Allen (Original Author)
Rhubarb 1951,Ag 31,12:2
Smith, Hal
Great Race, The 1965,S 16,00:0
Smith, Hal (Original Author)
Music in Manhattan 1944,O 7,11:2
Smith, Hal (Screenwriter)
Night Editor 1946,Mr 30,11:2
Smith, Hamilton (Original Author)
Man Unconquerable, The 1922,Jl 17,16:3
Smith, Harold Jacob (Original Author)
River's Edge, The 1957,Ap 12,20:2
Smith, Harold Jacob (Screenwriter)
River's Edge, The 1957,Ap 12,20:2
Defiant Ones, The 1958,S 25,29:1
Inherit the Wind 1960,O 13,41:1
Smith, Harry
Hell's Highway 1932,S 26,18:2
Smith, Harry B (Original Author)
Sweethearts 1938,D 23,16:2
Smith, Harry James (Original Author)
Tailor Made Man, A 1922,O 16,20:2
Smith, Helen Vreeland (Original Author)
Moon Over her Shoulder 1941,N 5,31:2
Smith, Henry
Bimbo the Great 1961,Je 29,26:1
Smith, Herbert
Taste of Honey, A 1962,My 1,33:3
Smith, Hinton (Miscellaneous)
In His Steps 1936,O 29,31:1
Smith, Howard
Her Kind of Man 1946,My 4,10:6
Kiss of Death 1947,Ag 28,28:2
Call Northside 777 1948,F 19,29:2
State of the Union 1948,Ap 23,28:1
Street with no Name, The 1948,Jl 15,26:6
Death of a Salesman 1951,D 21,21:3
Never Wave at a Wac 1953,Ap 24,30:2
Caddy, The 1953,S 18,16:6
Face in the Crowd, A 1957,My 29,33:1
Don't Go Near the Water 1957,N 15,37:1
No Time for Sergeants 1958,My 30,13:2
Brass Bottle, The 1964,My 21,42:1
Smith, Howard (Screenwriter)
Silver Slave, The 1928,Ja 3,28:2
Smith, Howard Ellis (Screenwriter)
Man Who Broke the Bank at Monte Carlo, The
1935,N 15,20:2
Professional Soldier 1936,Ja 30,14:2
It Had to Happen 1936,F 15,18:6
To Mary-With Love 1936,Ag 27,16:1
Think Fast, Mr Moto 1937,Ag 16,15:3
Smith, Howard I
Wind Across the Everglades 1958,S 12,21:1
Smith, Howard K
Best Man, The 1964,Ap 7,29:1
Smith, J Marshall
Born to Dance 1936,D 5,16:1
Smith, Jack
Mystery of the Hooded Horsemen, The
1937,Ag 13,13:2
On Moonlight Bay 1951,Jl 27,15:2
Illiac Passion, The 1968,Ap 19,40:1
Smith, James J
Happy Land 1943,D 9,33:3
Smith, Jamie
Faithful City 1952,Ap 8,35:2
Smith, Janet Adam (Miscellaneous)
Annapurna 1953,D 14,45:4
Smith, Jimmie
Trouble With Women, The 1947,Jl 14,14:4
Smith, Joanne
Sutter's Gold 1936,Mr 27,25:2
Smith, Joe
Manhattan Parade 1931,D 25,29:2
Heart of New York, The 1932,Mr 2,15:3
Two Tickets to Broadway 1951,N 22,47:2

Smith, John
Seven Angry Men 1955,Ap 2,15:2
Desert Sands 1955,N 19,22:7
Bold and the Brave, The 1956,My 26,15:2
Friendly Persuasion 1956,N 2,30:1
Fury at Showdown 1957,Ap 20,21:3
Circus World 1964,Je 26,34:2
Smith, Justin
Jazz Singer, The 1953,Ja 14,27:3
How to Succeed in Business Without Really
Trying 1967,Mr 10,30:1
Smith, Kate
Hello, Everybody 1933,Ja 30,9:4
This Is the Army 1943,Jl 29,11:6
Smith, Katherine
Intruder, The 1962,My 15,48:1
Smith, Kathleen
Incident, The 1967,N 6,65:1
Smith, Keely
Hey Boy! Hey Girl! 1959,Ag 6,18:3
Smith, Kent
Garden Murder Case, The 1936,Mr 2,13:2
Back Door to Heaven 1939,Ap 20,21:2
Cat People 1942,D 7,22:2
Hitler's Children 1943,F 25,27:1
Forever and a Day 1943,Mr 13,9:2
This Land Is Mine 1943,My 28,19:1
Three Russian Girls 1944,F 5,13:2
Curse of the Cat People, The 1944,Mr 4,11:1
Youth Runs Wild 1944,S 2,17:2
Spiral Staircase, The 1946,F 7,29:3
Nora Prentiss 1947,F 22,16:2
Magic Town 1947,O 8,29:2
Voice of the Turtle, The 1947,D 26,22:4
Jigsaw 1949,My 30,9:4
Fountainhead, The 1949,Jl 9,8:5
My Foolish Heart 1950,Ja 20,29:2
Damned Don't Cry, The 1950,Ap 8,9:2
This Side of the Law 1950,Jl 7,15:2
Paula 1952,Jl 16,21:2
Sayonara 1957,D 6,39:4
Sayonara 1957,D 6,39:4
Imitation General 1958,Ag 21,22:2
Badlanders, The 1958,S 4,33:1
Party Girl 1958,O 29,30:1
Mugger, The 1959,Je 25,20:7
Earth Is Mine, The 1959,Je 27,13:1
Strangers When we Meet 1960,Je 30,22:2
Susan Slade 1961,N 11,14:6
Moon Pilot 1962,Ap 6,30:2
Balcony, The 1963,Mr 22,7:1
Distant Trumpet, A 1964,My 28,40:1
Youngblood Hawke 1964,N 6,30:1
Young Lovers, The 1965,F 11,45:1
Trouble With Angels, The 1966,Ap 7,45:1
Games 1967,S 18,58:2
Smith, Kent (Narrator)
Design for Death 1948,Je 11,27:2
Smith, Kim
Little Ones, The 1965,S 16,55:2
Smith, Kitty (Original Author)
Code of the Wilderness, The 1924,Jl 1,21:4
Smith, Lew
To Please a Lady 1950,O 27,24:3
Smith, Lois
East of Eden 1955,Mr 10,33:1
Strange Lady in Town 1955,My 21,11:1
Smith, Loring
Shadow of the Thin Man 1941,N 21,23:2
Keep 'Em Flying 1941,N 27,29:2
Close-Up 1948,Ap 5,24:2
Citizen Saint 1948,My 28,28:2
Pat and Mike 1952,Je 19,32:6
Clown, The 1953,Ja 29,25:1
Happy Anniversary 1959,N 11,41:1
Cardinal, The 1963,D 13,41:1
Hurry Sundown 1967,Mr 24,22:1
Smith, Maggie
V I P's, The 1963,S 20,29:1
Pumpkin Eater, The 1964,N 10,58:1
Young Cassidy 1965,Mr 23,35:1
Othello 1966,F 2,24:1
Honey Pot, The 1967,My 23,52:1
Hot Millions 1968,S 20,42:1
Smith, Matthew
Barretts of Wimpole Street, The 1934,S 29,12:2
Smith, Maurice E (Producer)
Glory Stompers, The 1968,Mr 28,52:4
Smith, Mike
Having a Wild Weekend 1965,Ag 19,35:1
Smith, Mildred Joanne
No Way Out 1950,Ag 17,23:1
Smith, Minna Carolina (Original Author)
Rose of the Golden West 1927,S 26,27:1
Smith, Muriel
Moulin Rouge 1953,F 11,33:5
Crowning Experience, The 1960,O 24,25:3
Voice of the Hurricane 1964,Je 3,36:4
Smith, Muriel (Narrator)
Strange Victory 1948,S 27,27:2

Smith, Noel (Director)
Clash of the Wolves, The 1925,N 18,27:4
Over the Goal 1937,O 16,22:2
Mystery House 1938,Je 29,15:5
Secret Service of the Air 1939,Mr 2,19:2
Ladies Must Live 1940,S 6,25:3
Always a Bride 1940,N 21,43:3
Case of the Black Parrot, The 1941,Ja 10,23:3
Nurse's Secret, The 1941,Je 6,25:7
Burma Convoy 1941,O 7,26:7
Smith, Oliver
His Double Life 1933,D 16,12:3
Smith, Oscar
Marriage Clause, The 1926,S 28,30:2
Man Power 1927,Jl 26,17:1
Wizard, The 1927,N 28,18:5
Beau Sabreur 1928,Ja 23,18:3
At Yale 1928,Jl 30,21:2
Close Harmony 1929,Ap 29,29:2
Guilty as Hell 1932,Ag 6,14:5
Cocktail Hour 1933,Je 5,18:5
Hold 'Em Yale 1935,Ap 27,20:6
Hold 'Em Navy 1937,N 6,14:2
Smith, Pam
Misty 1961,Jl 18,33:2
Smith, Patricia
Spirit of St Louis, The 1957,F 22,25:1
Bachelor Party, The 1957,Ap 10,37:2
Smith, Paul
Retreat Hell! 1952,F 20,26:2
Smith, Paul (Composer)
Snow White and the Seven Dwarfs
1938,Ja 14,21:1 (In Addenda)
Smith, Paul Gerard (Miscellaneous)
Thrill of a Lifetime 1937,D 9,30:2
Smith, Paul Gerard (Original Author)
Son of a Sailor 1933,N 30,38:4
Hold 'Em Yale 1935,Ap 27,20:6
Just Around the Corner 1938,D 3,11:2
Private Buckaroo 1942,Je 25,27:4
Here We Go Again 1942,O 12,12:3
Smith, Paul Gerard (Screenwriter)
F-Man 1936,My 4,16:1
Turn off the Moon 1937,My 20,17:2
Conga Nights, La 1940,Je 5,33:5
Tanks a Million 1941,O 9,27:2
Hurry, Charlie, Hurry 1941,N 12,31:3
You're in the Army Now 1941,D 26,21:4
Jail House Blues 1942,F 6,23:2
Wild Bill Hickok Rides 1942,F 7,13:5
Give Out, Sisters 1942,Ag 28,22:3
Here We Go Again 1942,O 12,12:3
Untamed Fury 1947,Ap 26,10:6
Harpoon 1948,D 9,48:8
Smith, Paul J (Composer)
Pinocchio 1940,F 8,18:3
Victory Through Air Power 1943,Jl 19,13:1
Cinderella 1950,F 23,33:1
Smith, Queenie
Mississippi 1935,Ap 18,27:2
Show Boat 1936,My 15,29:4
On Your Toes 1939,O 21,12:2
From This Day Forward 1946,Ap 20,16:2
Killers, The 1946,Ag 29,24:2
Nocturne 1946,N 11,42:2
Long Night, The 1947,S 17,31:2
Sleep, My Love 1948,F 19,29:4
Great Rupert, The 1950,Ap 14,27:2
Emergency Wedding 1950,D 22,19:2
First Legion, The 1951,Ap 28,9:2
My Sister Eileen 1955,S 23,21:1
Smith, Reginald
Heart Song 1934,Je 6,24:6
My Song For You 1935,My 27,20:6
Smith, Robert
Call out the Marines 1942,Ja 26,18:3
Obliging Young Lady 1942,F 13,24:4
Smith, Robert (Original Author)
You Came Along 1945,Jl 5,7:2
Second Woman, The 1951,F 2,19:2
Buster Keaton Story, The 1957,Ap 22,31:6
Five Pennies, The 1959,Je 19,30:1
Smith, Robert (Producer)
Second Woman, The 1951,F 2,19:2
Magic Face, The 1951,O 1,19:2
Invasion USA 1953,Ap 30,39:4
Buster Keaton Story, The 1957,Ap 22,31:6
St Louis Blues 1958,Ap 12,13:1
Smith, Robert (Screenwriter)
You Came Along 1945,Jl 5,7:2
I Walk Alone 1948,Ja 22,36:3
Quicksand 1950,Je 16,28:4
Magic Face, The 1951,O 1,19:2
Sudden Fear 1952,Ag 8,9:2
Invasion USA 1953,Ap 30,39:4
99 River Street 1953,O 3,14:2
St Louis Blues 1958,Ap 12,13:1
Platinum High School 1960,My 26,37:3
Smith, Robert B (Original Author)
Sweethearts 1938,D 23,16:2

Smith, Robert Paul (Original Author)
Tender Trap, The 1955,N 11,29:6
Smith, Roberta
What a Life 1939,O 12,33:1
Girls Under 21 1940,N 11,22:4
Mayor of Forty-Fourth Street, The
1942,Je 11,27:4
Smith, Roger
Man of a Thousand Faces 1957,Ag 14,21:1
Operation Mad Ball 1957,N 21,38:1
Auntie Mame 1958,D 5,39:1
Never Say Anything Small 1959,F 12,23:1
Smith, Roger (Screenwriter)
Up the Junction 1968,Mr 14,51:1
Smith, S W (Producer)
Frightened Lady 1941,N 10,21:3
At Dawn We Die 1943,My 8,19:2
Smith, Salley
Young, The Evil and the Savage, The
1968,Ag 15,46:2
Smith, Sammy
Act One 1963,D 27,17:2
How to Succeed in Business Without Really
Trying 1967,Mr 10,30:1
Smith, Sara B (Original Author)
My Girl Tisa 1948,F 21,9:2
Smith, Sebastian
White Cargo 1930,F 24,18:1
Smith, Shawn
Long Wait, The 1954,Jl 3,9:2
Smith, Shelley (Original Author)
Running Man, The 1963,O 3,31:1
Smith, Shelley (Screenwriter)
Tiger Bay 1959,D 15,50:1
Smith, Shirley
Pretty Boy Floyd 1960,N 3,49:2
Smith, Sid
Ne'er Do-Well, The 1923,My 1,24:3
Smith, Stanley
Sophomore, The 1929,Ag 24,11:5
Sweetie 1929,O 26,15:1
Honey 1930,Mr 29,23:1
King of Jazz 1930,My 3,23:1
Love Among the Millionaires 1930,Jl 5,17:4
Queen High 1930,Ag 9,16:5
Good News 1930,S 6,9:2
Follow the Leader 1930,D 6,21:3
Stepping Sisters 1932,Ja 9,21:1
Flight Command 1941,Ja 17,21:2
Smith, Sydney
Frogmen, The 1951,Je 30,8:6
Fury at Showdown 1957,Ap 20,21:3
No Time for Sergeants 1958,My 30,13:2
Smith, Ted
We're Going to Be Rich 1938,Jl 4,10:2
Smith, Thorne (Original Author)
Night Life of the Gods 1935,F 23,14:6
Topper 1937,Ag 20,21:2
Topper Takes a Trip 1938,D 30,11:2
Turnabout 1940,Jl 27,17:6
Topper Returns 1941,Mr 28,26:6
I Married a Witch 1942,N 20,27:2
Smith, Truman
Phenix City Story, The 1955,S 3,9:1
Monte Carlo Story, The 1958,F 13,23:2
1 ▮ 1 1961,N 8,41:1
Smith, Tucker
West Side Story 1961,O 19,39:3
Smith, Vernon (Original Author)
Cohens and Kellys in Trouble, The
1933,Ap 17,16:4
Smith, Vivian
Hearts in Dixie 1929,F 28,30:3
Smith, Wallace (Original Author)
Not Quite Decent 1929,My 6,30:4
Big Time 1929,S 9,30:2
Beau Bandit 1930,Je 14,9:4
Captain Hates the Sea, The 1934,N 29,33:2
Smith, Wallace (Screenwriter)
Venus of Venice 1927,My 3,25:1
Silver Horde, The 1930,O 25,20:6
Captain Hates the Sea, The 1934,N 29,33:2
Bordertown 1935,Ja 24,22:5
Gay Desperado, The 1936,O 9,31:4
Her Husband Lies 1937,Mr 18,20:1
Smith, Wayne
Heart is a Lonely Hunter, The 1968,Ag 1,24:1
Smith, Webb (Screenwriter)
Snow White and the Seven Dwarfs
1938,Ja 14,21:1 (In Addenda)
Pinocchio 1940,F 8,18:3
Smith, Whispering Jack
Happy Days 1930,F 14,20:1
Smith, William A (Original Author)
Dark of the Sun 1968,Jl 4,13:1
Smith, Winchell (Original Author)
Saphead, The 1921,F 14,12:2
Turn to the Right 1922,Ja 24,11:1
Boomerang 1925,Jl 1,16:1
Lightnin 1925,Jl 22,14:4
Fortune Hunter, The 1928,Ja 10,28:4
Brewster's Millions 1935,Ap 8,23:3
Brewster's Millions 1945,Ap 27,23:2

Three on a Spree 1961,Ag 31,22:3
Smith, Winchell (Screenwriter)
Miss Brewster's Millions 1926,Mr 8,17:1
Smith, Winfield
Snafu 1945,D 26,15:2
Smith, Wonderful
Top Sergeant Mulligan 1941,N 12,31:3
Over my Dead Body 1942,D 26,15:2
Smithers, William
Attack! 1956,S 20,29:4
Smithson, Laura
Men Are not Gods 1937,Ja 19,28:1
Smitter, Wessel (Original Author)
Reaching for the Sun 1941,My 8,21:1
Smogyi, Ann
Szensacio 1937,Mr 1,15:2
Smoktunovsky, Innokenti
Letter That Was Never Sent, The 1962,N 19,39:2
Hamlet 1964,S 15,32:1
Nine Days of one Year 1964,D 29,19:1
Hamlet 1966,Mr 16,48:1
Smolik, Frantisek
Merry Wives, The 1940,N 12,28:3
Krakatit 1951,Ap 30,16:2
Sweet Light in a Dark Room 1966,Je 30,28:1
Smolinska, Janina
Song of the Flame 1930,My 7,24:5
Smordoni, Irene
Shoe-Shine 1947,Ag 27,19:2
Smordoni, Rinaldo
Shoe-Shine 1947,Ag 27,19:2
Smosarska, Jadwiga
Noc Listopadowa 1933,My 1,10:3
Ulan I Dziewczyna 1933,O 9,22:3
Prokurator 1934,My 22,28:4
Milosc Wszystko Zwycieza 1936,Ja 28,15:3
Love or a Kingdom 1937,D 4,21:1
Smutna, Dana
Sweet Light in a Dark Room 1966,Je 30,28:1
Smyrner, Ann
Journey to the Seventh Planet 1962,My 25,28:3
Code 7...Victim 5 1965,My 20,52:1
House of 1,000 Dolls 1968,Mr 14,51:4
Snayal, Pahari
Householder, The 1963,O 22,43:2
Snead, Sam
Follow the Sun 1951,Ap 26,34:4
Snegoff, Leonid
Broken Hearts 1926,Mr 3,26:1
Forbidden Woman, The 1927,O 31,22:1
Man Who Dared, The 1933,S 9,9:3
After Tonight 1933,N 3,23:2
Girl Without a Room 1933,D 7,26:3
Smoky 1934,Ja 1,28:2
Wedding Night, The 1935,Mr 16,19:1
Three Legionnaires 1937,Jl 10,18:2
Dangerously Yours 1937,O 18,14:2
Ride a Crooked Mile 1938,D 29,15:2
Barricade 1939,O 9,18:2
For Whom the Bell Tolls 1943,Jl 15,25:2
Song of my Heart 1948,Mr 5,17:3
Sneider, Vern J (Original Author)
Teahouse of the August Moon, The
1956,N 30,19:1
SNELL
See Also SCHNELL
Snell, Anthony
Breaking Through the Sound Barrier
1952,N 7,19:1
Gilbert and Sullivan 1953,O 28,36:3
Snell, David (Composer)
Born to Sing 1942,F 19,23:2
Snell, Earle (Original Author)
Branded Men 1931,D 12,23:3
Snell, Earle (Screenwriter)
On Your Toes 1928,Ja 9,20:1
Escape from Devil's Island 1935,N 25,22:2
King of the Royal Mounted 1936,S 29,35:2
Two in a Crowd 1936,O 5,25:1
Rainbow on the River 1936,D 18,31:4
Secret Valley 1937,Ja 25,22:2
It Happened Out West 1937,Je 7,22:3
Make a Wish 1937,S 23,33:1
Wide Open Faces 1938,Ap 15,23:2
Gladiator, The 1938,Ag 29,10:2
Homicide Bureau 1939,F 2,17:2
Taxi, Mister 1943,Ap 15,20:2
That Nazty Nuisance 1943,My 29,10:3
Prairie Chickens 1943,Jl 9,21:6
Snell, G H
Hurrah I'm Alive 1930,Je 16,25:3
Snelling, Leonard
Girl in the Street 1938,My 26,31:2
Snerd, Mortimer
You Can't Cheat an Honest Man 1939,F 20,13:2
Here We Go Again 1942,O 12,12:3
Snez, Nakai
Rocky Mountain 1950,N 4,13:2
Snoddy, Robert (Director)
Di que me Quieres; Say That You Love Me
1939,Ap 24,13:2

Snow, Edgar (Cinematographer)
China Story, The: One-Fourth of Humanity
1968,O 3,56:4
Snow, Edgar (Narrator)
China Story, The: One-Fourth of Humanity
1968,O 3,56:4
Snow, H A (Cinematographer)
Lost in the Arctic 1928,Jl 26,25:3
Snow, H A (Miscellaneous)
Hunting Big Game in Africa With Gun and
Camera 1923,Ja 9,27:1 (In Addenda)
Snow, Heber
Mystery of the Hooded Horsemen, The
1937,Ag 13,13:2
Snow, Sidney (Miscellaneous)
Hunting Big Game in Africa With Gun and
Camera 1923,Ja 9,27:1 (In Addenda)
Snow, Sidney A (Cinematographer)
Lost in the Arctic 1928,Jl 26,25:3
Snow, Sidney A (Miscellaneous)
Cougar, the King Killer 1933,My 22,18:6
Snow, Sidney A (Producer)
Cougar, the King Killer 1933,My 22,18:6
Snowden, Alec C (Producer)
Broth of a Boy 1959,D 28,18:1
Snowden, Caroline
First Year, The 1926,Mr 8,17:1
Marriage Clause, The 1926,S 28,30:2
Orchids and Ermine 1927,Ap 19,24:4
In old Kentucky 1927,N 21,20:1
Snowden, Leigh
Square Jungle, The 1955,D 31,17:2
All That Heaven Allows 1956,F 29,35:1
Creature Walks among Us, The 1956,Ap 27,21:6
I've Lived Before 1956,Ag 4,13:1
Snowdon, Roger
Othello 1960,My 16,39:1
Follow the Boys 1963,F 28,8:2
Snowflake
20th Century 1934,My 4,24:2
Lady by Choice 1934,N 17,12:1
Remember the Night 1940,Ja 18,27:2
Seventeen 1940,F 29,15:2
Biscuit Eater, The 1940,My 23,28:5
SNYDER
See Also SCHNEIDER
Snyder, Howard (Original Author)
It Happened Tomorrow 1944,My 29,18:2
In Society 1944,Ag 17,20:2
George White's Scandals 1945,O 11,26:2
Abbott and Costello Meet the Invisible Man
1951,Ap 13,18:6
Snyder, Howard (Screenwriter)
Almost Married 1942,Je 5,23:2
All by Myself 1943,Jl 16,20:3
George White's Scandals 1945,O 11,26:2
Abbott and Costello Meet the Killer Boris Karloff
1949,S 19,18:3
Snyder, L Dwight
Born to Dance 1936,D 5,16:1
Snyder, Robert (Director)
Blood Brothers 1953,F 21,10:7
Snyder, Robert (Miscellaneous)
Gods of Bali 1952,O 13,26:3
Snyder, Ted (Composer)
Young and Beautiful 1934,S 18,18:4
So-Jin
Thief of Bagdad, The 1924,Mr 19,19:1
Soafaer, Abraham
Stairway to Heaven 1946,D 26,28:1
Soall, Terence
Georgy Girl 1966,O 18,48:1
Soares, Rubens (Composer)
Blondie Goes Latin 1941,F 26,17:3
Sobell, Jack (Original Author)
Nora Prentiss 1947,F 22,16:2
Sobol, Louis
Copacabana 1947,Jl 12,7:2
Sobolevskaya, L
Girl With the Guitar, The 1960,F 1,22:4
Sobolevsky, N
Alone 1932,My 25,23:6
Sobolevsky, Peter
New Babylon, The 1929,D 2,28:2
Sniper 1932,Ag 26,20:3
We Are From Kronstadt 1936,My 2,11:1
In the Rear of the Enemy 1942,O 10,11:2
Moscow Skies 1945,Ja 22,22:5
Sobolyev, Sasha
Great Glinka, The 1947,D 22,30:2
Socher, Hylton
Summer Love 1958,Je 26,23:4
Sochevko, G
Poet and Tsar 1938,Ag 25,15:1
Sociar, Tridro (Director)
Incertidumbre 1936,S 21,26:5
Socias, I (Director)
Cinco Advertencias de Satanas, Las; Satan's Five
Warnings 1939,Ja 14,13:2
Socrate, Mario
Gospel According to St Matthew, The
1966,F 18,23:1

Soderberg, Hjaimar (Original Author)
Gertrud 1966,Je 3,33:1
Soderberg, Robert (Miscellaneous)
Born to be Bad 1950,S 29,31:5
Soderberg, Robert (Original Author)
Air Cadet 1951,My 11,32:3
Soderberg, Robert (Screenwriter)
Reckless Moment, The 1949,D 30,13:2
Soderblom, Holm
Kustens Glada Kavaljerer; Coast's Happy
Cavaliers, The 1939,My 23,27:2
Soderhjelm, Janine
Unstrap Me 1968,N 21,41:2
Soderholm, Margit (Original Author)
Sunshine Follows Rain 1949,S 29,39:2
Soderling, Walter
Woman Chases Man 1937,Je 11,26:2
Criminals of the Air 1937,O 28,29:2
St Louis Blues 1939,F 9,17:2
Gracie Allen Murder Case, The 1939,Je 8,31:3
Death of a Champion 1939,Ag 24,17:3
Men Without Souls 1940,My 13,21:2
When the Daltons Rode 1940,Ag 23,13:3
Slightly Tempted 1940,N 1,33:1
Penny Serenade 1941,My 23,25:2
Confessions of Boston Blackie 1941,D 8,31:2
Falcon in Hollywood, The 1944,D 9,21:2
So Dear to my Heart 1949,Ja 31,14:2
Soederbaum, Kristina
Verwehte Spuren; Covered Tracks
1939,O 14,13:3
Unsterbliche Herz, Das; Immortal Heart, The
1939,O 21,12:2
Jugend; Youth 1939,D 9,18:2
Reise Nach Tilsit, Die; Trip to Tilsit, The
1940,F 10,19:2
Soederblom, Aake
Klart till Drabbning; Cleared for Action
1937,D 10,33:3
Kustens Glada Kavaljerer; Coast's Happy
Cavaliers, The 1939,My 23,27:2
Rena Rama Sanningen; Nothing but the Truth
1939,O 7,11:2
Soehnker, Hans
Csardasfuerstin 1935,Ap 25,18:3
Grosse Chance, Die 1935,My 6,22:4
Ich Sing Mich in Dein Herz Hinein
1935,Je 3,22:3
Schwarzwaldmaedel 1935,O 12,12:3
Annette in Paradise 1936,Mr 7,11:4
Junge Graf, Der 1936,D 14,15:2
Unwiderst Ehliche, Der; Irresistable Man, The
1937,D 20,23:3
Eva, das Fabriksmaedel 1938,Ja 8,19:2
Mustergatte, Der; Model Husband
1938,My 19,11:3
Sie und die Drei; She and the Three
1938,D 10,13:3
Herbst-Monoever; Fall Manoeuvres
1939,Mr 18,9:3
Manner Mussen so Sein; Men Are That Way
1939,My 13,11:6
Tag Nach der Scheidung, Der; Day After the
Divorce, The 1940,Mr 2,9:5
Drei um Christine, Die; Three After Christine,
The 1940,My 4,13:2
Film Without a Name 1950,O 20,32:2
For the First Time 1959,Ag 15,8:7
Soencland, Senta
Reserve Hat Ruh 1932,Ap 11,19:2
Soenderby, Knud (Screenwriter)
Invisible Army, The 1950,Je 26,17:3
Soeneland, Senta
Hellseher, Der 1933,S 11,20:4
Drei von der Kavallerie 1935,Ap 13,11:4
Unbekannte Gast, Der; Unknown Guest, The
1935,Je 1,18:3
Soer, John
Dog of Flanders, A 1960,Ap 1,37:1
Soerensen, Annemie
Verkaufte Braut, Die 1934,Ap 27,25:2
Sofaer, Abraham
Dreyfus Case, The 1931,Ag 31,11:5
Wandering Jew, The 1935,Ja 14,11:3
Rembrandt 1936,D 3,31:1
Voice in the Night, The 1941,My 23,25:4
Christopher Columbus 1949,O 13,33:2
Quo Vadis 1951,N 9,22:2
Pandora and the Flying Dutchman 1951,D 7,35:2
His Majesty O'Keefe 1954,F 6,17:2
Naked Jungle, The 1954,Ap 3,19:2
Elephant Walk 1954,Ap 22,37:2
Bhowani Junction 1956,My 25,26:1
First Texan, The 1956,Je 23,20:2
Sad Sack, The 1957,N 28,57:1
Captain Sindbad 1963,Jl 4,9:1
Twice Told Tales (Rappaccini's Daughter);
Rappaccini's Daughter (Twice Told Tales)
1964,Mr 28,40:1
Greatest Story Ever Told, The 1965,F 16,40:2
Head 1968,N 7,51:1

Soffici, Mario (Director)
Cadetes de San Martin 1939,Jl 3,10:6
Viejo Doctor, El; Old Doctor, The
1940,Ap 13,21:3
Alma del Bandoneon, El; Soul of the Accordion,
The 1940,Ap 27,9:3
Sofia, Vinicio
Dead Woman's Kiss, A 1951,O 6,16:4
Soga, Masafumi (Producer)
Angry Island 1960,F 28,31:1
Sohma, I
Slums of Tokyo 1930,Jl 7,22:3
Sohmers, Barbara
Truth, The 1961,Je 27,23:2
Soifer, Alberto (Composer)
Radio Bar 1937,Ja 25,22:3
Soinzewa, Julie
Aelita: The Revolt of the Robots
1929,Mr 26,34:1
Sojin
Proud Flesh 1925,Ap 14,26:1
Sea Beast, The 1926,Ja 16,8:5
Road to Mandalay, The 1926,Je 29,21:2
Diplomacy 1926,S 13,18:1
All Abroad 1927,Ap 19,24:4
Old San Francisco 1927,Je 23,23:3
Devil Dancer, The 1927,D 19,30:1
Chinese Parrot, The 1928,Ja 2,28:1
Haunted Ship, The 1928,Ja 23,18:3
Streets of Shanghai 1928,F 21,19:3
Something Always Happens 1928,My 21,25:1
Rescue, The 1929,Ja 14,20:1
Careers 1929,Je 10,23:1
Unholy Night, The 1929,O 12,11:1
Show of Shows 1929,N 21,24:5
Sokal, H R (Director)
They Met on Skis 1940,D 23,23:2
Sokal, H R (Producer)
Slalom 1936,D 16,35:3
Ski Chase, The 1938,Mr 26,12:1
They Met on Skis 1940,D 23,23:2
White Hell of Pitz Palu, The 1953,N 14,14:2
Arms and the Man 1962,F 24,21:7
Sokatscheff, N
That Woman 1968,Jl 19,30:3
Sokic, Ruzica
Affair of the Heart, An 1967,S 23,20:3
Sokill, Maria
Cossacks in Exile 1939,Ja 28,19:2
Sokirko, V
Land, The 1955,Ap 11,29:3
Sokoler, Bob (Producer)
Wild, Wild World 1965,N 22,48:2
Sokoloff, Vladimir
Loves of Jeanne Ney, The 1928,Jl 10,17:3
Dreigroschenoper, Die; Beggar's Opera, The
1931,My 18,21:2
Grosse Tenor, Der 1931,My 29,26:5
Niemandsland; No Man's Land
1932,Ja 24,VIII,5:1
Teilnehmer Antwortet Nicht 1932,N 30,23:6
Hell on Earth 1934,Ja 29,10:2
Gehetzie Menschen 1934,Je 2,22:5
Life of Emile Zola, The 1937,Ag 12,14:2
Lower Depths, The 1937,S 11,20:1
Alcatraz Island 1937,O 14,22:2
West of Shanghai 1937,O 29,19:2
Conquest 1937,N 5,19:1
Beg, Borrow or Steal 1937,D 10,33:2
Expensive Husbands 1938,Ja 8,19:3
Arsene Lupin Returns 1938,Mr 9,21:1
Blockade 1938,Je 17,25:1
Amazing Dr Clitterhouse, The 1938,Jl 21,14:2
Spawn of the North 1938,S 8,27:1
Ride a Crooked Mile 1938,D 29,15:2
Juarez 1939,Ap 26,27:1
Song of the Street 1939,S 5,21:2
Real Glory, The 1939,S 15,26:2
Comrade X 1940,D 26,23:1
Compliments of Mr Iflow 1941,F 17,10:7
Love Crazy 1941,Je 6,25:5
Crossroads 1942,Jl 27,18:2
Road to Morocco 1942,N 12,30:1
Mission to Moscow 1943,Ap 30,25:2
For Whom the Bell Tolls 1943,Jl 15,25:2
Mr Lucky 1943,Jl 23,21:2
Song of Russia 1944,F 11,17:2
Passage to Marseille 1944,F 17,12:5
Till We Meet Again 1944,Ag 30,15:1
Conspirators, The 1944,O 21,15:2
Royal Scandal, A 1945,Ap 12,19:2
Back to Bataan 1945,S 13,26:3
Paris Underground 1945,O 20,8:2
Scarlet Street 1946,F 15,29:2
Scandal In Paris, A 1946,S 16,9:7
Cloak and Dagger 1946,O 5,13:2
Two Smart People 1947,F 15,20:4
To the Ends of the Earth 1948,F 13,26:2
Baron of Arizona, The 1950,Je 23,29:2
Macao 1952,My 1,34:2
While the City Sleeps 1956,My 17,37:1
Twilight for the Gods 1958,Ag 7,21:1
Man on a String 1960,My 21,15:1

Sokoloff, Vladimir— Cont
Threepenny Opera, The 1960,Jl 11,24:4
Magnificent Seven, The 1960,N 24,48:3
Mr Sardonicus 1961,O 19,39:3
Taras Bulba 1962,D 26,5:2
Sokolov, N
Ballad of Cossack Gloota, The 1938,F 28,19:1
Lenin in October 1938,Ap 2,18:1
Sokolova, L
Summer to Remember, A; (Seryozha)
1961,N 7,38:1
Sokolova, Natasha
Demon of the Steppes 1930,Ja 18,21:1
One Woman's Story 1949,My 18,33:2
So Long at the Fair 1951,Ja 22,14:2
Spider and the Fly, The 1952,Jl 29,17:3
Sokolovsky, Samyon
Skanderbeg 1954,Jl 5,6:4
Sola, Angel T
Pecados de Amor 1934,Ap 24,27:2
Sola, Catharine
Belle Americaine, La 1961,D 18,42:1
Champagne Murders, The 1968,Ap 25,53:1
Sola, Margarita
Riachuelo 1934,D 8,18:5
Solanis, Valerie
I, A Man 1967,Ag 25,28:1
Solar, Willie
Billy Rose's Diamond Horseshoe 1945,My 3,37:1
Solares, Gilberto Martinez (Director)
Senor Alcalde, El; Mayor, The 1939,My 20,11:2
Solari, Laura
Eravamo Sette Vedove; We Were Seven Widows
1940,F 16,23:4
Terra di Nessuno; Nobody's Land 1940,O 25,25:4
Roman Holiday 1953,Ag 28,13:1
Solbelli, Olga
Schoolgirl Diary 1947,O 18,9:2
Lost in the Dark 1949,My 14,9:2
Peddler and the Lady, The 1949,S 30,28:4
Tomorrow is too Late 1952,Ap 14,22:2
Lure of the Sira 1953,D 26,10:7
Theodora, Slave Empress 1955,Ja 12,24:2
Soldati, Mario
Professor, My Son 1949,Ap 18,18:4
Soldati, Mario (Director)
His Young Wife 1949,Mr 12,10:2
Flight Into France 1949,Jl 22,16:2
Of Love and Bandits 1953,Ja 17,12:4
O K Nero 1953,Je 20,8:6
Stranger's Hand, The 1955,F 16,24:5
Wayward Wife, The 1955,Ap 11,29:3
Of Life and Love 1958,O 7,40:2
Virtuous Bigamist, The 1959,My 28,34:3
Soldati, Mario (Original Author)
Of Wayward Love (The Serpent); Serpent, The (Of
Wayward Love) 1964,Mr 24,29:1
Of Wayward Love (The Soldier); Soldier, The (Of
Wayward Love) 1964,Mr 24,29:1
Of Wayward Love (The Women); Women, The
(Of Wayward Love) 1964,Mr 24,29:1
Soldati, Mario (Screenwriter)
Of Love and Bandits 1953,Ja 17,12:4
Wayward Wife, The 1955,Ap 11,29:3
Soler, Andres
Suprema Ley; Supreme Law 1938,Ja 15,19:2
Romeo and Juliet 1944,Je 17,10:3
Miserables, Los 1944,O 24,17:2
Soler, Domingo
Corazon Bandolero 1935,Mr 2,18:2
Chucho el Roto 1935,Mr 30,11:3
Tierra, Amor y Dolor 1935,Ag 10,16:5
Mujer del Puerto, La 1936,Ag 24,11:3
Mi Candidato; My Candidate 1938,O 31,12:3
Hombres de Mar; Men of the Sea 1938,N 7,23:6
Bajo el Cielo de Mexico; Beneath the Sky of
Mexico 1938,D 31,7:3
Vamonus con Pancho Villa; Let's Go With Pancho
Villa 1939,Ap 15,15:2
Senor Alcalde, El; Mayor, The 1939,My 20,11:2
A lo Macho; In Rough Style 1939,Je 3,11:3
Por Mis Pistolas; By My Pistols 1939,Je 10,14:3
Latigo, El; Whip, The 1939,Jl 1,11:3
Golondrina, La; Swallow, The 1939,Jl 31,9:3
Corazon de Nino; Heart of a Child
1940,Ja 1,29:4
Perfidia; Perfidy 1940,F 17,9:3
Reina del Rio, La; Queen of the River, The
1940,F 24,9:3
Odio; Hate 1940,Ap 6,13:2
Bestia Negra, La; Black Beast, The 1940,Je 3,11:2
Life of Simon Bolivar, The 1943,Je 18,16:5
El Conde de Monte Cristo 1943,N 9,26:2
Miserables, Los 1944,O 24,17:2
Hidden River 1950,D 1,31:2
Soler, Enriqueta
Mama 1933,Jl 8,14:6
Soler, Fernando
Chucho el Roto 1935,Mr 30,11:3
Celos 1936,Ap 15,25:2
Abnegacion 1938,My 31,8:3
Verbena Tragica; Tragic Festival, The
1939,Mr 13,12:3

Soler, Fernando— Cont
Por Mis Pistolas; By My Pistols 1939,Je 10,14:3
Papacito Lindo; Sugar Daddy 1939,N 18,22:6
Odio; Hate 1940,Ap 6,13:2
Bestia Negra, La; Black Beast, The 1940,Je 3,11:2
Creo en Dios 1943,Jl 17,8:3

Soler, Julian
El Escandalo 1934,S 22,12:3
Cruz Diablo 1935,Ap 6,10:1
Clemencia 1935,Ag 20,25:4
Bohemios 1935,S 16,15:3
Muertos Hablan, Los; Dead Speak, The 1935,N 25,22:2
Familia Dressel, La 1936,My 4,16:2
Mater Nostra 1936,S 9,32:4
Noches de Gloria; Glorious Nights 1938,Ap 23,19:3
Alma Jarocha 1938,Ap 30,18:2
Dos Cadetes, Los 1938,S 26,13:3
Supremo Sacrificio; Supreme Sacrifice 1938,N 29,27:2
Beso Mortal, El; Fatal Kiss, The 1939,Ja 21,19:3
Cobarde, El; Coward, The 1939,Mr 27,11:2
Estrellita; Starlet 1939,Ap 12,27:3
India Bonita, La; Pretty Indian Girl, The 1939,Ap 15,15:2
Por Mis Pistolas; By My Pistols 1939,Je 10,14:3
Latigo, El; Whip, The 1939,Jl 1,11:3
Soy Chato, Pero las Huelo; I Am Snub-nosed but I Can Smell 1939,Jl 22,12:3
Papacito Lindo; Sugar Daddy 1939,N 18,22:6
Odio; Hate 1940,Ap 6,13:2
Mi Madrecita; My Little Mother 1940,S 24,26:6
Life of Simon Bolivar, The 1943,Je 18,16:5

Soler, Mercedes
Asi es mi Tierra; Such Is my Country 1939,Mr 18,9:3

Solinas, Franco (Original Author)
Kapo 1964,Je 2,33:3
Big Gundown, The 1968,Ag 23,33:1

Solinas, Franco (Screenwriter)
Behind Closed Shutters 1952,Je 10,22:7
Beautiful but Dangerous 1958,F 6,24:1
Madame 1963,Mr 21,8:6
Kapo 1964,Je 2,33:3
Salvatore Giuliano 1964,S 18,28:1
Battle of Algiers, The 1967,S 21,56:1

Solis, Charito
Buddha 1965,Je 17,27:4

Solito, Giacinto (Director)
Gioconda, La 1958,O 13,33:4

Solito, Giacinto (Screenwriter)
Gioconda, La 1958,O 13,33:4

Sollima, Sergio (Director)
Of Wayward Love (The Women); Women, The (Of Wayward Love) 1964,Mr 24,29:1
Of Wayward Love (The Soldier); Soldier, The (Of Wayward Love) 1964,Mr 24,29:1
Of Wayward Love (The Serpent); Serpent, The (Of Wayward Love) 1964,Mr 24,29:1
Big Gundown, The 1968,Ag 23,33:1

Sollima, Sergio (Screenwriter)
Behind Closed Shutters 1952,Je 10,22:7
Big Gundown, The 1968,Ag 23,33:1

Solm, Fred
U-Boat 9 1929,Ja 22,23:1

Solntseva, Y (Director)
Life in Bloom 1949,My 9,20:4

Solnzeva, Y
Simple Tailor, The 1934,F 19,18:3

Solobevski, Peter
Island of Doom 1933,Jl 17,9:5

Solodova, E
Mistress, The 1954,My 31,9:2

Sologne, Madeleine
Eternal Return, The; Eternel Retour, L' 1948,Ja 5,15:2
Friend Will come Tonight, A; Ami Viendra Ce Soir, Un 1948,Jl 12,11:2
Just a big Simple Girl; Une Grande Fille Toute Simple 1949,O 28,29:2
Vautrin, the Thief 1949,N 11,31:2
Devil and the Angel, The 1949,D 3,8:6
Bernadette of Lourdes 1962,Ja 30,20:2

SOLOMON
See Also SALOMON

Solomon, B Rogow (Original Author)
Bowery, The 1933,O 5,24:2

Solomon, Ernest V (Screenwriter)
Corinna Darling 1958,Je 14,14:3

Solomon, J
Beachcomber, The 1938,D 26,29:3

Solomon, Joe (Producer)
Hells Angels on Wheels 1967,Jl 29,29:3
Name of the Game Is Kill, The 1968,Je 6,54:1

Solomon, Louis (Screenwriter)
Mr Winkle Goes to War 1944,Ag 3,16:1
Snafu 1945,D 26,15:2
Mark of the Renegade 1951,S 7,24:2

Solomon, William
Unidentified Flying Objects 1956,Je 13,46:2

Solon, Ewen
Rob Roy 1954,F 4,21:5
1984 1956,O 1,31:1

Hounds of the Baskervilles, The 1959,Jl 4,9:4
Jack the Ripper 1960,F 18,37:4
Sundowners, The 1960,D 9,39:1

Solorzano, Jesus
Ora, Ponciano; Come on, Ponciano 1937,D 18,18:2
Gavilan, El; Hawk, The 1940,Ja 22,11:2

Solouroglou, Christos
Barefoot Battalion 1954,My 29,13:4

Soloveyev, V (Original Author)
1812 1944,S 11,14:1

Soloveyev, V (Screenwriter)
Road to the Stars 1958,Je 5,39:2

Solovief, Alexander (Director)
Clown George 1932,Ag 24,21:4

Soloviev, L (Original Author)
Adventures in Bokhara 1944,Ag 21,9:4

Soloviev, V R
Mother and Sons 1938,S 15,29:2
Oppenheim Family, The 1939,My 24,29:2
Lenin in 1918 1939,Je 27,27:2

Soloviev, Vladimir
Ural Front, The 1945,Je 7,25:3
Days and Nights 1946,Ap 29,24:4
Vow, The 1947,Je 23,14:3
Life in Bloom 1949,My 9,20:4
No Ordinary Summer 1958,O 6,36:3

Soloviev, Yuri
Lullaby, The 1961,My 15,35:2
Sleeping Beauty, The 1966,My 4,50:1

Solovtzev, Valery
Fragment of an Empire, A 1930,Ja 27,18:4

Solovyev, V
Leningrad Symphony 1958,Je 23,19:6

Solovyov, A
Secret Brigade 1951,Mr 19,23:2
Wrestler and the Clown, The 1959,Ja 1,38:1

Solovyov, I
Admiral Ushakov 1954,Ja 18,19:2
Attack From the Sea 1954,Ap 19,19:4

Solovyov, L (Screenwriter)
Overcoat, The 1965,Mr 2,31:2

Solovyov, Vasily (Screenwriter)
War and Peace 1968,Ap 29,50:5

Solow, Eugene (Original Author)
Master of Men 1933,N 29,23:4

Solow, Eugene (Screenwriter)
Gentlemen are Born 1934,N 22,27:2
While the Patient Slept 1935,Mr 2,18:2
Crash Donovan 1936,Ag 10,10:3
League of Frightened Men, The 1937,Jl 2,25:1
Start Cheering 1938,Mr 17,17:3
Patient in Room 18, The 1938,Ap 22,15:6
Of Mice and Men 1940,F 17,9:2

Solt, Andrew (Miscellaneous)
Lovely to Look At 1952,My 30,11:2

Solt, Andrew (Original Author)
They all Kissed the Bride 1942,Jl 31,11:1
My Kingdom for a Cook 1943,O 15,15:3

Solt, Andrew (Screenwriter)
They all Kissed the Bride 1942,Jl 31,11:1
My Kingdom for a Cook 1943,O 15,15:3
Without Reservations 1946,Je 8,17:2
Jolson Story, The 1946,O 11,28:2
Joan of Arc 1948,N 12,30:5
Little Women 1949,Mr 11,33:2
Whirlpool 1950,Ja 14,9:2
In a Lonely Place 1950,My 18,37:2
Thunder on the Hill 1951,O 18,32:3
For the First Time 1959,Ag 15,8:7

Soltani, Serge
Winner's Circle, The 1957,My 6,25:2

Solthy, Gyorgy
Goose Boy, The 1951,O 13,9:2

Soltoft, Ole
Eric Soya's 17 1967,Ja 25,37:1

Solutseva, J (Director)
Ukraine in Flames 1944,Ap 3,18:2

Solvari, Laura
Moglie in Pericolo, Una; Wife in Danger, A 1940,Je 7,27:3

Solveg, Maria
Meistersinger 1929,D 16,34:2
Elisabeth von Oesterreich 1931,D 11,35:1
Voce del Sangue, La 1933,Ap 17,16:4
Ich Glaub' nie Mehr an Eine Frau 1933,O 13,25:4
Sohn der Weissen Berge, Der 1933,O 23,18:3
Luegen auf Ruegen 1934,Ja 1,28:2
Hochtourist, Der 1934,Ja 13,16:4

Solway, Clifford (Director)
Mr Kennedy, Mr Reagan and the Big, Beautiful, Beleaguered American Dream 1967,N 23,58:1

Solway, Clifford (Producer)
Mr Kennedy, Mr Reagan and the Big, Beautiful, Beleaguered American Dream 1967,N 23,58:1

Solyin, Vic
Cry of Battle 1963,O 12,27:2

Solyom, Kati
Age of Illusions 1967,Mr 30,55:1
Father 1967,S 29,53:1

Solyus, S
Horsemen, The 1951,Ja 29,14:5

Soma, Linda
Goddess, The 1958,Je 25,24:1

Sombert, Claire
Invitation to the Dance (Circus); Circus (Invitation to the Dance) 1956,My 23,35:7

Somerest, Pat
Body and Soul 1931,Mr 14,23:2

Somers, Brett
Bus Riley's Back in Town 1965,Ap 8,45:2

Somers, Esther
River Lady 1948,My 21,19:5
Canon City 1948,Jl 8,19:2
Snake Pit, the 1948,N 5,29:2
Portrait of Jennie 1949,Mr 30,31:2
Sun comes up, The 1949,My 13,29:2
People Will Talk 1951,Ag 30,20:1

Somers, Julian
Caravan 1949,Ap 21,30:4
Stranger in Between, The 1952,Ag 20,21:3
White Fire 1954,S 18,12:4
1954,S 18,12:4
Far From the Madding Crowd 1967,O 19,59:1

Somersalmis, Urho
Charlotte Loewenskoeld 1932,F 22,23:2

Somerset, Pat
Mother Machree 1928,Mr 6,20:3
Black Watch, The 1929,My 23,26:3
Men Without Women 1930,F 1,15:1
Born Reckless 1930,Je 7,10:4
Good Intentions 1930,Jl 26,16:4
Hell's Angels 1930,Ag 16,8:3
Devotion 1931,O 3,20:2
Murder in Trinidad 1934,My 16,22:2
Clive of India 1935,Ja 18,29:1
Here's to Romance 1935,O 3,29:2
To Mary-With Love 1936,Ag 27,16:1
Wee Willie Winkie 1937,Jl 24,12:1
I Cover the War 1937,Ag 2,10:2

Somerville, H B (Screenwriter)
Ashes of Vengeance 1923,Ag 7,20:2

Somerville, Mary
Mr Peabody and the Mermaid 1948,Ag 14,6:5

Somes, Michael
Royal Ballet, The (Ondine); Ondine (The Royal Ballet) 1960,O 5,45:2
Royal Ballet, The (The Firebird); Firebird, The (The Royal Ballet) 1960,O 5,45:2
Royal Ballet, The (Swan Lake Act II); Swan Lake Act II (The Royal Ballet) 1960,O 5,45:2
Romeo and Juliet 1966,O 6,55:1

Somio, Istvan
Zsivany Becsuelet 1935,O 30,16:3
Urilany Szobat Keres; Lady Seeks Room 1938,Mr 19,11:2

Somlay, Arthur
Budai Cukraszda 1936,Ja 2,21:5
Az uj Foeldesur 1936,S 22,30:5
Piros Bugyellaris; Red Purse 1939,Mr 11,21:2
Rozmaring; Rosemary 1940,F 10,19:3
Eb Ura Fako 1940,Mr 23,16:4
It Happened in Europe 1949,O 4,32:4

Somlo, Josef (Producer)
Fugitive, The 1940,Jl 23,22:2
Lady in Distress 1942,F 16,21:2
One Night With You 1949,F 21,20:2
Inheritance, The 1951,F 12,19:2
Man Who Loved Redheads, The 1955,Jl 26,29:2
Teckman Mystery, The 1955,Ag 22,18:2

Sommer, Edith (Miscellaneous)
From This Day Forward 1946,Ap 20,16:2

Sommer, Edith (Original Author)
Teenage Rebel 1956,N 17,17:6

Sommer, Edith (Screenwriter)
Perfect Strangers 1950,Mr 11,8:2
Born to be Bad 1950,S 29,31:5
Blue Denim 1959,Jl 31,21:1
Best of Everything 1959,O 9,24:2
Jessica 1962,Ap 20,20:2
Pleasure Seekers, The 1964,D 26,9:1
This Property is Condemned 1966,Ag 4,24:1

Sommer, Elke
Victors, The 1963,D 20,21:2
Prize, The 1964,Ja 24,21:1
Shot in the Dark, A 1964,Je 24,28:1
Why Bother to Knock 1965,F 4,24:2
Bambole; Dolls, The (Treatise on Eugenics); Treatise on Eugenics (The Dolls) 1965,Je 29,26:1
Art of Love, The 1965,Jl 1,34:1
Oscar, The 1966,Mr 5,16:1
Money Trap, The 1966,My 5,59:1
Boy, Did I Get a Wrong Number! 1966,Je 9,54:2
Venetian Affair, The 1967,Ja 19,41:2
Deadlier Than the Male 1967,F 22,21:1
Corrupt Ones, The 1967,F 23,41:3
Wicked Dreams of Paula Schultz, The 1968,Ja 4,28:1

Sommerfeld, Helga
Shadows Grow Longer, The 1962,Je 11,36:4

Sommerfeldt, Gunnar (Director)
Growth of the Soil 1929,S 30,23:1
Sommers, Jay (Screenwriter)
All Hands on Deck 1961,Ap 1,10:2
Sommers, Joanie
Everything's Ducky 1961,D 21,30:6
Lively Set, The 1964,O 15,54:1
Sommers, John
Ramparts We Watch, The 1940,S 20,27:1
Sommers, Julie
Pad, The (And How to Use It) 1966,Ag 18,27:2
Sommerville, I M (Miscellaneous)
Chappaqua 1967,N 6,65:2
Somnos, George (Director)
Girl in 419 1933,My 20,11:5
Midnight Club 1933,Jl 29,14:2
Wharf Angel 1934,Ap 21,12:1
Somogyi, Erzsi
Nem Elhetek Muzsikaszo Nelkuel 1936,F 21,21:2
Falu Rossza, A; Village Rogue, The 1938,Ap 18,11:2
Somov, Valeri
Italiano Brava Gente 1966,F 4,20:1
Somoza, Rafael
Molinos de Viento; Windmills 1940,F 26,11:2
Somr, Joset
Closely Watched Trains 1967,O 16,59:2
Sondergaard, Gale
Anthony Adverse 1936,Ag 27,16:1
Maid of Salem 1937,Mr 4,27:2
Seventh Heaven 1937,Mr 26,25:1
Life of Emile Zola, The 1937,Ag 12,14:2
Lord Jeff 1938,Jl 1,22:2
Dramatic School 1938,D 9,31:2
Juarez 1939,Ap 26,27:1
Cat and the Canary, The 1939,N 23,38:5
Mark of Zorro, The 1940,N 4,23:2
Letter, The 1940,N 23,12:6
Black Cat, The 1941,Ap 26,20:3
Paris Calling 1942,Ja 19,21:2
My Favorite Blonde 1942,Ap 2,27:2
Enemy Agents meet Ellery Queen 1942,Ag 22,16:2
Night to Remember, A 1943,Ja 1,27:2
Appointment in Berlin 1943,Jl 17,8:2
Strange Death of Adolf Hitler, The 1943,O 9,11:5
Spider Woman 1944,Ja 17,14:5
Invisible Man's Revenge, The 1944,Je 10,12:2
Christmas Holiday 1944,Je 29,16:1
Gypsy Wildcat 1944,O 5,18:6
Enter Arsene Lupin 1944,D 2,17:6
Climax, The 1944,D 14,28:5
Spider Woman Strikes Back, The 1946,Mr 23,8:3
Night in Paradise 1946,Je 6,16:3
Anna and the King of Siam 1946,Je 21,20:2
Time of Their Lives, The 1946,N 28,40:2
Pirates of Monterey 1947,D 17,41:4
Road to Rio 1948,F 19,29:3
East Side, West Side 1949,D 23,17:2
Sondergaard, Hester
Jigsaw 1949,My 30,9:4
Sondergaard, Nigel
Blue Bird, The 1940,Ja 20,11:2
Sondergaard, Quentin
This Property is Condemned 1966,Ag 4,24:1
Sondes, Walter
Should a Doctor Tell 1931,Ag 22,7:5
Iron Duke, The 1935,Ja 25,27:2
Sondheim, Stephen (Miscellaneous)
Gypsy 1962,N 2,24:1
Sondock, Mal
Town Without Pity 1961,O 11,53:1
Sonego, Rodolfo (Original Author)
Anna 1953,F 19,20:5
To Bed...Or not to Bed 1963,D 23,18:2
Sonego, Rodolfo (Screenwriter)
Tombolo 1949,D 31,9:4
Anna 1953,F 19,20:5
Rome, 11 O'Clock 1953,Ap 30,39:2
To Bed...Or not to Bed 1963,D 23,18:2
...And Suddenly It's Murder! 1964,Ja 24,21:1
Bambole; Dolls, The (The Soup); Soup, The (The Dolls) 1965,Je 29,26:1
Queens, The (Queen Marta); Queen Marta (The Queens) 1968,Mr 11,49:1
Queens, The (Queen Elena); Queen Elena (The Queens) 1968,Mr 11,49:1
Sonessa, Joseph
Take a Giant Step 1961,Mr 6,28:2
Soneya, Jiro
Revenge of General Ling, The 1938,F 21,15:1
Mutiny of the Elsinore, The 1939,F 16,17:2
Song, Soo Ah
Purple Plain, The 1955,Ap 11,29:1
Sonia, Giovanna Emery (Screenwriter)
Fear No Evil 1949,Mr 31,31:2
Sonja, Magda
Maria Stuart 1928,Mr 11,VIII,5:1
Mata Hari: The Red Dancer 1928,N 12,18:2
That Murder in Berlin 1929,Mr 12,26:2
Gehetzie Menschen 1934,Je 2,22:5
Robber Symphony 1937,Ja 27,17:2

Sonkur, Kalu K
Bwana Devil 1953,F 19,20:5
Sonnabend, Michael (Miscellaneous)
Titan-Story of Michelangelo, The 1950,Ja 23,16:2
Sonnemann, Emmy
Legend of William Tell, The 1935,O 2,27:1
Oberwachtmeister Schwenke 1936,My 5,26:7
Sonneveld, William
Silk Stockings 1957,Jl 19,11:1
Sonny
Good Times 1967,Ag 3,26:4
Sonoel
Bellman, The 1947,Ap 7,20:5
Sonoret, Octavio (Producer)
Goal 1967,Ja 19,26:1
Sons of the Pioneers
Hollywood Canteen 1944,D 16,19:2
My Pal Trigger 1946,Ag 17,16:3
Rio Grande 1950,N 20,21:2
Soo, Jack
Flower Drum Song 1961,N 10,40:1
Who's Been Sleeping in My Bed? 1963,D 26,33:2
Thoroughly Modern Millie 1967,Mr 23,25:1
Green Berets, The 1968,Je 20,49:1
Soo Hoo, Hayward
Big Bonanza, The 1945,F 26,14:5
Soohoo, Edward
Little Tokyo, USA 1942,Ag 7,13:2
Soong, Lucille
Darling 1965,Ag 4,20:1
Soos, Imre
Goose Boy, The 1951,O 13,9:2
Merry Go-Round 1958,Ap 3,23:3
Sophocles (Miscellaneous)
Oedipus the King 1968,S 19,62:2
Sophocles (Original Author)
Oedipus Rex 1957,Ja 8,26:1
Sorano, Daniel
Port of Desire 1960,N 3,49:2
Sordi, Alberto
His Young Wife 1949,Mr 12,10:2
Gran Varieta 1955,Ap 11,29:5
White Sheik, The 1956,Ap 26,37:4
Vitelloni 1956,O 24,43:1
Farewell to Arms, A 1958,Ja 25,14:1
Virtuous Bigamist, The 1959,My 28,34:3
Great War; (Grande Guerra, La) 1961,Ag 31,22:3
Best of Enemies, The 1962,Ag 7,35:2
Everybody go Home!; Tutti a Casa 1962,N 6,38:1
Day in Court, A 1963,My 11,15:2
To Bed...Or not to Bed 1963,D 23,18:2
...And Suddenly It's Murder! 1964,Ja 24,21:1
Mafioso 1964,Jl 1,42:1
Made in Italy 1967,My 1,44:2
Sordi, Alberto (Screenwriter)
Day in Court, A 1963,My 11,15:2
Sordi, Aroldo
Cavalcade of Song 1954,D 27,22:8
Sorel, Cecile
Pearls of the Crown, The 1938,Ap 12,26:2
Sorel, Gaby
Enemigos 1934,Ag 18,5:6
Sorel, George
Sing Me a Love Song 1936,D 26,15:2
Swiss Miss 1938,Je 4,18:2
Hitler-Dead or Alive 1943,Mr 31,23:3
Northwest Outpost 1947,Ag 8,10:2
Sorel, Guy
Thirteenth Letter, The 1951,F 22,27:2
Sorel, Jean
From a Roman Balcony 1961,O 16,33:5
View From the Bridge, A 1962,Ja 23,36:1
I Spit on Your Grave 1963,Je 29,13:5
Adorable Julia 1964,Ap 8,33:1
Disorder 1964,My 26,44:2
Bambole; Dolls, The (Monsignor Cupid); Monsignor Cupid (The Dolls) 1965,Je 29,26:1
Vaghe Stelle dell'Orsa; Of These Thousand Pleasures 1965,S 4,11:4
Sandra 1966,Ja 17,32:1
Made in Italy 1967,My 1,44:2
Queens, The (Queen Elena); Queen Elena (The Queens) 1968,Mr 11,49:1
Belle de Jour 1968,Ap 11,51:1
Weekend, Italian Style 1968,My 23,56:2
Sorel, Jeanne
American Madness 1932,Ag 6,14:5
Sorel, Michel
Pirates of Capri, The 1949,D 26,33:5
Sorensen, Paul
Steel Claw, The 1961,S 21,40:2
Sorensen, Rickie
Man of a Thousand Faces 1957,Ag 14,21:1
Tarzan's Fight for Life 1958,Ag 16,10:2
Soreze, Paul
Very Private Affair, A 1962,S 29,15:1
Sorges
Dr Knock 1937,My 1,16:4
Soria, Florentino (Original Author)
Rocket From Calabuch 1958,O 8,41:1
Soria, Gabriel (Director)
Chucho el Roto 1935,Mr 30,11:3
Martin Garatuza 1935,S 30,13:1

Soria, Gabriel (Director) — Cont
Muertos Hablan, Los; Dead Speak, The 1935,N 25,22:2
Mater Nostra 1936,S 9,32:4
Ora, Ponciano; Come on, Ponciano 1937,D 18,18:2
Virgin of Guadalupe, The 1943,My 15,13:3
Dama de las Camelias, La 1944,S 26,16:1
Soria, Gabriel (Producer)
Ora, Ponciano; Come on, Ponciano 1937,D 18,18:2
Soria, Gabriel (Screenwriter)
Virgin of Guadalupe, The 1943,My 15,13:3
Soria, Giovanna (Screenwriter)
Mad About Opera 1950,Ap 6,33:2
Young Caruso, The 1953,O 13,34:4
Beautiful but Dangerous 1958,F 6,24:1
Soria-Santander (Producer)
Virgin of Guadalupe, The 1943,My 15,13:3
Sorin, Louis
Mother's Boy 1929,My 8,34:6
Animal Crackers 1930,Ag 29,20:3
With These Hands 1950,Je 16,28:4
Sorina, Alexandra
Peter the Great 1923,Je 25,16:5
Hands of Orlac, The 1928,Je 5,21:1
Sorkin, Marc (Director)
Teilnehmer Antwortet Nicht 1932,N 30,23:6
Pasha's Wives, The 1942,Ap 6,19:2
Sorkin, Marc (Miscellaneous)
Pictura 1952,Ap 8,35:3
Sorkin, Marc (Producer)
drame De Shanghai; Shanghai Drama, The 1945,Ja 11,19:2
Soro, Alberto
Queens, The (Queen Marta); Queen Marta (The Queens) 1968,Mr 11,49:1
Sorokhtin, Igor (Director)
Conquerors of the Night 1933,Jl 31,16:3
Sorokin, K
Men of the Sea 1938,Je 20,11:2
Taxi to Heaven 1944,My 25,16:3
Train Goes East, The 1949,S 5,13:3
Bountiful Summer 1951,D 24,9:1
Taras Shevchenko 1952,Jl 28,12:6
Maximka 1953,O 12,30:4
Tiger Girl 1955,S 5,8:2
Heroes of Shipka 1956,S 3,10:5
Sorokin, Kiril
Song Over Moscow 1964,N 23,52:1
Sorokin, Konstantin
Twins 1947,Jl 28,12:2
Song Over Moscow 1964,N 23,52:1
Sorokina, Nina
Bolshoi Ballet 67 1966,S 30,54:1
Sorrell, Karen
Flight Into Nowhere 1938,My 2,13:3
Mysterious Mr Moto of Devil's Island 1938,S 19,16:2
Soshalsky, Vladimir
Sailor From the Comet, The 1959,Ag 3,21:2
Othello 1960,My 16,39:1
Soskin, Henry
Don't Raise the Bridge, Lower the River 1968,Jl 13,18:1
Soskin, Paul (Producer)
Quiet Wedding 1941,D 29,27:4
Avengers, The 1942,N 25,18:2
Randolph Family 1945,Mr 13,19:4
Weaker Sex, The 1949,Jl 11,13:2
High Treason 1952,My 21,23:3
Law and Disorder 1958,Ag 6,20:1
Happy is the Bride 1959,Je 30,27:2
Soskin, Paul (Screenwriter)
Weaker Sex, The 1949,Jl 11,13:2
Soslovsky, F A
Laughter Through Tears 1933,N 13,21:2
Sosor-Barma
Son of Mongolia 1936,N 21,21:4
Sosso, Pietro
Broken Wing, The 1932,Mr 26,17:2
Adam Had Four Sons 1941,Mr 28,26:6
Stranger, The 1946,Jl 11,18:2
Sota, Bruno Ve
Bait 1954,F 24,21:3
Sothern, Ann
Let's Fall in Love 1934,Ja 22,12:3
Melody in Spring 1934,Mr 31,8:2
Hell Cat, The 1934,Jl 7,16:5
Blind Date 1934,S 1,16:3
Kid Millions 1934,N 12,17:2
Folies Bergere 1935,F 25,13:2
Hooray for Love 1935,Jl 13,16:2
Girl Friend, The 1935,S 28,12:2
Grand Exit 1935,N 4,24:5
You may Be Next 1936,F 24,14:1
Don't Gamble With Love 1936,Mr 2,13:3
My American Wife 1936,Ag 21,12:3
Walking on Air 1936,S 12,20:2
Dangerous Number 1937,Mr 12,19:2
Fifty Roads to Town 1937,Je 5,21:1
There Goes my Girl 1937,Je 12,8:2
Super-Sleuth 1937,Jl 17,18:1
Danger-Love at Work 1937,D 11,22:2

Sothern, Ann— Cont
there Goes The Groom 1937,D 25,10:6
She's Got Everything 1938,Ja 14,21:3
Trade Winds 1939,Ja 13,17:2
Maisie 1939,Je 23,23:1
Hotel for Women 1939,Ag 26,20:2
Fast And Furious 1939,O 12,33:3
Joe and Ethel Turp Call on the President
1940,Ja 4,19:2
Congo Maisie 1940,F 8,18:4
Brother Orchid 1940,Je 8,18:2
Gold Rush Maisie 1940,S 2,19:2
Dulcy 1940,N 28,28:2
Maisie Was a Lady 1941,F 13,25:2
Ringside Maisie 1941,Ag 1,11:2
Lady Be Good 1941,S 19,27:1
Maisie Gets her Man 1942,Jl 16,23:2
Panama Hattie 1942,O 2,31:2
Three Hearts for Julia 1943,My 21,22:4
Swing Shift Maisie 1943,S 10,29:2
Thousands Cheer 1943,S 14,27:1
Cry Havoc 1943,N 24,16:2
Maisie Goes to Reno 1944,S 29,18:1
Up Goes Maisie 1946,Ja 25,26:7
April Showers 1948,Mr 27,10:2
Words and Music 1948,D 10,34:2
Letter to Three Wives, A 1949,Ja 21,24:2
Judge Steps Out, The 1949,Je 3,21:4
Nancy Goes to Rio 1950,Ap 7,22:2
Shadow on the Wall 1950,My 19,31:3
Blue Gardenia, The 1953,Ap 28,31:1
Best Man, The 1964,Ap 7,29:1
Lady in a Cage 1964,Je 11,27:1
Sylvia 1965,F 11,45:1
Sothern, E H
Chattel, The 1916,S 25,7:3
Enemy to the King, An 1916,N 27,9:1
Sothern, Harry
Tragedy of the East Side, A 1920,Ag 24,6:2
Sothern, Hugh
Buccaneer, The 1938,F 17,17:2
Dangerous to Know 1938,Mr 11,15:4
Oklahoma Kid, The 1939,Mr 11,21:1
Juarez 1939,Ap 26,27:1
Northwest Passage 1940,Mr 8,25:1
Mad Doctor, The 1941,F 27,23:4
Bad Men of Missouri 1941,Ag 16,18:2
Sothern, Sam
Eyes of Youth 1919,D 1,9:3
Sotiraki, Ioulietta
Wind of Hate; (O Anemos Tou Missous)
1958,N 17,37:2
Soto, Luchi
Morena Clara 1938,Je 18,18:3
Soto, Roberto
Tropic Holiday 1938,Je 30,21:2
Sotoff, Paul
Anthony Adverse 1936,Ag 27,16:1
Sottane, Liliane
Up the Creek 1958,N 11,26:2
Soubier, Clifford
Black Legion 1937,Ja 18,21:1
They Won't Forget 1937,Jl 15,16:1
Tovarich 1937,D 31,9:2
Soubiran, Andre (Original Author)
Doctors, The 1956,Ag 7,19:2
Soudeikin, Sergei (Miscellaneous)
We Live Again 1934,N 2,27:2
Soui, Roger
Tanga Tika 1953,O 6,34:4
Soukis, Robert (Miscellaneous)
No More Excuses 1968,My 22,53:1
Soule, Olan
Queen Bee 1955,N 23,18:2
Soulier
Claudine 1940,Ap 1,15:2
Sounds, Inc
Go Go Mania 1965,My 20,52:4
Souper, Kay
Dreyfus Case, The 1931,Ag 31,11:5
Souplex, Raymond
Manon 1950,D 26,19:1
Lady Paname 1951,Mr 20,35:4
Three Sinners 1952,Jl 8,23:2
Sour, Hilda
Divorcio en Montevideo 1940,Ap 8,15:3
Sourabian, Masha
Arshin Mal Alan; Peddler, Lover, The
1937,Mr 8,22:2
Sourza, Jane
French Touch, The 1954,S 2,18:2
Sousania, W
Yankee Clipper, The 1927,My 3,25:1
Soussanin, Nicholas
Swan, The 1925,Mr 2,14:1
Midnight Sun, The 1926,Ap 24,20:4
Hotel Imperial 1927,Ja 3,16:2
Gentleman of Paris, A 1927,O 3,20:1
Spotlight, The 1927,N 28,18:5
Last Command, The 1928,Ja 23,18:3
Yellow Lily, The 1928,My 21,25:1
Night Watch, The 1928,O 8,14:2
Woman Disputed, The 1928,N 10,20:8
Adoration 1929,Ja 14,20:1

Squall, The 1929,My 10,32:5
Criminal Code, The 1931,Ja 5,21:3
White Shoulders 1931,Je 5,26:5
Daughter of the Dragon 1931,Ag 22,7:5
Under Two Flags 1936,My 1,19:1
Those High Grey Walls 1939,O 19,27:2
Soussanin, Nicholas (Screenwriter)
Betrayal 1929,My 6,30:4
Soutar, Andrew (Original Author)
Love's Redemption 1922,Ja 9,15:2
Man Called Back, The 1932,Jl 30,16:5
Soutar, John (Screenwriter)
Last Journey, The 1936,Je 8,22:4
Souter, Farren
Iron Duke, The 1935,Ja 25,27:2
Southard, Ruth (Original Author)
No Sad Songs for Me 1950,Ap 28,26:2
Souther, John
Snafu 1945,D 26,15:2
Southern, Eve
Resurrection 1927,My 17,27:2
Gaucho, The 1927,N 22,32:2
Wild Geese 1927,D 5,26:2
Clothes Make the Woman 1928,Je 5,21:1
Haunted House, The 1928,D 17,23:1
Lilies of the Field 1930,F 22,13:1
Morocco 1930,N 17,29:1
Fighting Caravans 1931,Ja 26,21:1
Ghost Walks, The 1935,Mr 30,11:2
Southern, Terry (Original Author)
Candy 1968,D 18,54:2
Southern, Terry (Screenwriter)
Dr Strangelove or: How I Learned to Stop
Worrying and Love the Bomb 1964,Ja 31,16:1
(Incorrect in this edition; use 1964,Ja 30,24:1
elsewhere)
Loved One, The 1965,O 12,57:1
Cincinnati Kid, The 1965,O 28,48:1
Barbarella 1968,O 12,43:1
Southern, Virginia
Greater Glory, The 1926,My 4,31:1
Soutten, Ben
Under the Red Robe 1937,Je 1,27:2
Mutiny of the Elsinore, The 1939,F 16,17:2
Soutten, Graham
Sign of the Four, The 1932,Ag 20,7:4
Souvestre, Pierre (Original Author)
Fantomas 1934,Mr 13,27:4
Soviet Army Cameramen (Cinematographer)
Great Battle of the Volga, The 1963,My 20,36:1
Soviet Army Choir
I Love, You Love 1962,N 10,16:2
Soya, Karl Eric (Original Author)
Eric Soya's 17 1967,Ja 25,37:1
Soyuzkino (Producer)
Cities and Years 1931,Ap 4,23:1
Alone 1932,My 25,23:6
Spaak, Catherine
Easy Life, The 1963,D 23,18:2
Of Wayward Love (The Women); Women, The
(Of Wayward Love) 1964,Mr 24,29:1
Empty Canvas, The 1964,My 16,21:1 (Incorrect
in this edition; use 1964,My 16,12:1 elsewhere)
Night Watch, The; Trou, Le 1964,My 27,46:1
Crazy Desire 1964,Jl 3,13:2
Circle of Love 1965,Mr 25,42:4
Little Nuns, The 1966,Ap 28,49:1
Weekend at Dunkirk 1966,My 19,51:2
Hotel 1967,Ja 20,27:1
Made in Italy 1967,My 1,44:2
Man With the Balloons, The 1968,Je 25,33:2
Spaak, Charles (Miscellaneous)
Lower Depths, The 1937,S 11,20:1
Spaak, Charles (Miscellaneous)
Queen's Necklace, The 1947,My 17,8:5
Spaak, Charles (Miscellaneous)
Idiot, The 1948,F 5,26:2
Woman Who Dared, The 1949,Mr 19,10:7
Cartouche 1964,Jl 22,39:1
Spaak, Charles (Narrator)
Man to Men 1949,F 21,20:2
Spaak, Charles (Original Author)
Kermesse Heroique, La 1936,S 23,29:1
They Were Five 1938,Je 1,19:5
Great Temptation, The 1942,Jl 10,13:3
Woman Who Dared, The 1949,Mr 19,10:7
Justice Is Done 1953,Mr 3,23:2
Spaak, Charles (Screenwriter)
Pension Mimosas 1936,My 6,27:1
Grand Illusion 1938,S 13,28:2
Sacrifice d'Honneur 1938,D 2,27:2
Escape From Yesterday 1939,My 3,27:2
End of a Day, The 1939,S 12,28:4
Two Women 1940,N 2,19:3
Man of the Hour, The 1940,N 21,43:2
Hatred 1941,Ja 27,11:2
Heart of a Nation, The 1943,Ap 8,27:2
Jericho 1946,D 16,31:2
Spaak, Charles (Screenwriter)
Queen's Necklace, The 1947,My 17,8:5
Spaak, Charles (Screenwriter)
Panic 1947,N 27,50:2
Idiot, The 1948,F 5,26:2

Spaak, Charles (Screenwriter)— Cont
Who Killed Santa Claus? 1948,Ap 21,33:2
Blind Desire 1948,Je 10,28:4
Eternal Husband, The 1949,Ja 10,19:2
Man to Men 1949,F 21,20:2
Captain Black Jack 1952,O 22,31:3
Seven Deadly Sins, The (Avarice and Anger);
Avarice and Anger (The Seven Deadly Sins)
1953,My 12,31:3
Adorable Creatures 1956,Ja 11,36:2
We Are all Murderers 1957,Ja 9,27:2
Adulteress, The 1958,Ja 14,42:1
Crime and Punishment 1958,S 16,23:2
Paris Hotel 1959,S 12,12:3
Love and the Frenchwoman; (Francaise et
l'Amour, La) 1961,F 28,38:2
Magnificent Sinner 1963,Ap 25,38:1
Burning Court, The 1963,Ag 1,17:2
Two Are Guilty 1964,F 29,12:1
Spaak, M (Miscellaneous)
Justice Is Done 1953,Mr 3,23:2
Spaccarelli, Dan
Synanon 1965,My 6,44:1
Spaccarelli, Giorgio
Hell Raiders of the Deep 1954,Jl 3,9:2
Space, Arthur
Bugle Sounds, The 1942,Ap 3,25:2
Rio Rita 1942,My 8,27:3
Tortilla Flat 1942,My 22,27:1
Quiet Please, Murder 1942,D 22,31:1
Dancing Masters, The 1943,D 2,30:2
Whistling in Brooklyn 1944,Mr 24,17:3
Big Noise, The 1944,S 23,16:1
Boy's Ranch 1946,Ag 9,12:2
Black Beauty 1946,Ag 30,13:2
Cockeyed Miracle, The 1946,O 25,28:1
Red House, The 1947,Mr 17,27:2
Guilt of Janet Ames, The 1947,My 23,31:2
Crimson Key, The 1947,O 18,9:2
Invisible Wall, The 1947,N 1,11:2
Fuller Brush Man, The 1948,My 15,18:2
Silver River 1948,My 22,8:3
Fighter Squadron 1948,N 20,9:2
Southern Yankee, A 1948,N 25,47:2
El Paso 1949,Mr 24,35:2
Mary Ryan, Detective 1949,N 4,33:3
Tomahawk 1951,F 19,19:2
Yankee Pasha 1954,Ap 19,19:2
Foxfire 1955,Jl 14,19:1
Spirit of St Louis, The 1957,F 22,25:1
Spacey, John
Moon's our Home, The 1936,My 13,29:2
Thank You, Jeeves 1936,O 5,25:1
Parole Racket 1937,Mr 8,22:1
Who Killed Gail Preston? 1938,My 6,27:2
British Intelligence 1940,F 12,14:2
Spada, Maecello
Bertoldo, Bertoldino, Cacasenno 1937,D 22,32:3
Spada, Marcello
Lacrime e Sorrisi 1936,D 17,35:2
Scipio Africanus 1939,S 23,22:2
Spadaro, Giuseppe
Shoe-Shine 1947,Ag 27,19:2
Spadaro, Italia
Seduced and Abandoned 1964,Jl 16,23:1
Spadaro, Odoardo
Golden Coach, The 1954,Ja 22,30:2
Divorce-Italian Style 1962,S 18,34:1
Spadaro, Peppino
Mafia; (In Nome Della Legge) 1950,Mr 2,33:2
Ring Around the Clock 1953,My 19,36:2
Spadaro, Umberto
Foria 1948,Ja 21,30:2
Furia 1948,Ja 21,30:2
Difficult Years 1950,Ag 22,31:2
Angelo 1951,Mr 26,19:4
Women Without Names 1951,Ag 7,22:2
Brief Rapture 1952,F 28,23:2
Angelo in the Crowd 1952,O 4,15:2
Journey to Love 1953,O 9,32:8
Seduces and Abandoned 1964,Jl 16,23:1
Eye of the Needle, The 1965,Je 22,25:2
Spade, Marcello
Kif Tebbi 1929,My 20,22:6
Spade, Super
You Are What You Eat 1968,S 25,38:1
Spaeth, Merrie
World of Henry Orient, The 1964,Mr 20,27:2
Spafford, Robert (Director)
Heaven on Earth 1960,O 11,55:3
Spafford, Robert (Screenwriter)
Heaven on Earth 1960,O 11,55:3
Spagnoli, Genaro
Lost-a Wife 1925,Je 22,10:2
Honeymoon Hate 1927,D 31,31:1
Ruggles of Red Gap 1935,Mr 7,26:1
Spain, Fay
God's Little Acre 1958,Ag 14,23:2
Al Capone 1959,Mr 26,27:1
Beat Generation, The 1959,O 22,47:4
Welcome to Hard Times 1967,My 2,56:1
Spal, Jaromir
Bohemian Rapture 1948,F 16,16:2

SPALDING
See Also SPAULDING
Spalding, Harry (Screenwriter)
Surf Party 1964,Mr 12,40:4
Day Mars Invaded Earth, The 1964,Ap 2,28:3
Murder Game, The 1966,Mr 31,43:2
Spalla, Erminio
Deported 1950,N 2,39:3
Miracle in Milan 1951,D. 18,42:2
Sailor From Gibraltar, The 1967,Ap 25,38:2
Sparber, Isidore (Original Author)
Mr Bug Goes to Town 1942,F 20,21:3
Sparber, Isidore (Screenwriter)
Gulliver's Travels 1939,D 21,29:1
Mr Bug Goes to Town 1942,F 20,21:3
Sparemblek, Milko
Lovers of Teruel, The 1962,D 15,5:1
Lovers of Teruel, The 1962,D 15,5:1
Sparke, Pip
Father Goose 1964,D 11,55:1
Sparkin, Ned
Virtuous Vamp, A 1919,N 17,20:1
Sparks, Fay
Reflections in a Golden Eye 1967,O 12,59:1
Sparks, Martha Lee
So This Is London 1930,My 24,21:2
Daddy Long Legs 1931,Je 6,15:5
Sparks, Ned
His Supreme Moment 1925,Ap 13,24:1
Boomerang, The 1925,Jl 1,16:1
Seven Keys to Baldpate 1925,N 3,25:4
Bright Lights 1925,N 18,27:4
Only Thing, The 1925,N 23,25:4
Soul Mates 1926,Ja 4,16:1
Mike 1926,Ja 11,33:1
Auction Block, The 1926,F 15,16:4
Money Talks 1926,My 11,24:3
Secret Studio, The 1927,Je 15,31:4
Alias the Deacon 1927,Je 21,29:2
Alias the Lone Wolf 1927,S 20,32:2
Big Noise, The 1928,My 7,29:1
Magnificent Flirt, The 1928,Je 25,27:1
Strange Cargo 1929,F 18,28:1
Canary Murder Case, The 1929,Mr 11,22:2
Nothing but the Truth 1929,Ap 22,23:1
Street Girl 1929,Jl 31,17:3
Love Comes Along 1930,F 1,15:1
Double Cross Roads 1930,Ap 29,31:1
Devil's Holiday, The 1930,My 10,25:3
Fall Guy, The 1930,My 27,27:2
Leathernecking 1930,S 13,9:3
Kept Husbands 1931,Mr 24,31:2
Iron Man 1931,Ap 18,17:3
Secret Call, The 1931,Jl 13,13:5
Corsair 1931,N 19,27:5
Miracle Man, The 1932,Ap 21,25:2
Blessed Event 1932,S 3,16:2
Big City Blues 1932,S 10,18:5
Crusader, The 1932,O 8,15:4
42d Street 1933,Mr 10,19:3
Secrets 1933,Mr 16,21:2
Gold Diggers of 1933 1933,Je 8,22:3
Lady for a Day 1933,S 8,22:2
Too Much Harmony 1933,S 23,11:5
Going Hollywood 1933,D 23,19:2
Alice in Wonderland 1933,D 23,19:1
Hi, Nellie! 1934,F 1,15:5
Sing and Like It 1934,Ap 14,18:2
Private Scandal 1934,Je 15,26:2
Down to Their Last Yacht 1934,S 24,14:1
Servants' Entrance 1934,S 27,25:2
Marie Galante 1934,N 21,23:4
Imitation of Life 1934,N 24,19:1
Sweet Adeline 1935,Ja 7,13:2
Sweet Music 1935,F 21,23:2
George White's 1935 Scandals 1935,Ap 29,12:3
Collegiate 1936,Ja 23,25:2
One in a Million 1937,Ja 1,19:3
Wake up and Live 1937,Ap 24,16:2
This Way Please 1937,O 8,27:2
Hawaii Calls 1938,Ap 29,17:2
Star Maker, The 1939,Ag 31,14:2
Stage Door Canteen 1943,Je 25,13:2
Magic Town 1947,O 8,29:2
Sparks, Randy
Big Night, The 1960,F 18,37:4
Sparks, Robert (Producer)
So You Won't Talk 1940,O 17,33:2
Blondie Goes Latin 1941,F 26,17:3
Go West, Young Lady 1941,N 24,11:6
Easy Living 1949,O 13,33:3
Dangerous Profession, A 1949,D 12,29:4
Born to be Bad 1950,S 29,31:5
Walk Softly Stranger 1950,O 16,30:5
His Kind of Woman 1951,Ag 30,20:2
Las Vegas Story, The 1952,Ja 31,37:6
Son of Sinbad 1955,Jl 28,18:2
Sparkuhl, Theodore (Cinematographer)
Loves of Pharaoh 1922,F 22,13:3 (In Addenda)
Sparry, Willis Capt
Unidentified Flying Objects 1956,Je 13,46:2

Sparv, Camilla
Trouble With Angels, The 1966,Ap 7,45:1
Dead Heat on a Merry-Go-Round 1966,O 13,50:1
Murderers' Row 1966,D 22,40:3
Assignment K 1968,Jl 20,18:2
High Commissioner, The 1968,D 12,62:5
SPAULDING
See Also SPALDING
Spaulding, Bill
Jackie Robinson Story, The 1950,My 17,36:1
Spaulding, Harry (Producer)
Seven Women From Hell 1962,F 1,22:2
Spaulding, Kim
Off Limits 1953,Mr 30,25:5
Spaulding, Nellie Parker
Twenty-One 1924,F 18,13:1
Time, the Comedian 1925,D 14,18:2
Spaziani, Ello
Gospel According to St Matthew, The 1966,F 18,23:1
Speaker, Tris
Ninth Inning, The 1942,Ja 8,30:3
Speaks, John (Producer)
Dancing Pirate 1936,Je 18,19:1
Spear, Bernard
Bedazzled 1967,D 11,65:2
Speare, Dorothy (Original Author)
One Night of Love 1934,S 7,25:3
Spearing, James O (Original Author)
Devil Tiger 1934,F 9,23:2
Spearing, James O (Screenwriter)
Signal Tower, The 1924,Jl 21,14:4
Spearman, Frank H (Original Author)
Love Special, The 1921,Mr 21,11:3
Night Flyer, The 1928,Mr 13,23:3
Whispering Smith Speaks 1936,F 17,21:1
Whispering Smith 1949,F 15,28:2
Spector, Yiftach
Clouds Over Israel 1966,My 10,48:6
Speelmans, Herman
Voruntersuchung; Inquest 1931,My 24,VIII,4:1
Der Herr Finanzdirektor 1932,Je 25,18:2
Strich Durch die Rechnung 1934,Mr 3,8:6
Schuss im Morgengrauen 1934,S 29,12:3
Vier Musketiere, Die; Four Musketeers, The 1935,N 9,19:3
Herr Kobin Geht auf Abenteuer; Mr Kobin Seeks Adventure 1935,N 26,28:2
Graue Dame, Die; Gray Lady, The 1938,D 17,10:4
Seven Journeys 1951,Mr 12,20:2
Speelmans, Hermann
Schlacht von Bademuende, Die 1931,N 21,20:4
Hauptmann von Koepenick, Der 1933,Ja 17,22:6
Eine Tuer geht Auf 1933,F 6,11:5
Ein Gewisser Herr Gran 1934,F 24,18:5
Eines Prinzen Junge Liebe 1934,Mr 24,20:4
Zu Befehl, Herr Unteroffizier 1934,Je 16,20:3
Unsere Fahne Flattert Uns Voran 1934,Jl 7,16:6
Mann Will Nach Deutschland, Ein 1934,N 13,22:4
Ferien vom Ich 1935,Ap 1,17:2
Ganzer Kerl, Ein 1936,Ap 25,21:2
Seltsamer Gast, Ein 1937,Jl 10,18:2
Werf zum Graven Hecht, Die; Gray Pikes Wharf, The 1938,Ap 18,11:2
Musketier Meier III 1938,D 31,7:2
Dahinten in der Heide; Back in the Country 1939,Ja 21,19:3
Congo Express 1940,My 11,15:3
Ballerina 1958,My 10,19:2
Spehr, Albert
Great Commandment, The 1942,O 17,11:1
Speigel, Georgi
Taxi to Heaven 1944,My 25,16:3
Speight, Johnny (Original Author)
Privilege 1967,Jl 25,30:2
Spelling, Aaron
Vickie 1953,S 8,26:3
Three Young Texans 1954,Ap 17,8:2
One Foot in Hell 1960,O 20,42:2
Spelling, Aaron (Screenwriter)
One Foot in Hell 1960,O 20,42:2
Spellman, Martin
Boys Town 1938,S 9,25:1
Sharpshooters 1938,D 5,19:2
Let Us Live 1939,Mr 30,19:2
Santa Fe Stampede 1939,Ap 26,27:3
Streets of New York 1939,My 1,21:1
Meet the Chump 1941,F 27,23:4
Spelvin, George
Just Suppose 1926,Ja 18,26:2
Redemption 1930,My 3,23:1
Suzy 1936,Jl 25,16:1
Spence, Hartzell (Original Author)
One Foot in Heaven 1941,N 14,28:3
Spence, Ralph
Millions in the Air 1935,D 12,33:4
Spence, Ralph (Miscellaneous)
Oath, The 1921,Ap 11,9:1
His Darker Self 1924,Mr 26,19:2
Callahans and the Murphys, The 1927,Jl 12,29:3

Spence, Ralph (Miscellaneous) — Cont
Florodora Girl, The 1930,My 31,19:4
Silent Barriers 1937,Mr 26,25:1
Spence, Ralph (Original Author)
Gorilla, The 1927,N 21,20:1
Gorilla, The 1931,F 23,20:3
Tomorrow at Seven 1933,Jl 3,14:6
Poor Little Rich Girl, The 1936,Je 26,16:1
Gorilla, The 1939,My 28,6:2
Flying Deuces, The 1939,N 24,29:2
Down Argentine Way 1940,O 18,25:1
Around the World 1943,N 25,39:2
Plainsman and the Lady, The 1946,N 4,33:1
Spence, Ralph (Screenwriter)
Student Tour 1934,O 31,17:3
Band Plays on, The 1934,D 22,21:2
Winning Ticket, The 1935,F 11,14:2
Big Broadcast of 1936, The 1935,S 16,15:2
King Solomon's Mines 1937,Jl 3,18:1
Sh! The Octopus 1937,D 24,21:2
Flying Deuces, The 1939,N 24,29:2
Fleet's In, The 1942,Mr 12,24:2
Seven Days' Leave 1942,D 11,33:2
Around the World 1943,N 25,39:2
Higher and Higher 1944,Ja 22,8:4
Spencer, Clem (Composer)
Utah 1945,Mr 12,22:7
Spencer, Diana
Don't Give up the Ship 1959,Jl 9,22:1
Spencer, Douglas
Big Clock, The 1948,Ap 22,34:2
Bride of Vengeance 1949,Ap 7,38:2
Thing, The 1951,My 3,34:4
Redhead and the Cowboy, The 1951,Je 6,37:2
Place in the Sun, A 1951,Ag 29,20:1
Come Fill the Cup 1951,N 22,47:2
Monkey Business 1952,S 6,12:6
She's Back on Broadway 1953,Mr 12,24:2
Shane 1953,Ap 24,30:3
Trouble Along the Way 1953,My 7,37:2
Houdini 1953,Jl 3,10:2
River of no Return 1954,My 1,13:2
Kentuckian, The 1955,S 2,13:2
Three Faces of Eve, The 1957,S 27,16:6
Saddle the Wind 1958,Mr 21,17:1
Diary of Anne Frank, The 1959,Mr 19,40:1
Spencer, Elizabeth (Original Author)
Light in the Piazza 1962,F 8,25:1
Spencer, Franz G (Original Author)
Pacific Blackout 1942,Ja 15,25:2
Born to Sing 1942,F 19,23:2
Spencer, Franz G (Screenwriter)
Born to Sing 1942,F 19,23:2
Fighting Guardsman, The 1945,O 6,9:6
Masquerade in Mexico 1945,N 29,27:2
Spencer, Glenn (Composer)
Apache Rose 1947,Jl 23,19:3
Spencer, James
Adventure 1925,Ap 15,16:1
Spencer, Jeanne (Original Author)
Adventure in Washington 1941,Ag 1,11:3
Spencer, Joe
Bike Boy 1967,O 6,31:2
Spencer, Kenneth
Cabin in the Sky 1943,My 28,19:3
Bataan 1943,Je 4,17:2
Spencer, Lou
Call Me Mister 1951,F 1,21:2
Spencer, Marian
Weaker Sex, The 1949,Jl 11,13:2
Bond Street 1950,Mr 30,40:6
Intimate Relations 1954,F 22,15:4
Spencer, Mya Mya
Purple Plain, The 1955,Ap 11,29:1
Spencer, Norman (Screenwriter)
Hobson's Choice 1954,Je 15,37:1
Spencer, Ralph (Screenwriter)
Larceny Street 1941,Ja 6,11:2
Spencer, Ray (Screenwriter)
Crack-Up 1946,S 7,11:1
Spencer, Robert
Sea Hawk, The 1924,Je 3,22:1
Reported Missing 1937,S 3,12:2
Jury's Secret, The 1938,F 4,17:2
Spencer, Tim (Composer)
Utah 1945,Mr 12,22:7
Hit Parade of 1947 1947,My 5,32:8
Apache Rose 1947,Jl 23,19:3
Spenser, Jeremy
Anna Karenina 1948,Ap 28,32:2
Prelude to Fame 1950,N 10,35:3
Dancing Years, The 1951,Ja 29,14:4
Portrait of Clare 1951,D 26,19:6
Spider and the Fly, The 1952,Jl 29,17:3
Outpost in Malaya 1952,N 27,49:2
Edge of Divorce 1954,Jl 2,10:1
Summertime 1955,Je 22,25:1
Man Who Loved Redheads, The 1955,Jl 26,29:2
Prince and the Showgirl 1957,Je 14,22:2
Escapade 1957,Ag 6,30:2
It's Great to be Young 1957,D 26,23:3
Ferry to Hong Kong 1961,Ap 27,27:7
Roman Spring of Mrs Stone, The 1961,D 29,11:1
King and Country 1964,S 24,46:2

Spenser, Jeremy— Cont
King and Country 1966,Ja 28,20:4
Fahrenheit 451 1966,N 15,53:1
He Who Rides a Tiger 1968,S 10,39:1
Spentzoff, Sophia
Code 7...Victim 5 1965,My 20,52:1
Sperber, Milo
Mr Emmanuel 1945,Ja 8,15:2
End of the River, The 1948,Je 21,18:2
Billion Dollar Brain 1967,D 23,29:1
Speribauer, Fritz
Rosenkavalier, Der 1962,O 10,57:1
Sperling, Milton (Original Author)
Sing, Baby, Sing 1936,S 12,20:1
Happy Landing 1938,Ja 22,19:1
Court-Martial of Billy Mitchell, The
1955,D 23,14:2
Sperling, Milton (Producer)
Sun Valley Serenade 1941,S 6,20:1
I Wake up Screaming 1942,Ja 17,13:2
Rings on her Fingers 1942,Ap 24,21:4
Hello, Frisco, Hello 1943,Mr 25,25:1
Crash Dive 1943,Ap 29,25:2
Cloak and Dagger 1946,O 5,13:2
My Girl Tisa 1948,F 21,9:2
South of St Louis 1949,Mr 7,17:2
Three Secrets 1950,O 21,10:6
Enforcer, The 1951,Ja 26,19:2
Distant Drums 1951,D 26,19:3
Retreat Hell! 1952,F 20,26:2
Blowing Wild 1953,O 8,37:5
Court-Martial of Billy Mitchell, The
1955,D 23,14:2
Marjorie Morningstar 1958,Ap 25,32:2
Rise and Fall of Legs' Diamond, The
1960,F 4,34:1
Bramble Bush, The 1960,F 25,34:2
Merrill's Marauders 1962,Je 14,23:4
Battle of the Bulge 1965,D 18,36:1
Sperling, Milton (Screenwriter)
Sing, Baby, Sing 1936,S 12,20:1
Thin Ice 1937,S 4,8:2
I'll Give a Million 1938,Jl 16,7:2
Return of the Cisco Kid, The 1939,Ap 29,13:2
Here I Am a Stranger 1939,S 30,11:2
Great Profile, The 1940,O 18,25:1
Retreat Hell! 1952,F 20,26:2
Court-Martial of Billy Mitchell, The
1955,D 23,14:2
Bramble Bush, The 1960,F 25,34:2
Merrill's Marauders 1962,Je 14,23:4
Battle of the Bulge 1965,D 18,36:1
Spewack, Bella (Original Author)
Clear all Wires 1933,Mr 4,11:2
Solitaire Man, The 1933,S 23,11:5
Gay Bride, The 1934,D 19,27:2
Boy Meets Girl 1938,Ag 27,7:2
My Favorite Wife 1940,My 31,15:2
Kiss Me Kate 1953,N 6,23:2
Move Over Darling 1963,D 26,33:1
Spewack, Bella (Screenwriter)
Rendezvous 1935,O 26,12:2
Vogues of 1938 1937,Ag 20,21:1
Chaser, The 1938,Ag 2,15:3
Boy Meets Girl 1938,Ag 27,7:2
Three Loves Has Nancy 1938,S 2,21:2
My Favorite Wife 1940,My 31,15:2
Week-End at the Waldorf 1945,O 5,27:2
Move Over Darling 1963,D 26,33:1
Spewack, Samuel (Original Author)
Secret Witness, The 1931,D 21,28:4
Clear all Wires 1933,Mr 4,11:2
Solitaire Man, The 1933,S 23,11:5
Gay Bride, The 1934,D 19,27:2
Boy Meets Girl 1938,Ag 27,7:2
My Favorite Wife 1940,My 31,15:2
Kiss Me Kate 1953,N 6,23:2
Move Over Darling 1963,D 26,33:1
Spewack, Samuel (Producer)
World at War, The 1942,S 4,19:1
Spewack, Samuel (Screenwriter)
Rendezvous 1935,O 26,12:2
Vogues of 1938 1937,Ag 20,21:1
Chaser, The 1938,Ag 2,15:3
Boy Meets Girl 1938,Ag 27,7:2
Three Loves Has Nancy 1938,S 2,21:2
My Favorite Wife 1940,My 31,15:2
World at War, The 1942,S 4,19:1
Week-End at the Waldorf 1945,O 5,27:2
Move Over Darling 1963,D 26,33:1
Speyer, Erica
Sand Castle, The 1961,Ag 16,37:2
Speyer, Eve
Women Without Men 1928,N 12,18:2
Speyer, Rudolf
Moritz Macht Sein Glueck 1932,D 24,11:4
Speyer, William (Original Author)
Hat, Coat and Glove 1934,Jl 27,21:2
Night of Adventure, A 1944,Je 3,10:4
Speziali, Renato
Hours of Love, The 1965,S 4,11:5
Railroad Man, The; Ferroviere, Il 1965,O 25,46:2

Spice, Evelyn (Director)
Monkey Into Man 1941,My 31,14:1
Spiegel, Astrid
Echoes of Silence 1967,Ap 7,32:2
Spiegel, Ed (Director)
Justice and Caryl Chessman 1960,Mr 3,24:5
Spiegel, Georgi
Road Home, The 1947,My 2,28:3
Spiegel, Sam (Producer)
On the Waterfront 1954,Jl 29,18:1
Strange One, The 1957,Ap 13,12:3
Bridge on the River Kwai 1957,D 19,39:1
Suddenly, Last Summer 1959,D 23,22:1
Chase, The 1966,F 19,24:1
Spiehs, Carl (Producer)
How to Seduce a Playboy 1968,My 16,53:2
Spielman, Fred (Composer)
Bachelor's Daughters, The 1946,O 7,23:2
Torch Song 1953,O 13,34:2
Tom Thumb 1958,D 24,00:0
Spier, William (Director)
Lady Possessed 1952,F 15,17:2
Spies, Adrian (Screenwriter)
Dark of the Sun 1968,Jl 4,13:1
Spies, Walter (Director)
Wajan 1938,Ap 18,11:1
Spigel, Leonard (Original Author)
Silk Stockings 1957,Jl 19,11:1
Spigelgass, Leonard (Original Author)
I'll Fix It 1934,N 12,17:3
Unexpected Father 1939,Ag 11,12:2
Million Dollar Baby 1941,Je 7,20:2
All Through the Night 1942,Ja 24,13:2
They Got Me Covered 1943,Mr 5,20:2
Mystery Street 1950,Jl 28,12:5
Athena 1954,D 22,28:2
Ten Thousand Bedrooms 1957,Ap 4,37:1
Pepe 1960,D 22,18:1
Majority of One, A 1962,Ja 12,29:2
Spigelgass, Leonard (Screenwriter)
Letter of Introduction 1938,S 1,17:1
Service de Luxe 1938,O 24,13:2
Unexpected Father 1939,Ag 11,12:2
Private Affairs 1940,Jl 5,10:3
Tight Shoes 1941,Je 19,25:2
All Through the Night 1942,Ja 24,13:2
Butch Minds the Baby 1942,My 1,23:3
Big Street, The 1942,Ag 14,13:1
Youngest Profession, The 1943,Je 25,13:3
Perfect Marriage, The 1947,Ja 16,30:3
So Evil my Love 1948,Jl 22,27:2
I Was a Male War Bride 1949,Ag 27,7:2
Night Into Morning 1951,Je 11,20:7
Law and the Lady, The 1951,Ag 16,23:2
Because You're Mine 1952,S 26,18:2
Deep in my Heart 1954,D 10,35:2
Majority of One, A 1962,Ja 12,29:2
Gypsy 1962,N 2,24:1
Spiker, Ray
Our Daily Bread 1934,O 3,25:2
Brasher Doubloon, The 1947,My 22,34:5
Shane 1953,Ap 24,30:3
Spillane, Mickey
Ring of Fear 1954,Jl 29,18:3
Spillane, Mickey (Original Author)
I, The Jury 1953,Ag 22,8:2
Long Wait, The 1954,Jl 3,9:2
Spina, Harold (Composer)
Happy Landing 1938,Ja 22,19:1
Little Miss Broadway 1938,Jl 23,10:4
Just Around the Corner 1938,D 3,11:2
Spina, Howard (Composer)
Sally, Irene and Mary 1938,F 26,9:2
Spina, Maria Grazia
Cossacks, The 1960,S 6,41:4
Samson and the Slave Queen 1964,Mr 5,36:2
Successo, Il 1965,Ap 29,40:2
Bible, The 1966,S 29,60:1
Spindola, Robert
Ramona 1936,O 7,32:4
Firefly, The 1937,S 2,17:2
Spinelli
Moscow Nights 1938,My 3,19:3
Spinetti, Victor
Hard Day's Night, A 1964,Ag 12,41:1
Help! 1965,Ag 24,25:1
Taming of the Shrew, The 1967,Mr 9,43:1
Biggest Bundle of Them All, The 1968,Ja 18,46:1
Spingler, Harry
Perfect Lady, A 1918,D 2,11:3
Spinna, Harold (Composer)
New Faces of 1937 1937,Jl 2,25:1
Spinner, Marilyn
West Point of the Air 1935,Ap 6,10:1
Spinola, Paolo (Director)
Fuga, La 1966,Mr 22,33:1
Spinola, Paolo (Miscellaneous)
Fuga, La 1966,Mr 22,33:1
Spira, Camilla
Aftermath 1927,D 6,27:1
Mein Leopold 1932,Ap 1,17:4
Morgenrot 1933,My 16,15:2
Die Lustigen Musikanten 1933,My 27,11:6

Spira, Camilla— Cont
Ja, Treu Ist die Soldatenliebe 1934,Ap 28,11:4
Gehetzie Menschen 1934,Je 2,22:5
Judas von Tirol, Der 1935,Ap 27,20:7
Gruen ist die Heide 1935,O 14,21:2
Merry Wives of Windsor, The 1952,S 22,19:2
Grapes are Ripe, The 1953,O 15,43:2
Devil's General, The 1957,Ap 16,38:2
Sky Without Stars 1959,My 30,9:2
Roses for the Prosecutor; (Rosen fur den
Staarsanwalt) 1961,O 10,38:2
Spira, Fritz
Der Schrecken der Garnison 1932,Je 1,19:5
Feldherrnhuegel, Der 1934,Ap 20,17:2
Spira, Lotte
Liebeswalzer 1931,My 4,15:3
Leutnant Warst Du Einst bei den Husaren
1932,Mr 14,13:3
Hermine und die Sieben Aufrechten
1935,S 21,18:2
Kleine Nachtmusik, Eine 1940,Mr 2,9:5
Spira-Andresen, Lotte
Congo Express 1940,My 11,15:3
Spirina, Valentina (Screenwriter)
Gift for Music 1957,Jl 15,15:2
Grown-Up Children 1963,Ap 15,36:5
Spirit, Jiri
Distant Journey 1950,Ag 28,13:3
Spiro, Richard
His Woman 1931,D 5,21:2
Spitalny, Phil and his all-girl orchestra
Here Come the Co-Eds 1945,F 19,21:1
Spitz, Ernst (Original Author)
World and the Flesh, The 1932,My 7,11:5
Spitzer, Marian (Screenwriter)
Dolly Sisters, The 1945,N 15,24:6
Look for the Silver Lining 1949,Je 24,29:2
Spivak, Charlie and His Orchestra
Pin Up Girl 1944,My 11,25:6
Spivak, Charlie and orchestra
Follow the Boys 1944,Ap 26,24:6
Spivey, Cordelia
Forest Ring, The 1930,Ap 26,11:1
Spivey, Victoria
Hallelujah 1929,Ag 21,33:1
Spivy
Fugitive Kind, The 1960,Ap 15,13:1
Studs Lonigan 1960,D 15,59:1
All Fall Down 1962,Ap 12,41:3
Requiem for a Heavyweight 1962,O 17,35:1
Spletter, Carla
Letzte Rose 1936,O 10,21:3
Spohr, Vera
Ich Will Nicht Wissen Wer Du Bist
1933,F 16,23:2
Spolianski, Michael (Composer)
Gaiety Girls, The 1938,Mr 31,15:1
Spolianski, Michael (Miscellaneous)
Nie Wieder Liebe; No More Love
1931,O 4,VIII,7:1
Sanders of the River 1935,Je 27,16:1
Spoliansky, M (Composer)
My Song For You 1935,My 27,20:6
Spoliansky (Composer)
Evensong 1934,N 17,12:1
Spollone, Daniel
Steppe, The 1963,O 1,33:1
Spong, Hilda
Star Overnight, A 1919,N 17,20:1
Sponza, Mario
Stromboli 1950,F 16,28:2
Spooks (Dog)
Family Next Door, The 1939,Ap 28,31:2
Sposito, Carletto
Difficult Years 1950,Ag 22,31:2
Women Without Names 1951,Ag 7,22:2
Young Caruso, The 1953,O 13,34:4
Theodora, Slave Empress 1955,Ja 12,24:2
See Naples and Die 1959,Ag 31,16:2
Spotted Elk
Silent Enemy, The 1930,My 20,32:3
Spottiswoode, Raymond (Director)
3 Dimension 1953,F 4,32:2
Spotton, John (Director)
Memorandum 1967,S 26,54:4
Spottwood, James
Thunderbolt 1929,Je 21,17:2
Stadium Murders, The 1938,Ap 9,11:2
Sprague, Chandler (Director)
Not Damaged 1930,Je 9,23:3
Dancers, The 1930,N 15,15:3
Sprague, Chandler (Original Author)
Nuisance, The 1933,My 29,22:2
Early to Bed 1936,Jl 16,20:2
Chaser, The 1938,Ag 2,15:3
Guy Named Joe, A 1943,D 24,17:2
Sprague, Chandler (Screenwriter)
Menace 1934,N 22,27:2
Sprague, Milton
George Washington Carver 1940,Ap 17,26:4
Spring, B
White Hell of Pitz Palu, The 1930,S 27,21:3

Spring, Helen
To Please a Lady 1950,O 27,24:3
Emergency Wedding 1950,D 22,19:2
Something to Live For 1952,My 8,11:2
Spring, Howard (Original Author)
My Son, My Son! 1940,My 10,26:6
Fame Is the Spur 1949,N 8,34:2
Springer, Arthur (Original Author)
Wilderness Woman, The 1926,My 10,19:1
Springer, Norman (Original Author)
Blood Ship, The 1927,Jl 19,27:2
Submarine 1928,Ag 31,23:3
Devil's Playground 1937,F 15,12:5
Springfeld, Pavel
In the Rear of the Enemy 1942,O 10,11:2
Springfeld, Peter
Four Hearts 1946,F 25,21:5
Springs, Elliott White (Original Author)
Hard-Boiled Haggerty 1927,Ag 23,29:4
Young Eagles 1930,Mr 22,22:6
Springson, Sam
Mr Cohen Takes a Walk 1936,F 13,25:2
Springsteen, R G (Director)
Hellfire 1949,My 30,9:4
Red Menace, The 1949,Je 27,18:2
Singing Guns 1950,Je 5,19:3
Operation Eichmann 1961,My 4,40:7
He Rides Tall 1964,F 27,28:1
Taggart 1964,D 25,24:4
Black Spurs 1965,My 29,17:1
Johnny Reno 1966,Mr 10,26:3
Sprogoe, Ove
Journey to the Seventh Planet 1962,My 25,28:3
Crazy Paradise 1965,Ag 11,41:2
Sprotte, Bert
Jes' Call Me Jim 1920,My 24,20:3
O'Malley of the Mounted 1921,F 7,8:2
Soul of the Beast, The 1923,My 22,14:4
Rosita 1923,S 4,14:1
Wild Bill Hickok 1923,N 21,22:1
Singer Jim McKee 1924,Mr 24,13:1
Shooting of Dan McGrew, The 1924,Je 9,14:3
Little Robinson Crusoe 1924,S 3,17:1
His Hour 1924,O 7,26:1
Confessions of a Queen 1925,Mr 24,20:6
Private Life of Helen of Troy, The
  1927,D 10,14:7
Married in Hollywood 1929,S 23,24:3
Passport to Hell, A 1932,Ag 27,13:4
Song of the Eagle 1933,Ap 29,14:3
Pursuit of Happiness, The 1934,O 26,25:1
Spyri, Johanna (Original Author)
Heidi 1937,N 6,14:2
Heidi 1953,D 21,27:2
Heidi and Peter 1955,D 13,55:2
Heidi 1968,S 23,42:4
Spyropoulos, V (Screenwriter)
Anna of Rhodes 1950,Mr 23,34:2
Squier, Emma-Lindsay (Original Author)
Dancing Pirate 1936,Je 18,19:1
Squier, Lucita (Screenwriter)
Penrod 1922,F 20,7:1
Squinquel, Jose
Pasteur 1936,Ja 30,14:3
Squire, Anthony (Miscellaneous)
Breaking Through the Sound Barrier
  1952,N 7,19:1
Squire, Donald
Voice in the Night, The 1941,My 23,25:4
Squire, Harry E (Cinematographer)
Fang and Claw 1935,D 28,10:5
Squire, Katherine
Story of Page One, The 1960,Ja 14,28:1
Song Without End 1960,Ag 12,10:2
Squire, Ronald
Unfinished Symphony 1935,Ja 14,11:2
Rocking Horse Winner, The 1950,Je 9,29:2
While the Sun Shines 1950,Jl 1,9:2
No Highway in the Sky 1951,S 22,8:6
Encore (Winter Cruise); Winter Cruise (Encore)
  1952,Ap 3,45:1
My Cousin Rachel 1952,D 26,20:2
It Started in Paradise 1953,Jl 25,8:2
Always a Bride 1954,My 28,19:2
Scotch on the Rocks 1954,Je 14,18:2
Man With a Million 1954,Je 29,21:2
Footsteps of the Fog 1955,S 15,39:2
Around the World in 80 Days 1956,O 18,37:1
Raising a Riot 1957,My 8,44:1
Island in the Sun 1957,Je 13,37:1
Silken Affair, The 1957,O 31,41:1
Law and Disorder 1958,Ag 6,20:1
Inn of the Sixth Happiness, The 1958,D 14,2:7
Sheriff of Fractured Jaw, The 1959,Mr 14,27:4
Count Your Blessings 1959,Ap 24,23:1
Squire, William
Long Dark Hall, The 1951,My 10,38:3
Alexander the Great 1956,Mr 29,23:1
Srabo, Sandor
Hell's Island 1955,My 7,10:2
Srisurang, Luang
King of the White Elephant, The 1941,Ap 5,12:7

Srodka, S
Border Street 1950,Ap 26,35:2
Staal, Hetra
Dancing Heart, The 1958,Ja 18,10:3
Staal, Viktor
Donogoo Tonka 1936,Ap 13,15:2
Waldwinter 1936,N 14,23:3
Zu neven Ufern; To new Shores 1938,Ja 29,12:1
Gewitter im Mai; Storms in May 1938,Mr 5,11:3
Nacht im Mai, Eine; Night in May, A
  1938,N 12,10:3
Recht auf Liebe, Das; Right to Love, The
  1940,Je 15,12:3
Taiga 1959,Mr 17,42:4
Stabenau, Tony
Hold Everything 1930,Ap 23,24:1
Stabile, Dick
At War With the Army 1951,Ja 25,21:5
Stabler, Robert W (Producer)
Dayton's Devils 1968,O 3,56:4
Stack, Graham
Guns at Batasi 1964,N 17,47:1
Stack, Gunter
Torn Curtain 1966,Jl 28,23:1
Stack, Robert
First Love 1939,N 9,27:3
Mortal Storm, The 1940,Je 21,25:2
Little Bit of Heaven, A 1940,N 8,24:2
Nice Girl 1941,Mr 27,29:6
Badlands of Dakota 1941,S 9,27:6
To Be or not to Be 1942,Mr 7,13:2
Eagle Squadron 1942,Jl 3,12:5
Men of Texas 1942,Jl 13,18:3 (In Addenda)
Date with Judy, A 1948,Ag 7,8:2
Fighter Squadron 1948,N 20,9:2
Miss Tatlock's Millions 1948,N 25,47:2
Mr Music 1950,D 21,34:3
Bullfighter and the Lady, The 1951,Ap 27,19:2
My Outlaw Brother 1951,Ag 23,19:2
Bwana Devil 1953,F 19,20:5
Sabre Jet 1953,N 3,34:1
High and the Mighty, The 1954,Jl 1,21:2
House of Bamboo 1955,Jl 2,13:2
Good Morning, Miss Dove 1955,N 24,41:1
Great Day in the Morning 1956,My 19,12:6
Written on the Wind 1957,Ja 12,12:6
Tarnished Angels, The 1958,Ja 7,31:1
Gift of Love, The 1958,F 12,32:2
John Paul Jones 1959,Je 17,39:1
Last Voyage, The 1960,F 20,14:2
Caretakers, The 1963,Ag 22,19:2
Is Paris Burning? 1966,N 11,36:1
Corrupt Ones, The 1967,F 23,41:3
Stack, William
Sarah and Son 1930,Mr 13,22:4
Derelict 1930,N 22,21:3
Payment Deferred 1932,N 8,26:3
Charlie Chan's Greatest Case 1933,O 7,18:4
Tarzan and his Mate 1934,Ap 21,12:1
Fountain, The 1934,Ag 31,14:1
Hell in the Heavens 1934,D 12,28:2
Becky Sharp 1935,Je 14,27:2
Mary of Scotland 1936,Jl 31,22:2
His Brother's Wife 1936,Ag 15,6:2
Pennies From Heaven 1936,D 10,35:2
Stowaway 1936,D 19,16:1
Criminal Lawyer 1937,Ja 27,17:3
Soldier and the Lady, The 1937,Ap 10,11:1
Man-Proof 1938,Ja 14,21:1
Four Men and a Prayer 1938,My 7,18:1
Booloo 1938,Jl 30,10:2
So Ends our Night 1941,F 28,17:2
Stackpoole, H deVere (Original Author)
Man Who Lost Himself, The 1920,My 31,14:2
Blue Lagoon, The 1949,O 3,13:2
Truth About Spring, The 1965,Je 17,27:2
Stade, O B (Original Author)
Viva Villa! 1934,Ap 11,25:2
Stade, Signe
Here's Your Life 1968,D 20,60:1
Stader, Paul
Prince of Players 1955,Ja 12,24:2
Stadler, Marie
Head, The 1963,Je 20,29:1
Staemmle, R A (Director)
Raub der Sabinerinnen, Der 1937,Ja 16,21:1
Staffel, Jelly
Foresterchristl, Die 1931,Ap 27,25:1
Stafford, Bess
It Happened in New York 1935,Ap 6,10:1
Stafford, Bill
Too Late Blues 1962,Mr 1,27:4
Stafford, Frederick
OSS 117-Mission for a Killer 1966,O 13,50:3
Stafford, Grace
Dr Socrates 1935,O 3,29:2
I Married a Doctor 1936,Ap 20,17:1
Anthony Adverse 1936,Ap 27,16:1
Confessions of a Nazi Spy 1939,Ap 29,13:2
Indianapolis Speedway 1939,Jl 15,8:2
Flight Angels 1940,My 27,23:2

Stafford, Hanley
Lullaby of Broadway 1951,Mr 27,35:2
Girl in Every Port, A 1952,F 14,23:1
Just This Once 1952,Mr 18,22:3
Stafford, John (Director)
No Funny Business 1934,Mr 9,22:4
Revenge of General Ling, The 1938,F 21,15:1
Stafford, John (Producer)
Crouching Beast, The 1936,Ag 22,6:1
Candlelight in Algeria 1944,Jl 31,10:2
Golden Madonna, The 1949,S 5,13:4
Her Panelled Door 1951,Ag 28,18:2
Outpost in Malaya 1952,N 27,49:2
Stranger's Hand, The 1955,F 16,24:5
Across the Bridge 1957,O 30,24:1
Elephant Gun 1959,Je 20,11:2
Stafford, Tim
Donovan's Reef 1963,Jl 25,14:1
Hot Rods to Hell 1967,Ag 10,45:5
Stagnaro, Guido (Screenwriter)
World of Topo Gigio 1965,N 27,34:1
STAHL
See Also STOLL
Stahl, Ben (Original Author)
Blackbeard's Ghost 1968,Ap 11,51:3
Stahl, John M (Director)
One Clear Call 1922,Je 19,10:3
Dangerous Age, The 1923,Ja 29,11:1
Why Men Leave Home 1924,My 12,14:4
Husbands and Lovers 1924,D 9,23:3
Fine Clothes 1925,O 20,28:1
Memory Lane 1926,F 2,20:4
Lovers 1927,Ap 19,24:4
In old Kentucky 1927,N 21,20:1
Lady Surrenders, A 1930,O 4,15:2
Seed 1931,My 15,20:6
Strictly Dishonorable 1931,N 11,27:1
Back Street 1932,Ag 29,9:2
Only Yesterday 1933,N 10,25:1
Imitation of Life 1934,N 24,19:1
Magnificent Obsession 1935,D 31,11:2
Parnell 1937,Je 4,27:2
Letter of Introduction 1938,S 1,17:1
When Tomorrow Comes 1939,Ag 17,16:2
Our Wife 1941,S 18,31:1
Immortal Sergeant 1943,F 4,29:2
Holy Matrimony 1943,S 16,25:2
Eve of St Mark, The 1944,My 31,22:2
Keys of the Kingdom, The 1944,D 30,15:2
Leave Her to Heaven 1945,D 26,15:1
Foxes of Harrow, The 1947,S 25,35:4
Walls of Jericho, The 1948,Ag 5,16:2
Father Was a Fullback 1949,O 13,33:3
Oh, You Beautiful Doll 1949,N 12,8:4
Stahl, John M (Producer)
Parnell 1937,Je 4,27:2
Letter of Introduction 1938,S 1,17:1
When Tomorrow Comes 1939,Ag 17,16:2
Stahl, John M (Screenwriter)
Husbands and Lovers 1924,D 9,23:3
Memory Lane 1926,F 2,20:4
Stahl, Margaret
Boy on a Dolphin 1957,Ap 20,21:2
Stahl, Marvin D (Producer)
Big Fix, The 1947,My 3,10:3
Stahl, Philip (Narrator)
Will It Happen Again 1948,My 17,23:4
Stahl, Ray (Director)
Scarlet Spear, The 1954,Ap 10,11:4
Stahl, Ray (Original Author)
Scarlet Spear, The 1954,Ap 10,11:4
Stahl, Walter
I'll Take Romance 1937,D 17,33:2
Beasts of Berlin 1939,N 20,15:6
Stahl-Nachbaur, Ernest
Mother Love 1931,F 16,17:1
Stahl-Nachbaur, Ernst
Danton 1931,S 7,19:3
Ein Burschenlied aus Heidelberg 1931,S 14,15:3
M 1933,Ap 3,13:3
Stahle, Stina
Sun Over Klara 1944,My 1,20:8
Staidl, Ladislav (Composer)
Oratorio for Prague 1968,S 30,60:1
Staimmer, Peter
Yesterday Girl 1967,S 22,57:2
Stainaker, Charles
Custer of the West 1968,Jl 4,13:2
Stainton, Philip
Blue Lagoon, The 1949,O 3,13:2
Passport to Pimlico 1949,O 27,35:2
Mogambo 1953,O 2,18:1
Hobson's Choice 1954,Je 15,37:1
Ladykillers 1956,F 21,37:2
Moby Dick 1956,Jl 5,18:1
Cast a Dark Shadow 1957,N 28,57:1
Staiola, Enzo
Bicycle Thief, The 1949,D 13,44:2
Lucky Nick Cain 1951,Ap 23,21:2
White Line, The 1952,D 6,17:2
Volcano 1953,Jl 21,19:2
Journey to Love 1953,O 9,32:8
Times Gone By (The Old Book Stand); Old Book
  Stand, The (Times Gone By) 1953,D 30,16:2

Staiola, Enzo — Cont
Barefoot Contessa, The 1954,S 30,37:1
Stalenin, Ivan
Scandal? 1929,O 28,20:1
Staley, Joan
Belle Sommers 1962,My 31,23:2
New Kind of Love, A 1963,O 31,26:2
Roustabout 1964,N 11,38:1
Ghost and Mr Chicken, The 1966,S 22,57:2
Stalin, Josef
Soviets on Parade 1933,Mr 6,16:7
Liberation of Europe, The 1968,S 29,IV,7:1
Stall, Karl
Smiling Lieutenant, The 1931,My 23,13:4
Stallings, George (Screenwriter)
Victory Through Air Power 1943,Jl 19,13:1
Stallings, Laurence (Miscellaneous)
Jungle Book 1942,Ap 6,19:1
Stallings, Laurence (Original Author)
Big Parade, The 1925,N 20,18:1 (In Addenda)
What Price Glory 1926,N 24,26:4
Song of the West 1930,F 28,20:7
After Office Hours 1935,Mr 9,19:1
Christmas Eve 1947,N 28,30:2
What Price Glory 1952,Ag 23,10:2
Stallings, Laurence (Screenwriter)
Old Ironsides 1926,D 7,21:2
Show People 1928,N 12,18:2
So Red the Rose 1935,N 28,39:1
too Hot To Handle 1938,S 30,24:2
Man From Dakota, The 1940,F 22,29:2
Northwest Passage 1940,Mr 8,25:1
Jungle Book 1942,Ap 6,19:1
Salome, Where She Danced 1945,My 3,27:1
Christmas Eve 1947,N 28,30:2
Miracle Can Happen, A 1948,F 4,28:4
Three Godfathers 1949,Mr 4,25:2
She Wore a Yellow Ribbon 1949,N 18,35:2
Sun Shines Bright, The 1954,Mr 17,25:2
Stallmaster, Lynn
Steel Helmet, The 1951,Ja 25,21:5
Stallworth, Roscoe
Roots of Heaven, The 1958,O 16,46:1
Stalmaster, Hal
Johnny Tremain 1957,Jl 11,21:1
Stambaugh, Jack
Married in Hollywood 1929,S 23,24:3
Stamp, Terence
Billy Budd 1962,O 31,32:1
Term of Trial 1963,Ja 31,5:2
Collector, The 1965,Je 18,28:1
Modesty Blaise 1966,Ag 11,27:1
Far From the Madding Crowd 1967,O 19,59:1
Poor Cow 1968,F 1,28:2
Blue 1968,My 11,28:1
Stamp-Taylor, Enid
Candlelight in Algeria 1944,Jl 31,10:2
Wicked Lady, The 1946,D 23,19:5
Hatter's Castle 1948,Jl 3,8:6
Stamper, George Haymid
Emperor Jones, The 1933,S 20,26:2
Stanberger, Jack
One Potato, Two Potato 1964,Jl 30,16:1
Stanchina, Peter (Director)
Glaserne Kugel, Die; Glass Ball, The
1939,Je 17,12:3
Stander, Lionel
Scoundrel, The 1935,My 3,23:2
Hooray for Love 1935,Jl 13,16:2
Page Miss Glory 1935,Ag 29,25:2
Gay Deception, The 1935,O 11,31:1
If You Could Only Cook 1935,D 26,21:4
Soak the Rich 1936,F 5,14:2
Music Goes 'Round, The 1936,F 22,12:1
Milky Way, The 1936,Mr 26,27:2
Mr Deeds Goes to Town 1936,Ap 17,17:2
Meet Nero Wolfe 1936,Jl 16,20:1
They Met in a Taxi 1936,S 7,20:5
More Than a Secretary 1936,D 11,35:2
Star Is Born, A 1937,Ap 23,25:1
League of Frightened Men, The 1937,Jl 2,25:1
Last Gangster, The 1937,D 10,33:2
No Time to Marry 1938,F 23,27:2
Professor Beware 1938,Jl 14,17:1
Crowd Roars, The 1938,Ag 5,11:1
Ice Follies of 1939 1939,Mr 17,25:2
What a Life 1939,O 12,33:1
Bride Wore Crutches, The 1941,My 26,15:3
Hangmen Also Die 1943,Ap 16,24:2
Guadalcanal Diary 1943,N 18,29:1
Kid From Brooklyn, The 1946,Ap 19,25:2
In old Sacramento 1946,Ap 29,24:4
Specter of the Rose 1946,S 2,12:4
Unfaithfully Yours 1948,N 6,9:2
Mad Wednesday 1951,Ja 25,21:5
Loved One, The 1965,O 12,57:1
Promise her Anything 1966,F 23,46:1
Cul de Sac 1966,N 8,44:2
Dandy in Aspic, A 1968,Ap 3,40:1
Standing, Guy Jr
Titanic 1953,My 28,27:5

Standing, Guy Sir
Story of Temple Drake, The 1933,My 6,11:2
Eagle and the Hawk, The 1933,My 13,16:2
Midnight Club 1933,Jl 29,14:2
Cradle Song 1933,N 20,18:2
Hell and Highwater 1933,D 18,24:4
Death Takes a Holiday 1934,F 24,18:4
Witching Hour, The 1934,Ap 28,11:3
Double Door 1934,My 5,22:3
Now and Forever 1934,O 13,10:1
Lives of a Bengal Lancer, The 1935,Ja 12,12:2
Car 99 1935,F 23,14:7
Annapolis Farewell 1935,Ag 24,18:2
Return of Sophie Lang, The 1936,Jl 24,13:1
I'd Give my Life 1936,Ag 17,9:1
Lloyds of London 1936,N 26,39:1
Standing, Herbert
Through the Wrong Door 1919,Jl 21,12:3
Strictly Confidential 1919,O 6,15:1
Almost a Husband 1919,O 13,16:3
Judy of Rogues Harbor 1920,Mr 1,16:2
Masquerader, The 1922,Ag 14,12:4
Brown Derby, The 1926,Je 14,24:1
Standing, Joan
Pleasure Mad 1924,Ja 7,23:1
Happiness 1924,Mr 11,16:2
Three Weeks 1924,Ap 1,19:3
Women Who Give 1924,Je 3,22:1
Greed 1924,D 5,28:1
Dancers, The 1925,Ja 26,22:1
Memory Lane 1926,F 2,20:4
Campus Flirt, The 1926,S 22,31:1
Ritzy 1927,Je 20,25:3
College Hero, The 1927,N 22,32:2
Beau Sabreur 1928,Ja 23,18:3
Home James 1928,S 11,31:3
Fashions in Love 1929,Jl 1,31:2
Marriage Playground, The 1929,D 14,22:4
Street of Chance 1930,F 3,17:1
Lady's Morals, A 1930,N 8,21:3
Extravagance 1930,D 9,31:3
Ex-Flame 1931,Ja 24,15:1
Dracula 1931,F 13,21:3
Never the Twain Shall Meet 1931,Je 6,15:5
Man I Killed, The 1932,Ja 20,17:4
Little Lord Fauntleroy 1936,Ap 3,27:1
Standing, John
Pair of Briefs, A 1964,F 3,22:2
King Rat 1965,O 28,48:1
Walk, Don't Run 1966,Ag 25,42:3
Psycopath, The 1966,S 29,60:1
Standing, Percy
Flame of Love, The 1930,N 3,19:3
Standing, Wyndham
Out of the Shadow 1919,Ja 13,9:3
Marriage Price, The 1919,Mr 17,13:2
Temperamental Wife, A 1919,S 15,16:3
Witness for the Defense, The 1919,S 15,16:3
Isle of Conquest, The 1919,O 27,9:3
My Lady's Garter 1920,Mr 15,13:2
Earthbound 1920,Ag 11,9:4
Journey's End, The 1921,Jl 18,16:3
Iron Trail, The 1921,O 31,19:3
Little Johnny Jones 1923,Ag 13,16:1
Rejected Woman, The 1924,My 5,18:3
Vanity's Price 1924,O 8,16:2
Teaser, The 1925,Je 15,10:1
Dark Angel, The 1925,O 12,19:3
Canadian, The 1926,N 30,27:1
City Gone Wild, The 1927,D 6,27:1
Port of Missing Girls, The 1928,Jl 31,13:4
Widecombe Fair 1929,O 28,20:1
Hell's Angels 1930,Ag 16,8:3
Billy the Kid 1930,O 18,23:2
Silent Witness, The 1932,F 8,21:1
Study in Scarlet, A 1933,Je 1,15:3
Imitation of Life 1934,N 24,19:1
Limehouse Blues 1934,D 12,28:2
Clive of India 1935,Ja 18,29:1
Mary of Scotland 1936,Jl 31,22:2
Beloved Enemy 1936,D 26,15:2
Bulldog Drummond's Secret Police
1939,Mr 30,19:3
Rulers of the Sea 1939,N 9,27:1
Standing Bear, Chief
Sante Fe Trail, The 1930,O 18,23:2
Conquering Horde, The 1931,Mr 30,25:2
Standish, Pamela
Sixty Glorious Years 1938,N 18,25:2
Prime Minister, The 1942,F 4,23:2
Standish, Robert (Original Author)
Elephant Walk 1954,Ap 22,37:2
Standish, Schuyler
Little Men 1940,D 9,23:2
Standlee, Shirley
Patterns 1956,Mr 28,26:1
Stanfield, Ned
Stormy Weather 1943,Jl 22,15:1
Stanford, Stanley
Circus, The 1928,Ja 9,20:1
Stang, Arnold
Seven Days' Leave 1942,D 11,33:2
Man With the Golden Arm, The 1955,D 16,38:2

Stang, Arnold — Cont
It's a Mad, Mad, Mad, Mad World
1963,N 19,47:1
Stange, Hugh Stanislaus (Miscellaneous)
Chocolate Soldier, The 1941,N 1,20:2
Stange, Hugh Stanislaus (Original Author)
After Tomorrow 1932,Mr 7,13:5
Love Starved 1932,Ap 15,23:1
Seventeen 1940,F 29,15:2
Stangl, Rainer
Sky Without Stars 1959,My 30,9:2
Stanhope, Ted
Teen Age 1944,Je 19,17:1
Burning Cross, The 1948,F 20,19:1
High Noon 1952,Jl 25,14:2
Stanhope, Warren
Bedford Incident, The 1965,N 3,43:1
Staniewicz, Zbigniew
Maryjka 1934,D 3,15:2
Stanior, Marianne
Kabinett des Dr. Larifari, Das 1931,S 11,24:2
Stanislavsky, G
Amangeldy 1939,Je 16,27:4
Stanitsin, Victor
Men and Jobs 1933,Ja 3,19:3
Paris Commune 1937,Je 2,20:4
Jubilee 1945,F 22,31:3
First Front, The 1949,N 14,19:2
War and Peace 1968,Ap 29,50:5
Stankovski, Ernst
Cabaret 1957,N 9,31:2 (Incorrect in this edition;
use 1957,N 7,43:4 elsewhere)
Stanlaw, Penrhyn (Director)
Pink Gods 1922,S 25,10:2
Stanlaws, Penrhyn (Director)
Idols of Clay 1920,N 21,VI,2:3
At the End of the World 1921,Ag 15,14:3
Little Minister, The 1921,D 26,13:3
Law and the Woman, The 1922,Ja 22,VI,3:1 (In
Addenda)
Stanley, Aileen Jr
About Face 1952,My 24,15:3
Stanley, Art
Call Me Mister 1951,F 1,21:2
Stanley, Edwin
Amateur Daddy 1932,Ap 23,11:5
No Other Woman 1933,Ja 30,9:4 (In Addenda)
My Woman 1933,O 16,20:3
Life of Vergie Winters, The 1934,Je 15,26:1
You Belong to Me 1934,S 13,26:1
Hot Money 1936,Jl 25,16:2
Alcatraz Island 1937,O 14,22:2
Some Blondes Are Dangerous 1937,N 3,29:3
Wives Under Suspicion 1938,Jl 1,22:3
Missing Guest, The 1938,S 7,30:7
Unexpected Father 1939,Ag 11,12:2
Espionage Agent 1939,S 23,22:2
Eternally Yours 1939,O 7,11:2
20,000 Men a Year 1939,O 28,11:2
Youth Will Be Served 1940,N 15,25:2
Meet John Doe 1941,Mr 13,25:2
Man Betrayed, A 1941,Mr 27,29:5
Night of January 16th, The 1941,D 19,35:1
Man Who Came to Dinner, The 1942,Ja 2,25:2
Who Is Hope Schuyler 1942,My 22,27:1
Drums of the Congo 1942,Jl 20,16:4
Loves of Edgar Allan Poe, The 1942,S 21,19:2
Conflict 1945,Je 16,10:2
Stanley, Eric
Ringer, The 1932,Je 2,25:2
Over the Goal 1937,O 16,22:2
First Lady 1937,D 23,25:1
Sh! The Octopus 1937,D 24,21:2
Daredevil Drivers, The 1938,F 23,27:2
Slight Case of Murder, A 1938,F 28,19:1
Patient in Room 18, The 1938,Ap 22,15:6
When Were You Born? 1938,Je 9,27:2
Men Are Such Fools 1938,Je 17,25:1
Stanley, Fergal
Big Gamble, The 1961,S 2,19:2
Stanley, Florence
Up the Down Staircase 1967,Ag 18,36:2
Stanley, Forrest
Forbidden Fruit 1921,Ja 24,16:2
When Knighthood Was in Flower 1922,S 15,17:2
(In Addenda)
Pride of Palomar, The 1922,N 20,21:3
Tiger Rose 1923,D 3,14:1
Through the Dark 1924,Ja 8,27:1
Breath of Scandal, The 1924,N 26,17:3
Up the Ladder 1925,My 12,26:2
Climbers, The 1927,My 4,29:2
Cat and the Canary, The 1927,S 10,9:4
Drake Case, The 1929,S 16,30:1
Men Are Like That 1931,Ag 17,18:2
Stanley, Frederic
Lover Come Back 1931,Je 5,26:5
Dangerous Affair, A 1931,N 23,22:1
Stanley, Helene
Thrill of a Romance 1945,My 25,22:2
Holiday in Mexico 1946,Ag 16,19:3
My Dear Secretary 1949,F 14,15:4
All the King's Men 1949,N 9,37:2
Diplomatic Courier 1952,Je 14,12:2

Stanley, Helene — Cont

Wait Till the Sun Shines, Nellie 1952,Je 28,12:2
Dreamboat 1952,Jl 26,9:2
Snows of Kilimanjaro, The 1952,S 19,19:2
Carnival Story 1954,Ap 17,8:2
Davy Crockett, King of the Wild Frontier 1955,My 26,36:1
Circus of Love 1958,Ag 16,10:2

Stanley, Ken

Mouse That Roared, The 1959,O 27,40:1

Stanley, Kim

Goddess, The 1958,Je 25,24:1
Seance on a Wet Afternoon 1964,N 6,30:1

Stanley, Leo L (Original Author)

Six Thousand Enemies 1939,Je 9,26:2

Stanley, Louise

Paid to Dance 1937,D 6,19:1
Start Cheering 1938,Mr 17,17:3
Personal Secretary 1938,O 5,20:2

Stanley, Martha M (Original Author)

Scrambled Wives 1921,My 23,16:3

Stanley, Martha M (Screenwriter)

Teaser, The 1925,Je 15,10:1

Stanley, Maxfield

Great Love, The 1918,Ag 12,7:1
Twenty-three and a Half Hours' Leave 1919,O 27,9:3

Stanley, Pat

Ladies Man, The 1961,Jl 13,26:3

Stanley, Paul (Director)

Cry Tough 1959,S 17,48:4

Stanley, Phyllis

Sidewalks of London 1940,F 15,15:1
Next of Kin 1943,My 6,25:2
Law and the Lady, The 1951,Ag 16,23:2
Thunder on the Hill 1951,O 18,32:3
Take Me to Town 1953,Je 20,8:6

Stanley, Red

Cocoanut Grove 1938,Je 16,21:2

Stanley, Richard

King of Alcatraz 1938,O 7,21:2
Persons in Hiding 1939,Mr 2,19:2

Stanmore, Frank

Don Quixote 1934,D 24,17:1

Stannage, John

Pacific Adventure 1947,N 26,18:2

Stanngs, Laurence (Miscellaneous)

First World War, The 1934,N 8,27:1

Stano, Silvio (Director)

Alone in the Streets 1956,Je 28,33:2

Stano, Silvio (Screenwriter)

Alone in the Streets 1956,Je 28,33:2

Stanton, Betty

Troublemaker, The 1964,Je 23,25:1

Stanton, Dean

Proud Rebel, The 1958,Jl 2,23:4
Adventures of Huckleberry Fin, The 1960,Ag 4,17:1
Cool Hand Luke 1967,N 2,58:1
Day of the Evil Gun 1968,Ap 25,53:2

Stanton, Ernie

Thank You, Jeeves 1936,O 5,25:1
Case of the Black Parrot, The 1941,Ja 10,23:3

Stanton, Fred

Trifling With Honor 1923,My 30,10:4
When a Man's a Man 1924,F 5,20:1
Find Your Man 1924,S 23,26:1

Stanton, Helene

Big Combo, The 1955,Mr 26,13:2
New Orleans Uncensored 1955,Ap 30,10:8

Stanton, Mary

Pajama Game, The 1957,Ag 30,12:2

Stanton, Myra

Betrayal, The 1948,Je 26,10:5

Stanton, Pat (Cinematographer)

Here Is Ireland 1940,O 7,21:2

Stanton, Paul

Let 'Em Have It 1935,My 30,21:1
Red Salute 1935,S 30,13:1
Whipsaw 1936,Ja 25,18:4
It Had to Happen 1936,F 15,18:6
Every Saturday Night 1936,Mr 14,10:2
Charlie Chan at the Circus 1936,Mr 19,22:4
Half Angel 1936,My 30,7:3
Private Number 1936,Je 12,19:1
Sins of Man 1936,Je 19,17:2
Poor Little Rich Girl, The 1936,Je 26,16:1
Crime of Dr Forbes, The 1936,Jl 6,11:4
Road to Glory, The 1936,Ag 6,22:1
Sing, Baby, Sing 1936,S 12,20:1
Dimples 1936,O 10,21:2
Longest Night, The 1936,O 17,21:2
Night Waitress 1936,D 18,31:5
Crack-Up 1937,Ja 4,20:4
Black Legion 1937,Ja 18,21:1
Man of the People 1937,F 23,25:4
Star Is Born, A 1937,Ap 23,25:1
Make Way for Tomorrow 1937,My 10,23:1
Portia on Trial 1937,D 3,29:2
Paid to Dance 1937,D 6,19:1
City Girl 1938,F 4,17:3
Law of the Underworld 1938,Ap 28,27:2
Kentucky Moonshine 1938,My 21,9:2
Rascals 1938,My 27,12:2

Stanton, Richard (Director)

Checkers 1919,Ag 25,8:5
Thunderclap 1921,Jl 31,22:4

Stanton, Robert

Three Sons 1939,N 24,29:3
Abbott and Costello in Hollywood 1945,N 23,26:2

Stanton, Sylvia

Teen Age 1944,Je 19,17:1

Stanton, Will

Sadie Thompson 1928,F 6,12:3
True Heaven 1929,F 11,26:3
Mamba 1930,Mr 11,25:2
Cavalcade 1933,Ja 6,23:2
Sailor's Luck 1933,Mr 17,21:2
Hello Sister! 1933,My 6,11:2
White Hunter 1936,N 26,39:2
Lloyds of London 1936,N 26,39:1
Straight, Place and Show 1938,O 1,10:2
Little Princess, The 1939,Mr 11,21:1
Captain Fury 1939,My 26,20:2
Devil's Island 1940,Jl 12,11:4
Charley's Aunt 1941,Ag 2,18:2

Stanwood, Michael

Young Warriors, The 1968,F 8,36:1

Stanwyck, Barbara

Broadway Nights 1927,Je 28,29:4
Locked Door, The 1930,Ja 20,21:1
Ladies of Leisure 1930,My 24,21:2
Illicit 1931,Ja 19,25:1
Ten Cents a Dance 1931,Mr 7,17:2
Night Nurse 1931,Jl 17,23:4
Miracle Woman, The 1931,Ag 17,18:2
Forbidden 1932,Ja 11,28:5
Shopworn 1932,Ap 4,13:6
So Big 1932,Ap 30,19:3
Purchase Price, The 1932,Jl 16,5:5
Bitter Tea of General Yen, The 1933,Ja 12,20:6
Ladies They Talk About 1933,F 25,20:4
Baby Face 1933,Je 24,16:2
Ever in my Heart 1933,O 13,25:3
Gambling Lady 1934,Ap 5,25:2
Lost Lady, A 1934,O 4,19:1
Secret Bride, The 1935,F 2,10:1
Woman in Red, The 1935,Mr 23,11:3
Red Salute 1935,S 30,13:1
Annie Oakley 1935,D 24,10:5
Message to Garcia, A 1936,Ap 10,27:1
His Brother's Wife 1936,Ag 15,6:2
Banjo on My Knee 1936,D 12,15:1
Plough and the Stars, The 1937,Ja 29,15:1
Internes Can't Take Money 1937,My 6,23:2
This Is my Affair 1937,My 28,17:1
Stella Dallas 1937,Ag 6,21:1
Breakfast for Two 1937,N 20,21:2
Always Goodbye 1938,Je 25,7:2
Mad Miss Manton, The 1938,O 21,27:2
Union Pacific 1939,My 11,31:2
Golden Boy 1939,S 8,28:2
Remember the Night 1940,Ja 18,27:2
Lady Eve, The 1941,F 26,17:1
Meet John Doe 1941,Mr 13,25:2
You Belong to Me 1941,N 29,14:2
Ball of Fire 1942,Ja 16,25:2
Great Man's Lady, The 1942,Ap 30,14:3
Gay Sisters, The 1942,Ag 15,14:2
Lady of Burlesque 1943,My 14,17:2
Flesh and Fantasy 1943,N 18,29:1
Double Indemnity 1944,S 7,21:1
Hollywood Canteen 1944,D 16,19:2
Christmas in Connecticut 1945,Jl 28,7:2
My Reputation 1946,Ja 26,19:2
Bride Wore Boots, The 1946,Je 6,16:3

Stanwyck, Barbara — Cont

Strange Love of Martha Ivers, The 1946,Jl 25,18:4
California 1947,Ja 15,31:2
Two Mrs Carrolls, The 1947,Ap 7,20:1
Other Love, The 1947,My 15,32:4
Cry Wolf 1947,Jl 19,10:2
B F's Daughter 1948,Mr 25,35:2
Sorry, Wrong Number 1948,S 2,18:2
Lady Gambles, The 1949,My 21,9:2
East Side, West Side 1949,D 23,17:2
Thelma Jordon 1950,Ja 19,35:2
No Man of her Own 1950,My 4,32:3
Furies, The 1950,Ag 17,23:2
To Please a Lady 1950,O 27,24:3
Man With a Cloak, The 1951,N 28,37:2
Clash by Night 1952,Je 19,32:6
Jeopardy 1953,Mr 31,36:2
Titanic 1953,My 28,27:5
All I Desire 1953,Ag 29,10:1
Moonlighter, The 1953,S 23,37:2
Blowing Wild 1953,O 8,37:5
Witness to Murder 1954,Ap 16,16:4
Executive Suite 1954,My 7,19:1
Cattle Queen of Montana 1955,Ja 26,22:1
Violent Men, The 1955,Ja 27,17:2
Escape to Burma 1955,My 21,11:2
There's Always Tomorrow 1956,Ja 21,18:2
Maverick Queen, the 1956,Je 4,25:2
These Wilder Years 1956,Ag 18,11:2
Crime of Passion 1957,Ja 10,25:1
Trooper Hook 1957,Jl 13,11:2
Walk on the Wild Side 1962,F 22,20:1
Roustabout 1964,N 11,38:1
Night Walker, The 1965,Ja 21,22:1

Stanyukovich, K (Original Author)

Maximka 1953,O 12,30:4

Stapenhorst, Gunther (Producer)

Gaiety Girls, The 1938,Mr 31,15:1

Stapenhorst, Klaus (Producer)

Ballerina 1958,My 10,19:2
Flying Classroom, The 1958,Je 28,13:7

Staple Singers, The

Festival 1967,O 24,53:2

Stapleton, Jean

Damn Yankees 1958,S 27,12:7
Bells Are Ringing 1960,Je 24,31:2
Something Wild 1961,D 24,30:6
Up the Down Staircase 1967,Ag 18,36:2

Stapleton, John (Original Author)

Gentleman of Leisure, A 1923,Jl 16,14:2

Stapleton, Maureen

Lonelyhearts 1959,Mr 5,35:3
Fugitive Kind, The 1960,Ap 15,13:1
View From the Bridge, A 1962,Ja 23,36:1
Bye Bye Birdie 1963,Ap 5,27:3

Stapleton, Vivian

Young, The Evil and the Savage, The 1968,Ag 15,46:2

Stapley, Richard

Three Musketeers, The 1948,O 21,33:2
Little Women 1949,Mr 11,33:2
Strange Door, The 1951,D 10,34:6
King of the Khyber Rifles 1953,D 23,21:1
Target Zero 1955,N 16,43:2
D-Day, The Sixth of June 1956,My 30,13:1

Stapp, Marjorie

Gun for a Coward 1957,Ja 31,21:1
Kronos 1957,My 11,24:6
Battle at Bloody Beach, The 1961,Ag 17,18:2

Stapp, Philip (Director)

Symmetry 1967,Ja 21,35:1

Stapp, Philip (Screenwriter)

Animal Farm 1954,D 30,14:1

Star, Frederick

Riders of the Dawn 1920,My 3,18:1

Starbuck, Betty

Sap From Syracuse, The 1930,Jl 26,16:4

Starcic, Victor

Seventh Continent, The 1968,Jl 30,33:2

Starczewski, Jerszy (Director)

Wrzos; Heather 1938,N 7,23:4

Starenios, Dimos

Anna of Rhodes 1950,Mr 23,34:2
He Who Must Die 1958,D 29,21:1
Never on Sunday 1960,O 19,54:1
Casablan 1964,D 14,50:1
Oedipus the King 1968,S 19,62:2

Stark, Graham

Shot in the Dark, A 1964,Je 24,28:1
Alfie 1966,Ag 25,42:1
Those Fantastic Flying Fools 1967,O 19,59:2
Salt and Pepper 1968,S 19,62:3

Stark, Lothar (Producer)

Madame Wuenscht Keine Kinder 1933,Je 2,22:4
Judas von Tirol, Der 1935,Ap 27,20:7

Stark, Ray (Producer)

World of Suzie Wong, The 1960,N 11,36:1
Night of the Iguana, The 1964,Jl 1,42:1
Oh Dad, Poor Dad, Mamma's Hung You in the Closet and I'm Feeling so Sad 1967,F 16,32:1
Reflections in a Golden Eye 1967,O 12,59:1
Funny Girl 1968,S 20,42:1

Stark, Richard (Original Author)
Point Blank 1967,S 19,53:1
Made in U S A 1967,S 28,58:2
Split, The 1968,N 5,55:2
Stark, Traudl
Seine Tochter Ist der Peter; His Daughter is Peter
1938,Mr 28,19:3
Prinzessin Sissy 1939,Ja 14,13:2
Mutterliebe; Mother Love 1940,Mr 16,8:3
Leidenschaft; Passion 1940,S 24,26:6
Stark, Wesley
Royal Family of Broadway, The 1930,D 23,25:1
Stark, William
What Every Woman Knows 1934,O 27,20:2
Stark-Gstettenbauer, Gustl
Gretel and Liesel; (Kohlhiesel's Daughters)
1931,Ja 26,21:1
Wien Du Stadt der Lieder; (Vienna City of Song)
1931,Mr 20,29:1
Dolly Macht Karriere 1931,Jl 18,16:6
Kyritz-Pyritz 1932,Ag 9,20:5
Strich Durch die Rechnung 1934,Mr 3,8:6
Jungfrau Gegen Moench; Maiden vs Monk
1935,Mr 16,19:2
Edelweisskoenig, Der 1939,F 4,11:2
Stark-Gstettenbaur, Gustl
Hochzeit am Wolfgangsee 1934,N 17,12:2
Starke, Pauline
Life Line, The 1919,S 29,16:1
Soldiers of Fortune 1919,N 24,13:1
Eyes of Youth 1919,D 1,9:3
Connecticut Yankee in King Arthur's Court, A
1921,Mr 15,14:3
Snowblind 1921,My 23,16:3
Salvation Nell 1921,Je 27,16:3
Lost and Found 1923,Mr 19,22:2
In the Palace of the King 1923,D 3,14:1
Dante's Inferno 1924,S 30,27:3
Forbidden Paradise 1924,N 17,16:1
Devil's Cargo, The 1925,F 3,24:1
Man Without a Country, The 1925,F 12,16:1
Adventure 1925,Ap 15,16:1
Sun Up 1925,Ag 18,14:3
Bright Lights 1925,N 18,27:4
Perfect Sap, The 1927,Ja 11,18:2
Captain Salvation 1927,Je 27,25:2
Dance Magic 1927,Jl 13,21:2
Streets of Shanghai 1928,F 21,19:3
Man, Woman and Wife 1928,N 5,26:5 (In
Addenda)
Viking, The 1928,N 29,32:4
Starkey, Bert
Wild Geese 1927,D 5,26:2
Scarface, The Shame of the Nation
1932,My 20,22:3
Hell's Highway 1932,S 26,18:2
Starkovski, P
Lonely White Sail 1938,My 7,18:1
Starling, Lynn (Miscellaneous)
Impostor, The 1944,Mr 27,17:2
Starling, Lynn (Original Author)
Transatlantic 1931,Jl 31,15:2
Shanghai 1935,Jl 20,16:2
Starling, Lynn (Screenwriter)
President Vanishes, The 1934,D 8,18:5
Shanghai 1935,Jl 20,16:2
Give Us This Night 1936,Ap 6,18:1
More Than a Secretary 1936,D 11,35:2
Women of Glamour 1937,Mr 6,10:1
As Good as Married 1937,My 22,19:2
Three Blind Mice 1938,Je 18,18:2
Thanks for the Memory 1938,D 8,34:3
Cat and the Canary, The 1939,N 23,38:5
Night at Earl Carroll's, A 1941,Ja 23,19:1
Moon Over Miami 1941,Jl 5,14:2
Footlight Serenade 1942,S 10,30:3
Wintertime 1943,S 30,27:2
Climax, The 1944,D 14,28:5
It's a Pleasure 1945,My 4,23:3
Three Little Girls in Blue 1946,S 26,32:3
Time, The Place And The Girl, The
1946,D 27,14:3
Starling, Pat
Song of the Open Road 1944,Je 7,13:3
Black Angel 1946,S 26,32:4
Starnazza, Pippo
Organizer, The 1964,My 7,31:2
Starnes, Grady
I'd Climb the Highest Mountain 1951,My 10,38:1
Starostin, N
Ballad of Cossack Gloota, The 1938,F 28,19:1
Starr, Ben (Screenwriter)
Our Man Flint 1966,Ja 26,23:4
Pad, The (And How to Use It) 1966,Ag 18,27:2
Texas Across the River 1966,N 24,65:1
Busy Body, The 1967,Je 8,52:2
Starr, Dave
Singing in the Dark 1956,Mr 8,32:5
Starr, Dolores
Athena 1954,D 22,28:2
Starr, Frances
Star Witness, The 1931,Ag 4,19:5
Star Witness, The 1931,Ag 4,19:5

Five Star Final 1931,S 11,24:2
This Reckless Age 1932,Ja 9,21:1
Starr, Herman (Producer)
Pictura 1952,Ap 8,35:3
Leonardo Da Vinci 1952,N 21,21:5
Starr, Irving (Producer)
Nobody's Fool 1936,Je 4,27:2
Westland Case, The 1937,O 23,14:2
Black Doll, The 1938,F 7,10:2
Lady in the Morgue, The 1938,My 9,13:3
Last Express, The 1938,O 11,24:4
Last Warning, The 1938,D 8,34:4
Gambling Ship 1939,Ja 21,19:2
Witness Vanishes, The 1939,O 23,15:2
Time Out for Rhythm 1941,Jl 10,16:3
Fingers at the Window 1942,Ap 23,27:3
Sunday Punch 1942,My 11,19:2
Bataan 1943,Je 4,17:2
Swing Fever 1944,Ja 28,14:1
Four Jills in a Jeep 1944,Ap 6,27:2
Something for the Boys 1944,N 30,19:1
Cockeyed Miracle, The 1946,O 25,28:1
Gallant Blade 1948,O 13,31:3
Slightly French 1949,My 27,25:3
Johnny Allegro 1949,My 31,19:2
Starr, James A (Original Author)
Is Everybody Happy? 1929,N 2,14:6
365 Nights in Hollywood 1934,N 7,32:1
Corpse came C O D, The 1947,Ag 19,27:2
Starr, Jane
Fighting American, The 1924,My 13,24:1
Starr, June (Producer)
C'mon Let's Live a Little 1967,My 4,34:1
Starr, June (Screenwriter)
C'mon Let's Live a Little 1967,My 4,34:1
Starr, Ricki
Touchables, The 1968,N 21,41:1
Starr, Ringo
Hard Day's Night, A 1964,Ag 12,41:1
Help! 1965,Ag 24,25:1
Candy 1968,D 18,54:2
Starr, Ronald
Ride the High Country 1962,Je 21,26:2
Starr, Sally
So This Is College 1929,N 9,22:5
Not so Dumb 1930,F 8,12:5
Swing High 1930,Je 27,26:3
Sweetheart of Sigma Chi, The 1933,N 9,27:1
STARRETT
See Also STERRETT
Starrett, Charles
Fast and Loose 1930,D 1,21:1
Royal Family of Broadway, The 1930,D 23,25:1
Damaged Love 1931,Ja 19,25:1
Viking, The 1931,Je 17,32:5
Silence 1931,Ag 15,18:3
Age for Love, The 1931,N 13,27:2
Touchdown 1931,N 16,23:1
Sky Bride 1932,Ap 23,11:5
Lady and Gent 1932,Jl 16,5:5
Mask of Fu Manchu, The 1932,D 3,21:4
Our Betters 1933,F 24,13:2
Jungle Bride 1933,My 13,16:3
Sweetheart of Sigma Chi, The 1933,N 9,27:1
Mr Skitch 1933,D 23,19:1
This Man is Mine 1934,Ap 13,25:1
Call it Luck 1934,Jl 10,24:5
Desirable 1934,S 15,20:5
Gentlemen are Born 1934,N 22,27:2
Silver Streak, The 1935,Ja 16,21:1
Sons of Steel 1935,Ap 15,16:3
Shot in the Dark, A 1935,My 22,23:2
Make a Million 1935,N 9,19:3
So Red the Rose 1935,N 28,39:1
Outlaws of the Prairie 1938,Ja 29,12:1
Start Cheering 1938,Mr 17,17:3
Starrett, Vincent (Original Author)
Great Hotel Murder, The 1935,F 28,17:4
Starski, Ludwik (Original Author)
First Start, The 1953,F 2,17:3
Starski, Ludwik (Screenwriter)
Treasure, The 1951,Mr 29,24:4
Adventure in Warsaw 1955,O 24,22:2
Stass, Elga
That Woman 1968,Jl 19,30:3
Stass, Robert
Quiller Memorandum, The 1966,D 16,59:1
Stassino, Paul
Tiger Bay 1959,D 15,50:1
Roman Spring of Mrs Stone, The 1961,D 29,11:1
Malaga 1962,F 22,20:3
Stolen Hours 1963,O 17,39:1
Moonspinners, The 1964,N 4,47:1
Where the Spies Are 1966,Ja 27,29:1
Sands of Beersheba 1966,My 6,54:2
Magus, The 1968,D 11,57:1
State, Henry
Pickup on South Street 1953,Je 18,38:2
Stathatou, Dina
Mademoiselle-Age 39 1956,Mr 26,34:2
Santa Chikita 1959,My 11,30:1

Stather, Frank
Little Lord Fauntleroy 1914,Je 23,11:3
Staub, Ralph (Director)
Chip of the Flying U 1940,Ja 22,11:3
Staudte, Wolfgang (Director)
Murderers Among Us 1948,Ag 17,19:6
Tale of Five Women, A 1953,Ja 16,19:2
Sins of Rose Bernd, The 1959,Ja 24,13:4 (In
Addenda)
Always Victorious 1960,Ap 7,46:1
Roses for the Prosecutor; (Rosen fur den
Staarsanwalt) 1961,O 10,38:2
Ciske 1963,Ag 3,8:2
Staudte, Wolfgang (Screenwriter)
Murderers Among Us 1948,Ag 17,19:6
Roses for the Prosecutor; (Rosen fur den
Staarsanwalt) 1961,O 10,38:2
Ciske 1963,Ag 3,8:2
Staunton, Ann
Miracle on 34th Street 1947,Je 5,32:1
Hollow Triumph 1948,O 29,29:5
Stawinski, Jerzy (Screenwriter)
Kanal 1961,My 10,52:1
Eroica (First Episode) 1966,F 2,24:1
Eroica (Second Episode) 1966,F 2,24:1
Stayle, Stanly
Dear Wife 1950,F 2,31:2
Stead, Francis
Battle for Music 1945,O 15,13:2
STEADMAN
See Also STEDMAN
Steakley, Jim
Wild River 1960,My 27,22:1
Stearns, Johnny
Boomerang 1947,Mr 6,36:2
Stebbins, Bobbie
Strange Holiday 1945,O 20,8:2
Stebiov, Yevgeni
Meet Me in Moscow 1966,My 3,51:1
Steck, Joseph T (Screenwriter)
Waterhole #3 1967,O 11,41:4
Steckel, Leonard
Gitta Entdeckt Ihr Herz 1932,S 30,17:3
Ballerina 1958,My 10,19:2
Captain from Koepenick, The 1958,Jl 26,6:1
Eternal Waltz, The; (Ewiger Walzer)
1959,Jl 9,22:1
Visit, The 1964,O 22,44:1
STEDMAN
See Also STEADMAN
Stedman, Lincoln
Nineteen and Phyllis 1920,D 27,11:3
Old Swimmin' Hole, The 1921,F 28,16:2
Two Minutes to Go 1921,O 24,13:1
Black Oxen 1924,Ja 7,23:1
Captain January 1924,Jl 7,10:4
Wife of the Centaur, The 1925,Ja 7,33:5
Red Hot Tires 1925,O 20,28:1
One Minute to Play 1926,S 6,16:2
Let It Rain 1927,Mr 9,29:1
Rookies 1927,Ap 25,20:4
Harold Teen 1928,Ag 14,15:4
Woman Between, The 1931,O 24,20:3
Sailor Be Good 1933,F 27,11:2
Stedman, Myrtle
Silver Horde, The 1920,My 10,18:2
Concert, The 1921,F 21,16:1
Famous Mrs Fair, The 1923,Ap 23,18:3
Six Days 1923,S 24,5:4
Flaming Youth 1923,N 26,15:6
Lilies of the Field 1924,Mr 17,19:1
Woman on the Jury, The 1924,My 19,14:2
Bread 1924,Jl 21,14:4
Breath of Scandal, The 1924,N 26,17:3
If I Marry Again 1925,Ja 12,11:2
Goose Hangs High, The 1925,Mr 10,19:3
Sally 1925,Mr 16,16:1
Chickie 1925,Ap 27,15:2
Mad Whirl, The 1925,Jl 1,16:1
Alias the Deacon 1927,Je 21,29:2
Life of Riley, The 1927,S 5,13:2
Life of Riley, The 1927,S 11,VIII,5:1
Irresistible Lover, The 1927,O 19,24:4
Women's Wares 1927,N 15,27:1
Sporting Goods 1928,F 13,16:2
Jazz Age, The 1929,Ja 7,36:2
Wheel of Life, The 1929,Je 24,27:1
Lummox 1930,Mr 24,25:1
Little Accident 1930,Ag 4,13:4
Truth About Youth, The 1930,D 13,22:2
Green Light 1937,F 13,9:1
Stedman, Vera
Stop Flirting 1925,Je 18,16:3
Nervous Wreck, The 1926,O 12,30:2
Elmer and Elsie 1934,Ag 4,14:5
Steel, Alan
Samson and the Slave Queen 1964,Mr 5,36:2
Steel, Anthony
Amazing Mr Beecham, The 1949,D 26,33:4
Mudlark, The 1950,D 25,25:1
Wooden Horse, The 1951,Ag 29,20:2
Laughter in Paradise 1951,N 12,21:2
Another Man's Poison 1952,Ja 7,14:3

Steel, Anthony— Cont

Ivory Hunter 1952,Ag 19,19:1
Outpost in Malaya 1952,N 27,49:2
Hundred Hour Hunt 1953,Je 17,32:2
Master of Ballantrae, The 1953,Ag 6,16:2
Something Money Can't Buy 1953,O 1,34:3
Malta Story 1954,Jl 17,7:2
West of Zanzibar 1955,Ja 18,31:2
Storm over the Nile 1956,Je 9,14:2
Out of the Clouds 1957,Ag 1,20:4
Checkpoint 1957,S 19,25:2
Harry Black and the Tiger 1958,S 19,24:4
Question of Adultery, A 1961,Jl 6,18:2

Steel, Edward

Boy Cried Murder, The 1966,Ap 14,42:3

Steele, Barbara

Black Sunday 1961,Mr 9,23:1
Pit and the Pendulum, The 1961,Ag 24,25:3
Eight and One Half 1963,Je 26,36:1
Horrible Dr Hitchcock, The 1964,D 3,58:3
White Voices; Voci Blanche 1965,Ap 13,32:2
Hours of Love, The 1965,S 4,11:5
Young Torless 1967,S 25,56:2
Young Torless 1968,Jl 23,27:2

Steele, Bernard (Miscellaneous)

Back Door to Heaven 1939,Ap 20,21:2

Steele, Bob

Powdersmoke Range 1936,Mr 9,20:2
Of Mice and Men 1940,F 17,9:2
Big Sleep, The 1946,Ag 24,6:6
Killer McCoy 1948,F 12,31:2
South of St Louis 1949,Mr 7,17:2
Enforcer, The 1951,Ja 26,19:2
Lion and the Horse, The 1952,My 19,12:2
Steel Jungle, The 1956,Mr 10,9:5
Gun for a Coward 1957,Ja 31,21:1
Rio Bravo 1959,Mr 19,40:2
Pork Chop Hill 1959,My 30,9:2
Comancheros, The 1961,N 2,42:1
6 Black Horses 1962,Ap 25,30:1

Steele, Christopher

Tawny Pipit 1947,S 8,25:5
Quiet Week-End 1948,Ag 20,13:2

Steele, Fred

Pittsburgh Kid, The 1941,S 23,27:4
Hail the Conquering Hero 1944,Ag 10,14:2
Story of G I Joe 1945,O 6,9:6
Black Angel 1946,S 26,32:4
Foreign Affair, A 1948,Jl 1,19:3
Race Street 1948,Ag 23,13:3
Whiplash 1948,D 27,16:3

Steele, Geoffrey

Terror by Night 1946,F 9,9:2

Steele, Isobel Lillian

I Was a Captive of Nazi Germany
1936,Ag 3,11:2

Steele, Isobel Lillian (Original Author)

I Was a Captive of Nazi Germany
1936,Ag 3,11:2

Steele, Joseph Henry (Producer)

We're on the Jury 1937,F 10,18:5

Steele, Karen

Marty 1955,Ap 12,25:3
Toward the Unknown 1956,S 28,24:4
Bailout at 43,000 1957,Je 8,13:2
Rise and Fall of Legs' Diamond, The
1960,F 4,34:1

Steele, Lou

September Affair 1951,F 2,19:2

Steele, Marjorie

Bride Comes to Yellow Sky, The 1953,Ja 14,27:2

Steele, Michael

Command Decision 1949,Ja 20,34:2
Tanks are Coming, The 1951,D 6,42:4

Steele, Minnie

Darling of New York, The 1924,Ja 18,20:1

Steele, Pauline

Hurricane, The 1937,N 10,31:2

Steele, R V

Firing Line, The 1919,Jl 7,18:5

Steele, Richard

With Six You Get Egg Roll 1968,O 10,59:6

Steele, Tommy

Dream Maker, The 1964,Ap 23,34:1
Happiest Millionaire, The 1967,D 1,56:1
Half a Sixpence 1968,F 21,60:3
Finian's Rainbow 1968,O 10,59:5

Steele, Vernon

Little Lady Eileen 1916,Ag 14,7:6
Polly of the Circus 1917,S 10,11:3
Witness for the Defense, The 1919,S 15,16:3
His House in Order 1920,Mr 8,9:5
His House in Order 1920,Mr 8,9:6
King's Vacation, The 1933,Ja 20,21:2
Silk Express, The 1933,Je 28,24:2
Where Sinners Meet 1934,My 25,25:2
Great Flirtation, The 1934,Je 22,16:5
Captain Blood 1935,D 27,14:1
Lloyds of London 1936,N 26,39:1
Witness Vanishes, The 1939,O 23,15:2
They Were Expendable 1945,D 21,25:2
Lone Wolf in London, The 1947,N 22,10:3
To the Ends of the Earth 1948,F 13,26:2

Steele, Wilbur Daniel (Original Author)

Foot Falls 1921,S 9,18:3
Undertow 1930,Mr 1,23:1
Way to the Gold, The 1957,My 11,24:6

Steele, William

Fast Mail, The 1922,Jl 10,9:5
Last Man on Earth, The 1924,D 13,12:4
Flaming Frontier, The 1926,Ap 5,24:1
Dough Boys 1930,S 30,23:1

Steeman, S A (Original Author)

Murderer Lives at Number 21, The
1947,Ag 18,12:3
Jenny Lamour 1948,Mr 6,17:2
Inside a Girls' Dormitory 1956,F 6,27:7

Steeman, S A (Screenwriter)

Murderer Lives at Number 21, The
1947,Ag 18,12:3

STEEN

See Also STEIN

Steen, Anna

Murderer Dimitri Karamasoff, The
1931,Mr 1,VIII,6:7 (In Addenda)

Steen, Bodil

Crazy Paradise 1965,Ag 11,41:2
Eric Soya's 17 1967,Ja 25,37:1

Steen, Marguerite (Miscellaneous)

Man From Morocco, The 1946,N 25,38:2

Steen, Michael

This Property is Condemned 1966,Ag 4,24:1

Steenberger, Paul

Ciske 1963,Ag 3,8:2

Steer, Caroline

Rocking Horse Winner, The 1950,Je 9,29:2

Steers, Larry

Best People 1925,O 21,21:3
New Brooms 1925,N 4,17:4
Bride of the Storm 1926,Ap 5,24:1
Claw, The 1927,My 11,28:3
Redskin 1929,Ja 28,21:1
Wheel of Life, The 1929,Je 24,27:1
Let's Go Places 1930,Mr 1,23:1
Two Kinds of Women 1932,Ja 16,13:1
Cocktail Hour 1933,Je 5,18:5

Steers, Lary

Secret Call, The 1931,Jl 13,13:5

Stefanelli, Benito

For a Few Dollars More 1967,Jl 4,23:1
Big Gundown, The 1968,Ag 23,33:1

Stefaniai, Imre

Hello Budapest 1935,N 14,17:4

Stefanidou, Smaro

Santa Chikita 1959,My 11,30:1

Stefano, Joseph (Original Author)

Black Orchid, The 1959,F 13,33:2

Stefano, Joseph (Screenwriter)

Black Orchid, The 1959,F 13,33:2
Psycho 1960,Je 17,37:1
Fast and Sexy 1960,O 6,51:4
Naked Edge 1961,Jl 1,9:1

Stefansson, Vilhjalmur (Narrator)

Lost in the Arctic 1928,Jl 26,25:3

Steffans, Peggy

Hallelujah the Hills 1963,D 17,49:1

STEFFEN

See Also STEPHAN, STEPHEN

Steffen, Geary

Wintertime 1943,S 30,27:2

Stegger, Karl

Crazy Paradise 1965,Ag 11,41:2

Stehli, Edgar

Executive Suite 1954,My 7,19:1
Cobweb, The 1955,Ag 6,13:3
Spiral Road, The 1962,Ag 4,11:2
Twilight of Honor 1963,N 14,41:2
Seconds 1966,O 6,56:1

Stehli, Efgar

Brothers Karamazov, The 1958,F 21,18:2

Stehlik, Mitoslav (Screenwriter)

Girl With Three Camels, The 1968,Ag 13,45:2

Stehlik, Mitslav (Original Author)

Girl With Three Camels, The 1968,Ag 13,45:2

Stehll, Edgar

Atlantis the Lost Continent 1961,My 27,12:1

Stehnitzky, Nicholas

Marusia 1938,D 12,26:2

Steichen, Edward L (Director)

Fighting Lady, The 1944,D 28,12:2

Steiger, Rod

Teresa 1951,Ap 6,31:2
On the Waterfront 1954,Jl 29,18:1
Oklahoma! 1955,O 11,49:1
Big Knife, The 1955,N 9,41:2
Court-Martial of Billy Mitchell, The
1955,D 23,14:2
Jubal 1956,Ap 25,39:1
Harder They Fall, The 1956,My 10,26:3
Back From Eternity 1956,S 8,20:6
Run of the Arrow 1957,Ag 3,8:6
Across the Bridge 1957,O 30,24:1
Unholy Wife, The 1958,Mr 7,17:1
Cry Terror 1958,My 15,25:1
Al Capone 1959,Mr 26,27:1
Seven Thieves 1960,Mr 12,14:5

Steiger, Rod— Cont

Mark, The 1961,O 3,46:2
World in my Pocket, The 1962,My 10,30:2
13 West Street 1962,Je 7,31:2
Convicts 4 1962,O 4,44:2
Longest Day, The 1962,O 5,28:1
Hands Over the City 1964,S 18,28:1
Pawnbroker, The 1965,Ap 21,51:1
Loved One, The 1965,O 12,57:1
Time of Indifference 1965,O 13,50:1
Doctor Zhivago 1965,D 23,21:1
Time of Indifference 1966,O 13,50:1
In the Heat of the Night 1967,Ag 3,26:1
Girl and the General, The 1967,D 7,60:1
No Way to Treat a Lady 1968,Mr 21,56:1
And There Came a Man 1968,Ap 5,56:4
Sergeant, The 1968,D 26,53:5

Steimar, Jiri

Bohemian Rapture 1948,F 16,16:2

STEIN

See Also STEEN

Stein, Alexander

Brivele der Mamen, A; Little Letter to Mother, A
1939,S 15,26:4

Stein, Alexander (Screenwriter)

Attack From the Sea 1954,Ap 19,19:4

Stein, Daniel Michael (Original Author)

Wall of Noise 1963,S 5,27:1

Stein, Franz

M 1933,Ap 3,13:3

Stein, Gita

Catskill Honeymoon 1950,Ja 28,10:3

Stein, John

Paths of Glory 1957,D 26,23:2

Stein, Joseph (Original Author)

Enter Laughing 1967,Ag 1,24:1

Stein, Joseph (Producer)

Enter Laughing 1967,Ag 1,24:1

Stein, Joseph (Screenwriter)

Enter Laughing 1967,Ag 1,24:1

Stein, Leo (Composer)

Merry Widow, The 1952,S 25,38:1

Stein, Leo (Original Author)

Merry Widow, The 1934,O 12,33:1

Stein, Lotte

Kyritz-Pyritz 1932,Ag 9,20:5
Climax, The 1944,D 14,28:5
Mother Wore Tights 1947,Ag 21,33:2
Wallflower 1948,Je 12,8:5
Mr Belvedere Goes to College 1949,Ap 16,11:2
White Tower, The 1950,Jl 3,9:2
All I Desire 1953,Ag 29,10:1

Stein, Paul L (Director)

Red Peacock, The 1922,Ap 3,18:2
Don't Tell the Wife 1927,F 22,23:2
Climbers, The 1927,My 4,29:2
Forbidden Woman, The 1927,O 31,22:1
This Thing Called Love 1929,D 14,22:4
Her Private Affair 1930,Ja 11,21:3
One Romantic Night 1930,My 31,19:4
Sin Takes a Holiday 1930,N 28,23:1
Lottery Bride, The 1930,N 29,21:4
Born to Love 1931,Ap 25,23:4
Common Law, The 1931,Jl 20,20:4
Woman Commands, A 1932,Ja 28,13:2
Mimi 1936,Ja 10,16:3
Red Wagon 1936,Je 22,22:1
April Romance 1937,Ja 27,17:4
Heart's Desire 1937,Jl 12,20:4
Outsider, The 1940,Mr 18,13:2
It Happened to One Man 1941,F 24,11:6
Waltz Time 1946,F 11,25:2
Laughing Lady, The 1950,Ja 23,16:3
Lisbon Story, The 1951,S 6,39:4
Devil's Plot 1953,Je 19,18:1

Stein, Sammy

Lost Patrol, The 1934,Ap 2,13:2
Sing Your Worries Away 1942,My 15,25:2
Remember Pearl Harbor 1942,Je 4,22:4

Stein, Sheila

That Midnight Kiss 1949,S 23,28:2

Steinbeck, John (Original Author)

Grapes of Wrath, The 1940,Ja 25,17:2
Of Mice and Men 1940,F 17,9:2
Forgotten Village, The 1941,N 19,26:3
Tortilla Flat 1942,My 22,27:1
Moon Is Down, The 1943,Mr 27,8:6
Lifeboat 1944,Ja 13,17:1
Medal for Benny, A 1945,My 24,15:2
Pearl, The 1948,F 18,36:4
Red Pony, The 1949,Mr 9,33:2
East of Eden 1955,Mr 10,33:1
Wayward Bus, The 1957,Je 6,35:2

Steinbeck, John (Screenwriter)

Forgotten Village, The 1941,N 19,26:3
Pearl, The 1948,F 18,36:4
Red Pony, The 1949,Mr 9,33:2
Viva Zapata 1952,F 8,19:2

Steinbeck, Muriel

Pacific Adventure 1947,N 26,18:2
Wherever She Goes 1953,Ja 28,24:4
Long John Silver 1955,Ap 7,24:1

Steinbeck, Walter
Stolz der 3 Kompagnie, Der 1932,Jl 21,15:2
Week-End Im Paradies 1932,O 24,18:5
Eine Tuer geht Auf 1933,F 6,11:5
Ihre Majestaet die Liebe 1933,F 7,23:4
Blaue Vom Himmel, Das 1934,S 8,18:6
Heimat am Rhein 1934,D 11,29:4
Beiden Seehunde, Die 1935,Mr 9,19:2
Konjunkturritter 1935,Ap 29,12:4
Grosse Chance, Die 1935,My 6,22:4
Herr Kobin Geht auf Abenteuer; Mr Kobin Seeks
     Adventure 1935,N 26,28:2
Ganzer Kerl, Ein 1936,Ap 25,21:2
Oberwachtmeister Schwenke 1936,My 5,26:7
Schloss Vogeloed 1936,My 9,11:2
Selige Exzellenz, Die 1937,Je 15,26:2
Salon Dora Green 1937,Jl 26,15:3
Spiel in Sommerwind; Play in the Summer
     Breezes 1939,Ap 1,17:2
Kluge Schwiegermutter, Die; Wise Mother-in-Law,
     The 1939,O 9,15:3
Favorit der Kaiserin, Der; Favorite of the Empress,
     The 1939,D 25,29:3
Steinberg, Joe (Producer)
Cry of Battle 1963,O 12,27:2
Steinbicker, Reinhart (Director)
Liebe, Tod und Teufel 1935,My 25,12:2
Steiner, Dorothy
Joy of Living 1938,My 6,27:1
Steiner, Elio
Amore e Dolore 1937,My 13,31:4
Steiner, Estelle
Joy of Living 1938,My 6,27:1
Steiner, Jean
Persecution and Assassination of Jean-Paul Marat
     as Performed by the Inmates of the Asylum of
     Charenton Under the Direction of the Marquis
     De Sade, The 1967,F 23,41:1
Steiner, Max (Composer)
Stingaree 1934,My 18,27:1
Down to Their Last Yacht 1934,S 24,14:1
Star Is Born, A 1937,Ap 23,25:1
That Certain Woman 1937,S 16,29:1
Tovarich 1937,D 31,9:2
Gold Is Where You Find It 1938,F 14,20:6
White Banners 1938,Je 23,27:1
Dodge City 1939,Ap 8,19:1
Gone With the Wind 1939,D 20,31:2
Four Wives 1939,D 23,9:1
Gone With the Wind 1967,O 11,41:1
Steiner, Russell
Night of the Living Dead 1968,D 5,59:2
Steiner, Russell (Producer)
Night of the Living Dead 1968,D 5,59:2
Steiner, Sigfrit
Last Chance, The 1945,N 28,21:6
Village, The 1953,S 23,37:2
It Happened in Broad Daylight 1960,S 30,33:1
Steiner, Vicki Raw
Caught 1949,F 18,26:4
Steiner, Walter
Blonde Nachtigall, Die 1931,Ag 22,7:5
Steinert, Alexander
Too Young to Kiss 1951,N 23,32:2
Because You're Mine 1952,S 26,18:2
Steinhilber, Budd
Funnyman 1967,S 25,56:3
Steinhoff, Hans (Director)
Rosenmontag 1931,Mr 28,15:3
Wahre Jakob, Der 1931,Ag 7,20:2
Mein Leopold 1932,Ap 1,17:4
Ein Maedel der Strasse 1933,Ap 6,22:5
Madame Wuenscht Keine Kinder 1933,Je 2,22:4
Liebe Muss Verstanden Sein 1934,Mr 21,24:3
Unsere Fahne Flattert Uns Voran 1934,Jl 7,16:6
Freut Euch des Lebens 1934,N 3,20:3
Mutter und Kind 1934,N 30,22:3
Lockvogel 1935,Ja 5,20:3
Alte und der Junge Koenig, Der 1935,D 10,31:2
Keine Angst vor Liebe 1936,Ja 21,27:6
Frau Ohne Bedeutung, Ein 1938,Ap 16,17:2
Robert Koch 1939,N 25,13:2
Steininger, Franz (Composer)
Knickerbocker Holiday 1944,Ap 20,22:7
Steinke, Hans
Deception 1933,Ja 10,26:2
Island of Lost Souls 1933,Ja 13,19:2
People Will Talk 1935,Je 17,20:2
Once in a Blue Moon 1936,D 2,35:1
Buccaneer, The 1938,F 17,17:2
Steinpichier, Michael
Bible, The 1966,S 29,60:1
Steinrueck, Albert
Decameron Nights 1928,My 29,17:2
Eleven Who Were Loyal 1929,My 20,22:6
At the Edge of the World 1929,Je 18,29:4
Asphalt 1930,My 6,33:4
Stekel, Leonard
Ich Will Nicht Wissen Wer Du Bist
     1933,F 16,23:2
Stella, Enrico (Original Author)
Crazy Desire 1964,Jl 3,13:2

Steller, Hermine
Zwei Menschen 1931,D 23,27:3
Stelli, Jean (Director)
Blue Veil, The 1947,O 2,32:6
Stelli, Jean (Screenwriter)
It Happened in Gibraltar 1943,N 16,27:1
Stellina, Peppino
Alone in the Streets 1956,Je 28,33:2
Stelling, William
Hell in the Heavens 1934,D 12,28:2
Devil's Squadron 1936,My 11,16:2
Woman I Love, The 1937,Ap 16,27:2
Doomed to Die 1940,Jl 30,16:3
Flight Command 1941,Ja 17,21:2
Ghost and Mrs Muir, The 1947,Je 27,17:2
Stellman, Michael
Wastrel, The 1963,N 5,24:1
Stelper, Alexander (Director)
Wait for Me 1945,Mr 19,23:3
Stelzer, Hannes
Traumulus 1936,S 19,20:1
Abenteurer von Paris, Der 1937,My 29,20:3
Truxa 1937,Jl 26,15:2
Katzensteg 1938,Ja 22,19:2
Ein Hoffnungsloser Fall 1939,S 18,15:5
Kleine Nachtmusik, Eine 1940,Mr 2,9:5
Stemberg, Hans
Schwarzwaldmaedel 1935,O 12,12:3
Stemberger, Elisabeth
April 1, 2000 1954,F 17,27:2
Stemmle, Robert A (Director)
Glueckspilze 1936,O 26,21:1
Maedel mit Tempo, Ein 1937,Ag 23,22:2
Gleisdreieck 1938,Je 11,9:1
Volk Will Leben, Ein; People Wants to Live, A
     1939,Mr 27,11:2
Berliner, Die 1952,O 28,37:1
Stemmle, Robert A (Original Author)
Desire 1936,Ap 13,15:1
Stemmle, Robert A (Screenwriter)
Affair Blum, The 1949,O 18,35:2
Confess, Dr Corda 1960,O 24,25:5
Sten, Anna
Yellow Ticket, The 1928,D 10,25:1
Lash of the Czar, The 1929,F 12,23:1
When Moscow Laughs 1929,S 17,36:2
Karamazof 1931,S 21,20:2
Bomben auf Monte Carlo; Bombardment of Monte
     Carlo, The 1931,S 27,VIII,7:1
Salto Mortale 1931,O 25,VIII,6:1
Stuerme der Leidenschaft; Storms of Passion
     1932,F 14,VIII,6:1
Stuerme der Leidenschaft 1932,Mr 16,17:3
Trapeze 1932,My 3,25:2
Nana 1934,F 2,20:3
We Live Again 1934,N 2,27:2
Wedding Night, The 1935,Mr 16,19:1
Two Who Dared 1937,Jl 10,18:2
Exile Express 1939,Ag 16,21:3
Man I Married, The 1940,Ag 3,9:2
So Ends our Night 1941,F 28,17:2
Chetniks 1943,Mr 19,15:3
They Came to Blow up America
     1943,My 15,13:2
Three Russian Girls 1944,F 5,13:2
Let's Live a Little 1948,D 10,34:2
Soldier of Fortune 1955,My 28,7:4
Stendhal (Original Author)
Lovers of Toledo, The 1954,Ap 10,11:3
Rouge et Noir 1958,Ap 9,42:1
Stenermann, Salka
Seven Faces 1929,N 16,25:2
Stengel, Casey
Safe at Home 1941,N 26,31:2
Stengel, Christian (Director)
Dreams of Love 1954,Je 5,11:2
Stengel, Christian (Producer)
Dame de Pique, La 1944,O 19,19:2
Stengel, Leni
Half Shot at Sunrise 1930,O 11,21:3
Beau Ideal 1931,Ja 19,25:1
Cracked Nuts 1931,Ap 6,24:1
Road to Reno, The 1931,O 10,20:4
Beloved Bachelor 1931,O 17,20:1
Husband's Holiday 1931,D 25,29:2
Man About Town 1932,My 28,18:2
Hollywood Speaks 1932,Ag 12,18:2
Animal Kingdom, The 1932,D 30,14:2
Barbarian, The 1933,My 13,16:2
Stenhouse, J R Lieut-Commander
Explorers of the World 1931,D 18,29:3
Steni, Antonella
Tiger and the Pussycat, The 1967,S 21,56:4
Steni, Mario
Lorenzino de Medici 1936,Ap 14,19:3
Cieca di Sorrento, La 1936,Ag 3,11:3
Stenn, Ingrid
Third Sex, The 1959,Mr 26,27:1
Steno (Director)
Sins of Casanova 1957,O 7,23:2
Psycosissimo 1962,S 8,16:2
Day in Court, A 1963,My 11,15:2

Steno (Original Author)
Mad About Opera 1950,Ap 6,33:2
O K Nero 1953,Je 20,8:6
Steno (Screenwriter)
Mad About Opera 1950,Ap 6,33:2
O K Nero 1953,Je 20,8:6
Step Brothers, The
It Ain't Hay 1943,Mr 11,17:3
Step Brothers, The Four
Carolina Blues 1944,D 8,26:6
Stepanek, Karel
Hermine und die Sieben Aufrechten
     1935,S 21,18:2
Stronger Than the Rule 1937,S 25,10:2
Hotel Sacher 1939,Je 10,14:2
At Dawn We Die 1943,My 8,19:2
Captive Heart, The 1947,Ap 28,27:2
Fallen Idol, The 1949,N 16,39:2
Give Us This Day 1949,D 21,41:2
Conspirator 1950,Ap 28,26:2
State Secret 1950,O 5,38:2
Walk East on Beacon 1952,My 29,17:2
Affair in Trinidad 1952,Jl 31,14:2
Cairo Road 1952,N 1,17:2
City Beneath the Sea 1953,Mr 12,24:3
Never Let Me Go 1953,Je 11,37:2
Devil's Plot 1953,Je 19,18:1
Gay Adventure, The 1954,S 16,35:7
Prize of Gold, A 1955,O 15,19:2
Cockleshell Heroes, The 1956,Je 4,25:2
Anastasia 1956,D 14,35:6
Sink the Bismarck! 1960,F 12,22:3
I Aim at the Stars 1960,O 20,42:2
Operation Crossbow 1965,Ap 2,29:1
2nd Best Secret Agent in the Whole Wide World,
     The 1966,Ap 28,49:1
Frozen Dead, The 1967,N 16,58:1
Stepanek, Zdenek
Skeleton on Horseback 1940,F 5,13:3
Merry Wives, The 1940,N 12,28:3
Emperor and the Golem, The 1955,Ja 10,27:4
Transport From Paradise 1967,F 8,22:1
Stepanek, Zdenek (Original Author)
Merry Wives, The 1940,N 12,28:3
Stepankova, Jana
Death of Tarzan, The 1968,Jl 4,13:2
Stepanof, M
Cossacks of the Don 1932,Mr 19,11:2
Stepanov, Alexander
1812 1944,S 11,14:1
Winner, The 1947,D 1,27:2
Stepanov, V
Lad From our Town 1943,O 7,26:2
Miles of Fire 1958,N 10,36:6 (In Addenda)
Stepanova, Lidia (Director)
Inside the U S S R 1961,N 6,46:5
Stephael, Frederick (Screenwriter)
All the King's Horses 1935,Mr 9,19:1
STEPHAN
See Also STEFFEN, STEPHEN
Stephan, Aram
Love Is a Ball 1963,Ap 25,38:1
Bedtime Story 1964,Je 11,27:1
Stephane, Nicole
Strange Ones, The 1952,Jl 29,17:3
Stephane, Nicole (Producer)
To Die in Madrid 1965,S 16,00:0
Vie de Chateau, La 1967,Mr 21,35:1
Other One, The 1967,S 29,53:1
Stephani, Frederick (Original Author)
Love Is News 1937,Mr 6,10:1
We Have our Moments 1937,Ap 30,17:3
Sweet Rosie O'Grady 1943,O 21,30:2
It Happened on Fifth Avenue 1947,Je 11,33:2
That Wonderful Urge 1948,D 22,29:6
Stephani, Frederick (Producer)
Beg, Borrow or Steal 1937,D 10,33:2
Fast Company 1938,Jl 6,21:2
Fast and Loose 1939,Mr 9,18:1
Fast And Furious 1939,O 12,33:3
Sky Murder 1940,N 14,28:3
Born to Sing 1942,F 19,23:2
Tarzan's New York Adventure 1942,Ag 7,13:2
Stephani, Frederick (Screenwriter)
Between Two Women 1937,Ag 6,21:1
Sofia 1948,S 4,8:7
Johnny Holiday 1950,My 17,36:1
Stephanidou, Smaro
Mademoiselle-Age 39 1956,Mr 26,34:2
STEPHEN
See Also STEFFEN, STEPHAN
Stephen, Pierre
Three Waltzes 1939,Ap 25,19:2
Crazy in the Noodle 1957,D 15,45:4 (Incorrect in
     this edition; use 1957,D 17,45:4 elsewhere)
Stephen, Susan
Paratrooper 1953,D 31,9:3
His Excellency 1956,F 2,19:3
Barretts of Wimpole Street, The 1957,Ja 18,15:3
Value for Money 1957,Ag 1,20:4
Stephens, Ann
In Which We Serve 1942,D 24,18:1
Randolph Family 1945,Mr 13,19:4

Stephens, Ann— Cont
They Were Sisters 1946,Jl 24,24:2
Upturned Glass, The 1947,N 5,34:4
Man of Evil 1948,Mr 26,26:2
No Room at the Inn 1949,D 26,33:4
Eye Witness 1950,Ag 28,13:2
Franchise Affair, The 1952,Je 6,19:2

Stephens, Harvey
Cheat, The 1931,D 12,23:3
Paddy the Next Best Thing 1933,Ag 25,12:2
Worst Woman in Paris, The 1933,N 25,10:3
Jimmy and Sally 1933,D 16,12:3
Evelyn Prentice 1934,N 10,19:1
After Office Hours 1935,Mr 9,19:1
Let 'Em Have It 1935,My 30,21:1
Murder Man, The 1935,Jl 27,16:2
Orchids to You 1935,Ag 10,16:4
It's in the Air 1935,N 8,18:2
Whipsaw 1936,Ja 25,18:4
Tough Guy 1936,Mr 14,10:1
Robin Hood of El Dorado, The 1936,Mr 14,10:1
Absolute Quiet 1936,My 2,11:1
Three Wise Guys, The 1936,My 23,12:2
Sworn Enemy 1936,S 12,20:1
Maid of Salem 1937,Mr 4,27:2
Swing High, Swing Low 1937,Ap 15,19:1
King of Gamblers 1937,Jl 3,18:1
Night Club Scandal 1937,N 12,27:2
Dangerous to Know 1938,Mr 11,15:4
Tip-Off Girls 1938,Mr 25,15:3
Texans, The 1938,Jl 28,23:2
Oklahoma Kid, The 1939,Mr 11,21:1
You Can't Get Away With Murder
  1939,Mr 25,19:2
Grand Jury Secrets 1939,Je 29,19:2
Fighting 69th, The 1940,Ja 27,9:2
Abe Lincoln in Illinois 1940,F 23,19:2
Parole Fixer 1940,Ap 18,28:5
When the Daltons Rode 1940,Ag 23,13:3
Sergeant York 1941,Jl 3,15:1
Our Wife 1941,S 18,31:1
Joe Smith, American 1942,Ap 2,27:4
Courtship of Andy Hardy, The 1942,Ap 10,21:2
Lady is Willing, The 1942,Ap 24,21:2
George Washington Slept Here 1942,O 31,11:1
Lady in the Dark 1944,F 23,17:1
Three Young Texans 1954,Ap 17,8:2
In Love and War 1958,N 1,14:2
Diary of a Madman 1963,Je 6,39:1

Stephens, Helen
They Were Sisters 1946,Jl 24,24:2

Stephens, Jim (Narrator)
Smashing of the Reich 1962,O 3,44:4

Stephens, Kelley
Hoodlum Priest, The 1961,Ap 3,28:5

Stephens, Martin
Divided Heart, The 1955,Ag 4,16:1
Another Time Another Place 1958,My 3,10:4
Harry Black and the Tiger 1958,S 19,24:4
Count Your Blessings 1959,Ap 24,23:1
Touch of Larceny, A 1960,Mr 17,28:1
Village of the Damned 1960,D 8,43:3
Innocents, The 1961,D 26,15:2
Battle of the Villa Fiorita, The 1965,My 27,28:1

Stephens, Marvin
Man I Killed, The 1932,Ja 20,17:4
Trip to Paris, A 1938,Je 10,18:2
Safety in Numbers 1938,S 6,17:2
Speed to Burn 1938,S 9,25:1
Young as You Feel 1940,Mr 8,25:3

Stephens, Rachel
Bigger Than Life 1956,Ag 3,11:2
Oh Men! Oh Women! 1957,F 22,25:2
True Story of Jesse James, The 1957,Mr 23,17:2
Desk Set 1957,My 16,28:2

Stephens, Robert
Circle of Deception 1961,F 18,12:2
Taste of Honey, A 1962,My 1,33:3
Lisa 1962,My 25,28:1
Cleopatra 1963,Je 13,29:1
Small World of Sammy Lee, The 1963,Ag 14,28:1
Morgan! 1966,Ap 5,42:2
Roméo and Juliet 1968,O 9,41:1

Stephens, Roy
Dr Strangelove or: How I Learned to Stop
  Worrying and Love the Bomb 1964,Ja 31,16:1
  (Incorrect in this edition; use 1964,Ja 30,24:1
  elsewhere)

Stephens, Sheila
Backfire 1950,Ja 27,29:2
Caged 1950,My 20,8:6
Pretty Baby 1950,S 23,11:2

Stephens, William (Producer)
Meet Doctor Christian 1939,D 1,27:2
Dr Christian Meets the Women 1940,Ag 2,12:2
Deputy Marshal 1949,N 11,31:3

STEPHENSON
See Also STEVENSON

Stephenson, Bob
Anne of the Indies 1951,O 25,36:3

Stephenson, Carl (Original Author)
Naked Jungle, The 1954,Ap 3,19:2

Stephenson, Claude (Narrator)
Mein Kampf 1961,Ap 22,18:1

Stephenson, Henry
Spreading Dawn, The 1917,O 22,13:2
Men and Women 1925,Mr 30,21:3
Wild, Wild Susan 1925,Ag 5,12:4
Red Headed Woman 1932,Jl 1,19:3
Guilty as Hell 1932,Ag 6,14:5
Bill of Divorcement, A 1932,O 3,15:2
Cynara 1932,D 26,26:2
Animal Kingdom, The 1932,D 30,14:2
Tomorrow at Seven 1933,Jl 3,14:6
Double Harness 1933,Jl 21,20:2
Blind Adventure 1933,O 31,24:3
My Lips Betray 1933,N 4,18:3
Little Women 1933,N 17,22:3
If I Were Free 1934,Ja 5,25:2
Man of Two Worlds 1934,Ja 12,29:2
Mystery of Mr X, The 1934,F 26,21:3
Thirty Day Princess 1934,My 12,12:3
Stingaree 1934,My 18,27:1
One More River 1934,Ag 10,21:1
She Loves Me Not 1934,S 8,18:5
Richest Girl in the World, The 1934,S 21,29:2
What Every Woman Knows 1934,O 27,20:2
Outcast Lady 1934,N 3,20:3
Night is Young, The 1935,Ja 14,11:2
Vanessa: Her Love Story 1935,Ap 13,11:3
Reckless 1935,Ap 20,16:1
Flame Within, The 1935,Je 1,18:2
O'Shaughnessy's Boy 1935,O 5,18:2
Rendezvous 1935,O 26,12:2
Mutiny on the Bounty 1935,N 9,19:2
Perfect Gentleman, The 1935,D 19,33:4
Captain Blood 1935,D 27,14:1
Little Lord Fauntleroy 1936,Ap 3,27:1
Half Angel 1936,My 30,7:3
Hearts Divided 1936,Je 13,13:1
Walking on Air 1936,S 12,20:2
Give Me your Heart 1936,S 17,18:2
Charge of the Light Brigade, The 1936,N 2,24:1
Beloved Enemy 1936,D 26,15:2
When You're in Love 1937,F 19,15:2
Prince and the Pauper, The 1937,My 6,23:1
Emperor's Candlesticks, The 1937,Jl 9,18:1
Conquest 1937,N 5,19:1
Wise Girl 1938,Ja 10,13:3
Baroness and the Butler, The 1938,F 19,19:2
Marie Antoinette 1938,Ag 17,23:2
Suez 1938,O 15,21:2
Young in Heart, The 1938,N 4,27:2
Dramatic School 1938,D 9,31:2
Tarzan Finds a Son 1939,Je 15,27:2
Adventures of Sherlock Holmes, The
  1939,S 2,20:1
Private Lives of Elizabeth and Essex, The
  1939,D 2,21:2
Little Old New York 1940,F 3,9:2
It's a Date 1940,Mr 23,16:2
Spring Parade 1940,O 4,29:2
Down Argentine Way 1940,O 18,25:1
Lady From Louisiana 1941,My 15,27:2
Rings on her Fingers 1942,Ap 24,21:4
This Above All 1942,My 13,14:3
Mr Lucky 1943,Jl 23,21:2
Hour Before the Dawn, The 1944,My 11,25:6
Two Girls and a Sailor 1944,Je 15,16:1
Tarzan and the Amazons 1945,Ap 30,13:4
Green Years, The 1946,Ap 5,21:2
Heartbeat 1946,My 11,22:4
Of Human Bondage 1946,Jl 6,11:2
Night and Day 1946,Jl 26,16:2
Return of Monte Cristo, The 1947,Ja 3,16:4
Her Sister's Secret 1947,Ja 23,31:3
Locket, The 1947,Mr 20,38:2
Time Out of Mind 1947,Ap 7,20:1
Homestretch, The 1947,Ap 24,30:2
Dark Delusion 1947,Je 26,19:2
Song of Love 1947,O 10,31:2
Julia Misbehaves 1948,O 8,30:2
Enchantment 1948,D 27,16:2
Challenge to Lassie 1950,Ap 7,22:3
Oliver Twist 1951,Jl 31,17:2

Stephenson, James
When Were You Born? 1938,Je 9,27:2
White Banners 1938,Je 23,27:1
Cowboy From Brooklyn 1938,Jl 14,17:1
Boy Meets Girl 1938,Ag 27,7:2
Heart of the North 1938,D 21,29:2
King of the Underworld 1939,Ja 7,6:2
Torchy Blane in Chinatown 1939,F 3,13:2
Secret Service of the Air 1939,Mr 2,19:2
On Trial 1939,Ap 5,31:2
Confessions of a Nazi Spy 1939,Ap 29,13:2
Beau Geste 1939,Ag 3,15:2
Old Maid, The 1939,Ag 12,16:2
Espionage Agent 1939,S 23,22:2
We Are not Alone 1939,D 1,27:1
Private Lives of Elizabeth and Essex, The
  1939,D 2,21:2
Calling Philo Vance 1940,F 9,15:3
Murder in the Air 1940,Jl 4,12:2
Devil's Island 1940,Jl 12,11:4

Stephenson, James— Cont
Sea Hawk, The 1940,Ag 10,16:2
River's End 1940,Ag 26,11:4
Letter, The 1940,N 23,12:6
Dispatch From Reuters, A 1940,D 12,37:2
South of Suez 1940,D 19,33:2
Flight From Destiny 1941,Mr 28,26:7
Shining Victory 1941,My 31,14:1
International Squadron 1941,N 14,28:4

Stephenson, John
Teenage Rebel 1956,N 17,17:6
Careless Years, The 1957,N 28,57:3

Stephenson, Sandra
Money and the Woman 1940,O 4,29:2

Stepnickova, Jirina
Transport From Paradise 1967,F 8,22:1

Stepnickowa, Georgiana
Fremd im Sudetenland; Strange to the Sudeten
  Country 1938,N 5,15:3
Gottes Muehlen mahlen Langsam; Mills of the
  Gods, The 1939,F 18,12:4

Stepowski, K J
Tredowata 1936,D 31,21:2
Krawa Roza; Red Rose 1938,O 13,29:2
Znachor 1938,N 24,37:2

Steppat, Ilse
Marriage in the Shadows 1948,S 17,28:3
Confessions of Felix Krull, The 1958,Mr 5,38:1
Eighth Day of the Week, The 1959,Mr 24,45:2

Steppling, John
Madame Peacock 1920,O 25,18:1
Black Beauty 1921,F 21,16:1
Sin Flood, The 1922,O 30,11:1
Man Next Door, The 1923,My 29,10:3
Going Up 1923,O 10,16:2
Dramatic Life of Abraham Lincoln, The
  1924,Ja 22,17:3
Reckless Age, The 1924,Je 10,24:4
Fast Worker, The 1924,N 12,13:1
Cafe in Cairo, A 1925,Mr 18,19:2
California Straight Ahead 1926,Ja 12,27:5
Memory Lane 1926,F 2,20:4
Wedding Bills 1927,Je 29,29:3

Stept, Sam H (Composer)
Baby, Take a Bow 1934,Je 30,18:6
23 1/2 Hours Leave 1937,My 17,23:2
Hit Parade, The 1937,My 31,11:2
That's Right, You're Wrong 1939,N 30,25:3
Lullaby of Broadway 1951,Mr 27,35:2

Stept, Sam H (Miscellaneous)
Laughing Irish Eyes 1936,Ap 4,11:2

Sterke, Jeanette
Prisoner, The 1955,D 12,37:1
Lust for Life 1956,S 18,39:1

Sterler, Hermine
Strauss, The Waltz King 1929,Jl 22,17:1
Andere, Der 1932,Ja 15,24:4
Ich Geh' aus und Du Bleibst da 1932,N 21,21:1
Unfinished Symphony 1935,Ja 14,11:2
Dr Ehrlich's Magic Bullet 1940,F 24,9:2
Secret Agent of Japan 1942,Mr 23,19:3
Renegades 1946,Jl 11,18:2

STERLING
See Also STIRLING

Sterling, Andrew B (Composer)
Hold That Ghost 1941,Ag 8,13:3

Sterling, Bruce
In the Palace of the King 1923,D 3,14:1

Sterling, Ford
Stranger's Banquet, The 1923,Ja 1,18:1
Brass Bottle, The 1923,Jl 23,13:4
Hollywood 1923,Jl 30,11:4
Spoilers, The 1923,Ag 6,14:2
Day of Faith, The 1923,N 27,11:2
Wild Oranges 1924,Mr 3,22:3
Woman on the Jury, The 1924,My 19,14:2
Love and Glory 1924,Ag 5,10:2
He Who Gets Slapped 1924,N 10,20:1
So Big 1925,Ja 5,19:1
Daddy's Gone A-Hunting 1925,F 24,17:3
Trouble With Wives, The 1925,Ag 5,12:4
Stage Struck 1925,N 16,19:4
Mike 1926,Ja 11,33:1
American Venus, The 1926,Ja 26,25:2
Miss Brewster's Millions 1926,Mr 8,17:1
Good and Naughty 1926,Je 14,24:1
Show-Off, The 1926,Ag 23,9:1
Everybody's Acting 1926,N 8,19:2
Stranded in Paris 1926,D 13,27:1
Casey at the Bat 1927,Ap 4,30:5
For the Love of Mike 1927,Ag 24,27:5
Gentlemen Prefer Blondes 1928,Ja 16,24:1
Wife Savers 1928,Ja 17,23:2
Sporting Goods 1928,F 13,16:2
Chicken a la King 1928,Je 11,27:1
Oh, Kay! 1928,Ag 27,23:1
Fall of Eve, The 1929,Je 18,29:4
Sally 1929,D 24,14:4
Show Girl in Hollywood 1930,My 5,27:3
Bride of the Regiment 1930,My 22,32:6
Kismet 1930,O 31,20:1
Her Majesty, Love 1931,N 26,37:2
Alice in Wonderland 1933,D 23,19:1
Black Sheep 1935,Je 28,34:1

Sterling, Ford— Cont
Days of Thrills and Laughter 1961,Mr 22,37:1
Sterling, Harriet
Soul Fire 1925,My 6,26:3
Wilderness Woman, The 1926,My 10,19:1
Sterling, Jan
Johnny Belinda 1948,O 2,11:2
Caged 1950,My 20,8:6
Skipper Surprised his Wife, The 1950,Je 30,18:2
Mystery Street 1950,Jl 28,12:5
Union Station 1950,O 5,38:3
Mating Season, The 1951,Ap 12,41:2
Appointment With Danger 1951,My 10,38:2
Ace in the Hole 1951,Je 30,8:6
Rhubarb 1951,Ag 31,12:2
Flesh and Fury 1952,Mr 28,27:4
Split Second 1953,My 13,34:2
Pony Express 1953,Je 6,8:6
Alaska Seas 1954,Mr 6,13:5
High and the Mighty, The 1954,Jl 1,21:2
Return From the Sea 1954,Jl 10,7:3
Human Jungle, The 1954,N 26,24:6
Women's Prison 1955,F 3,18:5
Female on the Beach 1955,Ag 20,20:2
Man With the Gun 1955,D 23,14:2
Harder They Fall, The 1956,My 10,26:3
1984 1956,O 1,31:1
Slaughter on Tenth Avenue 1957,N 6,43:1
Female Animal, The 1958,Ja 23,24:3
High School Confidential 1958,My 31,6:6
Kathy O' 1958,S 25,29:2
Love in a Goldfish Bowl 1961,Jl 13,26:3
Incident, The 1967,N 6,65:1
Sterling, Lynn (Screenwriter)
Private Worlds 1935,Mr 28,25:2
Sterling, Philip (Miscellaneous)
Red Tanks 1942,Je 6,9:2
Day After Day 1943,N 6,16:3
Sterling, Robert
Gay Caballero, The 1940,O 25,25:3
Penalty, The 1941,Ap 10,29:3
I'll Wait for You 1941,Je 2,13:6
Get-Away, The 1941,Jl 17,23:4
Ringside Maisie 1941,Ag 1,11:2
Two Faced Woman 1942,Ja 1,37:2
Dr Kildare's Victory 1942,F 5,25:2
Johnny Eager 1942,F 20,21:2
Somewhere I'll Find You 1942,Ag 28,22:4
Secret Heart, The 1946,D 26,28:2
Roughshod 1949,Je 17,27:2
Sundowners, The 1950,My 5,17:2
Show Boat 1951,Jl 20,14:1
Return to Peyton Place 1961,My 6,26:1
Voyage to the Bottom of the Sea 1961,Jl 20,32:2
Global Affair, A 1964,My 7,31:2
Sterling, Rod (Screenwriter)
Patterns 1956,Mr 28,26:1
Sterling, Stewart (Screenwriter)
Having Wonderful Crime 1945,Ap 13,15:2
Sterling, Tisha
Name of the Game Is Kill, The 1968,Je 6,54:1
Coogan's Bluff 1968,O 3,56:1
Stern, Bernadette
Therese and Isabelle 1968,My 15,41:4
Stern, Bert (Director)
Jazz on a Summer's Day 1960,Mr 29,46:2
Stern, Bert (Producer)
Jazz on a Summer's Day 1960,Mr 29,46:2
Stern, Bill
Pride of the Yankees, The 1942,Jl 16,23:1
Stage Door Canteen 1943,Je 25,13:2
Here Come the Co-Eds 1945,F 19,21:1
Spirit of West Point 1947,O 3,31:2
Go, Man, Go 1954,Mr 10,29:5
Stern, Bill (Narrator)
Olympic Games of 1948, The 1948,S 25,11:2
Stern, David (Miscellaneous)
Francis 1950,Mr 16,40:2
Stern, David (Original Author)
Francis 1950,Mr 16,40:2
Francis in the Haunted House 1956,Jl 21,9:2
Stern, David (Screenwriter)
Francis 1950,Mr 16,40:2
Francis Goes to the Races 1951,Jl 25,19:2
Stern, Ernst (Miscellaneous)
Loves of Pharaoh 1922,F 22,13:3 (In Addenda)
Stern, G B (Original Author)
Long Lost Father 1934,F 19,18:2
Woman in the Hall, The 1949,Ja 24,16:2
Ugly Dachshund, The 1966,Ap 7,45:1
Stern, G B (Screenwriter)
Men Are not Gods 1937,Ja 19,28:1
Woman in the Hall, The 1949,Ja 24,16:2
Stern, George
Barricade 1950,Mr 25,8:6
Rogue River 1951,F 16,21:4
Stern, Isaac
Tonight We Sing 1953,F 13,17:2
Journey to Jerusalem, A 1968,N 18,59:1
Stern, Jack (Composer)
Wake up and Dream 1934,O 11,28:3
Folies Bergere 1935,F 25,13:2
One Rainy Afternoon 1936,My 14,29:2

Stern, Jack (Miscellaneous)
Little Miss Nobody 1936,Je 6,21:1
Stern, Jerome (Director)
Siren of Seville, The 1924,N 17,16:1 (In Addenda)
Stern, Leonard (Original Author)
Milkman, The 1951,Ja 1,13:6
Stern, Leonard (Screenwriter)
Abbott and Costello in the Foreign Legion 1950,Ag 14,14:4
Milkman, The 1951,Ja 1,13:6
Jazz Singer, The 1953,Ja 14,27:3
Three for the Show 1955,F 25,16:1
Stern, Louis
I Want my Man 1925,Ap 6,17:3
Wedding Bills 1927,Je 29,29:3
Where East Is East 1929,My 27,22:1
Stern, Mike
Sweet Bird of Youth 1962,Mr 29,28:2
Stern, Seymore (Screenwriter)
Dawn to Dawn 1933,D 27,23:5
Stern, Stewart (Original Author)
Teresa 1951,Ap 6,31:2
Stern, Stewart (Screenwriter)
Teresa 1951,Ap 6,31:2
Rebel without a Cause 1955,O 27,28:3
Rack, The 1956,N 6,30:1
James Dean Story, The 1957,O 19,16:7
Outsider, The 1962,F 8,25:1
Ugly American, The 1963,Ap 12,30:2
Rachel Rachel 1968,Ag 27,36:1
Stern, Tom
Hallelujah Trail, The 1965,Jl 2,17:1
Angels From Hell 1968,O 24,55:5
Sternberg, Hans
Because I Loved You 1930,Ja 25,13:2
Sterne, Morgan
No Exit 1962,D 6,55:2
Sterner, Martin
Sun Over Klara 1944,My 1,20:8
Sternhagen, Frances
Tiger Makes Out, The 1967,S 19,53:1
Sterns, Jack (Composer)
Young and Beautiful 1934,S 18,18:4
STERRETT
See Also STARRETT
Sterrett, Thomas Captain
Unbeliever, The 1918,F 12,9:2
Stessel, Ludwig
Great Sinner, The 1949,Je 30,19:2
Stettenberg, Stark
Volga, Volga 1933,D 15,28:3
Stettner, Willi
Madame Wuenscht Keine Kinder 1933,Je 2,22:4
Stettner, Willy
Schubert's Fruehlingstraum 1932,Je 22,19:4
Viktoria und Ihr Husar 1933,Ap 10,8:3
Quick, Koenig der Clowns 1933,D 9,18:3
Tausend Fuer Eine Nacht 1934,F 12,19:2
Tochter des Regiments, Die 1934,Mr 31,8:3
Steuermann, Salka
Anna Christie 1931,Ja 6,25:1
Steuwe, Hans
Heilige und Ihr Narr, Die; Saint and Her Fool, The 1935,N 29,24:2
Stevens, Angela
Naked Street, The 1955,O 1,11:2
Blackjack Ketchum Desperado 1956,Ap 5,26:2
Stevens, Anitra
Jazz Singer, The 1953,Ja 14,27:3
Egyptian, The 1954,Ag 25,23:1
Stevens, Carol
Good Sam 1948,S 17,28:2
Stevens, Charles
Where the North Begins 1923,Ag 27,14:3
Empty Hands 1924,Ag 18,8:2
Recompense 1925,Ap 20,22:1
Don Q, Son of Zorro 1925,Je 16,24:1
Son of his Father, A 1925,S 29,31:3
Vanishing American, The 1925,O 16,18:2
Black Pirate, The 1926,Mr 9,21:4
Mantrap 1926,Jl 12,24:4
Gaucho, The 1927,N 22,32:2
Stand and Deliver 1928,Ap 2,25:1
Iron Mask, The 1929,F 22,18:6
Insidious Dr Fu Manchu, The 1929,Jl 22,17:1
Virginian, The 1929,D 23,18:2
Big Trail, The 1930,O 25,20:3
Tom Sawyer 1930,D 20,20:6
Conquering Horde, The 1931,Mr 30,25:2
Cisco Kid, The 1931,O 24,20:3
Mystery Ranch 1932,Je 30,26:2
When Strangers Marry 1933,My 25,24:3
Lives of a Bengal Lancer, The 1935,Ja 12,12:2
Call of the Wild 1935,Ag 15,15:2
Ebb Tide 1937,N 18,27:2
Crime of Dr Hallet, The 1938,Mr 24,21:3
Renegade Ranger, The 1939,F 17,17:3
Girl and the Gambler, The 1939,Je 28,17:3
Frontier Marshal 1939,Jl 29,18:2
Wagons Westward 1940,Jl 8,13:2
Kit Carson 1940,N 15,25:3
Bad Man, The 1941,Ap 4,25:1

Stevens, Charles— Cont
Blood and Sand 1941,My 23,25:3
Tombstone, The Town too Tough to Die 1942,Jl 27,18:2
Pierre of the Plains 1942,Jl 30,17:3
Ambush 1950,Ja 19,35:2
Oh! Susanna 1951,Mr 30,28:5
Lion and the Horse, The 1952,My 19,12:2
Stevens, Charlotte
Tornado, The 1924,D 15,14:1
Mother 1927,My 4,29:2
Stevens, Connie
Rock-a-Bye Baby 1958,Jl 24,18:1
Parrish 1961,My 5,22:1
Susan Slade 1961,N 11,14:6
Palm Springs Weekend 1963,N 6,32:1
Two on a Guillotine 1965,Ja 14,44:3
Never too Late 1965,N 5,28:1
Way...Way Out 1966,O 27,55:1
Stevens, Craig
Dive Bomber 1941,Ag 30,10:2
Law of the Tropics 1941,O 10,26:5
Body Disappears, The 1942,Ja 31,13:2
Spy Ship 1942,Jl 11,8:2
Hidden Hand, The 1942,N 26,40:4
Secret Enemies 1943,Ja 1,27:3
Since You Went Away 1944,Jl 21,16:2
Doughgirls, The 1944,Ag 31,14:1
Hollywood Canteen 1944,D 16,19:2
Roughly Speaking 1945,F 1,18:4
God is my Co-Pilot 1945,Mr 24,22:6
Too Young to Know 1945,D 8,21:2
Humoresque 1946,D 26,28:1
Man I Love, The 1947,Ja 25,12:2
That Way With Women 1947,F 15,20:4
Love and Learn 1947,My 3,10:3
Night Unto Night 1949,Je 11,11:2
Lady Takes a Sailor, The 1949,D 17,15:2
Where the Sidewalk Ends 1950,Jl 8,7:4
Phone Call From a Stranger 1952,F 2,11:2
French Line, The 1954,My 15,13:2
Gunn 1967,Je 29,32:1
Stevens, Cy
Follow Me Quietly 1949,Jl 8,14:5
Stevens, Dodie
Hound-Dog Man 1960,Ap 28,29:1
Convicts 4 1962,O 4,44:2
Stevens, Dorinda
Night Train to Paris 1964,D 3,58:2
Stevens, Edwin
Unpardonable Sin, The 1919,My 3,11:3
Crimson Gardenia, The 1919,Je 16,11:2
Sahara 1919,Je 30,16:3
Lottery Man, The 1919,N 17,20:1
Hawthorne of the U.S.A. 1919,N 17,20:1
Man Unconquerable, The 1922,Jl 17,16:3
Voice From the Minaret, The 1923,F 5,18:2
Stevens, Everett
Too Late Blues 1962,Mr 1,27:4
Stevens, George (Director)
Cohens and Kellys in Trouble, The 1933,Ap 17,16:4
Kentucky Kernels 1935,Ja 5,20:2
Laddie 1935,My 6,22:3
Alice Adams 1935,Ag 16,11:3
Annie Oakley 1935,D 24,10:5
Swing Time 1936,Ag 28,21:2
Quality Street 1937,Ap 9,19:2
Damsel in Distress, A 1937,N 25,37:1
Vivacious Lady 1938,Je 3,17:3
Gunga Din 1939,Ja 28,19:2
Vigil in the Night 1940,Mr 9,19:2
Penny Serenade 1941,My 23,25:2
Woman of the Year 1942,F 6,23:2
Talk of the Town, The 1942,Ag 28,22:3
More the Merrier, The 1943,My 14,17:1
I Remember Mama 1948,Mr 12,29:2
Place in the Sun, A 1951,Ag 29,20:1
Something to Live For 1952,Mr 8,11:2
Shane 1953,Ap 24,30:3
Giant 1956,O 11,51:1
Diary of Anne Frank, The 1959,Mr 19,40:1
Greatest Story Ever Told, The 1965,F 16,40:2
Stevens, George (Producer)
Gunga Din 1939,Ja 28,19:2
Vigil in the Night 1940,Mr 9,19:2
Penny Serenade 1941,My 23,25:2
Talk of the Town, The 1942,Ag 28,22:3
More the Merrier, The 1943,My 14,17:1
I Remember Mama 1948,Mr 12,29:2
Place in the Sun, A 1951,Ag 29,20:1
Something to Live For 1952,Mr 8,11:2
Shane 1953,Ap 24,30:3
Giant 1956,O 11,51:1
Diary of Anne Frank, The 1959,Mr 19,40:1
Greatest Story Ever Told, The 1965,F 16,40:2
Stevens, George (Screenwriter)
Greatest Story Ever Told, The 1965,F 16,40:2
Stevens, George Jr (Producer)
John F Kennedy: Years of Lightning, Day of Drums 1966,Ap 11,41:1
Stevens, Gosta
I Am With You 1949,Mr 1,30:5

Stevens, Gosta (Director)
I Am With You 1949,Mr 1,30:5
Stevens, Gosta (Original Author)
Sara Laer Sig Folkvett 1938,F 16,17:1
Stevens, Gosta (Screenwriter)
Intermezzo, A Love Story 1939,O 6,31:1
En Enda Natt 1942,D 7,22:2
I Am With You 1949,Mr 1,30:5
Stevens, Inger
Man on Fire 1957,Ag 23,10:1
Cry Terror 1958,My 15,25:1
Buccaneer, The 1958,D 24,00:0
World, The Flesh and the Devil, The
1959,My 21,35:1
New Interns, The 1964,Ag 20,34:2
Guide for the Married Man, A 1967,My 27,16:1
Firecreek 1968,F 22,36:2
Madigan 1968,Mr 30,22:2
5 Card Stud 1968,Ag 1,24:1
Hang 'Em High 1968,Ag 8,27:3
Stevens, Ira
Little Princess, The 1939,Mr 11,21:1
Stevens, Jean
Over 21 1945,Ag 17,20:2
Mexicana 1945,N 17,14:6
Stevens, Jeffrey
On Moonlight Bay 1951,Jl 27,15:2
Stevens, Julie
Honeymoon Deferred 1940,F 16,23:4
Tear Gas Squad 1940,My 31,15:3
Carry on Cleo 1965,O 23,17:2
Stevens, K T
Kitty Foyle 1941,Ja 9,27:2
Great Man's Lady, The 1942,Ap 30,14:3
Address Unknown 1944,Ap 17,20:1
Port of New York 1950,F 3,29:2
Harriet Craig 1950,N 3,31:2
Vice Squad 1953,Ag 26,23:2
Missle to the Moon 1958,N 17,37:2
Stevens, Kay
New Interns, The 1964,Ag 20,34:2
Stevens, Kenneth
Winter Carnival 1939,Jl 28,14:2
Stevens, Landers
Trial of Mary Dugan, The 1929,Mr 29,21:1
Gorilla, The 1931,F 23,20:3
Hell Divers 1931,D 23,27:3
Rainbow Trail, The 1932,Ja 30,13:2
Swing Time 1936,Ag 28,21:2
That Girl From Paris 1937,Ja 1,19:1
We Who Are About to Die 1937,Ja 2,15:1
Stevens, Larry
Centennial Summer 1946,Jl 18,20:2
Stevens, Leslie (Director)
Private Property 1960,Ap 25,40:2
Stevens, Leslie (Original Author)
Marriage-Go-Round 1961,Ja 7,12:2
War Lord, The 1965,N 18,55:2
Stevens, Leslie (Producer)
Marriage-Go-Round 1961,Ja 7,12:2
Stevens, Leslie (Screenwriter)
Left Handed Gun, The 1958,My 8,36:2
Private Property 1960,Ap 25,40:2
Marriage-Go-Round 1961,Ja 7,12:2
Stevens, Louis (Miscellaneous)
Amazon Quest 1949,My 14,9:3
Stevens, Louis (Original Author)
State's Attorney 1932,My 6,15:3
Flying Devils 1933,Ag 26,14:3
Criminal Lawyer 1937,Ja 27,17:3
Streets of Laredo 1949,My 12,28:2
Santa Fe 1951,My 4,31:2
Horizons West 1952,N 22,16:5
Stevens, Louis (Screenwriter)
Ne'er Do-Well, The 1923,My 1,24:3
Mary Burns, Fugitive 1935,N 16,19:2
Special Investigator 1936,Ap 25,21:1
Texas Rangers, The 1936,S 24,29:1
Last Train from Madrid, The 1937,Je 19,20:2
Sinners in Paradise 1938,My 20,17:2
Massacre River 1949,Jl 15,17:2
Horizons West 1952,N 22,16:5
Stevens, Mallet (Miscellaneous)
New Enchantment, The 1926,Mr 15,18:3
Stevens, Mark
Within These Walls 1945,Jl 16,8:4
From This Day Forward 1946,Ap 20,16:2
Dark Corner, The 1946,My 9,27:3
I Wonder Who's Kissing Her Now
1947,Jl 24,27:2
Street with no Name, The 1948,Jl 15,26:6
Snake Pit, the 1948,N 5,29:2
Sand 1949,Ag 5,23:2
Oh, You Beautiful Doll 1949,N 12,8:4
Dancing in the Dark 1949,D 3,8:6
Please Believe Me 1950,Je 12,19:4
Between Midnight and Dawn 1950,O 2,19:2
Target Unknown 1951,Mr 5,24:2
Little Egypt 1951,Ag 30,20:3
Mutiny 1952,Mr 20,37:5
Torpedo Valley 1952,D 20,15:3
Jack Slade 1953,O 29,42:6
Cry Vengence 1955,F 19,18:3

Timetable 1956,Mr 17,13:2
September Storm 1960,O 29,26:7
Stevens, Mark (Director)
Cry Vengence 1955,F 19,18:3
Timetable 1956,Mr 17,13:2
Stevens, Mark (Producer)
Timetable 1956,Mr 17,13:2
Stevens, Morton
Lost Boundaries 1949,Jl 1,14:4
Stevens, Naomi
Black Orchid, The 1959,F 13,33:2
Apartment, The 1960,Je 16,37:2
Convicts 4 1962,O 4,44:2
Valley of the Dolls 1967,D 16,51:1
Stevens, Onslow
Radio Patrol 1932,Jl 14,24:2
Once in a Lifetime 1932,O 29,18:4
Nagana 1933,F 16,23:2
Peg o'my Heart 1933,My 20,11:4
Secret of the Blue Room, The 1933,S 13,22:1
Only Yesterday 1933,N 10,25:1
Counsellor-At-Law 1933,D 8,31:2
Bombay Mail 1934,Ja 6,18:2
This Side of Heaven 1934,F 10,21:2
I'll Tell the World 1934,Ap 21,12:2
In Love With Life 1934,My 12,12:3
Affairs of a Gentleman 1934,Je 23,16:7
Notorious Gentleman, A 1935,F 16,9:1
Three Musketeers, The 1935,N 1,25:1
Grand Exit 1935,N 4,24:5
Yellow Dust 1936,F 24,14:1
Under Two Flags 1936,My 1,19:1
F-Man 1936,My 4,16:1
Three on the Trail 1936,My 5,26:5
Murder With Pictures 1936,N 21,21:4
You Can't Buy Luck 1937,My 14,21:2
Flight From Glory 1937,S 11,20:1
there Goes The Groom 1937,D 25,10:6
When Tomorrow Comes 1939,Ag 17,16:2
Those High Grey Walls 1939,O 19,27:2
Man Who Wouldn't Talk, The 1940,Ja 12,13:3
Mystery Sea Raider 1940,Ag 26,11:4
Monster and the Girl, The 1941,Mr 20,25:3
Go West, Young Lady 1941,N 24,11:6
Appointment in Berlin 1943,Jl 17,8:2
House of Dracula 1945,D 22,16:3
O S S 1946,My 27,15:5
Angel on my Shoulder 1946,O 21,27:2
Gallant Blade 1948,O 13,31:3
Walk a Crooked Mile 1948,O 13,31:2
Night Has a Thousand Eyes 1948,O 14,38:3
Bomba, the Jungle Boy 1949,Ap 16,11:4
Red, Hot and Blue 1949,O 20,39:2
Mark of the Gorilla 1950,F 17,27:2
Sealed Cargo 1951,My 24,47:1
Sirocco 1951,Je 14,31:2
Lorna Doone 1951,S 21,19:4
San Francisco Story, The 1952,My 10,16:4
Charge at Feather River, The 1953,Jl 16,17:2
Lion Is in the Streets, A 1953,S 24,39:2
Them 1954,Je 17,36:2
New York Confidential 1955,F 19,18:1
Tribute to a Bad Man 1956,Mr 31,13:3
Buccaneer, The 1958,D 24,00:0
Lonelyhearts 1959,Mr 5,35:3
All the Fine Young Cannibals 1960,S 23,33:1
Couch, The 1962,F 22,20:3
Stevens, Paul
Exodus 1960,D 16,44:1
Mask, The 1961,O 28,12:4
Stevens, Rikki
Mister Buddwing 1966,O 12,36:1
Stevens, Rise
Chocolate Soldier, The 1941,N 1,20:2
Going my Way 1944,My 3,25:2
Carnegie Hall 1947,My 3,10:2
Stevens, Robert (Director)
To the Victor 1938,Ap 13,21:2
Big Caper, The 1957,Mr 29,16:1
Never Love a Stranger 1958,N 22,27:4
I Thank a Fool 1962,S 15,15:1
In the Cool of the Day 1963,My 30,20:1
Stevens, Ronnie
Pair of Briefs, A 1964,F 3,22:2
Stevens, Ruthelma
Life Begins 1932,Ag 26,20:3
Night Club Lady, The 1932,Ag 27,13:4
No More Orchids 1933,Ja 2,29:2
Grand Slam 1933,F 22,25:2
Mind Reader, The 1933,Ap 7,22:4
Working Man, The 1933,Ap 21,20:3
Circus Queen Murder, The 1933,My 9,20:5
Scralet Empress, The 1934,S 15,20:2
People Will Talk 1935,Je 17,20:2
Orchids to You 1935,Ag 10,16:4
Not Wanted 1949,Jl 25,11:4
Apache Drums 1951,My 7,22:2
Stevens, Stella
Say One for Me 1959,Je 20,11:2
Li'l Abner 1959,D 12,19:2
Man Trap 1961,N 30,40:4
Too Late Blues 1962,Mr 1,27:4
Courtship of Eddie's Father, The 1963,Mr 7,8:5
(Incorrect in this edition; use 1963,Mr 28,8:5
elsewhere)

Stevens, Stella— Cont
Nutty Professor, The 1963,Jl 18,15:2
Advance to the Rear 1964,Je 11,27:3
Synanon 1965,My 6,44:1
Secret of my Success, The 1965,N 4,57:2
Silencers, The 1966,Mr 17,35:1
How to Save a Marriage - And Ruin Your Life
1968,Ja 19,30:1
Where Angels Go-Trouble Follows
1968,Ap 11,51:1
Sol Madrid 1968,Je 14,43:1
Stevens, Virginia
Native Land 1942,My 12,16:3
Stevens, Warren
Frogmen, The 1951,Je 30,8:6
Mr Belvedere Rings the Bell 1951,Ag 2,18:1
Phone Call From a Stranger 1952,F 2,11:2
Deadline U S A 1952,Mr 15,8:2
Smoke Jumpers 1952,Mr 22,9:6
Wait Till the Sun Shines, Nellie 1952,Je 28,12:2
Gorilla at Large 1954,Je 12,13:2
Barefoot Contessa, The 1954,S 30,37:1
Black Tuesday 1955,Ja 1,16:2
Women's Prison 1955,F 3,18:5
On the Threshold of Space 1956,Mr 30,10:5
Forbidden Planet 1956,My 4,21:2
Hot Spell 1958,S 18,37:2
Intent to Kill 1959,Ap 1,43:2
40 Pounds of Trouble 1963,Ja 24,5:2
American Dream, An 1966,S 1,28:2
STEVENSON
See Also STEPHENSON
Stevenson, Burton E (Original Author)
Case of the Black Parrot, The 1941,Ja 10,23:3
Stevenson, Charles
Rustle of Silk, The 1923,My 8,22:4
Garrison's Finish 1923,My 28,18:2
Woman With Four Faces, The 1923,Je 18,13:5
Cheat, The 1923,Ag 27,14:3
Spanish Dancer, The 1923,O 8,20:1
Pied Piper Malone 1924,Ja 28,12:1
Hot Water 1924,O 27,27:1
Man Who Found Himself, The 1925,Ag 24,17:3
Doomsday 1928,Ap 2,25:1
Insidious Dr Fu Manchu, The 1929,Jl 22,17:1
Stevenson, Dick
Flower Thief, The 1962,Jl 14,11:5
Stevenson, Douglas
Janice Meredith 1924,Ag 6,13:3
Stevenson, Hayden
Trifling With Honor 1923,My 30,10:4
Acquittal, The 1923,D 12,24:5
Reckless Age, The 1924,Je 10,24:4
I'll Show You the Town 1925,Je 8,19:1
Behind the Front 1926,F 10,16:2
Man, Woman and Sin 1927,D 5,26:2
On Your Toes 1928,Ja 9,20:1
Fourflusher, The 1928,Ja 16,24:1
Red Lips 1928,O 16,29:2 (In Addenda)
College Love 1929,Ag 5,25:2
Stevenson, Houseley
Native Land 1942,My 12,16:3
Somewhere in the Night 1946,Je 13,24:2
Brasher Doubloon, The 1947,My 22,34:5
Dark Passage 1947,S 6,11:2
Thunder in the Valley 1947,N 28,30:1
Casbah 1948,My 3,27:4
Four Faces West 1948,Ag 4,18:3
Apartment for Peggy 1948,O 16,9:2
You Gotta Stay Happy 1948,N 5,29:2
Moonrise 1949,Mr 7,17:2
Lady Gambles, The 1949,My 21,9:2
Sorrowful Jones 1949,Je 6,15:2
Take one False Step 1949,Je 23,33:2
Colorado Territory 1949,Je 25,8:6
Calamity Jane and Sam Bass 1949,Jl 18,14:2
All the King's Men 1949,N 9,37:2
Edge of Doom 1950,Ag 4,13:2
Sierra 1950,S 15,31:2
Sun Sets at Dawn, The 1951,Ja 15,13:1
Hollywood Story 1951,Je 7,40:6
Wild North, The 1952,My 12,21:2
Stevenson, Houseley Jr
Atomic City, The 1952,My 2,21:1
War of the Worlds, The 1953,Ag 14,10:2
Caddy, The 1953,S 18,16:6
Stevenson, Janet (Screenwriter)
Counter-Attack 1945,My 17,15:2
Man From Cairo, The 1953,D 17,52:4
Stevenson, Margot
Smashing the Money Ring 1939,N 17,17:2
Invisible Stripes 1940,Ja 13,11:2
Calling Philo Vance 1940,F 9,15:3
Castle on the Hudson 1940,Mr 4,11:2
Flight Angels 1940,My 27,23:2
Stevenson, Philip (Screenwriter)
Counter-Attack 1945,My 17,15:2
Story of G I Joe 1945,O 6,9:6
Girl in White, The 1952,My 31,12:5
Man From Cairo, The 1953,D 17,52:4
Stevenson, Robert
White Heat 1934,Je 16,20:2
I Was a Male War Bride 1949,Ag 27,7:2

Stevenson, Robert (Director)
Tudor Rose 1936,My 24,IX,3:8 (In Addenda)
Nine Days a Queen 1936,O 3,21:1
Man Who Lived Again, The 1936,D 16,35:4
King Solomon's Mines 1937,Jl 3,18:1
Non-Stop New York 1937,N 29,19:2
Tom Brown's School Days 1940,Je 28,22:2
Back Street 1941,F 12,25:2
Joan of Paris 1942,Ja 26,18:2
Forever and a Day 1943,Mr 13,9:2
Young Man's Fancy, A 1943,D 4,11:2
Jane Eyre 1944,F 4,12:5
Dishonored Lady 1947,My 24,10:5
To the Ends of the Earth 1948,F 13,26:2
Woman on Pier 13, The 1950,Je 16,28:4
Walk Softly Stranger 1950,O 16,30:5
My Forbidden Past 1951,Ap 26,34:2
Las Vegas Story, The 1952,Ja 31,37:6
Johnny Tremain 1957,Jl 11,21:1
Old Yeller 1957,D 26,23:4
Darby O'Gill and the Little People 1959,Jl 1,26:1
Kidnapped 1960,My 19,44:3
Absent-Minded Professor, The 1961,Mr 16,44:2
In Search of the Castaways 1962,D 22,5:2
Son of Flubber 1963,F 9,5:2
Mary Poppins 1964,S 25,34:1
Monkey's Uncle, The 1965,Ag 19,35:4
That Darn Cat 1965,D 3,44:1
Gnome-Mobile, The 1967,Jl 20,30:2
Blackbeard's Ghost 1968,Ap 11,51:3
Stevenson, Robert (Original Author)
Nine Days a Queen 1936,O 3,21:1
Young Man's Fancy, A 1943,D 4,11:2
Stevenson, Robert (Producer)
Ware Case, The 1939,Jl 22,12:2
Forever and a Day 1943,Mr 13,9:2
Stevenson, Robert (Screenwriter)
Jane Eyre 1944,F 4,12:5
Kidnapped 1960,My 19,44:3
Stevenson, Robert Louis (Original Author)
Dr Jekyll and Mr Hyde 1920,Mr 29,18:1
Treasure Island 1920,Ap 12,13:1
White Circle, The 1920,Ag 23,9:2
Ebb Tide 1922,N 20,21:3
Dr Jekyll and Mr Hyde 1932,Ja 2,14:2
Treasure Island 1934,Ag 18,5:5
Trouble for Two 1936,My 30,7:2
Ebb Tide 1937,N 18,27:2
Kidnapped 1938,My 28,9:2
Living Dead, The 1940,D 17,33:2
Dr Jekyll and Mr Hyde 1941,Ag 13,13:2
Body Snatcher, The 1945,My 26,18:3
Adventure Island 1947,O 20,29:2
Black Arrow, The 1948,O 4,14:2
Treasure Island 1950,Ag 16,24:2
Strange Door, The 1951,D 10,34:6
Master of Ballantrae, The 1953,Ag 6,16:2
Kidnapped 1960,My 19,44:3
House of Fright 1961,Ag 24,25:4
Wrong Box 1966,Jl 20,46:1
Stevenson, Robert Louis 2d
Wedding Night, The 1935,Mr 16,19:1
Stevenson, Tom
Nine Loves Are not Enough 1941,O 30,27:2
Counter-Espionage 1942,S 28,13:2
Hidden Hand, The 1942,N 26,40:4
Gaslight 1944,My 5,17:2
Mr Skeffington 1944,My 26,23:2
Beginning or the End, The 1947,F 21,15:1
Swordsman, The 1947,O 17,18:4
Lone Wolf in London, The 1947,N 22,10:3
Mating of Millie, The 1948,Mr 13,12:2
Mr Peabody and the Mermaid 1948,Ag 14,6:5
When my Baby Smiles at Me 1948,N 24,20:2
Cargo to Capetown 1950,Mr 31,36:3
Stevenson, Venetia
Darby's Rangers 1958,F 13,23:2
Big Night, The 1960,F 18,37:4
Studs Lonigan 1960,D 15,59:1
Seven Ways From Sundown 1960,D 22,18:4
Horror Hotel 1963,Je 20,29:1
Stever, Hans
Pawns of Passion 1929,My 27,22:1
STEWARD
See Also STEWART, STUART
Stewardson, Joe
After You, Comrade 1967,Ap 11,54:1
STEWART
See Also STEWARD, STUART
Stewart, Alexander
Mickey One 1965,S 9,36:1
Only When I Larf 1968,O 24,55:3
Stewart, Alexandra
Exodus 1960,D 16,44:1
Passion of Slow Fire, The 1962,O 12,26:1
Season for Love, The 1963,My 9,40:2
Naked Autumn 1963,N 15,25:3
Fire Within, The 1964,F 18,27:1
Sweet and Sour 1964,D 28,34:2
And so to Bed 1965,Jl 31,11:3
Stewart, Anita
Girl Philippa, The 1917,Ja 1,10:2
Virtuous Wives 1918,D 30,7:3

Midnight Romance, A 1919,Mr 10,9:3
Mary Regan 1919,My 5,11:1
Her Kingdom of Dreams 1919,S 22,8:1
Mind-the-Paint Girl, The 1919,N 24,13:1
Fighting Shepherdess, The 1920,Mr 29,18:1
Love Piker, The 1923,Jl 16,14:2
Hollywood 1923,Jl 30,11:4
Great White Way, The 1924,Ag 4,10:1
Baree, Son of Kazan 1925,My 19,24:2
Boomerang, The 1925,Jl 1,16:1
Never the Twain Shall Meet 1925,Jl 29,24:4
Wild Geese 1927,D 5,26:2
Stewart, Anna Marie
Three Russian Girls 1944,F 5,13:2
Stewart, Athole
Speckled Band, The 1931,N 7,16:5
Faithful Heart 1933,Ag 15,20:2
Constant Nymph, The 1934,Ap 7,19:1
Loyalties 1934,O 26,25:1
Amateur Gentleman, The 1936,Ap 27,19:2
Dr Syn 1937,N 15,15:1
Tenth Man, The 1937,N 15,15:2
U-Boat 29 1939,O 6,31:3
Secret Four, The 1940,Ap 22,13:2
It Happened to One Man 1941,F 24,11:6
Stewart, Barry
Luck of Ginger Coffey, The 1964,S 22,44:1
Stewart, Blanche
Night at Earl Carroll's, A 1941,Ja 23,19:1
Stewart, Cevil and His Royal Rogues
Always Leave Them Laughing 1949,N 24,48:2
Stewart, David
Young Savages, The 1961,My 25,31:1
Stewart, David J
Silver Chalice, The 1954,D 27,22:5
Murder, Inc 1960,Je 29,26:6
Stewart, Dick
Glass Web, The 1953,N 12,37:5
Good Morning, Miss Dove 1955,N 24,41:1
Stewart, Donald Ogden
Not so Dumb 1930,F 8,12:5
Stewart, Donald Ogden (Miscellaneous)
Kitty Foyle 1941,Ja 9,27:2
Stewart, Donald Ogden (Original Author)
Finn and Hattie 1931,Ja 31,15:1
Rebound 1931,Ag 29,16:3
Forever and a Day 1943,Mr 13,9:2
Stewart, Donald Ogden (Screenwriter)
Tarnished Lady 1931,Ap 30,29:3
No More Ladies 1935,Je 22,18:5
Holiday 1938,Je 24,15:1
Marie Antoinette 1938,Ag 17,23:2
Love Affair 1939,Mr 17,25:2
Night of Nights, The 1939,D 28,17:1
Philadelphia Story, The 1940,D 27,22:2
That Uncertain Feeling 1941,My 2,25:1
Woman's Face, A 1941,My 16,21:2
Smilin' Through 1941,D 5,29:2
Tales of Manhattan 1942,S 25,25:1
Keeper of the Flame 1943,Mr 19,15:2
Without Love 1945,Mr 23,13:1
Life With Father 1947,Ag 16,6:6
Cass Timberlane 1947,N 7,20:2
Edward my Son 1949,Je 3,21:2
Stewart, Edmund
Ivory Hunter 1952,Ag 19,19:1
Stewart, Elaine
Everything I Have is Yours 1952,O 30,40:5
Bad and the Beautiful, The 1953,Ja 16,19:1
Young Bess 1953,My 22,31:1
Take the High Ground 1953,N 20,19:2
Brigadoon 1954,S 17,18:2
Adventures of Haji Baba, The 1954,O 9,8:7
Tattered Dress, The 1957,Mr 15,22:3
Night Passage 1957,Jl 25,28:1
Rise and Fall of Legs' Diamond, The 1960,F 4,34:1
Most Dangerous Man Alive 1961,Jl 5,29:2
Stewart, Eleanor
Trapped by G-Men 1937,N 4,29:1
Waterloo Bridge 1940,My 17,23:2
Stewart, Fred
Misleading Lady, The 1932,Ap 9,18:1
Splendor in the Grass 1961,O 11,53:1
World of Henry Orient, The 1964,Mr 20,27:2
Stewart, George
Silver Skates 1943,Mr 19,15:3
Stewart, Graham
Cockleshell Heroes, The 1956,Je 4,25:2
Man Upstairs, The 1959,Ag 11,23:2
Stewart, Hugh (Director)
Tunisian Victory 1944,Mr 24,17:2
Stewart, Hugh (Producer)
Tunisian Victory 1944,Mr 24,17:2
Gay Lady, The 1951,Ap 16,21:2
Night Without Stars 1953,Jl 14,19:4
Long Memory, The 1953,Jl 27,15:2
Make Mine Mink 1960,D 20,43:4
Stewart, Iva
Safety in Numbers 1938,S 6,17:2
Wife, Husband and Friend 1939,F 25,19:2
Mr Moto Takes a Vacation 1939,Je 19,12:6

Stewart, Jack
Operation Disaster 1951,Ja 15,13:1
Stranger in Between, The 1952,Ag 20,21:3
Brave Don't Cry, The 1952,N 6,37:2
Little Kidnappers, The 1954,S 2,18:1
Stewart, James
Murder Man, The 1935,Jl 27,16:2
Next Time We Love 1936,Ja 31,16:2
Rose Marie 1936,F 1,9:2
Wife vs Secretary 1936,F 29,11:1
Small Town Girl 1936,Ap 11,19:1
Speed 1936,My 16,11:2
Gorgeous Hussy, The 1936,S 5,7:1
Born to Dance 1936,D 5,16:1
After the Thin Man 1936,D 25,19:2
Seventh Heaven 1937,Mr 26,25:1
Last Gangster, The 1937,D 10,33:2
Navy Blue and Gold 1937,D 24,21:2
Of Human Hearts 1938,F 18,23:1
Vivacious Lady 1938,Je 3,17:3
Shopworn Angel, The 1938,Jl 8,11:2
You Can't Take It With You 1938,S 2,21:2
Made for Each Other 1939,F 17,17:2
Ice Follies of 1939 1939,Mr 17,25:2
It's a Wonderful World 1939,My 19,27:2
Mr Smith Goes to Washington 1939,O 20,27:2
Destry Rides Again 1939,N 30,25:1
Shop Around the Corner, The 1940,Ja 26,13:2
Mortal Storm, The 1940,Je 21,25:2
No Time for Comedy 1940,S 7,9:2
Philadelphia Story, The 1940,D 27,22:2
Come Live With Me 1941,F 28,17:3
Pot o'Gold 1941,Ap 4,25:2
Ziegfeld Girl 1941,Ap 25,17:2
It's a Wonderful Life 1946,D 23,19:2
Magic Town 1947,O 8,29:2
Miracle Can Happen, A 1948,F 4,28:4
Call Northside 777 1948,F 19,29:2
Rope 1948,Ag 27,12:4
You Gotta Stay Happy 1948,N 5,29:2
Stratton Story, The 1949,My 13,29:1
Malaya 1950,F 23,33:1
Winchester 73 1950,Je 8,38:2
Broken Arrow 1950,Jl 21,15:2
Jackpot, The 1950,N 23,55:2
Harvey 1950,D 22,19:1
No Highway in the Sky 1951,S 22,8:6
Greatest Show on Earth, The 1952,Ja 11,17:2
Bend of the River 1952,Ap 10,37:1
Carbine Williams 1952,My 8,37:2
Naked Spur, The 1953,Mr 26,37:3
Thunder Bay 1953,My 21,39:2
Glenn Miller Story, the 1954,F 11,33:2
Rear Window 1954,Ag 5,18:2
Far Country, The 1955,F 14,24:2
Strategic Air Command 1955,Ap 21,33:1
Man From Laramie, The 1955,S 1,20:2
Man Who Knew too Much, The 1956,My 17,37:1
Spirit of St Louis, The 1957,F 22,25:1
Night Passage 1957,Jl 25,28:1
Vertigo 1958,My 29,24:2
Bell, Book and Candle 1958,D 27,2:7
Anatomy of a Murder 1959,Jl 3,10:1
F B I Story, The 1959,S 25,23:1
Mountain Road, The 1960,Je 30,22:3
Two Rode Together 1961,Jl 27,23:3
Man Who Shot Liberty Valance, The 1962,My 24,29:2
Mr Hobbs Takes a Vacation 1962,Je 16,11:2
How the West Was Won 1963,Ap 1,54:1
Take Her, She's Mine 1963,N 14,41:1
Cheyenne Autumn 1964,D 24,8:1
Dear Brigitte 1965,Ja 28,20:1
Shenandoah 1965,Jl 29,18:3
Flight of the Phoenix, The 1966,F 1,26:1
Rare Breed, The 1966,Ap 14,42:3
Firecreek 1968,F 22,36:2
Bandolero 1968,Jl 18,26:2
Stewart, James (Original Author)
Miracle Can Happen, A 1948,F 4,28:4
Stewart, James C
Island of Allah 1956,Je 27,35:1
Stewart, Jerry
Servants' Entrance 1934,S 27,25:2
Stewart, Johnny
Boots Malone 1952,Mr 13,26:2
Stewart, Kay
What a Life 1939,O 12,33:1
Those Were the Days 1940,Jl 15,18:4
Life With Henry 1941,F 6,25:2
Private War of Major Benson, The 1955,Ag 3,27:2
Square Jungle, The 1955,D 31,17:2
Stewart, Larry
Yank in Korea, A 1951,Ap 2,29:2
Stewart, Lucile Lee
Bad Company 1925,Mr 16,16:1
Stewart, Maitland
Amazon Trader, The 1956,N 17,17:6
Stewart, Marianne
Right Cross 1950,N 16,39:2
Timetable 1956,Mr 17,13:2
Big Fisherman, The 1959,Ag 6,18:1

Stewart, Marianne— Cont

Facts of Life, The 1961,F 11,27:1
Stewart, Martha
Doll Face 1946,Mr 28,35:3
I Wonder Who's Kissing Her Now
1947,Jl 24,27:2
Daisy Kenyon 1947,D 25,32:1
Are You With It? 1948,Ap 15,31:2
In a Lonely Place 1950,My 18,37:2
Aaron Slick From Punkin Crick 1952,Ap 19,18:6
Stewart, Mary (Original Author)
Moonspinners, The 1964,N 4,47:1
Stewart, Maxine
Everything's on Ice 1939,O 6,31:1
Stewart, Nick
Carmen Jones 1954,O 29,27:2
Flame of the Islands 1956,F 25,12:4
Stewart, Nicodemus
Dakota 1945,D 17,17:2
Stewart, Paul
Citizen Kane 1941,My 2,25:1
Johnny Eager 1942,F 20,21:2
Mr Lucky 1943,Jl 23,21:2
Government Girl 1944,Ja 7,13:2
Champion 1949,Ap 11,29:2
Illegal Entry 1949,Je 11,11:2
Window, The 1949,Ag 8,10:5
Easy Living 1949,O 13,33:3
Twelve O'Clock High 1950,Ja 28,10:2
Edge of Doom 1950,Ag 4,13:2
Walk Softly Stranger 1950,O 16,30:5
Appointment With Danger 1951,My 10,38:2
Deadline U S A 1952,Mr 15,8:2
Lone Shark 1952,My 12,21:2
We're not Married 1952,Jl 12,16:2
Bad and the Beautiful, The 1953,Ja 16,19:1
Juggler, The 1953,My 6,39:2
Joe Louis Story, The 1953,N 4,29:4
Prisoner of War 1954,My 10,20:2
Deep in my Heart 1954,D 10,35:2
Chicago Syndicate 1955,Je 21,37:1
Cobweb, The 1955,Ag 6,13:3
Hell on Frisco Bay 1956,Ja 7,21:1
Wild Party, The 1956,D 22,13:1
Top Secret Affair 1957,Ja 31,21:1
King Creole 1958,Jl 4,15:2
Child Is Waiting, A 1963,F 14,5:6
Greatest Story Ever Told, The 1965,F 16,40:2
In Cold Blood 1967,D 15,60:1
Jigsaw 1968,Je 6,54:2
Stewart, Paul (Narrator)
World at War, The 1942,S 4,19:1
Stewart, Peggy
Wells Fargo 1937,D 30,15:2
Little Tough Guy 1938,Ag 18,23:3
That Certain Age 1938,N 5,15:2
Little Tough Guys in Society 1938,N 21,14:4
Back Street 1941,F 12,25:2
Utah 1945,Mr 12,22:7
Stewart, Peter (Director)
Adventure Island 1947,O 20,29:2
Miraculous Journey 1948,S 20,21:2
State Department-File 649 1949,F 21,20:2
Stewart, Ramona (Original Author)
Desert Fury 1947,S 25,35:4
Stewart, Ray
Sparrows 1926,S 20,21:3
Stewart, Richard
Mister Big 1943,Je 14,13:4
Stewart, Roy
Come Through 1917,Je 18,7:2
Westerners, The 1919,Ag 4,8:3
Riders of the Dawn 1920,My 3,18:1
Prisoners of Love 1921,Ja 17,9:1
Woman on the Jury, The 1924,My 19,14:2
Sundown 1924,D 1,17:3
Time, the Comedian 1925,D 14,18:2
You Never Know Women 1926,Jl 27,15:5
One Woman to Another 1927,S 19,30:3
Viking, The 1928,N 29,32:4
In old Arizona 1929,Ja 21,18:4
Men Without Women 1930,F 1,15:1
Born Reckless 1930,Je 7,10:4
Rough Romance 1930,Je 16,25:3
Fighting Caravans 1931,Ja 26,21:1
Mystery Ranch 1932,Je 30,26:2
Zoo in Budapest 1933,Ap 28,15:2
Stewart, Sally
Lady Vanishes, The 1938,D 26,29:1
Stewart, Sophie
Things to Come 1936,Ap 18,19:2
Murder in the Old Red Barn 1936,Ag 19,18:3
As You Like It 1936,N 6,29:3
Man Who Could Work Miracles, The
1937,F 22,13:1
Under the Red Robe 1937,Je 1,27:2
Return of the Scarlet Pimpernel, The
1938,Ap 11,12:2
Nurse Edith Cavell 1939,S 22,27:4
My Son, My Son! 1940,My 10,26:6
Inheritance, The 1951,F 12,19:2
Battle Hell 1957,Ag 22,23:1

Stewart, Ted
Courtship of Myles Standish, The 1923,D 31,9:3
Stewart, Virginia Lee
Friendly Enemies 1925,My 5,24:2
Sti, Rene (Director)
Porteuse de Pain, La 1936,Jl 1,29:5
Sti, Rene (Screenwriter)
Last Will of Dr Mabuse, The 1943,Mr 20,11:1
Stiberg, Eva
Unmarried Mothers 1956,F 23,32:5
Stick, Joseph T (Producer)
Waterhole #3 1967,O 11,41:4
Stickney, Dorothy
Wayward 1932,F 15,13:1
Murder at the Vanities 1934,My 21,20:2
Little Minister, The 1934,D 28,25:1
Moon's our Home, The 1936,My 13,29:2
And So They Were Married 1936,My 14,29:3
I Met my Love Again 1938,Ja 15,19:1
What a Life 1939,O 12,33:1
Uninvited, The 1944,F 21,19:3
Miss Tatlock's Millions 1948,N 25,47:2
Catered Affair, The 1956,Je 15,32:4
Remarkable Mr Pennypacker, The 1959,F 21,25:2
Stiebner, Hans
Weisse Sklaven 1937,Jl 31,6:2
Mit versiegelter Order; Under Sealed Orders
1938,Jl 30,10:2
Stief, Egon
Rubacuori 1932,Mr 5,11:2
Stiffi, Maria Vincenza
Don Bosco 1936,My 27,27:3
Stig
Surf, The 1949,D 17,15:2
Stiglic, France (Director)
Ninth Circle, The 1961,S 15,30:3
Stiglic, France (Screenwriter)
Ninth Circle, The 1961,S 15,30:3
Stignani, Ebe
Aida 1954,N 12,17:1
Stiles, Victor
Santa Claus Conquers the Martians
1964,D 17,50:2
Stiller, Mauritz (Director)
Hotel Imperial 1927,Ja 3,16:2
Woman on Trial, The 1927,S 26,27:1
Three Who Were Doomed, The 1928,Ja 10,28:4
Street of Sin, The 1928,My 28,23:2
Street of Sin, The 1928,Je 3,VIII,5:1
Legend of Gosta Berling, The 1928,O 29,29:1
Stillman, Frances
Guns of the Trees 1964,F 29,12:2
Stillman, John Jr (Producer)
Lady Says No, The 1952,Ja 7,14:3
Stillman, Robert (Producer)
Try and Get Me 1951,My 7,22:2
Americano, The 1955,Ja 20,35:1
Stinedorf, Louise A (Original Author)
White Witch Doctor 1953,Jl 2,19:3
STIRLING
See Also STERLING
Stirling, Edward
Eagle with Two Heads 1948,D 30,24:2
Stirling, Helen
Darling 1965,Ag 4,20:1
Stirling, Linda
Powers Girl, The 1943,Mr 26,14:2 (In Addenda)
Pretender, The 1947,Ag 12,26:2
Stirling, Pamela
Candlelight in Algeria 1944,Jl 31,10:2
Madness of the Heart 1950,O 12,43:2
To Paris With Love 1955,Mr 29,33:4
Divided Heart, The 1955,Ag 4,16:1
Elephant Gun 1959,Je 20,11:2
Stitt, Sonny
Jazz on a Summer's Day 1960,Mr 29,46:2
Stival, Giulio
Overcoat, The 1953,O 13,34:1
Stivan, Giulio
Frenesia; Frenzy 1940,Je 6,33:4
Stivanello, Anthony (Miscellaneous)
Cavalleria Rusticana 1953,D 28,17:2
Traviata, La 1953,D 28,17:2
Stix, John (Director)
Great St Louis Bank Robbery, The 1960,F 4,34:1
Stn, Augustin
Virgin of Guadalupe, The 1943,My 15,13:3
Stnkovski, Ernst
Good Soldier Schweik, The 1963,Ag 21,38:1
Stobart, Thomas (Cinematographer)
Conquest of Everest, The 1953,D 10,64:4
Stobrava, Ilse
Reiter von Deutsch-Ostafrika, Die 1935,Je 8,12:3
Lied vom Glueck, Das; Song of Happiness, The
1935,N 30,12:7
Stobrawa, Renee
Kreuzer Emden 1932,S 8,17:2
Hell on Earth 1934,Ja 29,10:2
Stock, Nigel
It Always Rains on Sunday 1949,F 14,15:5
Young Scarface 1951,N 8,35:2
Malta Story 1954,Jl 17,7:2
Night my Number Came up, The 1955,D 20,39:5

Stock, Nigel— Cont

Victim 1962,F 6,27:2
Damn the Defiant 1962,S 20,29:2
Password Is Courage, The 1962,D 22,5:2
Never Let Go 1963,Je 15,10:2
Nothing but the Best 1964,Jl 14,28:1
Night of the Generals, The 1967,F 3,38:1
Lost Continent, The 1968,Je 20,50:2
Lion in Winter, The 1968,O 31,54:1
Stock, Ralph (Original Author)
Gypsy Wildcat 1944,O 5,18:6
Stock, Valeska
Weavers, The 1929,O 7,22:1
Die Lustigen Musikanten 1933,My 27,11:6
Stock, Werner
Zweimal zwei im Himmelbett; Twice Two in a
Four-Post Bed 1939,F 5,19:3
Stockbridge, Fanny
Old Nest, The 1921,Je 29,10:3
Stockbridge, Henry
Dynamite 1929,D 28,11:1
No, No, Nanette 1930,Ja 4,21:1
Stockdale, Carl
Red Hot Romance 1922,Ja 23,11:4
Darling of New York, The 1924,Ja 18,20:1
Extra Girl, The 1924,Ja 21,20:1
Spirit of the U S A, The 1924,My 21,22:3
Cafe in Cairo, A 1925,Mr 18,19:2
Son of his Father, A 1925,S 29,31:3
Regular Fellow, A 1925,O 5,25:2
See You in Jail 1927,Ap 4,30:5
Shepherd of the Hills, The 1928,F 20,14:1
Carnation Kid, The 1929,F 25,16:1
Love Parade, The 1929,N 20,32:6
Hide Out 1930,Ap 12,23:1
Vampire Bat, The 1933,Ja 23,9:1
Dr Socrates 1935,O 3,29:2
Revolt of the Zombies 1936,Je 5,17:2
Rawhide 1938,Ap 25,19:2
Stockel, Vaclav
Firemen's Ball, The 1968,S 30,60:1
Stockfeld, Betty
Money for Nothing 1932,F 21,VIII,5:2 (In
Addenda)
Stockfield, Betty
Captivation 1931,S 28,17:4
Woman in Chains 1932,N 21,21:1
Farewell to Love 1933,N 25,10:2
Man Who Changed his Name, The
1934,O 17,26:2
Battle, The 1934,N 23,23:2
Beloved Vagabond, The 1937,F 8,12:5
Club De Femmes 1937,O 20,27:2
Slipper Episode, The 1938,My 19,25:2
Nine Bachelors 1942,F 9,19:2
Flying Fortress 1942,D 19,22:2
Edward and Caroline 1952,Ap 30,33:3
Lover's Net 1957,Jl 23,23:1
Stockley, Cynthia (Original Author)
Wild Honey 1922,F 28,17:4
Pink Gods 1922,S 25,10:2
Ponjola 1923,N 19,19:3
Female, The 1924,S 2,19:2
Claw, The 1927,My 11,28:3
Stockman, Boyd
Stage to Tucson 1951,My 5,14:2
Man From Laramie, The 1955,S 1,20:2
Stockton, Francis R (Original Author)
Tiger Lady, The 1928,Je 3,VIII,5:1
Stockton, John Arthur
Commandos Strike at Dawn 1954,Ja 14,25:1
Stockton, Sadie
Quiet One, The 1949,F 14,15:2
Stockwell, Dean
Anchors Aweigh 1945,Jl 20,15:2
Green Years, The 1946,Ap 5,21:2
Home Sweet Homicide 1946,S 12,5:7
Mighty McGurk, The 1947,Ap 4,19:4
Song of the Thin Man 1947,Ag 29,14:2
Romance of Rosy Ridge, The 1947,S 12,18:3
Arnelo Affair, The 1947,S 13,8:5
Gentleman's Agreement 1947,N 12,36:2
Deep Waters 1948,Jl 23,12:4
Boy With Green Hair, The 1949,Ja 13,26:2
Down to the Sea in Ships 1949,F 23,31:2
Kim 1950,D 8,40:4
Stars in my Crown 1950,D 22,19:1
Cattle Drive 1951,Ag 9,17:5
Gun for a Coward 1957,Ja 31,21:1
Careless Years, The 1957,N 28,57:3
Compulsion 1959,Ap 2,26:2
Sons and Lovers 1960,Ag 3,35:1
Long Day's Journey Into Night 1962,O 10,57:2
Rapture 1965,Ag 24,25:3
Psych-Out 1968,Mr 28,52:1
Stockwell, Guy
War Lord, The 1965,N 18,55:2
Blindfold 1966,My 26,55:2
...And Now Miguel 1966,S 8,43:1
Beau Geste 1966,S 8,43:1
Plainsman, The 1966,N 19,26:1
Tobruk 1967,F 9,33:2
Banning 1967,D 14,62:2

Stockwell, Harry
Broadway Melody of 1936 1935,S 19,28:1
Stoddard, Belle
Hangman's House 1928,My 14,25:1
Stoddard, Jean
You Only Live Once 1937,F 1,15:2
Stoddart, Dayton (Original Author)
Ruthless 1948,S 4,8:7
Stoeckel, Joe
Meisterdetektiv, Der 1934,F 13,23:2
Die Blonde Christl 1934,F 23,23:3
S A Mann Brand 1934,My 28,16:2
Mit dir Durch Dick und Duenn 1934,N 24,19:2
Bei der Blonden Kathrein 1934,D 3,15:2
Zwischen Himmel und Erde; Between Heaven and
Earth 1935,Ja 21,19:3
Johannisnact 1935,F 25,13:4
Ganzer Kerl, Ein 1936,Ap 25,21:2
Grobe Adele, Die 1937,My 15,23:5
Kampf mit dem Drachen, Der; Fight With the
Dragon, The 1939,N 6,20:3
1A in Oberbayern; 1A in Upper Bavaria
1939,N 18,22:6
Stoeckel, Joe (Director)
Dell Etappenhase 1938,Ja 1,11:3
Wenn Du eine Schwiegermutter hast; When You
Have a Mother-in-Law 1938,Ja 29,12:1
Musketier Meier III 1938,D 31,7:2
Starker als die Liebe; Stronger Than Love
1939,My 6,21:3
Arme Millionar, Der; Poor Millionaire, The
1939,D 30,9:2
Recht auf Liebe, Das; Right to Love, The
1940,Je 15,12:3
Stoeckel, Leonard
Salon Dora Green 1937,Jl 26,15:3
Stoeckel, Otto
Klein Dorrit 1935,O 19,21:2
Glueckskinder 1937,Je 5,21:1
Stoecker
Drama on the Threshing Floor 1937,O 30,22:3
Stoehr, Emil
Prinzessin Sissy 1939,Ja 14,13:2
Stoessel, Luise
Pantoffelhelden 1935,O 21,22:5
Stoger, Alfred (Director)
Lysistrata 1948,Je 19,19:2
Stoipe, Sven (Screenwriter)
Crime and Punishment 1948,Mr 1,17:2
Stoker, Bram (Original Author)
Dracula 1931,F 13,21:3
Horror of Dracula 1958,My 29,24:4
Stoker, H G
Channel Crossing 1934,My 24,28:3
Born for Glory 1935,O 21,22:4
Moonlight Sonata 1938,My 10,17:2
Man With 100 Faces 1938,N 1,27:2
Where's Charley? 1952,Je 27,18:3
Stokes, Al
Green Pastures, The 1936,Jl 17,20:1
Stokes, Dorothy
Society Scandal, A 1924,Mr 10,18:2
Butterflies in the Rain 1926,D 25,10:5
Stokes, Leslie (Original Author)
Oscar Wilde 1960,Je 21,28:2
Stokes, Sewell (Original Author)
I Believe in You 1953,My 5,34:3
Oscar Wilde 1960,Je 21,28:2
Stokowski, Leopold
100 Men and a Girl 1937,S 18,15:2
Carnegie Hall 1947,My 3,10:2
Stokowski, Leopold (Composer)
Fantasia 1940,N 14,28:2
Stokowski, Leopold and a symphony orchestra
Big Broadcast of 1937, The 1936,O 22,31:1
Stolarski, Ludwik (Screenwriter)
Border Street 1950,Ap 26,35:2
Stoliarov, S
Frontier 1935,D 28,10:5
Stolkonia, Eliza Radzin
Hamlet 1964,S 15,32:1
STOLL
See Also STAHL
Stoll, Georgie (Composer)
Toast of New Orleans, The 1950,S 30,13:3
Stollery, David
Darling, How Could You! 1951,N 9,22:4
Jack and the Beanstalk 1952,Ap 8,35:3
Her Twelve Men 1954,Ag 12,23:2
Storm Fear 1955,D 17,19:2
Stollgas, Koulis
Moussitsa 1960,O 31,25:2
Stolliar, Yakov (Miscellaneous)
Nightingale 1936,N 4,41:2
Stoloff, Ben (Director)
Circus Ace, The 1927,Jl 6,23:2
Gay Retreat, The 1927,O 10,24:1
Plastered in Paris 1928,S 24,25:1
Speakeasy 1929,Mr 11,22:2
Girl from Havana, The 1929,S 2,16:1
Happy Days 1930,F 14,20:1

New Movietone Follies of 1930, The
1930,Je 21,20:5
Three Rogues 1931,Ap 4,23:1
Goldie 1931,Je 29,20:3
Night Mayor, The 1932,N 25,19:2
Devil Is Driving, The 1932,D 16,25:5
Obey the Law 1933,Mr 13,18:3
Palooka 1934,F 28,23:2
Transatlantic Merry-Go-Round 1934,N 1,25:2
To Beat the Band 1935,N 23,23:2
Two in the Dark 1936,F 1,9:2
Don't Turn 'em Loose 1936,S 25,20:2
Sea Devils 1937,Mr 16,26:4
Super-Sleuth 1937,Jl 17,18:1
Fight for Your Lady 1937,N 20,21:2
Radio City Revels 1938,Mr 21,18:3
Affairs of Annabel, The 1938,O 13,29:2
Marines Fly High, The 1940,Mr 5,19:2
Hidden Hand, The 1942,N 26,40:4
Secret Enemies 1943,Ja 1,27:3
Mysterious Doctor, The 1943,My 20,26:4
Bermuda Mystery 1944,My 13,17:1
Take It or Leave It 1944,Jl 13,14:2
Stoloff, Ben (Producer)
Two O'Clock Courage 1945,Ap 14,13:3
Zombies on Broadway 1945,Ap 27,23:2
Radio Stars on Parade 1945,S 22,14:2
Big Fix, The 1947,My 3,10:3
Red Stallion 1947,N 27,50:3
Stoloff, Victor (Original Author)
Of Love and Desire 1963,S 12,32:1
Stoloff, Victor (Producer)
Of Love and Desire 1963,S 12,32:1
Stoloff, Victor (Screenwriter)
Volcano 1953,Jl 21,19:2
Stolpe, Sven (Original Author)
Interlude 1949,Ja 3,19:2
Stolper, A (Director)
Lad From our Town 1943,O 7,26:2
Days and Nights 1946,Ap 29,24:4
Far for Moscow 1951,Jl 2,16:6
Stolper, A (Producer)
Far for Moscow 1951,Jl 2,16:6
Stolyarov, Sergei
Heroes of the Sea 1941,Ap 28,11:2
Lucky Bride, The 1948,Ja 26,15:2
Sadko 1953,Je 1,18:6
Stolz, Hilda von
Krach und Glueckum Kuennemann; Row and Joy
About Kuennemann 1938,S 17,20:3
Stolz, Hilde von
Prater, Wiener 1938,D 3,11:3
Wiener Prater 1938,D 3,11:3
Ueber Alles die Treue 1939,F 13,13:3
Glaserne Kugel, Die; Glass Ball, The
1939,Je 17,12:3
Stolz, Robert (Composer)
Zwei Hertzen in Drei-Viertel Takt
1930,O 13,31:1
Hampelmann, Der 1931,S 8,38:7
Sein Liebeslied 1931,N 19,27:5
Liebling von Wien, Der 1933,Je 10,16:5
My Heart Is Calling 1935,Ap 15,16:3
Night of the Great Love, The 1937,O 1,19:5
Husaren Heraus 1938,Mr 19,11:3
Liebe im Dreiviertel Takt; Love in Waltz Time
1938,S 24,13:1
Herbst-Monoever; Fall Manoeuvres
1939,Mr 18,9:3
Spring Parade 1940,O 4,29:2
Stolz, Robert (Miscellaneous)
Das Lied ist Aus 1932,Ja 29,13:2
Liebeskommando 1932,Ap 27,13:6
Stomma, Z
Secret Brigade 1951,Mr 19,23:2
Stone, Allan
David and Bathsheba 1951,Ag 15,23:2
Stone, Andrew L (Director)
Girl Said No, The 1937,O 18,14:1
Stolen Heaven 1938,My 12,27:2
Say It in French 1938,D 1,29:1
Great Victor Herbert, The 1939,D 7,35:1
There's Magic in Music 1941,Je 5,27:2
Stormy Weather 1943,Jl 22,15:1
Hi Diddle Diddle 1943,S 24,26:2
Sensations of 1945 1944,Jl 7,13:2
Bedside Manner 1945,Je 23,9:6
Bachelor's Daughters, The 1946,O 7,23:2
Highway 301 1950,D 9,13:2
Confidence Girl 1952,Je 21,12:2
Steel Trap, The 1952,N 13,35:2
Blueprint for Murder, A 1953,Jl 25,8:2
Night Holds Terror, The 1955,S 15,39:2
Julie 1956,N 22,51:1
Cry Terror 1958,My 15,25:1
Decks Ran Red, The 1958,O 11,18:2
Last Voyage, The 1960,F 20,14:2
Ring of Fire 1961,Ag 17,18:2
Password Is Courage, The 1962,D 22,5:2

Stone, Andrew L (Director) — Cont
Secret of my Success, The 1965,N 4,57:2
Stone, Andrew L (Original Author)
Girl Said No, The 1937,O 18,14:1
Stolen Heaven 1938,My 12,27:2
Great Victor Herbert, The 1939,D 7,35:1
There's Magic in Music 1941,Je 5,27:2
Night Holds Terror, The 1955,S 15,39:2
Cry Terror 1958,My 15,25:1
Stone, Andrew L (Producer)
Girl Said No, The 1937,O 18,14:1
Say It in French 1938,D 1,29:1
Great Victor Herbert, The 1939,D 7,35:1
There's Magic in Music 1941,Je 5,27:2
Hi Diddle Diddle 1943,S 24,26:2
Sensations of 1945 1944,Jl 7,13:2
Bedside Manner 1945,Je 23,9:6
Bachelor's Daughters, The 1946,O 7,23:2
Confidence Girl 1952,Je 21,12:2
Night Holds Terror, The 1955,S 15,39:2
Cry Terror 1958,My 15,25:1
Last Voyage, The 1960,F 20,14:2
Ring of Fire 1961,Ag 17,18:2
Secret of my Success, The 1965,N 4,57:2
Stone, Andrew L (Screenwriter)
Sensations of 1945 1944,Jl 7,13:2
Bachelor's Daughters, The 1946,O 7,23:2
Highway 301 1950,D 9,13:2
Confidence Girl 1952,Je 21,12:2
Steel Trap, The 1952,N 13,35:2
Blueprint for Murder, A 1953,Jl 25,8:2
Julie 1956,N 22,51:1
Decks Ran Red, The 1958,O 11,18:2
Last Voyage, The 1960,F 20,14:2
Ring of Fire 1961,Ag 17,18:2
Password Is Courage, The 1962,D 22,5:2
Secret of my Success, The 1965,N 4,57:2
Stone, Arthur
It Must Be Love 1926,O 4,20:2
Silent Lover, The 1926,N 15,19:1
Affair of the Follies, An 1927,F 28,22:3
Patent Leather Kid, The 1927,Ag 16,31:2
Hard-Boiled Haggerty 1927,Ag 23,29:4
Valley of the Giants, The 1927,D 5,26:2
Burning Daylight 1928,Ap 23,20:2
Chicken a la King 1928,Je 11,27:1
Me, Gangster 1928,O 22,29:1
Captain Lash 1929,F 4,20:1
Thru Different Eyes 1929,Ap 15,22:6
William Fox Movietone Follies of 1929
1929,My 27,22:1
Vagabond King, The 1930,F 20,22:4
Vagabond King, The 1930,Mr 2,IX,5:1
Arizona Kid, The 1930,My 17,21:2
On the Level 1930,Jl 5,17:4
Girl of the Golden West, The 1930,O 27,17:1
Lash, The 1931,Ja 1,31:3
Conquering Horde, The 1931,Mr 30,25:2
Big Shot, The 1932,Ja 2,14:2
Broken Wing, The 1932,Mr 26,17:2
So Big 1932,Ap 30,19:3
Roar of the Dragon 1932,Jl 25,11:2
That's my Boy 1932,N 21,21:1
Bordertown 1935,Ja 24,22:5
Charlie Chan in Egypt 1935,Je 24,12:2
Fury 1936,Je 6,21:1
Go Chase Yourself 1938,Je 15,27:1
Ruthless 1948,S 4,8:7
Stone, Ben
Satan in High Heels 1962,Mr 24,15:6
Stone, Bobby
Gangster's Boy 1938,N 7,23:6
Streets of New York 1939,My 1,21:1
South of Pago-Pago 1940,Ag 2,12:2
Down Argentine Way 1940,O 18,25:1
Flying Wild 1941,Ap 12,19:3
Bowery Blitzkrieg 1941,O 1,24:5
Mr Wise Guy 1942,Mr 5,27:2
Stone, Carol
Freckles 1935,O 26,12:2
Stone, David C (Producer)
Hallelujah the Hills 1963,D 17,49:1
Brig, The 1964,S 21,37:4
Stone, David C (Screenwriter)
Hide and Seek 1964,Mr 12,40:3
Stone, Dorothy
Smiling Faces 1932,Ag 31,12:3
Revolt of the Zombies 1936,Je 5,17:2
Stone, Ezra
Those Were the Days 1940,Jl 15,18:4
Stone, Fred
Goat, The 1918,S 30,7:1
Under the Top 1919,Ja 6,11:3
Johnny Get Your Gun 1919,Mr 17,13:2
Smiling Faces 1932,Ag 31,12:3
Alice Adams 1935,Ag 16,11:3
Trail of the Lonesome Pine, The 1936,F 20,23:5
Farmer in the Dell, The 1936,Mr 7,11:4
Grand Jury 1936,Ag 1,16:3
My American Wife 1936,Ag 21,12:3
Hideaway 1937,S 25,10:2
Life Begins In College 1937,O 9,16:1
Westerner, The 1940,O 25,25:2

Stone, Gene
Rookies 1927,Ap 25,20:4
Fair Co-ed, The 1927,O 24,24:3
Stone, George E
Till I Come Back to You 1918,Ag 26,9:1
Seventh Heaven 1927,My 26,22:1
San Francisco Nights 1928,Ja 31,29:1
Tenderloin 1928,Mr 15,28:3
Clothes Make the Woman 1928,Je 5,21:1
State Street Sadie 1928,S 3,14:2
Weary River 1929,Ja 25,20:6
Naughty Baby 1929,F 5,26:3
Redeeming Sin, The 1929,F 16,14:6
Melody Lane 1929,Jl 16,23:5
Skin Deep 1929,S 30,23:1
Under a Texas Moon 1930,Ap 4,22:1
Little Casear 1931,Ja 10,19:2
Cimarron 1931,Ja 27,20:5
Front Page, The 1931,Mr 20,29:1
Spider, The 1931,S 5,7:4
Five Star Final 1931,S 11,24:2
Sob Sister 1931,O 3,20:2
Woman From Monte Carlo, The 1931,D 31,17:6
Taxi 1932,Ja 8,27:3
File No 113 1932,F 20,11:2
World and the Flesh, The 1932,My 7,11:5
Last Mile, The 1932,Ag 26,20:3
Phantom of Crestwood, The 1932,O 17,18:3
Vampire Bat, The 1933,Ja 23,9:1
Sailor Be Good 1933,F 27,11:2
42d Street 1933,Mr 10,19:3
Song of the Eagle 1933,Ap 29,14:3
Emergency Call 1933,Je 24,16:2
Big Brain, The 1933,Ag 5,9:5
Wrecker, The 1933,Ag 7,18:3
Sing Sinner Sing 1933,Ag 15,20:2
Penthouse 1933,S 9,9:2
King for a Night 1933,D 11,23:4
Frontier Marshal 1934,Ja 31,20:3
Viva Villa! 1934,Ap 11,25:2
Return of the Terror 1934,Jl 11,20:2
Dragon Murder Case, The 1934,Ag 23,13:3
Hold 'Em Yale 1935,Ap 27,20:6
Million Dollar Baby 1935,My 6,22:3
Public Hero No 1 1935,Je 8,12:2
Make a Million 1935,N 9,19:3
Frisco Kid 1935,N 25,22:1
Fish 1936,Ja 25,18:5
Freshman Love 1936,Ja 25,18:5
Man Hunt 1936,Ja 30,14:2
Bullets or Ballots 1936,My 27,27:1
Rhythm on the Range 1936,Jl 30,22:1
Jailbreak 1936,Ag 6,22:1
Anthony Adverse 1936,Ag 27,16:1
Polo Joe 1936,N 5,35:1
Here Comes Carter 1936,N 14,23:3
Back in Circulation 1937,O 4,17:1
Alcatraz Island 1937,O 14,22:2
Torchy Blane, The Adventurous Blonde
1937,D 18,18:1
Over the Wall 1938,Mr 28,19:2
Mr Moto's Gamble 1938,Ap 8,17:2
You and Me 1938,Je 2,19:1
Submarine Patrol 1938,N 19,9:2
You Can't Get Away With Murder
1939,Mr 25,19:2
Housekeeper's Daughter, The 1939,D 2,21:4
Night of Nights, The 1939,D 28,17:1
I Take This Woman 1940,F 16,23:3
Island Of Doomed Men 1940,Je 10,21:2
Slightly Tempted 1940,N 1,33:1
Cherokee Strip 1940,N 4,23:2
North West Mounted Police 1940,N 7,33:2
Face Behind the Mask, The 1941,F 7,23:2
Road Show 1941,F 19,25:2
Broadway Limited 1941,Je 16,11:6
Confessions of Boston Blackie 1941,D 8,31:2
Little Tokyo, USA 1942,Ag 7,13:2
Devil With Hitler, The 1942,O 19,15:2
Roger Touhy, Gangster 1944,Je 5,14:7
One Mysterious Night 1944,O 21,15:3
Suspense 1946,Jl 5,15:3
Abie's Irish Rose 1946,D 23,19:4
Girl in Every Port, A 1952,F 14,23:1
Bloodhounds of Broadway 1952,N 15,15:2
Pickup on South Street 1953,Je 18,38:2
Miami Story, The 1954,My 15,13:2
Guys and Dolls 1955,N 5,26:1
Man With the Golden Arm, The 1955,D 16,38:2
Slightly Scarlet 1956,Mr 17,13:2
Story of Mankind, The 1957,N 9,31:2
Some Like It Hot 1959,Mr 30,23:1
Pocketful of Miracles 1961,D 19,39:1
Stone, Grace Zaring Stone (Original Author)
Bitter Tea of General Yen, The 1933,Ja 12,20:6
Stone, Gregory (Composer)
Girls' School 1938,N 3,27:1
Stone, Harold J
Harder They Fall, The 1956,My 10,26:3
Somebody up There Likes Me 1956,Jl 6,16:1
Wrong Man, The 1956,D 24,8:1
Slander 1957,Ja 17,34:4
Man Afraid 1957,Ap 5,24:2

Garment Jungle, The 1957,My 16,28:2
House of Numbers 1957,S 13,15:2
These Thousand Hills 1959,My 7,36:1
Spartacus 1960,O 7,28:1
Chapman Report, The 1962,O 18,49:2
X - The Man With X-Ray Eyes 1963,O 24,37:1
Greatest Story Ever Told, The 1965,F 16,40:2
Girl Happy 1965,My 27,28:1
Big Mouth, The 1967,Jl 13,30:2
St Valentine's Day Massacre, The 1967,Jl 27,29:2
Stone, Henry
Saratoga 1937,Jl 23,16:3
Stone, Hilda (Original Author)
Passport Husband 1938,Ag 5,11:2
Girl in 313 1940,Je 14,25:3
Stone, Irving (Original Author)
President's Lady, The 1953,My 22,31:1
Lust for Life 1956,S 18,39:1
Agony and the Ecstacy, The 1965,O 9,5:6
Stone, Irving (Screenwriter)
Magnificent Doll 1946,D 9,34:2
Stone, Jack
Lilac Time 1928,Ag 4,7:2
Stone, James
Barefoot in the Park 1967,My 26,51:1
Stone, Jeffrey
Girl in the Kremlin, The 1957,My 22,29:2
Big Beat, The 1958,Je 26,23:4
Thing That Couldn't Die, The 1958,Je 28,13:7
Stone, Jennifer
Ladybug, Ladybug 1963,D 24,9:1
Stone, John
Weaker Sex, The 1949,Jl 11,13:2
Stone, John (Original Author)
Girl from Havana, The 1929,S 2,16:1
Salute 1929,O 5,22:5
Stone, John (Producer)
Mystery Woman 1935,Ja 9,22:2
Charlie Chan in Paris 1935,Ja 22,23:2
Great Hotel Murder, The 1935,F 28,17:4
Charlie Chan at the Circus 1936,Mr 19,22:4
45 Fathers 1937,D 11,22:2
Charlie Chan at Monte Carlo 1937,D 18,18:1
Rascals 1938,My 27,12:2
One Wild Night 1938,Je 3,17:2
Keep Smiling 1938,Ag 10,15:2
Charlie Chan in Honolulu 1938,D 31,7:3
Stone, Joseph (Original Author)
World in my Corner 1956,F 18,12:5
Operation Petticoat 1959,D 6,38:1
Stone, Leonard
Big Mouth, The 1967,Jl 13,30:2
Stone, Lewis
Rivers End, The 1920,F 23,11:2
Nomads of the North 1920,S 27,18:1
Concert, The 1921,F 21,16:1
Northern Trail, The 1921,Jl 4,10:2
Golden Snare, The 1921,Jl 11,9:3
Prisoner of Zenda, The 1922,Ag 1,14:3
Trifling Women 1922,O 4,23:4
Dangerous Age, The 1923,Ja 29,11:1
You Can't Fool Your Wife 1923,Ap 24,25:3
Scaramouche 1923,O 12,7:2 (Incorrect in this
edition; use 1927,O 1,7:2 elsewhere)
Stranger, The 1924,F 5,20:1
Why Men Leave Home 1924,My 12,14:4
Oytherea 1924,My 26,21:1
Husbands and Lovers 1924,D 9,23:3
Inez From Hollywood 1924,D 16,28:1
Cheaper to Marry 1925,F 2,14:1
Lost World, The 1925,F 9,15:3
Confessions of a Queen 1925,Mr 24,20:6
Talker, The 1925,My 12,26:2
Lady Who Lied, The 1925,Jl 7,24:2
What Fools Men 1925,S 29,31:3
Fine Clothes 1925,O 20,28:1
Girl From Montmarte, The 1926,F 25,26:2
Old Loves and New 1926,Ap 20,24:7
Midnight Lovers 1926,O 26,23:1
Blonde Saint, The 1926,N 23,27:1
Affair of the Follies, An 1927,F 28,22:3
Notorious Lady, The 1927,Ap 11,18:3
Prince of Head-Waiters 1927,Jl 11,23:5
Lonesome Ladies 1927,Ag 2,19:2
Private Life of Helen of Troy, The
1927,D 10,14:7
Foreign Legion, The 1928,Je 25,27:1
Patriot, The 1928,Ag 18,7:2 (In Addenda)
Woman of Affairs, A 1929,Ja 21,18:4
Trial of Mary Dugan, The 1929,Mr 29,21:1
Wild Orchids 1929,Ap 1,22:1
Madame X 1929,Ap 25,32:3
Wonder of Women 1929,Jl 22,17:1
Their own Desire 1930,Ja 25,13:2
Big House, The 1930,Je 25,31:2
Romance 1930,Ag 23,7:3
Office Wife, The 1930,S 27,21:3
Passion Flower 1930,D 22,16:2
Inspiration 1931,F 9,25:3
Father's Son 1931,F 21,15:2
My Past 1931,Mr 12,22:7
Secret Six, The 1931,My 2,23:4
Always Good-Bye 1931,My 23,13:4

Stone, Lewis— Cont
Bargain, The 1931,S 5,7:4
Sin of Madelon Claudet, The 1931,O 31,22:2
Strictly Dishonorable 1931,N 11,27:1
Phantom of Paris, The 1931,N 14,15:3
Mata Hari 1932,Ja 1,31:1
Wet Parade, The 1932,Ap 22,23:2
Letty Lynton 1932,Ap 30,19:3
Night Court 1932,My 27,27:5
New Morals for Old 1932,Je 24,15:3
Red Headed Woman 1932,Jl 1,19:3
Unashamed 1932,Jl 15,13:4
Divorce in the Family 1932,O 31,18:4
Mask of Fu Manchu, The 1932,D 3,21:4
Son-Daughter, The 1933,Ja 2,29:2
Men Must Fight 1933,Mr 11,18:3
White Sister, The 1933,Mr 18,9:3
Looking Forward 1933,My 1,10:2
Bureau of Missing Persons 1933,S 9,9:2
Queen Christina 1933,D 27,23:3
You Can't Buy Everything 1934,F 3,9:2
Mystery of Mr X, The 1934,F 26,21:3
Girl From Missouri, The 1934,Ag 4,14:6
Treasure Island 1934,Ag 18,5:5
David Copperfield 1935,Ja 19,8:1
West Point of the Air 1935,Ap 6,10:1
Vanessa: Her Love Story 1935,Ap 13,11:3
Public Hero No 1 1935,Je 8,12:2
China Seas 1935,Ag 10,16:4
Shipmates Forever 1935,O 17,29:3
Three Godfathers, The 1936,Mr 9,20:2
Unguarded Hour, The 1936,Ap 4,11:1
Small Town Girl 1936,Ap 11,19:1
Suzy 1936,Jl 25,16:1
Sworn Enemy 1936,S 12,20:1
Don't Turn 'em Loose 1936,S 25,20:2
Outcast 1937,Mr 3,27:2
Thirteenth Chair, The 1937,Je 18,25:3
You're Only Young Once 1938,Ja 3,16:2
Bad Man of Brimstone, The 1938,F 4,17:2
Judge Hardy's Children 1938,Ap 8,17:2
Stolen Heaven 1938,My 12,27:2
Yellow Jack 1938,My 20,17:2
Love Finds Andy Hardy 1938,Jl 22,10:2
Chaser, The 1938,Ag 2,15:3
Out West With the Hardys 1938,D 9,31:2
Ice Follies of 1939 1939,Mr 17,25:2
Hardys Ride High, The 1939,Ap 14,28:2
Andy Hardy Gets Spring Fever 1939,Jl 19,23:2
Joe and Ethel Turp Call on the President
1940,Ja 4,19:2
Judge Hardy and Son 1940,Ja 18,27:3 (In
Addenda)
Sporting Blood 1940,Jl 22,20:2
Andy Hardy Meets Debutante 1940,Ag 2,12:2
Andy Hardy's Private Secretary 1941,Mr 7,17:2
Life Begins for Andy Hardy 1941,Ag 22,19:4
Bugle Sounds, The 1942,Ap 3,25:2
Courtship of Andy Hardy, The 1942,Ap 10,21:2
Andy Hardy's Double Life 1943,Ja 12,23:3
Andy Hardy's Blonde Trouble 1944,My 5,17:3
Hoodlum Saint, The 1946,Je 27,29:1
Three Wise Fools 1946,S 27,19:2
Love Laughs at Andy Hardy 1947,Ja 8,28:2
State of the Union 1948,Ap 23,28:1
Sun comes up, The 1949,My 13,29:2
Any Number Can Play 1949,Jl 1,14:4
Key to the City 1950,F 2,31:2
Stars in my Crown 1950,D 22,19:1
Grounds for Marriage 1951,Ja 12,24:6
Night Into Morning 1951,Je 11,20:7
Angels in the Outfield 1951,O 18,32:1
Unknown Man, The 1951,N 17,9:5
It's a big Country 1952,Ja 9,25:2
Just This Once 1952,Mr 18,22:3
Scaramouche 1952,My 9,20:2
Prisoner of Zenda, The 1952,N 5,36:2
All the Brothers Were Valiant 1953,D 29,19:2
Stone, Marianne
Clouded Yellow, The 1951,N 13,33:2
Tiger Bay 1959,D 15,50:1
Lolita 1962,Je 14,23:2
Stone, Marshall (Director)
Come Spy with Me 1967,F 22,21:1
Stone, Milburn
China Clipper 1936,Ag 12,14:3
Man in Blue, The 1937,Ag 30,25:2
Atlantic Flight 1937,N 1,24:5
Federal Bullets 1937,D 27,11:1
Thirteenth Man, The 1938,Ja 1,11:2
Port of Missing Girls, The 1938,Ap 4,12:5
Crime School 1938,My 11,17:2
Sinners in Paradise 1938,My 20,17:2
Wives Under Suspicion 1938,Jl 1,22:3
Tail Spin 1939,F 11,13:2
King of the Turf 1939,My 8,21:2
Blind Alley 1939,My 23,27:2
Young Mr Lincoln 1939,Je 3,11:2
Tropic Fury 1939,S 8,28:4
Nick Carter, Master Detective 1939,D 14,35:2
Enemy Agent 1940,Ap 22,13:3
Great Plane Robbery, The 1940,N 15,25:2
Give Us Wings 1940,N 21,43:3
Frisco Lil 1942,F 12,27:2

Stone, Milburn— Cont

Captive Wild Woman 1943,Je 7,9:4
Sherlock Holmes Faces Death 1943,O 8,15:3
Mad Ghoul, The 1943,D 11,11:2
Gung Ho! 1944,Ja 26,23:2
Impostor, The 1944,Mr 27,17:2
Jungle Woman 1944,Jl 15,19:6
She Gets her Man 1945,F 9,20:5
Frozen Ghost, The 1945,Jl 28,7:3
Strange Confession 1945,N 8,17:3
Daltons Ride Again, The 1945,D 8,21:2
Spider Woman Strikes Back, The 1946,Mr 23,8:3
Inside Job 1946,Je 15,24:3
Michigan Kid 1947,F 22,16:3
Green Promise, The 1949,Je 24,29:2
Calamity Jane and Sam Bass 1949,Jl 18,14:2
Branded 1951,Ja 11,28:5
Atomic City, The 1952,My 2,21:1
Pickup on South Street 1953,Je 18,38:2
Second Chance 1953,Jl 23,20:2
Arrowhead 1953,S 16,38:6
Sun Shines Bright, The 1954,Mr 17,25:2
Siege at Red River, The 1954,Ap 3,19:2
Black Tuesday 1955,Ja 1,16:2
Long Gray Line, The 1955,F 11,19:2

Stone, Mildred

13 Hours by Air 1936,Ap 30,17:2
Shocking Miss Pilgrim, The 1947,F 12,34:2

Stone, N B Jr (Screenwriter)

Man With the Gun 1955,D 23,14:2
Ride the High Country 1962,Je 21,26:2

Stone, Paula

Treachery Rides the Range 1936,My 30,7:3
Case of the Velvet Claws, The 1936,Ag 29,16:3
Girl Said No, The 1937,O 18,14:1
Atlantic Flight 1937,N 1,24:5
Idiot's Delight 1939,F 3,13:1

Stone, Paula (Original Author)

Top Banana 1954,F 20,8:6

Stone, Peter (Original Author)

Charade 1963,D 6,40:1

Stone, Peter (Screenwriter)

Charade 1963,D 6,40:1
Father Goose 1964,D 11,55:1
Mirage 1965,My 27,28:1
Secret War of Harry Frigg, The 1968,Mr 5,34:5
Jigsaw 1968,Je 6,54:2

Stone, Phil (Director)

Wild Geese 1927,D 5,26:2
Marriage Forbidden 1938,Jl 16,7:2

Stone, Robinson

Stalag 17 1953,Jl 2,19:2

Stone, Virginia (Producer)

Cry Terror 1958,My 15,25:1
Last Voyage, The 1960,F 20,14:2
Ring of Fire 1961,Ag 17,18:2
Secret of my Success, The 1965,N 4,57:2

Stone, William (Original Author)

Devil Commands, The 1941,F 14,15:3
Pagan Love Song 1950,D 26,19:1

Stone-Barton Puppeteers

Road to Rio 1948,F 19,29:3

Stoneham, Charles Thurley (Original Author)

King of the Jungle 1933,F 25,20:3

Stonehouse, Ruth

Broken Barriers 1924,Ag 4,16:3
Fifth Avenue Models 1925,My 4,16:2

Stoney, George C (Screenwriter)

Birthright 1952,F 15,17:2

Stoney, Jack

Brasher Doubloon, The 1947,My 22,34:5
Woman on Pier 13, The 1950,Je 16,28:4

Stoney, Kevin

How to Murder a Rich Uncle 1957,O 26,19:2

Stong, Phil (Original Author)

State Fair 1933,Ja 27,13:2
Stranger's Return, The 1933,Jl 28,18:2
Farmer in the Dell, The 1936,Mr 7,11:4
Career 1939,Jl 28,14:2
State Fair 1945,Ag 31,14:3
State Fair 1962,Ap 12,41:4

Stooges, Three

Stop! Look! and Laugh! 1961,F 9,36:1
Snow White and the Three Stooges 1961,Jl 1,9:1
Three Stooges in Orbit, The 1962,Jl 12,19:4

Stoor, Mieczyslaw

Five From Barska Street 1955,Mr 14,29:4

Stopher, Harry C

Ramparts We Watch, The 1940,S 20,27:1

Stoppa, Paolo

Rossini 1948,Ja 31,14:2
Eternal Melodies 1948,F 14,17:3
Loves of Don Juan, The 1948,S 2,18:4
Iron Crown 1949,Je 11,11:2
Miracle in Milan 1951,D 18,42:2
Beauty and the Devil 1952,Ag 26,15:2
Of Love and Bandits 1953,Ja 17,12:4
Rome, 11 O'Clock 1953,Ap 30,39:2
Seven Deadly Sins, The (Avarice and Anger);
   Avarice and Anger (The Seven Deadly Sins)
   1953,My 12,31:3
Ring Around the Clock 1953,My 19,36:2
Times Gone By (The Idyll); Idyll, The (Times
   Gone By) 1953,D 30,16:2

Beauties of the Night 1954,Mr 23,23:5
Daughters of Destiny (Lysistrata): Lysistrata
   (Daughters of Destiny) 1954,Jl 6,19:1
House of Ricordi 1956,Mr 13,32:1
Return of Don Camillo, The 1956,Mr 27,41:1
My Seven Little Sins 1956,My 2,27:1
Gold of Naples (Pizza on Credit); Pizza on Credit
   (Gold of Naples) 1957,F 12,30:1
Miller's Beautiful Wife, The 1957,Je 12,40:2
Wife for a Night 1958,Je 12,35:2
Pepote 1958,D 2,46:1
Holiday Island; (Vacanzie a Izchia)
   1959,S 22,46:1
Where the Hot Wind Blows 1960,N 12,15:1
Carthage in Flames 1961,Ja 26,32:3
Rocco and his Brothers 1961,Je 28,40:2
Neapolitan Carousel 1961,O 12,41:3
From a Roman Balcony 1961,O 16,33:5
Leopard, The 1963,Ag 13,25:1
Becket 1964,Mr 12,40:2
Behold a Pale Horse 1964,Ag 14,16:1
Visit, The 1964,O 22,44:1
Male Companion 1966,F 15,33:2
After the Fox 1966,D 24,11:1

Storch, Arthur

Strange One, The 1957,Ap 13,12:3
Girl of the Night 1960,N 12,15:1

Storch, Larry

Last Blitzkrieg, The 1959,Ja 31,13:5
40 Pounds of Trouble 1963,Ja 24,5:2
Captain Newman, MD 1964,F 21,36:1
Wild and Wonderful 1964,Je 11,27:4
Bus Riley's Back in Town 1965,Ap 8,45:2
Very Special Favor, A 1965,Ag 26,40:3
Great Race, The 1965,S 16,00:0
That Funny Feeling 1965,O 21,57:2

Storck, Henri (Producer)

Masters of the Congo Jungle 1960,My 5,41:2

Storck, Henry (Director)

Rubens 1949,Ap 30,9:2

Storck, Henry (Producer)

Rubens 1949,Ap 30,9:2

Storer-Clouston, J (Original Author)

Bizarre, Bizarre 1939,Mr 21,27:2

Storey, David (Original Author)

This Sporting Life 1963,Jl 17,19:2

Storey, David (Screenwriter)

This Sporting Life 1963,Jl 17,19:2

Storey, Edith

Enemy to the King, An 1916,N 27,9:1

Storey, June

Girls' Dormitory 1936,Ag 29,16:2
In Old Chicago 1938,Ja 7,15:2
Island in the Sky 1938,My 14,18:1
Mickey, the Kid 1939,Jl 6,27:1
First Love 1939,N 9,27:3
Lone Wolf Takes a Chance, The 1941,Ap 7,13:2
Dance Hall 1941,Jl 19,16:2
Strange Woman, The 1947,F 24,16:4
Killer McCoy 1948,F 12,31:2
Miraculous Journey 1948,S 20,21:2
Cry of the City 1948,S 30,32:4
Snake Pit, the 1948,N 5,29:2

Storey, Ruth

Blue Gardenia, The 1953,Ap 28,31:1
Bells Are Ringing 1960,Je 24,31:2
Subterraneans, The 1960,Jl 7,26:1
In Cold Blood 1967,D 15,60:1

Storey, Thomas (Original Author)

Two in Revolt 1936,Ap 25,21:1

Stork, Hansi

Pfarrer von Kirchfeld, Der; Pastor of Kirchfeld,
   The 1939,Ap 22,15:3

Storm, Barry (Original Author)

Lust for Gold 1949,Jl 4,9:2

Storm, Carl

Sunshine Follows Rain 1949,S 29,39:2

Storm, Gale

Tom Brown's School Days 1940,Je 28,22:2
One Crowded Night 1940,Ag 27,17:2
Where Are Your Children? 1944,Ja 17,14:5
It Happened on Fifth Avenue 1947,Je 11,33:2
Stampede 1949,S 16,36:2
Abandoned Woman 1949,O 27,35:3
Kid From Texas, The 1950,Je 2,26:2
Underworld Story, The 1950,Jl 27,29:4
Curtain Call at Cactus Creek 1950,S 22,35:4
Between Midnight and Dawn 1950,O 2,19:2
Al Jennings of Oklahoma 1951,My 18,34:6
Texas Rangers, The 1951,Jl 14,7:2
Woman of the North Country 1952,Ag 30,6:2

Storm, Gilda

Jennie Gerhardt 1933,Je 9,20:2

Storm, Jane (Screenwriter)

Two for Tonight 1935,Ag 31,16:2
Millions in the Air 1935,D 12,33:4

Storm, Jerome (Director)

Girl Dodger, The 1919,F 24,11:3
Greased Lightning 1919,Ap 28,13:2
Busher, The 1919,My 26,19:4
Hay Foot, Straw Foot 1919,Je 23,10:3
Bill Henry 1919,Ag 18,9:2
Egg Crate Wallop, The 1919,S 29,16:1

Storm, Jerome (Director)— Cont

Red Hot Dollars 1919,D 29,7:2
Alarm Clock Andy 1920,Mr 15,13:2
Homer Comes Home 1920,Je 28,13:2
Village Sleuth 1920,S 13,12:1
Peaceful Valley 1920,O 11,19:3
Old Fashioned Boy, An 1920,N 1,13:2
Children of Jazz 1923,Jl 9,8:4
Goldfish, The 1924,My 20,15:2
Ladies at Ease 1927,O 5,31:1

Storm, Jerry

Give Me a Sailor 1938,Ag 11,31:1

Storm, John (Narrator)

Animal World, The 1956,My 31,21:6

Storm, Lesley (Miscellaneous)

Adam and Evalyn 1950,My 12,33:4

Storm, Lesley (Original Author)

Tonight and Every Night 1945,Mr 9,16:2
Tony Draws a Horse 1951,My 15,38:6

Storm, Lesley (Screenwriter)

Meet Me at Dawn 1948,My 18,26:2
Golden Salamander 1951,Mr 24,8:3
Personal Affair 1954,O 23,13:2
Heart of the Matter, The 1954,N 19,20:2
Spanish Gardner, The 1957,S 9,21:2

Storm, Rafael

Kiss and Make-Up 1934,Je 29,17:1
It Happened in New York 1935,Ap 6,10:1
Broadway Gondolier 1935,Jl 18,15:2
Lady Tubbs 1935,Jl 22,20:2
Here Comes Cookie 1935,O 12,12:2
Ultima Cita, La 1936,Ja 22,15:6
House of a Thousand Candles, The
   1936,Ap 2,29:2
Golden Arrow, The 1936,My 4,16:1
Wise Girl 1938,Ja 10,13:3
Straight, Place and Show 1938,O 1,10:2
When Ladies Meet 1941,S 5,19:2
Powers Girl, The 1943,Mr 26,14:2 (In Addenda)
Action in Arabia 1944,F 19,18:7
Hairy Ape, The 1944,Jl 3,8:3

Stormard, Debi

Eight on the Lam 1967,Ap 27,52:1

Storme, Sandra

Sophie Lang Goes West 1937,S 30,19:2
Clouds Over Europe 1939,Je 16,27:2

Stormoen, Harald

En Glad Gutt 1933,N 24,25:7

Storr, Otto

Head, The 1963,Je 20,29:1

Storrow, James J Jr (Producer)

Kid Rodelo 1966,F 23,46:1

Story, Jack Trevor (Original Author)

Trouble With Harry, The 1955,O 18,46:2

Story, Jack Trevor (Screenwriter)

Invasion Quartet 1961,D 11,41:2

Storz, Bill (Cinematographer)

This Is Your Army 1954,D 15,41:1

Stossel, Ludwig

Bockbierfest 1931,Mr 31,25:3
Skandal Um Eva 1931,Ap 21,35:2
Elisabeth von Oesterreich 1931,D 11,35:1
Strich Durch die Rechnung 1934,Mr 3,8:6
In Wien Hab' Ich Einmal ein Maedel Geliebt
   1934,My 26,12:3
O Schwarzwald, O Heimat; Oh Black Forest, Oh
   Home 1939,Ap 24,13:2
Four Sons 1940,Je 8,18:4
Man I Married, The 1940,Ag 3,9:2
Man Hunt 1941,Je 14,20:2
Underground 1941,Je 23,13:2
Great Guns 1941,O 3,27:2
Marry the Boss's Daughter 1941,D 4,33:4
All Through the Night 1942,Ja 24,13:2
Woman of the Year 1942,F 6,23:2
Pride of the Yankees, The 1942,Jl 16,23:1
Iceland 1942,O 15,27:1
Casablanca 1942,N 27,27:1
Who Done It 1942,D 3,35:2
Pittsburgh 1943,F 25,27:2
They Came to Blow up America
   1943,My 15,13:2
Action in the North Atlantic 1943,My 22,10:2
Hers to Hold 1943,Jl 22,15:1
Hitler's Madman 1943,Ag 28,15:1
Strange Death of Adolf Hitler, The 1943,O 9,11:5
Climax, The 1944,D 14,28:5
Lake Placid Serenade 1944,D 25,15:6
Dillinger 1945,Ap 26,26:2
Miss Susie Slagle's 1946,F 7,29:2
Cloak and Dagger 1946,O 5,13:2
Temptation 1946,D 25,33:6
Beginning or the End, The 1947,F 21,15:1
Song of Love 1947,O 10,31:2
Escape me Never 1947,N 8,11:2
This Time for Keeps 1947,D 5,33:4
Song Is Born, A 1948,O 20,37:2
Merry Widow, The 1952,S 25,38:1
No Time for Flowers 1952,D 26,20:3
Call Me Madam 1953,Mr 26,37:1
Sun Shines Bright, The 1954,Mr 17,25:2
Me and the Colonel 1958,Ag 27,33:1
Blue Angel, The 1959,S 5,11:4

Stothart, Herbert (Composer)
End of St Petersberg, The 1928,My 31,21:2 (In Addenda)
Barbarian, The 1933,My 13,16:2
David Copperfield 1935,Ja 19,8:1
Mutiny on the Bounty 1935,N 9,19:2
Night at the Opera, A 1935,D 7,22:1
Ah, Wilderness! 1935,D 25,30:2
Tale of Two Cities, A 1935,D 26,21:2
Rose Marie 1936,F 1,9:2
Good Earth, The 1937,F 3,27:1
Marie Antoinette 1938,Ag 17,23:2
Broadway Serenade 1939,Ap 7,25:2
Wizard of Oz, The 1939,Ag 18,16:2
Northwest Passage 1940,Mr 8,25:1
Stothart, Herbert (Miscellaneous)
San Francisco 1936,Je 27,21:1
Romeo and Juliet 1936,Ag 21,12:2
Maytime 1937,Mr 19,27:1
Firefly, The 1937,S 2,17:2
Girl of the Golden West, The 1938,Mr 25,15:2
Stouman, Tina
Windflowers 1968,F 23,43:1
Stoumen, Louis Clyde (Director)
Naked Eye, The 1957,Ap 22,31:6
Black Fox 1963,Ap 30,26:1
Image of Love 1965,Je 22,25:2
Stoumen, Louis Clyde (Original Author)
Naked Eye, The 1957,Ap 22,31:6
Stoumen, Louis Clyde (Producer)
Naked Eye, The 1957,Ap 22,31:6
Black Fox 1963,Ap 30,26:1
Image of Love 1965,Je 22,25:2
Stoumen, Louis Clyde (Screenwriter)
Black Fox 1963,Ap 30,26:1
Image of Love 1965,Je 22,25:2
Stout, George W (Producer)
Tundra 1936,D 3,31:2
Stout, Rex (Original Author)
Meet Nero Wolfe 1936,Jl 16,20:1
League of Frightened Men, The 1937,Jl 2,25:1
Stout, Royal G
Royal Family of Broadway, The 1930,D 23,25:1
Stout, Vernon (Screenwriter)
Three on the Trail 1936,My 5,26:5
Stout (Original Author)
Tundra 1936,D 3,31:2
Stovin, Jerry
Lolita 1962,Je 14,23:2
Stowe, Harriet Beecher (Original Author)
My Wife and I 1925,My 20,26:2
Uncle Tom's Cabin 1927,N 5,16:2
Stowe, Leslie
Tongues of Flame 1924,D 16,28:1
Mother's Boy 1929,My 8,34:6
Stowe, Lester
Copperhead, The 1920,F 9,10:3
Stowell, C W
Ramparts We Watch, The 1940,S 20,27:1
Stowell, William
Paid in Advance 1919,D 1,9:3
Stowers, Frederick (Original Author)
Nineteen and Phyllis 1920,D 27,11:3
Straat, Hans
Loving Couples 1966,S 20,38:1
Strabel, Thelma (Original Author)
Reap the Wild Wind 1942,Mr 27,27:2
Forest Rangers, The 1942,O 22,25:2
Undercurrent 1946,N 29,36:2
Strachey, Lytton (Original Author)
White Angel, The 1936,Je 25,24:1
Stradner, Rose
Ein Gewisser Herr Gran 1934,F 24,18:5
Hochzeit am Wolfgangsee 1934,N 17,12:2
One Hundred Days of Napoleon 1936,S 14,25:1
Postillon of Lonjumeau, The 1937,N 20,21:3
Last Gangster, The 1937,D 10,33:2
Blind Alley 1939,My 23,27:2
Keys of the Kingdom, The 1944,D 30,15:2
Straight, Beatrice
Phone Call From a Stranger 1952,F 2,11:2
Patterns 1956,Mr 28,26:1
Silken Affair, The 1957,O 31,41:1
Nun's Story, The 1959,Je 19,30:1
Young Lovers, The 1965,F 11,45:1
Straight, Clarence
Mrs Mike 1950,F 9,36:5
Strain, Thayer
Which Shall It Be? 1924,Ap 7,15:3
Strait, Howard E
Cease Fire! 1953,N 25,17:1
Strakosch, Avery (Original Author)
She Married an Artist 1938,F 25,15:2
Stram, Carl
Folket Pa Hogbogarden; People of the Hogbo Farm, The 1940,F 24,9:3
Strand, Paul (Cinematographer)
Wave, The 1937,Ap 21,18:1
Native Land 1942,My 12,16:3
Strand, Paul (Director)
Native Land 1942,My 12,16:3

Strand, Paul (Original Author)
Wave, The 1937,Ap 21,18:1
Strand, Paul (Producer)
Wave, The 1937,Ap 21,18:1
Strandberg, Eva-Britt
Masculine Feminine 1966,S 19,57:1
Strandmark, Erik
Unmarried Mothers 1956,F 23,32:5
Seventh Seal 1958,O 14,44:1
Strang, Harry
Hell Bound 1931,My 9,15:4
Air Hawks 1935,Je 4,26:5
Submarine Patrol 1938,N 19,9:2
Return of the Cisco Kid, The 1939,Ap 29,13:2
Mr Moto Takes a Vacation 1939,Je 19,12:6
Calling Philo Vance 1940,F 9,15:3
Kit Carson 1940,N 15,25:3
Phantom Submarine, The 1941,F 12,25:3
Buck Privates 1941,F 14,15:2
My Gal Sal 1942,My 1,23:1
Strange, Glenn
House of Frankenstein 1944,D 16,19:3
House of Dracula 1945,D 22,16:3
Abbott and Costello Meet Frankenstein 1948,Jl 29,17:2
Double Crossbones 1951,Ap 27,19:2
Comin' Round the Mountain 1951,Jl 27,15:2
Texas Carnival 1951,O 13,9:1
Strange, Mark
Isabel 1968,Jl 24,47:1
Strange, Philip
Ace of Cads, The 1926,O 18,18:1 (In Addenda)
Popular Sin, The 1926,D 20,28:3
Broadway Nights 1927,Je 28,29:4
Man Power 1927,Jl 26,17:1
Sporting Goods 1928,F 13,16:2
Loves of an Actress 1928,Jl 30,21:2
Rescue, The 1929,Ja 14,20:1
Behind That Curtain 1929,Jl 1,31:2
Wall Street 1929,N 25,22:1
Bright Lights 1931,F 10,24:4
Blame the Woman 1932,O 25,24:5
Loyalties 1934,O 26,25:1
Strange, Robert
Smiling Lieutenant, The 1931,My 23,13:4
Cheat, The 1931,D 12,23:3
Misleading Lady, The 1932,Ap 9,18:1
These Thirty Years 1934,My 24,28:3
Gambling 1934,D 4,22:3
Special Agent 1935,S 19,28:1
I Found Stella Parish 1935,N 4,24:4
Frisco Kid 1935,N 25,22:1
Murder of Dr Harrigan, The 1936,Ja 21,27:5
Walking Dead, The 1936,Mr 2,13:2
Trapped by Television 1936,Je 15,24:3
Beloved Enemy 1936,D 26,15:2
Stolen Holiday 1937,F 1,15:3
John Meade's Woman 1937,F 18,19:1
Sky Giant 1938,Jl 20,22:2
I Stand Accused 1939,Ja 5,17:1
They Made Me a Criminal 1939,Ja 21,19:2
Saint Strikes Back, The 1939,Mr 9,18:2
Story of Vernon and Irene Castle, The 1939,Mr 31,19:2
Spellbinder, The 1939,Ag 24,17:3
Angels Wash Their Faces 1939,S 4,16:2
Castle on the Hudson 1940,Mr 4,11:2
Strange, William
Mudlark, The 1950,D 25,25:1
Stranges, Judy
Dragoon Wells Massacre 1957,My 6,25:2
Stranks, Susan
Blue Lagoon, The 1949,O 3,13:2
Madeleine 1950,S 1,17:2
Stransky, Otto (Composer)
Opern-Ball, Der; Opera Ball 1931,N 6,28:3
Die oder Keine; Her or Nobody 1932,N 13,IX,4:2
Stransky, Otto (Miscellaneous)
Sein Scheidungsgrund 1932,F 20,11:2
Straram, Patrick
Take it All; A Tout Prendre 1966,Ap 26,55:1
Strasberg, Lee (Screenwriter)
Somewhere in the Night 1946,Je 13,24:2
Strasberg, Susan
Cobweb, The 1955,Ag 6,13:3
Picnic 1956,F 17,13:3
Stage Struck 1958,Ap 23,40:1
Scream of Fear 1961,Ag 23,29:1
Hemingway's Adventures of a Young Man 1962,Jl 26,17:1
Disorder 1964,My 26,44:2
Kapo 1964,Je 2,33:3
Trip, The 1967,Ag 24,43:1
Psych-Out 1968,Mr 28,52:1
Name of the Game Is Kill, The 1968,Je 6,54:1
Strassberg, Morris
Broken Hearts 1926,Mr 3,26:1
Power of Life 1938,Ap 29,17:2
Tevya 1939,D 22,15:3
Strasser, Alfred (Composer)
Dolly Macht Karriere 1931,Jl 18,16:6

Strassny, Fritz
Hands of Orlac, The 1928,Je 5,21:1
Stratas, Teresa
Canadians, The 1961,Je 1,31:1
Strate, Walter (Director)
Dance Of Life, The 1951,F 28,33:2
Violated 1953,D 12,23:8
Strate, Walter (Producer)
Dance Of Life, The 1951,F 28,33:2
Stratigos, Stefanos
Mademoiselle-Age 39 1956,Mr 26,34:2
Girl From Corfu, The 1957,My 20,28:2
Girl in Black, A 1957,S 17,39:2
Trouble for Father 1958,Ja 6,26:4
Horse and Carriage 1958,Je 30,23:3
Santa Chikita 1959,My 11,30:1
Astero 1960,Ap 25,32:2
Aunt From Chicago, The 1960,Je 6,33:6
Stratoberdha, Victor (Director)
Skanderbeg 1954,Jl 5,6:4
Stratton, Arthur
Ringer, The 1932,Je 2,25:2
Stratton, Chet
Greatest Story Ever Told, The 1965,F 16,40:2
In Harm's Way 1965,Ap 7,36:1
Track of Thunder 1968,F 1,28:4
Stratton, Gil
Girl Crazy 1943,D 3,27:2
Stratton, Gil Jr
Battle Zone 1952,N 1,17:2
Stalag 17 1953,Jl 2,19:2
Stratton, Inger
Playground, The 1965,O 4,00:0
Naked Runner, The 1967,Jl 20,30:2
Stratton, John
Mr Lord Says No! 1952,F 12,22:5
Cruel Sea, The 1953,Ag 11,18:5
Abandon Ship 1957,Ap 18,35:1
Third Key, The 1957,Je 3,30:2
Stratton-Porter, Gene (Narrator)
Keeper of the Bees, The 1925,O 28,29:2
Stratton-Porter, Gene (Original Author)
Keeper of the Bees, The 1925,O 28,29:2
Girl of the Limberlost, A 1934,N 9,24:6
Laddie 1935,My 6,22:3
Keeper of the Bees, The 1935,Ag 17,18:5
Freckles 1935,O 26,12:2
Harvester, The 1936,Jl 4,18:2
Straty, Ninon
Little Boy Lost 1953,S 22,38:2
Straub, Agnes
Alraune 1934,My 5,22:4
Vier Musketiere, Die; Four Musketeers, The 1935,N 9,19:3
Weisse Sklaven 1937,Jl 31,6:2
Fridericus 1939,F 25,19:2
Nanu, Sie Kennen Korff noch Nicht?; So, You Don't Know Korff Yet? 1939,My 22,15:3
Straub, Jean-Marie (Director)
Chronicle of Anna Magdalena Bach 1968,S 20,37:7
Straub, Jean-Marie (Screenwriter)
Chronicle of Anna Magdalena Bach 1968,S 20,37:7
Strauch, I
Prisoners of the Sea 1929,Ap 16,32:5
Straughn, Leslie
Native Son 1951,Je 18,19:2
Straukh, M
Leningrad Symphony 1958,Je 23,19:6
Straukh, Maxim
Two Soldiers 1944,Jl 27,14:2
STRAUS
See Also STRAUSS
Straus, Oscar (Composer)
Make a Wish 1937,S 23,33:1
Forbidden Music 1938,D 27,13:2
Three Waltzes 1939,Ap 25,19:2
Chocolate Soldier, The 1941,N 1,20:2
Straus, Oscar (Miscellaneous)
Si l'Empereur Savait Ca 1931,F 23,20:3
One Hour with You 1932,Mr 24,17:5
Straus, Oscar (Original Author)
Waltz Dream, The 1926,Jl 26,13:2
Married in Hollywood 1929,S 23,24:3
Straus, Sylvie
Act One 1963,D 27,17:2
STRAUSS
See Also STRAUS
Strauss, Eduard Jr
Eternal Waltz, The; (Ewiger Walzer) 1959,Jl 9,22:1
Strauss, Johann (Composer)
London 1926,O 25,15:1
Waltz Time in Vienna 1934,N 19,13:2
Andy Hardy's Private Secretary 1941,Mr 7,17:2
Fledermaus, Die; Bat, The 1948,Mr 15,26:2
Vienna Blood 1951,F 22,27:4
Fledermaus, Die 1964,F 8,15:2
Strauss, Johann (Miscellaneous)
Waltz Time 1933,S 29,24:2

Strauss, Johann Jr (Composer)
Three Waltzes 1939,Ap 25,19:2
Strauss, Johann Sr (Composer)
Three Waltzes 1939,Ap 25,19:2
Strauss, Johann 2d (Composer)
Great Waltz, The 1938,N 25,19:1
Strauss, Richard (Composer)
Rosenkavalier, Der 1962,O 10,57:1
Strauss, Robert
Native Land 1942,My 12,16:3
Sailor Beware 1952,F 1,17:1
Jumping Jacks 1952,Jl 24,30:2
Stalag 17 1953,Jl 2,19:2
Here Come the Girls 1953,D 26,10:1
Act of Love 1954,F 12,20:5
Money From Home 1954,F 27,11:3
Atomic Kid, The 1954,D 4,14:2
Bridges at Toko-Ri, The 1955,Ja 21,20:2
Seven Year Itch, The 1955,Je 4,9:1
Man With the Golden Arm, The 1955,D 16,38:2
Attack! 1956,S 20,29:4
Li'l Abner 1959,D 12,19:2
Wake Me When It's Over 1960,Ap 9,17:2
September Storm 1960,O 29,26:7
Last Time I Saw Archie, The 1961,My 29,9:6
George Raft Story, The 1962,Mr 22,40:1
Thrill of it All, The 1963,Ag 2,15:3
Wheeler Dealers, The 1963,N 15,25:2
Frankie and Johnny 1966,Jl 21,20:2
Fort Utah 1967,My 25,54:3
Strauss, Theodore (Miscellaneous)
Miss Susie Slagle's 1946,F 7,29:2
Strauss, Theodore (Narrator)
Russian Story, The 1943,Je 9,17:2
Strauss, Theodore (Original Author)
Moonrise 1949,Mr 7,17:2
Strauss, Theodore (Screenwriter)
Russian Story, The 1943,Je 9,17:2
California 1947,Ja 15,31:2
Isn't It Romantic? 1948,O 7,35:2
My Own True Love 1949,F 3,27:3
Four Days in November 1964,O 8,48:2
Strauss, William
North Wind's Malice, The 1920,O 18,13:1
Private Izzy Murphy 1926,N 10,25:1
Ankles Preferred 1927,Ap 18,21:2
Lucky Boy 1929,F 25,16:1
House of Rothschild, The 1934,Mr 15,27:2
Golden Boy 1939,S 8,28:2
Stravinskaya, Anya
Hello, Moscow! 1946,Je 15,24:4
Stravinsky, Igor (Composer)
Royal Ballet, The (The Firebird); Firebird, The
(The Royal Ballet) 1960,O 5,45:2
Straw, Jack
Pajama Game, The 1957,Ag 30,12:2
Don't Go Near the Water 1957,N 15,37:1
Big Beat, The 1958,Je 26,23:4
Strawn, Arthur (Screenwriter)
Man Who Lived Twice, The 1936,O 12,23:2
Lady From Nowhere 1936,D 21,19:2
Bad Men of Tombstone 1949,Mr 5,10:2
Hiawatha 1952,D 26,20:4
Strayer, Frank (Director)
Sweet Rosie O'Grady 1926,D 9,33:1
Rough House Rosie 1927,My 23,27:2
We're in the Air Now 1927,D 31,31:1
Partners in Crime 1928,Ap 30,18:3
Moran of the Marines 1928,O 15,16:1
Fall of Eve, The 1929,Je 18,29:4
Let's Go Places 1930,Mr 1,23:1
Murder at Midnight 1931,O 5,17:3
Crusader, The 1932,O 8,15:4
Vampire Bat, The 1933,Ja 23,9:1
El Rey de los Gitanos 1933,My 29,22:2
(Incorrect in this edition; use 1933,My 29,16:5
elsewhere)
Melodia Prohibida, La 1933,O 4,27:2
Dance, Girl, Dance 1933,O 25,23:3
Cruz y la Espada, La 1934,F 5,19:3
In Love With Life 1934,My 12,12:3
Las Fronteras del Amor 1934,D 4,23:3
Ghost Walks, The 1935,Mr 30,11:2
Off to the Races 1937,F 6,15:2
Big Business 1937,Je 1,27:2
Hot Water 1937,N 5,19:4
Blondie 1938,D 22,25:4
Blondie Meets the Boss 1939,Ap 27,31:1
Blondie Goes Latin 1941,F 26,17:3
Go West, Young Lady 1941,N 24,11:6
Street, David
Moonrise 1949,Mr 7,17:2
Street, James (Original Author)
Biscuit Eater, The 1940,My 23,28:5
Tap Roots 1948,Ag 26,16:3
Street, Julian (Original Author)
Don't Call it Love 1923,D 25,26:1
So's Your Old Man 1926,N 1,28:2
I'm From Missouri 1939,Mr 23,27:1
Streeter, Coolidge (Screenwriter)
Man From Beyond, The 1922,Ap 4,15:3

Streeter, Edward (Original Author)
Father of the Bride 1950,My 19,31:2
Father's Little Dividend 1951,Ap 13,18:5
Mr Hobbs Takes a Vacation 1962,Je 16,11:2
Streeter, Reginald
Cimarron 1931,Ja 27,20:5
Strehlen, Fritz
Der Falsche Ehemann 1932,O 17,18:3
Streinikov, N (Composer)
Poet and Tsar 1938,Ag 25,15:1
Streisand, Barbra
Funny Girl 1968,S 20,42:1
Streithorst, Erika
Liebe und Trompetenklang 1936,Ap 13,15:2
Strelby, Marianna
Wise Girl 1938,Ja 10,13:3
Strelich, Steve
Goodbye Broadway 1938,My 14,18:1
Strelkova, M P
Moscow Laughs 1935,Mr 25,12:2
Strelkova, Mme
Hour With Tchekhof, An 1933,S 6,24:4
Strelln, P
Idiot, The 1960,Jl 22,11:2
Stresa, Nino (Miscellaneous)
Island Sinner, The 1960,S 5,11:2
Stresa, Nino (Screenwriter)
Goliath and the Barbarians 1960,Ja 7,24:6
Queen of the Pirates 1961,Jl 27,23:4
Stribling, Melissa
Horror of Dracula 1958,My 29,24:4
Murder Reported 1960,Jl 12,39:1
League of Gentlemen, The 1961,Ja 25,30:4
Only When I Larf 1968,O 24,55:3
Strichewsky, Vladimir (Director)
Volga Boatman, The 1938,Ap 15,23:3
Strick, Joseph (Director)
Savage Eye, The 1960,Je 7,27:1
Balcony, The 1963,Mr 22,7:1
Ulysses 1967,Mr 14,55:1
Strick, Joseph (Producer)
Savage Eye, The 1960,Je 7,27:1
Strick, Joseph (Screenwriter)
Ulysses 1967,Mr 14,55:1
Strickland, Amzie
Slaughter on Tenth Avenue 1957,N 6,43:1
Strickland, Betty
32 Rue de Montmartre 1944,S 28,26:3
Strickland, Helen
Scoundrel, The 1935,My 3,23:2
Strickland, Robert
Girl Crazy 1943,D 3,27:2
Good News 1947,D 5,33:2
Stricklyn, Ray
Catered Affair, The 1956,Je 15,32:4
Somebody up There Likes Me 1956,Jl 6,16:1
Last Wagon, The 1956,S 22,20:2
Ten North Frederick 1958,My 23,29:2
Remarkable Mr Pennypacker, The 1959,F 21,25:2
Big Fisherman, The 1959,Ag 6,18:1
Lost World, The 1960,Jl 14,23:1
Young Jesse James 1960,Ag 25,25:1
Track of Thunder 1968,F 1,28:4
Stride, April
Master of Bankdam 1949,O 17,18:2
Striker, Joseph
Silver Wings 1922,My 18,14:4
Steadfast Heart, The 1923,D 25,26:1
Painted People 1924,Ja 29,16:1
I Am the Man 1925,Mr 6,23:1
Best People 1925,O 21,21:3
King of Kings, The 1927,Ap 20,29:2
Annie Laurie 1927,My 12,24:3
Cradle Snatchers 1927,My 31,25:2
Wise Wife 1927,N 1,21:1 (In Addenda)
Wrecker, The 1929,Ag 13,23:2
Strimpell, Stephen
Fitzwilly 1967,D 21,45:1
Strinati, Carlo
Man of Courage 1934,N 14,23:2
Strindberg, August (Original Author)
Miss Julie 1952,Ap 8,35:2
Of Love and Lust (Doll's House, A); Doll's House,
A (Of Love and Lust) 1959,My 26,31:2
Of Love and Lust (On Payment); On Payment (Of
Love and Lust) 1959,My 26,31:2
Stringer, Arthur (Original Author)
Unseeing Eyes 1923,O 22,17:1
Manhandled 1924,Jl 29,9:2
Empty Hands 1924,Ag 18,8:2
Story Without a Name, The 1924,O 6,25:1
Womanhandled 1926,Ja 5,25:2
Purchase Price, The 1932,Jl 16,5:5
Buck Benny Rides Again 1940,Ap 25,28:4
Stringer, Dewey
Beach Red 1967,Ag 4,18:1
Stritch, Elaine
Three Violent People 1957,F 11,34:2
Farewell to Arms, A 1958,Ja 25,14:1
Perfect Furlough, The 1959,Ja 22,27:4
Strizhak, Alexander (Director)
Her Way of Love 1929,Ag 19,22:1

Strizhenov, Oleg
Gadfly, The 1956,S 17,22:2
Mexican, The 1957,Ap 3,28:2
Forty-First, The 1957,Je 15,10:7
Captain's Daughter, The 1959,N 23,41:3
Journey Beyond Three Seas 1960,Ap 11,42:6
Queen of Spades 1961,S 4,10:1
Duel, The 1964,S 7,11:2
Last Game, The 1964,O 25,41:5 (Incorrect in this
edition; use 1964,O 26,41:5 elsewhere)
Strizhenova, M
Gadfly, The 1956,S 17,22:2
Gordeyev Family, The 1961,O 16,33:6
Sound of Life, The 1962,F 12,28:2
Strobye, Axel
Gertrud 1966,Je 3,33:1
I, A Lover 1968,My 4,46:2
Strock, Herbert (Director)
Gog 1954,Ag 14,8:2
I Was a Teenage Frankenstein 1958,Ja 30,19:4
Strode, Warren Chetham (Original Author)
Guinea Pig, The 1949,My 2,20:2
Strode, Warren Chetham (Screenwriter)
Two Who Dared 1937,Jl 10,18:2
Guinea Pig, The 1949,My 2,20:2
Strode, Woody
Gambler From Natchez, The 1954,Ag 14,8:2
Tarzan's Fight for Life 1958,Ag 16,10:2
Pork Chop Hill 1959,My 30,9:2
Last Voyage, The 1960,F 20,14:2
Sergeant Rutledge 1960,My 26,37:1
Spartacus 1960,O 7,28:1
Sins of Rachel Cade, The 1961,Ap 6,30:3
Two Rode Together 1961,Jl 27,23:3
Man Who Shot Liberty Valance, The
1962,My 24,29:2
Genghis Khan 1965,Je 24,28:2
7 Women 1966,My 5,59:1
Professionals, The 1966,N 3,45:1
Shalako 1968,N 6,32:1
Stroesco, Constantin
Million, Le 1931,My 21,33:2
Strohm, Egon D
Martin Luther 1953,S 10,22:1
Stroll, Edson
Snow White and the Three Stooges 1961,Jl 1,9:1
Three Stooges in Orbit, The 1962,Jl 12,19:4
McHale's Navy 1964,Jl 11,15:2
Strom, Carl
Karl Fredrik Reigns 1938,F 2,15:2
Kalle paa Spaangen 1940,Ja 27,9:3
Surf, The 1949,D 17,15:2
Lesson in Love, A 1960,Mr 15,46:1
Strom, Emy
Dear John 1966,Mr 9,46:1
Stromberg, Hunt (Director)
Roaring Rails 1924,O 15,27:3
Siren of Seville, The 1924,N 17,16:1 (In
Addenda)
Stromberg, Hunt (Producer)
Painted Veil, The 1934,D 7,29:1
Naughty Marietta 1935,Mr 23,11:2
Ah, Wilderness! 1935,D 25,30:2
Rose Marie 1936,F 1,9:2
Wife vs Secretary 1936,F 29,11:1
Great Ziegfeld, The 1936,Ap 9,21:2
Small Town Girl 1936,Ap 11,19:1
After the Thin Man 1936,D 25,19:2
Maytime 1937,Mr 19,27:1
Night Must Fall 1937,Ap 30,17:2
Firefly, The 1937,S 2,17:2
Marie Antoinette 1938,Ag 17,23:2
Sweethearts 1938,D 23,16:2
Idiot's Delight 1939,F 3,13:1
Women, The 1939,S 22,27:2
Another Thin Man 1939,N 24,29:1
Northwest Passage 1940,Mr 8,25:1
Susan and God 1940,Jl 12,11:2
Pride and Prejudice 1940,Ag 9,19:1
They Met in Bombay 1941,Jl 4,17:1
Shadow of the Thin Man 1941,N 21,23:2
I Married an Angel 1942,Jl 10,13:2
Guest in the House 1945,F 16,19:2
Young Widow 1946,Jl 29,12:8
Too Late for Tears 1949,Ag 15,12:3
Between Midnight and Dawn 1950,O 2,19:2
Mask of the Avenger 1951,Je 27,25:2
Stromberg, Hunt (Screenwriter)
Roaring Rails 1924,O 15,27:3
Stromberg, Soeren
Venum 1968,Ja 11,42:1
Strommerstedt, Monica
Inga 1968,N 21,41:2
Strong, Austin (Original Author)
Seventh Heaven 1927,My 26,22:1
Seventh Heaven 1937,Mr 26,25:1
Three Wise Fools 1946,S 27,19:2
Strong, Eugene
Border Legion, The 1918,Jl 29,9:3
Drop Kick, The 1927,S 20,32:2
Coney Island 1928,F 14,27:1 (In Addenda)
Crooks Can't Win 1928,My 29,17:2
Front Page, The 1931,Mr 20,29:1

Strong, John Mikale (Original Author)
No More Women 1934,Mr 15,27:4
Strong, L A G (Original Author)
Brothers, The 1948,My 5,30:4
Strong, L A G (Screenwriter)
Mr Perrin and Mr Traill 1949,Ja 17,15:2
Strong, Leonard
Little Tokyo, USA 1942,Ag 7,13:2
Bombardier 1943,Jl 2,15:2
Behind the Rising Sun 1943,O 14,26:2
Jack London 1944,Mr 3,19:3
Keys of the Kingdom, The 1944,D 30,15:2
Blood on the Sun 1945,Je 29,12:2
Back to Bataan 1945,S 13,26:3
First Yank into Tokyo 1945,O 25,18:2
Anna and the King of Siam 1946,Je 21,20:2
Dangerous Millions 1947,Mr 15,10:3
Jewels of Brandenburg 1947,My 24,10:5
Backlash 1947,My 24,10:5
Sword of the Avenger 1948,Ag 26,16:4
We Were Strangers 1949,Ap 28,28:2
Cargo to Capetown 1950,Mr 31,36:3
Atomic City, The 1952,My 2,21:1
Shane 1953,Ap 24,30:3
Destination Gobi 1953,My 30,7:1
Scared Stiff 1953,Jl 3,10:2
Hell's Half Acre 1954,F 27,11:3
Naked Jungle, The 1954,Ap 3,19:2
Prisoner of War 1954,My 10,20:2
Strong, Michael
Detective Story 1951,N 7,35:2
Dead Heat on a Merry-Go-Round
1966,O 13,50:1
Point Blank 1967,S 19,53:1
Strong, Porter
One Exciting Night 1922,O 24,17:3
White Rose, The 1923,My 23,18:3
Way Down East 1931,Mr 16,25:1
Strongheart (dog)
Silent Call, The 1922,Ja 30,16:2
Strongheart (Dog)
Love Master, The 1924,My 19,14:2
Stross, Raymond (Producer)
Frightened Bride, The 1953,Ag 20,18:5
Alligator Named Daisy, An 1957,O 7,23:2
Flesh is Weak, The 1957,N 9,31:2
Angry Hills, The 1959,Jl 16,31:3
Night Fighters, The 1960,D 15,59:1
Question of Adultery, A 1961,Jl 6,18:2
Leather Boys, The 1965,N 9,50:1
90 Degrees in the Shade 1966,N 16,52:1
Fox, The 1968,F 8,36:1
Strother, Bill
Safety Last 1923,Ap 2,22:1
Stroud, Claude
All About Eve 1950,O 14,13:2
Love Me or Leave Me 1955,My 27,14:1
Breakfast at Tiffany's 1961,O 6,28:1
Stroud, Don
Games 1967,S 18,58:2
Madigan 1968,Mr 30,22:2
What's so bad About Feeling Good?
1968,My 25,27:1
Coogan's Bluff 1968,O 3,56:1
Stroud, Gregory
Mikado, The 1939,Je 2,27:2
Stroyberg, Annette
Eye of the Needle, The 1965,Je 22,25:2
Stroyeva, E
Leningrad Symphony 1958,Je 23,19:6
Stroyeva, V (Director)
Petersburg Nights 1934,S 10,20:4
Boris Godunov 1956,Ja 23,21:4
Stroyeva, V (Screenwriter)
Boris Godunov 1956,Ja 23,21:4
Stroyeva, Vera (Director)
Revolutionists 1936,D 26,15:3
Grand Concert, The 1952,S 1,10:2
Variety Stars 1955,F 21,16:7
Khovanschina 1960,S 19,41:2
Stroyeva, Vera (Screenwriter)
Khovanschina 1960,S 19,41:2
Stroyevoy, V (Screenwriter)
Jew at War, A 1931,Jl 25,11:6
Strozzi, Kay
Ex-Lady 1933,My 15,16:2
Strucchi, Stefano (Screenwriter)
Revolt of the Slaves, The 1961,N 8,41:1
...And Suddenly It's Murder! 1964,Ja 24,21:1
Magnificent Cuckold 1965,Ap 20,42:1
Mandragola 1966,Je 7,50:2
Struchkova, Raisa
Cinderella 1961,D 19,39:1
Bolshoi Ballet 67 1966,S 30,54:1
Strudwick, Shepperd
Fast Company 1938,Jl 6,21:2
Congo Maisie 1940,F 8,18:4
Dr Kildare's Strange Case 1940,Ap 12,19:2
Flight Command 1941,Ja 17,21:2
Joan of Arc 1948,N 12,30:5
Fighter Squadron 1948,N 20,9:2
Enchantment 1948,D 27,16:2
Red Pony, The 1949,Mr 9,33:2

Chicago Deadline 1949,N 3,37:2
All the King's Men 1949,N 9,37:2
Reckless Moment, The 1949,D 30,13:2
Kid From Texas, The 1950,Je 2,26:2
Let's Dance 1950,N 30,42:2
Under the Gun 1951,F 23,33:2
Three Husbands 1951,Mr 9,30:2
Place in the Sun, A 1951,Ag 29,20:1
Eddy Duchin Story, The 1956,Je 22,15:1
Autumn Leaves 1956,Ag 2,21:2
Beyond a Reasonable Doubt 1956,S 14,27:2
That Night 1957,O 15,39:3
Sad Sack, The 1957,N 28,57:1
Psychomania 1964,F 15,14:3
Strueby, Katherine (Original Author)
Spitfire 1943,Je 14,13:2
Showtime 1948,My 20,35:3
Strueby, Katherine (Screenwriter)
Candlelight in Algeria 1944,Jl 31,10:2
They Were Sisters 1946,Jl 24,24:2
Showtime 1948,My 20,35:3
Eight O'Clock Walk 1955,Ap 30,10:6
Struewe, Hans
Prince of Rogues, The 1929,Jl 30,19:4
Strum, Hans
Monna Vanna 1923,S 25,8:2
Strumway, Lee
Bat, The 1926,Mr 15,18:3
Struss, Karl (Cinematographer)
Two for Tonight 1935,Ag 31,16:2
Struther, Jan (Original Author)
Mrs Miniver 1942,Je 5,23:1
Miniver Story, The 1950,O 27,24:2
Struthers, Burt (Original Author)
I Want my Man 1925,Ap 6,17:3
Strutton, Bill (Screenwriter)
Assignment K 1968,Jl 20,18:2
Stryker, Fred (Composer)
Pick a Star 1937,My 28,17:2
Everything's on Ice 1939,O 6,31:1
Strzhelchik, V
Garnet Bracelet, The 1966,My 28,11:6
STUART
See Also STEWARD, STEWART
Stuart, Aimee (Miscellaneous)
Wicked Lady, The 1946,D 23,19:5
Man of Evil 1948,Mr 26,26:2
Golden Madonna, The 1949,S 5,13:4
Stuart, Aimee (Original Author)
Irene 1936,D 13,XI,6:6 (In Addenda)
Jeannie 1943,S 13,14:2
Let's Be Happy 1957,My 25,25:1
Stuart, Angela (Original Author)
Northwest Outpost 1947,Ag 8,10:2
Stuart, Arlen
Kiss Me, Stupid 1964,D 23,22:2
Stuart, Barbara
Marines, Lets Go! 1961,Ag 16,37:2
Stuart, Binkie
Moonlight Sonata 1938,My 10,17:2
Stuart, Charles F (Cinematographer)
Soviet Russia Through the Eyes of an American
1935,S 28,12:2
Stuart, Don
Bride of the Storm 1926,Ap 5,24:1
Stuart, Donald
Beau Geste 1926,Ag 26,17:3
Lone Eagle, The 1927,D 20,33:2
Interference 1928,N 17,23:1
Silver King, The 1929,S 2,16:1
Derelict 1930,N 22,21:3
Devotion 1931,O 3,20:2
Man From Yesterday, The 1932,Je 25,18:2
Cynara 1932,D 26,26:2
Woman Accused, The 1933,Mr 13,18:2
Invisible Man, The 1933,N 18,18:4
Dancing Man 1934,Jl 16,11:3
First a Girl 1936,Ja 4,19:1
Yank in the R A F, A 1941,S 27,11:3
Destination Unknown 1942,O 29,19:3
Flying Fortress 1942,D 19,22:2
Immortal Sergeant 1943,F 4,29:2
Hour Before the Dawn, The 1944,My 11,25:6
Canterville Ghost, The 1944,Jl 29,16:2
Lucky Nick Cain 1951,Ap 23,21:2
Sheriff of Fractured Jaw, The 1959,Mr 14,27:4
Stuart, Eleanor
Oedipus Rex 1957,Ja 8,26:1
Stuart, Gil
Sound of Music, The 1965,Mr 3,34:1
Stuart, Gilchrist
Yank in the R A F, A 1941,S 27,11:3
Stuart, Gloria
Street of Women 1932,My 30,16:5
All American, The 1932,O 22,18:4
Old Dark House, The 1932,O 28,22:4
Air Mail 1932,N 7,20:3
Laughter in Hell 1933,Ja 2,29:2
Sweepings 1933,Mr 24,22:3
Private Jones 1933,Mr 25,13:3

Stuart, Gloria — Cont
Kiss Before the Mirror, The 1933,My 15,16:2
Girl in 419 1933,My 20,11:5
It's Great to be Alive 1933,Jl 8,14:6
Secret of the Blue Room, The 1933,S 13,22:1
Invisible Man, The 1933,N 18,18:4
Roman Scandals 1933,D 25,28:2
Beloved 1934,Ja 27,9:3
I Like It That Way 1934,Ap 18,23:3
I'll Tell the World 1934,Ap 21,12:2
Love Captive, The 1934,Je 8,18:1
Here Comes the Navy 1934,Jl 21,14:2
Gift of Gab 1934,S 26,17:6
Maybe It's Love 1935,F 11,14:2
Gold Diggers of 1935 1935,Mr 15,25:2
Laddie 1935,My 6,22:3
Professional Soldier 1936,Ja 30,14:2
Prisoner of Shark Island, The 1936,F 13,25:2
Poor Little Rich Girl, The 1936,Je 26,16:1
Crime of Dr Forbes, The 1936,Jl 6,11:4
36 Hours to Live 1936,Ag 15,6:3
Girl on the Front Page, The 1936,N 7,15:2
Wanted: Jane Turner 1936,N 30,24:7
Girl Overboard 1937,Mr 1,15:1
Life Begins In College 1937,O 9,16:1
Rebecca of Sunnybrook Farm 1938,Mr 26,12:1
Island in the Sky 1938,My 14,18:1
Keep Smiling 1938,Ag 10,15:2
Time Out for Murder 1938,O 7,21:2
Three Musketeers, The 1939,F 18,12:2
It Could Happen to You 1939,Je 9,26:3
Whistler, The 1944,Ap 29,12:2
Enemy of Women 1944,S 12,23:6
She Wrote the Book 1946,Je 20,20:3
Stuart, Grant (Screenwriter)
Chapman Report, The 1962,O 18,49:2
Stuart, Henry
When Duty Calls 1929,Ja 1,60:1
Sajenko, The Soviet 1929,Ja 15,22:4
Wrath of the Seas, The 1929,Ag 19,22:1
Stuart, Ian (Original Author)
Satan Bug, The 1965,Ap 15,38:1
Stuart, Iris
Stranded in Paris 1926,D 13,27:1
Casey at the Bat 1927,Ap 4,30:5
Wedding Bills 1927,Je 29,29:3
Stuart, Jane
Ramparts We Watch, The 1940,S 20,27:1
Stuart, Jeanne
White Face 1933,D 4,22:3
Bella Donna 1935,F 26,16:4
My Heart Is Calling 1935,Ap 15,16:3
Forever Yours 1937,Je 7,22:2
Kathleen 1938,Ja 24,17:1
Stuart, John
This Freedom 1923,N 28,15:1
Kitty 1929,Je 11,27:2
Fanny Hawthorn 1929,N 11,20:2
Atlantic 1930,Ja 26,VIII,6:2
Atlantic 1930,O 6,21:1
Children of Chance 1931,Ja 24,15:1
Wandering Jew, The 1935,Ja 14,11:3
Bella Donna 1935,F 26,16:4
In a Monastery Garden 1935,Mr 13,16:2
Abdul the Damned 1936,My 11,16:2
Ships With Wings 1942,My 25,11:2
Flying Fortress 1942,D 19,22:2
Courageous Mr Penn 1943,D 23,26:5
Madonna of the Seven Moons 1946,My 23,18:4
Mrs Fitzherbert 1950,My 11,37:2
Your Past Is Showing 1958,Jl 1,36:2
Stuart, Josephine
Oliver Twist 1951,Jl 31,17:2
Stuart, Kathryn (Screenwriter)
Career of Catherine Bush, The 1919,Ag 4,8:3
Stuart, Lillian
David Harum 1934,Mr 2,23:2
Stuart, Lily D
Such Women Are Dangerous 1934,Je 9,18:3
Stuart, Malcolm (Producer)
Way...Way Out 1966,O 27,55:1
Stuart, Mary
This Time for Keeps 1947,D 5,33:4
Adventures of Don Juan 1948,D 25,10:1
Stuart, Mel (Director)
Four Days in November 1964,O 8,48:2
Stuart, Mel (Producer)
Four Days in November 1964,O 8,48:2
Stuart, Michael
This Day and Age 1933,S 1,15:4
Stuart, Nick
Cradle Snatchers 1927,My 31,25:2
High School Hero 1927,O 24,24:3
Why Sailors Go Wrong 1928,Ap 9,18:2
News Parade, The 1928,My 29,17:2
River Pirate, The 1928,S 17,27:1
Girls Gone Wild 1929,Ap 22,23:1
Why Leave Home 1929,S 16,30:1
Swing High 1930,Je 27,26:3
Police Call 1933,Ag 22,20:3
Stuart, Philip (Original Author)
Irene 1936,D 13,XI,6:6 (In Addenda)

Stuart, Randy
Sitting Pretty 1948,Mr 11,35:2
Apartment for Peggy 1948,O 16,9:2
Dancing in the Dark 1949,D 3,8:6
Stella 1950,Ag 19,9:2
All About Eve 1950,O 14,13:2
I Can Get It for You Wholesale 1951,Ap 5,34:4
Room for One More 1952,Ja 16,21:2
Incredible Shrinking Man, The 1957,F 23,13:1
Stuart, Rudy
I Was a Male War Bride 1949,Ag 27,7:2
Stuart, William L (Original Author)
Where the Sidewalk Ends 1950,Jl 8,7:4
Stubbs, Chuck
They Shall Have Music 1939,Jl 26,17:2
Stubbs, Harry
Alibi 1929,Ap 9,29:1
Three Live Ghosts 1929,S 30,23:1
Locked Door, The 1930,Ja 20,21:1
Night Ride 1930,Ja 20,21:1
Truth About Youth, The 1930,D 13,22:2
Gang Buster, The 1931,Ja 24,15:1
Millie 1931,F 7,11:1
Fanny Foley Herself 1931,O 26,22:1
Her Majesty, Love 1931,N 26,37:2
Man Who Played God, The 1932,F 11,16:1
Mind Reader, The 1933,Ap 7,22:4
When Strangers Marry 1933,My 25,24:3
Invisible Man, The 1933,N 18,18:4
Now and Forever 1934,O 13,10:1
On the Avenue 1937,F 5,17:3
London by Night 1937,Ag 13,13:1
Love and Hisses 1938,Ja 1,11:1
Doctor Rhythm 1938,My 19,25:2
I Stand Accused 1939,Ja 5,17:1
Peck's bad Boy With the Circus 1939,Ja 11,17:4
Adventure in Diamonds 1940,Ap 4,27:2
Mummy's Hand, The 1940,S 20,27:2
Burma Convoy 1941,O 7,26:7
Stubbs, Ray
Raisin in the Sun, A 1961,Mr 30,24:1
Studdiford, Grace
Branded Woman, The 1920,S 6,10:5
Studer, Carl
Day and the Hour, The 1964,F 20,22:2
Doulos-The Finger Man 1964,Mr 3,31:1
Joy House 1965,F 18,29:1
Studstill, Pat
Paper Lion 1968,O 24,54:1
Study, Lomax
Boeing Boeing 1965,D 24,24:4
Caper of the Golden Bulls, The 1967,Je 22,46:1
Stuewe, Hans
Because I Loved You 1930,Ja 25,13:2
Caught in Berlin's Underworld 1930,F 10,20:4
Hungarian Nights 1930,Je 10,32:2
Verklungene Traume 1930,D 9,31:3
Barberina, Die Taenzerin Von Sans-Souci 1932,O 26,15:4
Walzerkoenig, Der 1932,D 5,21:2
Goethe's Jugendgeliebte 1932,D 26,26:2
Zapfenstreich am Rhein 1933,F 2,21:6
Die Frau von der Man Spricht 1933,Ap 22,16:4
Meisterdetektiv, Der 1934,F 13,23:2
Tannenberg 1934,Ap 3,26:6
Trenck 1934,Ap 7,19:2
Johannisnact 1935,F 25,13:4
Aschermittwoch; Ash Wednesday 1935,Mr 11,15:2
Private Life of Louis XIV, The 1936,Ja 9,25:2
Zu Strassburg auf der Schanz; At the Strassburg 1936,F 15,18:7
Schloss Vogeloed 1936,My 9,11:2
Heisses Blut 1936,S 26,11:2
Tiger von Eschnapur, Der 1938,Ap 30,18:2
Indian Tomb, The; Tiger von Eschnapur, Der 1938,My 14,18:2
Dahinten in der Heide; Back in the Country 1939,Ja 21,19:3
Drei Vater um Anna; Three Fathers for Anna 1940,Ja 20,11:3
Alle stehen Kopf; General Confusion 1940,Je 22,18:4
Leidenschaft; Passion 1940,S 24,26:6
Stuhldreher, Harry
Spirit of Notre Dame, The 1931,O 16,27:1
Stuhldreher, Harry (Original Author)
Band Plays on, The 1934,D 22,21:2
Stumar, John S (Director)
King's People, The 1937,My 12,27:1
Stumpf, Wolfgang
Bridge, The; (Bruecke, Die) 1961,My 2,42:1
Signs of Life; Lebenszeichent 1968,S 26,60:1
Sturdy, John Rhodes (Original Author)
Corvette K-225 1943,O 21,30:1
Cariboo Trail, The 1950,S 1,17:2
Sturdy, John Rhodes (Screenwriter)
Corvette K-225 1943,O 21,30:1
Sturgeon, Rolling S (Director)
Daughters of Today 1924,Mr 4,17:1
STURGES
See Also STURGIS

Sturges, John (Director)
Thunderbolt 1945,O 27,12:5
Sign of the Ram, The 1948,Mr 4,30:2
Capture, The 1950,My 20,8:6
Mystery Street 1950,Jl 28,12:5
Right Cross 1950,N 16,39:2
Magnificent Yankee, The 1951,Ja 19,21:2
Kind Lady 1951,Ag 8,21:2
People Against O'Hara, The 1951,S 6,39:3
It's a big Country 1952,Ja 9,25:2
Girl in White, The 1952,My 31,12:5
Jeopardy 1953,Mr 31,36:2
Escape from Fort Bravo 1954,Ja 23,11:2
Bad Day at Black Rock 1955,F 2,22:2
Underwater! 1955,F 10,27:2
Scarlet Coat, The 1955,Jl 30,14:2
Backlash 1956,Ap 21,11:2
Gunfight at the O K Corral 1957,My 30,23:2
Law and Jake Wade, the 1958,Je 7,11:1
Old Man and the Sea, The 1958,O 8,41:1
Last Train from Gun Hill 1959,Jl 30,31:2
Never so Few 1960,Ja 22,15:2
Magnificent Seven, The 1960,N 24,48:3
By Love Possessed 1961,Jl 20,32:2
Sergeants 3 1962,F 12,28:2
Girl Named Tamiku, A 1963,Mr 15,8:2
Great Escape, The 1963,Ag 8,19:1
Satan Bug, The 1965,Ap 15,38:1
Hallelujah Trail, The 1965,Jl 2,17:1
Hour of the Gun 1967,N 2,58:4
Ice Station Zebra 1968,D 21,49:1
Sturges, John (Producer)
Magnificent Seven, The 1960,N 24,48:3
Great Escape, The 1963,Ag 8,19:1
Satan Bug, The 1965,Ap 15,38:1
Hallelujah Trail, The 1965,Jl 2,17:1
Hour of the Gun 1967,N 2,58:4
Sturges, Mark
Synanon 1965,My 6,44:1
Sturges, Preston
Star Spangled Rhythm 1942,D 31,20:1
Paris Holiday 1958,My 10,19:2
Sturges, Preston (Composer)
One Rainy Afternoon 1936,My 14,29:2
Miracle of Morgan's Creek, The 1944,Ja 20,15:2
Sturges, Preston (Director)
Great McGinty, The 1940,Ag 15,23:1
Christmas in July 1940,N 6,35:2
Lady Eve, The 1941,F 26,17:1
Sullivan's Travels 1942,Ja 29,25:2
Palm Beach Story, The 1942,D 11,33:1
Miracle of Morgan's Creek, The 1944,Ja 20,15:2
Hail the Conquering Hero 1944,Ag 10,14:2
Great Moment, The 1944,N 13,15:2
Unfaithfully Yours 1948,N 6,9:2
Beautiful Blonde From Bashful Bend, The 1949,My 28,11:2
Mad Wednesday 1951,Ja 25,21:5
French They Are a Funny Race, The 1957,My 21,41:1
Sturges, Preston (Original Author)
Strictly Dishonorable 1931,N 11,27:1
Child of Manhattan 1933,F 13,11:4
Strictly Dishonorable 1951,Jl 12,21:6
Sturges, Preston (Producer)
Christmas in July 1940,N 6,35:2
Unfaithfully Yours 1948,N 6,9:2
Beautiful Blonde From Bashful Bend, The 1949,My 28,11:2
Mad Wednesday 1951,Ja 25,21:5
Sturges, Preston (Screenwriter)
Power and the Glory, The 1933,Ag 17,13:2
We Live Again 1934,N 2,27:2
Good Fairy, The 1935,F 1,18:1
Diamond Jim 1935,Ag 24,18:2
Easy Living 1937,Jl 8,20:1
Port of Seven Seas 1938,Jl 15,13:2
If I Were King 1938,S 29,31:1
Never Say Die 1939,Mr 9,18:1
Remember the Night 1940,Ja 18,27:2
Great McGinty, The 1940,Ag 15,23:1
Christmas in July 1940,N 6,35:2
Lady Eve, The 1941,F 26,17:1
Sullivan's Travels 1942,Ja 29,25:2
Palm Beach Story, The 1942,D 11,33:1
Miracle of Morgan's Creek, The 1944,Ja 20,15:2
Hail the Conquering Hero 1944,Ag 10,14:2
Great Moment, The 1944,N 13,15:2
I'll Be Yours 1947,F 22,16:2
Unfaithfully Yours 1948,N 6,9:2
Beautiful Blonde From Bashful Bend, The 1949,My 28,11:2
Mad Wednesday 1951,Ja 25,21:5
Birds and the Bees, The 1956,Ap 23,22:1
French They Are a Funny Race, The 1957,My 21,41:1
Sturges, Olive
Raven, The 1963,Ja 26,5:8
STURGIS
See Also STURGES
Sturgis, Eddie
After Midnight 1927,Ag 16,31:2
Big City, The 1928,Mr 26,26:2

Sturgis, Eddie— Cont
Fazil 1928,Je 5,21:1
Red Hot Tires 1935,Mr 1,16:3
Sturgis, Edwin
Seven Keys to Baldpate 1925,N 3,25:4
Outside the Law 1930,S 1,16:1
Sturm, Emmy
Zu Befehl, Herr Unteroffizier 1934,Je 16,20:3
Sturm, Hannes
Lost Shadow, The 1928,Mr 20,20:3
Sturm, Peter
Naked Among the Wolves 1967,Ap 19,54:7
Sturm, Yvonne
Christina 1951,Ja 15,13:1
Sturn, Hans (Original Author)
Ungetreue Eckehart, Der 1932,Ja 23,18:4
Sturrock, Dudley (Original Author)
Ourselves Alone 1937,Jl 31,6:2
River of Unrest 1937,N 27,21:2
Stutenroth, Gene
Game of Death, A 1945,N 24,22:4
Stuyvesant, Richard
Fistful of Dollars, A 1967,F 2,29:1
Styler, Burt (Screenwriter)
Call Me Mister 1951,F 1,21:2
Down Among the Sheltering Palms 1953,Je 13,11:2
Boy, Did I Get a Wrong Number! 1966,Je 9,54:2
Eight on the Lam 1967,Ap 27,52:1
Wicked Dreams of Paula Schultz, The 1968,Ja 4,28:1
Styles, Edwin
Hell Below 1933,Ap 26,13:2
Adam and Evalyn 1950,My 12,33:4
Penny Princess 1953,Mr 25,37:3
Styles, Herkie
Bellboy, The 1960,Jl 21,17:1
Styne, Jule (Composer)
Hold That Co-ed 1938,S 24,13:1
Hit Parade of 1941 1940,D 5,33:2
Rookies on Parade 1941,My 22,25:2
Priorities on Parade 1942,Jl 23,19:2
Powers Girl, The 1943,Mr 26,14:2 (In Addenda)
Hit Parade of 1943 1943,Ap 16,24:3
Heat's on, The 1943,N 26,29:2
Knickerbocker Holiday 1944,Ap 20,22:7
Step Lively 1944,Jl 27,14:1
Carolina Blues 1944,D 8,26:6
Tonight and Every Night 1945,Mr 9,16:2
Anchors Aweigh 1945,Jl 20,15:2
Tars and Spars 1946,F 15,29:2
Kid From Brooklyn, The 1946,Ap 19,25:2
Earl Carroll Sketchbook 1946,Ag 30,13:2
It Happened in Brooklyn 1947,Mr 14,28:5
It's a Great Feeling 1949,Ag 13,6:6
Gypsy 1962,N 2,24:1
Suarez, Hilda
Hand in the Trap 1963,Jl 2,16:2
Suarez, Jose
Lovemaker, The 1958,Mr 11,33:4
Carthage in Flames 1961,Ja 26,32:3
Suarez, Norberto
Terrace, The 1964,N 25,45:1
Suasa, Ruspoli di Poggio
Dolce Vita, La 1961,Ap 20,30:1
Suay, Ricardo Munez (Miscellaneous)
Moment of Truth, The 1965,Ag 10,18:1
Suberly, Sidney
Pawns of Passion 1929,My 27,22:1
Sublett, John W
Cabin in the Sky 1943,My 28,19:3
Subor, Michel
Anatomy of a Marriage; My Days With Jean Marc; My Nights With Francoise 1964,O 27,42:2
Petit Soldat, Le 1967,Ap 21,48:1
Subotsky, Milton (Original Author)
Horror Hotel 1963,Je 20,29:1
Subotsky, Milton (Producer)
Last Mile, The 1959,F 19,27:1
Psycopath, The 1966,S 29,60:1
Deadly Bees, The 1967,My 20,39:2
Danger Route 1968,Je 6,54:2
Torture Garden 1968,Jl 20,18:2
Birthday Party, The 1968,D 10,54:1
Subotsky, Milton (Screenwriter)
Last Mile, The 1959,F 19,27:1
Sucher, Henry (Original Author)
Mummy's Ghost, The 1944,Jl 1,10:7
Jungle Woman 1944,Jl 15,19:6
Frozen Ghost, The 1945,Jl 28,7:3
Sucher, Henry (Screenwriter)
Mummy's Tomb, The 1942,O 26,19:2
Captive Wild Woman 1943,Je 7,9:4
Mummy's Ghost, The 1944,Jl 1,10:7
Jungle Woman 1944,Jl 15,19:6
Frozen Ghost, The 1945,Jl 28,7:3
Suchy, Jiri
Audition 1968,Jl 4,13:2
Suckmann, Erich
Last ten Days, The 1956,Ap 12,26:1
Sucksdorff, Arne
Great Adventure, The 1955,My 24,34:6

Sucksdorff, Arne (Cinematographer)
Great Adventure, The 1955,My 24,34:6
Flute and the Arrow, The 1960,O 11,55:1
Sucksdorff, Arne (Director)
Great Adventure, The 1955,My 24,34:6
Flute and the Arrow, The 1960,O 11,55:1
Sucksdorff, Arne (Producer)
Great Adventure, The 1955,My 24,34:6
Sucksdorff, Arne (Screenwriter)
Great Adventure, The 1955,My 24,34:6
Flute and the Arrow, The 1960,O 11,55:1
Sucksdorff, Kjell
Great Adventure, The 1955,My 24,34:6
Sudakevich, A
Storm Over Asla 1930,S 8,17:1
Sudakevich, Annel
Yellow Ticket, The 1928,D 10,25:1
Sudermann, Hermann (Original Author)
Lily of the Dust 1924,Ag 25,16:2
Flesh and the Devil 1927,Ja 10,20:2
Sunrise 1927,S 24,15:3 (In Addenda)
Sunrise; Song of two Human Beings
  1928,Ja 29,VIII,6:2
Dame Care 1928,My 20,VIII,8:3
Song of Songs 1933,Jl 20,22:2
Katzensteg 1938,Ja 22,19:2
Magda 1938,S 10,20:2
Reise Nach Tilsit, Die; Trip to Tilsit, The
  1940,F 10,19:2
Johanns fever; St Johns' Fire 1940,Ap 6,13:2
Sudershan
Shakespeare Wallah 1966,Mr 23,40:2
Sudgeon, Leonard S Dr (Director)
Way up Yonder 1920,D 20,11:2
Sudin, Volodva
Adventure in Odessa 1954,Je 21,19:6
Sue, Eugene (Original Author)
Secrets of Paris 1923,Ja 8,22:1
Sue, Herbert Ah
Return to Paradise 1953,S 11,24:2
Suedo, Julie
White Sheik, The 1929,D 9,32:5
Human Monster, The 1940,Mr 25,11:2
Sues, Leonard
What a Life 1939,O 12,33:1
Suess, Dr (Original Author)
5,000 Fingers of Dr T, The 1953,Je 20,8:6
Suessenguth, Walther
City of Secrets 1963,Jl 27,10:2
Suetonius (Miscellaneous)
Cleopatra 1963,Je 13,29:1
Suey, Yee Chow
Fortune Hunters, The 1953,S 16,35:6
Suffel
Avocate d'Amour 1938,S 8,27:2
Suffel, Madeleine
Razumov 1937,Mr 9,27:2
Miquette 1951,F 5,18:2
Sufrin, Mark (Miscellaneous)
On the Bowery 1957,Mr 19,44:1
Sufy, Bernard
Inside Out 1964,S 25,32:1
Sugal, Ichro
Odd Obsession 1961,D 27,16:1
Suganuma, Tadashi
Ana-Ta-Han 1954,My 18,38:2
Sugar, Karoly
Und Es Leuchtet die Puszta 1934,Ja 30,17:2
Sugawa, Eizo (Director)
Challenge to Live 1964,Ap 8,33:1
Sugawara, Kenji
Golden Demon 1956,Ja 31,34:3
Street of Shame 1959,Je 5,17:2
Sugden, Leonard S Dr (Producer)
Lure of Alaska 1919,F 17,11:3
Untitled-Travel, Alaska 1919,F 24,11:3
Untitled-Travel, Alaska 1919,Mr 3,11:2
Sugie, Toshio
Saga of the Vagabonds 1964,O 7,31:1 (Incorrect
  in this edition; use 1964,O 7,51:1 elsewhere)
Sugimura, Haruko
Yang Kwei Fei 1956,S 11,41:2
She Was Like a Wild Chrysanthemum
  1960,Ja 22,15:2
Sugiyama, Shizeki (Producer)
Imposter, The 1955,Mr 23,27:1
Sugiyama, Shosaku
Zatoichi 1968,Je 28,37:1
Suglyama, Mitshuhiro
Flight From Ashiya 1964,Ap 23,34:1
Sujata
Merry Widow, The 1952,S 25,38:1
King of the Khyber Rifles 1953,D 23,21:1
Diamond Queen, The 1954,Ja 27,24:2
Sujata and Asoka
Salome 1953,Mr 25,37:1
Sukhanoff, Peter
Girl No 217 1945,S 3,17:2
Sukhanov, P
Tiger Girl 1955,S 5,8:2
Sukharevskaya, Ludmilla
Girl No 217 1945,S 3,17:2
Road Home, The 1947,My 2,28:3

Rimsky-Korsakov 1954,Mr 1,16:3
Sukhopolskaya, Z
Leningrad Symphony 1958,Je 23,19:6
Sul-Te-Wan, Madame
Kentucky 1938,D 24,12:1
Sul-Te-Wan, Mme
Ladies They Talk About 1933,F 25,20:4
Black Moon 1934,Je 28,26:2
Maid of Salem 1937,Mr 4,27:2
In Old Chicago 1938,Ja 7,15:2
Maryland 1940,Jl 13,16:5
Sul-Te-Wan, Mmme
Narrow Street, The 1925,Ja 5,19:1
Heaven on Earth 1931,D 19,16:4
Sulistrowski, Zygmunt
Amazon Trader, The 1956,N 17,17:6
Sullavan, Margaret
Only Yesterday 1933,N 10,25:1
Little Man, What Now? 1934,Je 1,29:1
Good Fairy, The 1935,F 1,18:1
So Red the Rose 1935,N 28,39:1
Next Time We Love 1936,Ja 31,16:2
Moon's our Home, The 1936,My 13,29:2
Three Comrades 1938,Je 3,17:1
Shopworn Angel, The 1938,Jl 8,11:2
Shining Hour, The 1939,Ja 20,15:2
Shop Around the Corner, The 1940,Ja 26,13:2
Mortal Storm, The 1940,Je 21,25:2
Back Street 1941,F 12,25:2
So Ends our Night 1941,F 28,17:2
Appointment for Love 1941,N 7,27:1
Cry Havoc 1943,N 24,16:2
No Sad Songs for Me 1950,Ap 28,26:2
Sullivan, A Edward (Director)
Burning Up 1930,F 8,12:5
Sullivan, Alan (Original Author)
Great Barrier, The 1937,F 5,17:5
Silent Barriers 1937,Mr 26,25:1
Sullivan, Arthur (Composer)
Mikado, The 1967,Mr 15,53:1
Sullivan, Barry
Lady in the Dark 1944,F 23,17:1
Woman of the Town, The 1944,Mr 6,17:2
Rainbow Island 1944,O 26,19:6
And Now Tomorrow 1944,N 23,38:2
Duffy's Tavern 1945,S 6,23:3
Getting Gertie's Garter 1946,F 4,21:2
Suspense 1946,Jl 5,15:3
Framed 1947,My 26,24:2
Gangster, The 1947,O 31,29:3
Bad Men of Tombstone 1949,Mr 5,10:2
Any Number Can Play 1949,Jl 1,14:4
Great Gatsby, The 1949,Jl 14,20:5
Tension 1950,Ja 12,32:4
Outriders, The 1950,Mr 9,25:2
Nancy Goes to Rio 1950,Ap 7,22:2
Life of her Own, A 1950,O 12,43:2
Grounds for Marriage 1951,Ja 12,24:6
Payment on Demand 1951,F 16,21:2
Three Guys Named Mike 1951,Mr 2,21:2
Inside Straight 1951,Mr 16,34:2
Cause for Alarm 1951,Mr 30,28:5
No Questions Asked 1951,Ag 10,13:2
Mr Imperium 1951,O 15,22:2
Unknown Man, The 1951,N 17,9:5
Skirts Ahoy! 1952,My 29,17:2
Bad and the Beautiful, The 1953,Ja 16,19:1
Jeopardy 1953,Mr 31,36:2
Loophole 1954,Mr 13,11:3
Playgirl 1954,My 15,13:3
Miami Story, The 1954,My 15,13:2
Her Twelve Men 1954,Ag 12,23:2
Strategic Air Command 1955,Ap 21,33:1
Queen Bee 1955,N 23,18:2
Maverick Queen, The 1956,Je 4,25:2
Julie 1956,N 22,51:1
Dragoon Wells Massacre 1957,My 6,25:2
Way to the Gold, The 1957,My 11,24:6
Another Time Another Place 1958,My 3,10:4
Purple Gang, The 1960,Ja 23,15:5
Seven Ways From Sundown 1960,D 22,18:4
Light in the Piazza 1962,F 8,25:1
Gathering of Eagles, A 1963,Jl 11,21:2
Man in the Middle 1964,Mr 5,36:1
My Blood Runs Cold 1965,Mr 25,42:4
Harlow 1965,My 15,18:1
American Dream, An 1966,S 1,28:2
Poppy is Also a Flower, The 1967,D 14,62:4
Sullivan, Billy
Sweepstakes 1931,Je 25,23:5
Sullivan, C Gardner (Miscellaneous)
If Marriage Fails 1925,Je 2,16:3
Sullivan, C Gardner (Original Author)
Sahara 1919,Je 30,16:3
Jackass Mail 1942,Jl 2,25:2
Sullivan, C Gardner (Screenwriter)
Hairpins 1920,Ag 2,12:2
Hail the Woman 1922,Ja 16,18:3
Soul of the Beast, The 1923,My 22,14:4
Human Wreckage 1923,Je 28,10:2
Only Woman, The 1924,N 3,20:1
Car 99 1935,F 23,14:7
Buccaneer, The 1938,F 17,17:2

Sullivan, C Gardner (Screenwriter) — Cont
Union Pacific 1939,My 11,31:2
North West Mounted Police 1940,N 7,33:2
Buccaneer, The 1958,D 24,00:0
Sullivan, Charles
Rookies 1927,Ap 25,20:4
Hit the Deck 1930,Ja 15,28:6
For the Defense 1930,Jl 19,7:5
Goodbye Broadway 1938,My 14,18:1
Sullivan, Ed
Mr Broadway 1933,S 14,26:3
Big Town Czar 1939,My 4,27:3
Bye Bye Birdie 1963,Ap 5,27:3
Singing Nun, The 1966,Mr 18,33:1
Sullivan, Ed (Original Author)
There Goes my Heart 1938,O 14,27:1
Big Town Czar 1939,My 4,27:3
Ma! He's Making Eyes at Me 1940,Ap 26,25:2
Sullivan, Edward Dean (Original Author)
Hell Bound 1931,My 9,15:4
Mad Game, The 1933,N 13,21:1
People's Enemy, The 1935,Ap 30,13:7
Sullivan, Elliott
They Won't Forget 1937,Jl 15,16:1
Accidents Will Happen 1938,Ap 25,19:2
Gangs of New York 1938,My 28,9:2
Racket Busters 1938,Ag 11,13:1
Next Time I Marry 1938,D 2,27:2
Spellbinder, The 1939,Ag 24,17:3
Smashing the Money Ring 1939,N 17,17:2
Saint's Double Trouble, The 1940,F 13,27:2
Millionaires in Prison 1940,Jl 16,21:3
Wild Bill Hickok Rides 1942,F 7,13:5
Lady Gambles, The 1949,My 21,9:2
Guilty Bystander 1950,Ap 21,18:2
Sergeant, The 1968,D 26,53:5
Sullivan, Francis L
Missing Rembrandt, The 1932,Mr 26,17:2
Wandering Jew, The 1935,Ja 14,11:3
Mystery of Edwin Drood, The 1935,Mr 21,27:1
Princess Charming 1935,Je 22,18:5
Two Who Dared 1937,Jl 10,18:2
Non-Stop New York 1937,N 29,19:2
Dinner at the Ritz 1937,D 4,21:1
Drums 1938,S 30,24:4
Citadel, The 1938,N 4,27:2
Climbing High 1939,Je 5,20:3
Ware Case, The 1939,Jl 22,12:2
Spy of Napoleon 1939,Ag 19,18:4
Secret Four, The 1940,Ap 22,13:2
21 Days Together 1940,My 23,28:4
Queen of Crime 1941,F 19,25:2
Mister V 1942,F 13,24:4
Avengers, The 1942,N 25,18:2
Young Man's Fancy, A 1943,D 4,11:2
Caesar and Cleopatra 1946,S 6,18:2
Great Expectations 1947,My 23,31:1
Smugglers, The 1948,Mr 29,17:1
Joan of Arc 1948,N 12,30:5
Take my Life 1949,Ja 19,34:2
Broken Journey 1949,My 26,34:3
Christopher Columbus 1949,O 13,33:2
Red Danube, The 1949,D 9,37:3
Laughing Lady, The 1950,Ja 23,16:3
Winslow Boy, The 1950,Je 7,34:4
Night and the City 1950,Je 10,11:2
Oliver Twist 1951,Jl 31,17:2
Behave Yourself 1951,N 8,35:2
My Favorite Spy 1951,D 26,19:3
Sangaree 1953,Je 5,19:1
Plunder of the Sun 1953,Ag 27,22:1
Drums of Tahiti 1954,Ap 24,14:5
Hell's Island 1955,My 7,10:2
Prodigal, The 1955,My 14,10:7
Sullivan, Fred
Winds of Chance 1925,Ag 17,10:3
Sullivan, Frederick
Beggar on Horseback 1925,Je 6,9:2
Murder by the Clock 1931,Jl 18,16:6
Blind Adventure 1933,O 31,24:3
You're Telling Me 1934,Ap 7,19:1
All the King's Horses 1935,Mr 9,19:1
Sullivan, G Gardiner (Original Author)
Tempest 1928,My 18,27:3
Cuban Love Song, The 1931,D 5,21:2
Sullivan, Gayne
Dementia 1955,D 23,14:4
Sullivan, Helene
Hell's Highroad 1925,Ag 26,14:2
Steel Preferred 1925,D 22,13:1
Claw, The 1927,My 11,28:3
Sullivan, Hugh
Persecution and Assassination of Jean-Paul Marat
  as Performed by the Inmates of the Asylum of
  Charenton Under the Direction of the Marquis
  De Sade, The 1967,F 23,41:1
Sullivan, Jean
Uncertain Glory 1944,Ap 8,9:2
Escape in the Desert 1945,My 12,10:2
Sullivan, John
Nobody Waved Goodbye 1964,S 17,52:1
Sullivan, John L
Legendary Champions, The 1968,O 29,54:1

Sullivan, John Maurice
Today 1930,N 17,29:1
Silence 1931,Ag 15,18:3
Strangers in Love 1932,Mr 5,11:2
Trial of Vivienne Ware, The 1932,Ap 30,19:3
Sullivan, Lee
Great John L, The 1945,Jl 9,14:6
Sullivan, Liam
One Man's Way 1964,Mr 12,40:3
That Darn Cat 1965,D 3,44:1
Sullivan, Mary
My Wife's Best Friend 1952,O 11,17:2
Sullivan, Maxine
St Louis Blues 1939,F 9,17:2
Sullivan, Michael (Producer)
Goal 1967,Ja 19,26:1
Sullivan, Sean
2001 A Space Odyssey 1968,Ap 4,58:1
Sullivan, Wallace (Original Author)
Laughing Irish Eyes 1936,Ap 4,11:2
Libeled Lady 1936,O 31,24:2
Four's a Crowd 1938,Ag 12,11:1
Big Guy, The 1940,Ja 1,29:2
Sabotage Squad 1942,Ag 5,16:1
Sullivan, Wallace (Screenwriter)
Sabotage Squad 1942,Ag 5,16:1
Sullivan, William
Courtship of Myles Standish, The 1923,D 31,9:3
Sully, Eve
Kid Millions 1934,N 12,17:2
Sully, Francois
Somewhere in France 1943,Jl 12,11:2
Sully, Frank
Mary Burns, Fugitive 1935,N 16,19:2
High, Wide and Handsome 1937,Jl 22,15:1
Daughter of Shanghai 1937,D 24,21:2
Hold That Co-ed 1938,S 24,13:1
Thanks For Everything 1938,D 10,13:2
Some Like It Hot 1939,My 25,31:2
Night of Nights, The 1939,D 28,17:1
Grapes of Wrath, The 1940,Ja 25,17:2
Doctor Takes a Wife, The 1940,Je 15,12:2
Cross Country Romance 1940,Jl 19,22:3
Return of Frank James, The 1940,Ag 10,16:4
Young People 1940,Ag 24,16:2
Submarine Zone; (Escape To Glory)
   1941,Ap 7,13:2
Girl, a Guy and a Gob, A 1941,Ap 24,25:3
Private Nurse 1941,Ag 29,13:3
Two Yanks in Trinidad 1942,Ap 6,19:4
Parachute Nurse 1942,Jl 27,18:2
Boogie Man Will Get You, The 1942,O 12,12:4
My Sister Eileen 1942,O 23,15:1
They Got Me Covered 1943,Mr 5,20:2
More the Merrier, The 1943,My 14,17:1
Two Senoritas From Chicago 1943,Ag 6,10:4
Thousands Cheer 1943,S 14,27:1
Secret Command 1944,Je 14,16:2
Two Girls and a Sailor 1944,Je 15,16:1
Along Came Jones 1945,Jl 19,8:7
Renegades 1946,Jl 11,18:2
Wild Harvest 1947,N 13,33:2
Bodyhold 1949,D 12,29:4
With a Song in my Heart 1952,Ap 5,20:2
Naked Street, The 1955,O 1,11:2
Sully, Robert
Heavenly Body, The 1944,Mr 24,17:3
Meet Me in St Louis 1944,N 29,20:2
Love Letters 1945,Ag 27,22:3
Sulochana
Jungle, The 1952,O 2,32:3
Sultan, Arne (Original Author)
Boys' Night Out 1962,Je 22,15:2
Promise her Anything 1966,F 23,46:1
3 on a Couch 1966,Jl 7,30:1
Sulyok, Maria
Szerelmi Almok 1937,Ja 5,19:2
Oeroek Titok, Az; Eternal Secret, The
   1940,Mr 9,19:3
Sulzberger, Cyrus L (Original Author)
Playground, The 1965,O 4,00:0
Sumac, Yma
Secret of the Incas 1954,My 29,13:3
Omar Khayyam 1957,Ag 24,12:4
Sumitra
Gyandev of India 1943,Ap 10,12:5
Summerfield, Eleanor
Dulcimer Street 1948,N 8,24:2
Laughter in Paradise 1951,N 12,21:2
Story of Mandy, The 1953,F 24,21:3
Both Sides of the Law 1954,Ja 12,19:2
Blackout 1954,My 22,8:2
Tears for Simon 1957,Ap 18,35:2
It's Great to be Young 1957,D 26,23:3
Cry From the Streets, A 1959,F 24,32:2
Running Man, The 1963,O 3,31:1
Operation Snafu 1965,My 22,18:1
Summers, Don
When Willie Comes Marching Home
   1950,F 18,9:2
Wagonmaster 1950,Je 19,17:2

Summers, George
Edge of the World, The 1938,S 12,13:2
U-Boat 29 1939,O 6,31:3
Summers, Hope
Inherit the Wind 1960,O 13,41:1
Couch, The 1962,F 22,20:3
Summers, James (Miscellaneous)
Hansel and Gretel 1954,O 11,33:1
Summers, Jeremy (Director)
Ferry Cross the Mersey 1965,F 20,16:2
Vengeance of Fu Manchu, The 1968,F 15,47:1
Summers, Jerry
Surf Party 1964,Mr 12,40:4
Summers, Richard (Original Author)
San Francisco Story, The 1952,My 10,16:4
Summers, Walter (Director)
Battles of Coronel and Falkland Islands, The
   1928,F 9,28:4
Battle of Mons, The 1929,Mr 18,30:6
Betrayal, The 1929,Ap 29,29:2
Lost Patrol, The 1929,D 16,34:2
Suspense 1930,N 8,21:3
Man From Chicago, The 1931,Ja 16,27:1
Flying Fool 1931,O 19,28:1
River of Unrest 1937,N 27,21:2
Summers, Walter (Original Author)
Flying Fool 1931,O 19,28:1
Summers, Walter (Screenwriter)
Dead Men Tell no Tales 1939,Jl 24,9:2
Human Monster, The 1940,Mr 25,11:2
Summerton, George (Cinematographer)
Ingagi 1931,Mr 17,34:3
Summerville, Amelia
Romola 1924,D 2,13:2
Great Deception, The 1926,Ag 9,10:3
Summerville, Slim
Beloved Rogue, The 1927,Mr 14,16:1
Chinese Parrot, The 1928,Ja 2,28:1
Last Warning, The 1929,Ja 7,36:2
Strong Boy 1929,Ap 1,22:1
Tiger Rose 1929,D 25,23:1
Troopers Three 1930,F 17,17:6
All Quiet on The Western Front 1930,Ap 30,29:1
Little Accident 1930,Ag 4,13:4
Spoilers, The 1930,S 20,15:4
See America Thirst 1930,D 12,35:3
Free Love 1930,D 15,29:1
Front Page, The 1931,Mr 20,29:1
Bad Sister 1931,Mr 30,25:2
Reckless Living 1931,D 5,21:2
Heaven on Earth 1931,D 19,16:4
Tom Brown of Culver 1932,Jl 30,16:5
Air Mail 1932,N 7,20:3
They Just Had to Get Married 1933,F 13,11:4
Out all Night 1933,Ap 8,16:2
Her First Mate 1933,S 2,14:5
Love, Honor and Oh, Baby! 1933,O 28,20:3
Their big Moment 1934,S 6,22:4
Life Begins at 40 1935,Ap 5,21:3
Farmer Takes a Wife, The 1935,Ag 9,21:2
Way Down East 1935,O 31,16:2
Country Doctor, The 1936,Mr 13,32:2 (Incorrect
   in this edition; use 1936,Mr 13,27:2 elsewhere)
Captain January 1936,Ap 25,21:1
White Fang 1936,Jl 18,18:2
Pepper 1936,Ag 24,11:2
Reunion 1936,N 27,27:1
Off to the Races 1937,F 6,15:2
Love Is News 1937,Mr 6,10:1
Fifty Roads to Town 1937,Je 5,21:1
Road Back, The 1937,Je 18,25:2
Rebecca of Sunnybrook Farm 1938,Mr 26,12:1
Kentucky Moonshine 1938,My 21,9:2
Five of a Kind 1938,O 31,12:2
Submarine Patrol 1938,N 19,9:2
Up the River 1938,D 3,11:2
Jesse James 1939,Ja 14,13:1
Charlie Chan in Reno 1939,My 31,27:2
Anne of Windy Poplars 1940,Ag 23,13:3
Gold Rush Maisie 1940,S 2,19:2
Western Union 1941,F 7,23:2
Tobacco Road 1941,F 21,16:2
Highway West 1941,Ag 8,13:4
Bride by Mistake 1944,S 16,20:2
Hoodlum Saint, The 1946,Je 27,29:1
Sumner, Cid Ricketts (Original Author)
Pinky 1949,S 30,28:2
Tammy and the Bachelor 1957,Je 15,10:7
Sumner, Geoffrey
Mr Potts Goes to Moscow 1953,S 3,15:2
Always a Bride 1954,My 28,19:2
Cul de Sac 1966,N 8,44:2
Sumner, Robin
Young Cassidy 1965,Mr 23,35:1
Sunasky, Irving (Miscellaneous)
Weddings and Babies 1960,O 6,51:3
Sundberg, Clinton
Undercurrent 1946,N 29,36:2
Love Laughs at Andy Hardy 1947,Ja 8,28:2
Mighty McGurk, The 1947,Ap 4,19:4
Hucksters, The 1947,Jl 18,21:2
Living in a Big Way 1947,O 10,31:4
Good News 1947,D 5,33:2

Sundberg, Clinton— Cont
Easter Parade 1948,Jl 1,19:3
Date with Judy, A 1948,Ag 7,8:2
Mr Peabody and the Mermaid 1948,Ag 14,6:5
Good Sam 1948,S 17,28:2
Kissing Bandit, The 1948,N 19,35:2
Words and Music 1948,D 10,34:2
Command Decision 1949,Ja 20,34:2
Barkleys of Broadway, The 1949,My 5,34:2
Big Jack 1949,My 23,27:4
In the Good Old Summertime 1949,Ag 5,23:2
Key to the City 1950,F 2,31:2
Father Is a Bachelor 1950,F 23,33:3
Annie Get Your Gun 1950,My 18,37:1
Duchess of Idaho 1950,Jl 21,15:3
Toast of New Orleans, The 1950,S 30,13:3
Two Weeks With Love 1950,N 24,31:2
Mrs O'Malley and Mr Malone 1951,F 23,33:2
On the Riviera 1951,My 24,47:1
Fat Man, The 1951,My 25,31:2
As Young as You Feel 1951,Ag 3,10:6
Belle of New York, The 1952,Mr 6,25:6
Girl Next Door, The 1953,S 5,7:4
Caddy, The 1953,S 18,16:6
Main Street to Broadway 1953,O 14,34:1
Birds and the Bees, The 1956,Ap 23,22:1
Bachelor in Paradise 1961,N 17,41:2
Hotel 1967,Ja 20,27:1
Sunderland, Nan
Sweepings 1933,Mr 24,22:3
Unconquered 1947,O 11,11:2
Sunderland, Scott
Pygmalion 1938,D 8,34:2
Goodbye Mr Chips 1939,My 16,27:2
Sundholm, Bill
Last Man, The 1932,S 17,18:4
Sundholm, Oscar W
Adventure's End 1937,D 20,23:2
Sundquist, Folke
One Summer of Happiness 1955,Mr 22,35:2
Wild Strawberries 1959,Je 23,37:1
Sundstrom, Florence
Rose Tattoo, The 1955,D 13,55:1
Vagabond King, The 1956,S 13,39:6
Spring Reunion 1957,My 6,25:2
Bachelor in Paradise 1961,N 17,41:2
Sundstrom, Frank
Song of my Heart 1948,Mr 5,17:3
Katrina 1949,N 18,35:3
Loving Couples 1966,S 20,38:1
491 1967,D 21,45:1
Sundstrom, Kurt-Olaf
Miss Julie 1952,Ap 8,35:2
Sunshine, Bunny
Mr Skeffington 1944,My 26,23:2
Superstar, Ingrid
I, A Man 1967,Ag 25,28:1
Bike Boy 1967,O 6,31:2
**** 1967,D 17,94:5
Supervia, Conchita
Evensong 1934,N 17,12:1
Suphaphongs, Ngamia
Bridge on the River Kwai 1957,D 19,39:1
Supplee, Cuyler
Spirit of the U S A, The 1924,My 21,22:3
Last Edition, The 1925,N 11,27:3
Surdez, Georges (Original Author)
South Sea Love 1928,F 7,30:3
Surgal, A M (Screenwriter)
Mickey One 1965,S 9,36:1
Surgutchoff, Ilya (Original Author)
Man Who Broke the Bank at Monte Carlo, The
   1935,N 15,20:2
If This Be Sin 1950,Jl 1,9:2
Surin, Fred (Director)
Bride Is Much too Beautiful, The 1958,Ja 21,35:1
Surina, Daniela
China Is Near 1968,Ja 9,37:1
Surovtsey, B
Sadko 1953,Je 1,18:6
Surranna
John Goldfarb, Please Come Home
   1965,Mr 25,42:4
Surtee Twins
Lord of the Flies 1963,Ag 20,37:1
Susa, Charlotte
Tiger von Berlin, Der 1930,S 15,29:3
D-Zug 13 Hat Verspaetung 1931,Ag 10,18:3
Zwei Menschen 1931,D 23,27:3
Hirsekorn Greift Ein 1932,Je 10,22:3
Koenigin der Unterwelt 1932,D 9,26:5
Zapfenstreich am Rhein 1933,F 2,21:6
Walzerparadies 1933,Mr 4,11:3
Alles um Eine Frau 1935,D 21,11:1
Erbe in Pretoria, Das 1936,Ap 18,19:3
Die Ganze Welt Dreht Sich um Liebe
   1936,N 27,27:2
Sie und die Drei; She and the Three
   1938,D 10,13:3
Henker Fraven und Soldaten; Hangmen, Women
   and Soldiers 1940,Ja 13,11:3
Susaki, Katsuya (Screenwriter)
None but the Brave 1965,F 25,24:1

Susann, Jacqueline
Valley of the Dolls 1967,D 16,51:1
Susann, Jacqueline (Original Author)
Valley of the Dolls 1967,D 16,51:1
Sushkevich, V
Resurrection 1963,O 7,35:2
Susini, Enrique T (Director)
Chrismosa, La; Gossiper, The 1940,Mr 30,11:2
Termina Siempre Asi; It Always Ends That Way 1940,S 3,21:3
Susini, Marie
Mouchette 1968,S 21,26:1
Susnin, A
Problem Child 1955,Ja 24,20:5
Suss, Bernard
True Confession 1937,D 16,35:2
Sussenguth, Walther
Schimmelreiter, Der; Rider of the White Horse, The 1935,F 25,13:3
Sussin, Mathilde
Waltz Dream, The 1926,Jl 26,13:2
U-Boat 9 1929,Ja 22,23:1
It's Easy to Become a Father 1929,Je 24,27:1
Susskind, David (Producer)
Edge of the City 1957,Ja 30,33:2
Raisin in the Sun, A 1961,Mr 30,24:1
Requiem for a Heavyweight 1962,O 17,35:1
All the Way Home 1963,O 30,46:1
Susskind, H W (Composer)
Crisis 1939,Mr 13,12:2
Sutch, Herbert
Scarlet Days 1919,N 10,18:2
One Exciting Night 1922,O 24,17:3
White Rose, The 1923,My 23,18:3
Sutherland, Anne
My Sin 1931,S 11,24:2
Sutherland, Dick
Masters of Men 1923,My 15,22:1
Shriek of Araby, The 1923,Je 11,16:2
Red Lily, The 1924,S 29,10:1
Tornado, The 1924,D 15,14:1
Beloved Rogue, The 1927,Mr 14,16:1
Claw, The 1927,My 11,28:3
Sutherland, Donald
Die! Die! My Darling 1965,My 20,52:1
Bedford Incident, The 1965,N 3,43:1
Dirty Dozen, The 1967,Je 16,36:1
Interlude 1968,Jl 3,26:1
Oedipus the King 1968,S 19,62:2
Split, The 1968,N 5,55:2
Joanna 1968,N 25,54:1
Sutherland, E J (Original Author)
Road to Yesterday, The 1925,D 1,22:4
Sutherland, Edward
Conrad in Quest of his Youth 1920,N 8,20:2
Sutherland, Edward (Director)
Coming Through 1925,F 18,17:3
Regular Fellow, A 1925,O 5,25:2
Behind the Front 1926,F 10,16:2
It's the old Army Game 1926,Jl 5,6:4
We're in the Navy Now 1926,N 8,19:2
Love's Greatest Mistake 1927,F 21,14:2
Fireman, Save My Child 1927,O 10,24:1
What a Night! 1928,D 24,11:1
Dance of Life, The 1929,Ag 16,18:6
Fast Company 1929,O 5,22:5
Saturday Night Kid, The 1929,N 16,25:2
Pointed Heels 1929,D 28,11:1
Social Lion, The 1930,Je 14,9:4
Gang Buster, The 1931,Ja 24,15:1
June Moon 1931,Mr 14,23:2
Palmy Days 1931,S 24,21:2
Sky Devils 1932,Mr 4,17:3
Mr Robinson Crusoe 1932,S 22,25:4
Secrets of the French Police 1932,D 12,18:4
Murders in the Zoo 1933,Ap 3,13:4
International House 1933,My 27,11:5
Too Much Harmony 1933,S 23,11:5
Mississippi 1935,Ap 18,27:2
Diamond Jim 1935,Ag 24,18:2
Poppy 1936,Je 18,19:1
Champagne Waltz 1937,F 4,17:2
Every Day's a Holiday 1938,Ja 27,17:2
Flying Deuces, The 1939,N 24,29:2
Boys From Syracuse, The 1940,Ag 1,25:2
Beyond Tomorrow 1940,S 27,27:1
One Night in the Tropics 1940,D 20,33:2
Invisible Woman, The 1941,Ja 9,27:2
Nine Loves Are not Enough 1941,O 30,27:2
Sing Your Worries Away 1942,My 15,25:2
Army Surgeon 1942,N 5,35:2
Navy Comes Through, The 1942,N 12,30:3
Dixie 1943,Je 24,26:2
Follow the Boys 1944,Ap 26,24:6
Secret Command 1944,Je 14,16:2
Having Wonderful Crime 1945,Ap 13,15:2
Abie's Irish Rose 1946,D 23,19:4
Sutherland, Edward (Producer)
Zenobia 1939,My 15,15:2
Abie's Irish Rose 1946,D 23,19:4
Sutherland, Ethel
June Moon 1931,Mr 14,23:2
Cock of the Air 1932,Ja 25,20:3

Sutherland, Grant
Edge of the World, The 1938,S 12,13:2
U-Boat 29 1939,O 6,31:3
Sutherland, Hope
Potash and Perlmutter 1923,S 24,5:4
Sutherland, James
Little Kidnappers, The 1954,S 2,18:1
Sutherland, John
Silver King, The 1919,Ja 13,9:3
Sutherland, John (Original Author)
Flight Command 1941,Ja 17,21:2
Sutherland, Sidney (Original Author)
Laughing Irish Eyes 1936,Ap 4,11:2
Allotment Wives 1945,N 22,39:3
Sutherland, Sidney (Screenwriter)
I Sell Anything 1934,D 27,25:2
Adventure's End 1937,D 20,23:2
Allotment Wives 1945,N 22,39:3
Sutherland, Victor
Lone Star 1952,F 2,11:4
Captive City, The 1952,Mr 27,34:2
We're not Married 1952,Jl 12,16:2
Powder River 1953,Jl 4,7:2
Donovan's Brain 1954,Ja 21,28:2
Sutro, Alfred (Original Author)
Society Scandal, A 1924,Mr 10,18:2
Laughing Lady, The 1930,Ja 4,21:1
Sutro, John (Producer)
Way Ahead, The 1945,Je 4,22:3
Glass Mountain, The 1950,My 18,37:3
Kisenga, Man of Africa 1952,Mr 7,18:2
Sutton, Charles
Democracy, The Vision Restored 1920,Ag 25,6:4
Sutton, Dolores
Where Angels Go-Trouble Follows 1968,Ap 11,51:1
Sutton, Dudley
Rotten to the Core 1965,Jl 20,39:2
Leather Boys, The 1965,N 9,50:1
Sutton, Frank
Marty 1955,Ap 12,25:3
Town Without Pity 1961,O 11,53:1
Satan Bug, The 1965,Ap 15,38:1
Sutton, George Jr (Original Author)
Framed 1927,Je 20,25:3
Sutton, Gertrude
Big News 1929,O 7,22:1
Anybody's Woman 1930,Ag 16,8:3
Sooky 1931,D 21,28:4
Sailor Be Good 1933,F 27,11:2
Working Man, The 1933,Ap 21,20:3
Say It in French 1938,D 1,29:1
Sutton, Grady
This Reckless Age 1932,Ja 9,21:1
Pack up Your Troubles 1932,O 1,10:4
Hot Saturday 1932,N 5,12:5
Only Yesterday 1933,N 10,25:1
Laddie 1935,My 6,22:3
Man on the Flying Trapeze 1935,Ag 3,16:2
Alice Adams 1935,Ag 16,11:3
My Man Godfrey 1936,S 19,18:1 (Incorrect in this edition; use 1936,S 18,18:1 elsewhere)
King of the Royal Mounted 1936,S 29,35:2
Valiant Is the Word for Carrie 1936,O 8,27:2
Pigskin Parade 1936,N 14,23:3
Waikiki Wedding 1937,Mr 25,29:1
We Have our Moments 1937,Ap 30,17:3
Turn off the Moon 1937,My 20,17:2
Love Takes Flight 1937,S 27,24:3
Stage Door 1937,O 8,27:2
Vivacious Lady 1938,Je 3,17:3
Having Wonderful Time 1938,Jl 8,11:2
Three Loves Has Nancy 1938,S 2,21:2
Mad Miss Manton, The 1938,O 21,27:2
Hard To Get 1938,N 14,15:2
You Can't Cheat an Honest Man 1939,F 20,13:2
It's a Wonderful World 1939,My 19,27:2
Angels Wash Their Faces 1939,S 4,16:2
Three Sons 1939,N 24,29:3
Torrid Zone 1940,My 18,11:3
Bank Dick, The 1940,D 13,29:2
She Knew All the Answers 1941,Je 20,28:4
Father takes a Wife 1941,S 5,19:3
Whispering Ghosts 1942,My 18,19:4
Lady Takes a Chance, A 1943,S 16,25:2
What a Woman 1943,D 3,27:2
Great Moment, The 1944,N 13,15:2
Royal Scandal, A 1945,Ap 12,19:2
Captain Eddie 1945,Ag 9,24:2
My Wild Irish Rose 1947,D 25,32:2
My Dear Secretary 1949,F 14,15:4
White Christmas 1954,O 15,16:3
Jumbo 1962,D 7,49:1
Sutton, Jan
Street Corner 1948,D 4,9:4
Sutton, John
Bulldog Drummond's Revenge 1937,D 17,33:2
Four Men and a Prayer 1938,My 7,18:1
Arrest Bulldog Drummond 1939,Ja 12,23:2
Susannah of the Mounties 1939,Je 24,13:2
Bulldog Drummond's Bride 1939,Jl 13,17:2
Tower of London 1939,D 12,37:2
Charlie McCarthy, Detective 1939,D 25,29:2

Sutton, John — Cont
Invisible Man Returns, The 1940,Ja 16,19:2
South to Karanga 1940,Ag 9,19:1
Hudson's Bay 1941,Ja 10,23:2
Yank in the R A F, A 1941,S 27,11:3
Moon Over her Shoulder 1941,N 5,31:2
My Gal Sal 1942,My 1,23:1
Ten Gentlemen From West Point 1942,Je 5,23:3
Thunder Birds 1942,O 29,19:2
Tonight We Raid Calais 1943,Ap 15,20:2
Jane Eyre 1944,F 4,12:5
Hour Before the Dawn, The 1944,My 11,25:6
Claudia and David 1946,Ag 15,19:2
Captain from Castile 1947,D 26,22:4
Adventures of Casanova 1948,Mr 22,18:3
Mickey 1948,Jl 19,11:2
Three Musketeers, The 1948,O 21,33:2
Fan, The 1949,Ap 2,12:2
Bride of Vengeance 1949,Ap 7,38:2
Bagdad 1949,D 24,11:4
Second Woman, The 1951,F 2,19:2
Payment on Demand 1951,F 16,21:2
Second Face, The 1951,Mr 2,21:3
David and Bathsheba 1951,Ag 15,23:2
Thief of Damascus 1952,My 8,37:2
Lady in the Iron Mask 1952,Jl 5,7:2
Golden Hawk, The 1952,O 18,16:4
My Cousin Rachel 1952,D 26,20:2
Sangaree 1953,Je 5,19:1
Death of a Scoundrel 1956,N 6,30:1
Amazon Trader, The 1956,N 17,17:6
Bat, The 1959,D 17,51:4
Sutton, Julia
Half a Sixpence 1968,F 21,60:3
Sutton, Kay
Saint in New York, The 1938,My 26,31:2
Smashing the Rackets 1938,Ag 9,22:5
I'm From the City 1938,Ag 19,13:4
Carefree 1938,S 23,35:1
Mad Miss Manton, The 1938,O 21,27:2
S O S Tidal Wave 1939,Je 22,19:3
Sutton, Paul
Spy Ring, The 1938,Ja 15,19:1
Shadows Over Shanghai 1938,D 1,29:2
Girl and the Gambler, The 1939,Je 28,17:3
Balalaika 1939,D 15,33:2
Little Old New York 1940,F 3,9:2
Ride on Vaquero 1941,Ap 19,20:2
Wild Geese Calling 1941,Ag 30,10:2
In old California 1942,Je 18,25:3
Sutton-Vane (Original Author)
Outward Bound 1930,S 18,28:3
Suttor, Betty
Jedda the Uncivilized 1957,F 28,18:7
Suyin, Han (Original Author)
Love Is a Many-Splendored Thing 1955,Ag 19,10:1
Suzanne, George
Seventh Cross, The 1944,S 29,18:1
Suzuki, Hideo (Director)
Girl in the Mist 1959,D 23,22:1
Walleyed Nippon 1963,S 3,36:1
Suzuki, Hyogo (Screenwriter)
Imposter, The 1955,Mr 23,27:1
Suzuki, Ikuzo (Miscellaneous)
Tokyo File 212 1951,Je 1,20:7
Suzuki, Kazuo
Angry Island 1960,F 28,31:1
Suzuki, Naoyuki (Screenwriter)
Bushido 1964,S 13,39:1
Svankmajer, Jan (Director)
Ravickarna 1968,Jl 19,30:1
Svanteidt, Tomas
To Love; Att Alska 1964,S 23,45:3 (Incorrect in this edition; use 1964,S 23,54:1 elsewhere)
Sved, Sandor
Hello Budapest 1935,N 14,17:4
Mother Love 1938,My 7,18:2
Svedlund, Doris
Devil's Wanton, The 1962,Jl 5,21:2
Svel, Josef
Firemen's Ball, The 1968,S 30,60:1
Svendsen, Sunja
Greenwich Village Story 1963,Jl 12,14:3
Svennberg, Tore
Stroke of Midnight, The 1922,Je 5,16:2
Dream Waltz, The 1930,D 27,16:3
Surf, The 1949,D 17,15:2
Sverdlin, L
University of Life 1941,F 26,17:1
Sverdlin, Leonid
In the Far East 1937,O 20,27:3
Sverdlin, Lev
Defense of Volotchayevsk, The 1938,Ag 11,13:3
Guerrilla Brigade 1942,Ap 14,17:2
Adventures in Bokhara 1944,Ag 21,9:4
Marriage 1945,F 22,31:3
Wait for Me 1945,Mr 19,23:3
Days and Nights 1946,Ap 29,24:4
Far for Moscow 1951,Jl 2,16:6
Sverdlova, R
Krasnaya Derevnya 1935,My 2,17:1

Sversson, Harald
Loerdagskvaellar 1936,F 13,25:3
Sveshnikova, Liubov
Country Bride 1938,Je 4,18:2
Svetlani, G
Mashenka 1942,N 21,10:7
Svetlanov, G (Director)
Songs Over the Dnieper 1958,Jl 24,18:1
Svetlov, B
Professor Mamlock 1938,N 8,26:2
Svetlov, M (Screenwriter)
If War Comes Tomorrow 1938,Jl 14,17:2
Svetlov, N
Dream of a Cossack 1952,F 18,15:2
Sveva, Carla
Giovanni De Medici, The Leader 1940,Ja 5,15:4
Svideteley, E (Miscellaneous)
Sadko 1953,Je 1,18:6
Svierkier, Anna
Day of Wrath 1948,Ap 26,27:2
Svilovoi, Elena (Director)
New China, The 1952,Mr 10,18:4
Svitak, J
Ecstasy of Young Love 1936,Mr 10,27:3
Svoboda, V
Victors and the Vanquished, The 1950,My 1,18:2
Svoboda, N K
Lenin in October 1938,Ap 2,18:1
Lenin in 1918 1939,Je 27,27:2
Svobodin, Nikolai
Great Glinka, The 1947,D 22,30:2
Svobova, Lena
Sailor From the Comet, The 1959,Ag 3,21:2
Svohodin, Nikolai
Sailor From the Comet, The 1959,Ag 3,21:2
Svormova, Libuse
Murder Czech Style 1968,Ag 20,33:1
Swain, Charles
Anna Lucasta 1959,Ja 15,27:1
Swain, John D (Original Author)
It's Great to be Alive 1933,Jl 8,14:6
Swain, Mack
Pilgrim, The 1923,F 26,15:1
Gold Rush, The 1925,Ag 17,10:3
Hands Up 1926,Ja 18,26:2
Ibanez's Torrent 1926,F 22,14:1
Sea Horses 1926,F 23,26:5
Kiki 1926,Ap 6,26:4
Footloose Windows 1926,Je 22,21:2
Nervous Wreck, The 1926,O 12,30:2
Her big Night 1926,O 13,21:1
Beloved Rogue, The 1927,Mr 14,16:1
See You in Jail 1927,Ap 4,30:5
Mockery 1927,Ag 22,21:3
My Best Girl 1927,N 7,26:4
Texas Steer, A 1928,Ja 2,28:1
Gentlemen Prefer Blondes 1928,Ja 16,24:1
Caught in the Fog 1928,D 4,29:1
Last Warning, The 1929,Ja 7,36:2
Cohens and the Kellys In Atlantic City, The
1929,Mr 18,30:6
Locked Door, The 1930,Ja 20,21:1
Finn and Hattie 1931,Ja 31,15:1
Gold Rush, The 1942,Ap 20,17:1
When Comedy Was King 1960,Mr 30,42:1
Swales, Frank
Surrender 1931,N 28,20:4
Swan, Buddy
Citizen Kane 1941,My 2,25:1
Sullivans, The 1944,F 10,19:2
Sweet and Low Down 1944,O 19,19:2
Centennial Summer 1946,Jl 18,20:2
Swan, Paul
Diana the Huntress 1916,Je 19,9:5 (In Addenda)
Illiac Passion, The 1968,Ap 19,40:1
Swan, William
Lady in a Cage 1964,Je 11,27:1
Swanbeck, Alex
Walls of Hell, The 1965,N 18,55:3
Swanger, Robert
I, The Jury 1953,Ag 22,8:2
Swanick, Peter
African Queen, The 1952,F 21,24:3
Swann, Bob
Emil and the Detectives 1964,D 24,8:3
Swann, Francis (Miscellaneous)
That Way With Women 1947,F 15,20:4
Swann, Francis (Original Author)
Gay Intruders, The 1949,Je 28,33:4
Swann, Francis (Screenwriter)
Shine on Harvest Moon 1944,Mr 11,10:2
Make Your own Bed 1944,My 27,12:2
Time, The Place And The Girl, The
1946,D 27,14:3
Love and Learn 1947,My 3,10:3
Gay Intruders, The 1949,Je 28,33:4
711 Ocean Drive 1950,Jl 20,21:2
Swann, Frank
Young People 1940,Ag 24,16:2
Swann, Frederick Albert (Original Author)
Man Who Broke the Bank at Monte Carlo, The
1935,N 15,20:2

Swanson, Audrey
Solid Gold Cadillac, The 1956,O 25,40:3
Swanson, Donald (Director)
Magic Garden, The 1952,F 6,24:2
Swanson, Donald (Producer)
Magic Garden, The 1952,F 6,24:2
Swanson, Donald (Screenwriter)
Magic Garden, The 1952,F 6,24:2
Swanson, Gloria
Don't Change Your Husband 1919,F 3,13:2
For Better, For Worse 1919,Ap 28,13:2
Male and Female 1919,N 24,13:1
Why Change Your Wife 1920,Ap 26,18:1
Something to Think About 1920,O 18,13:1
Great Moment, The 1921,Jl 25,8:3
Affairs of Anatol, The 1921,S 12,16:1
Don't Tell Everything 1921,D 12,20:2
Beyond the Rocks 1922,My 8,14:3
Impossible Mrs Bellew, The 1922,O 23,10:1
Prodigal Daughters 1923,Ap 17,26:3
Bluebeard's 8th Wife 1923,Ag 7,20:2
Zaza 1923,S 17,18:2
Humming Bird, The 1924,Ja 14,2:1
Society Scandal, A 1924,Mr 10,18:2
Manhandled 1924,Jl 29,9:2
Her Love Story 1924,O 7,26:1
Wages of Virtue 1924,N 24,15:3
Madame Sans Gene 1925,Ap 18,19:1
Coast of Folly, The 1925,Ag 31,19:3
Stage Struck 1925,N 16,19:4
Untamed Lady, The 1926,Mr 16,22:5
Fine Manners 1926,Ag 30,10:3
Love of Sunya, The 1927,Mr 12,12:2
Sadie Thompson 1928,F 6,12:3
Trespasser, The 1929,N 2,14:6
What a Widow 1930,O 4,15:2
Indiscreet 1931,My 7,21:4
Tonight or Never 1931,D 18,29:2
Perfect Understanding 1933,F 23,20:2
Music in the Air 1934,D 14,29:3
Father takes a Wife 1941,S 5,19:3
Sunset Boulevard 1950,Ag 11,15:2
3 for Bedroom C 1952,Je 27,18:3
When Comedy Was King 1960,Mr 30,42:1
Swanson, H N (Original Author)
Big Business Girl 1931,Je 12,27:1
Half-Naked Truth, The 1932,D 31,10:1
Swanson, Knut (Screenwriter)
Edge of Eternity 1960,F 25,34:2
Swanson, Maureen
Moulin Rouge 1953,F 11,33:5
Knights of the Round Table 1954,Ja 8,17:2
Spanish Gardner, The 1957,S 9,21:2
Town Like Alice, A 1958,S 22,27:1
Swanson, Neil H (Original Author)
Allegheny Uprising 1939,N 10,27:3
Unconquered 1947,O 11,11:2
Swanson, Ruth
So Big 1953,O 22,34:2
Swanson, Wendell V
Unidentified Flying Objects 1956,Je 13,46:2
Swanstroem, Karin
Doctor's Women, The 1929,Je 3,27:2
Nar Rosorna Sla Ut 1931,F 10,24:4
Troette Teodor 1932,Ja 18,18:4
Vi Som Gar Koeksvaegen 1933,O 7,18:5
Natt, En 1935,Ja 29,24:1
Swedenhielms 1935,S 6,12:3
Paa Solsidan 1936,Ag 26,16:3
Swanstrom, Arthur (Composer)
Take a Chance 1933,N 27,20:3
Swanton, Harold (Screenwriter)
Hellions, The 1962,Mr 15,28:2
Ballad of Josie, The 1968,Mr 14,51:2
Swanwick, Peter
Both Sides of the Law 1954,Ja 12,19:2
Murder Reported 1960,Jl 12,39:1
Invasion Quartet 1961,D 11,41:2
Trunk, The 1962,N 1,34:3
Swarthout, Gladys
Rose of the Rancho 1936,Ja 9,25:2
Give Us This Night 1936,Ap 6,18:1
Champagne Waltz 1937,F 4,17:2
Romance in the Dark 1938,Mr 21,18:2
Ambush 1939,F 9,17:2
Swarthout, Glendon (Original Author)
They Came to Cordura 1959,O 22,47:2
Where the Boys Are 1961,Ja 20,22:1
Swartz, Berman (Producer)
Duffy of San Quentin 1954,F 10,38:5
New Faces 1954,F 20,8:7
Swashenko, S
Soil 1930,O 21,34:4
Sweatt, A W
Star Is Born, A 1937,Ap 23,25:1
Swedo, Julie
Ireland's Border Line 1939,O 13,27:3
Sweell, Anna (Original Author)
Black Beauty 1921,F 21,16:1
Sweeney, Augustin
Sandra 1924,D 22,20:2

Sweeney, Bob
Last Hurrah, The 1958,O 24,40:1
Toby Tyler 1960,Ap 20,45:2
Moon Pilot 1962,Ap 6,30:2
Sweeney, Joseph
Soak the Rich 1936,F 5,14:2
Man in the Gray Flannel Suit, The
1956,Ap 13,21:1
Fastest Gun Alive, The 1956,Jl 13,23:3
12 Angry Men 1957,Ap 15,24:1
Sweeney, Robert
South Sea Woman 1953,Je 4,33:6
Sweet, Blanche
Thousand-Dollar Husband, The 1916,My 29,9:2
Storm, The 1916,O 9,12:1
Unpardonable Sin, The 1919,My 3,11:3
Quincy Adams Sawyer 1922,D 18,22:2
In the Palace of the King 1923,D 3,14:1
Anna Christie 1923,D 10,20:1
Those Who Dance 1924,Je 30,16:1
Tess of the D'Urbervilles 1924,Jl 28,12:2
His Supreme Moment 1925,Ap 13,24:1
Sporting Venus, The 1925,My 11,14:3
New Commandment, The 1925,N 10,25:3
Bluebeard's Seven Wives 1925,D 28,19:2
Diplomacy 1926,S 13,18:1
Singed 1927,Jl 12,29:3
Show Girl in Hollywood 1930,My 5,27:3
Silver Horde, The 1930,O 25,20:6
Sweet, Dolph
You're a Big Boy Now 1967,Mr 21,35:3
Swimmer, The 1968,My 16,53:1
Sweet, Harry
Fascinating Youth 1926,My 10,19:1
Hit the Deck 1930,Ja 15,28:6
True to the Navy 1930,My 24,21:2
Carnival Boat 1932,Mr 21,19:5
Sweet, John
Canterbury Tale, A 1949,Ja 24,16:2
Sweet, Kendrick (Producer)
Edge of Eternity 1960,F 25,34:2
Sweet, Sheila
Fuss Over Feathers 1954,D 27,22:6
Angel Who Pawned her Harp, The
1956,F 29,35:2
Swemmer, Arthur
After You, Comrade 1967,Ap 11,54:1
Swenson, Alice
Tanga Tika 1953,O 6,34:4
Swenson, Inga
Miracle Worker, The 1962,My 24,29:2
Advise and Consent 1962,Je 7,31:2
Swenson, Karl
Kings Go Forth 1958,Jl 4,15:2
Hanging Tree, The 1959,F 12,23:1
Gallant Hours, The 1960,Je 23,19:4
Ice Palace 1960,Je 30,22:1
One Foot in Hell 1960,O 20,42:2
North to Alaska 1960,N 11,36:1
Flaming Star 1960,D 17,19:1
Walk on the Wild Side 1962,F 22,20:1
Spiral Road, The 1962,Ag 4,11:2
Prize, The 1964,Ja 24,21:1
Swensson, Carin
Froeken Blir Piga 1937,Ag 12,8:3
Swerling, Jo (Miscellaneous)
It's a Wonderful Life 1946,D 23,19:2
Swerling, Jo (Original Author)
Ten Cents a Dance 1931,Mr 7,17:2
Behind the Mask 1932,My 2,13:2
Below the Sea 1933,Je 3,16:4
Defense Rests, The 1934,Ag 16,20:3
New York Town 1941,N 13,35:2
Lady Takes a Chance, A 1943,S 16,25:2
Guys and Dolls 1955,N 5,26:1
Swerling, Jo (Screenwriter)
Lady by Choice 1934,N 17,12:1
Whole Town's Talking, The 1935,Mr 1,16:2
Love Me Forever 1935,Je 28,24:1
Music Goes 'Round, The 1936,F 22,12:1
Pennies From Heaven 1936,D 10,35:2
Double Wedding 1937,O 22,27:2
Doctor Rhythm 1938,My 19,25:2
I Am the Law 1938,Ag 26,14:2
Made for Each Other 1939,F 17,17:2
Real Glory, The 1939,S 15,26:2
Westerner, The 1940,O 25,25:2
Blood and Sand 1941,My 23,25:3
Confirm or Deny 1941,D 19,35:2
Pride of the Yankees, The 1942,Jl 16,23:1
Crash Dive 1943,Ap 29,25:2
Lifeboat 1944,Ja 13,17:1
Leave Her to Heaven 1945,D 26,15:1
Thunder in the East 1953,F 4,32:2
King of the Roaring Twenties 1961,O 5,43:1
Swickard, Josef
Four Horsemen of the Apocalypse 1921,Mr 7,8:1
Eternal Struggle, The 1923,O 16,21:3
Boy of Flanders, A 1924,Ap 15,24:1
Men 1924,My 5,18:3
Maytime 1924,Je 2,14:3
Poisoned Paradise 1924,Ag 11,16:1
Dante's Inferno 1924,S 30,27:3

Swickard, Josef— Cont
Wizard of Oz, The 1925,Ap 14,26:1
Fifth Avenue Models 1925,My 4,16:2
Keeper of the Bees, The 1925,O 28,29:2
Desert Gold 1926,Mr 23,24:5
Senor Daredevil 1926,Ag 17,15:3
Four Horsemen of the Apocalypse, The
  1926,S 27,27:3
Senorita 1927,My 9,26:4
Time to Love 1927,Je 23,23:3
Old San Francisco 1927,Je 23,23:3
Get Your Man 1927,D 5,26:2
Sharp Shooters 1928,Ja 23,18:3
Street Corners 1929,S 2,16:1
Mamba 1930,Mr 11,25:2
Lost City, The 1935,F 21,23:3
Girl Said No, The 1937,O 18,14:1
You Can't Take It With You 1938,S 2,21:2
Swickard, Josey
Don Juan 1926,Ag 7,6:1 (In Addenda)
Swiderski, Jan
Eighth Day of the Week, The 1959,Mr 24,45:2
Swift, Allen (Narrator)
Slave Trade in the World Today 1964,N 24,44:1
Swift, David (Director)
Pollyanna 1960,My 20,26:1
Parent Trap, The 1961,Je 22,23:1
Interns, The 1962,Ag 9,17:5
Love Is a Ball 1963,Ap 25,38:1
Under the Yum Yum Tree 1963,N 21,43:2
Good Neighbor Sam 1964,Jl 23,19:1
How to Succeed in Business Without Really
  Trying 1967,Mr 10,30:1
Swift, David (Producer)
Good Neighbor Sam 1964,Jl 23,19:1
How to Succeed in Business Without Really
  Trying 1967,Mr 10,30:1
Swift, David (Screenwriter)
Pollyanna 1960,My 20,26:1
Parent Trap, The 1961,Je 22,23:1
Interns, The 1962,Ag 9,17:5
Love Is a Ball 1963,Ap 25,38:1
Under the Yum Yum Tree 1963,N 21,43:2
Good Neighbor Sam 1964,Jl 23,19:1
How to Succeed in Business Without Really
  Trying 1967,Mr 10,30:1
Swift, Don (Original Author)
Let's Sing Again 1936,My 9,11:2
Swift, Don (Screenwriter)
Thunder Mountain 1935,O 2,27:2
Calling of Dan Matthews, The 1936,Ja 25,18:4
Let's Sing Again 1936,My 9,11:2
Mine With the Iron Door, The 1936,Jl 11,11:3
Swift, Jonathan (Original Author)
Gulliver's Travels 1939,D 21,29:1
Three Worlds of Gulliver, The 1960,D 17,19:3
Swift, Kay (Original Author)
Never a Dull Moment 1950,N 22,20:2
Swiggett, Howard (Original Author)
Power and The Prize, the 1956,S 27,42:1
Swinburne, Mercia
Saraband 1949,Je 13,16:3
Swinburne, Nora
Perfect Understanding 1933,F 23,20:2
Man Who Won, The 1933,F 27,11:2
White Face 1933,D 4,22:3
Dinner at the Ritz 1937,D 4,21:1
Citadel, The 1938,N 4,27:2
It Happened to One Man 1941,F 24,11:6
Wings and the Woman 1942,O 8,31:1
Randolph Family 1945,Mr 13,19:4
Jassy 1948,F 20,19:2
Man of Evil 1948,Mr 26,26:2
Quartet (The Colonel's Lady); Colonel's Lady, The
  (Quartet) 1949,Mr 29,30:3
Blind Goddess, The 1949,Je 23,33:3
Christopher Columbus 1949,O 13,33:2
Good Time Girl 1950,S 25,18:5
Operation X 1950,D 11,31:2
River, The 1951,S 11,33:2
Quo Vadis 1951,N 9,22:2
Marry Me 1952,Mr 14,27:3
Landfall 1953,My 11,25:2
Betrayed 1954,S 9,36:1
End of the Affair, The 1955,Ap 29,28:2
Helen of Troy 1956,Ja 27,21:4
Third Man on the Mountain 1959,N 12,27:1
Conspiracy of Hearts 1960,Ap 8,24:1
Interlude 1968,Jl 3,26:1
Swingley, Bill
Luck of the Irish, The 1948,S 16,34:1
Swinley, Ion
Unwritten Law, The 1929,D 24,14:5
Swinstead, Joan
Adam and Evalyn 1950,My 12,33:4
Final Test, The 1954,Ja 26,21:5
SWITZER
See Also SCHWEITZER
Switzer, Carl (Alfalfa)
Wild and Woolly 1937,S 6,20:1
I Love You Again 1940,Ag 16,11:2
War Against Mrs Hadley, The 1942,N 26,40:2
Human Comedy, The 1943,Mr 3,19:2
Johnny Doughboy 1943,My 6,25:3

Courage of Lassie 1946,Jl 25,18:5
State of the Union 1948,Ap 23,28:1
Letter to Three Wives, A 1949,Ja 21,24:2
Pat and Mike 1952,Je 19,32:6
Track of the Cat 1954,D 2,38:2
Defiant Ones, The 1958,S 25,29:1
Switzer, Carl Alfalfa
Scandal Street 1938,F 5,19:2 (In Addenda)
Swope, Herbert B Jr (Producer)
Hilda Crane 1956,My 3,35:2
True Story of Jesse James, The 1957,Mr 23,17:2
Bravados, The 1958,Je 26,23:2
Swope, Herbert Bayard Jr (Producer)
Three Brave Men 1957,Mr 16,13:2
Swope, Margaret
Last Outpost, The 1935,O 5,18:2
Swope, Rusty
Teenage Rebel 1956,N 17,17:6
Swor, Bert
Why Bring That Up? 1929,O 5,22:5
Swor, Bert Jr
Carnation Kid, The 1929,F 25,16:1
Swor, John
Charlie Chan Carries On 1931,Mr 21,15:1
Quick Millions 1931,Ap 18,17:3
Swor, Mabel
For the Love of Mike 1927,Ag 24,27:5
Sybodinou, Anna
300 Spartans, The 1962,S 20,29:2
Sydes, Anthony
Claudia and David 1946,Ag 15,19:2
Sitting Pretty 1948,Mr 11,35:2
Chicken every Sunday 1949,Ja 19,34:2
Cheaper by the Dozen 1950,Ap 1,12:2
Shadow on the Wall 1950,My 19,31:3
SYDNEY
See Also SIDNEY
Sydney, Basil
Romance 1920,My 17,19:3
Red Hot Romance 1922,Ja 23,11:4
Transatlantic Tunnel 1935,O 28,16:2
Rhodes 1936,F 29,11:1
Amateur Gentleman, The 1936,Ap 27,19:2
Accused 1936,D 17,35:1
Talk of the Devil 1937,My 15,23:5
Crime Over London 1938,Jl 28,23:2
Secret Four, The 1940,Ap 22,13:2
Ships With Wings 1942,My 25,11:2
48 Hours 1944,Je 26,21:2
Caesar and Cleopatra 1946,S 6,18:2
Jassy 1948,F 20,19:2
Smugglers, The 1948,Mr 29,17:1
Meet Me at Dawn 1948,My 18,26:2
Hamlet 1948,S 30,32:2
Angel With the Trumpet 1951,D 21,21:5
Ivanhoe 1952,Ag 1,8:2
Magic Box, The 1952,S 24,40:2
Salome 1953,Mr 25,37:1
Hell Below Zero 1954,Jl 17,7:3
Simba 1955,O 22,24:2
Star of India 1956,Ag 28,11:1
Around the World in 80 Days 1956,O 18,37:1
Island in the Sun 1957,Je 13,37:1
Sea Wife 1957,D 5,45:2
John Paul Jones 1959,Je 17,39:1
Devil's Disciple, The 1959,Ag 21,12:1
Three Worlds of Gulliver, The 1960,D 17,19:3
Question of Adultery, A 1961,Jl 6,18:2
Sydney, Derek
Gentlemen Marry Brunettes 1955,O 31,31:5
Abandon Ship 1957,Ap 18,35:1
Hand in Hand 1961,F 7,41:3
Sydney, Gloria
Man of Evil 1948,Mr 26,26:2
Syfan, Thomas
I'd Climb the Highest Mountain 1951,My 10,38:1
Sykes, Eric
Invasion Quartet 1961,D 11,41:2
Coming-Out Party, A 1962,Jl 31,19:2
Kill or Cure 1962,N 13,43:4
Heavens Above! 1963,My 21,28:2
One Way Pendulum 1965,Mr 3,34:3
Those Magnificent Men in Their Flying Machines
  (Or How I Flew From London to Paris in 25
  Hours and 11 Minutes) 1965,Je 17,27:1
Rotten to the Core 1965,Jl 20,39:2
Liquidator, The 1966,O 29,34:1
Spy With a Cold Nose, The 1966,D 20,58:2
Shalako 1968,N 6,32:1
Sykes, Peter (Producer)
Tell Me Lies 1968,F 13,46:3
Sylba, Christina
Take Me Away, My Love 1962,Jl 30,15:5
Sylber, Charles
Guilty as Hell 1932,Ag 6,14:5
Syler, Athene
Passport to China 1961,Mr 23,28:1
Sylla, Cautier
Sextette (Part 5-Seducer's Fate); Seducer's Fate
  (Sextette) 1953,Mr 2,19:2
Sylva, Marguerita
Seventh Victim, The 1943,S 18,11:3

Sylvain
Passing of Joan of Arc, The 1928,Ag 12,VII,3:4
Passion of Jeanne d'Arc, The 1929,Mr 31,VIII,7:1
Sylvain, Claude
Rififi 1956,Je 6,37:1
If all the Guys in the World 1957,Ap 23,34:1
Man in the Raincoat, The 1958,Jl 15,21:2
Sylvain, Jean
Five Day Lover, The 1961,D 14,55:4
Sylvain, Jules (Composer)
Brokiga Blad 1931,N 30,16:2
Sylvain, M
Passion of Joan of Arc, The 1928,Ap 1,IX,5:5 (In
  Addenda)
Sylvain, Madeleine
Wild Oat, The 1956,Je 28,33:2
Sylvain, Marcel
Quebec 1951,Mr 16,34:2
Sylvaine, Vernon (Original Author)
Will any Gentleman? 1955,S 28,70:6
Sylvaine, Vernon (Screenwriter)
Will any Gentleman? 1955,S 28,70:6
Sylvan
Modesty Blaise 1966,Ag 11,27:1
Sylvere, Jacqueline
Dawn Over France 1945,Mr 17,17:2
Sylvester, Bill
Give Us This Day 1949,D 21,41:2
Sylvester, Robert (Original Author)
We Were Strangers 1949,Ap 28,28:2
Big Boodle, The 1957,Mr 12,38:1
Sylvester, Robert (Screenwriter)
Joe Louis Story, The 1953,N 4,29:4
Sylvester, William
Yellow Balloon, The 1954,O 13,28:2
Unholy Four, The 1954,N 20,10:2
Gorgo 1961,Mr 30,24:2
Ring of Treason 1964,My 28,40:3 (Incorrect in
  this edition; use 1964,My 29,15:1 elsewhere)
Man in the Dark 1965,Ja 21,22:1
2001 A Space Odyssey 1968,Ap 4,58:1
Sylvestre, Simone
Tainted 1950,Ja 21,10:2
Sylvia, Gaby
32 Rue de Montmartre 1944,S 28,26:3
Sylviano, Rene (Composer)
Moulin Rouge 1944,N 23,38:2
Sylvie
Crime et Chatiment; Crime and Punishment
  1935,N 13,25:3
End of a Day, The 1939,S 12,28:4
Pasha's Wives, The 1942,Ap 6,19:2
Corbeau, Le; Raven, The 1948,F 24,21:1
Passionnelle 1948,Mr 1,17:2
Angels of the Streets 1950,Ja 17,24:2
Under the Paris Sky 1952,My 6,35:1
Little World of Don Camillo, The
  1953,Ja 14,27:1
Ulysses 1955,Ag 18,17:2
Adulteress, The 1958,Ja 14,42:1
Forbidden Fruit 1959,F 23,19:1
Mirror Has two Faces, The 1959,My 27,31:1
Anatomy of Love 1959,S 29,46:2
Michael Strogoff 1960,My 21,15:1
Family Diary 1963,N 12,48:1
Chateau en Suede; Castle in Switzerland
  1964,O 14,51:1
Shameless Old Lady, The 1966,S 27,52:1
Sym, Igo
Handsome Gigolo, Poor Gigolo 1930,Ag 3,4:1
Wien Du Stadt der Lieder; (Vienna City of Song)
  1931,Mr 20,29:1
Alte Lied, Das 1931,S 11,24:2
Nur am Rhein 1931,S 25,28:7
Szpieg 1934,Mr 5,19:3
Symmes, John B
Manhunt in the Jungle 1958,Ap 12,13:1
Symo, Margit
Zigeunerblut 1935,Ap 8,23:5
Kein Wort von Liebe; Not a Word About Love
  1938,S 10,20:3
Nacht an der Donau, Eine; Night on the Danube,
  A 1938,N 19,9:3
Zigeunerweisen; Gypsy Ways 1940,My 11,15:3
Carmen de la Triana 1940,Je 15,12:2
Symon, Arthur (Original Author)
And Women Must Weep 1922,F 20,7:1
Symon, Burk
Bride for Sale 1949,N 21,29:4 (In Addenda)
Black Hand 1950,Mr 13,15:2
Symonds, Augustin
Four Feathers, The 1929,Je 13,35:4
Symonds, Henry (Original Author)
Forget Me Not 1922,Jl 24,10:2
College Hero, The 1927,N 22,32:2
Pacific Liner 1939,Ja 18,17:3
Sympson, Tony
Mutiny of the Elsinore, The 1939,F 16,17:2
Syms, Sylvia
Woman in a Dressing Gown 1957,S 13,15:2
Conspiracy of Hearts 1960,Ap 8,24:1
Expresso Bongo 1960,Ap 13,44:1
World of Suzie Wong, The 1960,N 11,36:1

Syms, Sylvia— Cont
  Desert Attack 1961,Mr 23,28:1
  Ferry to Hong Kong 1961,Ap 27,27:7
  Victim 1962,F 6,27:2
  Flame in the Streets 1962,S 13,32:1
  Quare Fellow 1963,F 20,6:1
  Operation Crossbow 1965,Ap 2,29:1
  Danger Route 1968,Je 6,54:2
Synek, Emil (Director)
  Jana, Das Maedchen aus dem Boehmerwald
    1936,Je 20,22:3
Synge, John Millington (Original Author)
  Playboy of the Western World, The
    1963,Mr 19,8:2
Syomina, Tamara
  Resurrection 1963,O 7,35:2
Syrett, Netta (Original Author)
  Woman Rebels, A 1936,O 30,27:2
Szablowski, Edmund L
  World Dances 1954,N 8,24:6
SZABO
  See Also SABO
Szabo, Istvan (Director)
  Age of Illusions 1967,Mr 30,55:1
  Father 1967,S 29,53:1
Szabo, Istvan (Screenwriter)
  Age of Illusions 1967,Mr 30,55:1
  Father 1967,S 29,53:1
Szabo, Laszlo
  Alphaville 1965,O 26,49:1
  Petit Soldat, Le 1967,Ap 21,48:1
  Made in U S A 1967,S 28,58:2
Szabo, Oskar
  Annette in Paradise 1936,Mr 7,11:4
Szabo, Pal (Original Author)
  Treasured Earth 1950,D 14,51:3
Szabo, Sandor
  Once in a Blue Moon 1936,D 2,35:1
Szaflarska, Danuta
  Treasure, The 1951,Mr 29,24:4
Szakall, Szoeke
  Why Cry at Parting 1930,F 4,28:3
  Zwei Hertzen in Drei-Viertel Takt
    1930,O 13,31:1
  Jumping Jack, The; Hampelmann, Der
    1931,My 24,VIII,4:1
  Hampelmann, Der 1931,S 8,38:7
  Susanne Macht Ordnung 1931,O 12,28:2
  Rendez-Vous 1932,Ap 30,19:3
  Melodie der Liebe; Melody of Love
    1932,Jl 31,IX,3:4
  Ihre Majestaet die Liebe 1933,F 7,23:4
  Ich Will Nicht Wissen Wer Du Bist
    1933,F 16,23:2
  Walzerparadies 1933,Mr 4,11:3
  Die Frau von der Man Spricht 1933,Ap 22,16:4
  Eine Stadt Steht Kopf 1934,Ja 29,10:2
  Pesti Szerelem 1934,My 10,25:3
  Melodie der Liebe 1934,S 17,20:3
  Mindent a Noert! 1934,O 17,26:3
  Frau wie Du, Eine 1934,D 24,17:3
  Kaiserwalzer 1934,D 29,11:2
  Graefin Mariza 1935,Ja 26,13:3
  Jo as a Haznal; Father Knows Best 1935,F 5,22:4
  Unbekannte Gast, Der; Unknown Guest, The
    1935,Je 1,18:3
  Baratsagos Arcot Kerek; Keep Smiling
    1936,O 5,25:2
  Schwebende Jungfrau, Die 1937,Ag 7,7:2
  Affairs of Maupassant, The 1938,F 12,20:2
Szakats, Zoltan
  Hello Budapest 1935,N 14,17:4
  Pokhalo 1938,My 7,18:2
Szaro, Henry (Director)
  Ulan I Dziewczyna 1933,O 9,22:3
  Pan Twardowski 1937,S 25,10:2
  Tkies Khaf; (Vow, The) 1938,S 15,29:3
  Dzien Upragniony; Anticipated Day, The
    1939,Mr 13,12:3
Szcepanski, Jan J (Screenwriter)
  Guests are Coming; Jada Goscie Jada
    1967,Ja 13,15:1
Szczepanska, L
  Milosc Wszystko Zwycieza 1936,Ja 28,15:3
Szczepkowska, Maria Morozowicz (Original Author)
  Dr Monica 1934,Je 21,28:2
Szekely, Hans (Original Author)
  Desire 1936,Ap 13,15:1
  Dramatic School 1938,D 9,31:2
Szekely, Hans (Screenwriter)
  Lie of Nina Petrovna, The 1938,Mr 30,19:2
Szekely, Ibolya
  Mother Love 1931,F 16,17:1
Szekely, Istvan (Director)
  Lila Akac 1935,My 15,26:3
  Csak Egy Ejszakara 1936,Mr 16,21:5
  Legy Jo Mindhalalig 1936,O 26,20:2
  Naszut Felaron 1937,F 13,9:2
  Dunaparti Randevu 1937,Mr 25,29:2
  Affair of Honor, An 1937,S 20,19:1
  Szerelemboel Noesueltem; I Married for Love
    1938,F 7,10:3
  Ket Fogoly; Two Prisoners 1938,D 31,7:3

Szekely, Steven (Director)
  Grosse Sehnsucht, Die 1931,O 8,22:6
  Piri Mindont Tud 1933,Ja 26,12:3
  My Wife, The Miss 1934,S 13,26:2
  Rakoczi Indulo 1934,N 21,23:4
  Buzavirag 1935,Ja 14,11:3
  Huszarszerelem 1935,Ap 23,24:5
  Szensacio 1937,Mr 1,15:2
  Segitseg Oeroekoeltem; Help, I'm an Heiress
    1937,O 28,29:2
  Pusztai Szel; Beauty of the Pusta 1938,Ja 10,13:4
  111-es Szobaban; In Room 111 1938,Ap 2,18:2
  Noszty Flu Este Toth Marival 1938,My 16,14:4
  Sziuel Szivert; Heart for Heart 1939,Ja 16,11:3
Szekely, William (Producer)
  Decameron Nights 1953,N 17,38:2
Szelecky, Zita
  Pillanatnyi Pezzavar; Temporarily Broke
    1939,My 20,11:3
Szeleczky, Lajos
  Keseru Mezeshetek; Bitter Honeymoon
    1939,O 9,15:3
Szeleczky, Zita
  Meltosagos Kisasszony, A; Superior Maiden, The
    1937,S 6,20:2
  Fekete Gyemantok; Black Diamonds
    1939,Ap 24,13:2
  Szegeny Gazdagok; Poor Plutocrats
    1939,D 4,18:4
  Gul Baba 1940,O 26,18:8
Szelubski, Jerzy (Director)
  Peace Will Win 1952,Ja 21,11:2
Szemes, Marika
  Goose Boy, The 1951,O 13,9:2
Szepes, Lia
  Mami 1938,F 19,19:5
  Majd a Zsuzsi 1938,O 22,14:3
  Marika 1938,N 19,9:3
Szereny, Eva
  Nagymama 1935,D 30,15:1
Sziatinay, Sandor (Director)
  Once a Week 1937,O 2,18:1
Szigeti, Joseph
  Hollywood Canteen 1944,D 16,19:2
Sziklai, Joseph
  Filleres Gyoers 1933,Mr 27,13:7
Sziklay, Serena F
  Harom Sarkany 1936,D 22,32:3
Szilassy, Laszlo
  Erik/a/Buzakalasz; Wheat Ripens, The
    1939,S 11,15:2
  Szegeny Gazdagok; Poor Plutocrats
    1939,D 4,18:4
  Uz Bence 1940,Ja 15,11:2
Szinetar, Gyorgy (Screenwriter)
  Goose Boy, The 1951,O 13,9:2
Szirtes, Adam
  Treasured Earth 1950,D 14,51:3
  Merry Go-Round 1958,Ap 3,23:3
Szivo, Antal
  Buzavirag 1935,Ja 14,11:3
Szkata, Harold
  Goldfinger 1964,D 22,36:1
Szokoll, Carl (Producer)
  Last ten Days, The 1956,Ap 12,26:1
  As the Sea Rages 1961,My 18,41:1
Szold, Bernard
  Lemon Drop Kid, The 1951,Mr 22,41:2
  M 1951,Je 11,20:7
Szombathely, Blanka
  Leanyvari Boszorkany; Witch of Leanyvar
    1939,N 25,13:2
Szoreghi, Julius V
  Modern du Barry, A 1928,Mr 19,26:2
Szorenyi, Eva
  Noszty Flu Este Toth Marival 1938,My 16,14:4
  Sziuel Szivert; Heart for Heart 1939,Ja 16,11:3
  Leanyvari Boszorkany; Witch of Leanyvar
    1939,N 25,13:2
Szozerbic, Joanna
  Barrier 1967,S 27,39:3
Sztankai, Istvan
  Dialogue 1967,O 14,13:2
Szulem, German (Producer)
  Terrace, The 1964,N 25,45:1
Szwbego, Stanislaw (Director)
  Ksiazatko; Lottery Prince, The 1937,D 27,11:2
Szyfer, J E (Miscellaneous)
  Yellow Cruise, The 1936,N 18,31:3

T

Taal, Marion
  Und Wer Kuesst Mich? 1935,Ja 28,10:5
Tabakin, Bernard (Producer)
  World for Ransom 1954,Je 5,11:2
Tabakov, Seryozha
  War and Peace 1968,Ap 29,50:5
Taber, Richard
  Sleeping City, The 1950,S 21,20:2
  Under the Gun 1951,F 23,33:2

Taber, Richard (Original Author)
  Is Zat So? 1927,My 17,27:2
  Two Fisted 1935,O 5,18:3
Tabet, Georges Andre
  Green Glove, The 1952,Ap 24,38:1
  Amazing Monsieur Fabre, The 1952,S 9,21:2
Tabet, Georges Andre (Miscellaneous)
  Counter Investigation 1949,D 30,13:2
Tabet, Georges Andre (Original Author)
  Folies Bergere 1958,My 28,37:2
Tabet, Georges Andre (Screenwriter)
  Snow Was Black, The 1956,O 16,36:5
  Folies Bergere 1958,My 28,37:2
  Girls of the Night 1959,Mr 21,13:2
  Sucker, The 1967,O 9,61:1
  Oldest Profession, The (Gay Nineties, The); Gay
    Nineties, The (The Oldest Profession)
    1968,N 8,42:1
  Oldest Profession, The (Gay Nineties, The); Gay
    Nineties, The (The Oldest Profession)
    1968,N 8,42:1
Tabliashvili, V (Director)
  Keto and Kote 1954,Ap 5,21:4
Tabor, Gunther
  Great British Train Robbery, The 1967,Ap 6,45:2
Tabor, Joan
  Teenage Millionaire 1962,Ja 12,29:2
Tabori, George (Original Author)
  Crisis 1950,Jl 4,10:2
Tabori, George (Screenwriter)
  Thunder in the East 1953,F 4,32:2
  I Confess 1953,Mr 23,28:2
  Chance Meeting 1955,Ap 20,38:1
  Journey, The 1959,F 20,19:1
  No Exit 1962,D 6,55:2
  Secret Ceremony 1968,O 24,55:1
Tabori, Paul (Screenwriter)
  Four Sided Triangle 1953,My 16,10:1
Taborko, Natalya
  Cinderella 1961,D 19,39:1
Tabunasov, N
  Frontier 1935,D 28,10:5
Tacchella, Jean Charles (Screenwriter)
  Crime Does Not Pay (The Man on the Avenue);
    Man on the Avenue, The (Crime Does Not
    Pay) 1962,O 17,35:2
  Crime Does Not Pay (The Fenayrou Case);
    Fenayrou Case, The (Crime Does Not Pay)
    1962,O 17,35:2
  Crime Does Not Pay (The Hugues Case); Hugues
    Case, The (Crime Does Not Pay)
    1962,O 17,35:2
  Crime Does Not Pay (The Mask); Mask, The
    (Crime Does Not Pay) 1962,O 17,35:2
Tachibana, Kamiko
  Three Stripes in the Sun 1955,N 24,41:2
Tachikawa, Hiroshi
  Yojimbo 1962,O 16,34:1
Tachikawa, Yoichi
  Throne of Blood 1961,N 23,50:2
Tade, Reginald
  Midnight Episode 1955,My 19,25:5
Tadic, Ljuba
  Steppe, The 1963,O 1,33:1
  Fury is a Woman 1964,S 28,19:1
Tadini, Giovanni
  Hell Raiders of the Deep 1954,Jl 3,9:2
Tadziemec, A (Original Author)
  Jews in Poland 1957,Ap 17,37:1
Taeger, Ralph
  X-15 1962,Ap 5,30:2
  Carpetbaggers, The 1964,Jl 2,24:4
  House is not a Home, A 1964,S 2,33:1
Taeger, Uta
  Goodbye Again 1961,Je 30,32:2
  Live for Life 1967,D 19,59:1
Taffarelt, Guiseppe (Screenwriter)
  Goliath and the Barbarians 1960,Ja 7,24:6
Taffel, Bess (Original Author)
  True to Life 1943,O 14,26:1
  Elopement 1951,D 21,21:3
Taffin, Tony
  Fire Within, The 1964,F 18,27:1
Tafler, Sydney
  No Room at the Inn 1949,D 26,33:4
  Lavender Hill Mob, The 1951,O 16,35:2
  Galloping Major, The 1951,D 17,27:2
  Hotel Sahara 1952,Ja 1,21:4
  Assassin, The 1953,Ap 18,17:2
  Hundred Hour Hunt 1953,Je 17,32:2
  Kid for two Farthings, A 1956,Ap 18,25:1
  Cockleshell Heroes, The 1956,Je 4,25:2
  Reach for the Sky 1957,My 1,40:1
  Too Many Crooks 1959,Ap 25,14:2
  Make Mine Mink 1960,D 20,43:4
  Follow a Star 1961,Ap 26,34:1
  Seventh Dawn, The 1964,S 3,24:1
  Alfie 1966,Ag 25,42:1
  Birthday Party, The 1968,D 10,54:1
Tafore, Sharmila
  Devi 1962,O 8,19:1

Taft, Billy
College Coquette, The 1929,Ag 26,17:1
Taftazani, Amid
Drums 1938,S 30,24:4
Tafur, Robert
We Were Strangers 1949,Ap 28,28:2
Secret of the Incas 1954,My 29,13:3
Green Fire 1954,D 25,7:1
Tag-a-Long
What's Cookin' 1942,F 26,15:5
Taggart, Ben
Silence 1931,Ag 15,18:3
Monkey Business 1931,O 8,22:6
Strangers in Love 1932,Mr 5,11:2
Million Dollar Legs 1932,Jl 9,7:5
Horse Feathers 1932,Ag 11,12:2
Notorious Sophie Lang, The 1934,Jl 21,14:2
Before I Hang 1940,O 3,31:3
Man Made Monster 1941,Mr 19,25:4
Lone Wolf Takes a Chance, The 1941,Ap 7,13:2
Escape From Crime 1942,O 12,12:3
Taggart, Errol (Director)
Longest Night, The 1936,O 17,21:2
Sinner Take All 1937,F 3,27:1
Taggart, George
No Greater Sin 1941,Ag 29,18:2
Taggart, James
Fabulous Dorseys, The 1947,My 30,25:3
Taggart, Tom (Screenwriter)
Gog 1954,Ag 14,8:2
Tagianossova, M
Professor Mamlock 1938,N 8,26:2
Tagliaferri, Ernesto (Composer)
Die Singende Stadt 1932,My 10,25:4
Tagliani, Renato
Love and Marriage (One Moment Is Enough); One
Moment Is Enough (Love and Marriage)
1966,Ag 5,20:1
Tagliavini, Ferruccio
Barber of Seville, The 1947,My 6,35:2
King's Jester, The 1947,Je 26,19:3
Anything for a Song 1947,Ag 5,26:2
Lady is Fickle, The 1948,F 7,10:4
I Cadetti di Guascogna 1952,O 6,22:2
Tagliavini, Ferrucio
My Heart Sings 1954,Mr 5,15:5
Tagore, Rabindranath (Original Author)
Two Daughters (The Conclusion); Conclusion, The
(Two Daughters) 1963,My 1,35:1
Two Daughters (The Postman); Postman, The
(Two Daughters) 1963,My 1,35:1
Charulata 1965,S 11,16:1
Tagore, Sharmila
World of Apu; Apur Sansar 1960,O 5,45:1
Tahl, Yoko
Ostrich Has two Eggs, The 1960,S 27,40:1
Taili, Carloni
White Sister, The 1923,S 6,10:2
Taillon, Gus
Top o' the Morning 1949,S 1,25:2
Taimanof, M
Beethoven Concerto 1937,Mr 24,29:1
Taini, Roma
Boliche 1935,My 28,30:2
Tairo, Olga
Niskavvoren Naiset; Women of Niskavuori
1938,N 21,14:5
TAIT
See Also TATE
Tait, Walter
Hallelujah 1929,Ag 21,33:1
Taits, L M
Greater Promise, A 1936,O 8,27:3
Tajo, Italo
Barber of Seville, The 1947,My 6,35:2
Lucia di Lammermoor 1947,N 1,11:3
This Wine of Love 1948,Ap 19,27:2
Faust and the Devil 1950,My 1,18:2
Taka, Miiko
Soyonara 1957,D 6,39:4
Sayonara 1957,D 6,39:4
Hell to Eternity 1960,O 13,41:1
Cry for Happy 1961,Mr 4,16:1
Operation Bottleneck 1961,S 7,40:2
Art of Love, The 1965,Jl 1,34:1
Walk, Don't Run 1966,Ag 25,42:3
Takada, Minoru
Battle in Outer Space 1960,Jl 9,10:5
Takada, Miwa
Majin 1968,Ag 10,15:5
Takagi
Town Like Alice, A 1958,S 22,27:1
Takagi, Kiyoshi
Madame Butterfly 1956,Ap 24,26:2
Takagi, Koichi (Producer)
Imposter, The 1955,Mr 23,27:1
Takagi, Masayuki (Producer)
Unholy Desire 1964,N 18,54:1
Burmese Harp, The 1967,Ap 29,25:1
Takahashi, Teiji
Ballad of Narayama 1961,Je 20,27:1

Takaishvil, A
Eagle of the Caucasus, The 1932,S 17,18:4
Takaishvilt, S
Scrapper, The 1959,D 14,42:2
Takaki, Kenji
Jungle Fighters 1962,Mr 15,28:2
High Wind in Jamaica, A 1965,Je 17,27:2
Takamine, Hideko
Mistress, The 1959,F 3,36:2
Carmen Comes Home 1959,D 23,22:1
Rikisha Man, The 1960,My 4,57:1
Happiness of Us Alone 1963,Ap 10,31:5
When a Woman Ascends the Stairs
1963,Je 26,36:4
My Hobo 1963,Jl 24,27:3
Could I but Live 1965,Ja 20,34:2
Takamura, Kiyoshi (Producer)
She Was Like a Wild Chrysanthemum
1960,Ja 22,15:2
Takano, Yasuaki
Hiroshima 1955,My 17,32:1
Takarada, Akira
Godzilla, King of the Monsters 1956,Ap 28,11:1
Walleyed Nippon 1963,S 3,36:1
Different Sons 1964,F 13,25:1
Honolulu-Tokyo-Hong Kong 1964,S 2,33:3
Gozdilla vs the Thing 1964,N 26,52:2
King Kong Escapes 1968,Jl 11,30:1
Takarazuka Kabuki dancers
Madame Butterfly 1956,Ap 24,26:2
Takase
Missing Rembrandt, The 1932,Mr 26,17:2
Takashima, Tadao
King Kong vs. Godzilla 1963,Je 27,23:4
Takasugi, May
Japanese War Bride 1952,Ja 30,22:6
Takata, Kokichi
Imposter, The 1955,Mr 23,27:1
Takee, Yoshio
Golden Demon 1956,Ja 31,34:3
Takei, George
Ice Palace 1960,Je 30,22:1
Green Berets, The 1968,Je 20,49:1
Takeyama, Michio (Original Author)
Burmese Harp, The 1967,Ap 29,25:1
Takhmasiv, Resa (Producer)
Arshin Takes a Wife 1950,Jl 31,13:6
Taki, Eiko
Flight From Ashiya 1964,Ap 23,34:1
Takiguchi, Yasuhiko (Original Author)
Harakiri 1964,Ag 5,24:2
Rebellion 1968,O 26,27:4
Takimura, Kazuo (Producer)
Samurai 1956,Ja 10,26:1
Samurai (Part II) 1967,O 21,16:1
Takizawa, Eisuke (Director)
Temptress and the Monk, The 1963,My 28,32:1
Takizawa, Osamu
Fires on the Plain 1963,S 25,39:1
Talamas, Shibley
Golden Mistress, The 1954,O 30,15:6
Talamo, Gino
Messalina 1924,Ag 25,16:2
Talan, Raul
Newspaper Boys, The 1937,N 6,14:3
Talankin, Igor (Director)
Summer to Remember, A; (Seryozha)
1961,N 7,38:1
Talankin, Igor (Screenwriter)
Summer to Remember, A; (Seryozha)
1961,N 7,38:1
Talarico, Vincenzo
Under the Olive Tree 1951,O 5,24:4
Talarico, Vincenzo (Miscellaneous)
Bigamist, The 1958,My 12,25:1
Talarico, Vincenzo (Screenwriter)
Scandal in Sorrento 1957,Je 13,37:1
Talavera, Frank
Salt of the Earth 1965,N 1,57:1
Talavera, Ramon
World Dances 1954,N 8,24:6
Talazac, Odetta
Million, Le 1931,My 21,33:2
Talazac, Odette
Maternite 1937,Je 8,30:2
Murderer Lives at Number 21, The
1947,Ag 18,12:3
Crime of Monsieur Lange, The 1964,Ap 4,15:5
TALBOT
See Also TALBOTT
Talbot, A (Screenwriter)
No Escape 1959,My 23,18:4
Talbot, Daniel (Producer)
Point of Order 1964,Ja 15,27:2
Talbot, Francis X (Screenwriter)
Through the Centuries 1933,D 2,9:8 (In
Addenda)
Talbot, Helen
Pistol Packin' Mama 1943,D 20,27:4
Talbot, Lyle
Love Is a Racket 1932,Je 11,9:3
Stranger in Town 1932,Jl 8,22:5
Purchase Price, The 1932,Jl 16,5:5

Talbot, Lyle — Cont
Big City Blues 1932,S 10,18:5
Three on a Match 1932,O 29,18:4
No More Orchids 1933,Ja 2,29:2
20,000 Years in Sing Sing 1933,Ja 10,26:2
Ladies They Talk About 1933,F 25,20:4
Girl Missing 1933,Ap 1,18:2
Life of Jimmy Dolan, The 1933,Je 14,22:3
Shriek in the Night, A 1933,Jl 24,11:2
She Had to Say Yes 1933,Jl 29,14:2
Mary Stevens, M D 1933,Ag 5,9:6
College Coach 1933,N 11,10:4
Havana Widows 1933,N 23,24:3
Mandalay 1934,F 15,15:6
Heat Lightning 1934,Mr 8,23:2
Fog over Frisco 1934,Je 7,26:2
Return of the Terror 1934,Jl 11,20:2
Dragon Murder Case, The 1934,Ag 23,13:3
One Night of Love 1934,S 7,25:3
Lost Lady, A 1934,O 4,19:1
Murder in the Clouds 1934,D 26,18:1
Red Hot Tires 1935,Mr 1,16:3
While the Patient Slept 1935,Mr 2,18:2
It Happened in New York 1935,Ap 6,10:1
Chinatown Squad 1935,My 30,21:1
Oil for the Lamps of China 1935,Je 6,25:2
Our Little Girl 1935,Je 7,24:4
Page Miss Glory 1935,Ag 29,25:2
Case of the Lucky Legs, The 1935,N 1,25:1
Broadway Hostess 1935,D 16,23:3
Boulder Dam 1936,Mr 30,17:5
Singing Kid, The 1936,Ap 4,11:1
Law in her Hands, The 1936,Je 6,21:2
Murder by an Aristocrat 1936,Je 13,13:2
Trapped by Television 1936,Je 15,24:3
Go West, Young Man 1936,N 19,31:3
What Price Vengeance 1937,My 26,30:3
Three Legionnaires 1937,Jl 10,18:2
Second Honeymoon 1937,N 13,11:2
Call of the Yukon 1938,My 6,27:1
One Wild Night 1938,Je 3,17:2
Gateway 1938,Ag 8,9:2
Arkansas Traveler, The 1938,N 17,29:2
I Stand Accused 1939,Ja 5,17:1
They Asked for It 1939,Je 30,17:4
Second Fiddle 1939,Jl 1,11:2
He Married his Wife 1940,Ja 20,11:2
Parole Fixer 1940,Ap 18,28:5
Mexican Spitfire's Elephant 1942,S 18,25:7
Up in Arms 1944,Mr 3,19:2
Falcon out West, The 1944,Mr 18,18:2
Sensations of 1945 1944,Jl 7,13:2
Are These our Parents? 1944,Ag 23,16:2
One Body too Many 1944,N 25,21:2
Vicious Circle, The 1948,Jl 22,27:2
Champagne for Caesar 1950,My 12,33:2
Jackpot, The 1950,N 23,55:2
With a Song in my Heart 1952,Ap 5,20:2
There's no Business Like Show Business
1954,D 17,37:3
Great Man, The 1957,Ja 2,28:2
She Shoulda Said No 1957,Ja 31,21:1
Sunrise at Campobello 1960,S 29,32:1
Talbot, Nita
Bundle of Joy 1956,D 20,36:1
I Married a Woman 1958,N 5,42:5
Who's Got the Action? 1962,D 26,5:4
Girl Happy 1965,My 27,28:1
Very Special Favor, A 1965,Ag 26,40:3
That Funny Feeling 1965,O 21,57:2
Cool Ones, The 1967,My 11,50:1
TALBOTT
See Also TALBOT
Talbott, Gloria
We're no Angels 1955,Jl 8,15:2
Crashout 1955,Jl 9,9:2
Lucy Gallant 1955,O 21,30:1
All That Heaven Allows 1956,F 29,35:1
Oklahoman, The 1957,My 15,39:1
Alias Jesse James 1959,My 18,31:2
Talchi, Vera
Walls of Malapaga, The 1950,Mr 21,34:2
Talen, Raul
Todo un Hombre 1936,Ja 6,20:5
Talent, Ziggie
Meet The People 1944,S 8,16:2
Talevera, Frank
Salt of the Earth 1954,Mr 15,20:2
Taliaferro, Hal
Man With Nine Lives, The 1940,Ap 29,12:3
Cherokee Strip 1940,N 4,23:2
Tombstone, The Town too Tough to Die
1942,Jl 27,18:2
American Empire 1943,Ja 14,25:4
Utah 1945,Mr 12,22:7
Fallen Angel 1946,F 7,29:4
Red River 1948,O 1,31:2
Brimstone 1949,O 7,35:3
Taliaferro, Mabel
Sentimental Tommy 1921,My 9,16:2
My Love Came Back 1940,Jl 13,16:5
Tallas, Gregg (Director)
Siren of Atlantis 1949,Ag 22,13:1
Prehistoric Women 1950,D 29,15:5

Tallas, Gregg (Director)— Cont

Barefoot Battalion 1954,My 29,13:4
Bed of Grass 1957,D 28,9:2

Tallas, Gregg (Miscellaneous)
Bed of Grass 1957,D 28,9:2

Tallas, Gregg (Producer)
Bed of Grass 1957,D 28,9:2

Tallas, Gregg (Screenwriter)
Prehistoric Women 1950,D 29,15:5

Tallchief, Maria
Million Dollar Mermaid 1952,D 5,35:2

Tallchief, Marjorie
Neapolitan Carousel 1961,O 12,41:3

Talley, Marion
Follow Your Heart 1936,O 22,31:1

Talley, Truman
News Parade, The 1928,My 29,17:2

Talley, Truman (Miscellaneous)
Baboona 1935,Ja 23,21:2
Borneo 1937,S 4,8:3

Tallichet, Margaret
Girls' School 1938,N 3,27:1
Stranger on the Third Floor 1940,S 2,19:2
It Started With Eve 1941,O 3,27:1

Tallier, Nadine
Please Mr Balzac 1957,N 18,37:2
Crazy in the Noodle 1957,D 15,45:4 (Incorrect in this edition; use 1957,D 17,45:4 elsewhere)
Folies Bergere 1958,My 28,37:2

Talma, Zolya
Rose Tattoo, The 1955,D 13,55:1

Talmadge, Constance
Veiled Adventure, The 1919,Jl 7,18:5
Fall of Babylon, The 1919,Jl 22,10:2
Temperamental Wife, A 1919,S 15,16:3
Virtuous Vamp, A 1919,N 17,20:1
Two Weeks 1920,Ja 26,16:1
In Search of a Sinner 1920,Mr 8,9:5
In Search of a Sinner 1920,Mr 8,9:6
Mamma's Affair 1921,Ja 24,16:2
Wedding Bells 1921,Ag 15,14:3
Woman's Place 1921,O 23,VI,4:1 (In Addenda)
Primitive Lover, The 1922,My 15,20:3
Dulcy 1923,S 17,18:2
Dangerous Maid, The 1923,D 11,26:2
Goldfish, The 1924,My 20,15:2
Her Night of Romance 1925,Ja 13,16:1
Learning to Love 1925,F 23,24:1
Duchess of Buffalo, The 1926,Ag 9,10:3
Venus of Venice 1927,My 3,25:1
Breakfast at Sunrise 1927,N 14,26:1
Venus 1929,O 14,20:2

Talmadge, Natalie
Isle of Conquest, The 1919,O 27,9:3
Our Hospitality 1923,D 10,20:1

Talmadge, Norma
Battle Cry for Peace, The 1915,Ag 7,8:3
Panthea 1917,Ja 8,9:2
De Luxe Annie 1918,My 20,9:7
Her own Way 1918,Ag 19,7:1
Forbidden City, The 1918,O 7,11:3
Heart of the Wetona, The 1919,Ja 6,11:3
New Moon, The 1919,My 12,11:4
Way of a Woman, The 1919,Jl 28,8:5
Isle of Conquest, The 1919,O 27,9:3
Woman Gives, The 1920,Ap 12,13:1
Yes or No 1920,Jl 5,12:4
Branded Woman, The 1920,S 6,10:5
Passion Flower, The 1921,Ap 4,18:1
Sign on the Door, The 1921,Jl 18,16:4 (In Addenda)
Love's Redemption 1922,Ja 9,15:2
Foolish Wives 1922,Ja 12,15:2
Smilin' Through 1922,Ap 17,22:3
Eternal Flame, The 1922,S 18,14:2
Voice From the Minaret, The 1923,F 5,18:2
Within the Law 1923,Ap 30,11:2
Ashes of Vengeance 1923,Ag 7,20:2
Song of Love, The 1924,F 25,13:1
Secrets 1924,Mr 25,25:2
Only Woman, The 1924,N 3,20:1
Lady, The 1925,Ja 27,11:2
Graustark 1925,S 8,29:1
Kiki 1926,Ap 6,26:4
Camille 1927,Ap 22,19:1
Dove, The 1928,Ja 3,28:2
Woman Disputed, The 1928,N 10,20:8
New York Nights 1930,F 1,15:1
Du Barry, Woman of Passion 1930,N 3,19:3

Talmadge, Richard
Cavalier, The 1928,O 31,28:4

Talman, William
Red, Hot and Blue 1949,O 20,39:2
Kid From Texas, The 1950,Je 2,26:2
Woman on Pier 13, The 1950,Je 16,28:4
Racket, The 1951,D 13,44:2
One Minute to Zero 1952,S 20,13:2
Hitch-Hiker, The 1953,Ap 30,39:3
City That Never Sleeps 1953,Ag 8,14:2
Big House U S A 1955,Mr 12,11:6
Crashout 1955,Jl 9,9:2
Ballad of Josie, The 1968,Mr 14,51:2

Talman, William (Screenwriter)
I've Lived Before 1956,Ag 4,13:1

Talqui, Vera
Little World of Don Camillo, The 1953,Ja 14,27:1

Talton, Alice
In a Lonely Place 1950,My 18,37:2
Great Jewel Robber, The 1950,Ag 4,13:2

Talton, Alix
Man Who Knew too Much, The 1956,My 17,37:1
Romanoff and Juliet 1961,Je 9,26:1

Talum, Walter
David and Bathsheba 1951,Ag 15,23:2

Tama, Matahiarri
Mutiny on the Bounty 1962,N 9,31:2

Tamaki, I
Three Stripes in the Sun 1955,N 24,41:2

Tamantin, Franca
Favorita, La 1953,O 30,27:4

Tamantini, Franca
Cinderella 1953,My 15,20:2

Tamara
Midsummer Night's Dream 1928,Ja 31,29:1
No, No, Nanette 1940,D 20,33:1

Tamara, Mary
Ich Sehne Mich Nach Dir 1936,S 9,32:4

Tamarez, Tom
Night World 1932,My 28,18:2

Tamarin, B
Red and White 1932,N 29,23:5

Tamarin, B P
Station Master, The 1928,Je 18,13:2
Prisoners 1937,F 20,9:2

Tamarin, Paul
Dr Strangelove or: How I Learned to Stop Worrying and Love the Bomb 1964,Ja 31,16:1 (Incorrect in this edition; use 1964,Ja 30,24:1 elsewhere)

Tamayo, Manuel (Screenwriter)
Mad Queen, The 1950,O 27,24:3

Tamayo, Marina
Alma Jarocha 1938,Ap 30,18:2
Guadalupe la Chinaca 1938,S 12,13:3
A la Orilla de un Palmar; At the Edge of a Palm Grove 1938,D 17,10:4
Perjura 1939,Ja 16,11:2
Su Gran Aventura; His Great Adventure 1939,Ap 3,11:6
Perfidia; Perfidy 1940,F 17,9:3
Life of Simon Bolivar, The 1943,Je 18,16:5

Tamba, Tetsuro
Bridge to the Sun 1961,O 18,50:1
Harakiri 1964,Ag 5,24:2
Seventh Dawn, The 1964,S 3,24:1
Kwaidan (Hoichi, The Earless); Hoichi, The Earless (Kwaidan) 1965,N 23,51:1
You Only Live Twice 1967,Je 14,40:1

Tamberlani, Carlo
Giovanni De Medici, The Leader 1940,Ja 5,15:4
Measure for Measure 1951,D 8,9:2
Alone in the Streets 1956,Je 28,33:2
Woman in the Painting, The 1959,Ja 15,27:1

Tamblyn, Eddie
Flood, The 1931,Ap 27,25:1
Sweetheart of Sigma Chi, The 1933,N 9,27:1
Shot in the Dark, A 1935,My 22,23:2

Tamblyn, Russ
Take the High Ground 1953,N 20,19:2
Seven Brides for Seven Brothers 1954,Jl 23,8:3
Many Rivers to Cross 1955,F 24,21:2
Hit the Deck 1955,Mr 4,17:1
Last Hunt, The 1956,Mr 1,37:2
Fastest Gun Alive, The 1956,Jl 13,23:3
Don't Go Near the Water 1957,N 15,37:1
Peyton Place 1957,D 13,35:1
High School Confidential 1958,My 31,6:6
Tom Thumb 1958,D 24,00:0
Cimarron 1961,F 17,12:2
West Side Story 1961,O 19,39:3
Wonderful World of the Brothers Grimm, The (The Dancing Princess); Dancing Princess, The (The Wonderful World of the Brothers Grimm) 1962,Ag 8,35:1
Follow the Boys 1963,F 28,8:2
How the West Was Won 1963,Ap 1,54:1
Haunting, The 1963,S 19,23:1
Long Ships, The 1964,Je 25,25:1

Tamblyn, Rusty
Kid From Cleveland, The 1949,S 5,13:2
Samson and Delilah 1949,D 22,29:2
Captain Carey U S A 1950,Mr 30,40:5
Father of the Bride 1950,My 19,31:2
Father's Little Dividend 1951,Ap 13,18:5
As Young as You Feel 1951,Ag 3,10:6
Retreat Hell! 1952,F 20,26:2
Winning Team, The 1952,Je 21,12:2

Tamburella, Paola W (Producer)
Shoe-Shine 1947,Ag 27,19:2

Tamburella, Paolo W (Director)
Ring Around the Clock 1953,My 19,36:2

Tamburi, Orfeo
Seven Deadly Sins, The (Envy); Envy (The Seven Deadly Sins) 1953,My 12,31:3

Tamez, Manuel
Tiburon 1934,Ap 18,23:3
Cruz Diablo 1935,Ap 6,10:1

Tamikawa, Suntaro (Narrator)
Tokyo Olympiad 1966,N 17,55:1

Tamiroff, Akim
Sadie McKee 1934,My 18,18:3 (Incorrect in this edition; use 1934,My 19,18:3 elsewhere)
Great Flirtation, The 1934,Je 22,16:5
Whom the Gods Destroy 1934,Jl 13,14:2
Chained 1934,S 1,16:2
Here is my Heart 1934,D 22,21:1
Lives of a Bengal Lancer, The 1935,Ja 12,12:2
Winning Ticket, The 1935,F 11,14:2
Naughty Marietta 1935,Mr 23,11:2
Black Fury 1935,Ap 11,27:2
Go Into Your Dance 1935,My 4,17:2
China Seas 1935,Ag 10,16:4
Big Broadcast of 1936, The 1935,S 16,15:2
Gay Deception, The 1935,O 11,31:1
Story of Louis Pasteur, The 1936,F 10,15:1
Woman Trap 1936,Mr 7,11:4
Desire 1936,Ap 13,15:1
Anthony Adverse 1936,Ag 27,16:1
General Died at Dawn, The 1936,S 3,17:2
Jungle Princess 1936,D 24,21:3
Her Husband Lies 1937,Mr 18,20:1
Soldier and the Lady, The 1937,Ap 10,11:1
King of Gamblers 1937,Jl 3,18:1
Great Gambini, The 1937,Jl 12,20:4
High, Wide and Handsome 1937,Jl 22,15:1
This Way Please 1937,O 8,27:2
Buccaneer, The 1938,F 17,17:2
Dangerous to Know 1938,Mr 11,15:4
Spawn of the North 1938,S 8,27:1
Ride a Crooked Mile 1938,D 29,15:2
Paris Honeymoon 1939,Ja 26,17:1
King of Chinatown 1939,Mr 16,27:2
Union Pacific 1939,My 11,31:2
Magnificent Fraud, The 1939,Jl 20,16:2
Honeymoon in Bali 1939,S 21,21:1
Disputed Passage 1939,O 26,27:2
Way of all Flesh, The 1940,Je 6,33:2
Untamed 1940,Jl 25,14:3
Great McGinty, The 1940,Ag 15,23:1
North West Mounted Police 1940,N 7,33:2
Texas Rangers Ride Again 1941,Ja 9,27:4
New York Town 1941,N 13,35:2
Corsican Brothers, The 1942,Ja 16,25:4
Tortilla Flat 1942,My 22,27:1
Five Graves to Cairo 1943,My 27,21:2
For Whom the Bell Tolls 1943,Jl 15,25:2
His Butler's Sister 1943,D 30,13:2
Miracle of Morgan's Creek, The 1944,Ja 20,15:2
Bridge of San Luis Rey, The 1944,Mr 4,11:1
Dragon Seed 1944,Jl 21,16:4
Can't Help Singing 1944,D 26,22:4
Pardon my Past 1946,Ja 28,15:5
Scandal In Paris, A 1946,S 16,9:7
Fiesta 1947,Je 27,17:3
Gangster, The 1947,O 31,29:3
My Girl Tisa 1948,F 21,9:2
Relentless 1948,Mr 6,17:3
Outpost in Morocco 1949,Mr 25,28:3
Black Magic 1949,N 9,37:2
Desert Legion 1953,My 9,13:2
Anastasia 1956,D 14,35:6
Battle Hell 1957,Ag 22,23:1
Touch of Evil 1958,My 22,25:2
Me and the Colonel 1958,Ag 27,33:1
Ocean's Eleven 1960,Ag 11,19:1
Romanoff and Juliet 1961,Je 9,26:1
Mr Arkadin 1962,O 12,26:1
Reluctant Saint, The 1962,D 4,47:2
Trial, The 1963,F 21,5:1
Topkapi 1964,S 18,25:1
Lord Jim 1965,F 26,18:1
Bambole; Dolls, The (Monsignor Cupid); Monsignor Cupid (The Dolls) 1965,Je 29,26:1
Alphaville 1965,O 26,49:1
Lt Robin Crusoe, USN 1966,Jl 14,28:1
Hotel Paradiso 1966,O 15,34:2
Liquidator, The 1966,O 29,34:1
After the Fox 1966,D 24,11:1
Vulture, The 1967,My 20,39:2
Rose for Everyone, A 1967,Je 30,30:1

Tamura, N Hezaburo (Original Author)
Daughter of Two Fathers, A 1929,Mr 12,26:3

Tamura, Nami
Love at Twenty 1963,F 7,5:6
Young Swordsman 1964,O 30,29:1

Tanaha, Tomoyuki (Producer)
Mothra 1962,Jl 12,19:4

Tanaka, Eiza
Mistress, The 1959,F 3,36:2

Tanaka, Haruo
Rikisha Man, The 1960,My 4,57:1

Tanaka, Kinuyo
Ugetsu 1954,S 8,40:3
Ballad of Narayama 1961,Je 20,27:1
Life of Oharu 1964,Ap 21,42:2
Alone on the Pacific 1964,S 24,46:2

Tanaka, Michiko
Madame Butterfly 1956,Ap 24,26:2
Tanaka, Shini
She Was Like a Wild Chrysanthemum
1960,Ja 22,15:2
Tanaka, Shinji
Island, The; Hadaka No Shima 1962,S 11,27:2
Tanaka, Tadashi (Cinematographer)
Tokyo Olympiad 1966,N 17,55:1
Tanaka, Tomoyuki (Producer)
Godzilla, King of the Monsters 1956,Ap 28,11:1
Sword for Hire 1957,S 5,32:1
Mysterians, The 1959,Jl 2,15:2
Battle in Outer Space 1960,Jl 9,10:5
Sanjuro 1963,My 8,34:2
Young Swordsman 1964,O 30,29:1
Ghidrah, The Three-Headed Monster
1965,D 16,63:3
Rebellion 1967,S 25,56:4
King Kong Escapes 1968,Jl 11,30:1
Rebellion 1968,O 26,27:4
Tanchuck, Nat (Screenwriter)
Hoodlum, The 1951,Jl 6,14:6
Garden of Eden 1957,D 18,45:3
Shuttered Room, The 1968,F 15,47:1
Tancred, Anthony
Forbidden Street, The 1949,My 14,9:2
Reluctant Widow, The 1951,S 8,8:6
Adventures of Sadie, The 1955,My 18,35:2
Tancredi, Italo (Producer)
Ten Commandments, The 1958,Ap 7,26:1
Tandrup, Harald (Original Author)
En Enda Natt 1942,D 7,22:2
Tandy, Jessica
Seventh Cross, The 1944,S 29,18:1
Valley of Decision, The 1945,My 4,23:2
Green Years, The 1946,Ap 5,21:2
Dragonwyck 1946,Ap 11,35:2
Forever Amber 1947,O 23,31:2
Woman's Vengeance, A 1948,Ja 30,19:2
September Affair 1951,F 2,19:2
Desert Fox, The 1951,O 18,32:1
Light in the Forest, The 1958,Jl 11,15:2
Hemingway's Adventures of a Young Man
1962,Jl 26,17:1
Birds, The 1963,Ap 1,5:5 (Incorrect in this
edition; use 1963,Ap 1,54:1 elsewhere)
Tang, Frank
Objective Burma 1945,Ja 27,15:2
Soldier of Fortune 1955,My 28,7:4
Tanguy, Annick
My Seven Little Sins 1956,My 2,27:1
Tanguy, Monique
Sinners of Paris 1959,Ap 24,23:1
Tanguy, Yves
8 X 8 1957,Mr 16,13:2
Tani, Yoko
Quiet American, The 1958,F 6,24:1
Wind Cannot Read, The 1960,Mr 10,36:1
Savage Innocents, The 1961,My 25,31:1
My Geisha 1962,Je 14,23:2
Marco Polo 1962,S 20,29:2
Who's Been Sleeping in My Bed? 1963,D 26,33:2
Tania
Pepe le Moko 1941,Mr 4,20:2
Tanizaki, Junichiro (Original Author)
Odd Obsession 1961,D 27,16:1
Tankard, Denis
That's Right, You're Wrong 1939,N 30,25:3
Tankuhn, Walter
Zigeunerblut 1935,Ap 8,23:5
Tannen, Charles
Educating Father 1936,Je 20,22:2
Submarine Patrol 1938,N 19,9:2
Jesse James 1939,Ja 14,13:1
Young Mr Lincoln 1939,Je 3,11:2
Drums Along the Mohawk 1939,N 4,11:2
Swanee River 1939,D 30,9:2
Grapes of Wrath, The 1940,Ja 25,17:2
Return of Frank James, The 1940,Ag 10,16:4
Cadet Girl 1941,D 11,39:1
To the Shores of Tripoli 1942,Mr 26,27:2
Little Tokyo, USA 1942,Ag 7,13:2
Footlight Serenade 1942,S 10,30:3
Manila Calling 1942,S 28,13:1
Quiet Please, Murder 1942,D 22,31:1
Crash Dive 1943,Ap 29,25:2
It Shouldn't Happen to a Dog 1946,S 7,11:2
Green Grass of Wyoming 1948,Je 10,28:3
Jackpot, The 1950,N 23,55:2
U S S Teakettle 1951,F 24,11:2
Dangerous Crossing 1953,S 30,37:2
Gorilla at Large 1954,Je 12,13:2
Bridges at Toko-Ri, The 1955,Ja 21,20:2
Voyage to the Bottom of the Sea 1961,Jl 20,32:2
Tannen, Julius
Half Angel 1936,My 30,7:3
Road to Glory, The 1936,Ag 6,22:1
36 Hours to Live 1936,Ag 15,6:3
Dimples 1936,O 10,21:2
Pigskin Parade 1936,N 14,23:3
Reunion 1936,N 27,27:1
Stowaway 1936,D 19,16:1

One in a Million 1937,Ja 1,19:3
Love Is a Headache 1938,Ja 28,17:3
Magnificent Fraud, The 1939,Jl 20,16:2
Christmas in July 1940,N 6,35:2
Miracle of Morgan's Creek, The 1944,Ja 20,15:2
Great Moment, The 1944,N 13,15:2
House of Frankenstein 1944,D 16,19:3
Unfaithfully Yours 1948,N 6,9:2
Tannen, William
Band Plays on, The 1934,D 22,21:2
She Couldn't Take It 1935,N 7,27:1
Crash Donovan 1936,Ag 10,10:3
When Love Is Young 1937,Ap 17,15:1
Sky Murder 1940,N 14,28:3
Flight Command 1941,Ja 17,21:2
I'll Wait for You 1941,Je 2,13:6
Big Store, The 1941,Je 27,14:4
Dr Jekyll and Mr Hyde 1941,Ag 13,13:2
Whistling in the Dark 1941,Ag 28,23:2
Woman of the Year 1942,F 6,23:2
Joe Smith, American 1942,Ap 2,27:4
Fingers at the Window 1942,Ap 23,27:3
Nazi Agent 1942,Je 13,11:2
Pacific Rendezvous 1942,Jl 8,27:4
Stand by for Action 1943,Mr 12,12:2
Air Raid Wardens 1943,Ap 5,15:5
Pilot No 5 1943,Je 25,13:4
Innocent Affair, An 1948,S 29,36:2
Yank in Korea, A 1951,Ap 2,29:2
Dangerous Crossing 1953,S 30,37:2
Sitting Bull 1954,N 26,24:4
Blackjack Ketchum Desperado 1956,Ap 5,26:2
Tannenbaum, Harold J (Cinematographer)
Memphis Belle, The 1944,Ap 14,1:2
Tannenbaum, Julius (Producer)
Black Like Me 1964,My 21,42:1
Tanner, Fred
Marie-Louise 1945,N 13,24:2
Heidi 1953,D 21,27:2
Heidi and Peter 1955,D 13,55:2
Shadows Grow Longer, The 1962,Je 11,36:4
Tanner, Gordon
Campbell's Kingdom 1960,Ja 11,35:5
Dr Strangelove or: How I Learned to Stop
Worrying and Love the Bomb 1964,Ja 31,16:1
(Incorrect in this edition; use 1964,Ja 30,24:1
elsewhere)
Return of Mr Moto 1965,D 2,48:1
Tanner, Tony
Pleasure Girls, The 1966,Ap 21,43:1
Stop the World-I Want to Get Off
1966,My 12,54:2
Tansey, Sherry
Over the Hill to the Poor House 1920,S 18,16:2
Steadfast Heart, The 1923,D 25,26:1
Tansill, Bob
Broadway Bill 1934,N 30,22:2
Tanska, Natasa
Krakatit 1951,Ap 30,16:2
Tantau, Giscia
Seven Journeys 1951,Mr 12,20:2
Tao (cat)
Incredible Journey, The 1963,N 21,43:2
Tapernoux, John (Miscellaneous)
Merlusse 1938,Mr 17,17:2
Tapley, Colin
Double Door 1934,My 5,22:3
Murder at the Vanities 1934,My 21,20:2
Pursuit of Happiness, The 1934,O 26,25:1
Lives of a Bengal Lancer, The 1935,Ja 12,12:2
Becky Sharp 1935,Je 14,27:2
Last Outpost, The 1935,O 5,18:2
Peter Ibbetson 1935,N 8,18:2
Sky Parade, The 1936,Ap 20,17:1
Early to Bed 1936,Jl 16,20:2
Return of Sophie Lang, The 1936,Jl 24,13:1
Thank You, Jeeves 1936,O 5,25:1
Crime Nobody Saw, The 1937,Ap 5,17:2
King of Gamblers 1937,Jl 3,18:1
Booloo 1938,Jl 30,10:2
If I Were King 1938,S 29,31:1
Storm Over Bengal 1938,D 8,34:4
Light That Failed, The 1939,D 25,19:1
Women in War 1940,My 30,21:2
Arizona 1941,F 7,23:3
White Fire 1954,S 18,12:4
Safecracker, The 1958,Mr 6,32:1
Tapley, Rose
Man Who Fights Alone, The 1924,Jl 28,12:2
Redeeming Sin, The 1925,Ja 20,18:2
Pony Express, The 1925,S 14,16:1
Resurrection 1931,Ja 24,15:1
Tappen, William
New Moon 1940,Jl 19,22:2
Tappert, Horst
Great British Train Robbery, The 1967,Ap 6,45:2
Taps, Georgie
52d Street 1937,N 15,15:1
Taps, Jonie (Producer)
Drive a Crooked Road 1954,Ap 3,19:3
Three for the Show 1955,F 25,16:1

Tarabarinov, Leonid
Poem of the Sea 1959,D 21,34:4
Taradash, Daniel (Director)
Storm Center 1956,O 22,25:4
Taradash, DAniel (Original Author)
Noose Hangs High, The 1948,My 29,8:6
Taradash, Daniel (Screenwriter)
Golden Boy 1939,S 8,28:2
Little Bit of Heaven, A 1940,N 8,24:2
Knock on any Door 1949,F 23,31:2
Rancho Notorious 1952,My 15,39:5
Taradash, DAniel (Screenwriter)
Don't Bother to Knock 1952,Jl 19,8:2
Taradash, Daniel (Screenwriter)
From Here to Eternity 1953,Ag 6,16:2
Desiree 1954,N 18,42:1
Picnic 1956,F 17,13:3
Storm Center 1956,O 22,25:4
Taradash, DAniel (Screenwriter)
Bell, Book and Candle 1958,D 27,2:7
Taradash, Daniel (Screenwriter)
Saboteur, The: Code Name-Mori Turi
1965,Ag 26,40:2
Hawaii 1966,O 11,54:1
Taranto, Nino
Eravamo Sette Vedove; We Were Seven Widows
1940,F 16,23:4
Tarasov, D (Screenwriter)
Wings of Victory 1941,N 17,15:2
Tarasov, Pavel
Gordeyev Family, The 1961,O 16,33:6
Tarasova, A K
Thunderstorm 1934,S 29,12:2
Tarasova, Alla
Peter the First 1937,D 25,10:4
Conquests of Peter The Great, The
1939,Ag 24,17:2
Tarasova, K I
Revolutionists 1936,D 26,15:3
Tarasova, Zenia
Wings of Victory 1941,N 17,15:2
Zoya 1945,Ap 16,18:6
Tarasovna, K
Petersburg Nights 1934,S 10,20:4
Taray, Ferenc
Szerelmi Almok 1937,Ja 5,19:2
Tardy, Danielle
Face to the Wind 1951,Ja 16,34:2
Targart, Gen
Newly Rich 1931,Jl 3,22:1
Targenson, Edwin Dial (Original Author)
Speed to Burn 1938,S 9,25:1
Tariacurl Trio
Ay Jalisco no te Rajes 1943,Ap 24,17:3
Tarita
Mutiny on the Bounty 1962,N 9,31:2
Taritch, Juri (Director)
Czar Ivan the Terrible 1928,Mr 12,26:1
Flames on the Volga 1929,Ap 2,28:4
Tarjan, Gyoergy
Egy ej Velencebzn 1935,D 27,14:2
Tarkhanof, M M
Diary of a Revolutionist 1932,Je 10,22:3
Thunderstorm 1934,S 29,12:2
Tarkhanov, M
Youth of Maxim, The 1935,Ap 20,16:1
Conquests of Peter The Great, The
1939,Ag 24,17:2
Tarkhanov, N
Peter the First 1937,D 25,10:4
Tarkington, Booth (Original Author)
Gentlemen from Indiana, The 1915,N 29,11:3
Conquest of Canaan, The 1921,Jl 11,9:3
Penrod 1922,F 20,7:1
Man From Home, The 1922,My 1,20:3
Clarence 1922,O 16,20:2
Flirt, The 1922,D 31,VII,2:2 (In Addenda)
Penrod and Sam 1923,Je 25,16:5
Boy of Mine 1923,D 24,12:1 (In Addenda)
Pied Piper Malone 1924,Ja 28,12:1
Fighting Coward, The 1924,Mr 17,19:1
Monsieur Beaucaire 1924,Ag 12,12:1 (In
Addenda)
Pampered Youth 1925,F 10,20:1
Man Who Found Himself, The 1925,Ag 24,17:3
Geraldine 1929,Mr 4,20:2
Cameo Kirby 1930,F 8,12:5
Father's Son 1931,F 21,15:2
Bad Sister 1931,Mr 30,25:2
Penrod and Sam 1931,S 26,25:3
Business and Pleasure 1932,F 13,23:4
Mississippi 1935,Ap 18,27:2
Alice Adams 1935,Ag 16,11:3
Gentle Julia 1936,Ap 11,19:1
Penrod and Sam 1937,Mr 29,14:3
Penrod and his Twin Brother 1938,Ap 18,11:1
Seventeen 1940,F 29,15:2
Father's Son 1941,F 13,25:3
Magnificent Ambersons, The 1942,Ag 14,13:3
Presenting Lily Mars 1943,Ap 30,25:3
Monsieur Beaucaire 1946,S 5,23:1
On Moonlight Bay 1951,Jl 27,15:2
By the Light of the Silvery Moon
1953,Mr 27,28:2

Tarkington, Booth (Screenwriter)
Edgar and the Teacher's Pet 1920,Mr 28,V,9:1
Edgar's Hamlet 1920,Ap 19,13:3
Edgar's Little Saw 1920,D 27,11:3
Edgar, The Explorer 1921,F 28,16:2
Get Rich Quick Edgar 1921,Mr 14,9:2
Tarkington, Rockne
Soldier in the Rain 1963,N 29,67:6 (Incorrect in this edition; use 1963,N 28,67:6 elsewhere)
Tarkovsky, Andrei (Director)
My Name Is Ivan (Ivan's Childhood) 1963,Je 28,25:4
Rublyov 1967,O 24,27:1
Tarkovsky, I
My Name Is Ivan (Ivan's Childhood) 1963,Je 28,25:4
Tarloff, Frank (Original Author)
Behave Yourself 1951,N 8,35:2
Guide for the Married Man, A 1967,My 27,16:1
Secret War of Harry Frigg, The 1968,Mr 5,34:5
Tarloff, Frank (Screenwriter)
Father Goose 1964,D 11,55:1
Guide for the Married Man, A 1967,My 27,16:1
Secret War of Harry Frigg, The 1968,Mr 5,34:5
Double Man, The 1968,My 2,57:1
Tarnow, Toby
Nobody Waved Goodbye 1964,S 17,52:1
Taro, Lotte
Weekend 1964,Ap 27,24:1
Tarola, Mary Jo
Affair With a Stranger 1953,Jl 11,8:2
Tarp, Lotte
Jokers, The 1967,My 16,50:1
Tarrazon, Michel
Naked Childhood 1968,S 28,36:1
Tarron, Elsie
Extra Girl, The 1924,Ja 21,20:1
Tarschys, Bernhard
To Bed...Or not to Bed 1963,D 23,18:2
Tarshis, Harold (Original Author)
Jail House Blues 1942,F 6,23:2
Tarshis, Harold (Screenwriter)
Fast Company 1938,Jl 6,21:2
Stop, Look and Love 1939,S 8,28:5
Jail House Blues 1942,F 6,23:2
Tarso, Ignacio Lopez
Macario 1961,S 28,48:6
Empty Star, The; Estrella Vacia, La 1962,Mr 28,36:4
Nazarin 1968,Je 21,48:1
Tarszyn, Andrei
Zygmunt Kolosowski 1947,N 13,13:3
Tartar, Mara
Mummy's Hand, The 1940,S 20,27:2
Tartchanof, M N
Dom Zhadnosti 1934,Ag 13,9:6
Tartovsky, Alexi (Director)
Violin and Roller 1962,Ag 20,18:2
Tartovsky, Alexi (Screenwriter)
Violin and Roller 1962,Ag 20,18:2
Tarvainen, Henry
Winter Kept Us Warm 1968,F 9,55:3
Tarver, Tony
Hamlet 1948,S 30,32:2
Tasca, Alessandro
Never Take No for an Answer 1952,Ap 29,32:2
Gospel According to St Matthew, The 1966,F 18,23:1
Tashlin, Frank (Director)
Son of Paleface 1952,O 2,32:3
Susan Slept Here 1954,Jl 30,9:1
Artists and Models 1955,D 22,20:1
Lieutenant Wore Skirts, The 1956,Ja 12,22:1
Hollywood or Bust 1956,D 24,8:1
Girl Can't Help It, The 1957,F 9,12:7
Will Success Spoil Rock Hunter 1957,S 12,37:5
Rock-a-Bye Baby 1958,Jl 24,18:1
Geisha Boy, The 1958,D 24,00:0
Say One for Me 1959,Je 20,11:2
Cinderfella 1960,D 17,19:2
Bachelor Flat 1962,Ja 13,14:1
It's Only Money 1962,N 22,43:1
Man From the Diners' Club, The 1963,Ap 18,39:1
Who's Minding the Store? 1963,N 29,67:6 (Incorrect in this edition; use 1963,N 28,67:6 elsewhere)
Disorderly Orderly, The 1964,D 24,8:3
Glass Bottom Boat, The 1966,Je 10,54:1
Alphabet Murders, The 1966,Jl 12,36:2
Caprice 1967,Je 8,52:2
Private Navy of Sgt O'Farrell, The 1968,My 9,54:1
Tashlin, Frank (Miscellaneous)
Woman of Distinction, A 1950,Mr 17,28:2
Tashlin, Frank (Original Author)
Delightfully Dangerous 1945,Je 9,17:3
Tashlin, Frank (Producer)
Girl Can't Help It, The 1957,F 9,12:7
Will Success Spoil Rock Hunter 1957,S 12,37:5
Say One for Me 1959,Je 20,11:2

Tashlin, Frank (Screenwriter)
Variety Girl 1947,O 16,34:4
Fuller Brush Man, The 1948,My 15,18:2
One Touch of Venus 1948,O 29,29:5
Paleface, The 1948,D 16,41:2
Kill the Umpire 1950,My 29,10:6
Good Humor Man, The 1950,Jl 14,17:2
Fuller Brush Girl, The 1950,O 6,23:2
Son of Paleface 1952,O 2,32:3
Artists and Models 1955,D 22,20:1
Lieutenant Wore Skirts, The 1956,Ja 12,22:1
Girl Can't Help It, The 1957,F 9,12:7
Will Success Spoil Rock Hunter 1957,S 12,37:5
Rock-a-Bye Baby 1958,Jl 24,18:1
Geisha Boy, The 1958,D 24,00:0
Cinderfella 1960,D 17,19:2
Bachelor Flat 1962,Ja 13,14:1
Who's Minding the Store? 1963,N 29,67:6 (Incorrect in this edition; use 1963,N 28,67:6 elsewhere)
Disorderly Orderly, The 1964,D 24,8:3
Caprice 1967,Je 8,52:2
Private Navy of Sgt O'Farrell, The 1968,My 9,54:1
Shakiest Gun in the West, The 1968,Jl 11,30:1
Tashman, Lilyan
Nellie, the Beautiful Cloak Model 1924,Ap 14,14:1
Manhandled 1924,Jl 29,9:2
Garden of Weeds, The 1924,N 4,24:1
Black Swan, The 1924,N 25,26:1
Parasite, The 1925,F 16,24:1
Declassee 1925,Mr 23,14:2
I'll Show You the Town 1925,Je 8,19:1
Pretty Ladies 1925,Jl 14,14:1
Seven Days 1925,Ag 31,19:3
Bright Lights 1925,N 18,27:4
Skyrocket, The 1926,Ja 26,25:2
So This Is Paris 1926,Ag 16,10:1
For Alimony Only 1926,S 21,33:1
Don't Tell the Wife 1927,F 22,23:2
Camille 1927,Ap 22,19:1
Prince of Head-Waiters 1927,Jl 11,23:5
Stolen Bride, The 1927,Ag 10,21:4
French Dressing 1927,D 13,33:2
Texas Steer, A 1928,Ja 2,28:1
Happiness Ahead 1928,Je 19,31:1
Take Me Home 1928,O 23,33:1
Manhattan Cocktail 1928,N 26,30:2
Craig's Wife 1928,D 4,29:1
Lone Wolf's Daughter, The 1929,Mr 4,20:2
Trial of Mary Dugan, The 1929,Mr 29,21:1
Bulldog Drummond 1929,My 3,23:2
Gold Diggers of Broadway, The 1929,Ag 31,13:4
Marriage Playground, The 1929,D 14,22:4
No, No, Nanette 1930,Ja 4,21:1
New York Nights 1930,F 1,15:1
Puttin' on the Ritz 1930,F 15,15:1
On the Level 1930,Jl 5,17:4
Matrimonial Bed, The 1930,Ag 25,14:2
Leathernecking 1930,S 13,9:3
Cat Creeps, The 1930,N 8,21:3
One Heavenly Night 1931,Ja 10,19:2
Finn and Hattie 1931,Ja 31,15:1
Millie 1931,F 7,11:1
Up Pops the Devil 1931,My 16,13:3
Murder by the Clock 1931,Jl 18,16:6
Mad Parade, The 1931,S 19,10:2
Road to Reno, The 1931,O 10,20:4
Girls About Town 1931,N 2,27:1
Wiser Sex, The 1932,Mr 12,19:5
Scarlet Dawn 1932,N 4,25:4
Mama Loves Papa 1933,Jl 24,11:2
Too Much Harmony 1933,S 23,11:5
Wine, Women and Song 1934,Mr 21,24:3
Riptide 1934,Mr 31,8:2
Tasker, Harold
Julius Caesar 1952,N 25,33:5
Tasker, Robert (Original Author)
John Meade's Woman 1937,F 18,19:1
San Quentin 1937,Ag 4,15:2
Tasker, Robert (Screenwriter)
Hell's Highway 1932,S 26,18:2
Notorious Gentleman, A 1935,F 16,9:1
Back Door to Heaven 1939,Ap 20,21:2
Secret Seven, The 1940,Ag 12,11:6
Dama de las Camelias, La 1944,S 26,16:1
Miserables, Los 1944,O 24,17:2
Taskin
Enemies of Progress 1934,Ja 11,19:2
Dom Zhadnosti 1934,Ag 13,9:6
Taskin, V
Pugachev 1938,Jl 4,10:2
Tasklu, V
In old Siberia 1929,Jl 22,17:1
Tasman, Charles
Massacre Hill 1950,D 14,51:3
Tasna, Rolf (Narrator)
Picasso 1955,D 23,14:4
Tasnady, Maria
Edes Mostoha 1935,N 21,27:2
Schlussakkord 1936,S 10,29:4
Streitum den Knaben Jo; Strife Over the Boy Jo 1938,D 10,13:2

Tasnady, Maria— Cont
Frau Sylvelin 1939,D 9,18:3
Das Erlebnis Geht Weiter; Another Experience 1940,F 3,9:3
Tassani, Riccardo
Loyalty of Love 1937,Mr 1,15:1
Tasse, Francois
Take it All; A Tout Prendre 1966,Ap 26,55:1
Tassie, Franz (Screenwriter)
Angel With the Trumpet 1951,D 21,21:5
Tassin, G M (Director)
Nazar Stodolya 1937,Ag 7,7:2
Tassin, George (Director)
Jimmie Higgins 1933,F 22,25:3
Tatar, George
Rich, Young and Pretty 1951,Jl 26,17:3
Tatar, George and Katrine
World Dances 1954,N 8,24:6
Tatar, Katrin
Rich, Young and Pretty 1951,Jl 26,17:3
Tatara, Jun
Rikisha Man, The 1960,My 4,57:1
TATE
See Also TAIT
Tate, Harry
Wings of the Morning 1937,Mr 12,19:1
Tate, John
Pacific Adventure 1947,N 26,18:2
On the Beach 1959,D 18,34:1
Tate, Kevin
7 Faces of Dr Lao 1964,Jl 23,19:1
Tate, Reginald
It Happened to One Man 1941,F 24,11:6
Next of Kin 1943,My 6,25:2
Way Ahead, The 1945,Je 4,22:3
Madonna of the Seven Moons 1946,My 23,18:4
Man From Morocco, The 1946,N 25,38:2
So Well Remembered 1947,N 5,34:3
Inheritance, The 1951,F 12,19:2
Story of Robin Hood, The 1952,Je 27,18:3
Malta Story 1954,Jl 17,7:2
Tate, Sharon
Don't Make Waves 1967,Je 21,36:2
Fearless Vampire Killers, The, or Pardon Me but Your Teeth are in my Neck 1967,N 14,52:1
Eye of the Devil 1967,D 7,60:1
Valley of the Dolls 1967,D 16,51:1
Tate, Sylvia (Original Author)
Woman on the Run 1950,N 30,24:2
Fuzzy Pink Nightgown, The 1957,O 31,41:1
Tatelman, Harry (Producer)
Underwater! 1955,F 10,27:2
Hot Blood 1956,Mr 24,14:2
Run for the Sun 1956,Ag 25,7:2
Tati, Jacques
Jour de Fete 1952,F 20,26:4
Mr Hulot's Holiday 1954,Je 17,36:2
My Uncle 1958,N 4,30:2
Tati, Jacques (Director)
Jour de Fete 1952,F 20,26:4
Mr Hulot's Holiday 1954,Je 17,36:2
My Uncle 1958,N 4,30:2
Tati, Jacques (Screenwriter)
Jour de Fete 1952,F 20,26:4
Mr Hulot's Holiday 1954,Je 17,36:2
My Uncle 1958,N 4,30:2
Tatic, Branco
Ninth Circle, The 1961,S 15,30:3
Tatler, Sydney
Third Key, The 1957,Je 3,30:2
Tattanelli, Pietro
Conjugal Bed, The 1963,S 17,30:1
Tattersall, Viva
Cynara 1932,D 26,26:2
Looking Forward 1933,My 1,10:2
Tattoli, Elda
China Is Near 1968,Ja 9,37:1
Tattoli, Elda (Screenwriter)
China Is Near 1968,Ja 9,37:1
Tatum, Clifford Jr
Room for One More 1952,Ja 16,21:2
TAUB
See Also TAUBE
Taub, Sam
Somebody up There Likes Me 1956,Jl 6,16:1
Taub, Walter
Transport From Paradise 1967,F 8,22:1
TAUBE
See Also TAUB
Taube, Aino
Familjen Som Var En Karusel 1937,My 22,19:3
En Saga 1938,Ja 8,19:2
Sara Laer Sig Folkvett 1938,F 16,17:1
Fram for Framgang; Head for Success 1938,N 28,11:3
En Enda Natt 1942,D 7,22:2
Secrets of Woman 1961,Jl 12,36:1
Taube, Mathias
Vaermlaenningarna 1932,N 18,23:2
Taube, Nicolai (Screenwriter)
My Daughter 1960,N 28,40:2
Taube, Sven-Bertil
Puss and Kram 1967,S 25,56:1
Guilt 1967,N 21,53:1

Tauber, Chaim
Motel, The Operator 1940,Ja 16,19:3
Tauber, Richard
Melodie der Liebe; Melody of Love
1932,Jl 31,IX,3:4
Das Lockende Ziel 1933,Je 19,18:2
Die Grosse Attraktion 1933,Jl 24,11:2
Ich Glaub' nie Mehr an Eine Frau
1933,O 13,25:4
Melodie der Liebe 1934,S 17,20:3
April Romance 1937,Ja 27,17:4
Heart's Desire 1937,Jl 12,20:4
Clown Must Laugh, A 1938,O 12,35:2
Forbidden Music 1938,D 27,13:2
Waltz Time 1946,F 11,25:2
Lisbon Story, The 1951,S 6,39:4
Tauber, Richard (Miscellaneous)
Heart's Desire 1937,Jl 12,20:4
Tauberova, Slavka
Fidlovacka 1931,Jl 7,27:5
Taubes, Frank (Screenwriter)
Mask, The 1961,O 28,12:4
Tauchen, Wilhelm
Jana, Das Maedchen aus dem Boehmerwald
1936,Je 20,22:3
Taurog, Norman (Director)
Lucky Boy 1929,F 25,16:1
Troopers Three 1930,F 17,17:6
Sunny Skies 1930,My 17,21:2
Follow the Leader 1930,D 6,21:3
Finn and Hattie 1931,Ja 31,15:1
Skippy 1931,Ap 4,23:1
Newly Rich 1931,Jl 3,22:1
Huckleberry Finn 1931,Ag 8,16:3
Sooky 1931,D 21,28:4
Hold 'Em Jail! 1932,Ag 20,7:4
Phantom President, The 1932,O 1,10:4
If I Had a Million 1932,D 3,21:4
Bedtime Story, A 1933,Ap 20,20:3
Way to Love, The 1933,N 11,10:3
We're not Dressing 1934,Ap 26,27:2
Mrs Wiggs of the Cabbage Patch 1934,O 29,14:2
College Rhythm 1934,N 24,19:1
Big Broadcast of 1936, The 1935,S 16,15:2
Strike Me Pink 1936,Ja 17,15:2
Rhythm on the Range 1936,Jl 30,22:1
Reunion 1936,N 27,27:1
Fifty Roads to Town 1937,Je 5,21:1
You Can't Have Everything 1937,Ag 4,15:2
Adventures of Tom Sawyer, The 1938,F 18,23:1
Mad About Music 1938,Mr 12,13:2
Boys Town 1938,S 9,25:1
Girl Downstairs, The 1939,Ja 26,17:1
Lucky Night 1939,My 5,29:3
Young Tom Edison 1940,Mr 15,27:2
Broadway Melody of 1940 1940,Mr 29,25:3
Little Nellie Kelly 1940,D 25,33:2
Men of Boys Town 1941,Ap 11,24:6
Design for Scandal 1942,F 6,23:3
Are Husbands Necessary? 1942,Jl 9,17:2
Yank at Eton, A 1942,O 16,23:1
Presenting Lily Mars 1943,Ap 30,25:3
Girl Crazy 1943,D 3,27:2
Hoodlum Saint, The 1946,Je 27,29:1
Beginning or the End, The 1947,F 21,15:1
Big City 1948,My 17,23:3
Bride Goes Wild, The 1948,Je 4,27:2
Words and Music 1948,D 10,34:2
That Midnight Kiss 1949,S 23,28:2
Please Believe Me 1950,Je 12,19:4
Toast of New Orleans, The 1950,S 30,13:3
Mrs O'Malley and Mr Malone 1951,F 23,33:2
Rich, Young and Pretty 1951,Jl 26,17:3
Room for One More 1952,Ja 16,21:2
Jumping Jacks 1952,Jl 24,30:2
Stooge, The 1953,F 5,19:2
Stars Are Singing, The 1953,Mr 12,24:2
Caddy, The 1953,S 18,16:6
Living It Up 1954,Jl 24,6:6
You're Never too Young 1955,Ag 26,10:2
Birds and the Bees, The 1956,Ap 23,22:1
Pardners 1956,Jl 26,20:2
Bundle of Joy 1956,D 20,36:1
Fuzzy Pink Nightgown, The 1957,O 31,41:1
Onionhead 1958,O 2,44:1
Don't Give up the Ship 1959,Jl 9,22:1
Visit to a Small Planet 1960,Ap 14,34:1
G I Blues 1960,N 5,28:1
All Hands on Deck 1961,Ap 1,10:2
Blue Hawaii 1962,F 22,20:2
It Happened at the World's Fair 1963,My 30,20:1
Palm Springs Weekend 1963,N 6,32:1
Tickle Me 1965,Je 24,28:3
Sergeant Deadhead 1965,O 23,17:3
Dr Goldfoot and the Bikini Machine
1966,F 17,29:3
Spinout 1966,D 15,60:1
Double Trouble 1967,My 25,54:2
Speedway 1968,Je 14,43:1
Tauzin, Maurice
Pied Piper, The 1942,Ag 13,15:3
Fighting Guardsman, The 1945,O 6,9:6
Bandit of Sherwood Forest, The 1946,Mr 23,8:4

Tarzan and the Huntress 1947,Ap 7,20:4
Tavernier, Albert
Too Many Kisses 1925,Mr 3,20:1
Tavernier, Gabriel
Diamond Queen, The 1954,Ja 27,24:2
Taviner, Reginald (Original Author)
Crime Ring 1938,Jl 22,10:3
Tavior, Ron
Nobody Waved Goodbye 1964,S 17,52:1
Tavoli, Jacques
Generals Without Buttons 1938,Mr 8,23:2
Tavoni, Eugenia
Wife for a Night 1958,Je 12,35:2
Tavrov, Y
Night Before Christmas, A 1963,D 16,44:4
Tayeb
Another Sky 1960,O 25,40:2
Taylor, Al
Lawless Nineties, The 1936,Je 29,11:1
Taylor, Alfred (Original Author)
Tell no Tales 1939,Je 2,27:3
Taylor, Avonne
My Best Girl 1927,N 7,26:4
Honor Among Lovers 1931,F 28,15:2
Taylor, Billy
Heads Up 1930,O 13,31:1
Taylor, Brad
Atlantic City 1944,Ag 14,11:4
Taylor, Brenda
Royal Ballet, The (Swan Lake Act II); Swan Lake
Act II (The Royal Ballet) 1960,O 5,45:2
Taylor, Buck
Wild Angels, The 1966,D 22,40:4
Taylor, Deems (Miscellaneous)
Louise 1940,F 3,9:4
Taylor, Deems (Narrator)
Fantasia 1940,N 14,28:2
Barber of Seville, The 1947,My 6,35:2
Taylor, Don
Winged Victory 1944,D 21,16:2
Song of the Thin Man 1947,Ag 29,14:2
Naked City, The 1948,Mr 5,17:2
For the Love of Mary 1948,S 23,37:2
Battleground 1949,N 12,8:4
Ambush 1950,Ja 19,35:2
Father of the Bride 1950,My 19,31:2
Target Unknown 1951,Mr 5,24:2
Father's Little Dividend 1951,Ap 13,18:5
Flying Leathernecks 1951,S 20,37:1
Blue Veil, The 1951,O 27,10:5
Submarine Command 1952,Ja 19,13:2
Japanese War Bride 1952,Ja 30,22:6
Girls of Pleasure Island, The 1953,My 16,10:1
Destination Gobi 1953,My 30,7:1
Stalag 17 1953,Jl 2,19:2
Johnny Dark 1954,Je 26,7:2
I'll Cry Tomorrow 1956,Ja 13,18:1
Bold and the Brave, The 1956,My 26,15:2
Taylor, Don (Director)
Battle for Music 1945,O 15,13:2
Everything's Ducky 1961,D 21,30:6
Ride the Wild Surf 1964,D 24,8:4
Jack of Diamonds 1967,N 11,26:3
Taylor, Don (Producer)
Battle for Music 1945,O 15,13:2
Foxhole in Cairo 1961,F 16,25:2
Sparrows Don't Sing 1963,My 7,46:2
Horror Hotel 1963,Je 20,29:1
They all Died Laughing 1964,Mr 16,37:2
Taylor, Don (Screenwriter)
Man in the Dinghy 1951,N 1,34:2
Foxhole in Cairo 1961,F 16,25:2
They all Died Laughing 1964,Mr 16,37:2
Taylor, Dub
You Can't Take It With You 1938,S 2,21:2
What's Buzzin Cousin 1943,Jl 23,21:4
Riding High 1950,Ap 11,26:2
Crime Wave 1954,Ja 13,26:2
No Time for Sergeants 1958,My 30,13:2
Hole in the Head, A 1959,Jl 16,31:2
Parrish 1961,My 5,22:1
Sweet Bird of Youth 1962,Mr 29,28:2
Hallelujah Trail, The 1965,Jl 2,17:1
Bonnie and Clyde 1967,Ag 14,36:1
Taylor, Dwight (Miscellaneous)
Head Over Heels in Love 1937,F 13,9:1
Taylor, Dwight (Original Author)
Numbered Men 1930,Je 9,23:3
Gay Divorcee, The 1934,N 16,27:1
Lady by Choice 1934,N 17,12:1
Paris in Spring 1935,Jl 13,16:2
Gangway 1937,Ag 21,7:3
Pickup on South Street 1953,Je 18,38:2
Taylor, Dwight (Producer)
Nightmare 1942,D 4,31:2
Taylor, Dwight (Screenwriter)
Top Hat 1935,Ag 30,12:2
Follow the Fleet 1936,F 21,21:2
Head Over Heels in Love 1937,F 13,9:1
Amazing Mr Williams, The 1940,Ja 19,15:2
Rhythm on the River 1940,Ag 29,23:2
Kiss the Boys Goodbye 1941,Ag 14,21:2
I Wake up Screaming 1942,Ja 17,13:2

Taylor, Dwight (Screenwriter) — Cont
Nightmare 1942,D 4,31:2
Thin Man Goes Home, The 1945,Ja 26,16:5
Conflict 1945,Je 16,10:2
Something to Live For 1952,Mr 8,11:2
We're not Married 1952,Jl 12,16:2
Vickie 1953,S 8,26:3
Boy on a Dolphin 1957,Ap 20,21:2
Taylor, Elaine
Casino Royale 1967,Ap 29,25:1
Half a Sixpence 1968,F 21,60:3
Anniversary, The 1968,Mr 21,57:2
Taylor, Elizabeth
Lassie Come Home 1943,O 8,15:4
White Cliffs of Dover, The 1944,My 12,15:2
National Velvet 1944,D 15,25:2
Courage of Lassie 1946,Jl 25,18:5
Life With Father 1947,Ag 16,6:6
Cynthia 1947,S 19,27:2
Date with Judy, A 1948,Ag 7,8:2
Julia Misbehaves 1948,O 8,30:2
Little Women 1949,Mr 11,33:2
Conspirator 1950,Ap 28,26:2
Father of the Bride 1950,My 19,31:2
Big Hangover, The 1950,My 26,20:3
Father's Little Dividend 1951,Ap 13,18:5
Place in the Sun, A 1951,Ag 29,20:1
Love Is Better Than Ever 1952,Mr 4,23:2
Ivanhoe 1952,Jl 1,8:2
Rhapsody 1954,Mr 12,17:1
Elephant Walk 1954,Ap 22,37:2
Beau Brummell 1954,O 21,31:5
Last Time I saw Paris, The 1954,N 19,20:2
Giant 1956,O 11,51:1
Raintree County 1957,D 21,22:1
Cat on a Hot Tin Roof 1958,S 19,24:1
Suddenly, Last Summer 1959,D 23,22:1
Butterfield 8 1960,N 17,46:1
Cleopatra 1963,Je 13,29:1
V I P's, The 1963,S 20,29:1
Sandpiper, The 1965,Jl 16,14:1
Who's Afraid of Virginia Woolf? 1966,Je 30,28:1
Who's Afraid of Virginia Woolf? 1966,Jl 10,II,1:5
Taming of the Shrew, The 1967,Mr 9,43:1
Reflections in a Golden Eye 1967,O 12,59:1
Comedians, The 1967,N 1,37:1
Doctor Faustus 1968,F 7,38:1
Boom! 1968,My 27,56:1
Secret Ceremony 1968,O 24,55:1
Taylor, Elizabeth (Producer)
Taming of the Shrew, The 1967,Mr 9,43:1
Taylor, Eloise
Damaged Love 1931,Ja 19,25:1
Taylor, Enid Stamp
Climbing High 1939,Je 5,20:3
Taylor, Eric (Original Author)
Fugitive at Large 1939,N 13,15:2
Outside the Three-Mile Limit 1940,Ap 8,15:2
Great Swindle, The 1941,My 14,25:4
Ghost of Frankenstein, The 1942,Ap 4,19:2
Crime Doctor's Courage, The 1945,Mr 3,11:3
Taylor, Eric (Screenwriter)
Lady in the Morgue, The 1938,My 9,13:3
Fugitive at Large 1939,N 13,15:2
Black Friday 1940,Mr 22,23:3
Ellery Queen, Master Detective 1940,D 19,33:1
Ellery Queen's Penthouse Mystery
1941,Mr 7,17:2
Black Cat, The 1941,Ap 26,20:3
Ellery Queen and the Perfect Crime
1941,Ag 11,17:3
Ellery Queen and the Murder Ring
1941,O 21,29:4
Enemy Agents meet Ellery Queen
1942,Ag 22,16:2
Phantom of the Opera, The 1943,O 15,15:2
Son of Dracula 1943,N 6,16:4
Whistler, The 1944,Ap 29,12:2
Shadows in the Night 1944,Jl 29,16:2
Crime Doctor's Courage, The 1945,Mr 3,11:3
Dick Tracy 1946,Ja 12,10:7
Spider Woman Strikes Back, The 1946,Mr 23,8:3
Truth About Murder, The 1946,Jl 27,12:6
Dick Tracy and Gruesome 1947,S 27,11:2
Prison Warden 1949,O 21,31:2
Taylor, Estelle
Tragedy of the East Side, A 1920,Ag 24,6:2
Foot Falls 1921,S 9,18:3
Monte Cristo 1922,Ag 15,20:3
Ten Commandments, The 1923,D 22,8:1
Tiger Love 1924,Je 16,18:3
Alaskan, The 1924,S 15,28:1
Don Juan 1926,Ag 7,6:1 (In Addenda)
New York 1927,Ja 31,13:1
Whip Woman, The 1928,F 13,16:2
Honor Bound 1928,Ap 30,18:3
Where East Is East 1929,My 27,22:1
Liliom 1930,O 4,15:2
Cimarron 1931,Ja 27,20:5
Street Scene 1931,Ag 27,22:5
Unholy Garden, The 1931,O 29,27:1
Call Her Savage 1932,N 25,19:2
Western Limited 1932,D 12,18:4
Southerner, The 1945,Ag 27,22:3

Taylor, Estelle— Cont

Show People 1967,O 2,58:2

Taylor, Evelyn
Oklahoma! 1955,O 11,49:1

Taylor, Ferris
Mr Dodd Takes the Air 1937,Ag 12,14:2
Jury's Secret, The 1938,F 4,17:2
You Can't Cheat an Honest Man 1939,F 20,13:2
Santa Fe Stampede 1939,Ap 26,27:3
Man of Conquest 1939,Ap 28,31:2
S O S Tidal Wave 1939,Je 22,19:3
Main Street Lawyer 1939,N 9,27:2
Chip of the Flying U 1940,Ja 22,11:3
Flight Angels 1940,My 27,23:2
Ladies Must Live 1940,S 6,25:3
Diamond Frontiers 1940,O 4,29:2
Mexican Spitfire out West 1940,O 30,29:3
Always a Bride 1940,N 21,43:3
She Couldn't Say No 1941,Ja 17,21:3
Saint in Palm Springs, The 1941,Ja 31,15:5
Man Betrayed, A 1941,Mr 27,29:5
Bringing Up Father 1946,N 22,27:3
Gunfighter, The 1950,Je 24,7:2
Two Flags West 1950,O 13,23:2
Prince of Peace, The 1951,Mr 24,8:3

Taylor, Forrest
Mystery of the Hooded Horsemen, The 1937,Ag 13,13:2
Chip of the Flying U 1940,Ja 22,11:3
Ghost Creeps, The 1940,Ag 19,13:3
Flying Wild 1941,Ap 12,19:3
Spoilers, The 1942,My 22,27:2
Rockin' in The Rockies 1945,Jl 5,7:2
Four Faces West 1948,Ag 4,18:3
Prince of Peace, The 1951,Mr 24,8:3
Park Row 1952,D 22,20:2

Taylor, Frank E (Producer)
Mystery Street 1950,Jl 28,12:5
Misfits, The 1961,F 2,24:2

Taylor, Grant
Forty Thousand Horsemen 1941,Ag 15,13:2
Massacre Hill 1950,D 14,51:3
Rats of Tobruk, The 1951,My 24,47:3
His Majesty O'Keefe 1954,F 6,17:2
Long John Silver 1955,Ap 7,24:1

Taylor, Grant (Original Author)
Terror Trail 1933,F 11,11:3

Taylor, Henry
Every Night at Eight 1935,Ag 3,16:2
You Only Live Once 1937,F 1,15:2

Taylor, Henry (Screenwriter)
Who Killed Gail Preston? 1938,My 6,27:2
Juvenile Court 1938,S 12,13:2

Taylor, Howard
Boom! 1968,My 27,56:1

Taylor, Jane
Cold Wind in August, A 1961,Jl 27,23:2

Taylor, Jean
Fighting Man of the Plains 1949,N 17,35:6

Taylor, Joan
Savage, The 1953,Ja 2,11:1
Off Limits 1953,Mr 30,25:5
Rose Marie 1954,Ap 2,22:2
Earth vs the Flying Saucers 1956,Ag 2,21:2
Omar Khayyam 1957,Ag 24,12:4

Taylor, John (Director)
Now Cinema! (Malcolm X: Struggle for Freedom); Malcolm X: Struggle for Freedom (Now Cinema!) 1968,Ap 9,56:1

Taylor, John (Miscellaneous)
Daybreak in Udi 1950,Je 2,26:2

Taylor, John (Producer)
Now Cinema! (Malcolm X: Struggle for Freedom); Malcolm X: Struggle for Freedom (Now Cinema!) 1968,Ap 9,56:1

Taylor, Joyce
F B I Story, The 1959,S 25,23:1
Atlantis the Lost Continent 1961,My 27,12:1
Ring of Fire 1961,Ag 17,18:2
13 Frightened Girls 1963,S 12,32:2
Twice Told Tales (Rappaccini's Daughter); Rappaccini's Daughter (Twice Told Tales) 1964,Mr 28,40:1

Taylor, Keith
Boy, Did I Get a Wrong Number! 1966,Je 9,54:2
Born Wild 1968,D 12,62:6

Taylor, Kent
Husband's Holiday 1931,D 25,29:2
Two Kinds of Women 1932,Ja 16,13:1
Forgotten Commandments 1932,Je 2,25:2
Merrily We Go to Hell 1932,Je 11,9:3
Lady's Profession, A 1933,Mr 25,13:3
I'm no Angel 1933,O 14,18:2
White Woman 1933,N 18,18:5
Cradle Song 1933,N 20,18:2
White Woman 1933,D 3,IX,9:4 (In Addenda)
Death Takes a Holiday 1934,F 24,18:4
David Harum 1934,Mr 2,23:2
Double Door 1934,My 5,22:3
Mrs Wiggs of the Cabbage Patch 1934,O 29,14:2
Limehouse Blues 1934,D 12,28:2
County Chairman, The 1935,Ja 19,8:1
Two Fisted 1935,O 5,18:3
My Marriage 1936,F 22,12:2

Sky Parade, The 1936,Ap 20,17:1
Florida Special 1936,My 29,15:2
Ramona 1936,O 7,32:4
Accusing Finger, The 1936,N 17,35:4
When Love Is Young 1937,Ap 17,15:1
Wings Over Honolulu 1937,My 29,20:1
Girl With Ideas, A 1938,Ja 1,11:2
Jury's Secret, The 1938,F 4,17:2
Last Express, The 1938,O 11,24:4
Four Girls in White 1939,F 23,19:3
Gracie Allen Murder Case, The 1939,Je 8,31:3
Five came Back 1939,Jl 5,20:2
Three Sons 1939,N 24,29:3
Sued for Libel 1940,Ja 19,15:3
I Take This Woman 1940,F 16,23:3
Two Girls on Broadway 1940,Ap 25,28:4
Girl in 313 1940,Je 14,25:3
Men Against the Sky 1940,S 12,31:2
I'm Still Alive 1940,O 11,25:4
Washington Melodrama 1941,My 26,15:3
Frisco Lil 1942,F 12,27:2
Tombstone, The Town too Tough to Die 1942,Jl 27,18:2
Army Surgeon 1942,N 5,35:2
Bomber's Moon 1943,Jl 31,8:2
Roger Touhy, Gangster 1944,Je 5,14:7
Daltons Ride Again, The 1945,D 8,21:2
Tangier 1946,Je 7,II,16:4
Deadline for Murder 1946,Je 29,22:7
Young Widow 1946,Jl 29,12:8
Dangerous Millions 1947,Mr 15,10:3
Second Chance 1947,S 20,12:4
Crimson Key, The 1947,O 18,9:2
Payment on Demand 1951,F 16,21:2
Playgirl 1954,My 15,13:3
Slightly Scarlet 1956,Mr 17,13:2
Harbor Lights 1964,F 13,25:3
Day Mars Invaded Earth, The 1964,Ap 2,28:3
Law of the Lawless 1964,Ag 27,28:2

Taylor, Kit
Long John Silver 1955,Ap 7,24:1

Taylor, Kressmann (Original Author)
Address Unknown 1944,Ap 17,20:1

Taylor, Larry
Alexander the Great 1956,Mr 29,23:1
King and Country 1966,Ja 28,20:4
Kaleidoscope 1966,S 23,45:1

Taylor, Laurette
Peg o'my Heart 1923,Ja 22,10:1
Happiness 1924,Mr 11,16:2

Taylor, Lawrence (Original Author)
Lady Without Passport, A 1950,Ag 4,13:2

Taylor, Lawrence (Screenwriter)
Jackie Robinson Story, The 1950,My 17,36:1

Taylor, Libby
Belle of the Nineties 1934,S 22,12:2
Mississippi 1935,Ap 18,27:2
Shanghai 1935,Jl 20,16:2
Fury and the Woman 1937,Je 22,26:2
Toy Wife, The 1938,Je 24,15:1
Great McGinty, The 1940,Ag 15,23:1
Howards of Virginia, The 1940,S 27,27:1
Flight From Destiny 1941,Mr 28,26:7
My Gal Sal 1942,My 1,23:1
Foxes of Harrow, The 1947,S 25,35:4
Another Part of the Forest 1948,My 19,30:2

Taylor, Lynn
Walk in the Shadow 1966,S 12,52:5

Taylor, Mary
Soak the Rich 1936,F 5,14:2
Lady of the Tropics 1939,S 8,28:3
Blossoms in the Dust 1941,Je 27,14:4

Taylor, Matt (Original Author)
All Abroad 1927,Ap 19,24:4
More Than a Secretary 1936,D 11,35:2
Road to Happiness 1942,Mr 27,27:4

Taylor, Megan
Ice-Capades 1941,S 25,29:1

Taylor, Nan
Pacific Adventure 1947,N 26,18:2

Taylor, P G Capt
Pacific Adventure 1947,N 26,18:2

Taylor, Phil
Howards of Virginia, The 1940,S 27,27:1
Ice-Capades 1941,S 25,29:1

Taylor, Ray (Director)
Return of Chandu 1935,Ap 15,16:3
Mystery of the Hooded Horsemen, The 1937,Ag 13,13:2
Frontier Town 1938,Mr 12,13:3
Rawhide 1938,Ap 25,9:2
West of Carson City 1940,My 7,31:3
Treat 'Em Rough 1942,Ja 19,21:3
Destination Unknown 1942,O 29,19:3
Daltons Ride Again, The 1945,D 8,21:2
Michigan Kid 1947,F 22,16:3
Vigilantes Return, The 1947,Jl 1,30:2

Taylor, Reeve (Screenwriter)
Midnight Episode 1955,My 19,25:5

Taylor, Renee
Producers, The 1968,Mr 19,38:1

Taylor, Rex (Miscellaneous)
Whispering Smith Speaks 1936,F 17,21:1

Taylor, Rex (Original Author)
Don't Tell the Wife 1927,F 22,23:2
High Gear 1933,Ap 15,16:2
Daytime Wife 1939,N 24,29:1

Taylor, Richard
Kill the Umpire 1950,My 29,10:6

Taylor, Robert
Handy Andy 1934,Ag 4,14:5
There's Always Tomorrow 1934,N 10,19:2
Wicked Woman, A 1935,Ja 1,24:1
Society Doctor 1935,F 4,11:3
Times Square Lady 1935,Mr 15,25:3
West Point of the Air 1935,Ap 6,10:1
Murder in the Fleet 1935,Je 3,22:2
Broadway Melody of 1936 1935,S 19,28:1
Magnificent Obsession 1935,D 31,11:2
Small Town Girl 1936,Ap 11,19:1
Private Number 1936,Je 12,19:1
His Brother's Wife 1936,Ag 15,6:2
Gorgeous Hussy, The 1936,S 5,7:1
Camille 1937,Ja 23,13:1
Personal Property 1937,Ap 11,27:2
This Is my Affair 1937,My 28,17:1
Broadway Melody of 1938 1937,S 3,12:1
Yank at Oxford, A 1938,F 25,15:1
Three Comrades 1938,Je 3,17:1
Crowd Roars, The 1938,Ag 5,11:1
Stand up and Fight 1939,Ja 27,17:2
Lucky Night 1939,My 5,29:3
Lady of the Tropics 1939,S 8,28:3
Remember? 1939,D 15,33:4
Waterloo Bridge 1940,My 17,23:2
Escape 1940,N 1,33:1
Flight Command 1941,Ja 17,21:2
Billy the Kid 1941,Je 20,28:2
When Ladies Meet 1941,S 5,19:2
Johnny Eager 1942,F 20,21:2
Her Cardboard Lover 1942,Jl 17,19:2
Stand by for Action 1943,Mr 12,12:2
Bataan 1943,Je 4,17:2
Youngest Profession, The 1943,Je 25,13:3
Song of Russia 1944,F 11,17:2
Undercurrent 1946,N 29,36:2
High Wall 1947,D 26,22:2
Bribe, The 1949,F 4,31:2
Ambush 1950,Ja 19,35:2
Conspirator 1950,Ap 28,26:2
Devil's Doorway 1950,N 10,35:1
Quo Vadis 1951,N 9,22:2
Westward the Women 1952,Ja 1,21:2
Ivanhoe 1952,Ag 1,8:2
Above and Beyond 1953,Ja 31,10:6
I Love Melvin 1953,Ap 10,18:4
Ride Vaquero 1953,Jl 16,17:2
All the Brothers Were Valiant 1953,D 29,19:2
Knights of the Round Table 1954,Ja 8,17:2
Valley of the Kings 1954,Jl 22,15:2
Rogue Cop 1954,S 18,12:2
Many Rivers to Cross 1955,F 24,21:2
Quentin Durward 1955,N 24,41:1
Last Hunt, The 1956,Mr 1,37:2
D-Day, The Sixth of June 1956,My 30,13:1
Power and The Prize, the 1956,S 27,42:1
Tip on a Dead Jockey 1957,S 7,12:7
Saddle the Wind 1958,Mr 21,17:1
Law and Jake Wade, the 1958,Je 7,11:1
Party Girl 1958,O 29,30:1
House of the Seven Hawks, The 1959,D 17,51:2
Killers of Kilimanjaro 1960,Ap 7,46:1
Miracle of the White Stallions 1963,My 23,31:2
House is not a Home, A 1964,S 2,33:1
Night Walker, The 1965,Ja 21,22:1
Johnny Tiger 1966,Je 16,53:4
Where Angels Go-Trouble Follows 1968,Ap 11,51:1

Taylor, Robert (Narrator)
Fighting Lady, The 1944,D 28,12:2
Secret Land, The 1948,D 2,39:2

Taylor, Robert Lewis (Original Author)
Silken Affair, The 1957,O 31,41:1

Taylor, Robert Lewis (Screenwriter)
Silken Affair, The 1957,O 31,41:1

Taylor, Rod
Long John Silver 1955,Ap 7,24:1
Virgin Queen 1955,Ag 6,13:2
Hell on Frisco Bay 1956,Ja 7,21:1
Catered Affair, The 1956,Je 15,32:4
Raintree County 1957,D 21,22:1
Separate Tables 1958,D 19,2:7
Ask any Girl 1959,My 22,32:1
Time Machine, The 1960,Ag 18,19:1
Birds, The 1963,Ap 1,5:5 (Incorrect in this edition; use 1963,Ap 1,54:1 elsewhere)
Gathering of Eagles, A 1963,Jl 11,21:2
V I P's, The 1963,S 20,29:1
Sunday in New York 1964,F 12,30:2
Fate Is the Hunter 1964,D 10,61:1
36 Hours 1965,Ja 29,25:2
Young Cassidy 1965,Mr 23,35:1
Do Not Disturb 1965,D 25,17:2
Glass Bottom Boat, The 1966,Je 10,54:1

Taylor, Rod — Cont

Liquidator, The 1966,O 29,34:1
Hotel 1967,Ja 20,27:1
Chuka 1967,N 2,58:3
Dark of the Sun 1968,Jl 4,13:1
Hell With Heroes, The 1968,S 3,54:2
High Commissioner, The 1968,D 12,62:5

Taylor, Rod (Producer)
Chuka 1967,N 2,58:3

Taylor, Rosemary (Original Author)
Chicken every Sunday 1949,Ja 19,34:2

Taylor, Ruth
Gentlemen Prefer Blondes 1928,Ja 16,24:1
Just Married 1928,Ag 13,23:2
College Coquette, The 1929,Ag 26,17:1
This Thing Called Love 1929,D 14,22:4

Taylor, S E V (Director)
Lone Wolf, The 1924,My 7,19:4

Taylor, Sam (Director)
Safety Last 1923,Ap 2,22:1
Girl Shy 1924,Ap 21,21:4
Hot Water 1924,O 27,27:1
Freshman, The 1925,S 21,12:4
For Heaven's Sake 1926,Ap 5,24:1
My Best Girl 1927,N 7,26:4
Tempest 1928,My 18,27:3
Woman Disputed, The 1928,N 10,20:8
Coquette 1929,Ap 6,14:4 (In Addenda)
Taming of the Shrew, The 1929,N 30,23:1
Du Barry, Woman of Passion 1930,N 3,19:3
Kiki 1931,Mr 6,16:1
Skyline 1931,O 5,17:3
Ambassador Bill 1931,N 14,15:3
Devil's Lottery 1932,Ap 2,13:2
Out all Night 1933,Ap 8,16:2
Cat's Paw, The 1934,Ag 17,12:2
Vagabond Lady 1935,Je 15,20:2
Nothing but Trouble 1945,Mr 10,14:1

Taylor, Sam (Original Author)
Girl Shy 1924,Ap 21,21:4

Taylor, Sam (Screenwriter)
Hot Water 1924,O 27,27:1
Freshman, The 1925,S 21,12:4

Taylor, Samuel (Original Author)
Sabrina 1954,S 23,43:2
Pleasure of his Company, The 1961,Je 2,36:1

Taylor, Samuel (Screenwriter)
Sabrina 1954,S 23,43:2
Eddy Duchin Story, The 1956,Je 22,15:1
Vertigo 1958,My 29,24:2
Pleasure of his Company, The 1961,Je 2,36:1
Goodbye Again 1961,Je 30,32:2
Rosie 1968,F 8,36:1

Taylor, Samuel A (Director)
Monte Carlo Story, The 1958,F 13,23:2

Taylor, Samuel A (Original Author)
Happy Time, The 1952,O 31,30:2

Taylor, Samuel A (Screenwriter)
Monte Carlo Story, The 1958,F 13,23:2
3 on a Couch 1966,Jl 7,30:1

Taylor, Samuel W (Original Author)
Man With my Face, The 1951,Je 15,27:5
Absent-Minded Professor, The 1961,Mr 16,44:2

Taylor, Samuel W (Screenwriter)
Man With my Face, The 1951,Je 15,27:5
Bait 1954,F 24,21:3

Taylor, Sidney
Light of Western Stars, The 1930,Ap 26,11:1

Taylor, Slats
Force of Arms 1951,Ag 14,20:2

Taylor, Slobhan
Dog of Flanders, A 1960,Ap 1,37:1

Taylor, Stanley
Guilty One, The 1924,Je 17,22:4
Ancient Highway, The 1925,N 11,27:3
Kosher Kitty Kelly 1926,S 28,30:2
Red Lips 1928,O 16,29:2 (In Addenda)
Home Towners, The 1928,O 24,26:4
Hottentot, The 1929,S 7,15:1

Taylor, Tony
Scandal at Scourie 1953,Je 16,24:2

Taylor, Totti Truman
Eight O'Clock Walk 1955,Ap 30,10:6
French They Are a Funny Race, The
1957,My 21,41:1

Taylor, Valerie
Berkeley Square 1933,S 14,26:2
48 Hours 1944,Je 26,21:2
No Place Like Homicide 1962,S 13,32:1

Taylor, Valerie (Screenwriter)
Take my Life 1949,Ja 19,34:2

Taylor, Vaughn
Up Front 1951,Mr 26,19:2
Meet Danny Wilson 1952,Mr 27,34:4
It Should Happen to You 1954,Ja 16,10:5
This Could Be the Night 1957,My 15,39:1
Jailhouse Rock 1957,N 14,41:1
Cowboy 1958,F 20,29:5
Cat on a Hot Tin Roof 1958,S 19,24:1
Andy Hardy Comes Home 1958,D 24,00:0
Warlock 1959,My 1,34:1
Blue Denim 1959,Jl 31,21:1
Psycho 1960,Je 17,37:1
Gallant Hours, The 1960,Je 23,19:4

Diamond Head 1963,F 21,5:2
Wheeler Dealers, The 1963,N 15,25:2
FBI Code 98 1964,Ap 9,25:6
Unsinkable Molly Brown, The 1964,Jl 17,15:1

Taylor, Wayne
Operation Secret 1952,N 6,37:2
Untamed Youth 1957,My 11,24:6

Taylor, Wilda
Roustabout 1964,N 11,38:1

Taylor, William
Outside the Law 1926,My 12,31:1

Taylor, William Desmond (Director)
Anne of Green Gables 1919,D 22,18:3
Judy of Rogues Harbor 1920,Mr 1,16:2
Nurse Marjorie 1920,My 24,20:3
Jenny, Be Good 1920,Je 28,13:2
Green Temptation, The 1922,Mr 20,10:3
Top of New York, The 1922,Je 19,10:3

Taylor, William Desmond (Producer)
Huckleberry Finn 1920,F 23,11:2
Soul of Youth, The 1920,Ag 16,8:2

Taylor, Wilton
Girl From Outside, The 1919,N 10,18:2
Alias Jimmy Valentine 1920,Ap 19,13:3
Drivin' Fool, The 1923,O 29,18:1

Taylor, Wright (Screenwriter)
When Tomorrow Comes 1939,Ag 17,16:2

Taylor-Smith, Jean
Rob Roy 1954,F 4,21:5
Weak and the Wicked, The 1954,Ag 21,10:3
Doctor in the House 1955,F 19,18:3

Taylor-Young, Leigh
I Love You Alice B Toklas! 1968,O 8,40:1

Tazaki, Jun
Tokyo File 212 1951,Je 1,20:7
Gate of Hell 1954,D 14,45:2
Blue Beast, The 1965,Ja 30,18:2

Tbileli, M
Scrapper, The 1959,D 14,42:2

Tchaikovsky, Peter Ilich (Composer)
Christmas Slippers 1945,D 24,19:2
Without Dowry 1946,Ap 15,22:2
Sleeping Beauty 1959,F 18,36:1
Eugene Onegin 1959,S 14,33:1
Royal Ballet, The (Swan Lake Act II); Swan Lake
Act II (The Royal Ballet) 1960,O 5,45:2
Queen of Spades 1961,S 4,10:1
Sleeping Beauty, The 1966,My 4,50:1

Tchakulayeva, A
Life is Beautiful 1933,F 13,11:5

Tchekhof
Man From the Restaurant, The 1930,Ja 6,30:5

Tchembarsky, L I
Polish Terror, The 1933,Mr 13,18:3

Tcherina, Ludmilla
Lover's Return, A; Revenant, Le 1948,Ja 26,15:2
Red Shoes, The 1948,O 23,9:2
Sign of the Pagan 1955,F 14,24:2
Lovers of Teruel, The 1962,D 15,5:1

Tcherkassky, Alexis
Cossacks in Exile 1939,Ja 28,19:2

Tcherkassof, N
Red Army Days 1935,O 21,22:4

Tchernia, Jean Richard Pierre
Belle Americaine, La 1961,D 18,42:1

Tchernia, M Pierre (Screenwriter)
Belle Americaine, La 1961,D 18,42:1
Counterfeit Constable, The 1966,N 22,32:2

Tcherpia, Pierre
War of the Buttons, The 1963,D 19,40:2

Tchertov, Guennady
Sons and Mothers 1967,O 2,58:1

Tcherviakov, Evgeni (Director)
Cities and Years 1931,Ap 4,23:1

Tchervyakof, Evgen
Conquerors of the Night 1933,Jl 31,16:3

Tchetchelazvili, G
Eagle of the Caucasus, The 1932,S 17,18:4

Tchin
Mr Wong, Detective 1938,N 21,14:4

Tchirkof, Boris
Three Women 1936,F 12,25:4
Defense of Volotchayevsk, The 1938,Ag 11,13:3

Tchistyakof, A
Storm Over Asia 1930,S 8,17:1
Life is Beautiful 1933,F 13,11:5
Patrioty 1933,S 25,18:5
Mother, 1905 1934,My 30,14:4
Deserter 1934,O 13,10:1
Thirteen, The 1937,Je 19,20:2

Tchornaya, Lala
Gypsies 1936,Jl 30,22:2

Tchugonof, K I
Rivals 1933,Ap 5,22:6

Tchurakovsky, N
Cossacks of the Don 1932,Mr 19,11:2

Tchuvelev, Ivan
Lash of the Czar, The 1929,F 12,23:1
Cities and Years 1931,Ap 4,23:1
Sibirsky Patrul 1932,My 14,11:5
Thunderstorm 1934,S 29,12:2

Tchverviakof
Czar and Poet 1928,Ja 15,VIII,5:2 (In Addenda)

Tchverviakof (Screenwriter)
Czar and Poet 1928,Ja 15,VIII,5:2 (In Addenda)

Tead, Phil
Fighting Blade, The 1923,O 15,15:4
Lightnin' 1930,N 29,21:4
Kiki 1931,Mr 6,16:1
Front Page, The 1931,Mr 20,29:1
Vice Squad, The 1931,Je 6,15:5
Final Edition, The 1932,F 22,23:2
Broadway Bad 1933,Mr 6,16:6
It Happened in New York 1935,Ap 6,10:1
Daring Young Man, The 1935,Jl 18,15:2
Music in My Heart 1940,Ja 4,19:2

Teagarden, Jack
Birth of the Blues 1941,D 11,39:1
Jazz on a Summer's Day 1960,Mr 29,46:2

Teagarden, Jack Orchestra
Birth of the Blues 1941,D 11,39:1

Teague, Anthony
How to Succeed in Business Without Really
Trying 1967,Mr 10,30:1

Teague, Frances
Iron Horse, The 1924,Ag 29,6:1
Last Edition, The 1925,N 11,27:3

Teague, John
Surfari 1967,Jl 19,26:2

Teal, Ray
Cherokee Strip 1940,N 4,23:2
Wild Bill Hickok Rides 1942,F 7,13:5
None Shall Escape 1944,Ap 7,23:2
Circumstantial Evidence 1945,Ap 21,18:3
Fighting Guardsman, The 1945,O 6,9:6
Bandit of Sherwood Forest, The 1946,Mr 23,8:4
Till the Clouds Roll By 1946,D 6,27:4
Michigan Kid 1947,F 22,16:3
Ramrod 1947,Je 30,25:6
Black Arrow, The 1948,O 4,14:2
Joan of Arc 1948,N 12,30:5
Streets of Laredo 1949,My 12,28:2
Blondie Hits the Jackpot 1949,S 9,28:3
Ambush 1950,Ja 19,35:2
Davy Crockett, Indian Scout 1950,Mr 17,28:3
Kid From Texas, The 1950,Je 2,26:2
Men, The 1950,Jl 21,15:2
Our Very Own 1950,Jl 28,12:5
Edge of Doom 1950,Ag 4,13:2
No Way Out 1950,Ag 17,23:1
Along the Great Divide 1951,My 17,38:3
Redhead and the Cowboy, The 1951,Je 6,37:2
Ace in the Hole 1951,Je 30,8:6
Tomorrow Is Another Day 1951,Ag 9,17:5
Distant Drums 1951,D 26,19:3
Captive City, The 1952,Mr 27,34:2
Wild North, The 1952,My 12,21:2
Lion and the Horse, The 1952,My 19,12:2
Carrie 1952,Jl 17,20:2
Jumping Jacks 1952,Jl 24,30:2
Montana Belle 1952,N 8,9:2
Turning Point, The 1952,N 15,15:2
Hangman's Knot 1952,D 11,45:3
Wild One, The 1953,D 31,9:2
Command, The 1954,Ja 16,10:5
About Mrs Leslie 1954,Je 28,16:2
Rogue Cop 1954,S 18,12:2
Run for Cover 1955,Ap 30,10:6
Desperate Hours, The 1955,O 6,25:1
Indian Fighter, The 1955,D 22,20:1
Burning Hills, The 1956,Ag 24,15:2
Band of Angels 1957,Jl 11,21:1
Saddle the Wind 1958,Mr 21,17:1
Home from the Hill 1960,Mr 4,19:1
Inherit the Wind 1960,O 13,41:1
One Eyed Jacks 1961,Mr 31,21:1
Judgment at Nuremberg 1961,D 20,36:1

Teal, Sonne
Poupee, La 1963,Ag 28,39:1

Tearle, Constance
Just a Woman 1925,My 26,24:2

Tearle, Conway
Virtuous Wives 1918,D 30,7:3
Way of a Woman, The 1919,Jl 28,8:5
Virtuous Vamp, A 1919,N 17,20:1
Mind-the-Paint Girl, The 1919,N 24,13:1
Two Weeks 1920,Ja 26,16:1
Forbidden Woman, The 1920,F 23,11:2
Oath, The 1921,Ap 11,9:1
Eternal Flame, The 1922,S 18,14:2
One Week of Love 1923,Ja 8,22:1
Bella Donna 1923,Ap 16,20:2
Rustle of Silk, The 1923,My 8,22:4
Ashes of Vengeance 1923,Ag 7,20:2
Common Law, The 1923,O 29,18:1
Dangerous Maid, The 1923,D 11,26:2
Black Oxen 1924,Ja 7,23:1
Lilies of the Field 1924,Mr 17,19:1
White Moth, The 1924,Je 16,18:3
Flirting With Love 1924,S 1,9:1
Great Divide, The 1925,F 11,19:4
Bad Company 1925,Mr 16,16:1
School for Wives 1925,Ap 1,21:3
Heart of a Siren, The 1925,Ap 8,24:3

Tearle, Conway— Cont
Mystic, The 1925,Ag 31,19:3
Dancing Mothers 1926,F 18,21:1
Dancers of Paris, The 1926,Mr 29,24:3
Greater Glory, The 1926,My 4,31:1
Gold Diggers of Broadway, The 1929,Ag 31,13:4
Evidence 1929,O 5,22:5
Lost Zeppelin, The 1930,F 3,17:1
Truth About Youth, The 1930,D 13,22:2
Lady Who Dared, The 1931,Je 6,15:5
Captivation 1931,S 28,17:4
Morals for Women 1931,N 16,23:1
Man About Town 1932,My 28,18:2
Her mad Night 1932,N 15,24:5
Day of Reckoning 1933,N 4,18:2
Should Ladies Behave? 1933,D 18,24:3
Stingaree 1934,My 18,27:1
Sing Sing Nights 1935,Ja 26,13:2
Klondike Annie 1936,Mr 12,18:2
Preview Murder Mystery, The 1936,Mr 21,13:2
Romeo and Juliet 1936,Ag 21,12:2
Tearle, David
Green Goddess, The 1930,F 14,20:1
Tearle, Godfrey
Salome of the Tenements 1925,F 24,17:3
Thirty-Nine Steps, The 1935,S 14,8:4
Last Journey, The 1936,Je 8,22:4
East Meets West 1936,O 31,24:2
One of our Aircraft Is Missing 1942,N 2,17:2
At Dawn We Die 1943,My 8,19:2
Gay Intruders, The 1946,Mr 18,24:2
Notorious Gentleman 1946,N 14,39:3
Beginning or the End, The 1947,F 21,15:1
White Corridors 1952,Jl 16,21:1
Story of Mandy, The 1953,F 24,21:3
I Believe in You 1953,My 5,34:3
Titfield Thunderbolt, The 1953,O 6,34:2
Decameron Nights 1953,N 17,38:2
Tearle, Noah
Over the Hill to the Poor House 1920,S 18,16:2
Teasdale, Verree
Syncopation 1929,Ap 8,32:1
Sap From Syracuse, The 1930,Jl 26,16:4
Skyscraper Souls 1932,Ag 5,11:2
Payment Deferred 1932,N 8,26:3
Luxury Liner 1933,F 3,21:3
They Just Had to Get Married 1933,F 13,11:4
Love, Honor and Oh, Baby! 1933,O 28,20:3
Roman Scandals 1933,D 25,28:2
Fashions of 1934 1934,Ja 20,12:2
Modern Hero, A 1934,Ap 20,17:1
Dr Monica 1934,Je 21,28:2
Desirable 1934,S 15,20:5
Madame Du Barry 1934,O 25,26:2
Firebird, The 1934,N 15,25:2
Midsummer Night's Dream, A 1935,O 10,31:1
Milky Way, The 1936,Mr 26,27:2
First Lady 1937,D 23,25:1
Topper Takes a Trip 1938,D 30,11:2
Fifth Avenue Girl 1939,Ag 25,12:2
I Take This Woman 1940,F 16,23:3
Turnabout 1940,Jl 27,17:6
Love Thy Neighbor 1940,D 18,32:5
Come Live With Me 1941,F 28,17:3
Tebaldi, Renata
Aida 1954,N 12,17:1
House of Ricordi 1956,Mr 13,32:1
Technik, Alfred (Original Author)
Devil's Trap, The 1964,Ag 14,16:1
Tecklenburg, Theo
Sunderin 1954,D 24,7:2
Teddy (Dog)
Boy of Flanders, A 1924,Ap 15,24:1
Teddy (Lion)
Extra Girl, The 1924,Ja 21,20:1
Tedemar, Sylvia
Good Morning and Goodbye! 1968,F 20,53:1
Tedeschi, Gianrico
Love a la Carte 1965,Ja 12,31:1
Fascist, The 1965,Je 18,28:3
Tedesco, Paolo
Gospel According to St Matthew, The 1966,F 18,23:1
Tedford, Charles (Miscellaneous)
Tanga Tika 1953,O 6,34:4
Tedlie, Charlotte
Luck of the Irish, The 1937,Ja 16,21:1
Tedrow, Irene
Moon and Sixpence, The 1942,O 28,26:4
Song of the Open Road 1944,Je 7,13:3
Hot Spell 1958,S 18,37:2
Thunder of Drums, A 1961,S 27,35:1
Teed, John
Young Woodley 1930,S 27,21:3
Teed, Phil
Glamour 1934,My 12,12:3
Teege, Joachim
Merry Wives of Windsor, The 1952,S 22,19:2
Teeman, Ann
Joe and Ethel Turp Call on the President 1940,Ja 4,19:2
Teetzmann, Horst
Paloma, La 1936,O 21,35:3
Stuetzen der Gesellschaft 1936,N 7,15:3

Teichman, Howard (Original Author)
Solid Gold Cadillac, The 1956,O 25,40:3
Teichman, Howard (Original Author)
Lonelyhearts 1959,Mr 5,35:3
Teilhet, Darwin L (Original Author)
No Room for the Groom 1952,Je 14,12:2
Teilou, Basil
Mrs O'Malley and Mr Malone 1951,F 23,33:2
Teitelbaum, Abraham
Wandering Jew, The 1933,O 21,11:2
Teitelbaum, Barbara
Come Back Baby 1968,Je 14,43:1
Teixeira, Virgilio
Man Could Get Killed, A 1966,My 12,54:2
Tel Aviv Philharmonic Choir
Journey to Jerusalem, A 1968,N 18,59:1
Tela-Tchal
Robber Symphony 1937,Ja 27,17:2
Telegina, Valentina
City of Youth 1938,S 5,30:4
New Teacher, The 1941,Ap 7,13:3
Frigid Sea, The 1955,N 21,23:4
House I Live in, The 1959,Ap 20,34:2
Farewell, Doves 1962,Mr 19,38:3
Telez, Manuel
Sombra de Pancho Villa, La 1934,Ja 8,20:3
Telfer, Dariel (Original Author)
Caretakers, The 1963,Ag 22,19:2
Telford, Frank (Producer)
Sergeant Ryker 1968,Mr 21,56:2
Tell, Alma
On With the Dance 1920,F 16,8:1
Right to Love, The 1920,Ag 23,9:2
Iron Trail, The 1921,O 31,19:3
San Francisco Nights 1928,Ja 31,29:1
Saturday's Children 1929,Ap 29,29:2
Tell, Olive
Chickie 1925,Ap 27,15:2
Womanhandled 1926,Ja 5,25:2
Prince of Tempters, The 1926,O 18,18:1
Summer Bachelors 1926,D 20,28:3
Slaves of Beauty 1927,Je 8,23:3
Soft Living 1928,F 27,16:2
Sailors' Wives 1928,F 28,18:4
Trial of Mary Dugan, The 1929,Mr 29,21:1
Hearts in Exile 1929,N 29,25:1
Cock O' the Walk 1930,Ap 12,23:1
Lawful Larceny 1930,Jl 12,16:4
Ten Cents a Dance 1931,Mr 7,17:2
Woman Hungry 1931,Mr 23,24:7
Right of Way, The 1931,Mr 24,31:2
Ladies' Man 1931,My 1,30:3
Devotion 1931,O 3,20:2
Delicious 1931,D 26,15:5
Strictly Personal 1933,Mr 20,18:2
Witching Hour, The 1934,Ap 28,11:3
Private Scandal 1934,Je 15,26:2
Baby, Take a Bow 1934,Je 30,18:6
Scralet Empress, The 1934,S 15,20:2
Shanghai 1935,Jl 20,16:2
Yours for the Asking 1936,Ag 20,14:2
In His Steps 1936,O 29,31:1
Polo Joe 1936,N 5,35:1
Tellegen, Lou
Unknown, The 1915,D 13,13:1
Maria Rosa 1916,My 8,7:2
Victory of Conscience, The 1916,Ag 28,7:5
World and Its Woman, The 1919,S 8,16:1
Flame of the Desert 1919,O 27,9:3
Woman and the Puppet 1920,Ap 5,20:1
Let Not Man Put Asunder 1924,Ja 15,16:1
Between Friends 1924,My 12,14:4
Single Wives 1924,Jl 29,9:2
Breath of Scandal, The 1924,N 26,17:3
Redeeming Sin, The 1925,Ja 20,18:2
Parisian Nights 1925,Je 2,16:3
After Business Hour 1925,Je 17,16:2
Sporting Chance, The 1925,Je 24,14:3
Enemies of the Law 1931,Jl 13,13:5
Tellegen, Mike
Down Under the Sea 1936,Ag 10,10:2
Teller, Eloise
Navajo 1952,F 21,24:4
Teller, Francis Kee
Navajo 1952,F 21,24:4
Teller, Linder
Navajo 1952,F 21,24:4
Teller, Mrs
Navajo 1952,F 21,24:4
Tellering, Michael
Fidelio 1961,My 13,10:1
Tellez, Christina
Castillos en el Aire; Castles in the Air 1938,My 21,9:3
Telli, Rina
Cavalleria Rusticana 1953,D 28,17:2
Tellini, Piero (Original Author)
Four Steps in the Clouds 1948,N 22,25:2
White Line, The 1952,D 6,17:2
Tellini, Piero (Screenwriter)
To Live in Peace 1947,N 25,37:2
Angelina 1948,Ap 6,27:2
Woman Trouble 1949,My 26,34:2

Tellini, Piero (Screenwriter)— Cont
Flesh will Surrender 1950,O 26,38:7
White Line, The 1952,D 6,17:2
Tale of Five Women, A 1953,Ja 16,19:2
Volcano 1953,Jl 21,19:2
Side Street Story 1954,Je 24,30:4
Utopia 1954,D 15,41:1
Virtuous Bigamist, The 1959,My 28,34:3
Tello, Sanchez
Rancho Grande 1938,D 2,27:2
Tello, Sanchez (Producer)
Corazon de Nino; Heart of a Child 1940,Ja 1,29:4
Tema, Muzaffer
Certain Smile, A 1958,Ag 1,13:2
Temba, Albertina
Cry, the Beloved Country 1952,Ja 24,23:2
Temerson, Jean
Devil Is an Empress, The 1939,D 4,18:4
S O S Mediterranean 1940,Ja 1,29:2
Personal Column 1941,F 3,13:2
Volpone 1947,D 27,9:3
Miquette 1951,F 5,18:2
Temoff, Serge
Devil Dancer, The 1927,D 19,30:1
Coffin Maker, The 1928,O 9,35:1
Tempe, Paul
Lower Depths, The 1937,S 11,20:1
Tempest, Marie
Moonlight Sonata 1937,Je 6,XI,4:4 (In Addenda)
Moonlight Sonata 1938,My 10,17:2
Temple, Joan (Original Author)
No Room at the Inn 1949,D 26,33:4
Temple, Lorraine
Pink Gods 1922,S 25,10:2
Temple, Shirley
Red-Haired Alibi 1932,O 24,18:5
Stand up and Cheer 1934,Ap 20,17:1
Change of Heart 1934,My 11,24:2
Little Miss Marker 1934,My 19,18:3
Now I'll Tell 1934,My 26,12:2
Baby, Take a Bow 1934,Je 30,18:6
Now and Forever 1934,O 13,10:1
Bright Eyes 1934,D 21,31:1
Little Colonel, The 1935,Mr 22,26:2
Our Little Girl 1935,Je 7,24:4
Curly Top 1935,Ag 2,22:3
Littlest Rebel, The 1935,D 20,30:1
Captain January 1936,Ap 25,21:1
Poor Little Rich Girl, The 1936,Je 26,16:1
Dimples 1936,O 10,21:2
Stowaway 1936,D 19,16:1
Wee Willie Winkie 1937,Jl 24,12:1
Heidi 1937,N 6,14:2
Rebecca of Sunnybrook Farm 1938,Mr 26,12:1
Little Miss Broadway 1938,Jl 23,10:4
Just Around the Corner 1938,D 3,11:2
Little Princess, The 1939,Mr 11,21:1
Susannah of the Mounties 1939,Je 24,13:2
Blue Bird, The 1940,Ja 20,11:2
Young People 1940,Ag 24,16:2
Kathleen 1941,D 19,35:3
Miss Annie Rooney 1942,Je 8,11:1
Since You Went Away 1944,Jl 21,16:2
I'll Be Seeing You 1945,Ap 6,20:6
Kiss and Tell 1945,O 26,16:2
Honeymoon 1947,My 19,27:2
Bachelor and the Bobby-Soxer, The 1947,Jl 25,12:5
That Hagen Girl 1947,O 25,13:2
Fort Apache 1948,Je 25,26:2
Mr Belvedere Goes to College 1949,Ap 16,11:2
Adventure in Baltimore 1949,Ap 29,27:2
Story of Seabiscuit, The 1949,N 12,8:4
Sound of Laughter, The 1963,D 18,44:2
Temple, Wilfred
Yellow Mask, The 1930,D 8,26:1
Temple, William F (Original Author)
Four Sided Triangle 1953,My 16,10:1
Temple-Smith, John (Producer)
It Takes a Thief 1963,Ag 15,24:7
Templeton, Alec (Composer)
Date with Judy, A 1948,Ag 7,8:2
Templeton, Dink
Night after Night 1932,O 31,18:4
Templeton, George
Make Me a Star 1932,Jl 1,19:3
Templeton, George (Director)
Sundowners, The 1950,My 5,17:2
Quebec 1951,Mr 16,34:2
Templeton, George (Original Author)
Saturday's Heroes 1937,O 16,22:2
Templeton, George (Producer)
High Lonesome 1950,D 8,40:4
Templeton, Harry
This Reckless Age 1932,Ja 9,21:1
Geronimo 1940,F 8,18:3
Templeton, William (Screenwriter)
Double Confession 1953,My 1,17:2
1984 1956,O 1,31:1
Templey, Marguerite
Avocate d'Amour 1938,S 8,27:2
Indiscretions 1939,My 1,21:1

Templin, Dan M (Original Author)
Boulder Dam 1936,Mr 30,17:5
Tempo, Nino
Red Pony, The 1949,Mr 9,33:2
Girl Can't Help It, The 1957,F 9,12:7
Temporance, Seven
Wrong Box 1966,Jl 20,46:1
Ten, Valentina
Igdenbu 1930,D 9,31:3
Ten Eyck, Lillian
Sandra 1924,D 22,20:2
Tena, Jose Tasso
Night Heaven Fell, The 1958,O 22,40:4
Tenario, Mario
Mujer de Nadie, La; Nobody's Wife
1938,F 7,10:3
Tenbrook, Harry
Danger Street 1928,S 25,29:4 (In Addenda)
Men Without Women 1930,F 1,15:1
Runaway Bride 1930,My 17,21:2
On the Level 1930,Jl 5,17:4
Donovan's Kid 1931,My 22,28:5
Terror Trail 1933,F 11,11:3
Rawhide 1938,Ag 25,19:2
They Were Expendable 1945,D 21,25:2
Mister Roberts 1955,Jl 15,14:1
Tendlar, David (Miscellaneous)
Mr Bug Goes to Town 1942,F 20,21:3
Tene, Avraham
Khamishia-Five Tales From Israel
1954,My 7,19:3
Tenenholtz, Nettie
Salome of the Tenements 1925,F 24,17:3
Tenes, Froilan
Juarez y Maximiliano 1935,F 16,9:2
Tengroth, Birgit
Ungkarlspappan 1936,Ja 4,19:1
Katrina 1949,N 18,35:3
Tenin, Boris
Pozor 1933,Mr 11,18:4
Grain 1936,Ja 16,25:2
Man With the Gun, The 1939,Ja 30,9:3
Without Dowry 1946,Ap 15,22:2
Hello, Moscow! 1946,Je 15,24:4
Tenin, E
Golden Mountains 1932,Ap 14,25:3
Tennant, Barbara
Circus Days 1923,Ag 6,14:2
Captain January 1924,Jl 7,10:4
Poisoned Paradise 1924,Ag 11,16:1
Tennant, Dorothy
Men With Wings 1938,O 27,27:2
Tennberg, Jean
Moment of Truth, The 1954,Ap 27,36:2
Tennberg, Jean-Marc
Fanfan the Tulip 1953,My 5,34:2
Adorable Creatures 1956,Ja 11,36:2
Love on a Pillow 1963,D 17,49:1
Tenney, Del
Satan in High Heels 1962,Mr 24,15:6
Tenney, Del (Director)
Horror of Party Beach, The 1964,Ap 30,30:1
Curse of the Living Corpse, The 1964,Ap 30,30:1
Tenney, Del (Producer)
Psychomania 1964,F 15,14:3
Curse of the Living Corpse, The 1964,Ap 30,30:1
Horror of Party Beach, The 1964,Ap 30,30:1
Tenney, Del (Screenwriter)
Curse of the Living Corpse, The 1964,Ap 30,30:1
Tennyson, Alfred E (Original Author)
Beggar Maid, The 1921,S 26,18:1
Tennyson, Gladys
Broadway After Dark 1924,My 20,15:2
Last Man on Earth, The 1924,D 13,12:4
Tennyson, Pen (Director)
Convoy 1941,Ja 17,21:2
Proud Valley 1941,My 17,19:2
Tennyson, Pen (Screenwriter)
Convoy 1941,Ja 17,21:2
Tennyson, Walter
Bride of the Storm 1926,Ap 5,24:1
Dress Parade 1927,O 31,22:1
Tenorio, Mario
Isla Maldita, La 1935,D 2,18:3
Mas Alla de la Muerta 1936,Mr 2,13:3
Sor Juana Ines de la Cruz 1936,Je 6,21:2
Tenser, Tony (Producer)
Conqueror Worm, The 1968,Ag 15,46:2
Teomi, M
Chalutzim 1934,Ap 2,13:3
Teomi, Oded
They Were Ten; (Heym Hayu Assara)
1961,Ap 18,44:2
Tepperman, Joy
Winter Kept Us Warm 1968,F 9,55:3
Terac, S H (Miscellaneous)
Honorable Catherine, The 1948,Ag 23,13:3
Terac, S H (Screenwriter)
Honorable Catherine, The 1948,Ag 23,13:3
Naked Woman, The 1950,Ja 21,10:2
Terac, Solange (Screenwriter)
Face to the Wind 1951,Ja 16,34:2

Terasaki, Gwendolen (Original Author)
Bridge to the Sun 1961,O 18,50:1
Terbois, Gilberte
Angels of the Streets 1950,Ja 17,24:2
Terekhina, Anna
Tanya 1942,Mr 5,27:1
Terentiev, V
On his Own 1939,S 13,31:3
Teresa, Maria
Tierra Brava 1938,O 29,15:6
Terhune, Albert Payson (Original Author)
Night of the Pub, The 1920,Ja 26,16:1
Lotus Eater, The 1921,N 28,16:1
Grand Larceny 1922,F 27,13:4
Knockout Reilly 1927,Ap 18,21:2
His Dog 1927,Ag 16,31:2
Whom the Gods Destroy 1934,Jl 13,14:2
Lad: A Dog 1963,My 2,40:2
Terhune, Max
Hit Parade, The 1937,My 31,11:2
Manhattan Merry-Go-Round 1937,D 31,9:3
Call the Mesquiteers 1938,Mr 19,11:2
Santa Fe Stampede 1939,Ag 26,27:3
Man of Conquest 1939,Ap 28,31:2
Terhune, William (Original Author)
Kelly the Second 1936,O 3,21:2
Terlo, Anthony
Woman Trouble 1949,My 26,34:2
Terno, Gerda Maria
Paradies der Junggesellen; Bachelors' Paradise
1940,Ap 13,21:3
Terol, Pedro
Odio 1935,Je 24,12:3
Heroes del Barrio, Los 1936,D 28,12:4
Molinos de Viento; Windmills 1940,F 26,11:2
Terra, Renato
Path of Hope, The (Il Cammino Della Speranza)
1952,Ag 5,15:5
Terra, Stefano (Screenwriter)
White Line, The 1952,D 6,17:2
Terrabust, Charlotte
Boy on a Dolphin 1957,Ap 20,21:2
Terracina, Giuseppi
Man of Courage 1934,N 14,23:2
Terranova, Dan
Blackboard Jungle 1955,Mr 21,21:5
Crime in the Streets 1956,My 24,27:4
Young Dillinger 1965,My 13,32:3
Terray, Lionel (Miscellaneous)
Annapurna 1953,D 14,45:4
Terrazzas, Ernest (Original Author)
Three Caballeros, The 1945,F 5,20:1
Terrell, Bill
Blue Grass of Kentucky 1950,Ja 27,29:2
Terrell, Ray
Hell's Five Hours 1958,Jl 24,18:1
Terrell, Steven
Tea and Sympathy 1956,S 28,24:4
Terrell, Yolande
Tell-Tale Heart, The 1934,Je 15,26:3
Terrett, Courtenay (Original Author)
Quick Millions 1931,Ap 18,17:3
Hush Money 1931,Jl 11,7:6
Famous Ferguson Case, The 1932,Ap 25,18:6
Made on Broadway 1933,Jl 8,14:5
Terrett, Courtenay (Screenwriter)
Castle on the Hudson 1940,Mr 4,11:2
Terribill, Giovanni
Messalina 1924,Ag 25,16:2
Terrill, Henry Maj
Big Country, The 1958,O 2,44:1
Terrill, Lucy Stone (Original Author)
Unguarded Women 1924,Je 24,18:2
Terrill, Patricia
Big Country, The 1958,O 2,44:1
Terris, Norma
Married in Hollywood 1929,S 23,24:3
Cameo Kirby 1930,F 8,12:5
Terriss, Ellaline
Atlantic 1930,Ja 26,VIII,6:2
Atlantic 1930,O 6,21:1
Iron Duke, The 1935,Ja 25,27:2
Secret Four, The 1940,Ap 22,13:2
Terriss, Tom (Director)
Lion and the Mouse, The 1919,F 17,11:3
Bandolero, The 1924,O 27,27:1
Terrot, Charles (Original Author)
Angel Who Pawned her Harp, The
1956,F 29,35:2
Alligator Named Daisy, An 1957,O 7,23:2
Terrot, Charles (Screenwriter)
Angel Who Pawned her Harp, The
1956,F 29,35:2
Terry, Alice
Four Horsemen of the Apocalypse 1921,Mr 7,8:1
Conquering Power, The 1921,Jl 10,VI,2:1 (In
Addenda)
Turn to the Right 1922,Ja 24,11:1
Prisoner of Zenda, The 1922,Ag 1,14:3
Where the Pavement Ends 1923,Ap 2,22:1
Scaramouche 1923,O 12,7:2 (Incorrect in this
edition; use 1927,O 1,7:2 elsewhere)
Arab, The 1924,Jl 14,11:5

Terry, Alice— Cont
Great Divide, The 1925,F 11,19:4
Confessions of a Queen 1925,Mr 24,20:6
Sackcloth and Scarlet 1925,Mr 25,24:2
Any Woman 1925,My 27,26:2
Mare Nostrum 1926,F 16,22:4
Four Horsemen of the Apocalypse, The
1926,S 27,27:3
Magician, The 1926,O 25,15:1
Lovers 1927,Ap 19,24:4
Garden of Allah, The 1927,S 3,13:5
Garden of Allah, The 1927,S 11,VIII,5:1
Terry, Don
Me, Gangster 1928,O 22,29:1
Valiant, The 1929,My 13,27:2
Untamed 1929,N 30,23:1
Border Romance 1930,My 26,25:3
Fight to the Finish, A 1937,Je 26,20:2 (In
Addenda)
Paid to Dance 1937,D 6,19:1
When G-Men Step In 1938,Mr 14,13:2
Who Killed Gail Preston? 1938,My 6,27:2
Mutiny in the Arctic 1941,My 3,20:5
Drums of the Congo 1942,Jl 20,16:4
White Savage 1943,Ap 26,15:2
Terry, Ellen
Bohemian Girl, The 1923,F 5,18:2
Terry, Ethel Grey
Crossroads of New York, The 1922,My 22,18:4
Under Two Flags 1922,S 25,10:2
Peg o'my Heart 1923,Ja 22,10:1
Garrison's Finish 1923,My 28,18:2
Wild Bill Hickok 1923,N 21,22:1
Unknown Purple, The 1924,Mr 24,13:1
Fast Worker, The 1924,N 12,13:1
What Fools Men 1925,S 29,31:3
Skinner's big Idea 1928,Mr 27,30:4
Terry, Ethelind
Lord Byron of Broadway 1930,Mr 8,21:1
Terry, Harry
Night Birds 1931,Ja 3,21:2
Sherlock Holmes's Fatal Hour 1931,Jl 13,13:5
Broken Melody, The 1934,O 31,17:3
Terry, J E Harold (Original Author)
Midnight Lovers 1926,O 26,23:1
Terry, Jack
West of the Water Tower 1923,D 31,9:3
Old Home Week 1925,My 25,21:3
Terry, Jean (Screenwriter)
Nana 1957,Ap 13,12:3
Terry, Joy
Naked Street, The 1955,O 1,11:2
Terry, Linda
Mad Miss Manton, The 1938,O 21,27:2
Parents on Trial 1939,S 18,15:5
Terry, Nigel
Lion in Winter, The 1968,O 31,54:1
Terry, Peggy
Air Hawks 1935,Je 4,26:5
Terry, Philip
Music in Manhattan 1944,O 7,11:2
Lost Weekend, The 1945,D 3,17:2
Explosive Generation, The 1962,F 15,24:2
Terry, Phillip
Navy Blue and Gold 1937,D 24,21:2
Yellow Jack 1938,My 20,17:2
Hold That Kiss 1938,Je 11,9:1
Four Girls in White 1939,F 23,19:3
Calling Dr Kildare 1939,My 12,25:4
On Borrowed Time 1939,Jl 7,13:2
Balalaika 1939,D 15,33:2
Those Were the Days 1940,Jl 15,18:4
Prison Camp 1940,Ag 3,9:3
Monster and the Girl, The 1941,Mr 20,25:3
Parson of Panamint, The 1941,Jl 26,18:2
Are Husbands Necessary? 1942,Jl 9,17:2
Sweater Girl 1942,Jl 13,18:3
Bataan 1943,Je 4,17:2
Ladies Courageous 1944,Mr 16,17:2
Pan-Americana 1945,Mr 23,13:2
George White's Scandals 1945,O 11,26:2
To Each his Own 1946,My 24,15:2
Born to Kill 1947,My 1,34:2
Terry, Robert
Renfrew of the Royal Mounted 1937,N 3,29:4
Terry, Ruth
Love and Hisses 1938,Ja 1,11:1
International Settlement 1938,F 12,20:3
Alexander's Ragtime Band 1938,Ag 6,7:2
Hold That Co-ed 1938,S 24,13:1
Wife, Husband and Friend 1939,F 25,19:2
Angel From Texas, An 1940,My 10,26:7
Slightly Honorable 1940,My 17,23:4
Blondie Goes Latin 1941,F 26,17:3
Rookies on Parade 1941,My 22,25:2
Appointment for Love 1941,N 7,27:1
Pistol Packin' Mama 1943,D 20,27:4
Lake Placid Serenade 1945,D 25,15:6
Cheaters, The 1945,Jl 21,7:2
Terry, Sheila
Week-End Marriage 1932,Je 4,9:2
Crooner 1932,Ag 20,7:4
Big City Blues 1932,S 10,18:5
Three on a Match 1932,O 29,18:4

Terry, Sheila— Cont
Scarlet Dawn 1932,N 4,25:4
I Am a Fugitive From a Chain Gang
1932,N 11,17:2
You Said a Mouthful 1932,N 18,23:2
Madame Butterfly 1932,D 26,26:2
Lawyer Man 1932,D 27,10:2
20,000 Years in Sing Sing 1933,Ja 10,26:2
Parachute Jumper 1933,Ja 26,12:2
Silk Express, The 1933,Je 28,24:2
Sphinx, The 1933,Jl 6,26:5
Private Detective 62 1933,Jl 7,20:2
House on 56th Street, The 1933,D 2,9:3
Murder on a Bridle Path 1936,Ap 11,19:2
Special Investigator 1936,Ap 25,21:1

Terry, Sonny
Festival 1967,O 24,53:2

Terry, Tex
Apache Rose 1947,Jl 23,19:3
Timberjack 1955,Mr 10,33:3

Terry, William
Stage Door Canteen 1943,Je 25,13:2
3 Is a Family 1944,D 20,20:3
It's in the Bag 1945,Je 11,12:1
Men in her Diary 1945,S 24,16:5

Terry-Lewis, Mabel
Scarlet Pimpernel, The 1935,F 8,27:2
Murder on Diamond Row 1937,N 12,27:2
They Came to a City 1945,F 19,21:3

Terry-Thomas
Private's Progress 1956,Jl 24,19:2
Green Man, The 1957,My 23,40:1
Brothers in Law 1957,Ag 20,22:1
Blue Murder at St Trinian's 1958,My 27,27:1
Your Past Is Showing 1958,Jl 1,36:2
Lucky Jim 1958,S 1,8:6
Tom Thumb 1958,D 24,00:0
Too Many Crooks 1959,Ap 25,14:2
Happy is the Bride 1959,Je 30,27:2
I'm All Right Jack 1960,Ap 26,40:2
Man in a Cocked Hat 1960,Je 15,50:2
School for Scoundrels 1960,Jl 12,39:1
Make Mine Mink 1960,D 20,43:4
Bachelor Flat 1962,Ja 13,14:1
Matter of Who, A 1962,Jl 25,29:2
Wonderful World of the Brothers Grimm, The
(The Singing Bone); Singing Bone, The (The
Wonderful World of the Brothers Grimm)
1962,Ag 8,35:1
Operation Snatch 1962,S 25,31:4
Kill or Cure 1962,N 13,43:4
Mouse on the Moon, The 1963,Je 18,32:1
It's a Mad, Mad, Mad, Mad World
1963,N 19,47:1
How to Murder Your Wife 1965,Ja 27,26:1
Strange Bedfellows 1965,Mr 11,38:1
Those Magnificent Men in Their Flying Machines
(Or How I Flew From London to Paris in 25
Hours and 11 Minutes) 1965,Je 17,27:1
Munster, Go Home 1966,Je 16,53:4
Bang, Bang, You're Dead 1967,Ja 19,41:2
Kiss the Girls and Make Them Die
1967,Ja 26,25:1
Guide for the Married Man, A 1967,My 27,16:1
Perils of Pauline, The 1967,Ag 3,26:3
Those Fantastic Flying Fools 1967,O 19,59:2
Don't Raise the Bridge, Lower the River
1968,Jl 13,18:1
Where Were You When the Lights Went Out?
1968,Ag 9,30:2
Danger Diabolik 1968,D 12,62:6

Terschack, F
Glass Mountain, The 1950,My 18,37:3

Tersersteeg, Gigspert
Dog of Flanders, A 1960,Ap 1,37:1

Tersieeg, Gijsbert
Last Blitzkrieg, The 1959,Ja 31,13:5

Terwin, Johanna
Tausend Fuer Eine Nacht 1934,F 12,19:2

Terzieff, Laurent
Cheaters, The; (Tricheurs, Les) 1961,Je 5,37:4
Notte Brava, La 1962,Ja 25,25:2
Kapo 1964,Je 2,33:3

Teschner, Mollie (Original Author)
Revolt of the Toymakers, The 1918,D 23,9:1

Teshigahara, Hiroshi (Director)
Woman in the Dunes; Suno no Onna
1964,S 17,52:1

Tessari, Duccio (Director)
My Son, The Hero 1963,S 19,23:1
Pistol for Ringo, A 1966,N 3,45:4

Tessari, Duccio (Screenwriter)
Always Victorious 1960,Ap 7,46:1
Last Days of Pompeii, The 1960,Ag 11,19:1
Carthage in Flames 1961,Ja 26,32:3
Revolt of the Slaves, The 1961,N 8,41:1
Marco Polo 1962,S 20,29:2
Duel of the Titans 1963,Ag 8,19:1
Pistol for Ringo, A 1966,N 3,45:4

Tessier, Robert
Glory Stompers, The 1968,Mr 28,52:4

Tessier, Valentine
Madame Borary 1934,N 19,13:2
Club De Femmes 1937,O 20,27:2

Abused Confidence 1938,D 1,29:1
Queen and the Cardinal, The 1944,Je 1,17:3
Justice Is Done 1953,Mr 3,23:2
Sins of the Borgias 1956,Mr 5,21:1
French-Cancan 1956,Ap 17,26:2
Snow Was Black, The 1956,O 16,36:5
Miracle of Saint Therese 1959,F 10,38:4 (In
Addenda)

Tessler, Robert
Born Losers, The 1967,Ag 19,16:2

Tester, Desmond
Tudor Rose 1936,My 24,IX,3:8 (In Addenda)
Nine Days a Queen 1936,O 3,21:1
Beloved Vagabond, The 1937,F 8,12:5
Woman Alone, The 1937,F 27,9:2
Non-Stop New York 1937,N 29,19:2
Drums 1938,S 30,24:4
Stars Look Down, The 1941,Jl 24,15:2

Tetahaimuai, Adeline
Tanga Tika 1953,O 6,34:4

Teter, Jack
In the Heat of the Night 1967,Ag 3,26:1

Teterin, E
Othello 1960,My 16,39:1

Teterin, V
Grasshopper, The 1956,Ap 23,22:1

Teterin, Yevgeni
No Ordinary Summer 1958,O 6,36:3

Teterin, Yevgeni (Director)
Mumu 1961,Je 5,37:4

Teterin, Yevgeni (Producer)
Mumu 1961,Je 5,37:4

Teti, Federico (Producer)
Aida 1954,N 12,17:1
Hercules 1959,Jl 23,32:2

Tetley, Dorothy
Blarney Kiss, The 1933,Ag 19,14:4

Tetley, Walter
Lord Jeff 1938,Jl 1,22:2
Boy Slaves 1939,F 9,17:3
They Shall Have Music 1939,Jl 26,17:2
Military Academy 1940,Ag 5,10:4
Thunder Birds 1942,O 29,19:2
Who Done It 1942,D 3,35:2
Gorilla Man, The 1943,Ja 15,21:4

Tetunic, Louis (Miscellaneous)
Farewell to Yesterday 1950,D 1,31:2

Tetzel, Joan
Duel in the Sun 1947,My 8,30:2
Paradine Case, The 1948,Ja 9,26:2
Thelma Jordon 1950,Ja 19,35:2
Hell Below Zero 1954,Jl 17,7:3
Joy in the Morning 1965,Je 10,38:1

Tetzlaff, Ted (Director)
World Premiere 1941,Ag 21,15:2
Riff-Raff 1947,Je 30,25:7
Fighting Father Dunne 1948,Je 25,26:2
Johnny Allegro 1949,My 31,19:2
Window, The 1949,Ag 8,10:5
Dangerous Profession, A 1949,D 12,29:4
White Tower, The 1950,Jl 3,9:2
Under the Gun 1951,F 23,33:2
Gambling House 1951,Mr 19,23:2
Son of Sinbad 1955,Jl 28,18:2
Seven Wonders of the World 1956,Ap 11,29:1

Teuber, Andreas
Doctor Faustus 1968,F 7,38:1

Teubler, Rudolf
Orphan Boy of Vienna, An 1937,S 9,19:2

Teuffen, Hantz Von
Flying Saucer, The 1950,Ja 5,28:3

Tevis, Carol
Once in a Lifetime 1932,O 29,18:4
Sing, Baby, Sing 1936,S 12,20:1

Tevis, Walter (Original Author)
Hustler, The 1961,S 27,35:1

Tevlin, C J (Producer)
Bat, The 1959,D 17,51:4

Tevlin, Eugene (Producer)
Bengazi 1955,O 8,13:4

Tewksbury, Peter (Director)
Sunday in New York 1964,F 12,30:2

Tex
Born Losers, The 1967,Ag 19,16:2

Texas, Temple
Kiss of Death 1947,Ag 28,28:2

Texera, Virgilio
Alexander the Great 1956,Mr 29,23:1
Boy Who Stole a Million, The 1960,D 22,18:3
Happy Thieves, The 1962,F 5,19:4
Return of the Seven 1966,O 20,52:5

Tey, Josephine (Original Author)
Girl Was Young, The 1938,F 11,27:2
Franchise Affair, The 1952,Je 6,19:2

Teynac, Maurice
Private Life of an Actor; En Scene 1948,S 7,21:3
Counter Investigation 1949,D 30,13:2
Night Without Stars 1953,Jl 14,19:4
Bedevilled 1955,Ap 23,23:1
Sans Famille 1959,S 5,11:4
Crack in the Mirror 1960,My 20,26:1
In the French Style 1963,S 19,23:1
Therese and Isabelle 1968,My 15,41:4

Tezuka, Shigeo
Angry Island 1960,F 28,31:1

Tgrachyov, Valya
Frigid Sea, The 1955,N 21,23:4

Thab, Joseph (Screenwriter)
Deception 1946,O 19,15:3

Thabault, Jean-Marc
Every Second Counts 1957,O 15,39:4

Thacher, Heather
Its a Boy 1933,Jl 23,IX,2:2 (In Addenda)

Thackeray, Eugene (Miscellaneous)
Artists and Models 1937,Ag 5,19:2

Thackeray, William Makepeace (Original Author)
Pendennis 1916,N 9,11:1
Vanity Fair 1923,My 7,19:3
Becky Sharp 1935,Je 14,27:2

Thackrey, Eugene (Screenwriter)
Unfinished Business 1941,S 2,20:2
Lady in a Jam 1942,S 11,25:2

Thalasso, Arthur
Strong Man, The 1926,S 7,44:2
Venus of Venice 1927,My 3,25:1
Behind the Headlines 1937,Je 1,27:2

Thalberg, Irving (Producer)
Biography of a Bachelor Girl 1935,Mr 2,18:2
Romeo and Juliet 1936,Ag 21,12:2

Thalberg, Sylvia (Screenwriter)
Montana Moon 1930,Ag 14,24:2
Prosperity 1932,N 26,11:4
Son Comes Home, A 1936,S 5,7:1

Thamar, Tilda
Red Angel, The 1950,N 4,13:2
Maid in Paris 1957,Jl 13,11:1
Paris Hotel 1959,S 12,12:3

Than, Joseph (Original Author)
Madame Spy 1934,F 10,20:1
Four Flights to Love 1942,Ap 13,12:2
None Shall Escape 1944,Ap 7,23:2

Than, Win Min
Purple Plain, The 1955,Ap 11,29:1

Thane, Edward
Almost a Honeymoon 1931,Ja 10,19:2

Thane, Gibson
Lady From Paris, The 1927,S 28,28:3

Thappar, Romesh
Householder, The 1963,O 22,43:2

Tharp, Grahame (Producer)
Virgin Island 1960,Mr 24,39:5

Thatcher, Heather
Plaything, The 1929,O 6,IX,9:4 (In Addenda)
But the Flesh Is Weak 1932,Ap 16,11:2
It's a Boy 1934,Je 8,18:2
Loyalties 1934,O 26,25:1
Thirteenth Chair, The 1937,Je 18,25:3
Tovarich 1937,D 31,9:2
Fools for Scandal 1938,Mr 25,15:3
If I Were King 1938,S 29,31:1
Girls' School 1938,N 3,27:1
Scotland Yard 1941,Ap 9,33:3
Man Hunt 1941,Je 14,20:2
Son of Fury 1942,Ja 30,23:2
We Were Dancing 1942,My 1,23:2
Moon and Sixpence, The 1942,O 28,26:4
Journey for Margaret 1942,D 18,36:7
Gaslight 1944,My 5,17:2
Anna Karenina 1948,Ap 28,32:2
Dear Mr Prohack 1950,Jl 15,7:2
Gay Lady, The 1951,Ap 16,21:2
Encore (Gigolo and Gigolette); Gigolo and
Gigolette (Encore) 1952,Ap 3,45:1
Hour of 13, The 1952,O 28,37:1
Will any Gentleman? 1955,S 28,70:6

Thatcher, Torin
Norah O'Neale 1934,O 25,26:3
Climbing High 1939,Je 5,20:3
U-Boat 29 1939,O 6,31:3
Let George Do It 1940,O 14,25:5
Major Barbara 1941,My 15,27:1
Frightened Lady 1941,N 10,21:3
Next of Kin 1943,My 6,25:2
Great Expectations 1947,My 23,31:1
Jassy 1948,F 20,19:2
Smugglers, The 1948,Mr 29,17:1
End of the River, The 1948,Je 21,18:2
Fallen Idol, The 1949,N 16,39:2
Affair in Trinidad 1952,Jl 31,14:2
Crimson Pirate, The 1952,Ag 28,21:2
Snows of Kilimanjaro, The 1952,S 19,19:2
Blackbeard the Pirate 1952,D 26,20:3
Desert Rats, The 1953,My 9,13:2
Houdini 1953,Jl 3,10:2
Robe, The 1953,S 17,32:6
Knock on Wood 1954,Ap 15,34:2
Black Shield of Falworth, The 1954,O 7,16:2
Bengal Brigade 1954,N 13,13:2
Love Is a Many-Splendored Thing
1955,Ag 19,10:1
Lady Godiva 1955,D 3,13:3
Diane 1956,Ja 13,18:1
Helen of Troy 1956,Ja 27,21:4
Istanbul 1957,Ja 24,34:1
Band of Angels 1957,Jl 11,21:1
Witness for the Prosecution 1958,F 7,16:1

Thatcher, Torin— Cont
Darby's Rangers 1958,F 13,23:2
Seventh Voyage of Sinbad 1958,D 24,00:0
Miracle, The 1959,N 13,25:4
Canadians, The 1961,Je 1,31:1
Jack the Giant Killer 1962,Jl 26,17:1
Mutiny on the Bounty 1962,N 9,31:2
Drums of Africa 1963,Jl 4,9:1
Sandpiper, The 1965,Jl 16,14:1
Hawaii 1966,O 11,54:1

Thaw, John
Bofors Gun, The 1968,S 23,42:3

Thaw, Russell
Redemption 1917,My 22,11:3

Thaxter, Phyllis
Thirty Seconds Over Tokyo 1944,N 16,19:1
Bewitched 1945,Ag 17,20:3
Week-End at the Waldorf 1945,O 5,27:2
Sea of Grass, The 1947,F 28,27:2
Living in a Big Way 1947,O 10,31:4
Sign of the Ram, The 1948,Mr 4,30:2
Blood on the Moon 1948,N 12,30:5
Act of Violence 1949,Ja 24,16:2
No Man of her Own 1950,My 4,32:3
Breaking Point, The 1950,O 7,10:6
Fort Worth 1951,Jl 13,12:7
Jim Thorpe - All American 1951,Ag 25,7:2
Come Fill the Cup 1951,N 22,47:2
She's Working her Way Through College
  1952,Jl 10,27:2
Springfield Rifle 1952,O 23,40:2
Operation Secret 1952,N 6,37:2
Women's Prison 1955,F 3,18:5
Man Afraid 1957,Ap 5,24:2
World of Henry Orient, The 1964,Mr 20,27:2

Thayer, Lorna
Lusty Men, The 1952,O 25,12:6

Thayer, Tiffany (Original Author)
Strangers of the Evening 1932,Je 4,9:2
Thirteen Women 1932,O 15,13:1
Call Her Savage 1932,N 25,19:2
King of Gamblers 1937,Jl 3,18:1
Chicago Deadline 1949,N 3,37:2

Thayer, Tina
Girls Under 21 1940,N 11,22:4
Yank at Eton, A 1942,O 16,23:1

Theadore, Ralph
Last Mile, The 1932,Ag 26,20:3

Thebom, Blanche
Irish Eyes Are Smiling 1944,N 8,27:1

Theby, Rosemary
Great Love, The 1918,Ag 12,7:1
Upstairs and Down 1919,Je 16,11:2
Heartsease 1919,Ag 25,8:5
Connecticut Yankee in King Arthur's Court, A
  1921,Mr 15,14:3
Shame 1921,Ag 1,8:3 (Incorrect in this edition;
  use 1921,Ag 1,6:4 elsewhere)
Rich Men's Wives 1922,Ag 21,6:2
Lost and Found 1923,Mr 19,22:2
Girl of the Golden West, The 1923,My 21,12:2
Slander the Woman 1923,My 28,18:2
Long Live the King 1923,D 4,24:1
Son of the Sahara, A 1924,My 27,14:1
Behold This Woman 1924,Jl 22,9:1
Red Lily, The 1924,S 29,10:1
So Big 1925,Ja 5,19:1
As Man Desires 1925,F 10,20:1
Fifth Avenue Models 1925,My 4,16:2
One Year to Live 1925,Jl 6,12:2
Port of Missing Girls, The 1928,Jl 31,13:4
Ten Nights in a Barroom 1931,F 28,15:2

Theek, Ingebord
Urlaub auf Ehrenwort; Furlough on Word of
  Honor 1938,Mr 28,19:2

Theil, Gunther
Third Sex, The 1959,Mr 26,27:1

Theilade, Nina
Sangen Till Henne; Song to Her, The
  1935,F 22,27:3
Midsummer Night's Dream, A 1935,O 10,31:1
Grosse Bluff, Der; Big Bluff, The 1937,S 6,20:2

Theilmann, Erika von
Ehestreik 1935,Ag 31,16:3

Theimer, Gretl
Zwei Hertzen in Drei-Viertel Takt
  1930,O 13,31:1
Leutnant Warst Du Einst bei den Husaren
  1932,Mr 14,13:3
Die Csikos Baroness 1932,Mr 28,11:2
Schubert's Fruehlingstraum 1932,Je 22,19:4
Schoen Ist die Manoeverzeit 1932,Ag 19,20:6
Wenn die Soldaten 1932,O 31,18:4
Holzapfel Weiss Alles 1933,Ja 7,11:3
Ihre Majestaet die Liebe 1933,F 7,23:4
Walzerparadies 1933,Mr 4,11:3
Tanzhusar, Der 1933,Ap 10,8:4
Viktoria und Ihr Husar 1933,Ap 10,8:3
Schuetzen Koenig, Der 1933,My 3,15:5 (In
  Addenda)
Drei Tage Mittelarrest 1933,My 18,17:4
Wiener Blut 1933,N 13,21:2
In Wien Hab' Ich Einmal ein Maedel Geliebt
  1934,My 26,12:3

Adjutant Seiner Hoheit, Der 1934,O 22,12:3
Einmal Eine Grosse Dame Sein 1934,O 27,20:3
Rosen aus dem Sueden; Roses from the South
  1935,Ap 23,24:5
Mein Liebster Ist ein Jaegersmann 1936,S 15,37:6
Ein Liebesroman im Hause Habsburg
  1936,O 12,23:2
Muede Theodor, Der 1936,O 24,23:2
Ein Lied, Ein Kuss, Ein Maeder 1936,D 12,29:4
Drei Maeoerl um Schubert 1937,Je 5,21:2
Landstreicher, Die; Hoboes, The 1938,N 26,18:1
Alles Fuer Veronika 1939,F 4,11:2
Kampf mit dem Drachen, Der; Fight With the
  Dragon, The 1939,N 6,20:3
Unsterblicher Walzer; Immortal Waltz
  1939,N 18,22:6

Thelander, Class
Matter of Morals, A 1961,Je 1,31:1

Thelin, Peter
Swedish Wedding Night 1965,N 15,48:1

Thellmann, Erika von
Toerichte Jungfrau, Die 1935,S 9,24:3
Weiberregiment 1936,S 14,25:2
Susanne im Bade; Susanna in the Bath
  1937,S 11,20:1
Unwiderst Ehliche, Der; Irresistable Man, The
  1937,D 20,23:3
Spiel in Sommerwind; Play in the Summer
  Breezes 1939,Ap 1,17:2
Opernball; Opera Ball 1940,O 15,29:2

Thellung, Francesco (Screenwriter)
Sign of the Gladiator 1959,D 3,46:1
Warrior and the Slave, The 1960,Mr 10,36:2
Sword and the Cross, The 1960,Jl 7,26:1

Themankar
Gyandev of India 1943,Ap 10,12:5

Theochari, Kyveli
Madame X 1960,O 3,34:5
Policeman of the 16th Precinct, The
  1963,Ap 22,23:2

Theodoli, Niccolo (Producer)
O K Nero 1953,Je 20,8:6

Theodoli, Niccolo (Screenwriter)
Bed, The (The Divorce); Divorce, The (The Bed)
  1955,Je 8,26:4

Theodore, Luke
Brig, The 1964,S 21,37:4

Theodore, Ralph
Dance of Life, The 1929,Ag 16,18:6
Angels Over Broadway 1940,N 18,23:2
Confessions of Boston Blackie 1941,D 8,31:2

Theodorelos, Anton
Bed of Grass 1957,D 28,9:2

Theodorou, Nelly (Original Author)
Stefania 1968,N 29,56:1

Thery, Jacques (Original Author)
Rhythm on the River 1940,Ag 29,23:2
Joan of Paris 1942,Ja 26,18:2
Between Us Girls 1942,S 25,25:3
Heavenly Body, The 1944,Mr 24,17:3
Yolanda and the Thief 1945,N 23,26:2

Thery, Jacques (Screenwriter)
Springtime in the Rockies 1942,N 12,30:2
To Each his Own 1946,My 24,15:2

Thesiger, Ernest
Old Dark House, The 1932,O 28,22:4
Ghoul, The 1934,Ja 27,9:2
Heart Song 1934,Je 6,24:6
My Heart Is Calling 1935,Ap 15,16:3
Bride of Frankenstein, The 1935,My 11,21:2
Man Who Could Work Miracles, The
  1937,F 22,13:1
Henry V 1946,Je 18,30:2
Caesar and Cleopatra 1946,S 6,18:2
Beware of Pity 1947,N 1,11:2
Smugglers, The 1948,Mr 29,17:1
Quartet (The Colonel's Lady); Colonel's Lady, The
  (Quartet) 1949,Mr 29,30:3
Winslow Boy, The 1950,Je 7,34:4
Last Holiday 1950,N 14,39:4
Laughter in Paradise 1951,N 12,21:2
Christmas Carol, A 1951,N 29,41:2
Man in the White Suit, The 1952,Ap 1,35:2
Robe, The 1953,S 17,32:6
Midnight Episode 1955,My 19,25:5
Quentin Durward 1955,N 24,41:1
Make Me an Offer 1956,F 29,35:2
Alligator Named Daisy, An 1957,O 7,23:2
Horse's Mouth, The 1958,N 12,41:1
3 Men in a Boat 1959,Jl 29,33:2
Battle of the Sexes, The 1960,Ap 19,40:4
Sons and Lovers 1960,Ag 3,35:1

Thevenet, Rene (Producer)
Sins of Youth 1960,D 24,8:2
Killing Game, The 1968,Ag 27,36:1

Theville, Roger
Mirages De Paris 1933,D 25,28:3

Thew, Harvey (Miscellaneous)
Transient Lady 1935,Mr 11,15:1

Thew, Harvey (Original Author)
Bedside 1934,Mr 7,23:4

Thew, Harvey (Screenwriter)
Flaming Barriers 1924,Ja 29,16:1
Calaboose 1943,Jl 30,19:2

Thibault, Jean-Marc
Sans Famille 1959,S 5,11:4
Belle Americaine, La 1961,D 18,42:1

Thiele, Eugen (Director)
Hellseher, Der 1933,S 11,20:4
Feldherrnhuegel, Der 1934,Ap 20,17:2

Thiele, Hertha
Maedchen in Uniform 1932,S 21,25:4
Mensch Ohne Namen 1932,N 7,20:3
Kuhle Wampe 1933,Ap 24,11:4
Anna und Elisabeth 1933,Jl 2,IX,2:2
Frau Lehmann's Toechter 1933,O 27,22:3
Reifende Jugend 1936,Ja 4,19:1
Anna und Elisabeth 1936,Je 13,13:1
Wiesse Majestat, Die; White Majesty
  1939,My 27,13:3

Thiele, Rolf (Director)
Rosemary 1960,Ja 19,40:2
Tonio Kroger 1968,Ja 16,24:1

Thiele, Rolf (Screenwriter)
Rosemary 1960,Ja 19,40:2

Thiele, Wilhelm (Director)
His Late Excellency 1929,Je 11,27:2
Hurrah I'm Alive 1930,Je 16,25:3
Liebeswalzer 1931,My 4,15:3
Drei von ver Tankstelle, Die 1931,Je 20,20:4
Fille et le Garcon, La; Girl and the Boy, The
  1932,Mr 27,VIII,6:2
Zwei Herzen und ein Schlag 1932,S 9,17:5
Bal, Le 1932,S 28,22:5
Waltz Time 1933,S 29,24:2
Jungle Princess 1936,D 24,21:3
London by Night 1937,Ag 13,13:1
Beg, Borrow or Steal 1937,D 10,33:2
Bridal Suite 1939,My 26,20:2
Tarzan Triumphs 1943,F 5,16:3
Tarzan's Desert Mystery 1943,D 27,23:3

Thiele, Wilhelm (Original Author)
Don't Get Personal 1936,F 22,12:1
Stablemates 1938,O 21,27:2
She Wouldn't Say Yes 1946,Ja 12,10:7

Thierree, Jean-Baptiste
Muriel 1963,O 31,26:1

Thierry, Clement
Au Grand Balcon 1951,My 5,14:2

Thierry, Marie-Louise
Naked Childhood 1968,S 28,36:1

Thierry, Paul
Operation Eichmann 1961,My 4,40:7

Thierry, Rene
Naked Childhood 1968,S 28,36:1

Thierte, Maurice (Composer)
Enfants du Paradis, Les 1947,F 20,32:2

Thiery, Fritz (Director)
Prinzessin Sissy 1939,Ja 14,13:2

Thiess, Ursula
Monsoon 1953,S 26,15:2
Bengal Brigade 1954,N 13,13:2
Americano, The 1955,Ja 20,35:1

Thigpen, Corbett H Dr (Original Author)
Three Faces of Eve, The 1957,S 27,16:6

Thigpen, Helen
Porgy and Bess 1959,Je 25,20:3

Thill, Georges
Louise 1940,F 3,9:4

Thimig, Hans
Story of Vickie, The 1958,Ja 30,19:2

Thimig, Helene
Mensch Ohne Namen 1932,N 7,20:3
Gay Sisters, The 1942,Ag 15,14:2
Moon Is Down, The 1943,Mr 27,8:6
Edge of Darkness 1943,Ap 10,12:4
Hitler Gang, The 1944,My 8,15:2
None but the Lonely Heart 1944,N 18,16:6
Hotel Berlin 1945,Mr 3,11:2
Isle of the Dead 1945,S 8,12:2
This Love of Ours 1945,N 1,20:2
Cloak and Dagger 1946,O 5,13:2
Locket, The 1947,Mr 20,38:2
Cry Wolf 1947,Jl 19,10:2
Escape me Never 1947,N 8,11:2
Decision Before Dawn 1951,D 22,12:2

Thimig, Hermann
Kleine Seitensprung, Der 1932,Ja 1,31:1
Mein Leopold 1932,Ap 1,17:4
Der Herr Buerovorsteher 1932,Je 17,24:1
Wenn die Soldaten 1932,O 31,18:4
Eine Nacht im Paradies 1933,F 20,11:6
Traum von Schoenbrunn 1933,Je 1,15:4
Eine Stadt Steht Kopf 1934,Ja 29,10:2
Blaue Vom Himmel, Das 1934,S 8,18:6
Marion, Das Gehoert Sich Nicht 1934,D 15,9:4
Viktor und Viktoria 1935,Ja 28,10:5
Liebe Dumme Mama; Stupid Mama
  1935,Mr 2,18:3
Himmel auf Erden, Der 1935,D 26,21:4
Karneval und Liebe 1936,Ap 4,11:2
Fahrt ins Gruene, Die 1936,My 23,12:2
Tanzmusik 1936,My 26,27:2
Fahrt in Die Jugend, Die 1936,Ag 31,19:2

Thimig, Hermann— Cont

Geheimnisvolle Mister X, Der; Mysterious Mr X, The 1939,Jl 1,11:2
Peter, Paul und Nanette 1940,My 25,20:1
Eternal Waltz, The; (Ewiger Walzer) 1959,Jl 9,22:1
Threepenny Opera, The 1960,Jl 11,24:4

Thimig, Hugo
Die Grosse Liebe 1932,F 22,23:2

Thimmig, Hans
Gluecklichste Ehe von Wien, Die; Happiest Married Couple in Vienna, The 1938,O 8,10:2

Thine, Armando
Mafioso 1964,Jl 1,42:1

Thirlwell, George
Fire Over England 1937,Mr 5,16:2

Thisse, Jean Pierre
Bouquets From Nicholas 1939,Mr 2,19:1

Thnat, Steve
In Like Flint 1967,Mr 16,53:2

Thoams, Frank M
Death of a Champion 1939,Ag 24,17:3

Thoeren, Robert
Und das Ist die Hauptsache; That's All That Matters 1931,My 24,VIII,4:1

Thoeren, Robert (Miscellaneous)
Summer Storm 1944,O 23,14:3

Thoeren, Robert (Original Author)
Big Jack 1949,My 23,27:4
Prowler, The 1951,Jl 2,16:6
Some Like It Hot 1959,Mr 30,23:1

Thoeren, Robert (Screenwriter)
Hotel Imperial 1939,My 11,31:3
Rage in Heaven 1941,Mr 21,19:2
Mrs Parkington 1944,O 13,16:1
Temptation 1946,D 25,33:6
Singapore 1947,S 17,31:2
Live Today for Tomorrow 1948,D 6,29:2
Fighting O'Flynn, The 1949,F 28,16:2
Captain Carey U S A 1950,Mr 30,40:5
Operation X 1950,D 11,31:2
September Affair 1951,F 2,19:2
Confessions of Felix Krull, The 1958,Mr 5,38:1

Tholsgaard, Verner
Girls are Willing, The 1959,My 11,30:1

THOM
See Also TOM

Thom, Robert (Original Author)
Wild in the Streets 1968,My 30,21:1
Legend of Lylah Clare, The 1968,Ag 23,33:1

Thom, Robert (Screenwriter)
Subterraneans, The 1960,Jl 7,26:1
All the Fine Young Cannibals 1960,S 23,33:1
Wild in the Streets 1968,My 30,21:1

Thomajan, Guy
Panic in the Streets 1950,Ag 5,9:2
Breaking Point, The 1950,O 7,10:6
Pink Panther, The 1964,Ap 24,25:1

Thomalla, Georg
Sky Without Stars 1959,My 30,9:2
Scampolo 1959,Ag 6,18:4

Thomas, A E (Original Author)
World's Champion, The 1922,F 27,13:4
Thirty Days 1922,D 11,22:1
French Doll, The 1923,S 5,15:3
Just Suppose 1926,Ja 18,26:2
Girl Habit, The 1931,Jl 4,11:5
No More Ladies 1935,Je 22,18:5

Thomas, A E (Screenwriter)
Everybody's Old Man 1936,Mr 26,27:2
Good Old Soak 1937,Ap 20,25:3

Thomas, Al
Massacre Hill 1950,D 14,51:3

Thomas, Amy Brandon
Java Head 1935,Jl 31,21:4

Thomas, Ann
Duffy's Tavern 1945,S 6,23:3
Walk East on Beacon 1952,My 29,17:2

Thomas, Augustus (Original Author)
Witching Hour, The 1916,D 11,7:3
Arizona 1918,D 16,13:3
In Mizzoura 1919,O 13,16:3
Copperhead, The 1920,F 9,10:3
Bonnie Brier Bush, The 1921,N 28,16:1
Men Are Like That 1931,Ag 17,18:2
Witching Hour, The 1934,Ap 28,11:3

Thomas, Basil (Original Author)
Please Turn Over 1961,Ap 29,12:2

Thomas, Bernard
Happy Land 1943,D 9,33:3
Pillow of Death 1946,Ja 26,19:3

Thomas, Bill (Original Author)
This Way Please 1937,O 8,27:2

Thomas, Brandon (Original Author)
Charley's Aunt 1925,F 9,15:3
Charley's Aunt 1930,D 26,18:4
Charley's Aunt 1941,Ag 2,18:2
Where's Charley? 1952,Je 27,18:3

Thomas, Bruce (Original Author)
Safecracker, The 1958,Mr 6,32:1

Thomas, Danny
Unfinished Dance, The 1947,O 31,29:2
Big City 1948,My 17,23:3
Call Me Mister 1951,F 1,21:2

I'll See You in my Dreams 1951,D 7,35:1
Jazz Singer, The 1953,Ja 14,27:3
Rendezvous in Space 1964,S 10,27:1

Thomas, Dick (Composer)
Sioux City Sue 1947,Jl 23,19:3

Thomas, Dylan (Screenwriter)
No Room at the Inn 1949,D 26,33:4

Thomas, Edna
Streetcar Named Desire, A 1951,S 30,27:1

Thomas, Edward
Tea For Three 1927,O 31,22:1

Thomas, Elton (Original Author)
Robin Hood 1922,O 31,15:4 (In Addenda)
Black Pirate, The 1926,Mr 9,21:4

Thomas, Elton (Screenwriter)
Thief of Bagdad, The 1924,Mr 19,19:1

Thomas, Evan
Girl From Maxim's, The 1936,S 16,29:1
Arrest Bulldog Drummond 1939,Ja 12,23:2
Little Princess, The 1939,Mr 11,21:1
Frenchman's Creek 1944,S 21,26:2
My Name is Julia Ross 1945,N 9,16:3
Dolly Sisters, The 1945,N 15,24:6

Thomas, Faith (Original Author)
Conspiracy 1939,Ag 23,19:2

Thomas, Frank M
Ex-Mrs Bradford, The 1936,My 28,19:2
Last Outlaw, The 1936,Je 15,24:1
Grand Jury 1936,Ag 1,16:3
M'liss 1936,Ag 8,5:2
Don't Turn 'em Loose 1936,S 25,20:2
Big Game, The 1936,O 24,23:1
Without Orders 1936,N 4,41:3
Wanted: Jane Turner 1936,N 30,24:7
We Who are About to Die 1937,Ja 2,15:1
Criminal Lawyer 1937,Ja 27,17:3
We're on the Jury 1937,F 10,18:5
Don't Tell the Wife 1937,F 19,15:2
Man Who Found Himself, The 1937,Ap 9,19:3
Soldier and the Lady, The 1937,Ap 10,11:1
China Passage 1937,Ap 16,27:2
Outcasts of Poker Flat, The 1937,Ap 27,18:3
You Can't Buy Luck 1937,My 14,21:2
Behind the Headlines 1937,Je 1,27:2
You Can't Beat Love 1937,Je 25,25:3
Meet the Missus 1937,Jl 2,25:2
Toast of New York, The 1937,Jl 23,16:2
Big Shot, The 1937,Ag 13,13:1
Forty Naughty Girls 1937,S 18,15:3
Danger Patrol 1937,N 19,27:3
Breakfast for Two 1937,N 20,21:2
Crashing Hollywood 1938,Ja 8,19:2
Law of the Underworld 1938,Ap 28,27:2
Blind Alibi 1938,My 20,17:2
Go Chase Yourself 1938,Je 15,27:1
Crime Ring 1938,Jl 22,10:3
Smashing the Rackets 1938,Ag 9,22:5
Mr Doodle Kicks Off 1938,S 28,29:4
Man to Remember, A 1938,N 7,23:2
Disbarred 1939,Ja 19,17:2
Secret Service of the Air 1939,Mr 2,19:2
They Made Her a Spy 1939,Mr 29,21:4
Society Lawyer 1939,Mr 31,19:2
Bachelor Mother 1939,Je 30,17:2
They all Come Out 1939,Ag 3,15:4
Geronimo 1940,F 8,18:3
Shooting High 1940,Ap 12,19:2
Women Without Names 1940,My 9,26:4
Brigham Young - Frontiersman 1940,S 21,13:2
Chad Hanna 1940,D 26,23:1
Monster and the Girl, The 1941,Mr 20,25:3
Among the Living 1941,D 13,25:2
Talk of the Town, The 1942,Ag 28,22:3
Hello, Frisco, Hello 1943,Mr 25,25:1

Thomas, Frankie
Wednesday's Child 1934,D 15,9:3
Boys Town 1938,S 9,25:1
Little Tough Guys in Society 1938,N 21,14:4
Angels Wash Their Faces 1939,S 4,16:2
Dress Parade 1939,O 28,11:2
Invisible Stripes 1940,Ja 13,11:2
Flying Cadets 1941,O 14,28:3
One Foot in Heaven 1941,N 14,28:3
Always in my Heart 1942,Mr 14,19:2

Thomas, Frankie Jr
Major and the Minor, The 1942,S 17,21:3

Thomas, Gerald (Director)
Circle, The 1959,Ap 16,29:2
Carry on Sergeant 1959,O 28,40:5
Carry on Nurse 1960,S 10,11:1
Please Turn Over 1961,Ap 29,12:2
Swingin' Maiden, The 1964,Ja 1,16:2
Carry on Cleo 1965,O 23,17:2

Thomas, Gilbert Travers (Screenwriter)
S O S Pacific 1960,O 13,41:3

Thomas, Gretchen
Marriage Forbidden 1938,Jl 16,7:2

Thomas, Gwydion
Doctor Faustus 1968,F 7,38:1

Thomas, Helga
Cinderella 1926,Ap 5,24:1
When Duty Calls 1929,Ja 1,60:1
Richthofhen: The Red Knight of the Air 1929,S 2,16:1

Thomas, Howard (Producer)
Elizabeth is Queen 1953,Je 29,20:4
Door in the Wall 1965,Ja 22,21:2

Thomas, Jack (Producer)
We'll Bury You 1962,O 25,48:3

Thomas, Jack (Screenwriter)
20,000 Eyes 1961,Je 19,30:1
Francis of Assisi 1961,Jl 29,8:2
We'll Bury You 1962,O 25,48:3

Thomas, Jameson
Chu Chin Chow 1925,F 11,19:4
Tesha 1928,S 16,IX,5:7 (In Addenda)
Woman in the Night, A 1929,Mr 11,22:2
Piccadilly 1929,Jl 15,25:1
High Treason 1929,Ag 25,VIII,4:7 (In Addenda)
White Sheik, The 1929,D 9,32:5
Farmer's Wife, The 1930,Ja 7,28:3
Hate Ship, The 1930,N 15,15:3
Extravagance 1930,D 9,31:3
Night Birds 1931,Ja 3,21:2
Lover Come Back 1931,Je 5,26:5
Three Wise Girls 1932,F 6,14:4
Trial of Vivienne Ware, The 1932,Ap 30,19:3
Phantom President, The 1932,O 1,10:4
No More Orchids 1933,Ja 2,29:2
Brief Moment 1933,S 30,18:5
Bombay Mail 1934,Ja 6,18:2
It Happened One Night 1934,F 23,23:2
Beggars in Ermine 1934,Ap 25,25:3
Scralet Empress, The 1934,S 15,20:2
Lost Lady, A 1934,O 4,19:1
Now and Forever 1934,O 13,10:1
Lives of a Bengal Lancer, The 1935,Ja 12,12:2
Sing Sing Nights 1935,Ja 26,13:2
World Accuses, The 1935,Mr 21,27:2
Mr Dynamite 1935,My 25,12:1
Charlie Chan in Egypt 1935,Je 24,12:2
Last Outpost, The 1935,O 5,18:2
Coronado 1935,D 19,33:4
Mr Deeds Goes to Town 1936,Ap 17,17:2
House of Secrets 1937,F 22,13:1
League of Frightened Men, The 1937,Jl 2,25:1
100 Men and a Girl 1937,S 18,15:2

Thomas, Jane
North Wind's Malice, The 1920,O 18,13:1
Heedless Moths 1921,Je 4,14:2
Silver Wings 1922,My 18,14:4
Town That Forgot God, The 1922,N 1,16:3
White Rose, The 1923,My 23,18:3
Hoosier Schoolmaster, The 1924,Mr 18,25:2

Thomas, Jerry (Producer)
African Manhunt 1957,Ap 20,21:4

Thomas, John Charles
Under the Red Robe 1923,N 13,25:3

Thomas, John Charles (Miscellaneous)
Under the Red Robe 1923,N 13,25:3

Thomas, Lonnie
Return of the Texan 1952,F 14,23:1

Thomas, Lowell (Cinematographer)
Out of this World 1954,Ap 16,16:2

Thomas, Lowell (Miscellaneous)
Mussolini Speaks 1933,Mr 13,18:3
Throne of the Gods 1933,D 22,25:3
Lion Has Wings, The 1940,Ja 22,11:2
Search for Paradise 1957,S 25,25:2

Thomas, Lowell (Narrator)
Blonde Captive, The 1932,F 29,21:3
Borneo 1937,S 4,8:3
Ski Champs 1951,D 15,11:2
Out of this World 1954,Ap 16,16:2
Seven Wonders of the World 1956,Ap 11,29:1
Search for Paradise 1957,S 25,25:2
Best of Cinerama, The 1963,D 26,33:2

Thomas, Lowell (Original Author)
Seven Wonders of the World 1956,Ap 11,29:1

Thomas, Lowell (Producer)
Out of this World 1954,Ap 16,16:2
Seven Wonders of the World 1956,Ap 11,29:1
Search for Paradise 1957,S 25,25:2

Thomas, Lowell (Screenwriter)
Search for Paradise 1957,S 25,25:2

Thomas, Lowell Jr (Cinematographer)
Out of this World 1954,Ap 16,16:2

Thomas, Lowell Jr (Narrator)
Out of this World 1954,Ap 16,16:2

Thomas, Lowell Jr (Producer)
Out of this World 1954,Ap 16,16:2

Thomas, Madoline
Girl in the Canal, The 1947,O 9,32:3

Thomas, Margot
Knack...and how to get it, The 1965,Je 30,42:1

Thomas, Mary
Great McGinty, The 1940,Ag 15,23:1
Kings Row 1942,F 3,23:2
Gay Sisters, The 1942,Ag 15,14:2

Thomas, Olive
Upstairs and Down 1919,Je 16,11:2

Thomas, Paul (Original Author)
Defector, The 1966,N 17,55:1

Thomas, Phil
School for Husbands 1939,F 7,16:2

Thomas, Powys
Luck of Ginger Coffey, The 1964,S 22,44:1
Thomas, Rachel
Proud Valley 1941,My 17,19:2
Captive Heart, The 1947,Ap 28,27:2
Tiger Bay 1959,D 15,50:1
Woman Who Wouldn't Die, The 1965,Je 10,38:1
Thomas, Ralph (Director)
Once Upon a Dream 1949,Jl 15,17:2
Clouded Yellow, The 1951,N 13,33:2
Island Rescue 1952,Jl 1,19:4
Assassin, The 1953,Ap 18,17:2
Doctor in the House 1955,F 19,18:3
Doctor at Sea 1956,Mr 1,37:3
Iron Petticoat, The 1957,F 2,12:2
Above Us the Waves 1957,Ap 18,35:2
Doctor at Large 1957,Jl 29,15:5
Checkpoint 1957,S 19,25:2
Tale of Two Cities, A 1958,Ag 5,23:1
Campbell's Kingdom 1960,Ja 11,35:5
Wind Cannot Read, The 1960,Mr 10,36:1
Conspiracy of Hearts 1960,Ap 8,24:1
39 Steps, The 1960,O 11,55:2
Upstairs and Downstairs 1960,D 2,53:4
No Love for Johnnie 1961,D 13,55:1
Doctor in Love 1962,Ap 27,27:2
Pair of Briefs, A 1964,F 3,22:2
Young and Willing 1964,F 27,28:1
No, My Darling Daughter 1964,Mr 28,13:5
Doctor in Distress 1964,Jl 8,38:2
Agent 8 3/4 1965,O 14,53:1
Deadlier Than the Male 1967,F 22,21:1
High Commissioner, The 1968,D 12,62:5
Thomas, Robert (Director)
Bonne Soupe, La 1964,Mr 16,37:1
Friend of the Family 1965,N 18,55:3
Thomas, Robert (Screenwriter)
Bonne Soupe, La 1964,Mr 16,37:1
Friend of the Family 1965,N 18,55:3
Thomas, Ted (Original Author)
Gallant Blade 1948,O 13,31:3
Thomas, Varley
Goldfinger 1964,D 22,36:1
Thomas, Virginia
Private Life of Helen of Troy, The
1927,D 10,14:7
Wild Party, The 1929,Ap 2,28:4
Thomas, Wilfrid (Narrator)
Queen in Australia, The 1954,Je 16,37:3
Thomas, William (Director)
Midnight Manhunt 1945,Ag 18,12:5
Special Agent 1949,Ag 22,13:1
Crosswinds 1951,D 7,35:4
Thomas, William (Original Author)
You're a Sweetheart 1937,D 25,10:5
Cowboy in Manhattan 1943,My 28,19:2
Thomas, William (Producer)
Power Dive 1941,My 29,15:4
I Live on Danger 1942,Ag 22,16:2
Aerial Gunner 1943,Je 26,10:2
One Body too Many 1944,N 25,21:2
Midnight Manhunt 1945,Ag 18,12:5
Fear in the Night 1947,Ap 19,11:3
Adventure Island 1947,O 20,29:2
Albuquerque 1948,Mr 1,17:2
El Paso 1949,Mr 24,35:2
Manhandled 1949,My 26,34:2
Special Agent 1949,Ag 22,13:1
Captain China 1950,Mr 2,33:2
Lawless, The 1950,Je 23,29:2
Eagle and the Hawk, The 1950,Jl 6,31:2
Tripoli 1950,N 10,35:2
Last Outpost, The 1951,Je 22,16:3
Passage West 1951,Ag 31,12:2
Crosswinds 1951,D 7,35:4
Hong Kong 1952,Ap 5,20:3
Sangaree 1953,Je 5,19:1
Those Redheads From Seattle 1953,O 1,34:2
Jivaro 1954,F 13,11:5
Run for Cover 1955,Ap 30,10:6
Hell's Island 1955,My 7,10:2
Far Horizons, The 1955,My 21,11:1
Lucy Gallant 1955,O 21,30:1
Big Caper, The 1957,Mr 29,16:1
Bailout at 43,000 1957,Je 8,13:2
Thomasjan, Guy
Boomerang 1947,Mr 6,36:2
Thomeray
Merlusse 1938,Mr 17,17:2
THOMPSON
See Also THOMSEN, THOMSON
Thompson, Beverly
With a Song in my Heart 1952,Ap 5,20:2
Thompson, Bill
Here We Go Again 1942,O 12,12:3
Thompson, Carlos
Flame and the Flesh 1954,My 3,21:2
Valley of the Kings 1954,Jl 22,15:2
Raw Wind in Eden 1958,S 20,10:6
Stefanie 1959,Je 18,36:1
Spessart Inn, The 1961,F 18,12:3
Vie de Chateau, La 1967,Mr 21,35:1

Thompson, Charlotte (Original Author)
Rebecca of Sunnybrook Farm 1932,Jl 30,16:5
Thompson, Clarence
Butterflies in the Rain 1926,D 25,10:5
Sensation Seekers 1927,Mr 16,28:2
Thompson, Clifford
20th Century 1934,My 4,24:2
Thompson, Creighton
Miracle in Harlem 1949,O 24,19:4
Thompson, Dee J
Once More, my Darling 1949,S 26,17:1
Killer is Loose, The 1956,Mr 3,17:2
Glass Bottom Boat, The 1966,Je 10,54:1
Thompson, Denman (Original Author)
Old Homestead, The 1915,D 27,9:1
Old Homestead, The 1922,O 9,10:2
Thompson, Donald
Quiet One, The 1949,F 14,15:2
Thompson, Donald (Cinematographer)
Blood-stained Russia 1917,D 10,15:4
Thompson, Duane
Sweet Rosie O'Grady 1926,D 9,33:1
Voice of the City, The 1929,Ap 29,29:2
Hollywood Hotel 1938,Ja 13,17:3
Thompson, Edward (Original Author)
Golden Girl 1951,N 21,20:3
Thompson, Evan
Chapman Report, The 1962,O 18,49:2
Thompson, Francis (Producer)
To the Fair 1965,F 13,10:2
Thompson, Fred (Original Author)
Charming Deceiver, The 1933,D 9,18:3
Sons o'Guns 1936,My 14,29:2
This'll Make You Whistle 1938,N 1,27:2
Thompson, Fred (Screenwriter)
Head Over Heels in Love 1937,F 13,9:1
Thompson, Gene
Kid From Left Field, The 1953,S 26,15:3
Thompson, George
Why Bring That Up? 1929,O 5,22:5
Thompson, Glenn
Kill the Umpire 1950,My 29,10:6
Thompson, Hal
Animal Crackers 1930,Ag 29,20:3
Thompson, Harian (Miscellaneous)
Rose of the Rancho 1936,Ja 9,25:2
Thompson, Harlan (Director)
Past of Mary Holmes, The 1933,My 1,10:3
Kiss and Make-Up 1934,Je 29,17:1
Thompson, Harlan (Original Author)
How to be Very, Very Popular 1955,Jl 23,10:1
Thompson, Harlan (Producer)
Early to Bed 1936,Jl 16,20:2
Wives Never Know 1936,O 31,24:2
College Holiday 1936,D 24,21:2
Champagne Waltz 1937,F 4,17:2
Big Broadcast of 1938, The 1938,Mr 10,16:2
Romance in the Dark 1938,Mr 21,18:2
Paris Honeymoon 1939,Ja 26,17:1
Magnificent Fraud, The 1939,Jl 20,16:2
Road to Singapore 1940,Mr 14,29:2
Thompson, Harlan (Screenwriter)
Girls Demand Excitement 1931,F 7,11:1
Here is my Heart 1934,D 22,21:1
Ruggles of Red Gap 1935,Mr 7,26:1
Thompson, Hilarie
How Sweet It Is 1968,Ag 22,47:1
Thompson, J Lee (Director)
Murder Without Crime 1951,D 26,19:6
Weak and the Wicked, The 1954,Ag 21,10:3
Yellow Balloon 1954,O 13,28:2
Blonde Sinner 1957,Ja 24,34:1
Woman in a Dressing Gown 1957,S 13,15:2
Alligator Named Daisy, An 1957,O 7,23:2
Tiger Bay 1959,D 15,50:1
Flame Over India 1960,Ap 30,14:1
I Aim at the Stars 1960,O 20,42:2
Desert Attack 1961,Mr 23,28:1
Guns of Navarone, The 1961,Je 23,19:1
Cape Fear 1962,Ap 19,35:2
Taras Bulba 1962,D 26,5:2
King of the Sun 1963,D 26,33:4
What a Way to Go! 1964,My 15,44:1
John Goldfarb, Please Come Home
1965,Mr 25,42:4
Return From the Ashes 1965,N 17,53:1
Eye of the Devil 1967,D 7,60:1
Thompson, J Lee (Original Author)
Murder Without Crime 1951,D 26,19:6
Thompson, J Lee (Producer)
Woman in a Dressing Gown 1957,S 13,15:2
Return From the Ashes 1965,N 17,53:1
Thompson, J Lee (Screenwriter)
For Them that Trespass 1950,S 27,37:2
No Place for Jennifer 1951,Jl 17,31:2
Weak and the Wicked, The 1954,Ag 21,10:3
Yellow Balloon, The 1954,O 13,28:2
Flame Over India 1960,Ap 30,14:1
Thompson, Jeff
Davy Crockett, King of the Wild Frontier
1955,My 26,36:1

Thompson, Jim (Miscellaneous)
Killing, The 1956,My 21,20:1
Thompson, Jim (Screenwriter)
Paths of Glory 1957,D 26,23:2
Thompson, Jimmy
Brigadoon 1954,S 17,18:2
Forbidden Planet 1956,My 4,21:2
Thompson, Johnny
In the Name of the Law 1922,Jl 10,9:5
Thompson, Julian (Original Author)
Warrior's Husband, The 1933,My 12,20:4
Thompson, Kay
Funny Face 1957,Mr 29,16:1
Thompson, Kay (Composer)
I Dood It 1943,N 11,29:1
Ziegfeld Follies 1946,Mr 23,8:3
Thompson, Kay and her radio choir
Manhattan Merry-Go-Round 1937,D 31,9:3
Thompson, Keene (Miscellaneous)
Paris in Spring 1935,Jl 13,16:2
Thompson, Keene (Original Author)
We're in the Air Now 1927,D 31,31:1
His Private Life 1928,N 12,18:2
Only the Brave 1930,Mr 8,21:1
War Correspondent 1932,Ag 13,18:6
Last Man, The 1932,S 17,18:4
Man Against Woman 1932,D 17,22:3
Mama Loves Papa 1933,Jl 24,11:2
Six of a Kind 1934,Mr 10,18:3
Wives Never Know 1936,O 31,24:2
Thompson, Keene (Screenwriter)
Wedding Bills 1927,Je 29,29:3
True to the Navy 1930,My 24,21:2
Love in Bloom 1935,Ap 20,16:2
Thompson, Kenneth
Secret Hour, The 1928,Mr 12,26:1
Doorway to Hell, The 1930,N 1,23:2
Lawyer Man 1932,D 27,10:2
Thompson, Larry
Sunday Dinner for a Soldier 1945,Ja 25,16:2
Too Young to Know 1945,D 8,21:2
Thompson, Leonard
Wrecker, The 1929,Ag 13,23:2
Thompson, Lotus
Folly of Vanity 1925,Ja 28,14:1
Thompson, Marian (Miscellaneous)
Shake Hands With the Devil 1959,Je 25,20:7
Thompson, Marshall
Clock, The 1945,My 4,23:2
Valley of Decision, The 1945,My 4,23:2
Twice Blessed 1945,Jl 7,7:5
They Were Expendable 1945,D 21,25:2
Bad Bascomb 1946,My 23,18:4
Cockeyed Miracle, The 1946,O 25,28:1
Gallant Bess 1946,D 6,27:6
Secret Heart, The 1946,D 26,28:2
Show-Off, The 1947,Mr 20,38:2
Romance of Rosy Ridge, The 1947,S 12,18:3
B F's Daughter 1948,Mr 25,35:2
Homecoming 1948,Ap 30,28:4
Words and Music 1948,D 10,34:2
Command Decision 1949,Ja 20,34:2
Roseanna McCoy 1949,O 13,33:2
Battleground 1949,N 12,8:4
Mystery Street 1950,Jl 28,12:5
Devil's Doorway 1950,N 10,35:1
Dial 1119 1950,D 4,32:6
Basketball Fix, the 1951,S 14,21:2
Tall Target, The 1951,S 28,26:2
My Six Convicts 1952,Mr 28,27:3
Caddy, The 1953,S 18,16:6
Port of Hell 1954,D 18,12:2
Crashout 1955,Jl 9,9:2
To Hell and Back 1955,S 23,21:2
Good Morning, Miss Dove 1955,N 24,41:1
Fiend Without a Face 1958,Jl 4,15:3
Flight of the Lost Balloon 1962,My 24,29:2
No Man is an Island 1962,O 11,49:2
Yank in Vietnam, A 1964,F 6,36:4
Clarence, the Cross-Eyed Lion 1965,Ag 5,15:3
Around the World Under the Sea 1966,Jl 21,20:2
Thompson, Marshall (Director)
Yank in Vietnam, A 1964,F 6,36:4
Thompson, Marshall (Original Author)
Clarence, the Cross-Eyed Lion 1965,Ag 5,15:3
Thompson, Morton (Original Author)
My Brother Talks to Horses 1947,Je 19,27:4
Not as a Stranger 1955,Je 29,24:1
Thompson, Morton (Screenwriter)
My Brother Talks to Horses 1947,Je 19,27:4
Thompson, Natalie
Ringside Maisie 1941,Ag 1,11:2
Vanishing Virginian, The 1942,My 28,13:3
Thompson, Nick
Snow Bride, The 1923,Je 12,22:2
Tongues of Flame 1924,D 16,28:1
Puppets 1926,Je 21,17:2
Corruption 1933,Je 20,22:7
Woman Rebels, A 1936,O 30,27:2
Blockade 1938,Je 17,25:1
Buffalo Bill 1944,Ap 20,22:6

Thompson, Patsy Ann
Tomorrow the World 1944,D 22,12:4
Thompson, Paul
Snows of Kilimanjaro, The 1952,S 19,19:2
White Witch Doctor 1953,Jl 2,19:3
Untamed 1955,Mr 12,11:6
Thompson, Peggy (Screenwriter)
King of the Newsboys 1938,Ap 2,18:2
Whirlpool; (Remous) 1940,O 8,31:2
Thompson, Peter
Wistful Widow of Wagon Gap, The
1947,N 21,36:2
Double Life, A 1948,F 20,19:1
Santa Fe 1951,My 4,31:2
Thompson, Polly
Deliverance 1919,Ag 19,10:1
Thompson, Ray
When a Man's a Man 1924,F 5,20:1
Enchanted Hill, The 1925,D 29,19:2 (In
Addenda)
Thompson, Rex
Young Bess 1953,My 22,31:1
Her Twelve Men 1954,Ag 12,23:2
Eddy Duchin Story, The 1956,Je 22,15:1
King and I, The 1956,Je 29,15:6
All Mine to Give 1959,Ag 4,32:5
Thompson, Roy Jr Captain
Cease Fire! 1953,N 25,17:1
Thompson, Slim
Green Pastures, The 1936,Jl 17,20:1
Thompson, Thomas (Screenwriter)
Saddle the Wind 1958,Mr 21,17:1
Thompson, Viola
Kisenga, Man of Africa 1952,Mr 7,18:2
Thompson, Virgil (Composer)
Spanish Earth, The 1937,Ag 21,7:2
River, The 1938,F 5,19:2 (In Addenda)
Thompson, Walter (Director)
Seven Wonders of the World 1956,Ap 11,29:1
Cinerama-South Seas Adventure 1958,Jl 16,26:1
Thompson, William
Comin' Round the Mountain 1940,S 26,27:3
Thompson, William (Miscellaneous)
Savage Splendor 1949,N 4,37:2
Thompson-Seton, Ernest (Original Author)
Legend of Lobo, The 1962,N 10,16:2
THOMSEN
See Also THOMPSON, THOMSON
Thomsen, Anne Werner
Young Have no Time, The 1959,N 23,41:2
Thomsen, Knud Leif (Director)
Venum 1968,Ja 11,42:1
Thomsen, Knud Leif (Screenwriter)
Venum 1968,Ja 11,42:1
Thomsen, Robert (Producer)
Unknown Man, The 1951,N 17,9:5
THOMSON
See Also THOMPSON, THOMSEN
Thomson, Beatrix
Dreyfus Case, The 1931,Ag 31,11:5
Old Curiosity Shop, The 1935,D 23,15:5
Thomson, Fred
Love Light, The 1921,Ja 10,9:1
Two-Gun Man, The 1926,Jl 13,19:3
Jesse James 1927,O 17,20:2
Thomson, Kenneth
Risky Business 1926,S 8,19:3
Corporal Kate 1926,D 15,30:4
Man Bait 1927,Ja 19,21:1
White Gold 1927,Ap 11,18:3
King of Kings, The 1927,Ap 20,29:2
Bellamy Trial, The 1929,Ja 24,30:5
Broadway Melody, The 1929,F 9,15:3
Girl from Havana, The 1929,S 2,16:1
Careless Age, The 1929,S 21,17:1
Notorious Affair, A 1930,Ap 26,11:1
Sweet Mamma 1930,Jl 12,16:4
Lawful Larceny 1930,Jl 12,16:4
Wild Company 1930,Jl 19,7:5
Reno 1930,N 4,36:1
Just Imagine 1930,N 22,21:3
Woman Hungry 1931,Mr 23,24:7
Murder at Midnight 1931,O 5,17:3
Bad Company 1931,N 7,16:5
Man Wanted 1932,Ap 16,11:2
Famous Ferguson Case, The 1932,Ap 25,18:6
70,000 Witnesses 1932,S 3,16:2
Movie Crazy 1932,S 15,19:3
Her mad Night 1932,N 15,24:5
Fast Life 1932,D 24,11:4
Daring Daughters 1933,Mr 25,13:4
Jungle Bride 1933,My 13,16:3
Hold Me Tight 1933,My 22,18:6
Little Giant, The 1933,My 27,11:5
Female 1933,N 4,18:3
From Headquarters 1933,N 17,22:4
Son of a Sailor 1933,N 30,38:4
Change of Heart 1934,My 11,24:2
Many Happy Returns 1934,Je 9,18:2
Behold My Wife 1935,F 18,19:3
Whispering Smith Speaks 1936,F 17,21:1

Thomson, Norman
Barbarian and the Geisha 1958,O 3,25:1
Thor, Jerome
55 Days at Peking 1963,My 30,20:1
Thor, Larry
Portland Expose 1957,S 27,16:6
Amazing Colossal Man, The 1957,O 26,19:2
Thorburn, June
Cruel Sea, The 1953,Ag 11,18:5
Touch and go 1956,Mr 20,13:2
Rooney 1958,Je 6,29:2
Tom Thumb 1958,D 24,00:0
Broth of a Boy 1959,D 28,18:1
Three Worlds of Gulliver, The 1960,D 17,19:3
Master Spy 1964,Ag 20,34:2
Why Bother to Knock 1965,F 4,24:2
Thordsen, Kelly
Desire in the Dust 1960,O 12,47:2
Sweet Bird of Youth 1962,Mr 29,28:2
Ugly Dachshund, The 1966,Ap 7,45:1
Boy, Did I Get a Wrong Number! 1966,Je 9,54:2
Good Times 1967,Ag 3,26:4
Thorgersen, Ed
Hit Parade, The 1937,My 31,11:2
Life Begins In College 1937,O 9,16:1
Maryland 1940,Jl 13,16:5
Thorgersen, Ed (Narrator)
Norway Replies! 1944,F 26,10:3
THORN
See Also THORNE
Thorn, Ronald Scott (Original Author)
Stop Me Before I Kill 1961,Je 22,23:4
Thorn, Ronald Scott (Screenwriter)
Stop Me Before I Kill 1961,Je 22,23:4
Doctor in Distress 1964,Jl 8,38:2
Thorn, William
Love Takes Flight 1937,S 27,24:3
Thornby, Robert T (Director)
Young Hollywood 1927,D 13,33:2
Thorndike, Lucille
Garden of Weeds, The 1924,N 4,24:1
Thorndike, Oliver
Story of Dr Wassell, The 1944,Je 7,13:2
Sign of the Cross 1944,D 21,16:3
Thorndike, Russell
Henry V 1946,Je 18,30:2
Thorndike, Sybil
Dawn 1928,Je 3,VIII,5:1
To What Red Hell 1929,O 6,IX,9:4 (In Addenda)
Nine Days a Queen 1936,O 3,21:1
Major Barbara 1941,My 15,27:1
Nicholas Nickleby 1947,D 1,27:2
Forbidden Street, The 1949,My 14,9:2
Stage Fright 1950,F 24,27:2
Wild Heart, The 1952,My 29,17:2
Melba 1953,Je 25,23:1
Prince and the Showgirl 1957,Je 14,22:2
Shake Hands With the Devil 1959,Je 25,20:7
Hand in Hand 1961,F 7,41:3
Big Gamble, The 1961,S 2,19:2
Thorndyke, Russell
Hamlet 1948,S 30,32:2
Thorndyke, Russell (Original Author)
Dr Syn 1937,N 15,15:1
THORNE
See Also THORN
Thorne, Anthony (Original Author)
So Long at the Fair 1951,Ja 22,14:2
Baby and the Battleship, The 1957,O 1,37:2
Thorne, Anthony (Screenwriter)
So Long at the Fair 1951,Ja 22,14:2
Bad Lord Byron, The 1952,Mr 20,37:5
Thorne, Lois
Odds Against Tomorrow 1959,O 16,27:1
Thorne, Robert
Janice Meredith 1924,Ag 6,13:3
Thorne, Teresa
Joe Macbeth 1956,Ap 7,13:1
Thorne, W L
Thunderbolt 1929,Je 21,17:2
Drake Case, The 1929,S 16,30:1
Abraham Lincoln 1930,Ag 26,24:1
She-Wolf 1931,My 28,30:6
Rainbow Trail, The 1932,Ja 30,13:2
Gold Racket, The 1937,Ag 2,10:3
Thornhill, Alan (Original Author)
Voice of the Hurricane 1964,Je 3,36:4
Thornhill, Alan (Screenwriter)
Crowning Experience, The 1960,O 24,25:3
Voice of the Hurricane 1964,Je 3,36:4
Thornton, Claudette
Redhead From Wyoming, The 1953,Ja 9,17:4
Thornton, Cyril
Thin Man, The 1934,Je 30,18:5
Barbary Coast 1935,O 14,21:1
Man About Town 1939,Je 29,19:1
Case of the Black Parrot, The 1941,Ja 10,23:3
Thunder in the Valley 1947,N 28,30:1
Thornton, Joan
Round Trip 1967,Jl 20,30:2
THORP
See Also THORPE

Thorp, Roderick (Original Author)
Detective, The 1968,My 29,20:3
THORPE
See Also THORP
Thorpe, Buddy
Joe Louis Story, The 1953,N 4,29:4
Thorpe, George
Adventure for Two 1945,D 14,24:5
Meet Me at Dawn 1948,My 18,26:2
Quiet Week-End 1948,Ag 20,13:2
Quartet (The Alien Corn); Alien Corn, The
(Quartet) 1949,Mr 29,30:3
Man on the Eiffel Tower, The 1950,Ja 30,12:2
Thorpe, Gordon
Iron Mask, The 1929,F 22,18:6
Bridge of San Luis Rey, The 1929,My 20,22:6
Abraham Lincoln 1930,Ag 26,24:1
Thorpe, Herbert
Irish and Proud of It 1938,O 31,12:3
Thorpe, Jerry (Director)
Venetian Affair, The 1967,Ja 19,41:2
Day of the Evil Gun 1968,Ap 25,53:2
Thorpe, Jerry (Producer)
Venetian Affair, The 1967,Ja 19,41:2
Day of the Evil Gun 1968,Ap 25,53:2
Thorpe, Jim
White Eagle 1932,S 24,18:4
My Pal the King 1932,O 4,26:4
Behold My Wife 1935,F 18,19:3
Treachery Rides the Range 1936,My 30,7:3
Wagonmaster 1950,Je 19,17:2
Thorpe, Richard
Barretts of Wimpole Street, The 1957,Ja 18,15:3
Thorpe, Richard (Director)
Border Romance 1930,My 26,25:3
Lawless Woman, The 1931,Je 8,21:1
Sky Spider, The 1931,Ag 31,11:5
Cross Examination 1932,F 27,22:1
Escapade 1932,My 28,18:2
Midnight Lady, The 1932,Jl 1,19:3
Strange People 1933,Je 17,16:5
I Have Lived 1933,S 6,24:4
Quitter, The 1934,Mr 14,23:3
Last of the Pagans 1936,Ja 9,25:2
Voice of Bugle Ann, The 1936,F 27,23:1
Tarzan Escapes 1936,N 20,27:2
Dangerous Number 1937,Mr 12,19:2
Night Must Fall 1937,Ap 30,17:2
Double Wedding 1937,O 22,27:2
Man-Proof 1938,Ja 14,21:1
Love Is a Headache 1938,Ja 28,17:3
First 100 Years, The 1938,My 13,17:2
Toy Wife, The 1938,Je 24,15:1
Crowd Roars, The 1938,Ag 5,11:1
Three Loves Has Nancy 1938,S 2,21:2
Huckleberry Finn 1939,Mr 3,21:2
Tarzan Finds a Son 1939,Je 15,27:2
Earl of Chicago, The 1940,Mr 14,29:3
Twenty-Mule Team 1940,My 10,26:6
Wyoming 1940,O 3,31:4
Bad Man, The 1941,Ap 4,25:1
Barnacle Bill 1941,Jl 25,12:4
Tarzan's Secret Treasure 1941,D 25,33:1
Joe Smith, American 1942,Ap 2,27:4
Tarzan's New York Adventure 1942,Ag 7,13:2
White Cargo 1942,N 27,27:2
Three Hearts for Julia 1943,My 21,22:4
Above Suspicion 1943,Ag 6,10:3
Cry Havoc 1943,N 24,16:2
Two Girls and a Sailor 1944,Je 15,16:1
Thin Man Goes Home, The 1945,Ja 26,16:5
Thrill of a Romance 1945,My 25,22:2
Her Highness and the Bellboy 1945,S 28,16:2
What Next Corporal Hargrove? 1945,D 26,15:2
Fiesta 1947,Je 27,17:3
This Time for Keeps 1947,D 5,33:4
On an Island With You 1948,Jl 30,13:2
Date with Judy, A 1948,Ag 7,8:2
Sun comes up, The 1949,My 13,29:2
Big Jack 1949,My 23,27:4
Malaya 1950,F 23,33:1
Black Hand 1950,Mr 13,15:2
Challenge to Lassie 1950,Ap 7,22:3
Three Little Words 1950,Ag 10,21:2
Vengeance Valley 1951,F 16,21:2
Great Caruso, The 1951,My 11,32:2
Unknown Man, The 1951,N 17,9:5
It's a big Country 1952,Ja 9,25:2
Carbine Williams 1952,My 8,37:2
Ivanhoe 1952,Ag 1,8:2
Prisoner of Zenda, The 1952,N 5,36:2
All the Brothers Were Valiant 1953,D 29,19:2
Knights of the Round Table 1954,Ja 8,17:2
Student Prince, The 1954,Je 16,18:2
Athena 1954,D 22,28:2
Prodigal, The 1955,My 14,10:7
Quentin Durward 1955,N 24,41:1
Ten Thousand Bedrooms 1957,Ap 4,37:1
Tip on a Dead Jockey 1957,S 7,12:7
Jailhouse Rock 1957,N 14,41:1
House of the Seven Hawks, The 1959,D 17,51:2
Killers of Kilimanjaro 1960,Ap 7,46:1
Honeymoon Machine, The 1961,Ag 24,25:2

Thorpe, Richard (Director) — Cont
Horizontal Lieutenant, The 1962,My 12,15:3
Tartars, The 1962,Je 21,26:2
Follow the Boys 1963,F 28,8:2
Fun in Acapulco 1964,F 20,22:4
Truth About Spring, The 1965,Je 17,27:2
That Funny Feeling 1965,O 21,57:2
Last Challenge, The 1967,D 28,25:1
Thorpe, Richard (Producer)
Last Challenge, The 1967,D 28,25:1
Thorpe, Ted
If a Man Answers 1962,N 22,43:1
Thorpe-Bates, Peggy
Georgy Girl 1966,O 18,48:1
Thorrent, Andre
Shameless Old Lady, The 1966,S 27,52:1
Thorry, Juan C
Caballo del Pueblo, El 1935,D 16,23:4
Thorson, Marilyn
Small Hours, The 1962,Ag 14,34:1
Thorson, Russell
Zero Hour 1957,N 14,41:1
I Want to Live 1958,N 19,45:1
My Blood Runs Cold 1965,Mr 25,42:4
Thorvaldson, Einar (Original Author)
Match King, The 1932,D 8,25:3
Threatt, Elizabeth
Big Sky, The 1952,Ag 20,21:1
Three Cheers
Hit Parade of 1943 1943,Ap 16,24:3
Three Dunhills
My Wild Irish Rose 1947,D 25,32:2
Three Hits and a Miss
Topper 1937,Ag 20,21:2
Three Stooges
It's a Mad, Mad, Mad, Mad World 1963,N 19,47:1
Three Stooges, The
Start Cheering 1938,Mr 17,17:3
Time Out for Rhythm 1941,Jl 10,16:3
Three Stooges Meet Hercules, The 1962,Ja 27,13:4
Threw, Harvey (Miscellaneous)
Trail of the Lonesome Pine, The 1936,F 20,23:5
Thring, Frank
Ben Hur 1959,N 19,50:2
King of Kings 1961,O 12,41:2
Throley, Victor
Young Don't Cry, The 1957,Jl 27,10:7
Throne, Malachi
Young Lovers, The 1965,F 11,45:1
Throwbridge, Charles
Crime School 1938,My 11,17:2
Thulin, Ingrid
Foreign Intrigue 1956,Jl 13,23:2
Wild Strawberries 1959,Je 23,37:1
Magician, The 1959,Ag 28,27:1
Brink of Life; (Nara Livet) 1959,N 9,36:2
4 Horsemen of the Apocalypse, The 1962,Mr 10,10:2
Winter Light 1963,My 14,32:1
Silence, The 1964,F 4,28:1
Return From the Ashes 1965,N 17,53:1
Guerre est Fini, La; War Is Over, The 1966,S 23,43:1
Night Games 1966,D 20,58:1
Guerre est Fini, La; War Is Over, The 1967,F 2,29:2
Thullier, Jean (Producer)
Man Escaped, A 1957,Ag 27,33:2
Testament of Orpheus 1962,Ap 10,48:1
Naked Autumn 1963,N 15,25:3
Thulstrup, Karl-Magnus
Lasse-Maja 1943,Mr 22,15:4
Thunberg, Olof
Winter Light 1963,My 14,32:1
Thunderbird, Chief
Annie Oakley 1935,D 24,10:5
Silly Billies 1936,Ap 6,18:1
Falcon out West, The 1944,Mr 18,18:2
Thundercloud, Chief
Ramona 1936,O 7,32:4
Renfrew of the Royal Mounted 1937,N 3,29:4
Typhoon 1940,My 23,28:4
North West Mounted Police 1940,N 7,33:2
Hudson's Bay 1941,Ja 10,23:2
Western Union 1941,F 7,23:2
Buffalo Bill 1944,Ap 20,22:6
Badman's Territory 1946,My 31,27:2
Senator Was Indiscreet, The 1947,D 27,9:2
Traveling Saleswoman 1950,Ja 6,25:3
Ambush 1950,Ja 19,35:2
Davy Crockett, Indian Scout 1950,Mr 17,28:3
Colt 45 1950,My 6,8:6
Thurber, James (Original Author)
Rise and Shine 1941,D 6,14:3
Male Animal, The 1942,Mr 28,11:1
Secret Life of Walter Mitty, The 1947,Ag 15,12:2
She's Working her Way Through College 1952,Jl 10,27:2
Battle of the Sexes, The 1960,Ap 19,40:4
Thurman, Mary
Bond Boy, The 1922,O 9,10:2
Zaza 1923,S 17,18:2

Fool, The 1925,Ap 13,24:1
Wildfire 1925,Je 10,18:2
Thurman, Wallace (Screenwriter)
High School Girl 1935,Mr 16,19:1
Thurn-Taxis, Alexis (Producer)
Rough, Tough and Ready 1945,Mr 24,22:7
Thursby, David
Black Swan, The 1942,D 24,18:3
Ghost and Mrs Muir, The 1947,Je 27,17:2
Thursby, DAvid
Thunder in the Valley 1947,N 28,30:1
Hills of Home 1948,N 26,32:2
Sealed Cargo 1951,My 24,47:1
Thursby, David
Virgin Queen, The 1955,Ag 6,13:2
Thurston, Carol
Story of Dr Wassell, The 1944,Je 7,13:2
Conspirators, The 1944,O 21,15:2
China Sky 1945,My 25,22:3
Swamp Fire 1946,Ag 26,21:4
Jewels of Brandenburg 1947,My 24,10:5
Rogues' Regiment 1948,D 20,31:2
Arctic Manhunt 1949,Ag 19,12:5
Thurston, Charles
Rolling Home 1926,Je 8,22:1
Chaser, The 1928,Ag 10,33:2
Big Shot, The 1932,Ja 2,14:2
Thurston, E Temple (Original Author)
Wandering Jew, The 1935,Ja 14,11:3
Thurston, Katherine Cecil (Original Author)
Masquerader, The 1922,Ag 14,12:4
Masquerader, The 1933,S 4,9:5
Thurston, Ted
Li'l Abner 1959,D 12,19:2
Thyssen, Greta
Terror is a Man 1960,Jl 14,23:1
Journey to the Seventh Planet 1962,My 25,28:3
Tiapkina, Elena
Moscow Laughs 1935,Mr 25,12:2
Soviet Border 1939,F 20,13:2
Tanya 1942,Mr 5,27:1
Wait for Me 1945,Mr 19,23:3
Tibbett, Lawence Jr
El Paso 1949,Mr 24,35:2
Tibbett, Lawrence
Rogue Song, The 1930,Ja 29,26:4
New Moon 1930,D 25,18:6
Prodigal, The 1931,Je 27,20:3
Cuban Love Song, The 1931,D 5,21:2
Metropolitan 1935,O 18,27:4
Under Your Spell 1936,N 7,15:2
Tibbetts, Martha
Ceiling Zero 1936,Ja 20,22:2
Tibbles, George (Composer)
If You Knew Susie 1948,F 23,19:2
Tibbles, George (Screenwriter)
Munster, Go Home 1966,Je 16,53:4
Tibbs, Casey
Thunder of Drums, A 1961,S 27,35:1
Tichenor, Edna
Drifting 1923,Ag 20,4:2
Silent Accuser, The 1924,N 25,26:1
Merry Widow, The 1925,Ag 27,14:1
London After Midnight 1927,D 31,31:1
Tichy, Gerard
King of Kings 1961,O 12,41:2
Cid, El 1961,D 15,49:1
Gladiators Seven 1964,My 7,31:2
Doctor Zhivago 1965,D 23,21:1
That Man in Istanbul 1966,My 19,51:2
Place Called Glory, A 1966,Ag 11,27:4
Tickelt, Jerrard (Original Author)
Island Rescue 1952,Jl 1,19:4
Tickelt, Jerrard (Screenwriter)
Island Rescue 1952,Jl 1,19:4
Tickle, Frank
Anna Karenina 1948,Ap 28,32:2
Escape 1948,Ag 16,12:2
Brandy for the Parson 1952,Ag 18,13:4
Tida, Choko
Honolulu-Tokyo-Hong Kong 1964,S 2,33:3
Tidblad, Inga
For Her Sake 1930,N 11,29:1
Haelsingar 1934,S 25,25:2
Foreign Intrigue 1956,Jl 13,23:2
Tiden, Selma
Old Home Week 1925,My 25,21:3
Tiedtke, A
Pension Schoeller 1932,S 20,26:3
Tiedtke, Jacob
Hilde Petersen, Postlagernd 1937,Je 26,20:3 (In Addenda)
Tiedtke, Jakob
Waltz Dream, The 1926,Jl 26,13:2
Luther 1929,Je 24,27:1
Drunter und Drueber 1932,D 19,19:5
Saison in Kairo 1933,D 25,28:2
Fraeulein-Falsch Verbunden! 1934,Ja 15,12:2
Tausend Fuer Eine Nacht 1934,F 12,19:2
Strich Durch die Rechnung 1934,Mr 3,8:6
Eines Prinzen Junge Liebe 1934,Mr 24,20:4
Ja, Treu Ist die Soldatenliebe 1934,Ap 28,11:4
Toller Einfall, Ein 1934,My 21,20:3

Tiedtke, Jakob — Cont
Blaue Vom Himmel, Das 1934,S 8,18:6
Heimat am Rhein 1934,D 11,29:4
Lockvogel 1935,Ja 5,20:3
Kalte Mamsell, Die 1935,Ja 12,12:2
Gretl Zieht das Grosse Los 1935,F 11,14:2
Liebe und die Erste Eisenbahn, Die; Love and the First Railroad 1935,F 18,19:4
Sonne Geht auf, die 1935,F 18,19:4
Doppelbraeutigam, Der; Double Fiance, The 1935,Mr 23,11:3
Grosse Chance, Die 1935,My 6,22:4
Fruehlingsmaerchen 1935,My 20,20:5
Schuechterne Felix, Der 1935,S 7,19:5
Frischer Wind aus Kanada 1935,S 21,18:2
Lied vom Glueck, Das; Song of Happiness, The 1935,N 30,12:7
Wenn am Sonntagabend die Dorfmusik Spielt 1935,D 9,25:3
Vetter aus Dingsda, Der 1936,F 1,9:3
Junge Graf, Der 1936,D 14,15:2
Besuch am Abend 1937,Jl 3,18:2
Nanu, Sie Kennen Korff noch Nicht?; So, You Don't Know Korff Yet? 1939,My 22,15:3
Verwehte Spuren; Covered Tracks 1939,O 14,13:3
Peter, Paul und Nanette 1940,My 25,20:1
Tiemroth, Edvin
Child of Man 1950,F 1,25:2
Tieri, Aroldo
When Love Calls 1948,O 9,12:6
Voice of Love, The 1950,Ja 7,11:2
Mad About Opera 1950,Ap 6,33:2
Streets of Sorrow 1952,N 18,37:4
Sins of Casanova 1957,O 7,23:2
Man Who Wagged his Tail, The 1961,S 19,39:1
Tiernan, Patricia
Battle Circus 1953,My 28,27:5
Scandal at Scourie 1953,Je 16,24:2
Dream Wife 1953,Jl 30,20:1
Tierney, Edward
Hoodlum, The 1951,Jl 6,14:6
Tierney, Gene
Return of Frank James, The 1940,Ag 10,16:4
Hudson's Bay 1941,Ja 10,23:2
Tobacco Road 1941,F 21,16:2
Belle Starr 1941,N 1,20:2
Shanghai Gesture, The 1941,D 26,21:2
Son of Fury 1942,Ja 30,23:2
Rings on her Fingers 1942,Ap 24,21:4
Thunder Birds 1942,O 29,19:2
China Girl 1943,Ja 21,27:2
Heaven Can Wait 1943,Ag 12,15:1
Laura 1944,O 12,24:1
Bell for Adano, A 1945,Jl 6,8:3
Leave Her to Heaven 1945,D 26,15:1
Dragonwyck 1946,Ap 11,35:2
Razor's Edge, The 1946,N 20,42:2
Ghost and Mrs Muir, The 1947,Je 27,17:2
Iron Curtain, The 1948,My 13,31:2
That Wonderful Urge 1948,D 22,29:6
Whirlpool 1950,Ja 14,9:2
Night and the City 1950,Je 10,11:2
Where the Sidewalk Ends 1950,Jl 8,7:4
Mating Season, The 1951,Ap 12,41:2
On the Riviera 1951,My 24,47:1
Secret of Convict Lake, The 1951,Ag 4,7:2
Way of a Gaucho 1952,N 5,36:2
Plymouth Adventure 1952,N 14,20:3
Never Let Me Go 1953,Jl 11,37:2
Egyptian, The 1954,Ag 25,23:1
Personal Affair 1954,O 23,13:2
Black Widow 1954,O 28,46:6
Left Hand of God, The 1955,S 22,34:5
Advise and Consent 1962,Je 7,31:2
Toys in the Attic 1963,Ag 1,17:2
Pleasure Seekers, The 1964,D 26,9:1
Tierney, Harry (Composer)
Half Shot at Sunrise 1930,O 11,21:3
Rio Rita 1942,My 8,27:3
Tierney, Harry (Original Author)
Irene 1940,My 24,23:3
Tierney, Lawrence
Ghost Ship, The 1943,D 25,19:4
Youth Runs Wild 1944,S 2,17:2
Dillinger 1945,Ap 26,26:2
Back to Bataan 1945,S 13,26:3
Badman's Territory 1946,My 31,27:2
Step by Step 1946,Ag 24,6:7
San Quentin 1947,F 10,24:3
Devil Thumbs a Ride, The 1947,Mr 22,10:2
Born to Kill 1947,My 1,34:2
Shakedown 1950,S 4,11:2
Hoodlum, The 1951,Jl 6,14:6
Best of the Badmen 1951,Ag 10,13:2
Greatest Show on Earth, The 1952,Ja 11,17:2
Singing in the Dark 1956,Mr 8,32:5
Custer of the West 1968,Jl 4,13:2
Tiesler, Hans (Screenwriter)
Fight for Peace, The 1938,My 14,18:1
Tiffany, Lylah
All the Way Home 1963,O 30,46:1

Tiffin, Pamela
Summer and Smoke 1961,N 17,41:1
One, Two, Three 1961,D 22,17:1
State Fair 1962,Ap 12,41:4
Come Fly With Me 1963,My 2,40:2
For Those Who Think Young 1964,Jl 9,27:1
Lively Set, The 1964,O 15,54:1
Pleasure Seekers, The 1964,D 26,9:1
Hallelujah Trail, The 1965,Jl 2,17:1
Harper 1966,Mr 31,43:1
Kiss the Other Sheik 1968,Jl 30,33:1

Tih, Betty Loh
Love Eterne, The; Liang Shan Po and Chu
Ying-lai 1965,Ja 16,14:1
Sons of Good Earth 1967,S 16,37:5

Tikhomirov, Roman (Director)
Eugene Onegin 1959,S 14,33:1
Queen of Spades 1961,S 4,10:1
Morning Star 1962,Ag 20,18:2

Tikhonov, N (Screenwriter)
Friends 1939,Ja 2,28:3

Tikhonov, Vacheslav
Young Guard 1949,D 26,33:6
Maximka 1953,O 12,30:4
House on the Front Line, The 1963,S 2,18:1
Optimistic Tragedy, The 1964,F 24,20:2
War and Peace 1968,Ap 29,50:5

Tikhonravof, S
Marionettes 1934,My 8,28:6
Childhood of Maxim Gorky 1938,S 28,29:3

Tilbury, Zeffie
Avalanche, The 1919,Je 30,16:3
Single Standard, The 1929,Jl 29,23:3
Ship From Shanghai, The 1930,Ap 26,11:1
Charlie Chan Carries On 1931,Mr 21,15:1
Mystery of Edwin Drood, The 1935,Mr 21,27:1
Werewolf of London, The 1935,My 10,25:2
Alice Adams 1935,Ag 16,11:3
Last Days of Pompeii, The 1935,O 17,29:2
Desire 1936,Ap 13,15:1
Gorgeous Hussy, The 1936,S 5,7:1
Give Me your Heart 1936,S 17,18:2
Under Cover of Night 1937,Ja 20,18:4
Maid of Salem 1937,Mr 4,27:2
It Happened in Hollywood 1937,O 2,18:1
Federal Bullets 1937,D 27,11:1
Bulldog Drummond's Peril 1938,Mr 18,23:2
Woman Against Woman 1938,Ag 23,20:6
Arrest Bulldog Drummond 1939,Ja 12,23:2
Story of Alexander Graham Bell, The
1939,Ap 1,17:2
Tell no Tales 1939,Je 2,27:3
Balalaika 1939,D 15,33:2
Grapes of Wrath, The 1940,Ja 25,17:2
Comin' Round the Mountain 1940,S 26,27:3
Tobacco Road 1941,F 21,16:2

Tilden, Jane
Blaufuchs; Blue Fox 1939,Mr 4,18:5
Blumen aus Nizza; Flowers From Nice
1939,Ap 1,17:3
Spiegel des Lebens, Der; Life's Mirror
1940,F 17,9:3

Tilden, William T
Music Master, The 1927,Ja 17,12:4 (In Addenda)

Till, Eric (Director)
Hot Millions 1968,S 20,42:1

Tiller, NAdia
Life and Loves of Mozart, The 1958,Ja 7,28:2
Rosemary 1960,Ja 19,40:2
Night Affair 1961,O 13,27:1
Portrait of a Sinner 1961,D 7,52:1
World in my Pocket, The 1962,My 10,30:2

Tiller, Nadia
Riff Raff Girls 1962,O 20,13:5
Burning Court, The 1963,Ag 1,17:2
And so to Bed 1965,Jl 31,11:3
Upper Hand, The 1967,Jl 29,29:3
Tender Scoundrel 1967,N 16,58:2
Poppy is Also a Flower, The 1967,D 14,62:4
Tonio Kroger 1968,Ja 16,24:1

Tillman, A C
All the King's Men 1949,N 9,37:2

Tillman, Fritz
Confess, Dr Corda 1960,O 24,25:5

Tillotson, David Leo
They Just Had to Get Married 1933,F 13,11:4

Tilsley, Frank (Original Author)
Damn the Defiant 1962,S 20,29:2

Tilton, Edwin Booth
Midnight Express, The 1924,N 19,19:3

Tilton, Martha
Sunny 1941,Je 13,22:2
Crime Incorporated 1945,Je 23,9:7
Benny Goodman Story 1956,F 22,22:1

Tilton, Roger (Director)
Jazz Dance 1954,S 21,24:1

Tilton, Roger (Producer)
Jazz Dance 1954,S 21,24:1

Tilvern, Alan
Bhowani Junction 1956,My 25,26:1
Triple Deception 1957,O 7,23:2
Chase a Crooked Shadow 1958,Mr 25,28:4
Khartoum 1966,Jl 14,28:1

Timar, Jozsef
Gyimesi Vadvirag; Wildflower of Gyimes
1939,O 21,12:3

Timberg, Sammy (Composer)
Gulliver's Travels 1939,D 21,29:1
Mr Bug Goes to Town 1942,F 20,21:3

Timblin, Charles
Mountain Music 1937,Je 24,30:3

Timbrooke, Harry
Play Girl, The 1928,Ap 23,20:2

Timchenko, N
1812 1944,S 11,14:1

Timofeyev, N (Composer)
Professor Mamlock 1938,N 8,26:2

Timofeyev, Nikolai
Lullaby, The 1961,My 15,35:2

Timofeyev, Nikolai (Composer)
Baltic Deputy 1937,S 4,8:2
Vasili's Return 1953,S 28,21:4
Tsar's Bride, The 1966,Mr 12,13:2

Timokhin, S D
Heroes of the Sea 1941,Ap 28,11:2

Timontayev, A
Diary of a Revolutionist 1932,Je 10,22:3
Kampf, Der 1936,S 11,29:3
On his Own 1939,S 13,31:3

Timoshenko, G
Fall of Berlin 1952,Je 9,19:2

Timoshenko, S (Director)
Sniper 1932,Ag 26,20:3
Island of Doom 1933,Jl 17,9:5
Leningrad Music Hall 1943,N 6,16:3
Boys From Leningrad, The 1955,My 2,16:5

Timoshenko, S (Miscellaneous)
Tovaristchi 1935,My 25,12:2

Timoshenko, S (Original Author)
Boys From Leningrad, The 1955,My 2,16:5

Timoshenko, Y
Variety Stars 1955,F 21,16:7

Timoshenko (Director)
Goal Keeper 1937,F 21,X,4:3 (In Addenda)

Timoteyeva, Nina
Bolshoi Ballet 67 1966,S 30,54:1

Timothy, Megan
Good Morning and Goodbye! 1968,F 20,53:1

Tinayre, Daniel (Director)
Games Men Play, The 1968,Mr 15,30:1

Tindall, Loren
Over 21 1945,Ag 17,20:2
Till the End of Time 1946,Jl 24,24:1
Good News 1947,D 5,33:2
Francis 1950,Mr 16,40:2

Ting, Li
Shepherd Girl, The 1965,S 2,36:3
Grand Substitution, The 1965,N 25,64:5

Ting-Liang-Tchao
Veil of Happiness, The 1928,My 1,33:3

Tingwell, Charles
Kangaroo 1952,My 17,22:7
Desert Rats, The 1953,My 9,13:2
Trouble in the Sky 1961,Jl 13,26:3
Murder She Said 1962,Ja 8,27:2
Murder at the Gallop 1963,Je 25,23:2
Murder Ahoy 1964,S 23,55:3
Murder Most Foul 1965,My 24,36:2

Tinling, James (Director)
Don't Marry 1928,My 21,25:1
True Heaven 1929,F 11,26:3
Flood, The 1931,Ap 27,25:1
El Ultimo Varon Sobre la Tierra 1933,Je 12,20:4
Arizona to Broadway 1933,Jl 22,14:3
Jimmy and Sally 1933,D 16,12:3
Call it Luck 1934,Jl 10,24:5
Senor Casada Necesita Marido 1935,F 11,14:3
Under the Pampas Moon 1935,My 31,11:1
Charlie Chan in Shanghai 1935,O 14,21:1
Every Saturday Night 1936,Mr 14,10:2
Champagne Charlie 1936,My 7,21:2
Educating Father 1936,Je 20,22:2
Pepper 1936,Ag 24,11:2
Holy Terror, The 1937,Ja 30,21:2
Angel's Holiday 1937,My 29,20:2
Sing and Be Happy 1937,Je 19,20:2
Great Hospital Mystery, The 1937,Jl 16,22:2
45 Fathers 1937,D 11,22:2
Mr Moto's Gamble 1938,Ap 8,17:2
Passport Husband 1938,Ag 5,11:2
Sharpshooters 1938,D 5,19:2
Deadline for Murder 1946,Je 29,22:7
Dangerous Millions 1947,Mr 15,10:3
Second Chance 1947,S 20,12:4
Roses Are Red 1947,N 15,11:2

Tinling, Joseph (Director)
Very Confidential 1927,N 29,31:1

Tinn, John
Purple Plain, The 1955,Ap 11,29:1
Windom's Way 1958,O 1,45:1

Tinschmann, Eva
Streitum den Knaben Jo; Strife Over the Boy Jo
1938,D 10,13:2

Tinsley, Louise
Captivation 1931,S 28,17:4
Man Who Won, The 1933,F 27,11:2

Tinsley, Theodore A (Original Author)
Panic on the Air 1936,Ap 20,17:1

Tinter, Hans (Director)
Cyankali 1930,Jl 13,VIII,4:2

Tinti, Gabriele
Heaven on Earth 1960,O 11,55:3
Flight of the Phoenix, The 1966,F 1,26:1
Wild Eye, The 1968,Ag 22,47:1
Legend of Lylah Clare, The 1968,Ag 23,33:1
Oldest Profession, The (Prehistoric Era)
Prehistoric Era (The Oldest Profession)
1968,N 8,42:1

Tintner, Hans (Director)
Kaiserliebchen 1931,N 12,30:2
Goethe's Jugendgeliebte 1932,D 26,26:2

Tinturin, Peter (Composer)
Under Western Stars 1938,Je 25,7:3

Tinturin, Peter (Miscellaneous)
Manhattan Merry-Go-Round 1937,D 31,9:3

Tiny Tim
You Are What You Eat 1968,S 25,38:1

Tiomkin, Dmitri (Composer)
I Live my Life 1935,O 12,12:2
Lost Horizon 1937,Mr 4,27:1
Our Russian Front 1942,F 12,27:2
Moscow Strikes Back 1942,Ag 17,19:2

Tiomkin, Dmitri (Miscellaneous)
Great Waltz, The 1938,N 25,19:1

Tip
Pepote 1958,D 2,46:1

Tip, Tap and Toe
You Can't Have Everything 1937,Ag 4,15:2
All by Myself 1943,Jl 16,20:3

Tiphaine, Bernard
Fire Within, The 1964,F 18,27:1

Tipot, V (Screenwriter)
Variety Stars 1955,F 21,16:7

Tipping, Tania
Woman in the Hall, The 1949,Ja 24,16:2

Tirado, Alfonso Ortiz
Su Ultima Cancion 1934,My 9,23:4

Tirado, Romualdo
Texan, The 1930,My 17,21:2
El Rey de los Gitanos 1933,My 29,22:2
(Incorrect in this edition; use 1933,My 29,16:5
elsewhere)
El Ultimo Varon Sobre la Tierra 1933,Je 12,20:4
Senor Casada Necesita Marido 1935,F 11,14:3
Vida Bohemia, La 1939,F 6,8:5

Tiroff, James
Brig, The 1964,S 21,37:4

Tirtof, Kostya
Ballad of Cossack Gloota, The 1938,F 28,19:1

Tischer, Bernd
Young Torless 1968,Jl 23,27:2

Tisort, Alice
Horse Ate the Hat, The 1931,S 1,30:6

Tisse, Edward (Cinematographer)
Soviet Russia Today 1935,Mr 5,23:4
Time in the Sun 1940,O 1,29:2

Tisse, Edward (Director)
Soviet Russia Today 1935,Mr 5,23:4
Immortal Garrison, The 1957,Mr 4,30:2

Tisse, Edward (Miscellaneous)
Thunder Over Mexico 1933,S 25,18:4

Tissen, Berthe
Lady Chatterley's Lover 1959,Jl 11,11:1

Tissier, Jean
Slipper Episode, The 1938,My 19,25:2
Courier of Lyons, The 1938,Je 3,17:1
Crossroads 1939,Mr 14,17:5
Symphonie d'Amour 1946,Mr 11,19:2
Her First Affair; (Children of Paradise)
1947,F 20,32:3
Shop-Girls of Paris; Au Bonheur de Dames
1947,Je 23,14:4
Murderer Lives at Number 21, The
1947,Ag 18,12:3
Loves of Casanova 1948,S 18,11:4
Strangers in the House 1949,O 13,33:3
Naked Woman, The 1950,Ja 21,10:2
Gigi 1950,Ja 31,20:2
Minne 1951,Ap 17,35:2
Strollers, The 1952,Jl 22,22:7
French Way, The 1952,S 6,12:6
Father's Dilemma 1952,S 23,25:1
Spice of Life, The 1953,D 29,19:3
Mama, Papa, the Maid and I 1956,Ag 28,31:1
And God Created Woman 1957,O 22,41:1
Hunchback of Notre Dame, The 1957,D 12,35:1
Candide 1962,N 20,39:1
White Voices; Voci Blanche 1965,Ap 13,32:2

Tissot, Alice
Cousine Bette, La 1928,Ag 12,VII,3:4
Mirages De Paris 1933,D 25,28:3
Maternelle, La 1935,O 15,19:1
Petits, Les 1936,D 30,17:2
Glory of Faith, The 1938,N 24,37:2
Last Desire 1939,D 22,15:2
Ces Dames aux Chapeaux Verts; Ladies in the
Green Hats, The 1945,Ap 5,26:2
Francis the First 1947,N 20,38:4
Ignace 1950,S 19,39:4

Tissot, Alice— Cont
Gates of Paris 1958,Ja 15,24:1
Tissot, Henri
Marriage of Figaro, The 1963,Ap 30,26:1
Devil and the 10 Commandments, The (Episode 2) 1963,O 15,44:1
Titchener, Lanham (Miscellaneous)
King's People, The 1937,My 12,27:1
Titheradge, Dion (Original Author)
Man Who Won, The 1933,F 27,11:2
Titterton, Frank
Waltz Time 1933,S 29,24:2
Titus, Harold (Original Author)
How Baxter Buttered In 1925,Je 23,24:3
Titus, Lydia Yeamans
Peace of Roaring River, The 1919,Ag 11,9:1
Strictly Confidential 1919,O 6,15:1
Nurse Marjorie 1920,My 24,20:3
Scaramouche 1923,O 12,7:2 (Incorrect in this edition; use 1927,O 1,7:2 elsewhere)
Boy of Flanders, A 1924,Ap 15,24:1
Tarnish 1924,O 13,21:1
Up the Ladder 1925,My 12,26:2
Talker, The 1925,My 12,26:2
Limited Mail, The 1925,S 1,18:2
Irene 1926,Mr 1,17:1
Two Lovers 1928,Mr 23,24:4
Water Hole, The 1928,S 3,14:2
While the City Sleeps 1928,O 22,29:1
Shanghai Lady 1929,N 11,20:2
Lummox 1930,Mr 24,25:1
Titus, Mickey
Junior Miss 1945,Je 18,15:4
Tiu, Vicky
It Happened at the World's Fair 1963,My 30,20:1
Tjernberg, Ove
Swedish Wedding Night 1965,N 15,48:1
Tkachuk, Yegor
Last Hill, The 1945,Je 26,13:2
Toal, Maureen
Ulysses 1967,Mr 14,55:1
Tobares, Alfredo
Terrace, The 1964,N 25,45:1
Tobey, Kenneth
I Was a Male War Bride 1949,Ag 27,7:2
Twelve O'Clock High 1950,Ja 28,10:2
Gunfighter, The 1950,Je 24,7:2
My Friend Irma Goes West 1950,Ag 3,20:2
Right Cross 1950,N 16,39:2
Flying Missile, The 1950,D 25,25:1
Rawhide 1951,Mr 26,19:2
Thing, The 1951,My 3,34:4
Angel Face 1953,Ap 25,11:5
Beast From 20,000 Fathoms, The 1953,Je 25,23:1
Bigamist, The 1953,D 26,10:4
Down Three Dark Streets 1954,S 4,6:4
Davy Crockett, King of the Wild Frontier 1955,My 26,36:1
Steel Jungle, The 1956,Mr 10,9:5
Man in the Gray Flannel Suit, The 1956,Ap 13,21:1
Great Locomotive Chase, The 1956,Je 27,35:1
Wings of Eagles, The 1957,F 1,28:1
Gunfight at the O K Corral 1957,My 30,23:2
Cry Terror 1958,My 15,25:1
Seven Ways From Sundown 1960,D 22,18:4
Tobey, Ruth
And One Was Beautiful 1940,Ap 11,32:4
Janie 1944,Ag 5,16:2
Delightfully Dangerous 1945,Je 9,17:3
Janie Gets Married 1946,Je 15,24:2
Tobias, Charles (Composer)
Life Begins In College 1937,O 9,16:1
You're a Sweetheart 1937,D 25,10:5
Shine on Harvest Moon 1944,Mr 11,10:2
Patrick the Great 1945,Ap 13,15:2
Love and Learn 1947,My 3,10:3
Tobias, Charles (Miscellaneous)
Gift of Gab 1934,S 26,17:6
Tobias, George
Maisie 1939,Je 23,23:1
They all Come Out 1939,Ag 3,15:4
Balalaika 1939,D 15,33:2
Hunchback of Notre Dame, The 1940,Ja 1,29:2
Music in My Heart 1940,Ja 4,19:2
Saturday's Children 1940,My 4,13:1
Torrid Zone 1940,My 18,11:3
Man Who Talked too Much, The 1940,Je 29,12:2
They Drive by Night 1940,Jl 27,17:5
River's End 1940,Ag 26,11:4
City for Conquest 1940,S 28,9:2
East of the River 1940,O 28,21:2
South of Suez 1940,D 19,33:2
Strawberry Blonde 1941,F 22,11:2
Affectionaly Yours 1941,My 24,18:2
Out of the Fog 1941,Je 21,20:2
Sergeant York 1941,Jl 3,15:1
Bride Came C O D, The 1941,Jl 26,18:2
Captains of the Clouds 1942,F 13,24:2
Yankee Doodle Dandy 1942,My 30,9:1
Juke Girl 1942,Je 20,9:2
Wings for the Eagle 1942,Ag 1,14:2
My Sister Eileen 1942,O 23,15:1
Air Force 1943,F 4,29:1

Mission to Moscow 1943,Ap 30,25:2
This Is the Army 1943,Jl 29,11:6
Thank Your Lucky Stars 1943,O 2,19:2
Passage to Marseille 1944,F 17,12:5
Between Two Worlds 1944,My 6,11:2
Make Your own Bed 1944,My 27,12:2
Objective Burma 1945,Ja 25,15:2
Mildred Pierce 1945,S 29,12:2
Her Kind of Man 1946,My 4,10:6
Nobody Lives Forever 1946,N 2,12:2
Gallant Bess 1946,D 6,27:6
Sinbad the Sailor 1947,Ja 23,31:2
My Wild Irish Rose 1947,D 25,32:2
Adventures of Casanova 1948,Mr 22,18:3
Set-Up, The 1949,Mr 30,31:2
Judge Steps Out, The 1949,Je 3,21:4
Everybody Does It 1949,O 26,32:2
Southside 1-1000 1950,N 3,31:2
Rawhide 1951,Mr 26,19:2
Mark of the Renegade 1951,S 7,24:2
Ten Tall Men 1951,O 27,10:5
Glenn Miller Story, the 1954,F 11,33:2
Seven Little Foys, The 1955,Je 30,18:2
Tattered Dress, The 1957,Mr 15,22:3
Silk Stockings 1957,Jl 19,11:1
Marjorie Morningstar 1958,Ap 25,32:2
New Kind of Love, A 1963,O 31,26:2
Glass Bottom Boat, The 1966,Je 10,54:1
Tobias, Harry (Composer)
Young and Beautiful 1934,S 18,18:4
One Rainy Afternoon 1936,My 14,29:2
Tobias, Harry (Miscellaneous)
Little Miss Nobody 1936,Je 6,21:1
Little Miss Nobody 1936,Je 6,21:1
Tobias, Sarett (Screenwriter)
She Wouldn't Say Yes 1946,Ja 12,10:7
Tars and Spars 1946,F 15,29:2
Tobin, Dan
Stadium Murders, The 1938,Ap 9,11:2
Black Limelight 1939,Je 26,12:2
Pittsburgh Kid, The 1941,S 23,27:4
Woman of the Year 1942,F 6,23:2
Undercurrent 1946,N 29,36:2
Bachelor and the Bobby-Soxer, The 1947,Jl 25,12:5
Big Clock, The 1948,Ap 22,34:2
Velvet Touch, The 1948,Ag 26,16:2
Sealed Verdict 1948,N 3,36:2
Miss Tatlock's Millions 1948,N 25,47:2
Dream Wife 1953,Jl 30,20:1
Catered Affair, The 1956,Je 15,32:4
Last Angry Man, The 1959,O 23,24:1
How to Succeed in Business Without Really Trying 1967,Mr 10,30:1
Tobin, Genevieve
Lady Surrenders, A 1930,O 4,15:2
Free Love 1930,D 15,29:1
Seed 1931,My 15,20:6
Up for Murder 1931,My 30,9:2
Gay Diplomat, The 1931,O 10,20:4
One Hour with You 1932,Mr 24,17:5
Hollywood Speaks 1932,Ag 12,18:2
Perfect Understanding 1933,F 23,20:2
Pleasure Cruise 1933,Ap 3,13:3
Infernal Machine 1933,Ap 8,16:3
Wrecker, The 1933,Ag 7,18:3
Good-Bye Again 1933,S 2,15:2
I Loved a Woman 1933,S 22,14:2
Easy to Love 1934,Ja 15,12:2
Dark Hazard 1934,F 23,23:3
Ninth Guest, The 1934,Mr 3,8:5
Success at any Price 1934,My 4,24:2
Kiss and Make-Up 1934,Je 29,17:1
Woman in Red, The 1935,Mr 23,11:3
Goose and the Gander, The 1935,S 12,29:2
Here's to Romance 1935,O 3,29:2
Case of the Lucky Legs, The 1935,N 1,25:1
Broadway Hostess 1935,D 16,23:3
Petrified Forest, The 1936,F 7,14:2
Snowed Under 1936,Mr 30,17:5
Great Gambini, The 1937,Jl 12,20:4
Dramatic School 1938,D 9,31:2
Zaza 1939,Ja 5,17:1
Yes, My Darling Daughter 1939,F 27,11:2
Our Neighbors-The Carters 1940,F 15,15:2
No Time for Comedy 1940,S 7,9:2
Queen of Crime 1941,F 19,25:2
Tobin, Michael
Yours, Mine and Ours 1968,Ap 25,53:1
Tobin, Vivian
Sign of the Cross, The 1932,D 1,25:1
If I Were Free 1934,Ja 5,25:2
This Man is Mine 1934,Ap 13,25:1
Bordertown 1935,Ja 24,22:5
World Accuses, The 1935,Mr 21,27:2
Tobis (Producer)
Nacht Gehoert Uns, Die; Night Belongs to Us, The 1930,My 11,IX,4:2 (In Addenda)
Tobisch, Lotte
Don Juan 1956,Mr 6,26:2
Last ten Days, The 1956,Ap 12,26:1

Toby, Dan
Man-Proof 1938,Ja 14,21:1
Toby, Ruth
Our Town 1940,Je 14,25:3
Toc Toc Girls
Hit Parade, The 1937,My 31,11:2
Tocci, Pedro
Nuestra Tierra de Paz; Our Land of Peace 1940,Je 1,12:3
Toch, Ernst (Composer)
Peter Ibbetson 1935,N 8,18:2
Ladies in Retirement 1941,N 7,27:1
Tock, Lou
Fabulous World of Jules Verne, The 1961,Je 29,26:1
Tod, Malcolm
Woman Tempted, The 1928,Ap 24,29:3
Daughter of Israel, A 1928,My 21,25:1
Todd, Ann
Ghost Train, The 1933,F 18,13:3
Murder on Diamond Row 1937,N 12,27:2
South Riding 1938,Ag 2,15:2
Stronger Than Desire 1939,Je 30,17:3
Zero Hour, The 1939,Jl 5,20:3
Intermezzo, A Love Story 1939,O 6,31:1
Destry Rides Again 1939,N 30,25:1
Blue Bird, The 1940,Ja 20,11:2
All This and Heaven, Too 1940,Jl 5,10:2
Brigham Young - Frontiersman 1940,S 21,13:2
Blood and Sand 1941,My 23,25:3
Bad Men of Missouri 1941,Ag 16,18:2
Private Nurse 1941,Ag 29,13:3
Men In her Life, The 1941,D 12,35:1
Remember the Day 1941,D 26,21:2
Kings Row 1942,F 3,23:2
Ships With Wings 1942,My 25,11:2
Dixie Dugan 1943,Ap 9,25:5
Roughly Speaking 1945,F 1,18:4
Pride of the Marines 1945,Ag 25,7:3
Seventh Veil, The 1945,D 26,15:1
My Reputation 1946,Ja 26,19:2
Vacation From Marriage 1946,Mr 15,27:2
Jolson Story, The 1946,O 11,28:2
Margie 1946,O 17,28:3
Paradine Case, The 1948,Ja 9,26:2
Showtime 1948,My 20,35:3
So Evil my Love 1948,Jl 22,27:2
One Woman's Story 1949,My 18,33:2
Daybreak 1949,Jl 4,9:2
Madeleine 1950,S 1,17:2
Breaking Through the Sound Barrier 1952,N 7,19:1
Green Scarf, The 1955,Ja 15,10:2
Time Without Pity 1957,N 23,11:2
Scream of Fear 1961,Ag 23,29:1
90 Degrees in the Shade 1966,N 16,52:1
Todd, Ann E
Three Daring Daughters 1948,F 13,26:3
Todd, Arthur (Cinematographer)
Deliverance 1919,Ag 19,10:1
Todd, Bobby
Original Sin, The 1950,Ag 21,15:2
Montpi 1959,Ap 21,40:1
Todd, Bobby (Screenwriter)
Original Sin, The 1950,Ag 21,15:2
Todd, Charles
Big Boodle, The 1957,Mr 12,38:1
Todd, Eula Guy
Society Girl 1932,Je 10,22:3
Todd, Harry
Jack-Knife Man, The 1920,Ag 2,12:2
Flaming Frontier, The 1926,Ap 5,24:1
Third Degree, The 1927,F 15,23:1
Broadway Bill 1934,N 30,22:2
Todd, James
Riders of the Purple Sage 1931,S 26,25:3
Charlie Chan's Chance 1932,Ja 23,18:4
Disorderly Conduct 1932,Ap 11,19:2
Careless Lady 1932,Ap 18,19:2
Luck of the Irish, The 1948,S 16,34:1
For the Love of Mary 1948,S 23,37:2
Trapped 1949,N 26,10:6
Francis 1950,Mr 16,40:2
Titanic 1953,My 28,27:5
Torch Song 1953,O 13,34:2
Wings of Eagles, The 1957,F 1,28:1
This Could Be the Night 1957,My 15,39:1
Buccaneer, The 1958,D 24,00:0
Todd, Lola
Harvester, The 1927,N 7,33:1
Todd, Lucas (Original Author)
Fury at Showdown 1957,Ap 20,21:3
Todd, Mabel
Varsity Show 1937,S 2,17:2
Over the Goal 1937,O 16,22:2
Hollywood Hotel 1938,Ja 13,17:3
Gold Diggers in Paris 1938,Je 2,19:2
Garden of the Moon 1938,S 24,13:1
Cowboy and the Lady, The 1938,N 25,19:3
Street of Missing Men 1939,Je 1,31:3
Todd, Michael (Producer)
Around the World in 80 Days 1956,O 18,37:1

Todd, Michael Jr (Producer)
Scent of Mystery 1960,F 19,23:1
Todd, Richard
Hasty Heart, The 1950,Ja 21,10:5
Stage Fright 1950,F 24,27:2
For Them that Trespass 1950,S 27,37:2
Lightning Strikes Twice 1951,Ap 13,18:7
Interrupted Journey 1951,My 29,20:2
Portrait of Clare 1951,D 26,19:6
Story of Robin Hood, The 1952,Je 27,18:3
Assassin, The 1953,Ap 18,17:2
Sword and the Rose, The 1953,Ag 20,18:3
Rob Roy 1954,F 4,21:5
Man Called Peter, A 1955,Ap 1,22:1
Bed, The (The Billet); Billet, The (The Bed)
1955,Je 8,26:4
Virgin Queen, The 1955,Ag 6,13:2
D-Day, The Sixth of June 1956,My 30,13:1
Saint Joan 1957,Je 27,21:1
Battle Hell 1957,Ag 22,23:1
Chase a Crooked Shadow 1958,Mr 25,28:4
Naked Earth 1958,Ag 29,18:1
Intent to Kill 1959,Ap 1,43:2
Breakout 1960,My 19,44:3
Jungle Fighters 1962,Mr 15,28:2
Hellions, The 1962,Mr 15,28:2
Longest Day, The 1962,O 5,28:1
Crime Does Not Pay (The Man on the Avenue);
Man on the Avenue, The (Crime Does Not
Pay) 1962,O 17,35:2
Never Let Go 1963,Je 15,10:2
Why Bother to Knock 1965,F 4,24:2
Operation Crossbow 1965,Ap 2,29:1
Battle of the Villa Fiorita, The 1965,My 27,28:1
Coast of Skeletons 1965,N 11,58:3
Love-Ins, The 1967,Ag 19,16:1
Todd, Robin
Portrait of Clare 1951,D 26,19:6
Todd, Sally
Frankenstein's Daughter 1958,N 17,37:2
Todd, Thelma
Fascinating Youth 1926,My 10,19:1
Rubber Heels 1927,Je 28,29:4
Shield of Honor 1927,D 13,33:2
Gay Defender, The 1927,D 26,26:6
Noose, The 1928,Mr 19,26:4
Heart to Heart 1928,S 10,29:2
Haunted House, The 1928,D 17,23:1
Naughty Baby 1929,F 5,26:3
Careers 1929,Je 10,23:1
Follow Thru 1930,S 13,9:3
Hot Heiress, The 1931,Mr 14,23:2
Maltese Falcon, The 1931,My 29,26:5
Monkey Business 1931,O 8,22:6
This is the Night 1932,Ap 16,11:2
Horse Feathers 1932,Ag 11,12:2
Speak Easily 1932,Ag 19,20:6
Call Her Savage 1932,N 25,19:2
Deception 1933,Ja 10,26:2
Air Hostess 1933,Ja 23,9:2
Cheating Blondes 1933,My 20,11:4
Devil's Brother, The 1933,Je 10,16:4
Mary Stevens, M D 1933,Ag 5,9:6
Son of a Sailor 1933,N 30,38:4
Sitting Pretty 1933,D 2,9:3
Counsellor-At-Law 1933,D 8,31:2
Hips, Hips, Hooray 1934,F 24,18:3
Palooka 1934,F 28,23:2
Bottoms Up 1934,Mr 23,29:2
You Made Me Love You 1934,My 30,14:3
Cockeyed Cavaliers 1934,Jl 25,22:2
Two for Tonight 1935,Ag 31,16:2
Toekes, Anna
Csak Egy Ejszakara 1936,Mr 16,21:5
Toerze, Jenoe
Okos Mama, Az 1936,Ap 13,15:2
Toerzs, Eugene
Meseauto 1936,N 10,31:4
Toerzs, Jenos
Elnoek Kisasszony 1935,O 12,12:3
Tofano, Sergio
Amore in Quarantena; Love in Quarantine
1938,D 13,31:2
Eravamo Sette Sorelle; We Were Seven Sisters
1939,Mr 3,21:3
Partner 1968,S 24,52:2
Toffei, Andre
Proud and the Beautiful, The 1956,My 29,32:2
Togami, Jatoro
Secret Scrolls-Part II; Ninjitsu 1968,My 23,56:3
Kojiro 1968,Ag 30,23:1
Tognazzi, Ugo
I Cadetti di Guascogna 1952,O 6,22:2
Psycosissimo 1962,S 8,16:2
Conjugal Bed, The 1963,S 17,30:1
Crazy Desire 1964,Jl 3,13:2
Ape Woman, The 1964,S 23,55:1
Magnificent Cuckold 1965,Ap 20,42:1
Fascist, The 1965,Je 18,28:3
High Infidelity (Modern People); Modern People
(High Infidelity) 1965,Jl 2,17:1
Hours of Love, The 1965,S 4,11:5
Very Handy Man, A 1966,D 15,60:1

Climax, The 1967,S 12,55:1
Barbarella 1968,O 12,43:1
Tognetti, Anne
Two Are Guilty 1964,F 29,12:1
Togo
Sign of the Four, The 1932,Ag 20,7:4
Togo, Haruko
Honolulu-Tokyo-Hong Kong 1964,S 2,33:3
Tohno, Eijiro
This Madding Crowd 1964,Je 17,48:1
Lost Sex 1968,Jl 23,27:2
Toidze, A
Poet and Tsar 1938,Ag 25,15:1
Dragonfly, The 1955,Je 27,18:2
Toinay, Klara
Okos Mama, Az 1936,Ap 13,15:2
Toinon
Heartbeat 1939,S 5,21:3
Toinon, Annie
Ways of Love (Jofroi); Jofroi (Ways of Love)
1950,D 13,50:2
Toiobeyev, Y
Inspector General, The 1954,My 3,21:2
Tokar, Norman (Director)
Big Red 1962,S 3,11:2
Savage Sam 1963,Ag 1,17:3
Tiger Walks, A 1964,Ag 27,28:2
Those Calloways 1965,Ap 15,38:2
Ugly Dachshund, The 1966,Ap 7,45:1
Follow Me, Boys! 1966,D 2,46:1
Happiest Millionaire, The 1967,D 1,56:1
Horse in the Gray Flannel Suit, The
1968,D 21,49:3
Tokarskaya, Mlle
Marionettes 1934,My 8,28:6
Tokes, Anna
Hotel Sunrise 1937,O 30,22:3
Az Ember Neha Teved; Man Sometimes Errs
1938,Mr 28,19:3
Tokunaga, Frank
Willow Tree, The 1920,F 2,10:1
Teahouse of the August Moon, The
1956,N 30,19:1
Escapde in Japan 1957,D 24,11:1
Tolan, Lawrence
Enforcer, The 1951,Ja 26,19:2
Inside the Walls of Folsom Prison
1951,My 28,17:4
Tolan, Michael
Hiawatha 1952,D 26,20:4
Greatest Story Ever Told, The 1965,F 16,40:2
Hour of the Gun 1967,N 2,58:4
Tolan, Michael (Narrator)
Witness, The 1967,N 7,47:1
Toland, Gregg (Cinematographer)
Citizen Kane 1941,My 2,25:1
Toland, Tor (Narrator)
Ski Champs 1951,D 15,11:2
Toland, Virginia
Let's Dance 1950,N 30,42:2
Tolchanov, I
Attack From the Sea 1954,Ap 19,19:4
Tolchanov, I M
Oppenheim Family, The 1939,My 24,29:2
Lenin in 1918 1939,Je 27,27:2
Toldy, John S (Original Author)
Arise my Love 1940,O 17,33:2
Toler, Sidney
Madame X 1929,Ap 25,32:3
White Shoulders 1931,My 5,26:5
Strictly Dishonorable 1931,N 11,27:1
Strangers in Love 1932,Mr 5,11:2
Is my Face red 1932,Je 11,9:3
Radio Patrol 1932,Jl 14,24:2
Tom Brown of Culver 1932,Jl 30,16:5
Speak Easily 1932,Ag 19,20:6
Blondie of the Follies 1932,S 2,19:2
Blonde Venus 1932,S 24,18:4
Phantom President, The 1932,O 1,10:4
Billion Dollar Scandal 1933,Ja 9,23:1
King of the Jungle 1933,F 25,20:3
World Changes, The 1933,O 27,22:3
Way to Love, The 1933,N 11,10:3
Massacre 1934,Ja 18,19:2
Dark Hazard 1934,F 23,23:3
Spitfire 1934,Mr 9,22:3
Trumpet Blows, The 1934,Ap 14,18:2
Upper World 1934,My 25,25:4
Here Comes the Groom 1934,Je 16,20:2
Operator 13 1934,Je 23,16:5
Romance in Manhattan 1935,Ja 18,29:2
Daring Young Man, The 1935,Jl 18,15:2
Orchids to You 1935,Ag 10,16:4
Call of the Wild 1935,Ag 15,15:2
Give Us This Night 1936,Ap 6,18:1
Gorgeous Hussy, The 1936,S 5,7:1
Longest Night, The 1936,O 17,21:2
Our Relations 1936,N 11,55:1
That Certain Woman 1937,S 16,29:1
Double Wedding 1937,O 22,27:2
Gold Is Where You Find It 1938,F 14,20:6
Wide Open Faces 1938,Ap 15,23:2
One Wild Night 1938,Je 3,17:2

Toler, Sidney— Cont
If I Were King 1938,S 29,31:1
Up the River 1938,D 3,11:2
Charlie Chan in Honolulu 1938,D 31,7:3
Disbarred 1939,Ja 19,17:2
King of Chinatown 1939,Mr 16,27:2
Kid From Kokomo, The 1939,My 20,11:2
Charlie Chan in Reno 1939,My 31,27:2
Charlie Chan at Treasure Island 1939,S 1,15:5
Charlie Chan in City in Darkness 1939,D 18,29:2
Charlie Chan's Murder Cruise 1940,My 3,17:5
Charlie Chan At the Wax Museum 1940,S 28,9:3
Dead Men Tell 1941,Ap 17,29:3
Night to Remember, A 1943,Ja 1,27:2
White Savage 1943,Ap 26,15:2
It's in the Bag 1945,Je 11,12:1
Tolerina, Ivan
Nine Days of one Year 1964,D 29,19:1
Tolhurst, Robin
Strange Affair, The 1968,Jl 25,26:2
Tolhurst, Stan
Overlanders, The 1946,D 20,31:2
Bush Christmas 1947,N 27,50:4
Tolkin, Mel (Screenwriter)
Last of the Secret Agents, The? 1966,Je 23,29:1
Toll, Lionel J (Producer)
Blonde Savage 1947,O 4,9:2
Tollaire, August
What Price Glory 1926,N 24,26:4
Monkey Talks, The 1927,Ap 5,30:7
Wife Savers 1928,Ja 17,23:2
Four Sons 1928,F 14,27:1
Plastered in Paris 1928,S 24,25:1
His Captive Woman 1929,Ap 3,26:4
Hot for Paris 1930,Ja 4,21:1
Passionate Plumber, The 1932,Mr 12,19:5
Girl Without a Room 1933,D 7,26:3
Toller, Ernst (Original Author)
Pastor Hall 1940,S 21,13:2
Tolley, Jean
Take It From Me 1926,N 2,35:1
Tolnay, A
Open City; Citta Aperta 1946,F 26,21:2
Tolnay, Klari
Legy Jo Mindhalalig 1936,O 26,20:2
Tisztelet a Kivetelnek 1937,Je 14,26:3
Az en Lanyom nem olyan; My Daughter Is
Different 1938,Ap 30,18:2
Doentoe Pillanat, A; Crucial Moment, The
1938,S 17,20:3
Kolcsonkert Kastely; Borrowed Castle, The
1938,D 17,10:4
Keseru Mezeshetek; Bitter Honeymoon
1939,O 9,15:3
Gyimesi Vadvirag; Wildflower of Gyimes
1939,O 21,12:3
Toprini Nasz; Wedding in Toprin 1939,N 6,20:2
Tiszavirag; Flower of the Tisza 1939,D 30,9:3
Father 1967,S 29,53:1
Tolney, Akos (Screenwriter)
White Warrior, The 1961,F 11,27:2
Tolo, Marilu
Marriage Italian Style 1964,D 21,42:1
Oldest Profession, The (Anticipation); Anticipation
(The Oldest Profession) 1968,N 8,42:1
Tolstova, V
Golden Taiga 1935,Ag 2,22:3
Tolstoy, Alexei (Original Author)
Peter the First 1937,D 25,10:4
Conquests of Peter The Great, The
1939,Ag 24,17:2
Golden Key, The 1939,D 21,29:3
Tolstoy, Alexei (Screenwriter)
Peter the First 1937,D 25,10:4
Conquests of Peter The Great, The
1939,Ag 24,17:2
Tolstoy, Countess
Streets of Sorrow 1927,Jl 6,23:2
Tolstoy, Ilya Count
Resurrection 1927,My 17,27:2
Tolstoy, Leo (Original Author)
Resurrection 1918,My 20,9:7
Polikushka 1927,Ja 17,12:4 (In Addenda)
Resurrection 1927,My 17,27:2
Power of Darkness 1927,Jl 27,27:4
Love 1927,N 30,22:4
Cossacks, The 1928,Je 25,27:1
Redemption 1930,My 3,23:1
Living Corpse, The 1931,Ja 4,27:2
Resurrection 1931,Ja 24,15:1
White Devil, The 1931,Ag 28,20:1
We Live Again 1934,N 2,27:2
Anna Karenina 1935,Ag 31,16:2
Kreutzer Sonata 1937,Mr 14,XI,4:6 (In Addenda)
Kreutzer Sonata, The 1938,My 28,9:3
Kreutzer Sonata, The 1938,D 20,30:2
Living Corpse, The 1940,S 23,21:4
Anna Karenina 1948,Ap 28,32:2
War and Peace 1956,Ag 22,26:2
White Warrior, The 1961,F 11,27:2
Resurrection 1963,O 7,35:2
War and Peace 1967,O 24,27:1
War and Peace 1968,Ap 29,50:5

Tolubeyev, Yuri
Return of Maxim, The 1937,N 2,33:1
Professor Mamlock 1938,N 8,26:2
New Horizons 1939,My 12,25:3
Girl From Leningrad 1941,D 20,25:2
Turning Point, The 1946,O 28,19:4
Don Quixote 1961,Ja 21,18:1
Hamlet 1964,S 15,32:1
Overcoat, The 1965,Mr 2,31:2
Hamlet 1966,Mr 16,48:1
Tolubeyeva, Z (Screenwriter)
Swan Lake 1960,Ja 26,25:2
TOM
See Also THOM
Tom, Konrad (Director)
Ksiazatko; Lottery Prince, The 1937,D 27,11:2
Mamele; Little Mothers 1938,D 26,29:1
Tom, Layne Jr
Charlie Chan at the Olympics 1937,My 24,23:1
Hurricane, The 1937,N 10,31:2
Charlie Chan in Honolulu 1938,D 31,7:3
Toma, Christian
Fantomas 1966,Ap 6,36:2
Tomack, Sid
Thrill of Brazil, The 1946,S 6,18:3
Framed 1947,My 26,24:2
Double Life, A 1948,F 20,19:1
My Girl Tisa 1948,F 21,9:2
Hollow Triumph 1948,O 29,29:5
Force of Evil 1948,D 27,16:2
House of Strangers 1949,Jl 2,8:2
Abandoned Woman 1949,O 27,35:3
Love That Brute 1950,My 27,10:6
Somebody Loves Me 1952,S 25,38:1
Sail a Crooked Ship 1962,F 3,12:6
Tomanelli, Carlo
Traviata, La 1953,D 28,17:2
Tomarchio, Ludovico
Swiss Miss 1938,Je 4,18:2
Tomasi, Andre
My Wife's Husband 1965,Ja 27,26:1
Tomassini, Giulio
Life of Donizetti, The 1952,Ap 26,19:2
Tomassini, Virgilio
Fear No Evil 1949,Mr 31,31:2
Tombes, Andrew
Moulin Rouge 1934,F 8,14:4
Born to be Bad 1934,My 31,22:6
Doubting Thomas 1935,Jl 11,24:2
Here Comes Cookie 1935,O 12,12:2
Thanks a Million 1935,N 14,17:1
King of Burlesque 1936,Ja 16,25:2
Country Beyond, The 1936,Ap 30,17:3
Hot Money 1936,Jl 25,16:2
Ticket to Paradise 1936,Ag 8,5:3
Stage Struck 1936,S 28,14:4
Holy Terror, The 1937,Ja 30,21:2
Time Out for Romance 1937,Mr 13,23:2
Turn off the Moon 1937,My 20,17:2
Charlie Chan at the Olympics 1937,My 24,23:1
Sing and Be Happy 1937,Je 19,20:2
Riding on Air 1937,Je 26,20:2 (In Addenda)
Easy Living 1937,Jl 8,20:1
Big City 1937,S 17,29:2
45 Fathers 1937,D 11,22:2
Sally, Irene and Mary 1938,F 26,9:2
Battle of Broadway 1938,Ap 25,19:2
One Wild Night 1938,Je 3,17:2
Five of a Kind 1938,O 31,12:2
Always in Trouble 1938,N 3,27:1
Vacation From Love 1938,N 10,33:2
Thanks For Everything 1938,D 10,13:2
What a Life 1939,O 12,33:1
Captain Caution 1940,O 21,21:3
Meet the Chump 1941,F 27,23:4
Meet John Doe 1941,Mr 13,25:2
Lady Scarface 1941,Ag 4,16:6
World Premiere 1941,Ag 21,15:2
Texas 1941,O 17,27:3
Louisiana Purchase 1942,Ja 1,37:1
Bedtime Story 1942,Mr 20,25:4
Larceny, Inc 1942,Ap 25,9:1
My Gal Sal 1942,My 1,23:1
They all Kissed the Bride 1942,Jl 31,11:1
Between Us Girls 1942,S 25,25:3
Road to Morocco 1942,N 12,30:1
Meanest Man in the World, The 1943,F 25,27:3
Hi 'Ya Chum 1943,F 26,17:4
It Ain't Hay 1943,Mr 11,17:3
Reveille With Beverly 1943,Ap 24,17:2
Coney Island 1943,Je 17,17:2
Let's Face It 1943,Ag 5,18:1
My Kingdom for a Cook 1943,O 15,15:3
I Dood It 1943,N 11,29:1
His Butler's Sister 1943,D 30,13:2
Swing Fever 1944,Ja 28,14:1
Phantom Lady 1944,F 18,15:2
Murder in the Blue Room 1944,O 28,12:2
Something for the Boys 1944,N 30,19:1
Lake Placid Serenade 1944,D 25,15:6
Can't Help Singing 1944,D 26,22:4
Bring on the Girls 1945,Mr 1,25:5
Patrick the Great 1945,Ap 13,15:2

Frontier Gal 1945,D 15,14:2
Badman's Territory 1946,My 31,27:2
Devil Thumbs a Ride, The 1947,Mr 22,10:2
Copacabana 1947,Jl 12,7:2
Two Guys From Texas 1948,Ag 28,8:6
Oh, You Beautiful Doll 1949,N 12,8:4
Jackpot, The 1950,N 23,55:2
How to be Very, Very Popular 1955,Jl 23,10:1
Tombragel, Maurice (Original Author)
Tropic Fury 1939,S 8,28:4
Hot Steel 1940,Je 21,25:3
Music in Manhattan 1944,O 7,11:2
Tombragel, Maurice (Screenwriter)
Legion of Lost Flyers 1939,O 30,13:3
Zanzibar 1940,Ap 1,15:3
Hot Steel 1940,Je 21,25:3
Horror Island 1941,Mr 31,11:3
Mutiny in the Arctic 1941,My 3,20:5
Two Senoritas From Chicago 1943,Ag 6,10:4
Moon Pilot 1962,Ap 6,30:2
Monkeys Go Home 1967,Mr 30,55:1
Tomei, Fausto
Forza del Destino, La 1952,O 17,33:1
Tomei, Giulio
First Opera Film Festival 1948,My 31,12:7
Tomelty, Joseph
Odd Man Out 1947,Ap 24,30:2
Breaking Through the Sound Barrier
 1952,N 7,19:1
Melba 1953,Je 25,23:1
Gentle Gunman, The 1953,O 1,34:3
Horse's Mouth, The 1954,Ja 20,33:4
Hobson's Choice 1954,Je 15,37:1
Hell Below Zero 1954,Jl 17,7:3
Tonight's the Night 1954,D 23,13:4
Front Page Story 1955,Ap 19,28:1
Chance Meeting 1955,Ap 20,38:1
Prize of Gold, A 1955,O 15,19:2
Simba 1955,O 22,24:2
Moby Dick 1956,Jl 5,18:1
John and Julie 1957,My 7,40:1
Day They Robbed the Bank of England, The
 1960,S 5,11:2
Upstairs and Downstairs 1960,D 2,53:4
Hell is a City 1961,Ja 19,26:3
Tomingas
Last Game, The 1964,O 25,41:5 (Incorrect in this
 edition; use 1964,O 26,41:5 elsewhere)
Tomiselli, Laura
Divorce-Italian Style 1962,S 18,34:1
Tomlin, Pinky
Times Square Lady 1935,Mr 15,25:3
King Solomon of Broadway 1935,O 19,12:2
Paddy O'Day 1936,F 8,19:2
Don't Get Personal 1936,F 22,12:1
Tomlin, Pinky (Composer)
King Solomon of Broadway 1935,O 19,12:2
Paddy O'Day 1936,F 8,19:2
Tomlinson, Daniel (Screenwriter)
Captain Lash 1929,F 4,20:1
Tomlinson, Daniel G
Bardelys The Magnificent 1926,N 1,28:1 (In
 Addenda)
Crowd, The 1928,F 20,14:1
Tomlinson, David
Quiet Wedding 1941,D 29,27:4
Mister V 1942,F 13,24:4
Johnny in the Clouds 1945,N 16,16:2
Journey Together 1946,Mr 4,16:5
My Brothers Keeper 1949,F 14,15:3
Easy Money (Episode 1) 1949,F 14,15:3
Sleeping Car to Trieste 1949,Ap 18,18:6
Miranda 1949,Ap 25,20:2
Broken Journey 1949,My 26,34:3
Master of Bankdam 1949,O 17,18:2
Fame Is the Spur 1949,N 8,34:2
Amazing Mr Beecham, The 1949,D 26,33:4
So Long at the Fair 1951,Ja 22,14:2
Wooden Horse, The 1951,Ag 29,20:2
Hotel Sahara 1952,Ja 1,21:4
Marry Me 1952,Mr 14,27:3
Secret Flight 1952,Jl 3,16:2
Magic Box, The 1952,S 24,40:2
Castle in the Air 1953,Ja 5,19:2
Landfall 1953,My 11,25:2
Ship Was Loaded, The 1958,Ja 20,20:1
Up the Creek 1958,N 11,26:2
3 Men in a Boat 1959,Jl 29,33:2
Tom Jones 1963,O 8,48:1
Mary Poppins 1964,S 25,34:1
War Gods of the Deep 1965,Je 3,24:3
Truth About Spring, The 1965,Je 17,27:2
Liquidator, The 1966,O 29,34:1
Tomlinson, Martin
Reach for Glory 1963,S 10,46:1
Tommy, Tony Chief
Classmates 1924,D 30,15:3
Tomoda, Jira (Miscellaneous)
Insect Woman, The; Nippon Konchuki
 1964,Jl 1,42:1
Tomolillo, Francesco
Path of Hope, The (Il Cammino Della Speranza)
 1952,Ag 5,15:5

Tomono, Hiroshi
Bridge to the Sun 1961,O 18,50:1
Tompkins, Connie
Miracle of Morgan's Creek, The 1944,Ja 20,15:2
Tompkins, Darlene
Blue Hawaii 1962,F 22,20:2
Tompkins, Juliet Wilbur (Original Author)
Heart to Heart 1928,S 10,29:2
Fanny Foley Herself 1931,O 26,22:1
Tomyakov, Nikolai
Stone Flower 1946,D 30,15:2
Tonayama, Taiji
Insect Woman, The; Nippon Konchuki
 1964,Jl 1,42:1
Toncray, Kate
Boots 1919,Mr 10,9:3
Peppy Polly 1919,Ap 7,11:5
Prisoners of Love 1921,Ja 17,9:1
Country Kid, The 1923,O 30,16:1
Narrow Street, The 1925,Ja 5,19:1
Daddy's Gone A-Hunting 1925,F 24,17:3
Tone, Franchot
Wiser Sex, The 1932,Mr 12,19:5
Gabriel Over the White House 1933,Ap 1,18:2
Today We Live 1933,Ap 15,16:2
Midnight Mary 1933,Jl 15,14:2
Stranger's Return, The 1933,Jl 28,18:2
Stage Mother 1933,S 30,18:5
Bombshell 1933,O 21,11:2
Dancing Lady 1933,D 1,23:2
Moulin Rouge 1934,F 8,14:4
Sadie McKee 1934,My 18,18:3 (Incorrect in this
 edition; use 1934,My 19,18:3 elsewhere)
World Moves On, The 1934,Je 30,18:5
Girl From Missouri, The 1934,Ag 4,14:6
Straight Is the Way 1934,Ag 29,13:2
Gentlemen are Born 1934,N 22,27:2
Lives of a Bengal Lancer, The 1935,Ja 12,12:2
Reckless 1935,Ap 20,16:1
No More Ladies 1935,Je 22,18:5
Mutiny on the Bounty 1935,N 9,19:2
Dangerous 1935,D 27,14:1
Exclusive Story 1936,Ja 18,19:2
Unguarded Hour, The 1936,Ap 4,11:1
King Steps Out, The 1936,My 29,15:2
Suzy 1936,Jl 25,16:1
Gorgeous Hussy, The 1936,S 5,7:1
Love on the Run 1936,N 28,13:3
Quality Street 1937,Ap 9,19:2
They Gave Him a Gun 1937,My 14,21:1
Between Two Women 1937,Ag 6,21:1
Bride Wore Red, The 1937,O 15,18:4
Man-Proof 1938,Ja 14,21:1
Love Is a Headache 1938,Ja 28,17:3
Three Comrades 1938,Je 3,17:1
Three Loves Has Nancy 1938,S 2,21:2
Girl Downstairs, The 1939,Ja 26,17:1
Fast And Furious 1939,O 12,33:3
Trail of the Vigilantes 1940,D 7,13:2
Nice Girl 1941,Mr 27,29:6
She Knew All the Answers 1941,Je 20,28:4
This Woman Is Mine 1941,O 13,21:2
Wife Takes a Flyer, The 1942,Je 19,19:1
Star Spangled Rhythm 1942,D 31,20:1
Five Graves to Cairo 1943,My 27,21:2
Pilot No 5 1943,Je 25,13:4
True to Life 1943,O 14,26:1
His Butler's Sister 1943,D 30,13:2
Phantom Lady 1944,F 18,15:2
Hour Before the Dawn, The 1944,My 11,25:6
Dark Waters 1944,N 22,25:2
That Night With You 1945,N 9,16:2
Because of Him 1946,Ja 25,26:6
Honeymoon 1947,My 19,27:2
Lost Honeymoon 1947,Je 20,25:6
Her Husband's Affairs 1947,N 14,29:2
Every Girl Should be Married 1948,D 24,14:2
Jigsaw 1949,My 30,9:4
Man on the Eiffel Tower, The 1950,Ja 30,12:2
Without Honor 1950,Jl 3,9:2
Here Comes the Groom 1951,S 21,19:2
Uncle Vanya 1958,Ap 29,26:2
Advise and Consent 1962,Je 7,31:2
Bonne Soupe, La 1964,Mr 16,37:1
In Harm's Way 1965,Ap 7,36:1
Mickey One 1965,S 9,36:1
High Commissioner, The 1968,D 12,62:5
Tone, Franchot (Director)
Uncle Vanya 1958,Ap 29,26:2
Tone, Franchot (Producer)
Uncle Vanya 1958,Ap 29,26:2
Tonelli, Elvira
Organizer, The 1964,My 7,31:2
Toner, Tom
Caper of the Golden Bulls, The 1967,Je 22,46:1
Toney, Jim
No Way Out 1950,Ag 17,23:1
Tong, J
Sable Cicada 1939,Ja 14,13:1
Tong, Kam
Across the Pacific 1942,S 5,9:2
Hidden Hand, The 1942,N 26,40:4
Love Is a Many-Splendored Thing
 1955,Ag 19,10:1

Tong, Kam— Cont
Flower Drum Song 1961,N 10,40:1
Mister Buddwing 1966,O 12,36:1
Kill a Dragon 1967,D 7,60:2

Tonge, Lillian B
Laughing Lady, The 1930,Ja 4,21:1

Tonge, Philip
His Double Life 1933,D 16,12:3
Miracle on 34th Street 1947,Je 5,32:1
Love From a Stranger 1947,N 28,30:1
Hans Christian Andersen 1952,N 26,20:2
House of Wax 1953,Ap 11,15:2
Scandal at Scourie 1953,Je 16,24:2
Elephant Walk 1954,Ap 22,37:2
Khyber Patrol 1954,S 20,19:2
Track of the Cat 1954,D 2,38:2
Prodigal, The 1955,My 14,10:7
Desert Sands 1955,N 19,22:7
Girls, Les 1957,O 4,27:2
Witness for the Prosecution 1958,F 7,16:1
Macabre 1958,Jl 24,18:1

Tonietti, Anne
Joker, The; (Farceur, Le) 1961,Ag 8,32:2

Toniolo, Edoardo
Gladiators Seven 1964,My 7,31:2

Tonkin, Phil (Narrator)
This Is Your Army 1954,D 15,41:1
Pilgrimage for Peace: Pope Paul VI Visits America, A 1966,Jl 21,20:2

Tonkonogy, Gertrude (Original Author)
Three-Cornered Moon 1933,Ag 12,14:2

Tonley, Akos (Screenwriter)
Golden Madonna, The 1949,S 5,13:4

Tonneli, David
Tomorrow Is my Turn 1962,F 2,24:2

Tono, Eijiro
Mistress, The 1959,F 3,36:2
Yojimbo 1962,O 16,34:1
Naked General, The 1964,D 16,51:2
Samurai (Part II) 1967,O 21,16:1

Tonomura, Taijil
Onibaba 1965,F 10,44:3

Tonoyama, Taiji
Island, The; Hadaka No Shima 1962,S 11,27:2

Tontini, Renato
Woman of Rome 1956,N 6,30:1

Tony (Horse)
My Pal the King 1932,O 4,26:4

Tony Jr
Terror Trail 1933,F 11,11:3

Tooker, William
Cradle Buster, The 1922,My 22,18:4
Lone Wolf, The 1924,My 7,19:4
Scarlet Letter, The 1926,Ag 10,19:2
White Black Sheep, The 1926,D 21,20:2
Tell It to Sweeney 1927,O 17,20:2
Two Girls Wanted 1927,N 14,26:1
Devil Dancer, The 1927,D 19,30:1
Ladies Must Dress 1927,D 31,31:1
Night Watch, The 1928,O 8,14:2
Woman of Experience, A 1931,Jl 9,26:5
It's a Gift 1935,Ja 5,20:2

Toombs, Alfred (Original Author)
Raising a Riot 1957,My 8,44:1

Toomey, Regis
Alibi 1929,Ap 9,29:1
Wheel of Life, The 1929,Je 24,27:1
Illusion 1929,S 28,17:3
Street of Chance 1930,F 3,17:1
Framed 1930,Mr 29,23:1
Light of Western Stars, The 1930,Ap 26,11:1
Shadow of the Law 1930,Je 7,10:4
Man From Wyoming, A 1930,Jl 12,16:4
Good Intentions 1930,Jl 26,16:4
Finn and Hattie 1931,Ja 31,15:1
Scandal Sheet 1931,F 9,25:3
Finger Points, The 1931,Mr 28,15:3
Other Men's Women 1931,Ap 20,16:3
Kick In 1931,My 25,17:1
Murder by the Clock 1931,Jl 18,16:6
Twenty-Four Hours 1931,O 3,20:2
Touchdown 1931,N 16,23:1
Under Eighteen 1931,D 26,15:5
Shopworn 1932,Ap 4,13:6
Midnight Patrol, The 1932,My 7,11:5
They Never Come Back 1932,Je 4,9:2
State Trooper 1933,Mr 27,13:6
Soldiers of the Storm 1933,My 17,15:3
Laughing at Life 1933,Jl 15,14:2
She Had to Say Yes 1933,Jl 29,14:2
Murder on the Blackboard 1934,Je 20,24:2
Redhead 1934,N 16,27:1
Shadow of Doubt 1935,Mr 11,15:1
G Men 1935,My 2,17:1
Great God Gold 1935,My 6,22:3
Big City 1937,S 17,29:2
Back in Circulation 1937,O 4,17:1
Shadows of the Orient 1937,O 11,26:6
Submarine D-1 1937,D 30,15:4
Invisible Menace, The 1938,F 14,20:6
Hunted Men 1938,My 21,9:2
Wings of the Navy 1939,F 4,11:1
Union Pacific 1939,My 11,31:2
Street of Missing Men 1939,Je 1,31:3

Indianapolis Speedway 1939,Jl 15,8:2
Hidden Power 1939,Jl 26,17:3
Thunder Afloat 1939,O 13,27:2
His Girl Friday 1940,Ja 12,13:2
Northwest Passage 1940,Mr 8,25:1
North West Mounted Police 1940,N 7,33:2
Arizona 1941,F 7,23:3
Meet John Doe 1941,Mr 13,25:2
Reaching for the Sun 1941,My 8,21:1
Nurse's Secret, The 1941,Je 6,25:7
Dive Bomber 1941,Ag 30,10:2
Law of the Tropics 1941,O 10,26:5
They Died With Their Boots On 1941,N 21,23:3
You're in the Army Now 1941,D 26,21:4
Bullet Scars 1942,Ap 24,21:4
I Was Framed 1942,Je 12,16:6
Forest Rangers, The 1942,O 22,25:2
Tennessee Johnson 1943,Ja 13,18:2
Destroyer 1943,S 2,15:3
Phantom Lady 1944,F 18,15:2
Jack London 1944,Mr 3,19:3
Follow the Boys 1944,Ap 26,24:6
Song of the Open Road 1944,Je 7,13:3
Doughgirls, The 1944,Ag 31,14:1
Murder in the Blue Room 1944,O 28,12:2
Betrayal From the East 1945,Ap 25,27:2
Spellbound 1945,N 2,22:2
Big Sleep, The 1946,Ag 24,6:6
Her Sister's Secret 1947,Ja 23,31:3
Big Fix, The 1947,My 3,10:3
Guilty, The 1947,My 19,27:2
Magic Town 1947,O 8,29:2
High Tide 1947,N 8,11:2
Bishop's Wife, The 1947,D 10,44:2
Boy With Green Hair, The 1949,Ja 13,26:2
Mighty Joe Young 1949,Jl 28,19:3
Come to the Stable 1949,Jl 28,19:1
Undercover Girl 1950,N 8,37:2
Frenchie 1951,F 12,19:2
Cry Danger 1951,F 22,27:3
Show Boat 1951,Jl 20,14:1
My Six Convicts 1952,Mr 28,27:3
Just for You 1952,O 9,40:6
High and the Mighty, The 1954,Jl 1,21:2
Human Jungle, The 1954,N 26,24:6
Guys and Dolls 1955,N 5,26:1
Great Day in the Morning 1956,My 19,12:6
Three for Jamie Dawn 1956,Jl 7,11:3
Dakota Incident 1956,N 10,14:2
Warlock 1959,My 1,34:1
Last Sunset, The 1961,Je 15,51:1
Voyage to the Bottom of the Sea 1961,Jl 20,32:2
King of the Roaring Twenties 1961,O 5,43:1
Man's Favorite Sport? 1964,F 20,22:1
Gunn 1967,Je 29,32:1

Toone, Geoffrey
Man Between, The 1953,N 19,41:2
Diane 1956,Ja 13,18:1
King and I, The 1956,Je 29,15:6
Zero Hour 1957,N 14,41:1
Once More With Feeling 1960,F 12,22:2
Dr Crippen 1964,F 15,14:1

Toones, Fred
Off to the Races 1937,F 6,15:2
Ride a Crooked Mile 1938,D 29,15:2

Toost, Michael
Eternal Waltz, The; (Ewiger Walzer) 1959,Jl 9,22:1

Tootikian, Karoun
World Dances 1954,N 8,24:6

Top
Pepote 1958,D 2,46:1

Topa, John
Red Planet Mars 1952,Je 16,15:2

Topart, Lise
Counter Investigation 1949,D 30,13:2

Topatan, Ahmet Danyal
Topkapi 1964,S 18,25:1

Topete, Jesus
Tropic Holiday 1938,Je 30,21:2

Topkins, F
Little Lord Fauntleroy 1914,Je 23,11:3

Topman, Murray Hill (Original Author)
Heaven on Earth 1960,O 11,55:3

Topol, Haym
Sallah 1965,O 13,39:1
Cast a Giant Shadow 1966,Mr 31,43:3

Toporkov, V
Devotion 1955,Ag 1,15:2

Toporkov, Vasily
Jubilee 1945,F 22,31:3

Toporow, Roman
Berlin Express 1948,My 21,19:3
Red Danube, The 1949,D 9,37:3
Kim 1950,D 8,40:4

Topper, Burt
War Is Hell 1964,Ja 23,26:1

Topper, Burt (Director)
War Is Hell 1964,Ja 23,26:1
Strangler, The 1964,Je 11,27:4

Topper, Burt (Producer)
War Is Hell 1964,Ja 23,26:1
Thunder Valley 1967,S 14,55:1

Topper, Burt (Producer)— Cont
Thunder Alley 1967,S 14,55:1
Devil's Angels 1967,O 5,46:1
Wild in the Streets 1968,My 30,21:1

Topper, Burt (Screenwriter)
War Is Hell 1964,Ja 23,26:1

Tor, Michael
Escape into Dreams 1950,Ap 13,34:5
Deported 1950,N 2,39:3
Side Street Story 1954,Je 24,30:4

Tora, Lia
Hollywood, Ciudad de Ensueno 1934,Ap 4,26:3
Sonadores de la Gloria; Dreamers of Glory 1938,D 10,13:3

Toraz, Jeno
111-es Szobaban; In Room 111 1938,Ap 2,18:2

Torberg, Frederick (Screenwriter)
Voice in the Wind 1944,Mr 16,17:2

Torbert, Bruce (Director)
Now Cinema! (Super Artist, Andy Worhol); Super Artist, Andy Warhol (Now Cinema!) 1968,Ap 9,56:1

Torbert, Bruce (Producer)
Now Cinema! (Super Artist, Andy Worhol); Super Artist, Andy Warhol (Now Cinema!) 1968,Ap 9,56:1

Tordesillas, Jesus
Mad Queen, The 1950,O 27,24:3
Spanish Affair 1958,F 6,24:1

Tordi, Pietro
Divorce-Italian Style 1962,S 18,34:1

Toren, Marta
Casbah 1948,My 3,27:4
Rogues' Regiment 1948,D 20,31:2
Illegal Entry 1949,Je 11,11:2
Sword in the Desert 1949,Ag 25,20:2
One Way Street 1950,My 12,33:3
Spy Hunt 1950,S 8,25:2
Deported 1950,N 2,39:3
Mystery Submarine 1951,F 2,19:2
Sirocco 1951,Je 14,31:2
Assignment-Paris 1952,O 25,12:6
Paris Express, The 1953,Je 6,8:6
House of Ricordi 1956,Mr 13,32:1

Torena, Juan
Gay Caballero, The 1932,Mr 26,17:2
Cruz y la Espada, La 1934,F 5,19:3
Nada Mas Que Una Mujer 1934,N 26,12:2
Crimen de Media Noche, El 1936,F 22,12:3
Message to Garcia, A 1936,Ap 10,27:1
Love Under Fire 1937,Ag 28,8:2
Vida Bohemia, La 1939,F 6,8:5
Verbena Tragica; Tragic Festival, The 1939,Mr 13,12:3
American Guerrilla in the Philippines 1950,N 8,37:2
My Man and I 1952,S 6,12:6

Toretzka, Ludmila
Men In her Life, The 1941,D 12,35:1

Torf, Silvia
Streets of Sorrow 1927,Jl 6,23:2

Torgerson, Edwin Dial (Miscellaneous)
One Wild Night 1938,Je 3,17:2

Torgerson, Skip
Mister Scoutmaster 1953,Ag 29,10:1

Torigi, Richard
Cavalleria Rusticana 1953,D 28,17:2

Torillo, Joe
Strictly Dishonorable 1931,N 11,27:1

Tork, Peter
Head 1968,N 7,51:1

Torme, Mel
Higher and Higher 1944,Ja 22,8:4
Good News 1947,D 5,33:2
Words and Music 1948,D 10,34:2
Duchess of Idaho 1950,Jl 21,15:3
Walk Like a Dragon 1960,S 16,24:1
Man Called Adam, A 1966,Ag 4,24:2

Torn, Rip
Time Limit 1957,O 24,37:2
Pork Chop Hill 1959,My 30,9:2
King of Kings 1961,O 12,41:2
Sweet Bird of Youth 1962,Mr 29,28:2
Critic's Choice 1963,My 2,40:2
Cincinnati Kid, The 1965,O 28,48:1
One Spy too Many 1966,D 8,64:1
You're a Big Boy Now 1967,Mr 21,35:3
Beach Red 1967,Ag 4,18:1
Sol Madrid 1968,Je 14,43:1
Beyond the Law 1968,S 30,60:4
Beyond the Law 1968,O 24,55:1

Tornblom, Stig
491 1967,D 21,45:1

Torniani, Pina
Avvocato Difensore, L'; Attorney for the Defense, The 1935,N 13,25:4

Torokczik, Mari
Merry Go-Round 1958,Ap 3,23:3

Toronyi, Imre
Igloi Diakok 1935,My 24,24:3
Nagymama 1935,D 30,15:1

Torre, Amelia de la
Bodas de Sangre; Bloody Wedding 1939,N 13,15:3

Torre, Janice (Composer)
Tom Thumb 1958,D 24,00:0
Torrebianca, Carmen
Isla Maldita, La 1935,D 2,18:3
Torrence, David
Inside of the Cup, The 1921,Ja 16,VI,2:1 (In Addenda)
Tess of the Storm Country 1922,N 13,12:1
Abysmal Brute, The 1923,Ap 18,24:5
Man Next Door, The 1923,My 29,10:3
Light That Failed, The 1923,N 27,11:2
Dawn of a Tomorrow, The 1924,Mr 26,19:2
Which Shall It Be? 1924,Ap 7,15:3
Tiger Love 1924,Je 16,18:3
Love's Wilderness 1924,D 22,20:2
Mystic, The 1925,Ag 31,19:3
Tower of Lies, The 1925,S 28,24:1
What Fools Men 1925,S 29,31:3
Auction Block, The 1926,F 15,16:4
Oh! What a Nurse! 1926,F 22,14:1
Brown of Harvard 1926,My 3,27:1
Forever After 1926,N 9,31:1
Third Degree, The 1927,F 15,23:1
Annie Laurie 1927,My 12,24:3
Rolled Stockings 1927,Jl 19,27:2
Big Noise, The 1928,My 7,29:1
Kentucky Courage 1928,My 14,25:1
Cavalier, The 1928,O 31,28:4
Strong Boy 1929,Ap 1,22:1
Black Watch, The 1929,My 23,26:3
Disraeli 1929,O 3,27:5
Hearts in Exile 1929,N 29,25:1
Raffles 1930,Jl 25,20:4
Scotland Yard 1930,O 20,28:2
Devil to Pay, The 1930,D 19,30:1
Bachelor Father, The 1931,F 2,23:1
East Lynne 1931,F 21,15:2
River's End 1931,Mr 7,17:2
Five Star Final 1931,S 11,24:2
Successful Calamity, A 1932,S 23,22:2
Smilin' Through 1932,O 15,13:1
Mask of Fu Manchu, The 1932,D 3,21:4
Voltaire 1933,Ag 23,21:2
Masquerader, The 1933,S 4,9:5
Berkeley Square 1933,S 14,26:2
Queen Christina 1933,D 27,23:3
Madame Spy 1934,F 10,20:1
Mandalay 1934,F 15,15:6
Charlie Chan in London 1934,S 13,26:1
What Every Woman Knows 1934,O 27,20:2
Black Sheep 1935,Je 28,34:1
Dark Angel, The 1935,S 6,12:2
Harmony Lane 1935,O 24,19:4
Captain Blood 1935,D 27,14:1
Country Doctor, The 1936,Mr 13,32:2 (Incorrect in this edition; use 1936,Mr 13,27:2 elsewhere)
Mary of Scotland 1936,Jl 31,22:2
Beloved Enemy 1936,D 26,15:2
Lost Horizon 1937,Mr 4,27:1
Ebb Tide 1937,N 18,27:2
Five of a Kind 1938,O 31,12:2
Stanley and Livingstone 1939,Ag 5,18:2
Rulers of the Sea 1939,N 9,27:1
Torrence, Ernest
Prodigal Judge, The 1922,F 5,VI,3:1 (In Addenda)
Trail of the Lonesome Pine, The 1923,Mr 20,24:3
Brass Bottle, The 1923,Jl 23,13:4
Hunchback of Notre Dame, The 1923,S 3,9:3
Ruggles of Red Gap 1923,S 10,15:4
West of the Water Tower 1923,D 31,9:3
Heritage of the Desert, The 1924,Ja 24,15:1
Fighting Coward, The 1924,Mr 17,19:1
Side Show of Life, The 1924,Jl 22,9:1
North of 36 1924,D 8,13:3
Peter Pan 1924,D 29,11:4
Dressmaker from Paris, The 1925,Mr 18,19:2
Night Life of New York 1925,Jl 14,14:1
Wanderer, The 1925,Ag 20,22:1
Pony Express, The 1925,S 14,16:1
American Venus, The 1926,Ja 26,25:2
Blind Goddess 1926,Ap 6,26:4 (In Addenda)
Rainmaker, The 1926,My 18,28:2
Mantrap 1926,Jl 12,24:4
King of Kings, The 1927,Ap 20,29:2
Captain Salvation 1927,Je 27,25:2
Twelve Miles Out 1927,Jl 26,17:1
Across to Singapore 1928,Ap 30,18:3
Steamboat Bill, Jr 1928,My 15,17:3
Cossacks, The 1928,Je 25,27:1
Desert Nights 1929,My 6,30:4
Bridge of San Luis Rey, The 1929,My 20,22:6
Speedway 1929,S 21,17:1
Unholy Night, The 1929,O 12,11:1
Untamed 1929,N 30,23:1
Officer O'Brien 1930,F 24,18:1
Sweet Kitty Bellairs 1930,S 6,9:2
Call of the Flesh 1930,S 13,9:3
Fighting Caravans 1931,Ja 26,21:1
Shipmates 1931,My 23,13:4
Sporting Blood 1931,Ag 15,18:3

Great Lover, The 1931,Ag 24,13:4
New Adventures of Get-Rich-Quick Wallingford 1931,O 10,20:4
Cuban Love Song, The 1931,D 5,21:2
Sherlock Holmes 1932,N 12,20:5
Hypnotized 1933,Ja 16,13:3
I Cover the Waterfront 1933,My 18,17:3
Torrente, Ugo
Divorce-Italian Style 1962,S 18,34:1
Torres, Antonio
Harbor Lights 1964,F 13,25:3
Torres, Carlos
Given Word, The 1964,Mr 25,47:1
Torres, Jose
Wild 90 1968,Ja 8,33:1
Torres, Marina
Goyescas 1944,My 29,18:3
Torres, Miguel C
Tribu 1935,Je 10,14:7
Paloma, La 1938,F 26,9:4
Golondrina, La; Swallow, The 1939,Jl 31,9:3
Torres, Miguel C (Director)
Noche del Pecado, La 1933,D 26,19:4
Sombra de Pancho Villa, La 1934,Ja 8,20:3
Juarez y Maximiliano 1935,F 16,9:2
No te Enganes, Corazon; Don't Fool Thyself, Heart 1937,D 14,33:6
Sonadores de la Gloria; Dreamers of Glory 1938,D 10,13:3
Golondrina, La; Swallow, The 1939,Jl 31,9:3
Mad Empress, The 1940,F 15,15:1
Life of Simon Bolivar, The 1943,Je 18,16:5
Pancho Villa Returns 1950,O 24,34:6
Torres, Miguel C (Original Author)
Pancho Villa Returns 1950,O 24,34:6
Torres, Miguel C (Producer)
No Mataras; Thou Shalt not Kill 1935,N 11,20:2
No te Enganes, Corazon; Don't Fool Thyself, Heart 1937,D 14,33:6
Paloma, La 1938,F 26,9:4
Mad Empress, The 1940,F 15,15:1
Pancho Villa Returns 1950,O 24,34:6
Torres, Miguel C (Screenwriter)
Mad Empress, The 1940,F 15,15:1
Life of Simon Bolivar, The 1943,Je 18,16:5
Torres, Miguel Contreras
Sonadores de la Gloria; Dreamers of Glory 1938,D 10,13:3
Torres, Nancy
Vida por Otra, Una 1933,F 11,11:3
Una Vida Por Otra 1933,F 11,11:3
Rebel Souls 1937,N 13,11:2
Torres, Pepe (Miscellaneous)
Marilyn 1963,Jl 18,15:1
Torres, Raquel
White Shadows of the South Seas 1928,Ag 1,13:3
Bridge of San Luis Rey, The 1929,My 20,22:6
Under a Texas Moon 1930,Ap 4,22:1
So This Is Africa! 1933,Ap 24,11:3
Woman I Stole, The 1933,Je 28,24:3
Duck Soup 1933,N 23,24:2
Red Wagon 1936,Je 22,22:1
Torri, Rosemary
Dark Odyssey 1961,Je 26,22:2
Torriani, Vico
Guitars of Love 1958,Jl 12,18:1
Torricella, Edoardo
Juliet of the Spirits 1965,N 4,57:1
Torrobo, Rafael Dr
Night Heaven Fell, The 1958,O 22,40:4
Torruco, Miguel
Massacre 1956,Je 2,13:5
Tors, Ivan (Director)
Rhino! 1964,Ag 27,28:2
Tors, Ivan (Producer)
Magnetic Monster, The 1953,My 14,32:5
Mask of the Himalayas 1953,Ag 12,22:3
Riders to the Stars 1954,Mr 20,10:7
Gog 1954,Ag 14,8:2
Flipper 1963,S 19,23:1
Flipper's New Adventure 1964,Ag 27,28:2
Gentle Giant 1968,Ap 20,26:1
Tors, Ivan (Screenwriter)
Song of Love 1947,O 10,31:2
In the Good Old Summertime 1949,Ag 5,23:2
That Forsyte Woman 1949,N 11,31:2
Watch the Birdie 1950,D 12,46:4
Magnetic Monster, The 1953,My 14,32:5
Mask of the Himalayas 1953,Ag 12,22:3
Tortosa, Jose Luis
Tango-Bar 1935,Jl 6,16:3
Dia que me Quieras, El; Day You Love Me, The 1935,Ag 27,23:3
Message to Garcia, A 1936,Ap 10,27:1
Tortosa, Manuel
Crimen de Media Noche, El 1936,F 22,12:3
Torvay, Jose
Border Incident 1949,N 21,29:2
Borderline 1950,Mr 6,17:2
Torch, The 1950,Ag 21,15:2
Brave Bulls, The 1951,Ap 19,39:2
My Outlaw Brother 1951,Ag 23,19:2
My Man and I 1952,S 6,12:6

Torvay, Jose— Cont
Hitch-Hiker, The 1953,Ap 30,39:3
Green Fire 1954,D 25,7:1
Strange Lady in Town 1955,My 21,11:1
Life in the Balance, A 1955,Jl 14,19:1
Littlest Outlaw, The 1955,D 27,31:1
Woman's Devotion, A 1957,Mr 22,26:1
From Hell to Texas 1958,Je 5,39:2
Torzs, Jeno
Iza Neni 1934,Je 5,28:6
Vasember 1935,D 9,25:3
Mami 1938,F 19,19:5
Fekete Gyemantok; Black Diamonds 1939,Ap 24,13:2
Toscanini, Arturo, and the NBC Symphony Orchestra
Hymn of the Nations 1946,Ap 22,26:2
Tosco, Otello
Verginita 1953,Ap 18,17:2
Tosi, Luigi
Earth Cries Out, The; Grido Della Terra, Il 1949,Ag 31,26:2
Tombolo 1949,O 31,9:4
Secret Conclave, The 1953,My 16,10:1
Strange Deception 1953,My 27,28:2
Night Heaven Fell, The 1958,O 22,40:4
Woman in the Painting, The 1959,Ja 15,27:1
Toso, Otello
Two Orphans, The 1950,O 19,40:6
Cliff of Sin, The 1952,N 22,16:5
What Price Innocence? 1953,My 2,13:3
Age of Infidelity 1958,Ag 19,23:2
Tossy, Helene
Game of Love, The 1954,D 15,41:1
Gervaise 1957,N 12,46:1
Tost, Peter
Flying Classroom, The 1958,Je 28,13:7
Tosti, Paolo (Composer)
Love in old Naples 1940,Ja 26,13:3
Toth, Endre de (Director)
Toprini Nasz; Wedding in Toprin 1939,N 6,20:2
Toth, Juliette
Women Without Names 1951,Ag 7,22:2
Toth, Mary
Noszty Flu Este Toth Marival 1938,My 16,14:4
Totheroh, Dan (Original Author)
Yellow Dust 1936,F 24,14:1
Deep Valley 1947,Ag 23,7:2
Totheroh, Dan (Screenwriter)
Dawn Patrol 1938,D 24,12:1
All That Money Can Buy 1941,O 17,27:2
Totman, Wellyn (Original Author)
Leathernecks Have Landed, The 1936,Mr 23,22:5
Down Under the Sea 1936,Ag 10,10:2
Totman, Wellyn (Screenwriter)
Dancing Feet 1936,Mr 28,11:2
Down Under the Sea 1936,Ag 10,10:2
Gangs of New York 1938,My 28,9:2
Wanted by the Police 1938,S 26,13:2
Toto
Side Street Story 1954,Je 24,30:4
Gold of Naples (The Racketeer); Racketeer, The (Gold of Naples) 1957,F 12,30:1
Law Is the Law, The 1959,My 11,41:2
Anatomy of Love 1959,S 29,46:2
Big Deal on Madonna Street, The 1960,N 23,20:1
Mandragola 1966,Je 7,50:2
Hawks and the Sparrows, The 1966,S 17,28:2
Hawks and the Sparrows, The; Uccellacci e Uccellini 1967,Jl 28,15:3
Treasure of San Gennaro 1968,F 27,36:1
Toto, Ecce Homo
King Solomon's Mines 1937,Jl 3,18:1
Toto (Dog)
Bringing Up Father 1928,Mr 19,26:2
Tottenham, Merle
Cavalcade 1933,Ja 6,23:2
Bondage 1933,Ap 24,11:3
Paddy the Next Best Thing 1933,Ag 25,12:2
Invisible Man, The 1933,N 18,18:4
Night Must Fall 1937,Ap 30,17:2
This Happy Breed 1947,Ap 14,24:2
Totter, Audrey
Main Street After Dark 1945,Ja 13,15:4
Dangerous Partners 1945,N 2,22:4
Sailor Takes a Wife, The 1946,Mr 1,17:2
Postman Always Rings Twice, The 1946,My 3,15:3
Cockeyed Miracle, The 1946,O 25,28:1
Lady in the Lake 1947,Ja 24,18:3
Beginning or the End, The 1947,F 21,15:1
Unsuspected, The 1947,O 4,9:2
High Wall 1947,D 26,22:2
Saxon Charm, The 1948,S 30,32:3
Alias Nick Beal 1949,Mr 10,35:2
Set-Up, The 1949,Mr 30,31:2
Any Number Can Play 1949,Jl 1,14:4
Tension 1950,Ja 12,32:4
Under the Gun 1951,F 23,33:2
Blue Veil, The 1951,O 27,10:5
Sellout, The 1952,My 31,12:7
Assignment-Paris 1952,O 25,12:6
Man in the Dark 1953,Ap 9,31:5
Mission Over Korea 1953,S 19,7:2
Women's Prison 1955,F 3,18:5

Totter, Audrey— Cont
Bullet for Joey, A 1955,Ap 16,12:1
Carpetbaggers, The 1964,Jl 2,24:4
Toudouze, Georges (Original Author)
Wanted Men 1936,Jl 8,15:2
Toughey, John
Steele of the Royal Mounted 1925,Je 18,16:3
Toulout, Jean
Miserables, Les 1926,Jl 9,17:1
Miserables, Les 1927,Ag 23,29:4
Three Masques, The 1929,N 24,X,8:4
Trois Masques, The 1929,N 24,X,8:4 (In Addenda)
Heroes of the Marne; (Famille Lefrancois, Le) 1939,Ap 24,13:2
Entente Cordiale 1939,D 26,23:2
Resistance; Peleton d'Execution 1946,Jl 5,15:3
Edward and Caroline 1952,Ap 30,33:3
Toumanova, Tamara
Days of Glory 1944,Je 17,10:2
Tonight We Sing 1953,F 13,17:2
Deep in my Heart 1954,D 10,35:2
Invitation to the Dance (Ring Around the Rosy); Ring Around the Rosy (Invitation to the Dance) 1956,My 23,35:7
Torn Curtain 1966,Jl 28,23:1
Tounsi, Larbi
Daughter of the Sands 1952,F 18,15:2
Tourain, Roland
Rules of the Game, The 1950,Ap 10,15:3
Rules of the Game, The 1961,Ja 19,26:1
Toure, Bachir
Roots of Heaven, The 1958,O 16,46:1
Tourel, Jennie
Journey to Jerusalem, A 1968,N 18,59:1
Tourjansky, V (Director)
Michael Strogoff 1926,D 6,28:3
Tales of 1,001 Nights 1927,Ja 24,14:1
Lie of Nina Petrovna, The 1938,Mr 30,19:2
Dark Eyes 1938,Ap 19,24:5
Verklungene Melodie; Dead Melody 1938,Je 25,7:2
Blaufuchs; Blue Fox 1939,Mr 4,18:5
Gouverneur, Der 1939,S 11,15:2
Postmaster's Daughter, The 1946,Ag 19,17:6
Tourjansky, V (Screenwriter)
Ordonnance, L'; Orderly, The 1933,O 22,IX,4:2
Dark Eyes 1938,Ap 19,24:5
Tourjansky, W (Director)
World's in Love, The 1937,My 19,27:2
Prisoner of the Volga 1960,Je 2,27:2
Pharaohs' Woman, The 1962,Ap 19,35:2
Tourjansky, W (Producer)
Cossacks, The 1960,S 6,41:4
Tourneur, Andree
Actress, The 1928,Jl 9,25:1
Tourneur, Jacques (Director)
They all Come Out 1939,Ag 3,15:4
Nick Carter, Master Detective 1939,D 14,35:2
Phantom Raiders 1940,Je 24,19:5
Cat People 1942,D 7,22:2
I Walked With a Zombie 1943,Ap 22,31:5
Leopard Man, The 1943,My 20,26:4
Days of Glory 1944,Je 17,10:2
Experiment Perilous 1944,D 30,15:2
Canyon Passage 1946,Ag 8,18:2
Out of the Past 1947,N 26,18:2
Berlin Express 1948,My 21,19:3
Easy Living 1949,O 13,33:3
Flame and the Arrow, The 1950,Jl 8,7:2
Stars in my Crown 1950,D 22,19:1
Circle of Danger 1951,Jl 12,21:6
Anne of the Indies 1951,O 25,36:3
Way of a Gaucho 1952,N 5,36:2
Appointment in Honduras 1953,N 19,41:4
Great Day in the Morning 1956,My 19,12:6
Nightfall 1957,Ja 24,34:1
Giant of Marathon, The 1960,My 26,37:3
Comedy of Terrors, The 1964,Ja 23,26:2
War Gods of the Deep 1965,Je 3,24:3
Tourneur, Maurice (Director)
Prunelia 1918,Je 3,9:3
Doll's House, A 1918,Je 10,9:3
Sporting Life 1918,S 16,9:3
Woman 1918,O 28,11:1
My Lady's Garter 1920,Mr 15,13:2
White Circle, The 1920,Ag 23,9:2
Last of the Mohicans, The 1921,Ja 3,20:2
Lorna Doone 1922,D 4,20:2
Christian, The 1923,F 12,13:4
Isle of Lost Ships, The 1923,My 14,18:2
Brass Bottle, The 1923,Jl 23,13:4
White Moth, The 1924,Je 16,18:3
Never the Twain Shall Meet 1925,Jl 29,24:4
Clothes Make the Pirate 1925,N 30,17:1
Old Loves and New 1926,Ap 20,24:7
Aloma of the South Seas 1926,My 17,19:1
Last Flight, The 1929,Je 17,29:1
Frochard et les Deux Orphelines, La 1934,F 7,16:2
With a Smile 1939,F 6,8:4
Katia 1939,D 23,9:2
Mad Emperor, The 1941,Mr 10,21:3
Carnival of Sinners 1947,Ap 8,34:2

Volpone 1947,D 27,9:3
Tourneur, Maurice (Producer)
White Heather, The 1919,My 5,11:1
Life Line, The 1919,S 29,16:1
Victory 1919,D 28,4:4
Treasure Island 1920,Ap 12,13:1
Great Redeemer, The 1920,O 25,18:1
Carnival of Sinners 1947,Ap 8,34:2
Tournier, Germaine
Marie-Louise 1945,N 13,24:2
Last Chance, The 1945,N 28,21:6
Tourreil, Georges
Bellman, The 1947,Ap 7,20:5
Tourtellot, Arthur B (Narrator)
Guns of August, The 1964,D 25,24:2
Toutain, Roland
Mystere de la Chambre Jaune, Le 1931,My 26,33:2
Lie of Nina Petrovna, The 1938,Mr 30,19:2
Sacrifice d'Honneur 1938,D 2,27:2
Great Temptation, The 1942,Jl 10,13:3
Eternal Return, The; Eternel Retour, L' 1948,Ja 5,15:2
Tovar, Lupita
East of Borneo 1931,S 26,25:3
Vidas Rotas 1935,Ag 3,16:3
Traidor, El 1938,Ap 9,11:3
Blockade 1938,Je 17,25:1
Alas sobre el Chaco; Wings Over the Chaco 1939,Mr 28,20:2
Maria 1939,Ap 10,13:4
Tropic Fury 1939,S 8,28:4
Crime Doctor's Courage, The 1945,Mr 3,11:3
Towb, Harry
30 Is a Dangerous Age, Cynthia 1968,Mr 5,34:1
Towers, Constance
Horse Soldiers, The 1959,Je 26,13:1
Sergeant Rutledge 1960,My 26,37:1
Shock Corridor 1963,S 12,32:1
Naked Kiss, The 1964,O 29,38:1
Towers, Donald
No Down Payment 1957,O 31,41:1
Towers, Harry Alan (Producer)
Code 7...Victim 5 1965,My 20,52:1
Bang, Bang, You're Dead 1967,Ja 19,41:2
Those Fantastic Flying Fools 1967,O 19,59:2
Vengeance of Fu Manchu, The 1968,F 15,47:1
Towers, Louis
Ride Back, The 1957,Ap 30,24:1
Towers, Tom
Unidentified Flying Objects 1956,Je 13,46:2
Town Criers
Radio Stars on Parade 1945,S 22,14:2
Towne, Aline
Highway 301 1950,D 9,13:2
Steel Trap, The 1952,N 13,35:2
Julie 1956,N 22,51:1
Send Me no Flowers 1964,N 13,30:1
Guide for the Married Man, A 1967,My 27,16:1
Towne, Charles Hanson (Screenwriter)
Fighting Roosevelts, The 1919,Ja 20,13:2
Towne, Gene (Original Author)
Billion Dollar Scandal, The 1933,Ja 9,23:1
Song of the Eagle 1933,Ap 29,14:3
I Love That Man 1933,Jl 10,11:7
Personality Kid, The 1934,Ag 1,14:2
Shanghai 1935,Jl 20,16:2
Girl Friend, The 1935,S 28,12:2
Grand Exit 1935,N 4,24:5
She Couldn't Take It 1935,N 7,27:1
Mary Burns, Fugitive 1935,N 16,19:2
You Only Live Once 1937,F 1,15:2
Ali Baba Goes to Town 1937,O 23,14:1
Towne, Gene (Producer)
Swiss Family Robinson 1940,F 9,15:3
Little Men 1940,D 9,23:2
Towne, Gene (Screenwriter)
Shanghai 1935,Jl 20,16:2
Every Night at Eight 1935,Ag 3,16:2
Mary Burns, Fugitive 1935,N 16,19:2
Case Against Mrs Ames, The 1936,My 28,19:2
Stand-In 1937,N 19,27:2
Joy of Living 1938,My 6,27:1
Eternally Yours 1939,O 7,11:2
Swiss Family Robinson 1940,F 9,15:3
Tom Brown's School Days 1940,Je 28,22:2
Top Banana 1954,F 20,8:6
Towne, George (Original Author)
History Is Made at Night 1937,Mr 29,14:2
Towne, Robert (Screenwriter)
Tomb of Ligeia 1965,My 6,44:1
Villa Rides 1968,Jl 18,26:3
Towne, Rosella
Patient in Room 18, The 1938,Ap 22,15:6
Cowboy From Brooklyn 1938,Jl 14,17:1
Secret Service of the Air 1939,Mr 2,19:2
Townes, Harry
Brothers Karamazov, The 1958,F 21,18:2
Screaming Mimi 1958,Je 26,23:3
Cry Tough 1959,S 17,48:4
Sanctuary 1961,F 22,31:1
Fitzwilly 1967,D 21,45:1

Townley, Jack (Director)
Pittsburgh Kid, The 1941,S 23,27:4
Townley, Jack (Miscellaneous)
Gangs of New York 1938,My 28,9:2
Townley, Jack (Original Author)
Cohens and the Kellys In Atlantic City, The 1929,Mr 18,30:6
Divorce Among Friends 1931,Ap 2,30:4
Strange People 1933,Je 17,16:5
Townley, Jack (Screenwriter)
Silly Billies 1936,Ap 6,18:1
Last Outlaw, The 1936,Je 15,24:1
Meet the Missus 1937,Jl 2,25:2
Mexican Spitfire out West 1940,O 30,29:3
Sis Hopkins 1941,My 1,27:5
Rookies on Parade 1941,My 22,25:2
Ice-Capades 1941,S 25,29:1
Great Gildersleeve, The 1942,D 18,36:8
Gildersleeve's Bad Day 1943,Je 11,23:1
Chicago Kid, The 1945,F 12,24:3
Utah 1945,Mr 12,22:7
My Pal Trigger 1946,Ag 17,16:3
Townley, Toke
Runaway Bus, The 1954,O 25,30:7
Cry From the Streets, A 1959,F 24,32:2
Chalk Garden, The 1964,My 22,42:2
Towns, Fred
Teen Age 1944,Je 19,17:1
Townsend, Casey
Synanon 1965,My 6,44:1
Townsend, Colleen
Janie 1944,Ag 5,16:2
Walls of Jericho, The 1948,Ag 5,16:2
Chicken every Sunday 1949,Ja 19,34:2
When Willie Comes Marching Home 1950,F 18,9:2
Townsend, Douglas
8 X 8 1957,Mr 16,13:2
Townsend, Edward W (Original Author)
Chimmie Fadden Out West 1915,N 22,12:3
Townsend, Leo (Miscellaneous)
Port of New York 1950,F 3,29:2
Townsend, Leo (Original Author)
Can't Help Singing 1944,D 26,22:4
Black Hand 1950,Mr 13,15:2
Townsend, Leo (Screenwriter)
It Started With Eve 1941,O 3,27:1
Seven Sweethearts 1942,N 13,28:1
Amazing Mrs Holliday, The 1943,F 22,20:2
Chip off the Old Block 1944,Mr 17,14:2
Night and Day 1946,Jl 26,16:2
That Way With Women 1947,F 15,20:4
Southside 1-1000 1950,N 3,31:2
Dangerous Crossing 1953,S 30,37:2
Siege at Red River, The 1954,Ap 3,19:2
White Feather 1955,F 17,23:1
Life in the Balance, A 1955,Jl 14,19:1
Running Wild 1955,N 12,23:2
Flight to Hong Kong 1957,Ja 3,28:2
Fraulein 1958,Je 9,27:2
I'd Rather Be Rich 1964,S 3,24:2
Bikini Beach 1964,S 17,52:6
Fireball 500 1966,N 24,65:4
How to Stuff a Wild Bikini 1967,Ja 12,48:1
Toy, Noel
How to be Very, Very Popular 1955,Jl 23,10:1
Toyada, Shiro (Director)
Illusion of Blood 1968,N 28,66:5
Toye, Geoffrey (Miscellaneous)
Mikado, The 1939,Je 2,27:2
Toye, Wendy (Director)
Three Cases of Murder (You Killed Elizabeth); You Killed Elizabeth (Three Cases of Murder) 1955,Mr 16,39:4
Three Cases of Murder (In the Picture); In the Picture (Three Cases of Murder) 1955,Mr 16,39:4
Three Cases of Murder (Lord Mountdrago); Lord Mountdrago (Three Cases of Murder) 1955,Mr 16,39:4
Teckman Mystery, The 1955,Ag 22,18:2
Raising a Riot 1957,My 8,44:1
Toyoda, Shiro (Director)
Mistress, The 1959,F 3,36:2
Toyuk
Igloo 1932,Jl 21,15:2
Tozer, Joseph
Clive of India 1935,Ja 18,29:1
Cardinal Richelieu 1935,Ap 19,24:2
Anna Karenina 1935,Ag 31,16:2
Hands Across the Table 1935,N 2,13:2
Dracula's Daughter 1936,My 18,14:2
Tozere, Frederic
Confessions of a Nazi Spy 1939,Ap 29,13:2
Hell's Kitchen 1939,Jl 3,10:5
Iron Curtain, The 1948,My 13,31:2
Live Today for Tomorrow 1948,D 6,29:2
Return of October, The 1949,F 23,31:2
Tozzi, Fausto
House of Ricordi 1956,Mr 13,32:1
Wonders of Aladdin, The 1961,D 23,16:1
Constantine and the Cross 1963,Mr 14,8:2

Trabaud, Pierre
   Antoine and Antoinette 1948,Ap 16,29:2
   War of the Buttons, The 1963,D 19,40:2
Trabauer, Karl
   Gottes Muehlen mahlen Langsam; Mills of the
      Gods, The 1939,F 18,12:4
TRACEY
   See Also TRACY, TREACY
Tracey, Emerson
   Mouthpiece, The 1932,Ap 21,25:2
Tracy, Don (Original Author)
   Criss Cross 1949,Mr 12,10:2
Tracy, Helen
   Twenty-One 1924,F 18,13:1
Tracy, Jack
   Robber Symphony 1937,Ja 27,17:2
Tracy, John
   Mister Buddwing 1966,O 12,36:1
   Drifter, The 1967,My 25,54:1
Tracy, Lee
   Big Time 1929,S 9,30:2
   Born Reckless 1930,Je 7,10:4
   Liliom 1930,O 4,15:2
   She Got What She Wanted 1930,D 29,18:1
   Strange Love of Molly Louvain, The
      1932,My 9,19:5
   Love Is a Racket 1932,Je 11,9:3
   Doctor X 1932,Ag 4,17:2
   Blessed Event 1932,S 3,16:2
   Washington Merry-Go-Round 1932,O 24,18:5
   Night Mayor, The 1932,N 25,19:2
   Half-Naked Truth, The 1932,D 31,10:1
   Clear all Wires 1933,Mr 4,11:2
   Private Jones 1933,Mr 25,13:3
   Nuisance, The 1933,My 29,22:2
   Dinner at Eight 1933,Ag 24,18:1
   Turn Back the Clock 1933,Ag 26,14:2
   Bombshell 1933,O 21,11:2
   Advice to the Lovelorn 1933,D 14,28:2
   I'll Tell the World 1934,Ap 21,12:2
   You Belong to Me 1934,S 13,26:1
   Lemon Drop Kid, The 1934,O 27,20:2
   Carnival 1935,F 16,9:1
   Two Fisted 1935,O 5,18:3
   Sutter's Gold 1936,Mr 27,25:2
   Wanted: Jane Turner 1936,N 30,24:7
   Criminal Lawyer 1937,Ja 27,17:3
   Behind the Headlines 1937,Je 1,27:2
   Crashing Hollywood 1938,Ja 8,19:2
   Fixer Dugan 1939,My 6,21:2
   Spellbinder, The 1939,Ag 24,17:3
   Millionaires in Prison 1940,Jl 16,21:3
   Betrayal From the East 1945,Ap 25,27:2
   High Tide 1947,N 8,11:2
   Best Man, The 1964,Ap 7,29:1
Tracy, Margaret
   Sign of the Ram, The 1948,Mr 4,30:2
Tracy, Spencer
   Up the River 1930,O 11,21:3
   Quick Millions 1931,Ap 18,17:3
   Six Cylinder Love 1931,My 16,31:3
   Goldie 1931,Je 29,20:3
   She Wanted a Millionaire 1932,F 20,11:2
   Sky Devils 1932,Mr 4,17:3
   Disorderly Conduct 1932,Ap 11,19:2
   Young America 1932,My 7,11:5
   Society Girl 1932,Je 10,22:3
   Painted Woman, The 1932,S 16,24:4
   Me and my Gal 1932,D 12,18:4
   20,000 Years in Sing Sing 1933,Ja 10,26:2
   Face in the Sky 1933,F 20,11:5
   Power and the Glory, The 1933,Ag 17,13:2
   Shanghai Madness 1933,S 23,11:6
   Mad Game, The 1933,N 13,21:1
   Man's Castle 1933,D 30,9:2
   Show-Off, The 1934,Mr 17,11:3
   Bottoms Up 1934,Mr 23,29:2
   Looking for Trouble 1934,Ap 12,27:2
   Now I'll Tell 1934,My 26,12:2
   Marie Galante 1934,N 21,23:4
   Murder Man, The 1935,Jl 27,16:2
   Dante's Inferno 1935,Ag 1,15:1
   Riffraff 1936,Ja 13,14:2
   Whipsaw 1936,Ja 25,18:4
   Fury 1936,Je 6,21:1
   San Francisco 1936,Je 27,21:1
   Libeled Lady 1936,O 31,24:2
   Captains Courageous 1937,My 12,27:1
   They Gave Him a Gun 1937,My 14,21:1
   Big City 1937,S 17,29:2
   Mannequin 1938,Ja 21,15:2
   Test Pilot 1938,Ap 16,17:1
   Boys Town 1938,S 9,25:1
   Stanley and Livingstone 1939,Ag 5,18:2
   I Take This Woman 1940,F 16,23:3
   Northwest Passage 1940,Mr 8,25:1
   Edison the Man 1940,Je 7,27:2
   Boom Town 1940,S 6,25:2
   Men of Boys Town 1941,Ap 11,24:6
   Dr Jekyll and Mr Hyde 1941,Ag 13,13:2
   Woman of the Year 1942,F 6,23:2
   Tortilla Flat 1942,My 22,27:1
   Keeper of the Flame 1943,Mr 19,15:2

   Guy Named Joe, A 1943,D 24,17:2
   Guy Named Joe, A 1944,Ja 9,II,3:1
   Seventh Cross, The 1944,S 29,18:1
   Thirty Seconds Over Tokyo 1944,N 16,19:1
   Without Love 1945,Mr 23,13:1
   Sea of Grass, The 1947,F 28,27:2
   Cass Timberlane 1947,N 7,20:2
   State of the Union 1948,Ap 23,28:1
   Edward my Son 1949,Je 3,21:2
   Adam's Rib 1949,D 26,33:2
   Malaya 1950,F 23,33:1
   Father of the Bride 1950,My 19,31:2
   Father's Little Dividend 1951,Ap 13,18:5
   People Against O'Hara, The 1951,S 6,39:3
   Pat and Mike 1952,Je 19,32:6
   Plymouth Adventure 1952,N 14,20:3
   Actress, The 1953,O 13,34:1
   Broken Lance 1954,Jl 30,9:1
   Bad Day at Black Rock 1955,F 2,22:2
   Mountain, The 1956,N 15,44:6
   Desk Set 1957,My 16,28:2
   Old Man and the Sea, The 1958,O 8,41:1
   Last Hurrah, The 1958,O 24,40:1
   Inherit the Wind 1960,O 13,41:1
   Devil at 4 O'Clock, The 1961,O 19,39:3
   Judgment at Nuremberg 1961,D 20,36:1
   It's a Mad, Mad, Mad, Mad World
      1963,N 19,47:1
   Guess Who's Coming to Dinner 1967,D 12,56:1
Tracy, Virginia (Original Author)
   Nero 1922,My 26,17:2
Tracy, William
   Brother Rat 1938,N 5,15:2
   Angels With Dirty Faces 1938,N 26,18:1
   Shop Around the Corner, The 1940,Ja 26,13:2
   Strike up the Band 1940,S 30,13:2
   Gallant Sons 1940,D 12,37:2
   Tobacco Road 1941,F 21,16:2
   Mr and Mrs Smith 1941,F 21,16:3
   She Knew All the Answers 1941,Je 20,28:4
   Tanks a Million 1941,O 9,27:2
   Cadet Girl 1941,D 11,39:1
   To the Shores of Tripoli 1942,Mr 26,27:2
   George Washington Slept Here 1942,O 31,11:1
   Fall In 1943,My 15,13:3
   Here Comes Trouble 1948,Ap 15,31:4
   Walls of Jericho, The 1948,Ag 5,16:2
Traeforou, M (Screenwriter)
   House on Stournara Street, The 1960,O 17,33:4
Trahey, Jane (Miscellaneous)
   Where Angels Go-Trouble Follows
      1968,Ap 11,51:1
Trahey, Jane (Original Author)
   Trouble With Angels, The 1966,Ap 7,45:1
Trail, Armitage (Original Author)
   Scarface, The Shame of the Nation
      1932,My 20,22:3
Traill, Peter (Original Author)
   Guilty One, The 1924,Je 17,22:4
Train, Arthur (Original Author)
   Blind Goddess 1926,Ap 6,26:4 (In Addenda)
   Illusion 1929,S 28,17:3
Train, Dean
   Tall Texan, The 1953,Ap 13,32:4
Train, Jack
   Showtime 1948,My 20,35:3
Trainer, Leonard
   Terror Trail 1933,F 11,11:3
Trakhtina, Mlle
   Enemies of Progress 1934,Ja 11,19:2
Tramel
   Crainquebille 1934,D 10,16:3
   Chasseur de Chez Maxim's, Le 1935,F 4,11:4
   Cognasse 1935,Ap 15,16:4
   Last Desire 1939,D 22,15:2
   Man Who Seeks the Truth, The 1941,O 7,26:6
   Well-Digger's Daughter, The 1946,S 30,21:4
Tramp Band, The
   Stormy Weather 1943,Jl 22,15:1
Trampe, Ray (Screenwriter)
   Mars Attacks the World 1938,N 8,26:3
Traney, Agnes
   Queen of the Night Clubs 1929,Mr 18,30:6
Tranter, Florence (Original Author)
   Suicide Legion 1940,My 6,13:3
Tranter, Florence (Screenwriter)
   Girl in the Street 1938,My 26,31:2
Tranter, Nigel (Original Author)
   Bridal Path, The 1959,D 21,34:2
Trantow, Cordula
   Bridge, The; (Bruecke, Die) 1961,My 2,42:1
   Tomorrow Is my Turn 1962,F 2,24:2
Trapani, Cesare
   Stranger on the Prowl 1953,N 10,38:1
Trapani, Enzo (Director)
   Brief Rapture 1952,F 28,23:2
Trapani, Enzo (Original Author)
   Brief Rapture 1952,F 28,23:2
Trapnell, Coles (Original Author)
   Within These Walls 1945,Jl 16,8:4
Trapszo, Tekla
   Mlody Las 1935,D 3,32:7

Trask, C Hooper
   Monte Carlo Madness 1932,Je 4,9:2
Trasker, Robert (Screenwriter)
   Accusing Finger, The 1936,N 17,35:4
Traub, Joe (Screenwriter)
   Earthworm Tractors 1936,Jl 25,16:1
Traube, Shepard (Director)
   Bride Wore Crutches, The 1941,My 26,15:3
Traube, Shepard (Screenwriter)
   Beasts of Berlin 1939,N 20,15:6
Traubel, Helen
   Deep in my Heart 1954,D 10,35:2
   Ladies Man, The 1961,Jl 13,26:3
   Gunn 1967,Je 29,32:1
Trauberg, Illya (Director)
   China Express, The 1930,Mr 10,24:1
Trauberg, Ilya (Director)
   Son of Mongolia 1936,N 21,21:4
Trauberg, L (Screenwriter)
   Flames on the Volga 1958,Ja 27,21:7
Trauberg, Leonid (Director)
   New Babylon, The 1929,D 2,28:2
   Alone 1932,My 25,23:6
   Youth of Maxim, The 1935,Ap 20,16:1
   Return of Maxim, The 1937,N 2,33:1
   New Horizons 1939,My 12,25:3
Trauberg, Leonid (Producer)
   We Will Come Back 1943,O 15,15:2
Trauberg, Leonid (Screenwriter)
   Youth of Maxim, The 1935,Ap 20,16:1
   Return of Maxim, The 1937,N 2,33:1
   New Horizons 1939,My 12,25:3
Traut, Walter (Cinematographer)
   Wedding of Palo, The 1937,Mr 2,17:1
Traven, B (Original Author)
   Treasure of Sierra Madre 1948,Ja 24,11:2
Traver, Robert (Original Author)
   Anatomy of a Murder 1959,Jl 3,10:1
Travernier, Albert
   Democracy, The Vision Restored 1920,Ag 25,6:4
Travers, Alfred (Director)
   You Can't Fool an Irishman 1950,D 7,45:4
Travers, Ben (Screenwriter)
   Chance of a Night Time, A 1931,Je 7,VIII,6:1
Travers, Bill
   Browning Version, The 1951,O 30,33:2
   Romeo and Juliet 1954,D 22,28:1
   Footsteps of the Fog 1955,S 15,39:2
   Bhowani Junction 1956,My 25,26:1
   Wee Geordie 1956,O 8,31:1
   Barretts of Wimpole Street, The 1957,Ja 18,15:3
   Seventh Sin, The 1957,Je 29,10:6
   Smallest Show on Earth, The 1957,N 23,11:2
   Bridal Path, The 1959,D 21,34:2
   Gorgo 1961,Mr 30,24:2
   Green Helmet, The 1961,Jl 20,32:2
   Invasion Quartet 1961,D 11,41:2
   Duel at Diablo 1966,Je 16,53:1
   Born Free 1966,Je 23,29:1
Travers, Celia
   Whistling in Dixie 1942,D 31,20:4
   Swing Shift Maisie 1943,S 10,29:2
   Mrs Parkington 1944,O 13,16:1
   Easy to Wed 1946,Jl 12,14:2
Travers, Douglas (Miscellaneous)
   Below the Sahara 1953,S 2,20:1
Travers, Henry
   Reunion in Vienna 1933,Ap 29,14:2
   Another Language 1933,Ag 5,9:5
   My Weakness 1933,S 22,14:1
   Invisible Man, The 1933,N 18,18:4
   Death Takes a Holiday 1934,F 24,18:4
   Born to be Bad 1934,My 31,22:6
   Maybe It's Love 1935,F 11,14:2
   After Office Hours 1935,Mr 9,19:1
   Four Hours to Kill 1935,Ap 11,27:3
   Escapade 1935,Jl 6,16:2
   Seven Keys to Baldpate 1935,D 14,11:2
   Sisters, The 1938,O 15,21:3
   You Can't Get Away With Murder
      1939,Mr 25,19:2
   Dodge City 1939,Ap 8,19:1
   Dark Victory 1939,Ap 21,27:2
   On Borrowed Time 1939,Jl 7,13:2
   Stanley and Livingstone 1939,Ag 5,18:2
   Rains Came, The 1939,S 9,11:2
   Remember? 1939,D 15,33:4
   Primrose Path 1940,Mr 23,16:2
   Edison the Man 1940,Je 7,27:2
   Anne of Windy Poplars 1940,Ag 23,13:3
   Wyoming 1940,O 3,31:4
   High Sierra 1941,Ja 25,11:2
   Bad Man, The 1941,Ap 4,25:1
   Girl, a Guy and a Gob, A 1941,Ap 24,25:3
   I'll Wait for You 1941,Je 2,13:6
   Ball of Fire 1942,Ja 16,25:2
   Mrs Miniver 1942,Je 5,23:1
   Pierre of the Plains 1942,Jl 30,17:3
   Random Harvest 1942,D 18,36:6
   Shadow of a Doubt 1943,Ja 13,18:2
   Moon Is Down, The 1943,Mr 27,8:6
   Madame Curie 1943,D 17,23:1
   None Shall Escape 1944,Ap 7,23:2

Travers, Henry— Cont

Dragon Seed 1944,Jl 21,16:4
Very Thought of You, The 1944,N 18,16:7
Thrill of a Romance 1945,My 25,22:2
Naughty Nineties, The 1945,Je 21,16:2
Bells of St Mary's, The 1945,D 7,26:2
Gallant Journey 1946,O 10,33:2
It's a Wonderful Life 1946,D 23,19:2
Yearling, The 1947,Ja 24,18:2
Flame, The 1948,F 20,19:2
Beyond Glory 1948,Ag 4,18:2
Girl from Jones Beach, The 1949,Jl 30,9:2

Travers, Linden

Lady Vanishes, The 1938,D 26,29:1
Stars Look Down, The 1941,Jl 24,15:2
Beware of Pity 1947,N 1,11:2
Jassy 1948,F 20,19:2
Quartet (The Colonel's Lady); Colonel's Lady, The
(Quartet) 1949,Mr 29,30:3
Christopher Columbus 1949,O 13,33:2
Master of Bankdam 1949,O 17,18:2
Mr Know-All 1950,O 11,42:1
No Orchids for Miss Blandish 1951,F 23,33:2
Bad Lord Byron, The 1952,Mr 20,37:5

Travers, P L (Original Author)

Mary Poppins 1964,S 25,34:1

Travers, Patricia

There's Magic in Music 1941,Je 5,27:2

Travers, Richard

Acquittal, The 1923,D 12,24:5

Travers, Roy

Q Ships 1928,S 17,27:1

Travis, June

Stranded 1935,Je 20,16:2
Broadway Gondolier 1935,Jl 18,15:2
Ceiling Zero 1936,Ja 20,22:2
Times Square Playboy 1936,My 2,11:2
Earthworm Tractors 1936,Jl 25,16:1
Bengal Tiger 1936,Jl 30,22:1
Jailbreak 1936,Ag 6,22:1
Big Game, The 1936,O 24,23:1
Case of the Black Cat, The 1936,D 26,15:4
Over the Goal 1937,O 16,22:2
Love Is on the Air 1937,N 12,27:3
Kid Comes Back, The 1938,F 7,10:2
Over the Wall 1938,Mr 28,19:2
Go Chase Yourself 1938,Je 15,27:1
Gladiator, The 1938,Ag 29,10:2
Mr Doodle Kicks Off 1938,S 28,29:4
Federal Man-Hunt 1939,F 2,17:3
Star, The 1953,Ja 29,25:1

Travis, Merle

From Here to Eternity 1953,Ag 6,16:2
World Dances 1954,N 8,24:6

Travis, Richard

Man Who Came to Dinner, The 1942,Ja 2,25:2
Big Shot, The 1942,Jl 18,8:2
Busses Roar 1942,S 25,25:4
Escape From Crime 1942,O 12,12:3
Truck Busters 1943,Ja 29,23:5
Mission to Moscow 1943,Ap 30,25:2
Backlash 1947,My 24,10:5
Jewels of Brandenburg 1947,My 24,10:5
Missle to the Moon 1958,N 17,37:2

Traylor, William

1 ■ 1 1961,N 8,41:1

TRAYNOR

See Also TRAINER

Traynor, John

Men of Tomorrow 1935,Ap 16,27:2

Treacher, Arthur

Gambling Lady 1934,Ap 5,25:2
Key, The 1934,My 30,14:3
Madame Du Barry 1934,O 25,26:2
Forsaking all Others 1934,D 21,18:1
Let's Live Tonight 1935,Mr 18,14:4
Woman in Red, The 1935,Mr 23,11:3
No More Ladies 1935,Je 22,18:5
Daring Young Man, The 1935,Jl 18,15:2
Curly Top 1935,Ag 2,22:3
Orchids to You 1935,Ag 10,16:4
Bright Lights 1935,Ag 15,15:2
Midsummer Night's Dream, A 1935,O 10,31:1
I Live my Life 1935,O 12,12:2
Remember Last Night? 1935,N 21,27:2
Splendor 1935,N 23,23:2
Magnificent Obsession 1935,D 31,11:2
Anything Goes 1936,F 6,23:3
Case Against Mrs Ames, The 1936,My 28,19:2
Hearts Divided 1936,Je 13,13:1
Satan Met a Lady 1936,Jl 23,24:2
Thank You, Jeeves 1936,O 5,25:1
Under Your Spell 1936,N 7,15:2
Stowaway 1936,D 19,16:1
Step Lively, Jeeves 1937,Ap 2,19:6
She Had to Eat 1937,Jl 24,12:1
You Can't Have Everything 1937,Ag 4,15:2
Thin Ice 1937,S 4,8:2
Heidi 1937,N 6,14:2
Mad About Music 1938,Mr 12,13:2
My Lucky Star 1938,S 10,20:2
Always in Trouble 1938,N 3,27:1
Up the River 1938,D 3,11:2
Little Princess, The 1939,Mr 11,21:1

Bridal Suite 1939,My 26,20:2
Barricade 1939,D 9,18:2
Brother Rat and a Baby 1940,Ja 27,9:4
Irene 1940,My 24,23:3
Star Spangled Rhythm 1942,D 31,20:1
Amazing Mrs Holliday, The 1943,F 22,20:2
Chip off the Old Block 1944,Mr 17,14:2
In Society 1944,Ag 17,20:2
National Velvet 1944,D 15,25:2
That's the Spirit 1945,Je 2,11:2
Delightfully Dangerous 1945,Je 9,17:3
Slave Girl 1947,Jl 18,21:3
That Midnight Kiss 1949,S 23,28:2
Love That Brute 1950,My 27,10:6
Mary Poppins 1964,S 25,34:1

TREACY

See Also TRACY, TRACEY

Treacy, Emerson

Once a Gentleman 1930,O 4,15:2
Okay America 1932,S 10,18:5
Give Me a Sailor 1938,Ag 11,31:1
Adam's Rib 1949,D 26,33:2
Wyoming Mail 1950,O 23,26:5
Prowler, The 1951,Jl 2,16:6
Fort Worth 1951,Jl 13,12:7

Treadway, Charlotte

Female Fugitive 1938,Ap 11,12:3

Treadwell, Laura

Accent on Youth 1935,Ag 12,10:3
Nobody's Baby 1937,My 20,17:3
Night of Nights, The 1939,D 28,17:1
Bringing Up Father 1946,N 22,27:3

Treatt, C Court (Cinematographer)

Struggle for Life 1935,Je 19,23:2

Treatt, C Court (Producer)

Stampede 1930,Ap 28,24:5

Trebaol, Children

Honest Hutch 1920,S 26,VI,2:1 (In Addenda)

Trebaol, Edouard

Oliver Twist 1922,O 30,11:1

Trebitsch, Gyula (Producer)

Rad Bizom a Felesegem; I Entrust my Wife to
You 1939,My 6,21:3

Treboal, Mrs

Design for Living 1933,N 23,24:2

Tree, David

Knight Without Armor 1937,Jl 9,18:1
Gaiety Girls, The 1938,Mr 31,15:1
Return of the Scarlet Pimpernel, The
1938,Ap 11,12:2
Drums 1938,S 30,24:4
Pygmalion 1938,D 8,34:2
Goodbye Mr Chips 1939,My 16,27:2
Clouds Over Europe 1939,Je 16,27:2
French Without Tears 1940,Ap 29,12:2
Major Barbara 1941,My 15,27:1

Tree, Dorothy

Husband's Holiday 1931,D 25,29:2
Life Begins 1932,Ag 26,20:3
Here Comes the Navy 1934,Jl 21,14:2
Friends of Mr Sweeney 1934,Jl 31,20:4
Side Streets 1934,Ag 15,13:5
Dragon Murder Case, The 1934,Ag 23,13:3
Case of the Howling Dog, The 1934,O 18,26:5
Madame Du Barry 1934,O 25,26:2
Firebird, The 1934,N 15,25:2
While the Patient Slept 1935,Mr 2,18:2
Woman in Red, The 1935,Mr 23,11:3
Four Hours to Kill 1935,Ap 11,27:3
Night at the Ritz, A 1935,My 16,20:2
Three Godfathers, The 1936,Mr 9,20:2
Great Garrick, The 1937,O 25,23:1
Trade Winds 1939,Ja 13,17:2
Confessions of a Nazi Spy 1939,Ap 29,13:2
Charlie Chan in City in Darkness 1939,D 18,29:2
Abe Lincoln in Illinois 1940,F 23,19:2
Knute Rockne-All American 1940,O 19,21:2
Sky Murder 1940,N 14,28:3
Singapore Woman 1941,My 12,13:6
Highway West 1941,Ag 8,13:4
Nazi Agent 1942,Je 13,11:2
Hitler-Dead or Alive 1943,Mr 31,23:3
Edge of Darkness 1943,Ap 10,12:4
Crime Doctor 1943,Jl 5,11:4
No Sad Songs for Me 1950,Ap 28,26:2
Asphalt Jungle, The 1950,Je 9,29:3
Men, The 1950,Jl 21,15:2

Tree, Herbert Sir

Macbeth 1916,Je 5,9:1

Tree, Joanne

Mad About Music 1938,Mr 12,13:2
Girls' School 1938,N 3,27:1
Girls Under 21 1940,N 11,22:4

Tree, Lady

Private Life of Henry VIII, The 1933,O 13,25:2
Girl From Maxim's, The 1936,S 16,29:1
Man Who Could Work Miracles, The
1937,F 22,13:1

Tree, Viola (Original Author)

Dancers, The 1925,Ja 26,22:1

Treen, Mary

Happiness Ahead 1934,O 11,28:2
Babbitt 1934,D 17,24:2

Treen, Mary— Cont

Red Hot Tires 1935,Mr 1,16:3
Traveling Saleslady 1935,Mr 29,26:2
Night at the Ritz, A 1935,My 16,20:2
Don't Bet on Blondes 1935,Jl 20,16:2
Page Miss Glory 1935,Ag 29,25:2
Shipmates Forever 1935,O 17,29:3
I Live for Love 1935,O 19,21:2
Case of the Lucky Legs, The 1935,N 1,25:1
Murder of Dr Harrigan, The 1936,Ja 21,27:5
Fish 1936,Ja 25,18:5
Freshman Love 1936,Ja 25,18:5
Colleen 1936,Mr 9,20:2
Brides are Like That 1936,Mr 23,22:5
Murder by an Aristocrat 1936,Je 13,13:2
Jailbreak 1936,Ag 6,22:1
Love Begins at 20 1936,S 19,20:1
God's Country and the Woman 1937,Ja 11,15:5
Fugitive in the Sky 1937,Ja 16,21:1
They Gave Him a Gun 1937,My 14,21:1
Ever Since Eve 1937,Je 25,25:2
Talent Scout 1937,Ag 20,21:3
Dance Charlie Dance 1937,Ag 26,25:2
Second Honeymoon 1937,N 13,11:2
Swing It, Sailor 1937,D 13,23:5
Sally, Irene and Mary 1938,F 26,9:2
Kentucky Moonshine 1938,My 21,9:2
First Love 1939,N 9,27:3
Double Alibi 1940,Mr 11,11:2
Girl in 313 1940,Je 14,25:3
Black Diamonds 1940,S 10,26:6
Kitty Foyle 1941,Ja 9,27:2
Father takes a Wife 1941,S 5,19:3
You Belong to Me 1941,N 29,14:2
Pacific Blackout 1942,Ja 15,25:2
Night Before the Divorce, The 1942,Ap 10,21:3
Great Man's Lady, The 1942,Ap 30,14:3
They all Kissed the Bride 1942,Jl 31,11:1
Between Us Girls 1942,S 25,25:3
They Got Me Covered 1943,Mr 5,20:2
Powers Girl, The 1943,Mr 26,14:2 (In Addenda)
Hit Parade of 1943 1943,Ap 16,24:3
Casanova Brown 1944,S 15,16:1
I Love a Soldier 1944,N 2,22:2
Don Juan Quilligan 1945,Jl 30,16:2
She Wouldn't Say Yes 1946,Ja 12,10:7
From This Day Forward 1946,Ap 20,16:2
It's a Wonderful Life 1946,D 23,19:2
Let's Live a Little 1948,D 10,34:2
Sailor Beware 1952,F 1,17:1
Let's Do It Again 1953,O 14,34:3
Birds and the Bees, The 1956,Ap 23,22:1
Sad Sack, The 1957,N 28,57:1

Treff, Alice

Eines Prinzen Junge Liebe 1934,Mr 24,20:4
Melodie der Liebe 1934,S 17,20:3
Hilde Petersen, Postlagernd 1937,Je 26,20:3 (In
Addenda)
Girls Behind Bars 1950,My 10,41:2
Seven Journeys 1951,Mr 12,20:2

Tregarthen, Jeannette

Holiday Camp 1948,Ja 24,11:2

Tregaskis, Richard (Original Author)

Guadalcanal Diary 1943,N 18,29:1
Force of Arms 1951,Ag 14,20:2
Mission Over Korea 1953,S 19,7:2

Tregaskis, Richard (Screenwriter)

Wild Blue Yonder, The 1952,Ja 2,20:1
Fair Wind to Java 1953,Ag 28,13:3

Tregl, Vaclav

Emperor and the Golem, The 1955,Ja 10,27:4

Trego, Charles (Cinematographer)

Isle of Paradise 1932,Jl 21,15:2

Treherne, Roger

Man Escaped, A 1957,Ag 27,33:2

Treichlinger, Wilhelm M (Screenwriter)

Heidi 1953,D 21,27:2

Trejean, Guy

Parisienne, La 1958,Jl 31,27:1

Trell, Max (Original Author)

Lawyer Man 1932,D 27,10:2
Just This Once 1952,Mr 18,22:3

Trell, Max (Screenwriter)

16 Fathoms Deep 1948,O 7,35:2
New Mexico 1951,Jl 14,7:2
Hell Below Zero 1954,Jl 17,7:3

Tremaine, Kathleen

Lady Vanishes, The 1938,D 26,29:1

Tremaybe, Les (Narrator)

M G M's Big Parade of Comedy 1964,S 24,19:1

Tremayne, Les

Racket, The 1951,D 13,44:2
Francis Goes to West Point 1952,Ag 23,10:2
It Grows on Trees 1952,N 29,11:2
I Love Melvin 1953,Ap 10,18:4
Dream Wife 1953,Jl 30,20:1
War of the Worlds, The 1953,Ag 14,10:2
Man Called Peter, A 1955,Ap 1,22:1
Lieutenant Wore Skirts, The 1956,Ja 12,22:1
Perfect Furlough, The 1959,Ja 22,27:4
Say One for Me 1959,Je 20,11:2
North by Northwest 1959,Jl 28:1
Angry Red Planet, The 1960,My 5,41:2
Story of Ruth, The 1960,Je 18,12:3

Tremayne, Les— Cont
Gallant Hours, The 1960,Je 23,19:4
Fortune Cookie, The 1966,O 20,52:1
Tremper, Will (Director)
That Woman 1968,Jl 19,30:3
Tremper, Will (Producer)
That Woman 1968,Jl 19,30:3
Tremper, Will (Screenwriter)
That Woman 1968,Jl 19,30:3
Trenaman, John
Conqueror Worm, The 1968,Ag 15,46:2
Treneva, N (Screenwriter)
Man of Music 1953,My 11,25:2
Trenholme, Helen
Case of the Howling Dog, The 1934,O 18,26:5
Firebird, The 1934,N 15,25:2
Treniers, The
Girl Can't Help It, The 1957,F 9,12:7
Don't Knock the Rock 1957,F 23,13:1
Trenk, William
Strange Death of Adolf Hitler, The 1943,O 9,11:5
White Tie and Tails 1946,N 8,28:2
I'll Be Yours 1947,F 22,16:2
Corpse came C O D, The 1947,Ag 19,27:2
Exile, The 1947,D 26,22:4
Trenk-Trebitsch, Willy
Eternal Waltz, The; (Ewiger Walzer)
1959,Jl 9,22:1
Trenker, Luis
Peak of Fate 1925,Je 13,10:5
Peaks of Destiny 1927,N 29,31:1
Fight for Matterhorn 1929,Jl 29,23:3
Doomed Battalion, The 1932,Je 11,9:3
Rebel, The 1933,Jl 25,17:2
Sohn der Weissen Berge, Der 1933,O 23,18:3
Kampf um Matterhorn 1938,Ap 18,11:2
Liebesbriefe aus dem Engadin; Love Letters From
the Engadine 1938,D 24,12:2
Challenge, The 1939,O 2,15:2
Giovanni De Medici, The Leader 1940,Ja 5,15:4
Trenker, Luis (Director)
Rebel, The 1933,Jl 25,17:2
Kaiser von Kalifornien, Der 1937,My 8,23:3
Liebesbriefe aus dem Engadin; Love Letters From
the Engadine 1938,D 24,12:2
Challenge, The 1939,O 2,15:2
Giovanni De Medici, The Leader 1940,Ja 5,15:4
Trenker, Luis (Original Author)
Doomed Battalion, The 1932,Je 11,9:3
Rebel, The 1933,Jl 25,17:2
Trenker, Luis (Producer)
Kaiser von Kalifornien, Der 1937,My 8,23:3
Liebesbriefe aus dem Engadin; Love Letters From
the Engadine 1938,D 24,12:2
Giovanni De Medici, The Leader 1940,Ja 5,15:4
Trenker, Luis (Screenwriter)
Giovanni De Medici, The Leader 1940,Ja 5,15:4
Trent, John
Chinese Parrot, The 1928,Ja 2,28:1
Sky Spider, The 1931,Ag 31,11:5
Doctor's Diary, A 1937,F 17,16:4
John Meade's Woman 1937,F 18,19:1
Great Gambini, The 1937,Jl 12,20:4
She's no Lady 1937,Ag 12,14:3
Blossoms On Broadway 1937,D 3,29:2
I Wanted Wings 1941,Mr 27,29:4
Trent, Karen Sue
Garden of Eden 1957,D 18,45:3
Trent, Lee
Falcon out West, The 1944,Mr 18,18:2
Trent, Peter
Earth Cries Out, The; Grido Della Terra, Il
1949,Ag 31,26:2
Dead Woman's Kiss, A 1951,O 6,16:4
Quiet American, The 1958,F 6,24:1
Gioconda, La 1958,O 13,33:4
Trent, Philip
Spy Ring, The 1938,Ja 15,19:1
Let Us Live 1939,Mr 30,19:2
Gangs Incorporated 1941,Ag 4,16:6
Bombay Clipper 1942,Ja 12,23:3
Trento, Guido
Shepherd King, The 1923,D 11,26:2
Street Angel 1928,Ap 10,33:2
Trenton, Pell
Willow Tree, The 1920,F 2,10:1
Treshchalov, Vladimir
Dimka 1964,Mr 21,13:5
Tressler, George (Director)
Merry Wives of Windsor, The 1966,F 28,21:1
Tressler, Hans Jurgel
Episode 1937,My 17,23:2
Tressler, Otto
Liebe und Trompetenklang 1936,Ap 13,15:2
Episode 1937,My 17,23:2
Prinzessin Sissy 1939,Ja 14,13:2
Story of Vickie, The 1958,Ja 30,19:2
Tressler, Wolf Dieter
Episode 1937,My 17,23:2
Tretiakov, V A
Lenin in 1918 1939,Je 27,27:2
Tretow, Annika
Naked Night, The 1956,Ap 10,27:5

Treul, John
Street Corner 1948,D 4,9:4
Trevarthen, Noel
Corruption 1968,D 5,59:1
Trevelyan, H B (Original Author)
Dark Angel, The 1925,O 12,19:3
Trevelyan, Una
Devil's Pass Key, The 1920,Ag 9,6:3
Treville, Roger
Parisian, The 1931,Ag 22,7:5
Slipper Episode, The 1938,My 19,25:2
Mr Peek-A-Boo 1951,S 19,37:1
Green Glove, The 1952,Ap 24,38:1
Happy Road, The 1957,Je 21,20:2
Bride Is Much too Beautiful, The 1958,Ja 21,35:1
Rue de Paris 1960,D 23,14:3
How to Steal a Million 1966,Jl 15,34:1
Trevino, George
Rosario 1936,Ap 20,17:2
Adventures of Casanova 1948,Mr 22,18:3
Brave One, The 1957,Mr 22,26:1
Ride Back, The 1957,Ap 30,24:1
Third Voice, The 1960,Mr 7,24:5
Trevor, Ann
Murder in the Old Red Barn 1936,Ag 19,18:3
Trevor, Austin
Mystery at the Villa Rose 1930,Je 2,25:4
Escape 1930,N 1,23:2
Man From Chicago, The 1931,Ja 16,27:1
Broken Melody, The 1934,O 31,17:3
Mimi 1936,Ja 10,16:3
Spy 77 1936,F 10,15:1
As You Like It 1936,N 6,29:3
Beloved Vagabond, The 1937,F 8,12:5
Knight Without Armor 1937,Jl 9,18:1
Dark Journey 1937,Ag 23,22:1
Goodbye Mr Chips 1939,My 16,27:2
Night Train 1940,D 30,21:1
Anna Karenina 1948,Ap 28,32:2
Champagne Charlie 1948,Ag 7,8:2
Red Shoes, The 1948,O 23,9:2
So Long at the Fair 1951,Ja 22,14:2
Lisbon Story, The 1951,S 6,39:4
To Paris With Love 1955,Mr 29,33:4
Abandon Ship 1957,Ap 18,35:1
Konga 1961,S 16,9:1
Day the Earth Caught Fire, The 1962,Mr 16,25:1
Trevor, Claire
Mad Game, The 1933,N 13,21:1
Jimmy and Sally 1933,D 16,12:3
Hold That Girl 1934,Mr 24,20:3
Baby, Take a Bow 1934,Je 30,18:6
Wild Gold 1934,Jl 24,20:2
Black Sheep 1935,Je 28,34:1
Dante's Inferno 1935,Ag 1,15:1
My Marriage 1936,F 22,12:2
Song and Dance Man 1936,Mr 12,18:2
Human Cargo 1936,My 16,11:2
To Mary-With Love 1936,Ag 27,16:1
Star for a Night 1936,S 5,7:2
Fifteen Maiden Lane 1936,O 17,21:3
Time Out for Romance 1937,Mr 13,23:2
King of Gamblers 1937,Jl 3,18:1
One Mile From Heaven 1937,Ag 19,23:1
Dead End 1937,Ag 25,25:1
Second Honeymoon 1937,N 13,11:2
Big Town Girl 1937,D 13,23:4
Walking Down Broadway 1938,Ap 1,17:3
Amazing Dr Clitterhouse, The 1938,Jl 21,14:2
Valley of the Giants 1938,S 10,20:2
Five of a Kind 1938,O 31,12:2
Stagecoach 1939,Mr 3,21:1
I Stole a Million 1939,Ag 7,11:2
Allegheny Uprising 1939,N 10,27:3
Dark Command 1940,My 11,15:2
Honky Tonk 1941,O 3,27:3
Texas 1941,O 17,27:3
Adventures of Martin Eden 1942,Mr 16,19:2
Crossroads 1942,Jl 27,18:2
Street Of Chance 1942,N 19,31:3
Desperadoes, The 1943,My 13,17:2
Woman of the Town, The 1944,Mr 6,17:2
Murder, my Sweet 1945,Mr 9,16:2
Johnny Angel 1945,D 28,12:2
Crack-Up 1946,S 7,11:1
Bachelor's Daughters, The 1946,O 7,23:2
Born to Kill 1947,My 1,34:2
Raw Deal 1948,Jl 9,11:4
Key Largo 1948,Jl 17,6:6
Babe Ruth Story, The 1948,Jl 29,17:2
Velvet Touch, The 1948,Ag 26,16:2
Lucky Stiff, The 1949,Ja 31,14:2
Borderline 1950,Mr 6,17:2
Hard, Fast and Beautiful 1951,Jl 2,16:6
Best of the Badmen 1951,Ag 10,13:2
Hoodlum Empire 1952,Mr 6,25:6
My Man and I 1952,S 6,12:6
Stop, You're Killing Me 1952,D 11,45:3
Stranger Wore a Gun, The 1953,Jl 30,20:3
High and the Mighty, The 1954,Jl 1,21:2
Man Without a Star 1955,Mr 25,19:3
Lucy Gallant 1955,O 21,30:1
Mountain, The 1956,N 15,44:6

Trevor, Claire— Cont
Marjorie Morningstar 1958,Ap 25,32:2
Two Weeks in Another Town 1962,Ag 18,10:1
Stripper, The 1963,Je 20,29:1
How to Murder Your Wife 1965,Ja 27,26:1
Trevor, Edward
Way Down East 1935,O 31,16:2
Charlie Chan's Secret 1936,Ja 18,19:4
Trevor, Elleston (Original Author)
Dunkirk 1958,S 11,42:2
Flight of the Phoenix, The 1966,F 1,26:1
Trevor, High
Dry Martini 1928,N 5,26:5 (In Addenda)
Trevor, Hugh
Skinner's big Idea 1928,Mr 27,30:4
Beau Broadway 1928,Jl 30,21:2
Red Lips 1928,O 16,29:2 (In Addenda)
Night Parade 1929,N 11,20:2
Cuckoos, The 1930,Ap 26,11:1
Midnight Mystery 1930,Je 2,25:4
Half Shot at Sunrise 1930,O 11,21:3
Pay-Off, The 1930,N 10,16:2
Royal Bed, The 1931,Ja 31,15:1
Trevor, Jack
Oberkellner, Der 1929,Jl 1,31:2
Rasputin: The Holy Devil 1930,Ag 25,14:2
Trevor, Norman
Romance 1920,My 17,19:3
Black Panther's Cub, The 1921,My 30,12:5
Jane Eyre 1922,Ja 29,VI,2:1 (In Addenda)
Wages of Virtue 1924,N 24,15:3
Man Who Found Himself, The 1925,Ag 24,17:3
Song and Dance Man, The 1926,F 1,16:1
Dancing Mothers 1926,F 18,21:1
Beau Geste 1926,Ag 26,17:3
Ace of Cads, The 1926,O 18,18:1 (In Addenda)
Music Master, The 1927,Ja 17,12:4 (In Addenda)
New York 1927,Ja 31,13:1
Afraid to Love 1927,Ap 12,25:3
Children of Divorce 1927,Ap 26,33:3
Sorrell and Son 1927,N 14,26:1
Wizard, The 1927,N 28,18:5
Mad Hour, The 1928,Ap 16,20:5
Restless Youth 1929,Ja 1,60:1
Tonight at Twelve 1929,S 23,24:3
Trevor, Spencer
Congress Dances 1932,My 12,23:2
April Romance 1937,Ja 27,17:4
Treynor, Albert (Original Author)
Rainmakers, The 1935,N 2,13:2
Always in Trouble 1938,N 3,27:1
Dancing Co-Ed 1939,N 10,27:3
Triana, Antonio
Lady and the Monster, The 1944,Ap 8,9:2
Triana, Juan F
Tesoro de Pancho Villa, El 1936,Ja 27,20:4
Trickett, David
Gay Intruders, The 1946,Mr 18,24:2
Trickett, Vicki
Pepe 1960,D 22,18:1
Gidget Goes Hawaiian 1961,Ag 10,17:4
Three Stooges Meet Hercules, The
1962,Ja 27,13:4
Cabinet of Caligari, The 1962,My 26,13:5
Tricoli, Carlo
Black Hand 1950,Mr 13,15:2
Lady Without Passport, A 1950,Ag 4,13:2
Triesault, Ivan
In our Time 1944,F 12,11:2
Uncertain Glory 1944,Ap 8,9:2
Hitler Gang, The 1944,My 8,15:2
Days of Glory 1944,Je 17,10:2
Cry of the Werewolf, The 1944,Ag 12,16:5
Counter-Attack 1945,My 17,15:2
Notorious 1946,Ag 16,19:2
Return of Monte Cristo, The 1947,Ja 3,16:4
Crimson Key, The 1947,O 18,9:2
Golden Earrings 1947,D 4,41:3
To the Ends of the Earth 1948,F 13,26:2
Johnny Allegro 1949,My 31,19:2
Kim 1950,D 8,40:4
Five Fingers 1952,F 23,7:5
Bad and the Beautiful, The 1953,Ja 16,19:1
Young Bess 1953,My 22,31:1
Her Twelve Men 1954,Ag 12,23:2
Buster Keaton Story, The 1957,Ap 22,31:6
Jet Pilot 1957,O 5,8:6
Fraulein 1958,Je 9,27:2
Amazing Transparent Man, The 1961,Mr 30,24:2
300 Spartans, The 1962,S 20,29:2
Barabbas 1962,O 11,49:1
It Happened in Athens 1962,N 15,46:2
Von Ryan's Express 1965,Je 24,28:1
Trieste, Leopoldo
White Sheik, The 1956,Ap 26,37:4
Vitelloni 1956,O 24,43:1
Farewell to Arms, A 1958,Ja 25,14:1
Divorce-Italian Style 1962,S 18,34:1
Seduced and Abandoned 1964,Jl 16,23:1
White Voices; Voci Blanche 1965,Ap 13,32:2
Successo, Il 1965,Ap 29,40:2
Eye of the Needle, The 1965,Je 22,25:2
Shoot Loud, Louder... I Don't Understand
1967,S 21,56:4

Trieste, Leopoldo — Cont
We Still Kill the Old Way 1968,F 29,28:1
Weekend, Italian Style 1968,My 23,56:2
Trieste, Leopoldo (Screenwriter)
Sky Is Red, The 1952,My 27,30:2
Trigger (Horse)
Hollywood Canteen 1944,D 16,19:2
Utah 1945,Mr 12,22:7
My Pal Trigger 1946,Ag 17,16:3
Apache Rose 1947,Jl 23,19:3
Trikonis, Gina
West Side Story 1961,O 19,39:3
Trikonis, Gus
West Side Story 1961,O 19,39:3
Unsinkable Molly Brown, The 1964,Jl 17,15:1
Trimble, A A
Great Ziegfeld, The 1936,Ap 9,21:2
You're a Sweetheart 1937,D 25,10:5
Trimble, Laurence (Director)
Silent Call, The 1922,Ja 30,16:2
Love Master, The 1924,My 19,14:2
Sundown 1924,D 1,17:3
Trind, Charles (Director)
Somewhere in France 1943,Jl 12,11:2
Trindade, Americo
Voyage of Silence 1968,S 12,54:1
Trinder, Tommy
Somewhere in France 1943,Jl 12,11:2
Champagne Charlie 1948,Ag 7,8:2
Trini, Maria
Desaparecido, El 1936,Je 2,25:3
Trinian, John (Original Author)
Any Number Can Win 1963,O 9,47:2
Trinkaus, Hans
Somewhere in Berlin 1949,Ag 16,19:3
Trintignant, Jean-Louis
If all the Guys in the World 1957,Ap 23,34:1
And God Created Woman 1957,O 22,41:1
Violent Summer 1961,My 20,12:1
Liaisons Dangereuses, Les 1961,D 19,39:1
French Game 1963,S 21,13:5
Easy Life, The 1963,D 23,18:2
Chateau en Suede; Castle in Switzerland 1964,O 14,51:1
Successo, Il 1965,Ap 29,40:2
Sleeping Car Murder, The 1966,Mr 8,45:1
Man and a Woman, A; Homme et une Femme, Un 1966,Jl 13,35:1
Trans-Europ-Express 1968,My 13,52:1
Biches, Les 1968,S 27,34:1
Trintiquart, Jean-Louis
Is Paris Burning? 1966,N 11,36:1
Triola, Anne
Without Reservations 1946,Je 8,17:2
Lullaby of Broadway 1951,Mr 27,35:2
Tripp, Paul
Christmas That Almost Wasn't 1966,N 24,65:2
Tripp, Paul (Composer)
Christmas That Almost Wasn't 1966,N 24,65:2
Tripp, Paul (Original Author)
Christmas That Almost Wasn't 1966,N 24,65:2
Tripp, Paul (Screenwriter)
Christmas That Almost Wasn't 1966,N 24,65:2
Triquet, Gaby
Serment, Le 1934,Mr 14,23:2
Maria Chapdelaine 1935,S 25,18:2
Miserables, Les 1936,O 28,31:2
Miserables, Les 1946,D 26,28:4
Trisault, Ivan
Mission to Moscow 1943,Ap 30,25:2
Trivas, Victor (Director)
Hell on Earth 1934,Ja 29,10:2
Song of the Street 1939,S 5,21:2
Head, The 1963,Je 20,29:1
Trivas, Victor (Miscellaneous)
Three Russian Girls 1944,F 5,13:2
Trivas, Victor (Original Author)
Song of Russia 1944,F 11,17:2
Stranger, The 1946,Jl 11,18:2
Trivas, Victor (Screenwriter)
Niemandsland; No Man's Land 1932,Ja 24,VIII,5:1
Song of the Street 1939,S 5,21:2
Mayor's Dilemma, The 1940,Ap 23,19:2
Where the Sidewalk Ends 1950,Jl 8,7:4
Secret of Convict Lake, The 1951,Ag 4,7:2
Head, The 1963,Je 20,29:1
Trivers, Barry (Original Author)
Big Broadcast of 1937, The 1936,O 22,31:1
Tars and Spars 1946,F 15,29:2
Trivers, Barry (Screenwriter)
Night Life of the Gods 1935,F 23,14:6
Lady Tubbs 1935,Jl 22,20:2
Three Kids and a Queen 1935,N 9,19:2
Three Cheers for Love 1936,Ag 1,16:2
Army Girl 1938,Ag 12,11:1
Girl in 313 1940,Je 14,25:3
River's End 1940,Ag 26,11:4
South of Suez 1940,D 19,33:2
Flight From Destiny 1941,Mr 28,26:7
Wagons Roll at Night, The 1941,My 10,20:4
International Squadron 1941,N 14,28:4
Flying Tigers 1942,O 23,25:2
Army Surgeon 1942,N 5,35:2

What a Woman 1943,D 3,27:2
Intrigue 1948,Ap 24,11:2
Trivers, Paul (Screenwriter)
Men In her Life, The 1941,D 12,35:1
Trnka, Jiri (Director)
Emperor's Nightingale, The 1951,My 14,29:1
Hand, The 1966,S 20,39:1
Trnka, Jiri (Miscellaneous)
Midsummer Night's Dream, A 1961,D 19,39:1
Trnka, Jiri (Producer)
Emperor's Nightingale, The 1951,My 14,29:1
Troell, Jan (Director)
Here's Your Life 1968,D 20,60:1
Troell, Jan (Screenwriter)
Here's Your Life 1968,D 20,60:1
Troesch, Robert
Kampf, Der 1936,S 11,29:3
Troglio, Pier Luigi
Fist in his Pocket 1968,My 28,40:1
Troiani, Amalia
Sandra 1966,Ja 17,32:1
Troisi, D (Original Author)
Eye of the Needle, The 1965,Je 22,25:2
Troitsky, S
Othello 1960,My 16,39:1
Troller, Beatrice
Cinerama Holiday 1955,F 9,31:1
Trombetti, Mario (Producer)
Barber of Seville, The 1947,My 6,35:2
Trombetti, Ugo (Producer)
Barber of Seville, The 1947,My 6,35:2
Tromm, Ilse-Nore
Vi Tvaa; We Two 1939,D 2,21:3
Tronson, Robert (Director)
Traitors, The 1963,Je 27,23:4
Ring of Treason 1964,My 28,40:3 (Incorrect in this edition; use 1964,My 29,15:1 elsewhere)
Troobnick, Gene
Harvey Middleman, Fireman 1965,Jl 13,39:1
Trooger, Margot
City of Secrets 1963,Jl 27,10:2
Heidi 1968,S 23,42:4
Trosper, Guy (Original Author)
Girl Trouble 1942,O 8,31:2
Pride of St Louis, The 1952,My 3,17:5
Trosper, Guy (Producer)
Birdman of Alcatraz 1962,Jl 19,19:2
Trosper, Guy (Screenwriter)
I'll Wait for You 1941,Je 2,13:6
Crossroads 1942,Jl 27,18:2
Eyes in the Night 1942,O 16,23:1
Stratton Story, The 1949,My 13,29:1
Devil's Doorway 1950,N 10,35:1
Inside Straight 1951,Mr 16,34:2
Americano, The 1955,Ja 20,35:1
Many Rivers to Cross 1955,F 24,21:2
Girl He Left Behind, The 1956,O 27,17:1
Darby's Rangers 1958,F 13,23:2
One Eyed Jacks 1961,Mr 31,21:1
Birdman of Alcatraz 1962,Jl 19,19:2
Spy Who Came in From the Cold, The 1965,D 24,24:1
Trotter, Charles (Cinematographer)
Mau Mau 1955,Jl 14,19:1
Trotter, John Scott
Rhythm on the River 1940,Ag 29,23:2
Kiss the Boys Goodbye 1941,Ag 14,21:2
Trotti, Lamar (Composer)
Judge Priest 1934,O 12,33:1
Trotti, Lamar (Original Author)
Man Who Dared, The 1933,S 9,9:3
You Can't Buy Everything 1934,F 3,9:2
Hold That Girl 1934,Mr 24,20:3
Wild Gold 1934,Jl 24,20:2
There's no Business Like Show Business 1954,D 17,37:3
Trotti, Lamar (Producer)
Thunder Birds 1942,O 29,19:2
Immortal Sergeant 1943,F 4,29:2
Ox-Bow Incident, The 1943,My 10,15:2 (In Addenda)
Colonel Effingham's Raid 1946,Ap 5,21:3
Mother Wore Tights 1947,Ag 21,33:2
Captain from Castile 1947,D 26,22:4
Walls of Jericho, The 1948,Ag 5,16:2
Yellow Sky 1949,F 2,36:1
You're my Everything 1949,Jl 23,7:2
Cheaper by the Dozen 1950,Ap 1,12:2
American Guerrilla in the Philippines 1950,N 8,37:2
I'd Climb the Highest Mountain 1951,My 10,38:1
As Young as You Feel 1951,Ag 3,10:6
With a Song in my Heart 1952,Ap 5,20:2
Stars and Stripes Forever 1952,D 23,17:2
Trotti, Lamar (Screenwriter)
Life Begins at 40 1935,Ap 5,21:3
Steamboat Around the Bend 1935,S 20,17:2
Gentle Julia 1936,Ap 11,19:1
Country Beyond, The 1936,Ap 30,17:3
Pepper 1936,Ag 24,11:2
Ramona 1936,O 7,32:4
This Is my Affair 1937,My 28,17:1
Slave Ship 1937,Je 17,19:2

Trotti, Lamar (Screenwriter) — Cont
Wife, Doctor and Nurse 1937,O 11,26:5
In Old Chicago 1938,Ja 7,15:2
Baroness and the Butler, The 1938,F 19,19:2
Alexander's Ragtime Band 1938,Ag 6,7:2
Gateway 1938,Ag 8,9:2
Kentucky 1938,D 24,12:1
Story of Alexander Graham Bell, The 1939,Ap 1,17:2
Young Mr Lincoln 1939,Je 3,11:2
Drums Along the Mohawk 1939,N 4,11:2
Brigham Young - Frontiersman 1940,S 21,13:2
Hudson's Bay 1941,Ja 10,23:2
Belle Starr 1941,N 1,20:2
To the Shores of Tripoli 1942,Mr 26,27:2
Tales of Manhattan 1942,S 25,25:1
Thunder Birds 1942,O 29,19:2
Immortal Sergeant 1943,F 4,29:2
Ox-Bow Incident, The 1943,My 10,15:2 (In Addenda)
Guadalcanal Diary 1943,N 18,29:1
Wilson 1944,Ag 2,18:1
Bell for Adano, A 1945,Jl 6,8:3
Razor's Edge, The 1946,N 20,42:2
Mother Wore Tights 1947,Ag 21,33:2
Captain from Castile 1947,D 26,22:4
Walls of Jericho, The 1948,Ag 5,16:2
When my Baby Smiles at Me 1948,N 24,20:2
Yellow Sky 1949,F 2,36:1
You're my Everything 1949,Jl 23,7:2
Cheaper by the Dozen 1950,Ap 1,12:2
My Blue Heaven 1950,S 16,12:6
American Guerrilla in the Philippines 1950,N 8,37:2
I'd Climb the Highest Mountain 1951,My 10,38:1
As Young as You Feel 1951,Ag 3,10:6
With a Song in my Heart 1952,Ap 5,20:2
O Henry's Full House (The Gift of the Magi); Gift of the Magi, The (O Henry's Full House) 1952,O 17,33:1
O Henry's Full House (The Last Leaf 1952,O 17,33:1
O Henry's Full House (The Cop and the Anthem); Cop and the Anthem, The (O Henry's Full House) 1952,O 17,33:1
O Henry's Full House (The Clarion Call); Clarion Call, The (O Henry's Full House) 1952,O 17,33:1
Stars and Stripes Forever 1952,D 23,17:2
Trotz, Adolf (Director)
Elisabeth von Oesterreich 1931,D 11,35:1
Tatras Zauber 1933,F 18,13:4
Troubetskoy
Savage Brigade 1948,D 3,33:4
Troubetzkoy, Youcca
Flower of the Night 1925,O 19,26:1
His Glorious Night 1929,O 5,22:5
Chasing Rainbows 1930,F 22,13:1
Trouche, Adolfo
Messalina 1924,Ag 25,16:2
Troughton, Patrick
Hamlet 1948,S 30,32:2
Treasure Island 1950,Ag 16,24:2
Chance of a Lifetime 1951,Mr 15,37:2
Black Knight, The 1954,O 29,27:2
Richard III 1956,Mr 12,1:4
Trouncer, Cecil
Guinea Pig, The 1949,My 2,20:2
Saraband 1949,Je 13,16:3
While the Sun Shines 1950,Jl 1,9:2
Troup, Bobby
High Cost of Loving, The 1958,My 17,12:1
Five Pennies, The 1959,Je 19,30:1
Troupe, Thomas
Big Fisherman, The 1959,Ag 6,18:1
Troupe, Tom
Sofi 1968,Mr 28,52:3
Troupe, Tom (Screenwriter)
Sofi 1968,Mr 28,52:3
Trout, Francis
Scattergood Baines 1941,Ap 4,25:2
Trout, Tom
Main Street After Dark 1945,Ja 13,15:4
Between Two Women 1945,Mr 29,18:3
Merton of the Movies 1947,N 7,20:3
Trovajoli, Armando
Yesterday, Today and Tomorrow (Part II-Anna Milan); Anna Milan (Yesterday, Today and Tomorrow) 1964,Mr 18,46:1
Trovato, Carmela
Path of Hope, The (Il Cammino Della Speranza) 1952,Ag 5,15:5
Trowbridge, Charles
Thais 1917,D 31,5:2
Damaged Love 1931,Ja 19,25:1
I Take This Woman 1931,Je 13,20:4
Secret Call, The 1931,Jl 13,13:5
Silence 1931,Ag 15,18:3
Rendezvous 1935,O 26,12:2
Exclusive Story 1936,Ja 18,19:2
Garden Murder Case, The 1936,Mr 2,13:2
Robin Hood of El Dorado, The 1936,Mr 14,10:1
Moonlight Murder 1936,Mr 28,11:2
We Went to College 1936,Jl 27,20:2

Trowbridge, Charles— Cont
Gorgeous Hussy, The 1936,S 5,7:1
Libeled Lady 1936,O 31,24:2
Dangerous Number 1937,Mr 12,19:2
They Gave Him a Gun 1937,My 14,21:1
Thirteenth Chair, The 1937,Je 18,25:3
That Certain Woman 1937,S 16,29:1
Sea Racketeers 1937,O 4,17:2
Alcatraz Island 1937,O 14,22:2
Fit for a King 1937,O 15,18:5
Saturday's Heroes 1937,O 16,22:2
Invisible Menace, The 1938,F 14,20:6
Patient in Room 18, The 1938,Ap 22,15:6
Gangs of New York 1938,My 28,9:2
Crime Ring 1938,Jl 22,10:3
Last Express, The 1938,O 11,24:4
Submarine Patrol 1938,N 19,9:2
Thanks For Everything 1938,D 10,13:2
Kentucky 1938,D 24,12:1
Cafe Society 1939,F 23,19:2
King of Chinatown 1939,Mr 16,27:2
Risky Business 1939,Mr 23,27:2
Sergeant Madden 1939,Mr 24,27:2
Story of Alexander Graham Bell, The
    1939,Ap 1,17:2
Each Dawn I Die 1939,Jl 22,12:2
Mutiny on the Blackhawk 1939,Ag 2,17:2
Lady of the Tropics 1939,S 8,28:3
Tropic Fury 1939,S 8,28:4
Swanee River 1939,D 30,9:2
Fighting 69th, The 1940,Ja 27,9:2
House of the Seven Gables, The 1940,Ap 15,21:3
My Love Came Back 1940,Jl 13,16:5
Mummy's Hand, The 1940,S 20,27:2
Cherokee Strip 1940,N 4,23:2
Trail of the Vigilantes 1940,D 7,13:2
Great Lie, The 1941,Ap 12,19:2
Strange Alibi 1941,Ap 28,11:2
Nurse's Secret, The 1941,Je 6,25:7
Sergeant York 1941,Jl 3,15:1
Dressed to Kill 1941,Ag 22,19:3
Great Guns 1941,O 3,27:2
Belle Starr 1941,N 1,20:2
Cadet Girl 1941,D 11,39:1
Who Is Hope Schuyler 1942,My 22,27:1
Ten Gentlemen From West Point 1942,Je 5,23:3
Over my Dead Body 1942,D 26,15:2
Tennessee Johnson 1943,Ja 13,18:2
Action in the North Atlantic 1943,My 22,10:2
Heavenly Days 1944,O 21,15:2
Mildred Pierce 1945,S 29,12:2
They Were Expendable 1945,D 21,25:2
Shock 1946,Mr 9,10:2
Hoodlum Saint, The 1946,Je 27,29:1
Undercurrent 1946,N 29,36:2
Beginning or the End, The 1947,F 21,15:1
Mr District Attorney 1947,F 28,27:3
Sea of Grass, The 1947,F 28,27:2
Tarzan and the Huntress 1947,Ap 7,20:4
Shoot to Kill 1947,My 17,8:5
Key Witness 1947,Jl 30,27:6
Black Gold 1947,S 5,16:4
Tycoon 1947,D 26,22:6
Song of my Heart 1948,My 5,17:3
Hollow Triumph 1948,O 29,29:5
Paleface, The 1948,D 16,41:2
Bad Boy 1949,Mr 23,35:2
Trowe, Gisela
Affair Blum, The 1949,O 18,35:2
Troy, Helen
Song and Dance Man 1936,Mr 12,18:2
Human Cargo 1936,My 16,11:2
Born to Dance 1936,D 5,16:1
Between Two Women 1937,Ag 6,21:1
Broadway Melody of 1938 1937,S 3,12:1
Big City 1937,S 17,29:2
Thoroughbreds Don't Cry 1937,N 26,27:4
Everybody Sing 1938,Mr 11,15:3
Kid Nightingale 1939,D 8,33:6
Troy, Louise
Swimmer, The 1968,My 16,53:1
Troy, Una (Original Author)
She Didn't Say No 1963,Jl 30,18:1
Troy, Una (Screenwriter)
She Didn't Say No 1963,Jl 30,18:1
Troyanofsky, N
Sadko 1953,Je 1,18:6
Troyanovsky, M
On his Own 1939,S 13,31:3
Chuk and Gek 1953,D 21,27:4
Othello 1960,My 16,39:1
Troyanovsky, M G
Childhood of Maxim Gorky 1938,S 28,29:3
Troyanovsky, Maek (Cinematographer)
Conquerors of the Arctic 1937,N 22,15:2
Troyanovsky, Mark
Miles of Fire 1958,N 10,36:6 (In Addenda)
Lullaby, The 1961,My 15,35:2
Troyanovsky, Mikhail
Guerrilla Brigade 1942,Ap 14,17:2
Stone Flower 1946,D 30,15:2
Troyat, Henri (Miscellaneous)
Fire in the Straw 1943,Jl 2,15:2

Troyat, Henri (Original Author)
Fire in the Straw 1943,Jl 2,15:2
Mountain, The 1956,N 15,44:6
Troyat, Henri (Screenwriter)
Sheep Has Five Legs, The 1955,Ag 10,19:2
Big Chief, The 1960,Ap 27,32:1
Truax, John
Fuzzy Pink Nightgown, The 1957,O 31,41:1
Truax, Maude
Up in Mabel's Room 1926,Je 29,21:2
Ten Modern Commandments 1927,Jl 11,23:4
Hula 1927,Ag 29,21:1
Two Against the World 1932,Ag 19,20:6
I Have Lived 1933,S 6,24:4
Dancing Man 1934,Jl 16,11:3
Trubshawe, Michael
Encore (The Ant and the Grasshopper); Ant and
    the Grasshopper, The (Encore) 1952,Ap 3,45:1
Brandy for the Parson 1952,Ag 18,13:4
Tonight at 8:30 (Ways and Means); Ways and
    Means (Tonight at 8:30) 1953,My 26,33:2
Something Money Can't Buy 1953,O 1,34:3
Titfield Thunderbolt, The 1953,O 6,34:2
Rising of the Moon, The (A Minute's Wait);
    Minute's Wait, A (The Rising of the Moon)
    1957,Jl 10,23:1
Law and Disorder 1958,Ag 6,20:1
Gideon of Scotland Yard 1959,My 20,38:2
Scent of Mystery 1960,F 19,23:1
Guns of Navarone, The 1961,Je 23,19:1
Best of Enemies, The 1962,Ag 7,35:2
Operation Snatch 1962,S 25,31:4
Mouse on the Moon, The 1963,Je 18,32:1
Reach for Glory 1963,S 10,46:1
True, Bess
Sailors' Wives 1928,F 28,18:4
True, Pauline
Desirable 1934,S 15,20:5
Trueman, Paula
Crime Without Passion 1934,S 1,16:2
One Foot in Heaven 1941,N 14,28:3
TRUESDALE
See Also TRUESDELL
Truesdale, Howard
Ashes of Vengeance 1923,Ag 7,20:2
Reno 1924,Ja 8,27:1
Why Men Leave Home 1924,My 12,14:4
Go West 1925,O 26,25:2
Burning Daylight 1928,Ap 23,20:2
TRUESDELL
See Also TRUESDALE
Truesdell, Frederick
Shadows 1919,F 10,11:3
Love Piker, The 1923,Jl 16,14:2
Pleasure Mad 1924,Ja 7,23:1
Truesdell, June (Original Author)
Accused, The 1949,Ja 13,26:2
Truex, Barry
Benny Goodman Story 1956,F 22,22:1
Truex, Ernest
Come On In 1918,S 23,7:1
Night of the Pub, The 1920,Ja 26,16:1
Whistling in the Dark 1933,F 5,IX,5:1
Warrior's Husband, The 1933,My 12,20:4
Start Cheering 1938,Mr 17,17:3
Swing That Cheer 1938,N 11,31:2
Ambush 1939,F 9,17:2
It's a Wonderful World 1939,My 19,27:2
Bachelor Mother 1939,Je 30,17:2
Under-Pup, The 1939,S 5,21:2
Little Accident 1939,N 24,29:3
His Girl Friday 1940,Ja 12,13:2
Slightly Honorable 1940,My 17,23:4
Lillian Russell 1940,My 18,11:2
Dance, Girl, Dance 1940,O 11,25:2
Christmas in July 1940,N 6,35:2
Unexpected Uncle 1941,S 25,29:1
Twin Beds 1942,My 1,23:4
Private Buckaroo 1942,Je 25,27:4
Star Spangled Rhythm 1942,D 31,20:1
Crystal Ball, The 1943,F 19,22:2
True to Life 1943,O 14,26:1
Chip off the Old Block 1944,Mr 17,14:2
Her Primitive Man 1944,Ap 1,11:1
Pan-Americana 1945,Mr 23,13:2
Men in her Diary 1945,S 24,16:5
Night in Paradise 1946,Je 6,16:3
Always Together 1947,D 11,46:1
Leather Saint, The 1956,Je 16,12:2
Twilight for the Gods 1958,Ag 7,21:1
Adventures of Marco Polo, The 1965,Ap 8,17:2
Fluffy 1965,O 21,57:2
Truex, Lizanne
Oklahoma! 1955,O 11,49:1
Truex, Philip
Trouble With Harry, The 1955,O 18,46:2
Trufanoff, Sergios
Fall of the Romanoffs, The 1917,S 7,9:2
Fall of the Romanoffs, The 1917,S 24,11:2
Truffaut, Francois
Love at Twenty 1963,F 7,5:6

Truffaut, Francois (Director)
400 Blows, The; (Les Quatre Cents Coups)
    1959,N 17,41:1
Jules and Jim 1962,Ap 24,32:1
Shoot the Piano Player 1962,Jl 24,19:1
Soft Skin, The; Peau Douce, La 1964,O 13,49:2
Fahrenheit 451 1966,N 15,53:1
Bride Wore Black, The 1968,Je 26,42:1
Truffaut, Francois (Miscellaneous)
army Game, The; Tire Au Flanc 1963,Ap 24,40:1
Bride Wore Black, The 1968,Je 26,42:1
Truffaut, Francois (Original Author)
Breathless 1961,F 8,26:1
Truffaut, Francois (Producer)
400 Blows, The; (Les Quatre Cents Coups)
    1959,N 17,41:1
Jules and Jim 1962,Ap 24,32:1
Truffaut, Francois (Screenwriter)
400 Blows, The; (Les Quatre Cents Coups)
    1959,N 17,41:1
Jules and Jim 1962,Ap 24,32:1
Shoot the Piano Player 1962,Jl 24,19:1
Army Game, The; Tire Au Flanc
    1963,Ap 24,40:1
Soft Skin, The; Peau Douce, La 1964,O 13,49:2
Fahrenheit 451 1966,N 15,53:1
Bride Wore Black, The 1968,Je 26,42:1
Truhitte, Daniel
Sound of Music, The 1965,Mr 3,34:1
Trujillo, Adelita
Newspaper Boys, The 1937,N 6,14:3
Truman, Michael (Director)
Touch and go 1956,Mr 20,13:2
Model Murder Case, The 1964,N 25,45:1
Truman, Michael (Producer)
High and Dry 1954,Ag 31,25:5
Divided Heart, The 1955,Ag 4,16:1
His Excellency 1956,F 2,19:3
Truman, Ralph
Mr Cohen Takes a Walk 1936,F 13,25:2
Dinner at the Ritz 1937,D 4,21:1
Father O'Flynn 1938,D 26,29:2
Saint in London, The 1939,Jl 19,23:3
Outsider, The 1940,Mr 18,13:2
Henry V 1946,Je 18,30:2
Beware of Pity 1947,N 1,11:2
Smugglers, The 1948,Mr 29,17:1
Christopher Columbus 1949,O 13,33:2
Mrs Fitzherbert 1950,My 11,37:2
Treasure Island 1950,Ag 16,24:2
Massacre Hill 1950,D 14,51:3
Interrupted Journey 1951,My 29,20:2
Oliver Twist 1951,Jl 31,17:2
Lisbon Story, The 1951,S 6,39:4
Quo Vadis 1951,N 9,22:2
Master of Ballantrae, The 1953,Ag 6,16:2
Golden Coach, The 1954,Ja 22,30:2
Malta Story 1954,Jl 17,7:2
Beau Brummell 1954,O 21,31:5
Night my Number Came up, The 1955,D 20,39:5
Man Who Knew too Much, The 1956,My 17,37:1
Ship That Died of Shame, The 1956,Ag 21,33:2
Third Key, The 1957,Je 3,30:2
Cid, El 1961,D 15,49:1
Trumbo, Dalton (Original Author)
Kid From Kokomo, The 1939,My 20,11:2
Lone Wolf Strikes, The 1940,F 5,13:2
You Belong to Me 1941,N 29,14:2
Remarkable Andrew, The 1942,Mr 6,17:2
Emergency Wedding 1950,D 22,19:2
Trumbo, Dalton (Screenwriter)
Road Gang 1936,F 24,14:1
Love Begins at 20 1936,S 19,20:1
Devil's Playground 1937,F 15,12:5
Fugitives for a Night 1938,S 21,30:4
Man to Remember, A 1938,N 7,23:2
Flying Irishman, The 1939,Ap 12,27:2
Five came Back 1939,Jl 5,20:2
Career 1939,Jl 28,14:2
Curtain Call 1940,Ap 19,25:2
Bill of Divorcement, A 1940,Jl 12,11:2
We Who Are Young 1940,S 13,27:2
Kitty Foyle 1941,Ja 9,27:2
Remarkable Andrew, The 1942,Mr 6,17:2
Guy Named Joe, A 1943,D 24,17:2
Tender Comrade 1944,Je 2,21:2
Thirty Seconds Over Tokyo 1944,N 16,19:1
Our Vines Have Tender Grapes 1945,S 7,21:2
Spartacus 1960,O 7,28:1
Exodus 1960,D 16,44:1
Last Sunset, The 1961,Je 15,51:1
Lonely are the Brave 1962,Je 28,21:2
Sandpiper, The 1965,Jl 16,14:1
Hawaii 1966,O 11,54:1
Fixer, The 1968,D 9,59:1
Trumbull, John
Spies of the Air 1940,Jl 4,12:3
Trumbull, Walter (Original Author)
Bits of Life 1921,O 17,18:1
Trumps (dog)
Winter's Tale, A 1922,Ja 23,11:4
Western Ways 1922,Ja 30,16:2

Trumps (Dog)
My Rural Relations 1922,D 24,VII,2:2 (In Addenda)

Trundy, Natalie
Careless Years, The 1957,N 28,57:3
Monte Carlo Story, The 1958,F 13,23:2
Mr Hobbs Takes a Vacation 1962,Je 16,11:2

Trustman, Alan R (Screenwriter)
Thomas Crown Affair, The 1968,Je 27,48:2
Bullitt 1968,O 18,41:2

Tryon, Glenn
Battling Orioles, The 1924,N 4,24:1
Painting the Town 1927,Ag 2,19:2
Two Girls Wanted 1927,N 14,26:1
Hero for a Night, A 1927,D 26,26:6
Thanks For The Buggy Ride 1928,Ja 23,18:3
Hot Heels 1928,My 22,19:3
How to Handle Women 1928,Je 18,13:2
Lonesome 1928,O 2,23:5
Broadway 1929,My 28,36:2
Skinner Steps Out 1929,D 7,19:3
Dames Ahoy 1930,Mr 29,23:1
King of Jazz 1930,My 3,23:1
Daybreak 1931,Je 1,15:1
Sky Spider, The 1931Ag 31,11:5
Big Pay-Off, The 1933,Ja 17,22:7
George White's Scandals 1945,O 11,26:2
Variety Girl 1947,O 16,34:4
Laurel and Hardy's Laughing 20's 1965,N 18,55:2

Tryon, Glenn (Director)
Two in Revolt 1936,Ap 25,21:1
Law West of Tombstone, The 1938,N 25,19:1
Beauty for the Asking 1939,F 10,19:1
That Nazty Nuisance 1943,My 29,10:3

Tryon, Glenn (Miscellaneous)
Roberta 1935,Mr 8,25:2
Daring Young Man, The 1935,Jl 18,15:2
Orchids to You 1935,Ag 10,16:4

Tryon, Glenn (Producer)
Devil With Hitler, The 1942,O 19,15:2
That Nazty Nuisance 1943,My 29,10:3
Calaboose 1943,Jl 30,19:2

Tryon, Tom
Three Violent People 1957,F 11,34:2
Unholy Wife, The 1958,Mr 7,17:1
Marines, Lets Go! 1961,Ag 16,37:2
Moon Pilot 1962,Ap 6,30:2
Longest Day, The 1962,O 5,28:1
In Harm's Way 1965,Ap 7,36:1

Trystan, Leon (Director)
Pietro Wyzej; Apartment Above 1938,Ja 10,13:4

Trzcinski, Edmund
Stalag 17 1953,Jl 2,19:2

Trzcinski, Edmund (Original Author)
Stalag 17 1953,Jl 2,19:2

Tsaganea, N
Loves of a Greek in Paris 1960,Ag 15,19:7

Tsaganea, Nitsa
Germans Strike Again, The 1949,Ap 14,29:4

Tsaganeas, Costas
Germans Strike Again, The 1949,Ap 14,29:4

Tsagareli, A (Original Author)
Keto and Kote 1954,Ap 5,21:4

Tsagareli, C (Original Author)
They Wanted Peace 1940,Ja 8,11:3

Tsahaneas, Christos
Wind of Hate; (O Anemos Tou Missous) 1958,N 17,37:2

Tsaref, M I
Thunderstorm 1934,S 29,12:2

Tsarlov, Mikhail
Poem of the Sea 1959,D 21,34:4

Tschechowa, Olga
Tatjana 1927,My 18,29:3
Aftermath 1927,D 6,27:1
When Duty Calls 1929,Ja 1,60:1
After the Verdict 1930,Ja 18,21:1
Liebe im Ring 1930,Ag 11,13:1
Darling of the Gods; Liebling der Gotter 1930,N 30,IX,6:5
Two Neckties; Zwei Kravatten 1930,N 30,IX,6:5
Maedel von der Reeperbahn, Das 1931,Ja 31,15:1
Grosse Tenor, Der 1931,My 29,26:5
Drei von ver Tankstelle, Die 1931,Je 20,20:4
Horse Ate the Hat, The 1931,S 1,30:6
Die Galavorstellung 1933,D 11,23:4
Ein Gewisser Herr Gran 1934,F 24,18:5
Trenck 1934,Ap 7,19:2
Heideschulmeister uwe Karsten 1934,Ap 14,18:3
Choral von Leuthen, Der 1935,Ja 21,19:4
Was Bin Ich Ohne dich? 1935,D 14,11:2
Zwichen Zwei Herzen; Between Two Hearts 1936,Ja 28,15:3
Liebelei 1936,F 28,18:2
Liebe und Trompetenklang 1936,Ap 13,15:2
Masquerade in Vienna 1937,Ja 26,16:4
Freuhling im Wien 1937,F 6,15:2
Vienna Burgtheater 1937,O 27,47:1
Seine Tochter Ist der Peter; His Daughter is Peter 1938,Mr 28,19:3
Rote Orchideen; Red Orchids 1939,Ap 15,15:2
Peer Gynt 1939,N 11,12:2
Favorit der Kaiserin, Der; Favorite of the Empress, The 1939,D 25,29:3

Befreite Hande; Freed Hans 1940,My 25,20:1
Leidenschaft; Passion 1940,S 24,26:6

Tschihaya, A
Slums of Tokyo 1930,Jl 7,22:3

Tschiya, Yasuo
Angry Island 1960,F 28,31:1

Tse, Fong Yi (Producer)
Maid of Formosa 1949,Ag 8,10:5

Tse-Hou, Lin
Maid of Formosa 1949,Ag 8,10:5

Tseitlin, M (Screenwriter)
One Day in Soviet Russia 1941,O 27,21:2

Tsekhanovsky, M (Director)
Leningrad Music Hall 1943,N 6,16:3

Tselikovskaya, Ludmila
Taxi to Heaven 1944,My 25,16:3
Four Hearts 1946,F 25,21:5
Ivan the Terrible, Part I 1947,Mr 10,25:2
Twins 1947,Jl 28,12:2
Grasshopper, The 1956,Ap 23,22:1

Tsenin, Sergei
Life in Bloom 1949,My 9,20:4

Tserodze, D
Magdana's Donkey 1958,Ja 27,21:7

Tsessarskaya, Emma
Village of Sin, The 1929,My 21,29:3
Grain 1936,Ja 16,25:2

Tsiang, H S
Black Gold 1947,S 5,16:4

Tsiang, H T
Purple Heart, The 1944,Mr 9,15:2

Tsien, Marie
Love Is a Many-Splendored Thing 1955,Ag 19,10:1

Tsiforos, M (Director)
Wind of Hate; (O Anemos Tou Missous) 1958,N 17,37:2

Tsiforos, N (Screenwriter)
Wind of Hate; (O Anemos Tou Missous) 1958,N 17,37:2
Castle in Greece 1960,D 12,38:2

Tsignadze, Vera
Ballet of Othello, The 1964,My 4,35:1

Tsishevsky, V
Peter Vinogradof 1935,Je 28,24:1

Tsitsishvill, Tsitsino
Stepchildren 1962,Jl 2,22:2

Tslang, H T
Chicken every Sunday 1949,Ja 19,34:2
Panic in the Streets 1950,Ag 5,9:2
Smuggler's Island 1951,My 24,47:2

Tsu, Irene
China 1943,Ap 22,31:2
How to Stuff a Wild Bikini 1967,Ja 12,48:1
Caprice 1967,Je 8,52:2
Green Berets, The 1968,Je 20,49:1
Green Berets, The 1968,Je 20,49:2

Tsuchiya, Yoshio
Magnificent Seven, The 1956,N 20,46:2
Red Beard 1968,D 20,60:4

Tsukamoto, Raynum K
Teahouse of the August Moon, The 1956,N 30,19:1

Tsukasa, Yoko
Girl in the Mist 1959,D 23,22:1
Challenge to Live 1964,Ap 8,33:1
Saga of the Vagabonds 1964,O 7,31:1 (Incorrect in this edition; use 1964,O 7,51:1 elsewhere)
Blue Beast, The 1965,Ja 30,18:2
Rebellion 1967,S 25,56:4
Kojiro 1968,Ag 30,23:1
Rebellion 1968,O 26,27:4

Tsukida, Masayuki
Hiroshima 1955,My 17,32:1

Tsukioka, Yumeji
Hiroshima 1955,My 17,32:1
Temptress and the Monk, The 1963,My 28,32:1

Tsuruta, Koji
Saga of the Vagabonds 1964,O 7,31:1 (Incorrect in this edition; use 1964,O 7,51:1 elsewhere)
Samurai (Part II) 1967,O 21,16:1
Secret Scrolls-Part I 1968,My 9,54:3
Secret Scrolls-Part II; Ninjitsu 1968,My 23,56:3

Tsuruta, Yosan
Tokyo Joe 1949,O 27,35:2

Tsuruya, Namboko (Original Author)
Illusion of Blood 1968,N 28,66:5

Tsushima, Keiko
Magnificent Seven, The 1956,N 20,46:2

Tsuyuguchi, Shigeru
Unholy Desire 1964,N 18,54:1

Tsuyuguchi, Shoichi
Insect Woman, The; Nippon Konchuki 1964,Jl 1,42:1

Tu, L
Fight to the Last 1938,D 22,25:3

Tua(orang_utan
Rango 1931,F 19,20:4

Tual, Denise (Director)
Days of our Years 1951,D 6,42:2

Tual, Denise (Producer)
Days of our Years 1951,D 6,42:2

Tual, Roland (Director)
Days of our Years 1951,D 6,42:2

Tual, Roland (Producer)
Angels of the Streets 1950,Ja 17,24:2
Days of our Years 1951,D 6,42:2

Tubb, Dick
Old Curiosity Shop, The 1935,D 23,15:5

Tubbs, William
Paisan 1948,Mr 30,26:2
Pirates of Capri, The 1949,D 26,33:5
Three Steps North 1951,Je 29,14:2
Quo Vadis 1951,N 9,22:2
Edward and Caroline 1952,Ap 30,33:3
Singing Taxi Driver 1953,My 16,10:1
Greatest Love, The 1954,Ja 12,19:2
Golden Coach, The 1954,Ja 22,30:2
Wages of Fear, The 1955,F 17,23:1

Tucherer, Eugene (Producer)
Cat, The 1959,Ap 13,35:1

Tuchman, Barbara W (Original Author)
Guns of August, The 1964,D 25,24:2

Tuchock, Wanda (Director)
Finishing School 1934,Ap 30,11:4

Tuchock, Wanda (Original Author)
Bed of Roses 1933,Je 30,20:3

Tuchock, Wanda (Screenwriter)
Hallelujah 1929,Ag 21,33:1
O'Shaughnessy's Boy 1935,O 5,18:2
Hawaii Calls 1938,Ap 29,17:2
Youth Will Be Served 1940,N 15,25:2
ThIs is the Life 1944,Ap 28,23:3
Sunday Dinner for a Soldier 1945,Ja 25,16:2
Nob Hill 1945,Jl 4,10:3
Within These Walls 1945,Jl 16,8:4
Homestretch, The 1947,Ap 24,30:2
Foxes of Harrow, The 1947,S 25,35:4

Tucker, Augusta (Original Author)
Miss Susie Slagle's 1946,F 7,29:2

Tucker, Ed
Broadway Bill 1934,N 30,22:2

Tucker, Forrest
Westerner, The 1940,O 25,25:2
New Wine 1942,F 2,11:2
Canal Zone 1942,Mr 30,21:2
Parachute Nurse 1942,Jl 27,18:2
Counter-Espionage 1942,S 28,13:2
Keeper of the Flame 1943,Mr 19,15:2
Renegades 1946,Jl 11,18:2
Never Say Goodbye 1946,N 23,12:2
Yearling, The 1947,Ja 24,18:2
Gunfighters 1947,Jl 25,12:5
Two Guys From Texas 1948,Ag 28,8:6
Plunders, The 1948,N 1,28:2
Last Bandit, The 1949,Mr 21,19:2
Hellfire 1949,My 30,9:4
Big Cat, The 1949,Jl 29,12:2
Brimstone 1949,O 7,35:3
Sands of Iwo Jima 1949,D 31,9:2
Nevadan, The 1950,Ja 13,19:4
Rock Island Trail 1950,Je 5,19:3
California Passage 1950,D 16,10:5
Oh! Susanna 1951,Mr 30,28:5
Fighting Coast Guard 1951,My 12,14:6
Warpath 1951,N 23,32:2
Crosswinds 1951,D 7,35:4
Wild Blue Yonder, The 1952,Ja 2,20:1
Bugles in the Afternoon 1952,Mr 5,32:2
Hoodlum Empire 1952,Mr 6,25:6
Hurricane Smith 1952,O 4,15:2
Montana Belle 1952,N 8,9:2
Pony Express 1953,Je 6,8:6
Flight Nurse 1954,Ja 30,9:6
Jubilee Trail 1954,My 1,13:3
Laughing Anne 1954,My 8,15:2
Trouble in the Glen 1955,Ap 11,29:2
Finger Man 1955,Jl 16,12:4
Three Violent People 1957,F 11,34:2
Auntie Mame 1958,D 5,39:1
Crawling Eye, The 1959,Ja 1,38:1
Cosmic Monster, The 1959,Ja 1,38:1
Night They Raided Minsky's, The 1968,D 23,43:1

Tucker, George Loane (Director)
Virtuous Wives 1918,D 30,7:3
Ladies Must Live 1921,N 21,20:1

Tucker, George Loane (Screenwriter)
Ladies Must Live 1921,N 21,20:1

Tucker, Harland
Kid Galahad 1937,My 27,21:3
Slim 1937,Je 24,30:2
Missing Witness 1937,D 10,33:3
Invisible Menace, The 1938,F 14,20:6
Patient in Room 18, The 1938,Ap 22,15:6
King of the Underworld 1939,Ja 7,6:2
Lone Wolf Strikes, The 1940,F 5,13:2
Road to Happiness 1942,Mr 27,27:4
Hit Parade of 1947 1947,My 5,32:8
Foreign Affair, A 1948,Jl 1,19:3
Beyond Glory 1948,Ag 4,18:2

Tucker, Jerry
Prosperity 1932,N 26,11:4
Hello, Everybody 1933,Ja 30,9:4
Sitting Pretty 1933,D 2,9:3

Tucker, Jerry— Cont

Captain January 1936,Ap 25,21:1
Federal Man-Hunt 1939,F 2,17:3

Tucker, Larry

Blast of Silence 1961,D 30,12:1
Shock Corridor 1963,S 12,32:1

Tucker, Larry (Producer)

I Love You Alice B Toklas! 1968,O 8,40:1

Tucker, Larry (Screenwriter)

I Love You Alice B Toklas! 1968,O 8,40:1

Tucker, Melville (Producer)

Black Shield of Falworth, The 1954,O 7,16:2

Tucker, Orrin

You're the One 1941,F 20,23:2

Tucker, Richard

Old Nest, The 1921,Je 29,10:3
Poor Men's Wives 1923,Ja 29,11:1
Broken Wing, The 1923,O 9,17:4
Beau Brummell 1924,Mr 31,20:1
Fast Worker, The 1924,N 12,13:1
Tornado, The 1924,D 15,14:1
Man Without a Country, The 1925,F 12,16:1
Air Mail, The 1925,Mr 17,18:1
Bridge of Sighs, The 1925,Mr 23,14:2
Golden Cocoon, The 1925,D 15,14:5
Blind Goddess 1926,Ap 6,26:4 (In Addenda)
That's My Baby 1926,Ap 12,18:4
Devil's Island 1926,Ag 2,21:2
Kiss in a Taxi, A 1927,Mr 15,29:2
Matinee Ladies 1927,Ap 13,29:4
Dearie 1927,Jl 4,20:3
Wings 1927,Ag 13,10:4
Desired Woman, The 1927,Ag 30,21:3
Jazz Singer, The 1927,O 7,24:4
Women's Wares 1927,N 15,27:1
Thanks For The Buggy Ride 1928,Ja 23,18:3
Beware of Married Men 1928,Ap 10,33:2
Loves of an Actress 1928,Jl 30,21:2
Show Girl 1928,N 5,26:1
On Trial 1928,N 15,26:5
My Man 1928,D 22,14:3
Captain Swagger 1928,D 24,17:7
Lucky Boy 1929,F 25,16:1
Dummy, The 1929,Mr 4,20:2
Squall, The 1929,My 10,32:5
This Is Heaven 1929,My 27,22:1
Puttin' on the Ritz 1930,F 15,15:1
Benson Murder Case, The 1930,Ap 12,23:1
Courage 1930,My 23,21:1
Safety in Numbers 1930,My 31,19:4
Shadow of the Law 1930,Je 7,10:4
Manslaughter 1930,Jl 24,26:4
Recaptured Love 1930,Ag 9,16:5
Brothers 1930,N 15,15:3
College Lovers 1930,N 28,23:1
Madonna of the Streets 1930,N 29,21:4
Bat Whispers, The 1931,Ja 16,27:1
Inspiration 1931,F 9,25:3
Too Young to Marry 1931,My 4,15:3
Hell Bound 1931,My 9,15:4
Seed 1931,My 15,20:6
Up for Murder 1931,My 30,9:2
Black Camel, The 1931,Jl 4,11:5
Holy Terror, A 1931,Jl 20,20:4
Deceiver, The 1931,N 23,22:1
Maker of Men 1931,D 19,16:4
Careless Lady 1932,Ap 18,19:2
Week-End Marriage 1932,Je 4,9:2
Guilty as Hell 1932,Ag 6,14:5
Crash, The 1932,S 9,17:5
Successful Calamity, A 1932,S 23,22:2
Iron Master, The 1933,F 4,11:3
Daring Daughters 1933,Mr 25,13:4
World Gone Mad, The 1933,Ap 15,16:3
Saturday's Millions 1933,O 14,18:3
Road to Ruin, The 1934,F 21,23:2
Countess of Monte Cristo, The 1934,Ap 2,13:2
Modern Hero, A 1934,Ap 20,17:1
Baby, Take a Bow 1934,Je 30,18:6
Paris Interlude 1934,Jl 28,16:5
Sing Sing Nights 1935,Ja 26,13:2
Shadow of Doubt 1935,Mr 11,15:1
Plot Thickens, The 1936,D 9,35:2
Flying Hostess 1936,D 14,29:4
Armored Car 1937,Jl 26,15:2
Something to Sing About 1937,S 21,29:4
Girl Said No, The 1937,O 18,14:1
Trapped by G-Men 1937,N 4,29:1
She's Got Everything 1938,Ja 14,21:3
Texans, The 1938,Jl 28,23:2
Sons of the Legion 1938,S 30,24:3
Risky Business 1939,Mr 23,27:2
Great Victor Herbert, The 1939,D 7,35:1

Tucker, Robert

Streets of New York 1939,My 1,21:1

Tucker, Sophie

Honky Tonk 1929,Je 5,32:3
Broadway Melody of 1938 1937,S 3,12:1
Thoroughbreds Don't Cry 1937,N 26,27:4
Follow the Boys 1944,Ap 26,24:6
Sensations of 1945 1944,Jl 7,13:2

Tucker, William

Streets of New York 1939,My 1,21:1

Tucker, William H

Purple Highway, The 1923,Jl 24,14:3 (In Addenda)

Tuckner, Robert (Original Author)

Moon Pilot 1962,Ap 6,30:2

Tudal, Antoine (Screenwriter)

Sundays and Cybele 1962,N 13,43:3

Tudewall, Robert

Jedda the Uncivilized 1957,F 28,18:7

Tuero, Emilio

Tras la Reja 1937,Ja 11,15:7
India Bonita, La; Pretty Indian Girl, The 1939,Ap 15,15:2
Juan Soldado, o Venganza; John the Soldier or Vengeance 1939,Jl 24,9:3
Dama de las Camelias, La 1944,S 26,16:1

Tufts, Sonny

Ambush 1939,F 9,17:2
So Proudly We Hail 1943,S 10,29:1
Government Girl 1944,Ja 7,13:2
I Love a Soldier 1944,N 2,22:2
Here Come the Waves 1944,D 28,25:2
Bring on the Girls 1945,Mr 1,25:5
Duffy's Tavern 1945,S 6,23:3
Miss Susie Slagle's 1946,F 7,29:2
Virginian, The 1946,Ap 18,22:2
Well Groomed Bride, The 1946,My 11,22:5
Cross my Heart 1946,D 19,42:3
Swell Guy 1947,Ja 27,17:2
Easy Come, Easy Go 1947,F 6,29:2
Blaze of Noon 1947,Mr 5,31:2
Crooked Way, The 1949,S 5,13:2
Easy Living 1949,O 13,33:3
Glory at Sea 1953,Mr 11,36:7
Cat-Women of the Moon 1954,Mr 20,10:7
Seven Year Itch, The 1955,Je 4,9:1

Tugelov, Nurdin (Miscellaneous)

Morning Star 1962,Ag 20,18:2

Tugend, Harry (Original Author)

Seven Sinners 1940,N 18,23:2
Pot o'Gold 1941,Ap 4,25:2
Caught in the Draft 1941,Je 26,27:3
Birth of the Blues 1941,D 11,39:1
Road to Bali 1953,Ja 30,25:1

Tugend, Harry (Producer)

Cross my Heart 1946,D 19,42:3
Trouble With Women, The 1947,Jl 14,14:4
Golden Earrings 1947,D 4,41:3
Darling, How Could You! 1951,N 9,22:4
Road to Bali 1953,Ja 30,25:1
Off Limits 1953,Mr 30,25:5
Public Pigeon No 1 1957,My 18,23:2

Tugend, Harry (Screenwriter)

King of Burlesque 1936,Ja 16,25:2
Captain January 1936,Ap 25,21:1
Poor Little Rich Girl, The 1936,Je 26,16:1
Sing, Baby, Sing 1936,S 12,20:1
Pigskin Parade 1936,N 14,23:3
Love Is News 1937,Mr 6,10:1
Wake up and Live 1937,Ap 24,16:2
You Can't Have Everything 1937,Ag 4,15:2
Ali Baba Goes to Town 1937,O 23,14:1
Sally, Irene and Mary 1938,F 26,9:2
Little Miss Broadway 1938,Jl 23,10:4
My Lucky Star 1938,S 10,20:2
Thanks For Everything 1938,D 10,13:2
Second Fiddle 1939,Jl 1,11:2
Little Old New York 1940,F 3,9:2
Caught in the Draft 1941,Je 26,27:3
Kiss the Boys Goodbye 1941,Ag 14,21:2
Birth of the Blues 1941,D 11,39:1
Lady Has Plans, The 1942,Mr 5,27:1
Beyond the Blue Horizon 1942,Je 25,27:2
Star Spangled Rhythm 1942,D 31,20:1
Let's Face It 1943,Ag 5,18:1
True to Life 1943,O 14,26:1
Cross my Heart 1946,D 19,42:3
Song Is Born, A 1948,O 20,37:2
Southern Yankee, A 1948,N 25,47:2
Take Me Out to the Ball Game 1949,Mr 10,35:2
Wabash Avenue 1950,Ap 29,8:3
Public Pigeon No 1 1957,My 18,23:2
Pocketful of Miracles 1961,D 19,39:1
Who's Minding the Store? 1963,N 29,67:6
(Incorrect in this edition; use 1963,N 28,67:6 elsewhere)

Tukiu

Kanchenjungha 1966,Jl 26,27:2

Tulley, Truman (Producer)

First World War, The 1934,N 8,27:1

Tulli, Marco

Beat the Devil 1954,Mr 13,11:2

Tully, Jim

Way for a Sailor 1930,D 13,22:2

Tully, Jim (Original Author)

Beggars of Life 1928,S 24,25:1
Laughter in Hell 1933,Ja 2,29:2

Tully, John

Against all Flags 1952,D 25,34:6

Tully, John (Screenwriter)

In the Wake of a Stranger 1961,Je 22,23:3

Tully, May (Original Author)

Mary's Ankle 1920,Mr 1,16:2

Tully, Montgomery (Director)

Murder in Reverse 1947,Ja 11,23:5
Mrs Fitzherbert 1950,My 11,37:2
Tale of Five Women, A 1953,Ja 16,19:2
Master Spy 1964,Ag 20,34:2
Battle Beneath the Earth 1968,S 12,54:3

Tully, Montgomery (Original Author)

Murder in Reverse 1947,Ja 11,23:5

Tully, Montgomery (Screenwriter)

Waltz Time 1946,F 11,25:2
Mrs Fitzherbert 1950,My 11,37:2
Master Spy 1964,Ag 20,34:2

Tully, Phil

All the King's Men 1949,N 9,37:2
Love That Brute 1950,My 27,10:6

Tully, Richard Walton (Original Author)

Bird of Paradise 1932,S 10,18:5
Rose of the Rancho 1936,Ja 9,25:2
Bird of Paradise 1951,Mr 15,37:2

Tully, Tom

Northern Pursuit 1943,N 26,29:2
Destination Tokyo 1944,Ja 1,9:2
Secret Command 1944,Je 14,16:2
Sign of the Cross 1944,D 21,16:3
I'll Be Seeing You 1945,Ap 6,20:6
Unseen, The 1945,My 14,20:5
Kiss and Tell 1945,O 26,16:2
Adventure 1946,F 8,23:2
Virginian, The 1946,Ap 18,22:2
Till the End of Time 1946,Jl 24,24:1
Lady in the Lake 1947,Ja 24,18:3
Killer McCoy 1948,F 12,31:2
Scudda-Hoo! Scudda-Hay! 1948,Ap 15,31:1
Intrigue 1948,Ap 24,11:2
Rachel and the Stranger 1948,S 20,21:2
June Bride 1948,O 30,10:2
Blood on the Moon 1948,N 12,30:5
Illegal Entry 1949,Je 11,11:2
Lady Takes a Sailor, The 1949,D 17,15:2
Where the Sidewalk Ends 1950,Jl 8,7:4
Branded 1951,Ja 11,28:5
Tomahawk 1951,F 19,19:2
Texas Carnival 1951,O 13,9:1
Return of the Texan 1952,F 14,23:1
Love Is Better Than Ever 1952,Mr 4,23:2
Lure of the Wilderness 1952,O 4,15:2
Turning Point, The 1952,N 15,15:2
Ruby Gentry 1952,D 26,20:2
Jazz Singer, The 1953,Ja 14,27:3
Trouble Along the Way 1953,My 7,37:2
Moon Is Blue, The 1953,Jl 9,18:3
Arrow in the Dust 1954,My 1,13:2
Caine Mutiny, The 1954,Je 25,17:1
Love Me or Leave Me 1955,My 27,14:1
Soldier of Fortune 1955,My 28,7:4
Ten North Frederick 1958,My 23,29:2
Wackiest Ship in the Army, The 1961,F 9,30:1
Carpetbaggers, The 1964,Jl 2,24:4
Coogan's Bluff 1968,O 3,56:1

Tulubyeva, Z (Director)

Swan Lake 1960,Ja 26,25:2

Tumaatura

Tanga Tika 1953,O 6,34:4

Tumiati, Giulio

Man With the Grey Glove, The 1953,Ja 3,11:2

Tumiati, Gualtiero

Casta Oiva 1937,O 5,29:2
Devotion 1953,Ja 31,10:6
Strange Deception 1953,My 27,28:2

Tun, Tun

Chamber of Horrors 1966,O 20,52:5

Tunberg, Karl (Original Author)

Sally, Irene and Mary 1938,F 26,9:2
My Lucky Star 1938,S 10,20:2
Hold That Co-ed 1938,S 24,13:1

Tunberg, Karl (Producer)

Masquerade in Mexico 1945,N 29,27:2
Imperfect Lady, The 1947,My 22,34:5
Up in Central Park 1948,My 27,29:3
You Gotta Stay Happy 1948,N 5,29:2
Count Your Blessings 1959,Ap 24,23:1
Seventh Dawn, The 1964,S 3,24:1

Tunberg, Karl (Screenwriter)

You Can't Have Everything 1937,Ag 4,15:2
Life Begins In College 1937,O 9,16:1
Rebecca of Sunnybrook Farm 1938,Mr 26,12:1
Hold That Co-ed 1938,S 24,13:1
Shipyard Sally 1940,Ja 18,27:3
I Was an Adventuress 1940,My 20,13:2
Public Deb No 1 1940,S 18,19:2
Down Argentine Way 1940,O 18,25:1
Tall, Dark and Handsome 1941,Ja 24,15:2
Yank in the R A F, A 1941,S 27,11:3
Week-End in Havana 1941,N 8,11:2
My Gal Sal 1942,My 1,23:1
Orchestra Wives 1942,S 24,23:2
Lucky Jordan 1943,Ja 25,10:8
Dixie 1943,Je 24,26:2
Standing Room Only 1944,F 23,17:2
Bring on the Girls 1945,Mr 1,25:5
Kitty 1946,Ap 1,23:1

Tunberg, Karl (Screenwriter) — Cont
Imperfect Lady, The 1947,My 22,34:5
Up in Central Park 1948,My 27,29:3
You Gotta Stay Happy 1948,N 5,29:2
Love That Brute 1950,My 27,10:6
Night Into Morning 1951,Je 11,20:7
Law and the Lady, The 1951,Ag 16,23:2
Because You're Mine 1952,S 26,18:2
Valley of the Kings 1954,Jl 22,15:2
Beau Brummell 1954,O 21,31:5
Scarlet Coat, The 1955,Jl 30,14:2
Seventh Sin, The 1957,Je 29,10:6
Count Your Blessings 1959,Ap 24,23:1
Libel 1959,O 24,12:4
Ben Hur 1959,N 19,50:2
Taras Bulba 1962,D 26,5:2
Seventh Dawn, The 1964,S 3,24:1
Harlow 1965,My 15,18:1
Where Were You When the Lights Went Out?
 1968,Ag 9,30:2
Tunberg, William (Original Author)
Garden of Evil 1954,Jl 10,17:1
Massacre 1956,Je 2,13:5
Tunberg, William (Screenwriter)
Old Yeller 1957,D 26,23:4
Savage Sam 1963,Ag 1,17:3
Tunc, Irene
Live for Life 1967,D 19,59:1
Tung-Foo, Lee
They Knew What They Wanted 1940,O 11,25:2
Tunick, Irve (Screenwriter)
Murder, Inc 1960,Je 29,26:6
Tunney, Gene
Legendary Champions, The 1968,O 29,54:1
Tuno, Eijiro
Secret Scrolls-Part II; Ninjitsu 1968,My 23,56:3
Tuominen, Yrjo
Jumalen Tuomio; Judgement of God, The
 1939,O 27,27:2
Tupou, Manu
Hawaii 1966,O 11,54:1
Tupper, Pearl
Hunchback of Notre Dame, The 1923,S 3,9:3
Tupper, Tristam (Original Author)
First Kiss, The 1928,Ag 20,21:3
Christina 1929,Ap 1,22:1
Salute 1929,O 5,22:5
Phantom Broadcast, The 1933,Jl 31,16:2
Red Hot Tires 1935,Mr 1,16:3
Tupper, Tristam (Screenwriter)
Red Hot Tires 1935,Mr 1,16:3
Tupper, Tristram (Screenwriter)
Girl Overboard 1937,Mr 1,15:1
Tur, Leonid (Screenwriter)
Military Secret 1945,Ag 2,16:2
Tur, Peter (Screenwriter)
Military Secret 1945,Ag 2,16:2
Tur Brothers (Screenwriter)
Devotion 1955,Ag 1,15:2
Turay, Ida
Rakoczi Indulo 1934,N 21,23:4
Koeszoenoem Hogy Elgazolt 1935,My 7,28:2
Zsivany Becsuelet 1935,O 30,16:3
Vasember 1935,D 9,25:3
Hotel Sunrise 1937,O 30,22:3
Pesti Mese; Tales of Budapest 1938,Ja 3,16:3
Kolcsonkert Kastely; Borrowed Castle, The
 1938,D 17,10:4
Pentek Rezi; Friday Rose 1939,D 23,9:2
Rozmaring; Rosemary 1940,F 10,19:3
Turcoff, Zigmund
Vilna Legend, A (Russian-Jewish Cast)
 1949,S 26,17:1
Tureau, Michel
Anatomy of a Marriage; My Days With Jean
 Marc; My Nights With Francoise
 1964,O 27,42:2
Turek, Ludwig (Screenwriter)
Our Daily Bread 1950,O 9,21:6
Turell, Saul J (Director)
Love Goddesses, The 1965,Mr 4,36:2
Turell, Saul J (Producer)
Love Goddesses, The 1965,Mr 4,36:2
Turell, Saul J (Screenwriter)
Love Goddesses, The 1965,Mr 4,36:2
Turfler, James
Down to the Sea in Ships 1923,F 19,10:1
Turgenev, Ivan (Original Author)
Fathers and Sons 1960,D 26,27:2
Mumu 1961,Je 5,37:4
Turgeon, Peter
Muscle Beach Party 1964,My 28,40:1
Dear Heart 1965,Mr 8,33:1
Turi
Difficult Years 1950,Ag 22,31:2
Turich, Felipe
Hombre Peligroso, Un; Dangerous Man, A
 1935,O 14,21:2
To the Victor 1948,Ap 17,11:2
Lawless, The 1950,Je 23,29:2
Wyoming Mail 1950,O 23,26:5
Short Grass 1951,Ja 13,10:4

Turich, Rosa
Rose of the Rio Grande 1938,Jl 9,10:3
Rangers of Fortune 1940,S 19,27:2
Kid From Texas, The 1950,Je 2,26:2
Turin, Viktor (Director)
Turksib 1930,My 26,25:3
Turk, Roy (Miscellaneous)
Sing and Like It 1934,Ap 14,18:2
Turkel, Ann
Paper Lion 1968,O 24,54:1
Turkel, Joseph
City Across the River 1949,Ap 8,31:3
Duffy of San Quentin 1954,F 10,38:5
Inside Detroit 1956,Ja 28,10:5
Killing, The 1956,My 21,20:1
Paths of Glory 1957,D 26,23:2
Boy and the Pirates, The 1960,N 24,48:3
Yellow Canary, The 1963,My 16,42:1
Sand Pebbles, The 1966,D 21,48:1
Turkow, Z
Purimspieler, Der 1937,D 6,19:2
Tkies Khaf; (Vow, The) 1938,S 15,29:3
Turkus, Burton (Original Author)
Murder, Inc 1960,Je 29,26:6
Turleigh, Veronica
Promoter, The 1952,O 29,36:2
Horse's Mouth, The 1958,N 12,41:1
Turman, Lawrence (Producer)
Young Doctors, The 1961,Ag 24,25:2
I Could go on Singing 1963,My 16,42:1
Best Man, The 1964,Ap 7,29:1
Flim Flam Man, The 1967,Ag 23,40:1
Graduate, The 1967,D 22,44:4
Pretty Poison 1968,O 25,55:1
Turnbull, Hector (Original Author)
Less Than the Dust 1916,N 6,9:2
Private Scandal, A 1921,Je 13,16:1
Cheat, The 1923,Ag 27,14:3
Cheat, The 1931,D 12,23:3
Turnbull, Hector (Screenwriter)
Heart of Nora Flynn, The 1916,Ap 24,11:2
Turnbull, John
Private Life of Henry VIII, The 1933,O 13,25:2
Lady is Willing, The 1934,Ag 11,16:5
Scarlet Pimpernel, The 1935,F 8,27:2
Passing of the Third Floor Back, The
 1936,Ap 29,19:2
Nine Days a Queen 1936,O 3,21:1
Rembrandt 1936,D 3,31:1
Man of Affairs 1937,F 20,9:2
So Well Remembered 1947,N 5,34:3
Daybreak 1949,Jl 4,9:2
Happiest Days of Your Life, The 1950,S 18,19:2
Turnbull, Lee
Farmer Takes a Wife, The 1953,Je 13,11:2
Come on, The 1956,Ap 7,13:1
Turnbull, Margaret (Original Author)
My Cousin 1918,N 25,11:3
Classmates 1924,D 30,15:3
Turnbull, Margaret (Screenwriter)
Bonnie Brier Bush, The 1921,N 28,16:1
Turnell, Dee
Words and Music 1948,D 10,34:2
Brigadoon 1954,S 17,18:2
Turner, Baby
Singer Jim McKee 1924,Mr 24,13:1
Turner, Barbara
Operation Eichmann 1961,My 4,40:7
Turner, Barbara (Screenwriter)
Deathwatch 1967,Je 28,38:1
Turner, Bowditch
Scaramouche 1923,O 12,7:2 (Incorrect in this
 edition; use 1927,O 1,7:2 elsewhere)
Turner, Claramae
Carousel 1956,F 17,13:1
Turner, Debbie
Sound of Music, The 1965,Mr 3,34:1
Turner, Don
Bullet Scars 1942,Ap 24,21:4
Turner, Doreen
Rosita 1923,S 4,14:1
Turner, Ethel (Original Author)
One Way Ticket 1936,Ja 1,35:2
Turner, Eugene
Iceland 1942,O 15,27:1
Silver Skates 1943,Mr 19,15:3
Turner, Florence
Dark Angel, The 1925,O 12,19:3
Padlocked 1926,Ag 2,21:2
College 1927,S 12,29:1
Chinese Parrot, The 1928,Ja 2,28:1
Turner, Fred
Jack-Knife Man, The 1920,Ag 2,12:2
Turner, George
White Cargo 1930,F 24,18:1
Well Groomed Bride, The 1946,My 11,22:5
Race Street 1948,Ag 23,13:3
Turner, George Kibbe (Original Author)
Those Who Dance 1924,Je 30,16:1
Street of Forgotten Men, The 1925,Jl 21,26:2
Tanz Geht Weiter, Der 1931,Ja 6,25:1
Tip Off, The 1931,O 26,22:1
Roar of the Dragon 1932,Jl 25,11:2

Turner, Jim
Operation Amsterdam 1960,Jl 7,26:1
Turner, John Hastings (Original Author)
It Happened to One Man 1941,F 24,11:6
Turner, Lana
They Won't Forget 1937,Jl 15,16:1
Great Garrick, The 1937,O 25,23:1
Love Finds Andy Hardy 1938,Jl 22,10:2
Rich Man, Poor Girl 1938,Ag 19,13:3
Dramatic School 1938,D 9,31:2
Calling Dr Kildare 1939,My 12,25:4
These Glamour Girls 1939,Ag 31,14:2
Dancing Co-Ed 1939,N 10,27:3
Two Girls on Broadway 1940,Ap 25,28:4
We Who Are Young 1940,S 13,27:2
Ziegfeld Girl 1941,Ap 25,17:2
Dr Jekyll and Mr Hyde 1941,Ag 13,13:2
Honky Tonk 1941,O 3,27:3
Johnny Eager 1942,F 20,21:2
Somewhere I'll Find You 1942,Ag 28,22:4
Slightly Dangerous 1943,Ap 2,17:2
Youngest Profession, The 1943,Je 25,13:3
Marriage Is a Private Affair 1944,O 27,17:7
Keep Your Powder Dry 1945,Mr 12,22:6
Week-End at the Waldorf 1945,O 5,27:2
Postman Always Rings Twice, The
 1946,My 3,15:3
Green Dolphin Street 1947,O 16,34:2
Cass Timberlane 1947,N 7,20:2
Homecoming 1948,Ap 30,28:4
Three Musketeers, The 1948,O 21,33:2
Life of her Own, A 1950,O 12,43:2
Mr Imperium 1951,O 15,22:2
Merry Widow, The 1952,S 25,38:1
Bad and the Beautiful, The 1953,Ja 16,19:1
Latin Lovers 1953,Ag 13,17:2
Flame and the Flesh 1954,My 3,21:2
Betrayed 1954,S 9,36:1
Prodigal, The 1955,My 14,10:7
Sea Chase, The 1955,Je 11,8:7
Rains of Ranchipur, The 1955,D 16,38:2
Diane 1956,Ja 13,18:1
Peyton Place 1957,D 13,35:1
Lady Takes a Flyer, The 1958,Ja 30,19:2
Another Time Another Place 1958,My 3,10:4
Imitation of Life 1959,Ap 18,18:1
Portrait in Black 1960,Jl 28,19:1
By Love Possessed 1961,Jl 20,32:2
Bachelor in Paradise 1961,N 17,41:2
Who's Got the Action? 1962,D 26,5:4
Love Has Many Faces 1965,F 25,24:1
Adventures of Marco Polo, The 1965,Ap 8,17:2
Madame X 1966,Ap 28,49:1
Turner, Mae
Spirit of Youth 1938,F 28,19:1
Turner, Maidel
Another Language 1933,Ag 5,9:5
Worst Woman in Paris, The 1933,N 25,10:3
Modern Hero, A 1934,Ap 20,17:1
Unknown Blonde 1934,Ap 24,27:2
Life of Vergie Winters, The 1934,Je 15,26:1
Whom the Gods Destroy 1934,Jl 13,14:2
Raven, The 1935,Jl 5,9:2
Sudden Death, And 1936,Jl 18,18:2
Make Way for a Lady 1936,D 12,15:1
Slim 1937,Je 24,30:2
State of the Union 1948,Ap 23,28:1
Here Comes the Groom 1951,S 21,19:2
Turner, Martin
Winter Carnival 1939,Jl 28,14:2
Turner, Maude
Wizard, The 1927,N 28,18:5
Turner, Michael
Othello 1966,F 2,24:1
Turner, Ray
Turnabout 1940,Jl 27,17:6
Turner, Raymond
Love Mart, The 1927,D 26,16:6
Synthetic Sin 1929,Ja 7,36:2
Weary River 1929,Ja 25,20:6
Naughty Baby 1929,F 5,26:3
Young Nowheres 1929,O 2,28:4
Turner, Robert Brooks
Breaking Through the Sound Barrier
 1952,N 7,19:1
Turner, Roscoe Colonel
Flight at Midnight 1939,S 7,29:2
Turner, Tim
Haunted Strangler, The 1958,Jl 4,15:3
Turner, Vickery
Prudence and the Pill 1968,My 24,37:1
Turner, Wendy
Summer Magic 1963,Ag 22,19:2
Turner, William (Screenwriter)
Mr Bug Goes to Town 1942,F 20,21:3
Turner, William H
Darling of New York, The 1924,Ja 18,20:1
Enemy Sex, The 1924,Jl 1,21:4
Garden of Weeds, The 1924,N 4,24:1
Pony Express 1925,S 14,16:1
Last Performance, The 1929,N 4,28:1
Love Me Tonight 1932,Ag 19,20:6

Turner, Yolande
Five Miles to Midnight 1963,Mr 21,8:6

Turney, Catherine (Screenwriter)
Mildred Pierce 1945,S 29,12:2
My Reputation 1946,Ja 26,19:2
Stolen Life, A 1946,My 2,27:4
One More Tomorrow 1946,My 25,12:2
Of Human Bondage 1946,Jl 6,11:2
Man I Love, The 1947,Ja 25,12:2
Man I Love, The 1947,Ja 25,12:2
Cry Wolf 1947,Jl 19,10:2
Winter Meeting 1948,Ap 8,31:2
No Man of her Own 1950,My 4,32:3
Japanese War Bride 1952,Ja 30,22:6

Turog, Ida
Az en Lanyom nem olyan; My Daughter Is
Different 1938,Ap 30,18:2

Turowski, W
Eve Wants to Sleep 1961,Je 6,42:2

Turpin, Ben
Small Town Idol, A 1921,Ap 17,VI,2:1 (In
Addenda)
Shriek of Araby, The 1923,Je 11,16:2
Hollywood 1923,Jl 30,11:4
Hogan's Alley 1925,N 24,28:4
Steel Preferred 1925,D 22,13:1
College Hero, The 1927,N 22,32:2
Show of Shows 1929,N 21,24:5
Swing High 1930,Je 27,26:3
Make Me a Star 1932,Jl 1,19:3
Million Dollar Legs 1932,Jl 9,7:5
Hollywood Cavalcade 1939,O 14,13:2
When Comedy Was King 1960,Mr 30,42:1
Days of Thrills and Laughter 1961,Mr 22,37:1

Turrou, Leon G (Original Author)
Confessions of a Nazi Spy 1939,Ap 29,13:2

Turtin, Claude
Forty Thousand Horsemen 1941,Ag 15,13:2

Turzhansky, W (Director)
Volga, Volga 1933,D 15,28:3

Tuscherer, E (Producer)
Star Without Light; Etoile Sans Lumiere
1947,Ag 4,14:2

Tusher, Betty (Original Author)
Psych-Out 1968,Mr 28,52:1

Tusher, Betty (Screenwriter)
Psych-Out 1968,Mr 28,52:1

Tusherer, Eugene (Producer)
Crossroads 1939,Mr 14,17:5

Tushingham, Rita
Taste of Honey, A 1962,My 1,33:3
Girl With Green Eyes 1964,Ag 11,37:2
Knack...and how to get it, The 1965,Je 30,42:1
Leather Boys, The 1965,N 9,50:1
Smashing Time 1967,D 21,44:1

Tushova, Maria
Country Doctor, The 1953,F 16,16:2

Tuson, Thelma
Chu Chin Chow 1934,S 22,12:2

Tustain, George
Three Weeks 1924,Ap 1,19:3

Tusukida, Masaya
Fires on the Plain 1963,S 25,39:1

Tutin, Dorothy
Importance of Being Earnest, The 1952,D 23,17:2
Beggar's Opera, The 1953,Ag 25,18:2
Tale of Two Cities, A 1958,Ag 5,23:1

Tutishkin, Andrei
Volga-Volga 1941,My 17,19:2
Military Secret 1945,Ag 2,16:2
Twins 1947,Jl 28,12:2

Tuttle, Day
Psychomania 1964,F 15,14:3

Tuttle, Eugenia
Boy of Flanders, A 1924,Ap 15,24:1

Tuttle, Frank (Director)
Cradle Buster, The 1922,My 22,18:4
Puritan Passions 1923,O 15,15:4
Dangerous Money 1924,O 14,21:5
Miss Bluebeard 1925,Ja 28,14:1
Kiss in the Dark, A 1925,Ap 7,17:3
Manicure Girl, The 1925,Je 15,10:1
Lucky Devil, The 1925,Jl 8,12:4
Lovers in Quarantine 1925,O 13,20:1
American Venus, The 1926,Ja 26,25:2
Untamed Lady, The 1926,Mr 16,22:5
Kid Boots 1926,O 11,18:2
Love 'Em and Leave 'Em 1926,D 8,24:3
Blind Alleys 1927,Mr 1,31:1
Time to Love 1927,Je 23,23:3
One Woman to Another 1927,S 19,30:3
Spotlight, The 1927,N 28,18:5
Easy Come, Easy Go 1928,My 8,25:3
Something Always Happens 1928,My 21,25:1
Varsity 1928,O 29,29:1
His Private Life 1928,N 12,18:2
Marquis Preferred 1929,Ja 21,18:4
Studio Murder Mystery, The 1929,Je 10,23:1
Greene Murder Case, The 1929,Ag 10,11:3
Sweetie 1929,O 26,15:1
Only the Brave 1930,Mr 8,21:1
Benson Murder Case, The 1930,Ap 12,23:1
True to the Navy 1930,My 24,21:2

Love Among the Millionaires 1930,Jl 5,17:4
Her Wedding Night 1930,S 29,19:1
No Limit 1931,Ja 17,23:1
Pays to Advertise, It 1931,F 21,15:2
It Pays to Advertise 1931,F 21,15:2
Dude Ranch 1931,Ap 25,23:4
This Reckless Age 1932,Ja 9,21:1
ThIs is the Night 1932,Ap 16,11:2
Big Broadcast, The 1932,O 15,13:1
Dangerously Yours 1933,F 23,20:3
Pleasure Cruise 1933,Ap 3,13:3
Roman Scandals 1933,D 25,28:2
Ladies Should Listen 1934,Jl 28,16:6
Here is my Heart 1934,D 22,21:1
All the King's Horses 1935,Mr 9,19:1
Glass Key, The 1935,Je 15,20:2
Two for Tonight 1935,Ag 31,16:2
College Holiday 1936,D 24,21:2
Waikiki Wedding 1937,Mr 25,29:1
Doctor Rhythm 1938,My 19,25:2
Paris Honeymoon 1939,Ja 26,17:1
I Stole a Million 1939,Ag 7,11:2
Charlie McCarthy, Detective 1939,D 25,29:2
This Gun for Hire 1942,My 14,23:2
Lucky Jordan 1943,Ja 25,10:8
Hostages 1943,O 11,23:2
Hour Before the Dawn, The 1944,My 11,25:6
Great John L, The 1945,Jl 9,14:6
Don Juan Quilligan 1945,Jl 30,16:2
Suspense 1946,Jl 5,15:3
Swell Guy 1947,Ja 27,17:2
Magic Face, The 1951,O 1,19:2
Hell on Frisco Bay 1956,Ja 7,21:1
Cry in the Night, A 1956,S 1,19:4

Tuttle, Frank (Producer)
Charlie McCarthy, Detective 1939,D 25,29:2

Tuttle, Frank (Screenwriter)
Cradle Buster, The 1922,My 22,18:4
Puritan Passions 1923,O 15,15:4
Something Always Happens 1928,My 21,25:1
All the King's Horses 1935,Mr 9,19:1

Tuttle, Lurene
Heaven Only Knows 1947,N 14,29:3
Mr Blandings Builds his Dream House
1948,Mr 26,26:2
Macbeth 1950,D 28,22:6
Goodbye, my Fancy 1951,My 30,14:2
Tomorrow Is Another Day 1951,Ag 9,17:5
Room for One More 1952,Ja 16,21:2
Don't Bother to Knock 1952,Jl 19,8:2
Niagara 1953,Ja 22,20:3
Never Wave at a Wac 1953,Ap 24,30:2
Glass Slipper, The 1955,Mr 25,19:2
Sincerely Yours 1955,N 3,37:1
Slander 1957,Ja 17,34:4
Untamed Youth 1957,My 11,24:6
Sweet Smell of Success 1957,Je 28,29:2
Psycho 1960,Je 17,37:1
Ghost and Mr Chicken, The 1966,S 22,57:2
Fortune Cookie, The 1966,O 20,52:1
Horse in the Gray Flannel Suit, The
1968,D 21,49:3

Tuttle, Margaretta (Original Author)
Feet of Clay 1924,S 22,16:1
Unguarded Hour, The 1926,Ja 5,25:2 (In
Addenda)

Tutyshkin, Andrei
Carnival in Moscow 1957,N 4,40:1

Tuzova, Z (Director)
American Farmers Visit Russia 1955,N 3,37:1

Tvinde, Lars
Boer Boerson Jr 1939,N 4,11:3

Twaha, Ali
Africa-Texas Style! 1967,Jl 13,30:2

Twain, Mark (Samuel Clemens) (Original Author)
Prince and the Pauper, The 1915,N 29,11:3
Huckleberry Finn 1920,F 23,11:2
Connecticut Yankee in King Arthur's Court, A
1921,Mr 15,14:3
Prince and the Pauper, The 1922,Ag 14,12:4
Tom Sawyer 1930,D 20,20:6
Connecticut Yankee, A 1931,Ap 13,17:1
Huckleberry Finn 1931,Ag 8,16:3
Connecticut Yankee at the Court of King Arthur,
A 1936,My 4,16:1
Prince and the Pauper, The 1937,My 6,23:1
Adventures of Tom Sawyer, The 1938,F 18,23:1
Huckleberry Finn 1939,Mr 3,21:2
Connecticut Yankee in King Arthur's Court, A
1949,Ap 8,31:2
Man With a Million 1954,Je 29,21:2
Adventures of Huckleberry Fin, The
1960,Ag 4,17:1

Twardowski, Hans von
Margin for Error 1943,Ja 25,10:7
Hangmen Also Die 1943,Ap 16,24:2

Tweddell, Frank
Claudia 1943,N 5,23:2
Claudia and David 1946,Ag 15,19:2
Undercover Man, The 1949,Ap 21,30:2
Tattooed Stranger, The 1950,F 10,18:6
I'd Climb the Highest Mountain 1951,My 10,38:1

Tweed, Frank
Puritan Passions 1923,O 15,15:4

Tweed, Tommy
Incredible Journey, The 1963,N 21,43:2

Twelvetrees, Helen
Ghost Talks, The 1929,F 18,28:1
Grand Parade, The 1930,F 1,15:1
Swing High 1930,Je 27,26:3
Her Man 1930,O 4,15:2
Cat Creeps, The 1930,N 8,21:3
Millie 1931,F 7,11:1
Painted Desert, The 1931,Mr 9,19:1
Woman of Experience, A 1931,Jl 9,26:5
Bad Company 1931,N 7,16:5
Panama Flo 1932,Ja 20,17:4
Love Starved 1932,Ap 15,23:1
State's Attorney 1932,My 6,15:3
Is my Face red 1932,Je 11,9:3
Unashamed 1932,Jl 15,13:4
Bedtime Story, A 1933,Ap 20,20:3
Disgraced 1933,Jl 15,14:2
My Woman 1933,O 16,20:3
King for a Night 1933,D 11,23:4
Now I'll Tell 1934,My 26,12:2
She Was a Lady 1934,Ag 22,21:2
Times Square Lady 1935,Mr 15,25:3
Hollywood Round-Up 1938,Mr 5,11:2

Twerp, Joe
Mary Burns, Fugitive 1935,N 16,19:2
Woman I Love, The 1937,Ap 16,27:2
In Old Chicago 1938,Ja 7,15:2

Twiss, Clinton (Original Author)
Long, Long Trailer, The 1954,F 19,24:3

Twist, Derek (Director)
End of the River, The 1948,Je 21,18:2
All Over the Town 1949,My 26,34:4

Twist, Derek (Producer)
Angels One Five 1954,Ap 30,28:2

Twist, Derek (Screenwriter)
All Over the Town 1949,My 26,34:4
Angels One Five 1954,Ap 30,28:2

Twist, John (Miscellaneous)
Pittsburgh 1943,F 25,27:2

Twist, John (Original Author)
Wanted: Jane Turner 1936,N 30,24:7
Men Against the Sky 1940,S 12,31:2
Army Surgeon 1942,N 5,35:2
Bombardier 1943,Jl 2,15:2
Sinbad the Sailor 1947,Ja 23,31:2
Operation Secret 1952,N 6,37:2

Twist, John (Screenwriter)
West of the Pecos 1934,D 29,11:2
Grand Old Girl 1935,F 26,16:4
Annie Oakley 1935,D 24,10:5
Yellow Dust 1936,F 24,14:1
Last Outlaw, The 1936,Je 15,24:1
We Who Are About to Die 1937,Ja 2,15:1
Sea Devils 1937,Mr 16,26:4
Outcasts of Poker Flat, The 1937,Ap 27,18:3
Toast of New York, The 1937,Jl 23,16:2
Flight From Glory 1937,S 11,20:1
Hitting a new High 1937,D 27,11:1
Law West of Tombstone, The 1938,N 25,19:1
Next Time I Marry 1938,D 2,27:2
Pacific Liner 1939,Ja 18,17:3
Great Man Votes, The 1939,Ja 20,15:2
Twelve Crowded Hours 1939,F 24,15:2
Saint Strikes Back, The 1939,Mr 9,18:2
Three Sons 1939,N 24,29:3
Reno 1939,D 21,29:2
Too Many Girls 1940,N 21,43:1
Parachute Battalion 1941,Ag 29,13:2
Navy Comes Through, The 1942,N 12,30:3
Bombardier 1943,Jl 2,15:2
Sinbad the Sailor 1947,Ja 23,31:2
Tycoon 1947,D 26,22:6
Colorado Territory 1949,Je 25,8:6
Dallas 1951,Ja 13,10:4
Fort Worth 1951,Jl 13,12:7
Best of the Badmen 1951,Ag 10,13:2
Big Trees, The 1952,F 6,24:2
So Big 1953,O 22,34:2
King Richard and the Crusaders 1954,Ag 23,20:5
Sea Chase, The 1955,Je 11,8:7
Helen of Troy 1956,Ja 27,21:4
Serenade 1956,Mr 24,21:1 (Incorrect in this
edition; use 1956,Mr 23,21:1 elsewhere)
Santiago 1956,Jl 14,13:2
Band of Angels 1957,Jl 11,21:1
Deep Six, The 1958,Ja 16,32:1
F B I Story, The 1959,S 25,23:1
Marines, Lets Go! 1961,Ag 16,37:2
Distant Trumpet, A 1964,My 28,40:1
None but the Brave 1965,F 25,24:1

Twitchell, Archie
Sophie Lang Goes West 1937,S 30,19:2
Hold 'Em Navy 1937,N 6,14:2
Daughter of Shanghai 1937,D 24,21:2
Tip-Off Girls 1938,Mr 25,15:3
Her Jungle Love 1938,Ap 14,27:2
Texans, The 1938,Jl 28,23:2
Give Me a Sailor 1938,Ag 11,31:1
Mickey, the Kid 1939,Jl 6,27:1

Twitchell, Archie— Cont
Geronimo 1940,F 8,18:3
Charlie Chan At the Wax Museum 1940,S 28,9:3
Behind the News 1941,Ja 16,25:3
I Wanted Wings 1941,Mr 27,29:4
West Point Widow 1941,S 11,21:5
Twitty, Conway
Platinum High School 1960,My 26,37:3
College Confidential 1960,Ag 22,23:1
Twohill, Pat
Forty Thousand Horsemen 1941,Ag 15,13:2
Twyford, Cyril (Screenwriter)
Triumph of Sherlock Holmes, The
1935,My 27,20:6
Tyagunov, Misha
Gift for Music 1957,Jl 15,15:2
Tyapkina, E
Boys From Leningrad, The 1955,My 2,16:5
Tyler, Beverly
Best Foot Forward 1943,Je 30,25:2
Green Years, The 1946,Ap 5,21:2
Beginning or the End, The 1947,F 21,15:1
My Brother Talks to Horses 1947,Je 19,27:4
Fireball, The 1950,N 10,35:4
Chicago Confidential 1957,Ag 31,19:1
Tyler, Dickie
Hotel Berlin 1945,Mr 3,11:2
It's in the Bag 1945,Je 11,12:1
Bells of St Mary's, The 1945,D 7,26:2
Tyler, Harry
Midnight Alibi 1934,Jl 4,18:3
Friends of Mr Sweeney 1934,Jl 31,20:4
Housewife 1934,Ag 10,21:2
Case of the Howling Dog, The 1934,O 18,26:5
Babbitt 1934,D 17,24:2
I Sell Anything 1934,D 27,25:2
Glass Key, The 1935,Je 15,20:2
Men Without Names 1935,Je 29,16:2
Lady Tubbs 1935,Jl 22,20:2
Three Wise Guys, The 1936,My 23,12:2
Two-Fisted Gentleman 1936,Ag 24,11:2
Pennies From Heaven 1936,D 10,35:2
Don't Tell the Wife 1937,F 19,15:2
Love Takes Flight 1937,S 27,24:3
Girl Said No, The 1937,O 18,14:1
Jesse James 1939,Ja 14,13:1
Story of Alexander Graham Bell, The
1939,Ap 1,17:2
Lady's From Kentucky, The 1939,Ap 27,31:1
Young Mr Lincoln 1939,Je 3,11:2
Gracie Allen Murder Case, The 1939,Je 8,31:3
20,000 Men a Year 1939,O 28,11:2
Grapes of Wrath, The 1940,Ja 25,17:2
Little Old New York 1940,F 3,9:2
Young People 1940,Ag 24,16:2
Behind the News 1941,Ja 16,25:3
Tobacco Road 1941,F 21,16:2
Mexican Spitfire Sees a Ghost 1942,Jl 31,11:2
Deep Waters 1948,Jl 23,12:4
Hellfire 1949,My 30,9:4
Traveling Saleswoman 1950,Ja 6,25:3
Bedtime for Bonzo 1951,Ap 6,31:4
Glass Web, The 1953,N 12,37:5
Witness to Murder 1954,Ap 16,16:4
Tyler, Judy
Jailhouse Rock 1957,N 14,41:1
Tyler, Lelah
Time Out for Romance 1937,Mr 13,23:2
She Had to Eat 1937,Jl 24,12:1
Babes in Arms 1939,O 20,27:2
Tyler, Leon
Mickey 1948,Jl 19,11:2
Just for You 1952,O 9,40:6
Monkey's Uncle, The 1965,Ag 19,35:4
Tyler, Poyntz (Original Author)
Fitzwilly 1967,D 21,45:1
Tyler, Richard
Father Was a Fullback 1949,O 13,33:3
Tea and Sympathy 1956,S 28,24:4
Blue Angel, The 1959,S 5,11:4
Tyler, Tim
Great Missouri Raid, The 1951,Ap 9,31:2
Tyler, Tom
Powdersmoke Range 1936,Mr 9,20:2
Last Outlaw, The 1936,Je 15,24:1
Frontier Marshal 1939,Jl 29,18:2
Mummy's Hand, The 1940,S 20,27:2
Westerner, The 1940,O 25,25:2
Cherokee Strip 1940,N 4,23:2
Valley of the Sun 1942,Mr 19,29:2
Talk of the Town, The 1942,Ag 28,22:3
San Antonio 1945,D 29,19:5
Badman's Territory 1946,My 31,27:2
Return of the Badmen 1948,Ag 5,16:2
Blood on the Moon 1948,N 12,30:5
I Shot Jesse James 1949,Ap 2,12:2
Younger Brothers, The 1949,My 28,11:2
Lust for Gold 1949,Jl 4,9:2
She Wore a Yellow Ribbon 1949,N 18,35:2
Tyler, William
Marines, Lets Go! 1961,Ag 16,37:2
Tynan, Brandon
Success 1923,Jl 10,22:5
Parnell 1937,Je 4,27:2

Sh! The Octopus 1937,D 24,21:2
Wells Fargo 1937,D 30,15:2
Girl of the Golden West, The 1938,Mr 25,15:2
Great Man Votes, The 1939,Ja 20,15:2
Lone Wolf Spy Hunt, The 1939,Mr 6,11:3
It all Came True 1940,Ap 6,13:2
Lucky Partners 1940,S 6,25:2
Rangers of Fortune 1940,S 19,27:2
Marry the Boss's Daughter 1941,D 4,33:4
Tyne, George
Walk in the Sun, A 1946,Ja 12,10:6
They Won't Believe Me 1947,Jl 17,16:2
Open Secret 1948,F 2,15:2
Sword in the Desert 1949,Ag 25,20:2
Thieves' Highway 1949,S 24,8:6
Sands of Iwo Jima 1949,D 31,9:2
No Way Out 1950,Ag 17,23:1
Not With my Wife, You Don't! 1966,N 3,45:2
Tyrand
Ways of Love (Jofroi); Jofroi (Ways of Love)
1950,D 13,50:2
Tyroler, William
Phantom of the Opera, The 1925,S 7,15:3
Tyron, Max
Greed 1924,D 5,28:1
Tyron, Tom
Story of Ruth, The 1960,Je 18,12:3
Cardinal, The 1963,D 13,41:1
Tyrrell, Ann
Bride for Sale 1949,N 21,29:4 (In Addenda)
Glass Menagerie, The 1950,S 29,31:5
Once a Thief 1951,Ja 19,21:3
Girl in White, The 1952,My 31,12:5
Seven Angry Men 1955,Ap 2,15:2
Tyrrell, Gerrard
Murder in the Old Red Barn 1936,Ag 19,18:3
Tyrrell, John
Legion of Terror 1936,N 2,24:2
Lady From Nowhere 1936,D 21,19:2
Counterfeit Lady 1937,Ja 11,15:6
Frame-Up 1937,Ag 9,23:2 (In Addenda)
Criminals of the Air 1937,O 28,29:2
Women in Prison 1938,Mr 1,19:3
Main Event, The 1938,Je 20,11:3
My Son Is Guilty 1940,Ja 15,11:2
Girls Under 21 1940,N 11,22:4
Face Behind the Mask, The 1941,F 7,23:2
Phantom Submarine, The 1941,F 12,25:3
I Was a Prisoner on Devil's Island
1941,Jl 28,16:4
Mystery Ship 1941,Ag 16,18:3
Canal Zone 1942,Mr 30,21:2
Sabotage Squad 1942,Ag 5,16:1
Cry of the Werewolf, The 1944,Ag 12,16:5
Tyson, Cicely
Man Called Adam, A 1966,Ag 4,24:2
Comedians, The 1967,N 1,37:1
Heart is a Lonely Hunter, The 1968,Ag 1,24:1
Tyson, Emma
...And Now Miguel 1966,S 8,43:1
Tyszkiewicz, Beata
Man With the Shaven Head, The 1966,S 21,42:2
Tytler, Jim
Shakespeare Wallah 1966,Mr 23,40:2
Tyzack, Margaret
Ring of Treason 1964,My 28,40:3 (Incorrect in
this edition; use 1964,My 29,15:1 elsewhere)
Whisperers, The 1967,Ag 1,24:1
2001 A Space Odyssey 1968,Ap 4,58:1
Tzagneas, Christ
We Have Only one Life 1963,Je 24,21:4
Tzavellas, George (Director)
Taxi Driver, The 1958,Mr 3,24:8
Lily of the Harbor 1958,Ap 16,38:3
Counterfeit Coin 1960,My 16,39:1
Grouch, The 1961,F 27,23:2
Antigone 1962,S 19,30:1
We Have Only one Life 1963,Je 24,21:4
Tzavellas, George (Screenwriter)
Taxi Driver, The 1958,Mr 3,24:8
Lily of the Harbor 1958,Ap 16,38:3
Counterfeit Coin 1960,My 16,39:1
Grouch, The 1961,F 27,23:2
Antigone 1962,S 19,30:1
We Have Only one Life 1963,Je 24,21:4
Tzelikovskaya, Ludmila
Spring Song 1942,S 12,9:2
Tzelniker, Meier
Mr Emmanuel 1945,Ja 8,15:2
Teckman Mystery, The 1955,Ag 22,18:2
Make Me an Offer 1956,F 29,35:2
A Night to Remember 1958,D 17,2:7
Expresso Bongo 1960,Ag 13,44:1
25th Hour, The 1967,F 17,45:1
Tzitzishvili, T
Dragonfly, The 1955,Je 27,18:2
Tzoi, G
Frontier 1935,D 28,10:5
Tzoylas, N
Phaedra 1962,O 19,24:1
Tzutzunava, T
Dragonfly, The 1955,Je 27,18:2

U

U S C Football Squad
Over the Goal 1937,O 16,22:2
Uaeckel, Antonie
Klein Dorrit 1935,O 19,21:2
Uberti, Mirella
Island Sinner, The 1960,S 5,11:2
Uccellini, Ugo
Romola 1924,D 2,13:2
Uchitel, Edvard (Director)
Panorama of Russia 1964,Jl 6,32:2
Ucicky, Gustav (Director)
Hocuspocus 1930,Ag 3,VIII,4:1
Immortal Vagabond, The 1931,Ag 3,15:5
Floetenkonzert von Sanssouci, Das
1931,O 17,20:1
Yorck 1932,Ja 31,6:1
Mensch Ohne Namen 1932,N 7,20:3
Yorck 1932,N 24,35:2
Voce del Sangue, La 1933,Ap 17,16:4
Morgenrot 1933,My 16,15:2
Fluechtlinge 1934,O 15,20:5
Maedchen Johanna, Das 1935,O 9,27:2 (In
Addenda)
Zerbrochene Krug, Der; Broken Jugi, The
1938,Ja 15,19:2
Macht der Berge, Die; Power of the Mountains,
The 1938,O 22,14:2
Aufruhr in Damaskus; Tumult in Damascus
1939,My 6,21:2
Mutterliebe; Mother Love 1940,Mr 16,8:3
Singing Angels 1952,Ja 16,21:2
Ucicky, Gustav (Original Author)
In Geheimdienst; In the Employ of the Secret
Service 1931,O 25,VIII,6:1
Udet, Ernst
White Hell of Pitz Palu, The 1930,S 27,21:3
Avalanche 1932,Mr 26,17:2
S O S Iceberg 1933,S 25,18:4
Ueda, Akinari (Original Author)
Ugetsu 1954,S 8,40:3
Ueda, Kichijiro
Rasho-Mon 1951,D 27,18:3
Uegusa, Kolnosuke (Screenwriter)
Drunken Angel 1959,D 31,12:1
Uehara, Ken
Honolulu-Tokyo-Hong Kong 1964,S 2,33:3
Uehara, Misa
Hidden Fortress The 1962,Ja 24,24:2
Ueicky, Gustav (Director)
Der Unsterbliche Lump 1932,My 20,22:3
Uemura, Kenjiro
Gate of Hell 1954,D 14,45:2
Uhl, Alfred (Miscellaneous)
This Is China 1937,O 6,29:4
Uhlig, Anneliese
Stimme des Blutes; Blood Bond 1937,D 28,29:2
Recht auf Liebe, Das; Right to Love, The
1940,Je 15,12:3
Uhse, Horst
Guitars of Love 1958,Jl 12,18:1
Uilsson, Anna Q
If I Marry Again 1925,Ja 12,11:2
Ukhov, Vsevolod
Sleeping Beauty, The 1966,My 4,50:1
Ukil, Sarada
Light of Asia, The 1928,My 12,8:4
Ulanova, Galina
Stars of the Russian Ballet (Swan Lake); Swan
Lake (Stars of the Russian Ballet) 1954,S 6,9:2
Stars of the Russian Ballet (The Fountain of
Bakhchisarai); Fountain of Bakhchisarai (Stars of
the Russian Ballet) 1954,S 6,9:2
Ballet of Romeo and Juliet, The 1956,Ap 3,31:2
Ulbricht, Walter (Screenwriter)
Sins of Rose Bernd, The 1959,Ja 24,13:4 (In
Addenda)
Uleha, Vladimir (Director)
Mizici Svet; Vanishing World 1935,My 30,21:2
Uleha, Vladimir (Producer)
Mizici Svet; Vanishing World 1935,My 30,21:2
Ulesova, Vera
Secret Agent 1949,F 10,37:3
Ulius, Betty (Screenwriter)
Psych-Out 1968,Mr 28,52:1
Ullman, Daniel B (Original Author)
Seven Angry Men 1955,Ap 2,15:2
Annapolis Story, An 1955,Ap 9,8:2
Man Afraid 1957,Ap 5,24:2
Ullman, Daniel B (Screenwriter)
Ringside 1949,S 17,10:8
Cavalry Scout 1951,Je 8,32:2
Maze, The 1953,Jl 11,8:2
Seven Angry Men 1955,Ap 2,15:2
Annapolis Story, An 1955,Ap 9,8:2
Warriors, The 1955,S 10,11:2
At Gunpoint 1956,F 4,24:5
First Texan, The 1956,Je 23,20:2
Oklahoman, The 1957,My 15,39:1
Mysterious Island 1961,D 21,30:6

Ullman, Elwood (Screenwriter)
Men in her Diary 1945,S 24,16:5
Sailor Beware 1952,F 1,17:1
Snow White and the Three Stooges 1961,Jl 1,9:1
Three Stooges Meet Hercules, The 1962,Ja 27,13:4
Three Stooges in Orbit, The 1962,Jl 12,19:4
Three Stooges Go Around the World in a Daze, The 1963,D 19,40:2
Tickle Me 1965,Je 24,28:3
Dr Goldfoot and the Bikini Machine 1966,F 17,29:3
Ullman, Frederic Jr (Producer)
ThIs is America 1933,Jl 20,22:2
I'm Still Alive 1940,O 11,25:4
Window, The 1949,Ag 8,10:5
Ullman, James Ramsey (Original Author)
White Tower, The 1950,Jl 3,9:2
Windom's Way 1958,O 1,45:1
Third Man on the Mountain 1959,N 12,27:1
Ullman, Robert
Lummox 1930,Mr 24,25:1
Ullman, William A Jr (Original Author)
Down Under the Sea 1936,Ag 10,10:2
Those High Grey Walls 1939,O 19,27:2
Ullman, William A Jr (Screenwriter)
Sergeant Madden 1939,Mr 24,27:2
Ullmann, Dan (Screenwriter)
Hiawatha 1952,D 26,20:4
Ullmann, Liv
Persona 1966,O 20,52:7
Persona 1967,Mr 7,46:2
Hour of the Wolf 1968,Ap 10,50:2
Shame 1968,D 24,14:1
Ullrich, Luise
Liebelei; Light Love 1933,Jl 2,IX,2:2
Liebe Dumme Mama; Stupid Mama 1935,Mr 2,18:3
Zwichen Zwei Herzen; Between Two Hearts 1936,Ja 28,15:3
Liebelei 1936,F 28,18:2
Fluechtling aus Chicago, Der 1936,Mr 16,21:4
Einmaleins der Liebe, Das 1937,Ja 2,15:2
Promise Me Nothing 1937,N 13,11:3
Wir Sind vom K u K Infantrie-Regiment 1938,N 19,9:2
O Schwarzwald, O Heimat; Oh Black Forest, Oh Home 1939,Ap 24,13:2
Tag Nach der Scheidung, Der; Day After the Divorce, The 1940,Mr 2,9:5
Schatten der Vergangeheit; Shadows of the Past 1940,Ap 20,14:2
Keepers of the Night 1953,Je 9,24:2
Shadows Grow Longer, The 1962,Je 11,36:4
Ulman, Daniel B (Original Author)
Under the Gun 1951,F 23,33:2
Ulmer, Edgar G (Director)
Black Cat, The 1934,My 19,18:4
Damaged Lives 1937,Je 14,26:2
Green Fields 1937,O 12,31:4
Singing Blacksmith, The 1938,N 3,27:1
Cossacks in Exile 1939,Ja 28,19:2
Wife of Monte Cristo, The 1946,Ap 8,31:2
Her Sister's Secret 1947,Ja 23,31:3
Strange Woman, The 1947,F 24,16:4
Carnegie Hall 1947,My 3,10:2
Ruthless 1948,S 4,8:7
Pirates of Capri, The 1949,D 26,33:5
Man From Planet X, The 1951,Ap 9,31:2
Babes in Bagdad 1954,Ap 5,21:3
Hannibal 1960,Ag 4,17:1
Cavern, The 1965,D 25,17:2
Ulmer, Edgar G (Original Author)
Damaged Lives 1937,Je 14,26:2
Wife of Monte Cristo, The 1946,Ap 8,31:2
Ulmer, Edgar G (Producer)
Light Ahead, The 1939,S 23,22:3
Americaner Shadchen; American Matchmaker 1940,My 7,31:3
Cavern, The 1965,D 25,17:2
Ulmer, Friedrich
Schloss Hubertus 1935,F 9,11:3
Csardasfuerstin 1935,Ap 25,18:3
Heilige und Ihr Narr, Die; Saint and Her Fool, The 1935,N 29,24:2
Klosterjaeger, Der 1936,Ja 3,13:7
Ulmer, Fritz
Waterloo 1929,Ap 16,32:5
Ulric, Lenore
Tiger Rose 1923,D 3,14:1
Frozen Justice 1929,O 26,15:1
South Sea Rose 1929,D 7,19:3
Camille 1937,Ja 23,13:1
Temptation 1946,D 25,33:6
Two Smart People 1947,F 15,20:4
Northwest Outpost 1947,Ag 8,10:2
Ulrich, Barbara
Cat in the Sack 1967,My 12,53:1
Ulrich, Kurt (Producer)
Roses for the Prosecutor; (Rosen fur den Staarsanwalt) 1961,O 10,38:2
Judge and the Sinner, The 1964,Je 6,14:2

Ulrich, Lenore
Heart of Paula, The 1916,Ap 3,11:4
Uluner, Y (Screenwriter)
Twins 1947,Jl 28,12:2
Ulvedy, Zsoka
Gyimesi Vadvirag; Wildflower of Gyimes 1939,O 21,12:3
Ulyanov, Mikhail
House I Live in, The 1959,Ap 20,34:2
Umecka, Jolanta
Knife in the Water 1963,O 29,31:2
Umeki, Miyoshi
Soyonara 1957,D 6,39:4
Sayonara 1957,D 6,39:4
Cry for Happy 1961,Mr 4,16:1
Flower Drum Song 1961,N 10,40:1
Horizontal Lieutenant, The 1962,My 12,15:3
Girl Named Tamiku, A 1963,Mr 15,8:2
Umurzakov, Elubai
Amangeldy 1939,Je 16,27:4
Uncle Willie
Sensations of 1945 1944,Jl 7,13:2
Unda, Emilia
Das Ekel 1932,Ja 30,13:2
Maedchen in Uniform 1932,S 21,25:4
Pappi 1936,My 16,11:3
Underdown, Edward
Inspector Hornleigh 1939,Je 15,27:3
Woman in the Hall, The 1949,Ja 24,16:2
Her Panelled Door 1951,Ag 28,18:2
Man on the Run 1952,F 27,22:5
Dark Man, The 1952,My 26,18:4
Beat the Devil 1954,Mr 13,11:2
Woman's Angle, The 1954,Ag 27,11:6
Camp on Blood Island, The 1958,S 18,37:2
Two-Headed Spy, The 1959,Mr 3,38:4
Day the Earth Caught Fire, The 1962,Mr 16,25:1
Khartoum 1966,Jl 14,28:1
Underdown, Robert
Murder Will Out 1953,Ap 6,24:2
Underdown, Teddy
Wings of the Morning 1937,Mr 12,19:1
Underwood, Betty
Dangerous Profession, A 1949,D 12,29:4
Underwood, Franklin
News Parade, The 1928,My 29,17:2
Underwood, Lawrence
Old Lady 31 1920,My 24,20:3
Passionate Youth 1925,Je 30,14:3
Underwood, Loyal
Dixie Handicap, The 1924,D 30,15:3
Ung, Lawrence
Thunder Birds 1942,O 29,19:2
Unger, Gladys (Original Author)
Goldfish, The 1924,My 20,15:2
Two Girls Wanted 1927,N 14,26:1
Breakfast at Sunrise 1927,N 14,26:1
Coming-Out Party 1934,Mr 17,11:3
Unger, Gladys (Screenwriter)
Mystery of Edwin Drood, The 1935,Mr 21,27:1
Alias Mary Dow 1935,Je 29,16:2
Sylvia Scarlett 1936,Ja 10,16:2
Daughter of Shanghai 1937,D 24,21:2
Unger, Gunnar
Youth 1927,N 30,22:4
Unger, Kurt (Producer)
Judith 1966,Ja 21,22:1
Unger, Oliver A (Producer)
Roosevelt Story, The 1947,Ag 22,11:2
Face of Fu Manchu, The 1965,N 11,58:3
Coast of Skeletons 1965,N 11,58:3
Mozambique 1966,F 10,33:1
Ten Little Indians 1966,F 10,33:1
Unger, Stella (Composer)
Date with Judy, A 1948,Ag 7,8:2
Ungewitter, Thomas
Inga 1968,N 21,41:2
Unicomb, Morris
Bush Christmas 1947,N 27,50:4
Unicombe, John
Rugged O'Riordans, The 1950,Ja 6,25:2
Unkel, Petra
Melodie der Liebe; Melody of Love 1932,Jl 31,IX,3:4
Ja, Treu Ist die Soldatenliebe 1934,Ap 28,11:4
Melodie der Liebe 1934,S 17,20:3
Aufforderung zum Tanz; Invitation to the Dance 1935,N 23,23:3
Heilige und Ihr Narr, Die; Saint and Her Fool, The 1935,N 29,24:2
Pappi 1936,My 16,11:3
Blinde Passagier; Stowaways 1937,Mr 6,10:1
Uno, Jukichi
Mistress, The 1959,F 3,36:2
Onibaba 1965,F 10,44:3
Unqvary, Laszlo
Varju a Toronyoran; Crow on the Tower 1939,N 18,22:6
Unsell, Eve (Screenwriter)
Three Men and a Girl 1919,Mr 31,11:3
Unterkircher, Hans
Last Laugh, The 1925,Ja 28,14:1

Unterkirchner, Hans
Song Without End 1960,Ag 12,10:2
Untershlak, J
Seeds of Freedom 1929,S 9,30:2
Uotila, Erkki
Jaakarin Morsian; Soldiers' Bride 1939,D 18,29:
Updegraff, Allan (Original Author)
Second Youth 1924,Ap 22,19:3
Upright, Blanche (Original Author)
Pleasure Mad 1924,Ja 7,23:1
Upson, William Hazlett (Original Author)
Earthworm Tractors 1936,Jl 25,16:1
Upton, Gabrielle (Screenwriter)
Gidget 1959,Ap 23,27:4
Escape from East Berlin 1962,D 6,55:3
Upton, Julian
To Hell and Back 1955,S 23,21:2
Urabe, Kumeko
Golden Demon 1956,Ja 31,34:3
She Was Like a Wild Chrysanthemum 1960,Ja 22,15:2
Ikiru; To Live 1960,Ja 30,13:5
Urail, Yoko
Enjo 1964,S 23,54:1
Uralsky, Vladimir
In the Far East 1937,O 20,27:3
Men of the Sea 1938,Je 20,11:2
Uraneff, Vadim
Sea Hunt, The 1926,Ja 16,8:5
Magic Flame, The 1927,S 19,30:3
Fazil 1928,Je 5,21:1
Friends and Lovers 1931,N 7,16:5
Uranoff, Vadin
Sea Beast, The 1926,Ja 16,8:5
Urasaliev, A
Fall of Berlin 1952,Je 9,19:2
Uray, Theodore
Az uj Foeldesur 1936,S 22,30:5
Salary, 200 a Month 1937,Ja 15,17:3
Segitseg Oeroekoeltem; Help, I'm an Heiress 1937,O 28,29:2
Sutyi, a Szerencseqyerek; Sutyi, the Lucky Child 1938,Ja 22,19:2
Szegeny Gazdagok; Poor Plutocrats 1939,D 4,18:4
Urban, Charles (Director)
Science of the Soap Bubbles 1921,Jl 4,10:2
Tortoise and the Hare, The 1921,Jl 4,10:2
Rare Animals 1921,Jl 4,10:2
From Egg to Chick 1921,Jl 4,10:2
Ancient Customs of Egypt 1921,Jl 4,10:2
Urban, Diana M
Mon Coeur Balance 1933,F 3,21:4
Urban, Dorothy
Fight for Life, The 1940,Mr 7,19:2
Urban, Joseph (Director)
Yolanda 1924,F 20,23:1
Urban, Joseph (Miscellaneous)
Restless Sex, The 1920,S 13,12:1
Buried Treasure 1921,F 14,12:2
Beauty's Worth 1922,Mr 27,12:1
When Knighthood Was in Flower 1922,S 15,17:2 (In Addenda)
Unseeing Eyes 1923,O 22,17:1
Urban, Maria
Journey, The 1959,F 20,19:1
Urban, Max (Composer)
Liaga, La; Torment, The 1937,O 4,17:2
Urban (Cinematographer)
Combatting the Elements 1921,My 30,12:5
Urban (Producer)
Four Seasons, The 1921,O 2,VII,3:1
Urbankova, Nada
Closely Watched Trains 1967,O 16,59:2
Urbanski, Evgeni
Ballad of a Soldier 1960,D 27,22:1
Letter That Was Never Sent, The 1962,N 19,39:2
Clear Skies 1963,N 27,30:1
Urbino, Vanna
Jules and Jim 1962,Ap 24,32:1
Urchell, Tony
Her Jungle Love 1938,Ap 14,27:2
Ure, Mary
Storm over the Nile 1956,Je 9,14:2
Windom's Way 1958,O 1,45:1
Look Back in Anger 1959,S 16,45:1
Sons and Lovers 1960,Ag 3,35:1
Mind Benders, The 1963,My 2,40:2
Luck of Ginger Coffey, The 1964,S 22,44:1
Custer of the West 1968,Jl 4,13:2
Urecal, Minerva
Her Husband's Secretary 1937,Mr 20,23:6
Oh, Doctor 1937,Je 19,20:3
Prison Nurse 1938,Mr 4,17:5
Start Cheering 1938,Mr 17,17:3
You Can't Fool Your Wife 1940,My 24,23:4
Ghost Creeps, The 1940,Ag 19,13:3
Murder by Invitation 1941,Jl 23,15:4
Man at Large 1941,O 11,21:4
Men in her Diary 1945,S 24,16:5
Wanderer of the Wasteland 1945,S 29,12:2
Apache Rose 1947,Jl 23,19:3
Lost Moment, The 1947,N 22,10:2

Urecal, Minerva— Cont
Good Sam 1948,S 17,28:2
Holiday in Havana 1949,O 14,33:5
Traveling Saleswoman 1950,Ja 6,25:3
Quicksand 1950,Je 16,28:4
Jackpot, The 1950,N 23,55:2
Aaron Slick From Punkin Crick 1952,Ap 19,18:6
Niagara 1953,Ja 22,20:3
Miracle in the Rain 1956,Ap 2,18:1
Mr Hobbs Takes a Vacation 1962,Je 16,11:2
Urena, Elena
Adelita, La 1938,O 12,35:2
Urgant, N
Tiger Girl 1955,S 5,8:2
Uribe, Justa
Arab, The 1924,Jl 14,11:5
Urinof, J I (Director)
Diary of a Revolutionist 1932,Je 10,22:3
Uris, Leon (Original Author)
Battle Cry 1955,F 3,18:1
Angry Hills, The 1959,Jl 16,31:3
Exodus 1960,D 16,44:1
Uris, Leon (Screenwriter)
Battle Cry 1955,F 3,18:1
Gunfight at the O K Corral 1957,My 30,23:2
Uris, Michael (Original Author)
Happy Go Lucky 1943,Mr 25,25:1
Plainsman and the Lady, The 1946,N 4,33:1
Urquhart, Molly
Wee Geordie 1956,O 8,31:1
Sundowners, The 1960,D 9,39:1
Urquhart, Robert
Knights of the Round Table 1954,Ja 8,17:2
Tonight's the Night 1954,D 23,13:4
Warriors, The 1955,S 10,11:2
Curse of Frankenstein, The 1957,Ag 8,15:5
Battle Hell 1957,Ag 22,23:1
Dunkirk 1958,S 11,42:2
Foxhole in Cairo 1961,F 16,25:2
Murder at the Gallop 1963,Je 25,23:2
Urruchua, Eduardo
Roots, The (The Cows); Cows, The (The Roots) 1957,S 3,23:2
Urruchua, Victor
El Escandalo 1934,S 22,12:3
Monjes, Des 1935,Ja 21,19:3
Clemencia 1935,Ag 20,25:4
Hoy Comienza la Vida 1936,Je 27,21:2
Supremo Sacrificio; Supreme Sacrifice 1938,N 29,27:2
Mi Madrecita; My Little Mother 1940,S 24,26:6
Urson, Frank (Director)
Roaring Road, The 1919,Ap 14,11:4
Love Special, The 1921,Mr 21,11:3
Too Much Speed 1921,Je 6,16:4
Changing Husbands 1924,Je 23,22:4
Forty Winks 1925,F 3,24:1
Night Club, The 1925,My 5,24:2
Chicago 1927,D 24,9:1
Urson, Frank (Producer)
Gentlemen of the Jury 1927,D 11,IX,6:2 (In Addenda)
Urueta, Chano (Director)
Profanacion 1934,Ja 31,20:4
Enemigos 1934,Ag 18,5:6
El Escandalo 1934,S 22,12:3
Jalisco Nunca Pierde; Jalisco Never Loses 1937,N 20,21:3
Cancion del Alma; Song of the Soul 1938,O 11,20:4
Mi Candidato; My Candidate 1938,O 31,12:3
Hombres de Mar; Men of the Sea 1938,N 7,23:6
Supremo Sacrificio; Supreme Sacrifice 1938,N 29,27:2
Maria 1939,Ap 10,13:4
Night of the Mayas 1941,Ja 14,16:7
Guadalajara 1943,Je 12,9:3
El Conde de Monte Cristo 1943,N 9,26:2
Urueta, Chano (Original Author)
Clemencia 1935,Ag 20,25:4
Urueta, Chano (Screenwriter)
Guadalajara 1943,Je 12,9:3
El Conde de Monte Cristo 1943,N 9,26:2
Urusevsky, S (Cinematographer)
Forty-First, The 1957,Je 15,10:7
Urzi, Rosetta
Seduced and Abandoned 1964,Jl 16,23:1
Urzi, Saro
Mafia; (In Nome Della Legge) 1950,Mr 2,33:2
Path of Hope, The (Il Cammino Della Speranza) 1952,Ag 5,15:5
Streets of Sorrow 1952,N 18,37:4
Mistress of the Mountains 1954,My 27,34:5
Seduced and Abandoned 1964,Jl 16,23:1
Facts of Murder, The 1965,Jl 1,34:1
Railroad Man, The; Ferroviere, Il 1965,O 25,46:2
US Dept of the Army Signal Corps
/(Cinematographer)
Untitled-News, Concentration Camps WW II 1945,My 2,3:7
Usellini, Guglielmo (Screenwriter)
Measure for Measure 1951,D 8,9:2

Usener, Heinz Dr
Signs of Life; Lebenszeichen 1968,S 26,60:1
Usenko, V
Pugachev 1938,Jl 4,10:2
Ushakov, Vladimir
Bride with a Dowry 1954,Ag 23,20:5
Ushakova, V
Boys From Leningrad, The 1955,My 2,16:5
Usher, Guy
Face in the Sky 1933,F 20,11:5
Fast Workers 1933,Mr 20,18:2
All of Me 1934,F 5,19:2
Good Dame 1934,Mr 17,11:4
Hell Cat, The 1934,Jl 7,16:5
Kid Millions 1934,N 12,17:2
It's a Gift 1935,Ja 5,20:2
Hold 'Em Yale 1935,Ap 27,20:6
Little Big Shot 1935,O 7,11:2
Grand Exit 1935,N 4,24:5
Make a Million 1935,N 9,19:3
Dangerous Waters 1936,Ja 22,15:5
President's Mystery, The 1936,O 19,22:1
Charlie Chan at the Opera 1936,D 5,16:2
Case of the Black Cat, The 1936,D 26,15:4
Sophie Lang Goes West 1937,S 30,19:2
Boots and Saddles 1937,N 8,19:2
Boy of the Streets 1938,Ja 24,17:1
Under Western Stars 1938,Je 25,7:3
Renegade Ranger, The 1939,F 17,17:3
Mister Wong in Chinatown 1939,Jl 31,9:2 (In Addenda)
Passport to Alcatraz 1940,Je 15,12:2
Doomed to Die 1940,Jl 30,16:3
No Greater Sin 1941,Ag 29,18:2
Lady for a Night 1942,F 12,27:2
Ushio, Mantaro
Odd Obsession 1961,D 27,16:1
Fires on the Plain 1963,S 25,39:1
Usovnichenko, P
1905 1956,Jl 9,27:2
Gadfly, The 1956,S 17,22:2
Ustinov, Peter
Odette 1951,Mr 28,33:2
Quo Vadis 1951,N 9,22:2
Hotel Sahara 1952,Ja 1,21:4
Plaisir, Le (The House of Madame Tellier); House of Madame Tellier (Le Plaisir) 1954,My 20,38:1
Egyptian, The 1954,Ag 25,23:1
Beau Brummell 1954,O 21,31:5
We're no Angels 1955,Jl 8,15:2
Spartacus 1960,O 7,28:1
Sundowners, The 1960,D 9,39:1
Romanoff and Juliet 1961,Je 9,26:1
Man Who Wagged his Tail, The 1961,S 19,39:1
Billy Budd 1962,O 31,32:1
Topkapi 1964,S 18,25:1
John Goldfarb, Please Come Home 1965,Mr 25,42:4
Lady L 1966,My 19,51:1
Comedians, The 1967,N 1,37:1
Blackbeard's Ghost 1968,Ap 11,51:3
Hot Millions 1968,S 20,42:1
Lola Montes 1968,S 23,42:6
Ustinov, Peter (Director)
Secret Flight 1952,Jl 3,16:2
Romanoff and Juliet 1961,Je 9,26:1
Billy Budd 1962,O 31,32:1
Lady L 1966,My 19,51:1
Ustinov, Peter (Narrator)
Women of the World 1963,Jl 3,14:1
Ustinov, Peter (Original Author)
Romanoff and Juliet 1961,Je 9,26:1
Ustinov, Peter (Producer)
Romanoff and Juliet 1961,Je 9,26:1
Ustinov, PEter (Producer)
Billy Budd 1962,O 31,32:1
Ustinov, Peter (Screenwriter)
Way Ahead, The 1945,Je 4,22:3
Secret Flight 1952,Jl 3,16:2
School for Scoundrels 1960,Jl 12,39:1
Romanoff and Juliet 1961,Je 9,26:1
Billy Budd 1962,O 31,32:1
Lady L 1966,My 19,51:1
Hot Millions 1968,S 20,42:1
Utecht, Siegfried
Somewhere in Berlin 1949,Ag 16,19:3
Utesov, Leonid
Moscow Laughs 1935,Mr 25,12:2
Utley, Betty
Pal Joey 1957,O 28,30:1
Party Girl 1958,O 29,30:1
Utsui, Ken
Great Wall, The 1965,D 16,63:2
Utyosov, Leonid
Variety Stars 1955,F 21,16:7
Uvanov, Boris
Sound of Life, The 1962,F 12,28:2
Uvarov, G
Golden Key, The 1939,D 21,29:3
Uvarov, Georgy
Cain and Artem 1930,Je 7,10:4

Uys, Jamie
Hellions, The 1962,Mr 15,28:2
After You, Comrade 1967,Ap 11,54:1
Uys, Jamie (Director)
Dingaka 1965,Jl 1,34:1
After You, Comrade 1967,Ap 11,54:1
Uys, Jamie (Producer)
Dingaka 1965,Jl 1,34:1
After You, Comrade 1967,Ap 11,54:1
Uys, Jamie (Screenwriter)
Dingaka 1965,Jl 1,34:1
After You, Comrade 1967,Ap 11,54:1
Uytterhoven, Pierre (Screenwriter)
Live for Life 1967,D 19,59:1
Uzelacova, Vera
Murder Czech Style 1968,Ag 20,33:1
Uzhvey, Natasha
Rainbow, The 1944,O 23,14:3
Uzhvi, N
New Horizons 1939,My 12,25:3
Uzhvy, N
Land, The 1955,Ap 11,29:3
Uzhvy, Natalya
Taras Shevchenko 1952,Jl 28,12:6
Uzvay, H M
Polish Terror, The 1933,Mr 13,18:3
Uzzeli, Corine
Woman's Experience, A 1918,N 11,13:3

V

Vaal, Erica
Journey, The 1959,F 20,19:1
Vaala, Valentin (Director)
Niskavvoren Naiset; Women of Niskavuori 1938,N 21,14:5
Vabbel, Marc
What Price Murder 1958,N 11,26:1
Vacarezzo, Alberto (Producer)
Murio el Sargento Laprida; Sergeant Laprida Died 1939,Mr 20,13:2
Vachek, Alois
Closely Watched Trains 1967,O 16,59:2
Vachon, Jean
For Sale 1924,Jl 14,11:5
Vacio, Natividad
Hitch-Hiker, The 1953,Ap 30,39:3
Green Fire 1954,D 25,7:1
Vadim, Annette
Blood and Roses 1961,O 12,41:4
Liaisons Dangereuses, Les 1961,D 19,39:1
Vadim, Roger
Sweet and Sour 1964,D 28,34:2
Vadim, Roger (Director)
And God Created Woman 1957,O 22,41:1
No Sun in Venice 1958,Je 10,40:2
Night Heaven Fell, The 1958,O 22,40:4
Blood and Roses 1961,O 12,41:4
Liaisons Dangereuses, Les 1961,D 19,39:1
7 Capital Sins (Pride); Pride (7 Capital Sins) 1963,Ja 17,5:2
Love on a Pillow 1963,D 17,49:1
Chateau en Suede; Castle in Switzerland 1964,O 14,51:1
Vice and Virtue 1965,Mr 18,25:1
Circle of Love 1965,Mr 25,42:4
Game is Over, The 1967,Ja 10,34:1
Barbarella 1968,O 12,43:1
Vadim, Roger (Original Author)
No Sun in Venice 1958,Je 10,40:2
Vadim, Roger (Producer)
Game is Over, The 1967,Ja 10,34:1
Vadim, Roger (Screenwriter)
And God Created Woman 1957,O 22,41:1
Please Mr Balzac 1957,N 18,37:2
Mam'zelle Pigalle 1958,Ap 19,10:4
Night Heaven Fell, The 1958,O 22,40:4
Blood and Roses 1961,O 12,41:4
Liaisons Dangereuses, Les 1961,D 19,39:1
Tales of Paris (The Tale of Sophie); Tale of Sophie, The (Tales of Paris) 1962,Ag 27,18:1
7 Capital Sins (Pride); Pride (7 Capital Sins) 1963,Ja 17,5:2
Love on a Pillow 1963,D 17,49:1
Chateau en Suede; Castle in Switzerland 1964,O 14,51:1
Vice and Virtue 1965,Mr 18,25:1
Vice and Virtue 1965,Mr 18,25:1
Game is Over, The 1967,Ja 10,34:1
Barbarella 1968,O 12,43:1
Vadim (Miscellaneous)
Naked Heart, The 1955,Mr 9,22:4
Vadis, Dan
Stranger Returns, The 1968,S 12,54:3
Vadja, Ernest (Original Author)
You Never Know Women 1926,Jl 27,15:5
Vadnay, Laslo (Original Author)
Josette 1938,Je 11,9:1
Seven Sinners 1940,N 18,23:2
Flesh and Fantasy 1943,N 18,29:1
Uncertain Glory 1944,Ap 8,9:2
Copacabana 1947,Jl 12,7:2

Vadnay, Laslo (Original Author)— Cont
  South Sea Sinner 1950,Ja 16,18:4
  I Love Melvin 1953,Ap 10,18:4
  Ten Thousand Bedrooms 1957,Ap 4,37:1
Vadnay, Laslo (Producer)
  Dime With a Halo 1963,Je 27,23:3
Vadnay, Laslo (Screenwriter)
  Tales of Manhattan 1942,S 25,25:1
  Uncertain Glory 1944,Ap 8,9:2
  Copacabana 1947,Jl 12,7:2
  Great Rupert, The 1950,Ap 14,27:2
  No Time for Flowers 1952,D 26,20:3
  Easy to Love 1953,N 27,99:9
  It Happened in Athens 1962,N 15,46:2
  Dime With a Halo 1963,Je 27,23:3
  Way...Way Out 1966,O 27,55:1
Vagabonds, The
  It Ain't Hay 1943,Mr 11,17:3
VAGHN
  See Also VAUGHAN
Vague, Vera
  Priorities on Parade 1942,Jl 23,19:2
  Lake Placid Serenade 1944,D 25,15:6
  Snafu 1945,D 26,15:2
  Earl Carroll Sketchbook 1946,Ag 30,13:2
Vail, Lester
  Beau Ideal 1931,Ja 19,25:1
  Dance, Fools, Dance 1931,Mr 21,15:1
  It's a Wise Child 1931,My 16,13:3
  I Take This Woman 1931,Je 13,20:4
  Murder by the Clock 1931,Jl 18,16:6
  Woman Between, The 1931,O 24,20:3
  Consolation Marriage 1931,O 30,26:4
Vail, Myrtle
  Myrt and Marge 1934,Ja 17,23:2
Vailati, Bruno (Producer)
  Giant of Marathon, The 1960,My 26,37:3
  Thief of Baghdad, The 1961,Ag 17,18:2
Vailati, Bruno (Screenwriter)
  Giant of Marathon, The 1960,My 26,37:3
  Thief of Baghdad, The 1961,Ag 17,18:2
Vailland, Roger (Original Author)
  Where the Hot Wind Blows 1960,N 12,15:1
  Naked Autumn 1963,N 15,25:3
Vailland, Roger (Screenwriter)
  Blood and Roses 1961,O 12,41:4
  Liaisons Dangereuses, Les 1961,D 19,39:1
  Naked Autumn 1963,N 15,25:3
  Day and the Hour, The 1964,F 20,22:2
  Vice and Virtue 1965,MR 18,25:1
Vajda, Ernest (Original Author)
  Grounds for Divorce 1925,Je 29,8:2
  Woman on Trial, The 1927,S 26,27:1
  His Private Life 1928,N 12,18:2
  Reserved for Ladies 1932,My 21,9:2
  Great Garrick, The 1937,O 25,23:1
  Stars and Stripes Forever 1952,D 23,17:2
Vajda, Ernest (Screenwriter)
  Crown of Lies 1926,Mr 30,20:6
  Service for Ladies 1927,Ag 15,22:5
  Serenade 1927,D 19,30:1
  Manhattan Cocktail 1928,N 26,30:2
  Marquis Preferred 1929,Ja 21,18:4
  Monte Carlo 1930,Ag 28,22:4
  Smiling Lieutenant, The 1931,My 23,13:4
  Woman Rebels, A 1936,O 30,27:2
  Personal Property 1937,Ap 11,27:2
  Great Garrick, The 1937,O 25,23:1
  Marie Antoinette 1938,Ag 17,23:2
  Dramatic School 1938,D 9,31:2
  He Stayed for Breakfast 1940,Ag 31,16:2
  They Dare not Love 1941,My 16,21:4
Vajda, J (Original Author)
  Acht Tage Glueck 1931,Jl 24,22:1
Vajda, Ladislao (Director)
  Hello Budapest 1935,N 14,17:4
  Ember a hid Alatt 1936,N 30,24:7
  Harom Sarkany 1936,D 22,32:3
  Revenge of General Ling, The 1938,F 21,15:1
  Az en Lanyom nem olyan; My Daughter Is
    Different 1938,Ap 30,18:2
  Doentoe Pillanat, A; Crucial Moment, The
    1938,S 17,20:3
  Magdat Kicsapjak; Magda Is Expelled
    1938,S 26,13:2
  Kolcsonkert Kastely; Borrowed Castle, The
    1938,D 17,10:4
  Pentek Rezi; Friday Rose 1939,D 23,9:2
  Golden Madonna, The 1949,S 5,13:4
  Her Panelled Door 1951,Ag 28,18:2
  Marcelino 1956,O 23,39:1
  Pepote 1958,D 2,46:1
  It Happened in Broad Daylight 1960,S 30,33:1
  Man Who Wagged his Tail, The 1961,S 19,39:1
  Shadows Grow Longer, The 1962,Je 11,36:4
Vajda, Ladislao (Screenwriter)
  Her Panelled Door 1951,Ag 28,18:2
  Marcelino 1956,O 23,39:1
  Pepote 1958,D 2,46:1
  Threepenny Opera, The 1960,Jl 11,24:4
  It Happened in Broad Daylight 1960,S 30,33:1
  Man Who Wagged his Tail, The 1961,S 19,39:1

Vakanov, V I
  Stars of the Russian Ballet (Swan Lake); Swan
    Lake (Stars of the Russian Ballet) 1954,S 6,9:2
Vala
  Return to Paradise 1953,S 11,24:2
Valaitis, V (Composer)
  Yolanta 1964,D 23,22:3
Valakou, Antigone
  Golfo-Girl of the Mountains 1958,My 19,19:5
  Horse and Carriage 1958,Je 30,23:3
Valbar, Robert
  Rasputin, The Holy Sinner 1929,Ja 15,22:4
  Thank You, Madame 1937,Ap 27,18:2
Valbel, Marc
  Tender Enemy, The 1938,Mr 31,15:2 (In
    Addenda)
Valberg, Birgitta
  Virgin Spring, The; Jungfrukallan 1960,N 15,46:1
Valbert, N
  University of Life 1941,F 26,17:1
Valcour
  Francois Villon 1950,Jl 3,9:2
Valderi, Xenia
  Woman of Rome 1956,N 6,30:1
  Red Desert 1965,F 9,43:1
Valdes, Miguelito
  Pan-Americana 1945,Mr 23,13:2
Valdis, Sigrid
  Our Man Flint 1966,Ja 26,23:4
Vale, Diedra
  Parachute Nurse 1942,Jl 27,18:2
Vale, Eugene (Original Author)
  Second Face, The 1951,Mr 2,21:3
  Global Affair, A 1964,My 7,31:2
Vale, Eugene (Screenwriter)
  Second Face, The 1951,Mr 2,21:3
  Francis of Assisi 1961,Jl 29,8:2
Vale, Martin (Original Author)
  Two Mrs Carrolls, The 1947,Ap 7,20:1
Vale, Michael
  Guerrilla Girl 1953,Jl 7,23:7
Vale, Nina
  Cornered 1945,D 26,15:1
Vale, Rita
  Thief, The 1952,O 16,37:1
Vale, Virginia
  Three Sons 1939,N 24,29:3
  You Can't Fool Your Wife 1940,My 24,23:4
  Millionaires in Prison 1940,Jl 16,21:3
  Crime Incorporated 1945,Je 23,9:7
Vale, Vola
  Alias Jimmy Valentine 1920,Ap 19,13:3
  White Oak 1921,O 31,19:3
  Soul of the Beast, The 1923,My 22,14:4
  Little Annie Rooney 1925,O 19,26:1
Valencia, Consuelo
  Cancion del Dia, La 1933,Ag 26,14:3
Valene, Nanette
  Lost Lady, A 1925,Ja 19,14:1
Valenska, Paula
  Bond Street 1950,Mr 30,40:6
  Gay Adventure, The 1954,S 16,35:7
Valenta, Vladimir
  Closely Watched Trains 1967,O 16,59:2
Valenti, Osvaldo
  I Tre Innamorati 1937,Je 17,19:2
  Avventura di Salvator Rosa, Un; Adventure of
    Salvator Rosa, An 1940,S 20,27:3
  Iron Crown 1949,Je 11,11:2
  Two Orphans, The 1950,O 19,40:6
Valentin, Albert (Director)
  Amphitryon 1937,Mr 24,29:1
Valentin, Albert (Screenwriter)
  Amphitryon 1937,Mr 24,29:1
  Sheep Has Five Legs, The 1955,Ag 10,19:2
  Nana 1957,Ap 13,12:3
  Female, The 1960,Ap 28,29:1
  Maxime 1962,O 25,48:3
  24 Hours in a Woman's Life 1968,S 25,39:1
Valentin, Karl
  Kirschen in Nachbars Garten 1937,My 15,23:6
  Thunder, Lightening and Sunshine
    1937,N 13,11:2
Valentina, Anna
  Never Let Me Go 1953,Je 11,37:2
Valentine, Barbara
  Carmen Baby 1967,O 11,41:2
Valentine, Grace
  Man's Home, A 1921,D 19,13:1
Valentine, John
  Lost Patrol, The 1929,D 16,34:2
Valentine, Leila
  Passers By 1920,Je 21,13:1
Valentine, Nancy
  30 1959,N 12,27:1
Valentine, Paul
  Out of the Past 1947,N 26,18:2
  House of Strangers 1949,Jl 2,8:2
  Special Agent 1949,Ag 22,13:1
  Love Happy 1950,Ap 8,9:4
  Something to Live For 1952,Mr 8,11:2

Valentine, Val (Miscellaneous)
  Weaker Sex, The 1949,Jl 11,13:2
Valentine, Val (Original Author)
  Notorious Gentleman 1946,N 14,39:3
  Waterloo Road 1948,D 25,10:3
Valentine, Val (Screenwriter)
  This Was a Woman 1949,Ja 5,22:2
  Miss Robin Hood 1953,Je 27,7:2
  Belles of St Trinian's, The 1954,D 23,13:4
  Constant Husband, The 1957,Jl 26,10:3
  Blue Murder at St Trinian's 1958,My 27,27:1
  Left, Right and Centre 1961,F 10,19:1
  Pure Hell of St Trinian's, The 1961,S 26,31:1
Valentini, Vincent (Original Author)
  Miracle in Harlem 1949,O 24,19:4
Valentini, Vincent (Screenwriter)
  War Is a Racket 1934,D 10,16:2
  Miracle in Harlem 1949,O 24,19:4
Valentino, Frank
  Traviata, La 1953,D 28,17:2
Valentino, Rudolph
  Four Horsemen of the Apocalypse 1921,Mr 7,8:1
  Conquering Power, The 1921,Jl 10,VI,2:1 (In
    Addenda)
  Sheik, The 1921,N 7,20:1
  Moran of the Lady Letty 1922,F 6,9:1
  Beyond the Rocks 1922,My 8,14:3
  Blood and Sand 1922,Ag 7,14:2
  Young Rajah, The 1922,N 6,13:1
  Monsieur Beaucaire 1924,Ag 12,12:1 (In
    Addenda)
  Sainted Devil, A 1924,N 24,15:3
  Eagle, The 1925,N 9,25:1
  Cobra 1925,D 7,19:1
  Son of the Sheik, The 1926,Jl 26,13:2
  Four Horsemen of the Apocalypse, The
    1926,S 27,27:3
Valenty, Lili
  Wild Is the Wind 1957,D 12,35:1
  In Love and War 1958,N 1,14:2
  Story of Ruth, The 1960,Je 18,12:3
  It Happened in Athens 1962,N 15,46:2
Valenzano, Carlo
  Leopard, The 1963,Ag 13,25:1
Valenzuela, Laura
  Cyrano and D'Artagnan 1964,S 26,16:1
Valere, Jean (Director)
  Time Out for Love 1963,Ap 23,31:2
Valere, Jean (Screenwriter)
  Time Out for Love 1963,Ap 23,31:2
Valere, Simone
  Loves of Colette 1949,D 3,8:6
  Beauty and the Devil 1952,Ag 26,15:2
  Night is my Kingdom, The 1953,S 30,37:1
  Grand Maneuver, The 1956,O 2,39:1
  Game is Over, The 1967,Ja 10,34:1
Valeri, Franca
  It Happened in the Park 1957,Ag 13,23:2
  Bigamist, The 1958,My 12,25:1
  ...And Suddenly It's Murder! 1964,Ja 24,21:1
Valeri, Marcella
  From a Roman Balcony 1961,O 16,33:5
  Viaccia, La 1962,S 21,35:1
Valeria, Babs
  Man in Grey, The 1945,N 30,18:6
Valerie, Jeanne
  Leda 1961,Jl 19,33:1
  From a Roman Balcony 1961,O 16,33:5
  Liaisons Dangereuses, Les 1961,D 19,39:1
  Red Lips 1964,Mr 19,28:2
  Adorable Julia 1964,Ap 8,33:1
  Let's Talk About Women 1964,S 29,52:5
  White Voices; Voci Blanche 1965,Ap 13,32:2
  Hired Killer, The 1967,Mr 2,30:3
Valerie, Joan
  Trip to Paris, A 1938,Je 10,18:2
  Submarine Patrol 1938,N 19,9:2
  Tail Spin 1939,F 11,13:2
  Daytime Wife 1939,N 24,29:1
  Man Who Wouldn't Talk, The 1940,Ja 12,13:3
  Young as You Feel 1940,Mr 8,25:3
  Free, Blonde and 21 1940,Ap 5,25:2
  Lillian Russell 1940,My 18,11:2
  Girl in 313 1940,Je 14,25:3
  Pier 13 1940,Ag 9,19:3
  Charlie Chan At the Wax Museum 1940,S 28,9:3
  Great Profile, The 1940,O 18,25:1
  Michael Shayne, Private Detective
    1940,D 19,33:2
  Rio Rita 1942,My 8,27:3
  Who Is Hope Schuyler 1942,My 22,27:1
  Just off Broadway 1942,Ag 29,18:4
Valero, Albano
  Loves of Ricardo, The 1926,Ag 16,10:1
Valery
  Parisian, The 1931,Ag 22,7:5
Valery, Anne
  Kind Hearts and Coronets 1950,Je 15,41:2
Valery, Olga
  Love in the Afternoon 1957,Ag 24,12:1
Valetti, Rosa
  Blue Angel, The 1930,D 6,21:3
  Das Ekel 1932,Ja 30,13:2

Valetti, Rosa— Cont
Raub der Mona Lisa, Der 1932,Mr 30,15:2
Hirsekorn Greift Ein 1932,Je 10,22:3
Zwei Herzen und ein Schlag 1932,S 9,17:5
Barberina, Die Taenzerin Von Sans-Souci
1932,O 26,15:4
M 1933,Ap 3,13:3
Valetty, Bruno (Director)
Amore che non Torna; Love That Doesn't Return
1938,Ag 15,11:2
Valewska, Zoe
Gaesschen zum Paradies, Das 1937,Ag 21,7:3
Valez, Kippee
Southside 1-1000 1950,N 3,31:2
Valio, Romulo
Great War; (Grande Guerra, La) 1961,Ag 31,22:3
Valk, Frederick
Night Train 1940,D 30,21:1
Suicide Squadron 1942,My 14,23:2
Thunder Rock 1944,S 15,16:1
Dead of Night 1946,Je 29,22:6
Frenzy 1946,Jl 20,10:3
Patient Vanishes, The 1947,My 23,31:2
Saraband 1949,Je 13,16:3
Mrs Fitzherbert 1950,My 11,37:2
Outcast of the Islands 1952,My 16,19:2
Magic Box, The 1952,S 24,40:2
Never Let Me Go 1953,Je 11,37:2
Mr Potts Goes to Moscow 1953,S 3,15:2
Zarak 1956,D 27,22:1
Colditz Story, The 1957,O 25,23:2
Valk, Johan
Ciske 1963,Ag 3,8:2
Valkis, Helen
Prince and the Pauper, The 1937,My 6,23:1
Talent Scout 1937,Ag 20,21:3
Valla, David
Inadmissible Evidence 1968,Je 24,44:1
Vallarino, Ramon
Perfidia; Perfidy 1940,F 17,9:3
Valle, David G
Silk, Blood and Sun 1943,Ja 30,10:6
Valle, Felix
Plastic Age, The 1926,Jl 19,13:1
Girl in Every Port, A 1928,F 20,14:1
Valle, Ricardo
Awful Dr Orlof, The 1964,D 3,58:3
Vallee, Maine
Jour de Fete 1952,F 20,26:4
Vallee, Marcel
Mirages De Paris 1933,D 25,28:3
Etoile Disparait, Une; Star Disappears, A
1935,F 9,11:3
Topaze 1935,F 16,9:2
With a Smile 1939,F 6,8:4
Schubert's Serenade 1940,S 3,21:2
Fric-Frac 1948,My 29,8:6
Topaze 1952,O 28,37:1
Vallee, Rudy
Vagabond Lover, The 1929,N 27,30:6
George White's Scandals 1934,Mr 16,24:2
Sweet Music 1935,F 21,23:2
Gold Diggers in Paris 1938,Je 2,19:2
Second Fiddle 1939,Jl 1,11:2
Time Out for Rhythm 1941,Jl 10,16:3
Palm Beach Story, The 1942,D 11,33:1
Happy Go Lucky 1943,Mr 25,25:1
It's in the Bag 1945,Je 11,12:1
Man Alive 1945,N 17,14:5
People Are Funny 1946,Ja 28,15:6
Bachelor and the Bobby-Soxer, The
1947,Jl 25,12:5
I Remember Mama 1948,Mr 12,29:2
Unfaithfully Yours 1948,N 6,9:2
My Dear Secretary 1949,F 14,15:4
Mother is a Freshman 1949,Mr 12,10:2
Beautiful Blonde From Bashful Bend, The
1949,My 28,11:2
Father Was a Fullback 1949,O 13,33:3
Admiral Was a Lady, The 1950,O 13,23:3
Gentlemen Marry Brunettes 1955,O 31,31:5
Helen Morgan Story, The 1957,O 3,33:2
How to Succeed in Business Without Really
Trying 1967,Mr 10,30:1
Vallee, Yvonne
Petit Cafe, Le 1931,Ja 25,VIII,5:6 (In Addenda)
Vallentin, Hermann
Trial of Donald Westhof, The 1928,F 18,11:2
Strange Case of Captain Ramper, The
1928,Je 4,13:2
Theaternaechte von Berlin 1932,Ja 11,28:5
Meine Frau, Die Hochstaplerin 1932,F 6,14:4
Hauptmann von Koepenick, Der 1933,Ja 17,22:6
Valles, Dave
Hot for Paris 1930,Ja 4,21:1
Vallette, Pierre (Miscellaneous)
Portrait of a Woman 1946,Ap 22,26:2
Valli, Alida
Sono Stato Io; It Was I 1940,My 10,26:7
Manon Lescaut 1941,Ap 14,23:5
Life Begins Anew; Vita Ricomincia, La
1947,Ap 7,20:5
Schoolgirl Diary 1947,O 18,9:2
Paradine Case, The 1948,Ja 9,26:2

Laugh Pagliacci 1948,Ja 31,14:2
Miracle of the Bells, The 1948,Mr 17,30:1
Third Man, The 1950,F 3,29:2
White Tower, The 1950,Jl 3,9:2
Walk Softly Stranger 1950,O 16,30:5
Two Orphans, The 1950,O 19,40:6
Lovers of Toledo, The 1954,Ap 10,11:3
Stranger's Hand, The 1955,F 16,24:5
This Angry Age 1958,Je 26,23:3
Night Heaven Fell, The 1958,O 22,40:4
Happy Thieves, The 1962,F 5,19:4
Grido, Il 1962,O 23,42:1
Long Absence, The 1962,N 16,23:2
Castilian, The 1963,O 3,31:1
Disorder 1964,My 26,44:2
Senso 1968,Jl 9,31:1
Valli, Joe
Wild Innocence 1938,N 11,31:2
Forty Thousand Horsemen 1941,Ag 15,13:2
Valli, Romolo
Girl With a Suitcase 1961,S 12,36:2
Viaccia, La 1962,S 21,35:1
Leopard, The 1963,Ag 13,25:1
Mandragola 1966,Je 7,50:2
Boom! 1968,My 27,56:1
Valli, Virginia
Village Blacksmith, The 1922,N 3,17:5
Wild Oranges 1924,Mr 3,22:3
Confidence Man, The 1924,Ap 15,24:1
Signal Tower, The 1924,Jl 21,14:4
Unknown, The 1924,N 18,22:1
K-The Unknown 1924,N 18,22:1
Up the Ladder 1925,My 12,26:2
Price of Pleasure, The 1925,My 26,24:2
Siege 1925,Je 16,24:1
Lady Who Lied, The 1925,Jl 7,24:2
Man Who Found Himself, The 1925,Ag 24,17:3
Evening Clothes 1927,Mr 21,10:4
Paid to Love 1927,Jl 25,25:3
Judgment of the Hills 1927,Ag 2,19:2
East Side, West Side 1927,O 18,33:2
Ladies Must Dress 1927,D 31,31:1
Escape, The 1928,My 7,29:1
Isle of Lost Ships, The 1929,O 26,15:1
Lost Zeppelin, The 1930,F 3,17:1
Guilty 1930,Ap 7,21:1
Vallier, Helen
Saadia 1954,Mr 20,10:5
Valliers, Renee
Don Quixote 1934,D 24,17:1
Vallin, Rick
Corregidor 1943,My 28,19:2
Northwest Outpost 1947,Ag 8,10:2
Last of the Redmen 1947,Ag 30,8:6
Jungle Jim 1949,Ja 1,9:2
Comanche Territory 1950,Ap 8,9:3
Vallman, Lillian
Song of Dolores 1951,Je 16,9:2
Vallon, Nanette
Brother Orchid 1940,Je 8,18:2
My Love Came Back 1940,Jl 13,16:5
Man Who Came to Dinner, The 1942,Ja 2,25:2
Vallone, Raf
Bitter Rice 1950,S 19,39:2
Under the Olive Tree 1951,O 5,24:4
Path of Hope, The (Il Cammino Della Speranza)
1952,Ag 5,15:5
White Line, The 1952,D 6,17:2
Anna 1953,F 19,20:5
Rome, 11 O'Clock 1953,Ap 30,39:2
Strange Deception 1953,My 27,28:2
Anita Garibaldi 1954,Mr 19,19:4
Daughters of Destiny (Lysistrata); Lysistrata
(Daughters of Destiny) 1954,Jl 6,19:1
Passionate Summer 1957,Jl 22,15:5
Adulteress, The 1958,Ja 14,42:1
Guendalina 1958,Je 30,23:2
Sins of Rose Bernd, The 1959,Ja 24,13:4 (In
Addenda)
No Escape 1959,My 23,18:4
Two Women; (Ciociara, La) 1961,My 9,43:2
Cid, El 1961,D 15,49:1
View From the Bridge, A 1962,Ja 23,36:1
Phaedra 1962,O 19,24:1
Cardinal, The 1963,D 13,41:1
Secret Invasion, The 1964,S 17,52:6
Secret Invasion, The 1964,S 17,52:5
Harlow 1965,Jl 22,24:1
Nevada Smith 1966,Je 24,28:1 (Incorrect in this
edition; use 1966,Je 30,28:1 elsewhere)
Kiss the Girls and Make Them Die
1967,Ja 26,25:1
Valmont, Vera
September Storm 1960,O 29,26:7
Valmy, Andre
Riptide 1951,Ap 7,9:2
Secret Document-Vienna 1954,Mr 29,22:4
Companions of the Night 1954,N 25,44:2
If all the Guys in the World 1957,Ap 23,34:1
Valnoha, Karel
Firemen's Ball, The 1968,S 30,60:1

Valnor, Lucy
Eternal Husband, The 1949,Ja 10,19:2
Valori, Bice
All the Other Girls Do! 1967,My 30,12:1
Valray, Louis (Director)
Thirteen Days of Love 1942,N 6,27:3
Valray, Louis (Original Author)
Thirteen Days of Love 1942,N 6,27:3
Valray, Maria
Bandolero, The 1924,O 27,27:1
Valsami, Nora
Stefania 1968,N 29,56:1
Valssiere, Professor
World Without Sun 1964,D 23,22:1
Valturri, Pat
Young, The Evil and the Savage, The
1968,Ag 15,46:2
Valva, John
Cleopatra 1963,Je 13,29:1
Valverda, Rafael
Loves of Carmen 1927,S 27,31:1
Quando el Amor Rie 1933,O 17,26:3
Valyano, N K
Greater Promise, A 1936,O 8,27:3
Van, Beatrice (Screenwriter)
Silk Stockings 1927,N 29,31:1
Van, Bobby
Because You're Mine 1952,S 26,18:2
Small Town Girl 1953,My 7,37:2
Kiss Me Kate 1953,N 6,23:2
Van, Connie
Far Country, The 1955,F 14,24:2
Van, Frankie
Kid Nightingale 1939,D 8,33:6
Van, Gus
Atlantic City 1944,Ag 14,11:4
Van, Jean
Fiesta 1947,Je 27,17:3
Van, Wally
Common Law, The 1923,O 29,18:1
Drivin' Fool, The 1923,O 29,18:1
Slave of Desire 1923,D 11,26:2
Barriers Burned Away 1925,Mr 12,17:2
van Aalten, Truus
Sajenko, The Soviet 1929,Ja 15,22:4
Nur am Rhein 1931,S 25,28:7
Susanne Macht Ordnung 1931,O 12,28:2
Hirsekorn Greift Ein 1932,Je 10,22:3
Pension Schoeller 1932,S 20,26:3
Teilnehmer Antwortet Nicht 1932,N 30,23:6
Eine Liebesnacht 1933,My 15,16:2
Bettelstudent, Der 1933,O 14,18:3
Van Alstyne, Egbert (Composer)
Broadway Rhythm 1944,Ap 14,24:6
Van and Schenck
Atlantic City 1944,Ag 14,11:4
van Antwerp, Albert
Chechahcos, The 1924,My 19,14:2
Van Atta, Lee
Second Wife 1936,Ag 29,16:3
Affairs of Annabel, The 1938,O 13,29:2
Van Atta, Winifred (Original Author)
Shock Treatment 1964,Jl 23,19:1
Van Beer, Stanley
Chance of a Lifetime 1951,Mr 15,37:2
Van Bergen, Ingrid
Aren't We Wonderful? 1959,O 16,27:1
Roses for the Prosecutor; (Rosen fur den
Staarsanwalt) 1961,O 10,38:2
Town Without Pity 1961,O 11,53:1
Counterfeit Traitor, The 1962,Ap 18,28:1
Escape from East Berlin 1962,D 6,55:3
van Brandenberg, Steye
Last Blitzkrieg, The 1959,Ja 31,13:5
van Bridge, Tony
Oedipus Rex 1957,Ja 8,26:1
Van Brunt, Ted
Big Clock, The 1948,Ap 22,34:2
Van Buren, A H (Director)
Hearts in Dixie 1929,F 28,30:3
Van Buren, Mabel
Conrad in Quest of his Youth 1920,N 8,20:2
Miss Lulu Bett 1921,D 25,VI,2:1
Light That Failed, The 1923,N 27,11:2
Dawn of a Tomorrow 1924,Mr 26,19:2
Top of the World, The 1925,F 17,18:1
Smooth as Satin 1925,Je 23,24:3
His Secretary 1925,D 21,27:2
Four Horsemen of the Apocalypse, The
1926,S 27,27:3
Craig's Wife 1928,D 4,29:1
Van Cleave (Composer)
Cinerama Holiday 1955,F 9,31:1
Van Cleef, Lee
High Noon 1952,Jl 25,14:2
Untamed Frontier 1952,Ag 23,10:2
Beast From 20,000 Fathoms, The 1953,Je 25,23:1
Arena 1953,Jl 23,20:2
Vice Squad 1953,Ag 26,23:2
Rails Into Laramie 1954,My 13,34:2
Dawn at Socorro 1954,Ag 28,8:2
Big Combo, The 1955,Mr 26,13:2
Conqueror, The 1956,Mr 31,13:3

Van Cleef, Lee — Cont
Tribute to a Bad Man 1956,Mr 31,13:3
Pardners 1956,Jl 26,20:2
China Gate 1957,My 23,40:2
Gunfight at the O K Corral 1957,My 30,23:2
Tin Star, The 1957,O 24,37:2
Young Lions, The 1958,Ap 3,23:1
Bravados, The 1958,Je 26,23:2
Man Who Shot Liberty Valance, The
  1962,My 24,29:2
For a Few Dollars More 1967,Jl 4,23:1
Good, The Bad and the Ugly, The
  1968,Ja 25,33:1
Big Gundown, The 1968,Ag 23,33:1
Van Cleve, Edith
Age of Innocence, The 1934,O 19,27:1
van Dapperen, R N N Lieut
Silver Fleet, The 1945,Mr 24,22:6
van Deele, Ed
Maternelle, La 1935,O 15,19:1
van Deele, Edmond
Napoleon 1929,F 12,23:1
6 1/2 x 11 1929,Ag 13,23:2
van den Berg, Gert
Zulu 1964,Jl 8,38:1
Code 7...Victim 5 1965,My 20,52:1
Naked Prey, The 1966,Je 15,40:1
van der Meersch, Maxence (Original Author)
Two Women 1940,N 2,19:3
Doctor and the Girl, The 1949,O 31,20:2
Van der Meersch (Original Author)
Maison dans la Dune, La; House on the Dune,
  The 1934,S 16,X,4:1 (In Addenda)
van der Most, Adelheid
Last Blitzkrieg, The 1959,Ja 31,13:5
van der Veer, Willard (Miscellaneous)
With Byrd at the South Pole 1930,Je 20,6:3
van der Velde, Dick
Ciske 1963,Ag 3,8:2
Van Der Vlis, Diana
X - The Man With X-Ray Eyes 1963,O 24,37:1
Incident, The 1967,N 6,65:1
Swimmer, The 1968,My 16,53:1
Van Dine, S S (Original Author)
Canary Murder Case, The 1929,Mr 11,22:2
Greene Murder Case, The 1929,Ag 10,11:3
Bishop Murder Case, The 1930,F 1,15:1
Benson Murder Case, The 1930,Ap 12,23:1
Kennel Murder Case, The 1933,O 30,14:2
Dragon Murder Case, The 1934,Ag 23,13:3
Casino Murder Case, The 1935,Ap 17,26:5
Garden Murder Case, The 1936,Mr 2,13:2
President's Mystery, The 1936,O 19,22:1
Gracie Allen Murder Case, The 1939,Je 8,31:3
Calling Philo Vance 1940,F 9,15:3
Van Dolson, Foy
Horror Island 1941,Mr 31,11:3
Van Dongen, Helen (Miscellaneous)
400,000,000, The 1939,Mr 8,19:2
Russians at War 1943,Ap 24,17:2
Van Doren, Mamie
Yankee Pasha 1954,Ap 19,19:2
Francis Joins the Wacs 1954,Jl 31,6:3
Ain't Misbehavin' 1955,Jl 2,13:2
Running Wild 1955,N 12,23:2
Second Greatest Sex, The 1956,F 11,12:2
Untamed Youth 1957,My 11,24:6
Teacher's Pet 1958,Mr 20,33:1
High School Confidential 1958,My 31,6:6
Beat Generation, The 1959,O 22,47:4
College Confidential 1960,Ag 22,23:1
Van Dorn, Mildred
Hold Your Man 1929,O 14,20:2
Son of the Gods 1930,Ja 31,24:1
Wild Company 1930,Jl 19,7:5
Liliom 1930,O 4,15:2
Iron Man 1931,Ap 18,17:3
Van Dreelen, John
13 Ghosts 1960,Ag 6,9:2
Von Ryan's Express 1965,Je 24,28:1
Madame X 1966,Ap 28,49:1
Van Druten, John
Main Street to Broadway 1953,O 14,34:1
Van Druten, John (Miscellaneous)
New Morals for Old 1932,Je 24,15:3
Van Druten, John (Original Author)
Young Woodley 1930,S 27,21:3
Unfaithful 1931,Mr 7,17:2
If I Were Free 1934,Ja 5,25:2
One Night in Lisbon 1941,Je 12,29:3
Forever and a Day 1943,Mr 13,9:2
Old Acquaintance 1943,N 3,20:2
Voice of the Turtle, The 1947,D 26,22:4
I Remember Mama 1948,Mr 12,29:2
I Am a Camera 1955,Ag 9,29:1
Bell, Book and Candle 1958,D 27,2:7
Van Druten, John (Screenwriter)
Night Must Fall 1937,Ap 30,17:2
Parnell 1937,Je 4,27:2
Raffles 1940,Ja 13,11:2
Lucky Partners 1940,S 6,25:2
My Life With Caroline 1941,O 30,27:1
Johnny Come Lately 1943,S 24,26:1
Old Acquaintance 1943,N 3,20:2

Gaslight 1944,My 5,17:2
Voice of the Turtle, The 1947,D 26,22:4
van Duinhoven, Ton
Last Blitzkrieg, The 1959,Ja 31,13:5
Van Duren, E
Figaro 1929,N 25,22:1
Van Duzer, Winifred (Original Author)
Good Bad Girl, The 1931,My 15,20:6
Van Dycke, Tom (Original Author)
Man Who Lived Twice, The 1936,O 12,23:2
Man in the Dark 1953,Ap 9,31:5
Van Dycke, Tom (Screenwriter)
Two-Fisted Gentleman 1936,Ag 24,11:2
Man Who Lived Twice, The 1936,O 12,23:2
Counterfeit Lady 1937,Ja 11,15:6
Van Dyke, Carol
Two for the Road 1967,Ap 28,36:2
Van Dyke, Dick
Bye Bye Birdie 1963,Ap 5,27:3
What a Way to Go! 1964,My 15,44:1
Mary Poppins 1964,S 25,34:1
Art of Love, The 1965,Jl 1,34:1
Lt Robin Crusoe, USN 1966,Jl 14,28:1
Divorce American Style 1967,Jl 20,30:2
Fitzwilly 1967,D 21,45:1
Never a Dull Moment 1968,Ag 15,46:2
Van Dyke, Jerry
Courtship of Eddie's Father, The 1963,Mr 7,8:5
  (Incorrect in this edition; use 1963,Mr 28,8:5
  elsewhere)
Palm Springs Weekend 1963,N 6,32:1
McLintock 1963,N 14,41:3
Love and Kisses 1965,D 23,21:4
Van Dyke, Marcia
In the Good Old Summertime 1949,Ag 5,23:2
Shadow on the Wall 1950,My 19,31:3
Van Dyke, W S (Director)
Forget Me Not 1922,Jl 24,10:2
Barriers Burned Away 1925,Mr 12,17:2
Ranger of the big Trees, The 1925,Jl 28,24:4
White Shadows of the South Seas 1928,Ag 1,13:3
Pagan, The 1929,My 14,29:1
Trader Horn 1931,F 4,21:3
Never the Twain Shall Meet 1931,Je 6,15:5
Guilty Hands 1931,Ag 29,16:3
Cuban Love Song, The 1931,D 5,21:2
Tarzan, The Ape Man 1932,Mr 28,11:2
Night Court 1932,My 27,27:5
Penthouse 1933,S 9,9:2
Prizefighter and the Lady, The 1933,N 11,11:3
Eskimo 1933,N 15,25:2
Manhattan Melodrama 1934,My 5,22:2
Thin Man, The 1934,Je 30,18:5
Hide-Out 1934,Ag 25,16:5
Forsaking all Others 1934,D 21,18:1
Naughty Marietta 1935,Mr 23,11:2
I Live my Life 1935,O 12,12:2
Rose Marie 1936,F 1,9:2
San Francisco 1936,Je 27,21:1
His Brother's Wife 1936,Ag 15,6:2
Devil is a Sissy, The 1936,O 17,21:2
Love on the Run 1936,N 28,13:3
After the Thin Man 1936,D 25,19:2
Personal Property 1937,Ap 11,27:2
They Gave Him a Gun 1937,My 14,21:1
Rosalie 1937,D 31,9:2
Marie Antoinette 1938,Ag 17,23:2
Sweethearts 1938,D 23,16:2
Stand up and Fight 1939,Ja 27,17:2
It's a Wonderful World 1939,My 19,27:2
Andy Hardy Gets Spring Fever 1939,Jl 19,23:2
Another Thin Man 1939,N 24,29:1
I Take This Woman 1940,F 16,23:3
I Love You Again 1940,Ag 16,11:2
Bitter Sweet 1940,N 22,27:1
Rage in Heaven 1941,Mr 21,19:2
Shadow of the Thin Man 1941,N 21,23:2
Feminine Touch, The 1941,D 12,35:3
Dr Kildare's Victory 1942,F 5,25:2
I Married an Angel 1942,Jl 10,13:2
Cairo 1942,N 6,27:2
Journey for Margaret 1942,D 18,36:7
Van Dyke, Willard (Producer)
Lonely Night, The 1954,Mr 29,22:2
van Essen, Lis
Eternal Waltz, The; (Ewiger Walzer)
  1959,Jl 9,22:1
van Everett, Maria
Echoes of Silence 1967,Ap 7,32:2
Van Every, Dale (Original Author)
Marianne 1929,O 19,22:6
East of Borneo 1931,S 26,25:3
Spirit of Notre Dame, The 1931,O 16,27:1
Tom Brown of Culver 1932,Jl 30,16:5
All American, The 1932,O 22,18:4
After Office Hours 1935,Mr 9,19:1
Men Without Names 1935,Je 29,16:2
Van Every, Dale (Producer)
Dr Cyclops 1940,Ap 11,32:3
Rangers of Fortune 1940,S 19,27:2
Van Every, Dale (Screenwriter)

Van Every, Dale (Screenwriter)
Desert Nights 1929,My 6,30:4
Those Three French Girls 1930,O 11,21:3
Air Mail 1932,N 7,20:3
Wings in the Dark 1935,F 2,10:1
Annapolis Farewell 1935,Ag 24,18:2
More Than a Secretary 1936,D 11,35:2
Captains Courageous 1937,My 12,27:1
Souls at Sea 1937,Ag 10,23:2
Sealed Cargo 1951,My 24,47:1
Van Every, Edward (Original Author)
Sweet Rosie O'Grady 1943,O 21,30:2
Van Eyck, Peter
Moon Is Down, The 1943,Mr 27,8:6
Five Graves to Cairo 1943,My 27,21:2
Impostor, The 1944,Mr 27,17:2
Address Unknown 1944,Ap 17,20:1
Sailor of the King 1953,S 3,15:2
Night People 1954,Mr 13,11:2
Wages of Fear, The 1955,F 17,23:1
Bullet for Joey, A 1955,Ap 16,12:1
Rawhide Years, The 1956,Je 16,12:2
Run for the Sun 1956,Ag 25,7:2
Attack! 1956,S 20,29:4
There's Always a Price Tag 1958,My 26,25:2
Snorkel, The 1958,S 18,37:2
Girl on the Third Floor, The; (Sophie et le Crime)
  1958,O 11,47:1 (Incorrect in this edition; use
  1958,O 11,18:4 elsewhere)
Flesh and Desire 1958,N 27,52:4
Glass Tower, The; (Glaserne Turm, Der)
  1959,Ag 27,24:4
Rosemary 1960,Ja 19,40:2
Rest Is Silence, The 1960,Ag 2,22:6
Foxhole in Cairo 1961,F 16,25:2
World in my Pocket, The 1962,My 10,30:2
Longest Day, The 1962,O 5,28:1
Mr Arkadin 1962,O 12,26:1
And so to Bed 1965,Jl 31,11:3
Spy Who Came in From the Cold, The
  1965,D 24,24:1
Shalako 1968,N 6,32:1
van Eyck, Tony
Hertha's Erwachen 1933,Mr 14,18:3 (Incorrect in
  this edition; use 1933,Mr 14,19:2 elsewhere)
Strich Durch die Rechnung 1934,Mr 3,8:6
Van Eyss, Edgar (Original Author)
I Was a Prisoner on Devil's Island
  1941,Jl 28,16:4
Van Eyss, Otto (Original Author)
I Was a Prisoner on Devil's Island
  1941,Jl 28,16:4
Van Eyss, Otto (Screenwriter)
Big Jack 1949,My 23,27:4
Van Eyssen, John
Four Sided Triangle 1953,My 16,10:1
Cockleshell Heroes, The 1956,Je 4,25:2
Horror of Dracula 1958,My 29,24:4
Man in a Cocked Hat 1960,Je 15,50:2
Van Fleet, Jo
East of Eden 1955,Mr 10,33:1
Rose Tattoo, The 1955,D 13,55:1
I'll Cry Tomorrow 1956,Ja 13,18:1
King and Four Queens, The 1956,D 22,13:7
Gunfight at the O K Corral 1957,My 30,23:2
This Angry Age 1958,Je 26,23:3
Cool Hand Luke 1967,N 2,58:1
I Love You Alice B Toklas! 1968,O 8,40:1
van Grove, Isaac (Miscellaneous)
I'll Take Romance 1937,D 17,33:2
Van Haden, Anders
Cheaters at Play 1932,F 27,22:1
Passport to Hell, A 1932,Ag 27,13:4
Best of Enemies 1933,Jl 17,19:5
Secret of the Blue Room, The 1933,S 13,22:1
Barbary Coast 1935,O 14,21:1
Van Hensbergen, Lo
Dog of Flanders, A 1960,Ap 1,37:1
Van Heusen, James (Composer)
Love Thy Neighbor 1940,D 18,32:5
Road to Zanzibar 1941,Ap 10,29:2
Playmates 1941,D 26,21:3
My Favorite Spy 1942,My 29,13:4
Road to Morocco 1942,N 12,30:1
Dixie 1943,Je 24,26:2
Lady in the Dark 1944,F 23,17:1
Going my Way 1944,My 3,25:2
And the Angels Sing 1944,Jl 13,14:2
Belle of the Yukon 1945,Mr 30,18:4
Duffy's Tavern 1945,S 6,23:3
Road to Utopia 1946,F 28,20:2
Road to Rio 1948,F 19,29:3
Anything Goes 1956,Mr 22,38:1
Pardners 1956,Jl 26,20:2
van Hoogstraten, Eleanore
Town Without Pity 1961,O 11,53:1
Van Khe, Tran
Town Like Alice, A 1958,S 22,27:1
Van Kye, Therese
State Secret 1950,O 5,38:2

Van Le, Le
Quiet American, The 1958,F 6,24:1
van Leeuwen, Piet
Ciske 1963,Ag 3,8:2
Van Lent, Lucille
Merry Widow, The 1925,Ag 27,14:1
Van Loan, H H (Original Author)
Great Redeemer, The 1920,O 25,18:1
Siren of Seville, The 1924,N 17,16:1 (In Addenda)
Noose, The 1928,Mr 19,26:4
Runaway Bride 1930,My 17,21:2
van Loewen, Jan
Life and Death of Colonel Blimp, The 1945,Mr 30,18:2
van Loon, Hendrik Willem (Narrator)
Fight for Peace, The 1938,My 14,18:1
van Loon, Hendrik Willem (Original Author)
Story of Mankind, The 1957,N 9,31:2
Van Loon, Robert
Paisan 1948,Mr 30,26:2
Van-Luy-Sian
Alone 1932,My 25,23:6
van Lyck, Henry
Signs of Life; Lebenszeichent 1968,S 26,60:1
van Maerlant, Jenny
Ciske 1963,Ag 3,8:2
Van Marter, George (Screenwriter)
Four Guns to the Border 1954,N 6,15:3
Van Norton, Denis
Cairo Road 1952,N 1,17:2
Van Nutter, Rik
Romanoff and Juliet 1961,Je 9,26:1
Thunderball 1965,D 22,23:1
Van Nuys, Laura Bower (Original Author)
One and Only Genuine Original Family Band, The 1968,Mr 22,55:1
Van Paassen, Pierre (Miscellaneous)
That They May Live 1939,N 7,31:2
Van Parys, Georges (Composer)
Avocate d'Amour 1938,S 8,27:2
Abused Confidence 1938,D 1,29:1
Van Patten, Joyce
Goddess, The 1958,Je 25,24:1
I Love You Alice B Toklas! 1968,O 8,40:1
Van Patten, Richard
Psychomania 1964,F 15,14:3
Van Praag, Van (Original Author)
Men in War 1957,Mr 20,32:4
Van Praag, William (Miscellaneous)
Roosevelt Story, The 1947,Ag 22,11:2
Van Riel, Raimondo
Quo Vadis 1925,F 16,24:1
Strange Case of Captain Ramper, The 1928,Je 4,13:2
Luci Sommerse 1936,Je 22,22:2
Scipio Africanus 1939,S 23,22:2
Van Riper, Kay (Miscellaneous)
Harvey Girls, The 1946,Ja 25,26:2
Van Riper, Kay (Original Author)
Blondie Meets the Boss 1939,Ap 27,31:1
Kathleen 1941,D 19,35:3
Van Riper, Kay (Screenwriter)
Family Affair, A 1937,Ap 20,29:2
You're Only Young Once 1938,Ja 3,16:2
Judge Hardy's Children 1938,Ap 8,17:2
Hardys Ride High, The 1939,Ap 14,28:2
Andy Hardy Gets Spring Fever 1939,Jl 19,23:2
Babes in Arms 1939,O 20,27:2
Van Ronkel, Rip (Original Author)
High Cost of Loving, The 1958,My 17,12:1
Van Ronkel, Rip (Screenwriter)
Destination Moon 1950,Je 28,32:2
High Cost of Loving, The 1958,My 17,12:1
Van Rooten, Luis
Hitler Gang, The 1944,My 8,15:2
Two Years Before the Mast 1946,S 25,39:2
To the Ends of the Earth 1948,F 13,26:2
Saigon 1948,Ap 1,30:5
To the Victor 1948,Ap 17,11:2
Big Clock, The 1948,Ap 22,34:2
Beyond Glory 1948,Ag 4,18:2
Night Has a Thousand Eyes 1948,O 14,38:3
City Across the River 1949,Ap 8,31:3
Detective Story 1951,N 7,35:2
My Favorite Spy 1951,D 26,19:3
Lydia Bailey 1952,My 31,12:5
Unholy Wife, The 1958,Mr 7,17:1
Fraulein 1958,Je 9,27:2
Van Roy, Erwein von
O Alte Burschenherrlichkeit 1932,Je 18,9:2
Van Scoy, W A (Cinematographer)
Dame Nature's Love 1918,O 14,15:1
Clouds that Smile 1918,D 9,11:4
Sunshine and Shadows 1919,Ap 7,11:5
Cloud, The 1919,Ap 21,13:4
Van Scoy, W A (Miscellaneous)
Teepe Town 1922,S 11,20:2
Van Sickel, Dale
Rogue Cop 1954,S 18,12:2
Van Sloan, Edward
Dracula 1931,F 13,21:3
Frankenstein 1931,D 5,21:2

Manhattan Parade 1931,D 25,29:2
Man Wanted 1932,Ap 16,11:2
Behind the Mask 1932,My 2,13:2
Forgotten Commandments 1932,Je 2,25:2
Thunder Below 1932,Je 20,11:2
Last Mile, The 1932,Ag 26,20:3
Mummy, The 1933,Ja 7,11:2
Death Kiss, The 1933,F 5,IX,5:3
Infernal Machine 1933,Ap 8,16:3
Working Man, The 1933,Ap 21,20:3
Trick for Trick 1933,Je 10,16:4
It's Great to be Alive 1933,Jl 8,14:6
Deluge 1933,O 9,22:3
Death Takes a Holiday 1934,F 24,18:4
Life of Vergie Winters, The 1934,Je 15,26:1
Scralet Empress, The 1934,S 15,20:2
I'll Fix It 1934,N 12,17:3
Grand Old Girl 1935,F 26,16:4
Shot in the Dark, A 1935,My 22,23:2
Air Hawks 1935,Je 4,26:5
Last Days of Pompeii, The 1935,O 17,29:2
Road Gang 1936,F 24,14:1
Dracula's Daughter 1936,My 18,14:2
Sins of Man 1936,Je 19,17:2
Penitentiary 1938,Mr 7,13:2
Doctor Takes a Wife, The 1940,Je 15,12:2
Secret Seven, The 1940,Ag 12,11:6
Before I Hang 1940,O 3,31:3
Van Steyn, Gilda Doorn
Tel Aviv Taxi 1956,D 31,10:7
Van Stralen, Anton
Jailbreakers, The 1961,Ja 5,27:2
Van Tuyl, Rellen
Titanic 1953,My 28,27:5
Van Upp, Virginia (Original Author)
Cafe Society 1939,F 23,19:2
Virginia 1941,Ja 29,21:2
Come Live With Me 1941,F 28,17:3
Affair in Trinidad 1952,Jl 31,14:2
Van Upp, Virginia (Producer)
Together Again 1944,N 24,19:2
She Wouldn't Say Yes 1946,Ja 12,10:7
Gilda 1946,Mr 15,27:2
Van Upp, Virginia (Screenwriter)
Poppy 1936,Je 18,19:1
My American Wife 1936,Ag 21,12:3
Swing High, Swing Low 1937,Ap 15,19:1
You and Me 1938,Je 2,19:1
Cafe Society 1939,F 23,19:2
Honeymoon in Bali 1939,S 21,21:1
Virginia 1941,Ja 29,21:2
One Night in Lisbon 1941,Je 12,29:3
Bahama Passage 1942,F 19,23:2
Crystal Ball, The 1943,F 19,22:2
Cover Girl 1944,Mr 31,26:1
Impatient Years, The 1944,S 20,20:1
Together Again 1944,N 24,19:2
She Wouldn't Say Yes 1946,Ja 12,10:7
Here Comes the Groom 1951,S 21,19:2
Van Vechten, Carl (Original Author)
Woman of the World, A 1925,D 14,18:2
Van Vleck, Gohr
Mystery Sea Raider 1940,Ag 26,11:4
Van Vliet, Jean
Ladies at Ease 1927,O 5,31:1
Van Vooren, Monique
Tomorrow is too Late 1952,Ap 14,22:2
Ten Thousand Bedrooms 1957,Ap 4,37:1
Happy Anniversary 1959,N 11,41:1
Van Voorhis, Westbrook (Narrator)
We Are the Marines 1942,D 14,19:2
Van Zandt, Philip
Citizen Kane 1941,My 2,25:1
Sherlock Holmes and the Secret Weapon 1943,Ja 5,15:2
Tarzan Triumphs 1943,F 5,16:3
Air Raid Wardens 1943,Ap 5,15:5
Big Noise, The 1944,S 23,16:1
House of Frankenstein 1944,D 16,19:3
Sudan 1945,Ap 19,22:8
Counter-Attack 1945,My 17,15:2
Thousand and one Nights, A 1945,Jl 12,8:2
Somewhere in the Night 1946,Je 13,24:2
Avalanche 1946,Jl 8,25:2
Slave Girl 1947,Jl 18,21:3
April Showers 1948,Mr 27,10:2
Vicious Circle, The 1948,Jl 22,27:2
Loves of Carmen, The 1948,S 3,16:2
Walk a Crooked Mile 1948,O 13,31:2
Lady Gambles, The 1949,My 21,9:2
Petty Girl, The 1950,Ag 18,17:2
Between Midnight and Dawn 1950,O 2,19:2
Copper Canyon 1950,N 16,39:2
Cyrano De Bergerac 1950,N 17,31:2
Where Danger Lives 1951,Ja 1,13:6
His Kind of Woman 1951,Ag 30,20:2
Submarine Command 1952,Ja 19,13:2
Thief of Damascus 1952,My 8,37:2
Yankee Pasha 1954,Ap 19,19:2
Gog 1954,Ag 14,8:2
Pride and the Passion, The 1957,Je 29,10:6

Van Zandt, Philip— Cont
Man of a Thousand Faces 1957,Ag 14,21:1
Vanaire, Jacques
Fashions in Love 1929,Jl 1,31:2
Jewel Robbery 1932,Jl 23,6:6
Road to Glory, The 1936,Ag 6,22:1
Vanbrugh, Irene
Catherine the Great 1934,F 15,15:6
Escape me Never 1935,My 24,24:2
Wings of the Morning 1937,Mr 12,19:1
Knight Without Armor 1937,Jl 9,18:1
Yank in London, A 1946,Ap 20,16:3
Vanbrugh, Violet
Captivation 1931,S 28,17:4
Pygmalion 1938,D 8,34:2
Vance, Dennis
Christopher Columbus 1949,O 13,33:2
Vance, Ethel (Original Author)
Escape 1940,N 1,33:1
Winter Meeting 1948,Ap 8,31:2
Vance, Jack
Criminal Code, The 1931,Ja 5,21:3
Vance, Jean (Screenwriter)
Shakedown, The 1961,Mr 16,44:2
Vance, Leigh (Screenwriter)
Flesh is Weak, The 1957,N 9,31:2
Dr Crippen 1964,F 15,14:1
Dream Maker, The 1964,Ap 23,34:1
Vance, Louis Joseph (Original Author)
Lone Wolf, The 1924,My 7,19:4
Married Flirts 1924,N 19,19:3
Alias the Lone Wolf 1927,S 20,32:2
Lone Wolf's Daughter, The 1929,Mr 4,20:2
Cheaters at Play 1932,F 27,22:1
Lone Wolf Returns, The 1936,F 4,25:5
Lone Wolf in Paris, The 1938,My 23,21:2
Lone Wolf Spy Hunt, The 1939,Mr 6,11:3
Lone Wolf Strikes, The 1940,F 5,13:2
Lone Wolf Meets a Lady, The 1940,Je 17,19:2
Lone Wolf Keeps a Date, The 1941,Ja 2,24:3
Lone Wolf Takes a Chance, The 1941,Ap 7,13:2
Counter-Espionage 1942,S 28,13:2
Vance, Vivian
Secret Fury, The 1950,Je 22,34:2
Blue Veil, The 1951,O 27,10:5
Great Race, The 1965,S 16,00:0
Vancura, Vladislav (Original Author)
Capricious Summer 1968,S 25,38:2
Vandal, Marcel (Producer)
David Golder 1932,O 20,24:2
Vandegrift, Monte
Private Worlds 1935,Mr 28,25:2
Seven Keys to Baldpate 1935,D 14,11:2
Woman Chases Man 1937,Je 11,26:2
Vandeleur, Iris
Love on the Dole 1945,O 13,11:2
Vandenbergh, Leonard J Dr (Director)
Wild Men of Africa 1920,Ja 10,9:1
Vandenbergh, Leonard J Dr (Producer)
Wild Men of Africa 1921,F 7,8:2
Vandenberghe, Paul (Original Author)
My First Love 1951,Je 11,20:7
Vandenberghe, Paul (Screenwriter)
My First Love 1951,Je 11,20:7
Vanderbilt, Cornelius Jr (Miscellaneous)
Hitler's Reign of Terror 1934,My 1,26:6
Vanderbilt, Cornelius Jr (Original Author)
Reno 1930,N 4,36:1
Vanderbilt, George (Producer)
Devil's Playground, The 1932,D 26,26:2
Vanderbilt, William K
Over the Seven Seas 1933,My 24,24:2
Vandercook, John W (Original Author)
Murder in Trinidad 1934,My 16,22:2
Caribbean Mystery, The 1945,Ag 20,22:4
Vanderveer, Elinor
Into her Kingdom 1926,Ag 10,19:2
Vanderwilt, Jean
Southerner, The 1945,Ag 27,22:3
Vandevere, Mike
Incident in an Alley 1962,My 17,31:1
New Interns, The 1964,Ag 20,34:2
Vandis, Titos
Astero 1960,Ap 25,32:2
Never on Sunday 1960,O 19,54:1
It Happened in Athens 1962,N 15,46:2
Island of Love 1963,Je 13,30:4
Topkapi 1964,S 18,25:1
Vandiver, Jerry
I'd Climb the Highest Mountain 1951,My 10,38:1
Vandyke, Truman
Daughters of Today 1924,Mr 4,17:1
Vane, Amy
Secret Cinema, The 1968,My 2,57:1
Vane, Charles
This Freedom 1923,N 28,15:1
Vane, Myrtle
Unknown, The 1924,N 18,22:1
K-The Unknown 1924,N 18,22:1
Vane, Sutton (Original Author)
Between Two Worlds 1944,My 6,11:2
Vaneck, Pierre
He Who Must Die 1958,D 29,21:1
Marianne of my Youth; (Marianne de ma Jeunesse) 1959,Ja 20,43:1

Vaneck, Pierre— Cont
Season for Love, The 1963,My 9,40:2
Is Paris Burning? 1966,N 11,36:1
Vanel, Charles
Waterloo 1929,Ap 16,32:5
Miserables, Les 1936,O 28,31:2
They Were Five 1938,Je 1,19:5
Flight Into Darkness (L'Equipage) 1938,O 17,12:1
Abused Confidence 1938,D 1,29:1
Crossroads 1939,Mr 14,17:5
I Give my Life 1941,S 1,18:4
Miserables, Les 1946,D 26,28:4
Savage Brigade 1948,D 3,33:4
Woman Who Dared, The 1949,Mr 19,10:7
Mafia; (In Nome Della Legge) 1950,Mr 2,33:2
Wages of Fear, The 1955,F 17,23:1
To Catch a Thief 1955,Ag 5,14:2
Diabolique 1955,N 22,41:1
Sinners of Paris 1959,Ap 24,23:1
No Escape 1959,My 23,18:4
Defend my Love; (Difendo il Mio Amore) 1959,O 8,48:7
Prisoner of the Volga 1960,Je 2,27:2
Truth, The 1961,Je 27,23:2
Steppe, The 1963,O 1,33:1
Symphony for a Massacre 1965,My 28,40:1
Vaness, Connie
Mugger, The 1959,Je 25,20:7
Vanicek, Eva
Rome, 11 O'Clock 1953,Ap 30,39:2
Vanin, A
Return of Maxim, The 1937,N 2,33:1
Vanin, V
Sibirsky Patrul 1932,My 14,11:5
Concentration Camp 1939,Mr 20,13:2
Vanin, V V
Lenin in October 1938,Ap 2,18:1
Lenin in 1918 1939,Je 27,27:2
Vanin, Vasili
Wings of Victory 1941,N 17,15:2
We Will Come Back 1943,O 15,15:2
Vanke, Elena
Cinderella 1961,D 19,39:1
Vanloo, Rolf E (Original Author)
Asphalt 1930,My 6,33:4
Vann, Jay (Screenwriter)
Tarzan's Revenge 1938,Ja 10,13:3
Vanna, Nina
Woman Tempted, The 1928,Ap 24,29:3
Youth Astray 1928,My 29,17:2
Vanne, Marda
Joanna 1968,N 25,54:1
Vanni, Renata
Westward the Women 1952,Ja 1,21:2
Hell on Frisco Bay 1956,Ja 7,21:1
Pay or Die 1960,My 27,22:2
Vanni, Vanna
Ho Perduto mio Marito; I Have Lost My Husband 1939,O 20,27:4
Re di Danari; Money King 1939,D 22,15:2
Vanni-Marcoux
Miracle des Loups, Le 1930,Jl 28,22:1
Vannoni, Emma
Tramplers, The 1966,D 8,64:1
Vanny, Ruos
Your Shadow Is Mine 1963,My 15,32:1
Vano, I (Director)
Magic Horse, The 1949,Je 20,14:7
Vanoni, Cesar
Texan, The 1930,My 17,21:2
Vanoni, Ornella
Duel of the Titans 1963,Ag 8,19:1
Vanoni, Pierre
World Without Sun 1964,D 23,22:1
Vanorio, Gabriele
Tarantella Napoletana 1954,Ap 19,19:3
Vansittart, Robert Sir (Screenwriter)
Sixty Glorious Years 1938,N 18,25:2
Vanstone, Richard
Strange Affair, The 1968,Jl 25,26:2
Vanucchi, Luigi
Tiger and the Pussycat, The 1967,S 21,56:4
Vanya, Elsie
Last Waltz, The 1927,N 14,26:1
Vanzi, Luigi (Director)
World by Night 1962,Ja 11,26:1
Vanzina, Stefano (Screenwriter)
Miserables, Les 1952,Mr 25,23:2
Var, Maria
Silent Dust 1949,D 30,13:2
Varas, Jean
Mr Orchid; Pere Tranquille, Le 1948,Mr 29,17:3
Devil in the Flesh 1949,My 10,29:2
Varconi, Victor
Triumph 1924,Ap 21,21:4
Changing Husbands 1924,Je 23,22:4
Poisoned Paradise 1924,Ag 11,16:1
Feet of Clay 1924,S 22,16:1
Worldly Goods 1924,N 3,20:1
Volga Boatman, The 1926,Ap 14,21:1
Silken Shackles 1926,My 25,25:1
For Wives Only 1926,D 1,24:5
King of Kings, The 1927,Ap 20,29:2

Fighting Love 1927,My 23,27:2
Forbidden Woman, The 1927,O 31,22:1
Angel of Broadway 1927,N 1,21:1 (In Addenda)
Chicago 1927,D 24,9:1
Tenth Avenue 1928,O 9,35:1
Divine Lady, The 1929,Mr 23,22:4
Eternal Love 1929,My 13,27:2
Doctors' Wives 1931,Ap 25,23:4
Captain Thunder 1931,My 11,15:4
Black Camel, The 1931,Jl 4,11:5
Men in her Life 1931,N 30,16:2
Safe in Hell 1931,D 19,16:4
Doomed Battalion, The 1932,Je 11,9:3
Rebel, The 1933,Jl 25,17:2
Roberta 1935,Mr 8,25:2
Mr Dynamite 1935,My 25,12:1
Feather in her Hat, A 1935,O 25,24:5
Dancing Pirate 1936,Je 18,19:1
Plainsman, The 1937,Ja 14,16:2
Trouble in Morocco 1937,Mr 15,27:1
Big City 1937,S 17,29:2
King of the Newsboys 1938,Ap 2,18:2
Suez 1938,O 15,21:2
Submarine Patrol 1938,N 19,9:2
Story of Vernon and Irene Castle, The 1939,Mr 31,19:2
Mr Moto Takes a Vacation 1939,Je 19,12:6
Everything Happens at Night 1939,D 16,12:6
Strange Cargo 1940,Ap 26,25:2
My Favorite Blonde 1942,Ap 2,27:2
For Whom the Bell Tolls 1943,Jl 15,25:2
Hitler Gang, The 1944,My 8,15:2
Unconquered 1947,O 11,11:2
Pirates of Monterey 1947,D 17,41:4
Where There's Life 1947,D 25,32:1
Varda, Agnes
Far from Vietnam 1967,O 2,58:1
Varda, Agnes (Director)
Cleo From 5 to 7 1962,S 5,43:4
Bonheur, Le; Happiness 1966,My 24,55:2
Creatures, Les 1966,S 16,31:2
Far From Vietnam 1968,Je 7,32:1
Varda, Agnes (Screenwriter)
Cleo From 5 to 7 1962,S 5,43:4
Bonheur, Le; Happiness 1966,My 24,55:2
Varda, Valerie
Mr Hobbs Takes a Vacation 1962,Je 16,11:2
Varden, Evelyn
Pinky 1949,S 30,28:2
When Willie Comes Marching Home 1950,F 18,9:2
Cheaper by the Dozen 1950,Ap 1,12:2
Stella 1950,Ag 19,9:2
Elopement 1951,D 21,21:3
Phone Call From a Stranger 1952,F 2,11:2
Student Prince, The 1954,Je 16,18:2
Desiree 1954,N 18,42:1
Athena 1954,D 22,28:2
Night of the Hunter, The 1955,S 30,23:1
Hilda Crane 1956,My 3,35:2
Bad Seed, The 1956,S 13,39:6
Ten Thousand Bedrooms 1957,Ap 4,37:1
Varden, Norma
Iron Duke, The 1935,Ja 25,27:2
East Meets West 1936,O 31,24:2
Shipyard Sally 1940,Ja 18,27:3
Earl of Chicago, The 1940,Mr 14,29:3
Scotland Yard 1941,Ap 9,33:3
We Were Dancing 1942,My 1,23:2
Random Harvest 1942,D 18,36:6
What a Woman 1943,D 3,27:2
White Cliffs of Dover, The 1944,My 12,15:2
National Velvet 1944,D 15,25:2
Bring on the Girls 1945,Mr 1,25:5
Hold That Blonde 1945,N 8,17:2
Green Years, The 1946,Ap 5,21:2
Searching Wind, The 1946,Je 27,29:1
Trouble With Women, The 1947,Jl 14,14:4
Thunder in the Valley 1947,N 28,30:1
Adventure in Baltimore 1949,Ap 29,27:2
Fancy Pants 1950,Ag 31,21:2
Strangers on a Train 1951,Jl 4,13:2
Thunder on the Hill 1951,O 18,32:3
Miserables, Les 1952,Ag 15,11:2
Young Bess 1953,My 22,31:1
Gentlemen Prefer Blondes 1953,Jl 16,17:2
Jupiter's Darling 1955,F 18,18:4
Witness for the Prosecution 1958,F 7,16:1
13 Frightened Girls 1963,S 12,32:2
Sound of Music, The 1965,Mr 3,34:1
Very Special Favor, A 1965,Ag 26,40:3
Doctor Dolittle 1967,D 20,55:1
Vardi, David
Tel Aviv Taxi 1956,D 31,10:7
Vardi, Sara
Blue 1968,My 11,28:1
Vardy, John
Children on Trial 1947,N 10,21:3
Vardy, John Mrs
Children on Trial 1947,N 10,21:3
Varela, Amanda
Falcon's Brother, The 1942,O 3,9:5

Varela, Nina
Viva Zapata 1952,F 8,19:2
President's Lady, The 1953,My 22,31:1
Love With the Proper Stranger 1963,D 26,33:1
Varela, Uvaldo
Arizona 1941,F 7,23:3
Varelli, Alfredo
Fear No Evil 1949,Mr 31,31:2
Quo Vadis 1951,N 9,22:2
Measure for Measure 1951,D 8,9:2
Stranger on the Prowl 1953,N 10,38:1
Man From Cairo, The 1953,D 17,52:4
Eye of the Needle, The 1965,Je 22,25:2
Varennes, Andre
Carnival of Sinners 1947,Ap 8,34:2
Varennes, Jacques
Criez-Le sur les Toits; Shout it From the Housetops 1935,Je 22,18:5
Bouquets From Nicholas 1939,Mr 2,19:1
Personal Column 1941,F 3,13:2
Mad Emperor, The 1941,Mr 10,21:3
Mlle Desiree 1948,N 19,35:2
Eagle with Two Heads 1948,D 30,24:2
Vautrin, the Thief 1949,N 11,31:2
Orpheus 1950,N 30,42:2
Three Sinners 1952,Jl 8,23:2
Diabolique 1955,N 22,41:1
Varesi, Gilda (Original Author)
Enter Madame 1935,Ja 12,12:1
Varga, Billy
Bodyhold 1949,D 12,29:4
Varga, Carol
Prince Who Was a Thief, The 1951,Jl 4,13:2
Varga, Joe
Magnificent Brute, The 1936,O 24,23:1
Vargas, Daniele
Successo, Il 1965,Ap 29,40:2
Stranger Returns, The 1968,S 12,54:3
Vargas, Edmund
Two Loves 1961,Je 22,23:2
Vargas, Juan Antonio (Screenwriter)
St Francis of Assisi 1947,Ap 5,12:5
Vargas, Myra
Forza del Destino, La 1952,O 17,33:1
Vargas, Pedrito
Littlest Outlaw, The 1955,D 27,31:1
Vargas, Victoria
Shadows 1961,Mr 22,37:1
Vari, John
Last Mile, The 1959,F 19,27:1
Variey, Beatrice
Horrors of the Black Museum 1959,Ap 30,37:2
Varini, Emilia
One Hundred Days of Napoleon 1936,S 14,25:1
Varkonyi, Michael
Queen of Sin and the Spectacle of Sodom and Gomorrah 1923,Mr 27,24:3 (In Addenda)
Varlamov, I (Director)
In the Circus Arena 1952,Ap 14,22:3
Varlamov, Leonid (Director)
Battle for China 1953,N 2,29:2
Varley, Beatrice
Squadron Leader X 1943,Jl 23,21:2
Man in Grey, The 1945,N 30,18:6
Wicked Lady, The 1946,D 23,19:5
Bedelia 1947,F 8,10:2
Lady Surrenders, A 1947,Je 20,25:6
So Well Remembered 1947,N 5,34:3
Holiday Camp 1948,Ja 24,11:2
Jassy 1948,F 20,19:2
Hatter's Castle 1948,Jl 3,8:6
Waterloo Road 1948,D 25,10:3
My Brothers Keeper 1949,F 14,15:3
Agitator, The 1949,Ag 19,12:5
Adam and Evalyn 1950,My 12,33:4
Good Time Girl 1950,S 25,18:5
Little Ballerina, The 1951,F 28,33:2
Melba 1953,Je 25,23:1
Room at the Top 1959,Mr 31,26:1
Varlin, Catherine (Screenwriter)
Le Joli Mai 1966,Je 10,54:2
Varnel, Marcel (Director)
Silent Witness, The 1932,F 8,21:1
Chandu the Magician 1932,O 1,10:4
Infernal Machine 1933,Ap 8,16:3
Dance Band 1936,Ja 4,19:2
Loves of Madame Dubarry, The 1938,Ap 4,12:5
Let George Do It 1940,O 14,25:5
Varneuil, Henri (Director)
Wild Oat, The 1956,Je 28,33:2
Varney, Reg
Miss Robin Hood 1953,Je 27,7:2
Varno, Roland
As You Desire Me 1932,Je 3,23:4
Private Jones 1933,Mr 25,13:3
Quality Street 1937,Ap 9,19:2
Balalaika 1939,D 15,33:2
Three Faces West 1940,Ag 19,13:2
Mystery Sea Raider 1940,Ag 26,11:4
Underground 1941,Je 23,13:2
Hostages 1943,O 11,23:2
Return of the Vampire, The 1944,Ja 29,10:1
Our Hearts Were Young and Gay 1944,O 12,24:2

Varno, Roland— Cont
Betrayal From the East 1945,Ap 25,27:2
My Name is Julia Ross 1945,N 9,16:3
Varro, Juan
Big Street, The 1942,Ag 14,13:1
Varsi, Diane
Peyton Place 1957,D 13,35:1
Ten North Frederick 1958,My 23,29:2
From Hell to Texas 1958,Je 5,39:2
Compulsion 1959,Ap 2,26:2
Sweet Love, Bitter 1967,Ja 31,50:1
Wild in the Streets 1968,My 30,21:1
Vartan, Sylvie
Friend of the Family 1965,N 18,55:3
Varte, Rosy
Every Second Counts 1957,O 15,39:4
Vartian, Setrag
Arshin Mal Alan; Peddler, Lover, The 1937,Mr 8,22:2
Varvarow, Feodor
End of St Petersberg, The 1928,My 31,21:2 (In Addenda)
Varvelle, Pearl
Smart Woman 1931,O 12,28:2
Varzi, Elena
It's Forever Springtime 1951,D 29,7:7
Path of Hope, The (Il Cammino Della Speranza) 1952,Ag 5,15:5
Rome, 11 O'Clock 1953,Ap 30,39:2
Strange Deception 1953,My 27,28:2
Vas Dias, Zelma
Lady Vanishes, The 1938,D 26,29:1
Vasa Folk Dance Group
World Dances 1954,N 8,24:6
Vasaroff, Michael
Paris 1926,Je 1,29:3
Vasary, Piri
Edes Mostoha 1935,N 21,27:2
Vaser, Vittorio
Gioconda, La 1958,O 13,33:4
Vasicek, Karel
Joseph Kilian 1966,Jl 19,34:1
Vasile, Turi (Screenwriter)
Verginita 1953,Ap 18,17:2
Vasilief, V
Beethoven Concerto 1937,Mr 24,29:1
Vasiliev, Georgy (Director)
Tchapayef 1935,Ja 15,22:1
Defense of Volotchayevsk, The 1938,Ag 11,13:3
Vasiliev, Georgy (Screenwriter)
Fortress on the Volga 1942,D 25,15:3
Queen of Spades 1961,S 4,10:1
Vasiliev, Sergei (Director)
Tchapayef 1935,Ja 15,22:1
Defense of Volotchayevsk, The 1938,Ag 11,13:3
Heroes of Shipka 1956,S 3,10:5
Vasiliev, Sergei (Screenwriter)
Fortress on the Volga 1942,D 25,15:3
Queen of Spades 1961,S 4,10:1
Vasilieva, Vera
Symphony of Life 1948,D 28,19:7
Chuk and Gek 1953,D 21,27:4
Bride with a Dowry 1954,Ag 23,20:5
Conflict 1955,D 26,23:4
Vasilyev, Vladimir
Little Humpbacked Horse, The 1962,O 8,19:1
Song Over Moscow 1964,N 23,52:1
Vasova, Marie
Thunder in the Hills 1947,My 24,10:5
Bohemian Rapture 1948,F 16,16:2
Emperor and the Golem, The 1955,Ja 10,27:4
Vasquez, Jose Luis (Mexicano)
Brave Bulls, The 1951,Ap 19,39:2
Vasquez, Matilde
Dona Francisquita 1935,Ap 27,20:6
Vassar, Queenie
Primrose Path 1940,Mr 23,16:2
Lady in a Jam 1942,S 11,25:2
Vasseli, Judith
Dance Magic 1927,Jl 13,21:2
Vassiliadou, Georgia
Germans Strike Again, The 1949,Ap 14,29:4
Astero 1960,Ap 25,32:2
Aunt From Chicago, The 1960,Je 6,33:6
Grouch, The 1961,F 27,23:2
Fortune Teller, The 1961,My 22,37:5
Midwife, The 1961,S 25,41:2
Vassiliev, D I (Original Author)
Alexander Nevsky 1939,Mr 23,27:1
Vassilieva, A I
Nazar Stodolya 1937,Ag 7,7:2
Vassilieva, Alexandra
Life in Bloom 1949,My 9,20:4
Vasszary, Janos (Director)
3:1 a Szerelem Javara; 3 to 1 for Love 1939,Mr 25,19:3
Vasudhara, Sunh (Director)
King of the White Elephant, The 1941,Ap 5,12:7
Vasyliev, V
Admiral Ushakov 1954,Ja 18,19:2
Vaszary, John (Director)
Mami 1938,F 19,19:5
Edes a Bosszu; Sweet Revenge 1938,S 10,20:3
Tokaji Rapszodia 1938,N 7,23:5

Rad Bizom a Felesegem; I Entrust my Wife to You 1939,My 6,21:3
Vaszary, Piri
Cimzett Ismeretlen 1936,F 7,14:2
Te Csak Pipalj Ladanyi; Keep On Smoking, Ladanyi 1938,My 18,9:3
Kolcsonkert Kastely; Borrowed Castle, The 1938,D 17,10:4
Varju a Toronyoran; Crow on the Tower 1939,N 18,22:6
Szegeny Gazdagok; Poor Plutocrats 1939,D 4,18:4
Eb Ura Fako 1940,Mr 23,16:4
Vatel, Martine
Muriel 1963,O 31,26:1
Vatori, Zeni
Magnificent Brute, The 1936,O 24,23:1
Vatteone, Augusto Cesar (Director)
Amor Manda, El; Love Commands 1940,My 18,11:3
Vattier
Three Waltzes 1939,Ap 25,19:2
Vattier, Nicole
Dawn Over France 1945,Mr 17,17:2
Vattier, Robert
Baker's Wife, The 1940,F 27,17:2
Carnival of Sinners 1947,Ap 8,34:2
Fanny 1948,F 13,26:2
Cesar 1948,O 28,36:2
Royal Affair, A; (Roi, Le) 1950,Mr 9,25:2
Letters From my Windmill (The Elixir of Father Gaucher); Elixir of Father Gaucher, The (Letters From my Windmill) 1955,D 19,33:1
Love Game, The 1960,N 9,44:1
Vaudry, Simone
Mystere de la Villa Rose, Le 1932,Ja 11,28:5
Vaugh, Robert
Caretakers, The 1963,Ag 22,19:2
VAUGHN
See Also VAGHN
Vaughan, Arky
Safe at Home 1941,N 26,31:2
Ninth Inning, The 1942,Ja 8,30:3
Vaughan, Bernard
Little Lord Fauntleroy 1914,Je 23,11:3
Vaughan, Beryl
Girls Under 21 1940,N 11,22:4
Vaughan, Edna
Ariane 1934,Mr 7,23:4
Vaughan, Frankie
Let's Make Love 1960,S 9,36:1
Right Approach, The 1961,My 18,41:1
Vaughan, Gillian
Horse's Mouth, The 1958,N 12,41:1
Cry From the Streets, A 1959,F 24,32:2
Vaughan, James (Screenwriter)
Good Times, Wonderful Times 1966,Jl 19,34:1
Vaughan, Peter
Die! Die! My Darling 1965,My 20,52:1
Naked Runner, The 1967,Jl 20,30:2
Hammerhead 1968,S 12,54:3
Bofors Gun, The 1968,S 23,42:3
Vaughan, Walter
C-Man 1949,My 28,11:4
Jigsaw 1949,My 30,9:4
Vaughan-Thomas, Wynford (Original Author)
Anzio 1968,Jl 25,26:1
Vaughn, Adamae
Courtship of Myles Standish, The 1923,D 31,9:3
Vaughn, Alberta
Drop Kick, The 1927,S 20,32:2
Skyscraper 1928,Ap 9,18:2
Forbidden Hours 1928,Jl 23,11:2
Dancers in the Dark 1932,Mr 19,11:2
Alimony Madness 1933,My 5,18:1
Vaughn, Dorothy
Times Square Playboy 1936,My 2,11:2
Love Begins at 20 1936,S 19,20:1
Black Legion 1937,Ja 18,21:1
That Man's Here Again 1937,My 6,23:3
Gambling Ship 1939,Ja 21,19:2
Unexpected Father 1939,Ag 11,12:2
First Love 1939,N 9,27:3
Bad Men of Missouri 1941,Ag 16,18:2
Lady Gangster 1942,Jl 10,13:2
Gentleman Jim 1942,N 26,40:3
That Brennan Girl 1946,D 9,34:3
Egg and I, The 1947,Ap 25,29:2
Vaughn, Hilda
Three Live Ghosts 1929,S 30,23:1
Manslaughter 1930,Jl 24,26:4
It's a Wise Child 1931,My 16,13:3
Susan Lenox; Her Fall and Rise 1931,O 17,20:1
Ladies of the Big House 1932,Ja 1,31:1
Phantom of Crestwood, The 1932,O 17,18:3
No Other Woman 1933,Ja 30,9:4 (In Addenda)
Today We Live 1933,Ap 15,16:2
No Marriage Ties 1933,Ag 4,18:2
Dinner at Eight 1933,Ag 24,18:1
Anne of Green Gables 1934,D 22,21:1
Wedding Night, The 1935,Mr 16,19:1
Men Without Names 1935,Je 29,16:2
Accusing Finger, The 1936,N 17,35:4

Vaughn, Hilda— Cont
Banjo on My Knee 1936,D 12,15:1
Charlie Chan At the Wax Museum 1940,S 28,9:3
Vaughn, Rees
Playground, The 1965,O 4,00:0
Vaughn, Robert
Young Philadelphians, The 1959,My 22,32:1
Magnificent Seven, The 1960,N 24,48:3
Big Show, The 1961,My 11,42:4
One Spy too Many 1966,D 8,64:1
Venetian Affair, The 1967,Ja 19,41:2
Bullitt 1968,O 18,41:2
Vaughn, Sammy
Born Wild 1968,D 12,62:6
Vaughn, William
Condemned 1929,N 4,28:1
Confessions of a Nazi Spy 1939,Ap 29,13:2
Conspiracy 1939,Ag 23,19:2
Vaughn-Hughes, Gerald (Screenwriter)
Sebastian 1968,Ja 25,33:2
Vausden, Val
Irish Destiny 1927,Mr 29,23:2 (In Addenda)
Vauthier, Jean (Screenwriter)
Abysses, Les 1964,N 24,44:1
Vautier, Elmire
Vivre 1928,Ag 12,VII,3:4
Mad Emperor, The 1941,Mr 10,21:3
Vautrot, Yvonne
Bell for Adano, A 1945,Jl 6,8:3
Vaverka, Anton
Phantom of the Opera, The 1925,S 7,15:3
Rolling Home 1926,Je 8,22:1
Love Parade, The 1929,N 20,32:6
Vavitch, Michael
Swan, The 1925,Mr 2,14:1
Graustark 1925,S 8,29:1
Crown of Lies 1926,Mr 30,20:6
Midnight Sun, The 1926,Ap 24,20:4
Valencia 1926,D 27,20:3
Hotel Imperial 1927,Ja 3,16:2
Third Degree, The 1927,F 15,23:1
Venus of Venice 1927,My 3,25:1
Two Arabian Knights 1927,O 24,24:3
Gaucho, The 1927,N 22,32:2
Devil Dancer, The 1927,D 19,30:1
Dove, The 1928,Ja 3,28:2
Glorious Betsy 1928,Ap 27,16:4
Woman Disputed, The 1928,N 10,20:8
Wolf Song 1929,F 25,16:1
Divine Lady, The 1929,Mr 23,22:4
Bridge of San Luis Rey, The 1929,My 20,22:6
Devil With Women, A 1930,O 20,28:2
War Nurse 1930,O 24,31:1
Vavor, Paul
Gul Baba 1940,O 26,18:8
Vavra, Otakar (Director)
Merry Wives, The 1940,N 12,28:3
Krakatit 1951,Ap 30,16:2
Vavra, Otakar (Producer)
Krakatit 1951,Ap 30,16:2
Vavra, Otakar (Screenwriter)
Merry Wives, The 1940,N 12,28:3
Krakatit 1951,Ap 30,16:2
Vaza, Opa
Germans Strike Again, The 1949,Ap 14,29:4
Vazhaev (Original Author)
Far for Moscow 1951,Jl 2,16:6
Vazquez, Jose A
Where Words Fail; Donde Mueren las Palabraso 1948,Ag 19,18:4
Vazquez, Jose Luis Lopez
Not on Your Life; Verdugo, El 1965,Mr 30,52:1
Vazquez, Roland
Midsummer Night's Dream, A 1967,Ap 18,32:1
Vaztan, Irena
Castle in Greece 1960,D 12,38:2
Vazzoler, Lisa
Fascist, The 1965,Je 18,28:3
Ve Sota, Bruno
Dementia 1955,D 23,14:4
Ve Sota, Jebbie
Dementia 1955,D 23,14:4
Veazie, Carol
Catered Affair, The 1956,Je 15,32:4
Cry in the Night, A 1956,S 1,19:4
Designing Woman 1957,My 17,20:2
Auntie Mame 1958,D 5,39:1
Baby, the Rain Must Fall 1965,Ja 14,44:1
Veber, Serge (Miscellaneous)
Amphitryon 1937,Mr 24,29:1
Fernandel the Dressmaker 1957,Jl 1,19:2
Senechal the Magnificent 1958,O 14,44:1
Veber, Serge (Screenwriter)
French Touch, The 1954,S 2,18:2
My Seven Little Sins 1956,My 2,27:1
Veber (Original Author)
Madame la Presidente 1916,F 7,9:3
Vebo, Sophia
Prosfygopoula; Girl Refugee, The 1938,S 27,25:3
Vecchietti, Alberto (Miscellaneous)
See Naples and Die 1959,Ag 31,16:2
Vecchietti, Alberto (Screenwriter)
See Naples and Die 1959,Ag 31,16:2

Vecheslov, S M
Last Night, The 1937,Ap 28,18:3
Vedder, Edward
Mozart Story, The 1948,N 15,21:5
Vedder, William
Paula 1952,Jl 16,21:2
Wild One, The 1953,D 31,9:2
Vedernikov, A
Tsar's Bride, The 1966,Mr 12,13:2
Vedey, Julian
Green Cockatoo, The 1947,Jl 19,10:2
Vedova, Elsso della
Never Take No for an Answer 1952,Ap 29,32:2
Vedres (Director)
Life Begins Tomorrow 1952,N 18,37:2
Vedres, Nicole (Screenwriter)
Paris 1900 1950,O 24,34:6
Life Begins Tomorrow 1952,N 18,37:2
Vee, Bobby
Play it Cool 1963,Jl 18,15:3
C'mon Let's Live a Little 1967,My 4,34:1
Veeck, Bill
Kid From Cleveland, The 1949,S 5,13:2
Vega, Rose
Loves of Ricardo, The 1926,Ag 16,10:1
Vegal, Fernando
Terrace, The 1964,N 25,45:1
Veidt, Conrad
Cabinet of Dr Caligari, The 1921,Ap 4,18:1
Three Way Works, The 1926,Mr 19,25:1
Beloved Rogue, The 1927,Mr 14,16:1
Impetuous Youth 1927,Je 13,17:1
Love Makes Us Blind 1927,Ag 23,29:4
Man's Past, A 1927,O 4,34:2
Husbands or Lovers 1927,N 22,32:2
Man Who Laughs, The 1928,Ap 28,12:3
Hands of Orlac, The 1928,Je 5,21:1
Two Brothers, The 1928,Ag 21,27:4
Lucrecia Borgia 1928,D 25,31:3
Man Who Cheated Life, The 1929,F 11,26:3
Last Performance, The 1929,N 4,28:1
Bride 68 1930,Ap 15,28:5
Thirteen Men and a Girl 1931,Ag 17,18:2
Congress Dances, The 1931,N 22,VIII,6:6
Congress Dances 1932,My 12,23:2
Die Letze Kompagnie 1932,Ag 26,20:3
Rome Express 1932,D 18,X,6:5
Schwartze Husar, Der 1932,D 23,20:1
Rome Express 1933,F 27,11:2
Ich und die Kaiserin 1933,My 28,IX,2:5 (In Addenda)
F P 1 1933,S 16,9:3
I Was a Spy 1934,Ja 15,12:2
Power 1934,O 5,29:3
Wandering Jew, The 1935,Ja 14,11:3
Bella Donna 1935,F 26,16:4
Legend of William Tell, The 1935,O 2,27:1
King of the Damned 1936,F 1,9:2
Passing of the Third Floor Back, The 1936,Ap 29,19:2
Under the Red Robe 1937,Je 1,27:2
Dark Journey 1937,Ag 23,22:1
U-Boat 29 1939,O 6,31:3
Devil Is an Empress, The 1939,D 4,18:4
Escape 1940,N 1,33:1
Blackout 1940,D 2,19:2
Thief of Bagdad, The 1940,D 6,28:2
Woman's Face, A 1941,My 16,21:2
Whistling in the Dark 1941,Ag 28,23:2
Men In her Life, The 1941,D 12,35:1
All Through the Night 1942,Ja 24,13:2
Nazi Agent 1942,Je 13,11:2
Casablanca 1942,N 27,27:1
Above Suspicion 1943,Ag 6,10:3
Veidt, Conradt
Mann der den Mord Beging, Der; Man Who Committed the Murder, The 1931,F 22,VIII,6:2
Veiga, Simao da
Gavilan, El; Hawk, The 1940,Ja 22,11:2
Veiller, Anthony (Narrator)
Tunisian Victory 1944,Mr 24,17:2
Veiller, Anthony (Original Author)
Tunisian Victory 1944,Mr 24,17:2
Veiller, Anthony (Producer)
Quarterback, The 1940,O 17,33:3
Victory 1940,D 23,23:2
New York Town 1941,N 13,35:2
Colorado Territory 1949,Je 25,8:6
Backfire 1950,Ja 27,29:2
Chain Lightning 1950,F 20,21:2
Dallas 1951,Ja 13,10:4
Along the Great Divide 1951,My 17,38:3
Fort Worth 1951,Jl 13,12:7
Force of Arms 1951,Ag 14,20:2
Red Planet Mars 1952,Je 16,15:2
Veiller, Anthony (Screenwriter)
Star of Midnight 1935,Ap 12,26:5
Break of Hearts 1935,My 17,24:3
Jalna 1935,S 14,8:4
Lady Consents, The 1936,F 6,23:4
Ex-Mrs Bradford, The 1936,My 28,19:2
Woman Rebels, A 1936,O 30,27:2
Winterset 1936,D 4,31:1

Soldier and the Lady, The 1937,Ap 10,11:1
Stage Door 1937,O 8,27:2
Radio City Revels 1938,Mr 21,18:3
Let Us Live 1939,Mr 30,19:2
Disputed Passage 1939,O 26,27:2
Her Cardboard Lover 1942,Jl 17,19:2
Assignment in Brittany 1943,Ap 22,31:2
Battle of Russia, The 1943,N 15,23:3
Adventure 1946,F 8,23:2
Stranger, The 1946,Jl 11,18:2
Killers, The 1946,Ag 29,24:2
State of the Union 1948,Ap 23,28:1
Red Planet Mars 1952,Je 16,15:2
Moulin Rouge 1953,F 11,33:5
That Lady 1955,Je 11,8:7
Safari 1956,Je 21,35:2
Solomon and Sheba 1959,D 26,7:2
List of Adrian Messenger, The 1963,My 30,20:1
Night of the Iguana, The 1964,Jl 1,42:1
Killers, The 1964,Jl 18,10:4
Veiller, Bayard
Red Planet Mars 1952,Je 16,15:2
Veiller, Bayard (Director)
Trial of Mary Dugan, The 1929,Mr 29,21:1
Veiller, Bayard (Miscellaneous)
Guilty Hands 1931,Ag 29,16:3
Veiller, Bayard (Original Author)
Within the Law 1917,Ap 30,11:3
Within the Law 1923,Ap 30,11:2
Woman With Four Faces, The 1923,Je 18,13:5
Smooth as Satin 1925,Je 23,24:3
Alias French Gertie 1930,Ap 14,24:2
Paid 1931,Ja 3,21:2
Thirteenth Chair, The 1937,Je 18,25:3
Within the Law 1939,Ap 6,31:2
Trial of Mary Dugan, The 1941,Mr 6,25:4
Veiller, Bayard (Producer)
Car 99 1935,F 23,14:7
Veiller, Bayard (Screenwriter)
Unseeing Eyes 1923,O 22,17:1
Guilty Hands 1931,Ag 29,16:3
Unashamed 1932,Jl 15,13:4
Veiller, Wilbur Anthony (Screenwriter)
Monkey on my Back 1957,My 30,23:2
Veillet, Claude (Original Author)
Greed in the Sun 1965,Ag 19,35:3
Veirazka, Vitezslav
Devil's Trap, The 1964,Ag 14,16:1
Veiro, Maria Teresa
Abnegacion 1938,My 31,8:3
Veit, Philipp
Grobe Adele, Die 1937,My 15,23:5
Veitch, Anthony Scott (Screenwriter)
Coast of Skeletons 1965,N 11,58:3
Vejar, Chico
World in my Corner 1956,F 18,12:5
Midnight Story, The 1957,Jl 5,14:2
Vejar, Harry J
Scarface, The Shame of the Nation 1932,My 20,22:3
Vejo, Carlos (Screenwriter)
Roots, The (The One-Eyed Boy); One-Eyed Boy, The (The Roots) 1957,S 3,23:2
Roots, The (The Filly); Filly, The (The Roots) 1957,S 3,23:2
Roots, The (The Cows); Cows, The (The Roots) 1957,S 3,23:2
Roots, The (Our Lady); Our Lady (The Roots) 1957,S 3,23:2
Vekroff, Perry N (Director)
Woman's Experience, A 1918,N 11,13:3
Velaise, Robert (Producer)
Ostrich Has two Eggs, The 1960,S 27,40:1
Velaro, Fred
Great Flamario, The 1945,Ja 15,15:5
Velasquez, Andres
Littlest Outlaw, The 1955,D 27,31:1
Velasquez, Ernest
Alla en el Rancho Chico; Out on the Little Ranch 1939,F 25,19:3
Salt of the Earth 1954,Mr 15,20:2
Velasquez, Jose
My Outlaw Brother 1951,Ag 23,19:2
Velasquez, Teresa
Castilian, The 1963,O 3,31:1
Velez, Jorge
Familia Dressel, La 1936,My 4,16:2
Jalisco Nunca Pierde; Jalisco Never Loses 1937,N 20,21:3
Tierra del Mariachi, La; Country of the Mariachi, The 1938,D 3,11:2
Alarma 1939,Ja 23,8:2
Ojos Tapatios 1939,F 13,13:3
Infidelidad 1939,My 8,21:3
Guadalajara 1943,Je 12,9:3
Velez, Jorge (Producer)
Dama de las Camelias, La 1944,S 26,16:1
Velez, Josephine
Drácula 1931,F 13,21:3
Quien Mato a Eva 1934,D 22,21:2
Velez, Lupe
Gaucho, The 1927,N 22,32:2
Stand and Deliver 1928,Ap 2,25:1

Velez, Lupe— Cont
Wolf Song 1929,F 25,16:1
Lady of the Pavements 1929,Mr 11,22:2
Where East Is East 1929,My 27,22:1
Tiger Rose 1929,D 25,23:1
Hell Harbor 1930,Mr 28,22:6
Storm, The 1930,Ag 23,7:3
East Is West 1930,N 1,23:2
Resurrection 1931,Ja 24,15:1
Squaw Man, The 1931,S 19,10:2
Cuban Love Song, The 1931,D 5,21:2
Broken Wing, The 1932,Mr 26,17:2
Kongo 1932,N 17,22:5
Half-Naked Truth, The 1932,D 31,10:1
Hot Pepper 1933,Ja 23,9:2
Palooka 1934,F 28,23:2
Hollywood Party 1934,My 26,12:2
Strictly Dynamite 1934,Jl 4,18:2
Morals of Marcus, The 1936,Ja 13,14:2
Zandunga, La 1938,My 14,18:2
Girl From Mexico, The 1939,Je 8,31:4
Mexican Spitfire 1940,Ja 10,16:4
Mexican Spitfire out West 1940,O 30,29:3
Six Lessons From Madame La Zonga 1941,F 19,25:2
Playmates 1941,D 26,21:3
Mexican Spitfire at Sea 1942,Je 26,16:5
Mexican Spitfire Sees a Ghost 1942,Jl 31,11:2
Mexican Spitfire's Elephant 1942,S 18,25:2
Ladies' Day 1943,Mr 26,14:3
Velez, Reina
Panama Flo 1932,Ja 20,17:4
Velez, Richard
Young Savages, The 1961,My 25,31:1
Velle, Lester (Miscellaneous)
Garment Jungle, The 1957,My 16,28:2
Velma Dawson Puppets
Falcon Strikes Back, The 1943,Ap 2,17:4
Velo, Carlos (Director)
Torero! 1957,My 22,29:2
Velo, Carlos (Miscellaneous)
Roots, The (The Filly); Filly, The (The Roots) 1957,S 3,23:2
Roots, The (The One-Eyed Boy); One-Eyed Boy, The (The Roots) 1957,S 3,23:2
Roots, The (Our Lady); Our Lady (The Roots) 1957,S 3,23:2
Roots, The (The Cows); Cows, The (The Roots) 1957,S 3,23:2
Velo, Carlos (Screenwriter)
Torero! 1957,My 22,29:2
Velox
Under the Pampas Moon 1935,My 31,11:1
Champagne Waltz 1937,F 4,17:2
Velox (Miscellaneous)
Rumba 1935,F 25,13:2
Velox and Yolanda
Pride of the Yankees, The 1942,Jl 16,23:1
Brazil 1944,N 20,25:2
Thrill of Brazil, The 1946,S 6,18:3
Velsa, Paul
Crise est Finie, La 1935,Mr 14,18:1
Velte, Louis
My Seven Little Sins 1956,My 2,27:1
Vembo, Sophia
Stella 1957,Je 11,40:1
House on Stournara Street, The 1960,O 17,33:4
Vemelyanov, Vladimir
No Ordinary Summer 1958,O 6,36:3
Venable, Evelyn
Cradle Song 1933,N 20,18:2
Death Takes a Holiday 1934,F 24,18:4
David Harum 1934,Mr 2,23:2
Double Door 1934,My 5,22:3
Mrs Wiggs of the Cabbage Patch 1934,O 29,14:2
County Chairman, The 1935,Ja 19,8:1
Little Colonel, The 1935,Mr 22,26:2
Vagabond Lady 1935,Je 15,20:2
Alice Adams 1935,Ag 16,11:3
Harmony Lane 1935,O 24,19:4
Star for a Night 1936,S 5,7:2
Racketeers in Exile 1937,Ap 12,15:3
Stadium Murders, The 1938,Ap 9,11:2
Female Fugitive 1938,Ap 11,12:3
Lucky Cisco Kid 1940,Je 24,19:5
He Hired the Boss 1943,Je 4,17:4
Venantini, Venantino
Galia 1966,D 20,50:4
Round Trip 1967,Jl 20,30:2
Sucker, The 1967,O 9,61:1
Vendell, Veronique
Becket 1964,Mr 12,40:2
Code 7...Victim 5 1965,My 20,52:1
Vendenberghe, Paul (Original Author)
Face to the Wind 1951,Ja 16,34:2
Vendeuil, Magali
Beauties of the Night 1954,Mr 23,23:5
Vendresse, Henry (Screenwriter)
Lucrezia Borgia 1937,O 13,27:2
Vendrey, Ferencz
Key Balvany, A 1933,Ap 18,13:6
Kek Balvany, A; Blue Idol, The 1933,Ap 18,13:6

Veneroni, Paola
His Young Wife 1949,Mr 12,10:2
Veness, Amy
Brewster's Millions 1935,Ap 8,23:3
Old Curiosity Shop, The 1935,D 23,15:5
Red Wagon 1936,Je 22,22:1
Beloved Vagabond, The 1937,F 8,12:5
Mill On the Floss, The 1939,N 15,19:3
Madonna of the Seven Moons 1946,My 23,18:4
They Were Sisters 1946,Jl 24,24:2
This Happy Breed 1947,Ap 14,24:2
Man of Evil 1948,Mr 26,26:2
Blanche Fury 1948,N 24,20:2
My Brothers Keeper 1949,F 14,15:3
Madeleine 1950,S 1,17:2
Good Time Girl 1950,S 25,18:5
Chance of a Lifetime 1951,Mr 15,37:2
Oliver Twist 1951,Jl 31,17:2
Tom Brown's School Days 1952,Ja 8,23:5
Vengay, Karin
Little Boy Lost 1953,S 22,38:2
Vengos, Thanasis
Moussitsa 1960,O 31,25:2
Policeman of the 16th Precinct, The
1963,Ap 22,23:2
Veniat, Jeanne
Prize, The 1952,Ap 30,33:2
Venina, Vera
Time to Love 1927,Je 23,23:3
Venner, Norman (Original Author)
Irish Luck 1925,N 24,28:4
Vensher, Ivan (Director)
Russia on Parade 1946,S 9,20:1
Ventura, Jacqueline
And God Created Woman 1957,O 22,41:1
Ventura, Lino
Razzi 1957,N 19,39:4
Crime and Punishment 1958,S 16,23:2
Grisbi 1959,Jl 13,23:1
Speaking of Murder 1959,O 12,14:1
Modigliani of Montparnasse 1961,Mr 1,27:3
Frantic 1961,Je 12,34:1
Devil and the 10 Commandments, The (Episode
3) 1963,O 15,44:1
Taxi for Tobruk 1965,Mr 30,52:1
Greed in the Sun 1965,Ag 19,35:3
Cloportes 1966,Ap 19,36:1
Great Spy Chase, The 1966,O 6,56:4
Ventura, Mary Ann
Bird of Paradise 1951,Mr 15,37:2
Ventura, Ray (Producer)
Monte Carlo Baby 1954,My 29,13:4
Stop Train 349 1964,N 12,40:2
Ventura, Viviane
High Wind in Jamaica, A 1965,Je 17,27:2
Battle Beneath the Earth 1968,S 12,54:3
Venturi, Lauro (Director)
Leonardo Da Vinci 1952,N 21,21:5
Venturi, Lauro (Miscellaneous)
Pictura 1952,Ap 8,35:3
Venturi, Tom
Illiac Passion, The 1968,Ap 19,40:1
Venturini, E D (Director)
El Principe Gondolero 1933,S 11,20:4
Venturini, E F (Director)
Gente Alegre 1933,S 19,26:4
Venturini, Edward (Director)
Headless Horseman, The 1922,D 25,21:1
Venturini, Giorgio (Producer)
Mistress of the Mountains 1954,My 27,34:5
Pharaohs' Woman, The 1962,Ap 19,35:2
Venturini, Livia
Strada, La 1956,Jl 17,19:2
Venuta, Benay
Repeat Performance 1947,Jl 2,19:2
I, Jane Doe 1948,Jl 5,8:4
Annie Get Your Gun 1950,My 18,37:1
Call Me Mister 1951,F 1,21:2
Fuzzy Pink Nightgown, The 1957,O 31,41:1
Venvenuti, Vittorina
Ho Perduto mio Marito; I Have Lost My
Husband 1939,O 20,27:4
Venzuella, Peter
Bad Man, The 1923,O 9,17:4
Veprik, A (Composer)
Last Night, The 1937,Ap 28,18:3
Vera, Maria
Goyescas 1944,My 29,18:3
Vera, Ricky
Leather Saint, The 1956,Je 16,12:2
Vera (Original Author)
Woman Tempted, The 1928,Ap 24,29:3
Vera-Ellen
Wonder Man 1945,Je 9,17:2
Kid From Brooklyn, The 1946,Ap 19,25:2
Three Little Girls in Blue 1946,S 26,32:3
Carnival in Costa Rica 1947,Mr 29,21:2
Words and Music 1948,D 10,34:2
On the Town 1949,D 9,37:2
Love Happy 1950,Ap 8,9:4
Three Little Words 1950,Ag 10,21:2
Happy Go Lovely 1951,Jl 26,17:2
Belle of New York, The 1952,Mr 6,25:6

Call Me Madam 1953,Mr 26,37:1
White Christmas 1954,O 15,16:3
Let's Be Happy 1957,My 25,25:1
Veras, Linda
General Della Rovere 1960,N 22,41:1
Verbes, Erno
Copper Canyon 1950,N 16,39:2
Vercel, Roger (Original Author)
Stormy Waters 1946,Je 17,32:2
Vercellone, Mario
Flight Into France 1949,Jl 22,16:2
Vercoe, Stephen
Knights of the Round Table 1954,Ja 8,17:2
Front Page Story 1955,Ap 19,28:1
Girls, Les 1957,O 4,27:2
Vercors, Helene
Blind Desire 1948,Je 10,28:4
Verdaguer, Juan
Inheritance, The; Herencia, La 1964,S 16,36:3
Verde, Valerie
New Kind of Love, A 1963,O 31,26:2
Verdelo, Alberto (Miscellaneous)
Grand Olympics, The 1964,Ap 22,57:2
Verdera, Clare
Annabel Takes a Tour 1938,D 29,15:3
Lady From Cheyenne, The 1941,Ap 18,18:2
Verdi, Giuseppe (Composer)
Lost One, The; La Traviata 1948,Mr 30,26:2
Trovatore, Il 1950,F 9,36:7
Forza del Destino, La 1952,O 17,33:1
Cavalleria Rusticana 1953,D 28,17:2
Traviata, La 1953,D 28,17:2
Aida 1954,N 12,17:1
Verdi, Giuseppe (Miscellaneous)
King's Jester, The 1947,Je 26,19:3
Verdi, Joe
Crime of Dr Crespi, The 1936,Ja 13,14:3
Vintage, The 1957,My 9,36:5
Verdier, Edward (Original Author)
Bride Wore Crutches, The 1941,My 26,15:3
Song of the Open Road 1944,Je 7,13:3
Delightfully Dangerous 1945,Je 9,17:3
Verdier, Edward (Screenwriter)
Bride Wore Crutches, The 1941,My 26,15:3
Seven Days Ashore 1944,Ap 26,24:7
Verdier, Julien
We Are all Murderers 1957,Ja 9,27:2
Verdon, Gwen
On the Riviera 1951,My 24,47:1
David and Bathsheba 1951,Ag 15,23:2
Farmer Takes a Wife, The 1953,Je 13,11:2
Damn Yankees 1958,S 27,12:7
Verdugo, Elena
Belle Starr 1941,N 1,20:2
Moon and Sixpence, The 1942,O 28,26:4
Rainbow Island 1944,O 26,19:6
House of Frankenstein 1944,D 16,19:3
Frozen Ghost, The 1945,Jl 28,7:3
Little Giant 1946,My 9,27:5
Song of Scheherazade 1947,F 27,26:2
Cyrano De Bergerac 1950,N 17,31:2
Thief of Damascus 1952,My 8,37:2
Verdy, Violette
Dream Ballerina 1951,Ap 16,21:2
Vere, Irene
This'll Make You Whistle 1938,N 1,27:2
Verea, Lisette
Night in Casablanca, A 1946,Ag 12,17:2
Verebes, Ernst
Paul Street Boys, The 1929,Jl 15,25:1
Bride 68 1930,Ap 15,28:5
Das Lied ist Aus 1932,Ja 29,13:2
Wenn die Soldaten 1932,O 31,18:4
Zapfenstreich am Rhein 1933,F 2,21:6
Walzerparadies 1933,Mr 4,11:3
Tanzhusar, Der 1933,Ap 10,8:4
Viktoria und Ihr Husar 1933,Ap 10,8:3
Traum von Schoenbrunn 1933,Je 1,15:4
Hellseher, Der 1933,S 11,20:4
Es Wird Schon Wieder Besser 1934,Ja 24,21:3
In Wien Hab' Ich Einmal ein Maedel Geliebt
1934,My 26,12:3
Blaue Vom Himmel, Das 1934,S 8,18:6
Es War Einmal ein Walzer 1934,O 15,20:5
Graefin Mariza 1935,Ja 26,13:3
Jo as a Haznal; Father Knows Best 1935,F 5,22:4
Zsivany Becsuelet 1935,O 30,16:3
Egy ej Velencebzn 1935,D 27,14:2
Marquise von Pompadour, Die 1936,F 3,21:3
Szensacio 1937,Mr 1,15:2
Magnificent Fraud, The 1939,Jl 20,16:2
To Be or not to Be 1942,Mr 7,13:2
Hitler Gang, The 1944,My 8,15:2
Climax, The 1944,D 14,28:5
Tangier 1946,Je 7,II,16:4
Northwest Outpost 1947,Ag 8,10:2
Outpost in Morocco 1949,Mr 25,28:3
Great Sinner, The 1949,Je 30,19:2
My Friend Irma 1949,S 29,39:2
Molly 1951,Mr 8,37:2
O Henry's Full House (The Cop and the Anthem);
Cop and the Anthem, The (O Henry's Full
House) 1952,O 17,33:1

Verebes, Ernst— Cont
Stars and Stripes Forever 1952,D 23,17:2
Verela, Amanda
Papa Soltero; Bachelor Father 1939,N 6,20:3
Chrismosa, La; Gossiper, The 1940,Mr 30,11:2
Verga, Giovanni (Original Author)
Cavalleria Rusticana 1947,D 20,21:2
Vergano, Aldo (Director)
Outcry 1949,Mr 14,15:5
Vergano, Aldo (Screenwriter)
Outcry 1949,Mr 14,15:5
Vergano, Serena
Family Diary 1963,N 12,48:1
Verhoeven, Michael
Judge and the Sinner, The 1964,Je 6,14:2
Verhoeven, Paul (Director)
Tag Nach der Scheidung, Der; Day After the
Divorce, The 1940,Mr 2,9:5
Palace Scandal 1949,Je 6,15:5
Eternal Waltz, The; (Ewiger Walzer)
1959,Jl 9,22:1
Judge and the Sinner, The 1964,Je 6,14:2
Verhoeven, Paul (Original Author)
Palace Scandal 1949,Je 6,15:5
Verhoeven, Paul (Screenwriter)
Palace Scandal 1949,Je 6,15:5
Verikh, Y
Fall of Berlin 1952,Je 9,19:2
Verlay, Alice (Composer)
Maternelle, La 1935,O 15,19:1
Verlay, Renaud
How Not to Rob a Department Store
1965,D 29,23:1
Verlier, Jacques
Girl With the Golden Eyes, The 1962,Ag 21,36:2
Verly, Michele
Legion of Honor, The 1928,Jl 20,8:4
Soul of France, The 1929,O 12,11:1
Vermehren, Isa
Seven Journeys 1951,Mr 12,20:2
Vermilyea, Harold
O S S 1946,My 27,15:5
Gentleman's Agreement 1947,N 12,36:2
Miracle of the Bells, The 1948,Mr 17,30:1
Big Clock, The 1948,Ap 22,34:2
Sainted Sisters, The 1948,My 20,35:2
Emperor Waltz, The 1948,Je 18,19:2
Beyond Glory 1948,Ag 4,18:2
Sorry, Wrong Number 1948,S 2,18:2
Manhandled 1949,My 26,34:2
Chicago Deadline 1949,N 3,37:2
Edge of Doom 1950,Ag 4,13:2
Born to be Bad 1950,S 29,31:5
Vermorel, Claude (Screenwriter)
Lovers of Toledo, The 1954,Ap 10,11:3
Vermoyal, Paul
Arab, The 1924,Jl 14,11:5
Verna, Gaetano
Man With the Grey Glove, The 1953,Ja 3,11:2
Young Caruso, The 1953,O 13,34:4
Vernac, Denise
Modigliani of Montparnasse 1961,Mr 1,27:3
Vernantini, Venantino
Nude Odyssey 1962,O 27,14:6
Vernay, Annie
Lie of Nina Petrovna, The 1938,Mr 30,19:2
Betrayal 1939,S 16,20:2
Mayor's Dilemma, The 1940,Ap 23,19:2
Vernay, Robert (Screenwriter)
Face to the Wind 1951,Ja 16,34:2
Verne, Jules (Miscellaneous)
Those Fantastic Flying Fools 1967,O 19,59:2
Verne, Jules (Original Author)
Twenty Thousand Leagues Under the Sea
1916,D 25,7:1
Mysterious Island, The 1929,D 21,17:1
Soldier and the Lady, The 1937,Ap 10,11:1
Untitled-Capt Grant's Children 1939,Ja 12,23:3
Captain Grant's Children 1939,Ja 12,23:3
20,000 Leagues Under the Sea 1954,D 24,7:2
Around the World in 80 Days 1956,O 18,37:1
From the Earth to the Moon 1958,N 27,52:2
Journey to the Center of the Earth
1959,D 17,51:1
Michael Strogoff 1960,My 21,15:1
Fabulous World of Jules Verne, The
1961,Je 29,26:1
Master of the World 1961,S 16,9:1
Mysterious Island 1961,N 21,30:6
Five Weeks in a Balloon 1962,Ag 27,18:1
In Search of the Castaways 1962,D 22,5:2
Up to his Ears 1966,My 18,37:1
Verne, Kaaren
Sky Murder 1940,N 14,28:3
Underground 1941,Je 23,13:2
All Through the Night 1942,Ja 24,13:2
Kings Row 1942,F 3,23:2
Sherlock Holmes and the Secret Weapon
1943,Ja 5,15:2
Seventh Cross, The 1944,S 29,18:1
Bullet for Joey, A 1955,Ap 16,12:1
Verne, Karen
Missing Ten Days 1941,Ap 21,15:5 (In Addenda)

Verne, M
Soul of France, The 1929,O 12,11:1
Verner, Hans
Judith 1966,Ja 21,22:1
Verner, Jean
Four Bags Full 1957,S 5,32:1
Verner, Lois
Girls Under 21 1940,N 11,22:4
Verneuil, Henri (Director)
Lover's Net 1957,Jl 23,23:1
What Price Murder 1958,N 11,26:1
Forbidden Fruit 1959,F 23,19:1
Paris Hotel 1959,S 12,12:3
Big Chief, The 1960,Ap 27,32:1
Love and the Frenchwoman; (Francaise et l'Amour, La) 1961,F 28,38:2
Cow and I, The 1961,Je 6,42:2
Maxime 1962,O 25,48:3
Monkey in Winter 1963,F 1,7:2
Any Number Can Win 1963,O 9,47:2
Weekend at Dunkirk 1966,My 19,51:2
25th Hour, The 1967,F 17,45:1
Guns for San Sebastian 1968,Mr 21,57:2
Verneuil, Henri (Original Author)
Sheep Has Five Legs, The 1955,Ag 10,19:2
Cow and I, The 1961,Je 6,42:2
Verneuil, Henri (Screenwriter)
What Price Murder 1958,N 11,26:1
Forbidden Fruit 1959,F 23,19:1
Paris Hotel 1959,S 12,12:3
Big Chief, The 1960,Ap 27,32:1
Maxime 1962,O 25,48:3
Any Number Can Win 1963,O 9,47:2
25th Hour, The 1967,F 17,45:1
Verneuil, Louis (Original Author)
Get Your Man 1927,D 5,26:2
Jealousy 1929,S 14,17:1
Love Habit, The 1931,F 2,23:1
True Confession 1937,D 16,35:2
With a Smile 1939,F 6,8:4
Mademoiselle ma Mere 1939,S 19,29:2
My Life With Caroline 1941,O 30,27:1
Deception 1946,O 19,15:3
Cross my Heart 1946,D 19,42:3
Verneuil, Louis (Screenwriter)
King, The 1941,O 23,29:3
Verneuil, M (Director)
Sheep Has Five Legs, The 1955,Ag 10,19:2
Verneuil, M (Screenwriter)
Sheep Has Five Legs, The 1955,Ag 10,19:2
Verney, Guy
This Happy Breed 1947,Ap 14,24:2
Anna Karenina 1948,Ap 28,32:2
Fame Is the Spur 1949,N 8,34:2
Martin Luther 1953,S 10,22:1
Vernillat, Francette
Seven Deadly Sins, The (Lust); Lust (The Seven Deadly Sins) 1953,My 12,31:3
Verno, Jerry
There Goes the Bride 1933,Mr 4,11:3
Ourselves Alone 1937,Jl 31,6:2
River of Unrest 1937,N 27,21:2
Non-Stop New York 1937,N 29,19:2
Girl Was Young, The 1938,F 11,27:2
Troopship 1938,Ap 26,18:2
Clown Must Laugh, A 1938,O 12,35:2
Chinese Den 1941,Mr 26,27:3
Vernon, Anne
Shakedown 1950,S 4,11:2
Affaire, L' 1950,N 13,23:2
Edward and Caroline 1952,Ap 30,33:3
Tale of Five Women, A 1953,Ja 16,19:2
Beautiful but Dangerous 1958,F 6,24:1
Diary of a Bad Girl 1958,My 30,13:2
General Della Rovere 1960,N 22,41:1
Umbrellas of Cherbourg, The; Parpapluis de Cherbourg, Les 1964,D 17,50:1
Friend of the Family 1965,N 18,55:3
Therese and Isabelle 1968,My 15,41:4
Vernon, Bobby
When Comedy Was King 1960,Mr 30,42:1
Vernon, Brownie
Widow by Proxy 1919,S 22,8:1
Vernon, Dorothy
Tenderloin 1928,Mr 15,28:3
Father O'Flynn 1938,D 26,29:2
Vernon, Glenn
Days of Glory 1944,Je 17,10:2
Youth Runs Wild 1944,S 2,17:2
Those Endearing Young Charms 1945,Je 20,26:5
Bedlam 1946,Ap 20,16:4
Woman on the Beach, The 1947,Je 9,26:6
Vernon, Howard
Secret Document-Vienna 1954,Mr 29,22:4
Sins of the Borgias 1956,Mr 5,21:1
Girl in the Bikini, The 1958,O 25,16:3
Secret Ways, The 1961,My 25,31:1
Awful Dr Orlof, The 1964,D 3,58:3
Alphaville 1965,O 26,49:1
Game is Over, The 1967,Ja 10,34:1
Vernon, Irene
Try and Get Me 1951,My 7,22:2

Vernon, John
Nobody Waved Goodbye 1964,S 17,52:1
Point Blank 1967,S 19,53:1
Vernon, Lou
Betrayal, The 1948,Je 26,10:5
On the Beach 1959,D 18,34:1
Vernon, Marilyn
Annapolis Salute 1937,O 2,18:1
Radio City Revels 1938,Mr 21,18:3
Vernon, Richard
Cash on Demand 1962,My 17,31:1
Servant, The 1964,Mr 17,30:2
Hard Day's Night, A 1964,Ag 12,41:1
Vernon, Richard (Producer)
Courageous Mr Penn 1943,D 23,26:5
Kiss the Blood off my Hands 1948,O 30,10:2
Vernon, Suzy
Last Waltz, The 1927,N 14,26:1
Schuldig 1928,Mr 11,VIII,7:6 (In Addenda)
Guilty 1928,S 18,33:2
Sajenko, The Soviet 1929,Ja 15,22:4
President, The 1929,Ja 21,18:4
Miche 1932,D 2,27:4
Chasseur de Chez Maxim's, Le 1935,F 4,11:4
Etoile Disparait, Une; Star Disappears, A 1935,F 9,11:3
Man and his Wife, A 1939,Mr 28,20:1
Vernon, Valerie
Gog 1954,Ag 14,8:2
Vernon, Virginia
Millionairess, The 1961,F 10,19:1
Vernon, Wally
Mountain Music 1937,Je 24,30:3
This Way Please 1937,O 8,27:2
Happy Landing 1938,Ja 22,19:1
Kentucky Moonshine 1938,My 21,9:2
Alexander's Ragtime Band 1938,Ag 6,7:2
Meet the Girls 1938,S 3,16:6
Sharpshooters 1938,D 5,19:2
Tail Spin 1939,F 11,13:2
Broadway Serenade 1939,Ap 7,25:2
Gorilla, The 1939,My 28,6:2
Charlie Chan at Treasure Island 1939,S 1,15:5
Sailor's Lady 1940,Je 29,12:2
Reveille With Beverly 1943,Ap 24,17:2
Tahiti Honey 1943,My 13,17:2
Pistol Packin' Mama 1943,D 20,27:4
Always Leave Them Laughing 1949,N 24,48:2
Beauty on Parade 1950,Ag 18,17:2
What Price Glory 1952,Ag 23,10:2
Bloodhounds of Broadway 1952,N 15,15:2
Affair With a Stranger 1953,Jl 11,8:2
What a Way to Go! 1964,My 15,44:1
Veronina, Vera
Why Cry at Parting 1930,F 4,28:3
Verrati, Ciro
Corsaro Nero, Il; Black Corsair, The 1939,My 8,21:3
Vershinin, Ilya (Original Author)
Counter-Attack 1945,My 17,15:2
Versini, Andre
Cat, The 1959,Ap 13,35:1
Versini, Andre (Miscellaneous)
Five Miles to Midnight 1963,Mr 21,8:6
Versini, Marie
Tale of Two Cities, A 1958,Ag 5,23:1
Paris Blues 1961,N 8,41:1
Young Racers, The 1963,O 10,49:3
Is Paris Burning? 1966,N 11,36:1
Verso, Eddie
West Side Story 1961,O 19,39:3
Versois, Odile
Man in the Dinghy 1951,N 1,34:2
Paolo and Francesca 1953,F 14,8:3
To Paris With Love 1955,Mr 29,33:4
Chance Meeting 1955,Ap 20,38:1
Checkpoint 1957,S 19,25:2
Room 43 1959,D 3,46:1
Nude in a White Car 1960,O 27,47:2
Cartouche 1964,Jl 22,39:1
Benjamin 1968,Mr 26,41:2
Vertes, Lajos
Csak Egy Ejszakara 1936,Mr 16,21:5
Vertinskaya, Anastasia
Hamlet 1964,S 15,32:1
Hamlet 1966,Mr 16,48:1
War and Peace 1968,Ap 29,50:5
Vertinskaya, L
Sadko 1953,Je 1,18:6
Don Quixote 1961,Ja 21,18:1
Vertinsky, A
Anna Cross, The 1954,O 25,30:7
Vertof, Dzega (Director)
Moscow Today 1929,My 13,27:2
Living Russia or the Man With the Camera 1929,S 17,36:2
Three Songs About Lenin 1934,N 7,32:1
Verushka
Blow-Up 1966,D 19,52:2
Very, M (Miscellaneous)
Perfectionist, The 1952,My 2,21:3

Very, Pierre (Miscellaneous)
Sans Famille 1959,S 5,11:4
Very, Pierre (Original Author)
Boys' School 1939,Je 6,26:2
Who Killed Santa Claus? 1948,Ap 21,33:2
Very, Pierre (Screenwriter)
It Happened at the Inn; Goupi Mains Rouge 1945,D 22,16:2
Room Upstairs, The 1948,S 4,8:6
Perfectionist, The 1952,My 2,21:3
Mama, Papa, the Maid and I 1956,Ag 28,31:1
Sans Famille 1959,S 5,11:4
Veselovskaya, Nina
Sisters 1959,My 25,33:2
Vesely, Karin
Suitor, The; Soupirant, Le 1963,S 18,35:1
Veshnivsky, Vladimir
Road to Life 1932,Ja 28,24:2
Vesnik, E
Othello 1960,My 16,39:1
Vespermann, Gerd
Guitars of Love 1958,Jl 12,18:1
Vespermann, Kurt
Bride 68 1930,Ap 15,28:5
Der Schrecken der Garnison 1932,Je 1,19:5
Pension Schoeller 1932,S 20,26:3
Keine Feier Ohne Meyer 1932,O 29,18:4
Schuss im Morgengrauen 1934,S 29,12:3
Kalte Mamsell, Die 1935,Ja 12,12:2
Konjunkturritter 1935,Ap 29,12:4
Unschuld vom Lande, Die 1935,My 13,18:6
Unbekannte Gast, Der; Unknown Guest, The 1935,Je 1,18:3
Erbe in Pretoria, Das 1936,Ap 18,19:3
Stimme der Liebe, Die 1936,My 16,11:2
Ist Mein Mann Nicht Fabelhaft 1936,D 8,31:3
Zwei im Sonnenschein 1937,Jl 31,6:2
Wenn Du eine Schwiegermutter hast; When You Have a Mother-in-Law 1938,Ja 29,12:1
Sie und die Drei; She and the Three 1938,D 10,13:3
Lustige Witwenball, Der; Merry Widows' Ball, The 1939,My 1,21:2
Verkannte Lebemann, Der; Unrecognized Man of the World, The 1939,S 16,20:2
Vessel, Edy
Thief of Baghdad, The 1961,Ag 17,18:2
Psycosissimo 1962,S 8,16:2
Eight and One Half 1963,Je 26,36:1
Vetluguin, Voldemar (Producer)
East Side, West Side 1949,D 23,17:2
Life of her Own, A 1950,O 12,43:2
Vetter, Charles Francis (Producer)
Green Helmet, The 1961,Jl 20,32:2
Vetter, Charles Jr (Producer)
Battle Beneath the Earth 1968,S 12,54:3
Vetterlund, Inga-Bodil
Sun Over Sweden 1938,Ap 9,11:2
Familjen Andersson; Anderson Family, The 1939,Ja 24,16:5
Kustens Glada Kavaljerer; Coast's Happy Cavaliers, The 1939,My 23,27:2
Vialla, A
Red Inn, The 1954,Je 8,25:2
Vianello, Raimondo
Psycosissimo 1962,S 8,16:2
Vians, Boris (Original Author)
I Spit on Your Grave 1963,Je 29,13:5
Vians, Boris (Screenwriter)
I Spit on Your Grave 1963,Je 29,13:5
Viard, Lucien (Producer)
Marie Octobre 1960,Ag 16,25:2
Viarisio, Enrico
Marcia Nuziale, La 1936,F 27,23:2
Milizia Territoriale 1936,Ap 6,18:2
Musica in Piazza 1936,My 7,21:3
Amo Te Sola 1936,Jl 20,11:2
Cappello a Tre Punte, Il 1936,S 28,14:5
Trionfo dell'Amore, Il; Love's Triumph 1938,Mr 29,18:4
Amore in Quarantena; Love in Quarantine 1938,D 13,31:2
Ho Perduto mio Marito; I Have Lost My Husband 1939,O 20,27:4
Amicizia; Friendship 1940,Mr 1,17:3
Al Vostri Ordini, Signora; At Your Orders, Madame 1940,My 25,20:1
Dama Bianca, La; Lady in White, The 1940,My 31,15:3
Lieutenant Craig-Missing 1951,My 19,9:4
Father's Dilemma 1952,S 23,25:1
Of Love and Bandits 1953,Ja 17,12:4
Viazemsky, Nikolai
Dark Is The Night 1946,Mr 18,24:3
Vibart, Henry
Kiss for Cinderella, A 1925,D 26,11:2
Just Suppose 1926,Ja 18,26:2
Dancers of Paris, The 1926,Mr 29,24:3
Wilderness Woman, The 1926,My 10,19:1
Prince of Tempters, The 1926,O 18,18:1
Vibert, Marcel
Garden of Allah, The 1927,S 3,13:5
Oppressed, The 1929,Jl 15,25:1

Vibert, Marcel — Cont
Mystere de la Chambre Jaune, Le
1931,My 26,33:2
Vicario, Marco
Alone in the Streets 1956,Je 28,33:2
Vicas, Victor (Director)
No Way Back 1955,My 19,25:5
Wayward Bus, The 1957,Je 6,35:2
Count Five and Die 1958,My 15,25:1
Vicas, Victor (Screenwriter)
No Way Back 1955,My 19,25:5
Stop Train 349 1964,N 12,40:2
Viccola, Giovanni
White Sister, The 1923,S 6,10:2
Vicenzoni, Luciano (Screenwriter)
For a Few Dollars More 1967,Jl 4,23:1
Vich, Antonio (Screenwriter)
Fedra, the Devil's Daughter 1957,O 26,19:2
Vickers, Martha
Big Sleep, The 1946,Ag 24,6:6
Time, The Place And The Girl, The
1946,D 27,14:3
Time, The Place And The Girl, The
1946,D 27,14:3
Man I Love, The 1947,Ja 25,12:2
That Way With Women 1947,F 15,20:4
Love and Learn 1947,My 3,10:3
Ruthless 1948,S 4,8:7
Bad Boy 1949,Mr 23,35:2
Alimony 1949,Jl 22,16:3
Vickers, Roy (Original Author)
Girl in the News, The 1941,My 5,13:2
Vickers, Sunny
Yank in Korea, A 1951,Ap 2,29:2
Vickers, Yvette
Hud 1963,My 29,36:1
Vico, Antonio
Patricio miro a una Estrella; Patricio Looked at a
Star 1938,N 12,10:3
Vida Hija del Panal, La; Warden's Daughter, The
1940,Ja 6,9:2
Marcelino 1956,O 23,39:1
Night Heaven Fell, The 1958,O 22,40:4
Pepote 1958,D 2,46:1
Vico, Manolo
Dona Francisquità 1935,Ap 27,20:6
Victor, Bernard (Producer)
China Story, The: One-Fourth of Humanity
1968,O 3,56:4
Victor, Charles
Hell's Cargo 1940,S 16,15:2
Blackout 1940,D 2,19:2
Invaders, The 1942,Mr 6,17:1
Ships With Wings 1942,My 25,11:2
Wings and the Woman 1942,O 8,31:1
Seven Days' Leave 1942,D 11,33:2
Silver Fleet, The 1945,Mr 24,22:6
Man From Morocco, The 1946,N 25,38:2
Meet Me at Dawn 1948,My 18,26:2
Showtime 1948,My 20,35:3
Temptation Harbor 1949,My 11,34:7
Broken Journey 1949,My 26,34:3
While the Sun Shines 1950,Jl 1,9:2
Man Who Cheated Himself, The 1951,F 9,21:2
Galloping Major, The 1951,D 17,27:2
Woman in Question, The 1952,F 19,24:2
Encore (The Ant and the Grasshopper); Ant and
the Grasshopper, The (Encore) 1952,Ap 3,45:1
Landfall 1953,My 11,25:2
Both Sides of the Law 1954,Ja 12,19:2
Prince and the Showgirl 1957,Je 14,22:2
Value for Money 1957,Ag 1,20:4
Victor, David (Producer)
One Spy too Many 1966,D 8,64:1
Victor, David (Screenwriter)
Trooper Hook 1957,Jl 13,11:2
Victor, Henry
White Monkey, The 1925,Je 9,16:3
Beloved Rogue, The 1927,Mr 14,16:1
Fourth Commandment, The 1927,Ap 6,25:1
Topsy and Eva 1927,Ag 8,10:3
Hate Ship, The 1930,N 15,15:3
One Heavenly Night 1931,Ja 10,19:2
Seas Beneath 1931,Ja 31,15:1
Suicide Fleet 1931,N 23,22:1
Freaks 1932,Jl 9,7:5
Mummy, The 1933,Ja 7,11:2
Scotland Yard Mystery, The 1936,Mr 16,21:4
Silent Barriers 1937,Mr 26,25:1
Confessions of a Nazi Spy 1939,Ap 29,13:2
Hotel Imperial 1939,My 11,31:3
Thunder Afloat 1939,O 13,27:2
Pack up Your Troubles 1939,O 27,27:2
Nick Carter, Master Detective 1939,D 14,35:2
Zanzibar 1940,Ap 1,15:3
Mystery Sea Raider 1940,Ag 26,11:4
To Be or not to Be 1942,Mr 7,13:2
Desperate Journey 1942,S 26,11:2
That Nazty Nuisance 1943,My 29,10:3
Victor, Herbert (Screenwriter)
Bedelia 1947,F 8,10:2
Kisenga, Man of Africa 1952,Mr 7,18:2

Victor, Jarl
Desert Sands 1955,N 19,22:7
Victoria, Queen (Original Author)
Story of Vickie, The 1958,Ja 30,19:2
Victrix, Claudia
Occident, L' 1928,D 16,IX,8:2
Vidacovich, Irvine
Panic in the Streets 1950,Ag 5,9:2
Vidal, Antonio
El Rey de los Gitanos 1933,My 29,22:2
(Incorrect in this edition; use 1933,My 29,16:5
elsewhere)
Buenaventura, La 1934,S 15,20:3
Cantante de Napoles, El; Singer of Naples, The
1935,F 25,13:4
Vidal, Armando (Director)
Heroes del Barrio, Los 1936,D 28,12:4
Vidal, Gene (Screenwriter)
Is Paris Burning? 1966,N 11,36:1
Vidal, Gil
Girls of the Night 1959,Mr 21,13:2
Sins of Youth 1960,D 24,8:2
Vidal, Gore (Original Author)
Left Handed Gun, The 1958,My 8,36:2
Visit to a Small Planet 1960,Ap 14,34:1
Best Man, The 1964,Ap 7,29:1
Vidal, Gore (Screenwriter)
Catered Affair, The 1956,Je 15,32:4
I Accuse! 1958,Mr 6,32:1
Scapegoat, The 1959,Ag 7,28:1
Suddenly, Last Summer 1959,D 23,22:1
Best Man, The 1964,Ap 7,29:1
Vidal, Henri
Damned, The; Maudits, Les 1948,Ap 26,27:2
Fabiola 1951,My 30,14:2
Strollers, The 1952,Jl 22,22:7
Naughty Martine 1953,Ap 13,32:4
Seven Deadly Sins, The (Gluttony); Gluttony (The
Seven Deadly Sins) 1953,My 12,31:3
Desperate Decision 1954,N 9,31:5
Gates of Paris 1958,Ja 15,24:1
Attila 1958,My 19,19:4
Parisienne, La 1958,Jl 31,27:1
What Price Murder 1958,N 11,26:1
House on the Waterfront, The 1959,F 21,25:2
Come Dance With Me!; Voulez-Vous Danser Avec
Moi 1960,N 8,32:6
Vidal, Vilma
Celos 1936,Ap 15,25:2
Cancion del Alma; Song of the Soul
1938,O 11,20:4
Hombres de Mar; Men of the Sea 1938,N 7,23:6
Vidalie, Albert (Original Author)
Night Heaven Fell, The 1958,O 22,40:4
Vidalin, Robert
Miserables, Les 1936,O 28,31:2
Sacrifice d'Honneur 1938,D 2,27:2
Vidi, Luce
Winner, The 1965,Jl 1,34:1
Vidocq, Eugene-Francois (Original Author)
Scandal In Paris, A 1946,S 16,9:7
Vidolazzi, Rocco
Rocco and his Brothers 1961,Je 28,40:2
Vidon, Henry
Secret Conclave, The 1953,My 16,10:1
Snorkel, The 1958,S 18,37:2
Mistress for the Summer, A 1964,Mr 28,13:5
Vidor, Catherine
Boheme, La 1926,F 25,26:2
Vidor, Charles (Director)
Double Door 1934,My 5,22:3
Arizonian, The 1935,Jl 27,16:2
Muss 'Em Up 1936,F 3,21:2
Doctor's Diary, A 1937,F 17,16:4
Great Gambini, The 1937,Jl 12,20:4
She's no Lady 1937,Ag 12,14:3
Romance of the Redwoods 1939,Ap 24,13:2
Blind Alley 1939,My 23,27:2
Those High Grey Walls 1939,O 19,27:2
My Son, My Son! 1940,My 10,26:6
Lady in Question, The 1940,D 10,33:2
Ladies in Retirement 1941,N 7,27:1
New York Town 1941,N 13,35:2
Tuttles of Tahiti, The 1942,Ap 30,14:1
Desperadoes, The 1943,My 13,17:2
Cover Girl 1944,Mr 31,26:1
Together Again 1944,N 24,19:2
Song to Remember, A 1945,Ja 26,16:4
Over 21 1945,Ag 17,20:2
Gilda 1946,Mr 15,27:2
Loves of Carmen, The 1948,S 3,16:2
It's a big Country 1952,Ja 9,25:2
Hans Christian Andersen 1952,N 26,20:2
Thunder in the East 1953,F 4,32:2
Rhapsody 1954,Mr 12,17:1
Love Me or Leave Me 1955,My 27,14:1
Swan, The 1956,Ap 27,21:5
Joker Is Wild, The 1957,S 27,16:6
Farewell to Arms, A 1958,Ja 25,14:1
Song Without End 1960,Ag 12,10:2
Vidor, Charles (Producer)
Loves of Carmen, The 1948,S 3,16:2

Vidor, Florence
Till I Come Back to You 1918,Ag 26,9:1
Lying Lips 1921,Mr 7,8:1
Hail the Woman 1922,Ja 16,18:3
Skin Deep 1922,O 23,10:1
Main Street 1923,Je 12,22:2
Marriage Circle, The 1924,F 4,23:3
Welcome Stranger 1924,O 14,21:5
Christine of the Hungry Heart 1924,D 8,13:3
Husbands and Lovers 1924,D 9,23:3
Are Parents People 1925,Je 9,16:3
Grounds for Divorce 1925,Je 29,8:2
Marry Me 1925,Jl 13,20:2
Trouble With Wives, The 1925,Ag 5,12:4
Enchanted Hill, The 1925,D 29,19:2 (In
Addenda)
Grand Duchess and the Waiter, The
1926,F 9,22:1
Sea Horses 1926,F 23,26:5
You Never Know Women 1926,Jl 27,15:5
Eagle of the Sea, The 1926,N 17,21:6
Popular Sin, The 1926,D 20,28:3
Afraid to Love 1927,Ap 12,25:3
One Woman to Another 1927,S 19,30:3
Honeymoon Hate 1927,D 31,31:1
Doomsday 1928,Ap 2,25:1
Magnificent Flirt, The 1928,Je 25,27:1
Patriot, The 1928,Ag 18,7:2 (In Addenda)
Chinatown Nights 1929,Ap 1,22:1
Vidor, King (Director)
Turn in the Road, The 1919,Mr 30,IV,6:1
Sky Pilot, The 1921,Ap 18,8:1
Peg o'my Heart 1923,Ja 22,10:1
Three Wise Fools 1923,Jl 23,13:4
Wild Oranges 1924,Mr 3,22:3
Happiness 1924,Mr 11,16:2
Wine of Youth 1924,Ag 11,16:1
His Hour 1924,O 7,26:1
Wife of the Centaur, The 1925,Ja 7,33:5
Proud Flesh 1925,Ap 14,26:1
Big Parade, The 1925,N 20,18:1 (In Addenda)
Boheme, La 1926,F 25,26:2
Bardelys The Magnificent 1926,N 1,28:1 (In
Addenda)
Crowd, The 1928,F 20,14:1
Patsy, The 1928,Ap 23,20:2
Show People 1928,N 12,18:2
Not so Dumb 1930,F 8,12:5
Billy the Kid 1930,O 18,23:2
Street Scene 1931,Ag 27,22:5
Champ, The 1931,N 10,29:4
Bird of Paradise 1932,S 10,18:5
Cynara 1932,D 26,26:2
Stranger's Return, The 1933,Jl 28,18:2
Our Daily Bread 1934,O 3,25:2
Wedding Night, The 1935,Mr 16,19:1
So Red the Rose 1935,N 28,39:1
Texas Rangers, The 1936,S 24,29:1
Stella Dallas 1937,Ag 6,21:1
Citadel, The 1938,N 4,27:2
Northwest Passage 1940,Mr 8,25:1
Comrade X 1940,D 26,23:1
H M Pulham, Esq 1941,D 19,35:1
American Romance, An 1944,N 24,19:1
Duel in the Sun 1947,My 8,30:2
Miracle Can Happen, A 1948,F 4,28:4
Fountainhead, The 1949,Jl 9,8:5
Beyond the Forest 1949,O 22,11:2
Lightning Strikes Twice 1951,Ap 13,18:7
Japanese War Bride 1952,Ja 30,22:6
Ruby Gentry 1952,D 26,20:2
Man Without a Star 1955,Mr 25,19:3
War and Peace 1956,Ag 22,26:2
Solomon and Sheba 1959,D 26,7:2
Show People 1967,O 2,58:2
Vidor, King (Original Author)
Turn in the Road, The 1919,Mr 30,IV,6:1
Crowd, The 1928,F 20,14:1
Texas Rangers, The 1936,S 24,29:1
American Romance, An 1944,N 24,19:1
Vidor, King (Producer)
Jack-Knife Man, The 1920,Ag 2,12:2
Our Daily Bread 1934,O 3,25:2
American Romance, An 1944,N 24,19:1
Ruby Gentry 1952,D 26,20:2
Vidor, King (Screenwriter)
Our Daily Bread 1934,O 3,25:2
H M Pulham, Esq 1941,D 19,35:1
War and Peace 1956,Ag 22,26:2
Vidov, Oleg
Hagbard and Signe 1968,My 17,56:1
Vienna, Philharmonic Orchestra
Rosenkavalier, Der 1962,O 10,57:1
Vienna, State Opera Co (Miscellaneous)
Rosenkavalier, Der 1962,O 10,57:1
Vienna Boys Choir
Singing Angels 1952,Ja 16,21:2
St Matthew Passion 1952,Ja 29,17:4
Vienna Hofburgkapelle
Singing Angels 1952,Ja 16,21:2
Viennese Singverein
St Matthew Passion 1952,Ja 29,17:4

Vierny, Dina
Youth in Revolt 1939,My 16,27:3
Viertel, Berthold (Director)
Uneasy Money 1928,D 11,35:3
One Woman Idea, The 1929,Je 10,23:1
Seven Faces 1929,N 16,25:2
Magnificent Lie, The 1931,Jl 25,11:6
Wiser Sex, The 1932,Mr 12,19:5
Man From Yesterday, The 1932,Je 25,18:2
Little Friend 1934,O 20,20:2
Rhodes 1936,F 29,11:1
Passing of the Third Floor Back, The
1936,Ap 29,19:2
Viertel, Peter (Screenwriter)
Saboteur 1942,My 8,27:2
Hard Way, The 1943,Mr 13,9:2
We Were Strangers 1949,Ap 28,28:2
Decision Before Dawn 1951,D 22,12:2
Sun Also Rises, The 1957,Ag 24,12:2
Old Man and the Sea, The 1958,O 8,41:1
Five Miles to Midnight 1963,Mr 21,8:6
Viertel, Salka (Original Author)
Queen Christina 1933,D 27,23:3
Viertel, Salka (Screenwriter)
Painted Veil, The 1934,D 7,29:1
Anna Karenina 1935,Ag 31,16:2
Conquest 1937,N 5,19:1
Two Faced Woman 1942,Ja 1,37:2
Deep Valley 1947,Ag 23,7:2
Prisoner of the Volga 1960,Je 2,27:2
Vieve, Jeanne
My Hustler 1967,Jl 11,29:2
Vignaud, J (Original Author)
Sirocco 1946,Ag 12,17:3
Vignaud, Jean (Original Author)
Venus 1929,O 14,20:2
Vigne, Odette
Spider, The 1946,Je 21,20:3
Vignola, Robert G (Director)
Louisiana 1919,Jl 21,12:3
World and his Wife, The 1920,Jl 19,16:3
Passionate Pilgrim, The 1921,Ja 3,20:2
Beauty's Worth 1922,Mr 27,12:1
When Knighthood Was in Flower 1922,S 15,17:2
(In Addenda)
Yolanda 1924,F 20,23:1
Married Flirts 1924,N 19,19:3
Declassee 1925,Mr 23,14:2
Cabaret 1927,My 2,26:4
Broken Dreams 1933,N 21,23:3
Perfect Clue, The 1935,Mr 14,18:1
Girl From Scotland Yard, The 1937,My 31,11:2
Vignola, Robert G (Original Author)
Way of a Girl, The 1925,Mr 30,21:3
Vignoli, Alicia
Puerto Nuevo; New Port 1937,F 20,9:3
Poor Perez 1937,N 1,24:6
Viejo Doctor, El; Old Doctor, The
1940,Ap 13,21:3
Vigny, Benno (Original Author)
Morocco 1930,N 17,29:1
Maedel von der Reeperbahn, Das 1931,Ja 31,15:1
Love in Morocco 1933,Mr 20,18:3
Vigo, Jean (Director)
Zero de Conduite 1947,Je 23,14:5
Atalante, L' 1947,Je 23,14:5
Vigo, Jean (Original Author)
Zero de Conduite 1947,Je 23,14:5
Vigran, Herbert
It all Came True 1940,Ap 6,13:2
Murder by Invitation 1941,Jl 23,15:4
Bedtime for Bonzo 1951,Ap 6,31:4
Night Into Morning 1951,Je 11,20:7
Just for You 1952,O 9,40:6
Susan Slept Here 1954,Jl 30,9:1
Midnight Story, The 1957,Jl 5,14:2
Vigrioli, Alicia
Dancing, El 1935,Ja 28,10:6
Viguie, Juan E (Director)
Romance Tropical 1934,O 15,20:5
Viguie, Juan E (Producer)
Romance Tropical 1934,O 15,20:5
Viguier, M
Amour Maitre des Choses, L' 1931,Mr 30,25:2
Viharo, Robert
Valley of the Dolls 1967,D 16,51:1
Villa Rides 1968,Jl 18,26:3
Vihrog, Jessie
Hurra! Ein Junge! 1932,Je 21,19:6
Der Falsche Ehemann 1932,O 17,18:3
Zwei Gute Kameraden 1933,D 4,22:3
Es Wird Schon Wieder Besser 1934,Ja 24,21:3
Freundin Eines Grossen Mannes, Die
1934,S 11,24:5
Lockvogel 1935,Ja 5,20:3
Sonne Geht auf, Die 1935,F 18,19:4
Keine Angst vor Liebe 1936,Ja 21,27:6
Annette in Paradise 1936,Mr 7,11:4
Paloma, La 1936,O 21,35:3
Friesennot 1936,O 26,20:1
Gilgi Eine Von Uns 1937,Jl 10,18:2

Vikhref, L
Zemlya Zhazhdet 1932,My 6,15:3
Vikland, O
Sadko 1953,Je 1,18:6
Don Quixote 1961,Ja 21,18:1
Vikovskaia, Nina
Sons and Mothers 1967,O 2,58:1
Viktorof, M
Pesnya O Stchasti 1935,Ap 8,23:4
Vikulin, Vladimir
Son of the Land, A 1931,My 23,13:4
Vilar, Antonio
Female, The 1960,Ap 28,29:1
Vilar, Jean
Gates of the Night 1950,Mr 16,40:2
Thirst of Men, The 1952,O 28,37:1
Vilar, Leonardo
Given Word, The 1964,Mr 25,47:1
Vilbert
Prize, The 1952,Ap 30,33:2
Vilbert, Henri
Adieux les Beaux Jours 1934,Ap 23,20:2
Savage Triangle 1952,S 30,38:2
Sins of Paris 1954,Ja 30,9:6
Letters From my Windmill (The Three Low
Masses); Three Low Masses, The (Letters From
my Windmill) 1955,D 19,33:1
Wild Oat, The 1956,Je 28,33:2
We Are all Murderers 1957,Ja 9,27:2
Pot Bouille 1958,O 28,39:1
Easiest Profession, The 1960,Mr 26,15:7
My Wife's Husband 1965,Ja 27,26:1
Vilches, Ernesto
Cascarrabias 1933,O 30,14:2
Noche del Pecado, La 1933,D 26,19:4
Desaparecido, El 1936,Je 2,25:3
113, El 1938,F 14,20:8
Vilden, Stanley
Blame the Woman 1932,O 25,24:5
Vildrac, Charles (Original Author)
Paquebot Tenacity 1934,Ag 12,IX,2:1
Vilie, Roberto
Two Orphans, The 1950,O 19,40:6
Villa, Claudio
See Naples and Die 1959,Ag 31,16:2
Villa, Roberto
Grande Appello, Il; Last Roll-Call, The
1939,Ap 11,18:6
Marco Visconti 1947,S 20,12:4
Operation X 1950,D 11,31:2
Villafranca, Carlos
Tarantos, Los 1964,Je 30,22:1
Village Dancers
World Dances 1954,N 8,24:6
Villalonga, J L
Tales of Paris (The Tale of Sophie); Tale of Sophie,
The (Tales of Paris) 1962,Ag 27,18:1
Magnificent Cuckold 1965,Ap 20,42:1
Villani, Tonino
Man of Courage 1934,N 14,23:2
Villard, Frank
Gigi 1950,Ja 31,20:2
Cheat, The 1950,O 2,19:3
Minne 1951,Ap 17,35:2
Savage Triangle 1952,S 30,38:2
Sextette (Part 4-Snow Queen); Snow Queen
(Sextette) 1953,Mr 2,19:2
Seven Deadly Sins, The (Lust); Lust (The Seven
Deadly Sins) 1953,My 12,31:3
Secret Document-Vienna 1954,Mr 29,22:4
Money, Money, Money 1962,Jl 18,20:1
Gigot 1962,S 28,26:1
Villarias, Carlos
Quando el Amor Rie 1933,O 17,26:3
Diablo Del Mar, El 1936,Ap 1,29:2
Irma la Mala 1936,O 6,28:7
El Misterio del Rostro Palido 1937,Ja 4,20:5
Nostradamus 1937,S 6,20:1
Ave sin Rumbo; Wandering Bird 1938,Ja 24,17:2
Pasado Acusa, El; Accusing Past, The
1938,O 15,21:4
Vida Bohemia, La 1939,F 6,8:5
Papa Soltero; Bachelor Father 1939,N 6,20:3
Villarino, Ramon
Circo Tragic, El; Tragic Circus, The
1939,Je 17,12:3
Villarreal, Carlos (Director)
Rosa de Xochimilco 1939,O 14,13:3
Villarreal, Julio
Una Vida Por Otra 1933,F 11,11:3
Vida por Otra, Una 1933,F 11,11:3
El Rey de los Gitanos 1933,My 29,22:2
(Incorrect in this edition; use 1933,My 29,16:5
elsewhere)
Ley Del Haren, La 1933,Je 17,16:7
Noche del Pecado, La 1933,D 26,19:4
Sagrario 1934,Ja 22,12:3
Profanacion 1934,Ja 31,20:4
Tiburon 1934,Ap 18,23:3
Sangre Manda, La 1934,My 15,18:2
Oro y Plata 1934,Ag 29,13:2
Tu Hijo 1934,D 17,24:3
Quien Mato a Eva 1934,D 22,21:2

Villarreal, Julio— Cont
Corazon Bandolero 1935,Mr 2,18:2
Chucho el Roto 1935,Mr 30,11:3
Vuelo de la Muerte, El 1935,Ap 16,27:3
Tribu 1935,Je 10,14:7
Pasado Acusa, El; Accusing Past, The
1938,O 15,21:4
Odio; Hate 1940,Ap 6,13:2
Mi Madrecita; My Little Mother 1940,S 24,26:6
Life of Simon Bolivar, The 1943,Je 18,16:5
El Conde de Monte Cristo 1943,N 9,26:2
Honeymoon 1947,My 19,27:2
Torch, The 1950,Ag 21,15:2
Plunder of the Sun 1953,Ag 27,22:1
Villas, Eduardo
Estrellita; Starlet 1939,Ap 12,27:3
Villasial, Luis
Cinco Advertencias de Satanas, Las; Satan's Five
Warnings 1939,Ja 14,13:2
Villasiui, Luis
Octavo Mandamiento, El; Eighth Commandment,
The 1937,Mr 1,15:2
Villatoro, Carlos
Monjes, Des 1935,Ja 21,19:3
Payasada de la Vida; Tricks of Life
1935,Mr 18,14:5
Fantasma del Convento, El; Fantasy of the
Monastery 1935,Ap 22,14:3
Tribu 1935,Je 10,14:7
A la Orilla de un Palmar; At the Edge of a Palm
Grove 1938,D 17,10:4
Virgen de la Sierra, La 1939,Mr 6,11:3
Villaume, Astrid
Venum 1968,Ja 11,42:1
Villegas, Lucio
Notorious Sophie Lang, The 1934,Jl 21,14:2
Nada Mas Que Una Mujer 1934,N 26,12:2
Goin' to Town 1935,My 11,21:2
Message to Garcia, A 1936,Ap 10,27:1
I'll Take Romance 1937,D 17,33:2
Renegade Ranger, The 1939,F 17,17:3
Only Angels Have Wings 1939,My 12,25:2
Villella, Edward
Midsummer Night's Dream, A 1967,Ap 18,32:1
Villers, Robert (Director)
Etoile Disparait, Une; Star Disappears, A
1935,F 9,11:3
Villi, Olga
Birds, the Bees and the Italians, The
1967,Ag 8,33:2
Villia, Celia
Dia que me Quieras, El; Day You Love Me, The
1935,Ag 27,23:3
Villiers, Alan Capt (Original Author)
Windjammer 1958,Ap 10,32:2
Villiers, Alan Capt (Screenwriter)
Windjammer 1958,Ap 10,32:2
Villiers, James
Operation Snatch 1962,S 25,31:4
Murder at the Gallop 1963,Je 25,23:2
Nothing but the Best 1964,Jl 14,28:1
King and Country 1964,S 24,46:2
Model Murder Case, The 1964,N 25,45:1
Eva 1965,Je 5,21:2
These Are the Damned 1965,Jl 8,35:1
Nanny, The 1965,N 4,57:2
King and Country 1966,Ja 28,20:4
Alphabet Murders, The 1966,Jl 12,36:2
Half a Sixpence 1968,F 21,60:3
Touchables, The 1968,N 21,41:1
Villiers, Kenneth
Mr Cohen Takes a Walk 1936,F 13,25:2
Broken Blossoms 1937,Ja 14,16:3
Villiers, Mavis
Lady's Morals, A 1930,N 8,21:3
Corridor of Mirrors 1949,Mr 23,35:3
Pool of London 1951,N 28,37:2
Suddenly, Last Summer 1959,D 23,22:1
Villoldo, Jorge
Way of a Gaucho 1952,N 5,36:2
Villy, Olga
Escape into Dreams 1950,Ap 13,34:5
Vilner, V (Director)
Simple Tailor, The 1934,F 19,18:3
Vilova
Black Angel 1946,S 26,32:4
Vimenet, Jean
Mouchette 1968,S 21,26:1
Vina, Victo
Carmen 1928,My 7,29:1
Vincenoni, Luciano (Screenwriter)
Birds, the Bees and the Italians, The
1967,Ag 8,33:2
Vincenot, Louis
Limehouse Blues 1934,D 12,28:2
Vincent, Allen
Mother's Boy 1929,My 8,34:6
This Reckless Age 1932,Ja 9,21:1
Street of Women 1932,My 30,16:5
Two Against the World 1932,Ag 19,20:6
Crooner 1932,Ag 20,7:4
No More Orchids 1933,Ja 2,29:2
Mystery of the Wax Museum, The
1933,F 18,13:3

Vincent, Allen— Cont

Broadway Bad 1933,Mr 6,16:6
Daring Daughters 1933,Mr 25,13:4
I Have Lived 1933,S 6,24:4
Success at any Price 1934,My 4,24:2
Return of Peter Grimm, The 1935,O 4,25:2
Bad Boy 1935,O 28,16:3
Chatterbox 1936,F 15,18:6
Sutter's Gold 1936,Mr 27,25:2
Family Affair, A 1937,Ap 20,29:2

Vincent, Allen (Screenwriter)
Face Behind the Mask, The 1941,F 7,23:2
Song of Love 1947,O 10,31:2
Johnny Belinda 1948,O 2,11:2
Girl in White, The 1952,My 31,12:5

Vincent, Anna
Mikado, The 1967,Mr 15,53:1

Vincent, Dominique
Rise of Louis XIV, The 1967,S 26,54:2

Vincent, Gene and his Blue Caps
Girl Can't Help It, The 1957,F 9,12:7

Vincent, Hilda (Original Author)
Danger Patrol 1937,N 19,27:3
Youth Will Be Served 1940,N 15,25:2

Vincent, June
Ladies Courageous 1944,Mr 16,17:2
Climax, The 1944,D 14,28:5
Can't Help Singing 1944,D 26,22:4
Here Come the Co-Eds 1945,F 19,21:1
That's the Spirit 1945,Je 2,11:2
Black Angel 1946,S 26,32:4
Mary Ryan, Detective 1949,N 4,33:3
Zamba 1949,N 7,33:2
Night Without Sleep 1952,S 27,13:2

Vincent, Leslie
Paris Underground 1945,O 20,8:2
Pursuit to Algiers 1945,O 27,12:2
Deadline for Murder 1946,Je 29,22:7

Vincent, May
Nuit est a Nous, La; (Night is Ours, The)
1931,F 21,15:2

Vincent, Mildred
Fast Worker, The 1924,N 12,13:1
Time, the Comedian 1925,D 14,18:2

Vincent, Romo
Turn off the Moon 1937,My 20,17:2
This Way Please 1937,O 8,27:2
Music for Madame 1937,O 23,14:1
Start Cheering 1938,Mr 17,17:3
Scene of the Crime 1949,Jl 29,12:2
Toast of New Orleans, The 1950,S 30,13:3
Stars and Stripes Forever 1952,D 23,17:2
Caddy, The 1953,S 18,16:6
Money From Home 1954,F 27,11:3
Naked Jungle, The 1954,Ap 3,19:2
Female on the Beach 1955,Ag 20,20:2
You're Never too Young 1955,Ag 26,10:2
Blueprint for Robbery 1961,F 2,24:3
Mister Buddwing 1966,O 12,36:1
Swinger, The 1966,D 15,60:1

Vincent, Russ
Apache Rose 1947,Jl 23,19:3

Vincent, Saylor
Albuquerque 1948,Mr 1,17:2

Vincent, Virginia
Helen Morgan Story, The 1957,O 3,33:2
I Want to Live 1958,N 19,45:1
Never Steal Anything Small 1959,F 12,23:1
Black Orchid, The 1959,F 13,33:2
Love With the Proper Stranger 1963,D 26,33:1
Tony Rome 1967,N 16,58:1

Vincent, Yves
Naked Woman, The 1950,Ja 21,10:2
Babette Goes to War 1960,Je 8,46:1
Anatomy of a Marriage; My Days With Jean
Marc; My Nights With Francoise
1964,O 27,42:2

Vincente, Armando de
Canillita y la Dama, El; Newsie and the Lady,
The 1939,F 18,12:2

Vincenti, Paul
Die Csikos Baroness 1932,Mr 28,11:2
Luegen auf Ruegen 1934,Ja 1,28:2

Vincenzoni, Luciano (Miscellaneous)
Seduces and Abandoned 1964,Jl 16,23:1

Vincenzoni, Luciano (Original Author)
Best of Enemies, The 1962,Ag 7,35:2
Birds, the Bees and the Italians, The
1967,Ag 8,33:2
Good, The Bad and the Ugly, The
1968,Ja 25,33:1

Vincenzoni, Luciano (Screenwriter)
...And Suddenly It's Murder! 1964,Ja 24,21:1
Seduced and Abandoned 1964,Jl 16,23:1
Railroad Man, The; Ferroviere, Il 1965,O 25,46:2
Good, The Bad and the Ugly, The
1968,Ja 25,33:1

Vinci, Jean
Wench, The 1949,Mr 14,15:5

Vinco, Ivo
Boheme, La 1965,O 20,51:2

Vinco, Jean
Don Juan 1956,Mr 6,26:2

Vine, Billy
Lucky Stiff, The 1949,Ja 31,14:2
Vagabond King, The 1956,S 13,39:6

Vine, Stanley
Man Who Changed his Name, The
1934,O 17,26:2

Viner, Edward
Little Lord Fauntleroy 1914,Je 23,11:3

Vinette
Robber Symphony 1937,Ja 27,17:2

Vineull, Laurent (Original Author)
Maternite 1937,Je 8,30:2

Vineull, Laurent (Screenwriter)
Maternite 1937,Je 8,30:2

Vingelli, Nino
Italiano Brava Gente 1966,F 4,20:1

Vinklar, Josef
Transport From Paradise 1967,F 8,22:1
Fifth Horseman is Fear, The 1968,My 7,52:1

Vinogradof, Misha
Zemlya Zhazhdet 1932,My 6,15:3

Vinogradov, N
Soviet Border 1939,F 20,13:2

Vinogradov, Vitya
Rainbow, The 1944,O 23,14:3

Vinogradova, B
Man of Music 1953,My 11,25:2

Vinogradsky, L (Screenwriter)
Fragment of an Empire, A 1930,Ja 27,18:4

Vinson, Gary
Majority of One, A 1962,Ja 12,29:2
McHale's Navy 1964,Jl 11,15:2
Nobody's Perfect 1968,Ap 4,58:3

Vinson, Helen
Jewel Robbery 1932,Jl 23,6:6
Two Against the World 1932,Ag 19,20:6
Crash, The 1932,S 9,17:5
They Call It Sin 1932,O 21,25:4
I Am a Fugitive From a Chain Gang
1932,N 11,17:2
Lawyer Man 1932,D 27,10:2
Second Hand Wife 1933,Ja 14,8:4
Grand Slam 1933,F 22,25:2
Little Giant, The 1933,My 27,11:5
Midnight Club 1933,Jl 29,14:2
Power and the Glory, The 1933,Ag 17,13:2
Kennel Murder Case, The 1933,O 30,14:2
As Husbands Go 1934,Ja 26,20:3
Life of Vergie Winters, The 1934,Je 15,26:1
Let's Try Again 1934,Je 22,24:1
Gift of Gab 1934,S 26,17:6
Captain Hates the Sea, The 1934,N 29,33:2
Broadway Bill 1934,N 30,22:2
Notorious Gentleman, A 1935,F 16,9:1
Wedding Night, The 1935,Mr 16,19:1
Private Worlds 1935,Mr 28,25:2
Age of Indiscretion 1935,My 18,21:2
Transatlantic Tunnel 1935,O 28,16:2
King of the Damned 1936,F 1,9:2
Reunion 1936,N 27,27:1
Love in Exile 1936,D 10,35:3
Vogues of 1938 1937,Ag 20,21:1
Live, Love and Learn 1937,N 19,27:2
In Name Only 1939,Ag 4,11:3
Married and in Love 1940,F 2,13:2
Curtain Call 1940,Ap 19,25:2
Enemy Agent 1940,Ap 22,13:3
Torrid Zone 1940,My 18,11:3
Beyond Tomorrow 1940,S 27,27:1
Nothing but the Truth 1941,O 23,27:1
Chip off the Old Block 1944,Mr 17,14:2
Lady and the Monster, The 1944,Ap 8,9:2
Are These our Parents? 1944,Ag 23,16:2
Thin Man Goes Home, The 1945,Ja 26,16:5

Vinti, Carlo (Director)
Traviata, La 1953,D 28,17:2
Cavalleria Rusticana 1953,D 28,17:2

Vinti, Carlo (Producer)
Cavalleria Rusticana 1953,D 28,17:2
Traviata, La 1953,D 28,17:2

Vinton, Arthur
Viking, The 1931,Je 17,32:5
Washington Merry-Go-Round 1932,O 24,18:5
Man Against Woman 1932,D 17,22:3
Laughter in Hell 1933,Ja 2,29:2
Blondie Johnson 1933,F 27,11:2
Central Airport 1933,My 4,20:5
When Strangers Marry 1933,My 25,24:3
Lilly Turner 1933,Je 15,21:2
Gambling Ship 1933,Jl 13,17:5
Avenger, The 1933,O 3,28:3
Son of a Sailor 1933,N 30,38:4
Cross Country Cruise 1934,Ja 20,12:3
Gambling Lady 1934,Ap 5,25:2
Man Trailer, The 1934,My 23,22:3
Personality Kid, The 1934,Ag 1,14:2
Dames 1934,Ag 16,20:2
Red Salute 1935,S 30,13:1
Little Big Shot 1935,O 7,11:2
King Solomon of Broadway 1935,O 19,12:2

Vinton, Bobby
Surf Party 1964,Mr 12,40:4

Viola, C G (Screenwriter)
Shoe-Shine 1947,Ag 27,19:2

Violet, E E (Director)
Veil of Happiness, The 1928,My 1,33:3

Violetto, Mina
Zappatore 1932,Mr 28,11:2

Violinov, Alexander
No Greater Love 1944,F 25,23:3

Viot, Jacques (Original Author)
Portrait of a Woman 1946,Ap 22,26:2
Long Night, The 1947,S 17,31:2
Dragon Sky 1964,Ag 25,28:2

Viot, Jacques (Screenwriter)
Daybreak 1940,Jl 30,16:2
Back Streets of Paris 1948,O 16,9:2
House on the Waterfront, The 1959,F 21,25:2
Black Orpheus 1959,D 22,41:1

Viotti, Gino
Quo Vadis 1925,F 16,24:1
Kif Tebbi 1929,My 20,22:6
Scipio Africanus 1939,S 23,22:2
Giovanni De Medici, The Leader 1940,Ja 5,15:4

Vipin, G
Twelfth Night 1956,Mr 5,21:1

Virana, Sveranta
Counterfeit Coin 1960,My 16,39:1

Virel, Andre (Cinematographer)
Gri-Gri 1956,S 29,12:2

Virgil, Helen
Temple of Venus, The 1923,N 1,24:3

Virgo, Peter
Body and Soul 1947,N 10,21:2
To the Ends of the Earth 1948,F 13,26:2
Shakedown 1950,S 4,11:2
Narrow Margin, The 1952,My 5,18:7
San Francisco Story, The 1952,My 10,16:4

Virido, Christiane
Cognasse 1935,Ap 15,16:4

Virlogeux, Henri
Any Number Can Win 1963,O 9,47:2
Day and the Hour, The 1964,F 20,22:2

Virogh, Jessie
Schloss im Sueden, Das 1936,F 24,14:2
Krach und Glueckum Kuennemann; Row and Joy
About Kuennemann 1938,S 17,20:3

Virtall, Nicholai (Screenwriter)
First Front, The 1949,N 14,19:2
Victors and the Vanquished, The 1950,My 1,18:2

Visaroff, Michael
Swan, The 1925,Mr 2,14:1
Valencia 1926,D 27,20:3
Camille 1927,Ap 22,19:1
Two Arabian Knights 1927,O 24,24:3
Last Command, The 1928,Ja 23,18:3
We Americans 1928,Mr 29,25:3
Ramona 1928,My 15,17:3
Tempest 1928,My 18,27:3
Plastered in Paris 1928,S 24,25:1
Night Bird, The 1928,O 2,23:5
4 Devils 1928,O 4,26:3
Marquis Preferred 1929,Ja 21,18:4
Disraeli 1929,O 3,27:5
Morocco 1930,N 17,29:1
Man Who Played God, The 1932,F 11,16:1
Strange People 1933,Je 17,16:5
We Live Again 1934,N 2,27:2
Mark of the Vampire 1935,My 3,23:4
Paddy O'Day 1936,F 8,19:2
Gay Desperado, The 1936,O 9,31:4
Champagne Waltz 1937,F 4,17:2
Soldier and the Lady, The 1937,Ap 10,11:1
Tropic Holiday 1938,Je 30,21:2
Paris Honeymoon 1939,Ja 26,17:1
Everything Happens at Night 1939,D 16,12:6
Four Sons 1940,Je 8,18:4
Charlie Chan At the Wax Museum 1940,S 28,9:3
Son of Monte Cristo, The 1940,D 5,33:1
Second Chorus 1941,Ja 16,25:2
For Whom the Bell Tolls 1943,Jl 15,25:2
Hostages 1943,O 11,23:2
Paris After Dark 1943,O 23,11:1
Intrigue 1948,Ap 24,11:2

Visaroff, Nina
Paddy O'Day 1936,F 8,19:2

Vischer, Blanca
Tango en Broadway, El 1934,D 29,11:3
Under the Pampas Moon 1935,My 31,11:1
Message to Garcia, A 1936,Ap 10,27:1
Bestia Negra, La; Black Beast, The 1940,Je 3,11:2

Visconti, Luchino (Director)
Bellissima 1953,My 18,26:2
Of Life and Love 1958,O 7,40:2
White Nights 1961,My 29,9:6
Rocco and his Brothers 1961,Je 28,40:2
Boccaccio '70 (The Job); Job, The (Boccaccio '70)
1962,Je 27,40:1
Leopard, The 1963,Ag 13,25:1
Vaghe Stelle dell'Orsa; Of These Thousand
Pleasures 1965,S 4,11:4
Terra Trema, La 1965,O 13,39:1
Sandra 1966,Ja 17,32:1
Stranger, The 1967,D 19,59:1
Senso 1968,Jl 9,31:1

Visconti, Luchino (Original Author)
Rocco and his Brothers 1961,Je 28,40:2
Visconti, Luchino (Screenwriter)
Bellissima 1953,My 18,26:2
White Nights 1961,My 29,9:6
Rocco and his Brothers 1961,Je 28,40:2
Boccaccio '70 (The Job); Job, The (Boccaccio '70)
1962,Je 27,40:1
Leopard, The 1963,Ag 13,25:1
Terra Trema, La 1965,O 13,39:1
Sandra 1966,Ja 17,32:1
Senso 1968,Jl 9,31:1
Vise, B J Professor
Conquerors of the Night 1933,Jl 31,16:3
Visentin, Angelo
Roof, The 1959,My 13,43:4
Vishnevetskaya, Sofiay (Screenwriter)
Optimistic Tragedy, The 1964,F 24,20:2
Vishnevsky, V (Screenwriter)
We Are From Kronstadt 1936,My 2,11:1
Vishnevsky, Vsevolod (Original Author)
Optimistic Tragedy, The 1964,F 24,20:2
Visotsky, Mikhail
Taras Family, The 1946,D 9,34:4
Vissentini, Gino (Screenwriter)
Bell Antonio 1962,Ap 3,43:2
Vissieres, Charles
Devil in the Flesh 1949,My 10,29:2
Little World of Don Camillo, The
1953,Ja 14,27:1
Return of Don Camillo, The 1956,Mr 27,41:1
Viswanathan, N
Kanchenjungha 1966,Jl 26,27:2
Vita, Alfio
Boccaccio '70 (The Raffle); Raffle, The (Boccaccio
'70) 1962,Je 27,40:1
Vita, Monique
Pot Bouille 1958,O 28,39:1
Bebo's Girl 1964,N 12,40:1
Vita, Perlo
Rififi 1956,Je 6,37:1
Vital
Crime in the Maginot Line 1939,My 8,21:2
Heritage 1940,N 5,33:2
Vital, G
Mystic Mountain, The 1936,Mr 31,17:2
Vital, Jean-Jacques (Producer)
Story of Monte Cristo, The 1962,N 7,48:1
Vital, Jean-Jacques (Screenwriter)
Dog, a Mouse and a Sputnik, A; Pied, a Cheval et
un Sputnik, A 1960,N 1,46:2
Vital, Mikhail
Poem of the Sea 1959,D 21,34:4
Vitale, Joseph
Days of Glory 1944,Je 17,10:2
Zombies on Broadway 1945,Ap 27,23:2
Lady Luck 1946,O 31,22:3
Where There's Life 1947,D 25,32:1
Road to Rio 1948,F 19,29:3
Paleface, The 1948,D 16,41:2
Connecticut Yankee in King Arthur's Court, A
1949,Ap 8,31:2
My Friend Irma Goes West 1950,Ag 3,20:2
Fancy Pants 1950,Ag 31,21:2
Stop, You're Killing Me 1952,D 11,45:3
Stranger Wore a Gun, The 1953,Jl 30,20:3
Square Jungle, The 1955,D 31,17:2
Vitale, Mario
Stromboli 1950,F 16,28:2
Island Sinner, The 1960,S 5,11:2
Vitale, Milly
Difficult Years 1950,Ag 22,31:2
Juggler, The 1953,My 6,39:2
Seven Little Foys, The 1955,Je 30,18:2
War and Peace 1956,Ag 22,26:2
Flesh is Weak, The 1957,N 9,31:2
Hannibal 1960,Ag 4,17:1
Breath of Scandal, A 1960,D 17,19:1
Vitallonga
Breakfast at Tiffany's 1961,O 6,28:1
Vitasova, Eleanor
My Beloved 1959,Je 15,31:4
Viteftot, N M
House of Death 1932,Ag 13,18:6
Vitelleschi, Stella
Ben Hur 1959,N 19,50:2
Vitiukov, B
Young Guard 1949,D 26,33:6
Vitkovitch, V (Original Author)
Adventures in Bokhara 1944,Ag 21,9:4
Vitol, A (Screenwriter)
Colt, The 1961,Je 5,37:4
Vitola, Cesare (Screenwriter)
Laugh Pagliacci 1948,Ja 31,14:2
Vitold, Michel
Tainted 1950,Ja 21,10:2
Francois Villon 1950,Jl 3,9:2
Judex 1966,Ap 26,55:1
Vitov, Alexander (Screenwriter)
Fathers and Sons 1960,D 26,27:2
Vitova, Hana
Merry Wives, The 1940,N 12,28:3

Vitrac, Roger (Original Author)
Vierge Folle, La 1938,D 30,11:3
Vitray, Georges
Tender Enemy, The 1938,Mr 31,15:2 (In
Addenda)
Vitry
Francis the First 1947,N 20,38:4
Vitsin, G
Boys From Leningrad, The 1955,My 2,16:5
Don Quixote 1961,Ja 21,18:1
Marriage of Baezaminov, The 1966,Je 11,20:2
Vitsoris
Voyage Surprise 1948,F 14,17:3
Vittes, Louis (Original Author)
Oregon Trail, The 1959,D 10,51:6
Vittes, Louis (Screenwriter)
Bengazi 1955,O 8,13:4
Oregon Trail, The 1959,D 10,51:6
Eyes of Annie Jones, The 1964,My 14,39:1
Vitti, Monica
Avventura, L' 1961,Ap 5,30:1
Night, The; Notte, La 1962,F 20,29:4
Eclipse 1962,D 21,5:1
Three Fables of Love (The Tortoise and the Hare);
Tortoise and the Hare, The (Three Fables of
Love) 1963,Ag 21,38:1
Deserto Rossa; Red Desert 1964,S 8,32:4
Chateau en Suede; Castle in Switzerland
1964,O 14,51:1
Sweet and Sour 1964,D 28,34:2
Red Desert 1965,F 9,43:1
Bambole; Dolls, The (The Soup); Soup, The (The
Dolls) 1965,Je 29,26:1
High Infidelity (The Victim); Victim, The (High
Infidelity) 1965,Jl 2,17:1
Modesty Blaise 1966,Ag 11,27:1
Queens, The (Queen Sabina); Queen Sabina (The
Queens) 1968,Mr 11,49:1
Vitti, Ralph
Somebody up There Likes Me 1956,Jl 6,16:1
Vitukhnovsky, M (Screenwriter)
Twins 1947,Jl 28,12:2
New Number Comes to Moscow, A
1959,Jl 6,23:1
Viva
Bike Boy 1967,O 6,31:2
Nude Restaurant, The 1967,N 14,52:1
Viva, Sim
Homme des Folies Bergere, L' 1936,Ap 18,19:3
Vivas, Eduardo
Indio, El 1939,My 13,11:5
Circo Tragic, El; Tragic Circus, The
1939,Je 17,12:3
Padre Mercader; Merchant Father 1939,Jl 15,8:3
Vivian, Jack
Dead Men Tell no Tales 1939,Jl 24,9:2
Vivian, Percival
Kiss in the Dark, A 1949,Mr 26,10:6
Prince Valiant 1954,Ap 7,40:2
Daddy Long Legs 1955,My 6,17:5
Vivian, Robert
Back Door to Heaven 1939,Ap 20,21:2
Vivian, Ruth
Man Who Came to Dinner, The 1942,Ja 2,25:2
Letter to Three Wives, A 1949,Ja 21,24:2
Vivian, Sidney
Key, The 1958,Jl 2,23:3
Vivien, L
Men of the Sea 1938,Je 20,11:2
Vivienne, Diane
Moonlighting Wives 1968,My 9,54:4
Vivier, Huguette
Shop-Girls of Paris; Au Bonheur de Dames
1947,Je 23,14:4
Murderer Lives at Number 21, The
1947,Ag 18,12:3
Vivier, Karl-Wilhelm (Screenwriter)
Bridge, The; (Bruecke, Die) 1961,My 2,42:1
Vivogradov, Valeri
Day the War Ended, The 1961,Ja 30,17:2
Vivyan, John
Imitation of Life 1959,Ap 18,18:1
Vizirenko-Klyavin, Robert
Lileia 1960,My 30,8:2
Vizvary, Mariska
Az en Lanyom nem olyan; My Daughter Is
Different 1938,Ap 30,18:2
Pentek Rezi; Friday Rose 1939,D 23,9:2
Vadroza; Wild Rose 1940,Ja 29,11:6
Vlachos, Anestis
Girl in Black, A 1957,S 17,39:2
Fear, The 1967,O 10,56:3
Vlacil, Frantisek (Director)
Devil's Trap, The 1964,Ag 14,16:1
Vlad, Roman (Composer)
Picasso 1955,D 23,14:4
Vladimorova, V
Apartment in Moscow 1962,My 28,25:5
Vladislavski, V
Lenin in October 1938,Ap 2,18:1
Vladislavsky, V
Anna Cross, The 1954,O 25,30:7

Vladislavsky, Vladimir
Girl No 217 1945,S 3,17:2
Admiral Nakhimov 1948,N 25,47:4
Vlady, Marina
Cavalcade of Song 1954,D 27,22:8
Sorciere, La 1956,D 28,17:2
Sins of Casanova 1957,O 7,23:2
Crime and Punishment 1958,S 16,23:2
Girl on the Third Floor, The; (Sophie et le Crime)
1958,O 11,47:1 (Incorrect in this edition; use
1958,O 11,18:4 elsewhere)
Nude in a White Car 1960,O 27,47:2
7 Capital Sins (Pride); Pride (7 Capital Sins)
1963,Ja 17,5:2
Conjugal Bed, The 1963,S 17,30:1
Steppe, The 1963,O 1,33:1
Don't Tempt the Devil 1964,Ap 28,43:1
Sweet and Sour 1964,D 28,34:2
Enough Rope 1966,Jl 15,34:3
Falstaff; Chimes at Midnight 1967,Mr 18,19:2
Two or Three Things I Know About Her
1968,S 26,60:1
Vlahopoulou, Rena
Girl From Corfu, The 1957,My 20,28:2
Vlahos, Anestis
Bed of Grass 1957,D 28,9:2
Vlahou, Persa
Anna of Rhodes 1950,Mr 23,34:2
Vlamos, James (Screenwriter)
Dark Odyssey 1961,Je 26,22:2
Vlarisio, Enrico
Four Steps in the Clouds 1948,N 22,25:2
Vlasek, June
Chandu the Magician 1932,O 1,10:4
Man Who Dared, The 1933,S 9,9:3
Vlasova, Olga
Carnival in Moscow 1957,N 4,40:1
Vockars, August
Zwei Hertzen in Drei-Viertel Takt
1930,O 13,31:1
Vocovits, Stelius
Phaedra 1962,O 19,24:1
Vodianitskaya, Galina
Zoya 1945,Ap 16,18:6
Vodnoy, Max
Green Fields 1937,O 12,31:4
Singing Blacksmith, The 1938,N 3,27:1
Voege, Gehard
Brand in der Oper 1932,Jl 11,11:4
Voelkner, Angeltka
Keepers of the Night 1953,Je 9,24:2
Vogan, Emmett
Two in Revolt 1936,Ap 25,21:1
Adventure in Manhattan 1936,O 23,27:5
Fly Away Baby 1937,Jl 9,18:2
Female Fugitive 1938,Ap 11,12:3
Beloved Brat 1938,My 2,13:2
Meet the Girls 1938,S 3,16:6
Secrets of an Actress 1938,O 8,10:2
Tail Spin 1939,F 11,13:2
Great Victor Herbert, The 1939,D 7,35:1
Thou Shalt Not Kill 1940,Ja 8,11:2
Horror Island 1941,Mr 31,11:3
Give Out, Sisters 1942,Ag 28,22:3
Whistling in Dixie 1942,D 31,20:4
Chatterbox 1943,Jl 2,15:3
Swingtime Johnny 1943,D 17,23:3
Are These our Parents? 1944,Ag 23,16:2
Enemy of Women 1944,S 12,23:6
Murder in the Blue Room 1944,O 28,12:2
She Gets her Man 1945,F 9,20:5
Utah 1945,Mr 12,22:7
Jolson Story, The 1946,O 11,28:2
Last of the Redmen 1947,Ag 30,8:6
Sorrowful Jones 1949,Je 6,15:2
Vogeding, Frederick
Murder on the Blackboard 1934,Je 20,24:2
Barbary Coast 1935,O 14,21:1
Charlie Chan in Shanghai 1935,O 14,21:1
House of a Thousand Candles, The
1936,Ap 2,29:2
Message to Garcia, A 1936,Ap 10,27:1
Cafe Metropole 1937,Ap 29,17:1
Charlie Chan at the Olympics 1937,My 24,23:1
Think Fast, Mr Moto 1937,Ag 16,15:3
Mr Moto Takes a Chance 1938,Je 13,15:4
Mysterious Mr Moto of Devil's Island
1938,S 19,16:2
Cowboy and the Lady, The 1938,N 25,19:3
Confessions of a Nazi Spy 1939,Ap 29,13:2
Charlie Chan in City in Darkness 1939,D 18,29:2
British Intelligence 1940,F 12,14:2
Four Sons 1940,Je 8,18:4
Man I Married, The 1940,Ag 3,9:2
Man Hunt 1941,Je 14,20:2
Vogeding, Fredrik
Below the Sea 1933,Je 3,16:4
Vogel, Daniel (Cinematographer)
Survival 1967 1968,Je 12,40:2
Vogel, Georg
Drei um Christine, Die; Three After Christine,
The 1940,My 4,13:2

Vogel, Jesse (Screenwriter)
Carmen Baby 1967,O 11,41:2
Therese and Isabelle 1968,My 15,41:4
Vogel, Mitchell
Yours, Mine and Ours 1968,Ap 25,53:1
Vogel, Nadine
Bizarre, Bizarre 1939,Mr 21,27:2
S O S Mediterranean 1940,Ja 1,29:2
Vogel, Nicholas
They Are not Angels 1948,My 22,8:3
Desperate Decision 1954,N 9,31:5
Vogel, Peter
Stefanie 1959,Je 18,36:1
Vogel, Rudolf
Story of Vickie, The 1958,Ja 30,19:2
Spessart Inn, The 1961,F 18,12:3
Heidi 1968,S 23,42:4
Vogelsang, George
Drei Vater um Anna; Three Fathers for Anna
1940,Ja 20,11:3
Vogler, Karl Michael
Those Magnificent Men in Their Flying Machines
(Or How I Flew From London to Paris in 25
Hours and 11 Minutes) 1965,Je 17,27:1
Blue Max, The 1966,Je 22,38:1
How I Won the War 1967,N 9,56:1
VOGT
See Also VOIGT
Vogt, Carl de
U-Boat 9 1929,Ja 22,23:1
Zu Strassburg auf der Schanz; At the Strassburg
1936,F 15,18:7
Fahrmann Maria; Ferryman Maria
1938,D 24,12:3
Vohs, Joan
Fort Ti 1953,My 30,7:1
Vice Squad 1953,Ag 26,23:2
Sabrina 1954,S 23,43:2
Cry Vengence 1955,F 19,18:3
Voice of Experience
Hit Parade, The 1937,My 31,11:2
Voight, John
Confessions of a Nazi Spy 1939,Ap 29,13:2
Beasts of Berlin 1939,N 20,15:6
VOIGT
See Also VOGT
Voinev, Konstintin (Director)
Sun Shines for All 1961,Jl 10,25:3
Marriage of Baezaminov, The 1966,Je 11,20:2
Voinev, Konstintin (Screenwriter)
Marriage of Baezaminov, The 1966,Je 11,20:2
Voit, Mieczyslaw
Joan of the Angels? 1962,My 8,43:6
Voitsik, Ada
Anna 1936,Jl 17,20:2
Gift for Music 1957,Jl 15,15:2
My Daughter 1960,N 28,40:2
Vojta, Jar
Ecstasy of Young Love 1936,Mr 10,27:3
Vokel, Elda
First Year, The 1932,Ag 22,20:2
Vokes, May
Janice Meredith 1924,Ag 6,13:3
Vokoloff, Vladimir
Mayerling 1937,S 14,27:1
Voland, Herbert
With Six You Get Egg Roll 1968,O 10,59:6
Volchek, Victor
Zoya 1945,Ap 16,18:6
Voleri, Jole
Manon Lescaut 1941,Ap 14,23:5
Volimoeller, Karl (Screenwriter)
Blue Angel, The 1959,S 5,11:4
Volk, George
To the Ends of the Earth 1948,F 13,26:2
Volker, Willi
Fremd im Sudetenland; Strange to the Sudeten
Country 1938,N 5,15:3
Volkie, Ralph
East of the River 1940,O 28,21:2
Bloodhounds of Broadway 1952,N 15,15:2
Volkof, R
Dubrovsky 1936,Mr 30,17:6
Volkoff, Alexander (Director)
Loves of Casanova, The 1929,Ap 30,33:2
Volkoff, Alexander (Screenwriter)
Casanova 1927,Je 23,23:3
Volkov
Last Game, The 1964,O 25,41:5 (Incorrect in this
edition; use 1964,O 26,41:5 elsewhere)
Volkov, F
Ski Battalion 1938,Mr 14,13:1
Volkov, N
Admiral Ushakov 1954,Ja 18,19:2
Volkov, Nikolai
Flying Carpet, The 1960,F 28,31:1
Volkov, Pavel
City of Youth 1938,S 5,30:4
New Teacher, The 1941,Ap 7,13:3
Turning Point, The 1946,O 28,19:4
Son of the Regiment 1948,Ap 29,27:3
Fate of Man 1961,Jl 11,28:1

Volkov, V
Poet and Tsar 1938,Ag 25,15:1
Volkov, Y M
Gobsek 1937,Jl 16,22:1
Vollmer, Lula (Original Author)
Sun Up 1925,Ag 18,14:3
Spitfire 1934,Mr 9,22:3
Vollmoeller, Karl (Original Author)
Song 1928,Ag 22,24:2
Lady of the Pavements 1929,Mr 11,22:2
Miracle, The 1959,N 13,25:4
Vollmoeller, Karl (Screenwriter)
Shanghai Gesture, The 1941,D 26,21:2
Vollmoeller, Karl Dr (Original Author)
Wasted Love 1929,D 30,16:4
Volmer, Helmuth (Producer)
Sunderin 1954,D 24,7:2
Liane, Jungle Goddess 1959,F 23,19:1
Third Sex, The 1959,Mr 26,27:1
Volmut, M Litvinenko
Natalka-Poltavka 1936,D 25,19:4
Volodin, Vladimir
Volga-Volga 1941,My 17,19:2
Tanya 1942,Mr 5,27:1
Winner, The 1947,D 1,27:2
Cossacks of the Kuban 1950,O 30,22:4
Volodina, Margarita
Optimistic Tragedy, The 1964,F 24,20:2
Volodina, Marina
Miles of Fire 1958,N 10,36:6 (In Addenda)
Volonte, Gian Maria
Magnificent Cuckold 1965,Ap 20,42:1
For a Few Dollars More 1967,Jl 4,23:1
We Still Kill the Old Way 1968,F 29,28:1
Violent Four, The 1968,Ag 15,46:2
Volonte, Gianmaria
Under ten Flags 1960,S 16,24:1
Voloshin, Alex
Ride a Crooked Mile 1938,D 29,15:2
Volpe, Frederick
Middle Watch, The 1930,D 20,20:6
Captivation 1931,S 28,17:4
Volpin, M (Screenwriter)
Hello, Moscow! 1946,Je 15,24:4
Horsemen, The 1951,Ja 29,14:5
Volrian, Peter
Big House U S A 1955,Mr 12,11:6
Volsky, M
Red Tanks 1942,Je 6,9:2
Voltaire (Original Author)
Candide 1962,N 20,39:1
Volti, Joe
Pacific Adventure 1947,N 26,18:2
Voltsik, A I
Oppenheim Family, The 1939,My 24,29:2
Volusia, Eros
Rio Rita 1942,My 8,27:3
Volz, Wolfgang
Funeral in Berlin 1966,D 23,17:1
von Alten, Ferdinand
Small Town Sinners 1928,N 27,34:1
Sajenko, The Soviet 1929,Ja 15,22:4
Man Who Cheated Life, The 1929,F 11,26:3
von Ambesser, Axel (Director)
Good Soldier Schweik, The 1963,Ag 21,38:1
von Arendt, Ekkehard
Wiener Blut 1933,N 13,21:2
von Baky, Josef (Director)
City of Torment 1950,Je 10,11:4
Last Illusion, The 1951,Mr 8,37:2
Dreaming Lips; (Traumende Mund, The)
1958,N 1,14:3
Stefanie 1959,Je 18,36:1
Confess, Dr Corda 1960,O 24,25:5
von Ballesko, Victoria
Our Daily Bread 1950,O 9,21:6
von Berne, Eva
Masks of the Devil, The 1928,N 26,30:2
von Bohlen, Fred
Mein Liebster Ist ein Jaegersmann 1936,S 15,37:6
von Bolvary, Geza (Director)
Zwei Hertzen in Drei-Viertel Takt
1930,O 13,31:1
Lustigen Weiber von Wien, Die 1931,Jl 10,22:2
Sein Liebeslied 1931,N 19,27:5
Das Lied ist Aus 1932,Ja 29,13:2
Raub der Mona Lisa, Der 1932,Mr 30,15:2
Liebeskommando 1932,Ap 27,13:6
Ich Will Nicht Wissen Wer Du Bist
1933,F 16,23:2
Liebling von Wien, Der 1933,Je 10,16:5
Winternachtstraum 1935,D 28,10:6
Schloss im Sueden, Das 1936,F 24,14:2
Ein Lied, Ein Kuss, Ein Maeder 1936,D 12,29:4
Schloss in Flandern, Das 1937,Ag 7,7:3
Charm of la Boheme, The 1938,Mr 19,11:2
Von Bolvary, Geza (Director)
Fledermaus, Die; Bat, The 1948,Mr 15,26:2
Von Borsody, Edward (Director)
Liane, Jungle Goddess 1959,F 23,19:1
von Borsody, Hans
Don Juan 1956,Mr 6,26:2
Cavern, The 1965,D 25,17:2

von Brincken, William
Mamba 1930,Mr 11,25:2
Hell's Angels 1930,Ag 16,8:3
Night Club Lady, The 1932,Ag 27,13:4
Passport to Hell, A 1932,Ag 27,13:4
Dracula's Daughter 1936,My 18,14:2
Prisoner of Zenda, The 1937,S 3,12:1
Thank You, Mr Moto 1938,Ja 3,16:2
International Crime 1938,My 16,14:4
Bulldog Drummond in Africa 1938,Ag 25,15:1
Pack up Your Troubles 1939,O 27,27:2
Four Sons 1940,Je 8,18:4
von Cetto, Gitta (Original Author)
Stefanie 1959,Je 18,36:1
von Cleve, Heinz
Abel Mit Der Mundharmonika 1934,S 1,16:3
Leichte Kavallerie 1936,F 8,19:2
von Collande, Volker
Waldwinter 1936,N 14,23:3
von Cube, Irmgard (Original Author)
They Shall Have Music 1939,Jl 26,17:2
von Cube, Irmgard (Screenwriter)
Song of Love 1947,O 10,31:2
Johnny Belinda 1948,O 2,11:2
von Cziffra, Geza (Director)
Tale of Five Women, A 1953,Ja 16,19:2
Fledermaus, Die 1964,F 8,15:2
von Cziffra, Geza (Screenwriter)
Fledermaus, Die 1964,F 8,15:2
von Dally, Ellinor
Karneval und Liebe 1936,Ap 4,11:2
von Deck, Wilhelm
Last Year at Marienbad 1962,Mr 8,26:1
von Diemen, Ursula
Andere, Der 1932,Ja 15,24:4
von Donegen, Frits
Dreaming Lips; (Traumende Mund, The)
1958,N 1,14:3
Von Eltz, Theodore
Tiger Rose 1923,D 3,14:1
Being Respectable 1924,Ag 4,16:3
On Thin Ice 1925,Mr 9,21:1
Sporting Chance, The 1925,Je 24,14:3
Red Kimono, The 1926,F 3,23:1
Great Mail Robbery, The 1927,Jl 20,29:3
One Woman to Another 1927,S 19,30:3
Rescue, The 1929,Ja 14,20:1
Four Feathers, The 1929,Je 13,35:4
Furies, The 1930,Ap 19,15:1
Arizona Kid, The 1930,My 17,21:2
Cat Creeps, The 1930,N 8,21:3
Beyond Victory 1931,Ap 6,24:1
Secret Six, The 1931,My 2,23:4
Up Pops the Devil 1931,My 16,13:3
Prodigal, The 1931,Je 27,20:3
Wicked 1931,S 19,10:2
Once a Lady 1931,N 9,22:4
Ladies of the Big House 1932,Ja 1,31:1
Hotel Continental 1932,Mr 21,19:5
Strangers of the Evening 1932,Je 4,9:2
Midnight Lady, The 1932,Jl 1,19:3
Red-Haired Alibi 1932,O 24,18:5
Luxury Liner 1933,F 3,21:3
Pleasure Cruise 1933,Ap 3,13:3
High Gear 1933,Ap 15,16:2
Jennie Gerhardt 1933,Je 9,20:2
Arizona to Broadway 1933,Jl 22,14:3
Dance, Girl, Dance 1933,O 25,23:3
Master of Men 1933,N 29,23:4
Change of Heart 1934,My 11,24:2
Call it Luck 1934,Jl 10,24:5
Bright Eyes 1934,D 21,31:1
Silver Streak, The 1935,Ja 16,21:1
Private Worlds 1935,Mr 28,25:2
His Night Out 1935,N 16,19:2
Magnificent Obsession 1935,D 31,11:2
High Tension 1936,Jl 11,11:4
Suzy 1936,Jl 25,16:1
Road to Glory, The 1936,Ag 6,22:1
Ticket to Paradise 1936,Ag 8,5:3
Beloved Enemy 1936,D 26,15:2
Under Cover of Night 1937,Ja 20,18:4
Sinner Take All 1937,F 3,27:1
Topper 1937,Ag 20,21:2
Westland Case, The 1937,O 23,14:2
Smashing the Rackets 1938,Ag 9,22:5
They Made Her a Spy 1939,Mr 29,21:4
Fifth Avenue Girl 1939,Ag 25,12:2
Legion of Lost Flyers 1939,O 30,13:3
Little Old New York 1940,F 3,9:2
Dr Ehrlich's Magic Bullet 1940,F 24,9:2
Great Plane Robbery, The 1940,N 15,25:2
Son of Monte Cristo 1940,D 5,33:1
Ellery Queen's Penthouse Mystery
1941,Mr 7,17:2
I'll Wait for You 1941,Je 2,13:6
Man in the Trunk, The 1942,O 23,25:1
Follow the Boys 1944,Ap 26,24:6
Bermuda Mystery 1944,My 13,17:1
Big Sleep, The 1946,Ag 24,6:6
Von Eltz, Theodore (Narrator)
Animal World, The 1956,My 31,21:6

von Esterhazy, Agnes Countess
Escaped From Hell 1929,Ja 29,27:1
von Friedl, Loni
Shadows Grow Longer, The 1962,Je 11,36:4
Blue Max, The 1966,Je 22,38:1
von Gegerfeldt, Erik
Sunshine Follows Rain 1949,S 29,39:2
von Gerlach, Arthur (Director)
At the Grey House 1927,N 8,33:1
Vanina 1928,Mr 20,20:3
von Gordon, Wolff (Screenwriter)
Merry Wives of Windsor, The 1952,S 22,19:2
von Goth, Rolf
Berlin After Dark 1929,My 28,36:2
Hirsekorn Greift Ein 1932,Je 10,22:3
Sehnsucht 202; Longing 202 1932,N 13,IX,4:2
Zirkus Leben 1932,D 28,14:7
Meisterdetektiv, Der 1934,F 13,23:2
Die Blonde Christl 1934,F 23,23:3
Es War Einmal ein Walzer 1934,O 15,20:5
Bei der Blonden Kathrein 1934,D 3,15:2
von Halmy, Tibor
Foresterchristl, Die 1931,Ap 27,25:1
Ein Prinz Verliebt Sich 1932,Ap 29,13:4
Gitta Entdeckt Ihr Herz 1932,S 30,17:3
Ihre Majestaet die Liebe 1933,F 7,23:4
Liebe in Uniform 1934,O 9,17:2
Rakoczi Indulo 1934,N 21,23:4
Ein Lied, Ein Kuss, Ein Maeder 1936,D 12,29:4
Csardas, Ihre Tollste Nacht 1937,Je 21,15:3
von Hamlay, Oskar
Moritz Macht Sein Glueck 1932,D 24,11:4
von Harbou, Thea (Original Author)
Metropolis 1927,Mr 7,16:3
At the Grey House 1927,N 8,33:1
Spies 1929,Mr 5,29:1
By Rocket to the Moon 1931,F 7,11:1
M 1933,Ap 3,13:3
Alte und der Junge Koenig, Der 1935,D 10,31:2
Journey to the Lost City 1960,D 8,43:3
von Harbou, Thea (Screenwriter)
Angelika 1954,S 25,10:7
von Hardenburg, William
Love Parade, The 1929,N 20,32:6
von Hartmann, Carl
Very Confidential 1927,N 29,31:1
Awakening, The 1928,D 31,9:1
Hell's Angels 1930,Ag 16,8:3
von Hofmannsthal, Hugo (Miscellaneous)
Rosenkavalier, Der 1962,O 10,57:1
von Hollay, Camilla
At the Edge of the World 1929,Je 18,29:4
von Kaufmann, Wilhelm Dr (Director)
Gretel and Liesel; (Kohlhiesel's Daughters) 1931,Ja 26,21:1
von Koczian, Johanna
Aren't We Wonderful? 1959,O 16,27:1
von Krusenstjerna, Agnes (Original Author)
Loving Couples 1966,S 20,38:1
von Lennep, Walter
Vetter aus Dingsda, Der 1936,F 1,9:3
Von Moio, Elisabeth
Situation Hopeless-But not Serious 1965,O 14,53:1
von Molo, Trude
Raub der Mona Lisa, Der 1932,Mr 30,15:2
Kadetten 1933,D 26,19:3
von Morhart, Hans
Pursuit of Happiness, The 1934,O 26,25:1
Beasts of Berlin 1939,N 20,15:6
Lady Has Plans, The 1942,Mr 5,27:1
Berlin Correspondent 1942,S 4,19:2
von Munchhofen, Helen
Survival 1930,Ja 13,21:1
Von Nady, Barbara
Journey, The 1959,F 20,19:1
von Newlinski, Herr
Sohn der Weissen Berge, Der 1933,O 23,18:3
von Nussbaum, Magdalena
Somewhere in Berlin 1949,Ag 16,19:3
von Oertzen, Jasper
Magic Face, The 1951,O 1,19:2
von Otto, Horst
Sunderin 1954,D 24,7:2
von Peterson, Friedhelm
Razzia 1948,Je 14,19:2
von Platen, Flokina
Strich Durch die Rechnung 1934,Mr 3,8:6
von Plessan, Victor Baron (Miscellaneous)
Wajan 1938,Ap 18,11:1
von Rezzori, Gregor
Very Private Affair, A 1962,S 29,15:1
Viva Maria 1965,D 20,48:2
Von Rue, Greta
Her Honor the Governor 1926,Jl 20,17:3
Von Salomon, Ernest (Screenwriter)
Liane, Jungle Goddess 1959,F 23,19:1
von Santer, Carl (Director)
City Without Jews, The 1928,Jl 9,25:1
von Schacht, Count
Isn't Life Wonderful? 1924,D 1,17:3

von Schwindt, Wolfgang
Finanzen des Grossherzogs, Die; Grand Duke's Finances, The 1935,Ap 6,10:3
von Seyffertitz, Gustav
When Knighthood Was in Flower 1922,S 15,17:2 (In Addenda)
Yolanda 1924,F 20,23:1
Lone Wolf, The 1924,My 7,19:4
Bandolero, The 1924,O 27,27:1
Red Dice 1926,Ap 16,20:3
Barbed Wire 1927,Ag 8,10:3
Magic Flame, The 1927,S 19,30:3
Student Prince, The 1927,S 22,33:2
Rose of the Golden West 1927,S 26,27:1
Gaucho, The 1927,N 22,32:2
Wizard, The 1927,N 28,18:5
Yellow Lily, The 1928,My 21,25:1
Mysterious Lady, The 1928,Ag 6,15:2
Docks of New York, The 1928,S 17,28:2
Me, Gangster 1928,O 22,29:1
Red Mark, The 1928,O 30,27:3
Woman Disputed, The 1928,N 10,20:8
Case of Lena Smith, The 1929,Ja 15,22:4
Canary Murder Case, The 1929,Mr 11,22:2
Dangerous Paradise 1930,F 16,III,8:1
Case of Sergeant Grischa, The 1930,Mr 8,21:1
Bat Whispers, The 1931,Ja 16,27:1
Dishonored 1931,Mr 6,16:1
Ambassador Bill 1931,N 14,15:3
Shanghai Express 1932,F 18,25:3
Roadhouse Murder 1932,Ap 29,13:4
Doomed Battalion, The 1932,Je 11,9:3
Afraid to Talk 1932,D 19,19:5
When Strangers Marry 1933,My 25,24:3
Queen Christina 1933,D 27,23:3
Change of Heart 1934,My 11,24:2
She 1935,Jl 26,18:2
Remember Last Night? 1935,N 21,27:2
Murder on a Bridle Path 1936,Ap 11,19:2
Mad Holiday 1936,N 26,39:2
Cipher Bureau 1938,D 14,32:6
Nurse Edith Cavell 1939,S 22,27:4
von Sternberg, Josef (Cinematographer)
Ana-Ta-Han 1954,My 18,38:2
von Sternberg, Josef (Director)
Salvation Hunters, The 1925,F 2,14:1
Underworld 1927,Ag 22,21:3
Last Command, The 1928,Ja 23,18:3
Drag Net, The 1928,Je 4,13:2
Case of Lena Smith, The 1929,Ja 15,22:4
Thunderbolt 1929,Je 21,17:2
Morocco 1930,N 17,29:1
Blue Angel, The 1930,D 6,21:3
Dishonored 1931,Mr 6,16:1
American Tragedy, An 1931,Ag 6,22:5
Shanghai Express 1932,F 18,25:3
Blonde Venus 1932,S 24,18:4
Scralet Empress, The 1934,S 15,20:2
Devil is a Woman, The 1935,My 4,17:2
Crime and Punishment 1935,N 22,18:2
King Steps Out, The 1936,My 29,15:2
Sergeant Madden 1939,Mr 24,27:2
Shanghai Gesture, The 1941,D 26,21:2
Macao 1952,My 1,34:2
Ana-Ta-Han 1954,My 18,38:2
Jet Pilot 1957,O 5,8:6
von Sternberg, Josef (Original Author)
Ana-Ta-Han 1954,My 18,38:2
von Sternberg, Josef (Screenwriter)
Salvation Hunters, The 1925,F 2,14:1
Street of Sin, The 1928,My 28,23:2
Dishonored 1931,Mr 6,16:1
Shanghai Gesture, The 1941,D 26,21:2
von Stolz, Hilde
Traumulus 1936,S 19,20:1
Masquerade in Vienna 1937,Ja 26,16:4
Abenteurer von Paris, Der 1937,My 29,20:3
Marriage in the Shadows 1948,S 17,28:3
von Stroheim, Edward (Producer)
Devil's Pass Key, The 1920,Ag 9,6:3
von Stroheim, Erich
Heart of Humanity, The 1918,D 22,17:3
Blind Husbands 1919,D 8,20:4
Wedding March, The 1928,O 15,26:1
Great Gabbo, The 1929,S 13,33:1
Three Faces East 1930,S 6,9:2
Friends and Lovers 1931,N 7,16:5
Lost Squadron, The 1932,Mr 11,15:4
As You Desire Me 1932,Je 3,23:4
Crimson Romance 1934,O 13,10:1
Crime of Dr Crespi, The 1936,Ja 13,14:3
Grand Illusion 1938,S 13,28:2
Alibi, L' 1939,Ap 10,13:3
Boys' School 1939,Je 6,26:2
Ultimatum 1940,F 5,13:2
I Was an Adventuress 1940,My 20,13:2
Thunder Over Paris 1940,Je 28,22:3
Personal Column 1941,F 3,13:2
So Ends our Night 1941,F 28,17:2
Five Graves to Cairo 1943,My 27,21:2
von Stroheim, ERich
North Star, The 1943,N 5,23:1

von Stroheim, Erich
It Happened in Gibraltar 1943,N 16,27:1
Lady and the Monster, The 1944,Ap 8,9:2
Storm Over Lisbon 1944,S 11,14:1
32 Rue de Montmartre 1944,S 28,26:3
Marthe Richard 1944,N 9,23:2
Great Flamario, The 1945,Ja 15,15:5
von Stroheim, ERich
Devil and the Angel, The 1949,D 3,8:6
von Stroheim, Erich
Sunset Boulevard 1950,Ag 11,15:2
von Stroheim, Erich (Director)
Blind Husbands 1919,D 8,20:4
Foolish Wives 1922,Ja 12,15:2
Greed 1924,D 5,28:1
Merry Widow, The 1925,Ag 27,14:1
Wedding March, The 1928,O 15,26:1
Wedding March 1965,S 13,42:1
von Stroheim, Erich (Original Author)
Between Two Women 1937,Ag 6,21:1
von Stroheim, Erich (Screenwriter)
Foolish Wives 1922,Ja 12,15:2
Wedding March, The 1928,O 15,26:1
Devil Doll, The 1936,Ag 8,5:2
Von Sydow, Clas S
Hawaii 1966,O 11,54:1
Von Sydow, Henrik
Hawaii 1966,O 11,54:1
von Sydow, Max
Seventh Seal 1958,O 14,44:1
Wild Strawberries 1959,Je 23,37:1
Magician, The 1959,Ag 28,27:1
Brink of Life; (Nara Livet) 1959,N 9,36:2
Virgin Spring, The; Jungfrukallan 1960,N 15,46:1
Through a Glass Darkly 1962,Mr 14,45:1
Winter Light 1963,My 14,32:1
Greatest Story Ever Told, The 1965,F 16,40:2
Reward, The 1965,S 16,55:1
Hawaii 1966,O 11,54:1
Quiller Memorandum, The 1966,D 16,59:1
Hour of the Wolf 1968,Ap 10,50:2
Shame 1968,D 24,14:1
von Tasnady, Maria
Young Caruso, The 1953,O 13,34:4
von Tempski, Armine (Original Author)
Hula 1927,Ag 29,21:1
von Thellmann, Erika
Good Soldier Schweik, The 1963,Ag 21,38:1
Von Tilzer, Albert (Composer)
Gift of Gab 1934,S 26,17:6
von Twardowsky, Hans
Scandal for Sale 1932,Ap 3,26:2
Private Jones 1933,Mr 25,13:3
Adorable 1933,My 19,20:2
Confessions of a Nazi Spy 1939,Ap 29,13:2
Espionage Agent 1939,S 23,22:2
Beasts of Berlin 1939,N 20,15:6
von Ungern-Sternberg, Wolfgang
Signs of Life; Lebenszeichent 1968,S 26,60:1
von Valetti, Ida
Moritz Macht Sein Glueck 1932,D 24,11:4
von Vaszarays, Gabor (Original Author)
Montpi 1959,Ap 21,40:1
von Vaszarays, Gabor (Screenwriter)
Montpi 1959,Ap 21,40:1
von Volvary, Geza (Director)
Pesti Szerelem 1934,My 10,25:3
von Wagner, Erika
Episode 1937,My 17,23:2
von Weike, Truus
Moritz Macht Sein Glueck 1932,D 24,11:4
Von Wohl, Ludwig (Original Author)
Slalom 1936,D 16,35:3
von Wymetal, Wilhelm Jr (Miscellaneous)
I'll Take Romance 1937,D 17,33:2
von Zedlitz, Hans
Ich Sing Mich in Dein Herz Hinein 1935,Je 3,22:3
Von Zell, Harry
Uncle Harry 1945,Ag 24,14:5
Till the End of Time 1946,Jl 24,24:1
Guilt of Janet Ames, The 1947,My 23,31:2
Where There's Life 1947,D 25,32:1
Saxon Charm, The 1948,S 30,32:3
Dear Wife 1950,F 2,31:2
Where the Sidewalk Ends 1950,Jl 8,7:4
Two Flags West 1950,O 13,23:2
For Heaven's Sake 1950,D 16,10:5
Call Me Mister 1951,F 1,21:2
U S S Teakettle 1951,F 24,11:2
I Can Get It for You Wholesale 1951,Ap 5,34:4
Son of Paleface 1952,O 2,32:3
Boy, Did I Get a Wrong Number! 1966,Je 9,54:2
Von Zerneck, Peter
13 Rue Madeleine 1947,Ja 16,30:2
Berlin Express 1948,My 21,19:3
Foreign Affair, A 1948,Jl 1,19:3
von Zynda, Henry
Beasts of Berlin 1939,N 20,15:6
Vonic, Gloria
Cimarron 1931,Ja 27,20:5

Vonn, Veola
Burma Convoy 1941,O 7,26:7
South Sea Woman 1953,Je 4,33:6
Phantom of the Rue Morgue 1954,Mr 20,10:5
Lafayette Escadrille 1958,Ap 19,10:4
Vorenina, Vera
Patriot, The 1928,Ag 18,7:2 (In Addenda)
Vorhaus, Bernard (Director)
Broken Melody, The 1934,O 31,17:3
Last Journey, The 1936,Je 8,22:4
King of the Newsboys 1938,Ap 2,18:2
Tenth Avenue Kid 1938,S 2,21:3
Fisherman's Wharf 1939,F 24,15:2
Way Down South 1939,Ag 18,16:4
Meet Doctor Christian 1939,D 1,27:2
Courageous Dr Christian, The 1940,Mr 29,25:3
Three Faces West 1940,Ag 19,13:2
Lady From Louisiana 1941,My 15,27:2
Bury Me Dead 1947,O 25,13:3
So Young, So Bad 1950,Jl 24,15:2
Pardon my French 1952,Mr 31,17:2
Vorhaus, Bernard (Screenwriter)
So Young, So Bad 1950,Jl 24,15:2
Vorkapich, Slavko (Director)
I Take This Woman 1931,Je 13,20:4
Vorkapich, Slavko (Miscellaneous)
Moscow Strikes Back 1942,Ag 17,19:2
Vorlova, Slavka
Bohemian Rapture 1948,F 16,16:2
Vorobyev, M
Train Goes East, The 1949,S 5,13:3
Vorobyov, Yevgeny (Screenwriter)
If Your Home Is Dear to You 1967,O 24,27:1
Vorobyova, Eugenia (Screenwriter)
Festival in Moscow 1958,F 17,19:1
Voronina, Vera
Whirlwind of Youth, The 1927,Je 6,27:2
Voroshilof, K E
Soviets on Parade 1933,Mr 6,16:7
Vosburgh, John
Red-Haired Alibi 1932,O 24,18:5
Voscherau, Carl
Sunderin 1954,D 24,7:2
Voselli, Judith
Kiss Me Again 1931,Ja 8,21:4
Voska, Vaclav
Bohemian Rapture 1948,F 16,16:2
Murder Czech Style 1968,Ag 20,33:1
Voskovec, George
World Is Ours, The 1939,Ag 14,11:5
Anything Can Happen 1952,Ap 4,21:1
Affair in Trinidad 1952,Jl 31,14:2
Iron Mistress, The 1952,N 20,39:2
12 Angry Men 1957,Ap 15,24:1
Uncle Vanya 1958,Ap 29,26:2
Bravados, The 1958,Je 26,23:2
Wind Across the Everglades 1958,S 12,21:1
Butterfield 8 1960,N 17,46:1
Hamlet 1964,S 24,46:1
Spy Who Came in From the Cold, The 1965,D 24,24:1
Mister Buddwing 1966,O 12,36:1
Voskovec, George (Screenwriter)
World Is Ours, The 1939,Ag 14,11:5
Voskresenskaia, Z (Screenwriter)
Sons and Mothers 1967,O 2,58:1
Vosper, Frank
Rome Express 1933,F 27,11:2
Power 1934,O 5,29:3
Man Who Knew too Much, The 1935,Mr 23,11:2
Strauss's Great Waltz 1935,Ap 8,23:3
Heart's Desire 1937,Jl 12,20:4
Spy of Napoleon 1939,Ag 19,18:4
Secret of Stamboul, The 1941,My 31,14:1
Vosper, Frank (Original Author)
Love From a Stranger 1937,Ap 19,27:2
Love From a Stranger 1947,N 28,30:1
Vosper, John
Perfect Marriage, The 1947,Ja 16,30:3
Magnetic Monster, The 1953,My 14,32:5
Voss, Aasta
Boer Boerson Jr 1939,N 4,11:3
Voss, Peter
Fight for Matterhorn, The 1929,Jl 29,23:3
Rosenmontag 1931,Mr 28,15:3
Tod Ueber Schanghai 1933,D 16,12:4
Mutter und Kind 1934,N 30,22:3
Reiter von Deutsch-Ostafrika, Die 1935,Je 8,12:3
Gruen ist die Heide 1935,O 14,21:2
Mein Leben fuer Maria Isabell; My Life for Maria Isabell 1935,N 5,33:5
Reifende Jugend 1936,Ja 4,19:1
Abenteurer von Paris, Der 1937,My 29,20:3
Kampf ums Matterhorn 1938,Ap 18,11:2
Fahrmann Maria; Ferryman Maria 1938,D 24,12:3
Voss, Richard (Original Author)
Zwei Menschen 1931,D 23,27:3
Vosselli, Judith
Prince of Tempters, The 1926,O 18,18:1
Rogue Song, The 1930,Ja 29,26:4
Reno 1930,N 4,36:1
Lady's Morals, A 1930,N 8,21:3

Today 1930,N 17,29:1
Sunny 1930,D 27,16:3
Inspiration 1931,F 9,25:3
Lady Who Dared, The 1931,Je 6,15:5
Under Eighteen 1931,D 26,15:5
Madame Butterfly 1932,D 26,26:2
Modern Hero, A 1934,Ap 20,17:1
Great Flirtation, The 1934,Je 22,16:5
Vostrcil, Jan
Loves of a Blonde 1966,O 27,55:1
Firemen's Ball, The 1968,S 30,60:1
Votrian, Peter
Hans Christian Andersen 1952,N 26,20:2
Her Twelve Men 1954,Ag 12,23:2
Hell on Frisco Bay 1956,Ja 7,21:1
Crime in the Streets 1956,My 24,27:4
Fear Strikes Out 1957,Mr 21,37:2
Votrian, Ralph
Bold and the Brave, The 1956,My 26,15:2
Tea and Sympathy 1956,S 28,24:4
Until They Sail 1957,O 9,41:2
Imitation General 1958,Ag 21,22:2
Voulgaris, Antonios
Barefoot Battalion 1954,My 29,13:4
Voutsinas, Andreas
Producers, The 1968,Mr 19,38:1
Vovsi, M
Day the War Ended, The 1961,Ja 30,17:2
Voyadjis, George
Zorba, The Greek 1964,D 18,25:1
Voyantiz, John
Guide, The 1965,F 10,44:2
Voyetekhov, Boris (Original Author)
Last Hill, The 1945,Je 26,13:2
Voyetekhov, Boris (Screenwriter)
Last Hill, The 1945,Je 26,13:2
Voynich, Ethel L (Original Author)
Gadfly, The 1956,S 17,22:2
Voytsik, Ada
Once There Was a Girl 1945,D 24,19:2
Voyuklakis, Alice
Shepherd's Daughter, The 1956,My 14,23:3
Astero 1960,Ap 25,32:2
Moussitsa 1960,O 31,25:2
Vrana, Speratza
Taxi Driver, The 1958,Mr 3,24:8
Vrbsky, Bedrich
Krakatit 1951,Ap 30,16:2
Vreeland, Helen (Original Author)
Danger Patrol 1937,N 19,27:3
Vrochota, R
Border Street 1950,Ap 26,35:2
Vroman, Mary Elizabeth (Original Author)
Bright Road 1953,Ap 29,33:5
Vronsky, Vakhtang (Director)
Lileia 1960,My 30,8:2
Vronsky, Vakhtang (Producer)
Lileia 1960,My 30,8:2
Vronsky, Vakhtang (Screenwriter)
Lileia 1960,My 30,8:2
Vronsky, Vitya
Adventure in Music 1944,Mr 6,17:3
Vroom, Frederick
Faith Healer, The 1921,Mr 14,9:2
Day of Faith, The 1923,N 27,11:2
Acquittal, The 1923,D 12,24:5
Sporting Youth 1924,Ap 2,16:1
His Hour 1924,O 7,26:1
Navigator, The 1924,O 13,21:1
General, The 1927,F 8,21:1
Vroom, Judith Ann
Love That Brute 1950,My 27,10:6
Vrstala, Jiri
Transport From Paradise 1967,F 8,22:1
Fifth Horseman is Fear, The 1968,My 7,52:1
Vrus, Iris
Seventh Continent, The 1968,Jl 30,33:2
Vubnik, A J
Laughter Through Tears 1933,N 13,21:2
Vuco, Olivera
I Even Met Happy Gypsies 1968,Mr 21,57:1
Vuisic, Pavlo
Steppe, The 1963,O 1,33:1
Vukotic, Dusan (Director)
Seventh Continent, The 1968,Jl 30,33:2
Vukotic, Dusan (Producer)
Concerto for Sub-Machine Gun 1968,Ja 20,21:3
Vukotic, Dusan (Screenwriter)
Seventh Continent, The 1968,Jl 30,33:2
Vulliamy, C E (Original Author)
They all Died Laughing 1964,Mr 16,37:2
Vuolo, Tito
Web, The 1947,Je 5,32:1
Mourning Becomes Electra 1947,N 20,38:2
Bishop's Wife, The 1947,D 10,44:2
Daisy Kenyon 1947,D 25,32:1
Mr Blandings Builds his Dream House 1948,Mr 26,26:2
Cry of the City 1948,S 30,32:4
Flamingo Road 1949,My 7,10:2
House of Strangers 1949,Jl 2,8:2
Great Gatsby, The 1949,Jl 14,20:5
Everybody Does It 1949,O 26,32:2

Vuolo, Tito — Cont
Between Midnight and Dawn 1950,O 2,19:2
Deported 1950,N 2,39:3
Enforcer, The 1951,Ja 26,19:2
Man Who Cheated Himself, The 1951,F 9,21:2
Up Front 1951,Mr 26,19:2
Saturday's Hero 1951,S 12,37:2
Racket, The 1951,D 13,44:2
Vydra, Vaclav
Skeleton on Horseback 1940,F 5,13:3
Merry Wives, The 1940,N 12,28:3
Vye, Murvyn
Golden Earrings 1947,D 4,41:3
Whispering Smith 1949,F 15,28:2
Connecticut Yankee in King Arthur's Court, A 1949,Ap 8,31:2
Road to Bali 1953,Ja 30,25:1
Destination Gobi 1953,My 30,7:1
Pickup on South Street 1953,Je 18,38:2
River of no Return 1954,My 1,13:2
Green Fire 1954,D 25,7:1
Escape to Burma 1955,My 21,11:2
Pearl of the South Pacific 1955,S 17,12:2
Best Things in Life are Free, The 1956,S 29,12:2
This Could Be the Night 1957,My 15,39:1
Al Capone 1959,Mr 26,27:1
Boy and the Pirates, The 1960,N 24,48:3
Andy 1965,Ja 22,21:2
Vylars, C (Original Author)
Frenzy 1946,Jl 20,10:3
Vyner, Margaret
Sailing Along 1938,Ap 16,17:1
Climbing High 1939,Je 5,20:3
Mr Emmanuel 1945,Ja 8,15:2
Patient Vanishes, The 1947,My 23,31:2
Encore (The Ant and the Grasshopper); Ant and the Grasshopper, The (Encore) 1952,Ap 3,45:1
Vyskobil, Ivan
Report on the Party and the Guests, A 1968,S 20,37:5
Report on the Party and the Guests, A 1968,S 28,37:1
Vysotsky, Felix (Cinematographer)
Ballet of Othello, The 1964,My 4,35:1
Vyvian, Jack
This Man Is News 1939,Jl 20,16:4
Vyvyan, Jennifer
Beggar's Opera, The 1953,Ag 25,18:2

W

Waag, Hanna
Karamazof 1931,S 21,20:2
Waltz Time in Vienna 1934,N 19,13:2
Wabschke, Emil
Hauptmann von Koepenick, Der 1933,Ja 17,22:6
Wachgold, Chaim
Dream no More 1950,Ja 6,25:2
Wachowlak, Maria
Partings 1962,N 28,44:1
Wachsberger, Nat (Producer)
Viscount, The 1967,My 11,50:1
Wachsberger, Nat (Screenwriter)
That Man in Istanbul 1966,My 19,51:2
Wachsmith, Fee
Children of no Importance 1928,Ap 3,33:2
Wada, Natto (Narrator)
Tokyo Olympiad 1966,N 17,55:1
Wada, Natto (Screenwriter)
Odd Obsession 1961,D 27,16:1
Fires on the Plain 1963,S 25,39:1
Enjo 1964,S 23,54:1
Alone on the Pacific 1964,S 24,46:2
Burmese Harp, The 1967,Ap 29,25:1
Wadams, Golden
Hotel Imperial 1927,Ja 3,16:2
Waddington, Patrick
Loyalties 1934,O 26,25:1
Loves of Madame Dubarry, The 1938,Ap 4,12:5
Journey Together 1946,Mr 4,16:5
A Night to Remember 1958,D 17,2:7
Waddle, Russell
Wrecker, The 1933,Ag 7,18:3
Wade, Frank W (Original Author)
Dirigible 1931,Ap 6,24:1
Wade, Lindy
All That Money Can Buy 1941,O 17,27:2
Syncopation 1942,My 29,13:3
Wade, Mary Ruth
Plunders, The 1948,N 1,28:2
Wade, Russell
Flying Hostess 1936,D 14,29:4
Gildersleeve's Bad Day 1943,Je 11,23:1
Bombardier 1943,Jl 2,15:2
Iron Major, The 1943,N 1,12:5
Ghost Ship, The 1943,D 25,19:4
Marine Raiders 1944,Jl 1,10:7
Tall in the Saddle 1944,D 15,25:3
Body Snatcher, The 1945,My 26,18:3
Game of Death, A 1945,N 24,22:4
Shoot to Kill 1947,My 17,8:5
Beyond Glory 1948,Ag 4,18:2

Wade, Vanita
When my Baby Smiles at Me 1948,N 24,20:2
Wademant, Annette (Miscellaneous)
Edward and Caroline 1952,Ap 30,33:3
Parisienne, La 1958,Jl 31,27:1
Wademant, Annette (Screenwriter)
Edward and Caroline 1952,Ap 30,33:3
Parisienne, La 1958,Jl 31,27:1
What Price Murder 1958,N 11,26:1
Women Are Weak 1959,Je 9,44:2
Come Dance With Me!; Voulez-Vous Danser Avec
Moi 1960,N 8,32:6
Love and the Frenchwoman; (Francaise et
l'Amour, La) 1961,F 28,38:2
Tales of Paris (The Tale of Antonio); Tale of
Antonio, The (Tales of Paris) 1962,Ag 27,18:1
Lola Montes 1968,S 23,42:6
Wadley, Mike (Cinematographer)
Mingus 1968,My 17,56:1
Wadner, Gunnel
Pimpernel Svensson 1953,F 6,16:4
Wadsworth, Henry
Applause 1929,O 8,24:5
Slightly Scarlet 1930,Mr 1,23:1
Fast and Loose 1930,D 1,21:1
Luxury Liner 1933,F 3,21:3
Soldiers of the Storm 1933,My 17,15:3
This Side of Heaven 1934,F 10,21:2
Show-Off, The 1934,Mr 17,11:3
Operator 13 1934,Je 23,16:5
Thin Man, The 1934,Je 30,18:5
Evelyn Prentice 1934,N 10,19:1
West Point of the Air 1935,Ap 6,10:1
Mark of the Vampire 1935,My 3,23:4
Big Broadcast of 1936, The 1935,S 16,15:2
Ceiling Zero 1936,Ja 20,22:2
Voice of Bugle Ann, The 1936,F 27,23:1
Doctor Rhythm 1938,My 19,25:2
Silver Skates 1943,Mr 19,15:3
Waern, Inge
Blood and Fire 1950,Je 24,7:4
Waescher, Aribert
Spiel mit dem Feuer 1934,N 26,12:2
Viktor und Viktoria 1935,Ja 28,10:5
Liebe, Tod und Teufel 1935,My 25,12:2
Maedchen Johanna, Das 1935,O 9,27:2 (In
Addenda)
Hoehere Befehl, Der 1936,Mr 31,17:3
Donogoo Tonka 1936,Ap 13,15:2
Seltsamer Gast, Ein 1937,Jl 10,18:2
Stronger Than the Rule 1937,S 25,10:2
Madame Bovary 1937,O 30,22:2
Man Between, The 1953,N 19,41:2
Waffles
Go West, Young Lady 1941,N 24,11:6
Wag, Hanna
Burning Heart, The 1930,My 12,27:3
Wagenheim, Charles
Two Girls on Broadway 1940,Ap 25,28:4
Charlie Chan At the Wax Museum 1940,S 28,9:3
Meet Boston Blackie 1941,F 26,17:2
Get-Away, The 1941,Jl 17,23:4
Sin Town 1942,O 17,11:2
House on Ninety-Second Street, The
1945,S 27,24:7
Dark Corner, The 1946,My 9,27:3
Pirates of Monterey 1947,D 17,41:4
Man-Eater of Kumaon 1948,Jl 2,24:2
Lady Without Passport, A 1950,Ag 4,13:2
House on Telegraph Hill, The 1951,My 14,29:1
Blackjack Ketchum Desperado 1956,Ap 5,26:2
Wager, Anthony
Great Expectations 1947,My 23,31:1
Hungry Hill 1947,O 11,11:2
Guinea Pig, The 1949,My 2,20:2
Fame Is the Spur 1949,N 8,34:2
Wind Cannot Read, The 1960,Mr 10,36:1
Wager, Michael
Hill 24 Doesn't Answer 1955,N 3,37:1
Exodus 1960,D 16,44:1
Waggner, Fernando
My Outlaw Brother 1951,Ag 23,19:2
Waggner, George (Composer)
Climax, The 1944,D 14,28:5
Waggner, George (Director)
Man Made Monster 1941,Mr 19,25:4
Horror Island 1941,Mr 31,11:3
South of Tahiti 1941,N 10,21:3
Wolf Man, The 1941,D 22,24:5
Climax, The 1944,D 14,28:5
Frisco Sal 1945,F 17,11:2
Shady Lady 1945,O 11,26:2
Tangier 1946,Je 7,II,16:4
Gunfighters 1947,Jl 25,12:5
Fighting Kentuckian, The 1949,S 19,18:3
Operation Pacific 1951,F 3,10:2
Waggner, George (Miscellaneous)
Keeper of the Bees, The 1935,Ag 17,18:5
Waggner, George (Original Author)
Sweetheart of Sigma Chi, The 1933,N 9,27:1
Three Legionnaires 1937,Jl 10,18:2
Idol of the Crowd 1937,D 4,21:1

Waggner, George (Producer)
Ghost of Frankenstein, The 1942,Ap 4,19:2
Sin Town 1942,O 17,11:2
Frankenstein Meets the Wolf Man 1943,Mr 6,8:3
White Savage 1943,Ap 26,15:2
Phantom of the Opera, The 1943,O 15,15:2
Cobra Woman 1944,My 18,17:2
Gypsy Wildcat 1944,O 5,18:6
Climax, The 1944,D 14,28:5
Frisco Sal 1945,F 17,11:2
Shady Lady 1945,O 11,26:2
Waggner, George (Screenwriter)
Nut Farm, The 1935,Ap 8,23:3
Don't Get Personal 1936,F 22,12:1
Three Legionnaires 1937,Jl 10,18:2
I Cover the War 1937,Ag 2,10:2
Idol of the Crowd 1937,D 4,21:1
Spy Ring, The 1938,Ja 15,19:1
Fighting Kentuckian, The 1949,S 19,18:3
Operation Pacific 1951,F 3,10:2
Return From the Sea 1954,Jl 10,7:3
Waggner, Shy
Fighting Kentuckian, The 1949,S 19,18:3
Wagnall, Mabel (Original Author)
Revelation 1924,Je 24,18:2
Wagner, Adelin
Tonio Kroger 1968,Ja 16,24:1
Wagner, Christiana
Jules and Jim 1962,Ap 24,32:1
Wagner, Elsa
Luther 1929,Je 24,27:1
Meistersinger 1929,D 16,34:2
Hertha's Erwachen 1933,Mr 14,18:3 (Incorrect in
this edition; use 1933,Mr 14,19:2 elsewhere)
City of Torment 1950,Je 10,11:4
Marriage of Figaro 1950,N 3,31:2
Wagner, Erika
Queen of Sin and the Spectacle of Sodom and
Gomorrah 1923,Mr 27,24:3 (In Addenda)
Wagner, Fernando
Pearl, The 1948,F 18,36:4
Tarzan and the Mermaids 1948,Mr 30,26:4
Sofia 1948,S 4,8:7
Garden of Evil 1954,Jl 10,17:1
Wagner, Fritz
Girls Behind Bars 1950,My 10,41:2
Seven Journeys 1951,Mr 12,20:2
Wagner, George
Iron Horse, The 1924,Ag 29,6:1
His Hour 1924,O 7,26:1
Wagner, Guyri
Odette 1951,Mr 28,33:2
Wagner, Harold
Paisan 1948,Mr 30,26:2
Wagner, Heinz
Das Ekel 1932,Ja 30,13:2
Wagner, Hilde
Burning Secret 1933,My 28,IX,2:5 (In Addenda)
Wagner, Jack (Original Author)
Medal for Benny, A 1945,My 24,15:2
Wagner, Jack (Screenwriter)
Dancing Pirate 1936,Je 18,19:1
Pearl, The 1948,F 18,36:4
Wagner, Margot
Pantoffelhelden 1935,O 21,22:5
Wagner, Max
World and the Flesh, The 1932,My 7,11:5
Under the Pampas Moon 1935,My 31,11:1
Charlie Chan in Shanghai 1935,O 14,21:1
Two in Revolt 1936,Ap 25,21:1
Dancing Pirate 1936,Je 18,19:1
Love Begins at 20 1936,S 19,20:1
Smart Blonde 1937,Ja 9,21:1
God's Country and the Woman 1937,Ja 11,15:5
Step Lively, Jeeves 1937,Ap 2,19:6
Border Cafe 1937,Je 8,30:2
Slim 1937,Je 24,30:2
Penrod and his Twin Brother 1938,Ap 18,11:1
Painted Desert 1938,S 14,26:5
Roaring Twenties, The 1939,N 11,12:1
You Can't Fool Your Wife 1940,My 24,23:4
Smoky 1946,Je 27,29:1
Mad Wednesday 1951,Ja 25,21:5
Wagner, Nicholas Captain
Adventure Girl 1934,Ag 9,14:5
Wagner, Paul
Unfinished Symphony 1935,Ja 14,11:2
Kamera den auf See; Comrades at Sea
1939,Ap 22,15:3
Wagner, Paul (Producer)
French They Are a Funny Race, The
1957,My 21,41:1
Wagner, Raymond (Producer)
Petulia 1968,Je 11,54:4
Wagner, Rob (Screenwriter)
R. S. V. P. 1921,D 12,20:2
Wagner, Robert
Halls of Montezuma, The 1951,Ja 6,9:6
Frogmen, The 1951,Je 30,8:6
Let's Make It Legal 1951,N 7,35:3
With a Song in my Heart 1952,Ap 5,20:2
What Price Glory 1952,Ag 23,10:2
Stars and Stripes Forever 1952,D 23,17:2

Wagner, Robert— Cont
Titanic 1953,My 28,27:5
Beneath the 12-Mile Reef 1953,D 17,52:2
Prince Valiant 1954,Ap 7,40:2
Broken Lance 1954,Jl 30,9:1
White Feather 1955,F 17,23:1
Between Heaven and Hell 1956,O 12,33:2
Mountain, The 1956,N 15,44:6
True Story of Jesse James, The 1957,Mr 23,17:2
Stopover Tokyo 1957,D 27,23:4
Hunters, The 1958,Ag 27,33:1
In Love and War 1958,N 1,14:2
Say One for Me 1959,Je 20,11:2
All the Fine Young Cannibals 1960,S 23,33:1
Sail a Crooked Ship 1962,F 3,12:6
Longest Day, The 1962,O 5,28:1
War Lover, The 1963,Mr 7,8:5
Condemned of Altona, The 1963,O 31,26:1
Pink Panther, The 1964,Ap 24,25:1
Harper 1966,Mr 31,43:1
Banning 1967,D 14,62:2
Biggest Bundle of Them All, The 1968,Ja 18,46:1
Don't Just Stand There 1968,S 3,54:2
Wagner, Robert (Director)
Two Wagons-Both Covered 1924,Ja 29,16:1
Wagner, Wende
Rio Conchos 1964,O 29,38:1
Covenant with Death, A 1967,F 16,32:3
Wagner, William
Rebecca of Sunnybrook Farm 1938,Mr 26,12:1
Wagstaff, Joseph
Let's Go Places 1930,Mr 1,23:1
Wagstaffe, Elsie
Appointment With Crime 1951,F 19,19:3
Saturday Night and Sunday Morning
1961,Ap 4,44:2
WAHL
See Also WALL, WOHL
Wahl, Evelyn
Parachute Nurse 1942,Jl 27,18:2
Jungle Siren 1942,O 10,11:3
Wahl, Walter Dare
Top Banana 1954,F 20,8:6
Wahl, Walter Dare and Company
Star Spangled Rhythm 1942,D 31,20:1
Wahl, Wolfgang
Scampolo 1959,Ag 6,18:4
Roses for the Prosecutor; (Rosen fur den
Staarsanwalt) 1961,O 10,38:2
Wahlberg, Gideon
Flickorna Fran Gamla Stan 1934,D 27,25:4
Tjocka Slaekten; Near Relatives 1935,My 20,20:5
Larsson I Andra Giftet 1935,O 19.21:3
Loerdagskvaellar 1936,F 13,25:3
Skaergaards-Flirt 1936,Ap 8,26:3
Soederkaakar 1936,D 19,16:2
Wahlberg, Gideon (Director)
Soeder om Landsvaegen 1937,Mr 10,27:3
Old Gods Still Live, The 1937,N 5,19:4
Baldvins Brollop; Baldwin's Wedding
1938,D 27,13:2
Skicka Hem Nr 7; Send Home No 7
1939,My 9,29:2
Wahlbom, Nils
Nar Rosorna Sla Ut 1931,F 10,24:4
Raggen, Det Aer Jag Det 1936,My 22,19:1
Ungdom Av I Dag 1936,Je 23,27:7
Vaaran Pojke 1936,O 10,21:3
Wahlgren, Ivar
Pimpernel Svensson 1953,F 6,16:4
Wain, Ann
Pure Hell of St Trinian's, The 1961,S 26,31:1
Wainwright, Marie
Polly With a Past 1921,Ja 10,9:1
Wainwright, Richard (Producer)
Crimson Circle, The 1936,D 28,12:3
Emil 1938,Ap 15,23:2
Queen of Crime 1941,F 19,25:2
Secret of Stamboul, The 1941,My 31,14:1
Madness of the Heart 1950,O 12,43:2
Waite, Genevieve
Joanna 1968,N 25,54:1
Waite, Malcolm
Hill Billy, The 1924,Mr 12,19:4
Gold Rush, The 1925,Ag 17,10:3
Lucky Horseshoe, The 1925,Ag 18,14:3
Kid Boots 1926,O 11,18:2
Monkey Talks, The 1927,Ap 5,30:7
We're in the Air Now 1927,D 31,31:1
Noah's Ark 1929,Mr 13,28:6
Vagabond Lover, The 1929,N 27,30:6
Twenty-Four Hours 1931,O 3,20:2
Waite, Marjorie
Red Hot Tires 1925,O 20,28:1
Waite, Ralph
Lovely Way to Die, A 1968,Jl 13,18:1
Waiter, Eugene
Eight and One Half 1963,Je 26,36:1
Wajan
Wajan 1938,Ap 18,11:1
Wajda, Andrzej
Love at Twenty 1963,F 7,5:6

Wajda, Andrzej (Director)
Kanal 1961,My 10,52:1
Ashes and Diamonds 1961,My 30,8:1
Fury is a Woman 1964,S 28,19:1
Lotna 1966,My 27,33:1
Wajda, Andrzej (Screenwriter)
Ashes and Diamonds 1961,My 30,8:1
Lotna 1966,My 27,33:1
Wakabayashi, Akiko
What's Up, Tiger Lily? 1966,N 18,33:1
You Only Live Twice 1967,Je 14,40:1
Wakabayashi, Eiko
Walleyed Nippon 1963,S 3,36:1
Bandits on the Wind 1964,Ja 15,27:3
Ghidrah, The Three-Headed Monster
1965,D 16,63:3
Wakao, Ayako
Phantom Horse, the 1956,Jl 25,16:1
Street of Shame 1959,Je 5,17:2
Great Wall, The 1965,D 16,63:2
Wakao, Tokuhei (Screenwriter)
Samurai 1956,Ja 10,26:1
Wakao, tokuhei (Screenwriter)
Samurai (Part II) 1967,O 21,16:1
Wakatsuki, Shigeru (Producer)
Human Condition, The 1959,D 16,56:1
Kwaidan (In the Cup of Tea); In the Cup of Tea
(Kwaidan) 1965,N 23,51:1
Kwaidan (Black Hair); Black Hair (Kwaidan)
1965,N 23,51:1
Kwaidan (Hoichi, The Earless); Hoichi, The
Earless (Kwaidan) 1965,N 23,51:1
Wakefield, Anne
300 Spartans, The 1962,S 20,29:2
Wakefield, Hugh
Aren't We All? 1932,Jl 1,19:3
Man they Couldn't Arrest, The 1933,Mr 14,19:3
Farewell to Love 1933,N 25,10:2
Man Who Knew too Much, The 1935,Mr 23,11:2
My Heart Is Calling 1935,Ap 15,16:3
Crimson Circle, The 1936,D 28,12:3
Forever Yours 1937,Je 7,22:2
Blithe Spirit 1945,O 4,27:2
One Night With You 1949,F 21,20:2
Caretaker's Daughter, The 1953,Ag 20,18:5
Man With a Million 1954,Je 29,21:2
Wakefield, Hugh (Screenwriter)
Caretaker's Daughter, The 1953,Ag 20,18:5
Wakefield, Oliver
Shipyard Sally 1940,Ja 18,27:3
Wakeham, Eliot
Mill On the Floss, The 1939,N 15,19:3
Wakely, Bryl
Bad Sister 1948,Je 11,27:3
Wakely, Jimmy
Arrow in the Dust 1954,My 1,13:2
Wakeman, Frederic (Original Author)
Hucksters, The 1947,Jl 18,21:2
Saxon Charm, The 1948,S 30,32:3
Kiss Them for Me 1957,N 9,31:2
Wastrel, The 1963,N 5,24:1
Wakeman, Frederic (Screenwriter)
Wastrel, The 1963,N 5,24:1
Wakhevitch (Miscellaneous)
Louise 1940,F 3,9:4
Walberg, Bobby
Adam Had Four Sons 1941,Mr 28,26:6
Walbridge, John (Miscellaneous)
Pinocchio 1940,F 8,18:3
Walbrook, Anton
Masquerade in Vienna 1937,Ja 26,16:4
Soldier and the Lady, The 1937,Ap 10,11:1
Victoria the Great 1937,O 29,19:1
Rat, The 1938,F 28,19:1
Sixty Glorious Years 1938,N 18,25:2
I Give my Life 1941,S 1,18:4
Invaders, The 1942,Mr 6,17:1
Suicide Squadron 1942,My 14,23:2
Life and Death of Colonel Blimp, The
1945,Mr 30,18:2
Man From Morocco, The 1946,N 25,38:2
Red Shoes, The 1948,O 23,9:2
Queen of Spades, The 1949,Jl 1,14:4
Angel Street 1952,N 11,25:2
Ronde, La 1954,Mr 17,27:2
Saint Joan 1957,Je 27,21:1
I Accuse! 1958,Mr 6,32:1
Lola Montes 1968,S 23,42:6
Walburn, Raymond
Laughing Lady, The 1930,Ja 4,21:1
Great Flirtation, The 1934,Je 22,16:5
Count of Monte Cristo, The 1934,S 27,25:2
Lady by Choice 1934,N 17,12:1
Broadway Bill 1934,N 30,22:2
Society Doctor 1935,F 4,11:3
I'll Love You Always 1935,Mr 30,11:2
She Married her Boss 1935,S 27,25:3
Thanks a Million 1935,N 14,17:1
Lone Wolf Returns, The 1936,F 4,25:5
Great Ziegfeld, The 1936,Ap 9,21:2
Mr Deeds Goes to Town 1936,Ap 17,17:2
Absolute Quiet 1936,My 2,11:1
Three Wise Guys, The 1936,My 23,12:2

King Steps Out, The 1936,My 29,15:2
They Met in a Taxi 1936,S 7,20:5
Craig's Wife 1936,O 2,29:3
Born to Dance 1936,D 5,16:1
Breezing Home 1937,Mr 20,23:5
High, Wide and Handsome 1937,Jl 22,15:1
It Can't Last Forever 1937,Jl 30,22:5
Broadway Melody of 1938 1937,S 3,12:1
Thin Ice 1937,S 4,8:2
Murder in Greenwich Village 1937,O 30,22:2
Start Cheering 1938,Mr 17,17:3
Battle of Broadway 1938,Ap 25,19:2
Professor Beware 1938,Jl 14,17:1
Gateway 1938,Ag 8,9:2
Sweethearts 1938,D 23,16:2
Let Freedom Ring 1939,Mr 10,19:2
It Could Happen to You 1939,Je 9,26:3
Under-Pup, The 1939,S 5,21:2
Eternally Yours 1939,O 7,11:2
Dark Command 1940,My 11,15:2
Millionaires in Prison 1940,Jl 16,21:3
Flowing Gold 1940,S 2,19:3
Christmas in July 1940,N 6,35:2
Third Finger, Left Hand 1940,D 12,37:2
San Francisco Docks 1940,D 26,23:3
Kiss the Boys Goodbye 1941,Ag 14,21:2
Rise and Shine 1941,D 6,14:3
Confirm or Deny 1941,D 19,35:2
Louisiana Purchase 1942,Ja 1,37:1
Man in the Trunk, The 1942,O 23,25:1
Dixie Dugan 1943,Ap 9,25:5
Desperadoes, The 1943,My 13,17:2
Dixie 1943,Je 24,26:2
Let's Face It 1943,Ag 5,18:1
And the Angels Sing 1944,Jl 13,14:2
Hail the Conquering Hero 1944,Ag 10,14:2
Music in Manhattan 1944,O 7,11:2
Heavenly Days 1944,O 21,15:2
Cheaters, The 1945,Jl 21,7:2
Lover Come Back 1946,Je 20,20:3
Breakfast in Hollywood 1946,Jl 15,21:1
Rendezvous With Annie 1946,S 23,29:3
Plainsman and the Lady, The 1946,N 4,33:1
State of the Union 1948,Ap 23,28:1
Red, Hot and Blue 1949,O 20,39:2
Key to the City 1950,F 2,31:2
Riding High 1950,Ap 11,26:2
Short Grass 1951,Ja 13,10:4
Mad Wednesday 1951,Ja 25,21:5
Excuse my Dust 1951,Je 28,21:2
Golden Girl 1951,N 21,20:3
She Couldn't Say No 1954,F 27,11:3
Spoilers, The 1955,D 24,10:2
WALCOTT
See Also WOLCOTT
Walcott, George
Swan, The 1925,Mr 2,14:1
Fury 1936,Je 6,21:1
Great Hospital Mystery, The 1937,Jl 16,22:2
Stella Dallas 1937,Ag 6,21:1
Cocoanut Grove 1938,Je 16,21:2
Forgotten Woman, The 1939,Ag 4,11:2
Quiet Please, Murder 1942,D 22,31:1
Walcott, Gregory
Mister Roberts 1955,Jl 15,14:1
McConnell Story, The 1955,S 30,23:1
Lieutenant Wore Skirts, The 1956,Ja 12,22:1
Steel Jungle, The 1956,Mr 10,9:5
On the Double 1961,My 20,12:1
Outsider, The 1962,F 8,25:1
Captain Newman, MD 1964,F 21,36:1
Walcott, Jacqueline
Shadows 1961,Mr 22,37:1
Walcz, Ethel
Cradle Snatchers 1927,My 31,25:2
Wald, Jane
What a Way to Go! 1964,My 15,44:1
Dear Brigitte 1965,Ja 28,20:1
Wald, Jerry (Original Author)
20 Million Sweethearts 1934,Ap 27,25:1
Gift of Gab 1934,S 26,17:6
Sweet Music 1935,F 21,23:2
Living on Velvet 1935,Mr 8,25:4
I Live for Love 1935,O 19,21:2
Hollywood Hotel 1938,Ja 13,17:3
Gold Diggers in Paris 1938,Je 2,19:2
Flight Angels 1940,My 27,23:2
Wald, Jerry (Producer)
Across the Pacific 1942,S 5,9:2
George Washington Slept Here 1942,O 31,11:1
Hard Way, The 1943,Mr 13,9:2
Action in the North Atlantic 1943,My 22,10:2
Destination Tokyo 1944,Ja 1,9:2
In our Time 1944,F 12,11:2
Very Thought of You, The 1944,N 18,16:7
Objective Burma 1945,Ja 27,15:2
Pride of the Marines 1945,Ag 25,7:3
Mildred Pierce 1945,S 29,12:2
Humoresque 1946,D 26,28:1
Possessed 1947,My 30,25:2
Unfaithful, The 1947,Je 28,10:2
Dark Passage 1947,S 6,11:2
To the Victor 1948,Ap 17,11:2

Wald, Jerry (Producer) — Cont
Key Largo 1948,Jl 17,6:6
Johnny Belinda 1948,O 2,11:2
Adventures of Don Juan 1948,D 25,10:1
One Sunday Afternoon 1948,D 27,16:3
John Loves Mary 1949,F 5,11:2
Flamingo Road 1949,My 7,10:2
Task Force 1949,O 1,8:6
Always Leave Them Laughing 1949,N 24,48:2
Inspector General, The 1949,D 31,9:2
Young Man With a Horn 1950,F 10,18:4
Perfect Strangers 1950,Mr 11,8:2
Damned Don't Cry, The 1950,Ap 8,9:2
Caged 1950,My 20,8:6
Glass Menagerie, The 1950,S 29,31:5
Breaking Point, The 1950,O 7,10:6
Storm Warning 1951,Mr 3,8:2
Blue Veil, The 1951,O 27,10:5
Behave Yourself 1951,N 8,35:2
Clash by Night 1952,Je 19,32:6
Lusty Men, The 1952,O 25,12:6
Miss Sadie Thompson 1953,D 24,9:1
Eddy Duchin Story, The 1956,Je 22,15:1
Affair to Remember, An 1957,Jl 20,8:5
No Down Payment 1957,O 31,41:1
Kiss Them for Me 1957,N 9,31:2
Peyton Place 1957,D 13,35:1
Long, Hot Summer, The 1958,Ap 4,16:1
In Love and War 1958,N 1,14:2
Mardi Gras 1958,N 19,45:2
Sound and the Fury, The 1959,Mr 28,11:1
Best of Everything 1959,O 9,24:2
Beloved Infidel 1959,N 18,46:1
Story of Page One, The 1960,Ja 14,28:1
Hound-Dog Man 1960,Ap 28,29:1
Sons and Lovers 1960,Ag 3,35:1
Let's Make Love 1960,S 9,36:1
Return to Peyton Place 1961,My 6,26:1
Wild in the Country 1961,Je 10,12:2
Mr Hobbs Takes a Vacation 1962,Je 16,11:2
Hemingway's Adventures of a Young Man
1962,Jl 26,17:1
Stripper, The 1963,Je 20,29:1
Wald, Jerry (Screenwriter)
Maybe It's Love 1935,F 11,14:2
Living on Velvet 1935,Mr 8,25:4
In Caliente 1935,Je 27,16:1
Little Big Shot 1935,O 7,11:2
I Live for Love 1935,O 19,21:2
Stars Over Broadway 1935,N 14,17:3
Sons o'Guns 1936,My 14,29:2
Sing Me a Love Song 1936,D 26,15:2
Ready, Willing and Able 1937,Mr 15,27:1
Varsity Show 1937,S 2,17:2
Hollywood Hotel 1938,Ja 13,17:3
Garden of the Moon 1938,S 24,13:1
Brother Rat 1938,N 5,15:2
Hard to Get 1938,N 14,15:2
Going Places 1939,Ja 7,6:1
Kid From Kokomo, The 1939,My 20,11:2
Naughty but Nice 1939,Je 23,23:2
On Your Toes 1939,O 21,12:2
Roaring Twenties, The 1939,N 11,12:1
Three Cheers for the Irish 1940,Mr 9,19:2
Torrid Zone 1940,My 18,11:3
They Drive by Night 1940,Jl 27,17:5
Million Dollar Baby 1941,Je 7,20:2
Out of the Fog 1941,Je 21,20:2
Manpower 1941,Jl 5,14:2
Navy Blues 1941,S 20,11:2
Wald, John
Lost Honeymoon 1947,Je 20,25:6
Wald, Malvin (Original Author)
Ten Gentlemen From West Point 1942,Je 5,23:3
Powers Girl, The 1943,Mr 26,14:2 (In Addenda)
Naked City, The 1948,Mr 5,17:2
Not Wanted 1949,Jl 25,11:4
Man on Fire 1957,Ag 23,10:1
Wald, Malvin (Screenwriter)
Naked City, The 1948,Mr 5,17:2
Outrage 1950,O 16,30:5
Al Capone 1959,Mr 26,27:1
Steel Claw, The 1961,S 21,40:2
Waldau, Gustav
Der Falsche Ehemann 1932,O 17,18:3
Saison in Kairo 1933,D 25,28:2
Eines Prinzen Junge Liebe 1934,Mr 24,20:4
Klein Dorrit 1935,O 19,21:2
Einmaleins der Liebe, Das 1937,Ja 2,15:2
Drei Maeoerl um Schubert 1937,Je 5,21:2
Schimmelkrieg von Holledau, Der 1938,Jl 19,15:4
Nacht an der Donau, Eine; Night on the Danube,
A 1938,N 19,9:3
Kleine Nachtmusik, Eine 1940,Mr 2,9:5
Eroica; (The Beethoven Story) 1951,O 29,19:2
Singing Angels 1952,Ja 16,21:2
Waldau, Ria
Meisterdetektiv, Der 1934,F 13,23:2
Waldekranz, Rune (Producer)
To Love; Att Alska 1964,S 23,45:3 (Incorrect in
this edition; use 1964,S 23,54:1 elsewhere)
Waldemar, Richard
Hirsekorn Greift Ein 1932,Je 10,22:3

Walden, Edgar E (Director)
Pickup 1951,Ag 31,12:2
Walden, Shandra
Next to no Time 1960,My 28,13:2
Walder, Ernest
Darling 1965,Ag 4,20:1
Walder, Nelia
Murder in the Blue Room 1944,O 28,12:2
Waldis, Otto
Exile, The 1947,D 26,22:4
Letters From an Unknown Woman
   1948,Ap 29,20:6
Berlin Express 1948,My 21,19:3
Fighting O'Flynn, The 1949,F 28,16:2
Border Incident 1949,N 21,29:2
Bagdad 1949,D 24,11:4
Bird of Paradise 1951,Mr 15,37:2
Anything Can Happen 1952,Ap 4,21:1
Knock on Wood 1954,Ap 15,34:2
Sincerely Yours 1955,N 3,37:1
Desert Sands 1955,N 19,22:7
Waldleitner, Luggi (Producer)
Rosemary 1960,Ja 19,40:2
Oasis 1960,Jl 7,26:1
Waldman, Frank (Original Author)
Our Hearts Were Growing Up 1946,Ag 12,17:2
Waldman, Frank (Screenwriter)
Bathing Beauty 1944,Je 28,20:1
High Time 1960,S 17,15:1
Love Is a Ball 1963,Ap 25,38:1
Party, The 1968,Ap 5,56:2
Inspector Clouseau 1968,Jl 25,26:1
Waldman, Lieble
Motel, The Operator 1940,Ja 16,19:3
Waldman, Myron (Miscellaneous)
Mr Bug Goes to Town 1942,F 20,21:3
Waldman, Tom (Screenwriter)
High Time 1960,S 17,15:1
Love Is a Ball 1963,Ap 25,38:1
Party, The 1968,Ap 5,56:2
Inspector Clouseau 1968,Jl 25,26:1
Waldmueller, Lizzi
Lachende Erben 1933,N 18,18:6
Waldo, Janet
Zaza 1939,Ja 5,17:1
Star Maker, The 1939,Ag 31,14:2
What a Life 1939,O 12,33:1
Our Neighbors-The Carters 1940,F 15,15:2
Waterloo Bridge 1940,My 17,23:2
Those Were the Days 1940,Jl 15,18:4
Waldock, Denis (Miscellaneous)
Dance Band 1936,Ja 4,19:2
Waldock, Denis (Screenwriter)
Dance Band 1936,Ja 4,19:2
Mimi 1936,Ja 10,16:3
Marry Me 1952,Mr 14,27:3
Waldow, Ernst
Wenn der Hahn Kraeht 1936,N 14,23:3
Meadehen von Gestern Nacht, Das; Girl of Last
   Night, The 1938,Je 18,18:2
Kleine Suenderin, Die; Little Sinner, The
   1938,D 3,11:3
Streitum den Knaben Jo; Strife Over the Boy Jo
   1938,D 10,13:2
Kluge Schwiegermutter, Die; Wise Mother-in-Law,
   The 1939,O 9,15:3
Affair Blum, The 1949,O 18,35:2
Waldow, Gustav
Sie und die Drei; She and the Three
   1938,D 10,13:3
Waldridge, Harold
Ruling Passion, The 1922,Ja 23,11:4
June Moon 1931,Mr 14,23:2
Sob Sister 1931,O 3,20:2
High Pressure 1932,F 1,22:3
Heart of New York, The 1932,Mr 2,15:3
Alias the Doctor 1932,Mr 3,22:3
Play Girl 1932,Mr 19,11:2
Strange Love of Molly Louvain, The
   1932,My 9,19:5
Strangers of the Evening 1932,Je 4,9:2
All American, The 1932,O 22,18:4
False Faces 1932,N 25,19:2
Death Kiss, The 1933,F 5,IX,5:3
Devil's Mate 1933,S 23,11:7
Easy to Love 1934,Ja 15,12:2
Private Scandal 1934,Je 15,26:2
Gigolette 1935,My 13,18:6
Dancing Pirate 1936,Je 18,19:1
Waldron, Charles
Mary Burns, Fugitive 1935,N 16,19:2
Crime and Punishment 1935,N 22,18:2
Great Impersonation, The 1935,D 14,11:1
Ramona 1936,O 7,32:4
Doctor's Diary, A 1937,F 17,16:4
Emperor's Candlesticks, The 1937,Jl 9,18:1
Navy Blue and Gold 1937,D 24,21:2
It's all Yours 1938,Ja 7,15:3
Kentucky 1938,D 24,12:1
On Borrowed Time 1939,Jl 7,13:2
Thou Shalt Not Kill 1940,Ja 8,11:2
Remember the Night 1940,Ja 18,27:2
And One Was Beautiful 1940,Ap 11,32:4

Dr Kildare's Strange Case 1940,Ap 12,19:2
Three Faces West 1940,Ag 19,13:2
Stranger on the Third Floor 1940,S 2,19:2
Case of the Black Parrot, The 1941,Ja 10,23:3
Devil and Miss Jones, The 1941,My 16,21:2
Nurse's Secret, The 1941,Je 6,25:7
Rise and Shine 1941,D 6,14:3
Gay Sisters, The 1942,Ag 15,14:2
Random Harvest 1942,D 18,36:6
Song of Bernadette, The 1944,Ja 27,15:2
Fighting Guardsman, The 1945,O 6,9:6
Big Sleep, The 1946,Ag 24,6:6
Waldron, Jack
Blindfold 1966,My 26,55:2
Waldron, Louis
Nude Restaurant, The 1967,N 14,52:1
Flesh 1968,S 27,36:1
Walds, Otto
Port of Hell 1954,D 18,12:2
Walerstein, Gregorio (Producer)
Living Idol, The 1957,My 3,18:1
Wales, Bert
Her Love Story 1924,O 7,26:1
Wales, Ethel
Miss Lulu Bett 1921,D 25,VI,2:1
Old Homestead, The 1922,O 9,10:2
Icebound 1924,Mr 3,22:3 (In Addenda)
Which Shall It Be? 1924,Ap 7,15:3
Bedroom Window, The 1924,Je 9,14:3
Revelation 1924,Je 24,18:2
Merton of the Movies 1924,S 8,15:3
Monster, The 1925,F 16,24:1
Beggar on Horseback 1925,Je 6,9:2
Go Straight 1925,O 6,30:1
Unknown Soldier, The 1926,My 31,10:2
Take It From Me 1926,N 2,35:1
Ladies at Play 1926,N 16,25:3
Loose Ankles 1926,N 21,VIII,7:3 (In Addenda)
Bertha, The Sewing Machine Girl 1927,Ja 4,21:1
Girl on the Pullman, The 1927,N 1,21:1 (In
   Addenda)
Wreck of the Hesperus, The 1927,N 28,18:5
Tenth Avenue 1928,O 9,35:1
Masks of the Devil, The 1928,N 26,30:2
Craig's Wife 1928,D 4,29:1
Doctor's Secret, The 1929,F 4,20:1
Donovan Affair, The 1929,Ap 29,29:2
Saturday Night Kid, The 1929,N 16,25:2
Tom Sawyer 1930,D 20,20:6
Criminal Code, The 1931,Ja 5,21:3
Flood, The 1931,Ap 27,25:1
Honeymoon Lane 1931,Ag 1,16:4
Maker of Men 1931,D 19,16:4
Love Me Tonight 1932,Ag 19,20:6
Gladiator, The 1938,Ag 29,10:2
Wales, Henry (Original Author)
You may Be Next 1936,F 24,14:1
Confirm or Deny 1941,D 19,35:2
Wales, Pauline
Mikado, The 1967,Mr 15,53:1
Waleska, Blanka
Distant Journey 1950,Ag 28,13:3
Walford, Gwen
Cleopatra 1963,Je 13,29:1
Walge, Arthur
Quo Vadis 1951,N 9,22:2
Walken, Ken
Blue Angel, The 1959,S 5,11:4
Walker, Aurora
Odio; Hate 1940,Ap 6,13:2
Vivire Otra Vez; I Shall Live Again
   1940,O 23,27:2
This Strange Passion 1955,D 5,34:2
Walker, Basil
Cadet Girl 1941,D 11,39:1
To the Shores of Tripoli 1942,Mr 26,27:2
Walker, Ben
Tracked by the Police 1927,Ap 27,22:5
Walker, Betty
Molly 1951,Mr 8,37:2
Middle of the Night 1959,Je 18,36:1
Exodus 1960,D 16,44:1
Walker, Bill
Killers, The 1946,Ag 29,24:2
Sand 1949,Ag 5,23:2
No Way Out 1950,Ag 17,23:1
Night Without Sleep 1952,S 27,13:2
Bloodhounds of Broadway 1952,N 15,15:2
Queen Bee 1955,N 23,18:2
Hot Spell 1958,S 18,37:2
Mask, The 1961,O 28,12:4
Wall of Noise 1963,S 5,27:1
Kisses for my President 1964,Ag 22,13:1
Walker, Charlotte
Trail of the Lonesome Pine 1916,F 14,11:2
Lone Wolf, The 1924,My 7,19:4
Classmates 1924,D 30,15:3
Manicure Girl, The 1925,Je 15,10:1
Great Deception, The 1926,Ag 9,10:3
Paris Bound 1929,S 21,17:1
South Sea Rose 1929,D 7,19:3
Double Cross Roads 1930,Ap 29,31:1
Three Faces East 1930,S 6,9:2

Walker, Charlotte— Cont
Lightnin' 1930,N 29,21:4
Scarlet Pages 1930,D 6,21:3
Salvation Nell 1931,Jl 6,24:4
Walker, Cheryl
Stage Door Canteen 1943,Je 25,13:2
3 Is a Family 1944,D 20,20:3
It's a Pleasure 1945,My 4,23:3
Walker, Clint
Fort Dobbs 1958,Ap 19,10:4
Yellowstone Kelly 1959,N 12,27:1
Gold of the Seven Saints 1961,Ap 6,30:3
Send Me no Flowers 1964,N 13,30:1
None but the Brave 1965,F 25,24:1
Night of the Grizzly, The 1966,Je 23,29:1
Maya 1966,Je 23,29:4
Dirty Dozen, The 1967,Je 16,36:1
Walker, Cub (Miscellaneous)
Wild Heart of Africa, The 1929,My 27,22:1
Walker, David (Original Author)
Wee Geordie 1956,O 8,31:1
Harry Black and the Tiger 1958,S 19,24:4
Walker, David Esdaile (Original Author)
Man Could Get Killed, A 1966,My 12,54:2
Walker, Dick Lion Act
Big Circus, The 1959,Jl 18,6:1
Walker, Eddy C
Man Without a Star 1955,Mr 25,19:3
Walker, Fiona
Far From the Madding Crowd 1967,O 19,59:1
Walker, Frank (Screenwriter)
Operation Kid Brother 1967,N 23,58:2
Walker, Gene
Casbah 1948,My 3,27:4
Walker, George
Redskin 1929,Ja 28,21:1
Walker, Gertrude (Original Author)
Damned Don't Cry, The 1950,Ap 8,9:2
Walker, Granville (Original Author)
Barricade 1939,D 9,18:2
Walker, Granville (Screenwriter)
Barricade 1939,D 9,18:2
Walker, Hal (Director)
Out of This World 1945,Je 7,25:2
Duffy's Tavern 1945,S 6,23:3
Stork Club, The 1945,D 20,18:2
Road to Utopia 1946,F 28,20:2
My Friend Irma Goes West 1950,Ag 3,20:2
At War With the Army 1951,Ja 25,21:5
That's My Boy 1951,Ag 2,18:1
Sailor Beware 1952,F 1,17:1
Road to Bali 1953,Ja 30,25:1
Walker, Harry
For the Defense 1930,Jl 19,7:5
Song of the Eagle 1933,Ap 29,14:3
Walker, Helen
Lucky Jordan 1943,Ja 25,10:8
Abroad With two Yanks 1944,O 26,19:7
Man in Half Moon Street, The 1945,Ja 20,16:2
Brewster's Millions 1945,Ap 27,23:2
Murder, He Says 1945,Je 25,20:3
People Are Funny 1946,Ja 28,15:6
Murder in the Music Hall 1946,Ap 15,22:2
Cluny Brown 1946,Je 3,27:3
Homestretch, The 1947,Ap 24,30:2
Nightmare Alley 1947,O 10,31:3
Call Northside 777 1948,F 19,29:2
My Dear Secretary 1949,F 14,15:4
Impact 1949,Mr 21,19:2
Big Combo, The 1955,Mr 26,13:2
Walker, Hugh
Criminal Code, The 1931,Ja 5,21:3
Walker, James (Chuckles)
Something to Shout About 1943,Ap 8,27:3
Walker, Jewel
Small Hours, The 1962,Ag 14,34:1
Walker, John
Over the Hill to the Poor House 1920,S 18,16:2
Walker, Johnnie
In the Name of the Law 1922,Jl 10,9:5
Third Alarm, The 1923,Ja 10,28:5
Red Lights 1923,S 10,15:4
Spirit of the U S A, The 1924,My 21,22:3
Wine of Youth 1924,Ag 11,16:1
Matinee Idol, The 1928,Ap 24,29:3
Girl of the Golden West, The 1930,O 27,17:1
Walker, Johnnie (Director)
Mr Broadway 1933,S 14,26:3
Walker, Johnny
Old Ironsides 1926,D 7,21:2
Ladies in Love 1930,Je 14,9:4
Enemies of the Law 1931,Jl 13,13:5
Walker, June
War Nurse 1930,O 24,31:1
Unforgiven, The 1960,Ap 7,46:1
Walker, Ken (Miscellaneous)
Wild Heart of Africa, The 1929,My 27,22:1
Walker, Lewis
Night Angel, The 1931,Je 11,28:4
Walker, Martin
Sanders of the River 1935,Je 27,16:1
Mimi 1936,Ja 10,16:3
Drums 1938,S 30,24:4
Hell's Cargo 1940,S 16,15:2

Walker, Martin— Cont

This England 1941,N 18,33:2
Love on the Dole 1945,O 13,11:2
Woman in the Hall, The 1949,Ja 24,16:2

Walker, Nancy

Best Foot Forward 1943,Je 30,25:2
Girl Crazy 1943,D 3,27:2
Broadway Rhythm 1944,Ap 14,24:6
Lucky Me 1954,Ap 10,11:2

Walker, Nella

Vagabond Lover, The 1929,N 27,30:6
Tanned Legs 1929,D 2,28:2
Seven Keys to Baldpate 1929,D 26,21:1
What a Widow 1930,O 4,15:2
Extravagance 1930,D 9,31:3
Hot Heiress, The 1931,Mr 14,23:2
Indiscreet 1931,My 7,21:4
Public Defender, The 1931,Ag 1,16:4
Daughter of the Dragon 1931,Ag 22,7:5
Lady With a Past 1932,F 22,23:2
They Call It Sin 1932,O 21,25:4
20,000 Years in Sing Sing 1933,Ja 10,26:2
Second Hand Wife 1933,Ja 14,8:4
Dangerously Yours 1933,F 23,20:3
Humanity 1933,Ap 22,16:3
Reunion in Vienna 1933,Ap 29,14:2
House on 56th Street, The 1933,D 2,9:3
Fashions of 1934 1934,Ja 20,12:2
Four Frightened People 1934,Ja 27,9:2
All of Me 1934,F 5,19:2
Ninth Guest, The 1934,Mr 3,8:5
Change of Heart 1934,My 11,24:2
Elmer and Elsie 1934,Ag 4,14:5
Madame Du Barry 1934,O 25,26:2
Big Hearted Herbert 1934,N 14,23:2
Behold My Wife 1935,F 18,19:3
McFadden's Flats 1935,Mr 13,16:2
Woman in Red, The 1935,Mr 23,11:3
Red Salute 1935,S 30,13:1
Coronado 1935,D 19,33:4
Small Town Girl 1936,Ap 11,19:1
Captain January 1936,Ap 25,21:1
Three Smart Girls 1937,Ja 25,22:2
Stella Dallas 1937,Ag 6,21:1
45 Fathers 1937,D 11,22:2
Crime of Dr Hallet, The 1938,Mr 24,21:3
Rage of Paris 1938,Jl 2,10:2
Young Doctor Kildare 1938,O 28,27:1
Three Smart Girls Grow Up 1939,Mr 18,9:2
In Name Only 1939,Ag 4,11:3
When Tomorrow Comes 1939,Ag 17,16:2
Saint Takes Over, The 1940,My 28,29:3
I Love You Again 1940,Ag 16,11:2
Kitty Foyle 1941,Ja 9,27:2
Back Street 1941,F 12,25:2
Buck Privates 1941,F 14,15:2
Girl, a Guy and a Gob, A 1941,Ap 24,25:3
Kathleen 1941,D 19,35:3
Hellzapoppin 1941,D 26,21:4
Kid Glove Killer 1942,Ap 17,21:4
We Were Dancing 1942,My 1,23:2
Air Raid Wardens 1943,Ap 5,15:5
Hers to Hold 1943,Jl 22,15:1
Take It or Leave It 1944,Jl 13,14:2
In Society 1944,Ag 17,20:2
Two Sisters From Boston 1946,Je 7,16:2
Beginning or the End, The 1947,F 21,15:1
Locket, The 1947,Mr 20,38:2
That Hagen Girl 1947,O 25,13:2
This Time for Keeps 1947,D 5,33:4
Nancy Goes to Rio 1950,Ap 7,22:2
Sabrina 1954,S 23,43:2

Walker, Nina

Misleading Lady, The 1932,Ap 9,18:1

Walker, Norman

Mozart 1940,O 4,29:2
Laburnum Grove 1941,D 2,29:2

Walker, Norman (Director)

Middle Watch, The 1930,D 20,20:6
Man Who Won, The 1933,F 27,11:2
Fires of Fate 1933,Ap 3,13:4
Suicide Legion 1940,My 6,13:3
Great Mr Handel The 1943,S 10,29:3

Walker, Norman (Producer)

Way Ahead, The 1945,Je 4,22:3

Walker, Patricia

Death of a Salesman 1951,D 21,21:3

Walker, Peter

If all the Guys in the World 1957,Ap 23,34:1

Walker, Polly

Hit the Deck 1930,Ja 15,28:6
Sleepless Nights 1933,Jl 22,14:2

Walker, Ray

Devil's Mate 1933,S 23,11:7
Thirty Day Princess 1934,My 12,12:3
Baby, Take a Bow 1934,Je 30,18:6
Million Dollar Baby 1935,My 6,22:3
Girl Friend, The 1935,S 28,12:2
Laughing Irish Eyes 1936,Ap 4,11:2
Hideaway Girl 1937,Ja 13,20:4
Her Husband Lies 1937,Mr 18,20:1
Angel's Holiday 1937,My 29,20:2
One Mile From Heaven 1937,Ag 19,23:1
Outlaws of the Orient 1937,S 25,10:2

Forgotten Woman, The 1939,Ag 4,11:2
Missing Evidence 1939,N 17,17:3
Hi 'Ya Chum 1943,F 26,17:4
Princess O'Rourke 1943,N 6,16:2
Crazy House 1943,D 16,33:3
Swingtime Johnny 1943,D 17,23:3
Jam Session 1944,My 3,25:3
Man From Frisco 1944,Je 16,14:7
Tars and Spars 1946,F 15,29:2
Step by Step 1946,Ag 24,6:7
Beast With Five Fingers, The 1946,D 26,28:3
Guilt of Janet Ames, The 1947,My 23,31:2
Unsuspected, The 1947,O 4,9:2
Black Bart 1948,Mr 4,30:4
April Showers 1948,Mr 27,10:2
Sainted Sisters, The 1948,My 20,35:2
Chinatown at Midnight 1949,N 18,35:3
Bodyhold 1949,D 12,29:4
Blue Gardenia, The 1953,Ap 28,31:1

Walker, Robert

Bataan 1943,Je 4,17:2
Madame Curie 1943,D 17,23:1
See Here Private Hargrove 1944,Mr 22,17:2
Since You Went Away 1944,Jl 21,16:2
Thirty Seconds Over Tokyo 1944,N 16,19:1
Clock, The 1945,My 4,23:2
Her Highness and the Bellboy 1945,S 28,16:2
What Next Corporal Hargrove? 1945,D 26,15:2
Sailor Takes a Wife, The 1946,Mr 1,17:2
Till the Clouds Roll By 1946,D 6,27:4
Beginning or the End, The 1947,F 21,15:1
Sea of Grass, The 1947,F 28,27:2
Song of Love 1947,O 10,31:2
One Touch of Venus 1948,O 29,29:5
Please Believe Me 1950,Je 12,19:4
Skipper Surprised his Wife, The 1950,Je 30,18:2
Vengeance Valley 1951,F 16,21:2
Strangers on a Train 1951,Jl 4,13:2
My Son John 1952,Ap 9,27:1

Walker, Robert Jr

Hook, The 1963,F 16,5:6
Ceremony, The 1964,My 14,39:1
Ensign Pulver 1964,Ag 1,13:2
Happening, The 1967,My 18,56:3
War Wagon, The 1967,Ag 3,26:3
Savage Seven, The 1968,Ag 22,47:1

Walker, Sid

Gift of Gab 1934,S 26,17:6

Walker, Stuart (Director)

Secret Call, The 1931,Jl 13,13:5
Misleading Lady, The 1932,Ap 9,18:1
Evenings for Sale 1932,N 12,20:5
Tonight Is Ours 1933,Ja 21,10:6
Eagle and the Hawk, The 1933,My 13,16:2
White Woman 1933,N 18,15:5
Romance in the Rain 1934,S 8,18:5
Mystery of Edwin Drood, The 1935,Mr 21,27:1
Werewolf of London, The 1935,My 10,25:2

Walker, Stuart (Original Author)

Seventeen 1940,F 29,15:2

Walker, Terry

Sudden Death, And 1936,Jl 18,18:2
23 1/2 Hours Leave 1937,My 17,23:2
Mountain Music 1937,Je 24,30:3
Blonde Trouble 1937,Ag 7,7:2
Federal Bullets 1937,D 27,11:1
Invisible Ghost, The 1941,My 8,21:2

Walker, Tippy

World of Henry Orient, The 1964,Mr 20,27:2

Walker, Turnley (Original Author)

Five Steps to Danger 1957,Ja 31,21:1

Walker, Virginia

Bringing Up Baby 1938,Mr 4,17:5

Walker, Walter

Reaching for the Moon 1930,D 30,24:2
Tailor-Made Man, A 1931,Ap 25,23:4
Annabelle's Affairs 1931,Je 29,20:3
Common Law, The 1931,Jl 20,20:4
Rebound 1931,Ag 29,16:3
New Adventures of Get-Rich-Quick Wallingford 1931,O 10,20:4
Tomorrow and Tomorrow 1932,Ja 30,13:2
Fireman, Save My Child 1932,F 18,25:3
Letty Lynton 1932,Ap 30,19:3
Rich are Always With Us, The 1932,My 16,19:5
Two Seconds 1932,My 19,25:3
Woman in Room 13, The 1932,My 21,9:2
American Madness 1932,Ag 6,14:5
Last Mile, The 1932,Ag 26,20:3
Life Begins 1932,Ag 26,20:3
Blessed Event 1932,S 3,16:2
You Said a Mouthful 1932,N 18,23:2
Kid From Spain, The 1932,N 18,23:2
Conquerors, The 1932,N 21,21:1
No Man of her Own 1932,D 31,10:1
Billion Dollar Scandal, The 1933,Ja 9,23:1
Great Jasper, The 1933,F 17,5:3
Our Betters 1933,F 24,13:2
From Hell to Heaven 1933,Mr 18,9:3
Jennie Gerhardt 1933,Je 9,20:2
I Loved a Woman 1933,S 22,14:2
I'm no Angel 1933,O 14,18:2
Female 1933,N 4,18:3

Walker, Walter— Cont

House on 56th Street, The 1933,D 2,9:3
Sitting Pretty 1933,D 2,9:3
You Can't Buy Everything 1934,F 3,9:2
Count of Monte Cristo, The 1934,S 27,25:2
Lost Lady, A 1934,O 4,19:1
Mrs Wiggs of the Cabbage Patch 1934,O 29,14:2
Gay Bride, The 1934,D 19,27:2
While the Patient Slept 1935,Mr 2,18:2
Sons of Steel 1935,Ap 15,16:3
Dangerous 1935,D 27,14:1
Magnificent Obsession 1935,D 31,11:2
Yours for the Asking 1936,Ag 20,14:2
Cowboy and the Lady, The 1938,N 25,19:3

Walker, William

Bright Leaf 1950,Je 17,7:2
Lydia Bailey 1952,My 31,12:5
Wait Till the Sun Shines, Nellie 1952,Je 28,12:2
Prince of Players 1955,Ja 12,24:2
Long, Hot Summer, The 1958,Ap 4,16:1
Our Man Flint 1966,Ja 26,23:4

Walker, Zena

Hellions, The 1962,Mr 15,28:2
Traitors, The 1963,Je 27,23:4
Model Murder Case, The 1964,N 25,45:1

WALL

See Also WAHL, WOHL

Wall, Faye

Hitler-Dead or Alive 1943,Mr 31,23:3

Wall, Geraldine

Winged Victory 1944,D 21,16:2
Boy's Ranch 1946,Ag 9,12:2
Love Laughs at Andy Hardy 1947,Ja 8,28:2
High Barbaree 1947,Je 6,27:2
Dark Delusion 1947,Je 26,19:2
Scudda-Hoo! Scudda-Hay! 1948,Ap 15,31:1
Green Grass of Wyoming 1948,Je 10,28:3
Beyond Glory 1948,Ag 4,18:2
Alias Nick Beal 1949,Mr 10,35:2
Green Promise, The 1949,Je 24,29:2
Everybody Does It 1949,O 26,32:2
Thelma Jordon 1950,Ja 19,35:2
Mister 880 1950,S 30,13:2
Appointment With Danger 1951,My 10,38:2
Man in the Gray Flannel Suit, The 1956,Ap 13,21:1
Affair to Remember, An 1957,Jl 20,8:5

Wall, Jean

Not Guilty 1948,Ap 23,28:2
They Are not Angels 1948,My 22,8:3
Blind Desire 1948,Je 10,28:4
Royal Affair, A; (Roi, Le) 1950,Mr 9,25:2
Ma Pomme 1951,O 15,22:2
Possessors, The 1959,Jl 21,24:1
Frantic 1961,Je 12,34:1

WALLACE

See Also WALLIS

Wallace, Babe

Stormy Weather 1943,Jl 22,15:1

Wallace, Beryl

Murder at the Vanities 1934,My 21,20:2
Kansan, The 1943,O 1,15:3
Woman of the Town, The 1944,Mr 6,17:2
Enemy of Women 1944,S 12,23:6

Wallace, Bryan (Screenwriter)

Strangers on a Honeymoon 1937,Mr 13,23:2
You're in the Army Now 1937,Ap 16,27:2
Murder on Diamond Row 1937,N 12,27:2
Inspector Hornleigh 1939,Je 15,27:3

Wallace, Catherine

Guilty One, The 1924,Je 17,22:4
Fourth Commandment, The 1927,Ap 6,25:1
Clothes Make the Woman 1928,Je 5,21:1

Wallace, Coley

Joe Louis Story, The 1953,N 4,29:4

Wallace, Dorothy

Merry Go Round 1923,Jl 2,16:2

Wallace, Edgar (Miscellaneous)

Should a Doctor Tell 1931,Ag 22,7:5

Wallace, Edgar (Original Author)

Terror, The 1928,Ag 16,25:3
Crimson Circle, The 1929,D 28,11:1
Yellow Mask, The 1930,D 8,26:1
Zinker, Der 1931,O 4,VIII,7:1
Calendar, The 1931,N 22,VIII,6:1
Menace, The 1932,Ja 30,13:2
Ringer, The 1932,Je 2,25:2
King Kong 1933,Mr 3,12:1
Before Dawn 1933,O 17,26:2
White Face 1933,D 4,22:3
Criminal at Large 1933,D 20,27:2
Return of the Terror 1934,Jl 11,20:2
Man Who Changed his Name, The 1934,O 17,26:2
Sanders of the River 1935,Je 27,16:1
Crimson Circle, The 1936,D 28,12:3
Strangers on a Honeymoon 1937,Mr 13,23:2
Murder on Diamond Row 1937,N 12,27:2
Dangerous to Know 1938,Mr 11,15:4
Human Monster, The 1940,Mr 25,11:2
Secret Four, The 1940,Ap 22,13:2
Queen of Crime 1941,F 19,25:2
Frightened Lady 1941,N 10,21:3
Coast of Skeletons 1965,N 11,58:3

Wallace, Edgar (Screenwriter)
Terror, The   1928,N 18,IX,7:6
Wallace, Francis (Original Author)
Touchdown   1931,N 16,23:1
Huddle   1932,Je 17,24:1
That's my Boy   1932,N 21,21:1
Big Game, The   1936,O 24,23:1
Rose Bowl   1936,D 2,35:2
Kid Galahad   1937,My 27,21:3
Wagons Roll at Night, The   1941,My 10,20:4
Kid Galahad   1963,Mr 7,8:5
Wallace, Fred
Sea God, The   1930,S 6,9:2
Doubting Thomas   1935,Jl 11,24:2
Every Saturday Night   1936,Mr 14,10:2
Wallace, Frederick William (Original Author)
Captain Salvation   1927,Je 27,25:2
Wallace, George
Japanese War Bride   1952,Ja 30,22:6
Wherever She Goes   1953,Ja 28,24:4
Arena   1953,Jl 23,20:2
Forbidden Planet   1956,My 4,21:2
6 Black Horses   1962,Ap 25,30:1
Wallace, Grace
Nix on Dames   1929,N 23,18:5
Wallace, Harry
Street Scene   1931,Ag 27,22:5
Night after Night   1932,O 31,18:4
She Done Him Wrong   1933,F 10,12:3
Wallace, Helen
Sioux City Sue   1947,Jl 23,19:3
Francis in the Haunted House   1956,Jl 21,9:2
Midnight Story, The   1957,Jl 5,14:2
Ten North Frederick   1958,My 23,29:2
Wallace, Ian
Tom Thumb   1958,D 24,00:0
Wallace, Inez (Original Author)
I Walked With a Zombie   1943,Ap 22,31:5
Wallace, Irving (Original Author)
West Point Story, The   1950,D 23,11:3
Split Second   1953,My 13,34:2
Chapman Report, The   1962,O 18,49:2
Prize, The   1964,Ja 24,21:1
Wallace, Irving (Screenwriter)
West Point Story, The   1950,D 23,11:3
Desert Legion   1953,My 9,13:2
Split Second   1953,My 13,34:2
Bad for Each Other   1953,D 24,9:3
Gambler From Natchez, The   1954,Ag 14,8:2
Sincerely Yours   1955,N 3,37:1
Burning Hills, The   1956,Ag 24,15:2
Bombers B-52   1957,N 23,11:2
Big Circus, The   1959,Jl 18,6:1
Wallace, Jack
Under Pressure   1935,F 4,11:3
Wallace, Jean
It Shouldn't Happen to a Dog   1946,S 7,11:2
Blaze of Noon   1947,Mr 5,31:2
When my Baby Smiles at Me   1948,N 24,20:2
Jigsaw   1949,My 30,9:4
Man on the Eiffel Tower, The   1950,Ja 30,12:2
Good Humor Man, The   1950,Jl 14,17:2
Native Son   1951,Je 18,19:2
Big Combo, The   1955,Mr 26,13:2
Storm Fear   1955,D 17,19:2
Star of India   1956,Ap 28,11:1
Sword of Lancelot   1963,O 10,49:2
Beach Red   1967,Ag 4,18:1
Wallace, Jo
Nice Women   1932,F 20,11:2
Wallace, John
Black Pirate, The   1926,Mr 9,21:4
Donovan Affair, The   1929,Ap 29,29:2
Wallace, Katherine
Illusion   1929,S 28,17:3
Wallace, Lew (Original Author)
Ben Hur   1925,D 31,10:5 (In Addenda)
Ben Hur   1931,D 4,28:2
Ben Hur   1959,N 19,50:2
Wallace, Maude
People Will Talk   1951,Ag 30,20:1
Elopement   1951,D 21,21:3
Wallace, May
Reckless Age, The   1924,Je 10,24:4
Midnight Madonna   1937,Jl 17,18:1
Wallace, Michael (Original Author)
Gold Diggers of 1937   1936,D 25,19:2
Wallace, Milton
Kiss and Make-Up   1934,Je 29,17:1
Wallace, Morgan
One Exciting Night   1922,O 24,17:3
Fighting Blade, The   1923,O 15,15:4
Dangerous Maid, The   1923,D 11,26:2
Pays to Advertise, It   1931,F 21,15:2
It Pays to Advertise   1931,F 21,15:2
Smart Money   1931,Je 19,21:1
Alexander Hamilton   1931,S 17,21:4
Women Go on Forever   1931,O 19,28:1
Unholy Garden, The   1931,O 29,27:1
Expensive Women   1931,N 14,15:3
Safe in Hell   1931,D 19,16:4
Hell's House   1932,F 12,24:5
Final Edition, The   1932,F 22,23:2

Grand Hotel   1932,Ap 13,23:2
Mouthpiece, The   1932,Ap 21,25:2
Lady and Gent   1932,Jl 16,5:5
Mama Loves Papa   1933,Jl 24,11:2
I Believed in You   1934,Ap 11,25:3
Trumpet Blows, The   1934,Ap 14,18:2
Many Happy Returns   1934,Je 9,18:2
We Live Again   1934,N 2,27:2
It's a Gift   1935,Ja 5,20:2
Murder on a Honeymoon   1935,Mr 4,12:2
Devil is a Woman, The   1935,My 4,17:2
Dante's Inferno   1935,Ag 1,15:1
Thunder Mountain   1935,O 2,27:2
$1,000 a Minute   1935,D 21,11:1
Love on a Bet   1936,Mr 5,25:2
Fury   1936,Je 6,21:1
House of Secrets   1937,F 22,13:1
Charlie Chan at the Olympics   1937,My 24,23:1
Under Suspicion   1937,D 20,23:2 (In Addenda)
Lady in the Morgue, The   1938,My 9,13:3
Woman Against Woman   1938,Ag 23,20:6
Mr Moto Takes a Vacation   1939,Je 19,12:6
I Love You Again   1940,Ag 16,11:2
Ellery Queen, Master Detective   1940,D 19,33:1
Dick Tracy   1946,Ja 12,10:7
Wallace, Oliver (Composer)
Dumbo   1941,O 24,27:2
Victory Through Air Power   1943,Jl 19,13:1
Cinderella   1950,F 23,33:1
Jungle Cat   1960,Ag 18,19:2
Wallace, Parnum
Our Mother's House   1967,O 10,56:1
Wallace, Paul
Gypsy   1962,N 2,24:1
Wallace, Ramsey
Voice in the Dark, A   1921,Je 6,16:4
Drivin' Fool, The   1923,O 29,18:1
Extra Girl, The   1924,Ja 21,20:1
Empty Hands   1924,Ag 18,8:2
Broken Laws   1925,Ja 21,19:3
Wallace, Ratch
Isabel   1968,Jl 24,47:1
Wallace, Regina
Adventures of Martin Eden   1942,Mr 16,19:2
Male Animal, The   1942,Mr 28,11:1
Crystal Ball, The   1943,F 19,22:2
Pillow to Post   1945,My 26,18:2
Because of Him   1946,Ja 25,26:6
Dark Corner, The   1946,My 9,27:3
Avalanche   1946,Jl 8,25:2
Rachel and the Stranger   1948,S 20,21:2
Wallace, Richard (Director)
Syncopating Sue   1926,N 2,35:1
Poor Nut, The   1927,Jl 19,27:2
American Beauty   1927,O 11,27:1
Texas Steer, A   1928,Ja 2,28:1
Butter and Egg Man, The   1928,Ag 28,27:4
Shopworn Angel, The   1929,Ja 1,60:1
Innocents of Paris   1929,Ap 27,16:5
Seven Days' Leave   1930,Ja 25,13:2
Right to Love, The   1931,Ja 2,25:1
Man of the World   1931,Mr 21,15:1
Kick In   1931,My 25,17:1
Road to Reno   1931,O 10,20:4
Tomorrow and Tomorrow   1932,Ja 30,13:2
Thunder Below   1932,Je 20,11:2
Masquerader, The   1933,S 4,9:5
Eight Girls in a Boat   1934,Ja 13,16:3
Little Minister, The   1934,D 28,25:1
Wedding Present   1936,N 19,31:3
John Meade's Woman   1937,F 18,19:1
Blossoms On Broadway   1937,D 3,29:2
Young in Heart, The   1938,N 4,27:2
Under-Pup, The   1939,S 5,21:2
Captain Caution   1940,O 21,21:3
Girl, a Guy and a Gob, A   1941,Ap 24,25:3
She Knew All the Answers   1941,Je 20,28:4
Obliging Young Lady   1942,F 13,24:4
Wife Takes a Flyer, The   1942,Je 19,19:1
Night to Remember, A   1943,Ja 1,27:2
Bombardier   1943,Jl 2,15:2
Fallen Sparrow, The   1943,Ag 20,13:1
My Kingdom for a Cook   1943,O 15,15:3
Bride by Mistake   1944,S 16,20:2
It's in the Bag   1945,Je 11,12:1
Kiss and Tell   1945,O 26,16:2
Because of Him   1946,Ja 25,26:6
Sinbad the Sailor   1947,Ja 23,31:2
Framed   1947,My 26,24:2
Tycoon   1947,D 26,22:6
Let's Live a Little   1948,D 10,34:2
Adventure in Baltimore   1949,Ap 29,27:2
Wallace, Richard (Producer)
Captain Caution   1940,O 21,21:3
Wallace, Robert (Original Author)
That Night   1957,O 15,39:3
Wallace, Robert (Screenwriter)
That Night   1957,O 15,39:3
Wallace, Royce
Take a Giant Step   1961,Mr 6,28:2
Wallace, William
Courage of Lassie   1946,Jl 25,18:5

Wallach, Eli
Baby Doll   1956,D 19,40:2
Seven Thieves   1960,Mr 12,14:5
Magnificent Seven, The   1960,N 24,48:3
Misfits, The   1961,F 2,24:2
Hemingway's Adventures of a Young Man
   1962,Jl 26,17:1
How the West Was Won   1963,Ap 1,54:1
Victors, The   1963,D 20,21:2
Act One   1963,D 27,17:2
Kisses for my President   1964,Ag 22,13:1
Moonspinners, The   1964,N 4,47:1
Lord Jim   1965,F 26,18:1
Genghis Khan   1965,Je 24,28:2
How to Steal a Million   1966,Jl 15,34:1
Tiger Makes Out, The   1967,S 19,53:1
Poppy is Also a Flower, The   1967,D 14,62:4
How to Save a Marriage - And Ruin Your Life
   1968,Ja 19,30:1
Good, The Bad and the Ugly, The
   1968,Ja 25,33:1
Lovely Way to Die, A   1968,Jl 13,18:1
Wallach, Ira (Original Author)
Don't Make Waves   1967,Je 21,36:2
Wallach, Ira (Screenwriter)
Boys' Night Out   1962,Je 22,15:2
Wheeler Dealers, The   1963,N 15,25:2
Don't Make Waves   1967,Je 21,36:2
Hot Millions   1968,S 20,42:1
Wallach, Lew
Up the Down Staircase   1967,Ag 18,36:2
Wallant, Edward Lewis (Original Author)
Pawnbroker, The   1965,Ap 21,51:1
Wallbridge, David
Take my Life   1949,Ja 19,34:2
Pink String and Sealing Wax   1950,O 4,38:2
Wallburg, Otto
Nacht Gehoert Uns, Die; Night Belongs to Us,
   The   1930,My 11,IX,4:2 (In Addenda)
Hampelmann, Der   1931,S 8,38:7
Bomben auf Monte Carlo; Bombardment of Monte
   Carlo, The   1931,S 27,VIII,7:1
Opernredoute; Opera ball   1931,O 4,VIII,7:1
Opern-Ball, Der; Opera Ball   1931,N 6,28:3
Kleine Seitensprung, Der   1932,Ja 1,31:1
Hochtourist, Der; Mountain Climber, The
   1932,Ja 17,VIII,6:1
Das Lied ist Aus   1932,Ja 29,13:2
Ronny   1932,Ap 14,25:3
Trapeze   1932,My 3,25:2
Zwei Herzen und ein Schlag   1932,S 9,17:5
Week-End Im Paradies   1932,O 24,18:5
Yorck   1932,N 24,35:2
Das Schoene Abenteuer   1932,D 8,25:3
Schwartze Husar, Der   1932,D 23,20:1
Ihre Majestaet die Liebe   1933,F 7,23:4
Friederike   1933,F 27,11:3
Die Frau von der Man Spricht   1933,Ap 22,16:4
Eine Liebesnacht   1933,My 15,16:2
Madame Wuenscht Keine Kinder   1933,Je 2,22:4
Heute Nacht-Eventuell   1933,Je 24,16:3
Wenn die Liebe Mode Macht   1933,O 30,14:3
Luegen auf Ruegen   1933,Ja 1,28:2
Hochtourist, Der   1934,Ja 13,16:4
Wie Sag' Ich's Meinem Mann?   1934,Ja 23,22:4
Strich Durch die Rechnung   1934,Mr 3,8:6
Tochter des Regiments, Die   1934,Mr 31,8:3
Inge und die Millionen   1934,Ap 13,25:1
Marion, Das Gehoert Sich Nicht   1934,D 15,9:4
Konjunkturritter   1935,Ap 29,12:4
Wer Nimmt die Liebe Ernst?   1936,F 10,15:2
Gruss und Kuss, Veronika   1936,F 24,14:2
Madonna, Wo Bist Du?   1936,Mr 21,13:3
Die Privatsekretaerin Heiratet   1936,D 5,16:4
Grosse Bluff, Der; Big Bluff, The   1937,S 6,20:2
Wallcks, Clara
Merry Widow, The   1925,Ag 27,14:1
Wallen, Sigurd
Brokiga Blad   1931,N 30,16:2
Roeda Dagen   1932,My 21,9:2
Pettersson & Bendel   1934,F 22,25:2
Karl Fredrik Reigns   1938,F 2,15:2
John Ericsson Victor of Hampton Roads
   1938,My 18,17:2
Familjen Andersson; Anderson Family, The
   1939,Ja 24,16:5
Med Folket Foer Fosterlandet   1939,F 21,14:2
Du Gamla, Du Fria; Thou old, Tho Free
   1939,Mr 21,27:2
Crime and Punishment   1948,Mr 1,17:2
Wallen, Sigurd (Director)
Mvetsoemma Adolf   1937,F 22,13:1
Adolf Armstrong   1937,O 1,19:5
Familjen Andersson; Anderson Family, The
   1939,Ja 24,16:5
Med Folket Foer Fosterlandet   1939,F 21,14:2
Waller, Eddy
Jesse James   1939,Ja 14,13:1
Return of the Cisco Kid, The   1939,Ap 29,13:2
Mutiny on the Blackhawk   1939,Ag 2,17:2
Legion of Lost Flyers   1939,O 30,13:3
Grapes of Wrath, The   1940,Ja 25,17:2
Geronimo   1940,F 8,18:3

Waller, Eddy— Cont

Gold Rush Maisie 1940,S 2,19:2
Devil's Pipeline, The 1940,N 11,22:4
Night Monster 1942,N 30,18:5
Kansan, The 1943,O 1,15:3
My Kingdom for a Cook 1943,O 15,15:3
Dakota 1945,D 17,17:2
Abilene Town 1946,Mr 4,16:5
Michigan Kid 1947,F 22,16:3
Black Bart 1948,Mr 4,30:4
Lust for Gold 1949,Jl 4,9:2
Traveling Saleswoman 1950,Ja 6,25:3
He's a Cockeyed Wonder 1950,O 20,32:4
Cavalry Scout 1951,Je 8,32:2
Far Country, The 1955,F 14,24:2
Foxfire 1955,Jl 14,19:1

Waller, Fats
King of Burlesque 1936,Ja 16,25:2
Stormy Weather 1943,Jl 22,15:1

Waller, Fred Jr (Miscellaneous)
Cradle Buster, The 1922,My 22,18:4

Waller, Lewis
Monsieur Beaucaire 1924,Ag 12,12:1 (In
  Addenda)

Waller, Marianne
Odette 1951,Mr 28,33:2

Wallerstein, Rose
Youth of Russia, The 1934,N 10,19:3

Walley, Deborah
Gidget Goes Hawaiian 1961,Ag 10,17:4
Bon Voyage! 1962,My 18,34:2
Summer Magic 1963,Ag 22,19:2
Young Lovers, The 1965,F 11,45:1
Ski Party 1965,O 23,17:3
Sergeant Deadhead 1965,O 23,17:3
Spinout 1966,D 15,60:1

Wallgren, Gunn
Crime and Punishment 1948,Mr 1,17:2

Walling, Richard
Slaves of Beauty 1927,Je 8,23:3
Walking Back 1928,Je 12,33:3

Walling, William
Village Blacksmith, The 1922,N 3,17:5
Temple of Venus, The 1923,N 1,24:3
Nellie, the Beautiful Cloak Model
  1924,Ap 14,14:1
Iron Horse, The 1924,Ag 29,6:1
Little Robinson Crusoe 1924,S 3,17:1
Man Without a Country, The 1925,F 12,16:1
Clash of the Wolves, The 1925,N 18,27:4
Jazz Singer, The 1927,O 7,24:4
Harvester, The 1927,N 7,33:1
Mating Call, The 1928,O 8,14:2
Welcome Danger 1929,O 21,30:1
Moby Dick 1930,Ag 15,20:5
Painted Desert, The 1931,Mr 9,19:1

Wallington, Jimmy
Start Cheering 1938,Mr 17,17:3
Stadium Murders, The 1938,Ap 9,11:2

WALLIS
See Also WALLACE

Wallis, Bertram
Wandering Jew, The 1935,Ja 14,11:3

Wallis, Hal (Producer)
Juarez 1939,Ap 26,27:1
Old Maid, The 1939,Ag 12,16:2
Dr Ehrlich's Magic Bullet 1940,F 24,9:2
'Til We Meet Again 1940,Ap 14,14:2
Torrid Zone 1940,My 18,11:3
Sergeant York 1941,Jl 3,15:1
Navy Blues 1941,S 20,11:2
Maltese Falcon, The 1941,O 4,18:2
Desperate Journey 1942,S 26,11:2
Now, Voyager 1942,O 23,25:3
Casablanca 1942,N 27,27:1
Air Force 1943,F 4,29:1
This Is the Army 1943,Jl 29,11:6
Watch on the Rhine 1943,Ag 28,15:1
Princess O'Rourke 1943,N 6,16:2
Passage to Marseille 1944,F 17,12:5
You Came Along 1945,Jl 5,7:2
Love Letters 1945,Ag 27,22:3
Saratoga Trunk 1945,N 22,39:2
Searching Wind, The 1946,Je 27,29:1
I Walk Alone 1948,Ja 22,36:3
So Evil my Love 1948,Jl 22,27:2
Sorry, Wrong Number 1948,S 2,18:2
My Friend Irma 1949,S 29,39:2
Paid in Full 1950,F 16,28:2
My Friend Irma Goes West 1950,Ag 3,20:2
Furies, The 1950,Ag 17,23:2
Dark City 1950,O 19,40:5
September Affair 1951,F 2,19:2
Peking Express 1951,Jl 19,20:2
That's My Boy 1951,Ag 2,18:1
Sailor Beware 1952,F 1,17:1
Red Mountain 1952,Ap 26,19:2
Jumping Jacks 1952,Jl 24,30:2
Come Back,Little Sheba 1952,D 24,13:2 (In Addenda)
Stooge, The 1953,F 5,19:2
Scared Stiff 1953,Jl 3,10:2
Cease Fire! 1953,N 25,17:1
Money From Home 1954,F 27,11:3
About Mrs Leslie 1954,Je 28,16:2

Three Ring Circus 1954,D 25,7:2
Rose Tattoo, The 1955,D 13,55:1
Artists and Models 1955,D 22,20:1
Rainmaker, The 1956,D 13,51:1
Hollywood or Bust 1956,D 24,8:1
Gunfight at the O K Corral 1957,My 30,23:2
Loving You 1957,Jl 18,19:2
Sad Sack, The 1957,N 28,57:1
Wild Is the Wind 1957,D 12,35:1
King Creole 1958,Jl 4,15:2
Hot Spell 1958,S 18,37:2
Don't Give up the Ship 1959,Jl 9,22:1
Last Train from Gun Hill 1959,Jl 30,31:2
Career 1959,O 9,24:1
Visit to a Small Planet 1960,Ap 14,34:1
G I Blues 1960,N 5,28:1
All in a Nights Work 1961,Mr 23,28:1
Summer and Smoke 1961,N 17,41:1
Blue Hawaii 1962,F 22,20:2
Girl Named Tamiku, A 1963,Mr 15,8:2
Wives and Lovers 1963,Ag 29,36:1
Fun in Acapulco 1964,F 20,22:4
Becket 1964,Mr 12,40:2
Roustabout 1964,N 11,38:1
Sons of Katie Elder, The 1965,Ag 26,40:3
Boeing Boeing 1965,D 24,24:4
Paradise, Hawaiian Style 1966,Je 16,15:3
Barefoot in the Park 1967,My 26,51:1
Easy Come, Easy Go 1967,Je 15,56:1
5 Card Stud 1968,Ag 1,24:1

Wallis, J H (Original Author)
Woman in the Window, The 1945,Ja 26,16:4
Strange Bargain 1949,S 30,28:3

Wallis, Jacquie
Kiss of the Vampire 1963,O 10,49:2

Wallis, Milton
Cheating Blondes 1933,My 20,11:4

Wallis, Norman
Racket Busters 1938,Ag 11,13:1

Wallis, Richard
I Thank a Fool 1962,S 15,15:1

Wallis, Shani
Oliver! 1968,D 11,57:1

Wallock, A Mark Rev (Original Author)
Prince of Peace, The 1951,Mr 24,8:3

Wallop, Douglass (Original Author)
Damn Yankees 1958,S 27,12:7

Walls, Tom
Blarney Kiss, The 1933,Ag 19,14:4
Just Smith 1934,Ap 23,20:2
Man With 100 Faces 1938,N 1,27:2
Half-Way House 1945,Ag 13,22:4
Johnny Frenchman 1946,O 21,27:3
Lady Surrenders, A 1947,Je 20,25:6
Spring in Park Lane 1949,S 21,38:2
Master of Bankdam 1949,O 17,18:2
Interrupted Journey 1951,My 29,20:2
Maytime in Mayfair 1952,Ap 23,23:5

Walls, Tom (Director)
Blarney Kiss, The 1933,Ag 19,14:4
Just Smith 1934,Ap 23,20:2

Walls, Tom Jr
Spring in Park Lane 1949,S 21,38:2
Galloping Major, The 1951,D 17,27:2

Wallsten, Robert
Soak the Rich 1936,F 5,14:2

Walmo, Luis
Terrace, The 1964,N 25,45:1

Walmsley, Jon
One and Only Genuine Original Family Band,
  The 1968,Mr 22,55:1

Walpole, Hugh
David Copperfield 1935,Ja 19,8:1

Walpole, Hugh (Original Author)
Vanessa: Her Love Story 1935,Ap 13,11:3
Mr Perrin and Mr Traill 1949,Ja 17,15:2
Kind Lady 1951,Ag 8,21:2

Walpole, Hugh (Screenwriter)
David Copperfield 1935,Ja 19,8:1
Vanessa: Her Love Story 1935,Ap 13,11:3
Little Lord Fauntleroy 1936,Ap 3,27:1

Walridge, Harold
Manhattan Parade 1931,D 25,29:2
Jewel Robbery 1932,Jl 23,6:6

Walsh, Adam
Spirit of Notre Dame, The 1931,O 16,27:1

Walsh, Arthur
This Man's Navy 1945,Ap 16,18:6
They Were Expendable 1945,D 21,25:2
My Darling Clementine 1946,D 4,44:5
You Gotta Stay Happy 1948,N 5,29:2
Last Hurrah, The 1958,O 24,40:1

Walsh, Bill (Original Author)
Misadventures of Merlin Jones, The
  1964,Mr 26,40:4

Walsh, Bill (Producer)
Davy Crockett, King of the Wild Frontier
  1955,My 26,36:1
Mary Poppins 1964,S 25,34:1
That Darn Cat 1965,D 3,44:1
Lt Robin Crusoe, USN 1966,Jl 14,28:1
Blackbeard's Ghost 1968,Ap 11,51:3

Walsh, Bill (Screenwriter)
Littlest Outlaw, The 1955,D 27,31:1
Shaggy Dog, The 1959,Mr 20,26:2
Toby Tyler 1960,Ap 20,45:2
Absent-Minded Professor, The 1961,Mr 16,44:2
Son of Flubber 1963,F 9,5:2
Mary Poppins 1964,S 25,34:1
That Darn Cat 1965,D 3,44:1
Lt Robin Crusoe, USN 1966,Jl 14,28:1
Blackbeard's Ghost 1968,Ap 11,51:3

Walsh, Dale
New Adventures of Tarzan, The 1935,O 15,19:3

Walsh, Dermot
Hungry Hill 1947,O 11,11:2
Jassy 1948,F 20,19:2
Desert Patrol 1962,Ja 18,23:5
Trunk, The 1962,N 1,34:3
Telltale Heart, The 1963,My 16,42:1
It Takes a Thief 1963,Ag 15,24:7

Walsh, Frank
America 1924,F 22,20:1
Joy Girl, The 1927,S 6,34:3

Walsh, George
Vanity Fair 1923,My 7,19:3
Rosita 1923,S 4,14:1
Slave of Desire 1923,D 11,26:2
Reno 1924,Ja 8,27:1
Me and my Gal 1932,D 12,18:4
Bowery, The 1933,O 5,24:2
Belle of the Nineties 1934,S 22,12:2
Under Pressure 1935,F 4,11:3
Klondike Annie 1936,Mr 12,18:2

Walsh, Jane
Man Who Found Himself, The 1937,Ap 9,19:3

Walsh, Jill (Screenwriter)
Bon Voyage! 1962,My 18,34:2

Walsh, Joey
Hans Christian Andersen 1952,N 26,20:2
Juggler, The 1953,My 6,39:2

Walsh, Johnny
Calling Dr Kildare 1939,My 12,25:4
Youth Runs Wild 1944,S 2,17:2

Walsh, Joseph
Anzio 1968,Jl 25,26:1

Walsh, Judy
Second Chance 1953,Jl 23,20:2

Walsh, Kay
Luck of the Irish, The 1937,Ja 16,21:1
Chinese Den 1941,Mr 26,27:3
Secret of Stamboul, The 1941,My 31,14:1
In Which We Serve 1942,D 24,18:1
This Happy Breed 1947,Ap 14,24:2
October Man, The 1948,Ap 16,29:2
Stage Fright 1950,F 24,27:2
Last Holiday 1950,N 14,39:4
Magnet, The 1951,F 27,22:6
Oliver Twist 1951,Jl 31,17:2
Encore (Winter Cruise); Winter Cruise (Encore)
  1952,Ap 3,45:1
Stranger in Between, The 1952,Ag 20,21:3
Magic Box, The 1952,S 24,40:2
Young Bess 1953,My 22,31:1
Lease of Life 1956,F 10,18:1
Cast a Dark Shadow 1957,N 28,57:1
Horse's Mouth, The 1958,N 12,41:1
Tunes of Glory 1960,D 21,38:2
Greyfriars' Bobby 1961,O 12,41:4
Reach for Glory 1963,S 10,46:1
Study in Terror, A 1966,N 3,45:3
Devil's Own, The 1967,Mr 16,53:2

Walsh, Maurice (Original Author)
Quiet Man, The 1952,Ag 22,13:1
Trouble in the Glen 1955,Ap 11,29:2

Walsh, Percy
Born for Glory 1935,O 21,22:4
Secret Four, The 1940,Ap 22,13:2
Pastor Hall 1940,S 21,13:2
Let George Do It 1940,O 14,25:5
Jeannie 1943,S 13,14:2
Adventures of Tartu, The 1943,S 24,26:1
Meet Me at Dawn 1948,My 18,26:2
Guinea Pig, The 1949,My 2,20:2
Fame Is the Spur 1949,N 8,34:2
Happiest Days of Your Life, The 1950,S 18,19:2

Walsh, R A (Director)
Kindred of the Dust 1922,Ag 28,14:1
Lost and Found 1923,Mr 19,22:2

Walsh, R A (Producer)
Oath, The 1921,Ap 11,9:1

Walsh, R H (Director)
Honor System, The 1917,F 13,9:4

Walsh, Raoul
Sadie Thompson 1928,F 6,12:3

Walsh, Raoul (Director)
Thief of Bagdad, The 1924,Mr 19,19:1
East of Suez 1925,Ja 24,22:1
What Price Glory 1926,N 24,26:4
Monkey Talks, The 1927,Ap 5,30:7
Loves of Carmen 1927,S 27,31:1
Sadie Thompson 1928,F 6,12:3
Red Dance, The 1928,Je 26,29:1
Me, Gangster 1928,O 22,29:1
In old Arizona 1929,Ja 21,18:4

Walsh, Raoul (Director)— Cont

Hot for Paris 1930,Ja 4,21:1
Big Trail, The 1930,O 25,20:3
Man Who Came Back, The 1931,Ja 3,21:2
Women of all Nations 1931,My 30,9:2
Yellow Ticket, The 1931,O 31,22:2
Me and my Gal 1932,D 12,18:4
Sailor's Luck 1933,Mr 17,21:2
Bowery, The 1933,O 5,24:2
Going Hollywood 1933,D 23,19:2
Under Pressure 1935,F 4,11:3
Every Night at Eight 1935,Ag 3,16:2
Klondike Annie 1936,Mr 12,18:2
Big Brown Eyes 1936,My 2,11:1
Spendthrift 1936,Jl 23,24:1
You're in the Army Now 1937,Ap 16,27:2
When Thief Meets Thief 1937,Je 15,26:2
Artists and Models 1937,Ag 5,19:2
Hitting a new High 1937,D 27,11:1
College Swing 1938,Ap 28,27:2
St Louis Blues 1939,F 9,17:2
Roaring Twenties, The 1939,N 11,12:1
Dark Command 1940,My 11,15:2
They Drive by Night 1940,Jl 27,17:5
High Sierra 1941,Ja 25,11:2
Strawberry Blonde 1941,F 22,11:2
Manpower 1941,Jl 5,14:2
They Died With Their Boots On 1941,N 21,23:3
Desperate Journey 1942,S 26,11:2
Gentleman Jim 1942,N 26,40:3
Background to Danger 1943,Jl 3,11:2
Northern Pursuit 1943,N 26,29:2
Uncertain Glory 1944,Ap 8,9:2
Objective Burma 1945,Ja 27,15:2
Horn Blows at Midnight, The 1945,Ap 21,18:2
Salty O'Rourke 1945,Ap 26,26:2
Man I Love, The 1947,Ja 25,12:2
Pursued 1947,Mr 8,10:2
Cheyenne 1947,Je 7,9:2
Silver River 1948,My 22,8:3
Fighter Squadron 1948,N 20,9:2
One Sunday Afternoon 1948,D 27,16:3
Colorado Territory 1949,Je 25,8:6
White Heat 1949,S 3,7:2
Along the Great Divide 1951,My 17,38:3
Captain Horatio Hornblower 1951,S 14,21:2
Distant Drums 1951,D 26,19:3
Glory Alley 1952,Jl 30,20:8
World in His Arms, The 1952,O 10,21:2
Blackbeard the Pirate 1952,D 26,20:3
Sea Devils 1953,Jl 31,11:5
Lion Is in the Streets, A 1953,S 24,39:2
Saskatchewan 1954,Mr 11,26:2
Battle Cry 1955,F 3,18:1
Tall Men, The 1955,O 12,36:2
Revolt of Mamie Stover, The 1956,My 12,12:7
King and Four Queens, The 1956,D 22,13:7
Naked and the Dead, The 1958,Ag 7,21:1
Sheriff of Fractured Jaw, The 1959,Mr 14,27:4
Private's Affair, A 1959,Ag 15,8:7
Esther and the King 1960,N 19,13:4
Marines, Lets Go! 1961,Ag 16,37:2
Distant Trumpet, A 1964,My 28,40:1

Walsh, Raoul (Producer)

Dark Command 1940,My 11,15:2
Esther and the King 1960,N 19,13:4
Marines, Lets Go! 1961,Ag 16,37:2

Walsh, Raoul (Screenwriter)

Hot for Paris 1930,Ja 4,21:1
Big Brown Eyes 1936,My 2,11:1
Spendthrift 1936,Jl 23,24:1
Esther and the King 1960,N 19,13:4

Walsh, Richard

Humoresque 1946,D 26,28:1

Walsh, Thomas (Original Author)

We're Only Human 1936,Ja 18,19:2
Don't Turn 'em Loose 1936,S 25,20:2
Union Station 1950,O 5,38:3
Pushover 1954,Jl 31,6:3

Walsh, William (Composer)

Fun and Fancy Free 1947,S 29,17:2 (In Addenda)

Walshe, Pat

Wizard of Oz, The 1939,Ag 18,16:2
Panic in the Streets 1950,Ag 5,9:2

Walsi, Katherine

Chase, The 1966,F 19,24:1

Walston, Ray

Kiss Them for Me 1957,N 9,31:2
South Pacific 1958,Mr 20,33:1
Damn Yankees 1958,S 27,12:7
Say One for Me 1959,Je 20,11:2
Tall Story 1960,Ap 7,46:1
Apartment, The 1960,Je 16,37:2
Portrait in Black 1960,Jl 28,19:1
Convicts 4 1962,O 4,44:2
Wives and Lovers 1963,Ag 29,36:1
Who's Minding the Store? 1963,N 29,67:6 (Incorrect in this edition; use 1963,N 28,67:6 elsewhere)
Kiss Me, Stupid 1964,D 23,22:2
Caprice 1967,Je 8,52:2

Waltari, Mika (Original Author)

Egyptian, The 1954,Ag 25,23:1

WALTER

See Also WALTHER, WOLTER

Walter, Bruno

Carnegie Hall 1947,My 3,10:2

Walter, Charlotte

Millie 1931,F 7,11:1

Walter, Chilton (Original Author)

Dress Parade 1927,O 31,22:1

Walter, Eugene (Miscellaneous)

Peak of Fate 1925,Je 13,10:5
Jealousy 1929,S 14,17:1

Walter, Eugene (Original Author)

Easiest Way, The 1917,Ap 9,13:4 (In Addenda)
Way of a Woman, The 1919,Jl 28,8:5
Trail of the Lonesome Pine, The 1923,Mr 20,24:3
Just a Woman 1925,My 26,24:2
Easiest Way, The 1931,F 28,15:2
No Other Woman 1933,Ja 30,9:4 (In Addenda)

Walter, Eugene (Screenwriter)

Woman Trap 1936,Mr 7,11:4

Walter, Herbert David (Original Author)

Dress Parade 1927,O 31,22:1

Walter, Jessica

Group, The 1966,Mr 17,35:1
Grand-Prix 1966,D 22,40:1
Bye Bye Braverman 1968,F 22,36:1

Walter, Karl Schmitt

St Matthew Passion 1952,Ja 29,17:4

Walter, Marcia

Close-Up 1948,Ap 5,24:2

Walter, Margot

Bockbierfest 1931,Mr 31,25:3
Wahre Jakob, Der 1931,Ag 7,20:2
Der Herr Bueroyorsteher 1932,Je 17,24:1
Schoen Ist die Manoeverzeit 1932,Ag 19,20:6
Barberina, Die Taenzerin Von Sans-Souci 1932,O 26,15:4
Koenigin der Unterwelt 1932,D 9,26:5
Zwel Gute Kameraden 1933,D 4,22:3
Die Galavorstellung 1933,D 11,23:4
Zu Befehl, Herr Unteroffizier 1934,Je 16,20:3

Walter, Paula

Mirele Efros 1939,O 21,12:2

Walter, W

Border Street 1950,Ap 26,35:2

Walter, Wilfred

To the Victor 1938,Ap 13,21:2
Human Monster, The 1940,Mr 25,11:2
Lady in Distress 1942,F 16,21:2

Walter, Wladyslaw

Moj Wujaszek Z Ameryki 1933,O 25,25:3
Parada Rezerwistow 1934,My 1,26:6
Kocha, Lubi, Szanuje 1934,N 3,20:4
First Start, The 1953,F 2,17:3

Walter-Ellis, Desmond

Maytime in Mayfair 1952,Ap 23,23:5
Penny Princess 1953,Mr 25,37:3

Walters, Betty

Teen Age 1944,Je 19,17:1

Walters, Bucky

Safe at Home 1941,N 26,31:2

Walters, Charles (Composer)

Torch Song 1953,O 13,34:2

Walters, Charles (Director)

Good News 1947,D 5,33:2
Easter Parade 1948,Jl 1,19:3
Barkleys of Broadway, The 1949,My 5,34:2
Summer Stock 1950,S 1,17:2
Three Guys Named Mike 1951,Mr 2,21:2
Texas Carnival 1951,O 13,9:1
Belle of New York, The 1952,Mr 6,25:6
Lili 1953,Mr 11,36:7
Dangerous When Wet 1953,Je 19,18:1
Torch Song 1953,O 13,34:2
Easy to Love 1953,N 27,99:9
Glass Slipper, The 1955,Mr 25,19:2
Tender Trap, The 1955,N 11,29:6
High Society 1956,Ag 10,9:2
Don't Go Near the Water 1957,N 15,37:1
Ask any Girl 1959,My 22,32:1
Please Don't Eat the Daisies 1960,Ap 1,37:1
Two Loves 1961,Je 22,23:2
Jumbo 1962,D 7,49:1
Walk, Don't Run 1966,Ag 25,42:3

Walters, Dickie

Carnival 1935,F 16,9:1

Walters, Dorothy

Confidence Man, The 1924,Ap 15,24:1
Man Must Live, A 1925,Ja 29,12:2

Walters, Elizabeth

Bill and Coo 1948,Mr 29,17:4

Walters, Ermadean

Song of Bernadette, The 1944,Ja 27,15:2

Walters, Glen

She Goes to War 1929,Je 10,23:1

Walters, Hal

Spies of the Air 1940,Jl 4,12:3

Walters, Hugh

Having a Wild Weekend 1965,Ag 19,35:1

Walters, Luana

Miss Pinkerton 1932,Jl 9,7:5
Algiers 1938,Jl 15,13:2
No Greater Sin 1941,Ag 29,18:2

Walters, Nancy

Bells Are Ringing 1960,Je 24,31:2
Green Helmet, The 1961,Jl 20,32:2
Blue Hawaii 1962,F 22,20:2

Walters, Patricia

River, The 1951,S 11,33:2

Walters, Polly

Smart Money 1931,Je 19,21:1
Expensive Women 1931,N 14,15:3
Blonde Crazy 1931,D 4,28:2
Manhattan Parade 1931,D 25,29:2
Taxi 1932,Ja 8,27:3
Union Depot 1932,Ja 15,24:4
Play Girl 1932,Mr 19,11:2
Beauty and the Boss 1932,Ap 2,13:2
Love Starved 1932,Ap 15,23:1
Mouthpiece, The 1932,Ap 21,25:2
Make Me a Star 1932,Jl 1,19:3
She Loves Me Not 1933,N 26,IX,1:1 (In Addenda)

Walters, Russell

Chance of a Lifetime 1951,Mr 15,37:2

Walters, Susan

Shoot to Kill 1947,My 17,8:5

Walters, Thorley

It Happened to One Man 1941,F 24,11:6
Waltz Time 1946,F 11,25:2
Gay Intruders, The 1946,Mr 18,24:2
Private's Progress 1956,Jl 24,19:2
Novel Affair, A 1957,Ag 28,22:1
Blue Murder at St Trinian's 1958,My 27,27:1
Man in a Cocked Hat 1960,Je 15,50:2
French Mistress, A 1960,D 19,34:2
Risk, The 1961,S 25,41:2
Pure Hell of St Trinian's, The 1961,S 26,31:1
Invasion Quartet 1961,D 11,41:2
Murder She Said 1962,Ja 8,27:2
Phantom of the Opera, The 1962,Ag 23,25:2
Ring of Treason 1964,My 28,40:3 (Incorrect in this edition; use 1964,My 29,15:1 elsewhere)
Psycopath, The 1966,S 29,60:1

Waltes, Cyril

I Believe in You 1953,My 5,34:3

Walthal, Anna May

As Man Desires 1925,F 10,20:1
Desert Flower, The 1925,Je 1,10:3

Walthall, Henry B

Great Love, The 1918,Ag 12,7:1
False Faces, The 1919,F 17,11:3
Birth of a Nation, The 1921,My 2,12:1
Birth of a Nation, The 1922,D 5,24:3
Gimme 1923,Ja 15,18:3
Boy of Mine 1923,D 24,12:1 (In Addenda)
Unknown Purple, The 1924,Mr 24,13:1
Woman on the Jury, The 1924,My 19,14:2
Single Wives 1924,Jl 29,9:2
Golden Bed, The 1925,Ja 20,18:2
Simon the Jester 1925,N 19,22:1
Three Faces West 1926,F 16,22:4
Barrier, The 1926,Mr 22,16:1
Unknown Soldier, The 1926,My 31,10:2
Road to Mandalay, The 1926,Je 29,21:2
Plastic Age, The 1926,Jl 19,13:1
Ice Flood, The 1926,O 19,26:2
Everybody's Acting 1926,N 8,19:2
Fighting Love 1927,My 23,27:2
Wings 1927,Ag 13,10:4
London After Midnight 1927,D 31,31:1
Love Me and the World Is Mine 1928,F 6,12:3
Jazz Age, The 1929,Ja 7,36:2
Speakeasy 1929,Mr 11,22:2
Bridge of San Luis Rey, The 1929,My 20,22:6
River of Romance, The 1929,Jl 29,23:3
Street Corners 1929,S 2,16:1
Trespasser, The 1929,N 2,14:6
Blaze O' Glory 1929,D 31,15:1
Temple Tower 1930,My 10,25:3
Abraham Lincoln 1930,Ag 26,24:1
Tol'able David 1930,N 17,29:1
Birth of a Nation, The 1930,D 22,16:2
Hotel Continental 1932,Mr 21,19:5
Fame Street 1932,Ap 2,13:2
Strange Interlude 1932,S 1,24:3
Cabin in the Cotton 1932,S 30,17:3
Chandu the Magician 1932,O 1,10:4
Central Park 1932,D 7,29:3
Me and my Gal 1932,D 12,18:4
42d Street 1933,Mr 10,19:3
Laughing at Life 1933,Jl 15,14:2
Headline Shooters 1933,O 23,18:3
Sin of Nora Moran, The 1933,D 13,29:3
Dark Hazard 1934,F 23,23:3
Viva Villa! 1934,Ap 11,25:2
Beggars in Ermine 1934,Ap 25,25:3
Men in White 1934,Je 9,18:2
Judge Priest 1934,O 12,33:1
Lemon Drop Kid, The 1934,O 27,20:2
Girl of the Limberlost, A 1934,N 9,24:6
Helldorado 1935,Ja 7,13:2

Walthall, Henry B— Cont
Dante's Inferno 1935,Ag 1,15:1
Tale of Two Cities, A 1935,D 26,21:2
Garden Murder Case, The 1936,Mr 2,13:2
Last Outlaw, The 1936,Je 15,24:1
Mine With the Iron Door, The 1936,Jl 11,11:3
Devil Doll, The 1936,Ag 8,5:2
China Clipper 1936,Ag 12,14:3

Walthall, Henry R
One Clear Call 1922,Je 19,10:3

WALTHER
See Also WALTER, WOLTER

Walther, Hertha von
Peak of Fate 1925,Je 13,10:5
Loves of Jeanne Ney, The 1928,Jl 10,17:3
Tiger von Berlin, Der 1930,S 15,29:3
Tannenberg 1934,Ap 3,26:6

Walther-Fein, Rudolf (Director)
Because I Loved You 1930,Ja 25,13:2
Korvettenkapitaen, Der 1933,Mr 20,18:3
Das Schicksal der Renate Langen 1933,N 4,18:4

Walton, Douglas
Secret of Madame Blanche, The 1933,F 4,11:3
Looking Forward 1933,My 1,10:2
Madame Spy 1934,F 10,20:1
Lost Patrol, The 1934,Ap 2,13:2
Murder in Trinidad 1934,My 16,22:2
Charlie Chan in London 1934,S 13,26:1
Count of Monte Cristo, The 1934,S 27,25:2
Bride of Frankenstein, The 1935,My 11,21:2
Dark Angel, The 1935,S 6,12:2
Garden Murder Case, The 1936,Mr 2,13:2
Mary of Scotland 1936,Jl 31,22:2
Thank You, Jeeves 1936,O 5,25:1
Camille 1937,Ja 23,13:1
Flight From Glory 1937,S 11,20:1
Marriage Forbodden 1938,Jl 16,7:2
Storm Over Bengal 1938,D 8,34:4
Story of Vernon and Irene Castle, The
1939,Mr 31,19:2
Bad Lands 1939,Ag 9,15:2
Raffles 1940,Ja 13,11:2
Northwest Passage 1940,Mr 8,25:1
Long Voyage Home, The 1940,O 9,30:2 (In
Addenda)
Too Many Girls 1940,N 21,43:1
Singapore Woman 1941,My 12,13:6
Hurry, Charlie, Hurry 1941,N 12,31:3
Picture of Dorian Gray, The 1945,Mr 2,15:2
Murder, my Sweet 1945,Mr 9,16:2
Dick Tracy vs Cueball 1946,N 23,12:2
High Tide 1947,N 8,11:2

Walton, Francis (Original Author)
Women in the Wind 1939,Ap 13,27:2

Walton, Fred
Fast Set, The 1924,N 18,22:1
New Brooms 1925,N 4,17:4
Splendid Crime, The 1925,D 17,27:1
His Dog 1927,Ag 16,31:2
Wise Wife 1927,N 1,21:1 (In Addenda)
Sin Takes a Holliday 1930,N 28,23:1
Kiki 1931,Mr 6,16:1
Big Gamble, The 1931,S 21,20:2
House of a Thousand Candles, The
1936,Ap 2,29:2
Dracula's Daughter 1936,My 18,14:2

Walton, George Col U S A R (Original Author)
Devil's Brigade, The 1968,My 23,56:2

Walton, Henry
Livingstone in Africa 1929,Mr 25,32:2

Walton, Herbert C
Take my Life 1949,Ja 19,34:2
Forbidden Street, The 1949,My 14,9:2
Little Ballerina, The 1951,F 28,33:2
I Believe in You 1953,My 5,34:3
Titfield Thunderbolt, The 1953,O 6,34:2
Hobson's Choice 1954,Je 15,37:1

Walton, William (Composer)
Henry V 1946,Je 18,30:2
Richard III 1956,Mr 12,1:4

Walton, William (Miscellaneous)
As You Like It 1936,N 6,29:3

Waltz, Calla
Union Pacific 1939,My 11,31:2

Waltz, Pat
Human Jungle, The 1954,N 26,24:6

Waltzmann, Runze
Escape from East Berlin 1962,D 6,55:3

Walzman, Max
Woman of Experience, A 1931,Jl 9,26:5

Wamala, Honey
Africa-Texas Style! 1967,Jl 13,30:2

Wampas Baby Stars
Young and Beautiful 1934,S 18,18:4

Wanamaker, Sam
My Girl Tisa 1948,F 21,9:2
Give Us This Day 1949,D 21,41:2
Mr Denning Drives North 1953,S 2,20:1
Battle of the Sexes, The 1960,Ap 19,40:4
Taras Bulba 1962,D 26,5:2
Man in the Middle 1964,Mr 5,36:1
Those Magnificent Men in Their Flying Machines
(Or How I Flew From London to Paris in 25
Hours and 11 Minutes) 1965,Je 17,27:1

Spy Who Came in From the Cold, The
1965,D 24,24:1
Warning Shot 1967,Je 8,52:2
Day the Fish Came Out, The 1967,O 3,57:1
Danger Route 1968,Je 6,54:2

Wanck, Maria
Anna und Elisabeth 1936,Je 13,13:1

Wanders, Skippy
Loves of Edgar Allan Poe, The 1942,S 21,19:2

Wandish, Ilka
Taras Bulba 1962,D 26,5:2

Wane, Tony
Sanders of the River 1935,Je 27,16:1

Wang, George
10th Victim, The 1965,D 21,46:1

Wang, James
Fighting American, The 1924,My 13,24:1
Yankee Clipper, The 1927,My 3,25:1
Singed 1927,Jl 12,29:3
Charlie Chan's Chance 1932,Ja 23,18:4
Last Man, The 1932,S 17,18:4

Wangel, Hedwig
Rasputin 1929,O 21,30:1
Pension Schoeller 1932,S 20,26:3

Wangenheim, Gustav
Nosferatu the Vampire 1929,Je 4,29:3
By Rocket to the Moon 1931,F 7,11:1
Danton 1931,S 7,19:3

Wangenheim, Gustav (Director)
Kampf, Der 1936,S 11,29:3

Wangenheim, Gustav (Original Author)
Kampf, Der 1936,S 11,29:3

Wangenheim, Gustav (Screenwriter)
Kampf, Der 1936,S 11,29:3

Wanger, Walter (Producer)
President Vanishes, The 1934,D 8,18:5
Big Brown Eyes 1936,My 2,11:1
Moon's our Home, The 1936,My 13,29:2
You Only Live Once 1937,F 1,15:2
Vogues of 1938 1937,Ag 20,21:1
52d Street 1937,N 15,15:1
Stand-In 1937,N 19,27:2
Blockade 1938,Je 17,25:1
Algiers 1938,Jl 15,13:2
Trade Winds 1939,Ja 13,17:2
Winter Carnival 1939,Jl 28,14:2
House Across the Bay, The 1940,Mr 22,23:2
Long Voyage Home, The 1940,O 9,30:2 (In
Addenda)
Sundown 1941,D 26,21:3
Eagle Squadron 1942,Jl 3,12:5
Arabian Nights 1942,D 26,15:1
We've Never Been Licked 1943,Ag 19,23:1
Gung Ho! 1944,Ja 26,23:2
Ladies Courageous 1944,Mr 16,17:2
Canyon Passage 1946,Ag 8,18:2
Smash-Up, The Story of a Woman
1947,Ap 11,31:2
Lost Moment, The 1947,N 22,10:2
Joan of Arc 1948,N 12,30:5
Tulsa 1949,My 27,25:2
Reckless Moment, The 1949,D 30,13:2
Lady in the Iron Mask 1952,Jl 5,7:2
Battle Zone 1952,N 1,17:2
Riot in Cell Block 11 1954,F 19,24:5
Adventures of Haji Baba, The 1954,O 9,8:7
I Want to Live 1958,N 19,45:1
Cleopatra 1963,Je 13,29:1

Wanka, Rolf
Toerichte Jungfrau, Die 1935,S 9,24:3
World's in Love, The 1937,My 19,27:2
Hilde Petersen, Postlagernd 1937,Je 26,20:3 (In
Addenda)
Kein Wort von Liebe; Not a Word About Love
1938,S 10,20:3
Sextanerin, Die; Erste Liebe; First Love
1938,S 12,13:3
Verliebte Herzen; Hearts in Love 1939,Je 10,14:2
S O S Mediterranean 1940,Ja 1,29:2
Recht auf Liebe, Das; Right to Love, The
1940,Je 15,12:3

Wanner, Hughes
Four Bags Full 1957,S 5,32:1

Wanzer, Arthur
Soldiers of the Storm 1933,My 17,15:3

War Eagle, John
Wild North, The 1952,My 12,21:2

Waram, Percy
One Third of a Nation 1939,F 11,13:2
Ministry of Fear 1945,F 8,15:2
Late George Apley, The 1947,Mr 21,29:2
It Had to be You 1947,D 8,35:2
Big Hangover, The 1950,My 26,20:3
Face in the Crowd, A 1957,My 29,33:1

Warbey, Christopher
Safari 1956,Je 21,35:2

Warbrick, Patrick
Land of Fury 1955,My 3,37:4

Warburton, John
Silver Lining, The 1932,My 30,16:5
Secrets of the French Police 1932,D 12,18:4
Cavalcade 1933,Ja 6,23:2
Study in Scarlet, A 1933,Je 1,15:3

Warburton, John— Cont
Charlie Chan's Greatest Case 1933,O 7,18:4
Let's Talk It Over 1934,Je 16,20:2
Partners of the Plains 1938,F 12,20:4
Captain Fury 1939,My 26,20:2
White Cliffs of Dover, The 1944,My 12,15:2
Dangerous Partners 1945,N 2,22:4
Confidential Agent 1945,N 3,11:2
Saratoga Trunk 1945,N 22,39:2
Tarzan and the Huntress 1947,Ap 7,20:4
Living in a Big Way 1947,O 10,31:4

Warcloud, Suni
Jim Thorpe - All American 1951,Ag 25,7:2

Ward, Alice
Skyline 1931,O 5,17:3
Rainbow Trail, The 1932,Ja 30,13:2

Ward, Amelita
Falcon in Danger, The 1943,Jl 23,21:2
Seven Days Ashore 1944,Ap 26,24:7
Rough, Tough and Ready 1945,Mr 24,22:7
Jungle Captive 1945,Jl 7,7:5
Slattery's Hurricane 1949,Ag 13,6:6

Ward, Bill
Amazing Mrs Holliday, The 1943,F 22,20:2
Experiment Perilous 1944,D 30,15:2
To Each his Own 1946,My 24,15:2

Ward, Bradley
Sinners in Silk 1924,S 8,15:3

Ward, Burt
Batman 1966,Ag 25,42:4

Ward, Carrie Clark
Why Smith Left Home 1919,O 13,16:3
Old Lady 31 1920,My 24,20:3
Scaramouche 1923,O 12,7:2 (Incorrect in this
edition; use 1927,O 1,7:2 elsewhere)
His Hour 1924,O 7,26:1
Awful Truth, The 1925,Jl 2,12:4
Eagle, The 1925,N 9,25:1
Rose of the World 1925,N 10,25:3
Only Thing, The 1925,N 23,25:4
Golden Cocoon, The 1925,D 15,14:5

Ward, Carrie Lee
Paliser Case, The 1920,F 16,8:1

Ward, Catherine Claire
Lilly Turner 1933,Je 15,21:2

Ward, Chance
Bat Whispers, The 1931,Ja 16,27:1

Ward, Craig
Our Hospitality 1923,D 10,20:1

Ward, D J
Beachcomber, The 1938,D 26,29:3

Ward, David
Adventures of Tartu, The 1943,S 24,26:1
Life and Death of Colonel Blimp, The
1945,Mr 30,18:2
Adventures, The 1947,Ap 4,19:2
Murder in the Cathedral 1952,Mr 26,35:2

Ward, Dervis
Loneliness of the Long Distance Runner, The
1962,O 9,44:1

Ward, Dorothy
Courage 1930,My 23,21:1

Ward, Edward (Composer)
No More Ladies 1935,Je 22,18:5
Night Must Fall 1937,Ap 30,17:2
Saratoga 1937,Jl 23,16:3
Mannequin 1938,Ja 21,15:2
Toy Wife, The 1938,Je 24,15:1
Shopworn Angel, The 1938,Jl 8,11:2
Broadway Serenade 1939,Ap 7,25:2
Gypsy Wildcat 1944,O 5,18:6
Climax, The 1944,D 14,28:5

Ward, Eric
World Dances 1954,N 8,24:6

Ward, Fannie
Cheat, The 1915,D 13,13:1
Each Hour a Pear! 1916,S 4,5:6
Yellow Ticket, The 1918,My 27,11:3
Common Clay 1919,Mr 3,11:2

Ward, Humphrey (Original Author)
Lady Rose's Daughter 1920,Ag 30,12:3

Ward, Humphrey Mrs (Original Author)
Missing 1918,Je 17,11:3

Ward, James
Night of the Iguana, The 1964,Jl 1,42:1
Kitten With a Whip 1964,N 5,50:4
Kiss Me, Stupid 1964,D 23,22:2
Red Line 7000 1965,D 9,60:4

Ward, James (Producer)
Where the Bullets Fly 1967,S 7,50:4

Ward, Jay
Reducing 1931,Ja 17,23:1
Pilgrimage 1933,Jl 13,17:5
Good-Bye Again 1933,S 2,15:2
Man Who Dared, The 1933,S 9,9:3
As Husbands Go 1934,Ja 26,20:3
Hold That Girl 1934,Mr 24,20:3
Big Hearted Herbert 1934,N 14,23:2
Stop, Look and Love 1939,S 8,28:5
Edison the Man 1940,Je 7,27:2

Ward, Jay (Producer)
Crazy World of Laurel and Hardy, The
1967,D 22,35:3

Ward, John
 Boots and Saddles 1937,N 8,19:2
Ward, Kathrin Clare
 Drag 1929,Je 21,17:2
 Call of the West 1930,My 27,27:2
 Conquering Horde, The 1931,Mr 30,25:2
 Three Girls Lost 1931,My 2,23:4
 Three Wise Girls 1932,F 6,14:4
 Make Me a Star 1932,Jl 1,19:3
 Vanity Street 1932,O 15,13:1
 Once to Every Woman 1934,Mr 26,22:3
Ward, Larry
 Distant Trumpet, A 1964,My 28,40:1
 Hombre 1967,Mr 22,41:1
Ward, Lita
 Aerial Gunner 1943,Je 26,10:2
Ward, Luci (Original Author)
 Santa Fe Stampede 1939,Ap 26,27:3
 Dick Tracy vs Cueball 1946,N 23,12:2
 Black Bart 1948,Mr 4,30:4
 Last Bandit, The 1949,Mr 21,19:2
Ward, Luci (Screenwriter)
 Law in her Hands, The 1936,Je 6,21:2
 Murder by an Aristocrat 1936,Je 13,13:2
 Mountain Justice 1937,My 13,31:2
 Melody for Two 1937,My 21,19:5
 Call the Mesquiteers 1938,Mr 19,11:2
 Santa Fe Stampede 1939,Ap 26,27:3
 Frozen Ghost, The 1945,Jl 28,7:3
 Badman's Territory 1946,My 31,27:2
 Black Bart 1948,Mr 4,30:4
 Return of the Badmen 1948,Ag 5,16:2
 Blackjack Ketchum Desperado 1956,Ap 5,26:2
Ward, Lucille
 Sixty Cents an Hour 1923,My 15,22:1
 Sporting Youth 1924,Ap 2,16:1
 Oh, Doctor! 1925,F 23,24:1
 His Majesty Bunker Bean 1925,S 15,12:1
 Woman of the World, A 1925,D 14,18:2
 California Straight Ahead 1926,Ja 12,27:5
 What a Man 1930,Jl 21,20:3
 Purchase Price, The 1932,Jl 16,5:5
 Rebecca of Sunnybrook Farm 1932,Jl 30,16:5
 Zoo in Budapest 1933,Ap 28,15:2
 Lilly Turner 1933,Je 15,21:2
 Little Miss Marker 1934,My 19,18:3
 Harvester, The 1936,Jl 4,18:2
 Mother Carey's Chickens 1938,Ag 5,11:1
 Sons of the Legion 1938,S 30,24:3
 First Love 1939,N 9,27:3
 Christmas in July 1940,N 6,35:2
Ward, Mackenzie
 Syncopation 1929,Ap 8,32:1
 Lady of Scandal, The 1930,Je 14,9:4
 Sunny 1930,D 27,16:3
 Student's Romance, The 1936,O 12,23:2
 As You Like It 1936,N 6,29:3
 Laughter in Paradise 1951,N 12,21:2
Ward, Malvin (Screenwriter)
 Dark Past, The 1948,D 23,25:2
Ward, Mary Jane (Original Author)
 Snake Pit, the 1948,N 5,29:2
Ward, Michael
 Sleeping Car to Trieste 1949,Ap 18,18:6
 Trouble in Store 1956,Ja 14,13:2
 Carry on Cleo 1965,O 23,17:2
Ward, Patricia
 Fan, The 1949,Ap 2,12:2
Ward, Penelope Dudley
 Citadel, The 1938,N 4,27:2
 Hell's Cargo 1940,S 16,15:2
 Convoy 1941,Ja 17,21:2
 Frightened Lady 1941,N 10,21:3
 Adventure for Two 1945,D 14,24:5
 Her Man Gilbey 1949,Je 9,35:2
Ward, Perry William
 Foxes of Harrow, The 1947,S 25,35:4
Ward, Polly
 Old Curiosity Shop, The 1935,D 23,15:5
 Sidewalks of London 1940,F 15,15:1
 It's in the Air 1940,D 10,33:2
 New Faces 1954,F 20,8:7
Ward, Richard
 Black Like Me 1964,My 21,42:1
Ward, Robert
 Fascinating Youth 1926,My 10,19:1
Ward, Ronald
 Passing of the Third Floor Back, The
  1936,Ap 29,19:2
 East Meets West 1936,O 31,24:2
 Sidewalks of London 1940,F 15,15:1
 This England 1941,N 18,33:2
 Operation X 1950,D 11,31:2
Ward, Roscoe
 West of Zanzibar 1928,D 31,9:1
Ward, S J H (Producer)
 2nd Best Secret Agent in the Whole Wide World,
  The 1966,Ap 28,49:1
Ward, Skip
 Voyage to the Bottom of the Sea 1961,Jl 20,32:2
 Is Paris Burning? 1966,N 11,36:1
 Hombre 1967,Mr 22,41:1
 Easy Come, Easy Go 1967,Je 15,56:1

Ward, Solly
 Flight From Glory 1937,S 11,20:1
 Danger Patrol 1937,N 19,27:3
 She's Got Everything 1938,Ja 14,21:3
 Blind Alibi 1938,My 20,17:2
 Conspiracy 1939,Ag 23,19:2
Ward, Tiny
 Waning Sex, The 1926,S 21,33:1
Ward, Trevor
 Fan, The 1949,Ap 2,12:2
 My Cousin Rachel 1952,D 26,20:2
Ward, Valerie
 Lady From Paris, The 1927,S 28,28:3
Ward, Walter
 Boy Slaves 1939,F 9,17:3
Ward, Warwick
 Madame Sans Gene 1925,Ap 18,19:1
 Variety 1926,Je 28,15:5
 Woman Tempted, The 1928,Ap 24,29:3
 Eva and the Grasshopper 1928,N 19,16:7
 Looping the Loop 1929,F 11,26:3
 Dancer of Barcelona, The 1929,N 25,22:1
 White Sheik, The 1929,D 9,32:5
 After the Verdict 1930,Ja 18,21:1
 Strange Case of District Attorney M, The
  1930,Mr 17,20:3
 Wonderful Lies of Nova Petrova, The
  1930,Je 30,27:2
 Yellow Mask, The 1930,D 8,26:1
 Perfect Alibi, The 1931,Ap 20,16:3
 F P 1 1933,S 16,9:3
 Ariane 1934,Mr 7,23:4
Ward, Warwick (Producer)
 Man From Morocco, The 1946,N 25,38:2
 Quiet Week-End 1948,Ag 20,13:2
 My Brother Jonathan 1949,Je 29,34:4
 Dancing Years, The 1951,Ja 29,14:4
Ward, Warwick (Screenwriter)
 Man From Morocco, The 1946,N 25,38:2
 Quiet Week-End 1948,Ag 20,13:2
 Dancing Years, The 1951,Ja 29,14:4
Ward and Van
 Crazy House 1943,D 16,33:3
Warde, Anthony
 Law of the Underworld 1938,Ap 28,27:2
 Affairs of Annabel, The 1938,O 13,29:2
 Mr Moto Takes a Vacation 1939,Je 19,12:6
 Chip of the Flying U 1940,Ja 22,11:3
 So You Won't Talk 1940,O 17,33:2
 Where Are Your Children? 1944,Ja 17,14:5
 Are These our Parents? 1944,Ag 23,16:2
 Allotment Wives 1945,N 22,39:3
 Black Market Babies 1946,Ap 1,23:1
 High Tide 1947,N 8,11:2
 Atomic City, The 1952,My 2,21:1
Warde, Beatrice
 Outrage 1950,O 16,30:5
Warde, Bobby
 Fabulous Dorseys, The 1947,My 30,25:3
Warde, Ernest C (Director)
 Bells, The 1918,S 16,9:3
Warde, Frederick
 Vicar of Wakefield, The 1917,F 26,10:2
Warde, Harlan
 State Department-File 649 1949,F 21,20:2
 It's a Great Feeling 1949,Ag 13,6:6
 Task Force 1949,O 1,8:6
 Prison Warden 1949,O 21,31:2
 No Sad Songs for Me 1950,Ap 28,26:2
 Man Who Cheated Himself, The 1951,F 9,21:2
 Operation Secret 1952,N 6,37:2
 Julie 1956,N 22,51:1
 Hot Spell 1958,S 18,37:2
Warde, Shirley
 Devil Commands, The 1941,F 14,15:3
Warde, Shirley (Original Author)
 Trick for Trick 1933,Je 10,16:4
Wardell, Jane (Screenwriter)
 Yank in Vietnam, A 1964,F 6,36:4
Warden, Bruno Hardt (Screenwriter)
 Student's Romance, The 1936,O 12,23:2
Warden, Jack
 U S S Teakettle 1951,F 24,11:2
 Man With my Face, The 1951,Je 15,27:5
 Frogmen, The 1951,Je 30,8:6
 Edge of the City 1957,Ja 30,33:2
 Bachelor Party, The 1957,Ap 10,37:2
 12 Angry Men 1957,Ap 15,24:1
 Darby's Rangers 1958,F 13,23:2
 Run Silent, Run Deep 1958,Mr 28,29:1
 Sound and the Fury, The 1959,Mr 28,11:1
 That Kind of Woman 1959,S 12,12:2
 Wake Me When It's Over 1960,Ap 9,17:2
 Escape from Zahrain 1962,Jl 12,19:3
 Donovan's Reef 1963,Jl 25,14:1
 Thin Red Line, The 1964,O 29,38:1
 Bye Bye Braverman 1968,F 22,36:1
Warden, Jonathan
 Greetings 1968,D 16,61:2
Wardenburg, Fred (Director)
 Have You Heard of the San Francisco Mime
  Troup? 1968,Je 28,37:1

Wardenburg, Fred (Miscellaneous)
 Have You Heard of the San Francisco Mime
  Troup? 1968,Je 28,37:1
Wardenburg, Fred (Producer)
 Have You Heard of the San Francisco Mime
  Troup? 1968,Je 28,37:1
Wardord, William
 Hoodlum Priest, The 1961,Ap 3,28:5
Wardwell, Geoffrey
 Taming of the Shrew, The 1929,N 30,23:1
 Challenge, The 1939,O 2,15:2
WARE
 See Also WEAR
Ware, Darrell (Original Author)
 Life Begins In College 1937,O 9,16:1
 Big Town Girl 1937,D 13,23:4
 Charlie McCarthy, Detective 1939,D 25,29:2
Ware, Darrell (Screenwriter)
 Wife, Doctor and Nurse 1937,O 11,26:5
 Second Honeymoon 1937,N 13,11:2
 Just Around the Corner 1938,D 3,11:2
 He Married his Wife 1940,Ja 20,11:2
 Public Deb No 1 1940,S 18,19:2
 Down Argentine Way 1940,O 18,25:1
 Tall, Dark and Handsome 1941,Ja 24,15:2
 Yank in the R A F, A 1941,S 27,11:3
 Week-End in Havana 1941,N 8,11:2
 My Gal Sal 1942,My 1,23:1
 Orchestra Wives 1942,S 24,23:2
 Lucky Jordan 1943,Ja 25,10:8
 Dixie 1943,Je 24,26:2
 Standing Room Only 1944,F 23,17:2
 Bring on the Girls 1945,Mr 1,25:5
 Kitty 1946,Ap 1,23:1
 Love That Brute 1950,My 27,10:6
Ware, Harlan (Miscellaneous)
 Artists and Models 1937,Ag 5,19:2
Ware, Harlan (Original Author)
 Jam Session 1944,My 3,25:3
 Too Young to Know 1945,D 8,21:2
 Pardon my Past 1946,Ja 28,15:5
 Come Fill the Cup 1951,N 22,47:2
Ware, Harlan (Screenwriter)
 Yours for the Asking 1936,Ag 20,14:2
 College Holiday 1936,D 24,21:2
 Turn off the Moon 1937,My 20,17:2
 Vacation From Love 1938,N 10,33:2
Ware, Helen
 Napoleon's Barber 1928,N 26,30:2
 Speakeasy 1929,Mr 11,22:2
 Half Way to Heaven 1929,D 7,19:3
 Virginian, The 1929,D 23,18:2
 Slightly Scarlet 1930,Mr 1,23:1
 She's my Weakness 1930,Je 21,20:5
 Abraham Lincoln 1930,Ag 26,24:1
 Tol'able David 1930,N 17,29:1
 One Night at Susie's 1930,N 24,26:5
 I Take This Woman 1931,Je 13,20:4
 Reckless Hour, The 1931,Ag 1,16:4
 Night of June 13th, The 1932,S 17,18:4
 Ladies They Talk About 1933,F 25,20:4
 Keyhold, The 1933,Mr 31,23:3
 Girl Missing 1933,Ap 1,18:2
 Warrior's Husband, The 1933,My 12,20:4
 Sadie McKee 1934,My 18,18:3 (Incorrect in this
  edition; use 1934,My 19,18:3 elsewhere)
 Romance in Manhattan 1935,Ja 18,29:2
Ware, Irene
 Chandu the Magician 1932,O 1,10:4
 Six Hours to Live 1932,O 22,18:4
 Humanity 1933,Ap 22,16:3
 My Weakness 1933,S 22,14:1
 Brief Moment 1933,S 30,18:5
 Orient Express 1934,F 28,23:2
 Let's Talk It Over 1934,Je 16,20:2
 You Belong to Me 1934,S 13,26:1
 Night Life of the Gods 1935,F 23,14:6
 Raven, The 1935,Jl 5,9:2
 Whispering Smith Speaks 1936,F 17,21:1
 O'Malley of the Mounted 1936,Ap 6,18:1
 Gold Diggers of 1937 1936,D 25,19:2
 Outside the Three-Mile Limit 1940,Ap 8,15:2
Ware, Linda
 Star Maker, The 1939,Ag 31,14:2
 Gangs Incorporated 1941,Ag 4,16:6
Ware, Mary
 Crack-Up 1946,S 7,11:1
Ware, Midge
 Prince Who Was a Thief, The 1951,Jl 4,13:2
Wareing, Lesley
 Iron Duke, The 1935,Ja 25,27:2
Waren, Helen
 Curse of the Living Corpse, The 1964,Ap 30,30:1
Warfield, Chris
 Take the High Ground 1953,N 20,19:2
 Student Prince, The 1954,Je 16,18:2
 Incident in an Alley 1962,My 17,31:1
 Diary of a Madman 1963,Je 6,39:1
Warfield, William
 Show Boat 1951,Jl 20,14:1
Warfield, William (Narrator)
 Masters of the Congo Jungle 1960,My 5,41:2

Warga, Robin
  Sunrise at Campobello 1960,S 29,32:1
Warhol, Andy
  Illiac Passion, The 1968,Ap 19,40:1
Warhol, Andy (Cinematographer)
  My Hustler 1967,Jl 11,29:2
  I, A Man 1967,Ag 25,28:1
  Bike Boy 1967,O 6,31:2
  Nude Restaurant, The 1967,N 14,52:1
  **** 1967,D 17,94:5
Warhol, Andy (Director)
  Chelsea Girls, The 1966,D 2,46:1
  My Hustler 1967,Jl 11,29:2
  I, A Man 1967,Ag 25,28:1
  Bike Boy 1967,O 6,31:2
  Nude Restaurant, The 1967,N 14,52:1
  **** 1967,D 17,94:5
Warhol, Andy (Producer)
  More Milk, Yvette 1966,F 9,32:3
  My Hustler 1967,Jl 11,29:2
  Bike Boy 1967,O 6,31:2
  Nude Restaurant, The 1967,N 14,52:1
  Flesh 1968,S 27,36:1
Warhol, Andy (Screenwriter)
  I, A Man 1967,Ag 25,28:1
  Bike Boy 1967,O 6,31:2
  Nude Restaurant, The 1967,N 14,52:1
Waring, Barbara
  Hungry Hill 1947,O 11,11:2
Waring, Frances
  One Woman's Story 1949,My 18,33:2
  Dear Mr Prohack 1950,Jl 15,7:2
Waring, Fred
  Varsity Show 1937,S 2,17:2
Waring, George J Mgr
  Pope Speaks, The 1933,Ap 17,13:3 (In Addenda)
Waring, Herbert
  Sleeping Partners 1930,D 13,22:2
Waring, Joseph
  Jumbo 1962,D 7,49:1
Waring, Richard
  Perfect Gentleman, The 1935,D 19,33:4
  Mr Skeffington 1944,My 26,23:2
Wark, Robert
  Private Property 1960,Ap 25,40:2
Warker, Alfred (Director)
  Double Cross Roads 1930,Ap 29,31:1
Warm, Hermann (Miscellaneous)
  Cabinet of Dr Caligari, The 1921,Mr 20,VI,2:1
  Passion Of Joan Of Arc, The 1929,Mr 29,21:1
  Passion of Jeanne d'Arc, The 1929,Mr 31,VIII,7:1
Warmington, S J
  Escape 1930,N 1,23:2
  Woman Alone, The 1937,F 27,9:2
Warnecki, J (Director)
  Noc Listopadowa 1933,My 1,10:3
  Kazdemu Wolno Kochac 1933,My 24,24:3
Warner, Anne (Original Author)
  Rejuvenation of Aunt Mary, The 1927,Jl 27,27:4
Warner, Astrid
  Glory Stompers, The 1968,Mr 28,52:4
Warner, David
  Tom Jones 1963,O 8,48:1
  Morgan! 1966,Ap 5,42:2
  Bofors Gun, The 1968,S 23,42:3
  Fixer, The 1968,D 9,59:1
  Sea Gull, The 1968,D 24,14:1
Warner, David (Narrator)
  King's Story, A 1967,My 25,57:2
Warner, Douglas (Original Author)
  Underworld Informers 1965,O 14,53:1
Warner, Franklyn (Producer)
  Shadows Over Shanghai 1938,D 1,29:2
  Cipher Bureau 1938,D 14,32:6
Warner, H B
  Raiders, The 1916,F 28,7:2
  Market of Vain Desire, The 1916,My 15,7:1
  Man Who Turned White, The 1919,Je 2,20:4
  One Hour Before Dawn 1920,Jl 12,12:4
  Zaza 1923,S 17,18:2
  Silence 1926,My 19,29:3
  King of Kings, The 1927,Ap 20,29:2
  Sorrell and Son 1927,N 14,26:1
  French Dressing 1927,D 13,33:2
  Man Made Women 1928,S 18,33:2
  Doctor's Secret, The 1929,F 4,20:1
  Conquest 1929,F 11,26:3
  Divine Lady, The 1929,Mr 23,22:4
  Trial of Mary Dugan, The 1929,Mr 29,21:1
  Gamblers, The 1929,Ag 24,11:5
  Argyle Case, The 1929,Ag 31,13:4
  Show of Shows 1929,N 21,24:5
  Tiger Rose 1929,D 25,23:1
  Green Goddess, The 1930,F 14,20:1
  Furies, The 1930,Ap 19,15:1
  Wedding Rings 1930,My 10,25:3
  Wild Company 1930,Jl 19,7:5
  On Your Back 1930,S 15,29:3
  Liliom 1930,O 4,15:2
  Princess and the Plumber, The 1930,D 23,25:1
  Woman of Experience, A 1931,Jl 9,26:5
  Reckless Hour, The 1931,Ag 1,16:4
  Five Star Final 1931,S 11,24:2

Expensive Women 1931,N 14,15:3
Charlie Chan's Chance 1932,Ja 23,18:4
Woman Commands, A 1932,Ja 28,13:2
Menace, The 1932,Ja 30,13:2
Cross Examination 1932,F 27,22:1
Tom Brown of Culver 1932,Jl 30,16:5
Crusader, The 1932,O 8,15:4
Phantom of Crestwood, The 1932,O 17,18:3
Son-Daughter, The 1933,Ja 2,29:2
Supernatural 1933,Ap 22,16:3
Jennie Gerhardt 1933,Je 9,20:2
Christopher Bean 1933,N 25,10:2
Sorrell and Son 1934,My 29,22:1
Grand Canary 1934,Jl 20,11:1
Behold My Wife 1935,F 18,19:3
Tale of Two Cities, A 1935,D 26,21:2
Rose of the Rancho 1936,Ja 9,25:2
Garden Murder Case, The 1936,Mr 2,13:2
Moonlight Murder 1936,Mr 28,11:2
Mr Deeds Goes to Town 1936,Ap 17,17:2
Lost Horizon 1937,Mr 4,27:1
Victoria the Great 1937,O 29,19:1
Girl of the Golden West, The 1938,Mr 25,15:2
Kidnapped 1938,My 28,9:2
Toy Wife, The 1938,Je 24,15:1
Army Girl 1938,Ag 12,11:1
Bulldog Drummond in Africa 1938,Ag 25,15:1
You Can't Take It With You 1938,S 2,21:2
Arrest Bulldog Drummond 1939,Ja 12,23:2
Let Freedom Ring 1939,Mr 10,19:2
Bulldog Drummond's Secret Police
    1939,Mr 30,19:3
Gracie Allen Murder Case, The 1939,Je 8,31:3
Bulldog Drummond's Bride 1939,Jl 13,17:2
Rains Came, The 1939,S 9,11:2
Nurse Edith Cavell 1939,S 22,27:4
Mr Smith Goes to Washington 1939,O 20,27:2
New Moon 1940,Jl 19,22:2
Topper Returns 1941,Mr 28,26:6
Ellery Queen and the Perfect Crime
    1941,Ag 11,17:3
All That Money Can Buy 1941,O 17,27:2
South of Tahiti 1941,N 10,21:3
Corsican Brothers, The 1942,Ja 16,25:4
Crossroads 1942,Jl 27,18:2
Hitler's Children 1943,F 25,27:1
Action in Arabia 1944,F 19,18:7
Woman in Bondage 1944,Mr 27,17:2
Enemy of Women 1944,S 12,23:6
It's a Wonderful Life 1946,D 23,19:2
High Wall 1947,D 26,22:2
El Paso 1949,Mr 24,35:2
Hellfire 1949,My 30,9:4
Judge Steps Out, The 1949,Je 3,21:4
Sunset Boulevard 1950,Ag 11,15:2
First Legion, The 1951,Ap 28,9:2
Here Comes the Groom 1951,S 21,19:2
Journey Into Light 1951,O 5,24:4
Ten Commandments, The 1956,N 9,35:2
Adventures of Marco Polo, The 1965,Ap 8,17:2
Warner, J Wesley
  Scarlet Days 1919,N 10,18:2
Warner, Jack
  Captive Heart, The 1947,Ap 28,27:2
  Holiday Camp 1948,Ja 24,11:2
  Dear Murderer 1948,My 8,12:2
  Easy Money (Episode 1) 1949,F 14,15:3
  My Brothers Keeper 1949,F 14,15:3
  It Always Rains on Sunday 1949,F 14,15:5
  Against the Wind 1949,Je 27,18:3
  Here Come the Huggetts 1950,D 25,25:3
  Hue and Cry 1951,Ja 9,25:2
  Blue Lamp, The 1951,Ja 9,25:1
  Christmas Carol, A 1951,N 29,41:2
  Valley of the Eagles 1952,Ap 11,19:2
  You Can't Beat the Irish 1952,My 1,34:4
  Tonight at 8:30 (Ways and Means)
    1953,My 26,33:2
  Hundred Hour Hunt 1953,Je 17,32:2
  Final Test, The 1954,Ja 26,21:5
  Ladykillers 1956,F 21,37:2
Warner, Jack L (Producer)
  This Is the Army 1943,Jl 29,11:6
  My Fair Lady 1964,O 22,41:1
Warner, Jack M (Producer)
  Man Who Cheated Himself, The 1951,F 9,21:2
Warner, Jerry (Screenwriter)
  Cat Creeps, The 1946,My 18,12:4
  Inside Job 1946,Je 15,24:3
  Bringing Up Father 1946,N 22,27:3
Warner, John
  Midsummer Night's Dream, A 1961,D 19,39:1
Warner, Marguerite
  Confessions of a Co-Ed 1931,Je 20,20:4
Warner, Richard
  Othello 1960,My 16,39:1
  Village of the Damned 1960,D 8,43:3
Warner, Walter
  Mouthpiece, The 1932,Ap 21,25:2
Warrander, Harold
  Convoy 1941,Ja 17,21:2

Warre, Michael
  Henry V 1946,Je 18,30:2
  Reach for the Sky 1957,My 1,40:1
Warren, A E
  Unholy Three, The 1925,Ag 4,14:3
Warren, Barry
  Kiss of the Vampire 1963,O 10,49:2
Warren, Betty
  Magic Bow, The 1947,Jl 7,13:2
  Champagne Charlie 1948,Ag 7,8:2
  Passport to Pimlico 1949,O 27,35:2
  So Long at the Fair 1951,Ja 22,14:2
Warren, Bruce
  Unfaithful 1931,Mr 7,17:2
  Body and Soul 1931,Mr 14,23:2
  13 Hours by Air 1936,Ap 30,17:2
  Heroes of the Alamo 1938,Ap 2,18:2
Warren, C Denier
  Clairvoyant, The 1935,Je 8,12:2
  Spy of Napoleon 1939,Ag 19,18:4
  It's in the Air 1940,D 10,33:2
Warren, C Denier (Screenwriter)
  She Shall Have Music 1942,O 31,11:2
Warren, C E T (Original Author)
  Above Us the Waves 1957,Ap 18,35:2
Warren, Charles Marquis (Director)
  Little Big Horn 1951,Jl 27,15:2
  Arrowhead 1953,S 16,38:6
  Flight to Tangier 1953,N 26,50:4
  Seven Angry Men 1955,Ap 2,15:2
  Trooper Hook 1957,Jl 13,11:2
Warren, Charles Marquis (Original Author)
  Oh! Susanna 1951,Mr 30,28:5
  Only the Valiant 1951,Ap 14,9:6
  Fighting Coast Guard 1951,My 12,14:6
  Redhead and the Cowboy, The 1951,Je 6,37:2
  Woman of the North Country 1952,Ag 30,6:2
  Day of the Evil Gun 1968,Ap 25,53:2
Warren, Charles Marquis (Screenwriter)
  Beyond Glory 1948,Ag 4,18:2
  Streets of Laredo 1949,My 12,28:2
  Little Big Horn 1951,Jl 27,15:2
  Springfield Rifle 1952,O 23,40:2
  Pony Express 1953,Je 6,8:6
  Arrowhead 1953,S 16,38:6
  Flight to Tangier 1953,N 26,50:4
  Trooper Hook 1957,Jl 13,11:2
  Day of the Evil Gun 1968,Ap 25,53:2
Warren, E Allyn
  Hungry Hearts 1922,N 27,18:1
  Courtship of Myles Standish, The 1923,D 31,9:3
  Outside the Law 1926,My 12,31:1
  Born to the West 1926,Je 30,18:1 (In Addenda)
  Sweet Rosie O'Grady 1926,D 9,33:1
  Trail of '98, The 1928,Mr 21,30:3
  Son of the Gods 1930,Ja 31,24:1
  Abraham Lincoln 1930,Ag 26,24:1
  East Is West 1930,N 1,23:2
  Du Barry, Woman of Passion 1930,N 3,19:3
  Fighting Caravans 1931,Ja 26,21:1
  Shipmates 1931,My 23,13:4
  Daughter of the Dragon 1931,Ag 22,7:5
  Hatchet Man, The 1932,F 4,25:2
  Tarzan, The Fearless 1933,Ag 12,14:3
  Limehouse Blues 1934,D 12,28:2
  Chinatown Squad 1935,My 30,21:1
  Devil Doll, The 1936,Ag 8,5:2
  They Won't Forget 1937,Jl 15,16:1
  Port of Seven Seas 1938,Jl 15,13:2
Warren, Gil
  Cyrano De Bergerac 1950,N 17,31:2
Warren, Gloria
  Always in my Heart 1942,Mr 14,19:2
Warren, Harry
  42d Street 1933,Mr 10,19:3
Warren, Harry (Composer)
  42d Street 1933,Mr 10,19:3
  Gold Diggers of 1933 1933,Je 8,22:3
  Footlight Parade 1933,O 6,21:3
  Roman Scandals 1933,D 25,28:2
  Moulin Rouge 1934,F 8,14:4
  Wonder Bar 1934,Mr 1,23:2
  20 Million Sweethearts 1934,Ap 27,25:1
  Dames 1934,Ag 16,20:2
  Sweet Music 1935,F 21,23:2
  Gold Diggers of 1935 1935,Mr 15,25:2
  Go Into Your Dance 1935,My 4,17:2
  Shipmates Forever 1935,O 17,29:3
  Stars Over Broadway 1935,N 14,17:3

Warren, Harry (Composer)— Cont

Colleen 1936,Mr 9,20:2
Sons o'Guns 1936,My 14,29:2
Hearts Divided 1936,Je 13,13:1
Marked Woman 1937,Ap 12,15:2
Melody for Two 1937,My 21,19:5
Singing Marine, The 1937,Jl 1,33:2
Mr Dodd Takes the Air 1937,Ag 12,14:2
Gold Diggers in Paris 1938,Je 2,19:2
Cowboy From Brooklyn 1938,Jl 14,17:1
Garden of the Moon 1938,S 24,13:1
Going Places 1939,Ja 7,6:1
Honolulu 1939,F 23,19:2
Naughty but Nice 1939,Je 23,23:2
Young People 1940,Ag 24,16:2
Down Argentine Way 1940,O 18,25:1
Tin Pan Alley 1940,N 22,27:3
That Night in Rio 1941,Mr 10,21:2
Great American Broadcast, The 1941,My 2,25:2
Sun Valley Serenade 1941,S 6,20:1
Week-End in Havana 1941,N 8,11:2
Orchestra Wives 1942,S 24,23:2
Iceland 1942,O 15,27:1
Springtime in the Rockies 1942,N 12,30:2
Sweet Rosie O'Grady 1943,O 21,30:2
Gang's All Here, The 1943,D 23,26:4
Billy Rose's Diamond Horseshoe 1945,My 3,37:1
Yolanda and the Thief 1945,N 23,26:2
Harvey Girls, The 1946,Ja 25,26:2
Ziegfeld Follies 1946,Mr 23,8:3
Pagan Love Song 1950,D 26,19:1
Lullaby of Broadway 1951,Mr 27,35:2
Artists and Models 1955,D 22,20:1
Rock-a-Bye Baby 1958,Jl 24,18:1

Warren, Harry (Miscellaneous)
In Caliente 1935,Je 27,16:1
Broadway Gondolier 1935,Jl 18,15:2
Cain and Mabel 1936,O 19,22:1
Gold Diggers of 1937 1936,D 25,19:2
Sing Me a Love Song 1936,D 26,15:2

Warren, Harry (Screenwriter)
Varsity Show 1937,S 2,17:2

Warren, James
Seven Sweethearts 1942,N 13,28:1
Wanderer of the Wasteland 1945,S 29,12:2
Badman's Territory 1946,My 31,27:2
Judge Steps Out, The 1949,Je 3,21:4
Fourteen Hours 1951,Mr 7,43:2
3 for Bedroom C 1952,Je 27,18:3

Warren, Janet
Double Life, A 1948,F 20,19:1

Warren, Jill
Over my Dead Body 1942,D 26,15:2

Warren, John
Up the Creek 1958,N 11,26:2

Warren, John (Original Author)
Up the Creek 1958,N 11,26:2
Rotten to the Core 1965,Jl 20,39:2

Warren, John (Screenwriter)
Up the Creek 1958,N 11,26:2
Two-Way Stretch 1961,Ja 24,20:3
Wrong Arm of the Law, The 1963,Ap 3,39:1
Rotten to the Core 1965,Jl 20,39:2

Warren, Julie
Powder Town 1942,Je 8,11:2

Warren, Katherine
Mary Ryan, Detective 1949,N 4,33:3
All the King's Men 1949,N 9,37:2
And Baby Makes Three 1949,D 23,17:3
Three Secrets 1950,O 21,10:6
Harriet Craig 1950,N 3,31:2
Mystery Submarine 1951,F 2,19:2
Night Into Morning 1951,Je 11,20:7
Prowler, The 1951,Jl 2,16:6
Force of Arms 1951,Ag 14,20:2
Tall Target, The 1951,S 28,26:2
ThIs Woman is Dangerous 1952,F 28,23:2
Washington Story 1952,Jl 2,22:3
Star, The 1953,Ja 29,25:1
Glenn Miller Story, the 1954,F 11,33:2
Caine Mutiny, The 1954,Je 25,17:1
Inside Detroit 1956,Ja 28,10:5

Warren, Kenneth J
Small World of Sammy Lee, The 1963,Ag 14,28:1
High Wind in Jamaica, A 1965,Je 17,27:2
25th Hour, The 1967,F 17,45:1

Warren, Leonard
Irish Eyes Are Smiling 1944,N 8,27:1

Warren, Leslie Ann
Happiest Millionaire, The 1967,D 1,56:1
One and Only Genuine Original Family Band,
The 1968,Mr 22,55:1

Warren, Philip
Her Jungle Love 1938,Ap 14,27:2
Prison Farm 1938,Jl 15,13:3
Give Me a Sailor 1938,Ag 11,31:1
King of Alcatraz 1938,O 7,21:2
Illegal Traffic 1938,N 17,29:3
Undercover Doctor 1939,Je 1,31:2
Geronimo 1940,F 8,18:3
Badman's Territory 1946,My 31,27:2
Criminal Court 1946,N 16,15:3
Trail Street 1947,Ap 10,35:2

Warren, Robert Penn (Original Author)
All the King's Men 1949,N 9,37:2
Band of Angels 1957,Jl 11,21:1

Warren, Ruth
Lightnin' 1930,N 29,21:4
Mr Lemon of Orange 1931,Mr 28,15:3
Doctors' Wives 1931,Ap 25,23:4
Six Cylinder Love 1931,My 16,31:3
Annabelle's Affairs 1931,Je 29,20:3
Guilty Generation, The 1931,N 21,20:4
Devil's Lottery 1932,Ap 2,13:2
Zoo in Budapest 1933,Ap 28,15:2
Mama Loves Papa 1933,Jl 24,11:2
Doubting Thomas 1935,Jl 11,24:2
45 Fathers 1937,D 11,22:2
Prison Farm 1938,Jl 15,13:3
Union Pacific 1939,My 11,31:2
Cisco Kid and the Lady, The 1939,D 25,29:2
Bodyhold 1949,D 12,29:4
In a Lonely Place 1950,My 18,37:2
He's a Cockeyed Wonder 1950,O 20,32:4
Man in the Dark 1953,Ap 9,31:5
Last Hurrah, The 1958,O 24,40:1

Warren, Tony (Original Author)
Ferry Cross the Mersey 1965,F 20,16:2

Warren, Yvonne
Murder Reported 1960,Jl 12,39:1

Warrender, Harold
Day Dreams 1930,F 4,28:3
Mimi 1936,Ja 10,16:3
Invitation to the Waltz 1938,Jl 2,10:3
Conspirator 1950,Ap 28,26:2
Scott of the Antarctic 1951,F 26,20:2
Pandora and the Flying Dutchman 1951,D 7,35:2
Ivanhoe 1952,Ag 1,8:2
Ivory Hunter 1952,Ag 19,19:1
Intimate Relations 1954,F 22,15:4

Warrenton, Lulu
Sin That Was His, The 1920,D 6,19:1
Ladies Must Live 1921,N 21,20:1

Warrick, Ruth
Citizen Kane 1941,My 2,25:1
Corsican Brothers, The 1942,Ja 16,25:4
Obliging Young Lady 1942,F 13,24:4
Forever and a Day 1943,Mr 13,9:2
Journey Into Fear 1943,Mr 19,15:3
Iron Major, The 1943,N 1,12:5
Secret Command 1944,Je 14,16:2
Mr Winkle Goes to War 1944,Ag 3,16:1
Guest in the House 1945,F 16,19:2
China Sky 1945,My 25,22:3
Perilous Holiday 1946,Je 1,10:4
Song of the South 1946,N 28,40:2
Swell Guy 1947,Ja 27,17:2
Daisy Kenyon 1947,D 25,32:1
Great Dan Patch, The 1949,N 9,37:2
Beauty on Parade 1950,Ag 18,17:2
Let's Dance 1950,N 30,42:2
Three Husbands 1951,Mr 9,30:2
Ride Beyond Vengance 1966,S 29,60:1

Warrington, George
Road to Glory, The 1936,Ag 6,22:1

Warrington, Kenneth
U-Boat 29 1939,O 6,31:3
Ireland's Border Line 1939,O 13,27:3

Wars, Henryk (Miscellaneous)
Manewry Milosne 1936,N 11,55:1

Warsch, Anne Waldman
Edge, The 1968,Mr 28,52:1

Warshawsky, Curtis B (Original Author)
Can't Help Singing 1944,D 26,22:4

Warshawsky, Samuel J (Original Author)
Can't Help Singing 1944,D 26,22:4

Wartel, Kerstin
I, A Lover 1968,My 4,46:2

Warth, Theron (Producer)
Design for Death 1948,Je 11,27:2
Blood on the Moon 1948,N 12,30:5
Captive City, The 1952,Mr 27,34:2
Return to Paradise 1953,S 11,24:2

Warwick, Granville (Screenwriter)
Hun Within, The 1918,Ag 26,9:1

Warwick, Henry
Cheat, The 1931,D 12,23:3

Warwick, James (Original Author)
Blind Alley 1939,My 23,27:2
Dark Past, The 1948,D 23,25:2

Warwick, John
This Man Is News 1939,Jl 20,16:4
Saint's Vacation, The 1941,Je 13,22:2
Frightened Lady 1941,N 10,21:3
Avengers, The 1942,N 25,18:2
Horrors of the Black Museum 1959,Ap 30,37:2

Warwick, Noel
High School Girl 1935,Mr 16,19:1

Warwick, Robert
Secret Service 1919,Je 23,10:3
In Mizzoura 1919,O 13,16:3
City of Masks, The 1920,Jl 12,12:4
Royal Bed, The 1931,Ja 15,15:1
Three Rogues 1931,Ap 4,23:1
Holy Terror, A 1931,Jl 20,20:4
Woman From Monte Carlo, The 1931,D 31,17:6

Warwick, Robert— Cont

So Big 1932,Ap 30,19:3
Rich are Always With Us, The 1932,My 16,19:5
Dark Horse, The 1932,Je 9,27:3
Unashamed 1932,Jl 15,13:4
Doctor X 1932,Ag 4,17:2
Afraid to Talk 1932,D 19,19:5
Silver Dollar 1932,D 23,20:1
Frisco Jenny 1933,Ja 7,11:2
Ladies They Talk About 1933,F 25,20:4
Pilgrimage 1933,Jl 13,17:5
Charlie Chan's Greatest Case 1933,O 7,18:4
Cleopatra 1934,Ag 17,12:1
Dragon Murder Case, The 1934,Ag 23,13:3
Night Life of the Gods 1935,F 23,14:6
Shot in the Dark, A 1935,My 22,23:2
Tale of Two Cities, A 1935,D 26,21:2
Whipsaw 1936,Ja 25,18:4
Tough Guy 1936,Mr 14,10:1
Sutter's Gold 1936,Mr 27,25:2
Mary of Scotland 1936,Jl 31,22:2
Romeo and Juliet 1936,Ag 21,12:2
Adventure in Manhattan 1936,O 23,27:5
In His Steps 1936,O 29,31:1
Prince and the Pauper, The 1937,My 6,23:1
Let Them Live 1937,Je 8,30:3
Road Back, The 1937,Je 18,25:2
Life of Emile Zola, The 1937,Ag 12,14:2
Counsel for Crime 1937,O 9,16:1
Conquest 1937,N 5,19:1
Awful Truth, The 1937,N 5,19:3
Spy Ring, The 1938,Ja 15,19:1
Adventures of Robin Hood, The 1938,My 13,17:2
Blockade 1938,Je 17,25:1
Come on Leathernecks 1938,S 15,29:3
Gangster's Boy 1938,N 7,23:6
Going Places 1939,Ja 7,6:1
Juarez 1939,Ap 26,27:1
Magnificent Fraud, The 1939,Jl 20,16:2
Private Lives of Elizabeth and Essex, The
1939,D 2,21:2
Murder in the Air 1940,Jl 4,12:2
Devil's Island 1940,Jl 12,11:4
Woman's Face, A 1941,My 16,21:2
I Was a Prisoner on Devil's Island
1941,Jl 28,16:4
Sullivan's Travels 1942,Ja 29,25:2
I Married a Witch 1942,N 20,27:2
Palm Beach Story, The 1942,D 11,33:1
Secret Enemies 1943,Ja 1,27:3
Tennessee Johnson 1943,Ja 13,18:2
Man From Frisco 1944,Je 16,14:7
Bowery to Broadway 1944,N 30,19:2
Princess and the Pirate, The 1945,F 10,16:2
Sudan 1945,Ap 19,22:8
Criminal Court 1946,N 16,15:3
Falcon's Adventure, The 1946,D 14,19:2
Gentleman's Agreement 1947,N 12,36:2
Pirates of Monterey 1947,D 17,41:4
Fury at Furnace Creek 1948,Jl 12,11:2
Adventures of Don Juan 1948,D 25,10:1
Impact 1949,Mr 21,19:2
Francis 1950,Mr 16,40:2
In a Lonely Place 1950,My 18,37:2
Tarzan and the Slave Girl 1950,Je 24,7:3
Vendetta 1950,D 26,19:1
Sugarfoot 1951,F 12,19:4
Sword of Monte Cristo, The 1951,Ap 23,21:2
Mark of the Renegade 1951,S 7,24:2
Mississippi Gambler, The 1953,Ja 30,25:1
Salome 1953,Mr 25,37:1
Chief Crazy Horse 1955,Ap 28,25:1
Lady Godiva 1955,D 3,13:3
While the City Sleeps 1956,My 17,37:1
Walk the Proud Land 1956,S 8,20:6 (In
Addenda)
Buccaneer, The 1958,D 24,00:0
Night of the Quarter Moon 1959,Mr 5,35:5
It Started With a Kiss 1959,Ag 20,14:2

Warwick, Virginia
My Own Pal 1926,Mr 15,18:3
Four Horsemen of the Apocalypse, The
1926,S 27,27:3

Wascher, Aribert
Berliner, The 1952,O 28,37:1

Waschneck, Erich (Director)
Docks of Hamburg 1930,Jl 7,22:3
Alte Lied, Das 1931,S 11,24:2
Zwei Menschen 1931,D 23,27:3
Abel Mit Der Mundharmonika 1934,S 1,16:3
Mein Leben fuer Maria Isabell; My Life for Maria
Isabell 1935,N 5,33:5
Liebesleute 1936,O 3,21:2
Die Ganze Welt Dreht Sich um Liebe
1936,N 27,27:2
Divine Jetta, The 1937,O 2,18:2
For Her Country's Sake 1937,N 27,21:3
Winter Stuerme; Winter Storms 1938,O 1,10:2
Streitum den Knaben Jo; Strife Over the Boy Jo
1938,D 10,13:2

Waschneck, Erich (Producer)
Love Is A Lie 1928,Je 26,29:1

Washbourne, Mona
Maytime in Mayfair 1952,Ap 23,23:5
Cash on Delivery 1956,S 1,19:3
Cast a Dark Shadow 1957,N 28,57:1
It's Great to be Young 1957,D 26,23:3
Cry From the Streets, A 1959,F 24,32:2
Count Your Blessings 1959,Ap 24,23:1
Brides of Dracula, The 1960,S 6,41:4
Billy Liar 1963,D 17,49:1
Night Must Fall 1964,Mr 19,28:1
My Fair Lady 1964,O 22,41:1
Ferry Cross the Mersey 1965,F 20,16:2
One Way Pendulum 1965,Mr 3,34:3
Collector, The 1965,Je 18,28:1
Third Day, The 1965,Ag 5,15:3
Washbrook, Don
Lonelyhearts 1959,Mr 5,35:3
Washbrook, John
Lonelyhearts 1959,Mr 5,35:3
Washburn, Beverly
Here Comes the Groom 1951,S 21,19:2
Juggler, The 1953,My 6,39:2
Lone Ranger, The 1956,F 11,12:1
Old Yeller 1957,D 26,23:4
Summer Love 1958,Je 26,23:4
Washburn, Bryant
Till I Come Back to You 1918,Ag 26,9:1
Way of a Man With a Maid, The 1919,Ja 20,13:2
Why Smith Left Home 1919,O 13,16:3
What Happened to Jones 1920,Ag 9,6:3
Hungry Hearts 1922,N 27,18:1
Common Law, The 1923,O 29,18:1
Try and Get It 1924,Ap 2,16:1
Parasite, The 1925,F 16,24:1
Wizard of Oz, The 1925,Ap 14,26:1
Wet Paint 1926,My 17,19:1
Young April 1926,Ag 31,15:3
Love Thrill, The 1927,My 10,24:5
Beware of Widows 1927,My 24,23:4
Breakfast at Sunrise 1927,N 14,26:1
Skinner's big Idea 1928,Mr 27,30:4
Swing High 1930,Je 27,26:3
Kept Husbands 1931,Mr 24,31:2
What Price Innocence? 1933,Je 26,16:3
Devil's Mate 1933,S 23,11:7
World Accuses, The 1935,Mr 21,27:2
Preview Murder Mystery, The 1936,Mr 21,13:2
Sutter's Gold 1936,Mr 27,25:2
Hollywood Boulevard 1936,S 21,26:4
Conflict 1937,Ja 18,21:2
Sea Racketeers 1937,O 4,17:2
Gangs Incorporated 1941,Ag 4,16:6
Sin Town 1942,O 17,11:2
Two O'Clock Courage 1945,Ap 14,13:3
Further Perils of Laurel and Hardy, The 1968,Ap 1,56:6
Washburn, Bryant Jr
Daring Daughters 1933,Mr 25,13:4
Washburn, Conway
Street Scene 1931,Ag 27,22:5
Counsellor-At-Law 1933,D 8,31:2
Washburn, Ralph
Passionate Youth 1925,Je 30,14:3
Washburn, Richard (Original Author)
Mad Whirl, The 1925,Jl 1,16:1
Washington, Blue
Blood Ship, The 1927,Jl 19,27:2
Haunted Ship, The 1928,Ja 23,18:3
Beggars of Life 1928,S 24,25:1
Washington, Booker T 3d
George Washington Carver 1940,Ap 17,26:4
Washington, Dinah
Jazz on a Summer's Day 1960,Mr 29,46:2
Washington, Ford L
Cabin in the Sky 1943,My 28,19:3
Washington, Fredi
Emperor Jones, The 1933,S 20,26:2
Imitation of Life 1934,N 24,19:1
One Mile From Heaven 1937,Ag 19,23:1
Washington, Hannah
Littlest Rebel, The 1935,D 20,30:1
Washington, Hazel
Imitation of Life 1934,N 24,19:1
Washington, Jurmann (Composer)
Night at the Opera, A 1935,D 7,22:1
Washington, Kenny
Foxes of Harrow, The 1947,S 25,35:4
Rogues' Regiment 1948,D 20,31:2
Rope of Sand 1949,Ag 4,19:2
Pinky 1949,S 30,28:2
Jackie Robinson Story, The 1950,My 17,36:1
Washington, Mildred
Hearts in Dixie 1929,F 28,30:3
Washington, Ned (Composer)
Night at the Opera, A 1935,D 7,22:1
Perfect Gentleman, The 1935,D 19,33:4
Hit Parade, The 1937,My 31,11:2
Romance in the Dark 1938,Mr 21,18:2
Pinocchio 1940,F 8,18:3
I Wanted Wings 1941,Mr 27,29:4
Brazil 1944,N 20,25:2
Mexicana 1945,N 17,14:6
Three for the Show 1955,F 25,16:1

Timberjack 1955,Mr 10,33:3
Washington, Ned (Miscellaneous)
Dumbo 1941,O 24,27:2
Wasilewska, Wanda (Screenwriter)
Rainbow, The 1944,O 23,14:3
Wasley, Andre
Devil's Daughter 1949,F 26,11:2
Forbidden Games 1952,D 9,43:2
Gervaise 1957,N 12,46:1
Wassam, Rebecca
Once to Every Woman 1934,Mr 26,22:3
Wassel, Dick
Pitfall 1948,Ag 25,31:2
Wassell, Dr (Original Author)
Story of Dr Wassell, The 1944,Je 7,13:2
Wasserman, Dale (Screenwriter)
Vikings, The 1952,Je 12,35:2
Quick, Before it Melts 1965,Ap 1,30:2
Mister Buddwing 1966,O 12,36:1
Wassermann, H (Director)
Fremd im Sudetenland; Strange to the Sudeten Country 1938,N 5,15:3
Wassermann, Jacob (Original Author)
Masks of the Devil, The 1928,N 26,30:2
Wassermann, W (Original Author)
Rheinlandmaedel, Das 1931,S 18,29:1
Wassil, Charles
Trap, The 1959,Ja 29,18:4
Wassmann, Hans
Meistersinger 1929,D 16,34:2
Schlacht von Bademuende, Die 1931,N 21,20:4
Der Storch Streikt 1932,My 2,13:2
Wastenson, Barbro
To Bed...Or not to Bed 1963,D 23,18:2
Wastenson, Monica
To Bed...Or not to Bed 1963,D 23,18:2
Waszynski, Michael (Director)
Parada Rezerwistow 1934,My 1,26:6
Prokurator 1934,My 22,28:4
Kocha, Lubi, Szanuje 1934,N 3,20:4
Dodek na Froncie 1936,Mr 30,17:6
Bedzie Lepiej 1937,Mr 30,20:1
Dybbuk, The 1938,Ja 28,17:2
Znachor; Miracle Man, The 1938,F 21,15:2
Znachor 1938,N 24,37:2
Rena 1939,Ja 27,17:3
Wata, Sussie
Veil of Happiness, The 1928,My 1,33:3
Watanabe, Misako
Kwaidan (Black Hair); Black Hair (Kwaidan) 1965,N 23,51:1
Water Waltzers
Artists and Models 1937,Ag 5,19:2
Waterfield, Robert (Producer)
Gentlemen Marry Brunettes 1955,O 31,31:5
Fuzzy Pink Nightgown, The 1957,O 31,41:1
Waterhouse, Keith (Original Author)
Billy Liar 1963,D 17,49:1
Waterhouse, Keith (Screenwriter)
Whistle Down the Wind 1962,Ap 23,34:2
Valiant, The 1962,Je 14,23:4
Kind of Loving, A 1962,O 2,46:1
Billy Liar 1963,D 17,49:1
Man in the Middle 1964,Mr 5,36:1
Matter of Innocence, A 1968,F 22,36:1
Waterman, Dennis
Up the Junction 1968,Mr 14,51:1
Waterman, Ida
Lady Rose's Daughter 1920,Ag 30,12:3
Love's Redemption 1922,Ja 9,15:2
Society Scandal, A 1924,Mr 10,18:2
Enchanted Cottage, The 1924,Ap 14,14:1
Swan, The 1925,Mr 2,14:1
That Royle Girl 1926,Ja 4,33:1
Social Celebrity, A 1926,Ap 19,24:3
Say It Again 1926,Je 7,23:2
Waterman, Willard
Riding High 1950,Ap 11,26:2
Mystery Street 1950,Jl 28,12:5
Louisa 1950,O 25,45:2
Rhubarb 1951,Ag 31,12:2
Auntie Mame 1958,D 5,39:1
WATERS
See Also WATTERS
Waters, Bunny
Broadway Rhythm 1944,Ap 14,24:6
Maisie Goes to Reno 1944,S 29,18:1
Dangerous When Wet 1953,Je 19,18:1
Pepe 1960,D 22,18:1
Waters, Ed (Screenwriter)
Man Trap 1961,N 30,40:4
Caper of the Golden Bulls, The 1967,Je 22,46:1
Waters, Ethel
On With the Show 1929,My 29,28:6
Gift of Gab 1934,S 26,17:6
Tales of Manhattan 1942,S 25,25:1
Cairo 1942,N 6,27:2
Cabin in the Sky 1943,My 28,19:3
Stage Door Canteen 1943,Je 25,13:2
Pinky 1949,S 30,28:2
Member of the Wedding, The 1952,D 31,10:2
Sound and the Fury, The 1959,Mr 28,11:1

Waters, Frank (Original Author)
River Lady 1948,My 21,19:5
Waters, George W (Screenwriter)
Why Must I Die? 1960,S 15,45:4
Waters, James
Anatomy of a Murder 1959,Jl 3,10:1
Waters, Jim (Producer)
Man Called Adam, A 1966,Ag 4,24:2
Waters, John (Director)
Born to the West 1926,Je 30,18:1 (In Addenda)
Two Flaming Youths 1928,Ja 2,28:1
Beau Sabreur 1928,Ja 23,18:3
Mighty McGurk, The 1947,Ap 4,19:4
Waters, Russell
Woman in the Hall, The 1949,Ja 24,16:2
Blue Lagoon, The 1949,O 3,13:2
Hidden Room, The 1950,Ja 9,19:2
Dear Mr Prohack 1950,Jl 15,7:2
Brave Don't Cry, The 1952,N 6,37:2
Miss Robin Hood 1953,Je 27,7:2
Mr Denning Drives North 1953,S 2,20:1
Turn the Key Softly 1954,F 4,21:6
Rob Roy 1954,F 4,21:5
Key, The 1958,Jl 2,23:3
Yesterday's Enemy 1960,Mr 4,19:1
Watkin, Lawrence Edward (Original Author)
On Borrowed Time 1939,Jl 7,13:2
Great Locomotive Chase, The 1956,Je 27,35:1
Watkin, Lawrence Edward (Producer)
Great Locomotive Chase, The 1956,Je 27,35:1
Watkin, Lawrence Edward (Screenwriter)
Treasure Island 1950,Ag 16,24:2
Story of Robin Hood, The 1952,Je 27,18:3
Sword and the Rose, The 1953,Ag 20,18:3
Rob Roy 1954,F 4,21:5
Light in the Forest, The 1958,Jl 11,15:2
Darby O'Gill and the Little People 1959,Jl 1,26:1
Watkin, Pierre
Dangerous 1935,D 27,14:1
It Had to Happen 1936,F 15,18:6
Nobody's Fool 1936,Je 4,27:2
Bunker Bean 1936,Je 27,21:2
Forgotten Faces 1936,Jl 4,18:2
Counterfeit 1936,Jl 20,11:1
Swing Time 1936,Ag 28,21:2
Green Light 1937,F 13,9:1
Devil's Playground 1937,F 15,12:5
Internes Can't Take Money 1937,My 6,23:2
Hit Parade, The 1937,My 31,11:2
Ever Since Eve 1937,Je 25,25:2
Stage Door 1937,O 8,27:2
Breakfast for Two 1937,N 20,21:2
Daughter of Shanghai 1937,D 24,21:2
Tip-Off Girls 1938,Mr 25,15:3
Mr Moto's Gamble 1938,Ap 8,17:2
There's Always a Woman 1938,Ap 29,17:2
Chaser, The 1938,Ag 2,15:3
Mr Doodle Kicks Off 1938,S 28,29:4
Young Doctor Kildare 1938,O 28,27:1
Girls' School 1938,N 3,27:1
Illegal Traffic 1938,N 17,29:3
There's That Woman Again 1939,Ja 6,25:4
Wings of the Navy 1939,F 4,11:1
Off the Record 1939,F 18,12:2
Risky Business 1939,Mr 23,27:2
They Made Her a Spy 1939,Mr 29,21:4
Society Lawyer 1939,Mr 31,19:2
Death of a Champion 1939,Ag 24,17:3
Mr Smith Goes to Washington 1939,O 20,27:2
Great Victor Herbert, The 1939,D 7,35:1
Geronimo 1940,F 8,18:3
Saint Takes Over, The 1940,My 28,29:3
I Love You Again 1940,Ag 16,11:2
Rhythm on the River 1940,Ag 29,23:2
Bank Dick, The 1940,D 13,29:2
Life With Henry 1941,F 6,25:2
Trial of Mary Dugan, The 1941,Mr 6,25:4
Meet John Doe 1941,Mr 13,25:2
Man Betrayed, A 1941,Mr 27,29:5
Naval Academy 1941,Je 5,27:3
She Knew All the Answers 1941,Je 20,28:4
Adventure in Washington 1941,Ag 1,11:3
Great Guns 1941,O 3,27:2
Adventures of Martin Eden 1942,Mr 16,19:2
Pride of the Yankees, The 1942,Jl 16,23:1
Whistling in Dixie 1942,D 31,20:4
Swing Shift Maisie 1943,S 10,29:2
Bermuda Mystery 1944,My 13,17:1
Dead Man's Eyes 1944,O 7,11:2
Over 21 1945,Ag 17,20:2
Dakota 1945,D 17,17:2
Little Giant 1946,My 9,27:5
Claudia and David 1946,Ag 15,19:2
Swamp Fire 1946,Ag 26,21:4
Shocking Miss Pilgrim, The 1947,F 12,34:2
Violence 1947,My 10,8:5
Sioux City Sue 1947,Jl 23,19:3
Red Stallion 1947,N 27,50:3
State of the Union 1948,Ap 23,28:1
Innocent Affair, An 1948,S 29,36:2
Zamba 1949,N 7,33:2
Story of Seabiscuit, The 1949,N 12,8:4
Blue Grass of Kentucky 1950,Ja 27,29:2

Watkin, Pierre— Cont

Big Hangover, The 1950,My 26,20:3
Rock Island Trail 1950,Je 5,19:3
Last of the Buccaneers 1950,D 15,43:2
Second Face, The 1951,Mr 2,21:3
Scandal Sheet 1952,Ja 17,23:1
Stranger Wore a Gun, The 1953,Jl 30,20:3
About Mrs Leslie 1954,Je 28,16:2
Maverick Queen, the 1956,Je 4,25:2

Watkins, Linda

Sob Sister 1931,O 3,20:2
Good Sport 1931,D 12,23:3
Charlie Chan's Chance 1932,Ja 23,18:4
Cheaters at Play 1932,F 27,22:1
Gay Caballero, The 1932,Mr 26,17:2
Ten North Frederick 1958,My 23,29:2
Parent Trap, The 1961,Je 22,23:1
Good Neighbor Sam 1964,Jl 23,19:1

Watkins, Maurine (Original Author)

Chicago 1927,D 24,9:1
Play Girl 1932,Mr 19,11:2
Strange Love of Molly Louvain, The
1932,My 9,19:5
Professional Sweetheart 1933,Jl 14,15:3
Search for Beauty 1934,F 10,20:2
Up the River 1938,D 3,11:2
I Love You Again 1940,Ag 16,11:2
Roxie Hart 1942,F 20,21:1
Easy to Wed 1946,Jl 12,14:2

Watkins, Maurine (Screenwriter)

Up the River 1930,O 11,21:3
Libeled Lady 1936,O 31,24:2

Watkins, Peter

War Game, The 1966,S 14,53:2

Watkins, Peter (Director)

Privilege 1967,Jl 25,30:2

Watkins, Peter (Producer)

War Game, The 1967,Mr 20,26:5

Watle, Sarita

Escuadron Azul, El; Blue Squadron, The
1938,Je 4,18:3

Watling, Jack

Adventure for Two 1945,D 14,24:5
Journey Together 1946,Mr 4,16:5
Easy Money (Episode 1) 1949,F 14,15:3
Quartet (The Facts of Life); Facts of Life, The
(Quartet) 1949,Mr 29,30:3
Under Capricorn 1949,S 9,28:3
Winslow Boy, The 1950,Je 7,34:4
Kathy's Love Affair 1952,Jl 3,16:2
White Corridors 1952,Jl 16,21:1
Naked Heart, The 1955,Mr 9,22:4
Reach for the Sky 1957,My 1,40:1
Gideon of Scotland Yard 1959,My 20,38:2
Sink the Bismarck! 1960,F 12,22:3
Three on a Spree 1961,Ag 31,22:3
Mr Arkadin 1962,O 12,26:1
Nanny, The 1965,N 4,57:2

Watson, Adele

Welcome Home 1925,My 18,12:1
Rolling Home 1926,Je 8,22:1
Jazz Heaven 1929,O 30,29:2
This Thing Called Love 1929,D 14,22:4
Street Scene 1931,Ag 27,22:5
Compromised 1931,N 7,16:5
Expensive Women 1931,N 14,15:3
Arrowsmith 1931,D 8,36:4
Purchase Price, The 1932,Jl 16,5:5
Pack up Your Troubles 1932,O 1,10:4

Watson, Ben

Across the Wide Missouri 1951,N 7,35:4

Watson, Billy

Little Minister, The 1934,D 28,25:1
Winning Ticket, The 1935,F 11,14:2
In Old Chicago 1938,Ja 7,15:2
Kidnapped 1938,My 28,9:2

Watson, Bobby

That Royle Girl 1926,Ja 4,33:1
Song and Dance Man, The 1926,F 1,16:1
Syncopation 1929,Ap 8,32:1
Follow the Leader 1930,D 6,21:3
Manhattan Parade 1931,D 25,29:2
High Pressure 1932,F 1,22:3
Moonlight and Pretzels 1933,Ag 23,21:2
Going Hollywood 1933,D 23,19:2
Wine, Women and Song 1934,Mr 21,24:3
Society Doctor 1935,F 4,11:3
Torchy Blane, The Adventurous Blonde
1937,D 18,18:1
You're a Sweetheart 1937,D 25,10:5
In Old Chicago 1938,Ja 7,15:2
Boys Town 1938,S 9,25:1
Kentucky 1938,D 24,12:1
Story of Alexander Graham Bell, The
1939,Ap 1,17:2
Dodge City 1939,Ap 8,19:1
On Borrowed Time 1939,Jl 7,13:2
Blackmail 1939,S 15,26:3
Everything's on Ice 1939,O 6,31:1
Wyoming 1940,O 3,31:4
Dr Kildare's Crisis 1940,D 19,33:1
Men of Boys Town 1941,Ap 11,24:6
Hit the Road 1941,Jl 3,15:3
Devil With Hitler, The 1942,O 19,15:2

Hitler-Dead or Alive 1943,Mr 31,23:3
That Nazty Nuisance 1943,My 29,10:3
Hitler Gang, The 1944,My 8,15:2
Hold That Blonde 1945,N 8,17:2
Paleface, The 1948,D 16,41:2
Copper Canyon 1950,N 16,39:2

Watson, Bruce

This Property is Condemned 1966,Ag 4,24:1

Watson, Caven

Vacation From Marriage 1946,Mr 15,27:2

Watson, Coy

Smart Set, The 1928,Mr 5,21:1
Restless Youth 1929,Ja 1,60:1

Watson, Debbie

Munster, Go Home 1966,Je 16,53:4
Cool Ones, The 1967,My 11,50:1

Watson, Delmar

Outside the Law 1930,S 1,16:1
Compromised 1931,N 7,16:5
Right to Romance, The 1933,D 15,28:2
Annie Oakley 1935,D 24,10:5
Silly Billies 1936,Ap 6,18:1
Old Hutch 1936,D 7,27:4
Heidi 1937,N 6,14:2
Hunted Men 1938,My 21,9:2
Kentucky 1938,D 24,12:1

Watson, Douglas

Soyonara 1957,D 6,39:4
Sayonara 1957,D 6,39:4

Watson, Fred

Children on Trial 1947,N 10,21:3

Watson, General Mrs

Festival 1967,O 24,53:2

Watson, Harry

Little Old New York 1923,Ag 2,10:3
Great White Way, The 1924,Ja 4,10:1
Zander the Great 1925,My 4,16:2
Old Hutch 1936,D 7,27:4
Penrod and Sam 1937,Mr 29,14:3
Damsel in Distress, A 1937,N 25,37:1

Watson, Henrietta

Collision 1932,F 21,VIII,5:2 (In Addenda)
Mister Hobo 1936,F 8,19:2

Watson, Jack

This Sporting Life 1963,Jl 17,19:2
Master Spy 1964,Ag 20,34:2
Hill, The 1965,O 4,00:0
Idol, The 1966,Ag 11,27:1
Grand-Prix 1966,D 22,40:1
Tobruk 1967,F 9,33:2
Devil's Brigade, The 1968,My 23,56:2
Strange Affair, The 1968,Jl 25,26:2

Watson, Justice

Death of a Scoundrel 1956,N 6,30:1

Watson, Lucile

What Every Woman Knows 1934,O 27,20:2
Woman Rebels, A 1936,O 30,27:2
Garden of Allah, The 1936,N 20,27:2
Three Smart Girls 1937,Ja 25,22:2
Young in Heart, The 1938,N 4,27:2
Young in Heart, The 1938,N 4,27:2
Sweethearts 1938,D 23,16:2
Made for Each Other 1939,F 17,17:2
Women, The 1939,S 22,27:2
Waterloo Bridge 1940,My 17,23:2
Florian 1940,Je 6,33:2
Mr and Mrs Smith 1941,F 21,16:3
Footsteps in the Dark 1941,Mr 15,13:2
Rage in Heaven 1941,Mr 21,19:2
Great Lie, The 1941,Ap 12,19:2
Model Wife 1941,Ap 24,25:3
Watch on the Rhine 1943,Ag 28,15:1
Uncertain Glory 1944,Ap 8,9:2
Till We Meet Again 1944,Ag 30,15:1
Thin Man Goes Home, The 1945,Ja 26,16:5
My Reputation 1946,Ja 26,19:2
Tomorrow Is Forever 1946,F 22,21:2
Razor's Edge, The 1946,N 20,42:2
Never Say Goodbye 1946,N 23,12:2
Song of the South 1946,N 28,40:2
Ivy 1947,Je 26,19:1
Emperor Waltz, The 1948,Je 18,19:2
Julia Misbehaves 1948,O 8,30:2
That Wonderful Urge 1948,D 22,29:6
Little Women 1949,Mr 11,33:2
Everybody Does It 1949,O 26,32:2
Harriet Craig 1950,N 3,31:2
Let's Dance 1950,N 30,42:2
My Forbidden Past 1951,Ap 26,34:2

Watson, Minor

Twenty-Four Hours 1931,O 3,20:2
Our Betters 1933,F 24,13:2
Another Language 1933,Ag 5,9:5
Pursuit of Happiness, The 1934,O 26,25:1
Charlie Chan in Paris 1935,Ja 22,23:2
Age of Indiscretion 1935,My 18,21:2
Mr Dynamite 1935,My 25,12:1
Lady Tubbs 1935,Jl 22,20:2
Annapolis Farewell 1935,Ag 24,18:2
Rose of the Rancho 1936,Ja 9,25:2
When's Your Birthday? 1937,Mr 19,27:2
Woman I Love, The 1937,Ap 16,27:2
Dead End 1937,Ag 25,25:1

Watson, Minor— Cont

That Certain Woman 1937,S 16,29:1
Saturday's Heroes 1937,O 16,22:2
Navy Blue and Gold 1937,D 24,21:2
Of Human Hearts 1938,F 18,23:1
Love, Honor and Behave 1938,Mr 21,18:2
Fast Company 1938,Jl 6,21:2
Boys Town 1938,S 9,25:1
Stablemates 1938,O 21,27:2
Touchdown Army 1938,O 28,27:2
While New York Sleeps 1938,D 22,25:3
Huckleberry Finn 1939,Mr 3,21:2
Flying Irishman, The 1939,Ap 12,27:2
Hardys Ride High, The 1939,Ap 14,28:2
Maisie 1939,Je 23,23:1
News Is Made at Night 1939,Jl 13,17:2
Angels Wash Their Faces 1939,S 4,16:2
Here I Am a Stranger 1939,S 30,11:2
Abe Lincoln in Illinois 1940,F 23,19:2
Viva Cisco Kid 1940,Mr 22,23:4
Twenty-Mule Team 1940,My 10,26:6
Young People 1940,Ag 24,16:2
Rangers of Fortune 1940,S 19,27:2
Gallant Sons 1940,D 12,37:2
Western Union 1941,F 7,23:2
Mr District Attorney 1941,Ap 17,29:3
Moon Over Miami 1941,Jl 5,14:2
Parson of Panamint, The 1941,Jl 26,18:2
Kiss the Boys Goodbye 1941,Ag 14,21:2
They Died With Their Boots On 1941,N 21,23:3
Birth of the Blues 1941,D 11,39:1
Woman of the Year 1942,F 6,23:2
Frisco Lil 1942,F 12,27:2
Remarkable Andrew, The 1942,Mr 6,17:2
To the Shores of Tripoli 1942,Mr 26,27:2
Yankee Doodle Dandy 1942,My 30,9:1
Big Shot, The 1942,Jl 18,8:2
Flight Lieutenant 1942,Jl 31,11:1
Enemy Agents meet Ellery Queen
1942,Ag 22,16:2
Gentleman Jim 1942,N 26,40:3
Crash Dive 1943,Ap 29,25:2
Mission to Moscow 1943,Ap 30,25:2
Princess O'Rourke 1943,N 6,16:2
Guadalcanal Diary 1943,N 18,29:1
Falcon out West, The 1944,Mr 18,18:2
Shadows in the Night 1944,Jl 29,16:2
God is my Co-Pilot 1945,Mr 24,22:6
You Came Along 1945,Jl 5,7:2
Bell for Adano, A 1945,Jl 6,8:3
Bewitched 1945,Ag 17,20:3
Courage of Lassie 1946,Jl 25,18:5
Boy's Ranch 1946,Ag 9,12:2
Southern Yankee, A 1948,N 25,47:2
Beyond the Forest 1949,O 22,11:2
Thelma Jordon 1950,Ja 19,35:2
Jackie Robinson Story, The 1950,My 17,36:1
Mister 880 1950,S 30,13:2
Bright Victory 1951,Ag 1,19:2
As Young as You Feel 1951,Ag 3,10:6
Little Egypt 1951,Ag 30,20:3
My Son John 1952,Ap 9,27:1
Untamed Frontier 1952,Ag 23,10:2
Bride Comes to Yellow Sky, The 1953,Ja 14,27:2
Star, The 1953,Ja 29,25:1
Trapeze 1956,Je 5,39:2
Rawhide Years, The 1956,Je 16,12:2
Ambassador's Daughter, The 1956,Ag 30,19:1

Watson, Moray

Grass is Greener, The 1960,D 24,8:2
Operation Crossbow 1965,Ap 2,29:1

Watson, Norman

Guinea Pig, The 1949,My 2,20:2

Watson, Wylie

Thirty-Nine Steps, The 1935,S 14,8:4
Gaiety Girls, The 1938,Mr 31,15:1
Jamaica Inn 1939,O 12,33:1
Waltz Time 1946,F 11,25:2
Years Between, The 1947,Mr 10,25:2
Tawny Pipit 1947,S 8,25:5
Dulcimer Street 1948,N 8,24:2
Don't Take it to Heart 1948,D 25,10:3
Fame Is the Spur 1949,N 8,34:2
No Room at the Inn 1949,D 26,33:4
Tight Little Island 1949,D 26,33:2
Girl in a Million, A 1950,Jl 24,15:2
Eye Witness 1950,Ag 28,13:2
Operation Disaster 1951,Ja 15,13:1
Magnet, The 1951,F 27,22:6
Happy Go Lovely 1951,Jl 26,17:2
Young Scarface 1951,N 8,35:2
Sundowners, The 1960,D 9,39:1

Watt, Harry (Director)

Target for Tonight 1941,O 18,22:2
Overlanders, The 1946,D 20,31:2
Massacre Hill 1950,D 14,51:3
Ivory Hunter 1952,Ag 19,19:1
West of Zanzibar 1955,Ja 18,31:2

Watt, Harry (Original Author)

Overlanders, The 1946,D 20,31:2
Ivory Hunter 1952,Ag 19,19:1

Watt, Harry (Screenwriter)

Target for Tonight 1941,O 18,22:2
Massacre Hill 1950,D 14,51:3

Watteaux, Giles
 Sextette (Part 3-The Key to Sin); Key to Sin, The (Sextette) 1953,Mr 2,19:2
WATTERS
 See Also WATERS
Watters, George M (Original Author)
 Swing High, Swing Low 1937,Ap 15,19:1
 When my Baby Smiles at Me 1948,N 24,20:2
Wattis, Richard
 Happiest Days of Your Life, The 1950,S 18,19:2
 Importance of Being Earnest, The 1952,D 23,17:2
 Mr Potts Goes to Moscow 1953,S 3,15:2
 Hobson's Choice 1954,Je 15,37:1
 Man Who Knew too Much, The 1956,My 17,37:1
 Iron Petticoat, The 1957,F 2,12:2
 Prince and the Showgirl 1957,Je 14,22:2
 Alligator Named Daisy, An 1957,O 7,23:2
 Silken Affair, The 1957,O 31,41:1
 Blue Murder at St Trinian's 1958,My 27,27:1
 Second to Hell 1959,Jl 18,6:3
 Captain's Table, The 1960,S 27,40:1
 Left, Right and Centre 1961,F 10,19:1
 Follow a Star 1961,Ap 26,34:1
 Nearly a Nasty Accident 1962,Je 28,21:2
 Coming-Out Party, A 1962,Jl 31,19:2
 Come Fly With Me 1963,My 2,40:2
 V I P's, The 1963,S 20,29:1
 Operation Crossbow 1965,Ap 2,29:1
Watts, Charles
 Just This Once 1952,Mr 18,22:3
 Wait Till the Sun Shines, Nellie 1952,Je 28,12:2
 Million Dollar Mermaid 1952,D 5,35:2
 Giant 1956,O 11,51:1
 Spirit of St Louis, The 1957,F 22,25:1
 Affair to Remember, An 1957,Jl 20,8:5
 Don't Go Near the Water 1957,N 15,37:1
 Big Circus, The 1959,Jl 18,6:1
 Ada 1961,Ag 26,15:1
 Something Wild 1961,D 24,30:6
 Lover Come Back 1962,F 9,21:1
 Jumbo 1962,D 7,49:1
 Wheeler Dealers, The 1963,N 15,25:2
 Baby, the Rain Must Fall 1965,Ja 14,44:1
Watts, Dodo
 Middle Watch, The 1930,D 20,20:6
 Almost a Honeymoon 1931,Ja 10,19:2
 Man From Chicago, The 1931,Ja 16,27:1
Watts, George
 Soak the Rich 1936,F 5,14:2
 One Crowded Night 1940,Ag 27,17:2
 Sky Murder 1940,N 14,28:3
 Angels Over Broadway 1940,N 18,23:2
 Mr District Attorney 1941,Ap 17,29:3
 Wild Geese Calling 1941,Ag 30,10:2
 Hurry, Charlie, Hurry 1941,N 12,31:3
 No Hands on the Clock 1941,D 22,24:6
 Remarkable Andrew, The 1942,Mr 6,17:2
 Talk of the Town, The 1942,Ag 28,22:3
Watts, Gwendolyn
 Billy Liar 1963,D 17,49:1
 Die! Die! My Darling 1965,My 20,52:1
Watts, James
 Lost Patrol, The 1929,D 16,34:2
Watts, Lyonel
 Outward Bound 1930,S 18,28:3
 Mr Emmanuel 1945,Ja 8,15:2
 So Well Remembered 1947,N 5,34:3
 Hidden Room, The 1950,Ja 9,19:2
Watts, Peggy
 Cock of the Air 1932,Ja 25,20:3
Watts, Queenie
 Poor Cow 1968,F 1,28:2
Watts, Twinkle
 Lake Placid Serenade 1944,D 25,15:6
Waugh, Alec (Original Author)
 Island in the Sun 1957,Je 13,37:1
Waugh, Evelyn (Original Author)
 Loved One, The 1965,O 12,57:1
Wax, Jane
 Voice of the Hurricane 1964,Je 3,36:4
Waxman, Albert
 Isabel 1968,Jl 24,47:1
Waxman, Franz (Composer)
 Heart Song 1934,Je 6,24:6
 Personal Property 1937,Ap 11,27:2
 Captains Courageous 1937,My 12,27:1
 Bride Wore Red, The 1937,O 15,18:4
 Three Comrades 1938,Je 3,17:1
Waxman, Philip A (Producer)
 Big Night, The 1952,Mr 20,37:5
 Young Don't Cry, The 1957,Jl 27,10:7
 Gene Krupa Story, The 1959,D 26,7:1
Waxman, Stanley
 Slattery's Hurricane 1949,Ag 13,6:6
Wayburn, Ned
 Great White Way, The 1924,Ja 4,10:1
Waycoff, Leon
 Murders in the Rue Morgue 1932,F 11,16:1
 Famous Ferguson Case, The 1932,Ap 25,18:6
 State's Attorney 1932,My 6,15:3
 Successful Calamity, A 1932,S 23,22:2
 Uptown New York 1932,D 10,19:3
 Silver Dollar 1932,D 23,20:1

Alimony Madness 1933,My 5,18:1
Man Who Dared, The 1933,S 9,9:3
I'll Tell the World 1934,Ap 21,12:2
Reckless 1935,Ap 20,16:1
Wayne, Billy
 Law in her Hands, The 1936,Je 6,21:2
 Reported Missing 1937,S 3,12:2
 Jury's Secret, The 1938,F 4,17:2
 Amazing Dr Clitterhouse, The 1938,Jl 21,14:2
 Tenth Avenue Kid 1938,S 2,21:3
 Missing Guest, The 1938,S 7,30:7
 Tail Spin 1939,F 11,13:2
 Eternally Yours 1939,O 7,11:2
 Castle on the Hudson 1940,Mr 4,11:2
 House Across the Bay, The 1940,Mr 22,23:2
 Star Dust •1940,My 4,13:1
 Hot Steel 1940,Je 21,25:3
 Young People 1940,Ag 24,16:2
 Bombay Clipper 1942,Ja 12,23:3
 Sin Town 1942,O 17,11:2
 Springtime in the Rockies 1942,N 12,30:2
 Jackie Robinson Story, The 1950,My 17,36:1
 Because of You 1952,D 4,47:3
Wayne, David
 Portrait of Jennie 1949,Mr 30,31:2
 Adam's Rib 1949,D 26,33:2
 Reformer and the Redhead, The 1950,Ap 10,15:2
 Stella 1950,Ag 19,9:2
 My Blue Heaven 1950,S 16,12:6
 Up Front 1951,Mr 26,19:2
 M 1951,Je 11,20:7
 As Young as You Feel 1951,Ag 3,10:6
 With a Song in my Heart 1952,Ap 5,20:2
 Wait Till the Sun Shines, Nellie 1952,Je 28,12:2
 We're not Married 1952,Jl 12,16:2
 O Henry's Full House (The Cop and the Anthem); Cop and the Anthem, The (O Henry's Full House) 1952,O 17,33:1
 Tonight We Sing 1953,F 13,17:2
 Down Among the Sheltering Palms 1953,Je 13,11:2
 How to Marry a Millionaire 1953,N 11,37:1
 Hell and High Water 1954,F 2,20:6
 Tender Trap, The 1955,N 11,29:6
 Three Faces of Eve, The 1957,S 27,16:6
 Sad Sack, The 1957,N 28,57:1
 Last Angry Man, The 1959,O 23,24:1
 Big Gamble, The 1961,S 2,19:2
Wayne, Fredd
 Crest of the Wave 1954,N 11,43:2
 Torpedo Run 1958,O 25,16:2
Wayne, Joanee
 To the Victor 1948,Ap 17,11:2
Wayne, John
 Big Trail, The 1930,O 25,20:3
 Girls Demand Excitement 1931,F 7,11:1
 Three Girls Lost 1931,My 2,23:4
 Men Are Like That 1931,Ag 17,18:2
 Maker of Men 1931,D 19,16:4
 Lady and Gent 1932,Jl 16,5:5
 Baby Face 1933,Je 24,16:2
 Lawless Nineties, The 1936,Je 29,11:1
 Conflict 1937,Ja 18,21:2
 I Cover the War 1937,Ag 2,10:2
 Idol of the Crowd 1937,D 4,21:1
 Adventure's End 1937,D 20,23:2
 Stagecoach 1939,Mr 3,21:1
 Santa Fe Stampede 1939,Ap 26,27:3
 Allegheny Uprising 1939,N 10,27:3
 Dark Command 1940,My 11,15:2
 Three Faces West 1940,Ag 19,13:2
 Long Voyage Home, The 1940,O 9,30:2 (In Addenda)
 Seven Sinners 1940,N 18,23:2
 Man Betrayed, A 1941,Mr 27,29:5
 Lady From Louisiana 1941,My 15,27:2
 Shepherd of the Hills, The 1941,Jl 31,13:2
 Lady for a Night 1942,F 12,27:2
 Reap the Wild Wind 1942,Mr 27,27:2
 Spoilers, The 1942,My 22,27:2
 In old California 1942,Je 18,25:3
 Flying Tigers 1942,O 23,25:2
 Pittsburgh 1943,F 25,27:2
 Reunion in France 1943,Mr 5,20:3
 Lady Takes a Chance, A 1943,S 16,25:2
 In old Oklahoma 1943,D 6,21:1
 Fighting Seabees, The 1944,Mr 20,14:2
 Tall in the Saddle 1944,D 15,25:3
 Flame of Barbary Coast 1945,My 28,22:2
 Back to Bataan 1945,S 13,26:3
 Dakota 1945,D 17,17:2
 They Were Expendable 1945,D 21,25:2
 Without Reservations 1946,Je 8,17:2
 Angel and the Badman 1947,Mr 3,28:4
 Tycoon 1947,D 26,22:6
 Fort Apache 1948,Je 25,26:2
 Red River 1948,O 1,31:2
 Wake of the Red Witch 1949,Ja 10,19:2
 Three Godfathers 1949,Mr 4,25:2
 Fighting Kentuckian, The 1949,S 19,18:3
 She Wore a Yellow Ribbon 1949,N 18,35:2
 Sands of Iwo Jima 1949,D 31,9:2
 Rio Grande 1950,N 20,21:2

Wayne, John— Cont
 Operation Pacific 1951,F 3,10:2
 Flying Leathernecks 1951,S 20,37:1
 Quiet Man, The 1952,Ag 22,13:1
 Big Jim McLain 1952,S 18,35:2
 Trouble Along the Way 1953,My 7,37:2
 Island in the Sky 1953,S 10,22:2
 Hondo 1953,N 27,99:9
 High and the Mighty, The 1954,Jl 1,21:2
 Sea Chase, The 1955,Je 11,8:7
 Blood Alley 1955,O 6,25:3
 Conqueror, The 1956,Mr 31,13:3
 Searchers, The 1956,My 31,21:4
 Wings of Eagles, The 1957,F 1,28:1
 Jet Pilot 1957,O 5,8:6
 Legend of the Lost 1957,D 23,18:2
 Barbarian and the Geisha 1958,O 3,25:1
 Rio Bravo 1959,Mr 19,40:2
 Horse Soldiers, The 1959,Je 26,13:1
 Alamo, The 1960,O 27,45:1
 North to Alaska 1960,N 11,36:1
 Comancheros, The 1961,N 2,42:1
 Man Who Shot Liberty Valance, The 1962,My 24,29:2
 Hatari 1962,Jl 12,19:1
 Longest Day, The 1962,O 5,28:1
 How the West Was Won 1963,Ap 1,54:1
 Donovan's Reef 1963,Jl 25,14:1
 McLintock 1963,N 14,41:3
 Circus World 1964,Je 26,34:2
 Greatest Story Ever Told, The 1965,F 16,40:2
 In Harm's Way 1965,Ap 7,36:1
 Sons of Katie Elder, The 1965,Ag 26,40:3
 Cast a Giant Shadow 1966,Mr 31,43:3
 Dorado, El 1967,Je 29,32:1
 War Wagon, The 1967,Ag 3,26:3
 Green Berets, The 1968,Je 20,49:1
 Green Berets, The 1968,Je 20,49:2
Wayne, John (Director)
 Alamo, The 1960,O 27,45:1
 Green Berets, The 1968,Je 20,49:1
Wayne, John (Producer)
 Angel and the Badman 1947,Mr 3,28:4
 Fighting Kentuckian, The 1949,S 19,18:3
 Bullfighter and the Lady, The 1951,Ap 27,19:2
 Alamo, The 1960,O 27,45:1
Wayne, Keith
 Night of the Living Dead 1968,D 5,59:2
Wayne, Ken
 Rugged O'Riordans, The 1950,Ja 6,25:2
 On the Beach 1959,D 18,34:1
Wayne, Mabel (Composer)
 King of Jazz 1930,My 3,23:1
 Dance Band 1936,Ja 4,19:2
Wayne, Mabel (Miscellaneous)
 Dance Band 1936,Ja 4,19:2
Wayne, Maude
 Behold my Wife 1920,O 11,19:3
 Song of Love, The 1924,F 25,13:1
 Fashions For Women 1927,Mr 28,26:4
Wayne, Michael (Producer)
 McLintock 1963,N 14,41:3
 Green Berets, The 1968,Je 20,49:1
Wayne, Naunton
 Lady Vanishes, The 1938,D 26,29:1
 Night Train 1940,D 30,21:1
 Girl Must Live, A 1942,Mr 24,25:2
 Quartet (The Facts of Life); Facts of Life, The (Quartet) 1949,Mr 29,30:3
 Passport to Pimlico 1949,O 27,35:2
 Hidden Room, The 1950,Ja 9,19:2
 Girl in a Million, A 1950,Jl 24,15:2
 Mr Know-All 1950,O 11,42:1
 Circle of Danger 1951,Jl 12,21:6
 Mr Lord Says No! 1952,F 12,22:5
 Double Confession 1953,My 1,17:2
 Titfield Thunderbolt, The 1953,O 6,34:2
Wayne, Nina
 Dead Heat on a Merry-Go-Round 1966,O 13,50:1
 Luv 1967,Jl 27,29:1
Wayne, Norman
 Yank in Korea, A 1951,Ap 2,29:2
Wayne, Patrick
 Eye Witness 1950,Ag 28,13:2
 Long Dark Hall, The 1951,My 10,38:3
 Long Gray Line, The 1955,F 11,19:2
 Mister Roberts 1955,Jl 15,14:1
 Searchers, The 1956,My 31,21:4
 Alamo, The 1960,O 27,45:1
 Comancheros, The 1961,N 2,42:1
 McLintock 1963,N 14,41:3
 Cheyenne Autumn 1964,D 24,8:1
 Shenandoah 1965,Jl 29,18:3
 Green Berets, The 1968,Je 20,49:1
Wayne, Richard
 Broadway Gold 1923,Jl 31,12:4
 Cheat, The 1923,Ag 27,14:3
 Reno 1924,Ja 8,27:1
 Unknown Purple, The 1924,Mr 24,13:1
 Cheaper to Marry 1925,F 2,14:1
Wayne, Robert
 Fashions in Love 1929,Jl 1,31:2
 Bitter Tea of General Yen, The 1933,Ja 12,20:6

Wayne, Velma
King and the Chorus Girl, The 1937,Mr 29,14:4
Wayne, Zissa
Alamo, The 1960,O 27,45:1
Wead, FRank (Original Author)
Hell Divers 1931,D 23,27:3
Wead, Frank (Original Author)
Midshipman Jack 1933,N 20,18:2
Fugitive Lovers 1934,Ja 13,16:3
I'll Tell the World 1934,Ap 21,12:2
Stranded 1935,Je 20,16:2
Ceiling Zero 1936,Ja 20,22:2
China Clipper 1936,Ag 12,14:3
Submarine D-1 1937,D 30,15:4
Test Pilot 1938,Ap 16,17:1
20,000 Men a Year 1939,O 28,11:2
Sailor's Lady 1940,Je 29,12:2
I Wanted Wings 1941,Mr 27,29:4
Dive Bomber 1941,Ag 30,10:2
International Squadron 1941,N 14,28:4
Destroyer 1943,S 2,15:3
Wings of Eagles, The 1957,F 1,28:1
Wead, Frank (Screenwriter)
Flying Fleet, The 1929,F 11,26:3
Air Mail 1932,N 7,20:3
West Point of the Air 1935,Ap 6,10:1
Murder in the Fleet 1935,Je 3,22:2
Ceiling Zero 1936,Ja 20,22:2
China Clipper 1936,Ag 12,14:3
Sea Devils 1937,Mr 16,26:4
Submarine D-1 1937,D 30,15:4
Citadel, The 1938,N 4,27:2
Tail Spin 1939,F 11,13:2
Moon Over Burma 1940,D 12,37:4
Dive Bomber 1941,Ag 30,10:2
Destroyer 1943,S 2,15:3
They Were Expendable 1945,D 21,25:2
Hoodlum Saint, The 1946,Je 27,29:1
Beginning or the End, The 1947,F 21,15:1
Blaze of Noon 1947,Mr 5,31:2
WEAR
See Also WARE
Wear, Ted (Screenwriter)
If Moscow Strikes 1952,Ap 30,33:4
Weatherly, Cliff
For Love or Money 1934,Jl 26,14:2
Weaver, Crawford
Legion of Terror 1936,N 2,24:2
Saturday's Heroes 1937,O 16,22:2
Danger Patrol 1937,N 19,27:3
Weaver, Dennis
Raiders, The 1952,D 13,19:2
Mississippi Gambler, The 1953,Ja 30,25:1
Dangerous Mission 1954,Mr 6,13:5
Seven Angry Men 1955,Ap 2,15:2
Storm Fear 1955,D 17,19:2
Touch of Evil 1958,My 22,25:2
Gallant Hours, The 1960,Je 23,19:4
Duel at Diablo 1966,Je 16,53:1
Way...Way Out 1966,O 27,55:1
Gentle Giant 1968,Ap 20,26:1
Weaver, Doodles
Behind the Headlines 1937,Je 1,27:2
Topper 1937,Ag 20,21:2
Swing That Cheer 1938,N 11,31:2
Girl, a Guy and a Gob, A 1941,Ap 24,25:3
Great Impostor, The 1961,Mr 30,24:1
Ring of Fire 1961,Ag 17,18:2
Tammy and the Doctor 1963,Je 27,23:2
Tiger Walks, A 1964,Ag 27,28:2
Weaver, Elvira
Swing Your Lady 1938,Ja 27,17:2
Weaver, Frank
Swing Your Lady 1938,Ja 27,17:2
Weaver, Fritz
Fail Safe 1964,S 16,36:1
Weaver, Fritz (Narrator)
Guns of August, The 1964,D 25,24:2
Weaver, Hannah
Unstrap Me 1968,N 21,41:2
Weaver, John (Screenwriter)
Adventures of Tom Sawyer, The 1938,F 18,23:1
Weaver, John D (Original Author)
Dreamboat 1952,Jl 26,9:2
Weaver, John V A (Miscellaneous)
Close Harmony 1929,Ap 29,29:2
Weaver, John V A (Original Author)
Love 'Em and Leave 'Em 1926,D 8,24:3
Crowd, The 1928,F 20,14:1
Saturday Night Kid, The 1929,N 16,25:2
Weaver, Leon
Swing Your Lady 1938,Ja 27,17:2
Weaver, Marjorie
China Clipper 1936,Ag 12,14:3
This Is my Affair 1937,My 28,17:1
Big Business 1937,Je 1,27:2
Hot Water 1937,N 5,19:4
Second Honeymoon 1937,N 13,11:2
Sally, Irene and Mary 1938,F 26,9:2
Kentucky Moonshine 1938,My 21,9:2
Three Blind Mice 1938,Je 18,18:2
I'll Give a Million 1938,Jl 16,7:2
Hold That Co-ed 1938,S 24,13:1

Young Mr Lincoln 1939,Je 3,11:2
Honeymoon's Over, The 1939,D 15,33:3
Cisco Kid and the Lady, The 1939,D 25,29:2
Shooting High 1940,Ap 12,19:2
Charlie Chan's Murder Cruise 1940,My 3,17:5
Maryland 1940,Jl 13,16:5
Michael Shayne, Private Detective
1940,D 19,33:2
Man at Large 1941,O 11,21:4
Man Who Wouldn't Die, The 1942,Ap 28,25:5
Just off Broadway 1942,Ag 29,18:4
Let's Face It 1943,Ag 5,18:1
Webb, Alan
Challenge to Lassie 1950,Ap 7,22:3
Third Secret, The 1964,Ap 29,27:1
Pumpkin Eater, The 1964,N 10,58:1
King Rat 1965,O 28,48:1
Taming of the Shrew, The 1967,Mr 9,43:1
Falstaff; Chimes at Midnight 1967,Mr 18,19:2
Interlude 1968,Jl 3,26:1
Webb, Charles (Original Author)
Graduate, The 1967,D 22,44:4
Webb, Clifton
Polly With a Past 1921,Ja 10,9:1
New Toys 1925,F 17,18:1
Heart of a Siren, The 1925,Ap 8,24:3
Laura 1944,O 12,24:1
Dark Corner, The 1946,My 9,27:3
Razor's Edge, The 1946,N 20,42:2
Razor's Edge, The 1946,N 20,42:2
Sitting Pretty 1948,Mr 11,35:2
Mr Belvedere Goes to College 1949,Ap 16,11:2
Cheaper by the Dozen 1950,Ap 1,12:2
For Heaven's Sake 1950,D 16,10:5
Mr Belvedere Rings the Bell 1951,Ag 2,18:1
Elopement 1951,D 21,21:3
Dreamboat 1952,Jl 26,9:2
Stars and Stripes Forever 1952,D 23,17:2
Titanic 1953,My 28,27:5
Mister Scoutmaster 1953,Ag 29,10:1
Three Coins in the Fountain 1954,My 21,18:2
Woman's World 1954,S 29,23:4
Man Who Never Was, The 1956,Ap 4,24:1
Boy on a Dolphin 1957,Ap 20,21:2
Remarkable Mr Pennypacker, The 1959,F 21,25:2
Holiday for Lovers 1959,Jl 25,10:2
Satan Never Sleeps 1962,F 22,20:1
Webb, Ferdinand (Screenwriter)
Magic Garden, The 1952,F 6,24:2
Webb, George
Alarm Clock Andy 1920,Mr 15,13:2
Below the Surface 1920,Je 7,20:3 (In Addenda)
Home Spun Folks 1920,O 4,14:3
Black Beauty 1921,F 21,16:1
Little Johnny Jones 1923,Ag 13,16:1
My Man 1924,F 11,18:3
Dude Ranch 1931,Ap 25,23:4
Webb, George R (Producer)
Webb Singing Pictures 1917,Ja 15,7:1
Webb, Jack
Men, The 1950,Jl 21,15:2
Sunset Boulevard 1950,Ag 11,15:2
Dark City 1950,O 19,40:5
Halls of Montezuma, The 1951,Ja 6,9:6
U S S Teakettle 1951,F 24,11:2
Appointment With Danger 1951,My 10,38:2
Dragnet 1954,Ag 21,10:2
Pete Kelly's Blues 1955,Ag 19,10:1
D I, The 1957,Je 6,35:2
30 1959,N 12,27:1
Last Time I Saw Archie, The 1961,My 29,9:6
Webb, Jack (Director)
Dragnet 1954,Ag 21,10:2
Pete Kelly's Blues 1955,Ag 19,10:1
D I, The 1957,Je 6,35:2
30 1959,N 12,27:1
Last Time I Saw Archie, The 1961,My 29,9:6
Webb, Jack (Producer)
D I, The 1957,Je 6,35:2
30 1959,N 12,27:1
Last Time I Saw Archie, The 1961,My 29,9:6
Webb, James (Original Author)
S O S Tidal Wave 1939,Je 22,19:3
Webb, James R (Original Author)
Woman in Hiding 1950,F 23,33:2
Webb, James R (Screenwriter)
South of St Louis 1949,Mr 7,17:2
Montana 1950,F 4,9:2
Raton Pass 1951,Ap 20,25:1
Big Trees, The 1952,F 6,24:2
Operation Secret 1952,N 6,37:2
Iron Mistress, The 1952,N 20,39:2
Charge at Feather River, The 1953,Jl 16,17:2
Phantom of the Rue Morgue 1954,Mr 20,10:5
Apache 1954,Jl 10,7:2
Vera Cruz 1954,D 27,22:4
Illegal 1955,O 29,12:6
Trapeze 1956,Je 5,39:2
Big Country, The 1958,O 2,44:1
Pork Chop Hill 1959,My 30,9:2
Cape Fear 1962,Ap 19,35:2
How the West Was Won 1963,Ap 1,54:1
King of the Sun 1963,D 26,33:4

Webb, James R (Screenwriter) — Cont
Cheyenne Autumn 1964,D 24,8:1
Guns for San Sebastian 1968,Mr 21,57:2
Webb, Janet
Funny Thing Happened on the Way to the Forum,
A 1966,O 17,48:1
Webb, Kenneth (Director)
Stolen Kiss 1920,Ap 5,20:1
Master Mind, The 1920,S 13,12:1
Salvation Neil 1921,Je 27,16:3
Secrets of Paris 1923,Ag 8,22:1
Beautiful City, The 1925,N 23,25:4
Just Suppose 1926,Ja 18,26:2
Lucky in Love 1929,D 14,22:4
Webb, Kenneth (Miscellaneous)
Gay Divorcee, The 1934,N 16,27:1
Webb, Mary (Original Author)
Wild Heart, The 1952,My 29,17:2
Webb, Millard (Director)
Black Swan, The 1924,N 25,26:1
My Wife and I 1925,My 20,26:2
Golden Cocoon, The 1925,D 15,14:5
Sea Hunt, The 1926,Ja 16,8:5
Sea Beast, The 1926,Ja 16,8:5
Affair of the Follies, An 1927,F 28,22:3
Love Thrill, The 1927,My 10,24:5
Naughty but Nice 1927,Jl 5,19:2
Drop Kick, The 1927,S 20,32:2
Gentlemen of the Press 1929,My 13,27:2
Glorifying the American Girl 1930,Ja 11,21:3
Her Golden Calf 1930,My 5,27:3
Webb, Millard (Original Author)
Glorifying the American Girl 1930,Ja 11,21:3
Webb, Millard (Screenwriter)
Love Thrill, The 1927,My 10,24:5
Webb, Percy Sergeant
Unbeliever, The 1918,F 12,9:2
Webb, Richard
I Wanted Wings 1941,Mr 27,29:4
Hold Back the Dawn 1941,O 2,29:1
Remarkable Andrew, The 1942,Mr 6,17:2
American Empire 1943,Ja 14,25:4
O S S 1946,My 27,15:5
Out of the Past 1947,N 26,18:2
Big Clock, The 1948,Ap 22,34:2
Isn't It Romantic? 1948,O 7,35:2
Night Has a Thousand Eyes 1948,O 14,38:3
My Own True Love 1949,F 3,27:3
Connecticut Yankee in King Arthur's Court, A
1949,Ap 8,31:2
Sands of Iwo Jima 1949,D 31,9:2
I Was a Communist for the F B I 1951,My 3,34:4
Starlift 1951,D 15,11:2
Distant Drums 1951,D 26,19:3
ThIs Woman is Dangerous 1952,F 28,23:2
Mara Maru 1952,Ap 24,38:1
Carson City 1952,Je 14,12:2
Three Hours to Kill 1954,S 4,6:4
Artists and Models 1955,D 22,20:1
Webb, Rita
Idol, The 1966,Ag 11,27:1
To Sir, With Love 1967,Je 15,56:1
Webb, Robert D (Director)
Caribbean Mystery, The 1945,Ag 20,22:4
Spider, The 1946,Je 21,20:3
Glory Brigade, The 1953,Ag 15,8:4
Beneath the 12-Mile Reef 1953,D 17,52:2
White Feather 1955,F 17,23:1
Seven Cities of Gold 1955,O 8,13:2
On the Threshold of Space 1956,Mr 30,10:5
Proud Ones, The 1956,Ag 11,10:2
Love Me Tender 1956,N 16,23:1
Way to the Gold, The 1957,My 11,24:6
Seven Women From Hell 1962,F 1,22:2
Webb, Robert D (Producer)
Seven Cities of Gold 1955,O 8,13:2
Webb, Roy (Composer)
Quality Street 1937,Ap 9,19:2
Abe Lincoln in Illinois 1940,F 23,19:2
Webber, Charles Rev
Native Land 1942,My 12,16:3
Webber, Herman E (Producer)
Canadians, The 1961,Je 1,31:1
Webber, Peggy
Macbeth 1950,D 28,22:6
Journey Into Light 1951,O 5,24:4
Submarine Command 1952,Ja 19,13:2
Webber, Robert
Highway 301 1950,D 9,13:2
12 Angry Men 1957,Ap 15,24:1
Stripper, The 1963,Je 20,29:1
Sandpiper, The 1965,Jl 16,14:1
Third Day, The 1965,Ag 5,15:3
Hysteria 1965,S 9,36:3
Silencers, The 1966,Mr 17,35:1
Harper 1966,Mr 31,43:1
Dead Heat on a Merry-Go-Round
1966,O 13,50:1
Hired Killer, The 1967,Mr 2,30:3
Dirty Dozen, The 1967,Je 16,36:1
Don't Make Waves 1967,Je 21,36:2
Weber, Andre
Great Spy Chase, The 1966,O 6,56:4

Weber, Franz
Beiden Seehunde, Die 1935,Mr 9,19:2
Marriage of Figaro 1950,N 3,31:2
Weber, Jean
Figaro 1929,N 25,22:1
Collier de la Reine, Le (Queen's Necklace, The) 1931,F 9,25:3
Weber, Joe
Friendly Enemies 1925,My 5,24:2
Weber, Karl
Walk East on Beacon 1952,My 29,17:2
Weber, Lois
Midnight Romance, A 1919,Mr 10,9:3
Weber, Lois (Director)
To Please one Woman 1920,D 20,11:2
What Do Men Want? 1921,N 14,18:1
Marriage Clause, The 1926,S 28,30:2
Sensation Seekers 1927,Mr 16,28:2
Angel of Broadway 1927,N 1,21:1 (In Addenda)
White Heat 1934,Je 16,20:2
Weber, Lois (Screenwriter)
To Please one Woman 1920,D 20,11:2
What Do Men Want? 1921,N 14,18:1
Weber, Pierre (Original Author)
Mademoiselle Gobette 1955,F 5,13:3
Weber, Tania
Day in Court, A 1963,My 11,15:2
Weber, Wayne
Illiac Passion, The 1968,Ap 19,40:1
Weber and Fields
Blossoms On Broadway 1937,D 3,29:2
Lillian Russell 1940,My 18,11:2
Webezirk, Gisela
Kabinett des Dr. Larifari, Das 1931,S 11,24:2
Webley, John
Mikado, The 1967,Mr 15,53:1
Webster, Al
Back Door to Heaven 1939,Ap 20,21:2
Webster, Ben
Twelve:Ten 1919,D 22,18:3
Old Curiosity Shop, The 1935,D 23,15:5
Prisoner of Zenda, The 1937,S 3,12:1
Lassie Come Home 1943,O 8,15:4
Webster, Frank
Tight Little Island 1949,D 26,33:2
Webster, Harry
Captain Boycott 1947,D 6,11:2
Webster, Henry Kitchell (Original Author)
What Fools Men 1925,S 29,31:3
Webster, Howard
Chechahcos, The 1924,My 19,14:2
Webster, Jack
Time Limit 1957,O 24,37:2
Webster, Jean (Original Author)
Daddy Long Legs 1919,My 12,11:4
Daddy Long Legs 1931,Je 6,15:5
Daddy Long Legs 1955,My 6,17:5
Webster, Joy
Panic in the Parlor 1957,D 18,45:1
Webster, M Coates (Original Author)
Man I Marry, The 1936,O 31,24:3
Double or Nothing 1937,S 2,17:3
My Favorite Spy 1942,My 29,13:4
Webster, M Coates (Screenwriter)
Isle of Destiny 1940,Ap 8,15:2
Singapore Woman 1941,My 12,13:6
He's my Guy 1943,Mr 12,12:3
Jungle Captive 1945,Jl 7,7:5
Strange Confession 1945,N 8,17:3
Webster, Mary
Delicate Delinquent, The 1957,Jl 4,16:1
Tin Star, The 1957,O 24,37:2
Eighteen and Anxious 1957,D 14,16:6
Master of the World 1961,S 16,9:1
Webster, Nicholas (Director)
Gone are the Days! 1963,S 24,43:2
Santa Claus Conquers the Martians 1964,D 17,50:2
Webster, Nicholas (Producer)
Gone are the Days! 1963,S 24,43:2
Webster, Patricia
How to Murder a Rich Uncle 1957,O 26,19:2
Webster, Paul (Composer)
Under the Pampas Moon 1935,My 31,11:1
Bad Boy 1935,O 28,16:3
Everything's on Ice 1939,O 6,31:1
Seven Sweethearts 1942,N 13,28:1
Presenting Lily Mars 1943,Ap 30,25:3
Thousands Cheer 1943,S 14,27:1
Hit the Ice 1943,S 23,27:2
Minstrel Man 1944,Jl 17,18:5
Timberjack 1955,Mr 10,33:3
Mardi Gras 1958,N 19,45:2
Webster, Paul (Miscellaneous)
Vogues of 1938 1937,Ag 20,21:1
Make a Wish 1937,S 23,33:1
Breaking the Ice 1938,S 23,35:3
Webster, Paul (Original Author)
Nora Prentiss 1947,F 22,16:2
Wechsier, Leon (Producer)
This Is China 1937,O 6,29:4

Wechsler, David (Original Author)
Search, The 1948,Mr 24,30:3
Wechsler, David(as) Fruh, Kurt (Original Author)
Village, The 1953,S 23,37:2
Wechsler, David(as) Fruh, Kurt (Screenwriter)
Village, The 1953,S 23,37:2
Wechsler, Lazar (Producer)
Marie-Louise 1945,N 13,24:2
Last Chance, The 1945,N 28,21:6
Search, The 1948,Mr 24,30:3
Four Days' Leave 1950,Je 9,29:4
Four in a Jeep 1951,Je 12,35:2
Village, The 1953,S 23,37:2
Heidi 1953,D 21,27:2
Heidi and Peter 1955,D 13,55:2
It Happened in Broad Daylight 1960,S 30,33:1
Shadows Grow Longer, The 1962,Je 11,36:4
Weck, Peter
Story of Vickie, The 1958,Ja 30,19:2
Almost Angels 1962,N 1,34:2
Cardinal, The 1963,D 13,41:1
Wedeking, J (Screenwriter)
Guitars of Love 1958,Jl 12,18:1
Wedell, Susan
Kiss Me, Stupid 1964,D 23,22:2
Wedenski, D
Living Corpse, The 1931,Ja 4,27:2
Wedgeworth, Ann
Andy 1965,Ja 22,21:2
Wedlock, Hugh (Original Author)
It Happened Tomorrow 1944,My 29,18:2
In Society 1944,Ag 17,20:2
George White's Scandals 1945,O 11,26:2
Abbott and Costello Meet the Invisible Man 1951,Ap 13,18:6
Wedlock, Hugh (Screenwriter)
Almost Married 1942,Je 5,23:2
All by Myself 1943,Jl 16,20:3
George White's Scandals 1945,O 11,26:2
Abbott and Costello Meet the Killer Boris Karloff 1949,S 19,18:3
Wedorn, Jose
Walzerparadies 1933,Mr 4,11:3
Fraeulein-Falsch Verbunden! 1934,Ja 15,12:2
Weedon, Harry
Never Take No for an Answer 1952,Ap 29,32:2
Weeks, Barbara
Party Husband 1931,My 16,13:3
Palmy Days 1931,S 24,21:2
Men in her Life 1931,N 30,16:2
Stepping Sisters 1932,Ja 9,21:1
Cheaters at Play 1932,F 27,22:1
Devil's Lottery 1932,Ap 2,13:2
White Eagle 1932,S 24,18:4
Deception 1933,Ja 10,26:2
State Trooper 1933,Mr 27,13:6
Soldiers of the Storm 1933,My 17,15:3
My Weakness 1933,S 22,14:1
Quitter, The 1934,Mr 14,23:3
Now I'll Tell 1934,My 26,12:2
Weeks, Jane
Innocent Affair, An 1948,S 29,36:2
Weel, Arne (Director)
Livet paa Hegnsgaard; Life on the Hegn Farm 1939,N 13,15:2
Weems, Walter
Anybody's War 1930,Jl 11,22:1
Weems, Walter (Screenwriter)
Hearts in Dixie 1929,F 28,30:3
Conflict 1937,Ja 18,21:2
Weff, Clarence (Original Author)
How Not to Rob a Department Store 1965,D 29,23:1
Wegener, Greta
Victoria the Great 1937,O 29,19:1
Sixty Glorious Years 1938,N 18,25:2
Wegener, Paul
Golem, The 1921,Je 20,17:2
One Arabian Night 1921,O 3,16:2
Loves of Pharaoh 1922,F 22,13:3 (In Addenda)
Monna Vanna 1923,S 25,8:2
Magician, The 1926,O 25,15:1
Lost Shadow, The 1928,Mr 20,20:3
Vanina 1928,Mr 20,20:3
Alraune 1928,My 20,VIII,8:4
Strange Case of Captain Ramper, The 1928,Je 4,13:2
Lucrecia Borgia 1928,D 25,31:3
Weavers, The 1929,O 7,22:1
Survival 1930,Ja 13,21:1
Inge und die Millionen 1934,Ap 13,25:1
Ein Liebesroman im Hause Habsburg 1936,O 12,23:2
Horst Wessel 1939,Mr 4,18:5
Starker als die Liebe; Stronger Than Love 1939,My 6,21:3
Unsterbliche Herz, Das; Immortal Heart, The 1939,O 21,12:2
Recht auf Liebe, Das; Right to Love, The 1940,Je 15,12:3
Living Dead, The 1940,D 17,33:2

Wegener, Paul (Director)
Golem, The 1921,Je 20,17:2
Freundin Eines Grossen Mannes, Die 1934,S 11,24:5
Mann Will Nach Deutschland, Ein 1934,N 13,22:4
August der Starke 1937,Ja 30,21:3
Krach und Glueckum Kuennemann; Row and Joy About Kuennemann 1938,S 17,20:3
Wegren, Dave
Barbary Coast 1935,O 14,21:1
Wegrostek, Oscar
No Time for Flowers 1952,D 26,20:3
Wegrzyn, Josef
Dziesieciu z Pawiaka 1932,Ap 21,25:2
Noc Listopadowa 1933,My 1,10:3
Rena 1939,Ja 27,17:3
Weguelin, Thomas
Congress Dances 1932,My 12,23:2
Monte Carlo Madness 1932,Je 4,9:2
Wehling, Bob (Screenwriter)
Sign of Zorro, The 1961,S 5,37:6
Wehmer, Marianne
Frauen vom Tannhof, Die 1936,F 18,27:1
Wehrer, Ann
Bike Boy 1967,O 6,31:2
Wei, Lo
Empress Wu 1965,Mr 16,42:2
Wei, Y L
Sable Cicada 1939,Ja 14,13:1
Weichand, Philipp
Fuerst Sepp'l 1937,Jl 17,18:1
Weichert, Richard (Director)
Two Neckties; Zwei Kravatten 1930,N 30,IX,6:5
Weidemann, Hans (Miscellaneous)
Verraeter; Traitors 1936,N 22,XI,4:2 (In Addenda)
Weidenmann, Alfred (Director)
Deadly Decision 1958,Ap 29,26:2
Scampolo 1959,Ag 6,18:4
Adorable Julia 1964,Ap 8,33:1
And so to Bed 1965,Jl 31,11:3
Weidenmann, Alfred (Producer)
Scampolo 1959,Ag 6,18:4
Weidler, Virginia
Mrs Wiggs of the Cabbage Patch 1934,O 29,14:2
Laddie 1935,My 6,22:3
Freckles 1935,O 26,12:2
Peter Ibbetson 1935,N 8,18:2
Timothy's Quest 1936,F 29,11:2
Maid of Salem 1937,Mr 4,27:2
Outcasts of Poker Flat, The 1937,Ap 27,18:3
Souls at Sea 1937,Ag 10,23:2
Love Is a Headache 1938,Ja 28,17:3
Scandal Street 1938,F 5,19:2 (In Addenda)
Mother Carey's Chickens 1938,Ag 5,11:1
too Hot To Handle 1938,S 30,24:2
Men With Wings 1938,O 27,27:2
Out West With the Hardys 1938,D 9,31:2
Great Man Votes, The 1939,Ja 20,15:2
Lone Wolf Spy Hunt, The 1939,Mr 6,11:3
Fixer Dugan 1939,My 6,21:2
Under-Pup, The 1939,S 5,21:2
Women, The 1939,S 22,27:2
Young Tom Edison 1940,Mr 15,27:2
All This and Heaven, Too 1940,Jl 5,10:2
Gold Rush Maisie 1940,S 2,19:2
Philadelphia Story, The 1940,D 27,22:2
I'll Wait for You 1941,Je 2,13:6
Barnacle Bill 1941,Jl 25,12:4
Babes on Broadway 1942,Ja 1,37:1
Born to Sing 1942,F 19,23:2
Youngest Profession, The 1943,Je 25,13:3
Best Foot Forward 1943,Je 30,25:2
Weidman, Charles
Arabian Duet 1922,My 15,20:3
Weidman, Jerome (Original Author)
I Can Get It for You Wholesale 1951,Ap 5,34:4
Invitation 1952,Ja 30,22:6
Weidman, Jerome (Screenwriter)
Damned Don't Cry, The 1950,Ap 8,9:2
Slander 1957,Ja 17,34:4
Weigel, Paul
Breath of the Gods, The 1920,Jl 26,9:5
Bluebeard's 8th Wife 1923,Ag 7,20:2
Which Shall It Be? 1924,Ap 7,15:3
Mademoiselle Midnight 1924,My 27,14:1
Silent Accuser, The 1924,N 25,26:1
Excuse Me 1925,Ja 27,11:2
Folly of Vanity 1925,Ja 28,14:1
Declassee 1925,Mr 23,14:2
For Heaven's Sake 1926,Ap 5,24:1
Blonde or Brunette 1927,Ja 11,18:2
Leatherneck, The 1929,Ap 22,23:1
Back Street 1932,Ag 29,9:2
Vampire Bat, The 1933,Ja 23,9:1
Great Dictator, The 1940,O 16,29:1
Joan of Paris 1942,Ja 26,18:2
Weight, Harmon (Director)
Ruling Passion, The 1922,Ja 23,11:4
Man Who Played God, The 1922,O 2,21:2
Ragged Edge, The 1923,Je 5,24:5
$20 a Week 1924,Je 10,24:4

Weight, Harmon (Director) — Cont
Drusilla With a Million 1925,My 25,21:3
Forever After 1926,N 9,31:1
Weihelm, Hans (Original Author)
Once a Thief 1951,Ja 19,21:3
Weijden, Bullan
Baldvins Brollop; Baldwin's Wedding
1938,D 27,13:2
Kalle paa Spaangen 1940,Ja 27,9:3
Weijden, Ruth
Loerdagskvaellar 1936,F 13,25:3
Weil, Richard (Original Author)
Shine on Harvest Moon 1944,Mr 11,10:2
Weil, Richard (Screenwriter)
Mysterious Doctor, The 1943,My 20,26:4
Shine on Harvest Moon 1944,Mr 11,10:2
Make Your own Bed 1944,My 27,12:2
Weill, Kurt (Composer)
Blockade 1938,Je 17,25:1
Lady in the Dark 1944,F 23,17:1
Knickerbocker Holiday 1944,Ap 20,22:7
Where Do We Go From Here? 1945,Je 7,25:2
Threepenny Opera, The 1960,Jl 11,24:4
Weils, Richard (Screenwriter)
Great Flamario, The 1945,Ja 15,15:5
WEIMAN
See Also WYMAN
Weiman, Rita (Original Author)
Madame Peacock 1920,O 25,18:1
Footlights 1921,S 9,IV,4:1
Acquittal, The 1923,D 12,24:5
Bluff 1924,Ap 28,18:2
Spotlight, The 1927,N 28,18:5
On Your Back 1930,S 15,29:3
Witness Chair, The 1936,Ap 18,19:2
President's Mystery, The 1936,O 19,22:1
Possessed 1947,My 30,25:2
Weimann, Matthias
Schimmelreiter, Der; Rider of the White Horse,
The 1935,F 25,13:3
Weinberg, Gus
Ne'er Do-Well, The 1923,My 1,24:3
Homeward Bound 1923,Jl 31,12:4
Weinberg, gus
Coming Through 1925,F 18,17:3
Weinberg, Gus
Soul Fire 1925,My 6,26:3
Weinberg, Herman G (Miscellaneous)
Golem, The 1937,Mr 22,27:2
Four Flights to Love 1942,Ap 13,12:2
It Happened in Gibraltar 1943,N 16,27:1
32 Rue de Montmartre 1944,S 28,26:3
Dame de Pique, La 1944,O 19,19:2
drame De Shanghai; Shanghai Drama, The
1945,Ja 11,19:2
Ces Dames aux Chapeaux Verts; Ladies in the
Green Hats, The 1945,Ap 5,26:2
Barge-Keeper's Daughter, The 1945,S 6,23:3
Open City; Citta Aperta 1946,F 26,21:2
Extenuating Circumstances; Circostances
Attenuantes 1946,S 24,41:3
Well-Digger's Daughter, The 1946,S 30,21:4
Shoe-Shine 1947,Ag 27,19:2
Enamorada 1949,D 3,8:6
WEINER
See Also WIENER, WINER
Weiner, Joshua
Dream no More 1950,Ja 6,25:2
Weinfeld, J (Producer)
We Live Again 1948,S 6,17:2
Weingarten, Lawrence (Producer)
Rendezvous 1935,O 26,12:2
Unguarded Hour, The 1936,Ap 4,11:1
His Brother's Wife 1936,Ag 15,6:2
Libeled Lady 1936,O 31,24:2
Last of Mrs Cheyney, The 1937,F 19,15:1
too Hot To Handle 1938,S 30,24:2
Balalaika 1939,D 15,33:2
Without Love 1945,Mr 23,13:1
Adam's Rib 1949,D 26,33:2
Invitation 1952,Ja 30,22:6
Pat and Mike 1952,Je 19,32:6
Actress, The 1953,O 13,34:1
Rhapsody 1954,Mr 12,17:1
Tender Trap, The 1955,N 11,29:6
I'll Cry Tomorrow 1956,Ja 13,18:1
Don't Go Near the Water 1957,N 15,37:1
Cat on a Hot Tin Roof 1958,S 19,24:1
Gazebo, The 1960,Ja 16,14:4
Honeymoon Machine, The 1961,Ag 24,25:2
Ada 1961,Ag 26,15:1
Period of Adjustment 1962,N 1,34:1
Signpost to Murder 1965,My 20,52:2
Impossible Years, The 1968,D 6,54:1
Weinrib, Lennie
Good Times 1967,Ag 3,26:4
Weinrib, Lennie (Director)
Wild Wild Winter 1966,Ja 6,20:2
Weinschenk, Pablo (Cinematographer)
Fury Over Spain 1937,Jl 21,19:2
Weinshtak, Vladimir (Director)
Rubicon 1931,S 21,20:2
Rubicon 1934,Mr 19,13:3

Weinstein, Abraham (Producer)
Long Is the Road 1948,N 12,30:5
Weinstein, Henry T (Producer)
Tender is the Night 1962,Ja 20,13:2
Joy in the Morning 1965,Je 10,38:1
Weinstock, V (Director)
Untitled-Capt Grant's Children 1939,Ja 12,23:3
Captain Grant's Children 1939,Ja 12,23:3
Weintenberger, Marguerite
Pecheurs d'Islande 1935,S 21,18:2
Weintraub, Rebecca
Tevya 1939,D 22,15:3
Weintraub, Sy (Producer)
Tarzan's Greatest Adventure 1959,Jl 9,22:1
Tarzan the Magnificent 1960,Jl 21,17:1
Tarzan Goes to India 1962,S 6,37:2
Tarzan and the Valley of Gold 1967,Mr 30,55:1
Weis, Don (Director)
It's a big Country 1952,Ja 9,25:2
Just This Once 1952,Mr 18,22:3
You for Me 1952,S 25,38:3
I Love Melvin 1953,Ap 10,18:4
Adventures of Haji Baba, The 1954,O 9,8:7
Gene Krupa Story, The 1959,D 26,7:1
Critic's Choice 1963,My 2,40:2
Billie 1965,S 16,55:3
Weis, Don (Producer)
Billie 1965,S 16,55:3
Weisbart, David (Producer)
Mara Maru 1952,Ap 24,38:1
Carson City 1952,Je 14,12:2
Charge at Feather River, The 1953,Jl 16,17:2
Thunder Over the Plains 1953,D 10,64:4
Command, The 1954,Ja 16,10:5
Them 1954,Je 17,36:2
Rebel without a Cause 1955,O 27,28:3
Target Zero 1955,N 16,43:2
Steel Jungle, The 1956,Mr 10,9:5
Between Heaven and Hell 1956,O 12,33:2
Love Me Tender 1956,N 16,23:1
Way to the Gold, The 1957,My 11,24:6
April Love 1957,N 28,57:2
Holiday for Lovers 1959,Jl 25,10:2
Private's Affair, A 1959,Ag 15,8:7
Flaming Star 1960,D 17,19:1
Follow That Dream 1962,Ag 9,17:7
Kid Galahad 1963,Mr 7,8:5
Rio Conchos 1964,O 29,38:1
Goodbye, Charlie 1964,N 19,49:1
Pleasure Seekers, The 1964,D 26,9:1
Valley of the Dolls 1967,D 16,51:1
Weisberg, Brenda (Original Author)
Little Tough Guy 1938,Ag 18,23:3
Scarlet Claw, The 1944,My 19,12:1
Lone Wolf in London, The 1947,N 22,10:3
Weisberg, Brenda (Screenwriter)
Little Tough Guy 1938,Ag 18,23:3
Hit the Road 1941,Jl 3,15:3
Mob Town 1941,N 20,39:3
Weird Woman 1944,Ap 1,11:1
Mummy's Ghost, The 1944,Jl 1,10:7
China Sky 1945,My 25,22:3
Girl's School 1950,F 3,29:2
Weisburd, Dan E (Screenwriter)
Dinosaurusi 1960,S 9,36:4
Weisenborn, Guenter (Screenwriter)
Tale of Five Women, A 1953,Ja 16,19:2
Weisenthal, Sam (Producer)
All Mine to Give 1959,Ag 4,32:5
Weiser, Grate
Frischer Wind aus Kanada 1935,S 21,18:2
Einer zu viel an Bord 1936,Ja 25,18:5
Letzte Rose 1936,O 10,21:3
Divine Jetta, The 1937,O 2,18:2
Liebe auf Umwegen; Love by Indirection
1937,D 18,18:2
Meine Freundin Barbara; My Firend Barbara
1938,Je 4,18:3
Alles Fuer Veronika 1939,F 4,11:2
Familie Schimek 1939,S 2,20:2
Verkannte Lebemann, Der; Unrecognized Man of
the World, The 1939,S 16,20:2
Our Little Wife 1940,Ja 27,9:2
City of Secrets 1963,Jl 27,10:2
Weisgerber, Anije
White Hell of Pitz Palu, The 1953,N 14,14:2
Weishart, David (Producer)
These Thousand Hills 1959,My 7,36:1
Weishaus, Mark
Come Back Baby 1968,Je 14,43:1
WEISS
See Also WISE
Weiss, Albert
Crime in the Maginot Line 1939,My 8,21:2
Weiss, Allan (Screenwriter)
Fun in Acapulco 1964,F 20,22:4
Roustabout 1964,N 11,38:1
Sons of Katie Elder, The 1965,Ag 26,40:3
Paradise, Hawaiian Style 1966,Je 16,15:3
Easy Come, Easy Go 1967,Je 15,56:1
Weiss, Arthur (Screenwriter)
Flipper 1963,S 19,23:1
Rhino! 1964,Ag 27,28:2

Weiss, Arthur (Screenwriter) — Cont
Around the World Under the Sea 1966,Jl 21,20:2
Weiss, Bill
Venetian Affair, The 1967,Ja 19,41:2
Weiss, Florence
Cantor's Son, The 1937,D 27,11:1
Singing Blacksmith, The 1938,N 3,27:1
Overture to Glory 1940,F 12,14:2
Weiss, George (Composer)
Fun and Fancy Free 1947,S 29,17:2 (In
Addenda)
Melody Time 1948,My 28,28:2
Weiss, Helmut
Fanny Hill 1965,D 2,48:1
Weiss, Jeff
Edge, The 1968,Mr 28,52:1
Weiss, Jiri (Director)
Before the Raid 1944,F 26,10:3
Sweet Light in a Dark Room 1966,Je 30,28:1
90 Degrees in the Shade 1966,N 16,52:1
Murder Czech Style 1968,Ag 20,33:1
Weiss, Jiri (Original Author)
Murder Czech Style 1968,Ag 20,33:1
Weiss, Jiri (Screenwriter)
Sweet Light in a Dark Room 1966,Je 30,28:1
Murder Czech Style 1968,Ag 20,33:1
Weiss, Peter (Original Author)
Hallucinations 1966,Ja 29,13:2
Mirage, The 1966,Ja 29,13:2
Studio of Dr Faust, The 1966,Ja 29,13:2
Faces in the Shadows 1966,Ja 29,13:2
Relief 1966,Ja 29,13:2
Persecution and Assassination of Jean-Paul Marat
as Performed by the Inmates of the Asylum of
Charenton Under the Direction of the Marquis
De Sade, The 1967,F 23,41:1
Weiss, Thea
Mozart Story, The 1948,N 15,21:5
Weissbach, Herbert
Berliner, The 1952,O 28,37:1
Weissberg, Louis
Tevya 1939,D 22,15:3
Weisse, A
Moon of Israel 1927,Je 29,29:3
Weisse, Hanni
Berlin After Dark 1929,My 28,36:2
WEISSMAN
See Also WISEMAN
Weissman, Dora
Shir Hashirim 1935,O 11,31:1
Guerrilla Girl 1953,Jl 7,23:7
Weissman, Herman (Screenwriter)
Bridge of San Luis Rey, The 1944,Mr 4,11:1
Weissmuller, Johnny
Tarzan, The Ape Man 1932,Mr 28,11:2
Tarzan and his Mate 1934,Ap 21,12:1
Tarzan Escapes 1936,N 20,27:2
Tarzan Finds a Son 1939,Je 15,27:2
Tarzan's Secret Treasure 1941,D 25,33:1
Tarzan's New York Adventure 1942,Ag 7,13:2
Tarzan Triumphs 1943,F 5,16:3
Stage Door Canteen 1943,Je 25,13:2
Tarzan's Desert Mystery 1943,D 27,23:3
Tarzan and the Amazons 1945,Ap 30,13:4
Tarzan and the Leopard Woman 1946,F 11,25:2
Swamp Fire 1946,Ag 26,21:4
Tarzan and the Huntress 1947,Ap 7,20:4
Tarzan and the Mermaids 1948,Mr 30,26:4
Jungle Jim 1949,Ja 1,9:2
Mark of the Gorilla 1950,F 17,27:2
Weissmuller, Johnny Jr
Andy Hardy Comes Home 1958,D 24,00:0
Weissner, Hilde
Lockvogel 1935,Ja 5,20:3
Finanzen des Grossherzogs, Die; Grand Duke's
Finances, The 1935,Ap 6,10:3
Pappi 1936,My 16,11:3
Traumulus 1936,S 19,20:1
Zwei lustige Abenteurer; Two Merry Adventures
1938,Ja 1,11:2
Ball im Metropol 1938,Mr 5,11:3
Maulkorb, Der 1938,Ap 9,11:3
Dahinten in der Heide; Back in the Country
1939,Ja 21,19:3
Weist, Dwight (Narrator)
Golden Age of Comedy, The 1957,D 27,23:4
Weitzenkorn, Louis (Original Author)
Five Star Final 1931,S 11,24:2
Men of Chance 1931,D 28,22:1
Weitzenkorn, Louis (Screenwriter)
King of the Newsboys 1938,Ap 2,18:2
Weizel, Heinz
Verraeter 1937,Ja 23,13:1
Welbeck, Peter (Original Author)
Code 7...Victim 5 1965,My 20,52:1
Bang, Bang, You're Dead 1967,Ja 19,41:2
Those Fantastic Flying Fools 1967,O 19,59:2
Welbeck, Peter (Screenwriter)
Face of Fu Manchu, The 1965,N 11,58:3
Ten Little Indians 1966,F 10,33:1
Vengeance of Fu Manchu, The 1968,F 15,47:1
WELCH
See Also WELSH

Welch, Charles
Gone are the Days! 1963,S 24,43:2
Welch, Eddie (Miscellaneous)
Las Vegas Nights 1941,Mr 20,25:2
Welch, Eddie (Screenwriter)
Hold 'Em Yale 1935,Ap 27,20:6
F-Man 1936,My 4,16:1
Scandal Street 1938,F 5,19:2 (In Addenda)
Her Jungle Love 1938,Ap 14,27:2
Prison Farm 1938,Jl 15,13:3
Welch, Elisabeth
Dead of Night 1946,Je 29,22:6
Welch, Harry
King of Burlesque 1936,Ja 16,25:2
Welch, James
Dramatic Life of Abraham Lincoln, The
1924,Ja 22,17:3
Iron Horse, The 1924,Ag 29,6:1
Tornado, The 1924,D 15,14:1
Welch, Jim
Trail of the Lonesome Pine, The 1936,F 20,23:5
Welch, Joseph N
Anatomy of a Murder 1959,Jl 3,10:1
Welch, Lester (Producer)
Seven Hills of Rome 1958,Ja 28,24:2 (Incorrect
in this edition; use 1958,Ja 31,24:2 elsewhere)
Gunfighters of Casa Grande 1965,S 2,36:1
Welch, Mary
Park Row 1952,D 22,20:2
Welch, Nelson
Thunder in the East 1953,F 4,32:2
Welch, Niles
Stepping Out 1919,S 22,8:1
Little Child Shall Lead Them, A 1922,S 2,10:4
From Rags to Riches 1922,S 25,10:2
My Man 1924,F 11,18:3
Wine of Youth 1924,Ag 11,16:1
Lying Wives 1925,Je 17,16:2
Rainbow Trail, The 1932,Ja 30,13:2
Cross Examination 1932,F 27,22:1
Night Club Lady, The 1932,Ag 27,13:4
Silver Dollar 1932,D 23,20:1
Zoo in Budapest 1933,Ap 28,15:2
Stone of Silver Creek 1935,Ap 8,23:3
Welch, Phyllis
Professor Beware 1938,Jl 14,17:1
Welch, Raquel
Fantastic Voyage 1966,S 8,43:1
One Million Years BC 1967,F 22,21:1
Shoot Loud, Louder... I Don't Understand
1967,S 21,56:4
Bedazzled 1967,D 11,65:2
Fathom 1967,D 14,62:1
Biggest Bundle of Them All, The 1968,Ja 18,46:1
Queens, The (Queen Elena); Queen Elena (The
Queens) 1968,Mr 11,49:1
Bandolero 1968,Jl 18,26:2
Oldest Profession, The (Gay Nineties, The); Gay
Nineties, The (The Oldest Profession)
1968,N 8,42:1
Lady in Cement 1968,N 21,41:1
Welch, Robert L (Producer)
Paleface, The 1948,D 16,41:2
Sorrowful Jones 1949,Je 6,15:2
Top o' the Morning 1949,S 1,25:2
Fancy Pants 1950,Ag 31,21:2
Mr Music 1950,D 21,34:3
Lemon Drop Kid, The 1951,Mr 22,41:2
Son of Paleface 1952,O 2,32:3
Welch, Robert L (Screenwriter)
Variety Girl 1947,O 16,34:4
Son of Paleface 1952,O 2,32:3
Welch, William
Over the Hill to the Poor House 1920,S 18,16:2
Price She Paid, The 1925,Ja 13,16:1
Welchman, Harry
Waltz Time 1946,F 11,25:2
Eight O'Clock Walk 1955,Ap 30,10:6
Welcker, Gertrude
Dr Nabuse 1927,Ag 10,21:4
Weld, Tuesday
Rally Round the Flag Boys! 1958,D 24,2:7
Five Pennies, The 1959,Je 19,30:1
High Time 1960,S 17,15:1
Return to Peyton Place 1961,My 6,26:1
Wild in the Country 1961,Je 10,12:2
Bachelor Flat 1962,Ja 13,14:1
Soldier in the Rain 1963,N 29,67:6 (Incorrect in
this edition; use 1963,N 28,67:6 elsewhere)
I'll Take Sweden 1965,Ag 12,30:4
Cincinnati Kid, The 1965,O 28,48:1
Lord Love a Duck 1966,F 22,14:6
Pretty Poison 1968,O 25,55:1
Welden, Ben
Missing Rembrandt, The 1932,Mr 26,17:2
Along Came Sally 1934,Je 16,20:3
Man Who Changed his Name, The
1934,O 17,26:2
Triumph of Sherlock Holmes, The
1935,My 27,20:6
King and the Chorus Girl, The 1937,Mr 29,14:4
Marked Woman 1937,Ap 12,15:2
Kid Galahad 1937,My 27,21:3

Another Dawn 1937,Je 18,25:3
Confession 1937,Ag 19,23:1
Varsity Show 1937,S 2,17:2
That Certain Woman 1937,S 16,29:1
Back in Circulation 1937,O 4,17:1
Alcatraz Island 1937,O 14,22:2
Love Is on the Air 1937,N 12,27:3
Missing Witness 1937,D 10,33:3
Happy Landing 1938,Ja 22,19:1
Prison Nurse 1938,Mr 4,17:5
Saint in New York, The 1938,My 26,31:2
Always Goodbye 1938,Je 25,7:2
Mystery House 1938,Je 29,15:5
Crime Ring 1938,Jl 22,10:3
Smashing the Rackets 1938,Ag 9,22:5
Tenth Avenue Kid 1938,S 2,21:3
Straight, Place and Show 1938,O 1,10:2
Federal Man-Hunt 1939,F 2,17:3
Lone Wolf Spy Hunt, The 1939,Mr 6,11:3
I Was a Convict 1939,Mr 23,27:2
Sergeant Madden 1939,Mr 24,27:2
Rose of Washington Square 1939,My 6,21:2
Star Maker, The 1939,Ag 31,14:2
Hollywood Cavalcade 1939,O 14,13:2
Outside the Three-Mile Limit 1940,Ap 8,15:2
Passport to Alcatraz 1940,Je 15,12:2
South of Pago-Pago 1940,Ag 2,12:2
City for Conquest 1940,S 28,9:2
Men of Boys Town 1941,Ap 11,24:6
Strange Alibi 1941,Ap 28,11:2
I'll Wait for You 1941,Je 2,13:6
Manpower 1941,Jl 5,14:2
Nine Loves Are not Enough 1941,O 30,27:2
All Through the Night 1942,Ja 24,13:2
Dangerously They Live 1942,Ap 11,9:2
Bullet Scars 1942,Ap 24,21:4
Stand by for Action 1943,Mr 12,12:2
Fighting Seabees, The 1944,Mr 20,14:2
Shadows in the Night 1944,Jl 29,16:2
Circumstantial Evidence 1945,Ap 21,18:3
Angel on my Shoulder 1946,O 21,27:2
Pretender, The 1947,Ag 12,26:2
Noose Hangs High, The 1948,My 29,8:6
Sorrowful Jones 1949,Je 6,15:2
Mary Ryan, Detective 1949,N 4,33:3
Buccaneer's Girl 1950,Mr 27,19:2
Lemon Drop Kid, The 1951,Mr 22,41:2
Weldman, Jerome (Original Author)
House of Strangers 1949,Jl 2,8:2
Weldman, Jerome (Screenwriter)
Eddie Cantor Story, The 1953,D 26,10:2
Weldon, Bunny
Broadway Nights 1927,Je 28,29:4
Weldon, Joan
System, The 1953,My 23,19:3
Stranger Wore a Gun, The 1953,Jl 30,20:3
So This Is Love 1953,Ag 12,22:1
Command, The 1954,Ja 16,10:5
Riding Shotgun 1954,Ap 2,22:2
Them 1954,Je 17,36:2
Deep in my Heart 1954,D 10,35:2
Day of the Badman 1958,Ja 30,19:2
Home Before Dark 1958,N 7,23:1
Weldon, Robert
Dead Men Tell 1941,Ap 17,29:3
Welf, Clarence (Screenwriter)
How Not to Rob a Department Store
1965,D 29,23:1
Welford, Nancy
Gold Diggers of Broadway, The 1929,Ag 31,13:4
Welisch, Ernst (Original Author)
Madame Pompadour 1927,Ag 2,19:2
That Lady in Ermine 1948,Ag 25,31:2
Welitsch, Ljuba
Arms and the Man 1962,F 24,21:7
Adorable Julia 1964,Ap 8,33:1
Well, Harry (Screenwriter)
Oliver Twist 1922,O 30,11:1
Weller, Jada
Betrayal 1929,My 6,30:4
WELLES
See Also WELLS
Welles, Beatrice
Falstaff; Chimes at Midnight 1967,Mr 18,19:2
Welles, Christopher
Macbeth 1950,D 28,22:6
Welles, Halsted (Screenwriter)
Lady Gambles, The 1949,My 21,9:2
3:10 to Yuma 1957,Ag 29,22:1
Hanging Tree, The 1959,F 12,23:1
Hell With Heroes, The 1968,S 3,54:2
Welles, Mel
Flight to Hong Kong 1957,Ja 3,28:2
Brothers Karamazov, The 1958,F 21,18:2
Welles, Meri
House is not a Home, A 1964,S 2,33:1
Welles, Orson
Citizen Kane 1941,My 2,25:1
Journey Into Fear 1943,Mr 19,15:3
Jane Eyre 1944,F 4,12:5
Follow the Boys 1944,Ap 26,24:6
Tomorrow Is Forever 1946,F 22,21:2
Stranger, The 1946,Jl 11,18:2

Welles, Orson— Cont
Lady From Shanghai, The 1948,Je 10,28:2
Black Magic 1949,N 9,37:2
Prince of Foxes 1949,D 24,11:2
Third Man, The 1950,F 3,29:2
Black Rose, The 1950,S 2,11:2
Macbeth 1950,D 28,22:6
Trent's Last Case 1953,N 27,99:9
Three Cases of Murder (Lord Mountdrago); Lord
Mountdrago (Three Cases of Murder)
1955,Mr 16,39:4
Trouble in the Glen 1955,Ap 11,29:2
Othello 1955,S 13,27:1
Moby Dick 1956,Jl 5,18:1
Royal Affairs in Versailles 1957,Mr 9,16:1
Man With a Shadow 1958,Ja 23,24:3
Long, Hot Summer, The 1958,Ap 4,16:1
Touch of Evil 1958,My 22,25:2
Roots of Heaven, The 1958,O 16,46:1
Compulsion 1959,Ap 2,26:2
Crack in the Mirror 1960,My 20,26:1
Ferry to Hong Kong 1961,Ap 27,27:7
David and Goliath 1961,O 7,14:3
Tartars, The 1962,Je 21,26:2
Mr Arkadin 1962,O 12,26:1
Trial, The 1963,F 21,5:1
Lafayette 1963,Ap 11,29:1
V I P's, The 1963,S 20,29:1
Is Paris Burning? 1966,N 11,36:1
Man for all Seasons, A 1966,D 13,60:1
Marco the Magnificent 1966,D 15,60:1
Falstaff; Chimes at Midnight 1967,Mr 18,19:2
Sailor From Gibraltar, The 1967,Ap 25,38:2
Casino Royale 1967,Ap 29,25:1
I'll Never Forget What's 'Isname
1968,Ap 15,51:1
Oedipus the King 1968,S 19,62:2
Immortal Story, The 1968,S 19,62:2
Welles, Orson (Director)
Citizen Kane 1941,My 2,25:1
Magnificent Ambersons, The 1942,Ag 14,13:3
Stranger, The 1946,Jl 11,18:2
Lady From Shanghai, The 1948,Je 10,28:2
Macbeth 1950,D 28,22:6
Othello 1955,S 13,27:1
Touch of Evil 1958,My 22,25:2
Mr Arkadin 1962,O 12,26:1
Trial, The 1963,F 21,5:1
Falstaff; Chimes at Midnight 1967,Mr 18,19:2
Immortal Story, The 1968,S 19,62:2
Welles, Orson (Narrator)
Masters of the Congo Jungle 1960,My 5,41:2
Finest Hours, The 1964,N 11,38:1
King's Story, A 1967,My 25,57:2
Welles, Orson (Original Author)
Mr Arkadin 1962,O 12,26:1
Welles, Orson (Producer)
Citizen Kane 1941,My 2,25:1
Magnificent Ambersons, The 1942,Ag 14,13:3
Lady From Shanghai, The 1948,Je 10,28:2
Macbeth 1950,D 28,22:6
Othello 1955,S 13,27:1
Welles, Orson (Screenwriter)
Citizen Kane 1941,My 2,25:1
Magnificent Ambersons, The 1942,Ag 14,13:3
Journey Into Fear 1943,Mr 19,15:3
Macbeth 1950,D 28,22:6
Touch of Evil 1958,My 22,25:2
Mr Arkadin 1962,O 12,26:1
Trial, The 1963,F 21,5:1
Falstaff; Chimes at Midnight 1967,Mr 18,19:2
Immortal Story, The 1968,S 19,62:2
Welles, Ralph
Night Ride 1930,Ja 20,21:1
Girls Demand Excitement 1931,F 7,11:1
Welles, Rebecca
Desire Under the Elms 1958,Mr 13,24:2
Welles, Virginia
Kiss and Tell 1945,O 26,16:2
To Each his Own 1946,My 24,15:2
Ladies' Man 1947,Ja 13,18:5
Dear Ruth 1947,Je 11,33:3
Francis in the Haunted House 1956,Jl 21,9:2
Wellesley, Charles
Don't Marry for Money 1923,Ag 21,17:3
Acquittal, The 1923,D 12,24:5
Oytherea 1924,My 26,21:1
Perfect Flapper, The 1924,Je 23,22:4
Lost World, The 1925,F 9,15:3
Unholy Three, The 1925,Ag 4,14:3
Skinner's big Idea 1928,Mr 27,30:4
Wellesley, Gordon (Director)
Silver Fleet, The 1945,Mr 24,22:6
Wellesley, Gordon (Original Author)
Night Train 1940,D 30,21:1
Wellesley, Gordon (Producer)
Lost People, The 1950,O 2,19:4
Reluctant Widow, The 1951,S 8,8:6
Wellesley, Gordon (Screenwriter)
Java Head 1935,Jl 31,21:4
Voice in the Night, The 1941,My 23,25:4
Flying Fortress 1942,D 19,22:2
Mr Emmanuel 1945,Ja 8,15:2
Silver Fleet, The 1945,Mr 24,22:6

Wellesley, Gordon (Screenwriter) — Cont
Reluctant Widow, The 1951,S 8,8:6
Green Scarf, The 1955,Ja 15,10:2
Passport to China 1961,Mr 23,28:1
Wellesley, William
Goldfish, The 1924,My 20,15:2
Wellman, Bill Jr
Darby's Rangers 1958,F 13,23:2
Lafayette Escadrille 1958,Ap 19,10:4
Pork Chop Hill 1959,My 30,9:2
Born Losers, The 1967,Ag 19,16:2
Wellman, Michael
High and the Mighty, The 1954,Jl 1,21:2
Wellman, Paul I (Original Author)
Cheyenne 1947,Je 7,9:2
Walls of Jericho, The 1948,Ag 5,16:2
Iron Mistress, The 1952,N 20,39:2
Apache 1954,Jl 10,7:2
Jubal 1956,Ap 25,39:1
Wellman, William A (Director)
Wings 1927,Ag 13,10:4
Legion of the Condemned, The 1928,Mr 19,26:2
Ladies of the Mob 1928,Je 18,13:2
Beggars of Life 1928,S 24,25:1
Chinatown Nights 1929,Ap 1,22:1
Man I Love, The 1929,My 28,36:2
Woman Trap 1929,Ag 31,13:4
Dangerous Paradise 1930,F 16,III,8:1
Young Eagles 1930,Mr 22,22:6
Maybe It's Love 1930,O 18,23:2
Other Men's Women 1931,Ap 20,16:3
Public Enemy, The 1931,Ap 24,27:1
Night Nurse 1931,Jl 17,23:4
Star Witness, The 1931,Ag 4,19:5
Safe in Hell 1931,D 19,16:4
Hatchet Man, The 1932,F 4,25:2
So Big 1932,Ap 30,19:3
Love Is a Racket 1932,Je 11,9:3
Purchase Price, The 1932,Jl 16,5:5
Conquerors, The 1932,N 21,21:1
Frisco Jenny 1933,Ja 7,11:2
Central Airport 1933,My 4,20:5
Lilly Turner 1933,Je 15,21:2
Midnight Mary 1933,Jl 15,14:2
Heroes for Sale 1933,Jl 22,14:3
Wild Boys of the Road 1933,S 22,14:1
College Coach 1933,N 11,10:4
Looking for Trouble 1934,Ap 12,27:2
Stingaree 1934,My 18,27:1
President Vanishes, The 1934,D 8,18:5
Call of the Wild 1935,Ag 15,15:2
Robin Hood of El Dorado, The 1936,Mr 14,10:1
Small Town Girl 1936,Ap 11,19:1
Star Is Born, A 1937,Ap 23,25:1
Nothing Sacred 1937,N 26,27:2
Men With Wings 1938,O 27,27:2
Beau Geste 1939,Ag 3,15:2
Light That Failed, The 1939,D 25,19:1
Reaching for the Sun 1941,My 8,21:1
Roxie Hart 1942,F 20,21:1
Great Man's Lady, The 1942,Ap 30,14:3
Thunder Birds 1942,O 29,19:2
Ox-Bow Incident, The 1943,My 10,15:2 (In Addenda)
Lady of Burlesque 1943,My 14,17:2
Buffalo Bill 1944,Ap 20,22:6
This Man's Navy 1945,Ap 16,18:6
Story of G I Joe 1945,O 6,9:6
Gallant Journey 1946,O 10,33:2
Magic Town 1947,O 8,29:2
Iron Curtain, The 1948,My 13,31:2
Yellow Sky 1949,F 2,36:1
Battleground 1949,N 12,8:4
Next Voice You Hear, The 1950,Je 30,18:2
Across the Wide Missouri 1951,N 7,35:4
Westward the Women 1952,Ja 1,21:2
It's a big Country 1952,Ja 9,25:2
My Man and I 1952,S 6,12:6
Island in the Sky 1953,S 10,22:2
High and the Mighty, The 1954,Jl 1,21:2
Track of the Cat 1954,D 2,38:2
Blood Alley 1955,O 6,25:3
Darby's Rangers 1958,F 13,23:2
Lafayette Escadrille 1958,Ap 19,10:4
Wellman, William A (Original Author)
Star Is Born, A 1937,Ap 23,25:1
Last Gangster, The 1937,D 10,33:2
Star is Born, A 1954,O 12,23:1
Lafayette Escadrille 1958,Ap 19,10:4
Wellman, William A (Producer)
Men With Wings 1938,O 27,27:2
Beau Geste 1939,Ag 3,15:2
Light That Failed, The 1939,D 25,19:1
Reaching for the Sun 1941,My 8,21:1
Great Man's Lady, The 1942,Ap 30,14:3
Gallant Journey 1946,O 10,33:2
Wellman, William A (Screenwriter)
Robin Hood of El Dorado, The 1936,Mr 14,10:1
Gallant Journey 1946,O 10,33:2
WELLS
See Also WELLES
Wells, Alan
Man Who Cheated Himself, The 1951,F 9,21:2
Beachhead 1954,Ap 17,8:2

Wells, Betty
Courtship of Andy Hardy, The 1942,Ap 10,21:2
Tortilla Flat 1942,My 22,27:1
Grand Central Murder 1942,My 23,8:8
Wells, Carole
Thunder of Drums, A 1961,S 27,35:1
Lively Set, The 1964,O 15,54:1
Wells, Carolyn (Original Author)
Countess Charming 1917,S 17,11:3
Woman Next Door, The 1919,My 19,20:5
Dearie 1927,Jl 4,20:3
Wells, Carveth
Jungle Killer, The 1932,N 26,11:4
Wells, Carveth (Narrator)
Hell Below Zero 1931,Je 27,20:3
Wells, Cyril
It's Love Again 1936,My 23,12:1
Wells, Dawn
New Interns, The 1964,Ag 20,34:2
Wells, Ethel (Pug)
Three Guys Named Mike 1951,Mr 2,21:2
Wells, George (Original Author)
Texas Carnival 1951,O 13,9:1
Wells, George (Producer)
Everything I Have is Yours 1952,O 30,40:5
I Love Melvin 1953,Ap 10,18:4
Dangerous When Wet 1953,Je 19,18:1
Jupiter's Darling 1955,F 18,18:4
Wells, George (Screenwriter)
Till the Clouds Roll By 1946,D 6,27:4
Show-Off, The 1947,Mr 20,38:2
Hucksters, The 1947,Jl 18,21:2
Merton of the Movies 1947,N 7,20:3
Take Me Out to the Ball Game 1949,Mr 10,35:2
Three Little Words 1950,Ag 10,21:2
Summer Stock 1950,S 1,17:2
Toast of New Orleans, The 1950,S 30,13:3
Excuse my Dust 1951,Je 28,21:2
Angels in the Outfield 1951,O 18,32:1
It's a big Country 1952,Ja 9,25:2
Lovely to Look At 1952,My 30,11:2
Everything I Have is Yours 1952,O 30,40:5
I Love Melvin 1953,Ap 10,18:4
Designing Woman 1957,My 17,20:2
Don't Go Near the Water 1957,N 15,37:1
Party Girl 1958,O 29,30:1
Ask any Girl 1959,My 22,32:1
Gazebo, The 1960,Ja 16,14:4
Where the Boys Are 1961,Ja 20,22:1
Honeymoon Machine, The 1961,Ag 24,25:2
Horizontal Lieutenant, The 1962,My 12,15:3
Penelope 1966,N 11,36:6
Three Bites of the Apple 1967,My 25,54:2
Impossible Years, The 1968,D 6,54:1
Wells, H G (Miscellaneous)
Man Who Could Work Miracles, The 1937,F 22,13:1
Wells, H G (Original Author)
Day Dreams 1930,F 4,28:3
Island of Lost Souls 1933,Ja 13,19:2
Invisible Man, The 1933,N 18,18:4
Things to Come 1936,Ap 18,19:2
Kipps 1942,My 25,11:2
Invisible Agent 1942,Ag 6,23:2
Invisible Man's Revenge, The 1944,Je 10,12:2
One Woman's Story 1949,My 18,33:2
Abbott and Costello Meet the Invisible Man 1951,Ap 13,18:6
History of Mr Polly, The 1951,O 25,36:3
War of the Worlds, The 1953,Ag 14,10:2
Time Machine, The 1960,Ag 18,19:1
First Men in the Moon 1964,N 26,52:2
Door in the Wall 1965,Ja 22,21:2
Half a Sixpence 1968,F 21,60:3
Wells, H G (Screenwriter)
Things to Come 1936,Ap 18,19:2
Wells, Ingeborg
Captain Horatio Hornblower 1951,S 14,21:2
Across the Bridge 1957,O 30,24:1
Wells, Jacqueline
Golden Bed, The 1925,Ja 20,18:2
Home Maker, The 1925,Ag 10,8:2
Classified 1925,N 2,20:1
Tarzan, The Fearless 1933,Ag 12,14:3
Tillie and Gus 1933,N 13,21:1
Black Cat, The 1934,My 19,18:4
Coronado 1935,D 19,33:4
Bohemian Girl, The 1936,F 17,21:1
Frame-Up 1937,Ag 9,23:2 (In Addenda)
Counsel for Crime 1937,O 9,16:1
Paid to Dance 1937,D 6,19:1
She Married an Artist 1938,F 25,15:2
When G-Men Step In 1938,Mr 14,13:2
Flight Into Nowhere 1938,My 2,13:3
Main Event, The 1938,Je 20,11:3
Highway Patrol 1938,Ag 4,15:2
Spring Madness 1938,D 1,29:3
Behind Prison Gates 1939,Ag 21,9:3
My Son Is Guilty 1940,Ja 15,11:2
Girl in 313 1940,Je 14,25:3
Wells, Jane
Little Lord Fauntleroy 1914,Je 23,11:3

Wells, Jerold
Masquerade 1965,Ap 29,40:2
Wells, Joan
Till the Clouds Roll By 1946,D 6,27:4
Yearling, The 1947,Ja 24,18:2
Wells, John
Fistful of Dollars, A 1967,F 2,29:1
Bobo, The 1967,S 29,53:1
30 Is a Dangerous Age, Cynthia 1968,Mr 5,34:1
Wells, John (Original Author)
30 Is a Dangerous Age, Cynthia 1968,Mr 5,34:1
Wells, John (Screenwriter)
30 Is a Dangerous Age, Cynthia 1968,Mr 5,34:1
Wells, Linton (Original Author)
Moran of the Marines 1928,O 15,16:1
Wells, Mae
Excuse Me 1925,Ja 27,11:2
Wells, Margaret
Spirit of West Point 1947,O 3,31:2
Pitfall 1948,Ag 25,31:2
Wells, Marie
Desert Song, The 1929,My 2,20:6
Song of the West 1930,F 28,20:7
Elmer and Elsie 1934,Ag 4,14:5
Scralet Empress, The 1934,S 15,20:2
Wells, Raymond
Yankee Senor, The 1926,Ja 28,14:4
Oh! What a Nurse! 1926,F 22,14:1
Tony Runs Wild 1926,Ap 28,28:3
Death Valley 1927,N 22,32:2
Wells, Raymond (Screenwriter)
Death Valley 1927,N 22,32:2
Wells, Sheilah
Love and Kisses 1965,D 23,21:4
Wells, Si
Three Cheers for Love 1936,Ag 1,16:2
Wells, Tom
Rookery-Nook 1930,Mr 23,IX,6:1
Wells, Veronica
Boom! 1968,My 27,56:1
Wells, William K (Miscellaneous)
New Movietone Follies of 1930, The 1930,Je 21,20:5
Wells, William K (Original Author)
Let's Go Places 1930,Mr 1,23:1
Wells, William K (Screenwriter)
New Movietone Follies of 1930, The 1930,Je 21,20:5
Wellton, Ollegard
Unmarried Mothers 1956,F 23,32:5
Welsch, Howard (Producer)
Daltons Ride Again, The 1945,D 8,21:2
Spider Woman Strikes Back, The 1946,Mr 23,8:3
Michigan Kid 1947,F 22,16:3
Vigilantes Return, The 1947,Jl 1,30:2
House by the River 1950,My 2,25:2
Woman on the Run 1950,N 30,24:2
Groom Wore Spurs, The 1951,Mr 14,41:2
San Francisco Story, The 1952,My 10,16:4
Rancho Notorious 1952,My 15,39:5
Montana Belle 1952,N 8,9:2
Bullet is Waiting, A 1954,N 12,17:2
Hot Blood 1956,Mr 24,14:2
WELSH
See Also WELCH
Welsh, Bill
Las Vegas Story, The 1952,Ja 31,37:6
Welsh, Jane
Sherlock Holmes's Fatal Hour 1931,Jl 13,13:5
Missing Rembrandt, The 1932,Mr 26,17:2
Condemned to Death 1932,Jl 14,24:2
Welsh, John
Lucky Jim 1958,S 1,8:6
Room at the Top 1959,Mr 31,26:1
Next to no Time 1960,My 28,13:2
Circle of Deception 1961,F 18,12:2
Francis of Assisi 1961,Jl 29,8:2
Mark, The 1961,O 3,46:2
Playboy of the Western World, The 1963,Mr 19,8:2
Welsh, Robert E (Producer)
Three Legionnaires 1937,Jl 10,18:2
Welsh, Robert E (Screenwriter)
Booloo 1938,Jl 30,10:2
Welsh, Ronnie Jr
Patterns 1956,Mr 28,26:1
Welsh, William
Mississippi Gambler, The 1929,O 28,20:1
Skinner Steps Out 1929,D 7,19:3
Welsh, William J
Ruggles of Red Gap 1935,Mr 7,26:1
Welton, Myron
Emergency Wedding 1950,D 22,19:2
Welzel, Heinz
D III 88, Die neue deutsche Luftwaffe greift an; D III 88, The New German Air Force Attacks 1940,F 17,9:3
Razzia 1948,Je 14,19:2
Wemper, Heinz
Unschuld vom Lande, Die 1935,My 13,18:6
Wencel, H (Director)
Pan Redaktor Szaleje; Mr Editor Is Crazy 1938,Je 14,17:3

Wences, Senor
Mother Wore Tights 1947,Ag 21,33:2
Wenck, Eduard
Lustige Witwenball, Der; Merry Widows' Ball, The 1939,My 1,21:2
Biberpelz, Der; Beaver Coat, The 1939,S 9,11:3
Wenck, Ewald
Herbst-Monoever; Fall Manoeuvres 1939,Mr 18,9:3
Wendell, Howard
Affair in Trinidad 1952,Jl 31,14:2
You for Me 1952,S 25,38:3
By the Light of the Silvery Moon 1953,Mr 27,28:2
Big Heat, The 1953,O 15,43:2
Black Dakotas, The 1954,O 2,21:2
Athena 1954,D 22,28:2
Stranger in my Arms 1959,Mr 4,34:2
Wendhausen, F R
At Dawn We Die 1943,My 8,19:2
Wendhausen, Franz (Director)
Familienparade 1937,Mr 20,23:5
Wendhausen, Frederick
Beware of Pity 1947,N 1,11:2
Wendhausen, Fritz (Director)
Peer Gynt 1939,N 11,12:2
Wendhausen, Fritz (Screenwriter)
1914: The Last Days Before the War 1932,S 5,9:6
Wendhousen, Frederick
Odette 1951,Mr 28,33:2
Desperate Moment 1953,S 1,19:4
Wendkos, Paul (Director)
Gidget 1959,Ap 23,27:4
Gidget Goes Hawaiian 1961,Ag 10,17:4
Angel Baby 1961,O 5,43:1
Gidget Goes to Rome 1963,S 12,32:2
Johnny Tiger 1966,Je 16,53:4
Wendkos (Director)
Attack on the Iron Coast 1968,Je 6,54:2
Wendlandt, Horst (Producer)
Tempestous Love 1958,N 22,27:4
Wendling, Maryse
Kermesse Heroique, La 1936,S 23,29:1
Wendorf, Ruben
Shir Hashirim 1935,O 11,31:1
Mirele Efros 1939,O 21,12:2
I Was a Male War Bride 1949,Ag 27,7:2
Wendt, Elisabeth
Kameradschaft 1932,N 9,28:5
Mutter und Kind 1934,N 30,22:3
Die vom Niederrhein; Lower Rhine Folks 1935,My 20,20:6
Seltsamer Gast, Ein 1937,Jl 10,18:2
Graue Dame, Die; Gray Lady, The 1938,D 17,10:4
Girls Behind Bars 1950,My 10,41:2
Wenger, John (Miscellaneous)
Blue Bird, The 1918,Ap 1,9:3
Wengraf, John
Convoy 1941,Ja 17,21:2
Paris After Dark 1943,O 23,11:1
Sahara 1943,N 12,25:2
Seventh Cross, The 1944,S 29,18:1
Tomorrow Is Forever 1946,F 22,21:2
Razor's Edge, The 1946,N 20,42:2
T-Men 1948,Ja 23,28:3
Sofia 1948,S 4,8:7
Five Fingers 1952,F 23,7:5
Desert Rats, The 1953,My 9,13:2
French Line, The 1954,My 15,13:2
Gambler From Natchez, The 1954,Ag 14,8:2
Gog 1954,Ag 14,8:2
Racers, The 1955,F 5,13:2
Oh Men! Oh Women! 1957,F 22,25:2
Pride and the Passion, The 1957,Je 29,10:6
Portrait in Black 1960,Jl 28,19:1
Judgment at Nuremberg 1961,D 20,36:1
Prize, The 1964,Ja 24,21:1
Ship of Fools 1965,Jl 29,18:1
Wengraf, Senta
Don Juan 1956,Mr 6,26:2
Wengren, David
Soft Living 1928,F 27,16:2
Wenham, Jane
Inspector Calls, An 1954,N 26,24:4
Teckman Mystery, The 1955,Ag 22,18:2
Wenkhaus, Rolf
Emil und die Detektive 1931,D 21,28:4
S A Mann Brand 1934,My 28,16:2
Wenman, Henry
Middle Watch, The 1930,D 20,20:6
Brewster's Millions 1935,Ap 8,23:3
Wenn, Clifton
Let Not Man Put Asunder 1924,Ja 15,16:1
Wenning, T H (Original Author)
Sophomore, The 1929,Ag 24,11:5
Wenrich, Percy (Composer)
Tin Pan Alley 1940,N 22,27:3
Wentworth, Marion Craig (Screenwriter)
War Brides 1916,N 13,11:1
Wentworth, Martha
Stranger, The 1946,Jl 11,18:2
Good Morning, Miss Dove 1955,N 24,41:1

Wentworth-James, Gertie (Screenwriter)
Wife Who Wasn't Wanted, The 1925,S 9,23:1
Wentz, Roby (Screenwriter)
Heroes of the Alamo 1938,Ap 2,18:2
Wenzler, Franz (Director)
Das Ekel 1932,Ja 30,13:2
Causa Kaiser; Kaiser Case, The 1932,F 14,VIII,6:1
Wenn die Liebe Mode Macht 1933,O 30,14:3
Gipfelstuermer, Der 1937,Ap 10,11:2
Horst Wessel 1939,Mr 4,18:5
Wepper, Fritz
Bridge, The; (Bruecke, Die) 1961,My 2,42:1
Question 7 1961,S 29,30:2
Miracle of the White Stallions 1963,My 23,31:2
Werbiseck, Gisela
Hairy Ape, The 1944,Jl 3,8:3
Wonder Man 1945,Je 9,17:2
Scandal In Paris, A 1946,S 16,9:7
Werden, Sybil
Desires 1954,Jl 2,10:2
Werfel, Franz (Original Author)
Juarez 1939,Ap 26,27:1
Song of Bernadette, The 1944,Ja 27,15:2
Me and the Colonel 1958,Ag 27,33:1
Embezzled Heaven 1959,Ap 24,23:1
Werich
World Is Ours, The 1939,Ag 14,11:5
Werich, Jan
Emperor and the Golem, The 1955,Ja 10,27:4
Werich, Jan (Original Author)
Emperor and the Golem, The 1955,Ja 10,27:4
Werich, Jan (Screenwriter)
Emperor and the Golem, The 1955,Ja 10,27:4
Werich (Screenwriter)
World Is Ours, The 1939,Ag 14,11:5
Werker, Alfred (Director)
Last of the Duanes 1930,S 13,9:3
Annabelle's Affairs 1931,Je 29,20:3
Heartbreak 1931,O 17,20:1
Gay Caballero, The 1932,Mr 26,17:2
Bachelor's Affairs 1932,Je 25,18:2
Rackety Rax 1932,N 5,12:5
It's Great to be Alive 1933,Jl 8,14:6
Advice to the Lovelorn 1933,D 14,28:2
House of Rothschild, The 1934,Mr 15,27:2
You Belong to Me 1934,S 13,26:1
Stolen Harmony 1935,Ap 20,16:2
We Have our Moments 1937,Ap 30,17:3
Wild and Woolly 1937,S 6,20:1
Big Town Girl 1937,D 13,23:4
City Girl 1938,F 4,17:3
Kidnapped 1938,My 28,9:2
Gateway 1938,Ag 8,9:2
Up the River 1938,D 3,11:2
It Could Happen to You 1939,Je 9,26:3
News Is Made at Night 1939,Jl 13,17:2
Adventures of Sherlock Holmes, The 1939,S 2,20:1
Reluctant Dragon, The 1941,Jl 25,12:2
Moon Over her Shoulder 1941,N 5,31:2
Whispering Ghosts 1942,My 18,19:4
A-Haunting We Will Go 1942,Ag 3,18:4
My Pal, Wolf 1944,O 9,17:2
Shock 1946,Mr 9,10:2
Repeat Performance 1947,Jl 2,19:2
Pirates of Monterey 1947,D 17,41:4
He Walked by Night 1949,F 7,15:2
Lost Boundaries 1949,Jl 1,14:4
Sealed Cargo 1951,My 24,47:1
Walk East on Beacon 1952,My 29,17:2
Devil's Canyon 1953,O 3,14:2
Three Hours to Kill 1954,S 4,6:4
At Gunpoint 1956,F 4,24:5
Young Don't Cry, The 1957,Jl 27,10:7
Werker, George P (Producer)
Young One, The 1961,Ja 19,26:1
Werkmeister, Lotte
Hampelmann, Der 1931,S 8,38:7
Zu Befehl, Herr Unteroffizier 1934,Je 16,20:3
Toerichte Jungfrau, Die 1935,S 9,24:3
Werkmeister, Vicky
Dolly Macht Karriere 1931,Jl 18,16:6
Wahre Jakob, Der 1931,Ag 7,20:2
Schlacht von Bademuende, Die 1931,N 21,20:4
Mein Leopold 1932,Ap 1,17:4
Schoen Ist die Manoeverzeit 1932,Ag 19,20:6
Werle, Barbara
Battle of the Bulge 1965,D 18,36:1
Werleteit, Bertil
Hawaii 1966,O 11,54:1
Werner, Dieter (Screenwriter)
Golden Plaque, The 1963,Ag 10,8:6
Werner, Gabriel
Last Year at Marienbad 1962,Mr 8,26:1
Werner, Ilse
Macht der Berge, Die; Power of the Mountains, The 1938,O 22,14:2
Drei Vater um Anna; Three Fathers for Anna 1940,Ja 20,11:3
Ihr Erstes Erlebnis; Her First Experience 1940,Je 8,18:3
Reaching for the Stars 1958,My 24,18:2

Werner, Jean
Heroes and Sinners; (Heros Sont Fatigues, Les) 1959,My 12,38:2
Werner, Lars (Producer)
Obession 1968,Ag 29,46:3
Werner, M (Director)
Prisoners of the Sea 1929,Ap 16,32:5
Werner, Oskar
Eroica; (The Beethoven Story) 1951,O 29,19:2
Angel With the Trumpet 1951,D 21,21:5
Decision Before Dawn 1951,D 22,12:2
Wonder Boy 1951,D 26,19:5
Last ten Days, The 1956,Ap 12,26:1
Life and Loves of Mozart, The 1958,Ja 7,28:2
Jules and Jim 1962,Ap 24,32:1
Ship of Fools 1965,Jl 29,18:1
Spy Who Came in From the Cold, The 1965,D 24,24:1
Fahrenheit 451 1966,N 15,53:1
Interlude 1968,Jl 3,26:1
Lola Montes 1968,S 23,42:6
Shoes of the Fisherman, The 1968,N 15,40:3
Werner, Walter
Kreutzer Sonata, The 1938,My 28,9:3
Marriage in the Shadows 1948,S 17,28:3
Werner-Hohle, Hugo
Mother Love 1931,F 16,17:1
Gruen ist die Heide 1935,O 14,21:2
Wernicke, Otto
Stuerme der Leidenschaft 1932,Mr 16,17:3
M 1933,Ap 3,13:3
Die Blonde Christl 1934,F 23,23:3
Verkaufte Braut, Die 1934,Ap 27,25:2
S A Mann Brand 1934,My 28,16:2
Zwischen Himmel und Erde; Between Heaven and Earth 1935,Ja 21,19:3
Knock-Out 1936,F 29,11:2
Stimme des Blutes; Blood Bond 1937,D 28,29:2
Gleisdreieck 1938,Je 11,9:1
Henker Fraven und Soldaten; Hangmen, Women and Soldiers 1940,Ja 13,11:3
D III 88, Die neue deutsche Luftwaffe greift an; D III 88, The New German Air Force Attacks 1940,F 17,9:3
Johannis fever; St Johns' Fire 1940,Ap 6,13:2
Maria Ilona 1940,Ap 20,14:3
Long Is the Road 1948,N 12,30:5
Werrenrath, Reinald
Vitaphone 1926,O 8,23:2
Werris, Snag (Screenwriter)
Four Jills in a Jeep 1944,Ap 6,27:2
Take It or Leave It 1944,Jl 13,14:2
If I'm Lucky 1946,S 20,41:3
Werth, Alexander (Miscellaneous)
Ukraine in Flames 1944,Ap 3,18:2
Werth, Barbara
Fast and Furious 1927,Jl 4,20:3
Wertimer, Ned
Impossible Years, The 1968,D 6,54:1
Werty, Quentin (Screenwriter)
Jigsaw 1968,Je 6,54:2
Dark of the Sun 1968,Jl 4,13:1
Wery, Carl
Heidi 1953,D 21,27:2
Desires 1954,Jl 2,10:2
Angelika 1954,S 25,10:7
Heidi and Peter 1955,D 13,55:2
Ballerina 1958,My 10,19:2
Wescott, Helen
Mr Belvedere Goes to College 1949,Ap 16,11:2
Charge at Feather River, The 1953,Jl 16,17:2
Wesener, Eduard
Stern von Valencia, Der 1934,Ap 21,12:2
Pantoffelhelden 1935,O 21,22:5
Traum vom Rhein, Der 1935,D 9,25:2
Alte Kameraden 1936,Ap 27,19:3
Unsterbliche Melodien; Immortal Melodies 1938,Ap 23,19:3
Kleines Bezirksgericht; Little Country Court 1939,F 18,12:4
Starker als die Liebe; Stronger Than Love 1939,My 6,21:3
Weske, Brian
Gay Intruders, The 1946,Mr 18,24:2
Quiet Week-End 1948,Ag 20,13:2
Fame Is the Spur 1949,N 8,34:2
Weske, J Victor
Tower of Terror 1942,Je 29,11:4
Wesker, Arnold (Original Author)
Kitchen, The 1961,N 2,42:1
Wesley, George
Fixed Bayonets 1951,N 21,20:2
Wesly, Claude
World Without Sun 1964,D 23,22:1
Wesolowski, Tadeusz
Moj Wujaszek Z Ameryki 1933,O 25,25:3
Wesoly, Luba
Overture to Glory 1940,F 12,14:2
Wessel, Dick
Arson Racket Squad 1938,Je 18,18:2
Missing Daughters 1939,Je 12,14:5
Street of Missing Women 1940,Ja 8,11:2
So You Won't Talk 1940,O 17,33:2

Wessel, Dick — Cont

Tanks a Million 1941,O 9,27:2
Action in the North Atlantic 1943,My 22,10:2
In old Sacramento 1946,Ap 29,24:4
Dick Tracy vs Cueball 1946,N 23,12:2
Bad Men of Tombstone 1949,Mr 5,10:2
Slattery's Hurricane 1949,Ag 13,6:6
Blondie Hits the Jackpot 1949,S 9,28:3
Watch the Birdie 1950,D 12,46:4
Texas Carnival 1951,O 13,9:1
Love Is Better Than Ever 1952,My 4,23:2
Belle of New York, The 1952,Mr 6,25:6
Young Man With Ideas 1952,Je 7,22:6
Wives and Lovers 1963,Ag 29,36:1

Wesselhoeft, Eleanor

Street Scene 1931,Ag 27,22:5
Madame Racketeer 1932,Jl 23,6:6
Cradle Song 1933,N 20,18:2
Black Moon 1934,Je 28,26:2
Wedding Night, The 1935,Mr 16,19:1
Boulder Dam 1936,Mr 30,17:5
Son Comes Home, A 1936,S 5,7:1
Ladies in Love 1936,O 29,31:1
Baroness and the Butler, The 1938,F 19,19:2
Intermezzo, A Love Story 1939,O 6,31:1
Everything Happens at Night 1939,D 16,12:6
Four Sons 1940,Je 8,18:4

Wessell, Dick

Slim 1937,Je 24,30:2
Brother Orchid 1940,Je 8,18:2
Merton of the Movies 1947,N 7,20:3
Unknown Island 1949,Ja 8,11:4

Wessell, Richard

Gazebo, The 1960,Ja 16,14:4

Wessely, Paula

Maskerade 1934,O 14,X,4:2 (In Addenda)
Masquerade in Vienna 1937,Ja 26,16:4
Episode 1937,My 17,23:2
Julika, Die 1939,D 23,9:1
Spiegel des Lebens, Der; Life's Mirror
1940,F 17,9:3
Maria Ilona 1940,Ap 20,14:3
Third Sex, The 1959,Mr 26,27:1

Wesson, Dick

Destination Moon 1950,Je 28,32:2
Breakthrough 1950,N 18,10:2
Inside the Walls of Folsom Prison
1951,My 28,17:4
Force of Arms 1951,Ag 14,20:2
Jim Thorpe - All American 1951,Ag 25,7:2
Starlift 1951,D 15,11:2
About Face 1952,My 24,15:3
Desert Song, The 1953,My 21,39:2
Charge at Feather River, The 1953,Jl 16,17:2
Calamity Jane 1953,N 5,40:2

West, Adam

Young Philadelphians, The 1959,My 22,32:1
Tammy and the Doctor 1963,Je 27,23:2
Robinson Crusoe on Mars 1964,Ag 27,28:2
Batman 1966,Ag 25,42:4

West, Algernon

Loyalties 1934,O 26,25:1

West, Bernie

Bells Are Ringing 1960,Je 24,31:2

West, Bert

Enemies of the Law 1931,Jl 13,13:5

West, Billy

Further Perils of Laurel and Hardy, The
1968,Ap 1,56:6

West, Brooks

Anatomy of a Murder 1959,Jl 3,10:1

West, Buster

Radio City Revels 1938,Mr 21,18:3

West, Charles

Bob Hampton of Placer 1921,My 2,12:1
Eternal Three, The 1923,O 12,7:2 (Incorrect in
this edition; use 1927,O 1,7:2 elsewhere)
Talker, The 1925,My 12,26:2
Road to Yesterday, The 1925,D 1,22:4
Nobody's Widow 1927,Ja 13,29:1
For the Defense 1930,Jl 19,7:5
Man Trailer, The 1934,My 23,22:3

West, Claudine (Original Author)

Forever and a Day 1943,Mr 13,9:2

West, Claudine (Screenwriter)

Good Earth, The 1937,F 3,27:1
Marie Antoinette 1938,Ag 17,23:2
Goodbye Mr Chips 1939,My 16,27:2
On Borrowed Time 1939,Jl 7,13:2
Mortal Storm, The 1940,Je 21,25:2
We Were Dancing 1942,My 1,23:2
Mrs Miniver 1942,Je 5,23:1
Random Harvest 1942,D 18,36:6
White Cliffs of Dover, The 1944,My 12,15:2

West, Dorian

Unstrap Me 1968,N 21,41:2

West, Edna

Half Way to Heaven 1929,D 7,19:3

West, Ford

Sherlock Jr 1924,My 26,21:1
Half Way to Heaven 1929,D 7,19:3

West, George

Alias the Deacon 1927,Je 21,29:2
On Your Toes 1928,Ja 9,20:1

West, H E

Night Tide 1963,Je 7,37:1
Best Man, The 1964,Ap 7,29:1

West, H St Barbe

Jaws of Hell 1931,Ja 5,21:3
Condemned to Death 1932,Jl 14,24:2

West, Henry

Sporting Life 1918,S 16,9:3
Speed Spook, The 1924,O 21,21:3
Crackerjack, The 1925,My 18,12:1
Men of Steel 1926,Jl 12,24:4
Girl on the Barge, The 1929,F 26,31:1

West, Isabel

Sainted Devil, A 1924,N 24,15:3
Old Home Week 1925,My 25,21:3

West, James

Happy Land 1943,D 9,33:3

West, James (Screenwriter)

Hey Boy! Hey Girl! 1959,Ag 6,18:3

West, Jessamyn (Miscellaneous)

Big Country, The 1958,O 2,44:1

West, Jessamyn (Original Author)

Friendly Persuasion 1956,N 2,30:1

West, Jessamyn (Screenwriter)

Stolen Hours 1963,O 17,39:1

West, Joseph (Screenwriter)

Man Made Monster 1941,Mr 19,25:4
Flying Cadets 1941,O 14,29:2

West, Judi

Fortune Cookie, The 1966,O 20,52:1

West, Lillian

Seventh Heaven 1927,My 26,22:1
Girls' Dormitory 1936,Ag 29,16:2
That's Right, You're Wrong 1939,N 30,25:3
Where Danger Lives 1951,Ja 1,13:6

West, Lockwood

High Treason 1952,My 21,23:3
Horse's Mouth, The 1954,Ja 20,33:4
Leather Boys, The 1965,N 9,50:1

West, Mae

Night after Night 1932,O 31,18:4
She Done Him Wrong 1933,F 10,12:3
I'm no Angel 1933,O 14,18:2
Belle of the Nineties 1934,S 22,12:2
Goin' to Town 1935,My 11,21:2
Klondike Annie 1936,Mr 12,18:2
Go West, Young Man 1936,N 19,31:3
Every Day's a Holiday 1938,Ja 27,17:2
My Little Chickadee 1940,Mr 16,8:2
Heat's on, The 1943,N 26,29:2

West, Mae (Original Author)

She Done Him Wrong 1933,F 10,12:3
I'm no Angel 1933,O 14,18:2
Belle of the Nineties 1934,S 22,12:2
Klondike Annie 1936,Mr 12,18:2

West, Mae (Screenwriter)

Goin' to Town 1935,My 11,21:2
Klondike Annie 1936,Mr 12,18:2
Go West, Young Man 1936,N 19,31:3
Every Day's a Holiday 1938,Ja 27,17:2
My Little Chickadee 1940,Mr 16,8:2

West, Martin

Man From Galveston, The 1964,Ja 23,26:3
Lord Love a Duck 1966,F 22,14:6
Harper 1966,Mr 31,43:1

West, Morris L (Original Author)

Crooked Road, The 1965,F 4,24:2
Shoes of the Fisherman, The 1968,N 15,40:3

West, Nathanael (Original Author)

Advice to the Lovelorn 1933,D 14,28:2
Lonelyhearts 1959,Mr 5,35:3

West, Nathanael (Screenwriter)

Ticket to Paradise 1936,Ag 8,5:3
President's Mystery, The 1936,O 19,22:1
Follow Your Heart 1936,O 22,31:1
Five came Back 1939,Jl 5,20:2
I Stole a Million 1939,Ag 7,11:2
Men Against the Sky 1940,S 12,31:2
Let's Make Music 1941,Ja 23,19:2

West, Pat

Ceiling Zero 1936,Ja 20,22:2
Turn off the Moon 1937,My 20,17:2
Thanks for the Memory 1938,D 8,34:3
Only Angels Have Wings 1939,My 12,25:2
Some Like It Hot 1939,My 25,31:2
His Girl Friday 1940,Ja 12,13:2
Geronimo 1940,F 8,18:3
To Have and Have Not 1944,O 12,24:1

West, Paul (Screenwriter)

Chattel, The 1916,S 25,7:3

West, Roland (Director)

Unknown Purple, The 1924,Mr 24,13:1
Monster, The 1925,F 16,24:1
Bat, The 1926,Mr 15,18:3
Dove, The 1928,Ja 3,28:2
Alibi 1929,Ap 9,29:1
Bat Whispers, The 1931,Ja 16,27:1
Corsair 1931,N 19,27:5

West, Roland (Original Author)

Unknown Purple, The 1924,Mr 24,13:1

West, Roland (Producer)

Nobody 1921,Jl 25,8:3

West, Samuel B (Screenwriter)

Captain Sindbad 1963,Jl 4,9:1

West, Wallace (Original Author)

Headline Shooters 1933,O 23,18:3

West, William (Director)

Flying Wild 1941,Ap 12,19:3

West-Larsen, Niels (Original Author)

Boy Who Stole a Million, The 1960,D 22,18:3

West-Larsen, Niels (Screenwriter)

Boy Who Stole a Million, The 1960,D 22,18:3

Westayer, Harry

Unguarded Women 1924,Je 24,18:2

Westbrook, John

Room at the Top 1959,Mr 31,26:1
Tomb of Ligeia 1965,My 6,44:1

Westbrook, Joline

Johnny Doughboy 1943,My 6,25:3

Westcoatt, Rusty

Yank in Korea, A 1951,Ap 2,29:2

Westcott, Edward Noyes (Original Author)

David Harum 1934,Mr 2,23:2

Westcott, Gordon

Enemies of the Law 1931,Jl 13,13:5
Guilty as Hell 1932,Ag 6,14:5
Love Me Tonight 1932,Ag 19,20:6
Heritage of the Desert 1933,Mr 11,18:3
Crime of the Century, The 1933,Mr 13,18:2
Working Man, The 1933,Ap 21,20:3
Lilly Turner 1933,Je 15,21:2
Private Detective 62 1933,Jl 7,20:2
Heroes for Sale 1933,Jl 22,14:3
Voltaire 1933,Ag 23,21:2
World Changes, The 1933,O 27,22:3
Convention City 1933,D 25,28:2
Fashions of 1934 1934,Ja 20,12:2
I've Got Your Number 1934,F 3,9:3
Dark Hazard 1934,F 23,23:3
Fog over Frisco 1934,Je 7,26:2
Circus Clown, The 1934,Je 30,18:6
Call it Luck 1934,Jl 10,24:5
Case of the Howling Dog, The 1934,O 18,26:5
6-Day Bike Rider 1934,N 3,20:3
Kansas City Princess 1934,N 5,23:1
Murder in the Clouds 1934,D 26,18:1
White Cockatoo, The 1935,Ja 16,21:1
Go Into Your Dance 1935,My 4,17:2
Night at the Ritz, A 1935,My 16,20:2
Front Page Woman 1935,Jl 12,15:1
Bright Lights 1935,Ag 15,15:2
Two Fisted 1935,O 5,18:3

Westcott, Helen

Adventures of Don Juan 1948,D 25,10:1
Girl from Jones Beach, The 1949,Jl 30,9:2
Three Came Home 1950,F 21,22:5
Gunfighter, The 1950,Je 24,7:2
Take Care of my Little Girl 1951,Jl 19,20:2
Phone Call From a Stranger 1952,F 2,11:2
Return of the Texan 1952,F 14,23:1
With a Song in my Heart 1952,Ap 5,20:2
Lone Shark 1952,My 12,21:2
Hot Blood 1956,Mr 24,14:2
God's Little Acre 1958,Ag 14,23:2
Last Hurrah, The 1958,O 24,40:1
Studs Lonigan 1960,D 15,59:1

Westerby, Robert (Original Author)

Spider and the Fly, The 1952,Jl 29,17:3
Cairo Road 1952,N 1,17:2

Westerby, Robert (Screenwriter)

Bad Sister 1948,Je 11,27:3
Broken Journey 1949,My 26,34:3
Prelude to Fame 1950,N 10,35:3
Spider and the Fly, The 1952,Jl 29,17:3
Cairo Road 1952,N 1,17:2
Golden Mask, The 1954,Mr 20,10:5
Fire over Africa 1954,N 22,29:5
War and Peace 1956,Ag 22,26:2
Trouble in the Sky 1961,Jl 13,26:3
Desert Patrol 1962,Ja 18,23:5
Three Lives of Thomasina, The 1963,D 12,46:1
Fighting Prince of Donegal, The 1966,N 10,64:1

Westerfield, James

Chase, The 1946,N 18,31:2
Undercurrent 1946,N 29,36:2
Whistle at Eaton Falls, The 1951,O 11,49:2
On the Waterfront 1954,Jl 29,18:1
Three Hours to Kill 1954,S 4,6:4
Violent Men, The 1955,Ja 27,17:2
Chief Crazy Horse 1955,Ap 28,25:1
Man With the Gun 1955,D 23,14:2
Three Brave Men 1957,Mr 16,13:2
Cowboy 1958,F 20,29:5
Proud Rebel, The 1958,Jl 2,23:4
Shaggy Dog, The 1959,Mr 20,26:2
Wild River 1960,My 27,22:1
Absent-Minded Professor, The 1961,Mr 16,44:2
Birdman of Alcatraz 1962,Jl 19,19:2
Blue 1968,My 11,28:1

Westergren, Hakan

For Her Sake 1930,N 11,29:1
Dream Waltz, The 1930,D 27,16:3
Brokiga Blad 1931,N 30,16:2
Troette Teodor 1932,Ja 18,18:4
Flickorna Fran Gamla Stan 1934,D 27,25:4

Westergren, Hakan— Cont
Swedenhielms 1935,S 6,12:3
Sara Laer Sig Folkvett 1938,F 16,17:1
Rena Rama Sanningen; Nothing but the Truth
 1939,O 7,11:2
Secrets of Woman 1961,Jl 12,36:1
Westerlund, Catrin
Swedish Wedding Night 1965,N 15,48:1
Westermeier, Paul
Kyritz-Pyritz 1932,Ag 9,20:5
Berlin-Alexanderplatz 1933,My 11,14:1
Morgenrot 1933,My 16,15:2
Bettelstudent, Der 1933,O 14,18:3
Wie Sag' Ich's Meinem Mann? 1934,Ja 23,22:4
Inge und die Millionen 1934,Ap 13,25:1
Stern von Valencia, Der 1934,Ap 21,12:2
Zu Befehl, Herr Unteroffizier 1934,Je 16,20:3
Vier Musketiere, Die; Four Musketeers, The
 1935,N 9,19:3
Was Bin Ich Ohne dich? 1935,D 14,11:2
Ich Sehne Mich Nach Dir 1936,S 9,32:4
Mutige Seefahrer, Der 1936,N 21,21:5
Falscher Fuffziger, Ein 1937,F 13,9:1
Meadehen von Gestern Nacht, Das; Girl of Last
 Night, The 1938,Je 18,18:2
Sein bester Freund; His Best Friend
 1938,Jl 2,10:4
Rote Orchideen; Red Orchids 1939,Ap 15,15:2
Aufruhr in Damaskus; Tumult in Damascus
 1939,My 6,21:2
Devil's General, The 1957,Ap 16,38:2
White Horse Inn, The 1957,D 4,50:3
Westerton, Frank H
Manon Lescaut 1914,Je 14,15:1
Westheimer, David (Original Author)
Von Ryan's Express 1965,Je 24,28:1
Westlake, Donald E (Original Author)
Busy Body, The 1967,Je 8,52:2
Westley, George Hembert (Original Author)
House of Rothschild, The 1934,Mr 15,27:2
Westley, Helen
Moulin Rouge 1934,F 8,14:4
Death Takes a Holiday 1934,F 24,18:4
House of Rothschild, The 1934,Mr 15,27:2
Age of Innocence, The 1934,O 19,27:1
Anne of Green Gables 1934,D 22,21:1
Roberta 1935,Mr 8,25:2
Melody Lingers on, The 1935,N 7,27:1
Splendor 1935,N 23,23:2
Show Boat 1936,My 15,29:4
Half Angel 1936,My 30,7:3
Dimples 1936,O 10,21:2
Banjo on My Knee 1936,D 12,15:1
Stowaway 1936,D 19,16:1
Cafe Metropole 1937,Ap 29,17:1
Sing and Be Happy 1937,Je 19,20:2
Heidi 1937,N 6,14:2
I'll Take Romance 1937,D 17,33:2
Baroness and the Butler, The 1938,F 19,19:2
She Married an Artist 1938,F 25,15:2
Rebecca of Sunnybrook Farm 1938,Mr 26,12:1
Alexander's Ragtime Band 1938,Ag 6,7:2
Keep Smiling 1938,Ag 10,15:2
Zaza 1939,Ja 5,17:1
Wife, Husband and Friend 1939,F 25,19:2
Lillian Russell 1940,My 18,11:2
All This and Heaven, Too 1940,Jl 5,10:2
Lady With red Hair 1940,D 6,28:2
Adam Had Four Sons 1941,Mr 28,26:6
Lady From Louisiana 1941,My 15,27:2
Million Dollar Baby 1941,Je 7,20:2
Sunny 1941,Je 13,22:2
Smiling Ghost, The 1941,S 26,26:5
Bedtime Story 1942,Mr 20,25:4
My Favorite Spy 1942,My 29,13:4
Westman, Lolita Ann (Original Author)
Runaway Bride 1930,My 17,21:2
Perfect Clue, The 1935,Mr 14,18:1
Westman, Nydia
Strange Justice 1932,O 20,24:2
King of the Jungle 1933,F 25,20:3
From Hell to Heaven 1933,Mr 18,9:3
Bondage 1933,Ap 24,11:3
Way to Love, The 1933,N 11,10:3
Little Women 1933,N 17,22:3
Cradle Song 1933,N 20,18:2
Trumpet Blows, The 1934,Ap 14,18:2
Success at any Price 1934,My 4,24:2
Ladies Should Listen 1934,Jl 28,16:6
One Night of Love 1934,S 7,25:3
Sweet Adeline 1935,Ja 7,13:2
Feather in her Hat, A 1935,O 25,24:5
Invisible Ray, The 1936,Ja 11,9:3
Gorgeous Hussy, The 1936,S 5,7:1
Craig's Wife 1936,O 2,29:3
Rose Bowl 1936,D 2,35:2
When Love Is Young 1937,Ap 17,15:1
Bulldog Drummond's Revenge 1937,D 17,33:2
Goldwyn Follies, The 1938,F 21,15:1
Bulldog Drummond's Peril 1938,Mr 18,23:2
First 100 Years, The 1938,My 13,17:2
When Tomorrow Comes 1939,Ag 17,16:2
Cat and the Canary, The 1939,N 23,38:5
Forty Little Mothers 1940,Ap 19,25:2

Hullabaloo 1940,D 19,33:1
Bad Man, The 1941,Ap 4,25:1
Chocolate Soldier, The 1941,N 1,20:2
They all Kissed the Bride 1942,Jl 31,11:1
Hers to Hold 1943,Jl 22,15:1
Her Primitive Man 1944,Ap 1,11:1
Late George Apley, The 1947,Mr 21,29:2
Swinger, The 1966,D 15,60:1
Westmeier, Paul
Ein Ausgekochter Junge 1932,My 3,25:5
Liebe und die Erste Eisenbahn, Die; Love and the
 First Railroad 1935,F 18,19:4
Westminster Choir
Hymn of the Nations 1946,Ap 22,26:2
Westmore, Lucy
Doctor Zhivago 1965,D 23,21:1
Westmore, Perc
Hollywood Hotel 1938,Ja 13,17:3
Weston, Cecil
Dude Ranch 1931,Ap 25,23:4
Huckleberry Finn 1931,Ag 8,16:3
Behold My Wife 1935,F 18,19:3
Banjo on My Knee 1936,D 12,15:1
This Land Is Mine 1943,My 28,19:1
Mr Belvedere Rings the Bell 1951,Ag 2,18:1
Weston, David
Becket 1964,Mr 12,40:2
Masque of the Red Death, The 1964,S 17,52:6
Heroes of Telemark, The 1966,Mr 10,26:1
Weston, Doris
Singing Marine, The 1937,Jl 1,33:2
Submarine D-1 1937,D 30,15:4
Chip of the Flying U 1940,Ja 22,11:3
Weston, Garnett (Original Author)
White Zombie 1932,Jl 29,18:2
Supernatural 1933,Ap 22,16:3
Preview Murder Mystery, The 1936,Mr 21,13:2
Daughter of Shanghai 1937,D 24,21:2
Pony Soldier 1952,D 20,15:2
Weston, Garnett (Screenwriter)
Daughter of Shanghai 1937,D 24,21:2
Bulldog Drummond in Africa 1938,Ag 25,15:1
Bulldog Drummond's Secret Police
 1939,Mr 30,19:3
Bulldog Drummond's Bride 1939,Jl 13,17:2
Mill On the Floss, The 1939,N 15,19:3
Crooked Road, The 1940,Je 11,33:4
Weston, George (Original Author)
Eyes of the Soul 1919,Ap 21,13:4
Weston, Jack
Stage Struck 1958,Ap 23,40:1
Please Don't Eat the Daisies 1960,Ap 1,37:1
All in a Nights Work 1961,Mr 23,28:1
Honeymoon Machine, The 1961,Ag 24,25:2
It's Only Money 1962,N 22,43:1
Palm Springs Weekend 1963,N 6,32:1
Incredible Mr Limpet, The 1964,Mr 26,40:4
Mirage 1965,My 27,28:1
Cincinnati Kid, The 1965,O 28,48:1
Wait Until Dark 1967,O 27,48:1
Thomas Crown Affair, The 1968,Je 27,48:2
Weston, Jay (Producer)
For Love of Ivy 1968,Jl 18,26:1
Weston, Joseph J
Over my Dead Body 1942,D 26,15:2
Weston, Leslie
Corridor of Mirrors 1949,Mr 23,35:3
Sleeping Car to Trieste 1949,Ap 18,18:6
Betrayed 1954,S 9,36:1
Stowaway Girl 1957,N 6,43:3
Weston, Margery
Virgin Queen, The 1955,Ag 6,13:2
Weston, Ruth
Public Defender, The 1931,Ag 1,16:4
Devotion 1931,O 3,20:2
Smart Woman 1931,O 12,28:2
Woman Between, The 1931,O 24,20:3
This Sporting Age 1932,O 1,10:4
Splendor 1935,N 23,23:2
Made for Each Other 1939,F 17,17:2
Weston, Sam
One Potato, Two Potato 1964,Jl 30,16:1
Weston, Sam (Producer)
One Potato, Two Potato 1964,Jl 30,16:1
Weston, William
Black Bird, The 1926,F 1,16:1
Westover, Russ (Original Author)
Tillie the Toiler 1927,Je 7,27:4
Westover, Winifred
Lummox 1930,Mr 24,25:1
Westrate, Edwin V (Miscellaneous)
Prison Farm 1938,Jl 15,13:3
Westrate, Edwin V (Screenwriter)
Shoot to Kill 1947,My 17,8:5
Westwood, John
Shepherd of the Hills, The 1928,F 20,14:1
Varsity 1928,O 29,29:1
Westwood, Patrick
Othello 1960,My 16,39:1
Westworth, Martha
Bowery Blitzkrieg 1941,O 1,24:5

Wethered, James
If Winter Comes 1948,Ja 23,28:4
Wetherell, M A
Livingstone in Africa 1929,Mr 25,32:2
Wetherell, M A (Director)
Somme, The 1928,N 27,34:1
Wetjen, Albert Richard (Original Author)
Way for a Sailor 1930,D 13,22:2
Wetra, Maris
Fruehlingsmaerchen 1935,My 20,20:5
Wetsterby, Robert (Screenwriter)
Greyfriars' Bobby 1961,O 12,41:4
Wette, Adelheid (Original Author)
Hansel and Gretel 1954,O 11,33:1
Wettergren, Gertrud
Karl Fredrik Reigns 1938,F 2,15:2
Wever, Ned
Some Came Running 1959,Ja 23,17:1
These Thousand Hills 1959,My 7,36:1
Anatomy of a Murder 1959,Jl 3,10:1
Prize, The 1964,Ja 24,21:1
Wexler, Haskell (Cinematographer)
Bus, The 1965,Ap 7,36:1
Wexler, Haskell (Producer)
Bus, The 1965,Ap 7,36:1
Loved One, The 1965,O 12,57:1
Wexler, Paul
Bloodhounds of Broadway 1952,N 15,15:2
Suddenly 1954,O 8,27:2
Kentuckian, The 1955,S 2,13:2
Wexler, Yale
Time Limit 1957,O 24,37:2
Stakeout on Dope Street 1958,Ap 24,38:1
Wexley, John (Miscellaneous)
City That Stopped Hitler--Heroic Stalingrad, The
 1943,S 6,21:3
Wexley, John (Original Author)
Last Mile, The 1932,Ag 26,20:3
Cornered 1945,D 26,15:1
Last Mile, The 1959,F 19,27:1
Wexley, John (Screenwriter)
Amazing Dr Clitterhouse, The 1938,Jl 21,14:2
Angels With Dirty Faces 1938,N 26,18:1
Confessions of a Nazi Spy 1939,Ap 29,13:2
City for Conquest 1940,S 28,9:2
Footsteps in the Dark 1941,Mr 15,13:2
Hangmen Also Die 1943,Ap 16,24:2
Cornered 1945,D 26,15:1
Long Night, The 1947,S 17,31:2
Weydner, Max
S A Mann Brand 1934,My 28,16:2
Erbe in Pretoria, Das 1936,Ap 18,19:3
Weyher, Ruth
Secrets of the Soul 1927,Ap 25,20:4
Midsummer Night's Dream 1928,Ja 31,29:1
Apaches of Paris 1928,D 11,35:3
Doctor's Women, The 1929,Je 3,27:2
Appassionata 1929,Jl 8,17:3
Weyman, Stanley (Original Author)
Under the Red Robe 1923,N 13,25:3
Under the Red Robe 1937,Je 1,27:2
Whale, James (Director)
Journey's End 1930,Ap 9,25:1
Waterloo Bridge 1931,S 5,7:4
Frankenstein 1931,D 5,21:2
Impatient Maiden, The 1932,Mr 4,17:3
Old Dark House, The 1932,O 28,22:4
Kiss Before the Mirror, The 1933,My 15,16:2
Invisible Man, The 1933,N 18,18:4
By Candlelight 1934,Ja 6,18:2
One More River 1934,Ag 10,21:1
Bride of Frankenstein, The 1935,My 11,21:2
Remember Last Night? 1935,N 21,27:2
Show Boat 1936,My 15,29:4
Road Back, The 1937,Je 18,25:2
Great Garrick, The 1937,O 25,23:1
Sinners in Paradise 1938,My 20,17:2
Wives Under Suspicion 1938,Jl 1,22:3
Port of Seven Seas 1938,Jl 15,13:2
Man in the Iron Mask, The 1939,Jl 14,11:1
Green Hell 1940,Ja 30,15:6
They Dare not Love 1941,My 16,21:4
Whale, James (Producer)
Road Back, The 1937,Je 18,25:2
Great Garrick, The 1937,O 25,23:1
Whalen, Michael
Professional Soldier 1936,Ja 30,14:2
Song and Dance Man 1936,Mr 12,18:2
Country Doctor, The 1936,Mr 13,32:2 (Incorrect
 in this edition; use 1936,Mr 13,27:2 elsewhere)
Poor Little Rich Girl, The 1936,Je 26,16:1
White Fang 1936,Jl 18,18:2
Sing, Baby, Sing 1936,S 12,20:1
Man I Marry, The 1936,O 31,24:3
Woman Wise 1937,Ja 23,13:1
Time Out for Romance 1937,Mr 13,23:2
Wee Willie Winkie 1937,Jl 24,12:1
Walking Down Broadway 1938,Ap 1,17:3
Island in the Sky 1938,My 14,18:1
Speed to Burn 1938,S 9,25:1
Time Out for Murder 1938,O 7,21:2
While New York Sleeps 1938,D 22,25:3
They Asked for It 1939,Je 30,17:4

Whalen, Michael — Cont
Ellery Queen, Master Detective 1940,D 19,33:1
Tahiti Honey 1943,My 13,17:2
She Shoulda Said No 1957,Ja 31,21:1
Elmer Gantry 1960,Jl 8,16:1
Whaley, Eddie Jr
Black Narcissus 1947,Ag 14,29:2
Wharton, Anthony (Original Author)
Two Weeks 1920,Ja 26,16:1
Wharton, Edith (Original Author)
Glimpses of the Moon 1923,Ap 3,23:4
Marriage Playground, The 1929,D 14,22:4
Age of Innocence, The 1934,O 19,27:1
Old Maid, The 1939,Ag 12,16:2
Whateley, Roger (Original Author)
Silver Streak, The 1935,Ja 16,21:1
Whateley, Roger (Screenwriter)
Silver Streak, The 1935,Ja 16,21:1
Wheat, Douglas
Kings Row 1942,F 3,23:2
Wheat, Laurence
Back Home and Broke 1922,D 25,21:1
Song of Love, The 1924,F 25,13:1
Confidence Man, The 1924,Ap 15,24:1
Inez From Hollywood 1924,D 16,28:1
Coming Through 1925,F 18,17:3
Old Home Week 1925,My 25,21:3
Not so Long Ago 1925,Jl 28,24:4
Irene 1926,Mr 1,17:1
Peck's bad Boy 1934,O 6,20:1
Public Hero No 1 1935,Je 8,12:2
Wheatcroft, Stanhope
Breath of the Gods, The 1920,Jl 26,9:5
Yankee Consul, The 1924,F 11,18:3
Iron Horse, The 1924,Ag 29,6:1
Women's Wares 1927,N 15,27:1
Notorious Sophie Lang, The 1934,Jl 21,14:2
Wheatley, Alan
End of the River, The 1948,Je 21,18:2
Corridor of Mirrors 1949,Mr 23,35:3
Sleeping Car to Trieste 1949,Ap 18,18:6
Appointment With Crime 1951,F 19,19:3
Devil's Plot 1953,Je 19,18:1
Diamond Wizard, The 1954,Jl 17,7:4
Simon and Laura 1956,Jl 3,17:2
Master Spy 1964,Ag 20,34:2
Wheatley, Dennis (Original Author)
Secret of Stamboul, The 1941,My 31,14:1
Lost Continent, The 1968,Je 20,30:2
Devil's Bride, The 1968,D 19,60:1
Wheedon, Gloria
Artists and Models 1937,Ag 5,19:2
Wheeler, Bert
Rio Rita 1929,O 7,22:1
Cuckoos, The 1930,Ap 26,11:1
Dixiana 1930,S 5,21:1
Half Shot at Sunrise 1930,O 11,21:3
Hook, Line and Sinker 1930,D 25,31:5
Cracked Nuts 1931,Ap 6,24:1
Too Many Cooks 1931,Ag 17,18:2
Caught Plastered 1931,S 12,15:4
Peach O'Reno 1931,D 24,20:8
Girl Crazy 1932,Mr 25,23:3
Hold 'Em Jail! 1932,Ag 20,7:4
So This Is Africa! 1933,Ap 24,11:3
Diplomaniacs 1933,Ap 29,14:2
Hips, Hips, Hooray 1934,F 24,18:3
Cockeyed Cavaliers 1934,Jl 25,22:2
Kentucky Kernels 1935,Ja 5,20:2
Rainmakers, The 1935,N 2,13:2
Silly Billies 1936,Ap 6,18:1
On Again-Off Again 1937,S 18,15:3
Las Vegas Nights 1941,Mr 20,25:2
Wheeler, Bert (Original Author)
Brown Derby, The 1926,Je 14,24:1
Wheeler, Burritt
Stella 1950,Ag 19,9:2
Wheeler, C (Original Author)
Bouquets From Nicholas 1939,Mr 2,19:1
Wheeler, Cyril
Matter of Who, A 1962,Jl 25,29:2
Wheeler, Harvey (Original Author)
Fail Safe 1964,S 16,36:1
Wheeler, Hugh (Screenwriter)
Five Miles to Midnight 1963,Mr 21,8:6
Wheeler, Joan
20 Million Sweethearts 1934,Ap 27,25:1
Desirable 1934,S 15,20:5
Madame Du Barry 1934,O 25,26:2
Wheeler, Lois
My Foolish Heart 1950,Ja 20,29:2
Wheeler, Rene (Director)
Winner's Circle, The 1957,My 6,25:2
Wheeler, Rene (Miscellaneous)
Young Girls Beware 1959,Ag 22,8:2
Wheeler, Rene (Original Author)
Cage aux Rossignols, La; (Cage of Nightingales,
A) 1947,Ap 3,31:2
Fanfan the Tulip 1953,My 5,34:2
Wheeler, Rene (Screenwriter)
Cage aux Rossignols, La; (Cage of Nightingales,
A) 1947,Ap 3,31:2
Jour de Fete 1952,F 20,26:4
Fanfan the Tulip 1953,My 5,34:2

Theodora, Slave Empress 1955,Ja 12,24:2
Rififi 1956,Je 6,37:1
Winner's Circle, The 1957,My 6,25:2
Young Girls Beware 1959,Ag 22,8:2
Wheeler, Steven
Johnny Tiger 1966,Je 16,53:4
Wheelis, Allen (Original Author)
Crazy Quilt, The 1966,O 4,50:1
Wheelwright, Ralph (Original Author)
Thunder Afloat 1939,O 13,27:2
Blossoms in the Dust 1941,Je 27,14:4
Two Smart People 1947,F 15,20:4
These Wilder Years 1956,Ag 18,11:2
Man of a Thousand Faces 1957,Ag 14,21:1
Wheelwright, Ralph (Producer)
Two Smart People 1947,F 15,20:4
Whelan, Albert
Man From Chicago, The 1931,Ja 16,27:1
Dance Band 1936,Ja 4,19:2
Candlelight in Algeria 1944,Jl 31,10:2
Whelan, Arleen
Kidnapped 1938,My 28,9:2
Gateway 1938,Ag 8,9:2
Thanks For Everything 1938,D 10,13:2
Young Mr Lincoln 1939,Je 3,11:2
Sabotage 1939,N 16,29:5
Young People 1940,Ag 24,16:2
Charley's Aunt 1941,Ag 2,18:2
Stage Door Canteen 1943,Je 25,13:2
Suddenly It's Spring 1947,F 27,26:2
Ramrod 1947,Je 30,25:6
Senator Was Indiscreet, The 1947,D 27,9:2
That Wonderful Urge 1948,D 22,29:6
Dear Wife 1950,F 2,31:2
Passage West 1951,Ag 31,12:2
Never Wave at a Wac 1953,Ap 24,30:2
Sun Shines Bright, The 1954,Mr 17,25:2
Whelan, Ron
Massacre Hill 1950,D 14,51:3
Kangaroo 1952,My 17,22:7
Greatest Story Ever Told, The 1965,F 16,40:2
Whelan, Tim (Director)
Its a Boy 1933,Jl 23,IX,2:2 (In Addenda)
It's a Boy 1934,Je 8,18:2
Along Came Sally 1934,Je 16,20:3
Murder Man, The 1935,Jl 27,16:2
Perfect Gentleman, The 1935,D 19,33:4
Divorce of Lady X, The 1938,Ap 1,17:2
Troopship 1938,Ap 26,18:2
Clouds Over Europe 1939,Je 16,27:2
Mill On the Floss, The 1939,N 15,19:3
Sidewalks of London 1940,F 15,15:1
Larceny Street 1941,Ja 6,11:2
Mad Doctor, The 1941,F 27,23:4
Missing Ten Days 1941,Ap 21,15:5 (In Addenda)
International Lady 1941,N 11,29:2
Twin Beds 1942,My 1,23:4
Nightmare 1942,D 4,31:2
Seven Days' Leave 1942,D 11,33:2
Higher and Higher 1944,Ja 22,8:4
Swing Fever 1944,Ja 28,14:1
Step Lively 1944,Jl 27,14:1
Badman's Territory 1946,My 31,27:2
This Was a Woman 1949,Ja 5,22:2
Whelan, Tim (Original Author)
Girl Shy 1924,Ap 21,21:4
Hold 'Em Jail! 1932,Ag 20,7:4
Out all Night 1933,Ap 8,16:2
Along Came Sally 1934,Je 16,20:3
Murder Man, The 1935,Jl 27,16:2
Larceny Street 1941,Ja 6,11:2
Whelan, Tim (Producer)
Seven Days' Leave 1942,D 11,33:2
Higher and Higher 1944,Ja 22,8:4
Whelan, Tim (Screenwriter)
Hot Water 1924,O 27,27:1
Freshman, The 1925,S 21,12:4
Murder Man, The 1935,Jl 27,16:2
Mill On the Floss, The 1939,N 15,19:3
Whelan, Tina (Original Author)
Peach O'Reno 1931,D 24,20:8
Wheler, R (Screenwriter)
Utopia 1954,D 15,41:1
Wherry, Daniel
Murder Will Out 1953,Ap 6,24:2
Wherry, Edith (Original Author)
Red Lantern, The 1919,My 5,11:1
Whiffen, Thomas Mrs
Barbara Frietchie 1915,N 29,11:3
Whiley, Manning
Saint's Vacation, The 1941,Je 13,22:2
Conspiracy in Teheran 1950,Mr 11,8:3
Inheritance, The 1951,F 12,19:2
Whipper, Leigh
Of Mice and Men 1940,F 17,9:2
Virginia 1941,Ja 29,21:2
Bahama Passage 1942,F 19,23:2
Vanishing Virginian, The 1942,My 28,13:3
White Cargo 1942,N 27,27:2
Mission to Moscow 1943,Ap 30,25:2
Ox-Bow Incident, The 1943,My 10,15:2 (In
Addenda)
Undercurrent 1946,N 29,36:2

Whipper, Leigh— Cont
Untamed Fury 1947,Ap 26,10:6
Lost Boundaries 1949,Jl 1,14:4
Shrike, The 1955,Jl 8,15:2
Young Don't Cry, The 1957,Jl 27,10:7
Whipple, Dorothy (Original Author)
They Were Sisters 1946,Jl 24,24:2
Whistler, Rudy
Fighting Father Dunne 1948,Je 25,26:2
WHITAKER
See Also WHITTAKER
Whitaker, Charles
Under Western Stars 1938,Je 25,7:3
Whitaker, Herman (Original Author)
Three Rogues 1931,Ap 4,23:1
Whitaker, Raymond
Case of Sergeant Grischa, The 1930,Mr 8,21:1
Whitaker, Slim
Rawhide 1938,Ap 25,19:2
Whital, Russ
Argentine Love 1924,D 23,16:2
Whitby, Gwynne
Quiet Week-End 1948,Ag 20,13:2
Mine Own Executioner 1949,Ja 19,34:2
Blue Lamp, The 1951,Ja 9,25:1
WHITE
See Also WHYTE
White, Alan (Original Author)
Long Day's Dying, The 1968,My 29,20:1
White, Alice
Satin Woman, The 1927,Ag 10,21:4
American Beauty 1927,O 11,27:1
Breakfast at Sunrise 1927,N 14,26:1
Private Life of Helen of Troy, The
1927,D 10,14:7
Gentlemen Prefer Blondes 1928,Ja 16,24:1
Mad Hour, The 1928,Ap 16,20:5
Big Noise, The 1928,My 7,29:1
Harold Teen 1928,Ag 14,15:4
Show Girl 1928,N 5,26:1
Naughty Baby 1929,F 5,26:3
Hot Stuff 1929,My 13,27:2
Show of Shows 1929,N 21,24:5
Girl From Woolworth's, The 1929,D 21,17:1
Playing Around 1930,Mr 31,24:3
Show Girl in Hollywood 1930,My 5,27:3
Sweet Mamma 1930,Jl 12,16:4
Widow From Chicago, The 1930,D 20,20:6
Naughty Flirt, The 1931,Ap 13,17:1
Murder at Midnight 1931,O 5,17:3
Employees' Entrance 1933,Ja 21,10:6
Luxury Liner 1933,F 3,21:3
Picture Snatcher 1933,My 19,20:3
King for a Night 1933,D 11,23:4
Cross Country Cruise 1934,Ja 20,12:3
Jimmy the Gent 1934,Mr 26,22:3
Gift of Gab 1934,S 26,17:6
Sweet Music 1935,F 21,23:2
Coronado 1935,D 19,33:4
Big City 1937,S 17,29:2
King of the Newsboys 1938,Ap 2,18:2
Annabel Takes a Tour 1938,D 29,15:3
Night of January 16th, The 1941,D 19,35:1
Flamingo Road 1949,My 7,10:2
White, Andy (Screenwriter)
Africa-Texas Style! 1967,Jl 13,30:2
Gentle Giant 1968,Ap 20,26:1
White, Barbara
Quiet Week-End 1948,Ag 20,13:2
This Was a Woman 1949,Ja 5,22:2
Mine Own Executioner 1949,Ja 19,34:2
While the Sun Shines 1950,Jl 1,9:2
All About Eve 1950,O 14,13:2
White, Betty
Advise and Consent 1962,Je 7,31:2
White, Bouck (Original Author)
Toast of New York, The 1937,Jl 23,16:2
White, Carol
Bon Voyage! 1962,My 18,34:2
Matter of Who, A 1962,Jl 25,29:2
Never Let Go 1963,Je 15,10:2
Playground, The 1965,O 4,00:0
Poor Cow 1968,F 1,28:2
I'll Never Forget What's 'Isname
1968,Ap 15,51:1
Fixer, The 1968,D 9,59:1
White, Carolina
My Cousin 1918,N 25,11:3
White, Cecil
Way Out 1967,O 26,54:3
White, Charles
Troublemaker, The 1964,Je 23,25:1
White, Christine
Macabre 1958,Jl 24,18:1
White, Crystal
Fighting Kentuckian, The 1949,S 19,18:3
White, Dan
Yearling, The 1947,Ja 24,18:2
Albuquerque 1948,Mr 1,17:2
Four Faces West 1948,Ag 4,18:3
Unknown Island 1949,Ja 8,11:4
Roseanna McCoy 1949,O 13,33:2
Rawhide 1951,Mr 26,19:2
Red Mountain 1952,Ap 26,19:2

White, Dan — Cont

Americano, The 1955,Ja 20,35:1
Rainmaker, The 1956,D 13,51:1
White, David
Sweet Smell of Success 1957,Je 28,29:2
Sunrise at Campobello 1960,S 29,32:1
Great Impostor, The 1961,Mr 30,24:1
Madison Avenue 1962,Mr 29,28:2
White, Dean
Return of the Badmen 1948,Ag 5,16:2
Race Street 1948,Ag 23,13:3
Stratton Story, The 1949,My 13,29:1
White, Dorothy
Give Me a Sailor 1938,Ag 11,31:1
Touch and go 1956,Mr 20,13:2
White, Ethel Lina (Original Author)
Lady Vanishes, The 1938,D 26,29:1
Unseen, The 1945,My 14,20:5
Spiral Staircase, The 1946,F 7,29:3
White, Fisher
Loose Ends 1930,O 18,23:2
Jaws of Hell 1931,Ja 5,21:3
Dreyfus Case, The 1931,Ag 31,11:5
As You Like It 1936,N 6,29:3
Dreaming Lips 1937,My 20,17:1
Under the Red Robe 1937,Je 1,27:2
Moonlight Sonata 1938,My 10,17:2
White, Frank
Royal Ballet, The (The Firebird); Firebird, The
(The Royal Ballet) 1960,O 5,45:2
White, George
George White's 1935 Scandals 1935,Ap 29,12:3
Rhapsody in Blue 1945,Je 28,22:2
White, George (Director)
George White's Scandals 1934,Mr 16,24:2
George White's 1935 Scandals 1935,Ap 29,12:3
White, George (Miscellaneous)
Duffy's Tavern 1945,S 6,23:3
White, George (Original Author)
Flying High 1931,D 12,23:3
George White's Scandals 1934,Mr 16,24:2
White, George (Producer)
George White's 1935 Scandals 1935,Ap 29,12:3
George White's Scandals 1945,O 11,26:2
White, Gloria Ann
Cisco Kid and the Lady, The 1939,D 25,29:2
White, Grace Miller (Original Author)
Tess of the Storm Country 1922,N 13,12:1
Tess of the Storm Country 1932,N 19,20:2
White, Harriet
Paisan 1948,Mr 30,26:2
Rapture 1950,D 14,51:3
White, Huey
Hush Money 1931,Jl 11,7:6
Female 1933,N 4,18:3
Convention City 1933,D 25,28:2
Gambling Lady 1934,Ap 5,25:2
Million Dollar Ransom 1934,S 19,15:2
Crash Donovan 1936,Ag 10,10:3
When G-Men Step In 1938,Mr 14,13:2
White, Irene
Wrecker, The 1933,Ag 7,18:3
White, Irving (Original Author)
Daughters Courageous 1939,Je 24,14:2
Always in my Heart 1942,Mr 14,19:2
White, Jack
52d Street 1937,N 15,15:1
White, Jack Palmer (Screenwriter)
Assignment-Paris 1952,O 25,12:6
White, Jacqueline
Air Raid Wardens 1943,Ap 5,15:5
Swing Shift Maisie 1943,S 10,29:2
Song of Russia 1944,F 11,17:2
Show-Off, The 1947,Mr 20,38:2
Crossfire 1947,Jl 23,19:2
Night Song 1948,Ja 29,27:5
Return of the Badmen 1948,Ag 5,16:2
Capture, The 1950,My 20,8:6
Narrow Margin, The 1952,My 5,18:7
White, James Gordon (Screenwriter)
Glory Stompers, The 1968,Mr 28,52:4
Mini-Skirt Mob, The 1968,O 24,55:5
Born Wild 1968,D 12,62:6
White, Jane
Town Like Alice, A 1958,S 22,27:1
White, Jennifer
L-Shaped Room, The 1963,My 28,32:1
White, Jesse
Harvey 1950,D 22,19:1
Bedtime for Bonzo 1951,Ap 6,31:4
Francis Goes to the Races 1951,Jl 25,19:2
Callaway Went Thataway 1951,D 6,42:1
Death of a Salesman 1951,D 21,21:3
Girl in White, The 1952,My 31,12:5
Million Dollar Mermaid 1952,D 5,35:2
Forever Female 1954,Ja 13,26:2
Hell's Half Acre 1954,F 27,11:3
Witness to Murder 1954,Ap 16,16:4
Not as a Stranger 1955,Je 29,24:1
Come on, The 1956,Ap 7,13:1
Back From Eternity 1956,S 8,20:6
Bad Seed, The 1956,S 13,39:6
Designing Woman 1957,My 17,20:2
Marjorie Morningstar 1958,Ap 25,32:2

Rise and Fall of Legs' Diamond, The
1960,F 4,34:1
Big Night, The 1960,F 18,37:4
On the Double 1961,My 20,12:1
Sail a Crooked Ship 1962,F 3,12:6
It's Only Money 1962,N 22,43:1
Yellow Canary, The 1963,My 16,42:1
It's a Mad, Mad, Mad, Mad World
1963,N 19,47:1
House is not a Home, A 1964,S 2,33:1
White, Jimmy
Rugged O'Riordans, The 1950,Ja 6,25:2
White, Joan
As You Like It 1936,N 6,29:3
White, Johnstone
Knock on Wood 1954,Ap 15,34:2
White, Jon (Original Author)
Camp on Blood Island, The 1958,S 18,37:2
White, Jon (Screenwriter)
Camp on Blood Island, The 1958,S 18,37:2
Crack in the World 1965,My 13,32:2
White, Jules (Director)
Stop! Look! and Laugh! 1961,F 9,36:1
White, Larry
Buster Keaton Story, The 1957,Ap 22,31:6
White, Lawrence G (Producer)
Guns of August, The 1964,D 25,24:2
White, Lee ('Lasses)
Scattergood Baines 1941,Ap 4,25:2
White, Leo
Rookie's Return, The 1920,D 27,11:3
Blood and Sand 1922,Ag 7,14:2
Rustle of Silk, The 1923,My 8,22:4
Why Worry? 1923,S 3,9:3
Sporting Youth 1924,Ap 2,16:1
Woman on the Jury, The 1924,My 19,14:2
Goldfish, The 1924,My 20,15:2
Masked Bride, The 1925,N 30,17:1
Ben Hur 1925,D 31,10:5 (In Addenda)
Devil's Island 1926,Ag 2,21:2
Blonde Saint, The 1926,N 23,27:1
See You in Jail 1927,Ap 4,30:5
How to Handle Women 1928,Je 18,13:2
Ben Hur 1931,D 4,28:2
All the King's Horses 1935,Mr 9,19:1
White, Leonard
Martin Luther 1953,S 10,22:1
White, Leslie T (Original Author)
Paid to Dance 1937,D 6,19:1
Strange Alibi 1941,Ap 28,11:2
Northern Pursuit 1943,N 26,29:2
Vice Squad 1953,Ag 26,23:2
Americano, The 1955,Ja 20,35:1
White, Leslie T (Screenwriter)
Behind Prison Gates 1939,Ag 21,9:3
White, Lester A (Miscellaneous)
If You Knew Susie 1948,F 23,19:2
White, Lionel (Original Author)
Killing, The 1956,My 21,20:1
Money Trap, The 1966,My 5,59:1
White, Marjorie
Sunny Side Up 1929,O 4,24:5
Happy Days 1930,F 14,20:1
Her Golden Calf 1930,My 5,27:3
New Movietone Follies of 1930, The
1930,Je 21,20:5
Just Imagine 1930,N 22,21:3
Charlie Chan Carries On 1931,Mr 21,15:1
Women of all Nations 1931,My 30,9:2
Black Camel, The 1931,Jl 4,11:5
Possessed 1931,N 28,20:4
Diplomaniacs 1933,Ap 29,14:2
Her Bodyguard 1933,Ag 7,18:2
White, Meredith
Beloved Brat 1938,My 2,13:2
White, Merrill G (Screenwriter)
Brave One, The 1957,Mr 22,26:1
White, Myrna
Funny Thing Happened on the Way to the Forum,
A 1966,O 17,48:1
White, Nelia Gardner (Original Author)
Sentimental Journey 1946,Mr 7,33:2
Gift of Love, The 1958,F 12,32:2
White, Patricia
Cry Wolf 1947,Jl 19,10:2
Undercover Man, The 1949,Ap 21,30:2
Tattooed Stranger, The 1950,F 10,18:6
White, Paul
Adventure's End 1937,D 20,23:2
Boy of the Streets 1938,Ja 24,17:1
Boy Slaves 1939,F 9,17:3
Scattergood Baines 1941,Ap 4,25:2
White, Pearl
Virgin Paradise, A 1921,Ag 4,18:3
Days of Thrills and Laughter 1961,Mr 22,37:1
White, Pudgie
Little Miss Marker 1934,My 19,18:3
Personality Kid, The 1934,Ag 1,14:2
White, Robb (Original Author)
Up Periscope 1959,Mr 5,35:4
Virgin Island 1960,Mr 24,39:5

White, Robb (Screenwriter)
Macabre 1958,Jl 24,18:1
House on Haunted Hill 1959,Mr 12,27:5
Tingler, The 1960,Mr 10,36:2
13 Ghosts 1960,Ag 6,9:2
Homicidal 1961,Jl 27,23:4
White, Robertson (Original Author)
Footloose Heiress 1937,O 9,16:2
Charlie McCarthy, Detective 1939,D 25,29:2
White, Robertson (Screenwriter)
Westland Case, The 1937,O 23,14:2
Torchy Blane, The Adventurous Blonde
1937,D 18,18:1
Patient in Room 18, The 1938,Ap 22,15:6
Lady in the Morgue, The 1938,My 9,13:3
Mystery House 1938,Je 29,15:5
My Bill 1938,Jl 7,22:4
Witness Vanishes, The 1939,O 23,15:2
Charlie Chan's Murder Cruise 1940,My 3,17:5
Dick Tracy and Gruesome 1947,S 27,11:2
White, Ruth
Edge of the City 1957,Ja 30,33:2
Nun's Story, The 1959,Je 19,30:1
To Kill a Mockingbird 1963,F 15,10:2
Baby, the Rain Must Fall 1965,Ja 14,44:1
Rage to Live, A 1965,O 21,57:1
Cast a Giant Shadow 1966,Mr 31,43:3
Up the Down Staircase 1967,Ag 18,36:2
Tiger Makes Out, The 1967,S 19,53:1
No Way to Treat a Lady 1968,Mr 21,56:1
Hang 'Em High 1968,Ag 8,27:3
Charly 1968,S 24,55:1
White, Sam (Director)
Officer and the Lady, The 1941,Ag 11,17:4
I Live on Danger 1942,Ag 22,16:2
People Are Funny 1946,Ja 28,15:6
White, Sam (Producer)
Reveille With Beverly 1943,Ap 24,17:2
Return of the Vampire, The 1944,Ja 29,10:1
People Are Funny 1946,Ja 28,15:6
White, Sammy
Show Boat 1936,My 15,29:4
Cain and Mabel 1936,O 19,22:1
Hit Parade, The 1937,My 31,11:2
Swing Your Lady 1938,Ja 27,17:2
711 Ocean Drive 1950,Jl 20,21:2
Pat and Mike 1952,Je 19,32:6
Bad and the Beautiful, The 1953,Ja 16,19:1
About Mrs Leslie 1954,Je 28,16:2
Living It Up 1954,Jl 24,6:6
Somebody up There Likes Me 1956,Jl 6,16:1
Helen Morgan Story, The 1957,O 3,33:2
White, Sandra
While the City Sleeps 1956,My 17,37:1
Solid Gold Cadillac, The 1956,O 25,40:3
White, Sheila
Here We Go Around the Mulberry Bush
1968,Mr 5,34:5
Oliver! 1968,D 11,57:1
White, Stewart Edward (Original Author)
Westerners, The 1919,Ag 4,8:3
Under a Texas Moon 1930,Ap 4,22:1
Shepper - Newfounder, The 1930,D 25,31:5
Mystery Ranch 1932,Je 30,26:2
Wild Geese Calling 1941,Ag 30,10:2
White, T H (Original Author)
Sword in the Stone, The 1963,D 26,33:3
Camelot 1967,O 26,54:1
White, Thelma
Wanted by the Police 1938,S 26,13:2
White, Theodore (Original Author)
Mountain Road, The 1960,Je 30,22:3
White, Valerie
Half-Way House 1945,Ag 13,22:4
Hue and Cry 1951,Ja 9,25:2
White, W L (Original Author)
Lost Boundaries 1949,Jl 1,14:4
White, Walter
Strange Holiday 1945,O 20,8:2
White, Wilfrid Hyde
Elephant Boy 1937,Ap 6,20:2
Meet Me at Dawn 1948,My 18,26:2
Forbidden Street, The 1949,My 14,9:2
Adam and Evelyn 1950,My 12,33:4
While the Sun Shines 1950,Jl 1,9:2
Browning Version, The 1951,O 30,33:2
Mr Denning Drives North 1953,S 2,20:1
Mr Potts Goes to Moscow 1953,S 3,15:2
Gilbert and Sullivan 1953,O 28,36:3
Man With a Million 1954,Je 29,21:2
Betrayed 1954,S 9,36:1
Quentin Durward 1955,N 24,41:1
Cash on Delivery 1956,S 1,19:3
Tarzan and the Lost Safari 1957,Ap 13,12:3
John and Julie 1957,My 7,40:1
Silken Affair, The 1957,O 31,41:1
Up the Creek 1958,N 11,26:2
Libel 1959,O 24,12:4
Flame Over India 1960,Ap 30,14:1
Let's Make Love 1960,S 9,36:1
Carry on Nurse 1960,S 10,11:1
Two-Way Stretch 1961,Ja 24,20:3
On the Double 1961,My 20,12:1

White, Wilfrid Hyde — Cont
Ada 1961,Ag 26,15:1
In Search of the Castaways 1962,D 22,5:2
Crooks Anonymous 1963,O 31,26:3
My Fair Lady 1964,O 22,41:1
Bang, Bang, You're Dead 1967,Ja 19,41:2
White, Will J
Hell's Five Hours 1957,Jl 24,18:1
Hell's Five Hours 1958,Jl 24,18:1
White, William C (Miscellaneous)
No Greater Love 1944,F 25,23:3
White, William C (Original Author)
Beg, Borrow or Steal 1937,D 10,33:2
White, William L (Original Author)
Journey for Margaret 1942,D 18,36:7
They Were Expendable 1945,D 21,25:2
White, Yolanda
All Mine to Give 1959,Ag 4,32:5
White-Lennon, Biddie
Ulysses 1967,Mr 14,55:1
White Spear, Chief
Iron Horse, The 1924,Ag 29,6:1
Whitefield, Raoul (Original Author)
Private Detective 62 1933,Jl 7,20:2
Whitehall, Henry B
Scarlet Letter, The 1926,Ag 10,19:2
Whitehead, Don (Original Author)
F B I Story, The 1959,S 25,23:1
Whitehead, G Z
Ulysses 1967,Mr 14,55:1
Whitehead, O Z
Scoundrel, The 1935,My 3,23:2
Grapes of Wrath, The 1940,Ja 25,17:2
My Brother Talks to Horses 1947,Je 19,27:4
Romance of Rosy Ridge, The 1947,S 12,18:3
Song Is Born, A 1948,O 20,37:2
Road House 1948,N 8,24:2
Ma and Pa Kettle 1949,Ag 12,13:2
For Men Only 1952,Ja 16,21:2
San Francisco Story, The 1952,My 10,16:4
Beware my Lovely 1952,S 13,10:5
Last Hurrah, The 1958,O 24,40:1
Rally Round the Flag Boys! 1958,D 24,2:7
Man Who Shot Liberty Valance, The
1962,My 24,29:2
Whitehead, Omar
Captain Blood 1924,S 9,19:1
Whitehead, Peter (Director)
London Scene, The (The Benefit of the Doubt);
Benefit of the Doubt, The (The London Scene)
1967,S 27,39:1
London Scene, The (Tonite Let's All Make Love
in London); Tonite Let's All Make Love in
London (The London Scene) 1967,S 27,39:1
Whitehead, Peter (Producer)
London Scene, The (Tonite Let's All Make Love
in London); Tonite Let's All Make Love in
London (The London Scene) 1967,S 27,39:1
London Scene, The (The Benefit of the Doubt);
Benefit of the Doubt, The (The London Scene)
1967,S 27,39:1
Whitehead, Verne (Original Author)
Reported Missing 1937,S 3,12:2
Whitelaw, Billie
Make Mine Mink 1960,D 20,43:4
Hell is a City 1961,Ja 19,26:3
No Love for Johnnie 1961,D 13,55:1
I Like Money 1962,My 19,18:2
Payroll 1963,My 11,15:2
Charlie Bubbles 1968,F 12,47:2
Whiteley, Jon
Stranger in Between, The 1952,Ag 20,21:3
Little Kidnappers, The 1954,S 2,18:1
Moonfleet 1955,Je 25,9:2
Spanish Gardner, The 1957,S 9,21:2
Whiteley, Thomas
Journey's End 1930,Ap 9,25:1
Merely Mary Ann 1931,S 12,15:4
Whitell, Josephine
Chinatown at Midnight 1949,N 18,35:3
Whiteman, Paul
King of Jazz 1930,My 3,23:1
Jazz King, The 1930,N 23,IX,6:2
Thanks a Million 1935,N 14,17:1
Strike up the Band 1940,S 30,13:2
Rhapsody in Blue 1945,Je 28,22:2
Fabulous Dorseys, The 1947,My 30,25:3
Whiteman, Paul and Orchestra
Atlantic City 1944,Ag 14,11:4
Whiteman, Paul Band
Thanks a Million 1935,N 14,17:1
Whiteside, John (Cinematographer)
Burma Chapter 1945,Ag 7,10:6
Whitespear, Greg
Water Hole, The 1928,S 3,14:2
Behold My Wife 1935,F 18,19:3
Whitfield, Anne
Gunfighter, The 1950,Je 24,7:2
White Christmas 1954,O 15,16:3
Whitfield, June
Spy With a Cold Nose, The 1966,D 20,58:2
Whitfield, Smoki
Another Part of the Forest 1948,My 19,30:2
Bomba, the Jungle Boy 1949,Ap 16,11:4

Second Woman, The 1951,F 2,19:2
Whiting, Barbara
Junior Miss 1945,Je 18,15:4
Centennial Summer 1946,Jl 18,20:2
Home Sweet Homicide 1946,S 12,5:7
Carnival in Costa Rica 1947,Mr 29,21:2
City Across the River 1949,Ap 8,31:3
I Can Get It for You Wholesale 1951,Ap 5,34:4
Beware my Lovely 1952,S 13,10:5
Dangerous When Wet 1953,Je 19,18:1
Whiting, Jack
Top Speed 1930,Ag 30,7:4
Life of the Party, The 1930,N 10,16:2
College Lovers 1930,N 28,23:1
Sailing Along 1938,Ap 16,17:1
Give Me a Sailor 1938,Ag 11,31:1
Whiting, John (Screenwriter)
Ship That Died of Shame, The 1956,Ag 21,33:2
Captain's Table, The 1960,S 27,40:1
Young Cassidy 1965,Mr 23,35:1
Whiting, Leonard
Romeo and Juliet 1968,O 9,41:1
Whiting, Margaret
Underworld Informers 1965,O 14,53:1
Whiting, Napoleon
Wall of Noise 1963,S 5,27:1
Whiting, Richard (Composer)
Adorable 1933,My 19,20:2
My Weakness 1933,S 22,14:1
Bottoms Up 1934,Mr 23,29:2
Call it Luck 1934,Jl 10,24:5
Transatlantic Merry-Go-Round 1934,N 1,25:2
365 Nights in Hollywood 1934,N 7,32:1
Bright Eyes 1934,D 21,31:1
Big Broadcast of 1936, The 1935,S 16,15:2
Here Comes Cookie 1935,O 12,12:2
Coronado 1935,D 19,33:4
Anything Goes 1936,F 6,23:3
Ready, Willing and Able 1937,Mr 15,27:1
Varsity Show 1937,S 2,17:2
Hollywood Hotel 1938,Ja 13,17:3
Cowboy From Brooklyn 1938,Jl 14,17:1
Whiting, Richard (Miscellaneous)
She Learned About Sailors 1934,Jl 30,9:4
Handy Andy 1934,Ag 4,14:5
Sing, Baby, Sing 1936,S 12,20:1
Whitley, Bert
Hard, Fast and Beautiful 1951,Jl 2,16:6
Whitley, Crane
My Favorite Blonde 1942,Ap 2,27:2
Enemy of Women 1944,S 12,23:6
Return of Monte Cristo, The 1947,Ja 3,16:4
Outpost in Morocco 1949,Mr 25,28:3
Crooked Way, The 1949,S 5,13:2
Red Mountain 1952,Ap 26,19:2
Whitley, Ray
Gun Law 1938,Je 24,15:1
Painted Desert 1938,S 14,26:5
Renegade Ranger, The 1939,F 17,17:3
Racketeers of the Range 1939,Je 8,31:4
Whitling, Townsend
Blanche Fury 1948,N 24,20:2
Whitlock, Lloyd
Scratch my Back 1920,Je 5,19:3
Private Scandal, A 1921,Je 13,16:1
Midnight Express, The 1924,N 19,19:3
Price She Paid, The 1925,Ja 13,16:1
Air Mail, The 1925,Mr 17,18:1
Home Maker, The 1925,Ag 10,8:2
Ancient Highway, The 1925,N 11,27:3
Sparrows 1926,S 20,21:3
Paradise 1926,O 4,20:2
Perfect Sap, The 1927,Ja 11,18:2
Hero for a Night, A 1927,D 26,26:6
Hot Heels 1928,My 22,19:3
Skinner Steps Out 1929,D 7,19:3
Cohens and the Kelleys In Scotland, The
1930,Mr 10,24:1
See America Thirst 1930,D 12,35:3
Cohens and Kellys in Africa, The 1930,D 20,20:6
Honeymoon Lane 1931,Ag 1,16:4
International Crime 1938,My 16,14:4
Arson Racket Squad 1938,Je 18,18:2
Whitman, Bede (Cinematographer)
Primitive Paradise 1961,My 27,12:1
Whitman, Ernest
Prisoner of Shark Island, The 1936,F 13,25:2
Green Pastures, The 1936,Jl 17,20:1
White Hunter 1936,N 26,39:2
Daughter of Shanghai 1937,D 24,21:2
Jesse James 1939,Ja 14,13:1
Congo Maisie 1940,F 8,18:4
Maryland 1940,Jl 13,16:5
Return of Frank James, The 1940,Ag 10,16:4
Third Finger, Left Hand 1940,D 12,37:2
Get-Away, The 1941,Jl 17,23:4
Pittsburgh Kid, The 1941,S 23,27:4
Among the Living 1941,D 13,25:2
Bugle Sounds, The 1942,Ap 3,25:2
Drums of the Congo 1942,Jl 20,16:4
Cabin in the Sky 1943,My 28,19:3
Stormy Weather 1943,Jl 22,15:1
My Brother Talks to Horses 1947,Je 19,27:4

Blonde Savage 1947,O 4,9:2
Whitman, Gayne
Love Hour, The 1925,S 2,21:3
Wife Who Wasn't Wanted, The 1925,S 9,23:1
His Majesty Bunker Bean 1925,S 15,12:1
Oh! What a Nurse! 1926,F 22,14:1
Night Cry, The 1926,Ap 7,26:6
Hell-Bent for Heaven 1926,My 4,31:1
Sailors' Wives 1928,F 28,18:4
Lucky Boy 1929,F 25,16:1
Big Jim McLain 1952,S 18,35:2
Dangerous Crossing 1953,S 30,37:2
Whitman, Katherine
Body Is a Shell, The 1957,S 9,21:2
Whitman, Philip H (Director)
Police Call 1933,Ag 22,20:3
Whitman, Stephen French (Original Author)
Drums of Fate 1923,Ja 15,18:3
Blonde Saint, The 1926,N 23,27:1
Whitman, Stuart
Rhapsody 1954,Mr 12,17:1
Darby's Rangers 1958,F 13,23:2
Ten North Frederick 1958,My 23,29:2
Decks Ran Red, The 1958,O 11,18:2
China Doll 1958,D 4,52:1
Sound and the Fury, The 1959,Mr 28,11:1
These Thousand Hills 1959,My 7,36:1
Hound-Dog Man 1960,Ap 28,29:1
Story of Ruth, The 1960,Je 18,12:3
Murder, Inc 1960,Je 29,26:6
Francis of Assisi 1961,Jl 29,8:2
Fiercest Heart, The 1961,Ag 3,13:5
Mark, The 1961,O 3,46:2
Comancheros, The 1961,N 2,42:1
Convicts 4 1962,O 4,44:2
Longest Day, The 1962,O 5,28:1
Day and the Hour, The 1964,F 20,22:2
Shock Treatment 1964,Jl 23,19:1
Rio Conchos 1964,O 29,38:1
Signpost to Murder 1965,My 20,52:2
Those Magnificent Men in Their Flying Machine
(Or How I Flew From London to Paris in 25
Hours and 11 Minutes) 1965,Je 17,27:1
Sands of the Kalahari 1965,N 25,64:5
American Dream, An 1966,S 1,28:2
Whitman, Walt
Heart of Humanity, The 1918,D 22,17:3
Long Live the King 1923,D 4,24:1
Whitmore, Annalee (Screenwriter)
Andy Hardy Meets Debutante 1940,Ag 2,12:2
Whitmore, James
Undercover Man, The 1949,Ap 21,30:2
Battleground 1949,N 12,8:4
Outriders, The 1950,Mr 9,25:2
Asphalt Jungle, The 1950,Je 9,29:3
Please Believe Me 1950,Je 12,19:4
Next Voice You Hear, The 1950,Je 30,18:2
Mrs O'Malley and Mr Malone 1951,F 23,33:2
It's a big Country 1952,Ja 9,25:2
Shadow in the Sky 1952,Jl 19,8:2
Because You're Mine 1952,S 26,18:2
Above and Beyond 1953,Ja 31,10:6
Kiss Me Kate 1953,N 6,23:2
All the Brothers Were Valiant 1953,D 29,19:2
Command, The 1954,Ja 16,10:5
Them 1954,Je 17,36:2
Battle Cry 1955,F 3,18:1
McConnell Story, The 1955,S 30,23:1
Oklahoma! 1955,O 11,49:1
Last Frontier, The 1955,D 8,45:1
Crime in the Streets 1956,My 24,27:4
Eddy Duchin Story, The 1956,Je 22,15:1
Young Don't Cry, The 1957,Jl 27,10:7
Deep Six, The 1958,Ja 16,32:1
Who Was That Lady? 1960,Ap 16,10:1
Black Like Me 1964,My 21,42:1
Waterhole #3 1967,O 11,41:4
Chuka 1967,N 2,58:3
Planet of the Apes 1968,F 9,55:2
Madigan 1968,Mr 30,22:2
Nobody's Perfect 1968,Ap 4,58:3
Split, The 1968,N 5,55:2
Whitmore, Stanford (Screenwriter)
War Hunt 1962,Ag 8,35:2
Your Cheatin' Heart 1965,My 20,52:2
Whitney, Beverly
Irish Eyes Are Smiling 1944,N 8,27:1
Whitney, Claire
Isle of Conquest, The 1919,O 27,9:3
Passionate Pilgrim, The 1921,Ja 3,20:2
Great Gatsby, The 1926,N 22,28:3
Chip of the Flying U 1940,Ja 22,11:3
Frisco Lil 1942,F 12,27:2
Mummy's Ghost, The 1944,Jl 1,10:7
Whitney, Dorothy
Breakfast at Tiffany's 1961,O 6,28:1
Whitney, Eleanore
Millions in the Air 1935,D 12,33:4
Timothy's Quest 1936,F 29,11:2
Three Cheers for Love 1936,Ag 1,16:2
Rose Bowl 1936,D 23,25:2
College Holiday 1936,D 24,21:2
Turn off the Moon 1937,My 20,17:2

Whitney, Eleanore— Cont

Blonde Trouble 1937,Ag 7,7:2
Thrill of a Lifetime 1937,D 9,30:2
Campus Confessions 1938,S 23,35:1

Whitney, Eve
Blonde Savage 1947,O 4,9:2

Whitney, Grace Lee
Irma la Douce 1963,Je 6,39:1

Whitney, Helene
Hunchback of Notre Dame, The 1940,Ja 1,29:2
Saint's Double Trouble, The 1940,F 13,27:2

Whitney, John
Objective Burma 1945,Ja 27,15:2
Bachelor's Daughters, The 1946,O 7,23:2
Calcutta 1947,Ap 24,30:2
I Was a Male War Bride 1949,Ag 27,7:2

Whitney, Lynn
Circumstantial Evidence 1945,Ap 21,18:3
Because of Him 1946,Ja 25,26:6
Storm Warning 1951,Mr 3,8:2

Whitney, Peter
Underground 1941,Je 23,13:2
Nine Loves Are not Enough 1941,O 30,27:2
Blues in the Night 1941,D 12,35:2
Valley of the Sun 1942,Mr 19,29:2
Rio Rita 1942,My 8,27:3
Spy Ship 1942,Jl 11,8:2
Busses Roar 1942,S 25,25:4
Whistling in Dixie 1942,D 31,20:4
Reunion in France 1943,Mr 5,20:3
Action in the North Atlantic 1943,My 22,10:2
Destination Tokyo 1944,Ja 1,9:2
Mr Skeffington 1944,My 26,23:2
Bring on the Girls 1945,Mr 1,25:5
Hotel Berlin 1945,Mr 3,11:2
Murder, He Says 1945,Je 25,20:3
Three Strangers 1946,F 23,20:2
Violence 1947,My 10,8:5
Northwest Outpost 1947,Ag 8,10:2
Iron Curtain, The 1948,My 13,31:2
Great Sioux Uprising, The 1953,Jl 18,6:2
Big Heat, The 1953,O 15,43:2
All the Brothers Were Valiant 1953,D 29,19:2
Gorilla at Large 1954,Je 12,13:2
Last Frontier, The 1955,D 8,45:1
In the Heat of the Night 1967,Ag 3,26:1

Whitney, Renee
Wild Party, The 1929,Ap 2,28:4
Play Girl 1932,Mr 19,11:2
Winner Take All 1932,Je 18,9:2
Picture Snatcher 1933,My 19,20:3
Baby Face 1933,Je 24,16:2
I've Got Your Number 1934,F 3,9:3
Return of the Terror 1934,Jl 11,20:2
Side Streets 1934,Ag 15,13:5

Whitney, Robert
Judge Hardy's Children 1938,Ap 8,17:2

Whitney, Susan
Miracle of Our Lady Fatima, The 1952,Ag 21,16:2

Whitson, Frank
Captain Blood 1924,S 9,19:1

Whitt, Wayne (Tiny)
Some Like It Hot 1939,My 25,31:2

WHITTAKER
See Also WHITAKER

Whittaker, Charles (Screenwriter)
Fires of Faith 1919,My 6,16:2
Partners of the Night 1920,Mr 1,16:2
Bond Boy, The 1922,O 9,10:2
Backbone 1923,Ap 30,11:2
Devil's Cargo, The 1925,F 3,24:1

Whittaker, W A (Producer)
Desert Attack 1961,Mr 23,28:1
Call Me Genius 1961,O 17,47:1

Whittell, Josephine
Caught Plastered 1931,S 12,15:4
Infernal Machine 1933,Ap 8,16:3
Life of Vergie Winters, The 1934,Je 15,26:1
Servants' Entrance 1934,S 27,25:2
It's a Gift 1935,Ja 5,20:2
Shanghai 1935,Jl 20,16:2
Follow Your Heart 1936,O 22,31:1
Women Are Like That 1938,Ap 11,12:2
Magnificent Dope, The 1942,Jl 3,12:5
Standing Room Only 1944,F 23,17:2
Enchanted Cottage, The 1945,Ap 28,19:2
Easy to Wed 1946,Jl 12,14:2
Adventure in Baltimore 1949,Ap 29,27:2
Molly 1951,Mr 8,37:2

Whitten, Delbert Emery
Tin Gods 1926,S 20,21:3

Whitten, Marguerite
Way Down South 1939,Ag 18,16:4
Cadet Girl 1941,D 11,39:1

Whittier (Original Author)
In School Days 1919,D 8,20:4

Whittingham, Jack (Miscellaneous)
Cage of Gold 1952,Ja 19,13:3

Whittingham, Jack (Original Author)
Clouds Over Europe 1939,Je 16,27:2
Thunderball 1965,D 22,23:1

Whittingham, Jack (Screenwriter)
Laughing Lady, The 1950,Ja 23,16:3
Dancing Years, The 1951,Ja 29,14:4
Lisbon Story, The 1951,S 6,39:4
Pool of London 1951,N 28,37:2
Case of Gold 1952,Ja 19,13:3
Stranger in Between, The 1952,Ag 20,21:3
Story of Mandy, The 1952,F 24,21:3
I Believe in You 1953,My 5,34:3
Devil's Plot 1953,Je 19,18:1
West of Zanzibar 1955,Ja 18,31:2
Divided Heart, The 1955,Ag 4,16:1

Whittinghill, Dick
Will Success Spoil Rock Hunter 1957,S 12,37:5
Moon Pilot 1962,Ap 6,30:2

Whittington, Harry (Original Author)
Desire in the Dust 1960,O 12,47:2

Whittington, Margery
Stage Struck 1925,N 16,19:4

Whittley, Crane
O S S 1946,My 27,15:5

Whitty, May Dame
Night Must Fall 1937,Ap 30,17:2
Thirteenth Chair, The 1937,Je 18,25:3
Conquest 1937,N 5,19:1
I Met my Love Again 1938,Ja 15,19:1
Lady Vanishes, The 1938,D 26,29:1
Raffles 1940,Ja 13,11:2
Bill of Divorcement, A 1940,Jl 12,11:2
One Night in Lisbon 1941,Je 12,29:3
Suspicion 1941,N 21,23:2
Mrs Miniver 1942,Je 5,23:1
Thunder Birds 1942,O 29,19:2
Forever and a Day 1943,Mr 13,9:2
Slightly Dangerous 1943,Ap 2,17:2
Crash Dive 1943,Ap 29,25:2
Stage Door Canteen 1943,Je 25,13:2
Constant Nymph, The 1943,Jl 24,8:2
Lassie Come Home 1943,O 8,15:4
Flesh and Fantasy 1943,N 18,29:1
Madame Curie 1943,D 17,23:1
Gaslight 1944,My 5,17:2
White Cliffs of Dover, The 1944,My 12,15:2
My Name is Julia Ross 1945,N 9,16:3
Devotion 1946,Ap 6,10:5
Green Dolphin Street 1947,O 16,34:2
This Time for Keeps 1947,D 5,33:4
If Winter Comes 1948,Ja 23,28:4
Sign of the Ram, The 1948,Mr 4,30:2
Return of October, The 1949,F 23,31:2

Whorf, David
Miracle Can Happen, A 1948,F 4,28:4

Whorf, Richard
Midnight 1934,Mr 10,18:3
Blues in the Night 1941,D 12,35:2
Yankee Doodle Dandy 1942,My 30,9:1
Juke Girl 1942,Je 20,9:2
Keeper of the Flame 1943,Mr 19,15:2
Assignment in Brittany 1943,Ap 22,31:2
Cross of Lorraine, The 1943,D 3,27:4
Impostor, The 1944,Mr 27,17:2
Christmas Holiday 1944,Je 29,16:1
Chain Lightning 1950,F 20,21:2

Whorf, Richard (Director)
Hidden Eye, The 1945,Ag 31,14:3
Sailor Takes a Wife, The 1946,Mr 1,17:2
Till the Clouds Roll By 1946,D 6,27:4
It Happened in Brooklyn 1947,Mr 14,28:5
Love From a Stranger 1947,N 28,30:1
Luxury Liner 1948,S 10,19:2
Champagne for Caesar 1950,My 12,33:2
Groom Wore Spurs, The 1951,Mr 14,41:2

Whorf, Richard (Producer)
Burning Hills, The 1956,Ag 24,15:2
Bombers B-52 1957,N 23,11:2

Whytalh, Russ Mrs
Tarnish 1924,O 13,21:1

WHYTE
See Also WHITE

Whyte, Patrick
Not Wanted 1949,Jl 25,11:4

Whytock, Grant (Producer)
Black Arrow, The 1948,O 4,14:2
Walk a Crooked Mile 1948,O 13,31:2

Wiard, Joyce
Mother Machree 1928,Mr 6,20:3

Wiata, Inia Te
Land of Fury 1955,My 3,37:4

Wiazemsky, Anne
Balthazar 1966,S 16,31:2
Chinoise, La 1968,Ap 4,58:2

Wibberley, Leonard (Original Author)
Mouse That Roared, The 1959,O 27,40:1
Mouse on the Moon, The 1963,Je 18,32:1

Wichey, Chet (Director)
Cafe in Cairo, A 1925,Mr 18,19:2

Wichura, E
Eve Wants to Sleep 1961,Je 6,42:2

Wick, Bruno
House on Ninety-Second Street, The 1945,S 27,24:7
Deep Waters 1948,Jl 23,12:4
Walk East on Beacon 1952,My 29,17:2

Wick, Charles (Producer)
Snow White and the Three Stooges 1961,Jl 1,9:1

Wickersham, Bob (Screenwriter)
Mr Bug Goes to Town 1942,F 20,21:3

Wickes, Mary
Man Who Came to Dinner, The 1942,Ja 2,25:2
Mayor of Forty-Fourth Street, The 1942,Je 11,27:4
Private Buckaroo 1942,Je 25,27:4
Now, Voyager 1942,O 23,25:3
Who Done It 1942,D 3,35:2
My Kingdom for a Cook 1943,O 15,15:3
Happy Land 1943,D 9,33:3
Higher and Higher 1944,Ja 22,8:4
June Bride 1948,O 30,10:2
Decision of Christopher Blake, The 1948,D 11,12:2
Anna Lucasta 1949,Ag 12,13:2
Petty Girl, The 1950,Ag 18,17:2
On Moonlight Bay 1951,Jl 27,15:2
I'll See You in my Dreams 1951,D 7,35:1
Young Man With Ideas 1952,Je 7,22:6
By the Light of the Silvery Moon 1953,Mr 27,28:2
Actress, The 1953,O 13,34:1
White Christmas 1954,O 15,16:3
Good Morning, Miss Dove 1955,N 24,41:1
Dance With Me Henry 1956,D 24,8:2
Don't Go Near the Water 1957,N 15,37:1
It Happened to Jane 1959,Ag 6,18:3
Sins of Rachel Cade, The 1961,Ap 6,30:3
How to Murder Your Wife 1965,Ja 27,26:1
Trouble With Angels, The 1966,Ap 7,45:1
Where Angels Go-Trouble Follows 1968,Ap 11,51:1

Wicki, Bernhard
Last Bridge, The 1957,Ag 21,22:2
Circus of Love 1958,Ag 16,10:2
Affairs of Julie, The 1958,D 10,53:1
Cat, The 1959,Ap 13,35:1
Eternal Waltz, The; (Ewiger Walzer) 1959,Jl 9,22:1
Night, The; Notte, La 1962,F 20,29:4
Of Wayward Love (The Serpent); Serpent, The (Of Wayward Love) 1964,Mr 24,29:1

Wicki, Bernhard (Director)
Bridge, The; (Bruecke, Die) 1961,My 2,42:1
Visit, The 1964,O 22,44:1
Saboteur, The: Code Name-Mori Turi 1965,Ag 26,40:2

Wicki, Bernhard (Miscellaneous)
Longest Day, The 1962,O 5,28:1

Wickland, Lyons
Miserables, Les 1935,Ap 22,14:2

Wicks, Florence
Enticement 1925,Mr 21,16:3

Widberg, Elsa
Crime and Punishment 1948,Mr 1,17:2

Widdeck, Martin
Return of Mr Moto 1965,D 2,48:1

Widding, Lars (Screenwriter)
Swedish Wedding Night 1965,N 15,48:1

Widdoes, Kathleen
Group, The 1966,Mr 17,35:1
Petulia 1968,Je 11,54:4
Sea Gull, The 1968,D 24,14:1

Widerberg, Bo (Director)
Raven's End 1965,S 10,40:1
Elvira Madigan 1967,S 30,26:1
Elvira Madigan 1967,O 31,37:2

Widerberg, Bo (Screenwriter)
Elvira Madigan 1967,S 30,26:1

Widerberg, Nina
Elvira Madigan 1967,S 30,26:1

Widmann, Ellen
M 1933,Ap 3,13:3

Widmark, Richard
Kiss of Death 1947,Ag 28,28:2
Street with no Name, The 1948,Jl 15,26:6
Road House 1948,N 8,24:2
Yellow Sky 1949,F 2,36:1
Down to the Sea in Ships 1949,F 23,31:2
Slattery's Hurricane 1949,Ag 13,6:6
Night and the City 1950,Je 10,11:2
Panic in the Streets 1950,Ag 5,9:2
No Way Out 1950,Ag 17,23:1
Halls of Montezuma, The 1951,Ja 6,9:6
Frogmen, The 1951,Je 30,8:6
Smoke Jumpers 1952,Mr 22,9:6
Don't Bother to Knock 1952,Jl 19,8:2
O Henry's Full House (The Clarion Call); Clarion Call, The (O Henry's Full House) 1952,O 17,33:1
Destination Gobi 1953,My 30,7:1
Pickup on South Street 1953,Je 18,38:2
Take the High Ground 1953,N 20,19:2
Hell and High Water 1954,F 2,20:6
Garden of Evil 1954,Jl 10,17:1
Broken Lance 1954,Jl 30,9:1
Cobweb, The 1955,Ag 6,13:3
Prize of Gold, A 1955,O 15,19:2
Backlash 1956,Ap 21,11:2
Run for the Sun 1956,Ag 25,7:2

Widmark, Richard — Cont

Last Wagon, The 1956,S 22,20:2
Saint Joan 1957,Je 27,21:1
Time Limit 1957,O 24,37:2
Law and Jake Wade, the 1958,Je 7,11:1
Tunnel of Love 1958,N 22,27:4
Trap, The 1959,Ja 29,18:4
Warlock 1959,My 1,34:1
Alamo, The 1960,O 27,45:1
Secret Ways, The 1961,My 25,31:1
Two Rode Together 1961,Jl 27,23:3
Judgment at Nuremberg 1961,D 20,36:1
How the West Was Won 1963,Ap 1,54:1
Flight From Ashiya 1964,Ap 23,34:1
Long Ships, The 1964,Je 25,25:1
Cheyenne Autumn 1964,D 24,8:1
Bedford Incident, The 1965,N 3,43:1
Alvarez Kelly 1966,N 17,55:2
Way West, The 1967,My 25,54:1
Madigan 1968,Mr 30,22:2

Widmark, Richard (Producer)

Time Limit 1957,O 24,37:2
Secret Ways, The 1961,My 25,31:1

Wieck, Dorothea

Maedchen in Uniform 1932,S 21,25:4
Teilnehmer Antwortet Nicht 1932,N 30,23:6
Theodor Koerner 1933,My 6,11:2
Anna und Elisabeth 1933,Jl 2,IX,2:2
Cradle Song 1933,N 20,18:2
Miss Fane's Baby is Stolen 1934,Ja 20,12:2
Trenck 1934,Ap 7,19:2
Toller Einfall, Ein 1934,My 21,20:3
Graefin Mariza 1935,Ja 26,13:3
Private Life of Louis XIV, The 1936,Ja 9,25:2
Anna und Elisabeth 1936,Je 13,13:1
Man on a Tightrope 1953,Je 5,19:1
Time to Love and a Time to Die, A
  1958,Jl 10,22:1

Wieder, Hanne

Rosemary 1960,Ja 19,40:2

Wiedmer, Walter L

Hoodlum Priest, The 1961,Ap 3,28:5

Wiehler, M (Miscellaneous)

Ada, to Nie Wypada 1937,My 4,29:1

Wieland, Guido

April 1, 2000 1954,F 17,27:2

Wieman, Mathias

Jolly Peasant, The 1929,Jl 1,31:2
Bride 68 1930,Ap 15,28:5

Wieman, MAthias

Rosenmontag 1931,Mr 28,15:3
Avalanche 1932,Mr 26,17:2

Wieman, Mathias

Mensch Ohne Namen 1932,N 7,20:3

Wieman, MAthias

Klein Dorrit 1935,O 19,21:2
Verlorene Tal, Das 1936,My 30,7:3
Anna und Elisabeth 1936,Je 13,13:1

Wieman, Mathias

Eternal Mask, The 1937,Ja 13,20:3
Togger 1937,Mr 14,XI,4:5 (In Addenda)

Wieman, MAthias

Patriots 1937,S 18,15:3
Unternehmen Michael; Private's Job, The
  1938,My 14,18:2
Winter Stuerme; Winter Storms 1938,O 1,10:2
Wir Sind vom K u K Infantrie-Regiment
  1938,N 19,9:2
Hochzeitsreise, Die; Wedding Journey, The
  1939,My 13,11:5

Wieman, Mathias

If all the Guys in the World 1957,Ap 23,34:1

Wiemann, Matthias

Graefin von Monte Christo, Die; Countess of
  Monte Christo, The 1932,My 15,VIII,4:2 (In
  Addenda)

Wiene, Conrad (Director)

Ein Walzer vom Strauss 1932,F 11,16:1
Ein Prinz Verliebt Sich 1932,Ap 29,13:4
Madame Blaubart 1933,My 11,14:2
Wiener Blut 1933,My 13,21:2

Wiene, Conrad (Producer)

Strauss, The Waltz King 1929,Jl 22,17:1

Wiene, Robert (Director)

Cabinet of Dr Caligari, The 1921,Mr 20,VI,2:1
Power of Darkness 1927,Jl 27,27:4
Guardsman, The 1927,S 7,35:2
Hands of Orlac 1928,Je 5,21:1
Scandal In Paris, A 1929,Je 10,23:1
Dancer of Barcelona, The 1929,N 25,22:1
Acht Tage Glueck 1931,Jl 24,22:1
Andere, Der 1932,Ja 15,24:4
Crown of Thorns 1934,Mr 28,27:6
Ultimatum 1940,F 5,13:2

Wiene, Robert (Producer)

Crime and Punishment 1927,Jl 13,21:2

Wiene, Robert (Screenwriter)

Strauss, The Waltz King 1929,Jl 22,17:1

WIENER

See Also WEINER, WINER

Wiener, Ed

My Hustler 1967,Jl 11,29:2
Bike Boy 1967,O 6,31:2

Wiener, Jean

Lady L 1966,My 19,51:1

Wiener, Jean (Composer)

Maria Chapdelaine 1935,S 25,18:2
Lower Depths, The 1937,S 11,20:1
Slipper Episode, The 1938,My 19,25:2
Escape From Yesterday 1939,My 3,27:2

Wiener, Paul

8 X 8 1957,Mr 16,13:2

Wier, William (Director)

Heiress, The 1949,O 7,35:2

Wier, William (Producer)

Heiress, The 1949,O 7,35:2

Wiere Brothers, The

Great American Broadcast, The 1941,My 2,25:2
Swing Shift Maisie 1943,S 10,29:2
Road to Rio 1948,F 19,29:3
Double Trouble 1967,My 25,54:2

Wierum, Howard

Storm Center 1956,O 22,25:4

Wiesenthal, Sam (Producer)

Cry Danger 1951,F 22,27:3
Second Chance 1953,Jl 23,20:2
Bengazi 1955,O 8,13:4

Wiesner, Arthur

Sins of Rose Bernd, The 1959,Ja 24,13:4 (In
  Addenda)

Wieter, George

Fidelio 1961,My 13,10:1

Wieth, Mogens

Invisible Army, The 1950,Je 26,17:3
Tales of Hoffmann 1951,Ap 5,34:2
Man Who Knew too Much, The 1956,My 17,37:1
Matter of Morals, A 1961,Je 1,31:1

Wifstrand, Naima

Sorciere, La 1956,D 28,17:2
Smiles of a Summer Night 1957,D 24,11:1
Wild Strawberries 1959,Je 23,37:1
Magician, The 1959,Ag 28,27:1
Dreams; Kvinnodrom 1960,Je 1,42:1
Night Games 1966,D 20,58:1
Hour of the Wolf 1968,Ap 10,50:2

Wigert, Sonja

Hennes Lilla Majestat; Her Little Majesty
  1940,Ap 20,14:2
Blood and Fire 1950,Je 24,7:4

Wiggam, Lionel (Miscellaneous)

Smash-Up, The Story of a Woman
  1947,Ap 11,31:2
Tap Roots 1948,Ag 26,16:3

Wiggam, Lionel (Original Author)

Very Thought of You, The 1944,N 18,16:7

Wiggin, Kate Douglas (Original Author)

Rebecca of Sunnybrook Farm 1932,Jl 30,16:5
Timothy's Quest 1936,F 29,11:2
Rebecca of Sunnybrook Farm 1938,Mr 26,12:1
Mother Carey's Chickens 1938,Ag 5,11:1
Summer Magic 1963,Ag 22,19:2

Wigren, Hans

Dear John 1966,Mr 9,46:1

Wigton, Anne (Original Author)

Great Flamario, The 1945,Ja 15,15:5

Wigton, Anne (Screenwriter)

Great Flamario, The 1945,Ja 15,15:5

Wikander, Ulla

Kryss med Albertina, Paa; Cruise in the Albertina,
  A 1940,Mr 25,11:3

Wilbert, Ruth

Girls of the Night 1959,Mr 21,13:2

Wilbur, Crane

High School Girl 1935,Mr 16,19:1

Wilbur, Crane (Director)

High School Girl 1935,Mr 16,19:1
People's Enemy, The 1935,Ap 30,13:7
Navy Spy 1937,Mr 22,27:3
Patient in Room 18, The 1938,Ap 22,15:6
Canon City 1948,Jl 8,19:2
Story of Molly X, The 1949,D 2,35:4
Outside the Wall 1950,Mr 15,34:8
Inside the Walls of Folsom Prison
  1951,My 28,17:4
Bat, The 1959,D 17,51:4

Wilbur, Crane (Original Author)

Her Husband's Secretary 1937,Mr 20,23:6
Navy Spy 1937,Mr 22,27:3
Crime School 1938,My 11,17:2
Blackwell's Island 1939,Mr 2,19:1
Hell's Kitchen 1939,Jl 3,10:5
Roger Touhy, Gangster 1944,Je 5,14:7
Adventures of Casanova 1948,Mr 22,18:3
Canon City 1948,Jl 8,19:2
He Walked by Night 1949,F 7,15:2
Solomon and Sheba 1959,D 26,7:2

Wilbur, Crane (Screenwriter)

Monster, The 1925,F 16,24:1
Dance Charlie Dance 1937,Ag 26,25:2
Alcatraz Island 1937,O 14,22:2
West of Shanghai 1937,O 29,19:2
Invisible Menace, The 1938,F 14,20:6
Over the Wall 1938,Mr 28,19:2
Crime School 1938,My 11,17:2
Girls on Probation 1938,O 21,27:3
Blackwell's Island 1939,Mr 2,19:1

Wilbur, Crane (Screenwriter) — Cont

Hell's Kitchen 1939,Jl 3,10:5
King of the Lumberjacks 1940,Ap 15,21:3
Night of Adventure, A 1944,Je 3,10:4
Roger Touhy, Gangster 1944,Je 5,14:7
Red Stallion 1947,N 27,50:3
Adventures of Casanova 1948,Mr 22,18:3
He Walked by Night 1949,F 7,15:2
Story of Molly X, The 1949,D 2,35:4
Outside the Wall 1950,Mr 15,34:8
I Was a Communist for the F B I 1951,My 3,34:4
Inside the Walls of Folsom Prison
  1951,My 28,17:4
Lion and the Horse, The 1952,My 19,12:2
Miracle of Our Lady Fatima, The
  1952,Ag 21,16:2
House of Wax 1953,Ap 11,15:2
Crime Wave 1954,Ja 13,26:2
Mad Magician, The 1954,My 20,38:2
Women's Prison 1955,F 3,18:5
Phenix City Story, The 1955,S 3,9:1
Bat, The 1959,D 17,51:4
Mysterious Island 1961,D 21,30:6
George Raft Story, The 1962,Mr 22,40:1
House of Women 1962,Ap 12,41:6

Wilcock, Rodolfo

Gospel According to St Matthew, The
  1966,F 18,23:1

Wilcox, Claire

40 Pounds of Trouble 1963,Ja 24,5:2
Wives and Lovers 1963,Ag 29,36:1

Wilcox, Collin

To Kill a Mockingbird 1963,F 15,10:2
Name of the Game Is Kill, The 1968,Je 6,54:1

Wilcox, Frank

Fighting 69th, The 1940,Ja 27,9:2
'Til We Meet Again 1940,Ap 14,14:2
Tear Gas Squad 1940,My 31,15:3
Murder in the Air 1940,Jl 4,12:2
River's End 1940,Ag 26,11:4
Santa Fe Trail 1940,D 21,21:2
Wagons Roll at Night, The 1941,My 10,20:4
Highway West 1941,Ag 8,13:4
They Died With Their Boots On 1941,N 21,23:3
Wild Bill Hickok Rides 1942,F 7,13:5
Bullet Scars 1942,Ap 24,21:4
Murder in the Big House 1942,My 8,27:3
Juke Girl 1942,Je 20,9:2
Lady Gangster 1942,Jl 10,13:2
Wings for the Eagle 1942,Ag 1,14:2
Across the Pacific 1942,S 5,9:2
Busses Roar 1942,S 25,25:4
Escape From Crime 1942,O 12,12:3
Hidden Hand, The 1942,N 26,40:4
Secret Enemies 1943,Ja 1,27:3
Truck Busters 1943,Ja 29,23:5
Conflict 1945,Je 16,10:2
Night Editor 1946,Mr 30,11:2
Beginning or the End, The 1947,F 21,15:1
Something in the Wind 1947,Ag 29,14:3
Gentleman's Agreement 1947,N 12,36:2
Miracle of the Bells, The 1948,Mr 17,30:1
Kid From Texas, The 1950,Je 2,26:2
Greatest Show on Earth, The 1952,Ja 11,17:2
Ruby Gentry 1952,D 26,20:2
Those Redheads From Seattle 1953,O 1,34:2
Never Say Goodbye 1956,Ap 14,20:1
Dance With Me Henry 1956,D 24,8:2
Majority of One, A 1962,Ja 12,29:2

Wilcox, Fred M (Director)

Lassie Come Home 1943,O 8,15:4
Courage of Lassie 1946,Jl 25,18:5
Three Daring Daughters 1948,F 13,26:3
Hills of Home 1948,N 26,32:2
Shadow in the Sky 1952,Jl 19,8:2
Forbidden Planet 1956,My 4,21:2
I Passed for White 1960,Ag 18,19:3

Wilcox, Fred M (Producer)

I Passed for White 1960,Ag 18,19:3

Wilcox, Fred M (Screenwriter)

I Passed for White 1960,Ag 18,19:3

Wilcox, Graham (Director)

Chu Chin Chow 1925,F 11,19:4

Wilcox, Harlow

Look Who's Laughing 1941,D 25,33:2

Wilcox, Herbert (Director)

Nell Gwyn 1926,Jl 19,13:1
London 1926,O 25,15:1
Madame Pompadour 1927,Ag 2,19:2
Decameron Nights 1928,My 29,17:2
Carnival 1931,N 22,VIII,6:1
Good Night, Vienna 1932,My 1,VIII,5:4
Magic Night 1932,N 3,25:3
Blue Danube 1934,N 8,27:1
Nell Gwyn 1935,Je 20,16:2
Peg of Old Drury 1936,Ap 13,15:1
Victoria the Great 1937,O 29,19:1
Girl in the Street 1938,My 26,31:2
This'll Make You Whistle 1938,N 1,27:2
Sixty Glorious Years 1938,N 18,25:2
Nurse Edith Cavell 1939,S 22,27:4
Torpedoed 1939,S 26,20:5
Irene 1940,My 24,23:3
No, No, Nanette 1940,D 20,33:1

Wilcox, Herbert (Director)— Cont

Sunny 1941,Je 13,22:2
Forever and a Day 1943,Mr 13,9:2
Yellow Canary, The 1944,Ap 14,24:7
Yank in London, A 1946,Ap 20,16:3
Piccadilly Incident 1948,Ag 5,16:2
Spring in Park Lane 1949,S 21,38:2
Odette 1951,Mr 28,33:2
Man in the Dinghy 1951,N 1,34:2
Maytime in Mayfair 1952,Ap 23,23:5
Kathy's Love Affair 1952,Jl 3,16:2
Trent's Last Case 1953,N 27,99:9
Laughing Anne 1954,My 8,15:2
Trouble in the Glen 1955,Ap 11,29:2

Wilcox, Herbert (Producer)

Loves of Robert Burns, The 1930,Mr 23,IX,6:1
Brewster's Millions 1935,Ap 8,23:3
Escape me Never 1935,My 24,24:2
Nell Gwyn 1935,Je 20,16:2
Wanted Men 1936,Jl 8,15:2
Victoria the Great 1937,O 29,19:1
Girl in the Street 1938,My 26,31:2
This'll Make You Whistle 1938,N 1,27:2
Sixty Glorious Years 1938,N 18,25:2
Nurse Edith Cavell 1939,S 22,27:4
Suicide Legion 1940,My 6,13:3
Irene 1940,My 24,23:3
No, No, Nanette 1940,D 20,33:1
Sunny 1941,Je 13,22:2
Forever and a Day 1943,Mr 13,9:2
Yellow Canary, The 1944,Ap 14,24:7
Yank in London, A 1946,Ap 20,16:3
Piccadilly Incident 1948,Ag 5,16:2
Spring in Park Lane 1949,S 21,38:2
Odette 1951,Mr 28,33:2
Maytime in Mayfair 1952,Ap 23,23:5
Kathy's Love Affair 1952,Jl 3,16:2
Beggar's Opera, The 1953,Ag 25,18:2
Trent's Last Case 1953,N 27,99:9
Laughing Anne 1954,My 8,15:2
Trouble in the Glen 1955,Ap 11,29:2

Wilcox, Herbert (Screenwriter)

Nell Gwyn 1926,Jl 19,13:1

Wilcox, Pamela (Screenwriter)

Man in the Dinghy 1951,N 1,34:2

Wilcox, Robert

Let Them Live 1937,Je 8,30:3
Armored Car 1937,Jl 26,15:2
Man in Blue, The 1937,Ag 30,25:2
Wild and Woolly 1937,S 6,20:1
City Girl 1938,F 4,17:3
Rascals 1938,My 27,12:2
Little Tough Guy 1938,Ag 18,23:3
Swing That Cheer 1938,N 11,31:2
Gambling Ship 1939,Ja 21,19:2
Undercover Doctor 1939,Je 1,31:2
Lone Wolf Strikes, The 1940,F 5,13:2
Island Of Doomed Men 1940,Je 10,21:2
Unknown, The 1946,Jl 20,10:3
Vigilantes Return, The 1947,Jl 1,30:2

Wilcox (Director)

Dawn 1928,Je 3,VIII,5:1

Wilcoxon, Henry

Cleopatra 1934,Ag 17,12:1
Princess Charming 1935,Je 22,18:5
Crusades, The 1935,Ag 22,21:3
Last of the Mohicans, The 1936,S 3,17:3
President's Mystery, The 1936,O 19,22:1
Two Who Dared 1937,Jl 10,18:2
Souls at Sea 1937,Ag 10,23:2
Prison Nurse 1938,Mr 4,17:5
Keep Smiling 1938,Ag 10,15:2
Dark Sands 1938,Ag 17,23:4
Mysterious Mr Moto of Devil's Island
  1938,S 19,16:2
If I Were King 1938,S 29,31:1
Five of a Kind 1938,O 31,12:2
Woman Doctor 1939,Mr 24,27:3
Tarzan Finds a Son 1939,Je 15,27:2
Free, Blonde and 21 1940,Ap 5,25:2
Earthbound 1940,Je 7,27:4
Crooked Road, The 1940,Je 11,33:4
Mystery Sea Raider 1940,Ag 26,11:4
That Hamilton Woman 1941,Ap 4,25:1
Lone Wolf Takes a Chance, The 1941,Ap 7,13:2
Scotland Yard 1941,Ap 9,33:3
South of Tahiti 1941,N 10,21:3
Corsican Brothers, The 1942,Ja 16,25:4
Man Who Wouldn't Die, The 1942,Ap 28,25:5
Mrs Miniver 1942,Je 5,23:1
Johnny Doughboy 1943,My 6,25:3
Unconquered 1947,O 11,11:2
Connecticut Yankee in King Arthur's Court, A
  1949,Ap 8,31:2
Samson and Delilah 1949,D 22,29:2
Miniver Story, The 1950,O 27,24:2
Greatest Show on Earth, The 1952,Ja 11,17:2
Scaramouche 1952,My 9,20:2
Ten Commandments, The 1956,N 9,35:2
War Lord, The 1965,N 18,55:2
Private Navy of Sgt O'Farrell, The
  1968,My 9,54:1

Wilcoxon, Henry (Producer)

Buccaneer, The 1958,D 24,00:0

Wilczowna, Janina

Halka 1938,Ja 17,11:3

Wild, Jack

Oliver! 1968,D 11,57:1

Wild, Katy

Evil of Frankenstein, The 1964,Je 18,29:2
Deadly Bees, The 1967,My 20,39:2

Wilda, Colette

Dame de Pique, La 1944,O 19,19:2

Wilde, Brian

Rattle of a Simple Man 1964,D 21,42:2
Jokers, The 1967,My 16,50:1

Wilde, Cornel

High Sierra 1941,Ja 25,11:2
Manila Calling 1942,S 28,13:1
Life Begins at Eight-Thirty 1942,D 10,35:2
Wintertime 1943,S 30,27:2
Song to Remember, A 1945,Ja 26,16:4
Thousand and one Nights, A 1945,Jl 12,8:2
Leave Her to Heaven 1945,D 26,15:1
Bandit of Sherwood Forest, The 1946,Mr 23,8:4
Centennial Summer 1946,Jl 18,20:2
Homestretch, The 1947,Ap 24,30:2
Forever Amber 1947,O 23,31:2
It Had to be You 1947,D 8,35:2
Walls of Jericho, The 1948,Ag 5,16:2
Road House 1948,N 8,24:2
Four Days' Leave 1950,Je 9,29:4
Two Flags West 1950,O 13,23:2
Greatest Show on Earth, The 1952,Ja 11,17:2
At Swords Point 1952,Ap 10,37:1
California Conquest 1952,Je 7,22:6
Operation Secret 1952,N 6,37:2
Treasure of the Golden Condor 1953,My 23,19:2
Main Street to Broadway 1953,O 14,34:1
Saadia 1954,Mr 20,10:5
Woman's World 1954,S 29,23:4
Passion 1954,D 11,11:1
Big Combo, The 1955,Mr 26,13:2
Scarlet Coat, The 1955,Jl 30,14:2
Storm Fear 1955,D 17,19:2
Hot Blood 1956,Mr 24,14:2
Star of India 1956,Ap 28,11:1
Beyond Mombasa 1957,My 31,14:2
Omar Khayyam 1957,Ag 24,12:4
Edge of Eternity 1960,F 25,34:2
Constantine and the Cross 1963,Mr 14,8:2
Sword of Lancelot 1963,O 10,49:2
Naked Prey, The 1966,Je 15,40:1
Beach Red 1967,Ag 4,18:1

Wilde, Cornel (Director)

Storm Fear 1955,D 17,19:2
Sword of Lancelot 1963,O 10,49:2
Naked Prey, The 1966,Je 15,40:1
Beach Red 1967,Ag 4,18:1

Wilde, Cornel (Producer)

Storm Fear 1955,D 17,19:2
Sword of Lancelot 1963,O 10,49:2
Naked Prey, The 1966,Je 15,40:1
Beach Red 1967,Ag 4,18:1

Wilde, Hagar (Original Author)

Bringing Up Baby 1938,Mr 4,17:5
Carefree 1938,S 23,35:1
Fired Wife 1943,O 1,15:2
Guest in the House 1945,F 16,19:2

Wilde, Hagar (Screenwriter)

Bringing Up Baby 1938,Mr 4,17:5
Unseen, The 1945,My 14,20:5
I Was a Male War Bride 1949,Ag 27,7:2
Red, Hot and Blue 1949,O 20,39:2
This is my Love 1954,D 25,7:3

Wilde, Heather

Bank Dick, The 1940,D 13,29:2
Immortal Sergeant 1943,F 4,29:2
Life With Father 1947,Ag 16,6:6
Last Holiday 1950,N 14,39:4

Wilde, Lee

Andy Hardy's Blonde Trouble 1944,My 5,17:3
Twice Blessed 1945,Jl 7,7:5
Look for the Silver Lining 1949,Je 24,29:2

Wilde, Lois

Hopalong Rides Again 1938,Ja 22,19:1

Wilde, Lyn

Andy Hardy's Blonde Trouble 1944,My 5,17:3
Twice Blessed 1945,Jl 7,7:5
Look for the Silver Lining 1949,Je 24,29:2

Wilde, Marty

Hellions, The 1962,Mr 15,28:2

Wilde, Oscar (Original Author)

Salome 1923,Ja 1,18:1
Lady Windemere's Fan 1925,D 28,19:2
Woman of No Importance 1936,D 13,XI,6:6 (In
  Addenda)
Frau Ohne Bedeutung, Ein 1938,Ap 16,17:2
Flesh and Fantasy 1943,N 18,29:1
Canterville Ghost, The 1944,Jl 29,16:2
Picture of Dorian Gray, The 1945,Mr 2,15:2
Ideal Husband, An 1948,Ja 15,28:2
Fan, The 1949,Ap 2,12:2
Importance of Being Earnest, The 1952,D 23,17:2

Wilde, Percival (Original Author)

Woman in Room 13, The 1932,My 21,9:2

Wilde, Sonya

I Passed for White 1960,Ag 18,19:3

Wilde, Ted (Original Author)

Girl Shy 1924,Ap 21,21:4

Wilde, Ted (Screenwriter)

Freshman, The 1925,S 21,12:4

Wilde Twins

Two Girls and a Sailor 1944,Je 15,16:1
Till the Clouds Roll By 1946,D 6,27:4

Wildenhain, Bernhard

Raub der Sabinerinnen, Der 1937,Ja 16,21:1

Wildenhain, Hilli

Muede Theodor, Der 1936,O 24,23:2

WILDER

See Also WYLER

Wilder, Alec

Sand Castle, The 1961,Ag 16,37:2
Open the Door and See all the People
  1964,Ap 2,28:1

Wilder, Billy (Director)

Major and the Minor, The 1942,S 17,21:3
Five Graves to Cairo 1943,My 27,21:2
Double Indemnity 1944,S 7,21:1
Lost Weekend, The 1945,D 3,17:2
Emperor Waltz, The 1948,Je 18,19:2
Foreign Affair, A 1948,Jl 1,19:3
Sunset Boulevard 1950,Ag 11,15:2
Ace in the Hole 1951,Je 30,8:6
Stalag 17 1953,Jl 2,19:2
Sabrina 1954,S 23,43:2
Seven Year Itch, The 1955,Je 4,9:1
Spirit of St Louis, The 1957,F 22,25:1
Love in the Afternoon 1957,Ag 24,12:1
Witness for the Prosecution 1958,F 7,16:1
Some Like It Hot 1959,Mr 30,23:1
Apartment, The 1960,Je 16,37:2
One, Two, Three 1961,D 22,17:1
Irma la Douce 1963,Je 6,39:1
Kiss Me, Stupid 1964,D 23,22:2
Fortune Cookie, The 1966,O 20,52:1

Wilder, Billy (Original Author)

Adorable 1933,My 19,20:2
Champagne Waltz 1937,F 4,17:2
Rhythm on the River 1940,Ag 29,23:2
Ball of Fire 1942,Ja 16,25:2
Emperor Waltz, The 1948,Je 18,19:2
Song Is Born, A 1948,O 20,37:2

Wilder, Billy (Producer)

Great Flamario, The 1945,Ja 15,15:5
Ace in the Hole 1951,Je 30,8:6
Stalag 17 1953,Jl 2,19:2
Sabrina 1954,S 23,43:2
Seven Year Itch, The 1955,Je 4,9:1
Love in the Afternoon 1957,Ag 24,12:1
Some Like It Hot 1959,Mr 30,23:1
Apartment, The 1960,Je 16,37:2
One, Two, Three 1961,D 22,17:1
Irma la Douce 1963,Je 6,39:1
Kiss Me, Stupid 1964,D 23,22:2
Fortune Cookie, The 1966,O 20,52:1

Wilder, Billy (Screenwriter)

Music in the Air 1934,D 14,29:3
Bluebeard's Eighth Wife 1938,Mr 24,21:2
Midnight 1939,Ap 6,31:1
What a Life 1939,O 12,33:1
Ninotchka 1939,N 10,27:2
Arise my Love 1940,O 17,33:2
Hold Back the Dawn 1941,O 2,29:1
Ball of Fire 1942,Ja 16,25:2
Major and the Minor, The 1942,S 17,21:3
Five Graves to Cairo 1943,My 27,21:2
Double Indemnity 1944,S 7,21:1
Lost Weekend, The 1945,D 3,17:2
Foreign Affair, A 1948,Jl 1,19:3
Sunset Boulevard 1950,Ag 11,15:2
Ace in the Hole 1951,Je 30,8:6
Stalag 17 1953,Jl 2,19:2
Sabrina 1954,S 23,43:2
Seven Year Itch, The 1955,Je 4,9:1
Spirit of St Louis, The 1957,F 22,25:1
Love in the Afternoon 1957,Ag 24,12:1
Witness for the Prosecution 1958,F 7,16:1
Some Like It Hot 1959,Mr 30,23:1
Apartment, The 1960,Je 16,37:2
One, Two, Three 1961,D 22,17:1
Irma la Douce 1963,Je 6,39:1
Kiss Me, Stupid 1964,D 23,22:2
Fortune Cookie, The 1966,O 20,52:1

Wilder, Gene

Bonnie and Clyde 1967,Ag 14,36:1
Producers, The 1968,Mr 19,38:1

Wilder, John

Until They Sail 1957,O 9,41:2
Summer Love 1958,Je 26,23:4
Imitation General 1958,Ag 21,22:2

Wilder, Marc

Can-Can 1960,Mr 10,36:1

Wilder, Margaret Buell (Original Author)

Since You Went Away 1944,Jl 21,16:2

Wilder, Margaret Buell (Screenwriter)
Stolen Life, A 1946,My 2,27:4
Young Widow 1946,Jl 29,12:8
Pirates of Monterey 1947,D 17,41:4
Wilder, Myles (Screenwriter)
Bluebeard's Ten Honeymoons 1960,N 8,32:6
Wilder, Patricia
Speed 1936,My 16,11:2
Bunker Bean 1936,Je 27,21:2
Wanted: Jane Turner 1936,N 30,24:7
That Girl From Paris 1937,Ja 1,19:1
New Faces of 1937 1937,Jl 2,25:1
On Again-Off Again 1937,S 18,15:3
Big Broadcast of 1938, The 1938,Mr 10,16:2
Little Miss Broadway 1938,Jl 23,10:4
My Lucky Star 1938,S 10,20:2
Wilder, PAtricia
Thanks for the Memory 1938,D 8,34:3
Wilder, Robert (Original Author)
Flamingo Road 1949,My 7,10:2
Written on the Wind 1957,Ja 12,12:6
Stranger in my Arms 1959,Mr 4,34:2
Sol Madrid 1968,Je 14,43:1
Wilder, Robert (Screenwriter)
Flamingo Road 1949,My 7,10:2
Big Country, The 1958,O 2,44:1
Wilder, Thornton (Original Author)
Bridge of San Luis Rey, The 1929,My 20,22:6
Our Town 1940,Je 14,25:3
Bridge of San Luis Rey, The 1944,Mr 4,11:1
Matchmaker, The 1958,Ag 13,22:1
Wilder, Thornton (Screenwriter)
Our Town 1940,Je 14,25:3
Shadow of a Doubt 1943,Ja 13,18:2
Wilder, W Lee (Director)
Pretender, The 1947,Ag 12,26:2
Vicious Circle, The 1948,Jl 22,27:2
Once a Thief 1951,Ja 19,21:3
Three Steps North 1951,Je 29,14:2
Bluebeard's Ten Honeymoons 1960,N 8,32:6
Wilder, W Lee (Producer)
Pretender, The 1947,Ag 12,26:2
Vicious Circle, The 1948,Jl 22,27:2
Once a Thief 1951,Ja 19,21:3
Three Steps North 1951,Je 29,14:2
Wildfire
It's a Dog's Life 1955,D 23,14:3
Wildhack, Robert
Broadway Melody of 1936 1935,S 19,28:1
Broadway Melody of 1938 1937,S 3,12:1
Back Door to Heaven 1939,Ap 20,21:2
Wildhagen, Georg (Director)
Marriage of Figaro 1950,N 3,31:2
Merry Wives of Windsor, The 1952,S 22,19:2
Wildhagen, Georg (Screenwriter)
Marriage of Figaro 1950,N 3,31:2
Merry Wives of Windsor, The 1952,S 22,19:2
Wilding, Michael
Convoy 1941,Ja 17,21:2
Kipps 1942,My 25,11:2
Ships With Wings 1942,My 25,11:2
In Which We Serve 1942,D 24,18:1
Randolph Family 1945,Mr 13,19:4
Ideal Husband, An 1948,Ja 15,28:2
Piccadilly Incident 1948,Ag 5,16:2
Her Man Gilbey 1949,Je 9,35:2
Under Capricorn 1949,S 9,28:3
Spring in Park Lane 1949,S 21,38:2
Stage Fright 1950,F 24,27:2
Law and the Lady, The 1951,Ag 16,23:2
Man in the Dinghy 1951,N 1,34:2
Maytime in Mayfair 1952,Ap 23,23:5
Kathy's Love Affair 1952,Jl 3,16:2
Torch Song 1953,O 13,34:2
Trent's Last Case 1953,Je 27,99:9
Egyptian, The 1954,Ag 25,23:1
Glass Slipper, The 1955,Mr 25,19:2
Scarlet Coat, The 1955,Jl 30,14:2
Zarak 1956,D 27,22:1
Breakout 1960,My 19,44:3
World of Suzie Wong, The 1960,N 11,36:1
Naked Edge 1961,Jl 1,9:1
Best of Enemies, The 1962,Ag 7,35:2
Girl Named Tamiku, A 1963,Mr 15,8:2
Sweet Ride, The 1968,Je 13,57:2
Wilding, Michael (Producer)
Man in the Dinghy 1951,N 1,34:2
Wildman, Jimmy
Ireland's Border Line 1939,O 13,27:3
Wilenchick, Clem
Last Warning, The 1938,D 8,34:4
Beasts of Berlin 1939,N 20,15:6
Flying Deuces, The 1939,N 24,29:2
Wilensky, Mike
Power of Life 1938,Ap 29,17:2
Wilentz, Max
Two Senoritas From Chicago 1943,Ag 6,10:4
Wiles, Gordon (Director)
Charlie Chan's Secret 1936,Ja 18,19:4
Two-Fisted Gentleman 1936,Ag 24,11:2
Lady From Nowhere 1936,D 21,19:2
Women of Glamour 1937,Mr 6,10:1
Gangster, The 1947,O 31,29:3

WILEY
See Also WILLEY, WYLIE
Wiley, Dwight Mitchell (Screenwriter)
Bride Wore Boots, The 1946,Je 6,16:3
Wiley, Hugh (Original Author)
Bits of Life 1921,O 17,18:1
Mr Wong, Detective 1938,N 21,14:4
Mister Wong in Chinatown 1939,Jl 31,9:2 (In Addenda)
Doomed to Die 1940,Jl 30,16:3
Wiley, Jan
She Wolf of London 1946,Ap 6,10:6
Wiley, Jean
These Thousand Hills 1959,My 7,36:1
Wiley, John
Great Locomotive Chase, The 1956,Je 27,35:1
Wiley, Manning
Mister V 1942,F 13,24:4
Wilhelm, Hans (Miscellaneous)
Loves of a Dictator 1935,Je 1,18:2
Wilhelm, Hans (Original Author)
Ein Burschenlied aus Heidelberg 1931,S 14,15:3
Three on a Week-End 1938,Je 2,19:3
Prison Without Bars 1939,Ag 10,13:2
On an Island With You 1948,Jl 30,13:2
Prowler, The 1951,Jl 2,16:6
Wilhelm, Hans (Producer)
Dime With a Halo 1963,Je 27,23:3
Wilhelm, Hans (Screenwriter)
Man Braucht Kein Geld 1932,N 16,15:3
Affair Lafont, The; Conflit 1939,O 9,15:2
Heartbeat 1946,My 11,22:4
On an Island With You 1948,Jl 30,13:2
No Time for Flowers 1952,D 26,20:3
Five Golden Hours 1961,O 19,39:3
Dime With a Halo 1963,Je 27,23:3
Wilhelm, Wolfgang (Original Author)
Troopship 1938,Ap 26,18:2
Dispatch From Reuters, A 1940,D 12,37:2
Voice in the Night, The 1941,My 23,25:4
Mister V 1942,F 13,24:4
Adventures, The 1947,Ap 4,19:2
Wilhelm, Wolfgang (Screenwriter)
Brewster's Millions 1935,Ap 8,23:3
Continental Express 1942,Ap 7,26:3
Squadron Leader X 1943,Jl 23,21:2
Captain Boycott 1947,D 6,11:2
End of the River, The 1948,Je 21,18:2
Wilhite, Prentice
No More Excuses 1968,My 22,53:1
Wilies, Jean
F B I Story, The 1959,S 25,23:1
McHale's Navy 1964,Jl 11,15:2
WILK
See Also WILKE
Wilk, Herbert
Lied der Wuste, Das; Desert Song 1940,F 3,9:3
Wilk, Max (Original Author)
Open Secret 1948,F 2,15:2
It Happened to Jane 1959,Ag 6,18:3
Don't Raise the Bridge, Lower the River 1968,Jl 13,18:1
Wilk, Max (Screenwriter)
Open Secret 1948,F 2,15:2
Close-Up 1948,Ag 5,24:2
Don't Raise the Bridge, Lower the River 1968,Jl 13,18:1
Wilk, Wiesla
First Start, The 1953,F 2,17:3
WILKE
See Also WILK
Wilke, Gisela
Fasching in Wien 1939,Mr 18,9:2
Wilke, Hubert
Great Deception, The 1926,Ag 9,10:3
Wilke, Robert
Kill the Umpire 1950,My 29,10:6
Las Vegas Story, The 1952,Ja 31,37:6
High Noon 1952,Jl 25,14:2
From Here to Eternity 1953,Ag 6,16:2
20,000 Leagues Under the Sea 1954,D 24,7:2
Far Country, The 1955,F 14,24:2
Strange Lady in Town 1955,My 21,11:1
Lone Ranger, The 1956,F 11,12:1
Backlash 1956,Ap 21,11:2
Rawhide Years, The 1956,Je 16,12:2
Raw Edge 1956,Jl 28,10:7
Written on the Wind 1957,Ja 12,12:6
Night Passage 1957,Jl 25,28:1
Tarnished Angels, The 1958,Ja 7,31:1
Never Steal Anything Small 1959,F 12,23:1
Spartacus 1960,O 7,28:1
Hallelujah Trail, The 1965,Jl 2,17:1
Tony Rome 1967,N 16,58:1
Wilkerson, Bill
Juarez 1939,Ap 26,27:1
Dr Cyclops 1940,Ap 11,32:3
Davy Crockett, Indian Scout 1950,Mr 17,28:3
Rock Island Trail 1950,Je 5,19:3
Broken Arrow 1950,Jl 21,15:2
Wilkerson, Guy
Mountain Justice 1937,My 13,31:2
Our Neighbors-The Carters 1940,F 15,15:2

Wilkerson, Guy— Cont
Untamed 1940,Jl 25,14:3
Spooks Run Wild 1941,N 1,20:3
Swamp Woman 1941,D 27,15:2
Great Missouri Raid, The 1951,Ap 9,31:2
Big Sky, The 1952,Ag 20,21:1
Stranger Wore a Gun, The 1953,Jl 30,20:3
Susan Slade 1961,N 11,14:6
Wilkerson, Martha (Screenwriter)
Hard, Fast and Beautiful 1951,Jl 2,16:6
Wilkin, Jeremy
Strange Affair, The 1968,Jl 25,26:2
Wilkins, June
Camille 1937,Ja 23,13:1
Bachelor Mother 1939,Je 30,17:2
When the Daltons Rode 1940,Ag 23,13:3
Wilkins, Martin
Congo Maisie 1940,F 8,18:4
Bomba, the Jungle Boy 1949,Ap 16,11:4
Sirocco 1951,Je 14,31:2
Lydia Bailey 1952,My 31,12:5
Wilkins, Reverend
Festival 1967,O 24,53:2
Wilkins, Vaughan (Original Author)
Dangerous Exile 1958,O 11,18:3
Wilkinson, G K (Original Author)
Monkeys Go Home 1967,Mr 30,55:1
Wilkinson, Geoffrey
Treasure Island 1950,Ag 16,24:2
Wilkinson, Penelope
River, The 1951,S 11,33:2
Wilkinson, Sam
Lost Patrol, The 1929,D 16,34:2
Battle of Gallipoli, The 1931,D 7,16:1
Jack Ahoy 1935,F 9,11:2
Last Journey, The 1936,Je 8,22:4
Dreaming Lips 1937,My 20,17:1
Wilkinson, Walter
Sea Hawk, The 1924,Je 3,22:1
Man Who Came Back, The 1924,S 1,9:1
Willans, Geoffrey (Screenwriter)
Bridal Path, The 1959,D 21,34:2
Willard, Edmund
Love Storm 1931,O 19,28:1
Iron Duke, The 1935,Ja 25,27:2
Legend of William Tell, The 1935,O 2,27:1
King of the Damned 1936,F 1,9:2
I Stand Condemned 1936,Jl 2,27:2
Troopship 1938,Ap 26,18:2
Pastor Hall 1940,S 21,13:2
Larceny Street 1941,Ja 6,11:2
Courageous Mr Penn 1943,D 23,26:5
Willard, Jess
Challenge of Chance, The 1919,Je 19,9:4
Legendary Champions, The 1968,O 29,54:1
Willard, John
Victims of Persecution 1933,Je 17,16:6
Willard, John (Original Author)
Cat and the Canary, The 1927,S 10,9:4
Cat Creeps, The 1930,N 8,21:3
Cat and the Canary, The 1939,N 23,38:5
Willard, Lee
Man With Nine Lives, The 1940,Ap 29,12:3
Willard, Leigh
Last Edition, The 1925,N 11,27:3
Fourth Commandment, The 1927,Ap 6,25:1
Willard, Winifred
Men Are not Gods 1937,Ja 19,28:1
Willat, Irvin (Director)
False Faces, The 1919,F 17,11:3
Behind the Door 1920,Ja 5,15:1
Yellow Men and Gold 1922,My 29,14:1
On the High Seas 1922,O 8,VI,3:1 (In Addenda)
Fog Bound 1923,My 29,10:3
Three Miles Out 1924,Ja 1,20:1
Heritage of the Desert, The 1924,Ja 24,15:1
Wanderer of the Wasteland, The 1924,Jl 8,14:2
Story Without a Name, The 1924,O 6,25:1
North of 36 1924,D 8,13:3
Air Mail, The 1925,Mr 17,18:1
Ancient Highway, The 1925,N 11,27:3
Enchanted Hill, The 1925,D 29,19:2 (In Addenda)
Back to God's Country 1927,O 24,24:3
Cavalier, The 1928,O 31,28:4
Isle of Lost Ships, The 1929,O 26,15:1
Damaged Love 1931,Ja 19,25:1
Willat, Irwin (Cinematographer)
Below the Surface 1920,Je 7,20:3 (In Addenda)
Willat, Irwin (Director)
Below the Surface 1920,Je 7,20:3 (In Addenda)
Willat, Joseph (Director)
Paradise 1926,O 4,20:2
Willecke, Detlef
Legend of William Tell, The 1935,O 2,27:1
Willemetz, Albert (Original Author)
Three Waltzes 1939,Ap 25,19:2
Willers, Irmgard
Horst Wessel; Hans Westmar 1934,F 4,IX,4:4
Willes, Jean
Chinatown at Midnight 1949,N 18,35:3
Woman of Distinction, A 1950,Mr 17,28:2
From Here to Eternity 1953,Ag 6,16:2
Lieutenant Wore Skirts, The 1956,Ja 12,22:1

Willes, Jean — Cont

Revolt of Mamie Stover, The 1956,My 12,12:7
King and Four Queens, The 1956,D 22,13:7
Desire Under the Elms 1958,Mr 13,24:2
No Time for Sergeants 1958,My 30,13:2
Ocean's Eleven 1960,Ag 11,19:1
Crowded Sky, The 1961,F 11,27:2
By Love Possessed 1961,Jl 20,32:2
Gypsy 1962,N 2,24:1

Willes, Peter

Call it a Day 1937,My 7,29:2
Dawn Patrol 1938,D 24,12:1
Idiot's Delight 1939,F 3,13:1
Adventures of Sherlock Holmes, The
    1939,S 2,20:1

WILLEY

See Also WILEY, WYLIE

Willey, Leonard

Prince and the Pauper, The 1937,My 6,23:1
Night Club Scandal 1937,N 12,27:2
Invisible Enemy 1938,Ap 30,18:2
Adventures of Robin Hood, The 1938,My 13,17:2
Tom Brown's School Days 1940,Je 28,22:2
Penny Serenade 1941,My 23,25:2

William, Warren

Honor of the Family 1931,O 17,20:1
Expensive Women 1931,N 14,15:3
Under Eighteen 1931,D 26,15:5
Woman From Monte Carlo, The 1931,D 31,17:6
Beauty and the Boss 1932,Ap 2,13:2
Mouthpiece, The 1932,Ap 21,25:2
Dark Horse, The 1932,Je 9,27:3
Skyscraper Souls 1932,Ag 5,11:2
Three on a Match 1932,O 29,18:4
Match King, The 1932,D 8,25:3
Employees' Entrance 1933,Ja 21,10:6
Mind Reader, The 1933,Ap 7,22:4
Gold Diggers of 1933 1933,Je 8,22:3
Good-Bye Again 1933,S 2,15:2
Lady for a Day 1933,S 8,22:2
Bedside 1934,Mr 7,23:4
Upper World 1934,My 25,25:4
Dr Monica 1934,Je 21,28:2
Cleopatra 1934,Ag 17,12:1
Dragon Murder Case, The 1934,Ag 23,13:3
Case of the Howling Dog, The 1934,O 18,26:5
Imitation of Life 1934,N 24,19:1
Secret Bride, The 1935,F 2,10:1
Living on Velvet 1935,Mr 8,25:4
Case of the Curious Bride, The 1935,Ap 5,21:3
Don't Bet on Blondes 1935,Jl 20,16:2
Case of the Lucky Legs, The 1935,N 1,25:1
Times Square Playboy 1936,My 2,11:2
Satan Met a Lady 1936,Jl 23,24:2
Case of the Velvet Claws, The 1936,Ag 29,16:3
Stage Struck 1936,S 28,14:4
Go West, Young Man 1936,N 19,31:3
Outcast 1937,Mr 3,27:2
Midnight Madonna 1937,Jl 17,18:1
Firefly, The 1937,S 2,17:2
Madame X 1937,O 25,23:1
Arsene Lupin Returns 1938,Mr 9,21:1
First 100 Years, The 1938,My 13,17:2
Wives Under Suspicion 1938,Jl 1,22:3
Lone Wolf Spy Hunt, The 1939,Mr 6,11:3
Gracie Allen Murder Case, The 1939,Je 8,31:3
Man in the Iron Mask, The 1939,Jl 14,11:1
Daytime Wife 1939,N 24,29:1
Lone Wolf Strikes, The 1940,F 5,13:2
Lillian Russell 1940,My 18,11:2
Lone Wolf Meets a Lady, The 1940,Je 17,19:2
Trail of the Vigilantes 1940,D 7,13:2
Lone Wolf Keeps a Date, The 1941,Ja 2,24:3
Arizona 1941,F 7,23:3
Lone Wolf Takes a Chance, The 1941,Ap 7,13:2
Wild Geese Calling 1941,Ag 30,10:2
Wolf Man, The 1941,D 22,24:5
Wild Bill Hickok Rides 1942,F 7,13:5
Counter-Espionage 1942,S 28,13:2
Private Affairs of Bel Ami, The 1947,Je 16,25:4

Williams

Parisian, The 1931,Ag 22,7:5

Williams, Ada

Common Clay 1930,Ag 2,16:4

Williams, Adam

Vice Squad 1953,Ag 26,23:2
Big Heat, The 1953,O 15,43:2
Crashout 1955,Jl 9,9:2
Proud and Profane, The 1956,Je 14,41:2
Rack, The 1956,N 6,30:1
Fear Strikes Out 1957,Mr 21,37:2
Darby's Rangers 1958,F 13,23:2
Badlanders, The 1958,S 4,33:1
North by Northwest 1959,Ag 7,28:1
Last Sunset, The 1961,Je 15,51:1
Convicts 4 1962,O 4,44:2
New Interns, The 1964,Ag 20,34:2

Williams, Alan (Original Author)

One Woman Idea, The 1929,Je 10,23:1
Pink Jungle, The 1968,O 17,52:1

Williams, Allie Mae

Birthright 1952,F 15,17:2

Williams, Andy

I'd Rather Be Rich 1964,S 3,24:2

Williams, Barbara

Smiling Faces 1932,Ag 31,12:3

Williams, Ben

Battle for Music 1945,O 15,13:2
Waterloo Road 1948,D 25,10:3

Williams, Ben Ames (Original Author)

Godless Men 1921,Ja 31,11:1
Across to Singapore 1928,Ap 30,18:3
Man to Man 1931,Ja 3,21:2
Too Busy to Work 1932,D 3,21:4
Small Town Girl 1936,Ap 11,19:1
Adventure's End 1937,D 20,23:2
Leave Her to Heaven 1945,D 26,15:1
Strange Woman, The 1947,F 24,16:4
All the Brothers Were Valiant 1953,D 29,19:2

Williams, Bill

Last Man, The 1932,S 17,18:4
Those Endearing Young Charms 1945,Je 20,26:5
Deadline at Dawn 1946,Ap 4,33:2
Till the End of Time 1946,Jl 24,24:1
Stratton Story, The 1949,My 13,29:1
Fighting Man of the Plains 1949,N 17,35:6
Dangerous Profession, A 1949,D 12,29:4
Blue Grass of Kentucky 1950,Ja 27,29:2
Cariboo Trail, The 1950,S 1,17:2
California Passage 1950,D 16,10:5
Great Missouri Raid, The 1951,Ap 9,31:2
Last Outpost, The 1951,Je 22,16:3
Son of Paleface 1952,O 2,32:3
Torpedo Valley 1952,D 20,15:3
Legion of the Doomed 1959,Mr 12,27:5
Hell to Eternity 1960,O 13,41:1
Tickle Me 1965,Je 24,28:3

Williams, Billy Dee

Last Angry Man, The 1959,O 23,24:1

Williams, Bob

Stars Are Singing, The 1953,Mr 12,24:2

Williams, Bob (Original Author)

Macao 1952,My 1,34:2

Williams, Bob (Screenwriter)

Treat 'Em Rough 1942,Ja 19,21:3
Stage to Tucson 1951,My 5,14:2

Williams, Bransby

Woman in Command, The 1934,My 29,22:2
At Dawn We Die 1943,My 8,19:2

Williams, Brock (Original Author)

Clouds Over Europe 1939,Je 16,27:2

Williams, Brock (Producer)

Tony Draws a Horse 1951,My 15,38:6

Williams, Brock (Screenwriter)

Mr Cohen Takes a Walk 1936,F 13,25:2
Blackout 1940,D 2,19:2
Prime Minister, The 1942,F 4,23:2
Flying Fortress 1942,D 19,22:2
Candlelight in Algeria 1944,Jl 31,10:2
Place of One's Own, A 1949,F 8,30:2
Tony Draws a Horse 1951,My 15,38:6

Williams, C B (Original Author)

Carnival Story 1954,Ap 17,8:2
Circus of Love 1958,Ag 16,10:2

Williams, Cara

Happy Land 1943,D 9,33:3
Something for the Boys 1944,N 30,19:1
Spider, The 1946,Je 21,20:3
Boomerang 1947,Mr 6,36:2
Saxon Charm, The 1948,S 30,32:3
Knock on any Door 1949,F 23,31:2
Girl Next Door, The 1953,S 5,7:4
Monte Carlo Baby 1954,My 29,13:4
Meet Me in Las Vegas 1956,Mr 14,39:2
Helen Morgan Story, The 1957,O 3,33:2
Never Steal Anything Small 1959,F 12,23:1
Man From the Diners' Club, The
    1963,Ap 18,39:1

Williams, Charles

Dance Team 1932,Ja 16,13:1
Strangers of the Evening 1932,Je 4,9:2
Devil Is Driving, The 1932,D 16,25:5
Gambling Ship 1933,Jl 13,17:5
Rhythm on the Range 1936,Jl 30,22:1
Wake up and Live 1937,Ap 24,16:2
Turn off the Moon 1937,My 20,17:2
Charlie Chan on Broadway 1937,S 20,19:1
Merry-Go-Round of 1938 1937,N 26,27:2
Love and Hisses 1938,Ja 1,11:1
Mr Moto's Gamble 1938,Ap 8,17:2
Stadium Murders, The 1938,Ap 9,11:2
Just Around the Corner 1938,D 3,11:2
Convoy 1941,Ja 17,21:2
Flying Cadets 1941,O 14,29:2
Time to Kill 1942,D 25,15:4
Where Are Your Children? 1944,Ja 17,14:5
Love on the Dole 1945,O 13,11:2
It's a Wonderful Life 1946,D 23,19:2

Williams, Charles (Original Author)

Third Voice, The 1960,Mr 7,24:5
Don't Just Stand There 1968,S 3,54:2

Williams, Charles (Screenwriter)

Joy House 1965,F 18,29:1
Don't Just Stand There 1968,S 3,54:2
Pink Jungle, The 1968,O 17,52:1

Williams, Clarence 3d

Cool World, The 1964,Ap 21,42:1

Williams, Clark

Transient Lady 1935,Mr 11,15:1
Werewolf of London, The 1935,My 10,25:2
Citizen Saint 1948,My 28,28:2

Williams, Cora

His Parisian Wife 1919,Ja 20,13:2
Womanhandled 1926,Ja 5,25:2
Sensation Seekers 1927,Mr 16,28:2

Williams, D J

Bride of the Lake, The 1934,S 11,24:5
Scrooge 1935,D 14,11:1
Murder in the Old Red Barn 1936,Ag 19,18:3
Wings of the Morning 1937,Mr 12,19:1
Elephant Boy 1937,Ap 6,20:2
Courageous Mr Penn 1943,D 23,26:5

Williams, Danny

Play it Cool 1963,Jl 18,15:3
Dream Maker, The 1964,Ap 23,34:1

Williams, David

Brimstone 1949,O 7,35:3
Circle, The 1959,Ap 16,29:2

Williams, Duke

Red Menace, The 1949,Je 27,18:2

Williams, Earle

Masters of Men 1923,My 15,22:1
Skyrocket, The 1926,Ja 26,25:2
Diplomacy 1926,S 13,18:1
You'd Be Surprised 1926,S 27,27:3

Williams, Ed

Cyanamide 1954,Mr 26,17:6

Williams, Edy

Pad, The (And How to Use It) 1966,Ag 18,27:2
Good Times 1967,Ag 3,26:4
Secret Life of an American Wife, The
    1968,Je 26,42:2

Williams, Elaine

Subject Was Roses, The 1968,O 14,53:2

Williams, Elmo (Director)

Tall Texan, The 1953,Ap 13,32:4
Cowboy, The 1954,Ag 3,14:2

Williams, Elmo (Producer)

Cowboy, The 1954,Ag 3,14:2

Williams, Emlyn

Criminal at Large 1933,D 20,27:2
Friday the 13th 1934,My 15,18:1
Evensong 1934,N 17,12:1
Iron Duke, The 1935,Ja 25,27:2
Men of Tomorrow 1935,Ap 16,27:2
My Song For You 1935,My 27,20:6
Loves of a Dictator 1935,Je 1,18:2
Broken Blossoms 1937,Ja 14,16:3
Citadel, The 1938,N 4,27:2
Dead Men Tell no Tales 1939,Jl 24,9:2
Jamaica Inn 1939,O 12,33:1
Girl in the News, The 1941,My 5,13:2
Major Barbara 1941,My 15,27:1
Stars Look Down, The 1941,Jl 24,15:2
This England 1941,N 18,33:2
Hatter's Castle 1948,Jl 3,8:6
Dolwyn 1949,Ag 30,18:4
Three Husbands 1951,Mr 9,30:2
Screen, The 1951,Ap 23,21:2
Another Man's Poison 1952,Ja 7,14:3
Ivanhoe 1952,Ag 1,8:2
Deep Blue Sea, The 1955,O 13,35:2
I Accuse! 1958,Mr 6,32:1
Wreck of the Mary Deare, The 1959,N 7,27:1
L-Shaped Room, The 1963,My 28,32:1
Eye of the Devil 1967,D 7,60:1

Williams, Emlyn (Director)

Dolwyn 1949,Ag 30,18:4

Williams, Emlyn (Miscellaneous)

Man Who Knew too Much, The 1935,Mr 23,11:2
Citadel, The 1938,N 4,27:2
Dead Men Tell no Tales 1939,Jl 24,9:2
This England 1941,N 18,33:2

Williams, Emlyn (Original Author)

Night Must Fall 1937,Ap 30,17:2
Life Begins at Eight-Thirty 1942,D 10,35:2
Corn is Green, The 1945,Mr 30,18:2
Night Must Fall 1964,Mr 19,28:1

Williams, Emlyn (Screenwriter)

Broken Blossoms 1937,Ja 14,16:3
Dolwyn 1949,Ag 30,18:4

Williams, Eric (Original Author)

Wooden Horse, The 1951,Ag 29,20:2

Williams, Eric (Screenwriter)

Wooden Horse, The 1951,Ag 29,20:2

Williams, Esther

Andy Hardy's Double Life 1943,Ja 12,23:3
Guy Named Joe, A 1943,D 24,17:2
Bathing Beauty 1944,Je 28,20:1
Thrill of a Romance 1945,My 25,22:2
Ziegfeld Follies 1946,Mr 23,8:3
Hoodlum Saint, The 1946,Je 27,29:1
Easy to Wed 1946,Jl 12,14:2
Fiesta 1947,Je 27,17:3
This Time for Keeps 1947,D 5,33:4
On an Island With You 1948,Jl 30,13:2
Take Me Out to the Ball Game 1949,Mr 10,35:2
Neptune's Daughter 1949,Je 10,32:2

Williams, Esther— Cont

Duchess of Idaho 1950,Jl 21,15:3
Pagan Love Song 1950,D 26,19:1
Texas Carnival 1951,O 13,9:1
Skirts Ahoy! 1952,My 29,17:2
Million Dollar Mermaid 1952,D 5,35:2
Dangerous When Wet 1953,Je 19,18:1
Easy to Love 1953,N 27,99:9
Jupiter's Darling 1955,F 18,18:4
Raw Wind in Eden 1958,S 20,10:6
Big Show, The 1961,My 11,42:4
Williams, Ezra
Return to Paradise 1953,S 11,24:2
Williams, Frances
Hollywood Party 1934,My 26,12:2
Williams, Francis
Magnificent Doll 1946,D 9,34:2
Her Sister's Secret 1947,Ja 23,31:3
Reckless Moment, The 1949,D 30,13:2
Show Boat 1951,Jl 20,14:1
Williams, Fred
Sandra 1966,Ja 17,32:1
Williams, Geneva
Little Colonel, The 1935,Mr 22,26:2
Williams, George B
Captain Blood 1924,S 9,19:1
Fifth Avenue Models 1925,My 4,16:2
Phantom of the Opera, The 1925,S 7,15:3
Midnight Sun, The 1926,Ap 24,20:4
Williams, Gladys
Betrayal, The 1948,Je 26,10:5
Williams, Gloria
Cocoanut Grove 1938,Je 16,21:2
Prison Farm 1938,Jl 15,13:3
Give Me a Sailor 1938,Ag 11,31:1
Williams, Grant
Written on the Wind 1957,Ja 12,12:6
Four Girls in Town 1957,Ja 17,34:5
Incredible Shrinking Man, The 1957,F 23,13:1
Susan Slade 1961,N 11,14:6
Couch, The 1962,F 22,20:3
PT 109 1963,Je 27,23:1
Williams, Guinn
Black Cyclone 1925,My 19,24:2
Ladies' Night in a Turkish Bath 1928,Ap 9,18:2
Burning Daylight 1928,Ap 23,20:2
My Man 1928,D 22,14:3
Noah's Ark 1929,Mr 13,28:6
Lucky Star 1929,Jl 22,17:1
Forward Pass, The 1929,N 29,25:1
Big Fight, The 1930,Je 28,9:2
Liliom 1930,O 4,15:2
College Lovers 1930,N 28,23:1
Bachelor Father, The 1931,F 2,23:1
Great Meadow, The 1931,Mr 14,23:2
Ladies of the Jury 1932,Ap 2,13:2
70,000 Witnesses 1932,S 3,16:2
You Said a Mouthful 1932,N 18,23:2
Devil Is Driving, The 1932,D 16,25:5
Heritage of the Desert 1933,Mr 11,18:3
Phantom Broadcast, The 1933,Jl 31,16:2
College Coach 1933,N 11,10:4
Palooka 1934,F 28,23:2
Cheaters 1934,My 12,12:4
Half a Sinner 1934,Je 23,16:5
Here Comes the Navy 1934,Jl 21,14:2
Romance in the Rain 1934,S 8,18:5
Flirtation Walk 1934,N 29,33:1
Silver Streak, The 1935,Ja 16,21:1
Private Worlds 1935,Mr 28,25:2
Glass Key, The 1935,Je 15,20:2
Miss Pacific Fleet 1935,D 7,22:2
Littlest Rebel, The 1935,D 20,30:1
Muss 'Em Up 1936,F 3,21:2
Powdersmoke Range 1936,Mr 9,20:2
Grand Jury 1936,Ag 1,16:3
Kelly the Second 1936,O 3,21:2
You Only Live Once 1937,F 1,15:2
Don't Tell the Wife 1937,F 19,15:2
Star Is Born, A 1937,Ap 23,25:1
Singing Marine, The 1937,Jl 1,33:2
She's no Lady 1937,Ag 12,14:3
Big City 1937,S 17,29:2
Wise Girl 1938,Ja 10,13:3
Bad Man of Brimstone, The 1938,F 4,17:2
You and Me 1938,Je 2,19:1
Professor Beware 1938,Jl 14,17:1
Army Girl 1938,Ag 12,11:1
Hold That Co-ed 1938,S 24,13:1
Dodge City 1939,Ap 8,19:1
Street of Missing Men 1939,Je 1,31:3
Six Thousand Enemies 1939,Je 9,26:2
Mutiny on the Blackhawk 1939,Ag 2,17:2
Bad Lands 1939,Ag 9,15:2
Blackmail 1939,S 15,26:3
Legion of Lost Flyers 1939,O 30,13:3
Fugitive at Large 1939,N 13,15:2
Fighting 69th, The 1940,Ja 27,9:2
Castle on the Hudson 1940,Mr 4,11:2
Alias the Deacon 1940,My 14,27:5
Wagons Westward 1940,Jl 8,13:2
Money and the Woman 1940,O 4,29:2
Dulcy 1940,N 28,28:2
Santa Fe Trail 1940,D 21,21:2

Six Lessons From Madame La Zonga
  1941,F 19,25:2
Billy the Kid 1941,Je 20,28:2
You'll Never Get Rich 1941,O 24,27:2
Swamp Water 1941,N 17,15:2
Mr Wise Guy 1942,Mr 5,27:2
Bugle Sounds, The 1942,Ap 3,25:2
Between Us Girls 1942,S 25,25:3
Silver Queen 1943,Ja 11,18:4
American Empire 1943,Ja 14,25:4
Desperadoes, The 1943,My 13,17:2
Belle of the Yukon 1945,Mr 30,18:4
Bad Men of Tombstone 1949,Mr 5,10:2
Brimstone 1949,O 7,35:3
Rocky Mountain 1950,N 4,13:2
Al Jennings of Oklahoma 1951,My 18,34:6
Springfield Rifle 1952,O 23,40:2
Hangman's Knot 1952,D 11,45:3
Southwest Passage 1954,S 11,11:2
Alamo, The 1960,O 27,45:1
Williams, Guinn (Narrator)
Mr Bug Goes to Town 1942,F 20,21:3
Williams, Guy
Mississippi Gambler, The 1953,Ja 30,25:1
Seven Angry Men 1955,Ap 2,15:2
Sincerely Yours 1955,N 3,37:1
Last Frontier, The 1955,D 8,45:1
Sign of Zorro, The 1961,S 5,37:6
Damon and Pythias 1962,S 6,37:2
Captain Sindbad 1963,Jl 4,9:1
Williams, Harcourt
Henry V 1946,Je 18,30:2
Hamlet 1948,S 30,32:2
Under Capricorn 1949,S 9,28:3
No Room at the Inn 1949,D 26,33:4
Eye Witness 1950,Ag 28,13:2
Gay Lady, The 1951,Ap 16,21:2
Young Scarface 1951,N 8,35:2
Case of Gold 1952,Ja 19,13:3
Cage of Gold 1952,Ja 19,13:3
Obsessed 1952,F 6,24:2
Roman Holiday 1953,Ag 28,13:1
Quentin Durward 1955,N 24,41:1
Around the World in 80 Days 1956,O 18,37:1
Williams, Harold (Cinematographer)
Ingagi 1931,Mr 17,34:3
Williams, Herb
Rose of the Rancho 1936,Ja 9,25:2
Williams, Herschel V Jr (Original Author)
Janie 1944,Ag 5,16:2
Janie Gets Married 1946,Je 15,24:2
Williams, Hope
Scoundrel, The 1935,My 3,23:2
Williams, Howard
Up the Creek 1958,N 11,26:2
Williams, Hugh
Charley's Aunt 1930,D 26,18:4
Rome Express 1933,F 27,11:2
Bitter Sweet 1933,Ag 24,18:2
White Face 1933,D 4,22:3
Sorrell and Son 1934,My 29,22:1
Outcast Lady 1934,N 3,20:3
David Copperfield 1935,Ja 19,8:1
In a Monastery Garden 1935,Mr 13,16:2
Let's Live Tonight 1935,Mr 18,14:4
Amateur Gentleman, The 1936,Ap 27,19:2
Last Journey, The 1936,Je 8,22:4
Wuthering Heights 1939,Ap 14,28:2
Inspector Hornleigh 1939,Je 15,27:3
Dead Men Tell no Tales 1939,Jl 24,9:2
Human Monster, The 1940,Mr 25,11:2
Ships With Wings 1942,My 25,11:2
One of our Aircraft Is Missing 1942,N 2,17:2
Avengers, The 1942,N 25,18:2
Ideal Husband, An 1948,Ja 15,28:2
Take my Life 1949,Ja 19,34:2
Blind Goddess, The 1949,Je 23,33:3
Girl in a Million, A 1950,Jl 24,15:2
Glory at Sea 1953,Mr 11,36:7
Holly and the Ivy, The 1954,F 5,16:1
Intruder, The 1955,Ja 26,22:1
Khartoum 1966,Jl 14,28:1
Williams, Hugh (Original Author)
Grass is Greener, The 1960,D 24,8:2
Williams, Hugh (Screenwriter)
Grass is Greener, The 1960,D 24,8:2
Williams, Ivory
Tarzan, The Ape Man 1932,Mr 28,11:2
Green Pastures, The 1936,Jl 17,20:1
Williams, J B (Director)
White Cargo 1930,F 24,18:1
Williams, J B (Screenwriter)
To the Victor 1938,Ap 13,21:2
Stars Look Down, The 1941,Jl 24,15:2
Dulcimer Street 1948,N 8,24:2
That Forsyte Woman 1949,N 11,31:2
Williams, Jack
Hit Parade of 1943 1943,Ap 16,24:3
Williams, Jay
Little Fugitive 1953,O 7,35:1
Williams, Jeffery
Saphead, The 1921,F 14,12:2

Williams, John
Emil 1938,Ap 15,23:2
Somewhere in France 1943,Jl 12,11:2
Woman's Vengeance, A 1948,Ja 30,19:2
Kind Lady 1951,Ag 8,21:2
Thunder in the East 1953,F 4,32:2
Dial M for Murder 1954,My 29,13:2
Student Prince, The 1954,Je 16,18:2
Sabrina 1954,S 23,43:2
To Catch a Thief 1955,Ag 5,14:2
D-Day, The Sixth of June 1956,My 30,13:1
Solid Gold Cadillac, The 1956,O 25,40:3
Island in the Sun 1957,Je 13,37:1
Will Success Spoil Rock Hunter 1957,S 12,37:5
Witness for the Prosecution 1958,F 7,16:1
Young Philadelphians, The 1959,My 22,32:1
Visit to a Small Planet 1960,Ap 14,34:1
Midnight Lace 1960,O 14,27:1
Dear Brigitte 1965,Ja 28,20:1
Harlow 1965,My 15,18:1
Last of the Secret Agents, The? 1966,Je 23,29:1
Double Trouble 1967,My 25,54:2
Secret War of Harry Frigg, The 1968,Mr 5,34:5
Flea in her Ear, A 1968,N 28,66:1
Williams, John (Original Author)
Sweet Love, Bitter 1967,Ja 31,50:1
Williams, Kate
Poor Cow 1968,F 1,28:2
Williams, Katherine
Where Sinners Meet 1934,My 25,25:2
Kiss and Make-Up 1934,Je 29,17:1
Williams, Kathlyn
We Can't Have Everything 1918,Jl 15,9:3
Conrad in Quest of his Youth 1920,N 8,20:2
Forbidden Fruit 1921,Ja 24,16:2
Private Scandal, A 1921,Je 13,16:1
Man's Home, A 1921,D 19,13:1
Clarence 1922,O 16,20:2
World's Applause 1923,F 4,VII,3:2 (In Addenda)
Broadway Gold 1923,Jl 31,12:4
Spanish Dancer, The 1923,O 8,20:1
Wanderer of the Wasteland, The 1924,Jl 8,14:2
Single Wives 1924,Jl 29,9:2
Locked Doors 1925,Ja 12,11:2
Wanderer, The 1925,Ag 20,22:1
Best People 1925,O 21,21:3
We Americans 1928,Mr 29,25:3
Our Dancing Daughters 1928,O 8,14:2
Single Standard, The 1929,Jl 29,23:3
Wedding Rings 1930,My 10,25:3
Road to Paradise 1930,S 30,23:1
Road to Paradise, The 1931,Ja 20,21:3
Daddy Long Legs 1931,Je 6,15:5
Other Love, The 1947,My 15,32:4
Williams, Kay
No Minor Vices 1949,F 26,11:2
Actress, The 1953,O 13,34:1
Williams, Kenneth
Beggar's Opera, The 1953,Ag 25,18:2
Land of Fury 1955,My 3,37:4
Carry on Sergeant 1959,O 28,40:5
Make Mine Mink 1960,D 20,43:4
Carry on Cleo 1965,O 23,17:2
Williams, Kenny
Irish Eyes Are Smiling 1944,N 8,27:1
Mother Wore Tights 1947,Ag 21,33:2
Slattery's Hurricane 1949,Ag 13,6:6
When Willie Comes Marching Home
  1950,F 18,9:2
Pride of St Louis, The 1952,My 3,17:5
Williams, L P (Composer)
Escape me Never 1935,My 24,24:2
Williams, Larry
Torchy Blane in Panama 1938,Ap 18,11:1
Garden of the Moon 1938,S 24,13:1
Girls on Probation 1938,O 21,27:3
Brother Rat 1938,N 5,15:2
Going Places 1939,Ja 7,6:1
Wings of the Navy 1939,F 4,11:1
Secret Service of the Air 1939,Mr 2,19:2
On Trial 1939,Ap 5,31:2
Waterfront 1939,Jl 17,10:2
Brother Rat and a Baby 1940,Ja 27,9:4
Williams, Lorraine (Original Author)
Cowboy, The 1954,Ag 3,14:2
Williams, Lottie
Twin Beds 1920,N 1,13:2
6-Day Bike Rider 1934,N 3,20:3
Murder by an Aristocrat 1936,Je 13,13:2
Dark Victory 1939,Ap 21,27:2
Fugitive From Justice, A 1940,Jl 8,13:3
Ladies Must Live 1940,S 6,25:3
Williams, Louis Sheldon
Our Mother's House 1967,O 10,56:1
Williams, Lucille
Half Way to Heaven 1929,D 7,19:3
Traveling Husbands 1931,Ag 8,16:3
Wicked 1931,S 19,10:2

Williams, Lyman
Glamour 1934,My 12,12:3
Damaged Lives 1937,Je 14,26:2
Williams, Mack
Command Decision 1949,Ja 20,34:2
Williams, Malcolm
First Kiss, The 1928,Ag 20,21:3
Williams, Margaret (Original Author)
Grass is Greener, The 1960,D 24,8:2
Williams, Margaret (Screenwriter)
Grass is Greener, The 1960,D 24,8:2
Williams, Marie
Eternal Struggle, The 1923,O 16,21:3
Williams, Maston
Subway Express 1931,My 2,23:4
Tillie and Gus 1933,N 13,21:1
Lost Jungle, The 1934,Je 8,18:1
Williams, Mervin
Salt of the Earth 1954,Mr 15,20:2
Williams, Michael
Persecution and Assassination of Jean-Paul Marat
as Performed by the Inmates of the Asylum of
Charenton Under the Direction of the Marquis
De Sade, The 1967,F 23,41:1
Williams, Milton
Miracle in Harlem 1949,O 24,19:4
Williams, Mona (Original Author)
Woman's World 1954,S 29,23:4
Williams, Norman (Producer)
Shakedown, The 1961,Mr 16,44:2
Dream Maker, The 1964,Ap 23,34:1
Williams, Percy
Black Oxen 1924,Ja 7,23:1
Goldfish, The 1924,My 20,15:2
Learning to Love 1925,F 23,24:1
Unholy Three, The 1925,Ag 4,14:3
London After Midnight 1927,D 31,31:1
Oh, Kay! 1928,Ag 27,23:1
Williams, Peter
Bridge on the River Kwai 1957,D 19,39:1
Williams, Quinn
Big Game, The 1936,O 24,23:1
Williams, Rebecca Yancey (Original Author)
Vanishing Virginian, The 1942,My 28,13:3
Williams, Rex
Escape From Crime 1942,O 12,12:3
Secret Enemies 1943,Ja 1,27:3
Gorilla Man, The 1943,Ja 15,21:4
Truck Busters 1943,Ja 29,23:5
Tarzan Triumphs 1943,F 5,16:3
Within These Walls 1945,Jl 16,8:4
Marrying Kind, The 1952,Mr 14,27:1
Williams, Rhys
How Green Was my Valley 1941,O 29,27:2
This Above All 1942,My 13,14:3
Remember Pearl Harbor 1942,Je 4,22:4
Mrs Miniver 1942,Je 5,23:1
Cairo 1942,N 6,27:2
Gentleman Jim 1942,N 26,40:3
Random Harvest 1942,D 18,36:6
No Time for Love 1943,D 2,30:1
Corn is Green, The 1945,Mr 30,18:2
Blood on the Sun 1945,Je 29,12:2
You Came Along 1945,Jl 5,7:2
Bells of St Mary's, The 1945,D 7,26:2
Spiral Staircase, The 1946,F 7,29:3
So Goes my Love 1946,My 2,3:7
Cross my Heart 1946,D 19,42:3
Easy Come, Easy Go 1947,F 6,29:2
Strange Woman, The 1947,F 24,16:4
Farmer's Daughter, The 1947,Mr 26,31:2
Imperfect Lady, The 1947,My 22,34:5
Moss Rose 1947,Jl 3,14:2
Trouble With Women, The 1947,Jl 14,14:4
If Winter Comes 1948,Ja 23,28:4
Black Arrow, The 1948,O 4,14:2
Hills of Home 1948,N 26,32:2
Bad Boy 1949,Mr 23,35:2
Crooked Way, The 1949,S 5,13:2
Tokyo Joe 1949,O 27,35:2
Fighting Man of the Plains 1949,N 17,35:6
Inspector General, The 1949,D 31,9:2
Kiss Tomorrow Goodbye 1950,Ag 5,9:2
Devil's Doorway 1950,N 10,35:1
California Passage 1950,D 16,10:5
Lightning Strikes Twice 1951,Ap 13,18:7
Sword of Monte Cristo, The 1951,Ap 23,21:2
Never Trust a Gambler 1951,Jl 20,14:2
Law and the Lady, The 1951,Ag 16,23:2
Light Touch, The 1952,Ja 17,23:1
Mutiny 1952,Mr 20,37:5
Okinawa 1952,Ap 24,38:3
Carbine Williams 1952,My 8,37:2
Miserables, Les 1952,Ag 15,11:2
World in His Arms, The 1952,O 10,21:2
Scandal at Scourie 1953,Je 16,24:2
Bad for Each Other 1953,D 24,9:3
Man in the Attic 1954,F 6,17:2
Johnny Guitar 1954,My 28,19:2
Black Shield of Falworth, The 1954,O 7,16:2
There's no Business Like Show Business
1954,D 17,37:3

How to be Very, Very Popular 1955,Jl 23,10:1
Scarlet Coat, The 1955,Jl 30,14:2
King's Thief, The 1955,Ag 13,7:2
Kentuckian, The 1955,S 2,13:2
Nightmare 1956,My 12,12:7
Fastest Gun Alive, The 1956,Jl 13,23:3
Raintree County 1957,D 21,22:1
Merry Andrews 1958,Mr 21,17:1
Midnight Lace 1960,O 14,27:1
Williams, Rhys (Cinematographer)
Knowing Men 1930,Mr 9,IX,6:1
Williams, Richard
Loss of Innocence 1961,N 22,27:1
Williams, Robert
Common Law, The 1931,Jl 20,20:4
Rebound 1931,Ag 29,16:3
Devotion 1931,O 3,20:2
Platinum Blonde 1931,O 31,22:2
Williams, Robert B
Cry of the Werewolf, The 1944,Ag 12,16:5
One Mysterious Night 1944,O 21,15:3
Dark Past, The 1948,D 23,25:2
Mary Ryan, Detective 1949,N 4,33:3
Lawless, The 1950,Je 23,29:2
Great Jewel Robber, The 1950,Ag 4,13:2
Groom Wore Spurs, The 1951,Mr 14,41:2
Lady Says No, The 1952,Ja 7,14:3
Revenge of the Creature 1955,My 14,10:7
Pork Chop Hill 1959,My 30,9:2
Williams, Robert Creighton (Screenwriter)
He Rides Tall 1964,F 27,28:1
Taggart 1964,D 25,24:4
Williams, Roger
Heroes of the Alamo 1938,Ap 2,18:2
Williams, Roy (Original Author)
Saludos Amigos 1943,F 13,8:2
Three Caballeros, The 1945,F 5,20:1
Williams, Rush
Rocky Mountain 1950,N 4,13:2
Frogmen, The 1951,Je 30,8:6
Williams, Shirley Hunter
Delightfully Dangerous 1945,Je 9,17:3
Williams, Sumner
On Dangerous Ground 1952,F 13,35:2
Running Wild 1955,N 12,23:2
Williams, Ted
Untitled-Baseball Technique 1941,Ja 17,11:3
Ninth Inning, The 1942,Ja 8,30:3
Williams, Tennessee (Original Author)
Glass Menagerie, The 1950,S 29,31:5
Streetcar Named Desire, A 1951,S 30,27:1
Rose Tattoo, The 1955,D 13,55:1
Cat on a Hot Tin Roof 1958,S 19,24:1
Suddenly, Last Summer 1959,D 23,22:1
Fugitive Kind, The 1960,Ap 15,13:1
Summer and Smoke 1961,N 17,41:1
Roman Spring of Mrs Stone, The 1961,D 29,11:1
Sweet Bird of Youth 1962,Mr 29,28:2
Period of Adjustment 1962,N 1,34:1
Night of the Iguana, The 1964,Jl 1,42:1
This Property is Condemned 1966,Ag 4,24:1
Boom! 1968,My 27,56:1
Williams, Tennessee (Screenwriter)
Glass Menagerie, The 1950,S 29,31:5
Streetcar Named Desire, A 1951,S 30,27:1
Rose Tattoo, The 1955,D 13,55:1
Baby Doll 1956,D 19,40:2
Suddenly, Last Summer 1959,D 23,22:1
Fugitive Kind, The 1960,Ap 15,13:1
Boom! 1968,My 27,56:1
Williams, Tunji
Kisenga, Man of Africa 1952,Mr 7,18:2
Williams, Valentine (Original Author)
Crouching Beast, The 1936,Ag 22,6:1
Dispatch From Reuters, A 1940,D 12,37:2
Williams, Van
Caretakers, The 1963,Ag 22,19:2
Williams, Walter
10th Victim, The 1965,D 21,46:1
Williams, Wayland
Gathering of Eagles, A 1963,Jl 11,21:2
Williams, Wirt (Original Author)
Ada 1961,Ag 26,15:1
Williams, Zack
Merry Widow, The 1925,Ag 27,14:1
Easy Pickings 1927,Mr 25,25:3
Yankee Clipper, The 1927,My 3,25:1
Hearts in Dixie 1929,F 28,30:3
Four Feathers, The 1929,Je 13,35:4
Gone With the Wind 1939,D 20,31:2
Williams Brothers, The
Something in the Wind 1947,Ag 29,14:3
Williamson, Alice M (Original Author)
Honeymoon Hate 1927,D 31,31:1
Williamson, E Stanley (Producer)
Track of Thunder 1968,F 1,28:4
Williamson, Howard
Mikado, The 1967,Mr 15,53:1
Williamson, J E (Director)
With Williamson Beneath the Sea 1932,N 24,35:2
Williamson, J E (Producer)
Wonders of the Sea 1922,O 16,20:2
With Williamson Beneath the Sea 1932,N 24,35:2

Williamson, Nicol
Inadmissible Evidence 1968,Je 24,44:1
Bofors Gun, The 1968,S 23,42:3
Williamson, Noah
Baby Doll 1956,D 19,40:2
Williamson, Robert
Bond Boy, The 1922,O 9,10:2
Williamson, Susan
Persecution and Assassination of Jean-Paul Marat
as Performed by the Inmates of the Asylum of
Charenton Under the Direction of the Marquis
De Sade, The 1967,F 23,41:1
Williamson, Thames (Original Author)
Bullet is Waiting, A 1954,N 12,17:2
Williamson, Thames (Screenwriter)
Cheyenne 1947,Je 7,9:2
Escape me Never 1947,N 8,11:2
Last Bandit, The 1949,Mr 21,19:2
Brimstone 1949,O 7,35:3
Bullet is Waiting, A 1954,N 12,17:2
Williamson, Thomas (Original Author)
Next Time I Marry 1938,D 2,27:2
Williamson Brothers (Producer)
Twenty Thousand Leagues Under the Sea
1916,D 25,7:1
Willinger, L (Original Author)
Tonight We Raid Calais 1943,Ap 15,20:2
Willingham, Calder (Original Author)
Strange One, The 1957,Ap 13,12:3
Willingham, Calder (Screenwriter)
Vikings, The 1952,Je 12,35:2
Strange One, The 1957,Ap 13,12:3
Paths of Glory 1957,D 26,23:2
One Eyed Jacks 1961,Mr 31,21:1
Graduate, The 1967,D 22,44:4
Willingham, Willard
Red Canyon 1949,Ap 28,28:2
Willingham, Willard (Screenwriter)
Battle at Bloody Beach, The 1961,Ag 17,18:2
Willis, Austin
Mouse That Roared, The 1959,O 27,40:1
Crack in the Mirror 1960,My 20,26:1
1 1 1 1961,N 8,41:1
Goldfinger 1964,D 22,36:1
Eight on the Lam 1967,Ap 27,52:1
Hour of the Gun 1967,N 2,58:4
Willis, Bill
Seed 1931,My 15,20:6
Willis, Constance
Mikado, The 1939,Je 2,27:2
Willis, F McGrew (Original Author)
Up in Mabel's Room 1926,Je 29,21:2
Costello Case, The 1930,N 4,36:1
Midshipman Jack 1933,N 20,18:2
Sis Hopkins 1941,My 1,27:5
Willis, Hubert
Hound of the Baskervilles, The 1922,S 11,20:2
Willis, Jack
Seed 1931,My 15,20:6
Willis, Jerome
Khartoum 1966,Jl 14,28:1
Willis, Leo
O'Malley of the Mounted 1921,F 7,8:2
Wild Bill Hickok 1923,N 21,22:1
Way of a Girl, The 1925,Mr 30,21:3
Kid Brother, The 1927,Ja 24,14:1
Six of a Kind 1934,Mr 10,18:3
Willis, Matt
Swamp Water 1941,N 17,15:2
Mysterious Doctor, The 1943,My 20,26:4
Swingtime Johnny 1943,D 17,23:3
Return of the Vampire, The 1944,Ja 29,10:1
Mark of the Whistler, The 1944,N 11,19:2
Walk in the Sun, A 1946,Ja 12,10:6
Yearling, The 1947,Ja 24,18:2
Blonde Savage 1947,O 4,9:2
Burning Cross, The 1948,F 20,19:1
So Dear to my Heart 1949,Ja 31,14:2
Breakthrough 1950,N 18,10:2
Inside the Walls of Folsom Prison
1951,My 28,17:4
Willis, Nat
Webb Singing Pictures 1917,Ja 15,7:1
Willis, Norman
Mary Burns, Fugitive 1935,N 16,19:4
Bullets or Ballots 1936,My 27,27:1
Lady From Nowhere 1936,D 21,19:2
Secret Valley 1937,Ja 25,22:2
That Certain Woman 1937,S 16,29:1
Girl With Ideas, A 1938,Ja 1,11:2
Prison Nurse 1938,Mr 4,17:5
Homicide Bureau 1939,F 2,17:2
Boy Slaves 1939,F 9,17:3
Blackwell's Island 1939,Mr 2,19:1
Forgotten Woman, The 1939,Ag 4,11:2
Johnny Come Lately 1943,S 24,26:1
Willis, Paul
Thunderclap 1921,Jl 31,22:4
Willis, Ted (Original Author)
It's Great to be Young 1957,D 26,23:3
Willis, Ted (Screenwriter)
Good Time Girl 1950,S 25,18:5
Trouble in Store 1956,Ja 14,13:2

Willis, Ted (Screenwriter) — Cont
Woman in a Dressing Gown 1957,S 13,15:2
It's Great to be Young 1957,D 26,23:3
Flame in the Streets 1962,S 13,32:1
Willm, Pierre-Richard
Carnet de Bal, Un 1938,Mr 26,12:1
Moscow Nights 1938,My 3,19:3
Betrayal 1939,S 16,20:2
Rasputin 1939,O 17,31:4
Wicked Duchess, The 1949,N 5,10:5
Dreams of Love 1954,Je 5,11:2
Willman, Noel
Androcles and the Lion 1953,Ja 15,23:2
Project M 7 1953,N 27,22:5
Beau Brummell 1954,O 21,31:5
Warriors, The 1955,S 10,11:2
Man Who Knew too Much, The 1956,My 17,37:1
Abandon Ship 1957,Ap 18,35:1
Across the Bridge 1957,O 30,24:1
Trouble in the Sky 1961,Jl 13,26:3
Never Let Go 1963,Je 15,10:2
Kiss of the Vampire 1963,O 10,49:2
Doctor Zhivago 1965,D 23,21:1
Vengance of She, The 1968,My 30,21:4
Willmas, James
Beware my Lovely 1952,S 13,10:5
Willmer, Catherine
Inspector Calls, An 1954,N 26,24:4
Willner, A M (Original Author)
Rogue Song, The 1930,Ja 29,26:4
Willner, A M (Screenwriter)
Strauss's Great Waltz 1935,Ap 8,23:3
Willock, Dave
Legion of Lost Flyers 1939,O 30,13:3
Priorities on Parade 1942,Jl 23,19:2
Let's Face It 1943,Ag 5,18:1
Gang's All Here, The 1943,D 23,26:4
Pin Up Girl 1944,My 11,25:6
Wing and a Prayer 1944,Ag 31,14:1
Spellbound 1945,N 2,22:2
Runaround, The 1946,Je 7,16:3
Fabulous Dorseys, The 1947,My 30,25:3
Chicago Deadline 1949,N 3,37:2
Call Me Mister 1951,F 1,21:2
Battle Zone 1952,N 1,17:2
It Came From Outer Space 1953,Je 18,38:2
Buster Keaton Story, The 1957,Ap 22,31:6
Second to Hell 1959,Jl 18,6:3
What Ever Happened to Baby Jane?
1962,N 7,48:1
Wives and Lovers 1963,Ag 29,36:1
Send Me no Flowers 1964,N 13,30:1
Willoughby, Barrett (Original Author)
Spawn of the North 1938,S 8,27:1
Alaska Seas 1954,Mr 6,13:5
Wills, Anneke
Pleasure Girls, The 1966,Ap 21,43:1
Wills, Beverly
George White's Scandals 1945,O 11,26:2
Mickey 1948,Jl 19,11:2
Some Like It Hot 1959,Mr 30,23:1
Wills, Bob
Go West, Young Lady 1941,N 24,11:6
Wills, Brember
Old Dark House, The 1932,O 28,22:4
Unfinished Symphony 1935,Ja 14,11:2
Wills, Chill
Racketeers of the Range 1939,Je 8,31:4
Allegheny Uprising 1939,N 10,27:3
Boom Town 1940,S 6,25:2
Westerner, The 1940,O 25,25:2
Tugboat Annie Sails Again 1940,N 9,20:2
Sky Murder 1940,N 14,28:3
Western Union 1941,F 7,23:2
Bad Man, The 1941,Ap 4,25:1
Honky Tonk 1941,O 3,27:3
Belle Starr 1941,N 1,20:2
Bugle Sounds, The 1942,Ap 3,25:2
Her Cardboard Lover 1942,Jl 17,19:2
Tarzan's New York Adventure 1942,Ag 7,13:2
Stand by for Action 1943,Mr 12,12:2
Best Foot Forward 1943,Je 30,25:2
See Here Private Hargrove 1944,Mr 22,17:2
Barbary Coast Gent 1944,S 29,18:2
Meet Me in St Louis 1944,N 29,20:2
Sunday Dinner for a Soldier 1945,Ja 25,16:2
I'll Be Seeing You 1945,Ap 6,20:6
What Next Corporal Hargrove? 1945,D 26,15:2
Leave Her to Heaven 1945,D 26,15:1
Harvey Girls, The 1946,Ja 25,26:2
Gallant Bess 1946,D 6,27:6
Yearling, The 1947,Ja 24,18:2
Sainted Sisters, The 1948,My 20,35:2
Raw Deal 1948,Jl 9,11:4
Saxon Charm, The 1948,S 30,32:3
Northwest Stampede 1948,D 10,34:3
That Wonderful Urge 1948,D 22,29:6
Family Honeymoon 1949,F 25,28:2
Red Canyon 1949,Ap 28,28:2
Tulsa 1949,My 27,25:2
Sundowners, The 1950,My 5,17:2
Rock Island Trail 1950,Je 5,19:3
Rio Grande 1950,N 20,21:2
High Lonesome 1950,D 8,40:4

Oh! Susanna 1951,Mr 30,28:5
Cattle Drive 1951,Ag 9,17:5
Small Town Girl 1953,My 7,37:2
City That Never Sleeps 1953,Ag 8,14:2
Man From the Alamo, The 1953,S 12,13:2
Francis Joins the Wacs 1954,Jl 31,6:3
Hell's Outpost 1955,F 26,13:3
Timberjack 1955,Mr 10,33:3
Santiago 1956,Jl 14,13:2
Giant 1956,O 11,51:1
Gun for a Coward 1957,Ja 31,21:1
Gun Glory 1957,Jl 20,8:7
From Hell to Texas 1958,Je 5,39:2
Alamo, The 1960,O 27,45:1
Where the Boys Are 1961,Ja 20,22:1
Gold of the Seven Saints 1961,Ap 6,30:3
Deadly Companions, The 1962,Ap 12,41:7
McLintock 1963,N 14,41:3
Wheeler Dealers, The 1963,N 15,25:2
Cardinal, The 1963,D 13,41:1
Rounders, The 1965,Ap 29,40:2
Fireball 500 1966,N 24,65:4
Wills, Drusilla
Non-Stop New York 1937,N 29,19:2
Girl Must Live, A 1942,Mr 24,25:2
Man in Grey, The 1945,N 30,18:6
Champagne Charlie 1948,Ag 7,8:2
Wills, Henry
Saskatchewan 1954,Mr 11,26:2
In Like Flint 1967,Mr 16,53:2
Wills, Lou Jr
My Wild Irish Rose 1947,D 25,32:2
Wills, Norma
Deadwood Coach, The 1925,Ja 21,19:3
Golden Princess 1925,S 7,15:3
Wills, Ross B (Original Author)
East of the River 1940,O 28,21:2
Wills, Si
Penrod and Sam 1937,Mr 29,14:3
Nobody's Baby 1937,My 20,17:3
Cipher Bureau 1938,D 14,32:6
Gay Intruders, The 1949,Je 28,33:4
Wills, Walter
Santa Fe Stampede 1939,Ap 26,27:3
WILLSON
See Also WILSON
Willson, Clyde
Andy Hardy Meets Debutante 1940,Ag 2,12:2
Willson, Dixie (Original Author)
Affair of the Follies, An 1927,F 28,22:3
Willson, Meredith (Composer)
Great Dictator, The 1940,O 16,29:1
Music Man, The 1962,Ag 24,14:1
Willson, MEredith (Composer)
Unsinkable Molly Brown, The 1964,Jl 17,15:1
Willson, Meredith (Original Author)
Music Man, The 1962,Ag 24,14:1
Willy, Suzy
Truth, The 1961,Je 27,23:2
Wilmar, Hugh (Cinematographer)
Jungle Cat 1960,Ag 18,19:2
Wilmar, Hugh A (Cinematographer)
White Wilderness 1958,Ag 13,22:1
Wilmer, Douglas
Richard III 1956,Mr 12,1:4
Pursuit of the Graf Spee 1957,D 27,33:2
Cleopatra 1963,Je 13,29:1
Fall of the Roman Empire, The 1964,Mr 27,14:2
Shot in the Dark, A 1964,Je 24,28:1
One Way Pendulum 1965,Mr 3,34:3
Khartoum 1966,Jl 14,28:1
Vengeance of Fu Manchu, The 1968,F 15,47:1
Wilmot, Gerry
Flying Fortress 1942,D 19,22:2
Wilmot, Ivan
Robber Symphony 1937,Ja 27,17:2
Clown Must Laugh, A 1938,O 12,35:2
Forbidden Music 1938,D 27,13:2
Wilms, Dominique
Every Second Counts 1957,O 15,39:4
Wilmsen, Max
Tiger von Berlin, Der 1930,S 15,29:3
Wilsen, Irma
Young as You Feel 1940,Mr 8,25:3
Wilsey, Jay
Way out West 1930,Ag 18,24:1
Terror Trail 1933,F 11,11:3
Wilshin, Sunday
Michael and Mary 1932,Mr 5,11:2
WILSON
See Also WILLSON
Wilson, Anne M
Winds of Chance 1925,Ag 17,10:3
Wilson, C H
Little Robinson Crusoe 1924,S 3,17:1
Wilson, Carey (Miscellaneous)
Sequoia 1935,F 23,14:6
Wilson, Carey (Narrator)
ThIs is Russia 1957,D 10,45:1
Wilson, Carey (Original Author)
Lost and Found 1923,Mr 19,22:2
Orchids and Ermine 1927,Ap 19,24:4
Bolero 1934,F 17,20:3

Wilson, Carey (Original Author) — Cont
Judge Hardy and Son 1940,Ja 18,27:3 (In Addenda)
Wilson, Carey (Producer)
Postman Always Rings Twice, The
1946,My 3,15:3
Dark Delusion 1947,Je 26,19:2
Green Dolphin Street 1947,O 16,34:2
Red Danube, The 1949,D 9,37:3
Scaramouche 1952,My 9,20:2
Wilson, Carey (Screenwriter)
So This Is Marriage 1924,D 23,16:2
Midshipman, The 1925,O 13,20:1
His Secretary 1925,D 21,27:2
Tender Hour, The 1927,Je 7,27:4
Stolen Bride, The 1927,Ag 12,21:2
American Beauty 1927,O 11,27:1
Why Be Good? 1929,My 6,30:4
Sequoia 1935,F 23,14:6
Mutiny on the Bounty 1935,N 9,19:2
Dangerous Number 1937,Mr 12,19:2
Judge Hardy and Son 1940,Ja 18,27:3 (In Addenda)
Wilson, Charles
Broadway Scandals 1929,O 29,35:1
Elmer the Great 1933,My 26,24:2
Mary Stevens, M D 1933,Ag 5,9:6
Kennell Murder Case, The 1933,O 30,14:2
Female 1933,N 4,18:3
Miss Fane's Baby is Stolen 1934,Ja 20,12:2
Fog over Frisco 1934,Je 7,26:2
Affairs of a Gentleman 1934,Je 23,16:7
Circus Clown, The 1934,Je 30,18:6
Hell Cat, The 1934,Jl 7,16:5
Dragon Murder Case, The 1934,Ag 23,13:3
Lemon Drop Kid, The 1934,O 27,20:2
St Louis Kid, The 1934,N 1,25:2
Broadway Bill 1934,N 30,22:2
Here is my Heart 1934,D 22,21:1
Murder in the Clouds 1934,D 26,18:1
Behold My Wife 1935,F 18,19:3
Car 99 1935,F 23,14:7
Great Hotel Murder, The 1935,F 28,17:4
Perfect Clue, The 1935,Mr 14,18:1
Four Hours to Kill 1935,Ap 11,27:3
Glass Key, The 1935,Je 15,20:2
Case of the Lucky Legs, The 1935,N 1,25:1
Fighting Youth 1935,N 2,13:3
Show Them no Mercy 1935,D 9,25:2
Strike Me Pink 1936,Ja 17,15:2
Panic on the Air 1936,Ap 20,17:1
Show Boat 1936,My 15,29:4
Mine With the Iron Door, The 1936,Jl 11,11:3
Satan Met a Lady 1936,Jl 23,24:2
Grand Jury 1936,Ag 1,16:3
I'd Give my Life 1936,Ag 17,9:1
Magnificent Brute, The 1936,O 24,23:1
Legion of Terror 1936,N 2,24:2
Pennies From Heaven 1936,D 10,35:2
Devil is Driving, The 1937,Jl 16,22:1
Roaring Timber 1937,Ag 19,23:1
Torchy Blane, The Adventurous Blonde
1937,D 18,18:1
Sally, Irene and Mary 1938,F 26,9:2
When Were You Born? 1938,Je 9,27:2
Tenth Avenue Kid 1938,S 2,21:3
Hold That Co-ed 1938,S 24,13:1
Rose of Washington Square 1939,My 6,21:2
Hotel for Women 1939,Ag 26,20:2
Here I Am a Stranger 1939,S 30,11:2
Smashing the Money Ring 1939,N 17,17:2
Return Of Doctor X, The 1939,N 23,38:5
He Married his Wife 1940,Ja 20,11:2
Girl in 313 1940,Je 14,25:3
Sandy Is a Lady 1940,Je 28,22:2
Face Behind the Mask, The 1941,F 7,23:2
Broadway Limited 1941,Je 16,11:6
Officer and the Lady, The 1941,Ag 11,17:4
Blues in the Night 1941,D 12,35:2
Lady Gangster 1942,Jl 10,13:2
Escape From Crime 1942,O 12,12:3
Two Senoritas From Chicago 1943,Ag 6,10:4
Shadows in the Night 1944,Jl 29,16:2
Wilson, Charles (Director)
Lucky Boy 1929,F 25,16:1
Wilson, Clarence
Dangerous Paradise 1930,F 16,III,8:1
Love in the Rough 1930,S 27,21:3
Front Page, The 1931,Mr 20,29:1
Amateur Daddy 1932,Ap 23,11:5
Winner Take All 1932,Je 18,9:2
Purchase Price, The 1932,Jl 16,5:5
Jewel Robbery 1932,Jl 23,6:6
Love Me Tonight 1932,Ag 19,20:6
Down to Earth 1932,S 2,19:2
Pick Up 1933,Mr 25,13:4
Girl in 419 1933,My 20,11:5
Tillie and Gus 1933,N 13,21:1
Son of Kong 1933,D 30,9:2
Unknown Blonde 1934,Ap 24,27:2
Now I'll Tell 1934,My 26,12:2
Old-Fashioned Way, The 1934,Jl 14,16:5
Count of Monte Cristo, The 1934,S 27,25:2
Wake up and Dream 1934,O 11,28:3

Wilson, Clarence— Cont
Lemon Drop Kid, The 1934,O 27,20:2
I'll Fix It 1934,N 12,17:3
Imitation of Life 1934,N 24,19:1
When a Man's a Man 1935,F 22,27:2
Great Hotel Murder, The 1935,F 28,17:4
Ruggles of Red Gap 1935,Mr 7,26:1
Little Miss Nobody 1936,Je 6,21:1
Educating Father 1936,Je 20,22:2
Love Begins at 20 1936,S 19,20:1
Case of the Black Cat, The 1936,D 26,15:4
Westland Case, The 1937,O 23,14:2
In Old Chicago 1938,Ja 7,15:2
Rebecca of Sunnybrook Farm 1938,Mr 26,12:1
Kentucky Moonshine 1938,My 21,9:2
Marriage Forbidden 1938,Jl 16,7:2
Texans, The 1938,Jl 28,23:2
You Can't Take It With You 1938,S 2,21:2
Some Like It Hot 1939,My 25,31:2
Drums Along the Mohawk 1939,N 4,11:2
Little Old New York 1940,F 3,9:2
We Who Are Young 1940,S 13,27:2
Melody Ranch 1940,D 26,23:3
Wilson, Claude
Cry of Battle 1963,O 12,27:2
Walls of Hell, The 1965,N 18,55:3
Wilson, Dana
Once a Thief 1951,Ja 19,21:3
Cry From the Streets, A 1959,F 24,32:2
Wilson, Dixie (Original Author)
God Gave Me Twenty Cents 1926,N 20,3:2
Wilson, Don
Wharf Angel 1934,Ap 21,12:1
Two Girls on Broadway 1940,Ap 25,28:4
Comin' Round the Mountain 1940,S 26,27:3
Roundup, The 1941,Mr 13,25:4
Thank Your Lucky Stars 1943,O 2,19:2
Out of This World 1945,Je 7,25:2
Radio Stars on Parade 1945,S 22,14:2
Kid From Brooklyn, The 1946,Ap 19,25:2
Chase, The 1946,N 18,31:2
Sailor Beware 1952,F 1,17:1
Niagara 1953,Ja 22,20:3
Stars Are Singing, The 1953,Mr 12,24:2
Wilson, Donald (Producer)
Miss Robin Hood 1953,Je 27,7:2
Wilson, Donald (Screenwriter)
Three Cases of Murder (Lord Mountdrago); Lord
  Mountdrago (Three Cases of Murder)
  1955,Mr 16,39:4
Three Cases of Murder (You Killed Elizabeth);
  You Killed Elizabeth (Three Cases of Murder)
  /1955,Mr 16,39:4
Three Cases of Murder (In the Picture); In the
  Picture (Three Cases of Murder)
  1955,Mr 16,39:4
Wilson, Donald B (Producer)
Prelude to Fame 1950,N 10,35:3
Wilson, Donald Powell (Original Author)
My Six Convicts 1952,Mr 28,27:3
Wilson, Dooley
My Favorite Blonde 1942,Ap 2,27:2
Night in New Orleans 1942,Jl 2,25:2
Cairo 1942,N 6,27:2
Casablanca 1942,N 27,27:1
Two Tickets to London 1943,Jl 3,11:2
Stormy Weather 1943,Jl 22,15:1
Higher and Higher 1944,Ja 22,8:4
Seven Days Ashore 1944,Ap 26,24:7
Come to the Stable 1949,Jl 28,19:1
Passage West 1951,Ag 31,12:2
Wilson, Dorothy
Age of Consent, The 1932,S 3,16:2
Lucky Devils 1933,F 20,11:5
Before Dawn 1933,O 17,26:2
Eight Girls in a Boat 1934,Ja 13,16:3
His Greatest Gamble 1934,Jl 18,20:2
White Parade, The 1934,N 10,19:1
When a Man's a Man 1935,F 22,27:2
Last Days of Pompeii, The 1935,O 17,29:2
Bad Boy 1935,O 28,16:3
Old Kentucky, In 1935,N 29,24:1
Milky Way, The 1936,Mr 26,27:2
Craig's Wife 1936,O 2,29:3
Wilson, Earl
Copacabana 1947,Jl 12,7:2
Wilson, Ed
Flaming Frontier, The 1926,Ap 5,24:1
Wilson, Elizabeth
Picnic 1956,F 17,13:3
Patterns 1956,Mr 28,26:1
Goddess, The 1958,Je 25,24:1
Tunnel of Love 1958,N 22,27:4
Happy Anniversary 1959,N 11,41:1
Child Is Waiting, A 1963,F 14,5:6
Tiger Makes Out, The 1967,S 19,53:1
Graduate, The 1967,D 22,44:4
Wilson, Elizabeth (Original Author)
Raw Wind in Eden 1958,S 20,10:6
Wilson, Elizabeth (Screenwriter)
Raw Wind in Eden 1958,S 20,10:6
Invitation to a Gunfighter 1964,O 28,51:3

Wilson, Elsie Jane
Oliver Twist 1916,D 11,7:3
Wilson, Everdinne
Porgy and Bess 1959,Je 25,20:3
Wilson, Forrest (Original Author)
Blessed Event 1932,S 3,16:2
Wilson, Frank
Emperor Jones, The 1933,S 20,26:2
Green Pastures, The 1936,Jl 17,20:1
Watch on the Rhine 1943,Ag 28,15:1
Wilson, Frank C
Devil is Driving, The 1937,Jl 16,22:1
Wilson, Frank J (Original Author)
Undercover Man, The 1949,Ap 21,30:2
Wilson, Frank R (Producer)
Blame the Woman 1932,O 25,24:5
Wilson, Garney
Guilty Bystander 1950,Ap 21,18:2
Wilson, George
One Minute to Play 1926,S 6,16:2
Wilson, Georges
Joker, The; (Farceur, Le) 1961,Ag 8,32:2
Long Absence, The 1962,N 16,23:2
7 Capital Sins (Gluttony); Gluttony (7 Capital
  Sins) 1963,Ja 17,5:2
Devil and the 10 Commandments, The (Episode
  6) 1963,O 15,44:1
Empty Canvas, The 1964,My 16,21:1 (Incorrect
  in this edition; use 1964,My 16,12:1 elsewhere)
Disorder 1964,My 26,44:2
Sweet and Sour 1964,D 28,34:2
Fascist, The 1965,Je 18,28:3
More Than a Miracle 1967,N 2,58:2
Stranger, The 1967,D 19,59:1
Wilson, Hal
Love Master, The 1924,My 19,14:2
Wilson, Harold (Producer)
Life Begins In College 1937,O 9,16:1
Danger-Love at Work 1937,D 11,22:2
Wilson, Harry
Native Land 1942,My 12,16:3
Some Like It Hot 1959,Mr 30,23:1
Wilson, Harry Leon (Original Author)
Man From Home, The 1922,My 1,20:3
Ruggles of Red Gap 1923,S 10,15:4
Merton of the Movies 1924,S 8,15:3
Oh, Doctor! 1925,F 23,24:1
Cameo Kirby 1930,F 8,12:5
Make Me a Star 1932,Jl 1,19:3
Ruggles of Red Gap 1935,Mr 7,26:1
Bunker Bean 1936,Je 27,21:2
Oh, Doctor 1937,Je 19,20:3
Merton of the Movies 1947,N 7,20:3
Fancy Pants 1950,Ag 31,21:2
Wilson, Howard
Ace of Aces 1933,N 11,10:4
Lost Patrol, The 1934,Ap 2,13:2
Car 99 1935,F 23,14:7
McFadden's Flats 1935,Mr 13,16:2
Wilson, Ian
How to Murder a Rich Uncle 1957,O 26,19:2
Happy is the Bride 1959,Je 30,27:2
Wilson, J Donald (Original Author)
Whistler, The 1944,Ap 29,12:2
Key Witness 1947,Jl 30,27:6
Wilson, James
Manhunt in the Jungle 1958,Ap 12,13:1
Wilson, Janis
Now, Voyager 1942,O 23,25:3
Watch on the Rhine 1943,Ag 28,15:1
Snafu 1945,D 26,15:2
Strange Love of Martha Ivers, The
  1946,Jl 25,18:4
Wilson, John (Original Author)
King and Country 1964,S 24,46:2
King and Country 1966,Ja 28,20:4
Wilson, Josephine
South Riding 1938,Ag 2,15:2
Lady Vanishes, The 1938,D 26,29:1
Quiet Week-End 1948,Ag 20,13:2
Chance of a Lifetime 1951,Mr 15,37:2
Wilson, Julie
Strange One, The 1957,Ap 13,12:3
This Could Be the Night 1957,My 15,39:1
Wilson, Katherine
New Toys 1925,F 17,18:1
Midnight 1934,Mr 10,18:3
Wilson, Lois
Why Smith Left Home 1919,O 13,16:3
City of Masks, The 1920,Jl 12,12:4
Midsummer Madness 1920,D 6,19:1
Lost Romance, The 1921,My 9,16:2
Miss Lulu Bett 1921,D 25,VI,2:1
Is Matrimony a Failure 1922,Ap 17,22:3
Manslaughter 1922,S 18,14:2
Bella Donna 1923,Ap 16,20:2
Only 38 1923,Je 11,16:2
To the Last Man 1923,Ag 28,12:1
Ruggles of Red Gap 1923,S 10,15:4
Call of the Canyon, The 1923,D 17,23:1
Pied Piper Malone 1924,Ja 28,12:1
Icebound 1924,Mr 3,22:3 (In Addenda)
Man Who Fights Alone, The 1924,Jl 28,12:2

Wilson, Lois— Cont
Monsieur Beaucaire 1924,Ag 12,12:1 (In
  Addenda)
North of 36 1924,D 8,13:3
Contraband 1925,Mr 24,20:6
Welcome Home 1925,My 18,12:1
Vanishing American, The 1925,O 16,18:2
Irish Luck 1925,N 24,28:4
Bluebeard's Seven Wives 1925,D 28,19:2
Let's Get Married 1926,Mr 2,22:1
Show-Off, The 1926,Ag 23,9:1
Great Gatsby, The 1926,N 22,28:3
New York 1927,Ja 31,13:1
Broadway Nights 1927,Je 28,29:4
Gingham Girl, The 1927,Jl 19,27:2
Alias the Lone Wolf 1927,S 20,32:2
French Dressing 1927,D 13,33:2
Coney Island 1928,F 14,27:1 (In Addenda)
Miss Information 1928,N 18,IX,7:6
Conquest 1929,F 11,26:3
Her Husband's Women 1929,Ag 13,23:2
Gamblers, The 1929,Ag 24,11:5
Show of Shows 1929,N 21,24:5
Lovin' the Ladies 1930,Mr 22,22:6
Furies, The 1930,Ap 19,15:1
Wedding Rings 1930,My 10,25:3
Once a Gentleman 1930,O 4,15:2
Age for Love, The 1931,N 13,27:2
Expert, The 1932,F 27,22:1
Crash, The 1932,S 9,17:5
Divorce in the Family 1932,O 31,18:4
Devil Is Driving, The 1932,D 16,25:5
Obey the Law 1933,Mr 13,18:3
Laughing at Life 1933,Jl 15,14:2
Deluge 1933,O 9,22:3
Female 1933,N 4,18:3
Show-Off, The 1934,Mr 17,11:3
No Greater Glory 1934,My 5,22:2
There's Always Tomorrow 1934,N 10,19:2
Bright Eyes 1934,D 21,31:1
Your Uncle Dudley 1935,D 12,33:4
Girl from Jones Beach, The 1949,Jl 30,9:2
Wilson, Lola
On Trial 1928,N 15,26:5
Wilson, Loy
Seed 1931,My 15,20:6
Wilson, Marie
Stars Over Broadway 1935,N 14,17:3
Miss Pacific Fleet 1935,D 7,22:2
Broadway Hostess 1935,D 16,23:3
Colleen 1936,Mr 9,20:2
Big Noise, The 1936,Jl 4,18:3
Satan Met a Lady 1936,Jl 23,24:2
China Clipper 1936,Ag 12,14:3
Melody for Two 1937,My 21,19:5
Great Garrick, The 1937,O 25,23:1
Invisible Menace, The 1938,F 14,20:6
Fools for Scandal 1938,Mr 25,15:3
Boy Meets Girl 1938,Ag 27,7:2
Broadway Musketeers 1938,O 14,27:1
Waterfront 1939,Jl 17,10:2
Virginia 1941,Ja 29,21:2
Rookies on Parade 1941,My 22,25:2
Broadway 1942,Je 5,23:2
Shine on Harvest Moon 1944,Mr 11,10:2
Music for Millions 1944,D 22,12:4
Young Widow 1946,Jl 29,12:8
No Leave, No Love 1946,O 18,29:2
Private Affairs of Bel Ami, The 1947,Je 16,25:4
My Friend Irma 1949,S 29,39:2
My Friend Irma Goes West 1950,Ag 3,20:2
Girl in Every Port, A 1952,F 14,23:1
Never Wave at a Wac 1953,Ap 24,30:2
Story of Mankind, The 1957,N 9,31:2
Mr Hobbs Takes a Vacation 1962,Je 16,11:2
Wilson, Maurice J (Producer)
Master Spy 1964,Ag 20,34:2
Wilson, Maurice J (Screenwriter)
Master Spy 1964,Ag 20,34:2
Wilson, May
Dulcy 1923,S 17,18:2
Wilson, Michael (Screenwriter)
Men In her Life, The 1941,D 12,35:1
Place in the Sun, A 1951,Ag 29,20:1
Five Fingers 1952,F 23,7:5
Salt of the Earth 1954,Mr 15,20:2
Sandpiper, The 1965,Jl 16,14:1
Salt of the Earth 1965,N 1,57:1
Planet of the Apes 1968,F 9,55:2
Wilson, Mitchell (Original Author)
Woman on the Beach, The 1947,Je 9,26:6
Wilson, Perry
Fear Strikes Out 1957,Mr 21,37:2
Matchmaker, The 1958,Ag 13,22:1
Wilson, Richard
I'd Climb the Highest Mountain 1951,My 10,38:1
Wilson, Richard (Director)
Man With the Gun 1955,D 23,14:2
Big Boodle, The 1957,Mr 12,38:1
Raw Wind in Eden 1958,S 20,10:6
Al Capone 1959,Mr 26,27:1
Pay or Die 1960,My 27,22:2
Wall of Noise 1963,S 5,27:1

Wilson, Richard (Producer)
Pay or Die 1960,My 27,22:2
Wilson, Richard (Screenwriter)
Man With the Gun 1955,D 23,14:2
Raw Wind in Eden 1958,S 20,10:6
Invitation to a Gunfighter 1964,O 28,51:3
Wilson, Robert
Big Game, The 1936,O 24,23:1
Wilson, Scott
In the Heat of the Night 1967,Ag 3,26:1
In Cold Blood 1967,D 15,60:1
Wilson, Sloan (Original Author)
Man in the Gray Flannel Suit, The
1956,Ap 13,21:1
Summer Place, A 1959,O 23,24:1
Wilson, Teddy and his band
Something to Shout About 1943,Ap 8,27:3
Wilson, Terry
Shakiest Gun in the West, The 1968,Jl 11,30:1
Wilson, Tom
Greatest Question, The 1919,D 29,7:2
Kid, The 1921,Ja 22,9:2
Two Minutes to Go 1921,O 24,13:1
Courtship of Myles Standish, The 1923,D 31,9:3
Fools in the Dark 1924,Ag 18,8:2
What Fools Men 1925,S 29,31:3
Best Bad Man, The 1925,D 2,23:1
California Straight Ahead 1926,Ja 12,27:5
Rainmaker, The 1926,My 18,28:2
Battling Butler 1926,Ag 23,9:1
When a Man Loves 1927,F 4,16:6
Riley, The Cop 1928,D 4,29:1
Strong Boy 1929,Ap 1,22:1
Big House, The 1930,Je 25,31:2
Vice Squad, The 1931,Je 6,15:5
Picture Snatcher 1933,My 19,20:3
Chief, The 1933,D 2,9:4
Love Begins at 20 1936,S 19,20:1
Devil's Island 1940,Jl 12,11:4
Wilson, Toni
Red Hot Romance 1922,Ja 23,11:4
Wilson, Violette
Moon Is Down, The 1943,Mr 27,8:6
Wilson, Ward (Narrator)
Golden Age of Comedy, The 1957,D 27,23:4
Wilson, Warren (Original Author)
You're a Sweetheart 1937,D 25,10:5
Cowboy in Manhattan 1943,My 28,19:2
Swingtime Johnny 1943,D 17,23:3
Wilson, Warren (Producer)
She Gets her Man 1945,F 9,20:5
Wilson, Warren (Screenwriter)
Tanks a Million 1941,O 9,27:2
Hellzapoppin 1941,D 26,21:4
Give Out, Sisters 1942,Ag 28,22:3
Good Morning, Judge 1943,Ap 30,25:4
Cowboy in Manhattan 1943,My 28,19:2
Swing Fever 1944,Ja 28,14:1
She Gets her Man 1945,F 9,20:5
She Wrote the Book 1946,Je 20,20:3
If You Knew Susie 1948,F 23,19:2
Wilstach, Frank J (Original Author)
Plainsman, The 1937,Ja 14,16:2
Wilstach, John (Original Author)
Under-Cover Man 1932,D 5,21:2
Wilton, Ann
Dead Men Tell no Tales 1939,Jl 24,9:2
Man in Grey, The 1945,N 30,18:6
Man of Evil 1948,Mr 26,26:2
Miniver Story, The 1950,O 27,24:2
Wilton, Eric
Silent Witness, The 1932,F 8,21:1
Masquerader, The 1933,S 4,9:5
Midnight Alibi 1934,Jl 4,18:3
Molly and Me 1945,My 26,18:2
Jolson Sings Again 1949,Ag 18,16:6
Valentino 1951,Ap 20,25:1
Three bad Sisters 1956,F 13,24:1
Wilton, Robb
It's Love Again 1936,My 23,12:1
Break the News 1941,Ja 2,24:2
Wiltshire, John
Massacre Hill 1950,D 14,51:3
Wherever She Goes 1953,Ja 28,24:4
Wiltshire, Maurice (Original Author)
My Brothers Keeper 1949,F 14,15:3
Wiltz, Walter
Carmen Baby 1967,O 11,41:2
Wiman, Anne-Mari
Wild Strawberries 1959,Je 23,37:1
Wimperis, Arthur (Miscellaneous)
Brewster's Millions 1935,Ag 8,23:3
Sanders of the River 1935,Je 27,16:1
Girl From Maxim's, The 1936,S 16,29:1
Wimperis, Arthur (Original Author)
Clouds Over Europe 1939,Je 16,27:2
Wimperis, Arthur (Screenwriter)
Private Life of Henry VIII, The 1933,O 13,25:2
Catherine the Great 1934,F 15,15:6
Scarlet Pimpernel, The 1935,F 8,27:2
Beloved Vagabond, The 1937,F 8,12:5
Forever Yours 1937,Je 7,22:2
Dark Journey 1937,Ag 23,22:1

Return of the Scarlet Pimpernel, The
1938,Ap 11,12:2
Drums 1938,S 30,24:4
Prison Without Bars 1939,Ap 10,13:2
Mrs Miniver 1942,Je 5,23:1
Random Harvest 1942,D 18,36:6
If Winter Comes 1948,Ja 23,28:4
Julia Misbehaves 1948,O 8,30:2
Red Danube, The 1949,D 9,37:3
Young Bess 1953,My 22,31:1
Wincelberg, Simon (Original Author)
On the Threshold of Space 1956,Mr 30,10:5
Winch, Elizabeth
Touch and go 1956,Mr 20,13:2
Winch, Frank (Original Author)
Buffalo Bill 1944,Ap 20,22:6
Winchell, Paul
Stop! Look! and Laugh! 1961,F 9,36:1
Winchell, Walter
Wake up and Live 1937,Ap 24,16:2
Love and Hisses 1938,Ja 1,11:1
Helen Morgan Story, The 1957,O 3,33:2
College Confidential 1960,Ag 22,23:1
Winchell, Walter (Original Author)
Broadway Thru a Keyhole 1933,N 2,18:3
Winchester, Barbara
Connection, The 1962,O 4,44:1
Winckler, Richard
Cow and I, The 1961,Je 6,42:2
Windeck, Agnes
Time to Love and a Time to Die, A
1958,Jl 10,22:1
Windheim, Marek
Something to Sing About 1937,S 21,29:4
I'll Take Romance 1937,D 17,33:2
She Married an Artist 1938,F 25,15:2
Hi Diddle Diddle 1943,S 24,26:2
In our Time 1944,F 12,11:2
Windish, Ilka
Magic Face, The 1951,O 1,19:2
Windom, William
One Man's Way 1964,Mr 12,40:3
Americanization of Emily, The 1964,O 28,51:1
Detective, The 1968,My 29,20:3
Windon, Lawrence C (Director)
Enemies of the Law 1931,Jl 13,13:5
Windsor, Adele
Girl from Havana, The 1929,S 2,16:1
True to the Navy 1930,My 24,21:2
Windsor, Barbara
Sparrows Don't Sing 1963,My 7,46:2
Study in Terror, A 1966,N 3,45:3
Windsor, Claire
To Please one Woman 1920,D 20,11:2
What Do Men Want? 1921,N 14,18:1
Grand Larceny 1922,F 27,13:4
One Clear Call 1922,Je 19,10:3
Fools First 1922,Jl 31,12:3
Rich Men's Wives 1922,Ag 21,6:2
Brothers Under the Skin 1922,N 13,12:1
Stranger's Banquet, The 1923,Ja 1,18:1
Rupert of Hentzau 1923,Jl 9,8:4
Eternal Three, The 1923,O 12,7:2 (Incorrect in
this edition; use 1927,O 1,7:2 elsewhere)
Acquittal, The 1923,D 12,24:5
Nellie, the Beautiful Cloak Model
1924,Ap 14,14:1
Son of the Sahara, A 1924,My 27,14:1
For Sale 1924,Jl 14,11:5
Dixie Handicap, The 1924,D 30,15:3
Denial, The 1925,Mr 10,19:3
Just a Woman 1925,My 26,24:2
White Desert, The 1925,Jl 8,12:4
Souls for Sables 1925,S 15,12:1 (Incorrect in this
edition; use 1925,S 15,29:1 elsewhere)
Dance Madness 1926,Ja 25,21:2
Money Talks 1926,My 11,24:3
Tin Hats 1926,N 29,16:3
Little Journey, A 1927,Ja 4,21:1
Claw, The 1927,My 11,28:3
Captain Lash 1929,F 4,20:1
Windsor, Duchess of (Narrator)
King's Story, A 1967,My 25,57:2
Windsor, Duke of (Narrator)
King's Story, A 1967,My 25,57:2
Windsor, Georgette
Black Book, The 1949,O 17,18:2
Windsor, Kirk
Having Wonderful Time 1938,Jl 8,11:2
Windsor, Marie
Song of the Thin Man 1947,Ag 29,14:2
Force of Evil 1948,D 27,16:2
Outpost in Morocco 1949,Mr 25,28:3
Hellfire 1949,My 30,9:4
Fighting Kentuckian, The 1949,S 19,18:3
Dakota Lil 1950,Mr 3,21:5
Frenchie 1951,F 12,19:2
Japanese War Bride 1952,Ja 30,22:6
Outlaw Woman 1952,Ap 5,20:3
Narrow Margin, The 1952,My 5,18:7
Sniper, The 1952,My 10,16:3
Jungle, The 1952,O 2,32:3
Tall Texan, The 1953,Ag 13,32:4

Windsor, Marie— Cont
Trouble Along the Way 1953,My 7,37:2
City That Never Sleeps 1953,Ag 8,14:2
So This Is Love 1953,Ag 12,22:1
Eddie Cantor Story, The 1953,D 26,10:2
Hell's Half Acre 1954,F 27,11:3
Cat-Women of the Moon 1954,Mr 20,10:7
Killing, The 1956,My 21,20:1
Story of Mankind, The 1957,N 9,31:2
Day of the Badman 1958,Ja 30,19:2
Unholy Wife, The 1958,Mr 7,17:1
Critic's Choice 1963,My 2,40:2
Day Mars Invaded Earth, The 1964,Ap 2,28:3
Bedtime Story 1964,Je 11,27:1
Mail Order Bride 1964,Je 11,27:3
Chamber of Horrors 1966,O 20,52:5
Windt, Herbert (Composer)
Legend of William Tell, The 1935,O 2,27:1
Windust, Bretaigne (Director)
Winter Meeting 1948,Ap 8,31:2
June Bride 1948,O 30,10:2
Perfect Strangers 1950,Mr 11,8:2
Pretty Baby 1950,S 23,11:2
Enforcer, The 1951,Ja 26,19:2
Bride Comes to Yellow Sky, The 1953,Ja 14,27:2
Winehouse, Irwin (Screenwriter)
Blueprint for Robbery 1961,F 2,24:3
Wineland, Sam K (Composer)
Samarang 1933,Je 29,22:2
WINER
See Also WIENER, WEINER
Winer, Elihu (Narrator)
Slave Trade in the World Today 1964,N 24,44:1
Wines, Carol
Three Rogues 1931,Ap 4,23:1
Winfield, Gil
Fiend Without a Face 1958,Jl 4,15:3
Winfield, Joan
Bullets for O'Hara 1941,Jl 28,16:4
Gorilla Man, The 1943,Ja 15,21:4
Stolen Life, A 1946,My 2,27:4
Winfried, Winna
Nuit du Carrefour; Night at the Crossroads, The
1932,Je 5,X,10:4 (In Addenda)
Wing, Mrs
Chinatown Nights 1929,Ap 1,22:1
Wing, Pat
Working Man, The 1933,Ap 21,20:3
Hi, Nellie! 1934,F 1,15:5
Wing, Rodric Red
Objective Burma 1945,Ja 27,15:2
Key Largo 1948,Jl 17,6:6
Wing, Toby
Search for Beauty 1934,F 10,20:2
Come on Marines 1934,Mr 24,20:3
Murder at the Vanities 1934,My 21,20:2
Kiss and Make-Up 1934,Je 29,17:1
True Confession 1937,D 16,35:2
Wing, Ward (Director)
Samarang 1933,Je 29,22:2
Wing, Wong
Dangerous Paradise 1930,F 16,III,8:1
Wing, Wong Mrs
Mr Wu 1927,My 16,24:2
Where East Is East 1929,My 27,22:1
Daughter of Shanghai 1937,D 24,21:2
Wingard, Karl G
Raggen, Det Aer Jag Det 1936,My 22,19:1
Wingardh, Carl-Gunnar
Tjocka Slaekten; Near Relatives 1935,My 20,20:5
Winge, Holger
Skanor-Falsterbo 1939,Ap 17,13:2
Winge, Oscar
Affairs of a Model 1952,Ag 7,12:8
Winge, Thorsten
For Her Sake 1930,N 11,29:1
Wingreen, Jason
Slender Thread, The 1965,D 24,24:2
Winkel, M
Dziesieciu z Pawiaka 1932,Ap 21,25:2
Winkelman, Michael
Indian Fighter, The 1955,D 22,20:1
Winkelstern, Marianne
Die Grosse Attraktion 1933,Jl 24,11:2
Hellseher, Der 1933,S 11,20:4
Winkler, Baby
Overture to Glory 1940,F 12,14:2
Winkler, Irwin (Producer)
Double Trouble 1967,My 25,54:2
Blue 1968,My 11,28:1
Split, The 1968,N 5,55:2
Winkler, Otti Dietze
Endstation 1937,Jl 17,18:1
Winkler, Robert
Bad Men of Missouri 1941,Ag 16,18:2
Winman, Dwight
Puritan Passions 1923,O 15,15:4
WINN
See Also WYNN, WYNNE
Winn, Albert C
Forty Thousand Horsemen 1941,Ag 15,13:2
Winn, Godfrey
Coming-Out Party, A 1962,Jl 31,19:2

Winn, Godfrey (Original Author)
Holiday Camp 1948,Ja 24,11:2
Winn, John R
Inheritance, The 1964,N 9,42:2
Winner, Michael (Director)
Play it Cool 1963,Jl 18,15:3
Girl-Getters, The 1966,Ap 13,37:6
Jokers, The 1967,My 16,50:1
I'll Never Forget What's 'Isname
1968,Ap 15,51:1
Winner, Michael (Original Author)
Jokers, The 1967,My 16,50:1
Winner, Michael (Producer)
I'll Never Forget What's 'Isname
1968,Ap 15,51:1
Winnerstrand, Olof
Ungkarlspappan 1936,Ja 4,19:1
John Ericsson Victor of Hampton Roads
1938,My 18,17:2
Torment 1947,Ap 22,34:2
Affairs of a Model 1952,Ag 7,12:8
Lesson in Love, A 1960,Mr 15,46:1
Night is my Future 1963,Ja 9,5:6
Winnicka, Lucyna
Joan of the Angels? 1962,My 8,43:6
Winninger, Charles
Pied Piper Malone 1924,Ja 28,12:1
Canadian, The 1926,N 30,27:1
Summer Bachelors 1926,D 20,28:3
Fighting Caravans 1931,Ja 26,21:1
Bad Sister 1931,Mr 30,25:2
God's Gift to Women 1931,Ap 18,17:3
Winninger, Charles
Gun Smoke 1931,Ap 24,27:1
Winninger, Charles
Night Nurse 1931,Jl 17,23:4
Children of Dreams 1931,Jl 20,20:4
Sin of Madelon Claudet, The 1931,O 31,22:2
Flying High 1931,D 12,23:3
Husband's Holiday 1931,D 25,29:2
Show Boat 1936,My 15,29:4
White Fang 1936,Jl 18,18:2
Three Smart Girls 1937,Ja 25,22:2
Cafe Metropole 1937,Ap 29,17:1
Go Getter, The 1937,Je 4,27:2
Woman Chases Man 1937,Je 11,26:2
You Can't Have Everything 1937,Ag 4,15:2
Nothing Sacred 1937,N 26,27:2
You're a Sweetheart 1937,D 25,10:5
Every Day's a Holiday 1938,Ja 27,17:2
Goodbye Broadway 1938,My 14,18:1
Hard To Get 1938,N 14,15:2
Three Smart Girls Grow Up 1939,Mr 18,9:2
Babes in Arms 1939,O 20,27:2
Destry Rides Again 1939,N 30,25:1
Barricade 1939,D 9,18:2
If I Had my Way 1940,My 6,13:2
My Love Came Back 1940,Jl 13,16:5
Beyond Tomorrow 1940,S 27,27:1
Little Nellie Kelly 1940,D 25,33:2
Pot o'Gold 1941,Ap 4,25:2
Ziegfeld Girl 1941,Ap 25,17:2
Get-Away, The 1941,Jl 17,23:4
My Life With Caroline 1941,O 30,27:1
Friendly Enemies 1942,Je 22,19:1
Coney Island 1943,Je 17,17:2
Hers to Hold 1943,Jl 22,15:1
Lady Takes a Chance, A 1943,S 16,25:2
Flesh and Fantasy 1943,N 18,29:1
Broadway Rhythm 1944,Ap 14,24:6
Sunday Dinner for a Soldier 1945,Ja 25,16:2
Belle of the Yukon 1945,Mr 30,18:4
State Fair 1945,Ag 31,14:3
She Wouldn't Say Yes 1946,Ja 12,10:7
Lover Come Back 1946,Je 20,20:3
Something in the Wind 1947,Ag 29,14:3
Living in a Big Way 1947,O 10,31:4
Give my Regards to Broadway 1948,Je 23,32:2
Father Is a Bachelor 1950,F 23,33:3
Torpedo Valley 1952,D 20,15:3
Sun Shines Bright, The 1954,Mr 17,25:2
Las Vegas Shakedown 1955,Je 18,14:2
Winogradoff, Anatol
Go, Man, Go 1954,Mr 10,29:5
Winogradowa, Marie
Last Stop, The 1949,Mr 22,31:2
Winsloe, Christa (Original Author)
Maedchen in Uniform 1932,S 21,25:4
Madchen in Uniform 1965,Ag 18,41:2
Winslow, Dick
Which Shall It Be? 1924,Ap 7,15:3
Tom Sawyer 1930,D 20,20:6
Seed 1931,My 15,20:6
So Big 1932,Ap 30,19:3
Laughter in Hell 1933,Ja 2,29:2
Human Side, The 1934,S 15,20:3
There's Always Tomorrow 1934,N 10,19:2
Mutiny on the Bounty 1935,N 9,19:2
Benny Goodman Story 1956,F 22,22:1
Francis in the Haunted House 1956,Jl 21,9:2
Do Not Disturb 1965,D 25,17:2

Winslow, George
Room for One More 1952,Ja 16,21:2
Monkey Business 1952,S 6,12:6
Gentlemen Prefer Blondes 1953,Jl 16,17:2
Mister Scoutmaster 1953,Ag 29,10:1
Artists and Models 1955,D 22,20:1
Summer Love 1958,Je 26,23:4
Winslow, Herbert Hall (Screenwriter)
Manon Lescaut 1914,Je 14,15:1
Winslow, Leah
She-Wolf 1931,My 28,30:6
Winslow, Thyra Samter (Original Author)
She Married her Boss 1935,S 27,25:3
Winsor, Kathleen (Original Author)
Forever Amber 1947,O 23,31:2
Winstanley, Jean
Sez O'Reilly to MacNab 1938,F 19,19:4
Winston, Bruce
Children of Dreams 1931,Jl 20,20:4
Private Life of Don Juan, The 1934,D 10,16:2
Man Who Could Work Miracles, The
1937,F 22,13:1
Thief of Bagdad, The 1940,D 6,28:2
Winston, Carl (Director)
Mann der Seinen Moerder Sucht, Der; Looking for
His Murderer 1931,Mr 15,IX,6:1
Winston, Helen (Producer)
Hand in Hand 1961,F 7,41:3
Winston, Helene
Send Me no Flowers 1964,N 13,30:1
Winston, Irene
Dear Brat 1951,Jl 5,21:2
My Son John 1952,Ap 9,27:1
Rear Window 1954,Ag 5,18:2
Winston, Irene (Original Author)
Bury Me Dead 1947,O 25,13:3
Winston, Laura
Victory 1919,D 28,4:4
Winston, Ron (Director)
Ambush Bay 1966,S 15,51:4
Don't Just Stand There 1968,S 3,54:2
Winston, S K (Director)
Adventure in Music 1944,Mr 6,17:3
Winston, S K (Miscellaneous)
Devil is a Woman, The 1935,My 4,17:2
Winston, Steve
Ghost Ship, The 1943,D 25,19:4
Winston, Vivian
Last Moment, The 1928,Mr 12,26:1
American Tragedy, An 1931,Ag 6,22:5
Winter, Christa
Wonder Boy 1951,D 26,19:5
Winter, Dale
Back Street 1941,F 12,25:2
Winter, David
Percy 1925,Mr 25,24:2
Winter, Donovan (Director)
Trunk, The 1962,N 1,34:3
Winter, Donovan (Screenwriter)
Trunk, The 1962,N 1,34:3
Winter, Jessie
Man of Affairs 1937,F 20,9:2
Winter, Keith (Miscellaneous)
Red Shoes, The 1948,O 23,9:2
Winter, Keith (Original Author)
Shining Hour, The 1939,Ja 20,15:2
Forever and a Day 1943,Mr 13,9:2
Winter, Keith (Screenwriter)
Chocolate Soldier, The 1941,N 1,20:2
Above Suspicion 1943,Ag 6,10:3
Uncle Harry 1945,Ag 24,14:5
Devotion 1946,Ap 6,10:5
Winter, Laska
Marriage Cheat, The 1921,Je 2,14:3
Tides of Passion 1925,Ap 20,22:1
Night of Love, The 1927,Ja 25,18:4
Tender Hour, The 1927,Je 7,27:4
Rescue, The 1929,Ja 14,20:1
Insidious Dr Fu Manchu, The 1929,Jl 22,17:1
Frozen Justice 1929,O 26,15:1
Rainbow Trail, The 1932,Ja 30,13:2
Painted Woman, The 1932,S 16,24:4
Winter, Margrit
Marie-Louise 1945,N 13,24:2
It Happened in Broad Daylight 1960,S 30,33:1
Winter, Peter M (Screenwriter)
Doll's House, A 1922,F 13,10:1
Winter, Philip
Rebecca 1940,Mr 29,25:2
Winter, Vincent
Little Kidnappers, The 1954,S 2,18:1
Warriors, The 1955,S 10,11:2
Bridal Path, The 1959,D 21,34:2
Gorgo 1961,Mr 30,24:2
Almost Angels 1962,N 1,34:2
Three Lives of Thomasina, The 1963,D 12,46:1
Winters, Bernie
Johnny Nobody 1965,N 24,35:1
Winters, Charlotte
His Woman 1931,D 5,21:2
Smart Blonde 1937,Ja 9,21:1

Winters, David
Last Angry Man, The 1959,O 23,24:1
West Side Story 1961,O 19,39:3
Winters, Gloria
Lawless, The 1950,Je 23,29:2
Gambling House 1951,Mr 19,23:2
Winters, Jonathan
It's a Mad, Mad, Mad, Mad World
1963,N 19,47:1
Loved One, The 1965,O 12,57:1
Russians are Coming the Russians are Coming,
The 1966,My 26,55:1
Penelope 1966,N 11,36:6
Oh Dad, Poor Dad, Mamma's Hung You in the
Closet and I'm Feeling so Sad 1967,F 16,32:1
Eight on the Lam 1967,Ap 27,52:1
Winters, Linda
Trade Winds 1939,Ja 13,17:2
Blondie Meets the Boss 1939,Ap 27,31:1
Street of Missing Women 1940,Ja 8,11:2
Winters, Roland
Cry of the City 1948,S 30,32:4
Once More, my Darling 1949,S 26,17:1
Dangerous Profession, A 1949,D 12,29:4
Malaya 1950,F 23,33:1
Captain Carey U S A 1950,Mr 30,40:5
Between Midnight and Dawn 1950,O 2,19:2
To Please a Lady 1950,O 27,24:3
West Point Story, The 1950,D 23,11:3
Raton Pass 1951,Ap 20,25:1
Follow the Sun 1951,Ap 26,34:4
She's Working her Way Through College
1952,Jl 10,27:2
So Big 1953,O 22,34:2
Bigger Than Life 1956,Ag 3,11:2
Top Secret Affair 1957,Ja 31,21:1
Jet Pilot 1957,O 5,8:6
Never Steal Anything Small 1959,F 12,23:1
Blue Hawaii 1962,F 22,20:2
Follow That Dream 1962,Ag 9,17:7
Winters, Shelley
Knickerbocker Holiday 1944,Ap 20,22:7
Double Life, A 1948,F 20,19:1
Larceny 1948,S 4,8:6
Cry of the City 1948,S 30,32:4
Take one False Step 1949,Je 23,33:2
Great Gatsby, The 1949,Jl 14,20:5
Johnny Stool Pigeon 1949,S 23,28:3
South Sea Sinner 1950,Ja 16,18:4
Winchester 73 1950,Je 8,38:2
Frenchie 1951,F 12,19:2
He Ran all the Way 1951,Je 21,24:2
Place in the Sun, A 1951,Ag 29,20:1
Behave Yourself 1951,N 8,35:2
Phone Call From a Stranger 1952,F 2,11:2
Meet Danny Wilson 1952,Mr 27,34:4
Untamed Frontier 1952,Ag 23,10:2
My Man and I 1952,S 6,12:6
Saskatchewan 1954,Mr 11,26:2
Executive Suite 1954,My 7,19:1
Playgirl 1954,My 15,13:3
Mambo 1955,Mr 31,23:3
I Am a Camera 1955,Ag 9,29:1
Night of the Hunter, The 1955,S 30,23:1
Big Knife, The 1955,N 9,41:2
I Died a Thousand Times 1955,N 10,45:2
Treasure of Pancho Villa, The 1955,N 25,38:2
Cash on Delivery 1956,S 1,19:3
Diary of Anne Frank, The 1959,Mr 19,40:1
Odds Against Tomorrow 1959,O 16,27:1
Let no Man Write my Epitaph 1960,N 11,36:2
Young Savages, The 1961,My 25,31:1
Lolita 1962,Je 14,23:2
Chapman Report, The 1962,O 18,49:2
Balcony, The 1963,Mr 22,7:1
Wives and Lovers 1963,Ag 29,36:1
House is not a Home, A 1964,S 2,33:1
Greatest Story Ever Told, The 1965,F 16,40:2
Time of Indifference 1965,O 13,50:1
Patch of Blue, A 1965,D 16,63:1
Harper 1966,Mr 31,43:1
Alfie 1966,Ag 25,42:1
Time of Indifference 1966,O 13,50:1
Enter Laughing 1967,Ag 1,24:1
Scalphunters, The 1968,Ap 3,40:1
Wild in the Streets 1968,My 30,21:1
Winterstein, Eduard von
Between Worlds 1924,Jl 7,10:4
Mystic Mirror, The 1928,O 1,23:1
Blue Angel, The 1930,D 6,21:3
Rosenmontag 1931,Mr 28,15:3
Grosse Tenor, Der 1931,My 29,26:5
Andere, Der 1932,Ja 15,24:4
Judas von Tirol, Der 1935,Ap 27,20:7
Letzte Rose 1936,O 10,21:3
Waldwinter 1936,N 14,23:3
Selige Exzellenz, Die 1937,Je 15,26:2
Unsterbliche Herz, Das; Immortal Heart, The
1939,O 21,12:2
Winterstein, Karl von
Zu Strassburg auf der Schanz; At the Strassburg
1936,F 15,18:7

Winther, Helle
Tjocka Slaekten; Near Relatives 1935,My 20,20:5
Winther, Karen
David Copperfield 1923,N 6,23:3
Wintle, Julian (Producer)
Dark Man, The 1952,My 26,18:4
Stranger in Between, The 1952,Ag 20,21:3
One That Got Away, The 1958,Ap 23,40:2
Coming-Out Party, A 1962,Jl 31,19:2
Crooks Anonymous 1963,O 31,26:3
Wintner, Nancy (Original Author)
Gang's All Here, The 1943,D 23,26:4
Winton, Barry
Man From Yesterday, The 1932,Je 25,18:2
Winton, Jane
Tomorrow's Love 1925,Ja 7,33:5
Why Girls Go Back Home 1926,My 18,28:2
Footloose Windows 1926,Je 22,21:2
Don Juan 1926,Ag 7,6:1 (In Addenda)
Beloved Rogue, The 1927,Mr 14,16:1
Monkey Talks, The 1927,Ap 5,30:7
Poor Nut, The 1927,Jl 19,27:2
Lonesome Ladies 1927,Ag 2,19:2
Sunrise 1927,S 24,15:3 (In Addenda)
Fair Co-ed, The 1927,O 24,24:3
Crystal Cup, The 1927,O 25,33:3
Patsy, The 1928,Ap 23,20:2
Burning Daylight 1928,Ap 23,20:2
Yellow Lily, The 1928,My 21,25:1
Melody of Love 1928,O 22,29:1
Captain Lash 1929,F 4,20:1
Scandal 1929,Ap 22,23:1
Bridge of San Luis Rey, The 1929,My 20,22:6
Furies, The 1930,Ap 19,15:1
Hell's Angels 1930,Ag 16,8:3
Winwood, Estelle
Quality Street 1937,Ap 9,19:2
Glass Slipper, The 1955,Mr 25,19:2
Swan, The 1956,Ap 27,21:5
23 Paces to Baker Street 1956,My 19,12:6
This Happy Feeling 1958,Je 19,28:2
Darby O'Gill and the Little People 1959,Jl 1,26:1
Misfits, The 1961,F 2,24:2
Cabinet of Caligari, The 1962,My 26,13:5
Notorious Landlady, The 1962,Jl 27,15:2
Dead Ringer 1964,F 20,22:3
Games 1967,S 18,58:2
Camelot 1967,O 26,54:1
Producers, The 1968,Mr 19,38:1
Wipf, Louis (Producer)
Oh, Amelia 1951,D 3,22:2
Wiren, Arne
Pimpernel Svensson 1953,F 6,16:4
Wirff, Signe
Sun Over Sweden 1938,Ap 9,11:2
Wirkus, Faustin (Producer)
Voodoo 1933,Mr 27,13:6
Wirth, Franz Peter (Director)
Arms and the Man 1962,F 24,21:7
Wirxon, Maris
Million Dollar Baby 1941,Je 7,20:2
Wisbar, Frank (Director)
Mozart Story, The 1948,N 15,21:5
Wisbar, Frank (Original Author)
Woman in Bondage 1944,Mr 27,17:2
Wisberg, Aubrey (Miscellaneous)
Horn Blows at Midnight, The 1945,Ap 21,18:2
Wisberg, Aubrey (Original Author)
So Dark the Night 1946,D 7,16:2
Heaven Only Knows 1947,N 14,29:3
Casanova's Big Night 1954,Ap 19,19:1
Wisberg, Aubrey (Producer)
Man From Planet X, The 1951,Ap 9,31:2
Wisberg, Aubrey (Screenwriter)
Submarine Raider 1942,Je 22,19:2
Counter-Espionage 1942,S 28,13:2
They Came to Blow up America 1943,My 15,13:2
Bomber's Moon 1943,Jl 31,8:2
Betrayal From the East 1945,Ap 25,27:2
Falcon's Adventure, The 1946,D 14,19:2
Big Fix, The 1947,My 3,10:3
Burning Cross, The 1948,F 20,19:1
Desert Hawk, The 1950,Ag 26,9:2
Man From Planet X, The 1951,Ap 9,31:2
Lady in the Iron Mask 1952,Jl 5,7:2
Son of Sinbad 1955,Jl 28,18:2
Wischmann, Marianne
White Horse Inn, The 1957,D 4,50:3
Wisdom, Norman
Trouble in Store 1956,Ja 14,13:2
Follow a Star 1961,Ap 26,34:1
Night They Raided Minsky's, The 1968,D 23,43:1
Wisdom, Norman (Screenwriter)
Follow a Star 1961,Ap 26,34:1
WISE
See Also WEISS
Wise, Robert (Director)
Curse of the Cat People, The 1944,Mr 4,11:1
Body Snatcher, The 1945,My 26,18:3
Game of Death, A 1945,N 24,22:4
Criminal Court 1946,N 16,15:3

Born to Kill 1947,My 1,34:2
Blood on the Moon 1948,N 12,30:5
Set-Up, The 1949,Mr 30,31:2
Two Flags West 1950,O 13,23:2
Three Secrets 1950,O 21,10:6
House on Telegraph Hill, The 1951,My 14,29:1
Day the Earth Stood Still, The 1951,S 19,37:1
Captive City, The 1952,Mr 27,34:2
Something for the Birds 1952,N 15,15:2
Desert Rats, The 1953,My 9,13:2
Destination Gobi 1953,My 30,7:1
So Big 1953,O 22,34:2
Executive Suite 1954,My 7,19:1
Helen of Troy 1956,Ja 27,21:4
Tribute to a Bad Man 1956,Mr 31,13:3
Somebody up There Likes Me 1956,Jl 6,16:1
This Could Be the Night 1957,My 15,39:1
Until They Sail 1957,O 9,41:2
Run Silent, Run Deep 1958,Mr 28,29:1
I Want to Live 1958,N 19,45:1
Odds Against Tomorrow 1959,O 16,27:1
West Side Story 1961,O 19,39:3
Two for the Seesaw 1962,N 22,43:1
Haunting, The 1963,S 19,23:1
Sound of Music, The 1965,Mr 3,34:1
Sand Pebbles, The 1966,D 21,48:1
Star! 1968,O 23,36:2
Wise, Robert (Producer)
Odds Against Tomorrow 1959,O 16,27:1
West Side Story 1961,O 19,39:3
Haunting, The 1963,S 19,23:1
Sound of Music, The 1965,Mr 3,34:1
Sand Pebbles, The 1966,D 21,48:1
Wise, Walter (Original Author)
Runaround, The 1946,Je 7,16:3
Wise, Walter (Screenwriter)
Sinner Take All 1937,F 3,27:1
WISEMAN
See Also WEISSMAN
Wiseman, Frederick (Director)
Titicut Follies 1967,O 4,38:1
Wiseman, Frederick (Producer)
Cool World, The 1964,Ap 21,42:1
Titicut Follies 1967,O 4,38:1
Wiseman, Joseph
With These Hands 1950,Je 16,28:4
Detective Story 1951,N 7,35:2
Viva Zapata 1952,F 8,19:2
Miserables, Les 1952,Ag 15,11:2
Silver Chalice, The 1954,D 27,22:5
Prodigal, The 1955,My 14,10:7
Three Brave Men 1957,Mr 16,13:2
Garment Jungle, The 1957,My 16,28:2
Unforgiven, The 1960,Ap 7,46:1
Happy Thieves, The 1962,F 5,19:4
Dr No 1963,My 30,20:1
Bye Bye Braverman 1968,F 22,36:1
Night They Raided Minsky's, The 1968,D 23,43:1
Wiseman, Nicholas Cardinal (Original Author)
Fabiola 1951,My 30,14:2
Wiser, Bud
Lulu Belle 1948,Je 21,18:3
Wish, Jerome (Screenwriter)
Angels From Hell 1968,O 24,55:5
Wishard, Scoville (Producer)
Voice of the Hurricane 1964,Je 3,36:4
Wishengrad, Morton (Screenwriter)
With These Hands 1950,Je 16,28:4
Wisher, Sally
Prison Without Bars 1939,Ap 10,13:2
Wisinger, Irene
Zwei Hertzen in Drei-Viertel Takt 1930,O 13,31:1
Wismer, Harry
Spirit of West Point 1947,O 3,31:2
Somebody up There Likes Me 1956,Jl 6,16:1
Wissler, Rudy
San Diego, I Love You 1944,N 10,25:1
Tomorrow the World 1944,D 22,12:4
Wisten, Roger
Living Dead, The 1940,D 17,33:2
Wister, Owen (Original Author)
Virginian, The 1929,D 23,18:2
Virginian, The 1946,Ap 18,22:2
Wiszniewska, Mira
Tredowata 1936,D 31,21:2
Wiszniewska, Tamara
August der Starke 1937,Ja 30,21:3
Dziewczeta z Nowolipek; Girls of Nowolipek 1938,N 25,19:2
Witensohn, A (Screenwriter)
Scrapper, The 1959,D 14,42:2
Withers, Bernadette
Trouble With Angels, The 1966,Ap 7,45:1
Withers, Charles
Hideaway 1937,S 25,10:2
Withers, Googie
Accused 1936,D 17,35:1
Gaiety Girls, The 1938,Mr 31,15:1
Crime Over London 1938,Jl 28,23:2
Lady Vanishes, The 1938,D 26,29:1
Haunted Honeymoon 1940,O 31,28:2

Withers, Googie— Cont
One of our Aircraft Is Missing 1942,N 2,17:2
Jeannie 1943,S 13,14:2
On Approval 1945,Ja 29,17:1
They Came to a City 1945,F 19,21:3
Silver Fleet, The 1945,Mr 24,22:6
Dead of Night 1946,Je 29,22:6
It Always Rains on Sunday 1949,F 14,15:5
Miranda 1949,Ap 25,20:2
Once Upon a Dream 1949,Jl 15,17:2
Night and the City 1950,Je 10,11:2
Pink String and Sealing Wax 1950,O 4,38:2
White Corridors 1952,Jl 16,21:1
Withers, Grant
Bringing Up Father 1928,Mr 19,26:2
Saturday's Children 1929,Ap 29,29:2
Time, The Place and the Girl, The 1929,Jl 8,17:3
Madonna of Avenue A 1929,Ag 12,22:2
Show of Shows 1929,N 21,24:5
Hearts in Exile 1929,N 29,25:1
Tiger Rose 1929,D 25,23:1
So Long Letty 1930,F 8,12:5
Second Story Murder, The 1930,My 3,23:1
Soldiers and Women 1930,My 12,27:3
Back Pay 1930,My 31,19:4
Dancing Sweeties 1930,Ag 16,8:3
Sinners' Holiday 1930,O 11,21:3
Scarlet Pages 1930,D 6,21:3
Other Men's Women 1931,Ap 20,16:3
Too Young to Marry 1931,My 4,15:3
Red-Haired Alibi 1932,O 24,18:5
Hold 'Em Yale 1935,Ap 27,20:6
Goin' to Town 1935,My 11,21:2
Sky Parade, The 1936,Ap 20,17:1
Let's Sing Again 1936,My 9,11:2
Border Flight 1936,Je 22,22:1
Lady, Be Careful 1936,O 10,21:1
Hollywood Round-Up 1938,Mr 5,11:2
Touchdown Army 1938,O 28,27:2
Mr Wong, Detective 1938,N 21,14:4
Mister Wong in Chinatown 1939,Jl 31,9:2 (In Addenda)
Doomed to Die 1940,Jl 30,16:3
Men Against the Sky 1940,S 12,31:2
Mexican Spitfire out West 1940,O 30,29:3
Billy the Kid 1941,Je 20,28:2
Get-Away, The 1941,Jl 17,23:4
Parachute Battalion 1941,Ag 29,13:2
Butch Minds the Baby 1942,My 1,23:3
Tennessee Johnson 1943,Ja 13,18:2
Gildersleeve's Bad Day 1943,Je 11,23:1
Lady Takes a Chance, A 1943,S 16,25:2
No Time for Love 1943,D 2,30:1
In old Oklahoma 1943,D 6,21:1
Fighting Seabees, The 1944,Mr 20,14:2
Utah 1945,Mr 12,22:7
Dangerous Partners 1945,N 2,22:4
Dakota 1945,D 17,17:2
In old Sacramento 1946,Ap 29,24:4
My Darling Clementine 1946,D 4,44:5
Gunfighters 1947,Jl 25,12:5
Wyoming 1947,Jl 25,12:5
Blackmail 1947,Ag 5,26:3
Tycoon 1947,D 26,22:6
Fort Apache 1948,Je 25,26:2
Old Los Angeles 1948,Jl 12,11:2
Plunders, The 1948,N 1,28:2
Wake of the Red Witch 1949,Ja 10,19:2
Last Bandit, The 1949,Mr 21,19:2
Hellfire 1949,My 30,9:4
Fighting Kentuckian, The 1949,S 19,18:3
Rock Island Trail 1950,Je 5,19:3
Tripoli 1950,N 10,35:2
Rio Grande 1950,N 20,21:2
Hoodlum Empire 1952,Mr 6,25:6
Woman of the North Country 1952,Ag 30,6:2
Fair Wind to Java 1953,Ag 28,13:3
Sun Shines Bright, The 1954,Mr 17,25:2
Run for Cover 1955,Ap 30,10:6
Lady Godiva 1955,D 3,13:3
Withers, Isabel
Paid 1931,Ja 3,21:2
Brother Rat 1938,N 5,15:2
Withers, Jane
Bright Eyes 1934,D 21,31:1
Ginger 1935,Jl 19,13:2
Farmer Takes a Wife, The 1935,Ag 9,21:2
Paddy O'Day 1936,F 8,19:2
Gentle Julia 1936,Ap 11,19:1
Little Miss Nobody 1936,Je 6,21:1
Pepper 1936,Ag 24,11:2
Holy Terror, The 1937,Ja 30,21:2
Angel's Holiday 1937,My 29,20:2
Wild and Woolly 1937,S 6,20:1
45 Fathers 1937,D 11,22:2
Rascals 1938,My 27,12:2
Keep Smiling 1938,Ag 10,15:2
Always in Trouble 1938,N 3,27:1
Pack up Your Troubles 1939,O 27,27:2
High School 1940,Ja 5,15:5
Shooting High 1940,Ap 12,19:2
Youth Will Be Served 1940,N 15,25:2
Johnny Doughboy 1943,My 6,25:3
North Star, The 1943,N 5,23:1

Withers, Jane— Cont
Giant 1956,O 11,51:1
Right Approach, The 1961,My 18,41:1
Captain Newman, MD 1964,F 21,36:1
Withers, Margaret
Blanche Fury 1948,N 24,20:2
Don't Take it to Heart 1948,D 25,10:3
Daybreak 1949,Jl 4,9:2
Encore (The Ant and the Grasshopper); Ant and
the Grasshopper, The (Encore) 1952,Ap 3,45:1
Murder on Monday 1953,O 7,35:2
Witherspoon, Cora
Peach O'Reno 1931,D 24,20:8
Ladies of the Jury 1932,Ap 2,13:2
Midnight 1934,Mr 10,18:3
Gambling 1934,D 4,22:3
Piccadilly Jim 1936,Ag 31,19:1
Libeled Lady 1936,O 31,24:2
On the Avenue 1937,F 5,17:3
Dangerous Number 1937,Mr 12,19:2
Quality Street 1937,Ap 9,19:2
Personal Property 1937,Ap 11,27:2
Big Shot, The 1937,Ag 13,13:1
Madame X 1937,O 25,23:1
Beg, Borrow or Steal 1937,D 10,33:2
Professor Beware 1938,Jl 14,17:1
Port of Seven Seas 1938,Jl 15,13:2
Marie Antoinette 1938,Ag 17,23:2
Three Loves Has Nancy 1938,S 2,21:2
Just Around the Corner 1938,D 3,11:2
Woman Doctor 1939,Mr 24,27:3
Dodge City 1939,Ap 8,19:1
Flying Irishman, The 1939,Ap 12,27:2
Dark Victory 1939,Ap 21,27:2
Women, The 1939,S 22,27:2
Charlie Chan's Murder Cruise 1940,My 3,17:5
I Was an Adventuress 1940,My 20,13:2
Bank Dick, The 1940,D 13,29:2
Over 21 1945,Ag 17,20:2
Colonel Effingham's Raid 1946,Ap 5,21:3
Young Widow 1946,Jl 29,12:8
I've Always Loved You 1946,S 7,11:1
Mating Season, The 1951,Ap 12,41:2
Just for You 1952,O 9,40:6
Withey, Chet (Director)
Hun Within, The 1918,Ag 26,9:1
New Moon, The 1919,My 12,11:4
Wedding Bells 1921,Ag 15,14:3
Richard the Lion-Hearted 1923,O 22,17:1
Withey, Chet (Original Author)
Her Honor the Governor 1926,Jl 20,17:3
Withington, Paul (Director)
Blonde Captive, The 1932,F 29,21:3
Witlock, Lloyd
Michigan Kid, The 1928,Jl 2,11:2
Witney, Michael
Way West, The 1967,My 25,54:1
Witney, William (Director)
Apache Rose 1947,Jl 23,19:3
Outcast, The 1954,Jl 3,9:2
Master of the World 1961,S 16,9:1
Witt, Claus Peter (Director)
Great British Train Robbery, The 1967,Ap 6,45:2
Witt, Peter Uwe
Tempestous Love 1958,N 22,27:4
Wittels, David G (Original Author)
I Dream too Much 1935,N 29,24:1
Wittgenstein, Goetz
Abel Mit Der Mundharmonika 1934,S 1,16:3
Wittler, Therese
Spitfire 1934,Mr 9,22:3
Wittlin, Joseph (Screenwriter)
Beyond Endurance 1946,My 20,18:8
Wittrisch, Marcel
Liebeskommando 1932,Ap 27,13:6
Stimme der Liebe, Die 1936,My 16,11:2
Witty, Christopher
Masquerade 1965,Ap 29,40:2
Witwer, H C
Great White Way, The 1924,Ja 4,10:1
Witwer, H C (Original Author)
Great White Way, The 1924,Ja 4,10:1
Alex The Great 1928,My 1,33:3
Cain and Mabel 1936,O 19,22:1
Witzig, Paul (Cinematographer)
Endless Summer, The 1966,Je 16,53:2
Wix, Florence
Secrets 1924,Mr 25,25:2
Missing Guest, The 1938,S 7,30:7
Wlach, Herrman
1914: The Last Days Before the War 1932,S 5,9:6
Wladon, Jean
One Million Years BC 1967,F 22,21:1
Wlaker, Nella
Don't Turn 'em Loose 1936,S 25,20:2
Wlesenthal, Sam (Director)
Americano, The 1955,Ja 20,35:1
Wodehouse, P G (Miscellaneous)
Step Lively, Jeeves 1937,Ap 2,19:6
Wodehouse, P G (Original Author)
Gentleman of Leisure, A 1923,Jl 16,14:2
Piccadilly Jim 1936,Ag 31,19:1
Thank You, Jeeves 1936,O 5,25:1
Damsel in Distress, A 1937,N 25,37:1

Anything Goes 1956,Mr 22,38:1
Wodehouse, P G (Screenwriter)
Damsel in Distress, A 1937,N 25,37:1
Wodson, Elaine
Angel Who Pawned her Harp, The
1956,F 29,35:2
Woegerer, Otto
Nacht mit dem Kaiser, Die 1937,Ag 14,16:5
Last ten Days, The 1956,Ap 12,26:1
WOHL
See Also WAHL, WALL
Wohl, Burton (Original Author)
Blues for Lovers 1966,S 8,43:1
Wohl, Burton (Screenwriter)
Cold Wind in August, A 1961,Jl 27,23:2
Third Day, The 1965,Ag 5,15:3
Blues for Lovers 1966,S 8,43:1
Wohlbruck, Adolf
Maskerade 1934,O 14,X,4:2 (In Addenda)
Wohlbrueck, Adolf
Trapeze 1932,My 3,25:2
Stolz der 3 Kompagnie, Der 1932,Jl 21,15:2
Melodie der Liebe 1934,S 17,20:3
Waltz Time in Vienna 1934,N 19,13:2
Viktor und Viktoria 1935,Ja 28,10:5
Zigeunerbaron 1935,S 14,8:5
Keine Angst vor Liebe 1936,Ja 21,27:6
Eine Frau die Weiss Was sie Will 1936,Jl 18,18:3
Wohlmuth, Robert (Director)
Kabinett des Dr. Larifari, Das 1931,S 11,24:2
Wojcik, Zbigniew
Eighth Day of the Week, The 1959,Mr 24,45:2
Wojzik, Anna
Flames on the Volga 1929,Ap 2,28:4
Wolbert, Burton
Guilty One, The 1924,Je 17,22:4
Wolbert, Clarence
Guilty One, The 1924,Je 17,22:4
Wolbert, Dorothea
Guilty One, The 1924,Je 17,22:4
Woman of the World, A 1925,D 14,18:2
Love and Learn 1928,F 20,14:1
Dangerous Paradise 1930,F 16,III,8:1
Friends and Lovers 1931,N 7,16:5
Expert, The 1932,F 27,22:1
Two Seconds 1932,My 19,25:3
Hallelujah, I'm a Bum 1933,F 9,15:2
Wolcik, Krystyn
Naked Among the Wolves 1967,Ap 19,54:7
WOLCOTT
See Also WALCOTT
Wolcott, Charles (Composer)
Saludos Amigos 1943,F 13,8:2
Three Caballeros, The 1945,F 5,20:1
Fun and Fancy Free 1947,S 29,17:2 (In
Addenda)
Wolcott, Charles (Miscellaneous)
Make Mine Music 1946,Ap 22,26:2
Wolcott, George
Born Reckless 1937,Jl 30,22:6
Wolcott, Jersey Joe
Harder They Fall, The 1956,My 10,26:3
Woldars, Robert
Beau Geste 1966,S 8,43:1
Tobruk 1967,F 9,33:2
WOLF
See Also WOLFE, WOLFF, WOLLF, WOOLF,
WULFF
Wolf, A Sanford (Screenwriter)
Blueprint for Robbery 1961,F 2,24:3
Naked Brigade, The 1965,Je 17,27:2
Wolf, Andreas
Sunderin 1954,D 24,7:2
Wolf, Frank
Stranger in Town, A 1968,Ap 25,53:4
Villa Rides 1968,Jl 18,26:3
Wolf, Friedrich (Original Author)
Cyankali 1930,Jl 13,VIII,4:2
Professor Mamlock 1938,N 8,26:2
Wolf, Friedrich (Screenwriter)
Professor Mamlock 1938,N 8,26:2
Wolf, Gusti
Kleines Bezirksgericht; Little Country Court
1939,F 18,12:4
Das Erlebnis Geht Weiter; Another Experience
1940,F 3,9:3
Wolf, Howling
Festival 1967,O 24,53:2
Wolf, John (Producer)
Oliver! 1968,D 11,57:1
Wolf, Millicent
Girl in a Million, A 1950,Jl 24,15:2
Wolf, Rennold (Screenwriter)
Perfect Lady, A 1918,D 2,11:3
Wolf, Simon
Mothers of Today 1939,Mr 2,19:2
Wolf, Thomas H (Screenwriter)
Fifty Years Before your Eyes 1950,Je 30,18:2
(Incorrect in this edition; use 1950,Je 28,32:3
elsewhere)
WOLFE
See Also WOLFF, WOLLF, WOOLF, WULFF,
WOLF

Wolfe, Bill
Poppy 1936,Je 18,19:1
Wolfe, Bud
Blackmail 1947,Ag 5,26:3
Man Who Cheated Himself, The 1951,F 9,21:2
Wolfe, David
Undercover Man, The 1949,Ap 21,30:2
House of Strangers 1949,Jl 2,8:2
Dangerous Profession, A 1949,D 12,29:4
Bagdad 1949,D 24,11:4
Kansas Raiders 1951,Ja 26,19:2
Screen, The 1951,Ap 23,21:2
Appointment With Danger 1951,My 10,38:2
Smuggler's Island 1951,My 24,47:2
Five Fingers 1952,F 23,7:5
Wait Till the Sun Shines, Nellie 1952,Je 28,12:2
Salt of the Earth 1954,Mr 15,20:2
Wolfe, Digby
Weaker Sex, The 1949,Jl 11,13:2
Wolfe, Edwin
All the Way Home 1963,O 30,46:1
Wolfe, Ian
Fountain, The 1934,Ag 31,14:1
Barretts of Wimpole Street, The 1934,S 29,12:2
Clive of India 1935,Ja 18,29:1
Raven, The 1935,Jl 5,9:2
Mutiny on the Bounty 1935,N 9,19:2
$1,000 a Minute 1935,D 21,11:1
League of Frightened Men, The 1937,Jl 2,25:1
Emperor's Candlesticks, The 1937,Jl 9,18:1
Devil is Driving, The 1937,Jl 16,22:1
Arsene Lupin Returns 1938,Mr 9,21:1
Blondie 1938,D 22,25:4
Fast and Loose 1939,Mr 9,18:1
Society Lawyer 1939,Mr 31,19:2
On Borrowed Time 1939,Jl 7,13:2
Allegheny Uprising 1939,N 10,27:3
Earl of Chicago, The 1940,Mr 14,29:3
Earthbound 1940,Je 7,27:4
We Who Are Young 1940,S 13,27:2
Son of Monte Cristo, The 1940,D 5,33:1
Hudson's Bay 1941,Ja 10,23:2
Secret Agent of Japan 1942,Mr 23,19:3
Saboteur 1942,My 8,27:2
Great Commandment, The 1942,O 17,11:1
Moon Is Down, The 1943,Mr 27,8:6
Holy Matrimony 1943,S 16,25:2
Her Primitive Man 1944,Ap 1,11:1
Seven Days Ashore 1944,Ap 26,24:7
Scarlet Claw, The 1944,My 19,12:1
Are These our Parents? 1944,Ag 23,16:2
Merry Monahans, The 1944,O 13,16:2
Murder in the Blue Room 1944,O 28,12:2
Zombies on Broadway 1945,Ap 27,23:2
Counter-Attack 1945,My 17,15:2
Brighton Strangler, The 1945,My 19,15:2
Fighting Guardsman, The 1945,O 6,9:6
Confidential Agent 1945,N 3,11:2
Bandit of Sherwood Forest, The 1946,Mr 23,8:4
Bedlam 1946,Ap 20,16:4
Searching Wind, The 1946,Je 27,29:1
Falcon's Adventure, The 1946,D 14,19:2
That Way With Women 1947,F 15,20:4
Mr Blandings Builds his Dream House
1948,Mr 26,26:2
Julia Misbehaves 1948,O 8,30:2
Younger Brothers, The 1949,My 28,11:2
Judge Steps Out, The 1949,Je 3,21:4
Colorado Territory 1949,Je 25,8:6
They Live by Night 1949,N 4,33:2
Please Believe Me 1950,Je 12,19:4
Petty Girl, The 1950,Ag 18,17:2
Copper Canyon 1950,N 16,39:2
Emergency Wedding 1950,D 22,19:2
Magnificent Yankee, The 1951,Ja 19,21:2
Mask of the Avenger 1951,Je 27,25:2
Place in the Sun, A 1951,Ag 29,20:1
Here Comes the Groom 1951,S 21,19:2
On Dangerous Ground 1952,F 13,35:2
Captive City, The 1952,Mr 27,34:2
Julius Caesar 1953,Je 5,19:1
Scandal at Scourie 1953,Je 16,24:2
Houdini 1953,Jl 3,10:2
Actress, The 1953,O 13,34:1
Seven Brides for Seven Brothers 1954,Jl 23,8:3
Her Twelve Men 1954,Ag 12,23:2
Moonfleet 1955,Je 25,9:2
King's Thief, The 1955,Ag 13,7:2
Rebel without a Cause 1955,O 27,28:3
Sincerely Yours 1955,N 3,37:1
Court-Martial of Billy Mitchell, The
1955,D 23,14:2
Gaby 1956,My 10,26:3
Witness for the Prosecution 1958,F 7,16:1
Lost World, The 1960,Jl 14,23:1
All in a Nights Work 1961,Mr 23,28:1
Wonderful World of the Brothers Grimm, The
1962,Ag 8,35:1
Diary of a Madman 1963,Je 6,39:1
One Man's Way 1964,Mr 12,40:3
Games 1967,S 18,58:2

Wolfe, Jane
Woman Next Door, The 1919,My 19,20:5
Men, Women and Money 1919,Je 16,11:2
Behold my Wife 1920,O 11,19:3
Wolfe, Janet (Screenwriter)
Bed, The (The Divorce); Divorce, The (The Bed)
1955,Je 8,26:4
Wolfe, Lawrence
Chafed Elbows 1967,Ja 5,30:1
No More Excuses 1968,My 22,53:1
Wolfe, Patrick
Beach Red 1967,Ag 4,18:1
Wolfe, Winifred (Original Author)
Ask any Girl 1959,My 22,32:1
If a Man Answers 1962,N 22,43:1
Wolfert, Ira (Original Author)
Force of Evil 1948,D 27,16:2
American Guerrilla in the Philippines
1950,N 8,37:2
Wolfert, Ira (Screenwriter)
Force of Evil 1948,D 27,16:2
WOLFF
See Also WOLLF, WOOLF, WULFF, WOLF,
WOLFE
Wolff, Albert (Miscellaneous)
Itto 1936,Ja 29,15:5
Wolff, Carl Heinz (Director)
Kyritz-Pyritz 1932,Ag 9,20:5
Frau Lehmann's Toechter 1933,O 27,22:3
Heideschulmeister uwe Karsten 1934,Ap 14,18:3
Tante Gusti Kommandiert 1934,My 4,24:4
Wackere Schustermeister, Der 1936,Jl 7,22:4
Wolff, Carl Heinz (Original Author)
Lumpenball 1931,Ap 27,25:1
Wolff, Christian
Third Sex, The 1959,Mr 26,27:1
Wolff, David (Narrator)
Return to Life 1938,Ag 4,15:1
Wolff, David (Screenwriter)
Native Land 1942,My 12,16:3
Wolff, Frank
America America 1963,D 16,44:1
Salvatore Giuliano 1964,S 18,28:1
Situation Hopeless-But not Serious
1965,O 14,53:1
Judith 1966,Ja 21,22:1
Wolff, Gerry
Naked Among the Wolves 1967,Ap 19,54:7
Wolff, Guido
Amazon Trader, The 1956,N 17,17:6
Wolff, Harald
'Night Affair 1961,O 13,27:1
Umbrellas of Cherbourg, The; Parpapluis de
Cherbourg, Les 1964,D 17,50:1
Wolff, Lothar
Kampf, Der 1936,S 11,29:3
Wolff, Lothar (Miscellaneous)
Story of the Vatican, The 1941,S 20,11:3
Wolff, Lothar (Producer)
Martin Luther 1953,S 10,22:1
Question 7 1961,S 29,30:2
Wolff, Lothar (Screenwriter)
Martin Luther 1953,S 10,22:1
Animal Farm 1954,D 30,14:1
Wolff, Ludwig (Original Author)
Mysterious Lady, The 1928,Ag 6,15:2
Wolff, Maritta (Original Author)
Whistle Stop 1946,Mr 18,24:2
Man I Love, The 1947,Ja 25,12:2
Wolff, Perry (Producer)
Smashing of the Reich 1962,O 3,44:4
Kamikaze 1962,O 3,44:4
Wolff, Perry (Screenwriter)
Kamikaze 1962,O 3,44:4
Smashing of the Reich 1962,O 3,44:4
Wolff, Peter
Ich Geh' aus und Du Bleibst da 1932,N 21,21:1
Wolff, PEter
Hauptmann von Koepenick, Der 1933,Ja 17,22:6
Wolff, Pierre (Miscellaneous)
Man Who Seeks the Truth, The 1941,O 7,26:6
Wolff, Pierre (Original Author)
Abused Confidence 1938,D 1,29:1
Bring on the Girls 1945,Mr 1,25:5
Room Upstairs, The 1948,S 4,8:6
Wolff, Pierre (Screenwriter)
Schubert's Serenade 1940,S 3,21:2
Man Who Seeks the Truth, The 1941,O 7,26:6
She Returned at Dawn; Retour a l'Aube
1947,Ag 1,21:5
Wolff, Willi (Director)
Carnival Crime, The 1929,Jl 8,17:3
Theaternaechte von Berlin 1932,Ja 11,28:5
Ein Liebesroman im Hause Habsburg
1936,O 12,23:2
Wolff, Willi (Producer)
Ein Liebesroman im Hause Habsburg
1936,O 12,23:2
Wolff, Willy (Director)
Marquise von Pompadour, Die 1936,F 3,21:3
Wolfit, Donald
Pickwick Papers, The 1954,Ap 5,21:2
Svengali 1955,S 26,18:2

Prize of Gold, A 1955,O 15,19:2
Satellite in the Sky 1956,S 4,32:7
I Accuse! 1958,Mr 6,32:1
Room at the Top 1959,Mr 31,26:1
House of the Seven Hawks, The 1959,D 17,51:2
Mark, The 1961,O 3,46:2
Portrait of a Sinner 1961,D 7,52:1
Lawrence of Arabia 1962,D 17,5:6
Dr Crippen 1964,F 15,14:1
Becket 1964,Mr 12,40:2
Life at the Top 1965,D 15,53:1
90 Degrees in the Shade 1966,N 16,52:1
Wolfsen, P J (Screenwriter)
Lady Consents, The 1936,F 6,23:4
Wolfson, David
Fixed Bayonets 1951,N 21,20:2
Wolfson, Martin
Act One 1963,D 27,17:2
Wolfson, P J (Director)
Boy Slaves 1939,F 9,17:3
Wolfson, P J (Original Author)
Night World 1932,My 28,18:2
Lady Consents, The 1936,F 6,23:4
Public Enemy's Wife 1936,Jl 9,17:2
Bullets for O'Hara 1941,Jl 28,16:4
Suddenly It's Spring 1947,F 27,26:2
Perils of Pauline, The 1947,Jl 10,17:2
Wolfson, P J (Producer)
Mad Miss Manton, The 1938,O 21,27:2
Boy Slaves 1939,F 9,17:3
Allegheny Uprising 1939,N 10,27:3
My Kingdom for a Cook 1943,O 15,15:3
Saigon 1948,Ap 1,30:5
Dream Girl 1948,Je 17,29:2
Wolfson, P J (Screenwriter)
Reckless 1935,Ap 20,16:1
Mad Love 1935,Ag 5,20:2
Rendezvous 1935,O 26,12:2
Love on a Bet 1936,Mr 5,25:2
Bride Walks Out, The 1936,Jl 10,15:1
That Girl From Paris 1937,Ja 1,19:1
Sea Devils 1937,Mr 16,26:4
Vivacious Lady 1938,Je 3,17:3
Allegheny Uprising 1939,N 10,27:3
Vigil in the Night 1940,Mr 9,19:2
He Stayed for Breakfast 1940,Ag 31,16:2
This Thing Called Love 1941,F 14,15:2
Submarine Zone; (Escape To Glory)
1941,Ap 7,13:2
Our Wife 1941,S 18,31:1
Pacific Rendezvous 1942,Jl 8,27:4
They all Kissed the Bride 1942,Jl 31,11:1
Suddenly It's Spring 1947,F 27,26:2
Perils of Pauline, The 1947,Jl 10,17:2
Saigon 1948,Ap 1,30:5
Wolfson, Victor (Screenwriter)
Finest Hours, The 1964,N 11,38:1
Rings Around the World 1967,D 7,60:3
Wolfstone, Billy
Penrod and Sam 1937,Mr 29,14:3
Wolgers, Beppe
Hugo and Josephine 1968,S 30,60:1
Wolheim, Dan
East Side, West Side 1927,O 18,33:2
Tenderloin 1928,Mr 15,28:3
Across to Singapore 1928,Ap 30,18:3
Fleet's In, The 1928,O 1,23:1
Sal of Singapore 1929,Ja 29,27:1
Hollywood Cowboy 1937,Jl 24,12:1
Wolheim, Louis
Little Old New York 1923,Ag 2,10:3
Unseeing Eyes 1923,O 22,17:1
America 1924,F 22,20:1
Story Without a Name, The 1924,O 6,25:1
Two Arabian Knights 1927,O 24,24:3
Sorrell and Son 1927,N 14,26:1
Tempest 1928,My 18,27:3
Racket, The 1928,Jl 9,25:1
Awakening, The 1928,D 31,9:1
Wolf Song 1929,F 25,16:1
Shady Lady, The 1929,Mr 25,32:2
Frozen Justice 1929,O 26,15:1
Condemned 1929,N 4,28:1
Ship From Shanghai, The 1930,Ap 26,11:1
All Quiet on The Western Front 1930,Ap 30,29:1
Silver Horde, The 1930,O 25,20:6
Danger Lights 1930,D 15,29:1
Gentleman's Fate 1931,Je 27,20:3
Wolkoff, Alexander (Director)
White Devil, The 1931,Ag 28,20:1
Secrets of the Orient 1932,Ja 4,27:3
Wolkonsky, Vadim
Dolce Vita, La 1961,Ap 20,30:1
Pigeon That Took Rome, The 1962,Ag 23,25:1
Woll
Battle of the Rails; (Bataille Du Rail)
1949,D 27,27:2
Wolle, Gertrud
Drei von ver Tankstelle, Die 1931,Je 20,20:4
Wahre Jakob, Der 1931,Ag 7,20:2
Annemarie, Die Braut der Kompanie
1934,D 8,18:6
Heisses Blut 1936,S 26,11:2

Wolle, Gertrud— Cont
Anton der Letzte; Anthony the Last
1940,Mr 30,11:2
Devil Makes Three, The 1952,Ag 30,6:2
Wollejko, Czeslaw
Young Chopin 1952,D 25,34:7
WOLLF
See Also WOOLF, WULFF, WOLF, WOLFE,
WOLFF
Wollf (Original Author)
Madame la Presidente 1916,F 7,9:3
Woloshin, Alex
His Private Life 1928,N 12,18:2
Case of Lena Smith, The 1929,Ja 15,22:4
Spawn of the North 1938,S 8,27:1
Wolper, David L (Producer)
Devil's Brigade, The 1968,My 23,56:2
Wolpert, Stanley (Original Author)
Nine Hours to Rama 1963,Ap 4,58:2
Wolston, Henry
Girl in the Street 1938,My 26,31:2
WOLTER
See Also WALTER, WALTHER
Wolter, Martha
Kuhle Wampe 1933,Ap 24,11:4
Wolter, Ralf
One, Two, Three 1961,D 22,17:1
Wolter, U (Original Author)
I Aim at the Stars 1960,O 20,42:2
Wolveridge, Carol
1984 1956,O 1,31:1
Wonacott, Edna May
Shadow of a Doubt 1943,Ja 13,18:2
Wonder, Tommy
Dance Charlie Dance 1937,Ag 26,25:2
Thrill of a Lifetime 1937,D 9,30:2
Gangster's Boy 1938,N 7,23:6
This Time for Keeps 1947,D 5,33:4
Wonderly, Frank
Great White Way, The 1924,Ja 4,10:1
Wonderly, W Carey (Miscellaneous)
That Girl From Paris 1937,Ja 1,19:1
Wonderly, W Carey (Original Author)
Broadway Gold 1923,Jl 31,12:4
Wong, Anna May
Bits of Life 1921,O 17,18:1
Toll of the Sea, The 1922,N 27,18:1
Thief of Bagdad, The 1924,Mr 19,19:1
Alaskan, The 1924,S 15,28:1
Peter Pan 1924,D 29,11:4
Forty Winks 1925,F 3,24:1
Mr Wu 1927,My 16,24:2
Old San Francisco 1927,Je 23,23.3
Devil Dancer, The 1927,D 19,30:1
Chinese Parrot, The 1928,Ja 2,28:1
Song 1928,Ag 22,24:2
Piccadilly 1929,Jl 15,25:1
Wasted Love 1929,D 30,16:4
Flame of Love, The 1930,Mr 23,IX,6:1
Flame of Love, The 1930,N 3,19:3
Amour Maitre des Choses, L' 1931,Mr 30,25:2
Daughter of the Dragon 1931,Ag 22,7:5
Shanghai Express 1932,F 18,25:3
Study in Scarlet, A 1933,Je 1,15:3
Chu Chin Chow 1934,S 22,12:2
Limehouse Blues 1934,D 12,28:2
Java Head 1935,Jl 31,21:4
Daughter of Shanghai 1937,D 24,21:2
Dangerous to Know 1938,Mr 11,15:4
When Were You Born? 1938,Je 9,27:2
King of Chinatown 1939,Mr 16,27:2
Ellery Queen's Penthouse Mystery
1941,Mr 7,17:2
Bombs Over Burma 1942,Ag 10,15:2
Impact 1949,Mr 21,19:2
Portrait in Black 1960,Jl 28,19:1
Wong, Barbara Jean
China 1943,Ap 22,31:2
Love Is a Many-Splendored Thing
1955,Ag 19,10:1
Wong, Beal
Purple Heart, The 1944,Mr 9,15:2
Samurai 1945,Ag 25,7:5
Wong, Bruce
Time to Kill 1942,D 25,15:4
Wong, Iris
Charlie Chan in Reno 1939,My 31,27:2
China 1943,Ap 22,31:2
Behind the Rising Sun 1943,O 14,26:2
Wong, Joe
Fancy Pants 1950,Ag 31,21:2
Wong, Linda
Five Gates to Hell 1959,D 10,51:6
Horizontal Lieutenant, The 1962,My 12,15:3
Wong, Mary
Good Earth, The 1937,F 3,27:1
Wong, P
Fight to the Last 1938,D 22,25:3
Wong, Victor
War Correspondent 1932,Ag 13,18:6
Son of Kong 1933,D 30,9:2
Shadows Over Shanghai 1938,D 1,29:2
Phantom Submarine, The 1941,F 12,25:3

Wong, Wing Mrs
East of Suez 1925,Ja 26,22:1
Wontner, Arthur
Sherlock Holmes's Fatal Hour 1931,Jl 13,13:5
Missing Rembrandt, The 1932,Mr 26,17:2
Condemned to Death 1932,Jl 14,24:2
Sign of the Four, The 1932,Ag 20,7:4
Triumph of Sherlock Holmes, The
1935,My 27,20:6
Thunder in the City 1937,Ap 23,25:2
Storm in a Teacup 1938,Mr 22,18:4
Queen of Crime 1938,Mr 19,25:2
Blanche Fury 1948,N 24,20:2
Brandy for the Parson 1952,Ag 18,13:4
Sea Devils 1953,Jl 31,11:5
Genevieve 1954,F 16,30:2
Three Cases of Murder (Lord Mountdrago); Lord
Mountdrago (Three Cases of Murder)
1955,Mr 16,39:4
Woo, W L (Cinematographer)
Fight to the Last 1938,D 22,25:3
Wood, A H (Original Author)
Lonely Wives 1931,Mr 16,25:1
Law of the Underworld 1938,Ap 28,27:2
Wood, A Voorhes
Prunelia 1918,Je 3,9:3
Wood, Allen
From Hell to Heaven 1933,Mr 18,9:3
Buck Benny Rides Again 1940,Ap 25,28:4
Wood, Brendan (Original Author)
Bowery Blitzkrieg 1941,O 1,24:5
Wood, Britt
Return of the Frontiersman 1950,Je 10,11:3
Wood, C
Should a Doctor Tell 1931,Ag 22,7:5
Wood, Cecelia
River, The 1951,S 11,33:2
Wood, Charles
Fame Is the Spur 1949,N 8,34:2
Wood, Charles (Screenwriter)
Knack...and how to get it, The 1965,Je 30,42:1
Help! 1965,Ag 24,25:1
How I Won the War 1967,N 9,56:1
Long Day's Dying, The 1968,My 29,20:1
Charge of the Light Brigade, The 1968,O 7,59:1
Wood, Cindi
Great Impostor, The 1961,Mr 30,24:1
Hoodlum Priest, The 1961,Ap 3,28:5
Wood, Clement (Screenwriter)
Barbarella 1968,O 12,43:1
Wood, David King
Unholy Four, The 1954,N 20,10:2
Wood, Diane
Prison Farm 1938,Jl 15,13:3
Wood, Donna
Pot o'Gold 1941,Ap 4,25:2
Wood, Dorothy
Daughters of Today 1924,Mr 4,17:1
Wood, Douglas
Bottoms Up 1934,Mr 23,29:2
Trumpet Blows, The 1934,Ap 14,18:2
Fountain, The 1934,Ag 31,14:1
President Vanishes, The 1934,D 8,18:5
Wedding Night, The 1935,Mr 16,19:1
Dangerous 1935,D 27,14:1
Prisoner of Shark Island, The 1936,F 13,25:2
Dracula's Daughter 1936,My 18,14:2
Parole 1936,Je 27,21:1
Great Guy 1937,Ja 1,19:2
On the Avenue 1937,F 5,17:3
This Is my Affair 1937,My 28,17:1
Over the Goal 1937,O 16,22:2
Dangerously Yours 1937,O 18,14:2
West of Shanghai 1937,O 29,19:2
I Am the Law 1938,Ag 26,14:2
Off the Record 1939,F 18,12:2
East Side of Heaven 1939,My 5,29:3
Eternally Yours 1939,O 7,11:2
20,000 Men a Year 1939,O 28,11:2
Man Who Wouldn't Talk, The 1940,Ja 12,13:3
Dr Ehrlich's Magic Bullet 1940,F 24,9:2
Private Affairs 1940,Jl 5,10:3
Honky Tonk 1941,O 3,27:3
H M Pulham, Esq 1941,D 19,35:1
Murder in the Big House 1942,My 8,27:3
Parachute Nurse 1942,Jl 27,18:2
What a Woman 1943,D 3,27:2
Adventures of Mark Twain, The 1944,My 4,25:5
Because of Him 1946,Ja 25,26:6
My Wild Irish Rose 1947,D 25,32:2
Petty Girl, The 1950,Ag 18,17:2
Harriet Craig 1950,N 3,31:2
Wood, Edna
Wanted for Murder 1946,D 12,38:4
Wood, Ellie
New Interns, The 1964,Ag 20,34:2
Wood, Ernest
Passionate Youth 1925,Je 30,14:3
Certain Young Man, A 1928,Je 11,27:1
Take Me Home 1928,O 23,33:1
June Moon 1931,Mr 14,23:2
Annabelle's Affairs 1931,Je 29,20:3
Sob Sister 1931,O 3,20:2

Ambassador Bill 1931,N 14,15:3
Parole Girl 1933,Ap 10,8:2
Bedtime Story, A 1933,Ap 20,20:3
Call it Luck 1934,Jl 10,24:5
Roaring Timber 1937,Ag 19,23:1
Wood, Freeman
Divorce 1923,Je 26,14:2
Fashion Row 1924,Ja 28,12:1
Female, The 1924,S 2,19:2
Price She Paid, The 1925,Ja 13,16:1
Dancers, The 1925,Ja 26,22:1
Wings of Youth 1925,Ap 20,18:1 (Incorrect in
this edition; use 1925,Ap 28,18:1 elsewhere)
Mannequinn 1926,Ja 12,27:5
Social Celebrity, A 1926,Ap 19,24:3
Taxi, Taxi 1927,F 15,23:1
Legion of the Condemned, The 1928,Mr 19,26:2
Garden of Eden, The 1928,Mr 19,26:2
Chinatown Nights 1929,Ap 1,22:1
Why Bring That Up? 1929,O 5,22:5
Lilies of the Field 1930,F 22,13:1
Young Eagles 1930,Mr 22,22:6
Ladies in Love 1930,Je 14,9:4
Kept Husbands 1931,Mr 24,31:2
Lady With a Past 1932,F 22,23:2
Wood, Gar
Abbott and Costello Meet the Killer Boris Karloff
1949,S 19,18:3
Wood, Gloria
Gaby 1956,My 10,26:3
Wood, Helen
My Marriage 1936,F 22,12:2
Champagne Charlie 1936,My 7,21:2
High Tension 1936,Jl 11,11:4
Charlie Chan at the Race Track 1936,Ag 15,6:2
Crack-Up 1937,Ja 4,20:2
Wood, Henry Mrs (Original Author)
East Lynne 1931,F 21,15:2
Wood, John
Last Days of Pompeii, The 1935,O 17,29:2
Housemaster 1939,Ap 10,13:2
Wood, Judith
Road to Reno, The 1931,O 10,20:4
Girls About Town 1931,N 2,27:1
Advice to the Lovelorn 1933,D 14,28:2
Looking for Trouble 1934,Ap 12,27:2
Crime Doctor, The 1934,My 11,24:3
Wood, Lana
Searchers, The 1956,My 31,21:4
For Singles Only 1968,Je 6,54:1
Wood, Leslie (Screenwriter)
Lilli Marlene 1952,Mr 29,19:2
Wood, Lynn
Jumbo 1962,D 7,49:1
Wood, Marjorie
Pride and Prejudice 1940,Ag 9,19:1
Excuse my Dust 1951,Je 28,21:2
Seven Brides for Seven Brothers 1954,Jl 23,8:3
Wood, Mary Laura
Valley of the Eagles 1952,Ap 11,19:2
Raising a Riot 1957,My 8,44:1
Scent of Mystery 1960,F 19,23:1
Wood, Montgomery
Pistol for Ringo, A 1966,N 3,45:4
Wood, Natalie
Tomorrow Is Forever 1946,F 22,21:2
Bride Wore Boots, The 1946,Je 6,16:3
Miracle on 34th Street 1947,Je 5,32:1
Ghost and Mrs Muir, The 1947,Je 27,17:2
Scudda-Hoo! Scudda-Hay! 1948,Ap 15,31:1
Chicken every Sunday 1949,Ja 19,34:2
Green Promise, The 1949,Je 24,29:2
Father Was a Fullback 1949,O 13,33:3
No Sad Songs for Me 1950,Ap 28,26:2
Our Very Own 1950,Jl 28,12:5
Never a Dull Moment 1950,N 22,20:2
Jackpot, The 1950,N 23,55:2
Dear Brat 1951,Jl 5,21:2
Blue Veil, The 1951,O 27,10:5
Just for You 1952,O 9,40:6
Star, The 1953,Ja 29,25:1
Silver Chalice, The 1954,D 27,22:5
One Desire 1955,S 3,9:1
Rebel without a Cause 1955,O 27,28:3
Searchers, The 1956,My 31,21:4
Burning Hills, The 1956,Ag 24,15:2
Cry in the Night, A 1956,S 1,19:4
Girl He Left Behind, The 1956,O 27,17:1
Bombers B-52 1957,N 23,11:2
Marjorie Morningstar 1958,Ap 25,32:2
Kings Go Forth 1958,Jl 4,15:2
Cash McCall 1960,Ja 28,26:1
All the Fine Young Cannibals 1960,S 23,33:1
Splendor in the Grass 1961,O 11,53:1
West Side Story 1961,O 19,39:3
Gypsy 1962,N 2,24:1
Love with the Proper Stranger 1963,D 26,33:1
Sex and the Single Girl 1964,D 26,9:2
Great Race, The 1965,S 16,00:0
Inside Daisy Clover 1966,F 18,23:1
This Property is Condemned 1966,Ag 4,24:1
Penelope 1966,N 11,36:6

Wood, Pamela
Macushla 1940,Ja 6,9:2
Wood, Peggy
Almost a Husband 1919,O 13,16:3
Wonder of Women 1929,Jl 22,17:1
Handy Andy 1934,Ag 4,14:5
Right to Live, The 1935,F 16,9:1
Jalna 1935,S 14,8:4
Star Is Born, A 1937,Ap 23,25:1
Call it a Day 1937,My 7,29:2
Housekeeper's Daughter, The 1939,D 2,21:4
Bride Wore Boots, The 1946,Je 6,16:3
Magnificent Doll 1946,D 9,34:2
Dream Girl 1948,Je 17,29:2
Story of Ruth, The 1960,Je 18,12:3
Sound of Music, The 1965,Mr 3,34:1
Wood, Philip
Room Service 1938,S 22,27:1
Our Town 1940,Je 14,25:3
Wood, Richard Carver (Director)
Unconquered, The; (Helen Keller in Her Story)
1954,Je 16,37:1
Wood, Robert
Whispering Smith 1949,F 15,28:2
Wood, Roland
Tiger Makes Out, The 1967,S 19,53:1
Wood, Sam (Director)
Double Speed 1920,F 2,10:1
Dancin' Fool, The 1920,My 3,18:1
What's Your Hurry? 1920,Ag 16,8:2
Peck's bad Boy 1921,Ap 25,9:2
Great Moment, The 1921,Jl 25,8:3
Don't Tell Everything 1921,D 12,20:2
Beyond the Rocks 1922,My 8,14:3
Impossible Mrs Bellew, The 1922,O 23,10:1
Prodigal Daughters 1923,Ap 17,26:3
Bluff 1924,Ap 28,18:2
Female, The 1924,S 2,19:2
Fascinating Youth 1926,My 10,19:1
One Minute to Play 1926,S 6,16:2
Rookies 1927,Ap 25,20:4
Fair Co-ed, The 1927,O 24,24:3
Latest From Paris, The 1928,F 27,16:2
So This Is College 1929,N 9,22:5
It's a Great Life 1930,Ja 18,21:1
Girl Said No, The 1930,Ap 5,23:3
Sins of the Children 1930,Jl 26,16:4
Way for a Sailor 1930,D 13,22:2
Paid 1931,Ja 3,21:2
Tailor-Made Man, A 1931,Ap 25,23:4
Man in Possession, The 1931,Jl 18,16:6
New Adventures of Get-Rich-Quick Wallingford
1931,O 10,20:4
Huddle 1932,Je 17,24:1
Prosperity 1932,N 26,11:4
Barbarian, The 1933,My 13,16:2
Hold Your Man 1933,Jl 1,16:6
Christopher Bean 1933,N 25,10:2
Stamboul Quest 1934,Jl 14,16:6
Let 'Em Have It 1935,My 30,21:1
Night at the Opera, A 1935,D 7,22:1
Whipsaw 1936,Ja 25,18:4
Unguarded Hour, The 1936,Ap 4,11:1
Day at the Races, A 1937,Je 18,25:2
Madame X 1937,O 25,23:1
Navy Blue and Gold 1937,D 24,21:2
Lord Jeff 1938,Jl 1,22:2
Stablemates 1938,O 21,27:2
Goodbye Mr Chips 1939,My 16,27:2
Raffles 1940,Ja 13,11:2
Our Town 1940,Je 14,25:3
Rangers of Fortune 1940,S 19,27:2
Kitty Foyle 1941,Ja 9,27:2
Devil and Miss Jones, The 1941,My 16,21:2
Kings Row 1942,F 3,23:2
Pride of the Yankees, The 1942,Jl 16,23:1
For Whom the Bell Tolls 1943,Jl 15,25:2
Casanova Brown 1944,S 15,16:1
Guest Wife 1945,O 18,21:2
Saratoga Trunk 1945,N 22,39:2
Heartbeat 1946,My 11,22:4
Ivy 1947,Je 26,19:1
Command Decision 1949,Ja 20,34:2
Stratton Story, The 1949,My 13,29:1
Ambush 1950,Ja 19,35:2
Wood, Sam (Producer)
For Whom the Bell Tolls 1943,Jl 15,25:2
Ivy 1947,Je 26,19:1
Wood, Victor
Moss Rose 1947,Jl 3,14:2
If Winter Comes 1948,Ja 23,28:4
Iron Curtain, The 1948,My 13,31:2
Hills of Home 1948,N 26,32:2
Kind Lady 1951,Ag 8,21:2
My Cousin Rachel 1952,D 26,20:2
Scandal at Scourie 1953,Je 16,24:2
Wood, Walter (Producer)
Hoodlum Priest, The 1961,Ap 3,28:5
Escape from East Berlin 1962,D 6,55:3
Wood, Walter A Lieut Col (Miscellaneous)
Annapurna 1953,D 14,45:4

Wood, Ward
Air Force 1943,F 4,29:1
Proud and Profane, The 1956,Je 14,41:2
Wood, Wilson
Show-Off, The 1947,Mr 20,38:2
High Tide 1947,N 8,11:2
Barkleys of Broadway, The 1949,My 5,34:2
Jumbo 1962,D 7,49:1
Woodard, Horace (Cinematographer)
Adventures of Chico, The 1938,F 26,9:2
Woodard, Horace (Director)
Adventures of Chico, The 1938,F 26,9:2
Woodard, Horace (Producer)
Adventures of Chico, The 1938,F 26,9:2
Woodard, Horace (Screenwriter)
Adventures of Chico, The 1938,F 26,9:2
Woodard, Stacy (Cinematographer)
River, The 1938,F 5,19:2 (In Addenda)
Adventures of Chico, The 1938,F 26,9:2
Woodard, Stacy (Director)
Adventures of Chico, The 1938,F 26,9:2
Woodard, Stacy (Producer)
Adventures of Chico, The 1938,F 26,9:2
Woodard, Stacy (Screenwriter)
Adventures of Chico, The 1938,F 26,9:2
Woodbridge, George
Tower of Terror 1942,Je 29,11:4
Escape 1948,Ag 16,12:2
Blanche Fury 1948,N 24,20:2
Fallen Idol, The 1949,N 16,39:2
Silent Dust 1949,D 30,13:2
Murder in the Cathedral 1952,Mr 26,35:2
Naked Heart, The 1955,Mr 9,22:4
Richard III 1956,Mr 12,1:4
Novel Affair, A 1957,Ag 28,22:1
Horror of Dracula 1958,My 29,24:4
Two-Way Stretch 1961,Ja 24,20:3
Heavens Above! 1963,My 21,28:2
Woodbridge, John
Robby 1968,Ag 15,46:3
Woodburn, Eric
Brave Don't Cry, The 1952,N 6,37:2
Little Kidnappers, The 1954,S 2,18:1
Battle of the Sexes, The 1960,Ap 19,40:4
Trial and Error 1962,N 17,17:2
Woodburn, James
Chinese Den 1941,Mr 26,27:3
Brothers, The 1948,My 5,30:4
Tight Little Island 1949,D 26,33:2
Woodbury, Joan
There Goes my Girl 1937,Je 12,8:2
Super-Sleuth 1937,Jl 17,18:1
Forty Naughty Girls 1937,S 18,15:3
Charlie Chan on Broadway 1937,S 20,19:1
Crashing Hollywood 1938,Ja 8,19:2
Algiers 1938,Jl 15,13:2
Passport Husband 1938,Ag 5,11:2
Always in Trouble 1938,N 3,27:1
Cipher Bureau 1938,D 14,32:6
While New York Sleeps 1938,D 22,25:3
Gangs Incorporated 1941,Ag 4,16:6
Confessions of Boston Blackie 1941,D 8,31:2
Dr Broadway 1942,Je 25,27:3
Hard Way, The 1943,Mr 13,9:2
Desperadoes, The 1943,My 13,17:2
Whistler, The 1944,Ap 29,12:2
Bring on the Girls 1945,Mr 1,25:5
Arnelo Affair, The 1947,S 13,8:5
Here Comes Trouble 1948,Ap 15,31:4
Woodbury, Woody
For Those Who Think Young 1964,Jl 9,27:1
Woode, Margo
Bullfighters, The 1945,My 12,10:3
Somewhere in the Night 1946,Je 13,24:2
It Shouldn't Happen to a Dog 1946,S 7,11:2
Moss Rose 1947,Jl 3,14:2
No Sad Songs for Me 1950,Ap 28,26:2
Woode, Metcalfe (Original Author)
Choosing a Wife 1919,Ag 11,9:1
Woodell, Barbara
Samurai 1945,Ag 25,7:5
Framed 1947,My 26,24:2
Force of Evil 1948,D 27,16:2
State Department-File 649 1949,F 21,20:2
I Shot Jesse James 1949,Ap 2,12:2
Baron of Arizona, The 1950,Je 23,29:2
Star, The 1953,Ja 29,25:1
Woodford, John
Success 1923,Jl 10,22:5
Woodhouse, Hugh (Screenwriter)
Nearly a Nasty Accident 1962,Je 28,21:2
Woodman, Martyn
All at Sea 1957,D 23,18:2
Woodman, Ruth
Man in Grey, The 1945,N 30,18:6
Woodruff, Bert
Greased Lightning 1919,Ap 28,13:2
Bill Henry 1919,Ag 18,9:2
Isle of Lost Ships, The 1923,My 14,18:2
Flowing Gold 1924,Mr 10,18:2
Sea Hawk, The 1924,Je 3,22:1
Worldly Goods 1924,N 3,20:1
Siren of Seville, The 1924,N 17,16:1 (In Addenda)

Paths to Paradise 1925,Je 30,14:3
Vanishing American, The 1925,O 16,18:2
Barrier, The 1926,Mr 22,16:1
Fire Brigade, The 1926,D 21,20:2
Life of Riley, The 1927,S 5,13:2
Spring Fever 1927,O 18,33:2
Speedy 1928,Ap 7,20:4
River, The 1928,D 24,11:1
Laughing Sinners 1931,Jl 4,11:5
Woodruff, Frank (Director)
Curtain Call 1940,Ap 19,25:2
Cross Country Romance 1940,Jl 19,22:3
Play Girl 1941,Ja 30,19:3
Lady Scarface 1941,Ag 4,16:6
Cowboy in Manhattan 1943,My 28,19:2
Two Señoritas From Chicago 1943,Ag 6,10:4
Pistol Packin' Mama 1943,D 20,27:4
Woodruff, Lewis B Mrs (Original Author)
Lady of the Light House, The 1915,Ap 6,4:3
Woodruff, Richard
Thunder Birds 1942,O 29,19:2
Woods, Alfred
Abdul the Damned 1936,My 11,16:2
Woods, Arthur
Lost Patrol, The 1929,D 16,34:2
Woods, Arthur (Director)
Spy 77 1936,F 10,15:1
Woods, ARthur (Director)
Haunted Honeymoon 1940,O 31,28:2
Woods, Arthur (Original Author)
Spy 77 1936,F 10,15:1
Woods, Arthur (Screenwriter)
Spy 77 1936,F 10,15:1
Red Wagon 1936,Je 22,22:1
Woods, Aubrey
Nicholas Nickleby 1947,D 1,27:2
Detective, The 1954,N 2,25:2
Woods, Craig
Destroyer 1943,S 2,15:3
Angel and the Badman 1947,Mr 3,28:4
Woods, Donald
As the Earth Turns 1934,Ap 12,27:2
Fog over Frisco 1934,Je 7,26:2
She Was a Lady 1934,Ag 22,21:2
Charlie Chan's Courage 1934,Ag 25,16:6
Sweet Adeline 1935,Ja 7,13:2
Case of the Curious Bride, The 1935,Ap 5,21:3
Florentine Dagger, The 1935,Ap 27,20:6
Stranded 1935,Je 20,16:2
Frisco Kid 1935,N 25,22:1
Tale of Two Cities, A 1935,D 26,21:2
Story of Louis Pasteur, The 1936,F 10,15:1
Road Gang 1936,F 24,14:1
White Angel, The 1936,Je 25,24:1
Anthony Adverse 1936,Ag 27,16:1
Son Comes Home, A 1936,S 5,7:1
Talent Scout 1937,Ag 20,21:3
Charlie Chan on Broadway 1937,S 20,19:1
Big Town Girl 1937,D 13,23:4
Black Doll, The 1938,F 7,10:2
Beauty for the Asking 1939,F 10,19:1
Girl From Mexico, The 1939,Je 8,31:4
Mexican Spitfire 1940,Ja 10,16:4
City of Chance 1940,Ja 22,11:3
If I Had my Way 1940,My 6,13:2
Mexican Spitfire out West 1940,O 30,29:3
I Was a Prisoner on Devil's Island
 1941,Jl 28,16:4
Gay Sisters, The 1942,Ag 15,14:2
Corregidor 1943,My 28,19:2
Watch on the Rhine 1943,Ag 28,15:1
Bridge of San Luis Rey, The 1944,Mr 4,11:1
Enemy of Women 1944,S 12,23:6
Hollywood Canteen 1944,D 16,19:2
Roughly Speaking 1945,F 1,18:4
Wonder Man 1945,Je 9,17:2
Never Say Goodbye 1946,N 23,12:2
Time, The Place And The Girl, The
 1946,D 27,14:3
Scene of the Crime 1949,Jl 29,12:2
Barbary Pirate 1949,O 28,29:3
Johnny One-Eye 1950,N 17,31:2
Mr Music 1950,D 21,34:3
Beast From 20,000 Fathoms, The 1953,Je 25,23:1
13 Ghosts 1960,Ag 6,9:2
Woods, Edward
Mothers Cry 1930,D 6,21:3
Public Enemy, The 1931,Ap 24,27:1
Local Boy Makes Good 1931,N 27,29:3
They Never Come Back 1932,Je 4,9:2
Hot Saturday 1932,N 5,12:5
Bondage 1933,Ap 24,11:3
Tarzan, The Fearless 1933,Ag 12,14:3
Dinner at Eight 1933,Ag 24,18:1
Beloved 1934,Ja 27,9:3
Shadows Over Shanghai 1938,D 1,29:2
Woods, Ernest
Washington Merry-Go-Round 1932,O 24,18:5
Woods, Frank (Screenwriter)
Old Homestead, The 1922,O 9,10:2

Woods, Franker
Hit the Deck 1930,Ja 15,28:6
Woods, Harry
Cafe in Cairo, A 1925,Mr 18,19:2
Jesse James 1927,O 17,20:2
Viking, The 1928,N 29,32:4
Palmy Days 1931,S 24,21:2
Monkey Business 1931,O 8,22:6
Law and Order 1932,F 29,21:3
Night World 1932,My 28,18:2
Radio Patrol 1932,Jl 14,24:2
Devil Tiger 1934,F 9,23:2
Shadows of Sing Sing 1934,F 21,23:2
Circus Clown, The 1934,Je 30,18:6
Belle of the Nineties 1934,S 22,12:2
St Louis Kid, The 1934,N 1,25:2
President Vanishes, The 1934,D 8,18:5
When a Man's a Man 1935,F 22,27:2
Rose of the Rancho 1936,Ja 9,25:2
Robin Hood of El Dorado, The 1936,Mr 14,10:1
Silly Billies 1936,Ap 6,18:1
Lawless Nineties, The 1936,Je 29,11:1
Conflict 1937,Ja 18,21:2
I Promise to Pay 1937,Ap 26,15:2
Crime Takes a Holiday 1938,N 28,11:2
Union Pacific 1939,My 11,31:2
Frontier Marshal 1939,Jl 29,18:2
Beau Geste 1939,Ag 3,15:2
Isle of Destiny 1940,Ap 8,15:2
West of Carson City 1940,My 7,31:3
South of Pago-Pago 1940,Ag 2,12:2
Tall in the Saddle 1944,D 15,25:3
West of the Pecos 1945,Ag 11,14:6
Wanderer of the Wasteland 1945,S 29,12:2
Trail Street 1947,Ap 10,35:2
Wyoming 1947,Jl 25,12:5
Tycoon 1947,D 26,22:6
Hellfire 1949,My 30,9:4
Colorado Territory 1949,Je 25,8:6
Fountainhead, The 1949,Jl 9,8:5
She Wore a Yellow Ribbon 1949,N 18,35:2
Short Grass 1951,Ja 13,10:4
Lone Star 1952,F 2,11:4
Woods, Harry M (Composer)
Evergreen 1935,Ja 11,29:1
Jack Ahoy 1935,F 9,11:2
It's Love Again 1936,My 23,12:1
Woods, Middleton
Indiscreet 1958,Je 27,18:2
Woods, T Frank (Producer)
Tall Texan, The 1953,Ap 13,32:4
Angel Baby 1961,O 5,43:1
Woods, Walter (Screenwriter)
Life of the Party, The 1920,N 22,13:3
One Glorious Day 1922,Ja 30,16:2
Is Matrimony a Failure 1922,Ap 17,22:3
Dictator, The 1922,Jl 3,8:6
Thirty Days 1922,D 11,22:1
Sutter's Gold 1936,Mr 27,25:2
Woods, William (Original Author)
Edge of Darkness 1943,Ap 10,12:4
Stowaway Girl 1957,N 6,43:3
Woods, William (Screenwriter)
Stowaway Girl 1957,N 6,43:3
My Six Loves 1963,Ap 4,58:4
Lively Set, The 1964,O 15,54:1
Woodson, William
One and Only Genuine Original Family Band,
 The 1968,Mr 22,55:1
Woodson, William (Narrator)
We'll Bury You 1962,O 25,48:3
Woodston, Ellen
So This Is London 1930,My 24,21:2
Woodsworth, Marjory
Double Life, A 1948,F 20,19:1
Woodthorpe, Georgia
Daddies 1924,F 11,18:3
Woodthorpe, Peter
Evil of Frankenstein, The 1964,Je 18,29:2
Woodville, Catherine
Young and Willing 1964,F 27,28:1
Underworld Informers 1965,O 14,53:1
Woodward, Henry
Last of the Mohicans, The 1921,Ja 3,20:2
Woodward, Joanne
Three Faces of Eve, The 1957,S 27,16:6
No Down Payment 1957,O 31,41:1
Long, Hot Summer, The 1958,Ap 4,16:1
Rally Round the Flag Boys! 1958,D 24,2:7
Sound and the Fury, The 1959,Mr 28,11:1
Fugitive Kind, The 1960,Ap 15,13:1
From the Terrace 1960,Jl 16,10:1
Paris Blues 1961,N 8,41:1
Stripper, The 1963,Je 20,29:1
New Kind of Love, A 1963,O 31,26:2
Signpost to Murder 1965,My 20,52:2
Big Hand for the Little Lady, A 1966,Je 9,54:2
Fine Madness, A 1966,Je 30,28:2
Rachel Rachel 1968,Ag 27,36:1
Woodward, Morgan
Cool Hand Luke 1967,N 2,58:1

Woodward, Neil
Two Loves 1961,Je 22,23:2
Woodward, W E (Original Author)
Evelyn Prentice 1934,N 10,19:1
Stronger Than Desire 1939,Je 30,17:3
Woodworth, Jane
Powder Town 1942,Je 8,11:2
Woodworth, Marjorie
Road Show 1941,F 19,25:2
Broadway Limited 1941,Je 16,11:6
Devil With Hitler, The 1942,O 19,15:2
Prairie Chickens 1943,Jl 9,21:6
Wave, A Wac and a Marine, A 1944,Ag 14,11:4
Salty O'Rourke 1945,Ap 26,26:2
Woodworth, Truman
Reluctant Dragon, The 1941,Jl 25,12:2
Woody, Jack
Thunder Over the Plains 1953,D 10,64:4
Woog, Robert (Producer)
Affaire, L' 1950,N 13,23:2
Strollers, The 1952,Jl 22,22:7
Woog (Cinematographer)
Sorciere, La 1956,D 28,17:2
Woog (Producer)
Love and the Frenchwoman; (Francaise et l'Amour, La) 1961,F 28,38:2
Wooland, Norman
Escape 1948,Ag 16,12:2
Hamlet 1948,S 30,32:2
All Over the Town 1949,My 26,34:4
Madeleine 1950,S 1,17:2
Quo Vadis 1951,N 9,22:2
Angel With the Trumpet 1951,D 21,21:5
Ivanhoe 1952,Ag 1,8:2
Edge of Divorce 1954,Jl 2,10:1
Romeo and Juliet 1954,D 22,28:1
Richard III 1956,Mr 12,1:4
Guns of Navarone, The 1961,Je 23,19:1
Portrait of a Sinner 1961,D 7,52:1
Barabbas 1962,O 11,49:1
Fall of the Roman Empire, The 1964,Mr 27,14:2
Walk in the Shadow 1966,S 12,52:5
Wooley, Sheb
Rocky Mountain 1950,N 4,13:2
Inside the Walls of Folsom Prison 1951,My 28,17:4
High Noon 1952,Jl 25,14:2
WOOLF
See Also WULFF, WOLF, WOLFE, WOLFF, WOLLF
Woolf, Edgar Allan (Original Author)
Broadway to Hollywood 1933,S 2,14:4
Everybody Sing 1938,Mr 11,15:3
What's Cookin' 1942,F 26,15:5
Woolf, Edgar Allan (Screenwriter)
Night is Young, The 1935,Ja 14,11:2
Casino Murder Case, The 1935,Ap 17,26:5
Moonlight Murder 1936,Mr 28,11:2
Mad Holiday 1936,N 26,39:2
Everybody Sing 1938,Mr 11,15:3
Ice Follies of 1939 1939,Mr 17,25:2
Wizard of Oz, The 1939,Ag 18,16:2
Woolf, Edgar Allen (Original Author)
Tough Guy 1936,Mr 14,10:1
Woolf, Edgar Allen (Screenwriter)
Tough Guy 1936,Mr 14,10:1
Woolf, Gabriel
Tom Brown's School Days 1952,Ja 8,23:5
Knights of the Round Table 1954,Ja 8,17:2
Woolf, Henry
Persecution and Assassination of Jean-Paul Marat as Performed by the Inmates of the Asylum of Charenton Under the Direction of the Marquis De Sade, The 1967,F 23,41:1
Woolf, James (Producer)
Room at the Top 1959,Mr 31,26:1
Term of Trial 1963,Ja 31,5:2
L-Shaped Room, The 1963,My 28,32:1
Of Human Bondage 1964,S 24,46:2
Pumpkin Eater, The 1964,N 10,58:1
King Rat 1965,O 28,48:1
Life at the Top 1965,D 15,53:1
Woolf, John (Producer)
Room at the Top 1959,Mr 31,26:1
Woolf, Leslie
Trouble With Harry, The 1955,O 18,46:2
Wooll, Edward (Original Author)
Libel 1959,O 24,12:4
Woollard, Kenneth (Original Author)
Operation Disaster 1951,Ja 15,13:1
Woollcott, Alexander
Gift of Gab 1934,S 26,17:6
Scoundrel, The 1935,My 3,23:2
Babes on Broadway 1942,Ja 1,37:1
Woolley, Monty
Live, Love and Learn 1937,N 19,27:2
Arsene Lupin Returns 1938,Mr 9,21:1
Everybody Sing 1938,Mr 11,15:3
Girl of the Golden West, The 1938,Mr 25,15:2
Three Comrades 1938,Je 3,17:1
Lord Jeff 1938,Jl 1,22:2
Young Doctor Kildare 1938,O 28,27:1
Midnight 1939,Ap 6,31:1

Man About Town 1939,Je 29,19:1
Dancing Co-Ed 1939,N 10,27:3
Man Who Came to Dinner, The 1942,Ja 2,25:2
Pied Piper, The 1942,Ag 13,15:3
Life Begins at Eight-Thirty 1942,D 10,35:2
Holy Matrimony 1943,S 16,25:2
Since You Went Away 1944,Jl 21,16:2
Irish Eyes Are Smiling 1944,N 8,27:1
Molly and Me 1945,My 26,18:2
Night and Day 1946,Jl 26,16:2
Bishop's Wife, The 1947,D 10,44:2
Miss Tatlock's Millions 1948,N 25,47:2
As Young as You Feel 1951,Ag 3,10:6
Kismet 1955,D 9,32:2
Woolley, Monty (Narrator)
Paris 1900 1950,O 24,34:6
Woolman, Harry
Time of Their Lives, The 1946,N 28,40:2
Woolner, Bernard (Producer)
Flight of the Lost Balloon 1962,My 24,29:2
Woolner, Lawrence (Producer)
Young, The Evil and the Savage, The 1968,Ag 15,46:2
Woolrich, Cornell (Irish, William) (Original Author)
Bride Wore Black, The 1968,Je 26,42:1
Woolrich, Cornell (Original Author)
Convicted 1938,Ag 22,9:3
Street Of Chance 1942,N 19,31:3
Leopard Man, The 1943,My 20,26:4
Mark of the Whistler, The 1944,N 11,19:2
Black Angel 1946,S 26,32:4
Chase, The 1946,N 18,31:2
Guilty, The 1947,My 19,27:2
Night Has a Thousand Eyes 1948,O 14,38:3
Window, The 1949,Ag 8,10:5
Rear Window 1954,Ag 5,18:2
Nightmare 1956,My 12,12:7
Boy Cried Murder, The 1966,Ap 14,42:3
Woolsey, Robert
Rio Rita 1929,O 7,22:1
Cuckoos, The 1930,Ap 26,11:1
Dixiana 1930,S 5,21:1
Half Shot at Sunrise 1930,O 11,21:3
Hook, Line and Sinker 1930,D 25,31:5
Cracked Nuts 1931,Ap 6,24:1
Everything's Rosie 1931,My 22,28:5
Caught Plastered 1931,S 12,15:4
Peach O'Reno 1931,D 24,20:8
Girl Crazy 1932,Mr 25,23:3
So This Is Africa! 1933,Ap 24,11:3
Diplomaniacs 1933,Ap 29,14:2
Hips, Hips, Hooray 1934,F 24,18:3
Cockeyed Cavaliers 1934,Jl 25,22:2
Kentucky Kernels 1935,Ja 5,20:2
Rainmakers, The 1935,N 2,13:2
Silly Billies 1936,Ap 6,18:1
On Again-Off Again 1937,S 18,15:3
Woon, Basil (Miscellaneous)
Showtime 1948,My 20,35:3
Woon, Basil (Screenwriter)
Voice in the Night, The 1941,My 23,25:4
Wooten, Rodney
Girl in Every Port, A 1952,F 14,23:1
Wooten, Steve
All Mine to Give 1959,Ag 4,32:5
Wooton, Sarita
Wuthering Heights 1939,Ap 14,28:2
On Your Toes 1939,O 21,12:2
Light That Failed, The 1939,D 25,19:1
Worden, Hank
Sainted Sisters, The 1948,My 20,35:2
Red River 1948,O 1,31:2
Yellow Sky 1949,F 2,36:1
Three Godfathers 1949,Mr 4,25:2
Wagonmaster 1950,Je 19,17:2
Sugarfoot 1951,F 12,19:4
Big Sky, The 1952,Ag 20,21:1
Indian Fighter, The 1955,D 22,20:1
Searchers, The 1956,My 31,21:4
Good Times 1967,Ag 3,26:4
Wordes, Smitty
One and Only Genuine Original Family Band, The 1968,Mr 22,55:1
Wordsworth, Richard
Time Without Pity 1957,N 23,11:2
Camp on Blood Island, The 1958,S 18,37:2
Worell, Herta
Schloss Hubertus 1935,F 9,11:3
Herbst-Monoever; Fall Manoeuvres 1939,Mr 18,9:3
Woringer, Bernard
Monkeys Go Home 1967,Mr 30,55:1
Worker, Adrian D (Producer)
Safari 1956,Je 21,35:2
Naked Earth 1958,Ag 29,18:1
Intent to Kill 1959,Ap 1,43:2
Workman, Jennie
Oklahoma! 1955,O 11,49:1
Worlock, Frederic
Miracles for Sale 1939,Ag 10,15:2
Lady of the Tropics 1939,S 8,28:3
Balalaika 1939,D 15,33:2
Strange Cargo 1940,Ap 26,25:2

Moon Over Burma 1940,D 12,37:4
Rage in Heaven 1941,Mr 21,19:2
Free and Easy 1941,Ap 3,29:4
Man Hunt 1941,Je 14,20:2
Dr Jekyll and Mr Hyde 1941,Ag 13,13:2
Yank in the R A F, A 1941,S 27,11:3
How Green Was my Valley 1941,O 29,27:2
International Lady 1941,N 11,29:2
Captains of the Clouds 1942,F 13,24:2
Eagle Squadron 1942,Jl 3,12:5
Pacific Rendezvous 1942,Jl 8,27:4
Pierre of the Plains 1942,Jl 30,17:3
Black Swan, The 1942,D 24,18:3
Air Raid Wardens 1943,Ap 5,15:5
Appointment in Berlin 1943,Jl 17,8:2
Sherlock Holmes Faces Death 1943,O 8,15:3
Lodger, The 1944,Ja 20,15:3
Hangover Square 1945,F 8,15:2
Woman in Green, The 1945,Je 16,10:3
Pursuit to Algiers 1945,O 27,12:2
Terror by Night 1946,F 9,9:2
She Wolf of London 1946,Ap 6,10:6
Dressed to Kill 1946,My 25,12:4
Imperfect Lady, The 1947,My 22,34:5
Last of the Redmen 1947,Ag 30,8:6
Singapore 1947,S 17,31:2
Lone Wolf in London, The 1947,N 22,10:3
Love From a Stranger 1947,N 28,30:1
Joan of Arc 1948,N 12,30:5
Hills of Home 1948,N 26,32:2
Notorious Landlady, The 1962,Jl 27,15:2
Worm, H (Miscellaneous)
Cabinet of Dr Caligari, The 1921,Mr 20,VI,2:1
Worms, Jean
Fantomas 1934,Mr 13,27:4
Abused Confidence 1938,D 1,29:1
Heart of Paris 1939,Ja 13,17:3
Song of the Street 1939,S 5,21:2
Rasputin 1939,O 17,31:4
Entente Cordiale 1939,D 26,23:2
Mayerling to Sarajevo 1940,O 30,27:6
I Give my Life 1941,S 1,18:4
Marked Girls 1949,Je 25,8:7
Worms, Rene
Etoile Disparait, Une; Star Disappears, A 1935,F 9,11:3
Wormser, Anne (Original Author)
West Point Widow 1941,S 11,21:5
Wormser, Richard (Original Author)
Sworn Enemy 1936,S 12,20:1
Let Them Live 1937,Je 8,30:3
Fugitives for a Night 1938,S 21,30:4
Tulsa 1949,My 27,25:2
Big Steal, The 1949,Jl 11,13:2
Wormser, Richard (Screenwriter)
Plainsman and the Lady, The 1946,N 4,33:1
Half Breed, The 1952,Jl 5,7:2
Crime Wave 1954,Ja 13,26:2
Outcast, The 1954,Jl 3,9:2
Wormster, Richard E (Original Author)
Frame-Up 1937,Ag 9,23:2 (In Addenda)
Worner, Hilda
All for a Woman 1921,D 5,20:1
Worrall, Dusty
King and I, The 1956,Je 29,15:6
Worsley, Wallace (Director)
Penalty, The 1920,N 15,12:2
Grand Larceny 1922,F 27,13:4
Blind Bargain, A 1922,D 4,20:2
Man Who Fights Alone, The 1924,Jl 28,12:2
Worth, Barbara
On Your Toes 1928,Ja 9,20:1
Worth, Barbara (Screenwriter)
Zamba 1949,N 7,33:2
Worth, Bobby (Composer)
Make Mine Music 1946,Ap 22,26:2
Fun and Fancy Free 1947,S 29,17:2 (In Addenda)
Melody Time 1948,My 28,28:2
Worth, Brian
Lion Has Wings, The 1940,Ja 22,11:2
Pastor Hall 1940,S 21,13:2
It Happened to One Man 1941,F 24,11:6
One Night With You 1949,F 21,20:2
Last Holiday 1950,N 14,39:4
Christmas Carol, A 1951,N 29,41:2
Tom Brown's School Days 1952,Ja 8,23:5
It Started in Paradise 1953,Jl 25,8:2
Inspector Calls, An 1954,N 26,24:4
Worth, Cedric (Miscellaneous)
When You're in Love 1937,F 19,15:2
Worth, Cedric (Screenwriter)
Ramparts We Watch, The 1940,S 20,27:1
Worth, Constance
China Passage 1937,Ap 16,27:2
Angels Over Broadway 1940,N 18,23:2
Meet Boston Blackie 1941,F 26,17:2
Crime Doctor 1943,Jl 5,11:4
Why Girls Leave Home 1945,Ag 4,7:3
Deadline at Dawn 1946,Ap 4,33:2
Worth, David
Three Rogues 1931,Ap 4,23:1
Romance in the Rain 1934,S 8,18:5

Worth, David— Cont
Fighting Youth 1935,N 2,13:3
Worth, Harry
Outlaws of the Orient 1937,S 25,10:2
Hopalong Rides Again 1938,Ja 22,19:1
Disbarred 1939,Ja 19,17:2
Honky Tonk 1941,O 3,27:3
Cairo 1942,N 6,27:2
Worth, Irene
One Night With You 1949,F 21,20:2
Orders to Kill 1958,N 18,41:2
Scapegoat, The 1959,Ag 7,28:1
Worth, Irene (Narrator)
To Die in Madrid 1965,S 16,00:0
Worth, Lillian
In Search of a Sinner 1920,Mr 8,9:5
In Search of a Sinner 1920,Mr 8,9:6
Docks of New York, The 1928,S 17,28:2
Dangerous Paradise 1930,F 16,III,8:1
Worth, Marvin (Original Author)
Boys' Night Out 1962,Je 22,15:2
Promise her Anything 1966,F 23,46:1
3 on a Couch 1966,Jl 7,30:1
Worth, Mary
Enchanted Cottage, The 1945,Ap 28,19:2
Worthing, Helen Lee
Janice Meredith 1924,Ag 6,13:3
Swan, The 1925,Mr 2,14:1
Crowded Hour, The 1925,Ap 27,15:2
Night Life of New York 1925,Jl 14,14:1
Flower of the Night 1925,O 19,26:1
Vanity 1927,Je 15,31:4
Worthington, William
Green Goddess, The 1923,Ag 15,21:1
Red Lights 1923,S 10,15:4
Kid Boots 1926,O 11,18:2
Good Morning, Judge 1928,Je 26,29:1
Man Who Came Back, The 1931,Ja 3,21:2
Shipmates 1931,My 23,13:4
No More Orchids 1933,Ja 2,29:2
Cardinal Richelieu 1935,Ap 19,24:2
Keeper of the Bees, The 1935,Ag 17,18:5
Worthington, William (Director)
Dragon Painter, The 1919,O 5,IV,5:3 (In Addenda)
Worts, George F (Original Author)
Once a Gentleman 1930,O 4,15:2
Phantom President, The 1932,O 1,10:4
Absolute Quiet 1936,My 2,11:1
Woslsey, Robert
Hold 'Em Jail! 1932,Ag 20,7:4
Wost, Nathaniel (Screenwriter)
Spirit of Culver 1939,Mr 9,18:1
Woszczerowicz, Jacek
Dzien Upragniony; Anticipated Day, The 1939,Mr 13,12:3
Wouk, Herman (Original Author)
Slattery's Hurricane 1949,Ag 13,6:6
Caine Mutiny, The 1954,Je 25,17:1
Marjorie Morningstar 1958,Ap 25,32:2
Youngblood Hawke 1964,N 6,30:1
Wouk, Herman (Screenwriter)
Slattery's Hurricane 1949,Ag 13,6:6
Woxholt, Greta
Sangen Till Henne; Song to Her, The 1935,F 22,27:3
Woytecki, W
Village, The 1953,S 23,37:2
Woznik, Wladyslaw
First Start, The 1953,F 2,17:3
Wragge, Edward
Ramparts We Watch, The 1940,S 20,27:1
Wraneff, Vadim
Blonde Saint, The 1926,N 23,27:1
Wrangell, Basil (Director)
Cinerama-South Seas Adventure 1958,Jl 16,26:1
Wrather, Jack (Producer)
Guilty, The 1947,My 19,27:2
High Tide 1947,N 8,11:2
Guilty of Treason 1950,Ap 11,26:2
WRAY
See Also REY, RAE, REA
Wray, Ardel (Screenwriter)
I Walked With a Zombie 1943,Ap 22,31:5
Leopard Man, The 1943,My 20,26:4
Isle of the Dead 1945,S 8,12:2
Wray, Fay
Legion of the Condemned, The 1928,Mr 19,26:2
Street of Sin, The 1928,My 28,23:2
Street of Sin, The 1928,Je 3,VIII,5:1
First Kiss, The 1928,Ag 20,21:3
Wedding March, The 1928,O 15,26:1
Four Feathers, The 1929,Je 13,35:4
Thunderbolt 1929,Je 21,17:2
Pointed Heels 1929,D 28,11:1
Behind the Makeup 1930,Ja 18,21:1
Texan, The 1930,My 17,21:2
Border Legion, The 1930,Je 30,22:6
Sea God, The 1930,S 6,9:2
Finger Points, The 1931,Mr 28,15:3
Conquering Horde, The 1931,Mr 30,25:2
Three Rogues 1931,Ap 4,23:1
Dirigible 1931,Ap 6,24:1
Captain Thunder 1931,My 11,15:4

Lawyer's Secret, The 1931,My 30,9:2
Unholy Garden, The 1931,O 29,27:1
Dirigible 1932,F 14,VIII,6:1
Doctor X 1932,Ag 4,17:2
Most Dangerous Game, The 1932,N 21,21:1
Vampire Bat, The 1933,Ja 23,9:1
Mystery of the Wax Museum, The 1933,F 18,13:3
King Kong 1933,Mr 3,12:1
Below the Sea 1933,Je 3,16:4
Ann Carver's Profession 1933,Je 9,20:2
Woman I Stole, The 1933,Je 28,24:3
Big Brain, The 1933,Ag 5,9:5
One Sunday Afternoon 1933,S 2,14:4
Shanghai Madness 1933,S 23,11:6
Bowery, The 1933,O 5,24:2
Master of Men 1933,N 29,23:4
Madame Spy 1934,F 10,20:1
Once to Every Woman 1934,Mr 26,22:3
Countess of Monte Cristo, The 1934,Ap 2,13:2
Viva Villa! 1934,Ap 11,25:2
Black Moon 1934,Je 28,26:2
Affairs of Cellini, The 1934,S 6,22:3
Richest Girl in the World, The 1934,S 21,29:2
Clairvoyant, The 1935,Je 8,12:2
Alias Bulldog Drummond 1935,S 10,26:2
They Met in a Taxi 1936,S 7,20:5
It Happened in Hollywood 1937,O 2,18:1
Murder in Greenwich Village 1937,O 30,22:2
Jury's Secret, The 1938,F 4,17:2
Adam Had Four Sons 1941,Mr 28,26:6
When Knights Were Bold 1942,Mr 31,29:2
Small Town Girl 1953,My 7,37:2
Treasure of the Golden Condor 1953,My 23,19:2
Cobweb, The 1955,Je 6,13:3
Queen Bee 1955,N 23,18:2
Hell on Frisco Bay 1956,Ja 7,21:1
Crime of Passion 1957,Ja 10,25:1
Tammy and the Bachelor 1957,Je 15,10:7
Summer Love 1958,Je 26,23:4
Wray, Fay (Original Author)
This is the Life 1944,Ap 28,23:3
Wray, Jane
Broken Laws 1925,Ja 21,19:3
Playing With Souls 1925,Ap 20,18:1 (Incorrect in this edition; use 1925,Ap 28,18:1 elsewhere)
Wray, John
New York Nights 1930,F 1,15:1
All Quiet on The Western Front 1930,Ap 30,29:1
Czar of Broadway, The 1930,Je 30,22:6
Quick Millions 1931,Ap 18,17:3
Silence 1931,Ag 15,18:3
Safe in Hell 1931,D 19,16:4
Woman From Monte Carlo, The 1931,D 31,17:6
High Pressure 1932,F 1,22:3
Miracle Man, The 1932,Ap 21,25:2
Mouthpiece, The 1932,Ap 21,25:2
Rich are Always With Us, The 1932,My 16,19:5
Miss Pinkerton 1932,Jl 9,7:5
Doctor X 1932,Ag 4,17:2
I Am a Fugitive From a Chain Gang 1932,N 11,17:2
Central Park 1932,D 7,29:3
Match King, The 1932,D 8,25:3
Death Kiss, The 1933,F 5,IX,5:3
After Tonight 1933,N 3,23:2
After Tonight 1933,N 3,23:2
Bombay Mail 1934,Ja 6,18:2
Big Shakedown, The 1934,F 12,19:2
Love Captive, The 1934,Je 8,18:1
Defense Rests, The 1934,Ag 16,20:3
I'll Fix It 1934,N 12,17:3
Captain Hates the Sea, The 1934,N 29,33:2
I am a Thief 1935,Ja 1,24:1
Great Hotel Murder, The 1935,F 28,17:4
Whole Town's Talking, The 1935,Mr 1,16:2
Stranded 1935,Je 20,16:2
Men Without Names 1935,Je 29,16:2
Bad Boy 1935,O 28,16:3
Frisco Kid 1935,N 25,22:1
Mr Deeds Goes to Town 1936,Ap 17,17:2
Poor Little Rich Girl, The 1936,Je 26,16:1
Son Comes Home, A 1936,S 5,7:1
Sworn Enemy 1936,S 12,20:1
Valiant Is the Word for Carrie 1936,O 8,27:2
President's Mystery, The 1936,O 19,22:1
We Who Are About to Die 1937,Ja 2,15:1
You Only Live Once 1937,F 1,15:2
Outcast 1937,Mr 3,27:2
Devil is Driving, The 1937,Jl 16,22:1
Making the Headlines 1938,Ap 1,17:2
Gangs of New York 1938,My 28,9:2
Tenth Avenue Kid 1938,S 2,21:3
Man to Remember, A 1938,N 7,23:2
Crime Takes a Holiday 1938,N 28,11:2
Pacific Liner 1939,Ja 18,17:3
Risky Business 1939,Mr 23,27:2
Each Dawn I Die 1939,Jl 22,12:2
Blackmail 1939,S 15,26:3
Remember the Night 1940,Ja 18,27:2
Amazing Mr Williams, The 1940,Ja 19,15:2
Swiss Family Robinson 1940,F 9,15:3
Man From Dakota, The 1940,F 22,29:2

Wray, John Griffith (Director)
Home Spun Folks 1920,O 4,14:3
Lying Lips 1921,Mr 7,8:1
Marriage Cheat, The 1921,Je 2,14:3
Hail the Woman 1922,Ja 16,18:3
Soul of the Beast, The 1923,My 22,14:4
Human Wreckage 1923,Je 28,10:2
Anna Christie 1923,D 10,20:1
Singed 1927,Jl 12,29:3
Gateway of the Moon, The 1928,Ja 9,20:1
Most Immoral Lady, A 1929,O 21,30:1
Wray, John Griffith (Producer)
Anna Christie 1928,D 23,VIII,7:1
Wrede, Ebba
Each Heart Has Its Own Story 1953,Mr 28,15:2
Wren, P C (Original Author)
Wages of Virtue 1924,N 24,15:3
Beau Geste 1926,Ag 26,17:3
Beau Sabreur 1928,Ja 23,18:3
Beau Ideal 1931,Ja 19,25:1
Beau Geste 1939,Ag 3,15:2
Beau Geste 1966,S 8,43:1
Wren, Sam
Dr Socrates 1935,O 3,29:2
I Married a Doctor 1936,Ap 20,17:1
Wright, Armand
To Be or not to Be 1942,Mr 7,13:2
Wright, Basil (Director)
Song of Ceylon 1937,Ag 16,15:1
Wright, Basil (Producer)
Children on Trial 1947,N 10,21:3
Wright, Ben
Power and The Prize, the 1956,S 27,42:1
Kiss Them for Me 1957,N 9,31:2
Wreck of the Mary Deare, The 1959,N 7,27:1
Journey to the Center of the Earth 1959,D 17,51:1
Operation Bottleneck 1961,S 7,40:2
Judgment at Nuremberg 1961,D 20,36:1
Mutiny on the Bounty 1962,N 9,31:2
Gathering of Eagles, A 1963,Jl 11,21:2
Sound of Music, The 1965,Mr 3,34:1
Wright, Betty Huntley
Strauss's Great Waltz 1935,Ap 8,23:3
Wright, Bob
Tall Story 1960,Ap 7,46:1
Wright, Bob (Composer)
Good Old Soak 1937,Ap 20,25:3
Saratoga 1937,Jl 23,16:3
Mannequin 1938,Ja 21,15:2
First 100 Years, The 1938,My 13,17:2
Three Comrades 1938,Je 3,17:1
Let Freedom Ring 1939,Mr 10,19:2
Music in My Heart 1940,Ja 4,19:2
Blondie Goes Latin 1941,F 26,17:3
I Married an Angel 1942,Jl 10,13:2
Kismet 1955,D 9,32:2
Wright, Bob (Miscellaneous)
After the Thin Man 1936,D 25,19:2
Maytime 1937,Mr 19,27:1
Firefly, The 1937,S 2,17:2
Sweethearts 1938,D 23,16:2
Broadway Serenade 1939,Ap 7,25:2
Wright, Cobina Jr
Moon Over Miami 1941,Jl 5,14:2
Week-End in Havana 1941,N 8,11:2
Footlight Serenade 1942,S 10,30:3
Something to Shout About 1943,Ap 8,27:3
Wright, Curley
Lawyer Man 1932,D 27,10:2
Sailor's Luck 1933,Mr 17,21:2
Wright, Derek (Cinematographer)
Antarctic Crossing 1959,My 11,30:1
Wright, Ellsworth
Go, Man, Go 1954,Mr 10,29:5
Wright, Ethel
Enchanted Cottage, The 1924,Ap 14,14:1
Wright, Florence
Great Dictator, The 1940,O 16,29:1
Wright, Gene (Original Author)
As Man Desires 1925,F 10,20:1
Wright, George D (Director)
Typical Mexican Aspects 1919,Ja 31,5:5
Wright, Gilbert (Miscellaneous)
Whispering Smith Speaks 1936,F 17,21:1
Wright, Gilbert (Original Author)
Thanks For Everything 1938,D 10,13:2
Utah 1945,Mr 12,22:7
Wright, Gilbert (Screenwriter)
Maya 1966,Je 23,29:4
Wright, Haidee
Blarney Kiss, The 1933,Ag 19,14:4
Power 1934,O 5,29:3
Wright, Harold Bell (Original Author)
When a Man's a Man 1924,F 5,20:1
Son of his Father, A 1925,S 29,31:3
Winning of Barbara Worth, The 1926,N 29,16:3
Shepherd of the Hills, The 1928,F 20,14:1
Eyes of the World 1930,Ag 15,20:5
When a Man's a Man 1935,F 22,27:2
Calling of Dan Matthews, The 1936,Ja 25,18:4
Mine With the Iron Door, The 1936,Jl 11,11:3
Secret Valley 1937,Ja 25,22:2

Wright, Harold Bell (Original Author)— Cont
It Happened Out West 1937,Je 7,22:3
Shepherd of the Hills, The 1941,Jl 31,13:2
Massacre River 1949,Jl 15,17:2
Wright, Helen
Dames Ahoy 1930,Mr 29,23:1
Wright, Hugh E
Better 'Ole, The 1919,F 24,11:3
Silver King, The 1929,S 2,16:1
Scrooge 1935,D 14,11:1
Wright, Humberstone
Garden of Allah, The 1927,S 3,13:5
Waterloo 1929,Ap 16,32:5
Fanny Hawthorn 1929,N 11,20:2
White Cargo 1930,F 24,18:1
In a Monastery Garden 1935,Mr 13,16:2
Wright, Huntley
Heart Song 1934,Je 6,24:6
Wright, Iris (Screenwriter)
Men Are not Gods 1937,Ja 19,28:1
Wright, John
McHale's Navy 1964,Jl 11,15:2
Wright, Kenneth (Director)
We Visit Moscow 1954,N 29,21:2
Wright, Kenneth (Narrator)
We Visit Moscow 1954,N 29,21:2
Wright, Kenneth (Producer)
We Visit Moscow 1954,N 29,21:2
Wright, Mabel
Alice in Wonderland 1931,D 28,22:1
Wright, Marie
Day Dreams 1930,F 4,28:3
Sixty Glorious Years 1938,N 18,25:2
Angel Street 1952,N 11,25:2
Wright, Maurice (Screenwriter)
Zanzibar 1940,Ap 1,15:3
Wright, Otis Pvt
Cease Fire! 1953,N 25,17:1
Wright, Pat
Good Morning and Goodbye! 1968,F 20,53:1
Wright, Paula Rae
Keep Smiling 1938,Ag 10,15:2
Wright, R C (Miscellaneous)
Scorched Earth 1942,S 12,9:2
Wright, Ralph (Director)
Perri 1957,O 2,27:5
Wright, Ralph (Original Author)
Saludos Amigos 1943,F 13,8:2
Three Caballeros, The 1945,F 5,20:1
Wright, Ralph (Screenwriter)
Perri 1957,O 2,27:5
Nikki, Wild Dog of the North 1961,S 5,37:6
Wright, Richard
Native Son 1951,Je 18,19:2
Wright, Richard (Miscellaneous)
Native Son 1951,Je 18,19:2
Wright, Richard (Original Author)
Native Son 1951,Je 18,19:2
Wright, Richard (Screenwriter)
Native Son 1951,Je 18,19:2
Wright, S Fowler (Original Author)
Deluge 1933,O 9,22:3
Wright, Tenny
Partners of the Night 1920,Mr 1,16:2
Wright, Teresa
Little Foxes, The 1941,Ag 22,19:2
Mrs Miniver 1942,Je 5,23:1
Pride of the Yankees, The 1942,Jl 16,23:1
Shadow of a Doubt 1943,Ja 13,18:2
Casanova Brown 1944,S 15,16:1
Best Years of our Lives, The 1946,N 22,27:2
Pursued 1947,Mr 8,10:2
Imperfect Lady, The 1947,My 22,34:5
Trouble With Women, The 1947,Jl 14,14:4
Enchantment 1948,D 27,16:2
Capture, The 1950,My 20,8:6
Men, The 1950,Jl 21,15:2
Something to Live For 1952,Mr 8,11:2
California Conquest 1952,Je 7,22:6
Steel Trap, The 1952,N 13,35:2
Count the Hours 1953,Je 24,30:4
Actress, The 1953,O 13,34:1
Track of the Cat 1954,D 2,38:2
Escapde in Japan 1957,D 24,11:1
Wright, Tony
Broth of a Boy 1959,D 28,18:1
In the Wake of a Stranger 1961,Je 22,23:3
Portrait of a Sinner 1961,D 7,52:1
Wright, Will
China Clipper 1936,Ag 12,14:3
Rookies on Parade 1941,My 22,25:2
World Premiere 1941,Ag 21,15:2
True to the Army 1942,Je 15,15:4
Parachute Nurse 1942,Jl 27,18:2
Night to Remember, A 1943,Ja 1,27:2
Reveille With Beverly 1943,Ap 24,17:2
Cowboy in Manhattan 1943,My 28,19:2
Murder in Times Square 1943,My 31,13:2
One Mysterious Night 1944,O 21,15:3
Salome, Where She Danced 1945,My 3,27:1
Bewitched 1945,Ag 17,20:3
Uncle Harry 1945,Ag 24,14:5
Road to Utopia 1946,F 28,20:2
Blue Dahlia, The 1946,My 9,27:3

Lover Come Back 1946,Je 20,20:3
Rendezvous With Annie 1946,S 23,29:3
Blaze of Noon 1947,Mr 5,31:2
Mother Wore Tights 1947,Ag 21,33:2
Cynthia 1947,S 19,27:2
Wild Harvest 1947,N 13,33:2
Relentless 1948,Mr 6,17:3
Green Grass of Wyoming 1948,Je 10,28:3
Walls of Jericho, The 1948,Ag 5,16:2
Live Today for Tomorrow 1948,D 6,29:2
Act of Violence 1949,Ja 24,16:2
Whispering Smith 1949,F 15,28:2
Little Women 1949,Mr 11,33:2
Impact 1949,Mr 21,19:2
Big Jack 1949,My 23,27:4
Lust for Gold 1949,Jl 4,9:2
Brimstone 1949,O 7,35:3
They Live by Night 1949,N 4,33:2
All the King's Men 1949,N 9,37:2
Adam's Rib 1949,D 26,33:2
Mrs Mike 1950,F 9,36:5
House by the River 1950,My 2,25:2
Ticket to Tomahawk, A 1950,My 20,8:6
No Way Out 1950,Ag 17,23:1
Dallas 1951,Ja 13,10:4
Vengeance Valley 1951,F 16,21:2
My Forbidden Past 1951,Ap 26,34:2
Excuse my Dust 1951,Je 28,21:2
People Will Talk 1951,Ag 30,20:1
Las Vegas Story, The 1952,Ja 31,37:6
Lydia Bailey 1952,My 31,12:5
Paula 1952,Jl 16,21:2
Lure of the Wilderness 1952,O 4,15:2
Happy Time, The 1952,O 31,30:2
Niagara 1953,Ja 22,20:3
Wild One, The 1953,D 31,9:2
River of no Return 1954,My 1,13:2
Tall Men, The 1955,O 12,36:2
Court-Martial of Billy Mitchell, The
1955,D 23,14:2
Wayward Bus, The 1957,Je 6,35:2
Alias Jesse James 1959,My 18,31:2
Deadly Companions, The 1962,Ap 12,41:7
Wright, William H (Producer)
Letter for Evie, A 1946,Je 28,17:4
Three Wise Fools 1946,S 27,19:2
Bride Goes Wild, The 1948,Je 4,27:2
Act of Violence 1949,Ja 24,16:2
Black Hand 1950,Mr 13,15:2
Skipper Surprised his Wife, The 1950,Je 30,18:2
Stars in my Crown 1950,D 22,19:1
Mrs O'Malley and Mr Malone 1951,F 23,33:2
People Against O'Hara, The 1951,S 6,39:3
Love Is Better Than Ever 1952,Mr 4,23:2
Young Man With Ideas 1952,Jc 7,22:6
Shadow in the Sky 1952,Jl 19,8:2
Clown, The 1953,Ja 29,25:1
Naked Spur, The 1953,Mr 26,37:3
Dead Ringer 1964,F 20,22:3
Distant Trumpet, A 1964,My 28,40:1
Wright, William H (Screenwriter)
Her Cardboard Lover 1942,Jl 17,19:2
Assignment in Brittany 1943,Ap 22,31:2
Adventure 1946,F 8,23:2
Sons of Katie Elder, The 1965,Ag 26,40:3
Wrixon, Maris
British Intelligence 1940,F 12,14:2
Flight Angels 1940,My 27,23:2
Ape, The 1940,N 28,28:3
Case of the Black Parrot, The 1941,Ja 10,23:3
Footsteps in the Dark 1941,Mr 15,13:2
Bullets for O'Hara 1941,Jl 28,16:4
Spy Ship 1942,Jl 11,8:2
Woman in Bondage 1944,Mr 27,17:2
Black Market Babies 1946,Ap 1,23:1
Wrubel, Allie (Composer)
Key, The 1934,My 30,14:3
Housewife 1934,Ag 10,21:2
Dames 1934,Ag 16,20:2
Happiness Ahead 1934,O 11,28:2
Flirtation Walk 1934,N 29,33:1
Sweet Music 1935,F 21,23:2
I Live for Love 1935,O 19,21:2
Broadway Hostess 1935,D 16,23:3
Life of the Party, The 1937,O 4,17:1
Radio City Revels 1938,Mr 21,18:3
Make Mine Music 1946,Ap 22,26:2
Melody Time 1948,My 28,28:2
Never Steal Anything Small 1959,F 12,23:1
Wrubel, Allie (Miscellaneous)
In Caliente 1935,Je 27,16:1
Bright Lights 1935,Ag 15,15:2
Toast of New York, The 1937,Jl 23,16:2
Music for Madame 1937,O 23,14:1
Wu, Honorable
Crime of Dr Hallet, The 1938,Mr 24,21:3
Mr Moto Takes a Vacation 1939,Je 19,12:6
Ellery Queen and the Perfect Crime
1941,Ag 11,17:3
Wuest, Gustav
Moritz Macht Sein Glueck 1932,D 24,11:4

Wuest, Ida
Last Waltz, The 1927,N 14,26:1
Bockbierfest 1931,Mr 31,25:3
Alte Lied, Das 1931,S 11,24:2
Ein Burschenlied aus Heidelberg 1931,S 14,15:3
Lindenwirtin vom Rhein, Die 1931,S 25,28:7
Bomben auf Monte Carlo; Bombardment of Monte
Carlo, The 1931,S 27,VIII,7:1
Die Csikos Baroness 1932,Mr 28,11:2
Mein Leopold 1932,Ap 1,17:4
Hurra! Ein Junge! 1932,Je 21,19:6
Schoen Ist die Manoeverzeit 1932,Ag 19,20:6
Wenn die Soldaten 1932,O 31,18:4
Man Braucht Kein Geld 1932,N 16,15:3
Walzerkoenig, Der 1932,D 5,21:2
Das Schoene Abenteuer 1932,D 8,25:3
Namensheirat 1933,Ja 9,23:1
Friederike 1933,F 27,11:3
Drei Tage Mittelarrest 1933,My 18,17:4
Lachende Erben 1933,N 18,18:6
Wie Sag' Ich's Meinem Mann? 1934,Ja 23,22:4
Eines Prinzen Junge Liebe 1934,Mr 24,20:4
Ja, Treu Ist die Soldatenliebe 1934,Ap 28,11:4
Zu Befehl, Herr Unteroffizier 1934,Je 16,20:3
Melodie der Liebe 1934,S 17,20:3
Es War Einmal ein Walzer 1934,O 15,20:5
Fluechtlinge 1934,O 15,20:5
Einmal Eine Grosse Dame Sein 1934,O 27,20:3
Freut Euch des Lebens 1934,N 3,20:3
Liebe und die Erste Eisenbahn, Die; Love and the
First Railroad 1935,F 18,19:4
Jungfrau Gegen Moench; Maiden vs Monk
1935,Mr 16,19:2
Csardasfuerstin 1935,Ap 25,18:3
Fruehlingsmaerchen 1935,My 20,20:5
So ein Maedel Vergisst Man nicht 1935,S 28,12:3
Private Life of Louis XIV, The 1936,Ja 9,25:2
Marquise von Pompadour, Die 1936,F 3,21:3
Annette in Paradise 1936,Mr 7,11:4
Bettelstudent, Der 1936,D 28,12:3
World's in Love, The 1937,My 19,27:2
Wenn Du eine Schwiegermutter hast; When You
Have a Mother-in-Law 1938,Ja 29,12:1
Husaren Heraus 1938,Mr 19,11:3
Kater Lampe 1938,Ap 23,19:3
Seefahrt die Ist Lustig, Eine; Merry Sea Trip, A
1938,O 22,14:2
Nacht an der Donau, Eine; Night on the Danube,
A 1938,N 19,9:3
Kleines Bezirksgericht; Little Country Court
1939,F 18,12:4
Diskretion-Ehrensache; Discretion with Honor
1939,Mr 13,12:3
Herbst-Monoever; Fall Manoeuvres
1939,Mr 18,9:3
Lustige Witwenball, Der; Merry Widows' Ball,
The 1939,My 1,21:2
Blonde Carmen, Die 1939,O 7,11:3
Kluge Schwiegermutter, Die; Wise Mother-in-Law,
The 1939,O 9,15:3
Wuest Ida
Burning Heart, The 1930,My 12,27:3
WULFF
See Also WOLF, WOLFE, WOLFF, WOLLF,
WOOLF
Wulff, Helge Prof
Wild Strawberries 1959,Je 23,37:1
Wunderlee, Frank
One Exciting Night 1922,O 24,17:3
Wurmser, Carl
Moritz Macht Sein Glueck 1932,D 24,11:4
Wurmser, Ernst
Lustigen Weiber von Wien, Die 1931,Jl 10,22:2
Ein Prinz Verliebt Sich 1932,Ap 29,13:4
Wurtenburger, Paul
Versuchen Sie Meine Schwester 1931,Je 20,20:4
Wurtzel, Sol M (Producer)
365 Nights in Hollywood 1934,N 7,32:1
Bright Eyes 1934,D 21,31:1
Life Begins at 40 1935,Ap 5,21:3
Black Sheep 1935,Je 28,34:1
Ginger 1935,Jl 19,13:2
Dante's Inferno 1935,Ag 1,15:1
Steamboat Around the Bend 1935,S 20,17:2
Paddy O'Day 1936,F 8,19:2
My Marriage 1936,F 22,12:2
Song and Dance Man 1936,Mr 12,18:2
Gentle Julia 1936,Ap 11,19:1
Country Beyond, The 1936,Ap 30,17:3
Little Miss Nobody 1936,Je 6,21:1
Crime of Dr Forbes, The 1936,Jl 6,11:4
Thank You, Jeeves 1936,O 5,25:1
Ramona 1936,O 7,32:4
Woman Wise 1937,Ja 23,13:1
That I May Live 1937,My 10,23:2
Think Fast, Mr Moto 1937,Ag 16,15:3
Thank You, Mr Moto 1938,Ja 3,16:2
City Girl 1938,F 4,17:3
International Settlement 1938,F 12,20:3
Mr Moto in Danger Island 1938,Mr 20,13:3
Walking Down Broadway 1938,Ap 1,17:3
Mr Moto Takes a Chance 1938,Je 13,15:4
Passport Husband 1938,Ag 5,11:2

Wurtzel, Sol M (Producer)— Cont

Mysterious Mr Moto of Devil's Island
1938,S 19,16:2
Five of a Kind 1938,O 31,12:2
Up the River 1938,D 3,11:2
Sharpshooters 1938,D 5,19:2
While New York Sleeps 1938,D 22,25:3
Mr Moto's Last Warning 1939,Ja 27,17:3
Mr Moto Takes a Vacation 1939,Je 19,12:6
Frontier Marshal 1939,Jl 29,18:2
Pack up Your Troubles 1939,O 27,27:2
20,000 Men a Year 1939,O 28,11:2
Escape, The 1939,N 3,17:4
City of Chance 1940,Ja 22,11:3
Charlie Chan in Panama 1940,F 23,19:3
Viva Cisco Kid 1940,Mr 22,23:4
Free, Blonde and 21 1940,Ap 5,25:2
Earthbound 1940,Je 7,27:4
Sailor's Lady 1940,Je 29,12:2
Pier 13 1940,Ag 9,19:3
Michael Shayne, Private Detective
1940,D 19,33:2
Romance of the Rio Grande 1940,D 25,33:4
Dance Hall 1941,Jl 19,16:2
Great Guns 1941,O 3,27:2
Secret Agent of Japan 1942,Mr 23,19:3
Man Who Wouldn't Die, The 1942,Ap 28,25:5
Whispering Ghosts 1942,My 18,19:4
Who Is Hope Schuyler 1942,My 22,27:1
A-Haunting We Will Go 1942,Ag 3,18:4
Just off Broadway 1942,Ag 29,18:4
Manila Calling 1942,S 28,13:1
Time to Kill 1942,D 25,15:4
Chetniks 1943,Mr 19,15:3
He Hired the Boss 1943,Je 4,17:4
Jitterbugs 1943,Je 5,12:2
Bomber's Moon 1943,Jl 31,8:2
Big Noise, The 1944,S 23,16:1
Deadline for Murder 1946,Je 29,22:7
Dangerous Millions 1947,Mr 15,10:3
Backlash 1947,My 24,10:5
Jewels of Brandenburg 1947,My 24,10:5
Second Chance 1947,S 20,12:4
Crimson Key, The 1947,O 18,9:2
Invisible Wall, The 1947,N 1,11:2
Roses Are Red 1947,N 15,11:2

Wuttig, Oskar (Screenwriter)
Tempestous Love 1958,N 22,27:4

Wyand, Paul (Cinematographer)
Royal Tour of Queen Elizabeth and Philip, The
1954,Je 22,24:2

Wyatt, Al
Sitting Bull 1954,N 26,24:4

Wyatt, Charlene
Valiant Is the Word for Carrie 1936,O 8,27:2
Untamed 1940,Jl 25,14:3

Wyatt, Eustace
Nightmare 1942,D 4,31:2
Journey Into Fear 1943,Mr 19,15:3
Ministry of Fear 1945,F 8,15:2

Wyatt, Florence
Notorious Landlady, The 1962,Jl 27,15:2

Wyatt, Jane
One More River 1934,Ag 10,21:1
We're Only Human 1936,Ja 18,19:2
Luckiest Girl in the World, The 1936,D 5,16:3
Lost Horizon 1937,Mr 4,27:1
Girl From God's Country 1940,S 9,18:5
Week End for Three 1941,O 24,27:4
Army Surgeon 1942,N 5,35:2
Navy Comes Through, The 1942,N 12,30:3
Kansan, The 1943,O 1,15:3
None but the Lonely Heart 1944,N 18,16:6
Bachelor's Daughters, The 1946,O 7,23:2
Boomerang 1947,Mr 6,36:2
Gentleman's Agreement 1947,N 12,36:2
Pitfall 1948,Ag 25,31:2
No Minor Vices 1949,F 26,11:2
Bad Boy 1949,Mr 23,35:2
Canadian Pacific 1949,My 20,32:4
Task Force 1949,O 1,8:6
House by the River 1950,My 2,25:2
Our Very Own 1950,Jl 28,12:5
My Blue Heaven 1950,S 16,12:6
Man Who Cheated Himself, The 1951,F 9,21:2
Criminal Lawyer 1951,Ag 24,11:4
Never too Late 1965,N 5,28:1

Wyatt, Whitlow
Safe at Home 1941,N 26,31:2

Wycherly, Margaret
Midnight 1934,Mr 10,18:3
Victory 1940,D 23,23:2
Sergeant York 1941,Jl 3,15:1
Crossroads 1942,Jl 27,18:2
Random Harvest 1942,D 18,36:6
Keeper of the Flame 1943,Mr 19,15:2
Moon Is Down, The 1943,Mr 27,8:6
Hangmen Also Die 1943,Ap 16,24:2
Assignment in Brittany 1943,Ap 22,31:2
Experiment Perilous 1944,D 30,15:2
Johnny Angel 1945,D 28,12:2
Yearling, The 1947,Ja 24,18:2
Something in the Wind 1947,Ag 29,14:3
Forever Amber 1947,O 23,31:2

Loves of Carmen, The 1948,S 3,16:2
White Heat 1949,S 3,7:2
Man With a Cloak, The 1951,N 28,37:2
President's Lady, The 1953,My 22,31:1

Wyckoff, Alvin (Director)
Peasant's Wedding, The 1939,Ap 19,20:5

Wycoff, Leon
That's my Boy 1932,N 21,21:1

Wyenn, Than
Good Morning, Miss Dove 1955,N 24,41:1
Beginning of the End 1957,Jl 4,16:1

Wykeham, Reg
Massacre Hill 1950,D 14,51:3

Wyks, Johann (Original Author)
Swiss Family Robinson 1960,D 24,8:4

Wyle, George (Composer)
Lullaby of Broadway 1951,Mr 27,35:2

WYLER
See Also WILDER

Wyler, Gretchen
Devil's Brigade, The 1968,My 23,56:2

Wyler, Michael
Close-Up 1948,Ap 5,24:2

Wyler, Richard
Ugly Ones, The 1968,D 12,62:5

Wyler, Robert (Miscellaneous)
Big Country, The 1958,O 2,44:1

Wyler, Robert (Screenwriter)
Last Train from Madrid, The 1937,Je 19,20:2
Sophie Lang Goes West 1937,S 30,19:2
Detective Story 1951,N 7,35:2

Wyler, Susan
Bye Bye Braverman 1968,F 22,36:1

Wyler, Trude
Certain Smile, A 1958,Ag 1,13:2

Wyler, William (Cinematographer)
Memphis Belle, The 1944,Ap 14,1:2

Wyler, William (Director)
Shakedown, The 1929,Ap 8,32:1
Hell's Heroes 1929,D 28,11:1
Storm, The 1930,Ag 23,7:3
House Divided, A 1932,Ja 9,21:1
Tom Brown of Culver 1932,Jl 30,16:5
Her First Mate 1933,S 2,14:5
Counsellor-At-Law 1933,D 8,31:2
Glamour 1934,My 12,12:3
Good Fairy, The 1935,F 1,18:1
Gay Deception, The 1935,O 11,31:1
These Three 1936,Mr 19,22:4
Dodsworth 1936,S 24,29:1
Come and Get It 1936,N 12,31:1
Dead End 1937,Ag 25,25:1
Jezebel 1938,Mr 11,15:2
Wuthering Heights 1939,Ap 14,28:2
Westerner, The 1940,O 25,25:2
Letter, The 1940,N 23,12:6
Little Foxes, The 1941,Ag 22,19:2
Mrs Miniver 1942,Je 5,23:1
Memphis Belle, The 1944,Ap 14,1:2
Thunderbolt 1945,O 27,12:5
Best Years of our Lives, The 1946,N 22,27:2
Detective Story 1951,N 7,35:2
Carrie 1952,Jl 17,20:2
Roman Holiday 1953,Ag 28,13:1
Desperate Hours, The 1955,O 6,25:1
Friendly Persuasion 1956,N 2,30:1
Big Country, The 1958,O 2,44:1
Ben Hur 1959,N 19,50:2
Childrens Hour, The 1962,Mr 15,28:2
Collector, The 1965,Je 18,28:1
How to Steal a Million 1966,Jl 15,34:1
Funny Girl 1968,S 20,42:1

Wyler, William (Producer)
Letter, The 1940,N 23,12:6
Detective Story 1951,N 7,35:2
Carrie 1952,Jl 17,20:2
Roman Holiday 1953,Ag 28,13:1
Desperate Hours, The 1955,O 6,25:1
Friendly Persuasion 1956,N 2,30:1
Big Country, The 1958,O 2,44:1
Childrens Hour, The 1962,Mr 15,28:2

WYLIE
See Also WILEY, WILLEY

Wylie, Constance
Only Thing, The 1925,N 23,25:4

Wylie, Evan (Original Author)
Joe Butterfly 1957,My 30,23:2
Nice Little Bank That Should Be Robbed, A
1958,D 11,17:4

Wylie, I A R (Original Author)
Man Must Live, A 1925,Ja 29,12:2
Four Sons 1928,F 14,27:1
Young Nowheres 1929,O 2,28:4
Evenings for Sale 1932,N 12,20:5
Pilgrimage 1933,Jl 13,17:5
Feather in her Hat, A 1935,O 25,24:5
That Man's Here Again 1937,My 6,23:3
Vivacious Lady 1938,Je 3,17:3
Young in Heart, The 1938,N 4,27:2
Under-Pup, The 1939,S 5,21:2
Four Sons 1940,Je 8,18:4
Keeper of the Flame 1943,Mr 19,15:2
Phone Call From a Stranger 1952,F 2,11:2

Wylie, I A R (Original Author)— Cont

Torch Song 1953,O 13,34:2

Wylie, Philip (Original Author)
Murders in the Zoo 1933,Ap 3,13:4
Come on Marines 1934,Mr 24,20:3
Second Honeymoon 1937,N 13,11:2
Under Suspicion 1937,D 20,23:2 (In Addenda)
Gladiator, The 1938,Ag 29,10:2
Charlie Chan in Reno 1939,My 31,27:2
Springtime in the Rockies 1942,N 12,30:2
Cinderella Jones 1946,Mr 16,9:6
Night Unto Night 1949,Je 11,11:2
When Worlds Collide 1952,F 7,30:2

WYMAN
See Also WEIMAN

Wyman, Jane
Smart Blonde 1937,Ja 9,21:1
Ready, Willing and Able 1937,Mr 15,27:1
King and the Chorus Girl, The 1937,Mr 29,14:4
Slim 1937,Je 24,30:2
Singing Marine, The 1937,Jl 1,33:2
Mr Dodd Takes the Air 1937,Ag 12,14:2
Spy Ring, The 1938,Ja 15,19:1
Wide Open Faces 1938,Ap 15,23:2
Crowd Roars, The 1938,Ag 5,11:1
Brother Rat 1938,N 5,15:2
Tail Spin 1939,F 11,13:2
Kid From Kokomo, The 1939,My 20,11:2
Kid Nightingale 1939,D 8,33:6
Brother Rat and a Baby 1940,Ja 27,9:4
Angel From Texas, An 1940,My 10,26:7
Flight Angels 1940,My 27,23:2
My Love Came Back 1940,Jl 13,16:5
Tugboat Annie Sails Again 1940,N 9,20:2
Honeymoon for Three 1941,F 8,19:2
Bad Men of Missouri 1941,Ag 16,18:2
You're in the Army Now 1941,D 26,21:4
Body Disappears, The 1942,Ja 31,13:2
Larceny, Inc 1942,Ap 25,9:1
My Favorite Spy 1942,My 29,13:4
Footlight Serenade 1942,S 10,30:3
Princess O'Rourke 1943,N 6,16:2
Make Your own Bed 1944,My 27,12:2
Doughgirls, The 1944,Ag 31,14:1
Hollywood Canteen 1944,D 16,19:2
Lost Weekend, The 1945,D 3,17:2
One More Tomorrow 1946,My 25,12:2
Night and Day 1946,Jl 26,16:2
Yearling, The 1947,Ja 24,18:2
Cheyenne 1947,Je 7,9:2
Magic Town 1947,O 8,29:2
Johnny Belinda 1948,O 2,11:2
Kiss in the Dark, A 1949,Mr 26,10:6
Lady Takes a Sailor, The 1949,D 17,15:2
Stage Fright 1950,F 24,27:2
Glass Menagerie, The 1950,S 29,31:5
Three Guys Named Mike 1951,Mr 2,21:2
Here Comes the Groom 1951,S 21,19:2
Blue Veil, The 1951,O 27,10:5
Starlift 1951,D 15,11:2
Story of Will Rogers, The 1952,Jl 18,10:5
Just for You 1952,O 9,40:6
Let's Do It Again 1953,O 14,34:3
So Big 1953,O 22,34:2
Magnificent Obsession 1954,Ag 5,18:4
Lucy Gallant 1955,O 21,30:1
All That Heaven Allows 1956,F 29,35:1
Miracle in the Rain 1956,Ap 2,18:1
Holiday for Lovers 1959,Jl 25,10:2
Pollyanna 1960,My 20,26:1
Bon Voyage! 1962,My 18,34:2

Wyman, Paul D (Producer)
Taming the Jungle 1933,Je 5,18:5

Wymark, Patrick
Operation Crossbow 1965,Ap 2,29:1
Repulsion 1965,O 4,7:6
Psycopath, The 1966,S 29,60:1
Woman Times Seven 1967,Je 28,38:1

Wymark, Patrick (Narrator)
King's Story, A 1967,My 25,57:2

Wymore, Patrice
Tea for Two 1950,S 2,11:2

Wymore, PAtrice
Rocky Mountain 1950,N 4,13:2

Wymore, Patrice
I'll See You in my Dreams 1951,D 7,35:1
Starlift 1951,D 15,11:2
Big Trees, The 1952,F 6,24:2
She's Working her Way Through College
1952,Jl 10,27:2
She's Back on Broadway 1953,Mr 12,24:2
Ocean's Eleven 1960,Ag 11,19:1

Wyn-Jones, Meurig
Abandon Ship 1957,Ap 18,35:1

Wynant, H M
Run of the Arrow 1957,Ag 3,8:6
Tonka 1959,Mr 26,27:1
It Happened at the World's Fair 1963,My 30,20:1
Slender Thread, The 1965,D 24,24:2

Wyndham, Dennis
Juno and the Paycock 1930,Je 30,22:6
Man they Couldn't Arrest, The 1933,Mr 14,19:3
Battle for Music 1945,O 15,13:2

Wyndham, Joan
Loyalties 1934,O 26,25:1
Juggernaut 1937,Jl 15,16:1
Wyndham, John (Original Author)
Village of the Damned 1960,D 8,43:3
Day of the Triffids 1963,My 11,15:2
Wyngarde, Peter
Alexander the Great 1956,Mr 29,23:1
Innocents, The 1961,D 26,15:2
Burn, Witch, Burn 1962,Jl 5,21:2 (In Addenda)
WYNN
See Also WINN, WYNNE
Wynn, Ed
Rubber Heels 1927,Je 28,29:4
Follow the Leader 1930,D 6,21:3
Chief, The 1933,D 2,9:4
Stage Door Canteen 1943,Je 25,13:2
Great Man, The 1957,Ja 2,28:2
Marjorie Morningstar 1958,Ap 25,32:2
Diary of Anne Frank, The 1959,Mr 19,40:1
Cinderfella 1960,D 17,19:2
Absent-Minded Professor, The 1961,Mr 16,44:2
Babes in Toyland 1961,D 15,49:1
Son of Flubber 1963,F 9,5:2
Mary Poppins 1964,S 25,34:1
Dear Brigitte 1965,Ja 28,20:1
Greatest Story Ever Told, The 1965,F 16,40:2
Those Calloways 1965,Ap 15,38:2
That Darn Cat 1965,D 3,44:1
Gnome-Mobile, The 1967,Jl 20,30:2
Wynn, Ed (Narrator)
Sound of Laughter, The 1963,D 18,44:2
Wynn, Helen
These Thirty Years 1934,My 24,28:3
Wynn, Keenan
For Me and My Gal 1942,O 22,25:1
See Here Private Hargrove 1944,Mr 22,17:2
Lost Angel 1944,Ap 10,14:1
Since You Went Away 1944,Jl 21,16:2
Marriage Is a Private Affair 1944,O 27,17:7
Without Love 1945,Mr 23,13:1
Between Two Women 1945,Mr 29,18:3
Clock, The 1945,My 4,23:2
Week-End at the Waldorf 1945,O 5,27:2
What Next Corporal Hargrove? 1945,D 26,15:2
Ziegfeld Follies 1946,Mr 23,8:3
Easy to Wed 1946,Jl 12,14:2
Thrill of Brazil, The 1946,S 6,18:3
No Leave, No Love 1946,O 18,29:2
Cockeyed Miracle, The 1946,O 25,28:1
Hucksters, The 1947,Jl 18,21:2
Song of the Thin Man 1947,Ag 29,14:2
B F's Daughter 1948,Mr 25,35:2
Three Musketeers, The 1948,O 21,33:2
My Dear Secretary 1949,F 14,15:4
Neptune's Daughter 1949,Je 10,32:2
That Midnight Kiss 1949,S 23,28:2
Annie Get Your Gun 1950,My 18,37:1
Love That Brute 1950,My 27,10:6
Three Little Words 1950,Ag 10,21:2
Royal Wedding 1951,Mr 9,30:2
Kind Lady 1951,Ag 8,21:2
Texas Carnival 1951,O 13,9:1
Angels in the Outfield 1951,O 18,32:1
It's a big Country 1952,Ja 9,25:2
Phone Call From a Stranger 1952,F 2,11:2
Belle of New York, The 1952,Mr 6,25:6
Holiday for Sinners 1952,S 20,13:2
Battle Circus 1953,My 28,27:5
Kiss Me Kate 1953,N 6,23:2
All the Brothers Were Valiant 1953,D 29,19:2
Long, Long Trailer, The 1954,F 19,24:3
Men of the Fighting Lady 1954,My 8,15:2
Glass Slipper, The 1955,Mr 25,19:2
Running Wild 1955,N 12,23:2
Shack out on 101 1956,Ja 10,26:2
Man in the Gray Flannel Suit, The
1956,Ap 13,21:1
Johnny Concho 1956,Ag 16,30:1
Great Man, The 1957,Ja 2,28:2
Joe Butterfly 1957,My 30,23:2
Fuzzy Pink Nightgown, The 1957,O 31,41:1
Don't Go Near the Water 1957,N 15,37:1
Deep Six, The 1958,Ja 16,32:1
Time to Love and a Time to Die, A
1958,Jl 10,22:1
Perfect Furlough, The 1959,Ja 22,27:4
Hole in the Head, A 1959,Jl 16,31:2
That Kind of Woman 1959,S 12,12:2
Crowded Sky, The 1961,F 11,27:2
Absent-Minded Professor, The 1961,Mr 16,44:2
King of the Roaring Twenties 1961,O 5,43:1
Son of Flubber 1963,F 9,5:2
Dr Strangelove or: How I Learned to Stop
Worrying and Love the Bomb 1964,Ja 31,16:1
(Incorrect in this edition; use 1964,Ja 30,24:1
elsewhere)
Man in the Middle 1964,Mr 5,36:1
Honeymoon Hotel 1964,Je 4,28:1
Patsy, The 1964,Ag 13,24:2
Bikini Beach 1964,S 17,52:6
Americanization of Emily, The 1964,O 28,51:1
Great Race, The 1965,S 16,00:0

Promise her Anything 1966,F 23,46:1
Stagecoach 1966,Je 16,53:1
Night of the Grizzly, The 1966,Je 23,29:1
Around the World Under the Sea 1966,Jl 21,20:2
Welcome to Hard Times 1967,My 2,56:1
Warning Shot 1967,Je 8,52:2
War Wagon, The 1967,Ag 3,26:3
Point Blank 1967,S 19,53:1
Finian's Rainbow 1968,O 10,59:5
Wynn, May
Caine Mutiny, The 1954,Je 25,17:1
Violent Men, The 1955,Ja 27,17:2
Wynn, Nan
Million Dollar Baby 1941,Je 7,20:2
Pardon my Sarong 1942,Ag 27,15:1
Princess O'Rourke 1943,N 6,16:2
Jam Session 1944,My 3,25:3
Wynn, Ned
Stagecoach 1966,Je 16,53:1
Wynn, Zoo
Larceny Street 1941,Ja 6,11:2
WYNNE
See Also WINN, WYNN
Wynne, Pamela (Original Author)
Dangerous Innocence 1925,Je 8,19:1
Devotion 1931,O 3,20:2
Wynter, Dagmar
Crimson Pirate, The 1952,Ag 28,21:2
Wynter, Dana
View From Pompey's Head, The 1955,N 5,22:5
D-Day, The Sixth of June 1956,My 30,13:1
Something of Value 1957,My 11,24:6
Fraulein 1958,Je 9,27:2
In Love and War 1958,N 1,14:2
Shake Hands With the Devil 1959,Je 25,20:7
Sink the Bismarck! 1960,F 12,22:3
On the Double 1961,My 20,12:1
List of Adrian Messenger, The 1963,My 30,20:1
If He Hollers, Let Him Go 1968,O 10,59:7
Wynters, Charlotte
Personal Maid 1931,S 5,7:4
Struggle, The 1931,D 11,35:1
Calling of Dan Matthews, The 1936,Ja 25,18:4
Girl Overboard 1937,Mr 1,15:1
Sinners in Paradise 1938,My 20,17:2
Reformatory 1938,Je 27,13:6
Cipher Bureau 1938,D 14,32:6
City of Chance 1940,Ja 22,11:3
Are Husbands Necessary? 1942,Jl 9,17:2
Falcon's Brother, The 1942,O 3,9:5
Lulu Belle 1948,Je 21,18:3
Woman of Distinction, A 1950,Mr 17,28:2
Foxfire 1955,Jl 14,19:1
Wynyard, Diana
Rasputin and the Empress 1932,D 24,11:4
Cavalcade 1933,Ja 6,23:2
Men Must Fight 1933,Mr 11,18:3
Reunion in Vienna 1933,Ap 29,14:2
Where Sinners Meet 1934,My 25,25:2
Let's Try Again 1934,Je 22,24:1
One More River 1934,Ag 10,21:1
Fugitive, The 1940,Jl 23,22:2
Voice in the Night, The 1941,My 23,25:4
Prime Minister, The 1942,F 4,23:2
Kipps 1942,My 25,11:2
Ideal Husband, An 1948,Ja 15,28:2
Tom Brown's School Days 1952,Ja 8,23:5
Angel Street 1952,N 11,25:2
Island in the Sun 1957,Je 13,37:1
Wysbar, Frank (Cinematographer)
Werf zum Graven Hecht, Die; Gray Pikes Wharf,
The 1938,Ap 18,11:2
Wysbar, Frank (Director)
Anna und Elisabeth 1933,Jl 2,IX,2:2
Hermine und die Sieben Aufrechten
1935,S 21,18:2
Anna und Elisabeth 1936,Je 13,13:1
Ball im Metropol 1938,Mr 5,11:3
Fahrmann Maria; Ferryman Maria
1938,D 24,12:3
Wysocka, Stanislawa
Tredowata 1936,D 31,21:2
Wyss, Alfredo U
Ramparts We Watch, The 1940,S 20,27:1
Wyss, Johann David (Original Author)
Swiss Family Robinson 1940,F 9,15:3

X

X, Mr (Original Author)
Little Child Shall Lead Them, A 1922,S 2,10:4
Xanrof, Leon (Original Author)
Love Parade, The 1929,N 20,32:6
Xenia, Maria
Casablan 1964,D 14,50:1
Xenidis, Stavros
Policeman of the 16th Precinct, The
1963,Ap 22,23:2
Xirgu, Margarita
Bodas de Sangre; Bloody Wedding
1939,N 13,15:3

Y

Ya-ching, Lee
Disputed Passage 1939,O 26,27:2
Yaari, Moshe
They Were Ten; (Heym Hayu Assara)
1961,Ap 18,44:2
Pillar of Fire, The 1963,Ap 8,35:2
Yabbarov, Anatoli
Red and the White, The 1968,S 21,26:1
Yablonsky, V
Return of Nathan Becker, The 1933,Ap 15,16:3
Yachigusa, Kaoru
Samurai 1956,Ja 10,26:1
Madame Butterfly 1956,Ap 24,26:2
Samurai (Part II) 1967,O 21,16:1
Yachnitski, A
General Suvorov 1941,S 20,11:2
Yacht Club Boys
Thanks a Million 1935,N 14,17:1
Stage Struck 1936,S 28,14:4
Pigskin Parade 1936,N 14,23:3
Artists and Models 1937,Ag 5,19:2
Thrill of a Lifetime 1937,D 9,30:2
Cocoanut Grove 1938,Je 16,21:2
Yacht Club Boys, The
Artists and Models Abroad 1938,D 22,25:3
Yacht Club Boys (Miscellaneous)
Pigskin Parade 1936,N 14,23:3
Yaconelli, Frank
Parade of the West 1930,Mr 3,18:4
Death Takes a Holiday 1934,F 24,18:4
Down Under the Sea 1936,Ag 10,10:2
East Side Kids 1940,F 19,21:6
Dr Cyclops 1940,Ap 11,32:3
Torrid Zone 1940,My 18,11:3
September Affair 1951,F 2,19:2
Serenade 1956,Mr 24,21:1 (Incorrect in this
edition; use 1956,Mr 23,21:1 elsewhere)
Yaconelli, Z
Amazon Quest 1949,My 14,9:3
Yacoubi, Ahmed ben Driss
8 X 8 1957,Mr 16,13:2
Yadas, Don Japanese Revue
I Love, You Love 1962,N 10,16:2
Yadin, Yosef
Four in a Jeep 1951,Je 12,35:2
Hill 24 Doesn't Answer 1955,N 3,37:1
Stop Train 349 1964,N 12,40:2
Yaffe, Ben
Fugitive Kind, The 1960,Ap 15,13:1
Yagi, James
Bridge to the Sun 1961,O 18,50:1
King Kong vs. Godzilla 1963,Je 27,23:4
Yagi, Yasutaro (Screenwriter)
Hiroshima 1955,My 17,32:1
Yagling, B (Screenwriter)
One Day in Soviet Russia 1941,O 27,21:2
Yahiro, Fuji (Screenwriter)
Buddha 1965,Je 17,27:4
Yainada, Isuzu
Yojimbo 1962,O 16,34:1
Yakhontov, Nikolai
Son of the Regiment 1948,Ap 29,27:3
Yakisch, Mara
Lustige Witwenball, Der; Merry Widows' Ball,
The 1939,My 1,21:2
Yakovehenko, M
Train Goes to Kiev, The 1961,Ap 10,26:1
Yakovlev, Sergei
House With an Attic 1964,D 21,42:5
Yakovlev, Yuri
No Ordinary Summer 1958,O 6,36:3
Idiot, The 1960,Jl 22,11:2
Ballad of a Hussar, The 1963,Jl 15,25:5
Yakovleva, K
Scandal? 1929,O 28,20:1
Yakovleva, S
Yellow Ticket, The 1928,D 10,25:1
Men and Jobs 1933,Ja 3,19:3
Yaltan, Jaron
Little Hut, The 1957,My 4,25:1
Yama, Yachuco
Operation Kid Brother 1967,N 23,58:2
Yamada, Isuzu
Hiroshima 1955,My 17,32:1
Throne of Blood 1961,N 23,50:2
Lower Depths, The 1962,F 10,12:5
Yamada, Minosuke
Ikiru; To Live 1960,Ja 30,13:5
Yamagata, Isao
Gate of Hell 1954,D 14,45:2
Rebellion 1968,O 26,27:4
Yamaguchi, Shirley
Japanese War Bride 1952,Ja 30,22:6
House of Bamboo 1955,Jl 2,13:2
Sword for Hire 1957,S 5,32:1
Yamamotn, R
Stray Dog 1964,Mr 4,32:7

Yamamoto, Fujiko
Golden Demon 1956,Ja 31,34:3
Utamaro, Painter of Women 1964,D 2,57:1
Buddha 1965,Je 17,27:4
Great Wall, The 1965,D 16,63:2
Yamamoto, Gaku
Showdown for Zatoichi 1968,O 5,40:1
Yamamoto, Reizaburo
Drunken Angel 1959,D 31,12:1
Yamamoto, Sanze (Director)
Magic Boy 1963,D 23,18:2
Yamamoto, Shugoro (Original Author)
This Madding Crowd 1964,Je 17,48:1
Yamamura, So
Yang Kwei Fei 1956,S 11,41:2
Barbarian and the Geisha 1958,O 3,25:1
Human Condition, The 1959,D 16,56:1
Country Doctor, The 1963,Ag 14,28:1
Yamanaka, Sadao (Screenwriter)
Saga of the Vagabonds 1964,O 7,31:1 (Incorrect
in this edition; use 1964,O 7,51:1 elsewhere)
Yamaoka, Iris
Petticoat Fever 1936,Mr 21,13:2
Yamaoka, Otto
Benson Murder Case, The 1930,Ap 12,23:1
Black Camel, The 1931,Jl 4,11:5
Hatchet Man, The 1932,F 4,25:2
Before Midnight 1934,Ja 10,24:3
We're Rich Again 1934,S 1,16:3
Petticoat Fever 1936,Mr 21,13:2
Libeled Lady 1936,O 31,24:2
Night Waitress 1936,D 18,31:5
Yamashita, Kikuji
She and He 1964,S 26,16:1
Yamato, Hiroshi
Barbarian and the Geisha 1958,O 3,25:1
Yamazaki, Tsutomu
High and Low 1963,N 27,30:1
School for Sea 1967,D 2,48:5
Yan, San Bo
China Express, The 1930,Mr 10,24:1
Yana
Cockleshell Heroes, The 1956,Je 4,25:2
Yanagi, Eijiro
Imposter, The 1955,Mr 23,27:1
Phantom Horse, the 1956,Jl 25,16:1
Idiot, The 1963,My 1,35:1
Yang, Marie
Satan Never Sleeps 1962,F 22,20:1
Yankin, Yura
Son of the Regiment 1948,Ap 29,27:3
Yanne, Jean
Inside Out 1964,S 25,32:1
Viscount, The 1967,My 11,50:1
Weekend 1968,S 28,36:1
Yannetti, Ettore
It's Forever Springtime 1951,D 29,7:7
Yanshin, M
Czar wants to Sleep, The 1934,D 10,16:3
Gypsies 1936,Jl 30,22:2
Prisoners 1937,F 20,9:2
Inspector General, The 1954,My 3,21:2
Safety Match, The 1955,Mr 28,24:5
Twelfth Night 1956,Mr 5,21:1
Yanukova, V D
Prisoners 1937,F 20,9:2
Yanushkevitch, R (Original Author)
Nightingale 1936,N 4,41:2
Yanushkevitch, Regina
Road to Life 1932,Ja 28,24:2
Yao, Tsung
Maid of Formosa 1949,Ag 8,10:5
Yaray, Hans
Lydia 1941,S 19,27:1
Carnegie Hall 1947,My 3,10:2
Yarbo, Lillian
Rainbow on the River 1936,D 18,31:4
Wives Under Suspicion 1938,Jl 1,22:3
You Can't Take It With You 1938,S 2,21:2
Family Next Door, The 1939,Ap 28,31:2
Way Down South 1939,Ag 18,16:4
Destry Rides Again 1939,N 30,25:1
Moon Over her Shoulder 1941,N 5,31:2
Wild Bill Hickok Rides 1942,F 7,13:5
Great Man's Lady, The 1942,Ap 30,14:3
Between Us Girls 1942,S 25,25:3
Swing Shift Maisie 1943,S 10,29:2
My Brother Talks to Horses 1947,Je 19,27:4
Night Unto Night 1949,Je 11,11:2
Look for the Silver Lining 1949,Je 24,29:2
Yarborough, Barton
Ghost of Frankenstein, The 1942,Ap 4,19:2
Unknown, The 1946,Jl 20,10:3
Yarbrough, Jean (Director)
Top Sergeant Mulligan 1941,N 12,31:3
Good Morning, Judge 1943,Ap 30,25:4
In Society 1944,Ag 17,20:2
Here Come the Co-Eds 1945,F 19,21:1
Naughty Nineties, The 1945,Je 21,16:2
House of Horrors 1946,F 23,20:3
She Wolf of London 1946,Ap 6,10:6
Inside Job 1946,Je 15,24:3
Holiday in Havana 1949,O 14,33:5

Jack and the Beanstalk 1952,Ap 8,35:3
Saintly Sinners 1962,Mr 29,28:2
Yarbrough, Jean (Producer)
Inside Job 1946,Je 15,24:3
Yarde, Margaret
Michael and Mary 1932,Mr 5,11:2
Scrooge 1935,D 14,11:1
Prison Without Bars 1939,Ap 10,13:2
French Without Tears 1940,Ap 29,12:2
Yardley, Herbert O (Original Author)
Rendezvous 1935,O 26,12:2
Yardley, Michael
Bush Christmas 1947,N 27,50:4
Yardley, Nicky
Bush Christmas 1947,N 27,50:4
Yarnell, Bruce
Irma la Douce 1963,Je 6,39:1
Yarof, M I
Thunderstorm 1934,S 29,12:2
Yarof, S K
Greater Promise, A 1936,O 8,27:3
Yaroslavtsev, V (Composer)
Yolanta 1964,D 23,22:3
Yarotskaya, M G
Last Night, The 1937,Ap 28,18:3
Yarotskayi, M
Train Goes East, The 1949,S 5,13:3
Yarov, Sergi
Wings of Victory 1941,N 17,15:2
Yarrow, Peter
You Are What You Eat 1968,S 25,38:1
Yarrow, Peter (Producer)
You Are What You Eat 1968,S 25,38:1
Yarson, Lilo
For Whom the Bell Tolls 1943,Jl 15,25:2
Yarus, Buddy
Mr Winkle Goes to War 1944,Ag 3,16:1
Objective Burma 1945,Ja 27,15:2
Yashwant
Gyandev of India 1943,Ap 10,12:5
Yasmina, Princess
Island of Allah 1956,Je 27,35:1
Yassine, Ismall
Little Miss Devil 1951,D 8,9:2
Yastrebitsky, A
Village of Sin, The 1929,My 21,29:3
Yastrebova, Nadia
Russian Ballerina 1947,S 11,31:2
Yasuda, Kimiyoshi (Director)
Zatoichi 1968,Je 28,37:1
Majin 1968,Ag 10,15:5
Yasui, Shoji
Burmese Harp, The 1967,Ap 29,25:1
Yasumi, Toshio (Screenwriter)
Chushingura 1963,O 4,26:1
Illusion of Blood 1968,N 28,66:5
Yasumiko
Winner, The 1965,Jl 1,34:1
Yates, Beverly
Bye Bye Birdie 1963,Ap 5,27:3
Yates, David
Night my Number Came up, The 1955,D 20,39:5
Yates, George W (Original Author)
Man From Frisco 1944,Je 16,14:7
Sinbad the Sailor 1947,Ja 23,31:2
Tall Target, The 1951,S 28,26:2
Them 1954,Je 17,36:2
Yates, George W (Screenwriter)
Falcon in Mexico, The 1944,Ag 5,16:2
Spanish Main, The 1945,N 7,20:2
Last Outpost, The 1951,Je 22,16:3
Tall Target, The 1951,S 28,26:2
This Woman is Dangerous 1952,F 28,23:2
Those Redheads From Seattle 1953,O 1,34:2
Saracen Blade, The 1954,My 15,13:4
Conquest of Space 1955,My 28,7:6
Earth vs the Flying Saucers 1956,Ag 2,21:2
Yates, Hal (Original Author)
Nobody's Baby 1937,My 20,17:3
Yates, Hal (Screenwriter)
Nobody's Baby 1937,My 20,17:3
Yates, Pauline
Darling 1965,Ag 4,20:1
Yates, Peter (Director)
One Way Pendulum 1965,Mr 3,34:3
Robbery 1967,S 28,58:2
Bullitt 1968,O 18,41:2
Yates, Peter (Screenwriter)
Robbery 1967,S 28,58:2
Yawitz, Paul (Original Author)
Confessions of Boston Blackie 1941,D 8,31:2
Walk Softly Stranger 1950,O 16,30:5
Black Scorpion, The 1957,O 12,23:2
Yawitz, Paul (Screenwriter)
Saturday's Heroes 1937,O 16,22:2
Breakfast for Two 1937,N 20,21:2
Crashing Hollywood 1938,Ja 8,19:2
Go Chase Yourself 1938,Je 15,27:1
Affairs of Annabel, The 1938,O 13,29:2
Fixer Dugan 1939,My 6,21:2
Little Accident 1939,N 24,29:3
Confessions of Boston Blackie 1941,D 8,31:2
One Mysterious Night 1944,O 21,15:3

Yawitz, Paul (Screenwriter)— Cont

Falcon's Alibi, The 1946,Ap 13,23:2
Models, Inc 1952,My 26,18:4
Yazumi, Toshio (Screenwriter)
Temptress and the Monk, The 1963,My 28,32:1
Ybarra, Ventura
Frontier Marshal 1939,Jl 29,18:2
Ye-chuan, Li
Last Woman of Shang, The 1964,D 15,56:2
Yearsley, Ralph
Village Blacksmith, The 1922,N 3,17:5
Hill Billy, The 1924,Mr 12,19:4
Desert Gold 1926,Mr 23,24:5
Kid Brother, The 1927,Ja 24,14:1
Rose-Marie 1928,F 13,16:2
Yeats, William Butler (Screenwriter)
Oedipus Rex 1957,Ja 8,26:1
Yeats-Brown, Francis (Original Author)
Lives of a Bengal Lancer, The 1935,Ja 12,12:2
Yeaworth, Irvin S Jr (Director)
Blob, The 1958,N 7,23:1
Dinosaurusi 1960,S 9,36:4
Way Out 1967,O 26,54:3
Yeaworth, Irvin S Jr (Producer)
Dinosaurusi 1960,S 9,36:4
Way Out 1967,O 26,54:3
Yeaworth, Jean (Screenwriter)
Dinosaurusi 1960,S 9,36:4
Way Out 1967,O 26,54:3
Yegiazarov, G (Cinematographer)
Poem of the Sea 1959,D 21,34:4
Yegorov, Y (Director)
Frigid Sea, The 1955,N 21,23:4
Yegorova, E G
Heroes of the Sea 1941,Ap 28,11:2
Yegorova, G
Nightingale 1936,N 4,41:2
Yegros, Lina
Octavo Mandamiento, El; Eighth Commandment,
The 1937,Mr 1,15:2
Yeldham, Peter (Screenwriter)
Code 7...Victim 5 1965,My 20,52:1
Mozambique 1966,F 10,33:1
Ten Little Indians 1966,F 10,33:1
Liquidator, The 1966,O 29,34:1
Bang, Bang, You're Dead 1967,Ja 19,41:2
Long Duel, The 1967,N 2,58:3
Yellen, Barry B (Producer)
Sound of Laughter, The 1963,D 18,44:2
Christmas That Almost Wasn't 1966,N 24,65:2
How to Seduce a Playboy 1968,My 16,53:2
Yellen, Jack (Composer)
King of Jazz 1930,My 3,23:1
George White's Scandals 1934,Mr 16,24:2
George White's 1935 Scandals 1935,Ap 29,12:3
King of Burlesque 1936,Ja 16,25:2
Captain January 1936,Ap 25,21:1
Happy Landing 1938,Ja 22,19:1
Rebecca of Sunnybrook Farm 1938,Mr 26,12:1
George White's Scandals 1945,O 11,26:2
Yellen, Jack (Miscellaneous)
Hell in the Heavens 1934,D 12,28:2
Our Little Girl 1935,Je 7,24:4
Sing, Baby, Sing 1936,S 12,20:1
Yellen, Jack (Original Author)
Sing, Baby, Sing 1936,S 12,20:1
Yellen, Jack (Screenwriter)
George White's 1935 Scandals 1935,Ap 29,12:3
Sing, Baby, Sing 1936,S 12,20:1
Pigskin Parade 1936,N 14,23:3
Love Is News 1937,Mr 6,10:1
Wake up and Live 1937,Ap 24,16:2
You Can't Have Everything 1937,Ag 4,15:2
Ali Baba Goes to Town 1937,O 23,14:1
Sally, Irene and Mary 1938,F 26,9:2
Little Miss Broadway 1938,Jl 23,10:4
My Lucky Star 1938,S 10,20:2
Hold That Co-ed 1938,S 24,13:1
Submarine Patrol 1938,N 19,9:2
Yemelyanov, V
Road to Life 1956,Je 11,26:6
Yen, Chen Yen
Song of China 1936,N 10,31:3
Love Eterne, The; Liang Shan Po and Chu
Ying-lai 1965,Ja 16,14:1
Lady General, The 1965,F 12,19:1
Grand Substitution, The 1965,N 25,64:5
Sons of Good Earth 1967,S 16,37:5
Yeniutina, V
Flames on the Volga 1958,Ja 27,21:7
Yeo, Leslie
Luck of Ginger Coffey, The 1964,S 22,44:1
Yeomans, Mary
Kitchen, The 1961,N 2,42:1
Yerby, Frank (Original Author)
Foxes of Harrow, The 1947,S 25,35:4
Golden Hawk, The 1952,O 18,16:4
Saracen Blade, The 1954,My 15,13:4
Yergin, Irving (Original Author)
Murder Game, The 1966,Mr 31,43:2
Yermilov, Seryozha
War and Peace 1968,Ap 29,50:5

Yermolayev, Alexei
Ballet of Romeo and Juliet, The 1956,Ap 3,31:2
Yeroleyev, P (Screenwriter)
House With an Attic 1964,D 21,42:5
Yershova, Yevgenia
Lileia 1960,My 30,8:2
Yesipova, Raisa
Woman's World 1933,Ja 23,9:2
Yetter, William
They Got Me Covered 1943,Mr 5,20:2
Yevsligneye, Evgeni
Welcome Kostya! 1965,N 22,48:2
Yezhkina, A
Overcoat, The 1965,Mr 2,31:2
Yezierska, Anzia (Original Author)
Hungry Hearts 1922,N 27,18:1
Salome of the Tenements 1925,F 24,17:3
Yguerbuchen, Mohammed (Composer)
Pepe le Moko 1941,Mr 4,20:2
Yi, Feng
Lady General, The 1965,F 12,19:1
Yiannacopoulos, Christos (Screenwriter)
Policeman of the 16th Precinct, The
1963,Ap 22,23:2
Yih, Chang
Song of China 1936,N 10,31:3
Yin-Yun, Chow
Maid of Formosa 1949,Ag 8,10:5
Ying-isol, Cheung
Empress Wu 1965,Mr 16,42:2
Yiotopoulos, Evangelos
Barefoot Battalion 1954,My 29,13:4
Yiouli, Smaro
Wind of Hate; (O Anemos Tou Missous)
1958,N 17,37:2
Fortune Teller, The 1961,My 22,37:5
Yip, Yee Tak
Ugly American, The 1963,Ap 12,30:2
Yisrael, Kol Symphony
Journey to Jerusalem, A 1968,N 18,59:1
Yoan, Nester
Way of a Gaucho 1952,N 5,36:2
Yoda, Yoshida
Horizontal Lieutenant, The 1962,My 12,15:3
Yoda, Yoshikata (Screenwriter)
Ugetsu 1954,S 8,40:3
Yang Kwei Fei 1956,S 11,41:2
Life of Oharu 1964,Ap 21,42:2
Taira Clan, The; Shin Heike Monagatari
1964,S 21,37:4
Yoda, Yoshio
McHale's Navy 1964,Jl 11,15:2
Yoke-Moon, Lee
Children of the Damned 1964,Ja 30,24:2
Yokel, Alex (Producer)
Skinnay's School and Scandal 1919,Ap 21,13:4
Yokomoka, Otto
Wedding Night, The 1935,Mr 16,19:1
Yokoo, Dekao
Tokyo File 212 1951,Je 1,20:7
Yolanda
Under the Pampas Moon 1935,My 31,11:1
Champagne Waltz 1937,F 4,17:2
Three Waltzes 1939,Ap 25,19:2
Yolanda (Miscellaneous)
Rumba 1935,F 25,13:2
Yoltz, Gretel
Girl in Every Port, A 1928,F 20,14:1
Hot Heels 1928,My 22,19:3
Yonaya, Rina
Tanya 1942,Mr 5,27:1
Yong, Soo
Painted Veil, The 1934,D 7,29:1
China Seas 1935,Ag 10,16:4
Klondike Annie 1936,Mr 12,18:2
Good Earth, The 1937,F 3,27:1
China 1943,Ap 22,31:2
Night Plane From Chungking 1943,My 31,13:2
Peking Express 1951,Jl 19,20:2
Big Jim McLain 1952,S 18,35:2
Love Is a Many-Splendored Thing
1955,Ag 19,10:1
Flight to Hong Kong 1957,Ja 3,28:2
Soyonara 1957,D 6,39:4
Sayonara 1957,D 6,39:4
Yonnel, Jean
Call, The 1938,Mr 29,18:3
Kreutzer Sonata, The 1938,D 20,30:2
Blind Desire 1948,Je 10,28:4
Marianne of my Youth; (Marianne de ma
Jeunesse) 1959,Ja 20,43:1
Miracle of Saint Therese 1959,F 10,38:4 (In
Addenda)
Thank Heaven for Small Favors 1965,Ja 14,44:2
Yordan, Caprice
Kiss Them for Me 1957,N 9,31:2
Yordan, Philip (Original Author)
Anna Lucasta 1949,Ag 12,13:2
Black Book, The 1949,O 17,18:2
Mara Maru 1952,Ap 24,38:1
Broken Lance 1954,Jl 30,9:1
Gun Glory 1957,Jl 20,8:7
Anna Lucasta 1959,Ja 15,27:1

Circus World 1964,Je 26,34:2
Yordan, Philip (Producer)
Anna Lucasta 1949,Ag 12,13:2
Harder They Fall, The 1956,My 10,26:3
Studs Lonigan 1960,D 15,59:1
Battle of the Bulge 1965,D 18,36:1
Yordan, Philip (Screenwriter)
Syncopation 1942,My 29,13:3
Dillinger 1945,Ap 26,26:2
Whistle Stop 1946,Mr 18,24:2
Suspense 1946,Jl 5,15:3
Chase, The 1946,N 18,31:2
Bad Men of Tombstone 1949,Mr 5,10:2
Anna Lucasta 1949,Ag 12,13:2
Black Book, The 1949,O 17,18:2
Edge of Doom 1950,Ag 4,13:2
Detective Story 1951,N 7,35:2
Mutiny 1952,Mr 20,37:5
Houdini 1953,Jl 3,10:2
Blowing Wild 1953,O 8,37:5
Naked Jungle, The 1954,Ap 3,19:2
Johnny Guitar 1954,My 28,19:2
Big Combo, The 1955,Mr 26,13:2
Conquest of Space 1955,My 28,7:6
Man From Laramie, The 1955,S 1,20:2
Last Frontier, The 1955,D 8,45:1
Joe Macbeth 1956,Ap 7,13:1
Harder They Fall, The 1956,My 10,26:3
Men in War 1957,Mr 20,32:4
No Down Payment 1957,O 31,41:1
Bravados, The 1958,Je 26,23:2
God's Little Acre 1958,Ag 14,23:2
Anna Lucasta 1959,Ja 15,27:1
Bramble Bush, The 1960,F 25,34:2
Studs Lonigan 1960,D 15,59:1
King of Kings 1961,O 12,41:2
Cid, El 1961,D 15,49:1
Day of the Triffids 1963,My 11,15:2
55 Days at Peking 1963,My 30,20:1
Fall of the Roman Empire, The 1964,Mr 27,14:2
Battle of the Bulge 1965,D 18,36:1
Yordon, Philip (Screenwriter)
House of Strangers 1949,Jl 2,8:2
York, Alvin C Sergeant (Original Author)
Sergeant York 1941,Jl 3,15:1
York, Andrew (Original Author)
Danger Route 1968,Je 6,54:2
York, B M
Yearling, The 1947,Ja 24,18:2
York, Carl
Pretty Boy Floyd 1960,N 3,49:2
Hustler, The 1961,S 27,35:1
York, Chick
Ramrod 1947,Je 30,25:6
York, David
Man From Colorado 1949,Ja 21,24:3
York, Dick
My Sister Eileen 1955,S 23,21:1
Three Stripes in the Sun 1955,N 24,41:2
Operation Mad Ball 1957,N 21,38:1
Cowboy 1958,F 20,29:5
Last Blitzkrieg, The 1959,Ja 31,13:5
They Came to Cordura 1959,O 22,47:2
Inherit the Wind 1960,O 13,41:1
York, Duke
Elmer and Elsie 1934,Ag 4,14:5
Pursuit of Happiness, The 1934,O 26,25:1
Strike Me Pink 1936,Ja 17,15:2
Topper Takes a Trip 1938,D 30,11:2
Fortunes of Captain Blood 1950,Je 10,11:3
Rogue River 1951,F 16,21:4
York, Gerald
Chuka 1967,N 2,58:3
York, Jeff
They Were Expendable 1945,D 21,25:2
Up Goes Maisie 1946,Ja 25,26:7
Postman Always Rings Twice, The
1946,My 3,15:3
Yearling, The 1947,Ja 24,18:2
Isn't It Romantic? 1948,O 7,35:2
Paleface, The 1948,D 16,41:2
Kill the Umpire 1950,My 29,10:6
Surrender 1950,O 9,21:5
Short Grass 1951,Ja 13,10:4
Lady Says No, The 1952,Ja 7,14:3
Demetrius and the Gladiators 1954,Je 19,9:1
Great Locomotive Chase, The 1956,Je 27,35:1
Johnny Tremain 1957,Jl 11,21:1
Old Yeller 1957,D 26,23:4
Savage Sam 1963,Ag 1,17:3
York, Katherine
Strange Woman, The 1947,F 24,16:4
York, Michael
Taming of the Shrew, The 1967,Mr 9,43:1
Accident 1967,Ap 18,33:1
Smashing Time 1967,D 21,44:1
Strange Affair, The 1968,Jl 25,26:2
Romeo and Juliet 1968,O 9,41:1
York, Powell
Disraeli 1929,O 3,27:5
York, Susannah
Tunes of Glory 1960,D 21,38:2
Loss of Innocence 1961,N 22,27:1

York, Susannah— Cont
Freud 1962,D 13,37:1
Tom Jones 1963,O 8,48:1
Seventh Dawn, The 1964,S 3,24:1
Sands of the Kalahari 1965,N 25,64:5
Kaleidoscope 1966,S 23,45:1
Man for all Seasons, A 1966,D 13,60:1
Sebastian 1968,Ja 25,33:2
Duffy 1968,S 17,50:3
Killing of Sister George, The 1968,D 17,58:4
Yorke, Carol
Letters From an Unknown Woman
1948,Ap 29,20:6
Yorke, Edith
Merry Go Round 1923,Jl 2,16:2
My Man 1924,F 11,18:3
Happiness 1924,Mr 11,16:2
Husbands and Lovers 1924,D 9,23:3
Excuse Me 1925,Ja 27,11:2
Capital Punishment 1925,F 5,23:3
Silent Sanderson 1925,Je 11,14:3
Wild Horse Mesa 1925,Ag 10,8:2
Phantom of the Opera, The 1925,S 7,15:3
Souls for Sables 1925,S 15,12:1 (Incorrect in this
edition; use 1925,S 15,29:1 elsewhere)
Oh! What a Nurse! 1926,F 22,14:1
Red Dice 1926,Ap 16,20:3
Born to the West 1926,Je 30,18:1 (In Addenda)
Sensation Seekers 1927,Mr 16,28:2
Valiant, The 1929,My 13,27:2
Seven Keys to Baldpate 1929,D 26,21:1
Yorke, Edithe
Below the Line 1925,S 21,12:4
Yorke, Oswald
Monsieur Beaucaire 1924,Ag 12,12:1 (In
Addenda)
Yorkin, Bud (Director)
Come Blow Your Horn 1963,Je 7,37:1
Never too Late 1965,N 5,28:1
Divorce American Style 1967,Jl 20,30:2
Inspector Clouseau 1968,Jl 25,26:1
Yorkin, Bud (Producer)
Come Blow Your Horn 1963,Je 7,37:1
Yoshida, Tetsuo (Screenwriter)
Majin 1968,Ag 10,15:5
Yoshida, Yoshio
Zatoichi 1968,Je 28,37:1
Yoshikawa, Eiji (Original Author)
Samurai 1956,Ja 10,26:1
Taira Clan, The; Shin Heike Monagatari
1964,S 21,37:4
Samurai (Part II) 1967,O 21,16:1
Yoshimura, Jitsuko
Insect Woman, The; Nippon Konchuki
1964,Jl 1,42:1
Onibaba 1965,F 10,44:3
Yoshinaga, George
Frogmen, The 1951,Je 30,8:6
Yoshiwara, Tamaki
Letter, The 1929,Mr 8,30:1
Cheat, The 1931,D 12,23:3
Yoshov, Valentin (Screenwriter)
Ballad of a Soldier 1960,D 27,22:1
Yost, Dorothy (Original Author)
Hills of Kentucky 1927,Mr 2,29:3
Blackmail 1939,S 15,26:3
Yost, Dorothy (Screenwriter)
Gay Divorcee, The 1934,N 16,27:1
Laddie 1935,My 6,22:3
Alice Adams 1935,Ag 16,11:3
Murder on a Bridle Path 1936,Ap 11,19:2
Bunker Bean 1936,Je 27,21:2
M'liss 1936,Ag 8,5:2
That Girl From Paris 1937,Ja 1,19:1
there Goes The Groom 1937,D 25,10:6
Four Girls in White 1939,F 23,19:3
Story of Vernon and Irene Castle, The
1939,Mr 31,19:2
Forty Little Mothers 1940,Ap 19,25:2
Sporting Blood 1940,Jl 22,20:2
Thunderhead 1945,Mr 16,21:2
Smoky 1946,Je 27,29:1
Big Cat, The 1949,Jl 29,12:2
Yost, Herbert
Fast and Loose 1930,D 1,21:1
Age of Innocence, The 1934,O 19,27:1
Yost, Robert (Original Author)
Illegal Traffic 1938,N 17,29:3
Yost, Robert (Screenwriter)
Dante's Inferno 1935,Ag 1,15:1
Preview Murder Mystery, The 1936,Mr 21,13:2
Forgotten Faces 1936,Jl 4,18:2
Thunder Trail 1938,F 5,19:3
Tip-Off Girls 1938,Mr 25,15:3
Prison Farm 1938,Jl 15,13:3
Illegal Traffic 1938,N 17,29:3
Grand Jury Secrets 1939,Je 29,19:2
Yost, Tibor (Screenwriter)
Desires 1954,Jl 2,10:2
Youlache
Sante Fe Trail, The 1930,O 18,23:2
Youmans, Vincent (Composer)
Song of the West 1930,F 28,20:7
Flying Down to Rio 1933,D 22,25:2

Youmans, Vincent (Composer) — Cont
No, No, Nanette 1940,D 20,33:1
Hit the Deck 1955,Mr 4,17:1
Youmans, Vincent (Original Author)
No, No, Nanette 1940,D 20,33:1
Tea for Two 1950,S 2,11:2
Young, Aida (Producer)
Vengance of She, The 1968,My 30,21:4
Young, Al (Miscellaneous)
Fight for Peace, The 1938,My 14,18:1
Young, Alan
Margie 1946,O 17,28:3
Chicken every Sunday 1949,Ja 19,34:2
Mr Belvedere Goes to College 1949,Ap 16,11:2
Aaron Slick From Punkin Crick 1952,Ap 19,18:6
Androcles and the Lion 1953,Ja 15,23:2
Gentlemen Marry Brunettes 1955,O 31,31:5
Tom Thumb 1958,D 24,00:0
Time Machine, The 1960,Ag 18,19:1
Young, Art
Alaskan Adventures 1927,My 10,24:5
Young, Arthur
Victoria the Great 1937,O 29,19:1
21 Days Together 1940,My 23,28:4
Murder by Invitation 1941,Jl 23,15:4
Inspector Calls, An 1954,N 26,24:4
Young, Arthur (Composer)
Dance Band 1936,Ja 4,19:2
Young, Arthur (Miscellaneous)
Dance Band 1936,Ja 4,19:2
Young, Audrey
George White's Scandals 1945,O 11,26:2
Wistful Widow of Wagon Gap, The
1947,N 21,36:2
Love Me or Leave Me 1955,My 27,14:1
Young, Babe
Safe at Home 1941,N 26,31:2
Young, Boez
Youth of Russia, The 1934,N 10,19:3
Tevya 1939,D 22,15:3
Young, Carleton
Pride of the Bowery 1941,Ja 24,15:2
Take It or Leave It 1944,Jl 13,14:2
Thunderhead 1945,Mr 16,21:2
Thrill of a Romance 1945,My 25,22:2
Smash-Up, The Story of a Woman
1947,Ap 11,31:2
Kissing Bandit, The 1948,N 19,35:2
Hard, Fast and Beautiful 1951,Jl 2,16:6
People Will Talk 1951,Ag 30,20:1
Day the Earth Stood Still, The 1951,S 19,37:1
Anne of the Indies 1951,O 25,36:3
Deadline U S A 1952,Mr 15,8:2
My Six Convicts 1952,Mr 28,27:3
Red Mountain 1952,Ap 26,19:2
Brigand, The 1952,Jl 26,9:2
Battle Zone 1952,N 1,17:2
Niagara 1953,Ja 22,20:3
Riot in Cell Block 11 1954,F 19,24:5
20,000 Leagues Under the Sea 1954,D 24,7:2
Cry Terror 1958,My 15,25:1
Last Hurrah, The 1958,O 24,40:1
Horse Soldiers, The 1959,Je 26,13:1
Sergeant Rutledge 1960,My 26,37:1
Armored Command 1961,O 7,14:3
Man Who Shot Liberty Valance, The
1962,My 24,29:2
Young, Carroll (Original Author)
Tarzan Triumphs 1943,F 5,16:3
Tarzan's Desert Mystery 1943,D 27,23:3
Tarzan and the Mermaids 1948,Mr 30,26:4
Jungle Jim 1949,Ja 1,9:2
Young, Carroll (Screenwriter)
Tarzan Triumphs 1943,F 5,16:3
Tarzan and the Leopard Woman 1946,F 11,25:2
Tarzan and the Mermaids 1948,Mr 30,26:4
Jungle Jim 1949,Ja 1,9:2
Mark of the Gorilla 1950,F 17,27:2
Jungle, The 1952,O 2,32:3
Young, Chic (Miscellaneous)
Blondie Hits the Jackpot 1949,S 9,28:3
Young, Chic (Original Author)
Blondie 1938,D 22,25:4
Blondie Meets the Boss 1939,Ap 27,31:1
Blondie Goes Latin 1941,F 26,17:3
Young, Clara Kimball
My Official Wife 1914,Jl 14,9:5
Easiest Way, The 1917,Ap 9,13:4 (In Addenda)
Cheating Cheaters 1919,Ja 27,11:4
Eyes of Youth 1919,D 1,9:3
Forbidden Woman, The 1920,F 23,11:2
Hush 1921,Ap 25,9:2
Charge It 1921,Ag 29,14:4
Lying Wives 1925,Je 17,16:2
Kept Husbands 1931,Mr 24,31:2
Women Go on Forever 1931,O 19,28:1
File No 113 1932,F 20,11:2
She Married her Boss 1935,S 27,25:3
His Night Out 1935,N 16,19:2
Three on the Trail 1936,My 5,26:5
Roundup, The 1941,Mr 13,25:4
Young, Clarence Upson (Original Author)
Law West of Tombstone, The 1938,N 25,19:1

Young, Clarence Upson (Screenwriter)
Plot Thickens, The 1936,D 9,35:2
Law West of Tombstone, The 1938,N 25,19:1
Girl and the Gambler, The 1939,Je 28,17:3
Bad Lands 1939,Ag 9,15:2
Hot Steel 1940,Je 21,25:3
Black Diamonds 1940,S 10,26:6
Devil's Pipeline, The 1940,N 11,22:4
North to the Klondike 1942,Mr 12,24:3
Strange Case of Dr Rx 1942,Mr 28,11:2
Night Monster 1942,N 30,18:5
Time to Kill 1942,D 25,15:4
Albuquerque 1948,Mr 1,17:2
Young, Clifton
Pursued 1947,Mr 8,10:2
Possessed 1947,My 30,25:2
Dark Passage 1947,S 6,11:2
My Wild Irish Rose 1947,D 25,32:2
Blood on the Moon 1948,N 12,30:5
Calamity Jane and Sam Bass 1949,Jl 18,14:2
Abandoned Woman 1949,O 27,35:3
Woman of Distinction, A 1950,Mr 17,28:2
Young, Collier (Original Author)
Act of Violence 1949,Ja 24,16:2
Young, Collier (Producer)
Outrage 1950,O 16,30:5
Hard, Fast and Beautiful 1951,Jl 2,16:6
Beware my Lovely 1952,S 13,10:5
Hitch-Hiker, The 1953,Ap 30,39:3
Bigamist, The 1953,D 26,10:4
Private Hell 36 1954,S 4,6:4
Mad at the World 1955,My 14,10:8
Huk! 1956,D 15,20:4
Young, Collier (Screenwriter)
Outrage 1950,O 16,30:5
Hitch-Hiker, The 1953,Ap 30,39:3
Bigamist, The 1953,D 26,10:4
Private Hell 36 1954,S 4,6:4
Young, Desmond
Desert Fox, The 1951,O 18,32:1
Young, Desmond (Original Author)
Desert Fox, The 1951,O 18,32:1
Young, Ed Fife and Drum Corps
Festival 1967,O 24,53:2
Young, Elizabeth
Queen Christina 1933,D 27,23:3
There's Always Tomorrow 1934,N 10,19:2
Young, Eric
Lord Jim 1965,F 26,18:1
Young, Evelyn
Girls of the Road 1940,Jl 22,20:2
Young, Francis Brett (Original Author)
Sea Horses 1926,F 23,26:5
Man About the House, A 1949,Mr 9,33:2
My Brother Jonathan 1949,Je 29,34:4
Young, Georgiana
Story of Alexander Graham Bell, The
1939,Ap 1,17:2
Young, Gig
Gay Sisters, The 1942,Ag 15,14:2
Air Force 1943,F 4,29:1
Old Acquaintance 1943,N 3,20:2
Escape me Never 1947,N 8,11:2
Woman in White, The 1948,My 8,12:2
Three Musketeers, The 1948,O 21,33:2
Wake of the Red Witch 1949,Ja 10,19:2
Lust for Gold 1949,Jl 4,9:2
Target Unknown 1951,Mr 5,24:2
Only the Valiant 1951,Ap 14,9:6
Come Fill the Cup 1951,N 22,47:2
Too Young to Kiss 1951,N 23,32:2
Holiday for Sinners 1952,S 20,13:2
You for Me 1952,S 25,38:3
Arena 1953,Jl 23,20:2
City That Never Sleeps 1953,Ag 8,14:2
Torch Song 1953,O 13,34:2
Young at Heart 1955,Ja 20,35:1
Desperate Hours, The 1955,O 6,25:1
Desk Set 1957,My 16,28:2
Teacher's Pet 1958,Mr 20,33:1
Tunnel of Love 1958,N 22,27:4
Ask any Girl 1959,My 22,32:1
Story of Page One, The 1960,Ja 14,28:1
That Touch of Mink 1962,Je 15,16:2
Kid Galahad 1963,Mr 7,8:5
Five Miles to Midnight 1963,Mr 21,8:6
For Love or Money 1963,Ag 8,19:1
Ticklish Affair, A 1963,Ag 22,19:2
Strange Bedfellows 1965,Mr 11,38:1
Shuttered Room, The 1968,F 15,47:1
Young, Gladys
Kathy's Love Affair 1952,Jl 3,16:2
Young, Gordon Ray (Original Author)
Hurricane Smith 1952,O 4,15:2
Young, Hariette
Irma la Douce 1963,Je 6,39:1
Young, Harold (Director)
Scarlet Pimpernel, The 1935,F 8,27:2
Woman Trap 1936,Mr 7,11:4
My American Wife 1936,Ag 21,12:3
Let Them Live 1937,Je 8,30:3
52d Street 1937,N 15,15:1
Little Tough Guy 1938,Ag 18,23:3

Young, Harold (Director) — Cont
Storm, The 1938,O 31,12:2
Newsboys' Home 1939,Ja 23,8:2
Forgotten Woman, The 1939,Ag 4,11:2
Sabotage 1939,N 16,29:5
Juke Box Jenny 1942,Ap 17,21:3
Mummy's Tomb, The 1942,O 26,19:2
Hi 'Ya Chum 1943,F 26,17:4
Three Caballeros, The 1945,F 5,20:1
Jungle Captive 1945,Jl 7,7:5
Frozen Ghost, The 1945,Jl 28,7:3
Citizen Saint 1948,My 28,28:2
Young, Howard Irving (Original Author)
Her Wild Oat 1928,F 6,12:3
Sez O'Reilly to MacNab 1938,F 19,19:4
Young, Howard Irving (Screenwriter)
Music in the Air 1934,D 14,29:3
Great Gambini, The 1937,Jl 12,20:4
Flying Saucer, The 1950,Ja 5,28:3
Young, Jack Captain
Yankee Doodle Dandy 1942,My 30,9:1
Young, James
Target Unknown 1951,Mr 5,24:2
Thing, The 1951,My 3,34:4
My Son John 1952,Ap 9,27:1
Young, James (Director)
Regular Girl, A 1919,N 11,13:3
Devil, The 1921,Ja 17,9:1
Without Benefit of Clergy 1921,Je 20,17:2
Masquerader, The 1922,Ag 14,12:4
Wandering Daughters 1923,Jl 2,16:2
Trilby 1923,Jl 30,11:4
Welcome Stranger 1924,O 14,21:5
Young, James R (Original Author)
Behind the Rising Sun 1943,O 14,26:2
Young, Janet
I Married a Doctor 1936,Ap 20,17:1
Young, Joan
Easy Money (Episode 2) 1949,F 14,15:3
Fallen Idol, The 1949,N 16,39:2
Good Time Girl 1950,S 25,18:5
Gay Lady, The 1951,Ap 16,21:2
Admirable Crichton, The 1957,D 15,45:4
  (Incorrect in this edition; use 1957,D 17,45:4
  elsewhere)
Suddenly, Last Summer 1959,D 23,22:1
Young, Joe (Composer)
Lullaby of Broadway 1951,Mr 27,35:2
Young, Joseph
Mighty Joe Young 1949,Jl 28,19:3
Young, Larry
Welcome Stranger 1947,Ag 7,15:2
Young, Lloyd (Original Author)
Mark of the Hawk, The 1958,Mr 6,32:1
Young, Lloyd (Producer)
Mark of the Hawk, The 1958,Mr 6,32:1
Young, Lloyd (Screenwriter)
Mark of the Hawk, The 1958,Mr 6,32:1
Young, Loretta
Laugh, Clown, Laugh 1928,My 28,23:2
Magnificent Flirt, The 1928,Je 25,27:1
Scarlet Seas 1928,D 31,9:1
Squall, The 1929,My 10,32:5
Fast Life 1929,Ag 17,5:3
Careless Age, The 1929,S 21,17:1
Show of Shows 1929,N 21,24:5
Forward Pass, The 1929,N 29,25:1
Man From Blankley's, The 1930,Mr 29,23:1
Second Story Murder, The 1930,My 3,23:1
Road to Paradise 1930,S 30,23:1
Kismet 1930,O 31,20:1
Truth About Youth, The 1930,D 13,22:2
Devil to Pay, The 1930,D 19,30:1
Beau Ideal 1931,Ja 19,25:1
Road to Paradise, The 1931,Ja 20,21:3
Right of Way, The 1931,Mr 24,31:2
Three Girls Lost 1931,My 2,23:4
Too Young to Marry 1931,My 4,15:3
Big Business Girl 1931,Je 12,27:1
I Like Your Nerve 1931,S 12,15:4
Platinum Blonde 1931,O 31,22:2
Ruling Voice, The 1931,N 5,29:3
Taxi 1932,Ja 8,27:3
Hatchet Man, The 1932,F 4,25:2
Play Girl 1932,Mr 19,11:2
Week-End Marriage 1932,Je 4,9:2
Life Begins 1932,Ag 26,20:3
They Call It Sin 1932,O 21,25:4
Employees' Entrance 1933,Ja 21,10:6
Grand Slam 1933,F 22,25:2
Zoo in Budapest 1933,Ap 28,15:2
Life of Jimmy Dolan, The 1933,Je 14,22:3
Midnight Mary 1933,Jl 15,14:2
Heroes for Sale 1933,Jl 22,14:3
Devil's in Love, The 1933,Jl 28,18:2
She Had to Say Yes 1933,Jl 29,14:2
Man's Castle 1933,D 30,9:2
House of Rothschild, The 1934,Mr 15,27:2
Born to be Bad 1934,My 31,22:6
Bulldog Drummond Strikes Back 1934,Ag 16,20:2
Caravan 1934,S 28,27:1
White Parade, The 1934,N 10,19:1
Clive of India 1935,Ja 18,29:1
Shanghai 1935,Jl 20,16:2

Young, Loretta— Cont
Call of the Wild 1935,Ag 15,15:2
Crusades, The 1935,Ag 22,21:3
Unguarded Hour, The 1936,Ap 4,11:1
Private Number 1936,Je 12,19:1
Ramona 1936,O 7,32:4
Ladies in Love 1936,O 29,31:1
Love Is News 1937,Mr 6,10:1
Cafe Metropole 1937,Ap 29,17:1
Love Under Fire 1937,Ag 28,8:2
Wife, Doctor and Nurse 1937,O 11,26:5
Second Honeymoon 1937,N 13,11:2
Four Men and a Prayer 1938,My 7,18:1
Three Blind Mice 1938,Je 18,18:2
Suez 1938,O 15,21:2
Kentucky 1938,D 24,12:1
Wife, Husband and Friend 1939,F 25,19:2
Story of Alexander Graham Bell, The
   1939,Ap 1,17:2
Eternally Yours 1939,O 7,11:2
Doctor Takes a Wife, The 1940,Je 15,12:2
He Stayed for Breakfast 1940,Ag 31,16:2
Lady From Cheyenne, The 1941,Ap 18,18:2
Men In her Life, The 1941,D 12,35:1
Bedtime Story 1942,Mr 20,25:4
Night to Remember, A 1943,Ja 1,27:2
China 1943,Ap 22,31:2
Ladies Courageous 1944,Mr 16,17:2
And Now Tomorrow 1944,N 23,38:2
Along Came Jones 1945,Jl 19,8:7
Stranger, The 1946,Jl 11,18:2
Perfect Marriage, The 1947,Ja 16,30:3
Farmer's Daughter, The 1947,Mr 26,31:2
Bishop's Wife, The 1947,D 10,44:2
Rachel and the Stranger 1948,S 20,21:2
Accused, The 1949,Ja 13,26:2
Mother is a Freshman 1949,Mr 12,10:2
Come to the Stable 1949,Jl 28,19:1
Key to the City 1950,F 2,31:2
Cause for Alarm 1951,Mr 30,28:5
Half Angel 1951,Je 16,9:2
Paula 1952,Jl 16,21:2
Because of You 1952,D 4,47:3
Young, Mary
This Is my Affair 1937,My 28,17:1
Watch on the Rhine 1943,Ag 28,15:1
Address Unknown 1944,Ap 17,20:1
Lost Weekend, The 1945,D 3,17:2
Stork Club, The 1945,D 20,18:2
Bride Wore Boots, The 1946,Je 6,16:3
Temptation 1946,D 25,33:6
Mating Season, The 1951,Ap 12,41:2
House on Telegraph Hill, The 1951,My 14,29:1
American in Paris, An 1951,O 5,24:2
Alias Jesse James 1959,My 18,31:2
Blue Denim 1959,Jl 31,21:1
Young, Ming
Toll of the Sea, The 1922,N 27,18:1
Young, Miriam (Original Author)
Mother Wore Tights 1947,Ag 21,33:2
Young, Nedrick
Bombs Over Burma 1942,Ag 10,15:2
Ladies' Day 1943,Mr 26,14:3
Swordsman, The 1947,O 17,18:4
Gallant Blade 1948,O 13,31:3
Lady Without Passport, A 1950,Ag 4,13:2
Gun Crazy 1950,Ag 25,17:5
Retreat Hell! 1952,F 20,26:2
Iron Mistress, The 1952,N 20,39:2
Seconds 1966,O 6,56:1
Young, Nedrick (Original Author)
Passage West 1951,Ag 31,12:2
Jailhouse Rock 1957,N 14,41:1
Young, Nedrick (Screenwriter)
Decoy 1946,N 2,12:2
Young, Noah
Safety Last 1923,Ap 2,22:1
Battling Orioles, The 1924,N 4,24:1
For Heaven's Sake 1926,Ap 5,24:1
Sharp Shooters 1928,Ja 23,18:3
Welcome Danger 1929,O 21,30:1
Feet First 1930,O 31,20:1
Newly Rich 1931,Jl 3,22:1
Young, Patrick
Spider and the Fly, The 1952,Jl 29,17:3
Young, Paul
Wee Geordie 1956,O 8,31:1
Young, Polly Ann
Masks of the Devil, The 1928,N 26,30:2
Sons of Steel 1935,Ap 15,16:3
Border Patrolman 1936,Je 29,11:2
Story of Alexander Graham Bell, The
   1939,Ap 1,17:2
Turnabout 1940,Jl 27,17:6
Road Show 1941,F 19,25:2
Invisible Ghost, The 1941,My 8,21:2
Young, R R (Screenwriter)
Waterhole #3 1967,O 11,41:4
Young, Raymond
Adam and Evalyn 1950,My 12,33:4
Midnight Episode 1955,My 19,25:5
Young, Rida Johnson (Original Author)
Captain Kidd, Jr 1919,Ap 21,13:4
Lottery Man, The 1919,O 6,15:1

Maytime 1924,Je 2,14:3
Brown of Harvard 1926,My 3,27:1
Mother Machree 1928,Mr 6,20:3
Glorious Betsy 1928,Ap 27,16:4
Hell Harbor 1930,Mr 28,22:6
Naughty Marietta 1935,Mr 23,11:2
Hearts Divided 1936,Je 13,13:1
Maytime 1937,Mr 19,27:1
Little Old New York 1940,F 3,9:2
Young, Robert
Black Camel, The 1931,Jl 4,11:5
Sin of Madelon Claudet, The 1931,O 31,22:2
Guilty Generation, The 1931,N 21,20:4
Wet Parade, The 1932,Ap 22,23:2
New Morals for Old 1932,Je 24,15:3
Unashamed 1932,Jl 15,13:4
Strange Interlude 1932,S 1,24:3
Kid From Spain, The 1932,N 18,23:2
Men Must Fight 1933,Mr 11,18:3
Today We Live 1933,Ap 15,16:2
Hell Below 1933,Ap 26,13:2
Tugboat Annie 1933,Ag 12,14:2
Saturday's Millions 1933,O 14,18:3
Right to Romance, The 1933,D 15,28:2
Carolina 1934,F 16,17:2
Spitfire 1934,Mr 9,22:3
House of Rothschild, The 1934,Mr 15,27:2
Lazy River 1934,Ap 4,26:2
Whom the Gods Destroy 1934,Jl 13,14:2
Paris Interlude 1934,Jl 28,16:5
Death on the Diamond 1934,S 24,14:1
Band Plays on, The 1934,D 22,21:2
West Point of the Air 1935,Ap 6,10:1
Vagabond Lady 1935,Je 15,20:2
Red Salute 1935,S 30,13:1
Remember Last Night? 1935,N 21,27:2
Bride Comes Home, The 1935,D 25,30:2
Three Wise Guys, The 1936,My 23,12:2
It's Love Again 1936,My 23,12:1
Secret Agent 1936,Je 13,13:1
Sworn Enemy 1936,S 12,20:1
Longest Night, The 1936,O 17,21:2
Stowaway 1936,D 19,16:1
Dangerous Number 1937,Mr 12,19:2
I Met Him in Paris 1937,Je 3,29:2
Emperor's Candlesticks, The 1937,Jl 9,18:1
Married Before Breakfast 1937,Jl 23,16:2
Bride Wore Red, The 1937,O 15,18:4
Navy Blue and Gold 1937,D 24,21:2
Paradise for Three 1938,F 16,17:1
Three Comrades 1938,Je 3,17:1
Josette 1938,Je 11,9:1
Toy Wife, The 1938,Je 24,15:1
Rich Man, Poor Girl 1938,Ag 19,13:3
Shining Hour, The 1939,Ja 20,15:2
Honolulu 1939,F 23,19:2
Bridal Suite 1939,My 26,20:2
Maisie 1939,Je 23,23:1
Miracles for Sale 1939,Ag 10,15:2
Northwest Passage 1940,Mr 8,25:1
Florian 1940,Je 6,33:2
Mortal Storm, The 1940,Je 21,25:2
Sporting Blood 1940,Jl 22,20:2
Dr Kildare's Crisis 1940,D 19,33:1
Western Union 1941,F 7,23:2
Trial of Mary Dugan, The 1941,Mr 6,25:4
Lady Be Good 1941,S 19,27:1
Married Bachelor 1941,O 16,25:3
H M Pulham, Esq 1941,D 19,35:1
Joe Smith, American 1942,Ap 2,27:4
Cairo 1942,N 6,27:2
Journey for Margaret 1942,D 18,36:7
Slightly Dangerous 1943,Ap 2,17:2
Sweet Rosie O'Grady 1943,O 21,30:2
Claudia 1943,N 5,23:2
Canterville Ghost, The 1944,Jl 29,16:2
Enchanted Cottage, The 1945,Ap 28,19:2
Those Endearing Young Charms 1945,Je 20,26:5
Searching Wind, The 1946,Je 27,29:1
Claudia and David 1946,Ag 15,19:2
Lady Luck 1946,O 31,22:3
They Won't Believe Me 1947,Jl 17,16:2
Crossfire 1947,Jl 23,19:2
Relentless 1948,Mr 6,17:3
Sitting Pretty 1948,Mr 11,35:2
Adventure in Baltimore 1949,Ap 29,27:2
That Forsyte Woman 1949,N 11,31:2
Bride for Sale 1949,N 21,29:4 (In Addenda)
And Baby Makes Three 1949,D 23,17:3
Second Woman, The 1951,F 2,19:2
Goodbye, my Fancy 1951,My 30,14:2
Half Breed, The 1952,Jl 5,7:2
Secret of the Incas 1954,My 29,13:3
Born Free 1966,Je 23,29:1
Young, Robert (Cinematographer)
Secrets of the Reef 1956,Jl 24,19:2
Young, Robert (Director)
Secrets of the Reef 1956,Jl 24,19:2
Young, Robert (Producer)
Nothing but a Man 1964,S 21,37:2
Young, Robert (Screenwriter)
Secrets of the Reef 1956,Jl 24,19:2
Nothing but a Man 1964,S 21,37:2

Young, Roland
Sherlock Holmes 1922,My 8,14:3
Unholy Night, The 1929,O 12,11:1
Bishop Murder Case, The 1930,F 1,15:1
Madam Satan 1930,O 6,21:1
New Moon 1930,D 25,18:6
Don't Bet on Women 1931,Mr 7,17:2
Prodigal, The 1931,Je 27,20:3
Annabelle's Affairs 1931,Je 29,20:3
Guardsman, The 1931,S 10,22:4
Squaw Man, The 1931,S 19,10:2
Woman Commands, A 1932,Ja 28,13:2
Lovers Courageous 1932,F 20,11:2
One Hour with You 1932,Mr 24,17:5
ThIs is the Night 1932,Ap 16,11:2
Street of Women 1932,My 30,16:5
They Just Had to Get Married 1933,F 13,11:4
Lady's Profession, A 1933,Mr 25,13:3
Pleasure Cruise 1933,Ap 3,13:3
Blind Adventure 1933,O 31,24:3
His Double Life 1933,D 16,12:3
Here is my Heart 1934,D 22,21:1
David Copperfield 1935,Ja 19,8:1
Ruggles of Red Gap 1935,Mr 7,26:1
Unguarded Hour, The 1936,Ap 4,11:1
One Rainy Afternoon 1936,My 14,29:2
Give Me your Heart 1936,S 17,18:2
Man Who Could Work Miracles, The
   1937,F 22,13:1
Call it a Day 1937,My 7,29:2
King Solomon's Mines 1937,Jl 3,18:1
Topper 1937,Ag 20,21:2
Ali Baba Goes to Town 1937,O 23,14:1
Sailing Along 1938,Ap 16,17:1
Young in Heart, The 1938,N 4,27:2
Topper Takes a Trip 1938,D 30,11:2
Yes, My Darling Daughter 1939,F 27,11:2
Here I Am a Stranger 1939,S 30,11:2
Night of Nights, The 1939,D 28,17:1
He Married his Wife 1940,Ja 20,11:2
Star Dust 1940,My 4,13:1
Irene 1940,My 24,23:3
Private Affairs 1940,Jl 5,10:3
Dulcy 1940,N 28,28:2
No, No, Nanette 1940,D 20,33:1
Philadelphia Story, The 1940,D 27,22:2
Topper Returns 1941,Mr 28,26:6
Flame of New Orleans, The 1941,Ap 26,20:2
Two Faced Woman 1942,Ja 1,37:2
Lady Has Plans, The 1942,Mr 5,27:1
They all Kissed the Bride 1942,Jl 31,11:1
Tales of Manhattan 1942,S 25,25:1
Forever and a Day 1943,Mr 13,9:2
Standing Room Only 1944,F 23,17:2
And Then There Were None 1945,N 1,20:2
You Gotta Stay Happy 1948,N 5,29:2
Great Lover, The 1949,N 24,48:2
Bond Street 1950,Mr 30,40:6
Let's Dance 1950,N 30,42:2
Young, Sen
Charlie Chan at Treasure Island 1939,S 1,15:5
20,000 Men a Year 1939,O 28,11:2
Night Plane From Chungking 1943,My 31,13:2
Betrayal From the East 1945,Ap 25,27:2
Young, Shaun Terence (Director)
One Night With You 1949,F 21,20:2
Young, Silvia
This Freedom 1923,N 28,15:1
Young, Skip
Cold Wind in August, A 1961,Jl 27,23:2
Young, Soo
Mad Holiday 1936,N 26,39:2
In Harm's Way 1965,Ap 7,36:1
Young, Stark (Original Author)
So Red the Rose 1935,N 28,39:1
Young, Stark (Screenwriter)
Uncle Vanya 1958,Ap 29,26:2
Young, Tammany
Checkers 1919,Ag 25,8:5
Regular Girl, A 1919,N 11,13:3
Bits of Life 1921,O 17,18:1
New Toys 1925,F 17,18:1
White Monkey, The 1925,Je 9,16:3
Roadhouse Nights 1930,F 22,13:1
Hallelujah, I'm a Bum 1933,F 9,15:2
She Done Him Wrong 1933,F 10,12:3
Gold Diggers of 1933 1933,Je 8,22:3
Tugboat Annie 1933,Ag 12,14:2
Bowery, The 1933,O 5,24:2
Six of a Kind 1934,Mr 10,18:3
You're Telling Me 1934,Ap 7,19:1
Little Miss Marker 1934,My 19,18:3
Gift of Gab 1934,S 26,17:6
Mighty Barnum, The 1934,D 24,17:1
It's a Gift 1935,Ja 5,20:2
Glass Key, The 1935,Je 15,20:2
Man on the Flying Trapeze 1935,Ag 3,16:2
Little Big Shot 1935,O 7,11:2
Young, Terence (Director)
Corridor of Mirrors 1949,Mr 23,35:3
Valley of the Eagles 1952,Ap 11,19:2
Frightened Bride, The 1953,Ag 20,18:5
Paratrooper 1953,D 31,9:3

Young, Terence (Director) — Cont
That Lady 1955,Je 11,8:7
Storm over the Nile 1956,Je 9,14:2
Safari 1956,Je 21,35:2
Zarak 1956,D 27,22:1
Action of the Tiger 1957,N 14,41:1
Black Tights 1962,F 21,54:2
Dr No, 1963,My 30,20:1
From Russia with Love 1964,Ap 9,25:1
Amorous Adventures of Moll Flanders, The
1965,My 27,28:1
Thunderball 1965,D 22,23:1
Triple Cross 1967,Jl 20,20:2
Wait Until Dark 1967,O 27,48:1
Poppy is Also a Flower, The 1967,D 14,62:4
Young, Terence (Screenwriter)
Fugitive, The 1940,Jl 23,22:2
Suicide Squadron 1942,My 14,23:2
Hungry Hill 1947,O 11,11:2
Bad Lord Byron, The 1952,Mr 20,37:5
Valley of the Eagles 1952,Ap 11,19:2
Young, Tex
Water Hole, The 1928,S 3,14:2
Virginian, The 1929,D 23,18:2
Young, Tony
He Rides Tall 1964,F 27,28:1
Taggart 1964,D 25,24:4
Young, Vernon
Matter of Morals, A 1961,Je 1,31:1
Young, Victor (Composer)
Breaking the Ice 1938,S 23,35:3
Everything's on Ice 1939,O 6,31:1
I Wanted Wings 1941,Mr 27,29:4
Timberjack 1955,Mr 10,33:3
Young, Victor (Miscellaneous)
Artists and Models 1937,Ag 5,19:2
Young, W W (Director)
Alice in Wonderland 1921,Mr 22,15:3
Young, Waldemar (Screenwriter)
Prince There Was 1921,N 14,18:1
Ebb Tide 1922,N 20,21:3
You Can't Fool Your Wife 1923,Ap 24,25:3
Lives of a Bengal Lancer, The 1935,Ja 12,12:2
Crusades, The 1935,Ag 22,21:3
Peter Ibbetson 1935,N 8,18:2
Desire 1936,Ap 13,15:1
Poppy 1936,Je 18,19:1
Plainsman, The 1937,Ja 14,16:2
Man-Proof 1938,Ja 14,21:1
Test Pilot 1938,Ap 16,17:1
Young, Walter
Alcatraz Island 1937,O 14,22:2
Torchy Blane, The Adventurous Blonde
1937,D 18,18:1
Youngdahl, William Rev
Time for Burning, A 1967,F 24,26:2
Younger, A P (Original Author)
While the City Sleeps 1928,O 22,29:1
Girl Said No, The 1930,Ap 5,23:3
Sunny Skies 1930,My 17,21:2
Single Sin, The 1931,Mr 17,34:3
Younger, A P (Screenwriter)
Abysmal Brute, The 1923,Ap 18,24:5
Slide, Kelly, Slide 1927,Mr 23,19:2
Younger, E
Peasants 1935,Ag 29,25:2
Youngman, Henny
Wave, A Wac and a Marine, A 1944,Ag 14,11:4
Youngson, Robert (Director)
Fifty Years Before your Eyes 1950,Je 30,18:2
(Incorrect in this edition; use 1950,Je 28,32:3
elsewhere)
Youngson, Robert (Producer)
Golden Age of Comedy, The 1957,D 27,23:4
When Comedy Was King 1960,Mr 30,42:1
Days of Thrills and Laughter 1961,Mr 22,37:1
30 Years of Fun 1963,D 26,33:4
M G M's Big Parade of Comedy 1964,S 24,19:1
Laurel and Hardy's Laughing 20's 1965,N 18,55:2
Further Perils of Laurel and Hardy, The
1968,Ap 1,56:6
Youngson, Robert (Screenwriter)
Golden Age of Comedy, The 1957,D 27,23:4
When Comedy Was King 1960,Mr 30,42:1
Days of Thrills and Laughter 1961,Mr 22,37:1
30 Years of Fun 1963,D 26,33:4
M G M's Big Parade of Comedy 1964,S 24,19:1
Laurel and Hardy's Laughing 20's 1965,N 18,55:2
Further Perils of Laurel and Hardy, The
1968,Ap 1,56:6
Youngstein, Max E (Producer)
Fail Safe 1964,S 16,36:1
Money Trap, The 1966,My 5,59:1
Welcome to Hard Times 1967,My 2,56:1
Youree, Charles
Thief in Paradise, A 1925,Ja 26,14:1
Yousekevitch, Igor
Invitation to the Dance (Circus); Circus (Invitation
to the Dance) 1956,My 23,35:7
Youskevitch, Igor
Invitation to the Dance (Ring Around the Rosy);
Ring Around the Rosy (Invitation to the
Dance) 1956,My 23,35:7

Youssef, Mohaud
Itto 1936,Ja 29,15:5
Youssoff, Ali
Smiling Faces 1932,Ag 31,12:3
Yovanovich, Ljubisha
Magic Sword, The 1952,N 19,37:2
Yowlachie, Chief
Red Raiders, The 1927,S 28,28:3
Senator Was Indiscreet, The 1947,D 27,9:2
Red River 1948,O 1,31:2
Paleface, The 1948,D 16,41:2
El Paso 1949,Mr 24,35:2
Ma and Pa Kettle 1949,Ag 12,13:2
Mrs Mike 1950,F 9,36:5
Ticket to Tomahawk, A 1950,My 20,8:6
Rose Marie 1954,Ap 2,22:2
Yuch-ting, Wang (Screenwriter)
Last Woman of Shang, The 1964,D 15,56:2
Yudin, Alexei
Dark Is The Night 1946,Mr 18,24:3
Yudin, G
Attack From the Sea 1954,Ap 19,19:4
Yudin, Gardin
Enemies of Progress 1934,Ja 11,19:2
Yudin, Gennady
Carnival in Moscow 1957,N 4,40:1
Yudin, K (Director)
Safety Match, The 1955,Mr 28,24:5
Wrestler and the Clown, The 1959,Ja 1,38:1
Yudin, Konstantin (Director)
Four Hearts 1946,F 25,21:5
Twins 1947,Jl 28,12:2
Horsemen, The 1951,Ja 29,14:5
Yudin, Pavel
Thirteen, The 1937,Je 19,20:2
Yueh, Wong
Maid of Formosa 1949,Ag 8,10:5
Yueh-ting, Wang (Screenwriter)
Empress Wu 1965,Mr 16,42:2
Yuin, G
Frigid Sea, The 1955,N 21,23:4
Yukhtin
Last Game, The 1964,O 25,41:5 (Incorrect in this
edition; use 1964,O 26,41:5 elsewhere)
Yukimura, Izumi
Bandits on the Wind 1964,Ja 15,27:3
Yukishiro, Keiko
She Was Like a Wild Chrysanthemum
1960,Ja 22,15:2
Yule, Joe
New Moon 1940,Jl 19,22:2
Boom Town 1940,S 6,25:2
I'll Wait for You 1941,Je 2,13:6
Billy the Kid 1941,Je 20,28:2
Kathleen 1941,D 19,35:3
Born to Sing 1942,F 19,23:2
Jackass Mail 1942,Jl 2,25:2
Bringing Up Father 1946,N 22,27:3
Yumatov, G
Road to Life 1956,Je 11,26:6
Heroes of Shipka 1956,S 3,10:5
Yung, Soo
Flower Drum Song 1961,N 10,40:1
Yung, Victor Sen
Shadows Over Shanghai 1938,D 1,29:2
Charlie Chan in Honolulu 1938,D 31,7:3
Charlie Chan in Reno 1939,My 31,27:2
Charlie Chan's Murder Cruise 1940,My 3,17:5
Charlie Chan At the Wax Museum 1940,S 28,9:3
Letter, The 1940,N 23,12:6
Dead Men Tell 1941,Ap 17,29:3
Yank on the Burma Road, A 1942,Ja 29,25:3
Secret Agent of Japan 1942,Mr 23,19:3
Moontide 1942,Ap 30,14:1
Across the Pacific 1942,S 5,9:2
Manila Calling 1942,S 28,13:1
China 1943,Ap 22,31:2
Crimson Key, The 1947,O 18,9:2
State Department-File 649 1949,F 21,20:2
Ticket to Tomahawk, A 1950,My 20,8:6
Breaking Point, The 1950,O 7,10:6
Woman on the Run 1950,N 30,24:2
Groom Wore Spurs, The 1951,Mr 14,41:2
Peking Express 1951,Jl 19,20:2
Forbidden 1954,Ja 23,11:2
Left Hand of God, The 1955,S 22,34:5
Blood Alley 1955,O 6,25:3
Men in War 1957,Mr 20,32:4
Flower Drum Song 1961,N 10,40:1
Yung-hua, Chen
Last Woman of Shang, The 1964,D 15,56:2
Yunger, E
Gadfly, The 1956,S 17,22:2
Yurenev, Vladimir (Director)
Lower Depths, The 1947,D 1,27:2
Yurief, Y
Untitled-Capt Grant's Children 1939,Ja 12,23:3
Captain Grant's Children 1939,Ja 12,23:3
Yuriko
King and I, The 1956,Je 29,15:6
Yurka, Blanche
Tale of Two Cities, A 1935,D 26,21:2
Queen of the Mob 1940,Jl 1,23:2

Yurka, Blanche — Cont
City for Conquest 1940,S 28,9:2
Escape 1940,N 1,33:1
Ellery Queen and the Murder Ring
1941,O 21,29:4
Lady for a Night 1942,F 12,27:2
Pacific Rendezvous 1942,Jl 8,27:4
Night to Remember, A 1943,Ja 1,27:2
Tonight We Raid Calais 1943,Ap 15,20:2
Hitler's Madman 1943,Ag 28,15:1
Song of Bernadette, The 1944,Ja 27,15:2
Bridge of San Luis Rey, The 1944,Mr 4,11:1
Cry of the Werewolf, The 1944,Ag 12,16:5
One Body too Many 1944,N 25,21:2
Southerner, The 1945,Ag 27,22:3
13 Rue Madeleine 1947,Ja 16,30:2
Flame, The 1948,F 20,19:2
Furies, The 1950,Ag 17,23:2
At Swords Point 1952,Ap 10,37:1
Taxi 1953,Ja 22,20:3
Thunder in the Sun 1959,Ap 9,37:2
Yuro, Bob
Satan in High Heels 1962,Mr 24,15:6
Yurushinkaya, Nina (Cinematographer)
In the Pacific 1958,My 5,24:1
Yusa, Akihiko
Phantom Horse, the 1956,Jl 25,16:1
Yutang, Lin Dr (Miscellaneous)
Kukan 1941,Je 24,17:2
Yutkevich, Sergei (Director)
Man With the Gun, The 1939,Ja 30,9:3
Hello, Moscow! 1946,Je 15,24:4
Othello 1960,My 16,39:1
Yutkevich, Sergei (Producer)
In the Rear of the Enemy 1942,O 10,11:2
Skanderbeg 1954,Jl 5,6:4
Yutkevich, Sergei (Screenwriter)
Othello 1960,My 16,39:1
Yutkevitch, Sergei (Director)
Golden Mountains 1932,Ap 14,25:3
Pozor 1933,Mr 11,18:4
Pageant of Russia 1947,Ag 11,17:3
Yvain, Maurice (Composer)
Queen and the Cardinal, The 1944,Je 1,17:3
Yves, Christiane
They Had to See Paris 1929,O 12,11:1
Slightly Scarlet 1930,Mr 1,23:1
What a Man 1930,Jl 21,20:3
Yzarduy, Mme De
Michael Strogoff 1926,D 6,28:3

Z

Zabala, Enrique
Vidas Rotas 1935,Ag 3,16:3
Zabboni, Ermete
Pearls of the Crown, The 1938,Ap 12,26:2
Zabczynski, Alexander
Manewry Milosne 1936,N 11,55:1
Krolowa Przedmiescia; Queen of the Market
Place 1937,D 29,17:2
Dyplomatyczna Zona 1938,O 24,13:2
Spelnione Marzenia; Fulfilled Dreams
1939,D 14,35:3
Zabotkina, Olga
Song Over Moscow 1964,N 23,52:1
Sleeping Beauty, The 1966,My 4,50:1
Zacarias, Miguel (Director)
Payasada de la Vida; Tricks of Life
1935,Mr 18,14:5
Rosario 1936,Ap 20,17:2
Baul Macabro, El; Macabre Trunk, The
1937,N 30,26:3
Cuna Vacia, La; Empty Cradle, The
1938,Mr 21,18:3
Rapsodia Mexicana 1938,N 26,18:2
Soy Chato, Pero las Huelo; I Am Snub-nosed but I
Can Smell 1939,Jl 22,12:3
Zacchini, Young Hugo
Big Circus, The 1959,Jl 18,6:1
Zacconi, Ines
Spirit and the Flesh, The 1948,N 1,28:2
Zacharewicz, Witold
Love or a Kingdom 1937,D 4,21:1
Halka 1938,Ja 17,11:3
Znachor; Miracle Man, The 1938,F 21,15:2
Krawa Roza; Red Rose 1938,O 13,29:2
Kosciuszki 1938,D 27,13:2
Zacharopoulou, Athina
Signs of Life; Lebenszeichent 1968,S 26,60:1
Zadora, Pia
Santa Claus Conquers the Martians
1964,D 17,50:2
Zafiriou, Helen
Girl in Black, A 1957,S 17,39:2
Madame X 1960,O 3,34:5
Moment of Passion 1960,N 21,34:1
Zafiriou, Nitsa
Lily of the Harbor 1958,Ap 16,38:3
Aunt From Chicago, The 1960,Je 6,33:6
Zago, Catherine
Your Shadow Is Mine 1963,My 15,32:1

Zagonara, Adelio
Lucia di Lammermoor 1947,N 1,11:3
Laugh Pagliacci 1948,Ja 31,14:2
Zagor, Michael (Screenwriter)
Man From Galveston, The 1964,Ja 23,26:3
Zagorsky, Alyosha
Dimka 1964,Mr 21,13:5
Zahipina, Natasha
Once There Was a Girl 1945,D 24,19:2
Zahn, Tommy
Cinerama-South Seas Adventure 1958,Jl 16,26:1
Zahorsky, Bohus
Thunder in the Hills 1947,My 24,10:5
Emperor and the Golem, The 1955,Ja 10,27:4
Happy End 1968,Je 11,54:4
Zaichikoff, Vassili
Girl No 217 1945,S 3,17:2
Zaichikov, V
We Are From Kronstadt 1936,My 2,11:1
Zaichikov, Vladimir
In the Far East 1937,O 20,27:3
Zajac, Credda
Gunfighter, The 1950,Je 24,7:2
Zak, Avenir (Screenwriter)
Lullaby, The 1961,My 15,35:2
Zakariadze, S
1812 1944,S 11,14:1
Zakhagladze, Sergo
Father of a Soldier 1966,F 21,51:1
Zakharov, Rostislav (Director)
Cinderella 1961,D 19,39:1
Zakharov, Rostislav (Miscellaneous)
Cinderella 1961,D 19,39:1
Zakharov, Rostislav (Producer)
Cinderella 1961,D 19,39:1
Zakharov, Rostislav (Screenwriter)
Cinderella 1961,D 19,39:1
Zakrzewska, Sylwia
Guests are Coming; Jada Goscie Jada
1967,Ja 13,15:1
Zakurenko, Vadin
Taras Family, The 1946,D 9,34:4
Zalata, Jane
Fabulous World of Jules Verne, The
1961,Je 29,26:1
Zalewski, Gerard (Director)
Guests are Coming; Jada Goscie Jada
1967,Ja 13,15:1
Zalmankova, Anicka
Mizici Svet; Vanishing World 1935,My 30,21:2
Zama, E (Producer)
Two Women 1940,N 2,19:3
Zama, Fleurette
Pied Piper, The 1942,Ag 13,15:3
Zamansky, V
Violin and Roller 1962,Ag 20,18:2
Zambrano, Enrique
Massacre 1956,Je 2,13:5
Zambuto, Gero
Avvocato Difensore, L'; Attorney for the Defense,
The 1935,N 13,25:4
Zambuto, Gero (Director)
Avvocato Difensore, L'; Attorney for the Defense,
The 1935,N 13,25:4
Zamiatine, E (Screenwriter)
Lower Depths, The 1937,S 11,20:1
Zamissi, Lucia
Messalina 1924,Ag 25,16:2
Zamitchkovsky, I
Polish Terror, The 1933,Mr 13,18:3
Zamkovoy, L (Director)
Break-Up, The 1930,N 29,21:4
Zamora, Saul
Desheredados, Los 1936,Mr 23,22:6
Calvario de una Esposa, El 1936,S 26,11:2
Zampa, Luigi (Director)
To Live in Peace 1947,N 25,37:2
Angelina 1948,Ap 6,27:2
Difficult Years 1950,Ag 22,31:2
White Line, The 1952,D 6,17:2
His Last Twelve Hours 1953,N 13,24:7
Woman of Rome 1956,N 6,30:1
Zampa, Luigi (Screenwriter)
Angelina 1948,Ap 6,27:2
Woman of Rome 1956,N 6,30:1
Zampi, Mario (Director)
Laughter in Paradise 1951,N 12,21:2
Mr Potts Goes to Moscow 1953,S 3,15:2
Tonight's the Night 1954,D 23,13:4
Your Past Is Showing 1958,Jl 1,36:2
Too Many Crooks 1959,Ap 25,14:2
Five Golden Hours 1961,O 19,39:3
Zampi, Mario (Producer)
French Without Tears 1940,Ap 29,12:2
Laughter in Paradise 1951,N 12,21:2
Mr Potts Goes to Moscow 1953,S 3,15:2
Tonight's the Night 1954,D 23,13:4
Your Past Is Showing 1958,Jl 1,36:2
Five Golden Hours 1961,O 19,39:3
Zampieri, Giuseppe
Rosenkavalier, Der 1962,O 10,57:1

Zander, Peter
Return of Mr Moto 1965,D 2,48:1
Zaner, Jimmy
Little Men 1940,D 9,23:2
Where Are Your Children? 1944,Ja 17,14:5
Zanetti, Cesare (Producer)
Cavalleria Rusticana 1947,D 20,21:2
Zanft, John (Miscellaneous)
When a Man's a Man 1935,F 22,27:2
Zang, Edgar (Narrator)
8 X 8 1957,Mr 16,13:2
Zanger, Jacob
Motel, The Operator 1940,Ja 16,19:3
Zangrilli, O
Greatest Love of All, The 1924,N 11,14:1
Zangwill, Israel (Original Author)
Nurse Marjorie 1920,My 24,20:3
We Moderns 1925,D 8,28:5
Perfect Crime, The 1928,Ag 6,15:2
Merely Mary Ann 1931,S 12,15:4
Crime Doctor, The 1934,My 11,24:3
Verdict, The 1946,D 13,29:4
Zann, Nancy
Sea Hawk, The 1924,Je 3,22:1
Zanoli, Maria
Sensualita 1954,Ap 29,40:2
Barefoot Contessa, The 1954,S 30,37:1
Zanolli, Angelo
Son of Samson 1962,S 27,33:4
Zanuck, Darryl F
At the Front 1943,Mr 19,15:5
Find Your Man 1924,S 23,26:1
Social Highwayman, The 1926,Je 15,23:3
Missing Link, The 1927,My 7,15:2
Old San Francisco 1927,Je 23,23:3
First Auto, The 1927,Je 28,28:4
Say It With Songs 1929,Ag 7,29:2
Zanuck, Darryl F (Producer)
Cardinal Richelieu 1935,Ap 19,24:2
Miserables, Les 1935,Ap 22,14:2
Metropolitan 1935,O 18,27:4
Thanks a Million 1935,N 14,17:1
Man Who Broke the Bank at Monte Carlo, The
1935,N 15,20:2
Show Them no Mercy 1935,D 9,25:2
King of Burlesque 1936,Ja 16,25:2
Professional Soldier 1936,Ja 30,14:2
Prisoner of Shark Island, The 1936,F 13,25:2
Country Doctor, The 1936,Mr 13,32:2 (Incorrect
in this edition; use 1936,Mr 13,27:2 elsewhere)
Message to Garcia, A 1936,Ap 10,27:1
Captain January 1936,Ap 25,21:1
Under Two Flags 1936,My 1,19:1
Half Angel 1936,My 30,7:3
Sins of Man 1936Je 19,17:2
White Fang 1936,Jl 18,18:2
Road to Glory, The 1936,Ag 6,22:1
Sing, Baby, Sing 1936,S 12,20:1
Pigskin Parade 1936,N 14,23:3
One in a Million 1937,Ja 1,19:3
On the Avenue 1937,F 5,17:3
Seventh Heaven 1937,Mr 26,25:1
Wake up and Live 1937,Ap 24,16:2
Lancer Spy 1937,N 4,29:1
In Old Chicago 1938,Ja 7,15:2
Happy Landing 1938,Ja 22,19:1
Kidnapped 1938,My 28,9:2
Josette 1938,Je 11,9:1
Three Blind Mice 1938,Je 18,18:2
I'll Give a Million 1938,Jl 16,7:2
Little Miss Broadway 1938,Jl 23,10:4
Alexander's Ragtime Band 1938,Ag 6,7:2
Hold That Co-ed 1938,S 24,13:1
Straight, Place and Show 1938,O 1,10:2
Submarine Patrol 1938,N 19,9:2
Just Around the Corner 1938,D 3,11:2
Thanks For Everything 1938,D 10,13:2
Kentucky 1938,D 24,12:1
Jesse James 1939,Ja 14,13:1
Tail Spin 1939,F 11,13:2
Little Princess, The 1939,Mr 11,21:1
Story of Alexander Graham Bell, The
1939,Ap 1,17:2
Return of the Cisco Kid, The 1939,Ap 29,13:2
Gorilla, The 1939,My 28,6:2
Young Mr Lincoln 1939,Je 3,11:2
Susannah of the Mounties 1939,Je 24,13:2
Second Fiddle 1939,Jl 1,11:2
Stanley and Livingstone 1939,Ag 5,18:2
Hotel for Women 1939,Ag 26,20:2
Hollywood Cavalcade 1939,O 14,13:2
Drums Along the Mohawk 1939,N 4,11:2
Daytime Wife 1939,N 24,29:1
Swanee River 1939,D 30,9:2
Blue Bird, The 1940,Ja 20,11:2
He Married his Wife 1940,Ja 20,11:2
Grapes of Wrath, The 1940,Ja 25,17:2
Little Old New York 1940,F 3,9:2
Johnny Apollo 1940,Ap 13,21:2
Star Dust 1940,My 4,13:1
Lillian Russell 1940,My 18,11:2
I Was an Adventuress 1940,My 20,13:2
Four Sons 1940,Je 8,18:4

Zanuck, Darryl F (Producer) — Cont
Maryland 1940,Jl 13,16:5
Man I Married 1940,Ag 3,9:2
Return of Frank James, The 1940,Ag 10,16:4
Public Deb No 1 1940,S 18,19:2
Brigham Young - Frontiersman 1940,S 21,13:2
Great Profile, The 1940,O 18,25:1
Down Argentine Way 1940,O 18,25:1
Tobacco Road 1941,F 21,16:2
Blood and Sand 1941,My 23,25:3
Yank in the R A F, A 1941,S 27,11:3
How Green Was my Valley 1941,O 29,27:2
Son of Fury 1942,Ja 30,23:2
To the Shores of Tripoli 1942,Mr 26,27:2
This Above All 1942,My 13,14:3
At the Front 1943,Mr 19,15:5
Purple Heart, The 1944,Mr 9,15:2
Wilson 1944,Ag 2,18:1
Winged Victory 1944,D 21,16:2
Dragonwyck 1946,Ap 11,35:2
Razor's Edge, The 1946,N 20,42:2
Gentleman's Agreement 1947,N 12,36:2
Pinky 1949,S 30,28:2
Twelve O'Clock High 1950,Ja 28,10:2
No Way Out 1950,Ag 17,23:1
All About Eve 1950,O 14,13:2
David and Bathsheba 1951,Ag 15,23:2
People Will Talk 1951,Ag 30,20:1
Viva Zapata 1952,F 8,19:2
Snows of Kilimanjaro, The 1952,S 19,19:2
Egyptian, The 1954,Ag 25,23:1
Man in the Gray Flannel Suit, The
1956,Ap 13,21:1
Island in the Sun 1957,Je 13,37:1
Sun Also Rises, The 1957,Ag 24,12:2
Roots of Heaven, The 1958,O 16,46:1
Crack in the Mirror 1960,My 20,26:1
Big Gamble, The 1961,S 2,19:2
Longest Day, The 1962,O 5,28:1
Zanuck, Darryl F (Screenwriter)
On Thin Ice 1925,Mr 9,21:1
Limited Mail, The 1925,S 1,18:2
Noah's Ark 1929,Mr 13,28:6
Zanuck, Richard D (Producer)
Compulsion 1959,Ap 2,26:2
Sanctuary 1961,F 22,31:1
Chapman Report, The 1962,O 18,49:2
Zanussi, Lucie
Maciste in Hell 1931,Je 29,20:3
Zanville, Bernard
Action in the North Atlantic 1943,My 22,10:2
Zany, King
Garden of Weeds, The 1924,N 4,24:1
Zapnoukayas, Ariadne
Dark Odyssey 1961,Je 26,22:2
Zapnoukayas, Nicholas
Dark Odyssey 1961,Je 26,22:2
Zappatti, Cesare
Dopo una Notte d'Amore; After a Night of Love
1935,O 29,16:5
Zara, Carolina
Piri Mindont Tud 1933,Ja 26,12:3
Zaramba, Paul
Appointment in Honduras 1953,N 19,41:4
Zarana, Zalla
Merry Widow, The 1925,Ag 27,14:1
Zaranova, Erika
Overture to Glory 1940,F 12,14:2
Zarchi, Natan (Miscellaneous)
End of St Petersberg, The 1928,My 31,21:2 (In
Addenda)
Zardi, Federico
Salvatore Giuliano 1964,S 18,28:1
Zaremba, John
Magnetic Monster, The 1953,My 14,32:5
Chicago Syndicate 1955,Je 21,37:1
Earth vs the Flying Saucers 1956,Ag 2,21:2
Zareschi, Elena
Ultima Nemica, L'; Last Enemy, The
1940,Ap 18,28:5
Loves of Don Juan, The 1948,S 2,18:4
Cossacks, The 1960,S 6,41:4
Zarkhi, Alexander (Director)
Baltic Deputy 1937,S 4,8:2
Last Hill, The 1945,Je 26,13:2
In the Name of Life 1947,O 20,29:2
Zarkhi, Alexander (Screenwriter)
Baltic Deputy 1937,S 4,8:2
Last Hill, The 1945,Je 26,13:2
In the Name of Life 1947,O 20,29:2
Zarkhi, Natan (Screenwriter)
Mother and Sons 1938,S 15,29:2
Zarubina, I
Thunderstorm 1934,S 29,12:2
Krasnaya Derevnya 1935,My 2,17:1
Three Women 1936,F 12,25:4
Peter the First 1937,D 25,10:4
Friends 1939,Ja 2,28:3
Conquests of Peter The Great, The
1939,Ag 24,17:2
On his Own 1939,S 13,31:3
Captain's Daughter, The 1959,N 23,41:3

Zarzhitskaya, A
Professor Mamlock 1938,N 8,26:2
Zastrzezynski, Waclaw
Ashes and Diamonds 1961,My 30,8:1
Zaval, Manolita
Papacito Lindo; Sugar Daddy 1939,N 18,22:6
Zavalia, Alberto de (Director)
Vida de Carlos Gardel, A 1940,Ja 6,9:2
Zavatta, Achile
Green Mare, The; Jument Verte, La
1961,O 24,41:2
Zavattini, Cesare (Original Author)
I'll Give a Million 1938,Jl 16,7:2
Four Steps in the Clouds 1948,N 22,25:2
Bicycle Thief, The 1949,D 13,44:2
Walls of Malapaga, The 1950,Mr 21,34:2
Miracle in Milan 1951,D 18,42:2
Father's Dilemma 1952,S 23,25:1
Bellissima 1953,My 18,26:2
His Last Twelve Hours 1953,N 13,24:7
Lucky Five, The 1953,N 27,22:5
Indiscretion of an American Wife 1954,Je 26,7:2
Hello Elephant 1954,S 10,18:5
Umberto D 1955,N 8,37:1
Awakening, The 1958,Mr 3,24:6
Zavattini, Cesare (Screenwriter)
Shoe-Shine 1947,Ag 27,19:2
Bicycle Thief, The 1949,D 13,44:2
Miracle in Milan 1951,D 18,42:2
It's Forever Springtime 1951,D 29,7:7
Sky Is Red, The 1952,My 27,30:2
Father's Dilemma 1952,S 23,25:1
Rome, 11 O'Clock 1953,Ap 30,39:2
Overcoat, The 1953,O 13,34:1
Lucky Five, The 1953,N 27,22:5
Indiscretion of an American Wife 1954,Je 26,7:2
Umberto D 1955,N 8,37:1
Gold of Naples (Theresa); Theresa (Gold of
Naples) 1957,F 12,30:1
Gold of Naples (Pizza on Credit); Pizza on Credit
(Gold of Naples) 1957,F 12,30:1
Gold of Naples (The Gambler); Gambler, The
(Gold of Naples) 1957,F 12,30:1
Gold of Naples (The Racketeer); Racketeer, The
(Gold of Naples) 1957,F 12,30:1
Awakening, The 1958,Mr 3,24:6
Roof, The 1959,My 13,43:4
Virtuous Bigamist, The 1959,My 28,34:3
Two Women; (Ciociara, La) 1961,My 9,43:2
Boccaccio '70 (The Raffle); Raffle, The (Boccaccio
'70) 1962,Je 27,40:1
Arturo Island 1962,D 22,5:2
Yesterday, Today, and Tomorrow (Part III-Mara
Rome); Mara Rome (Yesterday, Today and
Tomorrow) 1964,Mr 18,46:1
Yesterday, Today and Tomorrow (Part 1-Adelina
Naples); Adelina Naples (Yesterday, Today and
Tomorrow) 1964,Mr 18,46:1
Yesterday, Today and Tomorrow (Part II-Anna
Milan); Anna Milan (Yesterday, Today and
Tomorrow) 1964,Mr 18,46:1
Young World, A 1966,My 17,52:1
Woman Times Seven 1967,Je 28,38:1
Zavitz, Lee (Miscellaneous)
Gone With the Wind 1939,D 20,31:2
Zavlan, Mary
Hairy Ape, The 1944,Jl 3,8:3
Zavoli, Sergio (Narrator)
Blood on the Balcony 1964,Je 30,22:1
Zawadaki, J A
Aelita: The Revolt of the Robots
1929,Mr 26,34:1
Zayenda, Edmund
Mamele; Little Mothers 1938,D 26,29:1
Brivele der Mamen, A; Little Letter to Mother, A
1939,S 15,26:4
Zazucta, Enriqueta
Littlest Outlaw, The 1955,D 27,31:1
Zazvorkova, Stella
Happy End 1968,Je 11,54:4
Zbanatsky, Yuri (Screenwriter)
Ukrainian Festival 1965,N 1,57:1
Zbyszko, Stanslaus
Night and the City 1950,Je 10,11:2
Zea, James (Producer)
No Exit 1962,D 6,55:2
Zea, Maria Luisa
Sagrario 1934,Ja 22,12:3
Su Ultima Cancion 1934,My 9,23:4
Corazones en Derrota 1934,O 10,21:4
Juarez y Maximiliano 1935,F 16,9:2
Llorona, La 1935,Jl 20,16:2
Todo un Hombre 1936,Ja 6,20:5
Hoy Comienza la Vida 1936,Je 27,21:2
Irma la Mala 1936,O 6,28:7
Liaga, La; Torment, The 1937,O 4,17:2
Forgive Me, Son 1937,O 23,14:2
Zandunga, La 1938,My 14,18:2
Bajo el Cielo de Mexico; Beneath the Sky of
Mexico 1938,D 31,7:3
India Bonita, La; Pretty Indian Girl, The
1939,Ap 15,15:2
Juan Soldado, o Venganza; John the Soldier or
Vengeance 1939,Jl 24,9:3

Rosa de Xochimilco 1939,O 14,13:3
Virgin of Guadalupe, The 1943,My 15,13:3
Zebba, Sam (Director)
Fincho 1965,Je 2,39:2
Zebba, Sam (Producer)
Fincho 1965,Je 2,39:2
Zebba, Sam (Screenwriter)
Fincho 1965,Je 2,39:2
Zebrov, Dimitri
Lady With the Dog, The 1962,N 7,48:1
Zech, Georg (Director)
Schwarzwaldmaedel 1935,O 12,12:3
Zeffirelli, Franco
Angelina 1948,Ap 6,27:2
Zeffirelli, Franco (Director)
Boheme, La 1965,O 20,51:2
Taming of the Shrew, The 1967,Mr 9,43:1
Romeo and Juliet 1968,O 9,41:1
Zeffirelli, Franco (Miscellaneous)
Boheme, La 1965,O 20,51:2
Zeffirelli, Franco (Producer)
Taming of the Shrew, The 1967,Mr 9,43:1
Zeffirelli, Franco (Screenwriter)
Taming of the Shrew, The 1967,Mr 9,43:1
Romeo and Juliet 1968,O 9,41:1
Zegarac, Dusica
Ninth Circle, The 1961,S 15,30:3
Feverish Years, The 1967,S 22,57:2
Zeglio, Primo (Screenwriter)
Attila 1958,My 19,19:4
Morgan the Pirate 1961,Jl 20,32:2
Zeiden, Josef (Director)
God, Man and Devil 1950,Ja 23,16:2
Zeidman, B F (Producer)
Hell's House 1932,F 12,24:5
In His Steps 1936,O 29,31:1
Grand Central Murder 1942,My 23,8:8
Pacific Rendezvous 1942,Jl 8,27:4
Air Raid Wardens 1943,Ap 5,15:5
Youngest Profession, The 1943,Je 25,13:3
Zeilas
Dr Knock 1937,My 1,16:4
Zeisberg, Ingmar
Confession of Ina Kahn, The 1958,Ja 1,31:4
Always Victorious 1960,Ap 7,46:1
Zeisler, Alfred
House on Ninety-Second Street, The
1945,S 27,24:7
Bird of Paradise 1951,Mr ,37:2
What Price Glory 1952,Ag 23,10:2
Zeisier, Alfred (Director)
D-Zug 13 Hat Verspaetung 1931,Ag 10,18:3
Sein Scheidungsgrund 1932,F 20,11:2
Eine Tuer geht Auf 1933,F 6,11:5
Hochtourist, Der 1934,Ja 13,16:4
Strich Durch die Rechnung 1934,Mr 3,8:6
Stern von Valencia, Der 1934,Ap 21,12:2
Schuss im Morgengrauen 1934,S 29,12:3
Crime Over London 1938,Jl 28,23:2
Enemy of Women 1944,S 12,23:6
Alimony 1949,Jl 22,16:3
Zeisler, Alfred (Producer)
Viktor und Viktoria 1935,Ja 28,10:5
Zeisler, Alfred (Screenwriter)
Enemy of Women 1944,S 12,23:6
Zeitlen, Doris
Unstrap Me 1968,N 21,41:2
Zeitlin, Esther
Lady Without Passport, A 1950,Ag 4,13:2
Zeke and Anne
Thrill of a Lifetime 1937,D 9,30:2
Zelaya, Don
Girl From God's Country 1940,S 9,18:5
Hairy Ape, The 1944,Jl 3,8:3
Amazon Quest 1949,My 14,9:3
Macao 1952,My 1,34:2
Zeldin, V
Tsar's Bride, The 1966,Mr 12,13:2
Zeldin, Vladimir
They Met in Moscow 1944,Je 7,13:2
Symphony of Life 1948,D 28,19:7
Zeldis, Joshua
God, Man and Devil 1950,Ja 23,16:2
Zelenohorska, Jitka
Closely Watched Trains 1967,O 16,59:2
Zelichowska, Lena
Szpieg 1934,Mr 5,19:3
Jego Wielka Milosc 1936,Mr 24,27:5
Cabman No 13 1937,N 1,24:6
Love or a Kingdom 1937,D 4,21:1
Dyplomatyczna Zona 1938,O 24,13:2
Zelinka, Blancho
Echoes of Silence 1967,Ap 7,32:2
Zelitsky, Vladimir
Cossacks in Exile 1939,Ja 28,19:2
Zeller, Wolfgang (Composer)
Alte und der Junge Koenig, Der 1935,D 10,31:2
Zeller, Wolfgang (Miscellaneous)
Wajan 1938,Ap 18,11:1
Zellman, Tollie
Roeda Dagen 1932,My 21,9:2
Ungdom Av I Dag 1936,Je 23,27:7
Vaaran Pojke 1936,O 10,21:3

Zellman, Tollie— Cont
Rena Rama Sanningen; Nothing but the Truth
1939,O 7,11:2
Zellner, Lois (Original Author)
Nobody Home 1919,Ag 25,8:5
Zellner, Lois (Screenwriter)
Turning the Tables 1919,N 3,13:3
Zelnik, Friedrich (Director)
Weavers, The 1929,O 7,22:1
Crimson Circle, The 1929,D 28,11:1
Barberina, Die Taenzerin Von Sans-Souci
1932,O 26,15:4
Walzerparadies 1933,Mr 4,11:3
Die Galavorstellung 1933,D 11,23:4
Kaiserwalzer 1934,D 29,11:2
Zelnik, Friedrich (Producer)
Glass Mountain, The 1950,My 18,37:3
Zeltser, I (Screenwriter)
Heroes of the Sea 1941,Ap 28,11:2
Zelwerowicz, Alexander
Noc Listopadowa 1933,My 1,10:3
Zemach, Elizabeth
Savage Eye, The 1960,Je 7,27:1
Zeman, Karel (Director)
Fabulous World of Jules Verne, The
1961,Je 29,26:1
Journey to the Beginning of Time 1967,F 11,20:1
Zemina, Valentina
Son of his Father, A 1925,S 29,31:3
Zemkova, Libuse
Bohemian Rapture 1948,F 16,16:2
Zemlyankin, Vladimir
House I Live in, The 1959,Ap 20,34:2
Zeno, Norman (Miscellaneous)
Love and Hisses 1938,Ja 1,11:1
Zenovin, Alexander (Original Author)
Men of the Sea 1938,Je 20,11:2
Zenyakin, A (Director)
Inside the U S S R 1961,N 6,46:5
Zerbe, Anthony
Will Penny 1968,Ap 11,51:2
Zeretelli, N M
Aelita: The Revolt of the Robot
1929,Mr 26,34:1
Zerkalova, D
On his Own 1939,S 13,31:3
Zerlett, Hans H (Director)
Selige Exzellenz, Die 1937,Je 15,26:2
Truxa 1937,Jl 26,15:2
Es Leuchten die Sterne; Stars Shine, The
1938,My 21,9:3
Zerlini, Valerio (Screenwriter)
Guendalina 1958,Je 30,23:2
Zesch-Ballot, Hans
Ferien vom Ich 1935,Ap 1,17:2
Schloss Vogeloed 1936,My 9,11:2
Waldwinter 1936,N 14,23:3
Nacht mit dem Kaiser, Die 1937,Ag 14,16:5
Zeska, Phillip (Original Author)
World and the Flesh, The 1932,My 7,11:5
Zeske, Carl
Hirsekorn Greift Ein 1932,Je 10,22:3
Zessarskaya, Emma
Her Way of Love 1929,Ag 19,22:1
Zetterling, Mai
Torment 1947,Ap 22,34:2
Frieda 1947,Ag 15,12:3
Quartet (The Facts of Life); Facts of Life, The
(Quartet) 1949,Mr 29,30:3
Girl in the Painting 1949,Ag 22,13:1
Sunshine Follows Rain 1949,S 29,39:2
Lost People, The 1950,O 2,19:4
Bad Lord Byron, The 1952,Mr 20,37:5
Frightened Bride, The 1953,Ag 20,18:5
Desperate Moment 1953,S 1,19:4
Knock on Wood 1954,Ap 15,34:2
Prize of Gold, A 1955,O 15,19:2
Dance Little Lady 1955,D 26,23:3
Abandon Ship 1957,Ap 18,35:1
Truth About Women, The 1958,Ag 29,18:2
Of Love and Lust (Doll's House, A); Doll's House,
A (Of Love and Lust) 1959,My 26,31:2
Only Two Can Play 1962,Mr 21,33:2
Night is my Future 1963,Ja 9,5:6
Main Attraction, The 1963,Je 27,23:3
Zetterling, Mai (Director)
Loving Couples 1966,S 20,38:1
Night Games 1966,D 20,58:1
Zetterling, Mai (Original Author)
Night Games 1966,D 20,58:1
Zetterling, Mai (Screenwriter)
Loving Couples 1966,S 20,38:1
Night Games 1966,D 20,58:1
Zetterstrom, Sven (Screenwriter)
Incorrigible 1949,Jl 2,8:2
Zevaco, Lily Mme
Culte de Beaute, Le 1931,Je 8,21:1
Zevaco, Michael (Original Author)
Nostradamus 1937,S 6,20:1
Zevic, Stanley
Touch of Larceny, A 1960,Mr 17,28:1
Zguridi, A (Director)
Life in the Arctic 1953,S 7,15:2
In the Pacific 1958,My 5,24:1

Zhakov, O
Ski Battalion 1938,Mr 14,13:1
Professor Mamlock 1938,N 8,26:2
Great Citizen, The 1939,Ja 16,11:2
Zhakov, Oleg
Girl From Leningrad 1941,D 20,25:2
Road Home, The 1947,My 2,28:3
In the Name of Life 1947,O 20,29:2
My Daughter 1960,N 28,40:2
Zhakov, Otto
Baltic Deputy 1937,S 4,8:2
Zharikov, Y
My Name Is Ivan (Ivan's Childhood)
1963,Je 28,25:4
Zharky, A (Director)
Red Army Days 1935,O 21,22:4
Zharof, Mikhail
Tovaristchi 1935,My 25,12:2
Zharov, M
Return of Maxim, The 1937,N 2,33:1
Peter the First 1937,D 25,10:4
New Horizons 1939,My 12,25:3
Conquests of Peter The Great, The
1939,Ag 24,17:2
Vanka 1943,Mr 25,25:3
Road to Life 1932,Ja 28,24:2
Fortress on the Volga 1942,D 25,15:3
We Will Come Back 1943,O 15,15:2
Taxi to Heaven 1944,My 25,16:3
Ivan the Terrible, Part I 1947,Mr 10,25:2
Twins 1947,Jl 28,12:2
Life in Bloom 1949,My 9,20:4
Mistress, The 1954,My 31,9:2
Anna Cross, The 1954,O 25,30:7
Ivan the Terrible, Part II 1959,N 25,22:4
Girl With the Guitar, The 1960,F 1,22:4
Zharov, Peter (Screenwriter)
House I Live in, The 1959,Ap 20,34:2
Zhdanov, Yuri
Ballet of Romeo and Juliet, The 1956,Ap 3,31:2
Zheimo, I
Pesnya O Stchasti 1935,Ap 8,23:4
Red Army Days 1935,O 21,22:4
Zheimo, Yannina
Three Women 1936,F 12,25:4
Two Soldiers 1944,Jl 27,14:2
Zhelyabuzhsky, A (Director)
Red and White 1932,N 29,23:5
Zhenof, G
City of Youth 1938,S 5,30:4
Zhevago, I
Optimistic Tragedy, The 1964,F 24,20:2
Zhilin, Victor (Director)
My Daughter 1960,N 28,40:2
Zhilin, Victor (Producer)
My Daughter 1960,N 28,40:2
Zhilinsky, A
In old Siberia 1929,Jl 22,17:1
Zhitkova, Vera
Tanya 1942,Mr 5,27:1
Zhivankov, Svetland
Train Goes to Kiev, The 1961,Ap 10,26:1
Zhivankova, Svellana
Song Over Moscow 1964,N 23,52:1
Zhivanovich, Milivoye
Magic Sword, The 1952,N 19,37:2
Zhivotov, A (Composer)
Ski Battalion 1938,Mr 14,13:1
Zhizneva, Olga
Three Thieves 1933,O 30,14:3
Christmas Slippers 1945,D 24,19:2
Russian Ballerina 1947,S 11,31:2
Admiral Ushakov 1954,Ja 18,19:2
Ladies 1955,Je 27,18:2
No Ordinary Summer 1958,O 6,36:3
House With an Attic 1964,D 21,42:5
Garnet Bracelet, The 1966,My 28,11:6
Zhokovskaya, G
Springtime on the Volga 1961,D 25,27:4
Zhorzholiani, A
Dragonfly, The 1955,Je 27,18:2
Zhuenti, Suliko (Screenwriter)
Father of a Soldier 1966,F 21,51:1
Zhukov, A
Her Way of Love 1929,Ag 19,22:1
Krasnaya Derevnya 1935,My 2,17:1
Childhood of Maxim Gorky 1938,S 28,29:3
Zhukov, Georgi K
If Your Home Is Dear to You 1967,O 24,27:1
Zhukov, Igor
My Beloved 1959,Je 15,31:4
Zhukovskaya, Garen
Taras Shevchenko 1952,Jl 28,12:6
Zhukovsky, B E
Greater Promise, A 1936,O 8,27:3
Zhukovsky, Boris
Wings of Victory 1941,N 17,15:2
Zhuraviev, D
Poet and Tsar 1938,Ag 25,15:1
Zhutayef, A
Sibirsky Patrul 1932,My 14,11:5

Zibaso, W P (Screenwriter)
Ballerina 1958,My 10,19:2
Zichy, Count
Life and Death of Colonel Blimp, The
1945,Mr 30,18:2
Ziedner, Lili
Tjocka Slaekten; Near Relatives 1935,My 20,20:5
Ziegfeld, Florenz (Miscellaneous)
Show Boat 1929,Ap 18,32:3
Ziegfeld, Florenz (Original Author)
Wife Savers 1928,Ja 17,23:2
Rio Rita 1929,O 7,22:1
Whoopee 1930,O 1,26:3
Ziegler, Anne
Waltz Time 1946,F 11,25:2
Laughing Lady, The 1950,Ja 23,16:3
Ziegler, Hermine
Meadehen von Gestern Nacht, Das; Girl of Last
Night, The 1938,Je 18,18:2
Ziegler, Isabelle Gibson (Original Author)
Seven Cities of Gold 1955,O 8,13:2
Ziegler, Martha
Der Falsche Ehemann 1932,O 17,18:3
Zielinska, Lili
Kazdemu Wolno Kochac 1933,My 24,24:3
Ziemann, Sonja
Merry Wives of Windsor, The 1952,S 22,19:2
Affairs of Julie, The 1958,D 10,53:1
Eighth Day of the Week, The 1959,Mr 24,45:2
Secret Ways, The 1961,My 25,31:1
Matter of Who, A 1962,Jl 25,29:2
Ziemer, Bruno
1914: The Last Days Before the War 1932,S 5,9:6
Ziemer, Gregor (Original Author)
Hitler's Children 1943,F 25,27:1
Zier, Jerry
Dynamite 1929,D 28,11:1
Ziffren, Lester (Original Author)
Sharpshooters 1938,D 5,19:2
Ziffren, Lester (Screenwriter)
City Girl 1938,F 4,17:3
Man Who Wouldn't Talk, The 1940,Ja 12,13:3
Charlie Chan in Panama 1940,F 23,19:3
Charlie Chan's Murder Cruise 1940,My 3,17:5
Zigmit
Son of Mongolia 1936,N 21,21:4
Zikov, S D
Oppenheim Family, The 1939,My 24,29:2
Zilahy, Irene
Csardas, Ihre Tollste Nacht 1937,Je 21,15:3
Urilany Szobat Keres; Lady Seeks Room
1938,Mr 19,11:2
Zilahy, Lajos (Original Author)
Virtuous Sin 1930,N 2,VIII,5:2 (In Addenda)
Firebird, The 1934,N 15,25:2
Zilber, Oscar (Miscellaneous)
Life Begins Tomorrow 1952,N 18,37:2
Zile, Heinrich Professor (Screenwriter)
Slums of Berlin 1927,Ja 26,17:1
Ziliani, Alessandro
Koenigin der Liebe 1936,My 4,16:2
Zilly, John
Twelve O'Clock High 1950,Ja 28,10:2
Zilzer, Wolfgang
Primanerliebe 1928,Mr 13,23:3
Shadows of Fear 1928,N 6,35:1
Mata Hari: The Red Dancer 1928,N 12,18:2
Namensheirat 1933,Ja 9,23:1
Hochtourist, Der 1934,Ja 13,16:4
Underground 1941,Je 23,13:2
Appointment in Berlin 1943,Jl 17,8:2
Hitler's Madman 1943,Ag 28,15:1
Behind the Rising Sun 1943,O 14,26:2
In our Time 1944,F 12,11:2
Zimbalist, Al (Producer)
Cat-Women of the Moon 1954,Mr 20,10:7
Baby Face Nelson 1957,D 12,35:1
Watusi 1959,Jl 2,15:2
Drums of Africa 1963,Jl 4,9:1
Zimbalist, Don (Producer)
Young Dillinger 1965,My 13,32:3
Zimbalist, Don (Screenwriter)
Young Dillinger 1965,My 13,32:3
Zimbalist, Efrem Jr
House of Strangers 1949,Jl 2,8:2
Band of Angels 1957,Jl 11,21:1
Bombers B-52 1957,N 23,11:2
Deep Six, The 1958,Ja 16,32:1
Too Much, Too Soon 1958,My 10,19:2
Home Before Dark 1958,N 7,23:1
Crowded Sky, The 1961,F 11,27:2
Fever in the Blood 1961,Ap 20,30:4
By Love Possessed 1961,Jl 20,32:2
Chapman Report, The 1962,O 18,49:2
Harlow 1965,My 15,18:1
Reward, The 1965,S 16,55:1
Wait Until Dark 1967,O 27,48:1
Zimbalist, Sam (Producer)
Married Before Breakfast 1937,Jl 23,16:2
London by Night 1937,Ag 13,13:1
Navy Blue and Gold 1937,D 24,21:2
Paradise for Three 1938,F 16,17:1

Zimbalist, Sam (Producer)— Cont
Crowd Roars, The 1938,Ag 5,11:1
Tarzan Finds a Son 1939,Je 15,27:2
Lady of the Tropics 1939,S 8,28:3
Boom Town 1940,S 6,25:2
Tortilla Flat 1942,My 22,27:1
Thirty Seconds Over Tokyo 1944,N 16,19:1
Adventure 1946,F 8,23:2
Killer McCoy 1948,F 12,31:2
Side Street 1950,Mr 24,29:2
King Solomon's Mines 1950,N 10,35:1
Quo Vadis 1951,N 9,22:2
Too Young to Kiss 1951,N 23,32:2
Mogambo 1953,O 2,18:1
Beau Brummell 1954,O 21,31:5
Tribute to a Bad Man 1956,Mr 31,13:3
Catered Affair, The 1956,Je 15,32:4
Barretts of Wimpole Street, The 1957,Ja 18,15:3
I Accuse! 1958,Mr 6,32:1
Ben Hur 1959,N 19,50:2
Zimet, Julian (Original Author)
Saigon 1948,Ap 1,30:5
Zimina, Valentina
Boheme, La 1926,F 25,26:2
Woman on Trial, The 1927,S 26,27:1
Scarlet Lady, The 1928,Ag 15,19:4
Ziminska, Mira
Kazdemu Wolno Kochac 1933,My 24,24:3
Manewry Milosne 1936,N 11,55:1
Zimm, Maurice (Original Author)
Jeopardy 1953,Mr 31,36:2
Creature from the Black Lagoon 1954,My 1,13:4
Zimm, Maurice (Screenwriter)
Prodigal, The 1955,My 14,10:7
Zimmer, Bernard (Miscellaneous)
Carnet de Bal, Un 1938,Mr 26,12:1
Zimmer, Bernard (Screenwriter)
Kermesse Heroique, La 1936,S 23,29:1
Dame de Pique, La 1944,O 19,19:2
Marthe Richard 1944,N 9,23:2
Zimmer, Lee
Lonelyhearts 1959,Mr 5,35:3
Zimmerer, Toni
Monna Vanna 1923,S 25,8:2
Zimmerly, Stuart Cpl MP USAA
Tokyo File 212 1951,Je 1,20:7
ZIMMERMAN
See Also ZIMMERMANN
Zimmerman, Vernon (Director)
Lemon Hearts 1962,Ag 3,14:2
Zimmerman, Victor
Flight Angels 1940,My 27,23:2
Murder in the Air 1940,Jl 4,12:2
Bullets for O'Hara 1941,Jl 28,16:4
ZIMMERMANN
See Also ZIMMERMAN
Zimmermann, Franz
Soldaten-Kameraden 1936,O 5,25:1
Meine Freundin Barbara; My Firend Barbara
1938,Je 4,18:3
Zimovetz, Nikolai
Taras Family, The 1946,D 9,34:4
Zingarelli, Italo (Producer)
Sword and the Cross, The 1960,Jl 7,26:1
Gladiators Seven 1964,My 7,31:2
Zini, Malisa
Madreselva; Honeysuckle 1939,Ag 19,18:4
Alas de mi Patria; My Country's Wingo
1940,Je 4,19:4
Huella; Trial 1940,O 22,27:3
Zink, Ralph Spencer (Original Author)
Invisible Menace, The 1938,F 14,20:6
Zinneman, Fred (Director)
Wave, The 1937,Ap 21,18:1
Search, The 1948,Mr 24,30:3
Men, The 1950,Jl 21,15:2
Behold a Pale Horse 1964,Ag 14,16:1
Zinnemann, Fred (Director)
Kid Glove Killer 1942,Ap 17,21:4
Eyes in the Night 1942,O 16,23:1
Seventh Cross, The 1944,S 29,18:1
My Brother Talks to Horses 1947,Je 19,27:4
Act of Violence 1949,Ja 24,16:2
Teresa 1951,Ap 6,31:2
High Noon 1952,Jl 25,14:2
Member of the Wedding, The 1952,D 31,10:2
From Here to Eternity 1953,Ag 6,16:2
Oklahoma! 1955,O 11,49:1
Hatful of Rain, A 1957,Jl 18,19:2
Nun's Story, The 1959,Je 19,30:1
Sundowners, The 1960,D 9,39:1
Man for all Seasons, A 1966,D 13,60:1
Zinnemann, Fred (Producer)
Sundowners, The 1960,D 9,39:1
Behold a Pale Horse 1964,Ag 14,16:1
Man for all Seasons, A 1966,D 13,60:1
Zinner, Al (Miscellaneous)
Fun and Fancy Free 1947,S 29,17:2 (In
Addenda)
Zinny, Victoria
Viridiana 1962,Mr 20,43:4
Zinser, Leo
Panic in the Streets 1950,Ag 5,9:2

Zintel, Zagmunt
Eve Wants to Sleep 1961,Je 6,42:2
Joan of the Angels? 1962,My 8,43:6
Guests are Coming; Jada Goscie Jada 1967,Ja 13,15:1
Zirow, Margot
Hungarian Nights 1930,Je 10,32:2
Ziskin, Henry (Producer)
Tevya 1939,D 22,15:3
Ziubkof, K
Childhood of Maxim Gorky 1938,S 28,29:3
Zivolinovic, Bata
Three 1967,Je 30,30:1
I Even Met Happy Gypsies 1968,Mr 21,57:1
Zlatagorova, T (Screenwriter)
Lenin in 1918 1939,Je 27,27:2
Zlatkovien, Zora
Magic Sword, The 1952,N 19,37:2
Zlotnicki, J
Border Street 1950,Ap 26,35:2
Znicz, Michal
Co Moj Maz Robi W Nocy?; What Is my Husband Doing Tonight? 1935,N 29,24:2
Dodek na Froncie 1936,Mr 30,17:6
Krawa Roza; Red Rose 1938,O 13,29:2
Dyplomatyczna Zona 1938,O 24,13:2
Zocchi, Nella
Wife for a Night 1958,Je 12,35:2
Zocchi, Nietta
Romeo and Juliet 1954,D 22,28:1
Zoch, Georg (Director)
Ein Walzer fuer Dich 1936,S 29,35:2
Lachende Dritte, Der 1938,Ap 9,11:2
Zoch, George (Director)
Vetter aus Dingsda, Der 1936,F 1,9:3
Zochling, Leo (Miscellaneous)
Golden Twenties, The 1950,Ap 10,15:2
Zoeberlein, Hans (Director)
Stosstrupp 1917 1935,F 4,11:4
Zogg, David
Avalanche 1932,Mr 26,17:2
Zohr, Uri
Pillar of Fire, The 1963,Ap 8,35:2
Zohra
Shakuntala 1947,D 26,22:3
Zola, Emile (Miscellaneous)
Gervaise 1957,N 12,46:1
Zola, Emile (Original Author)
Nana 1928,Ja 22,VIII,7:7
Shadows of Fear 1928,N 6,35:1
Argent, L' 1929,Mr 3,VII,7:2 (Incorrect in this edition; use 1929,Mr 3,VIII,8:5 in film)
Assommoir, L 1933,Jl 30,IX,2:2 (In Addenda)
Nana 1934,F 2,20:3
Human Beast, The 1940,F 20,17:2
Shop-Girls of Paris; Au Bonheur de Dames 1947,Je 23,14:4
Passionnelle 1948,Mr 1,17:2
Nais 1948,Je 16,37:2
Human Desire 1954,Ag 7,7:2
Nana 1957,Ap 13,12:3
Adulteress, The 1958,Ja 14,42:1
Pot Bouille 1958,O 28,39:1
Game is Over, The 1967,Ja 10,34:1
Argent, L' 1968,S 23,42:5
Zola, Jean-Pierre
My Uncle 1958,N 4,30:2
Zoldou, Sonia
Naked Brigade, The 1965,Je 17,27:2
Zolen, Margaret
Paris Incident 1954,Ag 18,20:2
Zoli, Charles
Forty Thousand Horsemen 1941,Ag 15,13:2
Zolinikov, Yascha
House I Live in, The 1959,Ap 20,34:2
Zollo, Aldo
Romeo and Juliet 1954,D 22,28:1
Zolotow, Maurice (Original Author)
Let's Dance 1950,N 30,42:2
Zolotukhin, L
Resurrection 1963,O 7,35:2
Zolts, David
Thirteen, The 1937,Je 19,20:2
Zombory, Gyorgy (Producer)
Merry Go-Round 1958,Ap 3,23:3
Zonne, I
Professor Mamlock 1938,N 8,26:2
Zononi, Z
Rivals 1933,Ap 5,22:6
Zoppetti, Cesare
Richiamo del Cuore, Il; Appeal of the Heart, The 1931,Mr 2,19:1
Avventura di Giacomo Casanova 1938,D 2,27:3
Zoref, Peter (Producer)
Candy 1968,D 18,54:2
Zorin, Leonid (Screenwriter)
Peace to Him Who Enters 1963,N 25,23:5
Zorina, Vera
Goldwyn Follies, The 1938,F 21,15:1
On Your Toes 1939,O 21,12:2
I Was an Adventuress 1940,My 20,13:2
Louisiana Purchase 1942,Ja 1,37:1
Star Spangled Rhythm 1942,D 31,20:1

Follow the Boys 1944,Ap 26,24:6
Lover Come Back 1946,Je 20,20:3
Zoritch, George
Night and Day 1946,Jl 26,16:2
Escape me Never 1947,N 8,11:2
Zorrilla, Jose (Original Author)
Don Juan Tenorio 1937,D 28,29:3
Zorskais, Nina
Wait for Me 1945,Mr 19,23:3
Zotov (Cinematographer)
Moscow Today 1929,My 13,27:2
Zoumboulski, Voula
Stella 1957,Je 11,40:1
Zounds, Archibald Jr (Original Author)
Goliath and the Dragon 1961,Ja 5,27:2
Zrazhevsky, Alexei
Return of Maxim, The 1937,N 2,33:1
Great Citizen, The 1939,Ja 16,11:2
Turning Point, The 1946,O 28,19:4
Zsoldos, A (Original Author)
Acht Tage Glueck 1931,Jl 24,22:1
Zsoldos, Andor (Director)
Jo as a Haznal; Father Knows Best 1935,F 5,22:4
Zuardo, Leon (Screenwriter)
Sonny Boy 1929,Mr 9,24:3
Zubkov, Valentin
Cranes are Flying, The 1960,Mr 22,31:2
Sun Shines for All 1961,Jl 10,25:3
Home for Tanya, A 1961,Ag 14,28:5
My Name Is Ivan (Ivan's Childhood) 1963,Je 28,25:4
Zubof, A T
Mother and Sons 1938,S 15,29:2
Zubof, K
Marionettes 1934,My 8,28:6
Zucchi, Tina
Dottor Antonio, Il 1939,D 7,35:1
Zucco, Frances
Never Wave at a Wac 1953,Ap 24,30:2
Zucco, George
Dreyfus Case, The 1931,Ag 31,11:5
Autumn Crocus 1934,O 25,26:2
After the Thin Man 1936,D 25,19:2
Sinner Take All 1937,F 3,27:1
Man Who Could Work Miracles, The 1937,F 22,13:1
Parnell 1937,Je 4,27:2
Saratoga 1937,Jl 23,16:3
Souls at Sea 1937,Ag 10,23:2
London by Night 1937,Ag 13,13:1
Firefly, The 1937,S 2,17:2
Bride Wore Red, The 1937,O 15,18:4
Madame X 1937,O 25,23:1
Conquest 1937,N 5,19:1
Rosalie 1937,D 31,9:2
Arsene Lupin Returns 1938,Mr 9,21:1
Lord Jeff 1938,Jl 1,22:2
Fast Company 1938,Jl 6,21:2
Suez 1938,O 15,21:2
Vacation From Love 1938,N 10,33:2
Charlie Chan in Honolulu 1938,D 31,7:3
Arrest Bulldog Drummond 1939,Ja 12,23:2
Captain Fury 1939,My 26,20:2
Adventures of Sherlock Holmes, The 1939,S 2,20:1
Here I Am a Stranger 1939,S 30,11:2
Cat and the Canary, The 1939,N 23,38:5
Hunchback of Notre Dame, The 1940,Ja 1,29:2
New Moon 1940,Jl 19,22:2
Mummy's Hand, The 1940,S 20,27:2
Arise my Love 1940,O 17,33:2
Dark Streets of Cairo 1940,D 2,19:3
Monster and the Girl, The 1941,Mr 20,25:3
Topper Returns 1941,Mr 28,26:6
Woman's Face, A 1941,My 16,21:2
Ellery Queen and the Murder Ring 1941,O 21,29:4
International Lady 1941,N 11,29:2
My Favorite Blonde 1942,Ap 2,27:2
Mummy's Tomb, The 1942,O 26,19:2
Black Swan, The 1942,D 24,18:3
Mad Ghoul, The 1943,D 11,11:2
Mummy's Ghost, The 1944,Jl 1,10:7
Shadows in the Night 1944,Jl 29,16:2
Seventh Cross, The 1944,S 29,18:1
House of Frankenstein 1944,D 16,19:3
Having Wonderful Crime 1945,Ap 13,15:2
Sudan 1945,Ap 19,22:8
Midnight Manhunt 1945,Ag 18,12:5
Confidential Agent 1945,N 3,11:2
Hold That Blonde 1945,N 8,17:2
Imperfect Lady, The 1947,My 22,34:5
Moss Rose 1947,Jl 3,14:2
Lured 1947,Ag 29,14:4
Desire Me 1947,S 26,28:3
Where There's Life 1947,D 25,32:1
Captain from Castile 1947,D 26,22:4
Tarzan and the Mermaids 1948,Mr 30,26:4
Pirate, The 1948,My 21,19:2
Barkleys of Broadway, The 1949,My 5,34:2
Madame Bovary 1949,Ag 26,15:2
Let's Dance 1950,N 30,42:2
First Legion, The 1951,Ap 28,9:2

Zucco, George — Cont
David and Bathsheba 1951,Ag 15,23:2
Zuckerman, George (Original Author)
Whispering City 1948,My 10,25:5
Border Incident 1949,N 21,29:2
Trapped 1949,N 26,10:6
99 River Street 1953,O 3,14:2
Square Jungle, The 1955,D 31,17:2
Tattered Dress, The 1957,Mr 15,22:3
Zuckerman, George (Screenwriter)
Trapped 1949,N 26,10:6
Spy Hunt 1950,S 8,25:2
Under the Gun 1951,F 23,33:2
Iron Man 1951,Ag 20,14:2
Dawn at Socorro 1954,Ag 28,8:2
Square Jungle, The 1955,D 31,17:2
Written on the Wind 1957,Ja 12,12:6
Tarnished Angels, The 1958,Ja 7,31:1
Zuckerman, S (Miscellaneous)
Monkey Into Man 1941,My 31,14:1
Zuckert, William
Ada 1961,Ag 26,15:1
Shock Corridor 1963,S 12,32:1
Zuckmayer, Carl (Original Author)
Hauptmann von Koepenick, Der; Captain of Koepenick, The 1932,F 28,VIII,6:1
Hauptmann von Koepenick, Der 1933,Ja 17,22:6
Mayerling to Sarajevo 1940,O 30,27:6
Grapes are Ripe, The 1953,O 15,43:2
Devil's General, The 1957,Ap 16,38:2
Captain from Koepenick, The 1958,Jl 26,6:1
Zuckmayer, Carl (Screenwriter)
Escape me Never 1935,My 24,24:2
Rembrandt 1936,D 3,31:1
Grapes are Ripe, The 1953,O 15,43:2
Captain from Koepenick, The 1958,Jl 26,6:1
Blue Angel, The 1959,S 5,11:4
Zugsmith, Albert
Fanny Hill 1965,D 2,48:1
Zugsmith, Albert (Director)
College Confidential 1960,Ag 22,23:1
Zugsmith, Albert (Original Author)
Female Animal, The 1958,Ja 23,24:3
Zugsmith, Albert (Producer)
Invasion USA 1953,Ap 30,39:4
Top Banana 1954,F 20,8:6
Female on the Beach 1955,Ag 20,20:2
Square Jungle, The 1955,D 31,17:2
Raw Edge 1956,Jl 28,10:7
Written on the Wind 1957,Ja 12,12:6
Incredible Shrinking Man, The 1957,F 23,13:1
Tattered Dress, The 1957,Mr 15,22:3
Girl in the Kremlin, The 1957,My 22,29:2
Slaughter on Tenth Avenue 1957,N 6,43:1
Tarnished Angels, The 1958,Ja 7,31:1
Man With a Shadow 1958,Ja 23,24:3
Female Animal, The 1958,Ja 23,24:3
High School Confidential 1958,My 31,6:6
Night of the Quarter Moon 1959,Mr 5,35:5
Beat Generation, The 1959,O 22,47:4
College Confidential 1960,Ag 22,23:1
Fanny Hill 1965,D 2,48:1
Zugsmith, Alfred (Producer)
Touch of Evil 1958,My 22,25:2
Zuker, Ben
Without a Home 1939,Ap 1,17:3
Zukor, Adolph (Producer)
Midnight Alarm 1923,Ag 26,VI,4:1 (In Addenda)
General Died at Dawn, The 1936,S 3,17:2
Zukor, Eugene (Producer)
Mystery Sea Raider 1940,Ag 26,11:4
Zukowski, Feliks
Maryjka 1934,D 3,15:2
Zukrowswi, Woiciech (Screenwriter)
Lotna 1966,My 27,33:1
Zulch, Helga
Wozzeck 1962,Mr 3,13:1
Zur, Josef
They Were Ten; (Heym Hayu Assara) 1961,Ap 18,44:2
Zurawski, Saturnin
Partings 1962,N 28,44:1
Zuri, Virginia
Noche del Pecado, La 1933,D 26,19:4
Llorona, La 1935,Jl 20,16:2
113, El 1938,F 14,20:8
Dama de las Camelias, La 1944,S 26,16:1
Zurlini, Griffi (Director)
Girl With a Suitcase 1961,S 12,36:2
Zurlini, Griffi (Screenwriter)
Girl With a Suitcase 1961,S 12,36:2
Zurlini, Valerio (Director)
Violent Summer 1961,My 20,12:1
Family Diary 1963,N 12,48:1
Zurlini, Valerio (Screenwriter)
Violent Summer 1961,My 20,12:1
Girl With a Suitcase 1961,S 12,36:2
Family Diary 1963,N 12,48:1
Zuskin, Benjamin
Taras Family, The 1946,D 9,34:4
Zuskin, V L
Greater Promise, A 1936,O 8,27:3

Zuskin, Venimin
Jew at War, A   1931,Jl 25,11:6
Zuyeva, Anastasia
Tanya   1942,Mr 5,27:1
Jubilee   1945,F 22,31:3
Winner, The   1947,D 1,27:2
Zuzzo, George
There Goes the Bride   1933,Mr 4,11:3
Zvarik, Frantisek
Shop on Main Street, The   1966,Ja 25,47:1
Zvarikov, Helena
Shop on Main Street, The   1966,Ja 25,47:1
Zweig, Arnold (Original Author)
Case of Sergeant Grischa, The   1930,Mr 8,21:1
Zweig, Stefan (Original Author)
Marie Antoinette   1938,Ag 17,23:2
Beware of Pity   1947,N 1,11:2
Letters From an Unknown Woman
   1948,Ap 29,20:6
24 Hours in a Woman's Life   1968,S 25,39:1
Zweig, Stefan (Screenwriter)
Volpone   1947,D 27,9:3
Zwerling, Yetta
I Want to Be a Mother   1937,F 27,9:2
Motel, The Operator   1940,Ja 16,19:3
Zwickert, Bruno (Producer)
Herzensclieb; Heart Thief   1938,Jl 2,10:4
Zwobada, Andre (Director)
Francois Villon   1950,Jl 3,9:2
Daughter of the Sands   1952,F 18,15:2
Zwobada, Andre (Screenwriter)
Francois Villon   1950,Jl 3,9:2
Daughter of the Sands   1952,F 18,15:2